W9-BHO-426

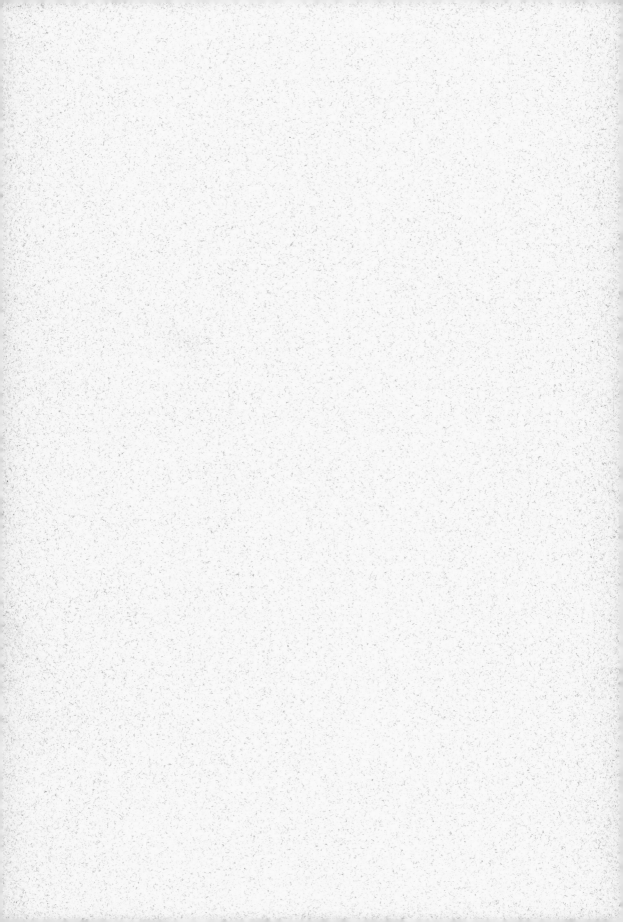

The International Bible Commentary

The International Bible Commentary

A Catholic and Ecumenical Commentary for the Twenty-First Century

Editor
William R. Farmer

Associate Editors
Sean McEvenue
Armando J. Levoratti
David L. Dungan

Map Editor
André LaCocque

A Liturgical Press Book

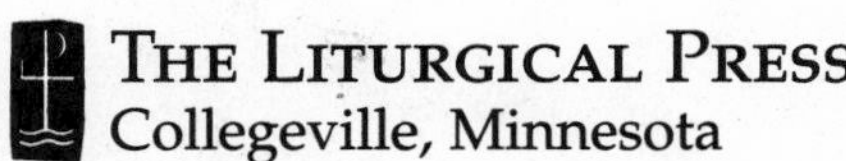

Nihil obstat: Robert C. Harren, *Censor deputatus.*

Imprimatur: ✠ John F. Kinney, Bishop of Saint Cloud, April 9, 1998.

Cover design by Ann Blattner. Jerusalem in the Fifteenth Century, from a manuscript illuminated for Philip the Good, Duke of Burgundy. Bibliothèque Nationale, Paris.

1 2 3 4 5 6 7 8

Library of Congress Cataloging-in-Publication Data

The international Bible commentary : a Catholic commentary for the twenty-first century / editor William R. Farmer . . . [et al.].

p. c.m.

Includes bibliographical references and index.

ISBN 0-8146-2454-5 (alk. paper)

1. Bible—Commentaries. 2. Catholic Church—Doctrines.

I. Farmer, William Reuben.

BS511.2.I57 1998

220.7—dc21 97-44829

CIP

The Editors
sincerely acknowledge their deep gratitude
for having the University of Dallas
as the academic base for their work together
on this ecumenical labor of love
during the seven-year period
1991–1998.

Contents

New Testament

About the Editors

William R. Farmer

Emeritus Professor of New Testament,
Perkins School of Theology

Research Scholar, University of Dallas

Farmer studied at Cambridge with C. H. Dodd while completing a degree in philosophy of religion and Christian ethics. His doctoral work at Union Theological Seminary was with John Knox. Farmer began writing on the social history of pre-70 Judaism and thereafter entered the field of synoptic studies. From 1965 to 1989 he worked closely with Albert C. Outler. His recent publications focus on the problem of Christian origins. Farmer is a Guggenheim fellow and a fellow of the International Institute for Gospel Studies. He was an invited visiting fellow at Fitzwilliam College, Cambridge, in the spring of 1995.

David Laird Dungan

Lindsay Young Distinguished Professor of Humanities, Department of Religious Studies, University of Tennessee

An ordained Presbyterian minister, Dungan was born in China, the son of Presbyterian missionaries. He completed a degree in theology at McCormick Theological Seminary in 1962 and obtained his doctorate from Harvard Divinity School in 1967, working with Krister Stendahl and Helmut Koester. His early writings focused on the sayings of Jesus in the letters of Paul and on ancient documents relevant to the study of the gospels. He is broadly published in synoptic studies and is the author of *The History of the Synoptic Problem,* forthcoming in 1999 from the Doubleday Anchor Bible Reference Library.

Sean McEvenue

Professor of Old Testament Theology,
Concordia University, Montreal, Canada

McEvenue's training with the Jesuits, mostly in Toronto, introduced him to biblical scholarship and the thought of the distinguished Jesuit theologian Bernard Lonergan. He completed his biblical studies at the Pontifical Biblical Institute in Rome, writing a doctoral dissertation in 1970 under the direction of Norbert Lohfink, S.J. His publications consist of books and articles centered primarily on the sources of the Pentateuch and focus on questions about truth and meaning of biblical texts. His main concern has been to exploit the clarity achieved in Lonergan's model of theological method in order to redefine the tasks of biblical interpretation.

Armando J. Levoratti

Professor of Old Testament,
Seminario Mayor, *La Plata, Argentina*

Levoratti is a member of the Pontifical Biblical Commission and the editor of *Revisita Bíblica,* the leading Latin American scholarly journal for biblical studies. With the assistance of his New Testament colleague Mateo Perdía he is the principal translator of the entire Bible from Hebrew and Greek published as *El Libro del Pueblo de Dios,* a version for the Argentinian people. He is also the editor-in-chief of *Santa Biblica,* an ecumenical study Bible published in 1995 by the United Bible Society and used throughout Latin America by both Protestants and Catholics. Professor Levoratti serves as a chief consultant of the United Bible Society.

Preface
A Catholic and Ecumenical Commentary

The idea of a Bible commentary that is both "Catholic" and "ecumenical" raises legitimate questions. From the outset the editors intended to produce "an ecumenical commentary for the twenty-first century" in the spirit of Vatican Council II (see Salvan Manifesto, 1990, reprinted below). The chief aim of this commentary was to give "scholarly assistance to pastors in all parts of the world."

Some believed that it was not yet possible to produce such a commentary. They said: "It is not possible to be Roman Catholic and ecumenical, at least not yet. . . ." Others thought we were involved in an "eschatological vision," that "the unity we seek still lies before us."

The difficulties which faced the editors were deeply felt. On the one hand they had become convinced that the participation of scholars who were not Roman Catholics was not only desirable, it was essential if the commentary was to be truly Catholic. On the other hand how would it be possible both to be faithful to the magisterial teaching of the Roman Catholic Church on the Bible and to invite the participation of scholars who owed no allegiance to the Roman Catholic magisterium? There was also a practical issue: how to produce a work that would be both faithful to Roman Catholic teaching and useful to all Christians everywhere.

In order to explore the feasibility of such a commentary and the principles on which it should be based the editors decided to schedule a "Symposium on Biblical Interpretation." This took place at the University of Dallas in January 1992. Participants included scholars from all communions, coming from Argentina, Brazil, Chile, England, Canada, Nigeria, and the United States, women and men, thirty in all. In the light of this symposium and the subsequent discussion and reflection Professor David L. Balás drafted a mission statement for the commentary project (reprinted below). The statement concluded with the expectation that the resulting commentary would be "a truly Roman Catholic, and also a truly ecumenical, commentary for all nations."

This "Statement of Mission," as a historical document, represents the ideal. How far the editors and contributors have approximated this ideal is for others to judge. Certainly the willingness of Protestant and Orthodox scholars to work with Roman Catholics to produce a truly Roman Catholic and a truly ecumenical commentary on the Bible is a sign of hope. To make this possible, great change had to take place in the hearts and minds of many.

We *are* involved in an eschatological vision; the unity we seek still lies before us.

A BRIEF HISTORY OF THE COMMENTARY PROJECT

The idea for this commentary was born in the mind and heart of Dom Bernard Orchard, O.S.B., of Ealing Abbey, London, in the spring of 1990. Orchard had served as editor of the first edition of *A Catholic Commentary on Holy Scripture* (London, 1953) and believed that the time had come to bring out a new edition. At that time Orchard and William R. Farmer were serving as co-chairmen of an ecumenical research society, the International Institute for the Renewal of Gospel Studies. Orchard wrote Farmer proposing that he consider assuming the editorship of this publishing project. In due time it became clear, however, that what was needed was not a new edition of an existing English commentary but a completely new and globally oriented commentary in the spirit of Vatican Council II.

In Salvan, Switzerland, on August 5, 1990, the fellows of the institute decided to endorse the proposal for "An Ecumenical Commentary for the Twenty-First Century," which, with Farmer as general editor, would have as its chief aim "scholarly assistance to pastors in all parts of the world." The fellows of the institute called upon all concerned for the support needed to bring this project to a successful conclusion within seven years, "to allow two full years for worldwide distribution in several major languages by the year 2000." Ben F. Meyer, a fellow of the institute, recommended his long-time friend and colleague Sean McEvenue of Concordia University in Montreal as the Old Testament editor.

The institute sought an academic base for the commentary project in a Catholic university with an excellent department of theology. The first choice of all concerned was the University of Dallas. For over twenty years this university had played an important role in a regional faculty research seminar on the Development of Early Catholic Christianity under the mentorship of Professor Albert Outler of Southern Methodist University. Basing the commentary at the University of Dallas would assure it the academic support of a large number of scholars in the Southwest who had learned to work together in the best ecumenical tradition of the post-Vatican II era.

The University of Dallas agreed expeditiously to the proposed arrangement. On January 13, 1991, on the campus of the university, a board of directors was formed "for the purpose of promoting and doing whatever shall be deemed necessary to complete and publish before the end of this century a new commentary on the whole Bible, after the manner of and in the spirit of *A Catholic Commentary on Holy Scripture* (1953). . . ."

In addition to the "Symposium on Biblical Interpretation" mentioned above there were two other conferences that deserve mention in this brief history.

(1) During February 18–20, 1994 a "Pilot Conference" was held on the campus of the University of Dallas. The purpose of this conference was to provide the opportunity for a limited number of contributors to have the first drafts of their work discussed by other scholars, including experts in related disciplines such a pastoral theology, patristics, history of doctrine, and liturgy.

(2) What was learned at the "Pilot Conference" was thereafter perfected and applied on a much wider scale eighteen months later at the Pontifical University of Nijmegen, in the Netherlands, during an extended conference held August 6–16, 1995. Through the ecumenical vision and generosity of a German Catholic missionary society it was possible for Protestant and Catholic contributors from Africa and Asia to join contributors from Europe in discussions that were illuminated by intercultural dialogue, which in turn facilitated and contributed to the formation of the first truly international Bible commentary. The editors met with twenty-six contributors from Asia, Africa, and Europe to discuss the latest drafts of each of their commentaries. This step was unusual; most commentaries are written with no communication among contributors. Contributors were divided into three groups, each meeting for three days. For each three-day session there was a special panel of experts representing related disciplines present to participate in the discussion of each commentary.

On the basis of these Nijmegen discussions the editors formulated guidelines for all the contributors working on their commentaries, in light of which they were urged to make final revisions. If there is a certain coherence and excellence by which the commentaries in this book are marked it is in no small measure due to the careful and lively collegial work carried out in these preparatory sessions (Dallas, 1992, 1994, and Nijmegen, 1995).

A Catholic and Ecumenical Commentary for the Twenty-First Century

Statement of Mission

The International Bible Commentary intends to be "Catholic." This last term is to be taken both with a capital "C," i.e., Roman Catholic, and with a lower case "c," i.e., universal. As universal it will not limit itself to the resources of any one nation or continent, but intends to be truly international, including contributors from around the world, and published simultaneously in English and Spanish and in other languages as well. Its ecumenical perspective implies that it intends to profit as fully as possible from the contributions of non-Catholic exegesis and exegetes.

The *Commentary* will be written not only (though also) for scholars; in fact it will address all the educated faithful, and especially pastors and teachers who should enable the faithful to find in the Bible the living and life-giving word of God.

As a "catholic" commentary in ecumenical perspective for the twenty-first century, it intends to make full, though not uncritical, use of all the resources of the human mind and of all the disciplines available to us today for an understanding of the writings of the Bible, such as philology, history, archaeology, literary criticism, philosophical hermeneutics, etc. For, as Vatican II's "Constitution on Divine Revelation" also affirmed, speaking of the Interpretation of Sacred Scriptures (chapter III, #12), "the exegete must look for that meaning which the sacred writers, in given situations and granted the circumstances of their time and culture, intended to express and did in fact express, through the medium of a contemporary literary form."

However, without detracting from the above task, and in accordance with a growing ecumenical consensus on the part of all exegetes who consider the Bible "Sacred Scripture" inspired by the Spirit of God, the *Commentary* intends to pay "no less attention . . . to the content and unity of the whole of Scripture" (ibid.) within which the individual writings and texts have their full "canonical" status and meaning. Furthermore, again in accordance with its catholicity and ecumenical perspective, the *Commentary* intends to seek a fuller understanding of the biblical writings, "taking into account the tradition"—and traditions— "of the entire church" (ibid.). The "Wirkungsgeschichte" of the Bible within the whole spectrum of Christian history (including not only its inexhaustible fruitfulness, but also its often conflicting interpretations—and misinterpretations) cannot be treated with any claim to completeness in a one-volume commentary, but the serious consideration of its essential lines belongs to its "Catholic" as well as "catholic" and ecumenical integrity.

Inasmuch as the *Commentary* intends to be authentically "Catholic" it will be guided by the teaching office of the Roman Catholic Church *(Magisterium),* with due attention, of course, to the varying degrees of authority with which such a teaching is proclaimed. It has to be kept in mind, however, that whereas the Catholic Church has a substantial body of definite teaching on the essential doctrinal content of the biblical message, "there are but few texts whose sense has been defined by the authority of the Church, nor are those more numerous about which the teaching of the Holy Fathers is unanimous" (Pope Pius XII, encyclical *Divino afflante Spiritu* [September 30, 1943] #47). Thus non-Catholic collaborators to the *Commentary* should feel assured that, within the framework of the general principles of interpretation described in the preceding paragraphs, they can proceed with full freedom. At the same time, they should have understanding for the duty of the editors to assure that, on those issues where definite Catholic teachings would be treated, the official Catholic view is clearly presented. General articles, e.g., on inspiration, canonicity, etc., will present faithfully the Catholic viewpoint(s), but include also a fair account of the main directions of the ecumenical spectrum.

Following these principles, *The International Bible Commentary* will be a truly Roman Catholic, and also a truly ecumenical, commentary for all nations.

The Salvan Manifesto

On the eve of the close of a century dominated by imperial conflict, worldwide expansion of communism, the Holocaust, and the nightmare of atomic annihilation, we look back on one bright moment of enduring hope—Vatican Council II. This reconciling event in the history of the Church has opened up promising possibilities for reducing meaningless conflict in human affairs. All who take their guidance from the decrees of this Council are bound together by the vision of a better future for the human family and its environment on this precious little planet in God's Great Universe.

Confident that God is in Christ reconciling the world unto himself, and that in Christ's holy Catholic Church of which we are baptized members, the world has its redemptive goal prefigured, we joyfully confess what we see with the eyes of faith. We see God's Holy Spirit at work in his Church in all its parts, but above all in the reforms of Vatican Council II. It is too soon for us to speak with confidence about the role of the Church's option for the poor in the unmasking and collapse of international communism. But the blood of Christ's martyrs shed on this altar marks a turning point in Church history and for us serves to validate the decrees of the Council. We take courage in a reforming Church chastened by the cries for justice raised against our human greed by the voices of the oppressed.

As fellows of an ecumenical institute chartered to contribute in a scholarly way to the renewal of Gospel studies in our time, we propose to cast our lot with the reforming Church of Vatican Council II. We believe that this Council was a gift of God to a lost world. In response to the work of the Holy Spirit through the reforms of this Council with its emphasis on the importance of the Scriptures, we propose to produce and publish "an ecumenical commentary for the twenty-first century." Drawing upon the best in evangelical and Catholic scholarship, we intend to produce a commentary which will have as its chief aim scholarly assistance to pastors in all parts of the world who seek to find in the Scriptures the spiritual resources they need as they face a hungry Church which assembles for worship with but one question in mind: "Is there any Word from the Lord?"

We call upon all concerned for the support that will be needed to bring this project to a successful conclusion. Work will begin in 1991 and is expected to be completed within seven years so as to allow two full years for worldwide distribution in several major languages by the year 2000.

—Salvan, Switzerland, August 5, 1990

David Dungan, William Farmer,
Ben Meyer, Bernard Orchard,
David Peabody, Philip Schuler
(Fellows of the International Institute
for Renewal of Gospel Studies)

Acknowledgments

In a project of the magnitude of this commentary the editors have received the help and support of more people than could possibly be fairly acknowledged here. However, in addition to the authors of the commentaries and articles, the editors would like to acknowledge a few individuals whose contributions have been invaluable. In no particular order we would like to express our thanks to the following persons:

Cynthia Stewart, our office manager, who coordinated the correspondence between the editors and the publishers and contributors, kept us within our budget, typeset a special edition of the commentary that was presented to the reigning pope, John Paul II, and to Bartholomew II, patriarch of Constantinople, and without whom many details that improved the quality of the final product would have fallen through the cracks.

Andrew Kolzow, O.P., prior, and the members of St. Albert's Priory, Irving, Texas, who initially gave the commentary project a home and who continued to support and participate in the life of the project after we had outgrown their office space and moved to other quarters.

Prof. Lyle Novinski, who among his many services to the commentary project designed the cover for the specially bound edition of the commentary for presentation to the Pope.

Daniel Van Slyke, who meticulously checked references to ensure that our volume would be reader friendly.

Prof. Erik Eynikel and the faculty of theology at the University of Nijmegen for arranging and hosting an international conference where contributors to the commentary from Africa, Asia, and Europe were able to meet and discuss each other's work for the mutual benefit of all. If there is a coherence to the contributions to this volume, it is due in no small part to the experience of the Nijmegen conference.

Our consulting editors: David Balás, O. Cist, History of Doctrine; Allan J. McNicol and Philip L. Shuler, New Testament; Enrique Nardoni, Spanish correspondence.

Past and present members of our board of directors: David L. Balás, O. Cist., David Dungan, Milam Joseph, † Ben F. Meyer, Dom Bernard Orchard, O.S.B., Robert F. Sasseen.

The publishing houses and their many individuals who have labored with us to make this commentary an international endeavor of the highest order. At press time of this edition the distinguished list of publishers includes The Liturgical Press, United States; Editorial Verbo Divino, Spain; Les Editions du Cerf, France; Verbinum, Poland; and Elle Di Ci, Italy.

Our families, for their patience and support through the past eight years when the commentary project consumed so much of our time and energy.

Abbreviations

Gen	Amos	Song	1–2–3–4 Macc	Gal
Exod	Obad	Eccl (*or* Qoh)	Pr Azar	Eph
Lev	Jonah	Lam	Pr Man	Phil
Num	Mic	Esth	Sir	Col
Deut	Nah	Dan	Sus	1–2 Thess
Josh	Hab	Ezra	Tob	1–2 Tim
Judg	Zeph	Neh	Wis	Titus
1–2 Sam	Hagg	1–2 Chr	Matt	Phlm
1–2 Kings	Zech	Add Esth	Mark	Heb
Isa	Mal	Bar	Luke	Jas
Jer	Ps (*pl.:* Pss)	Bel	John	1–2 Pet
Ezek	Job	1–2 Esdr	Acts	1–2–3 John
Hos	Prov	Jdt	Rom	Jude
Joel	Ruth	Ep Jer	1–2 Cor	Rev

AB — Anchor Bible
ABD — *Anchor Bible Dictionary*
ABRL — Anchor Bible Reference Library
ACW — Ancient Christian Writers. New York: Newman, 1946–.
AnBib — Analecta Biblica
ANET — James Pritchard, editor, *Ancient Near Eastern Texts Relating to the Old Testament* (Third Edition; Princeton University Press, 1969).
ANF — Ante-Nicene Fathers, ed. Alexander Roberts and James Donaldson. Buffalo: Christian Literature, 1885–1896; repr. Peabody, Mass.: Hendrickson, 1994.
ANRW — *Aufstieg und Niedergang der römischen Welt*
B.C.E. — Before the Common Era
BEThL — Bibliotheca Ephemeridum theologicarum Lovaniensium
BGBE — Beiträge zur Geschichte der biblischen Exegese
BHTh — Beiträge zur historischen Theologie

Bib.	*Biblica*
BIS	Biblical Interpretation Series
BJS	Brown Judaic Studies
BLS	Bible and Literature Series
BNTC	Black's New Testament Commentaries
BZNW	Beiehefte zur Zeitschrift für die Neutestamentliche Wissenschaft
CB	*Coniectanea biblica*
CBC	Collegeville Bible Commentary
CBH	Comentario Bíblico Hispanoamericano
CBQ	*Catholic Biblical Quarterly*
CBQ.MS	Catholic Biblical Quarterly Monograph Series
CCSG	Corpus Christianorum, Series Graeca. Turnhout: Brepols, 1977–.
CCSL	Corpus Christianorum, Series Latina. Turnhout: Brepols, 1953–.
C.E.	The Common Era
ClWS	Classics of Western Spirituality. London: 1978–.
CRI	Compendia rerum Iudaicarum ad Novum Testamentum
CSCO	Corpus scriptorum christianorum orientalium, ed. I. B. Chabot et al. Paris: Republicae; Leipzig: Harrasowitz; Louvain: Peeters, 1902–.
CSEL	Corpus scriptorum ecclesiasticorum latinorum. Vienna: Geroldi, 1866–.
EKK	Evangelisch-katholischer Kommentar
EstB	*Estudios biblicos*
FC	Fathers of the Church. Washington, D.C.: Catholic University of America Press, 1947–.
FOTL	Forms of the Old Testament Literature
FS	Festschrift
FzB	Forschung zur Bibel
GCS	Die griechischen christlichen Schriftsteller. Berlin: Akademie, 1897–.
GNO	Gregorii Nysseni opera. Leiden: E. J. Brill, 1960–.
GNS	Good News Studies
HNT	Handbuch zum Neuen Testament
HNTC	Harper's New Testament Commentaries
HThKNT	Herder Theologischer Kommentar zum Neuen Testament
HThR	*Harvard Theological Review*
ICC	International Critical Commentary
IDB	Interpreter's Dictionary of the Bible
IDBSup	Interpreter's Dictionary of the Bible, Supplements
Interp.	*Interpretation*
ITC	International Theological Commentary
IVP.NT	InterVarsity Press New Testament Commentary Series
JAAR	*Journal of the American Academy of Religion*
JB	Jerusalem Bible
JBL	*Journal of Biblical Literature*
JFSR	*Journal of Feminist Studies in Religion*

JPS	Jewish Publication Society
JSNT	*Journal for the Study of the New Testament*
JSNT.S	Journal for the Study of the New Testament, Supplement Series
JSOT	*Journal for the Study of the Old Testament*
KJV	King James Version (Authorized Version)
LB	Late Bronze Age
LeDiv	Lectio Divina
LFC	Library of the Fathers of the Holy Catholic Church, ed. E. B. Pusey, J. Keble, and J. H. Newman. Oxford, 1838–1888.
LHR	Lectures on the History of Religions
LThK	*Lexikon für Theologie und Kirche*
LXX	Septuagint
MB	Middle Bronze Age
MBC	Mercer Biblical Commentary
MD	*La Maison-Dieu*
MPG	Patrologia Graeca, ed. J.-P. Migne. Paris, 1857–1866.
MPL	Patrologia Latina, ed. J.-P. Migne. Paris, 1844–1864.
MSSNTS	Monograph Series. Society for New Testament Studies
MT	Masoretic Text (= Hebrew text)
NAB	New American Bible
NAC	New American Commentary
NCB	New Clarendon Bible
NCBC	New Century Bible Commentary
NCeB	New Century Bible
NEB	New English Bible
NIBC	New International Biblical Commentary
NIC	New International Commentary
NIGTC	New International Greek Testament Commentary
NIV	New International Version
NJB	New Jerusalem Bible
NJV	New Jewish Version
NKJV	New King James Version
Not.	*Notitiae*
NPNF	Nicene and Post-Nicene Fathers, ed. Philip Schaff et al. 2 series. New York: Christian Literature, 1887–1894; repr. Peabody: Hendrickson, 1994.
NRSV	New Revised Standard Version
NT	New Testament
NT	*Novum Testamentum*
NT.S	Supplements to *Novum Testamentum*
NTMes	New Testament Message
NTS	New Testament Studies
OBO	Orbis Biblicus et Orientalis

OT	Old Testament
OTL	Old Testament Library
ÖTK	Ökumenischer Taschenbuchkommentar
PLS	Patrologiae latinae Supplementum, ed. A. Hamman. Paris, 1957–1971.
PO	Patrologia Orientalis, ed. R. Graffin, F. Nau, et al. Paris: Firmin-Didot, 1907–.
PTA	Papyrologische Texte und Abhandlungen. Bonn: Habelt, 1968–.
PTS	Patristische Texte und Studien. Berlin: De Gruyter, 1964–.
REB	Revised English Bible
RGG	*Religion in Geschichte und Gegenwart*
RSV	Revised Standard Version
SBL.DS	Society of Biblical Literature. Dissertation Series
SBL.MS	Society of Biblical Literature. Monograph Series
SBS	Stuttgarter Bibelstudien
SC	Sources chrétiennes, ed. Henri deLubac, Jean Daniélou, et al. Paris: Cerf, 1942–.
SP	Sacra Pagina
StLi	*Studia liturgica*
TOTC	Tyndale Old Testament Commentaries
TSAJ	Texte und Studien zum antiken Judentum
TU	Texte und Untersuchungen. Berlin: Akademie, 1883–.
VT	*Vetus Testamentum*
WBC	Word Bible Commentary
WUNT	Wissenschaftliche Untersuchungen zum Neuen Testament
ZAW	*Zeitschrift für die alttestamentliche Wissenschaft*
ZNW	*Zeitschrift für die neutestamentliche Wissenschaft*

Prologue

The progress of biblical scholarship during the twentieth century has been impressive. Form and tradition criticism have demonstrated that behind the written records there was a long process by which each biblical tradition has come to its final form. Religious ideas and practices of each historical period have been illuminated by study of contemporary phenomena in the surrounding Near Eastern world. Comparative linguistics and semantic investigations, with ever more precise definitions of the changes in the meaning of words during the time, have brought us closer to the original import and significance of the texts. The history that forms the background of both Testaments has been reconstructed more accurately than ever before, often with the aid of striking archaeological discoveries. Textual criticism, in its search for the earliest form of the biblical texts, has received fresh impetus from the discovery at Qumran of manuscripts more ancient than any formerly available. An increasing sensitivity to the theological accent of different books has greatly broadened our appreciation of the rich polyphony that makes up the choir of Scriptures, and Old and New Testament scholars have been wrestling with problems inherent in the movement toward a more adequate hermeneutics.

An indispensable intellectual tool for the achievement of all this progress has been the so called *historical-critical method.* This method, it is true, has sometimes been used to assault the historical basis of Christianity and to undermine the authority of the Scriptures. It is also true that no method can be wholly divorced from certain philosophical presuppositions, and that in some cases the intertwining of method and content is so close that it is practically impossible to determine how much in certain biblical studies belongs to scientific method and how much is the projection of hypothesis, prejudice, desire, or subjective emotional attitudes. But the fact is that the Bible is a set of literary texts, and these texts come through to the modern reader as a message from a different group of cultures—those of ancient Israel and of the early Church. Moreover, the texts of Scripture bear a distinctive witness to a definite series of events at a particular place and time in history. As a consequence, the historical approach to the Bible is not only legitimate but also necessary. As the word of God set forth in human words of long ago the Bible can and must be read and studied against its proper historical backgrounds and within its contemporary social and cultural context, and since it narrates events that affected the lives of ancient Jews and early Christians it is reasonable to employ the tools and techniques of the historical method to better understand the segments of human history recorded in the Bible.

The texts of the Bible were written by different authors, for definite purposes, to historical communities that drew upon certain preexistent traditions. In general the biblical books give either direct or indirect information about their authorship, their destination, and the occasion and date of composition. Sometimes, however, this is not the case. For example, there is no certainty as to the identity of the person who wrote the letter to the Hebrews. All we know is that it was composed by an extremely gifted writer, fluent in Greek and well acquainted with the Judaic tradition. There is general agreement that the author is not Paul, but all attempts to identify an author so knowledgeable in both the Jewish and Greek traditions are ultimately guesswork. Now, if we ask about the authorship of this letter we are asking a historical and literary question. In a matter like this an appeal to canon and inspiration would not be an acceptable response. Hebrews, of course, is a part of the biblical canon, but the canonical status of a text does not settle the question of authorship, and because the lack of sources impedes making a clear decision regarding the author we can hardly do better than to accept the judgment of the great theologian Origen, who discussed the question early in the third century and concluded: "Who really wrote the letter is known to God alone" (Eusebius, *Hist. Eccl.* 6.25).

In biblical studies the word "criticism" does not imply captious faultfinding. The term is rather used in the etymological sense of scrutinizing and distinguishing in order to make an appropriate judgment. The historical method is called *critical* not because it criticizes the Bible or seeks to evoke skepticism about the truth of the biblical message but because in each of its steps it operates with the help of scientific criteria that seek to be as objective as possible. The process is essentially a rational reflection on the data supplied by literary, historical, or archaeological inquiry. As a scientific procedure it has no destructive intent and should in no way be viewed as dangerous, subversive, or disrespectful of the Christian faith. Whenever it is properly applied, far from being destructive, it helps to ascertain what the texts of Scripture meant when they were written or spoken in their original historical setting.

The historical-critical method, when used in an objective manner, implies of itself no *a priori.* Obviously an absolutely detached and value-neutral point of view is unreachable by a human interpreter, and if the practice of biblical criticism is accompanied by certain presuppositions or prejudices these are not something pertaining to the method itself, but to philosophical or hermeneutical choices that can be tendentious. In such cases a question may be raised as to whether certain faulty conclusions relate to the method itself or to the way it has been practiced since the Enlightenment.

There are still today basic unresolved disagreements between leading practitioners of historical criticism concerning its proper methodology. Nonetheless, many developments in biblical scholarship (including narrative, rhetorical, and reader-response criticism) have demonstrated the importance of the literary approach and the productivity of literary methods. In the case of the Bible, however, literary criticism can never be used in total isolation from a historical perspective, if only because the text is an ancient one from a foreign cultural context. In fact, without a knowledge of the history and cultures of biblical times the interpreter may easily distort the meaning of the texts, imposing on them an alien point of view, and it is precisely at this point that the results obtained by historical-critical investigation have been far reaching and have performed and still perform a highly valuable service to the Church. Placing Israelite and early Christian history in the larger context of the ancient Near Eastern and Mediterranean world shows that the biblical events, as they unfold first in Israel and then in Jesus and his Church, did not happen in an atmosphere of unreality or in a never-never land. On the contrary, this approach establishes the very real identity between the world of the Bible and the world in which we live day by day. Its courage to remove filters that custom and routine have laid over the reading of the Scriptures, as well as the attempt to bring the historical background of the biblical texts into sharper focus, have managed to provide fresh access to the Bible, opening "new possibilities for understanding the biblical word in its originality" (cf. the preface by Cardinal Joseph Ratzinger to the document of the Pontifical Biblical Commission on *The Interpretation of the Bible in the Church*). Such claims must not overlook the fact that the historical method is itself a historical phenomenon and as such must be subjected to the same scrutiny, criticism, and revision as any other part of human history, and yet even if a certain critique can be applied, and certain revisions can be made, this by no means implies that we should get rid of it completely and absolutely as no longer useful.

To begin with, we do not need to depreciate the importance of literary and historical research in order to recognize that the Bible is not merely literature, archaeology, and history. One example must suffice to clarify this point. The crucifixion of Jesus on its surface level was open to observation by anyone who happened to be in Jerusalem at that time. As a historical fact of the past it was a judicial execution that can be understood from the interplay of religious and political forces acting in Palestine at the beginning of the common era, when Pontius Pilate was the Roman prefect of Judea. But what are we to say, from a purely historical point of view, about the salvific value of the death of Christ? Here the historian is completely at a loss. Historians can report only what the early Church made of the cross, and affirm, for example, that Christians, contemplating the cross of Jesus, were moved to a remarkable self-abnegation and a courageous commitment of themselves to the extension of Jesus' mission. A historical judgment can neither confirm nor deny the claim that Jesus Christ lived, died, and rose from the dead to deliver us from sin and to confer upon us a new life. The divine, salvific meaning of historical events is not accessible to objective historical observation; it is revealed only to faith by the power of the Holy Spirit. Even if the historian is a believer he or she cannot, simply by reliance on literary and historical research, see that God was present and active in the event of the cross, bringing all human sin under judgment and reconciling a sinful humanity to God.

As a result a descriptive historical science will distinguish between history and theology, defining first the historical character of the event and then the meaning that the Church found in the event. We must, however, guard against opposing the historical facts to their theological interpretation. The theological content of Scripture is not something added to some untheological historical content. The biblical writers do not separate the historical event (Jesus' death on the cross) from its saving significance (Christ's death "for us"). They discern and experience a unique salvific event—"Christ died for our sins according to the Scriptures" (1 Cor 15:3)—and proclaim their experience in a great variety of theological expressions. The saving significance of Christ's death is not a subjective interpretation imposed on a plainly historical event. Rather than producing a soteriological interpretation, Christian faith is produced by the soteriological event of Christ's atoning death for us. Faith is doubtless needed to seize this meaning, but faith creates nothing: it is a mode of vision adapted to divine realities and simply recognizes and acknowledges them. Both elements—historical facts and theological understanding—are intrinsically bound up with one another, so that historical scholars who disclaim theological responsibility are simply closing their eyes to the theological aspects and implications of biblical research.

Biblical criticism asks only those questions that the method can answer, and deals only with those complexes of facts that are amenable to historical investigation. Its task is to reconstruct for us as accurately as possible the full human dimension of the biblical record, but it cannot penetrate beyond human actions, experiences, institutions, and ideas to perceive God's presence with God's people in the midst of history. Therefore we are warned not to expect of a descriptive historical science more than it is competent to achieve.

In other words: the text upon which historical criticism is focused is theological in character. The biblical writers wrote "from faith to faith," to bear witness to events that had led them to faith and to evoke or augment faith in their readers. They proclaim God's presence with God's people in the midst of history, illuminating their life situation, setting them free from their past, and opening a future before them. In this connection the gospel of John makes a statement that in a very real sense can be applied to the whole of the scriptural message: "these [signs] are written so that you may come to believe that Jesus is the Messiah, the Son of God, and that through believing you may have life in his name" (John 20:31).

If we realize, on the other hand, that the historical-critical method studies the biblical text in the same fashion as it would study any other ancient expression of human discourse we cannot but become aware of the inadequacy of historical criticism, at least in the form that has been widely accepted, to deal with Scripture as witness to a unique revelation of God to God's people of the Old and New Testaments, and to take account of the theological content of Scripture. By detaching the text from the stream of the Church's life it has hurled it into the abyss of an objectified past with nothing to say to the present. The biblical writers themselves never treated their own past in such a manner. Their past was rather a continual accosting, a challenge, and a confrontation.

There is another issue that deserves particular consideration in a prologue to an international Catholic bible commentary. The social context of biblical criticism is not the Church but the fellowship of biblical scholars; that is, not a community of faith but a peer group on the model of any professional guild, with an "expert" ethos and a highly technical language. In this way biblical scholarship sought to preserve intellectual liberty in order to pursue its work untrammeled by ecclesiastical interference and censorship. These scientists, indeed, have confidence in the body of scholarship; they are convinced that free and open discussion and scholarly criticism are the best means to prevent serious errors from gaining headway. If a fact has to be established as true, its truth must be tested by the criticism of their colleagues and not by an ecclesiastical authority.

One can understand this reluctance of many scholars to practice biblical exegesis in an ecclesial context. From its very beginning the application of a scientific methodology to the study of the Bible has been judged as improper by a wide section of the Church, and a deplorable result of this reciprocal mistrust was the lack of intimate relation between historical exegesis and the exposition of Scripture in the life of the Church. Thus one of the ironies of most recent Church history is the loss brought about by the separation of these two different and often antagonistic realms. In the realm of scholarship the investigation of the Bible has been prosecuted most scientifically, most vigorously, and with an international cooperation of scholars. These scientific investigations have not remained hidden in volumes accessible only to specially trained scholars; there is an immense literature now at the disposal of the nonspecialist for the understanding and interpretation of Scripture; but the knowledge that is available in that realm has somehow failed to inform the Church's preaching and teaching.

As a result of this particular situation we need a new reading of the Bible, made in the Church and as an essential part of ecclesial life. There are depths of meaning in the text of Scripture that remain hidden from the scholar until the text is preached by and to the Church. The ultimate content of Scripture is a word in which God comes in judgment and mercy, and that has to be proclaimed and heard and have its fruits in life before anyone, even the most accomplished scholar, can rightly understand its nature.

Therefore we propose as an alternative a Catholic or ecclesial exegesis; that is, a reading of the Bible that keeps the community of faith foremost in view during the task of scriptural interpretation. If the Bible is a written record that emerged out of the faith and life of the Church through the work of the Holy Spirit there must be an intimate relationship between Church and Bible. On the one hand Scripture grew out of the tradition of the believing community and became in its turn the word of God to the community; on the other hand the Church is a servant and witness of the living Word of God that has been transmitted from the apostles, and has the task of interpreting the Bible in the ever-new situations of its life, drawing from it ever new meaning, inspiration, and life. The Catholic communion of the Christian Church should be the hermeneutical locus and framework of the exegesis of Scripture.

The Bible and the Church stand together in a relation of mutual reciprocity. A community of faith cannot live as the Church of Jesus Christ apart from the spirit and force of God's word, and reciprocally this word is ultimately intended to create and sustain the community of faith. The Bible is dead letter unless it is read and lived in a living Church. Likewise the Church is a dead organization unless it is informed, strengthened, and constantly renewed by the living word of God. In the testimony of the Bible the Church finds the nourishment of its faith, the substance of its thought, and the guideline of its action. It remains alive, faithful, and active only to the extent that it listens to the Word.

God made Scripture a constituent element of the Church so that, with the assistance of the Holy Spirit, it could accomplish its mission of proclaiming to all the nations the saving power of the gospel. Thus the Church has an essential role to play in the interpretation of the sacred texts. The same Holy Spirit who inspired the sacred authors continues to work in the Church through diverse charisms, especially those of teaching and pastoral responsibility, and it would be misleading to oppose one authority to another. For the community the Bible is not an archive of the past. The human words of Scripture are but conduits of another Word, and the ultimate goal of an ecclesial interpretation is to hear that divine Word in those human words. Thus God's holy Spirit working through the Bible enables the Church to correct itself. The Church is to be thoroughly imbued with the spirit of the Scriptures by being a "listening community" attentive to the meaning of the biblical word and adapting it to present realities, unlocking the Bible from a past in which a pure historical reading has tended to seal it.

The truly Catholic approach to the Bible is one that is done in communion with the life of the Church and that draws its spirit and intent from a perspective of faith in the Scriptures as the word of God cast in thoroughly human terms. The Catholic interpreter takes seriously the entire canon of the Scriptures, so that no single biblical text can be taken in isolation from the entirety of biblical revelation. It views the entire message from a strong christological perspective, with the realization that ultimately all the Bible relates to the paschal mystery of Christ's death and resurrection. In this way of approaching the Scriptures the biblical text is viewed as belonging to a great stream of tradition—the life of the Church, with its momentous times of crisis and renewal—determining a flow of doctrinal developments and reformulations.

Although post-critical hermeneutics tries to reestablish continuity with a long tradition of biblical interpretation before the Enlightenment it does not represent a total rejection of historical-critical methods in favor of some impossible "return" to precritical times. If faith comes from hearing, and hearing through the word of Christ (Rom 10:17), fidelity to the Word requires a commitment to all that enhances the hearing of the word. Therefore we need a view of biblical interpretation that incorporates the gains made through historical study of the Bible while moving beyond this paradigm in an effort to deal with some of its inadequacies and to discover the form of interpretation most appropriate to the total content and ultimate meaning of the Bible. To define and acknowledge its limits is not to destroy the field of historical inquiry; rather it is to divine its true value and significance.

This Bible commentary is truly *international* and *ecumenical.* The Church of Jesus Christ has experienced very different histories as it expanded from the eastern Mediterranean to Europe and Africa, and then to Asia and America. In these nations and regions it suffered through and survived profound periods of crisis and redefinition. However, it has remained a powerful and vital force throughout the centuries because its universal message has been adapted, with the assistance of the Holy Spirit, to so many different peoples and cultures. It is obvious that the Christian faith has certain universal constants, but even the apostolic testimony to the Christ event was encased in the thought forms of the cultures of the first century of our era. God has never ceased to speak to God's people in the Holy Scriptures, but this message takes root in a great variety of terrain. The assumptions and attitudes of Christian believers are always influenced by their place in history and are expressed in categories that are part of a particular culture. Our interpretation bears the stamp of a particular time and culture, a particular set of traditions and experiences, and thus Christian faith always assumes a cultural form and takes shape in a particular historical time. This recognition helps us understand that the word of God transcends the cultures in which it has found expression and has the capability of reaching human beings in the particular cultural environments in which they live. It enables us also to see the gospel in many new and vitalizing ways.

Our conviction is that Christians of every particular Church have much to learn from their brothers and sisters living and working in other historical and cultural conditions. But even if doctrinal developments reflect the changing conditions of different times and cultures, the basic principle of Catholic and ecclesial interpretation remains the same: the exegetes who present the message of the Bible depend on sound scholarly work and try to incorporate the freshest fruits of scientific investigation; all biblical texts are most fully understood within the ongoing life and successive acts of (re)interpretation of the universal community of faith; but the works of the exegetes will be in some way a reflection of their own cultures.

Let us conclude this presentation with a general consideration about a most distinctive and characteristic feature of the Bible. The Bible is not a book of separate divine oracles or a mere collection of literary masterpieces. From Genesis to Revelation it is a great living unity insofar as it gives witness to God's redeeming and judging acts, of which for Christians the advent and work of Christ form the all-dominating center and focus. Jesus Christ is, for Christians, the bond who holds together the books of the Old and the New Testament and secures to the Christian Bible its unity. Everything beforehand was a preparation for him, and everything after—the reality of the Church, the preaching of the word, the sacraments, the charisms—is the way in which Christ encounters and becomes near to us here today. The common idea that sees in the OT exclusively the Law, and in the NT exclusively the Gospel, that speaks of the God of Israel as the holy Lawgiver and of the God of Jesus Christ as the loving Father is untrue to the Bible. It makes the Bible proclaim two different gods, or the same God revealed differently. However, "I am the LORD your God, who brought you out of the land of Egypt, out of the house of slavery" (Exod 20:2) is perhaps the most important word in the whole revelation of Sinai, for in it lies in promise the whole later divine revelation.

Truth is the whole. There is no inner canon within the canon of Scripture. While there are books that are central and books that are on the margin, not any of them should be considered irrelevant. Vivid and sometimes surprising witness to Christian truth can be found in apparently secondary writings like the book of Ruth or the letter to Philemon. Each book is there for the sake of the whole and for the interpretation of the whole. One part illuminates another, and cross-references to different books are necessary to elucidate the meaning of any given passage in any particular book.

Because they tend to be specialists, many biblical scholars do not address questions that relate to the Bible as a whole. They prefer, in any case, to expound the diversity and richness of the Bible. This is understandable because the Bible is indeed a very rich collection of diverse books, but at the same time the Church calls this collection of books "the Bible," signifying in this way that it has to be understood as itself a book.

One could begin reflection on the unity of the Bible by first sketching the narrative outline of the biblical story, or one could take one's lead from 1 Pet 1:10-12, perhaps the most comprehensive text in the New Testament about this theme. We purpose to initiate our reflections by taking another tack. Let us start by noting that beginning with the Gospel according to Matthew and ending with the Revelation of John we have a select set of distinctive Christian Scriptures that the Church has designated as the New Testament. To what, in this case, does the expression "New Testament" refer? Surprisingly enough it refers to something said by the prophet Jeremiah. So we find, right at the beginning of this reflection, an instance of what in contemporary literary criticism is called *"intertextuality."* Intertextuality is the experience of hearing echoes of one text in another, the discovery (or rediscovery, because the ancients knew it intuitively) that no text is ever truly autonomous; no text is ever produced and read apart from other texts. Every text is the absorption and transformation of other texts; it always implicates other texts within itself, and this is also apparent in the Bible. Later biblical writers and theologians make use of earlier Scriptures, creating "rereadings" *(relectures)* that develop new aspects of meaning. These intertextual relationships become particularly dense in the writings of the NT through multiple allusions to and explicit citations of the OT texts. A text makes explicit reference to older passages, whether to deepen their meaning or to make known their fulfillment, and this gives to the Bible, taken as a whole, an inner movement and interrelatedness of its parts (that is, an internal unity) that is unique of its kind.

The originating words of the phrase "New Testament" are found in Jer 31:31-34. (For the sake of clarity we should remember that the prophet uses the word *berith,* and that this Hebrew word can be translated into English either as "covenant" or "testament"; thus the phrase "New Covenant" is equivalent to the phrase "New Testament."):

> The days are surely coming, says the LORD, when I will make a new covenant with the house of Israel and the house of Judah. It will not be like the covenant that I made with their ancestors when I took them by the hand to bring them out of the land of Egypt—a covenant that they broke, though I was their husband, says the LORD. But this is the covenant that I will make with the house of Israel after those days, says the LORD: I will put my law within them, and I will write it on their hearts; and I will be their God, and they shall be my people. No longer shall they teach one another, or say to each other, "Know the LORD," for they shall all know me, from the least of them to the greatest, says the LORD; for I will forgive their iniquity, and remember their sin no more.

What is "new" about the new covenant is its theological character. The heart of the new covenant remains God's Law, but when God first gave the Law to Israel it was engraved on tablets of stone; this time, on the contrary, God will establish it in a more intimate fashion ("within them" and "on their hearts," v. 33). It will be even more intimate in another sense as well, because the condition upon which the new covenant is to be based is a special eschatological outpouring of divine forgiveness: "I will forgive their iniquity, and remember their sin no more" (v. 34).

The text of Jer 31:31-34 is cited in full in the NT (Heb 8:8b-12). This is a fact that no doubt influenced the Church in its decision to designate the Scriptures it added to its canon as "the New Covenant" or "the New Testament." This designation enabled the Church to identify the essential relationship of these Scriptures to those earlier Scriptures referred to by Jesus as "Moses and the Prophets." According to nomenclature provided by Jeremiah, the Law and the Prophets could in retrospect be designated as the books of the "Old Testament," or the "First Covenant." However, even more important in this regard is the fact that according to another tradition of the NT (cf. 1 Cor 11:23-27) Jesus connected his own passion with Jeremiah's new covenant.

From this perspective the unity of the Bible is grounded in God's unmerited grace. Jeremiah's promise of a new covenant based on divine compassion for the sinner must have made a profound impression on Jesus. This appears quite clear from the fact that, according to 1 Cor 11:23-25, on the night when Jesus was handed over he took bread and blessed it and then broke it and gave it to his disciples saying, "This is my body that is for you. Do this in remembrance of me." After the supper he likewise took the cup and said, "This cup is the *new covenant* in my blood."

Jeremiah himself, in his words about the new covenant, makes no reference to a sacrificial death, let alone blood. So we must look elsewhere in the Scriptures known to Jesus to find a text that enabled him to see the new covenant of Jeremiah in relationship to his forthcoming atoning death. This text is Isa 52:13–53:12. There Jesus read that it was the purpose of God to save Israel and all the nations through the atoning and redemptive suffering and death of God's servant. Recognizing the need to see the Scriptures in their deepest relationship to one another, Jesus read Jeremiah's promise of a new covenant based on the forgiveness of sins in the light of Isaiah's words concerning the suffering servant of the Lord.

> . . . he was wounded for our transgressions,
> crushed for our iniquities;
> upon him was the punishment that made us whole,
> and by his bruises we are healed.
> . . . you make his life an offering for sin . . .
> Therefore I will allot him a portion with the great,
> and he shall divide the spoil with the strong;
> because he poured out himself to death,
> and was numbered with the transgressors;
> yet he bore the sins of many,
> and made intercession for the transgressors
> (Isa 53:5-12).

In Jesus' days to be an effective leader in Israel required that one be an effective interpreter of Scripture. The pioneering role of Jesus as "interpreter of Scripture" explains why before he left his disciples it was necessary for him to gather them together and weld them into an indefectible *ecclesia* against which the gates of hell would not prevail (Matt 16:18). This he accomplished by instituting what the Church has come to refer to as "the Lord's Supper" (1 Cor 11:20). In light of this institution the gates of hell would not prevail against the *ecclesia* because wherever sin abides, there does grace much more abide (Rom 5:20).

Nowhere in the Bible is the internal relationship between the atoning death of Christ and Isaiah 53 more powerfully expounded than by the apostle Paul in Romans 3–5:

> . . . since all have sinned and fall short of the glory of God; they are justified by his grace as a gift, through the redemption that is in Christ Jesus, whom God put forward as a sacrifice of atonement by his blood, effective through faith (3:23-25).

> Jesus our Lord . . . was handed over to death for our trespasses and was raised for our justification (4:24-25).

> . . . God proves his love for us in that while we still were sinners Christ died for us (5:8).

By his memorable words and actions on the night he was offered up Jesus made clear to those who had eyes to see and ears to hear that his death was in accord with the Scriptures (cf. 1 Cor 15:3). The foregoing considerations help us understand why we experience the inherent unity of the Scriptures at its deepest level in the celebration of the Eucharist. Although every reading of Holy Scripture by a believer can mediate the revelatory action of God in his or her own life, the liturgical assembly is the most proper milieu for this occurrence. In the liturgical proclamation of the word of God the Christian community shares in knowledge with the people of God and the apostolic community that brought forth the Scriptures. The experience of God's revealing and redeeming love does not pertain to isolated individuals but to a community of faith, and we are grasped by the divine harmony of the Scriptures new and old. Every prayerful word, every word spoken in truth and charity is an aid to the effectiveness of the scriptural word and unveils even more clearly the God of love. We are united with the Law and the Prophets through our celebration of the benefits of the New Covenant by which, through the merits of Christ's death, we are bound to God.

The Eucharist focuses our attention on the central episode in the history of God's dealing with God's people (that is, the sufferings of Christ testified to in advance by Isaiah; cf. 1 Pet 1:11; Luke 24:44-46). This passion of our Lord is the strongest theological and narrative link in the intertextual chain that unites Moses and the Prophets with the books of the New Testament. It is in the celebration of the Eucharist that as baptized members of the body of Christ we face the life-or-death question whether to receive by faith the mystery of our unmerited salvation or not to receive it, to confirm or not confirm our membership in his body.

How to Use This Book

What You Will Not Find

(1) As this is an international and catholic commentary, you will not find here a uniform style or a set of articles written from a single perspective. Contributors have been encouraged to write their commentaries for their regular national readership, so that we can hear the tones of all the world cultures as they celebrate the Bible in real life today: The voices come from many different countries, continents, and languages, from South America, Europe, Africa, North America, India, Asia, the Philippines.

(2) You will not find a focused study of the history, geography, and archaeology of the Holy Land, but only a few maps and a selection of those facts and details that lead directly to an understanding of the biblical text.

(3) You will not find a biblical dictionary.

(4) You will not find a complete range of discussions dealing with all aspects of biblical study. Precise aspects have been selected for the general articles. The criterion of selection has been: what will readers engaged in pastoral concerns want to know in order to use the Bible well?

(5) You will not find sermons or applications of biblical ideas, as these would tend to be very specific and therefore of use only to relatively few individuals or local communities.

(6) You will not find interpretations of all the texts in the light of the whole biblical context. That is an ideal we espouse and a work that is begun here, as may be seen in several places where real light is drawn from the New Testament to the Old and/or from the Old Testament to the New, but this "intertextuality" is a relatively new discipline, and a difficult one.

What You Will Find

The purpose of the commentary is to enable readers to read the Bible with pleasure and profit by helping us to recover the ancient biblical truth with its precise meanings, its warmth, and its power, and to apply it to our own lives today. At every step it attempts to identify what necessary bits of information a modern reader will normally not have, or what biblical way of thinking a modern reader will not find obvious, and to help by providing the missing clues. Commentators will normally not say in their own words what the text means, but rather they will try to enable us to read the biblical text directly and experience its meaning in the Bible's own words. As with a cookbook, its main purpose is not to be read in itself (although some people do enjoy reading recipes), but rather to guide another activity. This commentary is a guide for reading the Bible. It will develop its full sense as you read the Bible.

The commentary contains a section of "General Articles" that treat selected questions about interpreting the Bible, questions that arise in a practical way in the minds of Bible readers. Many of these questions may already be in your mind. Others will certainly arise in the future. Times will come for any serious Bible reader when he or she will be happy to have these answers. There is no reason to bother with them until the questions have in fact arisen.

The body of the book consists of commentaries on the books of the Bible presented in the general order traditionally given those books in the first formative millennium of the Christian era. The biblical texts themselves are not printed in this volume. Each reader is invited to turn to the translation with which he or she is most familiar. (Many of these will present the biblical books in a different order and sometimes with slightly different divisions of chapter and verse, and often with a translation of a given verse that will differ from what the commentator suggests. With the help of indices, footnotes, and a little reflection readers will usually be able to solve these problems.)

Each commentary is divided into two major parts: "First Reading" and "Second Reading." For maximum benefit in using this commentary the reader should attempt to read the biblical book twice. The first reading is a rapid reading to see the book as a whole and to get the general idea (or a glimpse of the general idea), because that general idea is crucial in grasping the real context and sense of individual verses and chapters. The commentary will be an essential help in identifying that general context, as well as the historical background and spiritual meaning of the individual book. Many of the aberrations we have seen in the interpretation of Scripture over the past two millennia are directly due to neglecting this first step. The second reading then will be a slow reading, taking the book a bit at a time to be meditated and savored by the reader, filling up the general insight with the passionate details of poetry and preaching and history in which the writers originally discovered the shattering presence of God in their lives.

Finally, scattered throughout the commentaries there is a series of inserts that clarify key words and concepts, and provide explanations of things the biblical authors take for granted. These are located near the biblical chapters in which this key concept is first used or is most prominent, and cross references to them are made where they are most useful.

How to Use This Book

Clearly, then, the commentary is to be read not before reading the Bible, but while reading it. It is there to answer questions that arise in readers' minds as they read the Bible, or that have arisen in the past.

The best use of the commentary is to choose a biblical book and then to set aside time in order to read that book twice in the process of following the commentary. Often the book outline is given to the reader in the First Reading. This can be used to annotate one's own biblical text because it reveals the book's structure of communication and presents the book as expressing a unified grasp of reality in which God's love is revealed. Also in the first reading the actual subject matter of the book as a whole is identified: is it about something that happened? is it about an ethical value? is it about God's way of acting? about community? the presence of God? the nature of ultimate human wholeness? and so on. This sounds easy, but in fact it is in answering this question that we need the most help. Once the reader has identified the subject matter of the whole book it is possible to understand each verse or chapter as it was written, that is, as a reflection on that precise reality.

The commentary can, of course, be used more casually by someone who has to preach or comment on a specific text, in school, in church, or elsewhere. Such a reader can easily find the relevant book and then find the chapter and verse in the Second Reading section of the commentary on that book. However, that manner of proceeding is not the best way to benefit fully from this commentary. A specific text, taken in isolation from the rest of the Bible, may taste like pretty thin soup, and the Second Reading commentary, read in isolation from the general context of the First Reading, will often add only a salt that has little savor. Biblical books, which usually were written over decades and often over centuries by several authors and editors, are vital expressions of a central religious experience of a whole community. It is that central experience, identified in a First Reading, that gives substance and power to the ideas of specific verses. We may have heard many sermons that begin with a nod at the biblical text and then, apparently finding nothing spiritual in it, pass on to something else ("This reminds me of something that happened in the parish last month . . ."). The poor preacher understood all the words of the verses he or she had read, but did not grasp the biblical book as a whole and therefore had no notion of what central reality or mystery these verses illuminated.

Every reader approaching an individual verse or chapter may already have some understanding of the book as a whole from previous reading, and certainly will approach the reading with a personal gift of faith and a personal grasp of the divine mystery revealed in the Word of God. Still, the very best use of this particular commentary will be to begin with the First Reading and then to move to the Second Reading. This can be done in private study, in biblical study groups, in classrooms, in retreats, and so forth.

A second use of the book will be to consider the titles of the General Articles and to see which of these strike a chord. These are treatments of important topics helpful for understanding the Bible. These articles, taken together and read in conjunction with the information presented in the First Readings can serve as a competent and comprehensive introduction to the Bible.

A Guide to the Maps

André LaCocque, Map Editor,
with the assistance of Claire LaCocque

Introduction

IBC is "an ecumenical resource for the twenty-first century." In view of such a claim, significantly substantiated by the ecumenicity and international character of its contributors, it is worth recalling that we have entered an era of the visual. *IBC* takes its readers into a historically, and for most a geographically remote world. This may, from a romantic perspective, have a special appeal for some readers, but to those who are rightly unwilling to confuse the Bible with an assemblage of myths there is a need to know where the narrated events are taking place. This need can be met by carefully prepared historical maps. These should display a balanced amount of information, satisfying in terms of education but not cluttered with unnecessary details. In short, the *IBC* maps will provide, whenever possible, all necessary information in a reader-friendly way.

True, the Bible is no historical survey of the past, nor is it a précis of ancient Near Eastern geography. Nevertheless, it presents a repertoire of historical facts closely related to geographical sites in a land area stretching from the Indus river in the east to Spain in the west, and from modern Turkey in the north to Ethiopia in the south.

Physical maps of the region concerned will not suffice. Instead, the modern reader requires successive historical maps of the same area that together become a kind of cinematic display of the evolution of empires, with the birth of new cities and the disappearance of others. A comparison between the Davidic-Solomonic empire in the tenth-ninth centuries B.C.E., at the time when Israel reached its greatest expansion, and the tiny Persian province of Judah in the fifth century, when the population was reduced to some fifty thousand inhabitants dwelling in and around Jerusalem, is simply astounding. From such a comparison the reader will experience no difficulty in drawing far-reaching conclusions regarding the different levels of a multidimensional text deeply rooted in the "terrain." Something tremendous and earth-shattering has happened in the intervening centuries. Nehemiah's discourse could not possibly be the same as Solomon's!

Thus maps can make a powerful contribution to our understanding of the Bible with great economy of words. Within this perspective it is clear that a series of maps displaying general features such as the physical geography of the Near East or of Palestine will be of great interest to most readers of this commentary. These maps are grouped as a signature at the end of the book. They are meant to be both attractive and helpful, in general by their polyvalence and in particular by their precise response to the expectations of the reader of a specific book of the Bible.

Still, signature maps (SM) can only satisfy needs of a broad nature. More pointed needs arise with the reading of any dated document. For example, in the case of an invasion by an enemy coming from the north and met halfway through the country by national defense forces, the pictorial depiction of the events should be in close proximity with the text it illustrates. To this end the editors have inserted within the commentary a number of line-drawing maps (LD).

The reader will notice that cities on the maps are relatively sparse. Among those that are included, some are non-biblical. Often the Bible does not mention certain sites that are geographically and historically very important. Their presence on the maps will help the reader acquire a feel for the "world" of the Bible. The sheer enumeration of some of them will suffice: Ras Shamra/Ugarit, Ebla, Troy, Qumran, Tel-el-Amarna, Cairo, Aleppo, Mari, Boghazkoy. These and others will figure on one or more of the maps but will be identified as archaeological sites; their importance for understanding the Bible cannot be ignored by the cartographer. Also, one ought not be surprised to see such ancient archaeological sites situated, in some cases, at a distance from modern places with the same names. For example, Ashkelon used to be nearer the sea and farther north than it is presently.

A map "speaks" loudly to the informed reader, especially when aided by references to the biblical texts that illumine details of the map and are, in return, illumined by them. Such "reference bullets" serve another purpose as well. It has been said that the Bible was not written *ad narrandum sed ad probandum* ("not as history, but as apology"). Jesus' itinerary in Palestine according to the gospels, for example, may or may not be historically accurate. Thus a map retracing the steps of Jesus in Galilee or elsewhere is certainly useful, but the cartographer must clearly indicate the particular gospel on the basis of which such a reconstruction is made.

Thus the maps cease to be "mute" or simply one-dimensional. They acquire a life of their own. A map is both an urgent invitation to read the texts it illustrates and a synopsis of the historical and geographical information offered by the texts. For example, the drawing of the Israelites' journey in the desert after the Exodus from Egypt is highly problematic in spite of the relative abundance of place names the Bible provides. Even "Mount Sinai" is difficult to identify with any degree of certainty. Since the third century C.E. a strong tradition has placed it in the modern Sinai mountains, but some scholars think it was in the Arabian peninsula. The Israelite itinerary is, therefore, a reconstruction based on more or less reliable data. Alternative routes are sometimes given when the decisive facts are in doubt. It is important to trace the route of commercial roads if only to suggest in dramatic fashion that in the case of the Exodus story the escapees were led by their God away from the normal routes (Exod 13:21).

We have another example of such ambiguity in the division of the Promised Land among Israel's tribes according to the book of Joshua (somewhat corrected by the first chapter of the book of Judges). The cartographer has followed the information furnished by Joshua 13–24 as far as possible, but this depiction does not claim historical accuracy. The texts are not always consistent. Because of this anomaly the geographer is often struck with paralyzing trepidation when called upon to define the territorial limits of the tribes. The result can be both more scholarly (in terms of prudence) and less useful to the reader (as an explanation of the text). A necessary compromise leads us to consider cities attributed by the texts to two different tribes as border cities. As to Levi, that tribe does not receive contiguous sites but only scattered towns, forty-eight in all (Joshua 21). The levitical towns and the six cities of refuge (Josh 20:4, 7-8) can be identified by use of the code provided on the map.

These few examples will suffice for the purpose of this short introduction. Clearly maps serve as a deterrent to undisciplined imagination and can act as powerful pointers to the concreteness of the Bible. "Taanach, by the waters of Megiddo" (Judg 5:19) actually existed and is today an archaeological site in modern Israel. Bethlehem, Nazareth, Tiberias, Jerusalem—all are actual places on ancient and modern maps. Biblical religion is no dis-incarnated idea; it is a living reality and thus is inseparable from time and space, history and geography, politics and the occupation of a land. "In the beginning, the Word . . . became flesh and lived among us."

Culture and Commerce in the Ancient Near East of the First Millennium: SM 1

This map is an archaeological "plunge." One sometimes dubs such a view "The Crescent of Ancient Civilizations." It stretched between two diverse poles of culture: ancient Babylon and Egypt. The major highways ran from the Persian

Gulf to Egypt, through Ur, Babylon, Akkad, Mari, Aleppo, Qatna, Damascus, Palestine, Zoan, On, and from Ur to Susa, Nuzi, Asshur, Nineveh, Haran, Carchemish, Aleppo, etcetera. The route running east of Nuzi was sometimes called the Silk Road as it reached Afghanistan, India, and the Far East. It is on the basis of such commercial, strategic, and cultural arteries that it is possible to retrace Abraham's journey (see map SM 3 on Abraham). It can be immediately seen that Palestine's situation between north and south constituted a bridge as well as a bone of contention between major foreign powers, especially Egypt and Mesopotamia. As Jericho is most probably the oldest city in the world (existing as early as the seventh millennium B.C.E.) the Jordan valley may be considered a cradle of human civilization.

This map also illustrates the southern movement of the Hittite empire that occurred in 1900–1650 B.C.E. and, in a second wave, in the fourteenth century as far south as the Orontes river. As to the Hurrites, they were in the north of Mesopotamia, roughly in the Urartu region, a kingdom whose first known traces are from the ninth century B.C.E. The Hurrites were non-Semites. One finds them in the time of Abraham, indeed in the second millennium B.C.E. From their initial place they infiltrated the fertile plains of the southwest. Their code of laws is alluded to in Gen 21:10, for example.

Sumer is not on the map. In fact, Babylon took its place, but the Sumerian civilization maintained itself just the same, if only by its language and mode of writing.

Genesis 14 presents a king of Elam named Chedorlaomer. We do not know much about the Elamites of that time. Their historical capital was Susa (Neh 1:1; Esth 1:2; Dan 8:2, and elsewhere). That very ancient non-Semitic people is also mentioned in Jer 25:25; 49:35-39.

Mari on the Euphrates is a historical site that was first identified in 1933. Numerous tablets in cuneiform writing (numbering some 20,000) are shedding new light on the civilization of that time. A new discovery is the name of a clan, Banu-yamina, which is similar to the tribal name Benjaminites.

Excavations in Ur, the Chaldean metropolis where Abram/Abraham lived, have shown how remarkably civilized were the cities of that time. (See SM 3, "Abraham's Migration.")

Palestine: Physical Geography: SM 2

The deep depression of the Dead Sea and the Arabah (the plain) is clearly visible. It is the only sea in the world whose level is 1,306 feet below the oceans' level. The north-south depression that forms the Jordan River's bed divides the land. This natural division into Cisjordanian and Transjordanian territories has played a significant role in the history of settlement. The historically important tribes were located west of the river.

Right and left of the median depression the country appears very mountainous. Summits higher than three thousand feet are not uncommon. Principal peaks from north to south are:

Mt. Hermon	(9,232 ft.)	Mt. Carmel	(1,791 ft.)
Mt. Tabor	(1,929 ft.)	Mt. Gilboa	(1,758 ft.)
Mt. Ebal	(3,084 ft.)	Mt. Gerizim	(2,890 ft.)
Mt. Gilead	(4,091 ft.)	Mt. of Olives	(2,625 ft.)
Mt. Nebo	(2,690 ft.)	Mt. Seir	(5,200 ft.)

Some of these summits, such as Mount Hermon, are crowned with eternal snow. There are few plains; they too are named according to their biblical appellation: by the sea, Sharon and Shephelah; by the river, the plain of Jordan and the Arabah.

In the southern part of the country deserts are not scarce. In biblical times, they were for the most part steppes, which is to say that herds could more easily graze there than today. Consider, for example, "the Judean desert," "the Zin desert," "the Arabian desert."

The sea that the Bible calls "Great Sea" is obviously the Mediterranean. Its other biblical names are "the Sea" or "the Western Sea." There are, in all, three inner seas from north to south: Lake Huleh (or Semechonitis), the Sea (or Lake) of Chinnereth (or Galilee or Tiberias), and the Salt Sea (today called the Dead Sea because its waters contain so many minerals that fish cannot live in it). This sea's other names are Sea of the Desert, the Eastern Sea, the Sea of Siddim.

The Jordan River and the Dead Sea receive several streams; the principal ones are here indicated. From the east flow the rivers Yarmuk, Jabbok, Arnon, and Zered. Flowing into the Mediterranean Sea are several rivers: the Litani, the Kishon, the Yarkon, and the Besor. Farther to the south is the Brook of Egypt, which for a long time constituted the boundary between Egypt and Palestine. The reader should not get the false impression of a well-irrigated land; many streams have their flow interrupted during the summer (see the reflection in Deut 11:10-12).

Knowledge of the physical geography of Palestine helps us to realize the vital importance of rain (cf. Lev 26:4; Pss 68:10; 147:8; Prov 16:15; Isa 30:23; Ezek 34:26; Hos 6:3; Joel 2:23; Zech 10:1; Jas 5:7-18). This peculiarity of Palestine is underlined by contrast to Egypt and Mesopotamia that, watered naturally by their own rivers, did not need water from heaven.

Palestine, before being divided into tribes or administrative provinces, was sundered into natural regions, some of them eventually becoming actual countries. In Cisjordan (west of the Jordan), Phoenicia with its well-known cities of Sidon and Tyre; Galilee, the most fertile part of the land, with its famous Valley of Jezreel south of Nazareth, between the Kishon River and Beth-shean; Samaria, with its prestigious Mounts Ebal and Gerizim, the holy city of Shechem, future capital of the Northern Kingdom of Samaria; Judea, called to play a dominant role in the region because its confined geographical situation stimulated its vital energy. It was limited by the inimical Philistia to the west, by the rivalry of the northern tribes, the desolation of the Dead Sea to the east and of the desert to the south. Philistia on the west coast was a plain completely open to the conquerors called "people of the sea." The so-called Shephelah (literally "the Hollow") between Lakish and the Besor River was the granary of Judea and all the more at the mercy of the Philistines because it constitutes with their country the same geographical region. The Negeb (meaning "the South") is a place of large barren spaces, making it difficult to draw the southern boundaries of Judah.

In Transjordan (east of the Jordan) lies the Bashan, with its green pastures and its famous cattle breeding (cf. Amos 4:7; Ps 22:13). Gilead is in fact a chain of high mountains. Ammon, with its capital Rabbah, is a barren region. Moab, between the rivers Arnon and Zered, is very mountainous. Edom, south of the river Zered, is a desolate wasteland, but an important commercial route passed through it. Nabateans in the fourth century evicted the Edomites and controlled the caravan road to their advantage.

Abraham's Migration: SM 3

Excavations in Ur have shown how remarkably civilized were the cities of that time. Abraham thus left a prosperous and well-developed country for the desert and the unknown. Probably the Persian Gulf stretched as far north as Ur, which was at that time an important center of maritime activity. An approximate draft of the contours of the Gulf has been attempted here, taking into account the uncertainties of alluvial deposits.

Haran, the city to which Abraham came and in which he received his calling, is scarcely known to us today. (It has become a small Iraqi village.) It was once a religious center (of the moon god, like Ur) and was located at the crossing of two commercial roads, between the Hittite empire in the north and the Mediterranean Sea, and between Nineveh in the east and Carchemish in the west (cf. SM 1). Haran is mentioned also in Ezek 27:23; 2 Kings 19:12.

Abraham's itinerary was considerable for the time, taking into account that he covered approximately 1,400 miles with his family, tents, baggage, and animals. In order to imagine Abraham's journey we should consider that travelers had to go from town to town to trade their products. Therefore, although other roads are possible, the one that passes through Mari takes into account the archaeological discoveries made in that city that shed light on the commercial and political relations between Mari and Ur; the road then goes through Carchemish, Aleppo, and Qatna, and suggests that Abraham avoided the desert (through Tadmor/Palmyra).

The Exodus and Conquest of Canaan: SM 4

The itinerary of the Hebrews on their way out of Egypt (Exodus) is delineated with a precision that may appear audacious. The traditional hypothesis was that they passed north or south of the "Bitter Lakes," a viewpoint based on the identification made between "the Sea" (Exod 14:2-4) or "the Sea of the Reeds" (Exod 13:18) on the one hand, and the actual Red Sea on the other hand. This very identification is made already by the NT (Acts 7:36; Heb 11:29). The term "Red Sea" (in Greek *thalassa eruthra*) is based on the Greek translation of the Hebrew Bible (LXX). Quotations of the Bible in the Greek New Testament are for the most part based on the Septuagint text (third century B.C.E.). But the Hebrew text has *yam suph,* which literally means Sea of the Reeds or of the Rushes. Which is the Sea of the Reeds? Some Hebrew texts, such as Exod 23:31; Num 14:25; 21:4; Deut 1:40; 2:1; Judg 11:16; etcetera, use the term *yam suph* to designate the present Gulf of Aqaba and probably diverse bays covered with rushes. The sea crossed by the Hebrews is not the one mentioned by those texts. Exodus 14:2 as a matter of fact places the Sea of the Reeds at the very beginning of the Exodus and in the neighborhood of the cities of Pi-hahiroth, Migdol, and Baal-zephon. Pi-hahiroth cannot easily be located, but it was probably seated on one of the branches of the Nile. However, the location of Baal-zephon is clear, thanks to its temple which was situated on the lagoon in Lake Sirbonis. That temple was regularly visited by navigators sailing along the coast. Migdol, according to a traditional hypothesis, ought to be situated near the "Bitter Lakes," but an Egyptian papyrus called Anastasi I reveals that Migdol came immediately after Zilu on the road from the sea to Gaza. The same papyrus adds that an Egyptian fortress was situated there (note that Migdol means "fortified tower"). Exodus 15:22 indicates that after they came out of the sea the Hebrews were in the Shur desert, where they walked three days without finding any water. Therefore the Sea of the Reeds of Exod 13:18 ought to be located in the swampy strip of the northeast of the Nile delta, where papyrus (reed) was abundant. Moreover, this northern itinerary takes into account the Hebrew verb *sabab* (Exod 13:18) referring to a gyrating movement (see our line tracing through Baal-zephon). This thesis is further confirmed by another biblical text, Isa 11:15-16, which is a prophecy regarding the sea of Egypt and recalls the miraculous crossing of the sea by the Hebrews on the very day "when they came up from the land of Egypt." The text signals the "tongue" of the sea, an expression that illustrates very well the topography of the lagoon and its peninsula where Baal-zephon is located. On this see also Herodotus (fifth century B.C.E.), *History* II. 6 and 9. The people of Israel, guided by the column of smoke and fire (Exod 13:21), did not follow the normal commercial routes and caravan roads of the time, possibly because they were drawn far from them by fear of being intercepted.

At the time of the conquest Canaan looked like a chessboard whose squares were city-kingdoms. The correspondence between the Pharaohs and their vassal Canaanite kinglets that took place shortly before the Exodus in the thirteenth century B.C.E. has been discovered by modern archaeologists in the Tel-el-Amarna letters of the fourteenth century (El-Amarna is the ancient name of the city of Akhenaton on the Nile, some two hundred miles northwest of No-amon (modern Luxor). The letters mention over a score of city-kingdoms (and at least twice as many Canaanite cities). Such a situation explains to a certain extent the penetration of Israelite clans in a country deeply divided at a time of Egyptian weakness (the Canaanite appeals to Egyptian intervention in their affairs remained unheeded).

The Israelites, we are told, after avoiding Edom and Moab on their left (west), crossed the Jordan River near Jericho, in the mountainous region of the desert of Judah, where guerrilla warfare would be necessary (Num 20:14-21; Joshua 3). The first Canaanite city conquered was Gilgal, and it became the first confederation center of the Israelite tribes. According to the record in the book of Joshua the next stations were Jericho and Ai (for this there is no archaeological support, especially as regards Ai, whose name had probably been given to a heap of ruins—as the term in Hebrew indicates—hundreds of years before Joshua's time; cf. Joshua 8). The conquest of Shechem (cf. Josh 17:2) is confirmed by external evidence. The map shows three main lines of penetration: one northbound in Transjordan toward Edrei and beyond; one westbound, crossing the Jordan and bifurcating into two thrusts, northward and southward. Contrary to Joshua's description it is clear that the "conquest" was slow and a great deal less bloody and devastating than is indicated there.

Tribal Territories of the Israelites: SM 5

This map is based on the elaborate survey of the territories allotted to the different tribes according to Joshua and Judges, a review of which gives the following:

Judah (Joshua 15; Judg 1:8-18). Son of Leah. Settled in the Negeb with Simeon. It became the largest tribe, with 76,500 warriors according to Num 26:19-22. Its limits are described in Josh 15:1-12 and the list of its towns given in Josh

15:20-63. Its southern limit was the desert; it shared its northern border with Benjamin and Dan, and from there its border ran to the Mediterranean Sea. Joshua 15 gives a list of one hundred thirty-two cities in eleven districts (out of the original total of twelve?). Judah expanded at the expense of neighboring tribes and became a kingdom after Solomon's time. It embraced the Philistine territory, but not until the time of David was the Philistine spirit entirely destroyed. The Judean territory is very rugged and thus affords good natural defenses.

Simeon (Josh 19:1-9; 1 Chr 4:24-43). Son of Leah; allied with Levi (Gen 34:25-31), it is not mentioned in Moses' blessing (Deuteronomy 33). Its territory was swallowed by Judah (cf. Josh 19:1-9 with Josh 15:21-32). It initially had 22,200 men (Num 26:12-14).

Ephraim (Joshua 16; Judg 11:29). Son of Joseph and the Egyptian Asenath. Ephraim's southern border abutted Benjamin and Dan; in the north its limit was along the Kanah brook, but in the east the boundaries are less clear. No cities are named for Ephraim. It soon eclipsed its brother tribe, Manasseh, which it pushed back to the north (Genesis 48). Ephraim was the main rival of Judah (Isa 11:13) and became the head of the northern tribes, which sometimes are simply called "Ephraim." It numbered 32,500 men (Num 26:37). Its territory is very rugged.

Manasseh (Joshua 17; Judg 1:27-28.) Full brother of Ephraim. Half the tribe settled in the Amorite kingdom and reached the Lebanon border (1 Chr 7:14); the other half took over its domain with the help of Ephraim in Cisjordan (Josh 17:14-18). No list of cities is provided. Manasseh extended from the Sea to the Jordan River. Its southern limit coincides with northern Ephraim, while its northern border abuts Asher, Zebulon, and Issachar. Several cities, theoretically in its territory, were only conquered hundreds of years later.

Benjamin (Josh 18:11-28; Judg 1:21). Son of Rachel; 45,600 men (Num 26:38-41). Between Ephraim in the west and Judah in the south, it extended from the river Jordan to the hills overlooking the Aijalon Valley (in Dan). Twenty-six of its cities are listed. Being at the crossroads of several highways, Benjamin's territory was coveted by others and several battles took place there.

Zebulon (Josh 19:10-16; Judg 1:30). Son of Leah. It made its living from the sea (Gen 49:13 and Deut 33:18-19). At the beginning it numbered 60,500 men (Num 26:27) and was bordered by Asher, Naphtali, Issachar, and Manasseh. Fourteen cities are included with Sarid in the south and Rimmon in the north, the Valley of Iphtahel in the west down to the Kishon. Major commercial routes passed nearby, so that Zebulon was open to multiple outside influences.

Issachar (Josh 19:17-23). Son of Leah. Numbered initially 64,300 men (Num 26:23-25), two centuries later 58,600 men (1 Chr 7:1-4). Situated in eastern lower Galilee, between the Jordan River and the eastern portion of the Jezreel valley. Its southern limit followed the Harod valley from Jezreel to the Jordan River. Its relatively level ground was an invitation to invading armies.

Asher (Josh 19:24-31; Judg 1:31). Son of Zilpah, maidservant of Leah. On the western slopes of the Galilean mountains. Bounded by the Mediterranean Sea in the west, Naphtali in the east, Zebulon and Manasseh in the south, and Phoenicia in the north. This tribe led an almost independent existence (Judg 5:17) and had 53,400 warriors (Num 26:47) or perhaps 26,000 (1 Chr 7:40). Asher did not control important cities in the coastal plain (Judg 1:31) except briefly under David and Solomon (1 Kings 4:16). In Asher was the only natural harbor, Acco. A highway ran from there east to Damascus. The Phoenician cities of Tyre and Sidon were a thorn in the flesh of Asher.

Naphtali (Josh 19:32-39; Judg 1:33). Son of Bilhah, Rachel's maidservant. On the eastern slope of the Galilean mountains, with its capital at Kedesh (Judg 4:10). When they entered Canaan the tribe of Naphtali numbered 45,400 men (Num 26:48-50). It was bounded by Asher (west), Zebulon and Issachar (south), and the Jordan River (east); its northern limit is not indicated (probably the Litani River). It controlled the Jabneel Valley in the south. Its city list has nineteen towns. For a long period of time Canaanite cities like Beth-shemesh and Beth-anath could not be conquered (Judg 1:33). Three tribal boundaries (Naphtali, Manasseh, and Zebulon) met at Mount Tabor.

Dan (Josh 19:40-48; Judg 1:34-35, 17-18). Son of Bilhah. Dan could not hold its heritage alongside the Mediterranean Sea (Judg 1:34) and settled at the Jordan springs, near the town of Laish, which thereafter was renamed Dan (Judg 18:29). Dan is the northernmost Palestinian city, as can be seen also from the traditional expression "from Dan to Beersheba" (Judg 20:1; 1 Sam 3:20; 2 Sam 17:11). At the beginning they numbered 64,400 men (Num 26:43). The major north-south highway ran through Dan and was coveted by the Amorites, who pushed the tribe of Dan out to the north. The former territory theoretically belonging to Dan was briefly conquered under David and Solomon (1 Kings 4:9; 2 Chr 2:16).

Reuben and Gad. Gad (Josh 13:24-28; Num 32:34-36), son of the maidservant Zilpah, numbered 40,500 warriors (Num 26:15-18). Its constant fighting with Ammon makes its eastern boundaries imprecise. Situated north of Reuben, it extended to the Sea of Galilee (Josh 13:27), with the Jordan in the west and the Transjordan half-tribe of Manasseh settling north of the Jabbok in the Gilead and Bashan regions (up to Mount Hermon, Num 32:39-42; Josh 13:29-31). Reuben (Josh 13:15-23; Num 32:37-38), elder son of Leah, lost his birthright because of the sin he committed with Bilhah (Gen 49:4); this "explains" the insignificance of the tribe's role in Israel's history. It had 43,730 men (Num 26:5-11). Its proximity to the desert enemies of Ammon and Moab does not allow an exact delineation of its territory. Its eastern border was the Jordan River, and it extended from the Arnon Valley in the south to the city of Heshbon in the north.

Levi (Joshua 21; 1 Chr 6:54-81), third son of Leah, did not receive any territorial heritage, only scattered towns (forty-eight in number). The crude event mentioned in Genesis 34 explains why Jacob wanted to disperse Levi and Simeon throughout all of Israel (49:7). The offspring of Levi became in Moses' time the priestly tribe (Deut 33:8). Six "cities of refuge" were also designated where anyone guilty of manslaughter could find asylum and have his/her case impartially judged. In Cisjordan these were Kedem, Shechem, and Hebron; in Transjordan, Golan, Ramoth Gilead, and Bezer (see lists in Num 35:1-15 [P]; Deut 4:41-43; Josh 20:4-8).

Samuel and the Ark of the Covenant: SM 6

First displayed in the tribal shrine of Shiloh, the Ark was brought by the Israelites, threatened by a Philistine onslaught, as a divine palladium to Eben-ezer. The Philistine troops were gathered at Aphek, only a few miles away (1 Sam 4:1). During the ensuing confrontation the Ark was captured by the Philistines and carried as a trophy from Aphek to Ashdod. There it stood in the shrine of their god Dagon, but the image of Dagon repeatedly fell from its pedestal, and a plague broke out that was attributed to a bad spell attached to the Israelite Ark. It was therefore sent to another Philistine city, Gath (1 Sam 5:1-8). There also the Ark played havoc with the Gathites, and it was transferred to Ekron, but not for long: the Ekronites refused to harbor it and they were allowed to return the Ark to Israel (5:9-12). In all the Ark spent seven months among the Philistines (1 Sam 6:1).

Borne upon a chariot, the Ark arrived at Beth-shemesh in Israelite territory. As previously, it spread death and terror around it (1 Sam 6:19-20). Finally the people of Kiriath-jearim fetched it and set it up in the house of one Abinadab; his son Eleazar was appointed as its keeper (1 Sam 7:10).

Israel's Hegemony at the Time of David and Solomon: SM 7

David's trajectory starts in the territory of the Philistines, at Ziklag, where he took refuge from Saul's pursuit. David went from there to Hebron, where he was anointed by the elders of Judah (2 Sam 2:1-7, 11). Later, elders from northern Israel also came to David at Hebron and appointed him king of all Israel (ca. 1010 B.C.E.; 2 Sam 5:1-3; 1 Chr 11:1-3). Right away David took care of the Philistine threat (1 Chr 18:1) and captured the city of Jebus, which he made his capital with the name "City of David," someday to be called Jerusalem (2 Sam 5:6-10; 1 Chr 11:4-9). This "coup" was crowned by David's transferring the Ark from Kiriath-jearim (2 Samuel 6; 1 Chronicles 13). Jerusalem as capital had considerable advantages: not belonging to any tribe and being a natural stronghold in the Judean chain of mountains, it was now promoted to be the holiest place in Israel. It has occupied that historic status ever since.

David then progressively eliminated the Canaanite remnants of the pre-Israelite era (cf. Judg 1:21-35). A warrior since childhood (1 Samuel 17), David turned against Israel's restless neighbors. He subdued Ammon in spite of their hiring mercenaries, mainly Arameans (2 Sam 10:6-14; 1 Chr 19:6-15). Moab also was captured and treated with surprising harshness (2 Sam 8:2; 23:20; cf. 1 Sam 22:3-4). The Arameans themselves were defeated (2 Sam 10:15-19). The series of David's victories, however, is narratively interrupted (in 2 Samuel 11) by his horrendous behavior toward Uriah and his wife Bathsheba.

The Edomites knew the same fate as other enemies of David (1 Chr 18:12, 13), but their king Hadad fled to Egypt from which he would eventually return and lead a successful rebellion against Solomon (1 Kings 11:14-22). But it was especially in the north that David succeeded in expanding his sway. Damascus was garrisoned and paid tribute (2 Sam 8:5-6; 1 Chr 18:5-6). The Geshurites, at the east of the Lake of Galilee, escaped Israel's occupation by marrying their king's daughter to David. Absalom was the offspring of that marriage, and it comes as no surprise that Absalom fled to Geshur after his failed coup to seize his father's throne (2 Sam 13:37-39).

Historically, David's was the largest expansion of Israel's territory. Some texts make that clear (Numbers 34 [as a promise]; 1 Chr 13:5 ["from the Shihor River (in the Nile Delta) to Lebo-hamath (north of Aram-Damascus)"], or again 2 Sam 24:1-8 [census]). King David organized his kingdom by appointing governors of circumscriptions (1 Chr 27:25-31).

Solomon was anointed at the Gihon brook (2 Kings 1:11-48) and succeeded his father in 970. He reigned until 933. He consolidated David's empire with a network of constructions. During his reign the territory is said to have stretched from the river Euphrates to the border of Egypt (2 Chr 9:26). Solomon's hold on this large country was buttressed by the development at strategic points of store cities (2 Chr 8:4), such as Tadmor (later called Palmyra, here off the map), Hazor, Megiddo, and Gezer (1 Kings 9:15).

This king's policy of marrying foreign princesses as a way of keeping peace with the neighboring states is well known (see, for example, 1 Kings 11:1). His wealth is also notorious; the fact is that he controlled major commercial routes from Mesopotamia to Egypt and from Syria to the "Great Sea" (cf. 1 Kings 10:1-13; 2 Chr 9:14). The import-export business flourished (1 Kings 10:28-29). The exploitation of copper mines and the shipment of that metal from Ezion-geber (Elath) contributed to it (1 Kings 9:26).

The most ambitious building projects of King Solomon were the Temple of Jerusalem (966–959) and the royal palace (966–953) for which Solomon imported timber from Tyre (1 Kings 5:15-32; 2 Chr 2:3-16) in exchange for wheat and oil (1 Kings 5:11). Administrative provinces were created, often not respecting the traditional (tribal) divisions. Each of the twelve provinces, excluding Judah, had to provide taxes and compulsory work for a whole month by rotation (1 Kings 4:7, 19-20). This increasingly irritated the northern population groups and provoked Jeroboam's failed coup. Jeroboam fled to Egypt (an unfriendly gesture on the part of the Egyptians vis-à-vis Solomon; see the next paragraph) where he stayed until Solomon's death (1 Kings 11:26-40).

The biblical documents report some puzzling aspects of Solomon's reign. For instance, Gezer, a short distance northwest of Jerusalem, was captured by the then Pharaoh of Egypt (!) and burned. He gave the city to his daughter as a dowry when she married Solomon (1 Kings 9:16)! Similarly, how are we to understand the cession of twenty Galilean cities to Hiram of Tyre? If we add to that picture that Edom became increasingly restive (1 Kings 11:14-22), as did Aram under Rezon (11:23-25), it can be said that there were already at that time cracks in the structure of the Davidic-Solomonic empire.

The Two Kingdoms at the Time of Jeroboam II (787–747): SM 8

Shortly after the death of Solomon in 933 the kingdom split into two parts. Rehoboam, son of Solomon (933–926) upset the authorities of "all Israel" (that is, the tribes north of Benjamin with the exception of Gezer and Ajalon, which remained in Judah, while Jericho was occupied by Israel), and they refused to submit to him (1 Kings 12:1-20; 2 Chronicles 10). They rather enthroned Jeroboam I. The latter established his capital at Shechem (1 Kings 12:25), but soon moved it to Tirzah. The wars between north and south raged and followed diverse fortunes, with border towns alternately being annexed by Israel or Judah. Judah was in the uncomfortable position of being landlocked between Israel and the Philistines in the west, the Dead Sea and the desert in the south and east. It experienced both poverty and political stability down to the sixth century.

Rehoboam fortified fifteen cities, especially Lachish (2 Chr 11:5-12), but this did not prevent an Egyptian invasion of both Judah and Israel by Pharaoh Shishak (945–924) around 927 (1 Kings 14:25-28; 2 Chr 12:1-12; Shishak's Inscription at Karnak). The Pharaoh took all the riches accumulated by King Solomon in Jerusalem (in exchange, it appears, for not investing the city). Shishak's main aim was the control of trade routes in Palestine.

In 886 King Omri of Israel moved his capital to Samaria (a stroke of genius) and considerably increased the economic and cultural exchange with Phoenicia, thus bringing prosperity but also political and religious unrest (1 Kings 16:23-24).

King Ahab (875–853) married the Tyrian Jezebel. He built a huge stable for some five hundred horses at Megiddo, thus counting on a mobile force of intervention for the protection of his kingdom. He successfully repulsed an Aramean invasion (1 Kings 20:1-22). The dispute was over control of the commercial routes from east to west (from Damascus to Tyre) and from north to south (from Damascus through Transjordan to the Mediterranean ports or to Ezion-geber [Elath]). Several of the battles with the Arameans occurred in the vicinity of the strategic town of Ramoth-gilead. King Ahab was killed there in 853 (1 Kings 22:29-37; 2 Chr 18:28-34) in the battle of Qarqar against Shalmaneser II (see SM 9, The Assyrian Empire). This Assyrian king saw his invasion troops stopped by a coalition of Arameans and Israelites (!). This semi-success (the Assyrians were technically victorious) caused a lull in Assyrian expansion in that area, but when Ben-hadad of Aram attacked Gilead again, King Jehu of Israel appealed to Shalmaneser, who readily complied and set siege to Damascus and beyond. Shalmaneser's so-called "black obelisk" shows Jehu on his hands and knees paying tribute to the Assyrians (perhaps on Mount Carmel). Clearly in this way Jehu bought time for his country.

As the Assyrians were enmeshed in internal strife, however, the Arameans renewed their onslaught on Israel, going as far south as Aroer in Moab [controlled by Jehu] (2 Kings 10:32-33). They inflicted a crushing defeat on Jerusalem. But the Assyrian pressure on Aram mounted again and King Amaziah of Jerusalem (811–782) reclaimed Edom. However, things between north and south had worsened and Israel, under King Jehoash (803–787) invaded Judah, looting Jerusalem, its Temple and palace (2 Kings 14:8-14; 1 Chr 25:17-24). They then turned their belligerence toward Damascus, a venture that would eventually be completed by Jeroboam II.

Meanwhile in Judah, King Amaziah was assassinated and his son Uzziah enthroned (783). This able statesman was helped by favorable circumstances, namely the weakening of Aram—left bloodless by the Assyrians—the internecine strife in Assyria, and the persistent insignificance of Egypt. Uzziah would rule in Jerusalem for forty-one years (until 742). Jeroboam II in Israel would also have a long reign of forty years. Both kings helped to make the eighth century a period of remarkable prosperity in Palestine.

Jeroboam's domain included Lebo-hamath, far beyond Damascus (cf. Amos 6:13) in the north (2 Kings 14:25-29). As to Judah, it also controlled a vast territory down to Elath on the Red Sea. Uzziah of Judah set military/agricultural settlements in the Negeb (including Arad, Beersheba, and Hormah, cf. 2 Chr 26:2-10) down to Ezion-geber. He regained control of the trade routes (the Sea Route, the King's Highway, the Edom-Gaza Route).

It was during that glowing era that the prophet Amos denounced the triumphant materialism of the time (see references on the map). By contrast, 2 Kings 14:25 tells of the prophet Jonah ben Amittai of Gath-hepher prophesying to Jeroboam II great military successes in "restoring the border of Israel from Lebo-hamath as far as the Sea of the Arabah." That text, however, does not condone Jeroboam's "doing what was evil in the sight of the LORD" (v. 24).

The Assyrian Empire: SM 9

The northern kingdom of Israel fell into a state of chaos with the death of Jeroboam II in 746. No less than three kings reigned in succession in one year. In 745 Tiglat-pileser III succeeded to the Assyrian throne. He gave Assyria its greatest expansion, from the Persian Gulf to the valley of the Nile in Egypt. Tiglat-pileser inaugurated the policy of annexation of conquered territories and the deportation of local populations.

A coalition of states under the leadership of King Uzziah of Judah could not resist the Assyrian pressure (2 Kings 15:19-20). Later, Israel and Syria joined forces against the common enemy Assyria, but Jotham of Judah (740–735) refused to participate in the alliance. The same attitude was adopted by his son Ahaz (735–716?) in Jerusalem. Syria and Israel invaded Judah as far as Ezion-geber (to be captured a little later by the Edomites, who retrieved their independence). The Philistines also struck and captured Judean cities. Jerusalem itself was besieged. Then Ahaz resorted to an ill-fated appeal to Tiglat-pileser for help (2 Kings 16:5-10; 2 Chr 28:6-21).

Tiglat-pileser launched a series of three successive campaigns (734, 733, 732; 2 Kings 15:29). In 734 he moved down the coast to Egypt destroying Gezer and Gaza on the way. In 733 his aim was to neutralize Israel. Marching from the north through Galilee, the Assyrians captured the fortress of Hazor by storm and burned it to the ground. An Assyrian army took Acco and Dor. Another army occupied the Gilead region. A third prong of the Assyrian attack stormed the Great Plain of Megiddo and the latter was also utterly destroyed. On his third drive in 732 Tiglat-pileser captured Damascus and summoned Ahaz of Judah there to pay obeisance to him.

In 727 Tiglat-pileser died and Israel rebelled. The Assyrians laid siege to the city of Samaria for three years (724–721); in 721 Samaria fell and Israel was dismantled forever (2 Kings 17:4-46; 18:9-11). Israelites were deported by Sargon II to towns in Gozen on the Habor River, to Halah, just north of Nineveh, and to Media (2 Kings 17:6, 24; 18:10-11; 1 Chr 5:26). They were replaced by peoples from the region of Babylon (2 Kings 17:24). This mixed population was later known as "Samaritans."

In Judah, King Hezekiah (716–687) joined the anti-Assyrian coalition in 713–712. In preparation for the war he built the impressive water tunnel of Siloam to insure supply for Jerusalem during a siege (2 Kings 20:20; 2 Chr 32:30). He received Babylonian ambassadors in Jerusalem (2 Kings 20:12-19; Isa 39:1-8), and signed a treaty with Egypt, both in spite of the prophet Isaiah's opposition (Isa 30:1-5; 31:1-3).

In 701 Sennacherib of Assyria launched a major attack to the south. He destroyed Tyre, then Joppa, but was met by an Egyptian army at Eltekeh, which he routed. He then encircled Jerusalem, cutting it off from the rest of the world (cf. Isa 10:28-32). Capturing the stronghold of Lachish in the Shephelah, Sennacherib systematically devastated Judah. Hezekiah had no other choice, it seemed, but to surrender. The prophet Isaiah, however, urged Hezekiah to further resistance. Jerusalem would not fall (Isa 37:33). The prophet proved to be right, in spite of the contrary opinion of the prophet Micah of Moreshet-gath. Overnight the Assyrians fled after being decimated (by a plague epidemic?) (2 Kings 19:35; 2 Chr 32:22). But in consequence of those events Judah remained almost a bloodless corpse.

In 671–667 the Assyrians conquered Egypt, but in the second half of the seventh century that country broke away. Furthermore, Babylon and Media attacked Assyria. Nineveh fell in 612 to Nabopolassar of Babylon (cf. Nahum). Judah recovered its independence and prosperity under King Josiah (640–609; cf. 2 Kings 22:1–23:30; 2 Chronicles 34–35). Counseled by the prophets Zephaniah and Jeremiah, the king initiated religious reforms (2 Kings 22:3–24:28; 2 Chr 34:8–35:9). He succeeded in pushing back Judah's borders in both the south and north, in effect reunifying under his rule the territories of Judah and Israel.

The Babylonian Empire and the Conquest of Judah: SM 10

The Babylonians captured the Assyrian capital, Nineveh, in 612 (cf. Nahum). Pharaoh Neco in 609 rushed to the rescue of his former Assyrian enemies at Megiddo, but Judah refused passage to the Egyptians and King Josiah lost his life that year in the battle of Megiddo. The Egyptians, however, were routed by Nebuchadnezzar in 605 at Carchemish. The Babylonians extended their domination over Judah as well.

In 601 Jehoiakim of Jerusalem rebelled against Babylon, thus alienating Jeremiah the prophet who, for all practical purposes, appeared to be collaborating with the Babylonians. The king died in 598 and was succeeded by his son Jehoiachin. The latter, attacked also from the south by Edomites and perhaps other nations (cf. Jer 13:19), capitulated to the Babylonians in 597. He was replaced as king by his uncle Zedekiah (2 Kings 24:10-17; 2 Chr 36:6-10). Foolishly Zedekiah, encouraged by Egyptian promises of help, revolted in 589. Nebuchadnezzar devastated the whole country. The siege of Jerusalem lasted two years (cf. 2 Kings 25:21; Jer 39:4-9; 52:8-15). Some places were so utterly destroyed as to become forever uninhabitable. With exiles in the east and refugees in Egypt and other southern lands, the so-called Jewish Diaspora began. It seems that after all the massacres, exiles, and emigrations the Judean population was reduced from some 250,000 to about 20,000.

Gedaliah was appointed governor of Judah, to which he gave a semblance of restoration, but he was murdered in 586 by one Ishmael at the instigation of the king of Ammon. There was another flight from Jerusalem to Egypt, particularly by army officers who compelled Jeremiah to accompany them. These military men eventually became mercenaries in the Egyptian army and were garrisoned in Yeb (Elephantine) in the distant south of Egypt.

The Judeans who were deported to Babylonia remained for the most part grouped along the "Chebar River" (the so-called "rivers of Babylon" in Psalm 137), a canal running for some hundred miles between Babylon and Erech. There occurred among the exiles a major renaissance of spirituality and literary activity that transformed the disaster of exile into a religious peak in Israel's history.

In 550 the Persian Cyrus II ("the Great") conquered the Median capital city of Ecbatana, then Sardis, capital of King Croesus of Lydia, in 546. Cyrus conquered Babylon in 539, thus terminating what had been the Babylonian empire.

The Persian Empire: SM 11

Cyrus II (559–530) revealed himself as a tolerant monarch. In 538 he allowed the Jews to return to Zion and rebuild their Temple (2 Chr 36:22-23; Ezra 1:1-5; 6:3-5). The journey would be some thousand miles long (via the trade routes). There were successive waves of returnees, but their number remained small. The Judean country, a province of Persia, was no larger than forty miles by thirty, totaling some twenty-one villages. It stretched from the Jordan River at Jericho to the Mediterranean coast at Ono, and from Bethel in the north to Beth-zur in the south (north of Hebron, which was then held by the Edomites). Judea was part of the "fifth satrapy" called "Beyond the River [Euphrates]" ruled from Damascus by a governor. At the end of the sixth century the governor's name was Tattenai. Although the "second Temple" in Jerusalem would have much less imposing dimensions than the Solomonic one, internal and external difficulties delayed its completion. It was finally dedicated in 515.

Chief among the aforementioned difficulties was the menace of total assimilation of the returnees in the medley of populations, the outcome of the Assyrian and Babylonian shuffling of peoples. Realizing the danger, Nehemiah obtained permission to come to Jerusalem from Susa where he was serving the king. He reformed the Jewish community, dissolving mixed marriages and imposing the Torah of old as the state law in the province. Nehemiah rebuilt the city wall in fifty-two days (Neh 2:17–7:3). The area thus protected was considerably smaller than pre-exilic Jerusalem. Ezra, a Babylonian Jew, came in 428 (?) with contributions from his coreligionists for the Temple. Besides becoming governor of the Judean province he was a scribe who explained the meaning of the Law to the Jews.

Beginning in the fifth century commerce with Greece began to thrive; many Greek merchants settled in Syro-Palestine in harbors such as Acco, Dor, Ashdod, and Gaza. The ancient Edom became home to northwestern Arabs, later known as Nabateans, especially around Petra. The Edomites, pushed into the desert, settled around Beersheba and Hebron.

Meanwhile, the Persians conquered Egypt (522, then again in 519) and their empire extended from the Indus River to Upper Egypt and Libya, and to Thrace and Macedonia, being thus present on three continents. Under Darius I (522–486) the "Royal Road" was opened from Sardis in Lydia to Persepolis in Shushan, via Babylon and Susa. Concurrently a canal was dug connecting the Nile delta to the Gulf of Suez on the Red Sea.

Also during Darius's reign the Ionian cities revolted. The Persians suffered a major defeat at Marathon (490), but later Xerxes (486–464) was successful at Thermopylae while his fleet was destroyed at Salamis. On another front Egypt retrieved its independence in 459 and more decisively in 404. Artaxerxes III, however, reconquered it in 342; it remained under Persian control until Alexander the Great came on the scene. Darius III Codomanus (336–330) was the last

Persian king. He was killed by the Persian Bessus, and Persia fell into Alexander's hands.

The World of the Greeks (Fourth Century): SM 12

With the increase of their power mainland Greek cities began to covet the Aegean coast of Asia Minor, especially after defeating the Persians at Marathon (490) and Salamis (480). The heir of Macedonia, Alexander (356–323), was educated by Aristotle. After his accession to the throne he subdued first the independent Greek cities and then turned his attention to the east. He crossed over to Asia in 334 and began his irresistible conquest of Asia Minor and the Levant. He won a decisive battle at Issus over Darius III in 333. Pushing southward through Palestine, he invaded Egypt and founded on the Mediterranean coast the city of Alexandria that was to become a universal center of culture in the Greco-Roman world. As Samaria had revolted against the governor appointed there by Alexander, the latter destroyed the city and rebuilt it as a Greek *polis* with an important number of Macedonian colonists.

Alexander crossed the Euphrates and the Tigris to meet the regrouped army of Darius between Arbela and Gaugamela. The Persians were routed, thus opening up Alexander's way farther east: his fourteen-thousand-mile march ultimately took him to India. Under pressure from his own army, however, he changed course and turned back to the west through southern Persia to Babylon. There he died at the age of thirty-two.

From 323 to 301 the empire was in turmoil in the absence of a designated heir to Alexander; it was gradually parceled out among his generals. In 320 Ptolemy I of Egypt annexed Palestine, while Syria, Mesopotamia, and Persia were ruled by Seleucus I. The Ptolemaic rule in Egypt lasted from 323 to 30 B.C.E. The Egyptian administration was in Greek hands and the country submitted to an intensive process of hellenization.

In the north Seleucus I reigned over a vast empire. Palestine became a bone of contention between the Ptolemies and the Seleucids for most of the third century B.C.E. Under the Ptolemies the administration of Palestine was also in Greek hands, with the exception of the high priesthood in Jerusalem. Several cities were renamed according to Hellenistic tastes: Acco became Ptolemais; Ashod, Azotus; Beth-shan, Scythopolis; Rabbah of Ammon, Philadelphia. In 198 the Seleucids conquered Palestine in their turn, to the relief of many in Jerusalem. The Syrians created the province of Samaria that included Judea, Galilee, and Perea in Transjordan. To the south of it was the province of Idumea and to the east of it that of Galaaditis.

The powerful Seleucid king Antiochus III was defeated by the Romans at Thermopylae in 191 and in Magnesia in 190. By the treaty of Apamea he relinquished Asia Minor to the Romans and his son, the future Antiochus IV, was taken as hostage to Rome. The latter returned to Syria in time to usurp power over his brother in 175 and to take the throne of his father. A difficult period for Judea had begun, leading eventually to the Maccabean revolt.

Antiochus IV's (174–164) dedication to Hellenism led him to proscribe Judaism as an outdated superstition. Circumcision, Sabbath keeping, dietary laws, and Scripture reading were prohibited (1 Macc 1:41-64). In the Temple was installed the "abomination of desolation" (cf. Dan 11:31; 12:11), that is, the cult of Zeus Olympios (2 Macc 6:1-11). Dominating the Temple building, a fortress called the Acra was erected and manned with Syrians. Many Jews were killed or enslaved; others adopted Hellenism (2 Maccabees 4).

First Maccabees tells of the revolt of a priest by the name of Mattathias Hasmoneas and his five sons, John, Simon, Judas, Eleazar, and Jonathan, in Modein (about twenty miles northwest of Jerusalem). Mattathias was joined by many who were hostile to the hellenization of their country and religion. Judas "Maccabeus" ("Hammer") became their strategist, and a successful one at that. The country progressively passed under rebel control through guerrilla warfare, effectively cutting the main arteries to Jerusalem.

The Hellenized Jews in Jerusalem appealed to the governor of Syria (with jurisdiction over Judea) but his forces were foiled. In 165, for example, a military expedition with thousands of heavily armed men, led by Nicanor and Gorgias, was utterly defeated at Emmaus (1 Macc 3:27–4:25). Eventually Lysias' attack ended with a loss of five thousand men (1 Macc 4:26-35). Judas entered Jerusalem triumphantly and in December 164 rededicated the Temple and rekindled the holy lamps *(hanukkiah)* thus instituting the festival of Hanukkah (1 Macc 4:36-61). Nicanor was killed in 161 by Judas' men at Adasa, a victory celebrated thereafter as "Nicanor's Day" (cf. 1 Macc 7:26-50).

Lysias, however, returned with an enormous army. First Maccabees 6:28-30 speaks of 100,000 infantry, 20,000 cavalry, and 32 elephants. Following the Route of the Sea to the south and then turning north to Marisa and Hebron, Lysias launched a major attack to the north at Beth-zur. The Jews regrouped in Beth-zechariah but the war-elephants charged and Eleazar Maccabeus was killed under the mass of one of them. The Jews fled north toward Samaria. Lysias was victorious but he could not linger in Palestine; thus he struck a compromise treaty granting religious freedom (1 Macc 6:55-63). Alcimus, a Hellenized Jew, became high priest (2 Macc 13:3-8; on Alcimus see also 1 Macc 7:5-25).

Taking advantage of dynastic strife in Syria after the death of Antiochus IV, Judas resumed guerrilla activity, but the high priest Alcimus in Jerusalem appealed to the Syrians. General Nicanor took the lead in repeated attempts to quell the revolt. He died on the battlefield and his troops were severely routed. The Syrians then sent their best general, Bacchides, with a military elite corps. This time Judas himself was killed and his guerrillas were crushed. His brother Jonathan thereafter led the rebellion (160–143). Again the Hellenized Jews in Jerusalem called Bacchides to their help, but the battles remained indecisive and Bacchides, pressed by other military requirements at home, decided to negotiate and return to Antioch (156).

King Demetrius I of Syria saw his rule threatened by the dynastic claims of one Alexander Balas (152). Both he and Balas were anxious to get Jonathan as an ally and they outbid each other by granting him privileges, including the high priesthood, although Jonathan's genealogy did not warrant such an honor. Demetrius I died in battle with his rival, and Demetrius II, his son, tried to punish Jonathan for his support of Balas. The attempt failed and Demetrius, pressed by other concerns at home, confirmed Jonathan in all his powers (145).

Military successes piled up in Upper Galilee, even as far north as Hamath. Jonathan sided with Trypho, one of Alexander Balas' generals, against Demetrius II and was able to inflict repeated defeats on Demetrius. He even at some point entered Damascus in triumph. But Trypho betrayed him and had him killed. In order to regain the backing of the Jews, so treacherously double-crossed, Demetrius granted them full independence in 142 under Simon Maccabeus (143–134) "high priest commander and leader of the Jews." For the first time since 586 Judah was again a free state.

Simon conquered Joppa and Gerasa, expelling the Gentile population and turning the place into a military base. In 141 the Syrian garrison of the Acra in Jerusalem surrendered. All looked promising for Simon, but internally his high priesthood did not remain unchallenged (1 Macc 14:25-43).

In 139 the new Syrian king Antiochus VII wanted to reclaim Judea. Simon and two of his sons were treacherously murdered. John Hyrcanus, the surviving son of Simon, took over civil and religious power in Jerusalem (134–104). He considerably expanded Judea's borders, annexing part of Samaria (128) and all of Idumea (125). The Idumeans were coerced into accepting Judaism. Before his death John Hyrcanus divided powers into religious and secular, but his son Aristobulus I seized both when acceding to the throne. He conquered Galilee, whose non-Jewish population was coerced to convert to Judaism.

In 103 Aristobulus was succeeded by his brother Alexander Janneus (103–76). Under his reign (the Hasmoneans had by then proclaimed themselves kings in addition to being high priests) the kingdom nearly matched the extent of the Davidic empire of old, stretching from Dan in the north to Beersheba in the south, and from the Mediterranean coast to Transjordan. In the south, however, Alexander Janneus clashed repeatedly with a new enemy, the Nabateans, for the control of the south-north and east-west trade routes. The Nabateans were an Arab people who had evicted the Edomites from their land and made the rock-cut city of Petra their capital. Janneus, therefore, built impressive fortresses in the desert of Judah—Masada, Macherus and Hyrcania—and, in the mountains overlooking the Jordan River, Alexandrium.

Janneus favored Greek elements of the population and the Hellenistic style of cities. In 90 B.C.E. the Pharisees—a religious party in Judaism whose origins cannot be dated with precision, but that had already clashed with John Hyrcanus on religious grounds—rebelled; civil war erupted. Janneus, with the support of the Sadducees—another sect characterized by its attachment to the Temple, its aristocratic members, and its opposition to Pharisaism, especially to their claim of the existence of two Torahs (written and oral)—massacred six thousand Jews. The Pharisees, in 88 B.C.E., called on the Syrian troops. The conflict lasted six years, ending with the defeat of the Pharisees, of whom eight hundred were crucified while their wives and children were slaughtered before their eyes. Fifty thousand Jews had lost their lives. Janneus had been impressed, however, by the popularity of the Pharisees. He recommended to his wife and heir Salome Alexandra that she work closely with them in the future. Janneus died of alcoholism.

Salome did just as her husband had recommended. She inherited the civil rule (76–67) and appointed Alexander Janneus' son, Hyrcanus II, as high priest to the chagrin of his brother Aristobulus II. She turned over much of the internal governance of the land to the Pharisees. Many Sadducees were executed by Pharisaic courts. In 67, at her death, Aristobulus II swiftly defeated and ousted his brother and became himself high priest as well as governor (67–63). In response Hyrcanus II, who had fled to Petra for asylum, allied himself with Antipater II of Idumea and with Aretas, king of the Nabateans, to attack Jerusalem. But Rome, which was increasingly present on the scene in the Levant, confirmed Aristobulus as high priest.

The Roman Empire (ca. 150 C.E.): SM 13

Pompey, after his victory over Hannibal of Carthage, arrived in Damascus in 63 B.C.E. Rome had extended its hegemony over Macedonia and Achaia, then over Asia Minor and farther east to Bithynia and Pontus. Pompey undertook to campaign against the Nabateans with the help of Aristobulus II of Jerusalem, but during the concerted attack Aristobulus withdrew his troops. Pompey was incensed; he turned against Aristobulus, with the complicity of Jews who were backing Hyrcanus II as high priest. Twelve thousand Jews were killed and Pompey entered Jerusalem and the Temple (including the Holy of Holies). As expected he installed Hyrcanus II again as high priest (63–40). The independence of Judea came to an end after only about eighty years.

Pompey granted semi-independence to Samaria (which thus separated Judea from Galilee) as well as to the cities along the Mediterranean coast (thus cutting Judea off from access to the sea), and to cities east of the Jordan River that would be populated by Gentiles and form the Decapolis ("ten cities"). The Itureans received the Gaulanitis region. In short, the Judeans were "contained." All the Hasmonean achievements had been undone.

Meanwhile Julius Caesar was claiming leadership in Rome (49) and had overcome Pompey's opposition. When he pursued the latter in Egypt the high priest Hyrcanus II directed the Jews of Egypt to back Caesar. The latter was also helped by the Idumean Antipater, to whom in return he granted the title of procurator for the Palestinian region, while Hyrcanus was confirmed as high priest in Jerusalem (42).

Antipater's son Herod became governor of Galilee by Caesar's favor (see Josephus, *Ant.* 15.360), but he had first to quell rebellious elements. He levied heavy taxes to help the Roman Cassius, governor of Syria, in his opposition to Mark Antony. The latter gained the upper hand, however, and became ruler of the Roman holdings in the Levant. In Judea meanwhile there were repeated unsuccessful rebellions against Rome. Coming on the scene, Crassus, one member of the First Triumvirate in Rome, plundered the Jerusalem Temple, stealing great sums of money as well as the sacred vessels.

Crassus eventually died in battle against the Parthians, for in 40 B.C.E. the Parthians invaded Palestine. In Jerusalem Antigonus, son of Aristobulus II, took sides with the Parthians, who appointed him high priest and king in place of Hyrcanus II. As for Herod, he had fled to Rome where he was designated by the Senate as king of Judea, Samaria, and western Idumea. But Herod had to fight to take his "own," in particular from Antigonus in Jerusalem (the Parthians were already gone). Herod landed in Ptolemais in 39, captured Joppa with a mercenary army, then hurried south to Masada where his family had sought refuge in his absence. He then turned north to capture Sepphoris in Galilee. Jerusalem fell in 37 to the combined Roman and Herodian forces, and Antigonus was beheaded.

Herod faced strong opposition from the Pharisees and even from part of the aristocracy, but he systematically eliminated his enemies (some forty-five Sadducees were executed, for instance, and their properties confiscated). Herod's "Jewishness" was suspect to many because he was an Idumean (see LD map on the Hasmonean period). In a move to make himself more popular Herod married the Hasmonean Mariamne in 38 B.C.E. Her brother Aristobulus, although seventeen years old at the time, was appointed high priest and became very popular. Herod took umbrage at this and dispatched him to his death; eventually even Mariamne was executed in 29, along with her mother Alexandra and several members of the Hasmonean family.

Queen Cleopatra VII of Egypt connived with Antony and received from him large chunks of Herod's land in 35 B.C.E., including the coastlands of Philistia and Phoenicia except for the cities of Tyre and Sidon. Cleopatra also received Jericho on Herod's eastern border, but Antony was defeated in 31 by Octavian (Caesar Augustus) and he and Cleopatra committed suicide in 30. Herod had shifted allegiance to Octavian at the right time, after handing a crushing defeat to the Nabateans in Philadelphia in 31. Octavian returned to him his lost territories and added to them Samaria and the Mediterranean coast from Gaza to Strato's Tower (renamed Caesarea by Herod the Great; on this reversal of fortune see Josephus, *War* 1.398). With the passage of years other territories were granted to him by the Romans, so that the country stretched from Beersheba to Panias of the Itureans and included Perea in Transjordan and the Trachonitis and Auranitis in the northeast. His domain was bordered by the Nabateans in the south and the Decapolis in the central north (see SM 14, "Jesus in His Land").

Herod established military colonies, one in Gaba (or Gabae) overlooking the Jezreel Valley, another in Esbus (Heshbon) on the southeast border of his land, against invasions from the Nabateans. Herod built or rebuilt fortresses (from north to south: Cypros [by *Jericho*], *Hyrcania, Herodium, Macherus, Masada, Malatha* [names in italics figure on SM 14]). He attracted Gentiles to inhabit cities including Sebaste [Samaria] and Caesarea Maritima [Strato's Tower] which Herod developed into a major harbor, larger than the Greek facilities, with a temple dedicated to Augustus and other typically Greek edifices. The city grew in importance and became the capital of the country for the next six hundred years.

In Jerusalem Herod rebuilt the Temple on a magnificent scale. He likewise rebuilt the Antonia fortress overlooking the Temple precincts, as well as a theater, an amphitheater, and a stadium-hippodrome. Everywhere were traces of his ambitious constructions, in the new city of Phasaelis north of Jericho, at Hebron where he raised a massive shrine over the burial place of the Patriarchs, and elsewhere throughout the land.

Herod died in 4 B.C.E. He had executed two of his ten wives and three of his sons (Augustus once said, "I would sooner be Herod's pig than Herod's son!"), his brother-in-law, and his wife's grandfather [Hyrcanus II] (See Josephus, *War* 1.431–444; 1.551).

Jesus in His Land: SM 14

Herod's will divided his kingdom into three main parts (see Josephus, *Ant.* 17.317–318):

1. His son Archelaus received Judea, Samaria and Idumea.
2. Another of his sons, Herod Antipas, became tetrarch of Galilee and Perea, although these are not contiguous regions.
3. Philip was to be tetrarch over mainly non-Jewish territory to the northeast of the Lake of Galilee: Gaulanitis, Batanea, Trachonitis, and Auranitis. Salome, sister of Herod, received the cities of Jamnia and Azotus (Ashdod) on the Mediterranean shore, and Phasaelis on the Jordan River (see *Ant.* 1.321).

The three brothers rushed to Rome with conflicting claims while Jerusalem was in the grip of grave riots. The Roman governor of Syria, Varus, quelled the rebellion and left a legion in Jerusalem, but the Romans tried in addition to seize Herod's treasure and were successfully resisted by Archelaus's soldiers. The whole country became restless. Anarchy spread. Varus received considerable help from the Nabatean Aretas IV. Descending southward, they burned city after city from Sepphoris to Emmaus and recaptured Jerusalem (this was the so-called "war of Varus"). Two thousand Jews were crucified (see *Ant.* 17.295).

Archelaus was confirmed ruler (but not king) of Judea in 4 B.C.E., but because of his ruthlessness (see Matt 2:19-23), he was banished to Gaul in 6 C.E. (see *Ant.* 17.344). Samaria, Judea, and Idumea became the Roman province of Judea.

Herod Antipas ruled in Galilee and Perea for forty-three years (4 B.C.E. to 39 C.E.). He is mentioned twenty-four times in the NT as "Herod." Herod Antipas is notorious in the gospel for ordering the decapitation of John the Baptist and for his interrogation of Jesus before his crucifixion. John's execution occurred at Macherus (cf. *Ant.* 18.116–119). Herod Antipas's province stretched from the Esdraelon [Jezreel] valley to the cities of Gischala and Thella in the north, with the Jordan River as the eastern border and Chabulon the most western town (cf. Josephus, *War* 3.3.1–2 [35–43]). The region was very fertile and densely populated. Its principal cities were Sepphoris, Jotapata, Japhia, and Tiberias. Herod had built the last-mentioned city for his capital by the warm springs on the southwest shore of the lake, and called it Tiberias for the Roman emperor (see *Ant.* 18.2.3 [36–38]).

Nazareth lies between Sepphoris and Japhia. Some places around the lake mentioned in the gospel remain unidentified, such as Magadan (Matt 15:39) called Dalmanutha in Mark 8:9; some Matthew manuscripts have Magdala (apparently the native place of Mary Magdalene), while Josephus seems to call the same place Taricheae (*War* 3.10.1–10 [462–542]). Capernaum is on the northwest shore of the lake; it was probably a customs post near the border with Philip the Tetrarch's territory (Matt 9:9) and a garrison village for a centurion and his men (Matt 8:5-9). This centurion, although a Gentile, had built the city synagogue (Luke 7:5). An ancient Christian tradition has it that Tabgha (Heptapegon), lying between Capernaum and Gennesaret, was the site where the Sermon on the Mount occurred (Matthew 5–7), as well as the feeding of the five thousand (Matt 14:13-21) and the appearance of the risen Christ to his disciples (John 21).

Chorazin lies two miles to the northwest of Capernaum. There Jesus performed miracles (Matt 11:10-24). As to Bethsaida, also important in the gospel, its location is unsure. It may be the (Bethsaida) Julias at a short distance north of the lake, in an area where the distinction between Galilee and Philip's territory was somewhat fuzzy (John 12:21 "in Galilee"). Philip developed Bethsaida (the birthplace of Jesus' disciples Peter, Andrew, and Philip: John 1:44; 12:21) and married Salome, the very one who had demanded the head of John the Baptist.

A new Roman emperor, Caligula, banished Herod also to Gaul in 39 C.E.

Philip ruled his predominately Gentile region peacefully. He enlarged Panias as his capital and called it Caesarea Philippi. It was there that Peter confessed to Jesus that he saw in him the Messiah (Matt 16:13-20).

In spite of its name the Decapolis was composed at times of more than ten cities, mainly inhabited by a Gentile population. According to Mark 5:20 a formerly possessed man healed by Jesus went into the Decapolis to tell his story. The healing had occurred in "the region of the Gerasenes" or Gadarenes, or again Gergesenes (Matt 8:28; Mark 5: 1; Luke 8:26). Thus the site may have been Gerasa (today Jerash), but more probably Gadara as it lies closer to the lake, where the herd of swine hurled itself (Matt 8:32; swine are a sign that the area was occupied by non-Jews).

Jericho was a kind of royal estate with palaces, fortresses, aqueducts, plantations, palm trees, pools, and a well-traveled road to Jerusalem (setting of the parable of the Good Samaritan). This thoroughfare ran through Bethany, home of Mary, Martha, and Lazarus (John 11; hence it is called today el-Azarieh). From Bethany also Jesus rode on a donkey to Jerusalem and, later in the same week, to the "upper room" (Matt 21:1-11; 26:17-29). Jesus probably returned every night to Bethany.

Luke 17:11 speaks of an area "along the border between Samaria and Galilee" where Jesus healed ten lepers (among whom one was a Samaritan, 11:12-19). The precise location is uncertain, probably west-southwest of Scythopolis, in a town through which Galilean pilgrims on their way to Jerusalem would proceed. Josephus tells us that the pilgrims crossed the Esdraelon [Jezreel] valley and walked south for a minimum of three days (*Ant.* 20.118; *Life* 269), probably toward Shechem, Mount Gerizim, and Bethel. We are told that Jesus spoke with a Samaritan woman of the true living water (John 4:1-30). This may have been at Jacob's well near the town of Sychar (Shechem or its close vicinity).

Lying to the west of Jerusalem, Emmaus is mentioned as the place where Jesus appeared to two disciples after his resurrection (Luke 24:13-

35). The site is unknown although it might well be the modern village of Inwas.

Of course Jerusalem is also a central location in Jesus' history. (See LD "Jerusalem in the Time of Jesus" and LD "Jerusalem of the Old Testament.") First Jesus healed a hemiplegic man at the pool of Bethesda or Beth-zatha, north of the Temple mount near the Sheep Gate (John 5:1-14). On another occasion he healed a blind man whom he then sent to the pool of Siloam to purify himself (John 10). But Jerusalem is above all the site of the last events in Jesus' life.

These final occurrences must be prefaced with a note on Roman occupation of Palestine. Under Roman governors Judea, with Caesarea as its capital, lived in peace for a while. But in 26 C.E. a new governor arrived: Pontius Pilate, who proved to be a harsh ruler. The high priest of the time, Caiaphas, allied himself with Pilate for fear of provoking a direct intervention by Rome in Judea. It was under those circumstances that Jesus entered the Temple and knocked down the tables of money changers to the outrage of the "establishment," both religious and political. A few days later Jesus celebrated Passover with his disciples in the upper room (Matt 26:17-29; its location is unknown, although the Crusaders in the Middle Ages "identified" a structure still visited by pilgrims in the Old City of Jerusalem). After the meal they went to the garden of Gethsemane, at the foot of the Mount of Olives near the Kidron Valley. Arrested and condemned by Pilate (in Herod's palace?), Jesus was crucified and buried. A tradition that dates to the fourth century locates the tomb in a place now covered by the Church of the Holy Sepulchre.

Jesus had forecast the destruction of the Temple. Some years after his death, in 66 C.E., the "first Jewish revolt" erupted. Emperor Caligula had attempted to have his statue erected in the Holy Shrine. This was the last straw. Jerusalem and most of Judea threw off the Roman yoke. From 66 to 70, however, the Romans progressively quelled the rebellion. In 70 C.E. the Fifth, Tenth, and Fourteenth legions, about eighty thousand men, launched an attack against Jerusalem. The siege imposed a terrible hardship on the population. Late in July the Antonia fortress fell; then the Romans burned the Temple on the ninth of Ab (28 August). The city was entirely captured at the end of September of the same year. Josephus speaks of a million Jews killed and ninety-seven thousand taken captive. Titus ordered the city razed to the ground, save for three towers.

Paul's Movements Between His Conversion and the Jerusalem Conference (Gal 1:11–2:10): SM 15

This map shows the striking dynamism of the apostle Paul from his conversion "on the road to Damascus" to his return, after fourteen years of missionary work in Asia Minor and Achaia, to Jerusalem for the first Christian Council, the Apostolic Conference in Jerusalem (cf. Gal 2:1-10; Acts 15).

The arrows on the map follow the indications of Gal 1:11–2:10:

1. Paul goes to Arabia after his conversion. He spends an undetermined amount of time there.
2. He returns to Damascus.
3. After three years he goes to Jerusalem, where he spends fifteen days in the company of the apostle Peter ("Cephas" in Gal 1:18) and James, "the brother of the Lord" (1:19).
4. Paul leaves Jerusalem on his missionary journeys, beginning in the regions of Syria and Cilicia.
5. From these regions he proceeds to other parts of Asia Minor (modern Turkey) Thrace, Macedonia, and Achaia (north of the Pelopponese).
6. After fourteen years of missionary work in these areas Paul returns to Jerusalem for the Apostolic Conference.

Paul's Trip to Rome: SM 16

Between about 30 C.E., the approximate date of Jesus' death, and 70 C.E., the date of Jerusalem's destruction, the preaching of the gospel spread over the Roman world (Acts 13–28). The major figure among Christian missionaries was Saul of Tarsus, later renamed Paul. He studied in Jerusalem under Rabban Gamaliel (Acts 22:3) but adopted Christianity (Acts 9) and began to travel extensively, preaching the "Good News."

According to Acts Paul made three separate missionary journeys before his final journey to

Rome, drawn on this map. The cities marked with a triangle are cities Paul visited during these three early missionary journeys according to Acts.

Paul in Captivity (Acts 21–27)

According to the Acts of the Apostles, on his last visit to Jerusalem, when presumably he was carrying the contribution for the poor (Rom 16:25-26), Paul made a vow and went through certain purification rites in the Temple. He was arrested on the accusation of bringing a Gentile from Ephesus (Trophimus, Acts 21:29) into the Temple area. From Jerusalem Paul was transferred to a Caesarea prison where he spent two years (57–59). He appeared before two procurators in succession, Felix and Festus, and before the Jewish king Agrippa II. Finally Paul appealed to Caesar.

Sent to Rome at his own request, Paul was escorted by a centurion, Julius, and accompanied by a small group of believers, possibly including Luke. The ship proceeded to Sidon, Seleucia in Syria, and Myra in Lycia, and anchored in Cnidus (on the southwest coast of Asia Minor). But the sea became rough and, changing course, the ship sailed toward Crete, then along the southern side of the island until it reached Fair Havens. After this a "northeastern" wind drove the ship off course (Acts 27:14). It had to be undergirded with cords and unfreighted, eventually even untackled altogether (27:19). Paul promised the panic-stricken crew that no life would be lost. The ship wrecked, however, on the island of Malta; all 276 people on board were saved (27:37).

They wintered for three months in the island (Acts 28:11); then Julius and Paul continued with another ship to Syracuse (Sicily), Rhegium (southwestern tip of Italy), and landed at Puteoli, where a major thoroughfare led along the west coast to Rome. Local and Roman Christians came to greet Paul there and at the Three Taverns (28:15). Rome was inhabited by over a million people (half of them slaves and many more paupers). Augustine, later, spoke of Rome where the "lust of rule" was in the hands of a "more powerful few" while "the rest [were] worn and wearied" (*City of God* 1.30). Acts 28:30 says that Paul lived in Rome for two years (ca. 59–61). What happened after that is unknown. A letter of Clement of Rome (end of the first century) suggests that Paul was released and went to Spain. (In Rom 15:24-25 Paul mentions a plan to go to Spain). First Clement also says that after returning to Rome Paul was condemned and martyred.

Line Drawing Maps (LD)

Our Guide to the Maps would not be complete without some reference to the line drawing maps inserted within the various commentaries. Some of these are illumined by, and in turn illumine, the sacred text to which they are attached. Others, however, demand a minimum of historical survey to shed light on the whole and the details of a particular map. Some explanatory material on those few maps is therefore included here.

Table of Nations

This map is based on a striking list of peoples in Genesis 10 ("the descendants of Noah's sons"); see 1 Chr 1:4-23. The nations are distributed along three main divisions: the Semites, the Hamites, and the Japhetites. Geographically speaking, these represent Mesopotamia and Syro-Palestine; Egypt and Ethiopia, including Canaan in the north and Libya in the west; Greece and the Greek islands. The vantage point is clearly the land of Canaan.

Prophets of Israel and Judah

This map highlights places where prophets were born, where they exercised their vocation, or where special events occurred that had an influence on their ministry.

Beginning with Elijah, the following place names (from north to south) are evocative: Zarephath (jar of meal and cruse of oil, 1 Kings 17:16); Damascus; Mount Carmel (1 Kings 19); Jezreel (1 Kings 21:19); Samaria; Abel-meholah (where Elisha began to follow Elijah); Gilead (Elijah's birthplace); Gilgal; Jericho (2 Kings 2:11: Elijah is taken into heaven); Beersheba (Elijah is nourished by angels).

For Elisha we note Shunem (resurrection of a young man); Ramoth-gilead (anointing of Jehu); Dothan (the prophet guides Arameans from here to Samaria); Abel-meholah (Elisha's birthplace); Samaria (Elisha prophesies); Gilgal (miracles); Jericho (Elisha cleanses the waters); Jerusalem (Elisha is called "baldhead": 2 Kings 2:23); Arad (south of which Elisha prophesies the coming of a flood).

Significant for Amos are Tekoa (his point of departure); Jerusalem (references); and Bethel (Amos 7:10-17).

Jerusalem in the Time of Jesus

Jerusalem under Herod the Great (37–4 B.C.E.) expanded to the north, and under Herod Agrippa (41–44 C.E.) included Bezetha, a northern quarter, so that the city wall ran from the present-day Jaffa gate northwest to the present Russian Compound, then east to the Kidron Valley and south toward the Temple Mount where the wall stopped (see Josephus, *Bell.* 5.4.2-3 [147–160]).

For the line drawing maps within the commentaries on the gospels, see the notes above on map SM 14, "Jesus in His Land." For the map accompanying Paul's letters, see the notes on SM 15 and 16. For the map in Revelation of the seven churches of Asia Minor, see the notes on SM 16.

The Power of the Word of God

Armando J. Levoratti

> The word of God is living and active, sharper than any two-edged sword, piercing until it divides soul from spirit, joints from marrow; it is able to judge the thoughts and intentions of the heart. And before him no creature is hidden, but all are naked and laid bare to [his] eyes (Heb 4:12-13).

In this well-known biblical text the word of God is described as *living* and *active, sharper than any two-edged sword.* As God is the God who acts with power, God's word cannot fail to be active and powerful. Like a "sharp sword" or a "polished arrow" (Isa 49:2), it never fails to pierce through and through; there is no blunt side to it; it always cuts with one side or another, either saving or judging.

The piercing power of the word of God is such that it penetrates to the innermost depth of the human being. It scrutinizes and discerns *the thoughts and intentions of the heart.* The heart is here, as always in the Scriptures, the central seat of human personality, the deep font of human life in all its aspects, spiritual, intellectual, moral, and emotional. In the innermost center of personality where everyday choices as well as radical decisions are made the believer is regenerated by "the living and enduring word of God" (1 Pet 1:23). This is the place where the word must be received and kept; it is there that the word does its work, as it was experienced by the disciples on the road to Emmaus: "Were not our hearts burning within us while he was talking to us on the road, while he was opening the scriptures to us?" (Luke 24:32). But God's word does not take the shape only of a spoken or written word. An event can likewise be a word of God and must therefore be kept in the heart, as did Mary with the events of Jesus' infancy: "Mary treasured all these words and pondered them in her heart" (Luke 2:19; cf. 2:51).

The essential character and inexhaustible vitality and efficacy of the word of God is clearly defined in Isa 55:10-11: "as the rain and the snow come down from heaven, and do not return there until they have watered the earth, making it bring forth and sprout, giving seed to the sower and bread to the eater, so shall my word be that goes out from my mouth; it shall not return to me empty, but it shall accomplish that which I purpose, and succeed in the thing for which I sent it."

God's word is an invitation that cannot be met with indifference or silence, but must be accepted or refused. At the conclusion of the Sermon on the Mount, Jesus contrasts those who hear his words and put them into practice with those who hear but do not do them. The first are like someone who builds a house on rock; the others like one who builds a house on sand (Matt 7:24-26 // Luke 6:47, 49). These metaphors introduce a perspective of judgment. Each will be judged according to his or her attitude toward the word. Thus Christ proclaims, "the words that I have spoken to you are spirit and life" (John 6:63), but says of those who reject him, "on the last day the word that I have spoken will serve as judge" (John 12:48).

The Word of God in Creation and Salvation History

Even the words of everyday speech were for ancient Hebrews more than sounds conveying ideas. Words were not transient sounds that no longer exist when their vibrations cease. They were felt to be charged with the vital force of the speaker, and once uttered they continued to exert their power even in the speaker's absence. A deathbed curse or blessing was especially powerful; Isaac could not take back the blessing he had given by mistake to Jacob (Gen 27:27-40), and the words of the dying Jacob and Moses are represented as determining factors in the subsequent history of the Israelite tribes (Gen 49:1-27; Deut 33:1-29). Because of the active power of Balaam's word YHWH at first did not permit him to pronounce a curse against Israel (Num 22:12) and later changed his curse into a blessing (Deut 23:5; cf. Neh 13:2). To mention the name of God was all the more significant; it was not to be done lightly, as we are reminded in the fourth commandment. However, even though the Israelites conceived curses and blessings as necessarily producing their effects they did not attribute their efficacy in the last instance to the words themselves, but to the power of YHWH (cf. Num 23:8). Thus the word uttered through the prophet had the power of YHWH in it, and manifested its inherent potency in a given situation. Entirely in agreement with this conception, the centurion said to Jesus: "only speak the word, and my servant will be healed" (Matt 8:8).

The creative word of God is found at the beginning of everything. It both communicates and creates reality. By its unlimited power it gives existence to the beings it addresses. It is the powerful and fruitful source that brings into being: "he spoke, and it came to be; he commanded, and it stood firm" (Ps 33:9). "You spoke, and they were made. You sent forth your spirit, and they were created; there is none that can resist your voice" (Jdt 16:14). The universe, created by the word of God and subsisting only by it, also bears its imprint, its mark and traces. We see why the universe can be eloquent, and why "the heavens are telling the glory of God" (Ps 19:1[2]).

The psalmists like to describe the mastery of God's word over the forces of nature:

> He sends out his command to the earth;
> his word runs swiftly.
> He gives snow like wool;
> he scatters frost like ashes.
> He hurls down hail like crumbs—
> who can stand before his cold?
> He sends out his word and melts them (Ps 147:15-18).

But the word that at the beginning exerted its rule over the abyss of waters (Gen 1:1-13; Job 38:8-11; Sir 39:17) and imposed silence on the sea (Ps 65:7[8]; 89:9[10]; 107:29) shows its power also in the history of humankind (cf. Psalm 136). It sets in motion God's plan for humankind and directs it through every crisis. Without eliminating the free play of human action, God's word reveals the divine intentions for past, present, and future, and thus has an eminently prophetic import. It is the expression of God's will and purpose, the terms of God's covenant of grace, the warning of judgment against unfaithfulness. It is not dead letter, no utterance lost as soon as spoken in an unresponding void.

Sometimes the word precedes the interventions of God in history; it goes before and heralds; it "goes before the Lord to prepare his ways" (Luke 1:76; cf. Isa 40:3; Matt 3:2; Luke 1:17). In this way it announces more or less clearly what the future will be before God brings it to pass, and at the appointed time the power of the divine hand carries out the promise of God's word. Sometimes it comes later to interpret and illumine the depths of the meaning of the events now past.

In other cases the verbal communication of God with the human partner takes a dialogic form, showing in this way that whatever acts and encounters shaped the experience of God in the Bible, that experience crystallized in linguistic and literary statements. With Moses God speaks face to face, "clearly, not in riddles" (Num 12:7-8), as one speaks with a friend (Exod 33:11). In this verbal conversation the anthropomorphic aspect of the God of Israel is most profoundly retained, but at the same time the personal character of Israel's God is unambiguously asserted.

The whole Israelite people was set apart and privileged among all peoples because of the word God addresses to it: "He declares his word to Jacob, his statutes and ordinances to Israel. He has not dealt thus with any other nation; they do not know his ordinances" (Ps 147:19-20; cf. Rom 9:4). Israel was henceforth the privileged people of God because it listened to God's word and spoke it back in faith. The Law was not found in the unapproachable heights of heaven or beyond the seas: "No, the word is very near to you; it is in your mouth and in your heart for you to observe" (Deut 30:14). Paul applies this text to "the word of faith that we proclaim" and that must give rise to "believing in the heart" and "confession on the lips" (Rom 10:8-10).

The Word of God in Human Language

God speaks to human beings in human language, making use of the intelligent cooperation of some human servants and sending them to speak in God's name. The prophets were mouthpieces of YHWH. They had an irresistible impulse to proclaim the word they had heard when the "hand" of the Lord was upon them (cf. Ezek 37:1), and spoke in YHWH's name as spokespersons of YHWH's mind and will. The message and the commission to utter it were parts of the same overwhelming experience. Isaiah heard the voice of YHWH saying, "Whom shall I send, and who will go for us?" and he knew that the call was meant for him: "and I said, 'Here am I; send me!" (Isa 6:8). And YHWH declared to Jeremiah: "you shall go to all to whom I send you, and you shall speak whatever I command you" (Jer 1:7).

The narratives of prophetic vocation in the Bible are significant here. The word of God is wholly prevenient, a totally gratuitous initiative: the call surprises Moses in his solitude (Exod 3:1-14) and Samuel in his childish simplicity (1 Sam 3:1-18). Amos compares God's calling to the terrible roar of a lion: "The lion has roared; who will not fear? The Lord GOD has spoken; who can but prophesy?" (Amos 3:8). The vision of the Holy One terrified Isaiah because he knew himself as "a man of unclean lips," dwelling "among of a people of unclean lips" (Isa 6:5). In a deeply meaningful gesture God puts God's own words on the lips of Jeremiah (Jer 1:9) and tells him: "you shall serve as my mouth" (Jer 15:19; cf. 5:12-13; Luke 1:70; Acts 3:18, 21). God orders Ezekiel to eat the scroll that carries the prophetic message (Ezek 2:8–3:3), and he obeys the call even though he says "I went in bitterness in the heat of my spirit" (3:14). In proclaiming "Thus says the LORD" the messengers assert the commission they have received, their renunciation of their own words. Thus they become "filled with power, with the spirit of the LORD, and with justice and might, to declare to Jacob his transgression and to Israel his sin" (Mic 3:8).

The prophets gave testimony and explained their message in the situation in which they stood. With their new and disturbing message they threatened the prerogatives of those who held political, economic, and religious power. They risked their reputations and their lives by challenging the accepted standards of society, and faced their audience with the necessity of a moral decision. It was not a light matter to proclaim the prophetic word in such circumstances, always difficult, often disappointing, and sometimes dangerous (cf. Jeremiah 26). But with all their personal differences there was in all the prophets a characteristic common quality and a creative vitality, which accorded with their claim to speak the word of God.

The Word of Faith

The word of God is the "word of faith" (Rom 10:8). Faith is the expected human response to the preached word. We believe in the word (John 4:50; cf. Mark 1:15) but, being the object of faith, the word is also the source that gives rise to the very acceptance of itself. As prevenient grace, God's word carries within itself the grace of the beginning of faith: "faith comes from what is heard, and what is heard comes through the word of Christ" (Rom 10:17). So the believer accepts the message "not as a human word but as what it really is, God's word" (1 Thess 2:13). As for the apostolic word, given and received as the gospel of Jesus Christ, it is active and effective by virtue of what it proclaims: the word of reconciliation reconciles (2 Cor 5:18-20) and the word of salvation saves (Rom 1:16; 1 Cor 1:18); the word of grace brings grace (Acts 14:3; 20:32) and the word of life, or living word, communicates life (Heb 4:12). When received by the ear and welcomed into the heart, God's living word begets us a second time (1 Pet 1:23). As brought to birth by the word of truth we are the first fruits of the new creation (Jas 1:18).

The word constantly nourishes this faith, the growth of which will cease only with the end of our life on earth (Eph 2:8; cf. Rom 12:3). The nutritive character of the word is often taught in Scripture. Deuteronomy roundly declares that "one does not live by bread alone, but by every word that comes from the mouth of the LORD"

(Deut 8:3; cf. Acts 7:38), a text Christ will repeat during his temptations in the desert (Matt 4:4). The psalmist draws delight from the words of the promise: "How sweet are your words to my taste, sweeter than honey to my mouth!" (Ps 119:103; cf. 19:10[11]), and therefore seeks to find ever greater nourishment in them: "With open mouth I pant, because I long for your commandments" (Ps 119:131). Amid trials, contempt, and opposition Jeremiah reminds God how eagerly he had received God's word: "Your words were found, and I ate them, and your words became to me a joy and the delight of my heart" (Jer 15:16). In a vision and a gesture of startling symbolism God gives Ezekiel to understand that the divine word must be his food: "O mortal, eat what is offered to you; eat this scroll, and go, speak to the house of Israel. . . . I ate it; and in my mouth it was as sweet as honey" (Ezek 3:1, 3). Later the seer of Patmos will receive the same order from God's messenger (Rev 10:8-11).

The book of Wisdom makes the word of God superior to any earthly food: "O Lord . . . it is not the production of crops that feeds humankind but that your word sustains those who trust in you" (Wis 16:26). It is, consequently, a terrible divine punishment—a terrible hunger, said Amos—to be starved for God's word and not be able to find it:

> The time is surely coming, says the Lord GOD,
> when I will send a famine on the land;
> not a famine of bread, or a thirst for water,
> but of hearing the words of the LORD.
> They shall wander from sea to sea,
> and from north to east;
> they shall run to and fro, seeking the word of the LORD,
> but they shall not find it (Amos 8:11-12).

The word of God brings divine comfort to people in the depths of their being. That was the aim of Deutero-Isaiah: "Comfort, O comfort my people, says your God. Speak tenderly to Jerusalem, and cry to her that she has served her term, that her penalty is paid" (Isa 40:1-2). The psalmist, in turn, bases his dearest hopes in the word of God: "I wait for the LORD, my soul waits, and in his word I hope" (Ps 130:5; cf. 19:7-11[8-12]; 119:49-50), and Origen in turn says that "God's word is the soul's physician" (*On Exodus,* PL 12.269B).

In the Beginning was the Word

There is another consideration that deserves special attention. The OT emphasizes the dynamic, creative, and revealing character of the word of God. "I am now making my words in your mouth a fire, and this people wood, and the fire shall devour them," said the Lord to Jeremiah (Jer 5:14); and again: "Is not my word like fire, says the LORD, and like a hammer that breaks a rock in pieces?" (Jer 23:29). But when we turn to the NT we find that the activity that was characteristic of God alone is now shared by Jesus. To give effect to his will Jesus has only to utter it, and thus we are led to see that in Jesus is the power of the word of God. Jesus healed by a simple word (Matt 8:3; Mark 7:34; Luke 7:14); at a single word of command the demons were driven from the possessed (Matt 8:32); the winds and the sea obeyed his voice (Mark 4:39) and his words of forgiveness sufficed to blot out the sins of the paralytic (Matt 9:6; Mark 2:10-11).

In the synoptic gospels much attention is devoted to Jesus' preaching. It is carefully noted by Matthew that his audiences were astounded at the authority with which he taught (7:28), and a noticeable emphasis on his own words is indeed attributed by the evangelists to Jesus himself. Because the words of Christ have a self-realizing efficacy all the things that he has spoken must be fulfilled: "Heaven and earth will pass away, but my words will not pass away" (Matt 24:35).

A radically new conception of God's word enters with the gospel of John. John affirms the preexistence, the personality, and the divinity of the Word, and identifies it with Jesus Christ. Thus God completed in Jesus Christ the long process of revelation by enclosing the divine saving purpose in human flesh and blood.

In the prologue to his gospel John goes back to "the beginning," when apart from God nothing existed (1:1). Yet in that mysterious beforehand the Word was with God, mysteriously united with God as one person with another, and was itself God. Nothing was brought into existence without the creative intervention of the Word. It is the principle of all being, the source of all life, and the light that enlightens every human being. Yet it did not remain remote, a stranger to the world that is the Word's work: "The Word became flesh" (John 1:14), and its coming into the midst of our sin and death is the unsurpassable climax of the whole of God's revelation.

Jesus came into the world for the purpose of bearing witness to the truth (John 18:37). In the gospel of John there is no plurality of truths: Jesus himself is the Truth and he brings to the world this one and singular Truth of God in a decisive and definitive way. The "I" on the lips of Jesus has the same dignity as the "I" of YHWH: "No one has ever seen God. It is God the only Son, who is close to the Father's heart, who has made him known" (John 1:18).

Once the Word has been made flesh there can be only one "Word of God" in the strictest meaning of the term, namely the Word spoken by the Father from eternity and appearing on earth in flesh at one historical time. But it is clear that "he whom God has sent speaks the words of God" (John 3:34), and if the Word that is God was to come to all the world there had to be a process in which preached and written words would mediate belief in the risen Lord.

Word, Promise, and Covenant

God's word is revealed within a dispensation of *promise* and *covenant.* As a *promise* the word states today what God will do in the future for God's people. To promise is to pledge one's word; once uttered, the promise cannot be recalled. God cannot use divine power in such a way as to violate a promise God has made; that would mean unfaithfulness. Israel praises at length YHWH's fidelity to the oaths given to David, God's chosen one (Psalms 89; 132) and constantly reminds God of that promise, which is a source of courage and hope (Psalm 119). God's word will not pass away (Ps 119:140; cf. 19:8), has no alloy or deceit in it (Ps 18:30[31]). God's promise is true because God is faithful.

In *covenant* God enters freely into a bonded relationship with God's people, becoming their God as they become God's people. Israel was not a people already fully constituted that in addition became the people of God; Israel is only a people to the extent that it is the people of God. This is the value of the covenant: it establishes relationship with an interlocutor, a responsible partner who can respond in a genuine dialogue that cannot be avoided. God has "known" Israel (Amos 3:2); therefore Israel must "know" God (Hos 13:4; cf. 4:1). In the prophets the covenant takes on its rich conjugal meaning of intimacy, imitation, and mutual sharing. To be attuned to the alliance is to respond to a call, to consent to a vocation, to raise oneself to the level of dialogue.

The word is an act of one person addressing another; it is an invitation to some kind of personal interrelationship. Words separated from personal relationships eventually become stagnant and empty. The term of God's revelation is always a human being, the being who can respond consciously and freely to God's love. Therefore God requires and waits for the "yes" of the creature at every stage of the divine plan of salvation: the "yes" of the people at the making of the first covenant (Exod 24:3), its "amen" at the renewal of the covenant in the time of Ezra (Neh 8:6), the "let it be" of Mary at the dawn of the new dispensation (Luke 1:26-38), the "amen" that humankind, in Jesus Christ, says to God's glory (2 Cor 1:20-21), and the "Come!" that the Bride, taught by the Spirit, says to the Lord (Rev 22:17).

There is a sharing of creative powers; both God and the human partner are effectively involved in the process. God's creative power is certainly sovereign, but the future of the created order is made dependent in significant ways on the creaturely use of power. In creating the human being in the divine image and breathing into its nostrils the breath of life (Gen 1:26; 2:7) God creates a being who is able to hear and respond (cf. Exod 4:11), to understand the blessing that brings fruitfulness (Gen 1:28-30) as well as the commandment with regard to the forbidden fruit (Gen 2:16-17).

God's influence is effective to some degree in every event, but the future of creation depends in important ways on how the people respond with the power they have, and this entails a self-limitation with respect to divine sovereignty. Therefore one must speak of divine risk and vulnerability, beginning with creation. A text concerning the settlement of the Israelites in the promised land is representative in this connection:

> "Curse Meroz," says the angel of the LORD,
> curse bitterly its inhabitants,
> *because they did not come to the help of the LORD,*
> to the help of the LORD against the mighty (Judg 5:23).

The Acceptance of the Word: The Word and the Spirit

According to St. Paul the efficacy of the gospel is not due to the personality of the preacher or the manner in which it is presented (1 Cor 1:17). The gospel is "the power of God for salvation to everyone who has faith" (Rom 1:16), a vital reality capable of communicating its life to those who come into real contact with it. In the words of the gospel Christ is rendered present together with the redemptive power of his death and resurrection (1 Corinthians 15; cf. Rom 1:4). The "word of life" (Phil 2:16) really communicates the new life of grace; in the "gospel of your salvation" (Eph 1:13) salvation is conferred on those who hear it; and the "word of the cross" is sheer folly according to worldly standards but "the power of God and the wisdom of God" to those who are being saved (1 Cor 1:18, 24). Through faith the word of Christ dwells in the depth of the heart (Col 3:16), communicating to it the riches of salvation Christ has won by his cross and resurrection (cf. Eph 3:17).

Without denying the intrinsic dynamism of God's word and its salvific force Christian tradition has always insisted on the spiritual disposition of the person who approaches it. No one can understand God and God's word otherwise than by the event of faith, but at the same time no one can deeply penetrate the meaning of the inspired text of Scripture without being enlightened by the Holy Spirit. In the same way that the poetic work remains completely foreign to the person in whom poetic sentiment has never flourished, so the Bible will remain a partially closed book for readers or hearers who do not proceed in faith, under the guidance of the Holy Spirit, to discover the redemptive message: for Christians, the message of Christ. The true meaning of the Scriptures will certainly escape them; they will find in the text only a reflection of their own thought. Paul puts it simply and beautifully: "what human being knows what is truly human except the human spirit that is within? So also no one comprehends what is truly God's except the Spirit of God" (1 Cor 2:11).

The word is made known to us, and becomes for us a word of God, through the inner witness of the Holy Spirit. The Spirit is the correlative of the word. God works in two ways in us, *within by the Spirit* and *without by the word.* The Spirit causes the letter to live, so that the word spoken there and then becomes for us the word of God here and now. It is thus that the Bible never grows old but is always contemporaneous with us, receiving ever new life through the Spirit.

Although the light of the Holy Spirit is necessary to enter the specific domain of the Scriptures it would be a mistake to oppose the personal illumination of the Holy Spirit to the authentic interpretation of the Church's teaching authority. The witness of the Spirit together with the operation of the word of God is to be apprehended not only in the believing individual, but also in the believing community of the Church. The word acts with its power to constitute the community of believers (Acts 2:41; 6:7; 12:24; 19:20) and the Spirit of truth acts in the Church as its supporter and helper to lead it into the entire truth (John 16:13). Certainly the teaching of the Church does not replace the faith of its members, but it can and must guide the individual's faith and help each one to discern what really comes from the Spirit and what is nothing but fantasy. The role of the Church is to discern what springs from authentic faith and what is wild overgrowth in the complex mechanism of human imagination.

The Refusal of the Word

When we read the biblical texts that assert the power of the word of God we experience moments of joy and wonder, but when we look at our world many questions are raised. If the word of God is so powerful, why do we not experience it more deeply? Why all this darkness nearby? Why is it so easy to drift into wrongdoing and so hard to do the right?

These questions pose a problem that in last resort has to do with the mystery of God and God's communication with human beings. Thus we come to the very center of the problem of evil and any attempt to give an appropriate response exceeds the capacity of human understanding. God comes to the encounter with humanity always in some kind of obscurity, and even in manifestations of divine "glory" the phenomena that are seen—the light and the fire—are not God but only the signs of God's presence (cf. Exod 13:21-22; 33:17-23).

At this point we must confess that none of us has an adequate answer to the questions raised above. In the domain of faith we only see through a glass darkly (cf. 1 Cor 13:12) and all our knowledge is confined to a tiny illuminated area in the midst of darkness, for God is a "hidden God" (Isa 45:15) and God's hiddenness is not completely removed in divine revelation. Nevertheless, also in this case the word of God enlightens us in some measure (cf. Ps 119:105) and therefore we dare to say something about this difficult subject.

The initiative in the God-human relation has been God's. As we have seen, this is a covenant relationship. This covenant or mutually binding agreement involves God's gracious action and a joyful and free human response. God decides with sovereign liberty to grant allegiance, and makes known the divine will in such places as the Decalogue (Exod 20:1-17; Deut 5:6-21), the Golden Rule (Matt 7:12), the Great Commandment (Matt 22:36-40), or the prophetic words, "and what does the LORD require of you but to do justice, and to love kindness, and to walk humbly with your God?" (Mic 6:8).

This means that God did not choose to use power alone in order to achieve the divine purposes and to move forward God's salvific goals. The prevailing might of God has nothing to do with coercion. God has chosen to carry out the divine work in the world through dependence on human beings. The creature is given power to reject God, power to make the world other than what its Creator desires for it. This power to realize one's being with total independence and the utmost autonomy is the tragic greatness that accompanies human creatures throughout history.

Snow and heat, winter and summer, sun and stars, wind and storm "fulfill [God's] command" (Ps 148:8), but humans are free to refuse it. Some open their hearts to the word and believe in it. Others close their ears, harden themselves, and reject it. "He came to what was his own, and his own people did not accept him," says the gospel of John (1:11), and again, "the light has come into the world, and people loved darkness rather than light" (John 3:19).

Communication involves hearing as well as speaking. Jesus sensed this when several times he said to his hearers: "Let anyone with ears listen" (Matt 13:9). Knowing that the saving word of God can be received in different ways, Jesus said: "pay attention to *how* you listen" (Luke 8:18). These words are an echo of Psalm 95:

> O that today you would listen to his voice!
> Do not harden your hearts, as at Meribah,
> as on the day at Massah in the wilderness,
> when your ancestors tested me,
> and put me to the proof, though they had seen my work (Ps 95:7-9; cf. Exod 17:1-7; Num 20:1-13).

When over and over again Israel refused its divine vocation it could not be forced to repent. Israel's "no" to God could not be overpowered without violating the relationship between God and human beings. This is a characteristic of the divine helplessness to which the Bible bears witness:

> "O my people, what have I done to you?
> In what have I wearied you? Answer me!" (Mic 6:3).

The Triumph of the Word

There is another aspect of the mystery of God's word that must be taken into account: its definitive, irrevocable character. "The grass withers, the flower fades; but the word of our God will stand forever" (Isa 40:8; cf. Ps 119:89). What God wills, what God says, God does not retract (Ps 110:4), and Christ in his turn says: "Heaven and earth will pass away, but my words will not pass away" (Matt 24:35).

The NT is the eschatological covenant between God and the redeemed world in the crucified and risen Jesus. This covenant can be broken by particular persons insofar as they refuse to allow it to hold sway in their own lives, but it is the indefectible outpouring of God's love in covenant, and God's covenant with the Church cannot be broken.

Christ's coming to us is the final utterance of what God intended to say. Now God's word has been spoken in its fullness, and the Church is, in its innermost essence, the community of those who hear the word of God and heed it. As the "listening community of faith" the Church should experience the power of the word of God and unleash this power inside and outside its visible boundaries. As "the pillar and bulwark of the truth" (1 Tim 3:15) it must bring to light "under the suggestion of the Holy Spirit" all the original depths of the word of revelation. Especially in the eucharistic assemblies when the Scriptures are read and explained we should realize that God speaks to God's people as surely as they were ever addressed at Sinai or through the prophets. It is Christ himself who through his ministers proclaims God's gospel to a particular gathering and seeks of them the same response of loving faith he sought of those to whom he preached in Palestine.

To unleash the power of the word of God is the main responsibility of the "ministers of the word." Their function is to give an opportunity for the voice of Christ to be heard anew and to give a chance for each one to renew that response of faith by which the believer is joined to Christ's body. Through their voices the word of God should pierce like a two-edged sword, discerning the thoughts of hearts. It should offer new challenges to the generosity of God's people and make new demands on their charity. (See the article, "Unleashing the Power of the Bible.")

To help accomplish this task is the aim of this new biblical commentary.

How to Interpret the Bible

Armando J. Levoratti

The mission of the Church is to unite all human beings to God through incorporation into Jesus Christ. This incorporation into Christ is made real for individuals by their acceptance of the Christian message in a personal act of faith and baptism. And since "faith comes from what is heard, and what is heard comes through the word of Christ" (Rom 10:17) one of the things the Church must do to accomplish its mission is to proclaim the good news: "For 'Everyone who calls on the name of the Lord shall be saved.' But how are they to call upon one in whom they have not believed? And how are they to believe in one of whom they have never heard? And how are they to hear without someone to proclaim him?" (Rom 10:13-14).

In the NT the primary purpose of preaching (or proclamation) was to tell the good news to people who had never heard it before (Acts 2:14-42; cf. Rom 15:20-21). In our days the word preaching continues to carry this meaning, but it is now more commonly employed in connection with preaching inside the Church. Such a proclamation of the Word has played a central role in the life of the Church, and it would be hard to imagine the community of faith without the presence of preaching. The Church understands itself to be called to announce the content of Scripture both to its own members and to nonbelievers, and therefore preaching is an essential component in its pastoral ministry.

The explanation of the Word of God in preaching has Sacred Scripture as its first source. Scripture provides the starting point, and the task of the preacher is to derive from it a message that will be in effect word of God for a particular audience. But relating the Bible to life is not as easy as it could appear at first sight. Sometimes the application is relatively simple because there is a straight line between the biblical message and the present conditions of a living community. The world of the Bible is not unrelated to ordinary human experience. The Bible knows dishonesty in market speculation and crimes of all kinds; it shows children playing and dying in the streets and various situations of happiness, desperation, and distress. It tells the story of the people in the wilderness complaining about the food at the very moment God liberated them from slavery, and it is about disciples chosen to follow the very Son of God yet chronically dull and capable of desertion and denial. It is aware of conflicts in loyalties; it does not underestimate the complexity of responsible decisions and even grasps the ambiguities of both good and evil. While history never repeats itself, essential similarities endure. There is a clear analogy between many present situations and past biblical events and circumstances, and the events of the past can feed and illuminate those who attempt to live in faithful obedience to God's will in the present.

In more complex cases the bridging of the gap between "then" and "now" is not so easy. If we deal with a difficult biblical passage it would be impossible to translate its subject matter into our time without grasping the meaning of the text itself. Then an effort of interpretation is needed, and this requires more than a simple reading of the Scripture. In other words this actualization of the biblical message cannot be done without careful hermeneutical work, and that in turn requires a proper training if one is to rightly understand the biblical texts. Therefore hermeneutics should be a basic concern of all who are interested in letting the message of Scripture be heard in our time.

The function of the preacher in the Church is not to give personal views. The OT already shows awareness of this basic requirement in its debate about true and false prophetism. The unfailing complaint against the false prophets was that they proclaimed as coming from God what was only a human word, and did it to please the mighty or the crowd (Jer 14:13-16; 23:9-40; 28). True prophets, on the contrary, do not preach a word issuing *from* them, but a word coming *to* them. The way in which the word of God came to Moses, to Jeremiah, or to Jonah shows that far from the prophets' minds being identified with the word of God, their first inclination was to draw back and flee from it as from something surpassing human forces (cf. Exod 3:11; 4:10; Jer 1:6; Jonah 1:3). Jesus himself tells the truth he has heard from the Father (John 8:40) and the apostles cannot but speak of what they have seen and heard as witnesses of Jesus' life and resurrection (Acts 4:20).

In a similar way the Church can only dare to speak of God because God has spoken to it, and the word that the Christian preachers bring is the word of the Church, not their own. As God once acted through Christ, so now God acts through those who are "conformed to the image of his Son" (Rom 8:29; cf. 2 Cor 3:18). What Christ did in and for the world through his physical presence the community does now in and for the world. The word that Jesus spoke is not heard in our contemporary world unless it is proclaimed by the Church. The greatness of God's heralds consists in constantly dying to their own word in order to communicate with total fidelity the word of God (cf. 1 Cor 2:1-5; 2 Cor 4:2; 1 Thess 2:4-7).

Therefore it is in the line of John the Baptist that the "ministers of the word" should make their testimony. In the outstretched hand of the Baptist as he pointed to the Lamb of God (John 1:29), and in his stern "prepare the way of the Lord" (Matt 3:3) we discern the Christian preachers' and teachers' proper task, which is to point to, to witness for, and to make the paths straight for the coming of Christ. Christian preaching is the mission of the Church, the fellowship of those who have been addressed by the word of God, and entrusted with that word to proclaim to the world. That is why Paul warns his converts against the false notion that the word of God has its origin in them: "did the word of God originate with you? Or are you the only ones it has reached?" (1 Cor 14:36).

To describe this role the NT uses different metaphors, all of them designed to stress the idea that the preacher is the trustee and dispenser of another person's good. One metaphor is that of the "steward" *(oikonomos),* and implied in this concept is caring for the goods that have been placed in trust. Other metaphorical expressions are "herald" *(keryx)* and "witness" *(martys).* As stewards of Christ (1 Cor 4:1-2), preachers have the responsibility of "managing" the mysteries of God contained in the Scriptures and of "dispensing" them through the proclamation of the gospel; as heralds of God's word (1 Tim 2:7; 2 Tim 1:11) they are called upon to announce the message exactly as it was received; and as witnesses of the truth (Acts 1:8) they have to testify on behalf of Jesus Christ in the courtroom of the world (cf. Acts 20:24). The emphasis in all these metaphors is the same: the preacher's ministry is essentially a sincere and courageous service of the word that is to be proclaimed "with all boldness" throughout the world (Acts 4:29; Phil 1:14; cf. Acts 6:4; 8:4, 25; 13:5; 18:9-10; 1 Thess 1:8). Preachers are true to their mission in the measure that the kerygma is faithfully dispensed, heralded, and testified to (2 Cor 2:17; 4:2). To do so without distorting the intent of the text or using the sermon as a pretext to impose a personal point of view requires extraordinary care and discipline on their part.

This consideration helps us to understand that the chief problem in preaching is hermeneutical in nature. The critical hermeneutical issue for the "servants of the word" (Luke 1:2) is how to maintain the tension between carefully handling the biblical text and yet making it relevant in the present so that the biblical message can provide God's people comfort and guidance. On the one hand the modern historical method of exegesis requires us to interpret Scripture in its original intent; on the other hand we are gradually becoming more conscious of the distance that separates us from the text. The question is how to bridge the distance between the past of the text and the present of the Church. How can a given text be relevant in a completely changed situation?

The definition of hermeneutics is a much debated question. Whatever definition may be given, it can be said in a first approach that hermeneutics is a comprehensive word that embraces all the elements that enter into the interpretation of Scripture. Its full task is to move from a determination of the original meaning into contemporary language and thought forms. In fact, how the Scripture is interpreted determines in a very large measure the character of the gospel that is preached by and to the Church.

This does not mean, however, that biblical interpretation is to be related only to preaching. If the Bible is indeed the primary source of our knowledge about God's disclosure in Jesus Christ the reading and interpretation of the Bible takes on extraordinary importance in the whole life of the Church. The Second Vatican Council repeatedly declared that no biblical writing is "a matter of one's own interpretation" (2 Pet 1:20), but at the same time it recognized explicitly that the task of reading and interpreting the Bible belongs fundamentally to the whole body of the Church. In our days this reading and interpretation of Scripture is being carried out not only in formal situations of biblical research and magisterial teaching but in the ongoing liturgical, spiritual, and pastoral life of the Church. Scripture is being read (often in very original and enlightening ways) in Bible study groups, in base communities, in biblically based prayer movements, or by individuals seeking deeper union with Christ through biblical retreats and personal meditation. There is no question that much of this trend is the result of encouragement flowing from the Council's recognition of the centrality of Scripture for Christian life.

Recognition that the task of biblical interpretation belongs to the Church as community does not obscure the fact that not all believers are equally equipped to carry out this task. Therefore the Church needs biblical experts, preachers, and teachers, and a pastoral authority that stimulates and oversees the participation of believers, scholars, ministers of the Word, and pastors in the ongoing work of interpreting the Bible and making the biblical message relevant for the faithful in the world of today.

In 1993 the Pontifical Biblical Commission, with the explicit endorsement of Pope John Paul II, issued a document entitled *The Interpretation of the Bible in the Church.* This document takes its inspiration from Vatican II's *Dogmatic Constitution on Divine Revelation (Dei Verbum),* but goes beyond it in its attempt "to indicate the paths more appropriate for arriving at an interpretation of the Bible as faithful as possible to its character both human and divine." This document is an excellent hermeneutical guide and its reading is highly recommended. The following considerations are an attempt not to replace it, but to add some complementary ideas.

It goes without saying that the proper understanding and fruitful use of Scripture calls for more than hermeneutical probing with the critical tools of research. The great theologian Origen, early in the third century, rightly insisted that the interpreter of Scripture must be taught by the Spirit who inspired the biblical writers. The same Spirit, at work as the Scriptures were produced, continues to work as they are interpreted and proclaimed by the Church. Many centuries later this teaching of Origen was influential at Vatican II: the Sacred Scripture "is to be read and interpreted by the same Spirit by which it was written" (*Dei Verbum,* 12 [Abbott translation]).

This kind of reading requires going beyond a simplistic confidence in the possibility of disclosing the full meaning of the inspired texts from a purely historical, descriptive, or scientific standpoint, for the word of God finds no acceptance until it is sealed by the inward witness of the Holy Spirit, and the heart finds its rest in Scripture only through this inward testimony. The Spirit does not give new and hitherto unheard revelations. What the Spirit does is to confirm the teaching of the gospel in our hearts, according to the promise of Jesus: "When the Spirit of truth comes, he will guide you into all the truth; for he will not speak on his own, but will speak whatever he hears, and he will declare to you the things that are to come" (John 16:13).

Let us now establish some general principles of biblical interpretation.

I. First Principle: The Unity of the Bible

It is one and the same God who reveals the divine saving will and redemptive purpose in each of the testaments. Consequently there is a fundamental similarity between the OT and the NT that rests upon a community of ideas, beliefs, and language. All the great biblical themes—God, Temple, election, covenant, sacrifice, righteousness, redemption, sin—are present in both testaments, and it can be demonstrated that the presence of these common themes is not incidental but organic. These crucial terms have a distinctive character in the OT not found elsewhere, and they forged the context in which the NT equivalents, in the light of the Christ event, received more specific connotations. The Christ event is beyond all its anticipations, but there are always analogous realities in the OT. Certainly the OT writings did not reveal the love of God manifested in the Incarnate Son of God (cf. John 3:16); nevertheless, they show that God has condescended in some mysterious fashion to behave in humanly discernible and understandable ways, and therefore it is also a witness of the divine condescension: "I have loved you with an everlasting love; therefore I have continued my faithfulness to you" (Jer 31:3).

Wholly in agreement with the claim that the same God who spoke by the prophets is self-revealed through Jesus Christ, Christians from the start accepted the OT as the inspired word of God. That is to say that Christian use of the OT depends first of all on the belief that the One God of Israel is also the God and Father of Jesus Christ. Moreover, this belief was also indispensable for Christians because Jesus himself called the God of Scripture "Father," and discovered who he was in the reading of Scripture within a Jewish religious context (cf. Luke 4:16-21). In fact, Jesus was a literate Jew. His chief reading material was the Law and the prophets. As a Jew who called disciples to follow him Jesus preached, taught, and led, and from the effect of his teaching it is possible to tell how Jesus read the Law and the prophets. Taking a holistic approach to the Scriptures, he learned to read them through the eyes of the prophets, and especially through Isa 52:13–53:12. Within Scripture he found God's will for Israel, for himself as a son of Israel, and for his disciples. Thus the full impact of the words of Jesus is not grasped unless we hear them against the background of the history and prophecy, the wisdom and poetry of his own people.

Following the example of Jesus, the writers of the NT made constant appeal to Moses, the prophets, and the Psalms. They took for granted the authority of these Scriptures and used the prophecies to prove that Jesus was the Messiah promised to Israel and to present the Christian community as the true Israel of God. But this apologetic use was not their primary interest. The OT was essential to the early Church because it understood itself and the gospel of Jesus Christ as the fulfillment of the age-long purpose of God already at work in the history of Israel. Indeed, the OT was *the means by which the apostles themselves acquired the concepts and language in which they could preach the gospel.* For this reason familiarity with the Law and the prophets has always been a key to the understanding of the NT.

Now, if the NT looks back to the OT it is also true that the OT looks continually beyond itself, to the fulfillment of the divine promises. The history of Israel moved from promise to fulfillment, and as each fulfillment was only partial it pointed forward to another fulfillment yet to come. About the OT there hangs an air of something unfinished, and one has the impression that the mind steeped in these writings should be the first to admit it. Obviously the Hebrew Bible can be read as complete and unified in itself and understood in its own light, but it was generative of the hope of the Messiah, and this means that it points to something beyond itself to which Christians affirm that Jesus is the answer. In fact, the term Messiah is the Hebrew word for "anointed," and its Greek equivalent is *christos,* which becomes in English "Christ." By the time of Jesus there was in Israel a widespread expectation of the Messiah and in that age this word had become a technical term for the ideal king of the Davidic line who would restore the kingdom to Israel (cf. Acts 1:6). Jesus himself was very reluctant to be called the Messiah and had forbidden his disciples to speak of him by this name, but the early Church, by its application of the word to Jesus, recognized him to be the fulfillment of Israel's messianic hope. Thus for the Christian the OT cannot be *fully* understood without the NT.

As a consequence of all these considerations we can state the following hermeneutical principle: for Christians the OT receives its full meaning only in relationship to Christ whose coming it prepares, prefigures, and announces. The NT, on the other hand, can be understood only as the fulfillment of what God has begun during the history of the first covenant. Without the OT as its God-given interpreting milieu we would distort the NT according to our own categories. Without the NT the OT can easily be misconstrued as the revelation of a God who plays favorites with one nation, and its messianic expectations can be distorted into a secular messianism. The mystery of Christ was not made known to the former generations (Eph 3:4-5), but it was seen as from afar; and so deeply and subtly interwoven is the OT with the writings of the NT that no surgery can cut the two apart.

For the Christian the OT and the NT are movements of one great symphony, the one movement calling for the other. The prophetic message of salvation announces a fundamentally new saving act of God that points beyond the OT. Therefore the truly catholic approach to the Bible is one that takes seriously the entire canon of the Scriptures: on the one hand no single biblical text should be taken in isolation from the wholeness of the biblical message, and on the other hand the catholic interpreter must realize that the whole biblical message finds its ultimate meaning in relation to the paschal mystery of Christ's death and resurrection.

Because the Bible comes from the one God it is obvious that the end product would have some sort of unity, but the unity of the Bible is not a principle that should be taken for granted; rather it is something to be *sought;* it is not only a starting point but a goal of the process of study, of interpretation, and of theological reflection. In other words the comprehensive unity is something to be looked for in faith, and at the same time *something to be worked out and stated exegetically and theologically.*

II. Second Principle: Unity and Diversity in the Bible

Looking at the unity of the one God and at the inner dynamic of biblical faith that traces the disclosure of God's plan of salvation through space and time, we have considered the possibility of seeing the Bible as one. At the same time we should not underestimate the diversities and particularities of the biblical texts. This diversity is as startling as its unity, because it is not a unity that finds expression in uniformity but in great variety. The unity of the Bible is the unity of "so great a cloud of witnesses" (Heb 12:1). Moreover, it is not a static unity but the dynamic unity of a process. Scripture grew out of the history of God's dealing with God's people of the old and the new covenant, and its texts reflect all the diversity of history. Thus whenever we approach the Bible, and especially the OT, which covers such a long period of time, we are not concerned with one book whose sole author made of the whole a single unit. The Bible as a unity includes a plurality—*ta biblia,* "the books"—composed and edited in the course of more than ten centuries. Therefore in interpreting the biblical texts we should try to read everything first of all in the setting of its own age, and then in the context of the whole unfolding revelation of which it forms a part. This means that for a satisfying understanding of the whole Bible it is essential to retain the historical sense along with a perception of the continuous thread that runs through all the books of the OT and the NT. Diversity and unity must be perceived together in the Bible, and neither can be sacrificed to the other. It is impossible to reduce all to a flat uniformity, and the effort to make OT and NT say the same thing is to misrepresent both testaments.

Indeed, although the NT presents something new it is not altogether new. There is an important continuity that links the two testaments together, both in the manner and substance of God's revelation and in the ways people respond to that revelation. There are principles and ideas running through the whole, whose application would be differently pressed by different writers, yet still giving a real measure of unity to it all. The unity is the unity of a process and a development.

The two testaments together record the one history of God's dealing with humankind. However, God's purposes and will are seen with a greater clarity in the NT. This is quite understandable, because the OT bears witness to the saving action of God but the final and complete revelation waits for the end of the historical process, for the end of this age. The OT raises questions it never answers, and arouses hopes and expectations it never fulfills: hence that sense of inconclusiveness and expectation that is characteristic of the OT as a whole. In contrast, the NT proclaims that the expected event has actually taken place. God's covenant with humankind is sealed once and for all with Christ's death and resurrection. In the coming of Jesus Christ the eschatological hope of the prophets has been fulfilled and the reign of God is revealed, so that the work of Christ is a culmination rather than a denial of OT truth.

Theologians for centuries have tried to extract from the Scriptures a completely unified and consistent system of theology. They have also devised various measures by which to make all the texts speak with a single voice. But there will always be a diversity in biblical scholarship because of the diversity that exists in the Scriptures themselves. This diversity left very clear marks on the OT, and the tradition in the early Church was also preserved very differently in different branches. That means that we must guard against the idea that there is anything evil or perverse in biblical diversity. Unfortunately it has long been the dominant view, and in some areas of the Church it still is, that to admit the existence of any conflict of voices in Scripture or to permit any conflict of voices in the Church's interpretation of Scripture would be disastrous for the authority of God's word. A moment of reflection, however, makes clear that if God has anything to do with the witness to God's own self that is contained in the Scripture, God apparently has nothing against a diversity in the character of that witness.

Here we should remember what we said on the dynamic unity of the Bible. Each biblical writer has a perspective that is in some sense unique. Each was given certain fragments of truth. Since God is the unifying force in the midst of diversity we know that the diversity is just as important to God's purpose as the unity. In fact it may be said that the theological and practical pluralism within the Christian community had its origin in the pluralism of the biblical testimony regarding God.

Sometimes it is relatively easy to see the causes of divergence. In Rom 13:1-7, for example, Paul urges the Roman Christians to obey "the governing authorities"; the book of Revelation, on the contrary, has no respect for the Roman empire and its rulers. Whereas Paul thinks of the Roman authorities as God's agents working for the good of their people, the seer of Patmos looks at the Roman empire as an agent of Satan. These different attitudes were due to different situations. Paul, a Roman citizen, was writing at the time when the Roman empire was a power for law and order; John, an exile for the sake of the gospel, was writing at a period when Roman authorities had shown a strenuous opposition to the Christian faith. It is important to remember these different circumstances if we are to understand the teaching of the various authors—and this means, of course, that we cannot simply detach the teaching from its original context and apply it wholesale to our own situation.

It is most obviously true that the opening chapters of the Bible should not be read as the historical report of an eyewitness. Genesis 1 and 2 offer two different accounts of creation, and all the attempts to harmonize these two stories seem forced. In Genesis 1 the works of creation, eight in all, have been fitted into six days, resulting in a double assignment on the third and sixth days (Gen 1:9-13, 24-31). These six days of creative work, crowned by the rest on the seventh day, represent the liturgical week, and the point has been made that Sabbath is rooted in the created order of things. In Genesis 2 the order of events is different: humankind does not come last, but it is explicitly stated that there were no plants or animals in existence when Adam was created. Yet both accounts are witness to God as creator of all and to human beings as God's creatures having their life wholly from God. Genesis 1 and 2 testify that there is a difference between theological unity and theological uniformity. Both narratives need to be read in their own right for the information they give about God's creative work.

One further example may be added. The comparison of the Sermon on the Mount (Matthew 5–7) with Luke's Sermon on the Plain (Luke 6:17-49) shows many similarities between the two discourses, but whereas Matthew places Jesus on a hill, Luke puts him at its foot. A simple explanation of this discrepancy is that the interest of the evangelists in both cases is not geographical but symbolic. It is clear that Matthew intends a contrast with Moses. In describing how Jesus taught on the mountain he no doubt remembered that the ancient Law was given on Mount Sinai (Exod 19:20–24:2). For Luke the mountain does not have the same symbolic significance but it is possible that he also has the parallel with Moses in mind, since according to his account Jesus like Moses went into the hills to pray and then returned to the foot of the hill to teach there.

Our willingness to recognize the presence of discrepancies in the Scriptures is in accord with the example of Jesus. The discussion of marriage in Matt 19:3-9 indicates that Jesus thought Deut 24:1 needed to be corrected by Gen 1:27; 2:24, thus revealing an inconsistency between those two passages: "It was because you were so hardhearted that Moses allowed you to divorce your wives, but from the beginning it was not so" (Matt 19:8). In this way Jesus contrasts a human permission, which takes account of people's actual sinfulness, with the authentic will of God as it can be determined from the order of creation.

What we find in the Bible, and particularly in the NT, is far from being a systematic exposition of the Christian faith or a ready-made stock of answers to all our problems. What we have instead is a series of documents written under different circumstances. This is, of course, precisely what we would expect because the biblical authors are writing from their own situations, expressing their own experiences, and reflecting the ideas of their own background. Each of them bears witness to the truth in a particular historical context and speaks a word that is essential to the life of the people of God. We do not have to discard Qoheleth because he speaks in very different tones from those of Second Isaiah, or the letter of James because we question whether Paul would approve its teaching, nor should we reject the gospel of John because its description of Jesus' ministry fails to follow the pattern common to the synoptic gospels.

This polyphony must not be surprising. If we realize that the books of the Scripture were written in the course of more than a millennium, and in languages as diverse as Hebrew and Greek, we should be surprised if we do not discover in their pages many different voices. The amazing fact that emerges from familiarity with the Bible is its unity in depth under the surface of diversity.

A difficult hermeneutical task is at issue here. It is of course clear that not every biblical text will be equally appropriate in any given situation, but if the Church is conscious of being addressed by the living Word it will resist the temptation to recast God or Scripture for the sake of some concern for uniformity. What is offensive to one group may address another group's experiences powerfully.

III. Third Principle: God Acting in History

Revelation in and through history. Biblical scholars have emphasized God's self-disclosure in powerful acts of salvation, giving us in this way a deeper insight into the historical character of biblical revelation. Biblical religion is concerned with places, names, events. There is a revelation to be read by faith within certain historical facts. God is actively present in human history and significant events are actions of God, vehicles or channels of God's self-communication.

Whereas other religious documents primarily relate the exploits of the gods, the Bible is unique in its portrayal of actual events involving specific human beings. YHWH, the God of Israel, is not an eternal idea or an absolute ethical principle, but the God who heard the groaning of a people and remembered the covenant with Abraham, Isaac, and Jacob; the God who saw the plight of the Israelites in Egypt, took heed of it, and accomplished for them what they could not do for themselves (Exod 2:24-25). To know this God is to experience divine actions in the concrete affairs and relationships of people. If YHWH had chosen as the "holy nation" and YHWH's "own possession" (Exod 19:5-6) the Egyptian slavemasters instead of the Israelite slaves, then a completely different God would have been revealed. In a similar way the God of Peter, Paul, John, and James is known and worshiped as the God who raised Jesus from the dead.

According to the Bible only impious fools can say in their hearts: "There is no God" (Pss 14:1; 53:1[2]). "The heavens are telling the glory of God" (Ps 19:1[2]), and it is the presupposition of both the OT and the NT that there is no need to prove God's existence because the universe is sufficient testimony for anyone with an open mind and a docile heart (cf. Wis 13:1-9; Rom 1:19-20). Even the wicked fools are not atheists because they question the work of God, not God's existence. They do not deny the fact that God exists. What they are denying is that God becomes involved in human affairs, that God will act as Judge and Savior; hence their refusal to submit to the authority of God's word. But even if the Bible knows that the majestic power of God is discernible in the wonders of creation it knows also that nature cannot reveal the deepest mysteries of God's grace and love. The poet of Job 26 acknowledges God's sovereignty over nature in the wonders of earth, sea, and sky, but concludes:

> These indeed are but the outskirts of his ways;
> and how small a whisper do we hear of him!
> (Job 26:14)

The whole creation speaks of the striking and overwhelming supremacy of God. However, the most remarkable message of the Bible is not that there is a God, but that God has spoken to Israel and the Church in order to enter into a personal relationship with the whole of humankind (cf. Heb 1:1-2). The OT is based upon the belief that God is self-revealed in particular events of Israel's history. God is hardly ever described in the OT according to special divine attributes, but almost exclusively in terms of what God does and commands. Therefore YHWH's great deeds in the liberation of Israel from Egypt are basic for the knowledge of YHWH. The redemption from "the house of slavery" has become the pattern of YHWH's loving kindness and powerful aid: "I am YHWH your God, who brought you . . . out of the house of slavery" (Exod 20:2).

The Israelites accepted no god immanent in nature; their God is a transcendent and personal God, and human history as well as nature is wholly under God's control. History, in the Israelite conception, is a process governed by YHWH and moving toward an end intended by YHWH; it is God's chosen sphere of self-revelation and it can also be God's word. The book of Deuteronomy puts this attitude clearly in contrast with the religions of nature:

> And when you look up to the heavens and see the sun, the moon, and the stars, all the host of heaven, do not be led astray and bow down to them and serve them, things that the LORD your God has allotted to all the peoples everywhere under heaven. But the LORD has taken you and brought you out of the iron-smelter, out of Egypt, to become a people of his very own possession, as you are now (Deut 4:19-20).

At the pinnacle of God's dealing with Israel stands the incarnation of the Word: the Word that was present to God in the beginning and through whom all things came into being, the Word that had found a human voice in the Law and on the lips of the prophets, this same Word of God "became flesh and lived among us" (John 1:14). In the fullness of time it was not the historical event that became word: the Word itself became historical event. From that moment onward the expression "word of God" could have only one strict and primary meaning: the personal Word. Every other use of the expression is valid only insofar as it throws light upon the person of the Word made flesh.

Historical experience and knowledge of God. The most specific of Israel's "God consciousness" is a distillation from its historical experience, and accumulated experience deepened its knowledge. As the people entrusted themselves to their divine partner in dialogue the reality of God became clearer and at the same time their own destiny was clarified. In the Exodus, to take but one example, God is revealed as one who is caught up by the situation and is moved to take action: "I have observed the misery of my people who are in Egypt; I have heard their cry on account of their taskmasters. Indeed, I know their sufferings, and I have come down to deliver them out from the Egyptians" (Exod 3:7-8). Thus the early experience of Israel with its God has become constitutive for most of its subsequent reflections upon God and God's relationship with God's people (cf. Hos 11:1; Amos 2:10; Mic 6:1-5).

However, the experience of calamity and exile also taught Israel what God expected of the chosen people. When warnings of disaster often proclaimed by the prophets had become a reality and their words of doom had proven true, such human catastrophe was conceived as an instrument of divine wrath and a sort of theophany adapted for the sinner. Military defeat, invasion, and national disaster were the working out, through human agency, of YHWH's punishment for Israel's religious deviation. For the prophets the national disgrace was a call to communitarian and personal recommitment in light of a deeper understanding of God's acting in history (cf. also Prov 3:11-12; Heb 12:5-6).

That is why the secret of human destiny cannot be revealed in nature, where the mystery of disobedience does not come to a head. Snow and heat, winter and summer, sun and stars, wind and storm fulfill God's word (cf. Ps 148:8). Human beings, on the contrary, are free to turn away from the path of salvation and follow their own ways. Therefore the secret of human destiny must be sought in history, which began with an act of disobedience to God's command (cf. Genesis 3) and is now the scene of God's redemptive work in Christ.

History and word. The self-communications of God are firmly rooted in history, and none can be placed alone as an event separated from the whole. The validity of Christian faith depends on events, on the birth, death, and resurrection of Jesus Christ. If this did not happen there is no salvation and faith is vain (1 Cor 15:1-19). But an event is meaningless until it is interpreted by the eyes of faith. There is no full understanding of the facts until the interpretative words are spoken, and those words sometimes precede the redemptive acts of God to prepare their way (cf. Exod 3:7-10), and sometimes accompany or follow them to bring to light their meaning (cf. Exod 15:1-21). It is not surprising, therefore, that in God's dealing with God's people the continuing experience of divine activity raised up persons who spoke those words. These persons are the prophets and the apostles.

Prophecy is the necessary component of a history in which God takes part. Within the continuing intercourse of God and God's people the prophets (using this term in the broadest possible sense) have had a quite distinctive function. They received in any one of many ways the divine revelation (cf. Num 12:6-8) and were appointed to transmit that divine message to the people of God (Isa 6:9; Jer 1:7; Ezek 3:4; Amos 7:15). But prophecy is not the passive and inert reception of a hidden truth. Throughout their ministry the prophets were aware of being supported by God, of being God's mouthpiece even if not every "Thus says the LORD . . ." was a new supernatural communication. The prophets were rather those who with their spirit, their heart, and their entire life reflected the experiences of their people. Their personal vision of God, coupled with Israel's traditional faith, gave deep insight into God's will and plan in history. In this way they brought to light the meaning of the events, whether what was happening was a drought, or the invasion of a foreign army, or the fall of a great empire like Assyria and Babylon. The prophet, the mighty deed, and its meaning belong together. Israel was the people that was to see and understand the action of God in everything that happened and make a fitting reply.

The apostles, like the prophets, stand between God and God's people, between God and history, between God and the community of faith. They were chosen by Jesus to follow him during his lifetime on earth (Acts 1:21-22) and were witnesses of his resurrection (Acts 2:32; 10:40-41; 1 Cor 9:1-2; 15:5-8). The three synoptic gospels record that at least on one occasion Jesus sent them out on a mission to preach repentance in view of the coming reign of God and to heal the sick (Matt 10:1-21; Mark 6:7-13; Luke 9:1-6). This mission was an extension of Jesus' own ministry as expressed in the saying: "Whoever welcomes you welcomes me, and whoever welcomes me welcomes the one who sent me" (Matt 10:40; cf. Luke 10:16; John 13:20). After Jesus' resurrection the apostles were sent out by the risen Lord to "make disciples of all nations" (Matt 28:18-20; cf. Mark 16:15-16; Luke 24:45-49; John 20:21-23; Acts 1:8). Their witness to Jesus' teaching, and above all to his death and resurrection, was foundational for the Church. It provides the link between Jesus and the post-resurrection community of faith. The apostolic experience of Christ is the root that forever grounds the Church's life. The source of this apostolic testimony was certainly the words and acts of Jesus (Eph 3:3-5), but that knowledge was finally communicated in full "through the Spirit" (Eph 3:5). In the Acts of the Apostles the Spirit is given to the apostles in view of the testimony they are to render to Christ (Acts 1:8). The fourth gospel is still more precise: "When the Spirit of truth comes, he will guide you into all the truth" (John 16:13). Through the Spirit the word of God took form in the NT.

For anyone who engages in interpretation of the Bible it is important to understand correctly the relationship between word and deed. Every form of dualism is quite artificial. The acts of God are meaningful because they are set within a frame of verbal communication. The Lord "does nothing without revealing his secret to his servants the prophets" (Amos 3:7), and the prophet, that is, the human figure who mediates the word, announces the divine action that is to take place and at the same time interprets the relation of that action to the purpose of God. God's motivation and purpose are necessary components of the depiction of the divine intervention, and this purpose would remain unknown if the redemptive acts are not linked with a verbal communication.

Other channels of revelation. The Scripture as a whole, in spite of the immense variety of religious and theological viewpoints that are to be found within the biblical texts, sets before us the drama of God's dealing with human history. Every element in the Bible has its ultimate meaning in the context of that story. But we must also do justice to the complexity and many-layered character of the biblical traditions. Revelation through history is not the only category in which God's presence and reality are experienced. There is a wide diversity of ways in which the Bible portrays God's interaction with humanity, and alongside history we find other means of revelation, including cultic theophanies, visions, dreams, the universal imperative of the Law, and direct verbal communication between God and a human interlocutor such as Moses or the prophets. A prophet like Jeremiah could dialogue and even argue with God (cf. Jer 12:1-2) and he also speaks of being in God's divine council (Jer 23:18). His relationship with God was one of personal communion. Such a deep personal experience was also Isaiah's call (cf. Isa 6:5). God's self-disclosure in words and visions is not unrelated to divine self-disclosure through mighty acts, but there seems to be no cogent reason to unilaterally subordinate the former to the latter. In Num 12:6-8, for example, God is reported as saying to Aaron and Miriam: "Hear my words: when there are prophets among you, I the LORD make myself known to them in visions; I speak to them in dreams. Not so with my servant Moses; he is entrusted with all my house. With him I speak face to face—clearly, not in riddles; and he beholds the form of the LORD." In this way the Bible presents God as speaking to Moses "face to face, as one speaks to a friend" (Exod 33:11) and thereby bestowing intimate knowledge of God.

The realm of nature, as we have seen, is one of the most important modes by which God is manifested, and the Psalms praise God as the Creator as well as the Redeemer who acts in history (cf. Psalm 136). Furthermore, there is a valid way of talking and instructing about God that does not work by constant and immediate reference to a historical datum. The most obvious is the Wisdom literature. In works such as Job, Proverbs, and Ecclesiastes history can scarcely be regarded as the controlling category. In these writings there is no matter of subsequent interpretation of historical events; the concern is rather with ideas and practices that have survived the test of time and are rooted in an understanding of human experience.

IV. How to Interpret Narrative and Historical Texts

Biblical narrative. The Hebrew people and the early Church did not cultivate history for its own sake, but for the sake of recounting the wonders and redemptive acts that God had worked on behalf of God's people. If we look for history in its modern form we are looking for something the inspired authors, and therefore God, do not intend to give. So for example any reader of the Bible notices immediately that in the OT records YHWH is depicted as acting in the world and in human affairs. This representation was built on the cultural assumption of the ancient Near East that certain occurrences and concatenations of events were attributable to divine agency. Within this cultural tradition nature and history were viewed as divine spheres of activity. This was true, first of all, of odd, spectacular, catastrophic, or uncanny occurrences. It was taken for granted that natural disasters such as violent storms, earthquakes, droughts, plagues, or pestilence had divine agents. Unusual or extraordinary events such as an eclipse or the appearance of a comet were ascribed to direct divine interventions while the rise and fall of nations, social changes, wars, and fateful decisions were believed to be mediated acts of the gods. Not only marvelous or unexpected events were regarded as signs of divine intervention; dreams, as well as the sudden turns of fortune, were automatically ascribed to supernatural sources.

Few scriptural passages are so dominated and structured by divine interventions as the Exodus narratives. The course of events is so penetrated by this divine presence that we can say that YHWH proceeds step by step to procure the freedom of this people. YHWH decided to liberate the people from the land of bondage and bring them to the land promised to their ancestors, and to accomplish this purpose YHWH reveals an overwhelming supremacy over nature and human events (cf. Exodus 1–15).

This way of narrating events can be surprising for modern readers trained in modern scientific thought and interested in the interplay of natural and historical forces. Therefore readers of the Bible should take into account first of all that the belief that the Lord is a God who works wonders is essential to biblical faith, but at the same time they have to remember that this belief took its original form and was formulated for the first time in a world of different thought patterns. The biblical narratives are not the work of a dispassionate historian who knows all the techniques of modern historiography; they are part of a common Near Eastern way of expressing events and ideas. Their purpose was primarily to communicate a religious message, not to scientifically check or verify the accuracy of every source. The historical events are important insofar as they carry the revelation of God. Therefore it is salutary to ask whether the stress must be laid on the precise nature of the Egyptian plagues or on the significance of the Exodus as a redemptive event.

To put the hermeneutical principle briefly and at once: the unifying factor of the biblical story is the action of God in the course of human events. Therefore we must insist on the difference between the biblical storyteller and the modern historian. The ancient biblical storytellers were not historians in the modern sense; they were also "prophets" in their own way. The modern historians, on the contrary, concern themselves with records of "observable phenomena," and the action of God is not something that can be seen. Since it cannot be directly observed or measured it is outside the proper sphere of their discipline. Because it is something that is beyond the facts they can find in the historical sources they do not, as historians, deny or affirm it. If the historian affirms such activity it is as an act of faith rather than as a scientific conclusion. So too the unbelieving historian who denies the activity of God in Israel's history is not expressing a scientific conclusion but a judgment made on some other basis.

Different ways of narrating historical events. There are passages in the Bible that seem to relate historical events in a straightforward manner on the basis of eyewitness testimony. A good example of this can be found in the closing chapter of 2 Kings, where the story of the fall of Jerusalem is richer in its detailed account of events than in theological interpretation. But we are not to read all Scripture narratives as if they were eyewitness reports and ignore the imaginative form in which they are sometimes couched. In many cases a historical framework is filled out with a poetic and imaginative reenactment of history, as in Judg 5:20: "The stars fought from heaven, from their courses they fought against Sisera."

On the other hand it must be acknowledged that much of the narrative of the Bible can be called history only in a very loose sense. The Exodus event, for example, is firmly embedded in every layer of Israelite tradition but the nature of the traditions—epic, liturgical, confessional, poetic—rules out the possibility of a historic reconstruction that is fully satisfactory from the historical point of view.

The problem of historicity. To prevent misunderstandings we should make it plain that we are not denying the historical element in the Bible, nor do we intend to suggest, as some biblical scholars do, that the historical content of Christian faith is in fact minimal or nonexistent. The salvation event is part of earthly history, and to separate the *kerygma* from what really happened in history is to cut faith from its source, for if anything is clear from the reading of the Bible it is that the sacred authors were convinced that God had intervened in history to produce what we call historical events.

"Event plus interpretation" has become a byword in Bible study. While interpretation is all-important in that it gives us the meaning that is to be seen, the event is by no means secondary; without the event there could be no intervention of God, no interpretation, and therefore no revelation or redemption (cf. 1 Cor 15:12-20).

At this point a distinction must also be made between the biblical record and the actual historical occurrence. A narrative text without a historical referent (for example, a parable of Jesus) can provide basic concepts and categories for the Christian consciousness in its understanding of itself and the world. As far as the truth is concerned this can be conveyed to the reader in an equally effective manner by a fictive or a historical narrative. Indeed, there are fictional accounts (like the parable of the good Samaritan or the prodigal son) that are truer to life than a well documented but lifeless historical report.

These observations are meant to guard against a reductive tendency to equate truth with history. Narrative criticism corrects this assumption. Within the Bible truth is conveyed through a diversity of literary forms and genres, including psalms, prayers, parables, and proverbs. If we recognize that the operative word of God is concerned first of all with salvation we shall learn to see the Bible in perspective. We shall have no sense of shock if we read that Job, Tobias, Jonah, or Judith are literary figures rather than historical personages. Vivid and typical characters such as Hamlet or Don Quixote can disclose secret aspects of human existence that otherwise would remain hidden from human eyes. Therefore the first thing to be sought is the theological significance of the individuals depicted in the narrative texts, whether fictional or not.

The Bible as a Literary Work

Since the events and their interpretation come to us in a body of literature it is legitimate to use all the methods and techniques of literary investigation to seek out the Bible's message. Truth in literature cannot be reached without the reader's perception of words, phrases, lines, strophes, and other rhetorical aspects, and this requires not only intellectual understanding but also aesthetic involvement. Therefore the initial task of the readers of Scripture is to open their senses to the beauty and the distinctive features of the literary forms.

A literary work should be read as a unity. Its parts should first be interpreted from the literary whole that contains them and not from their immediate external referent. Thus the analysis of the language reveals in each case an articulation that is peculiarly suited to the organic unity of the literary work. In view of this organic unity the meaning of the work resides in the form and content as a whole. Form and semantic content merge to produce meaning. Change the arrangements and formal organization of the words, and you have something else.

As a literary work the Bible must be also interpreted in accord with the type of literature embodied in any particular passage. This means that it is necessary to take into account the various literary forms. Sometimes the genre of the whole text is absolutely vital for the proper interpretation of a text. Poetry cannot be interpreted as prose, parable as detailed theological writing, apocalyptic as history. The Bible speaks in hymns of praise to God, in the moral instructions and counsels of Israel's teachers, in the utterances of the prophets, in letters and occasional papers, but most of all in narrative texts. This wide variety of texts, with its emotional appeal and poetic beauty, reveals the skill of the biblical writers who shaped their message in an effective literary form. The spiritual depth and poetic beauty of the biblical texts is equally the reason why the Scriptures have always been the primary source of the language of prayer and liturgy.

When we try to define poetry we have the uneasy feeling that we are somehow missing something essential we cannot quite understand. However, the fact is that the impact of true poetry on feeling and imagination is much more intense than that of ordinary language. Moreover, the characteristic features of verse—rhythm, parallelism, alliteration, and the like—are the easiest vehicle for an oral culture in which memory (the keeping alive of tradition) is of paramount importance. It is not surprising, therefore, that much of the Bible is in poetry. Psalms, Job, the Song of Solomon, and Lamentations are all or nearly all in poetry; the prophets cast the larger part of their message in verse, and bits of earlier poetry are embedded in the prose narratives in such a way that the difference between the older poem and the later narrative is often clearly marked. That is why we should also let our aesthetic faculties respond to the countless lines of poetry found particularly in the OT, from Deborah's song (Judges 5) and David's lament (2 Sam 1:17-27) to the cosmic questions addressed to Job from the whirlwind (Job 38:31), or even the confessions of Jeremiah, the songs of the Suffering Servant, and the prophet's satire over the demise of the Babylonian potentate (Isa 14:12).

The most common type of poetry in the Bible is the lyric, which usually appears in the form of triumphal odes celebrating victories (cf. Exod 15:1-18) or as expressions of joy, pain, distress, thanksgiving, or praise, as in 1 Sam 2:1-10; Luke 1:46-55, 68-79, and the Psalms. However, the most typical of all biblical literary genres is narrative. It is in this form rather than in direct doctrinal formulation that biblical faith expresses itself. Several biblical books have a distinctly historical character but, as we have seen, the purpose of biblical storytellers was primarily to impart a religious message, not to scientifically check the accuracy of every source. The historical events are themselves important insofar as they carry the revelation of God. Moreover, not everything in biblical stories is factual, that is, not all the narratives have the same relation to real historical events. Particularly the OT contains several stories that are fictional yet true in the sense that they give us an accurate insight into the relationship between God and God's people.

The book of Judith, for example, is like a novella interlaid with some historical data (the invasion of the Assyrians). The event itself is fictional, but we already know that fiction can be a way to represent truth. The name of the leading character in the story, Judith, means "Jewess," and this Jewish woman personifies her whole nation in its reliance on God and its capacity to face persecution and grave risk. Thus the novel of Judith, by the agency of fiction, conveys a truth made clear by the centuries of Israel's struggles with its persecutors (see the commentaries on the books of Judith, Esther, and Jonah).

According to many forms of modern literary theory (particularly the so-called New Criticism) a literary work has to be understood in its own terms and in the form in which it stands before the actual reader, that is, as a closed system. It creates the "world" of the text with its own particular structure, its own symbolic coherence, and its own capacity to generate communication. Previous stages and editions, even if they can be discerned, are essentially irrelevant. The time of composition may not be very important either, because the work is to be understood neither by delineating the history of its formation nor by the recovery of the historical situation that brought forth its constituent parts. Even the intention of the author may be considered unimportant. Once produced, the literary work has its own independent life and takes on a meaning of its own. As such it should be interpreted within its own frame of reference, apart from either the historical or other facts to which it refers or the circumstances of its production and reception.

This method of analysis can be usefully employed in the study of the Bible insofar as the literary critic recognizes that this is not the only valid way of approaching the Scriptures. The great risk run by those who employ this kind of literary criticism is that of remaining on the level of formal study, failing to draw out the real message of the Bible (cf. *The Interpretation of the Bible in the Church* [1993] especially I. A. 1–4).

The Meaning of Scripture

Exegesis has generally been regarded as the task of disclosing the meaning of a particular text, especially when such a text, because of its antiquity, cultural diversity, or inherent difficulty needs to be read and analyzed with special care if it is to be correctly understood. As applied to the Holy Scriptures exegesis has been a permanent practice in the life of the Church, which from the first centuries has recognized, watched over, and faithfully transmitted the Bible as the word of God. Moreover, in this word the Church has found the principal nourishment for its faith and a guide for its moral life. As a result of this uninterrupted practice Christian exegesis has a long history. This history now shows that the methods employed in the interpretation of the Scriptures have always been closely related to the cultural conditions of different ages and places. Accordingly, biblical exegesis has changed from age to age, and it always exhibits the mark of its time.

As we have seen, the basis of modern scientific exegesis is the understanding of the precise meaning of a given biblical text. Therefore the question that ought to be asked in order to understand an OT or NT passage is one that concerns the understanding of any text whatsoever: "What does the text mean?" The believer and the nonbeliever can raise the same question, and honest research will serve to close any gap in how they understand the message in the text. Faith does not change the contents grasped and described in such a scientific inquiry, and up to this point believers and nonbelievers are constrained to reach agreement on the results even if they will differ about the value to be granted to or the truth of this message.

Obviously, to understand scientifically what a text means does not require any personal commitment of the exegete to the message of the text or any appropriation of it. This is to say that *understanding* and *appropriation* are different concerns, however closely related they may be. But if we believe that the biblical texts confront us with the God of Jesus Christ whose grace offers us justification and calls us to sanctification, another question should be raised: "What does the text mean to me here and now?" Appropriation is valid insofar as it is founded on understanding, because the literal meaning is at the same time the spiritual meaning, in its literalness and not in spite of it. In other words, the truth cannot be split up as if something was meant then and something else now; the biblical texts can be relevant *today* not in spite of but because of what was said *then.*

In this connection it is very important to say something about the *meaning* of the Bible. We can easily understand phrases like "each word has a meaning," "life has no meaning for me any more," or "music means a lot to me." But if we try to define the meaning of "meaning" we find that there are many disparate views about how "meaning" can be defined or even described. Sometimes dictionaries attempt to help readers by listing so-called synonyms of meaning (for example: purport, sense, reference, denotation and import), but those synonyms can only go so far in clarifying this issue.

Without wanting to get into the current debate about that difficult question we can say, for the practical purpose of helping the user of this biblical commentary, that *meaning is the significance the reader must apprehend in each word, sentence, or work in order to grasp them adequately.* But we should add immediately that the meaning of a text is expressed by the interrelation of its elements (words, sentences, images, etcetera), and that the precise meanings of all the elements of a text are determined not primarily from the linguistic, literary, and historical contexts that surround the text but rather from the interrelation of these elements within the text itself. Reading should begin by recognizing these interrelations. The text is to be first studied for the meaning it has developed within itself: its narrative or rhetorical structures, its logic and breaks in logic, the relation between meaning and image, and so on.

Most literary works worth reading have so many possible "meanings" (for example, intellectual, symbolic, or emotional) that to announce one extractable meaning can be quite misleading or at least confusing. Individual commentators will focus on one matter more than another, and one biblical book will invite the use of one method more than another. Still, the commentary will be richer insofar as the various possible modes of understanding a text are effectively embodied.

Literal Sense

The definition of the *sensus literalis* ("literal sense") is a perplexing question in the history of biblical exegesis. Even now the word "literal" is used in quite opposite senses. In ordinary speech about the Bible it suggests the idea of fundamentalism; indeed the average person, asked to define a fundamentalist, will say that he or she "is someone who takes the Bible literally." So, to take one of the best-known instances, a literal interpretation of the Genesis creation story would be that the world was created in six days, taking the word "day" literally as referring to ordinary days. However, a careful distinction should be made between the literal sense of a biblical text and the "literalist" sense to which fundamentalists are attached.

Literal sense is often defined as the sense the author *intends* and the words convey, with the further qualification that the intention of the author and the sense conveyed by the words cannot be separated. But this definition of the literal sense is inadequate. In fact it is extremely difficult, if not impossible, to interpret the author's intention without psychologizing and, on the other hand, it cannot be said that a text means only what its author consciously intended.

According to the document of the Pontifical Biblical Commission on *The Interpretation of the Bible in the Church* "the literal sense of Scripture is that which has been expressed directly by the inspired human authors. Since it is the fruit of inspiration, this sense is also intended by God, as principal author. One arrives at this sense by means of careful analysis of the text, within its literary and historical context." When a text is metaphorical its literal sense is not what flows immediately from a word-for-word translation (for example, "let your loins be girded" [Luke 12:35], but that which corresponds to the metaphorical use of these terms ("be ready for action"). When it is a question of a story the literal sense does not necessarily imply belief that the facts recounted actually took place, for a story does not belong necessarily to the genre of history but can instead be a work of imaginative fiction (*The Interpretation of the Bible in the Church* [1993] II. B. 1).

The foundation for all exegesis must lie in the understanding of the text as its author and its first hearers or readers understood it, governed by a historical sense and by the effort to place ourselves in the setting out of which it came. This means that the exegete must in the first place be a historian in order to understand the circumstances in which a certain language expresses the message for which he or she is looking. When the literal sense has been ignored exegesis loses its power, and biblical interpretation disappears in flights of gnostic or subjective speculation.

In order to utter their teaching the biblical writers spoke a language that may be identified historically and geographically; they used certain ideas familiar to their contemporaries and constitutive of their culture, such as the scientific, etiological, ethical, and mythical ideas of their time. Their assertions cannot be separated from the outdated language because they could not communicate in any other way than through their contemporary culture. But the important fact is that through patterns of culture and through themes common to the surrounding religions *a new message* is expressed in the Bible.

So, for example, the cosmogony of Genesis 1, where the first element of creation is water, agrees with the Babylonian myth known especially by the Israelites during the exile. But if we remember that the role of the Bible is not primarily to give a scientific explanation or to be a substitute for science we can realize that all this constitutes the *language* trying to express a *message.* In this case the scientific schema is merely an instrument of expression and has nothing to do with the faith and the message the author claims to bring. What is important is not that the world has been shaped from water; it is that, using the old cosmogonic data of which Genesis 1 contains a kind of residue, the writer asserts that the unique God created the world in the beginning by the divine all-powerful word.

Nevertheless, the maintenance of a historical sense does not mean that we read the Bible merely as a witness of the past. It only means that we read it as the word of God mediated in the context of a history—the history of Israel and of the early Church. We do not have to give up Genesis 1 because such science is outdated; neither do we have to try to reconcile Genesis 1 and the modern geological data by a sort of harmony according to which each of the six days corresponds to a geological era. The only thing to be kept in mind is that the Bible, using cultural elements as a channel of communication, gives us a revelation about God.

All that is *in* the text is not the meaning *of* the text, though the message is necessarily expressed through such language. It is impossible to divide the text in two, but it is possible at least to some extent to detach the truth revealed by God from its linguistic expression. When one has discovered the message of God in the language that expresses it a new task will appear: to understand how this message is valid for us today and how our language is able to express it for us today here and now.

The Spiritual Reading of Scripture

As we have seen, there are many ways of approaching the Bible: as literature, as a historical document, as the basis for Christian theology and behavior. Now let us consider two uses of the Bible: in the first, Scripture bears directly on the personal life of the reader, while the second is a more distinctively exegetical or theological use because in it the biblical texts bear directly on theological or historical argument. The second is the type to which most scholarly discussion is devoted, but the first involves most users of the Bible, that is, those who read the Bible to have communion with God, to renew themselves spiritually, and to find moral guidance for daily conduct.

In fact, the Bible was not given as a source for profound theological debates; rather it was given for us to know the living God and to have a living relationship with this God. In Sacred Scripture the truth of faith is immediately directed toward actual life. Christ is rendered present in the words of the gospel with the redemptive power of his death and resurrection. The "word of life" (Phil 2:16) in reality communicates the new life of grace, and in the "gospel of your salvation" (Eph 1:13) salvation is granted to those who hear it. So the word of God, having power of its own, enters directly into our personal lives in many and varied ways.

Certainly it is legitimate to examine this truth in a scientific manner in order to understand it better, but we cannot be faithful to the real nature of Christian truth if we forget the first intention of God in revealing it. Therefore to understand the biblical message in a truly comprehensive manner we must take the Bible for what it really is: *the word of God in human language.* The reader or hearer who ignores the human conditions of God's word remains on the outside of Scripture by introducing arbitrary interpretations; the reader or hearer who does not recognize in the words of Scripture the word of God also remains on the outer surface of the sacred book. Only in the event of faith, under the guidance of the Holy Spirit, is one able to existentially appropriate the redemptive message of Christ. Only in this way can be set up, on the foundation of an exegesis that takes into consideration every human factor of the biblical texts, a theological and spiritual exegesis that will disclose God's most profound intentions and teachings.

According to the Pontifical Biblical Commission the spiritual sense of Scripture can be defined as "the meaning expressed by the biblical texts when read, under the influence of the Holy Spirit, in the context of the Paschal mystery of Christ and the new life which flows from it" (*The Interpretation of the Bible in the Church* [1993] II. B. 2). The final purpose of Christian exegesis is the spiritual understanding of Scripture in the light of the Holy Spirit, but this spiritual sense can never be stripped of its connection with the literal meaning. The latter remains its indispensable foundation. As a consequence, the spiritual sense is not to be confused with subjective interpretation; rather it results from viewing the text in relation to real facts that are not foreign to it.

Spiritual reading, whether in community or in private, will uncover the spiritual sense only to the extent that it is kept within these perspectives. The close unity of the two approaches excludes any dichotomy between scientific exegesis and spiritual interpretation. A merely subjective inspiration is insufficient. The spiritual sense, to be recognized as the meaning of a biblical text, must offer proof of its authenticity. In this way one holds together three levels of reality: the biblical text, the paschal mystery, and the present circumstances of life in the Spirit.

In order to yield a perception of all the resonances of the word of God the spiritual reading of Scripture must be done in an attitude of prayer. This prayer can assume many forms, depending on the text that is read and the circumstances of life. There are prayers of praise, gratitude, repentance, and trust; there are also petitions for oneself and for others. Sometimes "we do not know how to pray as we ought, but that very Spirit intercedes with sighs too deep for words" (Rom 8:26).

Sensus Plenior

The defenders of the so-called *sensus plenior* see the need to go beyond the historical interpretation of some biblical texts. If there is basic continuity between the redemptive and revelatory acts of God in both testaments it would be correct to say that the prophets have seen "through a glass darkly" what later biblical writers, illuminated by a new revelation, could see more clearly. Often in prophecies the exegetes have a hard time figuring out what the prophets meant for their own times, and yet when the NT shows the fulfillment of a prophecy its sense becomes perfectly clear. Just as at each second the movement of an arrow is aimed at a target, so the OT texts were in a certain sense pregnant with the fulfillment that was to culminate in Christ and the Church.

The term *sensus plenior,* as the specific title of a biblical sense, is of rather recent vintage (dating back to about 1925). However, it has been argued that only the name is an innovation. In fact, the idea behind the term is supposed to be very ancient, reaching back to the exegesis of the Fathers and into the NT.

The *sensus plenior* has a direct relationship to the *literal meaning* of the biblical text, that is, to the meaning expressed by the human author, but at the same time it reveals an intention of God that the human author did not fully know. In other words, whereas the literal meaning is the sense of the words as intended by the hagiographers when they were inspired to compose a text in a particular stage of God's revelation, the fuller sense is the meaning that God, who knew from the start the whole plan of salvation, intended from the moment when the composition of the text was inspired. This deeper meaning, intended by God but not clearly perceived by the human author, was and is made clear in later times when the text was and is read in the light of a new revelation or a further development in the understanding of God's revelation. Although the hagiographer did not clearly intend that meaning it can legitimately be called a biblical sense since it was intended by God, who is the principal author of Scripture.

In the quest for a fuller sense there are guidelines to be observed. A legitimate *sensus plenior* is not a substitute for historical exegesis, but must be understood as a development from such exegesis. As a more profound meaning, the fuller sense must have a very real connection to the literal sense; it should be already present or latent in the text and flow from the text itself because a meaning can hardly become "fuller" until its historical literal sense has been determined. Any distortion or contradiction of the obvious meaning is not a *sensus plenior.* Therefore the shift from the literal meaning to the fuller sense can be compared to seeing a picture first in the very dim twilight of evening and then in the bright light of day. Nothing has changed or been added, but the daylight makes clear what before was not readily seen.

There are a number of OT passages that are used by NT authors in a way that seems to support the concept of *sensus plenior.* A typical example is the "sign of Immanuel" in Isa 7:1-17. In this case there is no indication that the prophet had some distant future event in mind; hence it is most difficult to conclude that he was speaking of Jesus Christ or of an unnamed Messiah. The point is not a virgin birth, but rather the sequence of events during the so-called Syro-Ephraimite coalition: a young woman is with child and will bear a son, and before this child is old enough to know good and evil the Lord will deal with the enemy kings. In the NT the context of Matt 1:23 gives a fuller sense to the prophecy of the *ʿalmah* by using the translation of the Septuagint: "The virgin *(parthenos)* will conceive."

Many objections have been raised against the recognition of the *sensus plenior* as a biblical sense. Some exegetes are reluctant to accept a scriptural sense that was unknown to the sacred writer, or to speculate about divine intentions in shaping the biblical language and its further developments. If the scriptural witness is the message that has been conveyed by the words of human authors it would be hazardous to assume that they were sometimes deficient instruments, moved to say something that only God intended fully. Therefore it has been argued that to speak of *sensus plenior* is not the best use of words. Perhaps it would be more accurate to speak of "re-readings" *(relectures),* that is, of subsequent readings of older texts that develop new aspects of meaning, sometimes different from the original sense (cf. Hos 11:1 and Matt 2:15; Deut 25:4 and 1 Cor 9:9; 1 Tim 5:18).

The Bible itself is thoroughly imbued with such re-readings, whether to deepen the meaning of older passages or to make known their fulfillment. In reading the NT, for example, we encounter multiple allusions and explicit citations of the OT, and the history of biblical interpretation shows us how the Church re-read the Bible in earlier and modern times.

An example may illustrate this point. It is generally agreed that the Jewish messianic tradition goes back to the oracle of Nathan (2 Sam 7:1-17) that promised David a dynasty and a throne that would last forever (v. 16). But this prophecy cannot be messianic in the strictest sense of the word because it promises the everlasting continuation of the dynasty of David, not the coming forth of a single new ruler. In other words, whereas the messianic passages look forward to a definitive final situation (peace without end), Nathan's oracle announces a succession of events related to David's dynasty. Yet nothing could be more obvious than the extinction of David's kingdom in 587 B.C.E. This catastrophe made clear to most people that the monarchy in Israel had been a failure, but Nathan's oracle continued to be re-read in the new historical situation. Thus the promise of an everlasting throne awakened hope in the restoration of the monarchy, and YHWH's salvific purpose with respect to Israel took the shape of a promised King Savior, a Messiah or anointed one.

In a similar way the early Church interpreted Jesus in the light of the Scriptures, and at the same time the Scriptures were re-read in the light of the Jesus event. By a sort of dialectical relationship between event and word Scripture reveals the meaning of events and events reveal the meaning of Scripture.

It is an open question whether the term "fuller sense" will survive and be useful or whether it will be taken up into a more adequate classification. The answer to that question will come from some creative development in biblical theology, no doubt, rather than from arguing over the term itself and its definitions.

Typology

Typological interpretation has been practiced in the Church from NT times to the present. So when Paul says (1 Cor 5:7) "For our paschal lamb, Christ, has been sacrificed" Jesus' redemptive death is interpreted in typological terms. The NT links Jesus Christ with the OT figures and events because the gospel fulfills what was present in promise in those prefiguring events.

This manner of reading the OT has also been used for various purposes among the Fathers of the Church. Sometimes they used typology for apologetic purposes, sometimes for edification or to set forth a particular theological truth. Against Marcion, who insisted upon the existence of a radical contradiction between the wrathful God of Israel and the Father of Jesus Christ, they defended the unity of the two testaments and resorted to typology and allegory to find a Christian meaning in some troublesome biblical passages.

Typology has been defined as an analogical way of thinking and speaking that focuses attention on two or more realities (for example, Adam and Christ) and in so doing apprehends the connection between them. In this attempt at finding typological correspondences between the OT and the NT the crucial word is *realities.* Typology concentrates on historical events, the center being the earthly life of Jesus Christ as the core event in the sequence of all the saving acts of God to which the Scriptures bear witness. However, the application of typology should not be restricted to correspondence between events. In the rich metaphorical and symbolic language of Scripture comparisons are made between persons (Moses and Jesus), institutions (Israel and the Church), laws (muzzling an ox and payment of ministers), buildings (the tent on earth and the heavenly tabernacle), and rituals (Passover and Easter). In particular the priestly work of Christ becomes more understandable set against the background of the Levitical priesthood (especially the role of the high priest, the structure of the sacrificial system, and the Day of Atonement).

In this kind of interpretation the significance of an OT figure is to be seen at two levels: its historical meaning and its typological implication in foreshadowing a future event. The final item is called the "type," and its earlier correspondence the "antitype." Typology thus adheres to historical exegesis, but at the same time it sees a similarity between two or more realities that God has purposely fixed so that the one is a prefiguring event and the other its continuation and fulfillment. Therefore typological interpretation has no intention of reverting to an unhistorical or uncritical viewpoint. The only presupposition that lies behind it is the conviction that "the time is fulfilled" (Mark 1:15) and that the meaning of a particular event in Israel's history is penetrated more deeply by placing it in relationship with its antitype in the NT (and vice versa). The first creation is completed by the new creation. The first man, Adam, made in the image of God to reflect God's glory, comes to his true destiny in the new Adam, Jesus Christ. In him God's glory is perfectly reflected and a new humanity is created. Nevertheless the OT types not only correspond to their NT antitypes; sometimes they can stand in antithesis to them, like Adam and Jesus Christ. Like Adam, Jesus is the representative of humankind, but unlike Adam, who brought death, Jesus brings forgiveness of sins and eternal life.

Whatever the NT writers meant by the term "fulfillment" they did not mean some perfect equation of past promise and present performance. No exact correspondence of details is to be looked for because the reality transcended the promise and went beyond anything that was to be found in the First Testament. The prophets did not write the gospel before the gospel. Their prophetic vision was obscure; they could hope only for a vague outline, peering out as through a fog to catch some sight of the period and pattern of the messianic day (cf. 1 Pet 1:10). Typological interpretation is aware that the redemptive benefits of the OT do not equal those of the new covenant; they were only "a shadow of the good things to come and not the true form of these realities" (Heb 10:1). That is why Christ could bless the eyes of his disciples that looked upon the things "many prophets and righteous people longed to see" (Matt 13:16-17).

A renewed emphasis on the unity of the Bible has created a revival of interest in typology among biblical scholars, but this revival of interest has not been without strong doubts about the existence of genuine correspondences between events that are separated in time and belong to different historical and religious conditions. However, the misunderstandings that have at various times attached to typological interpretations should not lead us to ignore the central place that this exegesis has had in the development of Christian thinking, and if the God who "long ago . . . spoke to our ancestors . . . by the prophets" is the one same God who "in these last days . . . has spoken to us by a Son" (Heb 1:1-2) it is legitimate to recognize that this God has left a mark also in the story of the OT covenant people.

The attempt to define the particular relationship between the testaments has often led to the use of *allegory.* However, those who most strongly uphold the validity of typological interpretation insist that there is a definite distinction between typology and allegory. Typological interpretation tries to establish remarkable analogies between events, persons, or things in the OT and similar events, persons, or things in the NT within the historical framework of revelation. Historical exegesis must precede and be the real basis for any typological interpretation. Allegorism, on the contrary, is the search for a hidden meaning underlying the obvious sense of a given text. This secondary sense discovered by allegorism does not necessarily have any connection with the historical framework of revelation. In fact the history of allegorical interpretation shows that most frequently it disregards the literal meaning and draws out a sense that has nothing to do with the original event.

Such a distinction is very useful for drawing the line between legitimate and illegitimate typology and for preventing a lush growth of extravagant interpretations, but it cannot be pressed very far because it is often difficult to distinguish between what is typological and what is merely allegorical. It is true that the relation to history is the main criterion that effects discrimination between typology and allegory, but it is also true that it is difficult to isolate the saving acts of God from the interpretation given in the biblical texts. So certain is this fact that the element that constitutes the type is not principally the person or the event considered in themselves, but this person or this event insofar as it is presented in Scripture and in the way that it is presented there. As a consequence a type may be purely scriptural, such as Melchizedek "without father, without mother" (Heb 7:3). Undoubtedly this royal priest of Jerusalem had parents, but the Bible's silence on this point is what constitutes him a type of the celestial generation of Christ.

Presuppositions

In a now famous essay Rudolf Bultmann once asked whether it was possible to do exegesis without any presuppositions, and his answer was "No." Every interpretation, he notes, incorporates a particular prior understanding. In fact, we bring to the task of interpretation too much of ourselves—our culture, our traditions, our theological assumptions—to make a presuppositionless exegesis feasible. No one encounters the world directly. Thought does not operate in a void. It is rooted in a whole complex of ideas, attitudes, sentiments, and interests of various kinds (both economic and political) that form the largely unconscious background of our thinking and acting. To be alive is to pursue certain values rather than others, and these values cannot be placed in a separate realm or region of their own. They are part of one's life, necessarily involved in the act of existing. Through them we face and interpret other objects, persons, or events. Moreover, every exegete or reader of the Bible approaches the text with specific questions and a certain idea of the subject matter with which the text is concerned. If that is true for the more purely historical and critical task of exegesis, how much more do our presuppositions play a key role in the larger hermeneutical endeavor of theological relevance and practical application. It is simply impossible for us *not* to bring our own experience of faith and Church to the biblical texts. The very *selectivity* of our hermeneutics is for the most part related to our traditions, not to our exegesis.

There is a risk in coming to the Bible with our experiential, cultural, and ecclesiastical assumptions because it is always possible to read into the text instead of reading out of the text. But this approach is not a bad thing in itself. Indeed, we cannot do otherwise. Everything we do involves certain presuppositions about the nature of what we are dealing with, and if every observer brings a body of assumptions and attitudes to the apprehension and interpretation of reality, so also does the interpreter of the Bible. This "pre-understanding" is not only an ever-present factor to be accounted for, it is also indispensable for the task of interpretation. Without it understanding would not be possible at all, because a message can be understood only by one who knows the language in which it is given. On the other hand only a vital involvement with the matter to be interpreted can establish a communication between the text and the interpreter and make possible a proper examination of the text. All interpretation proceeds on the condition that the interpreter has some prior understanding, however limited, of the thing to be interpreted, and the more we come to appreciate the value of that work the more accurately we can grasp what the text is saying.

This prior understanding is always present, but it functions in a variety of ways. Its negative influence is readily apparent when the interpreter deprives the Bible of its freedom to say anything that contradicts or is out of harmony with a definite point of view. As a result the theological wealth of the biblical message is narrowed; many of its essential features are thereby silenced and the rich polyphony of the biblical texts is reduced to a single monotonous or tendentious voice. Therefore the true beginning of hermeneutical wisdom is to be conscious, as far as possible, of the particular contours of our preconceptions. This self-consciousness allows us to check and control the negative influences of our own distinctive points of view.

Many examples in the history of biblical interpretation could illustrate this point, but there is one that is particularly striking. Jesus came into a world where there was already an authoritative Scripture and a community within which this Scripture was interpreted. The scriptural character of Judaism by this time is a historical fact, and it was the interpretation of Scripture that brought Jesus into conflict with the Jewish leaders and then to his death. Indeed, essential to Jesus' ministry and the origin of the Christian faith was a new way of understanding Scripture. This new hermeneutics (new and yet not totally new, for it was a recapturing of the centuries-old prophetic tradition) pursues the Law to its ultimate intention according to the will of God (cf. Matt 5:17-20). Jesus appears as the interpreter of the Torah who is able to bring to light its most profound significance. In some cases the biblical precept was extended in order to get at the root disposition beneath the forbidden action. Thus Jesus' disciples cannot be satisfied with merely avoiding murder; they must also curb the anger and insults that lead to murder (Matt 5:21-22). In other cases the radicalization was pushed so far that the letter of the Torah was revoked, as happens with divorce, vows, and retaliation (Matt 5:33-42; Mark 10:1-12). Jesus himself obeyed the Law (cf. Luke 10:25-28) and acknowledged the authority of the scribes and Pharisees to the extent that they were faithful to Moses (Matt 23:2), but when there was a conflict between the "letter" and the "spirit" the words of the Torah and the venerable traditions of his nation had to cede to the salvific will of God.

Unlike Jesus, some of the rabbis of the time of Jesus had a traditional method of interpretation that enabled them to find in the Scriptures the authoritative validation of the beliefs, practices, and general structure of their religious community. The Scriptures being regarded as infallible in every part, the same infallibility accrued to their interpretations of the Scriptures and the religious structures that were erected upon them. The consequence was that a community committed to such authoritative interpretations had no ears to hear John the Baptist or Jesus when in them the voice of the prophets began to speak afresh.

Jesus' teaching and behavior were a bold challenge to the established world of Jewish piety, and he did nothing to lessen the tension. The Law and the Prophets were to be fulfilled but the "traditions of the elders" did not enjoy the same privilege (Matt 15:1-9; Mark 7:5-8). For Jesus the doing of God's will was identified with love (Matt 22:34-40), but some leaders repeatedly defined it in terms of their legal prescriptions (Matt 12:1-14; Mark 7:1-5). Many of them saw in Jesus a threat to the future of the whole religion and social structure. Thus Jesus' behavior precipitated a conflict that resulted in his death.

Reader-Response Criticism

In connection with what was said about presuppositions we may refer now to what is called "reader-response criticism." This method of analysis focuses on the reader and the reading process, trying to establish the role actual readers play in the determination of literary meaning. A basic principle of this approach is the refusal to consider the literary text as a thing in itself, an object. Reading is indeed the actualization of meaning, and the study of literature must also be the study of ourselves as readers; it should enlarge the traditional critical discourses by including the individual reader's purposes, motives, attitudes, and feelings. Pursuant to these basic statements there is an increasing effort on the part of reader-oriented critics to redefine the aims and methods of literary studies.

In spite of the considerable attention paid to the act of reading, there is uncertainty regarding how to conceive the reader's response. More than a single trodden path, reader-response criticism seems to be a multiplicity of often divergent tracks. Nevertheless, common to all audience-oriented approaches is the assumption that meaning has no effective existence outside of its realization in the mind of a reader. There is no basic or neutral literary language uncolored by the perception and response of a particular reader. The reader, once relegated to the status of being unproblematic and obvious, has achieved a starring role.

On a table, on a shelf, in a bookstore a book is an object among others. Made of paper and ink, it lies where it is until someone comes and delivers it from its materiality, its immobility. There is only one way for the meaning of the book to be rendered actual in a living mind, and this is by an act of reading. Meaning comes to the reader in the course of reading, and because it is not available in or through the text, independent of the reader, it is necessary to take seriously the role of the reader in determining the meaning of the text. Reading is a dynamic, concrete, and temporal experience rather than the perception of a spatial form.

This attitude toward the process of reading relativizes the conventional view that the meaning of a text is like the content of a nut, simply awaiting its extraction by the reader. As a consequence reader-response criticism advocates a change in the understanding of meaning. Meaning is no longer considered as something ready-made; it is not a property of the text itself but rather a function of the experience of the reader in the act of reading the text. A shift is taking place, away from a static and objective meaning bound to the text to a more subjective meaning experienced by the reader in the temporal flow of the reading experience. In other words, meaning is *an event instead of a content.*

Radical reader-oriented approaches emphasize the indeterminance of the text. Literature, in this conception, is a "kinetic art," an art that refuses to stay still. The objectivity of the text is an illusion and meaning is a product of the reader. This opens the way for a great deal of subjectivity. The text itself is invented in the process of being read. The essential factor in meaning is not the spatial form of the text on the page but the temporal process of reading; consequently it is the reader who "makes sense." If meaning is no longer a property of the text but a product of the reader's activity the question to answer is not "What do poems mean?" but "What do poems do?" or even "How do readers make meaning?"

The weakness of this position is evident. It seems to involve a blurring of the distinction between *meaning* and *perception of meaning.* More importantly, it does not take into account the achievement of self-transcendence in reading. In the act of reading, the object of the reader's thought is the thought of another. The reader thinks a thought that belongs to another mental world. The experience of reading shows that the literary work lives its own life within the reader.

Less radical positions, while giving attention to the often neglected readerly aspect of literary communication, also take into account the characteristics of the text. The reader participates actively in the production of textual meaning but this necessary creative activity does not indicate that meaning is solely dependent on subjective perception. Even if it is important to interrelate the subjective and objective parts of reading it should be recognized that there are right and wrong, better and worse readings, and to become aware of the difference is the task of exegesis.

Reader-response criticism promotes self-reflecting reading. It provides an important step toward a self-conscious and self-reflective critical praxis. By removing the literary work from the center of attention and replacing it with the reader's cognitive activity it opens a new field of inquiry. As a critical practice that intends to help readers read with greater awareness and self-consciousness reader-response criticism can also help us to take account of important questions such as, "Do we read with more or less self-consciousness?" "Do we respond with more or less awareness and sensitivity?" As we become more aware of what we are doing when reading a text our reading and response to reading become more conscious of how text and reader affect one another. It is more desirable to have an acknowledged and controlled subjectivity than an objectivity that is finally an illusion. A critique, nevertheless, is not out of place. When we consider the internal processes through which literature realizes itself in the individual reading we are struck by the essential active-passive nature of the reader's role. Readers gain their experience by forgetting, forgoing themselves; dying, so to speak, in order that the text may live.

The Bible as a Whole

The biblical literature grew slowly over the centuries. As they composed their writings the biblical authors were relying on a variety of traditions, and thus most of the biblical texts were produced by more than one individual. The word was first proclaimed in oral form by poets, prophets, apostles, preachers, and epic historians, and then redactors and scribes edited the written word with the addition of their theological insight and commentary. The Pentateuch, for example, is a very extensive composition that incorporates many different genres and discrete units of material. Among its sources it quotes "The Book of the Wars of the Lord" (Num 21:14-15), where the term for "book" (Hebrew *sēfer*) refers to a written record (cf. Exod 32:32; Num 5:23; Deuteronomy 17–18; 24:3). On the other hand, in Num 21:27 a song about the fall of Moab is attributed to unidentified "ballad singers" (Hebrew *moshelim*), which does not necessarily imply a written source. Another source mentioned in the OT is "The Book of Jashar," from which were excerpted the song at Gibeon (Josh 10:13), David's lament (2 Sam 1:18), and Solomon's hymn (according to the Greek version of 1 Kings 8:13).

In the NT the gospels began as remembered deeds and teachings of Jesus shared among groups of disciples gathered to sort out what happened to their Master. Even Paul's letters, which did have a literary beginning, bear witness to and incorporate such oral traditions (1 Cor 11:23; 15:3-8).

From all of this it becomes clear that the Bible is a deposit of traditional material treasured by the community of faith. One cannot imagine a Christian community of faith without the traditions that help it to understand and sustain itself. The traditions shape the life of the community, and the community in turn interprets and reshapes the traditional materials. In this way the people of God and its Scriptures grew up alongside one another.

However, neither Israel nor the early Church was enslaved to its traditions. As new situations developed, old traditions were used in a new way, and even the same tradition could be reinterpreted quite differently. A simple comparison between the Beatitudes in Matthew and in Luke shows that not even the sayings of Jesus were regarded as immutable and unalterable. Luke has four Beatitudes balanced by four woes (6:20-26), and all take the form of direct address in the second person plural ("Blessed are you . . ."). Matthew has nine Beatitudes and no woes (5:3-12); all but the last of the Beatitudes are in the third person plural ("Blessed are the . . ."), and whereas Luke interprets poverty and hunger literally, Matthew understands them spiritually (for example, "poor in spirit," "hunger and thirst for righteousness"). The freedom with which the biblical authors used their traditional materials leads us naturally to ask which version is closer to the words of Jesus himself.

Since most biblical texts are the final product of a longer history of tradition the obvious implication is that it is legitimate to work backward from the text as we have it in order to identify its sources and reconstruct the process of its composition. In fact a great deal of energy and ingenuity has been expended in tracing the stages through which these traditions, originating in different circumstances and different localities (generally cult centers), have passed while being combined into a sequential and comprehensive narrative. Thus one can trace the development of specific traditions as they are reused by successive generations. The methods of historical and literary criticism are especially designed to recover an understanding of the formation of the biblical texts and, more importantly, to find out what a particular text meant to its author and its community.

This concentration on the small unit has considerable exegetical import, but at the same time the breaking of the text into its constituent parts can lead to the false conclusion that the recovering of the original historical context is the final step of the hermeneutical task. On the one hand, sometimes exegetes restricted themselves to the task of dissecting the biblical books in order to identify their sources and establish the date of composition of the various documents. On the other hand, there is in certain circles of biblical scholarship a tendency to place exaggerated value upon what is supposed to be original and early, as if this alone is authentic. The so-called "canonical approach," which has become an important aspect of biblical hermeneutics in recent years, rightly reacts against these tendencies.

Unlike the historical approach the canonical understanding of Scripture aims to carry out the *theological* task of biblical interpretation beginning with the statement that only the canonical perspective is authoritative for the Church. Inspired Scripture is precisely Scripture in that it has been recognized by the Church as the rule of its faith and life. Each of the individual books becomes biblical in light of the canon as a whole. Hence the starting point for ecclesial exegesis must be the Bible as it is, in its present form. A prophet may have addressed his or her words to the Israelites many centuries before the common era, but in the liturgy of the Church, as canonical Scripture, those words are addressed to the Christian community. Even if the book of Isaiah consists of three sections written more than two centuries apart, the interpretation of the whole must be done in light of Scripture received as the norm of faith by a community of believers.

As a consequence the canonical approach insists on focusing attention on the final form of the scriptural texts rather than on the isolated elements out of which they were formed. The emphasis falls not on the original form but on the book in its final form as it stands in the Bible. Whatever earlier developments may be observed within and behind the present text, only the latest theological perspective is authoritative for the Church. Canonical *texts* must be read within a canonical *context.* Single biblical passages are to be interpreted in the light of the whole Bible. Even when there is evidence that many sources have been used to create the extant whole (as is the case in the Pentateuch) we are committed to understanding this whole rather than simply elucidating the separate parts.

The relation between the testaments becomes a crucial part of the canonical approach. It takes seriously the Christian confession that OT and NT form the vehicle of God's revelation. Because the Church confesses that OT and NT *together* constitute its Sacred Scripture each of them is to be understood in the light of the other. This means more than establishing a historical connection. Within the framework of faith in the one divine purpose witnessed to in two testaments the canonical approach seeks to understand this divine reality by hearing the dual witness of the OT and NT.

This canonical perspective includes elements of undeniable value. It is doubtless true that the believing community provides the most adequate context for reading the Bible as Sacred Scripture. Because the sacred writings of the past are the medium through which God continues to make divine revelation contemporary, any attempt to approach the biblical text from some assumed neutral, objective starting point is inappropriate for understanding its theological import. Theological exegesis can only be done within a framework of faith. In an ecclesial stance, faith and the Holy Spirit enrich exegesis. Moreover, the Church accepts the harmony of the whole Bible stemming from its inspiration by God and its unity of testimony to the one revelation of God. One must seek the whole revelation in the whole Bible. The criterion for understanding parts of the Bible is the whole scriptural witness. This is a principle of the Church's catholicity.

But when advocates of the canonical approach state that the linking of exegesis to historical study jeopardizes the theological enterprise they posit a false alternative. A sound principle of biblical hermeneutics is to ascertain, at least as a first step in the process of interpretation, what the text meant in its original context. Whether or not we study a particular text in a canonical form we should try to recover the context in which it was written, and many biblical texts cannot really be understood unless we know something about their historical setting. Moreover, one must respect each stage of the history of revelation, and this means that the historical dimension of Scripture cannot be ignored. A completely unhistorical reading of the Bible leads to oversimplifications and arbitrary harmonizations. Continuous close dialogue between the historian and the theological exegete is mandatory, and such dialogue can scarcely be fruitful if the contribution of the historian is relegated to a relatively unimportant role.

Finally, there is another factor at work that deserves mention, namely the existence in the Bible of a plurality of theological traditions. Within these traditions there are doctrinal differences as well as different languages. As a consequence there can be, and in fact there is, a variety of biblical theologies. Different views not only of the final outlines of a biblical theology but also of the very principles upon which the subject can be approached have always existed and will always exist. This leads us again to express doubts about the absolutization of the canon as the only hermeneutical principle. No one approach is sufficient for the full task of biblical interpretation.

The fact of theological pluralism in the Bible as well as in the Church means that a canonical approach ought to be concerned with theological diversity as well as unity.

Scripture and Tradition

The apostolic tradition. It has always been recognized that Christianity did not begin with the NT. The Church began by living and confessing that "Jesus Christ is Lord" (Phil 2:11), and out of that life and faith scriptural texts emerged. Jesus and his apostles preached. By their speech the gospel was communicated and the new life flowing out from the apostolic communities spread ever wider and wider. The living word preceded all the written records of the gospel and continued alongside the written records, whose purpose was to express, to reflect, and to deepen the communal life in the Spirit. In a similar way the rest of the NT is the written testimony of the apostolic Church to God's revelation in Jesus Christ. It should be regarded as the precipitate of a previous preaching, as the *result* of God's revelation in Jesus Christ.

The Old Testament. The OT is also the product of a long process of formation and revision of traditions that antedate the canonical text. These traditions of the people of God were the memories and instructions that were passed down in various authoritative channels, including the circles of prophets and storytellers, of priests, and of sages. Many hands over a period of many years have joined together in bringing to completion the established text. Gradually the spoken traditions crystallized into written documents; the process of editing, compiling, and redaction drew toward a close, and thus books came to be formed. As time went on those books were recognized as Holy Scriptures.

Scripture and Tradition. On the other hand, the formation of the written Scriptures did not bring to an end the stream of Church tradition. What the existence of Scripture did was to alter the character of post-scriptural tradition. After the death of the apostles Scripture came to have an almost exclusive position as the authentic source coming from the biblical period. Therefore the ecclesial tradition assumed in large measure an interpretative function in relation to an antecedent segment of tradition, that is, the segment represented by the Scriptures.

For the Catholic faith, then, Sacred Scripture is so inseparable from tradition as to be, in fact, a part of it; even more than that, it is its most essential element. "Bible and tradition" does not mean the Scriptures plus a foreign element without which it would remain incomplete. Scripture and apostolic tradition are not two independent absolutes; they form a single unity because they have a single origin: God's unique revelation; they interpenetrate and explain one another. In other words tradition means the Bible replaced, or rather remaining, in its proper atmosphere, its original environment, its native light. If the Scriptures were to be torn from the living tradition of the Church, the Bible would become incomprehensible. It would be, in fact, separate from the very realities of which it speaks.

Scripture contains all the truths of Christian faith, at least germinatively. But Scripture needs tradition for its *right* interpretation. Tradition is not concerned with adding to the content of the biblical writings. It is closely identified with the life of the Church, and the understanding of the Church is indispensable to interpreting, clarifying, and applying the biblical message to the new circumstances of the Church and the world. Only in the context of this living tradition can the Bible be read and understood by the believing Church.

The example of Paul. Let us illustrate this assertion with the example of Paul. There can be no doubt that Paul was a great theologian, yet he wrote no "systematic theology" of the kind produced by later theologians. What he did was to write a series of letters addressed to particular communities and intended to deal with particular situations and difficulties that had arisen within the early Christian communities. Since Paul was writing to communities that had already "received his teaching" (1 Thess 4:1) he did not need to repeat the fundamental features of the Christian faith. Normally he could assume those basic beliefs, and he mentioned them only to clarify a particular point or correct a false understanding.

On the other hand Paul presents himself as a link in the chain of tradition reaching back to Jesus, whose authority remains present in the Church. He says to the Corinthians: "I handed on to you as of first importance what I in turn had received" (1 Cor 15:3), and again: "I received from the Lord what I also handed on to you" (1 Cor 11:23). The first statement pertains to a doctrinal summary regarding the death and resurrection of Christ. The second belongs to a liturgical account of the Last Supper. The object of the apostolic tradition consists, therefore, in actions as well as words. Thus the tradition of the apostolic age constituted the milieu in which revelation was progressing, insofar as the apostles explained the meaning of Jesus' words and actions.

This means that the communication of Paul with the believers was made inside the community of faith. His letters were originally intended to give Christians a deeper understanding of what they already believed. Even if he was truly an apostle by his special calling and by a revelation of the glorified Christ (Gal 1:15-16; cf. 1 Cor 9:1) he was concerned to preserve his communion with the Twelve, and especially with the "pillars" of the Church (Peter, James, and John: Gal 2:9). On the level of the basic, essential faith his preaching was determined by the gospel he had received and that he transmitted (1 Cor 15:1-11), and occasionally Paul's final argument was an appeal to the example and traditions of the first Christian communities in Judea (1 Cor 11:16).

Moreover, the Church's memory of what happened on the night Jesus was betrayed (1 Cor 11:23-27) was handed on to Paul by those who were apostles before him. The Pauline narrative is the earliest extant written form of this tradition, and this clearly indicates that the NT writings themselves are temporally preceded by what was known and preached from the beginning. In this sense tradition and Scripture began and continued to exist in the Church side by side in an intertwined relationship of life-giving mutuality.

To this can be added a brief reference to the issue that was at stake in Antioch, involving the unity of the Church itself. When the apostle Paul confronted the apostle Peter because he refused to continue eating with the Gentile Christians he did so because he believed that Peter was not walking in a straightforward manner with regard to "the truth of the gospel" (Gal 2:14). At that time none of the canonical gospels (Matthew, Mark, Luke, and John) was written down. Nonetheless the gospel as preached and lived was normative to the point that even the apostles were held accountable to its authority. The gospel according to whose truth Paul appealed was handed on (that is, "traditioned") orally, and only later was it given written form in the Church's gospels.

The testimony of the Fathers. The patristic evidence from the second and third centuries is unanimous in its insistence that what was preserved and must be preserved in the Church is the "apostolic tradition," that is, the body of essential truth that came down from the apostles and was contained in the Scriptures. Tradition and Scripture were clearly thought to exist in organic dependence on each other, while each had its own relative autonomy and its own particular authority: apostolic tradition because it was the Church's understanding of Christ's redemptive work; Scripture because of the permanence of the written word and the inspiration of the Bible. For Irenaeus, who wrote toward the end of the second century, the division of God's revelation into two partial sources—Scripture *and* tradition—would have been quite unthinkable, for there is only one tradition, apostolic in source and ecclesial in transmission. Scripture was regarded as the distilled essence of the apostolic teaching and there was no place for a rigid distinction between Scripture and tradition.

Scripture as the measuring rod of tradition. We cannot but deprecate the tendency to bring Scripture and tradition into confrontation. In fact they are different and yet organically bound together. Each has its own particular function. On the one hand our knowledge of the inspiration of Scripture and of its particular authority as mediator of the word of God depends on a tradition that came down from the apostolic Church. On the other hand tradition is dependent on Scripture for a continual reminder of and guidance to the full truth of the Christian faith.

It is fair to recognize, nevertheless, that one of the reasons why Scripture was fixed and separated from other traditions was, very likely, the sense that tradition was laid open to contamination. We know, on the other hand, how vulnerable the past is to loss and distortion. As the actuality of the present recedes from us it immediately begins to fade and become problematic. To avoid such negative effects it is indispensable to establish a clear distinction between tradition in the strictest sense and the broad stream of traditions that also took form in the course of the Church's history and that cannot claim the authority of God's self-revelation. In carrying out this discernment the Church rests confidence in the guidance and assistance of the Spirit promised by Christ (John 14:15-17; 16:5-15). This guidance was promised in a special way to those who have a teaching function in the Church, but, after all, even the apostolic tradition is handed on by fragile human beings who have a treasure of inestimable value "in earthen vessels" (2 Cor 4:7).

Moreover, words change their meaning in the course of history, and it can scarcely be denied that our religious formulas, many of them burdened by centuries of usage, stand in perpetual danger of corrosion. As a consequence the recasting of perennial themes in fresh language is a serious responsibility of the Church, and this means that the Church has to rethink and reformulate once and again the content of its faith. It should be clear, however, that proclamation is not a substitute for Scripture. On the contrary, any attempt at revival and renewal participates in the power of the inspiring Spirit only to the extent that it draws its substance and intention from the inspired Scripture.

This inevitably draws our attention to the relationship between tradition and biblical canon. When the Church formed the canon it committed itself to the rule of those particular written expressions of its faith. The tradition that became Scripture was not eliminated by the formation of Scripture, but henceforth Scripture was the measuring rod and touchstone of ecclesial preaching. As the permanent and divinely willed norm for all times in the Church, it is Scripture that measures and validates preaching, not preaching that measures the validity of Scripture. The Church submits itself to the authority of Scripture to maintain the purity of its faith and to criticize all other opinions, tendencies, and ideologies. In this way the whole ministry of the word is *under* Scripture.

The Church as authentic interpreter of Scripture. When we say, from the Catholic point of view, that the Church is the authentic interpreter of Scripture it does not mean that the Church will pronounce in an authoritative manner on matters of philology, literary criticism, archaeology, and other disciplines besides. Even more, the Church has rarely solemnly and positively defined the sense of particular biblical texts. As stated in the encyclical *Divino afflante Spiritu,* "among the many matters set forth in the legal, historical, sapiential, and prophetical books, there are only a few whose sense has been declared by the authority of the Church." The interpretation proposed by the Fathers is also a valid principle of Catholic hermeneutics, but "there are equally few concerning which the opinion of the holy Fathers is unanimous." As a consequence there are "many matters, and important matters, in the exposition and explanation of which the sagacity and ingenuity of Catholic interpreters can and ought to be freely exercised."

On the other hand the binding declarations of Church doctrine are obligatory for the faithful when they are concerned with truths that have been revealed by God *for our salvation.* Only when a biblical text has been investigated in order to discern its historically conditioned elements will it be possible to demarcate the salutary affirmation that will be valid for the Church of all times. Then a further effort must be made to reformulate the salvific truth in the language of today.

Actualization

If we take seriously the Bible's own claim to be the vehicle through which God speaks the divine living Word, we should conclude that God may speak through Scripture into our present life situation. Therefore we must not only seek to understand what the words of Scripture signified at the time they were written, but also to make clear their meaning for today. Exegesis is truly faithful to the proper intent of biblical texts when it attempts to link their message to the experience of faith in our present world: "Catholic exegetes must never forget that what they are interpreting is the *Word of God.* Their common task is not finished when they have simply determined sources, defined forms or explained literary procedures. They arrive at the true goal of their work only when they have explained the meaning of the biblical texts as God's words for today" (*The Interpretation of the Bible in the Church* [1993] III. C. 1).

There is a clear relationship between *inculturation* and *actualization.* Inculturation applies the biblical text to a different cultural setting; actualization applies it to a different time. In principle the liturgical homily epitomizes actualization, but it also takes place everywhere the word of God is made vitally alive and immediately present for a particular audience: in the readings of the liturgy and *lectio divina* (devotional, spiritual, meditative reading), in preaching, cathechesis, and evangelization. In this way the Bible and the sacraments are the privileged means used by God to build up the Church in every age.

Interpreting the contemporary meaning of Scripture must begin with a sound determination of the literal sense. This previous task is indispensable because we cannot speak of actualization if we do not perceive the distance between two moments in time, one corresponding to the cultural and historical setting of the biblical text, the other to the time and place of the interpreter. Indeed, this consciousness of a distance prompts the actualization, since it makes clear that the biblical texts were composed in response to past circumstances and in a language conditioned by the time of their composition. Two poles are thus clearly present, and the task of the interpreter is to bridge the historical gap.

The awareness of a distance between the biblical record and the present situation produces a dialectical movement from one pole to another. This movement begins with focusing our attention on a historical analysis of what a biblical text meant to its author when it was written. Then we return to our own time and try to express our understanding of the text in a manner that makes it relevant for today. At this point we shall recognize that many barriers separate us from biblical times and cultures, and it would betray a lack of honesty to minimize the intellectual difficulties we confront when we attempt to read the Bible. Then the crucial question to be asked is how a modern interpreter can appropriate writings as old, as foreign, and sometimes as disparate as those of the Bible in a manner that is relevant for a contemporary audience.

The Pontifical Biblical Commission offers some suggestions for actualization. After the determination of the literal meaning of a given text, the next step must be the hearing of the word from within one's own concrete situation. Then actualization that proceeds from faith in the context of the Church requires identification of those aspects of the present situation highlighted or put in question by the biblical text. In this way the community of faith will be able to draw from the fullness of meaning contained in the biblical text those elements that can illuminate the present situation in accord with the saving and judging will of God in Christ (cf. *The Interpretation of the Bible in the Church* [1993] IV. A. 1).

Actualization arises from the Church's faith, which receives the Bible as a message from God both to itself and to the entire world. Unlike a strict historical-critical method, it demands faith and concerns itself primarily with the theological meaning of the biblical message. Scripture is a voice both from the past and from the present. Its message is expressed in human words, in forms that are necessarily dependent on culture, but in the words of the prophets and the apostles reverberates the voice of the Holy Spirit, who tells us *today* "that truth which God, for the sake of our salvation, wished to see confided to the sacred scriptures" (*Dei Verbum* 11). The faithful must soberly assume the risk of actualizing the Christian message, in the knowledge that only thus can faith maintain its integrity. (For further treatment of inculturation, see "Inculturation of the Biblical Message.")

Insights into the History of Biblical Interpretation

Introduction

Biblical interpretation has been a permanent practice in the life of the Church. As a result of this uninterrupted practice, Christian exegesis has a history as long as that of the Church. This history shows that the methods employed in the interpretation of Scripture have changed from age to age, and exhibit always the marks of their time. Let us take a brief look at the history of exegesis, focusing on some of its most important aspects and starting with its anticipations in Qumran and rabbinic Judaism.

Biblical Interpretation in Qumran

Florentino García Martínez

Unlike the Christian conception of Scripture, which has a unified vision of the OT as a canonical or authoritative collection of revealed writings, we find in the Qumran writings, as in later rabbinic Judaism, a different attitude toward each of the three great parts of "the Bible": the Torah, the Prophets, and the Writings. This tripartite division seems to be implied in the famous line of 4QMMT 95: "to you we have wr[itten] that you must understand the book of Moses [and the words of the] prophets and of David." But since that same document elsewhere (103) speaks only of "[the book of] Moses . . . [the words of the prop]hets," and because David is certainly considered a prophet in the writings of Qumran (11QPsa XXVII, 11), and given that the Psalms are submitted to the same kind of interpretation *(pēsher)* as the writings of the prophets we can limit ourselves here to dealing only with the interpretation of "the books of the Torah" and "the books of the prophets" as they are designated in the Damascus Document (CD-A) VII, 15-17. The hermeneutical principles that govern the interpretation of each of these two parts are distinct and therefore each should be dealt with separately.

The basic attitude of the group to whom we owe the library of Qumran with regard to the Torah is expressed by the root *drš* and other words derived from it, including *midraš*. In later rabbinic literature these words clearly mean "interpreting," but in Qumran the basic meaning of the root word is not that of study, deduction, or interpretation of the Torah (although these elements are found implicitly) but rather of application, instruction, or decision about the exact fulfillment of the Law, and the meaning of the word *midraš* is this "manifest" collection (or book) of these applications.

One of the passages in the Rule of the Community (1QS VIII, 12-15) describes for us the group's plan to form a true community in the future, a community separated from the rest of Israel that concentrates all its energies on "preparing the way of [YHWH]." The passage provides us with a summary of the activities of that group, designated as the "study *[midraš]* of the Torah which he commanded through the hand of Moses, in order to act in compliance with all that has been revealed from age to age." This activity, *drš* of the Torah, by means of which the revealed text is applied to all circumstances of life, is a continuous and constant activity within the community once it has been established, as is indicated by the Rule of the Community (1QS VI, 6-8): "And in the place in which the Ten assemble there should not be missing a man to interpret the law *[doreš batorah]* day and night, always . . . . And the Many shall be on watch together for a third of each night of the year in order to read in the book, explain *[lidroš]* the regulation, and bless together." The judicial context of "explaining the regulation" *(mišpat)* defines the activity in relation to the Torah that makes it possible to work in agreement with it in all circumstances. The collection of these decisions is what is called *midraš*.

The authority to make these decisions resides in the priests, the "sons of Zadok," and in the members of the covenant, and this authority goes all the way back to the divine revelation. 1QS V, 7-9 explicitly says this: "He shall swear with a binding oath to revert to the Law *[torah]* of Moses with all that it decrees, with whole heart and whole soul, in compliance with all that has been revealed concerning it to the sons of Zadok, the priests who keep the covenant and interpret his will and to the multitude of the men of their covenant."

For the Qumran group the entire Torah has been proclaimed by Moses, but this Torah contains a double element: one part is accessible to all people because it has been revealed *(niglēh);* another part remains hidden *(nistār)* and is only manifested through activity within the community. This "hidden" element requires the mediation of the community's activity *(drš)* in order for it to be "revealed" to the members. In this way they may be completely faithful to the Torah and at the same time distinguish themselves from the rest of the people. One of the functions of the Instructor (1QS IX, 16-20) is precisely that of teaching the members "all that has been revealed"; the Instructor should "hide the counsel of the law in the midst of the men of sin" but at the same time should transmit to members the way to apply the Torah to daily life: "and he will teach them about all that has been discovered so that they can carry it out in this moment and so they will be detached from anyone who has not withdrawn his path from all wickedness."

Since the complete Torah is required for all, in its "revealed" part as well as in its "hidden" part, and since this "hidden" part is known only within the community, it is this *daraš* of the Torah that models the conscience of the group and brings them to separate themselves from all those who do not share in it (4QMMT 92-93). This *daraš* is required of all the members and anyone who separates himself or herself from it is punished. This punishment could even lead to expulsion from the inner circle (CD XX, 1-8).

The basic attitude of the Qumran group with respect to the Prophets (as well as the Writings insofar as we can speak of a tripartite division) is characterized by the use of the term *pēsher,* a word associated with the interpretation of dreams. In Qumran this is a technical term for pointing out the eschatologization to which the prophetic text is submitted and its application to the reality of the community that lives in the "last times." The clearest text is 1QpHab VII, 1-8. Here it is explained that the true meaning of the words of the prophet Habakkuk refers to the final period of history, the "last days," which are the present of the community although this meaning was not perceived by the prophet. It is also evident that this profound meaning of the text, which goes farther than what the sacred author had comprehended, is known only by the community and that the community owes this knowledge to the revelation received by the Teacher of Righteousness, "to whom God has disclosed all the mysteries of the words of his servants, the prophets."

In summary: in the Qumran community the interpretation of the biblical text has a central function in the foundation of the community; it is a constant activity, serving to formulate the specific identity of the group and differentiate it from others; it is authoritative and obligatory, and it has its definitive foundation in revelation. The person who does not accept it is driven from the group.

BIBLIOGRAPHY

Betz, Otto. *Offenbarung und Schriftforschung in der Qumransekte.* WUNT 6. Tübingen: J.C.B. Mohr, 1960.

Brewer, D. I. *Techniques and Assumptions in Jewish Exegesis Before 70 C.E.* TSAJ 30. Tübingen: J.C.B. Mohr, 1992.

Brooke, G. J. *Exegesis at Qumran. 4QFlorilegium in its Jewish Context.* JSOT.S 26. Sheffield: JSOT Press, 1985.

Bruce, F. F. *Biblical Exegesis in the Qumran Texts.* Exegetica III/1. Den Haag: Van Keulen, 1959.

Fishbane, M. "Use, Authority and Interpretation of Mikra at Qumran," in M. F. Mulder, ed., *Mikra.* CRI II/1. Assen: Van Gorcum, 1988, 339–377.

Gabrion, H. "L'interprétation de l'Ecriture dans la littérature de Qumran," in Wolfgang Haase and Hildegard Temporini, eds., *ANRW* II, 19/1. Berlin: Walter De Gruyter, 1979, 779–848.

García Martínez, Florentino. "Escatologización de los escritos proféticos en Qumran," *EstB* 46 (1986) 101–116.

Maier, Johann. "Early Jewish Biblical Interpretation in the Qumran Literature," in Magne Saebo, ed., *Hebrew Bible, Old Testament: The History of Its Interpretation. Volume I: From the Beginnings to the Middle Ages.* Göttingen: Vandenhoeck & Ruprecht, 1996, 108–129.

Patté, Daniel. *Early Jewish Hermeneutics in Palestine.* SBL.DS 22. Missoula: Scholars, 1975.

Trebolle Barrera, J. *La Biblia judía y la Biblia cristiana.* Madrid: Trotta, 1993.

Rabbinic Exegesis

Domingo Muñoz León

The date for the birth of rabbinic Judaism is usually situated at the beginning of the destruction of Jerusalem in the year 70 C.E. Prior to this time there had existed several groups in Palestine and in the Diaspora (Pharisees, Sadducees, Essenes [including Qumranites], Zealots, Samaritans, Apocalyptists, etcetera). After the destruction of Jerusalem the Sanhedrin was moved to Yavneh where, under the direction of Rabbi Yohanan ben Zakkai, there began a reorganization of Judaism in which the Pharisaic strain prevailed.

Once the Temple was destroyed, the written Torah (the Pentateuch) and the oral Torah became the central point of reference. Next to the Torah, the canon of the Prophets and Writings was established. The divine Word (the holy books) became the light that oriented everything in the new situation. The synagogue, already an important institution, came to be the place of worship and instruction, especially on Saturdays and feast days. What occupied central place within the structure of synagogical liturgy was the reading of the Torah, its translation into Aramaic (Targums) and the explanation of the biblical text (homilies). The meaning of the biblical text was studied in the Beth ha-Midrash, which continued collecting the opinions of diverse rabbis concerning interpretations. Thus there arose schools of interpretation that, at the beginning of the second century, were polarized around two great masters: Rabbi Akiva and Rabbi Ishmael. Their opinions have been incorporated into the later Midrashim. Other writers, such as the author of 2 Esdras, eagerly sought the answers to their current situation in the Scriptures (especially in the rereading of the Torah and in the fulfillment of the prophecy of Daniel).

Principles of Rabbinic Exegesis

For the rabbis the Scriptures are the authoritative norm of truth. It is the word of God, the revelation communicated to Moses and transmitted to the prophets. The Bible is to be understood as a whole; in it there is no before or after. It carries a plenitude of meaning that is crystallized in the expression: "There are seventy ways of looking at the Torah." On the other hand the Bible is meant for all times; consequently everything is contained in it.

Other important principles refer to the prevalence of the messianic meaning and to the choice of Israel as key factors in interpretation.

According to the rabbis, together with the written Torah Israel had received the oral Torah on Mount Sinai *(Torah she be ʿal peh)* which contains the entire divine will for Israel and is the guarantee of the true meaning of the biblical text. Jacob Neusner has spoken of the dual Torah as a way to express this symbiosis of the written and the oral revelation.

Methods of Rabbinic Exegesis

Although rabbinic exegesis has produced works of diverse character and in very diverse epochs of history there is a series of methods, procedures, and techniques that are common patrimony. Tradition has systematized them into a series of hermeneutic rules such as the seven rules of Hillel, the thirteen rules of Rabbi Ishmael, and the thirty-two rules of Rabbi Joseph the Galilean. For our purposes the following are important:

The argument from least to greatest or minor to major. The rabbis call it "Qal wahomer," "heavy and light." It is the first rule of Hillel.

The search for parallel places (within the same Bible) is also called "Gezerah shawah" ("equivalent principle"). It is the second rule of Hillel. This is the analogy between two texts or cases and is used to clarify the meaning of a passage or to draw a similar conclusion. The frequent substitution of "word" for "glory" and vice versa in the Targumim is based on this rule.

The different reading of a text vocalizing it or punctuating it in a different way (*al tikrah*: "do not read it thus . . . but rather").

The search for a second meaning (tartei mismah') puts into relief the richness of the text.

The securing of a principle (binyan) starting with two or more texts that afterwards are applied to many others (third and fourth rules of Hillel).

Attention to the context: the thing learned from within the text *(Dabar ha-lamed me'inyano).* This is the seventh rule of Hillel.

The study of gems or the numerical equivalent of the letters of one word that can be interpreted in the light of another word with the same equivalency.

Notarikon: The decomposition of a word, making of each letter the beginning of new words.

Allusion (remez): this procedure is very rich and can be based on words, personalities, or traditions.

Pešer: this is the search for an updated meaning, especially in prophetic texts. The procedure was used in the Qumran community.

Jewish hermeneutics has other dimensions as well, such as the use of allegory, the attribution of meaning to the least detail of punctuation in a biblical text (Rabbi Akiva), and in some cases speculations based on cabalistic calculations.

Jewish exegetical production is very rich. Even before the appearance of rabbinic Judaism we find many exegetical works such as the apocalyptic literature, the writings of Qumran, and the work of Philo. One must also presume the existence of targumic translations in the first century, although these have come down to us only in fragments from Qumran (in addition to the Targum of Job).

Among those written texts already edited during the formative period of rabbinic Judaism we ought to cite the following:

The Targumim. These are translations of the Bible made principally for the use of the synagogue. The translations are not mere versions but adaptations of the biblical text to the mentality and concerns of those attending the synagogue. Consequently they transform places of possible polytheistic significance; they use substitutions like "word" and "shekinah glory" to designate divine interventions in creation, apparitions, and salvific actions; they avoid anthropomorphisms; and they sometimes develop the meaning of the biblical text with extensive paraphrases. We have access to *Targum Neofiti,* the principal representative of the Palestinian Targum to the Pentateuch (written in Galilean Aramaic). A more official translation is *Targum Onqelos,* a translation of the Pentateuch written in Babylonian Aramaic. The so-called *Targum Pseudo-Jonathan* (or *Targum Yerushalmi*) to the Pentateuch is a later compilation, a mixture of the Palestinian Targum and *Targum Onqelos.* Likewise of great importance is *Targum Jonathan* to the Prophets, written in Babylonian Aramaic and recognized officially. There also exists a Targumic translation of the hagiographers.

The Midrashim. The exegetical commentaries of Judaism increased throughout the centuries. Here we will indicate the principal ones of the early period:

Tannaitic Midrashim (of halakhic tendency). These are the following: Mekhilta de Rabbi Ishmael (a commentary on Exodus); Sifra to Leviticus; Sifre to the books of Numbers and Deuteronomy. They were written in the second half of the third century and represent a great effort to expose the meaning of the text in accord with the Mishnah.

Exegetical Midrashim. The foremost among these is *Genesis Rabbah* at the end of the fourth century or beginning of the fifth. These commentaries try to give an answer to the situation of Israel, subject as it is to the Christian emperors. They indicate that in the end the triumph will be Israel's.

Homiletic Midrashim. Beginning with the fifth century there arose a series of commentaries that adopted the literary genre of a homily (the development of a textual base and illuminating it in light of another text). Generally the subjects are texts used on Saturdays or feast days. Many such writings exist: *Leviticus Rabbah, Pesikta de Rav Kahana, Tanhuma, Pesikta Rabbati,* etcetera.

The exegetical output continued in later Judaism, especially in the great medieval commentators (including Rashi and Maimonides). We cannot fail to mention, as well, the mystical exegesis whose most representative example is Zohar.

The Mishnah and Talmud. Although these are not works technically considered exegetical one finds in them the fruit of the exegesis done by the rabbis. The Mishnah (at the middle of the third century) with its six parts (Zeraim, Moed, Nashim, Nezikin, Qodashim, and Toharot) includes all of life and the religious and civil aspects of Israel. It is the expression of the oral Torah. The Talmud (with its twofold versions, Palestinian and Babylonian) is an encyclopedic commentary on the Mishnah and is the most impressive monument of Jewish literature.

In its totality rabbinic exegetical output constitutes an enormous effort to penetrate into the meaning of the Scriptures and apply them to the existing situation of the people of Israel. Its profound knowledge of biblical language and the symbiosis of the biblical text with the liturgical and social life of the people make the interpretations always replete with meaning. It is true that many of the procedures and techniques are artificial and do not respond to historical-critical criteria. The preeminence of the Law as the referent in aspects of ritual purity as compared with Christianity's affirming the fulfillment of the messianic prophecies has assured that there must be selective interpretation. Nevertheless, Jewish hermeneutics has great value in itself, and for a Christian exegete the knowledge of its points of view is of great help in the understanding of the biblical text. The document of the Pontifical Biblical Commission on *The interpretation of the Bible in the Church* (1993) indicates as one approach to the biblical text "recourse to the Jewish traditions of interpretation" (I. C. 2), and in the section on updating (IV. A. 2) it enumerates some of the methods used in Jewish exegesis.

BIBLIOGRAPHY

Muñoz León, Domingo. *Derás. Los caminos y sentidos de la Palabra divina en la Escritura. Primera Serie. Derás targúmico y Derás neotestamentario.* Madrid: C.S.I.C., 1987.

Neusner, Jacob. *Midrash in Context. Exegesis in Formative Judaism.* Philadelphia: Fortress, 1983.

____. *What is Midrash?* Philadelphia: Fortress, 1987.

Strack, Herman L. *Einleitung in Talmud und Midrasch.* 5th ed. Munich: C. H. Beck, 1921. English: H. L. Strack and Günter Stemberger. *Introduction to the Talmud and Midrash.* Translated by Marcus Bockmühl. Edinburgh: T & T Clark, 1991.

How has the Bible Exercised Power to Guide the Faithful in the Early History of the Church?

Charles Kannengiesser

With the spiritual power of the Bible at the core of its earliest expansion, the Church originated from the conversion undergone by Jesus' disciples in their understanding of Holy Scripture. They claimed to remain true to their traditional reading of the sacred books of their Jewish past, but their very encounter with Jesus let them find in those books a new message. The story of their experience, shared with fellow believers, became the New Testament. Such is the spiritual power of the Bible, that *it always produces unexpected newness in the mind of its readers if only their reading remains focused by the inner dynamic of what they read.* A short survey of Philo and patristic exegesis may illustrate the point.

Philo (c. 13–20 B.C.E.–c. 50 C.E.) was one of the most prominent members of the Jewish community in Alexandria. He was rich and politically influential, but what presented him with the ultimate challenge was to write his own Bible commentary. Single-handedly he created the very first continuous commentary ever written on the Torah. Starting with Gen 1:1 he composed thirty separate essays filled with an extensive account of what specific verses and passages of the Bible meant for him. Long after his death Philo's works came into the hands of a man called Pantaenos, the first known Christian teacher in Alexandria. Though written by a Jew, they became a vivid source of learning inside the local Christian community and they inspired Origen, the greatest of all Alexandrian interpreters of the Christian Bible.

Philo was deeply committed to his tradition of faith, which was reason enough for him to show that the religious tradition of his ancestors was compatible with the Alexandrian culture of his day. Therefore the wording of Torah inspired in him all sorts of reflections with reference to contemporary trends of thought and lifestyle. He called on the whole cultural and philosophical heritage proper to Alexandrian society in order to communicate the multifold meaning of Torah in appropriate ways. Such was the powerful inspiration Philo found for this task in the sacred writings that he could turn his words into a celebration of half a millennium of Greek culture and Greek spirituality without betraying a single conviction of religious Judaism. Philo thereby retrieved the cultural values he shared with his contemporaries, for the Bible as a source of inspiration is hermeneutical by nature. In other words *the Bible is a power engaging the biblical interpreters and their audiences into a renewed self-understanding and a new understanding of their own world.*

This is even more true when Christians become interpreters of Scripture. In the earliest centuries of the Church the innovative power of the Bible was at work like a nuclear source of energy producing increasingly new attitudes of faith in the believing mind, new sacral and social institutions inside faith communities, new procedures for inculturating the Bible itself. These spiritual chain reactions resulted in the building up of a whole new set of inspired writings, from the earliest gospel narratives to the book of Revelation.

The hermeneutical dynamics of Scripture specified the criteria for the canonical acceptance of NT writings, such as their unanimous reception in the main Church communities or their unquestionable message. For instance, twenty or more gospels circulated in the communities of the second century but only four were finally admitted into the so-called canon. *The Bible itself, by the inner requirements of its reception in Christian faith, decided about such admissions more than any external authority.*

The inspirational power of Scripture reshaped time and space for the believers in creating the world of the early Church. Liturgical festivals generated a new calendar. On the day of the Lord's resurrection, the third day after Friday according to the gospel account, a Eucharist began to be celebrated; it became our Sunday. The whole year started to culminate with Easter Sunday, with a preparatory period of Lent and a joyful prolongation until Pentecost. Epiphany, commemorating the baptism of Jesus and his "manifestation" as Christ, was another very old festival. Christmas came to be celebrated in Rome much later, in the fourth century. Soon religious festivals motivated by the Christian reading of Scripture punctuated the cycle of all seasons, just as they did in Jewish and other religious traditions.

Space also became aligned according to the new biblical imagination. Major urban centers of the Roman empire would be declared "Petrine," which means places with a Church tradition founded by Peter, such as Jerusalem, mother of all cities for the believers (Acts 2), Antioch (where a *Gospel of Peter, Acts of Peter,* and even an *Apocalypse of Peter* were written), Rome (where Peter was said to have been martyred according to a very ancient tradition), and Alexandria (where Mark, considered Peter's secretary, was venerated as the founder of the local church). From the time of the NT a biblical awareness would give the Church members a new sense for the *oikoumenē,* the whole inhabited world, to which Jesus had sent his disciples according to Matt 28:19: "Go therefore and make disciples of all nations . . . ." Thus the spiritual power of the Bible generated a worldwide space for Christian believers. In only a few generations merchants and soldiers would, at the cost of their lives, proclaim Christ all over the empire, from the northern ends of Europe to the shores of Roman Africa, and from deep in the Syrian Orient to the southern cities of Spain. Streaming through catechumenate and baptism into the Church of the earliest centuries came many thousands of new Christians finding a more serene access to a new type of social and political community spread all over the Roman world. In Roman Africa of the fifth century Augustine would celebrate the City of God, as he called it, established primarily on the powerful truth of Scripture.

Serving the ancient Church in their own sacralized space and time, Christian interpreters of the Bible would give believers a new sense of their human dignity. Parents ceased to practice exposure of newborn girls and abusive patriarchy. Church leaders, strongly based on Scripture, took over the task of early prophets in Israel as social reformers. They popularized arguments that encouraged good behavior and comforted the people of God with hope in a future predicted in Scripture. Even ascetic vocations were supported by Scripture. Women in early youth or prematurely widowed dedicated themselves to God according to biblical models. Soon male asceticism proclaimed itself as a replacement for martyrdom, and from the end of the third century a monastic youth movement followed the heroic times of persecutions. Scripture opened a space for many spiritual journeys not only into monasteries, but also on the level of educated thinking and the fine arts.

In other words *the Bible served as a hermeneutical power engaging the believing mind into a constant questioning and redefining of human values.* Received by popular demand as a message about afterlife, like most religious classics, the Bible actually transformed societies in such a way that the late Roman empire found itself christianized even as it stood at the brink of its own extinction.

The Power of the Bible in the Middle Ages

Willemien Otten

Introduction

The culture of the Middle Ages—the period extending roughly from the end of the Roman empire to the beginning of the Reformation (500 to 1500)—was a deeply biblical culture, perhaps more so than any other since the inception of Christianity. This is true not only for the theology of the medieval period, which for a long time coincided with the art of biblical exegesis, but also for the goals of medieval civilization at large. It becomes clearer when we realize how the medieval political and administrative ideals pertaining to prophetic leadership, kingship, and papacy ultimately climaxed in the spiritual-military enterprises of the crusades, which were aimed at the capture of Jerusalem, or when we look at the Romanesque and Gothic cathedrals, so sumptuously decorated with biblical motifs, that covered the medieval landscape under "a white garment of churches."

To call medieval culture a biblical culture in this general way helps to underscore that the biblical influence in this period was all-pervasive. But while the fact that the Bible played a foundational role in the Middle Ages can easily be illustrated with examples it is much more difficult to demonstrate the precise extent of biblical influence, since the Bible's centrality was often simply assumed without further explanation. Accepting as its basic premise that the Bible played a central role in all of medieval culture, this essay will analyze the prominence of the Bible in the Middle Ages by isolating those aspects that are more typical of medieval culture than of any other cultural phase in the West. The focus will be on:

(A) The Bible as Word of God, that is, as the embodiment of an immediate and powerful divine presence;

(B) The Bible as the highest source of truth, that is, as the receptacle of all wisdom, be it worldly or divine;

(C) The Bible as the highest theological authority, manifest in the exegesis and systematic theology of the Middle Ages.

I. The Bible as Word of God

While the Franks were the first to become Christianized in medieval Europe following the baptism of their king Clovis (c. 500), Europe was not restored to its former unity until the reign of Charlemagne (768–814). It is with the Carolingian renaissance that the incipient features of medieval culture took shape. Modelling himself after King David of the Old Testament and crowned emperor by pope Leo III in 800, Charlemagne displayed in his reign a combination of biblical and Roman aspects that would henceforth characterize medieval culture. Whereas the dominance of Roman culture remained clearly visible in the use of Latin as the language of the educated classes and in the development of Roman law, the role of the Bible speaks to the much deeper theological underpinning of medieval culture, which as a whole rested on the quest for eternal salvation. As the book containing the word of God, the Bible was important not only because it formed the most direct embodiment of divine authority but especially because it opened up the avenue to human salvation, which was mediated by the Church. In a society where literacy was not widespread and its value disproportionately enhanced, the Bible was essentially seen as a book from heaven with a message of transcendent truth.

Following their patristic predecessors, medieval readers thus saw the biblical text as deeply divine. Its interpretation was likewise considered sacred insofar as in matters of biblical exegesis medieval believers were trained to turn to the Church Fathers (especially the western Fathers Ambrose, Jerome, Augustine, and Gregory the Great) before venturing to give their own interpretation. The authority of the Church Fathers was second only to that of the Bible, the text of which was frequently read through excerpts in the Fathers. Together these powerful forces of the Bible and the Church Fathers came to form a textual chain of command that led the medieval believer from his or her contemporary setting all the way back to Adam's fate in Paradise. In the absence of much information about the historical origins of the biblical books the psychological impact of this chain was much stronger than seems possible today in our thoroughly modernized world. While the joint study of the Bible and the Church Fathers thus enabled medieval readers to preserve a bond of cultural continuity with the events described in the Bible, this was far outweighed by the bond of a transcendent spiritual continuity, which they also felt. If in Adam all people fell prey to sin, then in Christ all were redeemed. The heavenly salvation that medieval culture strove so hard to find, and for which it turned collectively and full of hope to the Bible as the Word of God, was concretely made available through the mediation of Christ in the context of the Church. Christ was therefore the central principle of all medieval biblical interpretation.

Reading biblical stories in the Middle Ages, both those in the OT and the NT, meant in the first place that one would read them as stages of a collective human journey that led from Adam's sin to Christ's salvation and on to the final judgment. But the aim was more than just digesting the words. Reading biblical stories allowed medieval believers the opportunity to participate in the biblical drama in such a way that the darkness of their own earthly existence would be shot through with the light of heaven. Naturally it is Christ who formed the hermeneutical hinge by which medieval believers were able not only to coordinate the interpretation of the OT with that of the NT but also to connect the fate of biblical figures such as Abraham, Moses, or John the Baptist directly to their own lives. Filtered through the mediation of Christ, the central message of the Bible as the concrete embodiment of divine authority thus inspired consolation and hope rather than awe and intimidation. And although many medieval believers would remain illiterate, there is no reason to disbelieve that this biblical message reached them, for it could also be found depicted above the doors or on the capitals of medieval churches. Biblical influence in the Middle Ages was indeed all-pervasive.

II. The Bible as Source of Truth

When Charlemagne brought a new degree of unity to European civilization by transforming it into a Christian empire the Bible by implication became his central book. While its principal role remained that of recording the promise of salvation, it could also be consulted for other purposes. In conformity with Christ's famous dictum "I am the way, and the truth, and the life" (John 14:6) medieval intellectuals generally felt encouraged to pursue their quest for wisdom, both sacred and secular, by using the Bible as a prime source of truth. The deep-rooted conviction that God equals Truth was the reason why there existed virtually no distinction between theology and philosophy until far into the twelfth century, as both disciplines used the Bible as their foundational document. It also goes far to explain why the Bible was also studied in the other disciplines of the liberal arts, ranging from grammar to astronomy.

Besides the Bible, other documents pertaining to philosophical truth were available as well, for example Plato's creation myth, the *Timaeus,* although they were less numerous than in patristic times. Following the patristic debate medieval thinkers revisited the old question whether the use of non-Christian sources should be permissible in a culture that claimed to be Christian. They resolved it by stressing the essential harmony of biblical and philosophical truth. To underscore their point that scriptural revelation and natural philosophy were not mutually exclusive, medieval thinkers resorted to the simile that the Book of Scripture and the Book of Nature contained identical truths. After all, God had revealed divine wisdom not only to all Christians, but to all of creation. The Bible itself intimated that creation could yield valuable knowledge of the divine, as is demonstrated by the words of Paul in Rom 1:20 that "ever since the creation of the world [God's] eternal power and divine nature, invisible though they are, have been understood and seen through the things he has made." Not just the Bible but all of creation was therefore deemed fit to reveal God's majesty. This parallelism of Nature and Scripture allowed medieval thinkers to coordinate the existing knowledge about nature, derived mainly from ancient philosophers such as Plato and Aristotle, with the truths received from the Bible. In their opinion they could freely do so without compromising the Bible's integrity or its epistemological priority as direct divine revelation.

With the discovery of more of Aristotle's works in the mid-twelfth century, however, the philosophical information about nature grew so sophisticated that it rapidly replaced the role formerly played by the Bible in that area. With the further development of philosophy and the rise of the universities there emerged more and more of a discrepancy between reason (that is, philosophy) and faith (that is, the simple adherence to biblical truths), although scholastic theologians like Thomas Aquinas strove hard to connect the two. The sciences moved steadily away from the Bible as an important source, and in its final stages even the development of scholastic theology was accompanied by a decrease of biblical authority, as lecturing on Peter Lombard's *Sentences* became more important than lecturing on the Bible. Nevertheless the analogy of the books of Nature and of Scripture remained generally intact throughout the entire Middle Ages, and so did the need to bring all philosophical wisdom in close contact with the underlying salvific truth of the Scriptures.

III. The Bible in Medieval Exegesis and Theology

By proclaiming Christ as the hermeneutical principle of biblical interpretation medieval thinkers confirmed an important strategy they had received from their patristic predecessors: typological exegesis. By interpreting the Bible through a christological lens they proved that the unity of the biblical message, especially of OT and NT interacting as prophecy and fulfillment, was crucial to them. This unity was nowhere more powerfully embodied than in the life and death of Christ as recorded in the gospels and reenacted in the ecclesial sacraments of baptism and Eucharist.

It is precisely because medieval biblical exegesis betrayed such a fundamental and unchangeable unity that it is possible to understand that it could also give rise to incredible diversity. Like their patristic predecessors medieval exegetes distinguished among various layers of exegesis, yet since all these were firmly rooted in the same underlying christological principle they did not violate the essential unity of the biblical message. The best-known exegetical division of the Middle Ages was a fourfold one, which a famous rhyme describes as follows:

> *littera gesta docet, quid credas allegoria,*
> *moralis quid agas, quo tendas anagogia,*

which may be translated as:

> "the letter teaches God's deeds
> the allegorical sense what to believe
> the moral sense how to act
> the anagogical sense for what higher goal to strive."

The fact that this fourfold exegetical division is rooted in the underlying christological unity of the medieval Bible, which was a cultural as well as a theological ideal, can explain why medieval exegetes and theologians could apply it with such playful flexibility. Instead of the complicated four levels they would often simply use a twofold division, namely that between the letter and the spirit of the text, or that between history and allegory. It is this basic distinction that underlies most biblical exegesis in the Middle Ages, although the moral or tropological sense remained prominent in monastic circles.

While the Middle Ages are justly celebrated as the age of spiritual exegesis this does not mean that medieval exegetes slighted the historical sense. The letter of the text was considered of paramount importance, since without it the other interpretations such as allegory would lack a firm basis. The literal or historical sense gained further prominence in the twelfth century. Its importance was enhanced even more when theology became a separate discipline at the new universities. Thus although modern historical-critical exegesis may have had its immediate origin in the ideals of humanism and the Renaissance, it resonates with certain medieval trends as well. Allegorical exegesis remained indeed prominent in the Middle Ages and the weight of certain authorities like Thomas Aquinas would always be treasured, but this was by no means intended to stifle the development of critical exegesis by precluding a probing but faithful inquiry into the literal meaning of the text.

The later Middle Ages saw a growing specialization of the exegetical trade. Yet the development of medieval exegesis differs from modern academic exegesis in that it always remained part of the larger medieval culturo-theological paradigm. The unity of this paradigm was represented by the Church. Although increasingly driven by the search for discursive truth, medieval exegetes remained generally focused on finding a higher, salvific truth, to the demands of which they were ready to submit their quest for scholarly knowledge. In this regard it is important to make mention of an important criterion of medieval biblical exegesis, namely that of *caritas* or love. According to Augustine's *On Christian Doctrine* (Book III. 10. 14) which served as the decisive exegetical handbook of the Middle Ages, only an exegesis that promoted love of God and neighbor was acceptable in the Christian Church. In adopting this principle medieval thinkers revealed not only that exegesis operates on a charitable basis in addition to an intellectual one but that the former ultimately surpasses the latter.

Biblical exegesis in the Middle Ages was predominantly practiced by clerics, as all learning was in fact in clerical hands. The early Middle Ages saw exegesis flourish in the monasteries and cathedral schools. Since the contacts between them were many, exegetical positions rarely became entrenched. With the definitive localization of intellectual learning in the universities and a concomitant growth and intensification of spiritual ideals outside the scholastic atmosphere different groups came to practice different kinds of exegesis. Monastic exegesis turned more and more inward as it focused increasingly on the individual soul. In scholastic exegesis, which had always been more sensitive to the literal sense, the trend to producing a systematic summary of the exegetical findings ultimately gave rise to the development of theology as an independent academic discipline. While the use of biblical material was highly valued, it now became incorporated in a self-enclosed theological discourse. An example is the *Summa Theologiae* of Thomas Aquinas. In it Thomas gives a prudent interpretation of his biblical material as he does of the Church Fathers, but his comprehensive theological system leads him at the same time beyond strictly exegetical and patristic concerns to deal with the full spectrum of sacred theology, from the nature and attributes of God to matters of eschatology. This is a far stretch from the biblical commentaries of the early Middle Ages whose interplay between exegesis and systematic theology sometimes resulted in a confused structure, but it is also different from today's complex interdependence between contemporary exegesis as a separate theological discipline in its own right and other theological disciplines such as systematic and moral theology, something recently analyzed by the Pontifical Biblical Commission. What binds all three together, however—namely early medieval biblical commentaries, Thomas Aquinas's *Summa Theologiae,* and modern Catholic academic exegesis—thereby providing the Catholic tradition with remarkable continuity, is the theme of *fides quaerens intellectum* as the motive behind the development of all theological and scriptural interpretation.

While Thomas Aquinas is a typical example of a scholastic exegete-as-theologian the Dominican order to which he belonged, together with its companion order the Franciscans, also inspired an important new use of the Bible, one that was geared more toward reaching a lay audience. Founded to help the poor in an urban environment and to prevent the spread of heresy, the mendicant orders of Dominic and Francis came to put a high value on preaching as an important element of their ministry. For the homiletic purposes of these orders acquiring biblical knowledge was of prime importance, as was the subsequent passing on of this knowledge to audiences that were largely deprived of pastoral care. Like the sculptured portals or the stained glass windows of the Gothic cathedrals, the fiery sermons preached by the mendicant friars of the later Middle Ages, when Latin was increasingly giving way to the vernacular, helped to spread knowledge of the Bible to all people. Important were also the mystery plays in which certain biblical scenes would be reenacted and performed for the public, and the mystical and devotional literature that influenced increasing numbers of private, educated citizens toward the end of the Middle Ages. Women constituted a large segment of this lay audience. It is their contribution to late medieval mysticism that shows us yet another vital appropriation of biblical themes, especially that of Christ's nourishing of the Christian community through his suffering.

While the late medieval period has often been criticized for the aloofness of its scholastic debates, it is by pointing to its importance in the maintainance of a culture of the Bible that the balance may be restored. For it is through the theological activities of lay people and clerics alike, namely their preaching, ministering, and writing to a growing audience in the later Middle Ages that the power of the Bible was kept very much alive so as to be able to generate new theological impulses until this day.

BIBLIOGRAPHY

Medieval Exegesis

Lubac, Henri de. *Exégèse médiévale: les quatre sens de l'Écriture.* Paris: Aubier, 1959–1964.

Smalley, Beryl. *The Study of the Bible in the Middle Ages.* Notre Dame, Ind.: University of Notre Dame Press, 1964.

The Bible in the Medieval World

Riché, Pierre, and Guy Lobrichon. *Le Moyen Age et la Bible.* Paris: Beauchesne, 1984.

The Bible as a Medieval Book

Gibson, Margaret T. *The Bible in the Latin West.* Notre Dame, Ind., and London: University of Notre Dame Press, 1993.

Interpretation of the Bible Within the Bible Itself

E. Earle Ellis*

I. The Character of New Testament Usage

1. General

Old Testament phraseology in the New Testament occurs occasionally as a part of the writer's own patterns of expression that have been influenced by the Scriptures (1 Thess 2:4; 4:5). Most often, however, it appears in the form of citations or intentional allusions. Lars Hartman ("Exegesis," 134) suggests three reasons for an author's citation of another: to obtain the support of an authority (Matt 4:14), to call forth a cluster of associations (Mark 12:1-2), and to achieve a literary or stylistic effect (Titus 1:12). He rightly observes that an allusion to the OT sometimes can be discerned only after the total context of a passage has been taken into account.

As might be expected in Greek writings, citations from the OT are frequently in agreement with the Septuagint ("seventy," LXX), the Greek version commonly used in the first century. But they are not always so, and at times they reflect other Greek versions, Aramaic paraphrases (Targums) or independent translations of the Hebrew text. Apart from the use of a different text-form they may diverge from the LXX because of a lapse of memory. However, this explanation is less probable than has been supposed in the past (Ellis, *Paul's Use,* 11–16, 150–152). More frequently, as will be detailed below, citations diverge from the LXX because of deliberate alteration—that is, by a free translation and elaboration or by the use of a different textual tradition, to serve the purpose of the NT writer. The textual variations in the quotation then become an important clue for discovering not only the writer's interpretation of the individual OT passage but also his perspective on the OT as a whole.

**The language found in this article at some points departs from the gender-inclusive usage of the publisher. It has been retained at the author's request as consistent with his theological understanding.*

2. Introductory Formulas

Formulas of quotation, which generally employ verbs of "saying" or "writing," correspond to those found in other Jewish works, such as the OT (for example, 1 Kings 2:27; 2 Chron 35:12), the Qumran scrolls (for example, 1QS 5.15; 8.14), Philo and the rabbis (for example, Philo, *Migr.* 118; *m. 'Abot* 3.7; Ellis, *Paul's Use,* 48–49). They locate the citation with reference to the book or writer or less frequently to the biblical episode, such as "in Elijah" (Rom 11:2) or "the story about the bush" (Mark 12:26). At times they specify a particular prophet (Acts 28:25), a specification that on occasion may be important for the NT teaching (for example, Mark 12:36; France, *Jesus* 101–102). When one book is named and another cited the formula may represent an incidental error that is no part of the teaching or, more likely, the cited text may be viewed as an interpretation (Matt 27:9) or elaboration (Mark 1:2) of a passage in the book named.

Introductory formulas often underscore the divine authority of the OT, not in the abstract but within the proper interpretation and application of its teaching. Thus the formula "Scripture *(hē graphē)* says" can introduce an eschatological, that is, "Christianized" summation or elaboration of the OT (John 7:38; Gal 4:30), and *graphē* can be contrasted to traditional interpretations (Matt 22:29). That is, it implies that the revelational, "word of God" character of Scripture is present within the current interpretation. In the words of Renée Bloch ("Midrash," 109), Scripture "always involves a living Word addressed personally to the people of God and to each of its members . . . ." B. B. Warfield (*Inspiration* 148) puts it similarly: "Scripture is thought of as the living voice of God speaking in all its parts directly to the reader." The formula "it is written" can also have the intended connotation of a specific and right interpretation of Scripture (Rom 9:33; 11:26) even though the connotation may not always be true (Matt 4:6).

Sometimes an explicit distinction between reading Scripture and knowing or hearing Scripture may be drawn. It is present in the story of the Ethiopian eunuch (Acts 8:30) and implicitly in Jesus' synagogue exposition at Nazareth (Luke 4:16-17, 21). It may be presupposed, as it is in rabbinical writings (Daube, *Rabbinic Judaism,* 433–436), in the formula "have you not *(ouk)* read?" That is, "you have read but not understood." This formula is found in the NT only on the lips of Jesus and usually within a scriptural debate or exposition (for example, in Matt 12:3, 5; 19:4; cf. Doeve, *Jewish Hermeneutics,* 105–107).

A few formulas are associated with specific circles within the Christian community (Ellis, *Old Testament,* 79–82). The nine *legei kyrios* ("says the Lord") quotations probably reflect the activity of Christian prophets. The *hina plērōthē* ("that it might be fulfilled") quotations, found especially in the gospels of Matthew and John, may have a similar origin. Both kinds of quotations contain creatively altered text-forms that facilitate an eschatological reapplication of the OT passages similar to that found in the Qumran scrolls (Ellis, *Paul's Use,* 139–147) to the experiences and understanding of the early Church. This is a kind of activity recognized in first-century Judaism to be appropriate to prophets as well as teachers (Ellis, *Prophecy,* 55–60, 130–132, 182–187).

Somewhat similar are the *pistos ho logos* ("faithful is the word") passages in the Pastoral letters (1 Tim 1:15; 4:9; 2 Tim 2:11-13; Ellis, "Pastoral Letters," 664). They appear to be instructions of Christian prophets (cf. 1 Tim 4:1, 6, *tois logois tēs pisteōs*) and/or inspired teachers used by Paul in the composition of the letters. Although they do not contain OT quotations some of these "faithful sayings" may refer to the exposition of the OT (for example, 1 Tim 2:13–3:1a; Titus 1:9, 14; 3:5-8; cf. Ellis, *Old Testament,* 82–83). They appear to arise out of a prophetic circle engaged in a ministry of teaching.

3. Forms and Techniques in Quotation

(a) *Combined quotations* of two or more texts appear frequently in a variety of forms: a chain of passages (Rom 15:9-12), a commentary pattern (John 12:38-41; Romans 9–11), and composite or merged citations (Rom 3:10-18; 2 Cor 6:16-18). With the exception of the last type these patterns were commonly employed in Judaism and in classical writings (Johnson, *Quotations,* 92–102). They serve to develop a theme and perhaps exemplify the principle in Deut 19:15 that two witnesses establish a matter. Sometimes (for example, in Rom 10:18-21) in the fashion of the rabbis they bring together citations from the Law, the Prophets, and the Writings. Such combinations usually were formed in conjunction with catchwords important for the theme (such as "stone" and "chosen" in 1 Pet 2:6-9).

(b) *Testimonia.* Citations "testifying" to the messiahship of Jesus were of special interest to the early Church. Sometimes they appear as combined quotations (Hebrews 1), combinations that possibly lie behind other NT citations (Ellis, *Old Testament,* 70–72). Such "testimonies" were primarily thematic combinations for instructional and apologetic purposes and as the *testimonia* at Qumran indicate (4QTest) some may have circulated in written form during the apostolic period. However, the hypothesis that they were collected in a precanonical "testimony book" used by the Church in anti-Jewish apologetic is less likely.

The "testimonies" apparently presuppose a worked-out christological understanding of the particular passages and are not simply proof texts randomly selected. The earliest Christians, like twentieth-century Jews, could not, as we do, simply infer from traditional usage the "Christian" interpretation of a biblical word or passage. Proof texts standing alone, therefore, would have appeared to them quite arbitrary if not meaningless.

According to a thesis of C. H. Dodd (*According to the Scriptures,* 78–79, 107–108) the "testimony" quotations were selected from and served as pointers to larger OT contexts that previously and as a whole had been christologically interpreted. For example Matt 1:23 in citing Isa 7:14 probably has in view the total section, Isa 6:1–9:7, as the additional phrase "God with us" (Isa 8:8, 10 LXX) and the frequent use of the section elsewhere in the NT indicate. Dodd (*According to the Scriptures,* 126) correctly perceived that the *testimonia* were the result of "a certain method of biblical study." But what precisely was that method? It may well have included, as Dodd thought, a systematic christological analysis of certain sections of the OT. Beyond this, however, the method probably corresponded to a form and method of scriptural exposition used in contemporary Judaism and known to us as midrash.

4. Quotation and Midrash

(a) The Hebrew term *midrash* means "commentary" (cf. 2 Chr 13:22; 24:27) and in the past it has usually been associated primarily with certain rabbinic commentaries on the OT. Recently it has been used more broadly to designate an activity as well as a literary genre, a way of expounding Scripture as well as the resulting exposition (Ellis, *Prophecy,* 188–192). Thus "the house of midrash" (*beth ha-midraš,* Sir 51:23) was a place where such exposition was carried on (and not a library of commentaries). According to Bloch ("Midrash," 32–33) the essence of the midrashic procedure was a contemporization of Scripture in order to apply it to or make it meaningful for the current situation. It can be seen, then, in interpretive renderings of the Hebrew text (= implicit midrash), as in the Greek LXX and the Aramaic Targums (Gooding, *Relics*). For example "Arameans and Philistines" in Isa 9:11(12) become in the LXX the contemporary "Syrians and Greeks." It appears also in more formal "text plus exposition" patterns (= explicit midrash), for example the rabbinic commentaries. Both kinds of midrash appear in first-century Judaism in the literature of the Qumran community.

(b) *Implicit midrash* appears in double entendre, in interpretive alterations of OT citations, and in more elaborate forms (Ellis, *Old Testament,* 92–96). The first type involves a play on words. Thus Matt 2:23 cites Jesus' residence in Nazareth as a "fulfillment" of prophecies identifying the Messiah as a *nazōraios* (Nazirite?—cf. Judg 13:5, 7 LXX) or a *neṣer* (= branch, Isa 11:1; cf. 49:6; 60:21; Betz, *Jesus der Herr,* 399–401). Possibly the double meaning of "lift up" in John 3:14; 12:32-34, that is, hang and exalt, alludes to an Aramaic rendering *(zeqaph)* of Isa 52:13, which carries both meanings; the terminology is clarified in the synoptic gospels where Jesus prophesies that he is to "be killed . . . and . . . rise" (Mark 8:31; cf. Luke 18:33). A similar double entendre may be present in Acts 3:22-26 where "raise up" apparently is used both of the Messiah's pre-resurrection ministry and of his resurrection.

The second type can be seen in Rom 10:11: "The scripture says, 'Everyone *(pas)* who believes in him shall not be put to shame.'" The word "everyone" is not in the OT text; it is Paul's interpretation woven into the citation and fitting it better to his argument (10:12-13). Similarly in the citation of Gen 21:10 at Gal 4:30 the phrase "son of the free woman" is substituted for "my son Isaac" in order to adapt the citation to Paul's application. More elaborate uses of the same principle will be discussed below.

More complex forms of implicit midrash occur (1) in making a merged or composite quotation from various OT texts, altered so as to apply them to the current situation, and (2) in the description of a current event in biblical phraseology in order to connect the event with the OT passages. Contemporized composite quotations appear, for example, in 1 Cor 2:9; 2 Cor 6:16-18. The use of scriptural phraseology to describe and thus to explain the meaning of current and future events is more subtle and reflects a different focus: the event appears to be of primary interest and the OT allusions are introduced to illumine or explain it. This kind of midrash occurs, for example, in the Lukan infancy narratives, in Jesus' apocalyptic discourse (Matt 24:15 // Mark 13:14 // Luke 21:20) and his response at his trial (Matt 26:64 // Mark 14:62 // Luke 22:69) and in Revelation where some seventy percent of the verses contain allusions to the OT (Ellis, "New Directions," 12–15).

In the infancy narratives the annunciation scene (Luke 1:26-38) alludes to Isa 6:1–9:7—for example to Isa 7:13-14 (v. 27, *parthenos, ex oikou David*); 7:14 (v. 31); 9:6-7 (vv. 32, 35)—a section of Isaiah that C. H. Dodd (*According to the Scriptures,* 78–82) has shown to be a primary source for early Christian exegesis. It probably also alludes to Gen 16:11 (v. 31); 2 Sam 7:12-16 (vv. 32, 35[?], *huios theou*); Dan 7:14 (v. 33b); and Isa 4:3; 62:12 (v. 35, *hagion klēthēsetai*). The Magnificat (Luke 1:46-55) and the Benedictus (Luke 1:68-79) appear to be formed along the same lines. It is probable that family traditions about the events surrounding Jesus' birth were given this literary formulation by prophets of the primitive Jerusalem church (Ellis, *Luke,* 27–29, 67–68).

The response of the Lord at his trial (Matt 26:64 // Mark 14:62 // Luke 22:69) is given by the gospels in the words of Ps 110:1 and Dan 7:13. It probably represents a summary of Jesus' known response, a summary in biblical words whose "messianic" exegesis either had been worked out in the Christian community or, more likely, had been taught to the disciples by Jesus. That Jesus made use of both Ps 110:1 and Dan 7:13 during his earthly ministry is highly probable (cf. France, *Jesus,* 101–103).

The apocalyptic discourse (Matthew 24 // Mark 13 // Luke 21), which also includes the use of Dan 7:13, consists of a midrash by Jesus on certain passages in Daniel, a midrash that has been supplemented by other sayings of the Lord and reshaped by the evangelists and their predecessors "into something of a prophetic tract" linked to the Church's experiences. In the course of transmission the midrash "lost many of its once probably explicit associations with the OT text" (Hartman, *Prophecy,* 242). If this reconstruction is correct it shows not only how teachings of Jesus were contemporized in a manner similar to the midrashic handling of the OT texts but also how the Lord's explicit midrash was modified so that the OT references, although not lost, were largely assimilated to the current application. The process is much more thoroughgoing than is the case in the composite quotations cited above.

These examples suggest that implicit midrash sometimes presupposes or develops out of direct commentary on the OT, that is, explicit midrash. We may now turn to that form of early Christian usage.

(c) *Explicit midrash* in the NT has affinities both with the *pesher* midrash at Qumran and with certain kinds of midrash found in rabbinic expositions. The ancient expositions of the rabbis are preserved in sources that are dated several centuries after the NT writings. However, in their general structure they provide significant parallels for early Christian practice since (1) it is unlikely that the rabbis borrowed their methods of exposition from the Christians and (2) similar patterns may be observed in the first-century Jewish writer Philo (for example, *Sacr. AC* 76–87; cf. Ellis, *Old Testament,* 96–101). They probably originated not only as "sermon" or "homily" but also as "commentary," that is, not only as the complement of synagogue worship but also as the product of the synagogue school. The type of discourse that finds most affinity with NT expositions is the "proem" midrash. As used in the synagogue it ordinarily had the following form:

The (Pentateuchal) text for the day
A second text, the proem or "opening" for the discourse
Exposition containing additional OT citations, parables, or other commentary and linked to the initial texts by catch-words
A final text, usually repeating or alluding to the text for the day.

The New Testament letters frequently display, with some variation, the general outline of this pattern (cf. Ellis, *Prophecy,* 155–157). The structure appears specifically in Rom 9:6-29:

vv. 6-7: Theme and initial text: Gen 21:12.
v. 9: Second, supplemental text: Gen 18:10.
vv. 10-28: Exposition containing additional citations (vv. 13, 15, 17, 25-28) and linked to the initial texts by the catchwords *kalein* and *huios* (12, 24-26, 27).
v. 29: Final text alluding to the initial text with the catchword *sperma.*

At Gal 4:21–5:1 the initial text of the commentary is itself a summary of a Genesis passage, an implicit midrash introducing the key word *eleuthera*. It is probably Paul's summation, but it might have been drawn from a Genesis midrash similar to Jubilees or the Qumran Genesis Apocryphon (cf. Ellis, *Prophecy,* 190–191, 224–226).

vv. 21-22: Introduction and initial text. Cf. Genesis 21.
vv. 23-29: Exposition with an additional citation, linked to the initial and final texts by the catchwords *eleuthera* (vv. 22, 23, 26, 30), *paidiskē* (vv. 22, 23, 30, 31), and *ben/huios* = *teknon* (vv. 22, 25, 27, 28, 30, 31).
4:30–5:1: Final text and application, referring to the initial text. Cf. Gen 21:10.

The pattern in 2 Pet 3:3-13 is similar, although less clear. As in Galatians 4 the initial "text" is a selective summary of a section of Scripture:

vv. 3-4: Theme: Cited Christian prophecy.
vv. 5-6: Initial text (with eschatological application). Cf. Genesis 1–7.
vv. 7-12: Exposition (with an additional citation: v. 8) linked to the initial and final texts by the catchwords *ouranos* (vv. 5, 7, 10, 12), *gē* (vv. 5, 7, 10), *apollumi* (vv. 6, 9, cf. v. 7). Cf. *hēmera* (vv. 7, 8, 10, 12).
v. 13: Final text and applications. Cf. Isa 65:17.

The above examples show how a composite, interpreted citation and an interpretive summary of a larger section of Scripture may serve as the "text" in a midrash. The use of short, explicit midrashim as "texts" in a more elaborate commentary pattern is only an extension of the same practice (for example, in Rom 1:17–4:25; cf. Ellis, *Prophecy,* 217–218). One instance of this appears in 1 Cor 1:18–3:20, which is composed of the following sections, all linked by catchwords such as *sophia* and *mōria:*

1:18-31: Initial "text."
2:1-5: Exposition/Application.
2:6-16: Additional "text."
3:1-17: Exposition/Application.
3:18-20: Concluding texts: Job 5:13; Ps 94:11.

The synoptic gospels also display exegetical patterns similar to those in the rabbis (cf. Ellis, *Prophecy,* 157–159, 247–252). Matthew 21:33-44 corresponds to an ancient form of a synagogue address:

v. 33: Initial text: Isa 5:1-2.
vv. 34-41: Exposition by means of a parable linked to the initial and final texts by a catchword: *lithos* (vv. 42, 44, cf. 35; Isa 5:2, *saqal*); cf. *oikodomein* (vv. 33, 42).
vv. 42-44: Concluding texts: Ps 118:22-23; Dan 2:34-35, 44-45.

In Luke 10:25-37 appears a somewhat different pattern, called in the rabbinic writings the *yelammedenu rabbenu* ("let our master teach us"), in which a question or problem is posed and then answered. Apart from the interrogative opening it follows in general the structure of the proem midrash:

vv. 25-27: Dialogue including a question and initial texts: Deut 6:5; Lev 19:18.
v. 28: A second text: Lev 18:5.
vv. 29-36: Exposition (by means of a parable) linked to the initial texts by the catchwords *plēsion* (vv. 27, 29, 36) and *poiein* (vv. 28, 37a, 37b).
v. 37: Concluding allusion to the second text *(poiein).*

Matt 19:3-8 is similar:

vv. 3-5: Question, answered by the initial texts: Gen 1:27; 2:24.
v. 6: Exposition linked to the initial text by the catchwords *duo, sarx, mia.*
vv. 7-8a: Additional citation (Deut 24:1) posing a problem, with exposition.
v. 8b: Concluding allusion to the (interpolated!) initial text *(apʾ archēs).*

As the gospels uniformly attest, debates with scribes, that is, theologians, about the meaning of Scripture constituted an important part of Jesus' public ministry. They were certainly more extensive than the summarized gospel accounts although they may have followed the same general arrangement. In any case a *yelammedenu* pattern known and used by the rabbis is the literary form often employed by the gospel traditioners. In the rabbinical writings the pattern is usually not a dialogue but the scriptural discourse of one rabbi. In this respect the exegetical structure in Romans 9–11 is closer to the rabbinic model than are the gospel traditions (cf. Ellis, *Prophecy,* 218–219).

Certain differences between rabbinic and NT exegesis should also be noted:

(1) The NT midrashim often do not have an initial text from the Pentateuch, that is, they do not employ the Sabbath text of the synagogue lectionary cycle.

(2) They often lack a second, proem text.

(3) They often have a final text that does not correspond or allude to the initial text.

(4) They have an eschatological orientation. Cf. Ellis, *Prophecy,* 163–165. Nevertheless in their general structure the NT patterns have an affinity with the rabbinic usage that is unmistakable and too close to be coincidental.

(d) A kind of exposition known as the *pesher midrash* appears in the Qumran writings, for example in the commentary on Habakkuk (1QpHab 3:1-3). It receives its name from the Hebrew word used in the explanatory formula, "the interpretation *(pesher)* is. . . ." This formula and its apparent equivalent, "this is" *(huah),* sometimes introduce the OT citation (CD 10.16) or, more characteristically, the commentary following the citation. Both formulas occur in the OT, the latter translated in the LXX by the phrase *houtos (estin).* Cf. Isa 9:14-15; Zech 1:9-10; Dan 5:25-26; 4QFlor 1.2-3; Ellis, *Prophecy,* 160, 201–205.

Besides the formula, the Qumran *pesher* has other characteristics common to midrashic procedure. Like the midrashim discussed above it apparently uses or creates variant OT text-forms designed to adapt the text to the interpretation in the commentary. It also links text and commentary by catchwords. It is found, moreover, in various kinds of commentary patterns: anthology (4QFlor), single quotations (CD 4.14), and consecutive commentary on an OT book (1QpHab).

More significantly for NT studies, the Qumran *pesher,* unlike rabbinic midrash but very much like early Christian practice, is both charismatic and eschatological. As *eschatological exegesis* it views the OT as promises and prophecies that have their fulfillment within the writer's own time and community, a community that inaugurates the "new covenant" of the "last *('aḥarit)* days," and constitutes the "last *('aḥaron)* generation" before the coming of Messiah and the inbreaking of the kingdom of God (cf. Jer 31:31; 1QpHab 2:3-7; 7:2).

This characteristic feature, the *pesher* formula combined with an eschatological perspective, appears in a number of NT quotations:

Rom 9:7-9: "In Isaac shall your seed be called" (Gen 21:12). That is *(tout estin)* . . . the children of the promise are reckoned for the seed. For this is *(houtos)* the word of promise. ". . . for Sarah there shall be a son" (Gen 18:10).

Eph 5:31-32: "On account of this shall a man leave father and mother and be joined to his wife, and the two shall be one flesh" (Gen 2:24). This is *(touto . . . estin)* a great mystery . . . for Christ and the Church.

Gal 4:22-24: It is written, "Abraham had two sons . . ." (cf. Genesis 21). These are *(hautai . . . eisin)* two covenants . . .

Acts 2:4, 16-17: They were all filled with the Holy Spirit and began to speak in other tongues . . . This is *(touto estin)* what was spoken by the prophet Joel, "I will pour out my spirit . . ." (Joel 2:28).

The Qumran *pesher* was regarded by the community as *charismatic exegesis,* the work of inspired persons such as the Teacher of Righteousness and other wise teachers *(maśkilim).* The OT prophecies were understood, as they are in the book of Daniel (9:2, 22-23; cf. 2:19, 24), to be a "mystery" *(raz)* in need of interpretation *(pesher),* an interpretation that only the *maśkilim* can give. Cf. 1QpHab 7:1-8; 1QH 12:11-13.

(e) From midrash to *testimonia:* "Words lifted from their scriptural context can never be a *testimonium* to the Jewish mind. The word becomes a *testimonium* for something or other after one has brought out its meaning with the aid of other parts of Scripture." With this perceptive observation J. W. Doeve (*Jewish Hermeneutics,* 116) goes beyond the thesis of C. H. Dodd mentioned above, to contend that "testimony" citations in the NT are derived from midrashim, that is, expositions of those particular OT passages.

In support of Doeve are several examples of a "Christian" interpretation of a text that is established in an exposition and presupposed elsewhere in a "testimony" citation of the same text (cf. 1 Cor 1:18-31 with 2 Cor 10:17; Ellis, *Prophecy,* 192–197, 213–218).

(1) The exposition in Acts 2:17-35 and that underlying Matthew 24 // Mark 13 // Luke 21 apply Ps 110:1 and Dan 7:13, respectively, to Jesus. This interpretation is presupposed in the use of the verses at Matt 26:64 // Mark 14:62 // Luke 22:69.

(2) Hebrews 2:6-9 establishes by midrashic procedures that Psalm 8 is fulfilled in Jesus; in 1 Cor 15:27 and Eph 1:20, 22 this understanding of Psalm 8 (and Psalm 110) is presupposed.

(3) Acts 13:16-41 is probably a (reworked) midrash in which 2 Sam 7:6-16 is shown to apply to Jesus. This interpretation of 2 Samuel 7 is presupposed in the *testimonia* in Heb 1:5 and 2 Cor 6:18.

The midrashic expositions in these examples are not, of course, the immediate antecedents of the cited *testimonia* texts, but they represent the kind of matrix from which the "testimony" usage appears to be derived. They show, furthermore, that the prophets and teachers in the early Church were not content merely to cite proof texts but were concerned to establish by exegetical procedures the Christian understanding of the OT.

We may proceed one step farther. Rabbinic parables often are found in midrashim as commentary on the OT texts. Christ's parables also occur within an exegetical context, for example in Matt 21:33-44 and Luke 10:25-37. Elsewhere, when they appear independently or in thematic clusters, they sometimes allude to OT passages (Mark 4:1-20 to Jer 4:3; Luke 15:3-6 to Ezek 34:11). Probably such independent and clustered parables originated within an expository context from which they were later detached. If so, their present context represents a stage in the formation of the gospel traditions secondary to their use within an explicit commentary format.

II. The Presuppositions of NT Interpretation

1. General

To many Christian readers, to say nothing of Jewish readers, the NT's interpretation of the OT appears to be exceedingly arbitrary. For example, Hos 11:1 ("out of Egypt I called my son") refers to Israel's experience of the Exodus; how can Matt 2:15 apply it to Jesus' sojourn in Egypt? In Ps 8:4-8 the bestowal of "glory" and "dominion" on the "son of man" *(ben ʾadam)* alludes to Adam or to Israel's king; how can Heb 2:8-9 and 1 Cor 15:27 apply the text to Jesus? If Gen 15:5 and 2 Samuel 7 are predictions of Israel's future, how can NT writers refer them to Jesus and his followers, who include Gentiles as well as Jews?

As has been shown above, the method used to justify such Christian interpretations of the OT represents a serious and consistent effort to expound the texts. The method itself, of course, may be criticized, but our modern historical-critical method is also deficient: although it can show certain interpretations to be wrong, it cannot achieve an agreed interpretation for any substantive biblical passage. "Method" is inherently a limited instrumentality and, indeed, a secondary stage in the art of interpretation. More basic are the perspective and presuppositions with which the interpreter approaches the text (cf. Ellis, *Prophecy,* 163–172; idem, *Old Testament,* 101–121).

The perspective from which the NT writers interpret the OT is sometimes stated explicitly; sometimes it can be inferred from their usage. It is derived in part from contemporary Jewish views and in part from the teaching of Jesus and the experience of the reality of his resurrection. Apart from its christological focus it appears to be governed primarily by four factors: a particular understanding of history, of man, of Israel, and of Scripture.

2. Salvation as History

Jesus and his apostles conceive of history within the framework of two ages, this age *(aiōn)* and the age to come (see, for example, Matt 12:32; Mark 10:30; Luke 20:34-35; Eph 1:21; Heb 9:26). This perspective appears to have its background in the OT prophets, who prophesied of "the last *(ʾaḥarit)* days" and "the day of the Lord" as the time of an ultimate redemption of God's people and the destruction of their enemies (see, for example, Isa 2:2; Dan 10:14; Mic 4:1). It becomes more specific in the apocalyptic writers, who underscored the cosmic dimension and (often) the imminence of the redemption and, with the doctrine of two ages, the radical difference between the present time and the time to come. This point of view is clearly present in the message of the Baptist that "the kingdom of God is at hand" and that the one coming after him, Jesus, would accomplish the final judgment and redemption of the nation (Matt 3:2, 10-12).

The *twofold* consummation of judgment and deliverance that characterized the teaching of apocalyptic Judaism becomes, in the teaching of Jesus and his apostles, a *two stage* consummation. As "deliverance" the kingdom of God that Judaism expected at the end of this age is regarded as already present within this age in the person and work of Jesus (Matt 12:28; Luke 10:9; Rom 14:17; Col 1:13). As "judgment" (and final deliverance) the kingdom awaits the second, glorious appearing of Messiah. This perspective may be contrasted with that of Platonism and of apocalyptic Judaism as follows:

Platonism and Gnosticism	Eternity ↑ Time			
Judaism	C −↓ I	This Age __________	P I	Age to Come __________
New Testament	C −↓ I	_ _ - - - - +↑ __________	P I ↓	 - - - - - - - -

Platonic and later Gnostic thought anticipated a redemption *from* matter and an escape from time and history at death. The biblical, Jewish hope was for a bodily resurrection, a redemption *of* matter within time: the present age, from the creation (C) and Fall (−↓) to the coming of Messiah (P) was to be succeeded by a future age of peace and righteousness under the reign of God. The NT's modification of Jewish apocalyptic rested on the perception that in the mission, death, and resurrection of Jesus the Messiah the age to come, the future reign or kingdom of God, had become present in hidden form in the midst of the present evil age, although its public manifestation awaited the parousia (P) of Jesus. Thus, in the words of Oscar Cullmann, for Jesus "the kingdom of God does not culminate a meaningless history, but a planned divine process" (*Salvation,* 233). Equally, for the NT writers faith in Jesus means faith in the story of Jesus, the story of God's redemptive activity in the history of Israel that finds its high point and fulfillment in Jesus.

For this reason the mission and meaning of Jesus can be expressed in the NT in terms of a *salvation history* "consisting of a sequence of events especially chosen by God, taking place within an historical framework" (Cullmann, *Salvation,* 25). Although the concept of *oikonomia* ("plan," "arrangement") as used in Eph 1:10 represents this idea, that is, a divinely ordered plan, the term "salvation history" does not itself occur in the NT. The concept is most evident in the way in which the NT relates current and future events to events, persons, and institutions in the OT. That relationship is usually set forth as a typological correspondence.

3. Typology

(a) Typological interpretation expresses most clearly the basic approach of earliest Christianity toward the OT. It is not so much a system of interpretation as a historical and theological perspective from which the early Christian community viewed itself. As a hermeneutical method it must be distinguished from the meaning of *typos* ("model," "pattern") as it was widely used in the Greek world.

Only occasionally using the term *typos,* typological interpretation appears broadly speaking as *covenant typology* and as *creation typology.* The latter may be observed in Romans 5 where Christ is compared and contrasted with Adam, "a type *(typos)* of the one who was to come" (5:14). The former appears in 1 Cor 10:6, 11, where the Exodus events are said to be "types [examples] for us," things that have happened "to serve as an example" *(typikōs)* and to have been written down "to instruct us, on whom the ends of the ages have come." Covenant typology accords with the Jewish conviction that all of God's redemptive acts followed the pattern of the Exodus; it is, then, an appropriate way for Jesus and his apostles to explain the decisive messianic redemption. More generally, covenant typology approaches the whole of the OT as prophecy. Not only persons and events but also its institutions were "a shadow of the good things to come" (Heb 10:1).

(b) New Testament typology is thoroughly christological in its focus. Jesus is the "prophet like Moses" (Acts 3:22-23) who in his passion and death brings the old covenant to its proper goal and end (Rom 10:4; Heb 10:9-10) and establishes a new covenant (Luke 22:20, 29). As the messianic "son of David," that is, "son of God" he is the recipient of the promises, titles, and ascriptions given to the Davidic kings (see, for example, 2 Sam 7:14; Ps 2:7; Amos 9:11-12; cf. John 7:42; Acts 13:33; 15:16-18; 2 Cor 6:18; Heb 1:5).

Because the new covenant consummated by Jesus' death is the occasion of the new creation initiated by his resurrection, covenant typology may be combined with creation typology: as the "eschatological Adam" and the "Son of Man," that is, "son of Adam" (Ps 8:4, 6-8; cf. 1 Cor 15:27, 45) Jesus stands at the head of a new order of creation that may be compared and contrasted with the present one. This combination in Paul and Hebrews finds its immediate background in the resurrection of Jesus, but it is already implicit in Jesus' own teaching, for example in his Temple saying (Matt 26:61 // Mark 14:58), his promise of "Paradise" to the robber (Luke 23:42-43), and his teaching on divorce based on Gen 2:24 (cf. Matt 19:3-9). It is probably implicit also in his self-designation as the Son of man (Matt 26:64 // Mark 14:62 // Luke 22:69), a designation that is derived from Dan 7:13-14, 27 with allusions to Psalm 8 and Ezek 1:26-28. "Son of man" in Psalm 8 refers not only to Israel's (messianic-ideal) king but also to Adam; likewise the Son of Man in Dan 7:13-14 is related not only to national restoration but also to the "dominion" and "glory" of a new creation. In apocalyptic Judaism also Israel was associated with Adam and the new covenant with a renewed creation (*T. Levi* 18; 1QS4.22-23). Jesus and his followers shared these convictions and explained them in terms of the mission and person of Jesus.

(c) The OT type not only corresponds to the new-era reality but also stands in antithesis to it. Like Adam, Jesus is the representative head of the race; but unlike Adam who brought death, Jesus brings forgiveness and life. Jesus is "the prophet like Moses," but unlike Moses' ministry of condemnation, that of Jesus gives justification and righteousness. Similarly the Law as an expression of God's righteousness "is holy and just and good" and its commandments (Exodus 20), actuated by an ethic of love (Lev 19:18), are to be "fulfilled" by the believer (Rom 7:12; 13:8; Gal 5:14). However, the (works of) the Law were never intended as a means of man's salvation and as such it can only condemn.

One may speak, then, of "synthetic" and "antithetic" typology to distinguish the way in which a type, to one degree or another, either corresponds to or differs from the reality of the new age. For example, Abraham represents synthetic typology (that is, his faith) but not antithetic (that is, his circumcision: Galatians 3). Moses and the Exodus can represent both (Heb 11:28-29; 1 Cor 10:1-4, 6-10; 2 Cor 3:9); so can Jerusalem (Gal 4:25-26; Rev 11:8; 21:2). The Old Covenant, that is, the Law, more often represents antithetic typology.

(d) Since the history of salvation is also the history of destruction (Cullmann, *Salvation,* 123) it includes a *judgment typology.* The flood and Sodom (Luke 17:26-30; 2 Pet 2:5-6; Jude 7) and probably the prophesied destruction of Jerusalem in 70 C.E. (Matt 24:3) become types of God's eschatological judgment. The faithless Israelite is a type of the faithless Christian (1 Cor 10:11-12; Heb 4:11); the enemies of Israel a type of the (Jewish) enemies of the Church (Rev 11:8; Rom 2:24) and, perhaps, a type of Antichrist (2 Thess 2:3-4; Rev 13:1-10).

(e) In a brilliant and highly significant contribution to NT hermeneutics Leonard Goppelt's *Typos* has set forth the definitive marks of typological interpretation. (1) Unlike allegory, typological exegesis regards the words of Scripture not as metaphors hiding a deeper meaning *(hyponoia)* but as the record of historical events out of whose literal sense the meaning of the text arises (pp. 17–18, 201–202). (2) Unlike the "history of religions" exegesis it seeks the meaning of current, NT situations from a particular history, the salvation history of Israel. From past OT events it interprets the meaning of the present time of salvation, and in turn it sees in present events a typological prophecy of the future consummation (pp. 194–205). (3) Like rabbinic midrash, typological exegesis interprets the text in terms of contemporary situations, but it does so with historical distinctions that are lacking in rabbinic interpretation (pp. 28–32). (4) It identifies a typology in terms of two basic characteristics, historical correspondence and escalation, in which the divinely ordered prefigurement finds a complement in the subsequent and greater event (p. 202).

In a masterly essay in *Exegetica* (Tübingen 1967, 369–380) Rudolf Bultmann rejected Goppelt's conclusion that salvation history was constitutive for typological exegesis and sought to show that the origin of typology lay rather in a cyclical-repetitive view of history (cf. *Barn.* 6:13). Although Judaism had combined the two perspectives, the NT, for example, in its Adam/Christ typology represents a purely cyclical pattern, parallels between the "primal time" and the "end time" (374).

However, Bultmann (pp. 369–370), in interpreting the NT hermeneutical usage within the context of the traditional Greek conception, does not appear to recognize that the recapitulation element in NT typology is never mere repetition but is always combined with a change of key in which some aspects of the type are not carried over and some are intensified. Exegetically Goppelt made the better case and established an important framework for understanding how the NT uses the Old.

4. Other Presuppositions

(a) In agreement with the OT conception, the NT views man in terms both of individual and corporate existence. It presents the corporate dimension, the aspect most difficult for modern Western man to appreciate, primarily in terms of Jesus and his Church (examples include Matt 26:26-28 // Mark 14:22-25 // Luke 22:19-20; Col 1:24). For the NT faith in Jesus involves an incorporation into him: it is to eat his flesh (John 6:35, 54), to be his body (1 Cor 12:27), to be baptized into him (Rom 6:3) or into his name (1 Cor 1:13; Acts 8:16), to be identified with him (Acts 9:5-6), to exist in the corporate Christ (2 Cor 5:17) who is the "tent" (Heb 9:11) or "house" (2 Cor 5:1) in the heavens, God's eschatological temple.

Corporate existence can also be expressed as baptism "into Moses" (1 Cor 10:2), existence "in Abraham" (Heb 7:9-10) or "in Adam" (1 Cor 15:22), and at its most elementary level the unity of husband and wife as "one flesh" (Matt 19:5 // Mark 10:7-8; Eph 5:29-32). It is not merely a metaphor, as we are tempted to interpret it, but an ontological statement about who and what man is. The realism of this conception is well expressed by the term "corporate personality" (cf. Ellis, *Old Testament,* 110–112).

The corporate extension of the person of the leader to include individuals who "belong" to him illumines the use of a number of OT passages. It explains how the promise given to Solomon (2 Sam 7:12-16) can be regarded as fulfilled not only in the Messiah (Heb 1:5) but also in his followers (2 Cor 6:18) and, similarly, how the eschatological temple can be identified both with the individual (Matt 26:61 // Mark 14:58; John 2:19-22) and the corporate (1 Cor 3:16; 1 Pet 2:5) Christ. It very probably underlies the conviction of the early Christians that those who belong to Christ, Israel's messianic king, constitute the true Israel (cf. Ellis, *Paul's Use,* 136–139). Consequently it explains the Christian application to unbelieving Jews of Scriptures originally directed to Gentiles (Acts 4:25-28; Rom 11:9-10) and, on the other hand, the application to the Church of Scriptures originally directed to the Jewish nation (2 Cor 6:16-18; 1 Pet 2:9-10).

Corporate personality also offers a rationale whereby individual, existential decision (Mark 1:17; 2 Cor 6:2) may be understood within the framework of a salvation history of the nation or the race. These two perspectives are considered by some scholars to be in tension or to be mutually exclusive. However, in the words of Oscar Cullmann (*Salvation,* 248), the "now of decision" in the NT is not in conflict with the salvation-historical attitude but subordinate to it: "Paul's faith in salvation history creates at every moment the existential decision." For it is precisely within the context of the community that the individual's decision is made: universal history and individual history cannot be isolated from one another.

The history of salvation often appears in the NT as the history of individuals: Adam, Abraham, Moses, David, Jesus; yet they are individuals who also have a corporate dimension embracing the nation or the race. The decision to which the NT calls everyone relates to them. It is never a decision between the isolated individual and God but is, rather, a decision to "put off the old man," Adam, and to "put on the new man," Christ (Eph 4:22-24*), to be delivered from the corporeity "in Moses" and "in Adam" (1 Cor 10:2; 15:22) and to be "immersed in" and "put on" Christ (Gal 3:27), that is, to be incorporated into the "prophet like Moses" and the eschatological Adam of the new creation in whom the history of salvation is to be consummated (1 Cor 15:45; cf. Acts 3:22-26).

(b) The early Christian prophets and teachers explain the OT by what may be called *charismatic exegesis.* Like the teachers of Qumran (see above) they proceed from the conviction that the meaning of the OT is a "mystery" whose "interpretation" can be given not by human reason but only by the Holy Spirit (1 Cor 2:6-16; cf. Matt 13:11; 16:17). On the basis of revelation from the Spirit they are confident of their ability

**Author's translation.*

rightly to interpret the Scriptures (Matt 16:17; Mark 4:11; Rom 16:25-26; Eph 3:3-6; 2 Pet 3:15-16). Equally they conclude that those who are not gifted cannot "know" the true meaning of the word of God (Matt 22:29; 2 Cor 3:14-16).

This view of their task does not preclude the NT writers from using logic or hermeneutical rules and methods, but it does disclose where the ultimate appeal and authority of their interpretation lie. Correspondingly, an acceptance of their interpretation of Scripture in preference to some other, ancient or modern, also will rest ultimately not on the proved superiority of their logical procedure or exegetical method but rather on the conviction of their prophetic character and role.

BIBLIOGRAPHY

Betz, Otto. *Jesus Der Herr der Kirche. Aufsätze zur biblischen Theologie II.* Tübingen: J.C.B. Mohr, 1990.

Bloch, Renée. "Midrash," in William S. Green, ed., *Approaches to Ancient Judaism.* Brown Judaic Studies 1. Missoula: Scholars, 1978, 29–50.

Cullmann, Oscar. *Salvation in History.* New York: Harper & Row, 1967.

Daube, David. *The NT and Rabbinic Judaism.* Peabody, Mass.: Hendrickson, 1994.

Dodd, C. H. *According to the Scriptures; the substructure of New Testament Theology*. London: Nisbet, 1952.

Doeve, J. W. *Jewish Hermeneutics in the Synoptic Gospels and Acts.* Assen: Van Gorcum, 1954.

Ellis, E. Earle. *The Old Testament in Early Christianity: Canon and Interpretation in the Light of Modern Research.* Tübingen: J.C.B. Mohr (Paul Siebeck), 1991.

____. "Pastoral Letters," in Gerald F. Hawthorne, et al., eds., *Dictionary of Paul and His Letters.* Downers Grove, Ill.: InterVarsity, 1993, 658–666.

____. *The Gospel of Luke.* Grand Rapids: Eerdmans, 1996 (1974).

____. *Paul's Use of the Old Testament.* Grand Rapids: Baker Book House, 1991.

____. *Pauline Theology: Ministry and Society.* Grand Rapids: Eerdmans, 1989.

____. *Prophecy and Hermeneutic in Early Christianity: New Testament Essays.* WUNT 18. Tübingen: Mohr, 1978.

____. "New Directions in the History of Early Christianity," in T. W. Hillard et al., eds., *Ancient History in a Modern University. FS E. A. Judge.* 2 vols. Grand Rapids: Eerdmans, 1997, 2:71-92.

France, R. T. *Jesus and the Old Testament. His Application of Old Testament passages to Himself and his mission.* London: Tyndale Press, 1971.

Gooding, David W. *Relics of Ancient Exegesis.* Cambridge and New York: Cambridge University Press, 1976.

Goppelt, Leonhard. *Typos: the typological interpretation of the Old Testament in the New.* Translated by Donald H. Madvig; foreword by E. Earle Ellis. Grand Rapids: Eerdmans, 1982.

Gundry, R. H. *The Use of the Old Testament in St. Matthew's Gospel. With special reference to the Messianic hope.* Leiden: Brill, 1967.

Hartman, Lars. "Scriptural Exegesis in the Gospel of Matthew and the Problem of Communication," in M. Didier, ed., *L'évangile selon Matthieu.* BEThL 29. Gembloux: J. Duculot, 1972.

____. *Prophecy Interpreted. The formation of some Jewish apocalyptic texts and of the eschatological discourse Mark 13 par.* CB.NT ser. 1. Lund: Gleerup, 1966.

Johnson, Franklin. *The Quotations of the New Testament from the Old: considered in the light of general literature.* Philadelphia: American Baptist Publication Society, 1896 (c1895).

Warfield, Benjamin B. *The Inspiration and Authority of the Bible.* Edited by Samuel R. Craig, with an introduction by Cornelius Van Til. Philadelphia: Presbyterian and Reformed Publishing Co., 1964.

Patristic Exegesis of the Books of the Bible

David L. Balás and D. Jeffrey Bingham

INTRODUCTION

Most articles on patristic exegesis address the approaches used by the Fathers through the progressive periods of the patristic era or in the regions or languages (East, West; Greek, Latin) associated with particular groups of Fathers. Others treat them according to whether the Father or group employed a method basically allegorical (Alexandrian) or literal (Antiochian). This article acknowledges and to some degree reflects the value of such approaches, but its interest is different. In a manner complementary to a commentary on the Bible it seeks to do two things. First, it provides for most books of the Bible an orientation to extant patristic commentaries and homilies in both critical editions and English translations when available. The reader will find a primary bibliography of these works after each discussion of the main divisions of biblical books within the canon, for example "Pentateuch," "Gospels and Acts." Second, this essay treats how the Fathers received, interpreted, and taught most books or corpora of the Bible. It provides selective insight into how Christians of the first six hundred years interpreted the Bible in their journey to understand God and their world, to worship God, to develop true doctrine, and to love God and neighbor. Through the Fathers' commentaries, homilies, theological treatises, and correspondence this article sets forth for the reader an idea of how Christians in a milieu other than our own read the very same text in a similar manner and yet also in a manner quite different. In this way it complements the international character of this commentary by demonstrating historically how Christian interpretation, though it shows elements of discontinuity among differing cultures, also reveals elements of continuity and permanence. It is hoped that these glimpses into patristic exegesis of biblical books will further the reader's understanding of the sacred text.

Some books (Leviticus, Ruth, 1 and 2 Chronicles, Ezra, Nehemiah, Esther, Micah, Nahum, Tobit, Judith, additions to Esther and Daniel, Letter of Jeremiah, 2 Peter, and Jude) were not treated due to space limitations within this essay and the more limited role of these books in the development of early Christian thought. The reader will find some helpful discussions on these books within the early Church in the commentaries that follow.

At the end of this introduction the reader will find a brief bibliography on patristic exegesis of the Bible. For helpful orientations and bibliographies to the development and history of patristic exegesis the reader will want to consult Denis Farkasfalvy's essay, "Interpretation of the Bible," in the *Encyclopedia of Early Christianity,* 2nd ed., edited by Everett Ferguson (Garland, 1997) and Manlio Simonetti's essay, "Exegesis, Patristic," in the *Encyclopedia of the Early Church,* edited by Angelo Di Berardino (Oxford, 1992). Further primary listings of the Fathers' sermons and homilies on the New Testament may be found in H. J. Sieben, *Kirchenväterhomilien zum Neuen Testament,* Instrumenta Patristica 22 (The Hague: Martinus Nijhoff International, 1991). For further secondary literature the following sources may be consulted: H. J. Sieben, *Exegesis Patrum,* Sussidi Patristici 2 (Rome: Istituto Patristico Augustinianum, 1983); *Bibliographia Patristica,* 32 vols., edited by Wilhelm Schneemelcher and Knut Schäferdiek (Berlin: de Gruyter, 1959–1994). Brief comments on liturgical perspective were greatly informed by J. P. Lang's *Dictionary of the Liturgy* (New York: Catholic Book Publishing, 1989). The authors wish to express their gratitude to Professor Pamela Bright and Professor Charles Kannengiesser for information they provided on the patristic interpretation of several Old Testament books. The authors also acknowledge their debt to John Brown, David Dickinson, Robert Judge, Bryan Litfin, Peter Martens, Beth Motley, and Jonathan Yates for their contributions to the completion of this essay.

GENERAL BIBLIOGRAPHY

On Patristic Exegesis of the Bible in General

The Cambridge History of the Bible. Vol. 1, *From the Beginnings to Jerome,* ed. P. R. Ackroyd and C. F. Evans. Vol. 2, *TheWest from the Fathers to the Reformation,* ed. G.W.H. Lampe. Cambridge: Cambridge University Press, 1969–1970.

Centre d'Analyse et de Documentation Patristique (Jean Allenbach et al). *Biblia Patristica: Index des citations et allusions bibliques dans la littérature patristique.* 6 vols. and supplement on Philo of Alexandria. Paris: Editions de C.N.R.S., 1975–1995.

Fontaine, Jacques, and Charles Pietre, eds. *Le monde latin antique et la Bible.* Bible de tous les Temps 2. Paris: Beauchesne, 1985.

Höpfl, Hildebrand, Athanasius Miller, Benno Gut, and Adalbert Metzinger. *Introductio specialis in Vetus Testamentum.* 5th ed. Rome: A. Arnodo, 1956. *Introductio specialis in Novum Testamentum.* 4th ed. Naples: M. d'Auria, 1949. Although these works are antiquated introductions, their bibliographies are still valuable for the commentaries of the ancient, medieval, and early modern periods.

La Bonnardière, Anne-Marie, ed. *Saint Augustin et la Bible.* Bible de tous les Temps. Paris: Beauchesne, 1986.

Lubac, Henri de. *Exégèse médiéval, Les quatre sens de l'Écriture.* 4 vols. Paris: Aubier, 1959–1964.

Margerie, Bertrand de. *An Introduction to the History of Exegesis.* 3 vols. Translated by Leonard Maluf, Pierre de Fontnouvelle, and Paul Duggan. Petersham, Mass.: Saint Bede's Publications, 1990–1994. English Translation of *Introduction à l'histoire de l'exégese.* 4 vols. Paris: Cerf, 1980–1990.

Mondésert, Claude, ed. *Le monde grec ancien et la Bible.* Bible de tous les Temps 1. Paris: Beauchesne, 1984.

Simonetti, Manlio. *Biblical Interpretation in the Early Church.* Translated by J. A. Hughes. Edinburgh: T & T Clark, 1994. English Translation of *Profilo Storico dell' Esegesi Patristica.* Rome: Augustinianum, 1981.

____. *Lettera e/o Allegoria: Un contributo alla storia dell'esegesi patristica.* Rome: Augustinianum, 1985. This is a much expanded and updated version of the preceding item.

New Testament in General

Sieben, Hermann Josef. *Kirchenväterhomilien zum Neuen Testament: ein Repertorium der Textausgaben und Überstzungen. Mit einem Anhang der Kirchenväterkommentare.* Instrumenta Patristica 22. The Hague: Martinus Nijhoff International; Steenburgis: Abbatia S. Petri, 1991. Indicates for all the books of the NT all the patristic homilies (including editions and translations) and commentaries (including editions).

PENTATEUCH

Genesis

The earliest Christian treatments of the Genesis material appear to have been commentaries and homilies on the first chapter's account of creation within six days. These works, *Hexaemera,* could be devotional, in praise of and wonder at God's creative majesty, or technical in explanation of the procedure of God's creative act. They were written by Melito of Sardis, Rhodo, Candidus, Apion, Maximus, Hippolytus, Victorinus of Pettau, Severian of Gabala, Basil of Caesarea, Gregory of Nyssa, Ambrose, and John Philoponos (Eusebius of Caesarea, *Ecclesiastical History* 4.26.2; 5.13.8; 5.27; Jerome, *Epistle* 84.7; *Lives of Illustrious Men* 61). Unfortunately, all but the last five and a fragment from Victorinus have been lost.

Exegetes of the early Church also produced several commentaries and homilies on the other material within Genesis. Among the Greek Fathers, in addition to comments on the *Hexaemeron* Hippolytus also treated the later narrative of Genesis, of which only fragments remain. Origen's thirteen books on Genesis are lost, but some fragments in *catenae* survive as do sixteen of his homilies. The commentaries of Eusebius of Emesa and Diodore of Tarsus are extant only in *catenae* fragments, but due to a fortunate discovery of papyri at Tura in 1941 Didymus of Alexandria's commentary is now known. In addition to providing his own interpretation Didymus presents and adheres to Origen's reading of chs. 1–3. The allegory is there along with the dualistic anthropology derived from the differing accounts of Adam's creation (Genesis 1, 2), and Adam and Eve before and after the Fall (Genesis 3). Two series of homilies on Genesis by John Chrysostom are extant: nine homilies preached in Lent of 386 and sixty-seven delivered during 388. The latter series provides almost a comprehensive commentary on the book. Of Theodore of Mopsuestia's commentary on Genesis, for the most part only selections of his reading of the first three chapters survive in fragmentary form. Cyril of Alexandria's seven books of *Elegant Comments (Glaphyra)* on Genesis offer a christological interpretation of chosen passages, where he employs a spiritual (typological) reading but also presents a literal one. Theodoret's commentary on the Octateuch (Pentateuch with Joshua, Judges, Ruth) is extant, while Gennadius's commentary on Genesis and Procopius's commentary on the Octateuch survive only in fragments.

The commentaries of the Greek Fathers are complemented by the works of the Latin Fathers, Jerome and Augustine, and the Syrian Father Ephraem. Jerome wrote a commentary that employed Origen's *Hexapla* and was informed by Hebraic issues and traditions. Augustine's three treatments evidence somewhat differing approaches. The first commentary, written against the Manichaean objections to the teachings and language of Genesis, was highly allegorical. The second, while still polemically focused against the Manichaean objections, was an attempt at literal exegesis. He only reached Gen 1:26 before abandoning the project in 393. From 401 to 415 he composed his final work on Genesis, a twelve-book composition exegetically treating the text up to Gen 3:24 with substantial theological explanation. This third commentary sought to be literal, but did entertain the allegorical sense. Augustine also addressed troublesome material in Genesis in his *Locutions on Genesis* and in the *Questions on Genesis*. Ephraem's commentary treats the early chapters of Genesis more extensively than the later ones, evidences connections to Rabbinic traditions, focuses attention on the theological question of free will, and is not slavishly typological.

Other interpretations of Genesis in addition to the *Hexamera,* commentaries, and homilies included specific works on events and persons within the narrative. Hippolytus expounded on Jacob's blessing of his sons in Genesis 49. Gregory of Nyssa and Basil of Caesarea (or Pseudo-Basil) both addressed the creation of humanity. Ambrose produced homilies and treatises on Paradise and the Fall, Cain and Abel, Noah, Abraham, Isaac, Joseph, and the Patriarchs. Rufinus of Aquileia also composed a commentary on Genesis 49, the blessings of the patriarchs.

Lawrence Boadt has very helpfully set forth some main categories under which the Fathers' interpretation of Genesis might be understood (see commentary text below). In particular, for example, the reader can note the use of the motifs of God as Creator in prayer and confession; the salvation of Noah from the flood in baptismal liturgy; the development of Adam in parallel and yet in contradistinction to Christ; the redemptive hope of humanity through the seed of Eve (Gen 3:15); and the patriarchs as types of Christ, Christians, and their faith as anticipatory models of the Church's faith.

In addition to these categories the reader may find the following patristic interpretations of Genesis valuable (see Jean Daniélou, *From Shadows to Reality: Studies in the Biblical Typology of the Fathers,* translated by W. Hibberd [Westminster, Md.: Newman, 1960] 11–149). Irenaeus, Tertullian, Cyril of Jerusalem, and Gregory of Nyssa saw the Church as the antitype of the Paradise of Genesis 2–3. From this Paradise (Church) unredeemed humanity is exiled, but baptized, spirit-indwelt humanity reenters it (Irenaeus, *Against Heresies* 5.10.1; Tertullian, *Against Marcion* 2.4; Cyril, *Procatechesis* 15, 16; Gregory of Nyssa, *On the Baptism of Christ*).

The early Church saw the sacrifice of Isaac as a type of the sacrifice of Christ (Gen 22:1-14). As Isaac is the only firstborn son, greatly loved, so too is Christ. As Isaac carries the wood for the sacrificial fire, so Christ is suspended from the tree (cross), nailed to the wood. As Isaac is delivered over by his faith, so too is Christ. And as a lamb (ram) in the end is offered for Isaac, Christ, the spiritual lamb, is offered for the world

(Gregory of Nyssa, *Homily on the Resurrection* 1; John Chrysostom, *Homily on Genesis* 47.3).

Some of the language of Genesis becomes quite important in doctrinal formulation. For Athanasius, Gen 1:26, "let *us* make humankind," shows that the Son was always with the Father in accordance with the Word's presence with God the Father in the beginning (John 1:1). It also shows that the Father through the Son created all things, all creatures (*Against the Arians* 2.31; 3.29). These ideas of the (eternal) presence of the Son with the Father and the Son as the Father's agent in creation counter the Arian thesis of the Son's creation. The First Sirmian Creed (351), though not in favor of Athanasius' return to his bishop's office in Alexandria and void of any mention of the Son being of the same substance *(homoousios)* as the Father, mentions Gen 1:26 in a way similar to Athanasius' language. According to Athansius, if anyone denies that in this text the Father addresses the Son or if anyone (Marcellus of Ancyra?) assumes that in this text God is but speaking to himself, that one is anathema (Athanasius, *On the Councils* 27.14). Germinius, who once sided with the Arians then moved doctrinally away, though he never confessed Nicaea, gave a different emphasis to Gen 1:26. He concentrated on the phrase "according to *our* image," pointing out that the wording is "our," not "my" or "your." This means, then, that any difference between the Son's and the Father's divinity is precluded (Hilary of Poitiers, *Historical Fragments* B V. VI. 1–2).

Genesis 19:24 would also receive attention: "the Lord rained . . . brimstone and fire from the Lord . . . ," because of the reference to two Lords, thought to be the Father and the Son. Athanasius cites it in order to show that already in the OT, before his resurrected exaltation, the pre-incarnate Son, Christ, was already everlastingly Lord and King (*Against the Arians* 2.13). Again the First Sirmian Creed cites it to teach that the two Lords are the Father and Son. It proclaims anathema upon anyone who believes God rained down judgment from himself (Athanasius, *On the Councils* 27.17). This interpretive distinction between Father and Son and the appellation of the title "Lord" to each seems to arise as early as Justin (*Dialogue with Trypho* 127.5). Both Irenaeus and Tertullian carry forward the tradition of distinction between Father and Son with common title (Irenaeus, *Against Heresies* 3.6.1; Tertullian, *Against Praxeas* 16.2). Eventually in Gregory of Nazianzus it will be used in specific support of the claim that the Father was never without the Word (Son) and therefore was always Father (*Theological Oration* 3.17 [*Oration* 29.17]).

Genesis is read during Lent, at the Easter Vigil, at Pentecost, Corpus Christi, in Ordinary time, and at Masses for baptism and marriage. It instructs believers about their dependence on God for life through creation, and redemption through covenant.

Exodus

From the beginning the Fathers devoted great attention to the book of Exodus. (Many of the following insights are indebted to Jean Daniélou, *From Shadows to Reality: Studies in the Biblical Typology of the Fathers.* Translation by Wulstan Hibberd [Westminster, Md.: Newman, 1960] 153–226.) Clement of Rome (*1 Clem.* 40–43, 53), *Barn.* 4.12.14-15, Justin's *Dialogue with Trypho* and Irenaeus, *Adv. Haer.* 4.30–31 all initiated and anticipated the extensive typological interpretation of the persons, events, and themes of Exodus as fulfilled particularly in Christ and the Church. In this regard the Fathers received the exegetical mantle from the Hebrew prophets and NT writers themselves, the former who anticipated a new exodus while in exile, the latter who understood the incarnation of the Son and the gift of the Holy Spirit as the fulfillment of this new exodus. Christological, ecclesiological, and moral interpretations of Exodus dominate.

For many of the Fathers Jesus was understood to be the second or new Moses, a theme already evident in Matthew's gospel. Eusebius, for instance, developed this interpretation (*Dem. Ev.* 3.2), understanding Christ as the supreme legislator. Christ ushered in new life and delivered believers from the idolatrous world into heaven, as typified in the new law he dispensed in the Sermon on the Mount. This paralleled the first Moses who was also a legislator (having received the law on Mount Sinai) and who delivered the Hebrews from the idolatry of Egypt to the promised land. Other parallels between Jesus and Moses seen by the Fathers included the following: as Moses fasted for forty days, so Jesus fasted in the wilderness; as God provided the miracle of the manna, so Jesus multiplied loaves; as Moses commanded the sea at the Exodus, so Jesus stilled the sea by his command; as the Hebrews crossed the Red Sea, so Jesus walked on the waters; as Moses' face shone after his encounter with God on Sinai, so was Jesus visibly glorified at his transfiguration on a high mountain; as twelve spies were commissioned, so were twelve apostles appointed; and as Moses called Joshua to assume the leadership of Israel, so Jesus called Simon Peter to lead the Church. To this extensive catalogue of comparisons one can add the powerful and prevalent typology of Moses praying with his hands extended in the battle with Amalek as a type of Jesus' cross with its extended arms (see, for example, *Barn.* 12.2; Justin, *Dial.* 90.4; Cyprian, *Testimonies* 2.21; 89; Tertullian, *Against Marcion* 3.18; Origen, *Homilies on Exodus* 11.4; Gregory of Nyssa, *Life of Moses* 2.147–151, 153).

The apostle Paul's spiritual interpretation of the Exodus in 1 Cor 10:1-4 included reference to Christ, the rock. In Exodus (17:6) Moses struck the rock at Horeb with his staff and water poured forth. For the Fathers the events of the Exodus bore a remarkable affinity to events in the life of Christ. For instance, when Christ the rock was pierced with the spear while on the cross, water too poured forth (cf. John 7:37; Cyprian, *Epistles* 63.8; Gregory of Elvira, *Tractate* 15). Another typology was the incident at Marah with its bitter waters (Exod 15:25) and the sweetening of the water by throwing in the wood, which was seen as a type of baptism. The emphasis here differed from the baptism that had as its type the crossing of the Red Sea. The "Marah" baptism emphasized the giving of life whereas at the "Red Sea" baptism the water was a symbol of judgment from which the baptized escape. Tertullian (*On Baptism* 9), Didymus (*On the Trinity* 2.14), and Ambrose (*On the Mysteries* 3.14) all comment on the Marah incident.

It comes as little surprise that the pivotal salvific incident in the Exodus, the Hebrew nation's passing through the Red Sea, became the dominant source for the Fathers' water-baptism typology, yet many of the Fathers' interpretations of baptism went beyond what the NT taught was fulfilled in Jesus Christ. They asserted a day-to-day fulfillment of the Exodus in the life of the Church, that is, in baptism and the Eucharist (drawn from the crossing of the Red Sea and the eating of manna). The crossing through the Red Sea was a type of baptism (see Paul above) that the Fathers associated with redemption—what God did once with water, God does in the life of the Church with water (Tertullian, *Bapt.* 8.9; Didymus, *Trin.* 2.14). In Didymus' work Egypt represented the world, the waters represented salvation and baptism, and Pharaoh and his soldiers were the Devil and his forces (also see Zeno of Verona, *Homilies* 7). Other exegetes would emphasize the superiority of the Christian sacraments over the types of the Exodus (Ambrose, *On the Mysteries* 3.13; *On the Sacraments* 1.4.12; Basil of Caesarea, *Treatise on the Holy Spirit* 14). For a wonderful catalogue of the extensive typological exegesis of the events surrounding the Exodus from Egypt see Augustine, *Against Faustus* 12.29–30.

A final theme for consideration is the set of moral, mystic, and ascetic interpretations that Exodus invited. Prominent here is Gregory of Nyssa's *Life of Moses*, which typologically illustrated the continual journey of the Christian soul toward perfection based on patterns and events in the life of Moses. Gregory interpreted Exod 20:21 (describing Moses' approach to God who was enshrouded in darkness) in terms of the soul's progress toward a vision of the enshrouded, inaccessible God through understanding (*Life of Moses* 2.162-169). With John Cassian the book of Exodus became a symbol for the monastic life as the way that led to God (*Conferences* 24.24-25): it provided examples of the monastic lifestyle (*Conf.* 3.3-4), admonitions against temptation (3.7), and spiritual combat (5.14–16). Increasingly the events of the Exodus came to be seen as a pattern for the spiritual life (see Gregory the Great's *Moral Discourses on Job* and Caesarius of Arles' *Sermons* 95–116).

The book of Exodus is used extensively in the Roman missal, notably at the Easter Vigil and at Pentecost, on Trinity Sunday and the third Sunday of Lent. In the Liturgy of the Hours it is likewise used in the first three weeks of Lent. The events of the Passover point toward Jesus, the new and great Passover lamb who has delivered his people from the bondage of sin.

Numbers

The book of Numbers was not used by the Fathers as frequently as other books of the Pentateuch. However, Origen *(Homilies on Numbers),*

Augustine *(Questions on Numbers),* Cyril of Alexandria *(Glaphyra on Numbers),* Theodoret *(On Numbers),* and Procopius of Gaza *(Commentaries on Numbers)* have all left substantial contributions.

There was also a handful of notable people and events frequently commented on. Balaam's fourth oracle, and especially Num 24:17, was to many of the Fathers a source of both inspiration and perplexity because Balaam was thought to have played the role of both prophet (Num 24:17 and the rising star from Jacob, a prophecy of the incarnation) and villain (Numbers 25, leading Israel into immorality at Baal Peor). Numbers 24:17 was a crucial passage for the Fathers: "I see him, but not now; I behold him, but not near—a star shall come out of Jacob, and a scepter shall rise out of Israel." From the earliest of the Church writings this verse was interpreted as a prediction of the incarnation of Christ. Justin (*Dial.* 106; 126) mentioned the verse, but not the name of Balaam who uttered the prophecy. Irenaeus (*Adv. Haer.* 3.9.2) saw the verse as christological, and both Athanasius (*Incarnation of the Word* 33) and Lactantius (*Divine Institutes* 4.13) attributed this verse not to Balaam, but to Moses. Cyprian (*Treatise* 12.2.10) and Augustine (*On Diverse Questions to Simplicius,* 2), however, mentioned Balaam as uttering the prophecy. The christological typology of this oracle functioned because of the connection made between "stars." That is, most of the Fathers thought the star that guided the magi who had come to visit the infant Jesus had been predicted by Balaam and his "star of Jacob" (although Augustine distanced himself from such an interpretation). Origen went so far as to attribute to Balaam the beginnings of the magi sect, including those who had come to see the infant Jesus (see Origen *Hom. in Num.* 13.7, 15.4; *Against Celsus* 1.59, 60). Some of the Fathers argued for Balaam's conversion as a type of the future Gentile conversion. His cry, "Let me die the death of the upright, and let my end be like his" (Num 23:10) was thought to signal his salvation—both Origen and Jerome saw in Balaam a model of Gentile salvation (Jerome, *Commentary on Ezekiel* 6).

In addition to the figure of Balaam, the incident with the bronze snake in Num 21:4-9 elicited the Fathers' response. Ignatius interpreted this event christologically (cf. John 3:14). For him the Word was raised up as the serpent was in the wilderness (*Smyrn.* 2). The same connection is made in *Barn.* 12 where the bronze serpent was seen as a type of Christ; the sinner would be restored by hope and belief in him. Tertullian also interprets this event as a foreshadowing of the passion of Christ, but with a different understanding. Moses hung a serpent on a tree as an instrument of healing for Israel. This was a prediction of the Lord's cross on which the devil (as serpent) was displayed so that everyone hurt by the serpent could turn to it and receive salvation (*Answer to the Jews* 10).

Another passage to which the Fathers had frequent recourse was Num 12:1-10, which served as a dual paraenesis: both Moses' humility and the attempted schism of Aaron and Miriam served as moral guides to the Church, the one positive, the other negative. The faithfulness of Moses, his humility in particular, drew great emphasis. *1 Clement* 43 spoke of Moses as the faithful one in all of God's house, and Ignatius (*Eph.* 1; *Magn.* 12), Irenaeus (*Adv. Haer.* 3.6.5), Cyprian (*Epistles* 51.16), the *Apostolic Constitutions* (7.1.7), and Gregory of Nazianzus *(To Cledonius)* all repeated this exhortation to be humble as Moses had been God's humble servant.

Miriam's illness that resulted from the attempted schism was noted by, among others, Irenaeus (frag. 31) and the *Apostolic Constitutions* (6.1.1), which likewise highlighted that those who create schisms are punished as had been the case with Miriam. The other notable schism in Numbers (ch. 16), the rebellion of Korah, Dathan, and Abiram and their attempted usurpation of the priestly roles served as a warning of the consequences of schism for the life and worship of the early Church. This incident was frequently referred to in the *Apostolic Constitutions* (2.3.10; 2.4.27; 3.1.11; 6.1.1; 7.1.10), and was discussed by Ambrose (*Ep.* 63.52-55) and Augustine (*On Baptism* 1.8-10; 2.9; 3.24).

Scenes depicting events in the life of Aaron and Miriam drawn from the book of Numbers find expression in the paintings of the Dura synagogue. In the liturgy, passages from Numbers are read in the Roman Missal in Ordinary Time and in the third week of Advent, the fifth week of Lent, and on several feasts including the Triumph of the Cross. Numbers is also read in the Liturgy of the Hours during the fourth week of Lent. The meaning of the book is that God's power and majesty are the focal points of believers' lives. Believers are not to wander away from God as the Israelites did.

Deuteronomy

The book of Deuteronomy did not attract the attention of the early Church Fathers, at least when the references to Deuteronomy were juxtaposed to another book of the Pentateuch such as Genesis. Yet this is not to say that Deuteronomy was entirely neglected. Deuteronomy 30:15 was a favorite passage in the early Church ("See, I have set before you today life and prosperity, death and adversity"); this message of choosing good as opposed to evil was associated with the similar theme in Genesis 2 expressed in the tree of the knowledge of good and evil in the Garden of Eden. Both Clement of Alexandria (*Stromata* 5.11) and Tertullian (*Exhortation to Chastity* 2.3) connected Genesis 2:9 with Deuteronomy 30:15.

Certain texts from Deuteronomy did find their way into christological discussions. The Shema of Israel, Deut 6:4, was a text used by the Arians to show how the Father alone was truly God in opposition to the Son who was subordinated to his Father. While Prov 8:22 was perhaps the most significant verse in the Arian controversies, the Arians found the declaration of God's unity in Deut 6:4 compelling. So, according to Athanasius, did the Arian argument proceed: "Behold, God is said to be one and only and the first, how do you say that the Son is God? For if he was God, he would not say, 'I alone' or 'God is one'" (*Orations against the Arians* 3.7).

Deuteronomy 6:4 was also important for the Cappadocians who had articulated the existence of the three hypostases (persons) of the Godhead. Unlike the Arians who denied the full divinity of the Son, Basil of Caesarea, his brother Gregory of Nyssa, and Gregory of Nazianzus were charged with abandoning the unity of God in favor of "three gods." To this criticism Gregory of Nazianzus repeatedly articulated both the unity of the Godhead and the diversity of persons. Gregory of Nyssa specifically cited Deut 6:4 in his argument for confession of only one God *(On Not Three Gods).*

The christological implication of Deuteronomy for the Fathers was not restricted to such dogmatic issues as trinitarian doctrines. For instance, in Eusebius' *Proof of the Gospel* (6.96-101) there are sixteen parallels drawn between the lives of Moses and Jesus, one example of which was Moses' promise of a holy land while Jesus offered the kingdom of God (also see the fuller treatment of the Moses/Jesus parallel above in *Exodus*).

Today Deuteronomy is frequently used in the liturgy, including several periods in Lent and Ordinary Time. It refers to God's salvation and blessing of the chosen people.

BIBLIOGRAPHY FOR THE PENTATEUCH

Primary Sources

Genesis

Ambrose. *Hexaemeron.* Edited by C. Schenkl. CSEL 32.1:3–261 (1897).

____. *Hexaemeron.* Translated by J. J. Savage. FC 42:1–283 (1961).

____. *De Abraham (libri duo).* Edited by C. Schenkl. CSEL 32.1:501–638 (1897).

____. *De Cain et Abel.* Edited by C. Schenkl. CSEL 32.1:339–400 (1897).

____. *On Cain and Abel.* Translated by J. J. Savage. FC 42:357–437 (1961).

____. *De Joseph.* Edited by C. Schenkl. CSEL 32.2:73–122 (1897).

____. *On Joseph.* Translated by M. P. McHugh. FC 65:189–237 (1972).

____. *De Isaac vel anima.* Edited by C. Schenkl. CSEL 32.1:641–700 (1897).

____. *On Isaac, or the Soul.* Translated by M. P. McHugh. FC 65:10–65 (1972).

____. *De Noe.* Edited by C. Schenkl. CSEL 32.1:413–497 (1897).

____. *De Paradiso.* Edited by C. Schenkl. CSEL 32.1:265–336 (1897).

____. *On Paradise.* Translated by J. J. Savage. FC 42:287–356 (1961).

____. *De Patriarchis.* Edited by C. Schenkl. CSEL 32.2:125–160 (1897).

____. *On the Patriarchs.* Translated by M. P. McHugh. FC 65:243–275 (1972).

Augustine. *De Genesi ad litteram liber imperfectus.* Edited by J. Zycha. CSEL 28.1:457–503 (1894).

____. *De Genesi ad litteram libri XII.* Edited by J. Zycha. CSEL 28.1:3–435 (1894).

____. *De Genesi contra Manichaeos.* MPL 34:173–220.

____. *Locutionum in Heptateuchum. Liber Primus. Locutiones Genesis.* Edited by J. Fraipont. CCSL 33:381–403 (1958).

____. *Quaestionum in Heptateuchum. Liber Primus. Quaestiones Genesis.* Edited by J. Fraipont. CCSL 33:1–69 (1958).

____. *The Literal Meaning of Genesis.* Translated by J. H. Taylor. ACW 41, 42 (1982).

____. *Two Books on Genesis Against the Manichees* and *On the Literal Interpretation of Genesis: An Unfinished Book*. Translated by R. J. Teske. FC 84 (1991).

Basil of Caesarea. *The Hexaemeron*. Translated by B. Jackson. NPNF, 2nd ser. 8:52–107.

____. *Homélies sur l'Hexaéméron*. Edited and translated by S. Giet. SC 26 (1968).

____. *Homilies on the Hexaemeron*. Translated by A. C. Way. FC 46:1–150 (1963).

____. *Sur l'origine de l'homme*. Edited and translated by A. Smets and M. Van Esbroeck. SC 160 (1970).

Catenae Graecae in Genesim et in Exodum 1, *Catena Sinaitica* and 2, *Colletio Coisliniana in Genesim*. Edited by Françoise Petit. CCSG 2, 15 (1977, 1986).

La Chaîne sur las Genèse. 3 vols. Traditio Exegetica Graeca 1–3. Edited by Françoise Petit. Louvain: Peeters, 1991–1995.

Cyril of Alexandria. *Glaphyrorum in Genesim Libri VII*. MPG 69:9–678.

Didymus of Alexandria. *Sur la Genèse*. Edited and translated by P. Nautin and L. Doutreleau. SC 233, 244 (1976, 1978).

Ephraem. *St. Ephrem the Syrian. Selected Prose Works: Commentary on Genesis, Commentary on Exodus, Homily on Our Lord, Letter to Publius*. Translated by E. G. Matthews, Jr., and J. P. Amar. FC 91 (1994).

____. *In Genesim et in Exodum commentarii*. Edited by R.-M. Tonneau. CSCO 152, 153 (1955).

Eusebius of Emesa. *In Genesim* (fragments). In *L'héritage litteraire d'Eusèbe d'Emèse: Etude critique et historique, Textes,* ed. E. M. Buytaert, 95–122. Louvain: Peeters, 1949.

Gregory of Nyssa. *Explicatio apologetica in Hexaemeron*. MPG 44:61–124.

____. *On the Making of Man*. Translated by H. A. Wilson. NPNF, 2nd ser. 5:387–427.

Hippolytus. *Benedictiones Isaac et Jacob*. In *Hippolytus de Rome. Sur les bénédictions d'Isaac, de Jacob et de Moïse*. Edited by M. Briere, L. Maries, and B. Ch. Mercier. PO 27.1–2:2-115 (1954).

____. *Fragmenta in Genesim*. In H. Achelis, ed., *Hippolytus Werke* 1.2. GCS 1:51–71 (1897).

____. *Fragments On Genesis*. Translated by S.D.F. Salmond. ANF 5:163–69.

Jerome. *Jerome's Hebrew Questions on Genesis*. Translated by C.T.R. Hayward. Oxford: Clarendon, 1995.

____. *Quaestiones Hebraicae in Genesim*. Edited by P. De Lagarde. CCSL 72:1–56 (1959).

John Chrysostom. *Homiliae 1–67 in Genesim*. MPG 53:21–54.

____. *Sermones 1–9 in Genesim*. PG 54:581–630.

____. *Homilies on Genesis*. Translated by R. C. Hill. FC 74, 82, 87 (1986, 1990, 1992).

____. *Sermones 1–9 in Genesim*. MPG 54:581–630.

John Philoponos. *De opificio mundi Libri VII*. Edited by G. Reichardt. Scriptores sacri et profani, fasc. 1. Leipzig: Teubner, 1897.

Origen. *Homélies sur la Genèse*. Introduced by H. de Lubac. Edited and translated by L. Doutrelaeu. SC 7. 2nd ed. 1985.

____. *Homilies on Genesis and Exodus*. Translated by R. E. Heine. FC 71 (1982).

Rufinus of Aquileia. *De Benedictionibus Patriarcharum*. Edited by M. Simonetti. CCSL 20:183–228 (1961).

Severian of Gabala. *Orationes sex in mundi creationem*. MPG 56:429–500.

Theodoret. *Quaestiones in Genesim*. MPG 80:77–225.

Victorinus of Pettau. *On the Creation of the World*. Translated by R. E. Wallis. ANF 7:341–343.

Exodus

Augustine. *Locutionum in Heptateuchum. Liber Secundus. Locutiones Exodi*. Edited by J. Fraipont. CCSL 33:404–423 (1958).

____. *Quaestionum in Heptateuchum. Liber Secundus. Quaestiones Exodi*. Edited by J. Fraipont. CCSL 33:70–174 (1958).

Catenae Graecae in Genesim et in Exodum 1, *Catena Sinaitica in Exodum*. Edited by Françoise Petit. CCSG 15:259–305 (1977).

Cyril of Alexandria. *Glaphyrorum in Exodum Liber I–III*. MPG 69:385–538.

Ephraem. "Commentaire de l'Exode par Saint Éphrem." Introduction, translation, and notes by Paul Féghali. *ParOr* 12:91–1131 (1984/1985).

____. *Sancti Ephraem Syri in Genesim et in Exodum commentarii*. Edited by R. M. Tonneau. CSCO 152–153 (1955).

____. *St. Ephrem the Syrian: Selected Prose Works: Commentary on Genesis, Commentary on Exodus, Homily on our Lord, Letter to Publius*. (See above.)

Gaudentius of Brescia. *Tractatus*. Edited by A. Glück. CSEL 68 (1936).

Gregory of Nyssa. *Life of Moses*. Translated by A. J. Malherbe and E. Ferguson. ClWS (1978).

____. *La vie de Moïse*. Edited and translated by J. Daniélou. SC 1 (1968).

____. *De Vita Moysis*. Edited by H. Musurillo. GNO 7.1 (1991).

Jacob of Sarug. *De sluier van Mozes. Metrische preek van Jakob van Sarug over de sluier van het Oude Verbond en de glans van het Nieuwe*. Edited and translated by A. Welkenhuysen, and L. Van Rompay. Brugge: Zevenkerken, 1983.

Origen. *Homilies on Genesis and Exodus.* Translated by R. E. Heine. FC 71 (1982).
____. *Origène. Homélies sur l'Exode.* Translated by Marcel Borrett. SC 321 (1985).
Procopius of Gaza. *Commentarii in Exodum.* MPG 87:511–690.
Theodoret. *In Exodum.* MPG 80:225–298.
Zeno of Verona. *Sermones.* Edited by Bengt Löfstedt. CCSL 22 (1971).
Only fragments remain of Diodore's commentary on Exodus.

Numbers

Augustine. *Locutionum in Heptateuchum. Liber Quartus. Locutiones Numerorum.* Edited by J. Fraipont CCSL 33: 432–444 (1958).
____. *Quaestionum in Heptateuchum. Liber Quartus. Quaestiones Numerorum.* Edited by J. Fraipont. CCSL 33:234–275 (1958).
Cyril of Alexandria. *Glaphyrorum in Numeros Liber.* MPG 69:589–642.
Origène, Homélies sur les Nombres. Translated by A. Méhat. SC 29 (1951).
____. *Selecta in Numeros.* MPG 12:575–584.
____. *Adnotationes In Numeros.* MPG 17:21–24.
Procopius of Gaza. *Commentarii in Numeros.* MPG 87:793–894.
Theodoret. *In Numeros.* MPG 80:350–400.

Deuteronomy

Augustine. *Locutionum in Heptateuchum. Liber Quintus. Locutiones Deuteronomii.* Edited by J. Fraipont. CCSL 33:445–453 (1958).
____. *Quaestionum in Heptateuchum. Liber Quintus. Quaestiones Deuteronomii.* Edited by J. Fraipont. CCSL 33:276–311 (1958).
Cyril of Alexandria. *Glaphyrorum in Deuteronomium Liber.* MPG 69:643–678.
Origen. *Adnotationes in Deuteronomium.* MPG 17:23–36.
____. *Selecta in Deuteronomium.* MPG 12:805–818.
Procopius of Gaza. *In Deuteronomium.* MPG 87:893–992.
Theodoret. *In Deuteronomium.* MPG 80:401–456.

HISTORICAL BOOKS

Joshua

Among the Fathers key events in the book of Joshua served as typologies for subsequent realities. Aside from certain events and themes in the book that encouraged these readings, in Greek Jesus' and Joshua's names were homonymous, providing obvious lexical resources for the frequent Joshua-Jesus typologies. Tertullian (*Against Marcion* 3.16), Jerome (*Ep.* 53), and Augustine (*Against Faustus* 12.322), among others, drew typological significance from the identical names.

The standard interpretation of Joshua taught the superiority of Jesus and the Gospel over Moses and the Law. As Moses could not lead the Israelites into the Promised Land and the privilege was granted to Joshua, so the Law that was unable to provide salvation was replaced with the Gospel of Jesus that ushered the spiritual Israel into the eternal Promised Land. Such interpretations are found in Origen's *Homily on Joshua* as well as Irenaeus's *Proof of the Apostolic Preaching* (40), Cyprian's *Testimonies* (2.21), and both Tertullian's *Against Marcion* (3.15, 18; 4.7) and *Against the Jews* (9, 10). In a similar vein Tertullian maintained (*Adv. Jud.* 4) that the seven-day march around Jericho pointed to the transitory status of the Sabbath as a day of rest.

Another typological reading of Joshua drew comparisons between Rahab's house and the scarlet cord hung from her window, treating them as types of the Church and Christ's blood respectively. Also Clement of Rome (*1 Clem.* 12) and Justin Martyr (*Dial.* 111.3-4) refer to Christ's blood. With Irenaeus (*Adv. Haer.* 4.20) and Origen (*Homilies on Joshua* 3.4-5) the ecclesiological dimension of this type was developed. A common interpretation was that as salvation from the Jewish conquest of Jericho could come from within Rahab's house, so also could salvation come only from those within the Church. Cyprian's interpretation was similar (*On the Unity of the Church* 8) as he quoted Josh 2:19, which reads "If any of you go out of the doors of your house into the street, they shall be responsible for their own death." Another interesting typology is that of baptism, which, following Paul in 1 Cor 10:2, the Fathers had traditionally associated with the Exodus and the crossing of the Red Sea (see, for example, Tertullian *On Baptism*). With Origen there is the explicit transformation of this typology so as to render the Exodus a type not for baptism, but for the entry of the catechumen into Christianity, while crossing the Jordan was a type of baptism (*Homilies on Joshua* 4.1). The subsequent Christian tradition, contrary to Origen, maintained the Exodus-baptism typology, but with Origen it also began to recognize the richness of the Jordan-baptism typology (for example, Gregory of Nyssa's *On the Baptism of Christ*). Along with this ecclesiological reading came the eschatological association of Jericho as a type of the world that would be destroyed, except for the Church (Rahab's house), at the end of the age (Hilary, *On the Mysteries* 2.9-10).

Episodes from the life of Joshua appear in the mosaic in S. Maria Maggiore in Rome, dating from the fifth century: scenes include the crossing of the Jordan, Rahab helping the spies, and the conquests of Jericho and Ai. Joshua is also read in the liturgy in Ordinary Time and on the fourth Sunday of Lent; it teaches the sovereignty of God as well as the need for active faith, and its expression in prayer, on behalf of believers.

Judges

The book of Judges infrequently called forth the attention of later Jewish (Sir 46:11–12) and NT writers (Heb 11:32), and the same can be said for the Fathers. There are, however, certain themes that can be discerned in the early Christian interpretation of Judges. When the Fathers wanted to emphasize Jewish waywardness, and especially the dangers of idolatry, the scenes depicting these recurring sins in Judges were recalled (see Tertullian, *Scorpiace* 3; Cyprian, *Treatise* 12.1.1; *Ap. Const.* 5.2.12). But there were also positive recollections of Judges. For Clement of Alexandria, Jewish history, including the period of the judges, demonstrated the superior antiquity of Hebrew thought even over that of Greek philosophy (*Stromata* 1.21). In the *Apostolic Constitutions* Jewish piety was commemorated in such figures as Joshua, Gideon, Manoah, Samson, and especially the prophet Deborah who appears to have served as a paragon for deaconesses in the early Church (*Ap. Const.* 7.2.37; 8.1.2; 8.3.20).

The early interpretation of the book of Judges also witnesses to the patristic inclination toward christological exegesis of the OT. One example is Origen's exegesis of Gideon and the sign of the fleece (Judg 6:36–40). For the first sign, in which the dew was only on the fleece, the dew represented the Word of God, the divine Law given to the people of Israel, the fleece. For the second sign, in which the dew fell only on the ground, the dew represented the first advent of Christ and the coming of the gospel through the apostles and evangelists to all the world, which was represented by the ground (*Homilies on Judges* 8.4). Interpreters before Origen, such as Irenaeus, were already making the distinction between the fleece as Israel and the ground as the rest of the world (*Adv. Haer.* 3.17.3).

The Church Fathers' penchant for moral exegesis can be seen in their reading of Judges. Perhaps the most demanding incident in the book of Judges from the perspective of tropological exegesis was Jephthah's tragic vow resulting in the sacrifice of his own daughter (Judg 11:30-40). Origen, in the sixth book of his *Commentary on John,* reflected on the significance of the deaths of martyrs. While realizing the difficulty of Jephthah's vow, as it suggested a cruel God, Origen concluded that martyrs' deaths, including that of Jephthah's daughter, in some manner thwarted the powers of evil. In this way their deaths eased the suffering of those believers who escaped martyrdom. This somewhat positive interpretation of Jephthah's action by Origen was challenged by Jerome who condemned the vow as rash (*Against Jovinian* 1.23). Subsequent interpreters took up Jerome's interpretation but also found praise for Jephthah in that he was at the very least faithful to the vow he had made (cf. Heb 11:32; Theodoret, *Investigations on Judges* 20; Ambrose, *On Virginity* 2.5–3.10).

As the Fathers recognized the faithfulness of God's judges in the face of Israel's disobedience, so the liturgy draws upon the theme of God's faithfulness in the book of Judges and challenges worshipers to the life of faith in the Holy Spirit. Judges is read in Ordinary Time, as well as on December 19 in the Roman Missal.

1, 2 Samuel and 1, 2 Kings

What are now two books of Samuel were originally one book that was divided by the compilers of the LXX for purposes of convenience because of its length. The same occurred for what is now 1 and 2 Kings. In the LXX all four books were grouped under one title, "Books of the Reigns." These four books contained themes that provided resources not only for the Chronicler, but also for the NT and the early Church's reflection on these books.

While material from Samuel and Kings was frequently used in the early Church there was seldom specific reference to these books. Nevertheless, patristic writers (not unlike the NT writers) were aware of the strong continuities between such persons as David, Elijah, Elisha, and Jesus. It comes as little surprise, then, that these OT personalities were interpreted allegorically with reference to Jesus. For example, David's anointing, his activity as shepherd, and his defeat of Goliath pointed to Jesus' baptism, his activity as a metaphorical shepherd, and his defeat of sin (extensive reflection on David can be found in commentaries on the Psalms by Origen, Athanasius of Alexandria, Eusebius of Caesarea, Hilary, Gregory of Nyssa, and Augustine). Also worthy of mention is the account of the witch of Endor who summoned Samuel from the dead (1 Samuel 28), an event that suggested to Origen that Samuel was a type of Christ inasmuch as both descended into Hades and made a return (*Second Homily on the Book of Kings* 6–8). Also, during the Donatist controversy (fourth c.), at the Conference of Carthage the Donatists argued that the "man of God" in 1 Kings 13 supported their position of nonparticipation in the sacraments of sinful priests. Jeroboam's rival worship, subsequent to the splitting of Israel into two kingdoms, was noted because this "schismatic" worship was not participated in by the "man of God," nor did he dine with Jeroboam. To the Donatists, even if sin could be cleansed the OT prophets still would not engage in the sacrifices of those who had committed certain sins—and Jeroboam was considered to be "in schism" (*Acts of the Conference of Carthage* 3.258).

First Samuel is read in Ordinary Time and on the fourth Sunday of Lent. It points to God's merciful actions in human history. Second Samuel is read in Ordinary Time and also on the fourth Sunday of Advent. It speaks of David as God's anointed king, anticipating Jesus Christ the Messiah who delivers God's people. First and Second Kings are read in Ordinary Time (2 Kings is also read in the third week of Lent) and both speak of God's covenant and of God's sending of prophets as indicators of right conduct.

1, 2 Maccabees

First and Second Maccabees were declared canonical by the councils of Hippo (393), Carthage (397), and, ultimately, Trent (1546). They were widely referenced in the works of early Christian writers such as Clement of Alexandria, Hippolytus of Rome, Tertullian, Cyprian of Carthage, Eusebius of Caesarea, Ambrose of Milan, Augustine, and Jerome. Second Maccabees was especially significant in that it contains an explicit scriptural affirmation of creation *ex nihilo* (2 Macc 7:28; Origen *On First Principles* 2.1.5; *Commentary on John* 1.17.103). It also contains a passage concerning prayers for the dead (2 Macc 12:43-45) important to the development and defense of the doctrine of purgatory. Moreover, the accounts of martyrdom in 2 Maccabees particularly resonated within the persecuted early Church. Gregory of Nazianzus, Eusebius of Caesarea, Augustine, John Chrysostom, Gaudentius, Eusebius of Emesa, and Leo the Great all wrote panegyrics to the Maccabean heroes, and Cyprian (*Exhortation to Martyrdom* 11) as well as Origen (*Exhortation to Martyrdom* 22–27) held these Jewish martyrs as models of fortitude and faithfulness to be imitated by Christians. Some have also seen echoes of 2 Maccabees in Ignatius' discussions of his impending martyrdom. The Maccabean martyrs were later canonized by the Church and a basilica established in their honor at Antioch, the site to which their deaths in Jerusalem had been hagiographically relocated. However, it was the anonymous mother of seven martyred sons who in particular was esteemed by the early Church. Her piety and faithfulness in the face of her septenary sacrifice moved Gregory Nazianzen to identify her as a prototype of Mary who would also lose a noble son for a righteous cause (*Oration* 15). The earliest commentary on Maccabees was written by Bellator at the behest of Cassiodorus during the sixth century, but this work is non-extant.

BIBLIOGRAPHY FOR HISTORICAL BOOKS

Primary Sources

Joshua

Augustine. *Locutionum in Heptateuchum. Liber Sextus. Locutiones Jesu Nave.* Edited by J. Fraipont. CCSL 33: 454–458 (1958).

____. *Quaestionum in Heptateuchum. Liber Sextus. Quaestiones Jesu Nave.* Edited by J. Fraipont. CCSL 33: 312–34. (1958).

Origen. *Homélies sur Josué.* Edited and translated by A. Jaubert. SC 71 (1960).

Procopius of Gaza. *Commentarii in Josue.* MPG 87:991–1042.

Theodoret. *Quaestiones in Josuam.* MPG 80:457–85.

Judges

Augustine. *Locutionum in Heptateuchum. Liber Septimus. Locutiones Judicum.* Edited by J. Fraipont. CCSL 33:459–465 (1958).

____. *Quaestionum in Heptateuchum. Liber Septimus. Quaestiones Judicum.* Edited by J. Fraipont. CCSL 33:335–377 (1958).

Isidore of Seville. *In Librum Judicum.* MPL 83:379–392.

Origen. *Origène: Homélies sur les juges.* Edited and Translated by P. Messié, L. Neyrand, and M. Borret. SC 389 (1993).

Procopius of Gaza. *Commentarii in Judices.* MPG 87:1041–80.

Theodoret. *Quaestiones in Judicum.* MPG 80:485–518.

1, 2 Samuel and 1, 2 Kings

Ambrose. *De apologia prophetae David.* MPL 14:891–960.

Basil of Seleucia. *Sermones.* MPG 85:182–225.

Cyril of Alexandria. *In Regum Libri I–IV.* MPG 69:679–98.

Gregory the Great. *Grégoire le Grand, Commentaire sur le Premier Livre des Rois.* Edited and translated by A. de Vogüe and C. Vuillaume. SC 351, 391 (1989, 1993).

John Chrysostom. *De Anna sermones.* MPG 54:631–674.

____. *De Davide et Saule homiliae.* MPG 54:675–708.

Origen. *Homélies sur Samuel.* Edited by Pierre Nautin and Marie-Thérese Nautin. SC 328 (1985).

____. *Homiliae in Regnorum libros.* Edited by W. A. Baehrens. GCS 33 (1925).

____. *Homilies on Jeremiah and 1 Kings 28.* Translated by J. C. Smith. FC 97 (1998).

Procopius of Gaza. *Catena in Octateuchum.* MPG 87:1147–1200.

Theodoret. *Quaestiones in libros Regnorum.* MPG 80:667–800.

WISDOM AND POETRY

Job

The book of Job was commented upon by many Fathers of the early Church. Though the book was important for many writers in the late first and second centuries, it is from the time of Clement of Alexandria and Cyprian that Job begins to play an ever-increasing role. The list of its commentators includes Origen (whose commentary is now lost), Athanasius of Alexandria, Didymus of Alexandria, Julian the Arian, John Chrysostom, Augustine, Julian of Eclanum, Hesychius of Jerusalem, and Gregory the Great. Early Christian writers (as well as iconographers) employed the story and persona of Job for both moral and doctrinal instruction. A few brief examples will be noted.

Numerous Fathers draw on Job as an example of humility, patience, kindness, and endurance in the midst of suffering (cf. Basil of Caesarea, *Homily* 20.7 *[Concerning Humility];* John Chrysostom, *Homily on 1 Corinthians* 10.4). So widespread is this moral understanding of Job that Christian iconography depicts him as a figure for major virtues, particularly patience and submission to God's will. Job was frequently portrayed covered with sores and sitting on a dungheap (Job 2:8).

Christian writers such as Tertullian, who wrote an entire work on the virtue of patience, developed this moral interpretation of Job. In *Of Patience* Tertullian declared to his readers that Job's story had been given as a testimony to the Christian community. He exhorted the Church to imitate Job since he was a victorious warrior whose reverence for God had not been undermined by Satan (*Pat.* 14). Ambrose too incorporated this major theme of Job as moral exemplar throughout his work *On the Prayer of Job and David.* For Ambrose, Job was like an athlete who had been judged victorious through suffering. The Lord had even intentionally preserved the life of his wife in order that she might serve as an additional source of temptation to him (Job 2:9-10; *Prayer* 2.4). His victory came as he was declared righteous by the Lord. The most prominent example of this moral interpretation of Job is Gregory the Great's thirty-five book ascetical treatise entitled *Morals on Job,* which both represents and develops the rich exegetical tradition surrounding the figure of Job. Gregory sees Job as a type of Christ; Job's suffering proved to be both cathartic and redemptive. Suffering should be welcomed, Gregory posited, since it purifies one's soul and simultaneously directs and focuses the sufferer on communion with God.

In addition to these largely moral interpretations of Job the early Church found specific doctrinal significance in Job 14:4-5, 19:25-26, and 41:1. Job 14:4-5 summarizes a larger discourse about humanity's sinfulness, weakness, and mortality. Augustine would appeal to it in order to support the idea of the infestation of all humans, of all ages, with sin and their need for the sacraments (for example, *Against Two Letters of the Pelagians* 4.4; cf. Origen, *Homilies on Leviticus* 8.3.5; *Homilies on Luke* 14.3.5). Job 19:25-26, for the early Church (both in literature and iconography), has Job proclaiming his own bodily resurrection. This passage will be used to teach the future resurrection of the dead (*1 Clem.* 26; Cyril of Jerusalem, *Catechetical Lectures* 18.15). Job 41:1, where God questions whether Job can subdue Leviathan, the dragon, becomes for the early Church a passage that teaches redemption through Christ's defeat of the devil (Origen, *On First Principles* 4.1.5; Gregory the Great, *Morals* 33.7.14).

Job is used liturgically in Ordinary Time and in the Masses for the Dead and the Anointing of the Sick. The book encourages Christians to bear adversity in trustful submission to God, to acknowledge the finitude of human understanding, and to hope confidently for salvation.

Psalms

For the authors of the NT, Psalms is the most frequently cited OT book. During the era of the Fathers the Psalter lost none of its importance. Prominent interpreters of the Psalms include Origen, Eusebius of Caesarea, Athanasius of Alexandria, Basil of Caesarea, Gregory of Nyssa, Ambrose, Jerome, John Chrysostom, Theodore of Mopsuestia, Augustine, Cyril of Alexandria, and Theodoret.

Many of the psalms repeatedly used by the authors of the NT also generated much interest among the Fathers. Key psalms shared by the exegetical traditions of both eras were 2, 22, 34, 51, 104, 110, 118, and 119. The messianic motif was central to the Fathers' reading of the psalms.

Several psalms to which the NT frequently referred, including Pss 69, 79, 98, 105, and 106, received relatively little attention in the patristic era. Conversely, other psalms, for example Pss 1, 45, and 50, were very frequently employed by the Fathers yet received little attention in the NT. Psalm 1 is a case in point. Though the psalm itself is never cited in the NT, the Fathers almost universally understood the "blessed one" of vv. 1-2 as referring to Christ, and consequently, to all Christians. Furthermore some, extrapolating from texts such as Rom 5:12-21 and 1 Cor 15:47, also regarded the "wicked [person]" of vv. 4-6 as referring to Adam, the original sinner (see, for example, Augustine's *Discourses on the Psalms* 21).

In early doctrinal formulation the psalms would inform pivotal elements of the Church's christology. Justin validated the dogma of Christ's bodily ascent into heaven by employing Ps 24:7-8. He understood the "gates" of these verses as referring to the gates of heaven and thus to Christ having passed through these gates into heaven (*Apol. 1,* 51). Later, for Irenaeus, Ps 132:11 would serve as testimony to Jesus' Davidic heritage, his kingship, and his birth from a virgin. Irenaeus employed this verse to complement his reading of Isa 7:14 (*Adv. Haer.* 3.21.5). Origen used Ps 16:10 to validate the interrelated doctrines of Christ's descent into hell and his resurrection. He reasoned that since Christ was uniquely (virgin) born and since he lived a unique (sinless) life, the phrase "[f]or you do not give me up to Sheol" must be applied to Christ since he was also unique in having been raised from the dead. For Origen it was Christ's uniqueness that prevented him from remaining permanently in Hades (*Commentary on John* 1.220). Although Origen wrote the first commentary on the Psalms, unfortunately only nine homilies on Psalms 36–38 and some fragments survive.

Cyprian of Carthage in composing an apology for his "son" Quirinus collated portions of Pss 45, 46, 68, and 82 to help support the idea that Christ was fully God. Psalm 45, in particular, provided Cyprian with evidence for Christ's divinity. He quotes from vv. 6-7: "Your throne, O God, endures forever and ever. Your royal scepter is a scepter of equity; you love righteousness and hate wickedness. Therefore God, your God, has anointed you with the oil of gladness beyond your companions" (*Three Books of Testimonies Against the Jews* 2.6).

Cyprian's use of Psalm 45 proved a foreshadowing of this psalm's significance. In the fourth century Psalm 45 was central to the Arian controversy. The Arians read vv. 6-7 to "prove" God the Son's subordination to God the Father. The statement that Christ was "anointed" by God, combined with the inference that he was thus elevated only because of his virtue and love of righteous conduct, surely meant that he was inferior to the Father. Athanansius of Alexandria, among others, provided a rejoinder. In the first of his *Four Discourses Against the Arians* Athanasius devoted a chapter to rebutting the Arians' understanding of this passage. The rebuttal proceeded by highlighting different elements of v. 6, "Your throne, O God, endures forever and ever," and v. 7, "God, your God." For him these texts made clear that the psalmist is granting eternality to another besides God the Father. Therefore these verses must be read as a statement that Christ is distinct from originated things (*Four Discourses* 1.12.46).

Theodore of Mopsuestia in his own commentary on the Psalms innovatively divided the Psalter into five broad categories: doctrinal psalms, praise psalms, prophetic psalms, didactic psalms, and exhortatory psalms (*Commentary on the Psalms,* Devreese edition 205–206). Theodore also considered King David to be the author of every one of the canonical psalms, and, in contrast to the common christological readings, believed only four psalms (2, 8, 45, 110) to be prophetic of Christ (Devreese edition 469–470).

Jerome, too, wrote a commentary on the Psalms and employed the Psalter as a basis for many homilies. Two examples from the homilies reflect the ways in which Jerome continued the tradition of using the psalms for christological and Trinitarian purposes. In *Homily 21,* which was composed using the text of Psalm 92, Jerome understands the line from v. 10 that reads "But you have exalted my horn like that of the wild ox" as being an allusion to the cross of Jesus through which he both triumphed over the devil and exalted the faithful. In *Homily 22,* on Psalm 94, Jerome understood v. 22 as conclusively refuting the error of the Arians. This verse reads "But the Lord has become my stronghold." Jerome reasons that since all agree that these words are written in reference to God the Father, and since they attribute to the Father the idea of having been "made" (the very thing that the Arians attributed to God the Son), the Arians' reasoning is proven to be thoroughly specious. Even Arians would never dream of ascribing anything less than eternality to God the Father.

Augustine, in addition to employing the Psalter as the subject of his longest commentary-like work, *Discourses on the Psalms,* also employed the Psalms as the basis for his public preaching and theological refutations. For example, in his *Treatise Against Two Letters of the Pelagians* (27.4), after having noted his agreement with a passage from Cyprian's *Testimonies,* Augustine also reminded his readers that Cyprian was an authoritative source for the doctrine of original sin. He followed this statement with a citation of Ps 51:5: "Indeed, I was born guilty, a sinner when my mother conceived me," already having noted that it was one of several texts the Pelagians could not adequately answer.

From the beginning of the Patristic era the Psalter figured prominently in the life of the Church. The celebration of the Eucharist, the liturgy of the word, the daily office, wedding ceremonies, and funeral services all came to be accompanied by the Psalms. Tradition holds that it was Ignatius of Antioch who introduced the antiphonal singing of psalms. More verifiable is the fact that the psalms were sung as part of the Church's worship by the middle of the second century. Clement of Alexandria refers to psalms being used at feasts (*Exhortation to the Heathen* 12; *Instructor* 2.4). Tertullian also confirms the presence of the Psalter in his church's worship. He wrote that at his church's love feasts each participant was required to stand up and sing a hymn from the Holy Scriptures (*Apol.* 39). These practices remained normative. At the turn of the fifth century Augustine wrote to defend the practice of the singing of psalms at the eucharistic celebration (*Against Hilary* 1, cf. *Retractations* 2.11).

With the rise of the monastic movement the psalms continued their great significance. It was during this era that the Psalter came to make up the principal part of the daily office. In the West there evolved three different schemes for using the psalms. Both the Roman (Gregorian) scheme and the Benedictine scheme allowed for the singing of the entire Psalter in one week, while the Ambrosian scheme normally sang all 150 over the course of two weeks. In the Eastern Church the psalms were normally recited in one week, though they were sung twice through in their entirety during the weeks of Lent.

It is also among the monastics that the psalms came to be used in the rite for sacred vows. For example, in the *Rule of Benedict* Ps 119:116 was included as a key portion of the ceremony through which novices were admitted as monks into the community. In the *RB* the initiate was required to place his written petition on the altar and quote aloud: "Receive me, Lord, according to your promise and I will live. Do not disappoint me in my hope" (58). This prayer was then repeated three times by the whole community.

The chanting of psalms at Christian burials dates back to at least the third century. One of the few psalms employed in this way is Psalm 114. It was used both in the *commendatio animae,* "the commendation of the soul" at the time of an individual's death and as part of the processional chant as the body was moved to the church and from the church to the grave.

By the late Patristic period memorization of all the psalms became a requirement for ordination. Both the second canon of the second Council of Nicea and Pope Gregory the Great made provision for excluding from office anyone who did not know the Psalter thoroughly.

As was also the case with the biblical wisdom literature, the psalms quickly became a source of moral and ethical guidance for early Christians. In introducing his translation of a portion of Origen's commentary on Psalms, Rufinus writes that "[Origen's] exposition of the thirty-sixth, thirty-seventh and thirty-eighth Psalms is ethical in its character, being designed to enforce more correct methods of life; and teaches at one time the way of conversion and repentance, at another that of purification and of progress" (*Rufinus' Preface to the Translation of Origen's Commentary on Psalms 36, 37, and 38;* trans. W. H. Fremantle, *NPNF,* 2nd ser. 3:566).

The psalms are read liturgically more than any other book of the Christian canon. They are present in each Liturgy of the Word, in the Mass, sacraments, vigils, and the Liturgy of the Hours. They edify believers through their anticipation of Christ fulfilled in the NT, their constant teachings on faith and hope, and their encouraging reminders of God's providence, compassion, and power. They exemplify prayer, confession, praise, and thanksgiving.

Proverbs

In patristic literature Proverbs, Ecclesiastes (Qoheleth), and the Song of Songs were considered as a group to form a symposium of Solomonic authorship on the various fields of human learning. The relationship among these three books is reflected upon in Origen's *Commentary on the Song of Songs.* The strong moral content of Proverbs provided resources for the Fathers' ethical exhortations but the book as a whole was infrequently commented on. Much of the exegesis that survives is in fragmentary form or in the *catenae.* Trends in the interpretation of Proverbs tend to correspond to the exegetical approaches of the individual authors—thus the allegorical and spiritual exegesis that Origen furnishes is scarcely surprising. Proverbs 22:20-21 LXX ("Do you portray them threefold in counsel and knowledge, that you might answer words of truth to those who question you": *First Principles* 4.2.4) provided Origen with a rationale for his hermeneutical approach, particularly his understanding of the Bible. These verses supported the notion of the multiple senses of Scripture: the literal (historical), moral, and spiritual (allegorical). To these corresponded not only his theological anthropology (body/soul/spirit), but also a threefold classification of Christians (the simple/those making progress/the perfect). Most notable of all the patristic writings on Proverbs that have survived are Basil of Caesarea's *Homilies on the Beginning of the Proverbs*—a highly prized commentary that was also frequently cited in the *catenae.* In his treatment of Prov 1:1-5 Basil's approach, not unlike many preceding him (such as Hippolytus' *On Proverbs*), was to emphasize and revere the moral teachings in the book that he demonstrated in his exposition of these verses.

The Antiochian exegete Theodore of Mopsuestia, while not denying the canonicity of Proverbs, reckoned to it a lower status of inspiration, a position condemned at Constantinople II (553 C.E.). However, Proverbs was to become the battleground for a far more serious and sustained controversy, namely that arising with Arius and his followers who postulated the ontological subordination of the Son to the Father. In Prov 8:22 personified Wisdom speaks: "The LORD created me at the beginning of his ways for his works" (LXX), and in 8:25 Wisdom again says of herself "[the LORD] brought me forth beyond all the hills." Justin, Origen, Tertullian and others looked to v. 25 as normative, emphasizing the "begotten-ness" or generation of Wisdom, and viewed v. 22 as expressing a similar idea (and thus downplaying any notion of the "creation" of Wisdom). Prior to Arius' interpretation, then, these verses were used to make a distinction between the Father and Son, and between the Son and the rest of creation. But for Arius v. 22 was decisive, teaching the "created-ness" (and not "begotten-ness") of Wisdom. Part of the issue here was the NT's close association of "wisdom" with Christ. References to the *logos* of John and Pauline references to Christ as "the wisdom of God" (1 Cor 1:24) and the "firstborn of all creation" (Col 1:15) provided impetus for the Arians to conclude that Christ was created, and by implication not eternal with the Father. Epiphanius, in fact, thought that Prov 8:22 was the text that initiated the Arian controversy (*Panarion* 69.12.1).

The first comprehensive rebuttal of this interpretation in the context of Prov 8:22 arose from Athanasius of Alexandria's theological treatise, *Four Discourses Against the Arians* (2.18–80). Against the Arians he advanced two possible interpretations: first, the Son was created *only* in the sense of his incarnation, and second, the creation of Wisdom was actually the creation of Wisdom's image in humans as they were themselves created.

Ecclesiastes

The book of Ecclesiastes receives no direct citation in the NT and the references to it by the Apostolic Fathers are sparse. In the third century the book enjoyed greater attention, and the first patristic commentaries were those of Hippolytus and Origen, both of whose works are extant only in fragmentary form. One of Origen's pupils, Gregory Thaumaturgos, wrote a paraphrase entitled *A Metaphrase of the Book of Ecclesiastes,* which is the earliest extant, complete work on Ecclesiastes. Gregory's paraphrase is important because it proposes a novel response to the seemingly heterodox statements in Ecclesiastes, particularly those tending to hedonism but also those expressing skepticism. What characterizes Gregory's work is a harmonization of these difficult passages, whether through the refashioning of the LXX text for his translation or through the concession of heterodox statements in the book. Gregory posited that these difficult statements represented either a younger, more foolish Solomon or a profane interlocutor. This hermeneutic, suggesting the presence of a hypothetical interlocutor, is called *prosopopoeia* and means "dramatization" or "the putting of speeches into the mouths of characters"; it has furnished many subsequent commentators, even those of modern times, with an interpretive approach to the tensions within Ecclesiastes.

Both Gregory of Nyssa's *Homilies on Ecclesiastes* and Jerome's *Commentary on Ecclesiastes* made use of *prosopopeia* to vindicate Solomon of "Epicurean" charges. Toward the end of the sixth century Gregory of Agrigentum wrote a massive *Explanation of Ecclesiastes* that stands along with Jerome's as among the best of patristic commentaries on this book. In the prologue Gregory cited Prov 30:33 LXX ("press milk and you will have butter") and identified milk with a more "obvious," literal reading of the text while the butter represents the "secret," or spiritual sense. Gregory used both interpretive approaches yet slavishly followed neither (the same could be said of Jerome's work). While an apologetic and moralizing tenor derived from earlier works (to offset the "hedonistic" teaching) was present in Gregory's commentary his proclivity toward a literal reading manifested itself in a greater acceptance of these passages.The other theme that troubled exegetes was Ecclesiastes' skepticism, which arose prominently in the opening lines of the book: "Vanity of vanities! All is vanity" (1:2). Verses such as this supported a *contemptus mundi,* a "contempt of the world" subsequently appropriated by the Church's ascetic tradition and articulated not only by the patristic writers previously mentioned but also by medieval commentators.

Song of Songs

The earliest extant Christian commentary on the Song of Songs comes from Hippolytus. In it we find the beginnings of a long tradition of allegorical interpretation in which Christ is viewed as the bridegroom and the Church as his bride. This nuptial theology, rooted in Ephesians 5, would come to dominate patristic interpretation after Origen's commentary and homilies on the Song of Songs. Origen sought to eliminate all interpretations that would reflect an earthly or carnal message, though he did not deny the book's literal meaning as a drama about marriage. For instance, he understood the Song's, "Let him kiss me with the kisses of his mouth!" in 1:2 as an appeal for the advent of the Bridegroom that surpasses the revelatory "kisses" of Moses and the prophets (*First Homily on the Canticle of Canticles* 2). Along with his christological and ecclesiastical exegesis Origen interpreted the Song as a picture of the soul's ascent toward union with God. Jerome would affirm Origenian exegesis; it was Jerome who, together with Rufinus's translation of the commentaries, preserved Origen's homilies and part of his commentary on the Song.

Allegorical interpretations thus became the norm in the early Church. Often the twin breasts of the bride in 4:5 and 7:8 were seen as representing the Old and New Testaments of salvation history. For Ambrose the flower of Song 2:1 was Christ who had sprouted from the virgin Mary to bring the fragrance of faith to the whole world (*On the Holy Spirit* 25.38). Cyril of Alexandria believed 3:1 described the women who sought the risen Savior on Easter morning, and 5:1 prefigured the Last Supper (*Commentary on the Canticle of Canticles,* respective verses). Gregory of Nyssa, Theodoret, and Aponius all continued the Origenian interpretation of the Church as Bride in their commentaries on the Song. Gregory highlighted the role of the Eucharist in the union between Christ and the Church. In North Africa, Origen's conception of the Church as an "unspotted" bride would give rise to controversy over the true extent of the Church in light of its impurity or capitulation to worldly pressures. The Song was also incorporated into the Church's liturgy.

In marked contrast to other interpreters, Theodore of Mopsuestia took a literal view of the Song of Songs in his commentary. Following Antiochian hermeneutical tendencies, he argued that it should not be understood as speaking of Christ and the Church but was instead to be read in a plain sense as an erotic song. Solomon wrote it in order to boldly extol the beauties of human love in the face of criticism for his marriage to an Egyptian princess. Thus possible use by Christians for edification was minimal. Theodore's view was condemned a century after his death by the Second Council of Constantinople in 553.

Sirach (Ecclesiasticus)

Allusions to this book, also known as the Wisdom of Sirach, appear early in the *Didache* (4.5), the *Letter of Barnabas* (19.9), Tertullian (*An Exhortation to Chastity* 2), and in Clement of Alexandria (*Miscellanies* 1.13) who suggested that the work was written by Solomon and had influenced the Hellenic philosopher Heraclitus (*Misc.* 2.5.24). Hippolytus (*On the Psalms* 1.7) and Eusebius (*Eccl. Hist.* 7.30.14) both quote from Sirach, and in the East it was cited by Christian writers such as Basil of Caesarea, Gregory of Nazianzus, Gregory of Nyssa, and John Chrysostom. Origen referenced Sirach frequently in his homilies as did Augustine, especially in his *Expositions on the Books of Psalms.* Sirach's authority was made explicit by the Councils of Hippo (393) and Carthage (397, 419), which officially established the book as canonical. In the sixth century Paterius compiled Gregory the Great's numerous references to Sirach into a quasi-commentary that two centuries later inspired similar efforts by Bede. It was not until the ninth century, though, that Rhabanus Maurus produced the first full-length commentary on this book.

Wisdom

Also known as the Wisdom of Solomon, this book was written pseudonymously by a Hellenistic Jew in the first century B.C.E., though many early Christian writers including Clement of Alexandria, Tertullian, and Cyprian accepted its self-professed Solomonic authorship. The book of Wisdom is first alluded to by Clement of Rome (*1 Clem.* 27.5) and possibly soon thereafter by Ignatius (*Magn.* 8.2b) and *Barnabas* (20.2). Other early witnesses include Irenaeus (*Adv. Haer.* 4.83.3), the Muratorian Canon (68–70), Tertullian (*Against the Valentinians* 2.2), Origen (*Against Celsus* 3.72), and Cyril of Jerusalem (*Catechetical Lectures* 9.15). Cassiodorus records both Ambrose and Augustine preaching on the book of Wisdom (*On the Institution of Divine Letters* 5), though these homilies are nonextant. Cassiodorus also commissioned Bellator to write a full-length commentary on Wisdom (the eight book *Exposition on Wisdom*), though this sixth century document has also been lost. In the seventh century Paterius compiled Gregory the Great's scattered comments on Sirach and Wisdom, and in the ninth century the Benedictine Rhabanus Maurus wrote the earliest extant full-length commentary on the book of Wisdom.

Though Jerome categorized Wisdom as pseudepigraphic, Clement of Alexandria and Augustine regarded it as canonical, an appraisal officially confirmed by the councils of Sardis (347), Carthage (397), Trullo (692), and Trent (1546).

While the nineteen chapters comprising this work provided a well of wisdom for the Fathers to plumb (Augustine alone refers to Wisdom of Solomon more than eight hundred times), Wis 7:22–8:1 in particular proved to be a favorite text for early Christian writers. In this passage Wisdom is personified and characterized by twenty-one attributes, including such theologically provocative statements as "For she is a reflection of eternal light, a spotless mirror of the working of God, and an image of his goodness" (Wis 7:26; cf. Heb 1:3), and "For she is a breath of the power of God, and a pure emanation of the glory of the Almighty" (Wis 7:25). On hundreds of occasions early Christian writers linked Wisdom 7 with such christologically significant NT passages as Col 1:15; 2 Cor 4:4; Heb 1:4; John 14:9, 10 (e.g., Origen *An Exhortation to Martyrdom* 35). This christological correspondence became especially important in the fourth century with the rise of Arianism, and the Arian debate also raised pneumatological questions to which the Wisdom of Solomon could speak. For example, Ambrose linked Wis 7:22, 23 with 1 Cor 2:6-16 to explain the Holy Spirit's role in dispensing and developing wisdom and discernment within the Church (*On the Holy Spirit* 3.6). The Donatist theologian Tyconius, a contemporary of Ambrose, made this same textual connection as well. Finally, this book was also important to the development of the martyrology of the early Church. The book of Wisdom linked righteous suffering with the gift of eternal life (Wis 1:12-16; 2:7–5:23; 10:1–19:22), and the author of the *Letter of the Martyrs of Lyon* (177) applied this relationship to Christian martyrs who in their suffering were united with the death and resurrection of Jesus Christ.

BIBLIOGRAPHY FOR WISDOM AND POETRY

Primary Sources

Job

Die älteren und griechischen Katenen zum Buch Hiob. 1: *Einleitung, Prologe und Epiloge, Fragmente zu Hiob 1,2–8,22,* ed. U. Hagedorn and D. Hagedorn. PTS 40 (1994).

Ambrose. *De interpellatione Iob et David.* Edited by C. Schenkl. CSEL 32.2:211–296 (1897).

____. *The Prayer of Job and David.* Translated by Michael P. McHugh. FC 65:329–355 (1972).

Athanasius. *Scolia in Iob (fragmenta in catenis).* MPG 27:1344–1348.

Augustine. *Adnotationes in Iob.* Edited by J. Zycha. CSEL 28.2:509–628 (1895).

Didymus of Alexandria. *Didymus der Blinde, Kommentar zu Hiob.* 4 vols. Edited by A. Henrichs, U. Hagedorn, D. Hagedorn, and L. Koenen. PTA 1–3, 33.1 (1968, 1985).

Gregory the Great. *Moralia in Iob.* Edited by M. Adriaen. CCSL 143, 143A, 143B (1979–1985).

____. *Morals on the Book of Job by S. Gregory the Great.* 3 vols in 4. Edited and translated by J. Bliss. LFC 18, 21, 23, 31.

Hesychius of Jerusalem. *Hésychius de Jérusalem, Homélies sur Job: Version arménienne.* 2 vols. Edited by C. Renoux and C. Mercier. PO 42.1–2 (1983).

John Chrysostom. *Commentarius in Iob (partim editus).* MPG 64:503–505.

____. *Fragmenta in Iob in catenis.* MPG 64:506–656.

____. *Kommentar zu Hiob.* Edited by U. Hagedorn and D. Hagedorn. PTS 35 (1990).

Julian the Arian. *Der Hiobkommentar des Arianers Julian.* Edited by D. Hagedorn. PTS 14 (1973).

Julian of Eclanum. *Expositio libri Iob.* Edited by L. DeConinck. CCSL 88:1–109 (1977).

Olympiodorus. *Olympiodorus Alexandria, Kommentar zu Hiob.* Edited by U. Hagedorn and D. Hagedorn. PTS 24 (1984).

Origen. *Homiliae in Iob* (fragments). MPG 12:1032–1049. MPG 17:57–105.

Psalms

Ambrose. *Expositio de psalmo CXVIII.* Edited by M. Petschenig. CSEL 62 (1913).

____. *Explanatio super psalmos XII.* Edited by M. Petschenig. CSEL 64 (1919).

Apollinaris. *Fragmenta in psalmos,* in Robert Devreesse, *Les anciens commentateurs grecs des Psaumes.* Studi e testi 141, 211–223. Vatican City: Biblioteca Apostolica Vaticana, 1970.

Arnobius the Younger. *Commentarii in Psalmos.* Edited by K. D. Daur. CCSL 25 (1990).

Asterius. *Homiliae in Psalmos.* Edited by M. Richard. In *Asterii Sophistae.* Oslo: Brogger, 1956.

Athanasius. *Expositiones in psalmos.* MPG 27:60–545.

____. *Epistula ad Marcellinum.* MPG 27:12–45.

____. "On the Interpretation of the Psalms (Letter to Marcellinus)." Translated by P. Bright. In Charles

Kannengiesser, ed., *Early Christian Spirituality.* Philadelphia: Fortress, 1986, 56–77.

Augustine. *Enarrationes in psalmos.* Edited by D. E. Dekkers and I. Fraipont. CCSL 38, 39, 40 (1956, 1990).

____. *Expositions on the Psalms.* Translated by S. Hegbin and F. Corrigan. ACW 29, 30 (1960).

Basil of Caesarea. *Homiliae super psalmos.* MPG 29:209–494.

Cassiodorus. *Expositio psalmorum.* Edited by M. Adriaen. CCSL 97, 98 (1958).

____. *Explanation of the Psalms.* Translated by P. G. Walsh. ACW 51–53 (1990–1991).

Cyril of Alexandria. *Expositio in Psalmos.* MPG 69:717–1273.

Didymus of Alexandria. *Didymos der Blinde, Psalmenkommentar (Tura-Papyrus).* 5 vols. Edited by L. Doutreleau, A. Gesché, and M. Gronewald. PTA 4, 6, 7, 8, 12 (1968–1970).

____. *Fragmenta in psalmos.* MPG 39:1156–1616, 1617–1622.

Diodore of Tarsus. *Commentarii in Psalmos.* Edited by J. M. Olivier. CCSG 6 (1980).

Eusebius. *Commentarius in Psalmos.* MPG 30:81–104. MPG 23:441–1221.

Evagrius of Pontus. *Scholia in psalmos.* MPG 12:1054–1686. MPG 27:60–545.

Gregory of Nyssa. *In inscriptiones psalmorum* and *In sextum Psalmum.* Edited by J. McDonough. GNO 5:24–193 (1986).

____. *Gregory of Nyssa's Treatise on the Inscriptions of the Psalms.* Translated by R. E. Heine. Oxford: Clarendon, 1995.

Hilary. *Tractatus super psalmos.* Edited by A. Zingerle. CSEL 22 (1891).

____. *Homilies on Psalms.* Translated by W. Sanday. NPNF, 2nd ser. 9:236–248.

Hippolytus. *In Psalmos* (fragments). Edited by H. Achelis. GCS 1:146–147, 153.

Jerome. *Commentarioli in psalmos.* Edited by G. Morin. CCSL 72 (1959).

____. *Tractatus lix in psalmos.* Edited by G. Morin. CCSL 78:3–352 (1958).

____. *Tractatum in psalmos series altera.* Edited by G. Morin. CCSL 78:353–447 (1958).

____. *Homilies on the Psalms.* Translated by M. L. Ewald. FC 48, 57 (1964, 1967).

John Chrysostom. *Expositiones in psalmos.* MPG 55:39–528.

Origen. *Excerpta in Psalmum I.* MPG 12:1076–1084, 1092–1096.

____. *Excerpta in Psalmum VI; XV; XVIII.* MPG 17:1076–1084, 1092–1096.

____. *Libri in Psalmos (Praefatio).* MPG 12:1053–1076.

____. *Libri in Psalmos (Fragmenta in diuersos Psalmos in catenis).* MPG 12:1085–1320, 1409–1686. MPG 17:105–149.

____. *Homélies sur les Psaumes 36 à 38.* Edited by Emanuela Prinzivalli. Translated by Henri Crouzel and Luc Brésard. SC 411 (1995).

____. *Homiliae de Psalmis.* MPG 12:1319–1410.

Prosper of Aquitaine. *Expositio psalmorum a centesimo usque ad cetesimum quinquagesimum.* Edited by P. Callens. CCSL 68A (1972).

Psalmenkommentare aus der Katenenüberlieferung. 1, 2; *Psalmenkommentare aus der Katenenüberlieferung* 3; *Untersuchungen zu den Psalmenkatenen.* Edited by E. Mühlenberg. PTS 15, 16, 19.

Theodore of Mopsuestia. *Le Commentaire de Théodore de Mopsueste sur Les Psaumes.* Edited by R. Devreesse. Vatican City: Biblioteca Apostolica Vaticana, 1939.

____. *Theodori Mopsuesteni Expositiones in Psalmos Iuliano Aeclanensi interprete.* Edited by L. DeConinck. CCSL 88A (1977).

____. *Fragments syriaques du Commentaire des Psaumes.* Edited by L. Van Rompay. CCSO 435–436 (1982).

Theodoret. *Interpretatio in Psalmos.* MPG 80:857–1997.

Proverbs

Basil of Caesarea. *Homilia in principium Proverbiorum.* MPG 31:385–424.

Evagrius Ponticus. *Scholies aux Proverbes.* Edited and translated by P. Géhin. SC 340 (1987).

Hippolytus. *In Proverbia.* MPG 10:615–628.

John Chrysostom. *Fragmenta in Salomonis Proverbie.* MPG 64:660–740.

Origen. *Fragmenta* and *Expositio in Proverbia.* MPG 17:149–252.

Ecclesiastes

Didymus of Alexandria. *Kommentar zum Ecclesiastes.* Edited by G. Binder, et al. 4 vols. Bonn: Habelt, 1969–1983.

Evagrius Ponticus. *Evagre le Pontique, Scholies sur l'Ecclésiaste.* Edited and translated by P. Géhin. SC 397 (1993).

Gregory of Agrigentum. *In Ecclesiasten.* MPG 98:741–1181.

Gregory of Nyssa. *In Ecclesiasten.* MPG 44:615–754.

____. *In Ecclesiasten Homiliae.* Edited by P. Alexander. GNO 5:277–442 (1986).

____. *Gregory of Nyssa: Homilies on Ecclesiastes: An English Version with Supporting Studies.* Edited by S. G. Hall. Berlin: de Gruyter, 1993.

Gregory Thaumaturgos. *Metaphrasis in Ecclesiasten.* MPG 10:988–1017.

____. *Gregory Thaumaturgos' Paraphrase of Ecclesiastes.* Translated by John Jarick. Septuagint and Cognate Studies 29. Atlanta: Scholars, 1990.
Jerome. *Commentarius in Ecclesiasten.* Edited by M. Adriaen. CCSL 72 (1959).

Song of Songs

Aponius. *In Canticum Canticorum expositionem.* Edited by B. de Vregille and L. Neyrand. CCSL 19 (1986).
____. *Commentaire sur le Cantique des cantiques.* Edited and translated by B. de Vregille and L. Neyrand. SC 420 (1997).
Cyril of Alexandria. *Fragmenta in Canticum Canticorum.* MPG 69:1277–1293.
Gregory of Nyssa. *In Canticum Canticorum.* Edited by H. Langerbeck. GNO 6 (1986).
Gregory the Great. *Expositio in Canticum Canticorum.* Edited by P. Verbraken. CCSL 144 (1963).
Hippolytus. *Interpretatio Cantici canticorum.* Edited by G. Garitte. CSCO 263:32–70; 264:23–53 (1965).
Origen. *The Song of Songs: Commentary and Homilies.* Translated by R. P. Lawson. ACW 26 (1957).
____. *Commentaire sur le Cantique des Cantiques.* Rufinus's text. Translated by L. Brésard, H. Crouzel, and M. Borret. SC 375, 376 (1991, 1992).
Theodore of Mopsuestia. *Fragmenta in Canticum.* MPG 66:699–700.
Theodoret. *Explanatio in Canticum Canticorum.* MPG 81:28–213.

MAJOR PROPHETS

Isaiah

Origen gave the Christian community its first commentary on Isaiah. Unfortunately this massive production of thirty books is no longer extant. However, nine of Origen's homilies on Isaiah were translated into Latin by Jerome and these still survive. Eusebius of Caesarea, a disciple of Origen, produced the earliest surviving commentary on the prophet. Also extant are the six homilies of John Chrysostom, the commentary of Pseudo-Basil of Caesarea on Isaiah 1–16, Jerome's commentary, Cyril of Alexandria's commentary, the commentary of Theodoret of Cyrus, Hesychius of Jerusalem's *scholia,* and Procopius of Gaza's *catena.*

In general the commentaries and homilies were composed by Christian minds reading the prophetic texts in light of the Christ-event. (For this insight we acknowledge our debt to R. L. Wilken's essay, *"In novissimis diebus:* Biblical promises, Jewish Hopes and Early Christian Exegesis," *Journal of Early Christian Studies* 1 [1993] 1–19.) The messianic age, to which even the Jews frequently believed much of Isaiah's material pointed, had come to pass in Jesus. For the Christians the Jewish messianic expectation contained in the Isaianic phrase "in days to come" (Isa 2:2) was a matter of contemporary experience. The promises of Isa 2:2-4 referred to the times of the Roman empire following Christ, the times of salvation, the times of the universal Church, the new community that brings the gospel to the world.

If early commentators read Isaiah with little interest in the original historical setting it was because a new historical setting now existed. But although the first sense was christological the commentators did treat the historical settings of the prophecies, sometimes extensively, and did use allegory for matters other than christology.

This same Christian newness to history would lead some early Christians to read other passages in Isaiah as prophecies of Jewish unbelief in Jesus. Origen (*Against Celsus* 2.8) and Cyprian (*Treatise* 12.1.3), for example, would read Isa 6:9-10 in this way. Cyprian (*Treat.* 12.1.3) would additionally understand Isa 1:2-4 to apply to the Jews in their misunderstanding of Jesus while Tertullian would apply Isa 1:2 to their unbelief in both Son and Father (*On Prayer* 2). The evangelization of the Gentiles and the misery of Israel after 70 C.E. provided a context for Christian interpretation of the prophet.

Yet in early Christian interpretation the material of Isaiah served a number of different ends. Isaiah 1:11-14 taught the lasting purity of inner virtues but the end of sacrifices (*Barn.* 2). From Isa 1:16-20 the Christian learned about the need for repentance (*1 Clem.* 8.4) and of the baptism in water that brought remission of sins (Justin, *Apol. 1,* 61). Clement of Rome in his ecclesiological concerns found prophetic warrant for the apostolic appointment of bishops and deacons in Isa 60:17 (*1 Clem.* 42.5), while Cyprian, in his own ecclesiological pressures, found Isa 2:12; 14:13-16 helpful in encouraging humility and the forsaking of *hubris* (*Ep.* 54.3). Of course the passage on the suffering servant, Isa 53:1-12, informed the Church's faith and practice. Clement of Rome would quote the entire passage to teach humility from the example of the Lord Jesus Christ (*1 Clem.* 16). Origen cites almost the entire passage in order to explain the prediction of the Savior's death for sinners, a death that would bring benefit, healing (*Against Celsus* 2.54-55). For Athanasius, too, 53:3-10 was a prophecy of Christ's death, a death of one of divine nature suffered for the salvation of all, and not for his own sake (*On the Incarnation* 34). Gregory of Nazianzus read 53:4, 5 in the sense of 2 Cor 5:21 and Gal 3:13. The Lord was made sin and a curse in the sense that he took them upon himself, bore them, and removed them from sinners (*Ep.* 101). For Augustine 53:7 sets forth the first lowly, hidden, silent coming of Christ to be followed by his exalted, manifested advent (*Tractate on the Gospel of John* 4.2).

In doctrinal conflict and development Isaiah's material would play many roles. Irenaeus would argue against Theodotion, Aquila, and the Ebionites that Isa 7:14 spoke of a *virgin* conceiving, not a young woman. God had superintended the translation of the Hebrew into Greek (LXX) and the translation was in accord with the apostolic faith (*Adv. Haer.* 3.21.1-4). Against the Gnostics who allegorized Isaiah's prophecies of the end time into ideas related to their *pleroma* Irenaeus would argue that they taught no such doctrine. Rather, in accord with Revelation they taught the times of the kingdom and the refashioning of the creation (*Adv. Haer.* 5.35.1–36.3). Also against the Gnostics Irenaeus would connect the prophecies of Isa 11:1-4 and 61:1-2 with the baptism of Jesus and the Spirit's descent upon him as recorded, for instance, in Matt 3:16-17. By doing so he opposed the Gnostic thesis that it was a spiritual "Christ" from the *pleroma* that descended upon Jesus (*Adv. Haer.* 3.9.3; 3.17.1).

Origen would see the Son and the Holy Spirit in the two seraphim of Isaiah 6 (*Homilies on Isaiah* 1.2; *First Principles* 1.3.4). This would evoke the anonymous (Pseudo-Jerome) anti-Origenist tractate *On the Vision of Isaiah* 6:1–7. Jerome, too, would object to Origen's interpretation in his *Commentary on Isaiah* (3.6.2) and in a letter to Damasus (*Ep.* 18A, 4.1–5.7). Jerome sees Christ as the Lord who is seated and who speaks and the seraphim as the two testaments.

Isaiah's role in theological discussion would not be limited to the dispute over the vision of ch. 6. Much material from the prophet would have an important place in trinitarian development. The Arians used Isa 1:2 to nullify the claim that the christological term "begotten" referred to the Son's sharing the Father's nature. For them the prophet made the term "son" applicable to those of dissimilar nature to God (Eusebius of Nicomedia, *Epistle to Paulinus of Tyre;* Alexander of Alexandria, *Epistle to Alexander of Thessalonica* 10–11; Athanasius, *Defense of the Nicene Definition* 9–10). Alexander of Alexandria, however, would explain that the passage referred to those adopted as God's sons, not the Son who was the Son by nature (*Epist. Alex. Thess.* 32). Isaiah 45:14 would be used by Athanasius to prove the divine essence of the Son, for there he is worshiped (*Against the Arians* 2.23), while Ambrose cited it to validate the unity of the divine substance (*On the Christian Faith* 1.3.27). For Basil the Great Isa 48:16 taught the Holy Spirit's divine nature (*Against Eunomius* 3.2.4; *On the Holy Spirit* 19.49). Isaiah 53:8 would be quite prominent. Alexander of Alexandria cited it twice in his *Epistle to Alexander of Thessalonica* (21, 46) to insist that the Son is begotten of the Father, but that his *hypostasis* and his generation are beyond human investigation. Thus Alexander sought to prevent Arian speculation into the Son's generation, but the Arians would use the text to prevent Nicea's language about the Son being the same substance as the Father from being taken too seriously; the Son was clearly subordinate (Sirmian Formula *[Blasphemia]* in Hilary, *On the Councils* 11). But Cyril of Jerusalem would see the Son's eternality in the prophet's words (*Catechetical Lectures* 11.5).

Isaiah's place in the Church's liturgical use of the OT is second only to Psalms. It is read during Advent, Christmas, Lent, and Holy Week. The readings remind the people of God that a holy, righteous God has provided a suffering, yet ultimately victorious, savior in the incarnate Son.

Jeremiah

From Origen's hand twenty homilies on Jeremiah are extant in Greek and fourteen in Latin. Fragments from Cyril of Alexandria's comments on the prophet can be found in *catenae,* and still extant is a commentary said to be authored by John Chrysostom, but it is spurious. Theodoret's commentary on Jeremiah treats the prophet as well as Lamentations and Baruch. Jerome's commentary on Jeremiah seems to have been his last. *Catenae* also preserve comments on Jeremiah by Ephrem (or Pseudo-Ephrem). Within Jeremiah the Fathers of the early Church would find material that informed them about their place in redemptive history, their ministry, their ethics and morals, and their theological questions.

Jeremiah 2:12-13, a passage in which the prophet chides the people for forsaking the Lord and digging broken cisterns, is a favored text for Christian self-definition against other groups. The opponents are contrasted with the Church, Christian faith, and may be Jews (Justin, *Dialogue with Trypho* 14.1; Tertullian, *An Answer to the Jews* 13) or heretics (Irenaeus, *Adv. Haer.* 3.24.1). An appeal by the prophet for the people to circumcise their hearts in accord with new covenant expectation (4:3-4) is used as a petition to Jews for Christian conversion (Justin, *Dial.* 28.2) and as warrant for the unity of the one God of both prophet and apostle of the new covenant (Tertullian, *Against Marcion* 1.20.4). Aphrahat will understand Jer 6:30 as teaching that the kingdom of God has passed away from the Jews, that they have been rejected (*Demonstrations* 5.21). Jeremiah echoes the Church's message and its self-understanding.

The prophet also provides moral teaching. Jeremiah 5:8 is used to compare lustful behavior to that of horses (Irenaeus, *Adv. Haer.* 5.8.3; Cyril of Jerusalem, *Catechetical Lectures* 9.13). Jeremiah 9:23-24 functions as an appeal to Christian humility (*1 Clem.* 13) and an exhortation to trust and glory in God (Cyprian, *Treatise* 12.3.10). For Origen, in a homily on the prophet, Jer 20:9 teaches the need to confess and repent of sinful words that burn in the sinner's heart (*Homily on Jeremiah* 19.8-9).

In the development of doctrine Jeremiah's material would play an important role. Irenaeus's explanation of Christ's divinity and humanity against those who assert that he was only a man is informed by Jer 17:9: "he (it) is a man and who can know him (LXX)." The text teaches the Lord's humanity, but also the unfathomable depth of his deity revealed only by God. He is Son of humanity and Son of God (*Adv. Haer.* 3.18.3; 3.19.2; 4.33.11). For Tertullian the same passage would contribute to the Christian teaching, against Marcion and the Jews, on the two advents of Christ, one lowly and the other glorious (*Against Marcion* 3.7).

In thinking about God, Gregory of Nazianzus would invest considerable space in explaining God's incomprehensibility from Jer 23:24 (*Oration* 2.8-11). Origen would be fascinated with Jer 20:7: "O Lord, you have deceived me and I have been deceived." It presents God as a parent or physician who may deceive the child or patient for his or her ultimate good. It should raise believers' awareness of their childlike, untaught state in which God teaches them as children, not as adults (*Homilies on Jeremiah* 19, 20).

In the Trinitarian controversy Athanasius would cite Jer 2:13 of the Father: "A fountain of living water." Since the Son is life (John 14:6) it is absurd for the Arians to suppose that "there was when he was not." This would make the Father a dry fountain void of life (*Defense of the Nicene Definition* 3.12; *Against the Arians* 1.19). The same bishop of Alexandria would cite Jer 9:10 (LXX 9:9) and 23:22 (LXX 23:18) in support of the Nicene formula's statement on the Son being of the Father's essence or substance (*Epistle to the Bishops of Africa* 4). Athanasius sees in the Greek wording of these texts *(hypostemati, hyparxis)* prophetic testimony to the language of Nicea.

Finally, since the early Christian community read the prophets in light of the new age introduced by the Christ-event, Jeremiah informed their vision of christology and soteriology. Origen read Jer 11:19 (LXX), "Come let us put wood into his bread," as indicating the Bread of Life's, the Teacher's, the Word's crucifixion at the hands of those people who opposed his teaching (*Homily on Jeremiah* 10.2). Likewise, Athanasius is found associating the tree or wood of 11:19 with the prophetic prediction of the cross (*On the Incarnation* 35). Of course the Fathers would give special place to Jer 31:31-34, the new covenant. Irenaeus emphasizes the newness, that is, its liberty, the blessing of the Spirit, the faith in Christ, the new manner of life that differs somewhat from the covenant of Moses, but he also stresses the unity of the God who gave both (*Adv. Haer.* 4.9.1; 4.33.14). In his *Treatises* Cyprian quotes the entire passage to teach the prophetic expectation of a new dispensation and covenant for the Gentile Church (12.1.11). For Jerome the passage teaches, in concert with others, that until the end comes humans will be incomplete in righteousness (*Against the Pelagians* 2.25-26), and for Augustine it emphasizes the blessing of power to fulfill the Law through the Spirit's writing it upon hearts. The fearful become those who delight in Law; the transgressor is made a lover (*The Spirit and the Letter* 32-42).

In the liturgy Jeremiah is read in Ordinary Time, Lent, and ritual Masses including those of Penance, Marriage, Baptism of Adults, Religious Profession, and Vocations. The words of the prophet remind the faithful to seek righteousness not through law written on stone but through a new heart written upon by God's Spirit.

Lamentations

Eusebius tells us that he possessed five books of Origen's *Commentary on Lamentations* (*Hist. Eccl.* 6.32.2). Unfortunately, of these only fragments have survived. Theodoret includes remarks on Lamentations in his *Commentary on Jeremiah.* Olympiodorus' comments on Lamentations also survive only as fragments in *catenae.*

As already helpfully noted in the commentary on Lamentations in this volume by Victor Manuel Fernández, Lam 4:20 was an important text to early Christians. In addition to reading the text as referring to Christ as the believer's spiritual food, early Christians would see the incarnation, cross, and passion prophesied in Lam. 4:20. Since the nose, the organ of breathing, stands out from the face, Justin believed a cross was traced in the center of the human visage. Thus Lam 4:20, "the breath of our nostrils is the LORD's anointed," anticipated Christ's crucifixion for Justin (*Apol. 1,* 55.1-6). Irenaeus, too, would see the Lord's passion in Lam 4:20, but he would emphasize both the reference to "breath" in 4:20a, which he translates "Spirit," and the reference to "his shadow" in 4:20c. This combination of terms prophesied the bitter, veiling incarnation (shadow) of the Spirit Christ (*Demonstration of the Apostolic Preaching* 71). For Origen as well the passage spoke of the first advent of the Lord Christ, that humble incarnation (*Homily on Joshua* 8.6). But the "shadow in which we live" could also refer to the mortality of the present age that clouded even the believer's partial experience of immortality in this life (*Commentary on Matthew* 15.12). Again the Alexandrian would read it in a positive, yet guarded manner of the Christian's present experience. "His shadow in which we live among the nations" is contrasted to the shadow of the Law in which the unredeemed live. In the shadow the believer has a share in Christ as the way, truth, and life, but it is dim. The believer still awaits a perfect, future redemption (*Commentary on the Canticles* 3).

The language of Lam 4:20, then, would serve the Christian's understanding of the present state in tension between two worlds, one of mortality and lament and one of immortality and exultation, a state reflective of the Lord's passion prior to glory. Such a theme would also be found in Lam 3:34, ". . . the prisoners of the earth." Gregory of Nazianzus would find here a reference to the body and carnality (earth) that obstructs the Christian's (prisoner) path to God (*Theological Oration* 2.12 [*Oration* 28.12]). The same theme of the Christian's struggle in the present state would be seen in Lam 3:27, 28, 30, 31. From these verses Jerome composed a description of the character of the ascetic life of the anchorites. Finally, early Christians would find in Lamentations anticipatory words of their own deep, relentless grief. At his *Funeral Oration on Meletius,* bishop of Antioch, Gregory of Nyssa would cite Lam 1:4, "The roads to Zion mourn." For Gregory, Jeremiah spoke these words long ago in reference to his grief over the demise of Jerusalem, but these words of lament were also realized and fulfilled in the community's mourning for Meletius.

Baruch

Frequently referred to by the Fathers as a part of Jeremiah, the book of Baruch supplied rich material for early Christian thought. Theodoret would include remarks on Baruch in his Jeremiah commentary and Olympiodorus would also provide commentary. Baruch would inform the Church's ideas on a broad range of questions from eschatology, revelation, and incarnation to Christian gnosis and sanctity in marriage.

Irenaeus, the earliest Father to cite Baruch, reads the address to Jerusalem in 4:36-37, 5:1-9 as Jeremiah's prophetic expectation of the rebuilt, eschatological Jerusalem in the kingdom prior to the new earth (*Adv. Haer.* 5.35.1-2). He also reads Bar 3:37[38], which speaks of God conversing with humanity on the earth, as fulfilled in the prophetic ministry of revelation mediated by the Father's Word and in the Word's own incarnate ministry of revelation (*Adv. Haer.*

4.20.4, 8). Tertullian will allude to the passage when he also discusses the Son of God's ministry of revelation throughout all redemptive history (*Against Praxeas* 16.3). Even later, in the fourth century, Bar 3:37[38] would be associated with the Son's incarnate life among humanity. It is here that God was conversing with humanity (Ambrose, *On the Christian Faith* 5.18.222). For Clement of Alexandria, Bar 3:13, which promises eternal peace to the one who walks in God's way, teaches the blessing that follows knowledge (*The Instructor* 1.10). Clement would also find in the language of Bar 3:10, which speaks of Israel's defilement in a strange country, a lesson against intimacy with a foreign (that is, a non-spousal) partner.

In their formulation of trinitarian doctrine Christians of the fourth century also turned to Baruch. In the same way that he had used Jer 2:13; 17:12 against the Arians, Athanasius would use Bar 3:12. If the Father is the "fountain of wisdom" he could never be without the Son, for this would make him a dry spring (*Defense of the Nicene Definition* 3.12; *Against the Arians* 1.19). Furthermore, Bar 4:20, 22 with its language about the eternity of God provided Athanasius with a basis for his argument on the Son's eternity. Against the Arians who said "there was when he was not," Athanasius argues that he who is the expression and revelation (cf., for example, Matt 11:27; John 14:8-9; Heb 1:3) of the Father who is eternal must himself be eternal (*Against the Arians* 1.12). With the same agenda to show the Son's deity and to show him as a distinct person from the Father, Hilary (*On the Trinity* 4.42) cites Bar 3:35[36]-37[38]. In contrast to an Arian usage of the text that would capitalize on the language about God's exclusive uniqueness in 3:35[36] in order to emphasize the Father's separation from the Son, Hilary takes another path. He emphasizes 3:35 [36]-37[38] in order to teach that the OT testified to the existence of the Son, "God," who dwelt among humanity on earth. Therefore the term "God" (3:35[36]) could not be assigned to the Father alone, for he was not incarnate on earth in conversation with humanity.

Ezekiel

In complement to the helpful discussion of the patristic commentaries on Ezekiel and the Fathers' use of Ezekiel 37 and 47 provided by Jesús Azurmendi Ruiz in his commentary in this volume, the following observations may be of interest.

The early Church would find the vision of God in Ezekiel 1 pivotal to its case for the partial, progressive nature of God's revelation of the divine essence to humanity. For Irenaeus the nature of the vision of ch. 1 is explained by Ezek 1:28: it was the vision of the *likeness* of God's glory. This contributes to his theme of the progression of humanity, in the advance of the economies, toward ever more immediate visions of God. The prophets did not see God as those who saw the Son would see God, and the incarnate vision anticipates the fuller vision of God in the eschatological kingdom. For Origen, too, the vision described in Ezek 1:15 is not a direct seeing of God. It is a vision of good things, the type of life that is available to the believer in the present age. Yet it is only a *shadow* of the full life available in the future glory when one is absent from the body and united with God and God's Son (*Dialogue with Heraclides* 173–174). Likewise, for Gregory of Nazianzus the vision of the prophet was not an observation of the essence or nature of God. No human being in the present state of things, prior to eschatological glory, has seen God's nature or essence (*Theological Oration* 2.19, cf. 17 [*Oration* 28.19]).

For the Alexandrians, Clement and Origen, Ezek 18:4, "the soul that sins shall die," provided a basis for meditation on sanctification and the nature of death. Clement (*On Spiritual Perfection* 3.14) would argue that the passage was addressing a Christian's putting aside of wicked passions in the same way that Paul speaks of the old human dying and being raised to life (Eph 4:22, 24). In this way one would be an acceptable sacrifice (cf. Rom 12:1). Origen, however, would read the passage differently. It is seen repeatedly in his discussions of the soul's death, mortality, and immortality. For him the passage teaches death as a soul's capitulation to sin. It addresses the exclusion of that soul from God, that is, life (*Homily on Leviticus* 9.11; *Dialogue with Heraclides* 168-172; *Commentary on John* 13.59).

For Gregory of Nyssa, who argued against an idea that the incarnation involved only human flesh and not the human soul, Ezek 18:20 was critical. He reasoned that if Christ came to save the lost he came to save their whole being.

Ezekiel 18:20 teaches the death of the sinning soul, as does 18:4, which in his mind took effect immediately at the Fall because there humanity was alienated from God; bodily death followed years afterward. Since, then, humanity dies in both soul and body the Saviour must have taken upon himself all that is lost (*Against Eunomius* 2.13).

Furthermore, for the early Christians ch. 18 would function prominently to inform them about repentance and steadfastness in the Christian life. Ezekiel 18:18-32, which teaches the Lord's preference for the sinner's repentance and righteousness rather than the sinner's death, and 33:11, which teaches the same, would be referred to repeatedly (e.g., Athanasius of Alexandria, *Ep.* 3 [Easter 331] 4; *Life of Anthony* 18; Basil of Caesarea, *Ep.* 41.2; Jerome, *Ep.* 122.1; 147.3). Illustrative of how differing theological climates can produce different readings and emphases from the same text is Tertullian's much earlier use of Ezek 33:11. Against the theological dualism of Marcion that sees two gods, one of goodness and one of justice, Tertullian turns to the Ezekiel passage. Here he finds one God who mercifully prefers a sinner's repentance but who justly and righteously will punish the sinner. This teaches one God who should be loved by the obedient, but feared by the sinner (*Against Marcion* 2.13).

Finally it would be important to note how the new covenant blessing of Ezek 36:25-27 was frequently understood by the early Church. The Lord promised Israel a cleansing with water, a new heart, and a new spirit. These promises would be realized for the early Christian in regeneration by baptism (e.g., Gregory of Nyssa, *On the Baptism of Christ*; Cyril of Jerusalem, *Catechetical Lectures* 3.15; 16.30).

In the Church's liturgy Ezekiel is read at the Easter Vigil and Pentecost, on the feast of Christ the king, on the fifth Sunday of Lent, and in Ordinary Time. The prophet encourages the community of believers concerning the blessings of the New Covenant, resurrection, the sanctifying ministry of the Holy Spirit, and the sovereign graciousness of God in salvation.

Daniel

Portions of the book of Daniel have had an important place in the Church's thought and practice. Daniel's material is discussed in theological, polemical, and apologetic treatises as well as in commentaries. Motifs from the stories within the prophetic book were also popular in the Church's iconography.

The behavior of Daniel and his companions in the first chapter exemplifies for Hippolytus, in his *Commentary on Daniel* (1.8, 12), the faithfulness and purity expected of Christians. It also validates for Origen the authenticity of Daniel as a true prophet of the Church in contrast to the false prophets of the pagans (*Against Celsus* 7.7).

The stone of Dan 2:34, 35 cut out from the mountain without human hands was interpreted christologically, covenantally, and ecclesiologically. It was seen to teach the virginal conception and the mysterious, divine incarnation of the Father's Son (Justin, *Dial.* 76.1; Ephrem, *Commentary on Daniel* 5.206); the glorious, powerful, destructive second coming of Christ against the temporal end time kingdoms in order to establish the eternal kingdom (Irenaeus, *Adv. Haer.* 5.26.1-2; Tertullian, *Adv. Iud.* 14); the coming of the new covenant, law that overtakes and ends the old law and replaces it with a new, spiritual circumcision (Tertullian, *Adv. Iud.* 3); and the Church, the body of Christ, which has tangibly filled the whole earth (Tyconius, *Book of Rules* 1) and therefore those who speak of a division and pollution of the Church (for example, the Donatists) hate their brother and stumble blindly against the mountain (Augustine, *Homilies on 1 John* 1.8, 13). These readings are frequently influenced by the rich scriptural images of "stone" and "mountain."

The three young Hebrews in the furnace of fire (Daniel 4) who are not burned provided a hopeful soteriological image reproduced in early Christian art. The common association of the fourth figure in the furnace with Christ the Son is present already in Irenaeus (*Adv. Haer.* 4.20.11) and Hippolytus (*In Dan.* 3.92). Nebuchadnezzar's subsequent repentance (Dan 4:25-37) serves as an example to stir others to repentance and restoration (Tertullian, *On Repentance* 11). Jerome in his *Commentary on Daniel* emphasized a historical and literal reading of Nebuchadnezzar's experience denying any symbolic reference.

The story of Daniel in the lions' den (Daniel 6) was rich soil for the early Church's meditation.

Daniel's response of prayer to the king's decree and his preservation was a model of how the Christian prays without ceasing and receives blessing (Origen, *On Prayer* 12.2; 13.2). His suffering at Darius' hands teaches that Christians are persecuted by wicked men and therefore should not rebel against one another (*1 Clem.* 45). To Cyprian, it teaches the place of the fear of God in faith and hope (*Treatise* 12.3.20). In the early Church's iconography the story was popularly depicted as a hopeful picture of salvation and resurrection.

The four beasts of Daniel 7 and the four parts of the image of Daniel 2 were of particular interest to early Christians. In most interpretations the first three were read as the empires of Babylon, Persia (Medo-Persia), and Greece. The fourth empire was commonly understood as Rome (Hippolytus, *In Dan.* 2.1-3; Jerome, *In Dan.* 7.1-7) with Cyril of Jerusalem stating that this interpretation was the Church's tradition (*Catechetical Lectures* 15.13). The Syrian commentators, however, offer some alternative readings of the fourth empire. Aphrahat's interpretation is somewhat difficult to clarify. On the one hand he seems to identify the fourth kingdom as Rome, yet on the other hand he appears to believe that the third and fourth kingdoms found their fulfillment together in Alexander, that is, in Greece (*Demonstrations* 5.19). Ephrem, in his *Commentary on Daniel* (5.206), sets the four kingdoms forth as those of the Babylonians, Medes, Persians (Cyrus), and Greeks (Alexander).

The "little horn" of Daniel 7, 8 was understood by the Fathers both historically and eschatologically. Hippolytus saw it in one place as referring to Antiochus Epiphanes (*In Dan.* 2.9-10), but in others as referring to Antichrist (*In Dan.* 2.2-3; 3.7.19). Jerome would stress against Porphyry the vanity of reading the little horn as Antiochus rather than Antichrist, but seems to allow for an orthodox reading that sees Antiochus as a proleptic fulfillment or type of Antichrist (*In Dan.* 7.7-8; 8.5, 9, 14). The Syrian commentators, as one would expect, prefer the historical interpretation. For Aphrahat (*Demonstr.* 5.20) and Polychronius, in his *Commentary on Daniel* (11), the little horn was Antiochus, in continuity with the identification of the fourth kingdom.

When it comes, however, to the interpretation of the Son of man in Dan 7:13 the Syrian reading is not so predictable. Polychronius gives no identity, Aphrahat (*Demonstr.* 5.21) rejects the interpretation that it is a reference to the Jews and applies it instead to Christ in his first advent, while Ephrem (*In Dan.* 5.215) applies it proleptically to the time of the Maccabees, but in its consummation to Christ. Commentators other than the Syrians read the passage christologically as well, and with both historical and eschatological perspectives. For Justin (*Dial.* 31) it refers to Christ's second advent, as it does for Irenaeus (*Adv. Haer.* 4.8.11) and Tertullian (*Adv. Iud.* 14). Lactantius connected the passage with Jesus' ascension into heaven in a cloud (*Epitome of the Divine Institutes* 47; cf. Acts 1:9). For Jerome the text is linked with Acts 1:11 and Phil 2:6-8. It refers, then, to the Son of man as the Son of God who is equal with God, who has taken human flesh and who will return from heaven (*In Dan.* 7.13, 14).

The late Middle Ages would show that disputes between ruler and Pope, dissident order and Pope, and reformer and Pope resulted in the Pontiff being identified with the Antichrist of Daniel and his acts equated with the abomination of desolation. The Protestant Reformation, particularly in the writings of Martin Luther, would continue this identification from Daniel. John Calvin's commentary on the prophet, however, would emphasize a historical interpretation, seeing the fourth kingdom as Rome and the little horn as Antiochus.

In the Church's liturgy Daniel is read, for example, on the thirty-third Sunday, the feast of Christ the King, and during the thirty-fourth week. It is also read in Lent and in Masses for persecuted Christians. The readings encourage God's people concerning God's sovereign control of events and their eventual victory over trial and adversity.

BIBLIOGRAPHY FOR THE MAJOR PROPHETS

Primary Sources

Isaiah

Pseudo-Basil. *Enarratio in prophetam Isaiam.* MPG 30:117–668.

____. *San Basilo. Commento al profeta Isaia.* Edited by P. Trevisan. Corona Patrum Salesiana. Series Graeca, 4–5 (1939).

John Chrysostom. *Jean Chrysostome. Commentaire sur Isaie*. Edited by J. Dumortier. Translated by A. Liefooghe. SC 304 (1983).

____. *Homiliae in Isaiam*. MPG 56:11–94.

____. "Chrysostom's *Interpretatio in Isaiam:* An English Translation with an Analysis of its Hermeneutics." Translated and analyzed by D. A. Garrett. Ph.D. diss., Baylor University, 1981.

Cyril of Alexandria. *Commentarius in Isaiam*. MPG 70:9–1449.

Eusebius of Caesarea. *Commentarii in Isaiam*. MPG 24:89–526.

____. *Der Jesajakommentar*. In *Eusebius Werke IX*, ed. J. Ziegler. GCS (1975).

Hesychius of Jerusalem. *Interpretatio Isaiae*. MPG 93:1369–1385.

____. *Hesychii Hierosolymitani interpretatio Isaiae prophetae*. Edited by M. Faulhaber. Freiburg: Herder, 1900.

Jerome. *In Isaiam*. Edited by M. Adriaen and F. Glorie. CCSL 73 (1963).

____. *Commentaires de Jerome sur le prophete Isaïe, I–IV*. Edited by R. Gryson and P.-A. Deproost. Freiburg: Herder, 1993.

Pseudo-Jerome (Theophilus of Alexandria?). *S. Hieronymi Stridonensis presb. tractatus contra Origenem de visione Esaiae*. Edited by A. M. Amelli. Monte Cassino: Tipografia di Montecassino, 1901.

Origen. *In Isaiam libri XXX* (fragments). MPG 13:217–220.

____. *In Isaiam homiliae*. MPG 13:219–254.

____. *In Isaiam homiliae*. Edited by W. A. Baehrens. GCS 33:242–289 (1925).

Procopius of Gaza. *Catena in Isaiam*. MPG 87:1817–2718.

Theodoret. *Commentaire sur Isaïe*. Edited and translated by J.-N. Guinot. SC 276, 295, 315 (1980, 1982, 1984).

Jeremiah

Jerome. *In Hieremiam*. Edited by S. Reiter. CCSL 74 (1960).

Theodoret of Cyrus. *Interpretatio in Ieremiam*. MPG 81:496–805.

Pseudo-Chrysostom. *Fragmenta in Ieremiam*. MPG: 64:740–1037.

Origen. *Homilae in Ieremiam*. Translated by P. Nautin and P. Husson. SC 232, 238 (1976, 1977).

____. *Homilies on Jeremiah and 1 Kings 28*. Translated by J. C. Smith. FC 97 (1998).

Lamentations

Olympiodorus. *Fragmenta in Jeremiae Lamentationes*. MPG 93:725–761.

Origen. *Fragmenta in Lamentationes in catenis*. Edited by E. Klostermann. GCS 6:235–279 (1901).

Baruch

Olympiodorus. *Commentarii in Baruch*. MPG 93:761–773.

Ezekiel

Gregory the Great. *Homélies sur Ezéchiel*. Vol. 1. Edited and translated by P. Morel. SC 327 (1986).

____. *Homiliae in Hiezechielem*. Edited by M. Adriaen. CCSL 142 (1971).

Jerome. *Commentarii in Ezechielem*. Edited by M. Adriaen and F. Glorie. CCSL 75 (1964).

Origen. *Homélies sur Ezéchiel*. Edited and translated by M. Borret. SC 352 (1989).

____. *Homiliae in Ezechielem*. Edited by W. A. Baehrens. GCS 33:319–354 (1925).

____. *Omelie su Ezechiele*. Edited by N. Antoniono. Collana di testi patristici 67. Rome: Citta Nuova, 1987.

Theodoret. *Interpretatio in Ezechielem*. MPG 81:807–1256.

Daniel

Ephrem. *Commentarii in Danielum*. In *Sanctus Ephraem Opera omnia quae exstant graece, syriace, latine* 2, ed. J. S. Assemanus, P. Benedictus, and S. E. Assemanus. Rome: Vatican, 1740.

Hippolytus. *Commentaire sur Daniel*. Introduced by G. Bardy. Translated by M. Lefevre. SC 14 (1947).

____. *Commentarius in Danielum*. Edited by G. N. Bonwetsch. GCS 1.1 (1897).

____. *Fragments from the Commentary on Daniel*. Translated by S.D.F. Salmond. ANF 5:177–194.

Jerome. *Commentariorum in Danielem, Libri* 3 (4). Edited by F. Glorie. CCSL 75A (1964).

____. *Jerome's Commentary on Daniel*. Translated by G. L. Archer. Grand Rapids: Baker Book House, 1958.

Polychronius. *Commentarius in Danielem*. In *Scriptorum Veterum Nova Collectio* 1, ed. A. Mai, 1–27. Rome: Vatican, 1825, 1831.

Theodoret. *Interpretatio in Danielem*. MPG 81:1255–1546 (1864).

MINOR PROPHETS

The twelve minor prophets (Hosea, Joel, Amos, Obadiah, Jonah, Micah, Nahum, Habakkuk, Zephaniah, Haggai, Zechariah, and Malachi) appeared early as a literary unit in Sir 49:10: "May the bones of the Twelve Prophets send forth new life." In canonical lists this custom of referring to these prophets as the "twelve" was common, yet the Fathers frequently cited them individually. Augustine gave us the appellation "minor prophets," this distinction being drawn because of their shorter length (*City of God* 18.29). Eusebius records (*Hist. Eccl.* 6.36.3) that there were at least twenty-five books of Origen dedicated to the twelve prophets, of which only fragments of Hosea now remain. Extensive expositions of these books were undertaken by Cyril of Alexandria, Theodore of Mopsuestia, Theodoret of Cyrrhus, and Jerome. Jerome's work, occupying the later years of his life, is of considerable erudition.

Hosea

For the patristic writers the issue of how to interpret Hosea's marriage was particularly troublesome. Julian of Eclanum, who, in addition to Cyril, Theodore of Mopsuestia, Theodoret, and Jerome, also wrote a commentary on Hosea, points out that the differences of interpretation on this matter were largely regional (*Commentary on Hosea* 1.2-5). The Alexandrians interpreted the command from God allegorically. This school claimed that a real marriage would have exposed Hosea to ridicule, and God nowhere else in the Bible demands a violation of formerly-revealed divine laws.

The Antiochians, in contrast, said an actual marriage did take place. Theodore (*Commentary on Hosea* 1.3) and Theodoret (*Interpretation of Hosea* 1.2) argued that literal names and places are attached to the marriage, and the woman is said to bear literal offspring. The point of the passage is not legalistic adherence to divine precepts but Hosea's unquestioning obedience to God's will for him (Theodoret, *Interp. Hos.* 1.4; cf. Julian, *In Hos.* 1.2-5). The prophet chose an absolute moral good. Even Cyril of Alexandria attempted to refute an unnamed interpreter who claimed the marriage must have been purely symbolic since Hosea would not have literally obeyed such a command from God. Like others, Cyril took note of the text's historical indicators such as actual names for actual offspring (*Commentary on Hosea* 1.15). Other directives from God, he points out, seem more repugnant than that a prophet should marry a prostitute (1.19-20). In fact, Christ himself associated with sinners, which is mystically pictured in Hosea's action (1.21-22). He rescued Gomer from her shameful position and gave her legitimate standing in society (1.22). While not depending on other commentators directly, Cyril's interpretation was consistent with Antiochians such as Theodore of Mopsuestia and Theodoret in the attempt to prove the historicity of Hosea's marriage.

Jerome notes that Apollinaris of Laodicea, Origen, and Pierius had written on Hosea (preface to *Commentary on Hosea*). His own work was intended to complete the brief commentary of Origen at the request of Didymus of Alexandria. However, Jerome is much more ambiguous when it comes to the appropriate hermeneutical method to be used. In the preface he states a predilection for an allegorical interpretation of Hosea's marriage because "God commands nothing but what is honorable, nor does he, by bidding men do disgraceful things, make that conduct honorable that is disgraceful" (preface to *In Hos.*), but his interpretation of Hos 1:2 seems to indicate that a literal marriage took place. Such variety in approach shows the flexibility with which the patristic interpreters came to the Scriptures, cautioning against a too-rigid distinction between the "Antiochian" and "Alexandrian" schools.

Joel

Origen brought his characteristic allegorical hermeneutical tendencies to his address to the book of Joel. For example, in his commentary on the book he finds multiple layers of meaning in 1:11-12, which predicts the withering of Judah's farms, vineyards, and orchards. Beyond the literal aspect the passage refers spiritually to the devastation of the Jews at the hands of the Romans for rejecting the Messiah, and tropologically to the soul, which is like a garden that blooms when virtue is pursued but shrivels from vice.

For Cyprian, Joel 2:12-16 was an important passage. He used it to demonstrate God's mercy toward those who had denied the faith but who then penitently sought reinstatement into the Church (e.g., *The Lapsed*, 36).

Because it is quoted in Acts 2, Joel 2:28-32 is one of the few passages from the Minor Prophets that the Fathers unanimously agreed must be read in light of the NT. In *Against Heresies* Irenaeus sees the unity of prophetic expectation and apostolic fulfillment in Peter's use of the prophet (3.12.1). Tertullian gives the passage a Montanistic flavor in *On the Resurrection of the Flesh* (63), a tendency also seen in the *Passion of Perpetua and Felicitas* (preface), which may bear his influence. Ambrose quotes 2:28 four times in *On the Holy Spirit* to prove that the outpouring of God's Spirit was predicted by the Hebrew prophets (1.18, 85, 92; 2.22; cf. *The Sacrament of the Incarnation of Our Lord* 6.59). Even Theodore of Mopsuestia understood Joel 2:28-32 in a christological sense by relating it to the day of Pentecost (*Commentary on Joel* 2:28-32).

Amos

Amos 4:13, "For lo, the one who forms the mountains, creates the wind, reveals his thoughts to mortals, makes the morning darkness, and treads on the heights of the earth—the LORD, the God of hosts, is his name!" was important for the church Fathers. It functioned pivotally in the trinitarian debate. The LXX contains the phrase "and declares his Anointed [= Christ] to humanity," which the orthodox patristic commentators used to teach the distinctiveness of the Son from the Father (Tertullian, *Against Praxeas* 28). Gregory of Nazianzus, however, highlighted the cooperation between Father and Son in the continuous upholding of the created order (*Oration* 30.11). Athanasius examined the verse in detail and found in it decisive proof against the Pneumatomachians who denied the divinity of the Spirit (*Letters to Serapion* 1.3; *On the Holy Spirit* 2.6). There is no cause for taking the created "wind" (*pneuma*) as a reference to the Holy Spirit, he argued, because Scripture uses the definite article when it wishes to indicate the Third Person of the Trinity. Ambrose also refuted the heretics' use of Amos 4:13 (*On the Holy Spirit* 2.6.48). The passage does not refer to the Holy Spirit but to the "thunder" of the incarnation, the Sons of Thunder (Jesus' brothers), and the voice of God at the Lord's baptism (2.6.54-57).

Amos was also important in christological and ecclesiological discussions. The coming darkness and mourning of Amos 8:9-10 were thought to foreshadow the dimming of the sun at the crucifixion of Christ. Irenaeus (*Adv. Haer.* 4.33.12), Tertullian (*An Answer to the Jews* 10.17, 19; 13:14; *Against Marcion* 4.42.5), Lactantius (*Divine Institutes* 4.19.3) and Cyprian (*Testimonies Against the Jews* 2.23) take this view. Basil, however, applies the verse to the persecution and confusion of the Eastern churches (*Letter to the Bishops of Italy and Gaul* 243).

Amos 9:11, which speaks of the fallen "booth of David," was interpreted as the body of Christ by Hilary of Poitiers (see commentary on Amos in this volume). Jerome, however, understood it as the demise of the Jewish synagogue, which has been superseded by the Church, to which all nations will be converted. Irenaeus had a similar view, arguing against the Marcionites that the God of the OT promised in the words of Amos to come to the Gentiles and raise up a new tabernacle of David (*Adv. Haer.* 3.12.14), but elsewhere he takes it as the resurrection body of Christ (*Proof of the Apostolic Preaching* 38, 62).

Obadiah

References to the Book of Obadiah are extremely scarce in the Church Fathers. As noted in the commentary on Obadiah in this volume, Theodore of Mopsuestia, Cyril of Alexandria, and Theodoret understood the book in light of the sibling rivalry between Esau and Jacob. "Edom," as the family and descendants of Esau, became a symbol of all who oppose Israel. From this the idea developed that "Edom" was the personification of the devil.

For the Latin Fathers Edom became a type representing worldly wickedness, the enemy of the Church and the soul. Augustine modifies the largely antagonistic interpretation of Edom by saying that as Esau was a "part" for the whole of Edom, so Edom was a part for the whole, the Gentile nations. Augustine interpreted Obadiah 21 as referring to Christians, and specifically the apostles, as those who "came up from Mount Zion" (Judea) to "defend" the mountain, that is, to preach to the Gentiles the gospel of salvation from the kingdom of darkness (*City of God* 18.31).

Jerome formally commented on Obadiah on at least two different occasions. While he was very young he composed a commentary on Obadiah that he would later disown. When he again took up the project (ca. 396 while in the midst of the Origenist controversy) he would regret his earlier attempt because of its excessive allegorization.

Jonah

Of the twelve minor prophets Jonah was the most frequently cited and artistically represented in the early Church. On this abundance of references Jerome wrote with perspicacity: "I know that older interpreters, both Greek and Latin, have said many things about this book, and have not so much uncovered many questions as they have obscured meanings" (*On Jonah;* CCSL 76:377).

In patristic thought the death and resurrection motif was frequently articulated both through the avenue of typological exegesis (Jonah being the "type" and Jesus the "antitype") and within the context of apologetic or theological writings defending or explaining the resurrection of Christ (e.g., Justin's *Dialogue with Trypho* 107 and Gregory of Nazianzus' *Oration* 2.106,109). Jerome captured this theme, as well as the universality of God's salvific plan, when he wrote of Jonah's "shipwreck prefiguring the passion of the Lord [that] calls the world to penitence; and in the name of Nineveh he announces salvation to the Gentiles" (*Ep.* 53).

Developing the theme of God's increasing scope of salvation, Jerome wrote elsewhere that Cyprian of Carthage was converted to Christianity by meditating on the book of Jonah. Particularly prominent interpretations of God's larger plan of salvation include Cyril of Alexandria's *On Jonah,* which propounded that the very reason for Jonah's mission was God's universal design. Theodoret *(On Jonah)* was more assertive in arguing that Jewish and Gentile salvations were correlatives under God's one rubric of salvation. Augustine, in commenting on Jonah's refusal to go to Nineveh, interpreted such reticence as a sign of Israel's jealousy toward Gentile salvation (*Ep.* 102.30-38).

The resurrection and salvation motifs also found expression in art. The story of Jonah was the most frequently depicted of OT scenes. He was most commonly displayed as being thrown into the sea and swallowed by the monster (which would allude to Christ's passion and resurrection), spewed out on dry land, and finally resting under a gourd. This later episode received various depictions. Sometimes Jonah was at ease, suggesting the Christian transformation of the pagan myth of Endymion who was transported to Elysium, paralleling Jonah's deliverance into Paradise. Other times Jonah appeared sad under the vine, underscoring his reluctance to spread God's message of salvation to the Gentiles.

In modern times Jonah has found extensive liturgical expression, being read both within Jewish (on the Day of Atonement) and Christian traditions. Since Vatican II, Jonah 3 is read in the first week of Lent, and chs. 1–3 are read during the twenty-seventh week in alternate years. Anglicans and Episcopalians cite Jonah 3–4 on the Sunday closest to September 21 and Lutherans refer to Jon 2:2-9 on Easter evening and Jon 3:1-5, 10 on the third Sunday after the Epiphany.

Habakkuk

For the Fathers, Habakkuk was usually interpreted in light of the NT. The phrase "but the righteous will live by faith" (2:4) was particularly important because of its use in Rom 1:17. Irenaeus, in light of Rom 1:17, understood the advent of Christ to be the fulfillment of the prophet's words (*Adv. Haer.* 4.34.2). The prophets and apostles, then, are from the very same God. For Tertullian, Habakkuk anticipated the kind of faith exercised by the woman who anointed Jesus' feet (*Against Marcion* 4.18; cf. Luke 7:36-50), or all who are justified by Christ (5.3). "Faith" in God was understood to open new avenues of understanding. Clement of Alexandria quoted Hab 2:4 to prove belief must precede the soul's "transcendental contemplation" of divine themes (*Stromata* 2.2). Likewise, Cyprian uses the verse to show that faith in Christ is necessary to understand the Scriptures (*Testimonies Against the Jews* 1.5) and to see great miracles achieved in one's life (3.42).

Zephaniah

The Book of Zephaniah was often interpreted eschatologically, especially in associating the terrors of the last judgment with the prophet's "Day of the Lord" motif. Cyprian links the inevitability of God's future wrath (Zeph 3:8) to

Jesus' command not to take vengeance since such belongs to God alone (*Three Books of Testimonies Against the Jews* 3.106; cf. *On the Advantage of Patience* 21). Origen, arguing against the view of Celsus that the peoples of the world could never be brought under the single reign of God, interprets Zeph 3:7-13 as a prophecy certain to be fulfilled (*Against Celsus* 8.72). Evil will be destroyed by God and human harmony will one day prevail. This eschatological reality will occur at the "consummation of all things." Zephaniah also contained christological references for the Church Fathers. For example, Cyprian understood 1:7, "the LORD has prepared a sacrifice," to be speaking of the crucified Jesus (*Against the Jews* 2.20).

Haggai

On the whole the little book of the prophet Haggai is seldom mentioned by the Church Fathers. It would, however, inform them on various issues. It addressed, for example, their views of theology, history, and morals.

Cyprian refuted his pagan opponent's premise that wars and famines continue because the ancient gods have been abandoned by Christians. He used Haggai's statement in 1:9 to prove the reverse: God's anger actually burns against those who continue to worship idols (*An Address to Demetrianus* 6; cf. *Three Books of Testimonies Against the Jews* 3.20). In book 10 of the *Ecclesiastical History*, where Eusebius was reflecting on the glories of the churches rebuilt after persecutions ceased, Paulinus of Tyre is likened to Zerubbabel. In this bishop's basilica Haggai's prophecy in 2:9 that the glory of the Jewish Temple will be restored "is no longer a word but a fact, for the last glory of this house has become and now truly is greater than the former" (*Eccl. Hist.* 10.4.45-46). Other historical readings would be much broader. The "shakings" of Hag 2:6-7 referred to the great epochs of salvation history for the Church Fathers. They reveal a movement from the former time of darkness to the new age of the gospel. Origen interpreted the "earth" as the era of lesser understanding under Moses and Plato and the "dry land" as the Christian land in which he now lives (*Against Celsus* 7:30; cf. 2.30). For Gregory of Nazianzus there were two "remarkable transformations of the human way of life in the course of the world's history," from idolatry to Law and from Law to Gospel, plus one "shaking" yet to come in the end times when this earth is transformed (*Theological Oration* 5.25 [*Oration* 31.25]).

The Book of Haggai was also used to provide moral instruction. For example, Clement of Alexandria interpreted 1:6 as a command for fiscal responsibility. The one who greedily hoards money or spends it wantonly will lose an eternal reward, putting the money into a "purse with holes" (*Christ the Educator* 2.3; *Stromata* 3.56.2).

Zechariah

The book of Zechariah was one of the Minor Prophets most widely quoted by the Church Fathers. This is because many of Zechariah's prophecies would come to be interpreted in the Christian tradition as references to Jesus' life and work. However, those who tended toward Antiochian exegesis, especially Theodore of Mopsuestia, were reluctant to give anything but a historical interpretation to passages that had important christological meaning for other patristic writers and the NT authors.

Zechariah 9:9, which describes the victorious king of Jerusalem riding "a colt, the foal of a donkey," was applied to the triumphal entry of Christ in Matt 21:4-5. Justin Martyr sees this as fulfillment of prophecy that proves Jesus is the Christ (*Dial.* 53). Clement of Alexandria, however, understands the colt as "high-spirited" Christians who are "unsubdued by wickedness" and are in need of Christ as a "trainer," (*Christ the Educator* 1.5.15). Theodore of Mopsuestia strictly limits the meaning of the verse to the return of Zerubbabel from exile (*Commentary on Zechariah* 9.9). The gospel application to Christ can be made only because Jesus displayed the same characteristics Zechariah described in Zerubbabel.

The prophet spoke of looking with regret on the "one whom they have pierced" in 12:10, and here the Church Fathers found another reference to Christ. Cyprian applied the verse to the historical event of Jesus' crucifixion, which was viewed by actual witnesses just as Zechariah predicted (*Testimonies Against the Jews* 2.20). Ignatius used the verse to refute the Docetic teaching that Jesus did not really assume human flesh (*Trall.* 10) and did not have a physical resurrection body (*Smyrn.* 3). At times the verse was given an eschatological interpretation. Irenaeus applied it to Christ's second coming in judgment, when sinners will be punished for their unbelief and rejection of the Son of man (*Adv. Haer.* 4.33.11). Tertullian does the same in attempting to show the error of the Jews and of Marcion in not understanding the two advents of Christ, one lowly, the other sublime (*An Answer to the Jews* 14; *Against Marcion* 3.7). Ambrose, however, focuses on the "pouring out of the spirit" in the verse, understanding it as a reference to the grace of the Holy Spirit (*The Holy Spirit* 1.12.127).

Tertullian gives Zech 13:7-9 a martyrological interpretation in which the striking of the shepherd and subsequent scattering of the sheep in v. 7 referred to clergy who abandon their congregations, and the purging fire of v. 9 is the "flame of persecution" that proves the steadfastness of the confessor's faith (*On Flight in Persecution* 11.3). Normally, however, the passage was understood to address the scattering of the disciples when Jesus was arrested for trial and put to death. Justin, for example, follows this interpretation (*Dial.* 53). Origen believed the "striking" of Christ the Shepherd was prefigured in the rock struck by Moses that brought forth flowing waters. In the same way water issued from Christ's side, which represents the Word of God (*Homily on Exodus* 11.2). Zechariah 14 was usually understood as a reference to Christ's second coming.

Malachi

As noted in the commentary text below, Mal 1:11, "in every place incense is offered to my name, and a pure offering," was understood by the Church Fathers to have eucharistic significance. For Justin, Irenaeus, and Cyril of Jerusalem the "unacceptable sacrifices" of v. 14 referred to Jewish worship, now replaced by the Christian meal. Tertullian also understood the text to speak of the Church's replacement of Israel, but in addition to the sacramental theme he interprets the sacrifices as spiritual offerings of praise and obedience, hymns of worship, and holy prayer (*An Answer to the Jews* 5; *Against Marcion* 3.22; 4.1).

The "messenger of the Lord" in 3:1 was understood to be either John the Baptist or Christ himself. Jerome interpreted the messenger as the Baptist and the "one coming to his temple" as Jesus. Irenaeus (*Adv. Haer.* 3.11.4) and Tertullian likewise understood John to be the messenger who is "angelic" in his Spirit-empowered ministry of witness (*Answer to the Jews* 9; cf. *Against Marcion* 4.18). Clement of Rome, however, interprets 3:1-2 as a promise of Christ's return (*1 Clem.* 23). In a similar fashion Cyril of Jerusalem takes the text eschatologically, not as a reference to the Second Coming alone but to both advents of Christ (*Catechetical Lectures* 15.2).

Malachi 3:6, "For I the LORD do not change," was used by the Fathers to teach the immutability of God. Origen refuted the Stoics who held that God is a body capable of change (*Against Celsus* 1.21). Even in condescending to become human God did not change as Celsus believed (4.14; cf. 6.62). Alexander of Alexandria, refuting the Arians, used the text to show there cannot be a time when the Father was without the Son (*Epistles on the Arian Heresy* 2.3). Hilary of Poitiers argued for the coequality of the Father and Son existing in constant immutability (*On the Trinity* 4.8; 7.27; 11.47).

The "sun of righteousness" in 3:20 (4:2) was understood christologically. As the true Sun, Jesus should be worshiped throughout the day, according to Cyprian (*On the Lord's Prayer* 35). For Origen, like the dawn, the Lord opened up a new day with the light of knowledge (*Homily on Exodus* 7.8; cf. *Homily on Leviticus* 9.10.2), as opposed to the mere "lamp" of the Law (*Hom. in Lev.* 13.2.1).

BIBLIOGRAPHY FOR THE MINOR PROPHETS

Primary Sources

Cyril of Alexandria. *Commentarius in xii prophetas minores*. Edited by P. E. Pusey. Oxford: Clarendon, 1868.

John Chrysostom. *Homélies sur Ozias = In illud, vidi Dominum*. Edited and translated by Jean Dumortier. SC 277 (1981).

Hesychius of Jerusalem. *In xii prophetas minores*. MPG 93:1339–1370.

Jerome. *Commentarii in prophetas minores*. Edited by M. Adriaen. CCSL 76, 76A (1969, 1970).

Julian of Eclanum. *Tractatus Prophetarum Osee, Iohel et Amos*. Edited by L. De Coninck. CCSL 88 (1977).

Origen. *In Ioel Liber* (fragments). In R. A. Reitzenstein, "Origenes und Hieronymus," *ZNW* 20 (1921) 90–94.

____. *In Osee commentarius* (fragments). In J. A. Robinson, *The Philocalia of Origen*. Cambridge: Cambridge University Press, 1893, 52–54.

Theodore of Mopsuestia. *Theodori Mopsuesteni Commentarius in XII prophetas*. Edited by H. N. Sprenger. Wiesbaden: Harrassowitz, 1977.

Theodoret. *Interpretatio in xii prophetas minores*. MPG 81:1545–1988.

GOSPELS AND ACTS

Matthew

In light of Irenaeus's reference to the four-gospel canon and his specific mention and exegesis of Matthew the early Church's use of the first gospel is certain. But evidence collected by Edouard Massaux (*The Influence of the Gospel of Saint Matthew on Christian Literature Before Saint Irenaeus*. 3 vols. New Gospel Studies 5.1-3, translated by N. J. Belval and S. Hecht [Macon, Ga.: Mercer University Press, 1990–1993]) and W.-D. Köhler (*Die Rezeption des Matthäusevangeliums in der Zeit vor Irenäus*. WUNT ser. 2, 24 [Tübingen: J.C.B. Mohr (Paul Siebeck), 1987]) argues strongly for the Church's use of Matthew in a variety of works by the end of the first or the beginning of the second century.

Although Jerome remarks that he knew of a commentary on the gospel (probably on the four gospels) by Theophilus of Antioch, he seems to question whether it is actually from Theophilus's hand (cf. *Lives of Illustrious Men* 25; *Ep.* 121.6; *Commentary on Matthew*, preface). The commentary under Theophilus's name first published in 1575, and discovered and set forth again by Zahn in 1883, is actually a fifth-century spurious assemblage of the comments of others. Jerome also reports that he knew the Greek commentaries on Matthew by Hippolytus of Rome, Origen, the Arian Theodore of Heraclea, Apollinaris of Laodicea, Didymus of Alexandria, and the Latin commentaries by Victorinus of Pettau, Hilary, and Fortunatian of Aquileia (*In Matt.* preface). Didymus's and Victorinus's commentaries are lost and only fragments of the others survive except for portions of Origen's twenty-five-book work and the short commentary of Hilary. Allegorical in focus, Hilary's *Commentary on Matthew* presents a Matthean interest in Jewish hostility toward Christ and his Church and the inclusion of the Gentiles. The extant portions of Origen's commentary consist of a treatment in Greek of Matt 13:36–22:33 and an anonymous Latin translation treating Matt 16:13–27:63. Eight homilies on Matthew falsely attributed to Origen also survive. His commentary, as Karen J. Torjesen has pointed out (*Hermeneutical Procedure and Theological Method in Origen's Exegesis*. Patristische Texte and Studien 28 [Berlin: de Gruyter, 1986] 105–107) is composed in such a way as to lead the reader from knowledge of Christ the Logos as human to the perfect understanding of him as divine. He does not ignore the literal sense of Matthew's account, but derives a spiritual teaching from it. For example, he acknowledges the historical significance of Jesus' transfiguration six days after the dialogue with the disciples on his identity and passion (Matt 16:21-28; 17:1-2), but the event teaches that the spiritual who wish a higher vision of the Logos must pass beyond the six days, which are the lusts and passions of the world since it was made in six days (*In Matt.* 12.36).

Other Greek works on Matthew's gospel include the *Scholia* of Athanasius of Alexandria, the ninety homilies of John Chrysostom, fragments of Cyril of Alexandria's commentary, and some homiletic fragments under the name of Ammonius of Alexandria. (These last are believed to be spurious.) Though a collection of homilies, Chrysostom's work offers the oldest surviving complete commentary on Matthew. Filled with moral teachings concerning the chaste, separate life of the Christian, Chrysostom's homilies also emphasize theological themes. Against the Manichaeans God's unity is developed, while in opposition to the Arians the Son's equality to the Father is treated in light of the weakness of his humanity.

Latin works on Matthew not mentioned in Jerome's list include the following: forty homilies and sixty tractates by Chromatius of Aquileia, an anonymous partial commentary on Matthew 24 attributed by some to Victorinus of Pettau or Ambrosiaster, an incomplete Latin commentary falsely ascribed to Chrysostom but actually written by an Arian of the fifth century, Jerome's own commentary which relies on Origen, and Augustine's two-book treatment of the Sermon on the Mount, his explanation of forty-seven problematic Matthean passages (and fifty-one Lukan), his argument for the concordance of the four gospels, and his explanation of seventeen passages in Matthew. Augustine also preached several sermons on Matthew.

The early Church commonly viewed Matthew as the earliest gospel, composed in Hebrew for Jews by the tax collector turned apostle and later translated into Greek. The tradition is first seen in Papias, and though later writers are indebted to a degree to his testimony, independent knowledge by some of the Fathers cannot be dismissed, and the combined testimony seems to extend beyond him (Papias in Eusebius, *Eccl. Hist.* 3.39.16; Irenaeus, *Adv. Haer.* 3.1.1; Origen in Eusebius, *Eccl. Hist.* 6.25.4; Eusebius, *Eccl. Hist.* 3.24.6; Cyril of Jerusalem, *Catechetical Lectures* 14.15; Jerome, *Commentary on Matthew* Preface, *Lives of Illustrious Men* 3).

For Irenaeus the original orientation of Matthew's gospel is seen immediately in the genealogy. He wrote to prove to the Jews that Christ was descended from David (frag. 27) and to develop the humble, gentle humanity of the incarnate Word (*Adv. Haer.* 3.11.8). To the catechumen, Cyril of Jerusalem was quick to explain that the notion of genealogy or generation in Matt 1:1 applied to his flesh. Christ was David's son "at the end of the age" (Heb 9:26), but God's Son before any age, for he is eternally begotten of the Father (*Catechetical Lectures* 11.5). Origen's reading of Matthew's first verse in his *Commentary on John* (1.22) points the reader to John's gospel. He, along with Irenaeus, notes its orientation toward the Jewish expectation of the Davidic Messiah, but from that point he asserts that only John's gospel emphasized Jesus' divinity. Matthew, Mark, and Luke, in his reading, await John's highlighting of the Word as God. However, although Irenaeus will see Jesus' humanity stressed in the genealogy and in other places throughout the gospel he has no difficulty finding strong testimony to Jesus' divinity. For instance, in *Against Heresies* 3.9.2 it is plain to him in the title Emmanuel, "God with us" (Matt 1:23) and the Magi's gift of frankincense (Matt 2:11).

The Sermon on the Mount (Matthew 5–7) would enter fully into the Church's theological and moral reflection. In Irenaeus's polemic against the Gnostics, Matt 5:17, "I have not come to abolish [the law and the prophets] but to fulfill them," would function pivotally. It informs his thesis of the unity between the acts and teaching of the Lord of the New Covenant and the revelation given under the old economy (*Adv. Haer.* 4.34.2). But the Lord's saying also, for the Bishop of Lyons, sets forth the Lord's extension of the prohibitions of the Old Covenant's Law. Jesus fulfills the Law by making explicit the Law's teaching concerning internal desires and thoughts. The Law does not prohibit merely external actions, but applies also to the interior part of the human being. Thus the teachings of Jesus regarding such things as anger and lust (murder and adultery, Matt 5:21-32) are his fulfillment, extension, expansion of the Law (*Adv. Haer.* 4.13.1, 3). Clement of Alexandria concurs. Fulfillment of the commands of the Law involves, for the Christian of true knowledge, separation from the desire for and mental anticipation of what is prohibited (*Miscellanies* 4.18.113). Within Irenaeus's polemic, which included a response to Marcion, his interpretation would provide the Christian community a positive understanding of the Lord's word. Such a reading would be needed, for Marcion, Tertullian reports, erased Matt 5:17 from the Lord's sayings and argued that Christ had come as the opponent of the Law and the prophets (*Against Marcion* 4.7, 9, 12, 36; 5.14). Tertullian himself shows how in his deeds and words Christ was true to the saying of Matt 5:17. Against the dualism of both Gnostic and Marcionite, Matt 5:17 demonstrates to the second-century Church a theological and covenantal continuity in salvation history. Later catechetical instruction would stress the same continuity between the Old and New Testaments on the basis of this Matthean text (Cyril of Jerusalem, *Catechetical Lectures* 4.33).

Another word of the Lord from Matthew's account of the sermon that would significantly inform early Christian thought was the beatitude of the pure, Matt 5:8: "Blessed are the pure in heart, for they will see God." Along with other biblical texts (e.g., Job 19:25-27; 1 John 3:1-2; 1 Cor 13:12) this beatitude would contribute to the Church's development of the hope of the vision of God. For Irenaeus the saying reflects the vision of God attained by humans in different degrees in different economies of revelatory history. Some in the past, under the Old Covenant, saw God figuratively, prophetically; some in the incarnation under the New Covenant see God adoptively; those in the times of the kingdom to come will see God immediately, paternally (*Adv.*

Haer. 4.9.2; 4.20.5). In his reading of the text, however, Origen emphasizes a mystical, spiritual vision, knowledge of God not through bodily eyes, but through the pure, undefiled mind and heart (*Against Celsus* 6.4, 69; 7.33, 45). Since God is by nature invisible, to see God is to know God and therefore the Lord's word applies to the intellectual faculty, not the faculties of sense (*First Principles* 1.1.8-9). There is for Origen a postmortem progressive ascent of mind and intelligence toward the perfect vision, knowledge of God by those of undefiled, spiritually-schooled, rational minds and intellects. These minds progress toward a perfect understanding of reasons and causes of God's ways (*Princ.* 2.11.6-7). Basil the Great, too, reads the text in reference to the inner person's contemplation, but for the Cappodocian there is a different focus. As the bodily parts that apprehend sensations need to be treated when they are injured, so the embodied, imprisoned mind needs to give heed to a proper faith. Contemplation of such a faith includes contemplation of the pure doctrine of the Trinity (*Ep.* 8.12). Through such trinitarian contemplation God is seen.

Matthean material outside the Sermon on the Mount would also inform the early Church's thinking. Matthew 11:27 and its Lukan parallel (10:22) would provide language critical to the development of orthodox theology and christology. The second phrase of this saying of the Lord, ". . . no one knows the Son except the Father, and no one knows the Father except the Son and anyone to whom the Son chooses to reveal him," aids Irenaeus in his polemic against the Gnostics. They teach two gods, the unknown, eternal Father and the wicked creator of the OT. They know the Lord's word recorded in Matt 11:27 (Luke 10:22), but they read " no one *knew* the Father except the Son" in order to emphasize the utter hiddenness of the Father until he was revealed by the Son's advent (*Adv. Haer.* 4.6.1). Before Christ the Gnostic's Father was unknown, and therefore he was not the known God of the OT. Irenaeus, however, does not read the saying as a temporal indicator of a specific moment of revelation. The saying emphasizes the Son as the true, perfect agent of the revelation of the Father, an agency he has been performing throughout redemptive history, even prior to his incarnation (*Adv. Haer.* 4.6.2-7). For Irenaeus, then, the Lord's word teaches against the Gnostics the one Father revealed in all times by the Word, the Son, and challenges the Jews to receive the Son along with the Father. Such emphasis on the unity of the God revealed exclusively by the Son is echoed by Clement of Alexandria (*Misc.* 8.10.58), while Origen claims the Word's appropriateness as the Father's revealer (*In Ioann.* 1.277-278), and Cyril of Jerusalem repeats the corollary between reception of the Father and reception of the Son (*Catechetical Lectures* 10.1).

Most fourth-century exegesis of Matt 11:27 // Luke 10:22, however, would concentrate on the saying's trinitarian implications. Cyril of Jerusalem in catechesis would emphasize the perfect, reciprocal knowledge between Father and Son as indicative of the Son's equal dignity with the Father in the Godhead (*Catechetical Lectures* 4.7; 6.6). Gregory of Nyssa, in polemic, set the Son's exclusive role as the Father's agent of revelation against Eunomius's subordinationism and saw in the Son's word of Matt 11:27 an affirmation of the Son's equality in essence and glory with the Father (*Against Eunomius* 1.32; 2.4). Athanasius of Alexandria wrote a tract countering the Arian interpretation of the Lord's word (*All Things Were Handed Over To Me* [Matt 11:27]). Whereas the Gnostics through their reading of the saying had focused Irenaeus's attention on the second part of the verse, the Arians began with the first line: "All things have been handed over to me by my Father . . . ." To the Arian this indicated a moment prior to the incarnation when the Son had been made Lord of creation. If this was so, they argue, he is not eternally of the Father for he would then have been Lord eternally. Therefore there must have been once when he was not, that is, the Son must be created (*All Things* 1; *Against the Arians* 3.26). Athanasius, however, argues that the saying applies to the Son's incarnation. The Son, being eternal with the Father, did not gain a lordship previously unearned. Rather, the "all things" refer to fallen humanity which the Father delivered over to the Son to be redeemed, healed through his saving incarnation (*All Things* 2-3). It is a deliverance to save, not rule, for the rule was already his. However, in another place Athanasius would explain the text differently. Again he insists that it does not refer to a prerogative being given to the Son, as if the Son did not have all glory eternally, but neither does he apply it to incarnation. Now he interprets it as a saying that discloses the distinction between the persons of Son and Father. Guarding against Sabellianism (Modalism) the Bishop of Alexandria emphasizes that the Lord's language simply explains the Son's relationship to the Father. It is a relationship in which he is eternal with the Father but in which he receives his inheritance of all things, as a Son, from the Father (*Against the Arians* 3.35-36). Such an understanding of the first line of the saying of Matt 11:27 applying to the Son's inheritance as the Father's only-begotten, obedient Son is seen also in Cyril of Jerusalem (*Catechetical Lectures* 7.5; 10.9). Although the Arian usage of the first line of Matt 11:27 would draw Athanasius's attention to that phrase of the saying, he also employed the second part in polemic against the Arians. The Son's statement that he knows the Father—the invisible, unoriginate One—sets the Son apart from creatures who are unable to see God's face and live (Exod 33:20), and associates him with the essence of the Father as they both share the omniscience peculiar to God (*Against the Arians* 2.22.44). Finally, the second phrase of Matt 11:27 informs Athanasius's view on the *Son's* eternal generation. For him, the Word did not become the Son at the incarnation. This would indicate, because of the saying's particular usage of the term "son," that until the incarnation the Word did not know the Father. But if the Father was being revealed to the people of the OT, and if the saying limits knowledge and revelation of the Father to the *Son*, the Word, then, must also have been Son before the incarnation (*Against the Arians* 4.23). Thus whether the purpose was anti-Gnostic or anti-Arian, the early Christian mind would emphasize the eternal nature of the Son's knowledge which he exercises throughout redemptive history.

Of course, any treatment of Matthew in the early Church must take account of the words of the Lord to Peter in Matt 16:18-19. An early developed presentation occurs in Cyprian's *The Unity of the Catholic Church* (4). In fact there exist two versions of Cyprian's treatise on the passage, commonly viewed as an early version and a later revision by his own hand. In both editions Cyprian's emphasis is on the unity of the Church through the unity of the bishops, which has as its paradigm the Lord's beginning the Church from *one* apostle, Peter. For Cyprian all the apostles are equal. There seems to be no supremacy apportioned to Peter or Rome, but this one apostle does function as the point of unity among different apostles from whom will derive diverse episcopal lines. In other exegesis of the passage the Fathers focus on the Lord's language, "upon this rock I will build my Church and the gates of Hades will not prevail against it," as indicative of several truths. It may indicate the Church's permanency in contrast to the OT economy (Athanasius of Alexandria, *Against the Arians* 4.34). It may indicate Jesus' divinity, for only as God could he on his own authority declare Peter to be the Church's foundation (Ambrose, *Exposition of the Christian Faith* 4.5.57). Or it may emphasize Peter's faith as the foundation of the Church, his confession of Jesus as "the Christ, the son of the living God (Matt 16:16)," by interpreting "upon this rock" as his christological belief (Augustine, *Homily on 1 John* 10.1). And though later Peter's confession, his faith, would not be minimized in the Church's interpretation of the passage (e.g., Leo the Great, *Ep.* 33.1; *Serm.* 62.2) the premier authority of the Roman see, as Peter's see, would be derived from the Lord's words to Peter. Sometimes linked with John 21:17 and Luke 22:31, the words were understood to give to Peter and his Roman successors, through his enduring ministry, an exalted identity, role, and authority (Leo the Great, *Serm.* 3.3; Gregory the Great, *Ep.* 7.37).

Finally we come to the role of Matt 28:19 in the faith and practice of the early Church. Already in Irenaeus's soteriology the Lord's words prior to his ascension, "Go therefore and make disciples of all the nations, baptizing them in the name of the Father, and of the Son, and of the Holy Spirit," have an important place. They teach that the trinitarian order of baptism commanded by the Lord is the power of regeneration apportioned to all nations (*Adv. Haer.* 3.17.1). Cyprian maintains the same soteriological significance of the Lord's words when he objects to reconciliation of the lapsed through certificates provided in the names of confessors and martyrs. Peace and forgiveness is available to the nations not through any name on a certificate, but through baptism in the name of the Trinity (*Ep.* 27.3). In like manner he emphasizes the necessity of baptism in the name of the Trinity against those who would diminish the relevance of the faith of the baptizer. He argues that if the faith of the baptizer is not trinitarian, the faith of the one baptized is in danger, and therefore so is the remission of sins (*Ep.*73.5-6). So, too, thinks Gregory of Nyssa. He claims the words of Matt 28:19 to be the mysterious word of the Christian's new birth, the transformation from being corruptible to incorruptible, mortal to immortal, after the likeness of the Godhead. But Gregory presses the trinitarianism of the words. The titles of Father, Son, and Spirit teach that these are the proper titles for the three persons and not the blasphemous ones proposed by the heretics. These titles, given by the Lord, the Word, are a rule of faith, truth, and piety, which lead the pious into a sufficient faith about God. The Lord says "name," singular, signifying immediately the unity of essence of the three persons. Gregory also asserts that the Lord never identified this one name. This is because the essence of Godhead is incomprehensible and therefore cannot be named (cf. Gregory of Nazianzus, *Oration* 40.45 [*On Holy Baptism*]). The Lord then spoke the three titles in order to set forth not a difference in nature or substance among the three, but their particular properties, so that a true faith in God is seen as a trinitarian faith. The titles divide the three in such a way that even in differentiation the three, Father, Son, and Spirit, are comprehended only in relation to each other. Thus, for example, faith in the Father calls forth faith in the Father's Son who is implied in the title "Father" (*Adv. Eunom.* 2.1-3). Augustine, in his prayer at the end of his *De Trinitate* 15.51, begins with a reference to Matt 28:19, echoing a later high regard for the place of the text in theological development. The Lord would not have spoken about our God as Father, Son, and Spirit unless God were Trinity, and the Lord would not have ordered baptism in the name of any who was not God.

Mark

Because of the greater detail in the other synoptic accounts, the gospel of Mark was given little individual attention in the patristic period. However, the Fathers did make selective use of Mark in their various writings.

The earliest attestation of Mark by a patristic writer is that of Papias, quoted by Eusebius (*Eccl. Hist.* 3.39). Papias associates Mark with the preaching of Peter, whose words Mark recorded with "great accuracy." That this gospel is a secondhand account explains why some events in Mark occur in a different order than an actual eyewitness might have recorded them, though nothing has been omitted or falsely stated. Clement of Alexandria recalls that Mark's gospel was undertaken at the urging of many Christians in Rome, with neither the encouragement nor discouragement of Peter (Eusebius, *Eccl. Hist.* 6.14). Tertullian also makes the connection between Mark and Peter (*Against Marcion* 4.2.5) as does Origen (Eusebius, *Eccl. Hist.* 6.25). Irenaeus places the writing of Mark at the time just after Peter's death (*Adv. Haer.* 3.1.1). He calls it a gospel with a "prophetical character," revealed by the Son of God through the Spirit that hovers over the Church, corresponding to the "creature like a flying eagle" of Rev 4:7 (*Adv. Haer.* 3.11.8). He believes this characterization is appropriate because the gospel begins with the Isaianic prophecy and because it is "compendious and summary," which prophecy tends to be. Origen agreed that Mark had produced some abridged versions of events (*In Ioann.* 6.129-131) and that Mark presented the gospel's "beginning" while John presented its completion through his emphasis on Jesus' divinity (*In Ioann.* 1.22).

Jerome's homilies on Mark (falsely ascribed to John Chrysostom) are the fullest extant treatments of the gospel by a Church Father. Fragments from Theodore of Mopsuestia's comments on Mark's gospel survive, as do sermons based on Markan passages written by such Fathers as John Chrysostom, Augustine, and Peter Chrysologus. Works on Mark erroneously attributed to Jerome and Theophilus have also survived.

Luke and Acts

As with Matthew, the early Church's use of Luke's gospel is certain at the point of Irenaeus's four-gospel canon, but even before the bishop of Lyons composed *Against Heresies* usage of the gospel is possibly evident in some Apostolic Fathers and Justin Martyr. Irenaeus relates that both Marcion and the Gnostic Valentinus knew Luke's gospel and were being inconsistent by taking parts of it and editing out other material (*Adv. Haer.* 3.14.3-4). Already in the second and early third centuries Luke's gospel is perceived as representative of Paul's (Gentile) gospel by both orthodox and heretic (*Adv. Haer.* 3.1.1; Tertullian, *Against Marcion* 4.2.5; Origen, *Homilies on Luke* 1).

The earliest known commentary on Luke was the fifteen-book work of Origen extant only in a few fragments. Fortunately, thirty-nine of his homilies on the gospel still survive. Jerome would translate them in 390. Of the other Greek Fathers, *scholia* on Luke from both Eusebius of Caesarea and Athanasius of Alexandria are extant, as are fragments of comments by Dionysius of Alexandria, Apollinaris of Laodicea, Theodore of Mopsuestia, and Titus of Bostra. Cyril of Alexandria's commentary on Luke's gospel, actually a series of 156 homilies, is complete in a Syriac version, while only three homilies exist complete in Greek and the rest survive in Greek only in fragments. In Latin there survive fragments of an Arian commentary on Luke's gospel, the *Tractate on Luke's Gospel*. Ambrose was the only Latin Father to compose a commentary on the gospel of Luke. The commentary appears to be his revised and edited compilation of selected homilies on the gospel. Though Augustine did not produce a commentary, he did explain fifty-one passages of Luke in his treatment of difficult texts in Matthew and Luke, and preached several times on Luke.

There are fragmentary remains of several Greek patristic commentaries and homilies on the Acts of the Apostles from several authors including Origen, Didymus of Alexandria, Theodore of Mopsuestia, and Cyril of Alexandria. The only substantial extant collection of homilies is a series of fifty-five sermons by John Chrysostom. From Chrysostom's hand eight additional homilies have survived: four on the beginning of the book and four on other passages including Paul's change of name. From the Latin Fathers it is important to mention Augustine's several homilies on Acts and the allegorical interpretive poem of Arator on the Acts of the Apostles.

John

From among the early Fathers, Ignatius of Antioch probably knew and used the Fourth Gospel; the same is practically certain of Justin Martyr. That he did not refer to it explicitly may be due to the fact that some Roman circles (called *"Alogoi"* by Epiphanius) opposed this gospel as heretical. Tatian, a disciple of Justin who later became an encratite, used the gospel of John as a framework for his four-gospel harmony, the *Diatesseron*. Melito of Sardis used it as well. Theophilus of Antioch in his *To Autolycus* (2.22) explicitly quotes it: "Hence the holy scriptures and all those inspired by the Spirit teach us, and one of them, John, says, 'In the beginning was the Logos, and the Logos was with God'" [John 1:1]. It is interesting to note that the catacombs of Rome contain representations of scenes from the gospel of John (in particular the raising of Lazarus) probably from the second century (F.-M. Braun, *Jean le théologien et son évangile dans l'Église ancienne*. Études bibliques [Paris: J. Gabalda, 1959] 149–156).

The Alexandrian Gnostic Valentinus, who moved to Rome (ca. 140), almost certainly used the gospel of John. The Valentinian *Gospel of Truth* (ca. 150?) contains numerous echoes of it. Ptolemy, an early disciple of Valentinus, wrote a commentary on its Prologue, attributing it to "John, the disciple of the Lord" (Irenaeus, *Adv. Haer.* 1.8.5). Heracleon, another Valentinian, authored the first known commentary on the gospel (ca. 170), extended fragments of which are quoted in Origen's commentary on John. Excerpts from the Valentinian Theodotus have been preserved by Clement of Alexandria.

The first explicit witness of the four-gospels canon, Irenaeus of Lyons, made extensive use of the gospel of John in his *Against Heresies* in refuting the Gnostics and Marcion and explaining the orthodox faith. His theological synthesis, emphasizing the unity of the history of salvation, treated almost all the major themes of the gospel of John. For example, he clearly perceived that the "life" or "eternal life" that presupposes faith in Jesus is not biological life or merely a continued existence of the soul, but communion with God the Father, through Christ, in the Holy Spirit.

Tertullian too made substantial use of the gospel of John, in particular in establishing the distinction of Father and Son within the Unity of God (see especially *Against Praxeas*). Hippolytus of Rome uses the gospel of John in a similar vein. Clement of Alexandria is reported by Eusebius as having written that ". . . John, last of all, conscious that the outward facts had been set forth in the Gospels, was urged on by the disciples, and, divinely moved by the Spirit, composed a spiritual Gospel" (*Eccl. Hist.* 6.14.7).

The first patristic commentary of which substantial parts have been preserved is that of Origen; Eusebius knew of thirty-two books (commenting on John 1–13), of which only approximately eight and a half are extant. For these, fortunately, we have the Greek text. The first five books were composed relatively early in Origen's life, while he was still in Alexandria, the rest being composed later in Caesarea. The first books of the commentary are extremely prolix: Book 1 is entirely on John 1:1, Book 2 arrives at John 1:7. These first verses of the Prologue of John offered Origen an opportunity to expose his christology and theology of the Trinity, and even some essentials of his comprehensive view of the created universe. There are manifold correspondences between the doctrines of these books of the commentary and those of *On First Principles* (a work written around the same time, but fully preserved only in Latin). Origen's "spiritual exegesis" is often quite congenial to the Fourth Gospel. "The kind of deeper meaning that he finds varies from the most arbitrary allegorising to a profound understanding of the symbolism of the Gospel" (M. F. Wiles, *The Spiritual Gospel: The Interpretation of the Fourth Gospel in the Early Church* [Cambridge: Cambridge University Press, 1960] 23). He is almost the only ancient commentator who systematically studied the key terms of John, such as "spirit," "truth," "life," "light," "knowledge," and "glory," and often penetrated their deeper meaning.

John's gospel played a key part in the trinitarian and christological discussions from their beginning, and therefore received special attention in the great controversies of the fourth and fifth centuries. Unfortunately, a good number of commentaries written in this context have been lost or survive only as fragments in *catenae* (see Wiles, *The Spiritual Gospel,* 4–5). Several important ones, however, have been preserved. The first of these is the series of eighty-eight homilies by John Chrysostom, preached in Antioch (ca. 391), and containing a careful exposition of the whole gospel. From the West, Augustine's *Tractates on the Gospel of John*, also covering the whole gospel, are extant. The work consists of 124 "sermons," some actually delivered, others merely dictated. Generally, the first group (1–54) is dated earlier (ca. 406–418) and the second (55–124) later (ca. 416–420). These works share a pastoral character and at the same time have substantial theological content. Chrysostom, though developing the teachings of the gospel against Arianism, is, in the spirit of Antiochian exegesis, more practical and less prone to explore the deeper symbolic meaning. Augustine's exegesis is more congenial to John's theology.

From the beginning of the fifth century two major Greek commentaries survive, those of Theodore of Mopsuestia and Cyril of Alexandria. Theodore's commentary, preserved in its entirety only in Syriac translation, is typical of the Antiochian school: its bent is practical and literal (though where the text clearly demands it he does give symbolic interpretations). His christology, too, reflects Antiochian tendencies. Cyril's monumental commentary is eminently theological, with ample use of spiritual interpretation. Doctrinally he fights against the Arians and the christology of Antioch, though Nestorius is not mentioned by name, and therefore the commentary is dated before 429. Fragments of several Greek commentaries are compiled in J. Reuss, ed., *Johannes-Kommentare aus der Griechischen Kirche*. TU 89 (1966). Commentaries represented are those by Apollinaris of Laodicea, Theodore of Heraclea, Didymus of Alexandria, Theophilus of Alexandria, Cyril of Alexandria (or Pseudo-Cyril), Ammonius of Alexandria, and Photius of Constantinople.

There are, of course, numerous commentaries of lesser importance from Byzantine theologians and Western medieval authors. From the golden age of Scholasticism, Thomas Aquinas's *Commentary on the Gospel of St. John* deserves special mention. Taken down from actual lectures in Paris by Thomas's secretary, Reginald of Piperno, it was corrected by Thomas himself and is considered to be one of his outstanding writings on sacred Scripture.

Due to the special interest and abundance of recent research on the patristic interpretation of John, as well as the immensity of the task of attempting to summarize the features of that interpretation, a secondary bibliography is offered to the reader.

BIBLIOGRAPHY FOR JOHN

Secondary Sources

Braun, F.-M. *Jean le théologien et son évangile dans l'Église ancienne.* Paris: J. Gabalda, 1959. This book contains a detailed study of all the traces of the Johannine *corpus* in the first two centuries by geographical regions (pp. 65–296), and an examination of the evangelist's "dossier."

Culpepper, R. Alan. *John, the Son of Zebedee: The Life of a Legend.* Columbia, S.C.: University of South Carolina Press, 1994.

Di Berardino, Angelo, ed. *Encyclopedia of the Early Church.* S.v. "John the Evangelist, Gospel of: use and interpretation in the Early Church," by T. E. Pollard.

Pollard, T. E. *Johannine Christology and the Early Church.* Cambridge: Cambridge University Press, 1970.

Schnackenburg, Rudolf. *The Gospel According to St. John.* Vol. 1. Translated by Kevin Smyth. New York: Herder and Herder, 1968. See pp. 192–217: "The Fourth Gospel in History."

Wiles, Maurice F. *The Spiritual Gospel: The Interpretation of the Fourth Gospel in the Early Church.* Cambridge: Cambridge University Press, 1960.

BIBLIOGRAPHY FOR THE GOSPELS AND ACTS

Primary Sources

Matthew

Pseudo-Ammonius. *Fragmenta in Matthaeum.* MPG 85:1381–1392.

Anonymous. "Anonymi chiliastae in Matthaeum XXIV fragmenta," in Giovanni Mercati, *Varia Sacra.* Studi e Testi 11, 1–49. Rome: Tipografia Vaticana, 1911; C. H. Turner, "An Exegetical Fragment of the Third Century," *JThS* 5 (1904) 218–241.

Athanasius of Alexandria. In Illud: *Omnia mihi tradita sunt* (Matth 11, 27). MPG 25:208–220.

____. *On Luke X.22 (Matt. XI.27).* Translated by A. Robertson. NPNF 2nd ser. 4:87–90.

____. *Scholia in Matthaeum.* MPG 27:1364–1389.

Augustine. *De consensu Evangelistarum libri IV.* Edited by Francis Weihrich. CSEL 43 (1904).

____. *De sermone Domini in monte libri II.* Edited by Almut Mutzenbecher. CCSL 35 (1967).

____. *The Harmony of the Gospels.* Translated by W. Findley and P. Schaff. NPNF 1st ser. 6:77–236.

____. *Our Lord's Sermon on the Mount.* Translated by W. Findley and P. Schaff. NPNF 1st ser. 6:1–70. Translated by John J. Jepson. ACW 5 (1948). Translated by D. J. Kavanagh. FC 11 (1951).

____. *Quaestiones Evangeliorum libri II.* Edited by Almut Mutzenbecher. CCSL 44B:7–118 (1980).

____. *Quaestionum septemdecim in Evangelium secundum Matthaeum liber I.* Edited by Almut Mutzenbecher. CCSL 44B:119–140 (1980).

____. *Sermons 51–94 on the New Testament,* in *The Works of Saint Augustine: A Translation for the 21st Century* 3.3. Edited by John E. Rotelle. Translated by Edmund Hill. Brooklyn, N.Y.: New City Press, 1991.

Chromatius of Aquileia. *Tractatus in Matthaeum.* Edited by R. Étaix and J. Lemarié. CCSL 9A:183–498 (1974).

____. *Tractatus XVII in Evangelium Matthaei.* Edited by Anselm Hoste. CCSL 9:389–442 (1957).

Fortunatus of Aquileia. *Commentarii in evangelia* (fragments). Edited by André Wilmart and Bernhard Bischoff. CCSL 9:365–370 (1957).

Hilary of Poitiers. *Sur Matthieu.* Edited and translated by Jean Doignon. SC 254, 258 (1978, 1979).

Hippolytus. *In Matthaeum* (fragments), in *Hippolytus Werke* 1.2. Edited by Hans Achelis. GCS 1 (1897) 195–209.

Jerome. *Commentarii in evangelium Matthaei.* Edited by David Hurst and Marc Adriaen. CCSL 77 (1969).

John Chrysostom. *Homilies on St. Matthew.* Translated by S. G. Prevost. Revised by M. B. Riddle. NPNF 1st ser. 10.

____. *In Matthaeum homiliae 1–90.* MPG 57:13–472. MPG 58:471–794.

Pseudo-Chrysostom. *Opus imperfectum in Matthaeum.* MPG 56:611–946.

Matthäus-Kommentare aus der griechischen Kirche. Edited by Joseph Reuss. TU 61 (1957). Contains the following:

- Apollinaris of Laodicea. *In Matthaeum* (fragments) 1–54.
- Cyril of Alexandria. *In Matthaeum* (fragments) 153–269.
- Photius of Constantinople. *In Matthaeum* (fragments) 270–337.
- Theodore of Heraclea. *In Matthaeum* (fragments) 55–95.
- Theodore of Mopsuestia. *In Matthaeum* (fragments) 96–135.
- Theophilus of Alexandria. *In Matthaeum* (fragments) 151–152.

Origen. *Commentaire sur l évangile selon Matthieu I.* Translated by Robert Girod. SC 162 (1970).

____. *Commentary on Matthew.* Translated by J. Patrick. ANF 10:409–512.

____. *Origenes Werke X. Origenes Matthäuserklärung* 1. *Die griechisch erhaltene Tomoi.* Edited by Erich Klostermann and Ernst Benz. GCS 40 (1935–1937).

____. *Origenes Werke XI. Origenes Matthäuserklärung* 2. *Die lateinische Übersetzung der Commentariorum Series.* First edition by Erich Klostermann and Ernst Benz (1933). Second edition by U. Treu. GCS 38 (1976).

____. *Origenes Werke XII, 1. Origenes Matthäuserklärung* 3. *Fragmente und Indices*. Edited by Erich Klostermann and Ernst Benz. GCS 41.1 (1941).

Pseudo-Origen. *Homiliae viii in Matthaeum.* MPL 95:1162–1167, 1189–1200. PLS 4:852–898. MPL 94:411–413.

Pseudo-Theophilus. *Commentarii sive alegoriae in quattuor evangelia.* PLS 3:1283–1329.

For specific listings of sermons and homilies see H. J. Sieben, *Kirchenväterhomilien zum Neuen Testament* 15–56.

Mark

Augustine. *Sermons* (From the Gospel of Mark). PLS 2:424–427. MPL 38:581–591; 1104–1107; 1112–1115; 1126–1133.

____. *Sermons* (From the Gospel of Mark). Translated by R. G. MacMullen. Edited by Philip Schaff. NPNF 1st ser. 6:406–413.

____. *Sermons 94A–147A on the New Testament*, in *The Works of Saint Augustine: A Translation for the 21st Century* 3.4. Translated by E. Hill. Brooklyn, N.Y.: New City Press, 1992. 24–39.

Jerome (Pseudo-Chrysostom). *Tractatus 10 in Marci Evangelium.* Edited by D. G. Morin. CCSL 78:449–500.

____. *Homilies on the Gospel of Mark*, in *The Homilies of St. Jerome*. Translated by M. L. Ewald. FC 57:121–192.

Pseudo-Jerome. *Commentarius in euangelium secundum Marcum.* MPL 30:589–644.

John Chrysostom. *Sermons* (From the Gospel of Mark). MPG 51:31–40. MPG 58:603–610; 757–767.

Peter Chrysologus. *Sermons* (From the Gospel of Mark). Edited by Alexandre Olivar. CCSL 24:102–105; 122–127; 167–172; 182–185; 186–190; 206–210; 269–273; 284–291 (1975). CCSL 24A:505–509; 511–516; 617–619 (1981). CCSL 24B:1040–1049; 1054–1058; 1060–1064; 1068–1072 (1982).

____. *Sermons* (From the Gospel of Mark). Translated by G. E. Ganss. FC 17:75–80; 133–137; 276–282 (1953).

Theodore of Mopsuestia. *Fragmenta in Marcum.* MPG 66:713–716.

Pseudo-Theophilus. *Allegoriae in euangelium secundum Marcum.* PLS 3:1308–1312.

For specific listings of sermons and homilies see H. J. Sieben, *Kirchenväterhomilien zum Neuen Testament,* 69–71.

Luke

Ambrose. *Expositio Evangelii secundum Lucam.* Edited by Marc Adriaen. CCSL 14 (1957).

____. *Expositio Evangelii secundum Lucam*, in *Sant' Ambrogio, Opere esegetiche* 11.1. Edited by Giovanni Coppa. Milan, 1978.

Athanasius of Alexandria. *Scholia in Lucam.* MPG 27:1392–1404.

Augustine. *Questiones Evangeliorum libri II.* Edited by Almut Mutzenbecher. CCSL 44B:7–118 (1980).

____. *Sermons 97A–116 on the New Testament*, in *The Works of Saint Augustine: A Translation for the 21st Century* 3.4. Translated by E. Hill. Brooklyn, N.Y.: New City Press, 1992, 40–208.

Cyril of Alexandria. *Commentarii in Lucam* (homilies 3, 4, 51, and *scholia* in *catenae*). MPG 72:476–950. MPG 77:1009–1016; 1040–1049.

____. *A Commentary Upon the Gospel According to St. Luke by St. Cyril, Patriarch of Alexandria.* 2 vols. Translated by R. P. Smith. Oxford: Oxford University Press, 1859; repr. Astoria, N.Y.: Studion, 1983.

____. *S. Cyrill: Alexandriae archiepiscopi Commentarii in Lucae evangelium quae supersunt syriace e manuscriptis apud Museum Britannicum.* Edited by Robert Payne Smith. Oxford: Typographeo Academico, 1858.

____. *S. Cyrilli Alexandrini commentarii in Lucam I.* Edited by J. B. Chabot. CSCO 70, Scriptores Syri 27 (1912).

Dionysius of Alexandria. *Exegetical Fragments on the Gospel According to Luke*. Translated by S.D.F. Salmond. ANF 6:114–120.

____. *Fragmenta in Lucam*. In *The Letters and other Remains of Dionysius of Alexandria.* Edited by Charles L. Feltoe. Cambridge: Cambridge University Press, 1904, 231–250.

Eusebius of Caesarea. *Scholia in Lucam.* MPG 24: 29–605.

Lukas-Kommentare aus der griechischen Kirche. Edited by Joseph Reuss. TU 130 (1984). Includes:

Apollinaris of Laodicea. *Fragmenta in Lucam,* 3–10.

Cyril of Alexandria. *Commentarii in Lucam,* 54–297.

Theodore of Mopsuestia. *Fragmenta in Lucam,* 12–14.

Origen. *Commentarii in Lucam* (fragments). In *Origène. Homélies sur S. Luc.* Edited and translated by Henri Crouzel, François Fournier, and Pierre Périchon. SC 87 (1962) 464–547.

____. *Commentarii in Lucam* (fragments), in *Origenes Werke IX. Die Homilien zu Lukas in der Übersetzung des Hieronmus und die griechischen Reste der Homilien und des Lukas-Kommentars.* 2nd ed. Edited by Max Rauer. GCS 49 (1959) 227–336.

____. *Homilies on Luke*. Translated by J. T. Lienhard. FC 94 (1996).

____. *In Lucam homiliae xxxix*, in *Origène. Homélies sur S. Luc*. Edited and translated by Henri Crouzel, François Fournier, and Pierre Périchon. SC 87 (1962) 99–459.

____. *In Lucam homiliae xxxix*, in *Origenes Werke IX. Die Homilien zu Lukas in der Übersetzung des Hieronymus und die griechischen Reste der Homilien und des Lukas-Kommentars* 2nd ed. Edited by Max Rauer. GCS 49 (1959) 3–222.

Theodore of Mopsuestia. *Fragmenta in Lucam*. MPG 66:716–728.

Titus of Bostra. *Commentarii in Lucam* (fragments), in *Titus von Bostra: Studien zu dessen Lukashomilien*. Edited by Joseph Sickenberger. TU 21.1 (1901) 143–245.

For specific listings of sermons and homilies see H. J. Sieben, *Kirchenväterhomilien zum Neuen Testament,* 61–86.

Acts

Arator. *Arator's De actibus Apostolorum*. Edited and translated by J. L. Roberts III, J. F. Makowski, and R. J. Schrader. Atlanta: Scholars, 1988.

John Chrysostom. *De mutatione nominum, homiliae 1–4*. MPG 51:113–156.

____. *Homilies on the Acts of the Apostles*. Translated by J. Walker, J. Sheppard, and H. Browne. Revised by G. B. Stevens. NPNF 1st ser. 11:1–328.

____. *In Acta apostolorum homiliae 1–55*. MPG 60:13–384.

____. *In principium Actorum, homiliae 1–4*. MPG 51:65–112.

For specific listings of sermons and homilies see H. J. Sieben, *Kirchenväterhomilien zum Neuen Testament,* 130–135.

John

Augustine. *In Johannis evangelium tractatus CXXIV*. 2nd ed. Edited by Radbodus Willems. CCSL 36 (1990).

____. *Lectures or Tractates on the Gospel of John*. Translated by J. Gibb and J. Innes. NPNF 1st ser. 7:7-452.

____. *Tractates on the Gospel of John*. Translated by J. W. Rettig. FC 78, 79, 88, 90, 92 (1988–1995).

Cyril of Alexandria. *Commentarii in Joannem*. MPG 73:9–1056. MPG 74:9–756.

____. (or Pseudo-Cyril). *Commentarii in Johannem* (fragments). In *Johannes-Kommentare aus der griechischen Kirche*. Edited by Joseph Reuss. TU 89 (1966) 188–195.

____. *Commentary on the Gospel According to John*. 2 vols. Translated by Philip E. Pusey and Thomas Randell. LFC 43, 48 (1832, 1835).

____. *Sancti patris nostri Cyrilli arch. Alexandrini in d. Joannis evangelium*. 3 vols. Edited by Philip E. Pusey. Oxford: Clarendon, 1872.

Didymus of Alexandria. *Kommentar zum Johannes-Evangelium, Kap. 6,3-33*. Edited by Bärbel Kramer. PTA 34:58–103 (1985).

Johannes-Kommentare aus der griechischen Kirche. Edited by Joseph Reuss. TU 89 (1966).

John Chrysostom. *Homiliae in Joannem*. MPG 59:29–482.

____. *Homilies on the Gospel of St. John*. Translated by Charles Marriott. Annotated by Philip Schaff. NPNF 1st ser. 14:1–334.

____. *Homilies on the Gospel of John*. Translated by T. A. Goggin. FC 33, 41 (1957–1960).

Origen. *Commentarii in Johannem*. In *Origenes Werke IV. Der Johanneskommentar*. Edited by Erwin Preuschen. GCS 10:3–480.

____. *Commentaire sur saint Jean*. Edited and translated by Cecile Blanc. SC 120, 157, 222, 290 (1966, 1970, 1975, 1982).

____. *Commentary on the Gospel According to John*. Translated by R. E. Heine. FC 80, 89 (1989, 1993).

____. *Commentary on the Gospel of John*. Translated by Allan Menzies. ANF 10:297–408.

Theodore of Mopsuestia. *Theodori Mopsuesteni commentarius in evangelium Johannis Apostoli*. Edited by J. M. Vosté. CSCO 115, 116 (1940). Syriac with Latin translation.

____. *Commentarii in Johannem* (fragments). In Robert Devreesse, *Essai sur Theodore de Mopsueste*. Studi e Testi 141. Vatican City: Biblioteca Apostolica Vaticana, 1948, 305–419.

For specific listings of sermons and homilies see H. J. Sieben, *Kirchenväterhomilien zum Neuen Testament,* 87–129.

PAULINE EPISTLES AND HEBREWS

In order to treat adequately the question of the patristic reception and interpretation of Paul it is necessary to recall the change in the state of the question that has occurred during the last few decades. As Professor William Babcock has written in his Introduction to *Paul and the Legacies of Paul* (Dallas: Southern Methodist University Press, 1990), which collected the papers presented at an international research conference, held in Dallas in 1987: "Over the past century and a half, especially among Protestant scholars, assessments of Paul's place and legacy in the early history of Christianity have tended to fall into a distressingly stereotyped pattern"

(p. xiii). According to Babcock this "pattern includes at least four elements" that can be summarized as follows:

(1) "That Paul's theology exercised its greatest appeal—and came closest to being rightly understood—among versions of Christianity that would turn out to be marginal or heretical by the standards of what would become the dominant tradition."

(2) That "the traditions that did ultimately give Christianity its enduring shape either ignored or misconstrued Paul . . ."

(3) That "only with Augustine, in the Latin West and at the turn from the fourth to the fifth century, did there emerge something like a recovery of the genuine central motifs in Pauline thought and in particular, a true sense for the great Pauline theme of justification by grace and faith . . ."

(4) That "the Greek Christian tradition never did—before or after Augustine—achieve an apt appreciation of Paul . . . ."

The cover copy indicates that "*Paul and the Legacies of Paul* presents a series of studies that paint a very different, and more complex picture . . ."—a picture confirmed by a whole series of studies cited in the bibliographies given below. "They suggest that Paul was by no means a negligible or marginal figure in what would become 'orthodox' Christianity, that the 'orthodox' reading of Paul was no mere domestication of his thought, and that Paul certainly had a formative significance for Greek as well as for Latin Christianity."

The reception and interpretation of the Pauline letters begins within the NT itself. The so-called Deutero-Pauline letters (according to most exegetes, 2 Thessalonians, Colossians[?], Ephesians, and the Pastorals), which were, of course, considered unquestionably Pauline by the Fathers, are here among the first examples (see their treatment in the present commentary below).

Among the Apostolic Fathers the letter of Clement to the Corinthians, the letters of Ignatius, and the letter of Polycarp to the Philippians reflect the influence of the Pauline letters. Surprising is the absence of the use of the Pauline letters in most of the Apologists. (The *Letter to Diognetus* is an important exception.) The following passage from that letter (with several others) undoubtedly shows the influence of Paul, especially the letter to the Romans:

> He himself gave up his own Son as a ransom for us—the holy one for the unjust, the innocent for the guilty, the righteous one for the unrighteous, the incorruptible for the corruptible, the immortal for the mortal. For what else could have covered our sins except his righteousness? In whom could we, lawless and impious as we were, be made righteous except in the Son of God alone? O sweetest exchange! O unfathomable work of God! O blessings beyond all expectation! The sinfulness of many is hidden in the Righteous One, while the righteousness of the One justifies the many who are sinners. (*Diogn.* 9.2-5, translated by E. R. Fairweather in *Early Christian Fathers*, LCC 1, edited by C. C. Richardson [Philadelphia: Westminster, 1953] 220–221.)

Of course several of the Gnostic writers appealed also to Paul. Marcion tried to support his rejection of the OT and his opposing to its creator "God" the good God of Jesus Christ on a collection of (often drastically mutilated) Pauline epistles.

For Irenaeus and Tertullian the Pauline corpus forms an integral part of the NT (substantially as we know it). It was especially Irenaeus who in his *Against Heresies* integrated the interpretation of practically the whole Pauline corpus (together with the other NT writings) into his own anti-Gnostic and anti-Marcionite theology (cf. R. Norris, "Irenaeus' Use of Paul in His Polemic Against the Gnostics," in *Paul and the Legacies of Paul,* 79–98).

From the third century on we have a considerable number of explicit commentaries on Pauline epistles ("from Jerome we know of some 20 Greek commentaries dedicated to various Pauline epistles . . . the majority of them unknown to us . . ." [Angelo Di Berardino, ed., *Encyclopedia of the Early Church*, s.v. "Paul III. Commentaries on the Pauline Epistles," by M. G. Mara]). In what follows only those commentaries and homilies will be mentioned that have been preserved entire or from which we have substantial fragments. (For detailed accounts and editions of the fragments see the bibliography on the patristic exegesis of Paul.)

Origen seems to have been the first to comment on all the Pauline epistles, although except for his commentary on Romans (in Rufinus's Latin translation, and partly in Greek) only fragments have been preserved. John Chrysostom left us a complete series of homilies on all the Pauline epistles and a commentary on Galatians, fortunately all preserved. From Theodore of Mopsuestia's commentaries only those on the "minor" Pauline epistles (that is, from Galatians to Philemon in the canonical order) are extant integrally in an early Latin translation, though we have numerous fragments of the Greek original. Theodoret's brief but systematic commentaries on all the Pauline epistles are preserved in the original Greek.

From among the Greek writers of the later patristic or Byzantine period we have commentaries or fragments of commentaries, for example by John of Damascus, Photius of Constantinople, Oecumenius of Tricca (10th c.), Theophylact (11th c.), and Euthymius Zigabenus (early 12th c.).

The first Latin patristic author who commented on the Pauline epistles is Marius Victorinus. We have only parts of his commentaries on Galatians, Ephesians, and Philippians. The writer called "Ambrosiaster" (an unknown author of the fourth century whose works have been falsely attributed to Ambrose) has left us substantial commentaries on all the Pauline epistles. From Jerome we have commentaries on Philippians, Galatians, Ephesians, and Titus. Pelagius, whose commentaries antedate his controversies with Augustine, commented briefly on thirteen of the Pauline letters.

From Augustine we have a commentary on Galatians and several incomplete treatments of Romans, both before and after his clash with Pelagius. Cassiodorus and his school left us orthodox reworkings of the commentaries of Pelagius.

In the Syrian Church, Ephrem (or Pseudo-Ephrem) commented on all the Pauline epistles. They have been preserved in Armenian, and indirectly in Latin.

Some of the major medieval authors who commented on the Pauline epistles were Hugh of St. Victor, Peter Lombard, Thomas Aquinas, and Dionysius the Carthusian.

From among the Protestant Reformers Luther's commentaries on Romans and Galatians have been foundational for his theology of justification and immensely influential. Calvin published commentaries on all the Pauline epistles (Strasburg, 1539). Catholic commentators of the sixteenth and early seventeenth centuries include Cajetan (Thomas de Vio), whose commentary on the Pauline epistles was published in Rome in 1529, and Cornelius de Lapide (Antwerp, 1614).

Due to the special interest and abundance of recent research on the patristic interpretation of Paul, as well as the immensity of the task of attempting to summarize the features of that interpretation, a secondary bibliography is offered to the reader. Also included is a bibliography informing the reader on the place of Hebrews in the early Church.

BIBLIOGRAPHY FOR PAULINE EPISTLES AND HEBREWS

Secondary Sources

Selected Studies on Patristic Exegesis of the Pauline Epistles

Babcock, W. S., ed. *Paul and the Legacies of Paul.* Dallas, Tex.: Southern Methodist University Press, 1990. Papers of an international conference on Paul in the early Church (including Augustine).

Cocchini, Francesca. *Il Paolo di Origene: Contributo alla storia della recezione delle epistole paoline nel III secolo.* Verba Seniorum n.s. 11. Rome: Studium, 1992. Includes a rich bibliography, 197–208.

Dassmann, Ernst. *Der Stachel im Fleisch: Paulus in der frühchristlichen Literatur bis Irenäus.* Münster: Aschendorff, 1979.

Di Berardino, Angelo, ed. *Encyclopedia of the Early Church.* S.v. "Paul II. Paulinism," by Ernst Dassmann.

____. *Encyclopedia of the Early Church.* S.v. "Paul III. Commentaries on the Pauline Epistles," by M. G. Mara.

Lindemann, Andreas. *Paulus im ältesten Christentum: Das Bild des Apostels und die Rezeption der paulinischen Theologie in der frühchristlichen Literatur bis Marcion.* BHTh 58. Tübingen: J.C.B. Mohr (Paul Siebeck), 1979.

Wickert, Ulrich. *Studien zu den Pauluskommentaren Theodors von Mopsuestia.* Berlin: A. Töpelmann, 1962.

Wiles, M. F. *The Divine Apostle: The Interpretation of St. Paul's Epistles in the Early Church.* Cambridge: Cambridge University Press, 1967.

Selected Bibliography for Romans and Hebrews

Romans

Fitzmyer, Joseph A. *Romans: A New Translation with Introduction and Commentary.* New York: Doubleday, 1993. Contains the most extensive and up-to-date bibliography on patristic commentaries and regularly refers to their interpretations of the text.

Schelkle, Karl Hermann. *Paulus Lehrer der Väter: Die altkirchliche Auslegung von Römer 1-11*. 2nd ed. Düsseldorf: Patmos, 1959. Detailed treatment of the exegesis of the epistle by the whole patristic tradition. Valuable summary of patristic exegesis of Romans, 413–441.

Hebrews

Greer, Rowan A. *The Captain of Our Salvation: A Study in the Patristic Exegesis of Hebrews*. BGBE 15. Tübingen: J.C.B. Mohr (Paul Siebeck), 1973. This is a substantial and balanced study, not limited to the commentaries. A brief conclusion (356–359) gives a summary characterization of the patristic exegesis of Hebrews.

Primary Sources

Extensive Interpretation of Pauline Epistles

Ambrosiaster. *Commentarius in xii epistulas Paulinas*. Edited by H. J. Vogels. CSEL 81.1–3 (1966–1969). Commentaries on all Pauline epistles.

Cassiodorus. *Expositio S. Pauli epistulae ad Romanos, una cum complexionibus in xii sequentes S. Pauli epistulas a quodam Cassiodori discipulo anonymo concinnatis*. MPL 68:415–686. Expositions on all Pauline epistles.

John Chrysostom. *Homilies on the Pauline Epistles*. Translated by J. B. Morris, W. H. Simcox, and revised by G. B. Stevens (Romans); T. W. Chambers (1, 2 Corinthians); Oxford translation revised by G. Alexander (Galatians, Ephesians), J. A. Broadus (Philippians, Colossians, Thessalonians), Philip Schaff (Timothy, Titus, Philemon). NPNF 1st ser. 11:338–13:557. Homilies on all Pauline epistles.

____. *Ioannis Chrysostomi interpretatio omnium epistularum Paulinarum* 1–6. Edited by Frederick Field. Oxford: Combe, 1845–1862.

John Damascene. *Commentarii in epistulas Pauli*. MPG 95:441–929, 997–1033. Commentaries on all Pauline epistles.

Pseudo-Oecumenius. *Catena Ps.-Oecumenii*. MPG 118:308–119:277. Commentaries on all Pauline Epistles.

Pauluskommentare aus der griechischen Kirche. 2nd ed. Edited by Karl Staab. NTA 15. Münster/Westfalen: Aschendorff, 1984. This work contains fragments from the writings of Didymus of Alexandria, Eusebius of Emesa, Acacius of Caesarea, Apollinarius, Diodore, Theodore of Mopsuestia, Severian of Gabala, Gennadius of Constantinople, Oecumenius, Photius, and Arethas on the epistles of Paul. Includes:

Oecumenius. *Commentarii in Pauli epistulas*, 423–461. Commentaries from Romans through 2 Timothy (no Titus or Philemon).

Severian of Gabala. *Fragmenta in epistulas s. Pauli*, 213–345. Expositions on all the Pauline epistles with the exception of Philemon.

Theodore of Mopsuestia. *Fragmenta in epistulam ad Romanos* and *Fragmenta in epistulam ad Corinthios i et ii*, 113–200. Contains the fragments on Romans, 1 and 2 Corinthians.

Pelagius. *Expositiones xiii epistularum Pauli*. Edited by Alexander Souter. TaS 9.1–2 (1922/1926). PLS 1:1113–1374. Expositions on all the Pauline epistles.

Theodore of Mopsuestia. *Commentarii in epistulas Pauli minores*. In *Theodori episcopi Mopsuesteni in epistulas B. Pauli commentarii* 1–2. Edited by H. B. Swete. Cambridge: University Press, 1880, 1882; reprint Westmead/Farnborough, Hants.: Gregg International, 1969. Contains commentaries on Galatians through Philemon.

Theodoret. *Interpretatio in xii epistulas s. Pauli*. MPG 82: 4–877. Interpretations of all Pauline epistles.

For specific listings of sermons and homilies see H. J. Sieben, *Kirchenväterhomilien zum Neuen Testament*, 136–173.

Interpretation of Individual Pauline Epistles and Hebrews

Romans

Augustine. *Augustine on Romans: Propositions from the Epistle to the Romans and Unfinished Commentary on the Epistle to the Romans*. Edited and translated by Paula Fredriksen Landes. Chico, Cal.: Scholars Press, 1982.

____. *Epistulae ad Romanos inchoata expositio*. Edited by Johannes Divjak. CSEL 84 (1971) 145–181.

____. *Epistulae quorundam propositionum ex epistula ad Romanos*. Edited by Johannes Divjak. CSEL 84 (1971) 3–52.

Cyril of Alexandria. *Fragmenta in epistulam ad Romanos*. MPG 74:773–856.

Origen. *Commentarii in epistulam ad Romanos*. MPG 14:833–1292.

____. "Exegesis of Romans VIII, 18–25." *JSL* 3rd ser. 12 (1860–1861) 410–420.

1 Corinthians

Cyril of Alexandria. *Fragmenta in primam epistulam ad Corinthios*. MPG 74:856–916.

Origen. *Fragmenta in epistulam primam ad Corinthios*. In C. Jenkins, "Origen on 1 Corinthians," *JThS* 9 (1908) 232–247, 353–372, 500–514; 10 (1909) 29–51.

2 Corinthians

Cyril of Alexandria. *Fragmenta in secundam epistulam ad Corinthios*. MPG 74:916–952.

Galatians

Augustine. *Epistulae ad Galatas expositio*. Edited by Johannes Divjak. CSEL 84 (1971) 55–141.

Jerome. *Commentarii in epistolam ad Galatas*. MPL 26:307–438.

Marius Victorinus. *Commentarii in epistulam ad Galatas*. MPL 8:1145–1198.

Origen. *Commentarii in Galatas* (fragments). MPG 14:1293–1298.

Ephesians

Jerome. *Commentarii in epistulam ad Ephesios*. MPL 26:339–554.

Marius Victorinus. *Commentarii in epistulam ad Ephesios*. MPL 8:1255–1294.

Origen. *Commentarii in Ephesios* (fragments). In J.A.F. Gregg, "The Commentary of Origen upon the Epistle to the Ephesians," *JThS* 3 (1902) 234–244; 398–420; 554–576.

Philippians

Marius Victorinus. *Commentarii in epistulam ad Philippenses*. MPL 8:1197–1256.

1 Thessalonians

Origen. *Commentarii in epistulam primam ad Thessalonicenses*. Edited by Isidore Hilberg. CSEL 55 (1912) 460–467.

Titus

Jerome. *Commentarii in epistulam ad Titum*. MPL 68:679–684.

Origen. *Commentarius in Titum*. MPG 14:1302–1306.

Philemon

Jerome. *Commentarii in epistulam ad Philemonem*. MPL 26:599–618.

Origen. *Commentarius in Philemonem*. MPG 14: 1305–1308.

Hebrews

Cassiodorus. *Expositio epistulae ad Hebraeos*. MPL 68:685–794.

Cyril of Alexandria. *Fragmenta in epistulam ad Hebraeos*. MPG 74:953–1005.

John Chrysostom. *Homilies on the Epistle to the Hebrews*. Translated by F. Gardiner. NPNF 1st ser. 14:363–522.

____. *In epistulam ad Hebraeos argumentum et homiliae 1–34*. MPG 63:13–236.

____. *Ioannis Chrysostomi interpretatio omnium epistularum Paulinarum* 7. Edited by F. Field. Oxford: Combe, 1862.

John Damascene. *Commentarii in epistolam ad Hebraeos*. MPG 95:929–997.

Oecumenius. *Commentarii in epistolam ad Hebraeos*. In *Pauluskommentare aus der griechischen Kirche* 2nd ed. Edited by Karl Staab, 462–469.

Pseudo-Oecumenius. *Commentarii in epistulam ad Hebraeos*. MPG 119:280–452.

Origen. *In Epistulam ad Hebraeos homiliae* (fragments). MPG 14:1308–1309.

____. *In Epistulam ad Hebraeos libri* (fragments). MPG 14:1307–1308.

Pseudo-Pelagius. *Fragmenta in epistulam ad Hebraeos*. PLS 1:1685–1687.

Theodore of Mopsuestia. *Fragmenta in epistulam ad Hebraeos*. In *Pauluskommentare aus der griechischen Kirche* 2nd ed. Edited by Karl Staab, 200–212.

Theodoret. *Interpretatio in epistulam ad Hebraeos*. MPG 82:673–785.

For specific listings of sermons and homilies see H. J. Sieben, *Kirchenväterhomilien zum Neuen Testament,* 174–178.

CATHOLIC EPISTLES

Eusebius of Caesarea informs us of Clement of Alexandria's *Outlines (Hypotyposeis),* eight books of interpretations of selected passages from the Old and New Testaments, including the Catholic Epistles, the *Epistle of Barnabas,* and the *Apocalypse of Peter* (*Eccl. Hist.* 6.14.1). Fragmentary comments on 1 Peter, Jude, and 2 John survive in Cassiodorus's Latin translation, *Outlines Concerning the Canonical Epistles*. Photius, in his *Library* (*Bibliotheca* Codex 109) would explain Clement's *Outlines* as reflecting both orthodoxy and impiety. In addition to these fragments of Clement's *Outlines* a few patristic commentaries are known and extant. Didymus of Alexandria, though his authorship had been questioned earlier in this century, composed a commentary treating James, 1 and 2 Peter, 1, 2, 3 John, and Jude. It survives in its complete form only in a Latin version. A commentary on the same epistles by Pseudo-Oecumenius also is extant as is one sometimes attributed to Hilary of Arles, but it is spurious and dates probably to the late seventh or early eighth century. Fifty fragments on the Catholic epistles survive in *catenae* under the name of John Chrysostom and thirty-eight *scholia* are ascribed to Cyril of Alexandria.

From Augustine, ten homilies developing the theme of charity within 1 John survive.

James

The epistle of James would inform early Christian morals and spiritual practice as it was used repeatedly to teach the virtues with which James was concerned. Origen would exhort Christians to pray that God would fulfill Jas 1:22 in their lives ("be doers of the word, and not hearers only") by cleansing them of sin and enlivening the good through Christ and the Spirit (*Homily on Genesis* 2.6). But he would also teach that Jas 4:17 taught personal responsibility to flee sin once the divine Word had begun to reveal to them the difference between good and evil (*On First Principles* 1.3.6). Valerius would dedicate a homily on Jas 4:6 to the virtue of humility (*Homily* 14). Augustine would preach sermons on James 1:19-22; 2:10; and 5:12.

Theologically, Jas 1:17, ". . . the Father of lights with whom there is no variation or shadow due to change" would provide language important to trinitarian discussion. Hilary of Poitiers states that the Arians would appeal to it to emphasize the Father's exclusive Godhead to the denial of the Son's divinity (*On the Trinity* 4.8). Athanasius, however, uses it differently. He deduces that the Arians erroneously make God a compound of quality and essence by saying the Son is like the Father only in virtue (quality). This conflicts with God's simplicity in essence, a simplicity he sees stated by James in 1:17 (*Epistle to the Bishops of Africa* 8). Cyril of Jerusalem cites the entire verse in his lecture on the Father, to show the eternal Fatherhood and a begetting of the Son that meant no alteration in the Godhead (*Catechetical Lectures* 7.5). Augustine, too, cites it in his discussion of the mystery of God's substance, the mystery of an immutable God who creates mutable things (*On the Trinity* 1.2-3). In the christological discussion Cyril of Alexandria would refer to Jas 1:17 to state his opposition to any notion of confusion of the divine Word with flesh. No change, no alteration could occur in the Word's divine nature (*Epistle to John of Antioch* 107e-108a).

The passage in James that would become somewhat troublesome in later soteriological thinking, Jas 2:14-26, usually found application without any apparent tension between Paul and James in the early Church. Gregory of Nazianzus taught the Christian that faith and works are each dead without the other (Jas 2:17). Therefore the Christian was to do good works upon believing the points of the faith (*Oration on Holy Baptism* 45). Ambrose would state simply that a proper faith in Christ is only profitable when crowned with good works (*Exposition of the Christian Faith* 2. Preface 14). For Augustine the faith that is set apart from that of the demons (Jas 2:19) is the faith that works through love by the Holy Spirit (*On the Trinity* 15.32).

Into the Middle Ages some tension would arise, and there would be attempts to reconcile perceived differences between Paul and James on faith and works. For example, Julian of Toledo would read Jas 2:24 as not so much dismissing justification by faith alone (cf. Rom 3:28), but as teaching the falseness of the idea that one could refuse good works (*Antithesis* 2.77). Later, in the Reformation, some opponents of the Reformers would set Jas 2:21-24 against their doctrine of justification by faith alone. John Calvin would reply that James is not treating the manner of justification, but imploring Christians to bring forth good works that prove and are the fruit of righteousness (*Institutes of the Christian Religion* 3.17.11-12).

James occurs in the liturgy, for example, on the third Sunday of Advent, in Masses for Various Needs and Occasions, in Ritual Masses for Reconciliation and in the Anointing of the Sick. It instructs the believer on the complementary relationship between faith and good works, especially the need to complement faith with love for neighbor, social justice, and moral purity.

1 Peter

Two passages within 1 Peter that would influence some formulations of the creed were 3:19 and 4:6: ". . . in which he went and preached to the spirits in prison"; "for this is why the gospel was preached even to the dead . . . ." These two passages would help inform the doctrine of Christ's descent into hell between his death and resurrection. For example, Origen would emphasize that Christ's ministry of preaching for conversion did not take place only in the body, but also when Christ's soul left the body and descended to preach to other bodiless souls (*Against Celsus* 2.43). Gregory of Nazianzus would read the significance of the descent to include rescue: when Christ descended he brought souls up from hell. Preaching was extended to triumphant deliverance of the dead (*Theological Orations* 3.20). Rufinus would see a somewhat more comprehensive significance. For him Christ descended to the dead to preach and to lead godly dead forth from corruption (*Commentary on the Apostles' Creed,* 28–29). Yet Clement of Alexandria had read the passages differently, in a manner unrelated to the creed's confession of Christ's descent into hell. The "spirits" and the "dead" referred to Christians who formerly were unbelievers, within whose spirits Christ became alive (*Commentary on 1 Peter* [fragments] 3:18, 20; 4:6).

In discussions of trinity and soteriology as well as moral instruction 1 Pet 2:22-33 would provide the early Church with rich language. The passage speaks of Christ's sinlessness and his faithful, quiet passivity in suffering as an example to believers in their own tribulation. Athanasius of Alexandria referred to the passage in his *Second Festal Letter* (5) for the precise purpose of exhorting Christian conduct in imitation of Christ, but for Gregory of Nyssa, in his treatise *Against Eunomius* (6.3), the passage defended the Son's sharing of the Father's essence even in incarnation. The heretics (Anomoeans) may argue that Christ is clearly distanced from the Father's unimpassioned nature in his taking upon himself human nature. But Gregory notes that the Son did not assume "passion" in the sense of a perverted nature, for "he committed no sin; no guile was found on his lips" (2:22). He only took upon himself the inconvenient attributes of body and soul. Also, Cyril of Jerusalem would refer to the passage (*Catechetical Lectures* 13.3-4). For him, however, the words of 1 Pet 2:22 need to be recognized first as the words of the prophet Isaiah (Isa 53:9), and then as words that reveal the true glory of the cross. Christ did not die for his own sins, but for the sins of others, and here is true redemption and salvation.

In christological matters, regarding the union of the two natures in Christ 1 Pet 4:1, "Christ suffered in the *flesh*," would be important. Cyril of Alexandria would set this text's language against those who would suggest a confusion of the Word's impassible divinity with flesh. Christ suffered not in the impassible nature of God, but in his own flesh (*Ep.* 39.107e-108b; to John of Antioch). Such an emphasis from 1 Peter's words were already set out by Athanasius of Alexandria in his theological work against the Arians. In his conception the Arians had become fixated upon the humanity of Christ to the point that they numbered him among the creatures. He counters this heresy by arguing that the phrase "in the flesh" of 1 Pet 4:1 demonstrates the weakness of Christ limited to the nature of flesh, that which belongs to humanity. One must recognize that the words of the apostle separate such creaturely attributes from the divine nature of the Word (*Against the Arians* 3.34-35).

And then, of course, there is the early Church's interest in the flood/baptismal passage of 1 Pet 3:20-21. For Cyprian the reference to the eight people in the ark saved through water teaches the necessity of the sacrament of baptism within the one, undivided Church (*Ep.* 73.11; 74.15; 75.2). Tertullian had already anticipated this typology between ark and Church in *On Idolatry* 24 and had developed the ark/flood, church/baptism typology in *On Rapture* 8. The earth is our flesh, the flood our baptism, the dove that returned to the ark the spirit of God that brings God's peace.

1 Peter is read, for example, in the Church's liturgy during the Sundays of the Easter Season, on the first Sunday of Lent, in Masses of the Chair of Peter, and on the feast of Mark the evangelist. It provides baptismal teaching and reminds the believer about the blessing of an enduring spiritual, heavenly inheritance, and of the need to be prepared to follow Jesus in suffering.

1, 2, 3 John

Whereas Raymond E. Brown (*The Epistles of John: Translated with Introduction, Notes, and Commentary*. AB 30. Garden City, N.Y.: Doubleday, 1982, 6–9 [see pp. 3–13 for an orientation to 1, 2, 3 John in the Church's tradition]) speaks of some "possible echoes" of 1 John in the early Christian literature of the second century, one finds probable use only in Justin (cf., for example, *Dial.* 123.9: "We who observe the commandments of Christ are called genuine children of God—and that is what we really are," compared especially with 1 John 3:1), and the *Letter to Diognetus* (cf. 10.2-3). According to the same author one would find "probative knowledge of one or more of the Johannine letters" for the first time in Polycarp's *Epistle to the Philippians* (cf. 7.1: "For everyone who does not confess Jesus Christ to have come in the flesh is Antichrist" compared with 2 John 7 and 1 John 4: 2-3). Irenaeus in his *Against Heresies* quotes explicitly from both 1 John and 2 John, but as if they were one letter (Brown, *The Epistles of John* 9–10). The third epistle of John appears in early Christian literature only by the middle of the third century, and it is only by the end of the fourth century that acceptance of all the three Johannine letters as canonical was slowly prevailing (Brown, *The Epistles of John* 11–13).

As for commentaries, a few Fathers who commented on the so-called "Catholic" epistles included also brief comments on 1–3 John (see the bibliography on Catholic epistles). A major commentary on 1 John has been preserved in the form of ten homilies preached by Augustine (six during the Easter Week of the year 415, the last four between Easter Week and the Feast of the Ascension). All manuscripts end with homily ten, covering 1 John 5:1-3, thus leaving 1 John 5:4-21 without comment. These homilies could also be called a treatise on charity: "there is no theme on which I would fainer speak than charity; and no other Scripture extols charity with greater warmth" (8.14; translated by J. Burnaby in *Augustine's Later Works*, 327–328). Augustine anchors charity (as does 1 John) in God's love for us, manifested especially in the incarnation of the Son and the sending of the Holy Spirit (cf. especially Homily 7), yet the major part of his homilies is an exhortation to brotherly and sisterly love that, paradoxically, includes also enemies as potential brothers and sisters (cf. Homily 8).

BIBLIOGRAPHY FOR CATHOLIC EPISTLES

Primary Sources

Augustine. *Commentaire de la Prèmiere Epître de S. Jean*. Edited and translated by Paul Agaësse. SC 75 (1984).

____. *Homilies on the First Epistle of John*. Translated by H. Brown. Revised by J. H. Myers. NPNF 1st. ser. 7:450–529.

____. *In Iohannis epistulam ad Parthos tractatus x*. MPL 35:1977–2062.

____. *Ten Homilies on the First Epistle General of St. John*. In *Augustine: Later Works*. LCC. Translated by John Burnaby. Philadelphia: Westminster Press, 1955, 259–348. Incomplete: there are intentional minor omissions of repetitive or less important passages.

____. *Tractates on the First Epistle of John*. Translated by J. W. Rettig. ACW 92 (1995) 121–277.

Clement of Alexandria. *Comments on the First Epistle of Peter, the Epistle of Jude, and the First and Second Epistles of John* (fragments). Translated by W. Wilson. ANF 2:571–577.

____. *Hypotyposes* (fragments). In *Clemens Alexandrinus* 3. *Stromata Buch VII und VIII. Excerpta ex Theodoto, Eclogae propheticae, Quis diues Saluetur, Fragmente*. 2nd ed. Edited by Otto Stählin, Ludwig Früchtel, and Ursula Treu. GCS 17 (1970) 195–215.

Cyril of Alexandria. *Fragmenta in Acta apostolorum et in epistulas catholicas*. In *Cyrilli archiepiscopi Alexnandrini in D. Ioannis evangelium* 3. Edited by Philip E. Pusey, 441–451. Brussels: Editions Culture et Civilisation, G. Lebon, 1965.

Didymus of Alexandria. *Didymi Alexandrini in epistulas canonicas brevis enarratio*. NTA 4.1. Edited by Friedrich Zoepfl. Münster: Aschendorffsche Verlagsbuchhandlung, 1914.

John Chrysostom (or Pseudo-Chrysostom). *Fragmenta in epistulas Catholicas*. MPG 64:1040–1062.

Pseudo-Oecumenius. *Commentarii in epistulas catholicas*. MPG 119:455–722.

For specific listings of homilies and sermons see H. J. Sieben, *Kirchenväterhomilien zum Neuen Testament,* 179–181.

REVELATION

There exists little consensus on possible traces of the book of Revelation in the Apostolic Fathers, but Justin testifies of his own knowledge of the prophecy (*Dial.* 81:15). Melito of Sardis, by Eusebius of Caesarea's record (*Eccl. Hist.* 4.26.2), composed a work *On the Devil and the Apocalypse of John*, no longer extant, and Theophilus of Antioch used Revelation in his work *Against the Heresy of Hermogenes* (Eusebius, *Eccl. Hist.* 4.24.1). Irenaeus uses Revelation frequently in his *Against Heresies*. He states that John the Lord's disciple wrote it (4.20.11; 4.30.4) at the end of Domitian's rule (5.30.3), and testifies to familiarity with several manuscripts of the book (5.30.1). It had, then, an early, broad circulation within the churches of Asia Minor, Syria, and Gaul. Within Gaul the churches of Lyons and Vienne certainly knew the language of Revelation and reflect it in their epistle to the churches of Asia and Phrygia (Eusebius, *Eccl. Hist.* 5.1.8-61). In the same time frame of the latter half of the second century it was also among the books accepted in Italy (*Muratorian Fragment*).

Hippolytus of Rome's *Apology for the Apocalypse and the Gospel of John*, now lost and extant only in fragments, shows continued Italian interest in the book into the turn of the century. Tertullian's numerous references as well as Origen's promised, but apparently unwritten, commentary indicate its honored place in North Africa. Fortunately some *scholia* of Origen on Revelation have survived, but the collection set forth by Harnack as Origen's *scholia* contains *scholia* from others, including Irenaeus and Clement of Alexandria.

The book of Revelation, however, was not without its questioners and opponents. Marcion rejected it (Tertullian, *Against Marcion* 4.5). Gaius of Rome attributed it to the Gnostic Cerinthus (Eusebius, *Eccl. Hist.* 3.28.1-2), among other possible reasons because of his distaste for chiliasm. The Alogoi, a second century sect of Asia Minor with anti-Montanist tendencies, also rejected Revelation (as well as John's gospel) and ascribed it to Cerinthus (Epiphanius, *Panarion* 51.3.116). They mocked the book for what they considered its impractical content—things like angels and trumpets (Rev 8:2)—and faulted it for its supposed erroneous reference (Rev 2:18-29) to a church in Thyatira (Epiphanius, *Panar.* 51.32.2–33.1). Dionysius of Rome was acquainted with such connections of Revelation to Cerinthus and of its history of rejection. He himself did not reject it, although he did not believe the author was John the apostle, but another John of Asia. The book was written, he thought, in a crude style and contained mysteries to which there must be a deeper, non-literal meaning. Significantly, these comments were evoked by the Egyptian bishop Nepos's book, *Against the Allegorists*, which taught a chiliasm drawn from Revelation (Eusebius, *Eccl. Hist.* 7.24-25).

Eusebius, who is our source for much of the above history, himself had a view of Revelation that was not enthusiastically positive. He does not reject the book outright, noting that opinion on its recognition is evenly split, but he will allow its placement among the spurious writings including texts such as the *Shepherd of Hermas, Barnabas*, and the *Teachings of the Apostles*. The hesitancy of Eusebius regarding acceptance of Revelation may be due to his rejection of chiliasm, which was popularly found in John's book. Such a futuristic, earthly, regal eschatology (not to mention the extreme, sensual version of Cerinthus) was unacceptable to his vision of Constantine's present Christian empire. Furthermore, the tension felt with regard to Revelation by Eusebius and those whose accounts he presents may be due to its possible connection to Montanism. Though much evidence is circumstantial, it is plausible that the Montanists used John's visions as models for their own visions and had a chiliast eschatology informed by Revelation.

Victorinus, bishop of Pettau (martyred ca. 304), wrote the earliest extant commentary on Revelation. The text of the original commentary was not established until 1916, and three recensions exist. Of the three the best known is that of Jerome, which improved the Latin, made other stylistic editorial changes, and altered or removed passages that revealed Victorinus's chiliasm. Though Jerome had identified him as a chiliast (*Lives of Illustrious Men* 18) and his commentary presents a literal reading of Revelation 20–21, the bishop of Pettau weaves in a remarkable amount of allegory and figurative reading throughout his comments. For example, as in Irenaeus (*Adv. Haer.* 3.11.8), the four living creatures of Revelation 4 are the four gospels. The twenty-four elders are the Law and the Prophets and the white robes of Rev 6:11 symbolize the Holy Spirit. The woman of Revelation 12 is the Church, ancient as the patriarchs, and the dragon is the devil, a murderer from the beginning (cf. John 8:44). This would be expected, for Jerome also writes of his being a follower of Origen (*Ep.* 62). For Victorinus the events of the seven bowls (Revelation 16) recapitulate the events of the seven trumpets (Revelation 7–8) more emphatically. The point is not order of events within Revelation, but their significance. They describe judgment and tribulation. Historically the beast of Revelation 13 was Nero, and eschatologically it is Nero resurrected from the abyss to be Antichrist. The first resurrection of Rev 20:4-6 is shown as parallel to the Pauline resurrections of 1 Thess 4:13-18; 1 Cor. 15:51-54. This resurrection enables those in the book of life, then immortal, to rule with Christ over all nations on the earth for a thousand years before the second trumpet. Jerome, of course, omitted this interpretation in his recension. He substituted instead a reading that emphasized the reign as the lawful, virginal purity of the believer. This is not surprising. Elsewhere, on the basis of the reference to the 144,000 who remained virgins (Rev 14:1-5), he argues that all who have not preserved their chastity are defiled (*Against Jovinian* 1.40).

Victorinus shows continuity with earlier chiliasts. Similar readings of Revelation 20–21 as a time of earthly blessing and renewal following a first literal resurrection and again followed by a second resurrection with judgment can be seen in Justin, *Dial.* 81; Irenaeus, *Adv. Haer.* 5.35.1–36.3; Tertullian, *On the Resurrection of the Flesh* 25; *Against Marcion* 3.25.

After the work of Victorinus the next commentary, extant only in fragments, is that of Tychonius, the Donatist. He follows Victorinus's notion of events recapitulated by future narration of events. The commentary's uniqueness rests in its strong ecclesiological focus. The millennium of Revelation 20 is the Church's present experience between Christ's two advents because Christ has already bound the devil (cf. Matt 12:29; Luke 11:22). Revelation 12 describes in general the incessant struggle between Christ and the devil, but more particularly it reveals the life of the Church (Donatist) that, pregnant with the gospel, gives birth to those in whom Christ is formed. The devil persecutes the Christians, the Church, Christ's body through the false Church (Catholic). Within Tychonius's commentary one can see at work several of the hermeneutical principles outlined in his *Book of Rules*. Tyconius's exegesis would provide a dominating paradigm for the Church's reading of Revelation in subsequent years.

Augustine, though he never wrote a commentary on Revelation, did adapt something akin to Tychonius's figurative-ecclesiological interpretation of Revelation 20 in his *City of God* (20.7-10).

The final Latin commentaries of the patristic period were those of Jerome, Primasius, and Apringius. Jerome's, as mentioned above, was one of several recensions of Victorinus's literal, chiliastic commentary. Primasius's commentary combines the thought of both Tychonius and Augustine. The manuscript of Apringius's work, published first in 1900, has only his comments on 1:1–5:7 and 18:6–22:21 surviving. The gap of 5:8–18:5 in the manuscript is filled with the material of Jerome and Victorinus. Cassiodorus's brief notes on Revelation have survived and evidence references to Tychonius and influence from both Victorinus and Augustine. Also Caesarius of Arles' nineteen homilies on Revelation are extant, though earlier they had mistakenly been classified as Augustine's *Exposition of the Apocalypse*. These homilies reflect the ecclesiological reading of Tychonius: the millennium of Revelation 20 is the Church's rule in the world; the first resurrection is regeneration; the descent of the new Jerusalem (Revelation 21) is the Church's universal dispersion.

The earliest surviving Greek commentary on Revelation is that of Oecumenius (sixth century) who with an appreciation for allegory reads the material as either referring to the past moment of Christ's incarnation, the present situation, or the end time. For him the woman and the male child to which she gives birth in Revelation 12 are Mary and Jesus. The woman and child are threatened by the dragon but the boy is saved by God while the woman flees into the desert for 1,260 days. That is, Satan stirs up Herod to murder Jesus but the heavenly Father gives Joseph a dream and the family flees to Egypt and remains there 1,260 days until Herod's death. Similarly, the millennium of Revelation 20 symbolically refers to the incarnation. Oecumenius, however, can still see Satanic persecutions through the Antichrist of the end time in Revelation. Andrew of Caesarea seems to know Oecumenius's commentary and employs it in his own. Andrew reads the material in an eclectic manner, finding an adequate interpretation through a literal, tropological, or allegorical sense. Unlike Oecumenius, for Andrew the woman and child of Revelation 12 are the Church and the Christians it brings forth, while the millennium of Revelation 20 is the time from Christ's first advent until the knowledge of God is universal. The first resurrection of Rev 20:4 is not eschatological, but refers to spiritual regeneration.

Revelation, as can be seen, informed the early Church concerning Christ's incarnation, the period between the incarnation and the end time of tribulation and eventual blessing, and the Church's life between those times. There was always discussion of the number 666 and the identity of Antichrist, both historical and eschatological, that ranged from highly speculative to soberminded and restrained treatment. The interpretations of the rich symbolism of Revelation could be very fanciful and very earthy. One's hermeneutical approach determined what one saw. But the history of Revelation in the early Church is not only a history of differing interpretations that at times led to differing opinions of the book's usefulness and even its canonicity. It is also a history of the ministry of the book to the faith of Christ's body in the first centuries.

In particular the language of Revelation contributed to the Church's reverent christology. The descriptions of the Lamb and the Word as "King of Kings and Lord of Lords" (Rev 17:14; 19:16) cause Origen to address Christ as the "treasure of treasures" (*Homily on Jeremiah* 8.5-6; cf. Col 2:3; Matt 13:46). Cyprian in his *Treatises* (12.2.26), cites John's vision of Christ in Rev 1:12-18 to address the everlasting power the Son received from the Father after his resurrection from the dead. Gregory of Nazianzus sees the divinity of the Son in the language of Rev 1:8, which he thinks is spoken of the Son ". . . who is and who was and who is to come, the Almighty" (*Theological Orations* 3.17 [*Oration* 29.17]). To the catechumen, Cyril of Jerusalem would present the Lord Jesus Christ as the Lion (Rev 5:5), not because he consumes humanity but because he is a steadfast, confident king who opposes and tramples the devil, that roaring, devouring, deceiving lion (*Catechetical Lectures* 10.3).

Revelation has a large role in the Church's liturgy. It is read on Holy Thursday, the Sundays of Easter season and on the feasts of the Assumption, All Saints, All Souls, Christ the King, and in Ordinary Time. The book encourages believers toward faithfulness and separation from wickedness in light of Christ's sure, ultimate triumph over sin, death, and the devil.

BIBLIOGRAPHY FOR REVELATION

Andrew of Caesarea. *Der Apokalypse-Kommentar des Andreas von Kaisareia*, in *Studien zur Geschichte des griechischen Apokalypse—Textes I*. Edited by Josef Schmid. Munich: Zink, 1955, 7–267.

Apringius of Beja. *Tractatus in Apocalypsin*. Edited by Marius Férotin. Paris: A. Picard, 1900.

Caesarius of Arles (Pseudo-Augustine). *Expositio in Apocalypsim*, in *Sancti Caesarii episcopi Arelatensis Opera omnia nunc primum in unum collecta*. 2 vols. Edited by Germanus Morin. Maredsous, 1937–1942, 2:210–277.

Cassiodorus. *Complexiones Apocalypsis Ioannis*. MPL 70:1405–1418.

Hippolytus. *De Apocalypsi* (fragments), in "Les fragments du De Apocalypsi d'Hippolyte," edited and translated by Pierre Prigent and R. Stehly. *ThZ* 29 (1973) 313–333.

Oecumenius. *The Complete Commentary of Oecumenius to the Apocalypse*. Edited and translated by H. C. Hoskier. Ann Arbor, Mich.: University of Michigan Press, 1928.

Origen. *Scholia in Apocalypsin*, in *Der Scholien—Kommentar des Origenes zur Apokalypse Johannis*. Edited by Constantin Diobouniotis and Adolf Harnack. TU 38.3 (1912) 4–44.

Primasius. *Commentarius in Apocalypsin*. Edited by A. W. Adams. CCSL 92 (1985).

Tychonius. *The Turin Fragments: Commentary on Revelation*. TS 7. Edited by Francesco LoBue and G. G. Willis. Cambridge: University Press, 1963.

Victorinus of Pettau and Jerome. *Commentarii in Apocalypsin Ioannis, editio Victorini et recensio Hieronymi: unacum posteriorum additamentis*. Edited by Johannes Haussleiter. CSEL 49 (1916) 11–154.

Victorinus of Pettau and Jerome. *Commentary on the Apocalypse*. Translated by R. E. Wallis. ANF 7:344–360.

For specific listings of sermons and homilies see H. J. Sieben, *Kirchenväterhomilien zum Neuen Testament,* 182–183.

Truth Told in the Bible: Biblical Poetics and the Question of Truth

Francis Martin and Sean McEvenue

The word "poetics" derives from a Greek word meaning "to make." Poetry "makes" reality out of words. This is true of that literary expression we usually call poetry and it is true as well of narrative, which "makes" an event and brings it present to us. When is this "making" process true? Simply put, the poetic function is true when it allows us to share in the intended reality. Thus a poem about the simultaneous greatness and fragility of human life is true if this aspect of reality is truly mediated to us. Look, for instance, at these lines from Job 14:

> A mortal, born of woman, few of days and full of trouble,
> comes up like a flower and withers,
> flees like a shadow and does not last.
> Do you [God] fix your eyes on such a one?
> Do you bring me into judgment with you?

In regard to narrative we may say that a historical narrative is true if it presents an actual event in a way that helps us understand what took place and brings us into real contact with this event.

When speaking of this poetic or "making" function of art, philosophers often use the term "imitation." We should be careful, however, to understand that by "imitation" they mean the act by which one form of reality is brought into another kind of existence. Cézanne's painting of landscapes takes the actually existing field, with its trees and backdrop of mountains, and gives it another way of existing as line and color made of oil. If, for instance, someone were to say to you, "imitate this chair" and you were to make another chair, you have not imitated the chair in the poetic sense, but rather you have reproduced it. If however, you were to take a photograph of the chair or compose a lyric poem about it, you have imitated the chair. Your imitation would be poetically true if it brings someone to real knowledge of the chair.

Much of the Bible is written in the form either of poetry or of stories, and virtually all of it is written in literary forms rather than in what literary critics have called "mimetic" forms. Unfortunately the words "story," "poetry," and "literature" often suggest something pleasurable rather than true, and even frivolous or ornamental rather than serious. But biblical literature consists of expressions of the word of God that are more true and more serious than any other writings. In what follows, the focus will be especially on biblical poetry in the first part and biblical narrative in the second.

Truth in Poetry

1. Meaning in Poetry

The difficulty with literary forms of writing and speaking is that they always require interpretation because they say one thing but actually mean another. For example one might say that "Abraham Lincoln was ten feet tall," or a eulogy at a funeral might begin "Mary Smith is still very much alive among us." In each case a speaker has said one thing but everybody knows it meant something different. In order to understand a literary piece, then, one has both to understand precisely what was said and to note all the intended differences between words and meanings in order to construct out of the totality of these differences what one thing was meant.

We carry out this mental activity day in and day out without thinking of it or finding it problematic. Someone who cannot manage it is said to be "literal minded" and is understood to be deficient. That is why, for example, if one asks what is the meaning of an insult, an answer consisting in definitions of the words of the insult would be deficient.

This distance between words and meaning is not a frivolity; it is due, rather, to human intelligence. We want to communicate realities that are far too complex and too subtle to be directly "said." In saying Abraham Lincoln was ten feet tall we meant (and expressed rapidly) a lot of ideas: something of his integrity and talent, something of his measure in comparison with other persons, something of his role in history, something perhaps of his monument in Washington, something of our personal feeling about him. If we did not want to use literary forms of expression but preferred "mimetic" forms, we would have had to write a very long and boring paragraph in order to say all that. Mimetic writing is a way of imitation in which words are individually defined to correspond precisely to defined parts of reality. Phone books are mimetic, and so are scientific writing, philosophical writing, legal writing. Mimetic language uses a sharply defined vocabulary of technical words rather than suggestive words, and its logic attempts to follow the exact contours of the object it is discussing in order to achieve precision, control, and objectivity. Mimetic writing avoids subjective horizons and it tends to be disjointed, without image or feeling, in order to be materially and quantitatively accurate. These are precious qualities for some purposes, but this kind of writing is incapable of asserting the kinds of truth that are most vital to us. Vital truths are often composite, including both subjective and objective perspectives, and often they include transcendent dimensions, requiring a language that suggests and connects rather than one that dissects and reduces. Mimetic prose could describe something about patriotism, for example, but it would not be an apt instrument to express what is easily expressed in singing one's national anthem. Philosophy can discuss "god" but its conceptual control system, refined as it is, leaves it mimetically tracing human thought patterns without ever lifting off into an interpersonal awareness of transcendence such as is expressed in the most primitive of the psalms.

For this reason there is a major difference in the appropriate ways of reading literary texts and mimetic texts. To understand mimetic texts one must begin by understanding the technical meaning given to each word either by convention or by the author's explicit definition, and on that basis slowly build a larger picture. To understand literary texts, on the other hand, one must begin with the larger picture: the form of the whole literary piece and all the relations between the words and images and feelings of that piece. From that general understanding one can proceed to define the precise meaning of each word in the whole. Of course in reality we oscillate between understanding the whole and understanding the individual word, but ultimately understanding of a poem comes from the whole down to the parts. It is for this reason that literary criticism lays so much stress on first establishing the exact extent of the text to be understood and on reading the whole text. And it is for this reason that our commentary leads the reader to do two readings of the biblical book: one reading to see the whole, and a second to go into the details of the parts.

There is a second dimension of "meaning" that is helpful to note in reading literature. Meaning resides not only in the relations of words but also in the relation between the speaker and the hearer. If a stranger approaches you and tells you endless names and stories about his family you might say quite truly that it "means" nothing to you. Were he talking to his sister the talk might well have been about shared information, adding to, reformulating, correcting, and so forth, and thus it would have much meaning. But to you it has no meaning. Because he and his topic have no relation to you, you understand everything he says, but nothing of what he means.

Now if, on the other hand, he talked on in a way that, apart from giving information, included universal qualities of beauty and values such that they aroused your anger or sympathy or admiration, and so forth, then it would mean something to you. He has said all this in a way that even a stranger can relate to. He has shaped his words so as to give them meaning, that is, something that is shared with another person, in this case even a stranger. Literature usually has this character. When we observe that some people are boring we mean that they like the sound of their own voice without providing meaning as a relationship with hearers.

With this understanding of literature, that is, that its meaning goes beyond what it says and is shared between writer and reader, we can now ask how we might effectively read biblical poetry. We will suggest three practical questions that can be addressed to any literary text, the answers to which should lead the reader to understand the text and respond to it.

2. First Step in Reading Poetry

The first step in understanding a poem is to determine where it begins and ends and then to see it as a unified "word," perceiving the forms of its parts and their relations to each other. This is the question of *form.* It is a first step because only in this way is the reader prevented from reading his or her own perspectives and logics into the text. Reading begins with self-denial: getting beyond oneself by patiently noting how someone else (particularly someone from a different culture and era) organizes discussion of this topic in a way very different from our expectations.

This single aspect of form study can change one's experience of a text radically. For example, Exodus 15 shows Moses and the people of Israel singing a song after the Egyptians have perished in the Reed Sea. Many readers tend to repudiate this song because they are immediately offended by its violent language. It begins in v. 1b:

> Let me sing to Yhwh
> Yeah, hurrah, hooray!
> Horse and rider he has slammed into the sea!*

This is the first strophe of a song that continues through vv. 17-18. At the end YHWH brings Israel into his own mountain, his abode, his sanctuary, where YHWH is king forever. Read in isolation, v. 1 evokes in the reader very negative reactions against a violent God who is vengeful and full of anger, and when one points out the whole song with its general context, students or faithful biblical readers often suspect one of trying to explain the text away rather than trying to help them to see the text as it simply is. Had they begun by answering the question of form, and seen this verse as part of a whole poem from the beginning, no problem would have arisen. The whole poem is in the context of a liturgy in the Jerusalem Temple. There is no army in attendance; there are no corpses lying about. The congregation is marveling about the mystery of their liberation and their privilege of praising God in Jerusalem. They recall the power of YHWH that brings them there by evoking an event that has happened at least three hundred years prior to this moment. They sing a song of Moses and Israel of old as we might sing a song of King Arthur in England, or Jeanne d'Arc in France, or Spartacus in Italy. Their song is one that glories in the power of God, not in the violence of war.

*Author's translation.

Of course the study of literary forms in the Bible goes far beyond the question of the extent and unity of texts, and in this century scholars have succeeded in identifying and accurately describing numerous literary forms found in biblical texts. These discoveries have been very useful in bringing many texts alive. Unfortunately this work has not yet found expression in many translations of the Bible into our modern languages. Certainly the traditional division into chapters is not a good guide. Even liturgical lectionaries have been drawn up without attention to this basic aspect of meaning. Readers can find some help in commentaries where these are available.

In practical terms, when reading the Bible every effort should be made, first, to find out at least where units begin and end, so that one can read the units as units. Second, if the piece is not too long it is well worth the trouble to write it out carefully in sense lines (that is, one clause per line) and to mark divisions, repetition, and correspondences with highlighters or colored pencils. Then patient meditation will eventually break open the form of a text so that the reader can see how the author has organized a unified "word." If one is to read a text effectively in the liturgy this practice is very important.

One important clue for reading biblical poetry is the observation that the biblical text is not marked by rhyme and rhythm as English poems are. Rather biblical poetry is marked by parallel structures in which each line is followed by an exact parallel and the two are to be read together.

Sometimes a third parallel is added and the three are to be read together. It is important to grasp this principle by working through some concrete instances. For example, it will be helpful to read the speech of Eliphaz in Job 22 and to take the time to note how each verse has two parallel lines (technically called "stichs").

Most poems are not as mechanically parallel as Job 22. It will be useful to read Psalm 104 at this point, and to note, first, that it begins with the phrase "Bless the Lord, O my soul!" without providing a parallel stich, but then the whole poem ends with the same phrase (v. 35). This technique of beginning and ending a unit with the same words is a figure of speech called "inclusion." It is frequently used in the Bible and it gives us an important clue about how far a text extends. To return to the figure of parallel stichs, it should be easy to observe that the rest of v. 1 is structured with two parallel stichs, and vv. 2 and 4 each have two parallel stichs. Verse 5 has two stichs, but the second does not have a content parallel to the first. Verse 8 is the same. Verses 3 and 15 each have three parallel stichs.

The parallel form, then, is not rigid, and yet noting the parallels and noting how the poet has broken with them is a key to understanding the poem. For example, in v. 1 to say "O LORD my God, you are very great" is of itself so banal and abstract that it can mean anything or nothing, but the parallel stich moves to concrete images: it suggests that God's greatness is expressed in something as visible as clothing. The second stich by itself is flat, and the first by itself is flat, but the two read together create a special excitement, an expectation in the reader. Then in v. 2 the two stichs with their two separate and irreconcilable images of cloth together evoke a sense of admiration, whereas separately they are not very suggestive. If one takes the juxtapositions of the first four verses together there is a suggestion of the sun image as the most powerful metaphor for God's presence in our life. This technique of juxtaposition through parallel stichs is perhaps the most important key to the structure of biblical poetry. It is never a waste of time to be attentive to it.

One feels that some biblical poetry is more expressive than other biblical poetry. The difference is to be found often in the brilliance of images, often in the poet's power of evoking earlier biblical texts, but most often in the skilled use of parallel stichs to express by juxtaposition what a continuous line could never express.

3. Second Step in Reading Poetry

After one has grasped the form of the text and seen what it says, along with its pattern of internal relations, as a unified word, the question of *meaning* arises. What is the text about?

This question sounds as if it should be easy, but we often are surprised at difficulties in answering it. What is the text about? Poetry and other literary pieces frequently assemble a number of seemingly disparate realities and leave them juxtaposed without stating in so many words what is meant. Usually there are clues, such as the length of treatment or number of repetitions. Where has the author made special effort? It will help if the reader can distinguish what elements in the piece are conventional materials and what elements are unique and specially worked over. Where has the author walked a thin line? Attentive sensitivity to the text is needed for this, just as it is often needed in daily conversations: for example, if one is to guess what one's parent or child or friend is worked up about or intent upon. The individual reader is not alone in being attentive, since the whole Church collaborates in attending to Scripture.

If we return to Exodus 15 we may ask: where does the author seem to have made a special effort? Two answers leap to the eye. First, the expressions of divine power are remarkable in the first part of the poem: the violent language in vv. 1 and 3 and the archetypal images of vv. 5, 8, 10, and 12. Equally remarkable is the fact that v. 21 repeats verbatim the words of v. 1. This figure of speech ("inclusion") serves to form and mark a literary unit. In this case it serves to unite the song with a story of Miriam and all the women singing. Why was this added? It is clear what it says, but what does it mean?

One might conclude that Exod 15:1-21 is focused on something about the power of YHWH as revealed at the Reed Sea on the one hand, and about singing on the other. The literary unit evokes in the reader (that is, it "means") feelings of rejoicing in the power of YHWH and of praise to YHWH, both for intervention in the past and immense power in the present.

Often in reading a biblical text we are at a loss about the meaning. We know, however, that any biblical text, whatever its original source or purpose, is to be understood as saying something about God and humankind. It is not secular literature. It is, therefore, justified and often helpful to ask the question: in what realm of meaning or in what *social institution* is God expected to intervene?

In Exodus 15 the social institution is no longer the Reed Sea at all, though that is what the text says. It is something that interests Israel centuries later in Jerusalem. The word "king" is used, but of YHWH, not of a human being. The word "steadfast love" occurs in v. 13, a word often found in the context of covenant, but it is not prominent. To say the text is about covenant would be reading something into the text that is hardly there. Similarly there is nothing about election. The poem is resolutely about God's acts of power in freeing Israel, guiding Israel, and establishing Israel in Judah and Jerusalem. The "realm of meaning or social institution" here is not the monarchy, or the Law, or family ethics, or even the cult; rather, God is expected to intervene in the realm of national security. The poem is about celebrating God's power and intention to do this. Once we have identified what the poem is about we must read it again, taking time to savor it, because each of its parts will now come alive for us with new life and light.

One more remark about meaning must be made here. In the frequent case in which one biblical text cites an earlier passage one must take the trouble to study the earlier passage in order to recover its complex meaning. The author (for whom the earlier text was a familiar Scripture) evokes it here as a context for understanding and expressing his or her present meaning and integrating it into the religious experience of his or her tradition. This suggestiveness of many biblical texts is the source of much of their power, and it implies a recognition that the same divine mysteries are revealed successively in a variety of expressions and experiences. A familiar example of this may be found in Luke 4:16-21, where Jesus cites Isa 61:1-2 and applies it to himself. In order to experience the simple meaning of these verses one would need to have in one's heart the whole word of Isaiah and of the prophetic tradition, because Jesus meant all of that. That is what these words are about!

4. Third Step in Reading Poetry

After one has come to understand the biblical text as forming a single "word," perceive what it says, and know some of the fullness of its meaning, there arises a question about *reality.* What do we really believe and assent to here? This is the "so what?" question.

As we said above, literary texts have a dimension of meaning that subsists between the author and the reader. Originally the text was addressed to readers in the ancient Near East, in some one specific historical context, but successive writing of the sacred texts has addressed them to a series of contexts, and the full biblical canon has been received by the Church for readers throughout the centuries. There is a meaning between the author and the reader of any era, including today, and this meaning is felt as a demand on the reader.

Once again, it is not always easy to answer the "so what?" question. It is all too easy to let the demand remain subliminal and to pass it by. Often we love one novel or movie and tell everyone about it, and just hate another and reject it without caring to identify the reason. Rejection may have diverse forms: we may simply feel anger about a book or author, or we may start fighting certain ideas, or we may even simply have difficulty in keeping our eyes open! When what we are reading is a biblical text we should take such reactions seriously. Scholars may train themselves to react to literature on aesthetic grounds alone, but for most readers, and particularly in regard to biblical texts, the reaction to literature, either of accepting or rejecting it, will be due mostly to the demands it makes upon us. The Bible always makes such demands, often personal demands for action, whether they be political or ethical or spiritual. Faithful "listening" to the biblical text as word of God entails attending to its demands, making decisions, and carrying them out.

Personal demands are a subjective reality as they depend not only on literary meaning, but also on the personal context of the individual reader. Only that person can feel them and identify them. When one is drawn to a given text, this may be the invitation of grace; or if one is left cold by a biblical text this may be personal resistance to grace. The demands of a biblical text are indeed the word of God for an individual reader, and for this reason it is important to reflect critically on the meaning we think we have uncovered in the text, and then to reflect on our reaction to it: what precisely is God asking me to do or to be? and how do I react to this demand? Subsequent discernment of this experience is an important topic in spiritual direction.

Truth in Narrative

Among the forms of literature, narrative holds a special place in the Bible and in theology. We shall, therefore, make a special effort toward understanding its forms and its truth.

Have you ever wondered why so much of the Bible consists of stories? There are laws, and wisdom reflections, and songs of praise; there are letters, and words of exhortation and warning; still, most of the Bible is narrative. We read and hear about the deeds and words of Adam and Eve, of Abraham, Deborah, Moses, David, and so many more, especially Jesus. In and through the words of the Scriptures we are brought into contact with events that are not only human history but the revelation of God as well. This is the way Vatican II's *Constitution On Divine Revelation* expresses it:

> It pleased God, in his goodness and wisdom, to reveal himself and to make known the mystery of his will (cf. Eph 1:9), which was that people can draw near to the Father, through Christ, the Word made flesh, in the holy Spirit, and thus become sharers in the divine nature (cf. Eph 2:18; 2 Pet 1:4). . . . The pattern of this revelation unfolds through deeds and words which are intrinsically connected: the works performed by God in the history of salvation show forth and confirm the doctrine and realities signified by the words; the words, for their part, proclaim the works, and bring to light the mystery they contain (*Dei Verbum* §2).

In what follows we are going to reflect on that mysterious process by which the words of the biblical narratives "proclaim the works [of God] and bring to light the mystery they contain." In so doing we will learn how to appreciate the one mystery that gives meaning to all the others, namely the presence among us and the continued saving action of Jesus Christ, our Lord. This is the "mystery of his will" spoken about in the text above, that is, the plan of God as revealed.

1. The Nature of Narrative

Let us begin with a definition of narrative. Narrative is a literary presentation of a completed action. There are many types of literature: there is lyric poetry that expresses an interior emotion, there is description that presents some reality, but not as it moves through time, and there is chronicle, which does, it is true, give a list of happenings, but does not link them to form a story. Only narrative presents the whole event with its "beginning, middle, and end" in a way that recaptures the flow of the event and enables us to appreciate it.

Consider this example. Catherine of Siena was a woman of deep prayer who had a flaming love for God and for others, who combined firm chastity with deep compassion, and who was courageous in her commitments. That is a brief description of Catherine of Siena. One could also write a lyric poem about this saint, mediating the depth of one's own admiration for her and the qualities God gave her. One might even give a list of the principal events of her life in a way that illustrates what was said in the description; that is, one could compose a chronicle of her life. Suppose, however, someone were to tell you this story:

> Catherine used to visit a young man who was in prison for murder. At first he mocked her efforts to speak to him of God's mercy, but then, won over by her repeated visits and her care for him, he listened and was reconciled to God. On the day of his execution Catherine accompanied him to the place where he was to be decapitated. As he mounted the stage he was overcome with fear. Catherine helped him kneel down and then held his head against her breast, consoling and strengthening him in his desire to give up his life in reparation to God. She thus held him as he died.

Catherine's gesture somehow reaches you through the words of the story, the narrative, and you can see for yourself what kind of a person she was. In that gesture you come to a direct and intuitive knowledge of this human being who manifests herself by her action. In the word of the Council, her deed and the story's words are "connected" and combine to reveal something of what God had made of this saint. A better storyteller might have mediated this action in more telling words, but the same deed, perhaps in that case more vividly represented, would reach you and affect you. This is the heart of narrative: it is, to repeat, a literary presentation of a completed action. Let us now consider other aspects of narrative.

2. The Levels of Narrative

If we could use an x-ray on a narrative text we would discover that lying underneath the actual text are several layers that, for our purposes, may be reduced to three: event, plot, and "organization." The *event* is "what happened"; it may be something the narrator makes up or borrows from the story tradition of the culture, or, as in our example, it may be a historical happening. The event, as you have just experienced, is somehow present in and through the words. In our example the event is the action of Catherine in winning the young man over, his reconciliation with God, and Catherine's consoling and helping him at his death. On the second level this event must be given shape, that is, its *plot* must be discerned and presented. The action had to be lifted out of the lives of both Catherine and the young man, its own beginning, middle, and end had to be grasped and then made the framework of the narrative. To do this well is the art of storytelling, as Aristotle observed long ago. Finally there is the more complex layer lying just below the surface of the narrative text. It may be called *organization.* Organization refers to the whole complex of images, allusions, resonances and associations, flow of thought and feeling created by the words. It is at this level that the narrative interprets the event in an important way. If *event* may be compared to a room, then *plot* is the architecture of the room and *organization* is its furniture.

The understanding of layers in narrative is very important in making out what the inspired authors are doing when they recount an event. Every narrator is an interpreter, and those whom the Holy Spirit instructed and inspired are no exception. In fact the ancients, who had a much more sophisticated understanding of this law of narrative than we do with our mechanical view of history writing, took their responsibility very seriously.

To illustrate this point let us take as an example the incident recounted in chs. 13 and 14 of the book of Numbers and compare it with the same event recounted in the book of Deuteronomy (Deut 1:19–2:1). We read in the book of Numbers that the Lord commanded Moses to send spies to reconnoiter the land the Lord had promised to give to the people. Upon their return they gave a vivid account of the fertility of the land but concluded that the inhabitants were too powerful for the Israelites: "We are not able to go up against this people, for they are stronger than we" (Num 13:31). Only Caleb urged the people to rely on the Lord and to go up and take the land in obedience to God's word. The people listened to the other spies and refused to go up. As a result they were condemned to wander for forty years in the desert.

The author of the book of Deuteronomy makes Moses the narrator of this event. In his speech to the people just as, finally, they are about to enter the land, Moses reviews their past. In recounting this event he tells it differently. This time the spies are sent because the people are reluctant to obey Moses. They are afraid simply to go and take the land God had promised them. The report of the spies is only in favorable terms: "It is a good land that the LORD our God is giving us" (Deut 1:25). Moses describes the people's reaction to this report: "But you were unwilling to go up. You rebelled against the command of the LORD your God; you grumbled in your tents" (Deut 1:26-27). It is only in the grumbling of the people that we hear of the difficulties reported by the spies. By having the people suggest the sending of spies and by omitting the negative part of the spies' report the narrator has interpreted the event, accenting the greatness of Israel's sin in refusing to trust the Lord. In other words, the *event* in the two narratives is the same, and so is the basic *plot;* the organization of the material, however, changes its accent and provides a striking interpretation.

The reader is invited to apply this mode of understanding to the gospels, especially the synoptics, where once again we may see the same *event* (this time in the life of Jesus) structured by the same *plot* and yet interpreted with different nuances because of the way in which each gospel author organizes the narrative. Look, for instance, at the story of the centurion's boy in Matt 8:5-13 and Luke 7:1-10. More remarkable still, compare the three narratives of the one event of the healing of Peter's mother-in-law (Matt 8:14-15; Mark 1:29-31; Luke 4:38-39). In these three brief anecdotes (Matthew's account has only thirty words!) we can see concentrated some of the theological principles that govern the whole of each individual gospel. Notice that only Matthew's account tells us that the house belongs to Peter, that Jesus needs no one to intervene on the woman's behalf, and that, once cured, she rises and serves only *him* (rather than the whole group as in Mark and Luke). Note as well that in Luke, Jesus' method of healing is not to take hold of the woman's hand (Matthew) and raise her up (Mark), but rather to rebuke the fever, treating it as he does demons in other parts of the gospel. Each of these differences, and there are several more, is part and parcel of the theological understanding of Jesus possessed by the individual evangelists. We will return to consider this more at length.

3. Point of View

When we go to see a film we seldom advert directly to the fact that the director has managed to tell the story not only through the actions and words of the actors but also, and to an important degree, by the angle or point of view he or she obliges us to take by his or her use of the camera: do we see a panoramic view as the hero rides on to the conflict, or do we see the expressions on the faces of the hero, the heroine, their adversary? Probably in a well-directed film we see all three in a mounting crescendo. This is part of the narrative art of the director. Literary stories also have a point of view; in fact, they have more than one. We can reduce to three the number of points of view that are important in understanding biblical narrative. There is first of all the *size of the action:* How much of the story should I tell? Then there is the *position of the narrator:* Where does the storyteller stand as he or she recounts the tale? Finally, in regard to nonfiction narratives, there is the *vision of history:* What is the place in history of the event being narrated? Let us say a few words about each of these.

The *size of the action* is determined by the narrator. One could imagine the story about Catherine being much longer and including more of the lives of Catherine and the young man, both before and, in the case of Catherine, after the incident. Actually, most narratives contain many incidents or episodes that are skillfully bound together to make up an overall action. A striking example of this is the Joseph story in chs. 37–50 of the book of Genesis. There each incident builds on its predecessor until the narrator lifts the veil and we see a divine perspective on a tawdry tale, one that anticipates the mystery of Jesus' betrayal and its consequences: "And now do not be distressed, or angry with yourselves, because you sold me here; for God sent me before you to preserve life" (Gen 45:5). Other long narratives are made up of anecdotes that could stand alone but in fact do not. Think, for instance, of the episodes in the books of Samuel and Kings, and especially those in the synoptic gospels.

In some narratives the one telling the story is clearly standing between us and what is being recounted; in others the narrator is hardly perceptible at all. We can describe this difference by speaking of "telling" a story or "showing" a story: this is what is meant by the *position of the narrator.* When an author "tells" a story he or she addresses us directly and we are conscious of the narrator's presence throughout: this is often the case in the two books of Maccabees. In a "showing" narrative we are concentrated upon the action and watch it unfold before our eyes, so to speak. This is the perspective most often adopted by biblical narratives because all the attention is fixed upon the act of God being manifested through the actions of the human beings involved in the event. Thus in ch. 17 of the first book of Samuel we read the story of David and Goliath. After a report that locates the warring camps Goliath steps upon the scene and we see him swagger and taunt, arrayed for war like few men before him. The action slows down to present the three sons of Jesse and explain the unexpected presence of young David in the camp; he hears of the challenge and the reward offered by Saul to the one who could kill Goliath. David's confident speech to Saul is framed by mentioning two obstacles: the angry attempt of David's brothers to prevent him from accepting the challenge and the encumbering equipment Saul tries to put on David. Then the pace of the story picks up. There on the battlefield between the two camps the giant, outfitted with all his profession provides, continues to boast and taunt and threaten while David, armed with his faith in God, runs toward him and slings his stone. Then the lens "zooms" and we watch as "the stone embedded itself in his brow" and the giant slumps to the ground. As David cuts off Goliath's head with the man's own sword we see played out before our eyes how "Some take pride in chariots, and some in horses, but our pride is in the name of the LORD our God" (Ps 20:7[8]). In the words of the narrative text, God is revealed in deeds.

One of the most remarkable aspects of biblical narrative is to be found in its *vision of history;* this is the third point of view we wish to discuss. For the world outside the Bible the past is past. The writing of history may be useful, but far less useful even than poetry (according to Aristotle) because it treats of individual events rather than general principles that alone are worth serious reflection. History for the extra-biblical world can be used to justify a present situation, the ascendancy of a certain people for example, but its greatest utility lies in preserving the achievements of great people who can serve as our examples. For this reason the most popular form of history was biography. Plutarch, one of the most prolific biographers of antiquity, says that he writes the lives of famous men because their virtues serve as a sort of looking glass in which he can see how to adjust and adorn his own life. Indeed, association in this way with these noble characters frees him from the ignoble and vicious impressions contracted by contact with lesser company, and he hopes it will do the same for his readers *(Life of Timoleon).* The principal purpose of history, then, is to serve one's efforts at self-improvement.

For the biblical world history is the theater where God and the divine plan of salvation stand revealed. The past is not merely past; it lives in the praise of God's people and continually makes present in their memory the great things God has done:

> things that we have heard and known,
> that our ancestors have told us.
> We will not hide them from their children;
> we will tell to the coming generation
> the glorious deeds of the LORD, and his might,
> and the wonders that he has done.
> He established a decree in Jacob,
> and appointed a law in Israel . . .
> that the next generation might know them,
> the children yet unborn,
> and rise up and tell them to their children,
> so that they should set their hope in God,
> and not forget the works of God (Ps 78:3-7).

In the biblical understanding of history to remember God's acts is to have them so present that they affect the actions of the present. To "forget the works of God" as the psalm expresses it does not mean that they slip one's mind; it means rather that what God has accomplished for the people no longer has an active role in changing them and determining their conduct: they no longer "set their hope in God."

Because of this different vision of history the point of view of biblical narrative manifests a unique understanding of reality. The principal protagonist of history is God, who is always present to God's people. Thus narratives of divine activity in the past are always endowed with a present actuality. This explains the role of liturgy in which God's acts are remembered and responded to in praise and sacrifice, and it also explains why narrative is the principal vehicle of transmitting revelation. Luke tells Theophilus that he is writing an "orderly account of the events that have been fulfilled among us" so that Theophilus "may know the truth concerning the things about which [he has been] instructed" (Luke 1:1-4), and John says that he wrote "so that you may come to believe that Jesus is the Messiah, the Son of God, and that through believing you may have life in his name" (John 20:31). These NT authors are firmly in the line of the ancient narrators who made the deeds of God present to their audiences in order that through faith, which is always a response to revelation, they might live in the knowledge of God and in obedience to God's will.

We see understanding of history not only in the narratives themselves but in the remarks, the asides the narrators make in order to be sure that their hearers and readers understand the purpose of what is being told them. When the story of David's adultery and his murder of Uriah is narrated, not only is the irony of David's calculated malice set out there for all to see, but the author from his faith perspective tells us, "the thing that David had done displeased the LORD" (2 Sam 11:27). Again the overriding power of God's direction of history is pointed out by highlighting the fulfillment of God's word: Hiel lost (by child sacrifice?) his firstborn son when he laid the foundations in rebuilding Jericho, and he lost his youngest son when he set up the gates, "according to the word of the LORD, which he spoke by Joshua son of Nun" (1 Kings 16:34; for the prophecy see Josh 6:26). The final act of the disaster that befell Israel is narrated in ch. 17 of the second book of Kings and is concluded by this remark: "The LORD removed Israel out of his sight, as he had foretold through all his servants, the prophets" (2 Kings 17:23). Examples of these directive remarks abound in OT narratives that still manage to maintain their "showing" point of view.

4. Summary Description of Narrative in the Bible

Before moving on to discuss the very special role of narrative in the gospels, and by way of preparation for that discussion, we will stop to consider here what we have learned about narrative and why it is such a powerful means of transmitting revelation.

First, about revelation itself: we have seen that it is accomplished through the action of God, making known and communicating both God's very self and a knowledge of the divine plan of salvation. This action is transmitted to us by words, honored in praise, described in moral exhortation, and re-presented in narrative. The real significance of this light of revelation can only be appreciated in the power of another light, namely that of faith, itself an act of God within us to which we yield. As the psalmist says: "In your light [of faith], we see light [of revelation]" (Ps 36:[9]10).

Next, narrative, because it presents an action, is particularly revelatory and this is the quality that makes it the most prominent form of literature in the Bible. Recall how Catherine "revealed" herself through the action told of her, and what is made known of God by narrating God's activity in the life of David and so many others whose stories are told in the Scriptures. The very thing that Aristotle thought was unimportant turns out to be the most important aspect of life. Human beings, and even God, communicate themselves most perfectly through individual actions and events.

Then, because narrative has many levels we can appreciate that for the biblical authors the retelling of an episode is the occasion of interpreting it by presenting the same event and plot by means of a differently organized narration. Regarding point of view, we have seen how the Bible is careful to sculpt individual narratives or anecdotes even when these form part of a larger action so that we can appreciate the ever-present activity of God in the midst of God's people. The stylistic characteristic of "showing" us the action rather than "telling" us about it adds to the revelatory power of biblical narrative. The humility and discretion of the authors allow us to come into direct contact with the action of God. Finally, the revealed understanding of the nature of history embodied in biblical narrative prepares us to receive the unique power of the Scriptures to make the Lord present to us. Now let us try to apply all this to the narrative dimension of the gospels.

5. The Narrative Time of the Gospels

The most important thing we must bear in mind about the gospel narratives is that they were not written to enshrine or promote or defend the memory of a dead and revered master but to put us in touch with the living Lord. Because he is risen from the dead, stories about Jesus are different from stories about any other person. It is true that God is present in the narratives of the OT that recount divine action through the great people and events of Israel's history, an action to be continued and fulfilled in a vaguely perceived future. However, Christians perceive that the presence of God in Jesus Christ is unique, and the fact that Jesus is alive means that he is both present to history and beyond it.

In order to understand the significance of this fact for the understanding of the gospel narratives we must bear in mind the fact that for Jesus in his humanity, as for any human being, death sets the seal on life. All that we have lived through, all the relations that we have in this life continue to be part of us after death. The fact that in our regard some of these events and relationships may still have the disorder of sin attached to them is the basis for the Catholic teaching about the need for purification after death. In fact it is only when we have been brought into the presence of God in a definitive and eternal manner that the events of our life take on their true significance. In the case of Jesus, of course, there is no question of sin, but there is the added fact that he exists now in a glorified and transformed humanity that nevertheless is the same humanity he had while on earth. All that makes his history is now part of his glorified existence.

That is why the book of Revelation speaks of him even now as a Lamb who still bears the marks of having been slain (Rev 5:6).

The importance of this fact for the interpretation of the narratives about Jesus is incalculable. Whereas both OT and NT narratives are written in ways that make their meaning applicable to subsequent generations, what is unique about the gospel is that it is about Jesus the Lord. All that Jesus Christ did and suffered still lives on in his glorified humanity and it is there that these events take on their full meaning. This fact was well known to the gospel writers who in subtle ways lead us to understand the significance of these events for us now as we are brought, through the text, into contact with the Lord who is alive. Let us consider some examples of this procedure. The disciples' cry for help during the storm at sea is recorded by Mark as a moment of panic: "Teacher, do you not care that we are perishing?" (Mark 4:38), but the same address to Jesus in Matthew is couched in liturgical terms, most probably those of Matthew's own community, still present in the Byzantine rite: *"Kyrie sōson:* Lord, save us! We are perishing!" (Matt 8:25). By having the disciples cry out in the prayer of his community Matthew establishes the link between them and every generation of believers who still relate to a Jesus who is alive.

Sometimes the words of Jesus are so contextualized that they are obviously intended by the author to apply to future generations. This can be appreciated, for instance, in the exhortation to vigilance found in Jesus' agony in the garden. It is not only the original disciples but every generation of believers overcome by somnolence, fear, and lack of understanding who hear the words of the now risen Christ: "Keep awake and pray that you may not come into the time of trial; the spirit indeed is willing, but the flesh is weak" (Mark 14:38). Sometimes what has been transmitted in the tradition is changed to show its application to the contemporary situation. This is exemplified in the Matthean version of traditional material also found in Luke 13:26-27. In Luke, Jesus, as part of his admonition about the narrow door, warns his listeners that even though "then" they will appeal to the fact that they ate and drank with him and that he preached in their streets, they will be rejected. In Matt 7:22-23 the same appeal to a special claim on Jesus is presented in terms that fit the post-Easter disciples: "Lord, Lord, did we not prophesy in your name, and cast out demons in your name, and do many deeds of power in your name?" The warning follows: judgment will be based on whether or not one has done the will of the Father.

An attentive reading of the NT will demonstrate the truth of the assertion that gospel writers have their gaze turned in two directions as they tell of the life of Jesus: they look backward to events as they occurred in the life of Jesus and they look upward where, in faith, they see these events now completed in the resurrected humanity of this same Jesus. If we apply what we have established about narrative we can see how the events narrated are revelation. In the narrative Jesus' actions are present to us, and in these actions—the healing of a blind man, the forgiving of a sinful woman, and many more—Jesus reveals not only himself but the Father as well: "Whoever has seen me has seen the Father" (John 14:9). Each NT theologian may interpret the events somewhat differently while mediating the same reality: this is the process we spoke about previously as "organization." You will notice the three dimensions of point of view in the various short narratives, each with an event to mediate, a "showing" mode of mediating it, and a vision of history that is unique to the Christian faith.

It is at this point that we can see how the narrative function of the gospel accounts coalesces with the Church's life of worship in the liturgy. As the year progresses we celebrate the various actions of Jesus: his birth, manifestation, temptations, suffering, death, resurrection, ascension, and sending of the Holy Spirit. All of these actions, because they exist in their completed and transformed state in the risen humanity of Jesus, are still sources of grace for us. The very center of this transformed historical activity is the act of love in which Christ died and in which he is now fixed forever. This is the secret of the liturgical life of the Church. In a similar way these actions, and especially the cross and resurrection, reach us in and through the gospel text. Both the liturgy and the sacred text lead us into the mystery, that is, into the plan of God as it was revealed in Jesus' earthly life and now shines gloriously in heaven even as it is being worked out in the successive generations of the Church until we all arrive at resurrection. Because of this mystery the action in the narrative makes both the past and the future present to us. Because of the risen humanity of Jesus Christ, who suffered so as to enter his glory, narrative, that most human mode of communication, has become a means of bringing us into contact with our living Lord who is the source of our life.

Unleashing the Power of the Bible

Introduction

Virgil Howard and Patricia LeNoir

Each separate part of this article deals in one way or another with the living and dynamic relationship between the Bible and the Church under the rubric: "Unleashing the power of the Bible." The assumption behind the title is that while most Christians would agree, however diverse their terminology, logic, and conclusions, that the Church is borne, guided, and nourished by the Bible, even to the point that it can speak of the Bible as "the word of God," there is nonetheless also some sense in which institutional churches can limit and distort this same Scripture in their effort to energize and norm the faith and ministry of the Church. How can this be and what can the Church do to reform its life in this matter?

Scripture and the Power of God

Paul speaks of Christ as "the power of God" (1 Cor 1:24), the One in whom God effects reconciliation between the creation and its Creator (Rom 5:10-11; 2 Cor 5:18-19; Col 1:20), right relationship between the world and God (Rom 3:21-26; 2 Cor 5:21; Phil 1:11), peace between God and humankind (Rom 5:1; 1 Cor 16:11; Eph 2:14, 17; 6:15), a new creation (2 Cor 5:17; Gal 6:15; 2 Pet 3:13; Rev 21:5). But he can use the same remarkable designation to describe the kerygma of the cross (1 Cor 1:18) and the gospel itself (Rom 1:16). In other words, what makes Christ present participates in the same divine power as what is at work in Christ. Small wonder, then, that the Church has recognized in Scripture this very same "power of God" at work, for in Scripture the Church has been entrusted with the transforming vision of God's healing of the creation. Whether recounted in stories of exodus and covenant or of crucifixion and resurrection, whether expressed in images of vineyard and *shalom* or the reign of God, whether creating and addressing the people of God in the form of Israel or the Church, the vision attested to in Scripture does not merely report and celebrate the new, restored creation, but embodies it in such a way that each new generation is able to experience it as call and gift and claim. The vision is made present in such a way that God can continue to work through it for the healing of creation. The vision of the new creation calls into question the world "as it is" and replaces it with the world in which "righteousness and peace will kiss each other" (Ps 85:10). The Bible, like Christ and the gospel, is the power of God at work for salvation, the restoration and renewal of the creation.

But if this is so, what sense can it make to speak of "unleashing" the power of the Bible? If the Bible really is the power of God, does Isaiah not speak the final word?

> For as the rain and the snow come down from heaven,
> and do not return there until they have watered the earth,
> making it bring forth and sprout,
> giving seed to the sower and bread to the eater,
> so shall my word be that goes out from my mouth;
> it shall not return to me empty,
> but it shall accomplish that which I purpose,

> and succeed in the thing for which I sent it
> (Isa 55:10-11).

Again a comparison with Jesus is instructive. The image of Jesus as the "incarnation" of God includes expressions both of authority and majesty (John 1:14-18; Col 1:19) and of powerlessness and vulnerability (Mark 6:5; Luke 13:34-35; Acts 10:37-39). Similarly, Scripture participates not only in the power of its Christ but also in his powerlessness, not only in his authority but in his abuse. Scripture shares the fate of its Christ insofar as it, too, is subject to misunderstanding, unbelief, rejection, and violence—and, as in the case of Jesus, all of this can happen not only at the hands of outsiders but also at the hands of those who profess faith and love. Unfortunately it is all too easy to point to historical instances in which the power of Scripture has been misused to justify wars, pogroms, and torture, especially against Jews, but also against other ethnic and religious groups; the evils of slavery and of continued violence against people of color; the preservation of economic and political privilege for the few and the misery of the many; the blessing of domestic violence against children and women; the denial of full human rights for women and persons with disabilities. Not as violent, but nearly as debilitating, is the purely formal and perfunctory use of Scripture one can frequently observe in churches, as well as the indifference to widespread ignorance of the Scriptures in some segments of the Church.

Perhaps, then, an initial step in liberating Scripture to accomplish its work of further empowering God's healing of the creation is for those of us who love Scripture and have been called to share it with those entrusted to our care to acknowledge our own power to facilitate *and* to frustrate Scripture in its mission. Such an acknowledgment, however, leads at once to the question of how those who guide the Church can help it more effectively to *join* Scripture in its redeeming work. How can we put ourselves more fully at the disposal of the power of God?

An initial response, perhaps not as self-evident as it might at first sound, is that *the Church will more fully participate with Scripture in God's redemptive work the more fully we are committed to the radicality and richness of the biblical vision of God's ministry to the creation.* This includes at least commitment to its holistic, transformative, and inclusive character.

(1) *The holistic character of the biblical vision.* One of the great gifts of the Bible is its stubborn insistence on the living and dynamic interrelatedness of all things. This begins already with the biblical perception of the relationship between God and the world and determines the way in which any particular aspect of reality is approached. Thus while both testaments are careful to distinguish between God and what God has created, they are also incapable of speaking about the one without the other. One finds no detached, scientific explanations of the world nor any merely utilitarian cataloging of "natural resources" because "the earth is the LORD's, and all that is in it" (Ps 24:1) and it is therefore unthinkable to say "earth" without at the same time saying "LORD." On the other hand, philosophical or theological speculation about God "as such" is equally foreign to the Bible since God is, after all, the One who feeds the birds and clothes the grass (Matt 6:25-33) and the One who observes misery and hears cries of oppression and knows sufferings and comes down to deliver (Exod 3:7-12) and it is therefore unthinkable to say "God" without at the same time saying "world." And every other aspect of creation participates in this fundamental interrelatedness of Creator and creation.

Nothing, then, is *either* sacred *or* secular, but everything is to be viewed in terms of the interdependence of both and each one's potential for serving as a vehicle of the other. Nothing is *either* physical *or* spiritual, but everything manifests both dimensions. No human being is *either* a social *or* an individual being, but each aspect qualifies and defines the other. It is not *either* Church *or* world for neither can live and flourish apart from the other and they find their fulfillment only in their relationship to each other. God's word for the creation is not *either* grace *or* judgment, for one without the other is distortion and only both together make clear the depth of the divine commitment to the creation. Whenever the Church gives in to the age-old temptation of dualistic thinking, its hearing is impaired and Scripture is pressed into the service of foreign philosophical and religious categories. Its vision of the rich and complex web of interrelatedness and interdependence and mutuality and wholeness becomes clouded and one-sided, ignoring important aspects of the world and God's activity in it. To read and honor the Bible's unitive vision of reality can help the Church to guard against the fragmentation of its own life. It is a way of welcoming Scripture to do its work and of anticipating that moment when God will finally "gather up all things in [Christ]" (Eph 1:10).

(2) *The transformative character of the biblical vision.* If it is true that Scripture is a manifestation of the power of God at work for the healing of creation, then the hermeneutical question: What does this passage of Scripture *mean?* must be accompanied by another question: What does this passage of Scripture *do?* And while there are certainly passages that seem to intend to establish and confirm the existing structures and practices, it is clear that the real dynamic in the Bible is toward transformation and renewal. The biblical writers did not understand themselves to be assembling and passing on religious information, though one can read many passages for that purpose and benefit from them. Nor did they regard themselves as historians in anything like the Enlightenment sense of the word, though again one can read the Bible for its interpretation of history and profit from it. Finally, the writers understood themselves to be recounting the Story of God and the creation, of God's dream for the earth and especially for the human family, of God's unceasing and gentle reclamation and restoration of a creation alienated from itself and its Creator. Along with tellings and retellings of the Story are meditations and sermons on it, celebrations of it and interpretations of it for daily living. All of these aim at placing the reader-hearer in the presence of the Story of God in a way that he or she is invited to become part of God's Story by claiming his or her part in it. The Bible never ponders whether or not the reader-hearer is included in the story; the only question is whether the reader-hearer will recognize her or his place in the story and claim it and live it. But that means to change worlds. To read-hear *as Scripture* "A wandering Aramean was my ancestor . . ." is to *become* one who has gone down into Egypt and been treated harshly and cried out and been brought out by the mighty hand of God, or to *become* one who treated the Aramean harshly, one from whom the ancestor had to be freed (Deut 26:1-15). In either case one is called to enter God's Story and ask what that means here and now for the way one makes decisions and values things. To read *as Scripture* that "Jesus came to Galilee, proclaiming the good news of God . . ." is to enter into a new time, one that is "fulfilled," that is full of God, and to ask what it means to now live completely in that gracious presence (Mark 1:14-15).

One way, then, to help unleash the power of the Bible is to practice hearing it as the invitation to rethink and realign our own story or time or world or self in light of the biblical vision, to participate in our own transformation into that new creation, to allow ourselves now to be moved by its values and commitments and hope. The interpreter, priest or pastor or teacher or preacher, who has learned to approach Scripture in full awareness of entering into a transformative moment will want to make that same kind of experience available to others.

(3) *The inclusive character of the biblical vision.* If the Bible's perception of God and creation is holistic and its intention is the transformation of this world into the new creation, then it is also clear that nothing can be excluded from its vision. Inclusiveness is not based in human good will or largesse but in the divine will for the creation. Thus while Israel constantly struggled to understand its relationship with other nations and as a socio-political entity was often at odds and even at war with them, it could never completely forget that its election was related to their well-being (Gen 12:3; Isa 49:6). The "stranger" enjoys special protection under the law (Deut 10:18-19; 16:11, 14; 24:19-21; cf. Ps 146:9; Job 29:16), and special attention is given to the most vulnerable in Israel's own society (Deut 24:17-21; Ps 68:5). The Church in the New Testament is described as a community of the Spirit in which distinctions because of gender, age, or social class (Acts 2:16-21 citing Joel 2:28-32; Gal 3:28) are set aside. Jesus is consistently portrayed as one who disregarded boundaries between clean and unclean, rich and poor, Jew and Gentile, men and women, in order to unite the human family in the reign of God. And the early Church struggled to find a faith language that could be shared by Jew and Gentile alike. In these and countless other ways Scripture refuses to allow any person or group of persons to fall outside the purview of God's radical love.

Nor does the radical inclusivity of the biblical vision stop with the human family, for "the creation itself will be set free from its bondage to decay and will obtain the freedom of the glory of the children of God" (Rom 8:21). While nature proclaims the glory of God (Pss 19:1-4; 104:5; 145:11) and gives God thanks (Ps 145:10), it also waits for "good news" and restoration (Isa 11:6-9; 35:1; Rev 22:1-2). (See article on "The Bible and Ecology.")

There are other ways to describe the richness of the biblical vision; these are intended to be suggestive. What is crucial for freeing Scripture to do its work is that the Church be constantly attentive for ways to commit itself to Scripture's vision of God's healing work. But what does that look like in the actual ministry of the Church?

Scripture and the Church

The ministry of the word takes many forms, including evangelization, catechesis, liturgical celebration, and theology (*General Catechetical Directory* 17). Scripture as "the church's support and strength, imparting robustness to . . . faith . . . , food for . . . souls . . . a pure and unfailing fount of spiritual life" (*Dogmatic Constitution on Divine Revelation* VI, 21) has a decisive voice in the definition of ministry and empowering of it.

Evangelization, the proclamation of the reign of God inaugurated by Jesus of Nazareth (Matt 4:17-23; Mark 1:14-15; Luke 11:20), is at the very core of the Church's mission. From the beginning the Church heralded to all the world the gospel of God's reign, God's reconciliation of the world to Godself (Matt 28:16-20; Rom 9:9-17; 2 Cor 5:16-20; 2 Tim 4:5). A major focus of evangelism is the sharing of the biblical story of God's grace with those who have never heard or appropriated that story for themselves. But evangelism in the biblical sense is inseparable from everything else the Church does, for sharing the gospel can mean sharing of healing (Matt 10:1, 8), food (Matt 14:13-21 and parallels), and forgiveness (Matt 9:8; Luke 24:47; John 20:23).

Catechesis, "that form of ecclesial action which leads both communities and individual members of the faithful to maturity of faith" (*General Catechetical Directory* 21), draws on a long biblical tradition. Study, learning, and teaching have always been a vitally important expression of faith for Israel (Deuteronomy 6; Psalm 119 are typical). Jesus carried on this emphasis, teaching his disciples as well as the crowds (Matt 5:1-2; 7:18; 9:35; 13:1-58) and called others into a ministry of teaching (Matt 13:51-52; 28:19-20; John 21:15-19). Paul regarded teaching as a gift of the Spirit (1 Cor 12:8, 29) and the author of 1 and 2 Timothy regards it as a fixed item of pastoral duties (2 Tim 4:2, 5). Because faith has a content and a tradition that deserve to be conserved and passed on, because the Christian community draws upon the stories of faith from the past to form its own character, because the people of God require tutelage in reading and praying the Scriptures for themselves and their families, Christian education is crucial.

Liturgical celebration is at the very heart of the Church's life. This was true for Israel as one can clearly see from the amount of material in the Hebrew Bible devoted to explaining the origins of worship (Exod 3:12; 12:1-32; 13:1-6) or describing patterns of worship (Deut 26:1-11; Isa 6:1-13) or warning against worship separated from the doing of justice (Amos 5:21-24; Mic 6:1-8; Isa 58:5-14). The same was true for the early Church (Acts 2:41-47; Rom 12:1-2; 1 Corinthians 11 and 14). In worship the Church experiences again the self-giving of God to the world supremely in Jesus Christ, and our own human response to God's gift in celebration and commitment to service. Along with the Eucharist, the homily serves as a major focal point for articulating this experience. (See article on "The Bible and Preaching.")

Theology in the more restricted sense of systematic and critical reflection on the truth of the Christian faith permeates both testaments. It is modeled in Acts 15 and enjoined in 1 Peter 3:15. The Church's theologians are servants of the word and of those who live by the word. The goal of theological reflection is to aid the faithful to think and speak and act more responsibly in light of faith. In other words theology leads to a more perfect love for God and God's creation.

Other phases of the Church's ministry could also be mentioned in the context of the ministry of the word. For example the ministry of *social justice and peace,* basic to and interwoven throughout all the ministries already named, represents also a major focus of ecclesial energy. There are very few writings in the Hebrew Bible that do not speak in one way or another about God's concern for justice and peace in the world (Exod 20:1-17; 2 Sam 12:1-15; Isa 58:5-14; Amos 5:21-24; Mic 4:1-4; 6:1-8). According to Luke's gospel Jesus defined his own ministry in terms of Isaiah's vision (Luke 4:18-19) and the Church attempted to embody this vision in its own life (Acts 6:1-6; Matt 25:31-46; Jas 1:26-27; 2:14-26). In its work for social justice the Church joins Jesus with the disprivileged and needy. *Pastoral care* to persons in various crisis situations, illness and death, bereavement and despair, marriage and family crises, is another way in which the Church joins Jesus in ministry. Jesus cared for persons in a variety of ways. He healed, taught, ate with sinners, and laid down his life for the sake of the world (Mark 2:1-11; John 10:11-30; 13:1-11). In imitation of him the Church of the New Testament cared for members of the Body of Christ (Matt 18:10-35; Acts 2:43-47; 1 Corinthians 12–14; Phil 2:5-11; 1 Tim 5:17-22). As members of Christ's body all Christians are called to live a life of caring for the other members of the Church and the whole human family.

No less than the ministry of the word, the Church's ministry of sacrament is shaped and energized and deepened by Scripture. Sacramental celebrations ritualize significant moments in the life of the faith community and in the lives of individual members. The people of God know that these are special moments. These are people gatherings around word, water, oil, light, bread, wine. These are people gatherings in which the faithful process, bless, stand, sit, kneel, respond, sing, pray, listen. These are people gatherings for the old, the young, the married, the single, the wanted and the unwanted, the joyful and the sorrowful. Scripture reminds the Church in its celebration of the Eucharist of the multifaceted richness of the sacrament: as an expression of *joyful thanksgiving* (Matt 26:26-27; cf. Mark 14:22-23; Luke 22:17-19; 1 Cor 11:24-25), of *commemoration* or *remembrance* (1 Cor 11:24; Luke 22:19 [longer text]), of *communion* (1 Cor 10:16-18), of *sacrifice* (Matt 26:28; Luke 22:20 [longer text]; 1 Cor 11:25; Heb 9:14; 13:15), of *Christ's presence* (Matt 26:26, 28; 1 Cor 10:16) of *proclamation* and *eschatological consummation* (1 Cor 11:26). Scripture offers a similar wealth of images in connection with baptism: *union with Jesus Christ* (Rom 6:1-11; Gal 3:27; Eph 1:13), *incorporation into the Church* (1 Cor 12:4, 13; Gal 3:28; 1 Pet 2:10), *gift of the Holy Spirit* (Acts 2:1; John 3:5; Titus 3:5; Eph 1:13), a washing symbolizing the *forgiveness of sin* (Acts 2:38; 22:16; 1 Cor 6:11; Heb 10:22), *new birth* (John 3:5; Titus 3:5), appeal to God (1 Pet 3:21). Other sacramental acts of the Church are privileged to draw on the same symbolic richness of the Scripture to help ensure that such acts are never allowed to become constricted or petty.

In all of these specific forms of ministry the Church is given the opportunity to be shaped and nourished by Scripture and to join with Scripture in embodying God's healing of the creation. But as we have also observed, the Church always has also the opportunity to ignore or misuse Scripture and thus impede God's ministry to the world through it. It is, then, critically important for those into whose hands the care of a parish has been committed to be continually sensitive to ways in which Scripture is employed. Is Scripture taken with sufficient seriousness in planning the work of ministry? This does not mean a wooden parroting of a sentence of Scripture after every statement or before every act of ministry but it does imply a deliberate and focused attempt to breathe the Scripture into every aspect of the Church's life and ministry. How are readings from Scripture selected for liturgical and pastoral events? How have particular texts already been given a specific interpretation by what is included and what is omitted in certain readings, or by the location given them in the lectionary and the Church year? How are readings introduced? by which liturgical formulas and by which contexting words? Since most hearing of Scripture happens in liturgical contexts, how are readers trained to read effectively? What provisions are made for seeing and hearing-impaired persons? How are lections typically treated in the homily and with what images are they surrounded in hymns and prayers? What opportunities are afforded the worshiper to meditate on scriptural images or sentences and to respond to them in a liturgical or personal way? All of these are very concrete ways of inquiring about the use of Scripture in the Church and whether such usage reflects the radicality and richness of the biblical vision of God's healing work.

In addition to this kind of inventorying of present practice there are things that a pastor or parish can undertake to further enhance the ministry of Scripture in the Church.

(1) We can work to create and nurture in the Church *a culture of Bible reading and study,* an ethos in which reading and study of Scripture is not remarkable but normal. The old image many Protestants (and not a few Roman Catholics) still have in mind when thinking and talking about the Bible in the Church is that of a Bible chained to the pulpit and accessible only to clergy. Adequate or not, such images have residual power and must be countered by positive action. It has been pointed out more than once that one of the most striking paragraphs in the *Dogmatic Constitution on Divine Revelation* is the one that begins: "Access to sacred Scripture ought to be widely available to the Christian faithful." In late antiquity it was understood that one read books in order to become a person of integrity and social deportment. A culture of pedagogy anticipated growth and transformation as a normal and expected result of reading. Medieval monasticism produced the practice of *lectio divina,* centering life around the reading of Scripture, again with the anticipation of spiritual growth and transformation of one's total being. Such an atmosphere will promote neither an idolization of the Bible nor a superficial or pious seeing and mouthing of the words of Scripture, but will encourage Christians to immerse themselves in the *study* of Scripture. The creation of such an atmosphere will be aided by the availability of certain things: for example, easy to read copies of the Bible in accessible places such as the sanctuary, the parish library, the homes of Church members. Braille and audio versions will be available for those with disabilities. Moreover, the Bible will be available in more than one good modern translation, preferably with good study notes. Access to Bible dictionaries, concordances, atlases, and appropriate commentaries is necessary. Even more important than these will be the availability of other Christian readers with whom to share questions and insights. Bible reading and study is dialogue with writers and interpreters and a group gives concrete expression to this dialogical character of Bible study. The experience of persons in Latin America who have participated in Bible study in the communal context of base communities has been one of life-changing insights. Groups may be helped by participating in one of the structured programs of Bible study now available (for example, the "Discipleship Bible Study" produced and distributed for the whole Church by the United Methodist Church, or the "Little Rock Scripture Study" program published by The Liturgical Press). Pastors and churches from a variety of ethnic and economic strata in the United States testify that they have been "turned around and turned on" in their mission in the world because significant numbers of members have been engaged in serious and systematic study of the Bible. This points to something else that must be available in a culture of Bible reading, and that is opportunity to respond to Scripture with one's life, that is, times and places where people have a chance to translate insights and energy gained from Bible study into significant service to Church and world. And there is one more thing that is crucial in the creation of such a culture within the Church.

(2) As priests, pastors, and teachers we can renew our own commitment to the role of rabbi in the congregation. A pastor's own commitment to regular and disciplined study of Scripture and the willingness to share such study with parishioners can be a powerful endorsement of their own practice. To know that one can go to one's spiritual leader with questions about the Bible or particular passages in it, or about important and sometimes painful issues that result from careful reading of Scripture: these can be of enormous comfort and incentive to a parishioner. Moreover, it is common among pastors who have been willing to encourage Bible study among Church members that they themselves have benefited both from what lay persons have taught them and from the study and reading to which the questions of lay persons have prompted them. To be involved with laity in the study of Scripture may encourage a pastor to do some "catching up" on translations and issues. It may mean investigating some more recent series of commentaries on the Bible. It may encourage one to become part of a lectionary discussion group of laity or clergy. There are numerous ways to reclaim the role of teacher and guide for the congregation and it is crucial for a spiritual leader to do.

None of this will be easy. There is much in the culture of the United States (and perhaps in others as well) that militates against such a subculture; even some remnants of our own Christian tradition, such as clericalism, seem to work against us. Therefore, to conclude, two words of encouragement and hope.

First, none of us is alone in this project. The unleashing of the power of the Bible in the Church is a collaborative undertaking in several senses of the word. Scripture is God's gift to the whole people of God and not to any special group or individual within the Church. Moreover, the origins, preservation, and interpretation of Scripture involve the writers and compilers of the biblical writings themselves and the communities they represent, those through the centuries who have studied and interpreted the Bible for the Church, the faithful of all ages who have read and interpreted Scripture with their lives and, working in and through all of these, the Spirit of God. The collaboration is sometimes full of tension and conflict, sometimes joyous and harmonious, seldom easy. Sometimes it surely sounds like rowdy drunkenness; and yet we have no reason not to trust that out of it the Spirit will yet bring about the miracle that the good news of God is spoken and heard (Acts 2).

Finally, we would do well to remind ourselves that working to free Scripture to better do its work of ministry in the world is, like anything else of genuine significance, ultimately a matter of love. Scripture, like those who interpret it, is born out of the love of God, sustained by that love daily, and will one day find its fulfillment in that divine love. This means that ultimately our work with Scripture depends less on our theology of revelation or our hermeneutical methods or homiletical techniques and more on our passion for being with it, listening to it and getting to know it, and being changed by it. To love Scripture passionately may not by itself be sufficient to free it from all neglect and abuse, but without that kind of love there is little hope of experiencing in it "the power of God for salvation" (Rom 1:16).

BIBLIOGRAPHY

Dyck, Elmer, ed. *The Act of Bible Reading. A Multidisciplinary Approach to Biblical Interpretation.* Downers Grove, Ill.: InterVarsity Press, 1966.

General Catechetical Directory. Washington, D.C.: United States Catholic Conference, 1971.

Green, Joel, ed. *Hearing the New Testament. Strategies for Interpretation.* Grand Rapids: Eerdmans, 1995.

Schneiders, Sandra M. *The Revelatory Text. Interpreting the New Testament as Sacred Scripture.* San Francisco: Harper, 1991.

Sugirtharajhah, R. S., ed. *Voices From the Margin. Interpreting the Bible in the Third World.* Maryknoll, N.Y.: Orbis, 1991.

White, James. *Sacraments as God's Self Giving. Sacramental Practice and Faith.* Nashville: Abingdon, 1983.

Wimberly, Edward P. *Using Scripture in Pastoral Care.* Nashville: Abingdon, 1994.

The Bible and Liturgy

Normand Bonneau

In Christian tradition the liturgy has always been considered the locus *par excellence* for the interpretation of Scripture. In liturgy, and particularly in liturgical proclamation (that is, the oral reading of a biblical passage in the context of a worshiping community), the Scriptures come into their own. They become fully what they are, the word of God active and present.

This vitality stems from the very nature of the liturgy itself. Liturgy is the ritualized expression of the ongoing drama of the relationship between the faithful and their risen Lord who configures them into the pattern of his death and resurrection. Presenting the fundamental characteristics of liturgical celebration is essential, therefore, for appreciating the particular way the Scriptures function and are interpreted in this setting. The main task of this article will be to describe the principles underlying the liturgical use of Scripture. The article will then demonstrate these principles at work through an examination of key aspects of the Sunday and Feast Day Lectionary.

Bible and Liturgy

Liturgical interpretation of the Bible is not an alien dimension added, as it were, from outside. In great part this is so because "the Bible and the liturgy show the same attitude of human beings to God, the same vision of the world and interpretation of history, so much so that there can be no liturgical life without an introduction to the Bible, while the liturgy in turn provides the Bible with a living commentary that enables it to manifest its full meaning" (Martimort, 140).

The close relationship between liturgy and Bible can be seen, for example, from their interaction as reciprocal sources. The Bible contains a multiplicity of passages that have liturgy as their source and setting (psalms, hymns, canticles). Liturgical practice has left traces on the shape and content of such foundational narratives as the Passover (Exod 12:1–13:6), the revelation of the covenant on Sinai (Exodus 19–24), the conquest of the promised land (Joshua, especially ch. 6), the baptism of Jesus, and the Last Supper in the gospels, to name only the most obvious. In yet other instances liturgical concerns have influenced the composition of entire books (for example, Joshua, Deuteronomy, perhaps Revelation). Finally, liturgical use was one of the decisive elements in the process that led to the defining of both Jewish and Christian canons of Scripture (van Olst).

In turn the Bible is one of the main sources of liturgy, as pointed out in the Vatican II *Constitution on the Sacred Liturgy:* "Sacred Scripture is of the greatest importance in the celebration of the liturgy. For from it are drawn the lessons which are read and which are explained in the homily; from it too come the psalms which are sung. It is from Scripture that the petitions, prayers and hymns draw their inspiration and their force, and that actions and signs derive their meaning" (III, 24). The eucharistic prayers, as well as most prefaces, are pastiches of scriptural texts and allusions. The blessing of baptismal water is a long rehearsal of God's mighty acts in salvation history. Even an incidental prayer such as that voiced by the assembly before receiving communion ("Lord, I am not worthy to receive you, but only say the word and I shall be healed") is adapted from the words of the centurion whose son (or servant) Jesus heals (Matt 8:8 = Luke 7:6-7) (Chauvet, 123).

The intricate interweaving of the Bible and liturgy has over the centuries created a rich tradition that continues to provide an inexhaustible source of new meaning for every generation of believers.

Liturgy as Context of Interpretation

Three main characteristics of liturgy determine how the Scriptures are appropriated and interpreted: (1) liturgy is an action, (2) it is Christocentric, and (3) it is pastorally oriented.

Liturgy is an action. I. H. Dalmais points out the essential nature of liturgy by comparing it to the theological enterprise, of which critical exegesis can be considered one branch. "Liturgy is an operation or action *(ergon);* it is not first and foremost a discourse *(logos).*" Liturgy and exegesis address different dimensions of human experience. While exegesis seeks to enhance the intelligibility of the biblical text, liturgy actualizes the story of salvation that the text proclaims.

Since they have different aims, liturgy and exegesis employ different modes of expression: "[Liturgy] takes symbol as its preferred mode of expression; it belongs to the world of poetic thought, which yields a product . . . ." Exegesis, as a form of theological investigation, deals in "conceptual or notional thought," that seeks to define and understand its object through reasoning and argumentation (Dalmais 229, 259). This fundamental distinction accounts for the fact that at times the liturgical performance of a biblical passage may differ from the interpretation proposed by critical exegesis.

Liturgy's action *(ergon)* is described in paragraphs 5, 6, and 7 of the Vatican II *Constitution on the Sacred Liturgy.* Salvatore Marsili summarizes the gist of these passages: "Liturgy is a sacred action through which, by means of ritual, the priestly work of Christ, that is, the sanctification of humankind and the glorification of God, is exercised and is continued in the Church and by the Church" (Marsili, 634). Two key aspects of this definition are particularly germane for grasping how the liturgy appropriates and interprets the Scriptures.

Liturgy is Christocentric. The primary focus of liturgy is Christ and his work of salvation. Through his self-offering on the cross as the perfect fulfillment of the Father's will Jesus embodied and realized God's passion for saving humankind. In the liturgy this saving mystery, called the paschal mystery because of Jesus' passage through death into the fullness of life, is actualized for and in the celebrating community. When applied to the proclamation of Scripture in the liturgy this realization leads the *Constitution on the Sacred Liturgy* to assert that Christ is present not only in the assembly, in the presider, and in the signs of bread and wine, but that he "is present in his word since it is he himself who speaks when the holy scriptures are read in church" (I, 7).

Liturgy is pastorally oriented. The work of Christ made present in the liturgy sanctifies humankind so that they might render true worship to God. This is the liturgy's pastoral orientation. The assembly of the faithful first of all benefits from God's action in Christ: through baptism, Eucharist, etcetera, they are redeemed, saved, reconciled, and sanctified. As a sanctified people the faithful then become the active subjects of the liturgy by offering glory to God in union with the risen Christ present in their midst. The relationship between the risen Christ and the assembly actualizes the story of salvation accomplished in the paschal mystery of Christ in and for the community here and now gathered. That is why the liturgy is the most explicit expression of the mystery of salvation as present event. As a result, when the Scriptures are proclaimed in this context the word of God becomes an event of salvation.

While these three fundamental aspects of liturgy—*God's action* in *Christ* for the *salvation* of humankind—permeate all liturgical use of Scripture they are most readily detected in the Sunday and Feast Day Lectionary, particularly in its principles of reading selection and its patterns of reading distribution.

The Sunday and Feast Day Lectionary

A lectionary can be defined as "an orderly sequence of selections from Scripture to be read aloud at public worship by a religious community" (Reumann, 116). The type and frequency of an assembly's public worship determines the selection and distribution of biblical passages.

Roman Catholic liturgy employs two basic kinds of lectionaries: lectionaries for use at eucharistic celebrations and lectionaries embedded in the Liturgy of the Hours. Of the six types of eucharistic lectionaries the Sunday and Feast Day Lectionary is the most important because of the preeminent place both of Sunday and of Eucharist in Christian tradition. The use of the Lectionary on Sunday and its use in a eucharistic celebration are the foundations from which emerge two of the principles for the liturgical use of Scripture: Christocentrism and pastoral orientation.

Christocentric Orientation of the Sunday Lectionary

1. The Sunday Eucharist

The importance of Sunday in Christian tradition cannot be overemphasized, as the *Constitution on the Sacred Liturgy* explains: "By a tradition handed down from the apostles, which took its origin from the very day of Christ's resurrection, the Church celebrates the paschal mystery every eighth day, which day is appropriately called the Lord's day or Sunday. . . . The Lord's day is the original feast day . . ." (V, 106). Because of the significance of Sunday, from the beginning Christians chose it as the most appropriate time to celebrate the Lord's Supper, the ritualized expression of the paschal mystery.

The resurrection of Jesus not only led the first generations of believers to assemble on the first day of the week. As the event inaugurating God's eschatological salvation, the resurrection of Jesus inspired Christians (1) to read the ancient Scriptures of Israel in a new light, as the gospel story of the disciples of Emmaus narrates so vividly (Luke 24:13-35, especially v. 27); (2) to interpret the paschal mystery and actualize it in their lives, as the New Testament letters witness; and (3) to record the story of Jesus in the gospels. Thus both the Sunday celebration of the Lord's Supper and the emergence of the writings that would become the New Testament spring from the paschal mystery of Jesus' death and resurrection.

There is evidence that by the middle of the second century the Scriptures were read as a standard feature at the Sunday Eucharist (see Justin's *First Apology,* 67). Based on this ancient tradition, the *Constitution on the Sacred Liturgy* describes the Sunday experience as follows: "For on this day Christ's faithful are bound to come together so that, by hearing the word of God and taking part in the Eucharist, they may commemorate the suffering, resurrection, and glory of the Lord Jesus, giving thanks to God who 'has given us a new birth into a living hope through the resurrection of Jesus Christ from the dead' (1 Pet 1:3)" (V, 106).

In such a highly Christ-charged setting as the Sunday Eucharist the gospels maintain pride of place. The revised Sunday and Feast Day Lectionary reflects this by its fundamental structure. It is organized in a three-year cycle of readings, with one of the three synoptic gospels assigned to each year, Matthew to Year A, Mark to Year B, and Luke to Year C (John's gospel appears primarily in the seasons of Lent and Easter). Three readings are provided for each Sunday and feast day, the first from the Old Testament (except for the Sundays of Easter when the first reading is drawn from Acts of the Apostles), the second from the apostolic writings, the third and most important from the gospels. In almost every instance the gospel passages set the tone for the liturgical seasons as well as for each Sunday and feast day.

Moreover, the Christic setting of the Sunday Eucharist lends a paschal interpretation to all three readings of each celebration. Every biblical text is illuminated by the paschal mystery, while every passage in turn deepens and broadens the understanding of this same mystery. No matter what their specific content, the three readings assigned to each Sunday and feast day always play the same liturgical roles. The first reading, from the Old Testament, contextualizes the gospel, relating it to the history of salvation whose center and fulfillment Christians find in Jesus. The second reading, from the apostolic writings, provides models of how the early Christians interpreted the paschal mystery of Jesus and appropriated it in their lives.

The paradigm for this fundamental unity of the readings appears in striking vividness at the Easter Vigil. The Old Testament readings, which offer a sweeping review of salvation history, are proclaimed in the light of the paschal candle, symbol of the risen Christ. The reading from Paul's letter to the Romans interprets the death and resurrection of Jesus in terms of baptism, through which, later in the service, new candidates appropriate this mystery. The gospel narrative of the discovery of the empty tomb announces the resurrection of Jesus, the central mystery of the faith the new candidates profess. Because all other celebrations are patterned after the paradigm offered in the Easter Vigil, all scriptural passages proclaimed in the context of the Sunday and feast day Eucharist bask in the light of the paschal mystery of Christ.

2. The Liturgical Year

The paschal orientation of the Sunday and Feast Day Lectionary emerges not only in the function of each of the three readings per celebration, but also in the way the Lectionary, by selecting and distributing biblical passages, articulates the various seasons that constitute the liturgical year. As a whole, the entire liturgical year flows out of and points to the paschal mystery of Christ. The liturgical seasons underline in a more elaborate and leisurely fashion various aspects of this mystery celebrated primarily on the Lord's Day. The liturgical year's Christ-centered orientation becomes evident when the overall structure and distribution of the readings in the current Lectionary is evaluated in light of other possible designs. The Vatican II committee in charge of Lectionary revision (*Coetus XI* of the *Consilium* on Liturgy), in crafting the Lectionary as it did

> . . . rejected, at least implicitly, other ways of going about its task. The lectionary was not to be ordered around a "history of salvation" motif (understood as a line running from the creation to the second coming), or around a systematic presentation of the theological teachings of the church, or according to a literary analysis of the parts of the Bible that were to be used. Nor were the readings to be chosen and ordered for the primary purpose of exhorting and encouraging people to lead more Christian lives. The lectionary was there to proclaim the passion, death, resurrection, and ascension of Christ, fully realized in him and being realized in us who, through faith and baptism, have been joined to him (Skudlarek, 33–34).

Accordingly, liturgical principles took precedence over exegetical, catechetical, paraenetic, or other principles in determining the selection and distribution of biblical passages in the Sunday Lectionary.

Pastoral Orientation of the Sunday Lectionary

Because the biblical readings contained in the Sunday and Feast Day Lectionary are embedded in the celebration of the Eucharist they have a pastoral orientation. They set in motion the very reason for the Church's being: to enable people to experience God's salvation in their own historical situation. Liturgy is concerned with the community here and now assembled. The "story" that the liturgy celebrates is salvation history actualized in the present, where the past and the future meet as memory and anticipation. Such is the case for every Sunday and feast, indeed for every liturgical celebration.

The liturgical year groups Sundays and feast days into liturgical seasons. The "narrative" of each liturgical season stresses a particular aspect of this pastoral orientation. The season of Lent tells the story of conversion and repentance culminating in the believers' appropriation of the paschal mystery through baptism and Eucharist at the Easter Vigil. The Easter season celebrates the story of the deepening communion of the faithful with the risen Lord who abides with his Church through the Spirit. The Advent-Christmas season unfolds the story of the community's patient waiting for the fullness of the kingdom still to come, a time of anticipation they fill with purposeful action until the consummation of the paschal mystery is revealed in them. The story actualized in the Sundays in Ordinary Time is that of Christians being shaped and molded into the death and resurrection of Jesus through the difficult fidelity of discipleship.

In each instance the readings selected for the Sunday Lectionary articulate and celebrate these overarching liturgical "narratives." Liturgy shapes the Lectionary: biblical passages are selected and distributed according to the needs of the liturgical story being lived out by the assembled community. The liturgy's pastoral orientation shapes the assembly of believers into the body of the risen Christ. Thus the Sunday Eucharist, which celebrates the paschal mystery, and the liturgical year, every aspect of which flows out of and points to the paschal mystery of Christ, fully determine the shape and content of the Sunday Lectionary.

How These Principles Work in the Sunday Lectionary

1. In Festal Seasons

The key feature of each festal season in the Lectionary is the architecture of readings as a whole. Such a design serves the particular liturgical narrative proper to that season. It is constituted through the interplay of four main principles of reading selection and reading distribution: harmony, thematic groupings, semi-continuous reading, and correspondence.

The following description of the first five Sundays of Lent shows the above liturgical and Lectionary principles at work. According to the *General Norms for the Liturgical Year and the Calendar* "Lent is a preparation for the celebration of Easter. The liturgy prepares the catechumens for the celebration of the paschal mystery by the several stages of Christian initiation; it also prepares the faithful, who recall their baptism and do penance in preparation for Easter" (27). The Lenten Lectionary selects biblical passages that highlight the paschal mystery, especially as it is reflected through the prism of baptism.

Because it is a festal season, Lent first employs the principle of *harmony* in its selection of biblical readings. Harmony means that biblical books or biblical passages are chosen in order to express the main themes of a liturgical season: select biblical passages are joined with specific liturgical actions. Accordingly the gospel of John, with its sublime way of articulating the paschal mystery, takes on special prominence during Lent. The tradition of using John in this season reaches back to the earliest centuries of the Church; the choice of the other readings for the first five Sundays of Lent is also guided for the most part by ancient tradition.

Once the Lenten gospel passages have been selected, the Lectionary then places them in *thematic patterns.* These are designed to move the community toward the mystery of baptism in the following manner. In all three Lectionary years the first two Sundays of Lent present the paschal mystery *in nuce.* On the first Sunday the gospels narrate the temptation of Jesus; the gospels on the second Sunday recount the transfiguration. Together these two Sundays constitute a prelude to the celebration of the passion, death, and resurrection of Jesus that takes place at the Triduum (the celebrations—lasting three days—extending from Maundy Thursday to Easter). The temptation conjures up the suffering and death of Jesus, yet with a note of triumph since he resists Satan's power. The transfiguration evokes the resurrection, confirming Jesus' prophecy that first he must go to Jerusalem to suffer, die, and on the third day be raised. Glorification comes only after suffering and death. This is the fundamental "Jesus pattern" into which all believers are initiated through baptism.

After this overture the three Lectionary years diverge slightly. In Year A the readings from John 4, 9, and 11 on the Third, Fourth, and Fifth Sundays respectively focus primarily on the candidates for initiation. In Year B passages from John's gospel for these three Sundays underscore Jesus' glorification through suffering and death. In Year C the selections from Luke and John all converge on the theme of penance leading to conversion. Over a cycle of three years, therefore, the assembly of the faithful celebrates three key aspects of Lent: initiation into the paschal mystery (Year A), a more profound assimilation of the pattern of death-resurrection in their own lives (Year B), and ever-growing receptivity to the mystery through penance and conversion (Year C).

The readings in Year A from John 4 (the Samaritan woman at the well), John 9 (the healing of the man born blind), and John 11 (the raising of Lazarus) play a critical role in the Lenten liturgy and invite special comment. These passages are paired with the scrutinies, an important stage in the catechumens' final preparation for baptism. Through these texts the Lenten liturgy prepares for the celebration of the paschal mystery, focusing on the experience of the candidates who will die and rise with Christ in baptism. In so doing they also remind all the baptized of their own commitment in agreeing to put on Christ. More specifically these three long passages from John announce what happens when someone meets the risen Lord, providing models by which the candidates can understand their own experience. Interpreted liturgically as crucial moments in the baptismal retreat of the catechumens the texts take on special significance: initiation into the paschal mystery of Christ means "passing over" from sin to grace (John 4), from darkness to light (John 9), from death to life (John 11). The Christocentric focus and the pastoral orientation of these passages are unmistakable; they serve the assembled community's liturgical celebration.

The Old Testament readings for the Sundays of Lent display a thematic pattern of their own. In each of the three Lectionary years, moving from the First to the Fifth Sunday, the Old Testament passages offer an overview of the history of salvation: First Sunday, an excerpt from primeval history (except in Year C); Second Sunday, an episode from the story of Abraham; Third Sunday, a key moment in the story of Moses; Fourth Sunday, stories from the time of monarchy; Fifth Sunday, a passage from one of the prophets. This rapid survey of salvation history anticipates the Easter Vigil readings from the Old Testament where a similar, yet more ample retelling takes place.

By virtue of their being selected for the Lenten Sunday Eucharists these Old Testament passages acquire a paschal-mystery orientation. They suggest that the death and resurrection of Jesus marks the climax toward which salvation history tends, a history that includes not only the people of Israel (evoked in the Abraham stories of the Second Sunday) but also all people from the creation of the world (evoked by the excerpts from Genesis read on the First Sunday). The overview of salvation history has a future orientation as well, for the prophetic texts of the Fifth Sunday look forward to Jesus' coming at the parousia to complete the kingdom already inaugurated in his death and resurrection. Pastorally these readings help the assembled community build up its identity as the people of God and assume its role as the contemporary witness to God's story of salvation.

Although there is no semi-continuous reading in Lent, *correspondence* between two or among all three texts assigned to a celebration is quite common. This is due in most instances to the second reading. The second readings during Lent reflect the main themes of the season. A good example of correspondence among all three readings appears on the First Sunday of Lent in Year A. Juxtaposed with the Matthean version of Jesus' temptation is the story of the temptation and fall of Adam in Genesis 2–3. The second reading from Romans 5:12-21 provides a bridge between the Genesis and the Matthew readings with its Adam/Christ typology: whereas the first Adam was tempted and succumbed, the new Adam was tempted but remained faithful even unto death; if Adam was the source of humanity in the first creation, the risen Christ is the source of the transformed humanity of the new creation. In the context of the Lenten liturgy's preparation for Easter, and more specifically in the context of Year A's stress on the catechumens, the proposed interpretation underscores Jesus' death and resurrection as God's intervention reversing the power of sin and its effects. These readings encourage the candidates as well as the assembly to see baptism as initiation into the community of faith, the sign of humanity freed from the power of sin and death, the avant-garde of the new creation in Christ.

On the First Sunday of Lent in Year B the first reading from Gen 9:8-15, the story of the renewal of the covenant with Noah and the survivors of the flood, is paired with 1 Pet 3:18-22, a segment of a baptismal sermon evoking Noah's ark as a type for baptism. The two readings correspond because both focus on water as a symbol of destruction and death, from which only God's power can save. They serve as an anticipation of the Easter Vigil when baptism is celebrated as God's salvation from the powers of sin and death through the paschal mystery of Jesus.

Again on the First Sunday of Lent, this time in Year C, the readings correspond. The Lukan narrative of the temptation appears with Deut 26:4-10, the ancient credo of Israel that was to be recited upon presenting to the Lord the first fruits of the harvest. The second reading from Rom 10:8-13 cites the fundamental creed of Christians: "if you confess with your lips that Jesus is Lord and believe in your heart that God raised him from the dead, you will be saved." The excerpt ends with the exhortation, "'Everyone who calls on the name of the Lord shall be saved.'" Both these texts, which correspond to each other through their use of creeds, shed light on the third reading. In the story of the temptation Jesus was able to repulse the attacks of Satan through his faith in God. In the context of the Lenten Year C readings, these three texts underscore faith and confidence in God as the means of conversion and therefore of salvation (Nocent, 139–140).

The Lectionary texts for the first five Sundays of Lent exhibit the same basic pattern in all three Lectionary years. Selected according to the principle of harmony, they are to be read both horizontally across the Sundays (thematic groupings of gospels and Old Testament) as well as vertically (correspondence between two or among all three readings per Sunday). The pastoral requirements of the Christ-centered ritualization of the drama of salvation, become present event for the worshiping community, determine their selection and distribution and, consequently, their interpretation. The same fundamental principles of reading selection and reading distribution operate in all the festal seasons.

2. In Sundays in Ordinary Time

Unlike the Sundays of the festal seasons (Advent, Christmas, Lent, and Easter), the Sundays in Ordinary Time do not have special focus. They are Sundays in a "pure state," Sundays celebrated very much the way each and every Sunday was celebrated in the earliest decades of the Church before solemnities of the Lord (such as Christmas, Easter, the Ascension, etcetera) and festal seasons developed. As a result the Lectionary selects and distributes scriptural readings somewhat differently. The two hallmarks of these Sundays are the principles of *semi-continuous reading* and *correspondence.* The gospel passages and the excerpts from the apostolic letters follow the first principle, each following their own independent tracks, while the Old Testament passage is selected in light of the gospel pericope of the day.

Semi-continuous reading, a modern adaptation of the ancient practice of *lectio continua,* intends to offer a significant exposure to a gospel or an apostolic letter. It relies heavily on modern exegesis, particularly form criticism, for the delimiting of pericopes, and redaction criticism for the decision to respect the unique contribution of each New Testament author.

Correspondence between the Old Testament reading and the gospel passage of the day can take a variety of forms: (1) the Old Testament passage is chosen because it is cited or alluded to in the gospel (as on the Seventh Sunday in Ordinary Time, Year A [= 7A] or the Eleventh Sunday in Ordinary Time, Year B [= 11B]); (2) the two relate a similar event or deed (e.g., 19A, 2B, 3C); (3) the Old Testament passage complements or supplements an idea or viewpoint expressed in the gospel (e.g., 33B, 15C); (4) the Old Testament reading provides background for the gospel (e.g., 11A, 6B); (5) the Old Testament reading offers a contrasting viewpoint to the gospel (e.g., 13C).

Since the liturgical "narrative" celebrated during the Sundays in Ordinary Time is apprenticeship for the kingdom, the passages selected enhance this aspect of the drama of salvation history. This demands exposure to the deeds and teachings of Jesus in his public ministry, an exposure to the way the earliest communities in the apostolic letters interpreted and appropriated the paschal mystery in their lives, and a constant evocation of the full sweep of the story of salvation, particularly in its Old Testament matrix.

Scripture and Liturgy: Creation of New Meaning

The above exposition of the principles determining the liturgical use of Scripture, particularly as they are articulated in the Sunday and Feast Day Lectionary, warrants three further comments.

(1) Liturgy presupposes familiarity with Scripture. The liturgy is selective in its use of Scripture. The Sunday and Feast Day Lectionary, for example, contains approximately fourteen percent of the entire Bible (five percent of the Old Testament and forty-two percent of the New Testament). Because it is so selective liturgy presupposes a basic familiarity with the stories, the kerygma, the symbols, the overarching plot, the characters of the Scriptures. As much as the revised liturgy of Vatican II, particularly through the lectionaries, offers a broader exposure to the Scriptures than had previously been the case, and as much as this exposure is aimed at fostering familiarity with the Scriptures, knowledge of the Bible must be supplemented outside of the liturgical experience. The Lectionary was not intended to provide a course in Scripture.

The selection itself, however, prompted as it is by the liturgy's desire to articulate the paschal mystery, illumines the whole of Scripture. Liturgy is the "school" showing how the Scriptures reveal Christ.

(2) The pairing of biblical passages creates new meaning. In the Lectionary, biblical passages are taken out of their biblical contexts and recontextualized with other passages in various settings and patterns, creating new meanings not originally found in the Scriptures. For example, at the Mass of the Lord's Supper the three proposed

Lectionary readings are Exod 12:1-8, 11-14 (instructions for the preparation and eating of the Passover lamb on the eve of crossing the Reed Sea), 1 Cor 11:23-26 (Paul's version of Jesus' words at the Last Supper), and John 13:1-15 (Jesus' washing of his disciples' feet on the eve of his crucifixion). This liturgically pregnant rapprochement sheds new light on all three passages. In the second reading, Jesus' blessing the two elements of bread and wine as his body and blood evokes the entire sacrificial economy of Israel: a key feature of animal sacrifices in Israel was the separation of the element of *blood* from the victim's *body*. Placing the Exodus 12 passage before 1 Corinthians 11 provides the background that adds a depth of significance to Jesus' words: in him the entire story of Passover is recapitulated and reconfigured to signify passage not only from slavery to freedom, but also from death to life. Finally, Jesus' enjoining the disciples to wash each other's feet in the gospel intimates that Eucharist, the thanksgiving sacrifice of the new covenant, is lived out through serving one another.

This interplay of passages is not an invention of the liturgy. It is in fact the oldest principle of interpretation in the Bible itself. Whether in the Old Testament alone or in the New Testament's re-reading of the Old this interplay can be seen at work. It is based on the premise that "later verbal symbols throw light on earlier ones in a cascade of imagery that conveys some sense of the divine" (Sloyan, 1977:133). Both in the Bible and in the liturgy meaning has never rested on the primary literal or historical sense of the text, at least not history as understood in the modern world: both Bible and liturgy eschew literalism and fundamentalism. Rather the biblical record of past events furnishes verbal symbols of the unseen God's presence, which, when juxtaposed with new events, transforms symbols for a new experience of that presence. Liturgy simply continues the process. That is why the liturgy does not hesitate to place Old Testament and New Testament texts side by side. Following the Bible's lead, the liturgy pairs texts according to "prophecy-fulfillment," not on the strictly historical level but in a play of symbols that appeals first and foremost to the imagination. The liturgy also employs the scriptural technique called typology, an interpretative approach founded on the recognition that new events, institutions, and characters find their depth of meaning in that they share the essential configuration of an earlier foundational event, institution, or character. Both in the Bible and in the liturgy texts call forth other texts that use similar symbols, and their juxtaposition transforms meaning into a new key.

(3) The interplay between ancient texts and the assembled community creates new meaning. The creation of new meaning results not only from the pairing of passages in the Lectionary. New meaning arises from the dialectic between the ancient texts and the lives of the worshipers here and now assembled. The believing community both writes itself into the text and in turn is shaped by the text. The result is a new "text" or narrative, a combination of old and new (Chauvet, 128). Never before has the specific interplay between these texts and these people occurred; never again will it occur in this particular way, for liturgy celebrates God's salvation made present and effective for this community here and now assembled.

In the end even the phrase "liturgical interpretation of the Scriptures" is perhaps inadequate to express the relationship between liturgy and Scripture, for it intimates that liturgy is a sort of "method" performing an analysis on the biblical text. Rather the liturgy is the atmosphere in which the Scriptures live, the air they breathe to come alive. Liturgy is the Bible in action; it is the Bible transformed from letter to spirit, from past record to present event, ever yielding new meaning out of the ancient text. Liturgy is the home of Scripture.

BIBLIOGRAPHY

Baldovin, John F. "The Bible and the Liturgy, Part 1: the Status of the Bible Today," *Catechumenate* 11/5 (1989) 12–19.

____. "The Bible and the Liturgy, Part 2: Their Interaction," *Catechumenate* 11/6 (1989) 2–10.

Beauchamp, Paul. "Exégèse d'aujourd'hui?" *Connaissance des Pères de l'Eglise* 51 (September 1993) 19–20.

Bonneau, Normand. *The Sunday Lectionary: Ritual Word, Paschal Shape.* Collegeville: The Liturgical Press, 1998.

____. "The Sunday Lectionary: Underlying Principles and Patterns," *Liturgical Ministry* 5 (1996) 49–58.

Chauvet, Louis-Marie. "What Makes the Liturgy Biblical?—Texts," *StLi* 22 (1992) 121–133.

Ciferni, Andrew D. "Scripture in the Liturgy," in Peter Fink, ed., *The New Dictionary of Sacramental Worship.* Collegeville: The Liturgical Press, 1990, 1144–1149.

Dalmais, Irénée Henri. "Theology of the Liturgical Celebration," in I. H. Dalmais et al., eds., *The Church at Prayer: An Introduction to the Liturgy, Vol. 1: Principles of the Liturgy.* Translated by Matthew O'Connell. Collegeville: The Liturgical Press, 1986–1987, 227–280.

Fontaine, Gaston. *"Commentarium ad Ordinem Lectionum Missae," Not.* 5 (1969) 256–282.

Gy, Pierre-Marie. "Le mystère pascal dans le renouveau liturgique: esquisse d'un bilan historique," *MD* 67 (1961) 23–32.

Jensen, Joseph. "Prediction-Fulfillment in Bible and Liturgy," *CBQ* 50 (1988) 646–662.

Keifer, Ralph A. *To Hear and Proclaim: Introduction to the Lectionary for Mass.* Washington D.C.: National Association of Pastoral Musicians, 1983.

Lathrop, Gordon W. *Holy Things: A Liturgical Theology.* Minneapolis: Fortress, 1993.

____. "A Rebirth of Images: On the Use of the Bible in Liturgy," *Worship* 58 (1984) 291–304.

Marsili, Salvatore. "Liturgie," in Domenico Sartore and Achille M. Triacca, eds., *Dictionnaire Encyclopédique de la Liturgie* 1 (A–L). French adaptation under the direction of Henri Delhougne. Turnhout: Brépols, and Montréal: Sciences et culture, 1992, 629–640.

Martimort, A. G. "The Dialogue Between God and His People," in Dalmais et al., eds., *The Church at Prayer 1,* 131–171.

Nocent, Adrien. "La parole de Dieu et Vatican II," in Pierre Jounel, Reiner Kacznski, Gottardo Pasqualetti, eds., *Liturgia, opera divina e umana: studi sulla riforma liturgica offerti a S. E. Mons. Annibale Bugnini in occasione del suo 70e compleano.* Roma: Edizione liturgiche, 1982, 133–149.

Nübold, Elmar. *Entstehung und Bewertung der neuen Perikopenordnung des Römischen Ritus für die Messfeier an Sonn- und Festtagen.* Paderborn: Bonifatius, 1986.

Reumann, John. "A History of Lectionaries: From the Synagogue at Nazareth to Post-Vatican II," *Interp.* 31 (1977) 116–130.

Roguet, A.-M. "Lectures bibliques et mystérè du salut," *MD* 99 (1969) 7–27.

____. "Qu'est-ce que le mystère pascal?" *MD* 67 (1961) 5–22.

Skudlarek, William. *The Word in Worship: Preaching in a Liturgical Context.* Nashville: Abingdon, 1981.

Sloyan, Gerard S. "The Bible as the Book of the Church," *Worship* 60 (1986) 9–21.

____. "Is Church Teaching Neglected When the Lectionary is Preached?" *Worship* 61 (1987) 126–140.

____. "The Lectionary as a Context for Interpretation," *Interp.* 31 (1977) 131–138.

____. A Treasure-House of Images," *Liturgy 90* 21/6 (August–September 1990) 7–9, 15.

Sodi, Manlio. "Célébration," in Sartore and Triacca, eds., *Dictionnaire Encyclopédique de la Liturgie* 1, 157–169.

Taft, Robert. "What Does Liturgy Do? Toward a Soteriology of Liturgical Celebration: Some Theses," *Worship* 66 (1992) 129–144.

Triacca, Achille M. "Bible et Liturgie," in Sartore and Triacca, eds., *Dictionnaire Encyclopédique de la Liturgie* 1, 129–144.

Van Olst, E. H. *The Bible and Liturgy.* Translated by John Vriend. Grand Rapids: Eerdmans, 1991.

Vasey, Michael. *Reading the Bible at the Eucharist.* Grove Worship Series, 94. Bramcote, Nottingham: Grove Books Ltd., 1986.

Verheul, A. "L'année liturgique: de l'histoire à la théologie," *Questions Liturgiques: Studies in Liturgy* 74/1 (1993) 5–16.

West, Fritz. *Scripture and Memory: The Ecumenical Hermeneutic of the Three-Year Lectionaries.* Collegeville: The Liturgical Press, 1997.

Wiéner, Claude. "The Roman Catholic Eucharistic Lectionary," *StLi* 21 (1991) 2–13.

The Bible and Preaching

Virgil Howard

For many Christians—Orthodox, Catholic, and Protestant—the Bible is an essential and empowering part of their daily prayer and worship of God; they read it regularly, perhaps using some form of daily lectionary or devotional literature. In the main Sunday services they hear and are nourished by Scripture not only in the form of the liturgical readings and the sermon or homily, but also in quotations and allusions in hymns, prayers, and liturgical rubrics. For many Christians, however, the Bible is experienced almost exclusively in the Sunday services and there primarily when it is being read aloud or is serving as the basis for the sermon. For both groups, then, and for all those Christians who find themselves somewhere between these two poles, the public reading of Scripture and the sermon are important forms in which the Bible has carried out its ministry to the Church. These are significant modes in which Scripture has manifested itself as "the power of God" working for the salvation of the world (cf. Rom 1:16; 1 Cor 1:18, 24). Many Protestant Christians, clergy and laity alike, regard the sermon as the high point of the Sunday service. Everything else, including the Lord's Supper, serves as preparation for or response to the preached word. By contrast, for Orthodox and Roman Catholic Christians as well as for those in the Anglican tradition the Eucharist has been the heart of the Sunday service with the homily serving the function of preparing believers for participation in the Paschal Mystery.

The latter half of the twentieth century has seen a renewed interest on the part of many Protestants in a regular and worthy celebration of the Eucharist. At the same time it has also seen an increased or renewed appreciation on the part of almost all Roman Catholics and many Orthodox and Anglicans for the integrity and importance of the sermon in Christian worship. Christians are indeed learning more and more from each other, but there remains much more to share and learn.

The purpose of this essay is neither to trace a history of Christian preaching nor to attempt to develop an ecumenical homiletical theory, but rather to offer reflections on the preaching ministry of the Church and some practical ways in which it can be further enriched and enlivened by the Bible and the Bible in turn further freed to bear its witness to God's work of redeeming the creation.

Preaching and the Bible

Preaching as a form of the Church's life and ministry goes back to Jesus himself. The Christian tradition remembers him as one who proclaimed the gracious presence of God (Matt 4:17; cf. Mark 1:14-15; Luke 4:18-19; Matt 9:35; 11:1; Mark 1:38-39 par. Luke 4:43-44; Luke 8:1; Eph 2:17) and commissioned his earliest disciples to do the same (Matt 10:7, 27; cf. Mark 3:14; 6:12; Luke 9:2, 60; Matt 24:14; Mark 13:10; Luke 24:47). Preaching is frequently referred to in the NT as a recognized aspect of the Church's ministry (Acts 4:2; 5:42; 1 Cor 1:23; 15:11; 1 Pet 2:9; 1 John 1:5).

Preaching aims to awaken faith in persons who have never heard the gospel ("evangelistic" preaching: Rom 10:14-17; cf. Matt 28:16-20; Luke 24:27) or to reawaken faith and nourish it among believers. In this case preaching usually occurs in the Christian community assembled for worship. Moreover, preaching is done by the whole community; it is not a solo performance by someone *for* the Church as much as it is an announcement in the words of one preacher but spoken together with all those who have preached and believed in the past and those in the present who hear and translate the sermon into their own experience. The preached word is a community word, moving from the hearing of one Christian to the hearing of other Christians, from one person's speaking from the pulpit to many persons' speaking in the world.

God calls certain persons to the ministry of preaching. Like all other forms of ministry to which Christians are called, preaching is sustained and guided by the knowledge that it is done in response to the divine will, that is, that it is a living out of *vocation.* Strengths and weaknesses of the person called to the ministry of preaching, family and social history, personal perceptions of worthiness or unworthiness are not decisive, but only God's determination to transform them into divine resources (Exod 3:1–4:17; Isa 6:1-13; 40:1-11; Jer 1:4-19; Luke 5:1-11; Acts 9:1-19; Gal 1:13-17). Though such divine calling may be articulated in many different ways by those who experience it, it always brings with it a sense of irresistible urgency (Jer 20:9; 1 Cor 9:16).

Christian proclamation, however, is done not only in the context of the Church's ministry and worship life. It occurs also in specific historical and social contexts. We will pay careful attention to these contexts since they exercise decisive influence over which issues the preacher will address in a given sermon. Moreover, such contexts influence what worshipers bring with them to the sermons and how they hear and appropriate the sermon in their own lives. Injustice and violence appear to be rampant in all cultures today, but the way they are experienced (or ignored) will vary from one social setting to another as will decisions made in response to the preaching of the Church. Some experiences are common to all members of the human family—birth and death and important moments of transition in between—but how such experiences are named and dealt with will vary and so will the preaching that seeks to address them and assist persons in coping with them. Hope will have its distinctive character depending on who is hoping and the situation in which hoping is done. The concreteness and specificity of any given historical and social context sits before the preacher, embodied in those who have gathered in the name of Christ with but one question uppermost in mind, "Is there a word from the Lord?"

For the vast majority of those who preach and those who listen to preaching, Christian proclamation is '"nourished and ruled by sacred scripture" (*Dogmatic Constitution on Divine Revelation* 21). This is the case in spite of the fact that there is enormous diversity in the way this statement is understood in various faith communities. Nor does this generalization mean that there is no such thing as authentic Christian preaching that takes as its point of departure and its authorization something other than a passage of Scripture, for example a topic of relevance to a congregation's life, a current event, a piece of literature or art, or a pastoral concern. But preaching that is most fully reflective of Christian tradition and most consistently helpful in nurturing the faith of the people is preaching that finds its authorization and substance in the Bible. Normally this takes the form of reading and interpreting a specific pericope (or collection of pericopes) for a specific group of Christians (see "The Bible and Liturgy").

In light of what has been said thus far one can think of Christian preaching as *the attempt by means of human speech to enable a particular biblical text and a particular hearer to engage each other in such a way that the hearer comes face to face with the gift and demand of God's love as that love is made explicit to the world in Jesus Christ.* The prayer and hope of every preacher is that the truth of the biblical text and the truth of a hearer's life will intersect and enter into dialogue with each other in such a way that the person will be led to recognize (again or for the first time) her or his life as having been born out of the creative love of God, sustained daily by that unbounded love, and destined ultimately to die into that same unfailing and mysterious love. Such an encounter may entail confronting all kinds of evidence and personal experiences that seem to contradict and ridicule such confidence, but those who preach and those who listen trust that the truth of the biblical word is able to cut through (Eph 6:17; cf. Matt 10:34; Rev 1:16; 2:12) alienation and guilt and mistrust and awful disappointment and usher the hearer into the transforming presence of divine love.

This understanding of preaching, emphasizing as it does the mediating role of preacher and sermon, requires that the preacher think in terms of dealing with two living, breathing, flesh and blood and spirit beings—text and hearer—rather than with a dead, archival document one must somehow resurrect and make palatable to an equally inert and passive worshiper. Thus whatever methods and techniques a preacher may employ in preparing to preach, it is essential that they be appropriate for dealing with living persons. When these methods and techniques are appropriate they will not be mechanical, manipulative, or violent, but will be ways of "being with" a biblical text and "being with" potential hearers so that a sermon emerges that will bring the two together in a redemptive encounter. One does not "work on" a passage of Scripture, one "waits on" (studies) it and "listens out" (exegetes) its truth in much the same way that one "waits on" (ministers to) a human being and "listens out" ("priests out") the truth of that person's life. What Nikos Kazantzakis says about all human words the preacher knows to be true in a special sense about biblical words; "every word is an Ark of the Covenant around which we dance and shudder divining God to be its dreadful inhabitant" (*The Saviors of God,* 94). And this rigorous, careful, patient waiting on and listening out is the homiletical definition of love.

Preaching begins, then, in silence: silence before God and before the text that will nourish and govern the sermon, a silence in which text, hearers, and the preacher's very self are placed in the hands of God.

Richer Preaching and Livelier Bible

Everyone who preaches has a typical way of going about preparing to preach, a way that is appropriate to that person's distinctive abilities and sensitivities. Normally this will include an exegesis of the biblical text: attention to literary issues such as context(s), literary genre and form, vocabulary and distinctive style, the meaning and use of specific words, a writer's use of earlier traditions; attention to historical issues such as authorship, audience, historical situation of various phases of the traditions contained in the text, the intention of the text and anticipated response of its earliest readers and hearers; and attention to theological issues such as assumptions about, images of, and claims that are being made regarding God, the faith responses being asked for from the reader, and practical, ethical implications. Preparation will also involve an exegesis of the socioeconomic realities of persons being addressed by the sermon. It will ask: Who are the intended hearers and in what circumstances do they live? With what issues are they struggling and where are their blind spots? Finally, preparation will involve making decisions about the *content* of this particular sermon for this particular group of Christians, the *form* in which the content will be presented, and the manner of *delivery* that will communicate most effectively. The suggestions that follow are not intended to replace anyone's current procedures for preparing to preach, but are rather offered as questions to be asked of the sermon at any point in the course of preparation in order to assess and, perhaps, to enhance the ways in which our preaching is "nourished and ruled" by Scripture.

How Will This Sermon Embody the Prophetic Word?

The word that comes to us in Scripture is always "prophetic" in that it challenges every other "word" the world has to speak or that we may speak to ourselves. In their own way various biblical writers stress the transcendence and freedom of God and the impossibility of reducing the divine mind and will to human thoughts, words, or categories (Isa 55:8-9; Rom 11:33-34; Matt 25:34; John 1:1). Similarly, the divine word that comes to the Church in the Scriptures shares in this transcendence and freedom of God and comes to us always as "other" than what we know, as "more" than we have been able to conceive or dream, as resistant to final decoding and classification. It calls into question radical evil and injustice posing under the guise of "the way things are," and announces the reign of God as righteousness and peace.

Nevertheless, prophets can be arrested, and the transcendence and freedom and otherness of the biblical word can be compromised when we allow it to be taken captive by our unquestioned perceptions and unchallenged values. Precisely this dangerous possibility, however, presents the preacher with a wonderful opportunity for a deeper engagement with the biblical text. The awareness of the risk of various forms of potential captivity allows the preacher to confront them explicitly and directly with the prophetic voice of the biblical text and thus challenge them, and out of such encounters may emerge not only the content of a sermon but new energy as well.

For example, rigorous, analytical study of biblical passages on which we intend to preach is crucial if we are to hear their witness and mediate it to other Christians. Historical, literary, and theological study of the kind presented in this commentary has been instrumental in freeing the Bible from a great deal of superstition and misuse as support for bigotry and oppression, and such gains are priceless. But what is invaluable as a means can become destructive when allowed to become an end. *Scholasticism* is that form of captivity in which the biblical text is reduced to an object of scientific inquiry and exegesis becomes an end in itself. Analytical skepticism can replace a trustful listening and debate takes precedence over obedience. When this happens sermons become vehicles for conveying information *about* the biblical text rather than embodiments *of* the biblical text.

Another potential form of captivity is *culturalism,* that is, the conscious or unconscious use of Scripture to legitimate and sanction the values of a given culture or society. The encounter between the Bible and the specific culture in which it is being read and proclaimed is important both for the culture and for Christian preaching. Often culture poses questions to which preaching must respond. The constant danger is that Scripture can be so co-opted by cultural assumptions and values that its unique voice is muted or lost and its words are pressed into the service of the dominant culture. In the United States, for example, it is not uncommon to hear the biblical invitation to enjoy God's good creation (Gen 1:26-31; Psalm 104; Eccl 5:18-19) used in the service of consumerism and comfort, or to hear divine providence described in terms of Western economic progress. The freedom of faith (Gal 5:1) is easily identified with Western democracy and salvation with mental health or social popularity. Those who preach in other cultural contexts will be aware of their own potential confusions and restrictions of the biblical witness. When Scripture is not free to be strange and other, to stand over against cultural values and practices, sermons can become appeals for the maintenance of the status quo instead of challenges to it. Preservation becomes the goal rather than transformation. The task of bringing the witness of Scripture to bear on one's cultural context instead of allowing it to be absorbed into the culture is even more complicated in societies which are struggling to emerge from oppressive regimes and institutions. (See the commentary on the gospel of Luke.) Which cultural values need to be challenged in the name of justice, and which ones need to be affirmed in support of liberation?

Moralizing is a constant reductionist temptation. The Bible is viewed as a collection of commandments and rules or of stories that have a "moral," and this usually leads to telling people what to do. It is, of course, true that the Bible speaks on every page of doing justice, loving kindness, and walking humbly with God (Mic 6:8), but rarely is this reducible to absolute moral axioms of good and bad, right and wrong, goodness and sinfulness. In fact, it is more frequently the case that prevailing standards for determining appropriate behavior are called into question and shown to be inadequate and it is precisely the "good" who are called to repentance. This becomes a paradigm in the gospel of Luke (cf. Luke 6:20-26; 7:36-50; 9:46-48; 10:25-37; 12:13-21; 15:1-32; 16:19-31; 18:18-30). Moralizing sermons tend to be judgmental, overloaded with imperatives and filled with good advice, whereas the biblical witness is permeated by expressions of God's graciousness in creation and redemption and invitations to radical transformation and participation in the good creation.

There is a way of interpreting biblical texts and preaching from them that confines their significance to one or another aspect of human existence and this *compartmentalism* silences what they may have to say about other aspects. A biblical passage can be pressed into the service of the "spiritual" in such a way that any relevance for earthly reality, bodily existence, or social and economic relationships is never explored. On the other hand Scripture is sometimes used in such a way that its witness is exclusively seen to involve social conditions and economic justice with no possible transcendent reference; or the Bible can be treated as a guide to emotional health and wholeness with psychological categories replacing theological ones. Over against all such attempts to compartmentalize human existence and the Bible's relevance to it, the Bible itself calls for recognition of the love of God that embraces *all* of human existence: heart (will and relationships), mind (emotional/psychological), soul (transcendent), and strength (physical) (cf. Mark 12:29). The biblical vision is of a new heaven and a new earth (1 Cor 5:17; Rev 21:1-5) where God's will is done (Matt 6:10). The inseparability of the physical and the spiritual is symbolized in Jesus' appearance to the faithful in the hungry and thirsty, the stranger, the rich, the naked, and the imprisoned (Matt 25:31-46: cf. Luke 6:20-21).

A particularly ironic form of captivity threatening the biblical witness is *biblicism,* a way of using the Bible that has the effect of elevating it above the gospel to which it is intended to bear witness. This happens when words or phrases or entire passages are quoted or strung together like pearls on a string and slowly but surely the Bible is made to turn inward upon itself, speaking only its own language and addressing only its own issues. It happens when literalism is allowed to rob the biblical texts of poetic elusiveness and symbolism, of irony and playfulness and ambiguity, of multivalence and mystery. It happens when harmonization is permitted to conceal tensions and contradictions, to smooth over struggle and conflict among various voices in the tradition, to obliterate, in other words, the human face of the Bible. Sermons governed by this kind of biblicism often sound more like calls to faith in the biblical words than to faith in the God to whom they testify and the Bible is preached rather than the gospel.

These are potential forms of captivity for the biblical word, and it could be salutary and invigorating for preaching to confront them directly with the passage or passages the sermon will embody. Is the truth of Scripture being blurred, distorted, or obscured by being forced into language and categories and ideologies that themselves badly need to be challenged and perhaps radically altered by the word of Scripture that comes as the transcendent questioner, the prophetic troubler? How does the sermon make present the challenging and transforming word of God?

How Does This Sermon Deal with Experience?

Whatever else the Bible is about, it deals with human experience—in its routine everydayness and its once-in-a-lifetime-ness, its regularity (Eccl 3:1-8) and its stunning newness (Isa 43:18-19). Human experience is the arena, the medium, the occasion of encounter with God, and one of the distinguishing qualities of the Bible is that it refuses to abstract the religious content from its experiential embodiment and present its reader with religious precepts and ideas. Instead the experience itself is preserved and treasured, recounted in stories and histories, recalled in commandments and instruction, reflected upon in proverbs and sermons, and celebrated in songs and prayers.

There is, for example, the experience of physical reality, beginning with bodily experience. The Bible is full of "body language" because, for one thing, it concerns real, living, flesh-and-blood human beings who experience the world through physical senses, who eat and drink and get hurt or sick and get well or die. Bodies are young and strong or old and frail. To tell a story about people is to tell a story about bodily reality. But sometimes physical experiences are themselves vehicles of religious meaning. Pain of childbearing and desire for it, hard work and sweat and death (Gen 3:16-19) speak of human relationship to God. A physical disability testifies to the nature of religious quest (Gen 32:22-32). That "the blind receive their sight, the lame walk, the lepers are cleansed, the deaf hear, the dead are raised, and the poor have good news brought to them" are signs of the presence of God's reign in the midst of this world (Matt 11:5). For Christians, of course, the singular and decisive bodily experience is that of Jesus himself in his passion and death on the cross, an experience echoed in Paul's attempt to come to terms with his own physical disability (2 Cor 12:1-10). Finally, bodily experiences can become metaphors for religious experience (Isa 6:6-7; John 9:1-41; 11:1-44).

The Bible is also attentive to people's emotional experience. One is struck by the wide range of emotions that are taken seriously. There are passages that express the experience of wonder at the magnificence of creation (Pss 8; 104; 145), of gratitude for the gift of the Law (Pss 19:7-13; 119), and of peace and oneness with God (Psalm 23). Some texts embody feelings of jubilation at liberation (Exod 15:1-18), deliverance (Psalm 138) and redemption (Rev 4:8, 11; 5:9-10, 12, 13). Christian existence knows not only the shout of ecstatic children but also the groaning of creation still being birthed and the sighs of those who lack the words to name their longing (Rom 8:15, 22, 26). But there are also passages in which very different feelings find expression, feelings of anger and frustration (Job) of betrayal and rage (Jer 15:10-18; 20:14-18), of confusion and abandonment (Psalms 22; 69), and of anguish (Luke 19:41-44; 22:39-46; Matt 27:45-50 par. Mark 15:33-37; Heb 5:7-8). Equally striking is the willingness of the Biblical writers to respect those feelings usually regarded as "negative" by allowing them full expression, not rushing past them in order to reach resolution. Doubt and anger and pain are given their full time on the way to doxology.

Then there is the dimension of social experience: the people whose experiences are narrated and reflected upon in the Bible are not isolated individuals but members of families and nations and tribes and peoples and languages (Rev 7:9). Human experience is linked with that of other human beings. Recall, for example, how intimately experiences of God are linked to family relationships: husbands and wives (first Man and Woman, Abraham and Sarah, Isaac and Rebecca, Jacob and Rachel, Joseph and Mary, and (symbolically) Christ and the Church in Eph 5:22-33, Rev 21:2); parents and children (Abraham and Isaac in 22:1-19; Hagar and Ishmael in Gen 16:1-15; 21:3-21; the widow of Zarephath and her son in 1 Kings 17:17-24; Naomi and Ruth in the book of Ruth; and parents of sick children in Matt 9:18-19, 23-26; 15:21-28; 17:14-20); and siblings (Jacob and Esau, Joseph and his brothers).

In all these forms of human experience and others the authors of the Bible took special care to preserve and pass on to others accounts of and reflections on the experiences of human beings. By paying attention to the details in stories, by honoring the breadth and scope of bodily, emotional, and familial experiences the writers made their experiences available to their contemporaries. And therein lies a crucial homiletical clue. One test of whether preaching is really *biblical preaching* or simply preaching on biblical ideas or themes is the question of how crucial the biblical texts themselves remain for the sermon. In biblical preaching the text is not "harvested" for ideas or a "point" to be made or doctrines to be formulated and then discarded. Rather the text with its recreation of or reflection on human experience of all kinds remains at the heart of the sermon. The hearer is enabled to experience the *truth* of the biblical text by *experiencing the biblical text itself.*

Even more importantly, however, the power of many biblical texts lies precisely in their ability to aid a reader or hearer in the recognition and articulation of her or his own experience. Those who listen to sermons bring with them their own experiences but the problem for many people is that they are unable to speak and thus to honor their own experiences. It may be that they have received the message that the body is at best irrelevant to faith in God and at worst inimical to it. Experiences of childhood abuse or awareness of society's inability to deal with physical disabilities may have taught them to be ashamed of their bodies. Certain of their emotional experiences may be too painful or too "negative" to be acknowledged and respected. Some come from family relationships that have been debilitating rather than nurturing and they find themselves trapped in rage or shame. All of these experiences are present but unarticulated and certainly not understood to be places where God wishes to meet them. By making the experiences (not just the conclusions or lessons) of biblical characters present and available in the sermon the preacher empowers persons to face, name, reclaim, listen to, and value their own experiences in such a way that they can become places of revelation, places to once again meet the God who has been waiting there all along.

How Does This Sermon Tell the Story?

The Bible is a storybook. It is itself a story and is filled with stories. The canon as a whole is structured as a narrative: "In the beginning" (Gen 1:1) . . . "the time is near" (Rev 1:3), telling the story of God and God's creation. "The story" of God is made up of "stories" of God and God's people. The formative experience of Israel, the Exodus from Egypt, and the reception of the commandments at Sinai make up one long story. Even ethical codes and commandments are made part of that story. In the same way the formative event for Christian faith, the life, death, and resurrection of Jesus, is available to the Church in the form of gospel narratives. Even one of the earliest Christian creedal statements suggests a narrative structure: ". . . Christ died for our sins in accordance with the scriptures, and . . . was buried, and . . . was raised on the third day in accordance with the scriptures, and . . . appeared to Cephas, then to the twelve" (1 Cor 15:3-5). There are even stories within stories: for example, the story of Jesus presents him as one whose favorite method of teaching was the parable. Finally, even the NT epistles in which narrative is not a major means of discourse permit us a glimpse of stories behind the present texts (1 Cor 1:10-17; 11:17-22; 1 John 2:18-19, and many other places). Story is the Bible's preferred mode of discourse.

Here is a story about stories:

When the great Rabbi Israel Baal Shem-Tov saw misfortune threatening the Jews it was his custom to go into a certain part of the forest to meditate. There he would light a fire, say a special prayer, and the miracle would be accomplished and the misfortune averted. Later, when his disciple, the celebrated Magid of Mezeritch, had occasion, for the same reason, to intercede with heaven, he would go to the same place in the forest and say: "Master of the universe, listen! I do not know how to light the fire, but I am still able to say the prayer." And again the miracle would be accomplished.

Still later, Rabbi Moshe-Leib of Sassov, in order to save his people once more, would go into the forest and say: "I do not know how to light the fire, I do not know the prayer, but I know the place and this must be sufficient." It was sufficient and the miracle was accomplished.

Then it fell to Rabbi Israel of Rizhin to overcome misfortune. Sitting in his armchair, his head in his hands, he spoke to God: "I cannot even find the place in the forest. All I can do is tell the story, and this must be sufficient." And it was sufficient.

God made man because he loves stories.

—*Elie Wiesel,* The Gates of the Forest

But it is not only God who loves stories: people do too, and so it is important to pay attention to the homiletical wisdom of Wiesel's story and consider the possibility that one way to enliven preaching is to tap into the power of biblical narrative. Over the past thirty years a significant body of homiletical literature has been produced advocating "narrative preaching." While narrative preaching is certainly not the only valid form of Christian proclamation it does present an attractive alternative to discursive, didactic, deductive sermons. Narrative preaching is not preaching that consists largely of stringing "illustrations" together around a "point" to be made, nor is it preaching that recaps a story, distills a lesson from it, and then discards the story to develop and apply the lesson or moral, nor, finally, is it preaching that explains or interprets a biblical narrative. Narrative preaching is preaching that focuses on a biblical story, an incident or parable, and maintains the form and style of the story as well as its major movements, direction, and intention. The story *is* the sermon. There are various ways to do this.

The preacher may choose to "tell the story," following the pericope along from beginning to end. This is a favorite method in the African-American preaching tradition in which a preacher is assessed in terms of his or her ability to "tell the story." Of course the preacher does not simply repeat the words of the biblical story, but fashions the story at certain points to help the listener hear the story as his or her own story. This is done by substituting contemporary language or images at certain points in order to cue the listener that though the story is being *told* in the past tense it is to be *heard* in the present tense. This can also be achieved by the preacher's expression of surprise at some part of the story, repetition of certain points, or pausing to ponder or meditate aloud at key points in the story. An alternative method is to begin the sermon by setting a context, for example, outlining an issue or crisis in the life of the Church or of a significant number of people, and thus "telling the biblical story" in such a way that it illumines or responds to the issue or crisis. Again narrative preaching will allow the story itself to provide the hearer with whatever answers or clues are necessary in dealing with the question or crisis. Another alternative, though somewhat less effective, is to "tell the story" first and then draw (brief!) conclusions from it. Finally, one can recast the biblical story completely in contemporary language and imagery. Whatever variant one chooses, the rule for narrative preaching is: *let the biblical story itself carry the message.*

Narrative preaching is, of course, an obvious option when the passage being preached from is itself narrative in form. But it could be helpful on occasion to "imagine" the story behind certain non-narrative texts. Instead of preaching a sermon listing some ways in which Christians distort the significance of the Lord's Supper and suggesting ways in which the celebration might be more worthily observed (1 Cor 11:17-34) one could "imagine" a story of contentious Christians who turn the meal into a competition for bigger shares so that even the sacrament is transformed into a status symbol.

Finally, preachers with more literary and poetic skills may occasionally create their own stories that totally recast the biblical story into a completely different story in terms of plot and characters while pursuing the same intention, or one might embody a biblical story in the form of a current event, a contemporary novel, play, piece of art, movie, or in the form of biography or autobiography.

Stories have the power to "enchant," to take people into another world, to help people make connections, envision wholeness. Narrative preaching can draw on the power of the biblical stories to assist a person to see her or his place in God's story. Feeling lost or alienated may mean that a person has lost any sense of a "beginning" and an "end" greater than his or her own, any sense that he or she is part of something larger than his or her own set of problems and fears and accomplishments. To hear a story from The Story may empower a person to remember and recover his or her own story—and that may be sufficient.

How Does This Sermon Offer the Guiding Image?

The Bible is a treasury of images. Much that was said about "story" could also be said about images, their prevalence and function in the Bible. "Image" here refers to anything: a word, picture, idea, or object that offers itself as a key to seeing and understanding things in a new way. Rather than speak of God in abstractions or by appending a list of adjectives to the word "God," the Bible images God, for example, as "rock" (Gen 49:24; Deut 32:4; 1 Sam 2:2; Pss 18:2, 31, 46; 19:14; 89:26) but also as "shepherd" (Gen 49:24; Ps 23:1; Isa 40:11; Heb 13:20) to name only two obvious possibilities among a multitude. The author of the gospel of John seems to have been at pains to offer as many images of Jesus as possible, beginning with that of "word" at the very outset, but especially in the "I am" pronouncements: bread (6:35, 41, 48, 51), light (8:12; 9:5), sheepgate (10:7) and shepherd (10:11), resurrection and life (11:25), way, truth, and life (14:6), vine (15:1, 5). Christians are not simply defined by what they believe and do, but are imaged as salt (Matt 5:13) and light (Matt 5:14), sheep (John 10:11-18), branches (John 15:5), saints (1 Cor 1:2; 2 Cor 1:1; Eph 1:1; Phil 1:1; Col 1:2, etcetera), and in many other ways. The cup and baptism are used as images of suffering and death (Mark 10:35-40), and the cross itself is not simply a physical instrument of execution, but becomes an image for the life of the Christian (Luke 9:23; cf. Matt 16:24; Mark 8:34).

The work of identifying and making images available to hearers requires that the preacher function with more of the mind than just intellect. The mind plays with images. Images require imagination, the ability to look below and beyond surface and literal meanings, to discern more than seems to be in a word. It is the ability to ask "What if . . . ?" and "How about . . . ?" Imagination is the drive to find ways of saying what cannot be fully expressed in human language and yet entrusts itself to human language.

Images have the power to offer new perspectives and possibilities, new ways of viewing the data of one's existence, and new ways of perceiving relationships and reality. In preparing to preach, the preacher may select from a passage of Scripture a dominant image, imagine a few associations called up by the image, explore a few paths into which an image may beckon, and then entrust the image to the listener to explore and ponder. A marvelous example of allowing an image to open up new ways of understanding one's life and relationships to God and others is the little book by Henri Nouwen published shortly before his death: *Can You Drink the Cup?* based on the cup image from Matt 20:20-23. The cup is a powerful biblical image. In offering biblical images in the sermon it is not necessary to exhaust all the possibilities inherent in a given image. Indeed, to do so would be to destroy the image since its power rests in part precisely on its open-endedness. Where it takes a person cannot be predicted; it can only be known in the experiencing of it by each individual. The task of the preacher is not to construct a new faith for anyone but to provide hearers with the resources for discerning and constructing and living their own faith. Valuable resources for this task are images offered in Scripture.

How Will This Sermon Become a Word of God?

The Bible is a book filled with miracles and anyone who preaches needs to be able to hope for the greatest miracle described in the Bible. It does not have to do with the sun standing still or walking on water or healing sick bodies, impressive and important as such signs undoubtedly are. Rather the greatest miracle, reported consistently and in many different forms throughout the Bible, is the miracle that God speaks and people hear, the word comes to human beings through other human beings *and is heard.* The miracle of God's speaking is completed by the miracle of human hearing. But it is, finally, God's work.

This essay has suggested some ways in which Christian preaching might be enhanced in its relationship to the Bible, questions that might be asked, ways of "being with" both the biblical text and the people for whom we preach. But when we as preachers have done all that we can humanly do to mediate the engagement between text and hearer that may result in a deepened awareness of God's incomprehensible love we can then only entrust our work to God and the listeners and trust in God's Spirit to grant the miracle of hearing.

BIBLIOGRAPHY

Brueggemann, Walter. *Texts Under Negotiation. The Bible and Postmodern Imagination.* Minneapolis: Fortress, 1993.

Buttrick, David. *Homiletic. Moves and Structures.* Philadelphia: Fortress, 1987.

____. *A Captive Voice. The Liberation of Preaching.* Louisville: Westminster/John Knox, 1994.

Craddock, Fred B. *Preaching.* Nashville: Abingdon, 1990.

Eslinger, Richard L. *Narrative Preaching. Preaching the Worlds That Shape Us.* Minneapolis: Fortress, 1995.

Gomes, Peter J. *The Good Book. Reading the Bible With Mind and Heart.* New York: William Morrow and Company, 1996.

Mitchell, Henry. *Celebration and Experience in Preaching.* Nashville: Abingdon, 1990.

Nouwen, Henri J. M. *Can You Drink the Cup?* Notre Dame, Ind.: Ave Maria Press, 1996.

Skudlarek, William. *The Word in Worship. Preaching in a Liturgical Context.* Nashville: Abingdon, 1981.

Smith, Christine M. *Preaching as Weeping, Confession, and Resistance.* Louisville: Westminster/John Knox, 1992.

Troeger, Thomas H. *Imagining a Sermon.* Nashville: Abingdon, 1990.

The Bible in the Charismatic Movement

Paul Hinnebusch

The Scriptures and the Recognition of God's Action in Our Hearts

Charismatics read and pray the Scriptures so avidly because they find that the Scriptures interpret for them what God is doing in their hearts. By the grace of "baptism in the Spirit," in fervent faith and love they have "come alive" to Christ and the Holy Spirit, and God is present to them, working in their hearts. The Emmaus story throws light on this way of using Scripture for prayer. "Were not our hearts burning within us while he was talking to us on the road, while he was opening the scriptures to us?" (Luke 24:32). The risen Lord works in our hearts for some time before we realize what is happening. Suddenly we realize that the Scriptures are speaking about what he is doing in our hearts, and through the Scriptures we come to understand something about his action in us. Usually we can respond to Scripture only because we have some degree of pre-reflective experience of his action in our hearts, the action of which the Scriptures speak. We find that the Scriptures put into words what the Lord is doing in us in a wordless way. Only because he is working these realities in our hearts through his Spirit do we understand what the Scriptures are saying.

When the scriptural mystery comes alive for us, when our hearts burn within us we are responding to the living presence of the Lord himself, not just to words. We are able to identify with the scriptural mysteries because they show forth the reality that the Lord is working in our hearts. The Lord is continuing among us his saving presence and action described in the scriptural words and events. His words to Thomas, for example, "do not doubt but believe," are his words to me, and I respond to them in the way Thomas did, "My Lord and my God!" (John 20:27-28). Thus we come to an understanding of Scripture only because, somehow, we are experiencing in our hearts what the Scripture is saying.

Thus when we hear or read Scripture our hearts often burn within us without our reflecting on what is happening, without our realizing that we are in communion with a living Person who is working in our hearts by an interior word of grace. Our listening to the Scriptures or reading them is already a prayer because our hearts, responding to the word, are responding to a person present with us through his word and Spirit. Where there is genuine Christian religious experience there will be insight into the Scriptures under the guidance of the Holy Spirit. Thus God speaks through the Scriptures even to ordinary people who know nothing about scientific historical exegesis.

This insight into the meaning of the Scriptures takes place not just on the level of the individual reader, but more fully and adequately in the Christian community. It is the community's experience of the divine mysteries that is expressed in the Church's traditional exegesis of the Scriptures. An individual's experience and insight needs to be discerned and evaluated in the light of the group's experience. The limits of a small group's experience and tradition can prejudice the evaluation of such experience. Hence the need to listen also to the broader Christian experience of the whole Church that has continued through the centuries. Our spiritual experience needs to be verified within the unbroken living experience and tradition of the Church from the beginning.

The Directive Use of Scripture

Scripture is directive for all Christians. It offers guidance for everyday life, for living the mystery of Christ. But does the Bible reveal the most minute details of our lives as some charismatics seem to expect?

Abuse of the practice of asking for "a word from Scripture" has been called "Bible roulette" or "cutting the pages," expecting the eyes to fall upon a passage which will be a direct word from God for the specific situation in which one finds oneself. The Scriptures are the revelation of the truths necessary for salvation. They should not be seen as a collection of ready-made answers to all of life's problems. Each person has the responsibility to make his or her mature decisions in the light of the general revealed truths. Even when God through divine goodness does give a word from Scripture in this way it should not be the sole principle of discernment. At best such a word should be seen as confirming or denying what is already going on in the heart of the person. Discernment and prudential judgment form a process of continual seeking and its accompanying confirmation. This involves careful study of the situation, gathering information, seeking counsel from others when necessary, reflection on one's past experience, and the like. Even if in humble sincerity one asks for the guidance of the Holy Spirit and then opens the Bible asking for a text to help make a decision, this text alone is not enough. It must be applied within the whole prudential process.

There is a right way of using the Bible for discernment in matters of personal guidance. A well-known example is found in the autobiography of Thérèse of Lisieux. Thérèse was confused about her vocation in the body of Christ, the Church. She searched the Scriptures for an answer. God spoke to her heart through 1 Corinthians 12–13. She did not recognize herself in the various members of Christ's body of whom Paul speaks there (apostles, prophets, teachers, etcetera). But as she went on to read Paul's great description of love she realized that the Body of Christ, made up of so many different members, needs a heart aflame with love. Thus she found her own place in the Body: "In the heart of the Church, my mother, I will be love."

Thérèse was not playing roulette, randomly seeking a text. She was studying a passage dealing explicitly with charisms in the Body of Christ. Of course she rightly expected guidance in finding her personal charism. Hers was an accurate exegesis and hermeneutic, and the Lord guided her to a true meaning implicit in that inspired text. Thérèse never had any instruction in scientific biblical exegesis. People like Thérèse, though they lack formal education, often find a richness of inspired meaning in the Scriptures that scientific exegesis may miss when it is divorced from the everyday Christian experience of ordinary people. Again we see how experience of the realities of which Scripture speaks leads to insight into the meaning of the Scriptures. The fact that a few charismatics play Bible roulette should lead no one to the universal conclusion that all charismatics misuse the Bible.

Unselfconscious Response to the Word

People sometimes say in disappointment, "When I pray for guidance, I never get a word from the Scriptures with an answer to my problem. It seems that the Lord never speaks a passage directly to me." Yet often it becomes clear that they have been prayerfully responding to the Lord in the Scriptures for a long time. Each time we use the Scriptures for prayer we need not expect a particular word concerning a mission we are to accomplish, or the answer to a problem. The Lord most often simply offers his presence to us, to be accepted with love and joy, in faith and simple trust. Most of the time the word he speaks to us is a word of love and communion rather than a word entrusting us with a great mission or a glamorous service. Those who are always looking for vivid words of mission or action tend to miss the delicate interior words of communion. The word of Scripture, as we said, is intended above all to bring us into intimate communion with God. With it comes the interior word that is God's presence, the indwelling Word in person who communicates wordlessly with us through his presence in our hearts. This is "the word of God fully known . . . this mystery, which is Christ in you" (Col 1:25, 27). This is the deeper reality the scriptural words cannot adequately express. Those words are but symbols opening us to this unspeakable Presence. Sometimes the only adequate response to this Presence is loving adoration and wordless self-surrender. If the Presence does not cause our hearts to burn within us, at least we respond to it in quiet waiting and expectant hope, ready to receive God's self-manifestation if and when God sees fit to give it. It cannot be forced. It is the free gift of love.

Experience Beyond Exegesis

Because the reality symbolized in the Scriptures is too big for human words people sometimes experience God speaking to them in a text in a way that seems to violate the rules of scientific exegesis. At times God may symbolize a spiritual experience to a prayerful person through scriptural words that in their literal inspired meaning do not speak of what the person is experiencing. The person may come across a portion of Scripture that seems to express perfectly a particular spiritual experience, then uses these words to express the experience to others, even though the biblical author was not thinking of that experience at all when writing the words under divine inspiration. When that happens God may indeed be speaking to the person through those particular scriptural words and clarifying the experience through them. But if the person tries to use this text to urge his or her own experience upon others, or to draw theological conclusions from the words as if his or her personal experience were universally valid for all, problems can result. Though it may be a valid interpretation of this one's personal religious experience it is not necessarily an exegesis of the inspired text appropriate for others.

Sometimes an experience of a spiritual reality and the symbol in which it is expressed to the understanding seem so inseparably one that for the person who has the experience the symbol is the reality. Something like this happened to Catherine of Siena. Jesus appeared to her and took her heart from her breast and replaced it with his own heart. Thus, in a striking mystical symbol, God accomplished in her the reality of which Ezekiel speaks: "A new heart I will give you, and a new spirit I will put within you; and I will remove from your body the heart of stone and give you a heart of flesh. I will put my spirit within you" (Ezek 36:26-27). The spiritual reality accomplished in this mystical experience was so vivid to Catherine that no one could convince her that Jesus had not literally replaced her heart with his own bodily heart. She was unable to distinguish the symbol from the divine reality that Christ accomplished in her, namely her total transformation in his own divine love, her perfect union with him, in which she lived his own life and loved with his own love. These, of course, are realities spoken of in Scripture.

Pastors, exegetes, and theologians should understand that this sort of experience of the Scriptures can be authentic even though it does not seem to correspond to rules of exegesis or theological reflection. No one experience of the Christian mystery exhausts that mystery. The ways of the Holy Spirit in our lives are multiple. There are many ways of expressing Christ in our lives, all of them in accord with the inspired meaning of the Scriptures.

Any misuse of the Scriptures among charismatics is not due to the charismatic phenomenon as such. By its very nature "baptism in the Spirit" inspires a deep love and reverence for Scripture and an openness to the Holy Spirit. The misuses are due rather to deficiencies in the particular Christian milieu in which the phenomenon takes place, such as ignorance of tradition and of exegetical principles. Much of the misuse of Scripture in the early days of the contemporary charismatic renewal came not from the charismatic phenomenon as such but from certain narrow fundamentalist groups that had a strong influence on the early charismatics in the mainline churches. The remedy for misuse is a better pastoral presentation of the Scriptures in response to specific needs of the charismatics, who are often uninstructed people with little or no theological or scriptural formation. Because of their God-given love of the Scriptures charismatics are eager for Bible study, and are usually open to solid exegesis when it is wisely presented to them. It is true that this openness to instruction is sometimes hindered by a mistrust of exegetes, who in the early days of the charismatic renewal were often scoffed at by charismatic leaders for "not knowing the Lord." In reality some of our best exegetes are men and women of profound faith who solidly interpret the Scriptures within the living tradition of the Church.

Much of the mistrust of exegetes is due to ignorance of such matters as literary genre. Some of it is due to the over-concentration by some exegetes on scientific literal exegesis to the neglect of interpretation in the light of religious experience and tradition. The case is not helped by those "retailers" of scientific historical exegesis who deliberately shock people by tearing down and ridiculing their primitive notion of Scripture without building them up by showing the revealed truths conveyed by the various literary genres.

Pastoral Applications

Since the mystery expressed in the Scriptures is the mystery of God-with-us, revealing the divine self to us in friendly communion, it is no surprise that people of living faith sometimes experience God's word addressed to them in a very personal way. Of course we are all open to deception in these matters. People of vivid imagination or those who succumb to wishful thinking can "hear" in the Scriptures what they want to hear. However, occasional deceptions and abuses should not lead us to conclude that everyone who tells of an experience of the word has been deceived. We should not automatically doubt people when they speak of these experiences but should rather apply the common rules for discernment.

People who have received authentic words from the Lord are also likely to receive deceptive words from Satan or from their own inflated ego. Satan quotes Scripture to Jesus himself in the desert. Paul warns that "even Satan disguises himself as an angel of light" (2 Cor 11:14) and fears that the Corinthians, who have been blessed so richly with charismatic graces, will fall away from their original faithfulness to Christ. "I am afraid that as the serpent deceived Eve by its cunning, your thoughts will be led astray from a sincere and pure devotion to Christ" (2 Cor 11:3). Because such falls do happen, pastors tend to doubt every case of hearing words from the Lord. This is tragic because it begets doubt in God's people and kills their expectation of hearing the Lord speak to them.

Here are a few pastoral suggestions:

(1) Expect that God's word will come alive in God's people. Do not let abuse by some cause you to doubt everyone.

(2) Realize the limits of your own spiritual experience and do not be surprised if God speaks to people in a way you have never experienced, or calls from them a response never asked of you.

(3) Use the ordinary rules for discernment of spirits.

(4) Teach people to use personal discernment by interpreting their experiences in the context of the whole of God's revelation and in the context of the continuing experience of God's people, that is, in the context of Christian tradition.

(5) Help them to realize the diversity of God's ways and not force their personal insights upon others who may have other valid insights, which respond to other aspects of the inexhaustible riches of Christ.

(6) Help them to avoid thinking that God speaks only through the Scriptures. Teach them to listen also to the Christian experience of the past and present. This age-old, continuing experience of the reality of which the Scriptures speak—God's real presence with us to work in our hearts—gives deeper insights into the Scriptures and reveals unexpected depths of meaning in them. Much of the Church's best understanding of the Scriptures is the result of reflection on its Christian experience through the centuries. The fruit of this experience and this reflection is expressed in Christian tradition, which helps us to discern the deeper meaning of the Scriptures.

The Bible in the Retreat Movement

Francis Martin

The title of this article already reveals the profound changes that have taken place in the Catholic Church as a result of the grace of the Second Vatican Council. There is first of all the fact that there is a "retreat movement," a genuine quest on the part of many in the Church for a deeper awareness of God and of the divine will for their lives. Then there is the fact that many aspects of this post-Vatican II movement are inspired by the same Council's insistence on the importance of the Bible for our life of faith. Speaking of the Scriptures, the Council says:

> For, since they are inspired by God and committed to writing once and for all time, they present God's own Word in an unalterable form, and they make the voice of the holy Spirit sound again and again in the words of the prophets and apostles. It follows that all the preaching of the church, as indeed the entire christian religion, should be nourished and ruled by sacred scripture. In the sacred books the Father who is in heaven comes lovingly to meet his children, and talks with them (*Dogmatic Constitution on Divine Revelation* 21).

For the purposes of our discussion the multiple dimensions of the retreat movement can be reduced to three: (1) group retreats led by someone who presents various topics for consideration and prayer, (2) directed retreats in which an individual is guided in prayer and seeking by someone else, and (3) a private retreat in which someone spends time alone with God seeking God and God's will.

The role of the Bible in group retreats is generally that found in all preaching, namely that it provides the message from God to be shared by preacher and audience alike. Endowed with the particular characteristics described in the text from the Council cited above, the biblical text has a special power: it is the word of God, "at work in you believers" (1 Thess 2:13). The most striking characteristic of group retreats since Vatican II has been the predominance of the biblical text in the conferences of the retreat leader and the reflection of the retreatants. After decades of hearing the word of God read aloud at the liturgy in their own language God's people are beginning to acquire a familiarity with the text and are able to identify with it in ever more personal ways. They are also, through private study and adult education classes, much more sophisticated in their instinctive appreciation of the historical setting for the sacred text, its literal meaning, and the divine "surplus" of enlightenment and empowerment it contains. One of the roles of commentaries such as this one is to enable both preacher and retreatants to enter more deeply into that capacity of the word to bring us in touch with the Father who comes to talk with us.

Directed retreats, a newer form, are most often characterized by the fact that the biblical text is read and meditated upon by the retreatant under the direction of someone else. Adapting some of the method of the *Spiritual Exercises* of Ignatius of Loyola, the retreat master proposes various texts to the retreatant who ponders them and then returns to discuss the way in which the text has an effect. A skillful director can discern in this discussion the way in which God is directing the retreatant and can suggest texts that will serve and further the divine action. In this way the word of the Lord is appropriated in a personal way by the retreatant who experiences the fact that this word is "living and active" (Heb 4:12), able to make present and personalize that activity by which God reveals God's very self and makes known the mystery of the divine will (See *Dogmatic Constitution on Divine Revelation* §2).

A private retreat uses the Scriptures in a way that is classically known as *Lectio Divina* or "Sacred Reading." In this activity the retreatant proceeds much in the same way as in a directed retreat except that the texts are chosen by the retreatant who seeks to hear from the Lord and be changed by what is heard. Most often it is advisable to read one book through rather than randomly reading separate passages. It is also recommended that the retreatant keep careful notes of what transpires in this activity so that, in regard to important decisions at least, it will be possible to share with someone else later and have one's discernment confirmed. What takes place in a private retreat, which may have a very specific goal, can take place every day when a Christian decides to take time to read what St. Gregory called a "letter from God."

BIBLIOGRAPHY

In addition to the articles on *Lectio Divina* in standard Catholic reference works and the literature given there, one may consult:

Fitzmyer, Joseph. *Spiritual Exercises Based on Paul's Epistle to the Romans.* New York: Paulist, 1995.

Stanley, David. *A Modern Scriptural Approach to the Spiritual Exercises.* Chicago: Institute of Jesuit Sources, 1967.

The Bible and Prayer in Africa

D. W. Waruta

Introduction

If there is one theme on which the biblical and African traditions converge it is that of prayer. The people of the Bible, like the Africans, are a praying people. Biblical and African spirituality are rooted in prayer and the theistic world of the Bible is not something new to the African people. Prayer includes attitudes, expressions, and exclamations of belief in God the creator and preserver of all things in general and the people who know God in particular. When the biblical story was told to the African people and whenever the Africans read the biblical story for themselves they heard and identified with the God of the Bible who loves people and listens to their prayers and supplications, and with the people of the Bible who like the Africans themselves did not believe it was possible to live and prosper without help from God. As John Mbiti (1975) observes, "the prayers, more than any other aspect of religion contain the most intense expressions of African traditional spirituality . . . a study of these prayers takes us to the core of African spirituality." It is therefore evident that in the praying act biblical and African religious heritage converge, and probably it is in this one aspect more than any other that Africans find the biblical religion not only acceptable but one they can call their own.

Prayer in the Bible

In both the Old and New Testaments the Bible is a book of prayer. In the OT the patriarchs, particularly Abraham and Jacob, are a praying people (Gen 15:2-6; 18:23-32; 24:12-14). The prayer of Abraham for an offspring is particularly significant and familiar to the African people. For the African the primary value of having children is brought to focus by the prayer of Abraham, the foremost of the biblical patriarchs (Gen 15:2-6). The prayerful promise and the seemingly bargaining vows to God expressed by Jacob at Bethel that "if God will be with me, and will keep me . . . and will give me bread to eat and clothing to wear, so that I come again to my father's house in peace, then the LORD shall be my God . . . and of all that you give me I will surely give the tenth to you" (Gen 28:20-22) is yet another familiar prayer to Africans. Africans go to God for security, protection, food, good health, prosperity, and peace, for indeed these can only come from God. The African people, like the patriarchs, regard God as one who will not fail to reward those who make and keep a covenant with God, believing that they will meet the expectations God demands from them and God in turn will bless them. Among the Agikuyu of Kenya one saying has it that *Kanya keru ni mwamukaniro* ("the calabash full of food is for exchanging"); that is, life is to give and receive. People cannot just receive from God without giving back as a token of their gratitude what God has given them. Jacob's prayer is therefore a very African prayer.

Rachel's earnest cry "Give me children, or I shall die!" (Gen 30:1) is a cry of many an African woman just as Leah's praise after bearing four sons "This time I will praise the Lord"

(Gen 29:35) is also a prayer of praise familiar to African mothers.

The lives of Moses, Samuel, and especially David are characterized by numerous prayers with which African people will identify. Moses' prayer for the people of Israel during their escape from Egypt is especially significant: "Remember Abraham, Isaac, and Israel, your servants, how you swore to them by your own self, saying to them, 'I will multiply your descendants like the stars of heaven, and all this land that I have promised I will give to your descendants, and they shall inherit it forever" (Exod 32:13-14). African prayer like the biblical one is rooted in the remembrance of God's promises to the people in the past especially during times when such promises seem to be obliterated by bad fortune or the people's rebellion. The priest in African tradition invokes God's promises and pleads to God on behalf of the people. Again the promises of offspring, land, and prosperity are central manifestations of God's blessings. The reference to and reverence for the ancestors are central to biblical and African prayers. Biblical communities, like African communities, worshiped and prayed to the "God of our ancestors."

Africans find much comfort in the Psalms. They are replete with expressions familiar in African prayer. "I lie down and sleep; I wake again, for the LORD sustains me" (Ps 3:5). "O LORD my God, in you I take refuge; save me from all my pursuers, and deliver me; or like a lion they will tear me apart; they will drag me away, with no one to rescue" (Ps 7:1-2). "I love the LORD, because he has heard my voice and my supplications. Because he inclined his ear to me, therefore I will call on him as long as I live" (Ps 116:1-2). "Sing to the LORD with thanksgiving; make melody to our God on the lyre. He covers the heavens with clouds, prepares rain for the earth, makes grass grow on the hills. He gives to the animals their food, and to the young ravens when they cry" (Ps 147:7-9).

The metaphors employed by the psalmists are familiar to African people and these prayers express the prayers of the heart, of the human spirit as it reaches out into the depths of God's power to save and bless those who call on God. The psalmists' praises are poetically memorable and African melodies, songs, and dances are full of such expressions. To pray is to plead, to praise, and to promise. This is evident both in the Bible and in African traditions. Examples of these are to be found throughout the OT. The books of the prophets, especially Isaiah, like the psalms, are replete with prayers Africans identify with at once. The African spirit, often cast down, is lifted up in a special way when the people read Isa 40:28-31. The creator, the almighty God will lift up those who cry. Those who wait for the Lord will "renew their strength" and will "mount up with wings like eagles."

While the OT expressions of prayer will probably be more familiar to the African people than those of the NT, Africans do identify with the prayer life of Jesus, the apostles, and the Christian community in the NT. The Lord's prayer is especially significant. It is a prayer of praise, pleading, repentance, and promise. Jesus calls God "Our Father." For Africans God is always "Our Father" in the beyond. Africans understand God as our Father, the source of all that God's children need.

In the Acts of the Apostles the Christian community prayed always in their homes and wherever else they met. When people came together whether in worship or for any other community gathering, prayer played a central role. This is not uncommon in Africa. Every gathering of people must include prayer, and the decisions people make are always subject to God's will, *mungu akipenda* ("if God wills"). It is God who brings and keeps people together. For Africans, people's gatherings are prayer gatherings. At the birth of a child, at initiation rites for the youth, at marriage ceremonies and funerals prayers play the central role in Africa. Africans through prayers recognize that it is God who brings and keeps the people together and prospers them. No one would dare make light of prayers in Africa. Even among the most secularized people in contemporary Africa no one will make light of prayers. In Africa the expression "let us pray" will often bring a rowdy mob to a reverent silence, even if they privately do not take prayers seriously. Nobody in Africa would dare question the efficacy and necessity of prayer.

Prayer in African Tradition and Contemporary Christianity

Prayer in African tradition is rooted in the theistic universe of African spirituality. For the African people the origin and existence of the entire creation are rooted in a creator God. All life springs from God and without God's help life cannot continue or prosper. While life flows from God resulting in blessings such as children, rain, harvest, fertility of the herds, health of the people, security, and happiness, Africans are also aware that there are other spiritual and human forces that frustrate this flow of life from God, resulting in barrenness, drought, famine, diminishing livestock, diseases, and general misery of the people. These negative forces, whether from angry ancestors, evil spirits, witches, sorcerers, or other anti-life, anti-human, and anti-social forces can cause great suffering to the people. African people seek to neutralize them through ritual sacrifices and prayers by enlisting the good spirits and the positive forces of life from God and restoring the normal flow of life throughout the community. Prayer in African tradition is therefore primarily concerned with keeping these anti-life forces at bay and keeping open the flow of life from God to the people. The anti-life forces or spirits may be powerful, but unlike God the creator and God's mediating agents they are not omnipotent. Only God is all-powerful and able to overrule and neutralize all other powers. When Africans see Jesus casting out demons, restoring sick people to health, and filling empty stomachs with food they see one who is pro-life and who stands as a channel of the flow of life from God. Thus praying in Jesus' name means invoking the name of the one who, like the revered ancestors, has access to life from God. When priests, pastors, and other agents of God pray for the people the African people see in them this flow of life being affirmed and at work for their own good. The connecting link between God and the people is facilitated not only through prayers but also through sacred agents of God whose task is to maintain the link between God's power and the people. Quite often God's power and the flow of life may be communicated through ordinary persons whom God chooses to engage. Through visions, dreams, and spiritual insight God may lift ordinary persons to the heights of the spiritual order and use such persons to bring warnings and blessings to the people. Prophets, seers, diviners, healers, and other visionaries are to be taken seriously, for they are able not only to inform people of the causes of their misery but also of what they must do in order to restore God's flow of life and its blessings.

African spirituality has had great influence within the African Independent Churches, which take the African cosmology as the basis of understanding the biblical message. In these churches prayer is central to worship and the role of the priests is considered very important while allowing for the participation of ordinary believers in communicating and mediating God's blessings. Even in the more westernized forms of worship African cosmology and prayer is evident particularly during times of crisis.

Conclusion

African Christians easily recognize continuity between the biblical and African world and only in very few instances do they notice some discontinuity. In fact the discontinuity is more often between African spirituality and historical denominational theologies from the West than the biblical world. Nowhere is the continuity between African spirituality and the Christian faith more evident than in the theme of prayer as expressed in the Bible, both in the Old and the New Testaments, and in Africa traditional spirituality.

BIBLIOGRAPHY

Dickson, Kwesi A., and Paul Ellingworth, eds. *Biblical Revelation and African Beliefs.* Maryknoll, N.Y.: Orbis, 1969.

____. *Theology in Africa.* Maryknoll, N.Y.: Orbis, 1984.

Mbiti, John S. *The Prayers of African Religion.* Maryknoll, N.Y.: Orbis, 1975.

____. *Bible and Theology in African Christianity.* Nairobi: Oxford University Press, 1986.

Shorter, Alyward. *Prayer in the Religious Traditions of Africa.* New York and Nairobi: Oxford University Press, 1975.

How Did We Get Our Bible?

Introduction

Erik Eynikel and William R. Farmer

The Bible is a book. This means that it has all the characteristics of literature. It is made of texts and these texts have a history. That history is explained in the following general articles, which consider first of all the history of the selection of literature, from oral tradition through written documents to the separate Bible books as we have them today. Periods of great crisis, particularly the Babylonian exile in 587 B.C.E. and the destruction of the Second Temple in 70 C.E., were very influential in this process. People started to write in order to explain what had happened, to keep the spiritual heritage that was left, and to build up a program for their future.

Second, these articles consider the history of the selection of the separate books in the Bible (OT and NT) leading to the present list or lists of canonical writings that the synagogue (OT) or the churches (OT and NT) consider Holy Scripture. Here too periods of crisis have played a major role in the various stages of the fixing of the biblical canon. God's people wanted, in turbulent times, to secure their spiritual foundations as preserved, according to them, in a selection of holy books. All this is explained in the articles "How the Bible Came to Us" and "The Deuterocanonical Writings."

Another aspect of the literary character of the Bible is that we most often read it in our own language. Most pastors are not familiar with the original languages of the Bible: Hebrew, Aramaic, and Greek. They read the Bible in a translation in their mother tongue. When they do so they can experience that different translations, even within one language, may deviate from each other. There are different reasons for this.

First, the translators do not always use the same translation technique. Sometimes they translate rather literally, using the "formal-equivalence" method. They may even use the "concordance" method, translating each instance of a particular word in the original language (Greek, for example) with only one word in the language of translation (English, Spanish, Polish, etcetera). In other translations the translators work more freely, producing "dynamic equivalence" versions that try to capture the "flavor" of the original language. All this depends on the target group the translators have in mind. More information on this can be found in the article "How the Bible Came to Us."

A second reason why translations can deviate is that there is not one text of the Bible, but many different texts. The original autographs of the authors of the biblical books are no longer extant. We only possess copies, or rather copies of copies of copies. For the OT the oldest complete manuscript (Codex Leningradensis 19B-A) dates from 1009 C.E. There are, however, fragments of older manuscripts (among them the Dead Sea Scrolls) and there are older complete manuscripts of translations of the OT made in antiquity. The most important is the Greek translation (Septuagint), a Jewish translation of the OT made in Alexandria in the third to first centuries B.C.E. We have manuscripts of this translation that predate the oldest complete Hebrew manuscript by many centuries. The translator of the Bible has to evaluate differences occurring in these versions and make a rational decision about the correct reading. However, since each translator can make his or her own choice, different readings occur. In the NT the situation is slightly different. There are now almost 5,500 manuscripts or fragments of manuscripts of the Greek NT. Therefore the ancient translations (in Latin, Syriac, Coptic, etcetera) are of less importance for the NT than are the translated versions of the OT. Nevertheless those approximately 5,500 manuscripts contain an estimated 300,000 to 400,000 variants, many of which, as in the study of the OT, must be critically evaluated by the translator, who must choose among the possible readings. More can be read about this in the articles "How Reliable is the Text of the Bible?" and "Text Criticism of the New Testament."

It is important for readers of our commentary to be aware of these issues because they can be confronted with them when comparing different Bible translations. After reading these articles the reader will understand that these differences, which are not very numerous and frequently of little importance, are due to the fact that God's word came to us through the mediation of many people, each with a unique history. Therefore it is to be expected that the reflection of these people on the word of God as written down in the biblical texts leaves all the marks of that ongoing history.

How the Bible Came to Us

Donald S. Deer

The English word "Bible" ultimately derives from the Greek word *biblia,* a plural meaning "books." "Bible," however, has come to designate that "book," in the singular, that brings together the books holding a special place in the life of the Church. The Bible came into being as the traditions reflected in each of its books were brought together in writing, then collected and selected, next copied, and finally translated. Central to the story of the Bible is God's revelation and God's people's response to that revelation.

How the Books of the Bible were Written

The earliest Christians did not have a Bible such as we have today, since parts of it had not even been written yet. Furthermore, it was not until much later that all the books could be bound together in one volume to become one book. Originally the different books of the Bible circulated separately as individual books, and only later as separate groups of books such as the collection of four gospels.

In the early part of the first century of our era, however, the only books of the Bible that Christians had in writing were the ones that made up the authoritative written literature, or "scripture(s)," in use by their Jewish contemporaries. This literature, later expanded to include other works, was eventually to be known to Christians as the Old Testament.

That Jewish literature itself had gradually come into existence over a period of more than a millennium, a period that had itself been preceded by a period of transmission of individual units of older traditions, such as the victory song found in Judges 5. In other words, the OT grew incrementally. We find a reference to a prior tradition in 2 Kings 22:8, which tells how the High Priest Hilkiah discovered "the book of the Law," which had been lost, in the Temple. Scholars have identified this lost-and-found book with at least part of the book of Deuteronomy. In the NT we are taken behind the scenes by one author to see how the editing of a gospel took place. In Luke 1:1-4 the author tells us that behind the editing was the tradition, including the oral proclamation, and behind the tradition the historical event, or events.

Irenaeus (ca. 130–ca. 200 C.E.), the bishop of Lyons, was the first person to use the term "New Testament" to designate the new Christian literature telling about Jesus and the emerging Church. This made it possible for the first time to talk about an "Old Testament." The designation of the two testaments as the "Bible" goes back to John Chrysostom (ca. 347–407 C.E.), bishop of Constantinople.

We do not know who wrote most of the books of the Bible, although later tradition was to assign names to them. What we do know, however, is that the writing took place not only over a period of more than a thousand years and in many different locations on different continents, but also in three different languages: the OT mostly in Hebrew but also in Aramaic (two words in Gen 31:47; Ezra 4:8–6:18; 7:12-26; Jer 10:11; and Dan 2:4b–7:28), and some deuterocanonical books of the OT and all of the NT in Greek.

Part of the backdrop to this writing was the domination of Palestine and the rest of the eastern Mediterranean region for a period of over a thousand years, up to and including the time of Christ and the early Church, by a succession of empires: Egyptian, Assyrian, Babylonian, Persian, Greek, and Roman. Thus the Bible reflects the hopes and aspirations of a small nation living under the domination of imperial powers. The God of the Bible is the God of people who seek freedom from the oppression of domination.

One legacy of the domination of this area of the world by the Greek-speaking Macedonian Alexander the Great and his successors was the spread of a form of Greek known as "Koine" (meaning "common"), that served as the common language down into the time of the Roman empire. Acts 21:37 describes a Roman official communicating with the apostle Paul in Greek. It was in this "common" Greek that Paul and all the other authors of the NT wrote, even though such books as the gospels depended at least in part on an earlier tradition transmitted orally in Aramaic.

Other defining moments in history also left a particular stamp on the writers and assemblers of the traditions found in the Bible: the exodus of the Hebrew people from Egypt under Moses and his receiving the Law at Sinai, the unification of the people of Israel under King David, the capture of the northern kingdom by Assyria, the destruction of the Solomonic Temple and the captivity of a large part of the population of the southern kingdom in Babylon and their return in the Persian period, the persecution of the Jews by the Syrian successors to Alexander the Great, and the capture of Jerusalem and the destruction of the Herodian Temple by the Romans in 70 C.E.

Those responsible for assembling the traditions in the Bible did not always eliminate overlapping traditions. The book of Psalms was originally five different books or collections of psalms, but when they were brought together in one collection both Psalm 14 (= Vulgate Psalm 13) and Psalm 53 (= Vulgate Psalm 52) were retained although they are essentially the same psalm. Since Matthew arranges Jesus' teaching in five discourses the presence of essentially the same teaching in Matthew 5:29-30 and 18:8-9 may be explained on similar grounds.

When a story was retold it was because the need was felt to recast the story in such a way as to meet the needs of a new situation in the life of God's people. The biggest block of repeated material in the OT is found in 1 Chronicles 10–2 Chronicles 36, which covers roughly the same ground as 1 Samuel 31–2 Kings 25, namely the story of the people of Israel from the death of Saul to the fall of Jerusalem.

In the NT it is the existence of four different gospels that constitutes the most notable example of multiple traditions. Each gospel tells about Jesus' life and ministry in its own way, as the example of the different timings of Jesus' action in the Temple demonstrates. The major convergence occurs in the narratives of the Passion.

There are smaller overlaps as well, including three different accounts of the giving of the ten (or more) commandments to Moses: not only in Exodus 20, but also in Exodus 34 and Deuteronomy 5. There are likewise three different accounts of Saul/Paul's conversion: in Acts 9, 22, and 26. Much of the material in Colossians is also found in Ephesians; similarly, many of the verses in Jude have parallels in 2 Peter.

Each community of faith produced literature in response to its needs, resulting in a variety of kinds of literature: history, prophecies, legal codes, proverbs, parables, fables, allegories, prayers, hymns, rituals, letters, apocalypses (visions of the future), speeches, traditional religious stories concerning origins, treatises, and even handbooks for church administrators.

For information on how each of the books of the Bible came into being, see the introductions to those books.

How the Books of the Bible were Collected and Selected

Not all the books that were written have survived. "The Book of Jashar," mentioned in Josh 10:13 and 2 Sam 1:18, is a case in point. There are still other books that used to be part of some Christian Bibles but are no longer included in most of our Bibles even though they have survived, such as the Letter of Barnabas, the Shepherd of Hermas, and 1 and 2 Clement. The Letter of Barnabas and the Shepherd of Hermas are found in Codex Sinaiticus dating from the fourth century, but are not in our current Bibles. First and Second Clement, however, which are found in Codex Alexandrinus, a fifth-century manuscript of the Bible, are included in the Coptic Orthodox Church's NT along with the "Apostolic Constitutions," making a New Testament of thirty books.

Still other books were slow to be accepted. Eastern Christianity was reluctant to accept Revelation (The Apocalypse), and Western Christianity was slow in accepting Hebrews. The other NT books that generated the most debate were James, 2 Peter, 2 John, 3 John, and Jude. The OT books that were most disputed were Esther, Proverbs, Ecclesiastes, Song of Songs, and Ezekiel.

To this day different branches of Christendom have different contents in their Bible. Roman Catholics in their official list ("canon") include seven OT books that they call "deuterocanonical" (meaning belonging to the second canon), namely Tobit, Judith, 1 and 2 Maccabees, Wisdom, Ecclesiasticus (Sirach), and Baruch. They are called "deuterocanonical" because they were not included in the Hebrew Bible, whose contents are designated as "protocanonical," or belonging to the first canon. The deuterocanonical books were included in the Greek translation known as the Septuagint (LXX), as well as in the Latin translation known as the Vulgate. Their inclusion makes an OT of forty-six books in Catholic Bibles. These deuterocanonical books, plus three others, 1 and 2 Esdras and the Prayer of Manasseh, and the additions made to the books of Daniel and Esther, are those that Protestants call "apocryphal," picking up on a designation introduced by Jerome. They were included in Protestant Bibles including the King James Version (Authorized Version), but in the nineteenth century it became popular among some Protestants to omit them from their Bibles. Protestants made no new translation of them into English between 1827 and 1939, but have made several since 1939. Many Protestant versions of the Bible are now available in two editions, one with and one without these books called the "Apocrypha." In Protestant Bibles all the books of the Apocrypha are grouped together between the OT and the NT instead of being interspersed among the books of the OT as in the Greek Septuagint.

There are also ecumenical versions of the Bible produced with the full involvement of representatives of different Christian communions at every level of the translation process. The French *Traduction oecuménique de la Bible* was produced by a joint effort of Catholics and Protestants, with Orthodox scholars involved in the checking. In an effort to communicate with Judaism as well, this version has the (protocanonical) OT books arranged in the order of the Hebrew Bible (which is different from that of our English Bibles), and includes many notes referring to Jewish traditions.

For Jews the only books to be included in their Bible, the "Hebrew Bible," were those that Catholics and Protestants call the "Old Testament," not including the "deuterocanonical" or "apocryphal" books. Although no final decision was made concerning the contents of this Bible until the second century of our era, the books that were included had been collected and selected a long time previous to that. These books were numbered in such a way as to make a total of twenty-four books and grouped into three divisions. The three divisions were not all accepted as Scripture by the Jews at the same time. The first division, or collection, made was known as "The Law," or "Torah," also called "The Five Books of Moses," or "Pentateuch." It contains the first five books of the Hebrew Bible: Genesis, Exodus, Leviticus, Numbers, and Deuteronomy. These books were considered the most important part of the Hebrew Bible. When they were later being translated orally into Aramaic the translation was only allowed to proceed at the rate of one verse at a time. The translation of the second division, the Prophets, however, could be done three verses at a time. "The Prophets" includes Joshua, Judges, 1 and 2 Samuel, and 1 and 2 Kings, as well as what Christians refer to as "the prophets": Isaiah, Jeremiah, and Ezekiel, and Hosea through Malachi.

In last place came the third division, "The Writings," including poetical books (Psalms, Job, and Proverbs), "five rolls" (Ruth, Song of Songs, Ecclesiastes, Lamentations, and Esther), prophecy (Daniel), and history (Ezra–Nehemiah and Chronicles). Note that the last book in this division is (2) Chronicles, which may explain the reference in Luke 11:50-51 to the period stretching from the creation of the world to the murder of Zechariah (2 Chron 24:20-22), which would correspond to an order beginning with Genesis and ending with (2) Chronicles. The acceptance of this third division came much later, and only gradually.

This "Hebrew Bible" is now numbered in English translations as thirty-nine books, and so is identical in content with the OT of the Protestant Bible although, as we have seen, the order of the books is not the same. The order of the books of the OT in Catholic and Protestant Bibles is close to, but not identical with, that of the Greek LXX. Note that what Catholics have traditionally called the "Apocrypha" is still another group of some sixty books including, for example, First (or Ethiopian) Enoch, referred to in Jude 14-15. These same books have come to be called the "Pseudepigrapha" by most Protestants.

In parallel development to the various collections of the OT came those collections of various categories of books that met different needs of the growing Christian Church: gospels, Acts, letters, and Revelation. The final decision as to the content of the (Catholic) Christian Bible was made by the Roman Catholic Church on April 8, 1546, at the Council of Trent. Eastern Orthodox churches decided the contents of their Bible in 1672 at the Synod of Jerusalem; they included most of the "deuterocanonical" books. The Eastern Orthodox Holy Synod held in 1950 added 3 Maccabees, 4 Maccabees (in an appendix), and Psalm 151. The New Revised Standard Version is available in an edition that includes all of these books and chapters.

Protestants have never made, and never would be able to make, any universally binding decision in this matter because there is no worldwide authority that can speak for all of them. Most Protestants tend not to use the "deuterocanonical" or "apocryphal" books of the OT, but readings from these books are included in the Anglican and Episcopal lectionaries. Roman Catholics, Protestants, and Eastern Orthodox agree, however, in having the same twenty-seven books in their NT: four gospels, Acts, twenty-one epistles or letters, and Revelation.

Not all Ethiopian Orthodox Bibles have the same books, although they always contain eighty-one, counting either forty-six OT books plus thirty-five NT books or fifty-four OT books plus twenty-seven NT books. When their NT has thirty-five books it includes the following eight: (four sections of) Sinodus, (two sections of) The Book of the Covenant, (one section of the three Epistles of) Clement, and the Didascalia.

Toward the end of the fourth century a significant portion of the Eastern Church used a twenty-two-book NT, omitting 2 Peter, 2 and 3 John, Jude, and Revelation. The Nestorian Churches have retained this twenty-two-book NT canon.

Each community of faith has retained those books that have best met its needs. As the Jewish community rebuilt its Temple and reestablished its religious life in Palestine during the restoration period following its return from exile in Babylon it did so on the basis of laws given by God through Moses. For that purpose it needed, and therefore made, a first collection and selection of those books that told the story down through Moses, namely Genesis to Deuteronomy; it made this choice no later, and possibly earlier, than 400 B.C.E. This collection of five books therefore came to be known as the Law, or the Books of Moses, and served as the most important guide for the faith and practice of the restored community, contributing to the definition of its identity. To this day the Samaritan community has these same five books as its only Bible.

When the identity of the Jews was further being tried, and needed to be affirmed in the religious, cultural, and political confrontation with Alexander the Great and his successors during the Hellenistic period, the Jewish community added a second division, "The Prophets" (around 200 B.C.E.). The final blow came with the capture of Jerusalem and the destruction of the (Second) Temple by the Romans in 70 C.E. Deprived of both homeland and Temple, the Jews gave increased attention and importance to their sacred books. By some time in the second century C.E. they were able to determine the shape of the third division, "The Writings," among which the book of Psalms has always had pride of place, as evidenced in Luke 24:44. Although the Jewish people had been dispersed they were to survive through the centuries, thanks to their common bond to a common text.

Christians appropriated the Jewish Scriptures as their own. At first the only Bible of the Greek-speaking Christians was the Greek LXX, which is the version usually quoted in the NT. They used this version so much, in fact, that the Jews felt obliged to produce further translations of their own into Greek in order to distinguish themselves from Christians. As the Christians used the Jewish Scriptures, however, they reinterpreted them in the light of the coming of Christ. The beginning of Christian interpretation of the Jewish Scriptures, which Jesus referred to as "Moses and the prophets," started with the way in which Jesus himself read these Scriptures. This way of reading "Moses and the prophets" was embraced by Jesus' disciples, who in turn handed it on and developed it for Christian use.

Eventually and inevitably, by analogy, Christians were to accord the same authority to their own Christian traditions as they had been giving to the Jewish Scriptures. As the original eyewitnesses were dying off, Christians felt the need to preserve the written accounts of Christ's words and deeds by collecting them. They also were obliged to do some selecting, eventually eliminating competing gospels such as the Gospel of Peter, which was still referred to by Origen (185–254 C.E.). By 200 C.E. there was a fourfold gospel canon, a collection of Paul's letters, Acts, 1 Peter, and 1 John. Later, but not necessarily in the following order, other books were added, notably those whose inclusion was delayed the longest: Hebrews, James, 2 Peter, 2 John, 3 John, Jude, and Revelation. As in the case of the OT, where the Law took precedence over the other divisions, so in the NT the four gospels were to occupy a preeminent place and letters attributed to Paul were to take precedence over later letters attributed to other apostles.

In the second century, however, (ca. 140 C.E.) Marcion had already decided to reduce the number of gospels to one. In his Bible he only included the gospel of Luke, as well as ten of Paul's letters, thereby excluding all the rest of the books of the NT and all of the Jewish Scriptures. He helped galvanize the Church into action, forcing it to defend the retention of "Moses and the prophets" and to decide which of the existing gospels to authorize for use in the Church.

A further reductionist attempt was made (ca. 160 C.E.) by a Syrian church leader named Tatian, who wove the four gospels into one continuous harmony called the *Diatessaron* ("four through one"), which continued to be popular in translations into various languages for centuries afterwards. The Church, however, continuing the witness of Irenaeus, has maintained the independent witnesses found in the fourfold gospel.

Other groups such as the Ebionites, the Gnostics, and the Montanists made their own choices of which books to "stand by," not all of them the same ones being used in the rest of Christendom. Since these groups were declared "heretical" this also forced the Church into defining the limits of its own Scriptures. More recently certain scholars have proposed that the gnostic Gospel of Thomas be included alongside the four traditional gospels, but this proposal has met with little approval. (See "The Church's Gospel Canon: Why Four and No More?")

Other factors also had an impact on, and hastened, the process of collection and selection (canonization) of the books of the NT. One was the need to provide guidance for the Church as it consciously settled down for the long haul after realizing that the end of time was going to be longer in coming than originally thought. Still more important was the need, in the face of persecution, to identify which books were worth dying for. In 303 C.E. the Roman Emperor Diocletian launched an empire-wide persecution of Christians during which some believers were put to death for refusing to turn over their Scriptures.

In earlier times the direct, or indirect, association of the various books of the NT with an apostle and the "correct" teaching in these books were seen as important factors contributing to their inclusion by the Church as part of "Scripture," but in time the greatest use of these books by the largest number of Christians over the widest area emerged as a primary consideration.

How the Books of the Bible were Copied

The decision about the order in which books were to be included between two covers of a complete Bible, with both Old and New Testaments, was not made and could not be made until Bibles began to take their present physical shape and all the books could be copied by hand onto leaves that could be bound together. All the time that the Jews were collecting and selecting their authoritative books, however, the standard format for these books was the scroll (roll), and no more than one of the larger of these "biblical" books could be copied onto one unwieldy scroll. Surviving NT manuscripts, including the earliest copies made on papyrus leaves, were with very few exceptions in the form of a "codex," essentially equivalent to our modern book format, but none of these "papyri" contains the entire NT. The oldest existing complete manuscripts in which all of the books of the Bible were bound together in one volume only go back to the fourth century; these were written on parchment, made from the skins of animals. Paper was introduced as a material to write on in the ninth century and became more common from the twelfth and thirteenth centuries onward.

All copies were made by hand until the invention of printing in the fifteenth century. The people who made these handwritten copies are called "scribes." We owe a great debt to such persons, most of them monks, for keeping the Bible "alive" through all the earliest centuries. Copying by hand, however, was slow and expensive, and each manuscript passed on its own set of errors. Furthermore, the number of copies was limited. The introduction of printed Bibles reduced the cost and therefore greatly increased access to the Bible.

The oldest texts of the Hebrew OT manuscripts contain consonants, but no vowels. In the oldest Greek NT manuscripts, while there are vowels, there is virtually no division into words and no punctuation. Contractions were commonly used for sacred names; in Greek the name of Jesus was contracted from six letters to two (the first and last), written $\overline{\text{IC}}$, or three (the first, second, and last), written $\overline{\text{IHC}}$.

Copying was done either visually or from dictation. Either way mistakes could be, and were, made. In Rev 1:5 *lusanti,* "freed," was misunderstood no later than the ninth century as *lousanti,* "washed," producing the reading found in the King James Version, "Jesus Christ . . . *washed* us from our sins in his own blood" or, in the New Jerusalem Bible, "Jesus Christ . . . has *washed away* our sins with his blood" instead of "Jesus Christ . . . *has freed* us from our sins by his blood" (New American Bible) or "By his . . . death . . . Jesus Christ . . . *has freed* us from our sins" (Good News Bible [also known as Today's English Version]).

Not all changes made by the scribes were unintentional; some were intentional rewordings of the text to avoid what appeared to be a compromising of cherished beliefs. In 2 Sam 12:14, the Hebrew text on which the King James Version was based talks about *"the enemies of* the LORD." The phrase "the enemies of" was apparently added to "the LORD" in order to avoid the reading we find translated in the NAB as "you have utterly spurned the LORD," and in the NRSV as "you have utterly scorned the LORD," a wording that was considered blasphemous.

Important discoveries of manuscripts in the nineteenth and twentieth centuries have put us in a much better position to get closer to the original wording of the texts of both the Old and New Testaments. The discovery, beginning in 1947, of the Dead Sea, or Qumran, scrolls, so called because they were found in caves used by the Qumran community near the Dead Sea, has led to hundreds of changes in the wording of our current translations of the Bible. These scrolls date from the third or second centuries B.C.E. to the first century C.E. The largest number of changes are to be found in Isaiah, but there are also changes in Genesis, Exodus, Deuteronomy, 1 and 2 Samuel, Psalms, Ecclesiastes, Jeremiah, Daniel, and Habakkuk. In Isa 21:8a, for instance, we now read *"The sentry* calls out" (Good News Bible), instead of "and he cried, *a lion"* (Authorized Version).

Among the more important NT manuscripts published in the nineteenth century we may cite Codex Sinaiticus and Codex Vaticanus, both originally written on parchment and both dating from the fourth century, and Papyrus 66 and Papyrus 75, both at least a century earlier and so called because they were written on papyrus leaves. John 5:3b-4 (the story of an angel stirring up the water) and John 7:53–8:11 (the story of the woman caught in adultery) are missing in all four of these manuscripts. John 5:3b-4 is also missing in Jerome's Latin Vulgate, and John 7:53–8:11 is also missing from the oldest Syriac and Coptic versions as well as from several manuscripts of the Old Latin version. Of the numerous manuscripts that do contain these verses, many are marked with an asterisk in the margin, indicating the scribes' recognition of their questionable nature. This evidence, combined with the differences in the vocabulary and style of these passages compared to that used in the rest of the gospel, has led most scholars to conclude that the stories were not originally a part of the text of the gospel of John even though some scholars think that they may contain genuine, independent traditions. Since the story of the woman taken in adultery was included by Jerome in the Vulgate, in any case, it is considered part of the Bible ("canonical") by the Catholic Church. The story of the angel stirring up the water, on the other hand, is not considered canonical since it was missing in Jerome's Vulgate, even though it was included in the (later) Sixto-Clementine Vulgate (1592–1598).

We depend, then, for our reconstruction of the original texts not only on ancient manuscripts of the OT in Hebrew and Aramaic, and of the NT in Greek, but also on versions (translations) of the OT in Greek, Aramaic, Syriac, and Latin, and on versions of the NT in Syriac, Latin, and

Coptic. Additional help is provided by quotations from rabbis or Church Fathers and from lectionary manuscripts in which texts of the Bible were arranged in separate units that could be read according to an order corresponding to liturgical practice.

An example of the help afforded by the versions is to be found in Hos 11:3 where the Syriac and Latin versions, and to some extent the Greek version, support the reading *"my* arms," as in the NJV, the Good News Bible, the NAB, the REB, and the NRSV, as opposed to *"their* arms" (Authorized Version), or *"his* arms," which is found in the traditional Hebrew text of this verse.

The chapter and verse divisions found in our modern translations were not in the original manuscripts. The chapter divisions we use today were introduced by Stephen Langton, later Archbishop of Canterbury, in the thirteenth century. The basic numbering of verses in the OT used today was worked out by the Dominican Sanctes Paginus in the sixteenth century. The verses in the NT are the work of a printer named Robert Stephanus (in French, Robert Étienne) who inserted them in his fourth edition of the Greek NT in 1551. The first Bible in English to have verse divisions was the Geneva Bible (NT, 1557; Bible, 1560).

It is to be noted that there is a difference in certain chapter numbers among Jewish, Catholic, and Protestant Bibles, and between some English Bibles and those in other languages, especially in the OT. There are also here and there differences in the verse numbering among the various versions. Sometimes we encounter differences in both chapter and verse divisions at the same time, especially in the Psalms. For example, the verse that is numbered Ps 53:3 in Knox and the French Maredsous version is the same verse as Ps 54:3 in all Jewish Bibles in both French and English, all Catholic and Protestant Bibles in French (except Maredsous), and some Catholic Bibles in English, such as the NAB, and is also the same verse as Ps 54:1 in other Catholic Bibles such as the NJB, and all Protestant Bibles in English. The reason for the difference in the chapter numbers in the Psalms is that Psalms 9 and 10 of the Hebrew Bible are only one psalm in the Greek LXX and in the version made from it, the Latin Vulgate (and in translations based on the Vulgate), and so are Psalms 114 and 115. On the other hand, the Greek and Latin divide both Psalms 116 and 147 into two. The result is that although there are 150 psalms in both Hebrew and Latin, the numbering of the chapters is different between the two from Psalms 9–10 through 147. The reason for the difference in verse numbers in the Psalms is that in some versions the introductory material is numbered, and in others it is not.

How the Bible has been Translated

It is not enough to know something of how the books of the Bible were written, collected and selected, and copied by hand in the earliest centuries. The Bible would still be inaccessible to us, a "closed" book, if it were not for translations made into our language. Translation of the Bible goes back at least to the time when most Jewish people no longer spoke Hebrew and required translation into Aramaic, at first oral, then written, of what was written in Hebrew. This practice may be reflected in Neh 8:7-8, where the Levites may have been giving a translation from Hebrew into Aramaic so that the people might understand the reading of the Law. Other Jews who were Greek-speaking produced translations of the whole OT into Greek. Still other translations were made into Syriac and Latin. The Latin Vulgate was the translation that was to become the official version of the Catholic Church and the basis for translation into many other languages until the middle of the present century. In fact, it was from Latin that the first translation of the Bible was made into English by at least two men associated with John Wyclif(fe).

The first Roman Catholic translation into English from the Latin Vulgate that was approved by the Church for Catholic readers was made by a group of English Catholic exiles associated with the English College in northern France, beginning during the reign of Queen Elizabeth I. Gregory Martin's translation of the NT, read and reviewed by his colleagues Cardinal William Allen and Richard Bristow, was published first in 1582, while the College was still located at Rheims, and so is known as the Rheims New Testament. It influenced the later King James Version (1611), known in England as the Authorized Version. Where the predecessor of the King James, the Bishops' Bible (1568–1602), had "moistnesse" in Luke 8:6, and "fat calf" in Luke 15:23, Rheims, followed by the King James, had the more modern "moisture" and the more familiar "fatted calf(e)."

The OT portion of this translation appeared too late to exert much influence on the Authorized Version. After Martin died in 1584 his work on the OT was completed by Allen and Bristow. It was not published until 1609–1610, when the College had moved back to its earlier location at Douay, which is why the complete Bible is known as the Douay-Rheims version. It was thoroughly revised again a century and a half later, beginning in 1749, by Bishop Richard Challoner, assisted by Francis Blyth. Since both men were converts from Protestantism it is not surprising that the Authorized Version had an influence on their revision of the Douay-Rheims version. It is this revision that was the principal version used by Roman Catholics until the second half of the twentieth century; it is sometimes known as the Douay-Rheims-Challoner version. It was authorized for use by American Catholics in 1810. Another version approved for Catholic readers was made in 1944–1949 by Monsignor Ronald A. Knox; it too was based on the Latin Vulgate, but had the advantage of using a much more modern idiom. It was authorized for use in Great Britain by the Roman Catholic hierarchy of England and Wales and the hierarchy of Scotland.

The first translation of the NT and parts of the OT from the original languages into English was made by William Tyndale, whose new translation of the NT (1526), Pentateuch (1530), and Jonah (1531) was followed closely by a long series of revisions through the King James, or Authorized, Version (1611), the Revised Standard Version (1946–1971), down to the New Revised Standard Version (1989). Modern-language versions made from the original languages and independent of the Tyndale/Authorized Version tradition date back to the beginning of this century, beginning with the Twentieth Century New Testament (1898–1904), many of whose innovations are to be found in such later versions as Goodspeed's New Testament (1923–1948), the New English Bible (1961–1970) and its revision, the Revised English Bible (1989), the Good News Bible (1966–1979), and the Contemporary English Version (1991–1995).

Roman Catholic translations based on the original languages owe their impetus to the publication of the papal encyclical *Divino Afflante Spiritu,* issued by Pius XII on September 30, 1943, as well as to the Constitution on Divine Revelation *(Dei verbum)* promulgated by the Second Vatican Council on November 18, 1965. This latter (6.22) states in part that "Access to sacred scripture ought to be widely available to the Christian faithful," and makes the point that ". . . the church . . . sees to it that suitable and correct translations are made into various languages, especially from the original texts of the sacred books." The two most important Catholic translations in the second half of the twentieth century growing out of the new situation created by these two documents have been the New American Bible and the (British) English translations found in the Jerusalem Bible (1966) and its revision, the New Jerusalem Bible (1985).

The New American Bible (1970–1986) is the standard Bible for American Catholics and is the product of American Catholic scholarship, with the collaboration of some Protestant scholars. A first translation of the NT, which had been sponsored by the Episcopal Committee for the Confraternity of Christian Doctrine, was published in 1941 as the Confraternity New Testament. It was a further revision of the Douay-Rheims-Challoner version and was based on the Latin Vulgate. With the publication of *Divino Afflante Spiritu* in 1943, however, the corresponding OT, which had already begun, was relaunched, no longer as a revision of Douay-Rheims-Challoner based on the Vulgate, but as a wholly new version based on the original languages; it was completed in 1969. A new translation of the NT, this time based on the Greek, was produced in time to be printed with the OT in a complete Bible in 1970. The NT was revised in 1986, the Psalms in 1991.

The translation into (British) English in the Jerusalem Bible (1966) leaned heavily on the French translation in the *Bible de Jérusalem,* but the translation of the New Jerusalem Bible (1985) was done directly from the original languages. The copious introductions and notes in both editions were based on the French *Bible de Jérusalem* (first edition, 1955; second edition, 1973). There are also imprimatur editions of the Revised Standard Version (1966), originally sponsored by the National Council of the Churches of Christ in the United States of America; and the Good News Bible (1979), originally sponsored by the American Bible Society. Both of these American versions have also appeared in British editions, with the appropriate adaptations to British English usage.

It is to be noted further that the Roman Catholic Churches in England and Wales, Ireland, and Scotland were among the churches that planned and directed the translation of the New English Bible and the Revised English Bible. "Evangelical" (conservative or fundamentalist) Protestants were originally often opposed for theological reasons to the idea of new translations or revisions, especially the RSV. In the past half century, however, they have produced several of their own new versions, such as the Modern Language Bible (1945–1969), the Amplified Bible (1959–1987), the New American Standard Bible (1963–1971), the Living Bible (1967–1976—based on other English versions rather than translated from the original languages) and its revision, the New Living Translation (1996—based on the original languages), the New International Version (1973–1984), the New King James Version (1979–1982), and the New Century Version (1987). A common tendency of these versions is to "harmonize" passages that appear not to agree with each other. Second Samuel 8:18b in most modern Protestant, Catholic, and Jewish versions says that "David's sons were *priests,*" a translation that all the "evangelical" versions are at pains to avoid since Num 3:10 states that only Aaron's descendants were qualified to serve as priests, and we know that David was not a descendant of Aaron.

Between 1962 and 1985 the New Jewish Publication Society came out with *Tanakh,* also known as the New Jewish Version. The dust jacket bills this version as "the standard Jewish Bible for the English-speaking world." Unlike Roman Catholic and Protestant versions of the OT it purposely has little recourse to readings found in the Dead Sea (Qumran) scrolls or to readings found in Greek, Latin, or Syriac versions of the Bible. Thus in Isa 21:8a it reads "[like] a *lion* he called out," with the traditional Hebrew text, rather than "the *sentry/watchman* calls out/cried," found in the Qumran text.

Translation involves five steps: (1) deciding what language to translate from, (2) determining what text in that language to translate, (3) understanding the meaning of that text, (4) choosing the proper translation theory for bridging the gap between the expression of the meaning in the source language and the expression of the equivalent meaning in the receptor language, and (5) finding the appropriate level of the receptor language in which to express that meaning. Versions differ from each other because of differences in the approach to translation in each of the above steps.

(1) Not all versions are always based on the original languages. Even some post-Tyndale Protestant versions show dependence on Latin, evidenced by their use of transliterations rather than translations of Latin, as in Isa 14:12a where some versions read "Lucifer," rather than "lightbearer," and in Luke 23:33, where some have "Calvary," rather than "Skull."

(2) Nor do all versions always use the same text in the original languages as the basis for their translations. Some Greek manuscripts read a Greek word in John 5:2 that is transliterated "Bethzatha" by the RSV/NRSV, the Good News Bible, and the Contemporary English Version. Other manuscripts, however, read a Greek word that is transliterated "Bethesda" by the NEB/REB, the NJB, the NAB, and the NIV. Still others read a Greek word that has come through the Latin Vulgate to Ronald Knox's English as "Bethsaida."

(3) Versions also vary in their understanding of the original languages. On the one hand the Hebrew word *ʾadam* could be either a common noun referring to an individual human being or a generic term referring to the human race, "humankind"; on the other hand it could be used as a proper name, "Adam." There is no unanimity as to the interpretation and translation of this term in certain verses. So, depending on which English version you are using, you may first encounter the proper name "Adam," rather than the common noun "the man," in Gen 2:19 (KJV, Knox, and New Living Translation, as in the Vulgate), or 2:20 (NJV, NIV), or 2:23 (Living Bible), or 3:17 (RSV), or 3:20 (Good News Bible), or 3:21 (NEB), or 4:25 (NJB, NAB, REB, and NRSV).

(4) Most versions may be conveniently categorized as (a) relatively literal, the so-called "formal-equivalence" versions, and (b) relatively freer in their renderings, the so-called "dynamic-equivalence" or "functional-equivalence" versions. The latter are less tied to the word order and structure of the original languages and

seek to avoid possible misunderstandings or unnecessary ambiguity. They give priority to the rendering of the sense, or meaning, of the original over the reproducing of the form of the original. The RSV's relatively literal translation of 1 Sam 26:12a—"So David took the spear and the jar of water from Saul's head, and they went away"—could be misleading. The reader could be led to ask (1) if Saul had water on the brain; (2) if David was a brain surgeon; and (3) where "the spear and the jar of water" went away to. The Good News Bible avoids these potential misunderstandings by rendering this verse as "So David took the spear and the water jar from right beside Saul's head, and he and Abishai left."

(5) Finally, versions differ in part because they represent different levels of language. The KJV contains archaic language that is misleading to the modern English-language reader; the "nephews" it refers to in Judg 12:14, for example, are "grandsons" in all modern versions.

The English language has not only evolved through the passage of time, it has also evolved through the dispersal of speakers of English in widely separated parts of the world, with the result that there are a variety of dialects of English that require the publishers of current translations to come out with different editions for different countries. The British edition of the Good News Bible reads "My . . . daughter is very ill" in Mark 5:23 in place of the American original's "My . . . daughter is very sick."

One of the concerns in many recent versions is the need to have "inclusive" language. Jesus' question in Mark 8:27 used to be translated "Who do *men* say that I am?" (Knox, RSV; compare Phillips, the NEB, the Translator's New Testament, and the NKJV). As long ago as 1904, however, the Twentieth Century New Testament, knowing that the Greek word used in this question did not refer exclusively to males, translated it as "Who do *people* say that I am?" It has been followed in this by Weymouth, Moffatt, Goodspeed, Montgomery, C. B. Williams, C. K. Williams, Rieu, Schonfield, the NASV, the JB/NJB, the Good News Bible, the NAB, the NIV, the New Century Version, the REB, the NRSV, and the New Living Translation.

In summary we may say that for a translation to accomplish its purpose it must faithfully render the meaning of the original and at the same time cause us to forget that it is a translation. In other words, it must be both accurate and readable.

The original authors of the books of the Bible composed their books in times, cultures, and languages quite different from our own, and without being conscious that these books would one day be collected into one book, the Bible. Neither could they be conscious of what would be involved in the copying of their books or the preservation of these copies, to say nothing of the ultimate necessity of removing errors that crept in during the process of copying and recopying these books by hand in the earliest centuries; nor could they imagine the herculean effort involved in providing meaningful translations of the Bible into the thousands of languages of the world today. So we may conclude that the fact that the record of God's revelation to God's people as preserved in the Bible has come down to us is nothing less than a miracle, for which we may be grateful.

The Deuterocanonical Writings

Reginald C. Fuller

The books and parts of books known by the above title are called Apocrypha by the churches of the Reformation. With one or two exceptions they are extant only in Greek and do not form part of the Hebrew canon. They are recognized as inspired and canonical Scripture by the Roman Catholic and (predominantly) the Eastern Churches following the early Christian tradition that accepted the Greek LXX as their Old Testament. These books are Tobit, Judith, Esther (Greek additions), Wisdom of Solomon, Sirach (Ecclesiasticus), Baruch 1–5, Letter of Jeremiah (Baruch 6), Daniel 3 (Song of the Three), Daniel 13 (Susanna), Daniel 14 (Bel), 1 and 2 Maccabees. The content and specific characteristics of these books are explained in full in the different commentaries on the books themselves, but it is relevant here to summarize a few important features.

Tobit is an edifying novella with freely adapted historical detail about the testings and blessings in the life of the pious family of Tobit in the Eastern diaspora under Assyrian rule. The work is transmitted in three different Greek recensions. The Semitic original is dated around 200 B.C.E.

In Judith the heroism and trust in God of an Israelite widow are glorified. The book is like a novella interlaid with historical data. It is only extant in Greek, in three different recensions, although it must originally have been written in Hebrew or Aramaic. It fits best in the second or first century B.C.E.

Wisdom of Solomon combines Jewish tradition with Greek thought and seeks to demonstrate the elevation of the wisdom of Israel in order to arm the Jews of the diaspora against the temptations of Hellenistic culture. It was originally written in Greek, in all probability in Alexandria, in the first century B.C.E.

Wisdom of Jesus ben Sirach is a compilation of proverbs typical of formative Judaism. It was originally written by Jesus ben Eleasar ben Sirach at the beginning of the second century B.C.E. and was translated into Greek by his grandson ca. 130 B.C.E. Two-thirds of the original Hebrew version has been reconstructed from Hebrew fragments from Cairo, Qumran, and Masada.

Baruch consists of different texts (in a variety of literary genres: history, wisdom poems, prayer of atonement, lamentation) of different dates. The several documents were originally written in Hebrew but the present collection under the name of Baruch is extant only in Greek and dates from the second or first century B.C.E.

The Letter of Jeremiah (Baruch 6 in the Vulgate) is a satire on idolatry. It is kin to passages such as Isa 44:9-20 and Jer 10:1-8. The connection to Jeremiah is probably inspired by Jer 29:1. Originally written in Hebrew in the second century B.C.E., it is only extant in a Greek version.

First and Second Maccabees describe the struggle of Mattathias and his sons, known as Maccabees, against Antiochus IV (175–164 B.C.E.) and his successors from 163 until 135. First Maccabees is obviously a translation from an original Hebrew text. Besides narrating the heroic struggle of Jewish guerrillas against a tyrant, it teaches that God's support will not fail if they remain faithful to God's law. Second Maccabees, stylistically quite different from 1

Maccabees, was originally written in Greek, probably by a Jew in Alexandria, and retells part of the history already given in 1 Maccabees. Second Maccabees stresses that salvation is more dependent on the direct intervention of God.

The additions to Daniel and Esther differ from the above because they do not consist of independent writings but are real additions within the text. The first addition to Daniel is the Prayer of Azariah and "Hymn of the Three Young Men" (sixty-eight verses), spoken by three martyrs who had been thrown into the fiery oven by Nebuchadnezzar because they refused to worship his golden image. The addition gives the content of their prayer. The second addition, the story of Susanna (sixty-four verses), is placed at the end, after the protocanonical book of Daniel. It tells the story of a beautiful and devout Jewish woman who was falsely accused of adultery by two rejected lovers. Daniel, however, inspired by an angel, saved her *in extremis.* He cleverly demonstrated the inconsistencies in the testimonies of the accusers and proved that the accusations were false. The third addition, also at the end of the book, is called "Bel and the Dragon" (forty-two verses); it contains two stories. In "Bel" Daniel demonstrates the fraud of the priests of Bel-Marduk, who request large quantities of food for the statue of their god but steal it at night. In "The Dragon" Daniel kills the divine Babylonian dragon by feeding it a mixture of pitch, fat, and hair. The Babylonians wanted to kill Daniel for that by throwing him into the lion pit, but Daniel was miraculously saved (cf. also Daniel 6).

The additions to Esther consist of six extended parts (numbered from A through G): Mordecai's dream (A), decree of pogrom against the Jews (B), Mordecai summoning Esther to go before the king (C), the prayers of Mordecai and Esther (D), Esther's audience with the king (E), the anti-decree counteracting the pogrom (F), and interpretation of Mordecai's dream (G). Peculiar to the additions to Esther, in contrast to the protocanonical book, is that God is named explicitly. In the protocanonical book God is present but in a hidden way (4:14; 6:13).

In general it can be said that the religious ideas of all the deuterocanonical books, despite their differences, witness to Jewish faith and the Jewish spirit as they were present in the last two centuries B.C.E. God is almighty, transcendent, and intolerant of idolatry. God miraculously saves the pious who suffer and even sacrifice their lives for their God and religion. The importance of the deuterocanonical books is that they reveal to us the spiritual climate at the end of the pre-Christian era, the period immediately preceding New Testament times.

Other books not recognized by the Roman Catholic Church are included in the canon of the Greek and Russian Orthodox Churches. They are 1 (3) Esdras, 3 Maccabees, Prayer of Manasseh, and Psalm 151. The Russian (Slavonic) canon also includes 2 Esdras (= 3 Esdras in Slavonic, = 4 Esdras in the Latin Vulgate appendix). This is not extant in Greek. First and Second Esdras and the Prayer of Manasseh are placed in an appendix to the Latin Vulgate Bible and 4 Maccabees is placed in an appendix to the Greek Bible.

It was Sixtus of Siena (d. 1599) who devised the titles "protocanonical" (p. c.) to indicate books of the Hebrew canon and "deuterocanonical" (d. c.) to indicate the other books, all (except 2 Esdras), found in the Greek LXX and included later in the canon. We shall use the abbreviations p. c. and d. c.

From the fourth century until the Reformation in the sixteenth century the Bible used throughout the Western world was the Latin Vulgate, consisting of Jerome's translation of the books of the Hebrew canon (the p. c.), the d. c. books, mainly in the Old Latin Version except for Tobit and Judith (newly translated by Jerome), and the NT mainly in Jerome's revision of the Old Latin. Though doubts were expressed over the centuries about some books, Luther was the first person in history to extract (for a variety of reasons) the d. c. books from their traditional order, largely that of the Greek LXX, and put them together as a group, after the books of the Hebrew canon, in his Bible of 1534. This change was followed by the Reformation churches; some indeed omitted those books altogether. In response the Council of Trent in its decree of 1546 declared that all the books, with all their parts, contained in the Latin Vulgate Bible were to be accepted as sacred and canonical. The title "Apocrypha," applied to these books, was used by Jerome to mean spurious or inauthentic, "not part of the canon." The name has continued in use by the Reformation churches to designate these books as "uncanonical," but with varying meaning.

It is probable that all but two of the d. c. books (Wisdom and 2 Maccabees) were originally written in Hebrew (or Aramaic), but the original texts have for the most part not survived and they continued in their Greek form as part of the Christian Bible. Most of the Hebrew text of Sirach was discovered in the Cairo Geniza in 1896 and at Qumran in 1947–1952, where fragments of Tobit, Judith, and the Letter of Jeremiah were also found. The general dating of these books is between 250 B.C.E. and the beginning of the Christian era, and the location of manuscripts so far discovered suggests free circulation not only in Egypt but also in Palestine.

The original Hebrew or Aramaic texts must have disappeared (that is, they were no longer copied) after 70 C.E. The Jews no longer used them, with one or two exceptions, and the overwhelming majority of Christians used the Greek LXX text. The theory that the Greek-speaking Jews of Alexandria recognized a canon longer than the Palestinian Hebrew canon has long been demolished. (See especially A. C. Sundberg, *The Old Testament of the Early Church,* 1964, passim.) It would have been inconceivable for the Jews of Alexandria to have usurped the authority of Jerusalem in so vital a matter. The legend of the origin of the LXX given in the Letter of Aristeas was surely devised to underline this dependence on Jerusalem. Moreover, this "Alexandrian" theory supposes that the Palestinian canon had been closed before the coming of Christ.

Josephus, writing about 93 C.E. (*Ap.* 1.8) asserts that the Hebrew canon was closed in the days of Artaxerxes, King of Persia, when the exact succession of prophets ceased, and that since that time no one has dared to add to or subtract from it or make any change in the text. This claim, however, does not bear examination. The imaginative account in 2(4) Esdras of Ezra's rewriting the Jewish Scriptures (supposedly destroyed by fire, 2[4] Esd 14:18) is even less worthy of credence. The book was in any case written about 100 C.E. We may not forget, however, that Josephus's intention was to defend the canon in use in his community in his day.

It is widely, though not universally, held today that many of the books of the Hebrew canon were written after Ezra's time: these include Chronicles, Daniel, Job, and many psalms. The book of Sirach (Ecclesiasticus) ca. 180 B.C.E., lists the prophets by name (48:22–49:12) but omits Daniel because that book did not yet exist in Sirach's day. The prologue to Sirach composed by the author's grandson (132 B.C.E.) speaks of "the Law (Torah), the Prophets, and the other writings of our ancestors." The Torah was, of course, the core and foundation, dating from before the schism of the Samaritans who recognize only these books as Scripture.

"The Prophets" were temporarily "complete" after the time when prophets ceased to appear among the people of Israel (1 Macc 9:27), evidently long before 200 B.C.E., but nothing is said in the records to suggest that this cessation was final. Indeed, the hope for and expectation of further prophets never died but grew steadily up to the time of Christ. "The Jews . . . have resolved that Simon should be their leader and high priest . . . *until* a trustworthy prophet should arise" (1 Macc 14:41).

"The [other] writings" does not suggest a clearly defined group but seems to indicate the books beginning to accumulate after the gap in the line of the prophets, and now being recognized as Scripture. There is no suggestion of a tripartite canon, nor indeed of any closure. There *was* a Canon in the sense of recognized sacred books, but it was an open-ended canon to which books could be added later. Though Josephus maintained that the text was preserved without change, Paul Kahle has shown that the text underlying the LXX differs notably from the manuscripts discovered at Qumran and also from the Masoretic text of a later time (*The Cairo Geniza* 138; and cf. F. J. Stendebach, "The Old Testament Canon in the Roman Catholic Church" in *The Apocrypha in Ecumenical Perspective,* 33).

We are led to the conclusion that the statements about closure, none of which are earlier than Josephus, were partly motivated by the growing Jewish disenchantment with the LXX Bible, which Christians used against them in arguing the claims of Jesus Christ. Other reasons, of later date, are given in the Talmud. We can say with W.O.E. Oesterley that the reasons adduced by the Jews for excluding the d. c. books from the Hebrew canon were "clearly artificial and contrary to fact" (*The Jews and Judaism During the Greek Period,* 48–49). Indeed, the word "canon" (= rule or standard) is used by Christians to mean "rule of faith" and is never used in the early centuries for a list of books that is closed. Though a collection of authoritative writings established itself in Judaism, nevertheless Judaism as such knew neither a concept of canon nor a process of canonization in the strict sense (James Barr, *Holy Scripture: Canon, Authority, Criticism,* Oxford, 1983, 49–50). One could add that the arbitrary choice of a total of twenty-two (the number of letters in the Hebrew alphabet) suggests a symbolic rather than an exact total, as can be seen from the various attempts to meet the total by combining or separating books—a sort of bed of Procrustes. Jewish tradition also proposes twenty-four as the total of books in the synagogal collection (cf. 2 Esd 14:18). Sirach was excluded, yet it continued as if it were still included (*t. Yad.* 2.13).

The requirement that a canonical book must have been composed in Hebrew (*t. Yad.* 4.5) was formulated later with a view to excluding the d. c. books on other grounds. One of the rabbis' aims was "to exclude the proliferating apocalyptic literature, whose syncretistic character threatened Judaism with disintegration" (Stendebach, "The OT Canon," 33). Then again a greater role was claimed for the proceedings at Jamnia than was actually the case. It is now agreed that there was no formal "synod" at Jamnia in the 90s C.E. at which decisions about the canon were made. This synod, however, could have provided the occasion for an examination of the records and the claims of certain books (Ecclesiastes, Song, Ruth) for inclusion. Besides these, doubts existed also about Ezekiel, Proverbs, and Esther well into the second century C.E. However, for practical purposes 100 C.E. is often given as a date of "completion" of the Hebrew canon.

The Jewish enumeration of the canonical books given in the Talmud, *B. Batra* 14b, dates probably from the third century C.E. at the earliest. Though Christians took their Scriptures from the Jews in the form of the Greek LXX we cannot speak about this with precision to any extent because only Christian manuscripts of the LXX have come down to us. Herbert Haag states that "The Church Fathers did not treat as canonical what they found in the LXX; what they treated as canonical came from the LXX." Thus, for example, different manuscripts contain 3 Ezra, 3 and 4 Maccabees, Psalms of Solomon, and the Prayer of Manasseh. (Herbert Haag, art. "Kanon," *Bibellexicon,* Einsiedeln, 1968, 915–922).

Are there any indications in the Bible itself? Do the actual books quoted give us some clue to the closure (if any) of the OT canon? Roger T. Beckwith suggests that we look at the gospels in an attempt to discover what books Jesus and his apostles regarded as Scripture before the break occurred. "For," he says, "if they teach us what their OT Canon was, do they not also teach us what, for Christians, the OT Canon ought to be?" (*The Old Testament Canon of the New Testament Church* 111). Beckwith chooses the text of Luke 24:44, "Moses, the prophets, and the psalms" as an indication that Jesus accepted the tripartite division of the Hebrew canon ("the psalms" indicating the hagiographa). But he omits to mention that in ten other places (See Matt 5:17; 7:12; 11:13; 22:40; Luke 16:16, 29-31; Acts 13:15; 24:14; 28:23; Rom 3:21) only *two* groups are mentioned: "the law and the prophets" (or "Moses and the prophets"). "By contrast, the threefold designation, 'the law of Moses, the prophets and the psalms' in Luke 24:44 is without parallel in NT literature" (John Barton, *Oracles of God,* 35). Again it is argued that, because all *direct* quotations of Scripture are from the Hebrew canon and only a small number of (implicit) references are made to the "Apocrypha," the latter should be regarded as non-canonical (d. c. quotations and allusions: Jas 1:19 with Sir 4:29; 1 Pet 1:6 with Wis 3:5-7; Heb 11:35 with 2 Macc 7:9, 11, 14, 23, 29, 36; Heb 1:3 and Col 1:15 with Wis 7:26; Rom 1:18-21 with Wis 13:1-9). But many other reasons suggest themselves as an explanation of this difference. All these books and parts of books are of more recent date than the Hebrew canon and we have already seen that the "canonization" process could take a long time. One consequence would be that many hearers would be less familiar (or even not at all familiar) with these books. But much more importantly this argument assumes that there was already a recognition of a closed canon. This, we have seen, is not sustained by the facts. Moreover, we may reasonably ask: Why suppose that the NT writers should be *obliged* to quote *every* inspired and canonical book? It is interesting to note that no less than nineteen of the thirty-nine books of the Hebrew canon (Joshua, Judges, 1 Samuel, 2 Kings, 1 and 2 Chronicles, Ezra–Nehemiah, Esther, Ruth, Ecclesiastes, Song of Songs, Ezekiel, Lamentations, Jonah, Obadiah, Nahum, Zephaniah, and Haggai) are not quoted by Jesus and the apostles. Does this cast doubt on their canonicity?

Last, Beckwith argues that since rabbinical interpretations (such as we find enshrined in the Talmud in the form of utterances by named teachers) do not change from generation to generation we are entitled to conclude that what is there stated can be taken as an indication of what was held generations earlier, not only in the time of Jesus but earlier still. R. T. Herford, *Judaism in the New Testament Period,* 82, agrees that one can go back as far as the NT period and "probably" earlier, but Beckwith (*Old Testament Canon,* 366) goes back much farther, at least as far as Maccabees. This is in effect the view of George Foot Moore in his *Judaism in the First Centuries of the Christian Era.* He says Judaism remained substantially the same from pre-Christian centuries down to Talmudic times. There was a kind of *normative* Judaism and this must be judged by rabbinic sources, not extraneous testimony. But this position is strongly questioned. W. D. Davies argues that the Dead Sea Scrolls show Judaism before 70 C.E. to be very different from the Judaism of subsequent periods. It was far more variegated and—more importantly—far more open to outside influences than Moore allows. "In short (the Dead Sea Scrolls) help further to destroy the view that pre-Christian Judaism was almost a monolithic structure" (Davies, *Christian Origins and Judaism,* 106). J. W. Bowker adds another consideration: "Rabbinic Judaism . . . in time became . . . the prevailing orthodoxy; this interpretation was then read back into the earlier periods, as though Pharisaic/rabbinic Judaism had always been 'orthodoxy'—whereas the earlier situation was far more open" (*The Targums and Rabbinic Literature,* 36 n.).

Since after 70 C.E. Christianity had broken away from Judaism, Christians were free to decide for themselves what books should be included in their Scriptures. However, this was not the main issue. The real bone of contention between Jews and Christians was not the exact contents of a canon but the *interpretation* of the Scriptures in terms of Jesus Christ, and hence the acceptance or rejection of him as the Messiah. In doing this Christians were doing what Jesus had himself done for the disciples on the road to Emmaus (Luke 24:27). But to the leaders of the Jews this was, of course, anathema: cf. Acts 4:2; 5:17-18; 6:11-12; 9:23; 12:1-3. It was at Jamnia, after 70 C.E., that the rabbis began to deal methodically with this threat, as they saw it, to their position. They accused the Christians of mistranslating the LXX or misinterpreting its meaning. "Considered from the point of view of moral right, the Christian appropriation of the Scriptures, the status, the very name of Israel, is a sheer act of usurpation, an outrage inflicted upon Judaism, among the most deadly of the long series of wrongs which Jews have suffered through the centuries at the hands of the Christian Church" (R. T. Herford, *Judaism in the New Testament Period,* 238).

Since the Christians almost invariably used the Greek LXX, it is easy to understand that the Jews turned more and more against that version and demanded a new, more literal translation from the Hebrew. Aquila's translation was completed about 140 C.E., that is, shortly after the cataclysmic revolt of Bar Kosiba. "The express purpose of Aquila's version was 'to set aside the interpretation of the LXX, in so far as it appeared to support the views of the Christian Church'" (H. B. Swete, *Introduction to the Old Testament in Greek,* 382). The LXX was banned altogether (Paul Kahle, *The Cairo Geniza,* 139). Henceforth the LXX was the basic Christian Bible (Old Testament).

The Early Church

The LXX Bible, now rejected by the Jews because of what they saw as misuse by the Christians, became an exclusively Christian text not only in terms of its use but also in that it contained the d. c. books now excluded by the Jews, though the exact number of books was not a matter of special concern to the community. Before the book form or codex was thought of, scrolls of various sizes were used, no one of which could contain the whole of the Scriptures, so occasional differences were inevitable. But there was a practical consequence of the Jewish rejection of the d. c. books that could not be ignored. Christian apologists were obliged to avoid quoting from them because their authority was not recognized by their opponents. The question had to be asked: which books should *not* be used in controversy with the Jews?

Melito, Bishop of Sardis (ca. 170 C.E.), made a collection of Scripture passages entitled "Selected

Texts from the Law and the Prophets Referring to Our Savior and Our Whole Faith." This was in response to a keen student called Onesimus who had asked him "many times" for this and for a list of OT books he could use. The latter request caused problems, as no Christian list existed, but Melito traveled to Palestine, "where these things were done and preached," and came back with the Jewish canon, the only list available. The rabbis were firmly established at Tiberias after moving from Jabneh (Jamnia) at the time of Bar Kosiba's revolt in 135 C.E., and a flourishing rabbinical school soon existed there beside the Lake of Galilee.

The list Melito sent to Onesimus (at least as recorded by Eusebius, *Hist. Eccl.* 4.26) gives the books not in the Hebrew order but in that of the LXX (being the order familiar to Christians) while omitting the d. c. books. Melito adds that he made his selection of Scripture passages from these books, but makes no comment on the difference between Bibles. It seems likely that he is giving Onesimus the Hebrew canon because only these books could be used in controversy with Jews. This was surely his purpose, rather than to give an "authoritative" list of a canon, which evidently had not been officially issued by the Church.

Nearly a century later Origen (d. 254) also gives a list of the Scriptures but makes it clear that the list is "as handed down by the Hebrews" (Eusebius, *Hist. Eccl.* 6.25). He adds, however, the books of Maccabees. Here and elsewhere he is careful to specify that it is the Hebrews' list. He frequently quotes the d. c. books in exactly the same way as he quotes the p. c., both (p. c. and d. c.) being contained in the Bibles in general use. "Origen saw no reason why the Church should be dispossessed of them [the d. c. books] just because the Jews did not acknowledge them. They were the Church's Scriptures" (M. F. Wiles, "Origen as a Biblical Scholar," *Cambridge History of the Bible,* 1.455–456).

Fourth Century

The exclusion of the d. c. books for purposes of controversy gradually led many scholars to believe that the difference in use implied a difference in status or authority. Books that could not be used in controversy to prove doctrine to the Jews were now thought to be books that did not have authority *in themselves* and so were not canonical Scripture.

Athanasius of Alexandria in his *Festal Letter 39* (367 C.E.) gives the Hebrew canon, plus Baruch, as sacred and divine, but specifies others (Wisdom, Sirach, Esther, Judith, and Tobit) to be read by "those just joining us." Maccabees are not included. Cyril of Jerusalem (d. 386) goes farther and assigns the d. c. to the apocrypha (*Catechesis,* 4.33, MPG 33.495). The views of these great men influenced many Latin writers of the time. Thus Rufinus of Aquileia (340–410), scholar, monk, and friend of Jerome, followed Athanasius and described the d. c. as "ecclesiastical," that is, to be read in church, but not authoritative in matters of faith (*Comm. in Symb. Apost.* 36–38). But like his predecessor he continued to use and quote the d. c. exactly as the p. c. Later (see below) he returned to the traditional view and attacked Jerome for excluding the d. c.

Jerome (Eusebius Hieronymus) (331–420) far outshone his contemporaries in Bible study. In his time there were "as many [Latin] versions as there were codices," to use Jerome's dramatic phrase. Pope Damasus wanted Jerome to revise and unify the text. This was the "Old Latin" translated from the LXX, not the Hebrew. In two years Jerome had revised the gospels and Psalms, as the books most in use. But to his astonishment he was widely attacked for "tampering with the word of God." At this point the Pope died, and as Jerome did not get on well with his successor (Siricius) he decided, in 385, to leave Rome. Eventually he settled in Bethlehem where he spent the rest of his life.

Here he took up again his work of revising the Latin Bible from the Greek, but at the same time studied Hebrew with a Jewish rabbi, Baraninas. Very soon Jerome came to the conclusion that nothing less than a new translation directly from the Hebrew was required. He gave as his reason that this was the only way to argue with the Jews, who were still criticizing the LXX and versions made from it. (See *Preface to Psalms* [Vulgate], MPL 28.1123–1128.) This led him eventually to reject not just the LXX as a translation but also the d. c. books contained in it. In the introduction to the books of Samuel and Kings (his *Prologus Galeatus* in which he defended his new translation from the Hebrew), Jerome declared the d. c. books to be uncanonical, *"non sunt in Canone"* (MPL 28.555–556). He went on (with Cyril of

Jerusalem) to term these books "Apocrypha." Jerome began his great work probably in the late 390s and completed it in 405/6. Needless to say, his view of the d. c. had great weight as that of the greatest biblical scholar of his age, and since the *Prologus Galeatus* was often included in Vulgate Bibles his views were widely publicized. It was not his intention to include the d. c. books, but under pressure he did make a beginning. He translated Tobit and Judith and the Greek additions to Esther, but we do not know exactly how much of the d. c. (as now contained in the Vulgate) we owe to him and how much to others. Augustine of Hippo, already famous, and now a bishop in 395, expressed his dismay at the new translation as it "cast doubt on the Greek LXX which for so long had been the authoritative Bible in the Christian Church" (*Letter to Jerome,* 5 [394/5]). Rufinus too (now, alas, alienated through controversy) accused Jerome of being persuaded by his Jewish rabbi, Baraninas, to discard the Greek LXX and cut out the d. c. books treasured in the Church (*Apology against Jerome,* 401 C.E.). Deeply affected by the opposition, Jerome seemed to back down in his reply to Rufinus. He said that in objecting to the parts of Daniel not in the Hebrew text he had only been giving the Jewish view, not his own! (*Apologia adversus libros duos Rufini,* 2.33 [MPL 23.476]). However, it is unlikely that he had changed his views.

It was at this point (396–397) that Augustine made an important contribution to the debate. In his *De Doctrina Christiana* 2.8 he sets out these criteria:

1. The Scriptures that are accepted by all Catholic churches will take precedence over those that are rejected by some.
2. Those books that are accepted by the majority and by the more important churches take precedence over those accepted only by a few or by less important churches.
3. If there is a book that the majority accept, but the more important churches reject (or vice versa) they should be regarded as of equal authority.
4. There follows a list of the whole OT canon, book by book, to show that, though they may in his view vary in authority, they are all included in the canon. The list corresponds with that issued by the councils of Carthage and confirmed by Pope Innocent I in his *Letter to Exsuperius of Toulouse,* 405 C.E.

Already Augustine had held a synod at Hippo in 393 at which a list of OT books was published, including the d. c., taken almost certainly from the Old Latin version. It is probable that Lamentations, Baruch, and the Letter of Jeremiah are intended to be included under "Jeremiah" and that the d. c. parts of Daniel and Esther are included under their respective names. A footnote was added to the effect that the *"ecclesia transmarina"* (that is, Rome) should be consulted with a view to approval of the list by the pope. The list was endorsed by the Third Council of Carthage in 397, but Pope Siricius died in 398. The list, together with the footnote, was sent to Pope Innocent I after his election in 402. The Pope incorporated the list in his 405 letter to Exsuperius, Bishop of Toulouse, a friend of Jerome, who had asked for guidance in light of the latter's well-known views. Innocent wrote: "Apart from the Canonical Scriptures, nothing must be read in Church, *under the title* of *the divine Scriptures."* There follows the list of books: five books of Moses, Joshua, Judges, 1–4 Kings (that is, Samuel and Kings), Ruth, sixteen books of prophets (four plus twelve), five books of Solomon (Proverbs, Ecclesiastes, Song of Songs, Wisdom, Sirach), Job, Psalms, Tobit, Judith, Esther, 1–2 Maccabees, 1–2 Esdras, 1–2 Chronicles. (See Mansi, *Concilia* 3.924.)

The Fourth Council of Carthage (417) sent this letter to the new Pope Boniface I in 419 with a cordial recommendation for its acceptance "because thus have we received it from the Fathers to be read in Church" (Mansi, *Concilia* 4.430). Jerome died the following year, aged 89. His version eventually won acceptance, except his psalter translated from the Hebrew. The faithful had been singing the Old Latin version too long to be willing to change. Jerome's earlier revision of the Old Latin known as the Gallican Psalter won general acceptance and is the psalter still in use today.

These councils had made abundantly clear what they considered to be the contents of the Christian canon, and though they were provincial, not general councils, the explicit approval of Pope Innocent I added greatly to their authority. In their view all the p. c. and d. c. books were part of the canon.

From Jerome to the Council of Trent

During the succeeding centuries voices continued to be raised emphasizing the distinction between the p. c. and d. c. books that the councils of Africa had so decisively dismissed. No doubt Jerome's influence was partly responsible for this reluctance to accept the councils' decision. Even Pope Gregory the Great (d. 604), for example, said it was quite in order to quote the d. c., though not canonical, because they were good for edification (*Moralia in lib. Job* 19.21 [MPL 76.119]), but Isidore, Archbishop of Seville (d. 636), later named Doctor of the Church, said "although the Hebrews do not accept them, the Church nevertheless numbers them among the canonical scriptures" (*In libros V. et NT Proemia* 7 [MPL 83.157]). The Council of Florence (1441) endorsed the Catholic canon as given at Carthage (Mansi, *Concilia* 31.13). Only a few years later Antoninus, Bishop of Florence (d. 1459) said the d. c. were canonical, but unequal in establishing matters in dispute. They have the same authority as Doctors of the Church: see his *Summa Theologica* 3.18.6 (Verona, 1740). Cardinal Ximenes, the renowned scholar who produced the Complutensian Polyglot Bible (published in 1522), prints in the preface Jerome's words on the d. c. books, *"non sunt in Canone."*

Erasmus (d. 1536), following Augustine *(De Doctrina Christiana),* favors an "order of authority" between the books. Thus the highest level belongs to those books of which there have never been any doubts in the Church: for example, Isaiah has more weight than Judith or Esther. Cardinal Cajetan (Thomas de Vio, d. 1534) expounded his views in his work *In omnes authenticos V.T. libros commentarii* (Paris, 1546) f. 481–482. He refers to Jerome's excluding the d. c. books from the canon and placing them among the Apocrypha and says that though in certain places one will find these books reckoned among the canonical books by councils or by Doctors, they are not authoritative *("regulares")* in matters of faith. They may, however, be termed canonical for the edification of the faithful, inasmuch as they are received and authorized for this in the canon of the Bible. Thus Cajetan recognizes both categories (p. c. and d. c.) as canonical but in a different sense: (1) those books that are authoritative in matters of faith, that is, divinely inspired (though Cajetan does not here mention inspiration), and (2) those that are received into the canon for the edification of the faithful but are not authoritative in matters of faith. These also are canonical. (See Seraphim Zarb, *De Historia Canonis Utriusque Testamenti,* 235.)

For Roman Catholics the decree of the Council of Trent (1546) authoritatively decided the status of the d. c. books. The council declared that all the books with all their parts that have been customarily read in the Catholic Church and are contained in the ancient Vulgate Latin edition are to be accepted as sacred and canonical. The decree states the reason, namely that God is the author of all the books of both the OT and the NT; consequently the Church receives and venerates these books with a like affection and reverence. Lest there be any doubt about which books are included, the Council gives a full list of the books, both OT (including the d. c.) and NT. Thus all these books are declared by implication to be *inspired,* since God is their author; they are all *canonical,* that is, included in the canon (d. c. as well as p. c.), and last, they are *authentic* and authoritative (as against the Reformers' idea that the d. c. cannot be used for proving doctrine). In all this the Council of Trent repeated and endorsed what was previously determined by earlier councils.

The Deuterocanonical Books in the East from Jerome to Modern Times

As in the West, so in the East the decisions of African councils even with papal confirmation did not conclude the matter. Though the great majority accepted these decisions and the d. c. continued to be quoted in the same way as the p. c., there were still those who dissented. Perhaps more significant was the practice of the Church in retaining the d. c. in its Bible as before, and distributed throughout the other books, as being apparently on the same level.

In the eighth century a series of writers including Andrew of Crete and Photius of Constantinople favored the full Catholic canon. On the other hand, John of Damascus (d. 754), a learned Christian who became a monk at St. Saba Monastery near Jerusalem, favored the Hebrew canon of 22 books: see *On the Orthodox Faith,* 4.17, but he regularly quoted the d. c. in the same way as the p. c. He was a strong defender of the faith and was later made a Doctor of the Church. This attitude, adopted by writers of East and West—that is, to favor the Hebrew canon but to continue to use and quote d. c. as if on the same level as p. c.—continued right up to the Reformation. In spite of the many differences that arose during this period between Rome and the Greek Church, they never argued about the content of the canon or the number of the books contained in it.

At the Council of Florence, which aimed at reunion between Christians of East and West, in face of the imminent fall of Constantinople to the Turks, the decree *Pro Jacobitis,* which contained a Bible list exactly corresponding with that of the councils of Africa, was promulgated. As a general council of course Florence had more authority than provincial councils and could expect more observance. After the Fall of Constantinople in 1453 and during the centuries of Turkish oppression the aim of the Eastern churches was to preserve the faith at all cost. Their theologians had to study in the West—there being no longer any facilities in the East—and an Orthodox College was established in Venice. Many joined the Uniate rites and the Greek College was founded in Rome about 1580 to train priests for the Greek rite, but this pressure to join Rome was strongly resisted and bad feeling arose among the Easterners. The support of Protestants against Rome was sought by some Orthodox. Thus Meletios Pegas, Patriarch of Alexandria, sent Cyril Lukaris (1572–1638) to Poland to strengthen the Protestants against Rome and especially to see if they would join the Orthodox Church. Cyril got on well with Protestants and went to Wittenberg and Geneva. In 1603, on the death of Pegas, Cyril became Patriarch of Alexandria. He now had Protestant contacts everywhere. His aim was not to start a new church, but to reform the Orthodox Church as Luther had tried to reform Rome! In 1620 Cyril Lukaris became Patriarch of Constantinople, partly through British influence. In recognition of this support Lukaris presented the Codex Alexandrinus to King Charles I.

At this time the Jesuits were making great efforts to convert the Orthodox, and the ambassadors of Britain and Holland were Cyril's supporters in Constantinople against this pressure from Rome. A modern Greek Bible, of an openly Protestant type, was printed in Geneva (Adrian Fortescue, *The Orthodox Eastern Church,* 265). In 1629 Cyril Lukaris published his *Oriental Confession of the Christian Faith,* Calvinist in tone. In a second edition in 1633 he included a Bible canon containing only the books of the Hebrew Bible. This was the breaking point. His numerous enemies succeeded in persuading Sultan Murad II that Cyril was stirring up rebellion. Murad deposed him and ordered the janissaries to put him to death. This was carried out. The *Confession* of Cyril Lukaris was condemned, shortly after his death, at a council in Constantinople (1638) presided over by Cyril II, the successor of Lukaris. Some time later Meletios Syrigos replied to the *Confession,* on the orders of Cyril II, saying that the heretics reject these d. c. books because they contain the invocation of saints and praying for the dead. A further Synod of Constantinople in 1642, though affirming Orthodox doctrine, tried to save Lukaris's reputation by denying that he wrote the *Confession.*

Also in 1642 a synod at Jassy in Moldavia made up of representatives of the Greek and Russian churches condemned the teachings of Cyril Lukaris and approved the Orthodox Confession of Peter Mogilev, Archbishop of Kiev. But Protestant influence was still active. In 1672 a Synod of Jerusalem was summoned by the renowned Dositheus, patriarch of that city, with the express purpose of counteracting the growing influence of Protestantism in the Greek Church. The synod was held in the Basilica of the Nativity in Bethlehem. The assembled Fathers, after affirming a number of doctrines in the Roman Catholic tradition, also declared that the (d. c.) books of Tobit, Judith, Sirach, and Wisdom are to be regarded as sacred and canonical.

In Russia, however, Peter the Great had other ideas. Having built his new capital city of St. Petersburg, he founded the Holy Synod in 1721 to govern the Church in Russia and he abolished the patriarchate of Moscow. The synod was composed of the metropolitans of Kiev, Moscow, and St. Petersburg (and the Exarch of Georgia, to ensure Russian domination there), but it was the Czar who ruled the Synod—though this was not openly acknowledged. During this time Protestant influence increased. In 1876 the Holy Synod approved a *Catechism for Young People* by Philaret Drozdov which recognized only twenty-two OT books. The author had, in his youth, been influenced by Prokopowicz, a friend of the Czar, who rejected the d. c. However, in 1876 the Synod approved a Bible containing both p. c. and d. c. This was in line with their normal usage.

Syria

At Antioch in Syria, former capital of the Seleucid kings, Greek was the dominant language, though in the countryside western Syriac (very like the Aramaic spoken in Palestine) generally prevailed. In Eastern Syria (around Edessa and the Euphrates valley) the people spoke a different dialect of Aramaic that we know as Syriac. This is quite distinct, with its own script, in which many of the Fathers wrote. The "Syriac" version of the OT known as the Peshitta (second–third c.) is written in this dialect and contains both p. c. and d. c. It was once thought to be of Christian origin because it contains the d. c., but it has now been shown to be the work of Jewish scholars (F. C. Burkitt, *Early Eastern Christianity,* 71). The d. c. were added later by Christians. But for what Jewish community was the version made? There is no evidence that the Jews of Edessa used it. Paul Kahle quotes Joseph Marquardt, who thinks the translation was made for the royal family of Adiabene, east of the river Tigris, who were converted to Judaism in the first century C.E. (Kahle, *The Cairo Geniza,* 2nd ed., 184. Cf. also Josephus, *Ant.* 20.2.3). The version later came into use by Christians of the area, who would have been less familiar with Greek. Thus Aphraates (d. 356) used Esther, Chronicles, 2 Maccabees, and Sirach, while Ephraem (d. 373) used Esther and 2 Maccabees, making no distinction between them and the p. c. books. Later, however, the Syrian Church became deeply influenced by the Monophysite heresy and, though many writers remained faithful to the full Catholic creed, others rejected the teaching of Chalcedon on the person of Jesus Christ. These Monophysites became the national Church of Syria and were known as Jacobites, after Jacob Beradaeus, their leader (d. 578) who traveled around founding Monophysite churches.

Ethiopia

The area we are concerned with, better known until recently as (part of) Abyssinia, has the city of Aksum (midway between Lake Tana and Asmara) as its political and religious center. The area's original name, "Habash," from which the name, Abyssinia is derived, is that of an Arab tribe in the Yemen, opposite modern Eritrea, who came to Ethiopia centuries before the Christian era and brought their Semitic language and way of life. With the spread of Greek culture over the whole area following the conquests of Alexander the Great the ancient Semitic title fell out of favor and the Greek name, Ethiopia (land of sun-burnt or black faces), was adopted. For the sake of clarity it is important to note that the "Ethiopia" of the Greek writers was not Habash, but farther north along the Nile valley, around Meroe in the area of the fourth cataract. This is the biblical Cush (Isa 18:1), better known as Nubia.

Aksum was already a kingdom when, according to Rufinus (*Hist. Eccl.* 1.9), two young Christian men from Syria, Frumentius and Oedesius, returning home along the Red Sea (ca. 330 C.E.) were captured by local bandits and taken to the king in Aksum where they could expect a life of slavery. But they made so favorable an impression on the king that he eventually set them free. Frumentius traveled to Alexandria where he urged Bishop Athanasius to send missionaries to Aksum. Athanasius then consecrated him bishop and sent him back to Ethiopia. For two centuries Christianity prospered, during which time many monks came there and founded monasteries. These monks, from Egypt and Syria, brought Bible texts with them, probably in Greek, the language used throughout the Middle East, and possibly some in Syriac. It is probable that some of these monks were Monophysites who left Syria after the Council of Chalcedon had condemned the doctrine in 451 C.E. Extant Bible manuscripts bear evidence that the earliest translation into Ge'ez, the ancient classical Ethiopic, dates back to the fifth century and was made from the Greek LXX. Ge'ez is a Semitic language, related to Arabic; it eventually became obsolete except in the liturgy and thus became a sacred language. Strangely, there are no extant manuscripts earlier than the thirteenth century. The damp climate would account for the absence of papyrus manuscripts, but all the existing manuscripts or codices are of goatskin or paper. No doubt the constant wars and invasions, with consequent destruction and pillage, would account in part for the absence of earlier records.

There is good reason to believe that the OT had been translated into Ge'ez by 600 C.E. (Edward Ullendorff, *Ethiopia and the Bible* [Schweich Lectures], 1968, 36ff.). The NT was translated into Ge'ez by about 500 or earlier. The Greek Bible would already be familiar to many before this date. This flourishing period of biblical history continued until the rise of Islam in North Africa. The invasion of Egypt by the Arabs in 640 C.E. began the breakup of Ethiopia's connection with the Christian world. Henceforth Egypt was a province of the Caliphate, with its center in Damascus, while Ethiopia maintained a precarious independence.

A second period of biblical activity began in 1268 with the accession of Yekueno 'Amlak as king. By this time Arabic had replaced Greek as the dominant language in the Middle East, and in Ethiopia the old Ethiopic Ge'ez was giving way to Amharic, the language south of Aksum. The Bible began to be translated into Amharic, this time not from Greek but (mainly) from Arabic. A profusion of Bible manuscripts now spread and multiplied, helped by the presence of many monastic institutions.

A striking feature of Ethiopian culture is that the entire surviving literature is Christian and largely biblical in inspiration, especially the Kebra Nagast or History of Ethiopia tracing the kings back to Solomon and the Queen of Sheba. In about 1500 the Arabs made themselves masters of most of Abyssinia. Ahmed, Emir of Harar, south of Djibouti, burned towns and villages, laid waste the countryside, destroyed churches and monasteries, slew every male adult, and enslaved the women. But salvation was at hand. Claudius succeeded to the throne in 1508 at the age of eighteen. A devout Christian, wise and fearless, he attacked Gran, as the Emir was called, and having killed him in battle won back his kingdom. He himself died in battle in 1540. Toward the end of his reign Portuguese and Italian missionaries began to come to Ethiopia and this gave a boost to the production of illuminated Bibles in which Byzantine influence is noticeable. A fine printed Ethiopian edition of the NT was published in Rome in 1548, made by three monks from the famed monastery of Debra Libanos, who brought Ethiopian manuscripts with them. In modern times the books of Enoch, Jubilees, and the Ascension of Isaiah have been critically edited in Europe, probably because their full versions are extant only in Ethiopic.

In 1820 the French consul in Cairo sponsored the translation of the whole Bible into Amharic by an Ethiopian, Abu Rumi, in succession to the Ge'ez Bible which few could now read. The work took ten years and was made from Arabic with the help of Hebrew, Syriac, Greek, and Latin (Vulgate). The handwritten text filled 9,539 pages. The translation was printed and published by the British and Foreign Bible Society in 1840. A translation into modern Amharic was sponsored by Emperor Haile Selassie and was completed in 1935, the year that Italy invaded Ethiopia. After World War II and the Emperor's return the text was collated with Hebrew and Greek texts, printed at the Emperor's own press, and financed by him. It finally appeared in 1960–1961.

The Ethiopian Bible has eighty-one books—forty-six in the OT and thirty-five in the NT—but totals vary. In the OT, besides the p. c. and d. c., one often finds also 1(3) Esdras, 2(4) Esdras (= the Apocalypse of Ezra), the Ascension of Isaiah, Enoch, Jubilees, the Gadla (Conflict) of Adam, and other lesser-known books. The books of Maccabees are sometimes omitted, possibly because Athanasius, who sent Frumentius to evangelize Aksum, did not include them in his canon. There are also lists of biblical books, for example in *Mashafa Berhan* which contains the *Canon of the Apostles* (fifth c.). This came to Ethiopia via Egypt about the tenth century. A more recent collection is in the *Canons of the Kings* (thirteenth c.), which has a list of the sacred books. These lists usually contain both p. c. and d. c. but vary in the extra books they include. (See Ignazio Guidi, *Fetha Nagast,* Rome, 1897.)

Martin Luther and the Apocrypha

Luther began his translation of the Bible into German during his stay in the Castle of Wartburg, 1521–1522, and completed the NT in March 1522. It was published in Wittenberg after his return there in the same year. The OT, with all its attendant problems, took nearly twelve years to complete and was finally published in the complete Bible edition of 1534. The Bible was divided into six parts of which the fifth was entitled "Apocrypha, that is books that are not held as equal to holy scripture, yet which are useful and good to read." Luther goes on to enumerate Judith, Wisdom, Tobias, Sirach,

Baruch, Maccabees, Parts of Esther, Parts of Daniel. Since he did not regard these books as holy Scripture he separated them from the other books and put them in an appendix after the OT. Luther had already published the five books of Moses in 1522, and with them a table of contents for the entire OT. This shows that he had already reached a decision about the canon, and the term "Apocrypha" now appears for the first time to describe those books as a whole, put together in one group. Never before had they been separated as a group from the books of the Hebrew canon. On the other hand Luther and Lutherans after him never entertained the idea of excluding them, that is, of publishing Bibles without them, in spite of powerful opposition to their inclusion.

On what grounds, then, did Luther hold his views of this group? For Luther "the canon by no means draws authority from the fact that it has established itself and been accepted in this form in the history of the Church." The decisive criterion for Luther is rather one of content. Nevertheless Luther's long familiarity with the Latin Vulgate, which he had read and recited for years, would not have been without influence, in addition to the Greek LXX, on his final choice of d. c. books. Part Five of his 1534 Bible has the title "Apocrypha," that is, books that are not held as equal to Holy Scripture but that are useful and good to read: Judith, Wisdom, "Tobias," "Syrach," Baruch, Maccabees, Esther (Greek additions), Daniel (Greek additions).

It is interesting to note that the Prayer of Manasseh, missing in the Aldine Greek LXX, which Luther probably used, is included in the Vulgate edition of Luther's time attached to the last chapter of 2 Chronicles. It was never included in the d. c. by Luther but he did esteem it highly and printed it in his Bible at the end. Luther's reordering of the d. c. books in place of the Vulgate order again indicates subjective choice. He thought highly of 1 Maccabees, which he considered worthy of inclusion among the p. c., but 2 Maccabees was different because 2 Macc 12:43-46 contains texts that were used to support the doctrines of purgatory, praying for the dead, and the intercession of the saints, doctrines with which he disagreed. In spite of disagreements, however, Luther's Bible always contained the d. c. books not only in his lifetime but for long afterwards. The earliest official statement on the subject of the canon is the "Formula of Concord" (1580) which briefly declares that the prophetic and apostolic writings of the Old and New Testaments are the only rule and guideline for teaching and teachers. No list is given but evidently the statement refers to the Hebrew canon and the twenty-seven books of the NT. By implication, therefore, the Apocrypha are excluded from the list of canonical books, as distinct from the Roman Catholic inclusion of those books in many conciliar decrees. First and Second Esdras (3 and 4 in the Vulgate Appendix) and 3 Maccabees were all included in Luther's "Apocrypha." Curiously, this was not by Luther's choice or direction, and they were omitted in later editions. Third Maccabees is today included in the Greek canon. The blurring of limits to the "Apocrypha" was bound to revive once the Bible became the court of appeal in place of the Church and everyone could decide its meaning for himself or herself (in principle at least), now that it was translated into the vernacular.

If Luther rejected Church tradition as a criterion for canonicity and rejected 2 Maccabees on the grounds of doctrinal statements (see above) we are entitled to ask for a clearer statement of criteria. D. S. Russell thinks that the Reformers rejected the d. c. books largely because Rome used them to support doctrines like the place of good works in attaining salvation, the invocation of the saints, prayers for the dead, and the doctrine of Purgatory (*Between the Testaments,* 88–89). In the 1708 Hamburg edition of Luther's Bible it was thought necessary to qualify the reasons for publishing the Apocrypha thus: "though not of divine origin and written by mere human beings without extraordinary divine impetus or special commission." It was during the eighteenth century that the move to omit the Apocrypha gained ground. Basically this was due to Puritan and Calvinistic influence, which as far as the United Kingdom is concerned became prominent in the Church of Scotland and in England during the Commonwealth under Oliver Cromwell.

The Deuterocanonical Writings in England

The first English Bible to put the d. c. books in a separate section was that produced in 1535 by Miles Coverdale, a former Augustinian friar who, like Luther, became a Reformer. This

Bible, made in exile, was based on the Latin Vulgate, Tyndale, and Luther's early work before he published his German Bible (1534). The d. c. were put by Coverdale after the OT (except Baruch, which he added to Jeremiah). Though he regarded the d. c. as on a lower level than the p. c. he evidently considered them to be in some sense Scripture when he said they were not "of like reputation with the other Scripture." He goes on to say why: because "there be many places in them that seem to be repugnant unto the open and manifest truth in the other books of the Bible." This could refer to doctrines that did not occur elsewhere in the Bible or doctrines with which the Reformers did not agree.

In 1562 and 1571 the Thirty-Nine Articles were promulgated by the Church of England; Article VI dealt with the Bible canon. It accepted as Scripture the canonical books of the OT and NT "of whose authority was never any doubt in the Church" (that is, the p. c.). Then it continued "the other books, (as Hierome saith) the Church doth read for example of life and instruction of manners" (that is, the d. c. or Apocrypha). Of course the argument was not conclusive as some books of the NT (for example, Hebrews and Revelation) had been doubted, but were not rejected. Nevertheless, as in Germany, the d. c., though placed separately, continued to be printed in most U.K. Bibles in spite of efforts to omit them. The 1611 Authorized or King James Version, which held the field right up to modern times, of course contained the d. c., though as early as 1619 editions without them appeared. As said above, such Bibles were cheaper, smaller, and more portable, and therefore easier to get into people's homes, but in England one could still be prosecuted for not including the d. c.

During the Commonwealth the "Westminster Confession of Faith" was drawn up and approved by Parliament in 1648 as the official religion of the "Three Kingdoms." This declared that "the Books commonly called Apocryphal, not being of divine inspiration, are no part of the Canon of the Scripture and therefore are of no authority in the Church of God, nor to be otherwise approved, or made use of, than other writings." At the Restoration in 1660 the Apocrypha reappeared, as did the Thirty-Nine Articles with Number VI on the Bible canon, so the division of opinion continued as many people had got used to Bibles without the Apocrypha.

The British and Foreign Bible Society, founded (in 1804) for the printing and distribution of the Bible at home and abroad, published the Scriptures in many languages but (in accordance with its constitution) without the Apocrypha. The German Bible Societies, however, had always included the Apocrypha, in harmony with their traditions, dating from Martin Luther's Bible of 1534. In spite of this the Württemberg Society produced a Bible without the Apocrypha in 1889, but "it was not any theological reason which had led to this result, . . . the theological significance of the Apocrypha was virtually never discussed" (W. Gundert, "The Bible Societies and the Deutero-Canonical Writings," 134). The main attraction was a commercial one. The lower price of the edition without the Apocrypha now proved irresistible, especially in times of economic depression.

Luther's Bible had a very clear title: *Biblia, i.e., the whole of Scripture, Old Testament and New Testament, translated into German by Dr. Martin Luther.* This contained the Apocrypha. Did Luther, after all, accord them a place in the canon though on a lower level of inspiration? Today Bibles with or without the Apocrypha are available from most Bible Societies including the B.F.B.S., now called "The Bible Society."

BIBLIOGRAPHY

Barr, James. *Holy Scripture: Canon, Authority, Criticism.* Philadelphia: Westminster, 1983.

Barton, John. *Oracles of God: Perceptions of Ancient Prophecy in Israel After the Exile.* New York: Oxford University Press, c1986.

Beckwith, Roger T. *The Old Testament Canon of the New Testament Church and Its Background in Early Judaism.* Grand Rapids: Eerdmans, 1985.

Bowker, John W. *The Targums and Rabbinic Literature: An Introduction to Jewish Interpretations of Scripture.* London: Cambridge University Press, 1969.

Burkitt, Francis C. *Early Eastern Christianity.* London: John Murray, 1904.

Davies, W. D. *Christian Origins and Judaism.* New York: Arno Press, 1973.

Fortescue, Adrian. *The Orthodox Eastern Church.* 3rd ed. London: Catholic Truth Society, 1911.

Guidi, Ignazio. *Il "Fetha Nagast," o "Legislazione dei re": codice ecclesiastico e civile di Abissinia.* 2 vols. Rome: Tipografia della Casa editrice italiana, 1897–1899; repr. Naples: R. Istituto Orientale, 1936.

Gundert, Wilhelm. "The Bible Societies and the Deutero-Canonical Writings" in Meurer, ed., *The Apocrypha in Ecumenical Perspective,* 134–150.

Haag, Herbert. art. "Kanon," *Bibellexikon.* Einsiedeln: Benziger, 1968, 915–922.

Herford, Robert T. *Judaism in the New Testament Period.* London: The Lindsey Press, 1928.

Kahle, Paul E. *The Cairo Geniza.* 2nd ed. Oxford: Blackwell, 1959.

Mansi, J. D. *Sacrorum conciliorum nova et amplissima collectio cujus Joannes Dominicus Mansi et post ipsius mortem florentinus et venetianus editores ab anno 1758 ad annum 1798, priores triginta unum tomos ediderunt . . . .* Paris: H. Welter, 1901–1927.

Meurer, Siegfried, ed. *The Apocrypha in Ecumenical Perspective,* translated by Paul Ellingsworth. Reading, England, and New York: United Bible Societies, 1992.

Moore, George Foot. *Judaism in the First Centuries of the Christian Era, the Age of the Tannaim.* 2 vols. New York: Schocken, 1971.

Oesterley, W.O.E. *The Jews and Judaism During the Greek Period.* London: SPCK, 1941.

Russell, D. S. *Between the Testaments.* Philadelphia: Fortress, c1965.

Stendebach, Franz Joseph. "The Old Testament Canon in the Roman Catholic Church" in Meurer, ed., *The Apocrypha in Ecumenical Perspective,* 33–45.

Sundberg, A. C. *The Old Testament of the Early Church.* Cambridge, Mass.: Harvard University Press, 1964.

Swete, Henry B. *An Introduction to the Old Testament in Greek.* Cambridge: University Press, 1902.

Ullendorff, Edward. *Ethiopia and the Bible.* The Schweich Lectures, 1967. London: Oxford University Press, 1968.

Wiles, Maurice F. "Origen as a Biblical Scholar." *The Cambridge History of the Bible.* London and New York: Cambridge University Press, 1963–1970. 1.455–456.

Zarb, Seraphim M. *De Historia Canonis Utriusque Testamenti,* editio secunda. Rome: Pont. Inst. Angelicum, 1934.

How Reliable is the Text of the Bible?

Albert Pietersma and Frederik Wisse

Most modern translations of the Bible include a limited number of notes to make the reader aware that some of the ancient manuscript witnesses add or omit certain verses, or have a variant reading that affects the meaning. Actually only a small fraction of the variant readings found in the manuscript tradition are listed in modern translations, though these tend to be the more important ones. During the centuries that the text of the OT and NT writings was transmitted by hand copying, hundreds of thousands of inadvertent and deliberate variant readings were created. The bulk of these are insignificant changes, such as scribal errors and orthographic differences, but a considerable number created alterations in the text of potential significance. This raises the question whether the text over the centuries may have been changed to such an extent that the original meaning in some places has been obscured or lost.

The Old Testament

Literary texts transcribed repeatedly and perforce imperfectly over a period of time by copyists and editors of varied ability and precision inevitably give rise to the need for textual criticism. Though criticism of the OT text has been practiced since the early centuries C.E., only scholarship from approximately the seventeenth century onward has gradually forged it into a semi-scientific tool—often labeled a hybrid of art and science—for study of the biblical text. The goal of textual criticism, whatever the impediments encountered by its practitioner, is to restore the original shape of a given piece of written literature, through the use of carefully honed procedures applied to all the textual evidence that has survived. Thus OT criticism may be said to aim at retrieving the original written text of the books included in this corpus. Some scholars have argued, however, that Hebrew OT criticism is *sui generis* in its aim, though such a claim results from a failure to distinguish between the theoretical goal of the discipline on the one hand and the practical limitations imposed by the evidence on the other.

Of great importance in the development of modern OT textual criticism were the polyglot (multilingual) Bibles of the sixteenth and seventeenth centuries, with their texts in different languages arranged in parallel columns for comparative use (Complutensian 1514–1517; Antwerp 1569–1572; Paris 1629–1645; London 1654–1657). Also influential, especially in Jewish society, were the so-called rabbinic Bibles, particularly the second Rabbinic Bible of Ben Hayyim (1524–1525), upon which almost all later editions were based. Not until the current century were editions produced that featured a single, known manuscript as their lemma text, for example Biblia Hebraica[3] (1929–1937) and Biblia Hebraica Stuttgartensia (1967–1977) and others. Clearly Hebrew OT textual criticism has developed in a direction distinct from its NT and Greek OT counterparts. While in the latter two fields fully critical editions have been produced, no such results have been achieved in the former. Indeed, some scholars maintain that a truly diplomatic edition must be viewed as the ideal version of the Hebrew OT. Others would argue, however, that the lack of critical editions must be attributed to the current state of text-critical evidence.

The history of modern Hebrew OT textual criticism is now commonly divided into pre-1947 and post-1947, since the discovery of numerous biblical manuscripts in the Judean desert has opened a new era in the discipline. The pre-1947 period was characterized by the unfolding monopoly of the so-called Masoretic text (MT), which began its dominance in the first and second centuries C.E. and left little rival evidence in its wake, with the exception of the Samaritan Pentateuch and the (Greek) Septuagint, the "Old Testament" of Christendom till the Protestant Reformation. Since all Masoretic manuscripts (numbered in the thousands), in spite of idiosyncrasies, nonetheless constitute a single family of witnesses, they cannot be deemed to give the critic a representative sample of Hebrew from pre-Christian times. Thus while a fully critical edition of the Masoretic text might be achievable (cf. Baer-Delitzsch [1869–1894] and Ginsburg [1926], who tried to retrieve the Ben Asher strand of MT), no such edition of the Hebrew OT itself could be responsibly produced: essentially three witnesses are extant for the Pentateuch and two elsewhere, one of those a translation into Greek. These three witnesses, MT, the Samaritan Pentateuch (SamP) and the Septuagint (LXX), are regarded by some scholars as three text-types (rather than individual texts). As a result the impression is created that they are reasonably representative of the entire spectrum of the OT text. Qumran, however, cannot be said to support this text-type theory.

The importance of the discoveries in the Judean Desert for OT text criticism can scarcely be exaggerated. They have furnished textual material in Hebrew form dating from ca. 250 B.C.E. to 135 C.E. for virtually every OT book, thus shifting the critic's chief attention away from the translations of the Hebrew favored by the Church and inner-Masoretic minutiae well known to Jewish scholars. Fragments of more than 190 biblical scrolls have thus far been identified, the text of which has been assigned to four major groups: proto-Masoretic, pre-Samaritan, Septuagint-related, and non-aligned texts (texts that show multiple relations rather than one dominant one). The picture Qumran therefore paints for the three pre-Christian centuries is one of textual plurality and diversity. While such variety *per se* might well give the textual critic an adequate cross-section of the evidence for the production of a critical (eclectic) edition of the Hebrew OT, it remains true that multiple attestation for individual passages is rare. Thus for the Hebrew OT the text critic's aim must remain unfulfilled, except in a sporadic manner in some critical biblical commentaries.

The impact of the Judean desert discoveries on the Greek OT has been similarly dramatic. Several fragments of the Pentateuch have been found at Qumran, and the Minor Prophets scroll from Nahal Hever has exercised far-reaching influence. Not only has the text-critical importance and reliability of the LXX (Old Greek) been enhanced, but the discoveries have helped defend its very existence, which had been the subject of vigorous debate in the so-called Kahle (multiple original translations into Greek) versus de Lagarde (single original translation) controversy. Most scholars currently espouse de Lagarde's view or a variation thereof. Greek OT textual criticism, like that of the NT but unlike that of the Hebrew OT, has long been engaged in reconstructing the closest possible approximation to the original text (*Septuaginta Vetus Testamentum Graecum* editio maior. Göttingen, 1931–). For much of the Greek OT the quantity of witnesses has been deemed adequate and their character sufficiently representative to warrant a critical edition. Major finds of pre-Byzantine manuscripts within living memory have furnished much early evidence. Nonetheless it should be borne in mind that the earliest witnesses typically postdate the original text by several centuries. Moreover, reconstruction of the original cannot be undertaken with equal confidence in all parts of the Greek OT. In sections of the historical books (Samuel–Kings) the entire received text appears to be a revision rather than the original Greek translation itself. Extant versions of Judges, Tobit, and Esther, for example, present a seemingly irreducible textual complexity. Efforts to harmonize the Greek text with the current Hebrew text, often dating back to the earliest stages of LXX transmission, continue to be a central problem for the realization of the text-critic's aim.

Nevertheless, in spite of the proven textual plurality of the pre-Christian centuries on the Hebrew front and the demonstrated textual value of the LXX, a basic dictum remains in force for the ancient translations: rival Hebrew readings should be posited only as a critic's last resort. Moreover, retroversion into Hebrew from non-Hebrew sources remains a controversial undertaking. Daughter versions of the LXX, though suffering from the same limitations as the Greek vis-à-vis its own source, can be of great text-critical value for the Greek OT but are of negligible worth for the Hebrew OT. A new English translation of the LXX, based on the NRSV, is currently being produced under the auspices of the International Organization for Septuagint and Cognate Studies.

An important distinction made by scholars in OT criticism is that between textual criticism and literary criticism. The former may be said to trace the transmission history of a finished product (a book) back to its pristine origin, while the latter may be described as dealing *inter alia* with the literary growth of a book-in-the-making. Thus typically textual criticism begins at the point where literary criticism leaves off. A comparison of the Hebrew OT and the Greek OT gives a number of examples, among which the two versions of Jeremiah are the best known. The relationship of the Masoretic version (supported by Qumran evidence) and the LXX version (also supported by Qumran evidence) falls within the domain of literary criticism, while the transmission history of each separately is the object of textual criticism. Though literary criticism may conclude that no single original composition of biblical books ever existed and in any case cannot be retrieved, such a conclusion is not necessarily of consequence for the textual critic. Textual criticism merely presupposes that *a* text existed. Precisely when a given written item is to be assigned to the one discipline or the other is, of course, often difficult to decide.

Textual scholars commonly distinguish two types of editions: (1) critical (evaluative) editions reconstructed (eclectically) from all available textual information, with secondary readings relegated to a so-called critical apparatus, and (2) diplomatic (non-evaluative) editions that print an actual manuscript, with competing evidence placed in the apparatus. While any text can be made into a diplomatic edition, a fully critical edition presupposes not only manuscript attestation in considerable quantity but also a reasonable assurance that the extant witnesses represent a fair cross-section of all witnesses that ever existed. While most scholars would agree that the bodies of evidence for both the Hebrew OT and the Greek OT easily fulfill the first of these requirements, few would grant that both meet the second to an equal degree, if indeed at all.

When the question of reliability is viewed from the perspective of textual criticism there is good reason for confidence with respect to the Greek OT, but less with regard to the Hebrew OT at the present time. This does not mean that the Greek OT is more reliable than the Hebrew OT, but only that at the present time scholars are in a better position to reconstruct the conjectural history of transmission of the Greek OT textual tradition than that of the Hebrew OT.

The New Testament

When, beginning in the eighteenth century, scholars became increasingly aware of variant readings among the Greek manuscripts of the NT they began to collect such readings and develop appropriate text-critical methods to choose from among them those readings that have the greatest claim to be original. The ultimate aim of the discipline of NT textual criticism is to establish a critical text of the Greek NT that approximates as closely as possible the original text and includes a critical apparatus that lists significant variants with their manuscript support.

A considerable number of critical editions of the NT have been published over the last 150 years. The most important and widely recognized of these is Novum Testamentum Graece, the so-called Nestle-Aland edition, which has been revised numerous times over the last hundred years. The critical text of the twenty-sixth edition (1979) is identical to the third (1975) and fourth (1993) editions of *The Greek New Testament* published by the United Bible Societies and intended for Bible translators. All important modern Bible translations are based on these editions of the critical text.

The manuscript attestation for the NT is far richer and more varied than that for any other ancient text. More than 3,100 manuscripts of the continuous Greek text are known, though all but forty-two contain only a part of the NT and not a few are fragmentary. The great majority date from the late Byzantine period, the five centuries before the invention of printing, but there are a few small papyrus fragments as early as the second century, and more substantial manuscripts and increasing numbers for the following centuries. Scholars distinguish among *papyrus codices* that date from the second to eighth century, *uncials,* written on parchment in capital letters and dating from the third to the tenth century, and *minuscules* written on parchment or paper in a cursive hand and dating from the ninth century onward. Apart from manuscripts of the continuous Greek text there are 2,403 Greek lectionary manuscripts, several thousand manuscripts of the ancient Latin, Syriac and Coptic versions, as well as a wealth of NT citations in the writings of the early Church Fathers. All this evidence is taken into account by textual critics in the reconstruction of the original text.

The canons (or rules) of textual criticism used by scholars to select the original reading from among the variants are based on the scribal tendencies evident in the manuscript tradition. Already from the earliest NT papyri it is apparent that some of the scribes took small liberties to "improve" the text. The excuse for this was apparently the assumption that the ambiguities or inconsistencies in sense and the difficulties in grammar or syntax they encountered were due to mistakes made by previous copyists. Thus the changes and additions they introduced were not meant to alter the text but rather to restore or enhance it. This process of misimprovements continued through the centuries with the consequence that the text of the great majority of the medieval manuscripts appears smoother and clearer than the text of manuscripts from the third and fourth centuries. Thus the most important canon is that the more difficult reading is likely the original one, since it explains the creation of variant readings. Other rules are a refinement of this basic one. Most textual critics also prefer the reading that is attested early in the tradition to the one with only late attestation, as well as readings from witnesses that have proved to be "good," that is, those whose variant readings appear to be more often original on text-critical grounds than those in other manuscripts. The most famous examples of such manuscripts are the fourth century codices Vaticanus and Sinaiticus.

The application of these principles during the latter part of the nineteenth century resulted in the rejection of the printed edition of the Greek text based on late medieval manuscripts that was dominant from the sixteenth to the nineteenth century, the so-called *Textus Receptus,* on which the translations of the Reformation and Counter-Reformation were based. A new consensus emerged, and continues to the present, in favor of a critical text based mainly on pre-Byzantine witnesses. The spectacular find of early papyrus manuscripts during this same period has tended to confirm the consensus. The fact that these papyri presented hardly any significant new variants suggests that the readings already known from the manuscript tradition offer the textual critic a more or less complete picture. Codex Vaticanus, the most important witness to the new critical text, even gained in stature, for its text of Luke and John was confirmed by a papyrus codex ($\mathfrak{P}^{75}$) from the beginning of the third century.

The present consensus allows a positive evaluation of the reliability of the text of the NT as reconstructed by scholars on the basis of the manuscript evidence. It appears reasonable to conclude that the evidence is more than adequate and the text-critical methodology sufficiently established to be able to recover the original text in the great majority of cases where there is variation. Not only does the task appear to be possible, but it would seem that it has already been accomplished. What is left to be done is mere fine-tuning.

Objections to this positive evaluation of the present state of affairs come from two directions. Some scholars, though basically supportive of the consensus position, are hesitant to consider the text-critical task substantially finished. They believe that particularly the early papyrus witnesses have not been sufficiently assessed, and that they may change our understanding of early scribal habits and indicate the existence of several basic text types in the earliest period of transmission. However, given the detailed analysis already spent on the papyri it is very doubtful that further study will change the present assessment significantly. A more radical objection comes from those who believe that the critical text recovered through textual criticism is not the original text but rather the text established by the orthodox hierarchy in the late second century. These scholars assume that earlier in the second century the text of the NT writings underwent extensive redaction, mainly through interpolations, to adapt them to changing ideological circumstances, and that all manuscript evidence for the original state of the text was suppressed by the orthodox establishment. Like any conspiracy theory, however, this claim is beyond proof or disproof. Not only is it highly improbable that during the first hundred years of the transmission of the text scribal interference was much different from the following centuries, but the manuscript evidence shows that the Church leadership was in no position to control the copying of the text until the Byzantine period. The many attempts to identify interpolations in the NT for which there is no manuscript evidence have proven to be at best inconclusive. The burden of proof is entirely on those who claim that the text of the NT as established on the basis of the available manuscript evidence is not a reliable witness to the original wording of the text.

Text Criticism of the New Testament

John Karavidopoulos

Introductory Remarks

By the phrase "text criticism of the New Testament" we mean mainly the endeavor made by scholars during the last two centuries to restore the original text of the NT exactly as it came from the quill of the sacred writers themselves. Such critical treatment of the text was performed in ancient times as well. Today specialists speak about three textual "recensions" of the NT that were made by about 300 C.E., each independently of the others, in Antioch, Alexandria, and Palestine. The first is attributed to the priest and martyr Lucian, the second to Hesychios, and the third to Pamphilos. We should add, however, that there is no unanimity in modern research concerning the existence of these three "recensions." One might speak about the Antiochean or Lucianic recension with less uncertainty. In any case the great number of variants in the manuscripts was destined to cause leaders of the Church and theologians to deal with the text very seriously with the intention of restoring it.

In the numerous manuscripts written in uncial or in minuscule letters, in Greek or in another ancient language, various errors were made during copying, due either to oversight of the scribe or to a deliberate effort to modify the text. One need not wonder how God's Providence could have allowed the creation of errors; the reason for that is that the *logos* of God, since entering human history, without losing at all the attributes of the *logos* of God, has accommodated to the course of the human factor. This explains, for example, why when two lines in the text end with the same word it is possible that when copying—particularly when the scribe due to fatigue happens to be less careful—the scribe might omit the second line. This phenomenon is called *homoioteleuton* (having the same ending). Furthermore, it is possible that a syllable might be dropped out when it looks like the previous one ("haplography" = single writing, as opposed to double writing), as it also happens that one syllable or some letter might be written twice ("dittography" = double writing). A deliberate effort to change the text is observed in passages that are obscure; the scribe has improved them with the addition or elimination of words or by harmonizing with a parallel text. This is more common in the synoptic gospels.

Classifications of Manuscripts by Types of Text

In the middle of the eighteenth century the number of variants in the text of the manuscripts led researchers to the idea that they might as well classify them in groups of similar text. First J. A. Bengel classified the various manuscripts in groups of families and then J. J. Griesbach distinguished three groups of manuscripts: Western, Alexandrian, and Constantinopolitan. The conclusions of B. F. Westcott and F.J.A. Hort constitute a significant milestone in the history of research on the text of the NT. After studying the NT manuscripts for twenty-eight years, in 1881 they completed a two-volume edition whose first volume contains the text of the NT and the second (written by Hort yet echoing the conclusions of both) constitutes the introduction. The two English critics, acknowledging Griesbach as their forerunner, divided the manuscripts of the NT into four groups, each presenting a special type of text. They are:

Neutral text: what the two English critics called the text preserved by the ancient codices Vaticanus and Sinaiticus, mainly the first. They considered this type of text as the most genuine and therefore based their edition on it. The title of their edition, *The New Testament in the Original Greek,* was typical of their certainty.

Alexandrian text came from linguistic improvements made to the neutral text by educated scribes of Alexandria. It is represented by the codices C, L, the Bohairic translation, and the Alexandrian theologians Clement, Origen (partly), Dionysius, and Cyril.

Western text prevailed among Church writers before the end of the third century. We find evidence for this text mainly in Justin, Tatian, Irenaeus, Tertullian, and Cyprian, in the codex D (Cantabrigiensis) and in the ancient Latin and Syriac translations. The corrections of this type of text are extensive and significant. They found their way into the first Syriac and Latin translations and were transferred to the West (thus the title "western text").

Syriac or Antiochean text prevailed from the time of John Chrysostom and thenceforth in the Byzantine empire. This text came from an authentic recension that aimed at the simplification of the linguistic difficulties and thus at a more understandable text. In addition, various conjunctions entered the text so that it might become more convenient, pronouns were replaced by proper nouns in many cases in order to avoid ambiguities or obscurities, and unknown grammatical types were replaced by more familiar ones. This recension was made in the fourth century, most probably by Lucian, and the improved text that came out of it soon prevailed in the empire. The *Textus Receptus* of the sixteenth and seventeenth centuries was based on this text.

Westcott and Hort did not consider this last type of text worthwhile for the critical restoration of the text of the NT since it was a more recent one. They also considered the "western" text of little worth; only on one occasion do they prefer the western text: namely in the passages in which this text, in spite of its general tendency to expand, is shorter than the neutral one. They called these passages "western non-interpolations," considering it to be the original. They thought the neutral text type the most ancient and genuine, and it was that on which they based their edition (1881).

Today, after the above distinction of types of the NT text by the two English researchers and a century of critical work by other specialists, manuscripts are distinguished in various groups depending on the type of text they contain. Of course the research continues, yet most scholars agree on the detection of the following four types of texts:

Alexandrian text. This text originates in Egypt and is witnessed by most papyri, by the uncial codices Vaticanus and Sinaiticus, by the Alexandrian theologians Clement and Origen, by the Bohairic translation and others. It includes and is restricted to the neutral text and the Alexandrian text of Westcott and Hort.

Western text. This text is called "western" not because it has its origin in the West but because it prevailed in the West during the second century, being witnessed by the ancient Latin and Syriac translations, the Latin fathers, Codex D (Cantabrigiensis), and in part certain papyri. Sometimes this text differs in a typical way from the rest of the tradition of manuscripts; this is most evident in the book of the Acts. More recent researchers have shown that certain variants of the "western" text were witnessed already in an earlier period in Egypt, and that is the reason why many accept Alexandria as the place of origin of this text.

Caesarean text. This is similar to the Alexandrian type of text and is witnessed by $\mathfrak{P}^{46}$, W (in Mark), Θ, λ, φ, as well as by the Gregorian translation. It is believed by many that Origen brought this text from Egypt to Caesarea in Palestine. (Scholarly consensus in favor of the existence of the Caesarean text is not as strong as for the other test-types. —*Ed.*)

Byzantine or Koine, or Ecclesiastical text. This comes from the recension by Lucian, priest and martyr of Antioch. It was transferred by John Chrysostom to Constantinople and prevailed throughout the Byzantine empire. It is also called Constantinopolitan or Imperial. After the fall of Constantinople it was transferred by Greek scholars to the West and became the basis of the *Textus Receptus.* This text was used in worship and presents a relative uniformity; it is witnessed in the works of the Fathers since the fourth century and in lectionaries and translations after the year 300.

Serious work is being done in the study of the manuscripts of the NT in recent decades at the "Institute for Research on the Text of the New Testament" in Münster, Germany, which publishes the critical text of the NT (the so-called "Nestle-Aland" editions). Despite the fact that a century has passed since the critical research of Westcott and Hort, the attitude of researchers toward the Byzantine or Ecclesiastical text has not changed. The advantage, however, that the researchers of the Institute have over the two English critics is the fact that in recent decades papyri of the third century and several minuscule manuscripts have come to light and are taken into account by the Nestle-Aland edition of the text of the New Testament.

The Contribution of the Ecclesiastical Text to Critical Research on the Text of the New Testament

Mention has already been made of a type of text that Westcott and Hort called Antiochean or Syriac and that later received various titles: Byzantine, Koine, Patriarchal, Imperial, Constantinopolitan, Ecclesiastical. The title that prevails today among critics is Byzantine (in the critical apparatus of the fourth edition of *The Greek New Testament* it is marked as Byz or Byz Lect and in the 27th Nestle-Aland it is contained within the calligraphic 𝔐 with which the text of the majority of the manuscripts is indicated). We prefer the title Ecclesiastical text, of course not with the meaning that it is the sole text that may justly bear this characterization—after all, the other types of text were used in the churches as well, for worship, for private study, or for catechetical instruction—but because it is preserved in a great number of manuscripts of running text with indications of use for liturgical purposes as well as in a multitude of lectionaries that are used in sacred worship. It could be called the Liturgical text as well.

Since the time when the absolute authenticity of the *Textus Receptus* was shaken, critical editions of the NT have been mainly based on uncial manuscripts (fourth century and later) that are dated earlier than the Byzantine manuscripts. In our day text critics depend more on the second- and third-century papyri than even the uncial manuscripts Vaticanus and Sinaiticus. Of course one cannot exclude the possibility of more ancient "ancestors" from which the Byzantine or ecclesiastical manuscripts originate. Even though the text of the latter is a product of recension and critical treatment with linguistic smoothings, improvements, and harmonizations, no one can deny the fact that this text preserves original readings, a fact that cannot be overlooked if one is doing critical work on the text. Those readings that agree in a typical manner with the papyri or the codices with uncial letters as well as those that are shorter than the other types of text should be considered original. Westcott and Hort referred to "western non-interpolations," the readings of the Western text that, in spite of the tendency of this text to expand and add, are shorter than the corresponding readings in the other text types. The English critics considered these readings as original and genuine. One might accept the same thing concerning the readings of the Byzantine text that present some treatment of harmonizing additions. They could even accordingly be named "eastern non-interpolations" and be considered undoubtedly original (e.g., Mark 3:13-14; 3:16; 3:32; 6:23; 16:18; Luke 10:21, etcetera).

It is a fact that the Byzantine or Ecclesiastical text has not been studied as much as it should be. We note also that several individual studies have been made in various parts of the world concerning the text of the NT in the fathers of the Church. The most significant effort to study the Byzantine text, especially the Byzantine lectionaries, was made during the third decade of our century by a team of NT scholars from the University of Chicago, led by professors E. C. Colwell and D. W. Riddle. The initial fruits of their research were made available in 1933 with the first volume of the series Studies in the Lectionary Text of the Greek New Testament. The initial volume is entitled *Prolegomena to the Study of the Lectionary Text of the Gospels.* Before the publication of this volume Colwell announced the entire scientific project in his preliminary article entitled "Is There a Lectionary Text of the Gospels?" (*HThR* 25 [1932] 73–84). In this article the American scholar argues for the existence of a defined text type that predominates among the lectionaries and that he calls the "lectionary text." Following the publication of this preliminary article the *Prolegomena* appeared, followed by an abundance of other studies in the series.

Some of the University of Chicago scholars' conclusions are of interest to us:

(1) The influence of the text of the lectionaries on the manuscripts of continuous text of the New Testament is often confirmed. For example, certain fixed introductory expressions to the pericopes found in the lectionaries (*tō kairō ekeinō, eipen ho kurios,* etcetera) also prevail in the manuscripts of continuous text. In addition, the placing of the pericope of the woman caught in adultery (John 7:53–8:11) in Luke and the placing of Luke 22:43 in Matthew is explained by the position these pericopes occupy in the lectionaries.

(2) The text of the lectionaries is essentially of the Byzantine type but is, generally speaking, more ancient than the *Textus Receptus.*

(3) Particular care was taken to keep the liturgical text intact during the process of copying from one lectionary to another. To this must be attributed the fact that many ancient readings of the lectionaries escaped the process of assimilation into the Byzantine text.

(4) Finally, the lectionaries are of great importance for the restoration of the history of the text of the NT since they may be considered noteworthy witnesses that confirm already existing readings of the ancient manuscripts.

Contribution of Orthodox Researchers

We turn now to the edition of the Greek New Testament that was prepared at the beginning of our century by the Orthodox Church and is based entirely on the lectionaries. This text of this edition, known also as the Patriarchal Edition (῾Η Καινὴ Διαθήκη ἐγκρίσει τῆς Μεγάλης τοῦ Χριστοῦ ᾿Εκκλησίας, Constantinople, 1904), continues to be reprinted by the Church of Greece (᾿Αποστολικὴ Διακονία) and by certain religious organizations and other publishing houses in Greece. In the prologue to the Patriarchal Edition the editorial committee cites one hundred sixteen manuscripts of gospels and epistles that represent the reading text for churches from the ninth to the sixteenth century. These manuscripts thus cover a span of some eight centuries, although the greater number of the more useful manuscripts come from the tenth through the fourteenth century. The Patriarchal Edition of 1904 constitutes the most serious attempt at a critical elaboration of the text of the NT by the Orthodox Church. The English critic Kirsopp Lake in particular suggested that this Patriarchal Edition be recognized as a more precise representation of the Byzantine text than the *Textus Receptus.* His proposal was not, however, accepted by his peers, perhaps for the following reasons: (a) the manuscript basis of the Patriarchal Edition is not very broad, (b) in certain passages, as V. Antoniadis notes in the prologue, non-Byzantine text readings were preferred, and (c) the edition was based almost exclusively on lectionaries and not on manuscripts of continuous text of the NT that do not agree exactly in many details with the text of the lectionaries (Kirsopp Lake, *The Text of the New Testament* [1928] 85).

In any case the Patriarchal Edition of 1904 constitutes the only edition of the Greek text of the NT in the Orthodox world. Since almost a century has passed, there is good reason for a new critical edition of the ecclesiastical text of the NT, an edition that (a) is based on a broader number of Byzantine manuscripts, (b) makes use of NT citations in the writings of the Church Fathers, and (c) is carried out in collaboration with all specialists in this area. It is the responsibility of Orthodox scholars to subject the liturgical text of their Church to a contemporary critical examination that, of course, follows the generally prevailing principles of textual criticism. It is within this framework that the collaboration of the author of this article with the United Bible Societies in the preparation of the fourth edition of *The Greek New Testament* (4th revised edition, ed. by Barbara Aland, Kurt Aland, Johannes Karavidopoulos, Carlo M. Martini, and Bruce M. Metzger, 1993) is to be placed. *The Greek New Testament* of the United Bible Societies coincides with the text of the 27th edition of Nestle-Aland, with, however, a different critical apparatus. The critical apparatus contains textual variants for some 1,438 passages.

In connection with the recently published fourth edition of *The Greek New Testament* a group of scholars from the University of Thessaloniki (Greece) undertook the editing of certain variants of the Byzantine lectionaries. Obviously it was impossible to take into account the 2,403 Byzantine lectionaries. Rather, a representative selection was made in collaboration with the Institute for Research on the Text of the New Testament at the University of Münster. The guiding principle in choosing the manuscripts was the desire to use representative manuscripts from various centuries (from the eighth to the sixteenth) as well as different text types. Thus manuscripts were chosen that contain the usual Byzantine text, others that often deviate from it, and still others that remain close to the Byzantine text. Still, the editorial committee decided it was necessary to have represented the text that is used today in the Greek Church (that is, the Patriarchal Edition of 1904) which, as we have already said, is based on the Byzantine lectionaries. Following the above criteria the group in Thessaloniki chose thirty manuscripts of the "gospels" (that is, gospel lectionaries) and forty manuscripts of the "epistles" (that is, *Apostolos* lectionaries), which are cited regularly in the critical apparatus. The work of collating the manuscripts was carried out in Thessaloniki over a span of four years while the compilation of the critical apparatus was done at Münster at a later date. Hence the fourth edition of *The Greek New Testament* has a more complete critical apparatus within which is represented the liturgical text of the Orthodox Church in the Greek original.

BIBLIOGRAPHY

Aland, Kurt, and Barbara Aland. *The Text of the New Testament,* translated by E. G. Rhodes. 2nd ed. Grand Rapids: Eerdmans, 1989.

Vaganay, Leon, C. B. Amphoux, and Jenny Heimerdinger. *An Introduction to New Testament Textual Criticism.* 2nd rev. ed. Cambridge and New York: Cambridge University Press, 1991.

Metzger, Bruce M. *The Text of the New Testament. Its Transmission, Corruption, and Restoration.* 3rd enlarged edition. New York and Oxford: Oxford University Press, 1992.

Epp, Eldon Jay, and Gordon D. Fee. *Studies in the Theory and Method of New Testament Textual Criticism.* Grand Rapids: Eerdmans, 1993.

Archaeology and the Bible

J. Maxwell Miller

Can archaeology, through excavation of biblical sites, prove the existence of Abraham or Solomon? date the exodus of the Israelites from Egypt? determine the exact time that the walls of Jericho fell? This article will attempt to explain what archaeology is about—its history, trends, and developments, what it can and cannot do, what archaeologists hope to accomplish when they excavate in the Middle East, and the value of archaeology to biblical study.

Archaeology

The term "archaeology" was coined by early Greek writers with reference to any sort of study of earlier times. Josephus' *The Antiquities of the Jews,* for example, is entitled literally *ioudaikēs archaiologias.* Although the term often is used rather loosely, especially in popular literature, it has a somewhat more narrow meaning today. Archaeology as practiced in the present may be defined as "the search for and study of the material remains of past civilizations." Let us examine the four elements of this definition in turn: "search for," "study of," "material remains," and "past civilizations."

Search for. Archaeologists search for clues regarding the identity and life style of people who have lived in times past. After selecting an area they want to explore, archaeologists conduct regional surveys where a great deal can be learned from the surface material remains that they find. This information is valuable in choosing where to excavate; indeed, because archaeological excavations require a great deal of time and are expensive only selected sites in a given region can be excavated. At the site of an excavation archaeologists dig into ruins, separate layers of debris, and examine systematically any remains that have survived.

Careful recording is crucial, especially when excavation is involved, because excavated remains can never be re-excavated. For that same reason archaeologists often record data they do not fully understand or that may not seem, at the moment, to offer particularly significant information about the past. Modern archaeology is a rapidly developing science that benefits constantly from improving scientific technology. Remains excavated today, therefore, if carefully and accurately recorded, may yield additional information to future archaeologists employing more advanced technology.

Study of. Archaeologists do not dig up "facts." They examine "sites," places where there is evidence of concentrated human activity in times past, and they excavate objects or "artifacts"—building foundations, floor surfaces, broken pieces of pottery, remnants of tools and weapons, and so forth. These sites and artifacts must be interpreted, which involves careful attention to their immediate context (geographical, topographical, ecological, stratigraphical), comparative analysis with similar sites and artifacts, and information derived from any available and relevant written records. Stratigraphy and typology figure prominently in the interpretation process and, as with other fields of research, there is always a degree of subjectivity.

When people live at one place over an extended period of time (for example, concentrated in a village or city), they produce occupational debris—broken pieces of pottery, seeds, coins, jewelry, tools, weapons, abandoned buildings, etcetera. In the ancient Middle East people tended to stay near water sources, agricultural land, and trade routes; thus when a village or city was destroyed or abandoned the same site often was chosen again for occupation at a later period of history. When the new settlers built over the debris from the earlier settlement they began a new phase of occupation during which they left behind another layer of debris at the site. Over time these different layers of debris would accumulate, with later stages of occupation deposited over earlier stages. The result is that city ruins in the Middle East often are high mounds, called "tells," consisting of many layers of debris ("strata") built up over hundreds and even thousands of years. Archaeological sites are "stratified," in other words, with each stratum representing a phase of occupation. Archaeologists, when they excavate a site, attempt to separate the strata and determine what the settlement (city, village, or whatever) was like at each stage of its occupation.

Objects fashioned by human hands (buildings, weapons, pottery, clothing, etcetera) reflect the behavioral patterns and stylistic preferences of the region and period of time in which they were produced. Styles gradually change over time, and other factors (such as technological developments) also influence the shape, decoration, and manufacture of artifacts. Archaeologists are especially attentive to these stylistic differences and changes ("typology") and find pottery ("ceramic typology") especially useful for dating. For example, if archaeologists isolate in a tell a stratified layer of debris that contains broken pieces of pottery known to be typical of the Roman period, naturally this stratum will be interpreted as representing the Roman phase of the city's history; other objects found in the stratum, even if their typology is less well known, can be dated to the Roman period also. Separating the occupational strata of ruins often is more difficult in practice than in theory, of course, and there often is room for disagreement in typological analysis. The latter is true especially when it comes to dating artifacts. It can be established from stratigraphy, for example, that a certain type of pottery was in use before another type (this is "relative dating"). Obtaining absolute dates, on the other hand, usually depends ultimately on written evidence.

Material remains. Archaeologists concentrate their attention on non-verbal material remains while historians work primarily with written texts. This distinction tends to break down, however, especially in the Middle East where some of the most important written records from ancient times have been discovered in the process of archaeological excavations. Moreover, non-verbal remains and written sources provide complimentary information about the past, so that it makes no sense to concentrate entirely on one and ignore the other. While the artifacts inform us about physical settings, settlement patterns, technological and stylistic trends, and so on, the written records provide names and details about specific peoples, individuals, and events. Thus archaeologists and historians have overlapping interests; they both depend to some degree on a combination of material remains and written records in their interpretations.

Both the material remains recovered by archaeologists and written records, each in its own way, offer somewhat biased information. Archaeological evidence is very selective. Only a small portion of the material culture from ancient times has survived; certain kinds of things are more likely to survive and thus are better represented archaeologically than others (for example, monumental stone architecture and pottery as opposed to mud huts and textiles), and archaeologists are able to examine only a sampling of the material remains that have survived. Written documents, on the other hand, often reflect ideological, propagandistic, and other sorts of biases. Interrelating material remains with written records moves beyond purely archaeological methodology, therefore, and calls for another level of subjective judgment. When it is reported in the news media that an archaeologist has found evidence pertaining to this or that historical person or event, one should attempt to determine exactly what material remains were discovered, why these have been interpreted as related to the particular historical person or event, and whether this is the only interpretation possible or even the most reasonable one.

Past civilizations. Archaeologists examine material remains fashioned by human hands as well as other traces of past human activity (such as carbonized seeds from crops and food preparation). Thus archaeology is to be distinguished from geology (which has to do with mountain formations, river beds, rocks, and other features of the earth's surface), paleontology (which has to do with fossils, bones, and other evidence pertaining to the physical structure of life forms including humans), and other scientific disciplines that seek clearer understanding of the past apart from human civilization. Here again, however, the distinctions are not rigid. Indeed, one of the characteristics of archaeology as practiced today is its multidisciplinary approach. An archaeological team surveying a region or excavating a site very likely will include a geologist, paleontologist, paleobotanist, and/or other specialists. Otherwise collected samples will be sent to these and other specialists for examination in their laboratories.

Biblical Archaeology

Archaeological research clearly is relevant for better understanding of the Bible, and the term "biblical archaeology" has come to be widely used. As will be explained below, there has been some objection to the appropriateness of this term. Nevertheless it calls attention to a legitimate area of research where biblical studies and archaeology overlap. Specifically, biblical archaeology may be defined as "the search for and study of material remains from the peoples of biblical lands during biblical times."

Antecedents to Biblical Archaeology

The Bible, timeless as it is, emerged from a particular geographical, cultural, and historical context. Moreover, the biblical writings are closely attentive to these contextual factors. In addition, the biblical narratives and poetry are full of references to the mountains, streams, and other topographical features of Palestine. Hundreds of place names are provided. Indeed, the biblical texts often seem to presuppose that the reader will be generally familiar with the land and its towns and villages. In Genesis 12–13 for example, in the description of Abram's arrival in Canaan, it is reported that

> Abram passed through the land to the place at Shechem, to the oak of Moreh. At that time the Canaanites were in the land. . . . From there he moved on to the hill country on the east of Bethel, and pitched his tent, with Bethel on the west and Ai on the east; and there he built an altar to the LORD and invoked the name of the LORD. . . . So Abram moved his tent, and came and settled by the oaks of Mamre, which are at Hebron; and there he built an altar to the LORD (Gen 12:6, 8; 13:18).

The familiar account in John 4 of Jesus' encounter with a Samaritan woman includes the following specifics:

> [Jesus] left Judea and started back to Galilee. But he had to go through Samaria. So he came to a Samaritan city called Sychar, near the plot of ground that Jacob had given to his son Joseph. . . . The woman said to him, "Sir, I see that you are a prophet. Our ancestors worshiped on this mountain, but you say that the place where people must worship is in Jerusalem" (John 4:3-5, 19-20).

No doubt the earliest audiences of these narratives were familiar with some or all of the places mentioned—a landmark tree near Shechem, a hill between Bethel and Ai, a grove of trees near Hebron, a village called Sychar at the base of a mountain sacred to the Samaritans—and these details would have added immediacy to the narratives for them. Other places mentioned in the biblical materials apparently were less widely known even in biblical times or required clarification for some reason. Thus one finds clarifying topographical notes embedded here and there in the biblical texts. Consider the following verses from the description of the Judah-Benjamin boundary in Joshua 15.

> . . . then the boundary goes up by the valley of the son of Hinnom at the southern slope of the Jebusites (that is, Jerusalem); and the boundary goes up to the top of the mountain that lies over against the valley of Hinnom, on the west, at the northern end of the valley of Rephaim; then the boundary extends from the top of the mountain to the spring of the Waters of Nephtoah, and from there to the towns of Mount Ephron; then the boundary bends around to Baalah (that is, Kiriathjearim); and the boundary circles west of Baalah to Mount Seir, passes along to the northern slope of Mount Jearim (that is, Chesalon), and goes down to Bethshemesh, and passes along by Timnah . . . (Josh 15:8-10).

Other biblical texts call the reader's attention to specific archaeological remains relating to biblical events. The account of Joshua's defeat of Ai concludes as follows:

> So Joshua burned Ai, and made it forever a heap of ruins [literally, a *"tel"*], as it is to this day. And he hanged the king of Ai on a tree until evening; and at sunset Joshua commanded, and they took his body down from the tree, threw it down at the entrance of the gate of the city, and raised over it a great heap of stones, which stands there to this day (Josh 8:28-29).

Thus the Bible itself sets a precedent for biblical archaeology. It recognizes that "tells" (*"tel"* is transliterated from Hebrew) are the remains of ancient cities (see also Deut 13:15-16; Josh 11:13, and elsewhere). Occasionally it calls the reader's attention to specific material remains relating to biblical events (see also Josh 4:9; 7:26; 1 Sam 6:18; etcetera).

If already in the OT there was a recognized need to clarify obscure place names this need only increased in post-biblical times, especially among Jews and Christians who lived elsewhere than Palestine. Indeed, it was an increased problem even for early Christians who still lived in the land. Place names change over time, especially when there is a new ruling elite that introduces a new official language. This happened in Palestine and throughout the Middle East following Alexander's conquests in the late fourth century B.C.E. For the next thousand years, until the expansion of Islam in the seventh century C.E., Greek (and to a lesser degree Latin) served as the official language of the Middle East. Consequently many of the old Semitic place-names, the ones used in the OT, were replaced with new names based on Greek and Latin.

Fortunately writers from Hellenistic and Roman times often noted the name changes, a very important example being Eusebius, bishop of Caesarea (ca. C.E. 264–340). Eusebius prepared Bible study aids for the clergy of his day. One of his works that has survived, known as the *Onomasticon,* is a list of the most important place names mentioned in the OT with notes indicating the contemporary names of these places (that is, contemporary with Eusebius) and their locations in terms of the Roman road system. Also there are occasional comments regarding current conditions of the site (for example, whether it was still occupied). Jerome regarded Eusebius's *Onomasticon* as important enough to translate into Latin almost a century later; he added further notes of his own.

Eusebius was contemporary with the emperor Constantine under whom Christianity became the official religion of the Roman empire. The next three hundred years would be a time of extensive church building, and typically the churches of this period had colorful mosaic floors. The early church community at Madaba, east of the Dead Sea, chose the lands of the Bible as the theme of its sanctuary floor—the mosaic floor is a map depicting the regions from the Egyptian delta to Syria and indicating places where important biblical events occurred. Dating from the sixth century and only partially preserved, this is the earliest map of Palestine and anticipates modern Bible atlases.

Jewish and Christian pilgrims were finding their way to Palestine at least a century before Eusebius, and European pilgrims were arriving in large groups by the ninth and tenth centuries. Naturally there was some reduction in the flow of Christian pilgrims from Europe after the Crusaders were expelled in the thirteenth century, yet the practice continued as it does today especially in the form of pre-packaged Holy Land tours. Many of the early pilgrims' travel accounts were collected, translated, and published between 1887 and 1897 by the Palestine Pilgrims' Text Society. In addition to the fact that their accounts provide information about circumstances in Palestine between biblical times and the present, these pilgrims and their present-day counterparts may be regarded as continuing the archaeological interest reflected in the biblical texts and providing a link to modern biblical archaeology. The difference of course (sometimes only a difference in degree) is that modern archaeologists seek to locate the places mentioned in the Bible and interpret whatever material remains have survived there by scientific means rather than depending on tradition and local guides.

Palestinian Archaeology During the Nineteenth and Twentieth Centuries

Napoleon's invasion of Egypt and Palestine in 1798, although it ended in failure from a military standpoint, was a key event for the modern archaeological "rediscovery" of the ancient world. It signaled three important developments that would unfold during the course of the nineteenth century. First his invasion turned the attention of the colonial powers toward the Middle East; thereafter they set about more deliberately establishing a presence in Egypt, Syria, Palestine, and Iraq by sending government representatives, merchants, and missionaries. With them came a new breed of explorers, scholars, and engineers (such as Ulrich Seetzen, Ludwig Burckhardt, Edward Robinson, Titus Tobler, H. V. Guerin, F. de Saulcy, Charles Wilson, Charles Warren, C. Clermont-Ganneau, Claude R. Conder, and H. H. Kitchener) who prepared accurate maps of most of Palestine and began systematic investigation of its antiquities. By the end of the nineteenth century several national organizations had been founded for the specific purpose of the exploration of Palestine. These included the Palestine Exploration Fund (British, founded in 1865), Deutscher Palästina-Verein (German, founded in 1887), École Biblique et Archéologique Française (French, founded in 1890), Deutsche Orient-Gesellschaft (German, 1898), and the American Schools of Oriental Research (United States, founded in 1900).

One of the most important contributions of these nineteenth-century explorers was their systematic examination of the topography and their mapping of Palestine. Napoleon's invasion signaled this process; his engineers prepared a scaled topographical map of the Palestinian coast. During the 1870s, sponsored by the Palestine Exploration Fund, Conder and Kitchener prepared a one-inch to one-mile scale map of Palestine west of the Jordan. By the turn of the century reasonably accurate maps were available for most of the region east of the Jordan also. It was recognized that the local Arabic place names often preserve ancient names (pronounced differently under Arabic influence) and Edward Robinson, drawing on his comparative examinations of place names in the biblical texts, local Palestinian topography, and local Arabic place names, published a masterful study (*Biblical Researches in Palestine, Mount Sinai, and Arabia Petraea,* 1841; expanded edition in 1856) that identified hundreds of biblical sites. Robinson has been called the "father of biblical archaeology" and current biblical atlases are heavily dependent on his pioneering work.

Napoleon's soldiers discovered the Rosetta Stone, which signaled another important development during the nineteenth century—the discovery of hundreds of written documents from the peoples of the ancient Middle East and decipherment of their ancient languages. The Rosetta Stone, a trilingual text in Egyptian hieroglyphics, Demotic, and Greek, provided the clues for deciphering Egyptian hieroglyphics in 1882. The Behistun Inscription, another trilingual text in Babylonian (Akkadian), Elamite, and Old Persian, played a similar role twenty years later in the deciphering of the cuneiform languages of Mesopotamia. Other important archives and languages would be discovered during the twentieth century (for example, Hittite archives discovered at Boghazköy in central Turkey in 1915, Canaanite archives discovered at Ras Shamra on the Syrian coast in 1929, Mari archives discovered at Tell Hariri on the Euphrates in 1933, and the Ebla archives discovered at Tell Mardikh in western Syria in 1975). However the first extensive epigraphical discoveries from ancient Israel's neighbors, and consequently those that had the initial influence on biblical studies, were made during the nineteenth century. Perhaps the major impact lay in the realization that the Israelites were relative latecomers to the scene of ancient history and civilization, that even in their own day they played a relatively minor role in international affairs, and that some of the materials in the OT had close parallels in earlier and contemporary literature.

Palestine has produced few epigraphical remains—occasional inscriptions, ostraca (writings on potsherds), seals, and seal impressions. Two of the most important inscriptions were discovered during the nineteenth century—the Mesha inscription found in 1868 at Dhibān east of the Dead Sea, and the Siloam inscription discovered in 1880 in the Siloam water tunnel in Jerusalem. These date from the ninth and eighth/seventh centuries B.C.E. respectively and are written in Canaanite alphabetic script. A comparable Aramaic inscription apparently from approximately the same time period was recently discovered at Tell Dan in northern Israel.

Actual excavation played a minor part in the nineteenth century; scholars focused their attention on topography and surface antiquities. It was only toward the end of the century, in fact, that they began to understand that "tells" were stratified ruins of ancient settlements. This had become clear by 1890, however, when Flinders Petrie, sponsored by the Palestine Exploration Fund, began the first excavation of a tell in Palestine, Tell el-Hesi.

Tell el-Hesi was the first of several major tells to be excavated in Palestine before World War I. Among others were Tell el-Jezer (ancient Gezer), Tell Ti'innik (Tannach), Tell el-Mutesellim (Megiddo), Tell es-Sultān (Jericho), Tell er-Rumeileh (Beth Shemesh) and Sebastiyeh (Samaria). When these sites were excavated, stratigraphical excavation techniques and ceramic typology for Palestine were still in their infancy. However with increased archaeological activity between the world wars archaeological methodology became more standardized and sophisticated. Ceramic typology was secure enough by the late 1920s to be useful for dating purposes. Carbon 14 dating became available in 1933. At Samaria, excavated in 1931–1935, Kathleen Kenyon pioneered what is now called the "Wheeler-Kenyon method" of excavation and recording, intended to insure better stratigraphical control. Most of the sites that had been excavated earlier were given further attention after the disturbances of World War I and many other sites were excavated as well, including Tell Beth Shean, Tell el-Balātah (Shechem), Tell en-Nasbeh, Beitēn (Bethel), et-Tell (Ai), Tell Beit Mirsim, Tell ed-Duweir (Lachish), and Ashkelon.

During the 1950s and 1960s—that is, after World War II and the political uncertainties of its immediate aftermath—archaeologists continued to focus on major tells and again revisited some of those that had been excavated earlier. Significant new trends became noticeable, gaining momentum during the 1970s and 1980s, and are characteristic of Syro-Palestinian archaeology as practiced today: (1) Israeli archaeologists as well as Jordanian and Syrian archaeologists (these last two groups not to the same extent) play a prominent role in exploring the antiquities of their respective countries. (2) Archaeological research today is more professionalized, multidisciplinary, and somewhat more closely aligned with the sciences than with the humanities. (3) Contemporary archaeologists tend to be more interested in sociological and anthropological kinds of questions than in historical kinds of questions. (4) Accordingly, while continuing to excavate large, multi-period tells contemporary archaeologists give more attention to smaller, single-period sites selected for specific problem-solving purposes. Also there is stronger emphasis on regional surveys. (5) Finally, as modern technology races ahead archaeological strategies change as well. Computers, satellite photography, Global Positioning Systems, neutron activation analysis, and other such technologies are revolutionizing the ways archaeologists go about collecting, recording, and interpreting data.

Biblical Archaeology During the Twentieth Century

While the archaeological research described above has been underway over the past century there also has been ongoing discussion regarding the relevance of archaeology for understanding the Bible. Obviously it is relevant in some ways, which no one would deny. Just as the results of the nineteenth-century explorations demonstrated that the Bible is anchored to a specific region that can be mapped, and that the mountains, streams, cities, and villages that turn up in its narratives were real places whose ruins can be located today, so has twentieth-century archaeology firmly anchored the Bible in its appropriate time frame and made tremendous strides toward isolating and illustrating the material culture of biblical times. The OT, for example, clearly is a product of the Iron Age. Accordingly, Early Iron Age houses and pottery vessels illustrate everyday life during the period of the separate kingdoms. There are occasions, moreover, when certain archaeological data can be reasonably correlated with a particular item in the Bible although the evidence inevitably will be circumstantial to some degree. For example, biblical chronology places Solomon in the tenth century B.C.E. The biblical account of his reign in 1 Kings depicts him as an extremely wealthy king with far-reaching international influence and reports that he built Hazor, Megiddo, and Gezer. Excavations at the tells of all three of these sites have revealed fortifications with impressive city gates from approximately the tenth century B.C.E. Thus some scholars regard it as reasonable to attribute these particular fortifications and gates to Solomon, rendering it possible in turn to date them a little more exactly than is possible on purely archaeological grounds.

Nevertheless the connection is circumstantial and open to challenge. Nothing about the fortifications themselves, or anything else found at Hazor, Megiddo, Gezer, or any other Iron Age site points specifically to a ruler named Solomon. While it is true, in other words, that the very existence and impressiveness of these fortification systems may be taken as suggestive of a strong centralized government, were we dependent on the archaeological evidence alone there would be no way of knowing that a king named Solomon ever lived. Thus the validity of the interpretation of the fortification systems as Solomonic depends ultimately on the historical accuracy of the biblical account of Solomon's fantastic accomplishments, and that account is not entirely convincing even to many biblical scholars, much less to secular historians. Moreover, while there is a possible "fit" between the biblical account of Solomon's reign and the fortification systems excavated at the three sites in question there seems to be a conflict between this account and another aspect of the archaeological evidence: namely, it is disconcerting in view of the biblical emphasis on Solomon's international influence and trade that the archaeological remains from the tenth century B.C.E. in Palestine present virtually no evidence of international contact (such as foreign trade items).

The example described above is typical of many correlations between the archaeological record and the biblical account made by contemporary archaeologists and biblical scholars. Recognizing that these correlations normally involve a degree of circumstantial evidence calls for three further observations. First, there is good biblical precedent for proposing "circumstantial" correlations of this sort. Consider again Josh 8:28-29 (quoted above) where the narrator explains that a heap of stones among the ruins of Ai relates to the Israelite conquest of the city and specifically the execution of the king. Probably there was nothing about the heap of stones itself that required the narrator's interpretation. Second, while one always wishes for firm "proof" much archaeological interpretation, whether or not it has to do with the Bible, is circumstantial. As emphasized above, archaeologists do not dig up "facts," they dig up "artifacts," silent material remains that must be interpreted. When evaluating archaeological interpretations such as the identification of the fortification systems as Solomonic, therefore, the appropriate question to ask is not whether the interpretation can be proven, but what exactly is the evidence and how strong and convincing is the interpretation placed upon it? The nature of the evidence and the "reasonableness" of the interpretation will vary from case to case, and it is not surprising that archaeologists and biblical scholars often disagree even among themselves. Third, in many cases pertaining to biblical history, such as the Solomonic fortifications, the issue boils down ultimately to one of confidence in the historical accuracy of the biblical materials. If one approaches the archaeological data with assurance that the biblical account of Solomon's reign is reasonably accurate—that is, that he was a powerful ruler and great builder who lived during the tenth century B.C.E.—then attributing the Hazor, Megiddo, and Gezer fortifications to him makes all the sense in the world. If one suspects, on the other hand, as some biblical scholars do, that the Solomonic Golden Age was largely a fabrication by late Judean priests and scribes, then he or she will be more receptive to other possible interpretations of the archaeological evidence and take more seriously aspects of this evidence that do not fit easily with the biblical account. This pattern and this tension have been central to discussions of archaeology and the Bible throughout the past century. Let us review some of the highlights of the debate as it has unfolded.

As indicated above, it was the mid-1920s before Palestinian ceramic typology had been worked out securely enough for pottery to play a determining role in dating the strata of Palestinian tells. This advance in pottery dating called for reconsideration of the tentative dates that had been assigned during earlier excavations. Accordingly C. Watzinger reviewed the pottery from Jericho that he and E. Sellin had excavated in 1907–1909 and concluded that the stratum of the tell they had associated with Joshua's conquest of the city actually belonged to a much earlier period. In fact, Watzinger concluded further, Jericho was not even occupied during Joshua's day; the biblical account of Joshua's conquest of Jericho must be, as some biblical scholars had already suspected, a legend. Watzinger's conclusions regarding archaeology, the Bible, and the historicity of the Israelite conquest of Canaan initiated a debate that continues today.

By the end of the 1930s two alternative approaches emerged that tended to dominate the discussion into the early 1970s. One approach, associated especially with Albrecht Alt and Martin Noth, placed heavy emphasis on historical-critical analysis of the biblical materials, was very cautious about the historicity of the biblical account of Israel's origins in its final form, and consequently also was cautious about interpreting archaeological remains to fit the biblical account. The other approach, associated especially with W. F. Albright and his students, placed more confidence in the biblical account (although they were far from literalists), and was more confident in making connections between archaeological remains and the Bible. It was during these mid-century decades, and especially under the influence of Albright and his students, that "biblical archaeology" became a widely accepted term and concept.

Since the 1970s, however, there has been some negative reaction to biblical archaeology among both archaeologists and biblical scholars. Essentially three objections have been raised: (1) Much of the mid-century biblical archaeology discussion focused on historicity questions: is there archaeological evidence that confirms the historicity of the patriarchs and clarifies the time periods in which they lived? Is there archaeological evidence for clarifying and dating the Israelite exodus from Egypt? Can one connect specific destruction levels excavated at key Palestine sites with the Israelite conquest of Canaan? As indicated above, Palestinian archaeologists are more interested nowadays in anthropological and sociological kinds of questions, and a similar trend is noticeable among biblical scholars. How did the people live in relation to their ecological environment? What were their social structures? (2) In their eagerness to correlate the archaeological record with the biblical account mid-century archaeologists and scholars often exceeded the reasonable limits of circumstantial evidence. They made connections that were possible, not necessarily compelling or even probable, and developed scenarios that involved multiple levels of circular argumentation. One still observes this sort of thing in popular journals and books, but especially since the mid-1970s there has been a strong reaction in the academic community against simplistic harmonizing of archaeology and the Bible. (3) Concern has been raised by both biblical scholars and Palestinian archaeologists, moreover, that the biblical archaeology agenda had an inappropriate influence on their respective fields. Seductive "archaeological solutions" to problematic biblical texts tended to sidetrack the search for other possible solutions, while the eager search for biblical connections tended to skew the agenda of Palestinian archaeology.

The Relevance of Archaeology for Bible Study

Along with the observation that there is a cautious mood at the moment among both archaeologists and biblical scholars regarding the interrelationship of their respective fields, it must be emphasized that this mood is in reaction to the excesses of biblical archaeology. Few would deny that archaeologists and biblical scholars have legitimately overlapping interests and that each of their fields of research is relevant to the other. Let us conclude this essay, therefore, with a summary of ways in which archaeology is relevant for Bible study.

(1) Biblical study begins with examination of manuscript evidence, and surely one of the most important modern developments in that regard was the discovery of the Dead Sea Scrolls in 1947 and afterward. The initial discovery was made by a local Beduin boy, but it was archaeologists who were able to establish that the scrolls date from the Roman period, who followed up the initial accidental discovery with systematic exploration of the region that turned up more scrolls, and who excavated Khirbet Qumran, which has been interpreted as a sectarian Jewish settlement whose inhabitants hid the scrolls in nearby caves.

(2) The biblical materials were written in the ancient Hebrew, Aramaic, and Greek languages which are fairly well understood today, but not entirely so. There are occasional rare words, grammatical forms, idiomatic expressions, and the like that puzzle the best philologists. Comparative study of other closely related ancient languages often sheds some light on the uncertainties of meaning and thus aids translation. Ugaritic, for example, has been especially helpful in the study of Hebrew vocabulary and grammar. Strictly speaking linguistic study is the bailiwick of philology and epigraphy rather than archaeology. However, the Ugaritic archive and most of the other first-hand written sources now available from ancient times were discovered by archaeologists.

(3) The biblical materials emerged from a particular geographical, chronological, and cultural context. Clarification of this context is perhaps the most important contribution that archaeology makes to biblical studies. Most of our Bibles today include printed maps, for example, and these are far more accurate and detailed than the Madaba mosaic or even the best maps available to Napoleon. Likewise Bible commentaries, dictionaries, and atlases are full of helpful information about lifestyles in biblical times, often illustrated with photographs and drawings supplied by archaeologists.

(4) Archaeology is less helpful, although certainly not irrelevant, for dealing with particular historical events described in the Bible. Where there are connections to be made the evidence usually is circumstantial and sometimes seems to be negative. For example, excavations at the sites mentioned in connection with the Israelite conquest of Canaan reveal that many of these were unoccupied at the time Joshua would presumably have lived. Indeed, much of the controversy that has surrounded biblical archaeology during the twentieth century has to do with archaeology and biblical history. While the difficulties in this regard cannot be ignored, neither should they detract from the other important ways in which archaeology contributes to better understanding of the Bible.

The Canonical Structure of the New Testament: The Gospel and the Apostle

François Bovon

In the following pages I will attempt to illuminate a theological structure that was determinative for primitive Christian faith: the Gospel and the Apostle. That structure may explain the construction of a bipolar canon in the second century; there will be no need, as in the past, to have recourse to external agency. Consequently, I would like to contradict the widely-accepted thesis that Marcion originated the New Testament canon. In my opinion the ship owner from Pontus was responsible neither for the idea of a collection nor for the bipolar structure of such a New Testament canon. A "New Testament" containing the gospels and epistles is the logical consequence and concrete expression of a revelation that articulates the event and its proclamation, involving Jesus and his disciples.

When he was caught up in controversy with his opponents at Corinth, Paul referred to the divine project of salvation, which he describes in terms of reconciliation (2 Cor 5:18-19). He refers not to one but to two actions whose relationship he carefully describes: "reconciliation" itself as an event, and the service of "reconciliation," that is, the effective proclamation of that event. Paul himself, inasmuch as he is an apostle, is the one responsible for proclaiming the gospel. The apostolic word serves as an indispensable complement to the act of redemption. The gospel has two faces, one with an event-character represented by Jesus and one with a language-character represented by the apostles.

The narrative tradition that has recalled, adapted, and given expression to the memories of Jesus up to the composition of the gospels, Matthew and Mark in particular, also attests, in spite of its concentration on the Master, to the existence of a bipolar structure. It likewise describes the division of functions within the cooperative endeavor.

In repeating the account of the institution of the group of the Twelve (Matt 10:1-4; Mark 6:7; 3:16-19; Luke 9:1; 6:13-16), their sending on mission (Matt 10:5-42 *parr.*), and their experiences of the Risen One (Matt 28:16-20; Luke 24:36-53; cf. Acts 1:1-8) the bearers of these traditions attest to the cooperation of the Lord and his disciples. The apostles constitute a group to whom responsibility has been given; although they are weak they have been made strong by the strength of Christ. Sent out two by two, they continue the work of Jesus, preaching the gospel of the reign of God and re-establishing human life by exorcisms and healings.

In the conclusion of Matthew, on the day of Easter, the disciples receive from the risen Christ a mission founded on a promise: "Jesus came to them and spoke to them" (Matt 28:18a). Although divine power belongs to Christ ("All power has been given to me in heaven and on earth," v. 18b), witness is the work of the disciples ("Go therefore, make disciples of all nations," v. 19). There is thus a division of roles just as there is a distinction of time periods. Because the Christ has gone away, they have to act. But, as in the prologue to the first letter of John (1 John 1:3), communion does not cease despite their separation: "And I will be with you always, to the close of the age" (Matt 28:20).

The Pauline school as we understand it from reading the Deutero-Pauline and Lukan writings maintains and refines the theological position of the master. In the prologue to his work Luke first mentions the origins, that is to say, "the things that have been accomplished among us" (Luke 1:1). For the evangelist as for the apostle, Christianity does not rest on an abstract revelation or a mystical experience, but on a history, a divine intervention in time and space. In order to be effective that saving event needs to be expressed and attested: that is why Luke hastens to add that there are ocular witnesses to the events who have become "witnesses and servants of the word" (Luke 1:2). Although the two poles are mutually indispensable they should not be confused with one another. One relates to the event, the coming of Jesus Christ, the other to proclamation, the apostolic testimony. But the first pole (as Luke immediately acknowledges) contains an element of language and the second an element of action: Jesus Christ himself is a witness to the word of God, and the gospel preached is communicated through apostles of flesh and blood. The gospel has two faces: gospel as christic event and gospel as apostolic proclamation, but each face in turn has two sides, a historical aspect and a verbal aspect. These aspects, and these faces, can neither be confused nor separated.

A comparison of the two prologues belonging respectively to the gospel and the first epistle attests the presence of a deliberate schema in another stream of primitive Christianity: the Johannine movement. Although the prologue of the gospel (John 1:1-18) sings of the coming of the Word, the second, in the form of an interpretive echo, forcefully augments it with an indispensable complement, the apostolic testimony. In the Johannine world as well it was necessary to exercise some theological diplomacy in order to defend the legitimacy of the Beloved Disciple by situating apostolicity at the side of the Revealer. In pictorial form, with the power that metaphors confer on language, the Johannine theologians present an initial course of revelation: from the Father to the Son and from the Son to the Beloved Disciple. As the Word resting in the bosom of the Father (John 1:18) knows the Father intimately, so the Beloved Disciple, whose head rested on Jesus' breast during the Last Supper (John 13:23, 25), is his hermeneut. Revelation is religious, but also historical and human because it comes through human persons and is expressed in their words. The Gospel and letters of John had to constitute, for a time, the canon of the Johannine communities: before the New Testament canon or the Marcionite canon they confirm the intrinsically Christian origin of the bipolar structure of Gospel and Apostle.

In my opinion the Gospel/Apostle structure that appeared in the first Christian generation prepared the way for the construction of a complement or counterpart to the existing Sacred Scriptures, principally the Septuagint. The formation of a New Testament canon was thus the logical materialization of that theological structure.

Protestant theology, which has always insisted on Jesus Christ and him alone, has often refused to grant the apostles their proper place in the economy of salvation. Thus many Protestant exegetes in the nineteenth and twentieth centuries have regarded the very existence of the Acts of the Apostles as an anomaly, if not a theological error. It unfortunately seemed even sacrilegious in their eyes to focus attention on the fate of the witnesses, who ought to disappear behind the christological message.

That opinion, rooted in polemic against the Catholic doctrine of apostolic succession, neglects the bipolar structure of Gospel and Apostle and unbalances the schema in favor of spiritual and divine realities. Thus Paul, for example, makes us understand that worship was the social and ecclesial root location of that fundamental structure. United in prayer, the first Christian communities praised God through the work of Christ, but they also rejoiced in the universal spread of the gospel (cf. Rom 1:8; 1 Tim 3:16). They address their petitions to God, asking God to protect and accompany the apostles and missionaries (cf. Acts 13:3; 20:36-38). They also recount the edifying stories of their travels and their successes (cf. 1 Thess 1:6-10). This explains the origin of the cycles of stories redacted by Luke in the book of Acts (cf. Acts 8:4-40; 9:32–11:18; 13–14).

The theological structure of Gospel and Apostle that underlies the progressive organization of ministries nurtured the appearance of a bipolar New Testament canon. No doubt it was built up unappreciably and irresistibly. The fact that Marcion chose one gospel and some epistles as the source and norm of his teaching does not, in my opinion, represent an innovation. Marcion's canon is one witness among others to the structuring power of the Gospel and the Apostle. The ecclesiastical authors around the year 200 recognized such a juxtaposition of gospels and epistles as a collection of the sacred writings of the new economy. But it should be noted that the theological structure of Gospel and Apostle meant more to them, on the whole, than the formal structure of the canon.

It is thus not surprising that in Christian liturgy the system of biblical readings has been established on the model of that theological structure. From the time of Justin and the *Acts of Peter,* Christian worship has included both pericopes from the Old Testament and readings drawn from the gospels and epistles. And while in the West we have adopted the custom of speaking of the gospel and the epistle, the East has preferred to speak of the gospel and the apostle. They represent the same reality, and in the title of this article I have taken my inspiration from the Eastern Orthodox formulation.

The New Testament canon, faithful to the underlying theological structure, relates revelation to history according to a logic that is unique to Christianity: it closely associates the gospel as founding event with the gospel as good news. In doing so it proclaims a historic beginning and claims an indispensable apostolic mediation.

The Eucharist in the New Testament

Roch Kereszty

The Eucharist sums up in itself the whole mystery of Jesus Christ: it reveals the purpose of his mission, recalls his redemptive death by allowing us to share in it, and makes present the risen Christ in his kingdom. The Eucharist is also the center of all the Scriptures where the unity of both testaments comes to light with astonishing clarity. Moreover in the eucharistic celebration the Scriptures reach their full actuality: no longer mere Scriptures, recorded history and past experience, they become "spirit and life"; they articulate for us the active, life-giving presence of the Word made flesh who remains with his Church until the consummation of history. For these reasons it seems most appropriate to treat the mystery of the Eucharist in a Catholic Bible commentary.

Origins

We find four texts in the NT that have traditionally been identified as the institution accounts of what later will be called the Eucharist by the early Church: Matt 26:26-29; Mark 14:22-25; Luke 22:15-20; 1 Cor 11:23-25. The Fourth Gospel has no institution account; however once its ecclesial dimension is recognized the Gospel of John has much to say about the Eucharist. It presents the multiplication of the loaves as a sign, and in the following discourse Jesus explains the sign's eucharistic import (6:1-59). The imagery and content of Jesus' farewell discourse at his last meal presupposes the synoptic institution account and in the allegory of vine and branches the Johannine theology of the Eucharist reaches its climax. A less obvious but nonetheless real connection can be detected between the breaking of the bread (one of the first names for the Eucharist) in the Christian community and the appearances of the risen Lord at the gatherings of the disciples (Luke 24:13-35; Acts 10:41 and perhaps John 21:12-14). In order to facilitate comparison I will arrange in parallel columns the four institution accounts and the central part of John's eucharistic discourse in a very literal translation.

The Eucharist in 1 Corinthians 11

Faced as we are with such a variety of texts of different provenance and date, the safest starting point for inquiring into the origin of the Eucharist is to analyze the earliest written source, 1 Cor 11:23-25. However, it needs to be examined in relation to its parallel texts since the earliest literary product may not necessarily reflect the earliest formulation.

A careful study of Galatians 1–2 indicates that it was crucially important for Paul to be in communion with the mother church in Jerusalem and with the reputed pillars of that church, James, Cephas, and John. While stressing his empowerment and apostolic mission directly from Christ himself Paul also explains that three years after his conversion he went up to Jerusalem "to visit Cephas"; as a measure of the importance of his visit, Paul adds that he "stayed with him fifteen days" (Gal 1:1, 18). After fourteen years he again returned to Jerusalem so that he might present his gospel to the "pillars" of the Church

1 Cor 11:23-26	Matt 26:26-29	Mark 14:22-25	Luke 22:15-20	John 6:51-58
[23]For I received from the Lord what I have also handed on to you, that the Lord Jesus on the night he was handed over, took bread, [24]and, after giving thanks, broke [it] and said, “This is my body for you. Do this in remembrance of me.” [25]In the same way, also the cup, after supper, saying, “This cup is the new covenant in my blood. Do this as often as you drink [it], in remembrance of me.” [26]For as often as you eat this bread and drink this cup, you proclaim the death of the Lord until he comes.	[26]While they were eating, Jesus, after taking bread and saying the blessing broke [it] and giving [it] to the disciples, he said, “take [it], eat [it]; this is my body.” [27]And after taking a cup and giving thanks he gave [it] to them saying, “Drink from it, all of you,” [28]for this is my blood of the covenant [which is] to be poured out for many for the forgiveness of sins. [29]I, however, tell you, from now on I do not drink from this fruit of the vine until that day when I drink it with you new in the kingdom of my Father.	[22]And while they were eating, after taking bread, saying the blessing, he broke [it] and gave [it] to them and said, “Take [it]; this is my body.” [23]And after taking a cup, giving thanks, he gave [it] to them and they all drank from it. [24]And he said to them, “This is my blood of the covenant [which is] to be poured out for many. [25]Amen I say to you that I do not drink from the fruit of the vine until that day when I drink it new in the kingdom of God.”	[15]And he said to them, “I desired with desire to eat this Passover with you before I suffer. [16]For I tell you that I do not eat it until it is fulfilled in the kingdom of God.” [17]And after receiving a cup [and] giving thanks, he said, “Take this and share [it] among yourselves. [18]For I tell you, from now on I do not drink from the fruit of the vine until the kingdom of God comes.” [19]And after taking bread [and] giving thanks, he broke [it] and gave [it] to them saying, “This is my body [which is] to be given for you; do this in remembrance of me.” [20]And likewise the cup, after supper, saying, “This cup [is] the new covenant in my blood [a cup which is] to be poured out for you.”	[51]“I am the living bread [that has] come down from heaven; whoever eats of this bread, will live forever; and the bread that I will give is my flesh for the life of the world.” [52]The Jews quarreled among themselves saying, “How can this one give us [his] flesh to eat?” [53]So Jesus said to them, “Amen, amen I say to you, unless you eat the flesh of the Son of Man and drink his blood, you have no life in you. [54]Whoever eats my flesh and drinks my blood has eternal life and I will raise him up on the last day. [55]For my flesh is true food and my blood is true drink. [56]Whoever eats my flesh and drinks my blood remains in me and I in him. [57]Just as the living Father sent me and I live because of the Father, so also the one who feeds on me will have life because of me. [58]This is the bread that came down from heaven. Unlike your fathers who ate and died, whoever eats this bread will live forever.”

[James, Cephas, and John] “to make sure that [he] was not running, or had not run, in vain” (Gal 2:1-2). Paul is firmly convinced that there is only one gospel for Jews and Gentiles (Gal 1:6-9; 2:7-8). Thus it is inconceivable that he would not want to be in agreement with the pillars of the church in Jerusalem on such a fundamental issue as the tradition of the Lord's Supper. (Farmer, "Peter and Paul, and the Tradition concerning the 'Lord's Supper' in 1 Cor 11:23-26," *One Loaf,* 35–55). It is then quite appropriate to seek a better understanding of 1 Cor 11:23-25 by comparing it to Matt 26:26-29 and Mark 14:22-25 which—according to a near consensus of exegetes—originated in the churches of Jerusalem and/or Galilee.

First Corinthians was written around 56 C.E. and in 11:23 Paul refers to his sojourn in Corinth that took place around 51 C.E. It was at that time that he had handed on to them what he had himself received from the Lord. "I received" *(parelabon)* and "I handed on" *(paredōka)* are technical terms in both rabbinic Judaism and the apostolic Church for receiving and handing on sacred traditions. When Paul refers to the summary of his gospel he preached to the Corinthians in the same year he uses the exact same terms, *paredōka* and *parelabon* (1 Cor 15:3). The expression "from the Lord" in this context means that according to Paul this tradition is not of human origin but comes from Jesus himself. In a similar vein Paul distinguishes his own recommendations to the Corinthians from what the Lord commands through him (1 Cor 7:8-12).

Moreover the literary analysis of 1 Cor 11:23-25 has shown conclusively that it is pre-Pauline in origin; Paul incorporates a preexisting account into his letter, with slight modifications. Among all the parallel institution accounts his text is closest to Luke 22:18-20.

We cannot determine the exact time when Paul received this tradition, but it must certainly have happened before he preached the gospel in Corinth, thus very early in his missionary career, at the latest in the forties. This, however, means that the churches with which Paul was acquainted had by this time developed a stylized, terse text relating what happened at the Last Supper, a text that was shaped by its constant use in the Church's liturgical celebration. Thus on purely historical grounds it is quite implausible that in about a decade after Jesus' death and resurrection the churches in Antioch and its surroundings, the churches with which Paul was in contact, could have invented on their own and spread successfully a rite of central importance for the Church while attributing its origin to Jesus himself.

The Lord Jesus on the Night When He was Betrayed Took a Loaf of Bread . . .

The beginning sentence inserts the institution into the larger context of the Passion of Jesus. The passive verb "he was betrayed" or "he was handed over" *(paredidoto)* refers not only to the betrayal of Jesus by Judas but also to God who allows Jesus to be delivered into the hands of his enemies that night. The Greek verb form echoes the LXX version of Isa 53:12: *paredothē eis thanaton hē psychē autou,* "his soul was handed over to death." (On the Hebrew wording of this verse see Ben F. Meyer, "The Expiation Motif in the Eucharistic Words: A Key to the History of Jesus?" *One Loaf, One Cup,* 19–21.)

At the same time the account emphasizes that the Lord Jesus, the risen, glorified Lord of his Church, is the same person who on that night was handed over to death. Thus the text implies an inseparable connection between Jesus' voluntary self-abasement unto death and his becoming Lord. In this way the risen Lord himself becomes the host, the chief celebrant at the Lord's Supper. In the act of remembering the Lord, his last supper, his passion and resurrection-exaltation are intrinsically united.

The phrase "on the night when he was betrayed" agrees with the synoptic chronology of the Last Supper. Whether the pre-Pauline tradition or Paul himself believed the Last Supper to be a Jewish Passover meal is uncertain. However, all the synoptics clearly identify it as a Passover meal and John's account of the farewell meal of Jesus is consistent with such a characterization (Matt 26:17; Mark 14:12; Luke 22:7-8). Nevertheless according to John Jesus was crucified on the day that ended at night with the celebration of the Passover supper (18:28; cf. also 19:14). None of the proposed theories has succeeded in resolving with certainty the apparent contradiction in synoptic and Johannine chronology, yet the most likely assumption seems to be that John is correct in stating that Jesus died in the afternoon of Nisan 14, before the time prescribed by the Law for the Passover meal. However, Jesus may have celebrated the Passover meal a day before, on Nisan 13, because he followed another calendar that was different from the official calendar of the Temple priesthood. An alternative explanation is that the huge number of pilgrims in Jerusalem during the festivities may have made it necessary to extend the allowed time for slaughtering the Passover lambs in the Temple to one day before the official date.

According to Matthew and Mark Jesus celebrated the Passover Meal with "the Twelve" (Matt 26:20; Mark 14:17), according to Luke with "the apostles" (22:14). For Luke, however, apostles was a technical term reserved for the Twelve (6:13). Even though John speaks about the disciples of Jesus rather than explicitly about the Twelve or the apostles he applies this term consistently and exclusively to the Twelve after the crisis that followed the eucharistic discourse (6:66-71).

That Jesus celebrates the Passover meal with the Twelve is theologically important for the synoptic authors. This Passover will serve as the covenant meal to seal the eschatological covenant in the very blood of Jesus with the "patriarchs" of eschatological Israel; the Twelve are now the leaders of a "little flock," a faithful remnant (Luke 12:32; cf. also Matt 19:28; Luke 22:30), yet seed for an innumerable multitude: "many [a multitude unlimited in number] will come from east and west and will eat with Abraham and Isaac and Jacob in the kingdom of heaven" (Matt 8:11). The remnant of faithful Israel represented by the Twelve is to become the center of salvation for the whole world.

And When He had Given Thanks, He Broke It . . .

The pre-Pauline account begins with this first important action of the Lord's Supper. But according to the synoptic accounts the blessing over the bread took place not at the beginning of the supper as was done at a usual meal, but "while they were eating." At the Passover meal there were two cups (the *kiddush* cup and the *haggadah* cup) served and drunk and a preliminary dish served before the blessing was spoken over the bread. The expression *eucharistēsas,* "when he had given thanks," is probably the Grecized equivalent in 1 Corinthians and in Luke of the Matthean-Markan *eulogēsas,* "after having said a blessing" (Matt 26:26; Mark 14:22). This refers to the Jewish blessing *(berakah):* at each meal the father of the family before breaking and distributing the bread blesses God for God's benefits and goodness.

And Said, "This is My Body That is for You."

At the question of the youngest in the family the *paterfamilias* explains the meaning of the unleavened bread at the Passover supper *(haggadah):* "this is the bread of affliction that our ancestors ate in Egypt. Whoever is hungry, come and eat. Whoever is in need, come and celebrate the Passover!" Here comes the first surprise in Jesus' last Passover meal. He does not identify the bread as the bread of past Egyptian slavery but as his body to be given "for you" (1 Corinthians, Luke) or "for many" (Matthew, Mark). While praising God, Jesus presents the bread as his own bodily self to be given up for them on the cross, breaks it and distributes it to be eaten by the disciples. The phrase "for you" is probably a cultic transformation of the more original Matthean-Markan "for many" that is associated there with the outpouring of Jesus' blood. The word "many" is a key word in the Fourth Servant Song (Isa 53:11, 12) and, determined by the context (Isa 52:14-15), it designates an unlimited multitude, all humankind, whose sins and punishment the one servant will bear; by his atoning "sin offering" (53:10) he will make sinners just in the sight of God.

The Hebrew or Aramaic word translated by the Greek *sōma* in the institution accounts is most probably *basar* in Hebrew, *bisra* in Aramaic. Its meaning is closer to flesh than to body. John's use of *sarx* in the eucharistic discourse then may be closer to the *ipsissima vox* of Jesus. Moreover in the Johannine statement "the bread that I will give for the life of the world is my flesh" the phrase "for the life of the world" accurately reflects in a more Hellenistic form the Matthean statement over the cup: the blood of Jesus is to be poured out "for many for the forgiveness of sins." The world as the object of Jesus' atoning sacrifice is more understandable for a Hellenistic audience than the phrase "for many" meaning "for all humankind."

"Do This in Remembrance of Me."

We will explain this text in conjunction with its repetition after the words over the cup.

In the Same Way He Took the Cup Also, after Supper, Saying . . .

This cup is probably the third cup of the Passover meal, the cup of blessing (cf. 1 Cor 10:16).

Only in 1 Corinthians and in Luke is it mentioned that the cup Jesus identified with his blood to be poured out was drunk at the end of the meal. In this detail they represent more accurately the historical situation at the Last Supper.

"This Cup is the New Covenant in My Blood."

This is the second surprise of Jesus' last Passover meal. Instead of simply blessing God while holding up the cup Jesus gives a new interpretation *(haggadah)* and relates the cup to the new covenant he is going to establish in his own blood. Some scholars argue that the pre-Pauline and Lukan traditions on the whole seem to be secondary and the Matthean-Markan text reflects better the original wording. Others opt for the priority of the pre-Pauline or pre-Lukan tradition. Space does not allow us to explain here the arguments for both sides. The quest, however, for the original wording will most likely remain open for the foreseeable future. In any case the Matthean-Markan formula ("this is my blood of the covenant, which is poured out for many for the forgiveness of sins") and the pre-Pauline tradition do not contradict one another; the difference concerns matters of emphasis rather than substance. The latter connects the sacrificial pouring out of Jesus' blood with establishing the new covenant as prophesied by Jeremiah. The former reflects more explicitly the tradition of Isaiah 53, which without doubt has strongly influenced Jesus.

"Do This, as Often as You Drink It, in Remembrance of Me."

The command to repeat the words and gestures of Jesus occurs twice in 1 Corinthians (after the thanksgiving over the bread and the cup) and once in Luke (after the words over the bread). The lack of this command in Matthew and Mark does not indicate the absence of the rite in the Palestinian churches. Implicit in Mark but explicit in Matthew is the understanding that what Jesus says and does determines the teaching and life of the Church.

The command "do this in remembrance of me" follows closely the pattern of the command to repeat the Passover celebration: "You shall observe this rite as a perpetual ordinance *(le zikkaron)* . . . you shall keep this observance" (Exod 12:24-25). The first Passover supper in Egypt is perceived as an effective anticipation of the saving event of the Exodus: YHWH kills all firstborn in Egypt but passes over the Israelites' firstborn because of the blood of the lamb smeared on their doorposts. Israel's yearly celebration of the Passover meal is more than a psychological effort to recall the saving event set in motion by that first supper. The descendants of Israel believe that they do share in this saving event: every member of the people, no matter how far removed in time from the first Passover, must consider himself or herself as personally having gone out of Egypt (*m. Pesahim* X,5). Moreover they also believe that the *shekinah*, the mysterious presence of YHWH, envelops them during the celebration.

Jesus' last supper was also the beginning of the eschatological saving event to be accomplished the next day on the cross. By his prophetic words and gestures Jesus not only explicated what was going to happen but effectively anticipated it. The OT context that helps us understand the gestures of Jesus is the whole complex of the sign actions of the prophets. A prophetic action "not only represents what it foretells but, in a certain way, produces it as well" (Jacques Dupont, "'This is my Body'" 21). Thus when the Church commemorates the Last Supper it is not a mere human effort to recall the past. By obeying the Lord's command to remember the Church participates in the eschatological salvation that the supper and the cross together have brought about.

However, unlike the injunction in Exodus the command of Jesus does not simply refer to repeating the celebration. He says : "Do this in remembrance of *me" (touto poieite eis tēn hemēn anamnēsin)*. We remember his person, not only his saving work. The appearances of the Risen One in the breaking of bread (a technical term designating the Eucharist in Acts) convinced the disciples that the crucified Jesus has been raised to a new life with God and has become the Lord of his Church and all creation. Therefore the pre-Pauline tradition implies that the Lord Jesus is the host of the meal. Not only does his redemptive work operate in the celebration but he himself is personally present. Much as the *shekinah* enveloped the celebrants of the Passover meal, so does the presence of the Risen One dominate the eucharistic celebration.

The pre-Pauline account ends with v. 25. Verse 26 is Paul's warning to the Corinthians who may have turned the Lord's supper into an enthusiastic and literally inebriating celebration (11:21) not to forget that the Lord's supper proclaims the death of the Lord. This proclamation is not added to the rite, but the rite of the Lord's supper itself celebrates his atoning death and resurrection. Paul also adds: "until he comes." By this reminder Paul places the Eucharist in the eschatological atmosphere that characterizes the synoptic accounts (Matt 26:29, Mark 14:25; Luke 22:16, 18).

The Eucharist in the Gospel of Matthew

Matthew provides a coherent presentation of Jesus' mission from a Jewish perspective. This Jewish perspective can hardly be the result of a late, secondary development after Mark's adaptation of the gospel to a Roman audience. Christianity was born in and spread from a Jewish matrix to a Roman and Hellenistic milieu; therefore Matthew's conception of the gospel (not his style, however, which shows a much better mastery of the Greek language than that of Mark) seems to reflect the primary perspective among the four evangelists from which we can most fruitfully approach the work and words of Jesus. For this reason I will first investigate the meaning of the Eucharist in the Matthean context.

In Matthew the Eucharist as the manna of the New Age that the messiah is going to give is adumbrated but does not become an explicit theme. The two multiplications of the loaves in the desert show Jesus as the creator and giver of bread. Even though two fish are also mentioned only the loaves of bread are said to have been distributed to the disciples who in turn give them to the crowds. When giving the bread Jesus repeats the gestures of the Last Supper: *"Taking* the five loaves and the two fish, he looked up to heaven, *and blessed* and *broke* the loaves, and *gave them* to the disciples, and the disciples gave them to the crowds" (14:19). The second multiplication (15:32-39) has some added eucharistic features: *eucharistēsas eklasen* ("after giving thanks he broke them"). Both terms, *eucharistia* and *klasis tou artou* (thanksgiving and breaking of bread) became technical terms for the Eucharist in the early Church. The large surplus of the remaining fragments (twelve and seven baskets respectively) also points to the abundance of the messianic food. However at the Last Supper the close connection with the blood of Jesus that is to be poured out for the forgiveness of sins points to the breaking of the bread not simply as a sign of the messianic banquet but as the anticipation of the self-sacrifice of the servant.

The unique feature of Matthew's eucharistic theology indeed centers on Jesus' outpoured blood as atonement for the sins of God's people Israel. When we compare Matthew with the other gospels the central role of blood and in particular the frequent mentioning of Jesus' blood (six times) becomes immediately evident; in Mark and Luke on the other hand Jesus' blood is not spoken about at all except in the words over the cup during the last supper.

According to Matthew, Joseph will call the son conceived in Mary by the Holy Spirit Jesus, Yeshua (or Yehoshua) meaning "YHWH saves" "for he will save his people from their sins" (1:21). The people is designated *ho laos,* the usual Greek term reserved for Israel as God's chosen people. Thus Jesus' mission centers on saving Israel, God's chosen people, from their sins. His whole public life is aimed at fulfilling this mission (9:10-13; 11:19). Before healing the paralyzed man he declares to him that his sins are forgiven (9:2). The physical healings then serve as the manifest sign that Jesus indeed has the power and the intention to treat not only the "symptoms," but the root cause of all illness, the sinful condition of his people. When reproached by the Pharisees for eating with sinners he replies: "Those who are well have no need of a physician, but those who are sick. . . . I have come to call not the righteous but sinners" (9:12-13).

Matthew alone sees all the healings and exorcisms of Jesus as the beginning of the vicarious sacrificial role of the servant. He heals not as an uninvolved divine visitor but by taking upon himself and carrying in himself our diseases and infirmities, ultimately our sins (8:17). However, Jesus' call for conversion, his invitation for his people to enter into the kingdom (with a few exceptions) falls on deaf ears; his free offer of forgiveness to all who would change their hearts, minds, and lives is rejected by official Israel. Thus "the good news risks turning into a condemnation" (Ben F. Meyer, *One Loaf,* 24; cf. also Rudolf Pesch, *Abendmahl,* 83–86). Jesus announces the impending judgment over Israel:

> You snakes, you brood of vipers! How can you escape being sentenced to hell? Therefore I send you prophets, sages, and scribes, some of whom you will kill and crucify, and some you will flog in your synagogues and pursue from town to town, so that upon you may come all the righteous blood shed *(pan haima dikaion ekchunnomenon)* on earth, from the blood of righteous Abel to the blood of Zechariah son of Barachiah, whom you murdered between the sanctuary and the altar. Truly I tell you, all this will come upon this generation (Matt 23:33-36).

This text constitutes the counterpoint to Matt 26:28; the two yield their meaning only in correlation to one another. The *pan haima dikaion ekchunnomenon* (all the righteous blood shed) on earth from the blood of righteous Abel to the blood of Zechariah calls out for vengeance to God, the protector and avenger of all innocent blood; God's condemning judgment threatens the present generation that contemplates the murder of the Innocent One par excellence. But over against all the righteous blood poured out and calling for vengeance is presented the blood of Jesus, the blood of the covenant that is to be poured out for the multitude for the forgiveness of sins (26:28: *to haima mou tēs diathēkēs to peri pollōn ekchunnomenon eis aphesin hamartiōn*). The one conceived by the Holy Spirit, the one whose innocence is attested by his betrayer Judas, his judge Pilate, and Pilate's wife (27:4, 19, 24) freely accepts the violent death to be inflicted on him and willingly pours out his innocent blood for the forgiveness of sins; primarily for the forgiveness of the sins of his own people, Israel, who alone accept responsibility for his death ("Then the people as a whole answered, 'His blood be on us and on our children" Matt 27:25), but ultimately for the forgiveness of all. (The "many" in Isa 52:14-15 refers to the Gentile peoples and their kings and so does the "many" in Isa 53:11-12). Moreover even though the mission of the earthly Jesus and his disciples is limited to the "lost sheep of Israel" Matthew envisions from the beginning a universal kingdom open to all nations, while the focus of the universal gathering remain "Abraham, Isaac, and Jacob" (8:11; cf. also 24:14). This universalist perspective of Matthew is confirmed by the universalism of the Servant Songs even outside the eucharistic institution account (12:21). Thus the mention of the name of Jesus at the beginning of the institution of the Eucharist in Matthew is charged with theological meaning, just as the title "the Lord Jesus" is theologically significant in the pre-Pauline tradition. While in 1 Cor 11:23 the designation "Lord Jesus" points to the risen Lord as the host of the eucharistic banquet, in Matthew the name "Jesus" reminds the readers that Jesus is about to accomplish the mission defined by his name Yehoshua: it is through his impending sacrificial death that YHWH will "save his people from their sins." Only the freely given blood of the innocent servant Jesus, who is the Son of God himself, can accomplish the impossible, namely to turn the worst crime of human history into a sacrifice of expiation that will result in a renewed offer of forgiveness for Israel and for all humankind. By anticipating at the Last Supper the outpouring of his blood as *the* expiatory sacrifice (Isa 53:10) the innocent servant pleads not for vengeance but for forgiveness. In Matthew's perspective this forgiveness of sins and the definitive covenant are offered first to Israel and then to all the nations. (This priority seems to be implied by the fact that according to Matthew the Jews alone, "the whole people" acknowledge responsibility for Jesus' death while Pilate tries to evade the consequences of his actions by hypocritically washing his hands from "this man's blood" [27:24]).

Even though forgiveness is offered in a special way to the people of Israel it does not "work" automatically. If God's people do not heed the preaching of the eleven disciples who are the patriarchs of the renewed Israel, if they do not observe all their teachings that include eating the body of Jesus and drinking his blood, Jesus' blood will call for a special divine judgment against them. Then the threat enunciated in 23:33-36 will indeed be realized. (The especially severe judgment on Israel does not mean that every Israelite of Jesus' generation is pronounced personally guilty of the blood of Jesus; even less can one construe personal guilt for subsequent Jewish generations on the basis of Matthew's gospel.)

It is remarkable that the most Jewish of all gospels insists in the most explicit way on taking and eating the body of Jesus and drinking his blood. In Israel the prohibition against drinking blood was absolute. Since both animal and human blood were seen as the seat of life, in fact life itself, they were considered the exclusive possession of God. No one was allowed to partake of blood:

> If anyone of the house of Israel or of the aliens who reside among them eats any blood, I will set my face against that person who eats blood, and will cut that person off from the people (Lev 17:10).

Originally the blood of all slaughtered animals was sacrificed to God, acknowledging that all life should return to the one who is the source of all life. Hence the belief in the atoning power of the blood of sacrificial victims:

> For the life of the flesh is in the blood; and I have given it to you for making atonement for your lives on the altar; for, as life, it is the blood that makes atonement (Lev 17:11).

This text has been the subject of many divergent interpretations. In our opinion the animal blood sprinkled on the altar symbolizes our own human lives, the right to which we have forfeited by our sins; the rite also expresses the offerers' desire to belong again to God by offering God the life of the animal in its blood. (Cf. the footnotes to Lev 17:11 in the *NAB*). In Matthew's perspective, however, not the blood of animals but only that of the servant who is the Son of God himself could actually obtain atonement for our sins by the free shedding of that innocent blood.

In this context the striking implications of Jesus' words begin to dawn on us: "this is my blood of the covenant. . . . Drink from it, all of you." Only the one who is Lord of the Sabbath, the Lord of all lives may renounce his sovereign right to his own life and offer it for us and to us. Without assuming the divine dignity of the One who says "drink from it, all of you" the command would appear a usurpation of God's exclusive right. The one to whom all life (all blood) belongs freely pours out his life (his blood) for us so that we may be truly atoned for, truly forgiven, and become worthy to partake in the final, irrevocable covenant. But Jesus is not satisfied to pour out his blood for us; he commands us to drink it. In this way He does not simply make us beneficiaries of his atoning death: in a Jewish context sprinkling with blood would have expressed this purpose more appropriately. Rather he wants to share with us the very source of atonement; let his blood speak in us "a better word than the blood of Abel" (Heb 12:24) and atone for our sins within us and through us. In other words it seems that by giving us what is most exclusively his own Jesus wants us to join him in his atoning work. He wants to atone to the Father in us and through us by giving us his own blood, his own life, which alone has genuine atoning power.

Thus at the Last Supper Jesus simultaneously reveals his divine dignity and his ultimate self-emptying for our sake. He alone has the absolute authority (*pasa exousia en ouranō kai epi tēs gēs:* 28:18) to conclude the definitive covenant, but he does so by making us share in his own blood that he freely and totally consecrated to God as an expiatory sacrifice. This sacred, innocent blood of the Son poured out for the sake of all and consumed by all believers atones for all sins and prepares us for the banquet in the Father's kingdom.

The Eucharist in the Gospel of Mark

The results of literary analysis are consistent with the data of tradition according to which the Second Gospel was composed by a Jewish interpreter of Peter. However, in contrast to Matthew neither tradition nor literary analysis point toward a Jewish audience. Even though Mark presents a traditional Jewish Christian christology he does not develop it from a Jewish perspective but rather makes an attempt to apply it to a Gentile and most probably Roman audience. Perhaps for this reason, unlike Matthew, Mark has no implicit "theology of blood." The expiatory sacrifice of the Servant is implied by the preservation of the Isaian subtext (Jesus' "blood is to be poured out for the many") but is not explained as a sacrifice for the forgiveness of sins. At the same time the great value of Mark vis-à-vis Matthew is the former's vivid portrayal of the unfolding drama of Jesus in which the institution of the Eucharist plays a pivotal role.

Both the solemn entry into Jerusalem and the Passover Supper are preceded by Jesus' prophetic instructions. First of all the disciples are to find a young colt on which no one has ever sat. (In Matthew the disciples are to find an ass with her colt, in John the colt of an ass. In both cases the messianic connotation is made obvious by reference to Zech 9:9: The messiah comes as a humble king who proclaims peace to the nations. Mark seems to miss the scriptural background for the prophetic sign, namely that Jesus was riding not simply a young colt, but the colt of an ass as prophesied by Zech 9:9.) It is on this colt that Jesus is to enter Jerusalem as the messianic king. Second, the disciples are to meet a man with a water jug who will show them a large upper room furnished and ready for the Passover meal for Jesus and the Twelve (11:2; 14:12-16). This second prediction may be based on a previously arranged sign between Jesus and the master of the house. Nevertheless the tone of the instructions has a prophetic solemnity. If Mark is closely linked to the oral preaching of Peter, as has again been recently proposed by Martin Hengel on the basis of impressive evidence, we have here an eyewitness recollection, and if Mark is identical with John Mark in Acts 12:12 this room may be the same upper room where according to Acts 1:13 the first disciples gathered. The solemnity of the preparations and the parallelism between the two stories suggest that in Mark's view Jesus' entry into Jerusalem and his Last Supper are two closely linked highlights of his history before the Passion: Jesus enters Jerusalem as the messianic king whose first major act is to purify the Temple. As he is blessing and praising God in thanksgiving at the Passover meal Jesus announces the meaning of his death: the atoning sacrifice for the sins of all that seals the definitive covenant between God and humankind. His shameful crucifixion, the betrayal, denial, and flight of his disciples, and even his apparent abandonment on the cross by his Father are the result of this voluntary self-surrender. At the same time the Last Supper not only announces but prophetically anticipates both his sacrifice and the joyous messianic meal in the kingdom of God.

The dramatic atmosphere of the last meal of Jesus is more emphasized in Mark than in the other synoptics. We learn from Mark that Jesus chose the Twelve primarily "to be with him" (3:14). We are also made aware that there is a warm human relationship between this elect group and Jesus. After the return of the disciples from a missionary journey Jesus expresses a personal concern for their exhausted state: "Come away to a deserted place all by yourselves and rest a while." Mark adds an explanatory note: "For many were coming and going, and they had no leisure even to eat" (6:31). The human closeness between the disciples and Jesus endures even though Jesus reproaches the disciples several times for their lack of faith. Dazed and gripped by anxiety the disciples are still loyally following Jesus on the road toward his Passion in Jerusalem (10:33). This atmosphere of personal intimacy is then shattered when Jesus announces at the beginning of his last Passover meal: "Truly I tell you, one of you will betray me, *one who is eating with me*" (14:18). At the anxious questioning of the disciples Jesus adds: "It is *one of the Twelve,* one who is dipping [bread] into the bowl with me" (14:20).

The italicized phrases are peculiar to Mark; the first Markan passage seems to be a modified version of Ps 41:9 that stresses the close table fellowship of Jesus with his betrayer, while the second passage points out that the traitor belongs to Jesus' inner circle, to the chosen patriarchs of the new Israel. Whether or not Judas actually partook of the first Eucharist Jesus points him out as the one who disturbs the intimacy of the table fellowship within which the institution of the Eucharist took place. Mark thus confronts us with the drama of Jesus' Passion: even in Jesus' closest circle one rejects the atoning sacrifice that alone could save him.

The Eucharist in Luke and Acts

In developing his understanding of the Eucharist Luke uses the data of the tradition common to Matthew/Mark and 1 Corinthians 11 while gathering additional information as he does for many other parts of his gospel. In his reconstruction of the history of Jesus and the apostolic Church the Eucharist appears at the juncture of two interrelated themes: Jesus' mission is a service of redemptive solidarity with sinners that prepares them for the eschatological banquet of the kingdom. Both themes occur also in other writings of the NT but Luke thematizes them with greater detail and depth.

Luke alone identifies sharing in the divine reign with eating bread in the kingdom of God (14:15). According to Luke this eschatological banquet is prepared only for those sinners who have accepted Jesus' call to conversion. (While the theme of banquet is more fully present in Luke than in any other gospel, in his attempt to eliminate doublets of what seemed to him the same event Luke describes only one multiplication of loaves.) Luke tells of Jesus' eating with sinners in the house of the converted tax collector Levi and also narrates the story of another tax collector, Zacchaeus. Jesus invites himself to dine in Zacchaeus's house, and through his conversion Zacchaeus enters into table fellowship with Jesus himself (19:1-10). In the parable of the prodigal son Jesus depicts the kingdom as a festive banquet the father arranges for his younger son who "was dead and is alive again . . . was lost and is found" (15:24). In the parable of the great banquet the poor (1:53; 6:20-21), the maimed, the blind, and the lame (considered unclean in Israel and excluded by the Qumran writings from the eschatological banquet) along with the Gentiles are to replace the originally invited who declined the invitation because they are attached to worldly possessions and enjoyments (14:16-24). Just the fact that someone is marginalized and despised in society or poor and starving does not by itself assure for him or her a privileged place in the banquet of the kingdom, but material poverty and the misery of sin call for God's "preferential" mercy and at the same time deprive the poor of any excuse not to accept the invitation. In order to belong to those who are truly blessed we have to renounce not only all our possessions but also our desire for wealth and become a follower of Jesus (6:20-21). Only those hungry people will be filled with the good things of the kingdom who do not worry about what to eat and drink but seek God's reign above everything else (12:22-31).

Just as in the other gospels the Lukan multiplication of the loaves is full of eucharistic allusions: it takes place after Jesus' preaching on the kingdom and after his healing of the sick. It is food for those who had already been instructed by Jesus' word and cured by him of the diseases that had signaled the dominion of sin and Satan over them. The story emphasizes that only Jesus can provide food for them, not the disciples (8:13-14). In multiplying the bread Jesus anticipates all the gestures of the Last Supper: he takes the loaves, says the blessing over them, breaks them, and gives them to his disciples. The overflowing abundance and the collection of the leftover fragments as well as the mediating role of the disciples between Jesus and the crowd also point out the similarity between this feeding of the multitude and the Church's Eucharist: "he . . . gave them to the disciples to set before the crowd" (9:16).

While being a preparation for the institution of the Eucharist the feeding of the multitude is also a proleptic sign of the eschatological banquet: all who ate were filled and the event takes place in the desert where the messiah of the end times is going to repeat the miracle of the manna (9:12, 17).

As we have seen above, the Lukan institution account stands in substantial agreement with the Matthean-Markan text, yet not only the account itself but also its immediate and mediate context shed new light on the Eucharist. Luke emphasizes the crucial importance of the last Passover supper of Jesus with the apostles (for Luke this term designates the Twelve) not only as Mark does by the special prophetic instructions (on how to find the prepared upper room) but also by Jesus' introductory words:

> "I have eagerly desired to eat this Passover with you before I suffer; for I tell you, I will not eat it until it is fulfilled in the kingdom of God." Then he took a cup, and after giving thanks he said, "Take this and divide it among yourselves; for I tell you that from now on I will not drink of the fruit of the vine until the kingdom of God comes" (22:15-18).

The Last Supper then is the climax of Jesus' celebration of communion with his disciples before his exodus, which is his deliverance from this world and assumption into heaven where he is going to sit at God's right hand. He is fully aware that one of them will betray him, that Peter will deny him, and that all of them are still unconverted: at this most solemn moment of Jesus' departure their main concern is "which of them was to be regarded as the greatest" (22:24). In spite of Jesus' awareness of the apostles' wretched condition the Lukan Jesus has the most personally intimate version of the eucharistic words. Jesus identifies the bread with his body "which is given for you": in other words "for you, my disciples, who are still concerned mainly about dignities, titles, and power, who will betray, deny, and abandon me in a few hours." "This cup that is poured out for you is the new covenant in my blood." Unlike Matthew and Mark in whose texts Jesus pours out his blood for the many, for all human beings, on the cross, Luke speaks about this cup being poured out for the concrete group of the disciples. For Luke the ultimate service of the one "who is seated at table" is the giving of his personal self *(sōma)* to his disciples in its entirety and pouring out his blood for them so that they may share in the new covenant.

By giving himself over to his disciples and delivering himself later into the hands of sinners Jesus begins the fulfillment of the Jewish Passover that is to be completed on the cross and at his ascension. Only by becoming the servant of his disciples and delivering himself into the hands of sinful people does he become consummated and ready to receive kingship from his Father that he will bestow on his disciples. "He . . . was numbered with the transgressors." This phrase from Isa 53:12 is the leitmotif of Jesus' Passion in Luke (22:37: "and he was counted among the lawless"); it marks the end of his farewell discourse at the institution of the Eucharist and explains the redemptive value of his Passion. Luke does not deny the Matthean understanding that we are saved by Jesus' blood; in fact his version of the words of Jesus affirms that the new covenant is established in Jesus' blood, yet he stresses another aspect of the saving event. The one who throughout his earthly life has always sought out sinners, who went after them, received them, and accepted table fellowship with them is now going to be reckoned as one of them. On Calvary he will suffer as a common criminal crucified between two evildoers; he will be surrounded by his executioners, the instruments of the power of darkness. It is through his complete solidarity with sinners that he will save the "good thief" by eliciting from him an act of faith. Rather than opposing his murderers he intercedes for them: "Father, forgive them; for they do not know what they are doing" (23:34).

The Last Supper anticipates Jesus' redemptive act accomplished by solidarity with sinners. Luke does not deny what Matthew emphasizes but he concentrates on another aspect: Jesus' death obtains forgiveness for us because he freely chooses to die the death of a sinner among sinners and personally intercedes for them. In the Eucharist Jesus makes a gift of himself through his body and blood to the apostles who are still sinners concerned about the first place in the kingdom and yet on their way to conversion.

The Lukan Last Supper narrative includes another "preferential Lukan theme," the kingdom as eschatological meal with Jesus. Jesus looks beyond the present weakness of the apostles to their future conversion and promises them table fellowship with himself in his kingdom:

> You are those who have stood by me in my trials; and I confer on you, just as my Father has conferred on me, a kingdom, so that you may eat and drink at my table in my kingdom (22:28-30).

This eschatological table fellowship begins in the eucharistic celebrations after Jesus' resurrection. In the Acts of the Apostles Peter testifies to the fact that the apostles indeed ate and drank with the risen Lord (Acts 7:56; 10:41). However, not only the apostles share in this table fellowship with Christ. The story of the two disciples going to Emmaus indicates Luke's conviction: in every eucharistic celebration, which must be preceded by an explanation of the Scriptures so that the disciples' faith be kindled, the risen Lord comes and manifests himself in the breaking of the bread (Luke 24:13-35). In this way Luke alone makes explicit that the Eucharist of the Church is not only the sacramental *anamnesis* of Jesus' sacrificial death but also an anticipated celebration of the eschatological glory, of the kingship of the risen Lord over the celebrating community and the whole world. As a fruit of Jesus' ultimate solidarity in death with us sinners and of his intercession for us we converted sinners, or rather still sinners on our way to conversion, may celebrate the presence of the risen Lord with joy and exultation.

A unique feature in the Lukan portrayal of eschatology is derived from the Lukan version of the parable of the faithful servant:

> Blessed are those servants whom the master finds awake when he comes; truly, I say to you, he will gird himself and have them sit at table, and he will come and serve them (12:37 RSV).

The eschatological Jesus is presented in this parable not as the Lamb worshiped together with God (Rev 5:8-13; 6:16) nor as the majestic and glorious judge (Matt 25:31-46) who separates the sheep from the goats but as the Lord waiting on his disciples at a heavenly banquet. However, from the account of the Last Supper we learn that even there he was among his disciples "as one who serves" (22:27) and he served them with his own sacrificed body. Thus in the Lukan perspective every Eucharist is an anticipation of the eternal table service of the heavenly Lord who feeds us with himself, while eternity is pictured as a fulfilled Eucharist. Hence the joy and intimacy at the breaking of the bread, the central act of worship in the Lukan community (Acts 2:46-47).

The Eucharist in the Gospel of John

The Context

The Gospel of John derives from a channel of eyewitness tradition that has developed in relative independence from the synoptic tradition, yet it presupposes in its audience the knowledge of the latter that it intends to complete, deepen, and selectively correct. The Fourth Gospel chooses from the earthly life of Jesus only a few events and presents them as seven "signs," miracles or prophetic parables in action, the meanings of which are clarified in a discourse attached to or interwoven with the narrative of the sign itself. Each sign within what C. H. Dodd calls the Book of Signs (chs. 1 through 12) anticipates and illustrates the mystery of Jesus' death and resurrection.

At the same time the seven episodes are meant to be not only anticipatory signs of the paschal mystery but also signs of its abiding presence in the Church, contemporaneous with its entire history. The risen Jesus who returns to his disciples in the Spirit continues his life-giving activity in the Church: he provides the new wine of the messianic wedding feast, distributes bread from heaven in the Eucharist, illumines the spiritually blind in baptism, and raises the dead to life through repentance. This ongoing, life-giving activity of Jesus in the Church derives from the paschal mystery and unites all believers to the person of the sacrificed and risen Jesus.

Why is There No Institution Account in the Gospel of John?

Many exegetes have attempted to answer the question why the Fourth Gospel contains no institution account of the Eucharist.

(a) The once popular answer of Bultmann explained it on the basis of the anti-sacramental theology of the original Johannine text to which the sacramental references would have been added later by an ecclesiastical redactor (John 3:5 "of water"; 6:51-58). However this hypothesis cannot explain why the allegedly later additions do not disrupt the unity of the Johannine text but appear as organic parts of a unified composition that in its entirety displays a sacramental dimension.

(b) C. H. Dodd and Joachim Jeremias explain the omission by positing the beginnings of a *disciplina arcani.* In order to protect the Eucharist from distorted rumors the author of the Fourth Gospel explained it in a manner obvious and helpful for Christians who participated in the eucharistic meal but not intelligible to outsiders. However, the eucharistic discourse in 6:51-58 contains such apparently scandalous statements about chewing on the flesh of the Son of Man and drinking his blood that they rather confirm than dissipate the suspicions of nonbelievers.

(c) Another hypothesis stresses the selective character of the Fourth Gospel. Presupposing knowledge of the synoptic tradition in his audience the author does not intend to give a full account of what Jesus said and did (20:30-31) but rather to develop in detail the meaning of some selected events from the life of Jesus (which he calls "signs"). John refers several times to persons and events the reader can understand only if he or she is in possession of some previous information. (For example 6:69 presupposes that the reader knows about the significance of the Twelve who appear in John without any explanation. John 20:1 presupposes that the reader knows who Mary of Magdala is.) The description of Jesus' last supper and his farewell discourse in John also assume the reader's knowledge of the institution of the Eucharist at that meal since John's text makes multiple references to it. For instance Jesus performs the washing of the feet *deipnou ginomenou* (during supper: 13:2; cf. also 13:4, 21:20). In the Christian circles of Ephesus where the Gospel of John was most probably composed and where Paul wrote in his letter to the Corinthians about the *kyriakon deipnon* (1 Cor 11:20) the word *deipnon* (supper) may have acquired a eucharistic connotation. The similarity to the Pauline phrase *kyriakon deipnon* is confirmed by the emphasis in John 13 on Jesus' dignity as *kyrios* at this *deipnon* (13:6, 9, 13, 14, 16). In John the Last Supper is indeed the Lord's supper. When the Johannine Jesus presents his betrayal by Judas as the fulfillment of the Scriptures he uses an otherwise unknown version of Ps 41:9 that seems to have been changed to echo the Johannine eucharistic discourse: "the one who ate (chewed) my bread has lifted his heel against me" (13:18). The words *trōgōn mou ton arton* refer back to John 6:35, 41, 48, 51, 54, 56. The one whose unbelief and future act of betrayal had been revealed after the eucharistic discourse (6:70-71) is going to betray him now, at the time of the eucharistic meal itself.

(d) Hypothesis (c) does offer a possible reason for the omission of an institution account. However we could find a more satisfactory answer through examining the theological perspective from which John treats the sacraments. What matters for him is not so much their institution by Christ as the way they derive from and unite us to his sacrificed and risen body. The Word became flesh so that he might give his flesh on the cross for the life of the world. The Spirit is enclosed "in the intestines" of Jesus during his earthly life and its life-giving waters will flow out of his pierced side only when Jesus is glorified on the cross and in his resurrection (7:37-39). In other words Jesus' flesh and blood become Spirit-giving food and drink, that is, true food and true drink for us, only on the cross. In this perspective then the Incarnation reaches its supreme goal in the Eucharist and the Eucharist is the fruit of the cross and resurrection. We may also view the Johannine Eucharist as the last stage in the mission of the Word. The Word becomes flesh at his birth, becomes Spirit-giving flesh in the paschal mystery, and enters into us fully in the Eucharist so that we may live by the Son for the Father. This Johannine perspective explains the strange division of exegetes over the presence of the Eucharist in the Gospel of John. Those who narrow their search to the eucharistic rite may conclude that the Fourth Gospel as a whole lacks a eucharistic dimension and that the eucharistic reference in 6:51b-58 is a foreign body inserted by an "ecclesial redactor" into the original anti-sacramental gospel. For those, however, who perceive that in John the final goal of the mission of the Word made flesh is to unite us to his incarnate person as branches are inserted into the vine and thus to make us one with the Son as the Son is one with the Father will discover the central place of the Eucharist in the whole of Johannine theology. Certainly this perspective in no way favors the ritualization and clericalization of the sacraments. However, as will become apparent later, John eliminates neither the ritual nor the role of apostolic mediation but makes them transparent since the sacraments unite us directly to the Spirit-giving flesh of Jesus himself.

The Bread of Life: Sign and Discourse (6:1-71)

The Feeding of the Five Thousand, 6:1-14

As we have seen before, the feeding of the multitude has eucharistic overtones in each of the synoptic gospels. However, in John the entire story becomes a sign, a symbolic anticipation of the Eucharist that is to be given in the Passover mystery and a symbolic representation of what continues to be celebrated in the Christian community. Thus most of the slight changes vis-à-vis the synoptic accounts are intended to accomplish this goal by establishing the OT background of the Eucharist and by preparing the discourse on the bread of life.

Only John mentions two details at the beginning of the story: Jesus "went up the mountain and sat down there with his disciples. Now the Passover, the festival of the Jews, was near" (6:3-4). The synoptics write several times that Jesus went up a mountain and they make these mountains important milestones in the ministry of Jesus. John, however, says only twice that Jesus went up a mountain, at the beginning and end of our story, so its unique occurrence and its use as a device of inclusion gives added importance to this detail. The mountain in the OT (just as in the religion of all peoples) symbolizes a privileged sphere of communication with God. God is powerfully present on Mount Horeb when giving the Law to Moses and on Mount Zion, God's holy mountain, where God dwells among the chosen people. While the Gospel of John relativizes the importance of the Temple on Mount Zion and even replaces the Temple by the body of Jesus it maintains the symbolic importance of the mountain. Closest to John's introductory image is Matt 5:1: Jesus goes up the mountain as the new Moses, his disciples come to him, and he begins to teach with absolute authority. Jesus' word is above the words of the Law that he does not abolish but fulfills by showing its real meaning. In John, however, Jesus goes up the mountain not to teach but to provide food for the people who came to be healed. He is not simply the new Moses, the prophet whom the people want to make king (6:14-15). His own identity and the nature of the food that the multiplied bread symbolizes will be revealed only in the account of the walking on water and in the subsequent discourse. Yet the facts that Jesus feeds the multitude from the mountain top and that the time is close to the Passover feast prepare what will be disclosed later, the transcendent origin of Jesus and that of the bread he will give. Jesus is more than a new Moses; the manna of the new Passover, the bread from heaven he provides, is his very self, Wisdom herself present in the flesh and blood of Jesus. According to the book of Sirach Wisdom dwelt in the highest heaven (24:4) and God made her set up her tent (*katepausen tēn skēnēn mou:* 24:8) in Jacob. John indicates to us that Jesus fulfilled this role. He is Wisdom who has pitched a tent among us (*eskēnōsen en hēmin:* John 1:14) and who now prepares food from on high to feed us.

Another detail peculiar to John is that Jesus does not use his disciples to distribute the food as is described in all the synoptics; he himself distributes the loaves (and only parenthetically the fish) after he has given thanks. The role of the disciples in the meal is restricted to making the people sit down so that they may be prepared to be fed by Jesus himself (6:10-11). On the other hand the gathering up of the fragments by the disciples receives a new emphasis in John. While in the synoptics the gathering up of the fragments seems to be a spontaneous activity and the subjects of the gathering activity remain unidentified, in John Jesus himself gives the order and gives it to his disciples: "Gather up the fragments left over [in abundance] so that nothing may be lost" (6:12). In the context of the bread of life discourse the symbolic meaning can hardly be missed: the eucharistic bread shows the overabundant generosity of the divine host and the disciples are in charge of this precious bread and must make sure that none of its fragments is lost.

The Walking on Water, 6:16-21

As explained above, the crowds do not perceive the meaning of what Jesus did. They see nothing more in Jesus than the promised messiah who will renew the miracle of the manna, but the disciples need to understand the sign character of the miracle as an anticipation and illustration of the Eucharist. Hence a second, "private" miracle takes place just for their sake.

The story of Jesus' walking on water shows the characteristics of a theophany. God's glory and power are especially revealed in treading over the sea, the symbol of uncontrollable, threatening chaos (Job 9:8). In Israel's history God's glory was most powerfully revealed in the Exodus when YHWH's "way was through the sea, your path, through the mighty waters . . . You led your people like a flock" (Ps 77:19-20; cf. also Isa 51:10). The remark at the beginning of the chapter that "the Passover, the festival of the Jews, was near" suggests that here the new and definitive Passover is anticipated. Just as before Jesus' Passion the big crowd greets him enthusiastically as the "king of Israel" (12:13) but misunderstands and ultimately rejects him, so does Jesus here abandon the politically agitated crowd and returns "to the mountain by himself" (6:15). Just as during the Passion the orphaned disciples are in danger of being overcome by the power of darkness and unbelief (12:35), so they are now alone in the midst of the raging sea, enveloped in darkness because "Jesus had not yet come to them" (6:17). But just as the anxiety and darkness of the Passion turns into seeing the risen Jesus as "Lord and God" (John 20:28) the disciples' lonely struggle on the stormy sea ends with the revelation of Jesus' divine majesty. Coming down from the mountain, the place of intimate communion with his Father, walking over the waves and drawing near to the buffeted boat, Jesus does not simply reassure the disciples; he reveals to them his divine identity: "It is I [lit.: I am]; do not be afraid!" (6:20). The one who saved them from the stormy sea and made them arrive in no time at the other shore is the very YHWH who had saved Israel from the Red Sea. Having experienced Jesus' divine majesty in his saving act the disciples are now better prepared to understand his discourse on the bread of life.

The Bread of Life Discourse: Structure and Content

Raymond E. Brown suggests the possible influence of a Christian Passover liturgy on the final shape of the discourse. This would explain the close connection between the first part of the discourse (vv. 35-51a) that stresses belief in Jesus as the source of eternal life and the second part that emphasizes eating his flesh and drinking his blood while expanding on the dimensions of this eternal life. At the same time Brown also agrees with those scholars who see here the influence of a Jewish Passover synagogue service that provides the OT substratum of texts for the discourse. Following most scholars we divide the discourse as follows: an introduction (vv. 25-34), the discourse itself consisting of two parts: (a) Jesus as the bread from heaven (vv. 35-51a) and (b) the explicitly eucharistic discourse (vv. 51b-59), and finally the reaction to the discourse (vv. 60-71).

In the introduction Jesus reproaches the crowd for not having perceived the sign in the multiplication of the loaves and challenges them to work not for perishable food but for the food that remains unto eternal life. At the question of the crowd he also explains that the only "work of God" expected of them is to believe in him whom the Father sent. When the Jews in turn challenge Jesus by quoting Ps 78:24 to ask a sign from heaven so that they may see and believe him Jesus uses this psalm verse, "He gave them bread from heaven to eat" to provide the summary and introduction to his whole discourse. It is not Moses who gave the Israelites bread from heaven, but his Father who gives them the true heavenly bread:

> For the bread of God is that which comes down from heaven and gives life to the world (v. 33).

The rest of the discourse is the unfolding of this summary statement. The first part of Jesus' speech (vv. 35-51a) centers on the first half of the psalm verse, the second part on the second half. Prefigured by the manna in the desert, Jesus himself is the bread of life insofar as he embodies and offers as food divine Wisdom herself. However, eating and drinking at Wisdom's banquet left those in the past still hungry and thirsty:

> Those who eat of me will hunger for more,
> and those who drink of me will thirst for more
> (Sir 24:21).

But Jesus offers Wisdom in such unheard-of abundance that

> Whoever comes to me will never be hungry,
> and whoever believes in me will never be thirsty
> (v. 35).

In the first part of the discourse partaking of Jesus as Wisdom means to come to him, to see him (with the eyes of faith) and believe in him. The role of the Father is to give people to Jesus or draw them to him. Those whom the Father has given to him listen to the Father's inner word, learn from the Father and come to Jesus (vv. 37, 39, 44). The result of believing in Jesus is to share in eternal life here and now and to be raised up by Jesus on the last day (vv. 39, 40, 44).

Only at the end of this section does Jesus speak about eating the bread of life that is himself rather than simply coming to him and believing in him (v. 50). The eating of the bread of life serves as a transition to the second part of the discourse that is directly eucharistic:

> I am the living bread that came down from heaven. Whoever eats of this bread will live forever; and the bread that I will give for the life of the world is my flesh (v. 51).

Up to now Jesus spoke about himself as Wisdom incarnate and it is by coming to him and looking at him in faith that our hunger is satisfied and our thirst quenched. Here a new theme is introduced and organically linked to the previous one. The living bread is not merely the person of Jesus insofar as he is the fullness of God's Wisdom but is also his flesh that he will give for the life of the world: "the bread that I will give for the life of the world is my flesh." These words most probably echo the words of the institution of the Eucharist in the Johannine liturgy. At the objection of the Jews, "How can this man give us his flesh to eat?" (v. 52) Jesus does not attempt to attenuate the harshness of his language but rather adds the necessity of drinking his blood, an even more outrageous scandal for the Jews. Nowhere else in the NT is the drinking of Jesus' blood so bluntly enjoined upon the disciples as in Matthew and John:

> Very truly, I tell you, unless you eat the flesh of the Son of Man and drink his blood, you have no life in you (v. 53).

A superficial comparison of the two parts of the bread of life discourse may lead us to conclude that Jesus attributes the same effects to faith in his person as to eating his flesh and drinking his blood. A closer look, however, reveals a genuine development of thought between the two parts of the discourse. We are instructed by Jesus that if we come to him in faith we must truly believe that his flesh is true food and his blood true drink (v. 55); we should also draw the consequences of this faith and feed on Jesus' flesh and drink his blood. Moreover it is only in the context of the Eucharist that the reality of eternal life is further explained as the mutual indwelling of Jesus and the communicant (v. 56) and communion with the Father: just as Jesus draws his life from the Father and lives for the Father so the one who feeds on his flesh and drinks his blood lives through Jesus and for Jesus. (The preposition *dia* in v. 57 indicates both cause and purpose). In the previous section the Father merely draws believers and teaches them in their hearts; in the eucharistic context the Father becomes the source and purpose of the communicant's life just as the Father is the source and purpose of Jesus' life. Thus in addition to the parallelisms between the two parts we must also underline an unfolding development that culminates in the second part of the discourse. Coming to Jesus in faith (part 1) leads to eating his flesh and drinking his blood (part 2). Just as coming to Jesus and looking at him in faith establishes the beginning of personal communion, feeding on his flesh and drinking his blood is its consummation.

The motive for the Eucharist and its effects are further expanded in the farewell discourse of Jesus within the implicit eucharistic setting of the Johannine Last Supper. Jesus gives his life for us because he loves his own (13:1) and loves the Father (14:31). The Father and the Son dwell in those who love Jesus and keep his word (14:23); the disciples are inserted into Jesus and are conduits of his life so that they will bear fruit just as the branches of the vine bear fruit as long as they remain united to the vine (15:1-8). They are to share in the love and glory that the Son has from the Father and are to be one just as the Father and the Son are one (17:1-26). All this takes place in the Holy Spirit whom Jesus will ask the Father to give to the disciples (14:15-28).

Returning now to ch. 6 we can better understand the words of Jesus by which he responds to the grumbling of his disbelieving disciples, "This teaching is difficult; who can accept it?" (v. 60).

> Does this offend you? Then what if you were to see the Son of Man ascending to where he was before? It is the spirit that gives life; the flesh is useless. The words I have spoken to you are spirit and life (vv. 61-63).

Although many commentators do not see the eucharistic perspective of the whole Fourth Gospel, Jesus' words refer not only to his opponents' first objection that questions Jesus' heavenly origin (vv. 41-42) but also to their consternation regarding the eating of the flesh and drinking of the blood of the Son of Man (vv. 52, 60). While v. 62 seems to respond directly to the first objection and v. 63 to the second, the two statements obtain their full meaning jointly just as the two parts of the discourse mutually complete and illuminate each other. Jesus is from above, from God's transcendent realm; therefore he does not speak about cannibalism. His flesh and blood, his humanity, become life-giving and spirit-giving only after he has consummated his "work" by being lifted up on the cross and ascending to the Father in his risen body. Only his sacrificed and risen humanity becomes for us the source of life in the spirit; only this spirit-filled and life-giving flesh and blood can become for us the way to the most intimate personal communion with Jesus in the Eucharist.

In the bread of life discourse, then, we encounter the same tension between flesh and spirit that permeates the whole Gospel of John: the eternal Word not only takes on flesh, he *becomes* flesh (1:14). It is literally from the "belly" *(koilia),* from the inside of Jesus' body that the living waters of the Spirit will gush forth at the crucifixion (7:37-39; 19:31-36). The same Jesus who is deeply shaken and crying at the tomb of Lazarus is "resurrection and life" itself (11:25, 33). He who is ever reclining at the Father's bosom reveals the secrets of his love to the disciple who reclines at his bosom (1:18; 13:23).

In the eucharistic doctrine of the Fourth Gospel, then, we see an even richer synthesis of OT themes than in the synoptics. Jesus is both Wisdom incarnate who invites us to his banquet and the Lamb of God who as the Suffering Servant and the true Passover lamb procures food and drink for us through consummating in himself the Passover mystery. The food and drink he provides is nothing less than his sacrificed and risen self and through himself a most intimate communion with the Father.

Real Presence of Christ in the Eucharist?

Evidently we cannot expect to find a direct answer to a question that in its precise formulation would only emerge much later: is the ultimate reality (substance) of bread and wine of the eucharistic celebration ontologically transformed (with an easily misunderstandable medieval term, "transubstantiated") into the body and blood of the living Christ? The Gospel of John does not directly speak about the bread and wine of the eucharistic celebration, let alone their transformation. Instead it stresses that Jesus himself is the bread of life; his flesh and blood, that is, his sacrificed and glorified humanity are true food and drink for us. It also insists that if we want to have eternal life we must eat the flesh of the Son of Man and drink his blood. However as Jacques Dupont points out, "These lines (verses 53-56) were written at the end of the first century for Christians who could not but refer them to the Eucharist" ("'This is my Body'" 25). Thus in the Johannine perspective Jesus himself teaches Christians (who alone can understand the eucharistic reference of his words) that he himself is their food and drink in the Eucharist. The Christian audience of the gospel could not fail to understand that by sharing in the bread and wine of the Eucharist they share in the only true food and only true drink, the spirit-giving, sacrificed and risen body-person of the Lord. In this way indirectly and globally, without later conceptual distinctions, the Johannine gospel nonetheless bears a forceful witness to the real presence as it was believed at the end of the first century in the Johannine communities.

The Eucharist in Pauline Theology

In all his letters except Romans Paul responds to the concrete problems of a community or communities to which he writes, yet, as usually happens, the practical issues that trouble the Corinthian church (such as divisions in the community according to leaders, fornication, sharing in pagan sacrificial meals, division between poor and rich at the Lord's supper, disorder because of the manifold charismatic gifts) prompt Paul (in what is called in the canon the First Letter to the Corinthians) not only to provide practical guidance but also to develop a theological rationale in order to inspire and shape attitudes and actions. Thus the participation of some Corinthian Christians in pagan sacrificial meals and the divisions between the poor and the rich at the *agape* meals (preceding the Lord's supper or more probably included in it) stir Paul to develop in writing those aspects of his eucharistic theology that bear on the Corinthian situation. On closer examination this eucharistic theology provides the key to understanding Paul's approach not only to these two issues but to most problems that plague the Corinthian church. According to Paul the manifold divisions in the church of Corinth and the dangers to its moral life and worship can be overcome only if the local assembly becomes aware of itself as the body of Christ. For Paul the Church as the body of Christ is not a vague metaphor in the sense in which we speak about a social or political "body." In Hebrew thinking the body of a person is the person himself or herself in his or her concrete tangible and visible reality; it is in and through the body that we are present in the world, act on it, and are acted upon by it. Nevertheless persons are not simply identical with their bodies: they possess them and thus they can give them over to immorality or to God. In a similar way the Church is the body of Christ, his visible and tangible manifestation in the world; Christ acts and is acted upon through his body the Church, yet Christ is not simply identical with the Church but has dominion over it and loves it as the bridegroom loves his bride; in fact he acquired the Church for himself by giving up his life for it "that she may be holy and without blemish" (Eph 5:25-27). Thus to belong to the Church means not only to possess "the mind of Christ" and to share his attitude of love and humility; the very bodies of Christians become "members of Christ," a visible extension and manifestation of Christ's personal life while preserving their individuality and freedom to become again separated from him. This is the ultimate reason why for Paul sexual relations with a prostitute are such a grave sin:

> Do you not know that your bodies are members of Christ? Should I therefore take the members of Christ and make them members of a prostitute? (1 Cor 6:15).

There is a mysterious mutual belonging between Christ and the body of the Christian:

> "Food is meant for the stomach and the stomach for food," and God will destroy both one and the other. The body is meant not for fornication but for the LORD, and the LORD for the body. And God raised the LORD and will also raise us by his power (1 Cor 6:13-14).

The conformation of our bodies to the body of Christ, then, will reach its perfection only in the resurrection when "he will transform the body of our humiliation that it may be conformed to the body of his glory" (Phil 3:21).

The Christian begins to belong to the body of Christ through baptism received in faith: "we were all baptized into one body" and "made to drink of one Spirit" (1 Cor 12:13). This initial belonging to the body of Christ is perfected by (sacramental) contact with the body and blood of the Lord, with his sacrificed and risen humanity in the celebration of the Lord's supper:

> The cup of blessing that we bless, is it not a sharing in the blood of Christ *(koinōnia tou haimatos tou Christou)?* The bread that we break, is it not a sharing in the body of Christ *(koinōnia tou sōmatos tou Christou)?* Because there is one bread, we who are many are one body *(sōma),* for we all partake of the one bread (1 Cor 10:16-17).

Paul's rhetorical question presupposes an already established belief among the Corinthians in the real presence of Christ in the Eucharist. In v. 16 Paul does not teach something new; he simply recalls their traditional understanding of the Eucharist in order to draw new conclusions from what they have believed from the beginning. The word *koinōnia* in the Pauline writings usually means different forms of personal communion that expresses itself in a commonality of views and values, in cooperation and solidarity (Rom 15:26; 2 Cor 6:14; 2 Cor 8:4; Gal 2:9), yet the word *koinōnia* always points to a deeper union than any natural fellowship, community, or commonality of views can produce. Its source is the Spirit and its result is such a unique communion of believers that even their bodies no longer belong to themselves but they together become the temple of the Holy Spirit (2 Cor 13:13; Phil 2:1; 1 Cor 3:16; 1 Cor 6:19; 2 Cor 6:16; Eph 2:21). Unique, however, in 1 Cor 10:16 is the sacrificial and cultic connotation of *koinōnia.* Paul does not simply speak about *koinōnia* with the Son (1 Cor 1:9) but with the blood and body of Christ. This participation in the blood and body of Christ is both compared to and contrasted with participation in pagan sacrifices in which the sacrificer enters into a real partnership with demons (10:20). This parallelism and contrast between the Lord's supper and pagan sacrifices (the "cup of the Lord" versus the "cup of demons," "the table of the Lord" versus "the table of demons" in 10:21) indicates that for Paul the Lord's supper is in some real way the sacrificial cult of the Church.

If we return now to Paul's central concern we see that the result of sharing in the blood and the body of Christ is that we though many become one body, the body of Christ (10:17). This communion with the body *(sōma)* of Christ in the Lord's supper builds up the one body (*sōma*) of Christ that is the Church. Thus according to Paul the *real* presence of Christ in the Eucharist causes the Church to be built up as the *real* body of Christ. To put it another way the *real presence of Christ in the Lord's supper is the foundation for Christ's real presence in the community of believers.* Here we touch upon the ultimate theological foundation for Paul's approach to the problems he had treated in the first part of 1 Corinthians. Since Christians commune with the very body and blood of Christ in the Lord's supper their bodies become members of Christ's body. For this reason one sins against the very body of Christ by fornication and by partaking of pagan sacrifices. Moreover, no one has the right to divide the Church by claiming allegiance to one leader over against another since Christ himself is not divided (1:13). Those who do not share their food with the hungry at the *agape* meals and therefore eat the bread and drink the cup of the Lord unworthily "will be answerable for the body and blood of the Lord" (*enochos estai tou sōmatos kai tou haimatos tou kuriou:* 11:27). To be guilty of someone's blood in Jewish thinking means to be held responsible for that person's death. This specific meaning becomes clear if we compare Deut 19:10 (LXX) with Paul's text: "and there will be no innocent blood shed in your land that the LORD your God is giving you as an inheritance and there will be [no one] among you [who is] guilty of blood *(haimati enochos).*

So Paul seems to point to two different ways of participating in the Lord's blood. If one participates with faith (by proclaiming the saving death of the Lord) one shares in the atonement the blood of Christ has acquired for us. If one drinks the blood of the Lord unworthily (which in this context refers primarily to sins against the unity of the Church, the one body of Christ), one becomes guilty of the Lord's blood; in other words, one shares in the guilt of his murderers. Thus we find a perspective in Paul on the mutually exclusive double effect of Christ's blood similar to what we have found in Matthew. As we have seen above, in Matthew the outpoured blood of Christ becomes a condemning judgment for those of his people who persevere in condemning him but a source of forgiveness for all believers who drink his blood in faith. In Paul this same double effect of condemnation or union (with Christ and with one another) is specifically applied to the members of the eucharistic assembly.

The connection is only implicit but nonetheless real between the orderly cooperation of the different charisms and the eucharistic body of Christ. Since sharing in the eucharistic body of Christ builds up the Church as the one body of Christ animated by the one Spirit of God, the diverse charisms of the members should cooperate for the harmony and peace of the one body rather than producing chaos and disorder (12:1–13:40).

Paul goes to great length to prove that neither baptism nor the Eucharist "works" magically for the Christian community. Unless they live the life that derives from baptism and the Eucharist they will perish just as their Israelite ancestors did who shared in the types of baptism and Eucharist:

> all were baptized into Moses in the cloud and in the sea, and all ate the same spiritual food, and all drank the same spiritual drink. For they drank from the spiritual rock that followed them, and the rock was Christ. Nevertheless, God was not pleased with most of them, and they were struck down in the wilderness (10:2-5).

Even though Paul deals with the Eucharist explicitly only in 1 Corinthians the Eucharist is the implied foundation for the Pauline understanding of the whole of Christian existence. Since we are the body of Christ through our participation in his eucharistic body we are also to participate in Christ's destiny. Just as out of love Christ gave up his body for us (2 Cor 5:14; Gal 2:20), in union with him we should also offer our bodies "as a living sacrifice, holy and acceptable to God" (Rom 12:1). This means not only spending our lives in God's service but a daily dying to our former sinful selves so that the life of the risen Christ may also manifest its energy and power in our existence. We should be "always carrying in the body the death of Jesus, so that the life of Jesus may also be made visible in our bodies" (2 Cor 4:10). The final fruit of sharing in the Lord's body and blood is our complete conformation to his sacrificed and risen body by uniting our death to his: "if we have died with Christ, we believe that we will also live with him" (Rom 6:8; cf. also 2 Tim 2:11 and Phil 2:17).

Conclusions

(1) By use of the criteria of multiple attestation and difference or discontinuity a strong case can be made on purely historical-critical grounds that the institution of the Lord's supper goes back to Jesus himself. Its origins derive from the Last Supper and from the risen Lord's appearances in the context of a meal.

(2) The texts of institution present the Last Supper of Jesus as a prophecy in action, a sacrificial meal effectively anticipating the sacrifice of the cross and concluding a definitive covenant. All eucharistic texts enclose the propitiatory aspect (the body given up, the blood to be shed for many) within the framework of *eucharistia,* thanksgiving: Jesus offers his body and blood for us to the Father in the spirit of thanksgiving. Paul and John make explicit the motive of love that animates Jesus' thanksgiving. Thus the Eucharist is a propitiatory sacrifice precisely as a sacrifice of thanksgiving: the two aspects stand or fall together.

(3) Both the Corinthian church and the Johannine churches interpreted the words of Jesus realistically: in and through the eucharistic bread and wine Jesus intended to establish for the duration of history a real participation in his sacrificed (flesh and body) person. Thus either both the Pauline and Johannine churches misunderstood the words of Jesus from the beginning or both correctly interpreted Jesus' intention that he himself wants to become and remain truly food and drink for us in the Eucharist.

(4) Under the humble signs of bread and wine in the rite of the "breaking of bread" the apostolic churches already anticipate the eschatological meal of the kingdom where Christ serves both as host and as food and drink for the meal.

(5) On the one hand worthy participation in the Lord's supper presupposes our belonging through faith and baptism to the body of Christ that is the Church and our acting as members of that body. On the other hand sharing in the eucharistic body of Christ increases our insertion and assimilation into Christ's ecclesial body. As

a result we are called to display in our own lives the pattern of the suffering, dying, and resurrection of the Lord, to give away our lives in humble service and conquer temptations through the power of his resurrection.

(6) The Lord's supper presents a shocking novelty that is not reducible to anything in the world of Old Testament and intertestamental Judaism, even less to rituals in the Hellenistic world. The eating of the body of Jesus and the drinking of his blood were misunderstood and received with consternation both by Jews and by educated pagans.

In spite of its newness the Lord's supper presents a unique synthesis and actualization of the central OT themes. What the chief redemptive events in the OT (the liberation from Egypt and from Babylonian captivity, the feeding with manna in the desert) foreshadowed, what the manifold sacrifices in the OT prefigured (in particular the sprinkling of the blood of bulls concluding the Mosaic covenant and the yearly offering of the Passover lamb) Jesus has brought to completion as the Son of God become servant of God by the free offering of his life. In this way he has fulfilled the Mosaic covenant (Matthew-Mark), inaugurated the unbreakable new covenant written in our hearts (Jeremiah and Ezekiel) and anticipated the joyful banquet of the kingdom (Isaiah). This banquet is prepared by divine Wisdom (Proverbs, Wisdom) incarnate as a flesh and blood human being who through his cross and resurrection offers himself to us as true food and drink for eternal life.

The Unfolding of the Biblical Themes in Early Christian Tradition

We can hardly give here more than an overview of selected texts to show the direction in which the biblical doctrine of the Eucharist developed in the second century. The last books of the NT had not yet been composed when the Letter of Clement in 96 already saw in the Eucharist not merely the fulfillment of some OT sacrifices (as the gospels and Paul do) but the fulfillment of *all* the sacrifices of the Old Law (*1 Clem.* 40, 41). It also reserves the offering of the Eucharist to the bishop-presbyters (*1 Clem.* 44.4).

As early as the first half of the second century the synoptic perspective and the Pauline and Johannine theologies of the Eucharist merged into a synthesis (*Didache,* the letters of Ignatius of Antioch, and the writings of Justin). The Eucharist is the presence in mystery of the kingdom since the risen Lord himself comes to us in the eucharistic assembly. It is there that the Church is gathered into the kingdom (*Did.* 9.4). The Johannine and Pauline eucharistic themes are united and further developed in the letters of Ignatius:

> Be careful therefore to use one Eucharist (for there is one flesh of our Lord Jesus Christ, and one cup for union with his blood *[eis henōsin tou haimatos autou],* one altar, as there is one bishop with the presbytery and the deacons my fellow servants) . . . (Ign. *Phil.* 4).

Using Johannine terminology (flesh = *sarx*) Ignatius stresses the Pauline idea of the unity of the Church as based on the Eucharist. Original to Ignatius, however, is the emphasis on the uniting power of the blood of Christ. The Johannine notion of the Eucharist as the source of eternal life is also linked to the one bread theme in Paul. Only for those who break one bread will the Eucharist become the medicine of immortality (Ign. *Eph.* 10.2). Paul as apostle claimed full authority over the manner and meaning of the eucharistic celebrations in Corinth. Ignatius attributes a similar authority to the local bishop with his presbyters and deacons. The Eucharist of the bishop is the visible manifestation of the unity of the local church (Ign. *Smyrn.* 8.1-2).

Ignatius insists on the identity of the crucified and risen body of Christ with his flesh in the Eucharist. He shows that the docetists are consistent: since they deny the true flesh of Christ they also abstain from the Eucharist: "they do not confess that the Eucharist is the flesh of our Savior Jesus Christ who suffered for our sins, which the Father raised up by his goodness" (Ign. *Smyrn.* 7.1). We see in this text a remarkably free conflation of Johannine theology ("flesh" = *sarx* instead of "body" = *sōma;* Jesus as Savior of the world) and the Matthean notion of Jesus' death as a sacrifice for sin. Because of his opposition to the docetists the eucharistic realism of Ignatius is even more explicit than that of John.

The two most striking aspects of Ignatius's eucharistic theology are his identification of faith and love with the flesh and blood of Christ and his interpretation of the eucharistic meaning of his martyrdom. He says more than we would expect: the crucified and risen body of Christ and his blood are not mere objects of faith and love or simply the source of these virtues. Ignatius encourages the Trallians in this fashion: "be renewed in faith, which is the flesh of the Lord, and in love, which is the blood of Jesus Christ" (Ign. *Trall.* 8.1). Such an identification between faith and the flesh of the Lord on the one hand and love and his blood on the other may be called symbolic but not less real for that reason. Ignatius seems to say that the reality of faith and love are inseparable from sharing in the real flesh and blood of Christ. In fact Ignatius intends to share not only in Christ's eucharistic flesh and blood but in the heavenly banquet that the Eucharist anticipates and to which martyrdom will lead him: "I desire the 'bread of God,' which is the flesh of Jesus Christ, who was 'of the seed of David,' and for drink I desire his blood, which is incorruptible love" (Ign. *Rom.* 7.3). Even more, through his martyrdom Ignatius himself yearns to become "a sacrifice for God," Eucharist in union with his Lord: "I am God's wheat, and I am ground by the teeth of wild beasts that I may be found pure bread of Christ" (Ign. *Rom.* 4.1, 2).

A similar tendency to identify the martyr's offering of his or her life with the Eucharist can be seen in the *Martyrdom of Polycarp*. Polycarp, "the great apostolic and prophetic teacher, the bishop of the catholic church in Smyrna" prays before his execution in a manner that resembles the great eucharistic prayers of Christian antiquity. He gives thanks for the grace of martyrdom, for sharing in the cup of Christ (14.1-3). His martyrdom is, as it were, taken up into the eucharistic sacrifice: when they light the pyre under him the body of the martyr was in the midst of the flames "not as burning flesh but as baking bread" (15.2).

In Justin's description of the Sunday liturgy we see for the first time the organic unity between the liturgy of the word (the "memoirs of the apostles," the gospels, or "the prophets" [the books of the OT] that were read, followed by an exhortation of the president and by prayers afterwards) and the liturgy of the Eucharist, a connection that has already been adumbrated in the Lukan story of the two disciples who encountered the risen Christ on the road to Emmaus (Luke 24:13-33; Justin, *Apol.* 1, 67.3-5). In Justin's description the words of institution do not follow exactly any of the written gospel accounts or 1 Corinthians 11. The words over the bread nevertheless resemble the Lukan version and the words over the cup that of Matthew, yet without any reference to the death or sacrifice of Jesus (66.3). That for Justin the Eucharist is also a sacrifice that fulfills those of the Old Law and a memorial of the Lord's Passion can be established only from his *Dialogue with Trypho* (41.70).

In Justin's account the Eucharist appears also as the source of all the charitable activity of the Church: voluntary contributions are made and from that collection the president takes care of the orphans and the widows, the sick and the prisoners, in short, of all who are in need (*Apol.* 1, 66.6).

The most important unfolding by Justin of the Johannine eucharistic theology is contained in the following passage:

> We call this food *Eucharistia;* and no one else is permitted to partake of it, except one who believes our teaching to be true and who has been washed in the washing which is for the remission of sins and for regeneration, and is thereby living as Christ has enjoined. For not as common bread nor common drink do we receive these; but since Jesus Christ our Savior was made incarnate by the word of God and had both flesh and blood for our salvation, so too, as we have been taught, the food which has been made into the Eucharist by the Eucharistic prayer set down by Him, and by the change of which our blood and flesh is nourished, is both the flesh and the blood of that incarnated Jesus (*Apol.* 1, 66. Translated by William A. Jurgens, *The Faith of the Early Fathers* [Collegeville: The Liturgical Press, 1970] 1.55).

The word pair "flesh and blood" so characteristic of John 6 dominates the text: it occurs three times, marking three crucial turning points in God's plan of salvation. Its first occurrence designates our humanity taken up by Jesus as his own. The second describes our humanity as nourished and transformed by the Eucharist; the third refers to the food that has become Eucharist, the flesh and blood of the incarnate Jesus. This last achieves the eschatological transformation of our humanity. The agent of both incarnation and eucharistic transformation is similar: in the first case it is the word of God *(logos theou);* in the second it is the word of prayer *(euchēs logos)* coming most probably from the *Logos* himself. Thus the whole mystery of Christ is summarized here in admirable simplicity: the goal of the incarnation is the Eucharist and the goal of the Eucharist is the eschatological transformation of humankind.

The scriptural foundation for Irenaeus's eucharistic theology is a combination of Pauline and Johannine elements and its context his refutation of the Marcionite and Gnostic errors. The bread and wine of this creation that are offered in the Eucharist would not become the body and blood of the Lord if the Lord Jesus were not the Son of the Creator. The Eucharist itself testifies against the Marcionites and Gnostics that the God of creation and Father of our Lord Jesus Christ is one and the same God (*Adv. Haer.* 4.18.4). Thus for Irenaeus the cosmic dimension of the eucharistic sacrifice receives a new emphasis: we offer to God in the Eucharist God's own creation of bread and wine that, receiving the word of God, become the body and blood of the Lord.

Moreover if the flesh were incapable of salvation we were not redeemed by the blood of the Lord, nor would the cup of the Eucharist be a communion with his blood or the bread we break a communion with his body (1 Cor 10:16). In reality, however, our bodies are nourished and increased by the eucharistic body and blood of the Lord for the future resurrection (John 6). Creation itself reaches its fulfillment in the Eucharist and the final effects of the Eucharist are our resurrected, glorified bodies (*Adv. Haer.* 5.18.5).

Pastoral Implications

(1) If the whole of salvation history centers on Christ as the fullness of God's revelation, if all the Scriptures ultimately prepare for him and witness to him, and if in the Eucharist the whole reality of the crucified and risen Christ is present to unite us to himself, then all Christian preaching should, directly or indirectly, lead to a deeper appreciation of the Eucharist. In the words of Luther "the Mass is part of the gospel; indeed, it is the sum and substance of it." After all, it is in the eucharistic celebration that every biblical text is actualized for the contemporary Christian community and individual, and our encounter with the Word of God leads us naturally to a full, personal, bodily communion with him in the Eucharist.

(2) If we adopt the perspective of the NT on the Eucharist we will not be tempted by the two extreme positions that threaten the Church's liturgical life today. We see on one side a preconciliar mentality that prefers or in its most extreme form idolizes the Tridentine Mass insofar as it promotes respectful individual worship; on the other side a more instinctive than conscious tendency aims at reducing the Eucharist to a joyful self-celebration of the Christian community that sees Christ primarily in the community and neglects if not practically ignores the source of his community-building presence under the signs of the eucharistic bread and wine. In the NT theology of the Eucharist (whether we start from Paul or John or from the synthesis of both as most Fathers did) the theocentric aspect of thanksgiving, worship, praise, and atonement and the community-forming aspect of the Lord's supper cannot be played one against the other. It is by sharing in the *real* body and blood of the Lord, sacrificed and risen, that we are built up as his *real* body the Church (Paul); Christ dwells in the individual and gives one eternal life only if one is inserted as a branch into Christ, the one true vine who joins the celebrants to himself and to each other (John). We can praise, thank, and plead with the Father for forgiveness only to the extent that we are united to Christ's ecclesial body. Vice versa, we live the life of Christ's ecclesial body only to the extent that we share in the Son's worship of the Father. Thus the ecclesial and worshiping aspects of the eucharistic celebration can only be promoted together rather than one at the expense of the other. The real presence of the sacrificed Christ in the Eucharist is the cause and guarantee of his growing presence in the body of the worshiping community.

(3) The biblical doctrine of the Eucharist should become the energizing source and pattern of all Christian living. As Hans Urs von Balthasar has shown convincingly, the Eucharist is the form of all Christian life. Just as Christ has become a gift both for the Father and for all humankind so should we, his members. We become truly ourselves, fully human and fully Christian in the measure that through him, with him and in him we become an acceptable gift to the Father and to our neighbors.

Just as Christ has become nourishing food by giving his flesh for the life of the whole world the Church cannot become a self-serving ghetto for its own members, but must serve the global human community in working for a civilization of love. This will, of course, lead to some positive results only through failure and persecution, a daily sharing in the cross of Christ.

(4) In the eucharistic theology of the NT the joy in the eucharistic meal does not derive primarily from the good feeling of human community; it is rather the joyful anticipation of the eschatological meal, a joy that transcends the boundaries of this life and conquers the fear of death. Thus a biblically based pastoral approach will shape the eucharistic celebration in such a way that it will simultaneously proclaim both Christ's death and his resurrection. It will encourage a daily dying with Christ to our earthly sinful selves so that we also daily experience the power of his resurrection. Any eucharistic celebration that centers on our earthly life alone stands in contradiction to the biblical witness.

Ecumenical Implications

(1) A greater unity in our understanding of the Eucharist can be achieved if, following the injunctions of Vatican II (*Dei Verbum* 21, 23, 24), Catholic preaching and theology of the Eucharist are increasingly nourished and ruled by Sacred Scripture, and if Protestant theologians continue in their search for the continuity between biblical faith, the faith of the Church Fathers, and the magisterial documents of the Catholic Church. Such a mutual rapprochement has already started and led to some significant breakthrough agreements in formulating what is common in our understanding of the Eucharist. Besides the documents produced by several joint commissions consisting of Catholic and Protestant theologians of different denominations the most important ecumenical document has been published by the Faith and Order Commission of the World Council of Churches: *Baptism, Eucharist and Ministry.* (The document was approved at the meeting of the Commission by more than one hundred theologians coming from the most important Christian traditions, Catholic, Orthodox, and Protestant. The meeting took place in Lima, Peru in 1982. See the text in *Search for Visible Unity. Baptism, Eucharist and Ministry,* edited by Jeffrey Gros, 1984, and cf. the official Vatican response to the document: "Baptism, Eucharist and Ministry: An Appraisal," *Origins* 17 [1987] 403–416.) Some form of real presence of Christ in the eucharistic celebration has been commonly expressed in the joint text: "the eucharistic meal is the sacrament of the body and blood of Christ, the sacrament of his real presence" (13). It has also been accepted that the "eucharist is the memorial of the crucified and risen Christ, i.e., the living and effective sign of his sacrifice, accomplished once and for all on the cross and still operative on behalf of all humankind" (5). The Faith and Order document also states that "the eucharist is . . . the foretaste of [Christ's] parousia and of the final kingdom (6).

However there are still disagreements on various points: (a) the Catholic and Orthodox doctrine that the bread and wine are ontologically transformed during the eucharistic celebration into the body and blood of Christ while retaining their empirical properties of bread and wine, (b) belief in the permanent presence of Christ under these signs, and (c) the doctrine of the propitiatory character of the celebration are still unacceptable for most Protestants.

(2) A more thorough reflection on the biblical doctrine in the light of the Church's tradition could bring us even closer to that unity of eucharistic faith that allows for a variety of complementary theologies. On the one hand Jesus declares "this is my body," "this is my blood of the covenant," thus identifying what he holds in his hands with his body and blood while he also calls his flesh that is to be sacrificed the bread of life. In a similar manner of speech the liturgy also identifies the consecrated bread and wine with the body and blood of the Lord but at the same time calls the consecrated elements "the bread of life" and "the cup of eternal salvation." In other words, the Church's teaching on ontological transformation (transubstantiation) presupposes that Jesus becomes *really present* but under the *real sign* of bread and wine. Thus bread and wine are not annihilated (analogously to the human person who offers himself or herself to God through Christ) but they rather reach their ultimate, God-intended perfection when becoming the effective signs of Christ's presence in the eucharistic consecration. Therefore Catholics should be more careful in defining the meaning of the

word "appearance" in eucharistic theology. God does not intend to deceive us by false appearances: the empirical qualities of bread and wine are needed to express Christ as true food and true drink for believers who still live in the world of sense experience. In this way the legitimate concern of the Protestant reformers would be acknowledged while at the same time the Catholic dogma of transubstantiation might be seen in a new perspective by Protestants as an organic development of scriptural doctrine rather than the outdated creation of what Luther called the "Aristotelian church."

Once the ontological transformation of the elements is accepted the permanent presence of Christ in the Eucharist naturally follows. This permanent presence (as long as the signs of bread and wine remain and point to Christ as our true food and drink) assures that Christ's eucharistic presence is prior to and does not depend on the faith of the celebrating community. Thus the priority of God's sovereign grace over human "works," a central concern of the Protestant reform (even if this human work happens to be an act of faith) receives an unexpected confirmation in a new understanding of Christ's abiding presence in the Holy Eucharist.

(3) Concerning the issue of the propitiatory character of the Eucharist Catholics can find a common basis with Protestants if they reflect together on the inseparable connection between the thanksgiving and propitiatory aspects of the Eucharist in the NT. One cannot declare the Eucharist a thanksgiving sacrifice while denying its propitiatory character nor can eucharistic atonement and expiation be stressed to the point of obscuring the source from which its efficacy derives: the divine love of the Son who gives himself over in thanksgiving to the Father in our place and for our sake. Moreover by common work we have to articulate the consequences of the simple biblical truth that the risen Christ is also the crucified one. According to John the risen Christ displays his wounds and according to the book of Revelation the victorious Lamb stands before the throne "as if it had been slaughtered" (John 20:20, 27; Rev 5:6; 13:8). This symbolic language shows that the risen Christ remains forever our propitiatory sacrifice even though he can no longer suffer or die. In the Eucharist we are not simply passive recipients of his atonement. Being united with him means being conformed to his state of sacrificial gift that is inseparably praise and atonement, thanksgiving for God's gifts and propitiation for our sins. Thus union with the eucharistic Christ calls for both sacramental and existential participation in Christ's sacrifice. Our participation adds nothing to the universal efficacy of his self-offering once and for all but allows us to share in its power of atonement and sanctification.

BIBLIOGRAPHY

Dupont, Jacques. "'This Is My Body . . . This Is My Blood'," in Raymond A. Tartre, ed., *The Eucharist Today.* Translated from French by C. O'Neill. New York: P. J. Kenedy, 1967, 13–28.

Rordorf, Willy, et al. *L'Eucharistie des premiers chrétiens.* Paris: Beauchesne, 1976. English: *The Eucharist of the Early Christians.* New York: Pueblo, 1978.

Feuillet, André. "The Principal Biblical Themes in the Discourse on the Bread of Life" in idem, *Johannine Studies.* Translated from French by Thomas E. Crane. Staten Island: Alba House, 1965, 53–128.

Jeremias, Joachim. *The Eucharistic Words of Jesus.* Translated from the revised 3rd German ed. by Norman Perrin. Philadelphia: Fortress, 1977.

Kereszty, Roch A. "The Eucharist in the NT," in *A Theology of Eucharistic Celebration* (forthcoming).

Léon-Dufour, Xavier. *Sharing the Eucharistic Bread.* Translated from French by Matthew J. O'Connell. New York: Paulist, 1987.

Meyer, Ben F., ed. *One Loaf, One Cup. Ecumenical Studies of 1 Cor 11 and Other Eucharistic Texts.* The Cambridge Conference on the Eucharist, August 1988. Essays by Otto Knoch, William R. Farmer, Otfried Hofius, Ben F. Meyer, Hans-Josef Klauck, and Alkiviadis C. Calivas. Introduction by Ben F. Meyer. Macon, Ga.: Mercer University Press, 1993.

Reumann, John. *The Supper of the Lord: The NT, Ecumenical Dialogues, and Faith and Order on Eucharist.* Philadelphia: Fortress, 1985.

The Bible and the Servant–Priest–Disciple

Timothy Gollob

Servanthood for some is a negative quality, but not for the Bible. Biblical servanthood is the state of being in union with the will of the Creator God. Jesus came with the mission of giving a new way of being faithful to this concept of servanthood. Those who wish to learn about this type of true following of Christ can gain much from a lecture, or from a book on the subject, or from the personal witness of a missionary or a great preacher, but each man or woman seeking a better understanding of what it means to be a faithful disciple must go to the books written under inspiration and find there the keys to understanding. A well-written commentary on the Holy Scriptures composed with the help of the rich and abundant sources that have become available since the Second Vatican Council will be a great tool for all sincere learners.

From the beginning of the Christian era every follower of Christ has been called away from the things of this world to be a person who witnesses to the reality of an otherworldly concept. Levi (Matthew) was called away from his tax business to be a witness to the truth that salvation is not bought; rather it is the gift of the saving power of a loving God that brings the possibility of salvation to all humans. Peter was called away from his father's fishing boat to be a witness to the fact that he was to net souls for God not by persuasive and educated sermons but by the witness of his words concerning what he had heard from the master on the shores of the Sea of Galilee. Also he was to witness with his very blood that he had followed his teacher to the ultimate conclusion of being a true disciple. Paul was called from his quest to impose Temple truth and discipline on the first Christians to be a witness that this new way was a cure for blindness of eye and of heart. He brought that witness to the ends of his world and sealed his testimony with the shedding of his blood in the Eternal City of Rome. In their turn each of the apostles and disciples of the early Church was asked to turn away from whatever had taken up his or her time and energy and become Jesus' followers in the new community of believers in the power of the word of one who claimed to be the Son of God.

In a very real way all of the early elders and presiders of the Church were called to turn away from the temptations that Jesus overcame in the desert at the beginning of his ministry. These were and are now the temptations that all have to face if they are to exchange temporal trinkets for eternal wealth. Thus each disciple is asked to accept the fundamental reality that Jesus calls the sinner-disciple to rejoice in the saving power of the Creator God and then to go out into the world re-membering the broken Body of Christ. This re-membering is accomplished by telling the story again and again of how Jesus called her or him away from darkness and into the wonderful life of grace. The Bible-oriented disciple is then always ready to let others know that there is no one who cannot gain the same gift, for God's love is infinite goodness.

> If we take a close look at what contemporary men and women expect from priests, we will see that, in the end, they have but one great expectation: they are thirsting for Christ. Everything else—their economic, social, and political needs—can be met by any number of other people. From the priest they ask for Christ! And from the priest

> they have the right to receive Christ, above all through the proclamation of the Word. As the Council teaches, priests "have as their primary duty the proclamation of the Gospel of God to all" (*Presbyterorum Ordinis,* 4). But this proclamation needs to have hearers encounter Jesus, especially in the mystery of the Eucharist, the living heart of the Church and of priestly life" (John Paul II, *Gift and Mystery: On the Fiftieth Anniversary of My Priestly Ordination* [New York : Doubleday, 1996] 85).

The priest, especially, will be called to remember the priestly obligation to invite to the feast of God's mercy all from the highways and byways and the hedges and edges of life. These are the chosen by God destined to be at God's eternal banquet. It is there that the bread of life is given to all who want it. In addition, those called to witness need strength since they are also called to be the martyrs of Christ: witnesses to the fact that death has no more dominion over those who put their trust in God.

Isaiah was the prophet who provided the touchstone Scriptures for Jesus. His prophecies set the program that was to form Jesus' ministry. So too the disciple must follow the same role as servant to the mysteries of the love of God for the poor and the sinner, for he or she, too, is one of the poor sinners of the world. One question is always on the mind of the person who strives to be a true disciple. What would Jesus have said or done in these circumstances? This is the question that keeps the witness of true believers alive to a world that is constantly changing and is always in need of a new praxis and a new hermeneutic. This question is the one that sends the disciple back to the Holy Scriptures again and again in search of a living word that will heal and save and lead all to grace. This is also the question that will inspire the seeker of truth to give hope to, and not take away the possibility of love for anyone, no matter how oppressed by external or internal hatred that person might be.

The Bible constantly challenges each reader to be willing to be like the master in proclaiming the truth that justice must come before peace can enter into our society. As with Jesus, the possibility of being misunderstood and being made to suffer must always be a factor in that witness.

> Since witnessing to the Resurrection of the suffering Servant is the nucleus of our ongoing examination of conscience and the test of priestly identity, the fundamental question always before us [priests] is this: whether or not we are prepared to wholeheartedly embody the suffering, compassionate, humble Servant in a spirit of joy that flames forth from our faith in Christ's and our own resurrection. Are people aware that it is our lived faith that is the source of our endurance, patience, and joy in the midst of affliction, illness, tension, and dissent? Reflection on the depth of our faith in the risen Christ, of necessity, turns our attention time and again to our own baptism in Christ, the humble, patient Servant of Yahweh" (Bernard Häring, *Priesthood Imperiled: A Critical Examination of Ministry in the Catholic Church* [Liguori, Mo.: Triumph Books, 1996] 54).

Likewise the disciple must be aware of the universal call to all to be a part of the priestly people of God by virtue of the sacraments of baptism and confirmation. Since Jesus wishes to continue his witness and service through his disciples he joins them to his life and mission, and also gives them a share in his priestly office, to offer spiritual worship for the glory of God and the salvation of the world (*Lumen Gentium* IV.34). Therefore all Jesus' disciples are called to participate in the redemptive mission of the Church, which is only whole and holy when each member takes up his or her priestly, prophetic, and royal role. Christ exercised his royal role through his obedience unto death. Thus the Christian rules through suffering and does not lord it over others who may be under his or her authority. The greatest among us will be the servant of all. As Heb 2:17 demands, the priestly person must be like his or her brothers and sisters in all things in order to be a more faithful witness in the service of God. This service is performed in a modern arena. To look back to the past will turn one into a pillar of salt!

Finally, the Bible unmasks the delusions of this world. Jesus clearly was tempted to be a false savior as he encountered the tempter in the desert. He foiled that plan by not wanting self-recognition, glory, riches, or honor for himself. He was to be the Servant suffering for the salvation of all. So too it is imperative that each disciple read and reflect on the Holy Scriptures so that the truths contained therein can unmask the temptations that have led astray many preachers and teachers and healers in the past and are alive and well in our modern world. No text may be taken out of its context. There can

The priesthood of Jesus Christ is based not upon human appointment, but upon being made perfect through the obedience to God that Jesus learned through innocent suffering (see commentary on Heb 5:7-15). Since Christ was made perfect through his suffering in obedience to God and thus was qualified to be a true high priest, every disciple of Jesus on the journey to Christian priesthood will be qualified through the Christ-like perfection that comes through innocent suffering in obedience to God. —*Ed.*

be no commentary that does not admit the universal love of God. There can be no compromise with the values of the world.

A commentary on the Bible is a tool in helping to relate old truths to modern times. Like an old letter put away in a desk drawer and rediscovered at a much later time, the Scriptures speak with personal and insistent love to the one addressed. On rereading the text one finds that old ideas take on a new life. The reader is led to believe once again that God is giving and forgiving. With encouragement the reader of God's Holy Scriptures can once again take up the task of witnessing to the love that inspired them to be written. That is the task that every person alive to the call of God's grace approaches on a daily, weekly, or monthly basis. What is the text telling me? What is the text saying to my community? What is the text asking of our world? What have others said about this text in the past? How does their response help us to make a modern response?

There is no prayer that can be better than a prayer for guidance from the Holy Spirit as the Holy Scriptures are opened so that they can light up new love and new forgiveness and new gifts for individuals and for the world. That is why we look to this new commentary to be a place where the faithful can learn the roots of the sacraments. The energy and the love that preceded the institution of the Eucharist can be experienced. So too we can appropriate for ourselves the focus that Jesus had in his approach to sinners.

Looking at the texts and understanding Jesus' Jewish background and the historical setting of the first members of the Church will be of assistance to all who wish to approach these mysteries today with the same intense faith that our first mothers and fathers in the Church had. That faith will be so alive that the sacraments will once again be sources of revitalization for the soul of the apostolate in each baptized person.

Since each of us is a beggar asking for grace, when we do receive it we have to go out and share that grace with our fellow poor. Whether it be the bread of life or the wine of rejoicing or the balm of forgiveness, each sacrament gives impetus to go out and bring the Good News to those who need it most. Thus the servanthood of Jesus Christ is kept alive and well in our world!

The Historic Jesus: God's Call to Freedom Through Love

William R. Farmer

Christian scholars and other believing Christians who are not professional exegetes often speak of biblical texts in very different ways; this may be especially true when the scholars are historians and the texts are the New Testament writings. Bringing different assumptions to the texts, these two groups are often hard-pressed to reap the benefits of the others' insights. For instance, most Christians read the NT and assume that the books are arranged more or less in the order in which they were written. Many further assume that the names traditionally associated with each text are the names of the authors (for example, that the gospel according to Matthew was written by the apostle Matthew, that all the Pauline letters were written by Paul, that Revelation was written by the apostle John, and so on).

Historians do not make these assumptions. They have argued persuasively that the letters were composed before the gospels were written. Further, the authorship of many of the NT writings, including all four gospels, has been questioned.

All of this scholarly debate can be quite confusing to ordinary Christians. It is important, therefore, to emphasize the points of connection between these two groups and to build upon them for the mutual benefit of both. It should be pointed out that there is widespread agreement among historians that many of the Pauline letters, including Romans, 1 and 2 Corinthians, and Galatians, were written by the apostle Paul. Further, while there is much debate over the "historicity" of many aspects of the gospels there is widespread agreement that many of the parables of Jesus reflect accurately what he had to say about God, our relationship to God, and our relationships with one another. These two points provide a starting place, acceptable both to scholars and to unsophisticated believers, from which to begin reflection on Jesus' message.

This article aims not only to reconstruct the message of Jesus but also to explain Jesus' teachings within the context of the development of his public career. To this extent it serves to demonstrate the possibility of a "history of Jesus" acceptable to historians, a history that is not essentially different from the story of Jesus familiar to us from the gospels.

The Origin and Development of the Gospel Tradition

The gospel tradition originated with Jesus and those who worked with him and experienced his saving influence. It developed in the earliest Christian communities where Jesus was remembered and worshiped as the crucified and resurrected Lord. This gospel tradition represents Jesus as he was remembered and worshiped in certain Christian communities a generation removed from the beginning of the Church. This is clear from the fact that the traditions concerning Jesus utilized by the evangelists include not only those originating with Jesus himself and his first associates but also many that reflect the needs of later Christian communities.

This means that between Jesus and the gospels stands the "traditioning" process by which the gospel stories and sayings of Jesus were handed on and in which they developed. These traditions were oral and written. They included sayings of Jesus originating both during his life and after his resurrection. They also included both material originating with eyewitnesses concerning the actions and character of Jesus of Nazareth and later modifications of this tradition made to meet the changing needs of different Christian communities.

The traditioning process has never ceased. It flourished up to and through the period when the gospels were written and achieved manifold expression during the second and third centuries. It achieved its normative form in the fourfold gospel canon through which in turn it has enhanced the literature and preaching of the Church. (See "The Church's Gospel Canon: Why Four and No More?")

An important methodological problem in writing about Jesus as a historical figure is the problem of chronology. Since the turn of the twentieth century critical theology has been aware of the historical uncertainty of the gospel chronologies. This has led to a virtual moratorium on the writing of "lives of Jesus" in the nineteenth-century mode.

The Historical Environment of the Gospel Tradition

Christianity began with Jesus and his disciples in Palestine and quickly spread among other nations of the Hellenized world. Thus we have a historical and cultural background that enables us to understand how the gospel tradition developed. The environment of Jesus of Nazareth was physically Palestinian, culturally Jewish, and temporally pre-Pauline. Therefore whatever Jesus did and said, however distinctive or even unique it may have been, would have been accommodated to those who shared this environment. Presumably tradition concerning Jesus' words and actions that achieved a stable form at a very early date would tend to reflect this environment both conceptually and pictorially. On the other hand the environment of the evangelists was extra-Palestinian and post-Pauline. Presumably what they wrote was accommodated accordingly. The other NT writings make clear that the social and theological forces set in motion by Jesus and his disciples broke out of the original Jewish-Palestinian environment at an early period. This transition is viewed in retrospect in the book of the Acts of the Apostles. More important, it is seen first-hand in the letters of the apostle Paul. Thus Paul's writings offer an important standard by which to distinguish between the environment of Jesus and that of the evangelists. It is clear from his letters that Paul engaged in a radical accommodation of Jesus' message. He saw carrying the gospel to the Gentiles as his special vocation. This vocation committed him to making lengthy journeys among people far removed from Palestine and to questioning the integrity of those who were apostles before him when they conducted themselves in a manner he viewed as prejudicial to the truth of the gospel (Gal 2:11-14).

The Historical Setting of Jesus' Public Ministry

Jesus was a Jew who lived in Palestine during the period of Roman occupation. The climax of his ministry came while Pontius Pilate was procurator of Judea. Pilate had at his disposal sufficient forces to support the collaborating Jewish regime. He could see that taxes were collected and police the rash of political discontent. Rome recognized the Law of Moses as the law of the land. The "established world of Jewish piety" was based on that Law. The Temple in Jerusalem and the synagogues in the land were the chief institutions of that establishment. The Pharisees who sat in Moses' seat were key figures in the established world of Jewish piety and were recognized by the Romans as legal authorities whose credibility with the people in the cities and towns of Galilee was their best hope for maintaining social stability.

Because of the strong place of the Temple cultus in Jewish Law and piety it was possible for Rome, by offering security to the Temple authorities and collaborating with the high priestly families in Jerusalem, to maintain a basis for its control over the nation as a whole. Only such Jewish groups as rejected the authority of the incumbent high priestly families were free from some measure of effective collaboration with Rome, and the price required for complete freedom was withdrawal from public life.

The benefits of the Pax Romana were felt not only by the educated and privileged classes but by the general populace. However, the Jews could not enjoy these benefits without suffering a far greater degree of domestic disruption than did some other ethnic groups within the empire. This was because of the peculiar heritage of the Jews, many of whose customs and laws needed to be liberally interpreted wherever and whenever the inevitable need for close contact with Gentiles arose. Alongside the laws governing Jewish life and practice, and inextricably bound up with them in the Scriptures of the Jews, were certain promises of God bearing upon the welfare of the covenanted people. These promises were conditional upon obedience to the Law. Thus on the basis of these promises less privileged classes were always capable of envisioning a relative improvement in their welfare if only more effective ways could be found to keep the Law. Out of this political and religious tension, and feeding upon heterogeneous messianic prophecies preserved in Jewish writings, came the eschatological and apocalyptic hopes that excited the populace whenever signs of the times indicated that God was about to redeem the people, and especially when an eschatological prophet like John the Baptist began to preach.

Collaborating elements of the Jewish populace (whose close cooperation was essential to the effectiveness of the Roman occupation) included those like the Pharisees who sought conscientiously to observe of the Mosaic Law as well as those who were, in this respect, more or less lax. Those willing at times to be somewhat flexible or even downright lax, especially in their attitude toward the dietary regulations and other levitical cleanliness rules, were sometimes preferred by persons in authority for some of the more important and lucrative positions in the complex fabric of Roman hegemony over Jewish life. In the parlance of those Jews who strictly observed the laws of Moses these nonobservant compatriots were sometimes referred to derogatively as "tax collectors and sinners." To the degree that they were not observant these Jews were regarded by observant Jews as having abandoned the covenant, as having sold their heritage for a mess of pottage. Observant Jews on the other hand were dependent on the guidance and support of legal experts like the scribes and Pharisees who could tell them what the Law did and did not require under ever-varying circumstances.

Consequently, at times when apocalyptic or messianic hopes were at a fever pitch non-observant Jews because of their fear of divine retribution would seek to return to the covenant in great numbers. In principle this would always present a special problem for Jews who were already righteous before the Law for in this kind of situation they would naturally question any sudden or last-minute repentance and object to any too-ready acceptance of sinners on the part of religious authorities, for even if the eschatological fulfillment of God's long-standing promises was at last about to be realized for all Israel, simple justice required the recognition of a real difference between those who had suffered deprivation and injustice because of their faithfulness to the Law and those who, having disregarded God's law, had profited thereby. The basic problem conditioning the situation of Jews in Palestine at this time, therefore, was that of the Law and its adequacy as a norm by which they could find a meaningful and satisfying existence within a life-affirming cosmopolitan culture that was constantly calling the separatist character of Jewish communal life into question.

The Development of Jesus' Message

There is general agreement (1) that Jesus' public ministry began with his baptism at the hands of John, whose identity is well established by the historian Josephus, and (2) that it ended in crucifixion in response to the fateful decisions of the procurator Pontius Pilate and the high priest Caiaphas, whose identities are also well established by Josephus. Between this beginning and end of Jesus' ministry there were two interrelated crises. Central to these crises was the fact that Jesus was opposed by the religious authorities, who felt challenged by his teachings and conduct including his practice of eating with tax collectors and sinners.

To share food with someone in eastern culture is a sacred act. It is hardly possible for this to take place where enmity or sins against one party or the other remain unresolved; forgiveness and reconciliation in such cases must precede eating together. It was one thing for Jesus to share his last supper with Judas knowing that Judas had sinned against him. That required only that Jesus in his great compassion for Judas was willing to forgive him his act of betrayal. It was quite another thing for Jesus to *publicly* welcome into the intimacy of his table fellowship people who were known to have sinned not only against family, but against God, whose Law they had flagrantly violated. Jesus, as a teacher, had no right to forgive such sins. Only God had this authority. There was, therefore, an outrageous presumption implied in Jesus' publicly receiving sinners and eating with them. Under these circumstances Jesus was claiming a role that entitled him to act on his revealed knowledge of God's eschatological forgiveness. Such messianic conduct represented a challenge to the religious authorities: both to the scribes and Pharisees, because they "[sat] on Moses' seat" (Matt 23:2) and were accorded the authority of interpreting God's laws governing procedures to be followed in benefiting from the provision for forgiveness through cultic sacrifice, and to priestly authorities whose *raison d'être* entailed presiding over the very sacrifices that were required for the forgiveness of sins.

Once it is recognized that the religious authorities felt threatened by Jesus it is possible to perceive a credible relationship between his ministry and his death and it is also possible to develop an intrinsic chronology for his earthly career. This can be done by arranging the sayings of Jesus and particularly his parables in relationship to these interrelated crises. For example a parable in which Jesus rebukes the attitude of self-righteousness on the part of those who resent God's mercy toward repentant sinners would have been occasioned by his decision to defend his action of eating with tax collectors and sinners against the criticism of the Pharisees. This decision would have come after a move on the part of some of the Pharisees to criticize such conduct, which in turn could have not been made before some tax collectors and sinners had repented of their sins and decided to accept Jesus' invitation to table fellowship. Their action in turn could not have taken place until after Jesus had invited repentant sinners into the intimacy of his table fellowship, and so on, back to Jesus' decision to leave the sparsely settled regions of the wilderness of Judea where he had been with John and to carry his eschatological call ("the kingdom of heaven has come near") to repentance into the more settled rural and urban areas of Israel.

Finally it is important to clarify another point. If a critic takes each parable and considers its theology in relation to the total corpus of Jesus' teaching it will be seen that the majority of them fall into one of two groups. The first group of parables coalesces around the theme of "the folly of postponing repentance." The second coalesces around the theme of "rebuking self-righteousness." Both groups of parables reflect a theology of grace. Absolutely central to this theology and distinctive of it is Jesus' prophetic power to unmask hypocrisy and self-righteousness. When the parables of Jesus preserved in the gospel of Matthew are analyzed theologically and compared to the parables of Jesus preserved in the gospel of Luke, in every case the theology of each parable in Matthew can be matched by the theology of one or more of the parables in Luke. Moreover, since we learn from Paul himself that the faith he preached was the faith of the Church he once persecuted (Gal 1:23), it follows that Paul began as a Christian by preaching a pre-Pauline faith. Thus the historian has no alternative but to conclude that the theology that is common to Paul and to the two streams of parable tradition preserved separately in Matthew and Luke goes back to Jesus. To imagine that these three streams of tradition converge in some unidentified pre-Pauline theologian would only serve to create for the historian a set of unnecessary problems.

One can thus reconstruct a sketch of the development of Jesus' message as follows:

1. Jesus followed John the Baptist proclaiming the imminent coming of the reign of God.
2. The initial stages of his message and movement consisted of:
   a. A gracious call to repentance.
   b. A positive response from "tax collectors and sinners."
   c. Jesus' rejoicing with sinners over God's gracious forgiveness of their sins, creating a new community of forgiven sinners that exists in anticipation of the coming kingdom.
3. Jesus' ministry is beset by internal and external crises. The internal crisis is compounded through interaction with the external.

a. An internal crisis develops among Jesus' followers because of the delay in the coming of the kingdom.
b. An external crisis develops because of the Pharisees' resistance to Jesus' message and his table fellowship with sinners. Jesus rebukes these Pharisees and declares that there is more joy in heaven over one repentant sinner than over ninety-nine self-righteous keepers of the Law. The attitude of the Pharisees toward Jesus becomes increasingly hostile and they plot his death. Like the Suffering Servant/Son of God messiah of Isaiah, Jesus is steadfast in his obedience to God, even at the risk of an ignominious and shameful death.
c. The external conflict with the Pharisees compounds internal uncertainty among the faithful, raising the question: Should we really allow sinners to share our fellowship? Jesus reassures his disciples that God will separate the just from the unjust. God alone will decide who is justified and who is not.

There are four major turning points in the development of the tradition leading from Jesus to the gospels:

First: Jesus' baptism by John, followed by the arrest, imprisonment, and death of the Baptist.

Second: The arrest, trial, death, and resurrection of Jesus, and the emergence of a post-Easter messianic community.

Third: Sectarian conflict and division within this Jewish messianic community over the means by which Gentiles were to be admitted to full membership.

Fourth: The inspiring renewal of unity following the Neronian persecution of Christians in Rome and in the aftermath of the divisive consequences of Jewish resistance to Roman oppression culminating in the destruction of the Temple in Jerusalem. The martyrdoms of the apostles Peter and Paul during the Neronian persecutions were central to this ecumenical development.

The central image of Jesus that emerges from this analysis of his ministry and message is that of a messianic prophet who issued a gracious call to repentance, and rejoiced with sinners over God's compassionate forgiveness of their sins. Moreover, he defended his act of sharing at table God's joy over the repentance of these sinners in the face of criticism and rebuked the self-righteous attitude of those who resented God's mercy toward repentant sinners.

Jesus' practice of couching his teaching in the formula "You have heard it said . . . but I say to you . . ." is of unquestioned importance for the historian. It is evidence that Jesus set himself above Moses. However, within the corpus of tradition that originated during the period of Jesus' ministry it is his parables, rather than his sayings concerning the Law, that afford the best key for understanding both his career and his character. There is in the parables of Jesus a theology of grace that, mirroring God's compassion, is ethically and morally concerned with the little ones, those who are excluded and victimized by the social and religious structures of their existence. From this theology comes a call to repentance and a promise of God's salvation to all who respond. In short, Jesus' parables demonstrate that his message provides a prophetic basis for Christian theology.

Jesus and the Gospel Tradition

1. Before Jesus' Baptism by John

Sayings of Jesus that bespeak a confident life within a world where human existence is fraught with personal anxiety may put us in touch with Jesus before his baptism by John. They reveal a prophetic detachment from the allurements of mammon.

> Do not worry about your life, what you will eat,
> or about your body, what you will wear.
> Is not life more than food,
> and the body more than clothing?
>
> Look at the birds of the air; they neither sow nor reap . . .
> and yet your heavenly Father feeds them.
>
> Therefore do not worry, saying, "What will we eat?" . . .
> or "What will we wear?"
> For . . . your heavenly Father knows that you need all these things (Matt 6:25-32 // Luke 12:22-30).

On the other hand a saying like:

> Do not think that I have come to bring peace to the earth;
> I have not come to bring peace, but a sword (Matt 10:34 // Luke 12:51).

seems to reflect a situation in which Jesus has made sharp-edged commitments and is calling on others to follow suit. Such sayings seem more likely to have originated in relation to Jesus' acceptance of John's baptism and especially after his decision to continue a public ministry following John's arrest, imprisonment, and death.

To be sure, irenic observations on life can be born in the midst of active engagement and conflict, but unless it is believed that Jesus came to John without previous experience or reflection there is no reason to imagine that such wise sayings originated only in the final period of his life. Their arresting beauty and abiding truthfulness, which assured their transmission in the early Church, would also have been sufficient reason for their use by Jesus during and after his discipleship to John. Once Jesus became a disciple of John it is unlikely that he would have rejected everything from his former mode of existence and then begun *de novo* to develop his theology as if by baptism his mind was washed clean of all that he had formerly believed and advocated.

Jesus presumably formulated some of his teaching around elements of the folk wisdom current among his hearers. This suggestion is based not merely on the *a priori* ground that such practice is a mark of real teaching. It is also supported by the fact that it is sometimes possible to recover from rabbinic literature teachings very close in thought and language to some of the teachings of Jesus. This suggests that Jesus himself sometimes selected and developed teachings. Therefore the subsequent selection and development of his teachings by those who honored his memory is not something entirely new or unnatural. As an example we may consider the following rabbinic sayings: "Did you ever in your life see an animal or a bird that had a trade? And they support themselves without trouble. And were they not created only to serve me? And I created to serve my maker. Does it not follow that I shall be supported without trouble?" (*Kiddushin* 4:14 R. Shim'on ben Eleazer).

2. Jesus and John the Baptist

Jesus, if we are to trust the earliest and most reliable tradition, saw himself in prophetic continuity with John in his commitment to the call for covenantal repentance in the face of the imminent coming of the reign of God (Matt 11:7b-19). But Jesus saw himself in radical discontinuity with John with regard to the basis for admission into that kingdom (Matt 11:18-19). John preached righteousness according to the Law (Matt 21:28-32). His strictures against the moral laxity of the people were uncompromising. The ostensible cause for his death was his denunciation of immorality in high places. With Jesus it was otherwise. Jesus came to save sinners, not to condemn them. As children of their Father in heaven they in turn were counseled to love their enemies even as God does (Matt 5:43-48 // Luke 6:27-28, 32-36). They were admonished not to put forgiveness on any calculating basis but to forgive freely, from the heart—not seven times, but seventy times seven (Matt 18:21-35 // Luke 17:4).

The fellowship of such a community of forgiven and forgiving sinners was poignant and joyful.

> There will be more joy in heaven over one sinner who repents than over ninety-nine righteous persons who need no repentance (Luke 15:7 // Matt 18:13).

Therefore Jesus ate with sinners and celebrated their repentance (Luke 15:1-10). Such radical doctrine and practice was difficult to justify by legal precedent from Jewish Scriptures. So revolutionary an attitude on the part of Jesus could irritate authorities whose importance rested on their mastery of the interpretive intricacies of an all-encompassing legal system.

3. The Heart of Jesus' Message

When certain parables of Jesus are interpreted within the context of his gracious call for repentance they serve as mirrors in which it is possible to delineate the mind of Jesus as he responded to the exigencies and difficulties he encountered. How was one to understand the delay in the coming of the kingdom that John had pronounced to be at hand—especially after John's arrest and execution? And if one were to continue to proclaim the coming of the kingdom how should one perceive this ministry? Was it to be understood as the work of God to be carried out during an extension of the period of grace in the face of the coming judgment? If so was it not reasonable to expect that in due season, failing fruits of repentance, this period of grace would come to a sudden and just end (Luke 13:6-9)?

Certainly parables that dramatically illustrate the folly of postponing repentance (Matt 22:1-10; 25:1-12; Luke 13:6-9) and teach the wisdom of living in ready expectation of God's gracious judgment (Luke 12:35-38) most probably originated in situations where such expectations had been enlivened and heightened, that is, in the period of Jesus' active ministry following his baptism into the movement of John and his decision to continue to proclaim the imminence of the kingdom following the arrest and death of John. Even within this period it is possible to delineate development. Presumably Jesus would have understood the lesson the authorities intended by John's execution. "A disciple is not above the teacher" (Matt 10:24). Jesus' decision to carry on would have been realistic only if he understood that he did so at great risk. While John had been beheaded, crucifixion was a more usual form of execution. For Jesus to say "take up your cross and follow me" (Matt 16:24 // Mark 8:34 // Luke 9:23) made clear that he had placed himself outside the discipline and protection of the established world of Jewish piety and was calling on others to do the same. This established world of Jewish piety derived its earthly jurisdiction from Rome. Thus in coming into conflict with the religious authorities Jesus risked the ultimate wrath of Roman power. Speaking in this way was a determined response to a policy of oppression that had been calculated to discourage dangerous rhetoric associated with messianic activity. Jesus was not intimidated by what the authorities did to John. Jesus continued to preach. "No one can serve two masters . . . Repent, and engage in the service of God . . . for the kingdom of heaven is at hand."

For Jesus to say "take up your cross and follow me" or for him to say "let the dead bury their own dead" (Matt 8:22 // Luke 9:60) was to take upon himself the full measure of messianic leadership. In such startling statements Jesus challenged others to free themselves from a paralyzing fear of human authorities, even those who sat in Moses' seat and those who represented the emperor. In the first saying Jesus unobtrusively clarified the all-important question whether he was naively calling his disciples into a course of action where the sacrifices being risked might be greater than he himself was prepared to bear.

> What will it profit [any]
> to gain the whole world
> if they lose their soul? (Matt 16:26*).
>
> Those who would save their souls
> must be prepared to give their lives (Matt 16:25 // Luke 9:24 // Mark 8:35*).

Such brave and bold words staved off the disintegrating effects of a temptation to abandon hope for the kingdom's coming once news of John's arrest and imprisonment was followed by confirmation of his death. Even so, such sayings do not seem to carry one to the heart of Jesus' message. They simply show that Jesus gave expression to qualities of leadership that help account for his emergence as a contender for the mantle of John.

As might be expected, some scribes and Pharisees objected to Jesus' practice of eating with tax-collectors and sinners; this led to a major crisis for Jesus. Succumbing to pressure to abandon this practice would possibly have brought Jesus favor. Instead he struck at the root of the problem, that is, the self-righteousness of a scrupulous religious establishment. When legal authorities neglected justice, mercy, and faith and emphasized the minutiae of the Law Jesus represented this as the council of "blind guides" (Matt 23:23-24). In any case Jesus himself came from a religious background so akin to Pharisaism as to command the respect of the Pharisees. Their anxiety over what he was doing was doubtless related to its implicit messianic character, yet in part it was also rooted in a perception that one of their own kind was endangering the interests of "the righteous." Jesus openly said that he did not come to call the righteous (Matt 13:9-13 // Mark 2:13-17 // Luke 5:27-32) and although he himself was known as a righteous man, in eating with sinners Jesus was breaking down the barriers by which many righteous Jews maintained the inner group strength necessary to withstand the external pressures to compromise religious scruples in the interests of achieving an improved economy and a more cosmopolitan society.

**Author's free rendering of the sense of the texts.*

Jesus' table fellowship with repentant tax collectors and sinners provided the nucleus of a new community based on the recognition that God is the Father of all. Indeed, if someone has a hundred sheep and one goes astray, does that person "not leave the ninety-nine in the wilderness and go after the one that is lost?" (Luke 15:3-6; cf. Matt 18:10-14). How much more will our heavenly Father rejoice over the return of a lost child (Luke 15:11-24), and therefore how appropriate that we celebrate the repentance of those lost children of Abraham who, once dead in trespasses, are now alive through God's merciful judgment (Luke 15:25-32; 19:1-10).

By such forceful imagery as this Jesus defended his practice of table fellowship with tax collectors and sinners. Such parables as "The Lost Son and his Elder Brother" (Luke 15:11-32) and "The Laborers in the Vineyard" (Matt 20:1-15) were first created in response to this crisis in Jesus' ministry. They were used to defend the gospel of God's unmerited and unconditional acceptance of the repentant sinner. Similarly the parable of "The Great Banquet" (Matt 22:1-10; Luke 14:16-24) serves to remind the righteous that they have no ground for complaint over the eschatological acceptance of sinners since they themselves have turned their back on the kingdom (cf. Matt 23:13 // Luke 11:52). Such love as God has for the sinner shows no lack of love for the righteous. "All that is mine is yours," says the father to his elder son, "but we had to celebrate and rejoice, because this brother of yours was dead and has come to life; he was lost and has been found" (Luke 15:32).

Other ethical teachings that have a strong claim to authenticity include the teachings on being angry with one's brother or sister (Matt 5:21-24); on the appropriateness of ethical surgery (Matt 5:29-30 and 18:8-9 // Mark 9:43-47); on retaliation (Matt 5:38-42); on serving two masters (Matt 6:24 // Luke 16:13); on doing good works to be seen by other people (Matt 6:2-4, 5-6, 16-18); on laying up treasures (Matt 6:19-21 // Luke 12:33-34); on the eye being the lamp of the body (Matt 6:22-23 // Luke 11:34); on not casting pearls before swine (Matt 7:6); on being wise as serpents and innocent as doves (Matt 10:16); on not fearing those who can kill the body but cannot kill the soul (Matt 10:28-31); on whoever would be greatest becoming the servant of all (Matt 20:26b-27 // Mark 10:43b-44, cf. Mark 9:35); on not presuming in matters of honor (Luke 14:8-10); on inviting as guests the poor and disadvantaged who cannot repay (Luke 14:12b-14a); on identifying with the "untouchables" and excluded and taking responsibility for their welfare even in the absence of ethnic obligation and at the risk of one's own security (Luke 10:30-35).

4. The Opposition to Jesus

In spite of the cogency of Jesus' defense of the gospel of God's mercy toward repentant sinners, opposition from the religious establishment stiffened. It was in this period that Jesus formulated his woes against the "scribes and Pharisees." These utterances are uncompromising. Israel was at the crossroads. Either it followed those Jesus characterized as "blind guides" who hypocritically held in their hands the keys of the kingdom but neither entered themselves nor allowed others to enter in (Matt 23:13) or it could follow him. Irony turns to bitter sarcasm in the judgment: "Woe to you, scribes and Pharisees, hypocrites! For you build the tombs of the prophets and decorate the graves of the righteous, and you say, 'If we had lived in the days of our ancestors, we would not have taken part with them in shedding the blood of the prophets.' Thus you testify against yourselves that you are descendants of those who murdered the prophets" (Matt 23:29-31).

Words like these sealed the fate of Jesus. By speaking them he unmasked what many in positions of privilege and power could not bear to have unmasked. Jesus penetrated the facade of goodness behind which people hid their lust for power. He presented them as being like "whitewashed tombs, which on the outside look beautiful, but inside . . . are full of the bones of the dead" (Matt 23:27).

The Pharisees were certainly not the only righteous Jews in Palestine. The Qumran community was also a haven for those who wanted to be right with God according to the Law of Moses. Jesus recognized the Pharisees as being righteous and alluded to them when his teaching required the example of a righteous person, but he perceived a difference between the righteousness practiced by some Pharisees and the obedience he taught his disciples to render God. A parable like "The Pharisee and the Tax Collector in the Temple" (Luke 18:9-14) was designed to heal. That particular Pharisee does not represent all Pharisees, and certainly not the ideal Pharisee. But in order to make his point that goodness can become demonic and destructive when it leads good people to place themselves above others in God's sight, Jesus chose a man from the most virtuous circle of Jewish society. Such people, no matter how moral, if they place their trust in their own righteousness and look down on others go from the house of God in a wrong relationship with God, whereas sinners who place their trust in the mercy of God return home in a right relationship to God.

Thus it is clear that one can give a credible account of the importance of the Pharisees for understanding the NT, and especially the importance of their opposition to Jesus' table fellowship with tax collectors and sinners, without settling the question as to the extent the priestly purity code was being extended to all Israelites in the time of Jesus. Certainly to the degree that the extension of the purity code was accepted in the time of Jesus, and to the extent that the Pharisees had any interest at all in gaining wide acceptance of this code among the laity Jesus' table fellowship with tax collectors and sinners could have been of added concern to the Pharisees, but a concern would have existed in any case, based simply on the explicit food laws. The Pharisees would not have been alone in this concern; it would have been shared by all righteous Jews to one degree or another.

5. The Outcome of Opposition to Jesus

To understand the consequences of the opposition to Jesus we must acknowledge that Jesus certainly challenged Jewish legal authority. As for Roman order, it was to be replaced by the kingdom of heaven. As a consequence the legal authorities were beside themselves to find some charge on which to get rid of Jesus. The compliance of high-priestly circles and the rest of the Jerusalem oligarchy was assured once Jesus made it clear that he called for changes not only in people's hearts but in the institutions of Zion, specifically within the central institution, the Temple itself (Matt 21:12-13 // Luke 19:45-46; cf. Mark 11:15-17). With the Pharisees, the high priests, and the elders of the people in concert, the Roman authorities, had they insisted on due process, could have done so only at the risk of at least a small tear in a delicately woven fabric of political collaboration. Ostensibly in the interest of maintaining Jewish Law and Roman order Jesus was executed. This was done in spite of the fact that Jesus programmatically insisted that he came "not to abolish [the Law] but to fulfill [it]" (Matt 5:17). Moreover he taught his disciples that unless their righteousness exceeded that of the scribes and Pharisees they would never enter the kingdom of heaven (Matt 5:20), yet it can hardly be doubted that in fulfilling the "law and the prophets" Jesus ran afoul of the scribes and Pharisees not only when he ate with tax collectors and sinners but in other matters as well, as for example Sabbath observance (Matt 12:1-8 // Mark 2:23-28 // Luke 6:1-5). So the die had been cast well in advance, and while by the standard of the kingdom of heaven Jesus died a righteous man he did not go to his cross innocent of breaking the Law as that was represented by the mores of the local populace. He was crucified in the end by the Romans as a political criminal. We can imagine the mixed feelings of anguish and relief on the part of responsible Jewish authorities. We are not in a position to know with certainty the motives of the principals who were involved in Jesus' death. Least of all are we in a position to apportion guilt.

This outline illustrates how tradition originating with Jesus comes alive against the historical background of the people of God in Palestine when Herod Agrippa was Tetrarch of Galilea and Perea, John the Baptist had been preaching a baptism of repentance in the Jordan valley, and Pontius Pilate was procurator of Judea.

The Character of Jesus

In retrospect and on the basis of what can be supported by historical inquiry is it possible to say something about the character of Jesus? Confining our inquiry to that nucleus of sayings and actions that beyond a reasonable doubt can be accepted as authentic we can draw some conclusions.

In rebuking self-righteousness and chiding those who resented God's mercy toward sinners Jesus disclosed something about the kind of person he was. His contemporaries could understand his concern for others, and many were moved by it. They saw his friendship for tax collectors and sinners and his concern for community. This compassionate but disconcerting and revolutionary stance of Jesus was a dynamic source of redemptive power that worked against any attempt of the established world of Jewish piety to structure human existence on the exclusivistic ground of the Mosaic covenant. This source of redemptive power also provided the basis for a distinctive style of life characterized by reaching out to the excluded with love instead of judgment. It was this stance, this personal structuring and restructuring of their historical existence, this shaping of the realities of their human environment, and the faith, love, compassion, and joy associated with this creative stance that sustained and gave theological depth and direction to their community. There is more to Jesus than this, but this understanding of his public career and character carries the investigator to the heart of what can be shown to be both essential and enduring in Jesus. The character of Jesus is the mark he "engraved" upon his disciples including the tax collectors and sinners admitted into the intimacy of his table fellowship. It was members of this community that heard Jesus gladly and remembered his words and actions, and from their number were drawn those who took responsibility for formulating and handing on to the earliest churches such authentic sayings of Jesus as have been preserved in the gospels.

The Character of Jesus' Community

It remains to show how in less dramatic ways the character of the community that emerged following the death and resurrection of Jesus was theologically pre-formed by other conflicts that beset Jesus during his earthly ministry. In situations where his disciples had different degrees of success and failure and where praise and blame based on results had led to invidious comparisons and dissension Jesus encouraged them to think of their work in relation to that of the sower who sows indiscriminately. Those who sow will neither be elated because of good results nor discouraged because of poor results. People sow, but the results are not in their hands. The one who does the work of God is not responsible for the response others make to that work. A disciple of Jesus is responsible only for how faithfully this work is done (Matt 13:3-9).

No amount of success either by Jesus or his disciples could completely overcome the anxiety of some of the faithful as the weeks and months passed and the full restoration of God's sovereign reign over Israel continued to be delayed. To meet the uncertainty that this delay caused, Jesus compared the reign of God to mustard seed and leaven to remind the disciples that great things come from small beginnings (Matt 13:31-33 // Luke 13:18-21 // Mark 4:30-32), the corollary of which would be that what is impressive and grand can be deceptive (cf. Matt 24:1-2). Jesus argued repeatedly from everyday examples that it is reasonable to be hopeful and to believe that the inbreaking of God's sovereign love into the lives of the disciples would be followed by the coming of God's kingdom. Therefore do not give up petitioning God: what God holds for the faithful in promise will be fulfilled, and what God has begun, God will complete (cf. Luke 18:1-8; 11:5-13; 14:28-33). Pray expectantly and with belief in your hearts:

> Your kingdom come.
> Your will be done,
> On earth as it is in heaven (Matt 6:10).

We are encouraged to imagine from the way Jesus' parables can be understood within the context of his earthly career that it was along such lines as these that he was able to reason with the disciples over the delay in the kingdom's coming in full eschatological force.

It appears likely that there was an additional factor compounding uncertainty over the delay of the kingdom. We ought not think that all the disciples of Jesus were equally reassured that it was correct for Jesus to eat with tax collectors and sinners. If it occurred to some of them to think that the scribes and Pharisees may be right in their insistence that Jesus was making them vulnerable by his relationships with the unrighteous, then it is not difficult to imagine that uncertainty among the disciples would have been compounded by this disturbing criticism from the pillars of Jewish piety. It is understandable that some of Jesus' disciples would have expressed concern over the presence of persons of questionable character within their fellowship. Jesus' parable of the wheat and the weeds (Matt 13:24-30) expresses a response to this kind of concern. This parable may be viewed as a Magna Carta for the Church, for in it Jesus teaches his disciples that God, not human beings, in due season will separate the just from the unjust. A similar teaching is given in the parable of the net (Matt 13:47-52). Here the reign of God is compared to a net cast out into the sea that includes within it fish that are both good and bad. What havoc would be wrought by fisherfolk who attempted to sort out the catch while the work of fishing was under way. No! that can be best done at the end of the day, after the net has been brought ashore. This self-understanding within Jesus' community—that is, that its members should not judge one another (cf. Matt 7:1-5 // Luke 6:37-38, 41-42, cf. Mark 4:24)—is an essential mark of the Church and means that the community of the Church, if it is faithful to this understanding, will be inclusive of sinners as well as saints.

This does not mean that there are no ethical norms that will characterize this community. Jesus' ethical teachings must have left a deep impression on his disciples because the Church has preserved for these sayings an important place in the earliest Jesus tradition and because the evangelists, especially Matthew and Luke, have given these ethical teachings a prominent place in their gospels. Jesus' teaching on love of enemies (Matt 5:43-48 // Luke 6:27-28, 32-36) seems to penetrate to the heart of his message and carries the hearer to the central core of the gospel. It has no other ground than the character of God. Because God loves God's enemies we should love our enemies.

The Relevance of This Historical Reconstruction

What is the relevance of this particular reconstruction? Surely opinions will differ. Just as every historical reconstruction of Jesus' life is a product of the interaction between the historian's mode of consciousness, the gospel literature, and the scholar's professional tools, so the response to this reconstruction will also be dependent on what is uppermost in the consciousness of a particular reader.

Many Christians are afflicted by the demonic structures of oppression in their society and the need for the active overthrowing of those structures. In that social and political context they will not find table fellowship with sinners the most adequate organizing principle for bringing about social change. For them, as for some liberation theologians, Jesus' confrontation of the status quo and the demand of God's just and righteous reign would be more attractive. Many others, however, are increasingly attracted to Martin Luther King, Jr., and Archbishop Oscar Romero, and a reconstruction like this could provide for them a much-needed impetus. These readers will observe how applicable is Jesus' behavior (and more specifically his table fellowship with sinners and tax collectors) to the tearing down of debilitating social discrimination based on racial, cultural, ideological, and even religious grounds. If one takes to heart the compassionate movement of the good Samaritan to the side of the stranger left half dead and the corresponding compassionate movement of the father toward his returning son, then the great liberating power of the gospel can begin to work among us.

Jesus taught his disciples to love their enemies. Any reconstruction that stumbles on that fact will not stand up to criticism. God is love, and this love should be the source of a movement of compassion, of servanthood, of risk-taking for the sake of the other; a divine movement from the privileged position of strength and power to the side of the weak and the excluded.

The historian, as historian, can only recapture a fragment of the real Jesus, but as this fragment shows, the real Jesus was not, as some historians claim, a different Jesus from the one proclaimed by the Church. Nor is the real Jesus simply a powerful moral forerunner of just any political martyrs. The real Jesus is a Savior whose redemptive death has turned human history completely around, from death to life, and prefigures a glorious future for the human family as children of God. All saints and martyrs of the Church, including Christians like Romero and King, share in the redemptive death of the chief martyr of the faith and witness to its continuing power in the world.

It is in this context that the historian can most fruitfully focus on the tradition that the apostle Paul passed on to his readers in the church at Corinth:

> The Lord Jesus on the night when he was betrayed took a loaf of bread, and when he had given thanks, he broke it and said, "This is my body that is [broken] for you. Do this in remembrance of me." In the same way he took the cup also, after supper, saying, "This cup is the new cove-

> nant in my blood. Do this, as often as you drink it, in remembrance of me" (1 Cor 11:23b-25).

This is the earliest tradition we have concerning the "Lord's Supper." Jesus' identifying his body with the bread and his blood with the cup is strongly supported in the parallel traditions preserved in the gospels of Matthew, Mark, and Luke. (See the article "The Eucharist in the New Testament.") This historical evidence indicates that Jesus consciously intended his death to be understood as a giving of himself on behalf of others. This is the essence of love. It is the kind of love that makes us free.

Jesus Christ

Jon Sobrino

To speak of Jesus Christ is possible only from a perspective that although concrete and for that very reason limited may more adequately introduce us into the totality of his mystery. In this study we will adopt the perspective of Latin America's liberation theology which we believe is similar to the perspective of the Christian Scriptures and that is certainly necessary in our present world reality. This presupposes (1) making the *reign of God* central to that theology, (2) having *liberation* as its goal (because of which this theology understands itself to be not only a theory of praxis but also a reflective understanding of love), and (3) assuming that the *poor,* as the *victims* of this world, are its theological locus. Starting from these presuppositions let us see how we gain access to Jesus Christ.

(1) Jesus of Nazareth appears in a constitutive relationship to the kingdom *(basileia),* and must always be understood as such. Nevertheless Jesus does not define that kingdom, and in order to know what he thought about the kingdom we might use the following three "ways."

The first is the *notional* or *imaginative way,* the presupposition being that Jesus inherits the OT tradition although correcting and completing it. According to that the reign of God is a utopia to which one responds with a hope that unfolds in three dimensions: (a) it is a historical hope, not merely a transcendental one; (b) it is a popular hope, the collective hope of the majority that responds to the needs of that majority; (c) it is a practical and not merely expectant hope, and it is dialectical since the reign of God does not grow from a *tabula rasa* but right in the midst of the anti-kingdom that is pitted against it. According to this method of research the kingdom is the utopia—generically speaking—in which a worthy and just life is possible for Israel in spite of its experiences of oppression both from external and internal sources and in spite of its failures with reference to God and others. What Jesus adds to this theory is that the reign of God is drawing near and this is taking place through grace.

The second way to discover what Jesus thought of the kingdom is to consider *the addressee.* What is most important about the reign of God is that it is announced to the poor, and ultimately only to the poor. These are they who live bowed down because life, in its material and social dimensions, is a heavy burden to them; they are the ones who do not have sufficient means to live, the marginated, the insignificant. If the kingdom is for them, then it is biased—the option for the poor is originally an option by Godself—and it is above all a kingdom of life. In the words of Oscar Romero, "The minimum of what we must defend is life, God's greatest gift."

The third way to understand the kingdom is the *way of praxis* under the assumption that the activity of Jesus is for the service of the kingdom. Through his healing, the expulsion of demons, the rescue of sinners, through his preaching, especially his parables, and through his feasts and celebrations one sees outlined what the reign of God is for Jesus. It is a society and a world of life and of liberty, a world free of the powerful who subjugate the poor, a world that does not create marginated or despised people but gathers them into its center where everyone can celebrate, especially the little ones. In consonance with this way of knowing, Jesus of Nazareth is the proclaimer and initiator of the reign of God. In summary he is the *prophet* who gathers together the hopes of the majority—in this case the poor among the people—and dedicates his life to fulfilling their hopes.

(2) Jesus also appears in a relationship of absolute trust with a God who is *Father* and he demonstrates absolute availability before a Father who continues being *God.* Jesus has the experience of a good God whom he calls *abba.* He experiences a God who does not terrorize because of his majesty, but rather attracts because of his tenderness and nearness to his people. The authority of Jesus derives from this, not as an authority that subjugates but as one that serves. And from here also his freedom—which has very little to do with a liberal freedom—comes to be a liberty that produces goodness: "nothing is an obstacle to doing good." Jesus believes in a good God and he is happy that God is God. That is what he communicates above all in the parables of mercy that are meant to defend, against God's adversaries, the divine posture of goodness toward those held captive by sinners who take issue with the goodness of God.

On the other hand, although Jesus is so close to his Father he does not possess him; rather he is completely available to his Father. Thus one can speak of the conversion of Jesus throughout his life. Kingdom, God, discipleship, miracles all mean different things for Jesus at the beginning and at the end of his life. Jesus changed, and that change did not occur quietly but rather through temptations and crisis (the more symbolic temptations in the desert and the more historical ones at the end of his life, the Galilean crisis). Jesus did not know the "day nor the hour" nor did he come to know in an unusual, forced manner. Throughout everything Jesus allowed God to be God.

If one combines confidence in a God who is *Father* with availability to a Father who is *God* then one can speak of the faith of Jesus. "To those who believe, all things are possible," Jesus says of himself in the gospel of Mark (9:23). Jesus is the one who has lived the faith originally and fully, says the letter to the Hebrews. Accordingly, then, Jesus is *Son,* the one who appears in personal relationship with a Father-God.

(3) Temptation was the internal climate of the life of Jesus and persecution was the external one. Although the chronology may not be exact, according to Mark's gospel Herodians and Pharisees were plotting against Jesus to put him to death soon after the beginning of his mission and at the end of the fifth controversy (Mark 3:6). Luke, perhaps remembering the village wrangling, says that they wanted to throw him off a precipice after his inaugural discourse in the synagogue at Nazareth (Luke 4:29). Whatever may have been the case, persecution permeates the life of Jesus, gradually as is apparent in Luke, and constantly as is evident especially in John's gospel.

Persecution culminates in the condemnation of Jesus to death. The high priests condemn him for blasphemy (a redactional addition). The true reason lies in Jesus' having rejected the plan to organize society around the Temple ("he wants to destroy the Temple," the religious, political, economic and financial center) precisely because this oppresses the majority. Before Pilate Jesus is accused of being a political agitator but Pilate condemns Jesus only when he is faced with the alternative "either Jesus or Caesar." This seems to indicate that Jesus is rejecting the *pax romana,* if only in an indirect way.

The death of Jesus demonstrates, then, that the mediators of the true God and of the false gods are in a fierce and mutually exclusive battle: it is the choice of either Jesus or the high priests and Pilate. And hidden behind the mediators is a similar struggle among the gods: it is a question of either the God of life or the gods of oppression. Jesus is executed by the gods of death for defending the God of life. It is clear that this way of framing his death is not unpremeditated.

During his life Jesus *debated* about the reality of the true God (whether this God does or does not allow the plucking of wheat from someone else's field in order to satisfy hunger because it is a primary right [Matt 12:1-8 // Mark 2:23-28 // Luke 6:1-5]), and *unmasked* the false gods, those who are the products of selfish human traditions, such as those that—in the name of God—do not permit the helping of parents in need (Mark 7:10-13). All this was raised to the level of a thesis: "no one can serve two masters"—that is, God and mammon, God and idols (Matt 6:24 // Luke 16:13).

This means that Jesus belonged to a movement to illuminate the reality of God, one that not only sought to demythologize divinity but to de-idolize false gods. Jesus affirms that the idols exist, that they are historical realities that clothe themselves in the characteristics of divinity. They claim to be transcendent and remote; they are self-justifying and untouchable; they offer salvation to their worshipers in exchange for a cult and an orthodoxy and like the mythical Moloch they demand victims for their subsistence (all of which continues to be a tangible reality). It is from here that Jesus demands orthopraxis for overcoming idolatry, as appears programmatically in the account of the final judgment and in the parable of the good Samaritan.

Because of all of this Jesus dies, executed on a cross, and although it may be practically impossible to know the details the most ancient accounts show him abandoned by God. In any case the death of Jesus is not a beautiful death; it is not a tranquil death like that of Socrates nor is it a euphoric death like that of some martyrs and heroes. In summary, Jesus is the *suffering servant* of YHWH, the one who dies bearing upon himself the sins of the world.

(4) After Jesus' death on the cross the disciples preach a bold message that we can formulate now as it appears paradigmatically in the first chapters of the Acts of the Apostles: "You killed the just one, but God raised him from the dead" (Acts 2:22-34). In this formulation the central subject of the scene is God who from that moment will receive a new name: "the one who calls forth things into being" (Rom 4:17). But it is crucial to understand that action as reaction. God is reacting to the murderous action of human beings. From this, a number of fundamental things may be deduced.

In the first place, God is the God who does justice: the executioner did not overcome the victim. God is directly the God of the victims, the biased God, and out of that bias God's universality will be unfolded. In the second place the victims can have a hope as can all human beings insofar as they analogously resemble the victims. Last, the truth of Jesus of Nazareth is revealed. Jesus is now the exalted one (there is a transformation of reality in the tradition of the Magnificat): from having been crucified by human beings he is brought back to life by God. Jesus is someone very especially related to God, so that at the end of time he will return as Son of Man to judge and gather Israel. (At this time there begins the dynamic of applying titles of dignity to Jesus in order to show his special reality.) Ultimately the life of Jesus is the true life. In summary it can be said that in Jesus all that is *truly human* and all that is *truly divine* are revealed.

(5) A relationship with Jesus, now risen, becomes a relationship of faith. In the most radical sense this means living and acting like Jesus until Christian existence itself is tantamount to a disciple's expressing in his/her life the life and praxis of Jesus. It is to be noted that this "following" takes on an epistemological dimension, viz., that in "being" like Jesus one is given the affinity that is necessary for confessing his otherness; thus the believer is required to make the leap of faith.

This faith expresses itself conceptually also, according to the theoretical models at hand, taken as they were from the Hebrew Scriptures and the surrounding religions. The expressions of faith use titles of dignity, calling Jesus high priest, Messiah, Son of God/servant, Word—but what is important about analyzing these titles is to catch a double movement. On the one hand, in order to express what was special about Jesus his followers applied a special title: "Jesus is Lord" (Phil 2:11; cf. Rom 10:9; 1 Cor 12:3). On the other hand one cannot presuppose what, before Jesus, was understood by saying that someone is "Lord." It is the Christian Scriptures that affirm the truth of that title: "Who is Lord? It is Jesus." Little by little these titles began affirming not only what would later be called the humanity and divinity of Jesus, but also what was the nature of Jesus' being truly human and truly divine. In this sense there would have to be a reformulation of dogmatic language and the affirmation not only of the fact that Jesus is *truly man and truly God* (as if Jesus fulfilled conditions we judge to be essential to being both human and divine), but also the affirmation of the fact that Jesus is *the true man* and *the true God,* that is, the unforeseen, scandalous, and blessed revelation of what is human and what is divine.

(6) What we have said starting from the life and destiny of Jesus of Nazareth can actually serve to transform us through faith in Christ. Above all we must follow Jesus in order to grow

in the conviction that when we walk historically, that is, make history while being on the side of victim peoples, life has "more" meaning and history gives "more" of itself. To put it in theological language: the conviction can grow that in following Christ we walk toward God, the ultimate mystery.

Second, we have to make, as Jesus did, the fundamental and theological option for the poor and the victims of this world who indirectly but effectively clarify for us who that Jesus is who gives himself up to them transcendentally.

Finally—since we are "poor examples of being Christ" as noted by Karl Rahner—we have to fashion in our own lives the life of Jesus (an essential act in Paul and John). It follows, then, that we will need to be (high) priests like him, helping God approach other human beings and other human beings approach God through mercy, fidelity, and surrender. And without adding anything more, it means that we ought to be "Christians" whether we are male or female, of different races, ethnic groups, or cultures (Gal 3:27-28). By virtue of that fact, just as we have "put on Christ, the Messiah," we must become messiahs to others without allowing that title to degenerate into a name that merely designates rather than signifies "the one who gathers together the peoples' hopes," the one whom liberation theology has called "liberator." We ought to allow ourselves to be formed by the Lord, but at the same time we ought to make him the Lord of history. That he is the Lord of history is not at all evident in our world, a fact that will necessarily lead us to the question of evil. In making us his body in history he has also left in our hands the need to respond to the question of evil. The Son in whom the plan of God is made manifest is the one to whom we ought to conform ourselves, disposing ourselves also to adopt the form of a servant. We ought to be word, sacrament of God for others, and gospel, good news for the poor.

In conclusion, to confess that Jesus is the true human being through whom is revealed the true God-being is a theoretical problem but it is ultimately clarified only in a practice, acting as Jesus did, in a way relevant to our day, within our historical moment. In that way we will be liberators of the poor of our times.

See BIBLIOGRAPHY FOR "LIBERATION."

Jesus Christ

Maria Clara Lucchetti Bingemer

Christian faith is fundamentally a faith in Jesus Christ. At the center of the Christian faith experience is the person of Jesus of Nazareth, acknowledged and proclaimed by the primitive community as the Christ of God, the exalted Lord seated at the right hand of the Father.

What we intend to do here is: (1) to reflect on the unity and tension between the historical Jesus and the Christ of faith in order to establish a clear idea of the identity of Jesus Christ; (2) to reflect on some titles given to Jesus by the first Christian generation, titles that provide indirect clues to reveal something about his mystery; (3) to draw some conclusions for our present Christian and ecclesial life from what was seen in the person of Jesus Christ.

The Christ of Faith: Meeting Point of a Tension

The question concerning the historicity of the figure of Jesus is of fundamental importance for christology, but this historicity is recognized within a historically situated community of believers. At the same time we recognize that christology does not develop only conceptually and speculatively. Therefore a merely positive historical and critical method does not account for all the complexity of the figure of Jesus of Nazareth and its meaning for Christian faith and theology. The community's endeavor to formulate in its own (socio-culturally determined) way the experience of its relationship with Jesus Christ expresses the significance of the person and work of Jesus, and at the same time defines the Christian existence of the community. Jesus Christ cannot be separated from his witnesses and this influences the directions that may be taken by faith in him and its subsequent reflection, namely christology.

On this basis we can say that the entire NT revelation is permeated by a dialectical tension between the "historical Jesus" and the "exalted Lord." This tension is perceived, believed, and revealed in the words of the witnesses when they profess their faith. The one who was "heard, . . . seen, . . . and touched with our hands" (1 John 1:1), the historical figure of Mary's son, the carpenter's son, whose brothers and sisters were known among the people and who died on the cross cannot be separated from the one who appeared risen and glorious, with power and divine authority.

The Christ of faith, therefore, is not a christological concept opposed to that of the historical Jesus; rather it integrates and assumes it in its totality. The dynamic unity between the historical Jesus and the risen and glorified Lord seated at the right hand of the Father is the Christ of faith. This is the one proclaimed in the words of the witnesses who have seen and testified. This is the central figure of the gospels and the whole NT.

The gospels are not biographies, nor is the NT as a whole a merely historical document. Instead, on a real and authentic historical basis the NT authors offer their faith interpretation of the historical and transcendent events that mark the life, death, and resurrection of Jesus. Therefore drawing near to him means coming close to the mystery of his person, his figure, and being challenged by it in every historical and cultural period in which humankind is called to live.

Because Jesus Christ is not merely a historical figure among others he is a reference for all people of all times and places. Because he is not just a projection of the early communities but is solidly rooted in history Jesus Christ can concretely help every man and every woman in their real and historical situation, in their spatial and temporal circumstances. The names and titles the witnesses gave to the one they professed as their Lord can help us understand more about his complex and fascinating identity.

Some Titles That Help to Identify Jesus Christ

The very first witnesses experienced the need to find names and titles to announce and proclaim the mysterious identity of this man they met one day, a man who completely changed their lives. Although within the limits of this article we cannot analyze all these numerous titles we will single out a few that may help us toward our objective of knowing the mystery of Jesus better, a mystery incorporating a fruitful tension between history and interpretation.

(1) Jesus the Messiah (= the Christ, *ho christos:* Christus is the Latin form of the Greek *christos*). This word corresponds to the Hebrew *mashiach* and designates someone who has been specially anointed to carry out a mission. The Hellenized form of the Hebrew word is *messias,* which appears only twice in the Greek NT and only in John (1:41; 4:25). Both times the evangelist himself translated it by *christos* and both references are to Jesus of Nazareth. Something essential must be said regarding the word *christos* in the NT, namely that the testimony of the NT concerning Jesus is consciously "christological" in spite of differences in detail from the messianic expectations of the Judaism of the time. Whenever the NT speaks of Jesus it is referring to him as the Christ, the Messiah. This implies that throughout the NT messiahship is no longer under the sign of expectation but under the sign of fulfillment. The Christ-event is mentioned everywhere in the past tense of the verb. To be sure, the evangelist's gaze is also directed to the future, rather intensely at times. However, the one who is expected as someone who is to come is in fact someone who is returning. He is not a stranger; he is as well known by his own people who are impatiently expecting him as they are known by him (cf. John 10:14, the gospel of the Good Shepherd).

For Christian faith the name of Jesus Christ encompasses much more than the messiahship of a certain Jesus of Nazareth in whom God fulfilled the promises made to the people of Israel. For the NT the whole salvation that God had planned and prepared for the world is related to Jesus as the Christ. And if Christ, a title of honor, became an integral part of the name of Jesus it is because the title expresses the essential aspect of his historical appearance that was, at the same time and inseparably, the presupposition of all his work as the mediator of salvation. This includes his obedient submission to the will of God, whom he calls *abba.* Along this same line, the "yes" of Jesus to his messianic vocation implied for the kerygma of the first Christian communities his journey to the cross and his resurrection and glorification. Jesus Christ is not a triumphant messiah; instead the most complete expression of his messiahship for christology is found in the so-called christological hymn that Paul incorporated in his letter to the Philippians (Phil 2:5-11). There Paul describes the way of Jesus in terms of *kenosis,* humiliation, and obedience until his exaltation at the right hand of God.

For the ecclesial community it is of fundamental importance to perceive and follow the way that was experienced by Jesus of Nazareth in the earthly stage of his life. This stage is characterized by self-emptying and service. In this stage the Christian community observes Jesus' attitudes, priorities, behavior, and preaching, all of which have paradigmatic value. Even though it is not a question of a literal imitation but of a creative and new following at every step, the community feels it is being led by the same Spirit who inspired Jesus during his lifetime, even though the circumstances in which this following will take place are different and can change every day.

The messiahship of Jesus Christ, although it is not something applicable to the present time that has already received the fulfillment of God's promises to the chosen people, reminds us that we must always be in tension toward the future, toward what is yet to come. This is because our Christian faith not only proclaims that the Messiah, so anxiously expected by the people, has already come but also that he will come again in glory. On the basis of the messiahship of Jesus, Christian existence is therefore called to be an ongoing proclamation of the Good News that the one who already came will come again and will recognize all his people and be recognized by them. In the meantime we have to follow him in obedience, humility, and constant selfless service.

(2) Jesus the Lord (= *kyrios:* the Greek term indicates a dominion that is legitimate and represents recognized authority). The designation of Jesus as *kyrios* corresponds to the way the earthly Jesus was addressed. It may refer to the title of *rabbi* (teacher), implying that Jesus was acknowledged as Lord and also that people were willing to obey him (cf. Matt 7:21; 21:28-32; Luke 6:46). This places Jesus above human and religious institutions like the Sabbath. It also gives what the earthly Jesus said an unquestionable authority for the community even after his death and resurrection. The faith invocation *kyrios,* which originated especially in the pre-Pauline Hellenistic community, means that the NT community submits to its Lord and confesses at the same time that he is the sovereign of the world (cf. Rom 10:9; 1 Cor 12:3; Phil 2:11). The glorified *kyrios,* Jesus Christ, rules over all humankind and over the universe. Before him all beings of the cosmos will bend their knees and at the same time glorify God the Father, at whose right hand Christ is seated (Eph 1:20; 1 Pet 3:22). In this way Jesus Christ receives the same titles as God (cf. 1 Tim 6:15; Dan 2:47). Thus in the NT period the idea of the relationship of Jesus Christ to God the Father was already present although it was not yet a profound and developed perception. The NT will be the basis on which the subsequent ecclesiastical doctrine of the Trinity will work.

Nevertheless there is something about the proclamation of Jesus Christ as Lord that makes it different from all other lordships and completes the profile of this Lord who is the center of Christian faith from the beginning until our own time. The dominion of Jesus Christ cannot be separated from his service. The exalted Lord is inseparably the servant of God and it is because of his condition as servant that he can be proclaimed as Lord. The concept of servant, present for example in Matt 20:27 // Mark 10:44, undoubtedly has Isaiah 53 as its background; that is to say it involves the *ʿebed yhwh,* the central focus of the songs of the servant of God that according to an ancient tradition were applied to Jesus. This theme permeates the synoptic gospels even though often it is expressed not by the terms for servant/slave *(doulos, pais)* but as *huios* (son) (cf. Matt 3:17 // Mark 1:11 // Luke 3:22, the baptism of Jesus, and Matt 17:5 // Mark 9:7 // Luke 9:35, the transfiguration). In John, Jesus is not called servant *(pais* or *doulos);* he is only called son *(huios).* However, in accord with the circumstances of the gospel we also find the thematic motif of the servant in the washing of the feet (cf. John 13:4-20), the humble service of a slave that is performed by Jesus at the threshold of his passion. In the Fourth Gospel Jesus also appears in the image of the Lamb of God *(amnos tou theou)* which has clear reference to the servant in Isaiah 53, one who "like a lamb that is led to the slaughter . . . did not open his mouth" (cf. vv. 4-7). Jesus is not only compared to a lamb; he *is* the Lamb of God (cf. John 1:29, 36; Acts 8:32; 1 Pet 1:19). This presentation of Jesus as the Lamb of God has a triple meaning: (a) Acts 8:32 underscores his patience in suffering; (b) with the expression "without defect or blemish" 1 Pet 1:19 emphasizes the impeccability and perfection of the sacrifice of Jesus; (c) John 1:29, 36 points out the expiatory power of Jesus' death that takes away, namely erases, the sin of the world.

Thus Jesus Christ, the Lord exalted at the right hand of God the Father, is inseparably the servant who empties himself of the glorious prerogatives of his divine condition to enter on a way of obedience that will lead him to the sacrifice of the cross (cf. Phil 2:5-11); he is the Lamb who by his sacrifice takes away the sin of the world (John 1:29, 36; Acts 8:32; 1 Pet 1:19). For all Christians this implies that entering on the way of Jesus Christ ineluctably means entering into his obedience, his humble service, his fidelity to the *abba* even to his death on the cross, and his love for his brothers and sisters to the point of giving his life for them. Only then will it be possible to participate in his glory to the extent determined by God's infinite wisdom and lordship.

Jesus Christ: Savior of the Present and the Future

In the NT the figure of Jesus Christ always unites present and future. He is not a dualistic figure locked in the opposition between the earthly and the heavenly realms. In the person of Jesus Christ we have the definitive reconciliation and successful synthesis of God and humankind, the Word and perfect listening, history and the interpretation of faith, earth and heaven, flesh and spirit. In consequence the one and only salvation is already totally present, affecting and saving the bodies of each individual, making them part of the body of society and of the human Church. But the promise of God is also eschatological. Just as the original creation realized by God in Christ is always present, so too heaven is already present on earth since the latter has been definitively invaded by heaven in the incarnation of the Word. So too will earth be eschatologically transformed by what is already given in the incarnation, life, death, and resurrection of Jesus Christ, by his presence that establishes a new network of relationships and inaugurates a new cosmos. It is a world in which the eucharistic banquet gathers all people in a loving interchange in which every member has a share without detriment to the rest. The metaphor of the banquet reveals in an excellent way the true nature of the salvation of Jesus Christ since in him we have not only the revelation of what God wants and does for humanity but also what God is, a mystery of communion that attracts and makes possible a profound communion with God through the person of Jesus Christ. This salvation takes place in a world riddled with conflict and death and as a result its signs are often precarious and fragile. However, by looking to Jesus Christ we can assume this difficult combat and merciless fight with the spirit of the servant of God who emptied himself and became obedient unto death, taking upon himself the violence and sin of the world. Thus Christians will have the strength to stand steadfast with their feet firmly planted in the present and their eyes full of hope, looking toward the horizon that is totally filled by Jesus Christ.

Jesus Christ

Jean Galot

From the perspective of Christian faith Jesus Christ is the name that expresses everything that the Law and the Prophets tended to announce and all that the NT places before our eyes. There would be no Catholic biblical commentary without Jesus Christ since we believe that the Christian Bible exists only for him and derives all its truth from him.

In its prologue the gospel of John makes us contemplate the incarnate Word as the center and summary of revelation. John presents him to us in his origin in eternity and later shows Jesus in his passage into our time: "In the beginning was the Word . . . and the Word became flesh and lived among us" (1:1-14). This is the divine Word from whom all the words of Scripture derive their meaning and value.

The prologue specifies that this Word is the Father's only Son through whom we are filled with grace and truth. Ever turned toward the Father in an everlasting contemplation, this Son has enabled us to see God; he has made us enter into the divine mystery. Such a Word is infinitely superior to all the words previously proclaimed because "long ago God spoke to our ancestors in many and various ways . . . but in these last days he has spoken to us by a Son" (Heb 1:1-2).

The difference between the two revelations was not understood by all Jesus' contemporaries. Jesus presented himself, according to the Fourth Gospel, as the divine person of the Son sent by the Father who received everything from the Father. He manifested his divine sovereignty by many miracles performed in his own name. He referred to himself as the "Son of Man," a figure filled with mystery who had come from heaven although he had all the concrete reality of a human being. In his prayer he called God Father, *"abba,"* with the assurance of complete familiarity with God like a child's familiarity with its father. He called himself the Good Shepherd in the way God had been acknowledged as the shepherd of the people. He led people to understand that his coming was that of the bridegroom according to the biblical image of the wedding of the Lord with his people, to the degree that his disciples were called the bridegroom's friends and were to rejoice in his presence. He spoke with sovereign authority, an authority that was peculiar to God, and he dared formulate precepts that modified and surpassed in excellence those that had been received from above in the first covenant: "You have heard . . . But I say to you . . ." (Matt 5:20-48). He intimated that divine wisdom was present in him (Matt 11:19; 12:42).

But when he asked his disciples the question "Who do people say that the Son of Man is?" (Matt 16:13; cf. Mark 8:27; Luke 9:18) the answer showed that most of the time Jesus was simply identified with one of the prophets. This is shown to be an insufficient answer because Jesus himself formulates a new question that requires a decisive stand on the part of his disciples: "But who do you say that I am?" (Matt 16:15; cf. Mark 8:29; Luke 9:20). The answer of Simon, the spokesman of the Twelve, is what the Master was expecting: "You are the Messiah, the Son of the living God" (Matt 16:16; cf. Mark 8:29; Luke 9:20). Thus we have the proclamation of the first profession of faith. It is the result of the testimony that Jesus has given of his identity, especially to those to whom "the secret of the kingdom of God" and the special revelation granted by the Father has been given (Mark 4:11; Matt 13:11; Luke 8:10). Jesus is the "Christ," the Messiah, though not just any messiah but the messiah who is the Son of God.

This profession of faith, immediately approved by Jesus, will become the permanent and definitive profession of faith of the Church. The gospel of Mark is presented as the "good news of Jesus Christ, the Son of God" (1:1). John says that he is writing "so that you may come to believe that Jesus is the Messiah, the Son of God, and that through believing you may have life in his name" (20:31).

When Jesus reveals himself as the Son he brings us to understand that he has received everything from the Father and possesses all that belongs to the Father. The resemblance is so perfect that seeing Jesus is seeing the Father (John 14:9). Nothing is lacking in Jesus' indissoluble oneness with the Father: "The Father and I are one" (John 10:30). In this communion with the Father, Jesus reveals himself as God. As Son he appropriates the name of God revealed to Moses long ago: "I am who I am" (Exod 3:14). He does not hesitate to claim this name as prior to Abraham's becoming: "Very truly, I tell you, before Abraham was, I am" (John 8:58).

It is once again this name of God that he attributes to himself in the supreme testimony to his identity in the course of his trial before the Sanhedrin. He not only admits that the high priest is right in asking the question: "Are you the Messiah, the Son of the Blessed One?" (Mark 14:61), he also answers it in the simplest and most solemn way by repeating the divine name: "I am" (Mark 14:62). Thus he removes any ambiguity, as is shown in the reaction of the high priest who denounces the blasphemy. By taking up this name in spite of the threat of imminent death hanging over him Jesus implies that his existence is assured of eternity. In addition he also announces the imminent coming of the Son of Man who will enlighten the future of humankind by establishing his kingdom in its midst.

The testimony that causes the condemnation receives a glowing divine affirmation in the decisive event of the resurrection. By appearing alive to his disciples the Savior makes them see his now glorious body with the wounds of his hands and feet. He tells them "It is I myself" (Luke 24:39). Moreover it is this "it is I" of the Risen One that will henceforth accompany the disciples in their daily lives: "And remember, I am with you always, to the end of the age" (Matt 28:20). This "I am" will guide the history of humankind to its end.

The assurance of an ongoing presence given to the disciples and to the Church shows the fundamental intention of love that animates the revelation of "I am." The revelation of being is also the revelation of love. The affirmation of "I am" addressed to the representatives of the Jewish religion is borne by a love determined to risk death and to offer itself in sacrifice.

The Son was not only sent by the Father on a mission of revelation. He also came on earth to accomplish a work of liberation: "For the Son of Man came not to be served but to serve, and to give his life a ransom for many" (Mark 10:45; Matt 20:28). His service already manifests a "gentle and humble" heart (Matt 11:29) and in the Son of Man's behavior this service reaches its culmination in the gift of his life. In this he expressed the fullness of love: "No one has greater love than this, to lay down one's life for one's friends" (John 15:13).

Saving love has its first origin in the Father. The Father gives his Son by sending him to be "the atoning sacrifice for our sins" (1 John 4:10). Jesus' heroic love expresses what was hidden in the Father's plan by obtaining the liberation of humankind by the ransom of his own life. The people whom sin had made "slaves" (John 8:34) receive true freedom from the Son. This is a superior freedom that makes them participants in the divine filiation.

Love pledged in sacrifice wins the victory and manifests its efficacy by the mystery of the resurrection. The risen Christ diffuses the new life he has acquired by his offering in the human community. He introduces this superior life in human hearts through the Holy Spirit. He undertakes the gathering of his Church and through it he transforms the destiny of men and women and of the universe.

Now Jesus makes his own proclamation: "And I, when I am lifted up from the earth, will draw all people to myself" (John 12:32). He exercises this attraction through the Spirit in order to build up his kingdom, a kingdom to which he communicates his love, the filial love for the

Father and a universal mutual love. The precept of mutual love he has left to his disciples is new because he is asking them to love one another as he himself has loved them and he excludes all restrictions or boundaries from love.

Through his Church Jesus constantly enables us to relive the mystery of his redemptive work. He wanted his disciples to reenact the ritual he accomplished at the Last Supper in memory of him. Through a sacramental action the unique offering of his passion is re-presented by tangible signs in the Eucharist. The meal in which he gives himself in his sacrificed and glorious body and blood nourishes and quenches the thirst of believers by filling them with the life of his resurrection.

His words continue to enlighten the faith of those who believe in him and to stimulate the faith of those who do not believe. Jesus himself has underscored the absolute value of his teaching: "Heaven and earth will pass away, but my words will not pass away" (Mark 13:31). The mission of the Holy Spirit is to remind the disciples of these very words so that they may understand them, and to guide them "into all the truth" (John 16:13).

The Holy Spirit has guided the effort of interpretation of the words entrusted to the disciples' memory and to the life of the Church. The first ecumenical councils have given us professions of faith concerning Christ's personal identity. In opposition to the error of Arius who claimed that the Son was a created being, the Council of Nicea (325) declared that the Son of God is not created but instead is begotten and "consubstantial" with the Father. The term "consubstantial" means that the Son is God as the Father is God and that with the Father he is one divine substance. The divinity of Jesus Christ was confirmed by the Council of Ephesus (431) that also acknowledged Mary as the mother of God.

The Council of Chalcedon (451) contributed an additional point by declaring that there is one person with two natures in Jesus. According to the context of the declaration the person is the divine person of the Son. The two natures are the divine nature and the human nature. The council achieved the synthesis of two currents, that of Alexandrian theology that stressed the unity and divinity of Christ and that of Antiochian theology with its emphasis on the duality and humanity of Christ. The council attributed unity to the person and duality to the natures. In this way the true humanity of Christ is guaranteed, a humanity that preserves all its attributes since the two natures are clearly distinct.

We have no reason to question the value of the Chalcedonian definition by stating that the concept of person used in its definition would not coincide with our present concept of person. The council did not borrow its concept of person from a particular philosophical theory. It simply took it from common usage. Even the term *"hypostasis,"* associated with the more usual term "person" *(prosōpon),* is used in the same sense with a more ontological emphasis. The council was referring to the common experience that people have of the person, namely their awareness of being persons and of living in relationships with persons. This common experience is universal and continues throughout the centuries. This is a sufficient reason to give all its value to the unity of person recognized in Christ.

Conciliar definitions provide us with trustworthy data, enabling us to have a better discernment of the Christ of our faith, who is identical with the Christ of history. They always invite us to a subsequent in-depth investigation that needs a constant reference to Scripture. As stated in the epistle to the Hebrews, it is true that "Jesus Christ is the same yesterday and today and forever" (13:8), but Christ is always new in the sense that his presence to us is always open to new discoveries. Christ revealed himself as a mystery that goes beyond all our human formulations and all our means of expression. This new biblical commentary will enable us to enter into that mystery.

The Life of Paul

Jerome Murphy-O'Connor

Youth and Education

Paul was an almost exact contemporary of Jesus of Nazareth. When interpreted in terms of the conventions of the time Paul's description of himself as "elderly" (Philemon 9) in a letter written about 53 C.E. would mean that he was then about sixty years old. His protestations regarding his Jewish identity (1 Cor 11:22; Phil 3:5; Rom 11:1) place his origins in the Diaspora and there is no reason to reject Luke's assertion that he was born in Tarsus in Cilicia (Acts 22:3).

According to Jerome (*Commentary on Philemon* vv. 23-24; *Famous Men* 5) his parents had been deported to Cilicia from the Galilean village of Gischala by the Romans. The source of this information is obscure but two points tend to confirm its accuracy, namely his own claim to be a "Hebrew born of Hebrews" (Phil 3:5; 2 Cor 11:22), that is, an Aramaic-speaking Jew, and Luke's note that he was a Roman citizen by birth (Acts 16:37; 22:25-29; 23:27). Village people would tend to be more at home in Aramaic than in Greek, and slaves or prisoners of war when liberated by a Roman citizen thereby acquired Roman citizenship (Philo, *Embassy to Gaius* 155). Paul inherited both a Semitic language and an internationally respected status.

Luke's interest in tying Paul closely to Jerusalem (Acts 1:8) makes his insinuation that Paul received all his education in the Holy City (Acts 22:3) suspect. The quality of Paul's secular education suggests that it was acquired in Tarsus, whose university was renowned (Strabo, *Geography* 14.5.13). His easy mastery of rhetorical techniques betrays profound study and long practice. In the same school of rhetoric he was exposed to the various strands of Greek philosophy, notably Stoicism, that were part of the intellectual equipment of every educated person.

During the whole of this formative period Paul would also have frequented the synagogue of Tarsus. There he deepened his knowledge of the Greek version of the Bible and was exposed to the traditions of hellenized Judaism whose towering figure was his contemporary Philo of Alexandria, and this perspective deeply impregnated his thought.

A Pharisee in Jerusalem

Only in Jerusalem could Paul have found the Pharisees, whose movement he joined (Phil 3:6; Gal 1:14). As a partly assimilated twenty-year-old whose motive for coming to Jerusalem was to discover the roots of his faith he would have been an ideal recruit for teachers who strove to inculcate a high standard of legal observance. Paul's total dedication to the study of the Law (Gal 1:14) explains his lack of awareness of Jesus' occasional presence in the city in the years 28–30 C.E. The complacency of Paul's ostentatious perfection makes it virtually certain that he was married. All his contemporaries understood "Be fruitful and multiply, and fill the earth" (Gen 1:28) as a binding precept, and the age of marriage was between eighteen and twenty (*m. Aboth* 5.21). The options of excluding (Jer 16:1) or deferring marriage (the cases of Josephus and Philo) were not open to a young stranger eager to make his mark in the competitive field of religious observance. Yet as a Christian missionary

Paul was single (1 Cor 7:8; cf. 9:5). What has happened? Why does he never mention a wife or children?

These questions remain as much unsolved mysteries as the reason why Paul, alone among the Pharisees, persecuted the church in Jerusalem. The clear implication of the letters that Paul undertook the persecution of the Church on his own initiative (Gal 1:13; Phil 3:6; 1 Cor 15:9) is confirmed by Luke (Acts 8:3; 9:1-2). The latter, however, should not be followed when he makes Paul the agent of the Sadducean chief priests (Acts 9:1-2; 26:10). Not only would such an alliance between Pharisees and Sadducees be most improbable but the authority of the Jewish leaders was limited to Judea proper. They could not have authorized Paul to arrest people in Damascus, which belonged to the Roman province of Syria. What Luke says must be understood in terms of his literary design to depict Paul as the perfect prosecutor before showing him to be the ideal apostle.

Conversion and Its Consequences

Why Paul went to Damascus is unclear. In its vicinity he had an encounter with Christ (Gal 1:15-16; 1 Cor 9:1; 15:8) that radically changed his life (2 Cor 5:16). His recognition that the crucified Jesus was risen from the dead threw an entirely new light on whatever else he had known about Jesus as a Pharisee. All Paul's values and perceptions were transformed. He now knew with utter certitude that Jesus was truly the Messiah with authority to relativize the Law. This insight he recognized as a revelation (Gal 1:11). If the Law was not an absolute, then Gentiles could be saved without first becoming Jews. In the moment of his conversion Paul also received his vocation as apostle to the Gentiles (Rom 11:13). This is verified by his first action, which was to preach the gospel among the Nabateans of Arabia (Gal 1:17). The political conditions there were not propitious to his ministry which, in consequence, was of very short duration.

On his return to Damascus Paul stayed three years (Gal 1:18). While not ignoring Jews (Acts 9:19-22), his ministry must have been concentrated among the Gentiles who flocked to the independent Greek city located on one of the great commercial crossroads of the ancient world. Since his attitude toward manual labor is not that of one who was born to it—he thinks of it as "slavish" (1 Cor 9:19) and "demeaning" (2 Cor 11:7)—one must assume that it was in Damascus that necessity forced him to learn a trade in order to support himself (1 Thess 2:9; 2 Thess 3:7-9; 1 Cor 4:12). Luke tells us that he became a tentmaker (Acts 18:3), a clever choice because the tools were easily portable and the skill in demand everywhere. Festivals needed booths for merchants and tents for visitors. Houses required awnings. Travelers called for stitches in leather sandals, cloaks, and harness.

The arrival of the Nabateans in Damascus some time in the latter part of 37 C.E. forced Paul into ignominious flight (2 Cor 11:32-33; contrast Acts 9:23-25). He escaped to Jerusalem where he spent two weeks with Peter (Gal 1:18). It is inconceivable that Paul did not use this time with an eyewitness of the whole ministry of Jesus to deepen his knowledge of what the latter had actually said and done. Paul preached the historical Jesus (2 Cor 11:4) and quoted his sayings (1 Cor 7:10-11; 9:14; 11:23-25). The parables provided the highly urbanized Paul with metaphors that reflect a rural environment and an agrarian culture (e.g., Rom 11:17-24).

The First Missionary Journeys

From Jerusalem Paul tells us only that he went to Syria and Cilicia (Gal 1:21). Nothing about his activities can be deduced from his letters until his first independent journey into Europe, which began sometime in the middle of the fourth decade of the first century. Acts goes a long way toward filling this gap and hints in the letters confirm some of its data.

Not long after its foundation (Acts 11:19-26) the church of Antioch suffered in 39-40 C.E. from the backlash of Jewish political agitation against the project of the emperor Gaius to erect a statue of himself as Jupiter in the Temple at Jerusalem. In order to resurrect the demoralized community the church in Jerusalem sent Barnabas, an experienced Jewish Christian from the Diaspora (Acts 4:36), to Antioch. He recruited Paul in Tarsus to assist him (Acts 11:25-26). For a community reeling from violence the symbolic value of a converted persecutor of the Church could not be overemphasized. The presence of Saul among the distressed believers of Antioch verified the power of grace, which the gospel promised. God was all-powerful. There was hope for the future. Once the situation had stabilized the church of Antioch sent Barnabas and Paul to evangelize Cyprus and a series of towns in the interior of Asia Minor (Acts 13–14). These towns—Antioch, Iconium, and Lystra—are listed in 2 Tim 3:11, and Paul certainly worked with Barnabas at one stage (1 Cor 9:6; Gal 2:1, 9). The fact that Paul never wrote to these churches suggests that Barnabas carried the primary responsibility for them.

Once Paul had served his apprenticeship he was commissioned by Antioch to operate independently in western Asia Minor. He selected Silas to accompany him (Acts 15:40) and from the believers in Lystra he chose Timothy, who was to become his closest collaborator (Acts 16:1-3). A serious illness brought Paul to the Galatians (Gal 4:13; Acts 16:6) where he probably spent from the fall of 46 C.E. to the spring of 48 C.E. That summer he trudged across northern Asia Minor to preach in Macedonia, spent a year in Philippi (Acts 16:12) and a year in Thessalonica (Acts 17:1). After persecution forced him out of Thessalonica he went to Athens (Acts 17:15) where he learned that he could not just found churches and move on. The Thessalonians needed his continuing care. He sent Timothy to check on their survival, and in response to the good news he brought Paul wrote his first letter, 1 Thessalonians (1 Thess 3:1-10).

In the spring of 50 C.E. Paul and his two assistants (2 Cor 1:19) set out for Corinth, which was to become his first great missionary base (Acts 18:1). He lived and worked with Prisca and Aquila (Acts 18:2). The city on two seas offered him unrivaled communications and if he could implant the gospel in a city of which it was said "Not for everyone is the journey to Corinth" (Strabo, *Geography* 8.6.20) its power would be evident to all. After a second letter to Thessalonica all Paul's energy was absorbed by Corinth. He stayed there for eighteen months (Acts 18:11) and encountered the proconsul L. Iunius Gallio in the late summer of 51 C.E., shortly before the missionaries returned to Antioch.

Jerusalem and Antioch

Paul found the community at Antioch deeply troubled. Its Law-free missionary practice was criticized by Jewish Christians from Judea who insisted on the necessity of circumcision. In order to clarify the situation Barnabas and Paul were sent to Jerusalem (Acts 15:1-2) just fourteen years after the latter's previous visit in 37 C.E. (Gal 2:1). Despite the strong case made by the Judaizers—Jews were the Messianic people; Jesus had been circumcised and encouraged observance of the Law—the leaders of the Jerusalem church agreed with Paul and Barnabas that circumcision was not necessary for Gentile Christians (Gal 2:9). A series of violent incidents revealed that anti-Semitism was on the increase in the Roman empire, and James felt that it was no time to dilute Jewish identity by incorporating into the chosen people Gentiles who would be no more than nominal Jews. It was this providential political judgment that enabled him to appreciate the action of the Spirit in the converts of Paul and Barnabas. Paul reciprocated by committing himself to sending financial relief to Jerusalem (Gal 2:10).

The nationalistic reasons that had led to agreement with Paul made it imperative for James to work to strengthen the Jewish identity of Christians of Jewish origin. This had a dramatic impact on the community at Antioch where Gentile and Jewish believers had worked out a satisfactory compromise regarding table-fellowship. A delegation from James insisted on stringent observation of Jewish dietary laws (Gal 2:11-14). This meant that Gentile members of the church effectively had to become Jews in order to maintain the unity of the community. The incident revealed to Paul that any acceptance of the Law inevitably led to legalism, which displaced Christ from the central position that was his right. For the first time Paul saw that the Law was a dangerous rival to Christ (Gal 2:15-21). Since Antioch no longer welcomed Gentile believers Paul could no longer be its representative. Henceforward his letters would insist that his apostolic commission had come through Christ from God (Gal 1:1; contrast 1 and 2 Thess 1:1).

The Years in Ephesus

Paul left Antioch for good in the spring of 52 C.E. On his way across Asia Minor he visited the Galatians and won their support for the collection for Jerusalem (1 Cor 16:1). He arrived in Ephesus at the end of the summer to find a community gathered by Prisca and Aquila (Acts

18:19). Paul had selected the capital of Asia as his next base because it was roughly equidistant from all his previous foundations. He had realized that for some time he must dedicate himself to nurturing existing communities. Expansion would be more efficient were it entrusted to visitors who would bring back the gospel to their home towns where they already had a network of family and friends—for example, Epaphras who founded the churches in the Lycus valley (Col 1:7; 4:12).

The next two years and three months (Acts 19:8-10) were to be among the most intense of Paul's career. Antioch decided to impose its new religious ethos on the daughter churches founded by Paul when he worked under its aegis. Thus Judaizing emissaries followed him to the west. The news of their presence among his converts in Galatia probably reached Paul in the spring of 53 C.E. In response he wrote Galatians, whose argument is really directed against the intruders who had the background to appreciate the sophistication and subtlety of his arguments rooted in the Law that they wished to impose. To the Galatians he insisted that they accept the responsibility of freedom.

Probably during the summer of 53 C.E. Paul was imprisoned while being investigated by the new proconsul of Asia. How long his incarceration lasted we do not know; perhaps several months. From a literary point of view it was most productive. He wrote a series of letters to Philippi that are now combined into our canonical epistle. One warned them of the dangers of the Judaizers (Phil 3:2–4:1) who he presumed would follow his tracks from Galatia to Macedonia. The arrest of Epaphras (Col 4:10) when, feeling incompetent to deal with an esoteric type of false teaching, he came to consult Paul obliged the latter to write Colossians. At the same time he penned Philemon to intercede for Onesimus who traveled to Ephesus to seek his mediation.

Relations with Corinth

During this period Apollos ministered in Corinth (1 Cor 3:6; Acts 19:1). His return to Ephesus (1 Cor 16:12) was probably the occasion of the now-lost first letter that Paul wrote to Corinth (1 Cor 5:9). In the spring of 54 C.E. further news came from Corinth in the form of a scandalized report by Chloe's people (1 Cor 1:11). In order to check the accuracy of what was no more than gossip Paul sent Timothy to Corinth (1 Cor 4:17; 16:10). No sooner had he left than an official delegation from Corinth arrived bearing a letter with the points the church there wanted discussed (1 Cor 7:1; 16:17). This enabled Paul to write a comprehensive response based on all his sources of information. It has been preserved as 1 Corinthians. The way he dealt with the problems alienated the Spirit-people, an influential group at Corinth who had been attracted by the teaching of Apollos.

Shortly after the dispatch of 1 Corinthians, Timothy returned to Ephesus to report that he had encountered a very hostile reception. This led Paul to change his plan to go to Macedonia (1 Cor 16:5). His presence in Corinth was imperative. In the event he was no more successful than Timothy. He was insulted by the Judaizers. They had reached Corinth far more quickly than he had anticipated and were given hospitality by the alienated Spirit-people. More important from Paul's perspective was the fact that the community failed to take his part (2 Cor 2:1-11; 7:5-16). In anger he left for Macedonia promising to return (2 Cor 1:16). On reflection he thought it would do more harm than good. When he returned to Ephesus he wrote the Severe Letter (2 Cor 2:4), which he sent with Titus.

The anxiety that consumed Paul as he waited for the response to the letter was exacerbated by the deteriorating situation at Ephesus. Eventually Paul was forced to leave the city (Acts 20:1). He founded a new church at Troas (2 Cor 2:12; Acts 20:6), an important link between his communities in Asia Minor and those in Europe. He broke off his ministry there as the end of the sailing season approached. If he missed the last boat to Europe he would have to wait for Titus' news until the following spring. Thus he crossed to Macedonia (2 Cor 2:13) where he finally met Titus. The latter's report was optimistic. The believers at Corinth had repented and professed themselves reconciled with Paul (2 Cor 7:8-9).

Still, not all the problems at Corinth were thereby resolved. The Judaizers might yet win over the Spirit-people. They shared common ground in admiration for Moses. The latter considered him the ideal wise man whereas for the former he was above all the legislator. More importantly the atmosphere in the community was being systematically poisoned by consistent sniping at Paul. He was being criticized as a flatterer because of his inconsistency (he had changed his travel plans twice). Above all his style of religious leadership was under attack.

Paul had the winter of 54-55 C.E. to plan the strategy of his response, and in the spring produced a masterpiece. In 2 Corinthians 1–9 he develops a profoundly christological vision of ministry in which suffering facilitates the visibility of grace (2 Cor 4:10-11). Its emphases were designed to drive a wedge between the Judaizers and the Spirit-people. Profiting by the reconciliation with the Corinthians Paul also raises the question of the collection for the poor of Jerusalem, which the troubles had pushed into the background.

Once 2 Corinthians 1–9 had been dispatched to Corinth, Paul felt free to venture into virgin mission territory, a pleasure he had not enjoyed for several years. He moved west along the Via Egnatia to Illyricum (Rom 15:19). There at the end of the summer, to his shock and dismay, bad news came from Corinth. His letter had ruined any chances the Judaizers had of converting the Spirit-people. In consequence they had redoubled their attacks on Paul's person. In particular they insisted that his refusal to accept benefactions from Corinthians was a sign that he did not love them. They also raised doubts as to whether the collection money would actually reach Jerusalem!

It was part of Paul's missionary strategy to accept financial help only when it came from a whole community. Thus he permitted Philippi to subsidize him when he was at Thessalonica (Phil 4:10-20). To accept gifts from wealthy individuals at Corinth, however, would make him the client of a multitude of patrons and would limit his freedom to reach out to the poor. His original statement of his position was ambiguous (1 Cor 9:18) and his enemies at Corinth found out that he was taking money from churches in Macedonia (2 Cor 11:7-11). Aware that there was some truth in the charges of dishonesty, Paul exploded with the anger of the guilty and dashed off 2 Corinthians 10–13. It is particularly in this letter that we see the quality of his rhetorical training.

Rome and Jerusalem

Before the winter of 55–56 C.E. set in Paul terminated his mission in Illyricum and undertook his promised visit to Corinth (2 Cor 12:14; 13:1). He appears to have effected a new reconciliation because Achaia came through with its commitment to the collection for the poor of Jerusalem (Rom 15:26). Nonetheless Paul decided that he had done what he could for Corinth. Henceforth he would look for new mission fields elsewhere. His choice settled on Spain, the limit of the known world (Gal 1:15; Isa 49:6). The technical term used in Rom 15:24 indicates that he wanted to be commissioned by Rome in the same way that he had once been commissioned by Antioch. The accusations of his enemies in Galatia and Corinth that he was an unrepresentative maverick had cut too close to the bone. Thus he sent Prisca and Aquila to Rome (Rom 16:3) to prepare a reception for him and to forward him some data on the composition of the community there to which he planned to write a letter.

In order to introduce himself, during the winter of 55–56 C.E. Paul wrote a letter to the Romans explaining his understanding of the relationship of Christianity to Judaism and of the process of salvation. In this sweeping document he distilled in diatribe form the insights of numerous discussions with Jewish and Gentile converts. Two points are of particular importance: his development of the concept of Sin as the false value system of society that distorts the individual (Rom 3:9) and his insight into how Law-observant Jews ultimately would be saved.

Paul had never wavered in his conviction that God could not deny God's own self and abandon the people who were divinely chosen and gifted (Rom 11:1-2). Paul recognized the truth of this in his own ministry. The book of Isaiah had always played a key role in his understanding of his apostolate to the Gentiles. He saw himself as part of the faithful remnant that proclaimed salvation to the nations, thereby fulfilling the eschatological obligation laid upon Israel (Isaiah 60). Not surprisingly it was in reading Isaiah that he realized the means whereby the Jews would be saved. In Rom 11:26, in order to support his thesis that "all Israel will be saved," he quotes "Out of Zion will come the Deliverer; he will banish ungodliness from Jacob. And this is my covenant with them" (Isa 59:20-21) "when I take away their sins" (Isa 27:9). Paul saw this as a prophecy of the parousia of Christ. The Jews, in other words, will be saved in exactly the same way as Paul was. His commitment to the Law had not only blinded him to the true role of Christ, but it had engendered bitter hostility. That attitude was changed by a completely unexpected encounter on the road to Damascus, where Christ took the initiative. So will it be for all Israel at the parousia when Christ appears in glory. Then the Jews will no more be capable of rejecting him than Paul had been.

After the dispatch of Romans in the spring of 56 C.E. Paul had to face the task of conveying the collection to Jerusalem. He was deeply apprehensive about the reception he would get (Rom 15:31) because his radical antinomianism must have been common knowledge. His letter to the Galatians certainly reached Antioch, which was in constant communication with Jerusalem. Eventually Paul became convinced that he might not escape with his life. Hence instead of going directly by ship to Palestine he made a circuit of the Aegean sea taking farewell of the communities he had founded (Acts 20:3–21:15).

In Jerusalem the community was divided on how Paul was to be received. James suggested that Paul demonstrate his acceptance of the Law by undergoing the purification required of Jews from Gentile lands who wished to enter the Temple (Acts 21:17-24). This Paul did, but he was arrested before he could present the collection. Roman intervention saved him from a Jewish mob in the Temple. On learning that Paul was a Roman citizen the tribune in Jerusalem, Claudius Lysias, transferred the responsibility to his superior in Caesarea, Felix, who had not disposed of the case when he was replaced by Festus. Eventually Paul claimed his right as a Roman citizen to be tried by the emperor and was sent to Rome (Acts 21:27–28:31).

The dating of these events is rather uncertain. According to Luke, Paul had been a prisoner for two years in Caesarea when the procurator Felix was replaced by Festus (Acts 24:27–25:1). This shift of authority is tentatively dated to 59 or 60 C.E. Hence Paul's arrest by the tribune Lysias (Acts 21:33) should be placed in 57 or 58 C.E. His transfer to Rome at his own insistence (Acts 25:11) must have occurred before the death of Festus in 62 C.E. There are no grounds to question Luke's assertion that Paul spent two years as a prisoner in Rome (Acts 28:30). Acts ends at this point.

The Last Years

What happened subsequently? The letters generally recognized as authentic are silent. Clement of Rome reports (ca. 95 C.E.) that Paul went to Spain (1 Cor 5:7) and Eusebius of Caesarea records a second imprisonment in Rome and martyrdom under Nero (*Eccl. Hs.* 2.25.8). This slight framework can be filled out if 2 Timothy is accepted as authentic, as it has every claim to be. It has been rejected not on internal grounds, but on the basis of arguments drawn from 1 Timothy and Titus in the context of an unwarranted assumption that the authenticity of the three Pastoral letters (1–2 Timothy and Titus) must be evaluated as if they were one letter!

The only place in Paul's life into which 2 Timothy can be inserted is a second Roman imprisonment (2 Tim 1:16-17). Prisca and Aquila were elsewhere when it was written (2 Tim 4:19), whereas they had been in Rome during his first imprisonment (Rom 16:3). In the interval he had enjoyed several years of freedom. The way in which Clement formulates Paul's journey to Spain makes it unlikely to be a historicization of the project laid out in Rom 15:24, 28. Indirect confirmation comes from the deterioration in Paul's relations with the Roman church. He is isolated and desperate for friendship (2 Tim 1:16-17; 4:11, 16). The most natural way in which this could have come about was a row about the Spanish mission. The Iberian peninsula was the most Romanized part of the empire, and Paul knew no Latin. To have any chance of succeeding he needed logistical, and above all linguistic support. The Roman church refused him this assistance, perhaps on the grounds that the evangelization of Spain was its responsibility or that the moment was inopportune. As Paul's ever more desperate appeals for volunteers fell on deaf ears his relations with the community soured.

Given Paul's ardent temperament, it is most probable that he pushed ahead anyway, and that he failed ignominiously. His silence now becomes understandable. The parallel with his abortive expedition into Arabia (Gal 1:17) needs no emphasis, particularly as regards the lack of planning. Where was he to go now? The only area in which he had unfinished business was Illyricum (Rom 15:19). He had been forced to break off his mission there in order to deal with the problems of Corinth. He owed the Illyrians the follow-up visit he had granted all his other foundations. If he followed his usual practice he would have spent at least a winter there before continuing east along the Via Egnatia. Second Timothy makes no mention of Thessalonica or Philippi. Paul next appears at Troas where he deposited his heavy winter cloak, books, and notebooks with Carpus (2 Tim 4:13). The great heat of summer made them an impossible burden. Subsequently he linked up with Timothy at Ephesus (2 Tim 1:18).

Beneath the surface of the letter one can detect Paul's unhappiness with Timothy's performance in Ephesus (2 Tim 1:6-7; 2:3; 4:5). As often happens, an excellent assistant proved to be an inept leader. Paul's reaction was to send him on a mission in the hinterland (2 Tim 4:12; 1:4), perhaps to Colossae or Galatia, while Paul himself took charge in Ephesus. Paul's sojourn there did not improve the situation. If "all who are in Asia . . . turned away from me" (2 Tim 1:15) he must have exacerbated whatever tensions wracked the community. There had always been opposition to Paul in Ephesus (Phil 1:14-18) and it is very likely that the church had developed in ways alien to the Pauline pattern during the seven or more years (from 54 C.E.) when Paul had been out of touch. The false teaching Paul exhorts Timothy to avoid probably reflects his personal experience at Ephesus on his last visit (2 Tim 2:14, 16, 23). It was the type of verbalism for which he had neither patience nor understanding.

Eventually Paul decided that his presence was doing more harm than good, and moved to Miletus (2 Tim 4:20). He assigned Tychicus (Col 4:7; Acts 20:4) to Ephesus where he would have the support of Prisca and Aquila (2 Tim 4:19; 1:18). Presumably Paul's intention was to reinforce the Pauline party in the church.

It is assumed by those who accept a second Roman imprisonment that it paralleled the first in that Paul was arrested in the East and conveyed to Rome under guard. A different scenario, I believe, is more compatible with the faint hints we have. Nothing in 2 Timothy insinuates that Paul was brought to Rome by force. His abandonment of Trophimus, who had come with him from Ephesus (Acts 21:29), in Miletus on grounds of illness (2 Tim 4:20) suggests that Paul left the port city in haste. There was a boat crossing to Corinth and it might be long before he found another. He lost a second companion on the other side of the Aegean sea when Erastus decided to stay in Corinth (2 Tim 4:20).

Even though no precise calculation is possible, it seems certain that Paul's abortive visit to Spain and his pastoral circle of the Aegean sea absorbed enough time to ensure that his return to Rome must have occurred after the great fire that raged in Rome for nine days (19-28 July) in 64 C.E. and destroyed ten of the fourteen quarters of the city. Rumors began to circulate that Nero had been responsible. In order to distract the mob he had Christians killed with atrocious cruelty. "Dressed in wild animals' skins, they were torn to pieces by dogs, or crucified, or made into torches to be ignited after dark as substitutes for daylight" (Tacitus, *Annals* 15.44). The news of Nero's bestial ferocity spread like wildfire through the empire. At least by the autumn of 65 C.E. it had reached the Pauline churches in Greece and Asia.

If the Roman church was to survive this vicious onslaught other communities had to come to its aid. Here we have a motive that adequately explains both the haste of Paul's departure from Miletus and the decision of Erastus to remain at Corinth; he thought the risk too great. Paul knew he was taking his life into his hands by going to Rome, but the need was imperative and he had once written "he died for all, so that those who live might live no longer for themselves, but for him who died and was raised for them" (2 Cor 5:15). To restore courage to the frightened Christians of Rome Paul was obliged to assume a rather high profile—unobtrusiveness was but a step away from apostasy—which eventually led to his arrest as a hardened criminal (2 Tim 2:9).

The latest limit for Paul's execution is the suicide of Nero on 9 June 68. The Armenian version of the *Chronicle of Eusebius* assigns the martyrdom to the thirteenth year of Nero (13 Oct. 66–12 Oct. 67), whereas Jerome's translation of the same work dates it to the fourteenth year (13 Oct. 67–9 June 68). The discrepancy may be insignificant. Those accustomed to counting in years beginning in January—as had been the case for the Romans since 153 B.C.E.—could easily be confused regarding the status of the last quarter of the year. In theory it was the beginning of the fourteenth year of imperial power, but it was the conclusion of a calendar year most of which belonged to the thirteenth regnal year of the emperor. It seems likely, therefore, that Paul died in the last quarter of 67 C.E. The manner of Paul's death, beheading (Eusebius, *Eccl. Hs.* 2.25), is understood to imply that he was condemned by a regularly constituted court. Where the execution took place and where he was buried are unknown.

BIBLIOGRAPHY

Bornkamm, Gunther. *Paul.* Translated by D. Stalker. New York: Harper & Row, 1971.

Bruce, F. F. *Paul. Apostle of the Free Spirit.* Exeter: Paternoster, 1977.

Davies, W. D. *Paul and Rabbinic Judaism. Some Rabbinic Elements in Pauline Theology.* London: Hodder & Stoughton, 1929.

Haenchen, Ernst. *The Acts of the Apostles. A Commentary.* Philadelphia: Westminster, 1971.

Hemer, Colin J. *The Book of Acts in the Setting of Hellenistic History.* Tübingen: J.C.B. Mohr, 1989.

Hengel, Martin, with R. Deines. *The Pre-Christian Paul.* London: SCM, 1991.

Hock, Ronald F. *The Social Context of Paul's Ministry. Tentmaking and Apostleship.* Philadelphia: Fortress, 1980.

Jewett, Robert. *Dating Paul's Life.* London: SCM, 1979.

Knox, John. *Chapters in a Life of Paul.* New York/Nashville: Abingdon-Cokesbury, 1950.

Légasse, Simon. *Paul Apôtre. Essai de biographie critique.* Paris: Cerf/Fides, 1991.

Lentz, John C. *Luke's Portrait of Paul.* Cambridge: Cambridge University Press, 1993.

Lüdemann, Gerd. *Paul, Apostle to the Gentiles. Studies in Chronology.* London: SCM, 1984.

Lyons, George. *Pauline Autobiography. Toward a New Understanding.* Atlanta: Scholars, 1985.

Murphy-O'Connor, Jerome. *Paul. A Critical Life.* Oxford: Clarendon, 1996.

Riesner, Rainer. *Die Frühzeit des Apostels Paulus. Studien zur Chronologie, Missionsstrategie, und Theologie.* Tübingen: J.C.B. Mohr, 1994. English: *Paul's Early Period: Chronology, Mission Strategy, and Theology.* Grand Rapids: Eerdmans, 1997.

Segal, Alan F. *Paul the Convert. The Apostolate and Apostasy of Saul the Pharisee.* New Haven and London: Yale University Press, 1990.

Taylor, Justin J. *Les Actes des deux apôtres, V. Commentaire historique (Act 9, 1-18, 22).* Paris: Gabalda, 1994.

Peter and Paul

Rudolf Pesch

Peter and Paul, whom the Church regards as princes of the apostles, together represent the unity of the Catholic Church made up of Jews and Gentiles. In the name of the one God, under the one Lord of the Church, and in the one Spirit through whom they were called, they are enduringly identified with the unanimity bestowed on the Church at Pentecost. This unanimity was carried forward by their apostolic partnership and canonized by their martyrdom.

Simon and Saul were Jewish men; in and of themselves they had little in common from a human perspective apart from the faith of Israel. The fact that they joined together in harmony on behalf of a single cause, that of Jesus of Nazareth, in order together to build up the Church as a communion of communities, the renewed people of God made up of Jews and Gentiles, is a miracle of common understanding that could never have been anticipated, but that sustains the Church even now and remains an effective impulse to Church reform.

Simon came from Galilee and was a Palestinian Jew. He was married—the gospels tell of the healing of his mother-in-law in Capernaum and legend speaks of his daughter. Saul came from Tarsus in Cilicia (now southern Turkey). He was a Jew of the Diaspora and a Roman citizen from birth; he remained unmarried.

Simon was a fisherman, Saul an artisan in leather, but the latter was also and primarily a scribe, educated by the Torah teacher Hillel in Jerusalem. Simon had learned Hebrew and Aramaic in the synagogue of his home town of Bethsaida on the northern shore of the lake of Galilee; in the streets of that somewhat Hellenized spot he may also have picked up a few words of Greek. Later, however, an old tradition tells us that he used an interpreter when he left Palestine. John Mark, who was associated with him from the earliest days of the community in Jerusalem, is supposed to have translated for him in Rome. Saul spoke Greek in Tarsus from childhood and later went beyond the synagogue to the house of studies in Jerusalem. His family bestowed on him the best education possible.

The provincial from Galilee and the world citizen from the Diaspora: here the head of a family in Capernaum who, with his brother Andrew, hoped to see renewal movements in Israel; there the strict Pharisee, the zealot for the traditions of the ancestors as they had been developed since the Exile in the scribal schools founded by Ezra. Nothing seemed to indicate that these two very different Jews would ever meet, let alone come to an understanding and work together in the same cause. And when Simon and Saul came together in the community of Jesus the Messiah as Peter and Paul, the road to agreement was still stony, rough, and weary enough—but all the more powerful in its potential.

The tombs of these two men in Rome, the one near Nero's circus on the Vatican hill, the other on the Tiber near the Porta Ostiense, became the focal point of the universal Church. The community there sees its bishop as the successor of both of them, for they were the founders of Rome's primacy in *agapē* and of the union of communities as a communion of friends who, like Jesus, surrender their lives for one another.

We can gather from the call narratives in the Fourth Gospel, which may give more accurate information than the synoptics, that Andrew, Simon's brother, had joined the reform movement of John the Baptist and met Jesus of Nazareth within the circle of John's disciples. Jesus had been baptized by John in the Jordan and in the oldest tradition he is called a disciple of John, one who "comes after John" (cf. John 1:27), that is, a student who walks behind him.

When Jesus separated from his teacher, John, whom he called the "greatest of those born of woman" (Matt 11:11) and began to work in Galilee at his own task of proclaiming the reign of God and the eschatological gathering of Israel, Andrew went with him and then brought his brother Simon as well. "We have found the Messiah" (John 1:41; cf. Matthew 16) said one brother to the other. Simon then—perhaps right away?—received the nickname "Cephas" ("Peter") from Jesus. It means a noble stone, a rock—after Easter it would become the supportive center of the new Jerusalem community, the foundation on which Jesus would build—unassailable by the gates of hell itself.

Simon may have been the first of those Jesus called to follow him and, especially in the group of the Twelve, to gather together as a new family; as such he clearly recognized that Jesus of Nazareth held the key to the definitive reform of Israel in his person, his faith, and his new theology that was a crucial corrective to that of John the Baptist. At Caesarea Philippi, at a decisive moment before the journey to Jerusalem, he acknowledged him as the Messiah. Tested by the Passion, matured by repentance after his denial, and blessed with the "protophany" (first appearance) of the Risen One, he accepted "the keys of the kingdom of heaven" (Matt 16:19): the commission and authority for the eschatological and universal gathering by which the People of God would achieve its full identity as a free community of brothers and sisters of equal dignity, chosen for universal service.

Jesus announced the good news to the poor: the reign of God is near and is now attaining its power among those who believe in him: power over the egoisms that separate and destroy, that disrupt community; power over the demons that make people ill, the idols and models of a society oriented to its own desires. Simon learned that God was fully engaged on behalf of God's people and thus for the nations of the world; as ruler of Israel, God now desires to be the Savior of the world. God is creating something new in the present moment. And for this new thing, Israel's renewal as a blessing for all nations, Simon desired to be a "fisher of people," as Jesus had promised (Mark 1:17).

What Israel had experienced and reflected on through 1,500 years of history, the words of salvation that had been given to it under the authority and in the name of Moses was enough, as Jesus explained. It only had to be carried out in confidence that the current already set in motion by God would carry the tradition along, and that this could already be experienced in following the way of Jesus. Jesus expressed this most clearly in his parable about the rich man and poor Lazarus, in which it was also evident that the proclamation of the gospel did not invalidate the Law and the prophets: "If they do not listen to Moses and the prophets, neither will they be convinced even if someone rises from the dead" (Luke 16:31).

Peter was called to follow the new path of Jesus, who came to establish a new center around which Israel would assemble. Peter's house in Capernaum, where he lived as a fisherman with his family, became Jesus' house, the base for his mission during the year, or several years, of his Galilean mission. Here he became a witness to Jesus' deeds of power, and by listening to him he became one of the crucial guarantors of the tradition of the Master's teaching.

The synoptic gospels present Peter as the first among Jesus' disciples to be called, and in all the lists of the apostles he is at the head of the Twelve whom Jesus called out from among the larger community of disciples and "created" as the center for the new gathering of Israel, its representatives and the "patriarchs" of the eschatological People of God, its "foundation stones" as is said in the vision of the new Jerusalem in the Revelation of John (cf. Rev 21:14). Jesus chose the Twelve to share their lives with him and to follow him in his mission. The narrative of the installation of the Twelve reads like a model project for the unbreakable unity of apostolic life and apostolic office (in the apostolic succession) for which the Church must continually struggle anew.

Peter appears repeatedly in the gospels and Acts as the speaker for Jesus' disciples, the

Twelve, and the initial community; he is the one who recognizes and confesses Jesus as the Messiah and the one who denies him at the crucial hour. What he, as the first among Jesus' disciples, had to learn was to think God's thoughts and not the contrary thoughts of human beings. The fact that the tradition had the courage to hand on the picture of Jesus' first disciple in such an unadorned fashion is probably due, in the first place, to the man himself.

It was through the existence and preaching of the Hellenist community, the Greek-speaking Jewish Christians around Stephen and Philip in Jerusalem that Saul came to know the Nazarene as the "Crucified One," the Messiah (about whom he had previously shared the opinion of the Temple officials: a condemned heretic, a man who led Israel astray). Jesus had been crucified by the Roman procurator at the request of the Temple officials; the title placed on his cross was "King of the Jews." The community of his followers believed that the Crucified was the true "king of the Jews," who validly represented YHWH's rule over Israel. But Paul as a persecutor of the Church may at first—as he seems to let slip in 1 Corinthians—have required people in the synagogues to say "Jesus is cursed" as a proof that they did not belong to the community of the Nazoreans (cf. 1 Cor 12:3). Only later did he understand that those who speak in the Holy Spirit can say nothing other than "Jesus is Lord" (ibid.).

Saul persecuted those who (as he at first thought) claimed to fulfill the Torah in the name of the deceiver from Nazareth but really abrogated it. They had long since adopted a "messianic" and "eschatological" interpretation of Torah that took them beyond the thought of the Pharisees, and they saw Jesus himself as *the* ultimate interpreter of Torah. At first Paul the persecutor was not in a position to recognize God's new action in Israel and the world, an act that had made "everything new" in the life of Jesus. Later, in his second letter to the community at Corinth, he wrote that he at first had known and condemned Christ "according to the flesh" (cf. 2 Cor 5:16-17)—before he himself became "a new creation" "in Christ" (that is, in his community). At that time he was one of those who, as the first letter to Timothy later said, "[desire] to be teachers of the Law, without understanding either what they are saying or the things about which they make assertions" (1 Tim 1:7). And he says of himself there: "I was formerly a blasphemer, a persecutor and a man of violence. But I received mercy because I had acted ignorantly in unbelief" (1 Tim 1:12-13).

All the more is it true for Paul that "the saying is sure and worthy of full acceptance, that Christ Jesus came into the world to save sinners—of whom I am the foremost. But for that very reason I received mercy, so that in me, as the foremost, Jesus Christ might display the utmost patience, making me an example to those who would come to believe in him for eternal life" (1 Tim 1:15-16).

In Jerusalem, Saul was first confronted with the messianic preaching of the "Hellenists" around Stephen, at whose stoning he served as a witness. Was the preaching of the Greek-speaking Jewish Christians from the Diaspora synagogues in Jerusalem not in fact an attack on the Torah and the Temple? What the "Aramaists" around Peter probably formulated more circumspectly, the Hellenists most likely said quite clearly: that the history, the life and death of Jesus had changed the meaning of Torah and Temple—not abrogated them, but transformed and gone beyond them. "More than the Temple is here" was one of the sayings they pronounced as a word from Jesus; but also "I have not come to abolish the Law and the prophets, but to fulfill them."

However, it was no longer Temple and Torah that the messianic synagogues in Jerusalem led by Peter regarded as the center of Israel; instead, it was a man who had been condemned in the name of "state and Church" and had died on the cross, of whom his followers said that he was living, that God had raised him up, and that the fulfillment of the prophetic promises to the People of God in the newly assembled community, the *ekklēsia* of God, was surety for it:

> Now the whole group of those who believed were of one heart and soul, and no one claimed private ownership of any possessions, but everything they owned was held in common. With great power the apostles gave their testimony to the resurrection of the Lord Jesus, and great grace was upon them all. There was not a needy person among them . . . (Acts 4:32-34).

What had been promised to and demanded of the *ekklēsia* of Israel at Sinai according to the covenantal declaration in the book of Deuteronomy was now being fulfilled: The community lived the great commandment, as Jesus had taught them and enabled them to do; it loved YHWH with its whole heart, soul, and strength, and for that reason there were no poor among them, the sick were healed, demons driven out, lepers brought back into the community and the dead raised, as the prophet Isaiah had promised and Jesus had commanded his disciples. The book of Acts depicts the healing power of the community, especially of the apostles, in the image of the curative shadow of Peter.

Simon and other followers of Jesus had had the courage to move the group of the Twelve (minus Judas), the women around Mary of Magdala, and soon afterward Mary, the mother of Jesus, from Galilee to Jerusalem, to bear witness there to the eschatological action of God in Israel. Simon Peter responded to God's election, which reached him definitively through the Crucified, by his exodus from the fishing village of Capernaum; in Jerusalem he became a "fisher of people," one who in the name of YHWH and the Messiah, Jesus, again cast the net to assemble Israel.

The community of one hundred twenty gathered in unanimity around Peter between the Passover feast and the first Feast of Weeks (Pentecost) after Jesus' execution. Peter interpreted recent events for them and proposed the restoration of the group of the Twelve through the election of Matthias; the fallen hut of Jacob should be restored, as James the brother of the Lord would later say at the Apostolic Council. The original community gathered around Peter and the Eleven was then, through the pentecostal Spirit, given the courage to invite all of Israel to join with them in realizing the saving history of the "New Covenant" in the universal spread of "redemption" that was now beginning.

Jesus was crucified and died on April 7 of the year 30. In that year Pentecost, the Feast of Weeks, fell on a Sabbath fifty days later; it was therefore a very special feast. While the hundred twenty in their assembly (probably in a house on Mount Zion) were celebrating the festival of the renewal of the covenant—the Torah-gift from Sinai in its spiritual power and universal validity—the Spirit-gift from the Father bestowed by their risen Lord fell on them, and they began in various tongues to praise God's wonderful works in creation and in the new creation of God's people through Jesus, the Messiah.

The many Jews from the Diaspora who came to see this, three thousand of whom were baptized, as is written, were already a sign of the universality of the "community of God" in Jerusalem. Probably Jewish pilgrims to the feast who remained in Jerusalem from Passover until the Feast of Weeks and had learned the story of Jesus from his disciples quickly began the mission in their home communities, so that Paul could soon move on to persecute the people in Damascus. The gospel was also spread by the Hellenists driven from Jerusalem after the stoning of Stephen, to which Saul had assented.

Peter by no means saw from the beginning that Gentiles also (without circumcision of males and without a comprehensive obligation to the whole Torah and all its prescriptions) could be called into the messianic community. Even though he had converted the first Gentiles, Cornelius and his household, at Caesarea Maritima, as Luke writes (Acts 10–11), Paul was ahead of him in building up the Church out of Jews and Gentiles: with new courage, deepened theological insight, refusal to compromise, and straightforwardness, as well as tireless zeal (a transferred gift from the Pharisaic tradition).

Saul, as he was called by his Jewish compatriots after the first king of Israel, or Paul, to use his name as a Roman citizen, became known as the apostle of the Gentiles, the missionary to the pagans. His conversion from bloodthirsty persecutor of the earliest communities to an apostle equal to Peter cannot be depicted in traditional categories. Paul himself declined to do so and spoke of a revelatory event rooted in God's eternal will ". . . when God, who had set me apart before I was born and called me through his grace, was pleased to reveal his Son to me . . ." (Gal 1:15-16).

Paul the outsider, the "abortion" (1 Cor 15:8) as his enemies called him, was no more expected to appear as an apostle than he had been expected earlier as a persecutor. He was introduced to the community in Damascus, and only three years later did he venture to Jerusalem to make the acquaintance of Cephas. He himself writes in Galatians that he remained fifteen days in Jerusalem and there got to know those who had been apostles before him, including Peter and James, the brother of the Lord.

Those who want to play down the importance of Paul's visit to Peter are certainly off the mark. Paul sought to associate himself with the tradition coming from Jesus himself and sustained by Peter in Jerusalem, a tradition to which Paul would later refer at important moments, e.g., when he wrote to the community in Corinth that he himself had received what he handed on to them, and then proceeded to quote the oldest "apostolic" creed (1 Corinthians 15), just as he had previously quoted the tradition of the Lord's supper (1 Corinthians 11). And certainly Paul also sought agreement with Peter himself, the first of the apostles, to whom, as Paul would later assert, the Risen One had first appeared.

We know of only two other encounters between Paul and Peter: at the "Apostolic Council" in Jerusalem and at the subsequent confrontation in Antioch, the so-called Antioch encounter.

Paul and Peter at Jerusalem had together secured the Gentile mission without circumcision and both had practiced it. The community in Antioch, which had originated in the flight of the Hellenists from Jerusalem, and whose growth had been fostered by Barnabas and Paul, had sent its two apostles as delegates to Jerusalem at the time when Peter was able to return from Rome to Jerusalem, after the death of Herod Agrippa, from whose prison he had escaped.

At Antioch, Jewish Christians from Jerusalem had provoked a quarrel over the question whether Gentiles could be received into the community of the followers of Jesus Messiah—in Antioch they were already called "Christians"—only on the condition that the men were first circumcised and that they agreed to obey the whole Torah. Chapter 15 of the Acts of the Apostles describes (probably in a redactional assimilation of two accounts, one of which told of the resolution of the later Antioch conflict through the so-called decree of James) how those responsible for the Church's beginnings were able to resolve the quarrel over the admission of Gentiles to the People of God. This was done through the interpretation of the "signs" of God's new action in recent history, something that was shown to be in full agreement with prophecy, that is, the promises of Scripture.

The handshake between Peter and Paul at the so-called Apostolic Council sealed an unplanned development that had unfolded through persecution, the flight of the "Hellenists" from Stephen's circle, and finally the conversion of Saul, the persecutor, in all of which many people had taken part; certainly Paul and Peter had played the most prominent roles, together with Barnabas and James, the brother of the Lord. They paved the way for the universal Church of Jews and Gentiles, even though they had to experience, with pain, the resistance of the majority of their own people. Paul later wrote to the community in Rome of the pain in his heart: "I have great sorrow and unceasing anguish in my heart. For I could wish that I myself were accursed and cut off from Christ for the sake of my own people, my kindred according to the flesh" (Rom 9:2-3).

Paul's new theology, which was able to interpret what was growing up in the *ekklēsia* of Jews and Christians as a working out of the action of God in the death and resurrection of Jesus, was accepted by Peter. In Jerusalem it was at first agreed that Peter would be chiefly responsible for the mission to the Jews, Paul for that to the Gentiles. But neither wanted to place limitations on his new partner, for obviously Paul continued to base his missionary activity in the synagogues, as the reports in Acts of his mission in the cities of Asia Minor and Europe show. And Peter also, at the latest with the conversion of Cornelius and his household in Caesarea Maritima (the time of which remains uncertain, as I have indicated above—before or after the Apostolic Council?) became a missionary to the Gentiles. It is true that he first had to acquire for himself the freedom that Paul claimed.

Paul was not shy about opposing Peter "to his face" (Gal 2:11) in front of the assembled community in Antioch. The former leader of the Jerusalem community had turned over leadership of that church to James, the brother of the Lord, after his own escape from King Agrippa's Jerusalem prison. After the Jerusalem agreement—at the latest—he himself, although responsible for the Jewish mission, became a missionary to the Gentiles. Back in Antioch he first bowed to the demands of emissaries from James, the Lord's brother, who wanted to separate the Jewish and Gentile Christians into different communities so that Jewish Christians could keep the purity code of the Torah and remove one of the reasons for the continuing denunciations directed at the Jerusalem community by the Diaspora Jews who asserted that the followers of Jesus Messiah were abolishing the Torah of Moses.

For Peter, loyalty to his successor in the difficult position of leadership of the Jerusalem community was especially important, for he knew that the life of the Jerusalem leaders was in constant danger; he himself had only escaped an early martyrdom there through a miracle. And later Paul himself got a whiff of the "climate" in Jerusalem when he was only rescued from a lynch mob by the intervention of the Roman soldiers in the Temple and then had to be conveyed to Caesarea Maritima by armed guards so that he would not fall victim to assassins who had sworn an oath against him, as his nephew revealed to the Roman commander in Jerusalem.

For Paul, however, Peter's anxious concern over the difficult situation of the Jewish Christians in Jerusalem was endangering the unity of the community of Jewish and Gentile Christians in Antioch, the one eschatological People of God newly won by God through the death of the Christ. For him, that was by far the greater good, because the international people of Jews and Gentiles was the proof that Christ is really "our peace," who has "broken down the dividing wall," as we read in a community hymn quoted by Paul in his letter to the Ephesians (cf. Eph 2:14-18).

The account of the conflict in Antioch that Paul gives in Galatians is only understood correctly if we read, as the result of the conflict, what Paul writes in "we"–form as a common conviction that firmly and unbreakably unites him with Peter: "we have come to believe in Christ Jesus, so that we might be justified by faith in Christ, and not by doing the works of the Law" (Gal 2:16). So Peter also says, according to the account in Acts, "we believe that we [Jews] will be saved through the grace of the Lord Jesus, just as they [Gentiles] will" (Acts 15:11).

The mutual relationship of Peter and Paul was a tension-filled combination, corresponding to the promised mutuality of lion and lamb. Three of the principal locations of the early Church—Jerusalem, Antioch, and Rome—were places where this relationship was realized, and after the martyrdom of Paul in Rome, around the year 60, and that of Peter in the same place around the year 67, the relationship of the leading apostles entered the canon through the intercession of the community there and its bishops.

The universal Church of Jews and Gentiles that grew out of the story of Jesus united Peter and Paul as the most important authorities for its New Testament canon. The gospels are under the authority of Peter, who is responsible for the story of Jesus, and in the Acts of the Apostles he is the protagonist until the Apostolic Council. Paul then, in the second part of the story of the earliest history of the Church, brings the gospel of Jesus Messiah to Rome, and in the canon this is followed by his letters, after which Peter's authority is again attested in two letters. In the second of these Paul and his letters are explicitly mentioned and defended against forgeries. Paul again presents Cephas as the responsible leader of the Jewish mission and himself as the apostle to the Gentiles: "I [was] entrusted with the gospel for the uncircumcised, just as Peter . . . for the circumcised" (Gal 2:7).

In Rome the two came together in the community to which Paul had written that he had received from Jesus Messiah "grace and apostleship to bring about the obedience of faith among all the Gentiles for the sake of his name" (Rom 1:5), and the Gentile Christians had the task of making the Jews "jealous" of the eschatologically renewed People of God (Rom 11:11), that is, attracting them to the place where the salvation of the world had become visible, where "all Israel" could be "saved" (Rom 11:26).

After his arrest in the Temple at Jerusalem, where the Romans protected him from the clutches of his zealous compatriots, and after two years of imprisonment in the Roman prefecture in Caesarea Maritima, Paul, having appealed to the emperor, was taken as a prisoner to Rome. He had often planned to visit the Christians in the capital of the world: "that I may reap some harvest among you as I have among the rest of the Gentiles. I am a debtor both to Greeks and to barbarians, both to the wise and to the foolish—hence my eagerness to proclaim the gospel to you also who are in Rome" (Rom 1:13-15). As a prisoner awaiting trial he was able to remain in his apartment, under guard, for two years, receiving visitors and so "proclaiming the kingdom of God and teaching about the Lord Jesus Christ with all boldness and without hindrance" (Acts 28:31).

Peter probably went to Rome for the first time immediately after his flight from Agrippa's prison in Jerusalem, in about the year 42. The Roman community has an old tradition of Peter's twenty-five-year episcopate in Rome.

When Paul wrote his letter to the Romans (about the year 56), and probably also when he came as a prisoner to Rome two or three years later, Peter was not there. When the community at Rome was made a scapegoat by Nero for his arson Peter seems to have escaped the pogrom, for the old legends tell how Nero's representatives crucified the apostle in Nero's absence and against his will because Nero would have preferred to torture Peter. Nero was out of the country for the last time in the year 67, attending the Isthmian games in Corinth where he appeared as a charioteer and singer. Peter is supposed to have been crucified head down, out of respect for the way his Lord died.

A quarter century later the community in Rome referred to the two apostles in a letter to the community in Corinth admonishing it to internal peace. They were not played off against each other until the modern era when the Church became divided: the "freedom" of Paul against the "office" of Peter. But for Paul and Peter freedom and unity in obedience, charism and office were never opposed.

Ignatius of Antioch wrote of the two apostles at the beginning of the second century in his letter to the Romans as united in authority and freedom: "I do not order you as did Peter and Paul; they were apostles, I am a convict; they were free . . ." (Ign. *Rom.* 4.3). The second letter of Peter has Peter speaking of "our beloved brother Paul" and "the wisdom given him" (2 Pet 3:15), and Paul himself did not permit the building up of parties through an appeal to himself or Cephas: "Now I appeal to you, brothers and sisters, by the name of our Lord Jesus Christ, that all of you be in agreement and that there be no divisions among you, but that you be united in the same mind and the same purpose. For it has been reported to me . . . that there are quarrels among you, brothers and sisters . . . that each of you says, 'I belong to Paul,' or 'I belong to Apollos,' or 'I belong to Cephas,' or 'I belong to Christ.' Has Christ been divided?" (1 Cor 1:10-13).

The unanimity of the community was also a unity with Peter and Paul, especially when a new task was given to the Church, as it was then given to Paul, and the task had to be carried out independently, as in Paul's case. Unanimity with Peter and Paul could not idly accept the initial division of the People of God, from which the apostles themselves also suffered, and it certainly could not cement it by persecuting the first persecutors. It was surely with a view to the persecutions of the Roman community by the synagogues, which were particularly strong there, that Paul wrote to the Roman Christians: "Bless those who persecute you; bless and do not curse them" (Rom 12:14).

Simon and Saul would never have come together if they had not, in complete freedom, allowed themselves to be called each by a new name and to be gathered to an eschatological work of God, the building up of the *ekklēsia* of Jews and Gentiles, the true "International" of the nations. Of this work Paul said in the synagogue in Antioch of Pisidia, with the prophet Habakkuk: "you will never believe [it], even if someone tells you" (Acts 13:41 with Hab 1:5).

Peter and Paul, if we take their witness seriously, show the Church that it only needs to take God's actions seriously and respond to them. Peter entrusted Paul with the mission to the Gentiles, as agreed, by telling him that "in the early days God made a choice among you" (Acts 15:7).

Paul knew that those who despised God's action and God's works could look, but not respond. He himself had been freed from the frozen rigor of the persecutor, and so he deprived everyone else of an excuse for refusing that freedom.

Liberation

Jon Sobrino

The Christian utopia consists of the divinization (participation in the life of God) of all that is, in order that God may come to be all in all. The personal destiny of a human being consists in being conformed to the heavenly Father, the *abba* of Jesus, and the destiny of all humanity is to make real the reign of God announced by Jesus. This eschatological utopia is also historical because it takes shape throughout an ongoing history. It is dialectical because it develops, not out of a *tabula rasa,* but against powerful forces. It is from this stance that the Christian faith may also announce its utopia as *liberation,* that is to say, as the overcoming of that which enslaves and works against divinization. Christian theology has treated this as salvation or redemption, while in Latin America especially it is treated as liberation, a concept that is more inclusive, more historical, and more biblical, in line with the Exodus event, the prophets, and Jesus.

Liberation is Historical and Social

The overwhelming fact in our world is the massive and cruel reality of injustice and oppression, leading to slow death due to poverty and violent death due to repression. This reality is historical in the sense that it is fundamentally the result of the structural configuration of the world, and it is social because it has to do not only with individuals but with entire peoples, two-thirds of humanity.

This crucified segment of humanity is *the* sign of the times that exposes the hidden truth of our world and demands a response to the plea that we take them down from the cross. It was with this view of reality that the meeting at Medellin began: "A voiceless clamor pours out of millions of human beings asking of their pastors a liberation that does not seem to come to them from anywhere" (14.2). That cry demands and indeed permits the primary and fundamental theologizing of reality in terms of liberation: "So just as the other Israel, the first people of God, experienced the salvific presence of God when he freed them from the oppression of Egypt, when he made them pass through the Red Sea and when he led them toward the Promised Land, so also we, the new people of God, cannot help but feel his healing presence when we are faced with that authentic development which, for each of us, is a passage from conditions of life that are less human to those which are more human" (*Introduction* 6).

Liberation is Integral

Christian liberation has customarily focused on (and been reduced to) the pardon of sins, to take one example; but more essential to liberation is an integral vision. So Paul speaks of liberation from sin, from death, and from the Law, as does liberation theology as well:

> Liberation is, above all, liberation from a deprivation of the basic necessities of life without whose assured satisfaction one cannot speak of human life, or, even less so, of a life worthy of the children of God. . . . Liberation is, in second place, liberation from the phantasms and realities that frighten and terrorize [humanity] . . .

> what ought to be called freedom from repression. . . . Presupposing these two liberations, but simultaneously with them, there is a kind of liberation that is as much personal as collective, viz., freedom from all kinds of dependencies . . . which militate against liberty when they are interiorized. . . . This is, finally, the liberation from one's self, i.e., from one's self as a totally absolute reality, (which one is not, of course), and which leads to possible idolatry (Ignacio Ellacuria, *Conversión de la Iglesia al reino de Dios* [San Salvador, 1985] 224–225).

This integrity or wholeness in liberation implies two important factors for faith. First, a human being is related to the totality, that is, with history as steward or sovereign, with other persons as brother or sister, and with God as child. Second, grace is connected with grace and the ethical exigency, "freed for the sake of freeing another" (Gustavo Gutierrez). Working out an integral theology from the viewpoint of liberation may mean dealing with all themes—God, Christ, Church, grace, and sin. This view holds significant possibilities for theology at large.

Liberation is Dialectical

Evil is not merely a lack of something good or the mere presence of something. Evil is a force that enslaves and produces victims. Liberation is, then, not only a matter of liberation *from,* but of liberation *against.* In history there is a struggle between God, the liberator, and the historical idols (the accumulation of riches and the doctrine of national security, in the words of Oscar Romero), between the kingdom and the anti-kingdom. Liberation presupposes struggle; it rediscovers the dialectical dimension of the prophets (against the profiteers and in favor of the orphan and widow). It also rediscovers the teachings of Jesus (the beatitudes and the curses) as well as those of John (the need to act against the evil one, the liar, and the assassin). But for that very reason liberating action leads to martyrdom beginning with the cross of Jesus unto the innumerable martyrs of today who are martyrs *in* the Church but no longer *of* the Church; they are martyrs of the reign of God, of justice, and of liberation.

Liberation Theology Focuses on the Locus of Redemption

Modern erudite theology rediscovered freedom but not liberation, even though the latter is an obvious reality in Scripture. The so-called theology of liberation has discovered liberation and the reason lies in the place where it allowed itself to be affected by reality. Just as freedom has been the important object of theology in secular societies where there is an abundance of goods, so also liberation has been discovered theologically in the world of oppression, the world of the poor and of victims.

It is in a particular social context that the sources of theology assume their determinate orientation. In the world of oppression, the necessity of liberation and its centrality in Scripture is rediscovered. If I am permitted the paraphrase, in the Third World there is a *Sitz im Leben* ("setting in life") but also a *Sitz im Tode* ("setting in death"). In the joining of the two realities what is central for Christian faith and theology is rediscovered, viz., the cruelty of oppression, the desire for liberation, the presence of God: crucified in the crucified people and liberator in their hope.

BIBLIOGRAPHY

Vatican Congregation for the Doctrine of the Faith. *Instruction on Certain Aspects of the "Theology of Liberation."* August 6, 1984. English in *Origins: NC Documentary Service* 14, no. 13 (September 13, 1984) 193–204.

Vatican Congregation for the Doctrine of the Faith. *Instruction on Christian Freedom and Liberation.* April 5, 1986. English in *Origins: NC Documentary Service* 15, no. 44 (April 17, 1986) 713–727.

To Heal and Transform: Women's Biblical Studies

Carolyn Pressler

Introduction

The emergence of feminist approaches to biblical interpretation is among the most significant developments in biblical studies today. Over the past three decades the number of interpreters reading the Scriptures explicitly from women's perspectives and for the sake of women and men's well-being has grown exponentially. Such interpreters both challenge and enrich the Church as it appropriates the Bible for its time.

Women's biblical studies are diverse and dynamic, reflecting the varying cultural, religious, and political realities of women's lives and their differing theological stances, training, and methods. Nonetheless, feminist biblical interpretations are distinguishable from traditional biblical scholarship. After briefly discussing the emergence of women's biblical studies I will attempt to sketch its distinguishing characteristics, its diversity, and its methods and contributions.

Any discussion of this multi-voiced, rapidly changing movement will necessarily be incomplete and open-ended. I wish to acknowledge three limitations of this essay. First, it focuses on Christian feminist interpretations. Second, while I have tried to take into account the global character of feminist biblical interpretation, the discussion will inevitably be shaped by my own social location, that of a North American, white, Protestant biblical studies teacher. Third, I have dealt primarily with the work of professional biblical scholars and pastors. Women in grassroots liberation movements are rereading the Bible in vigorous and powerful ways. The focus of this essay on academic and pastoral writings reflects the limits of its author and of the literature available, rather than a discounting of the significance of women's grassroots biblical interpretation.

Emergence of Women's Biblical Studies

Interpretation of Scriptures by women is not new. Women have interpreted Scriptures as long as there have been Scriptures. Even before the emergence of Israel and its sacred traditions women contributed to the compilation of the Scriptures of other cultures. A collection of hymns to her deity by the Sumerian priestess Enheduanna is believed to be the oldest known body of literature in the western world.

Miriam's song (Exod 15:21) and the Song of Deborah (Judges 5) are among the oldest passages in the Bible. Laying aside questions of historicity, these songs suggest the inclusion of women's traditions in the Bible (Brenner, 1993: 38–42). In the earliest churches the deacon Phoebe (Rom 16:1) and apostle Junia (Rom 16:7) surely interpreted and proclaimed the gospel traditions. The history of women's intellectual work in general and biblical interpretation in particular is poorly documented, but we can say with confidence that there is no time since its inception that women have not reflected on and interpreted the Bible.

Nor is it new for women to invoke the Bible from an advocacy position. Women have interpreted and challenged Scripture to assert their right to preach and speak publicly, to be educated, to lead. Kwok Pui Lan notes that Zhang

Zhujan, the first Chinese woman ever to preach from the pulpit, refuted Paul's injunction for women to remain silent in church (Kwok, 1993: 104). In the late eighteenth and early nineteenth centuries Euro-American Judith Sargent Murray bolstered her argument for girls' education with a nontraditional interpretation of Genesis 2–3 while Jarina Lee asserted her right to preach in the African Episcopal Church by arguing that the Savior had died for women as well as for men. The main roots of feminist approaches to biblical interpretation have been thoroughly grounded in political soil as women from various cultures have struggled for the right to participate fully in their communities (Gifford, 1985:11–33; Weems 1991:57–77). What is new is that women trained in biblical and theological disciplines are using their training to advocate for women.

Factors contributing to the growth of feminist interpretation differ in different parts of the globe. North American and European women (particularly white, middle-class women) have had earlier and more frequent access to graduate training, employment, and publishing opportunities. They were the first to develop sustained debate about feminist theology and biblical interpretation. British scholar Mary Grey notes three factors that contributed to the emergence of European feminist theology (Grey, 1996:102–104). The same factors fostered the development of North Atlantic feminist biblical interpretation.

First, contemporary secular women's movements raised the consciousness of women already trained and teaching in biblical studies. The earliest explicitly feminist biblical studies article, "Depatriarchalizing in Biblical Interpretation," was an effort by Phyllis Trible to "examine interactions between the Hebrew Scriptures and the Women's Liberation Movement" (Trible, 1973:30). Second, women's studies and gender studies as academic fields provided and continue to provide much of the theoretical foundation of feminist biblical interpretations. Third, the Second Vatican Council (1962–1965) served as a catalyst for several early feminist critiques of women's status in the Church. In 1964 Gertrude Heinzelman published her volume: *We Are Silent No Longer: Women Express Themselves about the Second Vatican Council* (Zurich: Interfeminas Verlag). Vatican II was also a factor leading Mary Daly to write *The Church and the Second Sex* (New York: Harper & Row, 1968).

During the 1980s feminist theology and biblical studies became more global as the work of women from Asia, Africa, and Latin America, as well as African-American, Hispanic, Asian-American, and Native American women began to be published. In 1979 Marianne Katoppo, an Indonesian scholar, published *Compassionate and Free: an Asian Woman's Theology* (Maryknoll, N.Y.: Orbis). The Asian women's theological journal, *In God's Image,* was established in 1982.

Asian, African, and Latin American feminist theologians point to the women's commission of EATWOT (the Ecumenical Association of Third World Theologians) as a decisive factor in development of feminist theologies on their continents. In 1983 women members of EATWOT organized themselves to deal with sexism of men of color and racism of white women (King, 1994:7–16). Consultations in Latin America (1985), Asia (1985), and Africa (1986) followed by an intercontinental conference in 1986 produced groundbreaking volumes of feminist theology (see NOTE at end of the bibliography).

Distinguishing Characteristics of Feminist Approaches to Biblical Interpretation

In all its rich variety, feminist biblical interpretation is distinguishable from traditional biblical studies in that it takes an advocacy stand for the survival and flourishing of all persons, particularly women. It is engaged, communal, and contextual.

Engaged

Feminist interpreters recognize that the Bible and biblical interpretation significantly shape ecclesial, social, and political relationships in large parts of the world. In the eyes of many the impact of the Bible on women has been both oppressive and emancipating but, for good or ill, it has been powerful.

Biblical interpretation is a political act. This is true whether the Scriptures are deliberately invoked for political purposes or not. The political ramifications of telling women that they cannot serve in certain positions because Jesus chose male disciples are obvious. The ramifications when preachers unintentionally depict men as God's ministers and women as recipients of ministry are equally political.

Biblical interpretation is political whether it involves logical argumentation or story and image. Carol Devens-Green analyzes nineteenth-century Christian missionary attempts to restrict the autonomy of Native American women. The missionaries invoked biblical injunctions that wives be submissive to their husbands (1 Pet 3:1-7; Col 3:1-18, Eph 5:22) to condemn the women's authority within marriage and society. They also used biblical stories and images to teach girls attitudes of humility and submission. The injunctions and the stories were equally antagonistic to Native American values (Devens-Green, 1993:130–139). Feminist interpreters have stressed that the Bible functions as powerfully when it shapes imagination as it does when it is used as a source of norms or data for constructing theological and ethical arguments.

The political nature of biblical interpretation is evident in what is not said as well as in what is said. Womanist scholar Clarice J. Martin coined the term "politics of omission" to describe the tendency of white exegetes to ignore or marginalize the presence of Africans in the Bible (Martin, 1989:105–135). Her phrase could also be used of the treatment of gender in much traditional biblical scholarship.

Whether biblical interpretation supports the well-being of women, attempts to restrict women's autonomy, or ignores women altogether, it is a political act. Feminist approaches to biblical interpretation seek to critique and resist ways in which the Bible is used to undergird female subordination and instead to interpret Scriptures in ways that heal and transform communities, explicitly including women.

Communal

Community is important as a source, methodological commitment, and goal of feminist biblical interpretation. The importance to feminists of their communities' experience as a theological source is illustrated in the report of the intercontinental conference of women theologians from the Third World: ". . . theologizing emerges as a specific manner in which women struggle for their right to life. Our theologizing arises from our experience of being discriminated against as women and as people of the Third World. . . . spiritual experience rooted in action for justice constitutes an integral part of our theology." The Bible is reread in and through their communities' struggles for liberation (Fabella, et al., 1988:186).

Working in consort with other women is an important methodological commitment for many feminist interpreters. This is striking in the work of the Women's Commission of EATWOT and in the collective interpretations of grassroots women. North American and European women's interpretation tends to be more individualistic. Even there, however, feminist theological collectives and round table discussions reflect a commitment to working communally.

The goal of feminist biblical interpretation is also communal. Mercy Oduyoye expresses this powerfully when she says that the aim of African feminist theologians is "to bring healing and transformation to our communities" (Oduyoye, 1996:112). Such healing includes, but is not limited to the healing and transformation of women and of gender relationships.

Contextual

Traditional historical critical methods of biblical study are intended to "let the text speak for itself," to ascertain as objectively as possible the history underlying a text and its meaning within that historical context. While many feminist interpreters affirm the value of the historical-critical approach they are among numerous groups of biblical critics currently challenging its presumed "value neutrality." They recognize that one's understanding of a text is integrally related to one's cultural and religious "location." What an interpreter sees, what she determines to be significant, and the models by which she orders textual and historical data are shaped by her social heritage and situation. Feminist interpreters have argued that claims of "objectivity" mask the particularity of the perspective of traditional scholarship, absolutizing the viewpoints of elite men.

Ironically the same charges of absolutizing their perspective have been rightly leveled at white North American and European women who dominated feminist biblical studies during its first decade. While their work was groundbreaking, it was flawed by a tendency to assume a nonexistent unanimity among women. Theologians from the Third World and scholars of color in North America challenge European and

Euro-American women's hegemonic claims and call for a multipronged analysis that takes into account ethnicity, class, and gender.

Diversity

The multiplicity of voices and perspectives raised in the past two decades makes it clear that feminist biblical interpreters are diverse. Discussion of their diversity for the most part has taken place along two axes: *ethnicity* and *theological stance.*

Ethnicity

The very term "feminist" for some North American women became so associated with white middle class perspectives that they developed their own terminology. African-American women have taken Alice Walker's term, "womanist," to name themselves (Walker, 1983:xi) while Hispanic theologians refer to their work as "mujerista" theology (Isasi-Diaz, et al., 1992: 105–125). Other women of color, such as African theologian Teresa Okure, continue to use the term "feminist" but fill it with their own content (Okure, 1993:76–85).

Womanist biblical scholar Renita Weems notes that the perspective of African-American women is shaped both by the multiple oppressions under which they live and by their heritage of a dynamic, critical approach to the Bible. African-American women were first introduced to the Bible via the preaching of slaveholders, which had its own definite agenda: inculcating submission. Slave women and men remembered and reappropriated the biblical stories to serve their own interests. According to Weems that history is reflected in suspicion of and resistance to interpretations antagonistic to black women and by freedom to retell biblical stories dynamically (Weems, 1991:57–77).

Euro-American feminist interpreters, by contrast, are often more bound to the biblical text, a characteristic that fosters precision but can create problems in its lack of flexibility. Belonging to the dominant race, class, and nation, Euro-American and European feminists have the dangerous luxury of ignoring those factors. At the same time their privileged status has granted them more access to academic arenas, enabling them to press the issue of gender.

Ada María Isasi-Diaz describes Hispanic women as heirs of a Christianity influenced by the Catholicism of the conquistadors in which the Bible had little role. Moreover, she asserts, they distrust a source that is too complicated to be understood easily and is therefore liable to be controlled by others. Isasi-Diaz believes that it is important to the survival of Hispanic women for them to learn to use the Bible, but acknowledges that it is not a large part of their heritage (Isasi-Diaz, 1990:261–69).

The final report of the Intercontinental conference sponsored by the women's commission of EATWOT identified main characteristics of women theologians working in Latin America, Africa, and Asia and articulated differences in the particular shapes of their struggles:

> In Latin America, women organize themselves around survival strategies. In Africa, the rebirth of women takes place in their struggle to overthrow the oppressive elements in traditional African cultures and religions and the evils of colonialism. In Asia, the struggle is centered in rediscovering the pride of being women, in building womanhood and humane communities, and in fighting against political, economic, and sexual injustices (Fabella, et al., 1988:186).

Recognition of the rich and varied contexts from which women interpret the Scriptures calls for an inductive, open-ended approach to others' interpretive work, attending to the integrity of genuinely differing readings.

Theological Spectrum

Women's varying critiques of the Bible and understandings of its authority form a wide theological spectrum. On one end of the spectrum are Evangelical feminists who hold that the Bible is the authoritative word of God in all matters, and believe that the Bible itself expresses God's will for women's well-being and equality. The problem, in their view, is not inherent in the text but stems from a long history of sexist misinterpretation and misuse of the Scriptures. At the other end of the spectrum are those who hold that the Bible is irredeemably misogynist and reject its authority for theology or spirituality. If they study the Bible at all they do so only to unmask its antagonism toward women.

Many, perhaps most feminist biblical interpreters view the Bible as oppressive of women and yet a source of liberating visions. The task of this last group of women is to hold in coherent tension critical appraisal of biblical values and stories that support male domination and constructive appropriation of its emancipatory themes and elements. That tension has generated a sustained debate about the locus and nature of authority. Many frankly identify the experience of their community as the primary locus of authority. Others understand the relationship between the authority of the Bible and that of their community dialogically. Euro-American theologian Rosemary Radford Ruether identifies a biblical prophetic-messianic principle that she correlates with women's experience (Ruether, 1983:12–46). Katharine Doob Sakenfeld locates authority "neither in the text or in the history that produced the text, but where *God is at work* in the whole life of the believing community, including its text production and its ongoing reflection on its texts" (Sakenfeld, 1989:166).

How to negotiate among different interpretations is a pressing question for feminist interpreters and, indeed, for the field of biblical studies in general. Given the multiplicity of interpretations, is it possible to exclude some and prioritize others? Feminist biblical scholars answer this question partly by affirming traditional criteria: that the interpretation take adequately into account textual and historical data; that it be coherent and consistent. In part they assess interpretations using ethical criteria. Those interpretations that support the powerful against the powerless are excluded, while those that enable the powerful to relinquish power and empower the most oppressed are granted priority.

The goal of dialogue is not to arrive at a richer approximation of *the* textual meaning, but rather to clarify and even sharpen differences in order to articulate varying positions in a more complex and nuanced way. Biblical teachers and scholars have a responsibility to explicate the different factors that make seemingly contradictory interpretations appropriate to their communities, not necessarily to resolve them.

Feminist Biblical Interpretation: Approaches and Contributions

Critique and Construction

For those who find the Bible both oppressive and liberating, the task of feminist interpretation has two prongs: *critique* and *construction.* The critical dimension involves analyzing ways in which the Bible functions to reinforce gender, racial, cultural, and economic domination of persons and peoples. Feminists investigate the presuppositions, methods, and conclusions of traditional interpretation as those serve to reinforce male dominance and female submission; they also critically examine the values and presuppositions of the biblical texts themselves as they relate to gender, race, and class.

Key terms used by feminist critics include "patriarchy" and "androcentrism." "Patriarchy," a term defined in various ways, may be understood as a hierarchically structured society in which power and status are determined by a number of factors including class, ethnicity, generation, and gender. In patriarchal society a woman in certain categories (e.g., mother, slaveowner) may have power over men in other categories (e.g., son, bondsman) but has less power and status than her male counterpart (e.g., the mother has less status than the father). "Androcentrism" refers to a perspective in which "male" is assumed to be normative.

The Scriptures are patriarchal to the extent that they reinforce the subordination of women and marginalized men, enjoining their submission (examples include the "household codes"), or uncritically narrating stories in which women are objectified or violated (for example, the story of "righteous" Lot offering his daughters to be raped). They are androcentric to the extent that they assume male agency and a male audience ("You shall not covet your neighbor's wife." "And those who ate were about five thousand men, besides women and children."). The critique is not limited to issues of gender. Feminists and womanists also analyze ethnocentric and religiously exclusivistic dimensions of the Scriptures and hierarchical or violent biblical concepts of power.

Engaging in the constructive dimension of feminist biblical studies, interpreters seek evidence of women's agency in Israel, early Judaism, and the early churches and lift up stories of powerful and godly women that can serve to subvert patriarchy in both biblical text and contemporary culture. They highlight narratives that portray human relationships characterized by mutuality and caring and find courage in stories of human resistance to oppression and in portrayals of God that emphasize divine vulnerability and divine commitment to the oppressed.

Specific Approaches

Feminists bring an array of methodologies to both the critical and the constructive dimensions of the interpretive task. Feminist biblical historians use historical-critical, anthropological, sociological, and archaeological methods to reconstruct the agency and oppression of women in ancient Israel, early Judaism, and the New Testament churches. Elisabeth Schüssler Fiorenza, an extremely influential biblical historian, finds evidence that in the telling and retelling of Christian traditions pressures to conform to the larger patriarchal culture erased stories of women's participation in the earliest churches. Drawing on the traces of female leadership that remain in biblical and extra-biblical sources, Schüssler Fiorenza reconstructs early Christianity as a pluralist and egalitarian movement (Schüssler Fiorenza, 1983).

Feminists use "new" literary and old storytelling methods to uncover androcentric values, identify women's genres, seek submerged female voices in the biblical texts, and call attention to neglected female images of God as Nurse, Housekeeper, and especially Mother and Wisdom Woman. Perhaps the most prevalent feminist interpretive method has been to retell stories of biblical women that have been neglected or distorted by traditional biblical scholarship. Stories of biblical heroes, leaders, prophets, and wise women provide models of women who can serve as a source of hope and provide a sense of heritage. A study of the Magnificat (Luke 1:26-55) by Ethiopian Coptic women illustrates the power of biblical models of women to evoke courage and the power of grassroots women to offer important insights to the Church. They see Mary as one like them, a refugee who fled to save her baby, a mother who watched the murder of her son. Young, unknown, the poorest of poor, she, like them, asks for justice, takes risks, and proclaims the reversal of the social order (Assaad, 207–208). Feminist interpreters also retell stories of biblical women whose lives reflect the suffering of contemporary women or conflict between women. Such stories call on women and men to understand, mourn, repent, and resist the violence that patriarchy inflicts.

Yet another method feminists use is to set in conversation biblical stories or practices on the one hand, and stories and practices indigenous to their own cultures on the other. Kwok Pui Lan, stressing the new and creative thought required to bridge the gap between stories from widely differing cultures, calls this process "dialogical imagination" (Kwok, 1989:30–34).

The theological articulation of liberating biblical dynamics, visions, and themes has been an important approach for many feminists. They point to the biblical assertion that female no less than male is created in the image of God, to the picture of a liberating God who hears the cry of the poor and accompanies them on their journey, to visions of a reign of justice when there will be neither male nor female, and especially to the teaching and praxis of Jesus who, in the words of Mercy Amba Oduyoye, is friend, healer, advocate, source of transformation, and breaker of boundaries (Oduyoye, 1996:113). These themes energize women's struggles and serve as norms by which to critique patriarchy in the Bible and in contemporary culture.

In addition to explicating particular biblical passages or themes, feminist biblical interpreters focus much attention on hermeneutics, that is, the theoretical bases for interpreting the Scriptures. Such reflections ask how the Bible is and should be appropriated by communities of struggle and faith. Feminist biblical interpreters have barely begun another important task, that of investigating the histories of women's biblical interpretation.

These approaches are not mutually exclusive. The tasks of rereading the Bible in ways that support the wholeness of women and the "healing and transformation" of communities are huge. The myriad insights and vigorous debate of feminists working from their many contexts and using a wide range of approaches are needed.

BIBLIOGRAPHY

Assaad, Marie. In Ursula King, ed., *Feminist Theology from the Third World: A Reader* (Maryknoll, N.Y.: Orbis, 1994) 204–206.

Baker-Fletcher, Karen. "Anna Julia Cooper and Sojourner Truth: Two Nineteenth-Century Black Feminist Interpreters of Scripture," in Elisabeth Schüssler Fiorenza, ed., *Searching the Scriptures.* Vol. 1: *A Feminist Introduction* (New York: Crossroad, 1993) 41–51.

Brenner, Athalya, and Fokkelien Van Dijk-Hemmes. *On Gendering Texts: Female and Male Voices in the Hebrew Bible.* Leiden: Brill, 1993.

Craven, Toni. *Artistry and Faith in the Book of Judith.* Chico, Cal.: Scholars, 1983.

Devens-Green, Carol. "Native American Women, Missionaries and Scriptures," in *Searching the Scriptures 1* (1993) 130–139.

Fabella, Virginia, and Mercy Amba Oduyoye, eds. *With Passion and Compassion: Third World Women Doing Theology.* Maryknoll, N.Y.: Orbis, 1988.

Fabella, Virginia, and Sun Ai Lee Park, eds. *We Dare to Dream: Doing Theology as Asian Women.* Maryknoll, N.Y.: Orbis, 1989.

Fewell, Danna Nolan, and David N. Gunn. *Gender, Power and Promise.* Nashville: Abingdon, 1993.

Gifford, Carolyn De Swarte. "American Women and the Bible: The Nature of Woman as a Hermeneutical Issue," in Adela Yarbro Collins, ed., *Feminist Perspectives on Biblical Scholarship* (Chico: Scholars, 1985) 11–33.

Gilkes, Cheryl Townsend. "'Mother to the Motherless, Father to the Fatherless': Power, Gender, and Community in Afrocentric Biblical Tradition," *Semeia* 47 (1989) 57–85.

Grey, Mary. "Feminist Theologies, European," in Letty M. Russell and J. Shannon Clarkson, eds., *Dictionary of Feminist Theologies* (Louisville: Westminster/John Knox, 1996) 102–104.

Isasi-Diaz, Ada María. "The Bible and Mujerista Theology," in Susan Thistlethwaite and Mary Potter Engle, eds., *Lift Every Voice: Constructing Christian Theologies from the Underside* (San Francisco: Harper & Row, 1990) 261–269.

____. *En La Lucha (In the Struggle): Elaborating a Mujerista Theology.* Minneapolis: Fortress, 1993 (= 1993a).

____. "La Palabra de Dios en Nosotras: The Word of God in Us," in *Searching the Scriptures 1* (1993) 86–97 (= 1993b).

Isasi-Diaz, Ada María, et al. "Mujeristas—Who We Are and What We Want," *JFSR* 8/1 (1992) 105–125.

King, Ursula, ed. *Feminist Theology from the Third World: A Reader.* Maryknoll, N.Y.: Orbis, 1994.

Kwok Pui Lan. "Discovering the Bible in the Non-Biblical World," *Semeia* 47 (1989) 30–34.

____. "Racism and Ethnocentrism in Feminist Biblical Interpretation," in *Searching the Scriptures 1* (1993) 101–116.

Martin, Clarice J. "A Chamberlain's Journey and the Challenge of Interpretation for Liberation," *Semeia* 47 (1989) 105–135.

Meyers, Carol. *Discovering Eve: Ancient Israelite Women in Context* (New York and Oxford: Oxford University Press, 1988).

Newsom, Carol A., and Sharon H. Ringe, eds. *The Women's Bible Commentary* (Louisville: Westminster/John Knox, 1992).

Oduyoye, Mercy Amba. "Feminist Theology, African," *Dictionary of Feminist Theologies* (1996) 112–114.

Okure, Teresa. "Feminist Interpretations in Africa," in *Searching the Scriptures 1* (1993) 76–85.

Pobee, John S., and Bärbel Von Wartenberg-Potter, eds. *New Eyes for Reading: Biblical and Theological Reflections by Women from the Third World* (Geneva: World Council of Churches, 1986).

Ruether, Rosemary Radford. *Sexism and God-Talk: Toward a Feminist Theology* (Boston: Beacon, 1983).

Sakenfeld, Katharine Doob. "Feminist Biblical Interpretation," *Theology Today* 46 (1989) 154–168.

Schüssler Fiorenza, Elisabeth. *In Memory of Her: A Feminist Theological Reconstruction of Christian Origins* (New York: Crossroad, 1983).

Tamez, Elsa, ed. *Through Her Eyes: Women's Theology from Latin America* (Maryknoll, N.Y.: Orbis, 1989).

Trible, Phyllis. "Depatriarchalizing in Biblical Interpretation," *JAAR* 41 (1973) 30–48.

____. *God and the Rhetoric of Sexuality* (Philadelphia: Fortress, 1978).

____. *Texts of Terror: Literary-Feminist Readings of Biblical Narratives* (Philadelphia: Fortress, 1984).

Walker, Alice. *In Search of Our Mother's Gardens: Womanist Prose* (New York: Harcourt Brace Jovanovich, 1983).

Weems, Renita. "Reading *Her Way* Through the Struggle: African American Women and the Bible," in Cain Hope Felder, ed., *Stony the Road We Trod: African American Biblical Interpretation* (Minneapolis: Fortress, 1991) 57–77.

____. *Just a Sister Away: A Womanist Vision of Women's Relationships in the Bible* (San Diego: LuraMedia, 1988).

NOTE: Elsa Tamez, ed., *Through Her Eyes: Women's Theology from Latin America* (Maryknoll, N.Y.: Orbis, 1989); Virginia Fabella and Sun Ai Lee Park, eds., *We Dare to Dream: Doing Theology as Asian Women* (Maryknoll, N.Y.: Orbis, 1989); Virginia Fabella and Mercy Amba Oduyoye, eds., *With Passion and Compassion: Third World Women Doing Theology* (Maryknoll, N.Y.: Orbis, 1988).

Family: An African Perspective

Mercy Amba Oduyoye

Family Structures and Ideals

The images evoked by the word "family" are many. It has never been a simple construct to define and now has become even more complex. The social sciences have worked with two main paradigms, the narrow definition of husband, wife, and unmarried children labeled "nuclear family" and the broader one of several generations and several nuclear families grouped together in a community dubbed "extended family." Families are made up of persons related by blood or affinity. Hence married persons belong to their blood or natal family as well as the family of affinity. Marriage results in a network of relationships: the members of the spouse's family are now one's in-laws. In Africa all in-laws are considered allies of one's family. These alliances as well as the phenomenon of household workers and live-in partners, apprentices, and guests broaden relationships within a family even further. The primeval family of mother and child is lodged firmly in shared life, womb and breast and blood, just as in the nuclear family naming and genealogy highlights the parenthood of the male progenitor, the father whose biological role science has helped to clarify. It takes a minimum of two persons to create a family. This makes relationship and relating to the other key in the meaning of family.

Families may have a common domicile called home or they may live in a single household, but they may not. What counts is the sense of belonging and the mutual caring and sharing. The family unit is a microcosm of the human community; it embodies the past and the future, the young and the old, female and male. A family is composed of individuals and yet it is one as a corporate body. Family is created by nature/biology and managed by culture: approved ways of the community in the sense both of the narrow community (that is, the family itself) and that of the wider community extending to the village, nation, and even the global community. Among one's kin one operates with a great deal of freedom and yet the bonds of restriction are never absent.

A family operates as a support unit that one can expect to be unfailing because of the covenantal relationships at its foundations. Yet this ideal is often shattered by quarrels and confrontations. For Africans family cannot be dissolved. Conflict in human relations is to be expected, just as the teeth and the tongue occupying the same space do quarrel but stay together and work together. Provision for making this promise of unity a reality is to be found in rituals of reconciliation that abound in African religious culture. Community cohesion and well-being are actively promoted; nevertheless, personal inclinations are not to be trampled on or taken for granted. A family incorporates both life and death. In a family opposites are held in tension and differences are viewed as opportunity for a diversity of contributions. For this reason family has become a symbol and a metaphor for understanding other human communities.

Patriarchal definitions of family yield paradigms like monogamy (one man with one wife) or polygyny (polygamy in which there is one man with more than one wife concurrently) living in one household or in dispersed domiciles. (The definitions are patriarchal because the crux is the man, the distinction depending on whether he has one wife or many.) Whatever form family takes, all cultures have definite paradigms for what constitutes a family unit.

Organization

Family is associated with words like mother, father, siblings, children, ancestors, and servants: terms that define human relations within a family. It is reasonable to assume that the original nuclear family was mother and child—the roots of matriarchy that gave way to patriarchy as human beings began to understand the role of the male in procreation. The mother-centered definition of a family that guides the Akan culture, while honoring fathers, posits that a person's social status derives from the mother who alone transmits blood, the life of a human being. Patriarchy gives the father not only the honor of being the source of life and naming but also the power to create the family unit; it is he who acquires a wife to procreate in his name and in some cultures even "pays" for her. (See Gen 31:15 for the *mohar,* or bride-price paid for Rachel and Leah; this corresponds to the African *lobola.*) In Africa the exchange of gifts and visits is the beginning of the alliance of families that a marriage initiates, a kinship, a network that contributes to the web of relationships among lineages that together makes up the African family.

The family as a social unit presents a variety of faces but its *raison d'être* has not been questioned. Whatever its structure, family is the context of much personal ritual surrounding marriage, birth, and death. These rituals, often featuring communal meals, make the family a religious unit. Rituals expand the family to include previous members now dead, the ancestors, and future generations yet to be born. Family members in Africa see themselves in the context of both their ascendants and descendants. Family does not function without friction: hence the evolution of rituals of arbitration and reconciliation. The rituals involved in all these events are passed on from generation to generation, creating a family religion that in some cultures develops its own symbols of altars, *teraphim* ("household gods," cf. Gen 31:19, 31) or ancestral pots as among the Igbo of Nigeria. Cemeteries and burial grounds become holy ground for the living. For some they are a reminder that the spirits of the physically departed are among us. These and other material possessions of the family unit may generate friction among its members as they confer power on the custodian.

Participation

Role assignments in a family tend to be regulated by the wider culture; hence to be a wife, a husband, a child, or a servant has implications beyond the family unit. Ancestors (ascendants) are venerated in many cultures, in some more than others. In Africa's Cosmic Religion there is a certain tension between the divinities and the ancestors since both are conceived as agents of the Supreme Being, God. Among the Urhobo (Nigeria) the divinities are not as prominent as the ancestors because the ancestors are said to be the agents of God *par excellence,* the intermediaries between humans and God. They participate fully in all aspects of family life and can reenter it physically as newborn babies.

Children are desired to ensure the continuity of the family and for the sustenance of the aged and their burial when the time comes for them to return to the ancestors. African resistance to the culture of family planning and infanticide has its roots here. Childlessness is a horror. Giving birth is the closest humans come to "creating" life and they desire to see that life mature; maltreatment of infants is therefore regarded as unnatural. Children are to be nourished and cared for till maturity. In Africa maturity is marked by mating rituals and family education in anticipation of the new birth that will replace the inevitable death of the aged.

Maturity brings one into the status of wife or husband. A mature man is expected to be husband and father and a mature woman should become wife and mother. In the prepatriarchal family age was a key determinant in power relations; older women were more respected than younger men. Moreover, a woman in a matrilineal society acquires a partner and collaborator when she marries. Patriarchy has changed this. Fathers have arrogated to themselves the status of sole head of the family, while brothers are one step above sisters in the hierarchy of power.

This situation is now portrayed as ordained by nature and by God. It is reflected in the symbolic uses of the family construct, as in the Hebrew analogy of the relation between Israel and YHWH. The challenges of the global women's movement may yet change this face of the family and transform it so as to eliminate patriarchy.

In some cultures the status of children as minors often includes exploitation and violation in the name of discipline and socialization. Contemporary sensitivities are challenging this view of children, making parents uncertain of their roles. The preference for boys over girls in some cultures is also being challenged. African Christians, like Christians everywhere, read into and out of the Bible many of the characteristics of the family as they themselves experience it.

The Family and the Bible

According to the Hebrew worldview the institution of marriage that creates families was inaugurated with the creation of a primordial heterosexual couple. They made up a family both monogamous and nuclear and produced two sons whose sibling rivalry resulted in fratricide. We are also presented with examples of "extended families" in the stories of Noah and of Abram and Lot with their households. Biblical families were polygamous, but prophetic reformers began to model marriage on the relationship between YHWH and Israel. This is a paradigm that favors monogamy and aligns with the meaning and implications of the Genesis stories of the creation of woman and man. (However, it has a distinct patriarchal bias.) In most parts of Africa polygyny continues side by side with monogamy. Polyandry (in which a woman has several husbands) is hardly known except where women "marry" other women for the purpose of acquiring progeny. The European and American Christian missions to Africa insisted that monogamy is the norm for Christianity. For African Christians both the Bible and African culture give mixed messages on this matter.

The Bible provides instances of the challenges of polygynous marriages without condemning the system itself. As all this is familiar to Africans and to Islamic communities there is a tendency to seek the support of the Bible and the Qur'an to back this age-old practice. Family organization and relationships in the Hebrew Bible provide a vivid illustration of how Africans have legitimized the practice of resorting to the Bible as if it were an archetype of divinely accepted behavior and a paradigm for the organization of human communities and relationships. There are instances in which polygyny has been found even where it is not intended, as in Eph 5:25: "Husbands, love your *wives* . . . ."

In the NT the family *par excellence* is that of Joseph, Mary, and their children. The nuclear family seems to be the norm although there are other households. From the NT Christianity has developed a marriage ceremony that is a supreme example of being unequally yoked, but that claims to be biblically based. It flies in the face of the discipleship of equals that one senses here and there in the Christian Scriptures. Galatians 3:28 and other egalitarian texts have been downplayed in favor of more androcentric passages now called "household codes" that describe the norms of Roman society of the early centuries of the Christian era with its patriarchal organization and male headship. (Examples include Eph 5:24-33; 1 Cor 11:3-10.) Such texts represent a changing social situation and are therefore unworthy of being set forth as unbending archetypes. For example, in such codes any concept of reciprocity in relations between spouses and between parents and children is often ignored (cf. Col 3:19-22).

Household slavery is legally over and few families can afford servants; the household codes in this respect offer little guidance concerning justice and companionship in human relations. Rather than operate as guidelines to promote solidarity of the family unit, they have become tinder for divorce as women reject the patriarchy that renders them anonymous appendages of a man's self-definition. Biblical language about marriage suggests that the wife, like the household slave, is the possession of the husband, who is the founder and owner of the family. This concept of family upholds the global system of patriarchy and is heightened by the provisions for divorce and advice concerning sexual abstinence in both testaments (see Num 30:1-15; 1 Corinthians 7). The covenant between spouses as an ideal for marriage is rendered problematic by the household codes: this constitutes a serious difficulty for the application of biblical teaching to the institution of the family in modern society. A second family-related issue that is problematic in the Christian Testament is divorce, to which we now turn.

Divorce

Whereas the African extended family cannot be dissolved, the nuclear family can. In Deut 24:1 we find the stipulation that a husband can issue a wife a bill of divorce. The reverse is not envisaged. It is always assumed that the wife is in the wrong (Isa 50:1; Jer 3:8). Matthew 5:31-32 gives an indication that this practice was in operation among the Jews in the NT period.

On the subject of divorce, once again both the Bible and African culture give a mixed response, and various Christian communities take varying attitudes toward the problem. This is further complicated by differences in national laws. In all cases, however, divorce is not an ideal; it is undesirable, but when it has to be, people take the step and then try to rebuild their lives as best they can. Affinal relations can break up, but kinship is by nature indissoluble. "Divorce does not destroy a nation," says an Akan adage.

In the biblical texts of both testaments the consequences of divorce for marriage and the institution of the family are not discussed; hence the callous way in which European and American missionaries to Africa tried to deal with polygyny in Africa by asking that wives be divorced before men could obtain full membership in the Christian community and the resistance of Africans to this solution. The anomaly of a religion that promotes family but causes the disruption of families has not escaped the African. According to Matt 5:31 the Church turned many wives into prostitutes by this demand (cf. Matt 19:9) while society made adultery a woman's crime (Mark 10:11-12; Luke 16:18). Completely discounting Mal 2:14, which counsels against dealing treacherously with the wife of one's youth, most of the divorce texts in both testaments are wholly androcentric.

Family as Symbol

The complex interpersonal relations in families make them a rich source of symbolism and paradigms. The family exhibits characteristics that we look for when human beings come together for a common purpose. People in community covenant together on the model of marriage. Persons with a common worldview and similar lifestyles come together. They grow together around their ideas and ideals. The community they create then binds them together in a discipleship of mutual sharing and caring. Families are organic, growing and adapting to new situations and the arrival of new members. In a family one expects the participation of all members according to their abilities. Family well-being and cohesion challenge all to mutuality in sharing, supporting, and caring. The weakest and most vulnerable receives the most attention. This interrelationship is facilitated by constant and open communication and a determination to uphold one another.

Both the material culture and the symbolic universe of a family serve this mutuality and cohesion and give a solid base from which to launch out in relationship to other individuals and other families. Extended families and kin groups provide models for how communities nurture and shape their members. Family supplies one with a name and gives one an identity that is distinctive. A family provides its members with the parameters of behavior and shapes their attitudes. Human collectivities are humanizing when they operate as a family does. Corporately they build up a group identity as well as shaping the individual members.

The extended family is a porous, flexible circle, expanding to include new arrivals: wives, husbands, servants, and guests. It is constantly renewing itself by making room for the new that comes with these persons while at the same time conscientiously passing down the cherished traditions of the past. This makes a family a very apt symbol of the dynamism of human relations and communities. The family is therefore a unit for education, not only teaching its own history and culture but socializing the young for harmonious and positive living within the wider community. It is an economic unit, a household, an *oikos,* managing its own estate and the well-being of its members as God does the whole universe and as the Church is meant to do for the whole Christian community.

Justice, Work, and Poverty

Enrique Nardoni

Justice, work and poverty are three significant concepts in the Bible. Justice is frequently associated with poverty, but work is—surprisingly—less often connected with justice and poverty. Because of the diversity of connections this article treats first the concepts of justice and poverty and then that of work.

Justice and Poverty

The concern for justice on behalf of the poor is not native to Israel. It goes back to the ancient Near Eastern cultures. Particularly important in this regard is the concept of justice in ancient Mesopotamia, a concept associated with the order established by divine power. Doing justice to a person was not only giving her what she deserved because of her achievement but also restoring her to the position she was designed to have in the society according to the divine will. Therefore in addition to commutative or distributive justice there was a liberating or restoring justice. The liberating justice occurred in the care shown by the king toward the poor, widows, orphans, and in the edicts of amnesty that the king periodically issued canceling debts or obligations, including restitution of confiscated property and manumission of slaves.

In ancient Israel the idea of liberating justice was applied first of all to the action of God toward Israel. The saving justice of God liberated Israel from Egyptian slavery in accordance with the order established by the promises given to the ancestors (Exod 6:6-8). The liberating deed of the Exodus became a paradigm of salvation because it assured the presence of the Creator in history on behalf of the chosen people. Second Isaiah and the psalmist refer to it when they ask God to liberate Israel from the Babylonian captivity (Isa 51:9-11; Ps 74:11-13). The concept of liberating justice has been expressed in the OT by the association of "justice" *(mishpat)* and "righteousness" (*ṣedeq* or *ṣedaqâ*) with "loving kindness" *(ḥesed)* and "faithfulness" *(ʾemet)*. (See Pss 89:14; 33:4-5; 37:28; 101:1; Jer 9:24; Mic 6:8; Hos 12:6. In the NT see especially Rom 1:17; 3:21-26.)

The liberation of Israel as an act of justice animated by compassion has been a foundational motivation for human relations inside the community. Thus the Book of the Covenant (Exod 20:22–23:33) demands compassion for the poor, the widow, the orphan, and the foreigner resident in the land. The motivation given is the compassion that God showed toward Israel when it was a foreigner in Egypt (Exod 22:21; 23:9). Deuteronomy, in addition to going deeply into the concern for the poor, the widow, the orphan, and the foreigner, extends the same compassion to the Levite in the land. This book exhorts the community to allow the poor to share the richness of the land.

The prophets were the social conscience of the nation in the name of the Lord, the God of the covenant. Their intervention in the social life became more prominent from the eighth century, when the differentiation of social classes increased substantially. They were the defenders of the poor and oppressed. Well known in this regard are the indictments of Amos and Hosea against Samaria. Amos, in the name of the Lord, rebuked the rich of Samaria because they sold the needy "for a pair of sandals" (Amos 2:6), and criticized their worship because of their lack of concern for the poor (5:21-24). In the name of the Lord Hosea entered a lawsuit against Israel. A basic charge was the breaking of social justice (Hos 4:1-4). Isaiah in Jerusalem echoed the social justice critiques of Amos and Hosea. For Isaiah, to do good is to "seek justice, rescue the oppressed, defend the orphan, plead for the widow" (Isa 1:16-17). Jeremiah took up from the former prophets the criticism of worship and the suit of the Lord against his own people. He predicted the destruction of Jerusalem, particularly on account of the social injustices of its inhabitants (Jer 7:5-6).

The punitive justice of God was not final in history, for once Israel suffered the punishment, God took the initiative to show the divine saving justice by liberating Israel from its oppressive enemies. Thus second Isaiah issued his oracles in which justice is parallel to salvation. "Let the skies rain down righteousness *(ṣedeq);* let the earth open, that salvation *(yesaᶜ)* may spring up, and let it cause righteousness *(ṣedaqâ)* to sprout up also" (Isa 45:8). The same concept of liberating justice animates the mission of the third Isaiah (Isa 61:1-2), and this writing was issued to inspire the observance of ethical obligations toward the afflicted.

The poor of the Psalms are the people who on the one hand suffer human injustice and oppression, and on the other hand trust deeply and experience gratefully the saving justice of God. In the Psalms anyone was poor who at the socio-economic level was weak, exploited, or oppressed by the rich or the powerful in the society. They did not have the resources to defend themselves from the exploitation and oppression of the powerful and rich whose goal was to accumulate power and wealth. But they did have the resources of their trust in the Lord (Pss 35:10; 37:5-6).

The book of Proverbs approaches poverty from another angle. Unlike the prophets who criticize the rich vehemently and see poverty as the result of injustice, the book of Proverbs has a different perspective: it stresses the responsibility of the people, emphasizing that one of the causes of poverty is laziness (Prov 10:4; 14:23; 21:5; 24:33-34). This book rarely issues a condemnation against the rich for exploiting the poor. In this regard Job is different. He sees poverty as one great example of injustice in the world (Job 24:2-12). Ecclesiastes in turn thinks that poverty and social injustice are endemic to this world (Eccl 5:7-8). All these sapiential books, although each has a different perspective, encourage the practice of philanthropic help.

Wisdom of Solomon introduces a new ingredient in the question of justice for the poor and the oppressed. It expresses a strong hope that the oppressed righteous will be rewarded with the immortality of the angels and from heaven will guide the people on earth to make a better humanity (Wis 3:7-8). A similar concept of the vindication of oppressed people is present in the apocalyptic literature such as the book of Daniel (12:1-3).

The NT stresses the saving justice of God that liberates the human being from the powers of this world (sin in all its dimensions, and death and its result) and transfers it to the divine realm. However, while stressing full redemption in the afterlife it does not leave aside the present world. It underlines the creation of a new community that anticipates the values of the eschatological world. It stresses the equality of all people, the responsibility of mutual service, and the obligation of compassionate and active love toward the needy. Christians have to imitate God's compassion, which restores humans to the position they are called to have according to God's merciful plan (Matt 18:32-33). Christians are required to serve Christ who identifies himself with the poor, the sick, the needy, and the rejected (Matt 25:40, 45). They are exhorted to follow the behavior of the good Samaritan (Luke 10:29-37) and are instructed to make it possible for the poor Lazarus to share the same table with the rich man (Luke 16:19-31). In Pauline theology, saving justice abolishes the differences of race, gender, social status, nationality, and culture in the sense that these differences do not control membership in the community. As Paul says: "There is no longer Jew or Greek, there is no longer slave or free, there is no longer male and female; for all of you are one in Christ Jesus" (Gal 3:28). There are different functions in the body of Christ but all of them are services for the whole community. The cancellation of barriers of separation and discrimination is part of the order established by the new creation that Christ brings about (Gal 6:15). The new creation effects in a sublime manner what the first creation intended for humanity. The marvelous manifestation of the justice of God is not only to vindicate those who are unjustly oppressed, but also to bring to completion the design of God to have every person sharing God's image in equal measure in the community of God's people.

Although the full establishment of justice and the total destruction of injustice do not seem to be possible in history, nevertheless Christians are called to nurture the utopia of a better world. They hold the conviction that the Creator is present in our history and cares about the present world. They themselves possess the power of the Spirit that moves people to create a society of peace and solidarity. They bear the responsibility of building a visible anticipation of the justice and peace that the consummated reign of God will bring about. As the Second Vatican Council in the Constitution on the Church in the Modern World, *Gaudium et Spes* ("Joy and Hope") 39, says: "Far from diminishing our concern to develop this earth, the expectation of a new earth should spur us on, for it is here that the body of a new human family grows, foreshadowing in some way the age which is to come. That is why, although we must be careful to distinguish earthly progress clearly from the increase of the kingdom of Christ, such progress is of vital concern to the kingdom of God, insofar as it can contribute to the better ordering of human society."

Work

The Bible begins with the story of God's work in the creation. God worked for six days and found the work rewarding (Gen 2:2-3). After the completion of this work, God rested. Although having rested on the seventh day, God continues working in the world (Ps 104:13; Isa 43:13; Jos 24:31). The importance of God's work in the six days of creation is that it is a model for human beings (Gen 2:2-3; Exod 20:9-10; 23:12), who have been created in the image of God and commissioned to conquer the earth and continue the work of God in the world (Gen 1:27-30). Although work is not the final objective of the creation of humanity—for the rest of God at the end of the creation is also a significant model and goal for human beings (Gen 2:2-3; Heb 4:3-11)—nevertheless work is a distinctive task of human beings on earth (Eccl 3:10).

A strong argument for the thesis that working is good is that God worked and found satisfaction in it (Gen 1:4, 10, 12, 18, 21, 25, 31). Unlike the myth of Atrahasis in which gods and goddesses decided to stop carrying the burden of the work they disliked and gave it to humanity to bear, in Genesis God is proud of this work and gives it to humanity as a model to follow. Another strong argument in this regard is that God placed Adam in the garden of Eden to work in it (Gen 2:15) as part of the human participation in the maintenance of God's garden and as action for the fulfillment of the human being. However, work in actual human existence is a mix of blessing and curse due to the assertive character of humans, who through their work look for absolute autonomy. The human being, indeed, received the blessing to subdue and populate the earth (Gen 1:28) and to create culture and civilization (Gen 4:17, 20-22; 10:1-31). As a matter of fact human beings created instruments to express their artistic skill (Gen 4:21) and developed metallurgy by extracting minerals from the underground (Job 28:1-6) and forging tools of bronze and iron (Gen 4:22). They built cities and created reigns and empires (Gen 4:17; 10:1-31; 11:3-4), and they are invited by the sage to work and prepare a comfortable future (Prov 6:6). But human work is not only a result of blessing. It is also mixed with toil (Gen 3:17c-19), violence, and revenge (Gen 4:1-16, 23-24; 6:11) and it can end with destruction and death (Gen 6:13-14; 11:6-9; Eccl 9:1-3). Work is an ambivalent reality. It can produce good and bad things. It means satisfaction and fulfillment for some, but for many it results in exploitation and oppression. While some are able to display their abilities in their work and to earn the appreciation of people as Bezalel and his companions did in the building of the tabernacle (Exod 38:22-23), others labor as slaves and do not obtain fulfillment and satisfaction from their toil: "They reap in a field not their own" (Job 24:6). "They tread the wine presses, but suffer thirst" (Job 24:11). While some celebrate with jubilation the achievement of the nation (Amos 6:4-6) a great part of the population is exploited, robbed, and oppressed in its work (Amos 4:1-5) or "sold for a pair of sandals" (Amos 2:6).

In the NT there are two series of texts relevant to the concept of work. The first refers to Paul who, after being called to apostleship, continued to work with his own hands and urged all Christians to do the same. His practice and exhortation run against the grain of Greco-Roman culture in which manual work was for slaves, not for free people. Paul's motives were to be self-sufficient so that he could avoid being a burden to others, and to be able to help others through almsgiving. He urged all Christians to do the same, especially those whose expectation of an imminent parousia led to idleness. He urges them to gain their own food and to keep busy; in this way they would avoid trouble and mind their own business (1 Thess 2:9; 4:11-12; 2 Thess 3:7-12; Eph 4:28). A second series of texts is related to "house rules" in which slaves are urged to be faithful and obedient to their masters and suffer injustice patiently. Christian motivations are given, and masters are urged to treat slaves with Christian care, but the only reward promised is in the afterlife (Eph 6:5-9; Col 3:17-25; 1 Pet 2:18-24).

Although the NT does not give any theology of work, the injunction to faithfulness and obedience to masters, along with the need to keep busy, would be used in the following centuries. Following the NT the Fathers of the Church emphasize the virtues that accompany work. Through work a person becomes self-sufficient, avoids idleness, gains humility, obedience, and submission, does penance, and imitates Jesus and Paul. The monastic movement broke the Greco-Roman association of work with slavery by showing monks practicing a balanced life of manual labor, intellectual life, and prayer: *Ora et labora* ("pray and work"). The Protestant Reformation transferred the practice of work from the monastery to the common life of the people. Calvinism especially inspired a worldly asceticism influential in following centuries, emphasizing austerity and the rewards of hard work as a sign of divine favor. The industrial era subjected workers to the tempo of the machine and the control of the manager and turned them into mindless automatons. Protest came from different quarters. Karl Marx issued his works of scientific socialism. Leo XIII initiated the modern social teaching of the Church with his encyclical letter *Rerum Novarum* ("Of New Things"), issued in 1891. The basis of the teaching of the social encyclicals issued by the popes in this century is a reflection on the human being who is a person created in the image of God and commissioned to conquer the world and to continue the work of God in it. As John Paul II says in his encyclical letter *Laborem exercens* 105–106: "The basis for determining the value of human work is not primarily the kind of work being done, but the fact that the one who is doing it is a person." The social dimension of work is expressed by the Second Vatican Council as follows: "By their work people ordinarily provide for themselves and their family, associate with others as their brothers and sisters, and serve them; they can exercise genuine charity and be partners in the work of bringing God's creation to perfection. Moreover, we believe by faith that through the homage of work offered to God humanity is associated with the redemptive work of Jesus Christ, whose labor with his hands at Nazareth greatly added to the dignity of work" (*GS* 67).

The theological affirmation of the positive value of work faces the reality of a world in which a multitude of people dislike the work they do; they work not for the sake of work but for the profit they can get from it. For many their professional work is different from what they want to make of their private life. However, the positive affirmation of human work renders a good service; it provides a basis for judging the ideologies that exploit human work for others' benefit and offers an ideal that helps those who suffer injustice to awake from their passive attitude dominated by the idea that their world cannot be changed. Affirmation of the value of work calls them to join the effort to change the oppressive situation of work that was not made by God but by the selfish interests of other human beings.

BIBLIOGRAPHY

Baum, Gregory. *The Priority of Labor: A Commentary on "Laborem Exercens," Encyclical Letter of Pope John Paul II.* New York and Toronto: Paulist, 1982.

Birch, Bruce C. *Let Justice Roll Down: The Old Testament Ethics and Christian Life.* Louisville: Westminster/John Knox, 1991.

Gillett, Richard W. *The Human Enterprise.* Kansas City, Mo.: Leaven Press, 1985.

Lohfink, Norbert F. *Option for the Poor.* Berkeley: Bibal, 1987.

Soelle, Dorothee. *To Work and To Love: A Theology of Creation.* Philadelphia: Fortress, 1984.

Violence and Evil in the Bible

Sean McEvenue

Many religious people are so offended by the violence of God as expressed, for example, in the notion of hell, or the notion of God as warrior, or presentations of God as angry, that they are profoundly troubled in reading the Bible or even reject it as source of their faith. Others try to resolve this problem by imagining that the angry God is in the OT only, whereas the NT reveals God as pure love. This problem is so real, and found in so many intelligent believers, that it merits some time and reflection.

The answer must have two parts: the first, in order to set the question in a realistic framework, will examine the notion that God should be only love, without anger. A second part will examine some specific biblical ideas and texts that frequently offer difficulties.

Violence in a Universe Ruled by a God of Love

The problem of violence is easily resolved in the precise logic of philosophers, but it is not easily resolved in the concrete thinking that arises in daily life. We experience or think of violence as any wild and destructive event that causes acute pain or lowers human living to an unacceptable level, removing all comfort and dignity. Violence is any radical damage to life that appears to be unnatural in our universe that is created and maintained by an all-powerful and loving God.

However, the harsh fact is that all life on earth is partly violent—not only because of criminality or insanity, but also because of the very nature of physical life. Everything that lives in space and time on earth dies. Death and the return to dust ends every life, thus making room for all the new plants, animals, and humans that are born daily. Facing that fact is often the beginning of maturity. And yet death is violent at whatever age it occurs, even if one is lucky enough to "pass away peacefully in one's sleep." Despite our most comforting words, death is not the fulfillment or culmination of life, but its final enemy. It is a breakdown of complex harmonious systems, and it is characterized by the onset of putrefaction. For humans it may occasion passage to a "better life," but in itself it is a radical and violent cutting off of this life.

Those who try to understand their mission in this world as though the violence of death were not part of it must elaborate a worldview that can only be called sentimental and illusory. If they include in that rosy picture a definition of God as the one who creates it they have formed their own little idol, a "God of love" who is illusory.

Of course God is love and nothing else, but not in the sense indicated above. That rosy illusion, if not supplemented with some further awakening, is escapist. Ultimately it is "taking God's name in vain" in the sense that it uses religion in order to escape from reality rather than as the basis for growth of faith, hope, and love within reality. God who created healthy infants and rosy sunsets and the laughter of lovers also created an order of nature in which one species lives by eating another, and in which hurricanes occur, and extended ice ages, and tropical heat and polar cold. The created universe is glorious and massive far beyond our imaginings, but its glory is not comfortable.

And Jesus, whom we know as "meek and humble of heart" and whom we follow because his "yoke is easy and his burden light" was tortured to death on the cross. Crucifixion is a major NT expression of the relation of human life to God the Father: not because the Father is cruel or angry, but because he is unlimited love, and because if limited humans are to share in that unlimited love we must first accompany Christ through the purification of death, both his and ours.

This touches upon the mystery of evil. It is important to distinguish suffering (violence that is natural in a physical environment) from evil (violence that results from absence of love).

Consider first natural suffering. The laws of nature include the experience of suffering pain as a useful warning of damage. It also includes the suffering that is due to many forms of conflict in which the fulfilling of one law conflicts with the fulfilling of another. In the end it is better that two trains colliding (or think of the trillions of atoms colliding this instant) should damage each other rather than annihilate the laws of nature. The good of order (i.e., the working of complex systems that maintain life and society) demands that natural laws function each time; thus conflict is statistically inevitable and even terrible destruction will occur from time to time. This is horrifying, but it is not really evil. The wisdom to distinguish between suffering and evil comes only through personal experience joined with prayer. When one contemplates the sufferings of one's loved ones or of people in war, particularly perhaps the suffering of children through starvation, abuse, and abandonment, it is not easy to affirm that God is love. Moreover, it is neither honest nor healthy to make such an affirmation until one has gone through all the denials and grieving and praying one needs, and until faith has been given to make real the sense of peace that is in fact true (cf. the couple at Emmaus in Luke 24:13-35, or the book of Job).

Evil, on the other hand, is the perverse will that seeks suffering and death for self and others. It is alienated psyche, and we all run into it at some time in our lives. Not only do we meet it in other people but we also participate in it, at least as a tendency—often with terror or loathing and yet some complicity—until we have been purified. Only God is pure love. Only God gets no pleasure whatsoever out of human suffering or death (Wis 1:12-15). Certainly some persons are evil, and probably we all suffer acutely because of their perversity. Faith is personal assent to the inner knowledge of the love of God, and the apex of the virtue of faith consists in remaining faithful to this assent even at times when we experience some truly evil intrusion into our lives.

Violence, then, whether it be natural violence or evil violence, is part of our universe, and it is as pervasive as life itself and human freedom. We know God as both creator and savior of our violent universe. It is inconceivable that God should not be present in violence, and associated with or opposed to violence in diverse ways. The Bible presents this relationship repeatedly, and the reader who is concerned about violence in the Bible must examine the text carefully in each case in order to perceive precisely how God and violence are related. For example, in Genesis 6 the reason given for the Flood is that all of life has become corrupt, and in v. 11 the corruption is characterized precisely as "violence." The divine solution that follows is depicted as a devastating flood, a return to primordial chaos, which is violence of a different sort, i.e., nature prior to life forms. In this case God allows the violence of nature to extinguish the evil violence of corruption. In Genesis 8 and 9 God undertakes never to do that again.

Some Difficult Biblical Ideas

Within this general context of thought we shall now turn to some particularly difficult biblical texts.

A. Asking God to Smash One's Enemies

In the OT punishment was often decreed according to the *"lex talionis,"* i.e., the notion that punishment should be measured by the crime: "an eye for an eye and a tooth for a tooth." The role of such expressions is partially that of "poetic justice," but also that of a rule of thumb for restricting the punishment so that the desire for revenge may not replace the desire for justice. However, many poetic texts in the prophets and in the psalms depict violent images of punishment of enemies where cruelty rather than measure appears to characterize the punishment. These are often offensive to our sensibilities.

This is one place where the Bible offers an important corrective to some contemporary thought. Western civilization, at least, has been steeped throughout this century in a heavily psychological way of viewing reality. This culture has developed profound and valuable advances in our understanding of human motivation, of the causes and meaning of human emotions, and of the possibilities of freeing oneself from various psychic forces such as compulsions and neuroses in the context of psychic transfer or other therapies, or through drugs.

One deceptive application of this growing insight has been the confusion of personal therapy with the notion of salvation, making psychological liberation equivalent to holiness. This way of thinking reduces to individual subjectivity notions that properly denote both individual subject and other reality: social reality (salvation) and/or a divine person (holiness). In the psychological way of thinking, the individual is often viewed as the supreme value. Communities such as nations or religious communities are seen as artificial conglomerates. Patriotism, for example, is treated as a suspect feeling and perhaps a delusion. Within this view a passion for social justice will not easily be presumed to have arisen out of healthy reasoning, but instead out of paranoia. It will be understood perhaps as fanaticism. Moreover, in this way of thinking, even at an individual level, if one is angry at an enemy one feels obliged to begin by freeing oneself from anger, and only then dealing with the "enemy." In addition one must presume that the other is an enemy only because, perhaps, my neuroses or paranoia make him or her that way (and then these afflictions are to be treated), or else the enemy is neurotic and should be given therapy. That is a cozy world in which we are all helpless children who live under treatment in a psychiatric ward.

Of course good psychologists do not get into this confusion, and even for armchair psychologists the radical failure of this paradigm for improving society has become evident in the intractable crime rate and the unabated violence around the world. The current swings toward the "right" may well be motivated by the desire to break out of flawed myth.

Moreover, within the myth that meaning is constituted by subjective feelings rather than by truth there easily develops the problem of "poor self-image." We constantly experience evil in one form or another. If we understand evil as a psychic problem to be cured by therapy we easily take it all upon ourselves, and a radical sense of failure may begin to characterize all our thoughts about the world. In recent years therapists have been at infinite pains to discover techniques for improving our self-image, often with little success. But the whole problem would not have arisen if one had accepted the reality of evil in this world and if one knew it as separate from oneself, as the enemy. At that point courage is required to face evil honestly, and then to oppose it actively. For this we invoke the presence of God.

The Bible proceeds in precisely this way, and it has offended many as a result. The psalmist, for example, frequently presents personal enemies as the enemies of God and asks God to destroy them: "As fire consumes the forest, as the flame sets the mountains ablaze, so pursue them with your tempest and terrify them with your hurricane. Fill their faces with shame, so that they may seek your name, O LORD" (Ps 83:14-16). The psalmist uses all kind of metaphors and stereotypes to identify the injustices, the enemies, and the punishments. But he does treat evil as real, and he respects the enemy as an adult. He recognizes the enemy as a spiritual being whom God knows and opposes. The enemy is real and responsible, as God is real and responsible. And evil matters: it merits our reaction! The psalmist feels unequal to the evil he experiences, and so he looks for the strength to stand up and face it by invoking God's help. He wants victory, and he uses every metaphor he can find to express this. His rhetoric is often imprecise but we can understand that he is after victory precisely over evil, over perverse and alienated psyche, since he identifies the enemy as enemy of God. Ultimately the victory is to be conversion of the enemy "so that they may seek your name."

Such psalms invite us who pray them to step out of our depressed dreamlands and face reality with God. Many people are embarrassed by the idea that God or anyone in God's place should be bashing anyone, friend or enemy. We were taught to hate the sin but love the sinner. But in our era many have stopped hating even the sin. We want to get through our lives without fighting, comfortably. The psalms challenge that passivity, and once prayer has enabled us to stand up and face evil in God's presence, to be confident in God's power, it becomes possible honestly to begin distinguishing between sin and sinner. Of course there are also therapies that encourage one to get one's anger out, expressing it in psychodramas or in various forms of controlled encounter. The psalms place us directly in the presence of God and invite us to express all our wildest emotions. These are moments of truth because our most hidden selves can come to the surface, and this happens in a context where we open our hearts to the presence and power of God the creator and savior of all.

Perhaps the most offensive verse in the Bible is the apparent curse against the Edomites at the end of Psalm 137: "Happy shall they be who take your little ones and dash them against the rock!" The Edomites here and in the prophecy of Obadiah are remembered as the final wanton destroyers of the sacred city of Jerusalem. Their act was sacrilege, to be viewed as a pyrrhic victory over YHWH. But the meaning even of this verse, when read as it is written, is not so much a curse against Edom but rather an imaging of Edom's crime in an attempt to come to terms with grief. This can be seen if one considers the preceding two verses. The psalmist recalls the horror of the last day in Jerusalem. He does not define or describe the crime, but he asks YHWH to remember the day and to punish. He then invokes the *"lex talionis"* according to which punishment should be of the same character as the crime: "Happy shall they be who pay you back what you have done to us!"(v. 8b). The crime has not been indicated in the text, but now in v. 9 it is shown in mirror-image, i.e., in the description of what would be the character of a fitting punishment: "Happy shall they be who take your little ones and dash them against the rock!" In this the psalmist is not sadistically tasting a foreseen revenge, but rather depicting the last day in Jerusalem as a mirror-image of someone smashing the heads of Israel's infants. The psalm pictures revenge as a literary technique expressive of the psalmist's grief, bitterness, and longing for Jerusalem. The psalmist can face this evil, and feel its bitterness once again, and be freed from despair only by invoking YHWH to be present as a companion in remembering.

Jesus, who most certainly distinguished between sin and sinner, has taught us about a proper relation to evil. Of course Jesus said that we should love our enemies and to do good to those who persecute us (Matt 5:43-45), and in dealing with his own enemies he did not ask his Father to destroy them, but rather forgave them because they did not know what they were doing (Luke 23:34). In such texts Jesus is usually seen as radically extending the familiar OT teaching that one should love one's neighbor as oneself (Lev 19:18), but this must not be taken as an instruction about how to face evil or enemies in that full sense. In the first case (Matt 5:43-45) the perspective does not include countering the evil by love (such as is suggested, for example, in Prov 25:21-22: "If your enemies are hungry, give them bread to eat; and if they are thirsty, give them water to drink; for you will remove the hot coals of anger from their heads" [author's translation]), but rather his focus is restricted to the spiritual advancement and eventual reward of the disciple. (See also Luke 6:35-36.) In the second case (Luke 23:34), forgiving those who did not know what they were doing is not a repudiation of violence in the face of evil, but rather a supreme application of discernment amid grave suffering. These adversaries were not evil.

Jesus' teaching about facing evil enemies, on the other hand, was shown in his direct attacks upon those scribes and Pharisees whose spiritual leadership he perceived as evil, in his taking a whip to the moneychangers who dishonored the Temple, or in his casting out demons. It was also shown in his advice that following him demanded absolute renunciation of self, and even that one must hate father and mother, wife and children, brothers and sisters (Matt 10:34-36; Luke 14:25-33), or in his instruction to cut off one's hand or pluck out one's eye if they were to be a scandal (Mark 9:42-50).

B. Hell

Many believers are offended by the NT notion of hell to the point that though they believe all else in the creed they will not believe that a loving God could ever say "You that are accursed, depart from me into the eternal fire prepared for the devil and his angels" (Matt 25:41). This notion may be understood as an eschatological expression of the cruel punishments promised for sin in Deut 28:15-26 and Lev 26:14-39.

The difficulty here may arise from the mentality we have just been describing. Once evil is reduced to psychological causation and therapy, then clearly there is no place for hell. However, when we break out of this myth the doctrine of hell is far from being an embarrassment; rather it should be an important biblical stumbling block calculated to make us face up to our real stature and dignity. It challenges us when we are tempted to forget that we are free and that there is real evil. For there is a temptation to want to think of humans as perpetual children involved in a game. It is easy to forget that we stand before the face of God and are truly children of God.

If one has freely chosen evil, how will one feel in the immediate presence of unlimited love? Will one want to remain there? Will one not welcome the invitation to depart from the Father? And will that departure not be bitter like an eternal fire?

One balks at the notion of eternal banishment, with not one more chance. Does anyone actually choose evil in that ultimate way? The Bible presents that as a real option. It dignifies and respects the human being as destined to stand up, to face God, and to make ultimate choices. However, it says little about just when such choices are made.

C. The God of the Bible as a Warrior

Throughout most of the history of ancient Israel there was the pervasive experience of war, of siege, of soldiers and death, of victory and defeat. The experience of war was as important to them as the experience of sports, of school, of jobs, of television, or of politics is to us. It was natural, therefore, that among the experiences of evil that were discussed in the Bible the evils of war played a prominent role, and that in those discussions God's protection of Israel was celebrated.

The question arises: should those who live under the NT embrace a doctrine of peace and simply reject those OT texts that make of God a warrior who gives victory to Israel on this earth? The answer is no, not only because Scripture is Scripture, but also because if one reads the OT texts attentively one discovers that they are equally compatible with embracing peace. Moreover, the NT has not changed this teaching.

Possibly the most striking text in this regard is the victory song that Exodus 15 has Moses sing after crossing the Reed Sea: "Let me sing for YHWH/Yea, hurrah, hooray:/Horse and rider/He has slammed into the sea!/My force and my song is Ya!/ . . . /YHWH is a man of war./YHWH is his name" [author's translation]. The next nine verses celebrate this revelation of God's power in the crossing of the sea. They are followed by eight more verses that rejoice in the fear other nations have of YHWH and recall the entry of Israel into the promised land and Israel's establishment on Zion: they are singing in the Temple where "YHWH will reign forever and ever."

We may be put off at first by this glorying in the death and fear of Israel's enemies. However, this results from misreading the song. Moses and then Miriam are imagined as singing the song, but the words recall the conquest of Canaan as already experienced (v. 13), and its setting is that of a time after the Temple has been built (v. 17), fully three or four centuries after Moses and Miriam! Moreover, the song nowhere suggests that Israel should be warlike or terrifying. Quite the contrary. Israel is at prayer, reading the Bible or singing in the Temple. The clear teaching of this song is that Israel does *not* have to be warlike: it has only to recall the unlimited power God has to protect it, a power that was revealed hundreds of years ago during the days of Moses and Miriam. Since God is omnipotent, Israel has only to walk through the parted waters with faith and say its prayers. God will strike terror in the heart of God's enemies.

This pacific approach to war is found throughout all the "holy war" texts in the Bible. While it is true that several of Israel's kings were successful in battle and that going to war was part of Israel's constant burden, it is also true that its spiritual tradition as retained in the Bible never extolled the cruel disciplines of the military and always presented victory as being totally in God's hands. For example, Deut 1:19-46 is a wonderfully constructed story that shows Israel being punished when it does not trust in God in the face of its enemies and subsequently being decimated when it trusts in itself to attack these same enemies.

This teaching remains unchanged in the NT. In NT times war was not a viable or sane option for Israel within the Roman Empire, so this imagery was not often associated with Jesus or with his disciples. In Gethsemane, however, Jesus is still depicted as victor in war. Jesus tells one of his disciples not to defend him with a sword because those who live by the sword die by the sword. But Jesus believes that his victory could be realized through God's power: "Do you think that I cannot appeal to my Father, and he will at once send me more than twelve legions of angels?" (Matt 26:53). John's gospel expressed the same belief in a different form, for he presents Jesus in the garden not as appealing to the Father but as taking upon himself the divine role. He names himself YHWH ("I am") and the enemy soldiers draw back and fall to the ground (John 18:3-6).

This is not the place to go into the vexed debates about just wars and about pacifism as a doctrine, questions that are not fully answered in the Bible but have been debated in the Christian churches for centuries. Changes in the technology of war have changed the nature of war and radically altered the debate about it. War is no longer a contest but rather a potential annihilation. What the Bible does teach with clarity is trust in God when faced by evil. It teaches that being a victim of cruelty is the result of one's own sin or the sin of the enemy. Evil and violence sometimes do come upon faithful individuals and faithful communities but it is never what God desires for God's children. God is a victorious warrior; when real danger is upon us we can believe in God and thus not succumb to evil.

D. The Annihilation of the Canaanites

One of the most troubling ideas in the Bible is the notion of the "ban," an idea that is found in many forms of tribal religion in the ancient Near East and in other parts of the world as well. Victory in war is given by God, and as a result all the spoils of war belong to God, not to the tribe. In some cases this was to be shown by the ritual killing of the conquered.

At one point in their history the tribes of Israel shared this view, and practiced it to some degree. Traces of it remain in the Bible. For example, in 1 Samuel 15 the prophet Samuel condemns Saul after his victory over the Amalekites because he had failed to kill the defeated king Agag, and because he had spared "the best of the sheep and of the cattle and of the fatlings, and the lambs, and all that was valuable" (1 Sam 15:9). All of that belonged to YHWH, but Saul spared it out of greed. It would be fascinating to explore how the ancients managed conquest and victory, but that would be irrelevant to the objectives of this article. We will restrict ourselves to observing how the Bible has converted these tribal traditions of the "ban" to its own purposes.

The most impressive text is perhaps Deuteronomy 7, where Moses foretells that in the promised land the Israelites will meet seven nations "mightier and more numerous than you," namely the Hittites, Girgashites, Amorites, Canaanites, Perizzites, Hivites, and Jebusites. And Moses tells the people that "when the LORD your God gives them over to you and you defeat them, then you must utterly destroy them. Make no covenant with them and show them no mercy" (v. 2). That is a shocking text when we first read it. Its absolute tone seems to leave no room for survival. As a result one is surprised to read, later in the same chapter: "If you say to yourself, 'These nations are more numerous than I; how can I dispossess them?' do not be afraid of them. Just remember what the LORD your God did to Pharaoh and to all Egypt . . . . The Lord your God will do the same to all the peoples of whom you are afraid. Moreover, the LORD your God will send [hornets] against them . . . . The LORD your God will clear away these nations before you little by little; you will not be able to make a quick end of them, otherwise the wild animals would become too numerous for you" (vv. 17-22). At the end it is evident that the command to execute them all has a meaning very remote from what we at first thought. It is obvious that the reality behind this text is not the black and white world of clear legislation, but rather the complex world of experience in which human activity, divine activity, and even the role of hornets and the relations between people and wild animals all play a role!

Scholarship has shown that this text came from the time, not of Moses, but rather of Josiah, seven hundred years later. At that time the famous seven nations, the Hittites, Girgashites, etcetera, were in fact no longer nations in Israel, but at most ethnic traces and memories. The writer and reader know that they are a dwindling memory. Moreover, they are no longer a danger to Israel in any way. They are no longer the object of fear.

So what fear is the text talking about? During the previous two hundred years the Israelites had been living in terror of the roaming armies from Assyria and Babylon and they had been intermittently oppressed and besieged by them. It never entered anyone's mind that Israel could attack, defeat, and annihilate these great empires. In 722 the northern kingdom of Israel was occupied, conquered, and exiled by Assyria, and within two or three decades of the writing of this text Jerusalem itself would be defeated by Babylon and later flattened. That is what the Israelites were afraid of, and that is the fear this text deals with. It must be read not as a command to wipe out foreign nations but as an exhortation to have no fear of them, an exhortation based on the memory of God's powerful intervention hundreds of years ago and on the evidence of the dwindling power of the Hittites and Girgashites and so forth since that time. The chapter seems to be talking about conquered nations but in fact it is urging oppressed Jews to maintain their identity through cultural and religious resistance. Israel must remain true to YHWH and bring no foreign idols into their houses: "Do not bring an abhorrent thing into your house, or you will be set apart for destruction like it" (v. 26).

Deuteronomy 7 is not a violent command to practice genocide but an encouraging exhortation to religious authenticity in the presence of truly terrifying enemies. This is a rhetoric of military violence, but its meaning is spiritual courage.

Conclusion

If the Bible were written in this century its mode of expression would be very different. It would be easier for us to understand, and it would be easier for us to enjoy. But its meaning would not be different.

However well one understands the biblical text it remains true that hope for us mortals, brothers and sisters of the Crucified, is not that we escape from death, but rather that we rise again.

Ecumenism

Jorge Mejía

Ecumenism is not an easy subject and the reader might even question the appropriateness of dealing with such a topic in a Bible commentary, even in a general article. However, there are many reasons not to ignore ecumenism in a commentary such as this. In the first place, the present commentary intends to be pastorally oriented—that is, helpful as far as possible to all those, be they priests and pastors or lay men and lay women, who minister daily to the spiritual needs of their fellow Christians everywhere, at the same time giving witness to the love of God in Jesus Christ for this world and all those who toil in it. In such a perspective ecumenism, the active commitment to the unity and union of all Christians, is not optional but a necessity. In fact the Church exists for unity (cf. Vatican Council II, Dogmatic Constitution on the Church, *Lumen gentium,* 1) and its witness to Christ presupposes unity and therefore requires at least a serious, convinced, persevering effort for unity (cf. Vatican Council II, Decree on Ecumenism, *Unitatis redintegratio,* 1). But this is not the only reason. Ecumenism understood in the sense just outlined is a biblical theme, very much present in the NT and not without roots and references also in the OT. I will only indicate some here, as an invitation to further study.

(1) Unity is a central concern in the Holy Scriptures. God is one and the human vocation, either personal or collective, is to be one. This is perhaps best illustrated by two biblical concepts about humanity and God's design for it. The first is the notion of family applied to the whole of the humankind. Whatever the historical and biological origin of the human race it is clearly seen in Scripture as coming from "one" (Acts 17:26 *ex henos*). This, I believe, is why the book of Genesis is structured as a series of "generations" *(toledot, sefer toledot),* coming forth from the first man and the first woman. We are all well aware (or should be) of the importance of this biblical notion with regard to the evil of racism, different forms of discrimination, and nationalism. Some kind of unity, even in the midst of all the diversity that distinguishes humanity and that we are only beginning to acknowledge, let alone accept, belongs to the nature and natural vocation of humankind.

Second, there is the couple, symbol and realization of unity between members of the human family: the small nuclear family intimating and preparing for the larger one. Creation begins and ends, or culminates, with a couple. Again the historical (or pre-historical) and biological facts regarding the origin of humankind are here quite secondary. The affirmation remains always valid: humanity is not a series of parallel, unrelated biological strands with no mutual connection whatsoever. On the contrary, it is appropriately described as flowing from a couple, man and woman, created one for the other, each in the fullness of humanity, which consists of both.

The same is found at the end. The last vision of Revelation is the "bride" coming down from heaven, adorned to meet her bridegroom (Rev 21:2). The same bride, further on, cries with the Spirit: "come" (Rev 22:17), calling her husband, the Lord. The bride is indeed the "city." But this only means that even in the diversity and plurality of humankind as saved, the proper expression of its definitive unity is always the couple—only this time the partner, and thus the cause of unity, is God.

(2) If there is a deep, radical relationship between creation and unity, in the sense that creation implies unity and therefore the movement toward union, the same can be said of redemption, which means that unity and union belong intrinsically to God's design. In fact, according to the gospel of John, in a section expressing the evangelist's own reflection on the mystery to which he witnesses, we read (John 11:51-52): "he [Caiaphas] prophesied that Jesus was about to die for the nation, and not for the nation only, but to gather into one *(en)* the dispersed children of God." The expression is admittedly very strong. It seems to presuppose that there is already a clear consciousness of division even among "the children of God" that is incompatible with the work of salvation. It is in the light of this central affirmation that the well-known verses of the so-called priestly prayer of Jesus in ch. 17 of the same gospel should be read and interpreted. Jesus prays and consecrates himself (John 17) that all may be "one" (again *en*), not only his immediate disciples but also those who will believe in him after them and because of them (John 20). It could be said with a nod to human psychology that unity, and therefore union (which presupposes separation or division) is a major concern of Jesus, and it would be true.

But there is much more here implied, as the following verse also reveals. As in ch. 11 union and unity are intimately related to the work of salvation, that is, to the mission of Jesus, sent to this world to gather humankind in itself and in relation to God through the offering of his life. This is the origin of the Church and the reason for its existence, but division creeps in, even among the "children of God." A first very painful division already separated Jews from Christians. Other divisions would tear asunder the seamless garment (cf. John 19:23), but the net will not be torn (John 21:11). The prayer and the sacrifice of the Lord Jesus are there to bring together again what humanity has divided (cf. Matt 19:6; Mark 10:9). This, however, will have to be done through the engagement of the Church (or churches), also in prayer and sacrifice, but first of all through repentance and mutual reconciliation.

(3) At this point it could be asked: which unity? and therefore: what process for union? Present-day ecumenism has its own answers, which will not be dealt with here. However, as intimated above, the same text in the gospel of John is very revealing about the kind of unity the Lord prays for and that we are called to help realize. That gospel speaks of the unity of the Father with the Son and the Son with the Father (cf. John 17:21-22). The same unity is affirmed in John 10:30 in the strongest possible terms: "The Father and I are one *(en)*." Unity among Christians (those who "believe"), and in the last instance unity in humankind, goes back to the unity in God, namely, unity between persons who are different in themselves but at the same time one in the supreme unity of the Godhead. It is quite obvious that if we are to attain such unity the "glory" of God must be communicated to us through the prayer and sacrifice of Jesus (John 17:24). In this way he will be in us as the Father is in him, for us to be finally consummated in one *(en)*, by the gift of the "glory" that is indistinguishable from God's very self. All this is done by love and through love.

The transcendent nature of unity, which we have tried to underline all along in this note, comes here to the fore. Unity belongs to the plan of God for humankind because it is the essence of the Godhead. The unity (and union or reunion) of Christians belongs to the same level. This is the reason why such unity and union are the necessary conditions for belief (John 17:21). One could gloss this by saying that union is the condition for salvation.

It is quite clear that John is not the only witness to such truth although he has expressed it most clearly in his own language and in the context of his own theology. The whole of the NT, and in particular the letters of Paul, is permeated by the same passion for unity, even in the midst of (necessary) diversity, and this in relation to the redemptive work of Christ (see especially Eph 2:14, with *en*) and God's design for humankind (1 Tim 2:5 and elsewhere).

Antisemitism in the Bible and After

Jorge Mejía

The subject I am asked to write about, albeit as such a rather recent one, has already produced almost a whole library of publications, some very learned, some less, some merely pamphlets.

I am thoroughly convinced that the first difficulty consists in the precise definition of the term "Antisemitism" (coined late in the last century, and certainly not in scholarly circles). If the term is given the very broad meaning of "critique of Jews and Judaism," whatever the motivations and content of such critique, then a good part of the OT (or Torah), particularly the major and so-called minor prophets, but also a not inconsiderable section of the historical books (or Former Prophets), could qualify for the label. The NT is a different problem but it could also be read in such an unfavorable light.

If, on the other hand, "Antisemitism" is held to mean a *vicious* attack on Jews and Judaism stemming from prejudice and intended to produce hate, moral or physical damage, including persecution and death, then the field narrows considerably. No one could seriously pretend that even the extremely harsh critiques of biblical Israel found, for example, in Hosea are Antisemitic, and if someone did he or she would not be taken seriously.

Further, a careful distinction must be drawn between the content of a writing or book and the use to which such writing or book can be put— or has been put. It must be openly admitted that the literary genre of the *"Adversus Judaeos"* treatises, either patristic or medieval (whether they are authentic or not being quite beside the point) and many other writings have made such use of Holy Scripture, of either Testament, as to make them appear Antisemitic, in the second sense just explained. This, however, is not a proof that the books concerned, or parts thereof, really deserve such blame. *Use* of biblical passages does not necessarily imply that such passages should be read the way they are (or have been) used, whatever the authority of those who have put them to such use. Hermeneutics is one thing; quite different are adaptation, accommodation, metaphorical sense characterized by figures of speech, etcetera, which sometimes verge on abuse.

The key, therefore, to evaluating Antisemitism in the proper sense in the Bible lies in hermeneutics. As this commentary makes obvious, hermeneutics means explaining, *not* explaining away. To this end the right principle or principles of interpretation should be sought.

Regarding the OT everyone will agree, I expect, that even the most severe, uncompromising condemnations of Israel are really appeals to conversion and are to be read and interpreted in the light of the unbroken promises to the patriarchs, exactly as Paul does in Rom 11:29: "for the gifts and the calling of God are irrevocable." These, like the rebukes, come from the same source, namely God's love for the people God has chosen (cf. Jer 31:3).

I believe that the same principle should be applied to the reading of the NT, as the citation of Paul has already indicated. There are, however, two problems here that must be faced squarely. The first consists in the rift that Jesus' preaching and actions created in Israel, already in his own time but more deeply and definitively afterward, a rift yet to be healed according to Paul's teaching in the passage quoted above. This is, of course, in relation to the OT (see for instance Matthew 23 and the parallel in Luke 11). The gospel of John seems to have been written with this division in mind, as is the fourfold story of the Passion.

Second, of course, is the problem of the texts themselves, including those to which I have just referred. Some state in clear terms the fact of the division and even present, or try to present, the responsibility for it (cf. 1 Thess 2:14-16). Other texts—too many indeed, in my opinion—have been quoted and analyzed in this connection. Some have been explicitly accused of being Antisemitic, including even the parable of the Good Samaritan (Luke 10:30-37), quite wrongly, to be sure. This commentary will certainly face the problems such texts raise. Here I shall limit myself to saying that there is in the NT, or in some strands of it, a *polemic* attitude toward the Jews contemporary with Jesus and the primitive Church, or at least some of them. A similar attitude is also traceable on the other side although the written witnesses for it are much later. This however should not prevent the careful reader and interpreter from performing the hermeneutical task indicated above with the help of the same principle: Israel as such has not been condemned or rejected or cursed or excluded from salvation (cf. Vatican Council II, Declaration on the Relation of the Church to Non-Christian Religions, *Nostra aetate,* 4) and the promises to Israel's ancestors are always valid (cf. Luke 1:72-75). So at the end the rift will be healed.

It is in this perspective that the NT should be read, notwithstanding the weight that some distorted readings of the past still carry. These we are called to redress or correct, not to say exorcise, with untiring effort. After all, Antisemitism is "a sin" (John Paul II, in Australia) and we are enjoined to avoid even the occasion and the appearances of sin.

Inculturation of the Biblical Message

R. J. Raja

Introduction

A neologism, the term inculturation as qualitatively different from accommodation, adaptation, or indigenization, "is the incarnation of Christian life and of the Christian message in a particular cultural context, in such a way that this experience not only finds expression through elements proper to the culture in question, but becomes a principle that animates, directs and unifies the culture, transforming and remaking it so as to bring about 'a new creation'" (Pedro Arrupe, *Inculturazione* 145). It implies a two-way process. As open to all cultures the Good News introduces something new into the receptor cultures and the cultures themselves bring something new to the richness of this Good News. "Through inculturation the Church makes the Gospel incarnate in different cultures and at the same time introduces people together with their cultures into her own community. She transmits to them her own values . . . at the same time taking the good elements that already exist in them and renewing them from within" (Pope John Paul II, *Redemptoris Missio* 52). Thus inculturation implies a dialectical relationship between gospel and culture. It denotes an existential dialogue between a living people and the living gospel that is already inculturated in its original attempt at communication to a particular people.

In this sense inculturation is less of a one-way process than a mutual enrichment. It is interculturation. "On the one hand, the treasures contained in diverse cultures allow the word of God to produce new fruits and, on the other hand, the light of the word allows for a certain selectivity with respect to what cultures have to offer: harmful elements can be left aside and the development of valuable ones encouraged" (*The Interpretation of the Bible in the Church.* Document of the Pontifical Biblical Commission, 1993; IV. B: Inculturation).

Without using the term inculturation, Vatican II long before underscored the necessity and importance of this double-pronged reality.

> . . . just as happened in the economy of the incarnation, the young churches, which are rooted in Christ and built on the foundations of the apostles, take over all the riches of the nations which have been given to Christ as an inheritance (see Ps 2:8). They borrow from the customs, traditions, wisdom, teaching, arts and sciences of their people everything which could be used to praise the glory of the Creator, manifest the grace of the savior, or contribute to the right ordering of Christian life (*AGD* 22; cf. also *LG* 13).

Theological Basis for Inculturation

Incarnation, the most human mode of God's presence in the world, is the primary motivation as well as a radical paradigm for inculturation (cf. *AGD* 3.10). Incarnation is not merely a *kenosis,* an "emptying [of God] from" something divine, but an "identification with" a definite socio-cultural milieu. If inculturation is thus a continuation in time and place of the enfleshment of God, of the dialogue of salvation initiated by God and brought to culmination when God uttered the divine Word in a concrete cultural context, then this enfleshment, this divine consideration *(synkatabasis)* and this dialogue must be prolonged in all their rich variety in the different cultures and diverse human experiences. The socio-cultural and historical links of the word of God to one distinct people, race, or culture must not make it culture-bound or limit it from assuming new cultural affinities or different linguistic modalities. "In his self-revelation to his people, fully manifesting himself in his incarnate Son, God spoke in the context of the culture proper to each age. . . . the church has been sent to all ages and nations and, therefore, is not tied exclusively and indissolubly to any race or nation, to any one particular way of life, or to any set of customs, ancient or modern. The church is faithful to its traditions and is at the same time conscious of its universal mission; it can, then, enter into communion with different forms of culture, thereby enriching both itself and the cultures themselves" (*GS* 58). The physical enfleshment of the Word of God (John 1:14) must continue to encounter human beings anywhere and at any time through a new mystical enfleshment "in such a way as to be able to reach all people in the cultural context in which they live" (*Interpretation of the Bible in the Church* IV. B) and at the same time make the word maximally intelligible as well as intimately and personally transformative.

This open-ended and universalistic outreach of the word is already affirmed in the very first pages of the Bible in the creation of humanity in God's own image and likeness (Gen 1:27-28), continued in the blessings extended to "all the nations of the earth" through Abraham and his offspring (Gen 12:3; 18:18) and confirmed in its extension to "all nations" through the proclamation of the gospel (Matt 28:18-20; Rom 4:16-17), making the cultures together with the people "co-heirs" *(synklēronomoi),* "co-members" *(syssōmoi)* and "co-sharers" *(symmetochoi)* of the promises of God in Christ (Eph 3:6).

Being bound to no single culture, the word is open to all cultures, is made accessible to every human person and society, and acquires a native face. Hence Vatican II urges the Christian faithful to "implant [themselves] among all these groups [cultures] in the same way that Christ by his incarnation committed himself to the particular social and cultural circumstances of the women and men among whom he lived" (*AGD* 10).

Besides, although the Greek verb *eskēnōsen in hēmin* used by John (1:14) to denote the enfleshment of the Word is closely related to the noun *skēnē* (tent) in Greek, the LXX links *skēnē* very often with the Hebrew term *mishkan,* which means a dwelling or living or "presence of the Eternal in time" (cf. Wilhelm Michaelis, art. *skēnoō, TDNT* 7, 385–386), and which in its dynamic equivalence bears the meaning "he became a human being and lived among us" (cf. *Good News Bible* ad loc). The incarnation then is a personal and visible presence of the Word as opposed to the unseen and awe-inspiring reality (cf. tent, Temple, etcetera, as in Exod 25:8; Num 35:34). It is a permanent and enduring reality and not a transitory or temporary presence. Thus when this personal and enduring presence of the Word becomes embedded in the heart of a culture it is like a buried seed that dies and rises, draws its sustenance from the earth around it and sprouts and grows to maturity. It is from this ground of local culture that the seed (of the Word) draws nourishing elements which it transforms and assimilates into itself "so that eventually it bears much fruit" (*AGD* 22) by contextualizing the message here and now in the actual life situation of the people.

Together with the incarnation both the paschal mystery and that of Pentecost are related to the reality of inculturation as complementary paradigms insofar as they bring to the word of God a creative newness and variegated richness in the Spirit (Luke 24:32-49). Thus the word acquires a new dynamism and a vivifying power to liberate the various cultures with which it comes in contact from all that keeps them subject to superstition, falsehood, and oppression of all kinds and at the same time to heal, ennoble, and perfect them to bring about the justice of the reign of God that is "the new heaven and the new earth" (Rev 21:1; Isa 66:22).

Inculturation of the word of God is the natural response of the command of the risen Lord: "Go into all the world and proclaim the good news to the whole creation" (Mark 16:15; Matt 28:19). It is responding to God's call in history to be authentic transmitters of the message of salvation. It is to be deeply aware of and alive to the Spirit and at the same time to be present fully to the socio-cultural and economic-political realities in which one lives. The risen Lord who is the Spirit gives us a freedom with which we shall be able to discern and perceive the glory of the Lord (2 Cor 3:17) present in the "many-colored robes" (Ps 45:14) of the nations and cultures enriching the one mystery with newer dimensions.

Since resurrection is the completion of the enfleshed commitment of the Word to the world and all humanity and not a hasty flight into the distant heavens it is in and through the resurrection that Jesus as well as his words are liberated from the shackles of local habitat as well as the vestiges of a monocultural clothing and becomes universally present to all the cultures and the whole of history. In fact resurrection is the fullness of the bodily encounter of the Word with each culture and every human being in the world and it thus becomes the dynamic force of inculturation at all times and everywhere.

Stages in the Process of Inculturation

1. Translations

Announcing the word of God to anyone takes place primarily through the medium of one's own mother tongue. Hence the first step in the inculturation of the Bible is the translation of the inspired Scripture into a local language that intimately touches the life of the hearer.

Already in OT times the Law of God written originally in Hebrew was translated by Nehemiah into Aramaic, the language of the people "so that the people understood the reading" (Neh 8:8-12). At a later time when Greek became the *lingua franca* of the people not only were the Hebrew Scriptures translated into Greek, but new ones (including some of the deuterocanonical books) were written in Greek. Similarly, the oral preaching of Jesus in his native Aramaic was written in Greek idiom (the *koinē* or "common language") for the sake of the people of the Diaspora.

But although literal translation of the message is already a step in inculturation, conveying the nuances of that message in an idiom peculiar to the receptor-language and culture is a *sine qua non* of authentic and relevant inculturation. The concepts, images, and symbols are not the same in every language. The cultural conditioning arising from the literary, linguistic, historical, geographical, social, political, economic, and religious worldview of the writers originating from a culture or cultures is different from our own. Hence the biblical message needs to be expressed and elucidated in each language through dynamic equivalents. Thus the translation itself becomes a new creation fully inculturated in the idiom of the people.

We may safely affirm that the Greek NT itself "is characterized in its entirety by a dynamic of inculturation. In its transposition of the Palestinian message of Jesus into Judeo-Hellenistic culture it displays its intention to transcend the limits of a single cultural world" (*Interpretation of the Bible in the Church* IV. B). The multiplicity of manuscripts of the Bible in Greek, Syriac, and Latin in the early times as well as the use of a multiplicity of literary forms and the rich variety of translations in each of the many modern languages are sure testimony to this inculturation thrust that is revealed in the dynamics of the transmission of the Good News.

2. Interpretation

However good a translation may be, it is only a first step in the process of inculturation. The Bible is a collection of writings composed and brought together more than two thousand years ago in contexts and languages quite different from those of today. The ways of feeling, thinking, living, and self-expression are proper to the local cultures in which the Bible was written. A translation may be apt and accurate, yet many of the idioms, expressions, modes of speech, the customs and habits, beliefs and tenets of the Bible are hard to comprehend by people of quite different languages, cultures, places, and times. Hence "whoever is to go among another people must hold their inheritance, language, and way of life in high esteem" (*AGD* 26).

Between the then and the now, between what it meant and what it means, between the ancient culture in which it was written and the strange new culture in which it is read there is always a deep chasm and a tension. The question "do you understand what you are reading?" and the reply "how can I, unless someone guides me?" (Acts 8:30-31) are ever old and ever new.

One must take into account also the new factors that have a bearing on the understanding of the biblical writings. Sciences such as archaeology, linguistics, philosophy, anthropology, sociology, and psychology have provided us with enormous amounts of data that shed new light on the understanding of the biblical world and its culture, with which no honest interpreter can dispense. Besides, the *Sitz im Leben* (the local, religious, and cultural context) of the people for whom the biblical message is intended plays a vital role in interpretation. Each people and society has its own mode of worship, liturgy, spirituality, prayer, myths, beliefs, philosophy, theology, law, art, customs, traditions, and more, all of which play an important role in any right interpretation of the Bible. The different gospels are in fact different attempts at inculturating the unique and original message of Jesus.

Already in NT times the Good News encountered successive cultures and environments and responded vitally to each of these new situations. (1) Palestinian Judaism was made up of Aramaic-speaking Jews who were fanatical about the Law and the Temple and intensely nationalistic and rabidly exclusive; (2) Hellenistic Judaism consisted of Greek-speaking Jews who were more open, universalistic, and tolerant toward other cultures and experiences; and (3) the Greco-Roman world was composed of Gentiles who were adherents of mystery religions and had a strong philosophical bent—but all were partners in dialogue with the gospel. The early Church responded to each of these new situations through appropriating a new language and a new lifestyle without compromising the core of the message.

This means that the interpreter must be a dialogue partner, and interpretation itself a dialogue in which there is legitimate inquiry, relentless search, mutual sharing, critical collaboration, and creative communion between cultures, religions, and peoples irrespective of their diversity. Thus the true interpreter (who is also an authentic inculturator) plays the role of a prophet insofar as he or she is able to bring about a convergence and communion between the then and the now, leading the reader ultimately to action in favor of community, human liberation, justice, and a preferential option for the poor, and thus help to actualize the reign of God here on earth.

3. Actualization

The formation of the local Christian community is the goal of all inculturation. Inculturation of the Good News must always mean evangelization of a culture with all its socio-political, religio-cultural, psychologico-spiritual, and economic structures. Each culture is built around a particular worldview, a definite system of values as well as a unique relationship in a community of people. No culture is neutral. Each has its positive, liberating, and humanizing characteristics as well as negative, alienating, and dehumanizing traits. This is true also for the cultures in which the Bible was written. It is the duty of the inculturator to listen to the voice of the Spirit and discern the values of the reign of God, namely peace, justice, and love as expressed or implied in these cultures.

Unfortunately there seems to have been a double disservice done in the Church in the past in the area of inculturation. Not only has the biblical word not been liberated from the narrow confines of a local culture or cultures in which it was written but also a new and strange culture of the country of origin of the inculturator/evangelizer has been added to it, and in some cases in Asia and Africa this process has been supported by both economic and military zealotry. It has now become the bounden duty of all those interested and involved in the inculturation of the word of God to quicken the process of liberation of the Good News from these twofold clutches and make it encounter the native culture that is also cleansed of all the unjust and ungodly values in which it may be enchained. The gospel freed from its cultural conditionings and the culture liberated from its oppressive limitations will form healthy partners in the task of inculturation.

To achieve such a result both biblical scholars and the people who are part of a particular culture must work hand in hand. Since cultures themselves change and evolve, the task of inculturation is a continued process that must move on progressively with time. "New local churches have to make every effort to convert the foreign form of biblical inculturation into another form more closely corresponding to the culture of their own land" (*Interpretation of the Bible in the Church* IV. B).

Attention must be paid here to the fact that inculturation is clearly not a one-way process. It is mutual rejection (of peripherals and asides) and mutual enrichment (of essentials and values). "Harmful elements can be left aside and the development of valuable ones encouraged" (*Interpretation of the Bible in the Church* IV. B). A creative gospel-culture encounter demands a constant dying to conditioned cultural expressions of the gospel as well as what is limiting and sinful in cultures and rising to new demands and challenges.

Two possible dangers must be guarded against. There may be a temptation first to water down the biblical message in order to suit it to the uncritical demands of the people. This will lead only to a superficial adaptation that neither serves the people nor is faithful to the message. Sacred Scripture as deeds and words that God has consigned to writing and as unfolded by the long tradition of the Fathers and the interpretation of the teaching authority of the Church (cf. *DV* 2, 8, 11, 17; *AGD* 22) has to be conveyed in all its stringent demands as well as radical challenges without any attempt at diluting it.

At the same time care should be taken also to avoid "every appearance of syncretism and false exclusiveness" (*AGD* 22) that may lead to unnecessary confusions and unreasonable compromises of the biblical revelation and make it even more irrelevant. "In any case, the risk of error does not constitute a valid objection against performing what is a necessary task, that of bringing the message of the Bible to the ears and the hearts of people of our own time" and of various cultures (*Interpretation of the Bible in the Church* IV. A, Actualization).

Last, since "people make culture and culture creates people" any attempt at inculturation must always take into account the whole of the human person with values that promote communion, human dignity, freedom, justice, and community. It must work for a transformation of the society to give it a human face that is also the face of God.

Conclusion

The need for inculturation, which in fact means interculturation, is urgent and pressing in every part of the world where the Good News is preached and accepted, more especially in the countries of Asia and Africa, and among the native peoples, the tribals and the aboriginals. Only a living dialogue and a committed encounter between the gospel culture and the native culture can make the Good News a liberative force—both liberated and liberating!

The driving force behind all inculturation will be the creative freedom that the Spirit of the risen Lord has poured upon us. The working model for all inculturation is always Jesus of Nazareth, son of a carpenter, who is at the same time the eternal Word of the Father (John 1:1), the perfect paradigm of inculturation.

BIBLIOGRAPHY

Amaladoss, Michael. *Making All Things New: Dialogue, Pluralism and Evangelization in Asia.* Maryknoll, N.Y.: Orbis, 1990. See especially "Inculturation," 121–130.

____. "Culture and Dialogue," *Vidyajyoti* 49/1 (1985) 6–15.

Arrupe, Pedro. "Sull' Inculturazione," in *Inculturazione.* Rome: Centrum Ignatianum Spiritualitatis, 1979.

Danielou, Jean. *The Gospel Message and Hellenistic Culture.* Philadelphia: Westminster, 1973.

Felix, Wilfred. "Inculturation as a Hermeneutical Question," *Vidyajyoti* 52/9 (1988) 422–436.

____. "Dogma and Inculturation," *Vidyajyoti* 53/7 (1989) 345–353.

____. "World Religions and Christian Inculturation," *Indian Theological Studies* 25/1 (1988) 5–26.

Fuller, Reginald H. *The Foundations of New Testament Christology.* London: Collins, 1969.

Heselgrave, D. J. *Communicating Christ Cross-Culturally.* Grand Rapids: Zondervan, 1979.

Jeevadhara. An Indian Theological Review 33 (1976). Allepey, Kerala, India. The entire issue is dedicated to the topic of inculturation.

Kraft, C. H. *Christianity in Culture: A Study in Crosscultural Perspective.* Maryknoll, N.Y.: Orbis, 1980.

Lobo, Lancy. "Towards an Inculturation in the Non-Sanskritic Tradition," *Vidyajyoti* 49/1 (1985) 16–28.

Nida, Eugene A., and W. D. Reyburn. *Meaning Across Cultures.* Maryknoll, N.Y.: Orbis, 1981.

Nida, Eugene A. *Customs and Cultures: Anthropology for Christian Missions.* Pasadena, Cal.: Harper, 1986.

Pieris, Aloysius. "Asia's Non-Semitic Religions and Mission of the Local Churches," *The Month* 15/3 (1982) 81–90.

____. *An Asian Theology of Liberation.* Maryknoll, N.Y.: Orbis, 1988.

The Bible and Ecology

Daniel G. Deffenbaugh and David L. Dungan

Introduction

Every day our newspapers, television programs, and radios bring us increasingly disturbing news of polluted rivers, poisoned lakes, clear-cut forests, eroding topsoil, a depleted ozone layer, global warming, and acid rain. People the world over are increasingly frightened and confused. Why is all this happening now? What does the future portend?

Environmental scientists are doing their best to grapple with these questions, but too often they treat the problems in a piecemeal fashion; the empirical method with its emphasis on scrutinizing the particulars of a phenomenon has now become acutely aware of its deficiencies. In short, traditional science lacks a holistic vision. Indeed, it may be that because of certain erroneous assumptions about nature as object, and human beings as manipulators and exploiters of this object, scientists are only making things worse. It would appear, then, that we need now to inquire about what the other disciplines, particularly Biblical hermeneutics and Christian theology, may have to offer in this context. It is our contention that the Bible has much to say about our present environmental predicament, and that perhaps the best place for Christians faithfully to address these issues is with reference to "the beginning" as it is recorded in the book of Genesis.

The Bible's Holistic Vision

In much the same manner as a modern geologist, the author of the Priestly creation account in Gen 1:1–2:4a looks back to the beginning stage of our planet and sees a situation in which the earth was not the beautiful, life-sustaining environment we know today but a bleak and lifeless wasteland:

> In the beginning when God created the heavens and the earth, the earth was a formless void and darkness covered the face of the deep, while a wind from God swept over the face of the waters (Gen 1:1).

The story goes on to tell how God intervenes in this chaos with a series of mighty acts, fashioning one aspect of our familiar world after another. God's hand was present in every facet of creation, and God delighted in what was made. There is a continuous and progressive development in the narrative: the fact that humanity is created on the same day as the animals (Gen 1:24-27), and that Adam is fashioned from the earth itself (Gen 2:7: "Adam" is a play on the Hebrew word for earth, *ʾadāmāh*) suggests a very intimate connection between humans and every aspect of creation, from the most basic to the most complex.

God establishes the whole of creation not as a stage upon which human salvation will eventually be played out, but as a profoundly interdependent community. We find three fundamental affirmations in Genesis 1–3:

1. *The entire creation is a harmonious community.* There is an intimate connection between living animals and what we moderns think of as senseless or inanimate objects like trees or the earth itself. God creates all

things in order that God may enter into relationship with them. All things are worthy of God's attention, which brings us to our second affirmation.

2. *All created beings are good in the sight of God.* There is no perceived dualism between good or valuable spiritual beings on the one hand and evil or valueless physical things on the other.
3. *Humans are made of precisely the same "stuff" as every other created being: ʾadāmāh or "earth."* There is one basic difference: humans, both male and female, are created in God's image; they alone have been appointed to tend and care for the rest of creation.

Let us examine each of these assertions in more detail.

The Entire Creation is a Harmonious Community

We may further develop our understanding of creation as a community of interrelated beings by referring to the Hebrew poets, especially those who fall within the Wisdom tradition. From these writers we get the distinct impression that humans are not the only creatures who worship God; all creatures worship and glorify the Creator in their own ways.

> The heavens are telling the glory of God;
> and the firmament proclaims his handiwork.
> Day to day pours forth speech,
> and night to night declares knowledge.
> There is no speech, nor are there words;
> their voice is not heard;
> yet their voice goes out through all the earth,
> and their words to the end of the world (Ps 19:1-4).

Another psalm depicts the earth and other creatures praising God for the just divine governance of the nations.

> O sing to the LORD a new song;
> sing to the LORD, all the earth . . .
> Let the heavens be glad, and let the earth rejoice;
> let the sea roar, and all that fills it;
> let the field exult, and everything in it.
> Then shall all the trees of the forest sing for joy
> before the LORD, for he is coming, . . . to govern the earth . . .
> with righteousness and the peoples with his truth (Ps 96:1, 11-13).

In addition to the poets, it was not uncommon for the Hebrew prophets to call upon the mountains and other members of God's creation to act as responsible and impartial witnesses in God's complaint against the wicked. Micah, for example, a prophet of both Judah and Israel (c. 715–687 B.C.E.), charges the unrighteous before God's created order:

> Hear what the LORD says:
> Rise, plead your case before the mountains,
> and let the hills hear your voice.
> Hear, you mountains, the controversy of the LORD,
> and you enduring foundations of the earth;
> For the LORD has a controversy with his people,
> and he will contend with Israel (Mic 6:1-2).

Similarly the prophet Isaiah, a contemporary of Micah, speaks of earth and sky acting as a sympathetic audience for God's complaint against the people of Israel:

> Hear, O heavens, and listen, O earth;
> for the LORD has spoken:
> I reared children and brought them up,
> but they have rebelled against me.
> The ox knows its owner,
> and the donkey its master's crib;
> but Israel does not know,
> my people do not understand (Isa 1:2-3).

Of course some may object that these poetic descriptions of the cosmos cannot be taken as metaphysical assertions about the nature of the universe. We would reply to this in two ways. First, we would agree that poetry cannot be appealed to in order to establish metaphysical principles, but at the same time all language, as the German philosopher Martin Heidegger argued, possesses an implicit metaphysic. In other words poetic references can only be recognized as such when they are consistent with the way in which those reading the poetry perceive and understand the cosmos. The words of such prophets as Micah and Isaiah were powerful, we would suggest, simply because they recalled the original affirmation of God's care for creation and humanity's moral obligation to be a faithful participant in the biotic community. The fact that Israel and Judah had taken the path of unrighteousness was an affront not only to God but to the community of which they had been a part since the beginning.

Second, the interdependence of God, humanity, and creation can be attested in other scriptural passages as well. The covenant established by YHWH with Noah after the flood bound YHWH not only to human beings but to *the whole of creation.* Notice the repetitious wording: it is as if the speaker (God) were trying to phrase this contract in the most sweeping way possible so that no living being of any kind would be left out.

> "As for me, I am establishing my covenant with you and your descendants after you, and with *every living creature* that is with you, the birds, the domestic animals, and every animal of the earth with you, as many as came out of the ark. I establish my covenant with you, that never again shall *all flesh* be cut off by the waters of a flood. . . . This is the sign of the covenant that I make between me and you and *every living creature* that is with you for all future generations; I have set my bow in the clouds, and it shall be a sign of the covenant *between me and the earth, . . . between me and you and every living creature of all flesh.* . . . When the bow is in the clouds, I will see it and remember the everlasting covenant *between God and every living creature of all flesh that is on the earth"* (Gen 9:8-16).

As in the creation of Genesis 1, Israel's priestly tradition explicitly stated in sweeping *legal terms* God's inclusive covenant with *all living beings,* that is, the entire created order, not simply the humans made in God's image. It is striking to observe these four traditions of the OT, the poetic, the prophetic, the priestly, and the legal, unanimously affirming a comprehensive interdependence between God, humans and all creation.

Humans Created in the Image of God

Historically Christian theology has placed considerable emphasis on one aspect of the creation narrative: the assertion that humans alone possess the image of God. Let us hear once more what the text says.

> Then God said: "Let us make humankind in our image, according to our likeness; and let them have dominion over the fish of the sea, and over the birds of the air, and over the cattle, and over all the wild animals of the earth, and over every creeping thing that creeps upon the earth." So God created humankind in his image; in the image of God he created them; male and female he created them (Gen 1:26-27).

It cannot be denied that humanity holds a privileged position in the midst of the biotic community created by God, but over the centuries too much emphasis has been placed on privilege and not enough on human responsibility. Christian theologians and lay people alike have chosen to read this account exclusively, with no reference to the subsequent chapter that elaborates the role of the human in the larger community. As Adam is made from the earth, so must Adam recognize the moral obligation that derives from the "roots" of creation. Adam must dress and keep the Garden, and must care for it.

> And the LORD God planted a garden in Eden, in the east; and there he put the man whom he had formed. . . . The LORD God took the man and put him in the garden of Eden to till it and keep it (Gen 2:8, 15).

A reading of the two narratives together, then, establishes a more richly nuanced perspective than if we were to focus on the Priestly account (Gen 1:1–2:4a) exclusively. While the latter describes human beings as created "in the image of God," and tends to lend support to an anthropocentric interpretation, the Yahwist narrative emphasizes the creation of humans out of the earth and their consequent obligation as caretakers, "dressers and keepers" of God's Garden.

The contention that humanity and earth are inextricably connected can be argued on the basis of the consequences of the Fall. Humanity's disobedience disrupts the essential *shalom* or wholeness of Eden, and its ramifications can be felt in every corner of creation. Adam and Eve must bear the burden of God's curse for their transgression of the divine prohibition against eating from the tree of the knowledge of good and evil.

> To the woman he said,
> "I will greatly increase your pangs in childbearing;
> in pain you shall bring forth children,
> yet your desire shall be for your husband,
> and he shall rule over you."
> And to the man he said,
> "Because you have listened to the voice of your wife,
> and have eaten of the tree
> about which I commanded you,
> 'You shall not eat of it,'
> cursed is the ground because of you;

in toil you shall eat of it all the days of your life;
thorns and thistles it shall bring forth for you;
and you shall eat the plants of the field.
By the sweat of your face
you shall eat bread
until you return to the ground,
for out of it you were taken;
you are dust,
and to dust you shall return" (Gen 3:16-19).

Note how Adam and Eve are not cursed apart from creation. God looks upon them as related intimately to the earth from which they were taken; their punishment is simultaneously a punishment of creation.

This same viewpoint shows up again a few chapters later when God beholds the corruption of creation (Gen 6:11) and decides to destroy the earth with a flood. Genesis 4–6 describes the spiral of human violence that followed after the Fall, first among humans and then engulfing the entire world. The words of Gen 6:5 relate God's reaction to the increasing violence and evil among humans.

> The LORD saw that the wickedness of humankind was great in the earth, and that every inclination of the thoughts of their hearts was only evil continually. And the LORD was sorry that he had made humankind on the earth, and it grieved him to his heart. So the LORD said, "I will blot out from the earth the human beings I have created . . ." (Gen 6:5-7a).

That much is understandable, but note how the story continues:

> . . . people together with animals and creeping things and birds of the air, for I am sorry that I have made them (Gen 6:7b).

Why would the biblical writer say that God intended to destroy all life on earth because of the wickedness of the humans? What did the animals do to offend God? The author of this account seemingly does not feel that this (to us outrageous) decision on God's part requires any justification, but the text does say that the earth had mysteriously become corrupt.

> Now the earth was corrupt (Heb. *šaḥat*) in God's sight, and the earth was filled with violence (Heb. *ḥāmās* = Greek *adikia*). And God saw that the earth was corrupt *(šaḥat);* for all flesh had corrupted its ways upon the earth. And God said to Noah, "I have determined to make an end of all flesh (Heb. *kol bāsār*); for the earth is filled with violence because of them; now I am going to destroy them along with the earth" (Gen 6:11-13).

Observe how this same all-inclusive approach continues. God commands Noah to build the ark and to take with him into the ark two of every kind of domesticated animal and two of every kind of wild creature from the fields and forests. Would not a modern storyteller have portrayed the humans just saving themselves and forgetting all about the wild animals? That certainly is not the case here. Above we saw that when Noah came out, the same community-of-living-creatures concept continued, as God made a covenant with him never again to destroy humans and all flesh by the waters of a flood.

In the biblical view the consequences of human sin never lead just to human-specific desolation; the community of living beings is simultaneously corrupted. Consider this marvelous example from the eighth-century prophet Hosea.

Hear the word of the LORD,
O people of Israel,
for the LORD has an indictment
against the inhabitants of the land.
There is no faithfulness or loyalty,
and no knowledge of God in the land.
Swearing, lying, and murder,
stealing and adultery break out;
and bloodshed follows bloodshed.
Therefore the land mourns,
and all who live in it languish;
together with the wild animals
and the birds of the air,
even the fish of the sea are perishing (Hos 4:1-3).

From a biblical standpoint, then, it seems absurd for humans to continue to pray for happy, healthy, and productive lives as long as we continue to do evil to the earth which is like an extension of our bodies, that out of which we were made and with which we continue to share our being.

Humans, the World, and Redemption

Of course, the good news connected with this renewed understanding of humanity in community with the world is the notion that as the earth is cursed through humanity's sin so will it be redeemed through humanity's justification and sanctification in Christ. This is no doubt the sense of Paul's affirmation of the "community of blessing" in Rom 8:18-21.

> I consider that the sufferings of this present time are not worth comparing with the glory about to be revealed to us. For the creation waits with eager longing for the revealing of the children of God; for the creation was subjected to futility, not of its own will but by the will of the one who subjected it, in hope that the creation itself will be set free from its bondage to decay and will obtain the freedom of the glory of the children of God.

This idea of the interdependence of humans and creation can be further supported by a close and critical reading of the Prologue to the Gospel of John. Here we are introduced to the notion of Christ as the *logos,* that through which the world *(ho kosmos)* was created.

> In the beginning was the *logos,*
> and the *logos* was with God,
> and the *logos* was God.
> He was in the beginning with God.
> All things came into being through him,
> and without him not one thing came into being.
> What has come into being through him was life,
> and the life was the light of all people . . . (John 1:1-4).

It is widely believed that the Greek term *logos* means "word" because that is the way it is usually translated. But much is lost in the transition from Greek to Latin to English. In fact, there is another Greek term that can be translated as "word": *rhema.* It can be found in such English words as rhetor (a person who uses words skillfully) and rhetoric (teaching people how to do the same). In any case, the Greek term *logos* did not refer primarily to our understanding of "word." Rather it had a wide range of meanings that generally convey the idea of order or pattern. Thus a *logos* can mean a legal argument, or the plot of a story, a building plan, a mathematical formula, a law or rule, and so forth. The typical Latin translation for *logos* was not *verbum* ("word") but *ratio* ("reason"), as when the Stoics used *ratio* to describe the ordered, rational structure of Nature. It gives us our word "logic."

When the term *logos* is used in the Prologue of John, stating that the *logos* is both God the creator of all things and the "light" of humans (John 1:4), we would suggest that the author is not drawing on the Greek philosophical tradition but rather has in mind the Hebraic Wisdom tradition in which *Ḥokmāh,* "Lady Wisdom," is God's partner in the creation of the universe and the guiding light of humans seeking to live righteous lives (see Proverbs 8, for example). She is described in reverential terms in Sirach 24:

> "I came forth from the mouth of the Most High,
> and covered the earth like a mist.
> I dwelt in the highest heavens,
> and my throne was in a pillar of cloud.
> Alone I compassed the vault of heaven
> and traversed the depths of the abyss.
> Over waves of the sea, over all the earth,
> over every people and nation I have held sway.
> Among all these I sought a resting place;
> in whose territory should I abide?
> Then the Creator of all things gave me a command,
> and my Creator chose the place for my tent.
> He said, 'Make your dwelling in Jacob,
> and in Israel receive your inheritance.'
> Before the ages, in the beginning, he created me,
> and for all the ages I shall not cease to be.
> In the holy tent I ministered before him,
> and so I was established in Zion.
> Thus in the beloved city he gave me a resting place,
> and in Jerusalem was my domain" (Sir 24:1-11).

If we interpret the term *logos* in John 1:14 in terms of the description of Divine Wisdom in Proverbs 8 and Sirach 24 and then apply this perspective to the material already discussed we get a clear and helpful vantage point from which we can understand the meaning of Genesis, the Psalms, and the Prophets. As Christians we can affirm that Christ, God's Wisdom, pervades the whole of creation. When the heavens proclaim the glory of God and the mountains bear witness to God's eternity and power, what else is this if not the "play of the Spirit" among the valleys and hills, the response of Christ/Lady Wisdom to God the Creator? In this divine celebration of Godself we humans—male and female—can also join. Humanity is the "principal violinist" in this wondrous "symphony of the universe."

Yet we know that a dissonance pervades the cosmos: sin. The harmony of creation is disrupted. But as Christians we affirm that Christ, God's Wisdom, came as "light [that] shines in the darkness, and the darkness did not overcome it" (John 1:5), and through our baptism we rejoice in our unity with him, having "clothed [ourselves] with Christ" (Gal 3:27). As justified and sanctified in the eyes of God we participate in God's compassion through divine Wisdom toward the whole world; we join with Christ in our desire to redeem the world. We can actively express and mediate Christ's compassion not just toward other human beings but to the world that is redeemed through him. "For God so loved the world *(ton kosmon)* . . ." (John 3:16).

Thus the obligation of Adam and Eve in the Garden, to till and keep it, is reaffirmed through Christ. We humans are simultaneously a part of creation and partners with the Triune God in caring for—and renewing—the beauty and order of the original ecological community. Scripture provides us with an inspirational vision, a model to attain through our sanctifying work.

The Redeemed Creation

The vision of the redeemed earth is perhaps best presented in Psalm 104 where, once again, Wisdom is a central motif.

> O LORD, how manifold are your works!
> In wisdom you have made them all;
> the earth is full of your creatures.
> Yonder is the sea, great and wide,
> creeping things innumerable are there,
> living things both small and great.
> There go the ships,
> and Leviathan that you formed to sport in it.
> These all [humanity included] look to you
> to give them their food in due season;
> when you give to them, they gather it up;
> when you open your hand, they are filled with good things.
> When you hide your face, they are dismayed;
> when you take away their breath, they die
> and return to their dust.
> When you send forth your spirit,
> they are created,
> and you renew the face of the ground.
> May the glory of the LORD endure forever;
> may the LORD rejoice in his works . . . ! (Ps 104:24-31)

The image of inter-species harmony here is exquisitely beautiful, resembling an ancient tapestry. Human beings in this vision are one part of the weave. As harmony is characteristic of God's creation, so is it foundational for the renewed sense of community that humans in their day-to-day existence must have as citizens of God's realm. Culture is not the singular concern here, but rather culture in cooperation with nature. It is a vision of God's *shalom* that we have seen before.

> In days to come
> the mountain of the LORD's house
> shall be established as the highest of the mountains . . . .
> Peoples shall stream to it,
> and many nations shall come and say:
> "Come, let us go up to the mountain of the LORD,
> to the house of the God of Jacob;
> that he may teach us his ways
> and that we may walk in his paths."
> For out of Zion shall go forth instruction,
> and the word of the LORD from Jerusalem.
> He shall judge between many peoples,
> and shall arbitrate between strong nations far away;
> they shall beat their swords into plowshares,
> and their spears into pruning hooks;
> nation shall not lift up sword against nation,
> neither shall they learn war any more;
> but they shall sit under their own vines and under their own fig trees,
> and no one shall make them afraid;
> for the mouth of the LORD of hosts has spoken (Mic 4:1-4).

Micah's vision reveals a yearning for the day when humans and nature have regained God's intended harmony. No longer is the pride of a man's life—his ability to fashion constructive things—taken away by making weapons of destruction. No longer is the glory of a woman's life—bringing children into the world—devastated when their young sons are conscripted by the army and taken away to learn the art of destruction, or when their daughters' lives are abused by similarly violent men.

Clearly the biblical writers understand God's creation to be harmonious, inclusive, beautiful, and good. Humans are given the responsibility within this community of caring for the earth and preserving its integrity. When humans deny this vocation and break God's covenant with them the ramifications are felt not only among fellow human beings but throughout the entire created order. However, when we accept our task in creation as caretakers the whole of creation is positively affected.

PEACE WITH ALL CREATION

In our day there is a growing awareness that world peace is threatened not only by . . . regional conflicts and continued injustice among peoples and nations, but also by a lack of due respect for nature, by the plundering of natural resources and by a progressive decline in the quality of life. The sense of precariousness and insecurity that such a situation engenders is a seedbed for collective selfishness, disregard for others and dishonesty.

Faced with the widespread destruction of the environment, people everywhere are coming to understand that we cannot continue to use the goods of the earth as we have in the past. The public in general as well as political leaders are concerned about this problem, and experts from a wide range of disciplines are studying its causes. Moreover, a new ecological awareness is beginning to emerge which, rather than being downplayed, ought to be encouraged to develop into concrete programs and initiatives. . . .

Certain elements of today's ecological crisis reveal its moral character. First among these is the indiscriminate application of advances in science and technology. Many recent discoveries have brought undeniable benefits to humanity. Indeed, they demonstrate the nobility of the human vocation to participate responsibly in God's creative action in the world. Unfortunately, it is now clear that the application of these discoveries in the fields of industry and agriculture have produced harmful long-term effects. This has led to the painful realization that we cannot interfere in one area of the ecosystem without paying due attention both to the consequences of such interference in other areas and to the well-being of future generations.

The gradual depletion of the ozone layer and the related "greenhouse effect" has now reached crisis proportions as a consequence of industrial growth, massive urban concentration and vastly increased energy needs. Industrial waste, the burning of fossil fuels, unrestricted deforestation, the use of certain types of herbicides, coolants and propellants: All of these are known to harm the atmosphere and environment. The resulting meteorological and atmospheric changes range from damage to health to the possible future submersion of low-lying lands.

While in some cases the damage already done may well be irreversible, in many other cases it can still be halted. It is necessary, however, that the entire human community—individuals, states and international bodies—take seriously the responsibility that is theirs.

The most profound and serious indication of the moral implications underlying the ecological problem is the lack of respect for life evident in many of the patterns of environmental pollution. Often the interests of production prevail over concern for the dignity of workers, while economic interests take priority over the good of individuals and even entire peoples. In these cases, pollution or environmental destruction is the result of an unnatural and reductionist vision, which at times leads to a genuine contempt for man.

On another level, delicate ecological balances are upset by the uncontrolled destruction of animal and plant life or by a reckless exploitation of natural resources. It should be pointed out that all of this, even if carried out in the name of progress and well-being, is ultimately to mankind's disadvantage.

Finally, we can only look with deep concern at the enormous possibilities of biological research. We are not yet in a position to assess the biological disturbance that could result from indiscriminate genetic manipulation and from the unscrupulous development of new forms of plant and animal life, to say nothing of unacceptable experimentation regarding the origins of human life itself. It is evident to all that in any area as delicate as this, indifference to fundamental ethical norms or their rejection would lead mankind to the very threshold of self-destruction.

Respect for life, and above all for the dignity of the human person, is the ultimate guiding norm for any sound economic, industrial or scientific progress.

The complexity of the ecological question is evident to all. There are, however, certain underlying principles which, while respecting the legitimate autonomy and the specific competence of those involved, can direct research toward adequate and lasting solutions. These principles are essential to the building of a peaceful society; no peaceful society can afford to neglect either respect for life or the fact that there is an integrity to creation. . . .

. . . the earth is ultimately a common heritage, the fruits of which are for the benefit of all. In the words of the Second Vatican Council, "God destined the earth and all it contains for the use of every individual and all peoples" (Gaudium et Spes, 69). This has direct consequences for the problem at hand. It is manifestly unjust that a privileged few should continue to accumulate excess goods, squandering available resources, while masses of people are living in conditions of misery at the very lowest level of subsistence. Today the dramatic threat of ecological breakdown is teaching us the extent to which greed and selfishness—both individual and collective—are contrary to the order of creation, an order which is characterized by mutual interdependence.

The concepts of an ordered universe and a common heritage both point to the necessity of a more internationally coordinated approach to the management of the earth's goods. In many cases the effects of ecological problems transcend the borders of individual states; hence their solution cannot be found solely on the national level. Recently there have been some promising steps toward such international action, yet the existing mechanisms and bodies are clearly not adequate for the development of a comprehensive plan of action. Political obstacles, forms of exaggerated nationalism and economic interests—to mention only a few factors—impede international cooperation and long-term effective action.

The need for joint action on the international level does not lessen the responsibility of each individual state. Not only should each state join with others in implementing internationally accepted standards, but it should also make or facilitate necessary socio-economic adjustments within its own borders, giving special attention to the most vulnerable sectors of society. The state should also actively endeavor within its own territory to prevent destruction of the atmosphere and biosphere by carefully monitoring, among other things, the impact of new technological or scientific advances. The state also has the responsibility of ensuring that its citizens are not exposed to dangerous pollutants or toxic wastes. The right to a safe environment is ever more insistently presented today as a right that must be included in an updated charter of human rights.

The ecological crisis reveals the urgent moral need for a new solidarity, especially in relations between the developing nations and those that are highly industrialized. States must increasingly share responsibility, in complementary ways, for the promotion of a natural and social environment that is both peaceful and healthy. The newly industrialized states cannot, for example, be asked to apply restrictive environmental standards to their emerging industries unless the industrialized states first apply them within their own boundaries. At the same time, countries in the process of industrialization are not morally free to repeat the errors made in the past by others and recklessly continue to damage the environment through industrial pollutants, radical deforestation or unlimited exploitation of non-renewable resources. In this context, there is urgent need to find a solution to the treatment and disposal of toxic wastes. . .

It must also be said that the proper ecological balance will not be found without directly addressing the structural forms of poverty that exist throughout the world. Rural poverty and unjust land distribution in many countries, for example, have led to subsistence farming and to the exhaustion of the soil. Once their land yields no more, many farmers move on to clear new land, thus accelerating uncontrolled deforestation, or they settle in urban centers which lack the infrastructure to receive them. Likewise, some heavily indebted countries are destroying their natural heritage, at the price of irreparable ecological imbalances, in order to develop new products for export. In the face of such situations it would be wrong to assign responsibility to the poor alone for the negative environmental consequences of their actions. Rather, the poor, to whom the earth is entrusted no less than to others, must be enabled to find a way out of their poverty. This will require a courageous reform of structures as well as new ways of relating among peoples and states.

. . . Despite the international agreements which prohibit chemical, bacteriological and biological warfare, the fact is that laboratory research continues to develop new offensive weapons capable of altering the balance of nature.

Today, any form of war on a global scale would lead to incalculable ecological damage. But even local or regional wars, however limited, not only destroy human life and social structures, but also damage the land, ruining crops and vegetation as well as poisoning the soil and water. The survivors of war are forced to begin a new life in very difficult environmental conditions, which in turn create situations of extreme social unrest, with further negative consequences for the environment.

Modern society will find no solution to the ecological problem unless it takes a serious look at its lifestyle. In many parts of the world, society is given to instant gratification and consumerism while remaining indifferent to the damage which they cause. . . . Simplicity, moderation and discipline, as well as a spirit of sacrifice, must become a part of everyday life. . . .

Today the ecological crisis has assumed such proportions as to be the responsibility of everyone.

At the conclusion of this message, I should like to address directly my brothers and sisters in the Catholic Church, in order to remind them of their serious obligation to care for all of creation. The commitment of believers to a healthy environment for everyone stems directly from their belief in God the Creator, from their recognition of the effects of original and personal sin, and from the certainty of having been redeemed by Christ. Respect for life and for the dignity of the human person extends also to the rest of creation, which is called to join man in praising God (cf. Ps 148:96).

In 1979, I proclaimed St. Francis of Assisi as the heavenly patron of those who promote ecology (cf. apostolic letter *Inter Sanctos:* AAS 71 [1979] 1509f). He offers Christians an example of genuine and deep respect for the integrity of creation. As a friend of the poor who was loved by God's creatures, St. Francis invited all of creation—animals, plants, natural forces, even Brother Sun and Sister Moon—to give honor and praise to the Lord. The poor man of Assisi gives us striking witness that when we are at peace with God we are better able to devote ourselves to building up that peace with all creation which is inseparable from peace among all peoples.

It is my hope that the inspiration of St. Francis will help us to keep ever alive a sense of "fraternity" with all those good and beautiful things which almighty God has created. And may he remind us of our serious obligation to respect and watch over them with care, in light of that greater and higher fraternity that exists within the human family. —*Pope John Paul II*

BIBLIOGRAPHY

Pope John Paul II. "The Ecological Crisis—A Common Responsibility." Message of His Holiness Pope John Paul II for the Celebration of the World Day of Peace 1 January 1990. Published as "Peace With All Creation," *Origins* 19:28 (Dec. 14, 1989) 465–468, and available also from the United States Catholic Conference, Department of Social Development and World Peace, Environmental Justice Program, 3211 4th Street N.E., Washington, D.C. 20017 (202-541-3182).

The U.S. Catholic Conference Environmental Justice Program is an integral part of a wider ecumenical effort known as the National Religious Partnership for the Environment. Its four member groups include the U.S. Catholic Conference, the National Council of Churches of Christ, the Evangelical Environmental Network, and the Coalition on the Environment and Jewish Life. These groups will be publishing suggestions for initiating parish programs, liturgical-homiletical-prayer helps, background information on the connection between social justice and environmental issues, parish bulletin inserts, videos (e.g., "Hope for a Renewed Earth"). For more information contact the local diocesan office or the U.S. Catholic Conference.

Barnes, Michael, ed., *An Ecology of the Spirit: Religious Reflections and Environmental Consciousness.* Lanham, Md.: University Press of America, 1990. A collection of essays on Christianity and the environmental movement. Contains particularly helpful essays on more recent movements such as ecofeminism and creation spirituality.

Berry, Wendell, *The Gift of Good Land.* San Francisco: North Point Press, 1981; *Home Economics* (1987); *What Are People For?* (1987). Though Berry is not a Christian theologian his reflections on the intimate relationship between people and land cannot be overlooked as a source for inspiration.

Cobb, John B., Jr., *Sustainability: Economics, Ecology, and Justice.* Maryknoll, N.Y.: Orbis, 1992. A helpful source that brings together issues of ecology and economics from the personal perspective of a process theologian.

David, Donald Edward. *Ecophilosophy. A Field Guide to the Literature.* San Pedro: R. & E. Miles, 1989. Still the most comprehensive annotated guide to the philosophical and theological discussion of the environment in English.

God's Earth Our Home. A Resource for Congregational Study and Action on Environmental and Economic Justice. National Council of Churches of Christ in the U.S.A. A collection of study pamphlets on key issues, together with suggestions for parish activities. For more information contact: WCC, 475 Riverside Drive, New York, NY 10115; Eco-Justice Working Group 212-870-2511.

Granberg-Michaelson, Wesley. *A Worldly Spirituality: The Call to Take Care of the Earth.* San Francisco: Harper & Row, 1984. An evangelical response to Lynn White's essay (see below).

Keeping and Healing the Creation. A Resource Paper prepared by the Presbyterian Eco-Justice Task Force. Louisville: Presbyterian Church USA, 1990. Contains an excellent analysis of biblical texts relating to environmental issues. Ties together worship, theology and environmental ethics in a clear, readable fashion. For more information contact: Presbyterian Church (U.S.A.) Committee on Social Witness Policy. 100 Witherspoon Street, Louisville KY 40202.

LaChance, A. J., and J. E. Carroll. *Embracing the Earth. Catholic Approaches to Ecology.* Maryknoll, N.Y.: Orbis, 1994. An excellent collection of fresh, imaginative essays; ideal for adult discussion groups.

Passmore, John. *Man's Responsibility for Nature.* New York: Charles Scribner's Sons, 1974. See ch. 1, "Man as Despot," for a treatment of the notion of human superiority.

Thomas, Keith. *Man and the Natural World: A History of the Modern Sensibility.* New York: Pantheon Books, 1983. An excellent historical survey of the idea of human superiority and how this has justified exploitation of the natural world.

White, Lynn, Jr. "The Historical Roots of Our Environmental Crisis," in Ian Barbour, ed., *Western Man and Environmental Ethics.* Reading, Mass.: Addison-Wesley, 1973. White's essay, originally published in 1967, was the clarion call for Christian theologians to respond to accusations that the environmental predicament in which the West was beginning to find itself is in fact a direct result of human actions justified by Christian theology. Interestingly, White proposes that Westerners begin following the model of a Christian saint, Francis of Assisi.

World Council of Churches, Programme Unit III: Justice, Peace and Creation; 150 route de Ferney, P.O. Box 2100, 1211 Geneva 2, Switzerland. See "Accelerated Climate Change. Sign of Peril, Test of Faith." This booklet lays out the elementary aspects of global warming, basic theological and ethical guidelines, realistic policy targets, and two chapters on the role of the churches.

The Christian and the State According to the New Testament and in the Early Church

Benedict Thomas Viviano

The early Christians related to the state on the basis of Jesus' preaching of the kingdom of God, which was soon to come in its fullness, as well as on the basis of their new life in Christ. Their hope for the coming of the kingdom relativized all purely human political powers in their eyes, but for help in concrete situations they also drew on the Hebrew and Greek Scriptures and their experience of life in the Roman empire and its vassal states.

The Scriptures of the past provided them with several models of government that seemed to have the approval of God. The first and perhaps the ideal model was the experience of direct divine rule (theocracy) mediated by charismatic prophet-type leaders of whom Moses was the supreme example. Philo presented Moses as prophet, priest, king, and legislator, and the Christians (for example, Gregory of Nyssa and Thomas Aquinas) eventually applied this description to Jesus as the new Moses. This model was then carried on by Joshua and the judges of Israel. It may be called the Sinai model, as opposed to the Zion model that comes with the monarchy (Saul, David, Solomon, and their successors). The theocratic or Sinai model is illustrated by the fable of Judg 9:8-15.

In the royal or Zion model the roles of king, prophet, and priest were ordinarily performed by different people. The prophets were usually critical of the kings and many doubted that the monarchy had any value whatsoever in God's sight. After the monarchies had been swept away by a series of world empires, Daniel was given a larger vision: God's plan of salvation could not be limited to a small state (historical Israel) but must be expressed by a universal regime called the kingdom of God (Dan 2:44; 7:13-14). But at just this time the Maccabees were setting up by force of arms a priestly state in Jerusalem, a Temple *polis.* In the meantime (exact dating is not possible at present), on the local level in the Jewish Diaspora, Jews began to organize in comparatively simple social institutions called synagogues, governed by councils of (lay) elders often composed of the wealthier, more influential members of the community, including women (compare Lydia in Acts 16:14, 15, 40; cf. Burtchaell, *Synagogue*). Women and older children are mentioned in the assembly for the first time in Neh 8:2. This semi-democratic model contrasted sharply with the Temple hierarchy whose membership was determined in principle by nobility of blood. After 70 C.E. a new model of leadership arose, that of academic leaders in the houses of study (the rabbinic academy or *yeshiva*). The academy functioned as legislature and court as well as school. In addition to these models there was also a side tradition of violent zeal for God and the Law. This zealot model is found in Phinehas (Numbers 25) and becomes associated also with Elijah (Hengel, *Zealots*). There were also texts of terror that advocated the extermination of Israel's enemies (e.g., Num 33:55). Paul claims to have been a zealot in some sense before his conversion (Gal 1:14).

Into this complex situation came Jesus of Nazareth with his message of the kingdom of

God, a kingdom that would consist of justice (Matt 6:33), peace, and joy (Rom 14:17) for all peoples, nations, and cultures (Matt 28:16-20; Dan 7:13-14). For Jesus this great hope was to be the object of prayer (Matt 6:10) and longing (Matt 6:33; cf. 2 Pet 3:12), but he never speaks of building the kingdom directly ourselves. It is to be the gift of God. Nevertheless, the kingdom remains the great social and political as well as personal and religious hope in the synoptic gospels.

Within this vision Jesus offers a radical interpretation of the commandment to love our neighbors (Lev 19:18); it is to include even our enemies. This nonviolent position, so remote from the traditional practice of states, can in part be explained by the political powerlessness of the early Christians. Until Constantine (325 C.E.) they did not have responsibility for the administration of the state (Gerhardsson, *Ethos*). But despite Jesus' action in the Temple (Mark 11:15-19) he meant his teaching to be the goal even of human society, and recent events seem to confirm the wisdom of his teaching. Even scholars who think Jesus was a kind of zealot against oppression admit that he was a nonviolent one (Horsley, *Spiral*).

Against this background certain texts of the gospels and other NT writings that address specific state issues take on more distinct contours. Thus the answer of Jesus to the Herodian test question about paying taxes to the emperor, "Give . . . to the emperor the things that are the emperor's, and to God the things that are God's" (Matt 22:21) can be interpreted as follows: Everything belongs to God, the creator and redeemer, to whom alone our ultimate allegiance belongs, but in the interim, before God brings the kingdom in its fullness, that is, before God's crown rights as creator are fully reestablished, everyone may pay taxes to the emperor, lest worse disorder arise (cf. *m. ʾAbot,* 3:2, 7).

This interpretation is strengthened by a somewhat similar passage, Matt 17:24-27. There, in connection with the Temple tax, the *didrachma,* Jesus teaches that the "children" (i.e., the heirs of the kingdom of God) are free, that is, exempt from the obligation to pay the tax. Nevertheless, Jesus continues, "so that we do not give offense to them . . . give it to them for you and me" (v. 27). So the followers of Jesus are not strictly bound, but for reasons of ecumenical or interfaith relations, pastoral expediency, and keeping the peace, they may pay the tax.

In the instructions Jesus gives to his apostles at the last supper, as recounted in Luke, there are some sayings peculiar to Luke that soften the radicalism of Jesus' teaching on nonviolence and poverty (Luke 22:35-38). Here Jesus instructs his disciples to provide for the situation after Easter when it will be necessary to carry money, and with the money to buy weapons when the circumstances call for it. This passage has helped the Church to come to terms with some of the compromises thought necessary to govern the state in history. We may call the two swords mentioned in v. 38 military tokenism. Today this may be transformed into metaphorical militarism—that is, wars are becoming unknown in advanced democratic societies but there are some permanent values traditionally associated with the military experience (courage, discipline, heroism, teamwork, camaraderie) that can be retained in a post-military era when the wisdom of Jesus' teaching on nonviolence prevails.

In Acts Jesus' reserved attitude toward human powers is shared by his disciples. Peter expresses it thus: "we must obey God rather than [i.e., before] any human authority" (Acts 5:29). He does not reject human authority, but God's authority is supreme. Conflict is foreseen as possible and does in fact occur. Luke stresses the boldness of the apostles, for example in Acts 4:23-31. Paul too shares the same limited and provisional loyalty to the Roman order. Luke shows Paul operating congenially within the framework of the Roman social order, yet also portrays him withholding his ultimate allegiance from it. Paul's use of the title "Lord" for Jesus has political implications in a world where the ruler is designated as "Lord" (see Acts 25:26; Cassidy, *Society and Politics*).

Turning now to the letters of Paul we notice first of all his teaching in 2 Cor 8:12-15 in connection with the collection for Jerusalem. Here he stresses the importance of equality in the community. (He bases his teaching loosely on the rules for the distribution of manna found in Exod 16:18.) This passage is the only one in the NT to provide a basis for the kind of egalitarian democracy known or striven for today.

Paul's most formal teaching on the Christian's duty to obey the state comes in Rom 13:1-7 and has had great influence particularly on Lutheran Christianity. Here Paul three times insists that all authority comes from God. Paul then draws the conclusion that Christians are to obey the civil authorities and submit to them, not only externally but as a duty of conscience (v. 5), and this includes paying taxes and showing respect. Such a sweeping endorsement has troubled Christian consciences that live under abusive regimes. Therefore it is first necessary to notice that Paul defines the authority as "God's servant *for your good*" and for the punishment of criminals (v. 4). From this definition we may conclude that when the state does not act as the servant of God and does not act for the good of the citizens, and becomes criminal itself, it is not able to command the same degree of allegiance as is envisaged in the definition. Paul himself does not yet draw this conclusion (see below on Revelation 13). He is here thinking in terms of the legitimate exercise of authority. But Paul also teaches that "our citizenship is in heaven" (Phil 3:20) where we share a common allegiance with the angels to the one Lord and God. This is an important limitation on Christian allegiance to earthly authorities because (a) some scholars think that Paul in Rom 13:1-7 is thinking primarily of those guardian angels who stand behind or over every nation according to Jewish apocalyptic (cf. Dan 10:13-14, 20-21, and Cullmann, *State*), and (b) in any case the fact that our primary citizenship is in heaven means that we are only bound in a limited way to earthly lords and leaders (Peterson, *Angels*), especially when they abuse their authority. The teaching of 1 Pet 2:13-17 is similar to Paul's; it is summed up in v. 17b: "Fear God. Honor the [king]" (this is the motto of Sweden).

The danger of abuse means that Paul's teaching, which explicitly looks only at the positive side of the state, must at times be balanced by another passage, Revelation 13, which was probably written in the aftermath of Nero's persecution of Christians in Rome in 64 C.E. It speaks of two beasts, the first of which combines features of the four beasts of Daniel 7, each standing for a world empire. The beast represents the state as uttering blasphemies, receiving worship (that is, divine honors) and persecuting Christians. All of this suffices to make the state demonic, even satanic. Christians must prefer death to such state idolatry, which has returned in modern times with totalitarian models of the state. The author probably thought of the beast as symbolizing the Roman empire under Nero. The second beast perhaps refers to the provincial elite that governed Asia Minor in the author's day and encouraged the cult of the emperor. Revelation 17–18 gives another very hostile description of the Roman empire.

We may safely conclude that the Christian, according to the witness of the whole NT, owes a penultimate obedience to the state when the state is exercising its powers lawfully and justly. But the Christian's ultimate loyalty is to God in Christ. Times arise when the Christian must resist a state that has become demonic. The Church in history lives in a perpetual dialectic between Romans 13 and Revelation 13.

After the close of the apostolic era Christians first had to endure over two centuries of state persecution, yet their faith continued to spread. Then to their surprise the emperor Constantine decided to refound the state as the Christian empire. Constantine called himself "equal to the apostles" and "bishop for external affairs" and convoked the first ecumenical council to settle disputes. This state patronage raised the ongoing danger of caesaropapism whereby the emperor ran the Church as if he were pope. The Church became a department of the state. In the eastern empire (Byzantium) this continued to be the case until 1453, and then in Moscow until 1917. The historian Eusebius was even briefly tempted to identify the Christian empire with the kingdom of God on earth, but Augustine soon put an end to such views in theology. In the western empire the Church struggled for independence from the suffocating embrace of the state. This struggle reached its climax in the prolonged investiture controversy. This long fight for freedom from state control continues to mark Roman Catholic Christianity to this day, despite occasional lapses. For a brief time the Church ran the risk of falling into the opposite extreme of a papal theocracy (Pope Innocent III). But the main danger continued to be state interference in Church affairs. Today, in the post-Constantinian era, most Christians are content when there is a fence (not a wall) of separation between Church and state. For Christians faithful to their biblical heritage patriotism is a real but subsidiary virtue. Their vision is global, embracing all nations (Matt 28:19) and on exceptional occasions calls for active resistance (Dietrich Bonhoeffer).

BIBLIOGRAPHY

Bammel, Ernst, and C.F.D. Moule. *Jesus and the Politics of his Day.* Cambridge: Cambridge University Press, 1984.

Burtchaell, James T. *From Synagogue to Church.* Cambridge: Cambridge University Press, 1992.

Cassidy, Richard J. *Society and Politics in the Acts of the Apostles.* Maryknoll, N.Y.: Orbis, 1987.

Cullmann, Oscar. *The State in the New Testament.* New York: Scribner, 1955.

Cunningham, Agnes. *The Early Church and the State.* Philadelphia: Fortress, 1982.

Daube, David. *Appeasement or Resistance.* Berkeley: University of California Press, 1987.

Farmer, William R. *Maccabees, Zealots and Josephus.* New York: Columbia University Press, 1956.

Gerhardsson, Birger. *The Ethos of the Bible.* Philadelphia: Fortress, 1981.

Harnack, Adolf von. *Militia Christi: The Christian Religion and the Military in the First Three Centuries.* Philadelphia: Fortress, 1981.

Hengel, Martin. *Christ and Power.* Philadelphia: Fortress, 1977.

____. *Victory over Violence. Jesus and the Revolutionists.* Philadelphia: Fortress, 1971.

____. *Was Jesus a Revolutionist?* Philadelphia: Fortress, 1971.

____. *The Zealots.* Edinburgh: T & T Clark, 1989.

Horsley, Richard A. *Jesus and the Spiral of Violence.* Minneapolis: Fortress, 1993.

Peterson, Erik. *The Angels and the Liturgy.* New York: Herder, 1963.

Rahner, Hugo. *Church and State in Early Christianity.* San Francisco: Ignatius, 1992.

Viviano, Benedict T. *The Kingdom of God in History.* Collegeville: The Liturgical Press, 1988.

Nationalism and Christian Faith

Benedict Thomas Viviano

The subject of nationalism and Christian faith is a delicate one because it is divisive. It can divide much of the OT from the NT; it can set Eastern Orthodox and state church Protestant Christians as nationalists against Roman Catholics and free church Protestants as internationalists—at least as far as their faith is concerned. As a theme of biblical theology nationalism has been comparatively little studied. Hence the present essay will have to be exploratory rather than definitive. Nationalism is not a purely rational subject. Even today it is capable of arousing tears of emotion (as during a parade or anthem) and inspiring heroic effort (as during war). The emotional reactions it evokes are often disproportionate to the limited object of affirmation, the nation.

I. Definition and Contexts

It is natural that one should be attached by affection to the place where one was born and grew up, whether that place is conceived of as a house, a landscape, a town, or a country. This attachment or loyalty is called patriotism. It is as natural as love of family, even if less intense. Patriotism is traditionally regarded as a virtue, even if only a secondary one. One can also be attached to the wonders of nature, such as oceans and mountains, as echoed in the psalms and biblical wisdom literature. Patriotism may be distinguished from nationalism in that nationalism is a more aggressive, destabilizing form of patriotism.

Some definitions may be helpful. Patriotism is defined as devoted love, support, and defense of one's country: national loyalty. Nationalism goes beyond this insofar as it is a desire for national advancement or independence (as from a multinational empire, for example from Austria before 1918, or from a colonial power such as France or Britain before 1960); it is the policy of asserting the interests of one's own nation viewed as separate from the interests of other nations or from the common interests of all nations. The assertion of one's national interests may further be viewed as incompatible with the interests of other nations and thus provide an argument for a war (Mark 13:8). The interests of the unity and self-determination of the nation are elevated to the status of the supreme value to which all other considerations must yield at all times.

Enlightenment futurologists and Marxist analysts failed to predict that nationalism would be even more important in the twentieth century than before. Their failure of vision blinded them to the fact that nationalism is not just a passing phase of social organization, even if an inevitable one, but a permanent temptation and danger. Four characteristics of modern nationalism are: (1) belief in the overriding need to *belong* to a nation (otherwise one is cut off from the trunk of life); (2) the *organic* relationships of all the elements that constitute a nation; (3) the value of our *own* simply because it is ours; (4) supremacy of the nation's claims to authority and loyalty over rival claims. This last point can lead to a belligerent, aggressive militarism that recognizes no overarching, supra-national standard like natural law, the charter of the United Nations, or the authority of revealed morality in the Bible and the tradition of the Church (Sir Isaiah Berlin).

In order to be better understood nationalism needs to be situated in a context. First it can be located in a spectrum of social attachments ranging from love of family to love of country (understood as a small nation-state) to a multinational empire to a Stoic philosophical embrace of the cosmos (to be cosmopolitan means to be a citizen of the world) and of all humanity or a religious faith and hope in the kingdom of God anticipated by Christians. Second it must be placed in connection with several related themes: land, war, racism, philosophy, politics, and the arts.

(1) Nationalism often takes the form of disputes over *land:* "unredeemed" border provinces like Alsace-Lorraine, Silesia, Trieste, South Tyrol, Gibraltar, Northern Ireland; or restoration of ancient nations like Greece, Italy, Israel; the conquest of colonies and the struggle of colonies to achieve independence (North and South America, Africa, parts of Asia). There are several biblical theologies of land (cf. the works of W. D. Davies and Walter Brueggemann).

(2) The rhetoric of nationalism needs to be emotional and extravagant because what it is often asking of young people is that they give up their lives in *war,* the supreme sacrifice. This asks much from their mothers and spouses as well. There are many battle texts in the OT, such as Exod 17:8-16.

(3) Sometimes nationalist aggression is justified by *racialist* arguments. Modern racism began with the Aryan theories of Count Gobineau but received a powerful reinforcement from Darwin's evolutionary doctrine about the survival of the fittest. Social Darwinism was developed by Thomas Huxley and others in a direction that ended in views of white supremacy over blacks and yellows and thus a justification for colonies and the wars they entail.

(4) Among modern *philosophies* that contributed (not always intentionally) to nationalism we may mention Herder's praise of the folk-soul of each people, Hegel's identification of the state with the Absolute in history, Sorel's glorification of violence, but especially Nietzsche's exaltation of war as an end in itself and his corresponding rejection of the ethical teaching of Jesus.

(5) Nationalists have tried to exploit all the major world *religions* for their purposes, Bismarck with German Protestantism, Maurras with Catholicism, Jabotinsky with Judaism, the Muslim Brotherhood with Islam, the Janata party with Hinduism.

(6) But essentially nationalism is a *political* doctrine, and a simple one at that, which can easily be made popular with simple people. Dr. Samuel Johnson once defined patriotism as the last refuge of a scoundrel. Had the word then existed he would rather have said this of nationalism. This doctrine has acquired a bad reputation because of its exploitation by unscrupulous politicians as a cover for their ends: militarism, personal gain, social manipulation, monarchism, revanchism, dictatorship of the right or of the left. Appeals to nationalism are made by people of every political tendency.

(7) Nationalism as political romanticism probably attained its best results in the *arts,* especially music. Many of the works of composers like Verdi, Wagner, Smetana, Liszt, and Chopin glorify national pasts real and imaginary and had concrete political results; so too the literary works of Sir Walter Scott, Lord Byron, Schiller, and many others.

Nation-states have been praised as intimate, organic, and creative in contrast with huge, impersonal, soulless empires. On the other hand, in the days of the global electronic village and world markets nation-states can appear petty, provincial, economically inadequate. In the past the excellent road system and security of the Roman empire made Paul's worldwide mission possible. When Christians of Egypt and Syria translated the classics of Christian theology from Greek into Coptic and Syriac this was not due to a schismatic nationalism but to a desire for greater *participation* in the goods of Greek Christian culture. Thus Coptic and Syriac became "languages of participation." (Attachment to a language can, however, be a force in nationalist movements or regionalism, as in Flanders or Quebec.) Associations of nations and armies such as the United Nations, the Organization of American States, the European Union, and the North Atlantic Treaty Organization relativize the claims of nations and regulate their possibilities for conflict.

II. Old Testament

The experience of the people of God in the Hebrew Scriptures can be read as a dialectical movement between universalism and particularism.

There is on the one hand the teaching of universal, transcendent values: there is one God, creator of heaven and the whole good earth, including all races and nations of humans (Genesis 1). This God transcends the distinction of gender and is to be loved above all else (Deut 6:4-5). God reveals the love of neighbor (Lev 19:18) and the Ten Commandments (Exodus 20; Deuteronomy 5) and international wisdom (Proverbs, Qoheleth, Job) to God's people. There is on the other hand the ever-expanding *election* of first an individual man, Abraham (Genesis 12) and his family, then a people under its prophetic-priestly leaders Moses and Aaron (Exodus–Deuteronomy), then a kingdom like that of other nations (1–2 Samuel, 1–2 Kings) under sovereigns like David or Solomon, in a land of their own, promised them by God and won either by conquest or by gradual settlement or by the uprising of oppressed local Canaanite populations. Then came the exile of the governing elite to Babylon, which deepened their attachment to the land they had left behind; cf. the nationalist piety of Ps 137:5-6 quoted on Israeli tanks in 1948. There followed the return from exile under the aegis of the mighty Persian empire, as a pitiful little vassal state built around its Temple in Jerusalem. Though this state was soon to be transformed into a Hellenistic *polis,* it possessed within itself a book, the Pentateuch in Hebrew, which would be able simultaneously to preserve a specific separate identity for this people (cf. Num 23:9b) and to give it a universal vision and mission (Genesis 10 P; Isa 2:1-5). And while the political reality shrank into insignificance its last major prophet, Daniel, would receive the crucial vision of the kingdom of God handed over to one like a human being "that *all* peoples, nations, and languages should serve him" (Dan 7:13-14). Israel's God thus reduced this people to one person whom Christians identify with Jesus Christ. From the blood and water of his pierced side (John 19:34) arose a new people of God (Matt 21:43). This new people receives a commission to make disciples of all nations/cultures (Matt 28:19), a commission realized by Paul and the other apostles (cf. Acts) down to the present day and until the return of Christ as "Son of Man" in glory who will bring the kingdom of God to completion with justice, peace, and love (Rom 14:17; Revelation 21). This is the line of salvation history as discerned for example by Oscar Cullmann, *Christ and Time,* and John Bright, *The Kingdom of God.* In it the nationalism of the kingdom of Israel is simultaneously canceled and elevated to the higher plane of the worldwide kingdom of God by passing through the narrow point of the death and resurrection of Jesus and the ever-widening Church.

Within this vast sweep of biblical history there is room for many circling currents. For example, national religions may be inferior to international/universal ones but they may also be superior in some sense to family religions, e.g., ancestor cults and local shrines. The OT moves in this direction (Mark S. Smith, "Yahweh and Other Deities," 221). Again the story of the tower of Babel (Gen 11:1-9 J) suggests that the division of humanity into different languages was a punishment for sin, yet this diversity is not evil in itself and can even be charming (variety can be of artistic and economic value, for example in tourism) so long as it is not overestimated and used as a basis for aggressive hostility to neighboring cultures. Again, according to the prophets (Jer 42:9-17; 50:41-43; Isa 47:5-7; 1 Kings 8:46-53; 2 Chr 36:15-21; Dan 4:19-27; Revelation 18) God may use the mighty Babylonian empire both to punish God's people and to show them mercy. In other words the nations can serve the divine plan (Walter Brueggemann, "At the Mercy of Babylon"). Finally, according to the latest radical reconstruction of Israelite history much of the pre-exilic history (especially of the time of Josiah) was given an ideal, semi-mythic form in post-exilic times in order to provide a model for a future independent state (see Liverani, "Nationality and Political Identity," *ABD*).

III. The New Testament

The NT for the most part is dominated by the perspective of the kingdom of God as described above. The universal sweep of the kingdom goes beyond all narrow nationalisms; it includes all people—*in their nations* (Dan 7:13-14; Acts 17:26). Nations are not destroyed but perfected and harmonized in a higher unity and synthesis. The great scene of judgment described in Matt 25:31-46 contains both a national and an individual, personal perspective: "All the *nations* will be gathered before him, and he will separate them [individuals] one from another" (Matt

25:32). This shift in perspective to the individual is supported by the rest of the passage.

Paul in his letters, especially that to the Galatians, and Luke in his Acts of the Apostles describe the struggle of the early Church, guided by divine revelation, to go beyond the restrictions of the Mosaic ceremonial law, especially the rules about circumcision and kosher foods (cf. Acts 10 and 15). In his worldwide mission Paul sets an example of missionary adaptation to different cultures (see "Inculturation of the Biblical Message") by using only references to the OT when preaching to Jews (Acts 13:16-41) and references to pagan poets and religiosity when preaching to Gentiles (Acts 17:22-31, especially vv. 23, 28). Acts concludes with Paul preaching the message of the kingdom of God in Rome, the capital of the then pagan empire. Within a few centuries, despite bloody persecution, the empire had become officially Christian. The emperor Constantine and his mother Helen have ever since been venerated in the East as equal to the apostles.

The Greek word for fatherland, *patris,* has a negative connotation in the NT: "Prophets are not without honor except in their own country *(patris)*" (Matt 13:54, 57; Mark 6:1, 4; Luke 4:23, 24; John 4:44). Paul's statement in Phil 3:20, "But our citizenship *(politeuma)* is in heaven, and it is from there that we are expecting a Savior" has been used to relativize the exaggerated claims of nationalist dictators in the recent past. The letter to the Hebrews, in its meditation on the faith of Abraham (Heb 11:13-16) contrasts his earthly homeland *(patris)* with a heavenly one where God has prepared a city for him. Then in Heb 13:14 the author adds: "here we have no lasting city, but we are looking for the city that is to come." The learned scholar convert Erik Peterson, writing his little *Book of the Angels* in Nazi Germany in 1936, argues slyly from the fact that Christians participate already now on earth in the heavenly liturgy of the angels as described in Revelation 4, especially in the threefold "holy" of the angels' song, to conclude that Christians have only one Lord, the risen Christ. This is the ultimate key to the question of nationalism and Christian faith. And yet Christians are bound to pray for their civil rulers (1 Tim 2:1-2; 1 Pet 2:17).

A complete study of the uses of *ethnos* (nation; plural *ethnē*) in the NT, not possible here, reinforces the international perspective of the NT that has already been indicated. But the NT never forgets its roots in the Jewish people. Note the combined perspective in John 11:48-53: "Jesus was about to die for the *nation,* and not for the *nation* only, but to gather into *one* the *dispersed* children of God" (vv. 51b-52; cf. Luke 7:5; Rom 1:16b). The link between the nation and the passion of Jesus is also found in Luke 23:2 and John 18:35. The delicate relation between Jewish roots and the Gentile mission is manifest in Acts 10:22; 24:2, 17; 26:4; 28:19. First Peter 2:9 applies Exod 19:6, Israel as a holy nation, to the Church. The universalistic perspective is visible in Acts 10:35; 17:26; Rev 5:9; 7:9; 13:7; 14:6. See the concordance for abundant further references to *ethnos* and also to *laos.*

The fathers of the Church shared this worldwide perspective on the Church. Ignatius of Antioch coined the phrase "catholic church." Irenaeus claimed that the faith was the same in the different nations of the empire. John Wesley thought of "the wide world" as his "parish." The Second Vatican Council, especially in its *Pastoral Constitution on the Church in the Modern World,* describes how Christians should cooperate in many areas in solidarity with the nations and peoples of the world, especially in the areas of the promotion of cultures (nos. 53–62) and of peace (nos. 77–90). Already in 1926 Pius XI, in a letter to missionary vicars in China (*AAS* 18 [1926] 305) spoke out against using missionary work as a means of extending the power of one nation over another: "The Church has always tried to prevent the infiltration of a nationalistic spirit among her missionaries, especially among her priests. . . . If ever a missionary acts contrary to this repeatedly stated policy, which only happens very rarely, she has not been slow to reprove such behavior and to take appropriate measures to correct it."

BIBLIOGRAPHY

Berlin, Isaiah. "Nationalism," in idem, *Against the Current: Essays in the History of Ideas.* Edited with a bibliography by Henry Hardy; introduction by Roger Hausheer. New York: Viking, 1980.

Brueggemann, Walter. "At the Mercy of Babylon," *JBL* 110/1 (1991) 3–22.

Davies, W. D. *The Gospel and the Land: Early Christianity and Jewish Territorial Doctrine.* Berkeley: University of California Press, 1974.

____. *The Territorial Dimension of Judaism.* Berkeley: University of California Press, 1982.

____. *Paul and Rabbinic Judaism: Some Rabbinic Elements in Pauline Theology.* 2nd ed. London: SPCK, 1955, ch. 4, "Nationalism," 58–85.

Moltmann, Jürgen. *The Trinity and the Kingdom: the Doctrine of God.* Translated by Margaret Kohl. New York: Harper & Row, 1981.

Murphy-O'Connor, Jerome. "Nationalism and Church Policy: Reflections on Gal 2,1-14," in Gillian R. Evans and Michel Gourgues, eds. *Communion et Réunion: Mélanges Jean-Marie Roger Tillard.* Leuven: Leuven University Press/Peeters, 1995, 283–291.

Shafer, Boyd C. *Nationalism: Myth and Reality.* New York: Harcourt, Brace, 1955.

Smith, Mark S. "Yahweh and Other Deities in Ancient Israel," in Walter Dietrich and Martin A. Klopfenstein, eds., *Ein Gott allein? JHWH-Verehrung und biblischer Monotheismus im Kontext des israelitischen und altorientalischen Religionsgeschichte.* OBO 139. Fribourg: Universitätsverlag; Göttingen: Vandenhoeck & Ruprecht, 1994, 197–234.

Also the appropriate articles in *IDB; ABD* (Mario Liverani, "Nationality and Political Identity," 4.1031–1037); *LThK; Catholicisme; RGG; Encyclopedia of Philosophy,* and the literature to which they refer.

Old Testament

The Pentateuch

Jean-Louis Ska

Introduction

The Pentateuch is a composite document, the result of the compilation of several texts that were originally independent and written at different times. It also bears the marks of several revisions. Reading the text in its present form is like visiting a city that has been rebuilt after repeated earthquakes. In this city a critical eye readily distinguishes three main types of structures: ancient buildings dating from different epochs and having survived the disasters entirely or in part; recent buildings raised after the earthquakes; composite buildings, partly old, partly new, where the restoration work has integrated ancient remnants into new structures. These composite buildings are a fitting image for the Pentateuch: it contains the basic writings that Israel saved from the destruction of Samaria and Jerusalem, recast or complemented in order to give the community of the Second Temple a text that could define its identity. What we have, therefore, is a sort of "fundamental law" or "constitution" that served as a guide in the work of restoration. Two principal tendencies underlie this work: continuity with the past and the need to update. There is continuity with the past because the Israel that rises from its ruins wants to claim identity with the pre-exilic Israel. There is updating because the post-exilic community must prove that the traditions of the past are still valid in the present circumstances. In theological terms this means that, on the one hand, the God of the post-exilic community is still and forever YHWH, the God of Abraham, Isaac, and Jacob, the God who appeared to Moses and led God's people from Egypt into the Promised Land, and that on the other hand this God of past traditions is also the God who directs the "present" history of Israel. In more historical terms the Pentateuch in its present form wants to assert that the history of Israel that began with Abraham does not end with the Exile. In juridical terms it declares that the Exile has not invalidated the codes of law and the institutions that rest on Moses' authority. All this explains the differences of style, the repetitions, the corrections, the additions, and the overall impression of mixing and mingling that numerous passages of the Pentateuch give the reader.

Ultimately the internal needs of the post-exilic community appear to us to be the determining factors in the formation of the Pentateuch; these are more important than certain external elements such as the politics of the Persian Empire that granted a relative autonomy to some of its provinces.

The Pentateuch

1. Description

The word "Pentateuch" comes from the Greek and means "five scrolls," that is, the five books that comprise it: Genesis, Exodus, Leviticus, Numbers, and Deuteronomy. In Hebrew the five books form the *tôrâ,* "Law." The Pentateuch is the most important part of the Hebrew Bible for several reasons. The narrated events have a foundational value and the codes of law have a normative value. The other historical books describe, roughly, what did not survive the Exile, such as the monarchic institution, or what became severely compromised, that is, possession of the Promised Land. The prophetic books and other writings do not have exactly a normative value, but rather an interpretative and hortatory value.

Without going into detail and as a first approach we can distinguish five main groupings in the Pentateuch:

1. Stories of the origins (Genesis 1–11)
2. Stories of the patriarchs (Genesis 12–50)
3. The departure from Egypt (Exodus 1:1–15:21)
4. The sojourn in the desert (Exodus 15:22–Numbers 33), with the important section on the sojourn at Sinai (Exodus 19–40; Leviticus; Numbers 1–10)
5. Moses' farewell before the people's entry into the Promised Land and the new legislation (Deuteronomy).

This division needs some corrections and the addition of particulars. First of all the patriarchs' history can easily be subdivided into three parts: the cycles of Abraham (Genesis 12–24) and Jacob (Genesis 25–35) and the story of Joseph (Genesis 37–50). Besides these three great figures we must mention a few lesser ones: Isaac (Genesis 26), Esau (Genesis 36), and Judah (Genesis 38). Then from Exodus 2 to Deuteronomy 34 the figure of Moses dominates the narrative, and this long section corresponds to his "biography" since he is born in Exodus 2 and dies in Deuteronomy 34. Therefore it is possible to reduce to three the five previous groupings: stories of the origins (Genesis 1–11), stories of the patriarchs (Genesis 12–50), and foundational experiences of the people of Israel under Moses' leadership (Exodus; Leviticus; Numbers; Deuteronomy) including narratives and laws. (Of course this last grouping can be subdivided into three of the sections we have listed above, numbers 3, 4, 5.) These three parts correspond to three main steps in the life of Israel: the world before the birth of Israel, the ancestors of Israel, and Israel as a people before their entrance into the Promised Land. We should also note that the separation of the three groupings is not as clearcut as it may seem at first sight. Hebrew literature masterfully practices the art of transition. Thus the story of the patriarchs probably begins in Gen 11:27. However, this verse can be understood only in connection with the genealogy of Gen 11:10-26, itself connected with the other genealogies in the account of the origins. The transition between the stories of the patriarchs and the rest of the Pentateuch, in particular the departure from Egypt, is announced as early as the story of Abraham (Gen 15:13-16); it begins with the descent of Jacob's sons into Egypt (Gen 46:1-5) and the death of Joseph (Gen 50:24-25). Exodus 1, and especially 1:1-7, 8, links the new episodes to what precedes and prepares for the coming of Moses on the scene. Exodus 13:17–14:31 (cf. 15:1-21) is a narrative that serves as a transition between the departure from Egypt and the sojourn in the desert. Exodus 15:22–18:27 contains the first episodes of the people's life in the desert; several other elements are a prelude to the Sinai pericope. Numbers 1–10 also has Mount Sinai for a setting but this section covers mainly the description of preparations for the march toward the Promised Land. The last chapters of Numbers already contain a few accounts of conquests (Numbers 21; 31–32) and directions for the apportioning of the land (Numbers 26; 34–35) and are therefore akin to the stories of the book of Joshua; the narrative of the appointment of a successor to Moses (Numbers 27) presages Deuteronomy and even Moses' death (Deuteronomy 34). All this allows us to understand the diversity of opinions concerning the beginnings and endings of the various sections.

In summary the Pentateuch uses the narrative form to present the main events of the history of Israel from the creation of the world to Moses' death. These events define the identity of the people. We must now see how this "foundational history" of Israel was read in the course of the centuries.

2. History of Interpretation

Rather than making an inventory of the various opinions that succeeded one another throughout the centuries we thought it preferable to define the principles that directed the reading of these five books and to see at what times and for what reasons these principles changed.

A. The First Centuries and the Patristic Period

Neither Judaism of this period nor the early Christians ever had the slightest doubt that

Moses was the author of the Pentateuch. In the NT it is possible to distinguish at least three positions concerning Moses and the Law. On the one hand certain writings consider Jesus the "new Moses" not because he replaces the old Law with the new but because he gives a new interpretation of the Law. In this Jesus belongs to a movement of constant reinterpretation already noticeable in the different codes of law of the Pentateuch, while exhibiting a greater authority than that of the scribes of his time. He is more than an interpreter of Moses. Matthew's gospel among other writings represents this first position in the Sermon on the Mount and in the theme of the fulfillment of the Scriptures (Matthew 5–7; see especially 5:17). On the other hand the NT in certain passages stresses the imperfection of the old Law compared to the gospel of Jesus Christ. The text that best illustrates this position is 2 Corinthians 3. Elsewhere Paul strongly insists on the fact that he does not want to invalidate in any way the Law of Moses (Rom 3:31). The letter to the Hebrews goes farther on the subject when it discusses the priesthood and cultic institutions: Christ's priesthood and sacrifice replace from now on the sin offerings of the old Law. Finally the third position maintains that the Law itself announces that some day it will be continued and fulfilled. There is continuity in the passage from the old order to the new. This position predominates in the work of Luke who shows Jesus as the fulfillment of the promises. It also underlies certain parts of Matthew and John who more than once present Jesus as a personage foretold and expected by the OT (see especially Matthew 1–2; John 5:45-47; 8:56; 12:41).

This question of the relationship between Old and New Testaments and particularly between Old and New Covenants remained the fundamental problem during the whole patristic era and until the end of the Middle Ages. The Christian reading of the Pentateuch owed a great deal to Jewish exegesis and Greek tradition. The two are joined in the work of Philo of Alexandria whose influence on the Christian world was determinative. Judaism was intent on actualizing its tradition without changing it; Greece developed, particularly in Plato's writings, a more philosophical method of reading that, when applied to texts of profane literature, sought to separate ideas from appearances, that is, from the language of poetry and epic.

The principles of Christian reading were systematically summarized in the *De doctrina christiana (On Christian Doctrine)* of Augustine (354–430). His *De catechizandis rudibus (The First Catechetical Instruction)* added some useful complements. Augustine's reading was based on a few axioms of Greek philosophy, especially Plato's. The fundamental distinction ruling the whole Augustinian system is that between *signum* ("sign") and *res* ("reality") which he compares to the Pauline distinction between "letter" and "spirit" (2 Cor 3:6). The sign does not have any reality in itself; its function is to indicate a reality. This distinction corresponds to a threefold division: the material and sensible world, the signs, and the real or supernatural world. God is the reality par excellence speaking to the sensible world through signs. The human mind travels in the other direction when it ascends from the sensible world through signs to God.

When he applies this theory to the Bible, Augustine defines the reality of the Scriptures in several complementary ways. The only true reality indicated by the signs is the Trinity. However, this reality is dynamic; it revealed itself in the mystery of Jesus Christ who is now present in the Church. This is why Augustine is able to define this reality of the Scriptures in a more anthropological and moral way, that is, the twofold commandment of the love of God and the love of neighbor. In his *First Catechetical Instruction* Augustine takes a further step: the heart of Scripture is before all else the revelation of God's love for us; our love is only a response to this divine love. This revelation proceeded in several steps of which the main ones are the OT and the NT, continued by the history of the Church (4.7). We must note that Augustine here introduces a historical and phenomenological category into his presentation of the reality of Scripture. As regards the Pentateuch, this results in paying more attention to the narrative than to the laws. The Jewish tradition is vastly different in this regard.

Concretely Augustine often has recourse to "allegory" and "figures" in order to show how to go from sensible signs to the reality of the Scriptures. For instance he holds that the OT contains the "figures" of the realities revealed in the NT.

B. The Modern Period and the Birth of Criticism

Several factors contributed to modify this way of reading the Scriptures. The growing influence of Aristotle, chiefly through the channel of Averroës's works, caused a waning of Platonist-inspired allegory. The monastic currents fostered individual piety centered on the humanity of Jesus Christ. The main Jewish commentators on the Bible showed a stronger and stronger preference for the "literal" meaning (see the evolution from Maimonides to Nachmanides, Ibn Ezra, Rashi, and Rashba). Renaissance scholars usually read the texts in the original language and within their context. Humanism is, by definition, more anthropocentric than theocentric. The discoveries of the modern era and the beginnings of technology changed the coordinates of human consciousness. All this explains how the two persons arose who strongly influenced the interpretation of the Pentateuch despite the inevitable limits of their work: Richard Simon (1638–1712) and Baruch Spinoza (1632–1677). Without going into detail let us simply say that they pleaded for a "rational" reading of Scripture and cast doubts on the Mosaic authenticity of the Pentateuch. This was the point of departure for the whole of modern criticism and the search for the human environment in which it was possible for the Pentateuch to develop.

With Richard Simon, who was a lawyer, interest in the legislation of the Pentateuch was reborn as was interest in the "juridical" aspects of questions, evidenced for instance by his theory of "public scriveners" as authors of certain parts of the Pentateuch. As for Spinoza, he emphasized the evolution of law and customs within the Scriptures, thus exhibiting a rather well-developed historical sense despite his static metaphysical rationalism. Finally we must mention that both Simon and Spinoza thought of Esdras as the author of the Pentateuch, without denying that certain portions of the book might go back to Moses himself.

C. The Contemporary Period

The new orientation of contemporary studies of the Pentateuch is the result of an increasing interest in history, which implies the idea of evolution, and the deciphering of documents originating in the ancient Near East (Egypt, Mesopotamia, and Syria).

The Documentary Hypothesis

The beginnings of the new method go back to H. B. Witter (1683–1715) in Germany and Jean Astruc (1684–1766) in France who independently made the same discovery: by comparing the first two chapters of Genesis they observed that the Hebrew text uses two different divine names *ʾĕlōhîm* ("God") in the first case (Gen 1:1–2:4a) and *YHWH ʾĕlōhîm* ("YHWH God") in the second (Gen 2:4b–3:24). In addition Astruc noticed that there are numerous doublets in Genesis and the beginning of Exodus and that these doublets use different names for God. Astruc's ideas were taken up in Germany by Johann Eichhorn (1752–1827). From then on scholars began to talk about "documents," one Yahwist that uses the divine name YHWH, and the other Elohist because it employs the divine name *ʾĕlōhîm.* The sigla are J (from the German form JHWH) for the one and E for the other. Naturally the Mosaic authenticity of the Pentateuch grew more and more faint. Three hypotheses were proposed by turns: the Pentateuch would be the final result of the compilation of several "documents," of the collection of "fragments," or of a lengthy process by which an original document would have received numerous additions or "complements." Based on the work of Eduard Reuss (1804–1891), Karl H. Graf (1815–1869), Abraham Kuenen (1828–1891), and Julius Wellhausen (1844–1891), the "documentary" theory was to gain acceptance for almost a century.

An important discovery was to prove decisive for this documentary theory. In 1805 Wilhelm De Wette published his *Dissertatio critico-exegetica (Critical-exegetical Dissertation)* in which he drew a parallel between the law of Deuteronomy and the reform of Josiah (2 Kings 22–23). This time the study was based on laws, not on narratives, and it made possible the dating of a document. The centralization of worship effected by Josiah (622 B.C.E.) corresponds on the juridical plane to the law of Deuteronomy 12. The laws and stories that do not suppose this centralization are therefore more ancient than Deuteronomy and those that suppose it are more recent. This "Archimedean point" allowed for a clearer distinction between the diverse components of the Pentateuch.

Gradually exegetes came to distinguish three groups of texts: (1) the ancient sources J and E,

(2) Deuteronomy, which forms a separate body, and (3) the priestly texts of the Pentateuch (siglum P). These last texts suppose the centralization of worship as early as the time of the sojourn in the desert through a sort of retrojection of institutions of the Second Temple to the beginnings of Israel. Therefore according to the documentary theory there exist several independent and complete documents that make up the Pentateuch.

The presuppositions of this method are those of the historiography of the time. The idea of evolution, applied to natural as well as human phenomena, the interest in origins and the preference for all that is "natural," and a negative view of all that is late, abstract, and legalistic are the main characteristics of this mindset. In this way Wellhausen and his disciples easily mixed value judgments with the conclusions of their critical work.

The School of Form Criticism (Formgeschichte)

This school continued rather than denied Wellhausen's direction. The neo-Romantic movement with its nostalgia for simple country life and aversion to industrial society caused a shift of interest from the writing itself to its antecedents, that is, oral tradition. The nascent taste for psychology and the history of religions also played a role in this evolution. Furthermore the researchers join artistic sensibility to critical sense. Hence their interest in "literary genres." A very large number of biblical texts are not original compositions, but make use of forms or schemes regularly employed in the same circumstances: for example, the liturgical recitation of traditions of the past. Finally, for these authors the forms or "literary genres" of oral tradition can be understood only if one knows in what concrete social and institutional context they grew and were transmitted *(Sitz im Leben).* The term *Sitz im Leben* (or *Volksleben*) ("existential context") was coined by one of the leaders of this new orientation, Hermann Gunkel (1862–1932). Although the research of this school focuses more on narratives than on laws it does not forget the latter. Studies on the *Sitz im Leben* of the pericope of Mount Sinai, the Ten Commandments, and the Covenant soon abounded.

Among the representative works of this period we must cite those of Gerhard von Rad (1901–1971) and Martin Noth (1902–1968). In his study of some texts he deems ancient (such as Deut 26:5b-9; 6:21-23; Josh 24:2b-13) von Rad observes that what we have here are "little creeds" that have a historical structure. He detects in these texts the outlines of the history of Israel as told in the Hexateuch (that is, the Pentateuch plus the Book of Joshua): the patriarchal stories, the sojourn in the desert, and the conquest of the Promised Land. Von Rad observes that none of these "creeds" mentions the Sinai legislation. He concludes that these two traditions were originally separated and had two different *Sitze im Leben.* For the "history of Israel" he postulates a liturgy at Gilgal during the time of harvest. As for the Sinai pericope, it originated in a feast celebrating the renewal of the covenant that took place in the fall at Shechem (Joshua 24) on the occasion of the Feast of Booths (Deut 31:10-11). This theory has been severely criticized and there are few who still defend it nowadays because these "little creeds" are regarded as late (deuteronomic) texts.

Von Rad's studies prepared for those of Noth, according to whom the first institution of Israel was an "amphictyony" or confederation of twelve tribes that met regularly in a central sanctuary at the time of the judges. In the course of these meetings the tribes participated in liturgies during which they recited the traditions they held in common. Noth distinguishes five main oral traditions shared by all tribes and more ancient than the monarchic period: the patriarchal stories, the Exodus, the stay at Mount Sinai, the sojourn in the desert, and the conquest. The two most ancient traditions are those of the Exodus and conquest. Like von Rad's, this theory has been criticized; however, the questions raised by these two authors remain relevant.

Finally we must cite, within the same current, the work on the covenant stimulated by George Mendenhall's published writings. The study of Hittite and later of Assyrian covenant treaties has led exegetes to look, particularly in the story of Mount Sinai and in Deuteronomy, for a pattern known throughout the ancient Near East. This pattern would have been used in the Pentateuch to describe the relationship between God and God's people. This pact is conditional: the suzerain, YHWH, promises protection to his vassal provided the latter respects the stipulations of the covenant, that is, the law promulgated by God on Sinai. This theology undergirds the

Deuteronomist's work (Joshua–2 Kings) and explains the destruction of Samaria and Jerusalem as the consequence of the unfaithfulness of the people to the Covenant. This theory was the occasion of much discussion on two points: In what texts do we find precisely this pattern? When did this theology develop?

Recent Developments

At present the situation is especially confused. First of all, the documentary theory and subsequent theories have been submitted to a critical examination that has left them shaken. To date there is no true consensus on any theory or method or on any way to reach an agreement. Some continue to defend the documentary theory; others modify it; still others propose different models. Some even go so far as to criticize the rationale of research on the genesis of texts (historical or diachronic study) in order to arrive at a better understanding of their content. Some forms of "synchronic" readings have been proposed: they read the text "as it is," "in its present form," or in its latest redaction, without any reference either to its authors or context or previous redactions or original addressees. In this type of interpretation readers are alone with the text and what they bring to it.

The causes of this confused situation are many. Let us mention especially the works recently published on the history of Israel that lead us to reexamine our knowledge of everything before the eighth century B.C.E.; the progress of archaeology and Middle Eastern studies; the growing interest in the study of times of crisis such as the Exile and the post-exilic period; an acutely critical philosophical climate—in the wake of the "masters of suspicion" (Nietzsche, Marx, and Freud)—in which every "certitude" is suspect; the advent of a pluralistic society, secularized and cosmopolitan, whose landmarks are often indistinct; the multiplication of diverse and divergent methods and approaches, caring little about establishing a dialogue between themselves because their hermeneutical principles define in very different ways the search for the "meaning" or "meanings" of a given text.

Nevertheless it is possible to classify the present tendencies within four overall categories. (1) A certain number of exegetes, especially in Germany, continue to uphold the documentary hypothesis either in its classical form or in more refined forms, by distinguishing numerous redactional levels. (2) Others take up the principal elements of the documentary hypothesis but change the dates and certain coordinates. To this group belong those scholars who date J from the exilic or even the post-exilic period (John Van Seters, Hans H. Schmidt, Martin Rose, and so on). (3) Still others prefer to make over the documentary theory completely and reconstruct the history of the composition of the Pentateuch on other data. The synchronic study of the text precedes the diachronic study; the analysis of the text in its coherent form precedes rather than follows the division into sources *(Literarkritik),* and the two pillars on which the entire Pentateuch rests are two "compositions," one deuteronomic (D) in inspiration, the other priestly (P). The most important names in this school are those of Rolf Rendtorff, Erhard Blum, Frank Crüsemann, and Rainer Albertz. (4) A fourth group, much more heterogeneous, finds its unity only in the more or less systematic rejection of the questions asked by the historico-critical method. These exegetes therefore favor the synchronic type of approach and show no interest in properly historical studies.

Within this last group we must distinguish three tendencies operating on quite different bases. In the first sub-group we would range the methods influenced by the contemporary literary schools (New Criticism, Readers-Response Criticism and Analysis, Narratology, Rhetorical Analysis, Deconstructionism). In the second group we would include the methods that take their inspiration from the human sciences, such as structuralism, sociology, psychology, feminism, and so on. Finally, the third group comprises methods intent on adopting a more explicitly theological language, including the canonical reading of Brevard Childs and related methods. Of course there are many intermediary forms and a whole gamut of nuances exists between the different groups and sub-groups we have just defined.

3. A Few Principles for Reading

The aim of this section is not to propose a new theory or method. Circumstances being what they are at present, it is possible only to broach a few essential topics and to propose to readers some courses their reflection might take.

As in Wellhausen's time, it is opportune first of all to set up a series of valid criteria for a serious reading of the Pentateuch. These are supplied us by the codes of law, in chronological order the covenant code (Exodus 21–23), the deuteronomic code (Deuteronomy 12–26), and the holiness code (Leviticus 17–26). Since De Wette, who linked Deuteronomy to the reform of Josiah (622 B.C.E.), the point of departure for study has been the relationship among these three codes of law and their relation to the narrative texts. They give us a sure point of departure. Without any doubt there is no complete agreement in this domain; however it seems to us that no honest discussion can elude the consideration of these relationships.

As far as the narratives are concerned, an easily recognizable block is Deuteronomy (D). The theological heirs of the original Deuteronomists are the people who during and after the Exile worked at what has been called the Deuteronomistic History (Joshua–2 Kings). Nowadays many exegetes hold that one or several Deuteronomists might also have contributed to the redaction of a fair number of passages or to the composition of certain ensembles in Genesis, Exodus, and Numbers. The topic remains the object of discussion, for the concepts of "deuteronomistic" and "Deuteronomist" remain difficult to define in a concrete way. However there is agreement on a few central ideas of Deuteronomy: its conception of a conditional covenant that gives us the key to Israel's history (hence the importance of deuteronomic law), and a theology of history that gives great importance to the Exodus and the Promised Land.

Next there is a significant agreement concerning the extent of the priestly document (P). Questions relative to its nature are more complex, but they have no direct bearing on either the extent or the date of the texts. On certain essential points P corrects D. For P, in contradistinction to D, the covenant is not conditional. God concludes a unilateral pact with Noah after the flood, a pact that concerns the whole of humankind (Genesis 9). God concludes another pact with Abraham and all his descendants, that is to say, the people of Israel (Genesis 17). This gives an indestructible foundation to the universe and the people of Israel. Therefore the sins that have caused the Exile have not nullified the divine promises, since for Israel the true covenant *(bĕrît)* is not that of Sinai but the oath sworn to Abraham. Just as the universe will never again be destroyed after the Flood, Israel will never disappear. In fact there is no covenant on Sinai according to P. The aim of the history of Israel is the creation of a people belonging to YHWH in the Promised Land, centered on sacred elements: the priesthood, the altar, and the tabernacle where the divine "glory" resides. This "glory" was manifested at the most important moments in the history of Israel: at the crossing of the Red Sea (Exodus 14), on Sinai (Exodus 24), and in the desert (Exodus 16; Numbers 14 and 20). History is divided into great periods, the first marked by the rhythm of the "genealogies" of Genesis and the second by that of the itineraries of the journey of Israel in the desert. Between the two the Exodus takes place (Exodus 1–15). As for the revelation of God, it is done in three steps: God is the creator of the universe (*ʾĕlōhîm,* "God": Genesis 1–10); the God of the patriarchs is called *ʾel shaddai* ("Powerful God": Gen 17:1; cf. Exod 6:3); and YHWH ("Lord") is the God of the Exodus who is revealed to Moses (Exod 6:3).

The great syntheses and theologies of Israel's history that contribute to make the Pentateuch a literary unit come from Deuteronomy and the priestly document (See Exod 6:2-8 [P]; Deut 26:5b-9; 6:21-23 [D]). The essential data of D and P are in their turn taken up and corrected in the holiness code ([H] Leviticus 17–26) taking into account the imperatives of the period of the Second Temple. Indeed, in its final redaction the holiness code attempts a synthesis between the dominant ideas of Deuteronomy and those of the priestly document; between the covenant of Deuteronomy and the holiness of worship, the purport of the priestly document; between the conditional covenant *(bĕrît)* of Sinai, a deuteronomic idea repeated in Lev 26:15, and the unilateral and unconditional pact (same word, *bĕrît)* with the patriarchs, a priestly idea found again in Lev 26:42. Some late texts of Deuteronomy had already spoken with the same meaning of a "covenant with the ancestors" (see Deut 4:23, 31; 7:8, 12; 8:18; 9:5). Thus the holiness code recognizes both the patriarchal traditions and that of Sinai; the possession of the land depends on faithfulness to the Law, but God will not forget the promise made to the patriarchs, and as a consequence the land can never be definitively lost. As far as holiness is concerned, Lev 19:1 (H), following Deuteronomy (see Deut 7:6; 14:2, 21; 26:19; Lev 19:2; 20:7, 8, 24, 26, 31-33), demands it of the whole people God has set apart from other nations (Lev 20:24, 26). The priestly document for its part limits holiness to the priesthood, the altar, and the tabernacle (Exod 29:43-46). The same idea is also found in the holiness code, which speaks of the particular holiness of institutions like the priesthood (Lev 21:6-8), the person of the high priest (21:12, 15), the Temple (24:9), and so on. According to Deuteronomy the people were holy by virtue of divine election; according to the holiness code the people are holy primarily by virtue of worship and the observance of the laws of ritual purity. This law is based on the rights of YHWH who has bestowed the land and liberated the people (Lev 25:38, 42, 55).

These few remarks allow us to propose another chronology that in its main steps is reliable enough: Deuteronomy, priestly document, holiness code. Deuteronomy dates back to Josiah's reform (622 B.C.E.); the priestly document goes back to the end of the Exile (538 B.C.E.) or the beginning of the return from the Exile (but certain exegetes speak of the time of Hezekiah, 716–687 B.C.E.). As for the holiness code, it is the fundamental writing from the period of the Second Temple, rebuilt about 520–515 B.C.E.). The three theologies correspond to three moments in the history of Israel: the end of the monarchy, the Exile and the beginning of the return, and the situation of Israel at the time of the Second Temple.

However, there are many unresolved questions. What are the texts of Genesis, Exodus, and Numbers that can be linked with certainty to one or the other deuteronomic redaction? What is properly speaking deuteronomic? What are the criteria that allow us to determine the texts that belong to a post-deuteronomic and post-priestly redaction akin to H (holiness code)? From what particular groups do these theologies emanate? At the same time the holiness code corresponds to the code of the covenant on more than one point: both presuppose a society without organized central power whereas D supposes the existence of a king.

It is equally difficult to go back farther in time and determine with precision what were the old, pre-exilic traditions preserved by the writers of the present-day Pentateuch. However we persist in thinking, along with many researchers, that the enterprise is not impossible. Deuteronomy and the priestly document already suppose known and fixed traditions. They utilize, invoke, and correct, disregard or reinterpret, but they do not invent. Furthermore, another question to be asked is that about the connections among these different blocks, especially between the patriarchal stories and all the cycles concerning the figure of Moses. The first text that suggests such a link is in Hosea 12 in an oracle that contrasts Moses with Jacob. This allows us at least to say that traditions existed side by side. But it is not before certain passages of Deuteronomy—whose date has been discussed—and especially of P (Exod 6:2-8) that Moses' mission and the Exodus are seen as the realization of the promises made to the patriarchs. Another question is that of the integration of the story of Joseph into the Pentateuch. However there are good reasons to believe that even before the Exile there existed traditions concerning Abraham, a first cycle of Jacob and his conflicts with his brother Esau and his uncle Laban, and a nucleus of the story of Joseph. The story of origins (Genesis 1–11) is more difficult to date but it supposes, even in its oldest parts, a rather sophisticated mentality.

Conclusion

The Pentateuch in its present state is the result of a compilation dating back to the Second Temple. In order to emphasize continuity with the past it does not eliminate the ancient texts. It introduces new elements to fit the present circumstances of a nation under foreign power that finds its identity especially in its sacred institutions. The present-day Pentateuch has two centers. One is internal, the whole of the revelation at Sinai (Exodus 19–Numbers 10) that supplies the essential part of the "constitution" of Israel as a people. The other center is external to it and it is the role of Deuteronomy to indicate, at the end of the Pentateuch, the direction one must follow to find it: we mean the land that before his death Moses contemplates from the heights of Moab without being able to enter it (Deuteronomy 34). This bipolarity is the key to the interpretation of all the rest. The stories of origins

(Genesis 1–11) root the history of Israel in a theology of creation: the God of Israel is the creator of the universe and the master of all nations. The patriarchal stories (Genesis 12–50) form "a narrative of the origins of Israel" of the genealogical type. Its goal is to insure the identity of Israel by blood ties; as a result it distinguishes Israel from its neighbors, the Moabites, Ammonites, Ishmaelites, and Edomites, and stresses its bonds with a certain land. The story of Joseph (Genesis 37–50) broaches the thorny subject of internal relationships among the different parts of the people of Israel. The story of the Exodus shows how Israel becomes a free people. The account of the stay at Mount Sinai defines Israel no longer by its origin but by its free commitments, the Law and the covenant on the one hand and worship on the other, both responses of a free people to the benefactions granted by YHWH, its sole liberator and only God. The stories and traditions of the desert depict the vicissitudes of a people on its way toward its land. The whole is unified by the long series of divine interventions on behalf of Israel. For the Jewish people the Pentateuch ends, like the Hebrew Bible, with a call to enter into or return to the Promised Land (Deut 34:4; 2 Chr 36:22-23). For Christians it contains the foundational experiences of their ancestors in the faith (cf. Rom 4:11-12) and the spirituality of a people on its way to the ultimate city (see Exod 15:17; Heb 13:14; John 14:1-10).

BIBLIOGRAPHY

Blenkinsopp, Joseph. *The Pentateuch. An Introduction to the First Five Books of the Bible.* ABRL. New York: Doubleday, 1992.

Campbell, Anthony F., and Mark A. O'Brien. *Sources of the Pentateuch. Texts, Introductions, Annotations.* Minneapolis: Fortress, 1993.

Noth, Martin. *A History of Pentateuchal Traditions.* Translated with an Introduction by Bernard Anderson. Chico: Scholars, 1981.

Pury, Albert de. *Le pentateuque en question. Les origines et la composition des cinq premiers livres de la Bible à la lumière des recherches récentes.* Geneva: Labor et Fides, 1989.

The Pentateuch as Torah in the Jewish Tradition

Anthony J. Saldarini

Though Jews and Christians both read and revere the Hebrew Bible/Old Testament as authoritative revelation from God, they value and interpret it differently. Jews cherish the Law revealed by God. Guided by the other biblical books and rabbinic literature, especially the Palestinian and Babylonian Talmuds, Jewish interpreters have developed profound insights into God and God's will for human life through the study of biblical Law. The Christian interpretation of the Law, as explained in Galatians and Romans, makes Christians' use of this portion of the Scriptures basically different from Jewish use.

"Torah," the Hebrew name for the Pentateuch, symbolizes the Jewish attitude toward the laws in the Pentateuch as the heart of the Bible and the core of divine revelation. Though the word *torah* is often translated as law it has a much broader range of meaning that includes wisdom and practice as well as law. The noun *torah* comes from the verb *yrh,* which means to teach (Lev 10:11). Both noun and verb refer to the content and process of teaching and instruction and to the rules, commands, and instructions that are the result of teaching and guidance. Torah occurs frequently in the Hebrew Bible in prophetic, wisdom, and legal texts. It may refer to instructions given by a priest, prophet, or teacher (Hag 2:11; Isa 1:10; Prov 13:14) or to a group of instructions in the Bible such as the law or teaching about the guilt offering (Lev 7:1) or the instructions for celebrating Passover (Exod 12:49). Torah can mean the judicial decision of a priest or judge (Deut 17:11). It also may refer to a larger body of teaching, such as the contents of the book of Deuteronomy: "This is the law [or instruction] that Moses set before the Israelites" (Deut 4:44). This instruction is defined as the testimonies, statutes, and ordinances that Moses taught Israel across the Jordan (Deut 4:45).

Later Jewish tradition cites as paradigmatic the story of Ezra the scribe who read "the book of the law *[torah]* of Moses, which the LORD had given to Israel" (Neh 8:1) to the people gathered in the square before the Water Gate in Jerusalem. The Levites interpreted the Law to the people who celebrated a festival in honor of the occasion (Neh 8:7-12), studied the Law, celebrated the feast of Booths as mandated by the Law (Neh 8:13-18) and renewed their commitment to the covenant with God (10:28-39). We do not know the contents and extent of this book of the Law in Nehemiah 8. Though it is often assumed to have been the Pentateuch it may have been an earlier collection that influenced biblical law. In any case the authority of this book of the Law, its effect on the people, and their acceptance and celebration of the Law and the covenant that underlies it encapsulate many of the characteristics of Torah and devotion to Torah in later Jewish practice and thought.

The route by which the Torah and the Bible as a whole took shape and gained authority in the Jewish community is poorly understood. Stories, royal annals, laws, prophecies, proverbs, and instructions were collected into longer sequences and further edited into the books of the Bible. This process of formation probably took place from the time of the Babylonian exile (586 B.C.E.) to about 300 B.C.E. In the second and first centuries B.C.E. the book of Sirach (also called Ecclesiasticus or Ben Sira) and the Dead Sea scrolls attest to the division of the Torah (or Law), the Prophets (including the historical books that are referred to as the Former Prophets in Jewish tradition) and less distinctly the Writings (including the Wisdom literature, Esther, Chronicles, and other books). The Greek preface to Sirach, written by the original author's grandson and translator in 128 B.C.E. in Egypt, refers to Ben Sira's study of "the Law and the Prophets and the other books of our ancestors" in order "to write something pertaining to instruction and wisdom, so that by becoming familiar also with [these things] those who love learning might make even greater progress in living according to the law." The Dead Sea scrolls refer to Moses and the prophets as communicators of God's will (*1QS* 1.2-3) and to the books of Moses (the Pentateuch), the prophets, David (the Psalms), and the chronicles of each and every generation (*4QMMT* C9–11). In general the Torah—that is, the Pentateuch—was the most sacred and authoritative division of the Hebrew Bible. Rabbinic literature generally attributes greater authority to the Torah than to the rest of the Bible. The Dead Sea scrolls and the New Testament, which stress God's future intervention in human history, treat the prophets and Psalms as equally authoritative.

During the Maccabean and early Roman periods (170 B.C.E.–70 C.E.) "the books of the Law,"—that is, the Torah—became a political and religious symbol for the Jewish way of life. When Antiochus IV Epiphanes wanted to suppress opposition to his rule in Judea he encouraged idolatrous worship and had the books of the Law torn to pieces and burned and their owners executed (1 Macc 1:56-57). Fidelity to the Law even to the point of martyrdom marked the Jew who was faithful to God (2 Maccabees 6–7) and rejection of the ancestral laws of Israel characterized those Jews who compromised too much with the Greek world.

Second Temple Jewish literature, including the deuterocanonical books, the Dead Sea scrolls, and the so-called apocryphal and pseudepigraphal books, testifies to the authority and lively influence of the Bible. Many of these works retell the biblical stories, reinterpret biblical law, or otherwise bring the Bible to bear on daily life or the crises facing the Jewish community. The Torah and its laws received a special emphasis in a number of the Dead Sea scrolls and other Jewish literature. New law codes gave guidance to the priests in the Temple and to people zealously committed to fidelity to God's will. The mid-second century B.C.E. book of Jubilees retells the narratives of Genesis and Exodus to promote strict observance of its understandings of Pentateuchal law. The Qumran Temple Scroll synthesizes and interprets laws and customs from the Pentateuch and later Jewish traditions. The Qumran "Halakhic Letter" *(4QMMT)* and a number of liturgical and legal texts adjudicate disputes over worship, purity, Sabbath observance, divorce, and many other biblical laws. The NT also witnesses to this legal agenda in the Second Temple period (for example, purity in Mark 12; divorce in Matthew 19; Sabbath in Matthew 12). Second Temple hymns and prayers grew from biblical models, mystical prayers and speculations deepened Israel's experience of God, and exhortations renewed the community's fidelity to the covenant. Apocalypses grew out of the prophetic heritage to encourage loyalty to the Law. Even after the destruction of the Temple in 70 C.E. the author of 2 Baruch turned to the covenant and the Law for renewal as he awaited apocalyptic divine intervention to restore Israel.

From the late first century C.E. onward a new group of learned teachers commonly referred to as "rabbis" in English and "sages" (literally, wise ones) in Hebrew gradually gained influence over the Jewish communities of the Near East. They created their own interpretation of the Bible, especially the Pentateuch, which was articulated in the Mishnah (200 C.E.), in the two great commentaries and expansions of the Mishnah known as the Palestinian and Babylonian Talmuds (fifth–sixth centuries), and in a series of exegetical texts called *midrashim* devoted to the interpretation of the Torah. For them Torah with its multiplicity of meanings and connotations became a central symbol for their whole way of life and system of thought. Because their views dominated Jewish thought and religious practice until the nineteenth century, Torah remains a cherished and powerful reality for Jews today.

The foundation of rabbinic literature is "Torah from Sinai," that is, the instruction revealed to

Moses by God on Mount Sinai (Exodus 19–24). Thus the first five books of the Bible, the Pentateuch, constitute Torah because they record the primary revelation given by God to Israel through Moses. The word Torah in this context becomes highly suggestive rather than just a name for a thing. The five Biblical books are called the Torah; they contain Torah which is instruction, guidance, commands (often referred to as law); they are the result of Torah, meaning God's instruction of the Israelites through Moses; and they are Torah, divine instruction par excellence, because they were revealed by God.

The rabbinic tradition came to use the term Torah as the word and symbol encompassing all that it taught and claimed for itself. Thus the term Torah encompasses all teaching believed to have its source in the Sinaitic revelation, including initially the Mishnah, which is a collection of laws based on the Bible, the *midrashim,* which are collections of Scriptural interpretations, and the two Talmuds. Torah in a still wider sense includes the commentaries on the Talmuds, the law codes derived from them, commentaries on Scripture, mystical writings, philosophy and, most generally, all Jewish learning in the rabbinic tradition. "Talmud Torah," literally "the study of Torah," refers to the study of all of rabbinic literature and teaching. By implication a person engaged in Talmud Torah is devoted to the contents of the whole tradition.

The Rabbis understood their interpretations of the Torah, including their exegeses, applications of laws, practices, and customs, as integral to the revelation received by Moses on Sinai. Thus they referred not only to the Torah, that is, the Pentateuch, but to Torah (without the definite article) by which they meant an oral Torah. According to this view, when Moses received the written Torah found in the Pentateuch on Sinai he also received oral teachings that were passed on by the leaders and prophets of Israel and finally authoritatively taught and recorded by the Rabbis. *Mishnah ʾAbot,* also known as *Pirke ʾAbot* or the "Chapter of the Fathers," traces the chain of tradition by which Torah was passed on. It does not explicitly mention oral Torah but implies that the teachings of the Rabbis were part of Torah given by God to Moses on Sinai. Third century Talmudic Rabbis began to use the term "oral Torah" to describe their teachings as a whole. Other Jewish groups had appealed to mystical or apocalyptic revelation or the guidance of a specially appointed teacher such as the Qumran Teacher of Righteousness or Jesus as the authority for their interpretations and traditions. The Rabbis, however, centered their teaching on Torah.

The focus on Torah in the rabbinic tradition has had liturgical, symbolic, and social consequences. The Torah scroll itself has become an object of reverence and enthusiasm and the reading of the Torah scroll in the synagogue a solemn moment of high honor. Though the evidence for the development of Sabbath observances, synagogues, and liturgical practices in the Second Temple and early post-Temple period is sparse, descriptions of Diaspora synagogues speak of regular readings from Torah on the Sabbath and early rabbinic documents imply regular readings on Sabbath, Mondays, and Thursdays. The Pentateuch was given pride of place in rabbinic synagogue practices and read on the Sabbath according to a three-year cycle in the land of Israel and a one-year cycle in Babylon. (This latter cycle is the one still used in traditional synagogues today.) Jewish tradition has developed detailed rules to govern the accurate and careful copying of Torah scrolls. From about the fourth century the scrolls have been kept in a cabinet, called an ark, at the front of the synagogue. They are covered with highly elaborate covers and decorated with other ornaments. In the Sabbath service the Torah scroll is carried around the synagogue to be reverenced by the congregation. To read the Torah to the community or to go up to the scroll to recite the benediction that precedes the reading are honors shared among the congregants. In sum, the Torah scroll is not only a written document to be read in the synagogue but the most sacred object and focus of the congregation's attention and sentiments. The Torah scroll functions as an object of reverence and as a religious symbol in a way analogous to the crucifix or the consecrated bread and wine in a Catholic church.

Torah also gives authority and status in the Jewish community. The person who knows Torah, meaning both the Bible and rabbinic literature, can speak authoritatively on community teachings and decisions. Being learned in Torah is a recognized community value that gives status to a religiously oriented Jew and motivates many to study the rabbinic tradition.

The common Christian assumption that Jewish Law is technical, dry and dead, and productive of a legalistic mentality is clearly incompatible with the living tradition of Jewish Torah. Devotion to Torah is based on God's choice of Israel and self-revelation in the Bible. The covenant relationship between God and Israel is the foundation for the laws, customs, and understandings of Scripture and tradition that constitute the substance of the Torah tradition. The living out of the covenant relationship and its laws in the Jewish community demands and promotes continued reflection on and interpretation of Torah.

For Jews the Pentateuch has the authority, centrality, and symbolic effect of the gospels for Christians. Jews look to God's revelation on Sinai in the same way that Christians look to Jesus Christ. As the teachings of Jesus in the gospels are interpreted, reinterpreted, pondered, and prayed over, the stories and laws of the Torah are memorized, interpreted, and meditated on by religious Jews. This creates a continuing dialogue between Jews and God, a dialogue within which the processes of revelation begun at Sinai are still active, resulting in new legal and theological insights. Both the Torah and the gospels are revered liturgically and privately and both exercise a similar authority over community teaching and practice. The reading of these books provides ongoing guidance and inspiration to each community and a symbolic focus for communal attention, prayer, and practice.

Genesis

Lawrence Boadt

FIRST READING

A. How to Approach Reading Genesis

1. Getting Started

Genesis needs no introduction. Its stories of creation, the garden of Eden, the flood, the great ancestors Abraham and Sarah and Isaac and Jacob, and the fate and fortune of Joseph in Egypt are among the best-known of world masterpieces. Indeed, they have influenced much of western society's literature. However, Genesis is far more familiar in the telling of individual stories than it is as a whole book. What it needs then is to be read!

This commentary is organized to help you read Genesis all the way through, to understand its plan and purpose, and still appreciate the wonder and beauty of each individual story. By looking at the book as a dramatic reading we will not only learn its religious message, but actually enjoy it.

So the first step is to read the entire book *once* from beginning to end, not studying it in detail, but getting a sense of what is in it and how each narrative flows into the next. Pay attention to major changes in the plot and note who are the main actors.

The second step is to back up and look at the table of contents of your Bible. Notice that Genesis begins a great collection of books that have been sacred to Jews and Christians. It is a beginning, and beginnings are important. But how diverse are the types of books it heads!

2. How Genesis Works as the Beginning

As we shall see, Genesis itself was collected from many different traditions. As the book gradually reached its present size and shape it had to play an increasingly important role in the growing collection of sacred books of Israel. It was the beginning of the Pentateuch, the sacred Torah or foundational basis for Israel's way of life. It was also the beginning of what we can rightly call the "Great Story," the narrative of divine guidance of the world from the day of creation to the end of the Israelite monarchy in the Babylonian exile, found in the first eleven books from Genesis through 2 Kings (Ruth was not originally part of this grouping). And it is the beginning of the entire Hebrew Scriptures as a sacred collection. At each of these three levels Genesis provides a powerful opening statement for the interpretation of all that follows.

Genesis as the Beginning of the Pentateuch

The Pentateuch is the fundamental building block of the Old Testament message. It begins in Genesis with the creation of all things in their place and a God who sees it all as good and can rest and take delight in contemplating its beauty (read Gen 1:31–2:4). But it ends with the Israelite people gathered on the border of the land of Palestine, hopeful of finding there a permanent home for themselves. In between, it is the story of a turbulent human journey where failures seem to be as frequent as successes. Many of the narrative stories seem to involve trial and testing, and many of the most positive stories are those of promise rather than completion. This gives the Pentateuch a kind of tentative quality. These men and women represent the human struggle to decide for God and against evil, and even the best of them must be constantly on guard. They all have clay feet at times, including Abraham and Moses! At the same time the Pentateuch has a very triangular shape: the action leads up to Mount Sinai at the center of the whole narrative, and then leads down and away from the mountain toward the promised land. On Mount Sinai is found the Torah (i.e., the Law). It becomes the focus of the Pentateuchal drama. Given in solemn manner and in great detail, extending from Exodus 19 to Numbers 10, it clearly is presented as the most complete expression of God's will for Israel. Genesis initiates these great events by telling us of the struggles of the first humans and the great tribal ancestors of long ago. It explains how Israel came to first meet and trust this God of Mount Sinai. It also matches the purpose of the final book of the five, Deuteronomy. Both books are written to convince the people that it is worth putting their trust in the divine word of promise.

Genesis as the Beginning of the Great Story

When exilic historians gathered the vast array of national stories and chronicles now found in the *Deuteronomic History* (Joshua, Judges, 1 and 2 Samuel, 1 and 2 Kings), they were not interested primarily in keeping the fame of kings and leaders alive for posterity, but in the lessons to be learned from their decisions. The so-called "history" is not a political chronology but the story of how God's word was obeyed or not obeyed in each generation, and how the preponderance of disobedience finally brought down God's judgment on the nation. This view is rooted in the message of Deuteronomy, placed as the last book of the Pentateuch, in which Moses warns the people to obey God's commandments given in the Law or they will be driven from the land (read Deut 30:15-20). Genesis in turn plays a crucial role in initiating this history: God creates a world in right order by the divine word, and that word inexorably maintains justice and right order through all ages. Thus the entire history becomes a history of that word spoken in Genesis 1.

Genesis as the Beginning of the Whole Bible

Just as Genesis has functioned to set up the "Great Story" of Israel's period of existence as an independent state on the land, so it also keys us to the manifold and wondrous works of God found in all of creation and through all ages of history. Genesis as a theme statement of the OT is echoed very clearly in the words of Israel's praise in Ps 104:24,

> How manifold are your works, O Lord!
> By wisdom you fashioned every one of them.

Genesis prepares us from the start to expect the wealth of books and their varied approaches that will make up the whole of the Hebrew Scriptures. They do not propose only one way of knowing God, but many. As a result they contain all kinds of literature: legal codes, royal chronicles, poetry, prophecy, wisdom sayings, model stories, and even love songs.

If we also include the New Testament in the vast plan of the Scriptures as a whole, then we can see that the book of Revelation ends with a new creation being established in perfection very similar to the first creation of Genesis. This even includes details found in Genesis 2 about the garden of Eden: precious stones, a river of life, a tree of life, the naming of all its dwellers, and the presence of the divine Spirit (see Revelation 21–22). The final words of the book of Revelation emphasize that this vision is a divine word of prophecy that will surely happen. It neatly rounds out the entire Scripture as the word of God spoken and active from the beginning of time, bringing about God's will, often despite human will and words that stand in contradiction to it.

In sum, this function of the Bible as the creative and discerning word of God is summarized by the author of the letter to the Hebrews:

> Indeed, the word of God is living and active,
> sharper than any two-edged sword (Heb 4:12).

B. The Literary Structure of Genesis

1. Major Divisions of the Book

The structure of the book reveals natural divisions of the material that make up our starting point for examination of the "plot" and literary purpose of the authors and editors. The first and most obvious characteristic of the book is that it tells the stories of different major figures that are said to have lived chronologically one after the other. Thus the book focuses mainly around persons: Adam and Eve, Cain and Abel, Noah, Abraham and Sarah, Isaac and Rebecca, Jacob and his wives Rachel and Leah, and finally Jacob's son, Joseph. This tells us already that at least part of its literary effect on readers will be as a history of humankind, a history that gets to be more and more selective. Secondly, it emphasizes these figures in key decisions and encounters with God so that they play decisive roles in the unfolding of the narrative (see, for example, Joseph's explanation of how he fulfills God's plan in Gen 45:4-8). A little like the main characters in Greek tragedies and comedies, the leading people of Genesis are not small nobodies in the eyes of the drama; they are significant individuals on whose decisions much depends. If not all heroes, they are at least all models of human response to the divine.

A third feature that stands out upon reading the text over several times is that there is quite a difference between chs. 1–11 and 12–50 (see how 11:32 marks the end of an èra, and 12:1-9 clearly begins a new call of God). In chs. 1–11 the time is very long ago before historical times; the events have to do with the origins of various human and divine actions. These stories have many likenesses to other Ancient Near Eastern religious tales of creation, stories we often identify as myths; and the ancestors involved are those of the entire human race. But in chs. 12–50 the narrative becomes much more specific, identifies the places, and names the known ancestors of Israel itself; their stories are tied together with a theme of the promise of land and nationhood in the future that is to be historical Israel as we know it. Above all, the families of Abraham, Isaac, Jacob, and Joseph are described in enough detail to be pictured as real people and not just as names attached to some event. These last thirty-nine chapters are not so much like classical myths about the time of creation as they are like legends, or even modern historical novels, that focus their interest on the personal dimensions of significant lives. Many scholars compare these narratives to the type of literature we know as "saga" from tenth- to eleventh-century Iceland, i.e., family histories that color the actual stories with the larger purpose of explaining the nation's character and identity.

2. A Diagram of the Literary Divisions

Genesis 1–11	**Genesis 12–50**
A. Genesis 1–3 The creation of the world and of human society, blessed by God but imperiled by sin.	*A′. Genesis 12–23* Abraham and his family receive divine blessing and struggle to get it established.
B. Genesis 4–5 Sin spreads even to hatred among brothers and between professions but God's blessing also builds.	*B′. Genesis 24–27* The blessing and promise pass to a new generation but the struggle persists to establish their place.
C. Genesis 6–9 Sin is so much greater than good that God must punish humanity, and start the blessing anew with Noah.	*C′. Genesis 27–36; 48–50* Jacob is blessed to carry on the promise despite his crookedness. God moves forward by setting up the twelve sons to be Israel.
D. Genesis 10–11 God renews the blessing by multiplying people, but human self-will in sin stays as bad as ever.	*D′. Genesis 37–47; 48–50* Joseph is used by God to lead the chosen sons to Egypt—it appears that the promised land is found.

3. The "Drama" of the Literary Narrative

The diagram above shows how the two parts of Genesis are carefully constructed to match one another, each with four steps of human history. By means of these stages the authors are able to underscore how God guides different ages and times, and how every generation affects the one that comes after. There is a sense of growing intensity created in Genesis by the inexorable movement forward of the various steps. Not only that, but, as many exegetes and commentators have noted, there seems to be an intentional enhancing of drama as the steps move forward. Thus for example in Genesis 1–11 the tension between God's close personal relationship to humanity in creation and humankind's sinful alienation and desire for autonomy from God grows steadily. At first humans are deceived into sin; then passion overwhelms Cain; then come sexual lust and habitual evil, then drunkenness and excess, until humanity finally becomes completely arrogant in the attempt to take heaven itself with a tower. Meanwhile the

God who had blessed human life with fertility and stewardship over the land constantly offers forgiveness and restores blessing after being forced to punish the recurrent sinfulness.

In chs. 12–50 the promise made to Abraham in 12:1-3 starts as a hope against hope, struggles to survive by producing even one child, grows to a clan of twelve, and finally moves into high gear with a descendant who becomes prime minister of the greatest land on earth and establishes the family in blessing—or so it seems! But God must also constantly fight against their doubt and their misguided actions in order to lead them forward. Clearly the drama won't end in Egypt!

C. Major Literary and Theological Themes

1. What Does One Look for in Genesis?

Although Genesis tells a story about the early history of the world and Israel's ancestors it never suggests it is primarily interested in verifying or teaching about the "facts" involved. The discussion above shows that its literary purpose was much more focused, first on what God intended for humans to be and to do, and then on the narrower but more awe-inspiring plan of God to choose Israel in a special way and to be with this people through thick and thin. Readers should not seek in Genesis a better explanation of astronomy or geology or the origins of the physical world than science today gives; nor should we hope to find an accurate and complete record of ancient history. The authors knew only so much of these things, and most of it was hearsay and limited by their culture's level of development. On the other hand they had a sharp vision of who God was and how humans were to act in relationship to this God. So we should expect that Genesis (and the Bible as a whole) will provide a very readable, literate, entertaining, and edifying series of stories, poems, laws, and other literary pieces that will *persuade* us of the truth about what God does and wills. Its purpose is religious, both on the level of making sense of what Israel believed and why, and on the level of personal commitment and conversion to God in worship and obedience.

2. Ten Significant Theological Themes in Genesis

Genesis is well-constructed as a unified drama, so we should expect to find its major themes woven skillfully throughout the book. The following selections do not exhaust all the themes of the narrative, and each will need to be explained in more detail in the commentary on individual passages below. But these ten provide most of the building blocks for the book's overall vision.

1. *Creation is divinely planned, ordered, and good.* Read again Genesis 1, noting its solemn claims about God's wise ordering.
2. *Humans are in God's image and are God's servants.* See especially Gen 1:26-30 and 2:15-17.
3. *God has blessed humanity.* Note how often blessing is given to people: 1:21 (the ground); 1:28 (all humanity); 5:2 (Adam); 9:1 (Noah); 12:3 (Abraham); 26:54 (Isaac); 27:29 (Jacob); 48:1-16 (Joseph).
4. *Sin is turning away from God.* Gen 4:1-12 is a meditation on the lure of sin and its hold over us.
5. *God, however, both punishes and forgives.* A very fine example of the recognition of divine punishment, forgiveness and renewed blessing can be found in Genesis 32 and the circumstances around Jacob's reconciliation to his brother Esau.
6. *Israel has been specially chosen by God.* Review Gen 12:1-3; 15:1-6; 17:1-8; 28:10-22.
7. *The story is a story of promise.* See such important episodes as the blessing of Isaac in Gen 27:27-29, and the promise to Jacob in 35:10-12.
8. *God uses crooked lines to write straight.* To see this lesson one only needs to reread Jacob's deception of Esau in Gen 25:27-34; 27:1-45.
9. *Genesis is a story of faith.* Gen 15:1-6 gives us the story of Abraham's trust that has always been central for biblical theology.
10. *Don't forget the importance of worship.* The union of the Sabbath rest with creation in Gen 2:1-3 sets the pattern for the Bible.

As we read the whole of Genesis we come upon these themes again and again in new ways. They are not expressed according to our modern ways of seeing reality, but because they speak in story form we can recognize the moment of human experience involved. It is important to remember that when these stories were collected from Israel's past traditions and written down they were never intended to be a complete historical record of Israel's significant moments, but were presented primarily as theological reflections that highlight the central themes crucial to Israel's understanding of a God who gave revelation and special election to Israel. Thus before we study the text of Genesis in detail we must face the question of how to go about interpreting it the best we can.

GENERAL CONSIDERATIONS ON THE INTERPRETATION OF GENESIS

A. The Nature of Interpretation

Genesis is easy to read, but hard to understand. The Pontifical Biblical Commission in its comprehensive document on *Interpretation of the Bible in the Church* (November 1993) underscores this in several ways. It begins by saying that "this study is never finished; each age must in its own way newly seek to understand the sacred books." It adds shortly after, "the interpretation of biblical texts continues in our own day to be a matter of lively interest and significant debate." We can conclude from this that before deciding on the best way to read Genesis we need to explore certain distinctions about the many *ways* one can interpret this text.

First, as part of the collection of sacred Scripture, Genesis claims to have divine revelation through its words; and the Church in its teaching role seeks to understand and define exactly what the content of the revealed truth is. This is not the same as endorsing its historical, scientific, or literal meaning as true, but only its religious message for our salvation and holiness. Such interpretation in the Church can take many forms, from theological arguments for doctrines rooted in the words of Genesis through pious or spiritual reflections on the text for the edification of the faithful to the liturgical proclamation of Genesis passages at the Eucharist or in prayer, a usage that often includes moral exhortation (sermons) and emphasizes some passages over others (e.g., the common stress on Abraham as "our father in faith").

Second, there is a critical study of the words of the text. This involves such important issues as: (1) How can we possibly recapture or know anything about the world of three thousand years ago culturally and intellectually? (2) How can we distinguish the ideology, the bias of the ancient writers from their recording of stories and events? (3) Since the words are in human language, how do we get beyond our own modern understandings of words and our own biases? (4) How do we recover any facts of history after they are long past? (5) Has not the Church's reading of Genesis so affected our understanding along Christian lines that we cannot know the original meaning of the text?

Between these two concerns, which reconstruction of the meaning of texts is better: that of the believer in prayer, or that of the university professor? Neither, for Catholic tradition employs both spiritual and scholarly methods of reading the meaning of Genesis. The two ways have different approaches and different short-range purposes while sharing the same long-range end of making both what *was* said and what *is* still valuable in Genesis clearer for us today. This means that interpreters are concerned both to recover what the biblical authors meant to say and to expound a text's relevance for believers in contemporary ways of thinking. In order to show the rich diversity of interpretations of Genesis we can review (1) early Jewish readings of the text in the biblical period; (2) the early and medieval Christian approaches; and (3) modern critical methods.

B. Early Jewish Readings of Genesis

Biblical interpretation was extremely active in the Jewish world of 100 B.C.E. to 100 C.E. and a whole book could be written on its richness of approach. Genesis received a great deal of attention from many quarters, but behind all of them stood an already well-established history of Torah teaching and preaching on the sacred text traditions. This can be seen above all where Genesis was known to writers of other biblical books, or at least the traditions behind the present narratives were known and alluded to. The first chapter of Zephaniah, for example, knows the Genesis order of the days of creation even as it declares that they are being undone, and Psalm 8 seems to reflect the theology of Genesis 1–2.

We should expect, therefore, that later interpreters were moving beyond the mere repeating of the text of Genesis. This is borne out by the treatments we possess.

(a) *Apocryphal Books.* Beginning in the second century B.C.E. a stream of books was produced that linked Genesis to the practices, and sometimes the messianic hopes, of Second Temple Judaism. The book of Jubilees (second to first centuries B.C.E.) retells the Genesis stories to show the patriarchs and matriarchs were faithful observers of the Mosaic Law. It glorifies their actions and denigrates any value in having contact with Gentiles (understood to mean Hellenistic Greeks). The Testaments of the Twelve Patriarchs (first century B.C.E. with many later additions) expands many Genesis incidents related to the twelve sons of Jacob, especially in Genesis 49. It also shows strong support for faithful observance of Jewish law as well as adding apocalyptic and messianic expansions. The book of Enoch (first century B.C.E. to third century C.E.), based on Gen 5:18-24, has the patriarch Enoch foretell much of what will happen at the end of time in a moralistic homily and a series of apocalyptic warnings. The Life of Adam and Eve (first century C.E.) tells everything you ever wanted to know about the secret lives of the first couple and were afraid to ask. These last two are *midrashic,* i.e., they interpret old texts as though written for the present moment.

(b) *Qumran Texts.* Among the Dead Sea scrolls from the Qumran caves are several related to Genesis. This indicates that the Qumran community had a lively interest in the implications of various questions based on the mysteries hidden in the book. First of all, fragments of the Hebrew text of Genesis were found in caves 1, 2, 6, and 8, but none very complete. Copies of Jubilees were also abundant, found in caves 1, 2, 3, and 11. Another work of the midrashic type, found in cave 1, was the Genesis Apocryphon, which contained some small sections on Genesis 1–11, and many expansions on the story of Abraham.

(c) *Philo of Alexandria.* A Jew of Alexandria in Egypt, Philo became the great apologist for the validity and truth of Jewish Law among the Hellenistic-thinking Jews of the diaspora. He lived from about 20 B.C.E. to 40 C.E. and wrote extensively. He was thoroughly knowledgeable in Greek philosophical thought and presented Moses and the narratives and laws of the Pentateuch in categories that were persuasive to Greek ways of thinking. One of his major works was the *Exposition of the Law,* written in nine treatises, five of which were discussions of Genesis: *On the Creation of the World; On Abraham; On Isaac; On Jacob; On Joseph.* All the patriarchs are presented as models of how the Law was to be lived. He turned again to expounding the meaning of Genesis in his extensive treatises on *The Allegory of the Jewish Law.* These are more inspirational in nature. He also wrote a major work of *Questions and Answers on Genesis and Exodus,* in which he explains individual verses first literally, and then allegorically or mystically. Philo gradually fell out of favor in Jewish tradition but became very influential on early Church interpreters who used not only his methods but often even his allegories themselves.

(d) *Flavius Josephus.* Josephus was a well-educated Jewish leader of the revolt against Rome in 66 C.E. Captured early, he saved his life by promising to chronicle the Roman war against the Jews. Later he wrote a full history of the Jews that he entitled *The Jewish Antiquities.* In general it is a loose retelling of the Bible with many other sources thrown in. Studies of his method of treating Genesis, for example, show he often expanded striking incidents to emphasize their importance, but almost as often gave condensed accounts of important sections such as the story of creation, perhaps because he had no important point to make. In the remaining parts he followed the text rather closely. This suggests Josephus was carefully choosing how to narrate the basic plot of the book in full while drawing out the particular lessons he wanted to make for his contemporary audience. But it does reveal that he felt he could reshape the text rather freely without being unfaithful to its meaning.

C. The Church's Reading of Genesis

1. Genesis and the Formation of the New Testament

All of our NT documents testify that the apostolic age preached that Jesus lived by and obeyed the Scriptures, meaning of course the OT texts. When NT writers report that Jesus used Genesis 2 to teach that there should be no divorce or adultery (Gen 2:24 cited by Matt 19:5; Mark 10:7-8; 1 Cor 6:16), they clearly understand that he is building on and extending the real meaning of Genesis in a new way. Thus when it came to deciding what constituted the sacred canon of Scripture for Christians, the church included not just NT books about Jesus but the whole of the OT, for without its testimony to what God did there would be no signs to reveal Jesus as the Christ who fulfills God's plan.

It is crucial to recognize how much emphasis the NT tradition places on Genesis stories because they are from the *beginning:* e.g., marriage is established in creation and reflects the love of Christ and the Church (Eph 5:31 commenting on Gen 2:24); also the claim that Christians live by Christ and his Spirit rather than by the law because they like Abraham are righteous apart from Law and believe in a promise that comes *before* any obligation of the law (Romans 4 and Galatians 3 on Abraham's faith; Hebrews 7 on Melchizedek in Gen 14:17-20; 2 Pet 1:17 on Isaac's sacrifice in Gen 22:2; or John 8 on the true followers of Abraham as Jesus' disciples).

There are thirty-eight direct quotations of Genesis or allusions to it in the NT. But other references can also be identified in a more general sense, such as when Jesus refers to Abraham in John 8:37-59 or to Noah in 1 Pet 3:20. The most popular references are to: (1) Gen 2:24, "a man shall leave father and mother and cling to his wife and they shall be one flesh" (Matt 19:5; Mark 10:7-8; 1 Cor 6:16; Eph 5:31); (2) Gen 15:6, "Abram put trust in the Lord, who reckoned it as righteousness" (Rom 4:3, 9; Gal 3:6; Jas 2:23); and (3) Gen 22:2, "Take your son Isaac, your only son, your beloved, and sacrifice him on a mountain" (Matt 3:17; 17:5; Mark 1:11; 9:7; Luke 3:22; 9:35; 2 Pet 1:17). From the NT uses of Genesis passages come many important Christian doctrines: original sin (Romans 5 and Genesis 3), the role of Melchizedek as a type of the priest and of the Eucharist (Genesis 14 and Hebrews 7); justification by faith (Genesis 15 and Romans 4, Galatians 3), and the figure of Christ as a new Adam (Genesis 2 and Romans 5).

2. Patristic Period Reading of Genesis

Because Christianity spread rapidly among the Gentile Hellenistic population and the strains with Judaism grew to the breaking point, Jewish exegesis of Scripture went its own way so that expositions of the legal requirements of the biblical Torah predominate in the Talmud and later writings. Christians instead focused on the aspects of how OT texts looked toward and found realization in the life and teaching of Jesus as presented in the NT. Christian methods grew out of the Jewish techniques mentioned above but quickly moved into fully Hellenistic/Roman ways of thinking.

The vast majority of scriptural reflections in the period from the second century to the twelfth were concerned to draw the christological implications from OT and NT alike. Writers saw a unity between the testaments that viewed the Old as promise and the New as its fulfillment or the events of the Old as *type* (prefigurement, image) and the New as *antitype* (reality). Genesis is particularly important in this regard, for as the beginning it serves as the prophetic type for all that is to come. This takes shape especially in innumerable reflections on such topics as the six days of creation, Adam and Eve, original sin, or Noah and the flood. To a lesser extent attention was called to the patriarchs Abraham, Isaac, and Jacob as types of faith, divine promise, and divine guidance. It is also important to note that such reflections are not limited to one area such as popular piety, but are found in liturgical practices, instructional catecheses, eucharistic homilies, theological treatises on the meaning of the texts (commentaries), and in religious art.

An important element in early Church exegesis was recognition of the multiple levels of meaning in every text. This method was already present in Jewish exegesis, especially in Hellenistic works like those of Philo of Alexandria, but became highly developed among Christian interpreters seeking for Christ in OT texts. Terms for the levels often differed, but by the Middle Ages four were clearly recognized: the *literal* meaning, the *spiritual* meaning hidden in the literal story (often referred to as the "allegorical" meaning), the *moral* lesson of the text, and the *anagogical* (i.e., the end purpose: getting to heaven). They are found in all biblical exegetes to a greater or lesser extent. Origen (184–253 C.E.) was the leading early master of such interpretation of Genesis. In commenting on Gen 1:26-27, that humans are made in the image and likeness of God, he notes the literal level in which it cannot mean our bodies are like God, but our spiritual faculties. He says that this must also be read on the spiritual level to mean we imitate Christ, firstborn of every creature (Col 1:15). Morally, it demands we obey God's commands to imitate the divine goodness and love; and anagogically it makes us realize that we are being transformed into the heavenly body of Christ's glory when we imitate Christ, and that our end as the divine image is to be a "citizen of heaven" *(Homily 1 on Genesis).*

Augustine (354–430), another master of spiritual interpretation, in his *The Literal Interpretation of Genesis* (ch. 3) asks "whether we should understand the words, 'In the beginning God created the heavens and the earth' only in accord with history, or whether they also signify something in figures?" He answers that the real spiritual meaning is how the words conform to the gospel and the Son as the first principle of all things.

We can sample typical patristic exegesis under ten categories:

(1) *The Liturgy.* Our earliest accounts of the Eucharist in 1 Cor 11:23-26 and the *Didache* focus on the paschal and messianic nature of the sacrament. But later eucharistic prayers regularly begin with the note of God's goodness in creation. Chapter 7 of the *Apostolic Constitutions* (no later than early fourth century) recites at length all the narrative events of Genesis 1–2 up to the expulsion of Adam and Eve from the garden and then moves directly to Jesus as the one who will restore us the life they lost. Other early eucharistic prayers such as the *Apostolic Tradition* of Hippolytus or the *Anaphora of Addai and Mari* cite creation in thanking God for sending the Word to us in the sacrament, "through whom you have created all things." Baptismal liturgies use similar themes. The prayer for the blessing of baptismal water in the *Euchology* of Serapion of Thmuis (360 or after) cites the prototype of the blessings of creation for God to renew blessing on these waters. In its liturgical prayers for repentance, the *Didascalia of the Apostles* (third c.) recites the names of Abraham, Isaac, and Jacob as models of people who were just before God and did not need rites of repentance as we do.

(2) *Baptismal Imagery.* The waters of creation were identified symbolically in many early Christian writers with the waters of baptism. The primordial waters prefigured the new creation by water in Christ at baptism. Tertullian, Ambrose, Cyril of Jerusalem, and Didymus of Alexandria all include this in their baptismal catechesis.

The symbolism of the dove for the Holy Spirit in the baptismal liturgy was identified both with the dove that hovered over Christ at his baptism in the Jordan and with the spirit that hovered over the deep in the act of creation (Gen 1:2), as well as with the dove that brought Noah a sign that the flood waters had receded (Gen 8:8-11).

Those to be baptized went naked into the water and Cyril of Jerusalem identifies this with the nakedness of Adam and Eve in the garden of Eden, innocent and without sin. Theodore of Mopsuestia notes the same symbolism in commenting on Gen 3:7, "and they knew they were naked." This imagery of Christ as the new Adam originates in Paul (Romans 5), and was very popular among early Church writers, especially in connection with reflections on Genesis 1–3.

An important part of the baptismal rite was the *sphragis,* or the marking of the baptismal candidate on the forehead with the sign of the cross. The Greek word *sphragis* generally meant a brand put on animals, or soldiers, or slaves. But Christian writers identified it with the mark of Cain (Gen 4:15) which was given to protect him.

The family of Noah saved in the ark was an almost universally used symbol of the baptized who were saved from sin's destructive waters by coming on board the ark of the Church. It is found in Tertullian's treatise *On Baptism,* and in Cyprian of Carthage, Justin Martyr, Didymus of Alexandria, Jerome, John Chrysostom, and Augustine. Ambrose wrote an entire treatise, *On Noah and the Ark,* on baptism and the flood symbolism. Even liturgical prayers such as the *Apostolic Constitutions* 2.149 drew on it. It had special force because the image was found originally in 1 Pet 3:18-20 in regard to baptism.

(3) *Sabbath Reflections.* The justification for the Christian change of the Sabbath from Saturday to Sunday required biblical symbolism as well. One favorite expression was that God established the day of the resurrection as an eternal Sabbath that replaces Saturday which is a mere temporal day of rest (Justin Martyr, *Dialogue;* Irenaeus, *Against all the Heresies;* Tertullian, *Against the Jews;* and Origen, *Homilies on Numbers*). A second reason was associated with reflections on Sunday as the eighth day of the week, i.e., the first day of a new week, reflecting the new creation established in the death and resurrection of Jesus. Since light was created on the

first day according to Gen 1:3-5, it is identified with the resurrection. Clement of Alexandria writes, "The seventh day, by banishing evils, prepares for the primordial day, our true rest. This is he who is the light brought forth first of all" (*Stromata* 6.16). Similar thoughts are found in Justin's *Apology,* Tertullian's *Apology,* and Eusebius, *The Preparation of the Gospel.*

(4) *Reflections on the Hexaemeron.* The term *hexaemeron* refers specifically to the account of creation in six days in Genesis 1. Philo devoted much attention to it, and two great works were produced in the fourth century by Basil in the Eastern Church and by Ambrose in the West. These two works were really a weekly series of talks during Lent and ranged far beyond a description of the text to thoughts about human nature in relation to God and our place in the scheme of the universe. The authors quote widely from the Scriptures, earlier church thinkers, and Latin and Greek poets and philosophers. Other examples of this genre are by Gregory of Nyssa (fourth c.); Bede (eighth c.); and Honorius of Autun (twelfth c.). The idea of the six days strongly influenced the Middle Ages: one need only think of the great mosaics of the hexaemeron on the walls of Monreale in Palermo from the twelfth century.

(5) *Theological and Exegetical Commentaries.* From Origen to the high Middle Ages great numbers of commentaries on Genesis were composed. The index in Migne's *Latin Fathers* (vol. 218) takes eight columns to list them, and at least two more columns in the index of the Greek Fathers. Commentators include the great Cappadocians Basil and Gregory of Nyssa; the Syriac Fathers such as Ephrem, the western theologians such as Ambrose and Augustine (who wrote at least three different ones plus his *City of God*); and many more during the Middle Ages, including Procopius, Isidore of Seville, Bede, Alcuin, Rabanus Maurus, Walafrid Strabo, Rupert of Deutz, Hugh of St. Victor and even Thomas Aquinas in his *Postilla seu expositio aurea in librum Geneseos,* right up to Nicholas of Lyra in the fifteenth century.

(6) *Homilies.* Many reflections on Genesis came in the form of baptismal preparation homilies or Lenten series. Those by Origen and John Chrysostom were perhaps the most famous. Chrysostom's work is far different from the treatises we have just been mentioning. A contemporary of the fourth century, Julian of Eclanum, said of him that his treatment of Scripture was "rather by exhortation than by exposition." The saintly bishop was very concerned with threats from contemporary situations and often introduces long and polemical asides into his treatment of passages even to the point of sounding angry or prejudiced to modern ears.

(7) *Adam and Eve.* Certain parts of Genesis have gotten more attention than others over the centuries. The first human couple were naturally significant as the type of all human beings to come. Special interest was shown in the contrast between the first Adam and Christ as the second or new Adam of a restored humanity, and in the idea of humans as the image of God, which was related to Christ by distinguishing image and likeness: "If we were made in the image (shadow) of God we must become in the likeness of Christ." Irenaeus of Lyons introduced a popular image of Christ as the new head of the human race. His idea of "recapitulation" was rooted in Paul's poem of Christ as the head of the body in Colossians 1.

Many Church writers noted the saving role of Eve in bringing forth Christ as her descendant. Gen 3:15, in which the serpent will bite her heel but her offspring will crush its head, was understood to look ahead from Eve to Mary and her son Jesus. Mary was the new Eve and Christ was the new Adam. Still later in the Middle Ages the painting of Eve nursing a child was familiarly identified with Mary's nursing the baby Jesus. Mary became like Eve, the mother of all the living.

(8) *Noah.* Origen devotes considerable time in his homilies to Noah and the ark. He sees in the triple-decked boat the three levels of Scriptural interpretation, the historical, the mystical or spiritual, and the moral, and applies it to the text as a kind of commentary on Christian life. Ambrose follows in this tradition as well.

(9) *Abraham and the Ancestors.* Abraham's significance for Paul led others to use the patriarch consistently as the example of faith for the Church. Since Abraham entertained the three angels in Genesis 18, and they then alternated with God's voice in the story, it was Abraham who was credited with first recognizing the Trinity. Isaac was also important not only as a prefigurement of Jesus who was led to execution willingly, but as the child of promise who replaced

Ishmael, as Christians would replace Jews in the scheme of salvation. So, too, since Jesus was the victim celebrated in the Eucharist, Isaac became a type of the Eucharist to come. Jacob also was a favorite of the Middle Ages, especially since it was Jacob who blessed Judah in Genesis 49 with the promise of the future messiah.

(10) *Genesis in Christian Art.* By the third century Christian art began to develop in frescoes and sarcophagus carving. Favorite themes of the early period included Adam and Eve naked, Noah and the ark, the sacrifice of Isaac, and Abraham entertaining the three angels. In the fourth century the new basilica of St. Mary Major in Rome was decorated with forty-four mosaic panels that told the entire story of Genesis. They remain the oldest complete artistic representation of Genesis in existence. In the Middle Ages masters of the art of illumination decorated Bibles and prayer books with popular scenes of the lives of Abraham and Jacob, and very frequently with scenes from the story of Joseph.

The same was true of cathedral decoration. Stained glass windows at Sainte Chapelle in Paris illustrate in detail all the books from Genesis to the Prophets. The south porch of Rouen cathedral carries the same motifs in small carved stone panels. And the cathedrals of Chartres, Bourges, Auxerre and Poitiers delight in telling the Joseph story in bas reliefs.

3. Medieval Developments in Interpretation

Throughout the medieval period biblical interpretation emphasized the allegorical meaning of texts. Two works were very influential in this beyond the treasury of early Christian patristic writers. Isidore of Seville's *Quaestiones in Vetus Testamentum* and his *Allegoriae quaedam Scripturae sacrae,* which was a list of all the important persons of the Bible and how they foreshadowed Jesus as messiah, provided a handbook from which most later writers drew. Somewhere between the ninth and eleventh centuries the *Glossa Ordinaria* emerged. It annotated the important verses of the Bible in order with the most widely accepted allegorical interpretations of the great patristic writers. It reinforced the conviction that every biblical passage of the OT had both a literal meaning and a Christian significance. Many seemingly remote connections were made, so that the scene of Isaac bearing the wood for the sacrifice in Genesis 22 or of Jacob blessing Joseph's two sons Manasseh and Ephraim with crossed arms in Genesis 48 both became signs of the crucifixion. The death of Abel was likewise identified as a type of the crucifixion. And if Isaac could be a figure of Christ, then Abraham was often seen as a model of God the Father. All of this pervaded Church art and architecture as well as the stories and mystery plays of the medieval world.

Love of the Scriptures was encouraged by the widespread leadership and example of the monastic communities and the practice of *lectio divina,* meditation upon the stories of the Bible and their spiritual meaning for life. Vivid imagination was cultivated so that when the well-loved biblical stories came up in the Mass liturgies or readings of the monks' daily office they were frequently acted out in choir. Thus drama was born in the West.

D. Modern Critical Methods of Reading Genesis

1. The Rise of Source-Critical Interpretation of Genesis

The introduction of knowledgeable Hebrew and Greek scholarship to the reading of OT texts in the periods of the Renaissance and the Reformation led to critical observations about discrepancies among the ancient manuscripts and between the methods of interpretation employed by Jewish exegetes versus their Christian counterparts. At first this led mostly to greater interest in the literal meaning of the texts and less reliance on allegorical ways of explaining difficult passages.

By the middle of the seventeenth century, however, keen observers were beginning to note that the literary style and content of Genesis had many seemingly contradictory aspects about them. The first to draw attention to such problems were the Jewish philosopher Baruch Spinoza and a Catholic priest in France named Richard Simon. In 1678 Simon observed that the quite different accounts of events in Genesis suggested that Moses may not have been the only author of the book of Genesis. Since this idea would have threatened the general belief that Moses had received the contents of revelation in Genesis directly through inspiration,

Father Simon's book was strongly criticized by theologians and was placed on the Index by the Church. Seventy-five years later another French scholar, Jean Astruc, suggested in his *Conjectures* of 1753 that Genesis 1 and 2 showed a different use of the divine name (*ʾelohim* in ch. 1; *yhwh ʾelohim* in ch. 2). He suggested that these came from two distinct documents that Moses had employed in putting together the book as a whole. This was the beginning of what became in another century the "documentary hypothesis" or "source theory." It also marks the birth of what we call today the "historical-critical method." The approach implicit in Simon's and Astruc's observations was to note and then search out the history of the development of our present book of Genesis. Scholars observed such phenomena as double accounts of the same story in the text (e.g., Abraham sending Hagar away in Genesis 16 and 21, or Abraham's seeming deception in passing off his wife Sarah as his sister instead in chs. 12 and 20) and attempted to trace how these texts had come to be included in the current arrangement and what original sources had been used by the final biblical authors in creating the present text of Genesis as we have it. See the article on "Pentateuch" for the full development of the "four-source" theory.

2. *Genesis According to the Source Critics*

The book of Genesis has usually been analyzed by the source critics as composed of only three of the traditional four sources: "J," "E," and "P." The "D" source (Deuteronomy) was thought to be found only in the book of the same name at the end of the Pentateuch. This view has been challenged today and many scholars are suggesting that D may be present as part of the final editing of Genesis. Some chapters such as Genesis 14 that did not fit any of the earlier sources are now often proposed as late Deuteronomic additions. But this has not received widespread acceptance yet, mainly because the only traces of such D material would be in sentences that are considered part of the final editing process; and whatever process was used it would certainly show signs of influence from both the P and D traditions from the exilic and post-exilic periods. Moreover there are few if any traces of continuous D narrative throughout Genesis. Thus we are left with the three primary sources. Certain characteristics of the Genesis text are fundamental to source criticism's conclusions about how the book came to be edited in its present form. (See also the introductory article, "The Pentateuch.")

(a) Genesis 1–11 seems to show two clearly different styles and therefore two separate sources interwoven throughout (see the table on p. 370). These have been identified as J and P. The J source portrays God's actions in very human terms, stresses humanity's weakness and tendency to fail, and uses stories that are closely related to the myths of neighboring peoples. P on the other hand portrays God's actions in solemn and majestic terms, uses lists and lengthy periods of time to establish God's plans, and stresses the divine blessing and covenant given to humans.

(b) Genesis 12–50 combines stories of great ancestors that reflect different regional concerns. The Abraham and Isaac narratives are largely set in Judah and the south, while Jacob (and his son Joseph by extension) mainly represent traditions from the area of the northern tribes. The majority of Abraham and Isaac traditions thus come from the J source, while most of the Jacob and Joseph stories are found in a separate E source from writers in the northern kingdom. However, source critics admit that all these traditions have been carefully combined so that many of the narratives could be read as either J or E. This is testimony to the skills of the ancient editing tradition. The P source, which was prominent in chs. 1–11, plays a smaller role in the second part, inserting key stories at important points in the development of the plot, e.g., at chs. 17, 23, and 49. This suggests that P filled in the existing combined narrative of E and J at the final stage of editing.

(c) Source critics generally identify J with royal scribes at the court of the Davidic monarchy in Jerusalem, perhaps even as early as Solomon's reign. Their perspective is built on the blessings God gave to Judah through David's achievements. In Genesis it is reflected in the mission given to Israel to bring blessing to other nations (Gen 12:1-3), especially through the kings of Judah (Gen 49:8-12). It pictures a God who remains close with those chosen to lead and is tolerant and forgiving when they fail (so Adam, Noah, Abraham, Jacob, and of course behind them all as a model of how they are presented, David, the favorite of God and frailest of humans.)

(d) The E source breathes an entirely different spirit. Where it is present, as in chs. 15, 20, 28, 31, 34–35, 40–42, God rarely appears intimate with leaders, interest centers not on Judah but rather on northern shrines such as Bethel or the tribal areas of Ephraim and Manasseh (identified as the sons of Joseph, Genesis 48), and there is a strong emphasis on the moral implications of human behavior, especially about "fear of God," i.e., faithful worship of God alone (Gen 20:11; 22:12), which may reflect northern Israel's struggle against the Baal cult in the ninth century B.C.E. typified by the prophet Elijah. Genesis 35:1-4, for example, shows a concern to put away all idols.

(e) When J and E were combined after the fall of the northern kingdom in 723/722 B.C.E. the two emphases of divine blessing on the house of Judah through the ancestors and obedient faithfulness to the Sinai covenant tradition were joined. Both, however, focused on a promise of prosperity while dwelling faithfully in the land. When the exile of 587 cast these claims into doubt the P source was systematically added to the J/E version of Genesis. Thus the story of creation in Genesis 1 gave to the existing story of Adam and Eve in chs. 2–3 a new emphasis on the eternal validity and purpose of God's words of creation and promise that overcame any fear that the divine promise would fail. The same note of confidence in the divine guidance of world events is found in other P texts of Genesis: the extremely lengthy lifespans of the genealogy of ch. 5; the emphasis on "God almighty" and an "eternal" covenant in ch. 17; the permanent title to property in Canaan for a burial place in ch. 23.

(f) Source critics have constructed a strong case for a gradual building up of the book of Genesis from written traditions stemming from different times and social settings in Israel's history. Theologies that reflect different stages of Israelite religious thinking have been sifted and combined to express a larger and deeper understanding of God's relationship and revelation to Israel in the finished product than any single earlier source had been able to express. Individual source-critical positions will be discussed in the following commentary whenever they can throw light on a particular section of Genesis.

However, source theory is being challenged and re-evaluated today by many scholars who think the same differences can be attributed to blocks of traditional material or to a variety of sophisticated theological echoes written into the style to recall other parts of the tradition. At the same time, many other methods have developed that add to or move in directions different from the source critical approach. These too can be very helpful in interpreting the meaning of the text and we can note a few before we turn to our second reading of the text by examining the individual passages.

3. Hermann Gunkel and Form Criticism

In 1901 Hermann Gunkel published his *Commentary on Genesis.* It was a revolutionary break from the procedures of Wellhausen and other pure source critics. Where Wellhausen had been interested only in the developed theological documents that told Israel's story from within the period of David and beyond, Gunkel argued that much of the biblical material was in fact based on long oral tradition and had been nourished and passed on perhaps for centuries before it came to be written down by the Yahwist and others. His study of Genesis led him to identify two major genres at work: "myth" in chs. 1–11 and "saga" or "legend" (i.e., "history-like story") in chs. 12–50. Neither of these should be understood to mean "fiction" or "not-true-to-life"; rather they are ancient ways of communicating the important stories and traditions of a people's past from a worldview that did not have the means for, nor seek after, exact accounts of "what actually happened" as the modern scientific and technologically-oriented mind does. This commentary will make frequent use of these categories to help us understand how creation was described or how the great cycles of ancestor stories can be made intelligible for us today.

4. Other Recent Historical-Critical Methods

(a) Martin Noth and Gerhard von Rad and most biblical scholars before 1970 combined source and form criticisms with historical and anthropological information such as the identification of the role of cultic centers and the use of genealogies in handing on family traditions to show how the materials in Genesis were collected and edited, from their first setting in the primitive beginnings of tribal Israel down through their final form in the book of Genesis. This is now sometimes called "tradition history."

(b) In recent years a great deal of further interest has been shown in applying social science models to the study of the ancient Israelite life situation behind the text of Genesis. Thus, for example, sociological models of how political, economic, cultural and religious values interact can suggest likely dynamics behind Jacob's relations with Laban, and cultural anthropology can throw light on the nature of tribes, clans, families, genealogical lists, etcetera.

(c) In the past century, our knowledge of ancient history has grown significantly; and archaeology and text decipherment have played an ever more important role in understanding the background of Genesis. Wherever historical information has added to understanding a particular passage, it is noted in the commentary below.

5. Literary Methods of Exegesis

No matter what the history of individual sections or passages might be, Genesis presents us with complete and finished texts that have been carefully crafted by their editor-authors to the shape we now find. Readers can only really understand the message and power of the text if they also understand its literary elements that create the response in the reader that the authors intended. Several methods are particularly helpful for understanding the book as a whole and are employed in remarks on individual passages. A few of them can be listed here.

(a) One important approach is *rhetorical criticism* which analyzes the stylistic devices and elements of rhetoric in the book.

(b) *Narrative analysis* studies the text in terms of plot, drama, expectations of the reader (e.g., as a believer) and the viewpoint of the real author or the imputed author (the viewpoint put into the story itself).

(c) *Structuralism* interprets meaning in texts by showing the relationships implicit in the grammatical logic of language. Behind its search for rules that explain meaning is a conviction that all language and grammar are ways that humans reconcile the deep opposites of our existence: life and death, male and female, fortunate and ill-fated, etcetera.

6. Contextual Methods of Analysis

Until now the methods we have discussed assume we are trying to find out what the *authors* of Genesis intended to say. Contextual methods focus instead on what modern *readers* ask from the text.

(a) *Feminist approaches* have shown the dangers of hidden male-domination values in stories of the garden of Eden or the great ancestors. They have also brought out important points about the contribution of female characters such as Sarah, Leah, or Tamar in Genesis 12–50 that had usually been overlooked in past exegesis.

(b) *Liberation theology* usually puts strong emphasis on the Exodus narrative and God's liberating role in it, but already in Genesis it highlights how God delivered the ancestors time and again from danger or the power of their own evil.

(c) *Fundamentalist approaches* read Genesis as a kind of scientific handbook on the origins of the material universe in a very literalistic manner. As the Roman document *On the Interpretation of Scripture* says, Catholics are not literalists. We can only remind ourselves that the Church has lived from its beginnings until now without needing such literalistic readings and has never felt the Bible's claims were endangered thereby. As Augustine once said when asked about why Genesis seemed to be at odds with other theories of how the world began, "Genesis was not written to tell us how the heavens were made, but how to get to heaven!"

(d) *Canonical criticism* traces how Genesis is to be read as the first book in a sacred collection of many books, how the community of Israel took the traditions in the book and formed them in view of its life and worship into the shape we have now, and how that shape affected the understanding of the synagogue and Church over the centuries.

(e) Another type of tradition-based interpretation of Genesis is to incorporate major important *Jewish ways of reading* the book, especially its development of legal interpretations and the many legendary stories about the lives of the main heroes. This is usually used as a supplement to other approaches.

(f) The Pontifical Biblical Commission's guidelines for biblical interpretation, *The Interpretation of the Bible in the Church,* evaluate a wide variety of other interpretive methods with their strengths and weaknesses in order to establish a sound Catholic approach to which methods are best used for understanding the Church's use of the Scriptures.

SECOND READING

A. Genesis 1–11

1. General Introduction

Genesis 1–11 is a unique body of literature in the Bible. These chapters contain a series of dramatic stories that have generally been classified as "myths" when myth is defined as stories about how the gods created and established the order of the world at the beginning. We can also note that the twelve episodes in these chapters do not proceed completely chronologically nor are they intended to show a specific progression in time. The authors have constructed a rough framework that moves from the day of creation through generations of human population expansion down to the real historical time of their direct ancestors in the family of Abraham, which begins in ch. 12. To fill this framework they used various ancient and respected mythological accounts or favorite tales that conveyed important information about human behavior in relation to God and God's divine purposes in creating the world as they knew it. Each story reveals a different aspect of God's mysterious intention in establishing good order in the cosmos and right ways of behavior for all created beings. This can help explain why we find a strong interest in "etiology," i.e., the explanation of why humans do certain things such as feel shame when naked, wear clothes, are attracted to the other sex, work for food, etcetera (in chs. 2–3). But the same stories also deal with human struggles against the limits set by God and our constant search for autonomy to the point of disobedience, as well as our hard-to-control passions in matters of sexuality and violence.

The combination of the themes of a good creation, spreading human sin, and a balance of divine punishment with compassion now produce a broad portrait of the real world of human existence and establish a fitting preparation and background for understanding why God initiated a second stage in the divine relationship to humanity by summoning Israel to be a special people. This new people would come to know and proclaim that only one God stood behind everything in the universe, a god of goodness, love, mercy, and justice. Thus these opening episodes of Genesis 1–11 also include a strong defense of monotheism against pagan polytheistic beliefs and no little bit of anti-Canaanite polemic in many of them.

Genesis 1–5

The first major stage of the drama focuses on the very beginning of the world and the place of humans in that scheme. There is a very *personal* dynamic in chs. 1–5: each natural object is lovingly created one by one and even the stories of human sin are largely centered on the individual responses of Eve, Adam, and Cain. They all contain the implicit claim that God was very near to the created world and communicated particularly with human beings even when they were blinded or disordered in their responses by their search for self-importance and freedom. The structure is chiastic, an orderly ABBA pattern: a list of created things, followed by two stories of sin, and completed by a second list of great ancestors. It underlines the point that divine blessing prevails and continues despite human failing.

A	Genesis 1:1–2:4	(P Source)	Blessing of Creation
B	Genesis 2:4–3:24	(J Source)	Sin begins
B'	Genesis 4:1-26	(J Source)	Sin spreads
A'	Genesis 5:1-32	(P Source)	Blessing reaffirmed

One Week of Creation (1:1–2:4)

(1) *The Prelude* (1:1-2). The great drama of creation opens with the affirmation that God did not have to "make" the universe by hand as a statue is made, but "created" (Hebrew *bara*ʾ) it by the unique divine power to will something and thereby achieve it. God works here on unformed matter of the world. The words describe it as empty and even chaotic and in the realm of darkness. This suggests that matter of itself is not subject to God "in whose light we find light" (Ps 36:10), but was originally outside of divine control. Then the divine power began to act. The "spirit of God" may mean God churning the waters in exercising control over their chaotic behavior or it may suggest a battle between the elements and God's purpose for them. In any case, it does *not* mean merely a strong wind, for the wording echoes the *Enuma Elish,* the Babylonian creation story known to the Israelites in exile, which described creation as a two-step process: first a battle between Marduk, the king of the gods, and Tiamat, the mother goddess (representing the ocean) who wished to destroy the gods of order. After Marduk's victory he formed and ordered each part of the physical universe. The "deep" *(tehom)* in v. 2 may well be intended to echo the sound of the name Tiamat.

(2) *The Six Days of Creation* (1:3-31). Instead of a struggle to the death with Tiamat, however, Genesis startles us with the miracle of a creation totally under God's guiding hand and completely organized so that chaos does not threaten. In this way it counters the power of the Babylonian creation myth to explain Marduk's superiority over the defeated and captured followers of YHWH. Instead God simply begins to speak and all things come to be. The power to create by the spoken word is not unique to Genesis. Examples occur in both Babylonian hymns and Egyptian creation stories. But the sense of sublime wisdom and harmony created by the narrative finds no other ancient parallel. Israel's God has a plan and it unfolds steadily and awesomely in a carefully balanced sequence that matches all Marduk's works of creation. But in Genesis that order is organized as a single week with a single focus, the making of human beings in the divine image. It is formed in two panels. On the first three days God makes the scenery and sets the staging; on days 4 to 6, the living actors are put in their proper places:

Day 1	*Day 4*
The creation of light	The specific lights are made
Day 2	*Day 5*
Water and air space are established	Fish and birds fill the water and the air
Day 3	*Day 6*
The dry land and vegetation are arrange	Land creatures and humans populate the land

All of this is recited in the style of a liturgical profession of faith or creed. The formulas have a solemn and deliberate pace to them: "And God said . . . and there was . . . and God saw that it was good . . . and God called (it X) . . . and it was night and morning . . . day Y." We might especially note the implications of these repeated phrases, e.g., that created things were unhesitatingly obedient to God's word and performed exactly as they were intended to; that everything created is good both in its substance and in God's plan for it; that there is a close connection between God's creative word and the power to name things. The second creation story in 2:4-25 will take up all these themes.

Finally, many scholars have pointed to the wisdom tradition at work in this chapter, particularly in the author's interests in different classifications of plant life and the ways humans are like God. We are seen to share God's likeness in the qualities of governing the world as a community of people who are fruitful and obedient and live in peace with all other creatures. The first humans are even commanded not to eat animal life (1:30). Many of these reflections echo concerns of the book of Proverbs (cf. Prov 3:19-26).

When all is finished, God looks over the whole of what has come to be and sees that it is very, very good!

(3) *God Rests* (2:1-4). The great hymn of creation ends with a seventh day to fulfill the

---

Summary of *Enuma Elish*

Book 1

Apsu and Tiamat create the first gods, but then regret it and plan to destroy them. The gods fight back, killing Apsu and challenging Tiamat herself. She prepares a fearsome army of monsters.

Book 2

The gods seek a hero who can stand up to Tiamat. All are afraid except Marduk, the young warrior son of Ea. He sets the condition that if he wins, the gods will name him to be king of the gods.

Book 3

The gods gather at a banquet to consider Marduk's demands. They are afraid and escape into drunken behavior.

Book 4

They accede to Marduk's terms. He proves his power by creating by his word alone, and they name him king. He gathers the weapons of storm: lightning, thunder, and wind to attack Tiamat. He slays her, takes from her the tablets of destiny, and makes the world from her body, splitting it in half to make sky and earth.

Book 5

Marduk establishes each god's role in the heavens.

Book 6

Marduk makes humans from clay and the blood of Kingu, the chief helper of Tiamat. They are to serve the gods. The gods in turn build Marduk a palace in Babylon. There he holds a banquet and declares his work done by hanging his weapons in the sky. The gods acclaim his power.

Book 7

The gods proclaim fifty great names of Marduk, giving him power over all things.

week. Symbolically the number seven (and thus, par excellence, the week) signifies wholeness and completion. God's "resting" suggests two different conclusions: the first is that God can sit back and contemplate all of creation with joy and satisfaction, knowing nothing is lacking to it; and second, God will leave it alone because it is complete and adequate for the creatures in it, especially humankind. God will not keep changing the world or its ground rules, and humans will have a certain autonomy by which they can exercise their stewardship and freedom in the image and likeness of God. They will have not only the power to govern in God's name; they will also have the power to make decisions, both good and bad. In v. 3 God then blesses and sanctifies the Sabbath day. This would be read by any believing Israelite as the basis for both the liturgical and personal observance of the Sabbath as commanded by the Law, especially as found in the ten commandments (cf. Exod 20:8-11).

The Special Creation of Humankind (2:5-25)

(1) The style of chs. 2–3 is far different from that of ch. 1. They use the term "YHWH God" where the first chapter uses simply "God." This second creation story is far less liturgical, solemn, and learnedly organized; instead it is more direct, intimate, and anthropomorphic (God thinks aloud or speaks to the human couple directly). In short, it is from an older source and more directly concerned with the primary place of humans in God's scheme of things. It has two movements: the making of the male (2:4b-17), followed by the making of the female (2:18-25). Although earlier, it fits superbly into the first chapter's concerns with how humans reveal their dignity as God's image when exercising dominion over the world and making free choices.

(2) *The First Man* (2:4b-17). The new opening in v. 4b stands out sharply by reversing the declaration about the "heavens and earth" that ends the first account in 4a and instead begins with "earth and heavens." This rhetorical reversal emphasizes a new starting point while preserving a continuation of the major theme of human origins. The earth is "dry," the equivalent of the first chapter's "empty and void," but water begins to rise from its midst. This is not just a "mist," but the primeval waters (related to Babylonian ideas of the cosmic waters of the deep—the word is the same in Hebrew and Babylonian, *ʾed*/*edu*). This "life-water" will mix with the dust of the earth and the breath of God to make the human being. Then God places this first man in a garden in the East, again using a Babylonian word, *edinu,* meaning a "well-watered plain." It is richly nourished by the greatest streams of the world. They should all probably be located in the Persian Gulf region rather than trying to get them to circle the earth, whether in Egypt or elsewhere. Thus "Cush" in 2:13 refers not to Ethiopia (as in Ezek 29:10) but to the Kassites of southern Mesopotamia. This garden has many trees, but two are named, a "tree of life" and a "tree of knowledge of good and evil" (2:9). Since the trees seem to play a role almost identical to one another (see 2:17 and 3:22) and the tree of which the couple eats in the next story is not directly identified the two are variants of one and the same tree symbolizing together that obedience to divine decrees means life. Throughout the Bible death is assumed as the natural state of humans, but here enduring life is connected to obedience. After they learn disobedience the tree of life will become inaccessible to humans.

This first account of Adam also ties him closely to the earth (there is a recurring pun in Hebrew made between *ʾadam,* "man" or "humankind," and *ʾadamah,* "ground") where he will find prosperity if he will be obedient. Since the water of life and tree of life are both connected with royal responsibility in the Babylonian myths there may be a royal role for humans intended by which they will rule God's dominion as long as they remain subject to their divine overlord.

(c) *The First Woman* (2:18-25). The message behind this second human creation is that humans need human community. Being alone is not good for humans. God creates animals and allows the man to name them and thereby enter into a living relationship with them, which includes stewardship over them. But none is "fit" for him. He needs a true partner, and to get one God initiates yet another act of creation. By putting the man into a deep sleep God assures the same autonomy to woman as to man—she depends directly on God for her being. The actual story may derive from an old folk tale that plays on the rib and its nearness to the heart. The heart is the source of both intellect and will in ancient thought and so God makes Eve as fully human as Adam. The description also plays on the attraction of love which draws men and women to each other from the heart. The fitting identity of the two human creatures is made complete by the little poem in v. 23—they are the same because he is *ʾish* and she is *ʾishah,* a pun in Hebrew that is like saying "man and wo-man" in English.

The Story of the First Sin (3:1-24)

(1) *The Serpent and the Tree* (3:1-7). This short drama is a fundamental lesson about the nature of human sin. The core of sin is the attempt to replace God as the determiner of morality. The serpent represents the twisting and insidious allurements and rationalizations we use in breaking moral limits to gain power or desirable ends for ourselves. Snakes had many connections to the mysterious powers of the underworld in ancient thought and are a fitting symbol of the power of evil in human life—even in times of blessing! Although the serpent deceived, Eve understood the command of God clearly enough. But both she and her husband desire to be like God, and agree to the sin. They are immediately aware of their lost innocence and the new strength of sexual passions in their life as they find themselves naked. Now they are indeed more knowledgeable than they were in 2:25, but it is the "practical" knowledge of sin's effects and its power in human actions.

(2) *The New Human Order of Sin* (3:8-24). The nakedness theme continues to carry the lesson forward. The couple cannot face God because of their shame, but God walks in the garden and still converses with them, thereby revealing the divine concern that will stay close to humans even in sin. Where life before had been guided by blessing with given limits that they could keep and thus avoid disobedience to God, now it has new rules. The human heart will always struggle with urges for the self over against God's will and evil acts will bring divine punishment in their wake. Gen 3:10 tells us the couple were afraid. This fear becomes a major factor in all subsequent human response to God. It may be the cause of sin when we act against others out of fear of their motives, or it may lead us to discover Israel's religious response to God through "fear of the Lord," i.e., loyalty to God's revealed ways coupled with faithful worship.

In vv. 12-19 the blame goes all around and the punishment follows. The writers have created a wonderful scene in which the action moves up and down a ladder. The man blames the woman, who blames the snake. God announces punishment in the reverse order, from snake to woman to man. The rhetorical inclusivity highlights the fact that the punishment of sin is complete and universal. The punishments themselves add a further dimension to the text by answering the questions of ancient audiences about why snakes and humans seem to be cursed in so many basic functions such as movement, work, or childbirth. Much of the pain or source of dread in daily life finds an explanation as the result of sin.

There are great similarities between Genesis 3 and well-known Babylonian stories such as *Adapa* or *Gilgamesh* in which human disregard of the gods ends in the loss of a gift of rejuvenation or even eternal life. However, Israel does not borrow these myths directly but tells its own story of human origins with its emphasis that the loss of a personal relationship of communion with God came by disobeying the divine word. Genesis 2–3 by itself is not a doctrine of *original sin* that would explain a humanity totally helpless before sin and in need of a savior. That must be built on NT texts (esp. Romans 5). As vv. 21-24 show, God continues to relate to and even help humanity, but they themselves will live with both the power of sin over them and its consequences in everything they do, the most dire of which is death.

Cain and Abel (4:1-16)

The story of Cain and Abel is placed after the garden as the second stage of human development, but must be seen as an independent tale. It, too, has many similarities to Mesopotamian discussions about the origins of work. The ancient conflicts between farmers, who desire fenced-in fields, and sheepherders, who need open rangeland, may lie behind the present story, but it is used by Israelite tradition to make a point about human moral decision making. *Cain* means "spear" and *Abel* means "puff of air," perhaps symbolic of the outcome of the narrative. No reason is given why Abel's sacrifice pleases God more than Cain's does, and we should not ask. The authors are more interested in Cain's reaction, which is the welling-up of hot anger and envy. It leads him to violence that is calculating and yet uncontrolled. The actual murder is described very sparely, for its horror is obvious. But the aftermath is given great attention. God expresses concern for the brother, and Cain's cynical reply is immediately rejected. God demands that we indeed be our brother's keepers—under pain of being cursed!

Yet even though we have a parallel here to the garden of Eden story in which the man is alienated from the soil (the *ʾadam/ʾadamah* pun of 2:4-17) and will bear the mark of sin's curse wherever humans go, God still shows mercy in the end when Cain is allowed a new start. But geography is a symbol. Just as Adam and Eve move farther East after being expelled from Eden, so Cain moves farther away from God than humanity was originally intended to be. The land of *Nod* in v. 16 suggests alienation as well as "wandering."

The Descendants of Cain (4:17-26)

This short narrative is built around a list of the great ancestral heroes who lived before the flood. The list has been shaped, however, by interest in Bedouin characteristics associated here with just two heroes: Cain and his descendant Lamech. Although Cain is a wanderer, he is attached to cities (v. 17), while Lamech's sons are identified as founders of the technologies of nomadic peoples: cattle and sheep herding, music (remember David and his lyre in 1 Sam 16:23), and blacksmithing. Cain's name identifies him with the nomadic Kenites who wandered the Sinai with Israel at the Exodus (Num 10:29-32), represented the fierce desert spirit, and even had cities (1 Sam 30:29), but never joined themselves to the Israelites. The authors of Genesis use this genealogy to show why. It climaxes in the legendary account of how Lamech's passion for revenge far outstripped even that of his ancestor Cain in 4:15, who was to be avenged sevenfold by God's justice. Clearly, this ironic distortion of divine justice in the poem of Lamech originated in an ancient song incorporated into the text as a lesson for later generations. In vv. 25-26, the authors make a transition to the "faithful" line of Adam that will lead to Abraham's family. The claim here that people called YHWH by name at such an early time is not factual, but signals the pledge of God's care for this particular family line, a pledge that is not really fulfilled until God reveals the name in Exod 3:13-15.

The Great Ancestors Before the Flood (5:1-32)

Chapter 5 consists of a formal list of the ten great ancestors who lived before the Flood, from Adam to Noah through the line of Adam and Eve's new son Seth. It is parallel to the listing of days of creation in ch. 1 and uses the same term for the list: it is a book of "generations" (Hebrew *toledot* in 2:4a and 5:1). Even the solemn liturgical style reveals the same P tradition already noted in ch. 1. It is also a much expanded and slightly different version of the list of ancestors in 4:17-24 (cf. *Methushael* and *Methuselah* in 4:18 and 5:25 as an example). We know of Assyrian "king lists" that name the great ancestral kings before what they call the "flood." It informs us that stories of long-lived ancestors have been connected to a flood narrative from ancient times. The earliest example is a Sumerian list of the third millennium B.C.E. In that tradition there are eight kings named and they live between 18,500 and 43,200 years each. Thus the very long lives granted ancestors in ch. 5, which range from 365 years for Enoch to 969 years for Methuselah, should also be interpreted as symbols. For the Genesis narrators these legendary lifespans indicated how much time had passed from creation to the flood and showed the reader literarily how divine blessing still ruled the earth in primeval times. They are part of the plan of Genesis 1–11 to organize the many stories that spoke about the mysterious ages before historical countries existed. But the flood was a major turning point. After the flood the continuation of the ancestor list in ch. 11 will drop the average age span to between 150 and 465 years. Later Abraham will live to be 175 years old (Gen 25:7); still later, Moses will live to be 120 (Deut 34:7). Within the Pentateuch, then, source critics believe the P editors consciously created an artificial shortening of lifespans to bring God's ways closer and closer to the readers' own times and experience. Ps 90:10 expresses this end point: "Seventy is the sum of our years, or eighty if we are strong." In addition, by choosing just ten ancestors of great age before the flood and another ten after it (in 11:10-26), the authors denote a privileged age of old when things happened that no longer can take place. The number ten is symbolic of completion, for after we count on ten fingers we run out.

The Sumerian King List

This list dates back to the end of the third millennium B.C.E. Its importance lies both in the great ages of these ancestors and also in the concluding remark that *the flood* then followed, just as in the Genesis account:

1. Alulim	28,800 year reign
2. Alalgar	36,000 year reign
3. Enmenluanna	43,200 year reign
4. Enmengalanna	28,800 year reign
5. Dumuzi	36,000 year reign
6. Ensipazianna	28,800 year reign
7. Enmenduranna	21,000 year reign
8. Ubartutul	8,600 year reign

The Flood

A Parallel to the Flood Narrative

The Babylonian story of *Gilgamesh* was one of the most popular mythological stories in the ancient world—copies have been found as far from Mesopotamia as Megiddo in Palestine and Anatolia in Turkey. A short sample of a section that is very close to Gen 7:24–8:17 follows: For six days and six nights the winds blew. On the seventh day, the raging storm subsided and the sea grew quiet. I felt the stillness and then realized that everyone else had drowned in the flood. I opened the hatch, and sunlight fell on my face. I bowed my face to the deck and wept with tears running down my cheeks. The ark ran aground on Mount Nisir. It remained grounded for six days, and then, on the seventh day I released a dove. It flew back and forth, but came back without finding a place to rest. Then I released a swallow, but it also returned without finding a place to rest. Finally, I released a raven. Because the flood waters had begun to subside, the raven fed, circled, cawed and flew away. Immediately I released the rest of the creatures from the ark and they scattered to the four winds.

(Taken from Victor Matthews and Don Benjamin, *Old Testament Parallels* [Mahwah, N.J.: Paulist Press, 1991] 38.)

Genesis 6–11

The cycle of stories in the next bloc of the primeval history centers on the great flood story, a type of narrative known throughout the ancient Near East and in many other world cultures as well. These stories address two perennial questions. First, why do major destructions wipe out whole peoples? Second, could human evil become so great that God would reject us and simply remove humans from the world? Babylonian versions such as the epics of *Gilgamesh* or *Atra-Hasis* both accept that the gods could change their minds about wanting humans at all. For Israel the issue was seen more in terms of how sin spread from individual to individual until all people increased their evil to intolerable levels so that God had to begin anew. Only after carefully preparing for the preservation of Noah and his family did God destroy the old order and renew the blessing with different ground rules. The stories that follow the flood in chs. 9–11 presume the workings of nation states and tribal peoples operating as societies. They also presume that God grants more leniency in allowing humans to eat the meat of animals, yielding to the desires of our appetites. But still sin persisted, and in the face of this larger social evil God will need to change directions again and build on one family's faithfulness. Yet as Genesis 6–11 unfolds it is clear that God foresaw this and guided human events toward Abraham's election all along.

The Wickedness of the Earth (6:1-8)

To prepare for the awful judgment of the Flood, the early J source is usually credited with the use of another ancient myth about how angels acted out of lust for human women, thus generating offspring who were grotesque giants. The story illustrates a fundamental disorder of the universe brought about through sinful desire. Immediately J adds God's own judgment upon human participation in such sin—that it pervaded the hearts of all people and only Noah remained faithful. More importantly, God's heart was wounded such that the bond of intimacy and patient forbearance shown toward this creature made in the divine likeness could no longer be sustained. The scene ends with foreboding, but the exact fate remains to be told.

The Great Flood (6:9–9:17)

The story of the flood is the longest episode in the primeval history. It can be divided into four acts: the preparation, the flood itself, the receding water, the aftermath. It is stately and full of repetitions and mysterious numbers that give it a dramatic flair perfect for community proclamation in both festive and catechetical situations. The reader should pay close attention to key turning points such as 6:13; 7:11; 8:1; 8:21; 9:8-9. They reveal the ironic twists in God's plans and how fragile is human destiny without God. Source critics point to the great number of inconsistencies in the narrative because two separate accounts from J and P have been woven together. There are dates built around seven- and forty-day periods; and others around months in a 365-day year. Sometimes there are seven pairs of clean animals (7:2) and at other times only one pair (6:19-20). And behind the entire account we know of Babylonian flood stories, most importantly the *Gilgamesh* epic. Similarities are so strong between the biblical version and Gilgamesh that we can be certain that both follow a common ancient Near Eastern tradition. But the authors of Genesis center their attention not on the question of immortality, as does Gilgamesh, but on human destiny and moral direction after the flood ceases.

(1) *The Preparation* (Gen 6:9-22). The preparatory stage opens with a notice that what follows is "the genealogy *(toledot)* of Noah." In Genesis as a whole, important stages are called *toledot.* There are ten in all. This is the third place so marked (see 2:4 and 5:1), and it tells us that the focus is on Noah's destiny as the survivor of the flood. For now, God sees all others as "corrupt and lawless" (6:11). This last word "lawless" *(hamas)* conveys that the entire order in creation has been undone by human sin, leading God to return the earth to the watery chaos from which it was called forth (cf. 1:9). Noah is introduced here as the only "just" person *(saddik)* on earth. To be *saddik* is to be right with God, loyal to divine command and intention. How Noah had proved himself to be just is not stated, but he clearly reveals it in what follows: he faithfully believes in and obeys God's seemingly irrational commands. People must have thought Noah a fool for constructing a boat 440 feet long on the dry land! Although human attitudes are not mentioned in 6:14-16 they were important to the NT authors of 2 Pet 3:5-7 who used this text to show how readily people scoff at coming judgment. 1 Peter 3:20-21 also refers to Gen 6:9-22 in speaking of Noah as the type of the baptized Christian: just as God delayed in bringing baptism to the world, so God was patient while Noah built the ark, but God saved both Noah and the baptized person before destruction.

In his preparations Noah must also save every species of animal. This confirms for readers that God's purpose is not to totally eliminate creation as such, but to remake it in a new direction after the flood.

(2) *The Flood Covers the Earth* (Gen 7:1-24). Noah enters the ark with the animals. The differences proposed between J and P are apparent in the two lists of vv. 3 and 9. J's greater number of clean animals may be intended to provide victims for sacrifices, or food for the time after the flood. The flood itself is described in cosmic terms. This is not ordinary rain: the waters that are gathered behind the firmament of heaven (the *mabbul,* 7:10) collapse on the earth, and the waters under the earth burst forth. The second and third days of creation are undone (Gen 1:6-9).

At this point in the drama the Lord shuts the door of the ark for Noah (7:16), showing that divine concern remains uppermost. The ark itself is said to be 30 cubits high, but since the water covered the highest mountains by only 15 cubits the keel of the ark fully laden must have barely scraped over the topmost peak. While all land animals perish, no mention is made of fish in the sea, so presumably they survived untouched since the focus of the drama is not on destroying everything but on the "ground" in relation to human life. The ground is cursed because of our sin and we are cursed in tilling it, according to Genesis 2–3. Now God cleanses the earth to prepare for a new relationship of humans to the land.

(3) *The Waters Recede* (Gen 8:1-19). Scene 3 opens with the stark but potent statement that the spirit of God began to work on the waters when God *remembered* Noah. Two theological claims are involved. First, from this point on in the story a new creation parallel to that begun in Gen 1:2 will unfold; second, God's "remembering" is the key to our lasting relationship of covenant. Salvation takes place in the Bible because God does not forget the covenant with Israel. This deliverance through the flood foreshadows the dramatic moment of remembering that triggers the Exodus liberation of Israel later (Exod 2:24).

Most of ch. 8 carefully details the peaceful receding of the waters, and borrows many details from the Gilgamesh tradition, especially in the sequence of birds that are sent forth. Mount Ararat was believed to be the highest point on earth. The name seems to reflect the ancient land of Urartu on the Turkish-Armenian border. For ancients, high mountains were always in the far north. It is the symbolic height from which redeemed humanity will go forth to fill the earth again in ch. 10.

(4) *The Aftermath as New Blessing* (Gen 8:20–9:17). The fourth and final scene has three subsections, but all represent a new blessing and promise to humankind. They complete the great drama of the flood that has moved from a judgment against the earth in ch. 6 to a renewed creation in ch. 9. Thus the whole drama takes shape much like the prophetic books of Isaiah or Ezekiel that arrange God's word dynamically moving from judgment to restoration.

(a) *8:20-22* reverses the judgment made in 6:5-8 despite the fact that the human heart will be no different after the flood than before. God's own heart will be more patient and more long-suffering. Indeed, the solemn promise of v. 22 intensifies God's promise to uphold creation. The narrator makes a point that Noah's first act was a sacrifice to God and the first object built on land was an altar. The altar will be the focal point of humanity's new relationship to God.

(b) *9:1-7* returns us to the blessing of the original creation in 1:28, and reestablishes all that God intended for human blessing at the beginning. And yet the next few verses modify the strict demands of that blessing by allowing humans to kill and eat animals as long as they respect the lifeblood of both animals and humans. This represents another foreshadowing for Israel, both in its practice of sacrifice and in its kosher food regulations (see Lev 17:10-14; Deut 12:16, 24-25). The solemn repetition of the blessing in 9:7 solidifies this new law.

(c) *9:8-17.* The covenant was predicted in 6:18, but only now does God actually initiate a covenant with humanity. This first covenant includes all living creatures but especially concerns our human family, for its sign will be the rainbow, symbolic of the archer's bow of the divine warrior. It is hung in the sky never to take aim at the whole earth and its people again. This is supported by the reaffirmation that God will always remember and save (just as Noah experienced so dramatically at 8:1!). Finally, God rests at the end of this new order of creation, matching the divine rest of Gen 2:1-3.

Noah's New Beginning (9:18-29)

Noah was not only the hero of the flood period; he must also become the link to the new start that humans will undertake on the earth. But despite his important roles as first farmer and first to be overcome by alcohol(!) the real purpose of the story is to show the roles of the three sons as the founders of all the diverse peoples across the world. This particular narrative picks up from where the list of sons left off in 5:32. There is a certain confusion in the plot about whether the sons should be Shem, Ham, and Japheth, or Shem, Japheth, and Canaan (with Ham added as "father of . . ."). Since the focus of the ancient poem in vv. 25-27 is clearly Canaan, an older story of Israelite polemics against the immorality and sexual improprieties of the Canaanites may have been fitted into the normative list of sons as given in 5:32 and 10:1.

Noah as the farmer fulfills the proper role of humans as tillers of the soil (1:28; 8:22). One of the gifts of God after the flood is wine to gladden the heart (see Song 1:2, 4; 7:9), but it also brings danger. Alcohol was often linked to Canaanite rituals involving sexual behavior. The remarks about Canaan looking on the nakedness of his father may thus mean that the son has sexual lust for Noah's wife, just as in the sexual regulations of Lev 18:1-19. Certainly their conclusion in Lev 18:24-27 intended such a condemnation of Canaanite sexual practices and saw them as totally alien to Israelite faith. The final poem of 9:25-27 envisions all three sons as groups living primarily in the land of Palestine. In this sense, Shem symbolizes the Israelites, while Japheth includes the Hittites, Hurrians, and other non-semitic peoples present in the land—perhaps in particular the Philistines.

The Map of All Nations (10:1-31)

This list forms the fourth "genealogy" division for the editors (see 2:4; 5:1; 6:9). This "map" is based on an older list from somewhere between the tenth and seventh centuries. All nations are related to one of the three sons and reflect the political realities more than any true ethnic connections. The "Japheth" nations include peoples to the North and West: Greeks, sea peoples and many nations in modern day Turkey. "Ham" includes native Canaanites, Egyptians, and certain groups in Arabia and Africa. Shem includes the semitic peoples of Mesopotamia, Arameans, Hebrews, and many Arabian tribes as well. This basic list takes up vv. 2-7, 20-23, and 31. But the authors have added two longer insertions into this plan: (1) vv. 8-19, on Nimrod of Cush and the Canaanite subfamilies; and (2) vv. 24-30, an expansion of the Shem list

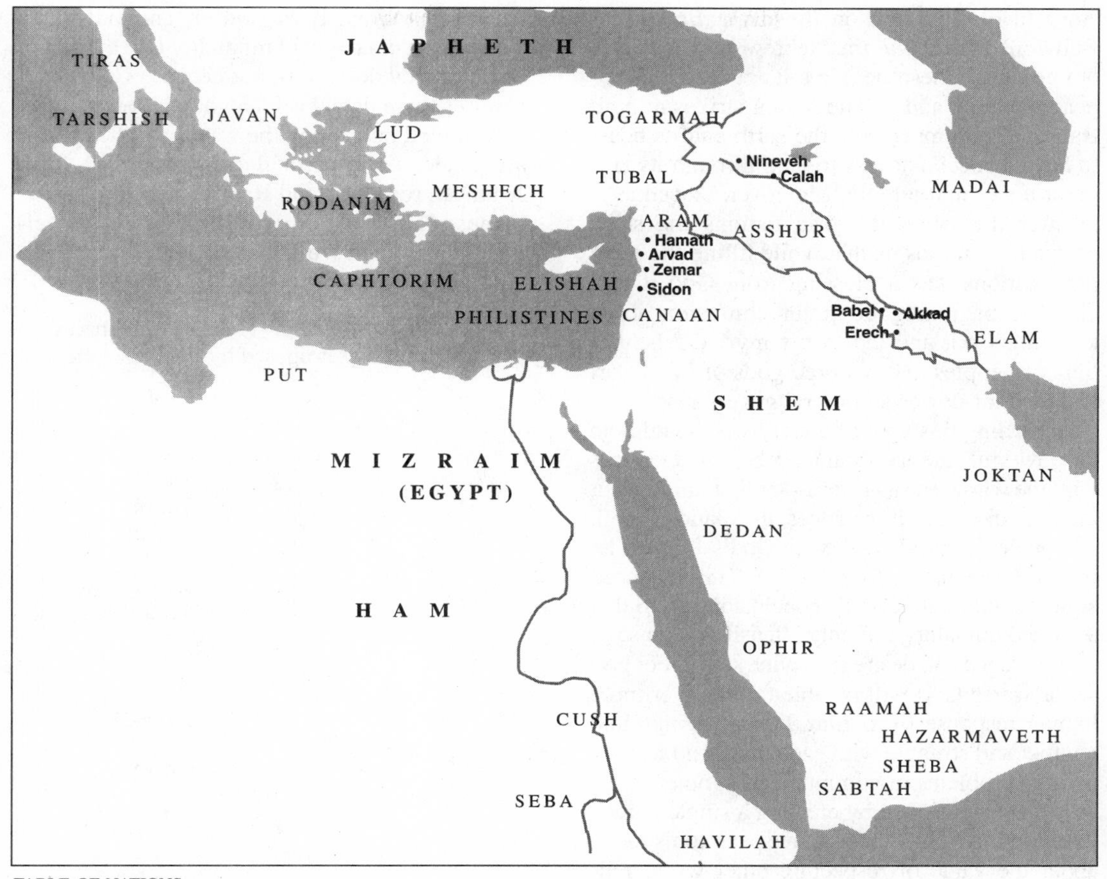

Gen 10;
1 Chr
1:1-27

TABLE OF NATIONS

which relates it to the upcoming line of Noah and Abraham in 11:10-26. The first insertion stands out as an addition by the fact that Egyptian Cush of v. 6 has become confused in v. 8 with Mesopotamian Cush (the Kassites; see the comment on 2:13 above). It is probable that the editors combined these older J notices with the basic three-part P list.

This genealogy functions at this point in the primeval history to show God's blessing in the post-flood period. But it emphasizes not just long-lived ancestors but well-developed tribes and nations. As many commentators have noted, it gives a world "map" that fulfills the command "to multiply and fill the earth" in 9:1. The narrative is preparing us for the calling of Abraham not to be a single hero among heroes, but to be the forerunner of a great nation among the nations of the world. His summons in 12:1 will have international implications, so the world stage is being prepared.

The Tower of Babel (11:1-9)

As the editors of chs. 1–11 approach the end of their account of the primal state of humankind they insert one last example of human opposition to God. The growth in population does not lead to greater obedience to God, but to greater joint efforts to be like God. What had been the evil tendency in individuals before the flood now becomes the collective energy of sin that gains control of human aspirations. This story is independent of the list of nations in ch. 10 which already recognized that peoples have different languages (10:5, 20, 31). It is generally attributed to the J source and shows a great interest in Mesopotamian things. It is even set in Babylon and has a strong polemical edge against Babylonian beliefs in the superiority of their religion and its god Marduk. The tower is reminiscent of the temple tower of Marduk at the center of Babylon, *Entemenanki,* which was believed to connect heaven and earth. The climax of the story involves a pun on the name *Babel* (for Babylon) with *balal,* the Hebrew verb meaning "to confuse" these people's languages that appears in vv. 7 and 9. The lesson strikes at both Babylon's claims to rule the earth and its boast to have a special access to God through its ziggurat tower and temple. Moreover, placed as it is after the table of world nations the story pointedly reminds us that while filling the earth with nations was a blessing from God it was also the beginning of major confusion about knowing God, and led to the myriad false beliefs of peoples that honored gods of every sort and level of power and moral governance.

In reading this gem of a story we should note its powerful literary drama. It begins and ends with the whole earth at stake—at first unified, but then in disarray. It balances the nations' call, "*Come* let us build . . ." with God's "*Come,* let us go down to confuse . . . ." This balanced structure highlights God's conclusion in v. 6 that a unified humanity can only intensify its sense of omnipotence and desire for divine status. For better or worse God will be able to win over more human response by putting human beings into conflict and struggle with each other and leaving us with problems of communication on even the most basic level than by creating a singleminded world family. This lesson may speak to us today about the value of respecting other world religions as an intended and important part of the divine plan and even a necessary matrix for the voice of Jewish-Christian revelation to be heard.

The Family Line from Noah to Abraham (11:10-32)

In one sense this family list of Noah and his son Shem is a straight continuation of the family list in ch. 5. But it is also more narrowly focused to bring the line of just one division of the nations down to the family of Abraham. In both the table of nations and the Babel story the message has centered on the worldwide breadth of God's blessing to humanity. Now the shift back to a single line of blessing recalls for us the major purpose of all eleven chapters: to set Israel's special vocation in the context of its being a part of the whole human race. What God will give to this one people and nation is not freedom from the temptations and troublesome dynamics belonging to all human beings but an invitation to know God more intimately and closely and to live in a partnership of covenant mutuality together—not because they deserve it, but because God freely chooses them. Israel is like other nations and yet it is singled out. Along the way two other points are made: their particularity is derived from Aramean roots (Ur and Haran), and Sarai's barrenness (11:30) forewarns that whatever develops for Abraham will be due to God's initiative.

Division of Genesis 1–11 into Two Sources as Commonly Proposed by Source Critics

P	*J*
1:1–2:4a	
	2:4b-25
	3:1-24
	4:1-16
	4:17-26
5:1-32	
	6:1-4
	6:5-8
6:9-22	
	7:1-5, 10
7:6-9, 11-16a	
	7:16b-23
7:24–8:5	
	8:6-12
8:13-19	
	8:20-22
9:1-17	
	9:18-27
9:28	
	10:1-32
	11:1-9
11:10-26	11:27-32

B. Genesis 12–50

1. Introduction

The second major division of Genesis introduces a four-part sweeping family history of four generations: Abraham, Isaac, Jacob, and Joseph. Their wives play an important part in each generation except for the last. These chapters stand in striking contrast to the world history that has just been completed for they are very particular in place, time, and the personal dimension of decision in every action. The series of stories that makes up the larger cycle in these family histories is intended to portray them as real people with whose experiences the reader can readily identify. Together they form one continuing family epic in three dramatic stages of divine planning: in chs. 12–25 the promises to Abraham and Sarah; in chs. 25–36 the emergence of Israel as an identifiable "people" under Jacob, Leah, and Rachel; and in chs. 37–50 the mysterious ways of divine purpose through Joseph. The fourth member and second generation bridge, Isaac, is not treated to a full cycle, but is sketched in incidents that link the Abraham and Jacob cycles together.

Where did the authors get their stories about the ancestors? There were older sources, to be sure. Some tales were no doubt passed down orally from ancestral tribal groups before the full nation called Israel emerged. Other stories would be shaped by later concerns to explain the ancestry of King David and the reasons why God blessed him with a great empire. Some "early" incidents can be related to typical hero legends and folk motifs; others may have combined these motifs in the literary category of *saga.* A saga is a kind of legendary family history that describes the great past of the nation through the deeds of individual members, especially leaders, many of whom were only vaguely remembered in the tradition.

Does this make Genesis merely a collection of tales or can we recover some historical basis for the lives of these ancestors? No independent archaeological or historical records have ever surfaced about anyone in Genesis 12–50 but there are a number of factors, such as treaty forms, the names of the patriarchs, inheritance laws that treat each son equally, etcetera, that fit best with the period of the Middle Bronze Age (1900–1600 B.C.E.). The Aramaic origins of the family and the setting of a semitic vizier, Joseph, in Egypt may also point to clear remembrances of a period before the Exodus. Many other elements in the narratives, however, suggest that these raw materials were reworked in the monarchy period: Abraham's links to "Salem" in 14:18 prefigure David and Jerusalem; Jacob honors Bethel, the future national shrine of the northern kingdom after 920 B.C.E. The best guess is that much older tradition has been reworked several times down through the monarchy period until it reached final form, but source critics believe that the key shaping was done by J and E before the fall of the northern kingdom in 722.

The final whole directs us to several important religious themes: (1) these stories are about the faith and obedience of individuals and their faults; (2) God's guiding hand must be seen behind all stages of the story; (3) the divine promise, despite apparent failure, will come true; (4) things are not always what they seem!

The Promises to the Ancestors in Genesis 12–50

The Promise to be a People	*The Promise of Land*
Gen 12:2 Become a great nation	Gen 12:1 Go to the land I say
Gen 15:5 Become a great people	Gen 12:7 Promise at Moreh
Gen 17:4 The "P" promise	Gen 13:14 When Lot departs
Gen 17:16 Promise of Isaac	Gen 15:18 The night dream
Gen 18:10 The three angels	Gen 17:8 The "P" covenant
Gen 18:18 Repeat of Gen 12:2-3	Gen 24:7 Abraham's servant
Gen 22:17 After Isaac sacrifice	Gen 26:4 Repeated to Isaac
Gen 26:4 Repeated to Isaac	Gen 28:4 Jacob at Bethel
Gen 27:29 Isaac's blessing	Gen 35:12 Second Bethel vision
Gen 28:14 Jacob at Bethel	Gen 46:4 Vision at Beersheba
Gen 35:11 Second Bethel vision	Gen 48:4 Bethel repeated
Gen 46:3 Vision at Beersheba	
Gen 48:4 Bethel repeated	
Gen 48:16 Blessing of Jacob	

---

2. The Abraham and Sarah Story

The various incidents about Abraham and Sarah hang together loosely around three themes: the promise to the couple, their faith and their doubt, and the final test that seals God's bond of trust with them. The promises are for a son and for a new land, and they are solemnly moved forward by a series of covenants with Abraham (chs. 15, 17) and already look forward to his and Sarah's descendants as a fully faithful people, Israel. This initial stage of the drama focuses primarily on the passing on of the promise to a legitimate heir. The promise is of utmost importance and in the end the couple proves strong and true. Because this cycle portrays Abraham's trust in God so simply and intimately, Abraham has always had a special place in Israel's piety as the father of the nation, in Islamic piety as the "friend of God," and in Christian piety of the NT as the man of faith (Rom 4:1-25; Gal 3:15-18; 4:21-31; Heb 11:8-19).

The Call of Abraham, 12:1-9

The account of Abraham's relationship with God begins with a simple "and God said to Abraham." Abraham's life is not portrayed as outside of or different from the human world of the first eleven chapters, but he stands out as one who actually listened to God. The call is starkly dramatic because it is both a summons away from his former life and an invitation to a new relationship that must be based entirely on trust. The call also contains a promise and a blessing. It has five points that provide the thematic outline for all that will follow in the history of this people, at least down to the time of King David: (1) I will show you a land; (2) I will make you a great nation; (3) you will be blessed and become a source of blessing; (4) I will bless your friends and curse your enemies; (5) other nations will benefit from your blessing.

As large as this promise is, it will not be achieved by a simple growth in power and population. It begins very modestly in vv. 4-9. Abram just goes as God commands. His assent is assumed and not expressed. But his subsequent actions reveal his complete dependence on God. He departs with all his family and possessions without holding back, and wherever he stops, he worships God and "consecrates" the new land. The "oak (or terebinth) of Moreh" must have been an old Canaanite shrine for it is described in Deut 11:30 and Judg 9:37 in just such a way. We are to picture Abraham replacing pagan worship with the cult of YHWH as he journeys through the whole land from north to south.

Abraham Puts Sarah at Risk, 12:10-20

The initial scene of profound trust by Abraham is followed by a deliberate counter-portrait of Abraham's weakness and occasional blindness. The basic plot about a journey to a foreign king, a lie about his wife's true relationship, and her deliverance through divine intervention is paralleled in chs. 22 and 26. All three versions may depend on an old folk story adapted to Abraham (and in ch. 26 to Isaac), or may possibly be based on second-millennium Hurrian legal precedents for a highborn man to also adopt his wife-to-be into his family inheritance. In its present use, however, the incident serves to underscore how much Abraham's destiny will depend on God's guidance and protection rather than on his own strength or cleverness. Without continuing divine education along the way, Abraham and his descendants risk falling back into a fear that will lead them to lose their courage to follow God's commands, resort to dishonesty and act only for their personal benefit. This scene points out the very close connection in the Bible between truth *(ʾemet)* and covenant loyalty *(ḥesed):* Pss 61:8; 25:10; 85:11; 86:15; 89:15; Exod 34:6; Josh 2:14, etcetera.

The juxtaposition of Abraham's sincere act of faith and his first failure in the beginning chapter should alert the reader to expect this same combination to recur throughout the coming narrative. The central focus of YHWH's control is made clear in the literary organization of the scene:

a. Abraham *acts* in going to Egypt;
b. Abraham's *speech* reveals his plans;
c. God *acts* to intervene;
b'. Pharaoh's *speech* reveals his intentions;
a'. Pharaoh *acts* to repair the damage.

The Blessing of God Continues, 13:1-18

The third incident in Abraham's adventures portrays the prosperity that God granted the patriarch and his clan. His nephew and special ward, Lot, also prospered. Abraham generously grants Lot whatever territory he should choose, and the two are pictured on the hill of Bethel surveying the whole land. The text describes the Jordan valley to below the area of the present Dead Sea as though the Sea were not yet there—all is a rich and fruitful plain. No wonder Lot chooses it. Abraham is left with the western half of Palestine from the central mountain spine to the seacoast. God blesses this separation and promises Abraham the land and a numerous progeny to fill it. Abraham then moves farther south and settles at Mamre, which is identified today about a mile and a half north of the modern city of Hebron at Ramet el Khalil. The ruins of a large Byzantine church still mark the spot. Meanwhile, vv. 10 and 13 hint at a devastating fate ahead for Lot and his presumably "better" choice of the river valley.

Early Israelite Sanctuaries

Shechem. Abraham's first stop in the land of Canaan is Shechem, where he offers a sacrifice to God at the "(holy) place" of the Oak of Moreh in Gen 12:6-7. The name *Moreh* suggests "teaching" or "divining" was done there by the local population. Later Jacob returns to Canaan in Gen 33:18-20 and erects an altar at Shechem to *El, God of Israel.* When forced to leave, Jacob buries the idols of his household there (Gen 35:1-4) thus signifying the abandonment of all pagan practices. At the return to the land under Joshua, once again the people meet at the oak of Moreh to renew their covenant with God, this time at the "sanctuary of YHWH" there (Josh 24:25-28). Joseph's bones were solemnly interred there at that time (Josh 24:32).

Bethel also plays a foundational role in the ancestor's claims to the land. Abraham made his second stop there and built an altar in Gen 12:8. Later, in Gen 28:10-22, Jacob has his vision of the ladder at the spot and erects a memorial stone as a pillar he anoints with oil. He also vows to build a sanctuary to YHWH and pay a tithe of his possessions at the place if he returns safely. Because of the vision he names the place *Beth-El,* the "house of God." He does return and builds a new altar and pillar in Gen 35:5-15.

Mamre. Gen 13:18 records Abraham building an altar at the "Oaks of Mamre" and then taking up residence there. It is mentioned again as the place of residence in Gen 14:13; 18:1; 23:17-19; 25:9; 35:27; 49:30; 50:13, but it is never referred to elsewhere in the Bible. Yet Josephus (*Ant.* 1.10.4) mentions the "Oak of Mamre" as a place of devotion in the first century, and large Roman and Byzantine ruins mark a major sanctuary at the spot today.

Penuel. Little is known of this place of divine encounter outside of the incident of Jacob wrestling with the unknown being in Gen 32:22-32. It appears in later lists of towns in the control of northern Israel (1 Kings 12:25) but its role as a shrine is now lost. Probably it was already a place famous for night spirits when Jacob arrived at it.

Beersheba. According to Gen 21:33, Abraham planted a tamarisk tree and prayed to God, calling on "YHWH *El-ᶜOlam,*" i.e., "YHWH, the Eternal God." This was the primary shrine of Isaac, who built an altar and prayed to God there (Gen 26:23-25). Jacob went there in Gen 46:1-4 to sacrifice to the god of his father Isaac and receive a vision.

Abraham Proves Himself Among Great Nations, 14:1-24

So far the text has portrayed Abraham as a herder of sheep and cattle, peacefully moving among the hills of Palestine. Suddenly we find a very different kind of story in which Abraham is swept up by an international attack on the settlements of the Dead Sea valley and reveals himself both as a warrior when necessary and as a noble sheik who comes to the rescue of his kinsfolk. The purpose of the incident is to portray Abraham as the equal of any king on earth. The final scene in which he encounters Melchizedek, the king of Salem (a prefigurement of Jeru-*salem;* see Ps 76:2), only confirms his destiny and that of his descendants to rule over the land (see already Gen 13:15-16). The meeting echoes Psalm 110 which links David and Melchizedek as rulers and priests of Jerusalem. Naturally enough all the promises made to Abraham that he would become a great people with extensive territory (12:1-3; 12:7; 13:15-16) were identified by the court writers of the monarchy with David's empire. Abraham shows all the resourcefulness, decisive strategies and humble reverence before God that characterized David himself.

The role of Abraham, however, seems added to an earlier account of a battle between great kings. The names and places fit best the Middle to Late Bronze Age (1700–1400) and may have derived from a very well known local story from the area just below the Dead Sea. Other touches also suggest a non-Israelite origin: Melchizedek, e.g., is a Hebrew version of the legendary Mesopotamian ruler Sargon of Akkad (both names mean a "righteous king"); and the name of God, El-Elyon (God the Most High) is well known from the Ugaritic and Phoenician culture of Syria and Lebanon. The name in this form occurs only here in the Bible, but many scholars think El-Elyon would have been the proper name of the deity of the pre-Israelite city of Jerusalem. Israel itself adopted it in the temple worship in a more orthodox fashion, using "YHWH (or Elohim) the Most High" in Pss 7:18; 21:8; 46:5; 47:3; 57:3; 78:56; etcetera. Only Ps 78:35 again uses El-Elyon. Later Christian authors of the letter to the Hebrews go even further to identify Melchizedek with Christ (see Heb 5:6-10; 7:1-28).

God's Covenant with Abraham, 15:1-21

Abraham not only received the promise of land but defended it in ch. 14. Now the narrators must face the bigger question of an heir. Gen 11:30 already warned the reader that Sarah was barren. How will God overcome that? Chapter 15 prepares the stage for the drama that will take us right up to ch. 22 by laying out two preliminary steps. In vv. 1-6 God renews the promise of a son and many descendants; in vv. 7-21 God concludes a solemn covenant with Abraham that includes both possession of the land and the certainty of children as key elements (see vv. 4-5, 7-8, 18-21). The traditional J and E sources are joined together here, and many scholars think that this chapter marks the beginning of the Elohist account. But if so, which parts belong to J and E cannot be separated any longer, for the whole is now a single literary account of the encounter between Abraham and his God. It results in a vision totally directed from God's side during which Abraham sleeps the deep sleep of Adam (see the comment on Gen 2:21). Although the covenant thus given is entirely a gift from God it comes in direct response to Abraham's faith expressed in vv. 1-6. This is a climactic moment toward which chs. 12–14 have been moving. From this moment on, the promise of a son will take concrete shape.

In vv. 1-6 the phrases "the word of the Lord" and "fear not" betray prophetic language. This may reveal the opening promise of E that parallels the J sources's version in 12:1-3. The conclusion of the dialogue between Abraham and God (in which Abraham objects at first but then concedes, just as Moses did at his call in Exod 3:11-15) declares Abraham's faith and is "reckoned to him as righteousness" (v. 6). This state of uprightness with God follows from Abraham's trust that God will fulfill the promise made. It is not tied to legal observance, even though that is a standard meaning of the expression in Lev 18:5, 19, 20, 22, 24; Ezek 13:17, 23, 28, etcetera.

The ritual of cutting the animals apart in vv. 9-11 was well-known in the eighth to sixth centuries B.C.E. It is mentioned in Jer 34:18 and in an Aramaic treaty that has survived from Sefire in Syria. The dismembering may either carry a threat that the same fate will be dispensed to the party who breaks the treaty or signify that the spilled blood seals the treaty. The mention of threatening birds in v. 11 may be an ominous sign that evil powers oppose the treaty. The symbol of God passing between the animals as fire is similar to that of the pillar of fire in the Exodus by which God led the people in the desert (Exod 13:21). All of these images confirm that this is a very solemn occasion indeed.

Abraham's First Son by Hagar, 16:1-16

Once again the authors have used an older story that may have originally been developed to explain either where the Ishmaelites lived or why the name of a site in the wilderness of Shur is "the well of the Living One (God) who sees me." But they have made it into a new dramatic moment in the fulfillment of God's promise of a son. We can note that Sarah takes the initiative and Abraham only reluctantly agrees to conceive a child through her maid. This step is legally permissible in the ancient world's law codes, but only with the free consent of the barren wife. So Sarah acts heroically, even though the baby will indeed be considered her legal child. Hagar was expected to humbly grant this right to her mistress. Instead she falls into the not-unexpected attitude of superiority over Sarah since childbearing was the most important marker of a woman's status. Sarah is perfectly within her rights to insist that Abraham take steps to insure both her honored place and Hagar's recognition of her own status as servant. The Law Code of Hammurabi, e.g., would order such a servant to be reduced to full slavery (law 146; eighteenth century B.C.E.).

Sarah instead sends Hagar away. This second stage of the drama extends God's plan to include a promise also to the Ishmaelites to become a great nation descended from Abraham. Ishmael is here identified with the Arabs, described as living wild and free in the desert. God gives Hagar the promise through an angel, perhaps to make the promise somewhat less than the one given Sarah. But Hagar must return home and carry on until the next stage of the drama for her in 21:9-21.

The Covenant Renewed and Extended, 17:1-27

Thirteen years pass in our series of incidents in Abraham's life. Then God takes a further initiative to enlarge the covenant. This whole chapter comes from the latest level of priestly writing and several separate P traditions may have been added together. They reflect an outlook developed in exile that emphasizes the enduring nature of the covenant despite periodic loss of community structures such as Temple and formal rituals.

(a) *God's Extended Covenant* (17:1-14). The first section is an extended description of the covenant in God's own speech. "El Shaddai" is an ancient divine name known even in Mesopotamia, but its meaning is not certain. From the first LXX translation it has been rendered "the Almighty." Verses 1-8 define the covenant by God's promise of a son and of land, while Abraham in turn will "walk before me and be whole," i.e., be faithful in keeping God's commands. The name change from Abram to Abraham is minor, but emphasizes the promise of *many* descendants. More significantly, the authors call it an "everlasting covenant." The covenant is not just with Abraham but with all generations after him. Thus the rules and terms must be studied carefully by all Israelites who read or hear this chapter. The earlier covenant with Noah was also called an "eternal covenant" (9:16) as will be the covenant at Sinai (Exod 31:16; Lev 24:8; Ps 105:10, all in the P tradition). No doubt the term derived from cultic use, and was popular during the Exile to reassure the captives that God had not abandoned them. In vv. 9-14 the requirement of circumcision, although an old rite of incorporation among many semitic peoples, receives special emphasis in this narrative because it represents a sign of commitment to the covenant that can be practiced even if all other formal expressions of worship are lost.

(b) *The Promise to Sarah* (17:15-27). Although God continues to speak to Abraham the topic is now Sarah and the miracle needed to open her womb despite her age and history of barrenness. This is no sudden whim of God, but the deliberate completion of a plan that God knew from the beginning and that was signaled to the reader just before the Abraham narratives began, at 11:30. God restates the promise of a son and gives the name of the destined child: Isaac. The chapter thus looks ahead to ch. 21 and back to ch. 16 while it ties the covenant into the whole series of promises from ch. 12 onwards.

Another Case of the Promise to Sarah, 18:1-15

This wonderful story of how God visited Abraham with the message of a son to be born almost exactly parallels the previous episode in 17:15-27. But it is by far the older version and has the wonderful quality of showing Abraham at his best, a generous and hospitable sheik who particularly shows kindness to strangers. The result is that they impart to him a gift of far greater value—announcing the coming birth of his long-hoped-for son by his beloved wife Sarah. It may well be based on a well known ancient folk legend, but the J tradition used it to show how even the best people are caught off guard. Just as Abraham laughed at the claim in 17:17, now Sarah laughs. The messengers of God sternly correct her. They may seem overly severe but it is a way to underscore that God laughs last, a point made explicit later at 21:6. The fact that the announcement comes by way of three messengers also adds to its importance. Early Church writers saw a prophecy of the Trinity in this passage.

God's Dialogue with Abraham, 18:16-33

The next dramatic scene involves first a soliloquy by God in vv. 16-19 and then a dialogue between Abraham and God in vv. 20-33. Both focus on the question of righteousness and serve as pointers to what lessons the reader needs to learn from these ancestors. By occurring in the very middle of the Abraham cycle this unit provides an interlude while preparing us for the coming action. As Abraham walks in the way of right behavior in vv. 16-19, so Sodom is guilty as charged, but God is willing to investigate further before punishing. Abraham's dialogue accents the importance God places on mercy alongside the unequivocal insistence on justice and right behavior. In this scene the ancestral traditions touch the concerns of the wisdom schools of Israel and their meditations on the ways of the just and wicked (see the book of Proverbs).

The Fates of Sodom and of Lot, 19:1-38

The contrast between chs. 18 and 19 is striking. Abraham and Lot both show generous respect for their guests, but the actions of the people of Sodom more than confirm the charges that God has heard raised against them (18:20-21). Although the description hints at sexual abuse by gang rape, Israelite tradition has always seen the sin of Sodom as total injustice and depravity toward God's laws (Isa 1:10; Jer 23:14). Many elements in the narrative suggest secondary interests played a part in how it developed: Lot's concern that Zoar should be spared; the wife turned into a pillar of salt like those that are often seen in the Dead Sea shore areas; the lack of any mention of Gomorrah until the very end despite the fact that elsewhere the prophets always combine "Sodom and Gomorrah" as paradigms of evil (Isa 1:9-10; Jer 49:18; Ezek 16:46-48; Hos 11:8, etcetera). These represent a number of older folk motifs that have been worked into a powerful moral story for Israel. The faith of Lot and his family is weak: he hesitates to obey the angelic commands to leave; his wife disobeys their command not to look back; and Lot nearly commits a crime against his daughters to save his guests (although we must remember that Israelite readers knew the ending of the story already, and knew God would not let it happen—this is the same storytelling dynamic behind Abraham's apparent willingness to sacrifice Isaac in ch. 22). Because of Lot's weaker faith his line will not share in the promise but will be moved offstage in the next episode. The judgment by fire is typical of prophetic descriptions (Isa 30:33; Ezek 38:22) but the stark conclusion of the story where Abraham views the smoking valley of death may also have struck the ancient readers as an explanation for why this valley still had a *dead* sea in it!

Lot and His Daughters, 19:30-38

Here again we have a very old tribal legend that may even have derived from the Moabite or Ammonite traditions that glorified their origins as wild and pure. Other scholars have suggested that early Israelite tribal conflicts with Moab and Ammon have led to these tales that mock and deride the foreigners and their pedigrees. But in the Abraham story this shocking incident plays a decisive role at this point by indicating how the line of Lot will not share in the promise but is to move elsewhere for its destiny. This is the final act in the series of Lot episodes begun in ch. 13, a series that has shown Abraham strong in faith and Lot less so.

Abimelech of Gerar, 20:1-18

This chapter is the duplicate of ch. 12 with the names and place changed. As the latter came from the J source, so this comes from another point of view, usually attributed to the E source. It explores the feelings of the parties, includes explanation of their attitudes, develops a more direct conversation between Abraham and Abimelech, and is mainly concerned with the guilt or innocence of both Abimelech and Abraham. In the ongoing saga of Abraham's character three themes are emphasized: (1) Abraham is a prophet whose righteousness can make him a healer and intercessor with God; (2) Abraham possesses a decisive "fear of God" in his life that is missing among the nations, even among good people like Abimelech; and (3) Abraham has deceived only because God has made him a wanderer on the earth. Without a set home he cannot provide security for his family. This last is crucial. It announces the next major step needed, to gain a permanent possession in the land for his son who is to be born.

Isaac and Ishmael, 21:1-21

The story now moves into high gear. Isaac is born according to the prediction in 17:15-21 with a strong emphasis on the importance of Sarah as the mother. At the same time the text picks up on the doubts that Abraham and Sarah had expressed in laughing at the promise (17:17; 18:12). The child is to be called Isaac, which can be translated "God laughed" to show the wonder and joy brought about by divine favor rather than by any strength, or goodness, or even the faith of the couple.

Side by side with this moment of joy, however, comes the tragedy of Ishmael's fate. Nowhere in the narratives of chs. 16 or 17 or here does God reject Ishmael as unworthy or evil. Indeed God also gives a promise of greatness to this first son: he will be a head of the nomadic peoples of the Sinai-Egyptian and Negev wilderness. The tale must have circulated independently from the previous stories because it portrays the boy as extremely young. But from hints in 16:16, 17:1, 18:10, 21:5 and 8 the boy must be 17 years old. In fact the present incident never even says that the child is Ishmael at all. The story has been included here for the same reason Lot's daughters were included, to separate out from the election of Israel all collateral lines of peoples related ethnically to Israel. The promise and the blessing come down in one particular family line—a very important point to stress for the readers who knew that Moabites, Ammonites, and Ishmaelites did not share Israel's faith in YHWH.

Early Israel's Neighbors in Palestine

Amorites. The name means "westerner" and often designates Semitic inhabitants of Lebanon and Palestine in Mesopotamian documents. Originally these Semitic peoples migrated from lower Mesopotamia to Syria and then were driven farther westward to the coastal areas.

Arameans. Gen 10:22-23 and 22:21 list an ancestral "Aram," and Genesis traces the ancestry of Abraham and his clan to their area of Syria. At a later time the Aramean kingdom, with its capital at Damascus, developed in the tenth to eighth centuries B.C.E. It was constantly at war with the northern kingdom of Israel in the ninth century (see 1 Kings 17 to 2 Kings 10).

Canaanites. Many scholars think that these are part of the Amorites that moved west around 2000 B.C.E. They occupied the lower coastal area of the Eastern Mediterranean and were in continuous struggle with the Israelites after the fourteenth century until David subdued them. Although they were the dominant population in the period of the ancestors they were heavily influenced and often controlled by the Egyptians.

Hittites. These were probably the same Hittite population that consisted of Indo-European conquerors of Anatolia. They moved with trade opportunities all over Western Asia and many settled in Palestine, perhaps as outposts of the Hittite empire. They are mentioned in Gen 10:15; 23:3-20; 27:46 and in most lists of national groups that live in the land. The word Hivite *may* also refer to Hittites.

Hurrians/Hivites. *Hivite* probably refers to the Hurrians who lived in upper Mesopotamia and southern Russia. They developed a powerful empire in the early second millennium and outposts were found throughout the Near East. Possibly the *Jebusites* who occupied Jerusalem were really Hurrian; so might also be the *Horites* who lived in Edom according to Gen 36:20-30.

Philistines. The Indo-European Doric invasion of Greece and Crete during the Late Bronze Age forced many native groups out across the Mediterranean, especially to the Eastern coastlands. Defeated by Pharaoh Rameses III in the Nile delta area about 1190, they were confined to the Palestine coast where they were the most dangerous foe of Israel until put under control by King David.

The Wells of Gerar, 21:22-34

The incident of the well is tied to the preceding story by the mention of the well at the end of Hagar's ordeal and forms the last of a series of "Abimelech and Gerar" tales that are collected in chs. 20–21. Like so many previous scenes this one probably uses several older folktales based on other themes, e.g., how did Beersheba get its name? Because it means both "well of the oath" and "well of seven."

The use of the tale, however, reinforces the *ḥesed* or "faithfulness" issue between Abimelech and Abraham. In vv. 22-25 they confirm how they will treat one another with *ḥesed,* and in the following conflict over the wells this is put to the test. In the end the *ḥesed* holds between them and Abimelech even concedes Abraham's right to the wells. This sets the stage for the acquisition of formal title to Canaanite property for which Abraham will negotiate in ch. 23. The Gerar cycle ends with Abraham settled in Beersheba and calling on the name of the "Everlasting God" (El Elyon) as in 14:18-20.

The Sacrifice of Isaac, 22:1-19

The story of the sacrifice of the only son is really another story of the testing of Abraham's rightness before the Lord. It is the climax of the entire dramatic life of Abraham. After this story the narrative winds down rapidly. Once again the authors may have adapted a well-known folk theme or cultic legend that explained how child sacrifice came to an end in the past, or how a particular mountain got its name, "the Lord provides." But these purposes have been transformed by one of the most tautly written, emotionally charged masterpieces of world literature. It begins simply enough. Despite all that Abraham has endured, God still tests him. No reason is given and Abraham asks for none. His obedience is greater than at any other moment in his entire history. Three times, at key points, he says trustingly, "here I am" (vv. 1, 7, 11). We ask how this could be. But the text does not probe reasons or inner thoughts. Indeed, its genius is that it tells the entire event in a stark narrative technique where all feelings are hidden below the surface. Suspense is created at every stage in the action before us, but also in every reader's mind—what was Isaac suspecting? Did Sarah know and agree? How much pain must have ripped Abraham's insides? But with just a few words per stage the drama marches inexorably forward. God's "test" brooks no argument against its clear purpose. God even admits Abraham must surrender his "beloved son" (v. 2).

Theologically, of course, the previous narrative has taught us that all things are unfolding according to God's guiding plan. There is a basic lesson here that the hopes and promises and plans for the future often fall under threat and often are lost. Abraham must first learn and relearn that only faith in God is the way to prosperity and success. Isaac was his one thin line of hope in the promise. His other relatives have been excluded one by one, and yet even so he must drop his plans and go where God sends him. Abraham of course passes the test, and God ends the scene with a new word in vv. 15-19, a word that confirms and establishes the promise of 12:1-3. Abraham has sought the "fear of God" among the peoples with whom he dealt (20:11) and now has proved himself the finest example. We can note for our sakes that the modern horror at the idea that God would command such an act is not reflected within the story itself. For just as our children already know "Little Red Riding Hood" almost from memory before they ask us to read it to them, so the Israelite audience already knows the ending of this most famous of all Abraham stories long before they read the text. It is a test, only a test, whose outcome is sure.

The Children of Abraham's Brother Nahor, 22:20-40

This short genealogy seems so out of place after the great scene preceding it, but the author has inserted this small piece of family information to prepare us for Isaac's marriage to Rebecca, the daughter of Bethuel, the son of Nahor, in ch. 24. This is a traditional fragment that does not entirely agree with later references to Laban as Nahor's son (29:5) instead of, as here, his grandson. Note, too, that in all Nahor has twelve sons, just as Ishmael will in 25:12-15, and Jacob will in 35:22-26. The number "twelve" probably symbolizes a full blessing from the Lord. All of Nahor's children reflect Aramean areas of Syria.

Sarah's Death and Burial, 23:1-20

Now Abraham's life is brought quickly to its conclusion. The last three chapters tell of Sarah's death, the purchase of a burial place for the family, the arrangement to gain a wife for Isaac, and the death of Abraham. The shift in focus stands out because God no longer appears as an active player in any of these events.

Sarah's death is stated realistically and naturally. The narrative is more concerned about the imperative need for a rightful burial place. Abraham negotiates in dignified and proper manner with the elders of the town of Hebron when they meet formally at the city gate. The text emphasizes the traditional manners of oriental politeness but also the completely legal nature of the transaction. For the first time Abraham actually owns a piece of the promised land. The price is high, it seems, but urgency leaves little room for maneuvering. Abraham accepts it willingly. This purchase, however, is never made the ground for Israel's claim to the land. Later, at the time of the Exodus, God grounds the gift once more in the *promise,* not the purchase. But the moment is a foreshadowing of what will come. It is made all the more solemn because Sarah (and soon Abraham) are to be buried there; even the local people honor Abraham as a "mighty prince" in their land.

The Courtship of Rebecca, 24:1-67

The great length and unified plot of the story of Rebecca's courtship stands apart from the necklace of individual incidents about Abraham and Sarah and their families that have made up all of chs. 12–23. This must be a somewhat later reworking of some old traditions about the Aramean family connections of Abraham, and focuses more on the attitudes and thoughts of the various individuals in the story than do earlier narratives. The action is carried by four long speeches that shape four stages of the betrothal process: vv. 1-9 in which Abraham charges the servant while reaffirming the promise of God as his guiding force; vv. 10-27 in which the servant relies on God's help in locating the girl and is more than rewarded; vv. 28-61 in which Laban guides the family decision to accept the offer; and vv. 62-67 in which the couple meet and love develops at first sight.

The text communicates two important messages to the reader. First, Israel is not to intermarry with the Canaanites; and second, Isaac (and every other Israelite) shall not return to Aram now that God has called them west to the promised land. The story is also a wonderful insight into how marriages are arranged in traditional clan tribal settings. More significantly it also reveals that even this new stage of the promise is being guided by the hidden hand of

God, a fact stressed all through the story by words such as "God made prosper, God blessed, God led," etcetera.

Abraham's Death, 25:1-18

The final portion of the Abraham narrative is divided into three short notices that complete the information needed about his life and relationships. Verses 1-6 note a new marriage after (?) Sarah's death that resulted in the Arabian tribes associated with Midian. They are relatives to Israel, but without the blessing. Verses 7-11 mark Abraham's death, which matches how he lived, full of blessing from God. Indeed, he dies exactly one hundred years after entering his new homeland. The final note in vv. 12-18 provides a twelve-son genealogy for Ishmael. These names also represent a variety of Arabian tribes, but they are narrated as a *toledot* ("genealogy") as have been creation (2:4), the pre-flood ancestors (5:1), Noah (10:1), and Terah (11:27). Together with the last named, this *toledot* now forms one of a pair of bookends around the great Abraham narrative.

3. The Jacob Story (25:19–36:43)

The next major block of narratives focuses on the story of how Isaac's *younger* son Jacob

Proposed Divisions of Genesis 12–50 into the Three Traditional Sources P, J, E

P	*J*	*E*	*P (cont.)*	*J (cont.)*	*E (cont.)*
	11:27-32			32:3-12	
	12:1-9				32:13-21
	12:10-20			32:22-32	
	13:1-18			33:1-17	?
14:1-24			33:18-20		
	15:1-6				34:1-31
	15:7-21	15:7-21			35:1-8
	16:1-16		35:9-15		
17:1-27					35:16-20 (21)
	18:1-16		35:22-29		
	18:17-33		36:1-43	(part)	(part)
	19:1-29			37:1-20	
	19:30-38				37:21-24
		20:1-18		37:25-28a	37:28b-36
		21:1-21		38:1-30	
	22:1-14, 19	22:1-14, 19		39:1-23	
	22:15-18				40:1-23
	22:20-24			(41:44-45)	41:1-57
23:1-20				(42:5, 27-28)	42:1-38
	24:1-67			43:1-34	(43:14, 23)
	25:1-6			44:1-34	
25:12-18	25:12-18				45:1-28
	25:19-34				46:1-5
	26:1-11		46:7-27		
	26:12-22			46:28-33	
	26:23-33			47:1-4	
26:34-35			47:5-11		
	27:1-45			47:12-26	
27:46			47:27-28	47:29-31	
28:1-9			48:3-6	48:2, 9-10a	48:1-2, 7-9
	28:10-22	28:10-22			48:10-12
	29:1-30			48:13-14, 17-19	48:15-16
	29:31–30:13			49:1-28	
		30:14-24	49:29-33		
	30:25-43			50:1-11, 14	
		31:1-55	50:12-13		50:15-26
32:1-2					

became the heir of the promise made to Abraham, and of how he acquired his large family that would become the foundation of the twelve tribes of later Israel. It is an adventurous tale with many surprising twists and turns that highlight the mysterious ways of God in directing the events of history. It gives considerable attention to the details of the patriarch's marriages to Rachel and Leah and the complicated birth relations of his children. These were important considerations for ancient peoples where blood lines and tribal connections were vital social realities. As with the Abraham narratives, behind the present dramatic plot lie many older cycles of stories that had belonged to Israel's oral tradition. The reader finds a mixture of *etiological legends* (i.e., stories to explain why a place was named this way, or why it is honored as a sacred shrine, etcetera), *genealogical lists* of tribes, *cultic texts* about the original events behind various shrines, and *tribal sagas* about the exploits of great ancestors. Many of these particular stories involve conflicts between groups: shepherds and hunters, Israelites and Edomites, Israelites and Arameans, Rachel tribes versus Leah tribes. The authors have skillfully made use of these to show God's favoring of one over another, and to affirm that even deceit and trickery can be turned to a good end in God's plan for the promise. At the same time, the conviction of a just retribution for every evil act is systematically maintained throughout. Other theological themes continue those we have already seen: the continuing divine blessing, the renewal of the covenant with the next generation, the promise of a son expanded now to include a whole tribe, and the possession of the land of Canaan to be the proper home of Israel in the future.

Isaac plays a very small part in these series of stories, just as he did in the Abraham cycle. In fact, there is no developed cycle of Isaac materials except for the few independent tales in chs. 24 and 26. It seems that the Isaac traditions may be the oldest of the lot (see the comment on 26:6-11) but have been absorbed into the more lively Abraham or Jacob cycles or replaced by them. We are rightly calling chs. 25–36 the "Jacob cycle" just as the final grouping in chs. 37–50 is the "Joseph cycle," but the biblical editors of Genesis have followed the traditional standard formula of listing the promises to "Abraham, Isaac, and Jacob" (Gen 50:25; Exod 3:6, 15, 16; 4:5; 6:3; and often) by ending each of these blocks with the death notice of the patriarch who came *before*. Thus Gen 35:29 brings the Jacob block to a close with the death notice of Isaac his father, and 49:33 ends the Joseph cycle with the death notice of Jacob.

The Birth of Jacob and Esau, 25:19-34

The editors signal a new beginning with the announcement of a *toledot* of Isaac. It will conclude in Gen 35:29 with Isaac's death. The special nature of the account is indicated by the hints that God responded to the prayers of Isaac and Rebecca at an important shrine. It is similar to the scene of Hannah, the mother of the prophet Samuel, praying for a child at the shrine of Shiloh in 1 Samuel 1. The descriptions of the two boys who are born show very old roots: Esau is red and hairy all over (a pun on the nation Edom because red in Hebrew is *ʾadom;* and hairy is *śeʿar,* which is very close to Edom's other name, Seir), while Jacob is smooth and already crooked in grabbing his brother's heel (the name Jacob means "The Lord protects," but it sounds like *ʿaqeb,* a "heel" or "crooked" thing). One is a hunter and crude, the other a shepherd and clever, even ambitious. We can no longer recover the ancient tribal humor or rivalries expressed in these word plays, or even the possibility that the very stories are versions of famous myths like *Gilgamesh,* where the clever king Gilgamesh has a wild and hairy friend named Enkidu. Instead the Israelite tradition has fashioned these older elements into a dramatic tale of the transfer of the promise from the older to the younger brother, and from possible rival nations such as Edom to the people of Israel (as suggested by the oracle in v. 23).

At this stage Jacob is pictured as industrious and prudent, while Esau is shown to be impetuous, rash and not careful of the future. His casual sale of his birthright, fortified by an oath, will ultimately justify Jacob's right to trick his brother out of the all-important blessing due the firstborn. As the story opens, both boys equally have the favor of one parent, but Jacob is showing the qualities that will lead to God's choice of him over Esau.

Isaac's Exploits, 26:1-35

The story of Jacob breaks off here and recommences at 27:1. It is interrupted by the seven short narratives about Isaac when he lived in the Negev desert, capped by a short notice about Esau in vv. 34-35. They originate from a different tradition cycle than do the Jacob materials in the rest of chs. 25–36 and center mostly on legends about certain wells around Beersheba. All seven episodes presuppose the semi-nomadic lifestyle of sheepherders who also do some farming and occasional trading with the local towns.

(1) Verses 1-5 establish a parallel between Abraham's actions and those of Isaac. The famine in Gen 12:10 drove Abraham to Egypt, but Isaac is told explicitly not to leave the promised land. Instead he duplicates a second Abraham event by traveling to Gerar (see ch. 10). (2) Verses 6-11 parallel the previous accounts of Abraham endangering Sarah by calling her his sister before a ruler who wants her for a wife. Here no special theological attention is paid to the moral guilt of either Abimelech or Isaac, and this may indicate that the present version is closer to the original simple legend form. The fact that an almost identical situation is repeated three times (12:10-20; 20:1-18; 26:6-11) indicates how valuable the authors found it as a lesson to show God's guiding hand that brings about the promise despite the shortsighted behavior of the ancestors themselves. (3) Verses 12-14 note that Isaac, like Abraham, manifested divine blessing by great wealth (see 13:2). The hundredfold of v. 12 endured as a symbol of success into the NT parables of Jesus (Mark 4:8). (4) Verses 15-16 repeat the basic episode in 21:25 of Abraham and the wells: Isaac has inherited Abraham's blessing. (5) Verses 17-22 reflect the struggles for land and water rights and end with Isaac achieving a clear claim to his own space. (6) Verses 23-25 are a theological reaffirmation of the promise to Abraham. (7) Verses 26-33 also connect Isaac to Abraham through Beersheba and the oath between him and Abimelech. The name Shibah suggests "well of the oath" as the meaning of the name Beersheba (rather than "well of seven," cf. 21:31). (8) Verses 34-35 are added to prepare for the coming rejection of Esau in 27:46.

Jacob's Deceitful Gain of the Blessing, 27:1-45

In a very skillful and suspense-laden narrative the story of Jacob's journey from being the youngest son to becoming the inheritor of the blessing and master of the promised land of Palestine is set in motion. The drama will carry through until the end of ch. 33 when Jacob returns as *Israel* to continue the claims of Abraham and Isaac, while Esau moves away permanently to Edom across the Jordan after having been fully reconciled to Jacob his brother. Behind the descriptions of Esau and Jacob in this contest to receive the blind father's blessing stands another of the ancient folktales of a contest between hunters and shepherds, but the theme has been interwoven into the artistic portrait of the ambitious plotting of Rebecca and her younger son. There is a somewhat comic element in the unlikely picture of Jacob covered over with sheep wool to fool his father, and yet the moral concern for honesty and rightful behavior are not treated lightly. Jacob deliberately lies to his father and triggers a fate for himself that will involve being deceived himself and deceiving others for many long years in the household of his uncle Laban before he can be healed and restored to God's full blessing. Esau himself articulates the tragic truth in v. 36 when he discovers he has been cheated a second time and exclaims bitterly that Jacob truly lives up to his name, which means "crooked." But the authors also make it clear that Esau brought this on himself by the irresponsible sale of his birthright in 25:33, his wanton intermarriage with Canaanite (Hittite) wives in 26:34-35, and his murderous rage in 27:41.

On the positive side, Jacob and Rebecca prove themselves clever and farsighted in setting in motion God's ultimate plan. This would have seemed obvious to readers in Israel's period of monarchy when they, the children of *Jacob,* flourished in the land while their kinspeople, the *Edomites,* still lived in a harsh and uncultivated wilderness. Esau's and Jacob's blessing by their father mirrors the historical reality.

The Vision at Bethel, 28:1-22

Verses 1-9 send Jacob on a journey to Laban that contradicts the reason proposed at the end of ch. 27. There Rebecca wanted to save Jacob from Esau's wrath; here the father wishes that he marry from their ancestral stock as he had himself in ch. 24. These nine verses are a later reflection similar to the Priestly thought of ch. 17 in which El Shaddai ("God Almighty") will bless and make Jacob into a multitude of nations

(17:1-4). The emphasis on not marrying a Canaanite may reflect exilic concerns over mixed marriages and their effects on proper Israelite Torah observance.

Verses 10-22 describe the first major theophany in Jacob's life. God appears to him in a dream to provide a glimpse at what lies ahead. This manifestation of God at Bethel has many repetitious lines and may combine both an Elohist and Yahwist account, but they have been crafted around a single focus: the promises made to his father and grandfather are now passed on directly to Jacob. The vision of a "ladder" is better understood as the main staircase or ramp to the top of a temple-tower or *ziggurat.* Mesopotamian ziggurats were artificial mountains that joined the heavenly realm of God to the earth. A small guest house for the god stood at the top but the main temple for public worship was located at the foot of the tower. The name that Jacob gives to the place, "Bethel," means "house of God" and fits perfectly the base temple of a ziggurat. For the peoples of Canaan and ancient Israel, however, a pillar or memorial stone could sufficiently represent such a sacred place. The vow to tithe reflects the practice of the later Bethel temple and was known to the prophet Amos (Amos 4:4). Jacob was closely associated with Bethel in ancestral tradition (e.g., Hosea, the only northern prophet, is also the only one who mentions the Jacob story; cf. Hos 12:3-4, 12; and comments below on Gen 35:1-15).

Jacob Gains a Family in Laban's Service, 29:1–30:24

The conflicts between Esau and Jacob over the inheritance now give way to a new series of traditions about the conflicts between Jacob and his Aramean relatives. The difficult personal and familial obstacles Jacob must overcome from a mistrustful and scheming uncle form the narrative context, but the purpose focuses on the remarkable wives and children who soon become the tangible sign of God's blessing to Jacob and will be the ancestral founders of Israel's twelve tribes and national identity.

(1) Verses 1-14 describe the opening scene in which everything starts with a positive unity between Laban and his nephew. The style of life is familiar to us: Laban and his clan are also sheepherders and semi-nomadic wanderers. The scene of Rachel at the well is very reminiscent of the earlier success of Abraham's servant in finding Rebecca. This time Jacob's love at first sight sets in motion a momentous period of conflict between branches of the same family. The final separation of Jacob from Laban in 31:54 will mark an end to any further connections of the Israelites with their Mesopotamian origins.

(2) Verses 15-30 quickly sketch Jacob's desire for Rachel, Laban's deceit in switching sisters, Jacob's acceptance of the weak excuse offered by his uncle, and his subsequent winning of Rachel as well; all at a cost of servitude to his uncle for fourteen years. Israelite storytellers were more than aware of the humorous aspects in this tragic situation but were also keenly interested in the fact that their entire nation supposedly developed from these two sisters and their two maids. Although Lev 18:8 forbids a man to marry two sisters, the authors knew that such laws did not apply to the great ancestors of old. Moreover, no one could miss the divine retribution at play in this scene of Jacob being tricked into taking the older over the younger, for his own deceit has been reversed upon himself.

(3) Verses 29:21-35 and 30:1-24 proceed to the center of the Jacob story: the birth of eleven sons and a daughter (with the twelfth son appearing in 35:16-19). The description of each son involves some humor created by the pun or word play on his name given by the mother. The point of these word plays is to carefully identify the proper mother and so establish the different interrelationships among the tribes. Although we cannot recover the origins of each of the twelve tribes completely, this type of genealogical distinction between the four mothers recalls that although all twelve qualified as "sons of Israel" they did not all originate equally. Later lists of the twelve tribes rarely agree on which tribes were original or on their birth order.

This lively account weaves the theme of the barren wife, so important already in the Sarah and Rebecca stories, with the competition between the two sisters to raise children to Jacob. Genesis constantly notes initial barrenness to emphasize that the resultant children are gifts from God and blessed with a special destiny. The entire drama climaxes in 30:22 when God seems finally to remember Rachel's hopes and Joseph is born. When God "remembers," great events begin to unfold (see Gen 8:1; Exod 2:23).

Old Testament Lists of the Twelve Tribes

Note the differences between different listings of the sons of Jacob or the tribes named after them. If Ephraim and Manasseh are included in the list, then Joseph (their father in Genesis 48) and Levi (who become a landless group) drop out. (Cf. also commentary on Judges 5:1-31.)

Genesis 29–31	*Numbers 1*	*Numbers 26*	*Joshua 13–19*
Reuben	Reuben	Reuben	Reuben
Simeon	Simeon	Simeon	Gad
Levi	Judah	Gad	Judah
Judah	Issachar	Judah	*Ephraim*
Dan	Zebulun	Issachar	*Manasseh*
Naphtali	*Ephraim*	Zebulun	Benjamin
Gad	*Manasseh*	*Joseph*	Simeon
Asher	Benjamin	Benjamin	Zebulun
Issachar	Dan	Dan	Issachar
Zebulun	Asher	Asher	Asher
Joseph	Gad	Naphtali	Naphtali
Benjamin	Naphtali	*Levi*	Dan

Jacob's Struggle with Laban to Leave, 30:25–31:55

Genesis 31:38 tells us that Jacob's time with Laban was twenty years in all. Since fourteen were used working for the right to his two wives Leah and Rachel, the events of this new section take six years. It is a tense drama in three acts in which Jacob finally turns the tables on Laban. Although Laban had won the last contest, this time Jacob receives his vindication by tricking Laban.

(a) *Jacob Wins Laban's Wealth* (30:25-43). The scene begins in the crafty conversation of two adversaries, each trying to gain the advantage. Laban thinks he has the upper hand because his nephew has no rights as a free man in Mesopotamia even though he acknowledges that he owes Jacob at least something. Jacob, on the other hand, offers what appear to be overly generous conditions for releasing him to return home. Laban then works hard to make sure that Jacob can gain little if he takes as his share only the goats and sheep born spotted or striped. Laban leaves Jacob only the all white sheep and all black goats so that mixed color young would be highly unlikely. But Jacob craftily resorts to a form of sympathetic magic based on the belief that what a person, or an animal in this case, sees at the moment of conception will permanently affect the new child. Since the animals look on striped poles as they mate, the lambs and kids become mostly spotted and striped. As a result, Laban's flocks become steadily fewer and Jacob's greater.

(b) *Jacob Flees in Secret* (31:1-21). Jacob is now *commanded* by God to depart for Canaan. All that follows will therefore be divinely blessed. But Jacob carefully takes all necessary legal steps to insure that his family freely chooses to accompany him and to separate themselves from the claims of Laban as head of their clan. To strengthen their resolve he reports the dream in which God directed his actions to gain the greater part of his uncle's flocks. It is tied to the promise he had received at Bethel in 28:10-22. Nevertheless he prudently leaves in secret lest Laban stop him by force.

(c) *Laban Confronts Jacob* (31:22-55). Jacob must move slowly with such a large party, and Laban soon catches up to him in Gilead just before he makes it to his homeland. A second dialogue ensues that matches the earlier duel in 30:25-43, both in its intensity and mutual efforts to gain the upper hand. But God's decision governs the outcome: Laban is warned not to stop Jacob, and Jacob relies on the obvious signs of God's blessing to both Laban and himself to justify his departure. Laban tries a final gambit when he accuses Jacob of stealing the *teraphim* ("family gods") which were most likely small human-shaped figurines needed in divination ceremonies when consulting the ancestral protective deities about major family decisions. Jacob is unaware that Rachel has taken them and vows a death sentence on whoever is found with them. Although Rachel hides them effectively and perhaps even a bit humorously, Jacob's oath has fated her to die in childbirth, another twist in a life where divine retribution follows every wrong. The scene also provokes Jacob to recite the whole list of wrongs done by Laban in contrast to his own uprightness and integrity through all twenty years. But the meeting ends happily with a classic ceremony of covenant-making, listing the terms of agreement, the curses against anyone who violates them, and the memorial mound and pillar. The place name points to a cultic site at Mizpah in Gilead where this event was celebrated in ancient times. Note that the God of Abraham is also called the god of his brother (and Laban's father) Nahor, but the god of Isaac receives a special title, "the Fear" or "the Awesome One," which hints at an older remembrance that Isaac and Abraham stories originally came from different circles of tradition, and their family gods were only later both identified with YHWH.

Jacob Reconciles with Esau, 32:1–33:20

Since the mystery of Jacob's selection to be the bearer of the promise began with deceiving and alienating Esau, the blessing cannot be made secure until this wound is healed and all is brought to a state of *shalom,* i.e., peace and stable prosperity for both sides. Like the previous confrontation between Laban and Jacob, this too has three acts.

(a) *Jacob Prepares to Meet Esau* (32:1-23). The dramatic meeting with his brother begins in a dramatic vision of the angelic armies (32:1-2). For Jacob, it reassures him that God is protecting his journey, and the name of the place, *Mahanaim,* "the two camps," reflects the strategy of dividing his family into two parts against Esau's possible vengeance. Jacob, however, initiates the reconciliation with his brother, thus in effect seeking forgiveness. Clearly the fear expressed at each step by Jacob comes from a recognition of long-ago guilt, as does his arrangement of elaborate gifts for his brother. Jacob displays all of his cleverness in this scene, as well as the courage he has shown by following God's guidance received in dreams. His prayer in vv. 9-12 is a masterpiece of Israelite piety, recalling God's love for his ancestors, the promise, his own unworthiness, his need for forgiveness, and his certainty that God will be with him, all of which leads him to petition God's help at this moment.

(b) *Jacob Wrestles with God* (32:24-33). The nighttime encounter with an angel, or even God in the form of a stranger, is one of the most powerful scenes in the entire OT. Here Jacob is subjected to a test not unlike Abraham's sacrifice of Isaac in ch. 22. A test in the darkest night is also similar to Jacob's first encounter with God's plans for him at Bethel in ch. 28. It signals the beginning of a new stage in his life. This short scene is filled with details that all had deep significance for Israel of old but have been long forgotten by later generations. The central focus is the change of name that also changes Jacob from just another hero blessed by divine favor to being the father of a chosen people. This story has strong elements of ancient folklore in it: Does it explain the name *Penuel* to mean "the face of God"? Or does it explain the name *Israel* as "he contended with God"? Or does it explain a dietary custom of not eating the thigh muscle because of Jacob's limp? Or is it a legend about night demons that lose power in the sunlight? These may all have played a role in the richness of the account, but ultimately the story asserts that Jacob was privileged to match God as a *partner* in strength. He lost by being wounded, but he prevailed in demanding and winning the blessing not just for himself but for Israel as a people to come. God retains the upper hand in not telling Jacob the divine name lest it be manipulated for favors, but Jacob receives the glory of encountering God and passing the test in honor. The whole scene stands as a preview of the covenant relationship still to come at Sinai.

(c) *The Reconciliation* (33:1-20). All's well that ends well. But who would have guessed that Esau would forgive and forget? The first divine blessing for the new man "Israel" is complete reconciliation with his wronged brother. Jacob even treats Esau as though the older brother did indeed possess the birthright, but the good will between them cannot hide God's decisive reversal of choice. As a result Jacob insists that they go their separate ways, even in opposite directions—Esau to Edom in the south, Jacob westward past Succoth and on to Shechem where Abraham first settled. There Jacob buys property, builds an altar, and declares it the land belonging to YHWH, just as Abraham had done before him.

Dinah and Shechem, 34:1-31

Jacob's arrival back in Canaan marks the climactic moment for the story of promise that began with Abraham's call in 12:1. "Israel" has

The Structure of the Jacob Narrative (Genesis 27–35)

A. ESAU AND JACOB	A'. ESAU AND JACOB
Gen 25:19-34 Gen 27:1-46	Gen 33:1-20 (Cf. Gen 28:1-9)
B. THEOPHANY	B'. THEOPHANIES
Gen 28:10-22	Gen 32:1-32 Gen 35:1-15
C. LABAN AND JACOB	C'. LABAN AND JACOB
Gen 29:1-30	Gen 30:25–31:55

D. THE BIRTH OF JACOB'S CHILDREN
Gen 29:31–30:24

NOTE: Other texts fill in the narrative traditions of interest:

Gen 26:	the Isaac cycle completed
Gen 34:	Dinah and the Shechemites
Gen 35:16-29	final notes on the family

multiplied children and taken possession of the land. The stories that follow in chs. 34 to 50 are not directly concerned with *whether* the promise can be fulfilled, but *how* it will be lived out now that it is fulfilled.

The first test case involves Israel and the Canaanite people of Shechem. The story itself has duplications and inconsistencies (does Hamor or his son Shechem speak in the name of the city?) that suggest older sources have been combined. It was originally an independent legend, for chronologically Dinah would be too young to be of marriageable age if we accept the ages given in 30:21. Jacob's role is so passive that scholars wonder whether he has been added to the narrative as an afterthought.

The story has been included in the Jacob cycle for two reasons, however. The first is to point out the dangers to the chosen people of intermarrying with Canaanites. Despite the artistically drawn portrait of Shechem's love for Dinah, her brothers constantly sound the theme of the sexual abuse involved. Even if foreigners take on circumcision as the sign of Israelite membership, it is not enough. A second reason is to explain to the reader why Levi and Simeon did not last as tribes with lands of their own: their violence did them in! Levi later became relegated to priestly roles scattered among other tribes; Simeon ended in the lower Negev and was absorbed by the tribe of Judah. This whole scene warns Israelites about two opposite dangers: being too attracted to Canaanite culture, and being too violent against its members who still live in the land.

Jacob in the Land, 35:1-29

Before leaving Jacob to tell the story of Joseph the authors include several important notices that are needed to complete the work of divine guidance up to this point and prepare for the next stage in Egypt.

(a) *Jacob Returns to Bethel* (35:1-15). In ch. 34 Jacob's sons have threatened the future of blessing in the land by their cruel violence to the people of Shechem. Jacob directs a rite of purification that includes putting away all idols and pledging loyalty to YHWH alone, and then leaves Shechem for good and returns to the place of his vision at Bethel. Jacob has a special association throughout his life with Bethel. No doubt the northern kingdom of Israel saw Jacob as their special ancestor whom they honored at their central cultic shrine when Jeroboam I set it up at Bethel in opposition to Jerusalem (1 Kings 12:39). Is it only a coincidence that Jeroboam himself both moved from Shechem to Bethel at that time and also rebuilt the shrine of Penuel (1 Kings 12:25-33)? The legend in vv. 1-8 may have played a major role in the liturgies of Bethel in the years up to the collapse of the northern kingdom in 722. The scene ends, however, in vv. 9-15 with the P summary of Jacob's call to be the ancestor of both Judah and northern Israel. It echoes and recaps the nearly parallel statements of the divine promise in 28:13-15 and the change of name and destiny in 32:28, both usually attributed to the older J and E traditions.

(b) *The Birth of Benjamin and the Death of Rachel* (35:16-21). One final son must be born, Benjamin. Like Joseph, he is the child of Jacob's favorite wife, Rachel, and will be special to his father. But he is born in tragedy since Rachel must die in the story as a result of her theft of her father's idols and Jacob's unwitting promise to have the culprit put to death. Jacob renames this child of a curse with a blessing; he will be the "son of his right hand," that is, a favored child.

(c) *Concluding Notes* (35:22-29). The final threads are tied up in listing the twelve sons in such a way as to emphasize both their common Aramean heritage and their distinctive mothers. A small, jarring note about Reuben's evil is inserted to prepare for the curse on him in Jacob's final words of 49:3-4. Finally, the death of Isaac is recorded with both sons present to bury him in the ancestral tomb—a sign that what had begun in the conflict of two brothers in 25:23 has now been settled in peace, with Jacob the one who succeeds his father.

Esau's Heritage, 36:1-43

Although Esau has been an ambiguous figure in the previous narratives, pictured partially as foolish, partially as violent, definitely as replaced by his brother in the promised inheritance, he has not been treated as an evil person and often we are led to be sympathetic with the unfortunate fate he must suffer. The final note of the Jacob cycle stands as a redemption of Esau—an assurance that although God's choice of Israel did not always respect the existing inheritance laws of the world and the political hierarchies in power, there was still divine blessing given to neighboring peoples. Six fragmentary and obscure lists of Edomite kings and family trees have been put side by side to impress the reader that Edom too is a great nation with its own blessing, one that took shape even before Israel's was capped by kingship (see v. 31).

The Generations of History in Genesis

Genesis has been literarily divided into ten sections by special lists of ancestors, each of which begins "These are the generations" *(Toledot):*

2:1	The history of the days of creation
5:1	The descendants of Adam
6:9	The family of Noah
10:1	The sons of Noah's descendants
11:10	The descendants of Shem
11:27	The family of Terah
25:12	The descendants of Ishmael
25:19	Isaac's family
36:1	Esau's family
37:2	Jacob's family

The Joseph Cycle, 37:1–50:26

The fourth and final great cycle of traditions in Genesis centers on the figure of Joseph, eleventh son of Jacob and great-grandson of Abraham. In style and content it is far different from anything that has gone before. It has few if any individual sagas or legends that circulated independently or were part of the repertory of an individual cultic shrine. Instead it is a continuous story whose every episode is essential to the narration of the next episode. For this reason the entire block from 37:1 to 47:27 (with the exception of two inserts: 38:1-30 and 46:1-27) has frequently been called the world's first novel. It has a plot that commences with the dreams of Joseph and follows out the suspenseful consequences until the dreams have all come true. Scholars can trace original parts of the narrative to the J or E written sources, but behind them there must still lie an earlier exciting tale of some hero who rose to great power in Egypt despite his lowly semitic background. The narrative contains remarkable literary allusions to Egyptian stories and quite a number of specific historical references to Egyptian customs, words, and attitudes. The earliest tale then must have predated Israel's own use of it. Probably Israelite religious circles connected to the Joseph tribes of Ephraim and Manasseh in the Shechem-Bethel area adapted the story with Joseph as its hero.

As a written narrative it is closest in style to the great story of David's kingship in 2 Samuel 9–20 and 1 Kings 1–2, and like that may also be dated to the period of the early monarchy in its JE versions, and to pre-exilic seventh-century Judah for the finished and polished literary masterpiece now before us. It was no doubt taken into the cycles about the great ancestors so that it would link the history of Israel's forbears in and around Canaan to the reason why they are found in servitude in Egypt when the book of Exodus opens. The story is tied into the family of Jacob in 37:1 and leads up to the final acts of the great patriarch in chs. 46–50.

Its *theological* message continues the key themes of the earlier chapters of Genesis such as the divine promise of protection for the leader who trusts in YHWH, and the mysterious ways of divine guidance that often turn human expectations upside down. But the earlier themes concerned with establishing progeny and a claim on the land of Canaan fade into the background and are simply hooked into the narrative at the end. Instead the story emphasizes the hidden ways of God in leading Joseph, the importance of dreams for knowing the future, and God's providential control over world events. These themes are well known in the wisdom tradition (see Prov 10:21; 22:29; 25:11; Sir 8:8 and often), and it is not inconceivable that sages under Hezekiah or even later had a major hand in the final writing of this section of Genesis. Certainly the final authors intended the reader to perceive that God never *directly* reveals anything to Joseph, unlike the experiences of his ancestors. Instead they propose a new way of relating to God, one much more like their ordinary experience of prayer and trust, and one with which they could relate very directly.

Joseph and the Treachery of His Brothers, 37:1-36

The new Joseph story opens with the tenth and final *toledot* notice of the priestly editors in 37:2. The chapter narrates quickly and ominously a series of scenes that lead to disaster for Joseph. The horror of what unfolds is mitigated only by the hint that the two dreams of the young man hold hope for a better future. Family conflict has been an enduring thread through all the ancestral narratives from ch. 12 onwards, but from a psychological viewpoint such brash dreams of power over one's older siblings are more than sufficient grounds for a deep resentment and even hatred to develop. This dislike would only be intensified by the obviously favored treatment Joseph gets from their father. Joseph's youthful boasting soon leads his brothers to murderous plotting, a fateful characteristic in them already seen in ch. 34. Far from the protection of Jacob, and proudly wearing his special coat ("long-sleeved"? or "covered with gold spangles"?), he falls into their trap. The weak efforts of Reuben and Judah to soften his fate prove of little help, but there seem to be two conflicting outcomes: in vv. 26-27 they sell him to Ishmaelite caravaneers going to Egypt; in v. 28 Midianite traders seem to have found him in the pit and taken him for sale as a slave. Source critics believe these slight differences reveal the older sources at work: E calls the father Jacob, has Reuben attempt the rescue, knows of Midianite traders, and has the boy sold to Potiphar; J has Israel as the father, Judah as the rescuer, Ishmaelite traders, and an unnamed "high official of Pharaoh" as the purchaser. But these inconsistencies are minor in the text and editors have usually blended them together, as, e.g., when they add that the Midianites sold him to the Ishmaelites in v. 28 to reconcile the discrepancy.

Finally, the brothers deceive their father about the fate of Joseph. Once again an act of deceiving has come back to haunt Jacob.

Judah and Tamar, 38:1-30

The story of how Judah's family line was established breaks into the dramatic story of Joseph, leaving us temporarily wondering what will happen to the boy in Egypt. No modern novelist would break up a good plot in this manner but we must reckon with a different mindset for ancient authors and with a larger purpose in Genesis to explain Israel's varied origins, not one of which is more crucial than the heritage of the tribe of Judah. Dramatically, it is placed here because of the mention of Judah's rescue efforts in the previous chapter, and because the results of deception played as great a role in Judah's history as they did in that of its great rivals, the Joseph tribes (Ephraim and Manasseh) in the northern kingdom.

The plot forms around a legal requirement that if a man dies without leaving children, especially a son, the brother or other near male relative must conceive a child with the widow. The child will bear the dead brother's name and inheritance. The law, later disused, is known as "levirate marriage" (see Deut 25:5-8) Thus Judah's son Er dies, and Onan, his brother, refuses this obligation to the widow so God allows him also to die. Judah rightly perceives that the widow Tamar may have a curse about her and refuses to allow his third and last son to marry her, lest he also die. Tamar deceives Judah by pretending to be a cult prostitute. But when he sleeps with her she conceives twins and slips away unrecognized with his personal seal and staff as pledges of payment. Naturally she is vindicated when the truth comes out, and Judah accepts her children as his own.

The purpose of the story is to indicate first how the tribe of Judah through its two main branches, the clans of Perez and Zerah, has Canaanite connections, and second how the patriarch Judah proved himself righteous as did the great ancestress mother Tamar. Judah is now rightly prepared to receive the blessing to be given in 49:9-12, when the "staff" of 38:18 suddenly takes on royal authority.

Joseph and the Wife of Potiphar, 39:1-23

Joseph's fate was slavery, but the authors emphasize that divine protection works behind the scenes by noting at the beginning and end of this single episode, "God was with him" (vv. 2-3 and 23). The plot is based on an old Egyptian folk story of the attempted seduction of a husband's younger brother by the wife. It can be found in the "Tale of Two Brothers" (*ANET* 23–25). As it is developed in the present version, Joseph is doing well for a slave—he so impresses his master that he becomes the steward of his household. Faced with the lust of the official's wife he shows true rectitude, abhorring adultery as the Law uncompromisingly required (Exod 20:14; Lev 18:20; Deut 22:22) and expressing complete loyalty to his master. But when he is betrayed by the woman herself his doom seems sure. Even at this point, however, God stays with him. Potiphar deals him a prison sentence rather than death. And God exceeds even that mercy by once more making Joseph favored in the prison with a position of importance. Five times in this short scene Joseph is referred to as a "Hebrew," a name used in the Bible normally only when comparing an Israelite with foreign peoples. It occurs in such similar scenes with foreigners as Exodus 1–10 and 1 Samuel 1–12. Generally, among themselves the chosen people are the "children of Israel."

Joseph in the Royal Prison, 40:1-23

The next scene is tightly bound to the previous one. Joseph has been condemned to the *royal* prison over which Potiphar has the supervision. And so he meets the butler and chief baker of the Pharaoh himself. The three-way dialogue about the meaning of their dreams contains a wonderful blend of pathos and humor. God's guiding hand is seen immediately in Joseph's ability to interpret such dreams about the future. The theological point is stated in v. 8: God alone gives the power to know such future-oriented portents. The interpretation itself seems simple enough even though we know nothing about any rules that might have been commonly employed in ancient dream analysis for explaining particular images. The key principle here is a word play on the expression. "to lift the head." For the butler, Joseph sees that it means the Pharaoh will raise the man's bowed head up in restored honor to look on the king's face; but for the baker it means his head will be lifted up off his shoulders. Each happens as Joseph had foretold. The lesson is that dreams are signs by which God's will can be known, but they are not open to human reasoning without specific divine inspiration. In each case they are God's preparation for what is yet to come. But unfortunately this episode ends with a hitch. The butler does nothing to help Joseph.

Joseph Enters the Pharaoh's Service, 41:1-57

The plot thickens. When the Pharaoh has troubled dreams about the future the restored butler suddenly remembers Joseph's ability. But the call to interpret the king's dreams brings both opportunity and grave danger. Failure, or even a correct identification that has an unfavorable prediction, could mean death. As usual the story makes use of an older Egyptian tale about seven good years and seven lean years (*ANET* 31), but it has been reworked as a lesson for Israel. This message is carried by the repeated assurances that God is guiding the outcome (41:16, 28, 32); and by Joseph's long explanatory speech which, in the best tradition of Egyptian and Israelite sages, proves he is not only farseeing but a trustworthy and competent advisor on royal policy. The king is so impressed that he bestows the full authority to accomplish Joseph's vision on Joseph himself—perhaps to the amazement of the members of the royal court. In this scene Joseph embodies the major ideals of the wise person: prudent in speech, calm and not hotheaded, able to plan and execute national policy. The "spirit" is on Joseph, and even Pharaoh acknowledges the power of his god (vv. 38-39). Joseph is invested with the symbols of office of the Grand Vizier (prime minister). The office is well known in Egyptian sources and authentically reflected here. It is possible that the small details mirror the Hyksos rule over Egypt in the eighteenth to sixteenth centuries B.C.E. but they need not, since the knowledge of Egyptian ways would have been quite current in the time of Solomon, for instance. Nevertheless, an original setting of the story at the time when Semitic invaders, called *Hyksos* ("foreign" or "nomad" kings) ruled Egypt, and even a lowly Semite might hope to rise to power, has much to commend it.

The First Visit of the Brothers to Egypt, 42:1-38

Temporarily the focus shifts from Joseph back to the family of Jacob. Just as famine once drove Abraham to Egypt, now famine drives Joseph's brothers. The scene of their first meeting with the great Egyptian vizier who has shown such wisdom and planning takes a foreboding turn when Joseph recognizes them and decides to put them to the test. The crux of the drama is that he controls the situation because he knows what they do not. He has become fully Egyptian in dress and manner and reveals no trace of his Hebrew origins. In turn their fear prevents them from even guessing the truth. Already in 41:45 we learned that Joseph has assumed an Egyptian name, and when in 41:51 he chooses the name *Manasseh* for his firstborn it could be interpreted to mean that Joseph has put his past in Canaan behind him. The genius of the narrator, however, is that at every stage we are made fully aware that, inside, Joseph has forgotten nothing and has a deep longing for his family in spite of everything they have done to him.

Reuben again stands out as a man of compassion, both in acknowledging the guilt they bore for selling Joseph and in expressing his father's grief. As a result Joseph softens his test and keeps only Simeon the second-oldest as a hostage, thus sparing Reuben as a reward for his efforts. The others he allows to return home. The additional demand for Benjamin to be brought back is the true test. Will they treat this second child of Rachel as badly as they treated Joseph? The chapter ends with Jacob being fully informed but refusing the request, thereby increasing the tension. Strangely, no one seems to care that Simeon remains incarcerated.

The Second Journey to Egypt, 43:1-34

In this new scene Judah re-emerges as the spokesperson of the brothers before Jacob. Chapters 43–45 may reflect a J version of the story. There seems to be no awareness at all that Simeon is in the prison, and the only reason for returning to Egypt is the severity of the famine. Jacob himself shows much of his old cunning in this scene in which he plots to win the favor of the vizier with gifts as once he won over his brother Esau. The subsequent complicated encounter in Joseph's palace reveals the best of a skilled storyteller at work. Every move raises the brothers' fears that Joseph is keeping close to them just so he can trap them. The scene in which Joseph catches the first sight of his younger brother is particularly powerful. Gradually even the brothers are lulled into thinking that for some reason the governor favors them because of Benjamin.

The Final Test, 44:1-34

But there must be a final test to see how deep their repentance goes. By now the brothers are fully convinced that their trials have been a punishment for the evil done to Joseph. Joseph knows this but also wants to see how they will treat Benjamin, the other favored child, if he is given special attention. Will their jealousy reemerge? Will they take the opportunity to leave the boy behind if this cruel governor would let them go free as a result? The test itself involves a serious charge. Theft is one thing, but taking the official divination cup by which a governor is expected to consult the will of the gods is another. The proper sentence would be death. Joseph's Egyptian steward insists, however, that the vizier is merciful and will simply make the guilty man a slave. This promise would be the perfect excuse for leaving Benjamin to his fate, much as they had once eased their consciences by selling Joseph instead of killing him. The steward seems to play the role of divine interpreter in this drama. Here, as in 43:23, he articulates the divine compassion that directs all of Joseph's actions. Judah once again steps forward to speak for the brothers. The very length of his address in vv. 18-34 signals its importance. It expresses in a deeply moving way the love Judah and the brothers now have for both Benjamin and their father. Judah does not mention any regret or sorrow for their treatment of Joseph in this speech, but that confession has already been partly made in Reuben's pleas to his brothers in 42:21-22. Judah proves his sincerity above all doubt by offering himself as a slave in place of Benjamin.

Joseph is Reconciled to His Brothers, 45:1-28

Judah's humble petition has confirmed that the brothers have changed in their hearts and Joseph can no longer control his yearning to be reconciled to them. The opening scene describes a poignant moment that catches the brothers off guard. Joseph then takes another step and reveals God's guiding hand behind everything that has happened to them as a family since the crisis began in 37:1. Verses 4-8 stand out as the theological focal point of the entire Joseph cycle. Joseph speaks as a prophet giving an oracle of deliverance: "Fear not!" He then describes the hidden plan of God that was operative at every stage: in showing mercy to Joseph in his trials, in guiding the brothers down to Egypt, and in directing and controlling Egypt, all in order to save their lives and preserve the promise.

Quickly the action shifts back to Jacob. Joseph gives elaborate directions for inviting him to live in Egypt and the Pharaoh extends this in royal fashion. An almost ceremonial procession returns to Canaan to bring the aged patriarch the good news. Jacob must be convinced, but his yes, when given, is definitive and fateful. He believes as Abraham once did, and moves his family to Egypt.

The land of Goshen was in the Eastern delta of the Nile, nearest Canaan, and Pharaohs often permitted Semitic groups to live on its edges in times of famine. The hint that Joseph's palace was near the area in v. 10 may reflect the older Hyksos setting of the tale since their capital was in this delta region at Avaris. Or it might simply imply that the task of gathering and dispensing grain made it imperative that Joseph be near the breadbasket of the country.

Jacob's Triumphant Entry into Egypt, 46:1-34

The focus has returned to Jacob. God again speaks to him directly in a vision after many long years. God not only confirms the divine purpose behind the move to Egypt but also foresees that Jacob's family will some day return to their homeland. This is an editorial foreshadowing of the rest of the Pentateuchal story. The triumphal journey to Egypt is interrupted in vv. 8-27 by a somewhat pedantic effort to account for Jacob's offspring and grandchildren so that they will number seventy. This may be an artificial attempt to match the statement to this effect in Exod 1:5, but it takes some twisting to get the numbers close. See also Deut 10:22 for the number seventy.

The journey to Egypt resumes in vv. 28-34 with the reunion of Jacob and his favorite son, Joseph. Joseph gives careful instructions to his family not to mention to Pharaoh that they are shepherds, but to call themselves cattle-tenders. The reason for this strange command is not altogether clear since they proceed to violate it immediately upon meeting Pharaoh in 47:3. There may be a wordplay between their role as shepherds and the hated name of Hyksos tyrants, whose name means "shepherd-nomads" or "foreigners."

Jacob and Joseph Together in Egypt, 47:1-31

This chapter serves as a wrapup of the great adventure that has begun in ch. 37 and is now resolved when both father and brothers bow down before Joseph as his dreams had once foretold. The remaining three chapters can all be considered appendices that belong to the Jacob and Joseph tradition but stand outside the plot of the crafted novella. But this concluding summary in ch. 47 has three acts: 47:1-12, 13-26, and 27-31.

Verses 1-12 describe the meeting between two great leaders. One rules the world's greatest empire, the other holds the divine blessing. The Pharaoh acts in a gracious and magnanimous manner befitting the master of this world's goods. Jacob, although wealthy in a nomadic fashion himself, describes a life filled with hardship, without a permanent home, and far too short despite his great age. This is a strange way to speak to a king who is your benefactor, but it is really intended to inform the reader that Israel's time in Egypt will not be made permanent, and a life of sojourning in the desert still lies ahead. Ironically, Jacob blesses Pharaoh rather than the other way around. This, too, is a foreshadowing: Israel will triumph over Egypt just a few chapters ahead when God delivers them from another Pharaoh's power.

Verses 13-26, in contrast, picture a shrewd Joseph in total command of Egypt's fate and using his skills to enhance the power and glory of Pharaoh. All in all, the story reflects the reality of Egyptian belief that the whole land of Egypt belonged at least nominally to the Pharaoh. The twenty percent tax was not exceptionally high by ancient standards, and the people are portrayed as genuinely grateful to Joseph and Pharaoh. It serves as a climactic portrait of the exemplary wisdom exhibited by Joseph, the ultimate proof that God's blessing had been with him all along.

Verses 27-31 solemnly note that Jacob makes Egypt his final home. In every way it would seem God had blessed the patriarch with the fruits of the promise—his children and grandchildren were numerous, he possessed the finest agricultural land anyone in his family had ever known, and his son has brought blessing on him and on Egypt and on all other peoples of a Near Eastern world stricken by famine. Was not each point of the promise to Abraham in 12:1-3 now fulfilled? Yes, but . . . it was not God's plan!

Jacob, wise through many long years of encounter with God's mysterious ways, insists that Joseph swear to return his body to Canaan where the promise really lay. The seriousness of this command to his son is emphasized by the insistence it be sworn on his genitals, the same solemn oath that Abraham demanded of his servant who was sent to bring a wife back from Mesopotamia for Isaac (Gen 24:2-9).

The Blessing of Joseph's Sons, 48:1-22

As if the promise exacted of Joseph at the end of ch. 47 was not enough, now Jacob performs an even more dramatic act of looking to the future. Jacob claims the two sons of Joseph for the land of Canaan. The future importance of these sons as tribes in the area of northern Israel is confirmed by the reversal in his blessing: Ephraim will surpass his older brother Manasseh. Historically the tribe of Ephraim did become the last surviving portion of northern Israel in the time of Hosea (see Hos 5:3, 5, 11, 13, etcetera). The blessings ignore Egypt's riches in order to promise the fruitfulness of Canaan to Joseph's future generations. The powerful tribes of Ephraim and Manasseh, however, never seemed to function in the promised land as a single "Joseph" tribe, but used their ancestor as a general name that signified a now-lost relationship between them. Chapter 48 integrates these two tribes into the family history by making their blessing one of the final acts of Jacob. The section concludes with a renewed insistence by the dying patriarch that Joseph remember that Shechem and not Egypt was his true home.

Jacob's Final Words to His Sons, 49:1-28

The independent poem in this chapter is very old. Even its Hebrew has many archaic words and usages that were no longer familiar in later writings. Since the poem on Judah appears to predict the rise of David we can place it perhaps in the early monarchy period (tenth century) but its various aphorisms about the individual tribes may go farther back into the period of the Judges. Most of the tribal descriptions are brief and probably humorous allusions to local characteristics, but a few are serious judgments explaining God's punishment for tribal actions in the past, and two are blessings for the future.

The judgments are on Reuben (see 35:22) and Simeon and Levi (see 34:1-31) for sins against Jacob's rights: their resulting sentences are the loss of their territorial heritage in Israel. The blessings are on Judah and Joseph, the two most powerful centers in the future nation of Israel, one the leading (and only) tribe of Judah, the other the most powerful center of the northern kingdom of Israel. Judah is described as prosperous and destined to rule (e.g., only a very rich man would tie an ass to a precious vine, since the ass will eat the plant). The lion was probably the symbol of the Davidic dynasty and predicts the kingship.

The blessing over Joseph combines a promise of prosperity in agriculture, military strength, and divine protection. This protection consists of the cosmic powers at Joseph's service; and divine blessing is enhanced by a string of divine titles, which reflect the previous ancestral narratives that so often addressed God as the God of their ancestors, "El Shaddai" (see 17:1; 43:14; 48:3), and the "God of your father." A new title appears: "the Mighty One of Jacob" (v. 24). Like the earlier use of "the fear of Isaac" (31:53) this may be the personal name of God used by Jacob's own immediate family. Only later, at the time of the Exodus, did the tradition declare that all of these titles were names for YHWH (see Exod 6:3).

For a fuller understanding of the remaining references to individual tribes, read Joshua and Judges, which narrate many old traditions about where tribes originally settled and what changes were forced on many of them by later circumstances of war or the need for better land. Chapter 49 ends with a renewed command by Jacob that he be buried in his homeland at Machpelah alongside Abraham, Isaac, Sarah, Rebecca, and Leah. The promise must not die with Jacob in the land of Egypt!

The Final Days of Jacob and Joseph, 50:1-26

This concluding chapter of Genesis narrates the end of an era. It is arranged in three acts: the death of Jacob (vv. 1-15), the final repentance of the brothers (vv. 16-21), and Joseph's death (vv. 22-26). Jacob's solemn burial at Hebron involves the whole clan and the consent of the Pharaoh, so that it becomes instead a formal claim on the future land.

The second scene in which the brothers fear that Joseph could still harbor hatred against them is psychologically compelling. They begin

The Name of the God of the Ancestors

Source Criticism received its first major impetus from the observation that Genesis 1 and 2 differed in the name used of God (*ʾelohim* versus *yhwh ʾelohim*). Scholars deduced that this was the sign of different original literary sources that regularly called God by quite different terms. This was taken a step farther when Albrecht Alt in the twentieth century noted that, although both *yhwh* and *ʾelohim* recur throughout the book of Genesis, these may not reflect the only early titles used of God. Drawing examples from pre-Islamic Arabic inscriptions mentioning the "God of the Ancestors" of different tribal groups, he pointed to the possibility that Genesis still preserved remnants of individual names for God proper to different ancestral tribes before they were forged into the people Israel at the time of the Exodus and settlement of Canaan. Even though Gen 4:26 says that people called on *yhwh* from primeval times, Exod 6:2-3 knows that Moses introduced the name *yhwh* to Israel instead of an earlier *ʾEl Shaddai.* Note the further examples in Genesis itself:

14:22	*ʾEl ʿelyon*	God most high
17:1	*ʾEl Shaddai*	God Almighty
21:33	*ʾEl ʿOlam*	The Everlasting God
28:3	*ʾEl Shaddai*	God Almighty
31:42	*Paḥad Isaac*	The Fearsome One of Isaac
31:53	*Paḥad Isaac*	The Fearsome One of Isaac
33:20	*ʾEl ʾElohe Israel*	El, the God of Israel
35:7	*ʾEl Beit-ʾel*	El, (God of) Bethel
43:14	*ʾEl Shaddai*	God Almighty
48:3	*ʾEl Shaddai*	God Almighty
49:24	*ʾAbbir Jacob*	The Mighty One of Jacob

Besides these, the term "God of your ancestors" is used in Gen 28:13; 31:42; 31:53; 32:9.

---

by finally seeking direct forgiveness for their wickedness from their victim, and he in turn reassures them that he did not act out of any personal animosity but is himself subject to God's plan for their good. Ironically, of course, what was good for them was also the very thing that they so hated, the dreams of a younger brother. Joseph's visions are now completely fulfilled as his brothers lie bowed down before him, dependent on his rule and beneficence.

The third scene states the final and necessary conclusion to the book. Joseph dies with the same rich life of blessing that his grandparents and parents had enjoyed. In an understated prophecy he does not so much ask as he tells his children that they will bring him home to the promised land. But for now he and they are "in Egypt" (*bemiṣrayim,* the final word in the book of Genesis).

4. An Afterword (Genesis 12–50)

There is a wonderful dramatic quality to the ancestral narratives of chs. 12–50. On the one hand the ancient stories of encounters with God had a supernatural edge to them that later Israel knew was no longer the way they worshiped God; on the other the narrators added hints and references to later events of their own time (such as the tribal lists in ch. 49). The result is a coherent narrative of faith that crosses generation after generation despite a history filled with terrible uncertainty and great difficulties. Later, in the NT, Heb 11:1-22 sees all of Genesis as a lesson in *faith.* But Genesis understood it primarily as a time of *blessing:* Abraham, Isaac, Jacob and Joseph all enjoyed much material blessing and success on one level and brought blessing to those around them. But above all this theme of blessing was tied to the problematic situation of the land of Canaan. They had been chosen and their election had survived the ups and downs of human history with its strange turns and often bloody conflicts, for evil was always a part of the story.

Emphasis on motifs such as God's choice of the younger over the older or the need for divine opening of barren wombs expressed for these storytellers the mystery of God's initiatives rather than their own. Genesis is what it says, "only the beginning," but it sets the stage for God's most astounding act of freedom, the liberation and covenant of partnership with God in the book of Exodus; and it sets this stage not just around itself, an insignificant country, but in the context of God's direction of kings and empires. No wonder then that this story of promise cannot be told without first including the primeval lessons for the world in chs. 1–11!

D. Reading Genesis Today

1. Theological Significance of Genesis

The importance of the narratives of Genesis for establishing the origins of belief in God and for laying out clearly the divine purpose in human history cannot be overestimated. The combination of the mythic stories of world origins with the particular traditions about the election of the great ancestors formed the two pillars of Israel's faith. The unique two-part shape of this book affirmed that God had created the world out of love and with the intention of forming an intimate relationship with humanity. But human sin moved through its own course in time and seemed to drive humanity ever farther apart from God. God then had to intervene with a new plan, to work through one faithful people as witnesses and heralds to all peoples.

Thus we can see in the creation stories of Genesis 1–11 a number of very definitive theological claims. These include affirmation that the world is not under the rule of chaos but is governed by a clear plan of divine wisdom and is good in all its parts. It also includes the recognition that God's word and spirit are active in the world, both shaping it and speaking to it. This lays the foundation for Israel's most important claim, that God does speak and is revealed in a general communication to the world, but even more so in a particular communication to Israel. History, not mythic time, becomes the stage for discovering God, and history both continues the plan of creation and provides new opportunities to repent, grow and hear more fully the God who speaks. History is never static. Although humans sin and disrupt God's goodness in creation, God can also return and heal those breaks. God thus allows humanity freedom to sin or to obey. This limits the divine omnipotence, but God compensates for such a limit by staying in communication and remaining present to the world.

This outlook on God's greater plan for all humankind is central to the treatment of Abraham and the ancestors in Genesis 12–50. Israel's election is through faith and trust in God's promises. This faith and trust is learned in encountering the living God, remembering from generation to generation, and training the next generation to know God and obey what God has commanded.

2. Genesis in the Liturgy

The Sunday lectionary of readings for the Eucharist in the Roman Catholic Missal has only thirteen selections from Genesis in its three-year cycle, and only three of these are repeated every year, none of them actually on a Sunday: two occur on Holy Saturday, Genesis 1 and Gen 22:1-18 (Abraham's sacrifice of Isaac); the third, Gen 11:1-9 (Tower of Babel) is read on the vigil of Pentecost. Of the thirteen passages, six are from the primeval history of Genesis 1–11, and seven are about Abraham. No text is read from Genesis 26–50, thus eliminating Jacob and Joseph from Sunday celebrations. Some attempt is made to read selections in order from the entire book of Genesis in the cycle of daily Mass readings for Year One. Eleven selections from Genesis 1–11 are read in the fifth and sixth weeks of the year; and eighteen selections from Genesis 12–50 take up the twelfth to fourteenth weeks. The result is a certain limited profile, especially to those who only hear the Sunday readings that from Genesis 1–11 emphasize God's grace and forgiveness and from the rest of the book mostly Abraham as a model of faith.

Because any OT lectionary passage is linked in some way to a passage from the gospels one can understand why the Church is interested in

Genesis in the Liturgical Readings for Sundays and Holy Week

Gen 1:1—2:2	Creation account	Easter Vigil
Gen 2:7-9; 3:1-7	Adam and Eve sin	1st Sunday Lent A
Gen 2:18-24	Marriage established	27th Sunday B
Gen 3:9-15	Punishment for sin	10th Sunday B
Gen 9:8-15	Blessing after Flood	1st Sunday Lent B
Gen 11:1-9	Tower of Babel	Pentecost Vigil
Gen 12:1-4	Call of Abraham	2nd Sunday Lent A
Gen 14:18-20	Melchizedek's blessing	Corpus Christi
Gen 15:5-12, 17-18	The Promise to Abraham	2nd Sunday Lent C
Gen 18:1-10	Promise of a son	16th Sunday C
Gen 18:20-32	Abraham pleads for Sodom	17th Sunday C
Gen 22:1-18	Sacrifice of Isaac	Easter Vigil
Gen 22:1-18	Sacrifice of Isaac	2nd Sun Lent B

highlighting the themes of grace and faith, both key to understanding God's action in Christ. On the other hand, this situation suggests that Catholics wishing to deepen their knowledge of God should make the effort to read and understand the whole book of Genesis as a literary unit with important emphases and purposes far beyond those that emerge in liturgical use alone.

3. The Relevance of Genesis for Contemporary Spirituality

Genesis offers rich themes for contemporary prayer and spirituality reflections. Because our age deals with many important decisions about the earth and its environment, as well as the motives, choices, and decision-making aspects of human society, Genesis seems particularly popular in biblical treatments of spirituality. Some key themes that might be suggested are:

(1) The development of creation spirituality, which inculcates a deep respect for all parts of nature and for their interconnectedness at the deepest level of existence. Reflections on ecology and the basic goodness of human beings belong here. (See also the article on "The Bible and Ecology.")

(2) The importance of equality in relationships between men and women, especially in their fundamental shared identity in God's plans.

(3) Awareness of the clear, yet hidden presence of God in all that happens, developing toward a renewed theology of divine providence that stresses the discovery of God's presence through modern psychological, scientific, and social developments and insights.

(4) A strong accent on faith and trust in a God who is with us in life decisions, especially when we are in conversation with God through prayer (Genesis 12–50).

(5) A fruitful development of reflection based on the ancestor narratives of the men and women of patriarchal society who shared in the bringing about of the promises. Even a passage such as Gen 16:1-5, where the patriarch Abraham has a second wife, would be read and understood in light of the earlier Genesis 2 in which the unity of man and wife is presumed. Thus the special position of Sarah would not be threatened. Even though the Bible includes many archaic practices, it rethinks them in light of a deeper relationship modeled on covenantal ideas and the election bond between God and Israel. It then puts them into tension by both preserving the past and at the same time reconceiving it within a broader and still developing understanding of God's revelation.

BIBLIOGRAPHY

Blenkinsopp, Joseph. *The Pentateuch: An Introduction to the First Five Books of the Bible.* Anchor Bible Reference Library. Garden City, N.Y.: Doubleday, 1992. See especially chs. 3–4.

Clifford, Richard J. *Creation Accounts in the Ancient Near East and in the Bible.* Washington, D.C.: Catholic Biblical Association, 1994.

Friedman, Richard Elliott. *Who Wrote the Bible?* New York: Summit Books/Harper & Row, 1987.

Gunkel, Hermann. *Genesis.* Translated by Mark E. Biddle. Macon, Ga.: Mercer University Press, 1997.

____. *The Stories of Genesis.* Vallejo, Cal.: Bibal Press, 1994; translation of 1901 original.

Levenson, Jon D. *Genesis as Myth and Other Essays.* New York: Harper & Row, 1988.

Matthews, Victor, and Don Benjamin. *Old Testament Parallels.* Mahwah, N.J.: Paulist Press, 1992.

Rad, Gerhard von. *Genesis, A Commentary.* Philadelphia: Westminster, 1972.

Scullion, John J. *Genesis: A Commentary for Students, Teachers and Pastors.* Old Testament Studies 6. Collegeville: The Liturgical Press, 1992.

Speiser, E. A. *Genesis.* AB1. Garden City, N.Y.: Doubleday, 1964.

Westermann, Claus. *Genesis* 1–11, 12–36, 37–50. 3 vols. Minneapolis: Augsburg, 1984–1987.

____. *Genesis: A Practical Commentary.* Text and Interpretation. Grand Rapids: Eerdmans, 1987.

Exodus: An Introduction

Milton Schwantes

When we approach the book of Exodus we are energized with the force that it had and has. Here is the Passover, that scenario in which the Exodus is anchored. It is vital food for worship in Synagogue and in Jewish homes. In the midst of a thousand persecutions and even during the Holocaust the hope of the departure narrated in the festival was always alive.

Jesus' Passover is emn Exodus bedded in the Passover of the Jewish people. It is a part of it, part of the way from servitude to freedom, from death to life.

The impact of Exodus and of Passover can be found everywhere in the Bible. When King Josiah made his effort to recover the best roots of Israel's history his endeavor culminated in the Passover of Jerusalem. The prophets lived in the remembrance of Exodus: Elijah went to Mount Horeb (1 Kings 19:1-18); Hosea refers to the Exodus "when Israel was a child" (11:1); Deutero-Isaiah describes the Lord as Israel's redeemer, ready to make a way in the desert for the exodus of God's people in exile (Isa 43:16-21). All these were but little drops of the river of living waters that, since the Exodus, irrigates and disturbs Israel's history and that of the communities of Jesus the Messiah. The Bible—in the first and the second testaments—has its ground in Exodus. Without it, what would become of its spirit?

In the Christian communities Exodus became especially meaningful in two similar and interrelated contexts. On the one hand members of European churches had recourse to Exodus in confronting fascism and in challenging the racism and anti-semitism in which the Church was immersed. Thus they rediscovered that Exodus is not a narrative among many others; it is a confession of faith. It is the paradigmatic testimony of God.

In Latin America during the '60s and in the years thereafter "liberation" became the key word for new ways and new hopes. Exodus is liberation! The book of Exodus was read and reread by Christian communities everywhere in Latin America. Many babies in the *favelas* received the names of Moses and Myriam. Exodus was the inspiring paradigm.

It is no accident that today, when the patterns of reading of the 1960s and 1980s have shown their weakness, people want to review their understanding of the Exodus. New approaches are necessary in the midst of these new times. The living water of this book needs new words in order that its capacity to assuage desperate thirst may abide and at the same time become new.

Exodus

John F. Craghan

FIRST READING

I. Getting Started

General Tenor of the Book of Exodus

In the beginning of the book, as the author of Exod 2:24 puts it, the God of Israel remembers the covenant with Abraham, Isaac, and Jacob. This is a backward glance at the book of Genesis and the promises to the patriarchs that their offspring will be numerous and that they will eventually inherit the Promised Land. The Joseph Story (Genesis 37–50) establishes Jacob and his twelve sons in the land of Egypt. One is poised, therefore, to wait for that moment when their descendants will begin the trek that will culminate in the promise becoming a reality. The opening verses of the book of Exodus set the stage for this event. Although the total number of Jacob's descendants is only seventy, at the beginning of the Exodus account the Israelites have become so prolific that the land of Egypt is filled with them (1:7).

The Exodus, or the going out from Egypt, lies at the very heart of Israel's faith experience. The God who acts on Israel's behalf is not an insignificant deity of the ancient Near East cut off from reality and relegated to the realm of mythical time. Rather, Israel's God dramatically enters the arena of real time and real people. As the introduction to the Ten Commandments expresses it, "I am the LORD your God, who brought you out of the land of Egypt, that house of slavery" (20:2). To mention the name of this God means to conjure up the image of a totally involved deity. To utter that name is to provide an identity. YHWH without the Exodus is no YHWH at all!

The Exodus identifies not only YHWH but also Israel. It is precisely in the Exodus that Israel emerges as God's people. That event implies that the former Egyptian slaves are different from all their contemporaries. The Exodus with its covenant experience at Sinai distinguishes them as YHWH's people. The going out, therefore, is a selection process. The author of Exod 6:7 succinctly captures that process in these words: "I will take you as my people, and I will be your God."

The biblical book that captures this twofold identity, the book of Exodus, is the biblical book *par excellence* for exposing Israel's roots. It is the glory of Israel's writers that those origins are presented in such a powerful and intimate way. The book of Exodus is not simply the record of Israel's itineraries. It is Israel's identity papers, the record of human interaction and divine grace, of human success and failure, and of divine assistance and forgiveness.

Major Sections of the Book

The broad outline of Exodus is relatively simple. It can be divided into three main sections on the basis of Israel's geographical location in the narrative: (1) Israel in Egypt (1:1–13:16); (2) Israel in the wilderness (13:17–18:27); (3) Israel at Sinai (19:1–40:38). Against this background the reader is first invited to read the following passages: (1) 1:1–20:26; (2) 24:1–25:8; (3) 32:1–34:35; (4) 35:1-9; (5) 40:1-38.

In this first introduction to the text the reader is invited to ponder the oppression of the Hebrews in Egypt, YHWH's defeat of Pharaoh and the Egyptians through the plagues, and the people's subsequent journey through the wilderness and encampment at Mount Sinai. At this juncture the reader is urged to focus on the making of the covenant at Sinai including the Ten Commandments. After noting the introduction of the Covenant Code in 20:22-26 the reader should look at other traditions of covenant making in 24:1-11. The reader should then consider 24:11–25:8, Moses' position on Mount Sinai and the initial instructions for the building of the sanctuary. In 32:1–34:35 the reader is challenged to reflect on Israel's apostasy (the golden calf incident) and the subsequent renewal of the covenant. The reader should then observe the introduction to the construction of the sanctuary (35:1-9) and the erection of that dwelling with the accent on God's abiding holiness (40:1-38).

Once readers have concluded these principal passages they are urged to read the omitted sections. The first of these is the Covenant Code in 21:1–23:33. The second section is 25:9–31:18, that is, all the instructions for the building of the sanctuary. The third and final section is 35:10–39:43, the actual carrying out of the instructions for the construction of the sanctuary. Hopefully readers will come to appreciate the details of the Covenant Code and especially the centrality of God's presence in the sanctuary. The careful articulation of the instructions and their equally careful execution reveal Israel's sensitivity to God's abiding presence in its midst.

Sense of Drama

The book of Exodus is not a haphazard collection of stories, laws, liturgical celebrations, etcetera. In its final form the book reveals a certain dramatic development. Even the instructions for building the sanctuary and their execution are calculated not to interfere with, but rather to enhance the development of the whole story.

Given the Egyptian reaction to Israel's burgeoning population, namely oppression and suppression (1:1-22), one eagerly awaits the arrival of Moses and deliverance from such imminent peril (2:1-22). Such deliverance begins to emerge with the different accounts of the commissioning of Moses (2:23–7:7). At this point the reader is ready to experience the divine response to Israel's predicament in the accounts of the plagues (7:8–13:16). The outcome of God's intervention is the eventual destruction of the Egyptian army and Israel's hymn of thanksgiving (13:17–15:21). Despite this great victory the people complain (15:22–17:7), yet also witness another military victory (17:8-16) and Moses' encounter with his father-in-law (18:1-27) that is intended to resolve some of the leader's conflicts.

For the rest of the book Israel is situated at Sinai (19:1–40:38). However, the sense of drama does not slacken. There is the solemn conclusion of the covenant (19:1–24:18) that includes the expression of God's will in the Ten Commandments (20:1-21) and the Covenant Code (20:22–23:33). This leads into Moses' sojourn on the sacred mountain for forty days and forty nights (24:12-18). Since God's presence is the overriding theme in the book, the next section responds to this need by having Moses receive all the instructions for the making of the sanctuary (25:1–31:18).

To overcome the reader's ennui with this profusion of cultic details, the book notes Moses' prolonged absence on the mountain. This sense of absence leads into the story of the golden calf, the tale of Israel's apostasy that results in punishment and the eventual renewal of the covenant (32:1–34:35). Once Israel is reinstated as YHWH's covenant partner the book concludes with the results of such reinstatement, the construction of the sanctuary that culminates in God's abiding presence.

Major Theological Themes in Exodus

Since Exodus possesses a keen dramatic sense it is hardly surprising that key theological themes are skillfully worked into the text. The following suggestions are not a complete list of those themes, but they do provide a sampling of some major points that the different theological traditions wish to emphasize. The commentary will develop such points at greater length.

Divine Presence

In 2:23-24 the author notes first the absence and then the presence of God. It is the groans and cries of the oppressed Israelite slaves that force God to recall the covenant with the patriarchs. God's commissioning of Moses and the divine intervention, especially in the plagues, clearly establish the priority of divine presence. Chapter 33 consists of four vignettes, each reflecting on the modes of God's presence in Israel.

Liberation

The two basic elements of Israel's creed are YHWH's bringing the people out of Egypt and bringing them into the Promised Land. The book of Exodus dramatizes and celebrates the first element of this creed. By acting on behalf of the oppressed slaves YHWH became known and trusted as the great liberator. The one phrase the OT uses most often to characterize the God of Israel is: "who freed you/us from the house of Egypt/slavery."

Centrality of Worship

Exodus understands Israel as a worshiping community. The enormous amount of space dedicated to the instructions for building the sanctuary and their execution (chs. 25–31; 35–40) makes the awareness of God's presence in worship a significant part of Israel's self-understanding. The directions for the celebration of Passover and the feast of Unleavened Bread (12:1-28, 40-51; 13:1-10) also accentuate Israel's call to acknowledge its God in liturgy.

Sense of Covenant

Covenant is that relationship between YHWH and Israel that is created on Mount Sinai. It is a personal bond by which Israel becomes YHWH's people and YHWH becomes Israel's God. It is this unique moral connection that gives Israel its identity among all the other peoples of the ancient Near East.

Law as Response to Covenant

In the Ten Commandments (20:1-21), the Covenant Code (20:22–23:33), the Dodecalogue (34:10-26), and other such codes Israel replies in a personal way to its covenant relationship. Law is received not as an imposition from without, but as an acknowledgment from within of the need to honor and respect both the God of the covenant and other people.

Prophecy

Moses functions in a unique way as Israel's prophet (see Deut 18:15-20). Moses must communicate God's word in a criticizing mode, that is, by telling it the way it really is (see, for example, 5:1-21). However, Moses must also share that word in an energizing mode, that is, by telling it the way it can be (see for example, 3:1-10).

YHWH as Lord of History

Exodus respects the tension between human liberty and divine initiative. Thus the God of Israel does not eliminate, for example, the freedom of Egypt's king. At the same time, however, the text makes quite clear that YHWH is the one who presides over Israel's destiny and will brook no opposition.

YHWH as Divine Warrior

Throughout its history Israel develops different perceptions of its God. While there are several such perceptions in the book of Exodus, one that commands center stage is that of YHWH as divine warrior. Thus the plagues are a demonstration of God's power in the holy war against Pharaoh and his people. YHWH's military exploits in Egypt's pursuit of Israel (14:1–15:21) also witness to this perception. In 15:3 YHWH is given the title "man of war" (= warrior) astonishing as this is to our ears.

Significance of the Covenant Mediator

Exodus understands the covenantal relationship between YHWH and Israel as contingent on the role of Moses as covenant mediator. He is the one who especially represents the people at the time of the making of the covenant (19:3-25; 20:18-21; 34:3-8). As covenant mediator Moses also functions as the loyal opposition when God seeks to wipe out the people after the golden calf incident and start a new community (32:7-14).

Complaint and Disobedience in the Wake of Celebration and Obedience

The book of Exodus depicts the revelation of Israel's God, not just through a people, but indeed through a sinful people. After the celebration of YHWH's victory over the Egyptians (15:1-21) the text immediately presents the people as murmuring and complaining against YHWH (15:22–17:7). After stating their intention to carry out all of YHWH's commands (19:8; 24:7), the people seriously offend God in the golden calf incident (32:1-6). Human sinfulness does not defeat the God of the covenant.

Role of Women

The passage in 1:8–2:10 shows that without the intervention of women Moses' life would not have been saved and the Exodus would never have become a reality. Again in 4:24-26 the quick action of Moses' wife Zipporah saves the leader and keeps intact the promise of deliverance. In 15:1-21 Miriam performs a cultic function as she leads the women in the song and dance honoring the exploits of the divine warrior. (Other passages in the Bible also support Miriam's central role in the life of the wilderness community.)

Challenge to Remember

While the book of Exodus mentions YHWH's remembering of the promises to the patriarchs (2:23-24; 6:5), the book also enjoins Israel's remembering of YHWH's involvement in the Exodus (12:26-27; 13:8). The God of Israel will not tolerate a generation gap. Israel must continue to share its story of deliverance so that the present generation locks arms with the original participants in going forth from Egypt.

II. The Book as a Whole

Detailed Outline of Contents

Above, the book of Exodus was divided into three major sections on the basis of Israel's geographical location in the narrative. In contrast, the following outline seeks to be more specific and detailed in order to enable the reader to better appreciate the dramatic development of the Exodus story.

Israel in Egypt, 1:1–3:16

- Israel's growth (1:1-7)
- Oppression of God's people (1:8-14)
- Suppression of God's people (1:15-22)
- Birth of the hero (2:1-10)
- Flight to Midian (2:11-22)
- Exodus as lament liturgy (2:23-25)
- Burning bush (3:1-6)
- Commissioning of Moses (3:7-15)
- Expansion of the commission (3:16-22)
- Moses' objections and subsequent signs (4:1-9)
- More objections, replies, and signs (4:10-17)
- Moses' return to Egypt (4:18-23)
- Circumcision (4:24-26)
- Meeting between Moses and Aaron (4:27-31)
- First audience with Pharaoh (5:1–6:1)
- P's commissioning of Moses (6:2-13)
- Genealogy of Moses and Aaron (6:14-30)
- Reassurance and compliance (7:1-7)
- Introduction to the plagues (7:8-13)
- Ten plagues (7:14–11:10)
- Passover ritual (12:1-20)
- Promulgation of the Passover (12:21-28)
- Death of the firstborn and departure (12:29-39)
- Chronology and further Passover regulations (12:40-51)
- Redemption of the firstborn (13:1-2, 11-16)
- Feast of Unleavened Bread (13:3-10)

Israel in the Wilderness, 13:17–18:27

- Israel on the march (13:17-22)
- Egypt's pursuit of Israel (14:1-10)
- Conquest of fear (14:11-18)
- Two traditions for the crossing of the sea (14:19-31)
- Song of the Sea (15:1-21)
- Grumbling at Marah (15:22-27)
- Quail and manna (16:1-36)
- Grumbling at Massah and Meribah (17:1-7)
- Battle with the Amalekites (17:8-16)
- Meeting between Moses and Jethro (18:1-27)

Making of the Covenant, 19:1–24:11

- Setting (19:1-2)
- Attitude toward the covenant (19:3-8)
- Two theophany traditions (19:9-20)
- Holiness of the mountain (19:21-25)
- Ten Commandments (20:1-17)
- Moses' appointment as mediator (20:18-21)
- Introduction to the Covenant Code (20:22-26)
- Law for slaves (21:1-11)
- Offenses punishable by death (21:12-17)
- Laws regarding bodily injuries (21:18-32)
- Laws regarding property damages (21:33–22:14)
- Social laws (22:15–23:9)
- Religious laws (23:10-19)
- Behavior in the Promised Land (23:20-33)
- Covenant-making and ceremonial meal (24:1-2, 9-11)
- Covenant-making and blood rite (24:3-8)

Instructions for the Building of the Sanctuary, 24:12–31:18

- Moses' ascent (24:12-15a)
- P's theophany (24:15b-18)
- Collection of materials (25:1-9)
- Plan of the ark (25:10-22)
- Table and lampstand (25:23-40)

Instructions for making the desert sanctuary (26:1-37)
Altar of holocausts (27:1-8)
Court of the sanctuary (27:9-19)
Oil for the lamps (27:20-21)
Priestly vestments (28:1-43)
Investiture of the priests (29:1-9)
Sacrifices of priestly consecration (29:10-37)
Daily sacrifices (29:38-46)
Further cultic ordinances (30:1-38)
Choice of the artisans (31:1-11)
Significance of the Sabbath (31:12-18)

Israel's Apostasy and the Renewal of the Covenant, 32:1–34:35

Making of the golden calf (32:1-6)
YHWH's wrath and Moses' mediation (32:7-14)
Twofold destruction (32:15-24)
Zeal of the Levites (32:25-29)
Atonement (32:30-35)
Orders for the departure (33:1-6)
Moses and the tent of meeting (33:7-11)
Moses' intercession (33:12-17)
Preparations for the theophany (33:18-23)
Theophany (34:1-9)
Dodecalogue (34:10-26)
Impact of the theophany (34:27-35)

Execution of the Instructions for the Building of the Sanctuary, 35:1–40:38

Start of construction and Israel's generosity (35:1–36:7)
Execution of the divine instructions (36:8–39:31)
Presentation of the work to Moses (39:32-43)
Erection of the sanctuary (40:1-33)
God's abiding presence (40:34-38)

Type of Literature

As the detailed outline suggests, the book of Exodus is popular literature, certainly not a sober historical treatise. In keeping with its character as popular literature, the book is the blending of different literary types to correspond to Israel's self-understanding by retaining a variety of literary genres. To express it negatively, Israel's sense of its origins and destiny cannot be exhausted by a paucity of literary forms.

The following offers a few examples of Israel's wealth of expression. In 2:1-10 Moses' infancy narrative is calculated to force the reader to focus on the future greatness of the hero as he grapples with seemingly insuperable forces. In the plague accounts there is clear evidence of literary art. Rather than simply a series of enormous catastrophes, the plagues are a series of disputes between Pharaoh and Moses about the greatness of Israel's God. In the crossing of the Reed Sea there is the high dramatization of an epic account. Fittingly in the Song of the Sea (15:1-21) Israel feels itself constrained to exalt the divine warrior in song and dance. In the rubrics for Passover the effects of liturgy are obvious. In the Covenant Code (20:22–23:19) the legal hand is at work. In the instructions for the construction of the sanctuary (25:1–31:18) and their execution (35:1–40:38) a priest's delight and celebration of remembered details is evident.

Different Authors

The book of Exodus offers evidence of a number of distinct theological traditions that have left their mark on its final form. While the entire question of Pentateuchal sources has recently been reopened by critical scholars (see below under modern literary critical approaches, and also the general article on the Pentateuch in this volume), the approach taken in this commentary follows an enduring and fruitful scholarly consensus. No really credible alternative hypothesis has been found, and however the historical questions are eventually settled through historical argument this traditional division of sources leads us to perceive precise aspects of the text's meaning that might otherwise pass unnoticed.

The first author is the Yahwist (= J) who writes perhaps in the tenth century B.C.E. during the heady days of the Davidic-Solomonic kingdom. J looks beyond the covenant making at Sinai by envisioning the occupation of the Promised Land (see 3:8, 17). For example, J's covenant tradition in 34:11 anticipates Israel's entrance into the Promised Land and its subsequent problems.

The second author is the Elohist (= E) who reflects a period of religious turmoil and syncretism in the eighth or ninth century B.C.E. For E the goal of the Exodus is Sinai itself (3:12). In E's version of covenant making Israel's God appears in the form of a fear-producing storm (19:16). At Sinai Israel appears as God's militia, ready to honor the will of the One whose presence is marked by the cloud over the mountain.

The third author is the Priest (= P) who struggles to offer a picture of hope during the debacle of the exile in the sixth century B.C.E. As used here P designates both the ancient materials used by this school as well as its shaping of the Exodus story. Not surprisingly P reworks the contributions of J and E to provide the viewpoint of the Jerusalem priesthood. The traditions in chs. 25–31 and 35–40 witness to this school's insistence on proper cult with its rituals and regulations.

In addition to some independent traditions (e.g., 19:3b-8) there are also some passages that reflect the theological stance and language of Deuteronomy (e.g., 13:1-16). Such texts tend to suggest part of a larger effort to rework the text of Exodus as well as Leviticus and Numbers to reflect the materials and ideas of the last book of the Pentateuch.

It would be a mistake for the reader to harmonize the sometimes conflicting views of these authors. Rather the reader is challenged to allow such diverse theologians the requisite freedom to interpret. Such a stance recognizes that these writers judge the past in the light of their present and with a view to the future needs of Israel. As the commentary will show, these writers have their distinct perspectives; inspiration does not neutralize the human tendency to impose one's view. Ultimately one must be as open as the Bible itself. It has canonized not one party line, but indeed a variety of party lines. [For another view see also the introductory article "The Pentateuch."]

III. Original Historical Setting

Although the biblical account provides no historical report in the modern sense of the term there are some indications of the setting. Many authorities place the Exodus around the middle of the thirteenth century B.C.E. during the reign of Ramses II (1290–1224 B.C.E.). This pharaoh of the oppression and the Exodus (despite 2:23) was well known for his building activities in the Nile delta and his use of *ʾApiru.* The latter are often described as displaced people, disturbers of the peace, malcontents who harassed the ancient Near East during the second and third millennia. It is likely that a process of assimilation took place: ancestors of the Israelites who had freely gone down to Egypt became assimilated to other *ʾApiru.*

The strongest argument for the Ramses II chronology is the testimony of 1:11 that refers to the supply city of Raamses. The Austrian Archaeological Institute has shown that Ramses II built the city of Raamses on the site of the Hyksos capital, Avaris, when it was accessible through one of the arms of the Nile. When that access was lost the city of Raamses was abandoned. According to this view the Exodus would have occurred in an area northeast of modern Cairo and west of the Suez Canal.

Not only were there several entries into Egypt over the centuries; there were also several departures. The text itself reflects an awareness of different routes (see the commentary on 13:17-22). However, from the vantage point of Israel's faith experience there is only *the* Exodus. This is the going out led by Moses that included the theophany at Sinai. It is likely that this group was relatively small (contrast the figures given in Num 1:46; 26:51). As this event was recited in worship and pondered by Israel's theologians it gradually took on epic proportions. The small band grew in both size and importance. At the same time it was not simply a question of mathematical enlargement; it was also a matter of faith perception. All Israel saw itself represented in the small yet expanding group that had managed to break free of Pharaoh's brickyards.

IV. Canonical Intertextuality

Since the Exodus is the central event in Israel's relationship with God it is hardly surprising that it enjoys an enormous influence on the rest of the Bible. This section is an attempt to offer a brief description of that influence in both the OT and NT. References to the events, themes, and theologies of the book of Exodus throughout the Bible confirm the centrality of this book.

Old Testament

Pentateuch

Exodus is, first of all, the beginning of the fulfillment of the promises to the patriarchs. The opening passage in Exodus speaks of the seventy descendants of Jacob and refers the reader back to Gen 46:8-27. However, Exodus looks farther back than the arrival of Jacob's descendants in Egypt. It evokes the divine command to increase, multiply, and fill the earth (Gen 1:28).

Indeed, it is the realization of that command that brings about the oppression of the Hebrews in Egypt. This opening verse in Exodus also recalls the promises to the patriarchs that they will become a great nation (Gen 12:2; 17:4; 28:14). The divine prediction of oppression in an alien land culminating in a grace-filled departure from that place (Gen 15:13-14) is particularly significant for establishing the links between Genesis and Exodus. Moses' carrying of Joseph's bones at the start of the journey from Egypt is tangible evidence of the intimate bond between the first two books of the Bible (see Gen 50:25; Exod 13:19).

Leviticus and Numbers reflect a similar unity. From the vantage point of geography Exodus overlaps with those two books since Israel is encamped at Mount Sinai from Exod 19:2 through Num 10:10. In addition, the consummation of the first sacrifice by fire in Lev 9:24 looks back to the divine manifestation at Sinai and the construction of the sanctuary. Moreover, the ordination ritual for Aaron and his sons (prescribed in Exod 29:1-46) is actually carried out in Lev 8:1–9:21. With its emphasis on the sinfulness of the wilderness generation Numbers forges a close link with Exodus. It is especially the disparaging of the Exodus event and the desire to return to Egypt that creates a tension between the two books (see Num 11:1-15; 14:1-10; 16:12-14).

The first eleven chapters of Deuteronomy reflect on and interpret the book of Exodus. In Moses' first address (1:1–4:49) there is mention of the appointment of the minor judges (Deut 1:9-18) and the revelation on Mount Sinai/Horeb (Deut 4:9-14). In Moses' second address (5:1–11:32) the Ten Commandments, the manna, and the golden calf incident all show the influence of the book of Exodus. The conclusion of the law book proper (12:1–26:15) is a ritual summary of the principal events of the Exodus experience (26:1-11). The recital of oppression and deliverance is at the very core of Israel's dealings with YHWH.

Deuteronomistic History

The book of Joshua with its emphasis on the crossing of the Jordan River (chs. 3–4) sees that event as parallel to Israel's crossing of the Reed Sea in Exodus. The Jordan crossing is thus the fulfillment of the series of key events initiated at the time of Israel's departure from Egypt. The setting up of the meeting tent at Shiloh (Josh 18:1) refers the reader to the erection of this building in Exod 40:1-3. (For a summary of the key episodes in the Exodus event see Josh 24:4-7.)

Phrases such as "who brought you/them out of the land of Egypt" often contrast YHWH's loving intervention on behalf of Israel with Israel's failure to keep the covenant relationship (see Judg 2:1, 12; 1 Sam 8:8). This phrase is particularly poignant when Jeroboam I of Israel sets up the two golden calves in the shrines of Dan and Bethel (1 Kings 12:28). For the deuteronomistic historian the erection of these calves is the fundamental flaw of the Northern Kingdom of Israel, and to that degree a denigration of God's activities in the Exodus.

Elijah's journey to the mountain of God (Horeb: see 1 Kings 19:8) recalls Moses' experience on the same mountain (Horeb = Sinai). One thus returns to the foundational event in Israel's history. At the same time there is a clear contrast. Whereas God is present to Moses in storms and fire (Exod 19:16, 18), God is not present to Elijah in wind, earthquake, or fire, but only in "a sound of sheer silence" (1 Kings 19:11-12). However, Elijah's veiling of his face (1 Kings 19:13) necessarily reminds the reader of Moses' experience of God's overpowering presence in the same locale (Exod 33:18-23).

Other "Historical" Books

The Chronicler's history (see 2 Chr 5:10; 6:2; Neh 9:9-19) as well as the books of Maccabees (1 Macc 4:9; 2 Macc 2:8) do make mention of central events in the book of Exodus, but one of the most interesting and indeed innovative adaptations of YHWH's intervention in the crossing of the Reed Sea occurs in the deuterocanonical book of Judith. Judith is Israel's female warrior who strikes the decisive blow against Holofernes and the Assyrians after the manner of YHWH. Just as YHWH's right hand shatters the Egyptians in Exod 15:6, it is the hand of Judith in the service of YHWH and Israel that confounds the Assyrians and assures her people of victory (Jdt 16:6).

Wisdom Books and Psalms

While Sirach speaks of the law that Moses commanded (Sir 24:23) and sings the praises of Moses and Aaron (Sir 45:1-17), it is most especially the book of Wisdom that exploits the traditions of the book of Exodus. Wisdom 11:2–19:22 is concerned with the problem of reward and retribution. According to the author of Wisdom it is the differences in the Exodus experience that determine concretely the fates of the just and the wicked. For this sage the first Exodus shows that YHWH does support and defend Israel. He argues that the YHWH of his time (first century B.C.E.) is no less faithful. That first Exodus is the unique event that determines the outcome of everything else. If one lives as a faithful Jew, YHWH's ongoing support stemming from the first Exodus can no longer be in question. The Psalms, as Israel's expression of praise *par excellence,* cannot avoid the Exodus as YHWH's unique choice of this people. While some passages in certain psalms mention the event as a whole in a brief way (Pss 81:6; 114:1) or speak of the Reed Sea deliverance (Pss 66:6[7]; 77:19[20]) or the plagues (Ps 135:8-9), other psalms develop the whole chain of happenings at some length. For example, Psalm 78 sings of God's overwhelming goodness in the Exodus despite Israel's ingratitude. Psalms 105 and 136 see God's awesome display of power in the Exodus as evidence of God's ongoing covenantal fidelity. Finally, Psalm 106 ponders these same events from the vantage point of Israel's memory of its sinfulness. Israel must frankly admit that it has not always remembered the generosity of its God.

Prophets

Among the eighth-century prophets the Exodus theme admits both positive and negative uses. Amos preaches that the Exodus is no guarantee of God's ongoing care. Indeed Israel's election in the Exodus must inexorably lead to Israel's punishment (Amos 3:1-2; see also 9:7). In a covenant lawsuit with God's people Micah employs the themes of the sending of Moses, Aaron, and Miriam and the deliverance from the land of bondage (Mic 6:4) to demonstrate the ingratitude of the Israelites. On the other hand, Hosea sees the entire Exodus experience as the basic demonstration of God's love and the precedent for God's forgiveness of Israel and its renewal. Indeed the time in the wilderness is the great moment of Israel's fidelity that can prompt future conversion (Hos 2:14-15[16-17]). Somewhat after the manner of Amos and Micah, Hosea contrasts the outpouring of God's affection in the Exodus with the covenantal infidelity of the people (see Hos 9:10; 11:1; 12:9, 14; 13:4-6).

To be sure, the composition of the book of Jeremiah is still the focus of ongoing scholarly dispute. However, taking the book as a whole one can find clear evidence of the centrality of the Exodus themes. Borrowing from his northern neighbor Hosea, Jeremiah speaks of the desert experience as a time of purity when Israel is YHWH's bride and the first fruits of God's harvest (Jer 2:2-3). Other phrases, such as "my beloved" (Jer 11:15), "the beloved of my soul" (Jer 12:7), "my heritage" (Jer 12:8-9), and "the LORD's flock" (Jer 13:17) capture the prophet's perception of Israel's earliest interaction with YHWH. At the same time the prophet is painfully aware of the conditional nature of the Sinai covenant. In Jer 31:31-34, fully conscious of Israel's obduracy, the prophet nonetheless speaks of a new covenant. YHWH will intervene directly so that Israel's covenantal recognition of YHWH will be so pervasive that teaching YHWH's law will no longer be required. Here (Jer 31:33) as well as elsewhere (Jer 7:23; 11:4; 24:7) the prophet uses the covenant formula, that is, "I will be your/their God and you/they shall be my people," that is so reminiscent of the Exodus experience (see Exod 6:7). (It is worth nothing that the book of Baruch also catches up the Exodus motif in the prayer of the exiles: see Bar 1:19-20; 2:11, 28.)

Whereas Hosea and Jeremiah can speak of the wilderness period as the time of Israel's fidelity to YHWH, the prophet Ezekiel has a radically different understanding. In order to demonstrate that owing to the people's sinfulness the destruction of Jerusalem is inevitable, Ezekiel deflates the flimsy theology of his compatriots in exile. While that audience contends that the Exodus from Egypt is the basis for all hope Ezekiel counters that from the very beginning of its history Israel was unfaithful to YHWH. In ch. 20 he elaborates the sin-filled reality of Israel's encounter with God. The Israelites sinned by their idolatrous practices while still in Egypt (vv. 6-9). Moreover, both the first (vv. 10-17) and the second (vv. 18-26) generations of Israelites sinned against their God in the desert. Hence YHWH has no choice but to punish Israel so that they will learn the true character of this God.

In an allegorical history of Jerusalem and Samaria Ezekiel preaches that at the very moment when Israel considered itself graced, at the very moment when it took root as God's people in the Exodus, Israel was unfaithful. Both Jerusalem and Samaria became prostitutes in Egypt when they were children (Ezek 23:1-8).

Second Isaiah, the anonymous prophet of the exile, emphasizes the Exodus theme in order to provide hope for his despondent audience. The new exodus, the return of God's people from Babylon to the land of Israel, is in continuity with creation and the first Exodus (Isa 51:9-10). Indeed, it is nothing less than a triumphal procession that will manifest God's glory in the desert (Isa 40:3-5). The miracles of the first Exodus will be repeated. The desert will have rivers and fountains as well as all sorts of trees (Isa 41:17-20). The God who conquered the Egyptians at the Reed Sea now opens a way in the sea and a path in the mighty waters so that the exiles may taste victory (Isa 43:16). Whereas the pharaoh in the first Exodus proved to be obstinate and intractable, the pharaoh of this new exodus, Cyrus, will be completely amenable to God's plans (Isa 44:24-28; 45:1-6).

While there is continuity with the first Exodus, this new exodus will be a radically new event that surpasses the original event not only in wonder but also in its saving meaning. "Do not remember the former things . . . I will make a way in the wilderness and rivers in the desert" (Isa 43:18-19). (The Exodus theme also appears in Isa 35:6, a link between First and Second Isaiah, and in Isa 63:11-12, part of the message of Third Isaiah.)

New Testament

The interpreters of Jesus and his message naturally looked to the OT as both source and inspiration when they sought to develop that message for a variety of conditions in their own communities. The extent of the use of the Exodus event in the NT witnesses both to the centrality of the book and to its enduring influence. In making use of this OT work these interpreters also enriched the significance of Israel's foundational event.

Synoptics in General

In identifying John the Baptist as the voice of one crying out in the desert (Matt 3:3; Mark 1:3; Luke 3:4) Matthew, Mark, and Luke expand the scope of Second Isaiah's use of the Exodus theme (see Isa 40:3). As the forerunner of Jesus, the Baptist appears in the wilderness and announces the Coming One. This adaptation of the new exodus implies a new phase in God's dealings with humanity, suggesting the setting in motion of a unique form of liberation/deliverance.

In Jesus' dispute with the Sadducees about the resurrection (Matt 22:23-33; Mark 12:18-27; Luke 20:27-40) the synoptics have Jesus refer to the episode of the burning bush. In order to show that the resurrection involves a new type of life excluding marriage and giving in marriage Jesus cites Exod 3:6. Since God is the God of Abraham, Isaac, and Jacob, that God is necessarily the God of the living, not the dead.

The feeding of the five thousand (Matt 14:13-21; Mark 6:34-44; Luke 9:10-17) refers back to the feeding of Israel with manna in the wilderness (but see also 2 Kings 4:42-44). Around the time of Jesus there was an expectation that the miracles of the Exodus would be repeated in the messianic age. At the same time this feeding looks forward to the Eucharist and the final banquet in the reign of God (see Matt 8:11; 26:29).

Since all three synoptics (Matt 26:17; Mark 14:12; Luke 22:7) have the Last Supper as a Passover meal they seem to be interpreting Jesus' death against the background of the Exodus. Hence just as the Passover celebrates the liberation of Israel from Egyptian bondage, the death of Jesus is the Passover that brings about liberty for all of humanity. Jesus' words over the cup at the Last Supper (Matt 26:28; Mark 14:24: "This is my blood of the covenant"; Luke 22:20: "This cup is the new covenant in my blood") recall the covenant-making event on Mount Sinai when Moses sprinkles the blood of the sacrificial animals on the Israelites, saying, "See the blood of the covenant that the LORD has made with you . . ." (Exod 24:8). Jesus' gesture, therefore, evokes the twin meanings of a new liberation and a new covenant. (For Jesus and the Ten Commandments see Matt 15:4; 19:18-19; Mark 7:10; 10:19; Luke 18:20.)

Matthew

In his infancy narrative Matthew describes Herod's threat to the life of Jesus after the manner of Pharaoh's threat to the life of Moses. In Matt 2:20 the angel instructs Joseph to return to the land of Israel, noting that those who sought the life of the child are dead. This phrase is a clear borrowing from Exod 4:19 where God tells Moses to return to Egypt. Matthew's phrase in 2:13 about Herod's desire to kill Jesus recalls Exod 2:15 where Pharaoh seeks to kill Moses. Matthew's borrowing of Hos 11:1 ("Out of Egypt I called my son," Matt 2:15) shows that Jesus relives the Exodus experience of Israel.

Jesus' ascent of the mountain in the Sermon on the Mount (Matt 5:1) suggests that Jesus is a new Moses who now gives God's final revelation (compare Matt 4:2 with Exod 34:28). In any event the antitheses in Matt 5:21-48 reflect the Matthean Jesus' interpretation of the Mosaic Law. Three of these antitheses accept the Mosaic Law but extend or deepen it (vv. 21-22, 27-28, 43-44) while another three reject the Mosaic Law entirely (vv. 31-32, 33-37, 38-39). The morality expounded by the Matthean Jesus goes beyond that communicated by Moses.

Luke–Acts

In his account of the transfiguration Luke has Moses and Elijah speaking with Jesus about his *exodos* or departure (Luke 9:30-31). While some interpret this in terms of Jesus' death, others refer it to Jesus' journey to Jerusalem that will culminate in his passion, death, resurrection, and ascension. If this second view is correct Luke understands Jesus' journey after the manner of Israel's departure from Egypt. In both cases it is a question of liberation.

In Acts, Luke has Stephen give a long discourse that focuses especially on God's way with Moses and the Israelites (Acts 7:17-41, 44). Luke's purpose is to demonstrate Israel's typical disobedience in rejecting prophets like Moses as the Church breaks away from its Jewish matrix. (For a briefer summary of the Exodus event see Paul's sermon in Pisidian Antioch in Acts 13:17-18.)

John

Early in his gospel John has the Baptist refer to Jesus as the Lamb of God who takes away the sin of the world (John 1:29). While the Baptist may have conceived of Jesus as the triumphant lamb who overcomes evil in the final times, the author of John thinks of Jesus, in part at least, as the lamb of the Christian Passover whose death frees the world from sin just as the blood of the Passover animal of Exodus frees the Israelites from the destroying angel (Exod 12:7, 13, 23). This usage fits in with the chronology of the Fourth Gospel. Unlike the synoptics, John places Jesus' death on the eve of Passover, that is, at that very time when the Passover lambs are being killed in the Temple (John 19:14). At the death of Jesus, John notes that the soldiers do not break his legs (John 19:33). This fulfills the prescription in Exod 12:46, that the bones of the Passover animal are not to be broken.

Like the synoptics, John relates the feeding of the five thousand (John 6:1-15). Unlike the synoptics, John has no institution of the Eucharist at the Last Supper. Instead, the feeding of the five thousand leads into the crowd's request for a sign (John 6:25-34) and the discourse on the bread of life (John 6:35-58). The Jews introduce the Exodus theme of manna in the desert (John 6:31). Jesus responds by noting that (according to Exod 16:6-15) it was not Moses who gave the bread from heaven (John 6:32). Rather, Jesus' Father gives the true bread from heaven. In John 6:35 Jesus solemnly announces, "I am the bread of life." The nourishing heavenly bread is Jesus' revelation (John 6:35-50), but Jesus is also the bread come down from heaven (the Eucharistic dimension of the discourse in John 6:51-58).

It is also significant that the Johannine Jesus uses a phrase that is a clear link to Exodus. In John 6:35 Jesus uses one of the "I am" formulas (see also John 8:12; 10:7; 11:25). This phrase is inspired by the Greek form of Exod 3:14 where YHWH communicates the divine name to Moses. The phrase in John therefore places Jesus on a level with God.

Paul

Paul employs the Exodus motif in a variety of ways in his letters. In 1 Cor 5:7 Paul brings together the feasts of Unleavened Bread and Passover. Pressing the sense of newness in the former, Paul moves on to interpret Jesus' death as the true Passover celebration that brings life. The life of the Corinthian community should reflect this newness and integrity. In the same letter (1 Cor 10:1-13) Paul describes the privileges of Israel during the wilderness wandering, but insists that those privileges do not guarantee God's ongoing pleasure. In 2 Cor 3:7, 12-14 Paul discusses the limitations of the Mosaic covenant, referring to the divine glory reflected in Moses' face (Exod 34:29-35). Paul argues that the Israelites of

Moses' time are like the Jews of his own time in that they do not acknowledge the passing character of Moses' glory. The veil covering Moses' face still persists when Moses is read in the synagogue. In the same letter (8:15) Paul cites the manner of collecting the manna in Exod 16:18 to demonstrate the proper measure of equality that is to be observed in contributing to the Jerusalem collection. Finally, in Romans Paul elaborates the principle of divine election in dealing with the Jews. In Rom 9:15 he quotes Exod 33:19, showing that the gift of faith is linked to God's compassion. In Rom 9:17 he cites Exod 9:16, demonstrating that the choice of Moses reveals divine mercy while the punishment of Pharaoh indicates divine severity.

In Romans 7 and Galatians 4 Paul reflects on a much larger issue, that of the Jewish Law and justification through faith, not works. While acknowledging the positive dimensions of the Jewish Law, Paul goes on to state that one becomes right with God only by the power of divine grace working through Jesus Christ. In Galatians 4 Paul presents the allegory of Hagar as Sinai, equating the Sinai covenant and the Mosaic Law with slavery.

Hebrews

For the author of this book the sacrifice of Jesus has superseded the old covenant, particularly the worship of that covenant. Borrowing from the description of the sanctuary in Exodus 25–26, the author teaches that the exclusion of the people from the Holy of Holies meant that they were not able to stand in God's presence (Heb 9:7-10). However, Christ, the high priest has entered the true sanctuary of heaven through his sacrificial death and has thus won eternal redemption (Heb 9:11-14). The author also discusses the blood of the covenant making in Exod 24:3-8 to contrast it with Jesus' own unrepeatable sacrifice.

In Heb 11:24-28 the author reflects on Moses' departure from Egypt in Exod 2:11-15. Like the Messiah, Moses chooses to share in his people's sufferings. In Heb 12:18-21 the author describes that terrifying theophany on Mount Sinai in order to contrast it with the covenant in Christ that gives access to God and makes one a child of God and a member of a sanctified people who have Jesus, not Moses, as their mediator (Heb 12:22-29).

First Peter and Revelation

The author of 1 Peter cites Exod 19:6: "But you are 'a chosen race, a royal priesthood, a holy nation . . .'" (1 Pet 2:9). For this writer the prerogatives of ancient Israel are more appropriately applied to Christians. As a chosen race they enjoy divine election. As a royal priesthood they continue the priestly functions of Jesus' life culminating in his passion, death, and resurrection. As a holy nation they are reserved for God in a unique way.

In two passages (Rev 1:6; 5:10) the author of Revelation also makes use of Exod 19:6 to the effect that all those who hear and obey God's word are truly priests. According to Rev 15:3 the martyrs who have escaped Satan's oppression sing the Song of Moses (Exod 15:1-21). There is a link, therefore, between the oppression of Satan and the oppression of Pharaoh and the Egyptians. The seven bowls in Rev 16:1-21 cause a succession of catastrophes after the manner of the plagues (Exod 7:14–11:10). The second bowl that turns the sea into blood (Rev 16:3) is especially reminiscent of the first plague perpetrated against the Egyptians (Exod 7:14-24). Finally the statement "his people/their God" (Rev 21:3) calls to mind the covenant formula in Exod 6:7.

V. History of Reception

One way to provide an overview of the history of interpretation of the book of Exodus is to concentrate by and large on the central human figure in the work, Moses. The different portraits and assessments of this unique man offer something of a barometer of the different approaches, biblical and otherwise, in the long history of interpretation. In general the literal meaning of the text was not the principal concern of interpreters until modern literary critical approaches.

Early Jewish Writings

In certain apocryphal writings the figure of Moses is central. While the *Testament of Moses* (written in the second century B.C.E.) focuses on Moses' death in Deuteronomy 34 it still provides some glimpses into the earlier career of the great leader. Early in the work Moses informs Joshua that from the very beginning of the world God designated him to be the mediator of the covenant. The book of *Jubilees* (second to first century

B.C.E.) is an expanded commentary on Genesis 1–Exodus 12. Moses is the one who receives this secret revelation on Mount Sinai, basically a history of the world from the time of creation to the time of the making of the covenant on that mountain. In this work the Mosaic era becomes the standard for the messianic age.

In his effort to counter false accusations against Judaism, Philo of Alexandria (ca. 20 B.C.E.–40 C.E.) produces a superhuman portrait of the great leader in his *Life of Moses.* Moses' experiences at the Egyptian court and in Midian prepare him to be the ideal king in the arduous task of engineering the Exodus. Moses also functions as a divinely inspired prophet who makes known what reason cannot understand.

In his *Jewish Antiquities* Flavius Josephus (ca. 37–95 C.E.) writes that Pharaoh becomes alarmed at the news of the approaching birth of the Hebrew savior. That news also fills the Egyptians with enormous dread. To resolve the situation Pharaoh decides to execute all the male Hebrew children, but God appears to Amram, Moses' father, in a dream and informs him that the child about to be born will escape Pharaoh's plans and eventually deliver the Hebrews from their bondage in Egypt.

Church Fathers

In his *Homilies on Exodus* Origen (185–254), the great Alexandrian scholar, sees in Moses' outstretched arms (Exod 17:11-12) the cross of Jesus and in the defeat of the Amalekites the victory over evil. This author also reflects on Moses' acceptance of advice from Jethro (Exodus 18). He concludes that this openness provides a warrant for eliciting knowledge from non-Christians who also have access to divine truth.

In *Letter 76* Gregory Nazianzen (ca. 330–390) discusses Moses' slaying of the Egyptian in Exod 2:12. Like other Church Fathers, including Tertullian and Ambrose, Gregory interprets Moses' action in a positive way.

In his *Life of Moses* Gregory of Nyssa (ca. 335–394) offers a guide to a life of virtue by providing an ideal portrait of Moses. In Moses' actions at the Reed Sea Gregory bypasses the biblical Moses to dwell on the symbolic value of the event. The defeat of the Egyptians portrays the need to drown all one's vices in the waters of baptism. The passage of the Israelites through the water is a passage from earthly to heavenly realities.

In several places in his vast literary output Augustine (354–430) takes up the topic of Moses in Exodus. In *Against Faustus* Augustine considers the question of Moses' authority to kill the Egyptian in Exod 2:12 despite the injustice involved. He finds that in this respect Moses is like Peter who also sinned in his impulsiveness. In this same work Moses' defeat of the Amalekites in Exod 17:8-16 is seen as a precedent upholding the "just war" theory. In his *Questions on the Heptateuch* Augustine considers Moses' request in Exod 32:32 to be blotted out of God's book. For Augustine Moses' request is a rather careless one stemming from his emotional involvement.

Medieval Jewish Commentators

In his *Commentary on the Pentateuch* Saadia Gaon (882–942) discusses Moses' vision of God in Exod 33:18-23. For this Jewish scholar Moses sees an appearance of light that God creates at the very moment of passing by. In turn, in his *Commentary on the Pentateuch* Rashi (1040–1105) reflects on different qualities of Moses. Commenting on Exod 2:11, Rashi observes that Moses looks upon his fellow Hebrews with a sympathetic eye, even to the point of being willing to share in their distress. In Exod 3:1 Moses leads the flock of his father-in-law Jethro across the desert. According to Rashi, Moses does this to keep the sheep away from private property so that they will not graze in fields belonging to others.

In his *Guide for the Perplexed* Maimonides (1135–1204) takes up the traditional concern about Moses' slaying of the Egyptian in Exod 2:12. Maimonides applauds Moses' decision, opining that his possession of the first degree of prophecy moves him to perform this action. Similarly in Exod 33:21 God wishes Moses to have a degree of divine or prophetic insight, not simply a place visible to the eye as the deity passes by. In his *Commentary on the Torah* Abarbanel (1437–1508) elaborates the qualities possessed by Moses in his slaying of the Egyptian. It is clearly an act of courage in that he refuses to accept insults perpetrated against his Hebrew brothers. In his discussion of Moses' function as covenant mediator Abarbanel underlines Moses' prophetic inspiration.

Medieval Christian Theologians

In his *Commentary on Dionysius' Mystical Theology* Albert the Great (ca. 1200–1280) discusses Exod 33:23, according to which God's face is not to be seen. If this means God's face in itself without any veil, then this is nothing less than the beatific vision. However, in Albert's opinion Moses views God's face in certain signs of divine effects. In going up the mountain in the company of Aaron, Nadab, Abihu, and the seventy elders (Exod 24:1-2, 9-11) Moses experiences the pinnacle of the divine ascent, but he does not contemplate the invisible God. Rather, he sees the place where God is located. In *The Soul's Journey into God* Bonaventure (1217–1274) proposes a threefold division of that journey: (1) being led in the path of God; (2) entering into the truth of God; (3) rejoicing in the knowledge of God. He then notes that this division corresponds to the three days' journey requested by Moses in Exod 3:18. For Bonaventure, Moses' vision of God in Exod 33:18-23 is indeed a perfect seeing of God that makes Moses blessed.

In his *Summa Theologiae* Thomas Aquinas (1225–1274) teaches that the name "He Who Is" communicated to Moses in Exod 3:14 is more properly the divine name than "God" since it looks to its source, namely existence. Thomas also comments on the deaths of the entire Egyptian army in Exod 14:28 and of the three thousand Israelites in the golden calf incident in Exod 32:28. His principle is that when the whole multitude sins, vengeance must be taken on them either in respect to the whole multitude (Exod 14:28) or part of the multitude (Exod 32:28).

In his *Postillae Perpetuae* Nicholas of Lyra (ca. 1270–1349) follows the interpretation of Rashi in Exod 33:18-23, that is, that Moses does not see the divine essence since no one can see God and continue to live (Exod 33:20). This scholar also attributes the divine attack on Moses in Exod 4:24 to a sin on Moses' part in not circumcising his son.

Reformation and Post-Reformation Commentators

In his *Preface to the Old Testament* Martin Luther (1483–1546), focusing on justification through faith, not works, states that the office of Moses is to make the Israelites aware of their sinfulness and thus pave the way for redemption through Christ. In a sermon on Exod 14:9-12 Luther develops the Israelites' complaint to Moses in the crossing of the Reed Sea. God tests the people by subjecting them to pressure in which faith in God can effect the impossible.

In his *Farrago Annotationum in Exodum* Ulrich Zwingli (1484–1531) understands the divine name communicated to Moses in Exod 3:14 not merely in terms of God's being but also in terms of God's governing and ruling the world. Zwingli also sees in the battle with the Amalekites a reflection of the struggle in leading the Christian life.

In his *Commentaries on the Four Last Books of Moses* John Calvin (1509–1564) asks why Moses does not express his real reason in seeking to return to Egypt (Exod 4:18-20). He suggests that humans find it difficult to speak of God, preferring to talk with greater ease about human feelings. For Calvin, Moses' upraised hands in the battle with the Amalekites (Exod 17:11-12) provide an example of how God delegates authority to God's servants who then operate as instruments of divine power.

In his *Commentaries on Sacred Scripture* the Catholic biblicist Cornelius Lapide (1567–1637) interprets the golden calf incident to mean that not all the Israelites apostatized. He suggests that their error lies in their profession of faith, not faith itself. His reading of God's hardening of Pharaoh's heart (Exod 7:3, 9:12) focuses, not so much on the meaning of the biblical text but on a refutation of Calvin's position regarding predestination.

Modern Literary-Critical Approaches

The periods of the Renaissance and Reformation gradually led to a greater interest in the literal meaning of the biblical text. By the middle of the eighteenth century scholars began to develop the historical-critical method of interpretation that eventually concentrated on the sources or documents in the Pentateuch. At the end of the last century and the beginning of this century commentators on the book of Exodus continued to approach the text in terms of the documentary hypothesis. Examples of this approach are the commentaries on Exodus by August Dillmann (1897) and Samuel R. Driver (1911). The latter, however, pointed out the presence of deuteronomic terminology in Exodus.

A significant development in the form-critical approach came from Hugo Gressmann in his *Moses and His Time* (1913) and *The Beginnings of Israel* (1922). He showed connections between the stories of Exodus and other ancient legends and sagas. Interpreting Sinai as a truly active volcano, he suggested that its location should be sought east of the traditional site in the Sinai peninsula.

In this century the documentary hypothesis took on several nuances. In his *History of Pentateuchal Traditions* (1948) Martin Noth posited a basic document from which the Yahwist and the Elohist drew their material. With regard to P there were other views. In his *Canaanite Myth and Hebrew Epic* (1973) Frank Moore Cross did not consider P an independent narrative but a final edition of the older material concluded around the end of the Babylonian exile in the sixth century B.C.E. In an article published in English in 1977 and in other publications Rolf Rendtorff denied the existence of a continuous P narrative source and an independent J source. In Rendtorff's view P and J simply reworked different blocks of material.

In his commentary on Exodus Umberto Cassuto reacted negatively to the various forms of the documentary hypothesis. He assumed an ancient heroic poem as the principal source of the book. Exodus, according to Cassuto, is a unified work that merits consideration in its final form.

Emphasizing the life setting that preserved the basic themes of the book of Exodus, Gerhard von Rad looked to Israel's worship in *The Form-Critical Problem of the Hexateuch* (1938). Since none of Israel's "creeds" (see Deut 6:20-24; 26:5-9) referred to the covenant making on Sinai von Rad concluded that the covenant was originally independent of the deliverance from Egypt and developed separately at a later date in a central Israelite shrine. Martin Noth took a similar approach in the work mentioned above, asserting that the traditions about Moses developed as later, secondary themes. Some of the Israelite tribes preserved the Exodus theme, but it was only at a later point in time that the Exodus emerged as the nucleus of Israelite faith.

The publication of Brevard Childs's *The Book of Exodus: A Critical Theological Commentary* (1974) represented a significant new plateau in commentaries on the book of Exodus by the sheer size of the undertaking. Childs concentrated on the final shape of the text, insisting that this final form is more than the sum of its various parts. His effort is a veritable history of interpretation of the text, including NT writers as well as other Christian and Jewish exegetes. Childs has forced readers to do theological reflection on Exodus as Sacred Scripture within the context of the Christian canon.

Two other works on Exodus deserve some mention. The first is the Jewish Publication Society's commentary on Exodus by Nahum Sarna (1991). (His earlier *Exploring Exodus* in 1986 is also a significant contribution.) Sarna's control of the text and the history of exegesis is commendable. What is central in this work is the religious meaning of the text. In *Theology in Exodus: Biblical Theology in the Form of a Commentary* (1994) Donald E. Gowan developed a new approach. As the subtitle indicates, this work asks only one question of the biblical text: what does this book say about God? It is a provocative work that evaluates Scripture and tradition in the light of modern needs.

Liberation Theology

The Exodus story continues to have an impact today, especially in Latin America, the locus of liberation theology. For liberation theologians the chief task is to reread the text in a new light, that is, against the background of exploitation that has characterized so much of Latin American history. In their view the ancient story of Israel's bondage and subsequent deliverance is as timely as ever. It shows that liberation is a process, not an acquired result. It is an ongoing human concern to uncover the manipulation of fellow humans and to proffer the means of genuine human transformation.

Liberation theologians who approach the biblical text from a variety of perspectives include Paolo Freire (*Pedagogy of the Oppressed,* 1970), J. Severino Croatto (*Exodus: A Hermeneutics of Freedom,* 1981), and George V. Pixley (*On Exodus: A Liberation Perspective,* 1987). For these and other liberation theologians the Exodus story underlines the need for the emergence of ever new prophets after the manner of Moses. It points up the task of such prophets to make people aware of the real malaise from which they suffer. Such prophets, therefore, must articulate the absence of genuine freedom that modern society so heartily encourages. There are ever new pharaohs whose claims to divinity must be unmasked. At the same time these prophets are bidden to speak a word of hope. They are called upon not only to transport their people from the brickyards but also to energize them to the radical possibility of genuine existence in which misery is known as evil and hope is recognized as attainable. Moses thus transcends the limitations of the thirteenth century B.C.E. to let God's word have an ever new impact.

Feminist Approaches

The book of Exodus has not escaped the attention of feminist theologians and exegetes. In 1983 J. Cheryl Exum wrote an article on the roles of the women in Exod 1:8–2:10. She has convincingly demonstrated how all these women are central to the whole thrust of the narrative. Listening to the voice of conscience and not Pharaoh's edicts, they practice civil disobedience and thus save the life of the future liberator of Israel. Without the compassion and courage of these women the Exodus event would never have taken place.

In 1987 Rita J. Burns published her doctoral dissertation: *Has the Lord Indeed Spoken Only Through Moses?* She has shown that the seven OT texts that mention Miriam by name testify to her leadership role in the wilderness community. Exodus 15:1-21 reveals Miriam, not Moses, as the first to interpret through song and dance the religious aspect of the Exodus event. In a 1989 article Phyllis Trible developed this approach, entitling her work "Bringing Miriam Out of the Shadows."

Two other works should also be mentioned. In 1992 Drorah Setel wrote the article on the book of Exodus for *The Women's Bible Commentary.* (edited by Carol A. Newsom and Sharon H. Ringe). She has adroitly presented the significance of women in the text despite the limited number of stories highlighting the roles of females. In 1993 Athalya Brenner edited a volume entitled *A Feminist Companion to Exodus to Deuteronomy.* It is not surprising that articles on Miriam command the lion's share of this timely volume.

Exodus in the Lectionary

The book of Exodus receives a fair amount of recognition in the Church's liturgical readings. No matter how many readings are chosen for the Easter Vigil, Exod 14:15–15:1 (the crossing of the Reed Sea) must always be read. On Holy Thursday the first reading is always Exod 12:1-8, 11-14. The selections from Exodus for the three-year Sunday cycle are as follows:

"A" Cycle

- Exod 17:3-7: Third Sunday of Lent
- Exod 34:4b-6, 8-9: Trinity Sunday
- Exod 19:2-6a: Eleventh Sunday in Ordinary Time
- Exod 22:20-26: Thirtieth Sunday in Ordinary Time

"B" Cycle

- Exod 20:1-17: Third Sunday of Lent
- Exod 24:3-8: Corpus Christi
- Exod 16:2b-4, 12-15: Eighteenth Sunday in Ordinary Time

"C" Cycle

- Exod 3:1-8b, 13-15: Third Sunday of Lent
- Exod 32:7-11, 13-14: Twenty-Fourth Sunday in Ordinary Time
- Exod 17:8-13: Twenty-Ninth Sunday in Ordinary Time

Selections from the book of Exodus for the weekday lectionary (Year I) are as follows:

- Fifteenth Week: Exod 1:8-14, 22; 2:1-5a; 3:1-6, 9-12; 3:13-20; 11:10-12, 14; 12:37-42.
- Sixteenth Week: Exod 14:5-18; 14:21–15:1; 16:1-5, 9-15; 19:1-2, 9-11, 16-20b; 20:1-17; 24:3-8,
- Seventeenth Week: Exod 32:15-24, 30-34; 33:7-11; 34:5b-28; 34:29-35; 40:16-21, 34-38.
- Optional reading for the Third Week of Lent: Exod 17:1-7
- Thursday of the Fourth Week of Lent: Exod 32:7-14

SECOND READING

Israel in Egypt: 1:1–13:16

The first part of Exodus provides the background for the departure from Egypt. The final editor of the book (perhaps writing around 400 B.C.E.) has pulled together the work of his principal sources (JEP) and perhaps some independent traditions. In a spirit of fidelity to these sources and traditions this final editor has chosen not to smooth out various repetitions and inconsistencies. Nevertheless there is a flow to the narrative.

In this first part of the work the final editor seeks to provide answers to the following questions: What brought about the misery experienced by the Israelites in Egypt? What are the credentials of the leader? How does this leader respond to God's call? In what ways does the leader attempt to deal with Pharaoh? What is the final catalyst that provokes the going out? How should Israel continue to celebrate this going out?

Israel's Growth (1:1-7)

The background of this introduction is Gen 46:1-4. This passage sums up the past by referring to the patriarchs, Isaac and Jacob (Israel). One is reminded as well of the sons of Jacob and their families living as special guests in the best land of Egypt (Gen 45:17-20). This passage also anticipates the future: Israel will become a great nation in Egypt and their God will lead them out. At the same time the passage creates tension and raises a problem. What will happen to God's people when they do leave Egypt? More fundamentally, how can such a small group become a great nations?

P is the author of this passage. Genealogies and lists are a favorite device for this writer (see Gen 5:1-32; 10:10-26). Moreover, the language of v. 7 reflects P's vocabulary ("fruitful," "numerous," "filled"). It is the fulfillment of the command in Gen 1:28: "Be fruitful and multiply; and fill the earth . . . ." Against the background of the exile this passage is intended by P to offer hope and encouragement to God's despondent people. Their temptation is to disparage the Promised Land and not return from exile (see Num 14:1-3, 5-10, 26-38). In its present position this passage explains how the small group developed into such a significant number.

The Oppression of God's People (1:8-14)

This section consists of J (vv. 8-12) and P (vv. 13-14). P states in a rather straightforward manner the results of Israel's fertility, namely their reduction to the slave labor of building. While this policy is only logical for the Egyptian autocratic state (compare Gen 47:13-26) it is totally opposed to Israel's tradition of freedom. J, however, is not content to register Egypt's usual attitude. He accentuates the threat that Israel poses and the opposite results of Egyptian oppression.

J notes the changed policy of the Egyptian government. With the emergence of a new king (whom the tradition chooses to leave nameless) there is a new manner of dealing with the prolific Israelites. Thus the oppression is directly related to the political threat that such numbers imply. One can legitimately ask whether the imposition of slave labor is really calculated to achieve the reduction of the Israelite population. With a certain irony, however, J wryly observes that the Egyptian plan is counterproductive. Instead of limiting the population, the policy only succeeds in encouraging its growth.

The Suppression of God's People (1:15-22)

E is generally thought to be the author of this doublet. (A doublet entails the repetition of substantially the same account in a somewhat different form.) The author prefers "God" to J's "YHWH" and also designates the political ruler "the king of Egypt" whereas J opts for "Pharaoh." Here the manner of defeating God's people is not oppression (the slave labor of building) but suppression (the killing of all the baby boys). While suppression would appear to be more apt than oppression for the purposes of population control, it flies in the face of political expediency. Rulers are not likely to deplete their labor force and thus endanger their building programs by killing off the supply of workers. However, in this popular literature it does provide a marvelous setting for resolving the dire situation. The final editor will link E's account with J's birth of the hero in the following chapter.

This scene is a well-constructed unit that pits the anonymous king of Egypt against the named midwives (Shiphrah and Puah). The beginning and end of the scene (vv. 16, 22) reveal the king and his followers as the agents of death, while the central section (vv. 17b, 18) presents the Hebrew midwives as the agents of life. At the center stands the decisive quality that motivates the civil disobedience of the women, namely fear of God. This fear is a profound respect for the person of God that implies obedience to this God's will. It should be noted that the civil disobedience of the women (who have no little ability to outwit the shrewd king) is not without its reward. Not only does the nation continue to increase and multiply (v. 20), but so do the offspring of the two midwives (v. 21). The setting of liberation clearly involves the courageous and daring actions of women.

The Birth of the Hero (2:1-10)

There is a natural desire to know something about the birth and youth of the hero (compare the theologically oriented infancy narratives of Jesus in Matthew 1–2 and Luke 1–2). Humans seek to find extraordinary signs that stamp a person as superhuman from the moment of birth. For example, Hercules strangles a snake in his cradle. Here J accedes to the needs of his own audience.

The ancient Near East provides certain analogues. Sargon, the great Semitic king who reigned in the twenty-fourth century B.C.E., is described in a legend as follows. His mother placed him in a basket of rushes that she sealed with bitumen. She then cast him into the river upon which he floated until drawn out. There is also an adoption account in which a child is found and then given to a nurse who is paid to keep it for three years. Afterward the child is adopted and trained as a scribe. Among Egyptian myths there is the account of the goddess Isis hiding the infant Horus in a delta papyrus thicket to keep him from death at the hands of Seth.

In its present form this account is linked with E's narrative of the suppression. Once again the story focuses on the roles of women; the men are notoriously absent. Moses' mother commits civil disobedience by building the basket. The account of its construction uses the same Hebrew word that appeared in the story of Noah's ark (see Gen 6:14). The mother's action leads to the safety of the future deliverer of Israel, just as Noah's action led to the preservation of humanity. Next Moses' sister serves as the link between mother and princess. His being placed at the riverbank also tones down the harshness of the exposure. Finally, the princess shows a degree of compassion that her father's edict would seem to deny. It is owing to the action of Moses' sister that the birth mother nurses the child. It is owing to the action of the princess that Moses is raised at the Egyptian court. Without the civil disobedience of all these women Moses would have perished and the liberation of Israel would never have taken place. It is women, therefore, who control the destiny of God's people.

Moses is an Egyptian name meaning "is born." In keeping with Israelite sensitivities the name of the Egyptian god is omitted. (Compare Thutmose, that is, "the god Thut is born.") This form of Egyptian name was given to children born on the god's anniversary. There is further evidence of Moses' Egyptian background in the Egyptian names borne by members of his family (see 6:16 for Merari and 6:25 for Phinehas). It is also noteworthy that Reuel's daughters in 2:19 refer to the hero as "an Egyptian." However, apart from these notices there is no further information about Moses' background.

The Flight to Midian (2:11-22)

J, the author responsible for this episode, endeavors to show Moses as a person interested in his own people. He is bent upon foreshadowing or anticipating a problem that will appear later. This problem is the question posed by the Hebrew in v. 14: "Who made *you* a ruler and judge over us?" It is precisely this question of credentials that Moses will have to face shortly. Moses' flight to Midian also foreshadows or anticipates other events. Just as Moses has to flee to the desert, so the people of Israel will head for the desert. Just as Moses encounters God at the mountain (3:1), so the people of Israel will experience God at the mountain (19:18).

The land of Midian, Moses' home for the time being, is a desert area in the Sinai peninsula. (Some authorities, however, place Midian east of the Gulf of Aqabah or Elath in northwestern Arabia.) In later traditions (see Num 25:6-9; Judg 6:1–7:25) these desert-dwelling Midianites will become the implacable enemies of Israel. In the present tradition, however, the Midianites and those associated with Moses are related tribes. (Reuel is a tribal name, not a personal name.) Chapter 18 will show how Moses learned many practical things from these Midianites.

J presents Moses as a man with a checkered background. Although J likes stories of wells (for example, the courting of Rebecca in Gen 24:15 and Rachel in Gen 29:10) he must introduce this woman at the well, Zipporah, as a non-Israelite. Thus Moses is an Israelite of the tribe of Levi (2:1) who is brought up as an Egyptian but must then flee his Egyptian home only to meet non-Israelites, one of whom he marries. These are hardly the best credentials. Hence the lingering question: With such credentials, will Moses be able to offset the oppression/suppression in Egypt?

Exodus as Lament Liturgy (2:23-25)

This description is not merely a passing note in the overall story. The text combines the long period of time (v. 23a, probably from E) with the miserable state of the people (vv. 23b-25, a P passage). This state is presented in lament language ("groaning" and "crying"). (Note the repetition of this language in 3:7, 9; 6:5.) The verb "to cry out" is the typical expression of the poor and disenfranchised; it is a cry that God cannot ignore. Lament is linked to covenant (v. 24). In covenant theology the people's problem necessarily becomes God's problem; the people's frustration necessarily become God's frustration. Liberation always begins with the recognition of the plight of the poor.

To this point one principal actor has been conspicuously absent: God. However, in this passage the name "God" appears five times in three verses. It is interesting that Israel's theologians make no attempt to explain the reason for God's delay in dealing with the sufferings of the people in Egypt. Both God's absence and God's presence are integral components of Israelite faith.

The Burning Bush (3:1-6)

This scene is a combination of J and E, though mostly J. (E is present in parts of v 1: for example, "Horeb, the mountain of God," and v. 4b.) This combination of sources is significant theologically since it indicates the diversity and richness of Israelite tradition. No one tradition could claim an exclusive right to tell the whole story. (This combination of sources will be very evident in the rest of ch. 3.) One should note that here (v. 1) Moses' father-in-law is named Jethro, whereas in 2:18 he is Reuel. Unlike "Reuel," "Jethro" is a personal name. (For further complications see Judg 1:16; 4:11.)

J probably chooses the term "bush" (in Hebrew *səneh*) in order to connect this scene with YHWH's mountain (in Hebrew *sīnai*). The burning of the bush is thus linked to the fire of the theophany of Sinai (see 19:18). Hence there is a close association of the Exodus and Sinai from the very start. What emerges from this scene for J is the twofold dimension of awe and historical continuity. Awe is expressed in Moses' gesture of removing his sandals because of the intrinsic holiness of the encounter with YHWH: YHWH's presence sanctifies the ground. Consequently, Moses hides his face. Historical continuity is articulated in v. 6. The God who speaks to Moses has been active over the centuries in caring for this people. The God of Moses is also the God of the patriarchs (see also 3:16).

The Commissioning of Moses (3:7-15)

This scene is intimately bound up with the divine revelation at the burning bush. The experience of God is thus related to Moses' function in Israel. Israel's theologians reflect the tradition that regards Moses as a prophet. He is, therefore, one who speaks on God's behalf to the people of Israel: he is God's spokesperson (see Deut 18:15-20). Faithful to the perception of Moses' prophetic office, J and E (and also P in ch. 6) employ the literary genre of call narrative. (See other examples of this form in Judg 6:11-21; Jer 1:4-10.) The narrative is not intended to be a detailed account of what actually transpired between God and Moses, as though citing Moses' diary. Rather it attempts to communicate the meaning of God's choosing a human person for a divine mission. The call narrative builds upon the human need for signs and reassurances.

Because of the unique importance of Moses, the final editor has retained all three call narratives with their similarities of form and differences of detail. The J and E texts he has interwoven here so that they can be heard as a two-part harmony in which sometimes J carries the melody and at other times E. We must read them in the biblical text as they stand together, but it is helpful to hear them separately as well. The basic structure is the same: (a) divine response to prayer that presupposes a given difficulty: 3:7 (J), 3:9 (E); (b) God's promise to save: 3:8 (J), 3:10 (E); (c) the commission: 3:16-17 (J), 3:10 (E); (d) Moses' objection: 4:1 (J), 3:11 (E); (e) overcoming the objection by a sign: 4:1-9 (J); 3:12 (E); (f) second objection: 4:10 (J), 3:13 (E);

(g) God's final or quasi-final answer: 4:13-16 (J), 3:14-15 (E), 4:17 (E?).

Both J (3:7) and E (3:9) begin by noting the plight of the people in lamentation language ("cry"). In developing the divine promise to save, J and E stress different dimensions of Moses' office. In 3:8 (J) YHWH is the one who intends to deliver the Israelites, while Moses in 3:16 (J) is dispatched to speak to the people. In 3:10 (E) Moses is sent specifically to bring the Israelites out of Egypt. Although the verb "to send" (vv. 10, 12, 13) designates the prophet as an envoy (see Jer 1:7; 26:12, 15) E appears to allot a much more substantial role to Moses. It is also interesting to note that E's phrase in 3:12 ("I will be with you") is elsewhere employed when the person commissioned faces peril or a task involving great risk of failure (see Jer 1:8, 19; 15:20; 20:11).

J emphasizes not only Israel's deliverance from the Egyptians but also the goal of that intervention: entrance into the Promised Land. "A land flowing with milk and honey" (3:8) is a stock expression that seems to refer to the raising of livestock and beekeeping, staple economies of the central hills of Israel. The reference to the Canaanites, Hittites, and others (vv. 8, 17) is to the pre-Israelite inhabitants of the land (for a seven-people enumeration see Deut 7:1). The Exodus, therefore, is not only a going out; it is also a going up, into the land formerly inhabited by these nations.

The proofs demanded by Moses in the E tradition are significant. In v. 12 the sign to provide credentials for Moses before Pharaoh and Israel is that the people will later meet to worship God on this very mountain. This is in keeping with the Elohist's concern for cult and cultic places. The sign, in this case, is a sign for Israelites contemporaneous with the Elohist as well as for the Israelites with Moses in the desert.

Moses still needs further proof for approaching the Israelites (v. 13). In the E tradition this proof is the disclosure of the divine name (vv. 14-15). It should be pointed out that for J this disclosure of the name YHWH demands no special scene. From the very beginning of his narrative (Gen 2:4b) J uses the personal name YHWH and from Gen 4:26 onward presumes that this name is known by humans. Up to this scene in ch. 3, E has simply employed the general term "God." As one might suspect, this scene is theologically central in E's scheme of things. (For P's use of divine names see 6:2.)

For Israel as well as for the ancient Near East names imply real existence. Something is a reality when one knows its name. The name implies a dimension of intimacy. By knowing someone's name one is on personal terms with that person. When one comes to the personal name of the God of Israel, however, there are two distinct issues.

The first issue is the etymology of YHWH. (The Hebrew text supplies only the four consonants: יהוה = YHWH.) The addition of the vowels "a" and "e" is already an attempt at interpretation.) The solutions to this etymological problem are legion and no one suggestion commands the field. A popular view is that the word means "he causes to be," hence "he creates." The second issue is the meaning that the author of the passage (E) intends. Here one stands on firmer ground, the context itself.

Verse 15 ("YHWH . . . has sent . . .") is the real answer to v. 13, since it provides the name Moses asks for. Verse 14 ("I am who am," that is, the name YHWH transposed into the first person) explains the name in terms of being: YHWH's being means active participation and involvement as well as free choice and unimpeded power. According to v. 10 the name means leading the people out of Egypt; according to v. 12 it means assisting Moses. Verse 14b ("I AM sent me to you") links v. 13 ("The God of your fathers has sent me") to v. 15 ("YHWH . . . has sent me"). YHWH is committed to act on behalf of the people.

Expansion of the Commission (3:16-22)

In this section from J, Moses is first commissioned to assemble the elders (v. 16), that is, the holders of political power in a tribal society. Moses is then directed to communicate the divine displeasure with the oppression of the Israelites. This commission is then expanded in vv. 18-22. Not only Moses but also the elders are to approach Pharaoh (v. 18). This expansion is not a useless appendage. The author is preparing the reader for a twofold notion of exodus: an exodus-flight and an exodus-expulsion. In v. 19 Pharaoh will not permit the people to go unless he is constrained; hence the people will be forced to flee. In vv. 21-22 YHWH will make the Egyptians well disposed toward the Israelites.

Indeed, the Israelite women will even receive gifts of jewelry and clothing. YHWH will so arrange matters that the Israelites will finally be expelled (see 12:35-36).

Moses' Objection and Subsequent Signs (4:1-9)

Like E in 3:11-12, J has his tradition of objection (v. 1) and signs (vv. 2-9). Signs are needed in order that Moses may authenticate himself to his people and thus substantiate his claims. The signs provided are a staff or type of magic wand (vv. 2-4) and a leprous sleight of hand (vv. 6-8). (The leprosy in this passage is not true leprosy. However, in the Bible leprosy is often seen as a sign from God of some fault or sin: see Miriam in Num 12:9-15.) It is interesting to note that P will later use the J rod-turned-serpent tradition in a different context (7:9-12). In any event, the signs mentioned are subsequently successful (4:31) and establish Moses' right to speak on behalf of YHWH.

More Objections, Replies, and Signs (4:10-17)

J heightens the enormity of the task given Moses by formulating a second objection. Moses now maintains that he does not possess the wherewithal for public relations because he really cannot communicate (v. 10). YHWH's reply focuses on divine omnipotence (v. 11). YHWH promises to provide two things: (a) help in oral delivery and (b) assistance with content (v. 12). These concessions notwithstanding, J's call narrative continues with a final effort on Moses' part to evade his vocation and a final reassurance on YHWH's part to support the wavering candidate. There is a certain audacity here, but an audacity consonant with the human penchant for escaping responsibility and passing it on to someone else (v. 13). YHWH's reaction is anger but, surprisingly, the anger is quickly suppressed so that Aaron becomes Moses' prophet (vv. 14-15). Thus Moses is to function after the manner of YHWH, and Aaron will be the divine spokesperson (v. 16; see Deut 18:18; Jer 1:9).

Concerning the staff (v. 17) one is naturally disposed to think of the J tradition in vv. 2-4 where the staff is *a* sign given to Moses to authenticate his mission and dispose the people to accept him. Here, however, the staff is linked to *signs.*

In this passage Aaron is called the Levite. This title anticipates Aaron's role as the ancestor of the levitical priests who presided in Jerusalem. Just as it is their obligation to hand on the Mosaic law (see Lev 10:11), so it is the responsibility of their ancestor to transmit the words of Moses.

Moses' Return to Egypt (4:18-23)

With the exception of vv. 18 and 20b this passage is from J. According to E, Moses makes the return trip to Egypt by himself (v. 18; see 18:5), but according to J, Moses makes this journey in the company of his wife and children (v. 20a). (The presence of Moses' wife and children will be important for the circumcision rite in vv. 24-27.) In view of Pharaoh's reluctance to let Israel go (the exodus-flight tradition) J has Moses exercise the office of prophet in vv. 22-23: (a) commission ("Thus you shall say to Pharaoh"); (b) messenger formulary ("Thus says YHWH"); (c) message ("Israel is my firstborn son"). Pharaoh's refusal to heed the prophetic word anticipates the death of the firstborn in the tenth plague (see 11:5).

The Circumcision (4:24-26)

This J scene, where YHWH tries to kill Moses, seems linked to the J story of Gen 32:24-32, where Jacob wrestles with YHWH. In both cases YHWH suddenly appears in the night as a threatening demonic power. Jacob is on his way to the land of promise, but he must first confront his hostile brother Esau. Moses, too, has received a promise, but he must first confront the hostile Pharaoh.

Zipporah is like Moses' mother and sister in that she saves her husband from death by quick and deliberate action. She thwarts the divine attack by carrying out a threefold ritual. She cuts off her son's foreskin, touches his feet (probably a reference to the genitals), and pronounces the words: "Truly you are a bridegroom of blood to me." The very fact that the author attempts to unravel this expression in v. 26b implies that its meaning was already unclear at the time of composition. The blood-smearing in this circumcision rite is like the Israelites' smearing of blood on their doorposts when the tenth plague threatens the life of their firstborn (12:12-13). Hence this scene looks to the tenth and final plague (12:29-32) and to the redemption of the Israelite firstborn (13:1-2, 11-16).

Meeting Between Moses and Aaron (4:27-31)

Aaron is a somewhat enigmatic character, yet this early tradition (J) seems constrained to associate him with Moses. In v. 30 it is Aaron who performs the signs, but according to the J tradition in 4:2-9 it is Moses who is to perform them. Nonetheless, the outcome is positive. In v. 31 the people are convinced and, rejoicing, they bow down and worship. J, however, feels compelled to express their fickleness or lack of real faith, for in the following scene the people will grumble. For J the people genuinely believe in YHWH and his servant Moses only in the aftermath of the Reed Sea event (see 14:31).

First Audience with Pharaoh (5:1–6:1)

Now that the Israelites have heard and accepted YHWH's message as presented by Moses and Aaron, it is time to have the leaders approach Pharaoh with a view to negotiating their release from Egypt. This well-constructed J story consists of six scenes. With one exception each scene opens with a verb of action.

The first scene (5:1-5) begins with the report that Moses and Aaron *went.* Verse 2 poses a question that the rest of the story will develop: Who is YHWH? The three-day journey into the desert is probably connected with the exodus-flight tradition. According to the tradition preserved in chs. 15–19 there are only three days or camps between Egypt and Sinai (15:27; 16:1; 17:1; 19:2). This scene provides a realistic attitude toward a labor force: one should prevent the slaves from getting away and so keep them at their work. Such an attitude rejects E's view of a suppression in 1:15-22.

The second scene (5:6-9) has Pharaoh speaking to the Egyptian taskmasters and the Hebrew foremen. (This deployment of foreign labor, whereby the taskmasters are Egyptian and the foremen members of the subject people, is historically accurate.) Unlike the rest of the scenes, here there is no verb of action, since one cannot expect the divine Pharaoh to go out to his underlings. The bricks in question are adobe: unburnt bricks dried in the sun.

The third scene (5:10-14) begins with a verb of action ("So the taskmasters . . . *went out*") and brings together the taskmasters, the foremen, and the people. The people are forced to look for straw while the foremen are flogged because the people cannot produce.

The fourth scene (5:15-19) has the Hebrew foremen before Pharaoh. Popular literature permits, indeed demands at times the interaction of the Pharaoh (who was a god in Egyptian belief) with such underlings, in this case the depressed foremen. Once again the scene opens with a verb of action ("Then the Israelite foremen came"). However, the outcome of the meeting is less than what the foremen hope for. The quota must remain the same, but still no straw!

The fifth scene (5:20-21) focuses on the foremen and Moses and Aaron. Once again there is a verb of action whereby the foremen bump into the two leaders ("they came upon . . ."). The less than accidental encounter does not augur well for the two leaders. They are the recipients of nothing less than a curse: "May YHWH look upon you and judge!" The start of Moses' grandiose plan is hardly auspicious: the future looks dismal indeed.

The sixth scene (5:22–6:1) has Moses appealing to YHWH. The verb of action is also present ("Moses turned again"). The scene depicts a discouraged Moses, indeed a typical Moses, who will not cease to badger YHWH with his complaints. One is hardly surprised, therefore, that he is hesitant about accepting his office. In any case Moses learns that YHWH will intervene dramatically. The reader is naturally awaiting the first plague. However, the editor chooses to review the call of Moses, taking it this time from the P source.

P's Commissioning of Moses (6:2-13)

In response to the people's lament in 2:23b-25 and in light of the setbacks in 5:1–6:1 the call of the prophet is the guarantee of support for God's chosen one and, at the same time, the overcoming of oppression/depression for God's chosen people. For P it is a question of both continuity and discontinuity. The God who speaks to Moses is the same God who appeared to the patriarchs. However, there is a difference: that God did not reveal the personal name YHWH to them. Instead, the deity employed the name "El Shaddai." (This is translated in a variety of ways, including "God the Almighty," "God of the mountain," "God of the steppe," "God of the breasts," etcetera. Some see El Shaddai as a member of a certain group of mountain gods or perhaps the presiding god of the assembly of mountain gods.) Unlike 3:14-15, this passage (see vv. 6-8) does not entail a personal honor for Moses that provides credentials. It is a special communication that looks to alleviating Israel's pain. For P there is only one covenant in question, the one made with Abraham in Genesis 17. This scene, therefore, creates tension between the ancient promise and the present lack of fulfillment. That lack will now be addressed.

For the commissioning of Moses P adopts the same basic call narrative as J and E: (a) divine response to prayer (v. 5); (b) God's promise to save (vv. 6-8); (c) the commission (vv. 9-11: the commission to the people is only alluded to); (d) Moses' objection (v. 12, repeated in v. 30); (e) overcoming the objection (7:1-5).

Verses 6-8 are an oracle of salvation, a literary genre at home especially in the prophetic literature of the sixth century B.C.E., the era in which the P source was written. Such an oracle provides hope and lays a new foundation for Israel's faith. It shows that the God who judges is also the God who delivers. More important, this bestowal of grace is not bound up with the success of institutions in the past. Paradoxically, Israel's lack of success cannot defeat God.

The expression "I am YHWH" is typical of P. This is royal style such as is used at the beginning of royal inscriptions. It was taken over and used as a self-introduction in liturgy (see 20:2). It suggests: "I am here, present and acting." It is a formula that calls for responsive action on Israel's part. (See the Holiness Code in Leviticus 17–26, for example at 19:4.)

Genealogy of Moses and Aaron (6:14-30)

P has interrupted the account of Moses' commissioning to insert this genealogy. (An indication of the insertion is the repetition after the insertion of the last line before the insertion: see vv. 13 and 26-27.) Although some tend to find genealogies rather boring and hence skip over them, one should observe their usefulness. They represent a form of survival: the tribe, for example, takes care of all its members. They provide identity: they tell a person who he or she is. They indicate status: for example, they inform kings and queens about their lineage. They structure history: they are the parameters of human and/or divine activity.

Here it is clear that P is really interested in the tribe of Levi. He rushes past Reuben and Simeon to get to Levi (vv. 14-15: all three were Leah tribes according to Gen 29:31-34). Both Moses and Aaron are sons of Amram (v. 20) and ultimately descendants of Levi. Although P makes Miriam the sister of both Moses and Aaron (v. 20), Exod 15:20 makes her the sister only of Aaron.

Originally "Levite" was a secular name meaning "member of the tribe of Levi." Only at the end of a long process was it changed into a designation for a somewhat lowly person who performs menial cultic tasks (see 28:1-43). By emphasizing Aaron P intends to establish a claim for the legitimacy of the group of priests that ultimately controlled the Temple in Jerusalem. (P has passed over other ancient priestly families such as the Mushites mentioned in v. 19.) For P, therefore, this genealogy has served to provide identity and undergird the status of Aaron's descendants.

Reassurance and Compliance (7:1-7)

In answer to Moses' objection about his speaking abilities (6:12, 30) P has YHWH reassure Moses that he will have a quasi-divine function. The outcome of divine intervention will be that YHWH will actually lead Israel out of Egypt (vv. 4-5). However, Egyptian recognition of YHWH is required. The rescue must be staged in such a fashion that it will demonstrate the power of Israel's God.

The literal translation of the beginning of v. 3 is "but I will harden Pharaoh's heart." For the biblical writers the heart is the organ of thinking and willing (see Isa 6:10; 29:13); use of this word focuses on the person as a thinking and willing subject. It should be noted that Exodus employs three different ways of expressing the hardening of Pharaoh's heart: (a) Pharaoh's heart was hardened (7:13, 14, 22; 9:7, 35); (b) Pharaoh hardened his (own) heart (8:15, 32[11, 28]); (c) YHWH hardened Pharaoh's heart (7:3; 9:12; 10:1, 20, 27). Exodus, therefore, admits both human freedom and divine omnipotence. Like the rest of the Bible, Exodus attempts no solution to the philosophical problem of reconciling human freedom with divine power.

Besides noting the compliance of Moses and Aaron in v. 6, P goes on to record the ages of the two leaders. According to P's chronological interests age indicates a milestone in one's journey through life. After the forty year wandering P later mentions that Moses dies at the age of 120 (see Deut 34:7).

Introduction to the Plagues (7:8-13)

In this scene P mentions the first demonstration of YHWH's power before Pharaoh, since for him this is the first meeting between Pharaoh and YHWH's emissaries (for J see 5:1–6:1). As noted earlier, P has changed Moses' staff from an authenticating instrument before the people (see J in 4:2-4) to a permission-seeking device before Pharaoh. Not surprisingly, Aaron has a key role to play. As YHWH has foretold (7:4), Pharaoh refuses to comply despite Aaron's serpent-consuming staff.

This introductory scene should serve as a guide of sorts in approaching the plagues. A staff turned into a serpent and a river changed to blood are indications of the world of folklore, not of scientific explanations. Nonetheless interpreters have sought a so-called natural explanation of the phenomena. According to the *cosmic* interpretation a comet made contact with the earth, bringing in its wake red dust, small meteorites, earthquakes, etcetera. According to the *geological* explanation a violent eruption of a volcano in the fifteenth century B.C.E. caused a tidal wave, the aftereffects of which brought about the plagues. According to a third view there was a natural succession of catastrophes beginning with an exceptionally large flooding of the Nile in July and August and culminating with a sirocco in March or April that killed off the remaining first fruits, not the firstborn. Ultimately, however, one must conclude that the biblical writers have only an imperfect knowledge of Egyptian matters. For example, locusts (the eighth plague) are known both in Egypt and Israel. However, the red Nile (the first plague) and frogs (the second plague) are known only in Egypt, while hail (the seventh plague) is exceptional in Egypt but not in Israel.

The biblical account itself contains doublets and inconsistencies, thus precluding a scientific exposition and suggesting a popular-literature approach. Thus the fourth plague (flies) is a doublet of the third plague (gnats). Similarly the sixth plague (boils, an epidemic affecting livestock and humans) is a doublet of the fifth plague (pestilence, that is, a livestock epidemic). With regard to consistency, one may raise some questions. If all the livestock are killed in the fifth plague (9:6), how can they be affected by boils in the sixth plague (9:10), hail in the seventh plague (9:25), and death of the firstborn in the tenth plague (12:29)? If frogs already cover the land of Egypt (8:6[2]), how can the magicians repeat the feat (8:7[3])?

Before moving on to the question of the literary arrangement of the plagues one should note that the presence of E is doubtful in these accounts. Hence one speaks more cautiously of JE, a combination of the Pentateuch's earliest sources without further distinction. As for distribution, there are five plagues from JE alone (the fourth, fifth, seventh, eighth, and ninth), two from P alone (the third and sixth), and three from a combination of JE and P (the first, second, and tenth).

The differences between JE and P touch on several points. With regard to roles, JE has Moses appear simply as a prophet whereas P has Aaron play the principal part, so that Moses is upstaged. Concerning formulae, JE has Moses employ the messenger formula while P has YHWH speaking to Moses, who then speaks to Aaron. Finally in terms of character, for JE the plagues are genuine afflictions to chastise Pharaoh for refusing to let the people go. For P, however, they are signs and wonders that legitimate Moses and Aaron as representatives of YHWH, not scourges as such. (Compare the P plague of gnats in 8:16-19[12-15] with the JE plague of flies in 8:20-32[16-28]).

The presence of the different biblical traditions raises some further questions: How does the final editor put everything together? Does this editor hope to attain something concrete, and if so, what indications are there? In seeking to answer these questions one must keep two points in mind. First, the plague account really begins in 7:8-13 because this scene contains the same outlook and vocabulary as the plagues themselves. Second, the tenth plague (the death of the firstborn) is excluded here since its makeup and literary characteristics are different.

The result is that there are ten episodes: the introduction in 7:8-13 and the nine plagues in 7:14–10:29. Moreover, they are arranged concentrically so that the introduction, the first plague, the second plague, etcetera, have counterparts of approximately the same length and with the same formula in the ninth plague, the eighth plague, etcetera. (Compare 8:16-19[12-15] with 9:8-12.) This concentric arrangement is not haphazard. It is intentionally designed to indicate definite progress as one reads the remainder of the story.

The plague account is not so much a series of devastations as it is a series of disputes between Pharaoh and Moses linked to the question in 5:2: "Who is YHWH, that I should heed him and let Israel go?" The failure of Moses and Aaron in these dealings with Pharaoh is not decisive since the story continues in the Reed Sea account. These dealings or plagues look to an even greater wonder at the sea.

First Plague: Water Turned into Blood (7:14-25)

Here there is a combination of JE (vv. 14-18, 20b-21a, 23-25) and P (vv. 19-20, 21b-22). According to JE it is the Nile, *the* river, that will be affected. Moreover, JE makes reference to the general death of the fish and the subsequent pollution. According to P, however, the waters of all Egypt are affected (v. 19), not just the Nile.

In terms of progress one must note that the Egyptian magicians are able to match the feat performed by God's emissaries (v. 22). With regard to Pharaoh, the recognition demanded of him is relatively simple: "By this you shall know that I am YHWH" (v. 17). As the plague account continues there will be significant differences on both scores.

Second Plague: The Frogs (8:1-15)

Both JE (8:1-4; 8:8-13a) and P (8:5-7, 15b) are unmistakably present in this account. As with the first plague, this episode reveals that the Egyptian magicians are still able to match the feats performed by Moses and Aaron (8:7). However, there are some differences. Now Pharaoh actively seeks out the intercession of Moses (8:8), although he remains adamant in the end (8:15). Besides, the recognition now demanded of Pharaoh is more embracing than in 7:17: "So that you may know that there is no one like YHWH, our God" (8:10).

Third Plague: The Gnats (8:20-32)

In this account, which is solely from P, there is clear evidence of progress. Unlike the first two plagues, this is one the Egyptian magicians are incapable of reproducing. In the magicians' report to Pharaoh there is the further observation: "This is the finger of God" (v. 19). However, as YHWH has predicted, Pharaoh chooses not to let Israel go.

Fourth Plague: The Flies (8:2-32)

This passage from JE seems to presuppose that the Egyptians are not very remote from the Israelites, since the former would be able to view the sacrifices offered by the latter (v. 26). This note is somewhat surprising since the author claims a distinction for the Israelites, namely that the plague will not affect the land of Goshen (v. 22). Hence the Egyptians and the Israelites do not live side by side. In any event the animal sacrifices of the Israelites would upset the religious sensitivities of the Egyptians. Perhaps this is because animals had a conspicuous place in Egyptian religion or because the sacrifice of whole animals was not the usual practice among them. What is significant here is, first of all, the required acknowledgment by Pharaoh that "I, YHWH, am in this land" (v. 22). Thus Pharaoh is to admit that YHWH is present in Egypt. Second, the permission for the three-day trip is for a point in the desert that is not too far away (v. 28). Once again Moses is to pray on behalf of the mighty ruler of Egypt. Clearly there is development in Pharaoh's character.

Fifth Plague: The Pestilence (9:1-7)

In this JE account one must observe that there is no negotiation between Pharaoh and Moses after the start of the plague, as in 8:25. However, in keeping with the preceding plague, there is a distinction between the Egyptians and the Israelites. The pestilence will strike Egyptian, not Israelite livestock. One can see that in this account Pharaoh takes pains to be assured that the distinction really exists (see vv. 6b-7a).

Sixth Plague: The Boils (9:8-12)

In this P account it is somewhat astonishing that Aaron plays a relatively minor role, that of Moses' assistant. In terms of development, what emerges is the downward spiral of the magicians. Although they were able to match the first two plagues they were unsuccessful in the third and were forced to admit the work as God's doing. Here the magicians are singled out for their lack of uniqueness. They too suffer from the skin disease and are unable to stand in Moses' presence (v. 11).

Seventh Plague: The Hail (9:13-35)

In this JE account there is an explanation given for the failure of the previous plagues to induce Pharaoh to relent. YHWH has acted this way to show power and to make that name resound throughout the earth (v. 16). One almost expects YHWH's final and decisive act here and now. While even this plague does not bring Pharaoh to grant the necessary permission to leave, it does contribute to the unfolding character of the divine ruler of Egypt. There is the notice in v. 14 that Pharaoh (as well as his subjects) is to confess that there is no one like YHWH anywhere on the earth. This is followed in v. 27 by the *mea culpa* of Pharaoh: "This time I have sinned; YHWH is in the right, and I and my people are in the wrong." This is truly a remarkable confession. Finally there is the statement that the plague of hail will induce an even greater confession, namely, that the earth is YHWH's (v. 29). The God of Israel is receiving a more fitting recognition from the mighty Egyptian god, Pharaoh himself.

Eighth Plague: The Locusts (10:1-20)

This JE account opens with an explanation of the hardness of heart of Pharaoh and his servants. This obduracy is calculated to demonstrate YHWH's might and to provide an ongoing tradition about those exploits in the Israelite community (vv. 1-2). The author makes special mention of Moses' actual going to Pharaoh and dwells on YHWH's vexation: "How long will you refuse to humble yourself before me?" (v. 3b). For the first time one learns that Pharaoh's servants are becoming exasperated to the point of urging their king to exercise restraint and be reasonable (v. 7). The result of this intervention is that Moses and Aaron are recalled to Pharaoh's court (v. 8). In this scene the author points out Pharaoh's suspicion that a conspiracy of sorts is underway, since Moses petitions for the whole Israelite community to take part in the desert worship (vv. 10-11).

The progress in depicting Pharaoh's change of character is clear in vv. 16-17. After the speedy summons there is the clear protestation of sin: "I have sinned against YHWH your God, and against you." Thus Pharaoh has advanced in his awareness of YHWH's presence and power from the time of the first plague. After the customary request for forgiveness and the successful outcome of that request there is nonetheless the concluding remark that Pharaoh remains adamant and so the people remain in Egypt.

Ninth Plague: The Darkness (10:21-29)

Many connect this darkness with a typical Near Eastern phenomenon, the *khamsin.* This is a hot wind that blows off the desert in March and April, bringing darkness and a very oppressive atmosphere in its wake. In the biblical account such darkness takes on a more foreboding character inasmuch as it suggests the evil powers of chaos. Such a character matches the tenor of this JE account. There is exasperation leading to the breaking off of any further negotiations (v. 28). Pharaoh is now willing to let all Israel leave for purposes of worship (contrast 10:11), but not the livestock (v. 24). Moses reacts to such permission rather ironically by pointing out that animal sacrifices are a part of Israel's worship and hence required. However, since the sacrificial animals can be determined only upon arrival at the place of worship it is necessary to bring all the livestock along. Pharaoh's response to Moses' ironic request is the cessation of all further negotiations. An impasse has been reached, one that will result in Moses' death if he should attempt to appear again before Pharaoh. A new way must be found to force Pharaoh's hand.

Tenth Plague: The Death of the Firstborn (11:1-10)

Given Moses' seemingly final appearance before Pharaoh, the reader expects a quick dash to the sea and then the trek in the desert. In other words, the writers up to this point have created suspense and the reader naturally anticipates the release of tension and denouement. Instead there is another (and final) plague, the character of which is completely different from that of the previous nine. (Actually the scene at the Reed Sea does not presuppose the tenth plague.) The reader now becomes bogged down not in a Sea of Reeds, but in a whirlpool of rubrics. There is the sudden command to prepare for liturgy, not the expected bolt for freedom. Presumably the biblical writers have a reason for the temporary demise of narrative and exaltation of liturgy.

The death of the firstborn does not come as a total surprise. In 4:23 YHWH addressed Pharaoh through Moses in these terms: "I said to you, 'Let my son go that he may worship me.' But you refused to let him go; now I will kill your firstborn son." Neither does the plundering of the Egyptians come as a complete surprise. In 3:21-22 the Israelites were assured that they would not leave Egypt empty-handed. However, 11:1-3 (either J or E), belonging to the exodus-expulsion tradition, assumes that this tenth plague is really the one and only plague. How else can the Israelites get silver and gold ornaments and clothing from the Egyptians? How else can one explain Moses' prestige with Pharaoh's servants and Egypt as a whole?

The literary arrangement of vv. 4-8 (from J; vv. 9-10 are from P) suggests that this plague is not linked to the previous nine. J usually informs the reader that Moses is to speak to Pharaoh but in v. 4 it is not clear to whom Moses delivers the divine message. Until v. 6 the recipient seems to be Israel, but in vv. 7-8 Pharaoh is addressed. At the end of v. 8 Moses leaves Pharaoh's presence in a rage, but according to 10:29 (JE) he was never again to appear before Pharaoh. Although some posit a historical link —an epidemic that struck the Egyptians and hence facilitated the departure of the Israelites —it is not unreasonable to conclude that the tenth plague has been contrived to connect with the feast of Passover.

The Passover Ritual (12:1-20)

In this rubrical section P provides details for a feast that was already old among semi-nomadic shepherds of the ancient Near East, an offering for the welfare of the flocks when the tribe set out to search for new pasture grounds. This was in the spring and indeed at a very critical time in the life of the flock, when the young of the sheep and the goats would be born. The antiquity of the feast is evident from the fact that there are no priests, no sanctuaries, and no altars.

Other details fit a pastoral context. The animal is roasted, not boiled (v. 9) since cooking utensils are at a minimum. Perhaps this explains why the bones are not broken (vv. 9, 46). The time is the twilight of the first full moon (v. 6). This coincides with the return of the shepherds to the camp on the brightest night of the month. The unleavened bread (v. 8) is the ordinary bread eaten by such shepherds, and the bitter herbs (v. 8) are the desert plants used by these shepherds for spices. The clothing and attire suit this background: "your loins girded, your sandals on your feet, and your staff in your hand, . . ." (v. 11). The blood rite (v. 7) is apotropaic in purpose. The smearing of the blood on the tent poles is intended to ward off all danger to the members of the tribe and especially to the young about to be born. This danger is personified in "the destroyer" (v. 23) who is prevented by the blood from striking humans and animals.

It is the blood rite that establishes the link between the tenth plague and the Passover. "The destroyer" is now given a new interpretation arising from Israel's history. YHWH will go through the land of Egypt striking down the firstborn of both humans and beasts (v. 12), but when YHWH sees the blood on the houses "the destroyer" will not be permitted to strike. Rather YHWH will "pass over" (v. 13).

While the etymology of "passover" is far from clear, the meaning of the term for Israel is abundantly evident. "To pass over" means "to spare, protect, deliver." What Israel does, therefore, is to interpret the ancient feast of semi-nomadic shepherds in terms of its own relationship with YHWH. The journey to be undertaken is no longer the quest for a temporary pasture but for the final pasture, the Promised Land itself. The ancient feast with its focus on change lends itself admirably to interpreting the change in Israel's destiny. The shepherds are now a people in flight (v. 11). (For the unleavened bread see 13:3-10.)

Promulgation of the Passover (12:21-28)

In this J passage (with the exception of P in v. 28) Moses approaches the elders, those leaders responsible for carrying out YHWH's command. Here the emphasis is principally on the blood rite. Hand in hand with the sprinkling is the prohibition against going outdoors until morning (v. 22) because of the nocturnal devastation.

The rubrics in vv. 24-27a are significant for Israel's abhorrence of any and every form of generation gap. Those taking part in the original Exodus and all subsequent Israelite communities are linked together in this pivotal experience. The question asked by the children in v. 26 is not one of mere historical interest. It is a contrived question designed to interpret the past in view of the present. To be sure, YHWH spares the Israelites but crushes the Egyptians, but the happenings of the thirteenth century B.C.E. affect the present community: "When he struck down the Egyptians [YHWH] spared *our* houses" (v. 27a). To celebrate the Passover means to span generations and coalesce in an experience explaining and unifying the entire people.

Death of the Firstborn and Departure (12:29-39)

J, the author of these vv., follows up the exodus-expulsion tradition of 11:1-3. The death of the firstborn has been so calamitous that Pharaoh summons Moses and Aaron at night (v. 31). There is no longer any hesitancy about allowing the livestock to go along (v. 32; see 10:24). Indeed, the devastation has been so severe that the Egyptians urge the Israelites to advance their timetable. The haste in this departure is reflected in the condition of the bread. The Israelites are so rushed that their dough is not leavened (v. 34); consequently they have to be satisfied with unleavened loaves (v. 39). (In 12:15 P gave no reason why the people would eat such bread for seven days.) Finally, in keeping with the exodus-expulsion traditions the Israelites ask the Egyptians for silver and gold articles as well as clothing, but in fact the despoiling goes far beyond such limitation. The Israelites ultimately get from the Egyptians whatever they want (v. 36).

J mentions the first destination and the number of people involved. Succoth lies thirty-two miles southeast of Raamses and is approximately in the middle of the isthmus between the Mediterranean Sea and the Gulf of Suez. J sets down the number as "about six hundred thousand men on foot, not counting the children" (v. 37). This would imply a population of some three million men, women, and children. While it is probable that the Hebrew word for "thousand" originally meant a subsection of a tribe and hence a total of five thousand or six thousand, the epic nature of this popular literature emphasizes the larger number. "A mixed crowd" (that is, a crowd of mixed ancestry) (v. 38) suggests that non-Israelite elements of the slave labor force also depart Egypt in the company of Moses.

Chronology and Further Passover Regulations (12:40-51)

In vv. 40-41 P reveals his penchant for chronology. He calculates the sojourn of the Israelites in Egypt as a period of four hundred thirty years (see Gen 15:13). The complexity of the biblical data, however, demands greater precision. In view of such data this sojourn is not necessarily continuous, made by the same group, and comprising the entire people. From a theological viewpoint P reveals a God absorbed in the real life of Israel. YHWH acts at a precise moment in time. Consequently YHWH's keeping vigil at that moment must be reflected in Israel's keeping vigil on this occasion each year.

P also provides additional Passover regulations relating chiefly to admission to the Passover celebration. (Such regulations presuppose a setting in which Israel is already leading an agricultural existence in the Promised Land.) Transient aliens (v. 45) and hired servants (v. 45) are excluded; their existence in the land is not so firmly rooted. Resident aliens (v. 48) and permanent slaves (v. 44) may take part in the celebration, provided the males have been circumcised (see Gen 17:13). The exodus celebration is further depicted as a domestic one (v. 46) that "the whole congregation of Israel" (v. 47) is to keep. This is a favorite P expression stressing the organization of Israel, especially in the desert, and emphasizing those responsible for this organization.

Redemption of the Firstborn (13:1-2, 11-16)

It is interesting to note that this tradition is not attached to the Passover account itself but to the deaths of the firstborn of the Egyptians. Similarly, other texts (see 22:28-29) do not link the redemption (or buying back) of the firstborn to the Exodus experience (v. 15). This practice of redemption of the firstborn reveals Israel's concern for human life and its special treatment of the firstborn. Although Israel was aware of the sacrifice of the firstborn among its Canaanite neighbors it revolted against such a practice (see Gen 22:1-19). The verb "to redeem" in vv. 13 and 15 refers to YHWH's ransoming Israel from slavery in Egypt. Israel views the firstborn of humans and animals as God's exclusive property; consequently they must be bought back.

Feast of Unleavened Bread (13:3-10)

Unlike Passover, which requires no sanctuary and is celebrated at home, Unleavened Bread is a pilgrimage feast that requires the attendance of the adult males at the sanctuary (see 23:15). Whereas Passover is the feast of semi-nomadic shepherds, Unleavened Bread is the feast of farmers. The feast expresses newness, noting the beginning of the barley harvest (the first crop to be gathered). For the first seven days of this harvest one has to eat bread made from the new grain. Such bread is unleavened or unfermented because it contains nothing of the previous year's harvest. Since this feast presupposes an agricultural environment it was adopted by the Israelites (probably from the Canaanites) some time after their desert experience. (It was only later that the feasts of Passover and Unleavened Bread were combined: see 2 Chr 35:17.)

Whereas J in 12:34 connects the unleavened bread to the haste of the Exodus, the author of 13:8 attaches a more personal note: "It is because of what YHWH did for *me* when *I* came out of Egypt." This flows from the concept of remembrance in 13:3. To remember means to say aloud, to relive, to make actual and meaningful now. Hence the feast is not a static recalling of the past but a dynamic reliving of it because of its repercussions for the present.

Israel in the Wilderness: 13:17–18:27

The first part of this section (13:17–15:21) raises these questions: What happens as Israel journeys to the Reed Sea? How does God intervene at the Reed Sea? The second part (15:22–18:27), however, is more of a summary of Israel's desert experience. For example, it deals with YHWH's protection in terms of providing food and drink (15:22–17:7), the defeat of Israel's enemies (17:8-16), and the organization of the people (18:13-27). At the same time this section foreshadows events that the book of Numbers will exploit. Hence the reader is not taken by surprise when the entire generation with the exception of Joshua and Caleb is forbidden to enter the Promised Land, but condemned to wander in the desert.

This section as a whole deals with the human symbol of wandering, a symbol that reflects life as a search for meaning both on the level of individuals and community. This symbol is also basic to other epic literature such as the *Odyssey,* the *Aeneid,* Melville's *Moby Dick,* and Dante's *Divine Comedy.* One is reminded of the Lukan Jesus who resolutely determines to make the journey to Jerusalem (Luke 9:51) and so capture the meaning of his own life and his community's by experiencing passion, death, and resurrection. In their present setting these chapters are the prelude to Israel's experience of covenant making at Sinai.

Israel on the March (13:17-22)

This passage, consisting of E in vv. 17-19 and J in vv. 20-22, brings up the problem of the route of the Exodus. While this question must remain open it is possible to offer a hypothesis as an effort to explain a number of the data contained in the biblical traditions. This hypothesis allows for two different routes by two different groups.

The probable translation of the body of water connected with the Exodus is "Reed Sea" or Sea of Reeds, not "Red Sea." The reed in question is a papyrus plant that is known to grow in the marshes at the north of the Nile delta (not in the Gulf of Suez or the Gulf of Aqabah). This name suggests a comparatively small body of water; its precise location is doubtful and not overly significant in dealing with the route of the Exodus. (The term "Red Sea" derives from the Greek translators of the Hebrew Scriptures. That term, however, includes even the Persian Gulf.)

The first possible route is the *northern* route. According to this itinerary, when the Israelites came out of Egypt they would have gone directly east, that is, across the northern part of the Sinai peninsula to Kadesh-barnea. However, the E tradition in v. 17 notes that the Israelites did not take the way of the Philistines, that is, the road along the Mediterranean Sea connected with the northern route. Still, the mention of Raamses (1:11), Succoth (12:37), Etham (13:20), and Pi-hahiroth in connection with Migdol and Baal-zephon (14:2, 9: all from J with the exception of the last two) tends to support this northern route.

The second suggested route is the *southern* route. According to this route the Israelites on leaving Egypt would have headed to the south or southeast to the lower part of the Sinai peninsula where they would have experienced the covenant making on Sinai. This would be the way of the desert mentioned by E in v. 18.

It is likely that these two traditions recall two different exodus experiences. Elements of the tribes of Reuben, Simeon, Levi, and Judah (the Leah tribes) were possibly the first to leave Egypt, taking the northern route. It is also likely that they are the group connected with the exodus-expulsion tradition who invaded the land of Canaan from the south (see the J tradition in Num 13:22-23; 14:24). Elements of the tribes of Benjamin, Ephraim, and Manasseh (the Rachel tribes) possibly left Egypt later under the leadership of Moses by means of the southern route. This group would have wandered in the desert, experienced YHWH at Sinai, and invaded the land of Canaan from the east (across the Jordan river). This group would be connected with the exodus-flight tradition. When the different entries into Canaan were combined in the final narrative these different exodus experiences were united as well.

In vv. 21-22 J distinguishes between a column of cloud by day and a column of fire by night, but in 14:24 J has one column of cloud and fire. Despite this variation, what is clear is the experience of God's presence. The cloud/fire is Israel's perception of its God's participation in the key events of the Exodus and desert wandering. This cloud/fire manifestation is not unlike YHWH's "angelic" presence (compare 3:2 with 3:4a).

Egypt's Pursuit of Israel (14:1-10)

The liturgical connection of Passover (and Unleavened Bread) with the Exodus by way of the tenth plague and the liturgical suture between the redemption of the firstborn and the tenth plague have now come to a close. The narrative resumes the action of the nine plagues in chs. 7–10 and after the exodus-expulsion interlude (see 11:1-3; 12:33-36) resumes the exodus-flight tradition (v. 5). The action now switches to the miracle at the sea, a military undertaking that does not presuppose the death of the firstborn.

This section contains both P (vv. 1-4, 8-10) and J or JE (vv. 5-7) traditions. For example, according to P Israel is trapped in the wilderness, but more accurately it is Pharaoh who is trapped into thinking thus. The reason P gives is that Pharaoh's absolute determination to pursue Israel will result in YHWH's definitive reception of glory through Pharaoh and his army. In the JE tradition Pharaoh has changed his mind, realizing full well the consequences of the loss of such an invaluable labor force. What is common to both traditions is that they have interpreted the crossing of the sea in terms of a holy war. A holy war is not merely the encounter between two opposing forces; it is a religious undertaking. For Israel this means that YHWH fights for Israel, not Israel for YHWH. A holy war has five elements: (a) sacrifices and oracles to consult YHWH (by reason of the pillar of cloud/fire YHWH already marches with Israel); (b) absolute confidence in YHWH (see 14:31); (c) ritual purifications (see 19:14-15); (d) fear put into the enemy by YHWH (see 14:24-25); (e) total destruction of the enemy (see 14:28, 30). For Israel's writers their commander-in-chief is no less than YHWH.

The Conquest of Fear (14:11-18)

In vv. 11-14 J takes up the all-too-human reaction to the Egyptian pursuit. It is fear that threatens to undermine the whole purpose of the Exodus. The people are tempted to prefer the resumption of slavery in Egypt to death in the desert. This murmuring motif is one that will reappear in Israel's wandering experience. Arguing from faith, Moses replies that such an either-or is invalid. Pressing the holy war theology, he makes a demand for renewed commitment (v. 13) and concludes with the assurance of victory. "YHWH will fight for you, and you have only to keep still" (v. 14).

In vv. 15-18 P responds to Israel's cry of frustration. YHWH's action consists of giving directions that will ensure the safe passage of the Israelites through the sea. Thus Moses is to lift his staff, stretch out his hand, and divide the sea in favor of Israel. As predicted in v. 4, the obstinate Egyptians will pursue Israel into the sea. Their corpses will then become mute yet eloquent witnesses to YHWH's power. The divine warrior will thus be duly acknowledged.

Two Traditions for the Crossing of the Sea (14:19-31)

The biblical traditions are unable to present an eyewitness account of what actually transpired at the Reed Sea because the required sources are wanting. However, Israel has chosen to interpret that event by dwelling on YHWH's military prowess. Holy war theology enables the traditions in this section to unfold the picture of a God who thinks resolutely on behalf of the fleeing Israelites. Liberation means not to be free *from* the ennui of Israel's laments, but to be free *for* the bewildered and beleaguered people.

According to J, YHWH is manifest in two ways: (a) the angel of God (v. 19a) and (b) the column of cloud (v. 19b). YHWH, in the form of a divine messenger and in the form of a cloud, now takes up a position between the Israelites and the Egyptians (v. 20). This position implies protection for Israel. Moreover, during the night YHWH drives back the sea with a strong easterly wind (v. 21b), thus making possible a passage on dry land. Just before dawn YHWH, present in the column of cloud and fire, startles the Egyptians with a glance that results in the loss of military discipline (v. 24). YHWH's panic-creating glance is now followed by the clogging of the Egyptian chariot wheels, that in turn leads to the sounding of retreat (v. 25). However, at dawn the sea resumes its normal depth. At this juncture YHWH hurls the retreating Egyptians into its midst (v. 27b). The outcome is that Israel acknowledges YHWH's intervention to the point of believing in YHWH and Moses, the servant of that God (vv. 30-31).

According to P Moses stretches out his hand over the sea (v. 21a). The result is a very special miracle. Dry land appears for the safe passage of the Israelites with the water forming something resembling walls to their right and left (v. 22). At this point the Egyptian forces pursue the Israelites on the dry land (v. 23). At YHWH's command Moses once again stretches out his hand over the sea (vv. 26-27a). The returning waters then engulf the entire Egyptian army (v. 28). P finally notes much more dramatically than J the Israelite passage on the dry land with the contained waters to the right and left (v. 29). In P Moses' gesture has replaced YHWH's strong easterly wind.

The Song of the Sea (15:1-21)

The earliest tradition about the crossing is found in this passage. Actually the tradition is twofold: one part (vv. 1-18) presents Moses and the Israelites singing a song that probably comes from the time of the monarchy. YHWH's intervention at the sea (vv. 1b-12) is linked to God's gift of the land and ongoing presence in the sanctuary (vv. 13-18). The second tradition (vv. 20-21 with transition in v. 19) introduces Miriam as leading the women in a victory celebration that includes singing, tambourines, and dancing. According to this tradition it is Miriam who gives expression to the religious aspect of the crossing. This is nothing less than the cultic celebration of the foundational event of Israel's religion. Miriam's relationship to Aaron (v. 20) implies that she is a cultic figure in the early days of Israel's existence. The other texts that mention Miriam associate her with the time of the wilderness experience and confirm the religious dimension of her role (see Num 12:1-15; 20:1; 26:59; Deut 24:8-9; 1 Chr 6:3; Mic 6:4). The anachronistic use of "prophet" (v. 20) is perhaps occasioned by the reluctance of later tradition to call Miriam a priest.

Grumbling at Marah (15:22-27)

This episode consists of three traditions: P (vv. 22a, 27), J (vv. 23-25), and an early deuteronomic addition (v. 26). P provides information after the manner of an itinerary: departure and arrival from stopping place to stopping place. Thus Moses leads the people from the Reed Sea through the desert of Shur to Elim. Verse 26 applies the basic theology of the book of Deuteronomy to this incident at Marah. Obedience to YHWH's will as expressed in commandments and precepts will prevent disastrous consequences such as the diseases inflicted by YHWH on the Egyptians.

The J tradition emphasizes God's generosity in meeting the needs of the desert community. After three days of travel the community comes upon water at Marah that, however, because of its bitterness is not drinkable. The people's predicament leads to Moses' cry to YHWH that, in turn, leads to YHWH's remedy for sweetening the water. Although J speaks of the people grumbling against Moses (v. 24) there is no indication at all that the people are in rebellion. Moreover, the content of the people's complaint is far from clear. According to v. 25 it is YHWH who puts Israel to the test, not vice versa (see 17:2). Thus, given a concrete need, YHWH generously responds.

This scene together with 16:1–17:7 underlines the femininity of YHWH. In the sociology of that day it is the task of the mother and wife to provide food and drink. Mother YHWH, therefore, senses the needs of her children in their plight and takes the necessary steps to alleviate the situation. The divine warrior who overcomes the mighty Egyptians at the Reed Sea is also the tender mother who quickly responds to family problems.

The Quail and the Manna (16:1-36)

This account focuses on two realities of the Sinai peninsula. The manna is the secretion of two insects that live on the tamarisk tree. The substance drops from the tamarisk to the ground where it hardens somewhat in the night air. This delicacy of central Sinai is prized by the Bedouin for its sweetness. The quail migrate to Europe in the spring and return in the fall. When they land exhausted on the northwest coast of the Sinai peninsula they can be easily captured. (For the quail as a replacement for the manna see Num 11:5-6, 31-33.)

P, who is the principal author in this account (J is probably to be found in vv. 4-5, 29-32) chooses to elaborate certain "spiritual" dimensions. Thus in vv. 17-21 there is just enough manna whether one gathers a large amount or a small amount. Moreover, any quantity kept over for the next day is summarily wormy and rotten. Similarly in vv. 22-26 there is a link between the manna and the Sabbath. On the sixth day one may gather twice as much in order to observe the complete rest required on the seventh. Whatever is left over from the sixth day is then used for the seventh. Indeed, those who venture out on the Sabbath to find manna are in violation of that sacred day, and besides, nothing is to be found then (v. 27).

The original tradition in this episode is God's gracious care of the people in the desert. Given the grumbling mentioned in vv. 2 and 7 one would expect that the sudden arrival of YHWH's glory (v. 11) would involve a punishment of sorts for the rebels. Instead, in v. 12 YHWH assures the people through Moses that their food needs will be met. If the people had rebelled against YHWH it would be rather surprising for YHWH to accede to the demands of the rebels. The simplest explanation, therefore, is the invocation of the graciousness tradition: the people are hungry and YHWH answers their petitions for bread and meat by supplying the manna and the quail (see Ps 105:40).

In view of the exile and an explanation of that debacle by reference to the rebellion of the desert generation, P has introduced the murmuring motif. This is expressed in the form of a death wish in v. 3: "If only we had died by the hand of YHWH in the land of Egypt, when we sat by the fleshpots and ate our fill of bread!" This death wish, however, contains the element of rejection of God's saving plan. By opting for an earlier death in Egypt they are rejecting the events that lead to the present impasse, the Exodus. It is not hunger pangs but theological despair that commands center stage on this level of the tradition. The reply of Moses and Aaron in v. 6 sustains this interpretation of the rebellion. It is a question of YHWH and the Exodus itself. The tradition of God's graciousness has thus been linked to a tradition about the sin of failing to believe that the God of Israel can indeed accomplish the divine plan.

Grumbling at Massah and Meribah (17:1-7)

This is a J narrative that is introduced by P's itinerary in v. 1a. Like the J story at Marah, this episode rests on the primary tradition of God's graciousness to Israel. Unlike the Marah tradition, this episode also contains the secondary tradition of Israel's contention with YHWH over the matter of the Exodus.

If one omits the people's attack on YHWH at the end of v. 2 the rest of that verse may be understood simply as a quarrel with Moses and a demand that he meet the needs of the people. Moses' cry to YHWH in v. 4 is not unlike his demand in 14:15 (P) that results in a positive answer from YHWH. Here the favorable reply is found in vv. 5-6 where Moses is commanded to strike the rock with his staff. (Contrast the different interpretation in Num 20:11-13.) The outcome is that YHWH once again meets the needs of the people—in this case the need for water. One should also observe that in v. 5 there is no indication of any punishment.

Verse 3 contains the secondary tradition of rebellion in this account. It is not really the thirst that is central; rather thirst serves as a backdrop for impugning the value of the Exodus: "Why did you bring us out of Egypt?" As in ch. 16, the Exodus is the object of attack because of the lack of water. On this level of the tradition there is rejection of the divine plan.

Battle with the Amalekites (17:8-16)

It is refreshing to come upon a narrative extolling a great human accomplishment in the midst of the awesome display of divine power. This J narrative is a legend whose purpose is to edify, in this instance to reflect the heroic stature of Moses. While salvation always involves the interplay of divine grace and human cooperation, it is reassuring to note a story where the limelight falls on the human protagonist.

Apart from the notices in vv. 14-15 explaining Israel's implacable hatred of the Amalekites and the origin of a particular altar, the entire movement centers on Moses, not YHWH. In v. 9 Moses commissions Joshua to make the battle preparations and adds that he (Moses) will take up his position on a nearby hill. While no details of the battle are given, there is a full description of Moses' contributions to the successful outcome. It is Moses' tenacity and steadfastness that win the day for Israel. The stamina displayed in keeping his hands raised, albeit with the support of Aaron and Hur (v. 12), is precisely what one would expect of such a giant. These heroic dimensions are captured by the expression "steady hands" in v. 12. The steadiness described in the account is the faithfulness shown in fulfilling an official task (see 2 Kings 12:16; 22:7). It is the courage of this one man that turns the tide of battle. For all his failings Moses retains his image as hero and superman (see Deut 34:7, 10-12).

The Amalekites who controlled the caravan routes between Egypt and Arabia lived in the Negeb, the southernmost section of Israel (see 1 Sam 15:7). Since they are linked to the tribe of Judah and are quite likely associated with the exodus-expulsion tradition the story is out of place here. However, as a portrait of the heroic qualities of Moses it is indeed most apropos in its present position.

Meeting Between Moses and Jethro (18:1-27)

This chapter, the work of E, contains two scenes: (a) the meeting between Moses and his father-in-law, culminating in a covenant meal (vv. 1-12); (b) the decentralization of judicial authority in Israel that results in the appointments of "minor" judges (vv. 13-27). It happens in the desert near the mountain of God (v. 5). Unlike the mountain of God in ch. 19, this mountain is not the scene of a theophany but of a meeting.

Jethro is hardly a new character in the story. In 2:11-22 J narrated Moses' marriage to his daughter. What is striking in the present account is E's concentration on Jethro. Although the latter does indeed bring his daughter and two grandsons to meet Moses (in 2:22 Moses has only one son, but see 4:20), the woman and the two sons play a rather unimportant role. In v. 7 Moses all but ignores his wife and family. Clearly Moses and Jethro are the central figures.

The meeting revolves around Moses' story of YHWH's exploits (v. 8), Jethro's joy-filled reaction to the story (vv. 9-11), and a covenant meal with Jethro on the one hand, and Aaron and the elders on the other (v. 12). Although some see Jethro's declaration as an indication of his conversion to Yahwism (v. 11; see 2 Kings 5:15) it is likely that Jethro merely recognizes that Moses' deity, YHWH, is more powerful than all other gods (see Josh 2:9-11). Although Jethro is called a priest (v. 1) and hence exercises a cultic office there is really no firm basis for suggesting that he is a priest of YHWH or that he shares his Yahwistic faith with Moses. In v. 12, as a matter of fact, Moses is conspicuous by his absence. Here Jethro accepts the sacrificial offerings, thereby indicating his acceptance of a mutual relationship with the Israelites. Given the subsequent enmity between Midianites and Israelites this tradition reflects an early friendlier association between the two groups.

Verses 13-27 presuppose a situation that developed after the desert experience, at a time when the population was large and sedentary. The distinction between the more important and less important cases (v. 22) indicates a decentralization of legal authority. According to some authorities it may suggest the judicial appointments during the time of King Jehoshaphat (871–848 B.C.E.: see 2 Chr 19:5-11). In any event, a subsequent situation has been read back into the desert experience and thus the later solution has been attributed to Moses. At the same time, however, the story provides another occasion for E to emphasize his fear-of-God motif (see 1:17, 21). Moses is instructed by his father-in-law to select God-fearing men (v. 21). This basic orientation of fear of God (that is, awe, transcendent awareness, radical trust) will ensure the common good, especially by the avoidance of bribes (see Deut 16:19).

Making of the Covenant: 19:1–24:11

Covenants are part and parcel of human social life. Since humans are drawn into relationships with other humans the terms of those relationships must first of all be clarified and then accepted. A covenant, therefore, is a relationship in which the moral bond between the parties involved is defined and then accepted. For example, in Gen 31:43–32:3 Jacob and Laban make a covenant. A significant element in that relationship is the sworn oath by both parties not to attack each other (31:52-53). Moreover, a pile of stones serves as a witness to the covenant (31:45-48). A ritual meal, finally, is also central to the relationship: "Jacob offered a sacrifice on the height and called his kinsfolk to eat bread" (31:54).

An obvious difference between the Jacob-Laban covenant and the Sinai covenant is the position of YHWH. YHWH is not an equal partner to the covenant; rather YHWH is the superior and Israel the inferior. Consequently YHWH is the one who promises to be loyal and issues commands, while Israel is the one who promises to be loyal and obey. Israel's pledged word to abide by the terms of the relationship is, therefore, essential to its existence as YHWH's chosen people. Covenant life is by definition the constant challenge to ongoing mutual fidelity.

Since the covenant on Sinai is *the* experience whereby this people becomes God's people it is only natural to assume that the scene at the mountain would be the logical meeting place for a variety of interpretations of this relationship. The variety of traditions reflects Israel's unrelenting efforts to fathom its unique position with YHWH. Hence YHWH and Israel can be perceived in various ways. At the same time these chapters witness to a certain conservatism. Israel is not content to employ one tradition and then discard it; instead it chooses to retain different traditions because each of them preserves a distinct value.

Despite all the distinctiveness of Israel's covenant traditions there is a basic outline for most of them. First of all there is the encounter with YHWH who overawes the people. Second, there is the expression of YHWH's will for this people. Moses is here the recipient of the terms of covenant existence. Third, Moses reports to the people the will of YHWH as he receives it, and then reports to YHWH the people's acceptance. This basic outline is also a testimony to Moses' unique position as the covenant mediator.

The Setting (19:1-2)

P continues his itinerary (see 16:1; 17:1), this time noting that the Israelites have arrived at Sinai. P's next tradition will come only in 24:15b; hence there is no tradition of covenant-making on Sinai comparable to J and E. For P there is only the one covenant made with Abraham that still perdures (see Gen 17:13). Nonetheless Sinai will become P's ideal place for many of Israel's cultic traditions.

The exact location of Sinai is not known. For those who follow the southern route of the exodus-flight tradition the mountain in question is often identified as Jebel Musa (Mount Moses). The size of the mountain (7,647 feet) is often thought to be imposing enough for the importance of the traditions associated with the biblical narrative. At the base of this mountain in the Sinai desert the Greek Orthodox monastery of St. Catherine's now stands.

Attitude Toward the Covenant (19:3-8)

The tradition embedded in vv. 3b-8 is an independent tradition drawn from the liturgy that is now introduced by v. 3a. Its purpose is to foster the proper attitude that should guide God's people. While it is clearly a proclamation, it is not a proclamation that provides precise rules of conduct; rather it is one that underlines the notion of word (v. 5: "if you obey my voice"). Israel is bidden to listen and thus act upon YHWH's word. The use of direct address ("I" and "you") adds both solemnity and power. Indeed, Israel is to learn from God's mighty deeds against the

Egyptians (v. 4) the nature of YHWH and the serious responsibility to heed that God's word.

There are other dimensions too. There is emphasis on intimacy. YHWH brings the people not just to a given destination in the desert but to this God's very person (v. 4). The covenant is specifically YHWH's (v. 5: "my covenant"), and the people belong to YHWH. The Hebrew word often translated "special possession" (v. 5) conjures up the notion of the personal private property of a king (see Deut 7:6; 14:2; 26:18). There is also stress on Israel's holiness (v. 6), hence its proximity to God. The expression "kingdom of priests" does not imply that every Israelite is a priest. Quite likely the totality of Israel is intended: a royalty of priests and a holy nation. Finally, there is the accent on liberty. Israel is not coerced to accept this relationship (v. 5: "Therefore, *if* you obey my voice"). In Israel YHWH is never a puppeteer who capriciously pulls the strings to control human behavior. Only a free response is a fitting response.

This liturgical tradition suggests an approach whereby YHWH can be considered the overlord and Israel the vassal. There are hints of such a conception here, hints that come to fruition in the book of Deuteronomy where the model of covenant is that of a treaty in which YHWH is the overlord and Israel is the vassal. Israel shows the ability to use political models to great advantage.

Two Theophany Traditions (19:9-20)

This section contains the J and E traditions of the Sinai theophany, God's manifestation on the mountain. (Verse 9 is a gloss that ties together the previous tradition with J and E.) For J (vv. 10-11a, 12-13a, 14-16a, 18, 20) the theophany is that of a volcanic eruption. It is a literary depiction that does not demand that one search for a now extinct volcano somewhere in Arabia. For E (vv. 11b, 13b, 16b-17, 19) the theophany is that of a fear-producing storm.

In the J account it is YHWH who selects Moses to hear the revelation and then share it with the people (v. 10). Moses is to prepare the people for a ceremony on the third day (vv. 11a, 15a; see also Hos 6:1-3 and 1 Cor 15:4 for the use of the third day in a covenant setting). The ceremony involves washing their clothes and continence (vv. 14b, 15b). While the mention of readiness (vv. 11a, 15a) is also part of holy war preparation, the accent is more on holy and less on war. What is expected of the people is that they will respect the limits of the mountain (v. 12) since YHWH will occupy it (v. 20). The power and majesty of this God are evident in the fire, smoke, and shaking of the mountain. It is the presence of this God that brings about the covenant. (The stipulations of this relationship in the J account are now found in ch. 34.)

In the E account it is the people who select Moses to be their spokesperson (20:19). It is the fear caused by the storm (v. 16b) that provokes their decision. It is also this fear that makes them willing to receive the will of the storm god. Unlike the J account, the E tradition has Moses organize a liturgical procession, but one that will place the people at the bottom of the mountain (vv. 13b, 17b). The tradition also alludes to meeting this God in the setting of a holy war. The camp in v. 17 need not be limited to a semi-nomadic camp; it is also a military camp. While the trumpet is a liturgical instrument (see Ps 47:5[6]), it is also a military instrument used for purposes of warfare (see Judg 7:20; also Joshua 6 where the ram's horn mentioned here in v. 13b is both liturgical and military). The Hebrew verb used in v. 17 ("they stationed themselves") also means to line up in battle array (see Judg 20:2). Israel at Sinai is thus God's militia, ready to accede to the will of this commander whose presence is also marked by the cloud over the mountain.

The Holiness of the Mountain (19:21-25)

In this passage J continues the theme of the holiness of the mountain first mentioned in vv. 12-13a. Realizing that the people will be tempted to see YHWH, J has Moses urge the people to observe a reverent distance. Not only are the people in general to sanctify themselves (v. 10) but also the priests (v. 22). Although Aaron is allowed to accompany Moses in his ascent to YHWH, the priests and the people are expressly forbidden (v. 24). YHWH's turf must be respected.

The Ten Commandments (20:1-17)

While the basic outline calls for the expression of the divine will following the encounter with YHWH, the condition of the biblical text is still somewhat disconcerting. In the J text of 19:25 Moses goes down the mountain to speak to the people. Next, in 20:1 God communicates the Ten Commandments rather abruptly. This is in turn followed by the remark in the E text of 20:19 that God's direct speaking to the people will result in death. Finally, in 20:22 YHWH speaks directly to Moses.

Both the Ten Commandments and the Covenant Code (20:22–23:19) have been associated with the E tradition. Most likely they are not E's personal work but independent traditions inserted by E at this point. At a first stage the fear experienced by the people (see E in 20:18) is the direct result of the storm theophany in ch. 19. Moses is consequently deputed to hear the entire revelation. At a second stage, because of the importance of the Ten Commandments, the people listen to this fundamental law. This listening leads to new fear. This, in turn, leads to Moses' receiving the rest of the legislation (the Covenant Code). This second stage clearly enhances the stature of the Ten Commandments since, unlike the Covenant Code, God communicates them directly to the people.

The form of the Ten Commandments is significant. It is a series of apodictic laws, that is, laws that impose a command directly on a person obliging that person to perform (or refrain from performing) some action that the legislator judges to be desirable (or harmful). Apodictic laws admit two formulations: (a) third person, as in Deut 17:6 ("a person must not be put to death on the evidence of only one witness"); (b) second person singular, as in Lev 18:8 ("You shall not uncover the nakedness of [that is, "thou shalt not have intercourse with"] your father's wife"). Although these apodictic laws are found rather exceptionally in the ancient Near East, they are characteristic of Israel. Moreover, second person singular formulations, insofar as they express the fundamental religious orientation of an entire people, are unique to Israel. (This form is found in the mouth of a patriarch establishing the culture of his family members in Jer 35:6-7.) There is, therefore, a dimension of intimacy, especially in these second person singular formulations, since YHWH speaks directly to the individual Israelite. Such laws are grounded in a person, not an impersonal legislative system.

With the exception of the first three, the Ten Commandments are originally a form of tribal wisdom. Before being united in their present form they circulated in different series of commands that the young of a tribe were expected to learn from their elders (see Leviticus 18; Tobit 4; Jeremiah 35). These tribal elders sought to provide for the common good and their position lent authority to the sayings. As is clear from v. 1, YHWH is the person behind this legislation. However, YHWH is more than a tribal elder. The identity of this God is evident in the central acts of the Exodus event. Using the liturgical introductory formula ("I am"), the text insists on the centrality of YHWH's role in the Exodus. Israel is bound to these commandments not only because they are for the common good, but also because this God has intervened decisively in its life. (Note how Deut 5:15 uses the Exodus tradition as motivation for the Sabbath observance rather than the creation tradition used here in vv. 9-11).

Moses' Appointment as Mediator (20:18-21)

The fear originally motivated by the theophany (19:16b) is now related to the divine proclamation of the Ten Commandments. (The smoking mountain in v. 18 harmonizes the traditions of J and E.) In this E passage Moses is deputed to hear the rest of the revelation (v. 19). Not surprisingly, E accentuates the fear-of-God motif in v. 20; such fear will be a help in avoiding sin. E concludes here by mentioning Moses' ascent in v. 21, an ascent that he will expand in 24:12-15a.

Introduction to the Covenant Code (20:22-26)

The legislation that Moses now hears by himself begins in 20:22 and concludes in 23:19. It is called the Covenant Code or the Book of the Covenant because in 24:3 the people agree to accept God's will, which is then specifically labeled "the book of the covenant" in 24:7. As with the Ten Commandments E has borrowed an independent collection or independent collections that he inserts at this point in the Sinai theophany. While this section of Exodus may strike some readers as being overly legal and perhaps legalistic and hence dry, one should nevertheless search for the values perceived by Israel. One such value is Israel's regard for the human person, a value that stands out when viewed against other ancient Near Eastern legal codes. Such an attitude stems from its religious convictions.

These opening verses continue the apodictic form of the Ten Commandments (v. 23 is in the plural, however, and v. 25 is a mixed form). Unlike the J and E traditions that associate God's presence in one form or another with the mountain, this independent tradition has God speak from heaven (v. 24). The prohibition against images stems from the fact the YHWH could not be seen and hence could not be represented. The law of the altar (vv. 24-26) presupposes Israel's early life in the land. More than one sanctuary is permitted—in fact, there are as many sanctuaries as there are places where God's presence is recognized. An elevated altar is forbidden since it may involve immodesty on the part of the sacrificer (see the precautions taken in 28:40-42).

The Law for Slaves (21:1-11)

Verse 2 introduces the casuistic or case section of the Covenant Code. (This section continues to 22:16.) This form of law is typical of the ancient Near East. By its nature casuistic law is pragmatic and evolves over time in the light of experience; the ethical principles implied in it are not articulated. The subject is simply reminded of the unpleasant consequences that will follow a violation of the law. In terms of obligation, case law binds the judge or judges who act for the legislator. The very core of these laws is the solution: if such and such has occurred, then such and such is the outcome. Although these laws have a personalistic overtone because of their setting at Sinai they are, apart from that important note, practical human laws written for the most part in the third person. Their background indicates a time in Israel shortly after the occupation of the land.

This section on slaves clearly distinguishes between slaves and slaveowners, although there are certain limitations on the slaveowners' rights. The situation described in v. 4 implies that women are the master's possession. Ideally (see Jer 34:8-22) the enslavement of Israelites is only temporary: six years for Israelite men (v. 2). (Deuteronomy 21:10-14 applies the same rule to Israelite women.) Verses 8-11 contain special legislation for occasions when there is a question of giving a female slave in marriage. In that case she enjoys certain rights as a wife.

Offenses Punishable by Death (21:12-17)

Although this section contains a mixture of legal forms, what makes it a unity is its subject: attacks on human life that involve the death penalty. While v. 12 establishes a general principle, vv. 13 and 14 make distinctions. In the case of unpremeditated homicide or accidental manslaughter ("an act of God") asylum is provided in a sanctuary. In the case of willful murder not even the sanctuary will avail. In reverence due to parents (vv. 15, 17) Israelite legislation is more demanding than that of the ancient Near East in general.

Laws Regarding Bodily Injuries (21:18-32)

Masters cannot dispose of their slaves at their mere whim. The cases mentioned in vv. 20-21 and 26-27 indicate limitations on the master's rights. Verses 23-25 enunciate the law of talion. This law intends to curb unbridled revenge by insisting on proportionate compensation. Slaves, however, do not enjoy this right because they receive only their freedom in compensation for the injury inflicted on them (vv. 26-27). Verse 32 is another indication of the plight of the slave. In the goring death of a slave the culpably negligent owner is obliged to pay the master the current price for a slave.

Laws Regarding Property Damages (21:33–22:14)

Israel never exacted the death penalty for crimes against property, something that the more progressive western nations did not acknowledge until the beginning of the last century. The general principle exemplified in this section is that an individual who has been wronged in a matter of property is to be compensated. The compensation is penal in character and usually greater than the damage caused. Thus someone who steals an ox or sheep and then slaughters or sells it must pay fivefold for an ox and fourfold for a sheep (21:37). A thief who cannot make full restitution for a crime is to be sold into slavery (22:2). Verses 6-10 have to do with divine adjudication. According to vv. 8[7] and 9[8] justice is administered before God, that is, in a holy place or a sanctuary. In the legal disputes expressed in these verses the manner of adjudication is best explained by v. 11[10]. The party or parties involved must swear by YHWH. This procedure reflects the sacredness of the divine name; to disparage the name is to disparage the person.

Social Laws (22:15–23:9)

(Although vv. 16-17 belong to the casuistic section of the Covenant Code they are grouped here because of their content.) The legislation in 22:18–23:19 constitutes the apodictic section of the Covenant Code. What is noteworthy about many laws here is the ethical sensitivity to the demands of charity toward one's fellow Israelite. By insisting so often on the obligations of love it transcends the Ten Commandments, which concern only the demands of justice.

The deflowering of an unbetrothed virgin implies serious financial problems for a father because it would be difficult for her to obtain a suitor. (For a father's worry over a daughter see Sir 42:9-14.) The law in 22:16 states that the seducer must marry her or, in the event of the father's unwillingness to give her, pay the customary marriage price for virgins. In ancient Israel a double standard existed. It is the status of the woman that determines adultery, not the status of the man. If the woman is either betrothed or married, and therefore the property of another man, the crime is adultery. If the woman is neither betrothed nor married it is not adultery, even if the man in question is married.

Both sorcery (22:18) and bestiality (22:19) involve the death penalty. Sacrifice to false gods (22:20), while a capital offense, is nuanced differently. Such a person is to be doomed: totally destroyed. Some think this destruction applies to the person's belongings as well.

The laws in 22:21-24 and 23:9 concern those who are legally helpless. Aliens (see 12:48) are foreigners who live in the midst of Israel and enjoy certain rights. Since they do not have full civic rights on a par with Israelites they are often victims of oppression. Verse 21 exhibits a peculiarity of Israelite jurisprudence, namely exhortation. Israel not only states the law but often provides reasons for its observance. In this instance Israel is to recall its own precarious existence in Egypt and thus treat the alien appropriately. Since the economy depends on the male heads of households, widows and fatherless children are exposed to the greatest dangers. To counteract these dangers the legislation in vv. 23-24 insists on divine involvement. YHWH will listen to the laments and take punitive action against the guilty. Israel's conviction is that a truly strong society provides for its weakest members.

Exhortation is also prominent in vv. 25-27. A cloak taken in pledge must be returned before sunset because this cloak also serves as bedding. The cry of such a cloakless Israelite merits prompt action from YHWH.

The material in 23:1-3, 6-8 looks to legal procedures. Those who compose Israel's popular courts are urged not to bear false testimony (v. 1), not to follow the majority view to the detriment of justice (v. 2), and not to accept bribes (v. 8). On the positive side they are to acquit the innocent and condemn the guilty (v. 7). Since it is unlikely that one would tend to favor the poor in court action, some emend v. 3 to read: "nor shall you be partial to *the wealthy* in a lawsuit." In any event, v. 6 clearly advocates due concern for the needy in litigation. Unfortunately Israel's prophets must decry the manipulation of the poor in the administration of justice (see Isa 1:23; 10:2; Ezek 22:29; Amos 5:10).

The provisions of 23:4-5 focus on one's personal enemy (some would identify this enemy in terms of an actual or imminent legal dispute). Allegiance to the covenant God takes precedence over personal antipathies; or better, such allegiance demands seeing one's enemy from a new perspective. In any event straying oxen or asses are to be returned to the proper owner and an overburdened ass is to be helped up.

Religious Laws (23:10-19)

Verses 10-12 refer to the sabbatical year and the Sabbath itself. According to vv. 10-11 the fields, vineyards, and olive groves are to lie fallow every seven years. The poor are envisioned as the primary beneficiaries of this institution (see also Lev 25:2-7; Deut 15:1-3). The mention of the Sabbath in v. 12 suggests that the sabbatical year is to take place at a fixed date, but there is little positive evidence to document its actual observance. With regard to the Sabbath the law in v. 12 declares that slaves, aliens, and even beasts are to benefit from the day of rest. (The word *shābbat,* "sabbath" in Hebrew suggests "to halt, stop." It is a day marked by rest when everyday activities stop.)

After mentioning the exclusive worship of God's name (and hence person) in v. 13 the Covenant Code considers the pilgrimage feasts to be observed in Israel, that is, feasts requiring male attendance at local sanctuaries. The feast of *Azymes* or Unleavened Bread celebrates the beginning of the barley harvest (see 13:3-10). It is here linked to the time when Israel came out of Egypt (v. 15). The feast of the grain harvest, or "Weeks" (Pentecost) that takes place about fifty days after Unleavened Bread marks the end of the wheat harvest. Finally, the feast at the end of the year, also called Tents or Tabernacles, celebrates the ingathering of all the produce of the field. Since these three pilgrimage feasts are agricultural they were celebrated only after the desert experience.

The Covenant Code concludes with several sacrificial injunctions. Since leavened bread implies a change it may have been deemed unfitting for use in sacrifice (v. 18a). Since the fat of an animal is considered the choicest part (see Lev 3:17) its being kept overnight would result in spoiling (v. 18b). Because YHWH is Israel's God, YHWH is worthy of receiving the first fruits of the soil at the local sanctuary (v. 19a). The prohibition against boiling a kid in its mother's milk (v. 19b), once thought to be a cultic practice among the Canaanites, is not clear. It seems to be a pagan practice whose specifics are not yet known.

Behavior in the Promised Land (23:20-22)

Some see this passage in light of Leviticus 26 and Deuteronomy 28, that is, as a list of blessings that flow from obedience to the terms of the code. Others regard it as a departure speech that is rather loosely linked to the code. Since these blessings are not closely related to the preceding stipulations, the second view is to be preferred. (The source of the tradition is not clear, however.)

The passage is a departure speech that aims at encouraging the people during the early monarchy in the tenth century B.C.E. (see the boundaries of the Davidic-Solomonic kingdom in v. 31). It is thus a time when Israel is threatened by Canaanite ways since it is now living side by side with the Canaanites as members of the one people of Israel. God is present through the messenger (vv. 20, 23). Such presence will mean protection, even against overwhelming odds. However, God's military action will be only gradual (vv. 30-31). During this entire time allegiance to YHWH and the covenant must be uppermost (vv. 21-22, 24, 32-33). Although they are to live with the Canaanites they are not to adopt their ways. It is obedience of this caliber that will bring about the blessings of abundance of food and drink, health, fertility, and long life (vv. 25-26).

Covenant-Making and the Ceremonial Meal (24:1-2, 9-11)

In the wake of the J and E traditions of the theophany and the subsequent legislation in chs. 20-23 there now come two more traditions of covenant-making: (a) vv. 1-2, 9-11 and (b) vv. 3-8. Most probably these are independent traditions. In the form of ritual actions they provide two more views of response to God's initiative. Although 24:1 is rather clumsily appended to the J and E traditions, and although 24:3 breaks up the initial tradition, still they preserve major values in terms of covenant making, values that Israel took pains to preserve.

In 24:1-2, 9-11 the text relates the celebration of a meal in God's presence. This quite simple but profound scene is a very ancient tradition stemming from Israel's perception of YHWH as tribal chief. By means of the meal YHWH takes the whole community, represented by the clan elders, into the family. The meal is the assurance and support given by the superior, YHWH, to the inferior, Israel. What is striking is that the clan elders do not accept any particular stipulations. What they do accept is the protection afforded them by the tribal chief. Israel's specific response to that gesture would be developed in subsequent traditions.

Covenant-Making and the Blood Rite (24:3-8)

Sacrifices (here communion sacrifices) effect covenant. In response to the people's willingness to accept YHWH's will (v. 3; see also v. 7), Moses writes down the stipulations (v. 4). After reading "the book of the covenant" he sprinkles the people with half of the blood of the slaughtered animals. For Israel blood is life. The sprinkled blood joins them to the blood splashed on the altar, which symbolizes God. A union has been created from this blood relationship. However, the terms for preserving that relationship are also spelled out. By living up to those terms Israel is assured of its ongoing union with YHWH. Unlike the ancient ceremonial meal this manner of covenant-making lays greater stress on the demands of the covenant God.

Instructions for the Building of the Sanctuary: 24:12–31:18

After the final traditions of covenant making (24:1-11) Moses ascends the mountain with Joshua to receive the tablets. This departure will set the stage for the golden calf story in ch. 32. Sandwiched in between these two texts is P's account of Moses' receiving divine instructions for the construction of the desert sanctuary. While P clearly rejects any covenant at Sinai he nonetheless finds this setting the ideal place for developing his cultic interests. Hence this section as well as chs. 35–40 may rightly be termed P's political document.

Recalling Israel's infidelity that provoked the sack of Jerusalem and subsequent exile in 586 B.C.E., P aims at underlining the nature of the restored community as a holy people. Concretely, holiness entails such institutions as priesthood and sacrifices, but the institutions are designed to achieve one purpose: God's presence. While Sinai is not, for P, the place of covenant making it is the place *par excellence* for YHWH's manifestation.

While P makes the desert sanctuary a portable replica of the Jerusalem Temple, it is wrong to regard all his cultic elaborations as a retrojection of that Temple into the desert experience. As a matter of fact P also employs older traditions, many of which are at home in ancient Canaanite religion. While P appropriates such Canaanite institutions he also confronts them, imposing upon them a theology of God's presence consonant with Israelite faith.

Moses' Ascent (24:12-15a)

This E passage expands the rather laconic statement of Moses' ascent in 20:21. Although it now introduces the P material, it originally served to position Moses on the mountain to receive the divine revelation (see 20:18-20). This revelation is linked to the tablets that YHWH will write. (In P the tablets are written by God's finger—see 31:18—whereas in J Moses writes them down: see 34:28.) It is interesting to observe that in the ancient Near East only Israel pictures its God as drafting or dictating legislation. For E the cloud is also significant as marking God's presence (see 19:16b; 20:21). Finally, the notion of additional judges in v. 14 is in keeping with E's "minor" judges in 18:21-26.

P's Theophany (24:15b-18)

For P this brief scene is not only an introduction to chs. 25–31; it is also a profound theological statement about the significance of Sinai. Here he links the divine manifestation on Sinai with the construction of the sanctuary (40:17, 33b) and the execution of the first sacrifice (Lev 9:1, 23-24). Just as the cloud covers the mountain and YHWH's glory settles there (vv. 15b-16a), so too the cloud covers the tent of meeting and YHWH's glory fills the sanctuary (40:34). In v. 16b YHWH calls Moses on the seventh day, and in Lev 9:1 Moses summons Aaron, his sons, and the elders of Israel on the eighth day. According to v. 17 YHWH's glory is viewed as a consuming fire, and according to Lev 9:24a fire comes from YHWH's presence and consumes the sacrifice. There is thus a clear parallelism between the manifestation on Sinai and the first act of worship after that manifestation. Hence Sinai becomes the model for worship.

Collection of Materials (25:1-9)

P's concept of YHWH's earthly dwelling borrows and reinterprets ancient Canaanite traditions. In that religion El, the head of the pantheon, has a tent on a mountain where he issues authoritative decrees or oracles (see 33:7-11). In v. 9 Moses is instructed to make a copy of the tent on the mountain. There is thus a similarity of form between the deity's earthly dwelling and its heavenly model. P employs two names for YHWH's place: (a) the more traditional "tent of meeting" (e.g., 40:34) and (b) his own special archaic "the dwelling." By using the latter term P understands the transcendent god of Israel who will meet with that people (see 29:42-43; 30:36). For P, YHWH will take up a permanent abode in the midst of the people (compare 33:7-11).

Unlike J and E, P provides directions for setting up the sanctuary and furnishing it (see also 36:8-38). Despite P's elaborations, modeled after the Jerusalem Temple, the basic reality is that of a portable sanctuary, a tent similar to Israel's own tents during the time in the desert.

This is similar to the practice of ancient Bedouin tribes who carried a small sacred tent made of red leather. During their journeys such tribes could experience the presence of their gods, owing to the stone idols carried in the tent. In human experience the presence of one's god is judged to be imperative.

Plan of the Ark (25:10-22)

After the manner of the practice mentioned above Israel can meet with its God because of the ark that is most likely housed by the tent. The ark is a rectangular wooden cabinet about four feet long, two and a half feet wide, and two and a half feet high that contains the stone tablets given to Moses by YHWH (vv. 16, 21)—hence the name "ark of the covenant" or "ark of the testimony." (In the ancient Near East it was a common practice to deposit treaties in a sacred place with a view to reading them at stipulated times.)

Although J and E do not associate the ark with the tent, P goes on to add that the ark has a propitiatory flanked by two cherubim. The propitiatory is the gold plate on top of the ark that is associated with divine forgiveness. From above the propitiatory YHWH can speak to Moses and thus to the Israelites. (For the role of the propitiatory on the Day of Atonement see Lev 16:15-16; note Rom 3:25.) It is likely that this propitiatory is a substitute for the ark, that is, the seat of God's presence or mercy after the ark itself was destroyed (see Jer 3:16). The original ark probably functioned as a support or pedestal for Israel's invisible God (see Num 10:35-36). Once the ark reached the Promised Land it served as YHWH's throne or footstool (see 1 Sam 4:4). The two golden cherubim, lesser deities borrowed from Israel's neighbors, provided protection for the throne and thus suggested the presence of Israel's God.

The Table and Lampstand (25:23-40)

The table contains the showbread (v. 30) that consists of twelve loaves of unleavened bread (see Lev 24:5-9), replenished every Sabbath and reserved to the priests. This bread serves as a reminder of God's covenant with the twelve tribes of Israel. The lampstand or *menorah,* although elaborately described, is somewhat baffling to scholars. In any event it is a candelabrum that holds seven lamps. It may have symbolized the fertility that derives from God. Some think that it represents a sacred tree, a frequent motif in ancient Near Eastern art. Today the term "menorah" is used for one of the best-known symbols of Judaism, the seven-branched candelabrum. (For the ten lampstands in Solomon's Temple see 1 Kings 7:49.)

Instructions for Making the Desert Sanctuary (26:1-37)

In P's conception the desert sanctuary is a collapsible temple that is exactly one half the size of Solomon's Temple (see 1 Kings 6:2, 16-17). First of all, wooden frames form a rectangular building that is approximately forty-five feet long, fifteen feet wide, fifteen feet high, and open on the east (vv. 15-29). Second, sheets of finely woven material are sewn together to make two large sheets. These sheets are joined together by means of loops and clasps and have the cherubim embroidered on them (vv. 1-6). Third, sheets woven of goat hair are stretched like a tent over the sanctuary. These sheets are slightly longer than those in vv. 1-6 and are left hanging down on both sides (vv. 7-13). Finally, ram skins dyed red cover the whole building, and *tahash* skins (light leather hides) cover the ram skins (v. 14).

This passage also mentions two veils. There is a veil over the entrance to the sanctuary (vv. 36-37) and one between the Holy of Holies and the Holy Place (vv. 31-32). The latter veil is more costly than the former. Behind the veil in the Holy of Holies (the most holy or most sacred area) stands the ark with the propitiatory (vv. 33-34). This is the area reserved to YHWH. Like the Temple (see 1 Kings 8:6, 8), the desert sanctuary reveals a gradation of holiness in its concentric structure with a most holy space at the center and areas of reduced holiness moving away from it.

The Altar of Holocausts (27:1-8)

This altar is basically a hollow wooden box about seven and a half feet long, seven and a half feet wide, and four and a half feet high that is plated with bronze. It is difficult to understand how it operates since the heat from these whole burnt offerings would destroy the altar. (Contrast the earthen altars in 20:24.) To resolve this problem some suggest that stones are placed on top of the altar for burning. This would imply a retrojection of the stone (and bronze) altar of a later period into the desert altar (see 1 Kings 8:64; 2 Chr 4:1). The four corners of the altar are provided with horns, a significant feature for those seeking asylum in the Temple (see 1 Kings 1:50; 2:28).

Court of the Sanctuary (27:9-19)

P now describes the rather elaborate courtyard for the desert sanctuary, approximately one hundred and fifty feet long, seventy-five feet wide, and seven and a half feet high (v. 18). As an integral part of the sanctuary the courtyard serves as the place for public ceremonies. A barrier of bronze columns and silver curtain rods (holding linen curtains) sets off the court from all other places. One is naturally reminded of Ezekiel's vision that pictures the Temple surrounded by a wall "to make a separation between the holy and the common" (Ezek 42:20).

Oil for the Lamps (27:20-21)

The pure olive oil is to come from the people but it is to be handled by the priests. The sanctuary light is obviously intended to be a perpetual reminder of YHWH's presence in the desert sanctuary. (There is no parallel for this instruction in chs. 35-40, but see Lev 24:1-4.)

The Priestly Vestments (28:1-43)

Some knowledge of the history of the priesthood in Israel is useful, if not necessary, to appreciate P's political document. Priesthood properly so called did not appear until there was considerable development of the social makeup of the community. (Note the lack of priests for the Passover in 12:1-20.) Two phenomena accompanied the rise of the monarchy: (a) erection of rival sanctuaries and (b) increased centralization at the Jerusalem Temple (see 1 Sam 2:27-36; 2 Sam 15:24-29). With the triumph of Deuteronomy's doctrine of only one sanctuary, Jerusalem, the priests serving the country sanctuaries were put out of work (see Deut 12:4-14). These country priests, many of whom were descendants of Levi, became second-class citizens in the Jerusalem Temple and were often the objects of charity, along with the widows, the fatherless, and the alien (see Deut 26:12). The only legitimate priests were the Jerusalem Zadokites —those descended from Zadok (see 1 Kings 2:26-27; 4:2), who were not descendants of Levi. In order to fulfill the deuteronomic ideal that all priests, regardless of lineage, should be descendants of Levi (see Deut 17:9) the originally non-levitical Zadokites claimed to be a special group of Levites, namely the Aaronites or those descended from Aaron. The outcome was that the Levites now became synonymous with inferior cultic employees who were subordinate to the sons of Zadok (see Ezek 44:10-31). In Exodus P reflects the claim of the Zadokites to be Aaronites.

This chapter endorses the claims of the Zadokites (v. 1). It focuses on Aaron, allotting only vv. 41-43 to his sons. Here it is worth noting that there is no ordination of priests as such in the OT. The word often translated "ordain" (v. 41) is, literally, "to fill the hand," a phrase whose original sense is not evident. In any event priests are made holy or sacred by reason of their work.

Of the vestments mentioned here the most interesting are the ephod and the breastpiece. Originally the ephod was a garment worn by the priests and attached to the breastpiece of judgment (v. 15). This breastpiece is of the same material as the ephod. It is a bag containing the sacred lots known as Urim and Thummim (v. 30). These lots provide "yes" or "no" answers for those seeking oracles from the priests (see 1 Sam 14:36-37; 28:6). With the ascendancy of prophetism, priests were no longer sought out to give oracles. In keeping with that development the Urim and Thummim, unlike the other priestly items, are merely mentioned but not elaborated. In the P description these originally oracular devices now contain stones engraved with the names of the twelve tribes (vv. 12, 29).

Investiture of the Priests (29:1-9)

This investiture involves three steps: purification, clothing, and anointing (see also Lev 8:1-36). As a result of the purification or washing the priest is enabled to enter the realm of the holy (see 30:17-21). The rite of anointing the high priest (v. 7) probably arose only after the exile when the high priest assumed a political position and consequently received the mark of royalty.

(According to 28:41 and other texts all priests are anointed.) This passage concludes by unequivocally stating the Aaronite claims of the Jerusalem Zadokite priests (see also v. 44).

The Sacrifices of Priestly Consecration (29:10-37)

There are three different types of sacrifice in this elaborate description. First, there is the sin offering, the bullock (vv. 10-14). Since the offering is for the sins of the priests they do not share in the victim. Second, there is the holocaust, the first ram (vv. 15-18). Third, there is the communion sacrifice, the second ram (vv. 19-26, 31-37). In v. 20 Moses consecrates the priests by rubbing the animal's blood on the extremities of the body of Aaron and his sons. In vv. 24-25 Moses then puts parts of the victims in their hands, has them perform the office of waving them before YHWH, and receives them back. As a result of this ritual gesture Aaron and his sons are invested with priestly power. (Verses 27-30 interrupt this ceremony. They determine the offering due the priests and make provision for handing down the priestly vestments.) Next the priests boil the flesh of this second ram and share it in a sacred meal. Since this meal is a sacred meal in connection with their priestly consecration, lay persons may not join them (vv. 31-35). This section concludes by noting the length of the ceremony. The exceptional holiness of the altar is underlined in the rubric of a daily sacrifice of a bullock for this seven-day period (vv. 35-37).

Daily Sacrifices (29:38-46)

The daily sacrifice of two yearling lambs (vv. 38-42) leads into a profound theological statement by P (vv. 43-46). The consecration of the altar, the sanctuary, and the priests looks to God's ongoing presence in the midst of Israel. Specifically, this God who dwells among them is none other than YHWH who brought them out of Egypt. Israel's cultic institutions are thus rooted in the Exodus and Sinai.

Further Cultic Ordinances (30:1-38)

The altar of incense (called the golden altar in 1 Kings 7:48) is perhaps a later priestly insertion, since it should logically be mentioned in ch. 25 and is not included in the incense-related episodes in the desert (see Num 16:6-7, 17-18; 17:11-12). Each morning and evening (vv. 7-8) a priest removes pieces of coal with a shovel from the altar of holocausts, sprinkles powder on the coals, and places them on the altar of incense (see Luke 1:8-9). Verses 34-38 provide the mixture for this absolutely sacred perfume. On the Day of Atonement (v. 10) the high priest takes this lifesaving smoke screen into the Holy of Holies and rubs the blood of the sacrificial animal on the horns of the altar of incense itself (see Lev 16:12-13, 18).

Census taking is construed as a dangerous undertaking (see 32:30-35; 2 Samuel 24). Everyone, therefore, twenty years of age or over who seeks to be enrolled and wishes to avoid the census plague must make a contribution to the sanctuary of a half-shekel (vv. 11-16; see Neh 10:33-35). Such a religious precaution is a fitting offering for the upkeep of YHWH's dwelling place.

Verses 17-33 enact further requirements for cultic personnel and objects. According to vv. 17-21 the priests must employ the laver (see 2 Chr 4:6) for washing their hands and feet prior to entering the sanctuary and when officiating at the altar. (All Muslims observe this rite before prayer in the mosque.) Since there is no mention of the laver in 38:29-31 and since it logically belongs with the altar of holocausts in 27:1-7 it is very likely a later priestly insertion. In addition to the washing, the priests (v. 30) and all the sacred furniture (vv. 26-28) are to be anointed with a very special holy oil (vv. 23-25). These rubrics indicate the unique character of cultic personnel and objects. They must be removed from everything that smacks of the profane (vv. 32-33). For P, however, the holiness of the sanctuary with its personnel is intended to have a sanctifying effect on the entire people.

Choice of Artisans (31:1-11)

The construction of a god's temple is not a haphazard decision. In ancient Canaanite literature the construction of Baal's temple falls to a special craftsman god. Against this background P has YHWH single out Bezalel and, as his assistant, Oholiab. P emphasizes that Bezalel's talent results from a divine spirit (v. 3; see also 35:31). This detail is central to P's plan of divine presence whereby the creation of the world, the construction of the desert sanctuary, and the erection of the permanent sanctuary are interrelated. Thus God's spirit in Gen 1:2 is linked to the spirit-filled architect of the desert construction (v. 3) who is, in turn, linked to the spirit-filled leader of the occupation forces, Joshua (see Num 27:18; Deut 34:9).

A key structural element in P is the execution of a command given directly or indirectly by God (see 7:6; 12:28). As noted in 25:1-9, it is eminently important to have exact correspondence between God's plan and its execution. Thus the divine command communicated through Moses to the artisans (vv. 6, 11) will be carried out exactly. In ch. 39 that execution will be noted in a context that also links the construction of the sanctuary to the creation of the world.

The Significance of the Sabbath (31:12-18)

Although P earlier connected Sabbath observance with the manna (16:23-30), he now develops the meaning of that institution for Israel. As in the other traditions of the Sabbath in Exodus there is the mention of cessation of work (see 20:9; 23:12; 34:21) and of the link to creation (see 20:11). In this passage, however, P underlines the sign value (vv. 13, 17) and the covenant significance (v. 16) of the Sabbath. Since YHWH sanctified the Sabbath (Gen 2:3) and rested (Gen 2:2) in the aftermath of creation (here in v. 17 YHWH enjoys ease and refreshment) Israel, through its observance, acknowledges the Holy One in its midst. Israel thereby enters into the whole rhythm of creation, celebrating anew its bond with the creator God and the created world. Israel is sacred and given over to YHWH (v. 13) just as the Sabbath is sacred and given over to YHWH (vv. 14, 15). Later (39:43) P will connect YHWH's action of blessing on the seventh day with Moses' blessing of the artisans.

Israel's Apostasy and the Renewal of the Covenant: 32:1–34:35

This section of Exodus bristles with enormous difficulties. The source division of chs. 32–34 is far from clear. The original event behind the story of the golden calf is not really apparent. Nevertheless despair should not control the general interpretation of the final text. Though the history of the traditions in these chapters continues to be elusive, what does emerge with clarity is Israel's understanding of itself as a covenanted people. The multiplicity of traditions, moreover, points to the centrality of this episode for Israel's self-understanding.

Not a few scholars are convinced that a real event stands behind the story of the golden calf and that it occurred during the wilderness experience. There may have been a group that opposed Moses and his ark-of-the-covenant symbol. Such a group under the leadership of Aaron may have broken away from allegiance to Moses and insisted on a bull figure as their symbol of the divine presence. However, to be more specific is to go beyond the evidence.

It should be noted that the golden calf does not violate the prescription of the Ten Commandments regarding false images (20:4-5). That prohibition concerns the person of YHWH, whereas the golden calf (actually a young bull) looks to an attribute of YHWH: strength. Such bulls could serve as supports for YHWH's throne (see the cherubim in 25:10-22). Israel's history, however, shows that the people did not always distinguish between the deity and the deity's attribute and so identified the young bull with YHWH (see Hos 13:2).

Jeroboam I (931–910 B.C.E.), the first ruler of the northern kingdom, set up such a young bull image in the cities of Dan and Bethel (see 1 Kings 12:26-32) as a cultic move against Solomon's Temple. Jeroboam's use of these images suggests that they were already an old tradition. Hence Exodus 32 need not be construed as directly condemning this king's cultic changes; however, it is likely that this chapter is an indirect condemnation of Jeroboam's cultic reforms.

In their present setting chs. 32–34 reflect a theology of covenant renewal. The elements in this theological construct are: (a) sin, which is generally apostasy; (b) punishment, (c) repentance, (d) restoration (see Numbers 13–14; Judg 3:7-11). This pattern is theologically significant. It implies that the revelation of YHWH is grounded not just in a people (which in indeed a plus), but in a sinful people. In this respect Israel considers itself a refuge of sinners.

Making of the Golden Calf (32:1-6)

The sin in this covenant renewal pattern is the desire of the people to get rid of Moses and so obtain a new leader (vv. 1, 4). This tradition is certainly non-priestly. In such traditions Aaron is never identified as a priest or an ancestor of priests; indeed, as here, he even opposes YHWH's chosen leader (see Num 12:1-8). Aaron readily accedes to the wishes of the people, constructs the young bull image, and calls for a celebration involving holocausts and communion sacrifices (vv. 2-5). It is not really clear that the reveling in v. 6 is some form of debauchery. Israel's sin of apostasy consists in rejecting Moses as leader and hence in rejecting YHWH.

YHWH's Wrath and Moses' Mediation (32:7-14)

Moses appears as a covenant mediator, one who intercedes for the people, here in the context of winning forgiveness that ultimately leads to covenant renewal. Israel, therefore, envisions a special role of intercession whereby the relationship of the people to YHWH is bound up with the relationship of certain endowed individuals to YHWH. It is also interesting to observe that Moses is able to oppose the God of Israel and still not be labeled disloyal.

YHWH's violent reaction is precisely the reverse of that envisioned by the young bull devotees. YHWH plans to wipe this people out and begin anew (vv. 7-10). Moses begins his mediatory role by pursuing the argument of continuity in history. To have the people die in the desert would only provoke ridicule from YHWH's enemies in Egypt. The action begun in Egypt should be carried on to completion. To abandon Israel now would be to renege on the promises to the patriarchs (vv. 11-13). In the end YHWH allows the persuasive Moses to win the argument (v. 14).

Twofold Destruction (32:15-24)

The tablets play a significant part in this story. In vv. 15-16 these tablets are unique. Although the custom is to have such inscriptions on only one side, these are on both sides. E's tradition is hinted at. (Joshua's presence in v. 17 has already been explained by E in 24:13.) The divine revelation that Moses was to have communicated to the people is now recast to tell the account of Israel's infidelity and so necessitate Moses' return to the mountain where he will receive new tablets. Although J has Moses inscribe the tablets (34:28), this tradition insists that God actually does the engraving (see also P in 31:18). The tradition, therefore, goes beyond the ancient Near Eastern understanding of divine writing whereby the deity does not produce the document physically. YHWH's writing, as a result, stresses the value and authority of these tablets. In the other direction, the breaking of the tablets is the breaking of the covenant relationship between YHWH and Israel. The action of the people in the construction of the young bull image results in the destruction of the covenant bond.

The destruction of the tablets is followed by the account of the construction and subsequent destruction of the golden calf. Although vv. 21-24 make a feeble attempt to exculpate Aaron in vv. 2-5 they are more interesting from the standpoint of making cultic objects. In ancient Canaanite literature, for example, cultic objects acquired their desired form by themselves. The palace of Baal is completed after a fire has worked on the silver and gold for six days. Aaron's reply in v. 24 that the image emerged by itself is thus readily intelligible. The destruction is even more interesting. According to v. 20 Moses employs mutually exclusive acts in undoing the image: burning and grinding. In ancient Canaanite literature Mot, the god of death, in undone in the same way. Anat, Baal's consort, burns, grinds, and scatters Mot. The final act of making the Israelites drink the image-polluted water (see also Deut 9:21) is similar to Anat's scattering of Mot's remains in the open fields where birds consume them. In Exodus the golden calf, like Mot, is utterly destroyed and made totally irretrievable.

The Zeal of the Levites (32:25-29)

There are two traditions for the punishment of the people. According to v. 35 YHWH smites the people for their sinful action. According to vv. 25-29 members of the tribe of Levi rally to Moses' call to arms and execute the Israelites who sacrificed to the golden calf, including their own relatives. This loyalty wins for them their priestly prerogatives (see Deut 33:9). This tradition does not condemn Aaron as the ancestor of the Aaronites. It expresses the reaction of the covenant-committed Levites who rejected the cult established by Jeroboam I at Bethel, one of the cities where this king erected a young bull image. This episode also condemns the action of the king in making priests from among the people who were not Levites (see 1 Kings 12:31).

The Atonement (32:30-35)

This tradition stresses Moses' identity with the people. If YHWH is unrelenting, then the mediator wishes to share the fate of the people. The concept of God's book was known in the ancient Near East and is at home in the notion of military conscription where the lives of those enrolled in the book were fraught with danger. In this section Israel adapts the tradition: an Israel that considers itself God's army. At the time of a census (see 30:11-16) there was a rite of expiation and the names of the Israelites were inscribed on tablets. Those so inscribed enjoyed the rights of a member of God's militia, for example, possession of the land and worship in the sanctuary. Anyone removed from the tablets was placed among the dead, that is, separated from the community.

Orders for the Departure (33:1-6)

This section pursues the thrust of 32:33-34, the continuation of the journey to the Promised Land with the aid of an angel. However, the angel in 32:34 merely affirms Moses' leadership role. The basic issue here is the personal presence of YHWH with Moses and the Israelites (vv. 2-3). An angel is not the same as YHWH. This bad news is reiterated in vv. 4-6 and is marked by a sign of Israel's repentance, the removal of all ornaments. The people now stand under God's judgment. One naturally wonders about the efficacy of Moses' mediation.

Moses and the Tent of Meeting (33:7-11)

This tradition, which is generally ascribed to E, takes up the question of divine presence already broached in vv. 1-6. However, the text itself is not a unity. According to v. 7 any Israelite can visit the tent, but according to v. 8 only Moses visits the tent while the people remain at their own tents in awe. According to v. 11b an official resides permanently in the tent, yet v. 11a presumes that the intimate dialogue between God and Moses precludes the presence of a third person. Verses 8 and 10 presume that the tent is placed in the middle of the camp (see P in 25:1-9), but v. 7 states that the tent is outside the camp and indeed at some distance from the camp.

It seems that E has introduced changes into an older tent tradition from Israel's desert experience in order to demonstrate that the tent theophany is a miniature reproduction of the revelation of Sinai. Both the mountain and the tent are outside the camp (v. 7; see 19:17). In both cases the people remain at a distance (v. 8; see 20:18). (In Hebrew the same verb is used for the people stationing themselves in 33:8 and 19:17.) In both cases a cloud indicates the divine presence (vv. 9-10; see 19:16ab). In both cases Joshua assists Moses (v. 11; see 24:13). Finally, in both cases Moses appears as God's intimate. Israel's relationship to YHWH hinges in no small measure on this unique mediator.

Moses' Intercession (33:12-17)

This section is linked to Moses' position vis-à-vis YHWH (v. 11a) and YHWH's order to lead the people on (v. 1a). According to v. 12 the implication is that an angel simply will not do. Appealing to his status as divine intimate, Moses argues on behalf of the people (v. 13). If the leader's status is genuine, the divine conclusion must be to provide for the people. Verse 14 shows that the appeal is successful. However, the response is directed only at Moses. Still dissatisfied, Moses presses his case by demonstrating that divine intimacy is real only if the people are included (vv. 15-16). The community-directed argument of Moses finally obtains divine approval (v. 17). The significance of this argumentation should not be overlooked. It implies that the welfare of the covenant people (here their renewal as God's people) is grounded in the love and trust between the covenant God and the covenant mediator.

Preparations for the Theophany (33:18-23)

With no little audacity Moses seeks further surety for his people, since the pronouncing of the divine name is the guarantee of presence and hence of compassion (for this compassion see 34:6-7). Divine name goes hand in hand with covenant. Because of the dangers connected with the direct display of God's glory Moses is to be set in the hollow of a rock and covered by God's hand (vv. 21-22). The viewing of God's back (but not the face) is both the limit and the proof of Moses' intimacy, but that intimacy is related to the well-being of the people. (For Elijah's similar theophany see 1 Kings 19:9, 11-13.)

The Theophany (34:1-9)

Most of this section is from J (vv. 1a, 2-4, 6a, 8). Indeed, together with most of the remaining material in ch. 34 this scene is the natural sequel of Moses' ascent of the mountain in 19:20 (J). In keeping with the basic outline of the covenant proceedings, an expression of God's will is expected in J's account. This expression has been removed from its natural place, that is, 19:20, because of Israel's infidelity in the golden calf incident. In other words, the expression of God's will in the initial encounter on the mountain (J) has become the expression of God's will in the second encounter of covenant renewal. According to the pattern of covenant renewal, restoration is now in order. The making of new tablets symbolizes the making of a new covenant. (References to the former broken tablets in v. 1b and to the cloud in v. 5 are editorial touches to make the J account fit its new setting.)

J's theophany first has Moses cutting the tablets and ascending the mountain alone (vv. 1a, 2-4). Next, YHWH passes before Moses (v. 6a). Finally, in deference to the divine presence, Moses bows down to worship (v. 8). Verses 6-7 and 9 are the conclusion of Moses' mediatorial role begun in 33:12-23. The theophany announced in 33:19 now takes place. The cultic saying in vv. 6-7 (see also 20:5-6) in its present position is a statement about divine forgiveness and divine punishment. The word often translated "merciful" in v. 6, as well as the verb "to grant mercy" in 33:19, derive from the Hebrew word for "womb." Thus Mother YHWH demonstrates the compassion for Israel that a mother is expected to show the child of her womb. At the same time YHWH will not let the guilty escape (v. 7). Ultimately the request for forgiveness (v. 9) is grounded once again in the relationship that Moses enjoys with YHWH. The covenant renewal can now proceed because Moses has identified with Israel.

The Dodecalogue (34:10-26)

There is no mention of Israel's explicit response to YHWH's overtures in this covenant renewal. Moses' intercession and the people's repentance seem adequate (see also 1 Sam 12:16-25). The opening verses (10-11) transcend the immediate setting by focusing on the dangers that will confront Israel in the Promised Land (note also 23:20-33). Sinai appears, therefore, as the apt place for anticipating those dangers by reason of the covenant bond that will distinguish Israel from its neighbors.

Although v. 28 speaks of the Decalogue or Ten Commandments, this series of laws is actually a Dodecalogue or Twelve Commandments. (The expression "Ten Commandments" in v. 28 is a later development.) The Dodecalogue is often labeled cultic or ritual in contradistinction to the ethical Decalogue (see the injunction for the pilgrimage feasts in v. 23 and the law of redemption in vv. 19-20.) However, the prohibitions of images (v. 17) and intermarriage with the Canaanites (v. 16) are patently ethical. Moreover, most of these commandments are second person singular formulations (see 20:1-17). For J this collection creates a healthy tension in his theological approach. According to Gen 12:1-3 Israel is to mediate blessings to the conquered nations. But a pagan environment can pose problems in mediating those blessings. This Dodecalogue, therefore, is J's form of insistence on fidelity to the covenant God in a pagan setting (vv. 12-15). It is rightly called by some YHWH's privilege law: a statement of YHWH's prerogatives grounded in the character of this God as the Jealous One (v. 14). The distinctiveness of Israel flows from the distinctiveness of YHWH.

The Impact of the Theophany (34:27-35)

J mentions the divine command to write down the terms of the covenant and the subsequent execution of that command on the mountain during a period comprising forty days and forty nights (vv. 27-28; see Deut 9:9, 18; Matt 4:2). J then narrates Moses' gathering of the people and his enjoining on them all that YHWH commanded on the mountain (vv. 31-32).

The tradition contained in vv. 29-30, 33-35 deals with Moses' shining face. It is linked to Moses' mediatorial position already noted in chs. 33 and 34. According to the tradition Moses must veil his face when he is not performing his official duties (vv. 33-34). Whatever the background of the veil itself, what is central to the biblical account is the radiant face of Moses insofar as it derives from God and is the symbol of his authority before God. The man who was rejected by the people (32:1, 4) is the man who has restored them in covenant and who now fittingly wears the symbol of his divine office. (See Paul's application of this tradition in 2 Cor 3:7–4:6.)

The Execution of the Instructions for the Building of the Sanctuary: 35:1–40:38

P now recounts the execution of the instructions given to Moses in chs. 25–31. It is tempting to construe chs. 35–40, together with ch. 34, as a type of restoration. Thus chs. 25–31 are a creation and chs. 32–33 a fall. In any event P uses the Sinai setting to develop his theology of divine presence.

The Start of Construction and Israel's Generosity (35:1–36:7)

P's basic structure here is the execution of commands given directly or indirectly by God. Thus there are divine commands for: (a) the observance of the Sabbath (35:1, including the prohibition against lighting fires in v. 3); (b) the collection of materials (35:4); (c) the call for artisans (35:10); (d) the start of work on the project (36:1). P goes on to note that the Israelites generously respond to YHWH's command (35:20-29). In fact, they are overzealous. Moses has to make a special appeal to stop the flow of contributions (36:2-6). The outcome is nonetheless an abundance of materials to complete the work (36:7). The spirit-endowed Bezalel and Oholiab (see 31:1-11) as well as the other artisans are also portrayed as responding to the divine command to execute all the work. It is rather interesting to compare this wholehearted response in P's ideal account with the reluctance to rebuild the Temple after the exile (see the prophets Haggai and Zechariah). The biblical record does not hesitate to register both the ideal and the real.

Execution of the Divine Instructions (36:8–39:31)

With the exception of 38:21-31 this section details how the divine instructions communicated to Moses in chs. 25–31 are in fact carried out. There is a difference, however, in the sequence. While the ark with the table and the lampstand (25:10-39) heads the list of instructions because of their greater importance, the tent (26:1-37) comes first in the order of execution. In this way there is progress from the outside inward. In general this section basically duplicates chs. 25–31, celebrating detail by detail with untiring delight how the final product corresponds to the initial directions. For the tent cloth, coverings, wooden frames, and veils (36:8-38) see 26:1-29, 31-37. For the ark with the propitiatory, table, and lampstand (37:1-24) see 25:10-39. For the altar of incense (37:25-28) as well as the anointing oil and fragrant incense (37:29) see 30:1-6, 23-25, 34-36. For the altar of holocausts and the court (38:1-7, 9-20) see 27:1-19. For the priestly and other vestments (39:1-31) see 28:1-43. The original text, describing the model tent and its furnishings in the Hebrew language, often has a light sing-song quality expressive of pleasure and admiration—a joyous chant that is not heard in translation.

In 38:8 P notes that the bronze laver (30:18-21) is made from the mirrors of the women who serve at the entrance of the sanctuary. These women reappear in a gloss of 1 Sam 2:22. Although women were probably involved in some ways with the worship of YHWH this male-controlled "official" story has so completely removed their presence from cultic matters that one can no longer be sure what the women's roles actually entailed.

The passage dealing with the amount of metal used (38:21-31) is a later insertion into the text. The sanctuary tax in v. 26 that draws on the first census of Israel (to be mentioned later in Num 1:45-46) apparently ignores the tradition of 35:21 and 36:3. According to this tradition Israel generously contributes on a voluntary basis. Verse 21 notes the position of Ithamar, son of Aaron, as head of the Levites. However, the Levites (see 28:1-43) are not instituted until Num 3:5-10 and Ithamar assumes his role as head only in Num 4:33.

Presentation of the Work to Moses (39:32-43)

Besides enumerating the finished cultic materials that are presented to Moses this section is especially telling for P's theology of God's ongoing presence. By a subtle use of structures P interconnects the creation of the world, the construction/erection of the desert sanctuary, and the establishment of that sanctuary in the Promised Land (for this last point see 40:1-33). Despite Israel's infidelity, God's plan will not be thwarted. The God who created in the beginning will continue to create in Israel's ongoing history. Cult, therefore, is the principal means by which the creative presence will be manifest among the Israelites.

P not only reintroduces his execution-of-command structure (see 35:1–36:7) but also embellishes it here with a more solemn formulation. Verse 32b may be translated literally: "And the sons of Israel did (it) according to everything that YHWH had commanded Moses. Thus they did (it)." Similarly v. 42: "According to everything that YHWH had commanded Moses, thus the sons of Israel did all the work." P also brings in a second structure, successful completion of work (v. 32a). In addition P has Moses make a judgment on the people's work. Verse 43a may be translated literally: "And Moses saw all the work, and behold, they had done it." Right after this judgment P has Moses bless the people (v. 43b).

The parallels with P's creation account are evident. In Gen 1:31 God looks at the whole work of creation and labels it very good. Genesis 2:1 observes that the heavens and the earth and all their array are finished. After concluding the six days of creation, God blesses the seventh day (Gen 2:3). Since God cannot issue a command to God, the creation account does not allow for the execution-of-command structure. As mentioned earlier (31:1-11), the spirit at work in creation (Gen 1:2) is also operative in Bezalel, the chief engineer of the sanctuary construction.

The Erection of the Sanctuary (40:1-33)

Here P minutely relates how Moses carries out YHWH's instructions in setting up the desert sanctuary. Besides pinpointing the time (vv. 2, 17) and accentuating the privileges of the Aaronites (vv. 13-15), P takes pains to highlight the significance of the event by means of his structures. The execution-of-command structure is mentioned no less than eight times (vv. 16, 19, 21, 23, 25, 27, 29, 32). Indeed, v. 16 has the more solemn form of the structure that may be translated literally: "And Moses did according to everything that YHWH had commanded him, thus he did (it)." The structure of successful completion of work is also in evidence. According to v. 33 Moses finishes everything.

P links not only creation and the erection of the sanctuary but also the setting up of that sanctuary in the apportioned Promised Land. In Num 27:18 and Deut 34:9 P describes Joshua as the spirit-filled leader and the architect of Israel's plan of occupation. In Josh 14:5, when narrating the division of the land, P employs the more solemn form of the execution-of-command structure. It may be translated literally: "As YHWH had commanded Moses, thus the sons of Israel did (it) and they divided the land." In the same book P also uses the successful-completion-of-work structure in narrating the final apportionment: (literally) "and they finished dividing the land" (Josh 19:51). This final act, moreover, takes place in front of the tent at Shiloh. In keeping with the divine command to subdue the earth (Gen 1:28), P states in Josh 18:1 that the earth was indeed subdued. In the same text he notes that the community of Israel gathered around the tent set up in Shiloh. For P, therefore, the event at Shiloh looks back to Sinai, which in turn looks back to the first creation. God's abiding presence in the land is the sacrament of hope for P's despairing exiles. In the final analysis the dull rubrics are charged with life.

The Abiding Presence (40:34-38)

For P, Sinai is the model of worship. According to 24:15b-16a the cloud covers the mountain and settles there. Here, too, the cloud covers the sanctuary and YHWH's glory fills it (v. 34). For P, therefore, the desert sanctuary captures the experience on Sinai and perpetuates it.

This tradition of the cloud's covering and settling is also the seal of approval on and legitimation of everything that Moses and the Israelites have done. YHWH here takes possession of the sanctuary. This is also Israel's experience when YHWH's glory fills Solomon's Temple and the priests are unable to minister because of the cloud (see 1 Kings 8:10-11). P's cloud theophany also anticipates Israel's ongoing trek through the wilderness. P's cloud, which now does duty for the tradition of the pillar of cloud and the pillar of fire (see 13:21-22; 14:19-20), also serves as a signal. It will indicate when and how long Israel will set up camp and when Israel is to strike camp (see Num 9:15-23).

In these concluding chapters P reveals himself as a truly pastoral theologian. For a people that experienced God's absence in the fall of Jerusalem and subsequent exile P now proclaims the good news of God's presence. Aware that Israel is deprived of Temple worship because it dwells in a foreign land, P announces that Israel will be restored to the land and indeed that the land will be sanctified by God's presence in the sanctuary. (For the conditions of return see Leviticus 26.) One thus returns to the gospel of creation. By careful and proper attention to cult, the Israelites are empowered to move from chaos to cosmos.

BIBLIOGRAPHY

Cassuto, Umberto. *A Commentary on the book of Exodus.* Jerusalem: Magnes, 1967.

Childs, Brevard S. *The Book of Exodus: A Critical, Theological Commentary.* Old Testament Library. Philadelphia: Westminster, 1974.

Clements, Ronald E. *Exodus.* Cambridge Bible Commentary. Cambridge: Cambridge University Press, 1972.

Driver, Samuel R. *Exodus.* Cambridge Bible. Cambridge: Cambridge University Press, 1911.

Durham, John I. *Exodus.* Word Biblical Commentary. Waco, Tex.: Word Publishing, 1987.

Fox, Everett. *The Five Books of Moses.* Schocken Bible. New York: Schocken Books, 1995.

Fretheim, Terence E. *Exodus.* Interpretation. Louisville: John Knox, 1991.

Gowan, Donald E. *Theology in Exodus: Biblical Theology in the Form of a Commentary.* Louisville: Westminster/John Knox, 1994.

Greenberg, Moshe. *Understanding Exodus.* New York: Behrman, 1969.

Hyatt, J. Philip. *Exodus.* New Century Bible. London: Oliphants, 1971.

Noth, Martin. *Exodus, a Commentary.* Philadelphia: Westminster, 1962.

Plastaras, James. *The God of Exodus: The Theology of the Exodus Narratives.* Milwaukee: Bruce, 1966.

Sarna, Nahum. *Exploring Exodus: The Heritage of Biblical Israel.* New York: Schocken, 1986.

____. *Exodus.* JPS Torah Commentary. Philadelphia: Jewish Publication Society, 1991.

Walzer, Michael. *Exodus and Revolution.* New York: Basic Books, 1985.

COVENANT

"Covenant" is more than "fidelity" or "solemnity." At Sinai a "contract" was made between God and a people. The Abrahamic covenant (Genesis 15, 17) was an oath-bound divine gift of the land to Abraham and his descendants. The Hebrew word is *berît* (= stipulation, contract). It is translated in the LXX with *diathēkē* (= stipulation, will); hence the English "testament." All express different aspects of the same thing.

Christians most often hear the word "covenant" in the words of Jesus at the Last Supper. The word over the cup (Matt 21:26-29 par.) refers to the blood (cf. Exod 24:6, 8) of the new covenant (cf. Jer 31:31-34) that will be shed for many (cf. Isa 53:11). In the Lord's Supper Jesus' death on the cross is made present. We are at the heart of the encounter between God and humanity. In many churches the sacrament of baptism is also regarded as a covenant between God and individual believers (cf. 1 Pet 3:21). Since marriage is a "covenant" between two people (cf. Mal 2:14) the idea of covenant has also shaped Christian spirituality of marriage. Our Bible has two parts corresponding to the two phases of salvation history, the old and new covenants (cf. Jer 31:31-34 par.; 2 Cor 3:3-4, 6; Heb 7:1-10, 18). The entire traditional hermeneutic of multiple meanings of Scripture rests on the relationship between the two "testaments" because it calls for reading them as a single unit. Christian-Jewish dialogue also depends on it. According to John Paul II the Jews of today are the people of the "old covenant never abolished" (cf. Rom 11:29). Are Christians and Jews members of *one and the same* or of different covenants? Are there perhaps *many* divine covenants, some of them with other religions? Can we regard the Noachic covenant (Gen 9:1-17; Isa 24:5) as one whose commandments continue to bind as the old covenant binds Israel, as long and insofar as the "nations" have not entered into the new covenant? On God's side the Noachic covenant is a promise never again to bring about a world-destroying flood. Hence the biblical Noachic covenant may be important for today's acute question of the protection of creation. But the central covenant in the Bible is God's covenant with the people of Israel, in Abraham and at Sinai, and the covenant with David, God's anointed, together with the prophetic promise of a new, eternal covenant.

The biblical idea of covenant is not captured within a single system of thought. The individual writings develop different points of view. Sometimes they propose entire systems of covenantal history, such as the deuteronomistic or priestly histories (and later the initiatives of "federation theology"). Sometimes the word is weakened to nothing more than "religion" or "faith." Sometimes the divine covenant is a mutual agreement and at other times it is a sovereign, unilateral institution by God. The New Testament also displays a variety of different views. Moreover, the Bible can speak of covenant without using the word itself, as in the covenantal formula: "I will be your God, and you shall be my people." The Old Testament speaks of many covenants, but at the canonical level the various expressions are interpreted together in such a way that one can truly speak of a single covenant for Israel. The commentaries on the individual books point out these nuances where they occur.

We can only speak in metaphors of the relationship between God and creatures, and metaphors can always be used in new ways. The metaphor of covenant makes an analogy between God's relationship to God's people on the one hand and certain relationships between human beings on the other: oaths, gifts, obligations, contracts. These are personal and often legal relationships. Some formulations of covenant theology can be traced to the language of diplomacy and contract in the ancient Near East. Other religious metaphors draw on nature or the fabrication of objects. The metaphor "covenant" is distinct from these latter because it refers to personal, social, historical experiences. It forces us to think "relationally." Making this personal metaphor so central was a major theological achievement of Israel. At the same time the Old Testament makes an effort not to depict God as a partner of human beings on their own level. Yet it was precisely this metaphor of covenant that paved the way for christology: Only when "relation" is no longer seen as an ontological accident, as for the Greeks, but as the trinitarian essence of Godself is it possible to think of incarnation (J. Ratzinger).

The biblical relationship between covenant and law (Torah) is important. Covenant is the comprehensive term: God establishes a relationship with God's people. Israel lives that relationship when it obeys God's will. Ultimately it cannot do it, but God's covenantal will is greater than Israel's failure. Here enters the Pauline doctrine of justification in Galatians where the covenantal promise to Abraham, fulfilled in Christ, is placed above the law of Sinai. The theology of the priestly document in the Old Testament already thought along analogous lines, making God's fidelity to the covenant independent of human obedience. The prophetic promise of a new covenant was another approach to the same thing: in the new covenant God will give a Torah that need not be taught because it is written in human hearts, never again to be broken by sin.

The promise of a new covenant in Jeremiah 30–31, associated with return from exile, is only for Israel: to that extent it had already been incipiently fulfilled before Jesus. But in the canonical layer of the psalter, in Pss 24 and 25, it was combined with the promise of the eschatological pilgrimage of the nations to Zion, when they will receive a share in Israel's covenant (Ps 25:14). As the promise of a new heart it was first completely fulfilled in the "heart of Jesus" that broke on the cross and began that new phase of salvation history in which the nations could also become part of Israel's covenant. The relationship between old and new covenant was already conceived in Jeremiah 31 as a contrast (*not* like the covenant at the exodus from Egypt!) and yet a continuation (*the same* Torah!). In the New Testament both aspects are also present, for example in 2 Corinthians 3 where both covenants have "glory," although in the new covenant the veil will be removed.

—*Norbert Lohfink*

Leviticus

Armando J. Levoratti

FIRST READING

On a first reading the book of Leviticus seems peculiarly out of touch with our spontaneous feeling. Its general topic is not one of wide appeal. With its detailed regulations of ceremonies such as the burning of animals and the sprinkling of blood it appears to be irrelevant and even repulsive. The practice of blood sacrifice seems downright barbaric, and many liturgical rites that accompanied sacrifices as well as its norms of hygiene and dietary rules make us ask under our breath: Does this book really contain the inspired word of God? Is there in it something more than meaningless ritual?

To make things more difficult for the reader (and for the preacher who would use these texts in a helpful way), the fact is that many moral and ceremonial rules that once governed Israelite life have come into question. Like all rules, the priestly regulations of Leviticus were embedded in a particular culture and changes in the historical and cultural context lead to the depreciation of certain values and the emergence of new ones. Slavery and war, for example, meant one thing in the biblical world, another in our own. Leviticus 25:42-46 gives the theological basis for not enslaving Israelites but permits the enslavement of non-Israelites since they were outside the boundaries of the covenant community. Likewise an easy victory over enemies is one of the blessings promised to those who keep God's commandments: "Five of you shall give chase to a hundred, and a hundred of you shall give chase to ten thousand; your enemies shall fall before you by the sword" (Lev 26:8). But in a time like the present, characterized by belief in the equality of all people, it is impossible to consider any kind of slavery as a morally acceptable institution, and in this nuclear age only a few of us would regard as a blessing the bloodshed of war, even if the blood poured forth is that of the enemies in a case of legitimate self-defense.

If our way of life is so different from that of ancient Israel that some of these laws are inapplicable nowadays, other commands in turn have lost any relevance for Christians because of the changed situation under the New Covenant. This is particularly clear in the case of unclean animals. Jesus "declared all foods clean" (Mark 7:19) and Paul had a clear perception that the Jewish dietary laws created a barrier that hindered the spread of the Christian faith in the pagan world. Of paramount importance is also the Christian belief that the OT sacrificial cult was brought to an end "through the offering of the body of Jesus Christ once for all" (Heb 10:10) "for it is impossible for the blood of bulls and goats to take away sins" (Heb 10:4). God does not take pleasure in sacrifices and burnt offerings (Ps 40:6; Heb 10:6). With the death and resurrection of Christ the sacrificial system of the First Covenant became obsolete for Christians and they have no need to offer burnt offerings for the atonement of their sins. Moreover "God is spirit, and those who worship him must worship in spirit and truth" (John 4:24).

All this is true, and it seems fair to acknowledge that the book of Leviticus in many of its detailed requirements appears remote from our cultural world and from our own religious needs. The minutiae of the ancient Jewish ceremonial law are little more than antiquarian lore for us. The wealth of detail with which they are presented is apt to kill the reader's interest. And yet, viewed in a broader light, the book has not a few points of attraction. Its basic and underlying doctrine has much to say even at the present time, and if readers pay close enough attention they will find sentences everywhere that are strikingly to the point even today. The only condition to meet in order to reach this wealth of doctrine is to penetrate the outward appearance and discern what lies below the surface.

First of all, the laws of Leviticus presuppose a lofty and spiritual conception of God. God is holy and the only fount of all holiness, and God's presence with Israel radiates this holiness to all close to God. Holiness, as something belonging to a mysterious, unapproachable, and unpredictable divine power, is an idea well known to many peoples. Such a power cannot be clearly defined but an impressive encounter with its reality can be experienced in lightning or earthquake, fertility of the soil or thundering waterfall, death-dealing plague or desolating fire. This primitive meaning of holiness, derived from elemental human experiences, is never completely absent in the OT (cf. 2 Sam 6:6-8; Isa 6:3-5), but the great contribution of Hebrew prophets was to infuse this idea with lofty ethical meaning. In agreement with the prophetic teaching this mature conception of God's holiness is conveyed with particular force in the book of Leviticus and is reflected there in the two refrains: "I the LORD, I who sanctify you, am holy" (21:8; cf. 20:8; 21:15, 23; 22:9, 16, 32) and "You shall be holy, for I the LORD your God am holy" (19:2; cf. 11:44-45; 20:26).

Furthermore a recurrent theme in biblical law is that the weakest members of society should receive special protection. The orphan and the widow, the poor and the immigrant are often singled out for special treatment. YHWH, the God of Israel, is the guardian of the poor and the oppressed, the avenger of those who have been unjustly treated. Therefore the Law prescribes a whole range of charitable attitudes and social measures to mitigate the suffering of the needy (cf. Exod 22:20-26; Deut 15:7-11).

A good example of this humanitarian concern for the poor is Lev 19:9-10, where the Lord commands that part of the harvest must be left so that those who are in need may glean it (cf. Ruth 2:2-3). If we take this demand in accordance with the strict meaning of the words it is obvious that it is inapplicable literally in our modern societies, but for Christian interpreters of the Bible it is not enough to understand what the words signified at the time when they were written. They must also seek to understand and communicate the meaning of the biblical message for today, and this requires us to pay special attention to the moral and religious principles underlying the legislation. In other words, Lev 18:9-10 challenges the reader to recognize the social dimension of the biblical faith and to adopt the point of view of the divine legislator, which is the preferential option for the poor. This option includes an active participation in the liberating work of God for justice, taking the path of solidarity and joining in the struggle for just social change. In the spirit of Leviticus 25, and as part of the jubilee of the year 2000, Pope John Paul II has called for a substantial reduction if not outright cancellation of the international debt of poor countries.

Another far-reaching belief that underlies the laws of Leviticus is that God is actually present with God's people. The laws of Leviticus continue the narrative of Exodus and an important theme in the final part of Exodus is God's intention to dwell among the people of Israel (Exod 25:8; 29:45-46). Therefore chs. 25–31; 35–40 of that book focus almost exclusively on the construction and furnishing of the Tabernacle as God's dwelling place. Following the erection of the Tabernacle a cloud covered it and the glory of the Lord filled it (Exod 40:34). YHWH now dwelt in the midst of Israel and the Tabernacle was designated "the tent of meeting" (40:35; cf. 27:21) because it was the place where God and the people communed together. Its portable nature ensured that the Lord would be with the people wherever they went.

YHWH was preeminently present in Israel's worship. All the cultic regulations, and especially those for the offering of sacrifices, indicate again and again that the ceremonies take place "before the LORD" and the food offerings make a "pleasing odor to the LORD" (Lev 1:9, 13, 17; 2:9; 3:5, and elsewhere). This presence of God with God's chosen people was permanent in the Tabernacle, but on special occasions the divine glory appeared in cloud and fire so that people could recognize the Lord's presence. The initial lawgiving at Sinai, the erection of the Tabernacle, and the ordination of the priests (9:24) were all marked in this spectacular fashion.

Moreover, the covenant of YHWH with Israel involved blessings and curses (Leviticus 26). If the people obeyed the Law they were to expect greater and greater prosperity. One of the blessings was the gift of rain at the right season; another, magnificent harvests. But the crowning blessing is God's presence: "I will place my dwelling in your midst . . . I will walk among you, and will be your God, and you shall be my people" (26:11-13).

There is another point worthy of note. In spite of its alien character to many contemporary readers, particularly in western society, Leviticus has always been central to Jewish life. Of the 613 commandments found in Scripture, 247 appear in this book, and so revered was an ancient commentary on Leviticus that it attained the unique designation *Sifra* ("The Book"). Jesus himself drew out the very core of the Law and the Prophets with a double quotation, one part from Deuteronomy and the other from Leviticus: "'You shall love the Lord your God with all your heart, and with all your soul, and with all your mind.' This is the greatest and first commandment. And a second is like it: 'You shall love your neighbor as yourself.' On these two commandments hang all the law and the prophets" (Matt 22:37-40 // Mark 12:30-31 // Luke 10:27; Deut 6:5; Lev 19:18).

We can add, finally, that the levitical code regulated the Israelite cult until the destruction of the Temple and the cessation of actual sacrifices in 70 C.E., but its theological background lived on and was a source of inspiration for the NT writers. The sacrificial system of Leviticus is no longer relevant for Christians, but from studying it we can learn a great deal about the nature of sin, the necessity of atonement, and the superiority of Christ's sacrifice. In particular the letter to the Hebrews refers again and again to the institutions of the first covenant to demonstrate that they were unable to bring about the complete removal of sins, using a series of contrasts to show that the high priesthood of Jesus is far superior to that of Aaron (Heb 9:24-28). The high priest in OT times never entered the Holy of Holies without blood, but the blood he sprinkled on the ark was the "blood of goats and bulls." Christ, acting as the high priest of the new and everlasting covenant, offered "his own blood" and his "once for all" sacrifice successfully "found eternal redemption." The repetition of Aaron's sacrifices was a constant reminder of the persistence of sin; Christ's once-for-all offering on the cross secured permanent forgiveness. Whereas the Aaronic priests served in the earthly Tabernacle, "a sketch and shadow of the heavenly one" (Heb 8:5), Christ entered "into heaven itself, now to appear in the presence of God on our behalf" (Heb 9:24). That is why the believers can "approach the throne of grace with boldness, so that we may receive mercy and find grace to help in time of need" (Heb 4:16).

Title and Literary Structure of the Book

As with other books of the Pentateuch, Jews title this book according to the word that stands at the beginning of the Hebrew text. Thus in Hebrew Bibles Leviticus is known as *Wayyiqra'* ("and he called"). Christians, however, have adopted a latinized form of the Greek word *levitikon,* which is the title given by the Septuagint (LXX).

The book of Leviticus is a literary unit within the larger Pentateuch. Even a casual reading of the Pentateuch detects a continuous body of legal materials running from Exod 25:1 through Num 10:10 (the so called "Sinai pericope"), but there are very significant signals within this pericope itself that alert us to the literary integrity of Leviticus. Exodus 25–40 is concerned essentially with the construction of the Tabernacle at the foot of Mount Sinai. Once this construction has been completed "the cloud covered the tent of meeting, and the glory of the LORD filled the tabernacle" (Exod 40:34). Only when the glory-cloud ascended from its resting place on the Tabernacle were the people of Israel to journey forth, and the people did so at the very end of the Sinai pericope (Num 10:11). Numbers 1–10 in turn is concerned primarily with the organization of the Israelite camp into marching order as it prepares to move forward to the conquest of Canaan. At this time there is a census of all those "able to go to war." In between, Leviticus discloses the constitutive precepts God gave from the place where the Tabernacle first stood. The distinctive content of Leviticus is thus identified concisely in the words of its double conclusion: "These are the statutes and ordinances and laws that the LORD established between himself and the people of Israel on Mount Sinai through Moses" (Lev 26:46); "These are the commandments that the LORD gave to Moses for the people of Israel on Mount Sinai" (Lev 27:34).

Most of this book has to do with worship. Dealing as it does almost exclusively with legislation ordering proper cultic practice, Leviticus is more unified in content than the books that surround it in the biblical canon; however, it is important to recognize that the laws of Leviticus are part of a historical narrative. Under the Sinai covenant Israel has been called to become "a priestly kingdom and a holy nation" (Exod 19:6) and these laws illustrate how God's purpose to make of Israel God's chosen people was worked out in an all-embracing system of religious service and social law.

The laws of Leviticus represent a stage in the development of Israelite worship and religion. They are presented as speeches of God to Moses (and sometimes also to his brother Aaron), but this is a literary device justified by the need to put all the Pentateuchal legislation under the authority of Moses. In its present form it is a priestly compilation made in Jerusalem about 500 B.C.E. and reflecting the ritual practice of the Second Temple (built in 515), although it contains earlier material.

Israelite Worship and the Book of Leviticus

The book of Leviticus is essentially a ritual: for sacrifices, for the ordination of priests, for the purification and expiation of sins. It communicates vital information for the understanding of worship in the Jerusalem Temple until its destruction in 70 C.E., but a ritual is intended to lead to the offering of specific forms of worship rather than to explain the significance of all its demands. Therefore a superficial reading of the book can give the impression that its content is no more than empty ritual without true personal devotion. Even more, it can reinforce the false conception that puts the priests in an unfavorable light compared with the prophets, the former being regarded as professionals of religion focused on externals and obsessed with material definitions of impurity, and the latter concerned with nobler spiritual teachings.

The best way of removing this wrong idea is to read the book of Leviticus against the background of the whole OT. In this way we realize that worship was the normal and most frequent manner in which the Israelites experienced YHWH. In addition we can see that, while the offering of sacrifices was a prominent part of ritual in Israelite circles, it would be erroneous to think that all of Israel's ritual was sacrificial in nature. So, for example, an important element of Israel worship hardly mentioned in Leviticus is that of prayer and song, even though many of the psalms were probably composed for use in Temple worship (cf. 1 Chr 16:4-36) and individuals would naturally go to the Temple to pray (cf. 1 Sam 1:9-18; 1 Kings 8:22, 27-30; Luke 18:10). Fasting, too, at least on particular occasions, was a condition of belonging to the people of God (Lev 23:29) and pious Israelites fasted out of personal devotion, whether for motives of purification, mourning, or supplication (cf. 2 Sam 12:6). The national liturgy had a "great fast" on the Day of Atonement and a special day of fasting was proclaimed in times of distress (Joel 1:14; Ezra 8:21; 2 Chr 20:3).

It is difficult to assess the influence of the cult in the formation and preservation of the Israelite faith, but the fact is that in the ancient world people could not think of a personal religion in an individualistic sense. What the people believed was professed by the group that assembled for the worship of YHWH. The Israelite prophets deviate sharply from the general patterns, but even they should not be considered apart from the cultic system in which they lived and in which they formed their basic ideas about YHWH.

The OT gives abundant space to cultic actions but it does not contain a systematic compendium of non-sacrificial rituals. Because of the elusiveness of the biblical tradition on this point one should be attentive to scattered references throughout all the biblical books. The following outline tries to draw out of the biblical texts some distinctive features of the Israelite cult and its development until Christian times.

In the traditions of the Pentateuch there are passages that depict the patriarchs offering sacrifices (Gen 22:13; 31:54; 46:1) or building an altar (Gen 12:7-8; 13:4; 26:25) or erecting and anointing with oil a pillar of stone (Gen 28:18; 35:14). This worship was not yet a realm set apart from the rest of life, but was fully integrated into the way of life of the wandering group. There were no priests or temples; the patriarchs themselves performed priestly functions at temporary altars built in the open.

The book of Exodus reports that Moses was sent to bring the people out of Egypt for the purpose of keeping a pilgrim feast and offering sacrifices in the wilderness (Exod 5:3) and that on the eve of the departure of the Israelites from Egypt he prescribed the Passover ritual: each family was to sacrifice a lamb, smear its blood on the doorposts, and celebrate a sacred meal at night, eating the flesh of the lamb. Moses further commanded the Israelites to repeat this rite each year and to explain its meaning to their children. In this way the Passover was linked with the memory of the deliverance from Egypt and was a perpetual reminder to Israel of what the Lord had wrought for them. In the days of the wandering, Jethro, Moses' father-in-law, was priest of Midian and "brought a burnt offering and sacrifices to God" (Exod 18:1, 12).

The unique element in Israelite worship, according to Pentateuchal traditions, was established by the theophany at Sinai. Here for the first time, on the way through the wilderness to the promised land, the group liberated from Egypt experienced the word of God coming to them from the theophany (Exodus 19; 24:15-18). In contrast to the patriarchal stories, the receiver of God's revelation is not an individual but the whole people. In this foundational event Moses becomes the mediator; to him alone God speaks after he has made his way to God.

According to the book of Joshua the first encampment of the Israelites after the crossing of the Jordan was at Gilgal (Josh 4:19). There they kept the first Passover in the Holy Land (Josh 5:10). Since an important sanctuary is known to have stood there it is probable that a YHWH shrine was established there at that time. Joshua 4:1-9, 20-24 tells of the carrying of stones from the Jordan to Gilgal, where they were set up as memorial stones (Hebrew *gilgal* means "circle" [of stones]) but that circle must have been in existence from a much earlier period than that of the Israelite conquest. A number of early traditions about Saul are set in Gilgal, and there he was proclaimed king (1 Sam 11:14-15). The sanctuary of Gilgal became an important place for sacrificial offerings (1 Sam 10:8; 11:15b; 13:8-10; 15:21) and the tribes rallied there from time to time on great occasions (Hos 4:15; 9:15; 12:11; Amos 4:4; 5:5).

In the time of the Judges the Israelites continued to offer their own sacrifices on simple outdoor altars (Judg 6:24-27; 13:19) but priests and temples were also known. Levites were considered the proper people to act as priests (17:13) and there was a temple at Shiloh where the ark of the Lord was kept until it was captured by the Philistines (1 Sam 4:11). But before the rise of the monarchy no uniformity existed because there was no central authority that could enforce it.

In the time of the monarchy the cult was given new energy with far-reaching effect when David brought the ark of the covenant to mount Zion, thus making Jerusalem the central shrine (2 Sam 6:12-19). The ark was venerated by all the Israelite tribes and its removal to Jerusalem lent enormous prestige to that center, making it the most important rallying point for Yahwism. David had thought of building a temple for YHWH but the prophet Nathan discouraged him from breaking with the ancient tradition of the tent shrine (2 Sam 7:5-7).

Solomon, David's son and successor to the throne of Jerusalem, carried out an extensive nationwide building program; his most memorable accomplishment was the construction of the Temple on Mount Zion. This Temple was a fitting edifice for housing the ark of the Lord, yet at the beginning it could not have won the favor of all. The fact that Solomon commissioned a Phoenician architect, Hiram of Tyre (1 Kings 7:13-14), is sufficient to indicate the alien character of this structure whose conception and decorations were typically Canaanite. A time would come when the Temple of Jerusalem would play a role in Israel's worship but at this stage it may have provoked prophetic hostility to Solomon, whose participation in international affairs brought to his kingdom many foreign religious practices. Nevertheless the existence of the Temple of Zion was nearly continuous for over a millennium although it did undergo two major reconstructions: one beginning in 520 B.C.E. following the exile, and the other as part of the vast building projects carried out by King Herod, who reigned in Palestine from 37 to 4 B.C.E.

During the period of the monarchy there was a wide variety of cultic rites in the different sanctuaries of Israel and Judah (cf. Hos 4:13, 15;

8:11; 9:15; Amos 3:14; 4:4-5; Jer 17:2-3). No single shrine was accorded absolute precedence over all others although Jerusalem was obviously the most significant of Israel's sanctuaries. Crowds of pilgrims made their journey to Jerusalem, drawn there by the splendor of its Temple, and the prestige of the City of David as a religious center strengthened the political unity of the kingdom. In the northern kingdom the importance of Jerusalem was openly disavowed (cf. 1 Kings 12:26-29). Jeroboam set up golden calves at Bethel and Dan as rivals to the Temple cult of Jerusalem, completing the political schism with a religious one.

The Canaanite environment was very influential. Every increase of our knowledge of the Canaanite cult has shown how deeply the Israelites were indebted to the Canaanites for the form of their worship. Before their use by Israel many sanctuaries had been used as temples of El and Baal. So heavy was this borrowing from Canaan that it is now beyond the powers of the historian to make any probable reconstruction of what the Israelite cult was like when the people first settled in Canaan. From Canaanite practices Israel drew its types of sacrifices and its calendar for the liturgical feasts. These feasts were later transformed in light of the faith of Israel and they became memorial celebrations of the saving deeds of Israel's God.

In spite of this influence the imageless worship of YHWH made Israel's faith unique in the ancient world. The prohibition of images is comprehensive, covering anything visible and susceptible of representation. The implication of this prohibition is that YHWH can be assimilated by nothing in the universe (Exod 20:4; Deut 5:8).

Further, it is a false understanding of ancient religion to suppose that its cult was only the performance of outward ceremonies and traditional rites. The worship of the shrines with its spoken words and visual symbolism, was not merely a way of access to God. In a culture where only a few attained literacy the sacred shrine was the single most powerful agency for the continuity of religion. The hereditary priesthood that normally carried out this worship passed on from one generation to another the holy lore that had been entrusted to it, and the personal piety of each Israelite was very much molded by the attitudes and traditions fostered by corporate worship at the local sanctuaries. At these religious shrines the earliest Scriptures of Israel were collected and kept in order.

Worship in Israel was not a performance undertaken before the throne of a passive divine spectator. The God of Israel was believed to be present in the Temple on Mount Zion in Jerusalem (cf. Ps 48:2-4) so that to worship before God was to stand in the divine presence and "behold the face of God" (cf. Ps 42:2). Moreover, to come into God's presence at God's holy place was to enter a sphere of sacred activity, to encounter a dynamic and powerful presence. But ritual law embraces repetitive ceremonial practices whose meaning and value easily elude the worshiper and it is more susceptible than other aspects of holy law to the charge of ritualism. Therefore the prophets often uttered violent attacks on Israel's worship. They contrasted the futility of sacrifices and other religious observances with obedience to YHWH and with doing right and acting justly. To the worshipers who regarded YHWH as an automatic provider of good things once the proper rites had been performed Amos said: "I hate, I despise your festivals" (5:21). Hosea, his slightly younger contemporary, issued a similar warning: "I desire steadfast love and not sacrifice, the knowledge of God rather than burnt offerings" (6:6). And Isaiah means the same thing when he says to those who appear before the Lord in the Temple: "Your hands are full of blood" (1:15; cf. Jer 6:20; 7:21-22; Mic 6:6-8).

This accusation against corrupt worship is probably the most typical reproach made by the prophets of Israel. Like no other, it accompanies the entire history of biblical prophecy on into the post-exilic period where we still encounter it in Trito-Isaiah and in Malachi. Such an impressive collection of passages seems to suggest that the pre-exilic prophets repudiated sacrifices and all cultic practices (Temple, sacrifices, festivals, altars, priests) in favor of a moral and non-cultic religion. However, the full evidence does not warrant such a drastic conclusion. What the prophets rejected was not the cult as such but the formalism of exterior worship when it has no corresponding interior dispositions (Isa 29:13). No elaborate formal worship can be a substitute for purity of heart, integrity of life, and obedience to YHWH. A religion without moral obedience, however elaborate in ceremonies and festivals, becomes an empty form and does not fulfill the demands of the holy God of Israel.

Therefore there is no reason to draw a sharp division between the prophetic religion of the spirit and the cultic religion of the priests as set forth in the Pentateuch, where sacrifice is enjoined and its ritual defined. When the prophet poses the question: "What does the Lord require of Israel?" (cf. Micah 6:6-8) the priestly response is: "You shall be holy, for I the LORD your God am holy" (Lev 19:2). The psalms and the wisdom books repeat the same lesson (cf. Ps 50:7-15; Prov 15:8; 21:3, 27). Out of a profound experience of penitence Psalm 51 declares that God will take delight in sacrifices and burnt offerings once the worshiper presents to God the acceptable sacrifice of a broken and contrite heart (vv. 10-12, 16-19).

When the last remnant of the state of Judah fell to the Babylonians in 587 B.C.E. a new phase of Israelite life came into being. Jews who had been deported to Babylon formed a community in exile and many of them cherished the hope of returning to their old homeland to reestablish the nation and restore the Temple cult. Meanwhile worship received a significant expansion in the captivity. Since sacrifices could not be offered it took the form of prayer and preaching. By the streams and canals of the Tigris and Euphrates rivers—"the waters of Babylon"—the exiles gathered for prayer and sad "remembrance" of Mount Zion and Jerusalem (cf. Psalm 137).

At the same time those who had escaped deportation made pilgrimages to the site of the ruined Temple. With shaved beards, torn garments, and gashed bodies they brought cereal offerings and incense to present to the Lord of Zion (Jer 41:4-5), and laments and ritual weeping could be heard on the road to the holy place (cf. Lam 1:4). Years later, even after the return of some exiles from Babylon, the anniversary of the burning of the Temple was still commemorated with fasting and mourning (Zechariah 7). Rather than rejoicing before YHWH the worshipers were to make atonement *(kipper)* for the guilt of the nation (cf. Nehemiah 9).

When the crisis of the exile was over and those who returned from Babylon dedicated themselves to the heavy task of rebuilding the life of the nation, the leaders of the restored community gave first place to the restoration of the Jerusalem Temple with its sacrifices, festivals, fast days, and above all the observance of the Sabbath. Suitable psalms became associated with these great occasions. In the great thoughts of the psalms, recited and sung, there was a strong safeguard against the too-easy tendency of ritual acts to degenerate into empty formality. The poet of Psalm 50, for example, speaks in the person of YHWH and tells the Israelites that he does not need sacrifices to satisfy his hunger. Instead of that, God prefers vows, prayers of thanksgiving, and sincere confession of need (cf. Ps 50:7-23; 51:19).

As the consecration of one day out of seven to God the Sabbath is certainly a distinctive Israelite observance; nothing like it is known elsewhere. However, the Sabbath is rarely mentioned in early texts; a few passages mention it in the period of the monarchy but by far the most references to it are post-exilic. One may say that rigorous Sabbath observance began with the Priestly codex in the post-exilic period and was developed with even greater rigor at Qumran and in the rabbinic period.

In the second century B.C.E. the Qumran community withdrew from the life of the nation and the Temple cult and established a kind of monastic way of life on the shores of the Dead Sea. In their view God had withdrawn from the Jerusalem Temple because the Maccabean high priests of that time were not legitimate, and as such had defiled the Temple and the whole land. The sect carried out the strictest holiness code and purity regulations in the desert, and its only worship was the "liturgy of the word." The priests offered no sacrifices but they preserved holiness for the presence of God on earth in the hope that God would soon inaugurate a new order in Israel and the world.

The Qumran texts contain a consistent temple symbolism. The community is represented as a new temple and sacrifice is seen as being spiritual in character, offered in the praise, the prayers, and the holy and pure lives of the members of the community. No direct parallel to this temple symbolism has been traced in Judaism but temple imagery is used in the NT to describe the body of Christ (John 2:21), the Christian community (1 Cor 3:16-17; Eph 2:19-22; 1 Pet 2:5-6), and the individual (1 Cor 6:19; 2 Cor 6:16).

With the destruction of Jerusalem by the Romans in 70 C.E. sacrificial worship came to an end, and the whole of Israel's religious life underwent a radical change. Without Temple and political autonomy the divinely revealed Torah (the Law) became the rallying force of the Jewish people. The prayers and teaching in the synagogues took the place of sacrifices in the Temple at Jerusalem and the liturgy was recast and readapted according to the needs of the time. The most prominent symbol in a synagogue is the ark in which the scrolls of the Torah are deposited and toward which worshipers in prayer turn their faces. Together with the exposition and observance of the Law, messianic hope also plays an important role.

The cult of the early Church was marked by the exuberance of joy. The Christian communities gathered "with glad and generous hearts" for praise and prayer, for instruction and "the breaking of bread" (Acts 2:46-47). Several NT texts report that the singing of hymns and songs inspired by the Holy Spirit was an important part of early Christian liturgy (Col 3:16; cf. 1 Cor 14:15; Eph 5:19). They met to worship "on the first day of the week" because it was the Lord's day, the day of the resurrection of Jesus. In the first stage of the Church's history worship was inspired by an effervescence of hope for the almost immediate return of the Lord. A characteristic liturgical word was Maranatha, "Our Lord, come!" (Rev 22:20; cf. 1 Cor 16:22). This practice must have issued from the first generation of Jewish Christians since the expression was preserved in its Aramaic original. The mood of the assemblies was mirthful because it was dominated by the remembrance of the past and the expectation of the future.

Christian worship is not confined to liturgical gatherings. In 1 Pet 2:5 the whole community is pictured as a temple of living stones and a priestly body that offers spiritual sacrifices in a life consistent with its faith, and Paul uses the language of the Israelite cult to describe the whole of Christian existence. Christians who strive to do what is right present themselves "as a living sacrifice, holy and acceptable to God" (Rom 12:1) and the preaching of the gospel, which is authentic worship of God, makes the offering of the Gentiles "acceptable, consecrated by the Holy Spirit" (Rom 15:16). If the Christian life is to be regarded as worship paid to God, the spreading of Christ's gospel is easily compared to the priestly service in such worship. Likewise in 2 Cor 2:14-16 Paul borrows two sacrificial terms—"fragrance" and "aroma"—and applies them to the proclamation of the gospel by the apostolic ministries.

Although the divine glory dwelt in the Temple of Jerusalem it remained a building of stone and wood. In the New Covenant, according to Christian belief, Jesus himself took the place of the Temple. As the incarnate Word of God he is the Tabernacle of God (cf. John 2:21). On the cross he achieved once and for all what the high priests of the First Covenant had attempted to do on the Day of Atonement (cf. Heb 10:1-18; Eph 5:2) and the Spirit given by Jesus is to animate worship "in Spirit and truth" (John 4:24) that replaces the sacrifices and cultic practices of the old Temple.

The Great Theme of Leviticus: Holiness

The laws of Leviticus are embedded in the historical narratives describing the conclusion of the covenant at Mount Sinai. It was there that Israel became a "holy people," that is, a people separated from the other nations and consecrated to the Lord (Exod 19:6). Israel's holiness, therefore, is the result of an act of divine grace, a gratuitous gift of God. But even though Israel was the very own people of YHWH by divine election and covenant it had to sanctify itself by its obedience to the will of God. Those made holy by God were expected to remain holy by doing nothing that would compromise their special status, and the moral and cultic laws of Leviticus were intended to show how they could keep their holiness.

As we saw at the beginning, holiness is a dominant topic in the book of Leviticus. God is holy (19:2) and God's holiness is supremely active and effective (cf. 10:1-3). Since God radiates holiness to all that is near, everything that was vowed or consecrated to God was to be removed from ordinary use. In fact "removed from secular use" is the original meaning of the word "holy" when applied to things, places, or ministers of the cult. The Tabernacle where God was present, the altar of sacrifice, and the days consecrated to divine worship were all holy, as were the vestments for religious rites, the oil for anointing, and the offerings and sacrificial victims. One did not touch or approach these holy things except on certain conditions of ritual purity.

Particularly holy were the priests, whose duty it was to perform the sanctifying rituals and teach the people the way of holiness (10:10). They in particular were near to God, for they drew near themselves (cf. 9:7-8) and brought near to the altar the victims of sacrifices (7:9;

21:6). Next to the priests in holiness were the Levites. Although they were prohibited from offering sacrifices they were allowed to eat from the sacred portions allocated to the priests.

In a particular way the book of Leviticus highlights the fact that human creatures are infinitely remote from the holy God and unworthy to stand in God's presence. It also has a deep sense of the separation between the perfect righteousness of God and the sinfulness of the human. Yet the infinitely holy God persists in seeking the sanctification of sinful creatures. Therefore alongside the texts that exalt God's transcendence Leviticus also teaches that the holy God desires to draw near to all creatures and bestow on them the very quality that is the unique divine prerogative: sanctity. Because God alone is holy the possibility and the degree of holiness in creatures depends on God's sanctifying action. Therefore God says to the people: "I am holy," and "I am the LORD; I sanctify you" (20:8).

Yet while Leviticus notes the divine side of sanctification it also emphasizes human commitment. Sanctification has two aspects: a divine act and human actions. The behavior of each member of the covenant people must mirror in his or her daily life that of God's very self (20:7). Their actions and attitudes are to take as a model God's purity and moral perfection. For this reason God's command to the Israelites, "You shall be holy, for I the LORD your God am holy" (19:2; cf. 11:44-45; 20:26) became the first imperative governing the people's behavior. This command looks not only for purity in worship but also for a lived holiness in familial, social, and economic contexts. Given the concern to regulate human activity by law, the main emphasis of the book is on what every member of the covenant people has to do to be really holy.

The Israelites were also to keep holy anything sanctified by God. This applies, for example, to the Sabbath day. Because God had sanctified it they were commanded to maintain its sanctity by refraining from all work (Lev 23:3; cf. Exod 20:8-11; Deut 5:12-15). In this way the priestly theology of Leviticus brings out two aspects of holiness that at first sight seem to be contradictory. God appears eager to communicate the divine holiness to Israel, but equally jealous to safeguard the divine sanctity. Holiness is a gift of God, not a result of human efforts. The people must, therefore, take great care not to attribute to themselves what is wholly a gift from above. At the same time Leviticus combines the "ought" with the "is" of the people of God. Holiness involves the total consecration of human life and labor to God's service. That is why Israel was constantly reminded that it was holy and had to remain holy, set apart for God's service. This holiness is attained by acting justly, loving mercy, and walking humbly with God (cf. Mic 6:8).

The opposite of holiness is uncleanness or impurity, regarded as an invisible, mysterious, and almost material substance attached sometimes to persons and things. Contact with a corpse, the involuntary flow of fluids from the sexual organs, suffering from certain types of skin diseases, or the eating of prohibited foods all caused an individual to become unclean. Both holiness and uncleanness were perceived by the ancient Israelites as being dynamic; that is, they had the ability to transmit their nature to other people or objects. As some holy objects made holy everything that touched them (6:11), so uncleanness was contagious and could be transmitted from some unclean things by simple contact (cf. 11:39-40). While impure, a person was enjoined from certain actions, primarily contact with the sanctuary and its cultic practices, and specific rites of purification were prescribed for various forms of ritual impurity. To defile the sanctuary by failing to make use of the available means of purification was to risk death.

Death and uncleanness are generally linked because they are the opposites of life and holiness. We are here in the realm of taboo, with the connotations of danger, interdiction, and prohibition that are usually associated with this term (cf. 2 Sam 6:6-7). But the distinctive Hebrew development of the concept of holiness gave a predominantly ethical basis to the primitive notion of uncleanness that the Hebrews retained in conjunction with other peoples. As a consequence of this shift from the ritual to the moral sphere the state of uncleanness results not only from involuntary causes (such as the menstrual flow and persistent skin diseases) but also from decisions that are under human control. These occur when people transgress any boundary established by God (cf. the commentary on Lev 13:1-59).

The duty of the priests was to maintain the ritual purity of Israel and its sanctuary by performing the rites that removed the last vestiges of impurity from the body and the consciousness of the worshipers. This was the case not only for individuals but also for the nation as a whole. The need for the nation to be purged of sin is vividly portrayed in the scapegoat ceremony of the Day of Atonement (Leviticus 16).

The Worldview of the Priestly Work

As a part of the Sinai pericope (Exod 25:1 to Num 10:10) Leviticus represents the culminating point of the story told by the Priestly work. That story culminates in YHWH's coming to dwell with Israel as their God; the ritual laws set out the terms on which God's presence may be a blessing to them. The worldview of these writings not only revolves around the ritual of the sanctuary but is dominated by a conception of order that extends through the cosmos, the sanctuary, and human society.

The vision of order underlying the Priestly work is a concentric one. In the center was the sanctuary, YHWH's dwelling place, as the source of holiness and blessing. Within the sanctuary there was a gradation of holiness: from the Holy of Holies (or Most Holy Place) where God's divine presence appeared above the ark, through the Holy Place, to the court and so to the camp in general. The outer boundaries of the camp formed a basic division between the areas affected by the holiness radiating from the Holy of Holies and the space outside the camp. The very fact that the Priestly work conceives Israel under the image of a military camp gathered closely around the Tabernacle implies a very high degree of connection between the holiness of the Tabernacle and the holiness of the people. It was for this reason that every kind of impurity (such as that of the leper or the scapegoat) was be sent out of the camp.

For each spatial grade there is a corresponding group of people: high priest, priests, Levites, Israelites. It is characteristic of the holiness code (but not exclusive to it) that the land of Israel must be seen as holy (Num 35:33-34; cf. Lev 18:24-30). Therefore people are warned against defilement of the land by bloodshed and sexual misconduct.

Patristic Interpretation

Patristic interpretation of the Bible had recourse fairly frequently to typological and allegorical methods as a way of eliminating the scandal that particular biblical passages could provide for certain Christians. This recourse to allegory with the pastoral and pedagogical purpose of explaining some major sacrificial and cultic themes of the Mosaic Law is especially notable in the main representatives of the Alexandrian tradition.

The so-called Letter of Barnabas is the most anti-Jewish of any of the early Christian writings. Its author's purpose is to show that the Mosaic Law was perfect as originally conceived but that the Jewish people, who were its first interpreters, completely misunderstood it because they interpreted it literally. Therefore Barnabas presents a "better understanding" (that is, an allegorical explanation) of the Mosaic Law. This allegorical exegesis shows obvious dependence on the Philonic tradition but Barnabas is even more allegorical than Philo; he completely rejects literal interpretation.

Barnabas's cult criticism was drawn from the prophets and psalmists (Isa 1:11-13; Jer 7:22-23; Ps 51:19). However, he overstated it by condemning not only the abuses but also the very institution of Jewish worship. According to Barnabas all the OT prescriptions concerning sacrifice, circumcision, and diet are to be understood not literally but in a higher spiritual sense. God was not pleased with material gifts or bloody sacrifices. The sacrifice God desires is the offering of one's heart in the form of repentance. Nor was God pleased with the kind of fasting practiced by the Israelites. The fast God cares for is abstention from injustice and the practice of charity. The laws regulating the Sabbath were equally misinterpreted by the Jews. The true Sabbath is the day of eternity, "the eighth day," which we commemorate in advance by our Sunday worship. Also the rules discriminating between clean and unclean foods (cf. Leviticus 11; Deut 14:3-21) were not meant to be taken literally. They conveyed a spiritual lesson about the various sins symbolized by unclean animals. Swine, for example, are numbered among forbidden animals because some people, like the swine, forget the hand that feeds them as soon as they are surfeited with food. Eagle, hawk, kite, and raven are prohibited because they are symbolic of those who seize upon their daily bread by rapine rather than earning it by honest toil and sweat (*Barn.* 10:4). Finally, the Jews erred in regard to the Temple. The true worship of God is not bound up with the Temple of Jerusalem "for, my brethren, the habitation of our hearts is a shrine holy to the Lord" (*Barn.* 6:15).

Clement of Alexandria follows Barnabas in totally rejecting any literal significance for the sacrificial code and follows Philo in viewing OT sacrifice as a symbol of the soul's progress toward God. In accordance with a well-established tradition Clement sees the community and the individual as the true temple of God. In a similar way the true altar is the congregation of those who pray and the individual soul from which arises the incense of holy prayer. This close association of prayer, incense, and altar (well known from the Old and New Testaments) characterizes also the sacrificial aspects of Jesus' high priestly activity: "If, then, we say that the Lord the great High Priest offers to God the incense of sweet fragrance, let us imagine that this is a sweet fragrance of incense; but let us understand it to mean, that the Lord lays the acceptable offering of love, the spiritual fragrance, on the altar" (*Paed.* 2.8).

This tendency to spiritualize the concept of sacrifice reaches its climax with Origen. He mentions sacrifice so frequently that he has been called "the great theologian of sacrifice." In his *Homilies on Leviticus* and other writings Origen explains the meaning of sacrifice for Christians of his own day based on a spiritual interpretation of Scripture. His basic presupposition is that each offering and sacrifice was a type and figure of Christ. One of the criticisms of the OT sacrificial rites is that they were only done in Jerusalem. Christ's sacrifice is superior because it also takes place in heaven. Christ is the true Passover lamb by whose blood we are reconciled to God. In his perfect and unique offering to the Father he is both high priest and victim, the suffering servant, and the definitive antitype of Isaac's self-immolation. Christians share in Christ's offering first and foremost by martyrdom, but beyond this Origen sees prayer, forgiveness, almsgiving, and all good works as sacrificial. Those who truly understand the Law offer spiritual, not physical sacrifices (see the commentary on Hebrews).

SECOND READING

I. Laws on Sacrifices: 1:1–7:38

The opening of Leviticus continues the narrative of Exodus. In the book of Exodus the covenant between God and Israel on Mount Sinai was followed by a series of instructions for the building of the Tabernacle (Exodus 26–27) and the ordination of the Aaronic priesthood (Exodus 28–29). The building of the Tabernacle was then carried out under the direction of Moses (Exodus 35–40) and God accepted it as a worthy place of worship by revealing the divine presence in the cloud of glory (Exodus 40:34-38).

After this historical narrative Leviticus 8–9 relates the carrying out of the divine instructions for the ordination of Aaron and his sons as priests and the offering of sacrifices to God at the altar of the newly-built Tabernacle. But before the inauguration of the cult could take place, it was necessary to set out instructions for the various kinds of sacrifices to be made at the new sanctuary. As usual Moses carries out his characteristic role of mediator between God and the people. While the Lord nearly always speaks to Moses alone (on a few occasions Aaron is also included: 11:1; 13:1; 14:33; 15:1) his words are intended for either the Israelites or the priests.

The other traditions of the Pentateuch include many narratives of animal sacrifice from Cain and Abel onward (cf. Gen 4:3-4; 22:13; 31:54; 46:1), but the Priestly story does not give any account of sacrifice until at Sinai the means are established whereby the glory of the Lord may be present in Israel and Israel may be God's people.

The extent of the manual on sacrifice is clearly marked by an introduction (1:1) and a conclusion (7:37-38). Perhaps not by accident similar conclusions occur seven times in the first half of Leviticus (7:37-38; 11:46-47; 12:7b; 13:59; 14:32; 14:54-57; 15:32-33).

The Sacrificial Cult

Chapters 1–7 contain a detailed description of various types of sacrifices and a definition of occasions on which they were to be offered. They include guidelines for those who bring the offerings as well as instructions for the priests who conduct the cultic ritual.

Sacrifice, as an act of worship, has a complicated history in biblical Israel. We hear reports of it from the beginnings of human history to the post-exilic period. The primeval history presents sacrifice as a response to God's blessing (the offering of the firstlings of the flock and the first fruits, Gen 4:3:4) and as a response to God's saving (Gen 8:20-22). Here the assumption is that sacrifice is one of the most widespread of all religious phenomena and not something peculiar to Israel's relationship to its God.

Different theories have been proposed to explain the purpose and meaning of sacrifices. According to some interpreters sacrifice is a gift to the deity: the worshiper gives a costly offering to the god to secure divine aid and to turn away divine wrath. Another group of interpreters considers sacrifices as instruments by means of which the life of the sacrificed victim is released to strengthen the life of both god and the offerer. Still another group views sacrifices as means of communion, instruments by means of which the gulf between god and human is overcome. Atonement or reconciliation is effected by the sacrifice; the worshiper is enabled to live and flourish because what separated him or her from communion with the god has been overcome.

In Leviticus we are confronted with a very elaborate system of sacrifices but it is impossible to find anything like a unified and coherent theory of sacrifice. It is even doubtful whether there is in biblical Hebrew any term exactly coextensive with our term "sacrifice." In the majority of cases "sacrifice" renders the Hebrew word *zebah,* but usually this term denotes a particular sacrifice to be distinguished from the holocaust *(ʿolah).*

In fact sacrifices are acts with many aspects and we must beware of simple explanations. It can be said, however, that the basic meaning of the sacrifices is the overcoming of the distance between God and human beings, the bringing of divine power to the people, the restoration of wholeness to the community. Sacrifices were inviting gifts to God; the word *minḥah* came to have the meaning "gift" in later Hebrew usage. Sacrifices were also meals in which God and human beings partook; they were offerings caused to ascend to the heavens to appease God's wrath, and in connection with sacrifices God made atonement (Heb. *kopher*).

In Leviticus sacrifice (or more precisely sacrificial blood) is regularly associated with cleansing and sanctification. Sacrifice can undo the effects of sin and human infirmity. Therefore the ritual of sacrifices reached its annual climax on the Day of Atonement when each part of the Tabernacle was smeared with blood to cleanse it and sanctify it from the uncleannesses of the Israelites (16:19).

Basic to this conception of sacrifice is the notion of substitution. The victim of the sacrifice substituted for an individual human life or for the lives of the members of the community in situations in which God could have exacted the life of the offender. Substitution could avert God's wrath, with sacrificial blood being especially instrumental because it was the symbol of life (cf. commentary on Lev 17:10-14). God accepted the blood of the sacrifice in lieu of human blood.

The Procedure of Sacrifice

The sacrificial rites included several stages. The offerers approached the sanctuary with the animal to be sacrificed, laid their hands on it, and slaughtered it. Then the priest performed a blood ritual (sprinkling, pouring out, applying), and burned the victim on the altar. The detailed rules for the final stages varied widely according to the kind of sacrifice that was offered. Whereas the victim of the holocaust was burned completely on the altar, the ritual of the peace offering included a sacred meal eaten by the people.

The separate role of priest and offerer are carefully defined. The offerers of the sacrifice were actively involved in the cultic act. They were convinced that something very significant was achieved through these acts and knew that their relationship with God was profoundly affected by the offering of the sacrifice.

The laying on of hands occurs frequently in the sacrificial cult. The obvious meaning of this symbolic gesture is the establishing of a close relationship between the worshiper and the victim. More difficult to determine is exactly what kind of relationship this was. It is generally agreed that in laying hands on the victim the offerer attested that the sacrifice that was going to be presented to God was offered in his or her name and that the benefits of this sacrifice should accrue to the worshiper. This interpretation is confirmed by the fact that it makes sense of the absence of the gesture with birds and cereal offerings (cf. 1:14-17; 2:1-16; 5:7-13). These offerings were small; they could be carried by the offerer in the hands and a simple presentation of them was sufficient to make known that they pertained to the offerer. The laying on of hands may also indicate that the animal was taking the place of the worshiper. The victim was a vicarious substitute for the donor who was offering himself or herself to God through the sacrificial victim. In this sacrificial context it cannot be said that sins were thereby transferred to the victim for expiation. It is true that in the ceremony of the scapegoat (Lev 16:21) the sins of the people were transferred to the goat by the same gesture, but precisely because the goat was thereby loaded with the sins of the people it was regarded as defiled and therefore unworthy to be sacrificed.

This act had other uses as well. For example, by laying on of hands a person in authority could invest other persons with offices of authority, as Moses laid his hands on Joshua when appointing him leader of the Israelite people (Num 27:18-23; Deut 34:9; cf. Num 8:10); cf. also Lev 24:10-16.

There are two kinds of sacrificial offerings: those that are optional and unscheduled (chs. 1–3) and those mandated for the removal of sin and culpability (chs. 4–5). The meaning of the different types of sacrifices continues to be actively discussed. One reason for this is that all the sacrifices have much in common and there may be a substantial overlap of meaning and function.

The Holocaust (1:1-17)

Leviticus is presented from the first verse and throughout as the direction of the Lord to Moses about the types and occasions of sacrifice. The Lord speaks from the Tent of Meeting (Heb. *ʾohel moʿed*), which is the name given to the portable tent structure that housed the ark and other cult objects. In other priestly texts this structural complex is called *mishkan,* a term that also means "tent." Conceived as God's earthly residence, this sanctuary served two principal functions: it was the sacred place where God communicated the divine word and it was a cultic site where God was worshiped through sacrifices.

The paradigmatic name for what is offered here is *qorban.* This Hebrew word denotes "that which is brought near" to God by presentation upon the altar, and is found exclusively in P and in Ezek 20:28; 40:43. It is a general term covering all the sacrifices that an Israelite could offer (burnt offerings, peace offerings, purification and reparation offerings) and it applies also to any sanctuary gift such as draft animals and carts (Num 7:3) or spoils of war (Num 31:50).

The first category of sacrifice mentioned in this section of Leviticus is the burnt offering. This was the commonest and most general sacrifice. It is mentioned throughout the Bible and played a major role in public worship (cf. Numbers 28–29), especially in rites of cleansing (Lev 12:6, 8; 14:19, 22; 15:15, 30; 16:24). It was a regular offering in the Temple of Jerusalem every morning and evening, and was also offered on great occasions such as the making of the Sinai covenant (Exod 24:3-8) or the entry into the promised land (Deut 27:6). The Hebrew name of the burnt offering is *ʿolah,* which probably means "ascending" or "that which ascends," implying that the offering is entirely turned to smoke.

The characteristic feature of this sacrifice is that the entire victim is burned; nothing except the skin was given back to the person who offered it, and the priest could not benefit from its flesh. This is why the LXX translates it "holocaust" (a Greek term meaning "wholly burnt"). Moreover the term *ʿolah* has sometimes been replaced by the word *kalil,* meaning a "total" sacrifice (1 Sam 7:9; Deut 33:10. Cf. especially Ps 51:19, where *ʿolah* is used alongside *kalil*).

The priest's role did not begin until the victim was brought into contact with the altar because the person making the sacrifice would cut the throat of the victim at some distance from the altar. When the victim was a bird the ritual was modified: the offerers did not lay their hands on it nor did they cut its throat. Instead, everything was done on the altar by the priest. Leviticus 5:7 and 12:8 show that these sacrifices were offered by the poor as a substitute for sacrifices of beasts, which only the rich could afford. For the same reason sheep and goats were more common offerings than cattle.

In Leviticus the burnt offering is assigned an expiatory function: "as atonement for you" (v. 4). Usually the expression *lekapper ʿal* means "to perform rites of expiation over, near, or with respect to" a person or a group of people, or an object (such as the altar). The atoning value of the burnt offering is also hinted at in Lev 14:20; 16:24, and even more explicitly outside the Law. Job offered burnt offerings every week for each of his seven sons and three daughters because he said: "It may be that my children have sinned" (Job 1:5; cf. also 42:8; Gen 8:21). These texts show that one function of the burnt offering was to prevent God's displeasure at the people's sin from being turned into punishment. Other texts, however, do suggest that it involved more than atonement.

The antiquity of the burnt offering is well established (Gen 8:20; 22:2, 7, 8, 13; Judg 6:26; 13:16; 1 Sam 7:9; 13:12). It was a gift with any number of goals in mind and it may originally have been the only sacrifice offered except the *shelamim,* which provided food for the table. With the advent of the Temple, however, it became imperative to devise specific sacrifices to purge the sacred house and its *sancta* of their contamination and desecration. Thus the purification and reparation offerings, respectively, were devised. These two sacrifices, once introduced into the sacrificial system, became the expiatory sacrifices *par excellence.*

The Grain Offering (2:1-16)

Most sacrifices involve the slaughter of an animal and the manipulation of its blood in some way. The chief exception is the grain offering, which was occasionally offered alone (Num 5:15) but generally accompanied blood sacrifices (Lev 23:13; Num 15:1-12). Together with the burnt offering and the peace offering it produced a "pleasing odor to the LORD" (Lev 1:9, 17; 2:2, 9, 12; 3:5, 16).

Fine flour or cakes of unleavened flour mixed with oil were the principal ingredients of the cereal offering. Salt and a pinch of incense had to be added, but yeast and honey were prohibited (v. 11; cf. Exod 23:18; 34:25). The priest was to take a good fistful of the flour and oil with all the incense and burn it on the altar. The remainder belonged to "Aaron and his sons" (that is, the priests) and is described as a "most holy part" (that is, it could not be taken out of the sanctuary and was to be eaten there only by the priests).

In these offerings the small part burned on the altar is called *ʾazkarah,* a technical term of the Priestly writings (Lev 2:2, 9, 16; 5:12; 24:7; Num 5:26) derived from the verb *zakar* ("to remember"). The precise meaning of the word is unclear. The traditional rendering is "memorial" or "memorial portion" but it can also be understood as "token" or "pledge." According to the first meaning the sacrifice "reminds" God of the person who offered it; the meaning "pledge" or "token" in turn suggests that the whole offering is in fact owed to God, but God is pleased to receive only a part, the rest being a perquisite of the Aaronite priesthood.

Special stress is given in v. 13 to the symbolic value of the salt of God's covenant (cf. Ezek 43:24; 47:11). Salt stands for permanence and incorruption. It was the preservative *par excellence* in antiquity and became a symbol of fidelity. Greeks and Arabs are known to have eaten salt when they concluded covenants, and a figurative extension of its preservative properties is the reference to Jesus' disciples as "the salt of the earth" (Matt 5:13). In the OT salt is connected with covenants on two occasions (Num 18:19; 2 Chr 13:5, where the "covenant of salt" binds the two parties in an irrevocable covenant). By the addition of salt to the offering the worshipers were reminded that they were in a perpetual covenant relationship with their God.

The prohibition of yeast or honey from the cereal offering should be noted. The association of these products with fermentation and putrefaction remains the most plausible cause of such an injunction (cf. 1 Cor 5:7-8: "Clean out the old yeast so that you may be a new batch, as you really are unleavened. For our paschal lamb, Christ, has been sacrificed. Therefore, let us celebrate the festival, not with the old yeast, the yeast of malice and evil, but with the unleavened bread of sincerity and truth"). Some interpreters think that the prohibition against honey represents a reaction against the widespread use of honey in pagan cults. In forbidding the use of honey on the altar the priestly laws may have been directed at eliminating pagan practices in Israelite sacrificial worship.

The Peace Offering (3:1-17)

The peace offering (Heb. *zebah shelamim*) is sometimes called *shelamim,* a term that would be connected with the root from which derives the Hebrew word *shalom* ("peace," "well-being"). This sense of peace suggests that these sacrifices were offered for the maintenance or restoration of good relations with God. After the slaughtering of the victim by the offerer of the sacrifice the blood and the fat went to the altar, the one to be cast against it and the other to be consumed by fire upon it because they belonged exclusively to God. Other parts of the flesh became the portion of priests, and the rest of the animal was eaten by the offerer with his or her family and guests (cf. Lev 7:15; 19:6-8). The most detailed description of this kind of sacrifice, apart from the priestly legislation, is found in 1 Sam 9:12, 14, 19, 22-25.

The *zebah shelamim* is sometimes called "communion offering" or "shared offering." This describes certain aspects of its character, for it included a sacred meal (cf. 1 Cor 10:18 "are not those who eat the sacrifices partners in the altar?"). The question can be raised whether these offerings were conceived of as shared with God in the sense that God was thought to partake of the food. It is probable that such an idea was once held, and the fact that the cereal offerings accompanied the animal sacrifice lends some credence to such an idea, but there is no evidence that it was held within the historical period of Israel's life. The Israelites were as aware as anyone that God did not physically eat food (cf. Deut 12:7, where it is said that the Israelites eat the *zebah shelamim* "in the presence of the LORD" and not "with the LORD").

The offering of peace offerings was an occasion for the common enjoyment of a meal before the Lord. It is likely that festivals and family trips to the sanctuary were an opportunity to feast. In 1 Sam 1:3-5 it is said as a matter of course that Elkanah would distribute sacrificial portions in his own household. At the time of the sacrifice to solemnize the covenant Moses, Aaron, Nadab, Abihu, and the seven elders are particularly said to behold God, eat, and drink, and that festive communion is most naturally associated with the *zebah shelamim* referred to in the text (Exod 24:4-11). The association obtains in royal provision for feasts combined with sacrifices, whether the king involved be David (2 Sam 6:17-19), Solomon (1 Kings 3:15; 8:62-65), or Hezekiah (2 Chr 30:22). The notion of a sacrifice that involves worshipers in a meal is attested in the patriarchal and Mosaic narratives. Jacob formalizes his treaty with Laban on that basis (Gen 31:51-54) and Jethro celebrates both the Lord's greatness and the presence of Aaron and the elders thereby (Exod 18:9-12).

These offerings were of three kinds: the thank offering, the offering in fulfillment of a vow, and the freewill offering (Lev 22:17-29; cf. Lev 7:11). The thank offering was an expression of gratitude to God for mercies received (Psalm 107 mentions four occasions for which a thank offering would be appropriate: successful passage through the desert, release from prison, recovering from a serious illness, or surviving a storm at sea); the votive offering was given to repay a vow (cf. 2 Sam 15:7-8) and the freewill offering needed no special occasion, being the spontaneous expression of the devotion of the offerer.

The Purification Offering (4:1–5:13)

This is the fourth type of sacrifice discussed in Leviticus. The most important feature of this rite is the sprinkling of the blood on the altar or the veil of the sanctuary. The text makes its ritual subdivisions not according to the sacrificial material (as in Leviticus 1–3) but according to the persons: the high priest (4:3-12), the whole congregation (4:13-21), the tribal leader (Heb. *nasiʾ*, 4:22-26), or the ordinary people (4:27-35). The instructions vary according to the rank of the person offering the sacrifice. The ritual highlights the very special role of the high priest in ancient Israel: because of his status in the community he was the representative of the nation and his sin was believed to contaminate the people as a whole (4:3).

The Hebrew term for this kind of sacrifice is *ḥattaʾt,* usually rendered as "sin offering." This seems to be the obvious translation because *ḥattaʾt* commonly means "sin" and its consequences (cf. Num 32:23). The difficulty with this translation is that the sacrifice is required in certain cases where no sin is involved (as in 12:6). On the other hand this translation hardly corresponds to the precise function of the sacrifice, because other sacrifices also have to do with sin and atone for sin.

Purification is the main element in this kind of sacrifice. It was designed to cope with a problem created by human sin: pollution and defilement. Sin not only angers God and deprives God of what is due; it also makes the sanctuary unclean, and a holy God cannot dwell amid uncleanness. The purification offering purifies the place of worship so that God may be present among the people. The proper means of purification was animal blood.

The Reparation Offering (5:14-19)

This kind of sacrifice concludes the list of sacrifices in Leviticus 1–5. The Hebrew name of this sacrifice is *ʾasham,* which means "compensation, equivalent." It was prescribed for two main types of offenses: trespass against "holy things" and trespass against God's holy name by uttering false oaths in court. What constituted an inadvertent sin against the Lord's "holy things" (sometimes translated as "sacred property") is not specified. Perhaps failing to fulfill a dedicatory vow or to present the tithe would have been an offense meriting a reparation offering. The penalty is in two parts: the worshiper has to restore to the priesthood that of which they have been deprived by mistake plus twenty percent, and must also bring a ram to be slain at the altar. In other cases this kind of sacrifice was due where damage had been done and loss had been suffered. The offerer had to compensate the offended person and acknowledge the sin before God by bringing the sacrificial ram.

As with the other sacrifices there has been much discussion about the function and purpose of the reparation offerings in Israelite worship. Many commentators take the reparation offering as a kind of sin offering, and vice versa. However, closer examination shows that the two sacrifices were quite distinct. Not only did the choice of the sacrificial animals differ but also the circumstances in which they were offered. Moreover, whereas the sin offering was due for unwitting offenses the reparation offering was designed to compensate for offenses where damage has been done and loss incurred, which in most cases can be assessed. Restitution seems to be the key idea in the reparation offering.

In spite of some ambiguities inherent in the Israelite sacrificial system the fact is that it presents different analogies to describe the consequences of sin and the way of remedying them. If the sin offering was intended to bring purification and remove the sinful barrier to the covenant relationship the reparation offering demonstrates that satisfaction or compensation is necessary to put ourselves right by paying for the wrongs we have done. Sin has a theological and a social dimension. It affects our relationship vertically with God as well as horizontally with our neighbor. The reparation offering brings reconciliation by making amends to those we have wronged.

Instructions for the Priests (6:1–7:38)

The material in these chapters is addressed to the priests who carried out the sacrifices. The principal theme is the eating of the sacrificial meat. In most cases only the priests could eat the sacrifices but lay persons could share in the peace offerings. In various respects these rules for the conduct of worship overlap with and to some extent duplicate the materials in chs. 1–5. A main concern in 6:8-13 is that the fire on the altar of burnt offering should never go out. The section closes with a brief summary of the main topics discussed (7:37-38).

The OT emphasizes that "to obey is better than sacrifice" (1 Sam 15:22), but never the reverse. Consequently sacrifice could never take the place of the observance of God's will in everyday life. However, the strong institutionalization of sacrifice arouses the question whether this cultic act corresponds to God's will at all. This question comes to sharp expression in Ps 51:15-17, which asserts that the true sacrifice, the one pleasing to God, is praise and a contrite heart; Ps 50:7-15 after an extremely thorough criticism of the sacrifice of animals declares that God's demand is not for sacrifices but thanksgiving and prayer. This way was prepared by the criticism prophets directed toward the sacrificial practices of their time. A far-reaching change in the concept of sacrifice is also shown by the fact that the death of the suffering servant is designated as a sacrifice of expiation ("an offering for sin," Isa 53:10).

II. The Initiation of Aaron and His Sons to the Priesthood: 8:1–10:20

Ordination of the Priests and Aaron's First Sacrifices (8:1–9:24)

Chapters 8 and 9 present a detailed description of the religious celebration marking the initiation of formal worship in ancient Israel. Unlike the other sections they are not legal in formulation but rather descriptive of special ritual events; they serve to describe the fulfillment of what was ordained in Exod 29:1-37 and also overlap in content with the final chapters of Exodus. The ceremony of priestly ordination is performed by Moses, who is assumed to have attained sufficient access to God to be able to institute the priesthood. In this way Moses continues his role as mediator between God and the Israelites. The recurrent formula "As the LORD commanded Moses" (8:9, 13, 17, 21, 29; 9:10) attributes Israelite modes of worship to divine command, not to custom and convention.

Of paramount importance in the priestly tradition is the distinction between the majority of the Israelites and the selected few who were divinely appointed as priests. However, the history of the Israelite-Jewish priesthood is obscure and uncertain. At the beginning of the OT stands the domestic priesthood of the patriarchs; at the end of the development, the hereditary post-exilic priesthood. The major offices of the priests were the offering of sacrifice, the rituals of purification, and the rituals of blessing (cf. Num 6:22-27). Clear in older texts but not mentioned in the Priestly code are the functions of giving oracles and instruction in the Torah (cf. Deut 33:7; Judg 18:5; 1 Sam 14:41; 28:6; Hos 4:6).

In the ceremony of priestly ordination Aaron and his sons were brought out from the midst of the community to be consecrated as priests (cf. Heb 5:1). There then followed a period of seven days during which they were not to leave the door of the Tent of Meeting (8:33-36). Since God radiates holiness to all that is close by, this symbolic action by the same token emphasized the separation of the priests from the rest of the people and confirmed their holy status. On the eighth day they were once again brought into contact with the rest of the community.

Ablutions (8:6) are a universal feature of religious ritual. Beyond the obvious hygienic advantages of water, its utilization in ritual also serves to purify symbolically. The ordination ceremony involving washing, clothing, and anointing endowed the priests with a degree of holiness that surpassed that of other Israelites. The fact that Aaron was treated differently from his sons shows that he was recognized as being even holier.

Most of ch. 8 is devoted to the description of two distinct yet related ceremonies: (1) the consecration of the altar and Tabernacle and of Aaron, the high priest (vv. 6-12) and the ordination of Aaron and his sons as priests, which was accomplished by a series of sacrificial and purificatory rites performed over a period of seven days (vv. 13-36). The ordination ceremony lasting seven days (Lev 8:33) parallels the seven days of creation and divine rest (Gen 1:1–2:3). Worship, which in accordance with the priestly view is the goal of creation, can therefore begin on the eighth day. On that day (9:1) the restoration of Aaron and his sons to society in their new role as priests takes place with further offerings. By recording that fire came out "from the LORD and consumed the burnt offering and the fat on the altar" (Lev 9:24; cf. 1 Kings 18:36-38), the author emphasizes that the ordination of the priests receives the seal of divine approval: God accepts Aaron and his sons as the community cultic representatives.

The high priest is presented as the bearer of a distinctive office. He wore special vestments not worn by ordinary priests, and he alone was anointed with the "oil of anointing," the same oil used to consecrate the Tabernacle, the altar, and the sacred vessels. At any time there could only be one high priest and each new appointee had to undergo a special consecration ritual. Of all the priests he alone was permitted to enter the Holy of Holies (cf. 16:1-22), but this permission was limited to one day in the year, the Day of Atonement. The eight vestments of the high priest are described in Exodus 28 and again in Exodus 39; here they are merely mentioned by name.

The turban (Heb. *miṣnephet*) and the diadem *(nezer),* as items of Aaron's apparel, were symbols of the royal authority given to the high priests in postmonarchical times. The ephod (8:7) was also a part of Aaron's sacred vestment. The Hebrew Bible mentions three (or four) kinds of ephods. In ancient times there was the linen ephod *(ʾephod bad),* an undergarment made of white linen that the priest wore to cover his genitals (cf. 1 Sam 2:18; 2 Sam 6:14, 20). A second type is the ephod that Abiathar carried in his hands when he escaped from the massacre at Nob (1 Sam 23:6). Possibly this was an embroidered garment used in connection with the casting of the sacred lot because Abiathar brought the ephod whenever David sought divine guidance (cf. 1 Sam 23:9). A third type is the high priest's ephod mentioned here and described in Exod 28:6-14; 39:2-7.

Judgment on Nadab and Abihu (10:1-20)

There are only two sections in Leviticus that narrate events rather than report God's words. This first one focuses on the sin of Nadab and Abihu, Aaron's sons, subsequent to the consecration of the priests. The other narrative passage deals with a man who blasphemes by cursing (24:10-16).

The short story of 10:1-7 has a didactic effect. While the whole narrative from 8:1–9:24 has led us to expect God's ministers to obey the law promptly and exactly, this story tells that on the very first day of Aaron's high-priestly ministry his two eldest sons died for infringing God's Law. In this way Leviticus highlights both God's power to sanctify and the danger posed by moral transgressions and ritual uncleanness associated with human behavior. The Nadab and Abihu incident is a good example of law in story form. The Priestly tradition (P) normally uses apodictic, casuistic, and other legal forms but it also includes many examples of story law: for example, Korah's rebellion (Num 16:1-35), the transfer of the priesthood to Eleazar (Num 25:1-8), and the punishment of the blasphemer (Lev 24:10-16). This way of teaching allows for ready recall of God's commandments and makes the principles concrete and easily understandable.

Nadab and Abihu were next in importance after Moses and Aaron, ranking even higher than the seventy elders (cf. Exod 24:1, 9-11). The nature of their sin is contained in the Hebrew words *ʾesh zarah* ("strange," that is, "not commanded or authorized" fire). This can only mean that instead of deriving from the altar (cf. 16:12; Num 16:46 [17:11]), the coals came from a source that was "profane" or "outside" (cf. 16:1 LXX; Num 3:4; 26:61).

According to some interpreters the story intends to invalidate all incense offerings outside the sanctuary, and more particularly the incense offering on the roofs of private homes (Jer 32:29; cf. Zeph 1:5). If the coals had to be taken from the altar it was impossible to burn incense outside the sanctuary. Archaeology seems to confirm this interpretation because many small censers were discovered in excavations conducted in all parts of Israel, and some of these utensils, dating mainly between the sixth and fourth centuries B.C.E., were found in private houses.

III. Uncleanness and Its Treatment

Clean and Unclean Animals (11:1-47)

After the sacrificial system has been established and inaugurated, the first thing that follows is the chapter on clean and unclean animals. These regulations (as well as those of chs. 12–15) come after the ordination tradition (Leviticus 10–11) because one of the tasks of the priests was to make a distinction between clean and unclean (10:10). Leviticus 11 is one of two major collections of dietary laws in the Torah, the other being Deut 14:3-21.

Clean and unclean animals are identified in each of four categories defined roughly by locomotion: beasts of the earth (vv. 2-8), creatures who live in the waters (vv. 9-12), flying creatures (vv. 13-23), and swarming creatures (vv. 29-31, 41-44). Although birds and winged insects appear to be treated in separate paragraphs, the Hebrew word meaning "bird" is applied to both. Interspersed with the definitions are instructions regarding how unclean animals make a person or an object unclean and how ceremonial cleanness may be restored (vv. 24-28, 32-40). After some general exhortations the entire discussion is summed up in vv. 46-47: "This is the law pertaining to land animal and bird and every living creature that moves through the waters and every creature that swarms upon the earth, to make a distinction between the unclean and the clean, and between the living creature that may be eaten and the living creature that may not be eaten."

In Leviticus 11 the key word is *tameʾ,* an adjective meaning "unclean" or "impure." By classifying certain living creatures under this "avoidance category" the Torah makes the observance of a dietary regimen essential to the attainment of holiness, but the text does not tell why some animals are to be shunned and others not, and this has given rise to conflicting interpretations, some ancient and some modern. Moreover in many cases we do not know which animals are actually meant. One expert estimates that only forty percent of the identifications can be stated with confidence.

What was the rationale underlying all these dietary regulations? A comprehensive explanation covering all the animals is most difficult to formulate. Various interpretations have been offered so far, but there is little agreement among the interpreters. Even in antiquity it was argued that the rules were purely arbitrary, designed by God simply to teach discipline to the Jews and set them apart (cf. Sifra Qedushim 11.22). By restricting their diet to clean animals the Israelites were reminded that they were called to be a holy nation. One must learn to obey God even in the absence of any rational justification (cf. Lev

20:24-26, "I am the LORD your God; I have separated you from the peoples. . . . you shall not bring abomination on yourselves by animal or by bird or by anything with which the ground teems, which I have set apart for you to hold unclean. You shall be holy"). Such a view also finds favor among modern scholars.

The Letter of Aristeas (third to second century B.C.E.) attempted to explain that the clean and unclean animals are symbols of human behavior: they were forbidden for food in order to teach moral qualities. Thus one should not act like "a filthy swine" but ought to imitate the lamb, which is clean and dependent on the shepherd. Such allegorical interpretations are quite ancient, occurring also in the Letter of Barnabas and in the writings of Clement of Alexandria, Origen, and other Fathers of the Church.

More recently it has been common to clarify these dietary rules in terms of hygiene: pork is a means by which trichinosis is transmitted to humans; shellfish were not eaten because they spoil quickly in a hot climate. But this popular modern explanation is not a likely one for ancient Semites, and in fact for many of the animals no health-related issue is discernible.

Some commentators suggest that the Israelites were instructed to avoid the unclean animals because they were connected with the cults of various deities either as sacrificial animals or as animals through which the power of the deity was manifest. Pork was eaten in Canaanite rites and Isa 66:17 says that "the flesh of pigs, vermin, and rodents" were consumed in secret ceremonies. Yet while some unclean animals were clearly used in the cultic rituals of Israel's neighbors it is impossible to demonstrate such use for all the animals designated unclean.

One of the major attempts to work out the meaning of the biblical system comes from the sphere of social anthropology. According to this approach the unclean animals were perceived as "abnormal" from one perspective or another. Certain animals were declared unclean because they did not fit major categories of the Israelite classification system for animals and were thus anomalous according to the worldview of ancient Israel. The "swarming things" (vv. 41-45), for example, were forbidden for food because their erratic movements seem to contradict order, and order was a part of God's creative activity (cf. our commentary on Lev 18:22). This approach is by far the most comprehensive and makes a good deal of sense from many points of view. However, it does not demonstrate the existence of a single principle at work behind the various prohibitions. The criterion shifts slightly from category to category.

Whatever the original reason (or reasons) for such prohibitions may have been, it belongs to a stage prior to the codification of the Priestly writings. Such regulations about purity and pollution may have arisen over many centuries and may have had different functions within the society at different times. At any rate the dietary laws have taken a central place in the self-understanding of Judaism throughout its history. The discrimination of clean and unclean flesh is part of its national and religious identity. While Jews have expressed their faithfulness to their God by the observance of all the laws it was the distinction between clean and unclean, along with circumcision and the Sabbath, that have most conspicuously enabled them to express their identity as Jews over against their neighbors and to resist assimilation.

Uncleanness of Childbirth (12:1-8)

In ancient Israel fruitfulness was a sign of divine favor and barrenness was regarded as a reproach (Gen 16:1-6; 1 Sam 1:1-18); the birth of a child was a joyous event (Jer 20:15) and a large family was looked on as a great blessing from God (Lev 26:9; Deut 28:11; Pss 127:3-5; 128:3-4). Reproduction is essential to the survival of humankind. The command to be fruitful is given in Gen 1:28 and renewed to Noah after the flood (Gen 9:1). Consequently it seems strange for the process of birth to render the mother "unclean" and to necessitate a sin or purification offering. The biblical text states that the act of giving birth to a child makes the mother temporarily inadmissible to worship but, as is usual for Leviticus, the rationale for this requirement is not stated. Probably what made the mother unclean was not the birth itself but the discharge that follows childbirth. In fact, three times her blood or discharge of blood is mentioned in this law (vv. 4, 5, 7). This uncleanness is obviously a ritual condition, not a moral one.

Such restrictions were not limited to Israel. In ancient societies in general women tended to be isolated during the period of childbirth. The process of procreation was surrounded by mystery and that of childbirth by fear.

At the conclusion of the period of isolation from ritual the mother was to bring two kinds of sacrifice: a burnt offering and a purification offering. Finally, the chapter concludes with a provision for the poor. These rituals are mentioned in Luke 2:22-24.

Unclean Diseases (13:1-59)

Levitical impurity can be a fact of biology, common to all persons, and also a result of specific moral or ritual offenses that anyone is liable to commit. The first forms of uncleanness (including specific skin diseases and certain bodily discharges) arise as a natural consequence of being human. These and other forms of impurity appear to be linked in one way or another to death.

The other forms of uncleanness occurred when individuals by their actions transgressed any boundary established by God. People who willfully ignore God's commands are a source of impurity and defile all that they touch. Their actions distance them from God and bring them under the domain of death.

In these chapters the Hebrew word *ṣaraᶜat* is a generic term that includes various skin diseases as well as blemishes affecting garments and buildings. It is impossible to find an English word to cover these diverse conditions. Inspired by the Greek translation *(lepra),* the traditional translation is "leprosy," but this is obviously inappropriate in the case of mold and mildew in clothes and houses. It seems likely that the Hebrew term denotes a scaly skin disease of some sort, such as eczema, psoriasis, and other more severe and damaging infections.

When the priest has confirmed that the skin disease is serious and defiling the "leper" shall wear torn clothes, untidy the hair, cover the upper lip and cry "Unclean, unclean," to prevent people from defiling themselves by touch. Furthermore, such a person shall dwell alone outside the camp (13:45-46). As persons permanently unclean, such people must separate themselves from the holy camp of Israel where God is present.

Leviticus 13:47-59 deals with infections that damage fabrics and worked leather. This is mold, mildew, or a fungus that appears in clothes worn without being washed for a long time in a tropical or semi-tropical climate. It can be found in all kinds of clothes, whether made of linen or wool or skin. The treatment is similar to that of persons: one seven-day period of isolation and then a second. If the fungus spreads after that period of time, the cloth must be destroyed.

Cleansing of Disease (14:1-57)

This chapter is intimately connected with the preceding. It divides into two halves: the first deals with the ritual cleansing of the persons whose skin disease has cleared up (vv. 1-32) and the second with the treatment of the *ṣaraᶜat* of houses.

The priests did not do anything to cure the sick persons. Their duty was to diagnose when a person was clean again and to perform the ritual cleansing after the cure. These rituals are termed by anthropologists "rites of aggregation," that is, ceremonies in which a person who is in an abnormal condition is reintegrated into ordinary society. Ablutions and sacrificial offerings are regular ingredients of such rites.

The laws relating to serious skin diseases close with a section on infected houses. Like garments, they too can be affected with mildew or possibly dry rot.

Unclean Discharges (15:1-33)

This chapter sets forth the procedures required when an Israelite male or female experiences discharges from the sexual organs. Most of the regulations deal with discharges that are the result of illness or infections, not to be confused with the normal menstruation of the female or the seminal emissions of the male. Such discharges of the male consisted of pus or some similar substance, which appeared as a clear liquid running from the penis. The abnormal vaginal discharges of the female as described here consisted of blood and persisted beyond, or outside, the menstrual period.

Chapter 15 also includes laws governing normal seminal emissions in the male and menstruation in the female. All the impurities dealt with extended to persons and objects that came in contact with the persons who experienced those normal or abnormal bodily discharges.

The Day of Atonement (Yom Hakippurim) *(16:1-34)*

All the sacrifices reached their annual climax on the Day of Atonement when each part of the Tabernacle was smeared with blood to "cleanse it and hallow it from the uncleannesses of the people of Israel" (16:19). The purpose of the scapegoat rite was to rid the community of the sins that were the cause of impurity in the sanctuary. The most striking phase of this ritual was the dispatch of the scapegoat into the wilderness. The symbolism of this last ceremony is transparent, as explained in vv. 21-22: the sins and transgressions of the whole people were dramatically transferred to the scapegoat, which was driven into the wilderness in order to remove them from the people and from the sanctuary.

Lots were cast for the two goats, one "for the LORD" and one "for Azazel" (v. 8). The latter goat was to be sent out "to Azazel into the wilderness" (vv. 10, 26). The evidence indicates that Azazel is the name of a demon. This is suggested first of all by the parallelism between the designation "for the LORD" and "for Azazel" (v. 8). As the former phrase refers to YHWH, so the latter should refer to a living creature. Second, the goat is sent out to the wilderness, which is a place of habitation for demonic characters. Third, in postbiblical literature Azazel appears as a full fledged demonic being (cf. 1 Enoch 8:1; 9:6; 10:4-8; 13:1).

Azazel's demonic nature must be sought primarily within the framework of the Priestly literature. Significantly this corpus says little about demonic issues. The general silence about demons in the Priestly theology led to the surmise that there is little room for active demons in Priestly theology. Consequently Azazel should be viewed as a demon, but perhaps an inactive one with no role to play in the rite except to indicate the place to which the sins are dispatched. In other words the goat does not appear to be a propitiatory offering for Azazel but only serves as a vehicle for transporting sins. Azazel, to whom the goat was sent, was apparently not an active personality. He was simply a ritual "place holder."

There is some evidence that demons dwell in inhabited places (cf. Isa 34:11-15). Why then was the goat sent out into the wilderness? This was done to remove it from populated areas so that as a bearer of contagious impurity it could do no harm. The meaning of *midbar,* "wilderness," shows this to be the case. The *midbar* is arid land endowed with little vegetation except grass for pasturage (Joel 2:22; Jer 9:10; 23:10; Joel 1:10; Pss 65:12; 78:52; Job 24:5; 1 Chr 5:9). Various wild animals—owls, jackals, ostriches, serpents, foxes—live in it and related places. Most important, though, is the fact that the *midbar* is not inhabited by human beings. Jeremiah 17:6 calls it an uninhabited "infertile land" (*lit.* "salt land"), and Job characterizes it as a place "empty of human life" (38:26). Thus when the scapegoat is sent to the wilderness it is sent to a place where impurity cannot threaten human populations.

Chapter 16 also ordains the use of sacrificial blood in unusual ways during the purification of the sanctuary. The main purpose of these expiatory rites was to cleanse the sanctuary from the pollutions introduced into it by unclean worshipers (16:16, 19) because an impure or defiled sanctuary would induce God to withdraw the divine presence from the Israelite community (cf. Ezek 10:1-22; 11:22-25). No ritual of purification was actually performed over the people (as was the case on other occasions), but the purification of the sanctuary was understood to extend to the people.

The ritual of this day was complex. The high priest could not enter "just at any time" into the innermost part of the Tabernacle (the Holy of Holies, where the ark was kept), but on the Day of Atonement, with proper precautions, he had to enter the holy place to sprinkle with the blood of the sacrifice the *kapporet,* that is, the golden plate that covered the ark of the covenant (cf. Exod 25:17-22). Because such entrance was fraught with danger the high priest, to protect himself from the wrath of God, had to prepare a censer full of hot charcoal taken from the altar of burnt offering in the outer court and put fine incense in it. The purpose of the incense smoke was perhaps to create a screen that would prevent him from gazing at the holy presence (Num 16:46 [17:11]; cf. Ps 141:2). He had also to wear a special set of vestments for most of the ceremony: not his proper high-priestly uniform described in Exodus 28, but a simple, less flamboyant dress.

In later Judaism, after the destruction of the second Temple of Jerusalem, the significance of

Yom Kippur became somewhat different from the ancient view. Atonement for the sins of the people replaced the purification of the sanctuary. This shift of emphasis is already suggested in v. 30: "For on this day atonement shall be made for you, to cleanse you; from all your sins you shall be clean before the LORD."

IV. Guidelines for Practical Holiness: 17:1–26:46

Because of its pronounced assertion of the divine holiness and its demand that Israel should likewise be holy (19:2; 20:26) this fourth section of Leviticus is usually called the "Holiness Code." Some interpreters maintain that the entire section once made up a separate collection of laws of an earlier date than the rest of the book. In contrast other scholars affirm that the laws manifest too little internal coherence to suggest a quite distinct document and betray no evidence of having belonged to any other unit than Leviticus and the priestly corpus of which it is part. More importantly these laws deal with every aspect of human life and provide a very instructive document concerning the close relationship between the demands of worship and holiness and the requirement of social justice. The holiness it calls for is not mere private piety, not even a fervent participation in public worship, but a total way of life involving every aspect of personal, family, and social commitment.

The Slaughter of Animals for Food (17:1-16)

The basic rationale of this chapter is stated in vv. 8-9: no sacrifices could be offered outside the Tabernacle. If the people of Israel wished to eat meat they had to bring the chosen animal to the entrance of the Tent of Meeting to offer it. The point made by this law is that no secular slaughter was permitted. This rule was just as binding on the resident alien, the foreigner who had settled in Israel, as on the native Israelite. The penalty for disregarding this rule was death (being cut off from the people). Verse 4 is still more explicit: blood guilt should be imputed to that person for having shed blood. Elsewhere the formula *shafak dam* ("he has shed blood") refers to homicide, usually intentional murder. This means that the offense is considered as serious as murder.

Surrounding this central provision are specific explanations and applications. The text of vv. 3-4 can be read as allowing the actual slaughter of an animal to occur in or outside the camp, requiring only that the victim and its blood be brought to the sanctuary. More probably the lawgiver is requiring that the animal be slaughtered at the entrance of the sanctuary, its blood drained and dashed upon the altar, and the fat from around the entrails (cf. Lev 3:3-4) burned on the altar as a "pleasing odor" to the LORD (3:5). The designation of the Tabernacle altar as "the altar of the LORD" (v. 6) is based on the view that there is only one legitimate altar at which the God of Israel may be worshiped.

The Deuteronomic law eliminates all local altars (cf. Deuteronomy 12), but it allows for secular slaughters because it would be unfeasible to require all Israelites to go to Jerusalem every time they wanted to eat meat. Leviticus contradicts this provision, specifying that even the slaughter of animals for meat must be treated as a sacrifice. This would have been feasible when all Israel was encamped about the shrine, but it would not have been when the Israelites were dispersed in the land and the Jerusalem Temple held the only legitimate altar.

The satyrs or goat-demons mentioned in v. 7 were probably demons who inhabited the wilderness and were thought to take the shape of goats. The slaying of sacrifices to them was a flagrant transgression of the first commandment ("you shall have no other gods before me," Exod 20:3; Deut 5:7).

There are several statements in the Torah forbidding the consumption of blood (Gen 9:4; Lev 3:17; 7:26-27; 19:26; Deut 12:16, 23-24). In Lev 17:10-14 the violation of this command carries the penalty of being "cut off" from the community of Israel. The notion that blood, a liquid, could be "eaten" rather than drunk is explicable assuming that the blood is consumed in the course of eating meat. Indeed, wherever the expression *ʾkal dam* ("eat blood") is met the context invariably shows that the blood is not drunk for its own sake but as a consequence of eating meat. The underlying conception here is the assumption that the life-force resides in the blood. In fact, living creatures cannot live without blood, and when a human or animal is bleeding it grows progressively weaker and weaker until it become lifeless. As such, blood can serve as a symbol for life.

To round off the discussion of meat eating the chapter includes some rules about hunting game and a provision for eating dead or torn animals. The blood prohibition applies only to wild game.

The prohibition of ingesting blood provides the scriptural basis for later regulations in Judaism governing the slaughter and preparation of meat. Meat could be consumed locally, provided the blood was properly removed (cf. Deut 12:20-25). Christianity, on the contrary, abandoned the concern for ritual slaughter, and the prohibition against consuming blood, retained for awhile (cf. Acts 15:28-29), within a few centuries was widely ignored.

Basic Principles of Sexual Behavior (18:1-30)

Chapter 18 outlines in detail which unions among relatives within the ancient Israelite clan were prohibited. It is the most systematic and complete collection within the Torah dealing with incest and other forbidden sexual unions. Chapters 18 and 20 act as complementary sections: the former lays down the prohibitions and the latter states the punishment for violating them. These chapters contain the largest hortatory sections in the Holiness Code. Leviticus 18:1-5, 24-30 and 20:22-24a are variations of the same theme: the Israelites should not imitate the doings of the land of Egypt and the land of Canaan. If they defile the land with such objectionable practices they will suffer the same fate as their predecessors.

The first section of laws (18:6-18) lists twelve degrees of kinship within the bounds of which it was forbidden to have sexual intercourse. The key expression "uncover nakedness" means "to have intercourse with." These prohibitions are addressed to an adult male and begin with the most immediate family: the addressee's mother. The other prohibitions are based on the principle of consanguinity or familial intimacy (vv. 12-14, for example, cover aunts by blood or marriage). We can assume that the law of levirate marriage (cf. Deut 25:5-10) was an exception here although it is not explicitly stated.

After the twelve prohibitions regarding the practice of sex within certain bounds of kinship there follow a prohibition of intercourse during the woman's menstrual period (18:19), a condemnation of adultery (18:20), and a prohibition of bestiality in the case of either a man or a woman (18:23). Leviticus 20:15-16 lays down the penalty for this last offense: both human and animal shall be put to death, for although the dumb creature is not morally responsible it has been irredeemably defiled by the perverse union.

Molech (v. 21) is the name or epithet of a deity to whom children were offered as sacrifices. Children were dedicated and burned to this god at Topheth in the Valley of Hinnom near Jerusalem. The offering of sons and daughters to Molech by "passing them through the fire" is mentioned only here and in Lev 20:2-5; 2 Kings 23:10; Jer 32:35. This practice without mention of Molech is found abundantly elsewhere (for example, Deut 12:31; 2 Kings 16:3; Jer 7:31; Ezek 16:21).

Sexual intercourse between men is one of the many sexual acts prohibited by the Holiness Code (v. 22). This prohibition is consistent with the worldview that underlies the Priestly story and legislation. As we have seen in the introductory section, Leviticus (like the whole Priestly tradition to which it belongs) is dominated by a conception of an order that extends through the cosmos, the sanctuary, and human society. The logic of this system can be seen in the priestly account of creation (Gen 1:1–2:4a), which orders, classifies, and defines the structure of the world as Israel saw it. God speaks and chaos becomes order. God puts apart the light and the darkness and establishes a calendar with times for work and rest (even God rests on the seventh day). The firmament separates "the waters from the waters" (v. 6), and the lights in the firmament separate the day from the night (v. 14). Birds, fish, and cattle are created in pure forms and put in their proper places—the heavens, the waters, and the land—with proper food and means of locomotion. In this way a hierarchy of created beings is established, with humanity in dominion over all (Gen 1:26-30).

Created in the image of God, humanity is composed of male and female. Sexual distinction is of divine origin, and as sexual distinction is part of the divine design of creation, so sexual activity is also part of God's good world. It is the duty of the sexually differentiated partners to be fruitful and multiply, and in fulfilling this duty they enjoy a special blessing.

In the light of this priestly worldview it is apparent that Leviticus envisages a world in which people, places, objects, and even periods of time are properly arranged. Holiness requires that individuals conform to the class to which they belong (that is, that they avoid mixing) and this principle of separation and distinction is to be extended to the smallest details: no mixture of domestic animals, no mixture of seed, not even a garment may be of mixed material (19:19).

According to this fairly simple purity system to "lie with a male as with a woman" is to perform a sexual act that is obviously "out of order." It transgresses the God-given boundaries, sowing a seed where it cannot grow and produce its fruit. Holiness means keeping distinct the categories of creation; it requires that individuals shall conform to the class to which they belong, without confusing the different classes of things. As a consequence it would be a great distortion for a man to be treated as a woman.

Principles of Neighborliness (19:1-37)

This chapter contains a long list of commands governing moral and cultic behavior. The list covers such a variety of topics that it is difficult to discover its logical organization. The material in it closely echoes the Decalogue and the collection of moral instructions found within the Book of the Covenant (Exod 22:21–23:9). All ten commandments are quoted or alluded to, and sometimes expounded or developed in a new way.

Broadly speaking vv. 1-8 concern religious obligations, vv. 9-18 include admonitions regarding duties toward one's neighbors, and vv. 19-36 (introduced by "You shall keep my statutes") deal primarily, although not exclusively, with pagan and superstitious practices that should be avoided (ingesting blood, witchcraft, prostitution, divination, and belief in the presence and power of evil spirits).

The imperative of v. 2, "You shall be holy, for I the LORD your God am holy," describes the ultimate basis of all law in Israel. In the Bible there is no divorce between theology and moral obligation. It consistently shows that human morality is ultimately justified by the holiness of God. To be holy is to live in a way that reflects the moral perfection of God. Theft, doing injustice, lying, false witness, cheating in weights and measures, hating, and taking vengeance are contrary to the will of God. Holiness begins at home with reverence to mother and father, and it includes certain religious obligations, but it is not confined to individual piety. It has a social dimension, and the signs of its presence are to be discerned in the whole of the people's life.

Note vv. 9-10, where a humanitarian concern for the poor is expressed. As we have seen in the introduction to the book of Leviticus, they give a good example of how to interpret the biblical law (and we can say the Bible in general) in the present circumstances. The command lays down as a rule not to gather up every stalk of grain but to leave an allotted portion "for the poor and the alien." If we take this law literally it is obvious that we cannot apply it to our modern societies where poor people usually live in urban centers far from the harvest fields. However the purpose of the law is crystal clear: we should devise the most effective means to help the poor of our age. It is the underlying principle that issues a challenge, not its specific application in the cultural setting of ancient Israel. The jubilee laws in Leviticus 25 again offer very relevant guidelines on issues of wealth and poverty.

After negative commands ("you shall not render an unjust judgment," "you shall not hate in your heart anyone of your kin," "you shall not take vengeance") this chapter seems to reach its pinnacle in v. 18, which Jesus and Paul cited as a summary of the divine requirements: "you shall love your neighbor as yourself" (Matt 22:39; Gal 5:14). What does it mean to "love one's neighbor?" In the rest of the chapter concrete examples are given: forbid exploitation of the weak and do not delay the payment of wages (v. 13), avoid spreading slander (v. 16), keep away from dishonest business relationships (vv. 11-12), and honor aged people (v. 32).

The ban of all mixtures in v. 19 (breeding together two different kinds of animals, sowing a field with two different kinds of seed, or blending together different materials in a garment) was concerned with upholding what Israel regarded as the divine order of life. Humanity was not to confuse what God has made distinct (cf. Gen 1:1–2:4a).

The great command to love one's neighbor is specifically extended to cover foreign residents (vv. 33-34). Israel should be particularly sensitive to the needs of resident aliens, "for you were strangers in the land of Egypt" (Deut 10:19).

Capital and Other Grave Crimes (20:1-27)

As we have seen, this chapter prescribes punishments of graduated severity for transgressing the rules of ch. 18. Some prohibitions of ch. 18 are not covered in this chapter, but it is obvious that they were subject to divine sanctions.

Rules for Priests and About Eating Sacrifices (21:1–22:33)

The previous chapters have dealt with the holiness of ordinary Israelites. Chapters 21–22 move on to consider the holiness of the priests. Higher standards are expected of them. These chapters divide into six sections, each of which closes with the formula "I am the LORD; I sanctify you/them" (21:8, 15, 23; 22:9, 16, 32; cf. 20:8).

It is no accident that these two consecutive chapters specify the imperfections that disqualify priests and animals for the altar. Each list of disqualifying priestly and animal blemishes (21:18-20; 22:22-24) contains twelve items, probably to achieve parity in the total. There are five identical items: blindness, overgrown limb, broken bones, sores, and scabs. The remaining items are difficult to match because they are mainly unidentifiable.

No castrated animals were to be offered under any circumstances (22:24), and men in similar condition were forbidden to officiate as priests. As a physical impediment debarred the priest from service in the Tabernacle, so any kind of blemish in an animal precluded its use in sacrifice. Although a blemished priest may not officiate himself, he may still eat the food of his God, that is, those parts of the sacrificial victims reserved for the sons of Aaron (21:22; cf. 2:3, 10; 6:10-11, 22).

Religious Festivals and Rules for the Tabernacle (23:1–24:9)

Like Exodus, Numbers, and Deuteronomy, the Holiness Code has a calendar of national feasts to be celebrated in the course of the year. This calendar parallels the others but contains more detail, adds some festivals, and fixes the exact dates for celebration.

At the beginning of the chapter there is a brief reference to the Sabbath (23:3), which was a weekly observance and not an annual festival requiring attendance at the central shrine. Whereas Deut 5:12-15 proposes the Sabbath rest as a humanitarian repose, the later priestly observance stresses the sacredness of the seventh day of the week (cf. Gen 2:3). The Sabbath is a day holy to YHWH: as persons and things could be consecrated and removed from profane use, so could a period of time be consecrated to the Lord. Work was a secular element that profaned the holy. The Sabbath was a day of religious assembly and the public sacrifices performed at the Tabernacle were to be increased on this day of solemn rest (cf. Num 28:9-10).

Passover and Unleavened Bread (23:4-8) were combined to form the first festival of the year. The numbering of the months was based on a year beginning in the spring (March or April). This ritual unites two originally different rites that can be derived from two ways of life, the nomadic and the sedentary.

On the fourteenth day (full moon) of the first month the Passover sacrifice was to be performed in the evening. In its origin this was not a Temple sacrifice. It was essentially a home festival though in later times the lamb was slaughtered in the Jerusalem Temple and the blood was not applied to the doorpost and lintel of the house, but passed up to the altar.

Many scholars argue that the Passover ritual (the killing of the lamb and the sprinkling of the blood on the doorposts) was originally an annual rite of semi-nomads practiced when the herders moved from the winter pasturages of the steppe to the summer pasturages of the cultivated lands. As a rite of shepherds it was not tied to a holy place and was not performed by priests at an altar but by the elders of the clan. Whatever the origin of the ritual, the Passover came to be linked with God's saving acts at the Exodus from Egypt. Therefore the recounting of the story of the Exodus deliverance was as important as the performance of the ritual. On the following day the feast of Unleavened Bread began and continued for seven days (vv. 6-8). Old, leavened bread was to be destroyed and unleavened bread eaten throughout the week.

Jesus invested the First Covenant cult, and particularly the Jewish Passover, with entirely new content. According to the gospel of John, Jesus was crucified on the day before the Passover (18:28; 19:14, 31) at the same hour the lambs were slaughtered in the forecourt of the Temple for the paschal meal. After his death the soldiers did not break his legs (19:33), and the evangelist sees in this fact the realization of a prescription of the ritual law (Lev 19:36; Exod 12:46). That is to say: Jesus is "the Lamb of God who takes away the sins of the world," as John the Baptist had pointed out at the beginning of the gospel (John 1:29; cf. also 1 Pet 1:19; Rev 5:6). Paul in turn refers to the festival of Unleavened Bread as an incentive to holiness: "Clean out the old yeast so that you may be a new batch . . . For our paschal Lamb, Christ, has been sacrificed. Therefore, let us celebrate the festival, not with the old yeast, the yeast of malice and evil, but with the unleavened bread of sincerity and truth" (1 Cor 5:7-8).

The sheaf of the first fruits and the Feast of Weeks (23:9-21) are associated with the grain harvest. At the beginning of the harvest season the first sheaf of grain cut was to be presented to the sanctuary, and at the end (fifty days later) two loaves of bread from the grain harvested were to be presented. The conclusion of this section (v. 22) paraphrases 19:9-10: the Israelites shall not reap their fields to the very border or gather the gleanings after the harvest; they shall leave them for the poor and the stranger. It omits the reference to the grape harvest because the grapes ripen much later.

The Feast of the Weeks was on the day after the seventh Sabbath, called the fiftieth day when counting inclusively (that is, including both the starting and the ending day). Hence in later times this day was given the Greek name *pentēkostē* ("fiftieth day"), from which derives the English Pentecost. According to Acts 2:1 the sending of the Holy Spirit on the Church fell on the day of Pentecost (the Feast of Weeks), the fiftieth day after Easter.

The first day of the seventh month (Tishri) was a holy day celebrated by the blowing of trumpets (23:23-25). Nothing is stated about this day except the command to do no work. Numbers 29:1-5 lists sacrifices to be offered on this holy day.

The tenth day of the seventh month was the Day of Atonement *(yom hakippurim)*. According to Lev 23:26-32 this day was a time of fasting and holy convocation (that is, of national gathering for public worship in the Temple). It was also a time of rest from work, and a special offering was to be made. Nothing more is said, but it is known that the ceremony of the two goats was associated with this day (cf. Leviticus 16).

The Feast of Booths or Tabernacles *(sukkoth)* was the final festival of the year, celebrated after the autumn harvest on 15–22 Tishri (23:33-36, 39-43). In this seventh month (September–October) the dry summer draws to an end; the grapes and olives are picked and the farmers look forward to the coming of the rains. The seventh month, then, marked the end of the agricultural year and the beginning of a new one. The first and eighth day of the festival were holy days on which no work was to be done. As a part of the joyful celebration the people were to live for a week in shelters made of palm leaves, tree branches, and willows. According to v. 43 this was a remembrance of Israel's wandering in the desert, when the people who came out of Egypt had to live in tents (Deut 7:12–8:20). Biblical scholars, however, are doubtful that the booths originally symbolized the desert sojourn, which was a dwelling in tents, not in booths. Therefore they direct attention to the agricultural origins of the feast, that is, to the common practice of the farmers who used to build temporary shelters (booths) in the fields to sleep in during the harvest so that they could make the best use of the daylight and keep the harvest under close watch until it was gathered. In later times this agricultural festival developed historical significance and was incorporated by the Israelites into the framework of their sacred history.

The destruction of the Temple by the Romans made it impossible to celebrate the various annual festivals as they were prescribed by the Law. Nonetheless, they were observed thereafter by the Jewish people in a modified form. At Passover the emphasis shifted from the sacrificial rite to the historical memorial of God's deliverance from oppression at the time of Pharaoh. Passover served to keep alive a hope for deliverance amid the oppressions of the present. The Feast of Weeks (Pentecost) was transformed into a commemoration of the gift of the Torah at Mount Sinai. The Day of Atonement is a day of repentance and prayer in the synagogue and is usually regarded as the holiest day of the year.

The Regular Service of the Sanctuary (24:1-9)

While the major events of Israel's worship took place at set festival times (cf. Leviticus 23) there was also a continuous kind of worship attended to by the priests. One part was the care of the lamp that was kept burning continually before the Lord. It served as the reminder of the abiding presence of God with Israel. The other feature was the setting of twelve cakes of freshly baked bread on a table before the Lord. This is elsewhere called the bread of the Presence or showbread (Exod 25:30; 1 Sam 21:6). It seems likely that the two piles of six loaves represented the twelve tribes of Israel, and their being set out in the sanctuary was a token of the perpetual covenant that bound Israel to God (v. 8).

A Case of Blasphemy (24:10-23)

This is the second section in Leviticus that narrates events rather than reporting words of the Lord. Its primary purpose is to affirm that the laws of Israel are binding upon resident aliens as well as Israelites. Foreign residents in Israel were expected to show respect for the Name (a substitute for the sacred name of YHWH). Misuse of God's name is condemned in the third commandment (Exod 20:7); cursing God is forbidden in Exod 22:28. The case of blasphemy, which was a capital crime in Israel, is perhaps singled out in the priestly legislation because of its cultic character.

This incident of blasphemy provided an occasion to spell out a series of moral and legal pronouncements. Verses 19-20 constitute one of the three passages in the OT setting out the so-called *lex talionis* or "law of retaliation" (eye for eye, tooth for tooth: cf. Exod 21:23-25; Deut 19:21). Though this fundamental principle of Near Eastern and biblical law sounds barbarous today, its original purpose was humanitarian; it was designed to regulate retaliation for damages and to mitigate blood vengeance: the punishment must be proportionate to the offense. In the Sermon on the Mount Jesus discusses the *lex talionis* (Matt 5:38-42) and urges his disciples not to turn this legal rule into a maxim for personal behavior.

Sabbatical and Jubilee Years (25:1-55)

The legislation associated with the Year of Jubilee presents the most radical program for continuous social reform to be found in the OT. The main purpose of these laws is to prevent the utter ruin of debtors. People who incurred debts they could not repay could be forced to sell off their land or even their personal freedom by becoming slaves. When left unchecked this process led to serious social division, with a class of rich landowners exploiting a mass of landless serfs (cf. Isa 5:8; Amos 2:6). Leviticus 25 prohibits all the people of Israel from selling themselves or their land permanently. The fundamental tenet of this commandment is expressed in vv. 23-24: "The land shall not be sold in perpetuity [or beyond reclaim], for the land is mine; with me you are but aliens and tenants. Throughout the land that you hold, you shall provide for the redemption of the land." Therefore Israelites may only rent out their land or their labor for a maximum of forty-nine years. At the end of that period those who have been enslaved return to their families, and the land sold during the preceding years was to be returned to the original owners or their descendants.

The word Jubilee is a rough transliteration of the Hebrew term *yobel,* which is usually supposed to mean "ram" or "ram's horn." The Jubilee began on the tenth day of the seventh month, on the Day of Atonement, and was inaugurated by sending abroad the loud trumpet throughout the land (v. 9). On such a day "liberty" was proclaimed. This word (Heb. *deror*) indicates the manumission of slaves, that is, of those Israelites who because of poverty had sold themselves either to fellow Israelites (vv. 39-43) or to non-Israelites dwelling in Israel (vv. 47-54). Hebrew *deror* is cognate with Akkadian *anduraru,* which designates an edict of release issued by ancient Babylonian kings and some of their successors. This edict was issued by a king on ascending the throne and was a feature of a more extensive legal institution known as *mesharum,* a moratorium declared on debts and indentures. In Ezek 46:17 "the year of liberty" is another name for the Jubilee.

The Jubilee laws begin with a reminder of the sabbatical year (vv. 2-7). Farmers know the benefits of leaving the fields uncultivated at stated intervals to alleviate the exhaustion of the soil and assure future fertility. In Israel this practice took on an added religious meaning: as the seventh day of the week (the Sabbath) was a day sacred to the Lord (Exod 20:8-11; Deut 5:12-15), so the seventh year "shall be a Sabbath of complete rest for the land, a sabbath for the LORD" (v. 4); that is, no one was permitted to plow or harvest the fields.

The Jubilee laws (vv. 8-55) combine the "ought" with the "is" of a society. There is an implicit recognition that some people prosper in their endeavors while others do not. If, for example, climatic conditions ruin people who farm in certain terrain or grow certain crops there seems to be an inevitable tendency toward the accumulation of land in the hands of those who are economically shrewd or politically powerful. In any case the Jubilee does not retreat to an eschatological age or utopian society; rather it seeks to affirm itself in the very existence of the real world. Nevertheless, modern interpreters have often wondered about the practicality of these regulations. Most scholars agree that the land reform system described in Leviticus 25 was never put into practice.

Epilogue to the Holiness Code (26:1-46)

The book of Leviticus is fittingly brought to a conclusion by a final appeal setting out the rewards of obedience to God and the punishment of disobedience. The covenant with YHWH from its inception contained a basic code of law that expressed the obligations imposed on the people as a whole and on each Israelite. Israel had become God's people because YHWH had set them free from slavery, breaking the bars of their yoke and enabling them to walk unbowed (v. 13). In response to this divine favor the people were summoned to live in accordance with the will of God, which embraced the whole of individual and social life. Obedience to God's will brings blessing, but the failure to fulfill its demands would result in the divine judgment falling upon the transgressors. The Law is itself part of the blessing God has conferred on Israel, but the Law also contains a curse on those who are disobedient to it (cf. Gal 3:10).

In biblical times major legal texts (such as a code of laws or a covenantal agreement) ended with such blessings and curses. The main section of Deuteronomy concludes in a similar way (Deuteronomy 28), and we also find this pattern in Exod 23:25-33 and Josh 24:20.

The blessings of obedience are the gift of rain at the right season and magnificent harvests (vv. 4-5), peace or easy victories over enemies, and numerous offspring (vv. 6-10). But the crowning blessing is God's presence: "I will place my dwelling in your midst," "I will walk among you," "I will be your God, and you shall be my people" (vv. 11-13).

As in Deuteronomy more space is devoted to the series of punishments that follow the breaking of the covenant (v. 15). The punishments that will ensue are physical and mental disease (v. 16, 25), drought and poor harvests (v. 20), military defeat (vv. 25, 33), wholesale slaughter (v. 30), destruction of cities and sanctuaries (v. 31), and exile (v. 33). Particularly significant is v. 34: the Lord will make the land desolate, and that long period of desolation will be the punishment for the land's not having been allowed to lie fallow every seventh year as was commanded in 25:1-7. Yet God's judgments are described as "discipline" (vv. 44-45). God punishes God's people not merely because they deserve it, but because God loves them and wants to correct their foolish ways. Therefore in spite of disasters the offer of salvation still remains. The condition of restoration is confession of sin and an earnest desire to amend their ways. Then God will remember the covenant with their ancestors of ancient times. The One who brought them out of Egypt will still be their God and will repeat the mighty deliverance of former days. What God did once, God can and will do again. (Cf. Prov 3:11-12: "My child, do not despise the LORD's discipline or be weary of his reproof, for the LORD reproves the one he loves, as a father the son in whom he delights"; see also Deut 8:5; Heb 12:5-6.)

A postscript (v. 46) serves as the conclusion to the entire Holiness Code: "These are the statutes and ordinances and laws that the LORD established between himself and the people of Israel on Mount Sinai through Moses." A similar statement appears in Lev 27:34 as the conclusion of the whole book (cf. also Num 36:13).

The Right to Redeem Gifts Dedicated to God (27:1-34)

In this appendix various rules are laid down concerning the making or promising of gifts to God that then became the property of the priests. When a person had made such a gift and then for particular reasons wished to take it back these laws stipulated the conditions upon which such a gift could be revoked. They highlight the need for caution and seriousness in making vows and promises to God. Rash promises may afterward be regretted, and Israel's law did not permit the person who had made a hasty promise to forget it (cf. Eccl 5:1-6).

To promise a person to the Lord (vv. 2-8) meant to vow time in service to the sanctuary, to be performed either by the person who made the vow or by members of the family (cf. Hannah's promise concerning her unborn son, 1 Sam 1:9-11). More frequently promises involved a specific animal, and if the animal was reckoned as "clean" (that is, suitable for sacrifice) any attempt to substitute for it was considered improper.

Verses 16-24 assume that the value of a property was in direct proportion to the number of years that had to elapse before the year of Jubilee. Exclusions included the firstborn, since they already belonged to the sanctuary (Exod 13:1-2). The amount of the commutation was to be determined by the priest in accordance with a fixed currency (the "sanctuary shekel").

The book of Leviticus comes to an end with a brief reaffirmation of the Mosaic authority of the laws contained in the book and their connection with the covenant of Mount Sinai (v. 34). The great priestly history of Israel's origins, which forms the narrative kernel around which Leviticus grew up, continued its story through the book of Numbers. In that book it tells of the period spent in the wilderness and Israel's progress to the eve of its entry into the promised land.

BIBLIOGRAPHY

Budd, Philip J. *Leviticus.* NCBC. Grand Rapids: Eerdmans; London: Marshall Pickering, 1996.

Douglas, Mary. *Purity and Danger.* London: Routledge, 1966.

Elliger, Karl. *Leviticus.* HAT 4. Tübingen: J.C.B. Mohr (Paul Siebeck), 1966.

Gerstenberger, Erhard. *Leviticus. A Commentary.* Translated by Douglas W. Stott. Louisville: Westminster/John Knox, 1996.

Levine, Baruch A. *In the Presence of the Lord: A Study of Cult and Some Cultic Terms in Ancient Israel.* Leiden: Brill, 1974.

Milgrom, Jacob. *Leviticus 1–16. A New Translation with Introduction and Commentary.* AB 3. New York and London: Doubleday, 1991.

Noth, Martin. *Leviticus. A Commentary.* Philadelphia: Westminster, 1965.

Vaux, Roland de. *Ancient Israel. Its Life and Institutions.* Translated by John McHugh. New York: McGraw Hill, 1961.

Wenham, Gordon J. *The Book of Leviticus.* Grand Rapids: Eerdmans, 1979.

Numbers

Olivier Artus

FIRST READING

I. General Characteristics of the Book of Numbers

The book of Numbers is often presented as a disparate collection, gathering without apparent order both legislative texts and stories. The first part of the book (1:1–10:10) consists exclusively of legislative texts. It is often placed in the same class as Exod 19:1–40:38 and the book of Leviticus—the whole of Exod 19:1 through Num 10:10 forming the "Sinai pericope." The second part of the book of Numbers (10:11–22:1a) describes the march of the people in the wilderness and the revolts that punctuate it. Finally, the last section of the book (22:1b–36:13) deals with preparation for the conquest of Canaan.

Although at first sight readers cannot help but be struck by this apparent lack of unity they can be offered two ways of looking at the book as a single whole.

(1) *Faithfulness of God to God's promise in spite of the unfaithfulness of the people.* The first section of the book of Numbers describes the organization of the people in view of the conquest of the Promised Land: a census is taken of the tribes and they are placed in order (chs. 1–2); the Levites are set apart and their functions are clearly defined (chs. 3–4); the cultic institutions are established (chs. 7–9). We have here a people that is organized, structured, and about to start in good order on its way to the Promised Land.

However, the entire people begins to doubt God's word: the arrangement agreed upon is questioned, and the authority of Moses and Aaron contested (chs. 12; 16–17). The Israelites refuse to undertake the conquest of the land of Canaan (chs. 13–14); even Moses and Aaron disobey (20:1-13). Despite these rebellions and revolts God never goes back on the promise; of course the guilty will be chastised, but Israel as a people remains heir to the Promised Land (15:1, 18), which it prepares itself to occupy (chs. 26–36).

(2) *The invitation to holiness and the condemnation of sin.* The exhortation in Num 15:40 ("So you shall remember and do all my commandments, and you shall be holy to your God") gives a key for the reading of the whole book: the Israelite community is called to live in closeness to God. But this closeness demands holiness, that is, respect for the laws and prescriptions enunciated in the legislative sections of the book as well as obedience to the divine project for God's people, the conquest of Canaan. The invitation to holiness concerns all domains of life; it is addressed both to individuals and to the community as such.

The people's disobedience entails its punishment: the first generation of Israelites dies in the desert because of its disobedience (ch. 14); Moses and Aaron are kept from entering the Promised Land (20:12). Alone in their generation Caleb and Joshua, who have remained faithful to God, benefit by the promise (14:24-38). It is the second generation of Israelites that prepares itself on the plains of Moab to enter Canaan and inherits the promise made to its ancestors.

The fate of the first generation thus takes on a paradigmatic value (32:8-15): the punishment that struck it serves as an example to all the following generations that, by pondering their ancestors' fate, can realize how costly it is to turn away from God. The central section of the book, a succession of descriptions of the rebellions of the people and the punitive sanctions they occasion, is of capital significance in the purport of the book: Israel is enjoined to remember definitively the events of the march in the desert, meditate on them, and from them draw lessons for its conduct.

These two ways of reading the book of Numbers show its unity: one single theological intention links the three sections (1:1–10:10; 10:11–22:1a; 22:1b–36:13) that can be clearly distinguished in the book thanks to the thematic criteria and topographical indications supplied by the text. This enables us to go beyond the classical distinction stories/laws; indeed, it is the same exhortation to holiness that is expressed in the legislative texts and in the stories, the latter illustrating and supporting the former by utilizing the same logic, a logic of the separation between the "holy" and the "profane," the "clean" and the "unclean," the "faithful" and the "unfaithful."

The overall theme of the book of Numbers invites contemporary readers to ask themselves two questions:

(a) What is the place of memory (and history) in the life of Christian communities? How are the experiences, failures, and successes of the past taken into account in the pastoral decisions bearing on the life of today's communities? What examples (or counter-examples) do we effectively remember and use as guides for our ecclesial life?

(b) What is our reaction to the image of a God who punishes, who holds us responsible for our actions, as in the accounts of Numbers 14; 16–17; 20:1-13; 21:4-9; 25? Literary and historical criticism of Numbers demonstrates that such an image was not unanimously accepted even at the time when the book was being written in its definitive form.

II. General Contexts of Interpretation

1. Original Historical Contexts

The present structure of the book of Numbers, and the theology it reveals, can be attributed to priestly authors. Priestly accounts were written on the basis of older (pre-exilic) sources. Thus in chs. 13–14 the priestly narrative depends on an ancient story describing the failure of a mission of exploration in the region of Hebron. The older story and the priestly story were blended at a later date. Other early traditions are apparent in chs. 11–12; 22–24. They were subsequently integrated into the continuum of the priestly narrative that links together the different pericopes of the book by means of notes on itineraries and/or topographical data.

The numerous legislative passages of the book can also be attributed to priestly writers. Certain priestly texts are more recent than others: for instance, the stories of chs. 16–17 and the laws of chs. 15; 18–19.

The structure and theology of the book of Numbers reflect a preponderant priestly influence, but certain texts betray different trends of thought: thus Moses' intercession in 14:13-19 develops a theology of sin and forgiveness akin to deuteronomic perspectives and therefore radically opposed to that expressed in the rest of this chapter. Whereas according to the priestly authors every voluntary fault brings on a punishment, the emphasis in 14:13-19 is on forgiveness. In the first case the history of Israel is regarded as the place from which the community draws the examples that dispose it to remain holy by obeying the commandments. In the second case the ethical imperative remains, but the rereading of history points out divine solicitude toward God's sinful people and thus gives rise to hope.

The book of Numbers thus bears the traces of a debate between two different conceptions of the relationship between God and humankind. Who are the protagonists in this debate? After the exile the priestly circles of the Temple of Jerusalem developed a theology intending to show the necessity of a separation between Israel and other peoples. For those who held this view the identity of the community demands such a separation and regards priests and worship as privileged mediations; this is obvious in the late texts of chs. 16–19.

This theology is undeniably dominant in the book of Numbers. Nevertheless, 14:13-19 attests to a radical challenge that may be attributed to lay circles; these deem that the history of Israel, and not its worship only, constitutes its identity inasmuch as it is a history of salvation.

Two particular points deserve to be developed:

a. The Plurality of Theological Perspectives in the Book of Numbers

The last redactors of Numbers did not seek to harmonize the contents of the book. The overall structure comes from priestly authors while a certain number of complements and late theological and historical additions, as well as harmonizations with Deuteronomy and the book of Joshua, reflect the influence of lay people upholding the deuteronomists' theology. Thus Numbers attests to a diversity of faith expressions within the same community. We too are challenged to assess our capacity to assume differences and divergences within our own communities.

b. Violence and Death in the Stories of the Book of Numbers

How are we to understand the violence of the punishments meted out, according to the priestly narratives of Numbers, to Israelites guilty of unfaithfulness to God, and the harshness of the sanctions listed in the legislative texts? Probably the best explanation is to be found in the political situation of the post-exilic period. The priestly class suffers from a relative powerlessness in the Judean society of the time, when Judea is under the control of a foreign empire (the Persians) and the priestly circles certainly do not command the right of life and death that their literature seems to suppose. Their theological preferences, their conceptions of religion and worship do not win unanimous acceptance. The radicalization of their utterances thus expresses their exasperation at a political state of affairs they are largely unable to control; it could be an admission of powerlessness.

This radical and violent manner of speech leads us to question our own way of presenting our faith, of communicating with those who do not share it or those who express it differently from us. By using God's name and figure in the service of their own conception of religion and their particular and contingent interests, did not the last priestly authors sin against the sanctity and the respect of God that are at the same time the center of their discourses? In any case, their literature confronts us: What is our ethical behavior, what are the means we use to advance our own opinions in the very midst of the Christian communities in which we live?

2. Canonical Context

Although the book of Numbers possesses a real autonomy on the literary plane and can be studied separately from the other books forming the Pentateuch it must also be placed within the whole dynamic movement of the Torah:

From a diachronic viewpoint: Many stories in Numbers belong to the priestly history (Pg) that begins in Gen 1:1-2, 4a and continues through the books of Genesis, Exodus, and Numbers. The priestly history is a coherent narrative that existed independently before being blended with other traditions. The priestly accounts of Numbers may therefore be read and interpreted as belonging to this larger whole, going beyond the limits of this one book. Besides, the legislative prescriptions—especially the cultic prescriptions—contained in Numbers complete those promulgated in Leviticus, which are probably earlier.

From a synchronic viewpoint: The book of Numbers illustrates the faithfulness of God to the promise in spite of the people's unfaithfulness; the promise made to the ancestors is not nullified by the sins of the people. To understand the stories in Numbers it is necessary to refer to the whole of the Torah: it is in Genesis that the promises made by God are formulated (chs. 12–24). It is in Exodus that the divine revelation to God's people, the sealing of the Covenant, and the construction of the Dwelling are recorded. Only familiarity with the stories of Exodus enables us to understand why the protests of the people, which in Exod 15:22–17:7 elicited salvific actions on God's part, provoke in the parallel narratives of Numbers (chs. 11; 20:1-13) God's wrath and punishment. Thus for instance in Exodus 16 the grumbling of the people leads to the gift of quails and manna. By contrast, in the parallel account in Numbers 11 the covetous people also receives meat, but is decimated by God. In all likelihood the explanation of the divergences between the two texts resides in the differences of their situation in relation to the revelation of Sinai. The manifestations of God, faithful to the promise, are salvific because they are necessary to the survival of the people: deliverance from Egypt, gift of water and food in the desert. But the full revelation takes place on Sinai; it is there that the people commits itself to God in a definitive covenant.

As a consequence the complaints of the people, which were legitimate before Sinai, become after Sinai signs of a lack of faith and a breaking of the Covenant; as such they are severely punished. This theological understanding, characteristic of the priestly authors, can be perceived only by reading the Pentateuch as a whole.

There is a rift between the books of Numbers and Deuteronomy. The difference in theology is such that it led Martin Noth to group the books of Genesis, Exodus, Leviticus, and Numbers under the name "Tetrateuch" in order to differentiate them from Deuteronomy. Deuteronomy rereads from its own theological viewpoint the whole of the history of Israel's origins. The narrative introduction to Deuteronomy contains numerous accounts parallel to the narrative traditions collected in Numbers (see Deuteronomy 1–3).

The last redactions of Numbers were intended to connect it to the historical books, particularly the book of Joshua. They highlight the personage of Joshua and contribute to the establishment of a certain narrative continuity between the Pentateuch and the historical books that follow it.

3. Intertextuality Within the Framework of the Canon of Scripture

In the book of Numbers the desert appears as a place of trial and temptation. Although widely diffused throughout the OT literature this negative image of Israel's sojourn in the wilderness is not found in all the books of the Hebrew Bible; thus Amos (see 2:10) alludes to the sojourn in the desert without mentioning the least unfaithfulness on the part of Israel. Hosea (see 12:15) presents the desert as a place of intimacy between God and Israel. The emphasis on Israel's unfaithfulness is a trait found in later traditions and in authors having to give an account of the catastrophe of the exile: Israel's infidelities in the desert are only a prefiguring of the infidelities that marked its whole history and brought about the Babylonian exile, seen as a divine punishment. Ezekiel agrees completely with such line of thought (see Ezekiel 20), which is akin to that of the priestly authors. Here it is possible to gauge the influence of concrete historical circumstances on the rereading and reinterpretation effected by writers on the traditions they inherit.

It is true that allusions to specific passages in Numbers are abundant in the NT, but it is 1 Cor 10:1-13 that represents the most systematic rereading of the march in the desert. Paul proposes a consistent typological rereading of the events described in Numbers; he finds in them a prefiguration of the revelation of Jesus Christ (1 Cor 10:4), a foreshadowing of the liturgy of the primitive Church (1 Cor 10:2-3), and finally a warning addressed to the Christian communities (1 Cor 10:6-13). Thus, as at the time of the return from the exile the events depicted in Numbers take on a paradigmatic significance, so they keep in Paul's eyes this same function of permanent admonition and appeal to conversion directed to Christian communities.

4. Intertextuality in the Framework of Patristic Exegesis

Patristic exegesis rereads Balaam's oracles (Numbers 22–24), in particular the fourth (24:17) as true prophecies announcing the coming of Christ. However, when they comment on the events narrated in the book of Numbers, the Fathers of the Church favor an ecclesiological interpretation: the selection of seventy elders foretells the institution of priests (see Hippolytus, *Apostolic Tradition* 7). This interpretation has been adopted in the liturgy of priestly ordinations. All those who are guilty of revolt and opposition against Moses and Aaron prefigure heretics and schismatics (see, for instance, *1 Clem.* 43–44). Such an interpretation is already present in the NT in the letter of Jude (v. 11).

The patristic readings of Numbers, which raise the questions of authority and distribution of gifts within the Church, open avenues to today's ecclesiological reflection. The many conflicts that punctuate Numbers lead us to examine our relationship to authority and to elucidate the causes of the dissensions that are not lacking in the life of the Church: disagreements in the field of ideas but also, as in Numbers 16–17, clashes among persons, rivalries and quarrels over the dominance of such and such a group. Besides, when we use Numbers to conduct a reflection on the Church we are unavoidably led to confront the fact of the imperfection of the Church—a human community subject to vicissitudes but inhabited by Christ as the Dwelling was placed in the community of the Israelites.

SECOND READING

III. General Historical Background of the Book

Whereas literary criticism succeeds in unearthing pre-exilic traditions subsequently integrated into a work that for the most part can be attributed to priestly authors, historical criticism is unable to reconstruct in any reliable manner the events that preceded the settling of Israel in Canaan. Similarly, archaeology does not offer sufficient data to reconstitute the Israelites' itinerary in the wilderness.

The information the text gives concerning the wanderings of the people in the desert—as described in the geographical notes that link the different narratives to each other, and as recapitulated in Numbers 33—cannot be regarded as historical data. The priestly authors structure the whole book by means of geographical indications that are a framework for their literary composition but cannot be trusted by historians. (Historical-critical analysis does succeed in connecting two toponyms with ancient literary traditions; these two are Hebron [13:22], a city whose name seems to be linked with the personage of Caleb, and Kadesh [20:1].)

The authors do not seek to reconstruct a bygone past through the geographical markers in their narrative; rather they deliver a message to their contemporaries. The time of the desert becomes a figure of the time of the exile, during which Israel was living far away from the Promised Land. The reluctance to enter Canaan shown by the community in Numbers 13–14 evokes the Israelites' unwillingness to come back from exile when the opportunity was offered them by the Persians. The warning against Moab in ch. 25 suggests that the fact of remaining, after the exile, in the midst of other peoples and without the benefit of any real political autonomy is a danger to the identity of Israel. Events and prefigurations of the desert thus are used to give the readers an understanding of the theological values at stake in the contemporary events, the exile and the return from exile.

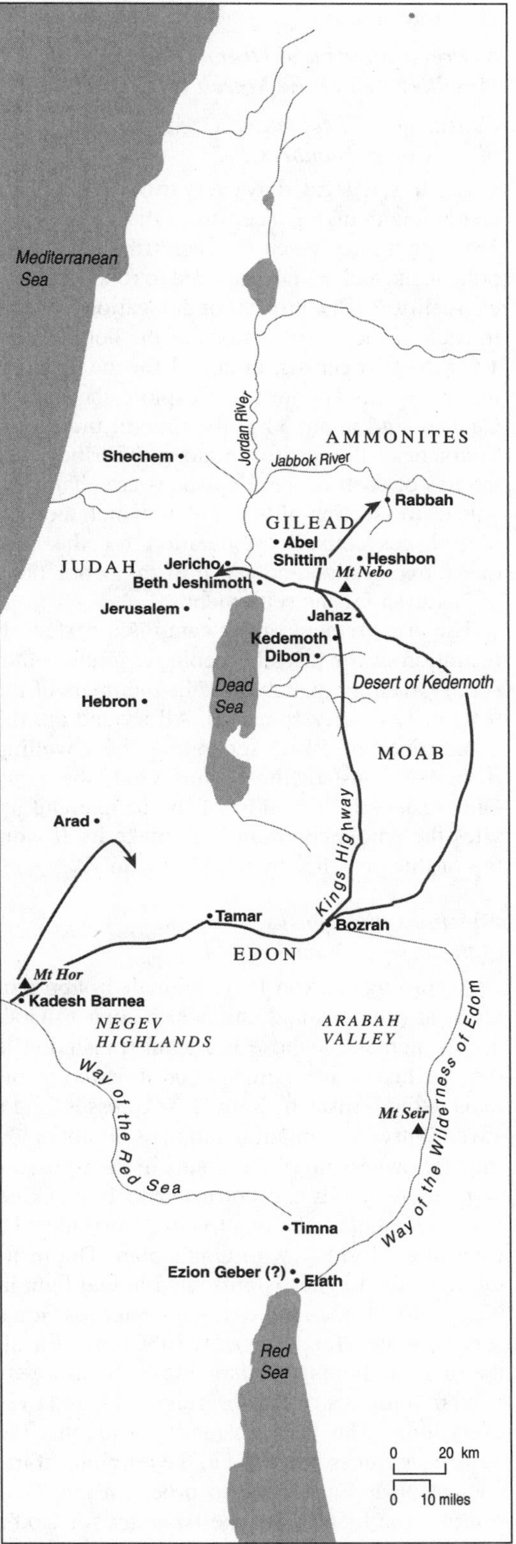

IV. Commentary

A. Preparations and Organization of the Israelites Before the March (1:1–10:10)

Census of the People and Organization of the Camp, Numbers 1–2

Leaders, delegated by every tribe of Israel, are charged with taking a census of the people (1:4-16). The figures given for each tribe have symbolic value and are not intended to reflect historical reality. Such a process of delegation is found in each of the main sections of the book: in ch. 1 for the first census, in ch. 13 for the designation of scouts appointed to explore the land of Canaan, and in ch. 34 at the time of the apportionment of the territory among the tribes. The themes of each of these episodes are characteristic of the section of the book in which they are placed: respectively preparation for the conquest, exploration and revolt of the people, and preparation for the settlement.

The arrangement of the camp is a perfect illustration of the priestly theology: in the center is the Dwelling, which only the members of the tribe of Levi may approach. All around are the other tribes of Israel separating the Dwelling from the non-Israelites. Thus God, the Holy One, resides in the midst of the people and invites the whole community to make itself worthy of this presence by remaining holy.

Functions and Census of the Levites, Numbers 3–4

According to Exod 13:12 all male firstborn of creation (humans and animals) belong to God. This statement—whose liturgical translation is the sacrifice of a certain number of firstborn animals in the Jerusalem Temple—expresses God's sovereignty over creation. Humans do not enjoy integral ownership of the goods in their possession; these goods are entrusted to humankind but fundamentally belong to God. They must be used in conformity with God's plan. The institution of the Levites is presented in that light in Num 3:40-51: the Levites are set apart for God's service (cultic functions) "as substitutes for all the firstborn among the Israelites" and as a permanent reminder of the sovereignty of God over everything. The OT constantly condemns the human sacrifices practiced in the religions of the ancient Near East. Thus to proclaim that God reserves the firstborn of the Israelites for God's self in no way means that God demands they be sacrificed. It means that they must be consecrated to God's service. The institution of Levites, setting apart a certain number of men for the divine service, dispenses the rest of the community from consecrating the eldest sons to that service and expresses the people's thankfulness to their God.

In their service the Levites are subordinated to the priests (4:1-33), a principle strongly repeated in the narrative of ch. 16 as well as in the legislative dispositions of ch. 18.

Diverse Legislative Prescriptions, Numbers 5–6

Chapters 5 and 6 contain the laws relative to varied aspects of the people's life:

(a) the incompatibility between certain types of uncleanliness (leprosy and other diseases) and dwelling in the community of the people of Israel regarded as a cultic community (5:1-4);

(b) the juridical and cultic reparation for wrongs inflicted on others (5:5-10);

(c) the procedure to follow in dubious cases of a woman's unfaithfulness (5:11-31);

(d) the nazirite vow, that is, the consecration of a person to God for a given period (6:1-21).

The unit formed by chs. 5 and 6 concludes with a blessing.

On the one hand these different laws show that the notion of "religion" covers all aspects of daily life: the wrongs caused to others are amended in a liturgy of restitution; litigious domestic cases are also decided within a ritual setting (5:11-31). On the other hand most texts stress the preeminent role of the priests in the implementation of the legislation and thus contribute to strengthening the primacy of the priestly function, already affirmed in ch. 4.

The law concerning the nazirite institution (*nāzir* is a word derived from the Hebrew verb *nazar,* "set apart," "separate") needs some additional remarks: the rules codified in the priestly text of Num 6:1-21 make use of elements from older traditions according to which persons consecrated to God abstain from wine and fermented beverages and no longer shave. Thus Samson (Judges 13–16), being consecrated to God, observes all these prescriptions. In the NT Luke shows John the Baptist keeping the nazirite rules. Beyond the material aspect of the ritual ordinances they describe, these different texts call the readers to discover their "spiritual" meaning:

consecration to God and conversion to the manner of living this consecration entails.

Establishment of Cultic Institutions, 7:1–9:14

These chapters of the book of Numbers report the dedication of the Dwelling, whose construction, recorded in the priestly account of Exod 35:4–40:33, is in complete harmony with the detailed instructions of the priestly text of Exod 25:1–31:11. The ritual of consecration appears as the liturgical rendition of the ordering of the people described in the first four chapters of Numbers. The animal and vegetable offerings of the tribes of Israel precede the consecration of the Levites, who are made the priests' auxiliaries for the service of the altar. The instructions contained in Num 9:1-14 concerning the liturgical calendar conclude the ritual of dedication of the Dwelling.

Last Instructions Before the Departure from Sinai, 9:15–10:10

Numbers 9:15-23 takes up again the elements already developed in Exod 40:34-38. The cloud that according to Exod 24:16-18 covered Sinai now settles on the Dwelling, the place of God's presence in the midst of the people. The cloud gives the signal for departure and marks the stages of the journey; God in person guides the people, a people called to absolute obedience. In the same way Num 9:15-23 already announces by its theme (the itinerary of the people and its stages) the second main section of the book, so the instructions of 10:1-10 concern the discipline that must reign in a people on their way from now on.

The first main section of Numbers can be attributed in its entirety to priestly writers: the figure of Israel at Sinai is used by these authors to expound the priestly theology. The texts of Num 1:1–10:10 are addressed to the community of the Israelites at the end of the Babylonian exile. They emphasize the preponderant responsibility of the priesthood in the preservation of the people's identity, an identity perceived and presented above all as a religious one, finding its expression in the worship at the Jerusalem Temple and the ritual precepts of daily life. They exhort Israel to obedience to God mediated by obedience to the whole body of legislative prescriptions.

Is such an obedience possible? What happens in cases of transgression? These two questions find their answers in the second section of the book in Num 10:11–22:1a.

B. The March in the Desert (10:11–22:1a)

A People in Good Order Prepares to Leave Sinai, 10:11-36

The pericope in Num 10:11-36 is a transition between the first and second sections of the book: after being numbered (chs. 1–2) and organized (chs. 3–4), and with the Dwelling at its center (chs. 7–8), the nation is ready to set out toward the Promised Land. The order described in 10:11-28 is willed by God: the community has obeyed God's instructions to the letter. The contrast between the stories of rebellion—recounted from Num 11:1 on—and the good order and serenity characterizing 10:11-36 is striking; this is the reason why certain commentators consider 11:1 to be the beginning of the second section.

Verses 29-32 add a universalistic dimension: the benefits of the Covenant are not the monopoly of the Israelites, and foreign peoples like the Midianites are invited to share in them.

First Revolts, First Punishments, Numbers 11

Numbers 11:1-3 opens the long series of episodes of the people's revolt. Every one of these murmurings betrays a lack of faith and an implicit questioning of the Covenant concluded at Sinai. The correction decreed by God has both a pedagogical function and a theological significance:

(a) The punishments incurred by Israel have an exemplary import; they call all future generations, all readers or hearers of the story to measure the risks involved in the forgetfulness of, the estrangement from, or the rejection of God.

(b) At a deeper level these punishments seek to demonstrate that humankind cannot live without God and that only a life centered on God is fruitful, whereas every distancing from God is deadly.

The narrative in 11:4-34 combines two ancient traditions: the giving of food in the desert and the institution of the seventy elders. The grumbling of the Israelites demanding meat is tantamount to a refusal of God's free gift. Indeed, the people have grown tired of the manna and are homesick for Egypt; thus the whole history of salvation is questioned, contested, negated.

Faced with the complaints of the people, Moses is at a loss. This is why God gives him seventy elders. This notion of sharing the pastoral charge has been adopted by the Catholic liturgy of ordination to the priesthood.

Verses 25-29 are read in the liturgy of the twenty-sixth Sunday of Year B in Ordinary Time and placed in parallel with Mark 9:38-48. Eldad and Medad prophesy in the camp although they are not among the seventy elders; the accent here is on the absolute sovereignty of God in the attribution of gifts as well as the gratuitousness of God's gift. (Joel develops a similar theology in ch. 3). The Spirit blows where it wills, beyond all human logic. God's gifts are not reserved for those who exercise an official charge in the community; all members are able to receive them.

Moses' Authority Questioned by Miriam and Aaron, Numbers 12

In contrast to the priestly texts that always juxtapose the figures of Moses and Aaron, ch. 12 highlights the person of Moses, recognized as superior to all prophets, and one whose intercession with God proves efficacious. The theme of this section confirms that of the preceding section: again God's freedom in the gratuitous attribution of the divine gifts is emphasized. Besides, just as the people's murmuring arouses God's anger in ch. 11, so here in ch. 12 Miriam's speaking against Moses earns her a severe punishment: by opposing any aspect of God's plan the dissenters in effect prefer their logic to that of God who, however, knows what is good for humankind. Far from overpowering people, God seeks to engage in a dialogue with them by choosing Moses as God's favored interlocutor given charge of representing the Israelites, and by responding to his intercession.

The story in ch. 12 may seem shocking to modern readers because Miriam and Aaron are guilty of the same sin but only Miriam is punished. The text supplies no explanation for this difference of treatment; nevertheless we may make two observations.

(a) When Aaron sees what is inflicted on Miriam, he implores Moses for her as well as for himself (vv. 11-12: "do not punish *us* for a sin that we have so foolishly committed"). Thus he regards Miriam's affliction as the first step of a punishment that could very well directly concern him also.

(b) The second remark is more conjectural. Inasmuch as the final redaction of Numbers was the work of priests it is plausible to hypothesize that such a redaction seeks to highlight the priestly personage of Aaron. As a consequence any mention of a punishment striking Aaron might have been deleted from the story.

Exploration of the Land of Canaan; Revolt of the People, Numbers 13–14

The present text of Numbers 13–14 results from the blending of two parallel narratives, one pre-exilic, the other priestly. This explains the many doublets and repetitions found in these two chapters. The older tradition, which can be identified in chs. 13–14, concerns the conquest of Hebron by the clan of the Calebites (13:22). This tradition was incorporated into a narrative of exploration of the southern part of the land, a narrative that ends with the people's refusal to undertake the conquest. The priestly account is based on this ancient story of exploration.

The later account is interested not so much in the action as in its theological significance: the Israelites rebel by murmuring against Moses and Aaron (14:2) and plan to return to Egypt; this is tantamount to rejecting God and God's design for the people. In ch. 14 the complaining is not the legitimate cry of a people who fear for their survival, as was the case in Exod 15:24 and 17:3. Here the grumbling reveals the distrust of the community for God and the leaders God has given the people. Such a lack of faith (14:11) occasions an exemplary punishment: the generation of adults who came out of Egypt will not see the Promised Land but will die in the desert.

Such a theology may shock today's readers: Who is this God who punishes God's own people so severely? To correctly interpret the text we must not lose sight of the concrete conditions in which it was written. The circumstances are those of the exilic and post-exilic times in which Israel has lost every shred of autonomy, every atom of political power. The violence of the priestly authors' language expresses their despair above all and is the pedagogical medium they believe to be best adapted to the situation they have to face.

Moreover, the priestly writers' understanding of the relationships between humankind and God does not win the unanimous agreement of the post-exilic communities. In 14:13-19 Moses' intercession—emanating from circles inspired by the deuteronomist theology (cf. Exod 32:11-14)

—reveals an understanding of forgiveness totally opposed to the priestly theology. Thus the study of chs. 13–14 uncovers a real debate between two schools of thought, that of the priests and that of the deuteronomists, that coexist within the community of Israel.

The failure of the people before Hormah (14:19-45) is the conclusion to the story in chs. 13–14. After having refused to enter Canaan on God's order and having planned to return to Egypt (14:3-4), the people now presume to conquer the land by relying on their own strength; this ends in catastrophe. In both cases the cause of the people's calamity is that they have forgotten God. The Israelites want to substitute their own human logic for the divine logic and thus negate the order that, according to priestly thought, had been established at creation.

Patristic exegesis is rich in commentaries on the stories of Numbers 13–14. For instance, Cyril of Alexandria (*Glaphyrorum in Numeri,* MPG 69, cols. 606–615) sees in the Promised Land the figure of the kingdom of heaven. Some people refuse to believe and are thereby excluded from the celestial banquet. This passage is read in the Liturgy of the Word on Wednesday of the eighteenth week of Ordinary Time in odd years.

Not "Exploring" According to the Lust of One's Heart (15:39), Numbers 15

The cultic prescriptions of Numbers 15 presuppose a sedentary life and therefore are an implicit reaffirmation of the promise made to the ancestors after the punishment meted out to the first generation that left Egypt: the people will come into the land God promised them (15:2, 18). As the story of Numbers 13–14 served as a warning to all generations of Israel, so the laws of ch. 15 are accompanied by a general caution: not "to explore" by following the lust of one's own heart (15:39). The same verb used to describe the mission of the spies in the priestly account of ch. 13 is here repeated in the legislative section of ch. 15; thus chs. 13–14 are an exemplary story, a "parable" confirming the commands of ch. 15, which are relevant to the present situation of Israel.

A Conflict About Competence in the Worship Services, Numbers 16–17

The three successive stories in this section of Numbers (16:1–17:5; 17:6-15; 17:16-26) have the common purpose of clarifying the respective functions of the community, the Levites, and the priests in worship services. The text in its present form contains numerous doublets and literary conflicts attesting to the complexity of the history of its composition. The figures of Dathan and Abiram (16:1, 12) belong to an ancient tradition that the priestly writers incorporated into the present narrative. The place of the Aaronic priesthood is highlighted in each of the three stories: only priests are authorized to approach the Dwelling and legitimately present offerings to God. Such an organization of the cultic service is based on a concept of holiness radically different from that of Deuteronomy. According to that book the whole people is chosen by God to become holy (Deut 7:6; 14:2, 21; 26:19; 28:9) whereas Numbers teaches that only priests chosen by God can aspire to holiness (16:3-7). There is definitely a theological debate going on and the priestly account in ch. 16 dialogues from a distance with Deuteronomy to refute its theology, summed up by Num 16:3a in these terms: "All the congregation are holy."

The stories in chs. 16–19 represent a late phase of the priestly literature: narrower preoccupation with the organization of worship and the preeminence of the priestly caste has been substituted for the universalist perspectives found in the priestly text of Gen 9:1-17.

Prescriptions Concerning the Respective Functions of Priests and Levites, Numbers 18

The legislative prescriptions of Numbers 18 agree with the stories of chs. 16–17. The primacy of the Aaronic priesthood asserted in the narratives is confirmed by the texts of the laws. As the stories in chs. 13–14 uphold the legislation in ch. 15, so those in chs. 16–17 illustrate the legislation expounded in ch. 18.

The Priests' Role in the Rituals of Cleanness, Numbers 19

The priestly theology contrasts the "holy" and the "profane," the "clean" and the "unclean." These concepts do not have just an ethical dimension; much more importantly they reveal a particular understanding of the religious sphere. Only clean objects and persons may stand in the presence of God, the Holy One *par excellence.* As a consequence life is punctuated by innumerable rituals of purification that enable the people to be in the state of cleanness necessary for living in God's presence. Priests play a specific role in the performance of these rituals. Unclean persons would be excluded from participating in the rites and worship that give rhythm and structure to the people's life.

Patristic exegesis has interpreted 19:1-10 allegorically. For instance, Cyril of Alexandria (see above) sees in the red heifer a figure of the sinless Christ, free and immolated so that the Church may live; the water used for purification is a figure of the baptismal water.

Moses and Aaron's Sin, 20:1-13

In the priestly narrative there is a correspondence between the people's sin, recounted in chs. 13–14, and the leaders' sin, exposed in 20:1-13. The punishment is the same: they will not enter the Promised Land. At first the reader of this passage might remain uncertain as to the nature of the sin committed by Moses and Aaron because the text has certainly been reworked; the doublets and literary ambiguities are many. Moses' and Aaron's sin consists in not having obeyed God's order to the letter: rather than speaking to the rock they strike it after having given the people a tongue-lashing. The story told in this passage is parallel to that of Exod 17:1-7, which is an earlier version on which the priestly writing is built.

The stories in the central section of Numbers show the failings of the people at all levels: The community rebels against its leaders (chs. 11, 13–14); the clan heads contest Moses' and Aaron's authority (ch. 16); even Moses and Aaron falter. No one is exempt from weaknesses and everyone appears with his or her humanity marked by sin. This sin does not cancel the promise made by God even though it delays its realization. God fulfills the divine plan for a chosen people, a people fallible and flawed; to God's faithfulness corresponds human unfaithfulness, but this asymmetry in the relationship does not entail its rupture.

Reading this text, Paul saw in the rock (Num 20:7) the figure of Christ (1 Cor 10:4). The water springing from it represents the water of baptism. This is an allegorical exegesis of Numbers whose principles surprise modern readers. The pericope from Numbers is reinterpreted to signify the symbolic and liturgical role of water in the young Corinthian community. Numbers 20:1-13 is read at the Liturgy of the Word on the Thursday of the eighteenth week of Ordinary Time in odd years.

On the Way to the Promised Land, 20:14–22:1a

After a lengthy stay in Kadesh (13:26; 20:1) the people set out on their journey toward Canaan. According to the story, the itinerary they follow skirts the eastern borders of the land and the Israelites arrive in the vicinity of Jericho near the place where the Jordan empties into the Dead Sea. This part of the journey is marked by Aaron's death (which follows the punishment announced in 20:12); the victory over Hormah (21:1-3), the counterpart of the defeat mentioned in 14:45; and the victories over Sihon, king of the Amorites, and Og, king of Bashan (21:21-35). These victories are celebrated and compared to the deliverance from Egypt in the liturgy of Pss 135:11 and 136:19-20; whether in Egypt or on the plains of Moab it is the same history of salvation that unfolds for Israel, which is invited to magnify in its liturgy from generation to generation God's deeds in its favor.

This victorious march toward the plains of Moab is interrupted by a fresh rebellion (21:4-9). Again the people grumble and only by Moses' intercession do they escape the scourge sent by God. The bronze serpent made by Moses to save the people is reminiscent of rites known in the ancient religions of the Near East; images of snakes, protectors of the people, were placed at the doors of temples. John's gospel sees in the lifting up of the serpent the prefiguration of that of Jesus, who came to save humankind on the cross (see John 3:14 and also 8:28; 12:32). The texts of Num 21:4-9 and John 8:21-30 are read in conjunction with one another in the Liturgy of the Word on Tuesday of the fifth week in Lent.

At the end of the second section of Numbers the people are at the threshold of the Promised Land, but they have experienced sin and the impossibility of living independently of God. The stories of the march in the desert serve as a warning in Israel's collective memory; they are exhortations to the people, their chiefs, and their leaders never to turn away from God. People, chiefs, leaders all are apt, yesterday as today, to forget God and prefer their own purely human logic to the logic of faith.

C. On the Plains of Moab; Preparations for the Settlement in Canaan (22:1b–36:13)

The Oracles of Balaam, 22:1b–24:25

The prophecies of Balaam, a person whose origin remains obscure (22:5), are grafted without any transition onto the narrative of Israel's arrival on the plains of Moab (22:1b). The one literary connection existing between the "Balaam pericope" and the texts preceding it is the repetition of the place-name "Moab." The Israelites reach the plains of Moab; the king of Moab asks Balaam to prophesy against Israel.

On the theological plane and in the present structure of the book the purpose of Balaam's oracles could be to reaffirm the promise of the blessing Israel enjoys (24:1) in spite of the people's rebellions and infidelities in the desert. On the literary plane Numbers 22–24 assembles ancient traditions, distinct traditions as attested by the different words for naming God (Elohim, YHWH) and also the inconsistencies in the story (for example the discrepancy between 22:20 and 22:22).

The story of Balaam's donkey (22:21-35), now part of chs. 22–24, is a popular tale forming a coherent unit all by itself. The text underscores the contrast between Balaam, a man whose reputation has spread beyond the boundaries of his country but who does not see the signs sent by God, and the donkey whose perspicacity stuns the reader. The lesson is that we must not be entrapped by appearances and conventions, which often blur our vision and distort our judgment. Augustine (*Quaestiones in Heptateuchum,* q. 50 *In Numeri*) sees in the episode of the donkey chosen by God a witness to God "who chooses what is least wise in the world in order to confound the wise."

The prophecies in Num 24:3b-9, 15b-24 can be read independently from the narrative because they form a whole by themselves. In contrast the prophecies of 23:7b-10, 19-24 are well blended into the narrative context to which they make reference. The theology expounded in Balaam's oracles emphasizes the election of Israel, a people set apart from other nations. This statement is the more effective because it is made by a foreigner who is literally forced into pronouncing, as God's spokesman, a blessing upon Israel.

Within the OT itself the figure of Balaam has been interpreted in a pejorative fashion, as in ch. 31 (especially vv. 8 and 16), a text written by priests. The NT takes up this unfavorable image in part (see, for instance, 2 Pet 2:15-16 and Jude 11). However, Balaam's figure probably inspired the much more positive image of the Magi coming from the East to announce Jesus' birth (Matt 2:1). The theme of the star, present in the prophecy of Num 24:15b, is also found in Matthew's story (Matt 2:1-10).

In their present form chs. 22–24 of Numbers concur in affirming the primacy of God's plans over human plans: Balak's designs are foiled; Balaam himself can only submit to the divine will. Therefore these chapters contribute to set forth anew—in a way different from that of 13:1–20:13—the invitation addressed by God to Israel and to the whole of humankind. For having turned a deaf ear to this invitation the people is punished once more; this is the topic of ch. 25. The blessing of 24:2-9 is read at the Liturgy of the Word on Monday of the third week of Advent.

Idolatrous Behavior and New Punishment of Israel, Numbers 25

The sin mentioned in ch. 25 is a new kind: the Israelites take part in idolatrous worship. The narratives of the march in the desert illustrated the sins that the people, left to themselves, were apt to commit: disobedience, transgression of cultic laws, lack of faith, covetousness. The story in ch. 25 shows still another danger, one arising from the proximity of foreign peoples who have their own deities, that is, the Baals, whose worship entails sacred prostitution. The purpose of the punishment striking the Israelites is to reaffirm the oneness of God. God is the only true God and demands an undivided love from the chosen people.

This story challenges our faith. Provided we succeed in getting beyond the violence of the text—probably an expression of the disarray in the priestly community during and after the exile, threatened as it was in its identity and forced to cohabit with populations that did not share the same faith—we are led to ask questions of ourselves concerning the way we view the religious and philosophical pluralism of the contemporary world. How can we avoid being engulfed by a general relativism? How can we affirm the Christian identity, demonstrate the positive contributions of Christianity while maintaining a dialogue with everybody and avoiding the stumbling block the priestly author did not overcome, that is to say, verbal violence that can lead to violence of other kinds?

New Census of the Israelites, Numbers 26

The census in Numbers 26 applies to the new generation that is about to enter the Promised Land. Indeed, as 26:64-65 underlines, the generation submitted to a census in ch. 1 has died in the desert (ch. 14), but the promise remains in force. The text of ch. 26 contains many proper names absent from ch. 1, which reinforces the impression that the people have been renewed. As in ch. 3, the Levites have a separate census.

Collection of Civil and Cultic Laws, Numbers 27–30

All the laws collected in Numbers 27–30 have in common the presupposition that the people are sedentary; they are given in view of the settlement in the Promised Land and this explains their place in the present structure of the book. Numbers 27:1-11 defines the right to inheritance in the absence of a male heir: daughters, too, are entitled to inherit. The exposition of the juridical rule is in the form of a brief story to serve as model.

Numbers 28:1–29:40 contains cultic legislation concerning offerings and sacrifices made to God in the sanctuary; a vegetable offering always accompanies the animal sacrifice. God must be honored by sacrifices offered in the sanctuary not only on feastdays and Sabbaths, but also every day of the week. The sacrifice consists in taking something from the goods (vegetable and animal) of creation and offering it to God. Offerings and sacrifices are thus signs that all can see, through which the community of Israel acknowledges God's sovereignty over all creation.

Numbers 30:1-16 gives legislation regulating vows made by women. The condition of women's dependence on their fathers and husbands is sure to shock modern readers, but it must be placed within the cultural context of the ancient Near East. It is important at the same time to note that women could and did make binding vows.

Within this legislative section 27:12-23 reports the story of Joshua's investiture as Moses' successor. Just as Eleazar had succeeded Aaron, so Joshua is called to succeed Moses. Along with the first generation that had left Egypt, Moses and Aaron lacked faith in God (see 20:12) and were condemned to die outside the Promised Land. However, in the present structure of the Pentateuch Moses' death is related only at the end of the book of Deuteronomy, in ch. 34.

War Against Midian and Victory for the Israelites, Numbers 31

Numbers 31 continues the narrative of ch. 25, from which in the present structure of the book it is separated by lists and collections of laws. The military campaign against the Midianites is linked to their responsibility for the debauchery in which Israel engaged (25:6-18). Although the text of ch. 25 does not explicitly mention it, it is possible that the Midianite woman of the story was—like the daughters of Moab in 25:1—a sacred prostitute. Then there would be two reasons why Israelites were forbidden to have sexual relations with foreign women: to maintain the identity of the people and to avoid idolatry. Besides, the priestly account of ch. 31 establishes a connection between the traditions about Balaam and those concerning the idolatry at Peor, which were originally independent. The figure of Balaam thus acquires a derogatory image (31:16), absent from the traditions of chs. 22–24.

Account of the Settlement of Several Tribes East of the Jordan, Numbers 32

The settlement of the tribes of Reuben and Gad and the half-tribe of Manasseh east of the Jordan encounters Moses' opposition; they must commit themselves to fight along with the rest of the Israel to conquer the land. Moses' admonition to these tribes centers around the events in the desert. As the people's refusal to enter Canaan (ch. 14) brought about their punishment, so now every new disobedience would have identical consequences (32:8-15). The events in the desert are presented as exemplary in the narrative of ch. 32: all the generations of Israel must keep them in their memory and regulate their behavior accordingly. Thus this story gives us a key for understanding the whole book. The first generation of Israelites who came out of Egypt, organized on the military and cultic levels according to God's instructions, paid for their disobedience with their lives. This sentence, the inevitable consequence of sin, shows to all following generations that the only choice sure to guarantee the survival and identity of the people is obedience to God's prescriptions transmitted through Moses.

This theology of God's absolute dominion over human history is characteristic of the priestly caste to which belong the authors of the book in its final form. Within the Pentateuch itself this theology is not unanimously received. For instance, the perspectives of Deuteronomy unambiguously differ from it (see also II, 1. Original Historical Contexts, above).

Israel's Itinerary, 33:1-49

This late priestly text attempts to retrace Israel's steps after the deliverance from Egypt. We must not see here a historical recapitulation of the people's itinerary, but rather a literary reconstruction picking up the principal data in Exodus and Numbers and introducing some new placenames; the text mentions sixteen names not otherwise known. The priestly authors symbolically divide the journey into forty stages and seek to date the events (vv. 3, 38).

Directions for the Conquest, 33:50–35:34

Numbers 33:50-56 recalls the risk of idolatry because of the cohabitation with foreign peoples; Israel must conquer the land and cleanse it from its idols (see 33:52).

Numbers 34:1-12 gives a theoretical sketch of the boundaries of the region. Written in a postexilic time during which Israel has lost its independence, this text offers an ideal vision of the Promised Land, whose borders are those described in Ezek 47:13-23; in fact, at no point in its history was Israel ever in control of all the territories enumerated in 34:1-12.

The process of apportionment of the land among the tribes—delegation of one leader per tribe (34:13-29)—recalls that used for the first census of the people in ch. 1 and also for the exploration of Canaan in ch. 13. This threefold repetition is a literary device the priestly authors used to signify the connection between the three main sections of Numbers (1:1–10:10; 10:11–22:1a; 22:1b–36:13).

The specification of cities for the Levites (35:1-8) is part of the legislation concerning the Levites, which covered every domain of their life: worship, offerings, division of the land.

The cities of refuge for those who have killed someone (35:9-15)—an identical law is found in the parallel text of Deut 19:1-11—are intended only for persons charged with unintentional homicide.

Additional Prescriptions Concerning Inheritance; Conclusion of the Book, Numbers 36

The laws expounded in Num 36:1-12 are a complement to those described in 27:1-11; they also insure the stability of the apportionment of the territory between the tribes described in 34:13-15: the land cannot pass by inheritance from tribe to tribe. Thus with every new situation arising in the life of the community appears a new codification willed by God and transmitted by Moses. The priests' text thus leaves open the possibility of an evolution of the Law. The only constant obligation is to apply in every detail the legislation presented as bearing the seal of divine right.

This possibility of an evolution of the Law in the Israelite community, as shown in Numbers, leads us to ask questions about the evolution of law and institutions in our own communities: When and how can we permit the law to evolve? How can we create unanimity concerning new institutions? How can we secure their establishment and their "reception" by the community?

The third part of Numbers concludes with 36:13, taking up the formula that opens the section at 22:1b, "in the plains of Moab by the Jordan at Jericho."

BIBLIOGRAPHY

Artus, Oliver. *Etudes sur le livre des Nombres.* Fribourg and Göttingen, 1997.

Levine, Baruch A. *Numbers 1–20. A New Translation with Introduction and Commentary.* AB 4. New York: Doubleday, 1993.

McEvenue, Sean E. *The Narrative Style of the Priestly Writer.* Rome: Biblical Institute Press, 1971.

Noth, Martin. *Numbers: A Commentary.* Translated by James D. Martin. Philadelphia: Westminster, 1968.

Olson, Dennis T. *The Death of the Old and the Birth of the New: The Framework of the Book of Numbers and the Pentateuch.* Chico: Scholars, 1985.

Deuteronomy

Yuichi Osumi

FIRST READING

General Character of the Book

1. Deuteronomy at a Religious Turning Point

In the ancient world a deity was worshiped by various names, each connected with a special power. When, for example, the lords of Shechem gathered the grapes, they celebrated in the temple of Baal-berith (Judg 9:4, 27), but when King Ahaziah lay injured he inquired of Baal-zebub of Ekron (2 Kings 1:2). Every local community had its own Baal and also its own Lord (YHWH). But Israel came to know that the Lord (YHWH), their God, had never had many names but only one (see Deut 6:4).

In Deuteronomy, formed as the farewell speech of Moses (see 1:1-5; 3:23-29; chs. 31–34), when Moses speaks of God to the people he calls God "the LORD, your (possessive singular or plural) God" or sometimes "the LORD our God." This is "the LORD, the God of Israel" as the deuteronomistic history (see the general article) often names God (Josh 8:30; 24:2; Judg 5:3, 5; 2 Sam 7:26-27; 1 Kings 8:15-26 and elsewhere). On the one hand, the title "your/our God" expresses the covenantal relationship between the Lord and Israel. The Lord makes the covenant with Israel: the Lord will be the God of Israel and Israel will be the people of the Lord (see especially Deut 26:17-19). "The LORD (YHWH)" is, on the other hand, a proper name written in only four letters "YHWH" and pronounced probably "Yahweh," but read always in the Jewish and Christian tradition as "Adonai = the LORD." This name expresses God's presence and power, by which Israel is elected (Deut 6:20-25; 7:6-8 and elsewhere) and on which the covenant of Israel is founded. Deuteronomy 6:4 says: "the LORD (YHWH) is one LORD (YHWH)." The Lord is not divided into many local or private deities (see the comment on 6:4). The Lord who is one, who rules the whole world and "who fills all in all" (Eph 1:23) became "your/our" God (Deut 10:14-15). YHWH cannot be your private God, but is totally directed to "you," to each one of "(all) Israel" (6:4; 9:1; see also 1:1; 5:1; 27:9; 29:2; 31:1, 11; 32:45; 34:12).

Sacrifice in local sanctuaries was no longer appropriate to the worship of the Lord, the one God. Deuteronomy required that the people destroy the local sanctuaries and centralize the cult at "the place which the LORD . . . will choose . . . to put His name—the name as the presence" (Deuteronomy 12; 14:22-29; 15:19-23; 16:1-17; 18:1-8, and elsewhere). The essential element of worship in each community was, therefore, no longer sacrifice but reading, meditating, or reciting the words of the book of the divine Law (see 6:6-9; 11:18-20; 30:11-14; also 17:18-20; 31:9-13). The focal point of daily life was the actualization of the words of God (6:4-15; 8:3; 12:28; 13:18; 15:5; 16:18-20; 17:8-13, 18-20; 18:15-22; 27:1-8, and elsewhere. In keeping with this it would be most appropriate to read the biblical text of Deuteronomy itself along with this commentary, and also the other texts of the Old and New Testaments that are cited).

The Jewish and Christian life that has its basis in Scripture finds here its origin. This meant that worship had to be changed from private cult in which everyone worshiped his or her own Lord to "common prayer" in the literal sense of the word, in which the whole of Israel prayed to the one God with the common words revealed in Deuteronomy.

In modern society, especially in the U. S. and also in Japan, religion is so privatized that there are as many religions as there are people and each Christian has his or her own private God, private YHWH, private Jesus (Robert N. Bellah, *Habits of the Heart* [Berkeley: University of California Press] 1985). See the comment on 5:8. Deuteronomy shows in this very situation the necessity of public worship offered to the one God. Our salvation is not that we are our own, but we belong unto our God, our faithful Jesus Christ (see *Heidelberg Catechism* §1).

2. Deuteronomy as the Second Law

Deuteronomy was in reality not written in the days of Moses but a few centuries after, when Israel was in a political crisis. Its authors put their readers on the plains of Moab, on the east side of the Jordan (1:1; 11:31; 27:2; also 9:1; 27:3, and elsewhere) and made them the audience of Moses. The people of Israel in Deuteronomy are just crossing the Jordan into the promised but unfamiliar land. Moses, however, is close to death. They need a new leader with whom they will pass through this crisis and new principles according to which they will live as the people of God. Deuteronomy makes clear by analogy that its readers are also at a historical turning point and that they must stand firmly on the words of God.

The title, "Deuteronomy," means "second law" or "repeated law." It derives from the LXX translation of Deut 17:18, which commands the king to write for himself "this second/repeated law" in a book to be read each day. In fact Deuteronomy refers to a second covenant made on the plains of Moab (29:1) and constitutes a law proclaimed through Moses that is in addition to the words of the first covenant, namely the decalogue (5:6-21). At the making of the first covenant, according to Deuteronomy, the Lord spoke to Israel "face to face" (5:4) at the mountain of Horeb ("Sinai" is called "Horeb" in the text of Deuteronomy). The Lord spoke only the Decalogue (see 5:22–6:1). Deuteronomy itself is the law revealed not to Israel directly but only to Moses at Horeb. However it should be given as the second law to the people when their situation is radically changed.

3. Deuteronomy as "Torah"

Modern English translations interpret the corresponding words of Deut 17:18 in the Hebrew (Masoretic) tradition as "a copy of this law." This is one of the possible translations. Deuteronomy calls itself as a whole "this law," or more precisely "this *torah*" (1:5; 31:9 and elsewhere). "Torah" originally meant individual "(revealed) instruction." Deuteronomy uses the word to refer to the book as a whole and introduces itself as the complete revealed instruction of the Lord to which the king also must be subject.

The one who speaks in Deuteronomy as "I" is, with a few exceptions, Moses, not the Lord. Moses, as mentioned above, died without going into the promised land (3:23-29; chs.31–34) but he speaks this *torah* in his farewell speech just before Israel crosses the Jordan (1:1; 9:1; 11:31, and frequently). This means also that Deuteronomy is the only representative of the last will of Moses, who is not present in person in the land from the beginning. No one even knows where Moses was buried (34:6). No one can therefore win Moses over to a particular side or claim to possess Moses' authority. Instead of his tomb Israel has the stele of the *torah* (27:1-8). Israel heard the *torah* even before the start of settlement; therefore the *torah* should be applicable anywhere in the land without exception.

4. Treaty Between God and God's People

Deuteronomy contains the literary elements of a covenant, or rather of a treaty comparable to those of the Hittites in the second millennium or the Assyrians in the first millennium: that is, a treaty between the great king and his vassals. Characteristic features of this form include:

(1) The vassal treaties began with a "preamble" that says: "the treaty with A . . . , the treaty that B, the king of X made with you . . . ." The preamble shows what this document is and who are the persons concerned. In Deut 1:1-5, the preamble of Deuteronomy, it is evident who made the treaty with Israel: it is the Lord. The content of the book is the whole *"torah"* (v. 5). Verse 1 makes clear who is the mediator of the treaty

and who must hear the *torah:* "these are the words that Moses spoke to all Israel."

(2) The fusion of history and law is most characteristic of the treaty form. The second section of vassal treaties is always a "historical introduction" describing what the great king did for the vassal: without the mercy of the great king the vassal could not have survived among the nations. This arouses fear and gratitude to the great king, thus motivating the vassals' loyalty. Deuteronomy has a historical review with exhortations (1:6–11:32) preceding the law (12:1–26:16). It describes not only how the Lord defeated enemies to lead this people to the promised land (2:24–3:22), or how the Lord protected them in the wilderness (8:2-4, 14-16) but also how Israel failed to trust the Lord (1:19-43) and what was the result of their faithlessness: they were defeated in war (1:44-45) and had to stay a long time in Kadesh (1:46). Hence they must fear the Lord. God's forbearance in spite of the apostasy of Israel is also made clear. Israel made the molten calf while Moses was on the mountain making the first covenant (9:7-24). The Lord accepted even the renewal of the treaty or the second covenant (9:25–10:11). "So now," the exhortation tells Israel, "fear [and] love . . . the LORD" (10:12-22; see also 8:1, 6-10, 11-14, 17-20).

(3) A third element is called a "basic stipulation." The basic stipulation of the treaty requires from the vassal a total and exclusive loyalty. The historical review of Deuteronomy contains the decalogue (ch. 5; these are the words of the first covenant) and the most important exhortation: "the LORD our God is one LORD. You shall love the LORD your God with all your heart, and with all your soul, and with all your might" (6:4-5; see Mark 12:28-34 and its parallels) as the basic stipulation of allegiance. Each law of Deuteronomy is an interpretation of this basic stipulation.

(4) A fourth element of vassal treaties is a set of detailed conditions for observing the treaty loyally. The conditions of the treaty in Deuteronomy are found in 12:1–26:16. After the proclamation of the conditions Moses cites the declaration of the covenant between the Lord and the people (26:17-19). Moses does not declare the covenant but only cites its words, because he is a mediator. Israel, one of the nations, a tiny people, became the people of God, the ruler of the whole world (see 7:7-8 and the introduction above). This relationship between the Lord and the people excludes the rule of the great kings of the earth.

(5) A treaty needs witnesses. The vassal treaty names divine beings as witnesses. Deuteronomy refers to the invocation of witnesses in 30:19 and 31:16–32:47 (especially 31:28; 32:1; see also 4:26) and calls to witness heaven and earth, not the deities. The Lord, however, is trustworthy and patient so that the treaty is never breached by the Lord but only by Israel (32:4-6, 18, 30-31, 37-42).

(6) Blessings and curses also motivate loyalty. Deuteronomy 28:1-68 is a list of blessings and curses. Israel, if obedient to the treaty, is blessed, and if disobedient, cursed. Blessings and curses, according to Deuteronomy, do not come from deities called to witness but from the Lord, one party to the treaty. Blessings and curses, therefore, are subject to divine mercy.

(7) The treaty requires periodic recitation and the depositing of its tablets. Deuteronomy refers to periodic recital in 31:9-13 and to the deposit in 31:24-26 (see also 10:1-5). Every seven years, in the year of remission (see 15:1), during the feast of Tabernacles, this book of the covenant shall be read. The year of remission reminds the people of their release from Egypt (15:15). The feast of Tabernacles was originally the thanksgiving for fruits (16:13-15) but Neh 8:13-18 shows the historical aspect of its meaning: the people redeemed from exile read the word of Torah in the feast of Tabernacles.

5. Structure of the Book

In general terms chs. 1–11 and 27–34 give a framework to the Deuteronomic Law (12:1–26:16). The Deuteronomic Law represents the constitutional law of Israel, which consists of three parts.

1. Part One (12:1–16:17) governs the religious life of Israel.
2. Part Two is the law for officials (16:18–18:22).
3. Part Three furnishes the rules for life in society (19:1–25:19).

Chapter 26 relates to Part One and closes the outer frame of the Deuteronomic Law. The theme of Part One appears also in Part Two (16:18–17:7; 18:9-14) and both parts are connected through concatenation of the keyword "eat"

(12:7, 13-27; 14:3-21, 22-29; 15:19-23; 16:1-8; 18:1, 8; see also 26:12, 14). This part of the book describes Israel as the community of communion (the community that eats together), comparable with the Church.

On the other hand Part Two is also connected to Part Three as witnessed by the concatenation of the keywords: "judge" and "judgment" (16:18-20; 17:8-13; 19:6, 17, 18; 21:2, 22; 24:17; 25:1, 2). The themes of religious life and social life therefore overlap with each other in Part Two, which thus forms the center of the Deuteronomic Law. The meaning of this structure is that the officials are assigned in Israel's social life (see Part Three) a decisive role for the actualization of the religious principle that appears at the beginning of the Deuteronomic Law.

The law of the king (17:14-20) occupies the central position in Part Two, which itself is the center of the whole Deuteronomic Law. The king as the highest official undertakes responsibility for the actualization of God's will, the *torah.* However, it is not a decisive issue for Israel whether a king shall be set over the people or not (compare with 12:30, and see the comment on 17:14-20).

General Contexts for Interpretation

1. Original Historical Contexts

Deuteronomy places the audience on the plains of Moab, on the east side of the Jordan. The settlement of Israel is dated generally in the thirteenth century B.C.E. This scene in Deuteronomy, however, reflects another historical situation. In 2 Kings 22–23 we find a historical account relating that in the eighteenth year of the reign of King Josiah (622 B.C.E.) a "book of the law *(torah)*" was found in the Temple in Jerusalem (22:8, 10-11). This book is also called the "book of the covenant" (23:2). Since the beginning of the nineteenth century C.E. it has been generally accepted that the book of the *torah* found in the Jerusalem Temple was the original book of Deuteronomy. The content of the law of Deuteronomy corresponds, in fact, to that of the reformation of the cult by King Josiah (2 Kings 23:4-14). He destroyed sanctuaries not only in the land of Judah but also in Samaria, the former territory of the northern kingdom, and centralized the cult in Jerusalem (23:5, 8-9, 15-20). In the days of Josiah the territory of David was subjected to his dynasty again. The reference not only to the centralization of the cult but also to the expansion of the land of Israel in Deuteronomy (especially 12:20-21) corresponds to the report on the Josianic reformation. Furthermore, according to Jer 22:15 the Josianic reformation intended also to establish social justice (see Deut 16:18–25:19).

The original book of Deuteronomy was, I believe, written as the program for the reformation of King Josiah. The reformation had probably started already when the book of the *torah* "was found" (see 2 Chr 34:3-8, 14). The reformation and the composition of its program were running side by side. The leaders of the reformation, namely the levitical priests and the scribes in Jerusalem (2 Kings 22:8), did not "discover" the book of the *torah* but wrote it anew as the constitution of Israel through a new interpretation of old principles "discovered" by them, the principles of the earlier laws of the kingdom. Deuteronomy refers to the old principles as the law of Exod 34:11-26 and the laws in the "Book of the Covenant" (Exod 20:22–23:33) as well as the decalogue. Accordingly we can also speak of Deuteronomy as "the second/repeated law." The situation in Deuteronomy, in which the people are just crossing the Jordan (9:1; 27:3), represents the situation of the reconstruction of Israel through which the whole land is to become subject to the *torah.* King Josiah may also be called the successor of Moses, like Joshua.

There is, however, one more crisis in which the book of Deuteronomy was revised and expanded. In the time of the exile the present form of the narrative framework (chs. 1–4; 29–34) and the expansion of the law formulated in the second person plural were provided by later "deuteronomistic" editors (see the general article on the "Deuteronomistic History" and the conclusion of the history, 2 Kings 25:27-30, which knows of the release of King Jehoiachin in 560 B.C.E. and his death). By this expansion, Deuteronomy was included in the history that ends in the exile from the promised land (Deuteronomy, Joshua, Judges, 1–2 Samuel, 1–2 Kings). Deuteronomy functions now as a criterion for judging the history of Israel. It shows that Israel was exiled not because the Lord, the national God of Israel, was defeated in the war, but because Israel breached the covenant with the Lord. The curses of Deuteronomy 28 were realized. Deuteronomy offers answers to the questions of whether and how the people of God can be restored (especially ch. 30).

2. Canonical Contexts

Deuteronomy was written to be recited publicly as the authoritative word (see especially 31:9-13). It stands at the starting point of the canonization of the whole Scripture. The process of canonization appears in Deuteronomy itself when it says that no one may add any word to the commandment and no one may take anything away from it (4:2; 12:32; see also Rev 22:18-19).

The promise that Israel will have a prophet like Moses (18:15, 18) opens a space for the "Former Prophets." On the other hand the statement that a prophet like Moses has never arisen in Israel since his death (34:10) establishes the rule of law or the rule of "Torah" also over the prophets. Deuteronomy therefore closes the Pentateuch while opening the Former Prophets and clarifying the priority of the Pentateuch, the Torah.

In the NT the words of Deuteronomy are very often cited. To obey the individual laws is in most cases no longer essential, but these words show what is the highest will of the Lord. The most important commandment (Mark 12:28-34 *parr.*) from Deut 6:4-5 (the *Shema*) and the decalogue (Matt 5:21, 27; Mark 10:19; Rom 13:9 and elsewhere) appear as representative of the whole Scripture. Just as the commandment to love one's neighbor (Lev 19:18) sums up the commandments of the second tablet of the decalogue (Matt 19:18-19; Rom 13:9), so also the commandment to love the Lord God sums up the first tablet (Matt 22:37-40 with Matt 19:18-19).

In Matthew's account of the scene depicting Jesus' temptation he cites words from Deut 8:3; 6:16; 6:13 (Matt 4:4, 7, 10). This answer of Jesus to Satan offers the basis for his mission. Jesus never pursued an earthly kingdom or earthly power or glory but only the kingdom, the power, and the glory of God.

From the standpoint of the NT the promise of a prophet like Moses (Deut 18:15, 18) was fulfilled by Jesus Christ (Acts 3:22; 7:37). Furthermore Christ, the master of the house of God, is prior to Moses, its servant (Heb 3:1-6). Hebrews 3:7-11, 15 cites Ps 95:7-11, recalling the history and exhortation of Deut 8:2-6; 10:16: "harden not your hearts" before Christ, the only Son of God (Heb 3:15; 4:7; Ps 95:7-8; Deut 10:16). If the Israelite cult was centralized in Jerusalem (Deuteronomy 12), the only temple in the world is now the body of Jesus Christ who said: "Destroy this temple, and in three days I will raise it up" (John 2:19; see also John 4:19-26; Hebrews 8–10).

Paul makes clear that righteousness comes not from one's deeds under the Law but from God; he cites Deut 30:11-14 not as the words of law but as the words of faith (Rom 10:5-8). For him, the one who became a curse hung on a tree (Deut 21:23) is for us Jesus the Christ (Gal 3:13). Christ is the end of the Law so that righteousness might be for everyone who believes (Rom 10:4).

3. Church Use

In the Jewish community the decalogue and the *Shema* were written on pieces of papyrus for devotional use, as the Nash Papyrus (dated second century B.C.E. or first century C.E.) shows (see Deut 6:6-9: "Bind them as a sign on your hand"). The words in the Nash Papyrus do not correspond strictly to the text of the Bible but indicate a type of devotional collection in the same way that the Lord's Prayer takes a particular liturgical style. In the ancient and medieval Church the reading of the decalogue in the liturgy was not common, but for Martin Luther the decalogue was the highest will of God so he decided to read it in the liturgy of his community. The catechetical tradition since Augustine, especially as preserved in the Reformed Church, uses the decalogue and the *Shema* as the sum of the instruction for the Christian life (e.g., *Heidelberg Catechism* §115).

When the words of the Law are in our mouth (30:14) we are in the presence of God. When, therefore, the confession of sin in the prayer of *1 Clem.* 60.2 puts the words of Deuteronomy (6:18; 12:28; 13:18; 21:9) on our lips it leads us toward the presence of the Lord. In the Liturgy of the Hours, especially in the time of Lent and around Trinity Sunday, we read texts from Deuteronomy to learn the highest will of the Lord. The "Song of Moses" (32:1-43) is one of the ten canticles used in the Liturgy of the Hours. Most of the texts from Deuteronomy in the lectionary are taken from chs. 4–11 and 26, 30, 32.

Many Church Fathers wrote commentaries on Deuteronomy (Origen, Jerome, Augustine, Cyril of Alexandria, Isidore of Seville, and Bede, among others). For them Deuteronomy was the last part of the one undivided Law given to Israel through Moses and should be interpreted only by analogy to the law of Exodus. Until the twentieth century little notice was taken of the unique meaning of Deuteronomy (as the basis of the deuteronomistic history, as the origin of the covenant theology, as the starting point of the religion of the book). Under the influence of the "theology of the word of God" the structure of Deuteronomy as covenant offered Gerhard von Rad the framework for his *Old Testament Theology.* In the latter half of this century many important commentaries appeared, including those by Gerhard von Rad, P. C. Craigie, A.D.H. Mayes, Georg Braulik, Moshe Weinfeld, and Duane L. Christensen.

SECOND READING

Preamble: 1:1-5

Moses speaks to "all Israel" beyond the Jordan (v. 1), namely in the land of Moab (v. 5), which is on the eastern side of the Jordan (see the first section above). The title of the people is "all Israel," which addresses Israel as a unity. Israel is one only because the Lord is one (see 6:4). The other place names in v. 1 are a mystery because they cannot be found in the land of Moab. Suph could be the Sea of Suph that Israel crossed over (the LXX, Targums, and other interpreters understood it so). Paran is often connected with Sinai (Horeb) and/or Seir (Deut 33:2; Hab 3:3). These place names reflect the itinerary from Egypt to Horeb. The speech of Moses is based on this history.

Verse 2 continues the itinerary, that is from Horeb to Kadesh-barnea. Kadesh-barnea is an oasis in the northern part of the Sinai peninsula, near to the promised land. Its distance from Horeb, eleven days, is contrasted with the length of the wandering of Israel, forty years (v. 3). Israel had to spend thirty-eight years between Kadesh-barnea and the Wadi Zered, the border between Edom and Moab (2:14). This serious retardation of its journey was caused by the faithlessness of Israel (see 1:19-46). The journey on the way of Mount Seir (v. 2) and the war against Sihon and Og (v. 4) are reported in 2:1-23; 2:24-37, and 3:1-11 respectively. The place names, Heshbon in the Moabite territory (Isa 15:4), Bashan north of Gilead (Amos 4:1), Edrei where Og was defeated (cf. Josh 12:4 "Og lived at Ashtaroth and at Edrei") reflect the history immediately preceding the speech of Moses (see 3:29). Moses explains "this *torah*" (v. 5), that is, the whole book of Deuteronomy (see the introduction above).

Historical Review: 1:6–4:43

The Journey from Horeb to the Eastern Coast of the Jordan (1:6–3:29)

The Command to Depart, 1:6-8

Now Moses starts to review the journey from Horeb to the eastern coast of the Jordan. On the name of God, "the LORD your God" and "the LORD our God" see the introduction above. The possession of the land by Israel was solely based on the covenant that the Lord had sworn to the ancestors of Israel (v. 8). At the starting point and the turning point of Israel's journey appears the word of the Lord (see also 2:3).

"The hill country of the Amorites as well as . . . the neighboring regions" (v. 7) are the whole land of Palestine, also designated "the land of the Canaanites." The Amorites and the Canaanites represent the inhabitants of the promised land. This expression of the range of the land is parallel to the expression "Lebanon, as far as the great river, the river Euphrates." These make up the ideal territory of the Davidic empire, which is based on the covenant of the Lord (2 Sam 8:3; Gen 15:18).

The Organizing Law of the People, 1:9-18

The phrase "at that time" (v. 9) relates the commandment of Moses (see also 1:16, 18; 3:18, 21, 23) or the possession of the land (see 3:8, 12) to a certain historical situation. "At that time," upon departure from Horeb, Moses made the people choose the heads of the tribes (v. 13), appointed them as commanders of the tribal army, installed officials (v. 15), and charged the judges to hear cases fairly (vv. 16-17, see also 16:19-20). The "officials" (see 16:18) were probably scribes of the law court but were also associated with the commander in the military system (20:9). On "alien" as sojourner, see 10:18. This section, which depends on the older tradition (see Exodus 18 and Numbers 11), attributes the establishment of the judiciary based on the system of the tribal army to Moses. This systematization was based on the idea that the promise of the Lord to the patriarchs (see Gen 15:5) had been realized and Israel had increased in population (vv. 10-11, see also 10:22). The organization of the people (1:9-18) and the land (4:41-43) constitute a cornerstone for the formation of Israel.

In Kadesh-barnea, 1:19-46

In Kadesh-barnea the people propose to send out spies (v. 22). According to Num 13:1-3 this was the order of the Lord. Deuteronomy, however, recognizes the faithlessness of the people in their proposal. Moses accepts it (v. 23). The apostasy of the people of God is not that they do not believe in God's existence but that they believe only their own judgment on their situation and will not put their trust in the word of God.

The spies reach the Valley of Eshcol (this means "cluster") near Hebron (v. 24, see Num 13:22-23) and bring back some of the fruit of the land (v. 25). The fertility of the land awes Israel because it indicates the power of the gods of the land. Further "the Anakim" were thought to belong to "the Rephaim," the descendants of giants (2:10-11, see Num 13:33; Gen 6:4).

Trust in the Lord (v. 29) should be based on salvation history: the Lord will fight just as in Egypt (v. 30): see 7:18, 21. The metaphor of parent and child (v. 31a), formulated in the second person singular and thus directed to each of the people personally, describes the love of the Lord (see also 8:5). "In fire by night, and in the cloud by day" the Lord showed the people the route (v. 33). The fire and the cloud indicate the power of the Lord (Exod 13:21-22; Num 14:14). Israel had, however, no trust in this God, their Lord.

Because of this apostasy the first generation of the Exodus was prohibited from entering into the promised land (v. 35). This includes even Moses (v. 37). There were two exceptions who trusted in the Lord: Caleb, son of Jephunneh (v. 36), and Joshua, son of Nun (v. 38). The former represents Judah, the southern kingdom (Josh 14:6-15), the latter is Ephraimite (Num 13:8) and represents the northern kingdom just as in Genesis 37–50 Joseph and Judah respectively symbolize the same territories (Genesis 38; 44).

Once more the Israelites rebel against the Lord when they begin the war without the Lord and they are defeated by the Amorites (vv. 41-46). The name "Hormah" (v. 44) sounds like "destruction" (see Num 21:3).

From Mount Seir to Moab, 2:1-23

Israel withdraws to the wilderness and skirts Mount Seir as instructed by the Lord (v. 1, see 1:40). The Lord then commands Israel to proceed northwards along the eastern side of Edom (vv. 3, 8), but prohibits them from fighting against the descendants of Esau because the Lord had given the territory of Seir (= Edom) to Esau, who was kin to Israel (vv. 4-5; see 23:7 and also Gen 32:4; 36). Israel buys water and food for money from them (v. 6), and lacks nothing (v. 7, see 8:3-4). The phrase "the LORD your God has blessed you in all your undertakings" reminds the people that every good thing comes from the hand of the Lord (see 14:29; 15:10, 18; 16:15, and elsewhere). The speech of the Lord clarifies that the allotment of lands or the rise and fall of peoples is in God's hand (see 9:5).

The Lord prohibits Israel from fighting against the Moabites and the Ammonites because the Lord had given Ar, the representative city(?) of Moab (see Isa 15:1) and the land of the Ammonites to the descendants of Lot (vv. 9, 19; see Gen 19:37-38). About the people of the land see Gen 14:5-6 and Josh 13:3-4. "Caphtorim, who came from Caphtor (Crete)" (v. 23) were Philistines (Amos 9:7), the rivals of Israel in the conquest of the promised land.

Between the speeches of the Lord, Moses emphasizes the retardation of the journey (v. 14) and the annihilation of the entire generation of warriors (v. 15) as the result of Israel's apostasy (see 1:19-46). On Wadi Zered, see the comment on 1:3.

The War Against Sihon, 2:24-37

Wadi Arnon (v. 24) divides the Israelite territory of Transjordan from the land of Moab. Israel comes at last into the land it is to conquer. "I have handed over to you King Sihon" and "when they hear report of you, they will tremble and be in anguish because of you" show that this is a war of the Lord: see Exod 15:14. The Moabites did not offer food and water and hired Balaam to curse Israel. (Deuteronomy mentions these events only in 23:3-6). While the narrative of Balaam in Numbers 22–24 describes how his curses were changed into blessings for Israel, Deuteronomy stresses that everything was in the plan of the Lord (2:30: cf. Exod 4:21). Israel defeats Sihon, destroys all the men, women, and children, appropriately for a war of the Lord (2:34; see

20:16-18), and conquers the territory as far as the Jabbok (2:36; cf. Num 21:24).

The War Against Og, 3:1-11

The process of this war—the command of the Lord (v. 2), handing over the enemy (v. 3), destroying them utterly (vv. 3-7)—is the same as that against Sihon (2:31-35). Israel does to Og as it did to Sihon (vv. 2, 6). "At that time" (see 1:9) Israel took from the two kings the land beyond the Jordan, from the Arnon to Mount Hermon (v. 8). Og was the last remnant of the Rephaim; there was therefore no longer any fear of revenge by the Rephaim (see 1:28). Og's bed (or sarcophagus) made of iron (or probably black basalt) was "kept in Rabbah," the capital of the Ammonites. Its dimensions were about thirteen or fourteen feet by six feet (v. 11).

Tribes in Transjordan, 3:12-22

"At that time" the Reubenites, the Gadites, and the half tribe of Manasseh were given the land of Transjordan. The allotment of the land is connected to the war of the Lord. "Pisgah" denotes the hills to the northeast of the Dead Sea (see 34:1). "At that time" the tribes that wished to stay in Transjordan were instructed to cooperate with the other tribes in the conquest of the promised land (vv. 18-20). The defeat of the two kings in Transjordan is the model for the conquest of the promised land (vv. 21-22).

Prayer of Moses, 3:23-29

The Lord refuses Moses' request to enter the promised land because of the sin of the people, not because of the sin of Moses himself (cf. 32:51; Num 20:12). "O Adonai (my LORD) YHWH" (v. 24) expresses the master and servant relationship between the Lord and Moses. Lebanon (v. 25) symbolizes the beauty of the land (Ps 72:16). See 31:1-8; 32:48-52; 34:1-12. Israel stayed in the valley opposite Beth Peor (see 1:1, also 4:46; 34:6). The place name reminds us of the apostasy (Num 25:1-9 and also Deut 4:3).

Sermon of Moses on the Revelation at Horeb (4:1-43)

Sermon of Moses, 4:1-40

"And now" (v. 1) begins an exhortatory speech on the basis of the preceding history (see also 10:12). This is a sermon describing the self-revelation of the Lord at Horeb and warning against idolatry. In the lectionary the words of 4:32-34, 39-40 are read on Trinity Sunday (Cycle B). These words show that the authority in heaven and on earth, given to Jesus Christ, the Son of God (Matt 28:16-20) is the revealed power of the only God, the Creator, and that we are the children of this Ruler of the world through the Holy Spirit (Rom 8:14-17). The revelation at Horeb is for us the preparation for the complete revelation through Christ (so we read Deut 4:1, 5-9 together with Matt 5:17-19 on Wednesday of the third week of Lent).

"Hear, O Israel" (or "Israel, give heed") introduces an important exhortation: see 5:1; 6:4; 9:1; 20:3; 27:9. We are the people of God not because of our goodness, but because of God's faithfulness. God loves us before we love God. Before we do something, God speaks a word to us. What we must do now is to listen. If we only hear God's word we are filled with it. If we accept it as the word of God it actualizes in ourselves.

The introduction (vv. 1-8) appeals for obedience to "statutes and ordinances." The phrase "statutes and ordinances" does not indicate two types of law but the singular rule of the *torah.* In v. 8 the "statutes and ordinances" are identified with "this entire law (this *torah*)." We should be obedient not to our own righteousness but only to that of the Lord; compare the words of Jesus: "you abandon the commandment of God and hold to human tradition" (Mark 7:8; cf. Mark 7:1-8, 14-15, 21-23, and the lectionary on the 22nd Sunday in Cycle B).

Being blessed for listening to the law of God is an idea found also in the wisdom tradition: Prov 3:1-2; see also Prov 2:21-22. The lesson is taken from what the Lord did in (or "against" according to the LXX) Baal Peor (Deut 4:3-4; cf. Num 25:1-9). The Law is proclaimed so that Israel may observe it in the promised land (v. 5; see the introduction above). Observance of the Law proves Israel's wisdom because the *torah* represents the knowledge of the whole world (see also Sir 24:25-27). The Lord is near whenever we call (v. 7) because God's word (see v. 8), namely the *torah,* is very near to us, in our mouth and in our heart (30:11-14).

"You must neither add anything . . . nor take away anything from it" (v. 2) is characteristic of the words used in a covenant but also teaches the proper attitude to the word of God (Rev 22:18-19) and is essential for the canon (see also Deut 12:32 and the introduction above). The presence of the Lord was revealed at Horeb to the assembled (v. 10) people (the germ of God's people) to make the covenant, the content of which was the decalogue (v. 13). The implication of the revelation out of the fire is that God revealed the divine self only by the sound of the word (v. 12). Idolatry is strictly prohibited (vv. 12, 15-24).

The commandment in vv. 15-24 amplifies the second half of the first commandment (see 5:8). The worship of the sun, the moon, the stars, and the host of heaven (v. 19) was forced on Israelites by the great kings of Assyria and Babylon. These are allotted to the other nations as divine beings by the Lord (v. 19), but "you," Israel, are the people of God's own "possession" (v. 20). This is an expression of the covenantal relationship between Israel and the Lord. The Lord who brought Israel out of Egypt, the iron-smelter, the terrible ordeal (v. 20; see Jer 11:4) is a devouring fire, a jealous God (v. 24; see the decalogue Deut 5:6, 9). The God of liberation is intolerant of our apostasy because of divine love.

If Israel forgets the covenant and provokes the Lord to anger it will be exiled from the promised land just like other nations (vv. 25-28; see 28:36-57). The heaven and the earth as enduring creatures testify to the warning of the Lord (v. 26; see 30:19 and the introduction above). Israel served idols, so it will be compelled to serve idols (v. 28), but there remains room for repentance (vv. 29-31; see 30:1-10). If Israel returns to the Lord "with all your heart and soul" (4:29; 6:5; 10:12; 11:13, and elsewhere) it will find God. The theme of repentance appears throughout the deuteronomistic history (Deut 30:2; Judg 3:9; 1 Sam 7:3; 2 Kings 17:13; 23:25, and elsewhere), because the Lord is a merciful God and will not forget the covenant (cf. v. 24 and see Exod 22:27).

Moses praises the Lord as the only God (vv. 35, 39) who has chosen Israel "by a mighty hand and an outstretched arm" (4:34; 5:15; 7:19, and frequently). The Lord drove out nations greater and mightier than Israel: see 7:1.

Organizing Law for the Land, 4:41-43

Moses sets apart in Transjordan "three cities to which a homicide could flee." The organization of the land corresponds to that of the people (1:9-18). The city of refuge guarantees that one who kills a person unintentionally will be given a fair trial. The land should not be ruled by personal grudges, but by the justice of God revealed in a fair trial (see 19:1-13).

Conclusion of the Historical Review: 4:44

This sentence relates not to the following but to the preceding history as a lesson.

Introduction to the Statutes and Ordinances: 4:45–5:1ab

The word "decrees" (v. 45) denotes the clauses of the covenant. For "the statutes and ordinances" see 4:1. Moses spoke these words to the Israelites "when they had come out of Egypt." Verses 46-49 sum up chs. 1–3.

History of Making the First Covenant and Exhortations: 5:1–11:32

Proclamation of the Decalogue (5:1-33)

Introduction, 5:1-5

The decalogue constitutes the articles of the first covenant (see 4:45), which was made at Horeb between the Lord and Israel (v. 2). The making of the covenant is not to be understood as a thing of the past but as effective for all time (v. 3). Moses calls to us all, "Hear, O Israel!" (5:1; see 4:1 and cf. 27:9). He functions as mediator, or rather interpreter of the awesome sound of the word (v. 5) which the Lord spoke to Israel face to face (v. 4).

The Decalogue, 5:6-21

The decalogue ("ten words" in English) begins with the self-revelation of the Lord (v. 6). When the Lord says "I am the LORD" God's overwhelming power is revealed. When we read this word we are in God's presence. God's self-introduction, "your God," emphasizes the covenantal relationship between God and us (see the introduction above). God is the One who set God's people free from bondage in Egypt. This is the prototype of our salvation by the Lord from exile and from sin.

The First Commandment: 5:7. If you are in my presence (v. 6), says the Lord, there should be for you no other god beside me (in Hebrew properly "against my face," "against me"). The

Lord declares that it is betrayal for us to have another God.

"A carved image": 5:8-9: cf. the "molten image" in Exod 34:17; 32:4; 1 Kings 12:28; see also Judg 17:3-4. The deities in Canaan were usually carved in human form. Those in heaven took the form of astral bodies (4:19) or birds (4:17), and those in the water under the earth that of fish (4:18) or of the great monster (Gen 1:21) that was thought of in the ancient world as a power opposed to creation. "You shall not bow down to them or worship them" (v. 9). We are not to let ourselves be drawn into the temptation of idolatry. This commandment is often, especially in the Reformed Church, understood as a prohibition not only against making idols but also against making an image of the Lord. This is not said without reason. God cannot be confined to an image (4:12). We may not make our own lord who answers our egocentric desire (see introduction above).

The first commandment is framed within the self-revelation of the Lord (vv. 6, 9). The second self-revelation is followed by the clause "I the LORD your God am a jealous God," one impatient and intolerant of our apostasy (see 4:24; 6:15; Exod 34:14; Josh 24:19; Nah 1:2). In Nah 1:2 the Lord does not punish Israel but takes revenge on its enemies. The intolerance of the Lord is an expression of divine love. "Ah, fondest, blindest, weakest, I am He Whom thou seekest! Thou dravest love from thee, who dravest Me" (Francis Thompson, "The Hound of Heaven").

For the iniquity of parents God punishes children to the fourth generation, namely all members of the clan (see 2 Kings 23:26). But the Lord shows steadfast love to thousands, namely all members of the clan (probably not "to the thousandth generation"), to those who love God (v. 10). Is this communal promise of God opposed to modern individualism? There can be in a family or community blessings through one member who loves the Lord and at the same time curses through another. In such a family each one can be responsible for oneself. This is therefore not opposed to the law of individual responsibility in Deut 24:16 and Ezekiel 18. However, it is true that our faith will save not only ourselves but also our household (Acts 16:31). Most Christians in Japan have converted individually to Christianity apart from their families and their conversion is not welcome in their family because every family has its own house god. Our wish is that our faith in Christ will lead our family to the same faith and salvation.

In Deuteronomy, to love the Lord is to keep the commandments (10:12-13; 11:1). The theme of this first part of the decalogue is our relationship to the Lord.

The Lord continues to speak but does so in the third person for the last clause of v. 10 ("those who . . . keep his commandments"). The commandments in vv. 11-16 constitute the second part of the decalogue. The theme of this part is also our relationship to the Lord but the commandments of the second part are actualized in our social life as are those of the third part.

The Second Commandment: 5:11. The misuse of the Lord's name could mean false witness in a lawsuit, but that problem is dealt with in the eighth commandment (v. 20). The situation more probably indicated here is magic. It suggests the possession of the power of God by calling on the divine name. We also often use the name of God or cite biblical passages to give authority to ourselves.

The Third Commandment: 5:12-15. The commandment of the Sabbath is linked to the preamble (v. 6) and to the last commandment (v. 21) through the reference to slavery. Sabbath means to stop all human work and live in the time of God. So Jesus says "the Son of Man is lord even of the sabbath" (Mark 2:28; see the lectionary on the ninth Sunday of the year, Cycle B). The Sabbath shall be kept in each family (v. 14). On the Sabbath, therefore, we can be in the presence of God everywhere, even without a Temple. While according to Exod 20:11 creation in seven days is the origin of the Sabbath, according to Deut 5:15 the people remember in the Sabbath observance their slavery in Egypt and their liberation from there.

The Fourth Commandment: 5:16. The motivation to honor parents is "so that your days may be long and that it may go well with you in the land." Such a motivation is preferred in the wisdom tradition (Prov 2:21; 3:2; 4:10; 9:11; 28:16, and elsewhere). At the same time the wisdom tradition honors not only the father but also the mother (Prov 1:8; 4:3; 6:20; 10:1; 20:20; 23:22, and elsewhere) because our father and mother are representative of the words of the Lord for us. Thus the theme of this commandment is a religious one. It implies also the parents' responsibility to educate their children to obey the Lord (see 21:18-21).

The third part of the decalogue begins with v. 17. Its theme is our social life. (Compare Matt 5:21-48 on the coming of the reign of God.) The fifth, sixth, and seventh commandments are prohibitions formulated without an object. The eighth, ninth, and tenth commandments have a key word: "your neighbor."

The Fifth Commandment: 5:17. This commandment did not prohibit war (see 20:10-20) or capital punishment (see 19:1-13; 21:18-21, 22-23; 22:20-27). The formulation without the object means protection of life without distinction as to sex or social stratum. Slaves were, for example, not treated as fully human beings (Exod 21:21), but their lives are to be protected. Jesus put anger and hatred, which exclude brothers and sisters from the community of life, in the category of murder (Matt 5:21-26; 18:6).

The Sixth Commandment: 5:18. This originally prohibited lying with a woman already married or engaged (see 22:22-29), but the sentence without the object leaves much room for interpretation (see 22:13-21; Leviticus 18 and 20); its observation will protect the purity of marriage and the honesty of the covenant between a woman and a man, especially from the violence of men (Matt 5:27-30).

The Seventh Commandment: 5:18. This could refer to kidnapping (cf. Exod 21:16, stealing of a person). The formulation, however, indicates stealing in general (Exod 22:1-9). In the OT a thief was never punished by death, but the theft often caused a more serious crime (see the comment on 19:14).

The Eighth Commandment: 5:20. "Neither shall you bear false witness against your neighbor." In those days a covenant was made and fulfilled or a dispute was reconciled before the elders of the community or the commander of the tribal army. In this "court" the witnesses had a decisive role. The Lord hates false witness (see Exod 23:1-8). In our life with our neighbors our words should not fail to be honest and trustworthy. In Jesus Christ, however, the promise of God and therefore our word also is always "yes" (2 Cor 1:20; see also Matt 5:33-37).

The Ninth Commandment: 5:21a. "Neither shall you covet your neighbor's wife." In Exod 20:17 the commandment not to covet a neighbor's house precedes, and the commandment not to covet a neighbor's wife or male or female slave and so on defines the "house" of the foregoing commandment. There the word "house" means "household." In Deut 5:21, on the other hand, to covet a neighbor's wife and to desire (not the same word as "covet") a neighbor's house and so on are different things. To covet a neighbor's wife is different from committing adultery (v. 18). The former is seeking a neighbor's wife during the absence of her husband, especially in wartime, or seeking the wife of one's debtor to enslave her as security.

The Tenth Commandment: 5:21b. "Neither shall you desire your neighbor's house, or field," and so on. This is also different from the commandment not to steal (v. 19). What is prohibited is to desire the neighbor's house during the absence of its master or to lend money at high interest. All acts that impoverish the neighbor shall be prohibited; these would include a war of aggression, indiscriminate deforestation or hunting, sponsoring gambling (also by governments), drug trafficking, pyramid marketing, and so on.

Post-Proclamation, 5:22-33

Because of God's holiness the sound of the divine words was so awful for Israel (vv. 23-26, cf. 4:24, 32-34) that the Lord decided to speak the Law only through a mediator with the exception of the decalogue (vv. 22, 28-33). The Lord knows human weakness and normally speaks to us in human words (preaching!).

Exhortations (6:1–9:7)

Introduction, 6:1-3

The exhortations are directed to the individual members of Israel to teach the principles of the reform. "This is the commandment—the statutes and the ordinances" Israel is to observe in the promised land (v. 1): see 4:1, 5. "A land flowing with milk and honey" indicates the grace of God (v. 3; see Exod 3:8, 17; 13:5; 33:3; Lev 20:24; Num 13:27; 14:8; 16:13-14 and frequently elsewhere).

The Most Important Commandment, 6:4-25

The section of exhortations begins with the call, "Hear, O Israel" (v. 4), and ends with the same call (9:1; see 4:1). "The LORD (YHWH) our God is one LORD (YHWH)" may be translated also "the LORD is our God, the LORD alone" or "the LORD is our God, the LORD is one" and could mean that the Lord is the only God for us, but it must be understood rather that the Lord is oneness and not divided into many local or personal deities (see the introduction above). The Lord directs all of the divine self to you; therefore "you shall love the LORD your God with all your heart, and with all your soul, and with all your might" (v. 5). Wealth or political power is included in the "might" (see 2 Kings 23:25). For love of God see Deut 5:10. Jesus said that this commandment is the most important of the OT (Matt 22:34-40; Mark 12:28-34; Luke 10:25-37). These words should be kept in the heart, memorized, and taught to children in every place and on all occasions throughout life, and they should also be written down (vv. 6-9). The land will be filled with the words of the Lord.

Being able to eat one's fill (v. 11) proves the grace of the Lord (8:10; 14:29; 26:12) but often causes ingratitude (8:12; 11:15; 31:20). We must be warned not to forget the Lord who gave us everything, and not to follow another god (6:10-14; see also 8:14) because the Lord is a jealous God (6:15; see 5:9). If we betray the Lord we must be wiped off of the land. Possession of the land is for us never an absolute right.

In vv. 16-19 another exhortation with a historical review is inserted: "Do not put the LORD your God to the test." It is God who tests us (cf. 8:2; Matt 4:7). We must do only "what is right and good in the sight of the LORD" (v. 18): see 12:25, 28; 13:19; 21:9. For Massah, see Exod 17:1-7 and cf. Num 20:1-13.

Deuteronomy offered a catechism to Israel with which to teach children the meaning of the decrees, statutes, and ordinances (vv. 20-25; cf. Exod 11:26-27; 13:8-9, 14-16). The motivation to observe the Law is the history that God's people were slaves in Egypt and were liberated from there by great and awesome signs and wonders of the Lord (cf. 5:6; 26:1-11).

Warning Against Foreign Influence, 7:1-26

Chapter 7 is constructed chiastically:

A The commandment not to allow any influences of the inhabitants of the land to remain: vv. 1-6 ("you must utterly destroy them . . . show them no mercy") (v. 2b)

B The Lord is the faithful God who maintains covenant loyalty (v. 9b)

C The Lord repays in their own person those who reject the Lord (v. 10a) //

C' The Lord repays in their own person those who reject the Lord (v. 10b)

D Observe the commandment, statutes, and ordinances "that I am commanding you today" (v. 11)

B' The Lord will maintain covenant loyalty (v. 12b)

A' The commandment not to allow influences of the inhabitants of the land to remain: vv. 16-26 ("you shall devour all the peoples . . . showing them no pity") (v. 16a)

The central principle is the observance of the revealed law of God (v. 11), not the extermination of other nations. Observing the Law is the same as not remaining under the influence of the inhabitants of the land and their gods (vv. 1-6, 16-26). Israel is a people holy to the Lord, namely God's chosen, treasured possession (v. 6; cf. Exod 19:5-6).

Seven nations are mentioned as inhabitants of the land (v. 1; see Josh 3:10; 24:11). Their habits of worship, namely the altars in their own style, the pillar of stone that was accepted also in Israel in the past (Gen 28:18; 34:14), *asherim* (the plural form of "Asherah," a wooden pole usually planted beside the altar: see 16:21) seemed good for asking a divine favor but they had to be destroyed (v. 5). Verse 2 itself does not command literal extermination but prohibits other nations (the Hittites, Girgashites, and so on) to live in Israel in their own way (see Exod 34:12-15). The Lord will drive them away from the land often without warfare (vv. 20-24; see Exod 23:27-31). So Israel should not be afraid of them even if they seem stronger, and should remember what the Lord did to Pharaoh (vv. 17-19; see 1:29-31 and cf. 8:2).

If we observe the Law the Lord blesses us (vv. 12-15). For the diseases of Egypt (v. 15) see 28:60; Exod 15:26; and cf. Exod 23:25: the blessing of the Lord includes the redemption of creation (see Rom 8:18-25). We were not elected because of our greatness but because of the Lord's loyalty to the covenant (vv. 7-8a; see the lectionary for the feast of the Sacred Heart, Cycle A, read with 1 John 4:7-16 and Matt 11:25-30).

Warning Not to Forget the LORD, 8:1-20

The first half of the chapter (vv. 2-10) tells a story similar to that in the second half (vv. 12-18).

The former tells its story to remind us of the grace of the Lord in the wilderness and to make us bless the Lord, while the latter tells its story to warn us not to be haughty and not to forget the Lord. It was the Lord who led the journey in the wilderness for forty years in order to humble the people of Israel, testing them to know what was in their heart, whether or not they would keep the divine commandments (v. 2; cf. v. 16). It was the Lord who gave them manna in the wilderness (v. 3; see Exod 16:1-36; Num 11:1-9). What is important is that the Lord fed Israel with heavenly bread. Therefore Israel had to journey in the wilderness forty years, but lacked nothing (v. 4; see 2:7). The Lord disciplined them as a parent disciplines a child (v. 5; see 1:31). It was the Lord who was leading them into a good land (vv. 7-9, 18). The Lord tested them to know them (v. 2), but it was they who came to know that one does not live by bread alone, but by every word that comes from the mouth of the Lord (v. 3; see Matt 4:4).

Satan tempted Jesus to change stones into loaves of bread (Matt 4:3). The people often follow a false leader who gives them bread. The Japanese emperor "Tennoh," originally the high priest of the Japanese sun goddess, made himself in the first half of the twentieth century the highest god of Asia and appeared to give the people bread. The Japanese people believed in him as the protector of their egocentric policy and insisted on their superiority over other nations. Even Christianity is often used as national idolatry for authorizing an expansion policy. The Lord as God of the whole world does not allow such a self-justification on the part of one nation. We must say that no one can serve two masters, God and wealth (Matt 6:24). The real heavenly bread, Jesus Christ, prohibits us from eating the bread of idols (1 Cor 10:16-17; see the lectionary for Corpus Christi, Cycle A). Do not forget God when you eat your fill and all that you have is multiplied (vv. 12-14, 17). If Israel betrays God they will be destroyed just like the inhabitants of the land who would not obey the voice of the Lord (vv. 19-20; see 6:15; 9:4-5).

Conclusion, 9:1-6

The conclusion of the exhortations in 6:1–9:6 begins with the call "Hear, O Israel" (v. 1). It draws attention to the situation of Israel as it is just crossing over the Jordan (see 1:1). It is the Lord who leads them into the land and drives the inhabitants away (v. 3; see 7:16-24), not because of the righteousness of Israel but because of the wickedness of the inhabitants of the land (vv. 4-6; see 8:17, 19-20) and because of God's loyalty to the promise (v. 5; see 7:8, 12b). The so-called "Gospel of Success" says: if you succeed in life you are loved by God; the poor, on the other hand, are not loved. This is far from the biblical message. The Lord loved poor Israel, so it should be humble before the Lord (6:15; 8:19-20). The One who is a devouring fire for them when they forget God (cf. 4:24) is a devouring fire that defeats enemies (v. 3).

Breaking and Renewal of the Covenant (9:7–10:11)

Breaking of the Covenant, 9:7-29

The history of breaking and renewal of the covenant continues after the story of the proclamation of the decalogue (ch. 5). It forms the frame of the exhortations in 6:1–9:6. "Remember and do not forget [cf. 6:12; 7:18; 8:2; 8:14] how you provoked the LORD your God to wrath." This is the history of Israel's continuous rebellion against the Lord. Even at Horeb when, according to Deuteronomy, the Lord gave them the tablets of the covenant, they were rebellious (vv. 8-11). The people Moses had brought out of Egypt cast for themselves an image of a calf (vv. 12-16; see Exod 32:1-14). The golden calf in Canaan usually did not represent a deity but was understood as a pedestal of the gods. It was prohibited as a foreign practice (7:25-26). Moses broke the two tablets of the covenant. This means that the covenant was abrogated (v. 17; see Exod 32:19).

Moses was before the Lord forty days and forty nights when he received the tablets of the covenant (vv. 9-11), so he had to stay before the Lord forty days and forty nights as mediator (vv. 18, 25); see Matt 4:2; Acts 1:3. In vv. 22-24 Moses reminds all the people of their rebellion at Taberah (Num 11:1-3), at Massah (6:16; Exod 17:1-7; Num 20:1-13), at Kibroth-hattaavah (Num 11:4-34), and further at Kadesh-barnea (1:19-46; Num 13:1–14:45).

Renewal of the Covenant, 10:1-5

The Lord alone decided to renew the covenant with the wicked people (10:1-2). "The day of the assembly" (v. 4) was the day when Israel was gathered before the Lord to hear the decalogue (see 4:10).

Aaron's Death and Consecration of the Levites, 10:6-9

This paragraph is formulated in the third person and inserted here as a note. Aaron died (cf. Num 33:30-31, 37-38). His son Eleazar succeeded him (see Exod 6:23 and elsewhere). The Lord consecrated the Levites (vv. 8-9; see 17:18; 31:9-13). The Levites have no allotment, but the Lord is their inheritance (v. 9; see 18:1-8).

Conclusion, 10:10-11

The Lord heard Moses' prayer and encouraged him to lead the people into the promised land (cf. Exod 33:1-6, 12-17).

Exhortations Before Crossing the Jordan (10:12–11:32)

Facing the promised land, Moses again gives exhortations in 10:12–11:32. "So now, O Israel": Moses begins an exhortatory speech on the basis of the preceding history (see 4:1). What the Lord requires of us is only to fear the Lord (6:13), to walk in all God's ways (5:33), to love God (6:5), to serve God (6:13): in short, to keep the Lord's commandments and statutes (10:12-13; see 6:24). The Lord is ruler of the universe (v. 14; see 8:10, 18).

"Yet the LORD set his heart in love on your ancestors" (10:15; see 7:7-8). "Circumcise, then, the foreskin of your heart" (v. 16). Circumcision of males was a sign of membership in the covenant community (Gen 17:9-14), but it is spiritualized here. What is important is inner conversion and openness to the Lord, so "do not be stubborn any longer" (see Jer 4:4 and cf. Deut 30:6). That the Lord is God of gods and Lord of lords means that God is not partial and takes no bribe, executes justice for the orphan and the widow, and loves the sojourners (vv. 17-18). Orphan, widow, and sojourner have no protection against the trespass of their social rights, but the Lord personally protects them. "Sojourner" means not only a foreigner but also a refugee from other Israelite tribes. The Lord loves them, so "you shall also love [them]" (v. 19; see 24:19-21) "for you were strangers in the land of Egypt" (see Exod 22:21; 23:9; cf. Deut 24:22).

For "holding fast" to God (v. 20) see also 11:22; 13:4; 30:20. Note also "he is your praise," that is, the object of Israel's praise (v. 21; see Ps 109:1). "Your ancestors went down to Egypt seventy persons; and now [cf. v. 12] the LORD your God has made you as numerous as the stars in heaven" (v. 22); see 1:10; Gen 15:5. "Remember this day that it was not your children" (here must be added: "who must make this covenant": see 5:3) "(who have not known or seen the discipline of the LORD your God), but it is you who must acknowledge [cf. v. 7] his greatness, his mighty hand and his outstretched arm" (see 4:34; 5:15; 7:19; 26:8). The summary of salvation history refers to the plagues in Egypt (11:3, 6:22; Exod 7:14–12:36), the miracle at the Sea of Suph (v. 4, Exod 14:1-31), the discipline in the wilderness (v. 5; 8:2-5, and elsewhere), and the punishment of Dathan and Abiram (v. 6; Num 16:12-15, 25-26, 27b-31, 33-34).

In 11:10-17 the clauses formulated in the second person plural and second person singular are juxtaposed. The latter represent the original text that promises the fertility of the land that Israel is about to enter, in contrast to the land of Egypt. This was the motivation of the exhortation to keep the entire commandment. The addition of the clauses in the second person plural (v. 10, "from which you have come," the dependent clause in v. 11a, vv. 13-14a, 16-17) in the time of the exile creates the structure of exhortation with blessing and curse: if they are obedient to the Lord they will be blessed in the good land, but if disobedient, perish from the land (see especially vv. 13-14a, 16-17). Verses 18-20 are the same exhortation as 6:6-9, and v. 21 reflects 6:2; 11:9. If the people then observe this entire commandment they can conquer every place on which they set foot (vv. 22-24; see 1:7), and cf. 11:25 with 7:24.

The conclusion for chs.1–11 says that the Lord sets before Israel a blessing and a curse (11:26). If the people obey the commandments of the Lord they are blessed (v. 27), and if they do not obey the commandments but turn from the way (see 9:12) to follow other gods, they are cursed (v. 28). The correspondence between obedience to the will of God and blessing, disobedience and curse is the key to restoration of the destroyed people of God (cf. Job 40:6-14; Rom 3:19-20, 21-25, 28; Matt 7:21-27; see the lectionary on the ninth Sunday of the year, Cycle A). "Other gods that you have not known" (11:28) refers to gods of the inhabitants, with which Israel has had no contact. Verses 29-30 connect the blessing and curse with Mount Gerizim and Mount Ebal: the blessing with Mount Gerizim and the curse with Mount Ebal because Mount Gerizim lies on the right hand side, namely on the south. These mountains are "beyond the Jordan." Israel is still on the eastern side of the Jordan. On the oaks of Moreh, see Gen 12:6.

Moses repeats the commandment to keep the statutes and ordinances in the promised land that Israel is about to enter (vv. 31-32).

The Deuteronomic Law: 12:1–26:16

Structure of Deuteronomic Law in Relation to the Decalogue

Deuteronomy contains a law book (12:1–26:16) as the detailed conditions of the treaty (see the introduction above). The themes of the decalogue, the basic stipulation of the treaty, are here repeated and amplified.

The religious principles in 12:1–14:29 form the counterparts of the first and second commandments (5:6-11). The law of the seventh year of release (ch. 15) is connected with the Sabbath commandment (5:12-15; see Exod 23:10-12). Although the Sabbath commandment itself is not in the deuteronomic law, the festival calendar in 16:1-17 cannot exist without it. This is the first part of the deuteronomic law (see the introduction above).

Although Martin Luther read the teaching to honor political authorities into the fourth commandment (5:16) the decalogue itself says nothing about the problem of government. However, the second part of the deuteronomic law (16:18–18:22) develops the law of the officials in place of the fourth commandment. (See also the *Catechism of the Catholic Church* §§2234–2243.)

The themes of the third part (19:1–25:19) correspond to those of the third part (the second tablet) of the decalogue (5:17-21).

The section 19:1–21:23, whose theme is protecting life, amplifies the fifth commandment ("you shall not murder": 5:17). The section 22:1–23:25 consists of two themes, namely adultery (see 5:18) and theft (5:19). The theme of protecting life appears also in 22:6-7, 8, and the theme of adultery was already dealt with in 21:10-14, 15-17. The theme of adultery is amplified and replaced by the more general concept, "purity of (social) life." In 23:17-25 the theme of purity (vv. 17-18, 21-23) and that of covetousness (vv. 19-20, 24-25) alternate. The section 24:1–25:19 corresponds to the commandments not to answer with false witness and not to covet the neighbor's wife or house, both of which have the key word "neighbor" (5:20-21). The theme of false witness appears in 24:8-9, 16, 17; 25:1-3, 13-16, but already in 17:6-7; 19:15-21.

First Part: Religious Principles (12:1–16:17)

Centralization of the Cult, 12:1-28

The most important religious principle of Deuteronomy is the centralization of the cult. Sacrifices to the Lord were permitted in only one place, for the Lord is one Lord (6:4; see the introduction above). Although Deuteronomy does not refer to the place by name it is apparently Jerusalem's Temple. No other place in the history of Israel was able to claim such an exclusive authority as Jerusalem (Pss 78:60, 67-71; 132:13-18). King Josiah destroyed all the sanctuaries in Judah (2 Kings 23:8-9) and Samaria (2 Kings 23:15-20) but not that in Jerusalem. It is just at this point that Deuteronomy connects with the Josianic reform (see the introduction above).

Instead of referring to the place by name Deuteronomy calls it "the place that the LORD your (sg./pl.) God will choose" ("out of all your tribes": 12:5, or "in one of your tribes": 12:14) "as his habitation" (12:5) or "to put His name there" (12:5, 21; 14:24) or "as a dwelling for his name" (12:11; 14:23; 16:2, 6, 11; 26:2). We can find a forerunner of this idea in Exod 20:24.

God's name represents the divine Self. In the place that the Lord chooses God puts only the divine name; *God* is in heaven, not in the sanctuary on the earth. This is "the theology of God's name." The existence of the Lord is not bound to the rise and fall of the nation or to the sin of the people, but God is available to God's people in the sanctuary only through the divine name. Cf. Ezek 20:9, 14, 22, 39, 44; 36:20-23, according to which the Lord redeemed Israel only for the sake of the divine name that Israel had profaned among the nations. For this reason also, taking the name of the Lord in vain is forbidden (see 5:11).

Jerusalem's Temple was destroyed in 587 B.C.E. by the army of Babylon (2 Kings 25:8-17) but was rebuilt in 515 B.C.E. after the time of the exile (Ezra 3–6) and expanded by King Herod from 20 B.C.E. onward (John 2:20). About this

Temple Jesus said: "Destroy this temple, and in three days I will raise it up" (John 2:19; see the introduction above). For us the name of Jesus Christ, the enduring temple (see the introduction above), is that by which alone we must be saved (Acts 4:12). We are baptized in his name (Acts 2:38) and we pray in his name (John 14:13-14; 15:16; 16:23-24).

Deuteronomy 12:1-12 is the introductory section formulated in the second person plural by the deuteronomistic school in the time of the exile (see the introduction above). The words of this section commanded the Israel that was about to come back from Babylon into the promised land to centralize its cult there (vv. 1, 9-10). Thorough destruction of the foreign sanctuaries when Israel enters the land (vv. 2-4), and not acting according to their own desires as they are doing "here" (v. 8) are emphasized because such false worship destroyed the country (see Deut 28:64; Neh 9:32-37). In Canaan, and also among the Israelites, sanctuaries were usually made on the mountain heights, on the hills, and under every green tree, the symbols of life (v. 2; cf. 1 Kings 14:23; 2 Kings 16:4; 17:10). For v. 3 see 7:5; 16:21-22.

Burnt offerings (v. 6) are to be wholly burnt by fire and thus devoted to the Lord. "Sacrifice" means slaughtering of an animal which is then to be shared by God and the worshipers as a communion meal. On the tithe see 14:22-29. Donations denote the portion of the sacrifice that is set apart as the share of the priests (Lev 7:14, 29-36). The votive gift is offered when a vow has been fulfilled (Judg 11:39). The freewill offerings are the other types of offerings besides the votive gift. On firstlings see 15:19-23. These are all offerings and sacrifices of Israel. However what is important here is not their definition but the commandment to eat them with all "your" household including "male and female slaves, and the Levites who reside in your towns," rejoicing in all the undertakings the Lord has blessed (vv. 7, 12; for the Levites see 10:8-9 and 12:19).

From v. 13 on the law of centralization is given in sentences formulated in the second person singular; this law regulates the process of cultic centralization in the Josianic reform. It legitimates only one place for the sacrifice of animals (vv. 13-14) but at the same time permits eating of flesh anywhere in the land and regulates the process of slaughtering (vv. 15-28). In the ancient world generally, and also in Israel, every slaughtering of an animal was a sacrifice. Deuteronomy confined the place of sacrifice to Jerusalem's Temple. This would have implied that the people would lose the right to eat meat in their home towns. A profane slaughter therefore had to be legitimated. Not only the clean, but also the unclean for worship may eat of it because the slaughter and eating of meat in itself are no longer sacrificial (v. 15). However, the people should not eat blood (v. 16).

The practice of pouring blood out when slaughtering an animal probably has its origin in a taboo. In Israel, however, it was believed that the life of the flesh was in the blood. The life belongs to the Lord. In eating blood the Israelite trespasses on the Lord's possession (Gen 9:1-7; Lev 17:10-16; also in the early Church see Acts 15:20-21, 29).

All offerings and sacrifices, whether flesh or crops, are to be brought to the chosen place (vv. 17-18). Important here also is to eat with the whole family (see v. 7). The Levites shall not be neglected (v. 19), not because they lost their work in the local sanctuaries through the centralization of the cult but because they devote themselves to actualization of the word of the Lord and thus have no allotment of land (14:29; 17:9, 18; 18:1, 6-8; 21:5; 24:8; 27:14).

"When the Lord your God enlarges your territory" (12:20; see 1:10-11; 10:22; 11:24; but especially 19:8-9) so that many Israelites reside far from the chosen place they must do the same (vv. 20-22 // v. 15; vv. 23-25 // v. 16; v. 26 // vv. 17-18; v. 27 // v. 16). On "what is right (and good) in the sight of the LORD" (v. 25, also v. 28) see 6:18; 13:19; 21:9.

Warning Against the Practice of Foreign Religion, 12:29-31

To follow the practices of foreign religions, the religions of the inhabitants, is absolutely prohibited (v. 30). The worship of the Lord shall be worship proper to the Lord (v. 31). For some deities even sons and daughters were offered by fire (see 2 Kings 3:27), but such is abhorrent to the Lord (see 7:25-26).

Warning Against Enticement, 12:32–13:18

The warning against enticement is connected to the commandment not to add to the word of the Lord and not to take anything from it (12:32b;

cf. 4:2). The people are to be always loyal to the Lord revealed in the Scripture, not in other texts. An enticement to follow another god destroys the covenant relation entirely. Three cases are dealt with.

The first case: A sign or wonder by a prophet or "those who divine by dreams" (see Num 12:6) shall never be a reason for Israel to follow another deity (13:1-3a). The God of Israel is the only Lord who brought Israel out of the land of Egypt (13:5, 10; see the decalogue at 5:6). The commandment "you (sg.) shall purge the evil from your midst" (v. 5) makes the individual Israelite responsible for the justice and purity of the people: see 17:7, 12; 19:19; 21:21; 22:21, 22, 24; 24:7. The Lord is testing the people's loyalty (13:3b-4). See also 18:19-22.

The second case: Even if it be one of the members of the family who entices the people secretly (that is, within the family) to follow another deity (vv. 6-7) that person shall be punished. We tend to spare members of our own family, but we must not conceal this secret enticement (v. 8). "Put them forward" (v. 9 LXX). Also, to conceal one who enticed the people is a breach of the covenant. Every Israelite is responsible for keeping his or her family loyal to the Lord, so "your own hand shall be first against them to execute them" (v. 9). "Then all Israel shall hear and be afraid, and never again do any such wickedness" (v. 11; see 17:13; 19:20; 21:21. In these passages it is also said: "you shall purge the evil from your midst"; cf. 13:5).

The third case concerns false worship in any of the towns in the promised land. The people are required first to inquire and make an investigation (13:12-14), then do what is right in the sight of the Lord (13:19; 12:25, 28).

Clean and Unclean, 14:1-21

The introduction (v. 1) is formulated in the second person plural but followed immediately by clauses in the singular (v. 2). "You shall not eat any abhorrent thing" (v. 3). The second person plural layer inserts in vv. 4-21 the list of animals allowed to be eaten and those prohibited. For the people in exile it was very important to know which animals they could eat.

To lacerate oneself and/or to shave one's forelock (v. 1) was a common practice as a mourning rite until the exilic time: see Jer 16:6; 41:5. The deuteronomistic historian (the second person plural layer) added the prohibition of this practice that seeks the power of the dead because it had, so he thought, destroyed the country. The law in the second person singular layer, on the other hand, emphasized that the holy people of the Lord, God's treasured people (see 7:6; 26:18) "shall not eat any abhorrent thing." Not boiling a kid in its mother's milk may have been originally a taboo or possibly a prohibition on humanitarian grounds (Exod 34:26; 23:19).

Not all the names of animals in the list in vv. 4-18 can be identified, but the number of animals may represent the completeness of nature. Animals edible and inedible are fourteen (2 x 7), birds inedible are twenty-one (3 x 7: in v. 13 we count three names): cf. Leviticus 11. We cannot know why some are edible and others are inedible, but for Israel this list shows an order in nature. Among the nations in the time of the exile only Israelites ate these and did not eat those. To eat anything that dies of itself is prohibited (v. 21) because its blood cannot be poured out (see the comment on 12:16).

For us those who eat, eat in honor of the Lord and those who abstain, abstain in honor of the Lord (Rom 14:6; see also Acts 10:9-16).

Tithes, 14:22-29

This section refers to a periodic offering of the tithe and may be the introduction to the following chs. 15:1–16:17 in which the periodic institutions are dealt with, but is more probably linked to the preceding section through the concatenation of the key word "eat" (vv. 3, 23, 26, 29; this key word is absent in the next section 15:1-18).

The tithe was a type of royal taxation (1 Sam 8:15, 17). The king collected the tithe for the upkeep of the royal sanctuary and as the priest's due. It was therefore not an offering the worshipers ate. In Deuteronomy, however, the emphasis of the law is on eating in the presence of the Lord (vv. 23, 26; see 12:18), so that "you may learn to fear the LORD your God always" (v. 23; see 17:19). The tithe shall be set apart from the first portion of the harvest, as also the firstlings of the herd and flock (v. 23; cf. 15:19-23). On "blessing" (vv. 24, 29) see also 26:15. If we support the weak in society we shall have no lack (vv. 26-29; see also 15:10, 18; 23:21; 24:19). Deuteronomy requires all the people of God to assemble around the communion table (see also 26:12-16).

The Law of Release, 15:1-18

Deuteronomy does not demand the cancellation of debts in the seventh year from their inception, but the establishment of a year of release in which all creditors in Israel shall cancel their claims (vv. 2, 9). "Every seven years" (v. 1): it seems obscure whether the time of release from debt is the beginning of the seventh year or the end, but the term ends at harvest time. The creditor collects interest or principal from the harvest of the year. The release has its basis in the community of the covenant people (vv. 2-3).

The Lord blesses the people, so that there will be no more poor among them (v. 4). But the law commands support of the poor and says, "there will never cease to be some in need on the earth" (v. 11). What does this mean? Poor people will never cease to exist. It is the constant condition of this world. We ought to support them because the blessing of the Lord is sufficient for us to share with the poor (v. 10; see the sharing of possession in the name of Jesus in Acts 3:44-45). Before the Lord we can see things differently. If we share our possessions with the poor we do not become poor, but the poor have enough to eat (2 Cor 8:13-15). As long as we observe the commandments of the Lord, therefore, the divine blessing is full in the land and there are no poor among us (v. 4), so that Israel will lend to other people but will not borrow from them: it is a blessing for Israel among the stronger nations (v. 6, see 28:12-13).

The release of the debt, however, brings about another difficulty for the poor. When the year of release draws near the rich will not lend to the poor (v. 9). This unkindness comes from lack of trust in the unlimited blessings of the Lord. If, therefore, the poor cry to the Lord against "you," you shall be found guilty (v. 9; see 24:15; Exod 22:23, 27; cf. Deut 10:17-18).

In v. 12 it seems that each Hebrew slave must serve six years and be released at (the beginning of) the seventh year of enslavement. Deuteronomy 15:12-18 is under the influence of Exod 21:2-11 in which the law regulates the process of release in the seventh year for each slave and deals with male slaves and female slaves differently. But according to the context of Deuteronomy 15 (see especially vv. 1, 17) the year of release is to be applied equally to male and female slaves. The manumission of slaves proclaimed by King Zedekiah (Jeremiah 34) was the release of all slaves in the land and Jeremiah cited Deut 15:1, 12 as the basis for the proclamation (Jer 34:14). When a slave is freed the master shall not send him or her out empty handed, just as the Lord blesses the people (vv. 13-14). Sympathy is important (v. 15). The slave's service was equivalent to the wages of a hired servant (v. 18). Deuteronomy did not condemn the institution of slavery, but dealt with slaves as sovereign before the Lord.

The release law appears not to benefit foreigners (vv. 2-3, 6-7, 12). At the outset the Law of the Lord applied to Israel, not to other nations, because they had their own gods. But this law is based on the unlimited blessings of the Lord (vv. 4-6, 10-11, 13-15). Moreover it is Israel's mission to be a blessing for all the families of the earth (see Gen 12:2-3). Similarly the Christian Church should be a blessing for all nations. On this basis, today for example, multinational companies operated by Christians should not enslave the people in poor countries but share the wealth with them. "[Christ] is our peace" (Eph 2:14) and all people are invited to be "filled with all the fullness of God" (Eph 3:19).

Firstlings, 15:19-23

The firstling represents all the offspring of livestock. The offering of firstlings shows that the Lord claims the privileged possession of all produce in Israel. Everything we have is the possession of the Lord (so we shall not oppress the poor!). But here emphasis is on eating the offering of firstlings in the chosen place together with all of one's family (v. 20; see also 26:1-11). The commandment in v. 21 seems to allow discrimination against the disabled, but that is not the case. Concerning this problem see 17:1. For vv. 22-23 see 12:15-16.

Festival Calendar, 16:1-17

Israel held three festivals a year, namely Passover (together with the feast of unleavened bread) at which time later the resurrection of Christ occurred, the feast of Weeks (= Pentecost), and the feast of Tabernacles.

The section 16:1-8 is constructed chiastically:

A "observe the month of Abib" (v. 1aa)
B keeping the Passover in the chosen place (vv. 1ab-2)
C unleavened bread related to the Exodus (v. 3)

D unleavened bread: "no leaven shall be seen" (v. 4a)
D' the Passover: "none of the meat . . . shall remain" (v. 4b)
C' the Passover related to the Exodus (vv. 5-6)
B' keeping the Passover in the chosen place (v. 7)
A' for six days . . . and on the seventh day (v. 8)

The framework of this section is the Sabbath law: see the expressions "observe (5:12!) the month of Abib" and "for six days . . . and on the seventh day" (A–A'), also see "keeping (5:15!) the Passover" (v. 1ab), "remember the day of your departure from the land of Egypt" (v. 3b, cf. 5:15), and "you shall do no work" (v. 8bb). In this framework the commandments for the Passover (see Exod 12:21-27; cf. Exod 12:1-13, 43-51) and for the feast of unleavened bread (see Exod 13:3-10; cf. Exod 12:14-20) are connected with each other through the reference to the Exodus (see especially C–C'), that is, the release from slavery. The Sabbath itself is connected with the Exodus (5:15).

The sacrifice of the Passover shall be slaughtered only in the chosen place (vv. 2, 5, 6, 7a), while one can eat the unleavened bread in his or her own tent (vv. 4a, 7b-8); in fact, however, the participants of the feast of unleavened bread are in or near Jerusalem for the Passover.

The feast of Weeks is celebrated at the end of harvesting (vv. 9-12). This festival is held on the day seven weeks (the fiftieth day = Pentecost) after the Passover. The whole family and the disadvantaged are to rejoice in the chosen place together (v. 11). This festival also reminds us of the Exodus (v. 12).

The feast of Tabernacles is held at the end of the season for gathering grapes and figs (vv. 13-15). It is held for seven days in the chosen place (vv. 13, 15). Also emphasized here is rejoicing with the family, the Levites, strangers, orphans, and widows (v. 14). Deuteronomy had to be read in this festival during the year of release (31:10-11). This feast is also connected with release from debt or bondage (see also the introduction above).

Three times a year all males in Israel (as representatives of their families in those days) are to appear before the Lord (v. 16; see Exod 34:23; 23:17). Many people went on a pilgrimage to Jerusalem from all over the country, and in the time of the Second Temple even from Babylon or Africa (see Acts 2:9–11; 8:27). The pilgrimage reenacted the Exodus. They are not to appear empty handed to make an offering to the Lord (vv. 16b-17; see Exod 34:20b; 23:15b). In Exodus 34 and 23 this commandment is connected only with the feast of unleavened bread, which is held at the beginning of the harvest without assurance of a sufficient crop.

Second Part: Officials (16:18–18:22)

This part constitutes the law of the officials: judges, king, priests, and prophets. The theme of the first part, the religious principle, appears in this part related to the tasks of the officials (16:21–17:7; 18:9-14). The officials are responsible for actualization of the religious principle in the social life of Israel. If the officials function adequately the promised land will be filled with the words of the Lord, the *torah*.

Judges, 16:18-20

A judge and an "official" (see 1:15, probably a scribe of the law court) is to be established in each town for each tribe (v. 18) and shall seek only fairness. That judgments should not be distorted, and that accepting bribes is strictly prohibited (v. 19; cf. 1:16-17; Exod 23:1-8) are self-evident principles (Prov 24:23-25). "Justice, and only justice, you shall pursue, so that you may live and occupy the land" (v. 20, cf. Prov 21:21).

Purity of Worship, 16:21–17:7

The levitical priests and the judges in the central sanctuary are responsible for social justice in the promised land (17:9-10), so that purity of worship is decisive for hearing the will of the Lord. To plant a tree as Asherah beside an altar and to set up a stone pillar were common practices in Canaan (see 7:5) and even in Jerusalem's Temple (see 2 Kings 23:4, 6-7, 14). The stone pillar probably symbolizes the sexual power of the man and Asherah is the consort of the god (Deut 16:21-22). It was believed that the sexual acts of the deities brought fertility to the land. The Lord, the Creator of the world, does not need a consort.

To sacrifice an animal with a defect is abhorrent to the Lord (17:1; see 15:21). We may be tempted to keep a strong animal for ourselves and select an animal with a defect as an offering. Although it may be eaten anywhere in the town like any other animal (15:22-23) one may not kill it arbitrarily because of its defect. The officials are responsible for protecting the altar from abhorrent things and for sacrificing animals.

The law in 17:2-7 deals with the religious theme but provides for legal procedures against apostasy. The people (or the judge) shall make a thorough inquiry to learn whether the charge is proved true (v. 4). A person must not be put to death on the evidence of only one witness (v. 6). The witnesses shall take responsibility for their testimony (v. 7; cf. 13:5).

The Court in Jerusalem, 17:8-13

In a case too difficult to judge in a local court (16:18-20) "you (sg.)," namely one (or more) of the parties or possibly the judge of the local court shall go up to the chosen place (that is, Jerusalem) to consult with the levitical priests and the judge who is in office at that time (vv. 8-9). The case is to be decided "between one kind of bloodshed [murder or other capital offense] and another, one kind of legal right and another, or one kind of [stroke] [of God's hand?] and another" (v. 8; see 2 Chr 19:10-11). The word "stroke" is generally translated "assault" [so NRSV] but denotes the case of murder or cursing in which the result is apparent but in which we cannot know the perpetrator. We can only refer the case to God (see 21:5). It is important to observe the judgment of the court in Jerusalem so that the will of the Lord is fulfilled all over the land (vv. 10-13; on v. 11 see v. 20).

The Law of the King, 17:14-20

The desire to set up a king "like all the nations that are around me" (v. 14) must be compared with the inquiry about the practice of worship of the surrounding nations (12:30). The latter is absolutely rejected, but the former is acceptable with a certain condition (17:15). Although the king indeed occupies the most important position in the state it is not a decisive point for Israel whether or not a king shall be set over the people. Most important is that the king is subject to the Law (vv. 16-20) and that the purity of religion be kept by him. The people may set a king over themselves but only from among their fellows in the community. It is the Lord who chooses a king (v. 15).

The king shall not multiply horses (= military power) for himself (v. 16aa). The additional warning (with the historical review in the second person plural layer) not to return the people to Egypt in order to acquire horses (v. 16ab-b) is related to the reliance of Israel on the political power of Egypt (see Isa 31:1-3; also Jer 2:18; 2 Kings 25:26). The king shall not multiply wives (have a harem) to symbolize the fertility of the land (see the comment on 16:21-22), nor shall he greatly multiply silver and gold (that is, engage in lavish finance: v. 17). He may not, therefore, be a typical king (cf. 1 Sam 8:11-18). He shall not rule the land with his own power, but with the Law of the Lord. As long as he is on the throne he shall have (a copy of) this (second) law written for him in the presence of the levitical priests and shall recite it each day (vv. 18-19). The role of the king is actualization of the entire Law *(torah)*. If he is obedient to the *torah* he cannot exalt himself above other members of the community or turn right or left from the commandments (see v. 11; 5:29; 28:14; Josh 1:7), but will learn to fear the Lord (see 14:23).

The Levitical Priests, 18:1-8

The priests in Deuteronomy are chosen only from the Levites. The levitical priests keep the book of the *torah* (17:18; 31:9, 25-26) and are responsible for judgment in difficult cases (17:9; 19:17; 21:5). They carry the ark of the covenant (10:8; 31:9, 25), stand before the Lord to minister and to bless in the Lord's name (10:8; 20:2-4). They devote themselves to actualization of the word of the Lord (18:5; "the LORD is their inheritance": v. 2) and therefore they have no allotment of the land (see 12:19). The Law (18:1-8) regulates which portion of the sacrifice they may eat ("eat" is the key word of the first and second parts of the law code: vv. 1, 8; see the introduction above). These directives are appropriate also for Christian pastors.

Not all the Levites are in the office of priest, but they have the qualifications for the priesthood (vv. 6-7). The Levite in the chosen place should be treated equally with other Levites in addition to what he receives from the sale of his patrimony (v. 8). He has probably sold what he inherited from his father and come to Jerusalem.

Purity of Worship, 18:9-14

Deuteronomy demands from us "completeness" before the Lord (v. 13); that is, we must be completely loyal to the Lord. All the prohibited practices (vv. 10-11) are connected with seeking an oracle. Today's "idolatry," especially expansionism or some forms of nationalism, seeks oracles that benefit their politics. Because of these abhorrent things the Lord drives the inhabitants out from the land (v. 12). We should seek oracles only from the Lord (see 6:6-9, 13) and never follow the practice of the inhabitants of the land (v. 14, see 12:29-31).

Prophets, 18:15-22

The Lord never permits giving heed to soothsayers and diviners (v. 14). From whom, then, should Israel hear the oracle of the Lord? The Lord spoke most of the divine word to Moses and commanded him to teach the people the statutes and ordinances the Lord spoke to him (vv. 16-18; see 5:22-31). Moses, however, will die. The Lord promises to raise up for the people a prophet like Moses from among them (vv. 15, 18). The will of the Lord is to be revealed in the divine word spoken by a prophet like Moses.

To distinguish a false prophet one should observe whether the thing spoken by him in the name of the Lord takes place and proves true (vv. 21-22). It is not for us to guess whether the prophet has magical power and can actualize whatever he or she has spoken (cf. 13:1-5). We must observe history. It is important whether the word spoken by the prophet takes place later in history. We must therefore judge whether or not the word of the prophet in our presence is based on history and the Law of the Lord revealed through Moses. Later Deuteronomy establishes the rule of law also over the prophets: "Never since has there arisen a prophet in Israel like Moses" (34:10). But we must say that never since has arisen a prophet like Moses until Jesus Christ (see the lectionary on the fourth Sunday of the year, Cycle B, which reads Deut 8:15-20 together with Mark 1:21-28).

Third Part: Community Life of the People (19:1–25:19)

The officials of Israel (16:18–18:22) are responsible for actualizing the religious principle (12:1–16:17) in the community life of the people. The laws in 19:1–25:19 make clear how the principle in 12:1–16:18 is to be actualized. The theme "judge/judgment" that is dealt with in the second part as an institution appears in the third part to establish fairness in community life (19:1-13, 14, 15-21; 21:1-9, 15-17, 18-21, 22-23; 25:1-3).

Protecting Life, 19:1–21:23

The commandment to choose the cities of refuge is comparable to 4:41-43, but the standpoint of the people is different. In ch. 4 Moses chose three cities in the Transjordan region, but now the people must first of all choose three cities in the promised land (v. 2) and then three more cities in the Transjordan when the Lord enlarges the territory of Israel (vv. 8-9; cf. Num 35:13-14). By choosing the cities of refuge Israel celebrates the blessings of the Lord. The case on one killing another at enmity (vv. 11-12) seems to assume only the case of a murder and not to include manslaughter. In that time, however, these were not as clearly distinguished from each other as in modern criminal law.

The prohibition against moving a boundary marker on the land (19:14; see 27:17; Prov 22:28; 23:10) follows the law of the cities of refuge. To move a land boundary threatens the right to life of one's neighbors, especially the socially weak (see Prov 22:23), or on the contrary often so angers them that it ends in the murder of the person who moves the landmark. This prohibition is, therefore, put in the section on "protecting life."

The sufficient evidence for judging a case is two or three witnesses. No suspected person shall be convicted of a crime with a single witness (19:15; see 17:6 and also the law of excommunication in Matt 18:15-17; *1 Clem.* 65). A false witness shall be excluded because he does harm especially to the right of the socially weak to live (see v. 14). The false witness shall suffer just what he had meant to do to the opponent: life for life, eye for eye, tooth for tooth, hand for hand, foot for foot (vv. 18-19, 21). "Life for life . . ." does not assume literal execution, but emphasizes equivalence between what the false witness meant to do and what shall be done to him.

The fifth commandment (5:17) did not prohibit war, but war is a serious issue for the protecting of life. The theme "war" appears in ch. 20 and in 21:10-14.

Israel's wars were wars of the Lord. Israel shall not be afraid of a larger enemy, for the Lord is with them (20:1; see 7:17-21). This does not allow self-justification by Israel; rather Israel's wars must be appropriate as wars of the Lord. The manner of war must be regulated strictly. If a given war is not appropriate to the name of the Lord, the Lord will not be with Israel and they will be defeated (see 1:41-45).

A war must begin with a worship service. The priest shall speak to the troops (20:2): "Hear, O Israel" (20:3; see 6:4; 9:1 and elsewhere) and encourage them (vv. 3-4). Then the officials (cf. 1:15; 16:18) make those go back home who have hesitation about going to war (vv. 5-8). Dedication of one's house, gathering of first fruits, and fulfilling one's obligation with a wife take precedence over military service. This is inconceivable in the "holy war" institutions of our modern countries that must have priority over everything. The expansionist country justifies its aggressive war in the name of holy war and requires all the people to take part in its army. Decisive, however, in the war of the Lord is reliance not on military force, but on the Lord.

Before a city is attacked, offering terms of peace shall be given priority (20:10). Enslavement of the defeated people and plundering were common in war (v. 14), not only in the ancient world but also in the modern age up to the nineteenth century. As for cities in the promised land, no one in them was to remain alive (vv. 16-17; see 7:2) because they would teach the people of the Lord to observe their religious practices, which would be abhorrent to the Lord (v. 18; see 7:25-26). In fact, however, these people remained in the promised land and served Israel as forced laborers (Judg 1:19, 21, and elsewhere; 1 Kings 9:20-21; see the comment on 7:2). When a town is besieged, its trees shall not be destroyed (vv. 19-20). This law assumes protection of the environment, which is most seriously destroyed in wars.

In the case of a murder in which the perpetrator is not known the guilt of innocent blood shall be purged from the promised land (21:1-9). The town nearest the murdered body is responsible for purging the guilt (21:2-8). By the rite described in vv. 3-8, which is to be done before the levitical priests (v. 5) who are responsible for judgment between one kind of stroke (of God's hand) and another (see 17:8), they wash away the guilt of innocent blood (vv. 8-9), into running water. The heifer is loaded with the guilt instead of pulling in the yoke. The people in the promised land must in any case be innocent of bloodshed.

It is women who suffer the most terrible damage from war. If anyone finds among the captives (20:14) a woman he wants to marry he must let her mourn for her father and mother a full month. After that he may marry her (21:10-13). She comes to his house, shaves her head, pares her nails, and discards her captive's garb. That is to say, she begins a new life as an Israelite. She is to be treated fully as a wife (v. 14). If the man is not satisfied with her he shall let her go free and not sell her for money, since he has dishonored her (see Exod 21:8). This law prohibited men from treating captive women cruelly without respect in the days when women were not equal to men.

Conflict between two wives and/or between their sons (21:15-17) is often caused by a marriage to a captive woman whom the husband loves and to whom he wants to give preference (see vv. 10-14). In any case the firstborn son shall have the preference (v. 16). The firstborn son shall be given "a double portion" (v. 17). He takes probably two-thirds of all the possessions of his father, regardless of the number of brothers (see Zech 13:8).

Parents have responsibility to the community for disciplining and teaching their children (21:18-21; see Prov 23:13-14; Deut 6:6-9, 20-25). This law appears here in relation to the theme "conflict between sons" (vv. 15-17). But if the sons and daughters follow discipline and teaching their days of life may be prolonged (see 5:16). The prototype of this discipline is discipline by the Lord (8:5). If a son will not heed his parents, the parents are to appeal to the community to punish him (21:19-20). But what parents, in fact, would request the execution of their son? This law requires parental discipline from early childhood in order that no son will become stubborn and rebellious.

The law in 21:18-21 refers to the death penalty, so the procedure for execution is also regulated (vv. 22-23). Hanging on a tree, however, does not describe the method of execution; it is the exposure of one already executed. This corpse shall not remain all night upon the tree, however, because anyone hung on a tree is under the curse of God (v. 23). Jesus Christ took upon himself this curse of God (see Gal 3:13). If the cursed body remained overnight its impurity was thought to spread over the promised land.

Purity of Life and Law of Possession, 22:1–23:25

The laws in 22:1–23:16 are ordered chiastically:

A A stray animal shall be returned to its owner (22:1-4)
B Law prohibiting mixing a certain thing with another (22:5)
C Law protecting life (22:6-8)
B' Law prohibiting mixing a certain thing with another (22:9-11)
D Make tassels on the four corners (skirt) of clothes (22:12)
E Law protecting the "virginity" of Israel (22:13-29)
D' Prohibition on uncovering one's father's skirt (22:30)
B" Law against mixing a certain person into the assembly and purity of the camp of the Lord (23:1-8; 23:9-14)
A' Slaves who have escaped from their owners shall not be given back to them (23:15-16)

In the chiastic structure of these laws the commandment to return a stray animal to its owner (22:1-4) and the prohibition to return a slave to his or her owner (23:15-16) correspond to each other (A–A'). Emphasis is on the latter. Not withholding help from a neighbor who loses his or her possession (21:1-3), or whose animal falls on the road (v. 4) is a matter of common sense (cf. Exod 23:4-5). But the law on the contrary stresses that slaves who have escaped from their owners shall not be given back to the owner (23:15-16). Deuteronomy rejects dealing with slaves by analogy with stray animals.

The link between 22:5, 9-11 and 23:1-8 (B–B'–B") is comparable to the link between 22:1-4 and 23:15-16 (A–A'). Not to mix a certain thing with another (22:5, 9, 10, 11) belongs to common knowledge (see Lev 19:19). By analogy with this common knowledge mixing certain persons into the assembly of the Lord is prohibited (23:1-8). Excluded from the assembly are those whose testicles are crushed or whose penises are cut off (v. 1). This does not refer to disabilities caused by disease or accident, but to religious practices. "Those born of an illicit union" are expelled even to the tenth generation (v. 2) because they are born as a result of cultic prostitution (see vv. 17-18). Excluded also are the Ammonites and the Moabites connected with the name of Balaam even to the tenth generation (vv. 3-6; see Numbers 22–24). Balaam is a warning to the assembly not to become accursed but to remain beloved children of the Lord (see 2 Pet 2:14-16). The children of the third generation born to Egyptians or Edomites (see 2:3-6) may be admitted to the assembly of the Lord (vv. 7-8). Important for formation of the assembly is sympathy: Israel also was a sojourner in Egypt (cf. Exod 22:21; 23:9) and in Edom (2:1).

"The assembly of the LORD" is connected with the military camp, so the law of the purity of the camp (23:9-14) follows the law of the purity of the assembly. Israel shall guard against any impropriety (v. 9) because wars are wars of the Lord and the camp is the camp of the Lord (v. 14; see ch. 20).

The law not to mix different things (22:5, 9-11), on the other hand, encompasses the law of protecting life (22:6-8). The law in vv. 6-7 will protect the environment (see 20:19-20). The Israelites made the roofs of their houses flat for resting in the evening. A parapet shall be made for the roof so as not to shed innocent blood (v. 8; cf. Exod 21:33-34).

Tassels shall be made for the four corners (skirt) of clothes (22:12) to weigh the skirt down so as not to bare the body (cf. Num 15:38-39). This law is parallel: 22:30 (D–D'). Emphasis is on the latter. "You shall not uncover your father's skirt." Marriage with a father's wife was even in Israel not uncommon (Amos 2:7) but is prohibited here.

At the central point of the chiastic structure 22:1–23:15 is the law protecting the "virginity of Israel" (22:13-29, E). This law corresponds properly to the prohibition of adultery in the decalogue (5:18). The prohibition against lying with the wife of another man itself, however, occupies here only the second position (v. 22). The law first of all intends to protect the "virginity of Israel" (vv. 13-21). The case described in vv. 13-17 is not a procedure to establish evidence of the virginity of the wife but to protect the honor of the Israelite woman from "slander" (v. 14). The theme of "virginity" appears in vv. 19, 23, and 28. The evidence of virginity (vv. 14, 15, 17, 20) is the cloths that were used as sheets on the wedding night. Both the man and the woman who violate the purity of marriage shall be put to death. "You shall purge the evil from your midst/from

Israel" (vv. 21, 22, 24), but the woman shall not be punished if there was no one to rescue her (vv. 25-27). If a man lies with a woman who is not betrothed he shall marry her, giving fifty shekels to her father (vv. 28-29). This means not a "bride-price" (cf. Exod 22:17 "thirty shekels"? cf. Lev 27:4), but a penalty. For 22:30–23:16 see the comments on 22:1-12.

Cultic prostitution (see 1 Kings 14:24; 15:12; 22:47; 2 Kings 23:7) is strictly prohibited (Deut 23:17-18). "A dog" denotes a servant of the temple who serves as a temple prostitute.

Everyone has responsibility for his or her vows before the Lord (vv. 21-23), but no one can be forced by another person to carry out a vow (v. 23; see 15:16-17 and 23:15-16).

Charging interest on loans to a member of the community is prohibited (vv. 19-20). It is a case of covetousness of a neighbors house (see the comment on the tenth commandment). One may take grapes from a neighbor's vineyard or grain from a neighbor's field for personal use (vv. 24-25; see 24:19-21). This constitutes an exception to the tenth commandment. These rules in vv. 15-16, 19-25 protect the rights of the socially disadvantaged.

False Witness and Covetousness, 24:1–25:19

Chapters 24–25 describe situations in which covetousness often arises, but 24:7 deals with the theme of theft and 25:1-3 refers to false witness. Deuteronomy 24:8-9, 16, 17; 25:13-16 may prohibit covetousness but also relate to false witness.

A man who divorces his wife shall not take her again after her second husband has divorced her or died (24:1-4). If she or her sons should bring the inheritance of her second man to the first man, the first would be seen as coveting his neighbor's house. The people, however, read this law as if it allowed divorce (by the husband). Jesus criticized their interpretation (Matt 19:3-9).

A man newly married shall be exempt from any public service for one year (24:5). Seeking a neighbor's wife during the absence of her husband was not uncommon, especially in wartime. The newly married couple is easy prey for coveters.

A mill or an upper millstone is itself not of great value and might be taken in pledge for a small debt, but for the debtor the burden of the pledge may be too heavy, for it is a necessity of life (24:6).

Kidnapping is the most extreme form of theft. The kidnapper shall be put to death (24:7; see Exod 21:16).

At the outbreak of a serious (contagious) skin disease the diagnosis and the isolation of the patient shall be decided carefully so as not to infringe on his or her human rights (24:8). What is important is the justice and righteousness of the judgment (see the eighth commandment: 5:20), for which levitical priests are responsible (see Leviticus 13–14). What the Lord did in the case of Miriam on the journey out of Egypt (v. 9) was to command that she be shut out of the camp for seven days (Num 12:14-15). The house whose master is shut out of the town must be guarded against covetousness, and thus the judgment of isolation shall be made carefully.

Sympathy is also a decisive factor in taking a pledge for a loan (24:10-11; cf. Exod 22:25a; for Deut 24:12-13 see Exod 22:26-27). To withhold the wages of poor and needy laborers is to covet their houses (24:14-15; see Lev 19:13). They might cry to the Lord against the employer (see Exod 22:23, 27).

The law protecting the rights of the socially weak (24:1-15, 17-22) with reference to the Exodus (vv. 9, 18, 22) encompasses the principle of personal liability (v. 16; cf. 5:9-10). If a coveter causes a weak neighbor to receive the death penalty by a false witness, and if the father or the son of the man to be punished must also be put to death, the house of the man to be punished loses its master and is at the disposal of the coveter. Compare with Ezek 18:20 which forbids the exiles to cast the blame on their parents for being in exile.

The justice due to a resident alien or an orphan ("an orphan of a resident alien"?) shall not be perverted, and a widow's garment shall not be taken in pledge (v. 17). A certain part of the harvest of field, trees, or vineyard shall be left for the socially weak (vv. 19-22). These rules constitute exceptions to the tenth commandment (see also 23:26-27). Resident alien, orphan, and widow are typical of the socially weak (see Exod 22:21-22; cf. Deut 10:18). In the case of famine the text of vv. 17-22 is to be read in the Liturgy of the Hours. The blessing of the Lord is sufficient if we share it with each other (see 15:10).

Judgment and execution must be just and righteous (25:1-3; cf. the number of lashes St. Paul received from the Jews: 2 Cor 11:24).

The commandment not to muzzle an ox while it is treading out the grain (25:4) means that a reward shall be paid to the person who works his ox for threshing for the sake of the whole neighborhood (cf. 24:14-15; 1 Cor 9:9-10).

One whose brother died without leaving a successor shall marry his brother's widow so that the property may not be lost to the family (25:5-10). Marriage with the brother's wife is in this case not contrary to the ninth commandment. The law, then, warns against destroying procreative ability (vv. 11-12). However, we know another meaning ("mystery"!) of marriage (Eph 4:32) according to which marriage is the relationship between a woman and a man to learn the relationship between Christ and Church.

To have two kinds of weights or two kinds of measures destroys the economic order, causes miscarriage of justice, and is, therefore, abhorrent to the Lord and thus strictly prohibited (25:13-16). One covets the neighbor's house by having such weights or measures. The case of Amalek is a typical example of covetousness (25:17-19).

Conclusion of the Deuteronomic Law (26:1-16)

The section 26:1-16 is connected with the first part of the law code through concatenation of the key words (on the key word "eat" see the introduction above; "bless" 26:15; 12:7b, 15; 14:24, 29; 15:4, 6, 10, 14, 18; 16:10, 15, 17) and through the relation of the themes ("first fruits" 26:1-11, see 15:19-23; "tithe" 26:12-15, see 14:22-29).

First Fruits, 26:1-11

Israel shall bring the first of the fruit of the promised land to the Lord and recite a formula of salvation history (vv. 5-10; cf. 6:10-25; Exod 13:1-16). Each one appears before the Lord and says personally, "my" ancestor was a wandering Aramean (v. 5), but now "I" bring the first of the fruit of the ground that *you,* O Lord, have given "me" (v. 10). The slavery in Egypt and the liberation from there are, on the contrary, the common experience of Israel: Egyptians treated "us" harshly, "we" cried to the Lord, the Lord brought "us" out of Egypt, and brought "us" into this place (vv. 6-9).

The words of this credal statement are read on the first Sunday of Lent when we also read that Jesus is the Lord (Rom 10:8-13), who triumphed over the temptations of Satan (Luke 4:1-13; lectionary Cycle C). If we celebrate the salvation history of the Lord we triumph over earthly temptation.

Tithes, 26:12-16

By the tithe the Israelites share the blessing of the Lord with each other. They come to an assembly around the communion table (see 14:22-29).

Most of the "statutes and ordinances" in 12:1–26:16 are not applicable literally today, but they teach us about the will of the Lord who will fill us with the divine word and invite us to share the divine blessings with neighbors. In the presence of God all of us are dealt with quite fairly, but a self-justification of our deeds is not allowed.

Declaration of the Covenant: 26:17-19

Moses cites the declaration of the covenant and certifies that the Lord and Israel are now bound to each other by treaty: Israel believes exclusively in the Lord as its God (v. 17; see 6:4-5), and the Lord makes Israel the only treasured people of God, holy to the Lord (vv. 18-19; see 7:6). The Lord, the ruler of the whole world, becomes "our God." In the same way Jesus, the only Son of God, emptied and humbled himself (Phil 2:6-11), giving us his body and the new covenant in his blood (1 Cor 11:23-26). Israel is high above all nations (v. 19) only because the Lord descended for it (see Eph 4:8-10).

The declaration of the covenant is the climax of the procedure to conclude a treaty. The conclusion of the treaty must be declared repeatedly: "today" (vv. 17, 18) the Lord concludes the treaty with us. The people answer that they will be obedient to the word of the Lord (v. 17). This treaty was declared by King Josiah on that day by these words (2 Kings 23:3). According to 31:10-13 Deuteronomy had to be read as the words of the treaty every seven years at the feast of Tabernacles. This signifies the renewal of the treaty. The treaty is concluded "today" between the Lord and us in Jesus Christ, and we are the children of the Lord (vv. 16-19 read together with Matt 5:43-48 in the lectionary on Saturday of the first week of Lent).

Blessings and Curses: 27:1–28:68

Exhortations Before Crossing the Jordan (27:1-26)

Israel shall set up the monument of "this *torah*" immediately upon arriving in the promised land (27:1-8). It is not clear whether the *torah* was to be written on the stone set up after crossing over the Jordan (v. 3) or on the stones of the altar (v. 8) and whether the stone was set up beside the river (v. 2) or on Mount Ebal (v. 4). The redactor in the time of the exile who formulated sentences in the second person plural put emphasis on the historical situation just after the crossing of the Jordan (vv. 2a, 4a). In Joshua 4, on the other hand, the people set up stones at Gilgal on the west side of the Jordan, and in Josh 8:30-35 they build a stone altar on Mount Ebal and write the *torah* on it. Also unclear is why the stones are set up on Mount Ebal, the mountain of curses (cf. 27:13; the Samaritan Pentateuch reads in v. 4 "Mount Gerizim," the holy mountain for the Samaritans). The monument of the *torah* was probably a warning to Israel not to incur the curses (see 27:9-26).

For the blessing of the people the tribes residing in the mid-Palestinian and Judean regions stand on the southern mountain (Gerizim, v. 12), and for the curse the tribes residing in the northern region and in the Transjordan stand on the northern mountain (Ebal, v. 13). The levitical priests declare the abominations that are to be expelled from the promised land (vv. 9, 14); "cursed be anyone who . . ." (vv. 14-26). The list of abominations begins with the religious principle (v. 15) and ends with the comprehensive clause calling down a curse on anyone who does not uphold and observe the words of "this *torah*" (v. 26). The curses against infringement of the right to live (v. 16, see 5:16 "that your days may be long"; see also 21:18-21; v. 17, see 19:14; v. 18; v. 19, see 24:17; v. 24, see 5:17; 21:1-9; v. 25, see 19:15-21) encompass the curses against sexual abominations (vv. 20-23, see 22:30; cf. Lev 18:8, 23, 9, 17). Bloodshed and sexual abomination harm the holy people most seriously.

Curses were much more meaningful among ancient people than in modern societies, but the declaration of abominations (27:14-26) and the list of blessings and curses (28:1-68) make us aware of our actions in the presence of the Lord. Before the divine court nothing can be hidden. When King Josiah heard the words of this *torah,* obviously including the curses, he tore his clothes to show his repentance (2 Kings 22:11). Faced with the curses, Josiah perceived the hidden sin of Israel as his own.

Blessings and Curses (28:1-68)

The promise of blessings and curses is a component characteristic of the vassal treaties of Assyria in the seventh century B.C.E. and also of those of the Hittites in the fourteenth and thirteenth centuries B.C.E. (see the introduction above, and cf. also Lev 26:3-39). Its content and rhetoric show many similarities to these treaties. It is, however, in Deuteronomy not the great king or the deities of the empire but the Lord who brings the people blessings and curses.

When the promised land is filled with the word of the Lord (vv. 1a, 2b, 9b, 13b, 14) it is filled with the blessings of the Lord (vv. 1-14). The Lord will make good the divine promise in the treaty (on v. 1, see 26:19; on v. 9, see 26:18-19). These blessings will make all people on earth glorify the Lord, by whose name we are called (v. 10; see Matt 5:16). On blessings, see 15:4-11.

Curses are carried out on the principle of "an eye for an eye, a tooth for a tooth." When Israel rejects the word of the Lord in the promised land it will be rejected and wiped out from the land (vv. 15-68). Verses 15-19 constitute the counterpart to vv. 1-6. Diseases and natural calamities visit the promised land (vv. 20-24) because the Lord is ruler of heaven and earth. The list of curses in vv. 25-35 that reflects a situation of war (on vv. 30-31, see 20:5-7) is parallel to the treaties of the Assyrian king Essarhaddon. Deuteronomy says that these disasters always attributed to the deities of Assyria do not come from them but from the wrath of the Lord. For the diseases of Egypt (vv. 27, 60), see 7:15.

Israel served other deities, so it shall be compelled to serve them (vv. 36, 64, see 4:28). On vv. 43-44, see v. 12. Verses 47-57 describe the distress of the besieged city. Israel did not serve the Lord, so it shall be compelled to serve its enemies (vv. 47-48). The critical situation described here is the same as that told by the prophet Jeremiah in the last days of the kingdom of Judah (vv. 48-49 // Jer 5:15-17; v. 48 // Jer

28:13-14; vv. 53-57 // Jer 19:9). If the people reject the words of "this *torah*," written "in this book" (see 17:18-19) all disasters, even those that are not written "in this book of the *torah*" will fall upon them (vv. 58-68). Israel will be plucked out of the promised land (v. 63) and the land will be purified.

Deuteronomy is not ignorant of the fact that a righteous person is not always happy (3:26, see also 2 Kings 23:29). However, at the historical crisis determining whether Israel might live long in the land or lose it (see introduction above) Israel faced the alternatives of obedience to the Lord or disobedience, blessings or curses.

If misfortunes are out of the control of the Lord, how can we overcome them at all? When Israel was defeated and destroyed by the great empire the list of blessings and curses made clear that it was the Lord who gave Israel into the hand of the great empire (vv. 7, 36-44, 47-57). If so, the key to restoring God's people was not lost. What they should do was turn to the Lord and renew their obedience (see 30:2-3!).

Making of the Second Covenant: 29:1–32:47

Title (29:1-2)

The title in 29:1-2 indicates that the history of the making of the second covenant on the plains of Moab begins here. This is the sequel to the history in chs.1–4. Chapter 31 is the story of the appointment of Joshua.

Historical Review (29:2-11)

The historical review sums up again the history from the eve of the Exodus to the eve of the crossing of the Jordan. On what the Lord did in the land of Egypt (29:2-3) see 6:21-22; 7:18-19; 11:3; 26:7-8. Moses led Israel forty years in the wilderness to make them know that the Lord is their God (vv. 5-6, see 8:2-5). On the war against Sihon and Og and the allotment of the Transjordan land to the Reubenites, the Gadites and the half-tribe of Manasseh (vv. 7-8) see 2:24–3:17.

Words of the Covenant (29:12-13)

Israel entered into covenant with the Lord, swearing by an oath. The Lord established Israel as God's people, and the Lord became Israel's God (see 26:17-19).

Exhortations (29:14–30:20)

Moses was making the covenant not only with those who were present at that time, but also with us who were not there (vv. 14-15; see also vv. 10-11). Anyone who serves the gods of other nations shall incur the curses written "in the book of this *torah*" (vv. 18-21; cf. 28:61). On poisonous and bitter growth (v. 18) see Jer 9:14; 23:15; Amos 5:7; 6:12. The complete destruction of Sodom, Gomorrah, Admah and Zeboiim (v. 23; cf. Gen 14:2, 8) was punishment for breach of covenant (Amos 4:11; Hos 11:8). All the nations will wonder, "Why has the LORD done this to this land?" (vv. 24-28; see Jer 16:10-13; 22:8-9).

The sentences in ch. 30 are formulated in the second person singular, but this chapter belongs to the plural layer in the time of the exile. "When all these things have happened to you" (v. 1); yes, these things have already happened. This chapter presupposes the destruction of Judah and Jerusalem in 587 B.C.E. and offers answers to the questions of whether and how the people of God can be restored. Israel can be restored if the people return to the Lord (vv. 2-5; see Jer 23:3; 29:13-14; 32:37-38). Moreover, it is the Lord who makes them return with all their hearts and with all their souls to the Lord (vv. 6, 10; see 2 Kings 23:25) and who will circumcise their hearts (v. 6; see 10:16; Jer 4:4; 9:24-25). We will be occupied with the word of the Lord, who will take delight in making us prosper (v. 9; cf. 28:63!) because the rule of the word of the Lord is restored. We may find here the gospel of Deuteronomy. The commandment is not too hard for us, nor is it too far away (v. 11) even if we are in exile. It is not in heaven, neither is it beyond the sea (vv. 12-13). The word of the Lord has already been uttered and it is in our mouths and in our hearts. If we are filled with God's word, God's will is actualized in us (v. 14). On the christological interpretation of this passage in Rom 10:6-8, see the introduction above. The lectionary understands that to remain close to the *torah* is to love one's neighbor. (This passage is read together with Luke 10:25-37 on the fifteenth Sunday of the year, Cycle C).

Before us the Lord has set blessings, namely life and prosperity, and curses, namely death and adversity (vv. 15, 19a; cf. 11:26-30; 27:12-13). The Lord cannot call to witness other deities and so calls upon heaven and earth and says to us before them that we are to choose life and obey the commandments of the Lord (vv. 16, 19b).

Appointment of Joshua (31:1-29)

The succession to the leadership of Israel requires the renewal of the covenant in the same way that the succession to the throne in Assyria required the renewal of the treaty, but the appointment of Joshua (31:1-8) reflects the crisis of the people of Israel that demanded a radical reinterpretation of the old principles. Deuteronomy constitutes the amplification and reinterpretation of the old principles represented by the decalogue (see the introduction above).

Moses wrote down "this *torah*" in a book and handed it over to the Levites. This book of the *torah* is to be recited as representative of the will of the Lord revealed through Moses before all the people every seventh year, in the year of remission (see 15:1), at the feast of Tabernacles (see 16:13), to make all the people know the *torah* (vv. 9-13; cf. 17:18-19). Nehemiah 8:13–10:40 may describe the procedure of the *torah* recital.

The Lord commissions Joshua in the tent of meeting (vv. 14-15, cf. Exod 33:7-11) and encourages him (v. 23; see vv. 7-8), but the Lord tells Moses that the people will soon betray their God and breach the covenant (vv. 16-21; see 6:10-15; 8:7-10). The Lord requires Moses to write a song to witness against the people (vv. 19, 21; see 32:1-43). Moses then calls heaven and earth to witness against the Levites (v. 28; 32:1) that they also will become rebellious toward the Lord (vv. 26-29).

The Song of Moses (31:30–32:44)

The Song of Moses (32:1-43) has in part the form of a lawsuit: summoning of witnesses (vv. 1-3), statement of the case (vv. 4-6), prosecution (vv. 7-14), indictment (vv. 15-18), judgment (vv. 19-25), but expanded with wisdom elements (vv. 1-2, 6-7, 19-20, 28-29). The song functions in this context, on the one hand, as a prophetic accusation against Israel, but on the other hand there is an important change between v. 38 and v. 39. The last part of the song expresses divine forbearance.

Moses appeals to heaven and earth as witnesses (v. 1; see 30:19) and claims that his teaching is to spread all over the earth (v. 2). Moses calls the Lord the Rock to praise God's justice and fidelity (v. 4). If Israel betrays God, God's fidelity declares Israel guilty (vv. 15, 18, 30-31, 37). The song describes the good action of the Lord and the close relation between the Lord and Israel: the Lord is our father who created us (v. 6). The Most High apportioned the nations, divided humankind, and fixed the boundaries of the peoples according to the number of the Israelites. The text from Qumran reads "the number of gods," and the LXX "the numbers of angels of God." These reflect the original meaning. But now the Most High is the Lord who possesses Israel as God's own people (vv. 8-9). The Lord led this people in the wilderness and gave them the fertile land (vv. 10-14), but Israel is foolish and has no understanding. "Jeshurun" (v. 15) is a title for Israel derived from the word "upright." It may be contrasted to the name "Jacob" ("swindler"). Jeshurun, however, abandoned God, the Rock of its salvation who made it (v. 15) and sought its salvation in another rock (vv. 17-18).

The Lord abandons the people (vv. 19-27). The people made the Lord jealous with what is no god, so the Lord makes Israel jealous with what is no people (v. 21). The Lord uses enemies as tools for punishment (vv. 22-27). Even Sheol cannot hide us before the wrath of the Lord (v. 22; see Amos 9:2). Enemies do not understand that their deities cannot save them from disaster, but harm them (vv. 28-35). The Lord punishes them (v. 35).

The Lord hands over Israel to what is no god (vv. 37-38), yet cannot stand to see Israel being destroyed. Israel learned in the exile that the Lord is only one God and jealous of all adversaries (5:7-10; Nah 1:2). "See now that I, even I, am he; there is no god beside me" (32:39; Isa 43:11, 13; 45:5-6, 18, 21-22; 48:12, and elsewhere). The sword of punishment is now turned to the enemies (vv. 40-43).

The Death of Moses: 32:48–34:12

Commandment to Ascend Mount Nebo (32:48-52)

The Lord commands Moses to ascend Mount Nebo (32:49), the top of which is called "Pisgah" (3:27). Moses must die there without entering into the promised land because of his sin

(vv. 50-52; see Num 20:1-13, but cf. Deut 3:26). On the death of Aaron, see Num 20:27-29.

Blessing of Moses (33:1-29)

A father imparts his blessing to his sons and daughters before death (see Gen 27:27-29; 49:1-28). So also Moses blesses each tribe (33:1-29). The blessing begins with the praise of the Lord who came from Sinai (not "Horeb": the origin of this song is not deuteronomistic), near Seir (Edom! cf. the very old song in Judg 5:4) and Paran as warrior (v. 2; see the comment on 1:2). On "Jeshurun" (v. 5), cf. 32:15. The conclusion of the song corresponds to this introduction: "There is none like God, O Jeshurun" (v. 26). The Lord appears there also as warrior. The status of tribes depends not on their own efforts, but on the power of God.

The blessing of each tribe is arranged from southeast to west and then northwards in a counter-clockwise order. The word of blessing reflects the present situation and status of each tribe. Reuben is on the brink of ruin (v. 6) and Simeon is no longer referred to. Even Judah is in crisis (v. 7), the crisis of isolation from other tribes. In the Pentateuchal tradition the Levites observed the word of the Lord even though their families were not in Massah or in Meribah (vv. 8-9), but in the wilderness of Sinai (Exod 32:26-29). They are responsible before the Lord for the oracle by lot ("Thummim and Urim" v. 8; see Exod 28:30 but not mentioned in deuteronomic law), for teaching the Law, and for sacrificing (v. 10; see 10:8; 17:9-11, 18-19). Benjamin resides in the protection ("shoulder" or "weapon") of God, namely in Jerusalem, the place chosen from the territory of Benjamin (see Josh 18:28). Joseph is the greatest tribe (vv. 16-17) and divided into two, Ephraim and Manasseh. These were the representative tribes of the northern kingdom. On God who dwells "in the bush" (v. 16) see Exod 3:2-6. A bull (v. 17) is a military image. Under the heading of Zebulun, Issachar is also mentioned (vv. 18-19; see Gen 30:18-20; 49:13-15). On the connection of Zebulun with the Mediterranean, see Gen 49:13. Verse 19 refers probably to Mount Tabor and the sanctuary on it (Judg 4:6; Hos 5:1). It was the Lord who expanded the territory of Gad into the Transjordan (vv. 20-21). Dan's military power is compared to a lion seeking livestock in Bashan (v. 22). The territory of Naphtali is called paradise because of its mild climate, so it is said that Naphtali is full of blessing (v. 23). The land of Asher is the most fertile in Israel (vv. 24-25; see Gen 49:20).

Death of Moses (34:1-12)

It is not very clear why Moses had to die without entering into the land: because of his own sin (Num 20:1-13; Deut 32:51-52), or because of the apostasy of the people (3:26). Nevertheless Moses had to die so that no one could win Moses over to one side or claim possession of Moses' authority (34:6, see the introduction above). Similarly Jesus had to ascend to heaven but the Holy Spirit came to us and brought us his word (John 16:5-15; Acts 1:8-9), for the letter kills, but the Spirit gives life (2 Cor 3:6).

Never since (save for Jesus Christ) has there arisen a prophet like Moses whom the Lord knew face to face (v. 10) and to whom the Lord spoke all of the *torah.* The *torah* is now written in Deuteronomy. Moses' role has been fulfilled.

BIBLIOGRAPHY

Clifford, Richard J. *Deuteronomy, with an Excursus on Covenant and Law.* Wilmington, Del.: Michael Glazier, 1982.

Crüsemann, Frank. *Torah. Theology and Social History of Old Testament Law.* Translated by Allan W. Mahnke. Minneapolis: Fortress, 1996.

Lohfink, Norbert. *Theology of the Pentateuch. Themes of the Priestly Narrative and Deuteronomy.* Translated by Linda M. Maloney. Minneapolis: Fortress, 1994.

Miller, Patrick M. *Deuteronomy.* Louisville: John Knox, 1990.

Noth, Martin. *The Deuteronomistic History.* JSOT.S 15. Sheffield: University of Sheffield, 1981.

Rad, Gerhard von. *Deuteronomy: A Commentary.* Translated by Dorothea Barton. Philadelphia: Westminster, 1966.

____. *Studies in Deuteronomy.* London: SCM Press, 1953.

Weinfeld, Moshe. *Deuteronomy and the Deuteronomic School.* Oxford: Clarendon Press, 1972.

_____. *Deuteronomy 1–11.* AB 5. New York: Doubleday, 1991.

Introduction to the Deuteronomistic History

Georg Braulik

Introduction: The Biblical Books Included in the Deuteronomistic History

The "deuteronomistic historical work" includes Deuteronomy, Joshua, Judges, 1 and 2 Samuel, 1 and 2 Kings, but not Ruth, which was first inserted into the canon of the Greek Bible, the Septuagint, between the books of Judges and 1 Samuel because the historical incidents it narrates fit there. However, its insertion disrupted an original connection established by the Hebrew canon. The succession of books in the LXX is also obscured by the other "historical" books that were added immediately after 2 Kings because they are of the historical genre, although in the older Hebrew canon they belonged to the third part of the canon, the "writings." In what follows, then, we will return to the older arrangement of the books, thereby focusing on an original literary collection that was not immediately perceptible even in the Hebrew canon.

What Justifies Us in Distinguishing the "Deuteronomistic Historical Work" from the "Former Prophets"?

In the Hebrew Bible there is a clear line of division between Deuteronomy and the book of Joshua, separating the "five books of Moses" (the Torah) from the former prophets. The books from Joshua to 2 Kings (except for Ruth) were understood within that canon as a *first* interpretation of the Torah, for according to the law concerning prophets in Deuteronomy 18 Israel will always have a prophet like Moses to interpret the Torah given once for all; that is, it will receive divine guidance through the ages. That is why these books are also called the "former *prophets.*" They show how Israel, in the promised land, sought to realize the Torah as its social order, ultimately in the form of a nation-state. The most illuminating figure that this group of books depicted, at its very center, was that of a "christ" (that is, an "anointed one")—David the king—and his kingdom. This experiment in realizing the Torah was doomed to failure; hence these are only the *"former* prophets."

They are contrasted within the Hebrew canon with a further group of books that immediately follows and makes a counter-statement: the *"latter* prophets." These books witness to a prophetic institution that expresses the collapse of the "state" experiment, the repentance in exile, and the promise of an entirely new and different action of God in Israel accompanied by a different realization of the Torah. In some sense this is a *second* interpretation of the Torah. Both interpretations are included in synagogue worship as selected texts comprising a second reading or *haftara* following the Torah. The Hebrew canon also includes other interpretations of the Torah that do not attain the status of *haftara.* That is, texts from that group can only be used for synagogue reading in special cases: these would include the five festival "rolls" or *megilloth.* The most important of these is the psalter because it most clearly expresses the hope for an "anointed one," a "christ" at the end-time. This group also includes the entirely new, strongly cult-oriented historical interpretation in Chronicles. The periods of history dealt with in Chronicles overlap for the most part with the epochs treated in the former prophets.

Because the historical presentations in the Hebrew canon are ultimately not at all interested in offering as complete information as possible about the past history of the world or of Israel, but instead intend to present a series of possibilities for commenting and interpreting the Torah, from the beginning of the Babylonian exile our Bible retains no continuing account of history covering the neo-Babylonian, Persian, Hellenistic, and Roman epochs. The experiments in Torah development made at that time apparently demanded types of literary treatment other than the historical if they were to say anything to the later community of the people of God. Of course this makes all the more interesting the kind of Torah interpretation that took the form of historical narrative: primarily, that is, the books to be discussed here.

It is true that in order to arrive at the original form of this historical presentation we have to go back even beyond the "former prophets." Only then will we encounter the "deuteronomistic historical work." That work existed as a connected literary reality even before the Pentateuch was brought together in the form in which we now have it. This is indicated by a number of narrative structures that begin within the framework of Deuteronomy and extend directly into the basic frame of the book of Joshua—for example, the description of the transfer of leadership in Israel from Moses to Joshua—but are also continued in the later books. Because Deuteronomy has influenced all these books we can speak of a "deuteronomistic" historical work. The common features include not only linguistic usage but also content, such as the worship of YHWH alone and observation of the Torah, structural concepts (e.g., the laws of history that lead to blessings or curses), and compositional schemata at various levels. When the Pentateuch was composed as the legal basis of the Temple community of Jerusalem/Judah existing within the Persian empire, Deuteronomy was accepted as the legal tradition that, as a program for historical depiction, had thus far constituted the beginning of that law.

With Deuteronomy as its concluding element, the Torah breaks off before the entry into the promised land. Everything is open. History had already begun twice at that point: once under Joshua, and again after the return from the Babylonian exile. What is laid down in the Torah could also unfold in the future, again and again, and in ever-new forms. What the deuteronomistic historical work described, following Deuteronomy, was now, in light of such new possibilities of development, only a kind of alternative picture that was already a tale of the past. Hence the Torah had a very different weight with respect to all the books that followed, and at this point the synagogal reading always begins again at the beginning. Christian interpretation and the liturgical order of the OT readings could learn a great deal from this precedence of the Torah over the other books of the OT, all of which are ultimately nothing but its interpretation.

At the same time the distinction of Deuteronomy at the canonical level and the revisions connected with it changed the text so little that even today we can see the books of the deuteronomistic historical work (from Deuteronomy to 2 Kings) as a literary unit. The central question is: Can the state take on the form of the people of God? To answer it, the time from the eve of the conquest of the land until its loss is described: from the last word of Moses before his death and the installation of his successor, Joshua, who is to conquer the land for Israel, to the fate of the last Davidic king, living in Babylonian captivity around 560 B.C.E.

The Structure of the "Former Prophets" Associated with Deuteronomy

The division of books plays an important role in shaping the canonical form of this body of text; this was not yet the case in the original deuteronomistic historical work. At the same time the separations between 1 and 2 Samuel on the one hand and 1 and 2 Kings on the other are due purely to the techniques of book production and are therefore of no importance. There thus are five books: Deuteronomy, Joshua, Judges, Samuel, and Kings—a "pentateuch." It is possible that the Torah's five-part structure was inspired by the already existing five-part deuteronomistic historical work.

The fundamental narrative structure of Deuteronomy depicts only the last days of Moses. The preceding history is described in retrospective narrative and brief references. The mass of material within the overall narrative consists of four speeches by Moses (chs. 1–4, 5–28, 29–32, 33).

His person not only shapes the book but is the prototype for all the prophets to come. According to the "place" of the action, Deuteronomy is still outside the land of promise. The next four books will take place within the land. Only at the end of the last one must Israel again quit its land.

Again in the book of Joshua the events are told in terms of a single person, the man Joshua. Still there are many more actions, persons, and constellations of events, and fewer speeches than in Deuteronomy. Joshua leads the entry into the land (chs. 1–12) by which Israel carries out the command of YHWH given in Deuteronomy, and he distributes the land among the tribes (chs. 13–21), thereby fulfilling the promise of YHWH that runs through Deuteronomy. At the end we find the farewell speech and death of Joshua (chs. 23–24).

The new book, Judges, that then begins (see chs. 1–2) spans a much longer period of time. It is shaped by the figures of "saviors" or "judges" whose stories the book tells, linking them into a chain of narratives. The individual narrative units run in a cycle announced at the beginning of the book: Israel's apostasy to other gods; punishment through enemies; YHWH sends a saving judge; protection against enemies as long as the judge lives; new apostasy from YHWH after the death of the judge (Judg 2:11–3:6). In the course of the book this cycle progressively collapses. At the end the people's existence without a state organization becomes a dead end. Beyond this, at the beginning of the next book (1 Samuel) the whole narrative cycle of the judges gives way to a single figure whose shadow stretches far into the period of the kings: Samuel.

Samuel is the last judge. 1 Samuel 7 tells how he saves Israel from the oppression of the Philistines. Only at this point do we find the concluding note about Samuel with which the period of the judges ends; the royal period begins with the people's demand for a king in 1 Samuel 8. In terms of content one would expect the book to end at this point, but the books are conceived in terms of individual figures. Samuel is such a figure; hence the story of his birth begins a new book.

The books of Samuel are oriented to three principal personalities: Samuel, Saul, and David. They sometimes act simultaneously or even together, but at least from 1 Samuel 13 onward interest is concentrated primarily on Saul, and from 2 Samuel 1 onward on David (whose death is narrated only in 1 Kings 2). The material relating to David can be divided in the sense of the book's form into two parts: David under the blessing (2 Samuel 2–8) and David under the curse (2 Samuel 9–24). The books of Samuel are framed by two psalms that clearly indicate the theme of this part of the historical work: the appearance of the kingdom and thus, because king equals "state," the new social shape of Israel in history. The two psalms are the thanksgiving song of Hannah (1 Samuel 2) and the thanksgiving song of David (2 Samuel 22) together with David's last words (2 Sam 23:1-7). In terms of the motifs, the two texts belong together and point to Nathan's promise in 2 Samuel 7: their proper theme is the messianic king. The books of Samuel are concluded with the composition found in 2 Samuel 21–24. The ascent of Solomon to the throne then inaugurates a new book.

In terms of content the books of Kings are divided into three parts: the story of Solomon (1 Kings 1–11) which, like that of David, is treated according to the schema of blessing (chs. 3–8) and guilt (chs. 9–11); the history of the kings of Israel and Judah to the end of the Northern Kingdom (1 Kings 12–2 Kings 17); the remaining history of the kings of Judah (2 Kings 18–25). The first two parts each end with a historical summary indicating a division. After the death of Solomon the narrative no longer focuses on a single personality but instead, as in the book of Judges, the phenomenon of a longer period of time reappears. However, there is not a repetitive cycle as in the case of the individual judges; instead the whole period of the kings is a single cycle drawn out to extraordinary length by the patience of God in view of God's promises. It reaches its negative high point not merely in oppression by enemies, but in the loss of the land that had been conquered under Joshua. With that the history breaks off, and it remains an open question whether God's mercy may again be experienced as had repeatedly happened during the shorter cycles of the time of the judges.

History of Research on the Time of Origin and Prior Stages of the "Deuteronomistic Historical Work"

(A) The scholarly father of the "deuteronomistic historical work" is Martin Noth. Before him there were three important attempts by scholars to explain and interpret these texts:

(1) The layers of the Pentateuch continue in a number of narrative threads into the books of Samuel and Kings (the thesis of Julius Wellhausen).

(2) Discoveries regarding the oldest, perhaps pre-literary forms of many narratives, especially in Joshua and Judges, contradict the possibility of such a continuation (exemplified by Albrecht Alt).

(3) There was a "deuteronomistic" edition (that is, connected to or influenced by Deuteronomy) from Joshua to Kings (posited in 1817 by W.M.L. de Wette). A. Kuenen (1861) showed that certain texts within the redactional framework of the books of Kings presuppose the Babylonian exile (1 Kings 9:1-9; 2 Kings 17:19-20; 20:17-18; 21:11-15; 22:15-20; 23:26-27; 24:2-4; 24:18–25:30) while others do not. He therefore distinguished between a pre-exilic editor who composed the books of Kings around 600 B.C.E. and an expanding and reinterpreting edition of the work at the time of the exile.

(B) Martin Noth (1943) made of the thus far rather vaguely understood "deuteronomistic" editors a single, genuine author. That author conceived his work so much as a whole and independent unit that the idea that he could have made ongoing use of Pentateuchal sources was no longer acceptable. The work was completed in Judea, not before the destruction of Jerusalem and shortly after the pardoning of King Jehoiachin by Evil-Merodach of Babylon in the year 561 B.C.E. as described at the end of the work. The deuteronomistic historical work was intended to show that the collapse of state and Temple was caused by the behavior of Israel during its national period, namely its continual disobedience to and apostasy from YHWH. It was a kind of justification of God, ending in wrath and to that extent containing no hope for the future.

Noth founded his theory of a *single* "deuteronomist" as author of the historical work primarily on four series of observations:

(1) the unique, stereotypical language throughout;

(2) the continual periodization and interpretation of the history of Israel through inserted speeches by important persons (Joshua at the beginning and end of the conquest of the land in Joshua 1 and 23; Samuel at the transition from the period of the judges to that of the kings in 1 Samuel 12; Solomon after the building of the Jerusalem Temple in 1 Kings 8) and through reflections by the "author" (listing of the conquered kings in Joshua 12; introduction to the history of the judges in Judges 2:11-23; fall of the Northern Kingdom in 2 Kings 17);

(3) a continuing chronological system (the key is found in 1 Kings 6:1: four hundred eighty years elapsed between the Exodus and the beginning of Solomon's construction of the Temple);

(4) the consistency of the supporting theological ideas.

Noth was only able to sustain his single deuteronomist either by explaining the relatively frequent dissonances in the text as discrepancies in source material that the author evaluated and incorporated or eliminating them by positing a relatively large number of later additions to the historical work. Later research chose to begin with these dissonances. The books of Kings were most frequently examined, followed by the books of Samuel.

(C) In spite of the skepticism in the major commentaries and introductory works, which appreciated the weight of previous research, Noth's theory was very quickly accepted throughout the world as the obvious frame of reference for the interpretation of these books. Since the 1960s the theory has been developed primarily in two forms ("layer" model and "block" model), later augmented by some "compromise" models. There is also a thesis that holds to Noth but surrenders the question of reconstructable sources and practically takes the books as historical fiction integrating many linguistic and material differences and composed in the post-exilic period. At present we are faced with a "polyphonic state of scholarship."

(1) Rudolf Smend (1971) and his "school" hold to Noth's unified work but posit a narrower scope and explain the dissonances (some of which had already been acknowledged by Noth) in terms of a number of re-editings of differing extent. The "deuteronomistic historian" (DtrH) composed the work as a whole, but it was greatly expanded by a "prophetic deuteronomist" (DtrP) and only properly outfitted with deuteronomistic theology by a number of "nomistic deuteronomists" (DtrN). In the latest works along these lines the number of sigla is almost inflationary.

In spite of many valuable individual observations, this trend in research has never sufficiently examined Noth's exilic dating of the oldest version of the entire work.

(2) Frank Moore Cross (1968) and his "school" posit the existence of two to four redactional blocks. They take their lead from a criticism by Gerhard von Rad correcting Noth's kerygma of hopelessness: YHWH's word was active not only to judge and destroy; in the promise to David that was constantly in process of fulfillment (2 Samuel 7) it acted also to save and forgive. Its steadily maintained messianism was not extinguished by the fall of Jerusalem (cf. 2 Kings 25:27-30). Cross considers both these analyses correct. In the deuteronomistic historical work there is apparently a tension between two kerygmata. He connects the kerygma of wrathful judgment and that of the hope that was not extinguished by the collapse of the state with the older proposal of two deuteronomistic redactions. The pre-exilic redaction was colored by the promise to David and climaxed in the figure and actions of Josiah (2 Kings 23:25); it did not expect a catastrophe. The second redaction reinterpreted and augmented this "triumphalistic" work after the destruction of Jerusalem in 586 B.C.E. and in light of that catastrophe. Its kerygma was what Noth first perceived. The Cross thesis does not simply return to positing two deuteronomistic redactions because (in agreement with Noth) for Cross and those who follow his lead the Josian deuteronomist (Dtr I) is the genuine author to a far greater degree than was the case for the scholars who wrote before Noth. The exilic deuteronomist (Dtr II) only created a new, edited version. The break in the redaction after 2 Kings 23:25 is evident from the fact that in 2 Kings 23:26–25:30 deuteronomistic phraseology is almost entirely absent.

(3) The result of the discussion of these two global theories has been that most scholars accept a pre-exilic deuteronomist but combine this initiative by Cross with some elements from the theories of the Smend school. In the opinion of the author of this article as well, we should reckon with a deuteronomistic historical writer in the last years of Josiah of Judah whose thoroughly "triumphalistic" work climaxed with this king. What materials were redacted in the process is uncertain. Perhaps there was a "prophetic history" from prophetic circles in the Northern Kingdom before this oldest layer of the deuteronomistic historical work. That would make a "DtrP" superfluous. There could also have been a preliminary version of the historical work from the time of Hezekiah. If the work of Dtr I did not extend from Deuteronomy 1 to 2 Kings 23 (which may be supported by a system of statements speaking of "bringing rest" and "*the* rest" of the Temple) the pre-exilic period would have seen the writing of a number of works on different epochs in somewhat the same style and spirit. Then there could have been a Deuteronomy–Joshua complex, for example the "deuteronomistic narrative of the conquest of the land" reconstructed by Norbert Lohfink, containing the basic elements of Deuteronomy 1 to Joshua 22 and legitimating the efforts of Josiah to extend his kingdom as well as his introduction of the deuteronomic law. Then came a book of the judges and a book of kings, probably already combined with a book of Samuel. In exile Dtr II would have combined these three works into a unit (if that had not already happened in the meantime), added the period between Josiah and the destruction of Jerusalem, but also made additions to Deuteronomy and in other strategically important places to interpret the collapse of the state as the result of the guilt of Judah and Jerusalem. Some other reworkings would have taken place at a later date, but probably not throughout the entire work. Thus Smend's "deuteronomistic nomist" would have inserted his commentary on the possession of the land and the destruction of its peoples, and obedience to the Law as its precondition, only in the books from Deuteronomy to Judges. Then still other minimal revisions would have been introduced in reaction to this, introducing a theology of pure grace, or a theology of repentance integrating grace and worthiness.

The Historical Work as a Source of Historical Information

The Special Character of Israel's Historical Writing

The most important formal elements in Israel's historical writing were already found in Hittite historiography; moreover, Israel's historical books resemble examples of Greek and late Babylonian historiography. From a theological point of view the gods of the surrounding nations reveal themselves, like YHWH, in historical events, in planned and goal-directed actions; they are moved by wrath, mercy, and justice. Nevertheless, Israel had a theology of history that was foreign to the ancient Near East; its norm was the nature of YHWH, YHWH's demand for exclusive allegiance, and Israel's experience of exodus. That is why only the OT attaches such an extensive and progressive chain of events to one and the same God. Finally, it is also unusual that in Israel's historical narratives it is usually the "people" that is the principal actor in history, often even when the subject is the history of the royal house.

The Relationship of the Former Prophets to the History and Its Sources

The authors of the former prophets, as we know, neither invented nor freely formulated the story from Joshua to the fall of Jerusalem; they relied on "sources," copied them out, and in many cases simply incorporated them in their work. Of course those sources stem almost exclusively from the national period. The deuteronomistic historical work would be unimaginable without the social constitution of a state that, in a sense, provided the raw material for this type of historical writing. Therefore the "historical" description of "pre"-national Israel is less "historical" in our sense. For example, Israel's "conquest of the land" is not to be imagined as taking place in the way described in the book of Joshua. In the post-exilic period a continuing historical narrative again breaks off.

The book of Joshua contains, among other things, individual etiological narratives and lists with the names of places and boundaries; the book of Judges incorporates heroic sagas. With regard to the sources for the books of Samuel and Kings that deal with the state but were not yet composed with an eye to a comprehensive history, we can distinguish three types:

(1) Documents needed for the independent functioning of a state; these would have been available in administrative archives. They would include, for example, lists of the highest civil servants (1 Kings 4:1-6) or the description of the technical details of the new governmental regulation of the tribal lands under the "provincial order" established by Solomon (1 Kings 4:7-19), probably also intended for proclamation. There would also be annals or general descriptions with the character of annals for the instruction of successive generations of civil servants and for a variety of state and governmental acts: hence the "chronicle" (literally "description of the events of the days," that is, the years of the reign) "of Solomon" (1 Kings 11:41); the "chronicle of the kings of Israel" (1 Kings 14:19) and the "chronicle of the kings of Judah" (1 Kings 14:29). Most of the information edited into the books of Kings probably stems from these sources. Hence the books of Kings form an important historical source for us. Also important for the development of the state were texts that recorded an event foundational to the state or institution. The genre of "royal novels" in Egypt served that purpose. They could have provided the model for the "oracle of Nathan" in 2 Samuel 7. Another text of related function would be the basic document underlying 2 Kings 22–23 on the discovery of the book of the Torah and the oath sworn by king and people in the eighteenth year of Josiah of Judah (622/21 B.C.E.). However, the account of the making of the covenant that was edited at that point may already belong to the next category.

(2) Texts from the realm of state propaganda. These are of the highest literary quality, perhaps the summit of biblical narrative. They include the "ark narrative" in 1 Sam 4:1–7:1; 2 Sam 6:2-23 that legitimated the Davidic state's transfer of Israel's center from central Palestine to Jerusalem. Also among these is the ancient narrative of the "story of the rise of David" (1 Sam 16:14–2 Sam 5:10) describing Saul's guilt and failure, David's innocence and God-given success, but also placing YHWH's "anointed" in a sacral sphere of immediate contact with God and, by placing a taboo on injury to him, extending the same taboo to the state he represented. The state was also served by what is probably the most magnificent major literary narrative, the "history of the succession to the throne" (2 Samuel 9–20; 1 Kings 1–2) that, although true to the king and to a certain extent "internal to the court" nevertheless used history to criticize Solomon.

(3) Texts from non-political contexts that, despite their critical attitude, still regarded the state as the natural framework for all social life. Here we find a rather large block of more or less popular narratives, often sagas and legends, most of them centering on a prophet (Samuel in 1

Samuel 1–3, Elijah and Elisha in 1 Kings 17–2 Kings 8; Isaiah in 2 Kings 19–20).

The horizon of the sources that were the building blocks of the deuteronomistic historical work was the state as solution to social problems. But the perspective from which, in its final form, it looked back at the state had been altered by the national collapse. Hence the deuteronomistic redaction subjected its material to a representational tendency that was rather more critical of the state than otherwise.

The Historical Work as Theological Proclamation

The final, exilic authors of the deuteronomistic history could only look back with the rage of those who have been duped at the time when Israel existed as a nation and then collapsed as a political state. Their work was a "look back in anger at the state" (Norbert Lohfink). Nevertheless, their ultimate interest is not in human anger, but in the divine wrath under which Israel had fallen. They thus attempted to unlock the mystery of this divine wrath that encompassed them. "Why has the LORD done thus to this land? What caused this great display of anger?" (Deut 29:24). That was the ultimate question that occupied these historians. The answer lay in Israel's apostasy to other gods and in the sins of its kings who led it astray into foreign cults. This line of thought runs through the redaction of the entire complex of books. Its clearest expression is found in two phrases used by the deuteronomistic historical work to refer to divine wrath: the "anger formula" ("the anger of YHWH was kindled against . . ." or "YHWH grew angry") and the "provocation formula" (some person, or Israel, "provoked YHWH"). There is talk about divine anger in all the books of the historical work, but it is especially frequent in Deuteronomy and the books of Kings; wrath is threatened at the beginning, and the end describes its appearance. The anger formula is typically found at climactic points in formulaic descriptions of Israel's apostasy from YHWH (for example, in Judg 10:6-7). In practice it means that the covenant has been broken (e.g., Deut 29:24-25; Josh 23:16; Judg 2:20; 2 Kings 17:15-18), and it is always combined with the notice that God will judge and punish. The provocation formula is not necessarily associated with divine punishment. The typical context for it is judgment on a king (as in 1 Kings 16:26; 22:53; 2 Kings 21:6). This theme of anger supports Martin Noth's interpretation of the historical work: it is a justification of God in light of the destruction of Israel.

Everything promised about the anger of God has been fulfilled. Then is this wrathful retrospect on a history gone awry—as preserved by the former prophets as a whole and judged in light of its end—the word that remains normative? The deuteronomistic historical work is planned in such a way that Moses and Samuel are the real interpreters of history. Samuel (in 1 Samuel 8 and 12; cf. the law for kings in Deut 17:14-20) interprets the establishment of the state as a road to catastrophe from the very beginning, even though this was one possible form that Israelite society might have assumed, had it obeyed the Torah. Thus the only prophecy for the future going beyond 2 Kings and not yet accomplished remains that of Moses at the beginning of the work, in Deuteronomy 4 and 30 (and in the song of Moses in Deuteronomy 32). These texts are among the last revisions and they quote words of Moses in which he develops the future of Israel in God's name. They therefore have a high degree of authority. Their perspective includes not only decline and exile, but also the conversion of Israel (Deut 4:23-31), its return, and the circumcision of its heart by God so that it will at last be able to keep God's commandment of love and the entire social order of Deuteronomy (Deut 30:1-10). With this incomparably wise and just (deuteronomic) Torah, Israel can be God's community even without a king or state. It will not even need a Temple because through the Torah YHWH is close to Israel to lend aid whenever and wherever it calls on its God (Deut 4:6-8).

The entire work with its proclamation of wrath should be read in light of texts like these. This is all the more obvious in the canon as we have it because Deuteronomy is now part of the Pentateuch and therefore has a still higher canonical status.

In this history we find no glorification of the state. In fact, the deuteronomistic historical work takes a critical stance toward the marriage of the people of God with a national state and at the end of the work develops the utopia of a people of God as a contrast society without political organization (unlike the societies organized as political units or states). In light of this we may ask how we should judge the major developments in Christian and Jewish history—from the theocratic Byzantine state through the Christian Middle Ages to the modern state of Israel as a quasi-theological entity. But also, how should we judge the initiatives of some kinds of "Christian social teaching" and theologies of liberation in light of the experiences of Israel as described in the deuteronomistic historical work?

Joshua

Edesio Sánchez Cetina

FIRST READING

To begin with: When you hear or read the name Joshua, what ideas or themes does the name evoke? I am, of course, referring to the book of Joshua and its protagonist. For most of us Joshua may be synonymous with Jericho and its tumbling walls. In many cases this immediate connection is due to the popularity of this account in ecclesiastical hymnology and in catechesis or Christian instruction. For others Joshua is the place to read the account of this extraordinary, astronomical phenomenon of the longest day in the history of the planet Earth. And for others still, perhaps a minority, Joshua is an obligatory theme in youth encounters. In the last case Joshua becomes a model for young Christians: he is a youth who puts all his trust in God, who eagerly studies the word and puts it into practice.

Joshua is obviously much more than all this. I suppose that you recall passages such as Achan's sin or the crossing of the Jordan River. You may also remember the name of Rahab, the prostitute who hid the spies. If you are familiar with several or all of these themes we will be starting on solid ground. For you, at least, Joshua is not the "great stranger." However, knowing isolated texts without being familiar with the entire book is like looking at the loose pieces of a jigsaw puzzle. It is necessary to have the complete picture in mind. And since we are speaking of puzzles I think it is important to point out the similarity that exists between reading Joshua and the process of solving a puzzle. In my family, every time we set up a puzzle we always start with the frame. It is only when the four sides have been set up that we continue with the rest. In order to have a beneficial and coherent reading of the book of Joshua it seems appropriate to do something similar, namely to begin with the frame. So I invite you to start by reading chs. 1 and 23–24. These passages will help you in placing the other parts of the book in the proper perspective. In addition to these texts it would also be useful to devote some time to 21:43-45 and to keep these lines in mind as you read the rest of the book, considering the following outline.

The Book as a Whole

In the first place the book of Joshua presents a theological framework on the basis of which the total message of the book can be understood. This theological framework is made up of chs. 1 and 22–24. These chapters, along with some passages interwoven in the body of the book (for example chs. 12; 21:43–22:6; 23), present the theological viewpoint of the deuteronomic author. The Deuteronomist is responsible for compiling and writing the history of Israel as it is narrated in the books of Deuteronomy, Joshua, Judges, 1 and 2 Samuel, and 1 and 2 Kings.

The two most important and extensive sections of the book, chs. 2–12 and 13–21, are centered within this theological framework. The first part focuses on the struggle for the land and the second on the division and distribution of the land. The first section is subdivided as follows: chs. 2 to 8, the conquest of several cities; chs. 10

and 11, the military campaigns in the two important regions of Canaan, the southern and the northern areas. In the middle there is a "hinge" episode (ch. 9) and at the end (ch. 12) the list of the kings conquered by the two important leaders of Israel: Moses (12:1-6) and Joshua (12:7-24). The second section (chs. 13 to 21) is subdivided as follows: 13:1-7, the introduction of the section; 13:8-33, the division of the land east of the Jordan; chs. 14 to 21, the division of the land west of the Jordan (a: chs. 14–15, the share of Judah; b: chs. 16–17, the share of the tribes of Joseph; c: chs. 18–19, the share of the remaining tribes; d: chs. 20-21, the cities of refuge and the cities for the tribe of Levi).

The book presents a varied collection of accounts of a cultic and etiological nature, lists of cities, and descriptions of tribal boundaries. It also contains some accounts that are considered sagas and a series of exhortations or parenetic sections typical of the deuteronomic author. We find at least one poetic passage and several legendary sections.

As a whole the book of Joshua presents a real tension between what God wants—a plan supported by the deuteronomic author—and the successes and failures of the "covenantal" people (from the Hebrew *berit* = covenant). Here is the key to understanding the contradictory appeals in the book. In the middle of the divine plan and what is "attained" by the people we find the key element of Joshua's theological teaching: fidelity to the word of God and to God's covenant. The tensions between obeying and failing to obey, both in terms of the total conquest of the land and its distribution, correspond to this theological principle whose goal is not historical memory *per se* but rather the parenesis, the teaching to the real audience of the book called to obey in a new historical situation, namely the context of Josiah's reform or the exilic community. It is also possible to speak of a tension between divine justice and divine grace. This tension is better understood when we place it against the backdrop of the theme of the privileged place that the poor, the marginalized, and the oppressed have in the eyes of God. The integration of Rahab in God's people and the rejection of Achan indicate not only obedience or disobedience to the word of God but also the way in which God's grace works. God shows this grace by making an immigrant foreigner, vulnerable and marginalized, a member of God's people, while at the same time God rejects those who have and want to have more simply out of the desire to become rich.

The relation between direct discourse (the words spoken by the Lord and by Joshua) and indirect discourse (the narrative that situates what is spoken by the protagonists in context) is one of the important clues to recognizing the theological nature of the book: YHWH and YHWH's spokesman, Joshua, present the requirements of the Law. The accounts involving the people show how they observed or failed to observe these requirements.

In general the book indicates that the three main protagonists of the book—YHWH, Joshua, and the people—acted in accordance with the stipulations found in the Book of the Law of Moses, requirements that were dictated by God through Moses. The strongest voice heard in Joshua is that calling for observance of the fundamental theological principles of Deuteronomy: one God, one Law, one people, and one land. Hence, just as in the book of Deuteronomy, the concept of totality is important in this book. At the beginning and end of the book the Lord, Joshua, and the people unite to profess this shared commitment to unity.

In terms of the foregoing, the following key theological themes of Joshua have to be considered: obedience to the word of God, the gift of the land, and leadership. All of them are intimately related by the unifying principle of the covenant: the Lord fulfills the divine promises because the people fulfill their part in their commitment to the covenant. For the people to do their part they need a leader who lives according to God's will and who deserves to be obeyed and emulated. Moses had fulfilled such requirements, and Joshua's leadership appears as a carbon copy of that of Moses. If the people and their leader work as one, God fulfills the promise to give the land to the people of God's choosing. As in Deuteronomy, so in Joshua the land is a vital theme. Some even call it the real protagonist of the book. The Lord has promised the land to the people's ancestors, has given it to the people, and has fought for it. The people will have to conquer and occupy it and live there forever. Their remaining in the land depends on the obedience and the fidelity of the people to the word of God: the Law of the Covenant.

Both Joshua and Deuteronomy present the theme of the land as a gift from God, not as a commodity or a source of riches. The Hebrew people are stewards of the land; they do not own it. The land constitutes an indissoluble part of being Hebrew. For the deuteronomic author possessing the land is strongly bound to fulfilling the stipulations of the covenant. When Israel broke the covenant it lost the land. Yet both Joshua and Deuteronomy present the theme of the land in conjunction with the theme of divine grace. The people who receive the gift of the land are represented by vulnerable foreigners, like Rahab and the Gibeonites, that is to say, people who do not possess anything. In Joshua the people who receive the land from God are not the powerful, the kings or the giants. It is important to observe that from ch. 13 on the land is distributed *according to families* rather than in terms of monetary capacity or in terms of social, military, or political position. All the members of the covenant people receive the possibility of having their share of land, their inheritance, as a family patrimony.

Original Historical Contexts

Although Joshua seems to be a book addressed to a community ready to take possession of the Promised Land for the first time, its first readers were the deuteronomic communities who read or listened to the message of the book during at least two periods of history: the time of the reform of King Josiah and the exile. [For a more detailed account of what follows, see also "Introduction to the Deuteronomistic History."] The sections that show the people and their leader in harmony with the deuteronomic principles probably correspond to the first deuteronomic writing. Joshua and Josiah appear as parallel figures: they both live in accordance with the Law of Moses (the book of Deuteronomy), they both celebrate the Passover, and they both consider the poor and the marginalized as objects of the divine justice and grace (cf. Jer 22:15-16 in the case of Josiah). The book of Joshua presents to that first audience the challenge of fidelity to the covenant and its principles, giving up other gods and focusing on a single place of worship. For that community the theme of the land is that of something that can be lost. In order to keep the land the people will have to emulate their leader, King Josiah.

For the community of the exile Joshua's message is like being drenched by a bucket of water. The people have lost the land and live the same experience as the people who had not yet possessed the land. In the book of Joshua the exilic community had the challenge to unite with a leader like Joshua or Moses. For that to happen they had to discover the theological core of Deuteronomy in Joshua: total fidelity to the Lord as the only God, and social justice. In fact, Joshua not only exhorts the people to abandon other gods and to follow YHWH alone; again and again Joshua reminds them that the model of Israel is to be found in Rahab, the Gibeonites, and the Levites. Israel's struggles against the pagan nations were not those of two imperial and military powers but instead those of a nation that had been enslaved and marginalized against kingdoms and giants seeking to perpetuate a society in which a few controlled the land and the power and most of the others lived unprotected in rural stretches of land as peasants and paid employees of those who were living under the protection of the city-states. To clarify this theme it is worth looking at what is presented in the exposition of Joshua 2 in the Second Reading below.

Readers may be surprised that not much emphasis, either here or in the rest of this commentary, is placed on the specifically historical and archaeological aspects that writers and readers of Joshua have found so interesting in the past. In fact, studies of historiography and archaeology related to Joshua are increasingly more cautious. Neither the strictly biblical material nor the contributions of archaeology have been able to present a clear and consistent picture of the historical period to which this book seeks to refer. An attentive reading of Joshua and a careful study of the contributions of archaeology will quickly show that the information provided in Joshua is more closely bound to a parenetic, theological intention than to the objective reports of modern historians.

What was said in the previous paragraph does not deny the fact that most of the accounts in Joshua have a historical foundation. The specific reality of Israel as an established nation in Palestine prevents us from thinking otherwise. No one denies the *what;* the major problems are the *how* and the *when.* Contemporary biblical studies tend to lean to the beginning of the thirteenth century B.C.E. as the date for the conquest or occupation of the Promised Land. There are at least three or four hypotheses concerning the way the occupation was carried out: a rapid and violent military conquest, a slow and peaceful occupation, a peasants' revolution, or the evolution of the nation starting with a group of tribes until it formed the kingdom of Israel.

In this work I have chosen to follow the sociological approach that is supported by several authors from different viewpoints. The struggles of the Lord for Israel are the decision of the God of the Exodus to grant the land of Canaan which was in the hands of monarchical and oppressive powers to a group of slaves liberated from Egypt and also to those masses of peasants and salaried people who were living outside the walled cities and were at the mercy of those urban elites. As we have already mentioned several times, in the book of Joshua it is Rahab and the Gibeonites who are the concrete models of God's people.

Canonical Intertextuality

Joshua appears as a work belonging to two periods or places in the OT canon. On the one hand it seems to have an undeniable place after the first part of the Bible known as the Pentateuch or the Law of Moses since its content completes the picture started in Genesis: the promise of the land (Genesis), the obstacles to taking possession of the land (the famine reported in Genesis, the oppression in Egypt narrated in Exodus), the Exodus (related in Exodus), the march through the wilderness and the covenant (narrated in Exodus, Leviticus, Numbers, and Deuteronomy) and entering and possessing the Promised Land (Joshua). From that perspective the Pentateuch is actually a "Hexateuch." According to this approach, outlined by Gerhard von Rad in particular, Joshua concludes a thematic unit made up of six books.

On the other hand Joshua has its place within what has been called deuteronomic history ever since Martin Noth. The deuteronomic history is a monumental work comprising the books of Deuteronomy, Joshua, Judges, 1 and 2 Samuel, and 1 and 2 Kings. Because of its position immediately following Deuteronomy, Joshua is a key work striving to show how the theory, present in Deuteronomy, becomes reality. Seen as a whole, Joshua is a song to total obedience to the Lord and a concrete confirmation of the theological principles of Deuteronomy. Thus Joshua attempts to show a marked contrast with the book of Judges, an account that forcefully shows a period of the history of Israel during which the covenant was gradually broken and all the theological foundations of Deuteronomy were taken apart. With Joshua the teaching of the OT has a document demonstrating that it is possible to live according to God's will in spite of the human flaws that are acknowledged in the book itself.

Finally, the book of Joshua is linked with the NT teaching in the sense that it offers us a figure of Jesus Christ. Not just in name but also in their lives and deeds, Joshua and Jesus offer parallel examples. Joshua, the "savior," is like Jesus, the liberator and spokesman of the will of God. In this aspect both recall the great figure of Moses. As the precursor of Josiah, Joshua reflects the royal image that Jesus also projected. Because he was the king who raised the banner of Joshua, Josiah better than anyone else projected the image of the ideal king: David. Joshua and Jesus are both responsible for leading God's people to their "rest" in the Promised Land.

SECOND READING

Theological Framework: 1:1-18

This chapter serves as the introduction to the entire book. With chs. 22 to 24 it forms a theological framework that directs the message of the whole book and of every section.

Joshua 1 is permeated by deuteronomic theological principles. The leader who succeeds Moses as well as the people must live in accordance with the guidelines of the word of God, the Book of the Law of Moses (6:24; 10:12-13; 28:1-2; 29:9; 31:12-13; cf. Pss 1:2; 119:165; Ezra 7:10). Obedience to the word of God is accompanied by success and prosperity. In Deuteronomy the reward is translated into obtaining the Promised Land and remaining there. The deuteronomic passages, which deal with the end of the two kingdoms, do point out the other side of the coin: disobedience to the divine word is equivalent to losing the land, exile and death (2 Kings 17:14-23; 18:11-12; 21:8-15).

Notice the number of times the word "land" and its cognates are found and also the verbs and the interaction of actor and recipient. We find the verb "give" nearly every time the word "land" is mentioned, and in every case except two God is the subject of the action. God is the principal subject of the giving of the land to the people. This is where the special theological emphasis of the book of Joshua emerges. The possession of the land depends essentially upon God who takes the initiative, giving it to the people; this corresponds to God's personal faithfulness to the divine word: ". . . that I swore to their ancestors to give them" (v. 6). Verses 3-5 are an obvious echo of Deut 11:24-25, thereby indicating the connection between Deuteronomy and Joshua as promise and fulfillment.

In order to possess the land and keep it forever, the people and their leader are only asked to be faithful and to obey the Book of the Law of Moses. God's gift of the land and obedience to God and God's word are key elements of the covenant between YHWH and Israel. This is why deuteronomic history is presented conditionally (cf. Deut 30:20). The successful conclusion of history depends on the fulfillment of the divine promises and on the obedience and fidelity of the people.

Here the themes of the divine word and of the land are joined with the theme of leadership. The fidelity of the people and the possibility for them to occupy the land and remain there depend on the quality of their leader. The leader's ministry is defined by God's presence in his life, being "strong and very courageous" (vv. 6, 7, 18; cf. Deut 1:38; 3:28; 31:7-8) and by his keeping and observing the Law of Moses (vv. 7-8). The people carry out the divine command through their leader's word: "All that you have commanded us we will do" (v. 16).

In this clearly deuteronomic chapter leadership is defined in terms of Moses. Joshua's leadership is a prolongation of that of Moses, whom Joshua 1 and the rest of the book acknowledge as "the servant of the Lord," *ʿebed YHWH* 8:31, 33; 11:12, 15; 16:6; 13:8; 14:7; 18:7; 22:2, 4, 5). It is only in 24:29, at the end of the book, that Joshua is called "the servant *(ʿebed)* of YHWH." In 1:1 he is called "Moses' assistant" *(meshārēt)*. Just as the Lord had been with Moses (vv. 5, 17; cf. Exod 3:12; Josh 3:7), so will God be with Joshua (vv. 5, 9, 17; cf. 6:27). The people are to obey Joshua just as they obeyed Moses. Like Moses (1:14-15; 13:8; 14:3) Joshua will distribute the land to the tribes (1:6; 13:6-7) and he will guide the people across the waters (v. 2). (See the section on the theme of leadership in the First Reading above.)

The structure of the chapter shows the order of authority by way of three direct discourses: (a) vv. 2-9, commands of the Lord to Joshua and definition of his vocation as a leader; (b) vv. 11-15, commands of Joshua to the people and definition of their task; (c) vv. 16-18, response of the people who promise to submit to Joshua's authority. In this chapter as a whole we also find a threefold commitment (on the part of God, Joshua, and the people) to bring the task of taking possession of the land to a successful conclusion.

The word "all" *(kol),* commonly used in Deuteronomy and in deuteronomic literature, reflects the theological aspect of totality and unity prevalent in the deuteronomic author. We find the expressions "all this people" (vv. 2, 14), "all the law" (vv. 7, 8, 16-18), and "that you may be successful wherever you go" (vv. 7-8).

Verses 5-9 reflect the teaching of Deut 17:18-20, which points to the obligation of the king to observe the law of Moses (cf. 1 Kings 2:2-4; 9:1-9). Thus we have the beginning of a series of suggestions depicting Joshua as a royal figure. According to several biblicists this figure is more clearly concretized in the person of King Josiah (compare Josh 8:30-35 with 2 Kings 23:1-3; Josh 1:7 with 2 Kings 22:2; Josh 5:10-12 with 2 Kings 23:21-23). Josiah was the king during whose reign, in my opinion, the first great deuteronomic redaction of Joshua was achieved.

Verses 1-9 have a strong sapiential flavor and reflect a literary structure characteristic of deuteronomic texts concerning a mission: (a) exhortation to be strong and steadfast; (b) description of the mission; (c) promise of divine assistance.

Verses 3-4 deal with the extent and boundaries of the Promised Land. Here and in other parts of the book the limits and boundaries correspond to a theological and pastoral perspective rather than to historically verifiable geographical criteria. We are almost certain that the geographical boundaries mentioned in the book of Joshua reflect the geography of the time of David and Solomon rather than that of the specific period of the conquest.

In this chapter, especially in vv. 2-9, we have the key elements that serve to subdivide the book: the occupation of the land west of the Jordan (vv. 3-5 correspond to chs. 2–12) and the distribution of that land (vv. 6-9, corresponding to chs. 13–21); the theme of fidelity to the Lord and the divine word is found in vv. 7-8 (corresponding especially to the last three chapters of the book, 22–24). The deuteronomic character of Joshua 1 is also underscored by the quotations from Deuteronomy in this chapter: vv. 3-5 = Deut 11:24-25; v. 4 = Deut 1:7; v. 5 = Deut 7:24; vv. 5, 6, 9 = Deut 31:6-8, 23; vv. 7-9 = Deut 17:14-20.

The Struggle for the Land: Joshua 2–12

In these chapters we first (in chs. 2–8) have accounts of the conquest of several cities; in the second part (chs. 10–11) the military campaigns in the two major areas of Canaan, the south and the north. In the middle we find a "hinge" episode (ch. 9) and at the end (ch. 12) the list of the kings conquered by the two major leaders of Israel: Moses (12:1-6) and Joshua (12:7-24). In chs. 2–12 YHWH is in fact the subject of the action: God is the one who gives and achieves the victory. Joshua will be the most prominent subject in chs. 13–22.

Rahab, a Foreigner, is the Model of a True Member of God's People (2:1-24)

Rahab? Is this the woman who appears in Jesus' genealogy (Matt 1:4)? It cannot be! A prostitute as a member of the people of the covenant, of God's royal realm, and in the genealogy of Jesus? In fact Joshua 2 (with Josh 6:17-25) relates the story of a morally despicable and socially marginalized woman who, through her courage and faith, obtains her own salvation and that of her family. Moreover, she becomes a heroine of faith and an everlasting testimony of salvation (Matt 1:5; Heb 11:31; Jas 2:25).

In this account several elements are worthy of our attention. In the first place it is surprising to observe that the section of accounts (chs. 2–12) begins with Rahab's story. The history of the conquest starts in Joshua 2 and with this story the theological and redactional guideline of the book is established. In this way Rahab—a woman and a foreigner, marginalized in society and by the Law (she is undoubtedly the OT counterpart of the Samaritan woman of John 4:5-42)—is presented as the prototype of the true member of the Lord's beritic people. The place of Rahab's story points out to us that all that is said about membership in God's people has to be considered in terms of that woman's figure.

In the second place Rahab's story has a great deal to tell us about the theology of the book of Joshua, the theological premises of deuteronomic history, the biblical concept of conquering a pagan land, and Israel's mission to the nations. Let us examine this on the basis of the following questions: Who is the enemy here? Who are the people on God's side who become the protagonists of the final part of the Exodus? Who are the people forming the *locus* of God's mission?

Those who form part of God's true people should not be defined on the basis of race, ethnicity, or blood. This means that the "clash" between Israel and Canaan is not the confrontation of two ethnic groups but rather the collision of a group of slaves liberated from Egypt and a group of socially and economically marginalized people with the landowners and the powerful of the city-states. The studies of George Mendenhall, Norman Gottwald, Walter Brueggemann, and others help us to understand that when the Bible speaks of the Canaanites it is referring to "those who are involved in social practices considered hostile by Israel's beritic vision. . . . The Canaanites form the 'urban elite' which controls the economy and enjoys a powerful political privilege to the detriment of the 'peasants' who produce the food and who define themselves as 'Israelites'" (Brueggemann, *Social Reading of the Old Testament* 49).

Rahab the prostitute represents the group of the marginalized who "were feeding and sustaining" the rich and powerful who were living under the protection of the great walls of the city-states. Gottwald says: ". . . prostitutes were one of several groups of marginalized occupations whose services were highly appreciated. However, because of the degrading nature of their work and the social taboos, codes and conventions, they carried the stigma of scapegoats and, as a result, their working conditions were poverty and marginalization. Among the groups of marginal people in ancient cities, we have . . . slaves, saddlers, butchers, barbers, midwives, prostitutes, buffoons, lepers . . ." (*Tribes of Yahweh* 557). It would not be an exaggeration to conclude that Rahab had to work as a prostitute in order to provide food and shelter for her family, just as is happening in several Latin American nations.

In the third place, if we ask the question concerning mission we will be able to say that the inclusion of "outsiders" in the midst of the beritic people has something to do first of all with God's "favorite people." Israel's first missionary concern involves those who, like Israel itself, have shared experiences of slavery, marginalization, vulnerability, and poverty. Rahab and her family find the doors of the kingdom wide open because their situation of helplessness makes them place all their trust in the Lord, the God of the poor and of the children.

Rahab's action and declaration not only correspond to the fact that she belonged to a group opposed to the powerful of Jericho. The text indicates that she acknowledged YHWH as her God (Josh 2:11-13). As she emerges from her vulnerable situation Rahab's trust in the Lord saves her from death. With regard to this it is interesting to look at the concentric structure in Josh 2:8-11. In the outer circles we have two statements by Rahab ("I know that the LORD has given you the land," v. 8; "the LORD . . . is indeed God in heaven above and on earth below," v. 11). In the intermediate circles the inhabitants or "rulers" *(yashab)* of the city are said to be melting in fear. And in the central circle we find the statement of the Exodus: "The LORD dried up the water of the Red Sea . . . when you came out of Egypt" (v. 10). In this way Rahab's professions of faith are in union with her faith in the God of the Exodus. The salvation of Rahab and her family is seen as a new Exodus. The action against Jericho is qualified as an exodus action in the same way as Israel's liberation from Egypt.

Like the Samaritan woman of John 4 and the Syro-Phoenician woman of Matthew 15, because of her faith Rahab earned her place among the beritic people and she shows God's radical mission in favor of the dispossessed. To the chagrin of many, Rahab becomes the ancestor of the Messiah and the only woman in the list of the heroes of faith in Heb 11:31 and Jas 2:25.

Here we also observe that salvation history has a few "detours" that teach God's people to remain open to divine surprises. Many "outsiders" are key instruments in God's salvific plan.

Liturgical Games, Not War Games (3:1–5:15)

In these three chapters we find a narrative whole that is highly liturgical. The word "priests" and the expression "the ark of the covenant" are used over and over in ch. 3. In ch. 4 there is a constant repetition of the term "stones" and for the first time in the book there is a mention of "Gilgal," the first important religious center of Israel where the stones will serve as a monument for the historical memory of the people. This is also the place where circumcision (5:2-9) and the Passover (5:10-12) will be celebrated. In both chs. 3 and 4 we find a major interaction between the actions of "passing," "crossing," and "standing still." The immobility and steadfastness of the priests and the ark of the covenant assure the people's passage and crossing. Even the date when the Jordan was crossed stresses the liturgical aspect of this unit (Josh 4:19; cf. Exod 12:3). Chapter 5 presents the liturgical actions of circumcision, the Passover, and Joshua's consecration in three stages.

All these chapters, situated prior to the conquest of Jericho (Joshua 6) and of Ai (Joshua 8), are making a powerful theological statement: the wars are the Lord's, the triumphs are the Lord's, and the war spoils belong to YHWH.

Chapters 3 and 4 should be read as one literary theological unit. Both combine discourses and narratives whose central theme is the crossing of the Jordan and the liturgical actions connected with that crossing. In the texts of both chapters we find deeds that seem to be out of context (e.g., 3:12) or already evoked, repeating actions that have already taken place before (e.g., 3:17 = 4:10-11). The actions and the liturgical elements present here form part of the semantics of holy war (Deut 20:1-20; 23:9-14; 1 Sam 21:4-6). This may explain the reason why the "officers" *(hashoterim)* appear commanding the people in 3:2-5 (cf. Deut 20:5).

In this blend of discourses and actions we observe the connection between order and obedience. The speaker, normally the one exercising authority, gives the order and the subordinate obeys: Joshua gives the priests the order to take up the ark and pass in front of the people and the priests obey (3:6). God gives the order to Joshua and he carries it out (3:8-9; 4:1-4; 4:10; 4:15-17). Joshua gives the order to the people and they carry it out (3:11-17; 4:5-8; 4:17-18). The Lord's supreme authority clearly stands out in this interaction. The main orders come from the Lord. It is the Lord who promises and who makes Joshua a great figure in Israel's midst (3:7; 4:14).

The Lord is the main actor and the one who causes the crossing of the Jordan (4:23; 5:1), the eviction of the enemy nations and the taking possession of the land (3:11-13). The Lord is the one who deserves the admiration of the nations of the earth and the acclaim of the people (4:24).

In these two chapters the crossing of the Jordan is shown as the great liturgical action that dramatizes and re-evokes the great deed of the Exodus. Just as the coming out of Egypt and the crossing of the Red Sea were accompanied by "wonders" (Exod 3:20; 34:10), the same happens here (3:5). As the Lord had dried up the Red Sea, so also with the Jordan: "the LORD your God dried up the waters of the Jordan for you until you crossed over" (Josh 4:23).

As in Deuteronomy (6:20-25), Josh 4:6-7, 21-24 speak of the instructional commitment of the present generation with future generations. In this way, not only the Lord's presence and the divine salvific actions are assured in the people's historical memory but the whole people in their historical extension also become sharers in the divine deeds. Here, just as in Deuteronomy (6:4-9), the home becomes the *locus* of something essential in the lives of the people. While in Deuteronomy the home is the center to which and from which the most central teaching of biblical faith (the *shema*ʿ) is imparted, in Joshua the home becomes the *locus* of the first liturgy and the first religious focus of the Promised Land.

Joshua 5:1-9 forms a unit that begins and ends with direct discourse: the Lord is the subject and Joshua is the addressee. The constant presence of the word "circumcising" and its various forms indicates that this is the central theme. Here the theme of the circumcision is related to slavery in Egypt, referred to as "the disgrace of Egypt" (v. 9), and to the Exodus. The passage tells us about a generation for whom the Exodus has not yet been fully realized. According to this text "the disgrace" (social situation) is not eliminated by the war but rather through a beritic ritual—the semantic connection between the two names of places mentioned here draws our attention: *Haʿaraloth* ("removing foreskins" and *Gilgal* ("removing" or "rolling back" the disgrace). This is not another action of social disruption but an act of obedience to God. Completing the Exodus consists in becoming a member of the covenant: this new generation become descendants of Abraham (inheriting the promise of Genesis 17) and they have a personal experience of the total Exodus. With regard to this it is interesting to consider the use of *goi* ("people," v. 8). The action of changing from "Gentile" *(goi)* to "people" *(ʿam)* is this twofold act that combines covenant and exodus.

Joshua 5:10-12 again centers the action in the liturgical context, but this time the action is eating. The word "Passover" appears twice, the word "manna" twice, and the expression "they ate the crops/produce of the land" three times. With the twofold action of eating the Passover and no longer eating the manna the Exodus actually comes to an end. The Exodus begins and ends with the Passover celebration; the wandering through the wilderness begins and ends with the manna. This finalization is also a beginning: the people are beginning to eat the produce of the land of Canaan. Thus life in the Promised Land starts by combining the twofold pastoral and agricultural reality of Israelite life. In this liturgical action of eating the Passover and the first fruits we also have a covenant action.

Once again Josh 5:13-15 presents a cultic act that combines worship and vocation as in the case of Isaiah. Like Moses, before fully dedicating himself to his task Joshua finds himself in the holy presence of God and receives his vocation from God. The direct discourse of 5:15 can continue almost without a break in 6:2-5. In the combination of these two texts Joshua's vocation becomes clearly parallel with that of Moses (Exod 3:1-15): like Moses, Joshua "saw" (v. 13); Joshua dialogued and questioned (vv. 13-14); Joshua was enveloped in an aura of worship and holiness (v. 14); Joshua clearly heard the definition of his mission (6:2-5).

The Conquest, a Great Liturgy (6:1-27)

This passage is a great lesson in understanding that the triumph over Jericho by way of the liturgy corresponds to the divine method of making God's plan a reality by means that are both surprising and disconcerting. With the model of Rahab (Joshua 2) and the conquest of Jericho and the integration of the Gibeonites (Joshua 9) we connect to God's "absurdities" in making a prophet out of a donkey (Num 22:27-34), a theologian and missionary out of a Samaritan woman (John 4), a child and descendant of Abraham out of a corrupt and thieving Zacchaeus (Luke 19:1-10), and privileged members of the reign of God out of children and the poor (Mark 10:14; Luke 6:20). If from the beginning of the account the Lord says: "I have handed Jericho over to you, along with its king and soldiers" (v. 2), the people and their leader had to obey and follow the strategy established by the Lord.

What was Jericho like? According to 6:1 it was a city "shut up inside and out." This means that it was one of those city-states of Canaan within whose walls the royal family, the rich and powerful landlords, and the members of the priestly and military classes lived. The poor were living on the walls or in the outskirts of the cities. Therefore the attack was against a clearly defined social group opposed to the spirit of the Exodus and the covenant with the Lord.

We have a liturgical ambience, and the acoustic aspect stands out: "trumpets of rams' horns," "sound of the trumpets," "shouts," "hearing" are terms constantly repeated in the chapter. The number seven appears often for the number of priests, horns, days, and marches around the city. This also serves to emphasize the religious and liturgical aspect of the event. In this atmosphere the Lord is the outstanding figure: the subject of the first direct discourse, the Lord promises to hand over Jericho (vv. 2 and 16) and gives the order to "charge straight ahead" (v. 5); the war spoils are for the Lord (vv. 17-19, 24) who keeps the promise to be with Joshua and make him famous (v. 27; cf. 1:5, 9; chs. 3–7). The acoustic aspect of this "fame" also stands out.

As in the case of Joshua 1, here too we find a sequence of authority: the Lord gives orders and Joshua obeys; Joshua gives orders and the people obey. Verses 5 and 20 show how a concrete order is followed by concrete obedience: "all the people shall charge straight ahead . . . the people charged straight ahead into the city."

Finally, the promise made to Rahab (2:12-20) is fulfilled in this chapter. Just as Rahab had fulfilled her part, Joshua and his people fulfilled the promise to save her along with her family (cf. Rahab's appeal for kindness, *ḥesed,* 2:12, 14). In all of Jericho neither the king nor those who symbolize power and wealth are saved; instead a prostitute is saved. Once again this marks the missionary projection of the Bible: a foreigner, a prostitute becomes the *locus* of divine salvation.

The Conquest of Ai, a Proof of Obedience and Fidelity (7:1–8:29)

This section is made up of six units (7:1-5; 7:6-9; 7:10-15; 7:16-26; 8:1-9; 8:10-29). The entire section indicates that warlike "muscle" is not the source of triumph; the crux is obedience to God versus disobedience. The unity of this section is marked in the framing structure *(inclusio)* which reveals an interesting sequence. Chapter 7 begins by stating that "the anger of the Lord burned against the Israelites" and concludes by indicating that "the Lord turned from his burning anger" (v. 26). Thus the first part of this section ends in a framing structure. However, since the complete section extends to Josh 8:29, here in 7:26 we have a phrase that will conclude the entire section: "to this day" (cf. 8:29).

Israel will have to conquer the city of Ai ("the ruin," "a heap of ruins," cf. Jer 26:18; Mic 1:6, 3:12; Ps 79:1) just as it did Jericho, without mishaps. Yet as this account shows, without God the people cannot even conquer "the ruin." Herein lies the irony of the story.

Infidelity Leads to Defeat, 7:1-5

Achan's action confirms that the Lord is the main protagonist in the "conquest" of the land. With its clearly exilic and post-exilic vocabulary, v. 1 situates the whole account in its authentic semantic context. Israel's inability to conquer the land is due to its "breaking faith" *(maʿal).* Its defeat does not really come at the hands of Ai's inhabitants, but from the "anger of the LORD." The following verses will demonstrate that Israel's defeat is not only due to Achan's sin; it is also due to bad strategy and self-confidence. The Israelites insisted on doing things their way.

Irony is evident in several parallels with Joshua 6. Joshua sends spies to look over the land and they come back with a plan of attack. The theme of the hearts of the people melting appears, except that now we are dealing with the Israelites, not with the inhabitants of the enemy city. Differently from the narrative of Joshua 6, in 7:1-5 the order of the Lord is nowhere to be found (cf. 9:14). In fact the seeming parallels show the reverse of the account of Joshua 6. We should also note that the divine promise of giving the land does not appear anywhere in all of ch. 7.

Joshua's Lamentation, 7:6-9

Why did you do this to us? Joshua's lamentation actually becomes a complaint and a reproach to the Lord. Why complete the Exodus if you are not on our side? What is said in v. 8 indicates that the divine promise made in 1:5, 9; 3:7 has been revoked.

The question of the fame (the "great name") of the Lord and of Joshua as the argument of the complaint-lamentation also appears. As Joshua sees it, the great name of the Lord depends on Israel's fame: "[the inhabitants] will cut off our name from the earth. Then what will you do for your great name?" (v. 9). A similar ideology is expressed in Deut 3:24. The verb "hear" frequently appears in the context of the theme of fame (Josh 2:10; 5:1; 9:1). There is a certain echo of Deut 9:11-29, a passage that relates Moses' intercession on behalf of the people. The literary style of the lamentation or complaint is not only shown in Joshua's action of tearing his clothes, falling face to the ground and putting dust on his head, along with the elders, but also by the question: "Ah, Lord GOD! Why . . ." (v. 7).

Deuteronomic literature places "the elders of Israel" (v. 6), the representatives of the twelve tribes, in the context of significant events of sacred history (cf. Josh 23:2; 24:1; 1 Sam 8:4-5; 1 Kings 8:1-3). In their normal functions they were responsible for the internal security of the community. They were in charge of legal matters dealing with crimes and family relationships. Moreover, they represented the community when they had contacts with other peoples or nations.

I Will be with You No More, 7:10-15

This short unit highlights its main theme by its framing structure—with the expression "[they have] transgressed my/the covenant" (vv. 10 and 15) at each end—and the constant repetition of the word "devoted things" (ban: *ḥērem*): the transformation of Israel from being the people protected by God to war spoil because of their breaking the covenant. The theme of the unit has its most radical point in the expression "I will be with you no more" (v. 12). In addition, the expressions "stand up" (vv. 10 and 13) and "[the Israelites] are unable to stand before their enemies" (vv. 12 and 14) are used twice.

By breaking the covenant Israel stands outside the privileges that are protecting it and becomes the enemy of God, a non-people. Thus it is just as exposed to extermination as the Canaanite people. Here we have one more argument to confirm that belonging to God's own people is not subject to racial or ethnic issues but is always bound to the stipulations of the covenant. In this sense our attention is drawn to the resemblance of the phrase, "I will be with you no more" to Hos 1:9, "I am not *(ehyeh)* your God."

Here we have the opposite situation to that in Joshua 2. There a foreign prostitute and her family become members of God's people and are saved. Here one of the "insiders" and his family remain outside of God's people and are destroyed. God's anger, caused by the people's behavior, is emphasized in the way sin is driven home and repeated: "Israel has sinned; they have transgressed my covenant . . . , they have taken some of the *ḥērem;* they have stolen, they have acted deceitfully, and they have put them among their own belongings" (v. 11). God's repeated order, "stand up" (vv. 10 and 13) indicates that there is a solution to the problem. The guilty one has to face divine punishment (v. 15).

Judgment and Punishment, 7:16-26

The order established by God in terms of judgment is the following: nation → tribe → clan → family → individual. In this way, although the sin was committed by one individual the entire nation has to "come near" *(qrb)* before the Lord.

The sin Achan confesses is committed in three steps that mirror the original sin (Gen 3:6): "I saw . . . I coveted . . . and took" (v. 21).

The presence of the word "all" in the last verses of the unit indicates the emphasis that is placed on the totality and unity of the people in the action of condemning and punishing.

The memory of this troubling experience *(ʿachar)* is preserved by the presence of a heap of stones and in the name of the place, "trouble" *(ʿAchor).* Note the play on words in Hebrew: *ʿāchār–ʿĀchor–ʿāchan* (it is important to note that in 1 Chr 2:7 the MT has *ʿāchār*). The "trouble" was the cause of the whole problem: Achan was troubled and he violated the covenant; Achan's sin troubled the peace of the people and their relationship with God; God troubled Achan and his family by eliminating them completely; the place is called the Valley of Achor.

See, I have Handed over to You the King of Ai, 8:1-9

The peculiar vocabulary of Joshua 6, with God as subject and Joshua and the people as addressees, reappears here in a clear contrast with Josh 7:1-6. Now we find the expression (twice, in vv. 1 and 7): "I [God] will give you" the enemy city. The first two verses are a direct discourse from the mouth of God presenting God's orders and promises, and v. 8 indicates again that the word that is to be obeyed is God's word. The orders issued by Joshua (vv. 4-9) are all subject to divine instructions. Verses 3 and 9 show how God's orders began to be carried out.

According to 8:1 Ai, like Jericho, is a city-state: it has a king and land connected with the city. Joshua 8:17 states that "they left the city open" which implies that it had walls. Verse 29 mentions the "gate" *(shaʿar)* of the city. Once again we verify that these attacked cities were mostly inhabited by landowners and a powerful elite.

The Divine Word is Obeyed; Triumph is Certain, 8:10-29

The verbs used at the beginning of this unit show that Joshua and his people were quick in carrying out God's order to the letter: "Joshua rose early . . . and went up" (cf. 8:1, "take . . . and go up"). The main action, which brings victory, has the Lord as its principal subject. The Lord orders Joshua to stretch out the sword in his hand and keep it that way until the end (8:18, 26). Here we note a parallel between Joshua and Moses (Exod 17:8-12). Verse 29 echoes the law of Deut 2:22-23.

Who are My People? (8:30-35)

Like ch. 1, this is another deuteronomic passage. It contains a strong liturgical flavor (the altar, the ark of the covenant, and the Levitical priests are mentioned) and it shows an evident observance of all the deuteronomic requisites (Deut 11:29-32; 27:1-26) with the participation of everyone, including "the women, and the little ones, and the aliens" (v. 35; cf. v. 33). At the same time Joshua is presented as the paradigm of the monarchy (cf. 2 Kings 23:1-3).

The passage speaks of the renewal of the covenant in which the orders of the Lord and the Book of the Law of Moses have a central place. There is also the acknowledged intention of making this event into a global experience: mention is made of all the words of the Law (three times) and all the assembly of Israel. This indicates the deuteronomic preoccupation with the unity and equality of the people. No one, not even aliens, will be excluded from the covenant with God or its benefits. Theologically speaking this passage compiles and verifies the direct concerns of the book to demonstrate the privileged membership of aliens, little ones, and women among the people (cf. chs. 2; 6; 9–10; 14:6-12; 15:18-19; 17:4).

In this unit the theological concern of the deuteronomic author surpasses and overshadows any other perspective, especially the viewpoints of geography and history. Here the author wants to solve a key question about the message of the book. Achan's sin, which brought "trouble" in the beritic relationship between God and the people, not only needed to show concrete punishment but also to manifest in a concrete and forceful way the bond between the people and YHWH based on the covenant. The covenant and its renewal are at the center. Only thus can we understand why, after the conquest of Jericho and Ai, the people are now in the area of Shechem. Theology is what matters; the instructions of Deuteronomy had to be fulfilled. This unit concludes the first major section of the book (chs. 2–8).

Saved by Cunning (9:1-27)

The news of the Israelites' arrival and their conquest of the land of Canaan spreads like wildfire (Josh 2:9-11; 9:1). In this chapter, as well as in chs. 10–11, Joshua's fame serves to generate the narrative. The three chapters start with the same expression, "When [he/they] heard . . . ." The people who had kings, namely those who lived under the protection of the city-states, sought to resolve the situation by declaring war on Joshua and his people (Josh 9:1-2). But the Gibeonites, an unprotected people without a king and thus probably without the protection of the city-states, found a cunning way to resolve their situation by staying on to live among the Israelites.

A group of Gibeonites pretended to be the emissaries of a people from "a far country" (vv. 6 and 9). The envoys presented themselves with donkeys (not horses), worn-out clothes, moldy food, and torn and mended wineskins (vv. 4-5; 12-13). Israel and its leaders fell into the trap. They shared their provisions (vv. 14-15) and agreed to enter into a treaty with the Gibeonites. The author of the text (vv. 1-5) assesses the situation in this way: "So the leaders partook of their provisions, and did not ask direction from the LORD" (v. 14).

When the deceit was discovered, it was already too late. The people's leaders had made a treaty with the Gibeonite leaders and they could not go back on their word. Thus the Gibeonites stayed to live among God's people forever. However, Joshua and Israel's leaders imposed a permanent burden on the Gibeonites: they would become "hewers of wood and drawers of water for all the congregation" (vv. 21, 23, and 27). Some are paying for their error for lying and the others for being overly trusting and forgetting their general leader, the Lord. It is interesting to read in a Canaanite text from Ugarit, the "Epic poem of Kirta," that cutting wood and drawing water were the tasks of women: ". . . the [women] hewers of wood swept from the country . . . the [women] drawers of water swept from the fountains" (Gregorio Del Olmo Lete, *Mitos y leyendas de Canaán, según la tradición de Ugarit* [Valencia: Institución San Jerónimo, 1981] 295).

This account appears as literary art of subtle irony and humor. The people who are supposed to be depending on God's will at all times are surprised by a foreign people who seem to be more familiar with the divine word: "because it was told to your servants for a certainty that the LORD your God had commanded his servant Moses to give you all the land, and to destroy all the inhabitants of the land before you" (v. 24).

If we were to read Joshua 9 without any other context, the end of the account would appear somewhat negative. These people's lives are saved, but they pay for this with their freedom. But this passage should be read in light of Deut 29:10-15: "You stand assembled today, all of you, before the LORD your God—the leaders of your tribes, your elders, and your officials, all the men of Israel, your children, your women, and the aliens who are in your camp, both those who cut your wood and those who draw your water—to enter into the covenant of the LORD your God, sworn by an oath, which the LORD your God is making with you today; in order that he may establish you today as his people, and that he may be your God . . . ."

In the spirit of deuteronomic theology, Joshua 9 is a proclamation of divine grace. Once again God opens the doors of the kingdom in order to incorporate among God's people "outsiders" who are presented here as "those from below." They are the ones who, by force, joined the ranks of a people of slaves who were seeking a place to live in the midst of the safety of the city-states of Canaan. The stories of Rahab and the Gibeonites emphasize the fundamental purpose of the divine mission: giving a place to live to the marginalized and the vulnerable, in this instance to dispossessed foreigners who start to form part of the covenant by way of their cunning and God's boundless grace and the divine word. This is the kind of grace that "rewards" a cunning falsifier like Jacob (Genesis 25–30) and "admires" a shrewd manager (Luke 16:1-9). Those "divine surprises" are certainly disconcerting for people like Robert Polzin (*Moses and the Deuteronomist* 120) who states rather creatively that "Deuteronomy is the literary shadow of Joshua 9 and Deuteronomy 9–10 is its theological setting."

The leadership theme, central in Joshua, is offered here in a negative manner: the people and their leader do things without paying attention to the voice of God and without demonstrating the virtue of all leaders, that is to say, suspecting and verifying. In fact Joshua plays a secondary role; he is almost "absent." As far as the structure of the passage is concerned, 9:3-15 is narrated from the Gibeonites' point of view, 9:16-27 from the Israelites' perspective (vv. 16-21 focus on the "leaders of the congregation" and vv. 21-27 focus on Joshua).

Translated as "moldy" in many versions, the last word of 9:5 could also be translated by "crumbled" or "reduced to crumbs." The last expression is the most plausible translation.

2 Samuel 21:1-4; 1 Kings 3:4-5 and 9:20-21 refer to the Gibeonites in the subsequent history of Israel.

Victory over the Southern Coalition (10:1-43)

Like 9:1 and 11:1, this account starts with the expression "when [he] heard" to indicate that Joshua's fame is the theme that introduces the narrative. The account is an example of the way the peace treaty signed by conquering and conquered people works. The strong party to the treaty is committed to assist and protect the weak party, while the latter submit as servants.

The interaction of protagonists and the verbs indicate that Joshua is the central agent of the narrative. Although in terms of authority the relation is God → Joshua → Israel → enemies, the account focuses on the person of Joshua. God gives him courage (v. 8): "Do not fear them." God commands (v. 40) and even "heeds" Joshua (v. 14). His enemies are frightened (vv. 1-2) and they give in to him (v. 8). The people of Israel are totally at Joshua's service. In fact, from v. 12 on, all the passages of direct discourse have Joshua as their subject. This is a clear example of how the promise of the people to Joshua in 1:16-18 is fulfilled and how God's promise to be with him and make him prosper is concretized (1:5-9).

The Gibeonites are Protected, 10:1-14

This unit begins and ends with the verb "hear." Adoni-zedek "heard" *(shmᶜ)* about Joshua's fame and the Lord "heeded" *(shmᶜ)* the voice of Joshua. God's direct participation is shown in the fact that it is God who hands the enemy over to Joshua (vv. 8, 12) and God is the one who on the one hand throws the enemy into a "panic" (v. 10) and on the other hand encourages Joshua "not to fear" the enemy (v. 8). Through a supernatural action the Lord is the one who inflicts a greater slaughter on the enemies than the entire people (vv. 10-11), and God is the one who makes "time" stand still for the sake of God's people (vv. 12-14).

Here we undoubtedly have an account of a holy war modeled on the divine deeds of Exodus characterized by the presence of wondrous events (cf. Exod 14:24; 23:27; Deut 2:15, 25; 11:25; Judg 4:15; 1 Sam 7:10; 2 Sam 22:15; 2 Chr 15:6; Ps 18:14-15). Here, as in other texts, it is said that "the LORD fought for Israel" (v. 14; cf. 23:10; Deut 3:22). The account, which starts with Joshua helping the Gibeonites, is transformed into the Lord's helping Israel. The triumph over the five kings was part of the plan of conquering the Promised Land. Once Gibeon submitted, the southern coalition was vulnerable.

In a slightly veiled manner v. 14 presents us with Joshua's parallel and paradigmatic figure: As on various occasions the Lord had done with Moses, so the Lord does now with Joshua (Num 12:8; Deut 9:26; the expression "there has been no . . . like it before or since" is repeated twice in 2 Kings 18:5 and 23:25 in reference to Josiah. In the first case Joshua emulates Moses' intercessory and prophetic role; in the second case Joshua appears as the royal precursor of Josiah.

In 10:1 we find the first mention of the city of Jerusalem in the Bible. In v. 2 the image of Gibeon, even though it was considered a city without a king, presents an enormous contrast with the image of ch. 9. This hyperbolic expression corresponds to the literary nature of this account and its purpose is to enhance the theme of Adoni-zedek's fear. In 10:10 we have the only example in Joshua of the verb *hamam* ("throw into a panic"). The poetic passage quoted in 10:12-13 was part of a collection of songs that celebrated the victories of heroes (cf. 2 Sam 1:18). It is used here as a literary device to explain Joshua's spectacular victory and God's supernatural participation. Verse 15 is textually the same as 10:43. In both cases it marks the conclusion of a narrative unit.

Utter Defeat, 10:16-28

The figure of Joshua dominates this unit. He is the only person who speaks and the actions are subject to his leadership. The Lord remains practically absent. The two quotations about God refer to a past action (v. 19) and a future action (v. 25). The extensive and detailed exposition indicates that this account is probably important to the author of Joshua.

The theme of leadership prevails here, more than any other key theme of the book. The interaction between Joshua's order and the people's obedience recalls the theme of leadership as it is presented in 1:16-18. It is interesting to note that the words used here by Joshua to encourage the people are the ones the Lord and the people used in ch. 1 to encourage Joshua (1:6, 7, 9, 18).

Verse 21 has some elements in common with Exod 11:7. The humiliation of the defeated is a frequent theme in the Bible (2 Sam 22:39 = Ps 18:39; 1 Kings 5:3; Ps 110:1; Isa 51:23). That humiliation is highlighted here in the action of hanging the bodies on posts or trees. Joshua's command in 10:27 echoes the command of Deut 21:23.

Total Conquest, 10:29-43

Based on a common formula, vv. 29-39 summarize the conquest itinerary that was followed by Joshua and the people of Israel. The actions are presented in a categorical way: all of Israel participates in the battle and all the enemies are annihilated. Verses 40-43 appear as a summary of the whole conquest of the south in response to the divine command. Joshua 10:43 closes the entire chapter in the same words that were used to close the unit in 10:15. In addition, v. 43 shows that it is a matter of conquest rather than occupation since this theme actually belongs in chs. 13 to 21. Even though the word *ḥērem* (ban, total destruction) does not appear, this unit echoes the ideology of total destruction as an offering to the Lord.

Goshen, mentioned in 10:41, does not refer to the Egyptian territory of Genesis but to a region probably located between the mountains and the Negeb desert.

Utterly Destroy Imperial Power! (11:1-15)

This unit begins like chs. 9 and 10: "when [he] heard." In fact, ch. 11 deliberately resembles ch. 10: a coalition of kings is formed, Joshua is ordered not to fear them, the coalition is defeated by divine action against the enemies. The editors intend to present parallel deeds to show that in the mission of the conquest the north has the same fate as the south. What is promised in Joshua 1 continues to be fulfilled to the letter.

The unit is divided into three clearly distinguishable parts: (a) list of the northern kings, vv. 1-5; (b) command and obedience, vv. 6-9; (c) destruction of the northern coalition, vv. 10-15.

The list of the kingdoms in 11:1-5 presents a very general framework that really corresponds to theological concerns. The geographical and historical details, although they are traceable, should not be viewed as direct reflections of the events and places that are at the root of this narrative.

Joshua and Israel will fight against kings whose military power is overwhelming. The mention of different ethnic groups shows that all the ancient people of Canaan were Joshua's enemies. They are clearly defined as imperial powers whose armies have countless horses and chariots. Here we find the only reference to "horses" in the book of Joshua. On the one hand it is a way of indicating that the type of terrain in question has changed, and on the other hand that Joshua and Israel will only be victorious thanks to the Lord's guidance and intervention.

The divine action is defined in vv. 6–9 as a combination of command (vv. 6, 9) and participation (v. 8). Verse 6 is the only direct discourse with the Lord as its subject. The divine command consists in destroying the military power of those kingdoms. In this way the Lord and the people are shown as a force that routs imperial, military, and oppressing powers. Israel's enemies are not the vulnerable inhabitants of villages and rural areas but instead are the royal forces of those who live under the protection of the city-states.

In this chapter and in other parts of the book the enemies are represented by giants (the "Anakim," Josh 11:21-22; 14:12-15; the "Rephaim," Josh 12:4; 13:12; 17:15) or the inhabitants of the city-states (cf. chs. 6 and 8). God orders their destruction. However, God asks the people of the Exodus from Egypt, Israel, whose real power is the Lord alone, to protect the marginalized, the underprivileged, and the vulnerable: women (Joshua 2) and aliens (Joshua 9). They are the ones the Lord invites to become part of God's people.

The tension between oppressing military powers and the vulnerable and needy people is also manifested in the references to animals. The horses (vv. 4, 6, 9), which are symbols of the oppressors' power, are destroyed. On the contrary, the livestock (v. 14) is kept to feed God's people, vulnerable people who protect those who are vulnerable like them.

The theme of the *ḥērem* is mainly found in vv. 10-15. In this way the author indicates that the war spoil belongs to God because the victory is also God's doing.

The theme of leadership reappears here according to the theological order presented in other parts of the book: the Lord commands Moses who, in turn, commands Joshua (v. 15).

In the case of Hazor, archaeology confirms the existence and destruction of a city on this site in the thirteenth century B.C.E, but there is discussion about when and how the destruction took place. Some attribute the destruction to Joshua and the Israelites, others to Deborah and Barak at the time of the judges, and still others to people from the sea.

Theological Summary of the Conquest (11:16-23)

These verses deal with Joshua's total triumph over the Promised Land. The geographical aspect of the list shows that Joshua's conquering task has already been completed. Verse 23 concludes the theological setting begun in 1:7.

The quotations in 11:20, 21-22 further emphasize the motive of the Lord's and Joshua's belligerent attitudes toward the kings and the Anakim. God did not want the people to have anything to do with imperial and oppressing nations. Like the city-states, the Anakim, descendants of giants, symbolized every power resisting the Lord and the divine salvific plan of creating a society in which all persons are considered equal. In this Joshua reflects the humanitarian aspect of Deuteronomy, a book that precisely relates the destruction of the land of the Anakim (Deuteronomy 2–3; 9:2-3).

The section dealing with the conquest of the land concludes with v. 23. Chapter 12 will be another unit summarizing and indicating key elements for the theology of the book and the great deuteronomic work. For the first time in Joshua (11:23) we find the Hebrew form of the word "inheritance" *(naḥelāh)* that will frequently reappear (some fifty times) from chs. 13 to 24. This theologically "loaded" term indicates that the land is more than the source of agricultural resources or the possibility of urbanization. In Joshua the land is the inheritance God gives to each family of God's people, for their survival rather than for their usufruct.

Moses' Conquests and Joshua's Conquests (12:1-24)

This passage, the work of a subsequent editor, makes a theological statement that places the theme of leadership at the center. The chapter is structured in such a way that the figures of Moses and Joshua are really parallel. Moses is the main subject of 12:1-6 and Joshua of 12:7-24. The main verbs of both units come in pairs, first concerning Moses and then Joshua. Thus both are united in their destiny and their serving the Lord: both, followed by Israel, destroy enemy kings; both give the land to the people of Israel. This will be seen again in 13:1–14:1.

Before entering to take possession of the territory that belongs to them, Israel and its leaders needed to defeat the imperial powers that "obstructed" the beritic people's historic task. In order to write their history, the history of the Lord, Israel and its leaders defeated the kings but protected the weak and the marginalized. The list of the defeated kings, sounding like a litany, asserts that the struggles of the conquest, the Lord's wars, are wars for justice. Their goal is to make room for communities and peoples who, under God's command, aspire to form part of societies of equals.

Beginning with ch. 12 we find a systematic use of the Hebrew term *gebul,* translated by limit, boundary, and territory. This word is used especially in ch. 13 and from chs. 15 to 19.

Taking Possession of the Land: Joshua 13–21

Chapter 13 marks the beginning of the second major section of the book and with it a new dynamic. Differently from chs. 2 to 12 where there is a struggle for the land, here the people are already living in the land. The theme of the destruction of the enemies is replaced by the theme of the distribution of the land. The lists of cities appear by themselves, no longer accompanied by the kings possessing them.

We are coming to a part of the book that is rather dry and apparently devoid of theological concern. It is a section that makes many readers lose interest because of the endless lists of cities and places allotted to one tribe or another. Yet attentive readers will discover theological geography here. Behind the lists of places and boundaries we find the teaching imparted by a God who wants to fulfill promises and a people who seek to become worthy of seeing the divine promises concretized. In spite of the prevailing presence of geographical data we should make it clear that here we also find tribal, folkloric, and legal material.

Borders, lists of cities, and other details will help readers in discovering the clues of the authors of Joshua who tell us about the real audience of these chapters. This is why they should not be read through the eyes of historians but rather through the eyes of believers who strive to discover what the word of God is teaching: tribal borders reflecting historical times prior to the monarchy are mixed with lists of cities pertaining to the time of King Josiah. In fact some of the limits of the territory reflect borders that only remained the ideal and the hope of ancient Israel.

Chapter 13 opens a section that curbs the exuberant and hyperbolic narrative of chs. 2–12: Joshua is already old and there is still a lot of land to apportion; large groups of non-Israelites are still sharing the Promised Land with the beritic people.

Joshua, Distribute the Land! (13:1-7)

This introductory unit consists almost entirely of a direct discourse of the Lord. Once again the theme of leadership has a predominant place. Now Joshua is in the same situation as Moses at the end of Deuteronomy. In his old age Moses distributed the land corresponding to the tribes of Reuben and Gad and the half-tribe of Manasseh. Now, in his own old age Joshua will have to do the same with the remaining tribes. The Lord reappears as the subject of the extermination of enemies. YHWH, not Joshua, is the "warrior." Joshua is simply the one who distributes the inheritance in obedience to the Lord's command.

Seen from the perspective of the exilic audience—because this section comes from the deuteronomic exilic redaction—the theme of leadership creates a negative image. During the monarchy, generally speaking, the people experienced false leaders who decided not to distribute the land equitably (as shown in the sad example of Naboth's vineyard, 1 Kings 21). For the new post-exilic generation Israel needs a leader like Joshua who, following the Law of Moses (namely Deuteronomy), would distribute the land with fairness.

The question of foreign people remaining among the beritic people is also important in these verses. The word "remains," repeated twice here, serves as the introduction to what will appear almost as a refrain in the entire section: there remained . . . (15:63; 16:10; 17:12-13; 18:1-3; 23:4-5, 12-13). This theme brings to the surface the key theme of Joshua and of deuteronomic literature, namely, fidelity to the Lord brings forth the fulfillment of all that God promised to their ancestors (Josh 21:43-45). The book of Judges will show the other side of the coin. Here the theme of the nations is not presented in the same way as in chs. 2–12 where the nations were eradicated from the land. Here (chs. 13–21) they remain as a warning to Israel that it can lose the land.

The territory listed in vv. 2-6 refers to the period of the kingdom of David and Solomon when Israel expanded its borders more than in any other period of history. The Hebrew word translated "allot the land" is only found twice in Joshua, at 13:6 and 23:4.

The issue of Joshua's being advanced in years is found in 13:1, 14:10, and 23:1. In fact, 23:1 is a copy of 13:1. This verse in turn seems to present an idea opposed to 11:23, which concluded the previous section (chs. 2–12).

Moses, Model of a Leader; Division of the Land East of the Jordan (13:8-33)

This unit seems to interrupt the natural sequence between 13:7 and 14:1. However, here we have the clear theological intent to show that Moses, the model of a leader, is also a model in terms of distributing the land. Joshua, who is about to carry out his mission of distributing the last parcel of land, follows the paradigm established by Moses, the model leader. The parallel is also found in the fact that Moses and Joshua did not drive out all the enemy nations from the land. The verbs "give," "defeat," "give an inheritance" are repeated throughout this section.

Another theological interest is in the preservation of the unity of the entire people at all costs. This is why some tribes are included although, for reasons of geography or history, they are not a natural part of the book of Joshua. All the people's yearning for unity is also shown in the mention of the Levites (vv. 14, 33; cf. 14:3-4). Thus, the twelve tribes that form the beritic people appear together. The mention of the Levites anticipates the theme of the Levitical cities (ch. 21).

Division of the Land West of the Jordan (14:1–21:42)

This part is introduced by 14:1-5. The Levites are mentioned again as the tribe that did not receive an inheritance of the land. However, they were given towns to live in as indicated in Josh 21:1-42. All this will be done in accordance with the Lord's command to Moses, a command his successor, Joshua, is fulfilling now.

The reference to the religious and civil leaders who accompany Joshua in 14:1, is a definite echo of the period of the exile (cf. Num 32:28; 34:17). The mention of Eleazar and the leaders also occurs in later texts of Joshua (19:51; 21:1). Joshua 14:1 and 19:51 have the same content and constitute a kind of framing structure *(inclusio),* thus pointing out that chs. 14–19 form a thematic unit whose subject matter is the distribution of the land west of the Jordan. These are considered priestly texts and they seem to indicate that, just as in chs. 2–12, the conquest and distribution of the land are religious and liturgical endeavors. Whenever Eleazar and Joshua appear together the priest is mentioned first.

For the first time in deuteronomic literature we find the term *gorāl* ("lot," "raffle") in 14:2. This is typical of later texts and of priestly contexts. We find the term twenty-eight times in Joshua, especially in chs. 14–19. It is also in these chapters that the words "land," "inheritance," and "territory" and the verbs "give," "inherit," and "distribute" constantly appear.

The Portion of Judah, 14:5–15:63

The first land distribution goes to Judah, thereby indicating its political priority. At the time of the Deuteronomist, Judah alone remains as a beritic nation. The redaction of this part of Joshua coincides with the time of Josiah, when Judah alone remained God's people.

Caleb, a Foreigner Who Inherits the Land, 14:6-15; 15:13-19

This unit marks the real beginning of the distribution of the land west of the Jordan. As in ch. 2 the main protagonists are foreigners. If in Joshua 2 a Canaanite, a woman and a foreigner, became a member of the beritic people, here another foreigner, a Kenizzite, an Edomite, is the first to receive his portion of land. Just as with Rahab, the person of Caleb marks the theological tone for the rest of the section: Who is acknowledged as a member of God's people? Who is worthy to receive a share in the Promised Land?

As in Rahab's case, Caleb becomes worthy of divine grace because of his total fidelity to the Lord (vv. 9, 14; cf. Deut 1:22-40). Just as with chs. 2 and 9, here we have to acknowledge that this is not a matter of ethnicity but rather of obedience and fidelity to God's word. Like Moses and Joshua, Caleb is ready to face the "giants" (v. 12, "the Anakim"). His confidence that he will triumph does not depend on his own ability or military power; it is rooted in divine assistance.

The expression "man of God," which is used here (14:6) for Moses, is a title applied almost exclusively to prophets. Thus it indicates that here Moses is viewed as a prophet (cf. Deut 33:1; 1 Kings 17:18; 2 Kings 4:7-9). Joshua 15:13-19 (cf. Judg 1:12-15) relates the concretization of Caleb's desire to defeat the Anakim. This brought about the allotment of the land to his female descendant and the appearance on the scene of the first judge of Israel, Othniel, the only judge coming from Judah (cf. Judg 3:9-11).

Boundaries and Cities of Judah, 15:1-12, 20-63

Verses 1-12 establish the boundaries of Judah: south, east, north, and west. The overwhelming presence of the words "boundary" and "going up" calls our attention: the boundaries are determined by going up. The verb "going down" is found only once. The boundaries not only include the tribe of Simeon (cf. 19:9) but also portions belonging to other people. These borders were only reached under King David.

From the first audience in Joshua's day to the last audience at the time of the exile, the challenge of faith, which is imposed by God, is the implied theological teaching. This passage shows that Israel's ideal limits exceeded the historical reality of the people. We learn, therefore, that there is always room for greater fidelity to God, an indispensable requisite to possess the land promised in its totality. Since that did not happen either at the time of Joshua or even less at the time of the exile, in the case of Judah to the south and also in the case of Ephraim and Manasseh to the north, portions of their territory remained in the hands of other ethnic groups.

Joshua 15:20-63 lists the cities belonging to Judah. The list is given according to regions (south, lowlands, Philistia, the hill country, and the wilderness), following a circular, clockwise movement. The list of the cities of Judah says a great deal about the editor and the redaction date. Joshua enumerates 358 cities. Of these, 144 belong to Judah and 38 to Benjamin. The other tribes have between 22 and 25 cities each. This is a period when the south completely dominates.

Boundaries and Cities of the Sons of Joseph, Joshua 16–17

Ephraim and Manasseh receive their portion of the territory in the northern part of the Promised Land. Unlike Judah (15:1-12) and Benjamin (18:11-20), here there is more "going down" than going up. This fact is significant if we consider the challenge presented by Joshua in 17:14-18. The two tribes of Joseph are not only invited to possess the land that "goes down" but also the portion that makes them go up: "go up to the forest . . ." (v. 15). To succeed in their conquest they will have to overcome the giants (v. 15) and fight against those who have "chariots of iron" (v. 18).

With regard to 17:3-6 (cf. Num 27:1-7) it has been noted that a genealogical list lies hidden within the geographical list. The names of Manasseh's granddaughters seem to be names of cities instead. Both chapters clearly point out that the tribes of Ephraim and Manasseh were unable to drive out several pagan nations from their territory (16:10; 17:12-13, 15-18).

Division of the Land Among the Seven Remaining Tribes, Joshua 18–19

The shifting of the important places in the history of Israel shows the change of religious centers in the history of the occupation of the land. The part dedicated to the conquest, especially in chs. 4 and 5, has its center in Gilgal. It is there that key events are celebrated, including the circumcision of the males of the wilderness generation, the celebration of the Passover, and the memorial of the crossing of the Jordan. The center of chs. 18 and 19 is Shiloh, where Joshua exhorts the people and apportions the land. Shiloh is important because it is there that the tent of meeting was established for the first time in the Promised Land. The third important place is Shechem, where the renewal of the covenant had been celebrated (8:30-35) and where it will be celebrated in future (Joshua 24). Thus the book of Joshua shows that from a very early period Israel is linked to the three most important religious centers of the pre-monarchic period.

Joshua 18:1-10 serves as the introduction to this whole unit and situates it in a theological perspective. God makes the taking possession of the land a reality (v. 3), but the people have to do their part: showing courage and steadfastness, being obedient and faithful to the Lord (v. 3). Moreover, the people's task is manifested in concrete actions: designated men will have to make a complete list of the non-assigned cities and villages of the area.

Our attention is drawn by the insistence in mentioning all the tribes of Israel even though the special situation of the Levites and the apportioning of the land to Reuben, Gad, and the half-tribe of Manasseh, Judah, Ephraim, and the other half-tribe of Manasseh had already been mentioned. This is due to the author's desire to maintain the unity and totality of the beritic nation. Remember that ch. 18 deals with a change of religious center and therefore a different historical reality. Not only are the names of the twelve tribes and of the Levites repeated, but once again we are told of the leadership in the parallel figures of Moses and Joshua: as Moses apportioned the land (v. 7), so would Joshua apportion it (v. 10). In Joshua's case he will apportion the land by "casting lots" (vv. 6, 8, 10).

Joshua 18:11-28 deals with the apportioning of the territory of the tribe of Benjamin and the number of towns assigned to it. Like Judah, the tribe of Benjamin occupies a privileged place with regard to the other tribes. Joshua 19:1-9 refers to Simeon's inheritance. The text reflects the period when the tribe of Simeon had already been assimilated by Judah. Joshua 19:10-51 presents the distribution of the land pertaining to the tribes of the Galilee region: Zebulun, Issachar, Asher, Naphtali, and Dan. The unit concludes by indicating that both Joshua and Eleazar received their respective inheritances. The final verse of this long unit (chs. 18–19) repeats several elements of the first verse, thereby closing the section and giving it a framing structure. If in 18:1 the "land lay subdued before" the people, in 19:51 the people "finished dividing the land."

The Cities of Refuge and the Levitical Cities, Joshua 20–21

The theme of the cities of refuge is presented in all of ch. 20 and in 21:13, 21, 27, 32, and 38 (cf. Num 35:6-15 and Deut 4:41-44; 19:1-4). The text of Joshua appears as the fulfillment of God's command to Moses in Deuteronomy. After referring to the distribution of the land, once again the book of Joshua returns to the spirit of justice and humanitarianism of Deuteronomy. The cities of refuge are intercalated with the cities of the Levites. This theme reminds us of an essential aspect of love in the biblical sense, namely loving our enemies, forgiving people who would otherwise meet with death. The cities of refuge offer a place for people who would not find a place in any other way, even immigrants (20:9). Here we find a glimpse, albeit in an incomplete way, of the message of Jesus Christ about loving our enemies (Matt 5:38-48; 6:9-15). Forgiveness is nuanced in the Deuteronomist's message. We still do not have the radical words of Jesus who is offering a loving place even to intentional enemies: "Father, forgive them; for they do not know what they are doing" (Luke 23:34).

With regard to the expression *goēl haddām* ("avenger of blood"), it is usually believed that this person is the close relative of the deceased who left a widow behind, or who lost some land. Nevertheless, some studies suggest that the law about revenge does not stipulate that a relative of the slain person is the one who avenges the dead person's life. The expression "avenger of blood" was applied to the individual designated by the city's leaders to hunt down and to kill the intentional murderer.

Joshua 21 deals with the cities given to the families of the Levites. The tribe of Levi, formed by priestly families, was not going to receive a clearly delineated territory as the other tribes did. In the deuteronomic spirit the book of Joshua insists on the fact that the inheritance of the Levites is the Lord. However, this chapter shows how the Levites received cities and holdings in all the Israelite territory. There is a practical reason for this. In this way all the citizens of Israel will have access to priests' services. This was undoubtedly an excellent provision during the exile, when Jerusalem had been destroyed as the center of worship. At the same time the people will have the opportunity to serve those who are vulnerable, like orphans, widows, and aliens. God is especially concerned about such people. It is interesting to note that in v. 3 as well as in v. 8 the Israelites, not their leaders, are the ones who do the giving.

The command of God to Moses (21:2), which is now being fulfilled, is found in Num 35:1-8.

All the Promises the Lord had Made Came to Pass (21:43-45)

These verses close the great section that started in ch. 13. The word *kol* ("all") is used six times, and unites these verses theologically: "the LORD gave to Israel all the land that he swore. . . , and having taken possession of it [all] . . . , all the good promises that the LORD had made . . . , all came to pass." This concept of "all" also involves the idea of rest in the land and peace in the presence of enemies.

This unit is totally permeated by the spirit of Deuteronomy. It is a theological summary that emphasizes the prophetic ideal rather than the objectivity of a historian. It serves as the conclusion of the section in chs. 13–21 and the introduction of the deuteronomic discourse of the following chapters. The Deuteronomist wants the entire book of Joshua to be read in light of these verses.

The theological themes indicated here are central in deuteronomic theology. However, they are presented in the opposite order of the way they appear in the book as a whole: (1) total possession of the land; (2) "rest" or peace; (3) total victory over the enemies; (4) the divine word and promise. These and other deuteronomic themes will be repeated again in the following unit.

Be Careful! You Can Lose the Land: Joshua 22–24

In these last three chapters we find the theme of fidelity to God's word coupled with an exhortation that is more like a warning than a proclamation. Israel can suffer the same fate as the other nations: that is to say, destruction and loss of the land.

At the beginning of the "Second Reading" we indicated that Joshua 1 and 22–24 form the theological framework around the entire book. Considering ch. 24 in relation to ch. 1 we observe that in the first chapter the Lord is challenging and inviting the leader, Joshua, to remain faithful and in union with God. In the final chapter the Lord and Joshua are challenging the people to remain faithful. Thus the book begins and ends with its central theological themes: fidelity to God and to God's word (the Book of the Law), the land, leadership, and also the concept of totality.

In the first chapter the danger of infidelity appears to come from a loss of courage and trust in the Lord and in the divine word. In ch. 22 the danger is the temptation to erect sanctuaries competing with the one chosen by the Lord. In ch. 23 the danger seems to be caused by mixed marriages and in ch. 24 it comes from serving other gods.

Faithful and Steadfast Brothers (22:1-8)

This passage relates the moment when Joshua allows the Reubenites, the Gadites, and the half-tribe of Manasseh to go back to their territory east of the Jordan. It is an opportune time to present another summary of the key theological principles of Deuteronomy that are repeated again and again in Joshua and now made a reality in the lives of these tribes:

1. Obedience to the command of the leaders, Moses and Joshua (22:2; cf. Num 32:20-32; Josh 1:12-15).
2. Carrying out the Lord's commands (22:3; cf. Deut 11:1; Josh 1:7).
3. Rest for the western tribes (22:4; cf. Deut 3:20; 12:9-10; 25:19; Josh 1:13, 15; 23:1).
4. God's gift of the land (22:4; cf. Deut 1:36, 39; 6:10; Josh 1:6, 13).
5. The Law of Moses (22:5; cf. Deut 4:44; 31:9; Josh 1:7-8; 8:32-34).
6. Moses, the "servant of the Lord" (22:4-5; cf. Deut 34:5; Josh 1:1, 13, 8:31).
7. Love of God (22:5; Deut 6:5; 10:12; Josh 23:11).
8. Serving God with all one's heart (22:5; cf. Deut 6:13; 10:12; Josh 24:14).
9. Abundance in the Promised Land (22:8; cf. Deut 7:13; 8:17; 28:4-14; Josh 8:2, 27).

With this summary Joshua confirms the unity of the Transjordan tribes not only in terms of solidarity but also in their fidelity to the Lord. The geographical separation does not mean a lack of union as long as theological harmony reigns. Thus the crisis presented in the following verses already has the seed of a solution in Josh 22:1-8.

The Altar Beyond the Jordan: Apostasy or Testimony? (22:9-34)

The profession of faith, which unites all the tribes, as observed in the two previous units, is now coming to a crisis. The Transjordan tribes have built a huge altar at the territorial frontier with other tribes. The western tribes are preparing to destroy their brothers (vv. 9-14). How ironic! Instead of receiving understanding, those who had fought shoulder to shoulder for the sake of the western tribes are now condemned.

Verses 15-20 do not show the conciliatory attitude of people who are seeking to inform themselves in order to resolve a dispute amicably. The words of Phinehas and his companions were condemning and threatening. In fact, they turned out to be selfish and presumptuous words. The sin of which the Transjordan tribes are accused is parallel to Achan's sin. The same word, infidelity [breaking faith] *(māʿal)* is repeated in both passages. Thus we have the twofold problem that accompanied Israel in its entire OT history: infidelity and division.

The explanation of the tribes of Reuben, Gad, and the half-tribe of Manasseh is clear and forceful. Once again it shows that the list from the deuteronomic creed (Josh 22:1-8) formed part of their daily lives. They were not apostates; they wanted to be faithful to the Lord with a clear vision of the future and the desire to preserve national harmony. Their pedagogical concern for future generations, typical of Deuteronomy (Deut 6:20-25; cf. Josh 4:6-7, 21-24) is a characteristic of these Transjordan tribes. Their wish is that their children remain faithful to the Lord and united like brothers and sisters in spite of the geographical separation.

Joshua 22:30-34 offers an opportune and peaceful solution. God's people can live in harmony and in fidelity: the dream of Deuteronomy made reality in God's people under Joshua's command. Let us note, however, that Joshua is the great absent one in the narrative part of ch. 22 (vv. 9-34). This may be an account depicting the living situation of a community after the exile. Under the priestly leadership this community is looking for ritual unity at any cost. It is worth reading Josh 22:9-34 in light of Deuteronomy 12 as well as glancing at 1 Kings 12.

Israel's History in a Nutshell (23:1-16)

The crucial moments of Israel's history until the exile are explained here theologically. Joshua 23 is a theological summary of Deuteronomy, and thematically as well as structurally it echoes the theology of the covenant. This theology emphasizes reading the history of Israel in the light of the first two commandments of the Decalogue. In other words, Joshua 23 is an exhortation to total fidelity to the Lord. In addition to this central theme Joshua presents other major deuteronomic themes, for example, the concept of totality (we find the word "all" twelve times) and the idea of goodness in connection with the land. This absolute fidelity is based on the experience of the Exodus, the wandering through the wilderness, and the occupation of the Promised Land. Being a nation of slaves and marginalized people, by its social position Israel is politically and militarily weak. It is only its reliance on the Lord that leads it to the victories related in Joshua 2–12. This idea is picked up in ch. 23 (vv. 3, 4, 5, 9, 13). Israel's future depends on the Lord. If Israel does not follow the stipulations of the covenant, especially with regard to the first two commandments, it will have the same fate as the neighboring nations: destruction and loss of the land (vv. 13, 15-16).

Verse 3 summarizes the content of chs. 2–12, and verse 4 the content of chs. 15-19. In addition, v. 6 echoes Josh 1:8; 8:31; 24:26. Verse 14 summarizes what is said in 22:43-45. In turn vv. 12-13 anticipate the people's experience in the book of Judges and vv. 15-16, like Deuteronomy 27–28, paint a picture of the Babylonian exile.

As chs. 22 and 24 do in their own way, this chapter indicates that although fidelity and obedience to the Lord and the divine word obtain the successes related in most of Joshua, the danger of forsaking the Lord is always present. This would bring, as a result, what is shown in the book of Judges and the latter part of the books of Kings: a people who did not conquer all the land and a people who were destroyed and expelled from the land. Here we have a good image of the community of the exile. Chapter 23 reminds the audience that a new history could be written, like that of Joshua 1–6; 8–21, if only the people remain faithful to the Lord and depend totally on God.

Joshua 23 resembles other discourses placed by the Deuteronomist in the mouths of the protagonists Moses, Samuel, and David.

Choose This Day Whom You Will Serve! (24:1-28)

Chapter 23 ends in such a way that we expect a more positive and climactic conclusion. This is what happens in ch. 24. This passage, which contains in summary all the theological teaching of the book, transcends the geographical and historical relativizations of the people of the covenant as the book has portrayed them. In fact, Joshua 24 appears as an event that can have its role in the history and current situation of any community accepting the challenge to make YHWH its only God and Lord.

As has been accurately said, Joshua 24 does not pretend to be the text of the covenant. Rather it shows how to establish a covenant between the Lord and a community seeking to become God's people. George Mendenhall's studies and others have related this passage to the vassalage treaties of the ancient Near East. Nevertheless, in Joshua 24 we should instead see a liturgical ceremony that must have been repeated in the Israelite ritual center of Shechem. We must also affirm with many other biblical scholars that Joshua 24 is not necessarily deuteronomic or post-deuteronomic. What we have here is most probably the echo of material that could have been the source of what would later become the deuteronomic tradition.

Total fidelity to the Lord is the central theme. The historical summary, which is embodied in vv. 2-13, is a great overture whose theme is similar to that of Deuteronomy 32 presenting the Lord, in the first person, as the one who accompanies Israel in its history. According to these verses the other gods remained "beyond [on the other side of] the River" (an expression used seven times in these verses). It was not they but the Lord who brought Abraham to the Promised Land (24:3; note here and throughout vv. 2-13 the constant repetition of the pronoun in the first person singular to refer to the Lord). It was not they but the Lord who gave the land to Abraham's descendants (v. 3); it was not they but the Lord who brought the people out of slavery in Egypt (vv. 6-7); it was not they but the Lord who brought the people to the Promised Land, taking the possessions of the pagan nations, and it was the Lord who gave the land to this, YHWH's people (vv. 8-13). This is why vv. 2 and 14, which serve to enclose this historical summary, speak not only of keeping the other gods "beyond the River" but also of keeping the people away from them: "put away the gods that your ancestors served beyond the River" (v. 14). However, fidelity to the Lord does not simply consist in staying away from other gods; it is also a question of trusting the Lord totally: ". . . it was not by your sword or by your bow" (v. 12).

The historical summary is followed by a series of verses (vv. 14-25) that contain seven commands: "revere, serve, put away, serve, choose, put away, incline." They all put pressure on the people to abandon the other gods (*ʾelohim,* referring to the other gods, is found seven times) and to cling to and serve the Lord alone (the Lord is mentioned eighteen times and *ʾelohim* is used in reference to God nine times). Of the sixteen times that the verb "serve" *(ʿbd)* is used, eleven refer to serving the Lord and five refer to the other gods. This is clearly the verb that is most repeated in this unit. The challenge consists in abandoning the other gods, no longer serving them, not abandoning the Lord, and serving YHWH alone. It is interesting to note that Egypt is called "the house of slavery" (*bēth ʿbādim,* v. 17). It is not only called that in this context because it was the place where God's people were enslaved and oppressed, but also because there the people's ancestors "served" other gods. The themes of "revering the Lord" (adoration, love, obedience) and "sincerity and faithfulness" (v. 14) also belong to the semantic context of service.

When they declare they will serve the Lord the people express the main reason for their vow of fidelity, namely that the Lord is the God of the Exodus and of the conquest (vv. 17-18). At the beginning and end of these two verses the people declare: "the Lord is our God." Joshua's answer (vv. 19-20) presents the other side of what God was and is for the people in the course of their history. YHWH is not only the God of the Exodus and the giver of the land but a "holy and jealous God." YHWH is a God who does not tolerate rebellion and infidelities; whoever breaks the covenant, especially by disobeying the first two commandments of the Decalogue, will undergo the same fate as the pagan nations, that is, exile and destruction.

This is why it is essential to renew or establish the covenant (v. 25). God's people need to live within the parameters of a covenant that keeps them united with their God, YHWH. Keeping the covenant means life; breaking it means destruction and death. The "Book of the Law" is the text that was to accompany the people in their journey through history; the guidelines of the covenant are stipulated in this book. Concerning the theme of the covenant, Joshua's words in v. 15, "as for me and my household, we will serve the LORD," verify that the covenant is established with each family rather than with the head of state and through the sovereign with all the nation. According to Joshua's testimony and other deuteronomic material, all heads of family take responsibility for their children's knowing the covenant and its stipulations. The home is the nucleus from which beritic teaching would expand to the entire nation (cf. Deut 6:4-9).

Here at the end of a book that presents the triumph of the fidelity of the leader and the people it is important to point out the context in which the people are invited to serve the Lord and be faithful to YHWH. Now that the people had already taken possession of the land and conquered it with the Lord's assistance, now that they had it all and no longer needed anything, according to Josh 24:18 ("the LORD drove out before us all the peoples, the Amorites . . .") they were asked to serve the Lord. The theological principle behind all this is that the Lord wants people who are free, not slaves. It is very difficult to serve God on the basis of freedom. Paul's letter to the Galatians and Jesus' constant struggles with several groups of his fellow Jews, as narrated in the gospels, attest to this reality.

The book of Joshua and its theological climax, ch. 24, present us with the challenge of being faithful servants of God as free rather than enslaved people. For the most part this ideal did not become a reality, yet the Bible tells us about Joshua, Josiah, and many others like Rahab who did accept this challenge of fidelity and they became heroes and heroines of the faith (Heb 11:1-40).

Farewell Joshua, Eleazar, and Joseph's Bones! (24:29-33)

The last verses offer three reports about the deaths of Joshua, Eleazar, and Joseph. The title "servant of the Lord," which the book had used only for Moses, is now applied to Joshua after his death. The quality of servant, now belonging to Joshua, is reaffirmed in the statement that "Israel served the Lord all the days of Joshua" (v.

31). Now Joshua is no longer merely the "servant of Moses"; he is "servant of the Lord." His age at the time of his death reminds us of other people who also died when they were advanced in years. Verses 29-31 are similar to Judg 2:6-10.

The lives of Joshua and the leaders who accompanied him are qualified by the phrase "all the days of Joshua, and all the days of the elders who . . . had known all the work that the LORD did for Israel." What a way to end the book and exalt the work of a great leader! Joshua's life is an integral part of the Lord's great redemptive work, namely the Exodus and the gift of the land. Thus the name of Joshua, the savior, characterizes a man who not only lived at the time of the salvation and formation of the beritic people but was also a protagonist in that work. Because of his participation, Joshua is a precursor of the Savior, Jesus.

The report of the burial of Joseph's remains is reminiscent of the last part of Genesis. The man who entered into Egypt and departed from it after his death also completed his "exodus" by resting with the remainder of the people in the Promised Land.

The last words tell of the burial of Eleazar, the priest who, with Joshua, played a major role in the division and distribution of the land among the tribes of Israel.

BIBLIOGRAPHY

Boling, Robert G. *Joshua. A New Translation with Notes and Commentary.* AB 6. Garden City, N.Y.: Doubleday, 1982.

Brueggemann, Walter. *Biblical Perspectives on Evangelism. Living in a Three Storied Universe.* Nashville: Abingdon, 1993.

____. *A Social Reading of the Old Testament. Prophetic Approaches to Israel's Communal Life,* edited by Patrick D. Miller. Minneapolis: Fortress, 1994.

Butler, Trent C. *Joshua.* WBC 7. Waco, Tex.: Word Books, 1983.

Coote, Robert B. *Early Israel. A New Horizon.* Minneapolis: Fortress, 1990.

Curtis, Adrian H. W. *Joshua.* Sheffield: Sheffield Academic Press, 1994.

Gottwald, Norman K. *The Tribes of Yahweh. A Sociology of the Religion of Liberated Israel, 1250–1050 B.C.E.* Maryknoll N.Y.: Orbis, 1979.

Mendenhall, George E. *The Tenth Generation. The Origins of the Biblical Tradition.* Baltimore: The Johns Hopkins University Press, 1973.

Mitchell, Gordon. *Together in the Land. A Reading of the Book of Joshua.* Sheffield: Sheffield Academic Press, 1993.

Polzin, Robert. *Moses and the Deuteronomist. A Literary Study of the Deuteronomic History. Part one: Deuteronomy, Joshua, Judges.* Bloomington: Indiana University Press, 1980.

Soggin, J. Alberto. *Joshua. A Commentary.* Philadelphia: Westminster, 1972.

Judges

Temba L. J. Mafico

FIRST READING

Interpretation of the Book of Judges

The book of Judges, like the book of Joshua that precedes it, is shocking to readers regardless of their religious inclinations. What is most distressing in Judges is the fact that God encourages wars and killings. The book presents a contradictory picture of the God who in Exod 20:13 and Deut 5:17 categorically enjoined the Israelites not to kill. Second, some readers find the book tedious because of its repetitious portrayal of Israel's apostasy and YHWH's relentless punishment of the Israelites through wars, defeats, and subjugation by their enemies. Third, a cursory reading of the book does not reveal the God of love, the God who has *ḥesed* and who forgives the Israelites and all humanity for their iniquities.

Is there any good news for the Christian Church in Judges? A careful reading of the book unfolds a profoundly rich message for humanity in general and for the Church in particular. Judges emphasizes what happens to the people of God and their community when they lack good leaders who minister to the people according to God's providence. In Israel judges and kings were endowed with the spirit of God by which they were to lead the people with equity and righteousness (Deut 1:16, 17). The judges and kings were responsible for the administration of the land and also for insuring that the commandments and statutes of God were obeyed. Whenever such leadership was lacking in Israel, "all the people did what was right in their own eyes" (Judg 17:6; 21:1) and not in the eyes of God. To unravel this profound message in Judges requires that the reader bear in mind its social, political, and religious contexts.

ISRAEL IN THE TIME OF THE JUDGES

Judges should never be treated as a historical record of events journaling the occupation of Canaan. It is a book intended to inspire faith in Israel. It is formulated around heroic stories of individuals like Deborah and Gideon and of tribes of Israel during the settlement of Canaan. These stories were reformulated to convey God's retributive justice to the people of Israel whenever they abandoned God and worshiped idols or made alliances with foreign nations.

The book of Judges was written for the Israelites of the eighth to the seventh centuries B.C.E. This was a time when the Israelites were experiencing serious religious apostasy, social upheavals, and political predicaments. The Northern Kingdom of Israel was facing serious military threats from Syria. Looming in the background for both Israel and Judah were military threats from the super power Assyria. In addition, Israel (or Samaria) was beleaguered by internal strife accentuated by rapid assassinations of kings and *coups d'état.* The people of Israel were desperate, wondering where the God of the forebears, the God who promised them the land flowing with milk and honey, had gone. Judges was written to provide an explanation of why God had plunged the Israelites into such dire political straits and to demonstrate how they should conduct their lives to regain God's favor. The author of Judges demonstrates with many examples that peace and national stability would return to Israel only when the Israelites once again trusted exclusively in YHWH as their forebears did under Joshua. For a full comprehension of the message of the book of Judges it is crucial that the reader should know the correct meaning and nuances of the key Hebrew verb *šāpaṭ* and the agent *šôpeṭ.*

The Term "Judge"

The word "judge" (Heb *šāpaṭ*) has many meanings. In the book of Judges it primarily means "to lead in battle." That is, *šāpaṭ* means "to deliver" or "to save" Israel from enemy oppression with the help of YHWH, the ruler of Israel (Judg 9:23; cf. Isa 33:32). The judges (Heb *šôpᵉṭim*) performed the task of delivering Israel on behalf of YHWH who clothed them with the divine spirit *(rûᵃch).* This meaning of the Hebrew root *špt* is corroborated by the fact that the deliverers are said to have judged (Heb *šāpaṭ*) Israel by going out to war. For example Othniel judged Israel by doing battle with Cushan-rishathaim (3:10). The authority and power he exercised were bestowed on him when the spirit of YHWH (*rûᵃch* YHWH) came upon him (Judg 3:10). The usage of the Hebrew root *špt* shows that the so-called judges served as deputies of YHWH, Israel's plenipotentiary ruler.

The Theme of Judges

The theme of the whole book of Judges is summarized in the introduction (Judg 1:1–2:23). In these two chapters the author opens the discourse by showing how the Israelites were able to inherit their land apportionment under the spiritual and military leadership of Joshua, a leader who was steadfast in the LORD and whose knowledge of God was able to keep the Israelites faithful to God. Israel's apostasy followed his death, as we read: "The people worshiped the LORD all the days of Joshua, and all the days of the elders who outlived Joshua, who had seen all the great work that the LORD had done for Israel" (2:7). Then Joshua died, as well as the elders and the whole generation of those who were familiar with God's great work of Israel's deliverance (2:8-10a), "and another generation grew up after them, who did not know the LORD or the work that he had done for Israel" (2:10b). The absence of a leadership group who knew of YHWH's salvific deeds plunged the Israelites into a faith crisis. They needed a leader but "in those days there was no king in Israel; [therefore] all the people did what was right in their own eyes" (17:6; 18:1; 19:1a; 21:25). Whenever the Israelites as individuals did what was good in their own eyes they lost the direction of divine providence and as a result "did what was evil in the sight of the LORD" (2:11; 3:7, 12, 4:1; 6:1; 10:6; 13:1).

According to the prophet Hosea who prophesied during a time of Israel's national instability Israel's sickness was caused by their ignorance of God. Hosea 5:4 reflects the degeneration of Israel's faith in YHWH.:

> Their deeds do not permit them
>   to return to their God.
> For the spirit of whoredom is within them,
>   and they do not know the LORD.

Instead of trusting in YHWH the Israelites had become so reliant on their kings that Yhwh through the prophet Hosea asked:

> Where now is your king, that he may save you?
> Where in all your cities are your rulers,
> of whom you said,
> "Give me a king and rulers"? (Hos 13:10).

For as long as the Israelites assumed that they could survive among the nations by their own efforts, skills, and schemes their political predicament would persist.

Judges is a book based on the theme of faith in God, a faith that must be based on the knowledge of God and God's work of salvation. The author demonstrates how the people of Israel were able to know and adhere to the LORD and God's commandments only when they had leaders who had the knowledge of God. The message that the author of Judges was giving is relevant to people of all generations. It warns leaders that they must be utterly familiar with God and God's plan of salvation for humanity if they are to inspire the people they lead to have faith in YHWH. Without this kind of leadership the people follow their own natural instincts that translate into rebellion against God. Teaching, encouraging, and admonishing in Israel was done by both word and example. This explains why the Israelites placed much weight on the leader's appointment. A leader was militarily, religiously, and politically accountable to God and to the people. However, the Israelites often forgot this point and supported bad leaders. To restore them, God punished them by military defeats. God used war because at the time the Israelites were concerned with and apprehensive about wars. Military threats managed to drive the message home. Therefore the author of the book of Judges employed military examples in order to demonstrate to the Israelites of a later generation who were preoccupied with military threats from superpowers that they must continue trusting in God. If they abandoned YHWH and followed their own instincts God would apply punishment.

On the basis of their interpretation of the principle of retribution the Israelites had come to believe that obedience to YHWH would lead to many benefits, especially victory in war, and that disobedience to the LORD would lead to military losses and natural disasters. Thus in reading Judges the reader must note the way the writer presents the working of divine retribution as the Israelites understood it. The reader should appreciate the fact that the message of Judges, particularly its retributive cycle, is still firmly held by many and is used to explain human situations, be they good or bad. At church revivals one will hear testimonies of how God blessed or punished according to one's deeds.

The Divine Formula of Retribution in Judges

The First Deuteronomistic Historian (Dtr 1)

To Judges are attributed two theological positions that are generally identified as originating with the first deuteronomist (Dtr 1) and the second deuteronomist (Dtr 2). Dtr 1 is a late preexilic theological perspective that informs the major portion of the so-called former prophets (Joshua, Judges, 1 and 2 Samuel, 1 and 2 Kings). [Cf. "Introduction to the Deuteronomistic History."] It was designed to support the institution of the monarchy and encourage faith in YHWH, especially during the reign of King Josiah of Judah who introduced religious reforms. These reforms were intended to eradicate the apostasy and Assyrian religious practices that King Manasseh, his father, had promoted. Dtr 1 also views the leadership of Joshua, Moses' successor, as a model for the subsequent leaders and kings of Israel. Joshua is selected and portrayed as having completely relied on YHWH, obeying God's statutes throughout his whole life and teaching the same to the people of Israel (Joshua 24). The conquest of Canaan in a short time is attributed to Joshua's complete obedience and faith in YHWH. Unlike the poor example of subsequent leaders like Saul, Jehu, and others, Joshua's good leadership and admonitions to the Israelites to obey and serve YHWH exclusively are emphasized (Josh 24:14-28; cf. 1 Sam 12:24-25).

To achieve his purpose Dtr 1 exaggerates the conquest of Canaan under the leadership of Joshua, portraying it as swift and decisive. The Israelites are reported to have killed *all* the Canaanites (Joshua 10–11) who believed in idols, while *no* single Israelite who believed in the LORD is reported to have died in all the battles against the Canaanites. The lesson communicated is that the Canaanites who trusted in Baal and the Asheroth—idol deities—and not in YHWH, were completely wiped out. "Joshua took [name of city] on that day, and struck it and its king with the edge of the sword; he utterly destroyed *every person* in it; he left *no one re-*

maining" (Josh 10:28, 39) or its variant, he "utterly destroyed all that breathed, as the LORD God of Israel commanded him" (Josh 10:40). Joshua "passed on from [a city or place of the slaughter of the Canaanites] and *all* Israel with him" (10:29, 31, 34, 36, 38, 43). It should be obvious that this statement was grossly exaggerated because in Joshua 13 and Judg 2:20–3:1-6 many Canaanite tribes were still occupying the land that in Joshua 1–11 was said to have been completely destroyed.

The book of Judges is placed after Joshua in order to show vividly that the time following Joshua was a period characterized by weak leadership, which in turn was the cause of rampant lawlessness, degeneration of society, and widespread apostasy. This political and religious decay is in sharp contrast to the ideal and orderly life the Israelites had enjoyed under Joshua, the life they would again enjoy if they could have good judges or god fearing monarchs of Joshua's calibre. But the fact that "there was no king in Israel," explains why "all the people [individually] did what was right in their own eyes" (Judg 17:6; 18:1; 19:1; 21:25). This statement is pregnant with very significant implications. It shows that the king's function in Israel was more than that of a mere ruler or military leader. He was anointed by YHWH to ensure the observance of the commandments of God by all Israel. The objective of the book of Judges was to influence the leaders and kings of Israel who reigned in the eighth to the sixth centuries B.C.E. to trust completely in God and stop relying on foreign alliances and foreign gods (Judg 2:20-21).

The Second Deuteronomistic Historian (Dtr 2)

Dtr 2 is a revision of the earlier deuteronomistic theology. The revision was necessitated by the changes wrought by the political vicissitudes that had rendered the formula of retribution as formulated by Dtr 1 dysfunctional. Dtr 2 provides answers to the nagging questions the Israelites were asking after the fall of Judah and the destruction of the temple of YHWH. This calamity was an enormous national disaster that, as it appeared, had nullified YHWH's covenant with David (2 Sam 7:9b-16). The eternal decree stated that David's dynasty would be perpetual on the throne regardless of the sins his offspring might commit (2 Sam 7:11b-16). YHWH had also promised that God's name would dwell in Jerusalem for ever (1 Kings 11:36). To the people of Judah the Temple represented Israel's invincibility because they believed that it signified Emmanuel, "God with us" (cf. Pss 89:20-38; 132:13-15; Isa 7:14). When the Babylonians defeated Judah, captured Jerusalem, razed the temple of YHWH, looted its holy vessels and took the elite into exile the Israelites were devastated and began to doubt YHWH's ability to protect them. They therefore called to YHWH, saying

> Awake, awake, put on strength
>   O arm of the LORD!
> Awake, as in days of old,
>   the generations of long ago! (Isa 51:9).

It was the task of the second deuteronomist to sustain the formula of retributive justice by demonstrating to the Israelites in exile how the nation's disobedience and unceasing rebellion had left YHWH no choice but to punish them severely (Ezek 5:7-17). They had spurned all the warnings YHWH had given them through the prophets (cf. Jer 2:9-13; 26:26-29). By means of the exile God was teaching them a lesson so that they might truly know God (Ezek 34:27, 30).

The Deuteronomistic Formula of Retribution

The deuteronomists formulated their theological message on a four-point cycle depicting the way the deuteronomists saw the vicissitudes of Israel's relationship with God during the time of the judges. With only minor variations in some accounts the divine retribution is repetitively presented in the following manner: (a) "The Israelites did what was evil in the sight of the LORD" (3:7a, 12, 4:1); (b) "Therefore the anger of the LORD was kindled against Israel, and he sold them into the hand of [the enemy who oppressed them]" (3:8a, 12b, 14a; 4:2); (c) "But when the Israelites cried out *(ṣāᶜaq)* to the LORD" (3:9a, 15; 4:3), (d) "the LORD raised up a deliverer *(môšîaᶜ)* for the people of Israel who delivered *(yāšaᶜ)* them" (3:9b, 15b). The Israelites would follow YHWH and obey the commandments for as long as their deliverer was alive. Thus the deuteronomist makes a strong connection between Israel's apostasy and the death of a leader. It was after the leader's death that the Israelites would do worse evil than even their forebears were capable of committing. The absence of a good leader who exemplified obedience to YHWH led to apostasy of all sorts.

Even though Judges makes it appear that the Israelites sinned as soon as they had been delivered from an enemy's oppression, a critical reading of the text contradicts this impression. Based on the length of time some of the judges governed the land, a long time elapsed before the Israelites abandoned YHWH and the retributive cycle began again. For example following their deliverance by Deborah and Gideon the Israelites remained faithful to YHWH for forty years in each case. During the judgeship of Ehud the Israelites are said to have been loyal to YHWH for a period of eighty years, that is, for two generations based on the life span in those days. There are periods when it is not reported that the Israelites committed any evil in the sight of YHWH, as is obvious during the succession of Jephthah (12:7), Ibzan (13:8-10), Elon (13:11-12), and Abdon (13:14-15).

What the deuteronomists did was transform historical stories and folktales they collected relating to the early Israelites' military victories against formidable enemies in order to show what contemporary Israelites could achieve militarily with YHWH's support. They were stressing that with strong leadership like that of Joshua, who was obedient to YHWH, the militarily beleaguered Israelites could rid themselves of the menace of their enemies if they would place their trust in YHWH. In other words the deuteronomists were campaigning for upright leadership like that of Joshua and the subsequent charismatic leaders. In Judg 2:7-10 it is clearly stated that "the people worshiped the LORD all the days of Joshua, and all the days of the elders who outlived Joshua, who had seen all the great work that the LORD had done for Israel. . . . Moreover, that whole generation was gathered to their ancestors and another generation grew up after them, who did not know the LORD or the work that he had done for Israel." It was at that point that the Israelites forgot YHWH and began worshiping other gods (2:11-12). Clearly the author is laying the blame for Israel's idolatry on the blind leadership of Israel. If only Israel had leadership that was full of insight everything would be fine. But "there was no king in Israel; all the people did what was right in their own eyes" (17:6; cf. 18:1 and *passim*).

The period of the judges provided a suitable demonstration of YHWH's retributive justice as summarized by the deuteronomists. They reviewed the history of the Israelites during the wars for the occupation of Canaan in order to show later generations that YHWH was always consistent in applying retribution. In the past God had blessed the Israelites whenever they obeyed the divine commandments by enabling them to conquer the land of Canaan and possess it, but whenever they had rebelled against YHWH and served other gods, God punished them repeatedly (Judg 3:7; 10:6; 8:33). The book was therefore intended to warn the Israelites of the dire consequences of rebellion and apostasy. The objective was to encourage the people to return to YHWH and live (Amos 5:4, 6). The book of Judges is a long sermon on the value of faith in YHWH. It does not literally portray the abiding image of God. With every change in Israel's historical context, so also did Israel's concept of God change.

Israel and the Unfolding Image of God

During the patriarchal period the Israelite clan ancestors regarded God as their patron deity. They referred to God as "the God of our ancestors." Each patriarch apparently had his main patron deity and local shrine. When the tribes of Israel finally united and became a nation the God of their progenitors was identified with YHWH, the deity who was known for the divine salvific activities. The Israelites' image of God had thus changed. They began to view God as their king (Judg 8:22-23) and judge (Judg 11:27). Since kings were the chief military commanders they regarded YHWH as their divine military succor, a deity with a convincing record of caring and securing victories for Israel (Josh 24:6-13; Judg 2:1-10; Deut 6:20-22; 26:5b-9; Isa 51:9-11). YHWH was expected to continue to defend the Israelites against surrounding nations and satisfy their needs, but only if they remained loyal to their God. The Israelites believed that among all the people of the earth they were the only people God had chosen and loved. Thus in the course of time their image of God changed. God would punish the Israelites for their own iniquities (Amos 3:2) and their sacrifices and vain worship would not avert God's wrath (5:18-20).

Israel's changing image of God should help the reader to realize that the God of the OT is not different from the God of the NT. What makes God appear different in Judges and in books of the OT is Israel's changing perspective in accordance with God's revelation through historical events.

General Context for Interpretation

The Theological Problem of Judges

Judges is generally known more for its martial stories of charismatic leaders like Deborah (4:1–5:31), Gideon (6:1–8:32), Jephthah (11:1–12:11), and Samson (13:1–16:31) than for its profound theology and teaching on Israel's conduct and divine retribution. These martial leaders are famous because they are credited with killing the inhabitants of Canaan in battles supported by YHWH. To reconcile God's commandment, "you shall not kill," with Israel's callous extermination of the Canaanites these wars have been called "holy wars," yet no matter what euphemism is applied to these wars, Judges is not normally used to generate sermons or to inspire meditation. Christians find its message very heavy and its image of God quite disturbing. It is not theologically clear why God promised the land of the Canaanites to the ancestors of Israel, and why God allowed the extermination of the Canaanites in order to fulfill the promise. The Canaanites, we are told, were to be dispossessed because their religion was very degenerate, encompassing temple prostitution, human sacrifice, and idolatry. Thus when the Israelites adopted their religion and practiced human sacrifice, they too were severely punished. Because of their incessant apostasy God ultimately dispossessed them from the land and exiled them to foreign lands. God did not show partiality. [See also the article "Violence and Evil in the Bible."]

There are other readers who find Judges tedious because of the Israelites' repetitive apostasy and YHWH's relentless punishment. The objective of Judges was to demonstrate that God's retributive justice does not change. According to the deuteronomist God would always reward the Israelites for their loyalty but would also punish them severely if they disobeyed God's commandments. The repetition in Judges accords with the ancient Near Eastern didactic method that facilitated mental retention of the essential objectives of the lesson. (Read Deut 6:6-9.) By their account of Israel's repetitive apostasy and God's corrective punishment the deuteronomists intended to make the Israelites realize why YHWH had abandoned them and allowed them to be exiled to foreign lands. For an appreciation of God's retributive justice as portrayed in the Bible it is important that the reader should be familiar with the book of Judges as a whole, particularly its main themes. As an African I also see some parallels between God's retributive justice in the book of Judges and the concept of God's justice as portrayed in African traditional religions, particularly in military matters. A brief account of the African spirit mediums and the role they played in tribal and subsequently in liberation wars will elucidate the point I am making.

The Judges and the African Spirit Mediums

The deuteronomists' portrayal of God and of the formula of retribution is not unique to the Israelites. It is also found in other religious traditions of the world such as African traditional religions. Central to African traditional religions is the belief that every good or bad situation has a divine cause and effect. (Africans did not believe in the existence of the devil or Satan.) This African belief is very similar to OT teaching as seen, for example, in Job's stern response to his wife: "Shall we receive the good at the hand of God, and not receive the bad?" (Job 2:10). This reinforces another statement in Job 1:21. Following the loss of his property Job said "Naked I came from my mother's womb, and naked shall I return there; the LORD gave, and the LORD has taken away; blessed be the name of the LORD."

In Zimbabwe the spirit mediums were consulted to declare the oracle of God when the land was experiencing disasters such as a severe drought, an epidemic, or pestilence (cf. Amos 4:4-7). God was summoned to declare whether or not the tribe should go to war or should forbear (cf. 1 Sam 28:3-25). In the case of a drought the tribe would ask their king to inquire of God through the tribal ancestral spirit, the *mhondoro,* about what was to be done to appease God. The king would call for a day of prayer and sacrifice to Mwari, "the Creator/God." This worship would be done at the sacred sanctuary on a high place such as a mountain like Mount Nyanga or Chimanimani in Mashonaland or the Matopo Hills in Matebeleland (cf. 1 Sam 9:12-14).

In the course of the ritual ceremonies, which were accompanied by singing, clapping of hands, and dancing, the spirit medium *(mhongo)* would become possessed and fall into a trance. The spirit medium would then declare why Mwari was angry with the people. On hearing about their wrongs the people would repent and promise to amend their ways and live according to divine providence (cf. 2 Kings 22:11; 23:1-3). To the people's joy the rains would soon fall again, ending the long drought. Spirit mediums, like the biblical judges and prophets, played a vital role during military encounters. They constantly reminded the people of the divine will manifested through the ancestral spirits.

It is a historical fact that in Mashonaland, a region to the south of Zimbabwe, there lived Chaminuka, a prophet who by analogy with biblical precedents was like a "prophet-judge" of the type of Deborah and Samuel. In 1883 he delivered the Shonas from Ndebele military intrigues and maneuvers. He also predicted that Lobengula, the king of the Ndebeles, would lose his land to the whites, a prophecy that eventually came true.

Before the coming of Christianity and westernization African society, like that of the Israelites, was religio-cultural. The African world was monitored by the ancestral spirits, *"vadzimu"* (sing. *mudzimu*) that were believed to be functioning under the authority of the supreme spirit, Mwari. Contact with these spirits was through the spirit mediums. The ancestral spirits functioned as intermediaries between humans and the metaphysical spirit world that included God. This datum is important because it reveals some of the similarities that exist between the spirit mediums and the biblical charismatic judges who delivered Israel and in peacetime appear to have admonished Israel to uphold the commandments of YHWH.

During the liberation of Zimbabwe from colonial rule (1972–1980) the intermediaries of the Mwari cult, namely the spirit mediums Mbuya Nehanda, Sekuru Kagubi and the prophet Chaminuka, inspired the militia to dislodge the oppressive white regime. The guerrilla leaders were able to rally the support of the general populace not only because of their valor but even more because of the divine assurance of success and support that was issued to them through the spirit mediums. This brief excursus is important because it places the religion of the Israelites during the period of the judges in relationship with contemporary religious beliefs of the African people. It is clear that African military practices and those of Israel before the classical prophets shared the same image of or perspective on God and war. The African tribal wars were very brutal and bloody. The defeated enemy was shown no mercy. In biblical terms the African tribal wars were like a *herem,* a "ban" applied by the judges during the so-called holy wars. Under the ban the enemy was annihilated: men, women, old people, children.

Did God really order this ghastly brutality against other people God created? From a Christian perspective of God the answer is certainly "no." What we find here is the image of God that the Africans and the Israelites held during their military campaigns. But in the classical period the divine image changed for the Israelites. They began to regard God as the deity who was no respecter of people. Similarly, with the coming of Christianity Africans no longer assume that God favors one tribe more than the other. It should be clear, therefore, that God did not change. What changed was the image of God as grasped by humans through historical events by which God revealed the divine nature.

Canonical Intertextuality

The formula of divine retribution permeates the OT and NT books. Whenever the Israelites experienced military and other setbacks they sought to identify the sin they, or an individual among them, had committed against YHWH (Josh 7:10-15; cf. Ps 7:3-5; John 9:2). Conversely when they were blessed with a bountiful harvest or had been triumphant in war they interpreted it as an indication that YHWH was rewarding them for their righteousness manifested through their obedience to God's commandments (Deut 9:4-6; cf. Pss 1; 18:20-24; 26:1-12; 28:1-5). Adherence to the formula of retribution naturally led to the problem of self-righteousness with which the prophets and, ultimately, Jesus had to deal.

The formula of retribution presented major problems with respect to the justice *(mishpat)* of God. In actual practice it was not always the case that the wicked were punished even when they directly challenged God (Habakkuk 1–2; Job 24; Ps 13:1-4). Those who considered themselves righteous because they adhered to God's commandments and statutes were devastated when they realized that God did not always bless or reward them (Job 22:3; 30–31). One reason why the book of Job was included in the canon was to challenge the inviolability of the deuteronomistic formula of retribution (Job 18:1-22; 21:1-26; 24:1-17; 27:1-6; 29:1-31, 40; cf. Hab 1:1–2:1). One of its objectives was to demonstrate the unpredictability of YHWH's actions. The book of Job questioned and modified the deuteronomistic formula of retribution by challenging its theological stance. The Israelites had finally discovered that YHWH was inscrutable, unfathomable, and unsearchable (Job 42:4-6). Holding to a monotheistic religion, they realized that the same God who did them good was also capable of doing what humans, from their perspective, consider evil (cf. Exod 4:11b; Job 21:7-33; Matt 5:45b; John 9:2-4). Thus the Israelites ultimately came to the realization that God and the way God does things could not be contained in a neat formula by which people could measure their spiritual achievements, declare their own righteousness, and demand their reward from God (cf. Ps 26:1-12). They finally turned the corner and found that God also loves the other nations and sent Jonah to prophesy to Nineveh, the capital city of the Assyrians, their archenemy (Jonah 1:1-2). They realized also that God could even send the Assyrians as divine agents to punish them (Isa 10:1-2), and Cyrus, the Persian king, to release them from exile (Isa 44:28; 45:1). The reader should attempt to see the whole picture of the development of the Israelites' concept of God and of God's revelation in historical events. The historical experiences of the Israelites served to amend their concept of God.

Israel's Need for a King

The judgeship of Samson is set over against the stories of the other judges like Gideon (Judg 6:1–8:5), Ehud (Judg 3:12-30), and Deborah (Judg 4:1–5:31), who obeyed YHWH's commands and delivered Israel (2:19). The Israelites only resorted to apostasy following their deaths. Furthermore the deuteronomistic framework (2:1-23; 3:7; 4:1; 6:1, 8:33; 10:6; 13:1) makes it clear that the judges were appointed by YHWH to fill the leadership vacuum that was created by the deaths of Joshua and the elders who had outlived him. To fill that vacuum YHWH raised up the judges to lead the Israelites in wars against their enemies and to admonish them to remain loyal to YHWH who had delivered them from their oppressors.

There is no doubt that the book of Judges is very concerned with the role good leadership plays in national stability and moral integrity. This assertion is supported by the fact that in the book of Jeremiah (e.g., 23:1-4, 11) YHWH is angry with the leaders of Israel for the apostasy of the nation. It is by their poor leadership and false prophetic utterances and priestly assurances that the people were led astray (Jer 6:14; 8:11; 23:25-32). In Jeremiah, therefore, it is made clear that ungodly and unenlightened leadership was the burden of the people (Jer 25:33). How truly that speaks of contemporary secular and, regrettably, in many instances, ecclesiastical leadership as well.

It appears that the deuteronomist concluded the narrative of the judges with Samson's degenerate leadership in order to highlight the effete state of later judges. Samuel's own sons, Abijah and Joel, who were judges at Beersheba, were so corrupt that the Israelites demanded a king to replace the judges (1 Sam 8:1-2). Corruption and misuse of divinely ordained power are the cardinal sins that forced the Israelites to demand a king "like other nations" (1 Sam 8:5-6).

SECOND READING

Prologue

The book of Judges is introduced with a summary of the events that culminated in the death of Joshua (1:1–2:5). The leadership and death of Joshua, the first leader of the Israelite confederacy, are highlighted in order to contrast them with the new era of the judges and kings. A brief recapitulation of Joshua's conquests is found in Judg 2:6-10, an account that has a striking similarity to Josh 24:28-31 although the account in Judges has been thoroughly revised to act as an introduction to the role of the judges. Judges 2:11-23 introduces the formula of divine retribution that characterizes the entire book.

Judges and Joshua Harmonized

The account in Judges 3 is an attempt to harmonize the conflicting accounts found in Joshua

1–11 and in Judges concerning the nature and pace of the conquest. In Josh 10:29–11:23 it is reported that the Israelites achieved a complete annihilation of the Canaanites; Joshua "left no one remaining, but utterly destroyed all that breathed," as YHWH had commanded (see Josh 10:40). The continuing existence of the Canaanites, Perizzites, Sidonians, Hittites, Hivites, Jebusites, and Amorites was not accidental, says the redactor. God left these people in order to train future generations of Israelites in the art of war. In other words these ethnic peoples were to act as "guinea pigs" for the later generation of Israelites to experience how to do battle by killing them (3:1-4). From the foregoing the reader would expect only pockets of these people who, by their paucity, would not give the Israelites much trouble. Evidence does not support this rosy picture. The fact that the Israelites were continuously tempted to adopt the Canaanite religion and culture must imply that the conquest was on the whole achieved by Israelite infiltration into the land of Canaan. The deuteronomistic redactors, writing for a community far removed from historical reality, idealized the ancient Israelite conquest in order to inspire faith in YHWH at a time when it was most needed. What should be obvious by now is that the deuteronomists were like preachers. They adapted folktales and with some embellishments were able to inspire hope and morale in the Israelites. This analogy should be borne in mind when one reads individual passages of the book of Judges.

Judges, Part One

Othniel (3:7-11)

Othniel ben Kenaz, the first of the judges, is very obscure. His prominence came when, because of the spirit of YHWH that entered him, he defeated Cushan-rishathaim in battle. According to the cycle of divine retribution the people of Israel had breached the commandments of God (3:7). To punish them God allowed Cushan to defeat and subject them (3:8). Instead of blaming their defeat on poor strategy or the superior strength of the enemy the Israelites attributed their dismal performance in battle to YHWH's retribution. Thus they rededicated their lives to YHWH and acknowledged their sin by crying to YHWH. YHWH, like a good parent, heard their appeal and raised *(qûm)* Othniel as "judge" to deliver them from the hand of Cushan. For eighteen years under Othniel's leadership Israel followed YHWH and enjoyed peace (3:11), but when Othniel died Israel had no leader to admonish them against apostasy and teach them to observe the commandments and statutes of YHWH. At any rate the deuteronomist intends to show that the Israelites were loyal to YHWH for eighteen years primarily because of Othniel's exemplary leadership.

Ehud (3:12-30)

Ehud's judgeship is intriguing. The people of Israel had again done what was evil in the sight of YHWH (3:12). Thus YHWH subjected them to the Moabites who imposed heavy tribute on them. To pay tribute to another king was very embarrassing and demoralizing to the Israelites. Thus the Israelites realized their sin and cried to YHWH for help. YHWH responded compassionately and, to give them relief, appointed Ehud as a *môšîaʿ*, a "savior" or "deliverer" (3:15). YHWH's commissioning of Ehud as judge took place while he was leading a group delivering tribute to Eglon, king of the Moabites (3:15). Ehud's unusual strength is evidenced by the fact that he was left-handed, a phrase that in Hebrew refers to dexterity (cf. 20:16). Nothing is mentioned of the spirit of God entering him at any point in his deliverance of Israel, but he is regarded as a judge notwithstanding the fact that he killed Eglon in cold blood. His audacity created a provocation that culminated in Israel's military victory against the Moabites (3:28-30). From the author's perspective Ehud became a *môšîaʿ*, a "deliverer" of Israel because YHWH was with him. Otherwise there is no other explanation the theocratic Israelites could have found to explain how they were freed from the Moabite oppression. Besides, the fact that Ehud subsequently governed Israel for eighty years was further proof of his divine calling.

Deborah and Barak (4:1-24)

The story of Deborah appears to serve several purposes. It takes the position that women were not inferior to men and could be called upon to deliver the Israelites. A woman like Deborah became even more gifted than men. She, unlike any man in Judges, was both a prophet and a deliverer. She decided (Hb *špṭ*) cases and the people

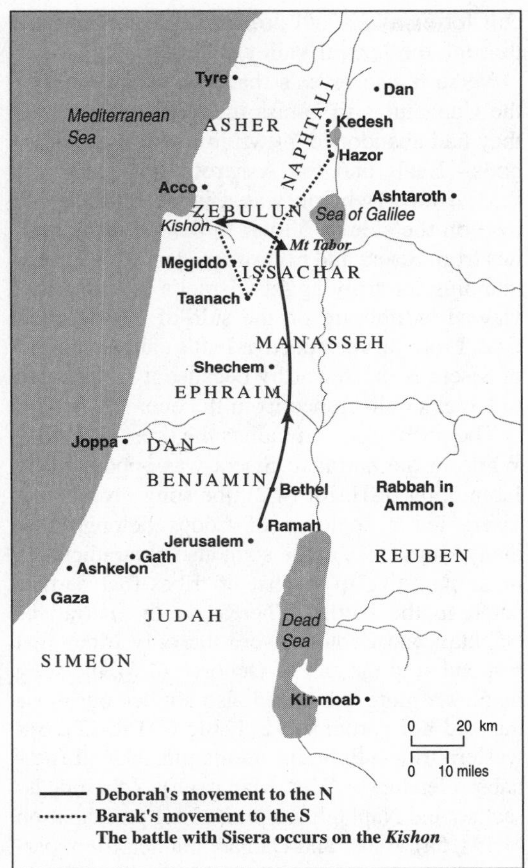

JUDGES 4–5

of Israel used to go to her for adjudication, which she rendered under a palm tree that bore her name, that is, the palm of Deborah (4:5).

The story of Deborah would find several parallels in Africa. A certain Mozambican woman called Machiweni was equally gifted. She was a diviner and an able arbitrator whose fame spread throughout Central and Southern Africa. Chiefs, headmen *(zᵉqēnîm)* and common people alike recognized her talents and sought her to decide cases and predict phenomena. Men, even those in high positions, went to her regardless of her gender because they recognized her power which they attributed to the spirit which was in her. No wonder, therefore, that a man of Barak's caliber would not go to battle unless Deborah, a woman, went with him.

In reading the story critically one gets the impression that the author deliberately qualified the role of Deborah as a judge who leads the army of Israel that was comprised of men. To establish her status and integrity as a leader the writer connected her to men. First he discloses that she was the wife of Lapidoth (4:4). When male judges delivered the Israelites the names of their spouses were not disclosed. The only attributes mentioned relate to their valor and strength (Judg 3:15; 6:12). Another prejudicial imputation is that as a woman she had to appoint a man, Barak, to conduct the military campaign against Sisera. However, because Barak was aware that Deborah was the charismatic judge he refused to go to war unless she also went with him (4:8-9). Because this victory was to prove the able leadership of women Barak would not be credited with the killing of Sisera. It was instead the deed of another woman, Jael, a Kenite (4:21). One also gets the impression that the Barak narrative was interpolated later to tone down the scintillating military leadership of women in a patriarchal society. Basically, however, this biblical text subtly and effectively highlights the contributions of women toward the establishment and stability of Israel as a state. A careful reading of other texts dealing with women like Sarah, Miriam, and the wise woman of Tekoa reveals how the narrators demonstrated women's ingenuity and strength in various situations.

Deborah's leadership was in many respects like that of Samuel. Deborah and Samuel were prophets and judges. They both had permanent places where people consulted them for a decision on cases they brought (Judg 4:4; cf. 1 Sam 7:15-17). Both inspired military leaders whom they accompanied to battle (Judg 4:6; cf. 1 Sam 7:8). Deborah appointed Barak to lead the army to liberate Israel (3:6) and Samuel anointed Saul to lead military campaigns against the Philistines (1 Sam 10:1).

The Song of Deborah (5:1-31)

The Song of Deborah is an important piece of Hebrew poetry that seems to reflect the actual manner in which the conquest of Canaan was achieved by the Israelites. Because of its archaic type it offers scholars access to the late twelfth and early eleventh centuries B.C.E. religion and polity of the Yahwist organization. The song celebrates the manifestation of YHWH to those who participated in the routing of the chariots of Sisera. The defeat of the Canaanites is attributed to YHWH because

> The stars fought from heaven
> from their courses they fought against Sisera (Judg 5:20).

The author's faith in YHWH is manifested by the metaphorical depiction of the stars leaving their courses to come to the aid of Deborah and Barak as they battled with Sisera. This is not the first time the deuteronomist shows faith in YHWH in this way. In the book of Joshua we read that Joshua spoke these words to the LORD on the day when the LORD gave the Amorites over to the people of Israel:

> Sun, stand still at Gibeon,
> and Moon, in the valley of Aijalon.
> And the sun stood still, and the moon stopped
> until the nation took vengeance on their enemies (Josh 10:13).

It seems clear that the battle against the Canaanites was not triggered by their provocation. Israel waged it in order to gain control of the plain of the Esdraelon valley. Now that the Israelites controlled the caravan routes in the highlands of Ephraim and Galilee (5:6b-7) Canaanite control of the plain had become an economic disadvantage. The Israelites believed that whatever was not good for them was also not good for their God. To possess the valley of Jezreel for economic purposes was regarded as a religious issue that YHWH must support for the sake of Israel or simply because YHWH was their God. As the patron of the nation God was like a loving parent who would never cheer for a neighbor's child when both are locked in a fight, regardless of who the aggressor was. This analogy correctly depicts how the Israelites regarded YHWH.

To develop a better understanding of the true nature of God, Israel had to wait until the time of the prophets, beginning with Amos. Until that time they felt that YHWH sanctioned anything they did simply because YHWH was their God. YHWH would never be concerned with other nations that worshiped other gods. Thus in v. 4 YHWH as the Divine Warrior of Israel marches from the region of Edom in full military gear. The earth trembles and the clouds drop water, a euphemism for uncontrollable urination due to fear. Also characteristic of the march of the Divine Warrior is the quaking of the mountains before YHWH, Mount Sinai in particular (v. 5). Verse 6 explains why the battle against Sisera was waged. The Canaanites had made it difficult for caravans and ordinary travelers to pass through the Jezreel Valley (v. 7).

Verse 6 also reveals that YHWH had allowed the Canaanites to harass the Israelites because they had abandoned YHWH in favor of the other gods—Baals and the Asheroth (cf. Judg 3:7; 8:33; 10:6). Deborah was a judge because she rose on the side of YHWH to deliver the Israelites from Sisera and his armies. Any leader commanding an army against Israel's enemies was viewed as fighting on the side of YHWH, their God. From this perspective Jael's callous murder of Sisera is praiseworthy because it contributed to Israel's deliverance from the enemy.

The poem also contradicts the prose narrative. While in the narrative Sisera was appointed by Jabin, king of Hazor (4:2), the song reveals that Sisera led a coalition of troops belonging to many kings (5:19). The song also contradicts the prose narrative in the list of tribes that participated in the battle. Whereas in the narratives Naphtali and Zebulun were the only tribes that responded to the call of Deborah (4:6), the song mentions more tribes and also singles out those that did not participate in battle (4:15b-17). Six western tribes: Ephraim, Benjamin, Machir (perhaps referring to West Manasseh), Zebulun, Issachar, and Naphtali are praised for participation (4:14-15a). Asher and Dan are blamed for apparently involving themselves with the Sea People (5:17). Reuben and Gilead (perhaps referring to East Manasseh) are blamed for staying at home and not taking part in the "holy war." No mention is made of Judah, Levi, and Gad. [Cf. list of tribes in Genesis commentary at Gen 30:25.]

The song was included to inspire faith in later generations of Israel. It shows the hopeless military situation in which the Israelites found themselves when they faced the coalition of Canaanite city states. Deborah's victorious leadership earned her the title "Mother of Israel." By means of effective contrast the writer ends the poem by showing that while Deborah the Mother of Israel is rejoicing in victory, the mother of Sisera, on the other hand, is anxious about her son's delay in returning from battle. The writer is sarcastic in showing the wise women of the Canaanites acting like false prophets, filling her with vain hopes. They tell her that Sisera's delay is because he is occupied with dividing the spoils of the defeated Israelites (4:29-30) when in fact he is dead.

The Lesson of the Song

God can call anyone, regardless of gender, to become a judge by whom God is able to deliver Israel. When a person has the divine gift of adjudication, prophecy, and military leadership he or she will be recognized by the people regardless of gender and other societal inhibitions. The song also reveals that the redactors were not necessarily interested in giving historical facts about the conquest of Canaan. Rather they were concerned about how they could raise the consciences of the people of Israel to have faith in YHWH. This explains why the account in the song contradicts the prose account. To the writer these were different views of the same event that underscored God's salvific activities for the Israelites when they were loyal to God.

Gideon (6:1–8:32)

The account of Gideon's judgeship appears to have undergone a series of interpolations. It has accumulated some elements that are characteristic of the call of Moses and those of some of the classical prophets. The description of the Midianite oppression and menace to the Israelites is more elaborate than that prefacing the account of any previous leader (6:1-6). Previously when the Israelites cried to YHWH because of enemy oppression YHWH simply raised a deliverer. In Gideon's case YHWH first sends a prophet to make an indictment against Israel. YHWH's grievance *(rîb)* was Israel's disloyalty to YHWH, the deity who delivered them from Egypt, drove out "all" the Canaanites and gave them the land (6:8-10). They had abandoned YHWH and served the gods of the Canaanites (6:7). Another major departure from the calls of the other judges is that the language used in the indictment is reminiscent of the covenant stipulations in Exod 20:1-4.

The seriousness of the Midianite menace is evident from the fact that even a strong man of Gideon's valor had to beat wheat in hiding, in the wilderness. It was while he was beating wheat that an angel of YHWH came to reassure him: "YHWH is with you, you mighty warrior" (v. 12). Gideon responded with a question: "If YHWH is with us, why then has all this happened to us?" (v. 13). By asking this question Gideon reveals that the prophetic indictment that precedes his call was originally not part of this biblical text. If it were, Gideon would not have asked the question. Furthermore, unlike the other judges when they were called, Gideon asks for a series of signs, the first of which he misconstrues as portending his imminent death (6:22-23). That same night YHWH instructs him to pull down the altar of Baal that his father owned and ministered for the city dwellers, and also to cut down the Asherah beside it. He is asked to replace it with an altar of YHWH and to make an offering there to YHWH. Even though he is afraid of the consequences of destroying Baal's altar he does not protest to the angel of YHWH about the instruction. Instead, with the aid of ten servants he destroys Baal's temple at night while the villagers are asleep. In the morning the men of the city are stunned to see Baal's altar destroyed and the Asherah cut down (6:28-32). They demand that Gideon be lynched. His father responds by demanding that Baal, if he is a living god, should defend his own altar.

There is a remarkable similarity between this episode and Elijah's contest on Mount Carmel in which Baal's failure to respond to a challenge by YHWH proves that he is not a living god (1 Kings 18:26-29). There are several complex problems in the story, however. Did the Israelites also worship Baal at Gideon's father's altar? If not, why do we not hear of the destruction of all the other Baal altars that the Israelites had also established? Why is Gideon's father not named? People of such significance are often named in the OT. If Gideon's father was an Israelite, how did he come to hold such a high position among the Baal worshipers who were Canaanite? The author of the story is silent on these questions because to ask them is to miss the objective of the narrative.

Hermeneutical Significance

It appears that Gideon's father was a chief priest of Baal ministering at an altar used by the villagers. He wielded great authority because his decision that Baal should contend for his own altar was accepted by the villagers. It is clear that Yahwism had been superseded by Baalism, which explains the Israelite plight before the Midianites. What is most remarkable is the fact that Gideon was called by God primarily because of his valor and not so much because he was a righteous person. He appears to have doubted YHWH's power, as reflected by his question, "If YHWH is with us, why then has all this happened to us?" (v. 13). What this statement demonstrates is that YHWH could use a Baal worshiper for the liberation of Israel just as God could use Cyrus of Persia to restore the Israelites in Judah (Isa 45:1). God calls different people and assigns them different tasks on the basis of natural gifts they already possess. God saw in Gideon great valor and appointed him to deliver the Israelites from oppression. The story also shows the nature of YHWH. No matter how far the Israelites had wandered away from YHWH, God was ready to receive them back as long as they remembered YHWH and cried to YHWH for deliverance.

The fact that the Israelites remembered YHWH and YHWH's salvific power when they were in dire straits demonstrates a common human phenomenon. It is when we are facing life's trials and tribulation that we seek God's presence in prayer. In several passages in Deuteronomy the Israelites are seriously warned that when they settle in the land and acquire good houses, and have eaten good food and are full, they should be careful not to forget YHWH their God. Finally, the story of Gideon's victory over the Midianites with only three hundred soldiers shows that it is not by human might and strategies that battles against our enemies are won; rather battles are won when God blesses the efforts no matter how little. This is the message that strengthened the Israelites when they were confronting many hostile nations surrounding them and when they were threatened with exile in foreign lands. While Judges encourages complete reliance on YHWH it also teaches that humans must ask God's guidance for strategies that would help them to overcome any adversity no matter how big. Prayer alone without a course of action is like having faith in God but without works.

The next episode in Gideon's career relates to his vendetta against the people of the Transjordan who did not accept Gideon as YHWH's appointee. Having captured the two kings, Zebah and Zalmunna, he brought them to Penuel and Succoth, two cities that belonged to them. After terrorizing their citizens before their very eyes he executes them. Why did Gideon do this? His action was in accordance with the laws of the *herem.* It was to act as a deterrent to other people who might have the propensity to rebel against Gideon, the person appointed by YHWH. Second, this account was included to show later generations the difference between Gideon who obeyed God's *herem* and Saul who disobeyed the *herem* by sparing two kings he had captured in battle.

The Israelites were so impressed with Gideon's military performance that they tried to persuade him to accept the idea of starting a royal dynasty (8:22). Again Gideon demonstrates his dependence on and loyalty to YHWH by declining the offer on the grounds that YHWH is the king of Israel (8:23). Gideon would rather obey God and not succumb to the temptation of acquiring power. (What a contrast to modern leadership in many countries!) It is for this reason that Samuel in 1 Sam 8:7 regarded the appointment of Saul as king of Israel to be a sign of Israel's rejection of YHWH's majesty.

Abimelech (9:1-57)

Although Gideon declined a dynasty an editorial text was inserted to link the next judge, Abimelech, to Gideon since he was his son by a polygamous marriage. He became a judge because when Gideon died at a ripe age the people of Israel again forgot the beneficent acts of YHWH and reverted to idolatry. They prostrated themselves before Baal-berith (8:29-32). Scholarly opinion based on archaeological data provides evidence attesting that Deborah and Barak were contemporaneous with or even later than Abimelech. If so, why did the redactor place the story of Abimelech out of sequence? The redactor's purpose was not to deceive. The material in Judges is arranged in such a way that it places the abortive attempt to introduce kingship in the middle of the book. It is also significant that this episode takes place at Shechem, the place where the covenant YHWH made with the Israelites at Sinai was renewed (Josh 24:1), but this time Shechem fails to unite the Israelites as a covenanted people. Instead it witnesses the bitterest civil war of all. In other words Abimelech's rule, like that of Solomon, divided the confederacy.

Abimelech's rise to judgeship parallels the kingship of Solomon in many ways. His mother was involved in negotiations with the Shechemite elite to crown Abimelech as king of Israel. On becoming king he in turn murdered his seventy brothers except the youngest, Jotham, who hid himself. At all events Abimelech was crowned king near an oak at the Shechem fortress (9:1-6). Jotham's escape from death was not an accident, according to the redactor. God had a prophetic purpose for him. It is Jotham who later told a fable to the same Shechemite elite admonishing the Shechemites that their crowning of Abimelech would invoke YHWH's retributive justice (9:15b-21). During Abimelech's judgeship the relationship between him and the Shechemite elite soured (9:26-29). In the ensuing battle Abimelech prevailed against Gaal; the rebel leader and his followers were killed (9:26-41).

Abimelech then mounted a fierce retaliatory action against the rebels, ambushing the Shechem peasants who were in the field and killing them. He razed Shechem and placed it under a curse (9:42-45). At this point the author reveals the moral of the story. Anything that humans achieve without YHWH will always end in disaster. Thus, having achieved this feat, Abimelech died an ignominious death. As he was engaged in some military mopping-up operation he drew too close to the tower of the stronghold of Thebez. A woman hurled a millstone from the tower and crushed his skull (9:50-54). The author shows that although Abimelech was king he had killed all his brothers but one, and had won great battles, nonetheless he was vulnerable because he was not endowed with God's spirit. Because of the lack of divine commissioning he was killed by a woman, a very shameful death for a strong man. Abimelech's death was followed by the disbanding of the Israelite militia (21:24), each person going to his own place (9:55). The Abimelech era came to an end very quickly, showing the execution of YHWH's justice on a wicked ruler and the fulfillment of Jotham's allegorical "prophecy."

Tola and Jair (10:1-5)

The redactor does not disclose the nature of these two judges because it would detract from the objective of the narrative. Following the illustrious administration of Gideon the redactor evidently wants to show that social conditions continued to deteriorate in order to justify the thematic refrain: "There was no king in Israel; all the people did what was right in their own eyes" (17:6; 19:1; 21:25). This suspicion is confirmed by the fact that judges like Jair appear to have had so much influence that thirty cities under his sons' charge were called Havvoth-jair "the villages of Jair" (10:4). Moreover, Jair and Tola judged Israel for forty-five years, much longer than Abimelech to whom much space in the text was devoted.

Prologue to Part Two of Judges: 10:6-16

Social, religious, and political conditions continued to degenerate. The Israelites are portrayed as being very much involved with the deities of their former oppressors. Whereas they were serving Baal and Asherah before, now they have added the gods of the Syrians, Sidonians, Ammonites, Moabites, and Philistines. In response to Israel's rebellious demeanor YHWH threatened no longer to respond to their cries until they had cleansed themselves of the abomination of these alien deities. With this description of Israel's prevailing situation the redactor has made a structural bridge to his or her second didactic discourse, intended to show that a life without YHWH is a life of social, political, and religious chaos.

Judges, Part Two

Jephthah (11:1–12:7)

Jephthah's judgeship serves a dual purpose. First, his rise to power is typical of the saying, "The stone that the builders rejected has become the chief cornerstone" (Ps 118:22). Jephthah was born into a rich family but was subsequently thrown out by his younger brothers because they alleged that he was the son of a woman whom their father had as a prostitute (11:1). He therefore became a renegade and went to live with a band of vagabonds at Tob where his might and military prowess were recognized (11:3). The Ammonite menace in the Transjordan had worsened and the Israelites were forced to summon Jephthah to be their *qāṣîn,* a low-ranking army officer (11:6), but Jephthah demanded a higher position and by a covenant made at Mizpah his wish was granted (11:4-11).

Jephthah's first act was to send messengers to the Ammonites to settle their claim to the land by diplomatic means (11:12-28), pointing out that the land the Israelites possessed was given to them by YHWH. He advised them to hold on to their own land that Chemosh, their god, had given them. Jephthah's argument confirms the point made earlier, that the people of the ancient Near East regarded deities as patrons of the nation. It is those gods who gave the land, and they guarded it against aggrandizement of the other nations supported by their gods. It is for this reason that Jephthah appealed to YHWH, the judge of the land under dispute, to decide the case (11:27). Because Jephthah appealed to the God of the Israelites the spirit of YHWH entered him (v. 29). In spite of Jephthah's stunning success and loyalty to YHWH the author minimizes the impact of Jephthah's military success by concluding his triumph with serious tragedy.

Before going to war Jephthah had made a vow before YHWH that he would sacrifice the first thing to meet him on his triumphant return (11:31). As fate would have it, it was his daughter, the only child he had, who joyfully came to meet him. She was dancing with timbrel to welcome her victorious father (11:34). Stunned and saddened by this event, Jephthah told his daughter about the vow; she accepted it and, unfortunately, it led to her death. This tragedy was followed by another involving a dispute between Jephthah's tribe and the Ephraimites who felt snubbed by not being invited to join battle against the Ammonites (12:1-2). The Ephraimites suffered heavy casualties when they tried to resolve the matter militarily (12:1-5). As they tried to escape they were met at the Jordan crossings and executed. They were identified by the accent with which they pronounced the word "Shibboleth" as "Sibboleth" (12:5-6). One thing is now clear: leaders who preceded Jephthah ended their governorship in peace lasting for many years, but now the situation is different. Jephthah's judgeship is followed by family tragedy and his military triumph plunges Israel into bitter civil war.

Three Minor Judges (12:8-15)

During this time of political and religious chaos no leader was able to judge Israel for a long time. Jephthah only judged for six years (12:7). He was followed by Ibzan who governed for seven years. Elon succeeded him and judged Israel for ten years. The last of these judges was Abdon who judged Israel for eight years. Why are the tenures of these judges now so short? Deborah and Gideon judged Israel for forty years each. As has been pointed out earlier, the redactor had a plan of God's retributive justice by which he or she arranged the stories used. By shortening their tenures and not providing the details of their judgeships the redactor was able to minimize the impact of these judges, leaving the impression in the mind of the reader that conditions in Israel continued to deteriorate. As a consequence God gave the Israelites to the Philistines for forty years. The next thing the redactor does to portray political chaos is to adapt a number of legendary folktales that developed around the figure of Samson.

Samson (13:1–16:31)

The birth of Samson is framed by the formula: "the Israelites again did what was evil in the sight of YHWH" (13:1a). In response YHWH delivers them into the hands of the Philistines for forty years (13:1b). Normally we would expect to read that the Israelites cried to YHWH and YHWH raised a deliverer. In the case of Samson there does not appear to be a connection between the Philistine oppression and Samson's solo attacks, which seem to be purely personal and intriguing.

The circumstances surrounding the birth and upbringing of Samson and Samuel are similar. Samson's mother was barren (13:1-7; cf. 1 Sam 1:11). Both Samson and Samuel were devoted to the service of God. (13:2; cf. 1 Sam 1:11). Both became judges of Israel (18:31; cf. 1 Sam 7:15).

That the story of Samson is more legendary than historical is manifested by several elements. The name of his father, Manoah, is mentioned, but not that of his mother, although she was the one who met the angel of YHWH twice. Several legendary stories of great people in biblical times are shaped according to the axiom: "Great things often have small beginnings." The birth of Isaac, the patriarch of Israel, is a typical example (Gen 18:9-15). He was born when his mother had become old and had ceased menstruation. The birth of Moses, the great lawgiver of Israel, took place at a time when Hebrew baby sons were being killed by the Egyptians (Exod 2:1-10) to curtail the Israelite population. When all hope is lost only God can deliver in the nick of time: after all, "Is anything too hard (lit. wonderful) for YHWH?" (Gen 18:14; cf. Isa 7:11).

Samson's mother was advised to live a disciplined life beginning with her child's conception

(Judg 13:4). She was to forego all intoxicants and other ritually forbidden foods. The storyteller appears to be intimating that if children are to become good citizens their parents' exemplary life must begin at the child's conception. Why is the father not included in this disciplined living for the sake of the child? Biblical teaching normally highlights the influence of the mother on the children more than that of the father, particularly when they are still young.

Leadership Without Divine Guidance

In spite of the fact that he was well reared Samson did not live up to expectations. He used his divine power more for personal control of the Philistines than for leading the Israelites in battles of liberation. The pretexts for his attacks on the Philistines were not related to their oppression of the Israelites; they were personal and related solely to his social life.

The Moral of the Samson Story

The story of Samson is told for multiple reasons and has a correspondingly wide variety of possible interpretations. The following are some possibilities. On the one hand the component stories underscore the grace of God manifested toward the Israelites who were born at the time when they had abandoned YHWH and were serving other gods. YHWH's retributive justice left no choice; they had to be subjected to the Philistines. But the same God who punishes also acts as the redeemer. The Israelites did not cry to the Lord because of the Philistines' oppression and yet God provided them with some occasional relief through Samson. Samson also acted as an example to the Israelites of how they could have routed the Philistines had they lived like Nazirites. For example Samson, who had been set aside to follow YHWH, had very unusual strength by which he single-handedly defeated the Philistines. What if there were more people like him? That God answers prayer is demonstrated by the fact that when he was thirsty Samson prayed to YHWH and God provided him with water. When he was oppressed by the Philistines, blinded and used for sport, Samson prayed to God who restored his lost strength and enabled him to inflict heavier casualties on the Philistines than he had ever inflicted in all his life. Samson became an example to the Israelites of later generations of how loyalty to YHWH could bring success.

Yet the story of Samson also taught some lessons that were illustrated by his own folly. The story of Samson shows how a great man chosen by God from his birth could lose direction by slighting the tradition of the elders, parental advice, and common sense. He loved Philistine women, daughters of the enemy whom God had "called" him to menace (14:1-3; 16:1, 4). This was in complete disregard of the commandment of YHWH that prohibited Israelite men from marrying foreign women (cf. 1 Kings 11:1-2). Samson ordered his parents to get him one of the Philistine women simply because "she pleases me well" (14:3). How often do we hear children defiantly answering their parents in this way while spurning good parental advice?

The story of Samson has been studied and interpreted by many scholars simply because it is intriguing. Some scholars regard Samson as a real person while others see him as a legendary figure. Some of his reported activities appear to have originated as etymological legends: for example, Samson's miraculous killing of the Philistines with a jawbone explains why the place was called Ramath-lehi, "the hill of the jawbone." When Samson became very thirsty, he entreated YHWH who, in response, provided him with water from a cleft in the earth. That also provided the etymology of the name of the well called En-hakkore, "the spring of one who called" (15:19). The story also fits several familiar motifs, one of which is that of the barren woman. The story of Samson is one of the clearest cases of redaction by means of interpolations for purposes of converting familiar folktales into lessons for Israel.

More Political and Religious Chaos

The deterioration of political leadership was concomitant with the acceleration of religious degeneration. The redactors disclose the religious and social decay that followed poor leadership by the last judges of Israel. The story of Micah was, in all probability, intended to show how crucial leadership was for a theocratic people like Israel. Without strong leadership of high moral calibre Israel plunged into political, religious, and social chaos.

Micah's Shrine (17:1–18:31)

This section of the book of Judges contains several independent stories that are joined together by skillful editorial devices. The theme that runs through these stories is: "there was no king in Israel" (17:6; 18:1; 19:1). The absence of the king is an issue that is used to prepare the reader for Israel's demand for a king during the judgeship of Samuel. The land of Israel had turned to anarchy (17:6b). Sons stole from their own parents (17:1-4). Public sanctuaries for the worship of YHWH had ceased to exist and private personal sanctuaries had replaced them (17:4). Micah, for example, had a sacred house in which he kept an ephod and teraphim and his son served as a priest (18:7-13). Later on he hired an itinerant Levite from Bethlehem to serve in his shrine. Just as Micah was rejoicing that YHWH would bless him now that he had a Levite as priest the Danites seized the shrine. There was nothing Micah could do to prevent this robbery or to regain his property because "there was no king in Israel; all the people did what was right in their own eyes."

A Levite's Concubine and the Sin of Benjamin (19:1-30)

The chapter appropriately opens with the words: ". . . there was no king in Israel" (cf. 17:6; 18:1). Anarchy and a complete disregard for tradition and custom were rife. Thus it happened that a Levite went to Bethlehem to bring back his estranged concubine who had escaped to her parental home (19:2). When he was returning with her to his own home the sun set on them at Gibeah, a town within Benjaminite territory (19:11). According to the tradition of the ancient Near East travelers, especially strangers, must be given hospitality, particularly at night (cf. Gen 18:1-8; 19:4-8). The city dwellers of Gibeah ignored the man, his servant, and his concubine in the center of the city square. An alien resident, an old man returning from his fields, saw the traveler in the open square and welcomed him and his concubine in his own house and entertained them. In the middle of the night, in an incident reminiscent of the story of the men of Sodom (Gen 19:4-5), the wicked men of Gibeah demanded that the old man hand the Levite over to them that they might know him (19:22). The old man entreated the men to take his virgin daughters instead of the visitor (19:23-24), but when they would not listen they were given the Levite's concubine whom they sexually molested all night. In the morning she was found dead at the door of the old man's house (19:26). The Levite took the corpse and, on reaching home, divided it into twelve parts and scattered them throughout the twelve tribes as a curse (19:29-30). By the concept of *pars pro toto* each tribe had become responsible for the death of the concubine. To show their innocence they were required to avenge this evil deed (cf. 1 Sam 11:5-11).

When the eleven tribes realized what had happened, they asked: "Has such a thing ever happened since the day that the Israelites came up from the land of Egypt until this day? Consider it, take counsel, and speak out" (19:30). They then united to wage war against the tribe of Benjamin (20:12-19). Of all the Benjaminites only six hundred men escaped to the mountains (20:47). In spite of the victory the eleven tribes of Israel lamented the fact that one of their own brothers was almost extinct (21:1). To reinstate Benjamin they raided Jabesh-gilead as a punishment for that town's not participating in the war against Benjamin, killing all the men and sparing only four hundred virgins. These were given to the Benjaminite men hiding in the mountains. The remaining two hundred Benjaminite men were advised to fetch their own wives by ambushing the virgins of Shiloh (21:16-23). With six hundred Benjaminite men having wives, the twelve tribes were now once again intact, but the major problem persisted. There was still no king in Israel.

The corruption of the judges had become so intense that even Samuel with all his integrity was not able to repair the image of the office of the judges. Besides, his own sons whom he had appointed judges at Beersheba were corrupt. Thus the Israelites demanded that they should have a king like all the other nations. They had become convinced that their political and military problems were the result of the corrupt judges.

Conclusion: The Teaching of Judges

Judges is basically made up of short stories, mainly of Israel's wars. Whenever the Israelites were defeated in battle they interpreted it as God's swift corrective punishment for their disobedience. The stories are told in order to inculcate in the minds of the nation of Israel, and its individual members, an attitude of obedience and trust in God. Obedience to God and compliance with cultural tradition are communicated by means of short stories such as those relating to Samson and his tragic marriages. The lesson from Samson's stories is that disobedience to God, flouting tribal tradition and ignoring good parental advice ultimately lead to personal disaster in this life regardless of one's status. Samson was a Nazirite, a man full of divine strength, but he died a blind prisoner among the Philistines, enemies of Israel whom he was inspired by YHWH to fight (Judg 13:5b). This happened because he had disobeyed God by violating the Israelite religious tradition of endogamous marriage (Deut 7:3) in spite of his parents' attempt to restrain him (Judg 14:3).

The book of Judges also stresses that whenever the Israelites did what was good in their own eyes and not in the eyes of their God they committed grievous sins against YHWH and humanity (Deut 12:8; Judg 17:6; 21:25; cf. 1 Kings 15:5, 11; 2 Kings 12:2; 14:3). It was only when the Israelites made choices that were consonant with God's providence that YHWH bestowed blessings on them. The issue is not whether an action looks good to a person, but rather whether an action is good according to God's providence. Thus only life lived according to divine principles will bestow blessings on the people of God.

The tragic story of Samson functions as a warning particularly to people who are called by God to perform ecclesiastical services. God endows people with power to preach, to counsel, to encourage, and to serve God and the people. However, so often their strong moral defenses collapse before temptation, often of a sexual nature. Samson, a Nazirite whose life had been devoted to God from childhood, violated his vow by yielding to his burning desire for women. Reading about Samson's tragedy brings to memory several stories of great political and religious giants who fell from grandeur because of their lustful sexual obsessions regardless of the desired partner's nationality, moral status, or religion. King David tarnished his illustrious monarchy because of Bathsheba (2 Sam 11:2–12:14). The deuteronomists also assert that Solomon fell from a glorious reign because of his desire for women, even foreign women from countries that were historically inimical to Israel (1 Kings 11:1-40). Thus Judges still has a message for the modern world. Unless humans learn to live according to God's providence for the world, taking care of the environment as the first human was commanded to do in the stories of creation, God will apply retributive justice.

BIBLIOGRAPHY

Boling, Robert G. *Judges.* AB 6A. Garden City, N.Y.: Doubleday, 1975.

Mafico, Temba L. J. "African Tradition and Jewish Culture," *Patterns of Prejudice* [London: Institute of Jewish Affairs] 16/3 (1982) 17–26.

____. "Were the Judges of Israel like African Spirit Mediums?" in Daniel Smith-Christopher, ed., *Text & Experience: Towards a Cultural Exegesis of the Bible.* Sheffield: Sheffield Academic Press, 1995, 330–343.

Moore, George Foot. *A Critical and Exegetical Commentary on Judges.* ICC 7. New York: Scribner, 1903.

Ranger, T. O. *Revolt in Southern Rhodesia, 1896–7: A Study in African Resistance.* London: Heinemann, 1967.

Soggin, J. Alberto. *Judges: A Commentary.* Translated by John Bowden. Philadelphia: Westminster, 1981.

Vaux, Roland de. *The Early History of Israel.* Translated by David Smith. Philadelphia: Westminster, 1978.

Ruth

Ofosu Adutwum

FIRST READING

According to the Talmud Ruth was the first book in the third section of the Hebrew Bible, the "Writings," but recent Jewish tradition places it with four other books (Song of Songs, Lamentations, Ecclesiastes, and Esther) to be read on certain festival occasions. Ruth is read at the Feast of Weeks, which concludes the wheat harvest. Ruth was probably linked with this festival because of its harvest setting, its strong element of fertility, and its pointer to ultimate triumph and joy.

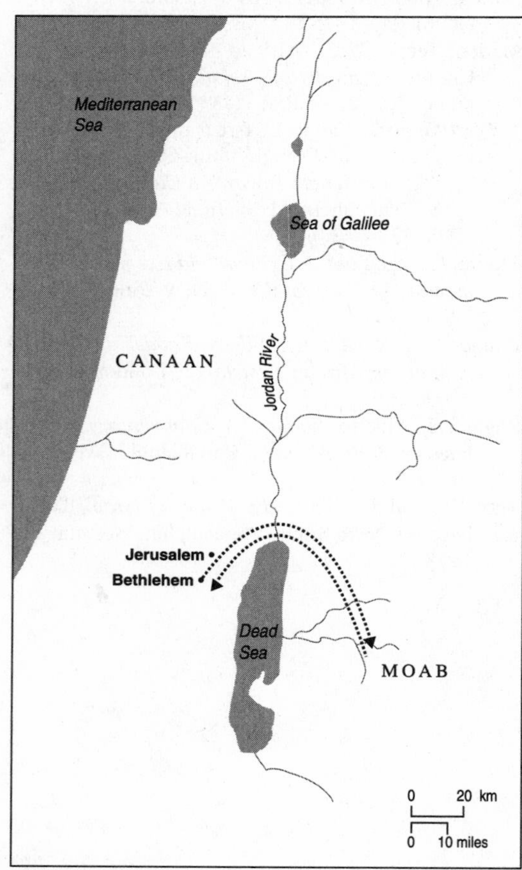

JOURNEYS IN RUTH

The Greek OT (the LXX), however, places Ruth after Judges, making it appear among the books in the second section of the Hebrew Bible, the "(Former) Prophets." This placement, probably dictated by the references of the contents of the two books to the same period, has been followed by the Latin Bible (the Vulgate) and Christian tradition. However, the placement of Ruth in the Hebrew Bible may be said to be original.

Jewish tradition assigns the authorship of Ruth to Samuel, but recent studies have suggested dates of composition of the book ranging from the early monarchical period to the post-exilic period. Reasons adduced for the various dates range from the location of Ruth in the Hebrew Bible through linguistic observations to its protest against the so-called nationalism and particularism of the Ezra–Nehemiah era. Lack of certainty with regard to the date and authorship of Ruth does not, however, notably affect appreciation of the content and message of the book.

The characters in the book are Elimelech of Bethlehem, Naomi his wife, their two sons Mahlon and Chilion, the Moabite wives of the two sons, Orpah and Ruth, and Boaz, a kinsman of Elimelech. The names of the characters are peculiar to the book and their meanings appear significant in its context. Elimelech, "my God is king," points to the period when Israel had no human king. Naomi has to do with delight or pleasantness; the bearer of the name had a bitter lot in life but this was in the end turned into great delight. Mahlon suggests weakness, and Chilion destruction or consumption; the two with these names died young, without offspring. Orpah has been connected with a Hebrew word meaning "back of the neck" or with a Semitic word meaning "cloud." In the story Orpah's love of and obedience to her mother-in-law do not permit her being seen in a negative light as this name seems to suggest.

Ruth probably derives from a word meaning "companionship" or from one meaning "refreshment." The life of Ruth was devoted to her mother-in-law. The meaning of Boaz has been derived from a Hebrew expression that means "in him is strength." As the story presents him Boaz is a man of wealth, commanding authority, and power; he is a man of moral and spiritual strength, firmly grounded in the strength of God. None of the characters, as the story testifies, deserves disapproval. They make good use of what is offered for common life.

Ruth, like the book of Jonah, has a broader outlook than the books of Ezra and Nehemiah. It engenders a universalistic spirit that is able to break down barriers created by alienation and prejudices and has a big welcoming heart for goodness wherever it is encountered. For the book of Ruth foreignness is not to be seen as intrinsically bad and repulsive. Humanity everywhere is God's creation and so an attitude of good will must be demonstrated toward all people.

Ruth is a good story that defies any attempt to see in it only one particular purpose. From whatever perspective one looks at the story one is unavoidably confronted with the fact of resilient perseverance and humanity. Nothing that is essential to bestow excellence on human life and conduct is lacking in the story. It is a story imbued with undying power to speak effectively in and to every human situation. The story itself is universal and transcendent in its sovereignty, a beautiful and powerful narrative about God, the source of all causalities, told for all time and every situation.

Patristic and Liturgical Use of Ruth

The Church Fathers Melito, Origen, Athanasius, and Jerome read Ruth, and Hippolytus of Rome wrote a commentary on it. The Fathers resorted to it mainly because of its universalistic spirit. Julius Africanus and Eusebius of Caesarea found in it a "historical" solution of the problem of the discrepancies between the two genealogies of Christ in Matthew and Luke.

Some sections of Ruth are read in the twentieth week of Ordinary Time in Year One. Ruth 1:1, 3-6, 14-16, 22 are read on Friday to quicken the assurance that even in dire circumstances God's care and human commitment do not fail. On Saturday 2:1-3, 8-11 and 4:13-17 are read to draw attention to human and divine magnanimity and the favor they bestow. Texts from Ruth are also popular selections for marriages and funerals.

How to Read Ruth

The concern of the book of Ruth is to bring into sharp focus the significance of community and the impact it has on human life and existence. Its interest is to demonstrate as clearly and powerfully as possible that the force sustaining human interrelationships to keep them strong and healthy in all the vicissitudes of life is what the German language powerfully captures in the word *Gemeinschaftstreue* (fidelity to community). To enable the reader to receive this as easily as possible and with great delight the author employs a narrative style. The reader is thus to approach the book having in mind that the author has something significant and interesting to offer, presented in the form of historical narrative.

One would urge the reader, before proceeding to the commentary, to read Ruth through at one go to capture the book's train of thought. This is not difficult, for the book is very short. The following commentary will then be seen to be what it is actually intended to be, a companion along the way to gaining a better grasp of the text as the reader studies it section by section.

SECOND READING

The Family of Elimelech and Naomi: 1:1-5

The first verse of Ruth tells in broad terms about the period in which the family of Elimelech lived and had its destiny unfold. It was the pre-monarchic period when judges ruled Israel. As the book of Judges presents them they were a little more than clan and tribal heads. Life ran not so much on legal rails as on the rails of practical sense of community and mutual trust.

The family of Elimelech migrates from home because of economic hardship. Famine is a severe affliction that compels people to leave home (Gen 12:10; 26:1). The family chooses to go to Moab, which is better placed than Judah in terms of natural resources. We see Elimelech and his family leave, trusting that they will be received in the place where they are taking refuge.

Verse 3 abruptly announces the death of Elimelech, the head and real stay of the family in their place of refuge. Naomi is left with her two sons, Mahlon and Chilion. They are her only source of consolation, security, and hope in a foreign land. The two sons take wives in Moab, Orpah and Ruth, Moabite women (v. 4). Joseph, Moses, and some other men of the Bible also took foreign wives (Gen 41:45; Exod 2:21; 2 Sam 3:3; 1 Kings 11:1-8). The natural sense of community implanted in human beings knows no boundaries. It is a transcending force naturally inclined toward welding humanity into a single community.

The marriages will, of course, be expected to enhance the strength and joy of the family, but fate does not allow this to happen. Mahlon and Chilion die. Verse 5 gives a graphic picture of the complete loneliness and privation that overwhelm Naomi. She is here described as "the woman," which throws into vivid relief her diminution and total helplessness. In this gloom she has virtually nothing to hold on to in spite of the presence of her two daughters-in-law. They are not here dismissed as useless, but the husband and the sons are "the arrows of the family quiver" (cf. Ps 127:3-5) and the three women are bereft of them.

Widowhood obviously is a very bitter experience. In some parts of the world the widow's state of loneliness, privation, and loss is made worse by certain soul-shattering widowhood rites she is made to go through. She is treated as though she were a death-dealing force of which the community must be purged. Scripture strongly urges that a widow's condition be made light and bearable (see, for example, Deut 24:17-21) and Christ sets us a shining example in Luke 7:11-15.

Naomi Returns to Bethlehem: 1:6-22

News reaches Naomi that the famine in Judah is over. God has "visited" the people and granted them prosperity (cf. Ps 85:1). God's "visitation" can be disastrous or favorable. It is disastrous when the divine kindness is not received with due respect and acknowledgment (Exod 20:5; Amos 3:2). Here, however, as in Gen 50:24; Exod 4:31; 1 Sam 2:21; Jer 29:10 the "visit" conveys God's goodness and favor granted out of mercy. It could be said that Naomi sets out to return home with confidence and hope although the cloud of misfortune still hangs over her.

Naomi's two daughters-in-law decide to go to Judah with her. It may be said, in the light of v. 8, that the decision of the two young widows is not dictated by any lack of security in their own country and home (cf. Gen 38:11; Lev 22:13; Judges 4:17-22). The decision of the young widows to leave home and chart a new course in life with their mother-in-law may be said to have been motivated by the life of the mother-in-law with them in Moab. Something of that life may be seen in vv. 8-13. Naomi sees the lives of the young widows ungrudgingly spent for her and the dead members of her family as a demonstration of what the Hebrews termed *ḥesed.* This word expresses the spirit that so values its object that it does for the object more than is normally required and does it with love, compassion, devotion, and at all cost.

Naomi appeals to God to show her daughters-in-law the divine counterpart of the spirit they have shown to her and the dead. The passage testifies that *ḥesed*—both human and divine—is universal. The practice of it by Ruth and Orpah in Moab may be seen as a clear expression of the conviction that human life everywhere is imbued with it. It is the will of God for human life in community, and through its practice by human persons God creates a healthy community life and grants a condition that generates mutual trust and faithfulness and radiates ease.

Naomi seeks only the best for her daughters-in-law. She prays that God grants each of them "rest" in the house of her husband. By "rest" *(menuḥah)* is meant here a permanent life of happiness, security, and contentment in a new marriage. Verse 13 does not need to be seen as an expression of complaint or accusation. Naomi is not resisting her present lot; she is rather presented as deeply concerned for the well-being of her daughters-in-law. She admits her helplessness to provide for them (although in a highly exaggerated manner). She does not thereby find fault with God. Her prayer in vv. 8-9 does not support the interpretation of her utterances in vv. 13 and 20-21 as an expression of accusation. Her consciousness of God requires that she explain the events of her life as coming from the economy of God because it is by that means alone that full sovereignty is ascribed to God and enduring satisfaction obtained. Verses 11-13 and 20-21 may be said to carry a classic expression of the humanity of Naomi and her commitment to God and God's ways with humanity.

Orpah accepts the advice of her mother-in-law and returns to her home (v. 14). Her return is not presented as meaning that she has little love for her mother-in-law. Naomi knows perfectly well that her two daughters-in-law hold her dear (v. 8). Orpah returns in obedience to and out of love for her mother-in-law, and with her blessing. No failure is pointed out in Orpah; she is a worthy woman. But Ruth clings to Naomi. She feels strongly bound to remain with her mother-in-law. Ruth's exceptional devotion to her mother-in-law (vv. 16-17) is an eloquent testimony to the power of faithfulness in community. It effects a voluntary change of identity and unforced submission to a new orientation. It calls forth commitment that defies the fear of the unknown and willingly accepts the consequences of the ultimate. Ruth seals her declaration of total devotion to her mother-in-law with a solemn oath made in the name of Naomi's God. The avowal is not one that in Israel is made and taken lightly (1 Sam 20:13; 14:44; 2 Sam 3:9; 1 Kings 2:23). Naomi is overwhelmed; she accepts Ruth in solemn silence.

Naomi arrives in Bethlehem with Ruth. The women of the town are excited about her return but Naomi thinks there is nothing to be happy about. She is in a state of bitterness because she has returned empty. She deserves the name "Mara" because it is one that fits her present circumstances. A change of name due to change in condition is not something unusual in Israel (Gen 41:45; 2 Kings 23:34; 24:17; Dan 1:7). Naomi's misfortune is attributed to God, but her statement of it rests on the belief that it is God who makes weal and creates woe (Isa 45:7). It is a statement of acceptance of the providence of God. This is confirmed by the positive note on which the chapter ends: "they came to Bethlehem at the beginning of the barley harvest," which recalls v. 6.

Ruth's Devotion Goes to Work: 2:1-23

The opening verse of ch. 2 is provided as a vital canvas on which the events of this chapter and the following ones will unfold. The verse introduces a blood relative of Elimelech named Boaz. He is a capable man, of good standing, a man of substance (*ish gibbor hayil:* cf. Judg 6:12; 1 Sam 9:1; 1 Kings 11:28; 2 Kings 15:20). All is not lost to Naomi.

Ruth does not delay in giving a practical demonstration of the genuineness of her devotion to her mother-in-law. She readily offers to go out to work in the harvest field for Naomi's livelihood (v. 2). She takes advantage of a custom requiring that the gleanings of a harvest field be left for the needy, including aliens (Lev 19:9-10; 23:22; Deut 24:19). Ruth is at first said to have arrived in the field of Boaz by accident, but v. 20 attributes her entry into that field to providence. It is the Lord who sees and directs (cf. Gen 22:13-14; Wis 16:17: "the universe defends the righteous"). Boaz visits his reapers. His greeting and the response of the workers (cf. Ps 129:8) readily reveal what they all believe to be the essential factor of life in community: the effective personal presence of God and the acknowledgment of God in all aspects of life.

Boaz notices Ruth in the field. His inquiry about her (v. 5) shows that to the ancients some information about the community to which an individual belongs is vital for knowledge and assessment of that individual (Gen 32:17; 1 Sam 30:13). The overseer presents Ruth as unpresumptuous, hard-working, and caring little for her own comfort and convenience (v. 7). Boaz is highly pleased with the overseer's description of Ruth. He welcomes her to glean in his field until the end of the harvest and grants her physical comfort and protection from harassment that could happen to her as a defenseless widow and foreigner (vv. 8-9). Boaz is thereby pictured as generous, magnanimous, and humane. Ruth bows down before Boaz in extreme gratitude, overwhelmed by his kindness to her, foreigner as she is (v. 10). Boaz says that Ruth's uncommon commitment to her mother-in-law, which made her willingly deprive herself of land and a circle of close relatives and friends to accept unknown conditions of existence among strange people, more than qualify her to lay claim to his kindness (v. 11), but the all-surpassing claim she has is her embracing the God of Israel with a faith so impressive and exceptional (v. 12; cf. Luke 7:9; Matt 8:10). Boaz sees very clearly that such an act of commitment cannot fail to receive the blessing and protective presence of God.

Naomi's Efforts for Ruth, and Ruth's Cooperation: 3:1-8

The well-being of Ruth is Naomi's fundamental concern. She will not unduly and selfishly take advantage of Ruth's exceptional devotion to her. She must seek a secure and independent future for Ruth. By his magnanimous treatment of Ruth the kinsman Boaz has paved a way for Naomi and given her courage to act in Ruth's interest. Naomi's advice and directions to Ruth (vv. 2-4) derive their motivation and strength from this and from her strong faith. Threshing is usually done from late afternoon till nightfall, a period when the winds are suitable for winnowing. The night is spent on the threshing floor to secure the grain against theft.

Ruth's readiness to cooperate with her mother-in-law is again demonstrated in v. 5. The cooperation is motivated by her *ḥesed* for her mother-in-law, not by self-interest. Ruth quietly draws near to Boaz when the latter is lying down in a state of composure and contentment (v. 7). She uncovers his feet and lies down. This action carries sexual overtones, but the character of Ruth shown throughout the book leads us to see that her action is well-motivated. It is not seduction but a positive move toward the realization of a socially and legally accepted good (cf. the action of Tamar and Judah's judgment of it in Genesis 38). This is confirmed by v. 9. Ruth invites Boaz to spread his cloak over her because he is next of kin.

Naomi, through Ruth and with the latter's full consent, is urging Boaz to ensure the fulfillment of the obligation of the next of kin to the dead. By her action Ruth demonstrates that she is ready to cooperate to make sure that the proper thing is done, that the honor due to the dead among the living is maintained, and that the support and protection due to the two widows are not denied them.

Boaz is much impressed by Ruth's strong sense of and faithfulness to community. This, to Boaz, is what attracts the blessing of God and the recognition and regard of the best of human judgment (*shaʿar ʿami,* "the assembly [lit. "gate'] of my people," v. 11: the "gate" is the place where the best of spirits and minds are exercised for the good of the community). The remark that Ruth is a woman of worth (v. 11) certifies that Ruth's forwardness (vv. 7-9) is not unbecoming; it is acceptable within the context of the legitimate customary practice of the day.

Boaz assures Ruth of his full cooperation in ensuring that the proper thing is done both to honor the dead and to secure protection and care for the widows. He makes Ruth aware that there is a kinsman whose claim to the right to take responsibility for her and Naomi is stronger than his and who must have the first opportunity. Boaz's delicate sense of community and faithfulness to it shines forth here.

The conduct of both Boaz and Ruth at the threshing floor proves that there is much in the human being that, coupled with the thought of God in human relationship, will bring recovery to humanity. The last word of the chapter is given to Naomi, and she uses it to express her confidence in Boaz. He is a trustworthy man and a reliable person. Through him Naomi is sure of victory for her cause and that of her loyal daughter-in-law.

After Toil Comes Rest: 4:1-17

Boaz keeps his promise to Ruth. He goes to the "gate," the place of deliberation, of business, of resolution of issues (Gen 23:17-18; Deut 22:15; Amos 5:10, 12-15). It is a place, as we have said, where the best of spirits and minds meet to seek the best for the community. There Boaz summons the nearer kinsman and ten of the heads of the leading families of the community. The elders bear authority in matters of both legal and social concern (Deut 19:12; 21:2-4; 25:7-9; 1 Kings 21:8-14). On them rests the rehabilitation of the community. In later Judaism ten of them must be present for the recital of the marriage benediction. The issue is the redemption of the property of Elimelech that Naomi has decided to sell. Boaz apparently sees this issue as one that should evoke grave concern and demand a solemn resolution. Boaz invites the nearer kinsman, in the presence of the elders, to ensure that no part of the family property is lost to the family (cf. Lev 25:23-25; Jer 32:8). The nearer kinsman accepts his obligation and undertakes to redeem the property, but on learning that with the responsibility of redeeming the property goes the responsibility of "buying" or "acquiring" Ruth in order to restore the name of the dead to his inheritance (v. 5) he declines to act as the nearest kinsman. The property, he realizes, will not come to augment his personal assets, for a son out of the union with Ruth will be the heir to the property. The ungenerous attitude and lack of sense of community of the kinsman are made to stand out clearly (v. 6). Boaz accepts the offer to redeem the property of Elimelech and take responsibility for Naomi and Ruth. The nearer kinsman and Boaz go through the formal process of transferring the rights and responsibility relating to the property and the widows, especially Ruth.

It is not clear whether in the rite of the sandal (v. 8; v. 7 is an explanatory note on the rite) it is the nearer kinsman or Boaz who removes his sandal. If it is the nearer kinsman, he does it to symbolize the transfer of the rights and responsibility. If, on the other hand, it is Boaz, he does so as a pledge of acceptance of the rights and responsibility (in Deut 25:7-9 the rite is used with a different significance).

Boaz, now wielding the full claim to all that belongs to the Elimelech family, turns to the elders and all those present for their ratification of the transaction (vv. 9-10). Here, as in v. 5, the verb "buy" is used in relation to acquiring Ruth. It is obvious that it is the commercial nature of the transaction that accounts for the use of this verb in connection with Ruth being taken by Boaz as wife. The use of the verb in the Mishnah in marriage contexts may be said to strengthen the observation. Verses 11-12 register the ratification of the transaction. There it is earnestly hoped that Ruth may come to be ranked among the mothers of Israel who built up the nation. It is also hoped that Boaz gains prominence in his community befitting his exceptional magnanimity.

The union of Boaz and Ruth is blessed with a son. Naomi now has a *go'el* to rehabilitate and resuscitate her and the family lineage of Elimelech. The action in v. 16 bears full testimony to the triumph of Naomi and its accompanying contentment. The son is her son not by the cold law of adoption but by the providence of God through a daughter-in-law who is more to her than seven sons. She who worked to find rest (*manoaḥ,* 3:1) for her daughter-in-law has, through her, been granted rest. The son is indeed born to Naomi, for whoever belongs to Elimelech belongs to Naomi. The involvement of the women of the neighborhood in the naming of the child (v. 17) may not be seen as unrealistic or unusual in light of their role in both 4:4-17 and 1:19 (cf. Luke 1:58-59). In the child's name, Obed, the point of the Ruth story is given in a word: service to God and the community.

Conclusion: 4:18-22

The writer concludes the story with a line of descent in which Obed stands. The last statement of v. 17 had already linked him with David; here further linkages are provided, probably to show the origin, significance, and importance of the line to which Obed belongs. In the line are true kinsmen dedicated to the security and future of the community. In the genealogy of Jesus in Matthew and Luke all the names mentioned here occur. In Matthew's version of the genealogy Obed is presented as the son of Ruth. Though a Moabite woman and a foreigner, Ruth has a place in the ancestry of David, and through him, of Jesus Christ. This is not seen as a source of embarrassment; rather, we are made to see in it the sovereignty of the providence of God that transcends and overcomes all barriers and prejudices and acts to weld humanity into a single community.

BIBLIOGRAPHY

Campbell, Edward F. *Ruth.* AB 7. Garden City, N.Y.: Doubleday, 1975.

Fewell, Danna N., and David Gunn. *Compromising Redemption: Relating Characters in the Book of Ruth.* Louisville: Westminster/John Knox, 1990.

Nielsen, Kirsten. *Ruth: A Commentary.* Translated by Edward Broadbridge. Louisville: Westminster/John Knox, 1997.

1–2 Samuel

Antony Campbell and Mark O'Brien

FIRST READING

General Character of 1–2 Samuel

At first sight 1–2 Samuel seem to contain a mass of past historical detail of little interest to the present day. On closer inspection we find they are struggling with three sets of issues that are well and truly alive today. First is the question of God's role in the shaping of society, second the question of the place and legitimacy of government in society, and third the intricacy of human living. Within these issues the biblical images of prophet and king are shaped—for Israel and for us. All of this is dealt with not in theological discourse but in the telling of stories. First and Second Samuel offer us both insight into the way ancient Israel went about its theological thinking and insight into the way God communicates with people within Scripture, then and now.

Strategy for Reading

In reading 1–2 Samuel it helps to do consciously what we all take for granted when reading our newspapers. We know automatically whether we are reading a front page piece and whether we are in the headlines or the body of the story; we know whether we are reading a news feature, a piece of investigative reporting, a columnist's piece of political opinion, or a writer's column gathering together the day's anecdotes, gossip, humor, bizarre episodes, etc. First and Second Samuel are just as diverse and demand the same decision making of their readers. When reading our newspapers we are aware of their political bias; ideally we make allowances for these biases. When reading Samuel we need to be aware that often our material comes to us from what we might call *David's Times*. It is important to realize that this material might look quite different had it come to us from *Saul's Post.*

All of this suggests that we do not read Samuel naïvely. The people who wrote these texts were not caught up in the pressured hustle of modern living, bombarded with more information than they could absorb, seldom stopping to reflect and digest. The thinkers contributing to 1–2 Samuel had reflection and digestion down to a fine art. To enjoy their texts and distill their meaning we need to be asking certain questions all the time. What sort of text is this: for example, is it story, report, or gossip? How has this text been put together: where do the emphases lie, what is passed over, what may be hinted at? What is the meaning of a text of this kind, written in just this way: how do I best understand what it is driving at?

Metaphors that may help—whether of painting, drama, or the storyteller's performance—will be introduced at the major structural moments in the books of Samuel: 1 Sam 1:1; 1 Sam 16:14; and 2 Sam 11:1.

General Contexts of Interpretation

The dating of the majority of biblical texts is a most uncertain science. For reading purposes it is reasonable to assume that 1–2 Samuel have their beginning in the time of the monarchy (i.e., the inauguration of national government) and that the experience they bring to expression reaches down to the exile and beyond. They cover about five centuries of a people's reflection on their experience of themselves and their God.

Some stages can be indicated in what is a complex process. First there are the oldest traditions that probably have their origins in David's time. The Story of David's Rise (1 Samuel 16–2 Samuel 5) contains clusters of detailed observations hardly likely to have survived without the concerted endeavor that produced such a narrative. The so-called Succession Narrative (better, The Story of David's Later Years; at least 2 Samuel 11–20) has such a veiled negativity toward David that it is difficult to point to a later context where it might credibly have been written once David had become the model hero king. Second, at some point there seems to have been considerable prophetic activity reshaping these early traditions. Some of this clusters around the figures of Elijah and Elisha and may have happened late in the ninth century. A third major impulse shaping 1–2 Samuel was the deuteronomic reform in the time of Josiah (late seventh century), with its forerunners under Hezekiah and the followup involved in digesting and giving a theological account of the experience of exile (sixth century). It does not help to try and graph these with precision here.

Historical, Social, and Intellectual Situations

The primary historical information to be kept in mind when reading 1–2 Samuel is the life-and-death relationship being played out between Israel and the Philistines at this time. The Philistines had been part of an ethnic migration southward down the Mediterranean coast under pressure of mass movements of people at the beginning of the twelfth century. Their southward movement was stopped by the Egyptians and they settled around the five cities of Ashdod, Ashkelon, Ekron, Gath, and Gaza—later giving their name to Palestine. Their power constituted a threat to nascent Israel just as the emerging nation of Israel presented a danger to them. One view of the rise of the monarchy in Israel is that the institutionalization of military force led by the king was necessary to survive the threat posed by the Philistines. Saul failed to achieve this, dying in battle against the Philistines on Mount Gilboa (1 Samuel 31). David achieved it, and in doing so transformed the nature of Israel.

Much of the text of 1–2 Samuel apparently reflects Israel's transformation from a loose association of tribes into a centralized nation governed by a monarch. For many nations of the ancient Near East monarchy was taken for granted as the natural social structure that had existed for all time. In Israel that was not so. Kingship and central government were a major disruption of the social structures under which the faith and religion of Israel had first developed. Israel's theological thinkers had to struggle with the new institution of the monarchy and its impact on the nation's life and faith.

The initial social milieu for many traditions is the royal court. Saul's court is not thought to have been highly developed. It is marked by the image of Saul haranguing his followers while seated under a tamarisk tree on the highest spot in Gibeah, his spear in his hand (1 Sam 23:6). The figures named at his court do not suggest a high level of institutionalization (see 1 Sam 14:49-52). David's court probably made substantial gains in sophistication (see the lists in 2 Sam 8:16-18; 20:23-26), but Solomon is the one who appears to have made his career in administration (see 1 Kings 4).

Prophetic concerns are mirrored frequently in 1–2 Samuel. We know very little of the social milieu in which such concerns could be securely situated. Certainly skilled storytellers were at home in the circles associated with the prophet Elisha (2 Kings 2–10). It is not unlikely that the great Elijah stories were preserved and shaped within these Elisha circles. They may well have been the ones responsible for writing some of the prophetic concerns into the Samuel texts. They claimed the anointing and commissioning of Jehu; they may well have given written form to the same claim for Samuel in relation to Saul and David, and differently for others. There is a sense of identity and social cohesion associated with the Elisha circle. Whether and in what way similar circles may have existed more widely in early times we do not know.

The concerns and context of the deuteronomic reform are too important to pass over in silence. The first five books of the Bible have long been seen as a unity, the Pentateuch, also called the Torah or the Law. It is only since 1943 that it has been argued that much of Deuteronomy and the six books that follow it (Joshua, Judges, 1–2 Samuel, 1–2 Kings) formed a single literary work, the Deuteronomistic History. Martin Noth made the proposal and the idea has gained wide acceptance although with an equally wide diversity of views about the number and timing of editions and revisions. According to this understanding circles associated with the reform based on the book of Deuteronomy interpreted the ups and downs of their people's history in relation to the law code of Deuteronomy (cf. 2 Kings 22:3–23:23). In their view when Israel observed the central spirit of these laws—fidelity to YHWH and centralization of worship in the Jerusalem Temple—all went well; when Israel failed to observe these laws they suffered breakdown and oppression.

A terminology has grown up reflecting these developments. Variations exist, but what we use here—widely used by others—can be swiftly summarized. "Deuteronomic" is used in reference to the law code, the book of Deuteronomy, and the reform under Josiah. "Deuteronomistic" is used in reference to the history (Deuteronomy–2 Kings). The people responsible for the history are referred to as "deuteronomists," or often in the singular, "the Deuteronomist." The language used in such circles can be stereotyped, marked by their ideology, concerned for fidelity to YHWH and for exclusive worship in Jerusalem. As examples see 1 Kings 9:3-9 and 1 Kings 11:11-13.

The theology of the deuteronomic circles is summarized powerfully in Deut 30:15-20. "See, I have set before you today life and prosperity, death and adversity. If you obey the commandments of the LORD your God . . . then you shall live and become numerous, and the LORD your God will bless you . . . . But if your heart turns away and you do not hear, . . . I declare to you today that you shall perish . . . ." It is critically important to recognize that such a theology can be interpreted in two totally different ways: the Law is either condition or consequence of the relationship. As *condition* observance of the Law is required for relationship with God and for the life and prosperity that flow from that relationship. As *consequence* the relationship with God is a gift that has been given and observance of the Law is the appropriate way to live out that relationship from which life and prosperity will flow. In our view the deuteronomic circles understood God's love to be unshaken by human sin: see Deut 7:7-8 and 9:4-7, 13-20 as well as the two deuteronomistic passages Exod 32:7-14 and Num 14:11-25. Individuals may die but the nation will survive; the covenant may be broken but the relationship remains. For the fruits of the relationship to flow, the Law as consequence of the relationship must be observed. Without the fruits the relationship remains. In our view, then, the primary understanding of the Law should be that it is a consequence of Israel's relationship with God—not a condition for that relationship.

First and Second Samuel are at a critical turning point in this Deuteronomistic History; they are at the interface between the judges and the kings. In the Deuteronomistic History Samuel is not only prophet but also judge. In 1 Samuel 7 like the deliverer judges before him he delivers Israel and, according to this chapter, they remain free from Philistine oppression all the days of his life. In 1 Samuel 8–12 he presides over the transition to the monarchy and in 1 Sam 13:1–16:13 he exercises the prophetic claim to designate and dismiss kings. The rest of 1–2 Samuel is devoted to the traditions of David, the king-figure *par excellence* in Israel.

For all this it is important to realize how little we know of the life and times of King David. Quite reasonably we might think that we have a fuller picture of David than of most figures from ancient Israel. We have the details of Jesse's youngest son and his anointing as king-to-be, of David's coming to the court of Saul, of David's military exploits and Saul's jealousy, of the civil war and David's final success, of the capture of Jerusalem, God's promise of a dynasty, the establishment of a kingdom that was almost an empire, and the complex events of David's later years. We know Joab was David's general; we know the members of David's administration (2 Sam 8:16-18; 20:23-26). We have reason to feel we are remarkably well informed. What comes as a stunning surprise is to realize, nevertheless, how little we know about David's life and career.

When we read 2 Samuel 21–24, especially the traditions in 21:15-22; 23:8-39, we discover that:

1. There are two elite groups at the top of David's military command structure that we have never heard about, called the Three and the Thirty.

2. The names of the Three are Josheb-basshebeth (Jeshbaal?), Eleazar, and Shammah (23:8-12)—and we have never heard of them elsewhere in the traditions of 1–2 Samuel.
3. Of all the names listed among the Thirty (23:24-39) we have only heard of two, the first and last listed, Asahel brother of Joab, killed by Abner (2 Sam 2:18-23), and the ill-fated Uriah the Hittite, killed by David's orders (2 Sam 11:14-25). We could add Abishai and Benaiah, named outside the list (23:18-23).

The conclusion is simple: David's organization was more complex than we know, and there were significant structures and individuals that we do not know about. The Three and the Thirty may be only the tip of the iceberg of our ignorance.

When we read the earlier part of 2 Samuel we discover that:

1. There had been a long civil war between the followers of Saul and David (2 Sam 3:1); we know almost nothing about it.
2. Absalom organized a significant revolution against David's rule and we know nothing about the support for it (2 Sam 15:1-12), yet it was powerful enough that David fled Jerusalem without striking a blow (15:13-15).
3. Israel and Judah are portrayed debating about David's return to power (2 Sam 19:40b-43); we know next to nothing about the nature of the political division involved.
4. Sheba ben Bichri's short-lived rebellion is reported and considered extremely dangerous (2 Sam 20:6); again we can only guess at the political forces in play.

When we read 1 Kings 1 we discover that:

1. In the competition between Adonijah and Solomon for David's throne "the prophet Nathan, and Shimei, and Rei, and David's own warriors did not side with Adonijah" (1:8). Shimei and Rei appear to be influential figures with power; yet we have never heard of them before.
2. Benaiah has been listed before as commander of the Cherethites and Pelethites (foreign mercenaries: 2 Sam 8:18; 20:23; 23:20-23). This is his first appearance in the main narratives (1 Kings 1:8). We may wonder sometimes at Joab's absences (e.g., from 2 Sam 14:33 to 18:2), but what has Benaiah been doing all this time?

Despite the apparent wealth of information available to us about David in the texts of Samuel–Kings we are forced to realize how little we know about David's rise to power and exercise of it. It is wise to be aware of our ignorance.

The passage about Shimei ben Gera is a good example of how these texts function. A reading of the text (2 Sam 16:5-13) suggests beyond any doubt that the episode is reported to bolster David's reputation for trust in God: "Let him alone, and let him curse; for the LORD has bidden him. It may be that the LORD will look on my distress, and the LORD will repay me with good for this cursing of me today" (vv. 11-12). David is presented as having an extraordinary capacity for faith and trust in God. The same episode, however, reveals the presence in Israel of a man—and probably others—who saw David as a murderer, a scoundrel, a usurper with responsibility for the blood of the house of Saul. The biblical text does not note that Shimei was wrong. In fact it notes David's remark that the LORD had bidden Shimei to curse (v. 11). It presents us with David's trust in God even in these most challenging of circumstances.

The text reminds us that there are at least two interpretations of the events of the books of Samuel. For David's followers God was with David (1 Sam 18:14); for Saul's followers David was a murderous usurper (2 Sam 16:7-8). We are invited to ponder and reflect and to accept the challenge of being enabled to discern God's presence and action within our lives today.

It comes as no surprise, then, that the image of David in 1–2 Samuel is as complex, uncertain, and ambiguous as any picture of a leader; a remarkable diversity of views is preserved in the biblical text. Along one pole David's success is a matter of divine destiny (e.g., 1 Sam 26:10-11); along the other pole David's success is a matter of murderous ambition (e.g., 2 Sam 16:7-8). David is presented as an extremely successful guerrilla commander (1 Samuel 22–30), as a monarch with unsurpassed military success in foreign affairs (2 Sam 8:1-15), as an incompetent and indecisive king in significant areas of domestic policy whose grip on all Israel is shown to be extremely fragile (2 Samuel 11–20).

Suspicion

At first sight it may seem a strange thing to say, but these texts in Samuel–Kings need to be treated with suspicion. We need to go beyond suspicion, yet we do not do that by avoiding it; there is no way out but through. In these texts at least two areas are significant for suspicion. The first has to do with "point of view"—where the observer stands, the place from which the writer perceives. The adage has it that "history is written by the winners." Whatever the truth of this, history is always written by people with a point of view and history looks different when written by others with a different point of view. The Story of David's Rise portrays David as a blameless man who came to royal power with perfectly clean hands; Shimei ben Gera, a connection of Saul's, portrays David as a man who killed his way to power with blood on his hands (2 Sam 16:5-8). We cannot read these texts responsibly without attempting to be aware of the point of view that dominates them. The issue is not what might have happened historically. The issue is our awareness of point of view—moral, political, social, theological, etcetera.

Biblical texts have a habit of portraying different views of the same realities without minimizing or reconciling the differences. For example the OT gives us three substantially irreconcilable insights into creation (one: Gen 1:1–2:4a; two: Gen 2:4b-25; three: Isa 51:9-10; Job 7:12; 9:13; 26:12-13; Ps 74:12-17 etc., these last involving mythic combat), two different stories of the flood (combined within Gen 6:5–9:17), at least two incompatible portrayals of the deliverance at the Reed Sea (combined within Exod 13:17–14:31) or of the occupation of the promised land (one: Joshua 1–12; two: Judges 1). We might say that in principle there is hardly a faith position taken in the OT that is not open to the possibility of being contradicted by another faith position that might equally be taken in the OT. There may be faith positions on the identity of God, the identity of Israel, the commitment of God to Israel, and so on that are not open to contradiction, but they are relatively few.

The recognition that contradictions exist is an immensely important insight into the nature of God's communication with us in the Bible. It seems that in the Bible God does not dictate what we should think, but rather invites us to thought. An example in Samuel–Kings is the presentation of the emergence of monarchy as the central government in Israel. Different views are involved. In 1 Samuel 8–12, for example, monarchy is endorsed either as God's gift for the political liberation of Israel or as God's response to popular demand for social justice after Samuel; these two traditions favoring monarchy were later opposed by editing that saw kingship as destructive for Israel, involving loss of faith and the rejection of God. These views are all presented in chs. 8–12; the biblical text does not adjudicate, unless the last writer is given the last word—a proposition that is patently absurd. The Bible demands our alertness to point of view; it invites us to read with suspicion and intelligent judgment.

If God's revelation came through history alone it would be the history that matters. If God's revelation was directly taught to us by every biblical text it would be the teaching in the text that matters. But God's revelation is not directly from history or text alone. If the presence of contrasting and differing texts in our Bible is an invitation to us to think and if God's revelation may be found in that thinking to which we are invited, it is essential that we are aware of the point of view of the texts we are thinking about. We may want to note, furthermore, that if communication reveals the communicator, the Bible's communication that invites us to thought reveals a communicating God who does not coerce or impose but rather invites. The invitation is to think, to use imagination, to search the Scriptures, to find where God is offering fullness of life—life and the joy of life that implies acceptance of being loved by God and does not exclude pain and suffering and heartache.

The second area significant for suspicion in these texts has to do with gender. For the Yahwist the man and the woman were created with complementarity and mutuality (Genesis 2). For the Priestly writer men and women were both created together in the image and likeness of God (Genesis 1). For centuries human cultures have fractured that harmony. In cultures where healing is in process and harmony is being recovered it is important to read Samuel–Kings with an awareness that they were written in a culture where males enjoyed substantially uncontested dominance. For women involved in the healing of humanity's fractured harmony, literature coming out of a male-dominant (patriarchal) culture can be a source of depression and indeed of oppression. The so-called hermeneutic of suspicion leads us in two directions: awareness that a male-dominant view is being heard; curiosity about what the female experience might have been and how that point of view might look if it was expressed. There are no magic guidelines that enable men to escape the trap of patriarchy. The only rule of thumb is to talk with and listen to women who are struggling with the issue. We measure the biblical text against the expression of other biblical texts and against the experience of today and we begin the process of discerning where life and creativity lie.

Impact on the Christian Community

When we look back on the thinking of our forebears in the Christian community we have to be both fair and honest. It is only honest to recognize how closely and insightfully great minds in the past have read the Scriptures. It is only fair to recognize that our reading of the Scriptures is usually very different from theirs.

In recent centuries historical awareness has been prized in Western European thinking and scholarship. "Historical awareness" is not primarily about the recovery of history. First and foremost it is an awareness of how each generation is conditioned by its place and its time, and an awareness that wide differences may exist between varying generations. We would be unfair if we sought to apply our historically aware understanding of Scripture to much earlier generations. From the beginning fine minds read the Scriptures closely with intelligence and insight. But they did not read them as we do.

For example, at the end of the first century Clement appeals extensively and with approval to the words of one of Job's friends: "There was no shape before my eyes, but I heard a breath and a voice. What! Can a mortal be pure before the Lord? . . ." (Job 4:16-18; 15:15; 4:19–5:5; *1 Clem.* 39). Clement does not cite Eliphaz; the introduction is simply "for it is written" (the text is from speeches of Eliphaz). What Clement does not say is that at the end of the book of Job the friends are emphatically disqualified by God, addressing Eliphaz: "for you have not spoken of me what is right, as my servant Job has" (Job 42:7, 8). For us it is odd to appeal with approval to a discourse that has been disqualified by God. To Clement it was probably not odd. Scripture was God's word and was available for the service of God's work. The personal revelation made to Eliphaz was helpful and right; probably it did not matter that the use made of it by Eliphaz to condemn Job was unhelpful and wrong.

In the early Church the Bible as printed book did not exist. Manuscripts were precious, treasured, and not widely available. Clement knew Job, but it is highly unlikely that he looked up the text of Job as we would. Introducing scriptural quotations as "someone has testified somewhere" or " for somewhere it is said" is a reminder of this reality (e.g., Heb 2:6; *1 Clem.* 15).

Clement is only one example, perhaps one of the earliest. Augustine is another, perhaps one of the greatest. As Peter Brown comments, "For Augustine and his hearers, the Bible was literally the 'word' of God. It was regarded as a single communication, a single message in an intricate code, and not as an exceedingly heterogeneous collection of separate books. Above all, it was a communication that was intrinsically so far above the pitch of human minds, that to be made available to our senses at all, the 'Word' had to be communicated by means of an intricate game of 'signs'" (*Augustine of Hippo* [London: Faber & Faber, 1967] 252).

We today have been schooled by the Bible not to regard it in this way. We see in it a variety of documents, a variety of writers, a variety of experiences, a variety of theologies—and above all a God who does not communicate with us in the "intricate game" of a code but through the clear expression of human beings. Augustine would not demur at the involvement of human beings: "Everything could well have been done by an angel, but the standing of the human race would have been devalued if God had seemed unwilling to let men act as the agents of His Word to men . . ." (*De doct. christ.* Proem. 6; Brown, ibid., 270–271). The issue is one of singularity versus variety, of code versus clarity.

The variety of views preserved in the biblical text and the processes discernible in the growth of this text suggest that a major role for the text is to serve as a model of the dialogue men and women must hold with God in the discernment of God's desire. The model is not one of divine revelation being handed down from on high; rather it reflects a process much closer to our experience today.

God's revelation does not come to us in the Bible through history alone or from the teaching of texts alone. Different views of individuals and institutions are expressed in different contexts. Many biblical texts provide us with reflections on the experience of life and the discerning of God within it. Not all these reflections sing the same song. A characteristic of the biblical text is the refusal to reduce this variety to any single view. No single faith stance prevails overall; no single model prevails for developing a faith stance. Then as now the development of faith and its proclamation were matters of delicacy and discernment. The invitation of God's word to us is to ponder these texts, enter into these reflections, and accept the challenge of being enabled to discern God's presence and action within our lives today. In brief, Scripture is not imposition of thought but invitation to thought. Reflection that is thoughtful demands some awareness of the context in which biblical texts are created and the point of view they express.

Selective use of Scripture is still very common. We all know that the devil can quote Scripture to his advantage (cf. Matt 4:6; Luke 4:10). In this respect few of us have not at some time been diabolical. It should be evident that we do not believe as true whatever we can quote from Scripture; rather we quote from Scripture what we believe to be true.

Against this background it is valuable to examine some of the points where the traditions of 1–2 Samuel have had and may continue to have impact on the Church. Intuitively the Christian community has sometimes recognized the significance of certain passages or aspects of the Scripture. Modern research can delight to confirm such intuitive understanding.

Hannah's Song and Mary's Magnificat

One such case is the reading of Hannah's song and the light it throws on belief in Jesus and the song of Mary, the Magnificat. As this commentary insists, the barrenness of Hannah and the birth of her child Samuel are portrayed in the text as powerfully evocative of a forthcoming change in the structures of Israel. This adds depth and intensity to our understanding of the Magnificat as a Christian evocation of momentous change.

Ark of the Covenant

Similarly, in the litany of Loreto Mary is given the title of "Arca Foederis," Ark of the Covenant. Presumably this is based on Mary's carrying of Jesus, the Word of God, in her body as the Ark carried within it the tablets of the decalogue, God's ten words. As this commentary insists, the story of the Ark is rich in symbolism and communicates an understanding of God's purpose for Israel. When the story of the Ark is given due weight the Ark is an even more fitting symbol for the incarnation, God's embodiment in Mary as *Theotokos,* Mother of God, the communication of God's purpose for the whole of humankind.

Move to Monarchy

Samuel–Kings prohibits any simplicity with regard to theory of government. Some texts paint the emergence of monarchy as God's saving gift; some texts paint it as rejection of Israel's saving God. Monarchy is seen as a response to the need for social justice and as a response to the need for national defense. Are kings seen to replace God in the mindset of a people? Are the evil influences that can and did come from kings seen as destructive of Israel? Are deliverance and justice to be sought from God's action, working through the people when needed? Their rich ambivalence allows both defenders and opponents of monarchy to appeal to these texts. For all their differences it is noteworthy that Catholic controversialists such as Bellarmine and Suarez believed that political authority derived proximately from the people and philosophers such as Hobbes and Locke were in agreement that the origin of authority was in the consent of the people.

The image of the king as God's anointed is not without its problems. Kings are anointed by the people or by priests. Only three kings—Saul, David, and Jehu—are portrayed as anointed by a prophet. There are serious doubts about the historicity of the prophetic anointings for Saul and David. The title of "messiah" or "anointed" has to reflect these various traditions and, in turn, is not affected by their historicity. In some psalms it is used as a royal title for southern kings. The image of the king as set apart as God's anointed leads to the affirmation of the "anointed" or "messiah" as set apart as God's instrument, whether that instrument is seen as earthly or eschatological.

King David as Model Figure

The more closely we look into the texts about David in 1–2 Samuel, the less likely candidate he becomes for model status. Yet in the biblical tradition David is a model figure of unquestioned standing. It is worth reviewing the factors that contribute to this understanding.

1. David beat off the Philistines and the threat they posed to Israel's existence.
2. David's success is consistently explained by the claim that the LORD was with him.
3. David forged Israel into a unified kingdom with Jerusalem as its unifying neutral capital.
4. David is portrayed without taint of denial or apostasy; he has a reputation for faith and trust in the LORD (cf. 1 Sam 24:9-15; 26:9-11; 2 Sam 7:2-3; 12:21-23; 16:10-12). Confronted with an episode of sexual and homicidal violence in his personal life, he confessed promptly and was equally promptly declared forgiven.
5. David expressed the desire to build a temple for the LORD in Jerusalem. Jerusalem is David's city; its Temple adds to David's luster. Before the Temple, the Ark of God came to Jerusalem—according to 2 Samuel 6 by God's permission, not David's ambition—a major sign of God's favor.
6. David was promised by God that, iniquity notwithstanding, his dynasty would always rule in Jerusalem—and it did until the destruction of Jerusalem in 587.
7. David's putative authorship of many psalms, perhaps especially Psalm 51, established his religious as well as his political reputation.

It is hardly surprising, then, that David is a national hero. What Abraham was to the people and what Moses was to the Law, David was to the kingdom. He was the first successful king of Israel, a great and heroic figure by comparison with Saul and Solomon. According to the tradition Saul failed because the spirit of the LORD abandoned him and Solomon failed because in the folly of his old age he abandoned the LORD. After Solomon the nation divided into northern and southern kingdoms and unity was lost. David alone stands out as having saved Israel from the Philistines and other threats and as having forged for the nation the unity of a single kingdom. Naturally when prophetic hope was expressed for the future one of the images was of a new king for the nation, a new descendant of David, a new savior and unifying king. Naturally the Christian community took up this image to express their understanding of their savior and their sovereign Lord, Jesus Christ. In Matthew, Jesus is son of David through Joseph (1:1-17) and son of God through Mary (1:18-25). These may appear to conflict, but Christian faith needed to claim both.

Jerusalem and New Jerusalem

David's capture of Jerusalem is widely noted as an act of political brilliance. There is a north-south tension within Israel that we may not fully understand. Jerusalem, in the border zone between Benjamin and Judah, was a neutral city. Captured, it became David's city (2 Sam 6:10, 12); neutral, it was the capital of David's kingdom. The coming of the Ark to Jerusalem (2 Samuel 6) is often presented as a coup for David. The text presents it as a move controlled by God. God's red light is symbolically expressed in the death of Uzzah and David's threefold reaction to it (vv. 7-10); God's green light is expressed in the blessing conferred because of the Ark (vv. 11-12). The Ark of God had been absent from the mainstream of Israel since the days of Shiloh (1 Samuel 4); its presence in Jerusalem is a sign of God's blessing and favor.

The building of the Temple is proposed by David and he is promised by God that his heir will build it (2 Sam 7:13). The beautiful response of God to Solomon's prayer expresses exquisitely the significance for Israel of the Jerusalem Temple: "I have consecrated this house that you have built, and put my name there forever; my eyes and my heart will be there for all time" (1 Kings 9:3). The Temple becomes symbolic of the bond between God and Israel: "my eyes and my heart will be there for all time."

It is no wonder that the Jerusalem Temple becomes a focus for the expression of Israel's hope after the disaster of exile. Ezekiel expresses hope for Israel's future through the vision of an architectural blueprint of the new Temple and its surroundings (Ezekiel 40–48). When at the end of the NT the new Jerusalem is seen by John "coming down out of heaven from God" (Rev 21:2) it is a symbol of future Jewish and Christian unity. It has a great high wall with twelve gates and on the gates are inscribed the names of the twelve tribes of the Israelites (v. 12). Entry into "the holy city, the new Jerusalem" is through the gates of the tribes of Israel. The wall of the city has twelve foundations, and on them are the names of the twelve apostles (v. 14). "The holy city, the new Jerusalem" is built upon the apostles. David's Jerusalem unified the divisions of Israel. "The holy city, the new Jerusalem" is, in an eschatological future, to unify the divisions of Israel and the Christian Church. Viewed in this light the deuteronomistic insistence on worship in Jerusalem is a powerful symbol for unity.

Davidic Covenant and Divine Commitment

Second Samuel 7 promises that instead of David's building a house for God, God will build a house or dynasty for David (vv. 11b-12). Furthermore, David's heir will build God's Temple and God will establish his dynasty (v. 13). The promise is unconditional: "When he commits iniquity . . . I will not take my steadfast love from him" (vv. 14-15).

This is one of the great expressions of God's commitment to Israel. It gives good insight into Israel's theologians at work. What Nathan as God's prophet here promises David is later offered by Ahijah, God's prophet, to Jeroboam—but subject to strict conditions (1 Kings 11:37-38). Throughout 1–2 Kings the deuteronomists place the condition of fidelity and obedience on this originally unconditional divine promise—but they never take away the promise of God's commitment to the Davidic dynasty in Jerusalem. At one point the deuteronomists appear to put a terminal limit on the promise, but even then it is indirect; because of apostasy it is threatened that the Temple will become a heap of ruins (1 Kings 9:8). So the texts and the theologians cling to the consequences of human fragility, yet the power of the promise overwhelms these cautions and points to a future beyond the collapse of 587.

David is said to have been promised a *nēr* or *nîr* (lamp or dominion/power) in Jerusalem (cf. 2 Sam 21:17; 1 Kings 11:36; 15:4; 2 Kings 8:19; 2 Chr 21:7; Ps 132:17). The origins of this promise escape us. It is again significant of faith in God's commitment to Israel, symbolized by David and the Davidic dynasty.

This expression of God's unconditional commitment is all the more remarkable when we remember that in the exile of the Ark (1 Samuel 4–6) God's commitment was indirectly put at stake—would God return to Israel or sojourn elsewhere? In two other passages of classic theological storytelling God's commitment to Israel is put at stake and dramatically affirmed: the relationship is unshakably strong (see Exod 32:7-14 and Num 14:10-25). When storytelling can vividly envisage the ending of a relationship its survival is expressive of the unconditional nature of the bond.

Conflict of Authority: King and Prophet

The figure of the prophet in 1–2 Samuel sets the tone for the whole prophetic literature, confronting king and people, calling for justice individually and socially, putting God's will as the paramount value in Israel and the prophet as God's mouthpiece controlling kings. Once again the complexity of the text prohibits any thought of simplicity. Most of the prophetic texts in 1–2 Samuel show evidence of having been overwritten. Such rewriting may clarify and highlight what was already there or it may write in what was not there, enhancing the prophetic claim in the light of later events. The clash of prophetic voices is not as evident in Samuel–Kings as it is in the prophetic books. However, any oversimplified application of prophetic authority to the events of today must be viewed with caution.

Text as Basis for Storytelling

Finally, many of the texts in Samuel–Kings point to an aspect that we need to take account of in our reflections today. We live in the post-Gutenberg age of the printed book and we need to make a massive imaginative leap even to envisage a world in which texts were written for other purposes than being distributed to a wide readership. We are probably better off to think of stories as written not to be read but to be heard or to be told—jarring as this may be to our sensibilities. It is quite possible that, for all their literary value even as condensed texts, the function such story texts served may have been as a base for more extended presentation—be it a storyteller's performance, a theologian's discourse, or a courtier's reflections on the art of conducting state affairs.

As the basis from which an artistic performance might begin the text may on occasion record variant ways in which a story might be told or give variant interpretations of an experience or preserve variant traditions and so on. Whoever used the text would have been expected to make an appropriate choice between the variants on offer in it. This procedure can be quite disconcerting to us, brought up in our era of the printed text; to those of the pre-print era of ancient Israel it may not have seemed surprising at all.

SECOND READING

An Invitation to Read

In working with any biblical commentary we always run the risk of reading the commentary and not the Bible. The more interesting and enlightening the commentary, the greater the risk. But it is the Bible we want to understand and interpret, not the commentary—not even this one.

So our readers here need to do what we try to do ourselves in our work: first read the biblical text, then read the commentary, then read the biblical text again. If closer study is wanted it comes after these first three stages of reading: Bible, commentary, Bible.

First identify the unit involved (for example, 1 Sam 1:1–2:11). Second, read the biblical text, 1:1–2:11. Third, read the commentary on 1:1–2:11. (In Samuel–Kings in this commentary it may also help to reread the larger introductory units pointing to metaphor and broader contexts—for example, 1 Sam 1:1–16:13.) Fourth, read the biblical text again. Now, and only now, it may be appropriate to settle down to some close study and comparative checking.

1 Sam 1:1–16:13

The Prophetic Role. Metaphor: Painting

If we wanted paintings of 1 Sam 1:1–16:13 we would be wise to count on commissioning four works of art. The first, "The Emergence of Samuel as a Prophet," could be a triptych (picture on three panels): (1) the birth of Samuel; (2) the contrast between the growing Samuel and the decadent Elide priesthood; (3) the emergence of Samuel on the national scene as a prophet recognized by all Israel (1 Samuel 1–3).

The second work would not feature Samuel but instead would focus on the Ark of the Covenant. We might be tempted to entrust the painting to someone with a touch for the bizarre within the ordinary—but it would have to be a work of serious religious significance. Again a triptych would be suitable: (1) the people's major religious symbol, the Ark of the Covenant, leaves their national territory, apparently the booty of a conquering enemy, the Philistines; (2) the Ark as clearly dominant among the enemy, a source of disease, death, and despair to be sent back as fast as possible to where it came from; (3) the return of Israel's Ark, the joy as it crossed the border and the sudden shattering of that joy in a disaster that leads to the Ark's being left permanently on the sidelines. The triptych would need a certain open-endedness, leaving us to ponder what all this might mean (1 Samuel 4–6).

The third commission would require an artist or two—perhaps more—with a feel for politics, popular opinion, and a theological sense of history. It would need an ability to work with sharply contrasting colors. Six canvases would be needed: (1) Samuel putting the Philistines to flight, conveying an overall sense of peace, well-being, and security; (2) an assembly at Ramah with Samuel and the elders in conflict over their demand for a king; (3) Saul coming for help to a prophet who turns out to be Samuel, and Samuel anointing the young man as king-to-be and future deliverer of Israel from the Philistine menace; (4) Samuel giving a theological lecture, casting lots to find the king among the tribes of Israel, and finally presiding over the coronation—a full and complex canvas; (5) a great portrayal of national passion with the burghers of Jabesh-gilead in search of a deliverer for their cruelly besieged city, the discovery of Saul and his strategic success in lifting the siege and saving the city, and the grateful nation's response in the mass acclamation of Saul as king; (6) Samuel as judgmental prophet-theologian holding forth on the wickedness of Israel but ending his discourse with some rays of hope (1 Samuel 7–12).

The fourth and final commission could well be accommodated in four canvases: (1) Saul dismissed as king after offering an unauthorized sacrifice, against the background of Philistine threat; (2) the rousing scene of Jonathan's guerrilla victory over a Philistine garrison, with Saul nearly spoiling the victory celebrations; (3) a second portrayal of Saul's dismissal as king after violating a strict order from Samuel; (4) the relatively peaceful scene of Samuel among the family of Jesse from Bethlehem, anointing his youngest son, David, as king-to-be in Israel—open-ended again since Saul is still king and no holder of the throne hands over power without a struggle (1 Sam 13:1–16:13).

Emergence of a Prophet (1 Samuel 1–3)

1:1–2:11

The triptych begins with the birth of Samuel. The picture has to radiate change and transformation. Central to it is the transformation of a woman from barrenness to fruitfulness, from despair and tears to hope and joy. Basic to it must be the symbolism of potential change for the whole people. The resonances are too strong for this to be simply the story of a barren woman's agony relieved in response to her vow. Among the mothers of Israel, Sarah and Rebekah and Rachel were barren. Each in her own way directed the course of the people's development. Sarah had Ishmael banished so that Isaac might be sole heir (Gen 21:10). Rebekah had her favorite Jacob blessed by his dying father, whose preference was for Esau, the firstborn twin (Gen 25:28; 27:5-17), and Israel is descended from Jacob. An old man's predilection for the two sons of his first-loved wife brought Israel into Egypt where it was kept alive in famine (Genesis 37–50). So here the birth of Samuel augurs the outbreak of something new in Israel.

This picture belongs to Hannah, mother of Samuel, a mother in Israel. In her is reflected what is felt for Israel. She is barren and in anguish, tormented by her rival. Her husband protests the depth of his love, but in this story his role is completely passive. The old priest, Eli, mistakes Hannah's silent vow for drunken folly. He makes amends with a prayer that brings her peace. It is the LORD, however, who hears her prayer and in so doing brings new hope to Israel. A son is born to Hannah; she names him Samuel. Once she had weaned him, in accordance with her vow she brings him to Eli at the sanctuary, to be given to God for life. At this moment, to borrow the NT metaphor, the new wine has been introduced into the old wineskin.

The song of Hannah celebrates this event. It was written later under the monarchy; note the reference to the anointed king (2:10). It may not be particularly apt as a song for a mother who has just given up a child to God; it is far more apt as the song for a woman who is a symbol of Israel on the brink of new life. It echoes Hannah's situation: "the barren has borne seven." It hymns God: "The LORD makes poor and makes rich; he brings low, he also exalts." It glorifies the king: "The LORD will judge the ends of the earth; he will give strength to his king, and exalt the power of his anointed." What this song celebrates is not simply the reversal of Hannah's situation. It is a portent of a major reversal in the situation of Israel, when the judges and the Elides will be replaced by Samuel and the kings. It is not surprising that in Christianity's experience of newness breaking into our world this song of Hannah should have been drawn on so substantially for the Magnificat of Mary.

2:12–3:18

The second panel is painted in dark, threatening colors broken up by the sharp contrast of pools of light. The light surrounds Samuel; the darkness envelops the Elides. First there is a portrayal of Eli's sons as sacrilegious. The sons of Eli were not content to take potluck; they took their pick according to their choice. Sacrificial service becomes an opportunity for profiteering and exploitation. A second sketch of Eli's sons contains a general accusation of evil, "all that his sons were doing to all Israel," and a specific charge of sexually abusive behavior with the women who served in the sanctuary. The old Eli's remonstrance is in vain. An ominous note is sounded: "for it was the will of the LORD to kill them." The Elide priesthood is doomed.

In contrast the images of Samuel are all sweetness and light. Framed between two references to Samuel at the sanctuary, the description of his significance is reflected in Hannah's fruitfulness—given to God, he is a source of new life. In a second pool of light Samuel is described as growing "both in stature and in favor with the LORD and with the people." The replacement figure for the Elides is at hand.

The doom of the house of Eli is swiftly sketched. First an anonymous man of God announces it: from their exalted dignity the Elides will be brought low. Many see the Elide crimes as the cause of the disaster in 1 Samuel 4. Such a reading may point to the human need to identify a cause for every calamity, but it is out of place here. The fate of Eli's two sons, dying on the same day, is a sign for him (2:34). A sign always points to the future; it is not itself the event it signifies. The Elides are caught up in the disaster of ch. 4; they alone are not its cause. The second announcement of doom for the house of Eli is pronounced by Samuel himself. It is not a call narrative, but the story of Samuel's first experience of the word of God. It is a fearful verdict.

3:19-21

The final panel depicts Samuel as a figure of renown to all Israel, from north to south, recognized as "a trustworthy prophet of the LORD." The "word of the LORD," the knowledge of God's will and purpose, is known to all Israel through Samuel.

Departure of the Ark (1 Samuel 4–6)

This second triptych demands great skill of its interpreter. Events that may strike us as bizarre are used to convey a message that is deadly serious. Samuel does not appear. In this narrative the Ark of the Covenant is the symbol through which the power and purpose of God are communicated. In the first panel of the triptych the Ark departs from Israel, a departure portrayed in language suggesting an active role for God: "the glory has departed from Israel" (4:21-22). In the second panel (5:1-12) the Philistine god is defeated and the Philistine people oppressed by the Ark. In the final panel (6:1–7:2a) the Ark returns to Israelite territory. Its return is not a cause of blessing but a source of death. In fear the people banish it to the border town of Kiriath-jearim, totally outside the mainstream of Israel's life and worship—but near to Jerusalem. A long wait is begun: "a long time passed" (7:2).

4:1-22

The interpreter's task is to grasp the meaning in the narrative's sequence and symbolism. The first panel of the triptych is full of the images of war. The conflict is between Israel and the Philistines. Israel loses two battles with a more than sevenfold increase in casualty figures (4:1b-2, 10-11).

Between these two battle scenes there is the dramatic picture of the elders asking why their God had defeated them: "Why has the LORD put us to rout today before the Philistines?" (4:3). The story has the Ark brought to the camp and the great joy expressed by Israel is authenticated by the corresponding fear among the Philistines (4:5-9). If it were not for that ominously worrying question "why has the LORD put us to rout today?" the storyteller would seem to be toying with us because the storyteller knows that—despite Israel's joy and the Philistines' fear—Israel loses the second battle decisively, loses the Ark too, and the two sons of Eli lose their lives that day.

Two vignettes illustrate the story and its meaning. Told the news, Eli dies. The fatality expresses finality. Told the news, his daughter-in-law dies giving birth. The name the dying mother gives her child interprets the defeat with foreboding: "the glory has departed from Israel" (4:21-22). The Ark has gone into exile from Israel; its return will be an opening to the new—with Samuel (1 Samuel 7) and with David (2 Samuel 6).

5:1-12

The second panel presents four scenes, varying in detail but expressing the same message. The first scene portrays the temple of the Philistine God, Dagon, in the Philistine city of Ashdod. There Dagon submits to the God of Israel—not once but twice. The second time Dagon's head and hands have been severed from his statue and gathered at the temple door; Dagon is powerless to think or act. The scene would be comic if it were not for its context. The army of Israel has just been decisively routed by the Philistines. In the religious logic of the day the army of the stronger god routs the army of the weaker god. But here in Dagon's temple the stronger god has been the God of Israel. So on the field of battle the stronger god must have been the God of Israel. As the question in 4:3 feared, the God of Israel did indeed put Israel to rout before the Philistines.

Three further scenes drive home the same message. In Ashdod, Gath, and Ekron disease and death accompany the coming of the Ark of the God of Israel. Philistine victory has become Philistine disaster. The God of Israel does not favor the Philistines. The Philistines are desperate to be rid of the Ark.

6:1–7:2

The final panel depicts the return of the Ark to Israel. The decision as to where the Ark will go is left to God in an act of divination. Against all odds two untrained cows leave their calves and pull the cart with the Ark straight to Israel. The symbolism is good for Israel: their God has not abandoned them, but has returned. Yet Israel's rejoicing is short-lived. A great slaughter breaks out around the Ark. The Ark may be back but it is not bestowing blessing. It must be taken away (6:20). Thus the Ark goes to Kiriath-jearim and there it will stay till David's day (2 Samuel 6). It is not God's purpose to abandon Israel, but the purpose of God for Israel's future remains unclear—at least as symbolized by the Ark. A long wait is begun: "a long time passed" (7:2). There has been a major rupture in the pattern of God's relationship with Israel, and the healing has not yet happened.

In the eyes of those for whom the Ark was of supreme symbolic significance these strange events conveyed the inner meaning of Israel's destiny as it unfolded. There would be a long wait for the last act in the drama. This text, focused on the Ark (chs. 4–6) has no place for Samuel. God's will and God's desire are manifested by the story of the movements and events associated with the Ark; they are not declared by a prophet. The Ark will not move again until 2 Samuel 6. From 1 Samuel 7 to 2 Samuel 5 it will be the prophet Samuel who declares God's will and God's desire to Israel.

Transition to Monarchy (1 Samuel 7–12)

The biblical text allows for many and various ways of finding God and discerning God's desire. With the Ark sidelined the focus returns to the prophetic figure of Samuel—in the middle of the Ark's long wait, as it were. Precisely because of its subject—the greatest social transformation in Israel's national history—the text here presents an immensely complicated pastiche (i.e., a work of art composed from various sources). Strongly contrasting views are expressed. The message of the chapters may not be so much in the particular theological views expressed. More significant may be the preservation of this radical diversity and the way the text has been built up through its preservation. It may help first to explore the individual scenes from the end back to the beginning and then, second, to follow the biblical text from the start. So first of all we will move from ch. 12 back to ch. 7 and then we will follow the biblical order from ch. 7 to ch. 12.

1 Samuel 12

The chapter portrays a very dark and stormy picture—and not just in v. 18. Samuel enters into judgment with Israel, looking back to the Exodus and down to the present day (vv. 7-12). The demand for a king is characterized as great wickedness (v. 17). However, the darkness is not total; the picture is chiaroscuro, contrasting light and shade. Shafts of light touch on the deliverance from Egypt (v. 8) and the deliverance under the judges (v. 11) and shine with some uncertainty into the future (vv. 19-24). In 1 Samuel 12 the demand for monarchy was inspired by fear of King Nahash, the Ammonite. So 1 Samuel 12 has a perspective reaching back in the far distance to the Exodus, in the middle distance to the judges, and in the near foreground to the Nahash episode.

1 Samuel 11

The picture of the Nahash episode is positive toward the monarchy. A city in the north of Israel, Jabesh-gilead, faces cruel humiliation by a besieging enemy. As the besieged inhabitants send "through all the territory of Israel" for help, the spirit of God comes powerfully upon Saul and he rallies the people and delivers the city. In response the people make Saul king "before the LORD" in the sanctuary at Gilgal. The picture is sunny: deliverance from extreme need by a deliverer empowered by the spirit of God. There is no indication of any demand for a king to replace the LORD. (NOTE: 11:14 has "renew the kingship"; as there is no trace of a king in vv. 1-11 this is read as an editorial adjustment in the compilation of the final text, replacing an original "establish the kingship.") Taken together, 1 Samuel 11 and 12 form a picture establishing monarchy in Israel as the result of a successful response to military peril. The scene in 1 Samuel 11 is full of light: the response was initiated by the spirit of God and the move to monarchy was initiated by Samuel. 1 Samuel 12, as we have seen, takes a different view and looks much more darkly on the matter.

10:17-25 and 1 Samuel 8

1 Samuel 10:17-25 offers a different scene in which Saul is made king. Samuel is depicted using two procedures to identify the king—first by lot (10:20-21), second by an oracle (10:22-23). Both procedures are ways of knowing God's will. Once identified Saul is duly appointed

king before the LORD (10:24-25). The issue here is the identification of the man who is to be king. The preceding episode, 9:1–10:16, is centrally focused on the identification of the king-to-be, brought by God to the prophet and duly anointed or commissioned. This factor eliminates 9:1–10:16 as the conventional lead-in to 10:17-25. For this we can look to 1 Samuel 8.

Before that, however, we should note that the choice of the king in 10:17-25 occurs within the setting of a national assembly at Mizpah. While the issue of monarchy in vv. 20-25 is painted in warm and sunny colors it is introduced by a veritable storm cloud of darkness in vv. 18-19a, which refer back as far as the Exodus and probably touch on the judges before characterizing the request for a king as rejection of God.

In 1 Samuel 8 we have another chapter of chiaroscuro. If we ignore the dark for the moment the demand for a king is motivated by the demand for justice—the area in which Samuel's sons have failed (8:1-3). Passing over the dark (i.e., Samuel's dialogue with God, 8:6b-10 and v. 18), we find that Samuel counters this demand with a litany of the burdens a king imposes on the people. Injustice is not necessarily among these burdens, so the people reiterate their demand and God tells Samuel to appoint a king (8:22). Thus we have an appropriate and adequate lead-in to 10:20-25.

Taken together 1 Samuel 8 and 10:17, 20-25 form a picture according to which monarchy was established in Israel as the result of a need for justice—despite the warning of burdensome royal taxes. In view of the demand for social justice God has commanded Samuel to appoint a king (8:22); Samuel appeals to God through the lot and the oracle to identify the king (10:17, 20-23); when Saul is identified he is made king (10:24-25).

Once this positive aspect has been noted we can then observe how the picture as it exists now has a much darker tone. Displeased by the demand (8:6a) Samuel prays to God and God's response portrays the demand in a totally negative light (8:6b-10 and v. 18). The demand for a king is a rejection of God, continuing a behavior pattern from the time of the Exodus and probably through the time of the judges. This is akin to the comment made in 10:18-19a. In both cases, it seems that a positive picture has been touched up and painted over to render it negative.

9:1–10:16 and 1 Samuel 7

A chance visit to a man of God has been painted over in the colors of a predestined visit to the prophet Samuel who has been given a day's notice of the guest God is bringing to him (9:15-17). Originally the "man of God" gave Saul a commission to "do whatever you see fit to do, for God is with you" (10:7). For Samuel this commission is made more precise. Saul is to be anointed king-designate and he is to deliver Israel from the Philistines, for Israel's cry has reached to God (9:16). From the people comes not a demand for a king but a cry for deliverance; from God, a king—or rather a king-designate.

The anointing as king-designate *(nāgîd)* requires Saul to be made king later. It makes most sense to associate this story with the coronation at Gilgal (11:15). Saul's being empowered by the spirit of God (11:6) is the result of the prophetic commission (in the original version) and Samuel's anointing (in the repainted picture). The reference to the Philistines in the repainted picture (9:16) must look beyond the Nahash affair to the long-term struggle against the Philistines—the struggle in which Saul ultimately failed.

This reference to the Philistines raises the contrasting image of 1 Samuel 7. There the Philistines constitute an immediate threat to Israel. Samuel's prayer brings God's thunderous intervention and victory. As a result "the Philistines were subdued and did not again enter the territory of Israel; the hand of the LORD was against the Philistines all the days of Samuel" (7:13). In this picture Samuel is portrayed acting with the power of a deliverer judge (Judges 3–9); there is no need for a king to defend Israel.

Review

Before we follow the biblical text from ch. 7 to ch. 12 a brief review is helpful. Overall, tradition preserved two accounts of the origin of monarchy in Israel, both of which were positive. One saw monarchy as a response to society's need for justice, the other as a response to society's need for defense. In the first the king was selected by lot or divine oracle; in the second the king-to-be was commissioned by a man of God or anointed by Samuel and then this commission was activated by the spirit of God in response to the threat from Nahash. Later in the history of the text there has been revision in highly negative terms (the dark tones)—restricted however to the first account.

Present Text

We can best grasp the final picture that has been created out of these basic images by looking first at the text before it has been retouched with the dark passages. In itself it is a complex text. It will be easier to take in if the dark retouches are momentarily ignored.

1 Samuel 7

The sunny images begin with an older story in 7:5-12 that has probably been repainted in deuteronomistic terms. Samuel is depicted as a deliverer judge with overtones of Moses and Elijah; by his simple intercession he is able to have God put the menacing Philistines to rout. The Philistine threat is removed for a generation; Samuel judges Israel "all the days of his life" (7:15).

1 Samuel 8

The picture changes. Samuel has been replaced by his sons and they are not assuring justice in Israel. The elders therefore ask Samuel for a king. At the original level Samuel points to the burdens involved in a monarchy without dissuading the people; they repeat their request for a king, adding defense to the demand for justice. When Samuel takes the matter to God he is told to appoint a king. The appointment of the king should follow next.

9:1–10:16

On the contrary, we do not have the appointment of a king but the identification and commissioning or anointing of a king-to-be. This could conceivably follow on 1 Samuel 8 if the king were not to be identified by Samuel through lot and oracle in 10:17-25. An attempt to harmonize 1 Samuel 9 and 10 risks making Samuel responsible for turning the ceremonies of the lot and the oracle into a charade. It is more sympathetic to the text to see that here two pictures of the origin of the monarchy are being preserved —one based primarily on social justice, the other on national defense. Rather than juxtapose the two separate pictures sequentially the text interweaves them. So before the king is identified and appointed in 10:17-25 the process of identification in the other story is introduced in 9:1–10:16 (along with some other themes).

10:17–11:15

The "justice" king is appointed in 1 Sam 10:17-25. The "defense" king is established in 1 Samuel 11, the commission/anointing of 1 Sam 9:1–10:16 becoming effective in 11:6 when "the spirit of God came upon Saul in power." The duplication here is overcome in the text by describing the second coronation as a renewal of the kingship (11:14). In this way two pictures of the origin of the monarchy in Israel are presented for consideration. Their interweaving expresses the unity of the monarchy; one and the same king is responsible for defense and for justice. Their separateness preserves different views that were current in Israel. In both pictures the monarchy is viewed positively. We may assume that they stem from times when the kings were seen as fulfilling their function of assuring justice and securing defense.

The dark retouches to the pictures of 1 Samuel 8 and 10 presumably come from a time when the kings were seen in a radically different light. Kingship was viewed as destructive when the centralized authority of the monarchy was believed to have eroded traditional values, destroyed traditional structures in society, and engaged in external affairs unprofitably. It cannot have been of God. The retouches express this view. In both cases the retouching of the text characterizes the older version as rejection of God, but it does not seek to form a coherent unified text with it. To have God command the rejection of God would be absurd. The dark retouches are not blended with the earlier traditions to express a single view; they express a different view and a different theology.

1 Samuel 12

This chapter is particularly significant because, although it characterizes the establishment of the monarchy as great wickedness, it offers guidelines for living successfully under the monarchy (12:14-15) and it assures Israel of God's fidelity and Samuel's intercession and instruction (12:20-24). The institution's destructive potential has the last word (12:25).

10:26-27 and 11:12-13

So far we have left these four verses undiscussed. They are an excellent example of how so much can be packed into so little. They also express forcefully how in an evolving situation yesterday's orthodoxy can become today's heresy. Before the institution of the monarchy "those whose hearts God had touched" were those who knew that it is God who saves; that was orthodoxy. Now "those whose hearts God had touched" are the ones who have gone with Saul; those who quote yesterday's orthodoxy are "worthless fellows" (10:26-27). Yesterday's embodiment of infidelity, the rejection of God, has become today's dispenser of clemency (11:12-13). Times have changed here and so has faith; times will change again and, as the negative passages have shown, so will faith.

Final Act of the Prophet Samuel: 13:1–16:13

1 Samuel 13

Of the four canvases in this collection, the first opens with a massively drawn picture of Philistine power—"thirty thousand chariots, and six thousand horsemen, and troops like the sand on the seashore in multitude" (13:5). Israel's weakness stands in stark comparison even if the figures given are only for the standing army—two thousand with Saul and a thousand with Jonathan (13:2). The text ends on much the same note, detailing the Philistine power to keep Israel in a state of technological inferiority, denying them weapons of iron (13:19-22).

Israel's weakness is highlighted by the intervening account of Samuel's condemnation and rejection of Saul (13:7b-15a). The text is likely to be secondary, offering a variant account of how Saul came to be dismissed by Samuel. The primary account is given in 1 Sam 15:1-35. In 13:7b-15a Saul is dismissed as king because he failed in total obedience to the prophet Samuel. In considerable anticipation, the anointing of another is foretold (13:14). Modern sympathies are likely to side with Saul. Samuel was late and the situation was serious. However, a text that has Samuel arrive just as Saul finishes the sacrifice is more concerned with principles and symbols than with strategy and fairness. The text expresses a prophetic claim to absolute obedience and the right to dismiss kings who fail in that obedience. A similar claim is expressed in 15:22-23—"to obey is better than sacrifice."

1 Samuel 14

In the second canvas it is possible that a story featuring an exploit by Jonathan has been combined with a tradition featuring a victory by Saul (for the Saul tradition, see 1 Sam 13:4-7a, 16-18; 14:20-23, 31-35; Klein, *1 Samuel*). Jonathan is portrayed in a daring act of valor, putting the precipitous terrain to strategic use in a raid on the Philistine garrison. In the present text Saul comes to Jonathan's aid and a victory is won. Despite the victory Saul is cast in an ill-fated light for imperiling his own son, the hero responsible for inspiring the victory. The pursuit of the Philistines is left unfinished (14:46). The story catches the typical in Saul: moments of folly nullify his moments of success.

Three vignettes depict Saul's reign: his battles fought for Israel (14:47-48); his family and associates (14:49-51); the keynote of his reign (14:52). As a summary of Saul's time this is more congenial to *Saul's Post* than to *David's Times.* Verses 47-48 particularly give a more favorable view of Saul than will be found in the following chapters; it is rather too good to be true.

1 Samuel 15

The third canvas in the collection features direct conflict between Saul and the prophet Samuel. In the context of his anointing (15:1) Samuel gives Saul God's command to exterminate the Amalekites. Saul boasts of complete compliance, Samuel is rightly suspicious, and Saul's confession is met with Samuel's rejection—"to obey is better than sacrifice" (15:22). The signal is given that another has been chosen (15:28). The dismissal is definitive; Samuel and Saul part, never to meet again.

There is probably an older story here that has been retouched to transform an original rebuke into outright rejection (the older story is in 1 Sam 15:1aα, 2-9, 13-15, 17a, 18-22, 24-25, 31-35a; see Campbell, *Of Prophets and Kings*). The annihilation of the Amalekites, one of Israel's arch-enemies, of course did not occur. In 1 Sam 30:1-20 the Amalekites are alive and well, engaged in their usual banditry—and four hundred escaped David's attack (30:17). We are allowed to assume the story of 1 Samuel 15 was composed with full knowledge of the story in 1 Samuel 30. The story of 1 Samuel 15 reflects concern for royal behavior when confronted with divine demand; it does not display interest in history. This attitude to story is significant for Joshua 1–12 and the conquest. The retouched version of the story expresses the prophetic claim to designate and dismiss kings. Saul is dismissed because he fails the prophetic demand for total obedience.

16:1-13

The final canvas depicts Samuel anointing David. It is the fulfillment of what has been anticipated earlier (13:14; 15:28). As with Saul's anointing, David's is directly ordered by God. The anointing is secret. It is concealed from Saul; although the Bethlehem elders are invited, their presence is not mentioned. The youngest and least likely of Jesse's sons is anointed. Prophetic power is again to the fore: "the LORD does not see as mortals see" (16:7). Once he is anointed, "the spirit of the LORD came mightily upon David from that day forward" (16:13). Samuel returns to Ramah. His task is done. The king-designate is on the scene; Samuel can retire from it. Events can be left to unfold.

1 Sam 16:14–2 Sam 8:18

The Realization in History. Metaphor: Drama

Samuel has dismissed Saul and designated David to be Israel's future king. The prophetic deed is done. It will take another twenty or more chapters for the political deed to be done, for David to achieve royal power and for Samuel's prophetic action to be realized in history. If we were to put 1 Sam 16:14–2 Sam 8:15 on stage the drama would be concerned with Saul's struggle to hold on to power as it slips away into David's hands. It is possible that an early document begins here, the Story of David's Rise. A five-act play would reflect its structure. Act One: single combat with the destiny of Israel at stake—and the victor becomes a threat to Saul's throne (1 Sam 16:14–18:16). Act Two: conflict at court between the increasingly suspicious Saul and the increasingly successful David (1 Sam 18:17–20:42). Act Three: open rupture, with David, the only person capable of saving Israel, hunted across the countryside by the luckless Saul (1 Sam 21:1–27:12). Act Four: the gathering storm and the ultimate failure of Saul (1 Sam 28:1–31:13). Act Five: David's assumption of royal power in place of Saul (2 Sam 1:1–8:18).

Act One: The Drama in Microcosm (16:14–18:16)

The story of David and Goliath is one of the best known Bible stories and not one of the best understood. The actual conflict opens with David pitted against "the Philistine champion," symbolizing Israel's life-and-death struggle with the Philistines. The narrative ends with succinct comments on the three players in the drama of Israel's throne: David had success; Saul stood in awe of him; all Israel and Judah loved David, for it was he who exercised military leadership among them (18:13-16; cf. 2 Sam 5:2). In between, Saul the anointed king quails and fails; David the anointed king-to-be braves the Philistine and saves the people. In this presentation David becomes king of Israel because the people recognized that he was the one to deliver Israel from the Philistine menace, something that Saul was manifestly unable to do. David could do it because the LORD was with him in all that he did. It was evident in the single combat; it was to be evident in the national struggle.

The opening scene goes back to a tormented Saul. The narrator knows that "the spirit of the LORD departed from Saul, and an evil spirit from the LORD tormented him" (16:14). His household knows that "an evil spirit from God" is tormenting him (16:15). We, the readers, know that this must be the result of Samuel's rejection of Saul. Saul's salvation is found in David the lyre-player who enters Saul's service and becomes his armor-bearer.

On the field of battle Saul faces the destiny for which he was anointed. The issue of Philistine dominance is put in the simple terms of the challenger (17:9). Saul, like all Israel, is "dismayed and greatly afraid"—rendered powerless by fear (17:11). David, standing beside Saul as his armor-bearer, offers to accept the challenge and fight the Philistine (17:32), putting his trust in his own experience (17:34-36) and his faith in God's power to save (17:37).

To appreciate this portrayal of David we need to recognize that an alternative version of David's emergence onto the scene of Israel's history is signaled here at three chief points in the present text: 17:12-31; 17:55–18:5; 18:17-30. Once this is seen David's courage in v. 32 stands in immediate juxtaposition with Saul's fear in v. 11. The alternative version will be discussed at the end of this section.

To return to the main story, David goes out to meet the Philistine. The combat is usually presented as most unequal, between a huge professional soldier and a "small, apparently defenseless" shepherd lad who has no real hope in force of arms. When we realize that in ancient Israel the sling was an accurate military weapon (see Judg 20:16; 2 Chr 26:14), suddenly the odds in this fight are radically changed. Like the English archers against French cavalry or the Molotov cocktail against the tank, the slinger is Israel's best chance against the lumbering, heavily armed foot soldier. As long as David gets his shot off before the Philistine gets his shield up, as long as David's nerve holds and his aim is good, the big Philistine is dead. Trust in God here is not God's supplying for David's weakness. Trust in God here means God's enabling David to do what David is quite capable of doing.

So David kills the Philistine and Saul's jealousy is aroused. David as a commander is successful and Saul's jealousy grows. Saul, who is unable to deliver either Israel or himself, seeks to be rid of the one man who can free Saul of his torment and Israel from the Philistines. When the time comes the people will turn to David to be their king and deliverer (2 Sam 5:1-3). In this view David came to power in Israel because he stepped into the vacuum left by Saul's failure against the Philistines. Theologically David's success is attributed to God's being with him when Israel was bereft of royal deliverance. It is a story of Saul's failure and David's success (Campbell, *Study Companion*).

The alternative version (signaled in part at 17:12-31; 17:55–18:5; 18:17-30) is also about David's rise to prominence in Israel. It portrays a different drama. God's role and Saul's failure are pushed into the background. Instead David seizes opportunity when it is offered. The Philistine's challenge offers him his chance and he grabs for it. Assured of royal favor as his reward (17:25-27), he kills the Philistine, enters Saul's court, and wins the hand of Saul's daughter in marriage. It is a story of singular chance swiftly seized.

Act Two: Conflict at Court (18:17–20:42)

As in so many stories of conflict, the boundaries of Saul's clash with David are fluid. Enmity begins to stir in Saul's mind in 18:6-9 and transfers to his action in 18:10-11. As well as being part of the conflict at court the offers of Merab and Michal in marriage can refer back to the reward assured David by the soldiers in 17:25. After the narrator's summary comment in 18:14-16 the drama can be set within the court of Saul.

The text opens with two anecdotal episodes and a comment (18:17-30). As we have just seen, this text concludes the alternative version of how David first emerged on the public stage in Israel. At the level of the present biblical text we can treat it here within the conflict at court between Saul and David.

The traditions of this conflict at court and of the following open rupture between David and Saul carry an immense burden of irony. David has been presented as the one who can deliver Saul from the evil spirit that torments Saul and that has come from God (16:14). David has also been presented as the one who can deliver Israel, which Saul is unable to do. In these traditions—which of course are formulated in a strongly pro-Davidic presentation—Saul is portrayed as energetically devoted to the destruction of David, Saul's own deliverer from torment and the potential deliverer of Israel. From Saul's point of view this is political necessity; rivals are to be eliminated. From the Davidic point of view this is a clear case of the sufferer wanting to kill the healer—and God is placed firmly on the side of the healer.

18:17-19

In the first of the sections offering an alternative version of the David and Goliath story (17:12-31) David was assured that the king "will give him his daughter" in marriage (17:25). In the opening episode of this conflict at Saul's court Saul does offer David his elder daughter, Merab, as a wife—as long as David will fight the Philistines for Saul so that the Philistines can kill David for Saul (18:17). It is not a nice deal in the first place, and Saul reneges on it when the time comes.

18:20-30

In a second anecdote Saul's daughter Michal falls in love with David. Again Saul makes the offer of marriage, this time with the explicit request for a marriage present of one hundred Philistine foreskins—to be sure that David gets himself killed (18:25). Naturally in a story like this David comes up with twice the number of foreskins asked and wins the hand of Michal as wife. Saul has baited the Philistine trap with his own daughters—in vain. The narrator's comment emphasizes the enmity that has been established between David and Saul (18:29) and the comparison between them that strongly favors David (18:30). Where before Saul feared the Philistine (17:11), now he fears David. The Philistines as the enemy have receded, replaced in Saul's distorted vision by a more immediate enemy, David.

19:1-7

From here on, with the enmity out in the open, the narrative piles up traditions of Saul's hostility until David flees Saul's court. In this anecdote Saul gives orders for David to be killed (19:1). Jonathan takes the role of David's protector: he sends David off to hide while he intercedes with Saul for David's life. An alternative version is signaled in vv. 2b-3a. David is to hide in a secret place evidently known to both Jonathan and David. Jonathan will go for a walk with Saul and pause within earshot of the place to argue David's case. In this way David will know Saul's mind. In the basic version Jonathan tells David that Saul has relented. Central to this tradition is the support for David given by Jonathan, Saul's eldest son and heir. David is no rebellious usurper; his chief backer is Jonathan.

19:8-10

A tradition follows of how the jealous Saul, under the evil spirit, threw his spear at David with murderous intent while David was playing music to soothe him (it is paralleled by 18:10-11). David fled into the night.

19:11-17

We have had Jonathan help David. Now Saul's daughter helps him. Michal recognizes David's peril and helps him escape through a window since Saul's soldiers are on watch for David. This text is a good example of the possibility noted in the introduction that some biblical texts served as a base from which storytellers began rather than being a record of what the storyteller actually said. The dummy in the bed is a stratagem to gain time. It is needed when Saul sends messengers "to see David for themselves" (v. 15a)—but it does not feature! When they come with orders to "bring him up to me in the bed" (v. 15b) it is too late for any stratagem. The story has been short-circuited in the text. From this brief plot summary a storyteller could spin an extensive tale. The essential is here: Saul has been deceived by his own daughter.

19:18-24

David is depicted as taking refuge with Samuel. In a patterned story with similarities to the pattern in 2 Kings 1:9-14 Saul ends up before Samuel—despite the view in 1 Sam 15:35. The story is used to account for the saying in the last verse, explained in a slightly different version in 10:10-13. There Saul succumbs to the power of the group; here Saul succumbs to the power of the person. The story here has its symbolism: Samuel's protection is given to David and Samuel's power abases Saul.

1 Samuel 20

David has left Saul's court. The final scene in the drama determines whether he can return there. Jonathan believes his father's hostility can be deflected as before; David is doubtful. David takes the initiative and hatches a plan to hide in the field while Jonathan ascertains Saul's mood. Again if we view this as a base for storytelling three versions may be preserved here. If Saul is hostile any message must be secret (vv. 9-10); Jonathan may be followed. In the first and simplest version Jonathan goes out for archery practice with an attendant whom he later sends back (vv. 35, 40); safely away from the city, Jonathan can meet David and they make their farewells (vv. 41-42). In a second version a coded signal is arranged (vv. 18-22), to be shouted in the vicinity of David's known hiding place. The third version can be found within the execution of the second: rather than a coded signal Jonathan shouts a direct message for David, concealed as a cry to the attendant (v. 38a). In all of these David is no usurper; his chief supporter is Saul's heir, Jonathan.

Act Three: Open Rupture with Saul (21:1–27:12)

Act Three is critical; it is the great divide in the drama of Saul and David. The rupture is out in the open. Only one can be leader; one must cede. The prophetic anointing is pitted against the power of office. The opening chapter anticipates the movement of the entire section. Separated from Saul, David ends up with the Philistines at Gath.

With ch. 22 major insight is offered into the way these traditions may have come together. At a number of points in the Story of David's Rise clusters of information occur that would hardly have survived independently (e.g., 1 Sam 22:1-5; 27:1-7; 2 Sam 2:1-4a, 8-9, 10b). These minor details of oral history appear to have been collected with a view to the compilation of a larger narrative, the story of how David came to be king in Israel. Understood in this way they point to an early date for the larger narrative.

1 Samuel 21

The drama opens with David alone. Jonathan has returned to the city; David is in the countryside without support. Successful guerrillas are resourceful, so David lies to Ahimelech, the priest of the sanctuary of Nob, just north of Jerusalem. First David gets food, the sanctuary bread. Then David gets weaponry, the sword of Goliath, which was among the sanctuary's treasures—a sword rich in symbol.

Perhaps the curtain should close here with David's flight from Saul. But a small scene has David flee to the court of King Achish of Gath. It sits a trace uncomfortably with David's reception by Achish in ch. 27. Storytellers could have handled the issue in various ways. In the present narrative the two episodes frame David's time as guerrilla chief. At the start he has to play the idiot to be rejected; at the end he is favored and respected. David is on the way up.

22:1-5

Before the narrative plays out a grand scene at the court of Saul we, the audience, are brought up to date on a series of small news items. David has attracted a guerrilla band of four hundred at Adullam, including his family and all the distressed, indebted, and discontented—a remarkable description of the supporters of Israel's future king (22:2). Obviously anticipating trouble, David sent his mother and father to Moab for safekeeping. On the strategic advice of the prophet Gad, David moved from the Philistine frontier to the interior of Judah. This cluster of details would be of little interest apart from the project of a Story of David's Rise. The rest of the stories in this third act of the drama are played out in Judah, between the Philistines to the west and the Dead Sea to the east.

22:6-23

The grand scene that follows has Saul holding court: "under the tamarisk tree on the height, with his spear in his hand" (22:6)—a rustic image that compares unfavorably with the later sophistication of the court of David. Saul is portrayed as suspicious of his own supporters. His plea for loyalty is cast in the pork-barrel language of the politician (22:7-8): what patronage does David have at his disposal as reward for you?

Only a foreigner, Doeg the Edomite, answers, betraying what he had seen at Nob. The priest's defense is to plead David's loyalty to Saul, his father-in-law—clever pleading in a narrative that favors David. Saul sentences "the priests of the LORD" to death. An incredible and stark scene follows. Saul's troops refuse their orders. Doeg, under Saul's personal order, single-handedly slaughters eighty-five priests, along with the men, women, and children of Nob, together with its livestock (22:18-19). Abiathar alone escapes to David with the ephod, source of guidance from God. At the end of the scene Saul is the sacrilegious butcher and the sole surviving priest is under David's protection.

1 Samuel 23

A new scene opens, centered around the Judean town of Keilah. The Philistines are robbing the threshing floors; the people of Keilah will starve. Through the ephod David is guided by God and against all odds defeats the Philistines and rescues the inhabitants of Keilah. David is portrayed in his role of deliverer in Israel. Informed of this, Saul rejoices for the wrong reason: not for the town's deliverance but because he believes David is delivered into his hand. Saul sets out to trap and destroy David, the deliverer. The LORD is with David and he and his band escape. The guerrilla band has grown to six hundred.

From walled town the scene changes to desert fastnesses, the Wilderness of Ziph west of the Dead Sea, a tough, arid country. The tone is set: "Saul sought him every day" (23:14). The dissonant note is struck that favors David. Jonathan, Saul's son and heir, visits David, encourages him, and pledges to be a loyal second to David when David is king over Israel (23:15-18). Then in the rocky desert mountains David, betrayed by some locals, moves his men along one side of the mountain while Saul and his men pursue along the other side of the mountain, closing the gap. Only a message about a Philistine raid saves the day for David—and reminds us why Saul was anointed: not to chase David, but to save Israel from the Philistines. We are also reminded that esteem for David was not universal; two groups betray him.

1 Samuel 24

Another scene opens with David near Engedi, the luxuriant spring on the west side of the Dead Sea. With three thousand picked men Saul sets out against David's six hundred. Relieving himself in a cave where David's men were hiding, Saul could have been killed by David who instead cut a corner off Saul's cloak.

As told, the story asks for a massive suspension of disbelief. In apparent daytime David follows Saul out of the cave and makes a passionate speech—in the presence of Saul's army. We have to trust the storyteller's skills to patch things up plausibly. Our task is to listen to David's plea. Against those who malign him David pleads his loyalty to Saul, displaying the corner of Saul's cloak as proof of his trustworthiness. The LORD is invoked as judge between the loyal David and the vindictive Saul. Saul replies with a confession of sin, an acknowledgment that David will be king, and a plea that his own descendants may be spared. It is a remarkable reply that only David's supporters could have composed. It appears to have been a favorite story in the Davidic camp (see ch. 26).

1 Samuel 25

Sandwiched between chs. 24 and 26 is the story of David, Nabal, and Abigail—a remarkable change of scene. We are in the vicinity of Carmel, still in the desert west of the Dead Sea. Guerrillas need to live off the land and David demanded payment for protection. His targets are typecast: "the woman was clever and beautiful, but the man was surly and mean" (25:3). Nabal, like any property owner, had no intention of feeding shiftless malcontents—remember David's people are in distress, in debt, discontented. But this story comes from David's people. David is not shiftless; he is the LORD's anointed.

While David's men are arming to take vengeance Abigail is loading up provisions to win favor. She meets David and wins him over with a speech of subtle flattery. Her plea to David to keep clear of blood-guilt is apt in the immediate circumstances; it is also appropriate to acquit David of the charge of bloodshed in his climb to power (cf. 2 Sam 16:8). The lives of David's enemies are to be slung out "as from the hollow of a sling" (25:29), recalling how Goliath died. She asks for David's protection: "when the LORD has dealt well with my lord, then remember your servant" (25:31). David is most gracious.

Nabal was feasting and drunk. Told the following day of the risk he had run, he died inside. Some ten days later he died indeed, struck by the LORD. David courted Abigail and she consented to become his wife. There is a moral to this story for Israel. Obstruct David and die; assist David and live regally, sharing in his success.

1 Samuel 26

The scene turns again to Saul, once more in pursuit of David, again with three thousand men. It is ch. 24 all over again except that this is the more likely story, set in the darkness of night. David spies out Saul's encampment. Under cover of darkness David and Abishai penetrate the camp and stand over the sleeping Saul. Abishai begs to pin Saul to the ground with a single stroke of his spear (26:8). David refuses, takes the spear and water jar by Saul's head, and leaves.

From across the valley David first abuses Saul's general, Abner, for incompetence in guarding the king. His voice recognized by Saul, David pleads not to be driven from his country. As before Saul replies with a remarkable confession: "I have done wrong . . . I have been a fool, and have made a great mistake" (26:21). David entrusts his own life to the LORD's protection. Saul blesses him and assures him of success. The scene closes with both going their separate ways again.

David's trust in God is to the fore in this scene, first by the sleeping Saul: "the LORD will strike him down; or his day will come to die; or he will go down into battle and perish" (26:10), then in his first reply to Saul: If it is the LORD who has stirred you up against me, may he accept an offering; a curse on those who drive me to serve other gods (26:19), and finally in his second reply to Saul: "The LORD rewards everyone for his righteousness and his faithfulness . . .

may my life be precious in the sight of the LORD" (26:23-24). The story has portrayed David as successful over against Saul and his incompetent army. Saul is in the wrong. David puts his trust in God and gets both promise and blessing from Saul. "Come back, my son David, for I will never harm you again, because my life was precious in your sight today" (26:21). This and the blessing are Saul's last words to David. The narrative gives Saul a gracious exit and final lines fit for a king. So David went his way; it is David's way that will lead to the throne of Israel.

1 Samuel 27

This third act closes with David's departure from Judah. Perhaps he does not serve other gods but he is driven to serve the Philistines. Fearing death from Saul, whose promises are not to be trusted (27:1), David enlists in the service of King Achish of Gath. His six hundred troops and his two wives are explicitly mentioned. So is the deal he cut with Achish and the sixteen months it lasted (27:5-7).

As presented here David could have written the chapter on ruthlessness for the guerrilla handbook. His supporters will admire his cunning; his foes will condemn his crimes; his victims have no voice. As later with both Bathsheba and Uriah, David's morality is no model. He raided the non-Israelite settlements on the way south toward Egypt; he took no prisoners and he left no survivors. All he took was livestock and clothing. With no survivors to contradict him he let Achish think he was raiding in the region of Judah. So Achish trusted David, assured of his loyalty. This trust will bulk large later. To whom is David loyal? To Achish? No. To Saul? Unlikely. To David? To Israel? To God? The passage is about the perception of David's life as a guerrilla leader and David's earning of the trust of a Philistine overlord, Achish. The moral judgment passed here is not modern; see for example Shimei (2 Sam 16:5-13) or Amos (Amos 1:3–2:3) or Hosea (Hos 1:4).

Act Four: Saul's Ultimate Failure (28:1–31:13)

With David out of the way can Saul win as king? The answer is to be no. The act opens on the eve of the decisive battle; God has doomed Saul to death. The scene then shifts back to the Philistine mobilization and the activities of David; he is not to be responsible for Saul's death. The final scene closes the career of Saul.

28:1-2

Achish continues to occupy the stage before the next major scene. The Philistines are mobilizing for war against Israel. Achish lays claim to David's loyalty. David's answer could be ambiguous. Achish reads it favorably and makes David his bodyguard for life (28:2). At stake is the critical question of David's reputation as a patriot. He commanded an effective and successful fighting force at a time when his country was under Philistine attack. Did David stand aside and let Saul die in defeat? Did David plan to play a subversive role within the Philistine force? Davidic storytellers are on thin ice in portraying this period of David's rise to power.

28:3-25

The next scene demands a darkened stage, low lighting, anything that reeks of ominous foreboding. Off stage we are aware of the noises of gathered armies: the Philistines at Shunem in the middle of the great valley of Esdraelon; all Israel at Gilboa on the southern edge of the valley. Center stage is Saul, lonely, fearful, isolated, the image of a man bereft of God. He has no answer from God. He has banished the unorthodox. So he goes to an illegal medium at Endor and asks to consult the dead Samuel.

Samuel is no comfort to Saul: "the LORD has turned from you and become your enemy" (28:16). Samuel harks back to what he had said in ch. 15. To the terrified Saul the dead Samuel says: "tomorrow you and your sons shall be with me" (28:19). So Saul is doomed; he has been since 16:14, maybe earlier. The woman prepares nourishment for him and he goes off into the night. He may be doomed, but he will die a brave man leading his troops. For all his failings Saul is not an ignoble figure.

This scene's gruesome reminder of God's will for Saul may function within the wider context to counteract a possible view among Saul's supporters (e.g., Shimei, 2 Sam 16:5-13) that David and his guerrilla warriors could have done more to help Saul at this critical juncture. Little of this is about history; much of it is about point of view. Then again, God's will is one thing; the way it is worked out is another.

1 Samuel 29

The scene flashes back to the Philistines gathering at Aphek on the coastal plain, somewhat north of Jerusalem. At issue still is David's reputation. As a Philistine ally at the time he played no role in the battle of Gilboa. He was trusted by Achish but not by the other Philistine lords. Might he have switched sides in the battle and helped Israel to victory? He might have; that was what the Philistine majority feared (29:4). So the narrative exonerates David: he was dismissed by the Philistines before any action was possible.

1 Samuel 30

The narrative stays with the flashback as David and his band journey back to Ziklag and find their camp has been raided by Amalekites (30:1). Their women and children have been taken captive. The emotion is elemental: David grieving his wives; the troops bitter enough to stone him. The narrator lifts the story to the plane of faith: David's trust in God, and Abiathar's ephod. God is not answering Saul but God answers David. The rescue force sets out and is totally successful. David's reputation soars. Wives, children, goods were all recovered. The Amalekite livestock were assigned to David as his spoil (30:20). New rules were decreed for the equal division of spoil and there was enough to send gifts to David's supporters in the areas of his Judean operations. As the curtain closes on this scene David is supremely successful.

1 Samuel 31

The curtain opens again on a totally different scene, a scene of battle back at Mt. Gilboa on the southern edge of the Esdraelon plain. The Philistines are victorious, the Israelites defeated. The Philistines kill Saul's sons Jonathan, Abinadab, and Malchishua; Saul and his armor-bearer take their own lives rather than fall into Philistine hands. The Philistines behead Saul's corpse, send his armor to one of their temples, and fasten his body to the city wall of Beth-shan. The bodies are rescued from this ultimate disgrace by the people of Jabesh-gilead who give them proper honors. Saul's career began by saving Jabesh-gilead (ch. 11); he held court beneath a tamarisk (22:6). It ends with his burial under the tamarisk tree in Jabesh (31:13). Act Four is at an end. King Saul is dead.

Act Five: David's Assumption of Royal Power (2 Sam 1:1–8:18)

With King Saul dead those familiar with the Bible might automatically assume that the story proceeds to the reign of King David. Saul's supporters and surviving sons would not have seen it that way at all. All royal families see themselves as dynasties (cf. 1 Sam 20:30-31) and dynasties do not disappear because a king has died. The royal house of Saul will cling to power. In the moves of this final act two dynamics are at work in these Davidic texts: denial and desire. There is the denial that David actively sought to be king. There is the desire that David be king, most evident in the long civil war between the house of Saul and the house of David (2 Sam 3:1).

1:1-27

David's elegy will put the figure of Saul to rest. The curtain opens on a messenger scene. David is at Ziklag. A messenger comes from the battle scene with the news of Saul's death; he admits having himself given Saul the coup de grace, and he has brought Saul's crown to David. The historical matters little here; the symbolic is all important. Saul's killer brings Saul's crown to David. It is a blood-stained crown.

David and his men mourn for Saul till evening. The messenger is executed. David proclaims his famous elegy for Saul and Jonathan. It is marked by the pathos of loss and the passion of love. As with so many public utterances, its sincerity escapes our verification. We may accept it or we may suspect it; the text presents it.

2:1-11

David's first move looks to the throne of Judah. The Philistines have defeated Saul and his army. David's guerrilla force remains an undefeated operational army of significance. After consulting the LORD David moves his troops to the neighborhood of Hebron. At this time Hebron may have had the central role in Judah that Shechem had in northern Israel. The presence of David's army backed an offer that could not be refused. The people of Judah anoint David their king. Two forces can be seen at work here. On the one hand David moves in obedience to God's instructions. On the other hand the Judeans could not have been immune to the political pressure of this army on Hebron's doorstep.

Once in power David honors those who honored the dead Saul (2:4b-7). It is a royal act; it concludes with the note that "the house of Judah has anointed me king over them." Abner establishes Ishbaal, Saul's son, as king over central Transjordan, Galilee, and much of the central hill country, summed up as "all Israel." The stage is set for civil war.

2:12–4:12

David's struggle with the heirs of Saul is an ugly civil war. We do not have the historical details of the war. What we have are stories from the opening and closing stages, little more. The grubby reality is not glossed over.

An initial combat between chosen champions is inconclusive. A fierce battle follows, and Abner's side loses (2:12-17). Three scenes detail the rout: Asahel killed in pursuit of Abner, the pain of civil war, and the return marches and casualty tallies (2:18-32). Between the opening and closing phases of the war we are told that it was a long war with David gaining the upper hand; David's sons born during the time at Hebron are noted (3:1-5).

The death of Abner is a complex scene (3:6-39). It is a struggle between two military men, Abner and Joab, for power within David's kingdom. The narrative is valuable for David's apologists. Abner, Saul's general, claims that God had sworn to give Saul's kingdom to David (3:9-10). The same Abner suggests the elders of Israel have wanted David as their king for some time (3:17) and reiterates God's promise that David will be Israel's deliverer from its enemies (3:18). The entire blame for the murder of Abner is placed on Joab (3:28-29, 37).

With Abner dead, Ishbaal's hopes are finished. Two of his commanders kill him and bring his head to David—and are executed for it (4:1-12). The story exonerates David of blame for the death of either Abner or Ishbaal.

5:1-5

David is enthroned over all Israel. Now that Abner and Ishbaal are dead, what Abner swore to do for David occurs anyway; all Israel rallies to David, makes a covenant with him, and makes him king (2 Sam 3:21; 5:1-3).

The tribes of Israel claim to be David's "bone and flesh." It has been said before (2:26-27); it will be an issue again (19:41-43). We cannot know what weight it carried. They appeal to David's leadership even under Saul, as the stories before this have attested (5:2a). They claim a divine word that is not in our texts (5:2b). The prophetic anointing by Samuel is to be understood as God's designation of David; the anointing at Hebron is its political realization in history.

5:6-25

A king needs a capital. In a stroke of political genius David captured Jerusalem, on quasi-neutral territory between Judah and Benjamin, south and north. As the "city of David" it remained the seat of his dynasty until the end of the kingdom in 587. The city seemed impregnable. David's troops may have used a vertical Jebusite water shaft to breach the defenses; early in this century a young British soldier made short work of the vertical climb.

Along with a capital, a king needs a palace and children and victory. Verses 11-25 provide all three. The Phoenicians built the palace. David is permitted the insight that God has made him king for the sake of Israel. This conviction, expressed in v. 10 also, is at the core of the Davidic tradition. What Saul wanted for Jonathan (1 Sam 20:31) God has given to David. In v. 10 or v. 12, we can suspect the end of what was probably an early document, the Story of David's Rise.

The two victories over the Philistines are definitive. They are of key significance, for the Philistines had been a threat to Israel's existence. David came to prominence by defeating a Philistine champion. Saul died, defeated by the Philistines. David, as king, delivers Israel from this foe. The Philistines never again appear as a serious threat.

6:1-23

The coming of the Ark symbolizes God's endorsement. For years the Ark has been in symbolic exile in Kiriath-jearim, at the bottom of the hills leading to Jerusalem. Second Samuel 6 has close affinities with 1 Samuel 4–6, where the Ark was central. Symbolism is again more significant than history. David brings the Ark in procession to Jerusalem but is stopped by the death of Uzzah at God's hands (6:1-11). The Ark is left with a foreigner, Obed-edom from Gath, who is blessed by God because of the ark. Given the news of this blessing—and not being a theological incompetent—David completes the Ark's journey to Jerusalem. The presence of the Ark sanctifies the previously non-Israelite city. But David did not bring the Ark to Jerusalem; God stopped that. The story makes the claim that the Ark came to Jerusalem through the power and purpose of God. God brought about Uzzah's death; God brought about Obed-edom's blessing; God brought the Ark to Jerusalem. God blesses the rule of David in Jerusalem.

Symbolic of the house of Saul, Michal despised David and, like her father's house, remained barren (6:16, 20-24).

7:1-29

The prophet expresses God's endorsement. This text received much attention in ancient times and even more from modern scholarship. As it stands now, David proposes to build a Temple to go with his palace and the proposal is welcomed by the prophet Nathan. Through Nathan, however, God promptly turns the offer down. Instead God will build a house or dynasty for David. David's offspring will build the Temple. He may be punished, but he will not be rejected as Saul was. David's dynasty (house, kingdom, throne) will be established forever (7:16). The significance of the promise is mirrored in David's prayer of thanksgiving (7:18-29).

Given the importance of David in the monarchy of Israel, in the hope of the prophets, and in NT proclamation, this text has been appealed to often. The temptation to be resisted is belief that here God is pinned down. It is true that Solomon built the Temple and the Davidic kingdom did not fall apart until after Solomon's death. It is also true that some later Israelite theologians took the unconditional promise of 2 Samuel 7 and attached conditional restrictions to it (cf. 1 Kings 2:4; 9:4-9; also 11:9-13). God cannot be trapped. What God has given, God can take away. For some, such expression of God's commitment cannot be totally divorced from human behavior.

The words of prophetic hope (unfulfilled unless radically re-understood—e.g., Isa 9:6-7; 11:1-9) were widely used to express the NT understanding of Jesus' significance. Since Jesus' kingdom "is not of this world" it is not a direct application of 2 Samuel 7. The Davidic dynasty in 2 Samuel 7 is of this world. In the texts of prophetic hope it moves toward the realm of metaphor and symbol. In the NT it has entered the realm of theology.

8:1-18

David's political achievements: an appendix. With David in uncontested possession of crown and capital, with the Ark in David's city, with God's promise of the Temple to come and a dynasty forever the drama of the story of David's rise is over. The epilogue merely rehearses a summary of David's achievements. The foreign affairs list claims most of the neighboring nations as integrated into the Davidic empire—Edom, Moab, Ammon, Philistines, Amalek, and the Syrians (8:12), ending with the theological affirmation that "the LORD gave victory to David wherever he went" (8:14). Domestically David is credited with administering "justice and equity to all his people" (8:15); a list of David's top officials is appended (8:16-18; cf. 2 Sam 20:23-26; 1 Kings 4:1-6).

Preparatory Supplement (9:1–10:19)

What we have here are a couple of traditions that provide information and a context for 2 Samuel 11–20. They do not have the same quality of storytelling and probably were not part of the great narrative that starts in 2 Samuel 11. They have been added here as the most appropriate place for such a supplement.

9:1-13

Mephibosheth has a role to play in the story of David's retreat from and return to Jerusalem (2 Sam 16:1-4; 19:24-30); hence the information given here. His words in 19:28, "For all my father's house were doomed to death before my lord the king" suggest that his siblings were still alive—the situation of 21:6-9. Here in 9:1-4 Mephibosheth alone remains. The sparing of Mephibosheth is narrated differently. These may be two different traditions.

The story to come requires Mephibosheth's position at David's table and his possession of Saul's lands under the stewardship of Ziba. Eating at David's table involves being under his close surveillance. There is a cruel irony here. The survivor of Saul's line is confined to David's table for the rest of his life. In 2 Kings 25:27-30 the survivor of David's line is confined to Evil-merodach's table for the rest of his life. As it ends for Saul shall it also end for David?

10:1-19

The story of David and Bathsheba is set within a siege of the Ammonite capital. These traditions portray a strategic victory over a Syrian-Ammonite coalition and the subsequent defeat of the Syrians and their allies (cf. 8:3-6). As the story ends the Syrians are afraid to help the Ammonites any more (10:19). The scene is set for Joab's siege.

2 Samuel 11–20

The Initial Experience of Monarchy. Metaphor: Storytelling

We have used the metaphors of painting and drama to explore the narrative of 1–2 Samuel. In this third great segment we will use the metaphor of storytelling as performance. It is not exactly a metaphor but rather a reminder to us that the text we have is not the storyteller's performance. Nor is it, in all likelihood, a polished literary text such as we are accustomed to in our age of print media. Polished text it is, a text that presents stories. We often think of it as "the story," but it is not. It is the text from which "the story" might be told. In our culture with its wide distribution of printed literature a story can be written to be read; in Israel's pre-print culture almost invariably a story was written to be told and heard. So we need to keep in mind the text, the storyteller, the story, and the audience—in this case ourselves, who happen to be readers. The difference between text and performance is important for all biblical narrative; we will give it special emphasis in this segment.

Perhaps because of this emphasis on storytelling as our "metaphor" the following section of this Samuel commentary is much more of a narrative itself, but it is a narrative that functions compactly as a commentary. It is an invitation to see the biblical narrative as we may not have seen it before. We can always see it for ourselves as we have seen it before. If the biblical text is "the text from which 'the story' might be told," there is more than one way in which the story might be told—although the text exercises its control and makes its suggestions. To get a feel for this, readers must read the biblical text as well as the commentary text. If not, our views will be accepted or rejected; the biblical views will not be seen.

If we were to have the story of 2 Samuel 11–20 told we would need a storyteller able to bring alive a remarkable text, a storyteller with a real sense for the complexities and ambiguities of human behavior and the functioning of political power in a monarchy. This part is often called the Succession Narrative, but the succession motif is not central; it is more appropriately called The Story of David's Later Years. The narrative revolves around three episodes; the first two lead up to the third.

In the first episode David remains in Jerusalem while the army is on campaign in Transjordan. David rapes the wife of one of his absent officers, invites the officer to cover David's tracks in the man's own marriage bed, and when he refuses David arranges for him to be killed at the front. A potentially stormy scene is quieted by the news for David that the man, Uriah, is dead. Nathan, God's prophet, confronts David with his crime. His punishment is to have infected his family with a fatal lust for homicidal and sexual violence (2 Samuel 11–12). Nathan's speech portrays this as punishment from God; the unfolding narrative opens the possibility that it is the consequence of David's crimes.

The second episode returns to the theme of rape and its consequences. It opens with a counselor in David's court advising Amnon, David's son and heir, how to have his way sexually with his half sister. Its first half ends with the same counselor informing David that only one of his sons has died in what David feared had been a massacre. In between there is the rape scene, with a despicable Amnon and an admirable Tamar, then David's passivity—angered but ineffectual—and Absalom's smoldering hate, and finally the banquet scene in which Absalom's servants stick the drunken Amnon like a pig. The second half has David passive again and Absalom absent in exile, and by the time a reconciliation has been achieved it is too late—Absalom is ready for rebellion (2 Samuel 13–14).

The final episode—David's major debacle—follows the rise and fall of Absalom in his political moves against his father. The storyteller would take us imaginatively into each of the scenes as David leaves Jerusalem to escape the triumphant forces of his rebellious son; along the way David is making moves that will help him to recapture his kingdom. The turning point is the battle and the death of Absalom. Then the story watches David retracing his steps in his return to power in Jerusalem—and explores the fragility of the coalition assembled around him. A northerner from Saul's tribe shatters the brittle unity of David's kingdom with a second rebellion. Uncertainty over command and loyalty at the head of the army is settled brutally by assassination. The wisdom of a woman saves a city from destruction. The leader of the rebellion is beheaded and the rebellion put down. The soldiers go home and the general returns "to Jerusalem to the king" (20:22). There the story can end. A list of David's officials serves as finale. The narrative could continue into 1 Kings 1–2 with the succession of Solomon, but four quite different chapters now separate it in the present text (2 Samuel 15–20).

We may ask whether these stories—David and Bathsheba, Amnon and Tamar, Joab and the wise woman, Absalom and revolt, Sheba and renewed revolt—were originally part of a group of semi-independent stories told for reasons that still largely elude us. Or did they constitute a single narrative? The prophetic focus in 2 Sam 12:7b-12 suggests an overview of a single narrative, but it could be a later perspective. The plots exist for a number of semi-independent stories. If we look closely at the links between these semi-independent stories, however, we see that the appropriate beginnings and endings that stories need for independence do not now exist. As it stands the text of 2 Samuel 11–20 has the shape of a single narrative.

Bathsheba, Uriah, and David (2 Samuel 11–12)

This apparently simple yet immensely complex story is framed within reports of the opening and closing stages of a military campaign against the Ammonite capital city of Rabbah across the Jordan. At the start of the campaign Joab is David's warrior, waging war for him; in the middle Joab is David's hatchet man, killing for him; at the end Joab is David's political minder, protecting his public image for him. In the background all the time, Joab is a constant and menacing reminder of the role of raw power in politics (see 2 Sam 19:1-8; 20:4-13).

Another aspect of power needs to be noted. The modern reader recognizes that this story and those that follow betray a male perspective. They look radically different when explored from a woman's point of view. Two actions stand out in this and the next story. Bathsheba sent and told David, "I am pregnant" (2 Sam 11:5). Tamar, raped and repulsed, went away "crying aloud as she went" (2 Sam 13:19). Both women placed what had happened to them outside the domain of private silence; both actions involved choices and grave consequences. A storyteller could pause over these moments. How differently their choices could be told. Neither is explored by the narrative. That too is something of the essence of these stories: they probe situations where options abound but they almost never plumb these options.

2 Samuel 11

This first story accuses David of two shocking crimes. First he summons Bathsheba to his bed and is guilty of rape—to say adultery would be to imply Bathsheba's consent, not suggested here (compare the different treatment in 1 Sam 25:39-42). Second, after a failed attempt at cover-up, he sends Uriah her husband to his death and is guilty of premeditated murder.

The narrative says nothing about David's options. There appears to be time for somebody to advise David against sending for Bathsheba. With Bathsheba pregnant his choices are limited: perhaps denial, since presumably only Bathsheba and we, the audience, know she was purifying herself after her period so that she was ready to conceive and the child was certainly David's; perhaps he might brazen it out with supercilious royal disdain, unless the moral climate in Jerusalem made that impossible. Other possibilities, such as a stay in the country for Bathsheba or a permanent posting in the city for Uriah, depended on their cooperation, which may have been most uncertain. A fatal accident for Bathsheba would have left a grieving Uriah —and perhaps too many people knew too much. The text leaves David's options uncanvassed; a storyteller might choose to explore them.

On the other hand we modern readers need to reflect on what the story leaves beneath the surface. Is David's presence in the capital a sign of indolence or of competent administration? Was David's view of Bathsheba while she washed unduly revealing? The text does not suggest it—a basin is more likely than a bath. The storyteller could inform us or leave us uninformed; the narrative is silent. Bathsheba informs David that she is pregnant. Why did she? It involved risk. Uriah, recalled from the front, refuses on grounds of pious principle to spend the night in his own house and so cover for David. Why did he deny his king? The refusal was not anticipated. David is told that Uriah had not gone down to his own house. Who reported this to David? How many people in the palace knew and how much did they know? David sent messengers to get Bathsheba; Bathsheba sent a message to David. How many were aware of the comings and goings or the message? Was Uriah aware? Was he guileless or aggrieved, innocent or scheming, angry or ambitious? No mention is made of children from Uriah. The text of the story opens every avenue and closes none. The surrounding circumstances are shrouded in silence.

Joab does David's killing for him. The report to David is subtle. Did Joab change David's order to a plan that was more sensible but cost more lives? The text has Joab anticipate anger from David at the strategic blunder involved. David's reaction is retarded for us while the message is delivered differently, and suddenly David is revealed as coldly callous. Loyal lives have been lost, but Uriah is dead. Joab is to be encouraged; "Do not let this matter trouble you." David is untroubled. "When the mourning was over, David sent and brought [Bathsheba] to his house, and she became his wife, and bore him a son."

2 Samuel 12

All seems to have gone smoothly for David. But God cannot be fobbed off like Joab: "the thing that David had done displeased the LORD" (11:27b). The prophet Nathan is dispatched and his parable traps David into indignant judgment. Nathan points to David. Because of murder the sword will not leave David's house—and in fact his three eldest sons, Amnon, Absalom, and Adonijah die violently. Because of rape David's own wives will be raped—and in fact this sordid act of political symbolism is done by Absalom. David confesses his sin, Nathan extends forgiveness promptly, yet the child will die. The text is complex; three punishments have been piled up, at least some of them offensive to our sensibilities. Acts have their consequences. Forgiveness may prevent punishment but cannot always dispense from consequences.

The story continues with David's intense prayer for his dying son and his surprising failure to grieve the death. Is this another example of David's fatalism? Another son is born to David by Bathsheba. Nathan reappears with the message of God's love for this son who is Solomon.

The campaign is concluded. David accepts the crown of Rabbah. David and all the people return to Jerusalem.

The story is ended; its interpretation will never be. The greatest and most revered of Israel's kings has been portrayed as a callous criminal, both a rapist and a killer. God's commitment to such a sinner is astounding. The prophet connects David's crimes with the deaths and disasters in his family. Where does the point of the story lie? Is its point ultimately in the decisions that David might have taken so differently?

Amnon, Tamar, and Absalom (2 Samuel 13–14)

2 Samuel 13

The biblical text takes us on beyond the private story of David into events unfolding ever more publicly in his life and the life of Israel. The impulse for the story comes from David's son and heir, Amnon. He has fallen in love with Tamar, the beautiful sister of David's son Absalom, and she seems to be out of his reach. The text says "for she was a virgin," apparently emphasizing her inaccessibility within the palace; at least the issue of blood-relationship ("his sister") is not stressed. Amnon made himself ill over his desire for Tamar.

Amnon has a friend, Jonadab, described as a very wise man. Some translations call Jonadab crafty. Hebrew has a word for crafty; it is used of the serpent in the garden (Gen 3:1). The word in Hebrew here is "wise": wisdom can be put to evil ends as well as good. Jonadab suggests a way that Amnon can get access to Tamar: pretend to be ill and ask for her to cook for you (13:5). Amnon takes the advice and asks David to send Tamar to him.

It is worth noticing that twice in the text Amnon puts stress on Tamar's physical closeness: she is to prepare the food *in his sight* that he may eat it *from her hand* (13:5, 6). The word for cakes even echoes the word for heart. Should

David have picked up these alarm signals? The text does not say, but the signals are there. Should David have wondered about his son's sickness? Should David have taken appropriate precautions for the protection of a virgin daughter in his palace? Is David portrayed as singularly unwise throughout this story? The text is silent, but the questions are there.

On Tamar's arrival Amnon has everyone ordered out—and they go. The text does not say who everyone was, but if they had not gone out in craven submission Tamar might not have been raped. The social solidarity that should have protected her failed her. There will be no point in her crying out later; those who could save her have already abandoned her. The text has two short sentences; a storyteller might have chosen to elaborate.

Once alone, Amnon propositions Tamar. Her response is the height of prudence and wisdom. She categorizes the rape as vile, unacceptable in Israel (v. 12). She points out its implications for her and for him (v. 13a). She suggests a way out: ask the king for my hand (v. 13b). The suggestion raises problems for us. We do not know the laws applicable in David's time and we do not know whether the king could clear the way for such a union. Amnon from the outset appears to set this aside, whether as impossible or undesirable we do not know. Nor do we know whether Tamar is playing for time, hoping for help, or offering a real possibility. For the verisimilitude of the story it cannot be out of the question; it has to have some plausibility.

Amnon does not listen and uses his superior physical force to rape Tamar. His lust turns to loathing and he orders her out. Again she speaks with wisdom and prudence: sending her away is an even greater wrong than the one just done (v. 16). With brutal callousness he orders her locked out. According to the law as we know it Amnon's options were marriage or payment (Exod 22:16-17; Deut 22:28-29). Marriage implies status and security in society.

Thrust into the street, Tamar faces a bitter choice: will her shame be silent or public? The text does not raise the option; her gestures of grief are public, her cries are continual (v. 19).

The narrative takes up the consequences of this sordid story of violent rape. Every action that follows is questionable. Absalom counsels silence (v. 20). David is very angry (v. 21); some ancient texts add that he does nothing because he is not willing to punish his firstborn. Absalom harbors a hatred for Amnon (v. 22).

Absalom nurses his hatred for two full years. Then he successfully organizes Amnon's murder at a shearing party. The text makes David almost an accomplice before the crime. Just as David sent Tamar to Amnon, so the text has David argue back and forth with Absalom for four full verses before sending his sons to the party—and Amnon to his death. After the killing the same Jonadab whose wisdom got Amnon into trouble at the beginning is there at the end to tell David exactly what has happened and why. We never hear of him again. We are left with the question: if Jonadab knew so clearly, why was David so totally in the dark? Whatever of that, the seeds sown by David's rape and murder have begun to sprout. Amnon has raped Tamar. Absalom has murdered Amnon. A harvest of evil has begun.

2 Samuel 14

Absalom flees for three years to his maternal grandfather (see 3:3), King Talmai of Geshur, northeast of the Lake of Galilee. David longs for Absalom but does nothing. Joab organizes a skilled piece of dramatic storytelling by a woman from Tekoa that persuades David to order Absalom's return. Her achievement is indicative of the high level of performance open to a woman at that time. Joab is commissioned to arrange Absalom's return to Jerusalem, but not to David's presence. Some personal references allow for the passage of time (14:25-27). After two full years Absalom still has not come into David's presence. Even to gain an audience with Joab he has to engineer a fire in Joab's fields. Eventually he is brought to David and a formal reconciliation is celebrated.

David's Final Debacle (2 Samuel 15–20)

For all the tactical and political skill attributed to David in this story, it recounts an event that should never have happened. It is one thing for a king to claw back his capital city and his kingdom when he has lost them. It is a far better and a far wiser thing not to lose capital city and kingdom in the first place. This is the story of David's major debacle. It passes through five phases: (1) Absalom's revolt, (2) David's retreat from Jerusalem, (3) David's recovery of his situation, (4)

David's return to Jerusalem, and (5) David's reestablishment of his power.

This great narrative is remarkable for what is dwelt on in fine detail and what is only sketched in broad outline. The actual revolt is only sketched. David's retreat from Jerusalem is followed in finest detail. Absalom's plans to retain power and David's arrangements to recover it are adequately treated. Apart from the four years of preparation for the revolt all this has not taken us beyond the first day. The preparations for the decisive battle go almost unreported. The battle story is focused on how Absalom died and how the news came to David—more satisfactory for storytelling then and now. David's journey of return is covered in fine detail. It helps to notice where much is left for storytellers to fill out.

For the storyteller David's major debacle is the core of the Story of David's Later Years. The two preceding stories lead up to it. David has himself woven a fabric of passion and murder in the case of Bathsheba and Uriah. He has allowed this weaving to extend farther into his family in the case of Tamar and Amnon and its consequences for Amnon and Absalom. Rape and murder by the king have been followed by rape and murder by his sons. Unpunished rape led to unpunished murder and unfinished reconciliation. Now the consequences come home to David. David behaved like a fool in the city; as a result he loses the city. In the field David behaves adroitly; as a result he will recover the kingdom.

1. Revolt, 15:1-12

The debacle begins with Absalom's revolt, a classic coup d'etat. From the text the storyteller needs to create the image of Absalom fomenting dissatisfaction in Israel (15:1-6), Absalom's interview with David (15:7-9), a series of flashes of Absalom's messengers putting out the word secretly throughout Israel (15:10), and finally the gathering in Hebron (15:11-12).

No sooner has David kissed Absalom (14:33) than Absalom is preparing to seize power (cf. Adonijah, "I will be king," 1 Kings 1:5). The reconciliation in the palace has been too little too late. David's administration of justice is faulty. Absalom does not kiss babies; he kisses disappointed litigants. Fomenting disappointment over injustice "Absalom stole the hearts of the people of Israel" (15:6).

The portrayal of the revolt itself is swift and incomplete. There is Absalom's interview with David, getting permission to go to Hebron. David was fooled by Amnon (13:6), fooled again by Absalom (13:24-27); he should not have been fooled a second time by Absalom, but he was: "The king said to him, 'Go in peace'" (15:9). We are told nothing of the revolt's organization, but it must have been extensive; the secret messengers went throughout all the tribes of Israel.

Of the coronation, too, we are told nothing, not even the reaction of the innocent invited guests. Apparently more important than the crowning was the defection of Ahithophel, David's counselor, whose counsel was "as if one consulted the oracle of God" (16:23). Maybe this is reported story; just give the bare bones and leave the details to the storyteller. Perhaps it is simply the hurried preliminaries to the main story to come.

2. Retreat, 15:13–16:14

When the news of Absalom's revolt is reported to David he is suddenly all action. "Get up! Let us flee, or there will be no escape" (15:14). Why David could not or would not defend his capital city, the impregnable Jerusalem, is a question not even raised. No council of war is called. The decision is immediate and effective. The entire royal household and the royal guards and mercenaries leave the city. Ten concubines are left to care for the palace; they will be victims of Absalom's sexual violence.

The unfolding scenes of David's retreat offer superb moments for the storyteller. At the last house above the valley of Kidron David passes his troops in review as they leave the city, the crack foreign mercenary Cherethites and Pelethites, even the newly arrived six hundred Gittites from Philistine Gath. For a moment the storyteller must close in on David's exchange with the leader of these six hundred. David offers his release; Ittai commits himself and his men to David (15:21-22). Is Ittai a man of simple loyalty or a consummately shrewd judge of political situations? We do not know. The narrative does not say; it just unfolds.

The storyteller needs to reach out again to catch the scene as the king crosses the Wadi Kidron. "The whole country wept aloud" (15:23). "The hearts of the Israelites" had gone after Absalom (15:13), but David too has his supporters.

Popular support is one thing, but not everything. As the retreating column wends its way across the wadi the narrative returns to a scene outside the city where two priests, Abiathar and Zadok, have been waiting with Levites and the Ark of the covenant of God. David orders the Ark carried back into the city; he is credited with a superb act of trust in God. It is typical Davidic theology to leave nothing to God except trust. Faith does not exclude good tactics, so David uses the priests and their sons to set up his lines of communication. The scene closes with the Ark being taken back into Jerusalem.

Our attention turns to the column working its way up the steep slopes of the Mount of Olives. The storyteller's gesture might sweep along its length before focusing on David again, weeping as he climbed, his head covered, his feet bare (15:30). David is told of Ahithophel's defection. It provokes a brief prayer, a rare event in this very secular narrative: "O LORD, I pray you, turn the counsel of Ahithophel into foolishness" (15:31).

The theme of counsel continues at the summit. David meets Hushai, a loyal courtier, and sends him back to act as secret agent against Absalom. David knows what he needs: "then you will defeat for me the counsel of Ahithophel" (15:34). Hushai is told how to get his messages out to the king. He returns to the city "just as Absalom was entering Jerusalem." In this narrative nothing happens by chance.

David still has two more encounters to go before he can splash his face in the Jordan. A little beyond the summit Ziba the servant of Jonathan's son Mephibosheth shows up with lavish gifts for David, skillfully selected supplies (16:1-2). According to Ziba, Mephibosheth is back in Jerusalem hoping that Saul's kingdom is going to fall into his lap. David promptly transfers all Mephibosheth's possessions to Ziba. Again the question: is Ziba a shrewd judge of the political situation and its likely outcome, or is he a rat-cunning opportunist making the best of the only chance he has? The narrative says nothing.

The second encounter is fascinating, a climactic highlight for David's retreat from Jerusalem. The storyteller's glance will pick up Shimei ben Gera emerging from the little village of Bahurim. His face is contorted with rage and hate. He is cursing and throwing stones as he comes. He is related to the house of Saul and he has no love for David. His curse gives voice to what the opposition in Israel believes of David: murderer, scoundrel, guilty of the blood of Saul's house, a man of blood who deserves the disaster that has overtaken him (16:7-8). The military, of course, do not take kindly to this and want Shimei's head. The king makes another of those extraordinary professions of faith that may be authentically Davidic. If the son of my own loins wants my life, why should this Benjaminite be different. "Let him alone, and let him curse; for the LORD has bidden him. It may be that the LORD will look on my distress, and the LORD will repay me with good for this cursing of me today" (16:11-12). It is a most remarkable comment.

So David and his men push on and Shimei keeps cursing and throwing stones. Finally the king and the people with him reach the Jordan and can clean up a bit and rest a little.

3. Recovery, 16:15–19:10

Now we have a total change of scene. The narrative takes us into Absalom's Jerusalem and the planning to secure the power that has been seized. The plans will be thwarted, Absalom will die in battle, and David will recover his place as king.

In Jerusalem, Absalom and his supporters are entering the city. Ahithophel is with Absalom. Hushai, David's agent, makes contact and makes his pitch for a place in Absalom's council. No immediate answer is given. Counsel, the advice given a king, is at the core of this narrative. Absalom asks counsel of Ahithophel. Once in Jerusalem what is the first move to make? Ahithophel's response is a reminder that war can be made a very dirty business. Loyalty is all. Israel must know that Absalom is totally committed to his rebellion. So David's ten concubines are to be led to a tent on the palace roof and violated by Absalom in the sight of all Israel. It may be good politics; it is hardly propitious in the storyteller's sight. But Ahithophel's counsel was held in very high esteem.

Counsel is to the fore in the next scene. Ahithophel proposes to pursue David at once that night, to catch up with him while he is still in shock, and to kill him—the king alone. So the people will return to Absalom and there will be peace (17:1-3). These are smart tactics, since David is waiting at the Jordan fords (15:28). Absalom sets up a counsel situation: thus says Ahithophel; what says Hushai? Hushai must have recognized the wisdom of Ahithophel's strategy because he argues against it urgently. David is too shrewd to fall into such a trap; in a night attack it is Ahithophel's troops who will panic. Needing breathing space for David, Hushai counsels assembling a mighty army to be led by Absalom to destroy David and his armed force. He is offering Absalom the security of a large army and the glory of a personal victory. Absalom falls for it and it is decided. The narrator adds a faith claim: this was God's doing. Ahithophel's counsel was good; God defeated it to bring down Absalom (17:14). David's prayer has been heard.

Hushai tells the two priests of Ahithophel's counsel and his own. His message for David: do not overnight at the fords but cross the Jordan at once. Why such a message if Hushai has prevailed? Some suggest an earlier version (Hushai as spy) and later version (Hushai as counter-counselor). Quite possibly Hushai regarded David's position as vulnerable anyway and perhaps feared Ahithophel's proposal might still be implemented. Alternatively Hushai was dismissed from the council before the decision was taken. A storyteller can choose between options; the text does not.

So the messengers are sent. In line with the best spy stories an extra courier has been introduced, the servant girl, to make the link with En-rogel in the valley south of Jerusalem (17:17). The Hebrew verbs suggest a regular pattern of communication. This may be a pointer to wider storytelling in which more extensive communications were maintained between Absalom's Jerusalem and David's camp. Any suggestion that regular communication back and forth via the girl and En-rogel took place during the afternoon of David's withdrawal disregards the limits of time and terrain.

The story here is thrilling but very dense (cf. Jos 2:3-7); it cries out to be expanded by the storyteller. A boy sees the two messengers and tells Absalom. The messengers hide in a well in Bahurim, over beyond the Mount of Olives. Where did the boy see them and how did he know to suspect them? How did they know that they had been seen and why did they choose to hide in Bahurim? Often the text only gives us the bare bones of a story. The messengers get through to David and Hushai's advice is followed.

Suddenly the narrative slows down. Up till now the events of David's retreat have all been crammed into one day. Now Ahithophel's suicide and burial are reported (17:23)—not a good omen for Absalom. Absalom's mobilization is passed over. The troop concentrations are reported across the Jordan: David at Mahanaim, Absalom in the land of Gilead. A change is mentioned in Absalom's high command; Amasa has replaced Joab. We have not heard of Joab since 14:33; shortly, he will turn up in David's command (18:2). Where have Joab's loyalties been? Only Joab knows.

Beyond the strategic details of location and command the narrative takes time to assess the support services in David's camp at Mahanaim. Three men, we may assume wealthy notables—Shobi, Machir, and Barzillai—have provided beds, basins, and vessels, and a grand variety of foods. The vignette is both human interest and political strategy. Clearly David has supporters in the area; he did not go to Mahanaim without good reason.

The death of Absalom receives close attention. The storyteller would need to create a plausible scene of dialogue between David and the army in which they persuade him not to accompany them. David impresses on the commanders his determination to spare Absalom: "Deal gently for my sake with the young man Absalom" (18:5). It does not matter that Absalom was ready to have David killed (17:1-4). It does not matter that David did not allow Absalom an audience for two full years in Jerusalem (14:28). Now, according to the story, David does not want him dead and everybody hears it (18:5).

The crucial battle is dealt with in three verses: Israel lost; David won. The story focuses on Absalom's death. How he got hung up in a tree matters little; what matters is that he was trapped and helpless. The soldier who found Absalom did not kill him and is eloquent as to why not. It is a fair assumption that if he had, Joab would have executed him on the spot (cf. 2 Sam 1:14-15; 4:8-12). Joab and his personal bodyguard make quite sure that Absalom is dead. The story may be trying to absolve David of guilt. It may be pointing to the political realism of Joab. Only with Absalom dead can all the people be at peace (cf. 17:3). With Absalom dead, Joab calls off any further fighting. That too is political realism.

With Absalom dead, the central interest for the storyteller is how David will take the news. In a brilliant heightening of tension the focus is on the runners who want to bring that news. The news of victory is not good news "because the king's son is dead" (18:20). The king's anxiety is mirrored in his waiting. Both runners report to the king with impeccable diplomacy. Deeply moved, David retires, weeping: "O my son Absalom, my son, my son Absalom! Would I had died instead of you, O Absalom, my son, my son!" (18:33).

Joab's realism gets the last word. Any worthwhile storyteller would give great weight to the dialogue with David: perhaps an initial awareness of the sullen and grieving troops, then full attention to the weeping king and the furious commander. Joab points out the realities of the situation with unsurpassed bluntness. At the end of his tirade he orders the king to go out and mingle with his troops. And David obeys Joab.

Absalom is dead. David is king. Royal power and popular loyalty are still live issues. Just as the storyteller sent our imaginations "throughout all the tribes of Israel" (15:10) organizing Absalom's revolt, so now we are invited to hear Absalom's supporters "throughout all the tribes of Israel" (19:9) disputing about David's merits, Absalom's death, and the need to recall David. The political factions within Israel will be a background for the rest of the story.

4. Return, 19:11–20:3

Factional politics are to the forefront as David plans his return. The storyteller has to be aware of giving the whole political background to David's return before turning to its more vivid and personal details. The critical commission is given to David's two agents in Jerusalem, the priests Zadok and Abiathar. First they are to appeal to the elders of Judah as David's flesh and blood. Why should Judah be the last to climb on the bandwagon of those gathering to bring David back? Second they are to bribe Amasa with the offer of Joab's job as commander of David's army. The storyteller may choose to indicate how strongly the bandwagon really was building. The narrative does not say. The appeal to Amasa suggests David was uncertain enough to need to play all his cards. Amasa is credited with winning over the loyalty of the people of Judah. So they come to Gilgal to bring David over the Jordan.

Significant figures from earlier in the story meet David before he crosses the Jordan. Three encountered him before in the story: Shimei ben Gera, Ziba, and Barzillai. One has not met him before in this story: Mephibosheth, son of Jonathan, grandson of Saul. Shimei is mentioned first. He came down with the people of Judah; he was in a hurry; he had a group from Benjamin with him. He is no longer a lonely figure but appears as a leader. Ziba, Mephibosheth's servant, is mentioned second. He had his sons and servants with him; he too was in a hurry. He appears the arch sycophant. Shimei gets the first interview. He asks for forgiveness, discreetly leaving his wrong unspecified—what he said or did or did not do. He is a shrewd politician with a strong political point to make: he is the first of northern Israel to support David. Abishai, a hothead and not a political strategist, wants to kill him. David extends an amnesty to Shimei "for do I not know that I am this day king over Israel?" (19:22; cf. Saul, 1 Sam 11:12-13). This gesture of fealty from Shimei, who had cursed David so bitterly, may be the first concrete sign that David will prevail and be restored as king.

Mephibosheth gets the second interview. David challenges him on his absence in David's hour of need (19:25). His response: Ziba deceived him, no details given. He places his fate in David's hands, noting that when all his father's house were doomed to death David had spared his life. Clearly Mephibosheth hopes David will spare him again. We do not know where the truth lies between Mephibosheth and Ziba. Neither apparently does David since he divides the land between them. What matters is that the last Saulide claimant to the throne has submitted to David (cf. 16:3). An aside: Mephibosheth's reference to how David had spared his life agrees with 2 Sam 21:7 against 2 Sam 9:1. This Story of David's Later Years begins in 2 Samuel 11, not 2 Samuel 9.

Barzillai is next. David invites the old gentleman to Jerusalem. Barzillai's refusal offers insight into the pleasures of court life; at his age he is in no position to appreciate fine cuisine and the delights of song (19:35). Barzillai wants to die in his ancestral home but he leaves one of his people with David. Here too is a pledge of loyalty.

Now the storyteller must draw these scenes to a close. The Jordan is crossed and Gilgal reached and David's return made a reality. The political reality also needs to be dealt with. All of Judah is represented; half of Israel is present (19:40).

Half is better than none but half is not all. We are not told the reality of the factions involved. So the story moves from the royal interviews and royal progress to the debate among the people. The people of Israel argue against the people of Judah. The people of Judah claim the king as kin. The people of Israel claim their ten shares; they have the tribes. They reinforce the earlier claim that they were the first to show loyalty. Yet Judah prevails in the debate. We do not know the background to these democratic debates. Later, under Jeroboam, the north will abandon the south over taxes (cf. 1 Kings 12:16). Here a Benjaminite rabble-rouser (according to the text) raises the same rallying cry: "to your tents, O Israel!" (20:1).

The story of David's return ends on a sour note. As David and the Judeans progress from Gilgal to Jerusalem the northerners, loyal to this Sheba ben Bichri, are heading home. All that is said of David's arrival in Jerusalem is the evocation of his shame; the ten raped concubines are placed in perpetual seclusion. The return has not ended on a happy note.

5. Reestablishment, 20:4-22, 23-26

Royal power must be reestablished. Amasa is sent out and given three days to raise the Judean troops. Can he be trusted? We are not told. When the three days are up David is alarmed that Sheba's revolt may be more dangerous than Absalom's. This is the measure of the issue. Abishai, Joab's brother, is given the job of going after Sheba—no mention of Joab. But of course Joab's men go along with Abishai (20:7); still no explicit mention of Joab, but he is there. At Gibeon, to the north of Jerusalem, Amasa appears on the scene and is promptly killed by Joab who has done this before (2 Sam 3:27). Is Joab a powerful hater, a power broker, or a soldier who knows Amasa is not loyal to David? The text does not tell us; a storyteller might.

The next scene associates Joab with loyalty to David (20:11). It seems that even in death Amasa commands some sort of loyalty, so his body is concealed. Joab now has the people's loyalty against Sheba ben Bichri.

Sheba has taken his forces into a walled city as David feared (20:6). A wise woman of the city holds parley with Joab, values the life of a whole city over the head of a single rebel, and takes her view to the citizens. Joab gets what he wants: the head of Sheba and the end of the revolt. The troops disperse. Joab returns to Jerusalem to the king.

The story ends—or this stage of it at least. It is a story of revolt, royal retreat, and return. It reflects human decisions and political power. It raises many questions and answers none. It is highly secular; the role given God is minimal. It reads ambivalently; interpreters have emphasized elements both favorable and unfavorable to David. Whether or not it was written for this purpose, the text certainly serves to raise major issues in which thoughtful counsel for the king was of crucial significance. Perhaps that is why the text does not answer the questions it raises; these are left for us to ponder. A storyteller might choose to hint at many of the answers; the text does not. We may ask where the basic drift of the stories is pointing. Do the stories refer ultimately to the decisions David might have taken so differently if only wise counsel had been heard at so many moments along the way?

We are left with a list of David's senior public servants (cf. 8:16-18). Joab commands the conscript army. Benaiah has charge of the mercenaries; he has not been mentioned since 8:18. Adoram is in charge of public works, Jehoshaphat is the recorder, Sheva the secretary; Zadok and Abiathar are the priests along with Ira the Jairite, a name unknown to us. We have more information about David than about any other figure in the OT—and how little we know.

2 Sam 21:1–24:25

Appendix

The last four chapters of 2 Samuel form a collection all on their own. It is tightly organized, with three categories of tradition arranged in concentric circles. At the center are two religious songs or psalms (22:2-51 [= Ps 18:2-50] and 23:1-7). On either side of these are two collections of David's warriors and their deeds (21:15-22; 23:8-39). Opening and closing the collection are two strange stories of the staying of divine threat (21:1-14; 24:1-25). All in all the collection is quite different from the surrounding text. It brings home to us in a startling way just how little we know of the life and times of this well-known royal figure, King David.

21:1-14

This strange story of expiating bloodguilt also showcases two acts of piety by David. He spares Jonathan's son Mephibosheth; he arranges the appropriate burial for Saul and Jonathan and seven impaled descendants of Saul.

There is a three-year famine. God identifies the cause as bloodguilt incurred by Saul with regard to the Gibeonites. The tradition is unknown to us. In expiation the Gibeonites demand seven of Saul's descendants for solemn execution "before the LORD at Gibeon on the mountain of the LORD" (21:6). It is then that David spares Mephibosheth. Rizpah, Saul's concubine, wins David's admiration by protecting the corpses from desecration, so David orders their burial together with the reburial of Saul and Jonathan. There is not a word about the bodies of Abinadab and Malchishua; the story may be legend. This scenario fits better with Mephibosheth's words in 2 Sam 19:28 than the earlier 2 Samuel 9 does.

21:15-22

This little collection lists episodes from David's wars with the Philistines in which four Philistine descendants of the giants, or special figures, were killed by David's men: Ishbi-benob (21:15-17); Saph (v. 18); Goliath (v. 19); and an anonymous six-fingered and six-toed one (vv. 20-21). Verse 17 both conflicts with and reinforces 2 Sam 18:3, but such legends abound about heroes. Goliath the Gittite (v. 19) may have given his name to the Philistine champion whose defeat propelled David to public fame (cf. 1 Samuel 17). Otherwise we know nothing about these traditions.

22:1-51

This lengthy hymn of thanksgiving is attributed to David "when the LORD delivered him from the hand of all his enemies, and from the hand of Saul" (v. 1). No single occasion suggests itself as appropriate. The sentiments are most apt for several stages in David's life. For closer study, see Psalm 18.

23:1-7

This short song rejoices in David's kingship, invoking strong northern elements (God of Jacob, Strong One of Israel) and delighting in the Davidic covenant (v. 5). As David's last words the boast of ruling justly (v. 3) sits uncomfortably with the charge given Solomon (1 Kings 2:5-9). But poetry is poetry and legend is legend.

23:8-39

This collection of Davidic traditions is fascinating for its revelation of structures in David's administration that are otherwise totally unknown to us and do not feature at all in the other Davidic narratives. These structures are the groups known as the Three and the Thirty. The Three were Josheb-basshebeth, Eleazar, and Shammah. Beyond this we know nothing of them or their exploits. The hero-worshiping story in vv. 13-17 now appears to be associated with these three warriors.

Where the Thirty are concerned we know four of the group's members, Abishai, Benaiah, Asahel, and Uriah the Hittite. The exploits attributed to Abishai and Benaiah are otherwise unknown to us. There is a clear distinction made between the Three and the Thirty. Abishai was commander of the Thirty but did not make it into the Three (v. 19). Benaiah was renowned among the Thirty but he too did not make it into the Three (v. 23). The total is given as thirty-seven (v. 39). Not all need have been members simultaneously; the number need not have been adhered to scrupulously.

These two apparently important groups, the Three and the Thirty, probably belonging to the early period of David's career, are passed over in absolute silence in the Davidic traditions apart from this collection. There is a tale to be told here but we have no key to unlock it.

2 Samuel 24

This is as strange a story as 2 Sam 21:1-14. It appears as the legend locating the place of the Temple, yet it is a disedifying story for so significant a role. As the text stands the story begins with God's anger against Israel and God's stirring up David against Israel by ordering a census. The Chronicler prefers to blame Satan (1 Chr 21:1). Joab resists; he and the army commanders are overruled (v. 4). Reasons are not offered. The census completed, David is remorseful and confesses to the LORD. The prophet Gad is sent to offer a choice of punishments: three years of famine, three months of defeat, or three days of pestilence. David chooses the shortest but articulates a different and pious reason. By a positive act of God's graciousness Jerusalem is spared the pestilence, which stops at the threshing floor of

Araunah the Jebusite (v. 16). An alternative version has the pestilence averted when under Gad's guidance David properly and publicly buys Araunah's threshing floor, builds an altar to the LORD, and offers sacrifice. The Chronicler identifies this site with the location of Solomon's Temple (2 Chr 3:1; see also 1 Chr 21:28–22:1).

There are tensions enough in the story; their resolution does not remove its mystery. If the Chronicler's tradition is correct, for better or worse David is identified with the origins of the Jerusalem Temple. Solomon may have built it, but David picked the place—with help from God through the prophet Gad.

BIBLIOGRAPHY

Anderson, Arnold A. *2 Samuel.* WBC 11. Dallas, Tex.: Word Books, 1989.

Brueggemann, Walter. *First and Second Samuel.* Interpretation. Louisville: John Knox, 1990.

Campbell, Antony F. *Of Prophets and Kings: A Late Ninth Century Document (1 Samuel 1—2 Kings 10).* CBQ.MS 17. Washington, D.C.: Catholic Biblical Association, 1986.

_____. *The Study Companion to OT Literature: An Approach to the Writings of Pre-Exilic and Exilic Israel.* Old Testament Studies 2. Collegeville: The Liturgical Press, 1989/1992.

Campbell, Antony F., and Mark A. O'Brien. *Sources of the Pentateuch: Texts, Introductions, Annotations.* Minneapolis: Fortress, 1993.

Hertzberg, Hans Wilhelm. *I & II Samuel.* OTL. London: SCM, 1964.

Klein, Ralph W. *1 Samuel.* WBC 10. Waco, Tex.: Word Books, 1983.

McCarter, P. Kyle Jr. *I–II Samuel.* 2 vols. AB 8–9. Garden City, N.Y.: Doubleday, 1980–1984.

Miscall, Peter. *I Samuel. A Literary Reading.* Bloomington, Ind.: Indiana University Press, 1986.

Noth, Martin. *The Deuteronomistic History.* JSOT.S 15. 2nd ed. Sheffield: Sheffield Academic Press, 1991. German original 1943.

1–2 Kings

Mark O'Brien and Antony Campbell

FIRST READING

General Character of 1–2 Kings

The first and second books of Kings tell the story of Israel's monarchy from the triumph of David's successor Solomon in Jerusalem to the exile of David's descendant Jehoiachin in Babylon. A chronological reckoning runs throughout the books; the narrative covers a period of about four hundred years. As in 1–2 Samuel, a central question in Kings is the role of God in the shaping of society. In the narrative the Jerusalem Temple and the prophetic word are the two great signs of God's guiding presence. Kings and people are judged by their fidelity to the exclusive worship of God at the Temple in Jerusalem and by their acceptance of the prophetic word.

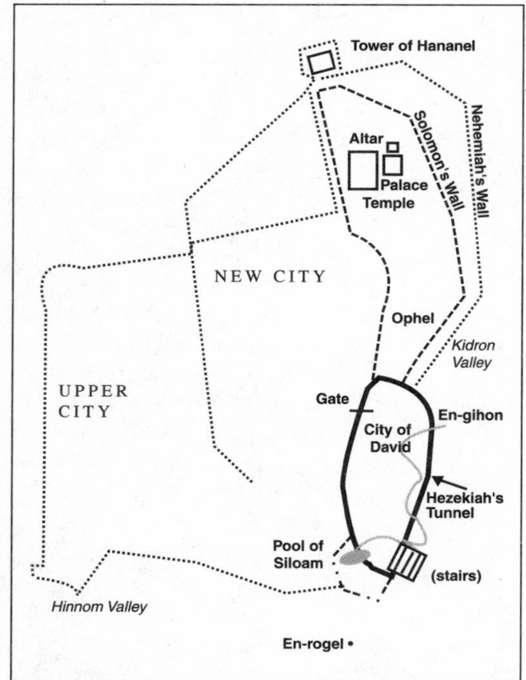

JERUSALEM OF THE OLD TESTAMENT

First and Second Kings are further examples of theology as narrative, although the interpretative element is more prominent than in 1–2 Samuel. This is due to the complex nature of the subject matter in Kings rather than evidence of a different way of expressing theological understanding. First and Second Kings may not be always historically accurate but they are not works of fiction. There is a genuine historiographic concern, evident in the construction of a chronology of the kings and the repeated citation of sources where a reader might have inspected the "rest of the acts" of any king. First and Second Kings develop their theological interpretation from a careful reflection on Israel's past insofar as it is available in the traditions and documents that survived. The narrative was not invented for the sake of the theology.

Strategy for Reading

In forming a strategy for reading 1–2 Kings it is worth reviewing what was said in preparation for reading 1–2 Samuel, in particular the need to be aware of the different ways in which stories, reports, speeches, and evaluative comments convey meaning. The books of Kings regularly make a point of referring the reader to a number of sources for consultation. The principal ones cited are the "Book of the Annals of the Kings of Judah" and the "Book of the Annals of the Kings of Israel." It is difficult to gauge accurately the precise official status of these annals; it is reasonable to assume that they were no freer of bias than similar documents in any other societies.

A panoramic view of 1–2 Kings reveals three distinct and different sections of text. The first covers the reign of Solomon from the story of his succession in 1 Kings 1–2 to the report of his death and burial in 1 Kings 11:43. After the death of Solomon, the second begins with the splintering of the kingdom in 1 Kings 12 into northern and southern factions, i.e., Israel and Judah, and traces the often turbulent story of these two kingdoms down to the Assyrian exile of Israel in 2 Kings 17. The third covers the story of the kingdom of Judah from the reign of Hezekiah in 2 Kings 18 to the Babylonian exile in 2 Kings 25.

For the reader who has just come from 1–2 Samuel the text is at first relatively familiar. The story of Solomon's succession in 1 Kings 1–2 has definite similarities to the Story of David's Later Years (or Succession Narrative) in 2 Samuel. Even though a significant portion of 1 Kings 3–11 is taken up with the building and consecration of the Temple the overall focus is on Solomon and his conduct as king, as in Samuel where the focus of the narrative was first Saul and then David. It is when one enters the area of 1 Kings 12 to 2 Kings 17 that matters become more complex. The narrative now has to chart a course through the labyrinth of two rival kingdoms with their respective kings and dynasties, the different lengths of their reigns, the tangled and often turbulent relationships between them and other ancient Near Eastern kingdoms.

It is welcome therefore to find the text's narrator offering signposts to point a way through the story of the divided kingdom. Each king's reign in 1–2 Kings is recounted within what has come to be called the "regnal framework" that shapes each account and directs the overall course of the narrative. A good spot to inspect the framework is 1 Kings 15 where seven key elements are easily identifiable: (1) the reigns of the respective northern and southern kings are synchronized (15:1); (2) the length of the reign of the king under consideration is given (15:2); (3) his capital is named (15:2); (4) an evaluation is made of his reign (15:3); (5) there is a reference to the relevant annals for the rest of the king's deeds (15:7); (6) the king's death and burial is reported (15:8); (7) his successor is named (15:8). For the kingdom of Judah the narrative also often supplies the king's age at his accession and the name of his mother (15:2).

The regnal framework will be discussed in more detail in the unit by unit commentary. Some of its components seem to be factual; others appear to be highly judgmental—the king did what was right or what was evil in God's eyes. The kings are described as doing right or evil according to their fidelity to the exclusive worship of God in the Temple and their acceptance of the prophetic word. To the modern mind this may seem unduly narrow; to the ancient narrator it was evidently central. The references given to the sources for the acts of the king appear to give confirmation to the judgments passed; at the same time the reference to external sources reveals an openness to control exercised by the evidence. The books of Chronicles show how a different judgment might be reached.

Historical, Social, and Intellectual Situations

The kingdom of Israel was a relatively late arrival on the stage of the ancient Near East. It was surrounded by already established monarchies. The raw newcomer made its presence felt when David successfully subdued the neighboring kingdoms, a conquest that occurred during a lull in hostilities between the great powers due to Assyria's decline. Israel had the good fortune to be on a number of the major caravan routes between the great powers of Mesopotamia and Egypt. This trade created the wealth needed to improve the standard of living, undertake building projects, and form favorable international agreements. But Israel also had the misfortune of being on the traditional invasion route between the great powers. A time of prosperity and peace could suddenly be shattered by war with its massive destruction and disruption of peoples' lives.

Israel did not enjoy its advantage for long. The rupture into northern and southern kingdoms after the death of Solomon allowed the subject nations to reassert their independence. The subsequent rise of the neo-Assyrian empire threatened the whole region over which David and Solomon once ruled. Northern Israel and Judah in the south, two small squabbling kingdoms among a number of other small squabbling kingdoms, were easy pickings for a superpower like Assyria. Israel succumbed to the might of Assyria in 722 B.C.E. (cf. 2 Kings 17), a fate that Judah managed to escape (cf. 2 Kings 18–19), but only for a time. A resurgent Babylon conquered Assyria and then challenged Egypt. Judah lay between them and was overrun by the Babylonian advance in 587 B.C.E.

We may point to five stages in this history that had most impact on Israel's thinking and the shaping of its traditions. First, Solomon's power and prosperity enabled him to develop a centralized royal administration and build the standard ancient Near Eastern symbols of royal power: a palace and a temple (c. 950). However, Israel was still a developing nation and Solomon had to seek foreign aid for these projects; from Egypt for his administration and from Tyre for his building program. This international traffic would have opened Israel to a range of new ideas and fashions. The second major impact on Israel's thinking was the breakup of the kingdom after Solomon's death (c. 930). The rival kingdoms of Israel and Judah not only had to contend with each other but also with neighboring kingdoms and, later on, the threat of Assyria. The Davidic dynasty continued to reign in Judah, but Israel experienced a number of more or less shortlived dynasties whose rule frequently ended in bloody coups. The extensive stories and traditions about Elijah and Elisha may well have emerged as a prophetic response to this turbulent period in the history of the northern kingdom. The third moment of impact was the conquest of northern Israel by Assyria (722). Many of Israel's citizens were taken into exile while others fled as refugees to Judah. The flood of refugees is believed to have had a profound effect on life and thought in Judah, probably bringing the seeds of deuteronomic theology with it. The fourth major impact was the deuteronomic reform under Josiah, believed by many to be the originating impulse for the creation of the Deuteronomistic History (622). The fifth and final impact was the exile of Judah at the hands of the Babylonians (587). Despite this catastrophe Judah managed, unlike northern Israel, to reestablish itself as an entity under the Persians who became the new masters of the ancient Near East (538).

As noted for 1–2 Samuel, a terminology has grown up reflecting developments associated with Josiah's reform and the exile. Variations exist, but what we use here—widely used by others—can be swiftly summarized. "Deuteronomic" is used in reference to the law code, the book of Deuteronomy, and the reform under Josiah. "Deuteronomistic" is used in reference to the history, the books of Deuteronomy through 2 Kings. The people responsible for the history are referred to as "deuteronomists," or often in the singular "the Deuteronomist." The language used in such circles can be stereotyped, marked by their ideology, concerned for fidelity to YHWH and exclusive worship in Jerusalem. As examples see 1 Kings 9:3-9 and 1 Kings 11:11-13.

Biblical and Theological Contexts

A common exegetical position is that circles associated with the deuteronomic reform gave 1–2 Kings their definitive shape and made them an integral part of the Deuteronomistic History. Opinions vary as to whether the major work was done during the reign of Josiah and revised during the exilic and post-exilic periods or whether it was a product of the exile as Martin Noth first proposed. In either case it is well to remember that the books we now have were produced in a Judean context although descendants of those refugees who fled to Judah may have had a hand in shaping them.

The task undertaken by the deuteronomists was a formidable one. Against the background of the promise of an enduring Davidic dynasty they had to explain the collapse of the united kingdom, the emergence of the northern kingdom with its own dynasties, and the fact that it endured for two hundred years. The Jerusalem Temple had become the focus of a massive investment of theology, liturgy, and tradition. Its destruction had to be explained against this background. Finally the deuteronomists' claims for the authority of the book of Deuteronomy had to be reconciled with the authority of the various prophets whose words and stories had been passed down in the tradition.

For the deuteronomists, David was the model for evaluating all the subsequent kings of Israel and Judah. In view of the diversity of views about David preserved in 1–2 Samuel it is highly significant that the deuteronomists singled him out as the measure of kingship without eliminating evidence of a contrary viewpoint in the books of Samuel. A careful reading of the relevant texts of 1–2 Kings indicates that despite his moral failings the deuteronomists saw David as a king who remained faithful to God, to worship in Jerusalem, and to the authority of the prophetic word. For this loyalty God gifted David with the promise of an enduring dynasty. The only other kings compared favorably with him without qualification are Hezekiah (2 Kings 18:3) and Josiah (2 Kings 22:2). Both are portrayed as faithful to God, to worship in the Jerusalem Temple, and to the prophetic word. The other kings of Judah and Israel are portrayed as failing to demonstrate such fidelity; this in the deuteronomists' eyes was a key factor in the collapse of both kingdoms.

Nevertheless, there is complexity within this deuteronomistic viewpoint. Despite the overall negative evaluation of the monarchy the promise of an enduring dynasty for David is not explicitly revoked (but see the implications of 1 Kings 9:6-9) and the story concludes with the exiled Judean king, Jehoiachin, being released from prison and enjoying favor in Babylon although still in exile (2 Kings 25:27-30). Moreover, responsibility for the collapse of Israel and Judah does not fall only on the kings. A number of texts exist in which it is the people who are blamed for the catastrophe.

It is reasonable to assume that the rupture of the united kingdom and the emergence of the rival states of Israel and Judah would have generated intense debate and reflection. The present text may preserve some of the more important elements of this debate. According to 1 Kings 12 it was Solomon's tax and labor policies and his son Rehoboam's threat to increase such burdens that fueled the northern breakaway. For the deuteronomists Solomon's involvement with foreign gods was the key factor in the rupture of the kingdom. The prophecy of Ahijah of Shiloh was reworked in order to drive home this view. The schism in the kingdom was identified as the divine retribution for Solomon's apostasy. The survival of the Davidic dynasty in Judah was seen as an act of mercy by God for the sake of David who had been promised an everlasting dynasty because of his loyalty.

The short poem in 1 Kings 8:12-13 that forms part of Solomon's dedication of the Temple is widely regarded as an ancient text. It expresses Israel's unshakable confidence that the Temple would always be the dwelling place of the divinity. The later deuteronomistic view was to insist that God cannot be contained by any structure but had chosen instead to place the divine name in the Temple (1 Kings 8:27-29). When the people called on the divine name God would hear in heaven and answer their prayer. The sins of the kings and the people ultimately provoked God to reject the Temple as a dwelling place for the divine name (2 Kings 23:26-27).

The deuteronomic name theology did not minimize the significance of the Temple. The building and dedication of the Temple is presented as the climax of Solomon's reign and the setting for a prayer that synthesizes key aspects of this theology (1 Kings 8:14-61). From this point fidelity to worship in the Jerusalem Temple becomes a central criterion in the evaluation of kings and people. The deuteronomists sought to provide an understanding of God's relationship to the Temple that could respond in an authentic way to the experience of the people. "My eyes and my heart will be there for all time" (1 Kings 9:3).

The deuteronomists were theologians attempting to come to grips with Israel's experience under the monarchy. The literary record they bequeathed suggests strongly that their endeavor was not just an intellectual exercise. They were advocates of deuteronomic theology and Deuteronomy is a book replete not only with reasoned argument but also passionate appeal and exhortation. They were immersed in the great tradition of Israelite storytelling, expert at reworking older material to make it speak with renewed vigor or creating new material from the treasury of Israel's traditions. The reader of 1–2 Kings will encounter the presence of the deuteronomists in all these areas: in the nuancing of a story, in the speech of a king like Solomon or a prophet like Ahijah, in the evaluations and explanations that are offered at strategic points throughout the narrative, and in the capacity to distill the highly complex issues of Israel's faith into a simple and intense credo.

Impact on the Christian Community

As we observed in the commentary on 1–2 Samuel, each generation is conditioned by its place and its time and wide variations can exist between different generations in their understanding of biblical passages. In the seventeenth century the divine right of kings generated heated debate in English-speaking society, involving prominent thinkers such as Thomas Hobbes and John Locke. The debate would be unlikely to interest most readers in modern democratic societies—even less the use of Scripture made during it. This does not mean that the portrayal of monarchy in 1–2 Kings has less significance for readers today. There is much in these books that is thought-provoking for anyone concerned with leadership and right government. By way of invitation and challenge, we will touch on a few key areas.

Monarchy

Even a casual reader of 1–2 Kings will be struck by their sustained critical appraisal of the conduct of kings in both the northern and southern kingdoms. The focus is on the figure of the king rather than monarchy as a form of government. Nowhere in 1–2 Kings is monarchy explicitly endorsed as a better form of government than others; nowhere is monarchy condemned as a worse form of government than others. This is not due to ignorance of alternatives to monarchy or its uncritical acceptance as the only conceivable form of government. The authors of 1–2 Kings did not share the ancient Near Eastern assumption that kingship was part of the divinely ordered structure of a nation. According to the Sumerian King List monarchy began "when kingship was lowered from heaven" long before the flood; immediately after the flood kingship was again "lowered from heaven" (*ANET* 265). The deuteronomists were well aware of the texts about judges in Israel when there were no kings. Monarchy emerged at a particular period in Israel's history: the commentary on 1–2 Samuel has discussed the various responses in the text to its emergence and the account of its successful establishment under David. First and Second Kings were completed in the Babylonian exile, when there were no longer kings. According to the deuteronomists monarchy could succeed brilliantly or fail disastrously. What made it work or fail, however, was not any inherent structural factor but the conduct of its kings and people. The deuteronomists saw David as the model king: they saw most of the subsequent kings as failures. The northern kingdom of Israel collapsed because of the sin of Jeroboam and its corruption of his successors and his people. The southern kingdom of Judah was preserved for a time for the sake of David. In the end it too collapsed, brought down by the weight of the sin of Manasseh and his corruption of the people. The deuteronomists understood the sin of both Jeroboam and Manasseh as apostasy, a turning away from God to other gods—the pursuit of power on one's own terms and for one's own gain. One might sum up the authors' attitude in modern terms by saying: blame yourselves, not the structure.

The books of Kings are rarely cited in the NT; when they are, it is principally in relation to prophecy. In Luke 4:25-27 Jesus reminds his listeners how Elijah in 1 Kings 17 and Elisha in 2 Kings 5 were empowered to help and heal foreigners instead of Israelites. In Rom 11:3 and 4 Paul quotes directly from the story of Elijah on Mt. Horeb (1 Kings 19:10 and 18). Despite the paucity of direct references it is reasonable to assume that the critical assessment of kings in these books was influential in the NT's understanding of the kingdom of God and of Jesus as king. The preaching of Jesus on the kingdom of God challenges any form of government, whether monarchical or democratic, to a profound self-appraisal.

Davidic Dynasty

A major feature of the story of Israel's kings is the promise of an everlasting dynasty to David (2 Samuel 7). As told in 1–2 Kings the story of David's dynasty is one of failure rather than triumph. Among his successors only Hezekiah and Josiah are singled out for favorable comparison with David without qualification. The others are either censured for tolerating worship at the high places or, in the case of Manasseh, condemned outright for apostasy. Ultimately the kingdom of Judah collapsed and the surviving members of the dynasty were taken into exile in Babylon. Despite this ignominious fate the promise of an everlasting dynasty is not revoked. In 1 Kings 9:6-9 Solomon is warned of Israel's doom and the destruction of the Temple but the dynasty is not explicitly included. Its future is left open. Even though it failed there is a sense of deep commitment to the dynasty and what it stood for. It is significant that the NT gives Jesus this flawed royal ancestry in the genealogy of Matthew's gospel. The books of Kings and Matthew's gospel affirm in different ways God's loyalty to those who have failed in their loyalty to God.

Jerusalem Temple

Loyalty to God is central in the books of Kings and worship in the Jerusalem Temple is its authentic expression. At first glance the emphasis on the Temple may appear fundamentalist and narrow. A careful reading reveals a more complex and subtle picture. The deuteronomists needed to come to terms with a standard feature of ancient Near Eastern society: the royal temple dedicated to the national god and under the patronage of the king. They sought to remove the Temple from royal control by proclaiming it as the place that God, not the king, had approved for worship (1 Kings 9:3). They made the Davidic dynasty custodian of Temple worship rather than its policymaker and censured members of the dynasty for tolerating rival places of worship (the "high places") or introducing rival forms of worship. A particularly striking example of the latter is the condemnation of Manasseh in 2 Kings 21:3-7. According to the authors of Kings the highest heavens could not contain God (1 Kings 8:27) but God could be invoked directly and intimately by pronouncing the divine name in the Temple (8:29). The sovereign freedom and transcendence of God was preserved while God's immanent presence to all who called on the divine name was assured. Even those unable to pray in the Temple because of famine, war, or exile would be heard as long as they prayed toward the Temple (1 Kings 8:37-50). This carefully nuanced theology is not without limitations. Its notion of centralized worship could be a powerful symbol of unity: the one nation worshiping the one God at the one shrine. By the same token the exclusive status of the Temple could provoke tension and rivalry. These surfaced after the northern kingdom broke away under Jeroboam (1 Kings 12:25-32). They arose again in the competing claims of Samaritans and Jews in the post-exilic and NT periods (cf. John 4:20). Jesus' teaching on worship "in spirit and truth" (4:23) sharpens the insight of 1–2 Kings that the transcendent God is present to all who proclaim God's name but goes beyond Kings by revoking any privilege for a particular place of worship.

Deuteronomistic Theology

In the Books of Kings the deuteronomists' theology is most evident in the evaluative comments on each king's reign: all are judged by their fidelity to the exclusive worship of God at the Temple. The steady rhythm of infidelity led to the catastrophe of the exile.

The repeated negative evaluation of the northern kings in particular creates a bleak and depressing impression. If we are to understand these texts it helps to reflect on what undergirded deuteronomistic thinking. Two foundational convictions stand out. The first was a profound awareness that God had chosen Israel, an insignificant people among the peoples of the earth (cf. Deut 7:7-8). For the deuteronomists this choice called for one response above all—unswerving fidelity to YHWH. In reflecting on Israel's history, therefore, it was inevitable that they would focus on the issue of fidelity to YHWH: other issues did not count or only made sense in the light of the paramount issue of fidelity.

The second conviction was belief in the act-consequence dynamic. Israel shared the ancient Near Eastern view that there was a definite and recognizable nexus between an action and its consequence. An evil deed will recoil banefully on its agent, a good deed beneficially. Proverbs 26:27 expresses the dynamic succinctly: "whoever digs a pit will fall into it, and a stone will come back on the one who starts it rolling." Numerous observations like this were invoked to undergird the act-consequence dynamic. For people of the ancient Near East, Israel included, it provided a foundational and persuasive response to the common human desire for order and meaning in life.

It was natural that Israel would apply the dynamic to aspects of its relationship with God. It is understandable that the deuteronomists would measure Israel's good and bad experiences under the monarchy against the kings' and peoples' fidelity or infidelity to YHWH. Because the deuteronomists were writing a history of their nation it is also understandable that they would target events of national significance as signs of divine reward or retribution: the successes or failures of kings, prosperity or penury, victory or defeat. A faithful response to God's gifts, as the deuteronomists claimed for David, resulted in beneficial consequences—a stable and prosperous kingdom, the promise of an eternal dynasty and a temple. Infidelity, of which the deuteronomists accused Solomon and most of the subsequent kings, resulted in negative consequences—the threat of disaster and its realization in the exile.

The deuteronomists' argument is intense and highly rhetorical, to the extent that religious language may have swallowed up underlying processes of act and consequence. To the modern reader their position may look unacceptably severe and biased, in particular the repeated condemnation of each apostate northern king from Jeroboam to Hoshea—none of Jeroboam's successors revoked his policies. Where the portrayal of the northern kings may strike a chord today is in relation to the deadly and long-term impact that evil policies have on a society if they remain unchallenged. The twentieth century is all too familiar with institutional and structural evil, the cultures of violence and death.

We may balk at the notion of divine retribution as presented by the deuteronomists and point to inadequacies in the act–consequence dynamic. The dynamic is limited by its parameters and by the sheer scope and complexity of human experience and divine mystery. The OT itself exposes the limitations of the dynamic in the books of Job and Ecclesiastes (Qoheleth). However, we can hardly ignore the deuteronomists' conviction that a proper relationship with God is foundational for the well-being of any society, whether monarchical or democratic.

Prophecy

The books of Kings also make extensive use of prophecy and the prophecy–fulfillment schema. In the text prophets approve kings or rebuke them for their conduct. They claim power to dismiss them and to designate new kings in their place: in 1 Kings 21 Elijah dismisses Ahab; in 2 Kings 9 Elisha's disciple designates Jehu. They prophesy the ultimate end of both kingdoms (cf. 1 Kings 14:15-16; 2 Kings 21:10-15). The authors of Kings shared the ancient Near Eastern view that the role of the king was "to promote the welfare of the people, . . . to cause justice to prevail in the land, to destroy the wicked and the evil, that the strong might not oppress the weak" (Prologue to the law code of Hammurabi [1727 B.C.E.], *ANET* 164). These authors condemned their kings when they failed to fulfill their role. They invoked prophetic authority to claim that the power enjoyed by Israel's kings was a gift from God for the good of the people; if they proved unworthy of the gift it would be taken away.

The prophecy–fulfillment schema comprises the prophecy itself plus the subsequent notice of its fulfillment. The schema may appear mechanistic at first glance. It is well to remember that it was constructed after the events described. The schema is an expression of the authors' belief in God's guidance of Israel's history, a guidance that does not inhibit human freedom. Taken in isolation the schema can create an impression of inevitability. However, the characters in the story framed by the schema are portrayed as free agents in a human drama. The authors who employed the schema claimed *that* the course of Israel's history was under God's guidance; they made no claim to know precisely *how* God brought this about. People down the centuries have searched the prophetic texts in the Bible for clues about the future and how God will operate. The deuteronomists' reserve provides a timely caution.

There is food for thought in another feature of prophecy in the books of Kings: the relationship between the prophetic word and its bearers. Prophets are portrayed as powerful figures authorized by God to confront the people and their leaders with their sins. But prophets too are portrayed as failures. Those who bear the word of God can be duped like anyone else (1 Kings 13); they can suffer a massive loss of faith (Elijah in 1 Kings 19); their prophetic insight can fail at a crucial moment (Elisha and the woman of Shunem in 2 Kings 4). Being a prophet does not preserve one from the limitations and failures of the human condition. There is a parallel in the NT's portrayal of Jesus' disciples, in particular their reaction to the crisis of his trial and crucifixion. It is a measure of God's commitment to humanity that it is these same flawed and fragile human beings who are called to be bearers of God's word.

SECOND READING

An Invitation to Read

We begin by recalling for our readers what was said in the commentary on 1–2 Samuel: when we are working with a biblical commentary there is always a risk that we read the commentary and not the Bible. As a way of minimizing this risk we recommend that the biblical text be read first, then the commentary, and then the biblical text again.

First identify the unit in the text that is under discussion (for example, 1 Kings 1–2). Second, read this portion of the text. Third, read the commentary on 1 Kings 1–2. Fourth, read the biblical text again. Now that an initial appreciation of the text under discussion has been established one can undertake a more searching analysis.

Metaphors are helpful to assist the reader's access to the biblical text. For 1 Kings 1–2 the metaphor is that of a drama; for the subsequent chapters of 1–2 Kings the metaphor is that of a national shrine. Each of these metaphors will be developed in the unit-by-unit commentary.

Reign of Solomon: 1 Kings 1–11

Establishment of Solomon as King (1 Kings 1–2)

If any metaphor is suited to these chapters it is the dramatic. The curtain opens on an aged king and closes on the final corpse. In between one pretender to the throne has failed and another succeeded; the aged king settles old scores and the successor strikes down his rival.

The drama opens with King David who is old and cold. The most lovely young woman in Israel is unable to rouse his passion. Instead it is the ambition of the crown prince that is roused (1:5). Adonijah moves swiftly to claim the crown. His entourage is the same as Absalom's at the start of a campaign that led to rebellion and the death of Absalom (2 Sam 15:1; 18:14-15). The narrative reflects the realities of politics: Adonijah's ambition was untamed; he had good looks and was next in line; he had solid support.

The drama intensifies with the intervention of Nathan the prophet, pitting the man of persuasive words against the man of impetuous action. Nathan creates a scenario with Bathsheba that challenges David to act. The move succeeds. In a display of royal authority that contrasts sharply with his enfeebled physical condition David invokes his oath and commands that Solomon be crowned immediately.

The climax of the succession drama is narrated by cleverly juxtaposing two powerful scenes. On the one side there is the stately procession and coronation of Solomon, exploding into a joyful and tumultuous celebration by the people (vv. 38-40). On the other side there is the feasting of Adonijah and his supporters that turns to apprehension and dismay as they hear the city in uproar and learn that Solomon has been crowned king in the presence of Zadok, Nathan, Benaiah and—significantly—David's warriors (vv. 41-48). Adonijah's supporters melt away, leaving him at the mercy of Solomon who leaves him in suspense, sparing his life and ordering him to his home.

Theologically Solomon's succession is identified as part of God's plan (cf. 1:48; 3:7). However, this divine plan is implemented by characters whose words and motives are difficult to assess. The question recurs: is this genuine concern or self-interest? truth or distortion?

With the coronation of Solomon and the dismissal of Adonijah the dramatic tension that began in v. 5 would appear to have eased. However, Solomon's instructions about Adonijah in v. 52 hint at the possibility of further conflict between these rival sons of David. In drawing the dramatic arc of the narrative in ch. 1 to a close the narrator provides an opening for the developments that take place in ch. 2.

David's deathbed scene with his farewell speech to Solomon is in two parts. In the first Solomon is charged to keep the Law of Moses in order to prosper and secure the future of the Davidic dynasty (2:1-4; see below at 1 Kings 9:1-9). In the second Solomon is instructed to see that Joab and Shimei pay for their treachery against David and that the sons of Barzillai are rewarded for their loyalty (2:5-9). The manner in which Joab and Shimei are to pay for their crimes is left to Solomon's wisdom. David dies and Solomon must now rule alone. He has regulated the case of Adonijah (1:52). He has received instructions from David about Joab and Shimei. He has been charged by David to keep the Law of Moses. As the story unfolds we find no report of how Solomon rewarded the sons of Barzillai. The narrative is firmly focused on the relationship between Solomon and his rivals.

There is no comment on whether Solomon acted either wisely or in accord with the Law of Moses in disposing of these rivals. The curtain closes on the corpse of Shimei. Is there a note of irony in the final remark: "So the kingdom was established in the hand of Solomon"? Solomon here is an ambivalent figure.

The following traditions explore this ambivalence: Solomon the visionary and wise; Solomon the administrator; Solomon the Temple builder; Solomon the lecher and idolater.

Review of the Kings. Metaphor: National Shrine

For any Israelite reader of 1–2 Kings the nation of Israel no longer existed as an independent state; the northern kingdom of Israel had been swallowed up by Assyria in 722 and Judah by Babylon in 587. A modern metaphor may deepen our appreciation, namely the guided tour of a national shrine where valuable stories, vital records, and other memorabilia have been carefully preserved and arranged. We moderns would think too of portraits, statues, and recordings. The deuteronomists were responsible for the arrangement and so they are the reader's guides. This is not a tour designed to leave one unmoved; there is too much at stake. Hence there are dramatic recitals of stories and briefer sketches that are designed to bring the past to vibrant life. There is a description of the Temple that allows one imaginatively to enter inside in awe and wonder. The speeches of kings and prophets reach across the centuries to address the present. The deuteronomistic evaluations of kings and people constantly drive home the importance of fidelity to God and integrity of worship.

The architecture of the shrine would reflect the layout of the text: two grand domes, one over the Temple in Jerusalem and one over the reform of Josiah, are linked by a gallery of the divided kingdom. The entrance hall displays Solomon's initial achievements; the final gallery, recording Judah's four last kings and Jerusalem's fall, brings the Israelite visitors back to the reality of their present life.

Establishment of the Temple (1 Kings 3–8)

The story of David's later years in 2 Samuel 11–20 and the story of the succession in 1 Kings 1–2 focused on the drama of relationships and intrigues within the royal family. In 1 Kings 3–8 there is a marked change; the text is comprised principally of accounts of Solomon's administration and his relationship with his subjects, with his court officials, and with international dignitaries. There are lists of provisions and reports of building programs. Key speeches are put on record. In the national shrine the visitor finds all the trappings of the state set out in impressive array.

3:1-3

The tour begins by outlining and explaining practices in the early part of Solomon's reign that might cause scandal when compared with later more prominent features. The explanations tell why Solomon accommodated his Egyptian wife in the city of David (v. 1) and why the people worshiped at the high places (v. 2). Verse 3 affirms that Solomon loved the LORD—"love" being understood in the deuteronomic sense of undivided loyalty—although it is admitted that he worshiped at the high places. Solomon's practice is in part covered by the explanation in v. 2; in part it prepares for the dream at Gibeon—*the great* high place. There is a signal here that the tension between Temple and high places will feature prominently as the story of the kings unfolds.

3:4-15

During one of Solomon's pilgrimages to Gibeon, God invited him in a dream to ask for whatever he wanted. Solomon requested an "understanding mind" to govern God's people (3:9), a request that won God's approval and the gift of surpassing wisdom. On waking Solomon did not sacrifice at Gibeon. Instead he returned to Jerusalem to sacrifice before the Ark of the Covenant (3:15).

The dialogue between God and Solomon in 3:4-15 echoes the deuteronomic understanding of covenant in which fidelity is the consequence of relationship with God, not a condition for it (cf. introduction to 1–2 Samuel). Solomon recognizes God's initiative in establishing him as David's successor. The consequence side of the deuteronomic understanding requires an appropriate response to this gift: here it is Solomon's desire to govern God's people rightly (3:8). His commitment to this and the recognition of his own inadequacy elicits a further divine initiative, the gift of wisdom that will enable him to fulfill this desire. According to the deuteronomic viewpoint the covenant with God develops and deepens as each divine gift brings corresponding responsibility in its train. The gift of wisdom ensures the welfare of the kingdom. Personal riches and honor are added. To "walk in my ways" (v. 14) is a condition—linked to the length of life for Solomon (cf. v. 11). The effects of these gifts will spread throughout the kingdom.

Solomon's return to Jerusalem to worship before the Ark may be the initial sign of God's gift at work: he abandons the high places in favor of worshiping exclusively in Jerusalem (3:15). If this is the case it is appropriate that the gift should first touch Solomon and then flow from him to others.

3:16–4:34

This narrative has been carefully arranged to evoke the powerful effect of Solomon's surpassing wisdom. In 3:16-28 there is the famous story of two mothers who claimed the same child. Solomon's handling of the case showed that the king who worshiped rightly—in Jerusalem—judged wisely. Respect for justice was established as news of his judgment spread and the people stood in awe of him. At the end 1 Kings 4:29-34 reports how the fame of Solomon's wisdom and understanding spread to all the nations. These two accounts frame a central section that describes the administration of his kingdom (4:1-28). The people enjoyed a standard of living marked by an increase in population with an abundance of food and drink, happiness, peace, and safety (vv. 20-25).

1 Kings 5

This chapter functions as the threshold to the Temple display. Careful arrangement of the material is again evident. Among the stream of visitors in Jerusalem from all the nations (cf. 4:34) the delegation from King Hiram of Tyre is singled out: he had always been a friend of David (5:1). Solomon's message to Hiram is a deuteronomistic interpretation of the significance of David's reign in relation to Solomon's. The demands of war prevented David from building a temple. The LORD gave him victory over his enemies and as a result Solomon enjoys peace and security. He judges that the time has now come to build a temple "for the name of the LORD" according to the promise God made to his father in 2 Sam 7:13. Hiram responds to the message by recognizing Solomon as a wise ruler. His decision to build a temple is therefore a further manifestation of God's gift of wisdom. Hiram and Solomon successfully negotiate arrangements for the supply of building materials and make a treaty to ensure peace (5:8-12). The building of the Temple is thus carried out in a spirit of harmony and cooperation. Within the larger horizon of the Deuteronomistic History the propitious signs pointed to by Solomon in 5:4 recall the conditions laid down in Deut 12:10-11 for worshiping at "the place that the LORD your God will choose as a dwelling for his name."

1 Kings 6–7

Within the metaphor of the national shrine the reader enters beneath the grand dome displaying the building of the Temple and its consecration. The text's description allows the visitor to visualize the beauty and grandeur of a building that in its innermost recess housed the Ark of the Covenant.

According to 1 Kings 6:1 the building of the Temple began in the four hundred eightieth year after the exodus from Egypt. According to Martin Noth this date forms part of the chronological schema of the Deuteronomistic History commencing with Deut 1:3. Noth believed the schema was constructed on the basis of traditional information and the Deuteronomist's own calculations. The historical accuracy of the chronology cannot be verified. First Kings 6:2-38 describes the Temple's construction; 7:13-51 tells how its special furnishings were made. In between there is a brief account of the construction of Solomon's palace (7:1-12). This arrangement, in which two extensive texts on the Temple frame a much shorter one on the palace, signals the preeminence of the Temple in the story of Solomon's reign. With 6:11-13 the description gives way to a speech that reflects deuteronomistic concerns. According to the later theology espoused in these verses Solomon's unswerving fidelity was necessary not only to ensure the fulfillment of the promise to David of an enduring dynasty but also the presence of God among the people. It is significant that God's presence is set "among the children of Israel"—wherever they might be; at the time of the exile the Temple was in ruins.

1 Kings 8

The dedication of the Temple and Solomon's speeches mark the high point of this part of the display. The text contains a variety of views about the Temple and its significance, a testimony to the massive investment of Israelite tradition in this institution. The way the text has been assembled reveals a fine sense of the special but limited nature of each tradition. Each one illuminates some aspect of the Temple and the mystery of God's presence. Each one is enriched through its relationship to the others. While the predominant view is deuteronomistic the text has been so arranged that each viewpoint enhances the overall effect without losing its distinctive features.

The narrative of vv. 1-11 describes the procession of the Ark from the city of David to the Temple. In 1 Samuel 4–6 the Ark is portrayed as the symbol through which God's power and purpose is communicated to Israel. Here in 1 Kings 8:9 the deuteronomistic understanding of the Ark comes to the fore; it contains the tablets of the covenant. The priestly symbolism is foregrounded in v. 10 when the cloud of glory fills the Temple where the Ark has been placed. It is a sign that God has taken possession of the Temple. The cloud as a symbol of the presence of the deity evokes the priestly account of the consecration of the sanctuary built by Moses in Exod 40:34-38.

Solomon's proclamation in vv. 12-13 is tantalizingly brief and in all probability ancient. In characteristically bold Hebrew style it captures the mystery and intimacy of God's presence by juxtaposing two parallel statements. The first foregrounds mystery by speaking of God dwelling in thick darkness (literally: dark cloud). The second foregrounds intimacy by speaking of God dwelling in the Temple as one dwells in a house.

In the extensive deuteronomistic composition that follows (vv. 14-53) the deuteronomists present a masterly exposition of their theology within the parameters described by the juxtaposed statements in vv. 12-13: namely God's transcendent mystery and immanent intimacy. In deuteronomistic terms God dwells in the heavens and God's presence on earth is expressed by the divine name that resides in the Temple.

The first section of this deuteronomistic composition looks to the past (vv. 14-21). Solomon begins by praising God who with the successful completion of the Temple has fulfilled the promises spoken to David. Solomon then addresses three issues related to the promise. First he explains that the Temple was an integral part of God's purpose for Israel from the time of the Exodus, a purpose that included the choice of David and the establishment of his dynasty. Second, he explains how the statement in v. 13 is not a presumptuous claim as it might appear to be if taken in isolation. The statement was made in response to the divine initiative, first promised to David and then realized through his son. Third, he stresses that the Temple was built for the name of God in accord with the promise.

Solomon then turns to the future (vv. 22-53): he prays first for the Davidic dynasty (vv. 23-26); second for the Temple as a place of prayer (vv. 27-30); third for the people (vv. 31-53). The prayer for the dynasty (vv. 23-26) is made within the framework of the deuteronomistic concept of the covenant in which God's initiative calls for a response of complete commitment. As noted at 1 Kings 2:4 the unconditional promise of 2 Samuel 7 has been shifted toward a promise involving the throne of all Israel—but conditional. The future security of the Davidic dynasty on the throne of Israel (the united kingdom) is contingent on the continued fidelity of David's descendants. In v. 25 Solomon prays for such fidelity. David is the model.

Solomon's prayer for the Temple (vv. 27-30) begins with a rhetorical question about God's dwelling place answered by the declaration that neither heaven nor the Temple can contain God. The declaration looks back to vv. 12-13 as well as forward to the remainder of the prayer. One may speak of God dwelling in the dark cloud as in v. 12 or in heaven as in v. 30. Nevertheless God cannot be contained by heaven or the cloud. Similarly God cannot be contained by the Temple whether one proclaims it as God's dwelling as in v. 13, or as the locus of the divine name as in v. 29. Having affirmed the mystery and freedom of the uncontainable divine presence the text moves to confirm the Temple as the exclusive locus of Israel's worship. This central claim is established in two steps: first by Solomon's request in v. 29; second by God's reply in 9:3.

Between this petition and its reply are seven situations of the people's need that Solomon asks God to look on favorably as long as those in need make their prayer in or toward the Temple: vv. 31-32, 33-34, 35-36, 37-40, 41-43, 44-45, 46-53. The predominant need has already been signaled in v. 30: forgiveness of sin. In only two situations, that of the foreigner in vv. 41-43 and of Israel being sent by God against its enemies in vv. 44-45, is the theme of sin and forgiveness not present. This emphasis and the absence of any reference to the king suggests that the collection of prayers in vv. 31-53 was made during the exile when the monarchy had collapsed; in their present setting, however, they can speak to any generation of Israelites.

The causal links between sin and defeat in war, sin and drought, or sin and plagues would not be endorsed by many today. Within OT theology, particularly that of Deuteronomy, they were accepted. The situations of affliction about which Solomon prays in vv. 31-53 recall the curses of Deuteronomy 28.

Verses 54-61 combine the motifs of praise and petition but within a larger horizon than the one in view in vv. 14-53. In vv. 14-21 Solomon praises God who has fulfilled the promises given to David. Here he praises God who has fulfilled the promises spoken through Moses. In vv. 22-26 he prays that God would be with the Davidic dynasty as with David. Here he prays that God may be with Israel as with their ancestors. In vv. 27-53 he prays that God would heed his prayer for the Temple and the prayer of the people in a number of critical situations. Here he prays that God may maintain his cause and the cause of the people "as each day requires" (v. 59). Verse 60 opens the horizon even further with a prayer that all peoples of the earth may know that "the LORD is God." Solomon concludes with a call for Israel's fidelity (v. 61).

Sin of Solomon (1 Kings 9–11)

The arrangement of chs. 9–10 is similar to that of chs. 3–8: a report of God's appearance to Solomon in a dream is followed by a description of Solomon's activities. In the terms of the metaphor it fashions a transition from the grand Temple display to the gallery of the divided kingdom. The sequence in which these activities are described in chs. 3–8 is reversed in 9:10–10:29. There the account of Solomon's wisdom in 3:16–4:34 preceded that of his building program in chs. 5–7. Here the information about his building program in 9:10-24 precedes the various accounts of his wisdom and wealth in 9:25–10:29. The change in sequence means that 9:10-24 provides a conclusion to the account of Solomon's building program that began in 1 Kings 5. The subsequent report of his international renown for wisdom provides a context for ch. 11. Foreign rulers like the queen of Sheba came to Solomon in search of wisdom. According to 11:1-8 it was Solomon's love of foreign women that led to his undoing.

1 Kings 9–10

God's message to Solomon in 1 Kings 9:1-9 is structured like the one at Gibeon in 3:11-14. God grants a request by Solomon and assures him of further blessings in return for complete loyalty. In 8:29 Solomon prayed that God's eyes might be open day and night toward "the place of which you said, 'My name shall be there.'" In 9:3 God promises that the divine name will be in the Temple "forever" and that "my eyes and my heart will be there for all time." A mark of the genius of deuteronomistic theology is its ability to hold together through the skillful use of metaphor two potentially exclusive forms of God's presence. God is present as the all-powerful creator and lord, expressed in the metaphor of dwelling in the heavens (8:30, 39, 43, 49). God is also present in the Temple as one who is close and attentive, expressed in the metaphors of the name and of the eyes and the heart (9:3).

God's commitment to the Temple is unconditional in 9:3. In 9:4-5, however, the Davidic dynasty's rule over the united kingdom of Israel is rendered conditional for the north. Solomon is charged to show "integrity of heart" like that of David so that the rule of the dynasty over all Israel may be secure.

God's commitment to the Temple and the people becomes conditional in 9:6-9. If the people abandon the LORD for other gods they will be cut off from the land and the Temple will be destroyed. This is the first time in the books of Kings that the sin of apostasy is explicitly mentioned. The focus on the people, the emphasis on sin, and the grim warning about the Temple suggest a later deuteronomistic revision, one that aimed to impress upon Israelites living in the wake of the exile the terrible legacy of infidelity. Although the focus is on the people there is no explicit exemption for the Davidic dynasty. Is it implied that the dynasty would share the fate of the people?

This deuteronomistic revision was nevertheless adamant that exile and the destruction of the Temple would not thwart God's purpose of becoming known and acknowledged among the nations. Israel's ruin would itself be a sign of God to the nations, an ironic answer to Solomon's prayer for the foreigner in 8:41-43.

First Kings 9:25 testifies to Solomon's commitment to the Temple, yet the preceding vv. 10-24 hint that all is not well: there is tension between Hiram and Solomon about the settlement of their contract, and the reader learns the real extent of Solomon's forced labor program—he used it to build whatever he desired "in Jerusalem, in Lebanon, and in all the land of his dominion" (v. 19).

In 1 Kings 9:26–10:29 reports of Solomon's wealth and military power are interwoven with accounts of foreign dignitaries who sought his renowned wisdom; the one singled out for special attention is the queen of Sheba. In the only speech in this account of Solomon as an international celebrity the queen of Sheba envies the happiness of Solomon's servants who continually hear his wisdom; she blesses Israel's God who has set Solomon on the throne of Israel "to execute justice and righteousness" (10:8-9) and she presents the king with lavish gifts. However there is no report of the people benefiting from Solomon's wisdom and wealth, as was the case in 3:28; 4:20, 25.

Solomon is not only the recipient of wealth as promised in 3:13; he acquires it in vast quantities through trade (9:26-28; 10:22) and taxes (10:15). He also amasses horses and chariots (10:26). It is difficult to tell whether the text portrays Solomon's acquisition of wealth and military power as further manifestations of the gift of wisdom or as signs of indulgence and greed.

1 Kings 11

Any subtle hints in 1 Kings 9–10 are barely sufficient to prepare the reader for the damaging assessment of Solomon in ch. 11. The accusations against him in vv. 1-8 provide a telling contrast to his portrayal in chs. 3–8. The statement in 3:3 that he loved God is followed by the account of his unblemished conduct and the description of how he built the Temple. Now in place of Solomon's love of God the reader finds his love of foreign wives and their gods (11:1-3). In place of his unblemished conduct there is breach of the deuteronomic law and the accusation that he did evil in the sight of the LORD (11:2-6). In place of his dedication to the building of the Temple there is a list of high places that he built for the gods of his foreign wives (11:7-8). So Solomon failed to remain faithful to YHWH and to the centralization of all worship in the Jerusalem Temple.

According to the deuteronomistic interpretation the fidelity displayed by Solomon won God's approval and blessing; his infidelity reaped God's anger and punishment. First Kings 11:9-13 portrays an angry God who confronts Solomon with his breach of the covenant and pronounces sentence. Verses 11-13 are similar in content to the subsequent prophecy of Ahijah in vv. 31-39. Both texts seek to explain the dissolution of the united kingdom in a way that would satisfy the requirements of deuteronomistic theology—a considerable challenge. There was the report of Solomon's infidelity that demanded retribution. There was the historical reality that Solomon ruled over the united kingdom until his death; it was only later under his son Rehoboam that the rupture took place. There was the fact that although Rehoboam lost the northern tribes to Jeroboam he retained control over Judah and the city of Jerusalem. There was also the unconditional promise in 2 Samuel 7 of an everlasting dynasty for David.

First Kings 11:11-13 takes up the challenge by invoking the deuteronomic principle of retribution for sin and then explaining how it applies to the factors outlined above. The principle is invoked in v. 11 where God declares that because of Solomon's infidelity the kingdom would be torn from him. Verse 12a explains why this did not take place during Solomon's lifetime: it was because of God's loyalty to the promise made to David. In v. 12b the requirement of retribution is satisfied by Rehoboam's loss of the united kingdom. The fact that Rehoboam (and after him David's descendants) continued to rule over Judah in Jerusalem is accounted for in v. 13 by appealing again to the promise to David, as well as to God's choice of Jerusalem (cf. Deut 12:5; 1 Kings 8:16). Thus the explanation appeals twice to the unconditional promise to David in order to accommodate the historical reality of

Solomon and Rehoboam within the deuteronomic understanding. The first is in relation to Solomon as ruler over the united kingdom; the second relates to the dynasty of David over Judah in Jerusalem. The episodes about Hadad and Rezon that follow, at least as introduced (cf. vv. 14, 23), go some way toward satisfying the need for divine retribution during Solomon's lifetime.

Ahijah of Shiloh

In 11:11-13 God speaks directly to Solomon and it is appropriate for the text to focus on him and the future of the Davidic dynasty. The one to whom God will give the kingdom is referred to once and is identified simply as "your servant" (v. 11b). It is only in 11:26-40, with the prophet Ahijah's dramatic gesture of tearing his new cloak and his accompanying prophecy, that the reader learns the identity of this "servant"—Jeroboam son of Nebat, from the northern tribe of Ephraim. It is Ahijah's prophecy that transforms Jeroboam from a trusted employee of Solomon into a man whom he saw as a threat and tried to eliminate.

Ahijah's prophecy in 11:31-39 interprets the symbolic action of tearing his garment in vv. 29-30. Verses 31-36 interpret it primarily in relation to the Davidic dynasty; vv. 37-39 interpret it primarily in relation to Jeroboam. Verses 31-36 share the deuteronomistic theology of 11:11-13, but with a level of complexity that points to more than one hand. It is to be expected that such a critical prophecy as Ahijah's would have been worked on and refined in the course of Israelite tradition.

In contrast to 11:11-13 the announcement of retribution—the sundering of the united kingdom—is placed first in Ahijah's prophecy (v. 31); the reasons for it are supplied in the subsequent verses. The different order allows Ahijah's opening words to interpret the symbolic action of tearing his cloak in v. 30. Once this different order is taken into account the reader can see that the prophecy applies the sin–retribution requirement much as did 11:11-13. It accommodates the reality of Solomon's uninterrupted reign, the rupture of the united kingdom under his son, the unconditional promise to David, and God's choice of Jerusalem. Verse 34 states that Solomon would be spared retribution not only because of God's loyalty to David but also because David was himself completely loyal to God. The portrayal of David as the model of loyalty is not explicit in 11:11-13 but it is required here as a preparation for v. 38 where Jeroboam is exhorted to be as loyal as David. The comparison with David as the model king becomes a prominent feature in the subsequent evaluation of the kings of Israel and Judah.

Verses 31-32 and 35-36 both deal with the distribution of the tribes. The duplication could be a sign of more than one hand at work. Verse 32 is not as essential as vv. 35-36. Verse 32 may be a later attempt to summarize the complex argument of the text that follows. Another sign of the complexity of this passage is the discrepancy between the twelve pieces of Ahijah's torn garment (v. 30) and the eleven tribes that are spoken of in the prophecy. No attempt was made within Israelite tradition to correct the discrepancy in the Hebrew text; the Greek text, however, speaks of two tribes in vv. 32 and 36, bringing the number to twelve.

Verses 37-38 constitute a remarkable reversal: what was given once to David is now promised to Jeroboam. Verse 37 expresses Jeroboam's designation as king over the ten tribes of Israel —God's prerogative. In order that Jeroboam's future and the future of his dynasty may be secure, v. 38 demands the same kind of fidelity to God that David demonstrated. Nevertheless there is a crucial difference between what was promised to David in 2 Samuel 7 and the promise in Ahijah's prophecy. David was given an unconditional promise of an enduring dynasty: God may punish the dynasty for its sins but will not revoke the promise (cf. 2 Sam 7:14 and also 1 Kings 11:39). With Rehoboam the Davidic rule survives in a substantially diminished form—just the south. When transferred to Jeroboam, however, the promise of an enduring dynasty becomes dependent on his fidelity. This distinction is an important factor in the deuteronomistic evaluation of the fate of these two dynasties.

Rupture of United Kingdom: 12:1-24

It is striking that in the actual story of the rupture of the kingdom the deuteronomistic viewpoint is not foregrounded. In place of ch. 11's emphasis on God's initiative the story in 12:1-20 highlights human initiative. The people assemble at Shechem to make Rehoboam king; the people confront Rehoboam over the tax burden; the people summon Jeroboam. In contrast to ch. 11 there is no mention or condemnation of Solomon's apostasy.

The account of Rehoboam's response to the people's demand is also presented in a way that highlights the human element rather than the divine. The old men who advised Solomon know the realities of royal politics: a king can only rule by first winning the allegiance of his people. Their counsel is rejected by Rehoboam who favors the view of his young friends that kingship means domination, not collaboration. He pays the penalty; the northern tribes reject him with a cry that echoes the earlier rejection of David by Sheba (2 Sam 20:1). They make Jeroboam king over Israel, with Judah alone remaining loyal to the house of David. This is the nearest thing to straightforward electoral politics in the OT.

The one explicit reference in 12:1-20 to the deuteronomistic viewpoint, presented so forcefully in ch. 11, is the claim in v. 15 that what took place was in fulfillment of the prophecy of Ahijah. This claim is important for the insight into deuteronomistic thinking that it provides. It is a logical development of belief in the book of Deuteronomy as the divinely sanctioned program for Israel's life in the land. Deuteronomy promised a prophet to guide Israel (Deut 18:15-22). The key prophetic speeches to come are heavily influenced by deuteronomistic language and thought. Notices throughout the history endorse this prophecy–fulfillment claim. Such texts do not mean, however, that deuteronomistic theology was advocating divine manipulation or coercion of human history. Rehoboam, his advisers, and the people are all portrayed as free agents within a very human drama. To put it another way, the bold claims of deuteronomistic theology are tempered by a profound reserve. The claim is made *that* the turn of events was brought about by God; there is no claim to know *how* God brought about this turn of events.

Verses 21-24 describe Rehoboam's mobilization for war against the breakaway north and God's intervention through Shemaiah that halts it. The inclusion of Benjamin in Rehoboam's realm is in contrast to both Ahijah's prophecy and the report in v. 20, which speak only of Judah. This may point to a different provenance for vv. 21-24. The story of the rupture of the united kingdom is framed by three speeches proclaiming that it was God's doing. Each is delivered to one of the key figures in the drama: God to Solomon in 11:11-13, Ahijah to Jeroboam in 11:31-39, and Shemaiah to Rehoboam in 12:23-24.

Gallery of the Divided Kingdom

The text has brought the visitor to the threshold of a new era. The kings of both Israel and Judah will be passed in review, with significant episodes highlighted. Incorporated under the royal reigns are substantial blocks of prophetic traditions—principally Elijah and Elisha, but also a number of others. It is as if the exhibits of the kings of Israel and Judah are displayed on opposite sides of extensive galleries; they are grouped for chronological comparison, with items from significant episodes included.

Reign of Jeroboam: 12:25–14:20

There is a certain similarity in the portrayals of Solomon and Jeroboam that catches the deuteronomistic perception of Israel's history. Both were invited into a relationship with God to which the proper response was fidelity. Both were accused of worshiping other gods and establishing other centers of worship beyond the Jerusalem Temple. The infidelity of both brought divine condemnation and retribution in keeping with the tenets of deuteronomistic theology. In order to account for the different fates of the two dynasties the deuteronomists invoked the unconditional promise to David of an everlasting dynasty, even if reduced from all Israel to Judah alone. Because of David's fidelity God would not revoke the promise despite Solomon's sin. Jeroboam was offered the same opportunity as David to secure an everlasting dynasty (11:38). He was unfaithful and his dynasty perished. When ultimately the exile overwhelmed the Davidic dynasty and Judah the deuteronomists then pointed to the equally overwhelming impact of Manasseh, a canker at the core of society (2 Kings 21:10-15; 23:26-27; 24:3-4).

The bulk of 1 Kings 12:25-32 is taken up with the details of Jeroboam's sin. Without prejudice to questions of redaction Jeroboam's reference in v. 28b can, at least at an early linguistic stage, be read to refer either to the one God of Israel or to more than one god (cf. 2 Sam 7:23 and 1 Chr 17:21). Given the singular reading (the one God of Israel), vv. 26-32 can be read as Jeroboam's move to counter the attraction of the Jerusalem Temple by establishing a cult of YHWH in Israel, chiefly at Bethel, as rival to Jerusalem. The prospect of his subjects going to Jerusalem to worship spelled political disaster for Jeroboam. In this understanding the golden calves were not an image of YHWH but symbols of the presence of YHWH, parallel in function to the Ark in the Temple. The deuteronomists, however, clearly understood Jeroboam's calves as signifying not YHWH but other gods. Note that in 14:9 Jeroboam is explicitly accused of apostasy. This portrayal of Jeroboam betrays a hostile attitude that is consistent with the highly negative evaluation of him by the deuteronomistic theologians in the subsequent chapters. For the deuteronomists statues of calves meant one thing—the worship of other gods. The famous parallel to 12:28 is in the story of the golden calf in Exodus 32 where the people make the same proclamation in v. 4 as Jeroboam—and where Aaron opts for the orthodox interpretation (v. 5).

The charge against Jeroboam is both nuanced and highly complex. It includes disobedience, the high places, the indiscriminate ordination of clergy, liturgical innovation, possibly apostasy, and certainly defiance of the law of centralization. Verse 30 implies that the people were willing accomplices in the sin of Jeroboam. The implication suggests an ironic contrast with ch. 12. The people freed themselves from the fiscal yoke of Solomon only to enslave themselves to the cultic yoke of Jeroboam. The subsequent deuteronomistic judgment formulas on each northern king regularly accuse Jeroboam of having caused Israel to sin. Such is the power of one ruler.

Two Prophetic Stories

The report of Jeroboam's initiatives is followed by two prophetic stories: first the story of the man of God from Judah in 13:1-32; second the story of Ahijah of Shiloh in 14:1-18. The story of the man of God is a classic example of the art of Israelite storytelling. It falls into two parts: vv. 1-10 and 11-32. In part one a man of God from Judah appears without warning and announces that a future Davidic king—Josiah—will desecrate the altar that Jeroboam has consecrated. The king's paralyzed hand and the shattering of the altar are dramatic signs verifying the authenticity of the prophetic word. In part two the focus shifts to the fate of the man of God. In a surprise development this prophet—who had seen the signs that so forcefully confirmed his mission and had expressed his complete commitment to God's directives—falls prey to a lie by a prophet of Bethel. This element of complication allows the story to open up the issue of the relationship between a prophet and God's word. The man of God disobeys the divine directives; while eating he is told by the Bethel prophet that he will pay for this disobedience. The strange manner of his death reveals the truth of the Bethel prophecy against him and in turn confirms the directives given him by God and the truth of his own prophecy. So the Bethel prophet has deceived a true prophet and himself prophesies truly twice (vv. 21-22 and 32). The manner in which the man of God silently goes on his way after hearing his doom and the assistance provided by the prophet who pronounces this doom lend poignancy to the story. Verses 11-32 probe the fragility of the bearers of the prophetic word and enhance its authority. Strangely, one prophet's lie and another's disobedience reveal the authenticity of God's word: they do not discredit it. All this serves in storytelling fashion to underscore the prophetic rejection of the altar in vv. 1-10, as v. 32 indicates. Verses 33-34 report that even this had no effect on Jeroboam; his refusal to repent resulted in the destruction of his dynasty.

First Kings 14:1-18 is a different kind of prophetic story in which brief narrative passages frame a long central prophetic proclamation. Jeroboam dispatches his disguised wife to the blind and aging prophet Ahijah to inquire about the fate of their sick child. His attempt at deception fails. The prophet identifies the visitor and tells her that because of Jeroboam's sins, above all the sin of apostasy (14:9), not only will their child die upon her return but Jeroboam's dynasty and Israel itself will ultimately perish. Bearing this message of doom Jeroboam's wife returns home and with cruel poignancy her child dies as she crosses the threshold of her house. The promise to Jeroboam had been conditional on his obedience (11:38); he disobeyed and, in ch. 14, he pays the price.

The stories in 1 Kings 13 and 14 tell of a prophet who rejected the altar that Jeroboam built in defiance of Jerusalem and of another prophet who condemned him for the sin of apostasy. Centralized worship in Jerusalem and exclusive fidelity to YHWH were the key criteria for the deuteronomistic evaluation of the kings of Israel and Judah. Jeroboam failed personally on both counts and, even worse, institutionalized this situation of sin in Israel—calves, priests, high places. The two stories are key elements of the deuteronomistic interpretation of the monarchy.

As in the case of 1 Kings 12:15 subsequent fulfillment notices support the interpretation. Chapter 15:28-30 claims that the conspirator Baasha's destruction of Jeroboam's dynasty fulfilled the prophecy of Ahijah. Second Kings 17:7-23 argues that the end of Israel was in accord with the word of all the prophets. Finally 23:15-20 reports how Josiah fulfilled the prediction of the man of God and destroyed the altar at Bethel as part of his program to restore centralized worship in Jerusalem.

Judean Kings During the Reign of Jeroboam: 14:21–15:24

It may come as a surprise to find that the text backtracks here to the reign of Rehoboam, last mentioned in 1 Kings 12:21-24. This backtracking technique is an organizational feature of the account of the kings of Israel and Judah. The technique is simple and follows the chronological system that records the length of reign of each king. Because Rehoboam, Abijam, and Asa of Judah came to the throne within the reign of Jeroboam it is convenient to treat them in sequence. In 15:25, the narrative backtracks to Nadab of Israel—who is first mentioned in 14:20—and begins a sequence of Israelite kings that reaches to 22:40. This is because all the Israelite kings concerned came to the throne within the forty-one year reign of Asa of Judah (cf. 15:10). From the point of view of coherence and unity this is an easier procedure than constantly switching from a king of Israel to a king of Judah or vice versa.

The technique of backtracking combined with the regnal framework (outlined in the "Strategy for Reading") enables the reader to follow the sometimes labyrinthine story of the divided monarchy until it ends with the exile of Israel in 2 Kings 17. With the help of the backtracking technique the reader can identify and compare Israelite and Judean kings of the same chronological era. In the metaphor of the national gallery it is as if the exhibits are arranged in bays on facing sides corresponding to the appropriate monarch of the other kingdom. The recurring elements of the regnal framework create an overall impression of unity and coherence as the visitor moves along the gallery while at the same time drawing attention to the distinctive features of each exhibit or collection.

The key element of the regnal framework is the evaluation of each king made according to the deuteronomistic criteria of exclusive fidelity to YHWH and centralized worship in Jerusalem. In the account of Rehoboam it is surprising to find the highly negative evaluation of Judah (14:22-24) instead of the expected evaluation of the king. These verses point to a difference between the portrayal of Israel and Judah. In 12:28-30 and again in 14:16 Jeroboam is accused of causing Israel to sin. As the deuteronomists saw it no king of Israel healed Jeroboam's breach of the requirements of fidelity and centralization. In Judah, by contrast, 14:22 states that it was the people themselves who sinned. No Judean king before Manasseh is accused of causing Judah to sin (cf. 2 Kings 21:9). As Jeroboam is blamed for northern Israel's end, so is Manasseh for Judah's.

In keeping with the deuteronomistic theology in the prophecy of Ahijah (11:31-39) each Judean king is compared with David as the model of kingship—negatively in the case of Abijam, positively in the case of Asa except for his failure to remove the high places (15:14, cf. 14:23). In deuteronomistic theology the survival of the Davidic dynasty in Jerusalem despite kings like Rehoboam and Abijam is explained as a legacy of the special relationship between God and David (15:4-5). The prophecy–fulfillment schema that surrounds the rise and demise of the northern dynasties of Jeroboam, Baasha, and Omri provides a telling contrast to the continuity of the Davidic dynasty in Judah, reinforcing the status of the promise to David. The combination of prophecy and the evaluation component of the regnal framework advances the deuteronomistic interpretation of history and give it a sense of overall unity. The evaluation formula also preserves the portrayal from the charge of determinism. The demise of each dynasty was prophesied but still had to be worked out in history: it came about because each king proved as guilty as Jeroboam.

As the story of Judah unfolds across these three reigns the picture provided by the deuteronomistic historians is of a troubled state, corrupted by sin and in need of reform, racked by civil war and at the mercy of the superpower Egypt. It survives on the strength of the bond alleged between God and David. Considering that these historians were most likely Judeans themselves their presentation shows a remarkable ability to look beyond tribal and national loyalties.

Israelite Kings During the Reign of Asa of Judah: 15:25–22:40

The narrative backtracks here to Jeroboam's son Nadab (cf. 14:20) in order to tell his story and those of a number of subsequent Israelite kings who came to the throne during the forty-one year reign of Asa of Judah. Between 15:25 and 16:28 the narrative describes the bloody demise of two Israelite dynasties (those of Jeroboam and Baasha), a seven day reign by Zimri, and the emergence of Omri as the founder of a new dynasty. The reign of Omri's son, Ahab, is the setting for a number of famous prophetic stories associated principally with Elijah. These stories occupy the bulk of the narrative between ch. 17 and the end of Ahab's reign in 22:40.

Nadab

The account of the reign of Nadab (15:25-32) is brief but of major importance for the deuteronomistic interpretation of the monarchy. Verse 26 records the first evaluation of a northern king as an integral part of the regnal framework. The evaluation is negative, accusing Nadab of behaving like Jeroboam his father and so perpetuating his corruption of the people. This same evaluation will be made in one form or another of every subsequent king of Israel; the sole unexplained exception is Shallum in 2 Kings 15:13-15 who receives none. The account of Nadab is also important because in v. 29 it completes the first prophecy-fulfillment schema for a northern dynasty. Baasha's murder of Nadab and the rest of the house of Jeroboam is identified as the fulfillment of Ahijah's prophetic condemnation of Jeroboam in 14:6-16. Similar prophecy–fulfillment schemas cover the dynasties of Baasha and Omri, and in a somewhat different manner, Jehu.

Dynasty of Baasha

The story of the short-lived dynasty of Baasha is told in 15:33–16:14. A negative evaluation in v. 34 is followed by a prophecy in 16:1-4 that condemns Baasha and proclaims the end of his dynasty; there is a clear echo here of the prophecy of Ahijah in 1 Kings 14. The violent death of Baasha's son Elah and his kin at the hand of Zimri is identified in v. 12 as the fulfillment of the prophecy. A feature of the account is the polemic emphasis on the sins of Baasha in v. 7 and again in v. 13; the latter includes the sins of his son Elah. This may betray later concern to stress that Baasha was an evil king in his own right and not just because he followed in the ways of Jeroboam as both the evaluation in 15:34 and the prophecy in 16:2 suggest. It is significant that 16:1-4 refers to Israel as "my people" twice. This provides a revealing insight into the deuteronomists who wrote in Judah after the collapse of the northern kingdom; censuring Baasha's grave infidelity, they affirm nevertheless that Israel remains God's special possession.

Dynasty of Omri

After a period of civil war Omri emerged victorious and brought a measure of stability to northern Israel. He built a new capital and founded a dynasty. His son Ahab married a foreign princess. From an economic and political perspective Omri would be judged a success. From the deuteronomistic perspective he was worse than his predecessors (16:25-26).

Ahab

According to the evaluation in 16:30-33 Ahab outstripped even his father in the gravity of his sins. Beyond the sins of Jeroboam he is accused of marrying Jezebel and worshiping Baal, evoking the condemnation of Solomon in 11:1-8. Ahab's wife Jezebel, from Sidon, would traditionally have worshiped Baal; her father, Ethbaal, was named after Baal. Verse 34 has Joshua's age-old and fearful curse on Jericho

(Josh 6:26) fulfilled in Ahab's time: a note of ominous foreboding.

Elijah and Baal (1 Kings 17–19)

The story of Ahab takes a dramatic turn in 1 Kings 17 with the appearance of the prophet Elijah. The contrast with the now familiar rhythm of the regnal framework is striking. He appears in the story without warning and with the minimum of identification—"Elijah the Tishbite, of Tishbe in Gilead" (v. 1). There is no information about his parents, no age, no chronology to show where he fits within the reign of Ahab. In the metaphor of the national shrine, the Elijah collection transforms one's perception of the whole Ahab exhibit.

We first see Elijah announcing to Ahab in 17:1 the coming of a drought that will end only on his say-so. The unfolding of this drama runs through to the end of ch. 18. It is followed by the narrative of Elijah's flight from Jezebel and his encounter with God on Mt. Horeb (Mt. Sinai). The final drama between Elijah and Ahab is the story of Naboth's vineyard in 1 Kings 21. Except for part of Elijah's prophecy in 21:20-24 there is little evidence of deuteronomistic language in this material. This suggests that the deuteronomists collected a number of traditional stories and arranged them with minimum reworking.

In 17:1 Elijah makes the bold claim that he is YHWH's messenger and that dew and rain—so vital for the fertility of the parched land of Israel—will fall only at his word. The verse looks back and forward. It looks back to 16:31-33 because Elijah's claim is a challenge to Ahab and Jezebel who follow Baal as the god of fertility. It looks forward to the subsequent narrative that will vindicate Elijah's claim. The story begins the process of vindication by describing the onset of the drought and portraying an Elijah who is true to his vocation. Elijah obeys God's direction to take refuge at the Wadi Cherith where there is water and God's ravens provide him with food (17:2-7). Elijah next obeys God's instruction to lodge with a widow in Zarephath of Sidon (17:8-16), a significant step because this is the territory of Jezebel and her god. In the homeland of Baal and in the face of the death-dealing drought God preserves the lives of Elijah and the widow. When Elijah raises her dead son to life in vv. 17-24 this foreign woman proclaims: "Now I know that you are a man of God, and that the word of the LORD in your mouth is truth" (v. 24). Her words form an adroit summary of the development of the story thus far. If one compares prophet and king this approval of the prophet contrasts with the deuteronomistic evaluation of the king.

In the third year of drought Elijah is commanded to go and tell Ahab that God will send rain (18:1). On the way Elijah meets Ahab's officer Obadiah and learns that the power of the state has been mobilized against him. Obadiah is himself at risk. Elijah is nevertheless true to his commission to meet Ahab. He confronts the king and in terms reminiscent of the earlier prophecies of Ahijah (14:6-16) and Jehu (16:1-4) charges Ahab and his father's house with apostasy (vv. 17-18). However instead of the accusation being followed by an announcement of doom as in the earlier prophecies of Ahijah and Jehu, Elijah here demands a confrontation with the prophets of Baal and Asherah on Mt. Carmel. Ahab complies and the scene is set for the drama that follows.

The core story (18:20-40) may have been originally independent: Ahab does not figure in it apart from summoning the people and the prophets; the abundance of water (vv. 33-35) contrasts starkly with the surrounding context of drought. The drama is a fine example of the storyteller's art. The one prophet of YHWH triumphs over the four hundred and fifty prophets of Baal. The trial of truth, with fire consuming the sacrifice, has no link to the context of drought—unless it evokes the imagery of lightning and storm. The long and elaborate liturgy by the prophets of Baal produces nothing; Baal is no god, a storm god who cannot produce a storm. Elijah's words express the meaning of the whole episode: the theophany of fire is a vindication. The trial is meant to demonstrate that YHWH alone is God and that Elijah alone is God's prophet and furthermore that it is God who has turned the hearts of the people back.

This theological claim is embedded in the movement of the narrative. In v. 21 the people will not even respond to Elijah's question. In v. 24 the people welcome the spectacle of a trial of fire. After watching the prophets of Baal the people respond to Elijah's invitation and move toward him; they even help him prepare his sacrifice. When the people see how God answers

Elijah they enthusiastically acclaim God and quickly respond to Elijah's command to seize the prophets of Baal. Elijah's execution of them is offensive to those modern readers for whom capital punishment is no longer acceptable; from the deuteronomistic perspective it is in accord with the requirements of Deut 13:1-5 and symbolic of the life and death struggle seen in apostasy. It is the reason for Jezebel's vow in 19:2 to have Elijah killed.

The final stage of the story is 18:41-46, which brings the narrative back to the ending of the drought. Ahab reappears in the narrative, invited by Elijah to eat and drink in anticipation of the coming of rain. With the subsequent approach of the rain Ahab is urged to leave immediately. In the midst of the storm the spirit empowers Elijah to run before Ahab's chariot all the way to Jezreel. The overriding impression is one of Elijah as a confident and power-filled prophet.

The contrast in 1 Kings 19 could hardly be more striking, with Elijah in full flight from a threatening Jezebel and plunged into suicidal despair. In chs. 17–18 Elijah gave strength and sustenance to those in need, was fearless in confronting Ahab, and triumphed over the prophets of Baal in spectacular fashion. Here he is fearful and despondent, powerless to sustain himself. The change evokes the theme of the fragility of God's messengers, seen earlier with the man of God in 1 Kings 13 and more distantly with Moses' despondency over the burden of leadership (Num 11:15). Elijah is revived by the angel's food; its marvelous qualities recall the food that sustained him and the widow in 17:14-16.

The scene on Mt. Horeb provides a fascinating contrast with the trial on Mt. Carmel. There Elijah questioned the people about their allegiance but they would not answer him, yet the theophany of fire transformed them from skeptics into believers. Here God questions Elijah who defends himself. Elijah experiences the power of God in wind, earthquake, and fire, but not yet God; then he encounters a uniquely real presence of God—beautifully captured in the phrase "a sound of sheer silence," the only occurrence of this phrase in the OT. None of this appears to change Elijah. His response to God's question is exactly the same as before (vv. 10 and 14). Despite the story's implication that Elijah was unaffected by this closely intimate encounter with the divine, the narrative goes on to a peak of prophetic claim. First, in the political realm, internationally Elijah is to anoint Hazael as king of Syria and nationally to anoint Jehu as king of Israel. Second, in the prophetic realm, Elijah is to anoint Elisha as his successor. The prophets claim the exercise of political power nationally and internationally, and they claim continuity in the exercise of that power. The consequences point to the dangers (vv. 17-18).

The narrative does not sustain this claim. Elijah finds Elisha, but instead of anointing him he throws his mantle over him—leaving it uncertain whether he is to be Elijah's successor or merely a replacement for the servant left behind in v. 3. Elisha encounters Hazael. Elisha's disciple anoints Jehu.

Ahab and Unnamed Prophets

Elijah does not feature in 1 Kings 20. Instead the reader finds a story in which unnamed prophets come to the assistance of Ahab who is under siege by an aggressive and arrogant Ben-hadad of Syria (Aram). When international diplomacy fails, God's prophets promise deliverance against the overwhelming power of the foreign king. The reason for the divine intervention is clearly stated before each battle: "and you shall know that I am the LORD" (vv. 13, 28). Israel is victorious and the roles are reversed: Ben-hadad is now in Ahab's power; Ahab spares Ben-hadad's life after he makes concessions that are advantageous to the Israelite king (v. 34). This seemingly practical and merciful manner of ending the war attracts prophetic condemnation in two stages. First the prophet who is killed by a lion for refusing to strike his fellow (v. 36) prefigures the fate of those who, like Ahab, disobey God's command (there is a parallel with 1 Kings 13:24). Second, the same prophet who demanded to be struck disguises himself and tricks Ahab into judging his own leniency as a dereliction of duty (vv. 35-43). For this Ahab's life and that of his people are forfeit. The story contained no instructions for Ahab about Ben-hadad.

Elijah and Naboth's Vineyard

Elijah reappears in 1 Kings 21 where the narrative switches to internal affairs in the northern kingdom and tells the famous story of how Jezebel took the lead role in plotting the death of Naboth so that Ahab could seize his vineyard. The unfolding of Jezebel's plot in vv. 8-14 invites reflection on the pervasive and destructive power of the state when it moves against its own citizens. She invokes the king's authority to gain the complicity of Naboth's fellow citizens. It is unclear whether they comply willingly or under duress. As instructed by Jezebel they arrange false witnesses, stage a show trial, and have Naboth executed. In v. 15 Jezebel commands Ahab to go and take the vineyard; in v. 17 God commands Elijah to go and tell Ahab that he will pay for the blood of Naboth with his own blood. When they meet Elijah pronounces doom for Ahab, his house, and his wife Jezebel (vv. 20-24) in a prophecy that echoes the earlier condemnations of the house of Jeroboam and the house of Baasha. In vv. 27-29 Ahab repents and God resolves to delay the destruction of his dynasty until the reign of his son. The theme of delay recalls Ahijah's prophecy against Solomon (1 Kings 11:31-39). There the delay was attributed not to Solomon himself but to the merits of his father David; here it is attributed to the repentance of Ahab himself.

Micaiah

In 1 Kings 22 Ahab invites Jehoshaphat of Judah to be his ally in a war against Syria. Before embarking on the campaign they consult their advisers. The story sets the one prophet of doom against the four hundred prophets who promise success and against king Ahab. The confrontation between Micaiah, Ahab, and Zedekiah, one of the four hundred, deals in storytelling fashion with the recognition of prophetic truth and obedience to it. The earthly royal court (v. 10) is set against its heavenly counterpart. Summoned for consultation, Micaiah vows to speak only what God tells him; surprisingly, on arrival he promises Ahab success as the four hundred have done. Just as surprisingly the king challenges the truth of this assurance (vv. 13-16). Menaced by the king, Micaiah reveals his knowledge of Ahab's doom and the source of his knowledge. He claims his presence in the heavenly court where God commissioned a spirit to go out and be a lying spirit in the mouths of the four hundred and so entice Ahab to his doom (vv. 19-23). Prophet is set against prophet: Zedekiah challenges Micaiah's claim to have the truth (v. 24); Micaiah retorts with a prophecy of doom for Zedekiah (v. 25). Prophet is set against king: Ahab sees through the false assurance and demands the truth from Micaiah (vv. 15-16); he is given it (vv. 17-23). Publicly Ahab refuses God's truth, ordering Micaiah jailed. Privately Ahab tries to evade God's word, arranging to disguise himself in the ensuing battle—in vain. He dies.

Although 1 Kings 20, 21, and 22 are three quite different stories they are bound together by their focus on Ahab and his downfall. It is announced first of all by the unnamed prophet in 1 Kings 20:42 who tells Ahab that he will forfeit his life because he spared Ben-hadad. It is proclaimed a second time in 21:20-24 where Elijah prophesies doom for the whole house of Ahab because of his evil deeds. It is proclaimed a third time by Micaiah in 22:19-23 after which the downfall of Ahab is told. Hence, 22:1-40 with its prophecies of doom for Ahab and the story of his death serves as a confirmation of Elijah's prophecy and the first stage in its fulfillment. The fulfillment is completed when Jehu destroys Jezebel (2 Kings 9:36-37) and the house of Ahab (10:17).

King Jehoshaphat of Judah: 22:41-50

In keeping with the procedure established earlier in the story of the divided monarchy, instead of passing immediately to the account of Ahab's successor, Ahaziah, the narrative backtracks to inform the reader about King Jehoshaphat who reigned in Judah during the time of Ahab. The evaluation of Jehoshaphat paints him in warm colors, matching the portrayal of him as a pious king in the story of the war with Syria (22:5-8). The report in v. 44 that he made peace with the king of Israel is probably based on the alliances in 1 Kings 22 and 2 Kings 3. Jehoshaphat is censured, like Asa before him, for failing to remove the high places and terminate worship there. This is a constant complaint against the kings of Judah until 2 Kings 18:4 where it is reported that Hezekiah removed the high places. The Davidic dynasty soldiers on as the Omride dynasty begins to crumble.

ISRAEL: NINTH CENTURY B.C.E.

Israelite Kings During the Reign of Jehoshaphat: 1 Kings 22:51–2 Kings 8:15

Besides Ahab two other members of the dynasty of Omri ruled over Israel during the reign of Jehoshaphat of Judah: Ahaziah and Jehoram. As with Ahab the account of their reigns is dominated by their relationship with prophets; for Ahaziah it is Elijah (2 Kings 1), for Jehoram it is Elijah's successor Elisha (2 Kings 3:1–8:15). Between the account of these two Israelite kings there is the story of the assumption of Elijah in the whirlwind and the transfer of his prophetic power to Elisha (2 Kings 2).

Ahaziah

The deuteronomistic evaluation of Ahaziah in 1 Kings 22:52-53 portrays him as a carbon copy of his evil father and mother. The account of Ahaziah's reign is almost completely occupied by the story of how he was condemned by Elijah for sending to the Philistine town of Ekron to consult Baal.

Elijah (1:2-17)

In this story Ahaziah is injured in an accident and sends messengers to inquire of Baal whether he will live. The angel of the LORD sends Elijah as a messenger to condemn Ahaziah for placing his life in the hands of Baal and not the LORD. Messenger meets messengers and in a foreshadowing of the outcome of the story the king's messengers return bearing Elijah's word instead of the word of Baal (2 Kings 1:6). Ahaziah's response is to dispatch soldiers to Elijah. For capture or consultation? The text is reticent—probably capture. There is a touch of irony in the contrast between the bedridden king and the prophet seated on the mountaintop. In the familiar three-stage structure of the folk story two companies of the king's soldiers are destroyed before the captain of a third company acknowledges the prophet's power and lives. In person Elijah delivers the same message as before. The king dies (v. 17a). King succumbs to prophet, idolatry to orthodoxy.

The information in 2:17b about Jehoram's succession is in conflict with that of 3:1. It is likely that 2:17b is a fragment from an alternative chronological scheme.

Elisha Succeeds Elijah (2 Kings 2)

Powerful insights into prophecy are expressed in the story of Elijah's departure and the transfer of his prophetic power to Elisha: independence of mind coupled with devotion to a master, the knowledge and authority required of a leader, the elusive quality of prophetic insight signaled by Elisha's need to see and the uncertainty as to what was seen.

Verses 2-8 portray Elijah responding to a series of commands from God that progressively separate him from his people and his land—from Bethel to Jericho to the Jordan. Three times Elijah tells Elisha not to follow him; three times Elisha disobeys, refusing to leave. Independence of mind is combined with devotion to the master. Three times bands of prophets are involved. Twice these question Elisha; twice he knows what they know and commands their silence. He has both the knowledge and the authority for leadership. The third time the prophets of Jericho witness silently as the two cross the river—into another realm.

Verses 9-12 tell how Elijah was separated from Elisha by the chariot and horses of fire and departed to heaven in a whirlwind. The text evokes the awesome yet elusive nature of the prophetic charism. Elisha requests a double share of Elijah's spirit (cf. Deut 21:17). For Elijah the request is "a hard thing" (v. 10): he may have extraordinary powers but he cannot create prophets. Instead Elijah offers a sign: if Elisha sees him departing, his request has been granted. In vv. 11-12 it is uncertain whether Elisha sees Elijah ascending in the whirlwind or only the chariot and horses of fire that separated them (cf. 2 Kings 6:17; 13:14). In vv. 13-14, Elisha strikes the water with Elijah's mantle and asks "where is the LORD, the God of Elijah?" The parting of the waters confirms that the prophetic charism has been transferred—whether at the sight of the departing Elijah, or at the sight of the chariots and horses, or at the grasping of Elijah's mantle, or at the striking of the water is left delicately opaque.

Elijah's mysterious departure outside the land recalls the mysterious death of Moses outside the land (Deut 34:6). The parting of the waters of the Jordan echoes the entry of Israel into the promised land in Joshua 3–4 and, more distantly, the crossing of the sea in Exodus 14.

In vv. 15-25 Elisha retraces the three stages of the earlier journey in reverse order: at the Jordan (vv. 15-18), at Jericho (vv. 19-22), and en route to Bethel (vv. 23-25). At the Jordan the prophetic band acknowledges that Elisha has received Elijah's spirit and nevertheless insists that a search party look for him. It returns empty-handed. Here we have the acceptance by the community and its confirmation when tested against experience. At Jericho deadly waters are made wholesome: those who revere Elisha are blessed. On the way to Bethel scoffing brats are mauled by she-bears. Animals and natural phenomena are commonly employed in storytelling cultures as signs of divine protection or punishment (cf. the lions in 1 Kings 13 and 20). Here the message is that those who ridicule a prophet like Elisha are cursed. Blessing and curse follow the prophet. The story ends with Elisha journeying to Mount Carmel, the site of Elijah's triumph, and then to Samaria, the seat of royal power.

Jehoram

Second Kings 3 begins with the standard introduction for a new king of Israel, in this case Ahab's son Jehoram. The evaluation in vv. 2-3 credits him with a measure of reform against the cult of Baal.

Elisha

Second Kings 3–8 is composed principally of stories of Elisha and his encounters with kings. These stories constitute a subtle critique of monarchy, contrasting the prophet Elisha and the ruling class. The focus is on Elisha's insight. He knows in advance what will happen and what should be done. He foresees the outcome of the Edomite campaign. He is aware of Naaman's needs and how to meet them. He knows the minds of kings and how to counter them. The story of the great lady of Shunem is different but again about great insight.

3:4-27

This is a complex story. At face value the present text pits an arrogant king against a powerful and ultimately less-than-forthright prophet. Jehoram forms a coalition with Jehoshaphat of Judah and the king of Edom to subdue Jehoram's rebellious vassal Moab and regain its valuable tribute. Water shortage causes a crisis. In his arrogance Jehoram promptly blames the LORD who, he claims, brought the coalition together. Jehoshaphat prefers to seek the LORD intentions from a prophet. Elisha is contemptuous of Jehoram but considerate of Jehoshaphat and with the aid of a musician he prophesies not only abundant water but also defeat for Moab and subsequent devastation. The water arrives—and deceives the Moabites. Israel devastates the Moabite countryside and traps its king in Kir-hareseth. In desperation he sacrifices his son on the wall of the city: a "great wrath" comes over Israel and they withdraw. In a surprising reversal the story ends with the army back in Israel, Moab still in revolt, its king still on the throne, and the source of Israel's tribute—the land of Moab—devastated.

The story can be read as a critical reflection on a ruler's claim to know God's mind. The claim is first voiced by Jehoram in v. 10 at the point where his campaign runs into trouble, and again in v. 13b. Elisha prophesies abundant water and also the devastation of Moab. Elisha's foreknowledge of events is a feature of these stories. The king assumes that the prophet sees what is good; the story allows for the possibility that what the prophet sees is the result of the king's folly. Moab is deceived by the water and becomes vulnerable to Israel. Jehoram pursues the short-term advantage and loses the long-term future. A storyteller would need to fill in some of the details here.

In relation to the campaign to regain control of Moab's wealth the question is: were Elisha's words a prophecy of victory or an ironic prediction that royal policy would lead to destruction of the very thing it hoped to possess? Supporting the ironic interpretation is the unexpected way in which the campaign ends (v. 27). The source of the "great wrath" is not identified, but the picture of Israel withdrawing from a devastated but now independent Moab provides a telling contrast to the beginning of the story. The king's campaign and his claim that God had summoned him leads to a train of events in which Israel ruins Moab's agriculture—the source of its tribute as a vassal—and loses control of Moab itself.

2 Kings 4

Moving from the international sphere to the domestic, this chapter comprises a number of traditions illustrating the prophetic response to people's need. Verses 1-7 tell how Elisha helped a widow of one of the prophets, empowering her not only to pay her debts but also to have the dignity of controlling her domestic affairs in the future (cf. 1 Kings 17:8-16, focused more on Elijah). Verses 8-37 provide the centerpiece with the moving story of Elisha and the Shunammite woman. Verses 38-41 and 42-44 give two further food traditions: Elisha makes the death-dealing to be life-giving (cf. 2 Kings 2:19-22) and the meager abundant (cf. 1 Kings 17:8-16).

The central story of Elisha and the Shunammite woman falls into three sections. The first describes how Elisha came to enjoy the hospitality of a "great lady" (Hebrew) of Shunem (vv. 8-10). The second tells how this hospitable woman who had no children and whose husband was old was promised a son by Elisha and in due course bore a son (vv. 11-17). The third section tells how her son died, how she sought Elisha's help, and how he restored her son to life (vv. 18-37). As the story unfolds the relationship between Elisha and the Shunammite woman recalls aspects of the relationship between Elijah and Elisha in 2 Kings 2. Elisha is now the prophet and the Shunammite woman cares for him. Like Elisha in ch. 2 she is a character of independent mind who makes her own decisions. Her hospitality prompts Elisha in v. 13 to ask what he can do for her in return, an echo of Elijah's offer to Elisha in 2:9. Her response indicates that she seeks no personal advantage. When Elisha promises her a son, her reply in v. 16 does not indicate that she expressly desires a child—a contrast to Sarah and other childless women in the OT.

Her reaction to the child's death is resolute and determined. She goes to Elisha and in a dramatic gesture of supplication brushes past his servant Gehazi and clasps his feet. In the story the gesture creates no discord with the earlier description of her as a "great lady"; it is a measure of her greatness that the death of her child produces such a response. Elisha dispatches his servant Gehazi to lay the prophet's staff on the dead child but the woman declares that she will not leave without Elisha. Her declaration may imply a deeper insight into events than that of the prophet; does she know in advance that Gehazi will fail? Her declaration also echoes Elisha's words to Elijah in 2:2, 4, and 6. Elisha hearkens to her word and follows her. The resuscitation of the child involves prayer followed by physical contact, as in the story of Elijah raising the widow's child in 1 Kings 17:17-24.

2 Kings 5

The story of Elisha and the "great lady" of Shunem is followed by the story of Elisha and Naaman, the "great man" of Syria (v. 1). Elisha the Israelite cures Naaman the Syrian of his leprosy. The prophet knows the cure for the military-political figure. Unimpressive procedures are effective where impressive ones were expected. The cure leads to faith in the God of Israel.

This narrative provides a penetrating exposé of the class divisions that permeated ancient Near Eastern society. Verses 1-5 give a cameo portrait of the society: the captured Israelite servant girl, the great man and his wife, and the king. Naaman enjoyed high favor with the king because through him the LORD delivered Syria. This is the narrator's comment. Naaman may not have known the LORD role in his life; this changes as the story unfolds. The great man is afflicted with leprosy but the servant girl assures him that he can be cured by the prophet in Samaria—a member of another class, the foreigner. Verse 5 indicates that the king and Naaman see the cure from the perspective of the ruling class; it will be a transaction between kings accompanied by the customary royal gifts.

Verses 6-19 tell how Naaman's encounter with the prophet leads to his deliverance from the barriers created by membership in the ruling class. In vv. 6-7 the arrival of Naaman with his letter of introduction exposes the powerlessness of the king of Israel. He responds by construing the letter as an impossible demand by the king of Syria seeking to cause trouble. This is the stuff of rulers. Elisha intervenes to retrieve a deteriorating international situation and to show that the prophet can do what the king cannot do. Naaman and his entourage arrive outside Elisha's house. Not the prophet but a messenger from the prophet instructs Naaman to bathe in the Jordan. Naaman's reaction in vv. 11-12 is vintage chauvinism: Elisha's less-than-personal touch and his instruction to take the Jordan waters is an insult to a Syrian of Naaman's class. The Israelite servant girl pointed the way to the cure; now Naaman's servants, wiser than their master, enable the cure to happen. With a deft piece of reasoning in v. 13 they retrieve the situation, convincing their master that Elisha's instructions are in reality justifiable; Naaman follows their advice and is cured.

A profound inner transformation follows the healing of Naaman's leprous flesh. He returns to Elisha professing that Israel's God is the only God and, in a surprising reversal, refers to himself as the prophet's servant (v. 15). When Elisha refuses a gift Naaman requests a gift from him—a load of earth. Before his cure Naaman despised the waters of Israel; now he seeks the soil of Israel, presumably on which to offer sacrifice to the God of Israel (v. 17). The barriers between Syrian potentate and Israelite prophet, between master and servant, have been broken down. The nationalism that expresses contempt for other countries has changed. One barrier remains: religion. Naaman is now a YHWH-worshiper in a society that worships Rimmon. Elisha's "Go in peace" implies that this is no barrier to the peace that the LORD brings.

Any comfortable conclusion that the rulers alone are the problem is demolished by telling the story of Elisha's servant Gehazi (vv. 20-27). He sees the cured Naaman departing and is filled with contempt and indignation. Naaman, "that Aramean," has been let off too lightly (v. 20). Gehazi proves as deft as the servants of Naaman in v. 13, but for his own selfish gain. He cleverly exploits his position as the servant of "my master" the prophet to become a master of deception, taking advantage of Naaman's generosity (vv. 22-24). The finale is fitting. Gehazi is exposed by his master; Elisha knows all ("Did I not go with you in spirit?"). Gehazi contracts Naaman's leprosy.

2 Kings 6–7

There are three distinct narratives in these chapters: the episode of the floating iron axe head (6:1-7); the story of an unsuccessful attempt by the king of Syria to capture Elisha (6:8-23); the story of the same king's attempt to take Samaria by siege and the raising of the siege (6:24–7:20). The relationship among the three narratives is at first sight obscure. In 6:1-7 Elisha restores a sunken axe head to a prophet by making iron do what it normally does not do: float. Just this aspect of Elisha's prophetic power features in the subsequent stories. Threatened with death in both cases, he turns the situations into life in unexpected ways.

In 6:8-23 Syria and Israel are at war; the story opens with Elisha as a spy who passes intelligence about the king of Syria's plans to the king of Israel. As the king of Syria learns from his officers in vv. 11-12, Elisha is an unusual type of spy; he is in Israel yet he knows the king's most intimate conversation. As happens with kings in other prophetic stories, the king of Syria is a slow learner. Faced with the devastating report of his officers he nevertheless responds in the way kings are accustomed to respond when their power is threatened; he sends a heavily armed unit to capture Elisha (the Hebrew in v. 14 points to a commando unit rather than a regular army). The irony of the situation can hardly escape the reader; the king plans the capture of a man who knows his every move.

In response to his attendant's alarm at the sight of the enemy surrounding Dothan, Elisha provides a reassuring word in v. 16 and a reassuring vision in v. 17: horses and chariots of fire (cf. 2:11; 13:14). The drama in the narrative is not about Elisha being in danger of capture but about what he will do to the enemy. In direct contrast to the time-honored practice of war Elisha does not unleash the horses and chariots of fire on the enemy to destroy them. Instead he temporarily blinds the enemy in order to prevent any violent action and then delivers Dothan by leading them away to Samaria (vv. 18-19). Once inside the capital their eyes are opened and the Syrians now see themselves surrounded. The malevolent Syrian king dispatched them to capture a prophet; this prophet now protects them from an equally malevolent Israelite king (vv. 21-22). Elisha commands that a feast be prepared for the Syrians before sending them home. The war ends without casualties. In a complete reversal of the way war is waged, the prophet brings peace where kings threaten death and destruction. The story has strong legendary traits.

Second Kings 6:24–7:20 is similar to the preceding story; it could be offering an alternative version. Elisha delivers Samaria from a dangerous siege in a way that completely upsets the expectations of how wars are won. On this occasion the situation is more critical than before; the king of Syria invades with his whole army (v. 24) and Samaria suffers extreme privation (v. 25). When a woman cries to him the king of Israel is powerless to provide anything "from the threshing floor or from the wine press" (v. 27). When the king learns of the gruesome pact between the woman and her companion he vows to execute Elisha (vv. 28-31). The king's hostility toward Elisha in v. 31 implies that he believes the prophet is the reason for Syria's invasion. As in the preceding story Elisha is portrayed in v. 32 as knowing exactly what the king plans. Elisha is not really in danger despite the hostile intentions of both the king of Israel and the king of Syria. This is evident in the way the subsequent narrative focuses on what Elisha does to deliver the city and the way in which this comes about.

Elisha, seated with the elders, calmly promises the frenzied king that within a day Samaria's privation will be completely reversed (7:1). When the king's captain expresses disbelief Elisha prophesies that he will see the abundance but not partake of it (v. 2). The narrative then tells the remarkable realization of Elisha's two prophecies. In vv. 3-8 four lepers resolve in desperation to desert to the enemy and on arrival discover an abandoned camp with everything still in place. The Syrians have vanished into thin air. Only the narrator and the reader know how the Syrians were panicked into fleeing the field (vv. 6-7). At first the lepers indulge in a frenzy of plundering but then repent and inform the city of the good news (vv. 9-10). Despite Elisha's prophecy (7:1) the king of Israel behaves as kings do in these texts: he is predictably skeptical and sends two horsemen to reconnoiter. For kings this is not the way wars normally end; there is no knowledge of how the Syrians abandoned the siege, no victory by Israel, no glory for the king. But there is the fulfillment of Elisha's prophecy when the plunder of the camp makes food plentiful and cheap. The fulfillment of Elisha's second prophecy against the skeptical captain involves a further reversal of the normal outcome of war. He is the only casualty; in an ironic echo of the earlier stampede of the Syrians he is trampled to death by his own people in their rush to get at the booty.

8:1-15

The text follows the arrangement of chs. 4–7: vv. 1-6 parallel ch. 4 by telling another story about Elisha and the Shunammite woman; vv. 7-15 parallel chs. 5–7 by telling another story about Elisha and the Syrians.

Verses 1-6 open with Elisha advising the Shunammite woman, whose son he raised to life in ch. 4, to leave Israel in order to escape famine. With the famine over, she returns to reclaim her property. This episode provides the setting for showing the transforming power of a story about Elisha. The king, listening to Gehazi's story about the prophet and the Shunammite woman, is moved to act on her behalf, ensuring that she regains her property and receives her revenue. Even unlikely characters such as the king of Israel can change under prophetic influence.

Verses 7-15 have Elisha in Damascus. Promptly the infirm Ben-hadad, king of Syria, sends Hazael to consult Elisha about his health. As in the preceding encounters with Syrians, Elisha is here portrayed as knowing what Hazael will do (vv. 11-12). The narrative draws an evocative contrast. There is the agony of Elisha, constrained by his prophetic calling to speak the truth yet weeping over the suffering that Hazael will inflict on the prophet's people. There is the cruel resolve of Hazael to kill. Ben-hadad dies as Elisha predicted (v. 10)—but at Hazael's hand. Hazael becomes king as Elisha foresaw (v. 13). Within the larger trajectory of 1–2 Kings, Elisha's encounter with Hazael fulfills in an unexpected way Elijah's commission to anoint Hazael king (1 Kings 19:15).

Judean Kings During the Reign of Joram of Israel: 8:16-29

The narrative recounts the reigns of the Judean kings Jehoram and Ahaziah, who came to the throne during the time of Joram. Three elements are of moment. The first is the accusation in vv. 18 and 27 that each followed the evil policies of the kings of Israel—the first time such an accusation has been made about Judean kings. The second is the claim in v. 19 that despite this evil the Davidic dynasty was preserved for David's sake (cf. 1 Kings 11:12-13, 34; 15:4): note however the weakening of Judah through the revolt of Edom (vv. 20-24). The third is the report in v. 29 that Ahaziah went to Jezreel to visit his wounded counterpart, Joram of Israel. This provides the setting for the story of Jehu.

Jehu: 2 Kings 9–10

These two chapters tell the story of Jehu's violent extermination of the house of Ahab—including Ahaziah king of Judah and his kin, tied to the house of Ahab by marriage—and his equally violent extermination of the cult of Baal. The story is followed by an evaluation of Jehu in 10:29-31. Both story and evaluation raise the vexed problem of evil and how to respond to it.

The story begins with Elisha instructing a disciple to anoint Jehu king (9:1-3) with the stipulation that when the job is done "open the door and flee; do not linger" (v. 3). Is this a hint at trouble to come? In keeping with the preceding stories is Elisha being portrayed here as a prophet who knows too well what kings do?

The disciple anoints Jehu and commissions him—in language reminiscent of 1 Kings 21:21-24—to eliminate the house of Ahab in retribution for the blood shed by Jezebel (9:4-10). When Jehu, anointed and commissioned, rejoins his colleagues the first question they ask is, "Is all well?" or "Is everything all right?" (the literal Hebrew of v. 11 is: "Is it peace?"). The same question is put three times by Joram: twice through his messengers (vv. 18 and 19) and then by himself when he meets Jehu at Naboth's property (v. 22). Finally Jezebel asks the question (v. 31). As the reader follows the furious pace of Jehu's revolt the question of peace reverberates through the narrative.

Is the question about peace in v. 11 to be taken simply as a conversation opener or does it touch the deeper issue of Jehu's purpose now that he has been commissioned? Joram's repeated question in vv. 18, 19, and 22 creates an air of tension. Jehu's reply is to claim there can be no peace while the baneful influence of Jezebel remains. He kills Joram and has the body thrown onto Naboth's property in order to fulfill what he claims is the word of God (vv. 25-26; a prophecy not mentioned before). Ahaziah, related to the house of Ahab through his mother (cf. 8:26), is also killed; however there is no claim that this is in accord with the word of God. Jezebel asks the peace question in v. 31 with biting sarcasm; she knows the answer and is prepared for her fate. Jehu claims that her demise is in accord with the word of God, this time attributed to Elijah (vv. 36-37; see 1 Kings 21:23).

In 2 Kings 10:1-10 Jehu orchestrates the extermination of Ahab's seventy sons in Samaria by terrorizing leading citizens into beheading them. His tactics recall those of Jezebel in 1 Kings 21. Their heads are brought to him in Jezreel where in an ambivalent statement he seems to disclaim any knowledge of the deed (v. 9b) and asserts that the deaths are in accord with Elijah's prophecy against the house of Ahab (v. 10; see 1 Kings 21:21-22, 24). This is the third time that Jehu proclaims the fulfillment of a prophetic word; surprisingly there is never mention of fulfilling his own commission (9:4-10).

More executions follow (vv. 11-17). According to Jehu's word to Jehonadab in vv. 15-16 this is done out of zeal for the LORD; according to the narrator in v. 17 it marks the fulfillment of Elijah's prophecy (cf. 1 Kings 21:21-24). Jehu follows up these seven deeds with a final act of zeal for the LORD witnessed by Jehonadab: the extermination of the cult and devotees of Baal, its prophets, priests, worshipers, pillar, and temple (vv. 18-27).

The story of Jehu's purge ends in 10:28. From this vantage point within the story the portrayal of Jehu appears ambiguous. He can be seen as a devoted Yahwist obedient to the prophetic commission to eliminate God's enemies. He can also be seen as a cunning and violent opportunist who conspired against his king (9:14), ruthlessly eliminated any potential threat to his power, and disclaimed responsibility for his deeds, justifying them by appeal to prophetic authority (cf. 10:9-10). Today's readers may find that the story of Jehu evokes modern ambivalences. Leaders of revolutions are acclaimed by some as liberators and peacemakers and reviled by others as killers and enemies of peace.

The deuteronomistic evaluation of Jehu (10:29-31) cuts through all ambiguity to make a clear statement: he did God's will but did not finish the job! The praise (v. 30) is sandwiched within an emphatic chiasm (vv. 29 and 31). First Jehu is condemned for not abandoning the sins of Jeroboam: the golden calves remained in Bethel and Dan (v. 29). Second, Jehu is praised for carrying out God's will in all that he did to the house of Ahab, the dynasty accused of promoting the cult of Baal (v. 30). Third, Jehu is again condemned for not following the Law of the LORD and not turning from the sins of Jeroboam, "which he caused Israel to commit" (v. 31). To have won the deuteronomists' unqualified approval Jehu would have had to complete his purge by razing the temples at Bethel and Dan, the symbols of Jeroboam's opposition to centralized worship in Jerusalem.

The deuteronomistic assessment of Jehu in 10:29-31 may strike us today, faced as we are with almost daily reports of violence at home and abroad, as inadequate and one-sided. It should be noted therefore that in Hos 1:4-5 the house of Jehu is condemned for the blood shed in Jezreel. Jehu's violent behavior in the story contrasts sharply with the disarming tactics of the prophet Elisha in the earlier war stories of 2 Kings 6–7 (cf. also 2 Kings 3). It also contrasts sharply with the controlled conduct of the priest Jehoiada in 2 Kings 11 (see below). It is a measure of the honesty of the ancient Israelites that they recorded conflicting responses to the problem of evil and did not try to conceal the conflict.

Athaliah's Attempt to Destroy the Davidic Dynasty: 2 Kings 11

This chapter provides a taut, dramatic account of how the violence that erupted in the northern kingdom under Jehu threatened to engulf the Davidic dynasty and Judah. The future of the dynasty and the security of Judah were preserved not by meeting violence with violence, but by the actions of a courageous woman, a loyal priest, and a faithful people. The contrast with 2 Kings 9–10 is unmistakable. Although 2 Kings 11 may have been slanted to Judah's advantage, this need not diminish the value of either story for reflecting on the vexed question of how to respond to evil.

Athaliah, mother of Ahaziah and daughter of Ahab, reacts to Jehu's execution of her son by attempting to exterminate the Davidic dynasty (v. 1). She seizes power for herself. Her attempt to bring the Davidic line to an abrupt end is thwarted by the intervention of Ahaziah's sister Jehosheba, who risks her life by hiding the infant Joash, Ahaziah's son, in the Temple for six years (vv. 2-3). Athaliah rules over Judah for these six years. The length of her reign is defined by the years Joash was hidden; the deuteronomists deny her even the acknowledgment of the regnal formulas.

In the seventh year the priest Jehoiada mounts a countercoup to reinstate the Davidic dynasty. Like Jehu, Jehoiada is a practical man who knows that conspiracies need the right support. He gets it by securing the loyalty of the guard (v. 4). Unlike Jehu, Jehoiada is portrayed wielding power not for himself but for the Davidic dynasty (vv. 5-16). He avoids bloodshed where possible and observes due propriety. Thus he arranges the changing of the guard to increase the protection afforded Joash. The arrangement also deprives the palace of military personnel, reducing the danger of a clash of arms. He has the heavily guarded Joash crowned king in the Temple according to proper custom. By the time Athaliah discovers the conspiracy her fate is sealed. The people are for the scion of David; she alone is executed, outside the Temple.

In v. 17 Jehoiada mediates two covenants: the first between the LORD and the king and the people, the second between the king and the people. In vv. 18-19 the people act in accord with these two covenants. They demonstrate their fidelity to the LORD by a purge of the cult of Baal; in contrast to Jehu they execute only its priest Mattan. They demonstrate their loyalty to the king by escorting him to the royal throne in the palace. The Davidic dynasty is restored, the cult is reformed, and Judah is spared an orgy of violence.

Joash of Judah: 2 Kings 12

Second Kings 12 is the account of Joash's forty year reign. The evaluation in v. 2 attributes his good conduct to sound instruction by Jehoiada the priest. Joash was seven when he became king and Jehoiada was presumably his tutor. Nevertheless the well-instructed Joash failed to abolish the cult of the high places—like his predecessors (v. 3).

The subsequent narrative points to a rather different relationship between the adult king and the priest. In vv. 4-16 Joash undertakes repairs to the Temple with apparent commitment; the portrayal evokes his mentor Jehoiada in 2 Kings 11. When the priests fail to carry out repairs it is Joash who turns instructor and Jehoiada and the priests who take instruction. In vv. 17-18 the contrast in Joash's behavior is striking. When threatened by Hazael of Syria, Joash buys peace by stripping the treasury of the Temple he so devotedly restored in vv. 4-16. His reaction recalls the earlier one of Asa in 1 Kings 15:16-20 when threatened by Ben-hadad of Syria. Joash's reign ends in assassination at the hands of his servants. The narrative does not comment; the reader may speculate whether his policy toward Syria was a factor in his violent death.

Israelite Kings During the Reign of Joash of Judah: 2 Kings 13

The Israelite kings here are Jehoahaz and Jehoash of the dynasty of Jehu. The way their stories are told is unique in the books of Kings: the story of Elisha's death occasions the closing and then reopening of the accounts of both kings. The account of Jehoahaz opens in v. 1 and closes in v. 9 with his death and the succession of his son Jehoash. The account of Jehoash opens in v. 10 and closes in v. 13 with his death and the succession of his son Jeroboam. To this point the text follows the normal arrangement for the account of a king's reign; after this the arrangement changes. Verses 14-21 tell how the dying Elisha gave two prophecies to Jehoash about Israel's struggle with Syria. Verses 22-24 then reopen the account of Jehoahaz but with no second closure. Verse 25 reopens the account of Jehoash; a second closure is to be found in 14:15-16 after the war between Jehoash and Amaziah of Judah. This arrangement makes the episode about Elisha in vv. 14-21 the central feature of ch. 13, framed on either side by accounts of Jehoahaz and Jehoash. Elisha is a key for understanding each king's reign.

According to 13:3-7 Israel was continually oppressed by Hazael of Syria and his son during the reign of Jehoahaz. Israel's oppression is mentioned again in v. 22 after the episode with Elisha. The repetition prompts the reader to recall the prediction made by Elisha to Hazael in 8:12; the prophet foresaw that trouble would come to pass. In 13:2-3 this is explained as divine retribution for Jehoahaz's adherence to Jeroboam's sins. The people's willing compliance is noted in v. 6. Two reasons are given for Israel's survival despite the oppression. According to vv. 4-5 it is God's compassionate response to Jehoahaz's prayer; the unidentified savior in v. 5 may be Jehoahaz himself. According to v. 23 it is God's loyalty to the covenant with Israel's ancestors.

The first section on Joash (Jehoash), 13:10-13, contains no report of these Syrian wars but alludes to Amaziah of Judah (see below). However, after the episode with Elisha in vv. 14-19 a report occurs in v. 25; Joash defeated Hazael three times as Elisha foretold. In v. 14 Joash recognizes that the dying Elisha still has the power that Israel so desperately needs (note the reference to chariots and horsemen). Elisha commands in detail the shooting of a victory arrow (v. 17); he commands with no detail the striking of the ground with arrows (v. 18). In the second case the king falls short of the unspoken prophetic expectation. Joash only strikes the ground three times and so is assured of only three victories. Israel's threatened situation will not be resolved. The strange little piece in vv. 20-21 about a resuscitated corpse draws attention to Elisha's life-giving power (ch. 4) that in future will no longer be available to Israel.

Amaziah of Judah: 2 Kings 14

Amaziah and Joash of Israel (14:1-22)

According to 14:1 Amaziah succeeded his slain father Joash of Judah in the second year of Joash of Israel. In line with most of the preceding Judean kings he is evaluated positively but censured for failing to remove the high places. Verse 3 claims that he modeled himself on his father but fell short of the model of all kingship—David.

On the domestic scene Amaziah's conduct mirrors that of his father. Verses 5-6 point out that Amaziah was careful to observe the "book of the law of Moses" (cf. Deut 24:16) in bringing his father's assassins to justice. His father showed a corresponding sense of propriety in the repair of the Temple (2 Kings 12). The international arena is another story. Initial success against Edom prompts Amaziah to challenge Joash. Amaziah is defeated and captured. Like any foreign conqueror Joash symbolically violates Jerusalem by breaking down part of the wall and ransacking the Temple. This war story is as much about Joash as about Amaziah, a factor that may explain the second closure of Joash's reign in vv. 15-16.

The spectacle of Israel and Judah at war does not augur well for the future. The peace that reigned between them since 1 Kings 22:44 has been ruptured; there is the danger of a return to the constant war that dogged their early relationship (cf. 1 Kings 14:30; 15:6, 16-22, 32). The reign of Amaziah ends with another parallel, this time ironic, between Amaziah and his father; he is assassinated, perhaps by the same faction that killed his father.

Jeroboam of Israel (14:23-29)

Jeroboam's accession marks the third generation of Jehu's dynasty and he receives the same negative evaluation as his predecessors. Verses 25 and 28 imply that Jeroboam enjoyed political success, something that is supported by the book of Amos which refers to the wealth of the capital Samaria during Jeroboam's time (e.g., Amos 6:4-6). According to vv. 26-27 this was not due to the power of Jeroboam but to a merciful God's preservation of Israel from destruction. In support of the argument that it was God's doing v. 25b claims that Jeroboam's success was the fulfillment of a prophecy by Jonah. Neither the books of Kings nor the later quite different book of Jonah contain this prophecy.

Israelite Kings During the Reign of Azariah of Judah: 15:1-31

Chapter 15 is dominated by the account of a number of Israelite kings who come to the throne during the fifty-two year reign of Azariah (Uzziah) of Judah, the second longest reign after that of Manasseh (2 Kings 21). The chapter begins with a brief account of Azariah. He is evaluated in the same way as most of his Judean predecessors: faithful to God but failing to enshrine centralized worship by removal of the high places (vv. 3-4).

The core of the chapter (vv. 8-31) tells of corruption, violence, and decay in Israel. Assassination is rife—Zechariah, Shallum, Pekahiah, Pekah; only Menahem and Hoshea escape. Zechariah lasts just six months (v. 12)—but long enough to fulfill the promise made to Jehu that his dynasty would rule for four generations. The first incursion by Assyria takes place during the reign of Menahem (v. 19). The superpower is bought off by taxing wealthy citizens, a politically risky move that suggests a desperate king. The situation worsens; Assyrian capture of Israelite territory and deportations occur during the reign of Pekah (v. 29). Pekah seizes power in the last year of Azariah and after a twenty-year reign is assassinated by Hoshea, Israel's last king. He will succumb to Assyria.

Judean Kings During the Reign of Pekah of Israel: 15:32–16:20

Two Judean kings come to the throne during the reign of Pekah: Jotham (15:32-38) and Ahaz (16:1-20). Of note in the account of Jotham is the report that God began to send Rezin of Syria and Pekah of Israel against Judah. Politically they were apparently attempting to press Judah into a coalition against Assyria. The text at 15:37 portrays this pressure as the LORD's doing, a sign of God's sovereignty over Judah's history, not dissimilar from earlier comments about Israel in 13:23 and 14:26-27. This crisis in Judah is the setting for the prophecy about Immanuel in Isaiah 7.

Ahaz receives the most negative evaluation of a Davidic king since Solomon (16:2-4). He not only followed the policies of Israel's kings as Joram (8:18) and Ahaziah (8:27) had done, but also passed his son through fire as the previous inhabitants of the land had done. The exact nature of the fire-ritual is debated, but clearly Ahaz has introduced to Judah an age-old abomination (see Deut 18:10 and 2 Kings 17:17; 21:6). According to 16:4 Ahaz was personally involved in worship at the high places, which previous Judean kings merely tolerated.

The narrative highlights two significant matters from Ahaz's reign. The first is his appeal to the Assyrians for help against Rezin and Pekah. The second is the construction of a new altar in the Temple modeled on one he saw in Damascus. Given the tone of vv. 2-4 a reader might expect an equally negative critique of these two actions. The narrative refrains from comment. The reader must weigh their meaning in the context. Did Ahaz's military policy expose Judah to Assyrian influence unnecessarily? According to v. 5, Rezin and Pekah could not conquer him. Was Ahaz prudently seeking the superpower's intervention for a speedy resolution of this regional conflict? Did Ahaz's altar enhance Temple worship or pollute it? The text implies that the altar was for the regular worship of the LORD (v. 15). Were the deuteronomists prepared to accept that even kings like Ahaz could be capable of some good?

Exile of Northern Israel: 2 Kings 17

The account of northern Israel's last king, Hoshea, and the catastrophic end of the kingdom is covered with surprising brevity: six verses in all. The text moves rapidly to the deuteronomistic explanation in vv. 7-23, the central feature of the chapter. The text then turns to the deported peoples brought in by Assyria to replace the exiled Israelites; Israel becomes a refugee, its land resettled by refugees displaced from other homelands.

The explanation unfolds in two principal stages. The first is introduced in v. 7 and concludes in v. 18. The second is introduced in v. 21 and concludes in v. 23. Verses 19-20 are an extension of vv. 7-18, providing a brief comment on Judah before reiterating the theme of v. 18. This is a complex text that draws together elements from the larger Deuteronomistic History; it may have been composed in several stages. Nevertheless there is an overall coherence to the interpretation.

The intensity and rhetorical power of vv. 7-18 evoke the metaphor of a trial. In vv. 7-11 the prosecution marshals evidence to show that the people acted in ways that were completely contrary to God's actions on their behalf; the prosecution concludes this part of its case by claiming that the people's actions provoked God to anger. Verse 12 takes another tack, arguing that their worship of idols was contrary to God's explicit teaching. Verse 13 anticipates the defense that ignorance excuses the accused by asserting that God had warned Israel and Judah by every prophet and seer; they had no excuse. Verses 14-17 then present evidence of the people's culpable rejection of God's teaching; the claim is again made that their conduct provoked God to anger. Because of all this God passed sentence of exile on Israel (v. 18). The collapse of Israel is thus explained in terms of the deuteronomistic understanding of sin and retribution—beneath it, the concept of act and consequence.

The sentence passed on Israel above is followed by a statement of Judah's sin, allegedly following Israel's example (v. 19). In the present text Israel's fate is reiterated as an example of the kind of retribution Judah faces (v. 20).

The trajectory of vv. 7-18 reaches from Exodus to Exile. Verses 21-23 focus on a critical part of this trajectory, the northern kingdom alone. They draw attention to two intertwined elements not covered in the earlier verses: the impact of Jeroboam's sin and the fulfillment of the prophetic word. The northern kingdom's sin is traced back to its first king, Jeroboam. The prophets announced that the kingdom would fall because of Jeroboam's sin; it happened as they foretold. The authority of prophecy invoked here reinforces the argument of vv. 7-18.

The interpretation of Israel's exile is followed by the account in vv. 24-41 of how the land was forcibly resettled by foreign deportees. The motif of marauding lions in vv. 25-26, found in some earlier prophetic stories, signals here that the LORD retains sovereignty over the land, a sovereignty that the king of Assyria acknowledges by returning a priest to teach the new population how to worship the LORD. The result, according to vv. 29-41, is syncretism. Normally such a thing is anathema but the reaction in this case is remarkably restrained. Instead of condemning these foreigners the text reminds the reader in vv. 35-40 of what it means to be an Israelite (with v. 40 referring to Israel, not the foreigners; cf. Nelson, *Kings*). The Samaritan sect with its own brand of Yahwism developed in the north; it is debated whether the text refers to this sect.

Hezekiah of Judah: 2 Kings 18–20

Judah survived the Assyrian onslaught that destroyed northern Israel, a factor that had a massive impact on Judean thinking. The extensive account of the reign of Hezekiah in Kings, the parallel account in Isaiah 36–39, and the version in 2 Chronicles 29–32 are a legacy of this thinking. A number of psalms celebrate the promise of an everlasting Davidic dynasty and the inviolability of Zion.

One might expect the deuteronomists to have seized the opportunity to drive home the view that sin brings divine retribution (the exile of Israel in 722) whereas fidelity is rewarded (the deliverance of Judah in 701). They do not; they tread gently. Certainly the introduction to the reign of Hezekiah could encourage this expectation. Hezekiah is evaluated as a righteous king who removed the high places that his ancestors had failed to remove, who terminated the worship there that his father Ahaz had actively promoted, and who trusted in God and kept the commandments (18:3-6). He was unique among the descendants of David. Verse 7 follows with the statement that God was with Hezekiah and that he prospered. The implication is that fidelity is rewarded.

The subsequent narrative, however, is more complex and nuanced. The text at 18:9-11 provides an account of Israel's exile parallel to 17:1-6. According to 18:12 the reason for the exile is Israel's disobedience of the commandments. Two differences from ch. 17 are noteworthy. Where ch. 17 speaks explicitly of divine punishment, 18:9-12 allows for natural consequences of corruption and decay within a society. Where ch. 17 speaks specifically of cultic sin, 18:12 speaks in broad terms that could include social injustice. Similarly Judah's deliverance from Assyria in 18:13–19:37 is not portrayed principally as God's reward for Hezekiah's fidelity. Reward is a factor but priority is given to seeing deliverance as a sign that the LORD alone is God (19:19). A similar theology is found in Exod 7:5 and 14:18 for God's deliverance of Israel from Egypt.

This story of Judah's deliverance is regarded by many scholars as a combination of three originally independent pieces. The first is a report in 18:13-16 of how Hezekiah paid the Assyrians to withdraw from Judah. The second (18:17–19:9a, 36-37) forms an envelope around a third (19:9b-35); they are prophetic stories with Isaiah playing a prominent role. They have a similar fourfold structure: (1) a speech from the Assyrian king, (2) Hezekiah's recourse to God, (3) a prophecy from Isaiah, and (4) realization of the prophecy. The three texts have been skillfully combined to create a story that maximizes dramatic and theological impact. It can be viewed as a drama in three acts or, in the metaphor of the gallery, as an exhibit in three sections.

The first section presents Hezekiah faced with the crisis of an Assyrian invasion and the capture of "all the fortified cities of Judah." His response is the time-honored one among Judean kings of buying peace by ransacking the treasury and Temple. This clashes with Hezekiah's image in vv. 3-8 as one who did right, trusted in God, and prospered. His policy of appeasement does not prosper for in v. 17 the crisis deepens with the Assyrians advancing against Jerusalem itself.

The second section covers the developments from Assyria's move against Jerusalem in 18:17 to a temporary lull in 19:8-9a; its conclusion (vv. 36-37) has been transferred to the end of the third section where it provides a suitable conclusion to the combined text. The Rabshakeh, a high Assyrian official, delivers two speeches from his king, one to Hezekiah (vv. 19-25) and the other to the citizens of Jerusalem (vv. 28-35). The speeches seek to undermine the trust in God of Hezekiah and the people. The first speech claims that because of Hezekiah's centralization policy God will not deliver Judah. The Assyrian implication is that God—like the people, presumably—is not pleased by Hezekiah's elimination of the high places. The king of Assyria claims that God has changed sides (v. 25). The second speech offers an Assyrian promise of land and prosperity and goes on to claim that God cannot deliver Judah. The background to the promise may have been the ongoing expropriation of land in Judah, condemned by the prophets. The Rabshakeh ends by asserting that the king of Assyria has never been overpowered by any god. The people should trust him—not Hezekiah, not God (v. 35).

Confronted by such power, Hezekiah proves a faithful king in contrast to his reaction in 18:13-16. He turns to the prophet Isaiah, asking that Judah, "the remnant that is left," be spared Assyria's mockery of God. The measure of true fidelity is to seek God's honor above all things. Isaiah as God's messenger assures Hezekiah of God's protection—"Do not be afraid"—and of God's sovereign power over the king of Assyria. His "Thus says the LORD" in 19:6 corresponds to the Rabshakeh's "Thus says the great king, the king of Assyria" in 18:19. Nevertheless his prophecy of what will take place is only partially fulfilled. There is an Assyrian withdrawal, apparently in response to information about Tirhakah of Ethiopia (19:9a; cf. also v. 7). But—in the present text, incorporating the third piece—the Assyrian king does not return to his land or fall by the sword. Instead he sends messengers to Hezekiah again to reassert his claim to power (vv. 9b-13).

The third section begins with what is now the third speech, dictated and delivered as a letter. This letter intensifies the assault on Hezekiah's trust in God by claiming that God has deceived him with empty promises of deliverance. Confronted by the taunt that his God is not only powerless but a liar, Hezekiah remains faithful. He turns directly to God, professing faith and praying for deliverance so that "all the kingdoms of the earth may know that you, O LORD, are God alone" (v. 19). His prayer is answered in a prophecy delivered by Isaiah. It comprises a refutation of the Assyrian king's arrogant claims (vv. 21-28), a sign that Judah and Jerusalem's future will be secure (vv. 29-31), and a promise of deliverance from the present threat (vv. 32-34). Jerusalem is symbolic. Here its deliverance and the survival of the Davidic dynasty are signs of God's favor (19:34). Later its destruction becomes a sign of God's wrath (21:10-15; 23:27).

The third section of the exhibit concludes with 19:35 fulfilling 19:32-34. With the Assyrian army destroyed there can be no attack on Jerusalem. The description of the army's destruction parallels elements of Exod 14:19-31. Transferred here, the concluding elements of the second section (vv. 36-37) report how the king of Assyria returned to Nineveh and was assassinated, fulfilling the prophecy in 19:7.

In the story of the Assyrian crisis Hezekiah proved a faithful king who trusted his God after an initial lapse. Second Kings 20 moves in the reverse direction, from fidelity to doubt. In a story of recovery from a near fatal illness Hezekiah is initially portrayed as a king whose prayer and protestation of fidelity lead to a prophecy's reversal and a promise of recovery. The text seems comfortable with the juxtaposition of prophecy and sound medical practice (v. 7). A doubting Hezekiah then demands a sign from God as assurance. God grants the sign and the shadow on the clock retreats but the demand has cast a shadow over the portrait of the king (vv. 1-11).

The shadow lengthens in vv. 12-19. Hezekiah gives a Babylonian delegation the grand tour of his realm; he is confronted by Isaiah who foresees the devastation that Babylon will one day visit on Judah and the Davidic dynasty. Because it does not affect him Hezekiah is unperturbed. His reaction highlights the difficulty kings have in seeing things the way prophets see them. Prophets see farther than kings.

Manasseh and Amon of Judah: 2 Kings 21

Manasseh

In the metaphor of the national shrine, the visitor now becomes aware that only one side of the gallery is lined with exhibits, those of Judean kings. In the text there is no synchronistic chronology to introduce the reign of Manasseh. The synchronisms were a consistent feature of the story of the two kingdoms.

Manasseh had the longest reign of any king of Israel or Judah—fifty-five years. According to the deuteronomists this was the king who set Judah on the path to destruction as Jeroboam had done earlier to northern Israel. There is no naming of Jeroboam in 2 Kings 21; nevertheless the parallels are unmistakable. Jeroboam, living in a divided kingdom by God's choice, chose to divide the kingdom religiously—by deuteronomistic standards. Manasseh, in a time of high material prosperity, opted for other gods, impoverished and barren religion—by deuteronomistic standards.

In vv. 2-7 Manasseh is portrayed implementing cultic innovations that destroyed what the deuteronomists regarded as authentic Israelite worship—just like Jeroboam. He contaminated its purity with foreign practices; he compromised its unity and centrality with a multiplicity of high places and altars; he used forms of mediation explicitly condemned in Deuteronomy (cf. 18:9-14); he profaned the Temple where God's name dwelt with an image of Asherah like the one Ahab had made. In vv. 8-9 the focus shifts to the people; they are accused of becoming willing disciples of Manasseh. Similarly in 1 Kings 12:30 the northern Israelites were accused of willingly adopting Jeroboam's cultic innovations.

In vv. 10-15 (probably a later text) the consequences of Manasseh's sins are spelled out, again paralleling Jeroboam. Because Jeroboam sinned and made Israel sin the prophet Ahijah pronounced judgment on him and the people (1 Kings 14:6-16). In the case of Manasseh an unnamed group of prophets declares that because Manasseh sinned and led Judah to sin, Judah will experience a fate similar to the northern kingdom's. The prophecy concludes by placing the people's sin within a larger trajectory of evil reaching back to the Exodus.

In v. 16 Manasseh is accused of being a mass murderer. Social justice is coupled with the emphasis on the cult. The primary concern is the cult, but it is not a blinkered view. A sharp awareness of social evil is evident here as in the earlier story of Naboth's vineyard (1 Kings 21).

Amon

Manasseh is succeeded by his son Amon who is portrayed as a carbon copy of his father. The implication is that the policies of Manasseh are firmly cemented in the kingdom of Judah.

Josiah of Judah: 22:1–23:30

In the metaphor of the national shrine, the gallery of the kings reaches the shrine's second grand dome where the monuments of the reign of Josiah, the final high point of the monarchy, are on display. Central is the book of the Law discovered in the Temple. The text of 2 Kings 22:3–23:30 is almost wholly taken up with the response of Josiah and the people to this book. There is little doubt that the book referred to is a partial version of Deuteronomy. According to 22:3 all that is recounted took place in the eighteenth year of Josiah's thirty-one year reign (cf. 2 Chr 34:3-8, differently). Except for the terse report of his death in 23:28-30 we have no other information about the events of his reign. The selective nature of the account is a measure of how deeply the deuteronomists were committed to the book of the Law.

There are two prominent themes in the text, and they are in tension. The first is the approval given to Josiah and his reform of Judah's cult in response to the discovery of the book of the Law. The approval in 22:2 is unqualified; it is reiterated in even more fulsome terms in 23:25. Of all the kings only Josiah and Hezekiah are compared favorably with David without qualification. The book of the Law is discovered during Josiah's program of repairs to the Temple; his devotion to the Temple existed even before the discovery of the book. On hearing the contents of the book Josiah consults Huldah the prophet, a move that recalls Hezekiah's recourse to Isaiah during the Assyrian crisis and David's consultation of Nathan in 2 Samuel 7. After receiving her prophecy Josiah and the people commit themselves wholeheartedly to the book in the covenant ceremony of 23:1-3. Josiah then purges the foreign cults introduced by his forebears, in particular Manasseh, and restores the pure worship of God in the Temple. He destroys Jeroboam's high place at Bethel, fulfilling the prophecy of the man of God in 1 Kings 13. He also destroys all other high places in the former northern kingdom. The restoration of authentic Israelite worship is marked by king and people with the celebration of Passover (23:21-23).

The second prominent theme is the surprising rejection of Judah, announced in Huldah's prophecy (22:15-20) and taken up in 23:26-27. It is only in these two texts that the two themes intersect. Huldah's prophecy announces the destruction of Judah because of its sins, with Josiah being spared the destruction because he was penitent and humble on hearing the words of the book. The passage in 23:26-27 declares that the reform has not altered the decree of destruction. It reinforces Huldah's prophecy; more explicitly it reinforces the prophecy of 21:10-15 that Jerusalem and Judah would be wiped out because of the sins of Manasseh.

It is quite likely that the theme of Judah's rejection was added at these two strategic points to an older text that hoped Josiah and his reform marked the dawn of a new era for Judah. The additions were made when that hope was dashed by Josiah's untimely death and the subsequent catastrophe of the exile. There are two pointers in this direction. One is in Huldah's prophecy to Josiah (22:18-20) that seeks to cast his violent death in a positive light by dissociating it from the punishment pronounced over Judah: he will be buried in peace. Before his unexpected death Huldah may have promised him blessing, given his fidelity to the book of the Law. Comment on and revision of prophecy is standard practice in the biblical text. The other pointer to later addition is that the people are reported to have participated fully in the covenant and the Passover. Yet these texts that speak of Judah's rejection have a very negative view of the people.

Granted that the story was revised to take account of Josiah's death and the exile of Judah, what meaning did the present text offer the reader who lived in the exilic or post-exilic periods?

There is no criticism of the reform as such. It remains a model of reform, of how king and people should worship God. Instead of seeing reform as a way of earning God's blessing there is a move to seeing it as an expression of devotion to the Law. The authority of prophecy is invoked to lend support to this move. According to the present text of Huldah's prophecy Josiah is to be spared Judah's destruction not because of his reform, but because of his penitent and humble heart at hearing the words of the book. The people are condemned by Huldah before the reform (22:15-17) and their condemnation is reaffirmed after it (23:26-27). The reform did not earn a pardon for the people. The real value of the reform is as a sign of commitment to the book of the Law and, through it, to God. This is fidelity for its own sake.

There is something noble, but also flawed, in this selfless commitment to the book. It accepts the view that the sins of parents, the impact of Jeroboam and Manasseh, are visited on subsequent generations, a view of limited application that Jeremiah and Ezekiel sought to correct for individuals (cf. Deut 24:16; 2 Kings 14:6; Jer 31:29-30; Ezek 18:1-32; 33:10-20). The treatment of Josiah's reform can erode confidence in the power of human beings to effect change and give the impression that God is capricious. Deuteronomistic theology provides a penetrating insight into Israel's relationship with God. Like any theology, however, it is limited by its parameters and by the sheer scope and complexity of human experience and divine mystery.

Last Four Kings and Exile of Judah: 23:31–25:30

After Josiah there is only the story of the end of Judean kingship, the short final gallery of the national shrine. Four kings reign, all descendants of Josiah. Their judgment formulas form a cluster differing notably from those before. The reform is abandoned. The narrative has been carefully arranged to portray the role of each king in Judah's decline and fall. Beyond the evaluation of each king the fulfillment of prophecies is noted at strategic points in the narrative. Close parallels to parts of 23:31–25:30 can be found in Jeremiah 39 and 52.

Jehoahaz

Josiah's son Jehoahaz foreshadows, in his vassalage to Egypt, the subsequent fate of the Davidic dynasty under the Babylonians. He becomes a pawn of Egypt, is eventually exiled there and dies. In 25:25-26 Judeans flee to Egypt after the assassination of the governor by Ishmael, a surviving member of the royal family. There may be a touch of irony in the way these two accounts of exile in Egypt frame the central account of exile in Babylon. Going to Egypt implies the reversal of the Exodus (cf. Deut 17:16).

Jehoiakim

Egypt installs Jehoiakim, son of Josiah, as the replacement vassal. When the Babylonians appear on the scene he is initially compliant, then rebellious. Their response is to send other vassal armies to bring Judah into line (24:2)—a familiar superpower tactic. The move is interpreted by the deuteronomists as the fulfillment of prophecy and as retribution for the sins of Manasseh (24:3-4). It is the beginning of the end for Judah.

Jehoiachin

Jehoiakim is succeeded by Jehoiachin, grandson of Josiah, who now has to face the Babylonian army itself. He and the royal household surrender; he survives and is taken to Babylon. It is reported in 25:27-30 that he enjoyed the king of Babylon's favor. This may be a vindication of Gedaliah's recommendation in 25:24. The Babylonians ransack the Temple and royal treasury, prompting a further claim about the fulfillment of prophecy (24:13). The reference is uncertain; it may be Isaiah's prophecy in 2 Kings 20:17.

Zedekiah

The Babylonians replace Jehoiachin with Zedekiah his uncle, who rebels, precipitating the third and final Babylonian invasion. Before the end is narrated it is foreshadowed that the disaster is divine retribution for the sins of Jerusalem and Judah (24:20). The Babylonians capture Zedekiah, execute his sons before his eyes, blind him, and take him into exile. For the Babylonians there will be no more kings of Judah.

The narrative of the fall of Judah is begun. The Babylonian chronology replaces the Judean one in 25:8, a sardonic allusion to a "new era" for Judah. The symbols of statehood—Temple, palace, city—are destroyed and key personnel executed. Nebuchadnezzar appoints Gedaliah as governor in Mizpah, not in Jerusalem. His policy is to "serve the king of Babylon, and it shall be well with you" (25:24). His assassination by Ishmael, a member of the royal family, leads to further disruption and flight. In contrast King Jehoiachin, who surrendered to the king of Babylon, enjoys favor in exile and dines at the royal table.

The story of Judah concludes without comment, in contrast to the long reflection on the end of the northern kingdom. Does this imply that the deuteronomists had not closed the book on Judah and that they looked to a future independent of Babylon? Were the declarations of Judah's end in 21:10-15, 22:15-20, and 23:26-27 regarded as enough? As regards the Davidic dynasty does the ambiguity of Jehoiachin's status in Babylon function as a sign of hope for David's dynasty in Jerusalem? The Deuteronomistic History concludes without cancellation of the promise to David of an enduring dynasty. Hope is not quenched. Nevertheless Jehoiachin's situation recalls that of Mephibosheth in 2 Samuel 9. The only survivor of Saul's line dined at David's table for the rest of his life. Is there a parallel to be drawn here? As it ended for the house of Saul, has it ended for the house of David?

BIBLIOGRAPHY

Brueggeman, Walter. *I Kings. II Kings.* Atlanta: John Knox, 1982.

Cogan, Mordechai, and Hayim Tadmor. *II Kings.* AB 11. Garden City, N.Y.: Doubleday, 1988.

DeVries, Simon J. *1 Kings.* WBC 12. Waco, Tex.: Word Books, 1985.

Holloway, Steven W. "Kings, Book of, 1–2." *ABD* 4.69–83.

Jones, Gwilym H. *1 and 2 Kings.* 2 vols. NCBC. Grand Rapids: Eerdmans, 1984.

Nelson, Richard D. *First and Second Kings.* Interpretation. Louisville: John Knox, 1987.

Noth, Martin. *The Deuteronomistic History.* JSOT.S 15. 2nd ed. Sheffield: Sheffield Academic Press, 1991. German original 1943.

O'Brien, Mark A. *The Deuteronomistic History Hypothesis: A Reassessment.* OBO 92. Fribourg, Switzerland: Universitätsverlag, 1989.

Walsh, Jerome. *1 Kings.* Berit Olam. Collegeville: The Liturgical Press, 1996.

Introduction to 1 and 2 Chronicles, Ezra–Nehemiah

Enzo Cortese

Introductory Questions

There are those who believe that these books constitute a single work, "The Chronicler's Opus" (Martin Noth). Today some specialists maintain that Ezra and Nehemiah are by a different author than that of Chronicles. While we are refraining from taking a definitive position concerning this stylistic-literary problem, we maintain that all of these books must be considered together, following the order given in the title and not that of the Hebrew Bible (Ezra, Nehemiah, Chronicles), for the reasons we shall present in the course of this study. The name "Chronicles" is more a translation of the Hebrew *dibre hajjamim* than of the Greek *paralipomenon* which means "things left out" (from the parallel books Samuel and Kings). The division of Chronicles into two books, done belatedly (in 1448), brings the first to a suitable close with the death of David and starts the second with the reign of Solomon. Ezra and Nehemiah are the titles of those books in Hebrew. The names they bear in the ancient versions have caused confusion.

In the Hebrew Bible, Ezra, Nehemiah, and Chronicles come after Daniel and are the last in the canon. In the Greek and Latin Bibles they come at the end of the historical books, before the deuterocanonical ones (Tobit, Judith, and finally 1 and 2 Maccabees) and Esther, and before the wisdom and prophetic books of the OT. [See also the article "The Deuterocanonical Writings."] These books, especially Ezra and Nehemiah, were found at Qumran, yet in antiquity they were rather the object of attention for scholars and were not used very much by the people, not even in the liturgy. For the Talmud and the Mishna, Chronicles is a book for the learned and not for the people; this judgment did not encourage access to it even in exegesis, whether Jewish or Christian, in the following centuries. Ezra and Nehemiah, then, together with Daniel, are the only books of the OT without a Targum.

Nonetheless, the personages of Ezra and Nehemiah are not ignored by Judaic tradition. Sirach, in his praise of David (Sir 47:8-11) shows his knowledge of Chronicles' version of events and, after praising the priest Jeshua and the reconstruction of the Temple, thereby displaying his knowledge of the book of Ezra, he cites more explicitly the memory of Nehemiah (49:13), lauding him for the rebuilding of the walls. It is true that he does not praise Ezra, but this should not arouse any special suspicion. The basic theme of these closing praises seems to be the material rebuilding of the Temple and the walls. It should also be kept in mind that, as a consequence of the redaction at hand, the two figures are not only made to be contemporaries but are even superimposed, at least in the actions dealing with mixed marriages, the proclamation of the Law, and the inauguration of the walls. Thus we can also find in the same period in Jewish tradition some who, favoring Nehemiah, also attribute to him the redaction of the Law, the specific work of Ezra (2 Macc 2:13) and apparently even the deeds of Zerubbabel (2 Macc 1:18-36!) and some who, suitably admiring Ezra as the great codifier of the traditions and institutions of Judaism, speak only and emphatically about him: for example, the two apocrypha of Ezra. The apocalypse describes Ezra as dictating for forty days all the books of the Hebrew canon and seventy other apocryphal books. There are also two other apocrypha of Ezra written by Christians (with a curse on the synagogue), which shows that he was an important personage for them as well. Flavius Josephus makes much use of Chronicles and of Ezra–Nehemiah, and keeps the books in the chronological order they have in the current version. [See also the article "Interpretation of the Bible Within the Bible Itself."]

In the modern era 1 and 2 Chronicles were often seen as a useless repetition of the Deuteronomic history and Ezra–Nehemiah as the manifestation of the closing of Judaism, set in contrast to the cultural and religious openness of Hellenism. Further difficulty was created by the great chronological and historical confusion existing in Ezra–Nehemiah and the trouble this causes for anyone not totally dedicated to deciphering it, as well as the long and frequent lists of proper names of persons or of geographical locations. In the original language they do not have the cadence and the classic style of the deuteronomic historical work or of the most ancient books. They are written in a new Hebrew of an Aramaicizing sort, and part of Ezra is even written in Aramaic (Ezra 4:8–6:18 and 7:12-26). Now, however, scholars have overcome doubts created by these difficulties and in recent decades have begun to study Chronicles, Ezra, and Nehemiah in depth. This is perhaps because of the desire to understand the Judaism of Jesus' time, something impossible without consideration of the premises of the preceding post-exilic centuries; or perhaps because it is perceived that the whole post-exilic epoch is an indispensable link in the chain that begins in the monarchic and even pre-monarchic era and reaches to present-day Judaism. Moreover, according to a very debatable recent vogue, the post-exilic epoch would be the principal phase not only for the redaction of the books of the OT but also for the emergence of traditions and even of prime documents that in reality should be considered much more ancient.

Content of Chronicles

The first book provides an ethnic-geographic framework over nine chapters, followed by the story of David. The second book in its first nine chapters recounts the history of the reign of Solomon, and then tells the whole history of the kingdom of Judah up to its destruction, without considering the northern kingdom. In order to grasp the specific message of Chronicles in relation to that of the deuteronomic historical work we can take the verb *drš,* understood in the sense of seeking God, as a thread of continuity. It appears frequently in Deuteronomy, but of the two parallel narratives only the Chronicler's makes it a fundamental element of its structure. Saul is condemned because he did not seek God in the right manner (1 Chr 10:13-14; 13:3). David continually urges the search for God (1 Chr 15:13; 16:11; 21:30; 22:19; 28:8-9). Solomon begins his reign in the same way (2 Chr 1:5). Before looking at the use of *drš* in this last phase of the story, by glancing ahead we notice that Ezra too uses this verb that is very meaningful to the Chronicler. Indigenous foreigners want to collaborate in the construction of the Temple because it helps them as well to seek God (Ezra 4:2). God is sought at the Passover after the rebuilding of the Temple (6:21). Ezra is praised for this (7:10). The other two texts (Ezra 9:12, 10:16), however, use the verb with a different meaning, on the one hand more generic and on the other more particular, as to a large extent in earlier biblical literature.

In the last section of the Chronicler's account a special use of *drš* begins, characterizing the laudable actions of Asa (2 Chr 14:3, 6b; 15:2, 12-13). However, his life is concluded with a criticism that uses the verb in the negative: 2 Chr 16:12. Even more abundant and always positive is its use in the evaluation of Jehoshaphat (17:3-4; 18:4, 6-7; 19:3; 20:3; 22:19). Then the verb disappears in the dark period of the alliances with the northern Omridians. After two cases in which the verb returns to its special meaning as in the ancient texts (2 Chr 24:6, 22) it reappears in the Chronicler's typical use: first in the negative, for Amaziah (2 Chr 25:15, 20), then in the affirmative for Uzziah/Azariah (2 Chr 26:5b). It is not used for Jotham and Ahaz, but reappears abundantly and only for Hezekiah (2 Chr 30:19; 31:21; in the other sense also in 31:9; 32:31) and Josiah (2 Chr 34:3, 21, 26).

From this literary feature alone it is possible to gain an idea of the Chronicler's concept of the history of the kingdom of Judah after Solomon. In general he does not differ much from the deuteronomic account in his evaluation of the kings. Among the principal differences we should above all point out the Chronicler's greater indulgence. We have already noted this in regard to Chronicles' silence on the faults of David and Solomon. Rehoboam, while being at fault for having embittered Israel and provoked the schism, becomes a patron for the Levites of the North and for all Israelites taking refuge in Jerusalem (2 Chronicles 11) and when he sins he does penance (2 Chronicles 12). For Abijah, in ch. 13, the corresponding deuteronomic condemnation (1 Kings 15:3) is lacking. Asa and Jehoshaphat are even more highly valued than in the deuteronomic text. For Asa the Chronicler adds nearly two whole chapters to the deuteronomic account (1 Kings 15:11-24), elaborating a positive judgment on him and transforming him in the account of a first great reform (2 Chronicles 14–15). In chs. 17 and 19, new in comparison with the deuteronomic story, a juridical-military reform based on the book of the Law and the Levites is attributed to Jehoshaphat. In another unique chapter (2 Chronicles 20), not found in the parallel deuteronomic story, a miraculous victory of his, achieved only by prayer, is described, embellished by the usual liturgical-musical contribution of the Levites. In substance the Chronicler's judgment on Amaziah, Uzziah/Azariah, Jotham, and Ahaz coincides with the deuteronomic one, apart from the new episodes of 2 Chr 25:5-10, 12-16 for the first, 26:6-20 for the second, and 28:5-15 for the fourth.

The greatest emphasis, however, is placed by the Chronicler on the figures of Hezekiah and Josiah. While the deuteronomic account is very brief in its description of the reform of worship by the former and verbose in recounting the siege of Sennacherib, where we find two parallel accounts (in 2 Kings 18–19), the Chronicler spends three whole chapters talking about the restoration of the Temple, other reforms (including yet another Levitical reorganization), the renewal of the covenant and of Passover (2 Chronicles 29–31). While a reproach is leveled at Hezekiah (32:25-30), in the Chronicler's view it is only to explain the king's illness, mentioned in one verse (32:24) corresponding to 2 Kings 20:1-11. The positive evaluation of the kings of Judah is especially evident with regard to Manasseh, for whom a conversion is devised as well as a reform in order to explain his long reign.

The deuteronomic reform of Josiah is divided into two by the Chronicler and made to begin with his restoration of the Temple. The reservation about Josiah in 2 Chr 34:21-22 is stated only to explain his tragic death. In the final chapter a positive attitude toward the last kings is not to be expected. There the Chronicler follows his source. Moreover, it can be said that he is more reticent in describing the destruction, particularly that accompanying the first deportation (as in 2 Kings 24:10-17) and the preceding invasions (2 Kings 24:2-7); everything is summarized in 36:16-20.

Another peculiarity of the Chronicler's history is the multiplicity of prophets and their interventions, all of which are indeed rather amorphous in comparison with those read in the parallel deuteronomic history. Here we provide a list only of the beginning of these new interventions, absent in the parallel deuteronomic history: Shemaiah (2 Chr 12:5, 7), Azariah (2 Chr 15:16); Hanani (2 Chr 16:7), Jehu of Hanani (2 Chr 19:1-2), Jahaziel (2 Chr 20:14), Eliezer (2 Chr 20:37), the letter of Elijah (2 Chr 21:12), Zechariah (2 Chr 24:20), two anonymous prophets (2 Chr 25:7 and 15), and Oded (2 Chr 28:9). In contrast to the deuteronomic account our author also cites Jeremiah (36:12), while the prophets he does not mention are those found in the deuteronomic history of the North, which he omits; among these only Elijah is recalled, through the device of the letter.

Ezra and Nehemiah

In Ezra there are two (or three) parts:

(a) The first repatriation, with the important list of Ezra 2 and the reconstruction of the altar (3:1-6) and the Temple (3:7–6:22).

(b) The repatriation and the work of Ezra, which extends at least from ch. 7 to ch. 10. We say "at least" because Ezra's activity is also mentioned in (c) Nehemiah 8. Also, the autobiography of Nehemiah—aside from Nehemiah 7, which is identical to Ezra 2 and probably an addition, in Nehemiah 8, for the reason indicated, and its appendixes (Nehemiah 9–10), can be divided into two parts corresponding to his two missions in Jerusalem. The first part (chs. 1–6) describes above all his repatriation and the emotion-filled rebuilding of the walls of Jerusalem; in chs. 11–12 is the conclusion (12:27-47), set amid long lists. His interventions in social matters in Nehemiah 5 are also important. Only ch. 13 speaks about the second mission.

While the summary of these two books is less complicated than that of the preceding ones, which also had to be compared to the parallel deuteronomic history, the literary and historical status and problems of Ezra–Nehemiah are in contrast very complicated. We will start with the main problem, something that requires a good deal of space.

According to the current arrangement of the material, the first personage to arrive in Jerusalem is Ezra (Ezra 7–9). Then Nehemiah arrives for the rebuilding of the city (Nehemiah 1–6). Ezra then promulgates the Law (Nehemiah 8) and Nehemiah is busy with the repopulating of the city and other problems (Nehemiah 11–13). Despite the recent and perhaps prevalent opinion that considers this order of things as settled, we prefer a different reconstruction of events, all the more so because another inversion of the true chronological order is also found in Ezra 4, and this time without debate; thus the redactors are not very concerned with the historical order of things. Indeed, after the building of the altar and the foundations of the Temple under Darius (Ezra 3), as the work is going on, in Ezra 4, an account is given of the difficulties posed by indigenous foreigners who wanted to collaborate in the undertaking; then mention is unexpectedly made in 4:6 of other obstacles raised by the indigenous foreigners who, by writing to Artaxerxes, want to hinder the reconstruction of the city walls. However, the obstacles that the context talks about are those of the reconstruction of the Temple, not of the walls, and they arise under Darius (4:5, 24) and not under Artaxerxes.

In Ezra 5–6 the account of the reconstruction of the Temple under Darius, at the urging of the prophets Haggai and Zechariah, continues. It is evident that some redactor has caused an anachronistic leap forward in the narration with the insertion of 4:6-23, because whichever Artaxerxes is in question we find ourselves at least twenty years after the epoch of Darius.

With respect to the other historical confusion, the main one, A. von Hoonacker in 1870 had proposed a reconstruction that we, prescinding from the lists intermingled among the accounts, reformulate in this manner:

(a) Ezra 1:1–4:5 + 5:1–6:22: under Darius I (522–486 B.C.E.) Zerubbabel rebuilds the Temple (520–510 B.C.E.).

(b) Nehemiah 1–6, 11–12: under Artaxerxes I (465–423 B.C.E.) Nehemiah carries out his mission. The episode narrated in Ezra 4:6-24 could be from this period.

(c) Ezra 7–10 and Nehemiah 8 (–10): under Artaxerxes II (404–358 B.C.E.) Ezra struggles against mixed marriages and (Nehemiah 8) promulgates the Law.

One probable cause of the chronological confusion created by the redactor is the misidentification of the two Artaxerxes. With this confusion in his head he has Ezra arrive first in Jerusalem, because in Ezra 7:1-10 it is stated that "in the reign of Artaxerxes" he departed from Babylon "in the [king's] seventh year" (vv. 7-8). He places Nehemiah afterwards, since in the memoirs it is stated that he came to Jerusalem in the twentieth year of Artaxerxes (Neh 2:1). The primitive book or document of Ezra probably already had the account of the rebuilding of the Temple, which occurred long before his mission. Now the redactor has thought it best to insert Ezra 4:6-23, namely the documents on the hostility of the indigenous people that existed during the Nehemian epoch and no longer during the time of Ezra, thus preparing the ground for the insertion of Nehemiah's autobiography.

The hypothesis presented here and the proposed explanation could find confirmation in the abovementioned apocryphal book of Ezra: there we find at the outset the final part of Chronicles (2 Chronicles 35–36) and Ezra 1:1-11. Immediately afterward comes Ezra 4:7-23 (and the apocryphal story of the contest among the pages of Darius: 3:1–4:63). The apocryphal book then provides (5:7-46) the list in Ezra 2 and continues narrating the rebuilding of the altar and the Temple and the tentative rebuff of the indigenous people from participating in the rebuilding (5:47-73), parallel to Ezra 3:1–4:5. Immediately afterward, in ch. 6, the apocryphal book recounts the rebuilding of the Temple at the urging of Haggai and Zechariah, as in Ezra 5–6, and continues with the remainder of canonical Ezra. It concludes with Neh 7:72–8:13. No other passage from Nehemiah is included in this apocryphal book.

This could confirm that the autobiography of Nehemiah was inserted by the redactor and that he, confusing the two Artaxerxes, has placed Ezra before Nehemiah and anachronistically anticipated, in a different location from that in the apocryphal work, the episode of the request of the indigenous people to participate in the reconstruction of the walls (Ezra 4:6-23) in the context of the reconstruction of the Temple. The shift of Ezra's arrival to the beginning of the fourth century enables understanding and better agreement with some points that otherwise create some problems. If we give credence to the tradition that presents Ezra as the great codifier of the law of Moses we should consider him the author of the redaction of the Pentateuch or at least of the Priestly Code, including its later redactions. A reading of the Law that lasts seven days, from first light until noon (Neh 8:3, 18) and in such a solemn manner, in the presence of the highest priestly and levitical authorities (8:4-7), indicates the desire to issue a text of extraordinary importance. It is historically evident that the Persian emperors wanted the states subject to them to codify their laws well. According to Plato, Darius I, the great lawmaker, ordered Ariandis in Egypt to set up a commission for compiling and codifying laws, and the undertaking was accomplished in sixteen years. This allows us to suppose that the Priestly Code, written probably during the exile, was edited beginning in the early post-exilic years.

The law brought from Babylon and proclaimed by Ezra, then, cannot be just any law. If the actions of this person are dated to the era of Nehemiah, the period for a definitive redaction of the Priestly Code or possibly of the whole Pentateuch is rather narrow. A final confirmation comes from the Elephantine papyri, which we will mention shortly.

History and Stages of Formation of the Books

It is impossible to trace the post-exilic history of Israel without the aid of Ezra–Nehemiah; moreover, our two books are enhanced and confirmed by extra-biblical archaeological and historical data, especially if we accept the hypothesis of chronological inversion demonstrated above. Working on the two fronts, that of our books and that of the extrabiblical data, we can better reconstruct this history. The background comes into better view thanks to the hypotheses of various authors, even though at times they do not agree. According to O. Plöger there was a theocracy, namely a government run by priests under Persian control, required to be vigilant to curb political and religious ferment aroused in prophetic circles. This theocracy would have been fully established by Ezra. This hypothesis does not seem very different from that of J. P. Weinberg, although he begins farther back: from the agrarian situation of the different regions of the Middle East under the neo-Babylonian empire and from the conflicts breaking out in Judea in Nehemiah's time between those who had settled there and the Jews brought back from exile (Nehemiah 5). Little by little a circle of people is created, lay and religious, supported by the Temple as a tacit instrument of imperial government. Through this circle the returnees slowly gain the advantage over those who had remained in the land. The former claim their rights and reestablish the society, structured according to tribal stocks, that in the centuries before the exile had attempted to oppose the monarchy.

Within this Jewish society there was conflict not only between the two groups mentioned. In the composite society that was being formed little by little after the exile there were also groups inspired by the deuteronomic law and awaiting eschatological events that might change the current unsatisfactory state of affairs. In that society there were also rather turbulent prophetic-messianic groups who were even more dissatisfied with the situation. The leadership group of this society was rigorously devoted to the Yahwist religion. It was already in action in pre-exilic history and almost all its members had gone into exile. Now, on its return it collided with the old syncretism, which itself was divided before the exile into the official religion, diplomatically open to the religions of the overlords, and the popular religion, still influenced by the old religion of Canaan. With the support of Nehemiah, radical Yahwism was imposed. It was here that Judaism was born, the religion to which, on our hypothesis Ezra himself would give the final refinement.

The Elephantine papyri, with material dating in large part to the fifth century B.C.E., document the syncretism in that Jewish military community. It was decisively condemned by the Priestly Code, written before Ezra but not yet in its full vigor, since Ezra, to whom its definitive redaction is probably due, had not yet imposed it. This was because he arrived in Palestine in 398 B.C.E. and the last Elephantine papyrus dates to 399. From these papyri we learn that under Darius II (423–404 B.C.E.) Johanan was the high priest. Indeed, it was to him and at the same time to Delaiah and Shelemiah, sons of Sanballat (Nehemiah's adversary: Neh 2:10, 19; 3:33; 4:1; 6:1) that the Jews of Elephantine sent their messages. According to Neh 12:23 Johanan was the grandson of Eliashib; from this must be deduced that Johanan and not Jonathan is the descendant of Eliashib listed in Neh 12:11. This Eliashib could then be the same who granted a room in the sacred zone to Tobiah, one of Nehemiah's old enemies (Neh 6:1). This was what outraged him on his second mission (Neh 13:4-9). However, Ezra withdrew to Johanan's room (Ezra 10:6). Thus the two high priests, respectively grandfather and grandson, Eliashib and Johanan, are matched respectively by Nehemiah and Ezra in two different and successive epochs.

Let us now summarize the post-exilic history, reducing it to four stages. At the start a first wave of repatriates succeeds in building the Temple a few years after 520 B.C.E. The impulse is provided by the prophets Haggai and Zechariah, and Zerubbabel, a descendant of David, and Jeshua, the high priest, take charge of the works.

The messianic hopes rekindled by the repatriation and by these events are gradually dulled. The descendants of David disappear from the scene, and the Persian government has surely taken away after Cyrus's edict many of the illusions it had created. Ancient passages from the third part of Isaiah, Zechariah, and Malachi probably reflect illusions and disappointments of those times, after which it seems there is a shift to another kind of prophecy consisting mainly in the eschatological reelaboration of preceding prophecies.

Therefore, almost a hundred years later, Nehemiah arrives (445 B.C.E.). He succeeds in rebuilding the walls of Jerusalem and repopulating the city. Hostility toward rebuilding, together with other ideological factors, pushes him to struggle for the separation of Jews from other inhabitants and from threatening neighbors. During his second mission the deuteronomic texts against Ammon and Moab are read (Neh 13:1-3) and he begins the struggle against mixed marriages (13:23-31; the prior narrative, in Nehemiah 10, would be a redactional text that originally referred to the later deeds of Ezra and not to those of Nehemiah cited anachronistically in 10:2; Nehemiah is also quoted in Neh 8:9 yet, as we have seen, in the parallel apocryphal book of Ezra his name does not appear).

Ezra, at the beginning of the fourth century (398 B.C.E.), achieves the definitive systematization of the sacred legislation (Nehemiah 8) and of the institutions of Israel and specifies measures for safeguarding them ethnically and religiously (Ezra 9–10). Ezra's measures may also have caused a suffocation of the liveliness of some religious groups, especially those inspired by the prophets. Still, these were able to continue living, albeit outside of official existence, perhaps in apocalyptic circles. Moreover, control by Ezra is indirectly control on the part of the Persians, who tolerate no messianic-political talk, something ultimately subversive of the empire.

In the last half of the fourth century the Oriental world fell under Macedonian dominion. After Alexander the Great, the Diadochoi contended over Palestine, worsening the economic-political situation. The Jews underwent a process of hellenization, especially in the second century when Palestine passed from the hands of the Ptolemies of Egypt and those of the Seleucids, and this finally led to the Maccabean revolt (167 B.C.E.). It was in this particularly sad situation that apocalyptic notions developed fully, and it was probably during this period that Qoheleth emerged.

Does the Chronicler's redaction date to this period? In order to try to answer this question it is necessary to attempt a reconstruction of the history of the formation of Chronicles, Ezra, and Nehemiah. If we proceed in chronological order we have to place the memoirs of Nehemiah at the start of the history. Before these there were the documents provided in Ezra 1–6, but it is too difficult to reconstruct them in their original tenor. We can only speak about a tradition that gave origin to the first draft of the book of Ezra. Basing ourselves on the above-explained inversion hypothesis which we accept, and taking into account that the work must have appeared after Ezra's mission, it could be dated around 350 B.C.E.

It is after this literary event that we can begin to speak about the Chronicler's redaction or redactions. We do not see the need to maintain that there were many of these, since there was also need to leave room for final touches and additions. Yet if we wish to defend the unity of the Chronicler's redaction we must resume the discussion of single authorship, mentioned at the beginning.

From everything we have said up to now it appears sufficiently evident that the two pairs of books are complementary. The current debate on the identity or diversity of the author(s) seems to be framed in the old manner: stylistic similarities are adduced as proof of identity and differences as contrary proof, on the thought that the two pairs of books each have a single author as many of our modern books have. In reality, here we may have to deal with a redactional school in which several persons are working; this would explain certain stylistic divergences. Moreover, we should keep in mind that this redactional complex comprises different works: the ancient documents contained in Ezra 1–6, the autobiographical memoirs of Nehemiah, the history of Ezra, and the reworking of the pre-exilic deuteronomic text, each one issued mainly in its own style.

There are at least four different styles, then, which the redaction has not been able to eliminate by leveling everything. We do not wish to enter into the details of likely stylistic differences since, while the diversity of authors can also be admitted, the two works are clearly complementary. Indeed, the one begins exactly where the other ends. Even if two different authors were involved, we would have to admit that the one wanted to complement the other.

In the history of the formation of these books, as we have hypothesized them, what we call the redactor or the redaction wanted to complete the history of Ezra at the start of a reworking of the deuteronomic history, so that he begins even farther back (Chronicles) and at the end, in reworking Ezra, inserts the memoirs of Nehemiah.

The so-called canonical argument does not hold true. This position is based on the fact that in the Hebrew canon we first have Ezra–Nehemiah and then Chronicles, as if the books of Chronicles had been added afterwards. It may indeed be the case that they were placed afterwards, as an appendix, because they are only a repetition, often pedantic, of the preceding deuteronomic history. Or else it could be that since the first period after Ezra the need was felt to replace the deuteronomic history of Israel, scarcely pleasing to the Persians and then to the Greeks, with our Chronicler's work. This work also connected the Tetrateuch with the primitive book of Ezra. In a later time the deuteronomistic history was set back in its place and our books, switching their order for the reasons mentioned above, finished at the end of the canon.

The date of this chronicler redaction cannot be very ancient. It must be before 300 B.C.E., that is, already in the Hellenistic epoch, but still not in the saddest period or when the hellenizing influence had reached such intensity as to provoke the revolt of the Maccabees. Indeed, neither pessimism nor a spirit of revolt against pagan overlords is found in these books. Moreover, there are descriptions of military equipment in Chronicles that are reminiscent of the Greek armies, already famous for their victories over the Persians: 1 Chr 12:9, 5; 2 Chr 11:12; 12:3; 14:7; 25:5; 26:9, 14-15. Also the civil economic restructuring attributed to Uzziah in 2 Chr 26:10 or the Davidic organization of public administration as in 1 Chr 27:25-34 would reflect the Hellenistic era.

Moreover, we should not go too far in dating the redaction: indeed, there are some lists in 1 Chr 3:17-24 of the post-exilic Davidic line and in Neh 12:12-21 of the post-exilic high priests, at the two extremes of the work (!), that do not run out until the end of the third century. If the redactors or perhaps those who added to the text were active so late they would not fail to provide more complete lists updated to their own time. Thus we say that the redaction of the work must have been substantially completed before the beginning of the third century and certainly before the disappointments suffered under the Seleucids and also before the early efforts at hellenizing Judaism, for this would not have failed to arouse reactions in spirits as solicitous for the institutions and the purity of the religion of Israel as were the authors and redactors of the Chronicler's work.

Conclusions and Perspectives for a Theological Reading

As we have observed, there are at least three periods, with the relative valorous personages or groups, that were determinative in Israel's post-exilic history. Perhaps they cannot be well distinguished one from another, but we can identify them as follows: the reconstruction of the Temple, the reconstruction of the city, the reconstruction of the religious life and of the nation. To the first correspond Zerubbabel, Jeshua, Haggai, and Zechariah, to the second Nehemiah, and to the third Ezra. The second and third periods might also be contemporaneous, as the current redaction and many modern authors propose. However, we may at least talk about different aspects.

The documents earlier than the chronicler's redaction that we have just dated each underscore the importance of those periods and those persons, an importance that is readily evident to us. Indeed, the events and persons of those stages of history made possible the continuing existence of Israel. It is through these events and persons that God continued salvation history, centered on the chosen people.

The chronicle redactors, gathering and elaborating these documents and transmitting their message, take a particular perspective. In reading their work we must strive to find this perspective and the message it brings. We are leaving to specific commentaries the task of the discovery and more precise definition of the different messages, including the particular differences between Chronicles and Ezra–Nehemiah, and their development in the various stages of the history of the formation of our books. Here we feature only some current themes of the liturgical message of our books.

(1) It is undoubtedly a much more vital, harmonious, aesthetically more valid and complete worship that the Chronicler's work presents to us. Moreover, it is an attempt at synthesizing the various cultic elements of the OT: the levitical institution in general, the sacrifices and reordering of the cult in the Priestly Code, the Psalms. It seems that the Chronicler is striving to present in his history all the facets of Israel's tradition and religious life. He does not forget another type of prayer in his work, particular those of various kings from David onward, up to the penitential prayers of Ezra (Ezra 9) and Nehemiah (Nehemiah 9). This is a liturgical effort worthy of imitation, especially since it teaches us to avoid improvisations in the liturgy that are the fruit of fantasy and personal whim, and instead to benefit from the wealth of tradition.

(2) Another reason for current interest is the theme of reconstruction. This word characterizes the stages of post-exilic history we have traced above. Nor can it be otherwise. If Judah wanted to begin living again it necessarily had to set out to rebuild, since everything had been destroyed. As we have seen, they started with the altar and the Temple since there lay the basis for Israel's life, and from there they must begin.

A necessary part of rebuilding was also ethnic. Which people should resume life in Palestine? The circumstances and the clashes press for an answer from the very beginning. The repatriates came across people who did not share their ideas, who accepted compromises with anyone even on religious questions of principle, who could go so far as to be enemies. Some had occupied the properties of the exiles; to regain them the returnees must now prove their origins and claim their own rights. Sometimes, as in the building of the Temple, it could be necessary to watch for intruders who apparently would want to cooperate but then would end by creating obstacles. These were evident from the beginning in the reconstruction of the walls of Jerusalem. At times Davidic-messianic political enthusiasms might have led to abuses or aroused fearful reactions on the part of the Persian empire, as can be read between the lines in Nehemiah's behavior (Neh 5:15-19).

Partly because of the industry of the repatriates and partly because of the unpleasant experiences of the early times after the return, or recalling the painful experiences of the final preexilic times, the will emerged to return to the Law, to be restored as a people radically based on it. The Persian empire facilitated the undertaking, especially if desires for political independence and for the Davidic monarchy were set aside. Yet the reborn rigor of interpreting the Law led not only to opposition to aliens, mingling with whom threatens the recovery. It also led to internal purifications. The problem arose already in Nehemiah's time, but becomes serious with Ezra. Rightly or wrongly it was formulated as a need to demonstrate the purity of their own stock. This caused the ancient genealogies to be seen in a new light. While they had earlier served to support the right to recover a piece of land, now they became the blade that cut off spurious branches at the trunk. This rigorism led to excesses, perhaps sometimes necessary. It almost seems that Ezra wanted nothing to do with anyone except the tribes of Judah and Levi and at most with that of Benjamin, and that he counted among enemies even those tribes that were always considered part of the people of Israel.

In reality the concern of Nehemiah and Ezra must be seen in the context of the concrete circumstances and difficulties they encountered in their efforts to get the reconstruction off to a good start and remove the feared obstacles, while delaying to future stages the interaction with the rest of Israel and its complete reconstitution. However, in the time of the redactor these internal tensions seem to have been overcome.

It is thought that in Chronicles a specifically anti-Samaritan attitude can be seen in the exclusion of events in the North, with the intention of dating them to the epoch of the Samaritan schism. To comprehend this apparent sectarian attitude it is helpful to clarify the terms of the question and clear the field of preliminary misunderstandings. First of all, there is uncertainty now regarding the date of this event. Even if we grant that the Samaritan schism occurred at the beginning of the Hellenistic epoch the aversion for the kingdom of the North had always existed in Judah ever since the ancient schism of Jeroboam and from the time when, after the Assyrian destruction of Samaria, the population had become mixed.

Chronicles basically follows the traditional tendency of the epoch of Ezra and Nehemiah. Abijah of Judah, who reproaches the North for its false priesthood and levitical practice before defeating it in battle (2 Chr 13:3-21); Jehu the seer, who rebukes Jehoshaphat for allying himself with the king of the North (2 Chr 19:1-11), a failed alliance reattempted by building a fleet (2 Chr 20:35-37) and that presages the future alliances with the Omridians by whom the South as well will be contaminated in the following decades; the warning of the anonymous man of God to Amaziah to dismiss the 100,000 men of Israel serving as soldiers in his army for the war against Edom (2 Chr 25:3-13)—all these are examples of this traditional attitude that cannot be regarded as a new sectarianism, just as Ezra's attitude is not a sectarianism. On the contrary, excesses of radicalism are called into question.

In all these post-exilic efforts at reconstruction one can perhaps already discern the tragic problem that continues to beset Jews today: what constitutes a Jew? What should be done to keep a people Jewish? These are very current questions not only for Israel today, but also for the Christian people and their communities. We recall that the ethnic-geographic reconstruction that Chronicles puts at the introduction of its history is a process already attempted in the preceding Priestly history in the Pentateuch and one that, at the end of the Bible, John too will follow in the book of Revelation. Revelation 7 describes the vision of the fully restored twelve tribes in a context of fearful selection: "Do not damage the earth or the sea or the trees, until we have marked the servants of our God with a seal on their foreheads" (7:3).

Chronicles strives to insert the monarchical structure into this traditional pan-Israelitic vision. Studies today bring out the emphasis with which the Davidic figure is presented by Chronicles, which seems to be due to a hidden interest in the messianic theme, the final point of its message that we wish to consider.

(3) One often hears it affirmed that the figure of the prophet is very important in the Chronicler's work. On this point and on the problem of messianism it is especially hard to state an exact judgment. Perhaps this work is difficult to judge because, contrary to the dominant opinion in the past, in its final redaction it aims at holding together several tendencies expressed in Israel in different currents. While remaining mainly the expression of the ideas of what we have called, following Plöger, a theocratic community, the work does not intend to close the door to the deuteronomic and prophetic currents or to their eschatological-messianic discourse. As we have noted, however, it does not become the mouthpiece for their explicit message; this is for diplomatic reasons: namely, so as not to irritate the supreme political authority or other people with whom the survivors had to live, perhaps some of the Jews themselves, whether religious or lay. To evaluate the importance given by Chronicles to prophetism or messianism is a task for tightrope walkers. There is always the risk of overly denying or affirming it, thus losing balance on one side or another.

We indeed cannot say that the prophetic figures in Chronicles are rare. They are relatively more numerous than those of the deuteronomic historical work, if it is taken into account that in it many prophets, and especially the two classic figures of Elijah and Elisha, work in the kingdom of the North, the history of which is systematically ignored in Chronicles. At the same time we cannot deny that the prophetic figures in Chronicles are very dull, both those with a deuteronomic parallel and those proper and exclusive to Chronicles, the list of whom was given above. If indeed the prophets had been of great interest to Chronicles or the preceding post-exilic history that it elaborates, it could have talked about Amos, Micah, Nahum, Zephaniah, Habakkuk, or Ezekiel. It is true that they do not appear in the deuteronomic historical work on which it depends. Yet even Haggai and Zechariah, named in it at the end of the parallel deuteronomic history, are dealt with in few words (Ezra 5:1-2). Isaiah is given much more space and importance in the deuteronomic parallel. Jeremiah, not cited in the deuteronomistic history, is mentioned only in the condemnation pronounced on Zedekiah (2 Chr 36:12-13), and incorrectly in speaking about Cyrus's edict (2 Chr 36:20 = Ezra 1:1). Chronicles recalls Elijah, but in a very reduced manner (2 Chr 21:12-15) and without relating any of his deeds. In general the prophetic interventions narrated by Chronicles are reduced to simple discourses, without other deeds or symbolic actions. They serve solely to emphasize the thesis of divine retribution, whether individual (especially for specific kings) or collective. This is a thesis that absolutely does not take into account the doubts that moved Job or Ecclesiastes. In these interventions at times greater emphasis is given to the condemnation of the behavior of the kings in the deuteronomic parallels that aim to justify the punishment of the two kingdoms. Yet in the prophetic interventions of Chronicles a clearly eschatological thought flourishes, a characteristic of the prophets, at least of the post-exilic era.

It cannot really be said that the interest of Chronicles in prophetism is great, nor that this makes Chronicles very different from Ezra and Nehemiah. Already, after the final illusions of the epoch of Nehemiah (and of Trito-Isaiah), the majority had ceased to believe that the eschatological prophecies would be realized in the time and the way that at first had been thought. Thus the Temple and the walls of Jerusalem, during whose rebuilding there had been much enthusiasm, become the sole pledge for the future salvation proclaimed by the prophets. The theology of Zion and the related psalms become the only fortress for refuge amid disappointment. Within the walls of Jerusalem there can still be felt the achievement of the promise of the Immanuel (= God with us), the prophecy of Isa 7:14, with a veiled repetition in Hag 1:13 and 2:5; Zech 8:23 and 10:5, and proclaimed again in the Chronicler's work in 1 Chr 22:18; 2 Chr 13:10-12; 15:2, 9; 20:17, and elsewhere. Yet the walls of Zion, understood in this new light, are like the frame for the messianic picture. Can we say that in our Chronicler's work there is the theme of the Messiah? Gerhard Von Rad affirmed it, but later denied it.

It is not true, however, that the Chronicler has reshaped the promise of Nathan or that the figure of the Messiah now becomes just a collective figure. We have seen that the monarchic figure has a central place in the Chronicler's work right from the introduction. We should recall that the pre-exilic messianic psalms continue to be recited after the exile and, even though the collective sense is sometimes joined to them, this does not cancel the individual sense: prayer continues for the future king.

The disappointments after the mysterious disappearance of Zerubbabel were certainly great. People no longer knew from which genealogical lineage they should expect the Messiah (1 Chr 3:17-24). Yet this bewilderment manifests hope, a hope that Nehemiah and Ezra do not want to inflame too much and that the priests have frozen, so to speak, by placing the High Priest in the place of the king, as turns out from the reelaborations of the prophecies. This is done so as not to raise further concerns in the Persian government, by whom our personages were invested with religious-political responsibilities.

The attitude of the Chronicler, like that held in the preceding stages of post-exilic history, is one of prudence and caution. The many efforts made by persons passing here in review and by those who carried out the Chronicle redaction in these books do not aim at combating hopes aroused by the prophets and, before them, by the whole ancient history of Israel. If anything they are born of these hopes and attempt to preserve them. This attempt should teach us something as well, especially constancy in times of trial when we are unable to see signs of hope in our life or in our history.

BIBLIOGRAPHY

Ackroyd, Peter R. *I & II Chronicles, Ezra, Nehemiah.* London: SCM, 1973.

Allen, Leslie C. *1, 2 Chronicles.* The Communicator's Commentary. Waco, Tex.: Word Books, 1987.

Becker, Joachim. *Messianic Expectation in the Old Testament.* Translated by David B. Green. Philadelphia: Fortress, 1980.

Blenkinsopp, Joseph. *Ezra–Nehemiah: A Commentary.* OTL. Philadelphia: Westminster, 1988.

Eskenazi, Tamara. *In an Age of Prose: A Literary Approach to Ezra–Nehemiah.* Atlanta: Scholars, 1988.

Hayes, John H., and J. Maxwell Miller. *Israelite and Judaean History.* Philadelphia: Westminster, 1977.

Hengel, Martin. *Jews, Greeks, and Barbarians: Aspects of the Hellenization of Judaism in the Pre-Christian Period.* Translated by John Bowden. Philadelphia: Fortress, 1980.

Laato, Antti. *Josiah and David Redivivus. The Historical Josiah and the Messianic Expectations of Exilic and Postexilic Times.* CB.OT 33. Stockholm: Almqvist & Wiksell, 1992.

Plöger, Otto. *Theocracy and Eschatology.* Translated by S. Rudman. Richmond, Va.: John Knox, 1968.

Smith, Morton. *Palestinian Parties and Politics that Shaped the Old Testament.* LHR n.s. 9. New York: Columbia University Press, 1987; 2nd, corrected ed. London: SCM, 1987.

Williamson, H.G.M. *Israel in the Books of Chronicles.* Cambridge and New York: Cambridge University Press, 1977.

____. *1 and 2 Chronicles.* NCBC. Grand Rapids: Eerdmans, 1982.

____. *Ezra, Nehemiah.* WBC 16. Waco, Tex.: Word Books, 1985.

Wilson, Robert R. *Genealogy and History in the Biblical World.* New Haven: Yale University Press, 1977.

1 Chronicles

Luca Mazzinghi

Genealogies: 1 Chronicles 1–9

The first nine chapters contain a list of genealogies that begin with Adam and extend to David: the text for the most part excludes narrative elements, limiting itself to a long series of names. These names mirror not only those of persons but also names of populations, of territories, or of cities that reflect in reality the historical situation of the time in which the Chronicler is writing. The material used in these chapters comes in part from earlier biblical texts, especially Genesis 5, and is partly enriched with elements drawn from other sources unknown to us. While some still dispute whether these chapters are to be attributed entirely to the Chronicler or to a later redactional effort, in any case analysis of the text, although it is at times in bad condition, reveals the existence of a precise theological plan that justifies its reading, something often tiresome for the modern reader.

The series of names opens with Adam and lists names from him to Abraham, and from Abraham to the twelve sons of Jacob/Israel; at the center of the list are the tribe of Judah, of which King David is a descendant, and the priestly tribe of Levi. The other tribes are relegated to the second level, as are celebrated personages such as Noah, Abraham, and Moses. The Chronicler thus presents God's plan for creation and humanity: from the first human being all history converges on David, the priesthood, and an Israel united around the tribe of Judah. The long series of names becomes in this way a message of hope: the future of Israel is already anticipated by its past. The review of the tribes of Israel begins in ch. 2, along the lines of Joshua 13–21. Chronicles, however, begins with Judah.

The Tribe of Judah and the House of David (2:3–4:23)

The text contains at its center a genealogy of the house of David (ch. 3), framed by two genealogies relating to the tribe of Judah, 2:3-55 and 4:1-23. In this way the Davidic dynasty becomes indissolubly tied to this tribe (cf. 1 Chr 28:4). 1 Chronicles 2:3-55 is concerned with the sons of Judah, the principal line of which follows the descent of the two sons born of Tamar, Perez and Zerah; of the other sons, Er and Onan have no issue (cf. v. 3), while only 1 Chr 4:21-23 is concerned with Shelah; thus the attention of the Chronicler is concentrated on the principal line represented by Hezron and Jerahmeel, son and grandson of Perez.

In the genealogy of David foreign elements are also included; there is mention of Bath-shua, the Canaanite wife of David (cf. 3:5). The mention of the fate of Er (cf. Gen 38:7) and of Achan (cf. Josh 7:16-26) introduces within the Davidic genealogy two negative elements: belonging to the line chosen by the Lord (who is named for the first time in v. 3) is not a guarantee of immunity. Noteworthy in this connection is the pun on Achan who appears with the name of Achar (2:7), from the verb *ʿakar,* "to bring misfortune." Here appear the first distinct references to the theme of God's justice, one of the theological constants of the Chronicler.

The House of Judah (3:1-23)

This chapter presents in succession the lists of the sons of David (vv. 1-9), of the kings of Judah (vv. 10-16), and of the descendants of David after the exile (vv. 17-24). Many modern authors consider this chapter a redactional addition to the Chronicler's work; if, however, the text is authentic the list of vv. 17-24 that describes the post-exilic descent of the house of David leads us to date the whole Chronicler's work to around 320 B.C.E. The chapter's chronological scope takes the reader far beyond the exile and opens up to the hope of a restoration of the Davidic monarchy.

In the list of the sons of David (3:1-9) the Chronicler follows 2 Sam 3:2-5 and 5:14-16; there is no mention of Athaliah, the pagan usurper (cf. 2 Kings 11). The list of the descendants of David after the exile is proper to the Chronicler; the other biblical sources are concerned with Zerubbabel alone, who must be considered as something of a messianic figure (cf. Hag 1:1; 2:23; Zech 4:6-13; Ezra 3:2, 8, etcetera).

Supplements to the Genealogies of Judah (4:1-23)

This section, supplementing the genealogies of Judah already introduced in ch. 3, again underscores the importance that tribe has for the Chronicler. The lists are very fragmentary and the text is in poor condition (for example, the beginning of v. 3 is missing). The material is certainly pre-exilic, scarcely reworked by the Chronicler. The names of various personages stand in large part for localities in southern Judea.

Simeon and the Transjordanian Tribes (4:24–5:26)

After Judah are presented the tribe of Simeon (4:24-43), which is tied to Judah, and the tribes of Transjordania (5:1-26): Reuben, Gad, and part of Manasseh. In reality these were deported in 734 B.C.E. by Tiglath-Pileser (2 Kings 15:29), but the Chronicler confuses this deportation with the one following the destruction of Samaria in 721 at the hands of the Assyrian king Shalmaneser (2 Kings 17:6); Pul, the king cited in v. 26, is one of the names of the same Tiglath-Pileser. The Chronicler thus ignores the deportation of 721, which marks the end also of the other tribes of the North whose genealogy appears in the following chapters, and limits the episode just to the Transjordanian tribes, for whom alone there seems to be no pardon (cf. "to this day," which concludes v. 26). Thus at the time of the Chronicler the right to all Palestine remains, with the sole exclusion of Transjordania.

Sin is described by the familiar image of prostitution to other gods; also derived from prophetic preaching is the idea that God makes use of foreigners to punish God's own people.

The Tribe of Levi (6:1-81)

The importance this tribe has in the Chronicler's plan is already evident from the number of verses dedicated to it, a good eighty-one, scarcely fewer than those dedicated to Judah. About half of the material contained in this long section comes from biblical texts, while the rest derives from sources unknown to us or attributable to the Chronicler's work. The three levitical clans are Gershom, Kohath, and Merari.

The text is concerned above all with the posterity of Kohath, the line from which Aaron comes and from him the high priests up to the time of the exile. The continuation of the list for the period following the exile is found in Neh 12:1-26. This list, which omits several names that are found elsewhere (cf. 2 Kings 11:15, Jehoiada and Uriah; 2 Chr 26:17, Azariah), has little historical value, and its very belonging to the Chronicler's work has been disputed. The list of high priests serves rather to confirm the continuity of priestly service in Israel and especially the legitimacy of the Zadokite priesthood, given that Zadok, a priest in Solomon's time (cf. 1 Kings 2:26-27, 35), is inserted within the Aaronide line even though he did not belong to it. Then, in 6:16-30, we have all three clans and the relative lists respond to the need to prove the legitimacy of the levitical families' belonging to the lineage of Levi after the return from the exile.

In the list of the sons of Kohath the prophet Samuel is inserted, although actually he belonged to the tribe of Ephraim (cf. 1 Sam 1:1), perhaps because of the priestly functions he developed (1 Sam 2:11, 26; 3:15; 7:9-10).

The importance of liturgical chant is emphasized by vv. 31-47. The temple cantors are linked to the lineage of Levites through three genealogies going back to the three descendants of

Levi: Heman, Asaph and Ethan/Idutun (whose names appear in the titles of Psalms 50, 70–83, 88, 89). The service of singing praise within the Temple is, for the Chronicler, the greatest expression of worship, since the institution is traced back even to David (1 Chr 15:1–16:43). In a brief historical parenthesis (16:37-42) the Chronicler underscores, by linking it to David's time, the differentiation of tasks between the Levites, dedicated to service in the Temple and to praise, and the priests, sons of Aaron, responsible for the offering of sacrifice and incense, the service within the Holy of Holies, and the expiatory rite for the sins of the people.

The chapter on Levi closes with a long list of towns belonging to the tribe of Levi that repeats the information given in Joshua 21. The towns listed are found in the territory of all the other tribes; thus the whole land is filled with the presence of the Levites. The bond of the Levites with David, the reorganizer of liturgical chant and of worship, is linked to the bond with the promised land. To the Levites, then, David himself entrusts the most important task, the divine service.

The Other Tribes (7:1–8:40)

These chapters contain very summary remarks on the remaining tribes of Israel: Issachar (vv. 1-5), Benjamin (vv. 6-12 and again 8:1-28), Manasseh (vv. 14-19), Ephraim (vv. 20-29) and Asher (vv. 30-40). Almost nothing is said about Naphtali, while Dan and Zebulun are not even named; these three tribes of the North had ceased to exist for some time before the Chronicler's era. Some authors think they find a mention of Dan in v. 12, and they attribute to Zebulun the genealogy of Benjamin, which is repeated in ch. 8 and followed, in 8:29-40, by the genealogy of Saul. The traditions belong to the Davidic epoch and, as usual, the author draws his information both from biblical texts and from sources that in this case were of military origin, as can be noted by the language employed.

In ch. 8 we have a new list of Benjaminites arranged by locality of residence, a different list from the preceding one (7:6-12) and made up of material mainly of extra-biblical derivation; it is difficult to understand to what historical period it refers, for the deportation recorded in vv. 6-7 reflects some tribal conflict of an uncertain period. The genealogy of the Benjaminites has some importance for the Chronicler since the tribe of Benjamin is tied to Gibeon (v. 29), the place where the Ark was located before David's reign (1 Chr 21:29; cf. 1 Chr 9:35), and above all to Jerusalem (vv. 28, 32) and finally to King Saul (v. 33). In this way the reader is prepared to turn attention to Jerusalem, the city of David (ch. 9), and to Saul, the protagonist of ch. 10.

The Inhabitants of Jerusalem (9:1-44)

This chapter serves the function of concluding the lists of chs. 2–8 and preparing the following narration of the reign of Saul, introduced, in 9:35-44, by the repetition of the genealogy of Saul recorded earlier in 8:33-40. The structure of the text is clear and is of great theological interest: after an introduction relating to the exile and the return (vv. 1-2) the inhabitants of Jerusalem are listed in this order: the Israelites before all (vv. 4-9), followed by the priests (vv. 10-13), and the Levites (vv. 14-16). Finally there is a long section dedicated to the gatekeepers of the Temple and to other levitical functions (vv. 17-34). In this manner the Chronicler clearly distinguishes the people (the laity) from the clergy, listed in order of importance. Thus Jerusalem appears as the city of worship, where the very existence of the people is subordinated to the presence of priests and Levites; the priests are called fighting men (v. 13) so that their service is comparable to that of soldiers who fight for God. Verses 2-34 are parallel to the text of Neh 11:2-23, where the inhabitants are clearly those of the post-exilic period. Our text, however, by placing the list in the Davidic context seems to want to tie these lists to the period preceding the exile itself; the aim is to show the continuity existing within the community of Israel before and after the exile. Among the inhabitants of Jerusalem, besides the tribes of Benjamin and Judah, the northern tribes of Ephraim and Manasseh (9:3-9) are recalled, although they still did not live in Jerusalem; thus the center appears as the ideal center of Israel.

The class of gatekeepers (9:17-34) acquires great importance in the books of Chronicles (cf. also 1 Chr 26:1-19). In Neh 11:19 the gatekeepers appear distinct from the Levites, while our text is concerned to underline the descent of the tribe of Levi. Moreover the text aims at establishing the importance of the gatekeepers by linking their origin to the tent of the time of the Exodus (v. 19), even though they are not mentioned in the texts of the Pentateuch. In this way the gatekeepers acquire an importance equal to that of the levitical cantors (cf. vv. 33-34) whose institution is traced back to David. Beginning with v. 22 the Chronicler describes the situation at the time of David, although with the purpose of justifying—through this double hook both to the Exodus tent and to David—the preeminence that the class of gatekeepers had at that time. They are praised for their loyalty (vv. 22, 31); starting in v. 24 their tasks are described in relation to the custody of the Temple and the care of the sacred objects (vv. 28-34). In 9:35-44 Saul's genealogy is presented again (cf. 8:29-38); more than as an addition, we may regard this as a deliberate contrast between the loyalty of the Levites and the figure of the unfaithful king, to be dealt with in ch. 10.

The Kingdom of David: 1 Chronicles 10–29

We are at the core of the Chronicler's work. The history of David's reign is presented through small literary units, each of which deals with a specific event. These units can be grouped around four basic events: the beginning of the Davidic kingdom (chs. 10–12); the transfer of the Ark to Jerusalem and the beginning of divine worship (chs. 13–17); the wars of David (chs. 18–20); and finally the internal organization of the kingdom (chs. 21–29). The Chronicler often strays from the texts of 1–2 Samuel, at times expanding them on the basis of other sources or changing their meaning on the basis of his own theological perspective, at times omitting significant episodes such as David's sin with Bathsheba (2 Samuel 11) as well as the whole lively narration of David's ascent to the throne of Saul (1 Samuel 13–30) and again the dramatic story of Absalom's rebellion (2 Samuel 13–20). The Chronicler is convinced that David is the ideal king whose reign becomes a plan to follow and a near-messianic sign of hope for the postexilic community.

The Beginnings of the Kingdom (1 Chronicles 10–12)

After the elimination of Saul by the Philistines' actions, along the lines of 1 Sam 31:1-13, Chronicles immediately advances to describe the enthronement of David. Chapters 11 and 12 form a literary unit structured around a central idea: the enthronement of David as king of all Israel. All the material coming in large part from the text of 2 Samuel is thus selected and rearranged by the Chronicler in this new context. In this way a new composition emerges that guides the reader, who already knows the story of David as it was narrated in the deuteronomic work, to a new comprehension of the story itself.

David King at Hebron, 11:1-3

The beginning of ch. 11 is the direct continuation of 1 Chr 10:14: by the omission of the long narration of the ascent to the throne as contained in 1 Samuel, David is presented in the act of receiving royal dignity that he has not sought but that is a gift from God (cf. 11:1b, 3b). The Chronicler takes the text of 2 Sam 5:1-3, but omits vv. 4-5: in the book of Chronicles, David appears as king of all Israel but no mention is made of a preceding reign of seven years at Hebron. The basic idea of Chronicles is the presentation of an Israel united and compact, gathered around David. To this end v. 1 modifies the verb of 2 Sam 5:1: "the Israelites came" becomes "the Israelites gathered," where the verb *qabaṣ* recalls the gathering of the people in return from exile (cf. 1 Chr 16:23). The conquest of Jerusalem (11:4-9) is not, for the Chronicler, just one of David's many exploits, as in 2 Samuel 5–7, but rather is the inaugural episode of his reign.

The list of David's followers (11:10-47) depends, up to v. 41a, on the similar list of 2 Sam 23:8-39, from which it differs by omitting the name of Uriah, detrimental to David's honor, and by adding in vv. 41b-47 a list not contained in 2 Samuel. With the list of 12:1-24, not contained in the deuteronomic source (2 Samuel 23–24) yet probably ancient at least up to v. 23, we go back again in time to the men who supported David when he was not yet king. The list includes people of the tribes of Benjamin (vv. 1-8), Gad (vv. 9-16), Benjamin again, Judah (vv. 17-19), and Manasseh (vv. 20-23). In this way the Chronicler returns to the idea of unity, showing an Israel then compact around David even before he became king.

1 Chr 12:24-41 appears to be more directly the Chronicler's work, based on some ancient source unknown to us. The thirteen tribes (including

Levi as well) are numbered by geographical criteria to show the help each one has given to the kingdom. The numbers are hyperbolic but they go back to the Chronicler's intention to glorify David further. There is a recurrence of the theme of the unanimity of the people (v. 39) that carries out a specific word of the Lord (v. 24; cf. 1 Chr 11:10). The list concludes (vv. 39-41) with the mention of a great feast celebrated at the act of David's enthronement; the dryness of the lists is transformed in the celebration of joy over the attained goal (v. 40), according to a theme dear to the Chronicler (cf. 2 Chr 23:13, 21; 29:36; 30:23, 25-26). No religious element is expressly mentioned with regard to David's enthronement; the author reserves this theme to the following chapters (1 Chronicles 13–16) dedicated to the transport of the Ark to Jerusalem.

The Transfer of the Ark to Jerusalem (1 Chronicles 13–17)

Starting from the text of 2 Sam 6:1-23 the Chronicler notably expands the account of the translation of the Ark to Jerusalem, to which he attributes great importance. The narration proceeds in two different stages: a first tentative one, then the definitive transfer of the Ark to Jerusalem with the inauguration of the levitical service (chs. 15–16); the two stages are separated by an intermezzo (ch. 14). The conclusion of the section contains the celebrated prophecy by Nathan (ch. 17). In this way the Chronicler presents the second stage of the consolidation of the Davidic kingdom; after the political stage, presented in the preceding section, the accent falls now on the religious aspect: the heart of the kingdom are the Ark, the sign of God's presence, the worship that is conducted around it, and the Temple, announced prophetically by Nathan in ch. 17; this same text also contains the promise relating to the stability of the Davidic monarchy. In contrast with the figure of David presented in 2 Samuel, the religious work of the king emerges in a dominant manner: the Chronicler dedicates a good 323 verses to the religious aspect of the Davidic kingdom as compared to scarcely 77 in 2 Samuel.

In 13:1-14 the text, beginning with v. 6, follows almost to the letter the account of 2 Sam 6:2-11. Verses 1-4 introduce a theme dear to the Chronicler: while in one way everything appears to be the work of David he does not act without having consulted the people, involving them in the decisions to be taken (cf. also 2 Chr 30:5-10; 34:33; 35:18). This sort of democratic perspective, intentionally idealized in regard to David, may represent a reaction of the Chronicler against the pretensions of the priesthood of his time. The procession of v. 8, in which all Israel takes part, is a sign of the joy that issues from what the Ark represents: the presence of God in the midst of the people.

After the interlude of 14:1-17, Chronicles narrates in 15:1–16:3, with an abundance of detail, the preparations carried out by David for the transport of the Ark, mentioning in particular the Levites who were responsible for the task (vv. 5-15) and especially the levitical cantors (vv. 16-24); beginning with v. 25 the procession to Jerusalem is described. While this last section depends on the text of 2 Sam 6:12b-18, the first twenty-four verses appear to be the Chronicler's original work. The transfer of the Ark is transformed into the gratifying display of a choral liturgy; the emphasis placed on the role of the Levites (cf. Deut 10:8 and 18:5) with a secondary role given to the priests is a sign of the fact that the Chronicler in reality wants to describe the organization of worship as it was in his time when the Levites had assumed greater importance. Verse 13 offers proof that the episode of Uzzah (1 Chr 13:10-11) was tied to the violation of the liturgical norms, which now are fully respected. Among these the importance of singing and music (with cymbals, harps, lyres and trumpets) emerges again; the tradition that attributed to David the composition of the Psalms already existed in the Chronicler's time. The procession of the Ark takes place in an atmosphere of joy and feasting, the fruit of God's help (v. 26; cf. also 16:1-3), an atmosphere scarcely disturbed by the episode of Michal, whose punishment the Chronicler does not state (cf. 2 Sam 6:20-23); Michal, appearing here for the first time, is the representative of the house of Saul, of those who have no care for the Ark (cf. 1 Chr 13:3).

Inauguration of Levitical Service, 16:4-38

The Chronicler constructs with great skill a text at whose center a psalm of praise is found, framed by the description of the liturgical service inaugurated around the Ark (vv. 4-7, 37-38).

Again the emphasis is on the primary task of the Levites, the praise of God, which nearly substitutes for the sacrificial cult proper to the priests; thus the Chronicler continues to attribute to David the organization of worship as it is in his time. The psalm contained in vv. 8-36 is in fact made up of parts of other psalms: vv. 8-22 correspond to Ps 105:1-15, vv. 23-33 to Ps 96:1-13, and vv. 34-36 to Ps 106:1, 35-36; this involves a process recognized within the psaltery itself (cf. Psalm 108). Psalm 105 is a thanksgiving psalm for the marvels performed by the Lord in the history of the people; the Chronicler omits all reference to Exodus, stopping (v. 22) at the mention of the Patriarchs; in this way he puts the accent on the covenant (vv. 15-16), which allows him to tie the psalm to the episode of the transport of the Ark of the Covenant. Psalm 96 is used to move from the historical recollections to universal praise; the final verses (34-36, cf. Psalm 106), linking this praise with the prayer for the exiled people, bring the reader to reread in the situation of his or her own time a text that the Chronicler places in David's mouth. Our author's skill, therefore, is to use texts from different sources in a new context (the Davidic one) that is still constantly being realized.

At the conclusion of the inauguration of worship in Jerusalem, mention is made of that at Gibeon (16:39-42). The sanctuary at Gibeon is spoken of here in relation to the Tent in the desert (cf. Ezra 29:38-42; Num 28:3-8) and the role of the priesthood of Zadok. In this way the Chronicler can justify the presence of Solomon in this place (2 Chr 1:1-13); moreover, the memory of the Tent in the desert allows him to affirm the continuity of worship in Israel.

Nathan's Prophecy, 17:1-15

The texts of Nathan's prophecy and the following prayer of David depend closely on the text of 2 Samuel 7 with few, albeit meaningful, changes. The text omits 2 Sam 7:1, yet more important are the insertion in v. 11 of the reference to Solomon ("one of your own sons," absent from 2 Sam 7:12) and the omission of the text of 2 Sam 7:14 regarding the possible sins of David's descendants. The prophecy of Nathan in the Chronicler's version places value on the monarchical institution, which disappears again when the Chronicler is writing, becoming the point of departure for royal messianism (cf. the Christian rereading in Luke 1:31-32 and Heb 1:5). The following prayer of David (17:16-27, cf. 2 Sam 7:18-29) enables the Chronicler to describe the king's sentiments; it displays a tone of supplication and reconciliation rather than one of joy and thanksgiving. The Chronicler skillfully expresses David's feeling of smallness before the majesty of God, and David's request that the divine promises might be confirmed (cf. v. 23). The concluding verse modifies the text of 2 Sam 7:29: the plea for a blessing is transformed into David's certainty of already having received it.

David's Campaigns (1 Chronicles 18–20)

These three chapters gather into one pericope all the material regarding David's wars; in a very brief text the Chronicler summarizes 2 Samuel 8–21, omitting everything that might hurt the image of an ideal David (the killing of Amnon, the revolts of Absalom and of Sheba) and keeping only the passages of a military nature that, compiled together in this chapter, help to highlight the greatness of David as a military commander. This prepares the explanation of the reasons why construction of the Temple was not accomplished by David; cf. 1 Chr 22:8; 28:3. Chapter 18 is a collection of various items (cf. 2 Samuel 8); from 19:1–20:3 David's campaigns against the Ammonites are mentioned (cf. 2 Samuel 10) and finally, in 20:4-8, the text relates some episodes relating to the war against the Philistines (cf. 2 Sam 21:18-22). In this last case the three acts of heroism achieved by David's champions are each in some manner attributed to him (cf. 20:8b).

The Kingdom's Internal Organization (1 Chronicles 21–29)

Only ch. 21 depends on the text of 2 Samuel 24, but it too is transformed into one of the preparatory actions for the construction of the Temple. However, the remaining chapters, from 22 to 29, have no parallel in the narration of 2 Samuel and seem to be an original contribution of the Chronicler. The basic theme is very clear: the preparations made by David, before his death, in order to be assured of a successor (Solomon) and for the building of the Temple. Two central points are involved in the divine promise declared in 1 Chr 17:11-12; in this way the Chronicler describes what for him is the culminating point of the reign of David: the preparation for the construction of the Temple and the organization of worship. Chapters 22–29 are organized according to a clear concentric structure: at the beginning (ch. 22) and at the end (chs. 28–29) we find David's arrangements for Solomon, while at the center (chs. 23–27) there is the internal organization of the kingdom, with special reference to worship. It is possible that the Chronicler is using authentic sources at least in part, sources ignored by or unknown to the narrator of 2 Samuel.

Preparations for the Construction of the Temple, 22:2-19

The text comprises three distinct sections: David's preparations (vv. 2-5), the testament addressed to Solomon (vv. 6-16), and the discourse addressed to the leaders of Israel (vv. 17-19); the discourses are the most evident characteristic of the chapter as a basic theme emerges, namely the preparations for the construction of the Temple, named a good ten times in different ways (vv. 2, 5, 6, 7, 8, 10, 11, 14, 19 twice) and emphasized by intentionally hyperbolic numbers and figures. Moreover, the chapter seeks to explain why David was not personally able to construct the Temple (cf. 22:8) despite the greatness of his kingdom: the matter evidently requires a theological explanation, which the Chronicler furnishes by picking up material from 1 Kings 8:18 and Deut 12:10. David's wars, although willed by God and conducted with God's help, are the obstacle because of which David must forsake building the Temple. This can only be done in a time of peace and by a "man of peace" (cf. v. 9); this constitutes a tragic paradox for David's life. Although in chs. 18–20 the military ideal of David as a warrior appears, the Chronicler does not maintain that war in itself is a good (cf. 2 Chr 16:9); it is often a sign of divine punishment and stands in contrast to the situation of peace that the Temple presupposes. The democratic tendency of Chronicles is to be noted in the description of the passing of power from David to Solomon (vv. 17-19) in contrast to 1 Kings 1:23-27: the organization of the clergy and the kingdom.

These chapters, dedicated to the organization of the kingdom and in particular of its worship, constitute a text that has no parallels in 2 Samuel and, according to many authors, is a later insertion that does not reflect the Chronicler's thought; the text of 23:1 indeed finds its natural continuation in 28:1. Nevertheless the five chapters form a unit; the disharmony and internal inconsistencies can be traced to the diversity of sources employed by the Chronicler. He identifies the worship conducted in his time with that established by David; in this manner, by revealing a deep meaning of the tradition, he wants to summon his readers to the careful observance of cultic norms.

The Levites, 23:1-32

The section dedicated to the Levites has a clear internal structure: after the introduction in vv. 1-5 containing the Davidic decree on the subdivision of the Levites' duties (vv. 3-5), a first part (vv. 6-23) presents a genealogy of the levitical families while vv. 24-32 give a description of their duties. The different information about the age of the Levites (cf. vv. 3, 6-7, 24, 27 with Num 4:3, 23:29, etcetera) can be explained by looking to textual alterations or real variations occurring in different periods regarding the admission of Levites to service; even the exaggerated number of Levites (v. 3), compared with Num 4:58, is part of that process of ideal amplification to which the Chronicler subjects the whole Davidic epoch. The role of the Levites (cf. 1 Chronicles 6) eclipses even the figure of Moses (vv. 14-15), whose sons are no longer considered priests (as in Judg 18:30; 1 Sam 2:27) but rather Levites. In vv. 24-32 the Chronicler explicitly affirms the newness of the levitical duties (see also 1 Chronicles 15) that he, in contrast with the theology of the Pentateuch (cf. v. 25 and Numbers 3–4), attributes directly to David. Accurately distinguishing the task of the Levites from that of the priests, the Chronicler stresses in particular two totally new levitical functions that will be seen again in later chapters: the gatekeepers (vv. 28-29 and 1 Chronicles 26) and the cantors (vv. 30-31 and 1 Chronicles 25); the chant is considered so important that v. 5 attributes ideally to David even the making of musical instruments.

Priests and Levites, 24:1-31

This chapter is clearly divided into two parts: vv. 1-19 are dedicated to the priests while vv. 20-31 constitute a new list of Levites that does not agree with the one provided in 1 Chr 23:6-24; this is surely a later insertion into the Chronicler's work that reflects a changed historical situation. Although the Chronicler acknowledges the theological primacy of the priests (v. 5), all his sympathies lie with the Levites, to whom he gives more space. The part dedicated to the priests has its center of interest in the system of the division of the clergy into twenty-four classes that once again the Chronicler backdates to David. In reality this system emerged only after the return from exile, when the elevated number of priests necessitated a rotation in the turns of service in the Temple, achieved precisely through the subdivision of the clergy into twenty-four classes. Nehemiah 11:10-14 testifies already to a subdivision into four classes (cf. 1 Chr 9:10-13) that in Neh 12:1-7, 12-20 become twenty-two. The division into twenty-four classes becomes normative in the Judaism of the second Temple, in the times of the NT (cf. Luke 1:5). The ordering of the priestly classes presupposes an irenic attempt to resolve the conflict between the descendants of Abiathar, excluded from the priesthood by Solomon (1 Kings 2:26), and those of the pure line of Zadok, whose family the priests returning from exile claimed. Both are linked with Aaron through the two sons Eleazar and Ithamar (cf. vv. 2-6); the purpose of the creation of this subdivision in classes may have been the attempt to resolve the differences among the various priestly families.

The Musicians, 25:1-31

The levitical cantors get special attention, since their subdivision into twenty-four classes (vv. 9-31) repeats that of the priests (1 Chronicles 24). The list of cantors is not historically likely and is absent from the texts of later Judaism; it is presented rather as an ideal subdivision proposed by the Chronicler. The last nine names of the sons of Heman, listed in v. 6, in reality form, when read in Hebrew, a word play on the probable beginning of a psalm that could be translated in this way:

> Grant me favor, Lord, grant me favor;
> you are my God,
> I have exalted and celebrated (your) aid;
> in adversity I said, give visions generously.

It must be pointed out that in vv. 1-3 the Chronicler uses the verb "to prophesy" to describe the cantors' activities; the cantor Heman in v. 5 is called "seer" (cf. 2 Chr 35:15). For one thing, this expresses the remembrance of an ecstatic activity proper to prophetic groups (cf. 1 Sam 10:5); for another, the role of the cantors is considered that of composing the psalms, seen as compositions inspired by God for singing in the liturgical service. Moreover, to associate singing with prophecy means to consider it as the privileged expression of worship and the path through worship to understanding the will of God.

The Gatekeepers, 26:1-19

For the third time, after 1 Chr 9:17-26 and 16:37-43, the Chronicler furnishes a list of gatekeepers: in contrast with Ezra 2:42, 70; 7:24; 10:24; Neh 10:28; 11:19 they are assimilated into the Levites; this is a sign of an evolution of the gatekeepers in the Chronicler's time and of greater importance attributed to their function. In vv. 14-19 the talk is about their duties, presupposing an already constructed Temple as it existed in the Chronicler's time; we are looking at a theoretical and ideal presentation that reflects the typical model of the organization of worship as the Chronicler imagines it. It should be noted that in v. 17 (cf. 1 Chr 24:4 and 25:1) the service of the Temple is compared to military service.

Other Levitical Functions, 26:20-32

This section presents two lists referring to the treasury Levites and their responsibilities (vv. 20-28) and to the civil functionaries and judges, drawn also from among the Levites (vv. 29-32). In no other part of the Bible are judges spoken of as Levites; although the institution of judges as it is presented in the text can of course be authentic and attributable to the Davidic era their levitical status is surely a creation of the Chronicler, in whose time the growing importance of the Levites had touched even civil roles.

Military and Civil Offices, 27:1-34

This chapter comprises four sections: the lists of army commanders (vv. 1-15), tribal chiefs (vv. 16-22), administrators of the king's goods (vv. 25-31), and his seven councilors (vv. 32-34). Despite the contrary opinion of many commentators who consider it an addition, the chapter seems well integrated in its current context with the exception of vv. 23-24, a later interpolation for the purpose of softening David's responsibility in the census related in 1 Chronicles 21. From a historical viewpoint the Chronicler uses sources that, at least in part, are probably authentic and may actually reflect the situation in David's time. The first list attributes to David the system of twelve prefectures that 1 Kings 4 ties to Solomon; the second list has a more artificial character and reflects the typical vision of the Chronicler of an Israel harmoniously divided into the twelve tribes; moreover, the tribes of Gad and Asher are lacking, while a strange tribe of Aaron is introduced and that of Manasseh is counted twice. The third and fourth list reflect probably authentic situations. The list of David's councilors, in particular, follows a different source from that of 1 Chr 18:15-17 (cf. 2 Sam 8:16-18; 20:23-26); nothing is said about the roles of Ahithophel and Hushai during Absalom's revolt (2 Sam 15:12, 31, 37; 16:17, 23, and elsewhere). The placement of these lists at the end of the levitical and priestly lists serves the Chronicler's theology: the aim is to show the solidity of the Davidic kingdom and above all to affirm that the civil functions are in some way ordered to the religious organization. There is a certain analogy with the description of the ideal Jerusalem of Ezekiel (cf. Ezekiel 47–48): what Ezekiel projects into a distant future the Chronicler attributes to David's era.

David Places Solomon in Charge of Building the Temple, 28:1–29:25

This section is not based on 1 Kings 1–2. It constitutes a literary unit whose basic theme is the enthronement of Solomon. After a brief introduction (28:1), vv. 2-10 contain David's testament, followed (28:11-21) by David's entrusting to Solomon the construction plans for the Temple; then follow a description of the offerings brought by the people (29:1-12), David's thanksgiving prayer (vv. 10-20), and finally the solemn enthronement of Solomon (vv. 21-25). Everything takes place in the sight of the people, and David addresses his discourse to them: the people participate actively with offerings brought to the Temple. Solomon, however, remains totally passive.

The core of David's discourse in 28:2-10 dwells on the theme of the construction of the Temple, in view of which Solomon becomes king. The Temple is defined as a home of repose for the Ark (cf. Deut 12:10; 2 Sam 7:1; 1 Chr 22:9); the idea, very ancient (cf. Num 10:35-36) is developed in the sense that the Temple is not directly the house of God but the place where the Ark reposes (cf. the same idea expressed in Ps 132:7-8, 14). The Temple is the main purpose of the Davidic-Solomonic monarchy; for this Solomon was predestined before his birth, and his ascent to the throne is presented by the Chronicler as free from the many intrigues and acts of bloodshed described by 1 Kings 1–2. Verse 5, with an expression unique to the Chronicler, makes it clear that the kingdom really is God's. Verse 8 (textually uncertain) introduces a theme of deuteronomic theology, the possession of the land: while in deuteronomic texts this possession is described as a reality still to be attained (cf. Deut 4:5; 9:4, etcetera), here it appears as an already present reality, contingent however on faithfulness to the will of God: vv. 9-10 are thus understood as an exhortation addressed to Solomon to be inwardly faithful to God, written again in the Deuteronomist's style.

The plan for the Temple (28:11-21) that David hands over to Solomon and, through him, to all the people (v. 21), contrary to 1 Kings 6–7, appears as a direct divine revelation (vv. 12 and 20), as in the case of the tent in the desert (Ezra 25:9) and Ezekiel's ideal Temple (Ezek 40:14). The Temple is described in its architectural details, hard for us to reconstruct. Verses 14-18 are taken up with a list of sacred vessels of the Temple and their value: outstanding among these is the golden chariot of the cherubs (v. 18), a unique expression to designate the Ark that calls to mind the vision of Ezekiel 1. Verse 20 is an exhortation in deuteronomic style that recalls the appeals of Moses to Joshua in Deut 31:6, 8; Josh 1:5.

The quantity of offerings for the Temple (29:1-9) is intentionally exaggerated; in v. 7 the mention of the darics, the money coined by Darius, king of Persia (521–486 B.C.E.) is an obvious anachronism, as is the mention of the treasury of the Temple in v. 8, which existed then but here reflects a typical usage of the Judaism of the Second Temple (cf. Luke 21:1). In v. 9 a typical feature of the Chronicler's theology is expressed: an attitude of joy in the service of God.

The final prayer of David is the seal placed by the Chronicler on the long narrative devoted to his kingdom. Even though it is composed of loans from different preceding biblical texts (for example, the beginning—v. 10b—is similar to

Ezra 7:27; Neh 9:5; for v. 11 cf. Dan 3:52 and Ps 89:11; for v. 15, Gen 23:4; Ps 39:12, and Job 8:9) the prayer seems well anchored in the context where it is inserted. Stylistically the Chronicler uses a prose form, avoiding poetic writing; in this way the prayer of the king differs from the psalms, reserved to the levitical cantors in the Temple. At the center of the prayer is the figure of God, invoked in the second person and closely tied to David and the people through constant use of possessive adjectives and pronouns. In this way the prayer appears as the expression of a profound personal relationship existing between God, the king, and the people. God, described emphatically through the accumulation of a series of attributes, appears as the one from whom everything comes and before whom the human being is nothing (vv. 14-17; these verses lack any indication of a life after death, a theme missing from the Chronicler's entire work). The gifts of the people then appear as a return to God of divine blessings. Verses 18-19 express the realization of the Chronicler's religious ideal, projected onto the conclusion of the reign of David: complete adherence to the will of God, seen however as God's own work.

The enthronement of Solomon (29:21-25) is presented in a completely different way from that depicted in 1 Kings 1–2, from which the Chronicler takes only the text of 1 Kings 2:12, quoted in vv. 26-27; the event appears as a choral act of the gathered people in which also the "leaders" and the "sons of David" (v. 24) collaborate with the new king.

BIBLIOGRAPHY

See pages 653–654.

2 Chronicles

Luca Mazzinghi

The Reign of Solomon: 2 Chronicles 1–9

In these chapters the Chronicler presents from his particular perspective the history of the reign of Solomon already contained in 1 Kings 1–11. In the first place the account in Chronicles omits anything that casts a bad light on the king or that does not suit his grandeur: the bloody episodes that preceded his ascent to the throne (1 Kings 1–2), the judgment of Solomon over the two prostitutes (1 Kings 3:16-27), Solomon's unfaithfulness in his old age (1 Kings 11:1-13), his political and economic difficulties (1 Kings 11:14-40). The Chronicler accordingly omits the account of the construction of the royal palace (1 Kings 7:1-12) so as to concentrate his full attention on the building of the Temple, to which he dedicates a full five chapters (2 Chronicles 2–7). Within this last section there are important additions to the deuteronomic opus (cf. 2 Chr 5:11-13; 6:41-42; 7:1-3) in which the Chronicler returns again to the importance that worship and prayer have for him. Solomon, like David before him, now appears as a figure far back in royal history and is described as the ideal king. He is the king who, by building the Temple, fulfills his father's plan. Chapters 1–9 open (1:14-17) and close (9:1-28) with the celebration of the riches and wisdom of Solomon, who for the Chronicler shines with undimmed glory.

The Dream at Gibeon and the Riches of Solomon (1:1-17)

The Chronicler opens the account of Solomon's reign by taking the episode of the dream at Gibeon from 1 Kings 3:4-15 and modifying it according to his own theological prospective. In the Chronicler's telling, the presence of Solomon at Gibeon no longer constitutes an act of private worship; reference to the dream is left out, while vv. 2 and 3 present the king in public, together with the whole assembly of Israel, according to a vision dear to the Chronicler. Moreover, the Chronicler places at Gibeon the tent ordered by Moses to be made in the desert; in this way he justifies the presence of Solomon in a sanctuary different from the one in Jerusalem and shows that a close bond exists between the Temple and the Mosaic institutions of worship. The Chronicler is probably conserving the remembrance of authentic traditions connected to the tent in the desert that become somehow justified here by tying them to the traditions regarding the Ark (cf. v. 4). The first act of Solomon's reign is therefore a genuine liturgical act rather than a political one; the wisdom requested by the king (vv. 7-10) is not due to his inexperience (cf. 1 Kings 3:7) and consists not so much in the ability to govern as in the ability to lead the people to God through the construction of the Temple. In this context references to Solomon's profane knowledge are excluded (cf. 1 Kings 3:16–5:14).

Construction of the Temple (1:18–5:1)

In the account of the pact with King Huram and the preparations for construction the Chronicler omits the narrative contained in 1 Kings 3:15–5:14 and passes directly to describing the *raison d'être* for Solomon's reign, namely the building of the Temple; he makes only a single fleeting allusion to the royal palace (2 Chr 2:11). In chs. 3 and 4 the Chronicler, on the basis of 1 Kings 6–7, describes the building erected by Solomon (ch. 3) and its furnishings (ch. 4). With respect to the text of 1 Kings the Chronicler's narrative is shortened; more attention is given to the worship that should be celebrated in the Temple (cf. chs. 5–7) than to the building as such. He has no scruple over using exaggerated numbers and measures, especially the stated quantities of gold. Finally, some particulars show that in reality our author had in mind the Temple of his era, the one rebuilt after the return from the exile; the veil mentioned in v. 14 is actually typical of the second Temple; the mention of the second month (v. 2) is a reminder of the reconstruction of the Temple after the exile, which also occurred in the second month (cf. Ezra 3:8).

Inauguration of the Temple (5:2–7:22)

These three chapters constitute a literary unit centered on the theme of the dedication of the Temple that, in the Chronicler's view, constitutes the peak of Solomon's reign. To this end the text broadens and modifies the account of 1 Kings 8:1–9:8 that had been shortened in the preceding section, dedicated to the building of the Temple (2 Chronicles 2–4). At the same time the Chronicler strives to harmonize the account of 1 Kings with the cultic practices peculiar to his time.

Transfer of the Ark, 5:2–6:2

The transfer of the Ark to Jerusalem and its entrance into the Temple constitute an important event in the narrative of Solomon's reign, an event in which all Israel is described as participating (vv. 2-3). The Chronicler follows 1 Kings 8:1-13 closely; only vv. 11-13 constitute an addition. In v. 4 the bearers of the Ark are considered no longer to be priests (1 Kings 8:3) but rather Levites, in accordance with the importance that these have in the Chronicler's eyes, yet also in accordance with the priestly prescriptions of Num 3:31 (cf. 1 Chr 23:13-14). It should be noted that the Ark was no longer in existence at the time of Chronicles. The text of the prayers (6:3-11, 12-42) follows 1 Kings 8:15-21, 22-53, but with a more universalist outlook (vv. 32-33).

The description of the feast of the dedication (7:1-10) depends on 1 Kings 8:54-66. Verse 6 constitutes a special addition by the Chronicler, again with respect to liturgical singing by the Levites. In vv. 8-10 the Chronicler modifies the chronology of the feast as contained in 1 Kings 8:64-66. The feast of the dedication (from the 8th to the 14th of the seventh month) appears linked to the pilgrimage feast *par excellence,* the feast of booths (from the 15th to the 21st) and both are concluded by a solemn assembly (on the 22nd), followed by the dismissal of the people on the 23rd of the month.

Exploits and Fame of Solomon (2 Chronicles 8–9)

In the account of some of Solomon's exploits and of the visit of the queen of Sheba, Chronicles follows 1 Kings 9:10-28 and 10:1-13 with some modifications. The campaign conducted against Hamath (8:3) by the king in Lebanon is historically probable. The description of Solomon's fame (9:13-28) closely follows the text of 1 Kings 10:14-29. At the conclusion of Solomon's reign (9:29-31), however, Chronicles omits the whole passage of 1 Kings 11:1-40, which contains the harsh judgment on the end of his reign, just as at the beginning he had omitted 1 Kings 1–2. The ideal figure of Solomon is in this way removed from any possible criticism. Verse 29 cites three different sources to which the Chronicler refers the reader: to the "Acts of Solomon" mentioned in 1 Kings 11:41 he adds the writings of the prophet Nathan (cf. 1 Chr 17:1-15), of Ahijah of Shiloh (cf. 2 Chr 10:15; 1 Kings 11:29-39), and of Iddo, probably the same Iddo of 2 Chr 12:15; 13:22. We have no knowledge of any of these writings; however, the Chronicler's theological perspective is worth noting: the writing of history is considered to be a task entrusted to prophets; understanding history indeed means discovering in it the mystery of the divine plans.

The Kings of Judah Until the Exile: 2 Chronicles 10–36

The final part of the Chronicler's work is dedicated to the history of the Kingdom of Judah beginning with the division of the two kingdoms at the death of Solomon (931 B.C.E.): on principle, the author has no interest in the Northern

Kingdom and limits the narration to the kings of Judah; these represent all Israel, according to the expression used several times in the text. The Chronicler does not conceive of a divided Israel; behind this idea it is possible to discern as well an anti-Samaritan polemical point. In presenting the kings of Judah the Chronicler seeks to highlight the positive aspects, excusing their unfaithfulness in some instances (cf. the case of Manasseh); the evaluating criterion for each king is the constant presence of the typical expression "to seek God/the Lord," that expresses the need to be faithful to God. Four ideal figures emerge as models of this faithfulness: Asa, Jehoshaphat, Josiah, and especially Hezekiah. Alongside the kings the prophets constantly appear. Their proclamation is condensed in warnings and urgent calls to faithfulness to the Lord. In this way the Chronicler reads in the history of the kings of Judah a message of hope addressed to the post-exilic community: despite the disappointments suffered at the time of return and the difficulties experienced in rebuilding, the past history teaches, for the Chronicler, how to recognize God's action on Israel's behalf and invites people to respond by seeking God.

The Revolt of the Northern Tribes (10:1–11:4)

The account of the division of the kingdom of Solomon and the schism of the northern tribes after the king's death reworks the text of 1 Kings 12:1-24; here Jeroboam's rebellion is presented as a punishment for the sins of Solomon, narrated in 1 Kings 11:1-13, that the Chronicler has nonetheless ignored. Moreover, he presupposes that the rebellion of Jeroboam is known to his readers, as well as the episode of the prophet Ahijah of Shiloh (2 Chr 10:15) narrated in 1 Kings 11:29-40. In this way the complaint of the northern tribes and their demands on Jeroboam (v. 4) appear baseless; Solomon, in the Chronicler's view, would not have imposed any heavy yoke on Israelites like that described in 1 Kings 5:27-28, a text that the Chronicler omits. The schism of the North looks rather like the rebellion of a servant against a master (cf. 2 Chr 13:6); the religious aspect of the schism (1 Kings 12:23-36) is practically ignored. Only in part do Rehoboam's ineptitude and stubbornness (cf. vv. 10-11 with Ezra 5:7-8) constitute an explanation for the schism, about which the Chronicler is obliged to speak. Yet the schism clearly does not enter into his theological perspective of a united and faithful Israel.

Rehoboam and Abijah (11:5–13:23)

The history of the reign of Rehoboam (11:5–12:16) stands as an original work of the Chronicler that only in part follows the narration of 1 Kings 12–14. As an introduction to the narrative the Chronicler provides a probably authentic list (11:5-12) of cities that the king would have fortified, in reality only after the invasion of the Pharaoh Sheshonk (= Shishak, 12:1-12). The chronological inversion depends on theological considerations: the invasion, seen as a punishment for the unfaithfulness of Israel, destroys what little good was accomplished in the first three years of the king's faithfulness (cf. 11:17). The next section (11:13-17) also lacks parallels in 1 Kings, with the exception of a fleeting mention of Jeroboam's schismatic cult (cf. 1 Kings 12:26–13:14) that, however, is compared to a real act of idolatry (cf. the mention of "goat-demons"). In this text the Chronicler refers to the migration (probably highly idealized) from the northern kingdom of priests, Levites, and Israelites faithful to Jerusalem, where alone the worship and priestly functions can be practiced. The list of Rehoboam's wives and children (11:18-23) also seems to be authentic, and his harem is considered to be a violation of the norm of Deut 17:17.

The long narrative of the reign of Abijah (13:1-23) is one of the best examples of the method employed by the Chronicler: taking as a basis the sparse details contained in 1 Kings 15:1-8, which give a negative view of the reign of Abijah, the Chronicler re-elaborates the history in a totally new perspective. He renders the king, who at this point has reigned only three years, as a faithful man of God and a worthy successor of David and Solomon. The war declared by Abijah against Jeroboam appears in open contradiction to the order of the prophet Shemaiah in 2 Chr 11:3-4. This therefore is a reference to an actual event that becomes in this case the occasion for setting forth the Chronicler's own theological vision of the events through the improbable and surely fictitious discourse delivered by Abijah to the northern tribes (vv. 4-12).

Asa (2 Chronicles 14–16)

The three chapters dedicated to the reign of Asa constitute an original development by the Chronicler on the basis of sparse details furnished in 1 Kings 15:9-24. In the deuteronomic work the figure of Asa is presented positively; his inglorious end, however, leaves the Chronicler perplexed, and he rereads Asa's history in his own particular theological perspective. The reign of Asa is clearly divided into two parts: a time of prosperity (ch. 14) due to the religious reform effected by the king (ch. 15), and a time of misfortune due to Asa's prevarication (ch. 16). In this manner his reign becomes a paradigmatic text, a living sermon on the theology of retribution, that is, on how God rewards the just and punishes the wicked; it is also a new invitation to religious faithfulness. In these chapters the Chronicler makes use of sources unknown to us that at least in part might have a guarantee of historical authenticity. The war against Zerah (14:8-14) is a report first found in Chronicles; although many critics go so far as to consider it a total invention, many details lead one to think it an authentic episode, albeit broadly reworked in terms of the Chronicler's theology.

The history of the religious reform effected by Asa (15:1-19) is an original composition by the Chronicler that only at the end of the chapter (vv. 16-19) is tied to the text of 1 Kings 15:13-16. Asa's reform, already mentioned in 2 Chr 14:2-4, has some historical foundation, but here it becomes a further occasion for the Chronicler's preaching. The discourse of the prophet Azariah (a prophet otherwise unknown in the Bible) in vv. 2-7 is just a rereading of the events in the light of our author's own theology of history. Using quotations from earlier prophets (cf. Hos 3:4; 5:15–6:1; Ezek 38:21; Hag 2:22; Jer 29:13-14), Azariah calls the people to repent and seek God, the fundamental condition for prosperity. The war against Baasha, king of Israel (16:1-11), is based on 1 Kings 15:17-22, while vv. 7-10 (the prophet's intervention) are the Chronicler's original contribution. The discourse of the prophet Hanani, recorded nowhere else in the Bible, is based on the prophetic accusations of Isa 31:1-3; Hos 6:13; 7:11; 12:2. Verse 9, with the language of Zech 4:10, reaffirms faith in divine retribution.

Jehoshaphat (2 Chronicles 17–20)

The narrative of the reign of Jehoshaphat broadens and modifies in large part the text of 1 Kings 22:1-59, where the figure of the king of Judah is presented in a rather colorless way. The deuteronomic story is concerned more with Ahab, king of Israel during those years and, alongside Ahab, with the long and important cycle of the prophet Elijah (cf. 1 Kings 17–20). Neither Ahab nor Elijah is recalled by the Chronicler, who is interested solely in the history of the kingdom of Judah. The figure of Jehoshaphat is described in an exemplary manner: a faithful king and reformer who enjoyed a long period of peace, another example for our author's contemporaries.

The reform of Jehoshaphat (17:7-9) is similar to that of Nehemiah (Neh 8:9-12; cf. Ezra 7:25) and probably reflects a typical usage of the Persian period when the teaching function had already passed from the priests to the Levites and the teachers of the Law, who are lay persons. In this way the Chronicler projects a typical usage of his own time many centuries into the past. The description of Jehoshaphat's military power (vv. 12-19), although notably expanded, is probably based on authentic sources. In the episode of the alliance with Ahab (18:1–19:3) the Chronicler follows, often to the letter, the text of 1 Kings 22, up to v. 36. The final scene (19:1-3; cf. 2 Chr 14:14–15:1) constitutes a theological reflection proposed by the Chronicler: his "seeking God" (v. 3; but cf. the beginning of the narration in 18:4, 6, 7) saves Jehoshaphat from a possible punishment for having been allied with the impious Ahab.

Judiciary Reforms, 19:4-11

The judicial reform achieved by Jehoshaphat is not narrated in 1 Kings; many critics think that it never happened and that the Chronicler is simply attributing an institution proper to his own time to the epoch of Jehoshaphat. In reality a reform of the judiciary system created by David cannot be excluded *a priori,* particularly the creation of a double system of local tribunals and a "supreme court" in Jerusalem. The distinction between civil cases and religious cases and the affinity to the ideas of Deut 16:18-20; 17:8-13 are also interesting. What is peculiar to the Chronicler, however, is the theological framework into which the narrative of the judiciary reform is inserted.

The account of the war against the Moabites and the Ammonites (20:1-30) is an original composition of the Chronicler and represents the most detailed military narrative contained in 1–2 Chronicles. Behind the text lies a real event, probably a campaign conducted against Judah by a coalition of Transjordanian tribes (Moab, Ammon, and the perhaps Edomite tribe of Meunites) that attacks by coming out of the Dead Sea but is defeated first in an ambush (cf. v. 22) and then in a series of mutual clashes (cf. v. 23). These events are narrated by the Chronicler in line with his own method of inserting them into a broad theological framework that makes examples of them for readers of his time.

The liturgical framework is important: cf. vv. 18-19. Verses 21-22 show the battle starting with sacred singing by the Levites; the account ends with the solemn procession to the Temple (vv. 27-28). All this constitutes a message that the Chronicler sends to his contemporaries: the salvation of the community, in case of danger, lies not in political skill or military power, but in faithfulness to God expressed through worship.

The conclusion to the reign of Jehoshaphat (20:31-37) is taken from 1 Kings 22:41-45. Nevertheless, v. 33 contradicts what is stated in 2 Chr 17:6; this tension is due to the sometimes uncritical use the Chronicler makes of his sources; moreover, v. 33, in contrast with the piety and success of Jehoshaphat, expresses again the difficulty felt by the Chronicler: the ideal of a people who "seek God" is far from being fully attained. With this key it is also possible to understand the negative end of Jehoshaphat (vv. 35-37): by inverting the order of events found in 1 Kings 22:49-50 the Chronicler sees in the failure of the maritime expedition undertaken by Jehoshaphat the punishment for his alliance with the North. Once again it is a prophet (v. 37) who shows the theological meaning of events; the Chronicler in fact claims (v. 34) to be using a prophet as his source.

From Jehoram to Ahaz (2 Chronicles 21–28)

With the reign of Jehoram (21:1-20) the Chronicler enters into the darkest period of the kingdom of Judah, part of it exile, a period that culminates in the reign of Ahaziah and particularly the regency of Queen Athaliah, who is succeeded, thanks to a popular revolt, by Joash and then Amaziah, Uzziah, and Ahaz.

The alliance of Jehoshaphat with the northern kingdom (cf. 2 Chr 20:35) opens the doors to the attempt by the kingdom of Israel to destroy the Davidic dynasty: all this is seen by the Chronicler as a punishment for the sins of Jehoram and Ahaziah. The attempt, however, fails because God is faithful to the house of David (cf. 2 Chr 21:7; 1 Kings 11:36; 15:4; 2 Kings 8:19). The history of Jehoram, Athaliah, and the successive kings follows the text of 2 Kings 8 with significant modifications and additions, above all of a theological character, especially the introduction of some prophetic figures. Among these the curious mention of the letter of Elijah creates problems of chronology; indeed, according to 2 Kings 3:1 Elijah vanishes before the reign of Jehoram.

For the reign of Joash (24:1-16) the Chronicler departs very little from the account of 2 Kings 12:1-17; the changes made in the text are nonetheless significant. According to 2 Kings 12:18-22, after the restoration of the Temple ordered by Joash as a reaction to damages probably caused by Athaliah the king comes to an inglorious end; the Chronicler feels the need to justify this by introducing, in the second part of ch. 24, the mention of a sin of Joash that is the cause of his punishment. In this manner the whole first part of his reign is described as a happy period. The dividing point, for the Chronicler, is the death of the priest Jehoiadah (vv. 15-17). Verse 2 is enlightening in this regard compared with 2 Kings 12:3: Joash did God's will only as long as Jehoiada was alive. This highlights the importance of the high priest.

After the death of Jehoiada (24:17-22) the sending of the prophets and particularly of Zechariah is a further example of the theology of the Chronicler regarding the prophets: they have the task of "warning" (v. 19; cf. 2 Chr 19:9-10) so that sinners might convert if they want. The public stoning of Zechariah, condemned to the penalty of blasphemers, taking place moreover within the Temple, is the sign of rejection of the king and, for the Chronicler, the moment of his definitive condemnation. The episode is probably the one referred to, with minor variants, in Matt 23:35.

The history of the reign of Amaziah (25:1-28) is narrated by the Chronicler in a way similar to that of Joash: the text of 2 Kings 14:1-22 posed a theological problem: how to reconcile the defeat by Israel and the inglorious death of a basically good king? The Chronicler responds with two long additions, vv. 5-10 and 13-16 (cf. also v. 20) that, just as in the case of Joash, show the fate of Amaziah according to the canons of divine justice (cf. the quotation from Deut 24:16 in v. 4; see Jer 31:10; Ezek 18:20): his end is due to his sin. Nevertheless, the events recorded by the Chronicler concerning the recruitment of Israelite mercenaries and the description of the war of aggression against Edom need not be totally lacking in foundation.

King Uzziah (26:1-23) is none other than Azariah who is briefly the subject in 2 Kings 15:1-4, 6-7, who nonetheless reigned all of fifty-two years; the brevity of the deuteronomic account is clearly unsatisfactory to the Chronicler, who therefore provides a much fuller and elaborate narration. The Chronicler's theological intent is clear: as in the case of Jehoiada and Joash (cf. 2 Chr 24:2) he juxtaposes Uzziah to a teacher, Zechariah, probably a priest. The second part of the narrative (vv. 16-21) thus passes unexpectedly from the historical plane to the theological: in a highly dramatic scene the sin of the king is described as having arrogated to himself priestly prerogatives by burning incense in the Temple. While this was considered normal in the early times of the monarchy (1 Kings 8:64; 2 Kings 16:13) it was no longer permitted for a lay person under priestly legislation after the exile: cf. Exod 30:7-9; Num 18:1-7; Lev 10:2; 1 Chr 23:13.

The reign of Jotham (27:1-9) is dealt with in a few verses, as already in 2 Kings 15:32-38, to which the Chronicler adds some original material (vv. 3b-6).

The history of the reign of Ahaz (28:1-27) is an original exposition by the Chronicler, very different from what is recounted in 2 Kings 16:1-20 and Isaiah 7–8; it is based on sources unknown to us. Although elaborated theologically, the events told still seem to retain a historical core. The height of Ahaz's faults is attained, according to the Chronicler, in the closing of the Temple doors (v. 24), that is, in the abolition of daily worship (cf. 2 Chr 29:7).

The account of the war against the Arameans and the northern kingdom (known as the "Syro-Ephraimite war") is an original composition by the Chronicler (28:5-15), of extreme interest for understanding his vision with respect to Israel. Absent from the narrative are the Chronicler's usual themes such as the description of the battle, the recourse to God, and the miraculous intervention by the Lord. Rather the core of the account is the brotherhood that should exist between Israel and Judah: this concept is expressed as usual through the intervention of a prophet, Oded (vv. 9-11), who invites Israel to repent and to acknowledge the inhabitants of Judah as kin (v. 11); the prohibition against enslaving Israelites is contained in Lev 25:29-43. The intervention of the northern leaders (vv. 12-13) constitutes a surprising admission of their own faults. The attitude of the Chronicler toward the North (and therefore toward Samaritans who were his contemporaries) is much less negative than is often believed: Israel and Judah should be brothers and sisters even though they have sinned against each other. Judah's defeat, narrated in v. 6, is not corroborated by historical documents; it is rather a sign of what happens when kinship is shattered.

Hezekiah (2 Chronicles 29–32)

The Chronicler dedicates four long chapters to the reign of Hezekiah, thus making of this king a figure of the first rank in comparison with the other sovereigns of Judah after David and Solomon. The Chronicler transmits almost entirely the text of 2 Kings 18–20, omitting only 2 Kings 18:9-12; however, he inserts a number of original texts: 2 Chr 29:3-36, the purification of the Temple and the restoration of worship; 2 Chr 30:1-27, the celebration of Passover; 2 Chr 31:1-19, the reorganization of the clergy; 2 Chr 32:27-30, the prosperity of Hezekiah. It is evident from these additions that the Chronicler's interest has shifted entirely to the religious aspect of Hezekiah's reign: our author dedicates nearly three chapters to developing the short text of 2 Kings 18:4. Hezekiah is presented as a religious reformer superior even to Josiah, so much so that the Chronicler is held to have transferred to Hezekiah some elements that belong to the subsequent Josian reform. As in the previous history of Ahaz (2 Chronicles 28) the absence of the prophet Isaiah (mentioned only in 2 Chr 32:20) is striking: the Chronicler's attention is concentrated entirely on the king and the people, and the faithful Hezekiah requires no prophet to admonish him.

In the context of the religious reform (29:1-36) the importance of the Levites with respect to the priests emerges in the purification of the Temple; indeed, it is the Levites whom the king addresses with the singular appellation "my sons," while the priests are explicitly reproached in v. 34 for their lack of zeal. All this gives testimony to the situation created in the post-exilic era: the growth of levitical prerogatives advanced to the detriment of the priests' role. Amid the tensions arising from this the Chronicler takes the side of the Levites, underlining the importance of their role. An interesting new feature in ceremony is, still in full accordance with the style of the Chronicler, the presence of sacred music (vv. 25-30) inspired by the levitical cantors listed in vv. 12-14 and by joy (v. 30b).

The Solemn Celebration of Passover, 30:1-27

This constitutes for the Chronicler the second act of the reign of Hezekiah who, in v. 26, is explicitly compared to Solomon. A characteristic feature of this text is the invitation to the feast expressly extended to the northern tribes and the actual participation of some of them (v. 11). Hezekiah also allows those who are not ritually pure to celebrate Passover (vv. 17-20; cf. Lev 7:19-21). The purity of inner dispositions is seen as superior in comparison to legal purity, which is still considered to be important (cf. in the NT Matt 15:1-20; Mark 7:1-13). Finally, vv. 23-27 describe a second feast whose characteristic appears as joy and spontaneity in celebration, born of enthusiasm and popular faith.

Reorganization of Worship and of the Priesthood, 31:1–32:33

Concluding the presentation of Hezekiah, the Chronicler takes over the text of 1 Kings 18:4-6, dividing it into two sections: v. 4 corresponds to 2 Chr 31:1, vv. 5-6 to 2 Chr 31:20-21. Between the two parts, the first relative to the religious reform of Hezekiah, and the second containing a flattering judgment on his work, the Chronicler inserts vv. 2-19, dedicated to the last act of the king's work: the restructuring of the clergy and the reorganization of levitical and priestly service (cf. 2 Chr 8:14-15 and 23:18-19). In particular, norms are set for the contributions and offerings of the people and the king; the latter's are regulated in accordance with the prescriptions of Ezek 45:22-24; 46:2.

The episode of the invasion by Sennacherib, king of Assyria (32:1-23) is a development of the text of 2 Kings 18–19: in accordance with his own style the Chronicler shortens the deuteronomic account, omitting many of its parts (18:7-8; 14-16; 19:3-4, 6-9, 15-34) and adding some original texts; in this latter case our author makes use of sources unknown to us but probably worthy of credence. Among the preparations for the siege (vv. 3-6) it is interesting to note the concern for water resources (see vv. 3-4 and 30; cf. 2 Kings 20:20 and Isa 22:9-11), which in part has been confirmed by archaeology with the discovery of the famous "Hezekiah's tunnel." This tunnel still diverts water from the well of Gihon outside the walls to within the city in order to guarantee water in the event of a siege.

The words the Chronicler places in the king's mouth as he exhorts the people (32:7-8) take on special importance. The end of v. 7 contains an allusion to the Isaian oracle of Immanuel, God with us (Isa 7:14). It is significant that this prophetic exhortation is placed in the mouth of the king rather than that of the prophet Isaiah. The latter is strangely absent (with the exception of 32:20) even in the account of the message of Sennacherib (vv. 9-23). Contrast his prominence in the parallel text of 2 Kings 19. This absence can be explained by the tendency to exalt Hezekiah, who needs no prophet alongside him as other kings do, but who lives in direct relationship with God. Hezekiah, and along with him the whole people, thus appear in a different light: no longer frightened by the Assyrians, but fully trusting in God's action.

Regarding the final years of Hezekiah (32:24-35), the disappearance of the episode narrated in 2 Kings 20:1-11 is striking. It deals with Hezekiah's illness, to which the Chronicler alludes only in v. 24, excluding as well any reference to Isaiah (see above).

Manasseh, Amon, and Josiah (2 Chronicles 33–35)

The figure of Manasseh (33:1-20) is presented in 2 Kings 21:1-18 in an unfailingly negative light. Yet the exceptional length of his reign, all of fifty-five years, has of course created problems for the Chronicler who sees in the king's longevity a divine reward, utterly unthinkable in the case of an evildoer like Manasseh. Therefore after the negative presentation of the king in line with the deuteronomic presentation (2 Chr 33:1-9), in vv. 10-11 he introduces a new theme: the punishment of Manasseh, namely exile to Babylon, imposed on him by the Assyrians. From some Assyrian texts we know that Manasseh indeed had to go to Nineveh as a vassal of the kings Esarhaddon and Ashurbanipal, perhaps at the time of the revolt against the latter stirred up in 652–648 B.C.E. by one of his brothers, and in which Manasseh might have participated. This forced journey may have been read by the Chronicler as a true "exile" and therefore interpreted as a divine punishment. Thus even Manasseh's return to his country is reinterpreted by the Chronicler as a sign of his conversion (vv. 12-13), which leads him to change his attitude, as is narrated in vv. 14-17. An apocryphal psalm of the Hellenistic epoch, the "Prayer of Manasseh," found also in the Latin Bible (the "Vulgate"), pauses to reflect on the "conversion" of this king just as the Chronicler tells it. The Chronicler transfers to Amon (33:21-25, based on 2 Kings 21:19-24) the wickedness for which the text of 2 Kings associates him with his father Manasseh.

Josiah (2 Chronicles 34–35)

According to the text of 2 Kings 22:1–23:30 Josiah is the greatest king of Judah after David and Solomon. The Chronicler reserves this honor, however, to Hezekiah: the tragic death of Josiah is for him in some way a sign of divine disapproval. The text of 2 Chr 35:20-25 indeed relates this even much more extensively than does 2 Kings 23:29-30. The Chronicler presents the reform of Josiah in a different way than do the books of Kings, not as a single act that would have occurred after the discovery of the "Book of the Law" and would have come to pass as a radical cleansing of every trace of idolatry infesting the Temple during the reign of the impious Manasseh. After mentioning a reform of Manasseh himself (2 Chr 33:15-17) the Chronicler reads the action of Josiah rather as a much blander and more gradual reform commenced at the beginning of his reign (2 Chr 34:3-7). This shift of the Josian reform to the early times of his reign and, at the same time, the redimensioning of the reform itself, many elements of which are retrodated by the Chronicler to Hezekiah, possess, according to many modern historians, serious guarantees of authenticity. The struggle against alien cults can be seen besides as the religious expression of the desire to be free of vassalage to the Assyrian empire, already weakened in the last years of King Ashurbanipal.

The Chronicler sets the beginning of Josiah's reform (34:1-7) between 628 and 626 B.C.E., namely in the final years of the Assyrian king Ashurbanipal. Verses 3-7 have no parallels in 2 Kings: Josiah is presented as a monarch who since his youth (at age sixteen) was committed to the radical religious reform that the deuteronomic account attributes to his mature years (cf. 2 Kings 22:3 and the preceding paragraph of this essay). The Chronicler's main concern is to underscore the range of the operation, which extends well beyond the confines of the kingdom of Judah (vv. 6-7). This will be repeated again in 2 Chr 34:9, 21, 33, and 35:17-18: the extension of the Josian reform to the northern territories is probably historical in a period when Assyrian power was in decline. What interests our author is still the ideal range of this event: in the Josian reform all Israel will find itself united, according to the Chronicler's cherished ideal. The account of the discovery of the "Book of the Law" (34:8-33) follows closely the text of 2 Kings 22:3–23:3 with some significant changes, especially the mention of the Levites and the cantors.

After the description of the covenant, that is, the commitment made by Josiah to observe the Law together with the people (vv. 29-32), the Chronicler resumes in v. 33 the reform recounted in 2 Kings 23:4-20, which our author has shifted to the early years of the reign of Josiah (cf. 2 Chr 34:3-7). Nineteen verses (35:1-19) are dedicated to the celebration of Passover as arranged by Josiah, while it is told in only three verses in 2 Kings 23:21-23. Here as well the Levites are highlighted and their role is emphasized. After only one verse dedicated to the priests (v. 2; cf. 2 Chr 31:2-3) the king personally addresses the Levites (vv. 3-6), defining their tasks precisely. Outstanding among these is the role of "teachers of the people" (cf. Neh 8:7), which in the immediate post-exilic period belonged instead to the priests (2 Chr 15:3; Hag 2:11; Zech 7:3; Mal 2:7). Verses 7-9, beyond their hyperbolic numbers—more than forty thousand head of cattle sacrificed for four hundred thousand participants—show that the Passover, as a family feast (Ezra 12:2-3), is now characterized as a great national feast in which everyone is called to participate generously. The Passover ritual described in vv. 10-17 comprises not just the immolation of lambs but also holocausts and sacrifices of communion in which all the people can share. All this establishes the newness of the Passover proclaimed by the Chronicler in vv. 18-19.

Death of Josiah, 35:20-27

Here we have a narrative that is more extensive than its matching text in 2 Kings 23:29-30. It is confirmed by the discovery of the "Babylonian Chronicles." The tragic death of the king while still young creates a theological problem for the Chronicler that he resolves by presupposing a grave sin on Josiah's part that caused his ruin (note the similarity to the death of Ahab in 2 Chr 18:33-34). Surprisingly the sin is described as a refusal to listen to the word of God pronounced by Neco (v. 22): in this way a pagan (as earlier Balaam in Numbers 22–24) is considered on a par with prophets and the words he pronounces in the name of his god are reread as genuine words of the God of Israel. The lament for the death of Josiah (v. 25) is said to be taken from Lamentations; it may be that the Chronicler is thinking about the book of Lamentations or else the text of Zech 9:12-14.

The Last Kings of Judah: Exile and Return (2 Chronicles 36)

In its last chapter Chronicles provides a very quick summary of the events that occurred from the death of Josiah until the Babylonian exile. In only twenty-one verses he sets down what is related, with abundant detail, in 2 Kings 23:31–25:30 (cf. Jeremiah 39 and 52); in particular the Chronicler omits the whole of 2 Kings 25, which describes the destruction of Jerusalem by Nebuchadnezzar. It is evident that the Chronicler's intention is to consider the exile as a tragic event, but one that has concluded and is remote in time: the edict of Cyrus, which will be mentioned at the very end of the work (2 Chr 36:22-23), opens Israel to a new hope. Jehoahaz (36:1-5; cf. 2 Kings 23:31-35) is the last king chosen by the people.

With regard to Jehoiakim (36:5-8) Chronicles records an imprisonment of the king in Babylon (v. 6), omitted by 2 Kings yet mentioned in Dan 1:1-2 and historically probable, after the victory of Nebuchadnezzar at Carchemish in 605 B.C.E. against the Pharaoh Neco.

In the brief description of the destruction of Jerusalem and ruin of the Temple in 586 B.C.E. (2 Chr 36:11-21) there is significance in the final comment of v. 21, which combines the texts of Jer 25:11; 29:10 with Lev 26:33-35. The exile is considered to be the fulfillment of the prophecies of Jeremiah (the number of seventy years is symbolic) but at the same time it is the sign of fulfilling the law of the Sabbath year (Leviticus 26); the land that has been contaminated by its inhabitants must "rest" while they are in exile so that life might return there. In this way the Chronicler expresses awareness of the temporal limits of the exile (cf. the nod to the Persians: 2 Chr 36:22-23) yet, at the same time, according to the priestly tradition he reaffirms the importance of the Sabbath law, the observance of which becomes, for the Israel of his time, a sign of faithfulness to the Lord.

The Chronicler's work ends in 36:22-23 with an explicit quotation from Ezra 1:1-4 that in turn contains a version, probably reworked, of the edict of Cyrus by which the king of Persia, in 538 B.C.E., allowed the return of the Jewish exiles to Jerusalem. By ending his work with this text the Chronicler expresses the certainty that even a pagan king can be sent by God, as happened with Neco (2 Chr 35:22) and Nebuchadnezzar (2 Chr 36:17-21). It is significant that the Chronicler interrupts the words of Ezra 1:1-4 at v. 3a with "Let him go up." The edict of Cyrus does not signify, as in Ezra, the beginning of the hard work of rebuilding, but is like a shout of triumph and liberation. While 2 Kings 23–25 ends with Israel still in exile, the Chronicler opens the doors to hope.

BIBLIOGRAPHY

See pages 653–654.

Ezra–Nehemiah

Giuseppe Bettenzoli

Preface

The first impression anyone receives on setting out to read the books of Ezra–Nehemiah is that one is looking at a historical account organic in its parts and coherent in its logic. However, a deeper reading shows the text to be full of contradictions even from the strictly historical point of view. Indeed, Ezra–Nehemiah is a collection of texts, heterogeneous in their structure and literary genre as well as in their diversity of historical, environmental, and social situations, and in the linguistic connotation specific to them. This refers not so much to the use of different languages (Hebrew and Aramaic) as to the different asyntactic and lexemic forms present in the various texts that surely can be traced to different times and social environments.

In order to provide more adequate tools for understanding the compositional history of these texts while also analyzing them for greater practicality in their current redactional sequence, we have brought them back, with appropriate annotations, into homogeneous groupings according to their linguistic, literary, and thematic characteristics. In this way five cores of texts can be identified:

(1) A core of diaristic (autobiographical) texts comprising the personal memoirs of Ezra and Nehemiah, written in the first person and having in common the explicit consciousness that the mission of the protagonists is accomplished only through particular protection on the part of God and the Persian king.

(2) Complementary texts to this original core (autobiographical additions), adapting at least partially their style and literary forms; they too generally contain a relatively ancient documentation.

(3) A core of liturgical-narrative texts whose homogeneity is shown above all in introductory and concluding formulas as well as in the theme.

(4) Documents of the administrative archive not included in the preceding texts but not redactionally reworked in other contexts.

(5) Redactional texts primarily intended for the historical integration of events and persons. To these texts are of course added all the introductory and concluding formulas and the insertions that can be attributed with confidence to the work of the final redactor.

This subdivision into homogeneous cores is not conceived as a chronological distribution assuring that one text is anterior or posterior to another, but is proposed solely according to a logical viewpoint. The dating should be sought, where possible, within the texts themselves; moreover, their insertion into the unified set could have happened either through successive stages or only at the time of the final redaction.

Every text is substantially analyzed in its literary, linguistic, and thematic characteristics so as to permit a more objective evaluation of its original historical and theological meaning. This is then verified or not in the context of the final redaction, in which it may have undergone changes or transformations. The final redactor indeed organizes the texts on the basis of his historical-theological evaluation so as to display the providential design of YHWH in the work of social and religious reconstruction of the Jewish community. The events are then grouped in the following thematic units:

Ezra 1–6: return from exile and reconstruction of the Temple despite Samaritan opposition. This ends positively with the solemn celebration of Passover and Unleavened Bread in 515 (Ezra 6:19-22).

Ezra 7–10: the moral and religious organization of the Jewish community as the work of Ezra, who calls for respect for the Torah especially to eliminate mixed marriages, seen as a danger for social integrity and the purity of faith in YHWH. The conclusion contains a list of those who repudiate their foreign wives together with their children as an example of submission to YHWH (Ezra 10:18-44).

Nehemiah 1–7: the civil organization of the Jewish community as the work of Nehemiah, who promotes and completes the reconstruction of the walls of Jerusalem despite the opposition of the authorities of Samaria. The conclusion of this part presents the picture of the repopulation of Jerusalem and the list of inhabitants.

Nehemiah 8–12: the birth of Judaism with the solemn reading of the Torah by Ezra, with a grand ceremony of expiation and the solemnly signed agreement of the religious and civil leaders to respect the prescriptions of the Torah. This section is concluded with a series of lists of the inhabitants of the territories of Judah and with the feast of dedication of the walls of Jerusalem (Nehemiah 11–12); to this is added an overall picture of the work of reconstruction, seen as the ideal epoch in the life of the Jewish community (Neh 12:44-47).

Nehemiah 13: this speaks of the second mission of Nehemiah and the social difficulties springing up in Jerusalem for which Nehemiah must provide a remedy.

In this rather complex work of redactional stitching the original purpose of each text was of course modified: the texts are removed from the historical context in which they were formed and are bent to the redactor's ideological design in support of a particular demonstrative thesis. However, the redactor's skill does not prove to be particularly refined, since the result is not an acceptable coherence. The defect probably lies in an excessive yielding of the redactor to the literal expression of the compiled texts. This is a defect in the redaction, but an advantage for us: because of it we can more easily reconstruct the events in their historical setting.

In reading the various texts we must therefore inquire into a double interpretive dimension: the original, tied to the formation of the text (how and why the text was created) and the redactional, touching the problems and ideology of the redactor's time (how and for what purpose the text was used). This distinction is very important for a correct historical inquiry and also for evaluating texts in our daily experience.

A particular problem is posed by the massive presence in this book of lists of names. At a first reading these lists become rather tiresome, if not annoying and incomprehensible in the dynamic of the narrated events. It must be said first of all that it was part of the mentality of the epoch and the literary style of the chronicle redactors to insert lists of names drawn from various administrative archives. Some lists in Ezra–Nehemiah surely serve as historical documentation, witnessing to the historicity of the events. Such, for example, are the list in Ezra 2:1-70 // Neh 7:6-72, a census of the inhabitants of Judea, and the lists inserted in the autobiographical texts (Ezra 8:16-20; Neh 3:1-32).

Nevertheless, there are many other lists, added after the first redaction, that incongruously interrupt some literary units, such as Ezra 8:1-14; 10:18-44; Neh 12:33-36, 41-42, or else they are a confused pile of different lists, more or less justifiable at the time when the redactors inserted them. For example, their purpose may have been to confirm the reconciliation among rival priestly families (Ezra 8:1-14) or to denounce families guilty of having contracted mixed marriages, thus placing them outside the pale of Jewish society (Ezra 10:18-44), or to legitimize the right of many families to reside in Jerusalem or in various cities of Judea (Neh 11:1-36), or finally to highlight the ancestors of priests and Levites who in some way had distinguished themselves in the service of the Temple (Neh 12:1-26, 33-36, 41-42).

With these lists, added at a later time, we therefore depart from the historical-theological sphere and descend to interests that are more contingent and internal for the chronicle redactors' contemporary society: that is, we descend to the level of legitimizing acquired rights. We therefore are looking at an undeniable sign of decay of religious ideals in Jewish society, which thus finds itself far from the narrated historical phase both from the temporal and cultural points of view. Indeed, we perceive in the redactors of Ezra–Nehemiah an evident feeling of nostalgia for the heroic epoch of reconstruction when there was readiness and enthusiasm on the part of the Jewish people in adhering to the Torah and displaying their own social and religious identity (cf. Neh 12:44–13:3). Now, however, they find themselves faced with a new ferment of ideas and deeds that tend to put into crisis the social and religious model that had been affirmed during the Persian empire. Very probably we are in the years following the exploits of Alexander the Great, in the last part of the fourth century, and of the first expansion of Hellenistic culture, with everything positive and negative that it brought under both economic and cultural aspects. The very awareness that the time for rebuilding was irremediably past must have led the chronicle redactors to draft the post-exilic history in Ezra–Nehemiah in such a way as to present to their contemporaries a reference model to incite them to maintain uncontaminated their religious identity, the indispensable premise for their proper activity in history. [See also the article "Introduction to 1 and 2 Chronicles, Ezra–Nehemiah."]

I. Ezra

Cyrus Decrees the Liberation (Redactional Text) (Ezra 1:1-11)

By "redactional text" we mean here a literary unit that did not exist before the chronicle redactor, but was created by him specifically in order to frame properly, from a historical viewpoint, the literary material compiled by him. Naturally he may have made use of sources from elsewhere, but the text in itself can be considered his creation.

Ezra 1:1-11 is an example of a redactional text, set as a historical introduction to all the material compiled in Ezra–Nehemiah. Verses 1-3a are a literary duplicate of 2 Chr 36:22-23, citing the text of the edict of Cyrus, and completed in vv. 3b-4 by the invitation that the Persian king issued to the exiles to restore worship in Jerusalem. The response to the edict is given in vv. 5-6 in the positive reply of the families of Judah and Benjamin, of priests and Levites, to whom the other exiles entrust the donations for the Temple of YHWH. To this introductory account is added the documentation of the treasures of the Temple, confiscated by Nebuchadnezzar in his time, that are given back by Cyrus into the hands of Sheshbazzar, "the prince of Judah" (vv. 7-8). Its exact inventory is stated (vv. 9-11a) and the passage concludes with a final annotation summarizing the preceding theme (v. 11b).

Lists of Repatriates (Administrative Texts) (Ezra 2:1-70 // Neh 7:6-72)

An especially important early document is the list of repatriates in the time of Zerubbabel in Ezra 2:1-70, so important that it has been reintroduced with some slight variants in Neh 7:6-72. Only the redactional usage of this text changes: in Ezra 2 it serves to underscore the return of the exiles, and in Nehemiah 7 to document the repopulation of Jerusalem (cf. the redactional introduction to this latter document in Neh 7:4-5). The list is arranged partly by family but primarily by city, and for every city the total number of residents is noted (Ezra 2:5-58; Neh 7:8-60). There is a separate registry of the Temple personnel: priests, Levites, singers, gatekeepers, and "oblates," or servants.

In Ezra 2:59-63 // Neh 7:61-65 there follows a list of priestly families that were unable to document their Israelite origin and were therefore excluded from the priesthood. Finally, Ezra 2:64-67 // Neh 7:66-69 state the total number of individuals in the worship assembly *(qāhāl)* together with their beasts of burden. In addition there are donations of money and objects for the Temple from some family heads (Ezra 2:68-69 // Neh 7:70-71). This all ends with a general observation on the place of residence of the Temple personnel (Ezra 2:70 // Neh 7:72).

This document is composed of various parts with different origins: the first section is specifically a census of the inhabitants of Judah, while the rest is drawn from the Temple archives regarding personnel in service. All this is used by the redactor for completely different narrative purposes, as noted above.

Reconstruction of the Temple Altar (Liturgical-Narrative Text) (Ezra 3:1-13)

The limits of the literary unit in question are easily recognizable: it begins in v. 1a with a dating by the month and a brief historical-social setting ("the Israelites were in the towns") followed in v. 1b by the reference to the assembly of the people in Jerusalem; it ends in v. 13, in which the introductory term *ʿām* (people) recurs, recapitulating the assembly's ambivalent behavior (joy and weeping) during the liturgical ceremonies and underscoring the great clamor that could be heard from a distance.

The body of the excerpt speaks about the consecration of a provisional altar by Zerubbabel and Jeshua, and about the preparations for and organization of the tasks of rebuilding the Temple. The text's narrative development is hardly linear: v. 3 repeats substantially the same concepts as v. 2 in making some remarks on fear of enemies and the kind of sacrifices offered. Likewise v. 6 returns to the theme of sacrifices from v. 4b in specifying their continuity in time as well as the absence of the structure of the Temple. These are both clarifications that disturb the linearity of the presentation and respond to didactic-cultic requirements extraneous to the original narrative intent.

Verses 7-10 dwell on the modalities of Temple construction: the procurement of wood, the direction of the works entrusted to the Levites, the list of those in charge of the works and the start of the foundations of the *hēkal,* the most sacred part of the Temple. At that point the festive celebrations begin (v. 10), with Davidic songs (Ps 100:5 is quoted in v. 11) that arouse contrasting emotions: the elders remember the first Temple and weep out of nostalgia for past grandeur while the young exult with joy, satisfied with what has been accomplished (v. 12). This is clearly a text of the narrative sort, yet with everything centered on the renewal of worship in Jerusalem. The author dwells especially on liturgical details, highlighting their importance and their conformity with the Mosaic Law.

Hostility over the Rebuilding of the Temple (Redactionally Reorganized Administrative Texts) (Ezra 4:1-6, 22)

This literary unit is a composite, and certainly went through redactions at different times. However, we consider it here as a unit because of its theme. In its context it serves as an anti-Samaritan document. Parts of it, perhaps the older ones, are in Aramaic, and parts in Hebrew; the latter appear as a historical and redactional completion of the former. We speak of "parts" in the plural because the Aramaic text is composed of two different documents probably drawn from the royal archives: 4:8-23 represents the correspondence carried on between Rehum, the governor of Samaria, and King Artaxerxes concerning the rebuilding of the walls of Jerusalem; these works are interpreted as an act of rebellion against the king and therefore are interrupted by a royal ordinance. However, 4:24–6:18 speaks about the reconstruction of the Temple under Zerubbabel and Jeshua, always within the correspondence between the governor Tattenai and King Darius; Tattenai's report is detailed and bureaucratically correct: he asks that the archives be searched to see if there was an ordinance of Cyrus for the rebuilding of the Temple. Cyrus's document is indeed found and quoted in the king's reply, asking the governor to actively facilitate the practice of the cult of YHWH.

This last unit is especially developed literarily: it has its evident redactional introduction in 4:24, recapitulating the status of the work on the Temple up to the second year of Darius. This is followed in 5:1-2 by a historical context that allows the continuation of reconstruction. Later there is a full historical conclusion in 6:14-18 where mention is made of the completion of the works and of the feast of the dedication of the Temple with the official installation of the priests.

The unit in 4:8-23, however, is a much more meager document, copied from the archives almost without change except for an introduction (v. 8) and conclusion (v. 23) that remain within the bureaucratic style. Strangely, it is set before 4:24–6:18, thereby causing a lack of congruence from a historical-chronological point of view. This supposes that the redactor did not know the chronology of the narrated events, or else more likely that he organized the documentary material according to a logical and thematic order; on this basis the problem of the city walls precedes the building of the Temple, which represents the completion of social life in Jerusalem. Moreover, the redactor adds to this the account in Hebrew of the celebration of Passover (6:19-22), the climax of Judah's recovery of its socio-religious identity.

The introduction to the whole literary unit (4:1-7) can be attributed to the same redactional hand (cf. the definition of the Jews as "exiles": 4:1; 6:19, 20). This too is in Hebrew, and it has the evident purpose of completing the historical context of Samaritan opposition, going back to the time of Zerubbabel and Jeshua (vv. 1-4) and under the rule of Cyrus and Darius (v. 5) as well as of Xerxes (v. 6). Then v. 7 is an introduction in Hebrew to the Aramaic document of 4:8-23 examined above.

Clearly this literary unit has gone through a rather complex redactional history that has led to inconsistencies or superimpositions of historical data. It is not that the redactors did not realize this, but rather that their intent was ideological and thematic: to show the continual opposition of the Samaritans, who still are not successful in their aim of stopping the works of reconstruction. They have included two Aramaic documents that in reality do not so much show opposition as rather administrative correctness on the part of the authorities in Samaria.

Ezra Returns to Jerusalem (Redactional Text) (Ezra 7:1-10)

This text functions as a literary hinge and introduction to the figure and activity of Ezra. The formula "after this" (v. 1a) ties the ensuing content to what had previously been said. Moreover, Ezra's genealogy is presented, going back to Aaron (vv. 1b-5) to bring out his authority as an interpreter of the Law on whom the favor of both God and the king converge (v. 6). In vv. 7-10 there then follows a brief panorama of Ezra's work with its two purposes. This anticipates the themes of the documents compiled in the chapters that follow.

Letter of Artaxerxes (Administrative Text) (Ezra 7:11-26)

After the list in Ezra 2 a second important document is contained in Ezra 7:12-26, written in Aramaic, preceded by an introduction in Hebrew (v. 11) that repeats in general the beginning of the document itself. This is the letter of King Artaxerxes to Ezra, conferring upon him the charge of applying the Law of YHWH in Judah, in the version approved by the Persian authorities (cf. v. 26) and delivered into Ezra's hands (cf. vv. 14, 25). One of the political aims of the kings of Persia was indeed to promote clear legislation for each subject people, respecting its religious traditions and beliefs. Ezra is granted full administrative and judicial powers (v. 26), supported by subsidies from the central treasury (cf. vv. 21-24). It is evident that this document is drawn from the archives of the Persian court and is fundamental for understanding the role actually played by Ezra as the king's commissioner with political power over Judah to bring the Yahwist Law into application, which over time had become the law of the king of Persia for the people of Judea.

Prayers of Ezra (Ezra 7:27-28)

See below, Ezra 8:15-36.

Another List of Repatriates (Administrative Text) (Ezra 8:1-14)

This text is inserted inappropriately into the literary unit Ezra 7:27-28; 8:15-36, interrupting its narrative logic. This shows that its placement is to be attributed to a later redactor who wanted to complete the account of Ezra's return with the list of exiles who accompanied him. There is no reason, however, not to believe that the document quoted has its own antiquity and historical validity, even though it probably has been reinterpreted and modified.

The list begins with two priests belonging to two formerly rival families: the Zadokites and the posterity of Abiathar, who had been removed from the Temple (cf. 1 Kings 2:27). Naming them together indicates their reconciliation. The list continues with the names of family heads, to which are added the numbers of males accompanying each of them. While there is a clear introduction in v. 1, a literary conclusion is lacking at the end of the list, a sign that as a literary text it is strictly redactional.

Preparations for Ezra's Journey (Autobiographical Text) (Ezra 8:15-36)

This text is a narration in the first person of the repatriation to Jerusalem achieved by Ezra with a retinue of exiles, particularly priests and

Levites. The recounting of events is introduced at vv. 7:27-28 with thanks to God for the favor gained from the king and from the authorities of the Persian kingdom, and with a statement of the theme of repatriation (v. 28b). In this last verse there appears the expression "for the protective hand of God was upon me," which recurs in the text (cf. 8:18, 31) and provides a thematic thread for this whole literary unit.

The introductory verb for this narrative, "and I gathered" (v. 28b), is repeated in 8:15 and specified by data both geographical ("by the river that runs to Ahava") and bureaucratic (record of the identities of the exiles). From these opening remarks the actual account flows (vv. 16-34). It alternates between bureaucratic reports (vv. 16-20, 24-30) and narrative parts (vv. 21-23, 31-34). Verses 16-20 tell in detail about the search for Levites for service in the Temple, citing meticulously the names of persons and localities with the precise number of Levite volunteers ready to return to Jerusalem. This bureaucratic style is also evident in vv. 24-30, which speak of the choice of priests responsible for the custody of treasures donated by the royal court and by Israelites for transport to the Temple. An exact inventory of these treasures follows, with the statement of their delivery, together with a discourse of Ezra in which he assigns responsibilities to the priests and Levites. The narrative parts, however, are more interesting to read and deal with the preparations for the journey (vv. 21-23) through a propitiatory fast for divine protection. This contrasts with the refusal of the military protection offered by the king. The actual account of the return (vv. 31-34), however, is very abrupt, barely a series of notes that tell of the consignment of the treasures for the Temple into the hands of the priest Meremoth and their being scrupulously weighed and registered.

Verses 35-36 bring the whole literary unit to a conclusion with the thank offerings made by the repatriates at the Temple, detailed by the type and number of animals sacrificed, and with accreditation to the authorities of the province of Transeuphrates ("Beyond the River") through presentation of the king's ordinances. This analysis also brings out the strong bureaucratic character of the text. The narrative parts as well, limited in their historical development, seem conceived not as the supporting element but as preparatory to the bureaucratic report. Indeed, the original purpose of this text seems to have been to give a report to Persian authorities of Ezra's actions in carrying out the king's arrangements. It is not without reason that the introduction and conclusion make reference to these arrangements. A certain religious-nationalist pride shines through here and there (cf. v. 22), expressing consciousness of the historic importance of the return and safety under divine protection, but this element does not succeed in correcting the substantially official character of this document.

Mixed Marriages (Autobiographical-Theological Text) (Ezra 9:1-15)

This is comparable to the previous text since both have in common the subject speaking in the first person; however, it represents a different literary genre, evident both in its formulation and in its theme. In v. 1a we find a formal introduction, probably of redactional origin and designed to connect the text with the preceding chapter ("after these things had been done"); this is followed by the statement of the theme for the whole passage (v. 1a, b) in the form of a denunciation of the mixed marriages on the part of the chiefs *(sārīm):* the accused are, in order, the people in general and more specifically the priests and Levites. Verse 2 aims at underscoring the illegality of these marriages, but in the second half of the verse a contradiction of v. 1 appears: the accused are no longer the religious authorities but the *sārīm* themselves, with the magistrates, who nonetheless remain the authors of the charge. At least v. 2b thus seems to be a subsequent adjustment, all the more because the concept of a *zeraʿ haqqodeš* (holy race) is inserted here inconsistently.

This general introduction is followed in vv. 3-5 by an analysis of Ezra's reactions of distress and despair that in turn prepare and introduce Ezra's prayer. This (vv. 6-15) constitutes the central body of the literary unit and is structured internally according to symmetrical elements as shown by the conjunction *weʿattāh* (vv. 8, 10, 12). Acknowledgment of guilt, seen as a continuation of past behavior (vv. 6-7), is matched by a new acknowledgment of guilt consequent upon the quotation of Deut 7:3 on the obligation of abandoning the practice of mixed marriages (vv. 12-13).

The acknowledgment of God's kindness, of which the favors on the part of the king of Persia are a sign (vv. 8-9), is contrasted with the human inconsistency that is nonetheless redeemed by the divine promises, quoted from Lev 18:24-25 (vv. 10-11). The prayer concludes in vv. 14-15 with a rhetorical question on the meaning of a fault that could lead to destruction, and with yet another act of faith in God's mercy.

This, then, is a text of decidedly theological character, elaborated according to a dualistic scheme that sees a negative aspect in human action, dominated by sin and inconsistency (cf. v. 6b), and as a counterweight the supreme kindness of God who comes to the aid of human misery. Ezra's whole discourse is aimed at arousing awareness of the normative value of the Torah (v. 14). The observance of the Law is seen as a threshold for a definitive break with the past and for establishing a new relationship with YHWH.

Ezra's Reform (Additional Biographical Text) (Ezra 10:1-17, 19, 44b)

As part of the core of integrative texts we also count Ezra 10:1-17, 19, 44b, which speaks about the people's oath of faithfulness to the Law. It is tied thematically to ch. 9 but differs literarily by being written in the third person and by a different lexemic choice (cf., for example, "from the peoples of the lands" in 9:1; "from the peoples of the land" in 10:2, 11) that presupposes a different cultural context.

The fulcrum of this literary unit is the convocation and conduct of an assembly (*qāhāl:* vv. 7-17) that must resolve the problem of the mixed marriages. All repatriated Jews are obliged to participate in it under pain of confiscation of goods and excommunication (v. 8). Preparation for it comes in a motivational speech by Shecaniah addressed to Ezra (vv. 2-4), who makes the chiefs of the priests and Levites swear faithfulness to the Law and prepares himself with a fast for the task of having the Law fulfilled by the people (v. 5-6). During the assembly the people accept Ezra's call almost unanimously, although they bring up the difficulty of carrying it out in a short time (vv. 12-14). The assembly concludes with the naming of an examining commission to carry out the appropriate judicial procedures (vv. 15-17).

The passage probably has its dual conclusion in v. 19, with the oath of repudiation of the foreign women, and in v. 44b, in which this repudiation is effected. This is a text to be counted in the juridical-religious genre: emphasis is placed on juridical procedures and precise dates are stated (vv. 9, 17); the religious setting is moreover recognizable in the term *qāhāl* (vv. 1, 8) and by the principal interlocutors of Ezra, who are priests and Levites (v. 5).

List of Mixed Marriages (Administrative Text) (Ezra 10:18-44)

Ezra 10:18-44 is a document whose literary formation has a redactional origin. It also is inserted within a literary unit (Ezra 10:1-17, 19, 44b) and lacks a conclusion: there is just a brief introduction in v. 18, indispensable for its insertion into the text. This is a list of those who have become guilty of marriages with foreign women: it begins with priestly families and goes down, in descending hierarchical order, to the Levites, cantors, and gatekeepers, and down at last to the people. Comparing this list with Ezra 2 // Nehemiah 7 and Ezra 8 shows agreement between some names; these were probably not original to the archival document but rather were inserted by the redactor for purposes of harmonization.

II. Nehemiah

At Susa, Nehemiah Prays (Autobiographical Text) (Neh 1:1b-11)

This text is autonomous with respect to what follows in Neh 2:1-4, 17; 6:1–7:3: its own dating gives evidence of this, even though it is incomplete in its reference to the sovereign. Its conclusion in vv. 11-12 is syntactically not very consistent, and inappropriately anticipates the theme of 2:1. The body of this passage is represented by a prayer of Nehemiah to YHWH (vv. 5-11b), a text rich in deuteronomic themes and expressions (Deut 30:1-4 is expressly cited); it is an admission of guilt as well as a plea for mercy.

The prayer is introduced in vv. 2-4 by a request for information on the situation in Judah, followed by a psychological crisis on Nehemiah's part. This is the premise for his reconsideration of his own conduct. More than a narrative unit, this can be defined as a meditation and a realization by the people of their own historical guilt that has led to a catastrophic social situation. The narrative parts (vv. 2-4) are a situational introduction to this meditation.

The final redactor places this text as an introduction to the memoirs of Nehemiah in order to give them a scheme of dualistic reading, already seen in Ezra 9: the situation of human sin is compared with the mercy of YHWH, concretized in the gift of the Torah (vv. 8-9); the purpose of the text is to advance the political-religious rehabilitation of the people of Israel.

Nehemiah is Sent to Jerusalem and Rebuilds and Organizes It (Autobiographical Text) (Neh 2:1–4:17 and 6:15–7:3)

This is the largest literary unit within the books of Ezra–Nehemiah; it is also the most consistent both from a literary and a historical viewpoint. It is a first-person account of the rebuilding of the walls of Jerusalem and the opposition on the part of the authorities of Eber-Nahar, the political region of the Transeuphrates. The text has a suitable introduction in 2:1 consisting of a precise dating and the narrator's historical-social setting as a cupbearer in the court of King Artaxerxes I. The events leading up to the reconstruction of the walls are explained in 2:2-8, in the narration of the conversation between Nehemiah and the king. This takes the form of a verbal sparring that ends with the satisfaction of Nehemiah's requests and the action taken by one whose protection is divine ("the gracious hand of my God was upon me,"): this expression, found in Ezra 7:27-28; 8:15-36, and repeated in the text of Nehemiah at 2:18 and, in another form, at 6:16, is the premise as well as the definitive motivation for the success of the work of reconstruction. The account unfolds in accordance with contrasting thematic elements: the positive act of the rebuilding of the walls in its various phases (2:11-18; 3:1-32, 38; 4:4-8, 10-17; 6:15) is in contrast to the negative and obstructionist attitude of the authorities of the Transeuphrates (2:10, 19-20; 3:33-37; 4:1-3, 9; 6:1-14, 16-19). These latter parts are marked literarily by "and he heard" // "and it happened that he heard," which indicate a contrast with what preceded and represent a refrain aimed at underscoring the rigidity and irrationality of the behavior of the Persian authorities, namely Sanballat, Tobiah, and their functionaries.

The phases of reconstruction of the walls are:

(1) Inspection of the walls and presentation of the restoration project to leading citizens (2:11-18).

(2) Organization of the work, with families listed by specific tasks assigned to them (3:1-32). This list is probably taken from some

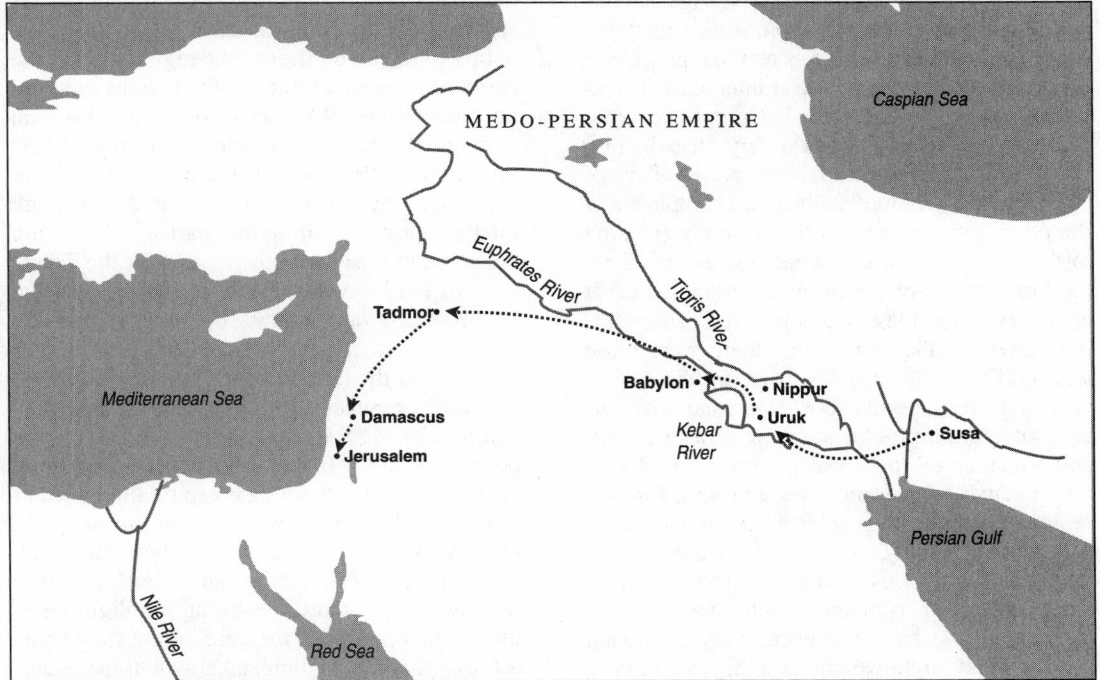

JOURNEY OF NEHEMIAH

administrative archive, but it is fully inserted into the arrangement of this literary unit; thus it should be considered as part of the original text.

(3) Progress of the work to half the height of the walls (3:38).

(4) Moments of psychological despondency owing to false alarms of enemy attack, and Nehemiah's speech of encouragement (4:4-8).

(5) Reorganization of the people for the task and for the defense of Jerusalem (4:10-17).

(6) Date of completion of the walls (6:15).

The text concludes at 7:1-3: after the completion of the walls, the closing of the doors and suitable vigilance are arranged.

Even a superficial reading of this literary unit reveals a gripping narrative rich with unexpected events and enhanced by personal considerations (cf. 2:6-7, 12-13, 17-19) that render it an original and personalized text. We are far removed here from the bureaucratic style seen in Ezra 8:15-36. This text is probably conceived rather as a personal reflection on the meaning of the task achieved as well as a testimony to the people on the correctness of the protagonist's behavior.

Social Problems in Jerusalem (Additional Autobiographical Text) (Neh 5:1-19)

Another literarily autonomous passage, yet one complementary to the narration of the rebuilding of the walls, is Nehemiah 5, a text that provides a general summary of the social interventions carried out by Nehemiah during his term as governor of Jerusalem. This text has a very clear literary structure that is balanced in its parts: after the opening statement in v. 1 (the main complaints of the people) three sections follow, corresponding to three homogeneous themes: vv. 2-5 set forth the principal problems of an economic sort that are the object of the complaints, each of which is introduced by the expression "there were those who said" (vv. 2, 3, 4); vv. 6-13 are the central core of the passage and show Nehemiah's actions to resolve these problems: he convenes the civil authorities as the principal parties accused and, after a harsh rebuke, proposes a general forgiveness of debts; the proposal is accepted and sealed with an oath; finally, vv. 14-18 draw a picture of the ideal behavior of an administrator based on the example of Nehemiah, who as governor (*peḥām:* v. 14) has renounced every economic privilege that might weigh upon the shoulders of the people. The passage concludes in v. 19 with an invocation to YHWH after the model of Neh 13:31b. Although written in the third person, the text here examined has the air of being rethought later in time to depict the ideal behavior of an administrator of the State; such was Nehemiah, a man concerned for the economic problems of those who are less than prosperous.

Neh 6:1–7:3

See above, 2:1–4:17.

Neh 7:6-73

See Ezra 2:1-70.

Ezra Proclaims the Law (Liturgical-Narrative Text) (Neh 8:1-18)

Neh 8:1-18 is very similar to Ezra 3:1-13 both in its liturgical context and above all from a literary point of view. The introduction starts properly in 7:73b and includes 8:1a: it is identical to Ezra 3:1 without thereby giving the impression of being a later interpolation or simply foreign to its context. The theme is set in v. 1b (the request made of Ezra to read the Mosaic Law) which is paralleled by v. 2 as the people's request is satisfied. At this point the ceremony begins; it is solemnly described in vv. 3-8 respecting all the rules of ceremonial, from the listing of the authorities to the registration of the people's reverent attitude in the various required postures. Verses 9-12 speak of Ezra's proposal (Nehemiah's name was added later; indeed, it is missing in the Greek translation of the LXX) to appoint a day for a feast; the Levites through their singing take an active part in convincing the people to celebrate the reading of the Torah.

With v. 13 the text unfolds a second part that is introduced much like v. 1b: on the second day there is a new request to study the Law, and in this context the leaders of the people rediscover the feast of Succoth (v. 14). This is then proclaimed (v. 15) and put into practice by the people (vv. 16-17). The conclusion of the second part comes in v. 18 with a recapitulation both of Ezra's reading and of the feast of Succoth. Dominant notions in the text include the Torah of Moses, feast/sacred day, and *qāhāl.* Together with the theme and the constant highlighting of the various points of the ceremonial they characterize, this text in unmistakably within the cultic and liturgical sphere.

Penitential Function and Solemn Commitment (Liturgical-Juridical Text) (Neh 9:1–10:40)

This literary unit begins at 9:1a with a dating according to the day and the month, followed by the usual formula in v. 1b (cf. Ezra 3:1b; Neh 8:1a) "the people of Israel were assembled," coupled with the penitential attitude of the people. This indeed constitutes the theme of the whole passage: a penitential liturgy.

The liturgy begins at v. 2 with the acknowledgment of the people's guilt, especially for the practice of mixed marriages; this is followed by the reading of the Torah (v. 3). In this very solemn narrative the singing Levites are heard intoning the choral prayer (vv. 4-5): a prayer of thanksgiving *(berākāh)* occupies the remainder of the chapter (vv. 6-37). It is a prayer filled with quotations from the Pentateuch; it reviews the whole history of Israel, a history that sees YHWH granting the most extraordinary favors and the people neglecting their God and transgressing the Torah. The prayer finishes with an acknowledgment of the people's sins and of divine justice (vv. 33-35) and with recognition of their political state of dependence, a consequence of past guilt (vv. 36-37).

The ceremony ends with a written agreement signed by priests, Levites, leaders of the people, and the rest of the population, respecting a hierarchical order (10:2-29), to put the Mosaic Law into practice in its totality (v. 30). More precise commitments are specified, largely relating to the post-exilic situation: renunciation of mixed marriages (v. 31), respect for the Sabbath rest (v. 32), rendering of offerings to the Temple for the carrying out of worship (vv. 33-34), and supplying of firewood needed for sacrifices (v. 35). These commitments are concluded at v. 40c, which summarizes them in the fundamental point: duties toward the Temple shall not be neglected. Verses 36-40b are very probably a later interpolation, inserted into the text in order to respond to some uncertainties with regard to the placement of offerings within the Temple: this is a liturgical text differing in character from the preceding one, not so much historical-narrative as decidedly juridical.

List of Inhabitants of Jerusalem and the Province (Administrative Texts) (Neh 11:1-36)

We are in the presence here of a rather complex text that bespeaks a redactional history of several phases. Even a cursory reading will show its many leaps of argument and different introductions, giving an overall impression of a rather confused text. In seeking to bring order out of this confusion we can discern a more properly narrative part in vv. 1-2, 20, 25a, and 36, where in general the residential distribution in Jerusalem and the province is described. Within this text some lists of various sorts have been inserted: vv. 4-19, furnished with their own introduction at v. 3, give a list of the residents of Jerusalem, distinguishing them into the tribes of Judah and of Benjamin and into priests, Levites, and gatekeepers; vv. 25b-35, however, consider the distribution in the province of residents still belonging to the tribes of Judah and Benjamin; finally, vv. 21-24 are additional notes on the residence of the "oblates" or servants of the Temple and on the identity of the leaders of the Levites of Jerusalem.

List of Repatriated Priests and Levites (Administrative Texts) (Neh 12:1-26)

Equally complicated is the structure of Neh 12:1-26, which can be considered as a single literary unit insofar as it is delimited by an introduction at v. 1 ("These are the priests and the Levites"), which is matched by a similar formula in v. 26 ("These were in the days of . . ."). Within it, however, there is still evidence of several documents, somehow harmonized with each other, but revealing their independent origins and purposes.

First of all, vv. 1-9 give the list of priests and Levites at the time of Zerubbabel and Jeshua. The conclusion of this list is probably to be found in v. 7b which, for reasons that escape us, has been otherwise displaced. Then comes, without any literary warning, the posterity of Jeshua, that is, the list of the High Priests from 520 to 405 B.C.E. (vv. 10-11). Next follows the list of the heads of the priestly families at the time of Joiakim, the son of Jeshua (vv. 12-21). For the heads of the priestly families in the times of the successive High Priests the reader is referred instead to the Book of the Annals of the Temple (vv. 22-23). Finally, the heads of the Levites at the time of the priest Joiakim are listed in vv. 24-25.

All these documents, with the partial exception of the last, are recorded in a rather dry manner, without setting or comments: it almost seems that they serve as fillers, texts with the sole function of filling gaps in the historical narration, or more probably of not neglecting families that in the redactor's time had acquired renown and power.

Inauguration of the Walls (Liturgical-Narrative Text) (Neh 12:27-43)

This text in Neh 12:27-43 can be compared to previous ones in Ezra 3:1-13 and Nehemiah 8–10 for similarity of theme and literary arrangement. It refers to the feast of the dedication of the walls of Jerusalem, as specified in the opening statement of the passage in v. 27a; for this purpose all the Levites are summoned to Jerusalem (v. 27b). Moreover, in v. 28 the usual formula "and they gathered" is found again, announcing the beginning of the account of the ceremony.

The singers gather in Jerusalem from the surrounding villages (vv. 28-29), while a rite of purification is conducted for the priests, the Levites, the people, and even for the gates and walls of the city (v. 30). After the purification is finished, the processions take place: the heads of Judah and the people are divided into two groups that, leaving from the same place, make their way around the walls of the city in two opposite directions (left and right) and come together at the Temple, where the ceremony is solemnly concluded. Verses 31-32 and 37 describe the first processional train and its path, vv. 38-39 depict the second train, and v. 40 marks their arrival at the Temple. Verses 33-36 incongruously interrupt the stated narrative logic by introducing a list of priests present in the first train, just as vv. 41-42 give a list of the priests leading the second train. Both lists respond to record-keeping logic, extraneous to the narrative-liturgical intent of the original.

Verse 43 brings the whole text to a conclusion: the ceremony ends with the offering of sacrifices and the feast of the people, whose clamor is heard even from far away. It should be noted that this last observation is similar to Ezra 3:13 and is placed in both texts as a literary conclusion. Moreover, all these texts of the liturgical core show literary similarities that are surely not accidental, from the introductory formula to the concluding one. These, together with the theme, make it one of the most recognizable literary cores in its homogeneity. It would be no wonder were they to prove to come from the same social setting.

Ideal Picture of the Epoch of Zerubbabel and Nehemiah (Redactional Text) (Neh 12:44–13:3)

One last text of redactional character is Neh 12:44–13:3: in it is drawn an ideal picture of the epoch of Zerubbabel and Nehemiah, forgetting all the problems connected with it. Some points (for example, the offerings at the Temple or the mixed marriages) are even in stark contradiction with the text of Neh 13:4-31.

To sketch this picture the redactor has drawn abundantly from chronicle material: v. 45 even refers to the levitical legislation of 1 Chronicles 23–26, especially 2 Chr 8:14; v. 46 for its part refers to 2 Chr 29:30. In 13:1-2 Deut 23:4-6 is quoted in order to make evident the prompt response of faithfulness on the part of the Jews, who remove from the community any foreign element: this is an integralist behavior that was not required by Deuteronomy, but that the author offers as a model of a society perfectly reconciled with YHWH. Very probably this text had been conceived as the conclusion of the whole narrative of post-exilic events, but for reasons unknown to us it has received a less compelling placement: it follows the feast of the dedication of the walls (Neh 12:27-43) which represented the beginning of a fully structured society.

This ideal picture, however, precedes a text (Neh 13:4-31) with which it stands in contrast in many aspects: from our historical point of view it is an unfortunate and unjustifiable inconsistency. This can be explained only by the redactor's theological purpose that saw the past age of social and religious reconstruction of Israel as an ideal point of reference. Beyond all problems he saw as positive the enthusiasm of that historical age and the zeal for conforming to the Torah. These are characteristics that he probably did not see put into effect in his own time by a society ridden with innovative ferment in which he did not share.

New Problems Faced at Jerusalem by Nehemiah (Autobiographical Text) (Neh 13:4-31)

One text that is very close to Neh 2:1–4:17; 6:1–7:3, both in literary arrangement and in theological content, is Neh 13:4-31, which takes as its subject improper behaviors of the Jews. The introduction to the text is recognizable in

vv. 4-9 through a marked literary incipit ("Now before this") and through the story of the abuses by the priest Eliashib in the Temple for Tobiah's benefit, while Nehemiah was away from Jerusalem. He had returned to the king's court in Persia and so had lost control of the situation in Judah. When he decided to return to Jerusalem he learned of these abuses; he took suitable measures and evicted Tobiah from the Temple (vv. 8-9). With that the theme is set for the whole passage, which is divided into three different sections that match three forms of incorrect behavior involving respectively Levites (vv. 10-14), civil authorities (vv. 15-22), and the people in general (vv. 23-29).

Each section is introduced by the perception of a problem, shown by the verb "I found out" (v. 10) or by the expression "in those days I saw" (vv. 15, 23), and develops into an accusatory speech on Nehemiah's part (cf. *wā'ārībāh:* vv. 11, 17, 25) and the adoption of appropriate measures (vv. 12-13, 19-22a, 28). The problems concern contributions for the Levites, who otherwise cannot carry out their functions in the Temple, the market open in Jerusalem even on the Sabbath, and the practice of mixed marriages, seen as abandonment of traditions, especially of the Hebrew language. Each section closes with an invocation by Nehemiah to YHWH to remember the merits acquired by Nehemiah (vv. 14, 22b, 29). The whole concludes in vv. 30-31 with a recapitulation of the principal measures taken by Nehemiah, with yet another invocation to YHWH. This recurrent invocation of YHWH is what characterizes this text, as well as Nehemiah 2–4 and 6–7, as personal reflection, a witness to the protagonist's commitment to regulate the social life of Jews.

Conclusion

This study has shown the characteristics of the individual literary units representing documents of differing provenance, with their specific original purposes. The work of the redactor or redactors of Ezra–Nehemiah was one of stitching them together in order to document the history of the reconstruction of Jerusalem and the Temple. The way in which this redactional task was carried out nonetheless reveals the dominant ideas that guided the redactional group. These can be summarized as follows:

(1) The guiding notion of the two fundamental autobiographical texts, Ezra 8:15-36 and Neh 2:1–4:23; 6:1–7:3, is: "The gracious hand of my God was upon me." The redactors are aware that the work of reconstruction was possible solely through the presence of YHWH in that historical phase and through YHWH's continuing help in overcoming the thousands of difficulties the people encountered, especially from the opposition of the Persian authorities of Samaria.

(2) The dualistic scheme that contrasts human and divine was evident in religious thinking: human sin is matched by God's mercy, as the destruction and dispersion of the people for their sins is matched by the reconstruction and social recomposition of Israel, which is above all God's work.

The texts that mark these notions are distributed to the strategically most important points of the account: Ezra 9:1-15, before the repudiation of the mixed marriages; Neh 1:1b-11, at the beginning of the reconstruction of the walls; Neh 9:1–10:39, at the conclusion of the reading of the Torah.

(3) In the eyes of the redactor or redactors worship assumes special importance: the liturgical texts are relatively numerous (Ezra 3:1-13; Neh 8:1-18; Neh 9:1-10, 40; Neh 12:27-43) and are placed at the beginning and end of every work of material and social reconstruction, so as to embody the historical events in the worship and give full meaning to them. The events are therefore seen as a grand liturgy in which it is God who acts and in which human beings must make themselves available to carry out God's will.

This is worship that is done, however, not just with liturgical ceremony, but above all is characterized by the will to conform to the Torah, seen as the only point of assembly around which Judah can rebuild its own social identity (see the problem of mixed marriages) and religious identity (for example, the rediscovery of the feast of Succoth).

The social aspect of problems, marginal yet not overlooked, is dealt with only in Neh 5:1-19, involving economic inequalities and abuse of power. What actually matters more to the redactor are duties toward the Temple, to which contributions must be directed for the exercise of its religious functions (cf. Ezra 1:6; 8:31-36; Neh 10:33-35; 13:10-14).

There is no doubt, then, that the authors/redactors belong by cultural formation and interests to the circle of Temple personnel, and that they see it as an indispensable structure for the social and religious development of Judah. In a time of economic and cultural innovation at the beginning of the Hellenistic period they fear that the cultural and religious specificity that had enabled Jews to bring forth their own identity and their own historical role may be growing weaker or even being lost along with the guiding role of the Temple. On that account they portray for the people the example of the period of reconstruction as a call to recover the initial enthusiasm, to remain faithful to the Torah, understood above all as participation in the liturgies of the Temple. It is clearly an ideological choice that the chronicle authors make, yet certainly it is not the only one possible within the same Israelite tradition.

Indeed, alongside this official religion based on the Temple and the worship connected with it a parallel religious practice that we can term "popular" also develops in Judah. This expresses itself especially in apocalyptic literature and is particularly concerned with the social problems of the most disadvantaged classes. This kind of religion, rather than putting forth the old model again and striving to remain faithful to the past, proposes to turn its sights toward the future, to that Kingdom of God that will overturn the established social order and definitively dry the tears of the weak and oppressed.

BIBLIOGRAPHY

See pages 653–654.

Tobit

Irene Nowell

FIRST READING

Getting Started

The book of Tobit is most profitably read as a short story. The reader's delight in the story will be enhanced by approaching it somewhat like a tale from the Brothers Grimm. There is an angel and a demon, a magical fish and a faithful dog, a journey and a lady in distress. Even as one enjoys the imaginative progress of the story, however, one is caught by the depth of its meaning.

It may be initially distressing to some readers to recognize that the story is fiction. However, it is through the vehicle of the story that the author conveys the theological message. A few centuries after the writing of this book Jesus used the same method to get his point across. He told stories of runaway sons and lost sheep, of kings and banquets, of sowing seed and kneading bread. The function of his stories was not to tell his listeners facts about current events, but rather to reveal the deeper meaning of God's realm and reign. Just so, the author of this book uses his story to tell his audience about God's care for faithful people. [See the article "Truth Told in the Bible: Biblical Poetics and the Question of Truth."]

The Book as a Whole

The book of Tobit is a short novel about a pious family that survives tragedy through God's providential care. It was written in Aramaic in the early second century B.C.E. and later translated into Greek. Because the book was not included in the Hebrew Bible, the Aramaic version ceased to be copied and was lost. Three different forms of the story survived in Greek. Most current translations depend on the one of these three Greek forms that shows the greatest similarity to a Semitic language (such as Aramaic or Hebrew). This Greek form of the story, found in a manuscript at a monastery on Mount Sinai, is used as a basic text and then supplemented by the other two. Fragments containing a substantial portion of the book in Aramaic and Hebrew were found with the Dead Sea Scrolls at Qumran. Future translations will certainly depend largely on these fragments. [See also the article "The Deuterocanonical Writings."]

At the beginning and end of the story there are historical notes concerning various rulers in Assyria, their wickedness and their collapse. These historical notes provide a foil for the main story. The murder of an Assyrian king (ch. 1) and the eventual destruction of Assyria's capital city, Nineveh (ch. 14), demonstrate that God punishes the wicked, even if for a time they seem to prosper.

Between the historical notes there are two stories sandwiched into each other. There is the story of Tobit, a good man who has been struck with blindness, and the story of Sarah, a good woman who has lost seven husbands. The journey of Tobit's son Tobiah joins the two stories and brings both to a happy ending. The healing and eventual prosperity of Tobit's and Sarah's families demonstrate that God blesses faithful people, even if for a time they may suffer.

A first reading will reveal the story and the deft twists of the plot. Later readings may focus on character development or characteristic imagery.

Readers may want to keep two questions in mind as they read the book of Tobit: What is the image of God portrayed here? What is said about the lives of God's faithful?

Original Historical Contexts

The book of Tobit was written in the early second century B.C.E. At this time Israel was under the control of the Seleucid kings of Syria. The Jews had not known independence since the sixth century when the Babylonians had conquered and exiled the southern kingdom, Judah. A remnant of the exiled people had returned to Judah in the last half of the sixth century, but they remained under the control of the Persians. In the fourth century they came under the domination of the Greeks. When Alexander's empire was divided they first fell under the Ptolemies in Egypt and then in the second century under the Seleucids. A great number of the people were also scattered in other places, particularly in Mesopotamia and Egypt.

The second-century author sets his story of Tobit in an earlier time that paralleled his own, the eighth–seventh centuries B.C.E. The major political power of that period was Assyria, a country of northern Mesopotamia, where Iraq is today. During these centuries the Assyrians gradually swallowed up or dominated all the little countries of the Fertile Crescent and eventually defeated even Egypt. The Assyrians were cruel conquerors. They tortured and killed many of the inhabitants of defeated lands. They also took many citizens captive to other countries and resettled the land with other conquered peoples. Thus there was little chance that the deportees could retain their national identity and even less possibility that they might regain strength and take back their native land. One such conquered people were the Israelites. In 722 B.C.E. Sargon II, king of Assyria, defeated Israel, the land of the ten northern tribes, and deported many of its citizens. Tobit is portrayed as one of the deportees.

The author of the book of Tobit tells the story in order to illustrate how faithful people can live according to God's law outside the land of Israel. Just as the exiled Tobit lived a holy life in the eighth century, so the author's second-century audience can live holy lives wherever they may be. The chosen people experience God's providential care in every land.

Canonical Intertextuality

The author of the book of Tobit knew most of the books that would later be included in the Hebrew Scriptures. There are many allusions to these books, especially Genesis and Deuteronomy. The ideals of family life, the care for burying the dead, the journey to find a proper wife all reflect the Genesis stories. The concept of retribution found in the book of Deuteronomy, the idea that God rewards the good and punishes the wicked, is basic to the theology of the book of Tobit. Tobit also reflects an interest in parental responsibility for the instruction of children similar to that found in the wisdom literature, especially the books of Proverbs and Sirach. The life of Job also reflects in many ways the life of Tobit.

The book of Tobit is not quoted directly in the NT but many of its main themes, such as generosity to the poor, hospitality, and the vision of the new Jerusalem, are developed further in the NT.

History of Reception

The book of Tobit is not included in the Hebrew canon, and thus not in Protestant Bibles. It is, however, part of the OT for Orthodox and Roman Catholic traditions. The Roman Catholic canon of the Bible is based on the Latin Vulgate, translated from the Hebrew and Greek by St. Jerome. Jerome did not want to translate Tobit since it was not part of the Hebrew canon but some friends of his who were bishops persuaded him to translate the story for them. In a preface to the book Jerome claims that he translated it in one day, dictating his Latin translation to a secretary as an assistant translated the book aloud from Aramaic to Hebrew. Jerome's translation contains significant additions to the book as it is represented in the Greek telling of the story and the fragments from Qumran. Modern translations do not use Jerome's Latin version but translate directly from the Greek or from the Aramaic fragments where they are available. [See the article "The Canonical Structure of the New Testament: The Gospel and the Apostle."]

The book of Tobit is a resource for Christian theology of angels. Origen, a third-century Christian writer, uses this book to describe God's assignment of particular tasks to particular angels: "as to Raphael, the work of curing and healing; to Gabriel, the conduct of wars; to Michael, the duty of attending to the prayers and supplications of mortals" (*De Principiis* 1.8.1). He says these angels are named "appropriately to the duties which they discharge in the world" (*Contra Celsum* 1.25). So Raphael is named "God heals."

Another angelic task described by Origen is to present our prayers to God. "It is not only the High Priest who prays with those who truly pray, but also the angels who have joy in heaven upon one sinner that does penance . . . . This is clear from the case of Raphael offering a rational sacrifice to God for Tobit and Sarah" (*De oratione* 11.1; cf. 14.4). It is especially when we pray together that the angels carry our prayer to God: "And if Raphael says of the one man Tobit that he offered as a memorial his prayer and that of Sarah, who later became his daughter-in-law when she married Tobiah, what are we to say when many assemble in the same mind and in the same judgment and together form one body in Christ?" (*De oratione* 31.5).

The book of Tobit presents examples of holy living. Cyprian of Carthage, another third-century theologian, holds up Tobit as the model of a faithful man who is praised by an angel after he suffers in patience (*De mortalitate* 10). He says that Tobit, "who after the sublime works of his justice and mercy, was tried with the loss of his eyes, in proportion as he patiently endured his blindness, in that proportion deserved greatly of God by the praise of patience" (*De bono patientiae* 18).

Tobit's faithfulness in giving alms is also noted by Cyprian. Tobit's life demonstrates that prayer without good works is not enough: "Those who pray should not come to God with fruitless or naked prayers. . . . The one who will give us on the day of judgment a reward for our labors and alms, is even in this life a merciful hearer of one who comes to him in prayer" (*De dominica oratione* 32). The angel Raphael teaches Tobit about almsgiving. "He shows that our prayers and fastings are of less avail unless they are aided by almsgiving; that entreaties alone are of little force to obtain what they seek, unless they be made sufficient by the addition of deeds and good works" (*De opere et eleemosynis* 5). Tobit in turn teaches his son: "Be such a father to your children as was [Tobit]. . . . command your children what he also commanded his son," to give alms (*De opere et eleemosynis* 20).

The book of Tobit has had a significant influence on Christian understanding of marriage. From the Middle Ages to the present, Raguel's blessing of Tobiah and Sarah (Tob 8:15-17) has been used as part of the nuptial blessing. A tenth-century blessing reads: "May he who sent the Archangel Raphael to prepare the marriage of Tobiah and Sarah send his holy angel from his heavenly throne to comfort you in his holy service, show you the path of righteousness and protect you forever from all evil."

Jerome's translation of the book of Tobit (the Vulgate) led to a questionable custom, abstaining from intercourse for the first three nights of the marriage, the so-called "Tobias-nights." The Vulgate reads: "Then Tobias exhorted the virgin and said to her: Sarah, arise and let us pray to God today, and tomorrow, and the next day, because for these three nights we are joined to God, and when the third night is over, we will be in our own wedlock" (Tob 8:4, Vg). Raphael also instructed Tobiah to wait until after the third night to "take the virgin with the fear of the Lord" (Tob 6:16-22, Vg). These passages are not found in the Aramaic fragments, nor in the Greek tradition of the story, nor in any other version. Because of the universal use of the Vulgate, however, and because it was the only authorized version for Roman Catholics from the Reformation until Vatican II, this version of the marriage of Tobiah and Sarah was the most widely known among Catholics. Modern translations based on the Greek (and the Aramaic) make it clear that Tobiah and Sarah consummated their marriage on the first night.

Two selections from the book of Tobit are among the OT choices in today's Lectionary for weddings: the story of the wedding, Tob 7:9-10, 11-15, and the prayer on the wedding night, Tob 8:5-7. God's blessing of Tobiah and Sarah still echoes in today's formula for blessing the newlyweds. They are good models for today's couples: Their marriage is surrounded by prayer, mutual tenderness, and healing. Their marriage joins two families and their children are hope for the future.

Selections from the book of Tobit are also read during Week 9 of Year 1 in the Lectionary, and Tobit's song of praise (ch. 13) is used as a canticle in the Liturgy of the Hours.

SECOND READING

General Background

There are several discrepancies in the historical information given in the book of Tobit. The succession of Assyrian kings is wrong: Sargon II, who succeeded Shalmaneser, is omitted (Tob 1:15). Tobit's lifetime is impossible: he was a young man when the kingdom divided (922 B.C.E., Tob 1:4), was persecuted by Sennacherib (705–681 B.C.E, Tob 1:18-20), was blinded under Esarhaddon (681–669 B.C.E., Tob 2:1), and lived another fifty years (cf. Tob 14:2). His son sees the fall of Nineveh (612 B.C.E.) before he dies (Tob 14:15). This freedom with historical data indicates that the author is not intending to convey historical truth but rather truth about God's action in the lives of faithful people.

The outline of the plot is based on two ancient folktales that have been told for thousands of years all across the Near East and Eastern Europe: the story of the Grateful Dead and the story of the Monster in the Bridal Chamber. In the story of the Grateful Dead a traveler comes upon an unburied corpse and uses his own resources to bury the man. Shortly after this event he is joined on his journey by a stranger who promises to serve him. The stranger's wages will be half of whatever the traveler gains on the journey. The stranger advises the traveler how to gain wealth, saves the traveler from some disaster, and reveals himself as the grateful dead man whom the traveler buried. In the story of the Monster in the Bridal Chamber a young woman is afflicted by a demon who kills her bridegrooms. When this story is joined to the Grateful Dead it is the stranger who saves her from the demon and arranges her marriage to the traveler.

Another resource used by the author is the story of Ahiqar, a story several centuries older than the book of Tobit that is found preserved in several languages. The hero of this ancient Assyrian tale is an official in the king's court. He raises his orphaned nephew and trains him for royal service. The nephew, however, is ungrateful. He accuses his uncle of treason and Ahiqar is condemned to death. The executioner saves Ahiqar because Ahiqar had once saved his life. He hides Ahiqar until the king repents of his death. Then Ahiqar is restored to his former position and the nephew is in turn condemned to death.

The similarities between these stories and the story of Tobit are evident. Tobiah's journey protected by Raphael, and his marriage to Sarah who is afflicted by a demon resemble the two folktales. The story of Tobit himself, a just man who suffers and then is restored, is similar to that of Ahiqar. Ahiqar is even made a relative of Tobit and many of the sayings of Ahiqar are found in Tobit's speech to Tobiah (ch. 4).

The differences between the book of Tobit and these stories are also evident. The purpose of the book of Tobit is not to spin a tale but to tell of God. God's care for people is demonstrated through the care of an angel and the courage of a young man. God's justice is demonstrated through the healing of righteous people. The message of the book is to trust in God.

Tobit's Ordeals (1:3–3:6)

In this first section the title character is introduced and the conflict presented. Tobit is portrayed as a righteous and charitable man who has been scrupulous in observance of the Law. His strict observance is illustrated by his tithing. His practice is based on the Law found in the Pentateuch. Leviticus prescribes a tithe to support the priests and Levites and to maintain the sanctuary (27:30-33; cf. Num 18:21-32). Deuteronomy prescribes that a tenth of everything that is grown be brought to the temple and eaten there in a great festal banquet (Deut 14:24-27). In the third year the tithes are put into community storage for the poor and landless in the community (Deut 14:28-29; 26:12). Tobit has taken all this legislation very seriously. He gives one tithe to the priests and Levites, a second tithe to the poor in Jerusalem, and uses a third tithe (or one tithe in the third year) for the banquet to which the poor are invited. His virtue is also evident in his charitable deeds: almsgiving and burying the dead. He is presented as a very holy man.

Paradoxically it is Tobit's goodness that causes the conflict of the story. It seems that the more he tries to live a good and holy life the more he suffers. His suffering brings suffering to his family as well. His neighbors, who mock his efforts, seem to live well enough. But the king, who causes the most distress, comes to a bad end. Is human suffering inevitable whether one is virtuous or wicked? Is it simply a matter of arbitrary fate? Is it better just to get by? Should one ignore the injustices of the political system and the persecution of the powerless? Where is God in the story of this holy man?

Sarah's Plight (3:7-17)

The literary device of simultaneity links two suffering people who are separated by many miles. "On that very day" the grief of Raguel's daughter Sarah also reaches the breaking point. Sarah is afflicted by a demon who has killed her seven bridegrooms on the wedding night. The servants taunt her with the accusation that it is she who kills them. Tobit and Sarah are separated in human eyes, but we will see that their lives are linked in the sight of God.

Like Tobit, Sarah turns to prayer. Prayer is a major element in this story. There are prayers at every major turning point: Tobit in his affliction (3:2-6) and at his healing (11:14-15); Sarah in her affliction (3:11-15); Tobiah and Sarah on their wedding night (8:5-8); Raguel in thanksgiving for Sarah's healing (8:15-17). The book moves toward conclusion with Tobit's great prayer of praise (13:1-18). It is in answer to their prayer that Raphael is sent to heal Tobit and Sarah. After their healing the angel informs them that it was he who presented their prayer to God (12:12).

Sarah is afflicted by a demon, Asmodeus. The demon has a Persian name, *aeshma daeva,* meaning "demon of wrath." There is no explanation for the demon's presence. Sarah and her family are good people. In every other way the family seems to prosper. On the literary level the demon is an element of the folktale. On the human level the demon represents life's inevitable and incomprehensible sufferings. On the theological level the demon demonstrates that there are evils in our lives that cannot be conquered without God's help. In the NT Jesus will tell us that such evils can be cast out only by prayer and fasting (Tob 12:8; cf. Mark 9:29).

A Father's Instruction (4:1-21)

Chapter 4 is in the form of a farewell discourse. In this form the head of the family or group senses that he is going to die and thus calls everyone together for his final instructions. See, for example, Jacob's farewell discourse in Genesis 49 or Jesus' farewell discourse in John 14–17. In the course of this book Tobit will give two such discourses, Tob 4:3-21 and 14:3-11. The theological message of the book is spelled out in these discourses.

Throughout Deuteronomy parents are exhorted to teach their children to keep God's law (cf. Deut 4:9-10; 6:7). Tobit instructs his son as he himself was instructed by his grandmother Deborah (Tob 1:8). He encourages him to respect family ties. Tobiah is to honor his parents, especially his mother, and give them a respectful burial. He is told to follow the Jewish custom of the time in marrying a woman from his own clan. The custom of marriage within one's own clan is based on the example of the ancestors, especially Isaac and Jacob (Tob 4:12; Gen 24:3-4; 27:46–28:5).

The primary topic of Tobit's instruction is almsgiving, a major theme of this book. Almsgiving, care for the most helpless people in the society, is a major concern in Deuteronomy (cf. Deut 10:17-19; 24:17-21; 26:12-13). The developed theology of almsgiving in the book of Tobit is similar to that found in Sirach, also written in the second century B.C.E. Generosity to the needy is presented as a great virtue. Such generosity, however, should be according to one's means (cf. Sir 18:15-18; 35:9-10). There is no encouragement to impoverish oneself, but only to be always ready to give at least a little. Sirach emphasizes that almsgiving delivers from sin (Sir 3:30-31) and is equivalent to offering sacrifice (cf. Sir 34:18–35:4) and lays up a treasure against the day of need and delivers one from death (cf. Sir 29:10-13; 40:17, 24).

The book of Tobit, written only a few centuries before the NT, reflects the broad sweep of theology that formed the basis of Judaism in Jesus' time. Thus we find much of the material in this book echoed in the NT. Many of the statements in Tobit's instruction to Tobiah (ch. 4) resemble NT exhortations to give generously to the poor (e.g., Matt 6:20-21; 25:35-36; 2 Cor 9:7). The "Golden Rule" (Matt 7:12; Luke 6:31) is a positive restatement of Tob 4:15: "Do to no one what you yourself dislike." Tobit's instructions to his son correspond to the measure by which people will be judged worthy of the reign of God: "I was hungry and you gave me food, I was thirsty and you gave me drink, a stranger and you welcomed me, naked and you clothed me" (Matt 25:35-36). In the gospel we are told that it is Christ himself who receives the charitable gift.

The Angel Raphael (5:1–6:1)

The chapter in which Raphael is hired as young Tobiah's guide is characterized by alternating movement from Tobit's house to the street and back again. The opening scene (5:1-4), which is inside Tobit's house, presents the need: Tobiah, sent by his father to recover the money invested in Media, does not know how to get there. The closing scene (5:17–6:1), which is set outside, presents the solution: Unaware of the truth of his words, Tobit says twice that a good angel will go with Tobiah. The intervening scenes—outside (5:4-8), inside-outside (5:9-10), inside (5:10-17)—describe the encounter and conversation with the angel.

Throughout the story there is an ironic ignorance in the human characters as they deal with the angel. The readers are given clues the characters do not have. Neither man recognizes that Raphael is an angel, but the narrator tells the reader right away. Both men ask Raphael his origins and he identifies himself as Azariah, a kinsman. The name he gives means "YHWH helps." The reader knows that this name describes Raphael's mission—to bring God's help. The reader also knows that Raphael is a kinsman only as one of God's children. Both men ask if Raphael knows the way to Media. His answer reveals the excellence of angelic knowledge: "I know *all* the roads." Throughout the journey the characters will refer to him as Azariah, the name he gave them, and the narrator will call him Raphael or "the angel."

The characters in the book of Tobit entertain an "angel in disguise." There is a long tradition of God's help coming through these messengers. Their appearance is often hidden and sometimes troubling. Three visitors come to tell Abraham and Sarah of the impending birth of their son Isaac (Gen 18:1-15). Sarah laughs at the news, but is assured that nothing is impossible to God. Manoah, the father of Samson, is slow in recognizing the angel who has spoken to his wife and then is certain he will die because he has seen him. In contrast his wife understands that God would not have sent the angel if they were not intended to carry out the message he brought (Judg 13:21-23). Mary is troubled by the appearance of an angel and accepts his message only after being assured that it is from God. The letter to the Hebrews reflects on the story of Abraham and Sarah (Genesis 18) and advises: "Do not neglect hospitality, for through it some have unknowingly entertained angels" (Heb 13:2). Those who trust in God's help may not recognize right away the messenger God sends. They may suffer initial distress, but instinctively they will say yes to the living presence of that help in the guide provided by God for the journey.

Journey (6:2-18)

The activity of the angel becomes evident during the journey. The angel is what the word "angel" implies, a messenger. The angel first of all guides Tobiah on the journey. The angel instructs the young man in catching the fish and then in the uses of its entrails for the healing of others. Just as Abraham's servant was helped by an angel in finding a bride for Isaac (Gen 24:7), so Tobiah will be aided by an angel in finding his bride. The angel exhorts Tobiah to marry Sarah in fulfillment of his father's injunction to marry a near relative. When Tobiah hesitates because he has heard the fate of Sarah's previous husbands, the angel teaches him to exorcise the demon by means of the fish liver and heart and then to pray that God will bless and protect them both.

The angel in this story is named Raphael, "God heals." The name itself is a reminder that the angel does not act on his own authority but rather in the power of God. The angel also does not usurp the activity proper to the human characters. The angel simply instructs, exhorts, and encourages. It is Tobiah who must perform the actions and God who heals through him.

This is a fictional story told to carry a deeper meaning (see "Getting Started" above). The forces of good and evil are larger than life. There are angels active in this story; there are also figures of evil who must be faced. The fish who tries to swallow Tobiah's foot functions as the dragon of the folktale. In the biblical context the fish is the great sea monster who symbolizes chaos, the serpent who attempts to lead human beings away from their true destiny (cf. Gen 1:1-2; Pss 74:13-14; 89:9-10; Isa 27:1; Amos 9:3). In the book of Revelation the dragon is identified with "Satan, the deceiver of the whole world" (Rev 12:9). The angels throw him down to earth and he is finally cast into the lake of fire and sulphur to remain there forever (Rev 20:10; cf. 20:2-3).

Meeting and Wedding (7:1-17)

Tobiah's conversation with Raguel and Edna is modeled on Jacob's conversation with the shepherds in Haran (Gen 29:4-6). The almost verbatim use of the Genesis passage leads the reader to identify the characters in this story with the patriarchs. Just as Jacob travels to his mother's home to find a bride for himself, so Tobiah comes to his father's relatives. Just as Jacob's marriages give rise to the people of Israel, so Tobiah's marriage is a sign of the birth of the new Israel. He and Sarah will have seven sons (a perfect number) and will leave Nineveh (Tob 14:3-4, 15). Thus he becomes a sign of hope that the Israelites will eventually return to their land (Tob 14:5-7).

The wedding ceremony is one of the few described in later books of the OT. The marriage formula resembles one found in a fifth-century document from Egypt. The Contract of Mibtahiah's Third Marriage says, "She is my wife and I am her husband from this day forever." The formula is significant not only because it reveals details about Israelite marriage customs, but also because it reflects the covenant formula between Israel and God: "I will be your God and you will be my people forever."

Marriage in the OT is an image of the relationship between God and the chosen people (cf. Hos 2:21-25). In the NT it is an image of the relationship between Christ and the Church (Eph 5:23-33). Married people are a living symbol for all believers of the tender, strong, life-giving love of God. In their relationship they are a sacrament of God's presence with us.

All the characters involved in the wedding of Tobiah and Sarah exhibit courage and openness to the will of God in the circumstances of their lives. Tobiah, who has let Raphael make the decisions during the journey, now takes responsibility for his own life. Raguel and Edna risk giving Sarah in marriage for the eighth time. Sarah agrees to yet another marriage.

Healing of Sarah (8:1-18)

The happy wedding night of Tobiah and Sarah is filled with prayer. Tobiah begins with a prayer of petition that their marriage will be blessed. His prayer begins in traditional Jewish fashion with praise of God. Then he recalls God's wonderful works of the past. Only after these two elements of prayer does he move to petition. The traditional Roman Collect, the opening prayer of the eucharistic liturgy, is based on this same pattern.

Tobiah's telling of the creation story is unique in the OT. This is the only passage outside of Genesis where Eve is mentioned. His interpretation focuses on the blessings of the creation story—God's gift of Adam and Eve to each other for mutual support and the gift of their fruitfulness—but there is no mention of the grief in the garden. Tobiah's prayer presents Adam and Eve as the patron saints of marriage and the bringing forth of children. His petition asks that he and Sarah may be like them, that they may have a long life together and be blessed with children. Sarah, who is silent throughout the book, joins in the Amen.

Raguel's prayer of thanksgiving also begins by blessing God. Then he proclaims his gratitude for God's abundant mercy. The word "mercy" appears four times in his brief prayer! In his prayer Raguel represents both sets of parents as he thanks God for a happy wedding and calls down a blessing on the marriage.

The two prayers present a healthy theology of marriage and a worthy example to follow. Marriage is seen as a gift from God. God gave Adam and Eve to each other; God has had mercy on the "two only children," Tobiah and Sarah. Perseverance and ongoing joy in marriage is also God's gift and children are a blessing. The prayer of the newlyweds is certainly a good beginning for a marriage. Their delight in each other overflows in gratitude to God; their hope for the future is entrusted to God. Mark Twain has captured their hope in an imaginative recreation of the Genesis story. He tells of Adam saying after Eve's death, "I did not know that wherever she was was Paradise."

Final Details in Media: Feast/Money (8:19–9:6)

Marriages are family and community events. They do not involve only the bridal couple. In a manner reminiscent of Abraham (cf. Gen 18:1-15) Raguel and Edna prepare a great feast, twice as long as the ordinary seven-day celebration. From the amount of food to be prepared one can imagine a large number of guests. Gabael and Raphael too are in attendance. The whole community celebrates because the marriage is a blessing on the whole community.

The marriage is a joining of two families. Raguel and Edna tell Tobiah that they are now Tobiah's father and mother. Sarah is called his sister, a common term of endearment in the OT (cf. Song 4:9, 12; 5:1-2). Raguel instructs Sarah to honor Tobiah's parents because now "they are as much [her] parents as the ones who brought [her] into the world" (10:12). The two families have become one.

Marriage also has economic implications. Raguel gives Tobiah and Sarah half his possessions at the time of the wedding. The other half will belong to them when Raguel and Edna die. Tobit's estate will also come to Tobiah and Sarah after Tobit and Anna die (14:13). The joining of the families is a joining of their resources.

The best-known wedding guest in the NT is Jesus at the wedding feast of Cana (John 2:1-11). His presence is a blessing for the married couple. His gift is a miraculous enhancing of their resources. Marriage is a family and community event. In the end we all hope to be invited to the great wedding feast of the kingdom (Rev 19:7-9).

Return Journey (10:1-14)

Tobit and Anna represent the worry of all parents about their children. Tobit counts the days and imagines all sorts of disasters. Anna, the more vocal of the two, announces that her son is dead and then proceeds to spend all her time watching for him. Tobiah, for his part, knows his parents and understands their worry. When the wedding feast is over he insists on leaving promptly for home. The love of all the members of this family for each other is evident even when it is not directly expressed.

The farewell in Nineveh is a ceremony of blessing. Raguel blesses Tobiah and Sarah in turn. Edna blesses Tobiah and kisses him and Sarah. Tobiah blesses Raguel and Edna and promises to honor them. He also blesses God for giving him so much delight.

The book of Tobit is a resource for the blessing of travelers. As Tobit blessed Tobiah with the prayer that "a good angel" would accompany him (5:17; cf. 5:22), we pray that the angels will accompany us on our travels and that we too may return home in peace and health and joy (10:11-12; cf. 5:17).

Healing of Tobit (11:1-18)

Many of the themes of the book of Tobit recur in the final chapters. The second healing occurs at the end of the journey. The angel, the "messenger," gives the instructions; the human character must carry them out in order to be the instrument of God's healing. This creates the occasion for yet another prayer of gratitude.

The double welcome repeats motifs from previous chapters. The tenderness of Anna toward her husband is shown when she announces Tobiah's arrival to him. She has consistently referred to Tobiah as *"my* son," but now she says to the blind Tobit, *"Your* son is coming." Tobit's subsequent welcome of Sarah recalls the theme that marriage joins the two families. Tobit calls Sarah "daughter" four times when he meets her. There is a second wedding feast of seven days. Ahiqar and his nephew are among the many guests. All the Jews of Nineveh celebrate the family's good fortune.

Tobiah's reunion with his parents recalls other such reunions. Anna's words to Tobiah echo Jacob's exclamation when he is reunited with Joseph whom he thought was dead: "At last I can die, now that I have seen for myself that Joseph is still alive" (Gen 46:30). In contrast to Tobit who can only stumble through the gate, the father of the prodigal son runs out to meet him (Luke 15:11-32). In all these stories there is a great celebration.

Raphael (12:1-22)

Chapter 12 is the revelation of Raphael's angelic identity. The folktale theme of paying the guide half of everything leads to the angel's farewell discourse. Raphael identifies himself as one of the seven angels who stand before God (cf. Rev 8:2, 6; 15:1-8; 16:1; 17:1; 21:9). His words describe the functions of angels: guidance and protection, instruction, testing, mediation of prayer. As spiritual beings angels have no need of food and drink; Raphael only appeared to be taking nourishment. The point Raphael makes most clearly is that angels serve only at the will of God. Angels are not to be worshiped; thanksgiving is due to God, not to the angel.

Raphael continues his function of instruction. He exhorts Tobit and Tobiah to praise God and to give witness concerning God's goodness to them. Repeating one of the major themes of the book, he declares the benefits of giving alms. He also reiterates the theme of retribution: "Do good and evil will not find its way to you." Then, his mission accomplished, the angel ascends to the one who sent him.

Angels are frequent visitors in the NT. They perform the same functions described by Raphael. They give information and carry messages (Matt 1:20, 24; 28:5; Luke 1:11-19, 26-38; 2:9-15). They guide and protect (Matt 2:13, 19; 18:10; Acts 5:19; 8:26; 12:7-11), encourage and strengthen (Matt 4:11; Luke 24:23). They test (Matt 13:41, 49; Acts 12:23). They assist in prayer (Rev 8:2-4). Never, however, do they usurp God's place (Matt 24:36). Nor do they take away from human beings the responsibility for their own lives.

Song of Praise (13:1-18)

Chapter 13 is the longest prayer of the book. The first section (13:1-8) is Tobit's final hymn of gratitude for what God has done for him. The second section (13:9-18) is a hymn of praise for the new Jerusalem. The first section echoes several themes from the psalms (see Psalms 93, 95–100, 145); the second section echoes the prophetic description of the new Jerusalem (Isa 54:11-12; cf. Isaiah 60).

The first section states clearly the theology of retribution upon which the book is based: God punishes the wicked and blesses the just. The theology of retribution is described in the book of Deuteronomy, especially the list of blessings and curses in Deuteronomy 28. But Deuteronomy also states that retribution is not automatic. The wicked may prosper for a time; the just may suffer (Deut 8:2-16).

Tobit reflects this theology as he uses his own story as a model for the story of his people. He is a righteous person who suffers for a time but now rejoices in God's blessing. Israel, however, is in exile because of sinfulness. In either case, whether suffering comes because of human sin or for reasons hidden in the mysterious wisdom of God, everything happens through the power and mercy of God. Tobit does not attribute pain and affliction to a third figure such as Satan. Therefore there is nowhere to turn except to God. It is God who will have mercy and raise up again.

In the second section Tobit sees himself as an image of Jerusalem. Just as Tobit has suffered and has now been lifted up by God, so Jerusalem has been afflicted but will be again rebuilt by God's mercy. The theme of his song is joy. The description of the new Jerusalem in Revelation (21:10-21) is also a hymn of joy for the city that symbolizes our unity as God's people. With Tobit we await the day when God will make all things new.

Epilogue (14:1-15)

In Tobit's second farewell discourse he reiterates the major themes of the book: the eventual blessing of the righteous and punishment of the wicked, and the sure value of almsgiving. The political realm is the primary example of God's retributive justice: Wicked Nineveh will be destroyed as the prophets said. Israel too will be punished for its sinfulness, but God will have mercy and it will be restored. Ahiqar and his nephew are a second example that the wicked are punished and the good, even if they suffer for a time, are saved. Therefore Tobit tells his children to live faithfully and especially to be zealous in giving alms. It is mercy to others that calls down God's mercy in return.

The heart of Tobit's message is that of Jesus: "Give and gifts will be given to you; a good measure, packed together, shaken down, and overflowing, will be poured into your lap. For the measure with which you measure will in return be measured out to you" (Luke 6:38). Those who are generous with what they have will find that God in turn is not lacking in generosity (cf. Luke 14:13-14).

Judith

R. J. Raja

FIRST READING

The book of Judith portrays in a nutshell the common belief that the God of Israel is one who cares for God's own people, especially in time of distress (cf. Jdt 13:17; Exod 3:7-14, etcetera). In divine concern for the liberation of the nation this God makes use of ordinary people (cf. Exod 4:10; Isa 6:5, etcetera) like Judith, a widow, in order to prove that "God's weakness is stronger than human strength" (1 Cor 1:25). God will deliver Israel "by the hand" of a defenseless woman (Jdt 8:33) from the man who said, "what I have spoken I will accomplish by my own hand" (2:12). Indeed it is the only deuterocanonical book that hails a woman as the sole hero. Not without reason is Judith (the name means "a Jewess") called a female David. The presentations of Judith and David and their exploits form a close parallel, as shown below.

Composition

The book of Judith is divided into two distinct parts, the first (chs. 1–7) dealing with the war preparations of the Assyrians against the Jews and the second and more important (chs. 8–16) describing the deliverance of the Jews by the hands of Judith. Both parts are arranged in inverted parallelisms (chiasms). The first opens with an introduction of the two principal antagonists of the Jew in the story, Nebuchadnezzar (1:1-16) and the army general Holofernes (2:1-

	Judith		**David (1 Samuel 17)**
2:4	Holofernes is the chief general of the Babylonians.	17:4	Goliath is the champion of the Philistines.
8:4	Judith is a widow.	17:14	David is the youngest boy.
8:7	Judith is beautiful and very lovely to behold.	17:42	David is ruddy and handsome.
8:9-34	Judith tells Uzziah and the others to take courage.	17:32	David tells Saul not to lose heart.
9:1-14	Judith prays to God.	17:45	David goes in the name of God.
9:7	Judith's God is the Lord who crushes wars; the Lord is his name.	17:45-47	David's God is the God of armies. The battle is the Lord's.
9:10	God will win the war through the hand of a woman.	17:46-47	God will give the enemy into the hand of David.
13:6-8	With the sword of Holofernes himself Judith cuts off his head.	17:50-51	With the sword of Goliath David cuts off his head.
13:15	Judith brings the head of Holofernes to Bethulia.	17:54	David brings the head of Goliath to Jerusalem.
15:1-7	The army takes flight and Israel plunders the camp.	17:52-53	The Philistines flee and Israel takes possession of the booty.

13). The rest of the first part can be outlined as follows:

- a. 2:14–3:10: Holofernes begins his campaign against the nations and the people surrender.
- b. 4:1-15: Israel prepares for war.
- c. 5:1–6:11: Holofernes talks with Achior.
- c'. 6:12-21: Achior talks with the people of Israel.
- b'. 7:1-5: Holofernes prepares for war.
- a'. 7:6-32: Holofernes begins a campaign against Bethulia and the people wish to surrender.

The second part, which focuses its attention mainly on Judith, follows a similar pattern:

- a. 8:1-8: Introduction of Judith.
- b. 8:9-10: Judith plans to save Israel.
- c. 10:9-10: Judith leaves Bethulia.
- d. 10:11–13:10a: Judith overcomes Holofernes.
- c'. 13:10b-11: Judith returns to Bethulia.
- b'. 13:12–16:20: Judith plans to destroy Israel's enemies.
- a'. 16:21-25: Conclusion about Judith.

The force of the chiasms is such that the reader is not viewing a story told as it unfolds before a still camera but an action-packed drama. In the first chiasm (2:14–7:32), the words of Holofernes to Achior (6:2-9), full of pride and haughtiness, are contrasted with a simple narration of the truth to the people by Achior (6:17) that leads them to a humble confidence in God (6:19). In the second chiasm (8:1–16:25) the whole narrative focuses the reader's attention on Judith's conquest of Holofernes. The entire chiastic arrangement is made to revolve around this central portion (10:11–13:10a) where both Judith's beauty (10:14, 19, 23; 11:21, 23; 12:16) and the power of her hands (12:4; 13:4 [11:22]) are repeatedly highlighted. Thus the chiasms through a highly sophisticated arrangement emphasize the key points of the story.

Literary Genre and Historical Truth

There are many exaggerations in the story with regard to numbers (1:4, 16; 2:5, 15; 7:2, 17). Chronological, historical, and geographical errors abound in the book: Nebuchadnezzar is portrayed as king of the Assyrians (1:1) whereas he was ruler of the Babylonians from 604 to 562 B.C.E. He is said to have ruled in Nineveh which was destroyed by his father seven or eight years before he began to reign (612 B.C.E.), and his capital was Babylon. King Arphaxad is mentioned neither in the Bible (cf. Gen. 10:22) nor in secular history. The city of Ecbatana was built by Deioces around 700 B.C.E. and conquered by Cyrus the Great (in 550 B.C.E.) and not by Nebuchadnezzar. All these howlers are in the very first verse of the book! Besides these, the immense army of Holofernes is made to cover a distance of three hundred miles in three days (2:21). Of the eight Israelite districts mentioned in 4:4, Kona, Belmain, Choba, Aesora, and the valley of Salem are completely unknown. The location of Bethulia (4:6), probably meaning "House of YHWH," is still a mystery. The rebuilding of the Temple (4:13) is dated about a century early. The post-exilic system of government by the high priest and Sanhedrin (4:6-14; 15:8) is introduced into the pre-exilic story (cf. 1 Macc 10:20). Such glaring anachronisms do not speak well for the historicity of the narrative.

In the words of Martin Luther, the book of Judith is an allegorical passion play that depicts "the victory of the Jewish people over all their enemies, which God at all times wonderfully vouchsafes. . . . Judith is the Jewish People represented as a chaste and holy widow, which is always the character of Gods's People. Holofernes is the heathen, the godless or unchristian Lord of all ages" (Preface to the book of Judith in Luther's translation of the Bible, 1534).

On the other hand there are a number of specific dates (1:13; 2:1), exact periods of time (1:16; 3:10; 7:20; 8:4, etcetera), individual names well known in history (Nebuchadnezzar, Holofernes, Joakim, Uzziah, etcetera), an abundance of well-attested geographical names (Nineveh, Damascus, Esdraelon, Samaria, Sidon, Tyre, Cilicia, Scythopolis, Euphrates, Jerusalem, etcetera), a genealogy of Judith with sixteen known ancestors (8:1), and the absence of divine or miraculous interventions, all of which argue for a historical nucleus at the root of the narrative. Hence the story could claim "a certain historicity" in which real historical persons and places are associated with fictional incidents. However what lies behind this narrative is the theology it wants to convey, namely that in any confrontation between a foreign nation and Israel there is an encounter that transcends all history, the encounter between alien gods and YHWH. In the Exodus narrative (Exod 5:1-2) the contest is between YHWH and Pharaoh's non-recognition of YHWH. Sennacherib's siege of Jerusalem (2 Kings 18–19; Isa 36–37) is a sign of Assyria's refusal to accept YHWH. In the same way Nebuchadnezzar's confrontation with Judith is Babylon's confrontation with YHWH. It is the encounter between "anti-YHWH forces" and "YHWH forces," the affirmation of eternal truth and not historical truth that is represented in all these stories.

The book of Judith is a concrete example of such a resistance story. It is history in parabolic form. It is the history of every generation or rather a historical novel that transcends every time and place and at the same time embraces every period of history where confrontation takes place between evil and good. It is the Exodus story of all times. The persons mentioned in the story are real people who lived in history but the factual details may not be true to history.

Exodus Relived

Since for Israel liberation always meant exodus every act of deliverance of Israel from its enemies was always modeled on the story of the Exodus. In Judith, especially in the second part of the book and more so in the song of Judith (16:2-17) much of the description and imagery, as shown below, replays and reflects the Exodus:

Historical Context

The author exhibits a more accurate knowledge of the geography of Palestine where the central events of the story (chs. 4-–6) take place. The LXX (Greek) text of the story constantly gives the impression of a strong substratum of Hebrew terms, idioms, and syntax. Besides one cannot but notice in the story an emphasis given to various religious concepts such as the covenant (9:13) and its interpretation in deuteronomistic terms (5:17-21; 8:20; 11:10); the Temple (4:2-3; 8:21, 24; 9:8-13; 16:20), the holy city of Jerusalem (4:2; 10:8; 11:19; 15:9; 16:18, 20), priesthood (4:6, 14-15), tithing (11:13), sacrifices and offerings (4:14; 9:1; 16:18) and a variety of titles for God closely linked to Israel (cf. 4:2; 6:21; 7:19, 28; 9:2, 12; 10:1; 12:8, etcetera). There is thus much to be said in favor of the anonymous author's being a Palestinian Jew and a Pharisee with a radical adherence to the Mosaic Law although sympathetic to the Samaritans (4:4-5; 15:3-5). The use of the terms "Israelites" (4:1) and "Hebrews" (10:12) instead of "Judeans" (cf. Acts 22:3, 30) to denote the Jews would lead one to think of the place of writing as the Diaspora.

Although the composition of the book could be dated any time before the Christian era back to the fifth century B.C.E, political and religious elements displayed in the book allow us reasonably to hazard a guess that most probably it was composed during the later part of the reign of

Judith		**Exodus**
4:9, 12, 15	The cry of the people	2:23-24; 3:7
8:33; 9:10; 12:4	Deliverance by "the hand"	3:19-20; 6:1; 9:22-23; 10:21-22; 13:3, 14; 15:6; 17:11-12
9:3-4	The Lord strikes the enemy	11:5-6
9:7	The Lord of War	15:3
9:8-9	The wrath of God	15:7
11:7; 6:2	Who is God?	5:1-2; 8:10, 22; 9:29
12:5	Until midnight . . . morning watch	14:24-25, 27; 16:6-7
Song of Judith		**Exodus**
15:14	Leading the women in song	15:20
16:2-3	The Lord is God, a warrior	15:2-3
16:3-4	The Lord is victor over enemies	15:4-5
16:6	Victory by the hand	15:6
16:10	Enemy is frightened	15:14-16
16:13	Song of the Lord	15:1
16:14	Creation subject to the Lord	15:8, 10

John Hyrcanus I (135–104 B.C.E.) or the early part of the reign of Alexander Janneus (103–76 B.C.E.). The setting of the story may go back to the Persian era, but its written form may be assigned to the Hasmonean period.

Canonical Context

The original text of Judith comes from the Greek manuscripts of the LXX. Jerome claims that he has made use of an Aramaic text for his translation in the Vulgate, but until now no original Aramaic or Hebrew manuscript has been discovered. Known only in the Greek translation, the book did not form part of the Hebrew canon. In spite of the fact that unlike the book of Esther it propounds the basic tenets of Palestinian Judaism it was considered an "outside book" by the rabbis since it fostered a universalistic attitude, contradicted the Pentateuchal injunction that neither an Ammonite nor a Moabite may become a member of the Jewish community (cf. Deut 23:3-4; Jdt 14:10), extended a favorable attitude to Samaritan cities, and portrayed Judith as a radical woman, something quite difficult for the rabbis to digest.

In the early Church the reaction to Judith was mixed. While the Eastern Church with the exception of Clement of Alexandria (150–215?) and the Council of Nicea (325) denied it canonicity (cf. Melito of Sardis, Origen, Cyril of Jerusalem, Gregory Nazianzus) in the Western Church it was usually accorded canonical status (by, e.g., Hilary of Poitiers, Augustine, Cassiodorus, and others).

In later times the Protestant churches followed Martin Luther in denying it canonical status while the Roman Catholic Church accepted it and numbered it among the deuterocanonical books.

Patristic Usage

Although Judith is nowhere cited in the NT a few Fathers of the Church make reference to it for political and religious reasons. The author of 1 Clement cites Judith as an example of courage and bravery and as one who had "performed many deeds of manly valor" (*1 Clem.* 55:45). Others however, like Tertullian (*De Monogamia* 17, *PL* 2.252), Ambrose (*De Virginibus* 1.2.4, *PL* 16.213), and Methodius (*Convivium decem Virg., Oratio* 11.2, *PG* 18.212), portray her as one who "accomplished by virtue of chastity what the whole people of the Israelites were powerless to do" (Fulgentius, *Ep.* 2:29).

Liturgical Use

Of the very few texts that find their place in the Lectionary or Breviary (8:2-8, 2lb-23; 13:18-20; 15:9; 16:2-3a, 13-15) the two that are used with reference to Mary (13:18-20, alternative responsorial psalm for Masses in honor of Our Lady and 15:9, one of the five antiphons for the Saturday Office of Our Lady) seem to be of importance since these are *relectures* that bring new nuances to the text. Judith is seen as a prototype of Mary. Elizabeth's praise of Mary (Luke 1:41-45) is a *relecture* of the blessings given to Judith by Uzziah, Joakim, and the people.

Other examples of typology in Judith. There seems to be a strong intertextual link between Sarah (Genesis 12–23) and Judith, so much so that it is possible to think of the portrayal of Judith as a *relecture* of Sarah.

Sarah	Judith
Gen 12:11: Sarah is beautiful.	*8:7:* Judith is beautiful.
Gen 12:14-15: The Egyptians and Pharaoh's officials admire Sarah for her beauty.	*10:14, 19, 23; 11:21, 23:* The Assyrian guards and attendants of Holofornes marvel at the beauty of Judith.
Gen 12:13: Pharaoh is tricked by deceit.	*9:10-13:* Holofernes will be cheated by deceitful words.
Gen 12:17: Lust of Pharaoh for Sarah brings plague upon him and his people.	*12:16-20:* Evil intention of Holofernes brings about his downfall.
Gen 12:16: God blesses Abraham because of Sarah.	*13:4, 14-16:* God blesses the people through the help of (by the hand of) Judith.
Gen 12:17: God afflicts Pharaoh.	*16:16:* God (through the hand of Judith) foils the enemy.
Gen 17:16: Sarah is mother of nations and of Israel.	The name Judith means "a Jewess," a representative of Israel.

From this *relecture* it becomes clear that both Sarah (canonical) and Judith (deuterocanonical) are types that symbolize the importance of women in salvation history. Genesis 12 is the first realization of the promise that YHWH will bless those who bless Israel and curse those who curse them. The book of Judith is one of the last books of the OT to bear witness to this same truth. While in Genesis 12 God takes the lead, in Judith it is the woman who takes the lead, but of course with God's help (16:6).

Judith for Our Times

The name Judith itself is not without significance. She represents all Israelite women known for their piety, wisdom, and action. She stands in the line of Miriam the prophet who led Israel to sing the praises of YHWH after their liberation from Egypt (Exod 15:20-21; Jdt 15:13; 16:13); she represents Deborah who encouraged Israel to fight against the onslaught of the enemies (Judg 4:4-9; Jdt 14:2-4); she reminds us of Jael the brave woman who murdered Sisera, her people's enemy (Judg 4:17-22; Jdt 13:6-8); she parallels the ingenious woman of Abel of Bethmaacah who by her wise counsels helped to cut off the head of David's adversary (2 Sam 20:15-22; Jdt 8:11-36; 11:20-23); she evokes the beauty and the boldness of Esther (Esth 2:7; 5:1-4 MT; Jdt 10:3-4, 7, 10, 14, 18-19, 23). One sees in her a harmonious blending of a soldier and a seductress, of wisdom and charm, of masculinity and femininity; a veritable androgyne!

In portraying Judith in such a fashion the author of the story stands in stark opposition to the prevalent thinking and culture of the times. His dissenting voice breaks asunder the enslaving prison walls of male chauvinism and lets into the narrative the gentle breeze of a legitimate and much desired feminism. The woman is shown as equal to and in some sense even superior to men! Is not Judith one of the biblical forerunners of a healthy feminism?

Further Judith presents herself as a person for others, a model for human liberation. Her total reliance on God for victory over evil (8:11-27; 9:2-14; 13:4-5, 7) does not in any way diminish her initiative, determination, courage, and selflessness (13:20). As in the case of all who are toiling for others, personal considerations take a back seat in her thinking before community concerns. She so identifies herself with the anguished cause of her people that she neither takes refuge behind pious platitudes or in any angelic intervention, nor is she afraid to go against the demeaning plans of the male society. Her identity with the wider community makes her take a middle course to bring about the liberation of that community.

Thus Judith becomes the model for all who are engaged in works of liberation. Her story is a continuous cry that breaks through narrow nationalistic parameters and reaches out to every place and time challenging every one—big and small, strong and weak, male and female—to join hands with YHWH the God of the slaves (and Jesus the servant of the least, the last, and the lost) in the amelioration of the lot of the oppressed and the marginalized.

Judith is also a lesson in faith that can move mountains (Matt 17:20). The might of the Assyrian empire collapses at the hand of a woman with practical wisdom and a deep faith in God. It is her profound faith in YHWH that goads her to be different and to act differently. She dares to be different from her people and from her own sex and proves eloquently that anyone who wants to achieve anything worthwhile must be different. Judith teaches also that a genuine love for one's people, country, and culture need not come under the condemnation of narrowmindeness. For Judith faithfulness to the covenant implies true patriotism. The means she employs can be justified from the standpoint of morality since, given the irredeemable situation, she used the means at hand. We may see behind the action of Judith God's own reaction to sin. It is God who through the hand of a woman (13:4-14; 16:6) has executed divine justice.

Judith in the Arts and Literature

The visual arts in the early Middle Ages delighted in portraying Judith as a heroine with sword and/or the head of Holofernes. In the high Middle Ages, however, Judith was presented as an antetype of Mary, a woman victorious over Satan. It was the Renaissance sculptors such as Donatello and painters like Botticelli, Mantegna, Allori, Michelangelo, and others who immortalized Judith in stone and canvas. English writers like Chaucer and Gower have sung the praises of Judith as a model of strength and chastity. Theatrical versions by Basley Aldrich in 1904 ("Judith of Bethulia") and Arnold Bennett in 1919 ("Judith") and dance portrayals by Martha Graham and others have also embellished the story of Judith with romantic themes and subplots. Thus Judith has achieved her rightful place in Christian iconography down the ages.

SECOND READING

Part One: 1:1–7:32

Nebuchadnezzar Conquers Arphaxad (1:1-16)

The first chapter narrates the plan of Nebuchadnezzar (604–562 B.C.E.) to wage war against Arphaxad to bring him under subjection. The story opens in 593 B.C.E., a pseudo-historical date, and with fictitious identifications. Nebuchadnezzar himself stands for all the powerful but irreligious enemies of the people of God. The western nations regarded Nebuchadnezzar only as a mortal man (1:11) and not as divine as he presumed himself to be (3:8; 6:2); hence they refused to join him and help him in his battles. But in 588 B.C.E., the seventeenth year of his reign, he waged war against Arphaxad and defeated him.

Holofernes Marches Against the West (2:1-28)

The second chapter brings out the high pretensions of Nebuchadnezzar; he is portrayed as making himself equal to YHWH, "the lord of the whole earth" (Jdt 2:5; Josh 3:11; Zech 6:5). His army of 120,000 foot and 12,000 cavalry (Jdt 2:5-15) will cover "the whole face of the earth" (Jdt 2:7; Ps 59:13; Isa 41:5) and "what [he] has spoken [he] will accomplish by [his] own hand" (Jdt 2:12; Deut 32:39; Isa 43:13). He swears with the phrase "as I live"(2:12) which is usually attributed to YHWH (cf. Deut 32:40; Isa 49:18; Jer 22:24; Ezek 5:11, and elsewhere). Already Nebuchadnezzar is thus set in opposition to YHWH.

The dates—the eighteenth year of Nebuchadnezzar and the twenty-second day of the first month (2:1)—are significant insofar as they refer to 587 B.C.E., the year in which Jerusalem was devastated (cf. Jer 52:29) and the end of the Passover festival which falls on the twenty-second of Nisan (cf. Exod 12:2, 18), both calling to the mind of the reader the agony as well as the ecstasy of Israel.

Holofernes (the name is Persian), "the chief general of [Nebuchadnezzar's] army" (2:4) is entrusted with the campaign against the West with a vast army. The geographical details are confused and unknown except for some that are mentioned in the table of nations in Genesis 10. The battle is drawn already in anticipation between gods (Nebuchadnezzar against YHWH) and their human agents (Holofernes against Judith!). The words of Nebuchadnezzar, "what I have spoken I will accomplish by my own hand" (2:12) are ironical pointers to the hands of Judith (8:33; 9:9-10, and elsewhere) and those of YHWH (cf. Exod 3:19-20; Isa 10:5-16) which will execute judgment on Nebuchadnezzar himself.

The Western Nations Surrender (3:1-10)

As the army of Holofernes marches on all the peoples of the seacoast (the West) surrender to him without resistance. He devastates the nations and destroys all the shrines of the local gods "so that all nations should worship Nebuchadnezzar alone, and that all their dialects and tribes should call upon him as a god" (3:8), a direct affront against YHWH. Till then no Assyrian, Babylonian, or Persian king had ever claimed divinity. It was only later that the Egyptian king Ptolemy V (203–181 B.C.E.) and the Syrian king Antiochus IV (175–164 B.C.E.) both called themselves "Epiphanius," that is, "God Manifest."

Israel Mounts Its Resistance (4:1-15)

Chapter 4 is a clear example of the dictum, "Work as though everything depends on God and pray as though everything depends on you." On the one hand the Israelites had prepared themselves for war by fortifying their villages and storing up food enough to enable them to hold out; on the other hand they had taken themselves much more earnestly to YHWH the omnipotent Lord (cf. 8:13; 15:10; 16:6, 17) in continual prayer (4:9, 12, 15; "cried out"), "much fasting" (4:9, 13), and penances expressed through the symbols of ashes and sackcloth (4:10, 11, 12, 14). Although sackcloth as a sign of penance was customary mainly in Israel it was even put on the resident aliens, slaves, and cattle to express the intensity of the struggle as well as the solidarity of one and all (cf. Jon 3:8). Even the altar is draped with it (4:12). The belief that God is at the heart of everything is the basis of their prayer. Hence it becomes existential and passionate, informed with strong faith, hope, and responsibility in the concrete reality of the situation in which they live.

Two historical inaccuracies need to be noted here: the rededication of the Temple (4:3) might refer to some time after the return from exile (515 B.C.E.) or still later, at the time of the Maccabees (164 B.C.E.) after the Temple was profaned by Antiochus IV, but not to the time of Nebuchadnezzar (604–562 B.C.E.). The writer makes Nebuchadnezzar the symbol of hard times endured by Israel. Second, the senate of the people of Israel as understood by the term *gerousia* (4:8; 15:8) never existed in the time of the events in the story. It is of later Greek vintage and comes from the time of the Maccabees (cf. 2 Macc 11:27). Joakim (= may YHWH establish) may be a representative figure of the priesthood in general (cf. Bar 1:7-9; Neh 12:26). Further, Bethulia although mentioned here and elsewhere as a geographical location occupying a key defensive position (cf. 4:6; 6:10-12; 8:21; 10:10, etcetera) has never been identified. It may stand for Jerusalem and its sanctuary (cf. 4:2-3; 5:19; 8:24; 9:8, 13; 10:8; 13:4; 15:9; 16:18). Judith may therefore represent the whole of Israel as identified with the very heart of Judaism, namely Jerusalem, the Temple, and the sanctuary.

Holofernes Acts Against the Prophecy of Achior (5:1–6:21)

When Holofernes asks Achior, the Ammonite leader, for information about the Israelites he prophesies (6:2) that Israel cannot be defeated except by the will of its own God. He narrates the whole history of Israel in terms of the acts of God (cf. Psalms 78; 105; 106; Acts 7, etcetera) from Abraham to the return from the Babylonian exile (5:6-21). The underlying current in the whole narrative is the deuteronomistic theology (cf. Deuteronomy 28–30) that when Israel is faithful to YHWH it is blessed and when unfaithful it is cursed (Jdt 5:17-19). The clear implication that it was YHWH and not Holofernes who would be the cause of Israel's success or downfall is above the comprehension of Holofernes. He does not understand that YHWH in person, "their Lord and God will defend them" (5:21) and if they are destroyed "they [will be] utterly defeated" (5:18) by YHWH alone. So against the prophetic counsel of Achior, Holofernes not only declares war against Israel but also against YHWH. In the option between Nebuchadnezzar and YHWH, Holofernes chooses the former. Not being satisfied with that, he also passes a death sentence on Achior and orders him to be handed over to the people of Bethulia to be killed. But since the Bethulians resist the attempt of the slaves of Holofernes to bring Achior up the mountain they leave him bound at the foot of the mountain. Holofernes makes the statement, "you shall not see my face again" (6:5); ironically Achior will see the face of Holofernes, but severed from his body (14:6).

The people of Bethulia, however, bring Achior to Bethulia. Uzziah (= YHWH is my strength), of the tribe of Simeon like Judith herself (9:2), and Chabris and Charmis, all of them magistrates, together with the people of the town, hear from Achior about the plans of Holofernes and cry out to YHWH in prayer for their deliverance (6:18-19).

Holofernes Lays Siege to Bethulia (7:1-32)

In addition to the soldiers and cavalry already mentioned (cf. 2:5, 15) Holofernes adds 50,000 more foot soldiers, lays siege to Bethulia, and takes possession of the springs that supplied water to the Israelites (cf. 7:7, 12, 17), thus intending to kill all of them with thirst while suffering no casualties in his army. This was done at the advice of the Edomite and Moabite chieftains, traditional enemies of Israel (cf. Numbers 20–23), and others. The siege lasted thirty-four days (7:20), at the end of which the Israelites began to lose faith both in God (7:25; cf. Ps 44:12; Judg 3:8; 4:2; 10:7) and in themselves (7:28). Their situation was similar to that of their ancestors in the wilderness (cf. Exod 14:10-12; 16:3; Num 14:2-4). But Uzziah exhorted them to be patient for five more days during which he expected YHWH's help, a miracle indeed, since they could not expect any rain in the summer months that follow the harvest (4:5; 7:20).

There may be some significance in the number of days mentioned here. The thirty-four days of the siege of Bethulia may point to the four days Judith spent in the camp of the Assyrians (12:10) and the thirty days during which Israel plundered the camp of the enemy (15:11). The thirty-four days of siege and the five days stipulated by Uzziah (7:30), adding up to thirty-nine, approximated the number forty, the traditional number of days (the forty days of fast by Moses on Sinai: Exod 24:18; Num 13:25, etcetera), months (the forty months of mourning: Jdt 8:4), or years (the forty years of Israel's wandering in the wilderness: Num 14:33; 32:13) symbolic of suffering.

Part Two: 8:1–16:25

Judith Comes on the Scene (8:1-36)

Judith (the name occurs also in Gen 26:34) is now introduced into the picture with a genealogy unparalleled among female characters in the Bible. She is a widow (8:4), a member of a group for whom YHWH normally has special concern (cf. Ps 68:5; Sir 35:14; Deut 10:18; 14:29; 16:11; 24:17-21; 26:12-13, etcetera). She is a model of Jewish piety, faithful to the practices of prayer (8:5, 8; cf. Matt 6:5-13), penance, and fasting (8:6; cf. Matt 6:17-18). The practice of almsgiving (cf. Matt 6:2-4) is omitted here since it does not fit into the story. Judith is beautiful (8:7), something extraordinary in her that YHWH will use as a foil against Holofernes. Besides this she is portrayed as a wealthy woman (8:7).

Judith is alarmed at the despair of her people (cf. 7:23-32) and sends her maid (*abra* meaning "graceful one" 8:10, 33; 10:2, 5; 13:9; 16:23) to call the elders to her. When they come she upbraids them for their theological misjudgments, their lack of faith in YHWH, and putting God to the test (8:12; cf. Deut 6:16; Matt 4:7). God's ways are not human ways, she says; God is free and must be allowed to be God and not be manipulated by human means (cf. 8:12-17). Besides, not acting on the deuteronomistic theory of retribution, God is only testing them (cf. Deut 8:2-5; Judg 2:22-23, etcetera) as with their ancestors (8:26). Since such testing goes hand in hand with YHWH's loving concern they have reason to hope in and be faithful to YHWH (8:17). When the long (8:11-27) and forthright speech of Judith, the only female theologian in the OT, ends, Uzziah defends his way of acting and implores her to pray for rain. She responds by saying that God will deliver Israel by her own hand (8:33), a motif that will be repeated several times later by the writer (cf. 9:9-10; 12:4; 13:4, 14, 15; 15:10; 16:6). As with Moses, God's hand will now be with Judith, and as with the story of Exodus her exploits "will go down through all generations of our descendants" (8:32). The wavering attitude and lack of faith of the elders (men) are used by the author as foils to the brave and believing Judith (a woman). Judith's spiritual authority is thus validated.

Judith Prays for Success in Her Efforts (9:1-14)

Having exhorted her people to put their trust in God, Judith now takes herself to prayer. It is the official time for prayer (9:1). She puts on sackcloth and ashes, symbols of penance, prostrates herself, and prays for three favors from God. Reminding God of all the mighty divine deeds in the past, she implores God first to listen to the prayer of the widow that she is (9:2-6). Her next petition is that God break down the might of the enemy (9:7-8; cf. Ps 149:7-8). Last she begs for strength for herself that she may destroy the Assyrian power with her own hand and her deceitful words (9:9-10, 12-13), motivated of course by noble intentions. The content of her prayer displays the three basic principles of holy war: trust in God (cf. 9:2-6; Ps 20:8-9), the absolute power of God (cf. 9:7-10; 15:3-7) and victory for the powerless and the oppressed (cf. 9:11; 1 Sam 2:4). One finds in this prayer a litany of ten titles for God of which the three in v. 11 expressing the religion of the *anawim* (Zeph 2:3) are also found in the song of Moses (Exod 15:2).

Judith Uses Her Beauty to Ensnare Her Enemy (10:1-23)

The whole of this chapter is built around the beguiling charm of Judith (10:4, 7, 14, 19, 23). After prayer (ch. 9) she has recourse to her second aid, namely her ravishing beauty (10:4). From the prayer room she moves on to the beauty parlor. Her inner beauty (ch. 9) is now matched by her outer beauty. She prepares herself in such a way as "to entice the eyes of all the men who might see her" (10:3-4). Taking a bag of ritually clean food, and accompanied by her maid (10:5, 10) she meets the elders of the town who pray to God for success in her efforts (10:8). Not only the elders (10:7) but all of Holofernes' men and Holofernes himself are struck by her breathtaking beauty (10:14, 19, 23). Female beauty and male power face each other in the tent of Holofernes. Power is vanquished by beauty. Strong men fall victim to a "defenseless" widow! There is touch of irony in the words of the soldiers who tell Judith that she has saved her life by coming to meet Holofernes (10:15). She in fact will save her life and that of her people while Holofernes will lose his. Captive Judith will capture her very captors. The soldiers deliver her into the hands of Holofernes (10:15) but God will deliver Holofernes into the hands of Judith (13:14-15).

Judith Meets Holofernes (11:1-23)

The dialogue between Holofernes and Judith provides the matter for this chapter. Ravished by the latter's beauty, Holofernes exhorts her repeatedly to take courage (11:1, 4). Judith in fact had taken courage not, as Holofernes believes, because she had chosen to serve "Nebuchadnezzar, king of all the earth" (11:1, 7) but because she already serves YHWH the true sovereign of all the earth. Judith now adds wisdom to her beauty (11:20-23) and answers him in double talk, mixing truth and deceit in her speech. Both humor and irony punctuate her speech (11:5-6, 8, 10-16, 19). Wisdom prevails over brute power.

By telling Holofernes that "God will accomplish something through you, and my lord will not fail to achieve his purposes" (11:6) she refers to YHWH by the terms "God" and "my Lord," but he takes them to refer to Nebuchadnezzar. Again she deceives him by saying that the people would violate the Law by eating unclean food and not offering the first fruits and the tithes to the Levites and the priests (11:11-15), which is not true. Further her words "things that will astonish the whole world" (11:16) mean for Holofernes the capture of Bethulia, but for Judith victory by the Bethulians over the mighty Assyrian empire. Last, the words "there I will set up your throne" (11:19) mean for Holofernes victory and the power to be judge over Israel, but for Judith they mean that Holofernes will be judged and condemned.

The speech of Judith is so convincing and her beauty so hypnotic (11:21, 23) that Holofernes is ready to accept her God as his (11:23). But her words: "I will say nothing false to my lord" (11:5), which are a real protestation of truth, have to be understood both in the context of the patriarchal age (cf. Gen 27:1-25; 34:13-29; 37:32-34) and from the background of the wars of YHWH in the time of the judges (cf. Josh 2:1-7; Judg 3:20-21; 4:17-22, etcetera). We may note here that the "lies" of Judith are confined to chs. 10–13 and that she lies only to men outside the covenant.

Judith Makes Ready for "The Greatest Day" (12:1-20)

As an observant Jew Judith keeps to the dietary laws, goes apart for prayer, and follows the norms of ritual purification (12:1-9). The irony continues in the words of both Judith and Holofernes. When Judith says that her food will not run out "before the Lord carries out by [her] hand what he has determined" (12:4) it means one thing for her (victory for Israel) and quite another for Holofernes (victory for the Assyrians). When Holofernes says that there will be no Jew in the camp to bring her food when the supply runs out (12:3) the reader knows that there will be a multitude of Jews in the camp before such a thing happens!

After three days of delay and suspense Holofernes is overcome with passion for Judith (12:12) and sends the eunuch Bagoas (a Persian name like Holofernes) to invite her to a banquet. Dressed in all her finery she approaches the tent of Holofernes. Her presence makes him burn with lust and the heavy drinks bring him to stupor (12:15-16, 20). The words of Judith, "today is the greatest day in my whole life" (12:18), a day that would bring joy (12:14), remind the reader of what the Lord will carry out through her hand (12:4), namely the victory of Israel. "YHWH's hand is stretched out and who will turn it back?" (Isa 14:24-27). As in the book of Esther (chs. 5–7) the fate of Israel is settled at a banquet.

Judith Murders Holofernes and Returns to Bethulia with Her Booty (13:1-20)

After all the guests have left the tent and the doors are shut Judith implores the Lord repeatedly to give her strength (13:4-5, 7), approaches Holofernes' bed, takes hold of his sword, chops off his head, puts it in the food bag, and marches off with her maid outside the camp as was her custom, to go out for prayer (13:10). She rushes to the gates of Bethulia and cries out, "God, our God, is with us" (13:11). As the people of the city gather she praises God who had shattered their enemies through her hand (13:11, 14). Then showing them the head of Holofernes and the canopy of his bed, she tells them how the Lord had protected her from the lust of Holofernes and saved the people by her hand (13:15-16). The people and Uzziah bless God and Judith for the great victory by a threefold beatitude (13:17-18) that is applied to Mary in the Roman Catholic liturgy (see above).

Judith's Victory is Revealed to the Assyrian Army (14:1-19)

Judith now orders the Bethulians to hang the head of Holofernes on the city wall and march against the Assyrian camp. When Achior sees the head of Holofernes he falls at the feet of Judith and blesses her (14:7-8). After hearing the story from her lips he professes belief in the God of Israel who has brought about this victory. Against the prohibition that "No Ammonite or Moabite shall be admitted to the assembly of the Lord" (Deut 23:3) he is circumcised and becomes a member of the Israelite community.

As the Assyrian army sees the Israelites marching against them they ask Bagoas to find out from Holofernes what his plan of action is. When Bagoas enters the tent he finds to his dismay only the headless body of the general, and Judith nowhere in the tent (14:14-17). At his news that "One Hebrew woman has brought disgrace on the house of King Nebuchadnezzar" (14:18), the whole army goes into complete disarray (15:1-2).

Judith Conquers the Enemy (15:1-14)

The Israelites pursue the enemy into the camp, causing heavy losses. Uzziah calls on all Israel from Jerusalem in the south to Damascus in the north and Gilead in the east to fall upon the enemy, kill every one of them, and despoil them. The conquest over the enemy is complete with Israel amassing an enormous amount of booty. To the victor belong the spoils: Joakim the high priest and the council (cf. 4:6, 8) come to Bethulia to acclaim God for the exploits performed through the hands of Judith (15:8), the savior of Israel. She is eulogized as "the glory of Jerusalem," "the great boast of Israel," and "the great pride of our nation" (15:9-10; see above for the application to Mary). After looting the camp for a month the Israelites celebrate their victory, the women crowning themselves with olive leaves in the manner of the Greeks and dancing (cf. Exod 15:20), and the men wearing garlands and singing. Judith joins them in their celebration.

Judith Praises God for Victory (16:1-20)

While the prayer of Judith in ch. 9 is spontaneous and personal, the song of praise in ch. 16 is one of corporate worship. The theme of the song "The Lord is a God who crushes wars" (9:7-8; 16:2) is the same as that of the canticle of Miriam (cf. Exod 15:3 LXX), and the latter perhaps was the prototype of Judith's canticle. The song teems with vividness and irony (16:5-10). The introductory verse is a call to praise God (16:1), followed by reasons for praise (vv. 2-12) and the conclusion is a "new song" (16:13) with further reasons for praise (16:13-17). The first part of the song (vv. 2-12) deals mainly with the Assyrian threat and the rescue of the oppressed by God through the hand of Judith (16:5-6) as well as her beauty (16:6-9). The "new song" (16:13-17) praises God as the Lord of all creation (16:13-15) as opposed to Nebuchadnezzar who claimed to be "the lord of the earth" (2:5). Thus in the whole of this hymn YHWH is hailed as both the deliverer of the people and the creator of the whole universe (in a pattern similar to that of Pss 97–98). What may be considered "new" in the song (16:13) is that the victory over the Assyrians is a pointer to the eschatological victory (cf. 16:17; Pss 48; 98; 99) that will bring about "the new heaven and the new earth" (cf. Isa 66:22-23; Pss 96:11-13; 98:7-9) when God will be sovereign over all and everything.

Epilogue: Judith's Last Days (16:21-25)

After three months of celebration in Jerusalem (16:20) Judith returns to Bethulia. Despite many proposals of marriage she remains faithful to the memory of her husband and lives her widow's life till the age of 105, an age similar to that of the heroes of the patriarchal times. She grows more and more in fame (16:21b-23), sets her maid free, distributes her wealth to her kin, and dies honorably. Judith's age corresponds also to the Maccabean period that lasted exactly 105 years.

Judith is buried in the same place as her husband Manasseh and the whole of Israel mourns her for seven days. The book closes with the statement: "No one ever again spread terror among the Israelites during the lifetime of Judith, or for a long time after her death" (16:25), a fitting acclaim repeatedly recalled by Israel after their victory over enemies (cf. Judg 3:11, 30; 5:31; 8:28 and elsewhere). The Vulgate adds at the end: "The anniversary of this victory is celebrated by the Hebrews and ranks as one of the holy days. The Jews have observed it from that time to the present day." This may be a reference to the feast of Hanukkah (cf. Esth 9:27-28; 1 Macc 7:48-49), which is celebrated in the month of Adar.

BIBLIOGRAPHY

Craghan, John F. *Esther, Judith, Tobit, Jonah, Ruth.* OTMes 16. Wilmington, Del.: Michael Glazier, 1982.

Craven, Toni. *Artistry and Faith in the Book of Judith.* SBL.DS 70. Chico: Scholars, 1983.

Enslin, Morton S. *The Book of Judith.* Jewish Apocryphal Literature 7. Leiden: E. J. Brill, 1972.

Moore, Carey A. *Judith.* AB 40. Garden City, N.Y.: Doubleday, 1985.

Esther

Samuel Pagán

FIRST READING

The episodes narrated in the book of Esther take place in Susa (Neh 1:1), one of the capitals of the Persian empire, during the reign of Ahasuerus or Artaxerxes, also known as Xerxes I (Ezra 4:6). This work presents the origin of the feast of Purim (Esth 9:16-32) which celebrates the salvation of the Jewish community in a period of persecution and national crisis.

The following outline offers a summary of the book:

I. Feasts and intrigues in the palace: Esth 1:1–2:23
 a. Queen Vashti defies Artaxerxes: 1:1-22
 b. Esther is proclaimed queen: 2:1-18
 c. Mordecai denounces a conspiracy against the king: 2:19-23

II. Persecution of the Jews: Esth 3:1–5:14
 a. Haman plots the destruction of the Jews: 3:1-15
 b. Esther promises to intercede for her people: 4:1-17
 c. Esther invites the king and Haman to a banquet: 5:1-14

III. Salvation and liberation of the Jews: 6:1–9:15
 a. Haman is forced to honor Mordecai 6:1-14
 b. Haman is hanged: 7:1-10
 c. Artaxerxes' decree in favor of the Jews: 8:1-17
 d. The Jews destroy their enemies: 9:1-15

IV. Regulations for the feast of Purim: Esth 9:16–10:3
 a. The feast of Purim: 9:16-32
 b. Mordecai's greatness: 10:1-3

Canonicity

The canonicity of the book of Esther has been questioned by Jews and also by Christians. The most quoted motive for this questioning is the lack of an explicit reference to the name of God.

In the first century of the common era the book of Esther became recognized in the Jewish community. The Talmud (*B. Batra* 14a-15a) and Flavius Josephus (*Ant.* 11) mention it as part of the canon and the so-called "Council of Jamnia" (ca. 90 C.E.) must have acknowledged its religious value for several reasons: the book appears to be a historical work about a time of persecution and it justifies the existence of a popular Jewish feast. In addition, after the destruction of the Jerusalem temple in 70 C.E. Jews probably saw the heroic deed of Mordecai and Esther as an example for situations of crisis.

Among Christians there have been various doubts concerning the canonicity of the book of Esther: the account offers a vague and superficial set of religious values and the name of God is absent from the narrative (the Greek text includes an important series of additions that not only mention God's name but also enhance the religious value of the book). Moreover, Esther is not mentioned in the NT and it does not appear in several ancient lists of canonical books. In the final analysis the objective of the book of Esther is to present "the historical basis" for the feast of Purim which is not included in the Christian calendar.

All these factors contributed to make the Eastern churches very slow to include this book in the biblical canon. The Western churches accepted Esther's canonicity by the fourth century C.E.

No fragments of Esther have been found among the Qumran manuscripts. Some scholars think that this is the result of a historical accident: the book may have been known in the community but no scrolls of Esther were kept in caves. According to other scholars theological rejection of the book by the community is due to the fact that God is not mentioned. Perhaps the absence of God's name and Esther's initial refusal when Mordecai asks her to intercede for the Jews were factors that prevented the religious authority of the book from being accepted there. In fact, the Qumran liturgical calendar only included the feasts described in the Pentateuch and the feast of Purim is not one of them.

Esther has been found in different places within the canon of Scripture, depending on the criteria for the particular canonical organization. [See the article "How We Got Our Bible."] Chronological, logical, and theological criteria can be identified.

MT	**Talmud**	**LXX**
Minor Prophets	Minor Prophets	Job
Psalms	Ruth	Wisdom
Job	Psalms	Sirach
Proverbs	Job	*Esther*
Ruth	Proverbs	Judith
Song of Songs	Ecclesiastes	Tobit
Ecclesiastes	Song of Songs	Minor Prophets
Lamentations	Lamentations	Isaiah
Esther	Daniel	Jeremiah
Daniel	*Esther*	Baruch
Ezra	Ezra	Lamentations
Nehemiah	Nehemiah	Letter of Jeremiah
Chronicles	Chronicles	Ezekiel

The Feast of Purim

Josephus (*Ant.* 11.6.13 [Loeb 11.269-296, especially 281, 286, 292, 295]) mentions the feast that was celebrated on the fourteenth and fifteenth of the month of Adar (February–March) to commemorate the deliverance of the Jews at the time of Mordecai in the Persian empire. In 2 Maccabees (cf. 15:36) there is a reference to the feast of Nicanor that was celebrated on the thirteenth day of Adar, "the day before Mordecai's day." The Talmud, in turn, describes the ceremonial details of the Purim festival which included manifestations of enthusiasm, happiness, and carnival feasts. In addition there were banquets, drinks, and exchanges of gifts among relatives and friends. The book of Esther was also read. The feast of Purim has both secular and religious aspects.

Attempts to assign a Jewish origin to the feast of Purim have been fruitless. The very name of the feast betrays its non-Jewish origin. The word "Purim" the singular of which is *pur,* means "lots" and it may be related to the Babylonian word *puru* whose most frequent use has the same meaning.

Several theories about the origin of the feast of Purim have been proposed. Some researchers link the story of Esther to Babylonian myths and festivities: Mordecai and Esther could be identified with the divinities Marduk and Ishtar, Haman and Vashti with the Elamite gods Humman and Mashti. However, a more probable theory links the origin of the Jewish feast to the New Year celebrations in the Persian empire. Esther presents various rites and traditions that were common in the celebrations of New Year in Persia and other ancient cultures.

Author and Date of Composition

Determining the date of the composition of Esther depends on an internal analysis of the book. From the linguistic point of view the text should be situated in the Persian or the early Hellenistic period for three fundamental reasons. The Hebrew used in Esther has little in common with the Hebrew discovered in Qumran; the text of Esther does not reflect the Greek influence that characterized the Hellenistic period and the books with which Esther has some literary and linguistic affinity belong to the Persian period. To this linguistic argument should be added the fact that the account shows deference and sympathy toward the Persian king and, moreover, speaks of a Jew who attained a prestigious position in the empire. Such affinity suggests the period of Persian hegemony. The year 400 B.C.E. has been suggested as the approximate composition date for most of the book.

The author, who remains anonymous throughout the narrative, must have been a Jew who was familiar with Persian language, customs, and traditions, but one who also expresses respect for the ancient traditions of the Jewish people.

Literary Analysis

The plot of the story includes a series of events in which intrigues and suspense fulfill a specific function (4:11–5:2; 5:4, 8, 14; 6:6). Frequently we also find the use of irony, especially manifested by a series of contrasts. The destiny of Haman, the implacable persecutor of the Jewish people, is particularly ironic: he recommended (for himself) the honors to be paid to his enemy, Mordecai (6:6-9) and he was hanged on the gallows he had ordered prepared for his adversary (7:9-10).

The characters' concrete actions are more eloquent than the analysis of their feelings and motivations. The author likes repetitions and delights in duplicating events, objects, and characters: there are two royal banquets (1:3, 5), two lists of seven names (1:10, 14), a second house (2:14), and a second group of candidates to be queen (2:19); Esther offers two banquets (5:5; 7:1). Haman discusses his concerns with his wife and friends on two occasions (5:14; 6:13) and Esther risks her life twice by appearing before the king (5:2; 8:3).

The narrative presents a series of thematic aspects that show biblical intertextuality. The author has undoubtedly read the stories of Joseph since we find common aspects in both accounts. The protagonists are living in situations of conflict and crisis. In spite of their humble origin they attain positions of power and prestige in a foreign empire and from that position they succeed in delivering their people from mortal danger. Another possible thematic influence is the account of the Passover and of Israel's liberation from slavery in Egypt. In the book of Esther the Jews are saved from the danger of death as the Hebrews were liberated at the time of the Exodus. Esther acts as a new Moses: although she was in the royal court she did not forget her roots; at the opportune time she responded to the clamor of the people.

The analysis of the entire structure of the work shows a process that establishes parallelisms and contrasts between events, themes, characters, and sentences. This type of literary structure is called "chiasmus."

The king's insomnia is placed at the center of the narrative. According to Esth 6:1 King Artaxerxes is unable to sleep and asks that the book in which the history of the Persian empire is written be brought and read to him. The reading of the document shows him that Mordecai has been faithful to the empire and should be rewarded. This event changes the course of the narrative and establishes a clear contrast between the first five and the last five chapters. The first five chapters relate that the Jewish community in the city of Susa is in mortal danger, while the last five chapters deal with their liberation, thanks to Queen Esther's intervention.

Other details are added to the parallelism of events and themes. Three banquets occur in each section (cf. 1:3, 5; 5:4; 6:14; 8:17; 9:17) and the annals of the kings are mentioned (2:23; 10:2). The reference to these annals marks the structural center of the work (6:1) since the future of the Jewish people changed radically after King Artaxerxes had the daily records read to him on the night he could not sleep (cf. 6:1-3). This chiastic arrangement also serves to emphasize divine providence.

The following diagram illustrates the chiastic structure of the work:

A. Beginning: presentation of the king and the Persian court (1:1-22)
B. First royal decree (2:1–3:15)
C. Conflict between Haman and Mordecai (4:1–5:14)
X. Center of the work. Crisis (6:1-3)
C'. Triumph of Mordecai over Haman (6:1–7:10)
B'. Second royal decree (8:1–9:15)
A'. Conclusion: Mordecai's position at court (10:1-3)

This structural analysis allows us to see that in the first part the A, B, and C components describe the danger facing the Jewish community, and in the second section A', B', and C' show the people's deliverance and the recognition of Mordecai. The episode that marked the beginning of the salvation of the Jews is at the center of the work. Thus the importance of God's providence for the salvation of the people is implicitly manifested.

Greek Additions to the Book of Esther

The Greek translation (LXX) of the book of Esther includes a series of additions without parallel in the Hebrew text. These additions, which append 107 verses to the 167 of the MT, are also found in the Latin Vulgate. They can be catalogued in six sections:

(A) Mordecai's dream (11:2–12:6): this includes two important incidents, namely an apocalyptic dream and the discovery of the plot to kill the king.

(B) Artaxerxes' decree (13:1-7): this adds the text of Artaxerxes' decree against the enemies of the empire at Haman's instigation.

(C) Mordecai's and Esther's prayers (13:8–14:19): these underline the religious aspect of the book and are prayers for the liberation of the Jews.

(D) Esther appears before the king (15:1-16): this addition describes how Esther appeared before the king and adds an important theological statement: "God changed the spirit of the king to gentleness."

(E) Artaxerxes' decree favoring the Jews (16:1-24). This text includes the content of the royal decree issued in favor of the Jews.

(F) Interpretation of Mordecai's dream (10:4–11:1) relating Mordecai's dream to the narrative of the book of Esther. This addition includes an appendix with details on the origin of the book and the composition date of the Greek version.

Of the Greek additions, the one identified by the letter C has special religious value. A Greek-speaking Jewish reader may have added these prayers to reinforce the religious element. These prayers declare God's kindness toward Israel and include references to Abraham and to the liberation from Egypt (4:17f-g, 17y). The other additions add a note of mystery to the account and emphasize the power of God manifested in history.

Historical Aspects

Some scholars interpret the book as a historical and truthful account while others view it as an essentially fictitious narrative, the product of the author's literary imagination. Between these two extremes, most contemporary experts regard it as a "historical novel." This literary genre is based on some historical events and develops the plot in a creative and ingenious way to obtain its objectives.

The author based the narrative and content of the book on historical figures and specific events but reinterpreted the events and created new episodes for the purpose of promoting the celebration of the feast of Purim in the entire Jewish community. In this type of literature one's attention does not focus on the accuracy of the historical details but rather on the plot, the presentation, and the objective of the story.

The thematic and contextual connection of the story of Vashti (ch. 1) with a tale from the "Thousand and One Nights" has attracted the attention of Esther scholars. Both narratives show life in an Eastern harem with its customs and intrigues. Vashti's story may have had an independent origin and later been incorporated into the book of Esther to illustrate the character of the king and to describe life in the Persian palace.

Theology

Even though the Hebrew text of Esther does not mention the name of God even once, God's liberating action is evident. God intervenes in history and radically changes the future and fate of the Jews. In a situation of crisis and mortal danger the divine intervention transforms the threat of death into a celebration of life. God alters the course of events and inverts the destiny of the characters: that is, the Jews receive the king's favor and Haman receives death. According to the account of the origin of the feast of Purim the Jews "got relief from their enemies" (Esth 9:16). This relief was the result of God's saving action (cf. Ps 95:11; Deut 12:9; 1 Kings 8:56). The liberating action of God is similar to God's major interventions in the history of Israel (cf. Exod 3; 12-15; Josh 6; Judg 14-15). These actions are celebrated in the Psalms (Ps 126:1-6), in a few poems (1 Sam 2:7-8; Luke 1:51-53) and in many accounts (Exodus 1–2; Luke 1–3).

In face of Esther's ambivalence Mordecai speaks one of the most famous phrases of the book: "If you keep quiet at such a time as this, help and protection will come to the Jews from another quarter" (4:14). According to Mordecai the queen had the responsibility to intercede and to do something for the sake of her people. However, even Esther's inaction would not endanger the salvation of the people. In the final analysis the liberating action depends on God, not on Esther's decision.

However, human intervention is not superfluous. The whole narrative presupposes a natural relation of cooperation between God and human agents. The protagonists do their part and contribute to God's will becoming a reality. The preservation of life, respect for human dignity, affirmation of human rights, and the destruction of the forces of evil are a religious responsibility, a theological duty, and an existential prerogative.

Thus the feast of Purim celebrates an act of liberation and salvation. The Jews rejoice when they recall that Haman, who represents hostile and merciless forces assailing God's people, was finally defeated. The celebration is also a source of hope. In the presence of persecution and holocaust there is always the hope of redemption.

Contextualization

The book of Esther contains a message for today's believers. The struggles and vicissitudes of the Jews who were persecuted in Persian society are particularly significant for communities of exiles, immigrants, and foreigners. Esther, the heroine of the story, who belongs to an ethnic minority, has to struggle to preserve the lives of her compatriots.

At the beginning of the narrative Queen Vashti proclaims the value of personal dignity. Women are not objects to be used or manipulated. The queen publicly defies the king's whim, obedience to which was probably the rule in harem society (cf. Matt 4:1-12; Mark 6:14-29). Personal dignity and in particular the dignity of women are more important than honors, wealth, and prestige.

The presence of Esther and Mordecai in the Persian empire is a symbol of hope for human groups in times of crisis. They exemplify a model of prudence and energy in the struggle against oppression and injustice. Even though Esther became a queen and enjoyed the power provided by her position, she neither denied that she was Jewish nor forgot her roots. On the contrary, at the opportune time the power she had enabled Esther to do something for her people.

We should note that the steps taken by Esther occurred in the political arena rather than in the religious one. Her commitment to God, to the people, and to justice manifested itself in concrete political deeds. For Esther the task of saving the people from persecution and from the holocaust was a political action with an ethical and religious foundation. These instructions challenge contemporary society with the problem of anti-Semitism and even more with the political and moral problem posed by the marginalization and destruction of entire communities because of ethnic or racial hatred.

Haman is the prototype of the oppressive despot who has no regard for human rights. His policy of persecution and extermination represents a typical reality that has happened over and over again in the history of humankind, not only through deplorable deeds against the Jews but in any policy that prevents dissidence and promotes deportations, exiles, mass killing, and fratricidal wars. By contrast, Mordecai is an example of fidelity to the customs, traditions, and values of his people. His conduct makes believers see that at critical times they should not be passive spectators. Instead, they ought to be God's agents in the process of salvation and liberation of people in danger of death.

In the tradition inaugurated by this biblical account, in the seventeenth century Latin America received the poetic and literary contribution of an exemplary woman. The Mexican poet, Sister Juana Inés de la Cruz, followed the example of Vashti and Esther. She burst into the literary world and into the milieu of critical reflection when male dominance was overcoming all attempts to do justice to women. One of her most widely read poems is a quatrain addressed to men in which she criticizes the macho attitude of those who offend and discredit the honor of women after having subjected them to their sexual drives and violence. Sister Juana Inés denounced the hypocrisy of such an attitude and proclaimed the moral value and rights of women.

The book of Esther provides us with a guideline for action. Today large sectors are profoundly affected by discrimination, manipulation, sexual harassment, and persecution, especially manifested in the use of women as objects and sexual symbols. Vashti's valiant and dignified attitude may help in giving women the place to which they are entitled in contemporary society. Esther's conduct, which is a blend of common sense, courage, and prudence, shows that the practice of faith is more important than making an eloquent religious discourse. In addition, the book of Esther offers a great challenge to Church theologians: namely, how to translate theological discourse into actions that are liberating for humankind.

SECOND READING

Queen Vashti Defies King Artaxerxes: 1:1-22

The actions described in this first chapter can be divided into three acts as in a drama. The first act (vv. 1-9) situates the reader in King Artaxerxes' court and presents the events that preceded the arrival of Esther at the royal palace. The second (vv. 10-12) presents the king's order and Queen Vashti's disobedience. The third act (vv. 13-22) describes the consequences of the queen's attitudes.

At the very beginning of the work a subtle tone of irony becomes evident. In spite of being rich and valiant, the King of Persia was also a weak person. His wife disobeys him in the presence of subordinates and he needs advice even in intimate and family matters. Though he demanded his wife's obedience, in the end Artaxerxes is manipulated by Memucan's advice (vv. 16-17) and he issues a ridiculous decree.

The account starts with the description of two great banquets. King Artaxerxes offered the first to his "friends and other . . . nobles" (v. 3) and the second "for the people of various nations who lived in the city" (v. 5). The economic power of the empire and the lifestyle of the king are manifested in these two feasts. The author is interested in showing the splendor of the palace and the power of the king because this royal power will later be a decisive factor in the salvation and liberation of the Jews (8:1-17).

As in the historical books of the Bible, the narration starts with the expressions "It was after this that . . ." (v. 1) and "In those days . . ." (v. 2). In this way the author is adapting to the models of Hebrew literature in order to provide a historical validation for the feast of Purim, which was the specific objective of the book.

Verse 1 determines the period and place where the plot of the work unfolded. King Artaxerxes ruled over an empire that extended "from India to Ethiopia." This empire had been established by the conquests of Cyrus (539–529), Cambyses (529–522), and Darius (521–486).

The first of the banquets took place in the acropolis or citadel of Susa (vv. 2-4). "The third year of his reign" (483 B.C.E.) was a very important moment for Artaxerxes because he had already defeated Egypt and was preparing for other military campaigns. At the end of this festivity the king organized another banquet for seven days. It was an extraordinary happening considering the fact that all the people "of various nations" (v. 5) who lived in Susa were invited and the guests were drinking out of gold cups (vv. 7-8).

Queen Vashti appears for the first time in v. 9. While the king was celebrating his banquet in the pavilion, the queen was giving a drinking party for the women. As a rule celebrations in the Persian empire included men and women (cf. Neh 2:6). In this narrative, however, the separation was needed for the objectives of the plot. The name "Vashti," which has not been found in available non-biblical sources, may have been an honorary title that was given to any queen. It could also be connected with a Persian word that means "the best," "the beloved," or "the desired one."

The second part of the first episode (vv. 10-12) presents a contrast filled with irony: Queen Vashti publicly disobeys and defies King Artaxerxes. On the seventh day of the banquet, under the influence of wine (v. 10), King Artaxerxes, who had made a show of his political power and economic ability, wished to show off the queen's beauty. By the reference to the "royal crown" the targums of this passage infer that the queen was supposed to appear before the king without clothes, wearing only the crown. However, the MT does not suggest that idea. Whatever the situation may have been, the queen provoked the king's fury by defying his order (v. 12).

The seven eunuchs mentioned in v. 10 were officials of the king who had administrative and military responsibilities. The royal "diadem" (v. 11) was a blue and white turban adorned with jewels and precious stones.

The third section (vv. 13-22) narrates the consequences of the queen's refusal. Vashti's firm reaction upset the king and confused his advisers because of the grave repercussions it could have caused in the whole empire. The narrative underlines the powerlessness of the king and his very famous administrative system in the face of the queen's strong will and this act of personal dignity.

Artaxerxes consults the wise men for their "ruling and judgment" (v. 13). They were probably astrologers who interpreted the motion of the stars and advised the king according to such interpretations (cf. Gen 41:8; Dan 2:27; 5:12). They were also familiar with the laws and the operation of the government. The recommendation of the royal advisers, all men, comes by way of Memucan. If the queen's disobedience is not punished it could serve as a model for all the women of the empire (v. 17). The queen must be deposed. Thus male superiority would be asserted not only in the royal court but also in the intimacy of the home.

Esther is Proclaimed Queen: 2:1-18

Verses 1-18 show how Esther became queen in the Persian empire. The account can be divided into three parts, separated by two explanations by the narrator. First, the place left vacant by Queen Vashti has to be filled (vv. 1-4); then Esther is introduced as one of the candidates to be queen (vv. 8-11); finally, the king places the royal diadem on Esther's head (vv. 15-18). Verses 5-7 explain Mordecai and Esther's presence in Susa and indicate the relationship between the two characters. Verses 12-14 reveal some of the customs of the Persian harem.

The account of the selection of Esther as queen of the empire is simple, without intrigues or suspense. There is a striking parallel to the tale of the "Thousand and One Nights." Although it is difficult to confirm the historical value of that famous tale, similar situations may have happened rather frequently in antiquity (cf. 1 Kings 1:1-4).

After his anger abated the king "no longer was concerned about Vashti" (v. 1). Some scholars think that the monarch may have regretted dictating such a harsh sentence but that he could not revoke the royal decree. The selection of a new queen included a kind of beauty contest throughout the empire in order to present "beautiful young virgins" (vv. 2-3) to the king. The virgins were taken to Susa, to the "women's house" or harem. The criterion for becoming queen was to "please the king."

Verses 5-7 momentarily interrupt the narrative to introduce two new protagonists: Mordecai and Esther. Mordecai was a Benjaminite who was taken captive to Babylon by King Nebuchadnezzar (2 Kings 24:10-16; 2 Chr 36:10). His name is a Hebraic form of Marduka, which includes a reference to the name of the Babylonian god Marduk. In Mordecai's genealogy there are references to several of his distant ancestors. Kish was the father of King Saul (1 Sam 9:1) and Shimei was "a man of the family of the house of Saul" (2 Sam 16:5). This family reference contrasts Mordecai's relatives with those of Haman the Agagite, a descendant of Agag, one of Saul's enemies (cf. 1 Samuel 15; Esth 3:1).

The mention of Mordecai's father, Jair, a classic Hebrew name (cf. Num 32:41; Deut 3:14; Josh 13:30; Judg 10:3) and especially the reference to the deportation that took place in 597 B.C.E. present a historical difficulty. If Mordecai had been one of the deported people, then at the time of Artaxerxes he would have been 120 years old. Esther, who was twenty or thirty years younger than her uncle and adoptive father, would have been between 90 and 100 years old and her age would have made it very difficult for her to win a beauty contest. The deportation may have included Jair but not Mordecai who must have been born in the Diaspora. The note that Kish "had been carried away with King Jeconiah" is a reference to the social dignity and nobility of Mordecai's family (cf. 2 Kings 24:12).

The Hebrew name Hadassah (v. 7) evokes the aroma of the myrtle bush. Esther is the non-Hebrew name that was given to the queen, perhaps on the day of her crowning. Verses 10-11 emphasize that Esther obeys Mordecai as well as her uncle's concern for his cousin and adoptive daughter. Esther's decision not to disclose "her people or kindred" is necessary for the development of the work. We must not forget that the book of Esther is referring to a period of persecution against the Jews.

Before she was taken to the king, a girl's preparation lasted about twelve months (v. 12). During that time she submitted to a rigorous diet and a beauty treatment. Once this phase was completed, the girl was included in the group of women presented to the king. When the young Jewish girl's turn came, the king "loved Esther . . . of all the virgins she won his favor and devotion" (v. 17) and he appointed her queen in Vashti's place. To celebrate the occasion the king prepared a banquet in honor of the new queen and invited "all his officials and ministers" (v. 18). Moreover, in a benevolent gesture he granted a remission of taxes in all the provinces.

The name of Esther's father, Aminadab [Abihail], is very common in the OT and is used for both men and women (cf. Num 3:35; 1 Chr 2:29, 5:14; 2 Chr 11:18). The month of Tebeth [Adar] of the seventh year of Artaxerxes' reign corresponds to December–January of the years

479–478. Finally, the king's generosity (v. 18) included a time of rest and the distribution of gifts and food (cf. Gen 43:34; Jer 40:5).

Mordecai Denounces the Plot Against the King: 2:19-23

When Mordecai discovers a plot to assassinate the king (v. 21) he informs Queen Esther (v. 22). She, in turn, reveals it to the king who orders an investigation (v. 23). In this section Esther's submission to Mordecai is emphasized once again (v. 20; cf. 2:10; 4:8-17). Verses 19-23 prepare the atmosphere for the sequence of events that is described in ch. 6.

Verse 19 is one of the most difficult to translate in all the book of Esther. According to the Vulgate text, the "virgins were reassembled a second time." This is incomprehensible since Esther had already been selected to be the queen of the empire. It is important to note that the first selection (vv. 2-3) had been done to elect the queen and not to expand the harem of concubines.

Mordecai's presence in the king's "courtyard" or at the king's "gate" (vv. 19 and 21) seems to indicate the official position he assumed after Esther was named queen. As an official rather than a visitor to the palace he was able to discover the plot against the king. The subsequent investigation led to the hanging of the conspirators (cf. v. 23). According to ancient historians Xerxes used to impale those condemned to death, but in the book of Esther (5:14; 7:9) we find repeated reference to the gallows.

Plot Against the Jews: 3:1-15

The third chapter of Esther can be divided into two sections: the first (vv. 1-6) presents the confrontation between Haman and Mordecai, while the second (vv. 7-15) develops the theme of the conspiracy against all the Jews living in Persia. Verse 7 presents the theme that gives the motive for the entire book, namely the feast of Purim.

The phrase "after these events" (v. 1) refers to the period between Esther's crowning "in the seventh year" (2:16) and the "twelfth year" of Artaxerxes (3:7). During that time the king honored Haman and appointed him second in command in the empire. The account does not explain the reason for this appointment. The term "Agagite," in reference to Haman, was probably a Persian or pagan title. Yet in the memory of the Israelites the name was identified with the descendants of Agag, the Amalekite, enemy of Saul (cf. 1 Sam 15:8-33). Thus from the beginning of the story there is opposition between Haman and Mordecai, whom the text has already connected with Saul's family.

In addition to his royal appointment Haman also receives the honors of his position. These include the explicit order for "all who were at court" (v. 2) to kneel and bow before him. This practice was known in various ancient communities, including the Jewish (cf. Gen 33:3; 1 Sam 20:41; 24:8). Mordecai, however, disobeyed the king's command and refused to bow before Haman. He did not want to humiliate himself before a descendant of Agag and the Amalekites, a people conquered and almost exterminated by Israel (cf. 1 Sam 15; 30). Agag represented a historic enemy for the Jewish people (cf. Exod 17:8-16; Deut 5:17-19; 1 Chr 4:43).

When the king's servants informed Haman of Mordecai's attitude, Haman "became furiously angry" (v. 5). This marks the beginning of the plot to exterminate the Jews in the Persian Empire (v. 6). If because of his condition as a Jew Mordecai could disobey the king, the whole Jewish community could imitate his conduct. This is why Haman "plotted to destroy all the Jews under Artaxerxes' rule." As was shown in the case of Vashti (1:19), disobeying the king was a major crime that had to be drastically punished.

Verse 7 gives an important detail concerning the general purpose of the book, namely, the expression that gave rise to the name of the feast of Purim. A word of Babylonian origin, *pur* means "lot." During the first month of the year, known as Nisan, Babylonians attempted to divine the future. Thus they could organize themselves and make plans for the whole year. One of the ways of knowing the future was casting "lots." The lot cast before Haman fell on the thirteenth day of the twelfth month, that is to say, the month of Adar. This may have been the best moment to exterminate the Jews.

In his dialogue with King Artaxerxes (vv. 8-11) Haman denounces a "certain nation scattered among the other nations" in all the provinces of the empire, with their own laws and customs, a people who did not observe Persian laws and had to be destroyed (v. 8). Moreover, the enemy of the Jews was ready to pay a considerable amount of money to obtain the total extermination of the Jewish community. Haman's proposal seemed good to the king who authorized him to execute his genocidal plan against the Jewish people. The royal "signet ring" (v. 10) was a symbol of authority.

Verses 12-15 present the result of Haman's step. Corresponding instructions were prepared on the thirteenth day of the first month and sent to all the provinces of the empire by royal couriers (v. 13). By order of the king all the Jews were to be destroyed, slaughtered, and exterminated, and their goods were to be plundered. This massacre was to take place on a given day, the thirteenth day of the twelfth month, which is Adar.

The promulgation of this decree almost a year in advance attracts attention. During that time the persecuted community had ample time to organize to confront the crisis. Some exegetes think that this prolonged period was supposed to increase tension in the Jewish community and contribute to the development of an anti-Jewish spirit in the Persian community. Verse 15 concludes the chapter on a note of irony. Artaxerxes and Haman sat down to carouse together thinking that the extermination of the Jews was a fait accompli. However, the "city of Susa was thrown into confusion."

Esther Promises to Intercede for Her People: 4:1-17

The narrative continues the plot that began in the previous chapter when Haman made plans to destroy the Jewish people. The chapter can be divided into two sections: the first (vv. 1-3) presents the reaction of Mordecai and the Jewish community to the plan of extermination that was decreed by the king; the second (vv. 4-17) includes a series of communications between Esther and Mordecai (vv. 8-11).

The reaction of Mordecai and the Jewish community in the Diaspora is one of humiliation, contrition, and protest. The gesture of "tearing one's clothes" (v. 1) is a traditional way of expressing grief (cf. Gen 37:29; 2 Kings 18:37; Job 7:5). Putting on "sackcloth and ashes" expresses the idea of humiliation (2 Sam 13:19), compunction (Dan 9:3), or mourning (Job 2:8). Mordecai's "loud shouting" (v. 1) is a shout of protest, not a funeral lamentation. The LXX text correctly interprets the expression and adds the phrase, "an innocent nation is being destroyed!" Mordecai goes "as far as the king's gate" (v. 2) with his protest but imperial laws prevent him from going farther.

The Jews in the provinces have the same reaction as that of Mordecai. The community responds with "a loud cry of mourning and lamentation," fasting, and putting "on sackcloth and ashes" (v. 3). The people add a fast to their grief and sorrow. The text of Esther makes no explicit reference to God and yet it mentions the fast, a religious practice that was generally accompanied by prayer (cf. 1 Sam 7:6; Ezra 8:21, 23; Neh 9:1; Joel 2:12; Jonah 3:8).

The second section (vv. 4-17) presents the communications between Mordecai and Esther in three scenes (vv. 4, 5-9, 10-17). Each scene presupposes the previous one and discloses once again the close relationship of the protagonists. The queen sends clothes to Mordecai so that he can come to the palace but her adoptive father refuses the offer. He wants to continue to demonstrate his grief and protest since what caused them has not been overcome (v. 4). Then the queen sends one of her eunuchs to find out what is happening to Mordecai. In the conversation that takes place in the city square Mordecai manifests his preoccupation and protest and asks the queen to intercede before the king for the sake of her people (v. 8). The final scene (vv. 10-17) describes Esther's response to Mordecai somewhat dramatically (vv. 11, 13-14, 16).

An important detail about the Persian royal protocol stands out in Esther's initial reaction. The queen refuses to accede to Mordecai's petition because access to the king was controlled. Mordecai's response is direct and firm (vv. 13-14). Before the queen's fearful attitude Mordecai acts with authority. According to the story Mordecai treats Esther as his cousin and adoptive daughter and not as the queen of Persia (2:7; 10, 22). He reminds her that the royal decree is directed against all the Jews, including her (v. 13).

The frequently quoted v. 14 includes an affirmation of hope. If Esther does not intervene to save the Jews, their liberation will take place in some other way. Mordecai may have in mind another official of the empire or another Jewish person capable of obtaining the king's favor, or he may simply be contemplating an armed response of the Jewish community in self defense. However, his rhetorical question "who knows whether it was not for such a time as this that you were made queen?" identifies Esther with Mordecai's hope. In the phrase "from another quarter" (v. 14) some have seen an allusion to God. The courageous "even if I must die" (v. 16) shows the queen's solidarity with her people.

The theme of disobedience emerges once again in Esther's attitude. The queen is willing to speak with the king to plead for her people although it is "contrary to the law" (v. 16). Following a moral imperative is more important than obeying the laws of the empire.

Esther Hosts a Banquet: 5:1-14

There are two major sections in this chapter. The first (vv. 1-8) relates Esther's strategy to obtain the king's attention and favor in order to intercede for the Jewish people. The second (vv. 9-14) emphasizes details of Haman's personality. The central theme of the work, that is, the persecution and subsequent salvation of the Jews, is momentarily set aside to focus on the conflict between Mordecai and Haman (chs. 5–7).

For such an important occasion Esther presents herself in splendid attire (v. 1) and wins the favor of the king who receives her cordially. The raising of the royal scepter, a visible sign of the king's absolute power (v. 2), was a benevolent gesture the queen had to accept. More than a license to make unlimited demands of the king, the expression "even to half of my kingdom" (v. 3) is an example of exaggeration in Eastern courtesy (Esth 5:6; cf. Mark 6:23).

Esther bypasses two good opportunities to intercede for her people (vv. 4-8). During the banquet which she has prepared in honor of the king, he orders that Esther's desires be granted (v. 5). Then, when they are drinking wine (v. 6), again the king tells the queen that her petition will be granted. In response to this invitation Esther limits herself to requesting the presence of the king and Haman at another banquet that will be organized the following day to honor them both (v. 8).

The narrative does not specify why Esther does not make her petition known to the king during the royal audience. The queen may have been waiting for a more appropriate and intimate moment to deal with a matter as delicate as that of the royal decree. Her reason for inviting Haman is not explained either. The author may have wanted to add an element of intrigue to the account. Moreover, Haman's fall occurs in the middle of a banquet prepared by the queen. In any case there is a certain degree of irony here. While the Jews are preparing for persecution and a possible slaughter by fasting, others in the empire are celebrating at banquets.

After Haman leaves the banquet with the royal family the joy of the celebration is changed into anger and resentment. At the palace gate Haman sees Mordecai who does not get up or make a move to pay homage to him. Haman contains his anger until he arrives home. There he consults his friends and his wife Zosara [Zeresh] about what he should do with Mordecai. Their recommendation is to kill the Jew.

There is an interesting discourse by Haman in the presence of his wife and friends. For him there is nothing more important than having wealth and many children, attaining a high political and social position, and enjoying the approval of the royal family (vv. 11-12). His successes are an indication of his values. According to the story, riches take priority over children. The recommendation of Zosara and of advisers is related to Haman's anger and hostility toward Mordecai. The Jewish leader should not only be killed but publicly humiliated. The gallows, fifty cubits high (about seventy-five feet), should be visible in the whole city of Susa (v. 14). In addition Mordecai's death would be a public anticipation of what was awaiting the whole Jewish community.

Haman is Forced to Honor Mordecai: 6:1-14

The expression "that night" (v. 1) connects ch. 6 with ch. 5. While Haman is thinking about hanging Mordecai, during a night of insomnia King Artaxerxes realizes that he had not properly rewarded Mordecai for having saved his life (v. 2; cf. 2:21-22).

The theme of royal insomnia is frequently found in the Bible (cf. Dan 6:18). In this case it is used as a literary technique to increase the suspense and introduce a touch of irony in the account: in other words, while Mordecai's death is being prepared in Haman's house his exaltation is being organized in the royal palace. Important events in the life of the empire (Ezra 4:15; cf.

Mal 3:16) were recorded in the "book of daily records" (v. 1).

The irony increases even more when Artaxerxes asks Haman what should be done for a person whom the king wishes to honor. Believing himself to be the person in question, Haman responds according to his personal desires and aspirations. This is what should be done for a person whom the king wishes to honor! Haman's petitions reflect his ambitions and his value system. Not only must the horse that he requests be part of the royal cavalry, but it has to be the very horse on which the king rides. This petition could be interpreted as Haman's aspiration to the throne (cf. 1 Kings 1:33).

The translation of the latter part of v. 8 is complex since the reference to the royal robe could apply either to the king or to the horse. The text is probably alluding to some adornment that was borne by Persian royal horses. It was made of turbans placed on the animal's head and interlaced with its mane. Another possible translation would be: "and a horse like the one your majesty rode when the royal crown was placed on your head."

Starting with v. 10 Haman's luck changes drastically. His plot against Mordecai has failed since it is transformed from a shameful death (5:14) to public tribute. It is important to note that in the royal decree Artaxerxes acknowledges Mordecai as a Jew (v. 10). On the one hand the story identifies Haman as the "enemy of the Jews," (3:10) and on the other hand the king orders Haman to honor "Mordecai the Jew" (6:10). Verse 13 contains an expression of confidence and assurance allowing the voice of the Jewish Diaspora to be heard: if Mordecai is of the Jewish people, Haman will not be able to defeat him but instead Haman will fall in defeat before him.

Verse 14 is the transition from ch. 6 to ch. 7. While Zosara and the friends are talking with Haman the king's eunuchs arrive to take him to the banquet hosted by Esther. Escorting guests to celebrations was an ancient custom (cf. Luke 14:17).

Haman is Hanged: 7:1-10

Haman's death is related in this new chapter. The enemy of the Jews is executed on the same gallows he had ordered erected to kill the Jewish leader. Various scenes describe the fall of this personage. Now Haman does not take any initiative. Instead, he is completely excluded from the conversation and in the end he is condemned to die (7:1-10).

The account does not indicate the time of the banquet (v. 1). It probably takes place in the afternoon rather than at night since the events that occur must have taken some time. The reference to the "second day" (v. 2) alludes to the second banquet prepared by Esther (cf. 5:8).

When the king tells Esther to request what she wants, the queen asks for her life and the life of her people since their extermination had been decreed. In making this request she shows that she is aware of the decree against the Jews since she uses the terms of the royal decree: "destroyed, plundered, and made slaves" (v. 4; cf. 3:13). She also insinuates that she is aware of the economic transaction connected with the Jews. When Artaxerxes asks her who is the person who "would dare to do this thing" Esther responds clearly: "Our enemy is this evil man Haman!" (v. 6). When the king hears her answer he is disturbed because he did not know that the plan to annihilate the Jews had also included the queen. Moreover, he cannot condemn Haman for issuing a decree he himself had authorized and signed.

In verse 7 the irony of the narrative reaches its climax: the enemy of the Jews is pleading at the queen's feet because the only person who can save his life is one of the people he had wanted to destroy. In his despair Haman fails to observe the rules of the royal harem or the proper protocol with the queen, and this becomes the immediate motive of his condemnation.

The final verses describe the dramatic outcome. Once he is condemned to be hanged Haman dies in his own house where he had prepared the gallows for Mordecai. He dies with his face covered, since in antiquity those condemned to death had their faces covered (v. 8). With this execution "the anger of the king abated" (v. 10).

The Decree of Artaxerxes in Favor of the Jews: 8:1-17

Chapter 8 deals with the exaltation of Mordecai (vv. 2, 7-8) and Esther's petition to the king for the sake of the Jews (vv. 3-6). There is also a description of the content of the new decree favoring the Jews (vv. 10-15) and an additional commentary on the reaction of the city of Susa, every province, and every city regarding the fate of the Jews (vv. 16-17).

After Haman's death (7:10) Esther is given his properties and belongings by the king, no doubt to compensate her for all the harm she had suffered. Then Mordecai is summoned by the king after Esther has told the king that she is related to the Jewish leader. The expression "was summoned by the king" places Mordecai in the inner circle of those who have direct access to the king (cf. 1:14). The giving of the ring (v. 2) means that Mordecai is to take over Haman's position. For her part Esther appoints him administrator "over everything that had been Haman's" so that he will have the necessary wealth and power required by his new position in the Persian empire.

Verses 3-6 describe Esther's petition for the sake of the Jewish community. Her first gesture is to fall at the king's feet [weeping] (cf. v. 3) to obtain the cancellation of the decree that Haman had prepared against the Jews. The queen weeps only on this occasion. Before such emotion the king "extended his golden scepter" (v. 4) as a sign of compassion so that Esther would rise to her feet (cf. 5:3; 6:6).

In her petitions Esther does not implicate the king in the anti-Jewish plot: the decree was planned and written by Haman (v. 5). She includes several clauses that highlight the king's dignity: "if it pleases the king," "if I have found favor," "if the thing seems right before the king" and "if I have his approval." The objective of Esther's petition is to obtain the revocation of the letters authorizing the slaughter of the Jews even though royal decrees could not be revoked according to Persian imperial laws (v. 8; 1:19). Finally, Esther's request assumes a more intimate and personal character: the queen is concerned about the "ruin of her people" and the destruction of her "ancestral nation" (v. 6).

The king authorizes Esther and Mordecai to write a new decree, "what they think best" (v. 8). The decree would have the royal seal (cf. 3:10), a symbol of its irrevocable character. The royal secretaries (v. 9) write down what Mordecai commands regarding the Jews, to be sent to the satraps, governors, and administrators (3:12). The decree is to reach all the provinces of the empire, from India to Ethiopia (1:1). The documents are to be given in writing and in the language of each community (v. 9).

The date of the writing of the decree is interesting: the twenty-third day of the month of Nisan. From the date of Haman's decree (3:12) until the decree prepared by Mordecai two months and ten days or seventy days have gone by. The author may have wanted to allude to the seventy years of the exile in Babylon (cf. Jer 25:12; Dan 9:2) to show that Haman's decree was a calamity similar to that of the deportation endured by the Jewish people at the hands of Nebuchadnezzar (cf. 2 Kings 25; Jer 39:1-7; 52:3-11; 2 Chr 36:17-21).

Verses 10-12 emphasize the urgent need to communicate the decree (v. 10) and its content (vv. 11-12). It gives all the Jews the right to defend themselves from any attack (v. 11). The confiscation of their enemies' property is also authorized. Moreover, there is a reference to the possible day of the killing or "the thirteenth of the twelfth month, which is Adar" (cf. 3:7).

The decree contains a reference to "children and women" (v. 11) that is difficult to accept today. Since the phrase was also included in Haman's decree, Mordecai may have included it to authorize measures similar to those previously taken by the enemy of the Jews.

As soon as the decree is written it is sent by couriers to all the provinces of the empire and to Susa (v. 14). Mordecai leaves the king's presence. His royal robe represents the empire's colors (v. 15). The "gold crown" (v. 15) was a symbol of authority and nobility. The purple color of the linen robe was a symbol of distinction (Dan 5:7, 29; 1 Macc 10:20, 62, 64; Luke 16:19). It is important to note the symbolic value of the protagonists' clothes. Mordecai put on sackcloth and ashes to emphasize his grief and protest (4:1); Esther used her royal dress to appear before the king in order to intercede for the Jews (5:1); finally, the king acknowledges Mordecai and changes his clothing (8:15).

The people of Susa rejoice when they see Mordecai being honored (v. 15; cf. 3:15). For the Jews there was "light and gladness, joy and honor" (v. 16), "a banquet and a holiday" (v. 17). In addition many Gentiles became Jews (v. 17).

Light is a sign of prosperity (Pss 27:1; 36:9) and well-being (Pss 97:11; 139:12; Job 22:28; 30:26). The holiday refers to a religious festival (cf. 9:19). The conversion of the Gentiles may include those who sympathized with the vindication of the Jews and those who sincerely embraced Judaism as their official religion. The fear that fell upon the Gentiles probably evokes the experience of the inhabitants of Canaan (Josh 2:9), Transjordania (Exod 15:16), and Egypt (Ps 105:38) in the days of the Exodus and the conquest of the Promised Land.

The Jews Destroy Their Enemies: 9:1-15

The final part of the book may be divided into three sections: the first describes the slaughter the Jews carried out on the thirteenth and fourteenth days of the month of Adar (9:1-15); the second (9:16-32) refers to Mordecai's and Esther's letters concerning the rules for the day of Purim; the third reaffirms Mordecai's importance in the Persian empire (10:1-3).

The narrative style of these chapters does not have the same literary level as the rest of the book. There are some inconsistencies in the narrative (cf. commentary on vv. 1-3) and some unnecessary repetitions (cf. vv. 24-25). Another strange aspect involves the variants concerning the observance of the day of Purim (vv. 20-22, 29-32). In the view of some exegetes the entire final section is made up of later additions to the original narrative.

Chapter 8 concludes the narrative of the tension between the Jewish community and the Persian empire (8:10-12; 17). The two royal decrees are in force. Yet in the narrative of ch. 9 generally the reference is only to the decree favoring the Jewish community. It is important to note that according to the decree prepared by Mordecai (8:10-12) the Jews were authorized to organize and defend themselves against attackers but not to attack their enemies. The emphasis in ch. 9 is on the Jewish offensive. According to the narrative the Jews meet in the various imperial provinces and organize a plan to "lay hands on" (cf. 2:21; 3:6; 6:2) those who caused their woes (v. 2).

The Persian community reacts with fear at this Jewish aggressiveness (vv. 2-3). The origin of that fear may be varied. On the one hand the conversion of many Gentiles (8:17) must have produced a sense of respect for and fear of the Jewish community. Moreover, the change in the Persian administration and the figure of Mordecai in the leadership of the empire must have increased the fear of the community (v. 3). We should also note that the princes, satraps, governors, and officers of the king were supporting the Jews.

The figure of Mordecai stands out in v. 4. He has made an important contribution to the Persian empire and his fame extends to all the Persian provinces (cf. 10:2-3).

Verses 5-10 emphasize the Jews' slaughter of their enemies. The purpose of the description is to emphasize the Jews' absolute victory. They execute eight hundred men in Susa (vv. 6, 15) and kill seventy-five thousand in the rest of the provinces (v. 16). Haman's ten sons are among the dead in the capital of the empire. They may have sought to avenge their father's death (7:10) and desired to recover his properties and inheritance (8:1-2). It is important to observe that the account does not mention killing women and children (cf. 8:11). Such an extraordinary number of dead clearly shows that here the book of Esther is not dealing with an event that really took place but rather is following the conventions of the novel. It is almost impossible that the Jews could have annihilated so many people without causing any reaction.

On three occasions the narrative indicates that in their triumph the Jews did not touch their enemies' properties (vv. 10, 15, 16). Perhaps the narrative seeks to point out an important moral value. The objective of the Jewish aggression is self-defense, not getting rich. Yet a complete evaluation of the book of Esther can connect Jewish behavior and especially this account with the story of Saul's treatment of Agag the Amalekite (cf. 1 Samuel 15). According to that story the consequences of having taken the Amalekites' possessions were disastrous for Saul. With this perspective in mind the author of this chapter probably included this ethical note in the account.

Verses 11-12 include the report to the king about the number of people killed by the Jews in the capital of the empire as well as the king's report to Queen Esther. It is important to observe that the reports do not mention the Jewish losses but only those of the enemies of the Jews who had died. Among the dead there must have been some belonging to the king's entourage (cf. 1:3-5). However, the king is only interested in pleasing Esther and granting her desires.

Esther's response to the king's courtesy and interest is surprising. For no apparent motive the queen requests one more day to continue the slaughter of the enemies of the Jews. The original decree of resistance, organization, and self-defense (8:10-12) only included the thirteenth day of the month of Adar but now the queen wants an extension of the permission. Moreover, she requests the hanging of Haman's sons who were already dead! (v. 13). In the first place it was not fitting to request an extension of the day of revenge of the Jews (8:13). In the Persian empire all people could defend themselves against an enemy attack. The motivation of Mordecai's decree (8:10-12) was Haman's previous decree (3:9-11). The Jews did not require royal authorization to repel an attack against them during another time of the year. But the author of this account is only interested in the second decree in favor of the Jews.

The reason for asking that the bodies of Haman's sons be hanged was the public humiliation of the dead (v. 14). The king's authorization was needed for that type of action (cf. 5:14). Once the Jews of Susa have obtained the royal authorization they kill another three hundred men on the fourteenth day of the month of Adar (v. 15).

The Feast of Purim: 9:16-32

Verses 16-19 continue the theme of the previous section (9:1-15). On the thirteenth day of the month of Adar the Jews "gain relief from their enemies" and "destroy" fifteen thousand of them. The expression "gain relief from their enemies" is probably referring to an ideal state of peace and prosperity (cf. Deut 3:20; 12:9). This was the aspiration of the Jews in the Diaspora. On the fourteenth day the Jews of the provinces would celebrate a day of rest with a banquet and gladness (cf. v. 15). According to v. 18 the Jews who were living in Susa celebrated their feast on the fifteenth day of the same month of Adar. This is the reason why two holidays were celebrated in connection with the Jews' victory in the Persian empire (v. 19). As part of the celebrations Jews "gave presents to one another" or "sent gifts of food to one another" (v. 19). Gifts express their joy and their concern that no one would be prevented from celebrating the triumph because of lack of food and economic means.

Verse 20 starts a new section (vv. 20-28). Its purpose is to confirm the celebration and regulate the annual feast. Mordecai writes to all the Jews of the Diaspora (v. 20) telling them to celebrate the feast on the fourteenth and fifteenth days of the month of Adar (v. 21). These days will be remembered as the days "the Jews gained relief from their enemies" and as the month during which their lot changed radically. Verse 22 reaffirms that the celebration is to include gladness, feasting, gifts, and "presents to the poor." The Jews accept Mordecai's recommendation (v. 23).

Verses 24-25 provide a brief summary of the plot of the book of Esther. It was important to remind the Jews of the Diaspora of the historical origin of the celebration. Haman is identified as "the enemy of all the Jews" (cf. 3:10; 8:1; 9:10, 24) so that "all the Jews" (vv. 20, 30) may celebrate his death. This account may have formed part of Mordecai's letter.

In vv. 24, 26, and 28, there are further references to the name *pur,* and the feast of Purim is explicitly mentioned (cf. commentary on 3:7). Jews pledged that they would observe the feast of Purim for all generations and everywhere (v. 28).

In vv. 29-32 we have a new and possibly independent section of the work disclosing the sending of another letter to the Jews of the Diaspora to confirm (v. 31) the previous communication sent by Mordecai (v. 20). The authority of Queen Esther is emphasized (vv. 29, 31-32) and the regulations concerning the feast are said to have been recorded in a book (v. 32).

The reference to "Queen Esther, daughter of Aminadab [Abihail]" in relation to "the Jew Mordecai" (v. 29) underlines once again the importance of the queen in the story. The letter is sent "wishing peace and security" (v. 30) and with "full written authority" (v. 29). The author may have thought that Mordecai's previous letter (v. 20) had not reached its objective and found the new letter firm, cordial, friendly, and sincere. Finally, Esther's letter is presented as a "command" (v. 32).

Exaltation of Mordecai: 10:1-3

The final section of the book of Esther (10:1-3) may have been a subsequent addition similar to the two previous ones. Perhaps one of the editors of the work was not satisfied with the importance given to Queen Esther in vv. 29-32 (cf. 2 Macc 15:36) and added these phrases on Mordecai's exaltation. In any case the work that includes the historical background of the feast of Purim is known as "the Book of Esther," not "the Book of Mordecai."

The book concludes with the distinction conferred on Mordecai (v. 3). The Jewish leader becomes second in command in the empire; in other words, he is the main administrator of the Persian empire and he responds only to the king's orders. Mordecai "was powerful among the Jews and popular with his many kindred." The honors he received are related to his administration for the peace and for the well-being of the community.

Two different ways of governing are contrasted in the final perspective of the book. King Artaxerxes levies heavy taxes on land and on the islands of the sea (cf. 10:1). On the contrary, Mordecai is concerned for the well-being and peace of his people. If Artaxerxes has many subjects, Mordecai is esteemed by all his "kindred" (cf. 10:3). The indication that Artaxerxes levied taxes even on "the islands of the sea" alludes to the extension of his power and rule.

The Greek Text of Esther

The Greek version of the book of Esther was written around 114 B.C.E., after the Maccabean wars. The victory of Judas Maccabeus over the Greek general Nicanor, an event that took place precisely on the thirteenth of Adar (2 Macc 15:36) was a crucial moment in that struggle for the political and religious freedom of the Jewish people. In this historical and political context the recent persecution of the just and their struggle were re-read in light of the conflict between Haman and Mordecai. This is why Haman is no longer called the "Agagite" but instead "a Macedonian." One of the motives that could have influenced this re-reading was the coincidence in terms of dates: the thirteenth of Adar, the day of the struggle according to Esther's Hebrew text and the day of Judas Maccabeus's victory. Another noteworthy influence on the Greek version comes from apocalyptic literature, which served to confirm the faith of persecuted people and encourage them to resist.

BIBLIOGRAPHY

Berg, Sandra Beth. *The Book of Esther: Motifs, Themes and Structure.* SBL.DS 44. Missoula, Mont.: Scholars, 1978.

Brockington, Leonard H. *Ezra, Nehemiah and Esther.* London: Nelson, 1969.

Clines, David J. A. *Ezra, Nehemiah, Esther.* Grand Rapids: Eerdmans, 1984.

Coggins, Richard J., and S. Paul Re'emi. *Israel Among the Nations: A Commentary on the Books of Nahum and Obadiah.* ITC. Grand Rapids: Eerdmans, 1985.

Costas, Orlando E. *Liberating News: A Theology of Contextual Evangelization.* Grand Rapids: Eerdmans, 1989.

Gordis, Robert. *Megillat Esther.* New York: Ktav, 1974.

Levenson, Jon D. *Esther. A Commentary.* Louisville: Westminster/John Knox, 1997.

Moore, Carey A. *Daniel, Esther and Jeremiah: The Additions.* AB 44. Garden City, N.Y.: Doubleday, 1977.

____. *Esther.* AB 7B. Garden City, N.Y.: Doubleday, 1971.

____. *Studies in the Book of Esther.* New York: Ktav, 1982.

Pagán, Samuel. *Esdras, Nehemías y Ester.* CBH. Miami: Caribe, 1992.

Van Wijk-Bos, Johanna W. H. *Ruth, Esther, Jonah.* Atlanta: John Knox, 1986.

1 Maccabees

Humberto Jiménez G.

FIRST READING

I. General Character of the Book

The books of Maccabees have not received much of a welcome from Christian readers. The Evangelical churches regard them as apocryphal. Nor do Jews consider them to be inspired, even while attaching great importance to them as historical works. The books have not fared better in the Catholic Church, which has rather neglected them, perhaps because their subject, a rebellion of Jews against Greek domination, does not elicit much interest. In addition the bellicose character of the religion displayed in these books awakens hostile sentiments in many who have no use for war, even a war of self-defense. Furthermore the foreign setting of the events, the unfamiliar names, and the out-of-the-way places tend to put off potential readers.

First Maccabees is a translation of a work almost certainly written originally in Hebrew. Its author was a Jew of Jerusalem who was very knowledgeable about the OT and Palestine and a devoted supporter of the Maccabean cause. However, no fragment in Hebrew or Aramaic has been discovered in the caves at Qumran. This is not surprising, inasmuch as the Essene sect had arisen precisely out of the opposition between these rigid observers of the Law and the Maccabees, who had ended by compromising with the Greeks. Neither did the Pharisees look kindly on the Maccabees or have any interest in preserving copies of the book. The version that we have today is written in a Greek that is very like that of the historical books in the LXX translation.

The final redaction must have occurred in the last years of the second century B.C.E., in the time of John Hyrcanus (134–104 B.C.E.) before Jerusalem was captured by Pompey. The focus of the book is on the dynasty of Mattathias and his five sons, their military feats, and their skill as statesmen. The author seeks to connect the Maccabean family with the house of David and the great heroes of Israel's past; to this end he shows the activity of the Maccabean dynasty as in continuity with the words and deeds of the ancient personalities of the Hebrew Bible.

II. General Context of the Interpretation

1. Original Historical Context

In order better to understand these books, and especially the first, we must have an overall view of them. A first, rapid reading is easy because the author knows how to maintain the tension of the story and keep the reader's interest; the problems of interpretation are not great and the doctrinal content is fairly simple. The difficulties that arise have to do with historical details of less importance. The trickiest point is the matter of violence, and we shall discuss this in its proper place. We shall try, then, to locate the books in their setting, their period, and the circumstances that saw them come into existence and influenced their composition.

Palestine could not avoid political changes. After the exile King Cyrus had allowed the Jews to return to their homeland. They did not regain their political autonomy but they were able to organize as a religious community that had the Temple for its center. The conquests of Alexander the Great had a strong influence on the regions he controlled. Greek culture spread rapidly and became the cultural movement known as Hellenism. Alexander seems to have been well disposed toward the Jews.

At Alexander's premature death his generals, known as the Diadochi, divided up the empire among themselves. With our eye on the Bible our interest is, first, in the dynasty founded by Seleucus, who held dominion over Asia Minor and extended his rule as far as the Punjab in India, and, second in the dynasty of the Lagids or Ptolemies, founded by Ptolemy, who controlled Egypt, Cyrenaica (modern Libya), Cyprus, and some of the Cyclades.

When this division was made Palestine remained under the authority of the Ptolemies, who were tolerant in religious matters, so that the Jews encountered no major problem. The situation changed when Antiochus III, a Seleucid, defeated the Egyptian general Scopas in 199 B.C.E. and Palestine passed into other hands. Initially Antiochus granted the Jews a certain autonomy in following their religion, but soon relations between the Seleucids and the Jews began to deteriorate. The reasons seem to have been the difficulties experienced by the Seleucid economy, which was pounded by wars; the desire of Antiochus to carry out a religious reform; and internal divisions in Judaism.

Two parties sought to control Palestine: one favored Hellenistic culture because the separatist attitude of the Jews caused the Greeks to despise and resent them; the other party was more inclined to a rigid and conservative traditionalism. The struggles narrated in the Books of the Maccabees were in large part the result of the rivalry between these two parties.

The confrontation between the Greek and Jewish cultures did not take place solely on the philosophical and religious levels since Hellenism reached the Near East in the form of an intrusive military and political power. When the Jews resisted Hellenism they were not simply exercising a personal choice of a way of life and kind of thinking; they were also adopting an attitude toward the political authorities.

The crisis turned violent when Antiochus IV Epiphanes ascended the Seleucid throne. He was a complex personality; some scholars regard him as having been unbalanced, a megalomaniac, a prototypical persecutor. He spent six or seven years in Rome as a hostage and the power and organization of the empire made a permanent impression on him; while there he learned much from his enemies. A great deal of his politics and his religious outlook can be explained by this experience.

Supported by the Hellenizing party, he began to take various measures against the traditional Jews. In order to meet the state's shortage of money Antiochus sold the office of high priest to the highest bidder among the Hellenizing Jews: first to Jason in 174 B.C.E. and later to Menelaus in 171 B.C.E.

The decision to replace the Jewish Law as the political constitution of Judea and to turn Jerusalem into a Greek-style city alarmed the majority of the people. With the help of the Seleucid army, the Jewish Hellenists carried out radical reforms in religious matters: they suppressed the traditional rites and prohibited the sacrifices in the Temple as well as the observance of the Sabbath and circumcision; all copies of the Law were to be destroyed under pain of death; the Temple was turned into a pagan sanctuary by erecting in it a statue of Olympian Zeus. Some scholars, however, think that the reference was not to a statue or image of Zeus but to a meteor, that is, one of those stones fallen from the sky that the ancients worshiped and venerated. In this interpretation Antiochus' intention would have been to change the "traditional" Jewish religion by introducing the worship of the sky-god; or better still, the king wanted to introduce into Jerusalem a syncretistic divinity in which Jews, Syrians, and Greeks could see an emanation from a supreme God.

To this religious explanation others oppose an economic explanation. In Jerusalem, Hellenism was linked to the wealthy families of the Jewish aristocracy. Jason received permission from Antiochus to turn Jerusalem into a Greek city to be called Antioch (2 Macc 4:9-10). This radical project (it is claimed) caused the ordinary people under the leadership of the Maccabees to rebel against the Jewish aristocracy; Antiochus' persecution was his response to this revolt of the lower orders.

A politico-economic interpretation has also been offered. In this view the revolution had for its purpose to win political and economic power.

Antiochus IV was concerned to consolidate his power and assure himself of a source of revenue in the territory of Israel as part of his plan to turn his kingdom into another Rome. The rebellion began in the countryside. The military engagements were led by Mattathias together with his sons John, Simon, Eleazar, Judas (known as "the Maccabee"), and Jonathan. Jews faithful to the Law (and known as the Hasideans) combined to defend the religion of their fathers in this time of danger; they used their weapons against both the Seleucid troops and the Jewish Hellenists. This civil and religious war divided the country.

Taking advantage of the difficulties in which the Seleucid kingdom found itself, Judas organized a guerilla struggle and defeated the Greeks. He succeeded in recapturing Jerusalem except for the military citadel, the Acra; he cleansed the Temple and reconsecrated it. The crisis seemed to be ended by the cleansing of the Temple, the suppression of pagan worship, and the amnesty granted by Antiochus IV. But Judas and his brothers continued the rebellion and turned the war into a family heritage, to be continued until Judea became autonomous once again. Pious Jews, for their part, refused solidarity with the actions of the Maccabees and were content with the religious freedom they had recovered.

At the death of Judas, Jonathan assumed the leadership. He was a skilled negotiator and obtained the high priesthood from Demetrius II. This displeased not a few, who withdrew to the shore of the Dead Sea and formed the Qumran community or community of Essene monks. When Jonathan was treacherously murdered in 142 B.C.E. his brother Simon continued the struggle, and a more or less representative assembly conferred on him the highest priestly, civil, and military offices. The Greeks were unable to oppose him and had to accept the situation. Thus the Maccabean or Hasmonean dynasty was born.

During the Maccabean period two different systems of dating were used for the Seleucid era. One was the Macedonian-Seleucid system, which started with the autumn of 312 B.C.E. The other, the Babylonian-Seleucid system, began in the spring of 311 B.C.E. In 1 Maccabees it is impossible at times to decide which chronology is being followed in a particular passage.

It is worth noting that the author leaves women completely out of the picture. The only woman mentioned is Cleopatra, daughter of Ptolemy, whom the latter gave in marriage to Alexander Balas in order to strengthen the alliance between the Maccabees and the Ptolemies. This reflects the situation of women in Hebrew society at that time. It should be noted that the books of Judith and Esther, which are contemporaneous with 1 Maccabees, have female protagonists who save Israel. However, 1 Maccabees is a work written by men, and it relates the history from a masculine perspective.

2. Context in the Canon

The books of the Maccabees are not included in the Hebrew canon. One of the criteria used by Jews for determining canonicity was that the book must have been written before the Persian period; since the books of the Maccabees are from a later time they were not recognized as inspired. Moreover the Pharisees, a group that came into existence during the Maccabean struggles and opposed the Maccabees, did not admit these books into the canon. The cessation of prophecy, which the author of 1 Maccabees acknowledges (4:46; 9:27; 14:41), was the excuse given for not pronouncing on the canonicity of any books; it kept the Jews from accepting this book among the inspired books.

Flavius Josephus, a representative of Pharisaic thought, allows only twenty-two books (the number of letters in the Hebrew alphabet) to be inspired, and implicitly excludes the books of the Maccabees when he says: "Events have been narrated from the time of Artaxerxes to our own day, but these books are not allowed the same authority as the earlier ones, inasmuch as the succession of prophets has not been clearly established." The Alexandrians were more broadminded and did not agree that inspiration was barred either by age or by the Greek language; they were therefore not reluctant to include more recent books written in Greek with the older books, which had likewise been translated into Greek. The Catholics and the Orthodox have adopted the Alexandrian canon while the churches born of the Reformation follow the Hebrew canon. [See also the article "The Deuterocanonical Writings."]

Among Christian writers there have been divergent views on the canonicity of the books of the Maccabees. Origen calls them Scripture; Melito of Sardis, Athanasius, and Cyril of Jerusalem cite them frequently; Jerome does not include them in his translation, but he does cite them in his commentaries. By the fourth and fifth centuries they were included in all Western and Eastern lists of biblical books. They are listed in the Decree of Gelasius, the canon of the African Church, and the Apostolic Canons. Codex Sinaiticus, despite having been mutilated, includes 1 and 4 Maccabees.

3. Canonical Intertextuality

The author of 1 Maccabees cites many passages of the OT, sometimes directly, sometimes implicitly, and rereads them in the light of the situation he is experiencing. He tries in this way to shed light on present events and give them a religious meaning by showing that his history is simply a continuation of the religious history narrated in the inspired books.

The behavior of Mattathias and his sons in rebelling against authority is fully justified in the OT. Exodus 22:20 commands: "Whoever sacrifices to any god, other than the Lord alone, shall be devoted to destruction." The author compares the action of Mattathias with that of Phinehas who, filled with zeal, executed Zimri (Num 25:6-15). When he was dying, Mattathias reminded his sons of the example given by Abraham, Joseph, Phinehas, Joshua, Caleb, David, Elijah, Hananiah, Azariah, Mishael, and Daniel, who merited a reward for their lives and deeds. In both word and deed our author has taken the Phinehas episode as a model. The mention of Joshua and Caleb is also calculated, since while all Israel was unfaithful these two remained faithful to the Lord (Num 14:8).

The flight of Mattathias and his sons to the mountains recalls the time when David was a fugitive (1 Sam 11:7-19). There is also a parallel between the two slayings of the innocent: the slaying of the priests of Nob, murdered by Saul (1 Sam 22:6-23) and the murder of the priests by Antiochus (1 Macc 2:29-38). The priests killed at Nob belonged to a rejected line of high priests (1 Sam 3:11-14). God had no pity on these pious men who were killed but did pity Mattathias, who rebelled. First Maccabees 3:19 echoes 1 Sam 14:6, where it is said that it is the Lord and not the number of combatants that ensures victory. First Maccabees 3:46 mentions Mizpah where, according to 1 Sam 7:5-6, there was a place of prayer for Israel. In 1 Macc 3:55-56 Judas repeats the recommendations of Deut 20:5-9 with regard to the laws of war. First Maccabees 4:34 cites Psalm 118:1-3 in thanksgiving for victory. First Maccabees 4:40 alludes to David's fight against Goliath (1 Samuel 17) and Jonathan's against the Philistines (1 Sam 14:1-23).

Psalm 74:2-7 inspires the description of the condition of the Temple before its purification by Judas. Unhewn stones are used in repairing and purifying the altar in accordance with the prescriptions of Exod 20:25. Objects used in worship are made in accordance with Exod 25:23-30, 31-39, and 30:1-10. The language of 1 Macc 5:40-41 on Timothy's strategy recalls 1 Sam 14:9-10. The reference to a sabbatical year in 1 Macc 6:49 is explained by Lev 25:1-17. The death of the Hasideans who have been deceived by Alcimus and Bacchides is described in the words of Ps 79:2-3. The prayer of Judas before the battle against Nicanor refers to what happened in the time of Hezekiah when Sennacherib besieged Jerusalem (2 Kings 18:17–19:37; Isaiah 36–37).

First Maccabees 9:73 likens Jonathan to the ancient judges (cf. Judg 3:10). In the eulogy of Simon (ch. 14) there are reminiscences of older texts: 14:6 (cf. Exod 34:24), 14:8 (cf. Zech 8:12), 14:9 (cf. Zech 8:4-5), and 14:12 (cf. 1 Kings 5:5). Finally the last verses of the book (16:23-24) imitate the formula with which the Book of the Kings of Judah closes the account of each reign.

As is clear, the books most often cited are the historical books and among these the books of Samuel. The Pentateuch is also used: when all is said and done the Maccabees are fighting on behalf of the Law.

Strange though it may seem, the book of Daniel is a good introduction to the study of the books of the Maccabees. Daniel belongs to the genre of apocalypse and is written in code so that we cannot understand it without having the key. If the book of Daniel had described events clearly and directly Antiochus' agents would not have allowed it to circulate freely; but because it was written in code, it threw the persecutors off the track. As a result, amid the destruction of the sacred books ordered by Antiochus, this book remained safe.

The book of Daniel deals with the period of persecution by King Antiochus and mirrors the events that took place at that time, but the facts are presented as if they had happened in the time of Daniel. Nebuchadnezzar represents Antiochus IV who ordered that the dietary prohibitions of the OT be ignored. Daniel and his companions prefer to eat vegetables and this regimen proves more beneficial for him and his friends than the diet followed by those who ate food from the king's table. The fact that Daniel and his companions obeyed the dietary laws to the letter and yet had a healthy appearance was a call to the Jews of the Maccabean age to remain faithful to the Law.

The statue Nebuchadnezzar ordered to be erected on the plains of Babylonia and to be worshiped under pain of death alludes to the image of the god Jupiter (or the aerolith) that Antiochus IV placed in the Temple. Just as the three young men were miraculously delivered from the flames, so the Lord will rescue those who refuse to bow down to the idol of Antiochus IV. We could go on looking for such correspondences, which are not accidental but intentional. [See also the article "Interpretation of the Bible Within the Bible Itself."]

4. Patristic Interpretation

Not a few writers of antiquity cite or use the books of the Maccabees. Among others there are Clement of Alexandria, Hippolytus, who cites 1 Maccabees to prove the truth of what is written in Daniel, Tertullian, who uses them to show that there can be exceptions to the law of the Sabbath and Origen, who mentions them in several of his works.

We may add the names of Cyprian, Eusebius of Caesarea, Theodoret, and Jerome, who in his famous *galeatus* ("armored") prologue denies that the book is inspired. Finally Augustine says that the Church accepts these books and not without profit even while he acknowledges the doubts about their inspiration.

5. Liturgical Use

Not many passages of 1 Maccabees are used in the liturgy: 1:11-16, 43-45 is read on Monday of Week 33 (uneven years); 2:15–29 appears on the Thursday of the same week, 4:36-37, 52-59 on Friday, and 6:1-13 on Saturday. This is the week in which the book is most often read, together with some passages from the second book. The readings come at the end of the liturgical year and are meant as exhortations to trust in the midst of persecutions. In the Mass for Persecuted Christians 1 Macc 2:49-52, 57-64 is one of the readings that may be used. No passage from this book appears in any Sunday liturgy.

In the fourth volume of the breviary readings from the two books of Maccabees appear in the thirty-second week and half of the thirty-third, with responsories taken from the same two books.

6. Use Throughout History

The heroic deeds of the Maccabee brothers have inspired not a few works of art. In music there is George Frederick Handel's oratorio *Judas Maccabeus,* written to celebrate the victory of George II, Duke of Cumberland; the work, well known for the epic spirit the author was able to infuse into it, has never ceased to be popular.

7. Contemporary Meaning

Some revolutionary groups of our day have assigned importance to the work, using it as justification for armed rebellion against governments they regard as unjust. The book in fact raises numerous questions: Is war justified in some cases? Can the behavior of the Maccabee brothers be taken as a model by Christians who see no course of action available except revolt? Was all the bloodshed worthwhile? Were the results what was expected or were many people disillusioned? When all was said and done, did the Maccabean monarchy have a happy outcome? These questions touch on the problem, so often debated, of violence in the Bible and the moral judgment that should be passed on it. Are the books of the Maccabees simply a story of struggles and revolts, acts of valor and heroism, or do they have a religious value that makes them worth reading? Is their message simply the way God protects God's own or is there something deeper than appears on the surface?

The struggle that was begun in a deeply religious spirit and for the purpose of defending the people's dearest traditions soon lost its clearly religious aim and became a political struggle, not only against the Seleucids but against the Hellenizing Jews. Divisions arose and the religious and political principles that inspired the early struggles were betrayed. The awaited prophet did not come to answer the questions raised by the situation (1 Macc 4:46) and interpret events from the viewpoint of God. Had such a prophet come the movement would have avoided the ambiguities into which it fell.

Although 1 Maccabees claims to describe the Maccabean rebellion of all Israel and leave other Jews aside as though they were people outside the Law it is clear that there were other parties besides the Maccabean and that the whole of Israel did not join it. Both Jason and Menelaus had followers among the Jews. The Hasideans and the devout Jews who observed the Sabbath formed two other groups that were outside the Maccabean orbit, and surely some of the soldiers in the citadel were Jews.

Revolutions often carry within them the seeds of their own undoing. The alliance with Rome and the concentration of power in the Maccabean dynasty were factors leading to failure. The history of the Maccabees justifies Lord Acton's famous claim: All power corrupts, and absolute power corrupts absolutely. The Maccabees reached the point of accepting civil authority and priestly office from the hands of those against whom they had taken up arms. For this reason they drew upon themselves the hatred and enmity of many of their countrymen. The Maccabean dynasty that began so gloriously ended with the rule of Herod, the Idumean of such tragic memory.

8. Sources of 1 Maccabees

The author of 1 Maccabees uses as a source an apocryphal work, *The Testament of Moses,* and he agrees with it that the persecution was a punishment for the sins of the Hellenists. This is an apocalypse that also bears the title, *The Assumption of Moses.* In it Moses, before dying, prophetically tells Joshua the future history of Israel from the destruction of the first Temple down to Herod, but he also promises Israel future happiness.

Also used are some passages from 1 Enoch (55–90), a book that provides a schematic vision of history from the creation onward. In 1 Macc 9:7-10 there is an allusion to this work (1 Enoch 90:9-36), whose author thought that Judas was immortal and would see the fulfillment of God's glorious promises. In some passages of 1 Maccabees it can be seen that the author knew Daniel 7–12; he also used a pagan source that recounted the history and established the chronology of the Seleucid kingdom.

The author also introduced discourses and compositions of his own. The biblical historians, like the Greek and Roman historians, took a great deal of liberty in composing discourses and poems. In some instances it is not easy to distinguish these compositions from an authentic text, but the documents of the Seleucid kings and of the Romans and Spartans that dealt with their relations with the Jews hewed so close to the real situation that there is no difficulty in accepting them as trustworthy sources and not as products of the historian's imagination. The same cannot be said of the letters that appear in 5:10-15 and 10:52-56, 70-73, or of all the discourses cited there. There is no sufficient reason for thinking that these texts were preserved in Jewish archives; they are in fact not authentic documents but literary compositions of the author.

SECOND READING

First Maccabees can be read at several levels: literary, historical, political, and religious. The Bible is not a book to be read hastily, but calmly and thoughtfully; successive readings of the same passage open new perspectives and yield the secrets of a purposeful book.

From the historical viewpoint our author is fairly reliable. Although his conception of history differs a good deal from ours (since he is writing a history that is sympathetic to his heroes), the topographical, geographical, and chronological data are basically objective. The outline of the book is rather straightforward: 1–2: Beginning of persecution, rebellion of Mattathias; 3:1–9:22: Judas Maccabeus; 9:23–12:52: Jonathan; 12:53–16:22: Simon. Each brother falls in the breach; but each carries on the struggle according to his temperament and with his own methods.

The religious point of view is the most important one. The work presents the Maccabee brothers as "the family of those men through whom deliverance was given to Israel" (5:62). It also makes the Law central: the Law divides people into two camps. The rivalry is not so much between the Seleucids and the Hasmoneans as between those who observe the Law and those who oppose it.

Historical Introduction: 1 Maccabees 1–2

The introduction takes the form of an artistically presented diptych in which the advance of ungodliness (ch. 1) and the growing resistance to it (ch. 2) are contrasted. On the one side is the Hellenism personified by Alexander; on the other are heroes who defend the Law.

The author situates the history of Israel in the framework of universal history. He emphasizes the pride of Alexander and the events that follow on his death. The history of Alexander's successors can be summarized in a sentence: They filled the earth with disasters; according to our author everyone feared the spread of Greek culture. The evil has two main causes: Antiochus IV Epiphanes and the apostate Jews he supports.

The setting up of a gymnasium in Jerusalem had both political and religious implications. First of all a gymnasium was a center for the spread of Greek customs and ideas. On the other hand it was associated with the worship of pagan gods and with depraved practices. In addition the Jewish men who took part, naked, in the gymnasium exercises concealed their circumcision by means of a painful surgical operation; to the faithful this amounted to a rejection of the covenant. As during the exile, so now external signs were important as a way of asserting one's identity at a time when the very being of the nation was endangered. There was a confrontation between the traditionalists and the progressives, the latter being supporters of a radical reform.

a. The Sacking of the Temple (1:16-40)

Antiochus' plan to take possession of Egypt was frustrated by Rome, which was beginning to cast its shadow on Asia Minor. On his way back from Egypt, Antiochus IV sacked the Temple and the city of Jerusalem, murdered a great many Jews, and deported a large number of them. The looting and other crimes of Antiochus deeply grieved the Jews. Our author utters a lament (1:25-28) that recalls certain poetic passages of the OT. (Cf. Psalm 78, which was perhaps composed at this same period.)

The fortress built by the king—Acra was the Greek name—was a permanent threat and a symbol of the oppression suffered by the city. Many Jews fled lest they fall victim to persecution by the soldiers of the citadel.

b. Persecution of the Jews (1:41-64)

In order to advance the integration of the Jews into the new social order Antiochus decided to suppress Jewish worship. Supporters of the Greeks looked to this integration as a source of prosperity. The king directed his efforts against the external symbols of Judaism—worship, circumcision, dietary laws—in the expectation that without these the religion would die out. He even went so far as to set up an idol (Zeus? a meteorite?) on the Temple altar. This was the "abomination of desolation" of which Daniel speaks (Dan 9:27). Many Jews yielded to the king's orders; others fled to the wilderness in order not to be defiled and to be able to observe the Law.

c. Mattathias and His Sons (2:1-14)

Mattathias began the rebellion with a deed that recalled that of Phinehas (Num 25:6-15). A holy war flared up; Jewish resistance was not passive, and once violence was accepted there was no stopping it.

d. Mattathias in the Wilderness (2:27-38)

Mattathias and his followers fled to the desert where they organized a guerilla war. However not everyone followed him in adopting violence. Some went into the wilderness in order to be able to live according to the Law; when they were attacked on the Sabbath and had to choose between dying and defending themselves with arms but thereby violating the Sabbath they chose not to defend themselves; they called on heaven and earth as witnesses to their innocence and left revenge in God's hands. The Maccabees adopted a pragmatic outlook. In their eyes the people were more important than the Law; the Sabbath was made for human beings, not human beings for the Sabbath.

Mattathias and his followers not only attacked unbelievers but coerced apostate Jews into keeping the Law, thereby denying their fellow rebels the religious freedom they sought for themselves. Given the difficult circumstances in which the people were living, this course of action was perhaps justified from the Maccabees' point of view; their attitude is problematic from our modern viewpoint.

e. Mattathias' Testament and Death

The testament names a series of persons who were models in the history of Israel; it also appoints Judas, who was not the greatest but was the bravest. The list of names includes those most important for the time Jews were now living through. Mattathias speaks of their merits and their rewards: their merit was their trust and faith in the Lord; their reward was that the Lord never failed them at any time.

In describing the death of Mattathias the author takes the description of Jacob's death (Genesis 49) as his model. Like Jacob, Mattathias predicted the future of his sons and, after telling them their responsibilities, died. The mourning rites were observed and he was buried in the tomb of his ancestors.

Judas and His Early Victories: 3:14–4:34

Judas succeeded his father. To the Jews he seemed like a second Joshua. In these chapters we hear the echo of motifs from the wars of YHWH in the books of Joshua and Judges. Judas faces three armies, the first of them commanded by Apollonius, a district leader, and the second by Seron, a provincial general. Finally the king himself intervened and appointed Lysias, a distinguished man and a relative of the king, to carry out the mission of reducing the Jews to subjection. Lysias assigned Ptolemy to direct the campaign against Palestine.

The book is sparing in its description of the first two battles, but in Judas's speech before the second the author explains the meaning of this war and revives some traditional elements of the holy war. When Judas's soldiers saw how far more numerous the enemy troops were he encouraged them: "It is easy for many to be hemmed in by few, for in the sight of Heaven there is no difference between saving by many or by few. It is not on the size of the army that victory in battle depends, but strength comes from Heaven" (3:18-19).

In the description of Judas there are traits that remind us of David: Judas takes the sword of the dead Apollonius (3:12) as David had taken the sword of Goliath; the forty thousand infantry and the seven thousand cavalry sent by Lysias are not real numbers since so many horsemen would have been useless in the rough territory of Judea, but are taken from 1 Chr 19:18 where David annihilated the same number of Syrian soldiers. It is at Mizpah that Judas prepares for the battle with the soldiers sent by Lysias; there, too, at an earlier time, Samuel had gathered the Israelites for the battle with the Philistines. Before entering on the struggle Judas offers a prayer in which he recalls how David conquered the Philistine giant (4:30).

Among the rituals carried out was a consultation of the Law. Perhaps the sacred book was opened at random in order to find the Lord's will expressed in it (3:48). The original text is confused here and lends itself to various interpretations. One is that the people sought in the sacred text what pagans sought from their idols. Another could be that pagans also endeavored to use the sacred text in order to find a legitimation of the worship Antiochus was trying to force on the Jews. In any case the passage recalls the action of Hezekiah when he spread before the Lord in the Temple the letter Sennacherib had sent to him.

Judas does as prescribed in Deut 20:5-8: men recently married, those who had planted a vineyard or were building a house, and those who were fainthearted were sent home.

Gorgias and Nicanor, the generals sent by Lysias, were defeated at Emmaus, and Lysias himself lost the battle at Beth-zur. The first phase of Judas's campaign reached its climax in the dedication of the Temple which he rebuilt on Mount Zion. Mountains had a great religious importance for the ancients; they were privileged places for meetings with the divinity. Moreover each country regarded its mountain as the center of the earth and even the navel of the world, the point around which the earth had been formed. The sight of their desecrated Temple was an insult to Jews; it also represented a danger since the right order of the world depended on the state of the Temple. For this reason the battles won would not have achieved their goal if the Temple continued to be profaned. Three years to the day from the desecration Judas celebrated the new dedication. The Temple had been consecrated several times in the course of history: first it was dedicated under Solomon (1 Kings 8); then it was purified by Hezekiah (2 Chronicles 29); and it had to be rebuilt after the exile.

On the twenty-fifth of Chislev in the year 164 B.C.E. the Temple was dedicated in a ceremony that lasted eight days. Judas, his brothers, and the assembly decided that the feast of the dedication should be celebrated annually for eight days. This is the festival known as Hanukkah, a word that means "celebration." In the course of time the festival has been given various names: Dedication (1 Macc 4:59); Purification (2 Macc 2:9); the Festival of Lights because of the many lamps illumining the Temple or else because on this occasion lamps were lit in all the homes.

The action of dedicating the rebuilt Temple had numerous religious implications. First it was a decision of Judas and his people. All of Israel's previous feasts had been prescribed in the Scriptures, and no feast had ever been instituted by human decision. Not even the restoration of the Temple after the exile was solemnized by the establishment of a commemorative day, so that the step taken by Judas was an unprecedented innovation. In acting in this way Judas was imitating the customs of his enemies but at the same time integrating these into Judaism. This was the first step on the long road of the Maccabees' historical mission: to introduce Greek practices into Judaism without sacrificing the religion of the ancestors.

War with Hostile Neighbors: 5:1-64

Judas's victories aroused the antagonism of the neighboring peoples; especially the rebuilding of the Temple inflamed them and unleashed a series of local persecutions of the Jews. This was not the first time that this happened; in the time of Ezra and Nehemiah there had likewise been strong opposition to the restoration of the sanctuary (Ezra 4–5). Those who had to endure the blows were the Jews living in pagan cities. Judas had to intervene: he divided his forces and undertook a rapid series of skirmishes, which our author describes in an order that is more thematic than chronological.

The campaigns took place especially in Galilee and Gilead. Judas acted in accordance with the law of war in Deuteronomy 20, which distinguishes between near and distant cities. To the former the law of anathema or complete extermination was to be applied. In distant cities, on the other hand, only the males were to be eliminated. This cruel approach of Judas was justified in his eyes because his wars were not wars of conquest but wars in defense of religion.

This part of the campaign ended with the great march that brought the scattered Jews back to Judah and led them up Mount Zion. The Temple thus fulfilled once again its mission of drawing and uniting those who were scattered.

The author believes that in some sense Judas was the chosen one and that only he and his family could win victories. Proof of this was the episode of Joseph and Azariah who wanted to make war on the neighboring peoples in order to cover themselves with glory but were defeated. Their defeat is not interpreted as a punishment for their ambition but is attributed to the fact that "they did not belong to the family of those men through whom deliverance was given to Israel" (5:62).

Death of Antiochus: 1 Maccabees 6

The death of Antiochus raises a series of problems. We have at least six accounts of it: two are extrabiblical, three are biblical, and there is a prophetic reference to it in Daniel. Each has differences in the details surrounding the death of the persecutor. According to Polybius, a Greek historian, Antiochus died mad at Tabae after sacking the temple of Artemis at Elymais in Persia. The other account is by Appian, an Alexandrian official, who links the death of Antiochus with the robbery of the temple of Venus, which was also in Elymais.

First Maccabees describes the death of Antiochus (6:1-6) as taking place after the dedication of the Temple in Jerusalem and in connection with the attempted robbery of a temple in Persia. Frustrated by the failure of his attempt to sack the temple in Elymais, Antiochus returned to Babylon where he received news of events in Judea (6:5-7). The news made him ill. He died after having appointed Philip as regent for his son Antiochus V, who was still a minor. Here the death of Antiochus is not the result of sacking the temple in Persia but of an arrogant and defiant attitude toward Jerusalem.

According to 2 Macc 1:13-17 Antiochus died at the hands of the priests of the goddess Nanea when he tried to loot her temple. The different names given to the goddess are not a difficulty; they are in fact different names for the same divinity. There is a very poignant account of Antiochus' death in 2 Maccabees 9, but the passage represents a theological literary genre rather than a historical narrative. The author is presenting events in a dramatic form, using the literary genre of a persecutor's death such as we have, for example, in the book of Wisdom (5:1-15). We read something similar in the account of Herod Agrippa's death (Acts 12:21-23). The differences between 2 Maccabees 9 and the other accounts can be explained by the different viewpoint the author adopts there. He wants to make it clear that Antiochus died the death of a persecutor.

There is an enigmatic reference to the death of Antiochus in Dan 11:40-45. Here it takes place in the holy land. But the several accounts agree on the fundamental point: Antiochus died in Persia as a result of an attack on a temple. Which temple? The extrabiblical writers say that of Artemis or of Venus; 2 Maccabees 1 says Nanea. Second Maccabees 9 and First Maccabees 6 connect the death with the Temple of Jerusalem. Both are trying to teach the lesson that retribution is inevitable: tyrants meet a fearful end. The death of Antiochus must have occurred in the spring of 164 B.C.E., but the exact date cannot be determined.

War Between Judas and Lysias: 6:18-63

Up to this point the results of the war were favorable to Judas. However he felt the presence of the citadel as a thorn that tormented him. He decided to take advantage of the youth of King Antiochus V, called Eupator, and attack the citadel. Some in the citadel managed to break through the encircling Jews by night and tell the king of the situation. The king organized a strong army that was equipped with the most advanced tools of the day; its elephants were like the armored tanks of today. Judas was defeated, although our author does not use this word nor does he give any religious explanation for the failure. Eleazar performed a heroic but futile action when he attacked and killed the elephant on which he thought the king was riding; the enormous animal crushed him when it fell.

The author's gift for storytelling shows in the description of the battle, for he gives a vivid picture of an army and its mighty weapons. He sounds more like a war correspondent delighting in the event than a Jew telling of his people's defeat, although he does suggest this in the most tactful way possible.

Now master of the field, Antiochus was in a position to attack Jerusalem on the one hand and Beth-zur on the other. He first conquered the latter, whose stores had run out because it was a sabbatical year (Lev 25:1-7). He then attacked Jerusalem where the siege of the citadel had gone on for too long. The author lists in detail the various machines used in attacking Jerusalem: crossbows, assault machines, flamethrowers, catapults, scorpions (machines for hurling little arrows), and slings. The situation in Jerusalem was not good.

Fortunately for Jerusalem the king had to lift the siege because he heard that Philip (v. 14) had returned and was determined to press his right to the title of regent, given him by King Antiochus IV, against Lysias, the acting regent. The possibility that Demetrius too was attempting to claim the throne (7:1) was a further reason for reaching an agreement with the Jews. Oddly enough the Maccabees are not mentioned in these negotiations. We must admire the author's honesty in describing events with great objectivity. God did not always intervene even when the Maccabees were fighting for the people of the covenant.

The Jews gained their religious freedom, but not political autonomy. The Maccabean revolt did not yield a political base. In the eyes of the king the Maccabees were simply one party seeking a rigid interpretation of their ancestral laws.

Demetrius and Alcimus: 7:1-25

At his death Seleucus IV Philopator left as his heir young Demetrius, then nine years old, whom he had sent to Rome as a hostage. At that point Antiochus IV, brother of Seleucus, took the reins of the kingdom. When Antiochus IV died in turn he left his son, Antiochus V, as heir, but Demetrius thought with good reason that he was the legitimate heir. Outwitting his Roman guards he took ship for the coast of Phoenicia, landed at Tripolis, gathered an army, and assembled a fleet. His generals put Antiochus V and Lysias to death.

Demetrius' attitude to the Jews was not significantly different from that of the other Syrian kings. He took the part of the Hellenists and sought to end Judas's rebellion.

The Alcimus episode throws some light on the various divergences within the Jewish resistance movement. As a result of the agreement between Lysias and Judas the Maccabees were free to settle accounts with the apostate Jews, who were persecuted, harassed, and forced to leave Palestine. Alcimus (a Hellenized version of the Jewish name Iaqim) belonged to the priestly line but not to the family of the high priest Onias. The line of high-priestly succession had been interrupted during the early years of Antiochus Epiphanes, when the Hellenist reform took place. Menelaus, the previous high priest, whom 1 Maccabees does not mention, was not a member of the high-priestly family. Alcimus, who was chosen to accompany Bacchides, was a priest in the line of Aaron, and some Jews accepted him as high priest since he seemed to them a man of peace.

The Hasideans, who had joined Judas at the beginning of the struggle, now wanted to lay down arms. Their aim seems to have been to restore a legitimate priesthood and worship. They were soon disillusioned, however, in their supposition that a legitimate priest would not harm them. The fact that a man had been born a priest and was discharging this office was no guarantee of his fidelity to the Law. The Hasideans had not kept in mind what had happened when Jason filled this office; now Alcimus betrayed them.

Judas and his followers were not so naïve and did not fall into the trap set by Alcimus. Why was he offering proposals of peace while protected by a fully equipped and hostile army? Bacchides left Alcimus and a supporting army behind to fight Judas and his followers, but Judas managed to remain in power. Alcimus lost the support of the army but could not submit to the Maccabean.

Demetrius and Nicanor: 7:26-50

Demetrius gave Nicanor the task of reducing Judas to submission. Nicanor went to Jerusalem with seemingly peaceful intentions; he suggested that instead of having recourse to arms he and Judas Maccabeus have a meeting. In the beginning the conversations had positive results and a peace treaty was signed. Nicanor dismissed his soldiers and struck up a friendship with Judas. But Alcimus accused Nicanor to the king of working against the interests of the nation; the king ordered Nicanor to hand Judas

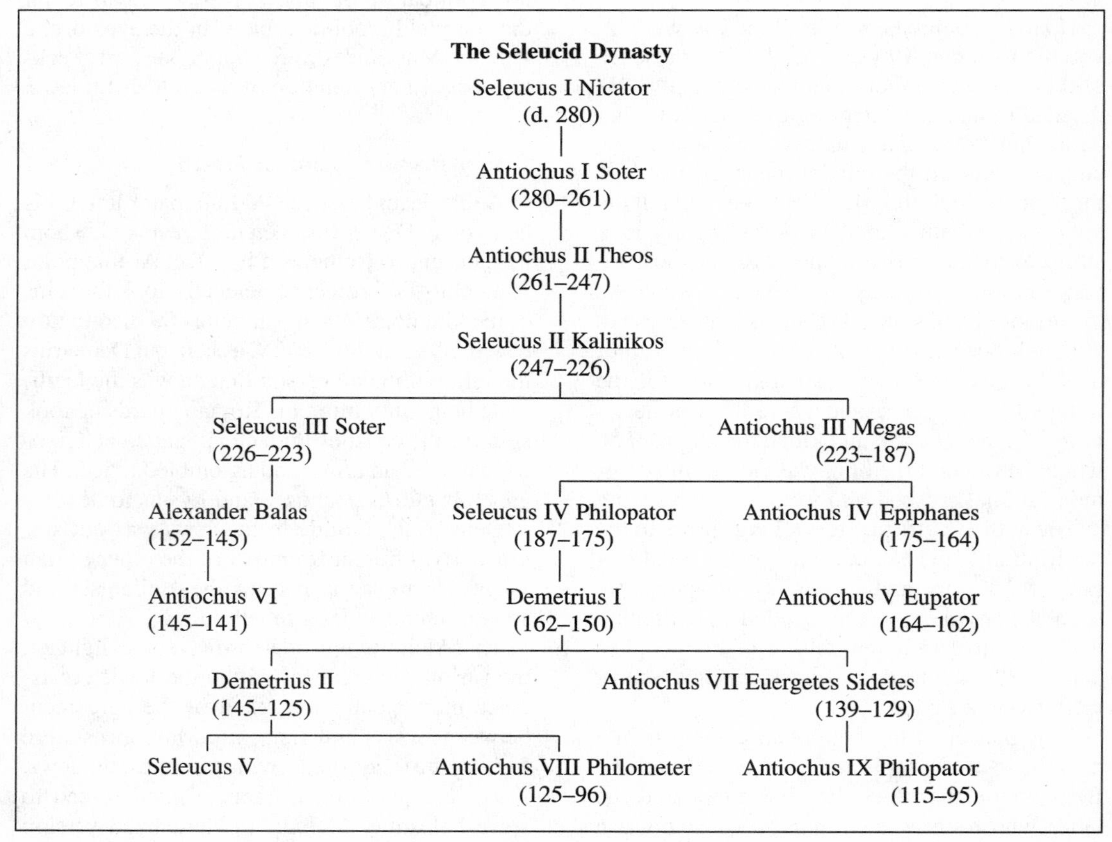

over. Nicanor's attitude to Judas changed. The two met in battle at Capharsalama, where five thousand soldiers of Nicanor's army fell. Nicanor then showed contempt for the Temple and its priests. His threat to destroy the Temple was understandable since the sanctuary was a religious symbol the destruction of which would have seriously damaged the Maccabeans, more so than it would priests like Alcimus.

The opposing armies met at Adasa, northeast of Beth-horon, an hour and a half from Jerusalem at a point where the road narrowed as it passed between the hills. Judas's army proved its superiority. Nicanor died and his soldiers were scattered. His defeat is presented as a direct consequence of the prayer of the priests (7:36-38). The Jews believed that anyone who desecrated the Temple would not escape punishment. Judas's own prayer recalls the deliverance of Jerusalem by an angel of the Lord when it was besieged by the Assyrians. Now, however, there was no angel of the Lord coming to give aid; the sword of the Jews, through whom God was acting, accomplished everything.

If we compare 1 Maccabees 7 and 2 Maccabees 14–15 we meet with some problems. The two stories are parallel to some extent and the main line of the narrative is the same. There are, however, divergences that call for an explanation: for example, Alcimus' betrayal of the Hasideans (1 Macc 7:8-25); the suicide of Razis (2 Macc 14:37-46); and the dream-vision of Judas before the battle. Various explanations are possible but none is completely satisfactory. The most acceptable one is that the two authors know the main outline of the story but tell it in different ways.

The Jews cut off the head of Nicanor and the right hand with which he had sworn to destroy the Temple and dedicate it to the god Bacchus (1 Macc 7:47; 2 Macc 14:33); they hung these trophies on the wall of the citadel. David had done the same with Goliath (1 Sam 17:54) and Judith with Holofernes (Jdt 14:11), as prescribed by the laws of warfare at the time.

This great victory was celebrated with special solemnity. The date was March 13 of the month of Adar (March 28, 161 B.C.E.). The people agreed in democratic fashion that the popular Feast of Nicanor should be celebrated annually on this date (1 Macc 7:48; 2 Macc 15:36). Later the feast fell into disuse because it was so close to the Feast of Purim; from 70 C.E. on it disappeared from the calendar.

At this point 1 and 2 Maccabees cease to be parallel. The author ends this chapter with the traditional formula from the book of Judges: "So the land [of Judah] had rest for . . ." but here the time of peace was much shorter. The death of Judas was near.

The Romans Come on the Scene: 1 Maccabees 8

The description of the Romans is an enthusiastic one but in some respects it is naïve, exaggerated, and inaccurate. The Jews now enjoyed religious freedom; the Hasideans laid down their weapons; the people wanted a breath of fresh air, the end of their isolation, relations with other peoples. By entering into a treaty with Rome the Maccabees gained a powerful ally in their struggle with their immediate enemies but they also became increasingly dependent on a power that would in the end destroy them.

Rome's policy in the Middle East was not to intervene directly except in extreme cases. It preferred to support the efforts of rebellious states to make things difficult for their rulers, in this case Demetrius. Although the prophets had always opposed alliances with foreign peoples, especially with Assyria and Egypt, Solomon had set a precedent when he entered into agreements with pagan nations and turned Israel into a splendid nation.

Judas sent an embassy consisting of Eupolemus, a man with a Hellenized name but nonetheless faithful to the principles of Yahwism, and Jason, whose name was the Greek form of the Hebrew Joshua or Jesus, to establish relations with Rome. The journey was long and difficult since the men might well fall into the hands of the Syrian police; they probably traveled by sea.

It was customary that international treaties be engraved on bronze; the original of treaties with Rome was in Latin, which was then translated into Greek. The Latin copy was deposited on the Capitol while the other was sent to the state with which the treaty was being made. The treaty here made with Rome followed the same pattern. Our author translated it into Hebrew and from this was made the Greek translation we have today. The preamble is deliberately omitted in order not to mention the Roman god named in it (Jupiter Capitolinus).

Death of Judas: 1 Maccabees 9

These events of this chapter follow directly on those of the seventh, the alliance with the Romans being a parenthesis. On the other hand it was Judas's major success, the treaty with Rome, that brought his downfall. As long as Judas was simply a guerilla leader he did not disturb Antioch, but now he became a danger since he was supported by the Romans. Quick action was needed, and Demetrius supplied it.

Despite the enthusiasm roused by the victory over Nicanor, Judas's troops were disheartened by the disproportionately large army of the Seleucids. Many of his soldiers deserted and only eight hundred loyal men remained. Judas did not listen to his advisers who urged him to avoid battle; he himself was not sure he could win but he preferred dying in battle to cowardly flight. Honor urged him to continue the struggle. He made a personal decision that ran counter to what others wanted; neither did he ask the aid of heaven, as he did on other occasions (1 Macc 4:10, 30-33; 7:41-42). He died fighting bravely, and the author does not try to give a theological explanation of the meaning of his death and defeat.

We do not find in 1 Maccabees the faith in resurrection that is expressed in 2 Maccabees. The people's lament for Judas is inspired by David's elegy for Saul and Jonathan. The death of Judas was not a great tragedy for the Maccabean movement since his brothers continued the struggle.

The story of Judas ends like that of the kings of Israel and Judah (2 Kings 10:34-35; 12:20-22; 13:8-9, 12-13). "Savior of Israel" (9:21) echoes what was said of the judges of Israel.

Jonathan Continues the Struggle: 9:13-73

At the death of Judas the rebels quieted down for a while. Now Jonathan became active; he is described according to the model of the Judges. The people were in a serious crisis aggravated by famine. Their anxiety was like what they had felt when the prophets disappeared; the situation called for a rescuer.

The people wanted Jonathan to take the position of authority left vacant by the death of Judas. Jonathan's political skill revived the Maccabean revolution after the death of his brother. He was known as Apphus, "the crafty," a nickname given to him as a result of the ambush he laid for the sons of Jambri who had murdered his brother John (1 Macc 9:37-42).

Profiting by the power vacuum, the transgressors of the Law took power once again. Bacchides and Alcimus took advantage of this to damage their opponents. Their reprisals led to a movement of protest among the Jews. Jonathan began a guerilla campaign in which he attacked and withdrew. Looking for a secure base, he took refuge with his men in the wilderness of Tekoa, to which David had likewise fled. In order to feel freer and have greater freedom of action he asked his brother John to request the protection of the Nabateans, but an Arabic tribe, the family of Jambri, attacked and killed him. Jonathan's response was terrifying and cruel but it must be seen in the context of the age.

Although Jonathan avoided the trap set for him near the Jordan by Bacchides, the latter kept control of the greater part of Judea. Meanwhile, in the year 153 of the Seleucid Era (159 B.C.E.), Alcimus began to renovate the Temple. He tore down the wall that was said to have been built by Haggai and Zechariah and separated the Jews from the Gentiles. In this manner he suppressed the differences between the two groups. This caused his death. The story of his end recalls the end of the wicked in other books of the Bible.

Jonathan changed his guerilla tactics, leaving the wilderness and taking refuge in a fortress that allowed him to make bold raids without exposing himself too much. Bacchides encircled him but Jonathan escaped. Seeing himself frustrated, Bacchides returned to his country and vented his wrath on his Jewish advisers who had brought him to defeat. He made peace with Jonathan, who was able to live in peace for five years and profited by the time to work to his own advantage.

Jonathan and Alexander Balas: 10:1-14

Alexander, who claimed the Seleucid throne, was surnamed both Balas and Epiphanes. He asked for recognition as a son of Antiochus IV but according to many authors he was an impostor from Smyrna. He was supported by the kings of Cappadocia, Pergamum, and Egypt; he also won the friendship of Rome. Jonathan now found himself in an advantageous situation. Both Demetrius and Alexander courted him, each wanting him as an ally. Both needed him in order keep the throne, and both made him tempting offers. Demetrius authorized him to gather troops and Alexander conferred on him the office of high priest. Was it legitimate to accept the priesthood from a king whose own legitimacy was in doubt? The Seleucids had in the past bestowed the high priesthood on Jason, Menelaus, and Alcimus; Alexander was taking advantage of this precedent. Jonathan changed sides and joined Alexander because the latter did not persecute Jews and was offering him the high priesthood.

In 152 B.C.E. Jonathan officiated as high priest at the festival of Booths (1 Macc 10:15-21). Thus did a member of the Maccabean family reach the highest office of the nation. But some Jews did not look benignly on what they regarded as a usurpation by Jonathan; they opposed him and withdrew to the hills near the Dead Sea where they formed the Qumran community. Some scholars think that when the Dead Sea scrolls speak of a wicked high priest they are referring to Jonathan or Simon.

Jonathan and Demetrius: 10:22-50

Alexander Balas's offers to Jonathan reached the ears of Demetrius, and in a display of generosity he tried to go beyond them. He offered the Jews many advantages if they would take his side; among these was the closing of the Acra fortress, the last redoubt of the Seleucids within Jerusalem proper. But Jonathan realized that Demetrius was not sincere and he remained faithful to Balas. Shortly afterwards Demetrius lost a battle and his life.

Alexander, Ptolemy, and Jonathan: 10:51-66

In order to strengthen the security of his kingdom and win the social standing he did not have due to his plebeian origin Alexander decided to acquire a relationship by marriage with Ptolemy, and he asked for the hand of the latter's daughter, Cleopatra. Alexander invited Jonathan to the wedding, which was celebrated in Ptolemais, and granted him the titles of "King's Friend," "Strategos," that is, commander of the troops in Judea, and "Meridarch," that is, governor of Judea. Thus religious, military, and civil authority were united in the one person of Jonathan.

Apollonius, Demetrius II, and Jonathan: 10:67-89

Within three years Alexander had brought disgrace on himself by his orgies and cruelty. The elder son of Demetrius reckoned that the time had come to restore the Seleucid line to the throne of Antioch. Apollonius, governor of Coelesyria, sided with him. Jonathan did battle with Apollonius and won. In recompense Balas bestowed new honors on him and sent him a golden clasp for his purple cloak.

Death of Alexander and Its Consequences: 11:1-37

Shortly after, Ptolemy of Egypt and Alexander died. Jonathan profited by the situation to gain further advantages for the chosen people. Demetrius II, now king, decided to make a friend of Jonathan before conquering him by arms. Jonathan adopted the same diplomatic attitude and succeeded in extending his domain and receiving once again the title of "Chief Friend of the King."

The royal treasury was in a critical state. To remedy the financial situation Demetrius II dismissed his troops except those originating in the islands of the nations. This step lost him the favor of the soldiers who had supported him so enthusiastically. After assessing the situation Trypho met with Imalkue the Arab and pressed him to surrender Antiochus, the son of Alexander Balas.

Jonathan tried to benefit from the precarious situation in Syria. A rebellion was started in Antioch and Jonathan helped Demetrius to put it down after being promised the abolition of the Acra and the surrender to him of Beth-zur, the last Judean city belonging to the hellenizing party. Once the rebellion was crushed Demetrius did not keep his promises. On learning of this Antiochus sent letters to Jonathan reaffirming his friendship with him, confirming him as high priest, and giving his brother Simon the title of "Strategos" of the region from the Ladder of Tyre to the borders with Egypt. Jonathan accepted the friendship of Antiochus and fought openly against Demetrius' generals.

This chapter of 1 Maccabees ends with a victory over the forces of Demetrius near Hazor in northern Israel. Initially the Jews were routed, but after Jonathan prayed the fortunes of battle changed. This episode is reminiscent of Joshua tearing his garments and praying after the defeat at Ai (Josh 7:6-9) but in 1 Maccabees there is no hint that the defeat was due to the sins of Israel. In this author's mind, defeats never have theological explanations, but victories do. In all these struggles among the various claimants to the Seleucid throne the author seeks to give the impression that these were wars of Jews against Gentiles in which God was on the side of Israel.

Jonathan took control of Beth-zur, began the rebuilding of the ramparts of Jerusalem, and cut off the Acra from the rest of the city.

Rome and Sparta: 12:1-23

As Judas had done before him Jonathan sent an embassy to Rome, but with the intention of gaining political recognition and status rather than receiving concrete aid. He also sent an embassy to Sparta to confirm the brotherhood between the Spartans and the Jews. The promise that had made Abraham the father of nations could be seen as justifying the insertion of some descendants of Japheth into the line of Shem.

Seizure of Jonathan: 12:39-53

The broad powers that Jonathan possessed and his diplomatic influence were an obstacle to the ambitions of Trypho, who decided to get rid of him. When their armies were about to engage, Trypho resorted to trickery; he pretended to be a friend of Jonathan and invited him to dismiss his troops and come to Ptolemais. There he seized Jonathan and slaughtered his personal escort. Jonathan thus fell victim to intrigue and the shifting loyalties among which he had successfully maneuvered for twenty years. There was an irony in his own loyalty to Alexander and Antiochus VI, successors of Antiochus IV, yet the results of Jonathan's policies were due to his own opportunism in entering into agreements with those who best suited his desires.

Exaltation of Simon: 1 Maccabees 13

When Simon was recognized as successor to his brother, Trypho offered to give back Jonathan if Simon would send him one hundred talents of silver and two of Jonathan's sons as hostages. Although Simon knew the offer was deceitful, he agreed lest his own people become suspicious of him. Trypho did not keep his word; on the contrary, he tried to make contact with the Acra but was unsuccessful because of a heavy snowfall. Foiled in this undertaking, he withdrew to Syria; on the way he killed Jonathan and his two sons at Baskama. This was at the beginning of 142 B.C.E. Simon recovered his brother's body and buried it at Modein, his native city, where he erected a sumptuous mausoleum that seems to have been inspired by Greek models of that period.

The murder of Jonathan was followed by the murder of Antiochus VI; Trypho's treacherous nature was clear. Demetrius II was not any more trustworthy but Simon turned to him, and Demetrius, driven by the threat from Trypho, received him gladly. He granted Simon exemption from taxes, a general amnesty for all hostile actions of the Maccabean forces, and permission to continue fortifying Judea. As a result of this peace treaty Israel was delivered from all forms of enslavement and recovered its freedom and independence (1 Macc 13:41). This was in the year 170 of the Seleucid calendar (142 B.C.E.) and Simon's first year as high priest, Strategos (general), and Hegoumenos (leader), which were the titles granted him by Demetrius. After twenty-five years of struggle and negotiation the line of Mattathias seemed more stable than that of the Seleucid kings since the latter were constantly threatened by the various claimants to the throne.

Free now from harassment by Demetrius and Trypho, Simon decided to take control of Gazara (Gezer) and of the citadel in Jerusalem, two troublesome enclaves occupied by foreigners and apostate Jews. He laid siege to Gazara, took it, and treated its inhabitants humanely. The place was of great strategic value because it controlled the route from Gaza to Jerusalem. In the spring of 141 Simon conquered the Syrian garrison in Jerusalem, the siege of which had been begun by his brother Jonathan. The citadel symbolized Syrian control of the Jews' most sacred place. A festival commemorated the event. The purification of Gazara and the citadel was called for by the presence there of idols; it highlights the religious character of the occupation.

Simon strengthened the fortifications of the Temple and the citadel in which he now lived with his family. He appointed his son John as supreme military commander and thereby introduced the dynastic principle. John, who would become king with the name John Hyrcanus, set up his general quarters at Gazara.

Eulogy of Simon: 14:4-15

The author idealizes the situation although it must be acknowledged that the peace the Jewish people enjoyed under Simon surpassed that of previous times. Simon gave Israel a seaport by his definitive annexation of Joppa; he extended the frontiers of the realm. The eulogy of Simon is interwoven with echoes of the prophets and the Pentateuch: Zech 8:4, 12; Ezek 34:27; Mic 4:4; and Lev 26:4).

The reign of Simon resembled a messianic age. The promises had been fulfilled; the people were no longer living a dream or an impossible utopia.

Renewal of Treaties: 14:16-24

In the period of peace that followed the recognition of Simon as supreme leader of Israel he proved his qualities as a ruler. He maintained the relations Jonathan had established with Sparta and Rome. He was allowed to wear purple and to engrave his exploits on bronze tablets attached to the pillars of Mount Zion. On these tablets his father and brothers were also named.

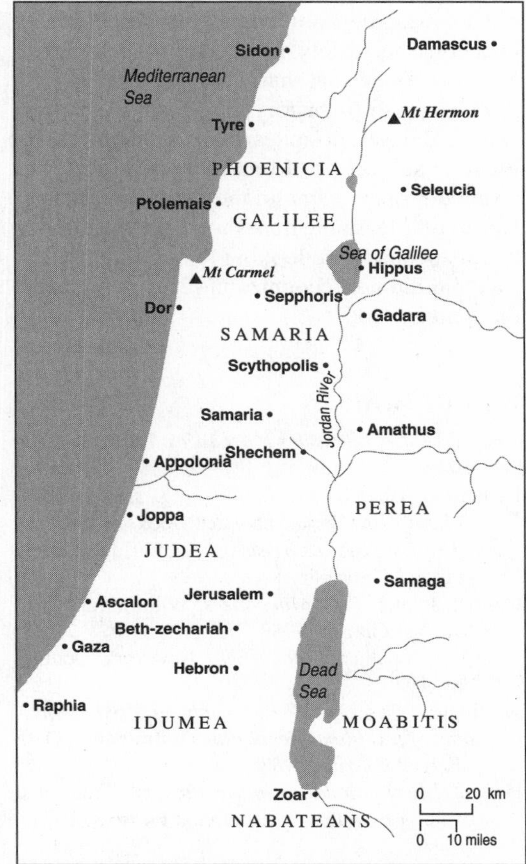

ISRAEL IN THE TIME OF THE HASMONEANS

In 140 B.C.E., Demetrius II had been taken prisoner during a campaign against the Parthians (14:1-3). His brother, Antiochus VII Sidetes, took the throne and during his struggle with Trypho made an agreement with Simon in which he ratified the privileges previously granted him and authorized him to coin money. Trypho's cause was lost and he committed suicide.

Antiochus Sidetes then demanded that Simon restore the territories he had conquered, especially Gazara and Joppa. In response Simon asserted the right of the Jews to recover "the inheritance of our ancestors" that had been unjustly wrested from them. As for Gazara and Joppa, he explained that these cities had harmed the Jewish people; he did, however, acknowledge that Antiochus had some right to them and so he offered compensation, but not as large as the Seleucid had demanded. The report brought back by Athenobius, brother of Antiochus, angered the king, who ordered his general, Cendebeus, to harass Judea.

Defeat of Cendebeus: 16:1-10

Simon's words to his sons John and Judas recall those of Mattathias to his sons at the time of his death (1 Macc 2:48-68) and have several parallels in the book (1 Macc 12:15; 13:3; 14:26).

The Maccabean army now included cavalry. John's crossing of a stream recalls Joshua at the Jordan and John's own uncle, Judas, in similar circumstances (1 Macc 5:43). Simon was now too old to fight, but his son John won the victory. This episode shows that peace was not completely assured. Only after the death of Antiochus Sidetes in a campaign against the Parthians could the Jews regard themselves as independent.

Death of Simon: 16:11-24

Ptolemy (the name was a Hellenized form of a Semitic name) was possibly an Idumean, more or less allied with the Jews, and sufficiently important to be a son-in-law of Simon. His ambition led him to the assassination of the high priest. Simon died a violent death as had his brothers

Judas, Jonathan, and Lazarus, the difference being that his death was due to treason and occurred when he was drunk. The author offers no religious reflection on this fact. Simon's son John managed to escape and continued the monarchy.

The book ends with the formula customary in the book of the kings of Judah (1 Kings 11:41; 14:19; 15:23). The author thereby confirms the traditional character he sought to give to his work and also places John in the line of the kings of Judah. David's monarchy had not ended: John, called Hyrcanus because he conquered the Hyrcanians, reigned for thirty-one years, from 135 to 104. The annals of his reign have been lost.

Did the disappearance of the Maccabean dynasty also mean the disappearance of its ideals? Did the seeds it sowed fall on barren ground and produce no fruit? Did the various movements and revolts that took place under Roman domination have anything to do with the spirituality of the Maccabees or were they independent events with purely external and accidental points of contact? In particular did the violent opposition to Rome that culminated in the capture of Jerusalem and the destruction of the Temple in 70 C.E. have any connection with the Maccabean revolt?

Josephus, the great Jewish historian, concludes that the similarities between the Maccabees and the rebels of his own day were merely superficial. The victory of the Maccabees over the Seleucids was a sign that they were a devout people. But not wanting to incur the dislike of his Roman friends, Josephus depicts the rebels of his time as inauthentic Jews, people who acted at variance with the law of God. In addition Josephus was somehow related to the Maccabees and therefore could not allow that there was any connection between them and the leaders of his bitter enemies, the rebels against Rome.

Nevertheless it can be shown that there was a connection between the two groups. First of all there are the traits common to both revolutionary movements; furthermore, the example and teaching of the Maccabees had a great influence on the Jews of the first century.

When the revolt against Rome burst out after a period of relative peace the motives that had inspired the Maccabees reappeared. From the religious and political points of view they were similar: in both cases people were fighting for their God, the Law, and the Temple; they were resisting pagans and their idolatry.

At the same time, however, there were distinguishing factors. The power of Rome could not be compared with that of the Seleucids. Moreover, the Maccabees were able to turn to their advantage the struggles between the different Greek pretenders to the throne; as a result their struggle was crowned with victory. Those who took arms against Rome were deeply divided among themselves. The idea that God was going to intervene in their cause as he had in the Maccabean aroused false hopes.

It must be noted that in the time of Jesus there were no revolutionaries in the proper sense of the word. From 6 B.C.E. to 42 C.E. there was relative calm in Palestine. At that time the word "zealot" did not have the connotations it acquired later on; at this period there was no organized movement against Rome. Jesus was not crucified as a zealot; before 66 C.E. this word did not mean opposition to Rome. Nor did Jesus condemn the zealots, for the simple reason that they did not exist at that time.

The course of history continued. The Maccabean dynasty disappeared and the people remained subject to Roman domination. The awaited prophet came in the person of Jesus of Nazareth. Messianic hopes were fulfilled in him but the people were looking for a political Messiah and did not recognize in Jesus of Nazareth one sent by God.

BIBLIOGRAPHY

Abel, F. M. *Les Livres des Maccabées.* Paris: Gabalda, 1949.

Bickerman, Elias J. *From Ezra to the Last of the Maccabees.* New York: Schocken Books, 1962.

____. *The Jews in the Greek Age.* Cambridge, Mass.: Harvard University Press, 1988.

Collins, John J. *First Maccabees.* Wilmington, Del.: Michael Glazier, 1989.

Goldstein, Jonathan. *I Maccabees.* New York: Doubleday, 1976.

Harrington, Daniel J. *The Maccabean Revolt: Anatomy of a Biblical Revolution.* Wilmington, Del.: Michael Glazier, 1988.

Hengel, Martin. *Judaism and Hellenism.* Translated by John Bowden. Philadelphia: Fortress, 1974.

2 Maccabees

Gonzalo Aranda Pérez

FIRST READING

This book is called "The Second Book of Maccabees" because of the place it holds within ancient codices that have transmitted it to us: it follows the First Book of Maccabees in the Alexandrian (fifth century) and Venetian (eighth century) codices as well as in the versions. As to its content, however, it is not a continuation of 1 Maccabees; it spans practically the same period as 1 Maccabees 1–7. Clement of Alexandria at the end of the second century called it the "epitome of Maccabean history" because, beginning with ch. 3, it is a résumé of a previous work written by Jason of Cyrene. Prior to the summary and the preface that introduces it (2:19-32) there are two transcribed letters sent by the Jews in Jerusalem to those in Egypt, inviting them to celebrate with them the feast of the purification of the Temple (1:1–2:18). If 1 Maccabees tries to justify the Hasmonean dynasty, and if Daniel 11–12, where the same happenings appear, announces the immediate irruption of the reign of God, then 2 Maccabees proposes to show the sanctity of the Temple of Jerusalem purified by Judas Maccabeus with the extraordinary help of God.

The author of the summary makes himself responsible for the content of the book and must be considered the inspired author. We know nothing more about Jason of Cyrene. The letters, since they were probably translated from Hebrew or Aramaic by the same author or attached to the summary at a later date, also form a part of the final text of the work. The text was originally written in Greek just as was its source. One of the letters is dated in the year 124 B.C.E. Thus the book in its present form was published at the end of the second century or the beginning of the first century B.C.E., in any case before Pompey's invasion in 63 B.C.E.

After the letters at the beginning (1:1–2:18) the author of the book lays out his plan and proposal (2:19-32) and then continues to tell the story of the Jews of Jerusalem from the times of Seleucus IV (187–175 B.C.E.) until the time of Demetrius I (161–150), some fifteen years in all. The first part (3:1–10:9) culminates in the purification of the Temple that took place in the year 164. It includes first the punishment of Heliodorus in which the holiness of the Temple and the divine protection over it are clearly manifested (3:1-40); then there is an account of the introduction of pagan customs into Jerusalem, customs that brought down the punishment of God upon Israel (4:1-50), the profanation of the Temple (5:1–6:17), and the martyrdom of Eleazar and the seven brothers with their mother (6:18–7:42). Finally we have the account of the initial acts of Judas (8:1-36), the death of Antiochus IV (9:1-29), the purification of the Temple and the institution of a feast that would commemorate that event (10:1-8). The second part, showing a certain parallelism with the first, exposes the successive deeds of Judas under the reign of Antiochus V (10:9–13:26) and culminates with the death of Nicanor who, though Demetrius I was then in power, had begun a new persecution and launched terrible threats against the Temple. Judas, after winning a great victory, inaugurates an annual feast, "the day of Nicanor" (14:1–15:36).

The narration includes more time than the author indicates in the preface to his work (2:19-20) and concentrates on some particular episodes that act as a background to a historical context that is not always very precise. The comparison with 1 Maccabees shows that some acts are incorrectly located as to time, such as the campaign against Lysias during the reign of Antiochus V when in reality it took place during the reign of Antiochus IV (11:1-21; 1 Macc 4:26-35). This phenomenon is not inimical to the historical veracity of 2 Maccabees. It can be explained either by the author's combination of deeds for the sake of emphasizing their religious dimension, or because he is following the calculation of years according to an oriental or Babylonian form of the Seleucid calendar, or because he accepts facts from his source without altering them, as in the case of the letter that narrates the unusual way in which Antiochus IV died (1:11-17). Attention is not diverted to the exactitude of the dates (2:24-25) but instead the text puts into relief the action of God who guided those happenings. During the Hellenistic period writers frequently used a form of narration known as "the sympathetic style of writing history," a form that seeks above all else to delight and convince the reader. The Second Book of Maccabees seeks to edify its readers in their Jewish faith, recalling for them the beautiful examples given by those who defended the cause of God and showing them the rewards that await those who are disposed to give their lives for their faith.

The reading of the book can be done independently of 1 Maccabees or in combination with that book while selecting some of the representative passages such as the first letter (1:1-9), the punishment of Heliodorus (3:1-40), the providential meaning of the persecution (6:12-17), the martyrdom of Eleazar and of the seven brothers with their mother (6:18–7:42), Judas' commanding a sacrifice to be made on behalf of those who had died in combat (12:39-45), or the final battle against Nicanor (15:1-36).

General Context for Interpretation

Original Historical Context

The work of Jason of Cyrene could have been composed about the year 160 B.C.E., after the death of Nicanor, or perhaps later if he continued with the story of Judas's brothers (2:19). The Second Book of Maccabees as it has come down to us was written during the epoch of the Hasmonean or Maccabean family, after the reign of John Hyrcanus (134–104), and reflects the differences within Judaism at that time. It could have been written in Alexandria since the letters are directed to the Jews in Egypt, but it could also have been written in any other Greek city of the Diaspora or even in Palestine, given its interest in the Temple. The author wishes to distance himself positively from the governing body of the Hasmoneans and to show that the salvation of the people and of Judaism is linked to the Temple and its holiness, not to the successors of Judas Maccabeus. The latter appears especially as the leader of those devout ones whom God protects and makes invincible, but in reality it is the prayer, purity, and fidelity of the martyrs that moves God to act in favor of God's people. It is interesting that the brothers of Judas are scarcely mentioned (8:22; 14:17) and that not even the name of their father, Mattathias, appears. These silences cast doubt on the legitimacy of the successors of Judas and their exercise of the high priesthood. On the other hand the author exalts the high priest, Onias III (3:1; 4:1-6, 32-38; 15:12) and expounds doctrines that resemble those of the Pharisees, especially the resurrection of the dead (7:9; 12:44; 14:46) and the existence of angels (11:6; 15:22).

The letters directed to the Jews of Egypt endeavor to strengthen the communion between them and the Jews of Jerusalem. We know from Flavius Josephus (*Bell.* 1.1–33; *Ant.* 13.62–73) that about the year 150 B.C.E. Onias IV, following the assassination of his father Onias III (2 Macc 4:34), fled to Egypt and constructed in Leontopolis, twenty-eight kilometers north of Cairo, a reproduction on a small scale of the Temple of Jerusalem, although the Law prohibited such an act (Deut 12:5-14). The Second Book of Maccabees does not mention this deed nor does it explicitly condemn that temple or the one in Gerizim although it does condemn the inhabitants of the latter place (6:2). When the Temple of Jerusalem is referred to as the most famous or the holiest (2:22; 5:15; 14:31), perhaps that is the acceptance in some way or other of the existence of other temples, or it may be a rhetorical form of speech. What was intended was indeed to give encouragement and confidence to the Jews in Egypt who again found themselves in serious trouble after the death of Ptolemy VI Philometer (180–145 B.C.E.) who had favored the Jews, and the advent of Ptolemy VII Euergetes II Phiscon (145–116 B.C.E.) who endlessly pursued them.

Canonical Context

Together with 1 Maccabees, 2 Maccabees is to be situated at the end of the historical books of the Hebrew Scriptures. Old Testament historiography reaches its peak with 2 Maccabees not only because it narrates the history of Israel up to the Christian era, but also because it explicitly interprets that history as the story of salvation. The Law (or laws) to which the author makes reference some thirty times is the theme that runs through the book. It deals with the Law of Moses (7:30) whose message holds the greatest authority and claim to observance (2:11; 7:11). Also there is explicit reference to Jeremiah, "prophet of God" (15:14) and transmitter of the Law (2:2). The Second Book of Maccabees is supported by "the Law and the Prophets" (15:9) and by the "holy book" (8:23). Therein the protagonists find strength and courage.

Perhaps unlike any other book of the Hebrew Scriptures, 2 Maccabees reflects the progress of revelation in some important aspects. It clearly teaches the resurrection of the dead (7:11, 14, 23, 29, 36; 12:38-45[46]; 14:4-6) as the response to the problem of the retribution of the righteous. This response from 2 Maccabees can be joined to other such responses given throughout the Bible during the same epoch: the one from the book of Daniel that affirms the resurrection of the just and of sinners to receive either reward or punishment (Dan 12:2-3) and the response from the book of Wisdom that teaches about the immortality of the soul (Wis 3:1). But 2 Maccabees uniquely affirms the resurrection of the just. The sufferings of the just, in agreement with what Isiah says about the suffering servant (Isa 52:13–53:12), have salvific and expiative value insofar as they may hold back the punishment of God from the people (7:38). Finally, in 2 Maccabees Gen 1:1 is explicitly interpreted as describing creation out of nothing (7:28).

In the Bible as a whole 2 Maccabees illumines the historical context of Judaism in which Jesus Christ lived and in which the primitive Church developed. In it are elucidated themes such as the resurrection of the dead and the expiatory value of the death of martyrs who will, from a Christian perspective, receive their definitive light with the revelation of Jesus Christ (Matt 22:23-33 // Mark 12:18-27 // Luke 20:27-40; Rom 3:21-26). The Christian Scriptures directly allude to 2 Maccabees and the heroic example of the martyrs (7:1-42) only once, in Heb 11:35.

Use in the Church

Some passages from 2 Maccabees have held special attraction since the earliest times. The apostolic Fathers already allude to the martyrdom of the seven brothers (2 Maccabees 7). This passage acquires great prominence among the Fathers when they speak of martyrdom (e.g., Cyprian of Carthage in the third century in his work *Ad Fortunatum de exhortatione martyrii*) or when they treat of the resurrection (e.g., Methodius of Olympus in his treatise on the resurrection in which he defends the identity of the resurrected body with the earthly body) or, finally, when they write about the virtue of patience (e.g., Athanasius of Alexandria commenting on the psalms). Eusebius of Cesarea in addition to his abundant use of 1 and 2 Maccabees in his historical works has recourse to 2 Macc 7:28 in his *De ecclesiastica theologia* as the important source for proving the fact of creation out of nothing. In the same sense and with greater flourish Epiphanius of Salamis uses it in his *Panarion.* Likewise 2 Maccabees has influenced the stories of martyrs in rabbinic literature.

Although there is no complete commentary on 2 Maccabees from the patristic period (the first one was done by Rabanus Maurus in 840) the passages on the resurrection and martyrdom have often been addressed. Although Jerome did not consider this a canonical book both he and Augustine spoke of the brothers and their mother as true martyrs. Gregory Nazianzen and John Chrysostom composed homilies in honor of Eleazar and the martyr brothers with their mother on the occasion of their feast day, celebrated in Antioch where their relics were honored (*PG* 49.617–623; *PG* 62.660). A work narrating the deeds of the Maccabees has been erroneously attributed to Ambrose of Milan; this work was probably of medieval origin. Commentaries from the Middle Ages, among which Thomas Aquinas's stands out, treat the two books of the Maccabees jointly.

Catholic theology has had recourse to 2 Maccabees as a scriptural proof for affirming the resurrection of the dead, the existence of purgatory, the advisability of offering sacrifices for the deceased, and God's creation of the world out of nothing. The Second Vatican Council cites 2 Macc 12:45 to show the relationship between the pilgrim Church on earth and the Church in heaven (*LG* 50). The *Catechism of the Catholic Church* turns to 2 Macc 6:30 to clarify the meaning of the term "soul" as "the spiritual principle" of the human being (no. 363), to 2 Macc 7:9, 14, 29 to show the progress of revelation on the theme of the resurrection (no. 992), to 2 Macc 7:22-23, 28 to explain that the world was created out of nothing (no. 297), to 2 Macc 10:29-30 and 11:8 to teach about the existence and function of the angels (no. 333), and finally to 2 Macc 12:45 to reaffirm the advisability of praying for the dead and the reality of Purgatory (nos. 958, 1031–1032).

In the Lectionary for Mass there are two passages from 2 Maccabees (6:18-33 and 7:1, 20-31, followed by Psalms 3 and 17, respectively). These two passages are inserted into the semicontinuous reading of 1 Maccabees during uneven years, on ferial days 3 and 4 of the thirty-third week in Ordinary Time. The reading from both books is offered as a unit. On the 32nd Sunday, cycle C, 2 Macc 7:1-2, 9-14 is read and followed by Psalm 17 as a Hebrew scriptural reading corresponding to the Gospel that proclaims the teaching of Jesus on the resurrection of the dead (Luke 20:27-38). That same reading is offered as a possible choice in the Lectionary for the Common of Martyrs, but followed by Psalm 124; there also is found 2 Maccabees 6 followed by Psalm 34 and part of 2 Maccabees 7 followed by Psalm 31. Finally 2 Macc 12:43-45, followed by Psalm 103, figures as a possible Hebrew scriptural reading in the Masses for the Dead. Within the Liturgy of the Hours only 2 Macc 12:32-45 is read in the Office of Readings for Friday of the 31st Week in Ordinary Time.

Contemporary Use

Together with other sources, 2 Maccabees continues to be a valid and indispensable testimony for the history of the Maccabean disturbance and for information on how Judaism continued to develop into the diverse groups that endured into the Christian era. In addition this book puts before the reader the true values of human existence, that is, fidelity to God and God's commandments above everything, including one's own life. It goes on uncovering the providence of God present in political and social happenings and interpreting them from a religious point of view. In face of a regime that denies religious liberty and a culture contrary to religion and the Law of God, 2 Maccabees invites one to rebellion. What the author really wants is to be faithful to his religious convictions and to be able to follow them in peace and freedom.

The Christian reader will discover negative aspects: the excessive and unnecessary violence of Judas Maccabeus, praised by the author (8:33; 15:32-34), and an image of a God who does not pardon the enemies of Israel even though they repent of their behavior—this as the inexorable accomplishment of the law of "an eye for an eye" (9:13). One should not forget the rhetorical style of the book. [See also the articles "The Deuterocanonical Writings" and "Violence and Evil in the Bible."]

SECOND READING

Letters to the Jews in Egypt: 1:1–2:18

Apparently there are two letters: one (1:1-9) written in 124 B.C.E. (188 of the Seleucid era) in which is reproduced a prior letter (1:7-8) sent in 143 B.C.E. (169 of the Seleucid era), and a second letter (1:10–2:18), undated and presented as a letter sent by Judas himself. Both conclude with the same message: the invitation to the Jews in Egypt to celebrate the feast of the purification of the Temple. In the letter sent in 143 notice was given concerning the renewal of sacrifice after the tribulation. The second letter does not appear authentic; a part of it might also be considered a prolongation of the first letter.

The First Letter (1:1-9)

This text throws into relief the bonds of race and religion that unite the Jews in Egypt and those in Jerusalem; they are "kindred" (1:1). Peace means being participants in the blessings of the covenant even though in a foreign land

(Lev 26:41-45). It means receiving from God the propensity for fulfilling the Law (1 Chr 28:9; Deut 5:29) and it means being reconciled with God. The concept of "reconciliation" *(katallagē)* is peculiar to 2 Maccabees (5:20; 7:33; 8:29); those of "conversion" and "pardon" dominate in other books of the Hebrew Scriptures. There is an underlying invitation to move away from the Jewish temple in Leontopolis and to celebrate the feast of the purification of the Temple in Jerusalem, supposing that this Temple was recognized as the only legitimate sanctuary just as the Law indicated (Deut 12:5-14) and thus to maintain religious communion with the Judaism of Jerusalem. The letter cited contains the oldest allusion to the rite of lighting lamps (1:8). The tribulations suffered because of Jason will be treated in 4:7-17 (= 1 Macc 1:11-15). "The festival of booths in the month of Chislev" distinguishes it from the festival of booths that was celebrated before and from the many other feasts similar to it (Lev 23:33-34; 1 Macc 10:21). St. Paul in some way imitates the style of this letter when he uses the concept of "reconciliation" and applies it to the new relationship with God through Jesus Christ (Rom 5:10; Eph 2:16; Col 1:21-22).

The Second Letter (1:10–2:18)

From the opening section of the letter (1:10-17) we learn that Judas Maccabeus would communicate with a famous Alexandrian Jewish philosopher and teacher of Ptolemy VI Philometor (180–145 B.C.E.) concerning the deeds and death of Antiochus IV. The data about the death of the king do not correspond with the facts narrated in 9:1-29 (1 Macc 6:1-17), perhaps because they express what were basically the first rumors of a death or because the author of the letter confused this death with that of Antiochus III in the temple of Bel in Elimaida. The goddess Nanea may be Artemis. In 1:18 this second letter connects with the theme of the first. It is a document artificially elaborated, marginal to the content of 2 Maccabees, that was to complete that of the first letter, projecting the notice about the celebration of the feast (1:18; 2:16) at the time of its being instituted.

The account of the sacred fire and the crude oil or naphtha serve to show the continuity of the sacrifices offered upon the return from exile with those offered before the exile. In spite of the fact that the presence of God had temporarily abandoned the Temple (Ezek 10:18-22; 43:1-9) this Temple continued being the "place" or the "holy place" (2:18). God had again shown the divine presence through the fire as in the sacrifices offered by Elijah (1 Kings 18:20-40), by Moses and Aaron (Lev 9:22-24) and by Solomon (2 Chr 7:1). Thus it was taught by Moses. If neither the Ark of the Covenant nor the altar of sacrifices was there any longer it was because Jeremiah had hidden them and their appearance was to be reserved for eschatological times (2:1-7). Then the presence of God would be manifest visibly as it was to Moses (2:8; Exod 24:16) and Solomon (1 Kings 8:10-14). The length of the festival (2:16; 1 Macc 4:56-59) was to follow the example of Solomon (1 Kings 8:65-66). The author of the letter indicates the sources of the information he has provided (2:13-15) without assigning any value other than purely informational. There is a final summary that admirably points to the consciousness of the choice and holiness of the people (2:17; Exod 19:5-6) as well as the hope for a proximate divine intervention of an eschatological nature (Deut 30:3-5; Isa 66:18-19; Ezek 34:11-13) joined to the fact that the Temple has been purified (2:18). In the Christian Scriptures the same inseparable relationship between the "election" and "sanctification" of the people is celebrated, now realized through and in Jesus Christ (Rom 8:28-30; Eph 1:4; Titus 3:4-8; Rev 1:6; 1 Pet 2:9). In like manner the relationship established in 2:18 between the purification of the Temple and the action of God helps to uncover the eschatological meaning behind the gestures of Jesus during the purification of the Temple (John 2:13-22). The one time that the feast of the Dedication is mentioned in the Christian Scriptures (John 10:22-24) serves as context for openly posing the question of whether or not Jesus is the Messiah and to offer Jesus himself the opportunity to reveal himself as the Son of God, one with the Father (John 10:30, 38).

Author's Preface: 2:19-32

The author unburdens himself of the responsibility of exactitude in reporting historical information, a task proper to a historian, and situates himself in the position of proclaimer or announcer. It is the only case in the Hebrew Scriptures in which a hagiographer speaks of how he has composed his work. In the Christian Scriptures, Luke will do so again (Luke 1:1-4). Both passages give evidence of the fact that the inspiration hagiographers enjoyed did not save them from needing the skills proper to any writer. In 2 Maccabees for the first time the term "Judaism" appears (8:1; 14:38), meaning the religion and form of life opposed to "Hellenism" (4:13). This terminology continues to be used in the Christian Scriptures (Gal 1:14).

Part I: The Profanation of the Temple and the Subsequent Purification: 3:1–8:36

This story corresponds along general lines, except for ch. 3, to what was narrated in 1 Macc 1:10–4:61, with discrepancies on some questions of a historical nature. The Second Book of Maccabees explains the transcendent religious sense of each and every happening. God punishes the whole people for the sin of some of the people, that is, their passing over to Hellenism and abandoning Judaism, and this under the guidance of the high priests (ch. 4). Punishment overtakes the Temple that was so intimately joined to the fate of the people (5:19-20), and also afflicts the martyrs (6:18–7:42), but this punishment is healthy, a passing correction (6:12-16). The fidelity of the martyrs causes the anger of God to cease and be transformed into mercy: God gives victory to Judas (8:1-36), chastises the impious (9:1-29), and allows the Temple to be renewed and purified (10:1-5). The festival of the Dedication was set up as a feast to be celebrated by all Jews (10:6-8).

The Frustrated Attempt of Heliodorus (3:1-40)

This pericope focuses on the holiness and richness of the Temple of Jerusalem as well as God's miraculous protection of the edifice. The event occurred about the year 178 B.C.E. during the time of Seleucus IV Philopator (187–175). The money deposited for particular needs in the Temple as a secure place attracted the greed of the governors and its amount—perhaps exaggerated in the narration—raised suspicions about the legitimate use of public money (i.e., for sacrifices). The comparison is made between the piety and sincere concern of the high priest Onias III for the people (4:5-6; 15:12) and the ungodliness, personal greed, and betrayal of the Temple on the part of Simon who perhaps intended to establish markets in the style of the Greeks. Onias was the legitimate high priest, son of that Simon II praised in Sirach 50:1-21, of the family of Zadok (Ezra 2:36; 1 Chr 24:1-6; 2 Sam 8:17). The sorrow and anguish in the prayer of the high priest together with his people, described in a narrative filled with pathos, moved God to act in a miraculous way. The apparitions of celestial horses and horsemen are a way of describing the powerful action of God (5:1-4; 10:29-30; 11:8) and take up again an image already present in Zechariah 1:8-10; 6:1-3. The same representation will appear later in the Revelation of John to express divine actions whether for the purpose of punishing the world and humankind (Rev 6:2-8) or for saving it through Jesus Christ (Rev 19:11-16). The story of the encounter of Paul with Christ on the road to Damascus in some ways coincides with this passage from 2 Maccabees (Acts 9:8; 2 Macc 3:27).

The Corruption of the High Priests (4:1-50)

Taking up again the story line of the former chapter the author emphasizes the moral stature of the legitimate priest, Onias III. When Onias approached the king seeking peace, the king had already been assassinated by Heliodorus (4:1-6). Antiochus IV Epiphanes upon coming to the throne in 175 B.C.E. (1 Macc 1:10) made a strong thrust toward the hellenization of Palestine. The first culpable ones for the author of 2 Maccabees were, nevertheless, some Jews (1 Macc 1:11-15), especially Jason and Menelaus who usurped the high priesthood. Both had obtained it by a bribe (4:7-9, 23-25). Never before in Israel had this been attempted against the legitimate high priest. According to Flavius Josephus, Jason—who had renounced his Jewish name Joshua—received the responsibility of being high priest after the death of Onias III since the son of Onias IV was still a child (*Ant.* 12.5.1). But 2 Maccabees tries to accent the illegitimacy of the high priesthood of Jason. He is the restorer of Hellenism in Jerusalem, making it a city in the Greek style with all its consequences (4:10-20), although in some grave cases he did not receive full support (4:18-20). He put the gymnasium next to the sanctuary and young athletes wearing the *petasos,* the winged hat of Hermes, were trained for the Olympic games (4:12). Menelaus with his brother Lysimachus (4:29) dedicated himself to robbery and to plotting the murder of Onias III (4:30-38). In order to kill Onias they violated the right of asylum in the temple of Apollo in Daphne and his death deeply disturbed even Antiochus himself (4:37). The author of 2 Maccabees wanted to show how those who do evil are victims of their own sin (4:16, 26, 38, 42) and in one case this happened—though not immediately—because of the great power of the bribe (4:43-50).

The Pillage of the Temple and the Brutal Repression of Judaism (5:1-27)

This section of 2 Maccabees connects the acts mentioned with a second expedition of Antiochus to Egypt (5:1), perhaps because the author assumed that the first expedition took place when he visited Jerusalem (4:21-22). First Maccabees, however, situates these events after the first expedition in the year 169 B.C.E. and the placement of the statue of Zeus in the Temple two years later in the year 167. Daniel 11:25-30 alludes to the two expeditions, both of which were followed by severe retaliation against the people of Jerusalem. The sack of the Temple surely happened after the first expedition (Dan 11:28), the abominable introduction of the worship of Zeus after the second (Dan 11:30-31). Second Maccabees presents all these abuses in a single literary framework (5:1–6:11) showing that God had permitted it because of the sins of the people (5:18-20) although it surely could have been avoided as on prior occasions (5:18-20; 3:1-40). As the author had announced (2:21), he first tells of the appearances that came from heaven to foretell such disgraces (5:2-4), then the historical circumstances that produced them (5:5-11), and finally the disgraces themselves, clarifying once more the true reasons of a religious and transcendent order (5:12-26). The heavenly appearance responds to the literary conventions of the time (3:25). The way in which Jason dies, that is, without being able to get the protection of the Spartans who were close "acquaintances" of the Jews, at least politically (5:9; 1 Macc 12:21), indicates how the law concerning the final end of evildoers is fulfilled (5:9-10; 4:17). In the eyes of God the most valiant ones are God's people (5:19) who always suffer the cruelty of the impious (5:6, 12-14, 25-26). Philip will again appear in 6:11; 8:8. Concerning Apollonius, chief collector/despoiler for the Seleucid army, see 1 Macc 1:29-37. In the midst of all that evil the author presents the figure of Judas Maccabeus as the open door to hope (5:27). Within the Christian Scriptures we find an echo of the expression of 5:19 when it is applied by Jesus to the Sabbath and human beings (Mark 2:27). The similar fate experienced by the Temples of Jerusalem and Gerizim (5:23; 6:3-5) is sign of the provisional character of both. This will again be evident in the dialogue of Jesus with the Samaritan woman (John 4:5-30) although always affirming the primary legitimacy and holiness of the Temple in Jerusalem (John 4:22).

The Profanation of the Sanctuary and the Heroism of the Martyrs (2 Maccabees 6–7)

The author sees in these happenings the culminating point of the evils described in the former chapter (6:3). He displays in detail what was told in a more general manner in 1 Macc 1:44-53. He seeks to show to what point the impurity in the inner sanctuary manifested itself (6:4-5) and what levels of violence were involved in imposing the Greek religion by force (6:6-9) and repressing Jewish customs in so bloody a fashion (6:10-11; 1 Macc 1:60-61; 2:32-38). Anticipating the possible scandal in the mind of the reader, the author once again gives the profound explanation of these happenings (6:12-17). Jerusalem was dominated by the Syrian troops on the Akra (1 Macc 1:33). Antiochus tried to impose on all a common religion of a syncretic nature and in the style of the Greeks. To do this he sent an Athenian expert, "Geron," perhaps a "senator" or an "elder." The worship of YHWH was replaced by that of Olympian Zeus in the year 167 B.C.E. The Temple was converted into a place of banquets and sacred prostitution as in the temples of Syria (6:4-6). The monthly celebration of the king's birthday brought with it its own political identification (6:7). The popular cult of Dionysius was imposed and new laws affected all the Jews of the empire, a sign that the Jewish people everywhere represented opposition to Hellenism (7:8-9). The two cases told in 6:10-11 are the same as those referred to in 1 Macc 1:60-61 and 2:32-38.

The reflection in sapiential style of 6:12-17 is consonant with the tradition of Israel: God punishes the people in order to teach them, but does not remove the divine mercy (Deut 8:5; Isa 54:7-8; Prov 3:12; Tob 13:5). As for the other nations, however, God allows them "to reach the full measure of their sins" so that they might be punished with greater severity. The author of the book of Daniel judges that sin reached its full measure precisely in the impieties of Antiochus IV (Dan 8:23; 9:24). The idea of a delay in divine punishment is rooted similarly in the biblical tradition (Gen 15:16) and in sapiential reflection (Wis 11:9-19). In the Christian Scriptures it appears again as applied to the scribes and Pharisees who reject Christ (Matt 23:32) and to the Jews who impede St. Paul from preaching the gospel (1 Thess 2:16). Nevertheless in the Christian Scriptures the conviction predominates that God delays punishment while waiting for the conversion of all (Rom 2:4-5; 2 Pet 3:9), and in the Christian Scriptures the present tribulations carry the same meaning, that is, parental correction on the part of God (Heb 12:6; Rev 3:19).

The martyrdom of Eleazar (6:18-30) is narrated as "an example of nobility and a memorial of courage" (6:31). It teaches that fidelity to the Law of God is of supreme value. Even though this passage treats of a dietary law (Lev 11:7-8) now transcended in the Christian Scriptures (Mark 7:19), the conduct of Eleazar continues to be a model of faith, courage, and hope (Heb 11:35). Attention is likewise given in this story to the impact of good example and the evils that can result socially from conduct that causes scandal even though that conduct may be correct (6:24-25). The words of Eleazar reflect the certain knowledge of a divine judgment after death (6:26) carried out with "holy knowledge" (6:30) infinitely superior to that which rules in human judgments. The story of the martyrdom of Eleazar is taken up again in 4 Maccabees 5–7 where the protagonist, presented as a priest and philosopher, dies asking God to accept his death as expiation for the sins of the nation as did the last of the brother martyrs in 2 Macc 7:38. In the Christian tradition Eleazar is considered the "teacher" of those brothers and is venerated, together with them, as a martyr of the Old Covenant.

The martyrdom of the seven brothers with their mother (7:1-41) shows the effects of the example of Eleazar (6:28). Neither place nor date is mentioned. The presence of the king in this moment of the plot can be rhetorical in character, as are the discourses and the form of the narration including the number "seven" which indicates perfection and fullness. The martyrdom of the seventh brother is delayed because the author introduces the words of the mother beforehand (7:20-29). Her faith in the resurrection is supported by the words of Moses in Deut 32:36 (cf. 2 Macc 7:6) and the powerful action of God in creation, especially in the marvelous gestation of a child in the womb of its mother (7:22-23), a theme that always inspires a profound wonder in the Scriptures (Ps 139:13-15; Job 10:8-12; Eccl 11:5). The concept of the resurrection extends beyond that of the revitalization of the people (Isa 26:19) or the healing of a mortal illness (Job 19:26-27); it means the physical reanimation of the body and its members after death (7:11, 23). The Semitic mind does not understand life outside the body. Thus the resurrection takes place as alluded to in Psalm 16:10, Ezek 37:10, and Job 19:25. For the first time in the Bible the creation of the world out of nothing, literally "not out of things that existed" (7:28) is affirmed, though indeed this affirmation had already been suggested in Genesis 1 and Isa 44:24. The author makes an apologia for martyrdom, basing it on theological arguments. In the schema of the book the cruel death of the seven brothers and their mother, like that of Eleazar, serves to explain the new turn of events, that is, that these martyrs move God to desist from punishing the people (7:38).

In the Christian Scriptures a similar prominence is given to the number seven. In Revelation there is also a hiatus before the appearance of the seventh element (Rev 6:12–8:1; 9:13–11:15). On a deeper level Jesus ratifies faith in the resurrection from the dead, a truth the Pharisees also taught (Acts 23: 6-10), but he purifies it of an excessively materialistic interpretation (Mark 12:18-27 par.; 1 Cor 15:35-46). Creation out of nothing is assumed in Heb 11:3, and in John 1:3 creation is contemplated as the work of the Word of God. The salvific dimension of the death of the martyrs is full and efficacious for all in the death of Christ, but Christ not only stays the merited punishment but makes the sinner just before God (Rom 3:21-26). Those who plot against the preaching of the gospel are the ones who now struggle against God (Acts 5:39; 26:14-15). Ample space is given to the martyred brothers in 4 Maccabees where they are presented, along with their mother, as proof that reason—in this case, reason illumined by faith —surpasses the strongest of human inclinations (4 Maccabees 8–17). The Christian tradition gave to these brothers and their mother the name of "Maccabees" and considered them "martyrs of the Old Covenant." According to testimony gathered in the fourth century the relics of the martyrs were venerated in Antioch on the supposition that they had died in that city. From there they passed to Constantinople and Rome. The Roman martyrology celebrates their feast on the first of May.

The Reaction and the Victories of Judas (8:1-36)

Identical happenings are related in 1 Macc 2:43-48 and 3:38–4:25 but 2 Maccabees omits the topographical and chronological data and even inserts happenings that occurred in other historical moments (8:30-33; 1 Macc 5:6; 7:8). Judas is invincible not only because of his good military strategies (8:21-22) but because "the wrath of the LORD had turned to mercy" (8:5). He begins his maneuvers in the manner of guerillas (8:1-7) forcing Philip, the local governor of Jerusalem, to ask for help from the military leaders of the region, "the friends of the king" (1 Macc 3:38). Among these we are especially reminded of Nicanor (8:9), who will be the leader of the army in a later period, because he "hated and detested Israel" (1 Macc 7:26) and was "thrice-accursed" (2 Macc 8:34). The attitudes of Nicanor and Judas are contrasted. Nicanor, placing his hope in his own strength and ignorant of the divine designs (8:9-11), believed victory would be his. On the other hand Judas, even though he was the leader of a well organized army (8:5, 16), depended principally upon prayer and confidence in God. As if to move God to act Judas prays in detailed fashion and presents all the disgraces suffered by the people (8:2-4). His confidence in God is supported by the remembrance of the former deeds of the Jews (8:19-20; 2 Kings 19:35) and is confirmed by the reading of the Law (8:23), which now carries the strength and purpose of a prophetic word (1 Macc 3:48). Nicanor suffers the very humiliation he had foreseen for the Jews (8:25-29, 34-35); he is even made to recognize that God is helping them, thus justifying his own defeat (8:36). The moral greatness of Judas is shown in his use of booty gained to help those in need (8:28) and also in his organizing public prayer times to ask God to forgive the people (8:29).

Punishment of the Persecutor, Antiochus IV: 9:1-29

It is not certain whether the death of the king occurred before or after the purification of the Temple; both events took place by the end of 164 B.C.E. It is certain that the announcement of the king's death must have arrived in Jerusalem after the Temple had been purified. Thus the distinctive order of 2 Maccabees can be explained. The author wants to emphasize that the liberation of the Temple was the result of divine favor (10:1) and not a concession of peace on the part of the Seleucid potentate. But given the fact that this concession was indeed given at the time of Antiochus IV and after the battle of Judas against Lysias (1 Macc 4:28-35) the author of 2 Maccabees postpones this battle and its consequences (11:6–12:9) and takes special interest in narrating the death of that king prior to the purification of the Temple. Neither dates nor exact places are given; on the other hand a detailed description is given of the sentiments of the king before and after being wounded by God with so terrible an affliction. Pride in the man brought him to the point of considering himself to be God (9:8; Isa 40:12; Job 38:8-11; Ps 65:7-8) but this pride was brought low when the true God decided to intervene (9:5-6, 10, 12). Sorrow made the attitude of the king change to the point where he was disposed to everything, including the act of "becoming a Jew" (9:11-18). But Antiochus had filled up the measure of his sins and was consequently no longer able to receive mercy (9:13, 18). This passage, which represents a terribly severe judgment on the part of God, is understandable given the fact that Antiochus was only looking to elude punishment and that the author of the book was thinking according to the law of "an eye for an eye and a tooth for a tooth." Under the law of talion punishment corresponded to the evil either realized or planned by the impious (9:9; Sir 7:17). Besides, his form of death is a foretaste of the later destiny of Antiochus (Isa 66:24) and comes to be the common motif in the death of tyrants such as Herod the Great (Josephus, *Ant.* 17.6.5) and Herod

Agrippa (Acts 12:23). The king's letter recommending his son, Antiochus V Eupator (9:19-27), could originally have been directed to each one of the villages that formed the empire; it would have been sufficient to change only the first sentence. (For further information on the courtier Philip see 1 Macc 6:55-56, 63; 2 Macc 13:23). With an expression similar to that of 9:12 in a number of the Greek manuscripts and versions, i.e., "to make one's self equal to God" St. Paul describes the attitude of Christ who, in a position completely opposite that of Antiochus, humbled himself even though he was truly "equal to God" (Phil 2:6-8).

The Recovery and Purification of the Temple: 10:1-9

With this particular action the first part of the narration reaches its high point just as the author had proposed (10:9; 2:19). Likewise the requests within the letters (1:9; 2:16) have a basis; 1 Maccabees offers a fuller account. In contrast the author mentions here the new sacred fire lit from a flint (10:3; Lev 10:1) indicating that God was not acting now as in other times (2 Macc 1:19-22; 2:10-11). The interest in the fire can be related to the rite of lighting lamps proper to this feast (1:8). We recall the prayer, full of compunction and humility (10:4; Ps 44:26), and the fact that the new feast is connected to the festival of Booths (10:6-7; 1:9; Lev 23:34-43). Here also the author puts into relief the similarities to the inauguration of the Temple built by Solomon (1 Kings 8:62-66). The palm branches and adornments were a reminder of the ivy crowns that had to be worn at the festival of Dionysius (6:7) and the lamps of the incense burnt at the doors of the houses (1 Macc 1:55). The decree to celebrate the festival is directed to all the Jews (10:8; 1:9; 2:16). The Second Book of Maccabees does not record the year of the purification as does 1 Macc 4:52 but it does clarify that it occurred at the same time as the death of Antiochus (10:9). Nevertheless it points out that two years elapsed without sacrifice (10:3) instead of the three that can be deduced from 1 Maccabees (1 Macc 1:54; 4:52). The reasons for this computation are not clear from 2 Maccabees. Perhaps the author mixes two forms of counting years, the oriental or Babylonian and the occidental or Macedonian.

Part II. Judas Secures the Safety of the Jews: 10:10–15:36

As was announced (2:20), the narration continues with the wars of Judas against Antiochus V Eupator (164–162). First Judas had to fight against the local military leaders (Gorgias and Timothy), then against the highest military authority (Lysias) and even the king himself until he obtained peace treaties that would assure the freedom of Judaism (10:14–13:26). Perhaps by establishing a parallelism with Part I of this work, the author continues his narration up to the institution of a festival, the day of Nicanor, that fell during the reign of Demetrius I (14:1–15:36) and continued up to the moment when "the city [came into the possession] of the Hebrews" (15:37).

New Victories and a Peace Treaty (10:10–11:38)

Ptolemy Macron is distinct from the Ptolemy of 4:45; 8:8. Here the struggles of Judas with the surrounding villages are brought together with the first campaign of Lysias against Judea. These events had taken place before the death of Antiochus IV and the purification of the Temple (1 Macc 5:3-8; 4:26-35) and after the victories of Judas over Gorgias and Nicanor as narrated in 8:8-29, 34-36, at the precise time when the king was occupied with the wars in the East (9:1), having left Lysias as teacher to his son and in charge of the western part of his empire (1 Macc 3:32-36). Faced with the resistance of Judas and his own need to be in Antioch as well as the pressure put on him from Rome, Lysias decided to stop the persecutions and come to a peace accord allowing the Jews to live according to their own laws. The three letters dated in the Seleucid year 148 (164 B.C.E.)—the letter from Lysias in 11:16-21, the second letter from the king in 11:27-33, and the one from the Romans in 11:34-38—all respond to that moment of relative peace and freedom that permitted Judas and his followers to occupy the Temple and purify it. The battles against Timothy (10:24-38) are combined with the capture of the city of Gazara carried out by Simon and took place much later (1 Macc 13:43-48; 2 Macc 12:10-25). The second letter from the king, which carries no specification of date, responds to another context (2 Macc 13:18; 1 Macc 6:48-63).

The people's prayer (11:6) is supported in the book of the Law, and concretely in what God had promised to the Hebrew people before entering into the Promised Land (10:26; 11:6; Exod 23:20-23) and is now fulfilled in Judas when he enters into combat (10:29, 30). The description of the warrior angel responds to the imagery already seen (3:25-26). The fact that Lysias may be seeking reconciliation with the Jews is interpreted as a recognition of the power of God (11:13-14). In the Christian tradition help from heaven against the enemies of the faith is also represented by the image of the horseman dressed in white: thus James the apostle was so represented as he entered battle against Islam in Spain in the tenth century.

Other Local Wars and the Sacrifice for the Dead (12:1-45)

Except for the battle at Joppa (12:3-9) these other skirmishes are also narrated in 1 Maccabees 5. They occurred at the end of 164 and throughout 163. Judas acted in defense of his brothers (12:30-31) in fulfillment of the law of talion (12:16). The explanation for why those soldiers died in the battle of Jamnia, that it was because of their sin (12:40-41), is different from the explanation given in 1 Macc 5:61-62. The resurrection is again affirmed and this belief is now attributed to Judas himself (12:42-43). Likewise the practice of offering prayer and sacrifice for the dead is praised (12:44-45). It is not only a matter of the sacrifice sustained by a total community when it discovers the sin of any one of its members (Lev 4:13-14), but also its faith in the communion that exists between the living and the dead and in the possibility of helping the former in the expiation of their sins. The presupposition is that there is a space after death and before the final resurrection on the last day for personal purification. Christian tradition has made abundant use of this passage for affirming the existence of Purgatory and the value of prayer offered for the dead. This doctrine was being shaped little by little in the light of 2 Maccabees and other texts of the Christian Scriptures as well as by the words of Jesus about there being some sins that cannot be pardoned either in this life or in the next (Matt 12:32) and by Paul's saying that although evil works will be burned up by fire, the person will be saved (1 Cor 3:15). Augustine experiences the comfort of these truths on the occasion of the death of his mother (*Confessions* 9.11-13; *City of God* 21.26). The Council of Lyons in 1245 confirmed the term "purgatory" to designate that state of the soul in need of purification. When this doctrine together with the one relating to indulgences was denied by reformers the Council of Trent reaffirmed it in 1563 and advised that the eucharistic sacrifice be offered for the dead. Vatican Council II as well as the *Catechism of the Catholic Church* both appeal to this passage for support.

The Recognition of Judas as the Authority Among the Jews (13:1-26)

These events correspond to 1 Macc 6:18-63 and the year indicated for their occurrence is 163 B.C.E. The text is silent, however, about the fact that it was Judas who had besieged the citadel in Jerusalem (1 Macc 6:20), perhaps to remove the responsibility of Judas for the king's attack or because in fact the king had not actually taken the citadel (1 Macc 6:54). The hidden though real dimension of the deeds (13:3) as well as the punishment of the impious (12:5-9) are, however, abundantly clear. The prayer of Judas and his confidence in God are again emphasized (12:10-14) and valued more highly than the quality of his strategies (12:13, 15). All the battles are won with the protection of God (13:17). The victory of Judas seems magnified (1 Macc 6:48-54); in reality it was the rebellion of Philip against the king that obliged the latter to stop the war and make peace with the Jews (2 Macc 13:23; 1 Macc 6:55-63). In fact Judas is recognized as governor of Judea. Some Latin codices, perhaps depending on a change in Greek from Hegemonides to *hegemona,* say that he governed over the Mediterranean coast. The title "king of kings" (applied also to God in Deut 10:17; 1 Tim 6:15) is given to Jesus Christ in Rev 17:14.

Under Demetrius I. Threats Against the Temple and the Death of Razis (14:3-46)

The arrival on the throne of the new king (14:1; 1 Macc 7:1) raises the desire of the pro-Hellenist Jews to clothe themselves anew with power in Jerusalem and with the office of high priesthood, officially vacant since the death of

Menelaus (13:3-8). This brings with it new and serious difficulties for pious Jews. The description in 2 Maccabees has a different tone from that in 1 Macc 7:1-37. Concerning the name of "Hasideans" (14:6), see 1 Macc 2:42. The intrigues and avarice for power on the part of Alcimus disrupt the good understanding between Judas and the new Seleucid authorities (14:26-29). Again disgrace comes because of the sin of some Jews. Nicanor fears the warlike valor of Judas (14:18), not that of Simon (14:17) and, infuriated at not being able to fulfill the order of the king (14:31), he hurls threats against the Temple (14:32-33) that remind one of what Antiochus IV had done. Moreover the persecution against Judaism begins with one of its most venerable representatives, Razis (14:37-46). This episode, unique to 2 Maccabees, recalls the death of the martyrs in 6:18–7:42. The author gives us the key to the moral interpretation of the suicide of Razis in 14:42, taking perhaps as his model the death of Saul as narrated in 1 Sam 31:4.

Victory over Nicanor (15:1-36)

The author now displays all his rhetorical narrative skill in recreating a situation with tones almost apocalyptic. In contrast to the brief account in 1 Macc 7:39-50, here we see the development of themes such as the holiness of the Sabbath (15:1-4), the confidence and courage that imbue the Sacred Scriptures—the Law and the Prophets—(15:9), the help which those just ones now dead give to the living (15:12-16), the power of the prayer that remembers divine help on similar occasions (15:22-24; 2 Kings 19:35), and the courage and piety of Judas (15:30). The spaciousness in the description of interior attitudes contrasts with the brevity used in giving an account of the battle (15:25-27), although this passage emerges as one of the most beautiful expressions of the book. The treatment given to the dead body of Nicanor (15:32-35), which no doubt wounds the sensibilities of today's reader, must be understood within that historical context and in the light of its relationship to sin. Here punishment controls the entire work. The fortress of Jerusalem was still not in the power of the Jews (1 Macc 13:21). Concerning the festival of Nicanor, see 1 Macc 7:49 and for "Mordecai's day" or the feast of Purim, see Esther 9.

Epilogue: 15:37-39

This final pericope corresponds to the preface (2:19-32). Jerusalem was completely in the hands of the Jews in the year 141 B.C.E. once Simon, the brother of Judas, took the fortress. The genre of the book is clear: the author concludes with an expression of hope that the reader has found enjoyment in it.

BIBLIOGRAPHY

Bickermann, E. J. *The God of the Maccabees.* Leiden: E. J. Brill, 1979.

Doran, Robert. *Temple Propaganda: The Purpose and Character of 2 Maccabees.* CBQ.MS 12. Washington, D.C.: Catholic Biblical Association, 1981.

Goldstein, J. A. *II Maccabees: A New Translation with Introduction and Commentary.* AB 41a. Garden City, N.Y.: Doubleday, 1983.

Kampen, John. *The Hasideans and the Origin of Pharisaism. A Study in 1 and 2 Maccabees.* Atlanta, Ga.: Scholars, 1988.

Tcherikover, Avigdor. *Hellenistic Civilization and the Jews.* Philadelphia: Jewish Publication Society, 1959.

Wisdom: A Way of Thinking About God

Sean McEvenue

Introduction

Theology has been defined since the eleventh century as "faith in search of understanding" *(fides quaerens intellectum).* Thus theology has always been a bridge from knowledge based on faith to knowledge based on reason. Theology develops not so much because of new revelation as because of new human knowledge that asks new questions of faith and allows new answers to emerge. For this reason the university is an apt place for theology, because it is there that new human knowledge is collected and formulated.

If theology builds bridges from faith to reason, the question arises: is there any study that builds bridges from reason to faith *(intellectus quaerens fidem)?* The answer is that Wisdom, as proposed in many texts of the OT, plays that role. Biblical Wisdom is an invitation to science to extend itself toward faith.

Wisdom as Faith, but Also as Reason

Wisdom as Faith

The OT in some texts clearly presents Wisdom as something akin to faith, a pure gift of God. In these texts Wisdom is often understood in terms of the human activity involved in acquiring or possessing "wisdom," but at other times in terms of the transcendent object that is thus acquired or possessed. First, then, in terms of human activity Wisdom is presented as a unique divine gift that Solomon received (1 Kings 3:3-14). It is a more than human talent (2 Sam 14:17; 16:23; 19:27). It is rooted in, or equivalent to, the "fear of the Lord," which in turn is akin to what we would call faith (Prov 1:7; Sirach 1).

Second, as transcendent object Wisdom is perhaps most clearly presented in the book of Wisdom where Wisdom is defined as a spiritual being that is understood as the world soul pervading all creation (7:22-24) or as the breath of God (7:25-26) or as present in human spirits (7:27-28) or as consort of God (8:3-4). This teaching is an elaboration of the simpler expression of the same ideas in Prov 8:22-31. Similarly, Wisdom is presented as a spiritual woman in the heavenly court in Sirach 24.

Proverbs 1–9 repeatedly presents Wisdom as the object of desire in the form of a voice of a woman crying in the streets, inviting all to seek her and learn from her. Job 28 depicts this search as a successful activity in terms of technological advance (Job 28:1-6) and yet one that is ultimately frustrated, and he recommends that one abandon the search for Wisdom as transcendent object and revert to Wisdom as a divinely graced but human activity: "the fear of the Lord, that is Wisdom, and to depart from evil is understanding" (Job 28:28). Whether Wisdom is understood as a divinely inspired human activity or the divine object of that activity, in all these texts we see Wisdom as a reality that relates to human reason but remains divine in origin.

Wisdom as Reason

However, when we see Wisdom at work it often has a totally secular face. For example in Job 28:1-6, as mentioned above, it is seen simply as technological advance, and certainly Solomon's wisdom is depicted in terms of activities we would assign to reason, and his unique success was measured in terms of a competition in the mode of a Nobel prize: "Solomon's wisdom surpassed the wisdom of all the people of the east, and all the wisdom of Egypt . . . wiser than Ethan the Ezrahite, and Heman, Calcol, and Darda, children of Mahol . . . . He composed three thousand proverbs, and his songs numbered a thousand and five. He would speak of trees, from the cedar that is in the Lebanon to the hyssop that grows in the wall; he would speak of animals, and birds, and reptiles, and fish" (1 Kings 4:30-33). In this description of Wisdom it sounds very much like the lore of an excellent school teacher—very much in the realm of common reason rather than that of faith. This impression is borne out by the stories told to prove Solomon's wisdom. They show sagacity and skill and *savoir faire,* but nothing in the realm of faith. The Queen of Sheba, for example, is astounded at the elegance of his servants and the refinement of his table and his skill in solving riddles (1 Kings 10:1-5).

Similarly the Wisdom exercised by Hushai and Achitophel appears to be purely secular: it can only be described as political sagacity combined with a talent for deception (2 Sam 15-17). The Wisdom of the wise woman of Tekoa turns out to be no more than skill in courtly wheedling. It consists of carrying out the orders of general Joab in order to implement his political manipulation: in effect she prepares the disastrous return of Absalom to the court by verbally outfoxing David (2 Samuel 14). Such verbal and diplomatic skills are often not much admired in our culture, and they certainly seem remote from faith. But they clearly were admired in ancient times. Many of the Proverbs, for example, are clever observations, or astute advice, or clever use of language without any apparent faith dimensions. The whole of Proverbs 26 could have been written by Alexander Pope or François Duc de la Rochefoucault rather than by a religious leader. Even Jesus is depicted sometimes as surpassingly clever in a secular sense, though the transcendent dimension is also present. For example, in answer to the tangled trap question about the religious implications of paying taxes, he evades the trap with a slogan: one should render to Caesar what is Caesar's, and to God what is God's (Matt 22:21). In the context this is not a supernatural insight into political science; it is verbal adroitness used by Jesus to return to his eschatological theme. Similarly Jesus' advice to take the lowest chair in a banquet so as to end up being promoted (Luke 14:10), like the lessons in table manners proposed by Ben Sirach (31:12-18), is not an exhortation to self-denying humility or to Christian charity. It is a bit of shrewd advice on the level of secular one-upmanship turned to the service of an eschatological theme.

Wisdom as the Bible Defined It: Prov 1:2-7

Despite, or because of, the divergence of these two views of Wisdom in the Bible as faith or as reason, the introduction to the book of Proverbs provides a complex definition of Wisdom that is constructed so as to unite the two into a single reality. It says that the purpose of this book is to enable people to know Wisdom and understand its language (Prov 1:2), and then it proceeds to enumerate the contents of this topic. The enumeration of contents opens with "righteousness" (which is a very broad category of general holiness including all the personal relationships of an individual with neighbor, family, government, and God) and ends with "fear of the Lord," which appears roughly equal to what we might call "faith, hope, and charity." In between are listed a number of items in the realm of virtue and skill and diplomacy, ending with the verbal skills of understanding proverbs and figures of speech and riddles. All of these items pertain to Wisdom. What is the a common denominator? What is Wisdom itself?

This question can be addressed in two ways, corresponding to our two approaches to Wisdom. First, we shall ask whether there is a single or unified human activity (that is, mental or psychic activity) that is common to all these kinds of knowledge. Second, we shall consider the transcendent object of this activity: is there any single reality corresponding to the spiritual woman who awakens our desire by calling in the streets? The answer to both will be yes.

First, then, human activity. The most surprising item listed, both here and in the list of Solomon's qualities admired by the Queen of Sheba (1 Kings 10:1), is perhaps the ability to solve riddles. The ancients attributed greater power to words and concepts than we do, and the ability to solve riddles was in their eyes directly linked with the power to resolve confusion in reality. (One has only to think of the riddle of the Sphinx in *Oedipus Tyrannus,* or the many practices of magic.) Proverbs 16:1, 10; 25:2-3 reveal something of the direction of thought involved: "The plans of the mind belong to mortals, but the answer of the tongue is from the Lord. . . . Inspired decisions are on the lips of a king; his mouth does not sin in judgment. . . . It is the glory of God to conceal things, but the glory of kings is to search things out. . . . the mind of kings is unsearchable." Words, thoughts, and outer reality are all plunged in the same mystery, and the king (both wise and empowered by the Lord) has a charism equally of knowing, saying, and doing the right thing. The essence of a riddle is that it invites inquiry, puzzling with words, putting things rightly together. I would suggest that dedication to inquiry is the common denominator contained in all the items mentioned in Prov 1:2-7. It is the supreme value and virtue named by the word "wisdom."

Wisdom is cleverness in every realm. Of course, in the realm of courtly life cleverness will consist of adroit diplomacy; in the realm of faith cleverness will consist of fearing the Lord. But the dichotomy between secular and religious cleverness is one the Bible did not know, and that the Bible in fact refuses to admit. Inquiring about the meaning of words or literary figures is a practice that is extolled. It is an inquiry that, unless artificially curtailed, does not stop at words but goes on to psychic states, human relations, questions of diplomacy and political theory, questions about justice, questions about ultimate reality and salvation. Inquiry of itself is limitless. It was only an artificial decree of the Enlightenment that declared inquiry into "objective" data to be totally different (that is, because it is valid) from inquiry into "subjective" data, or inquiry into material reality totally different from inquiry into spiritual reality. If one is conscious of this appetite within oneself one will realize that it is unlimited. The "why?" of a young child exhausts parents precisely because it is tireless and insatiable and without limit. This same appetite continues to fill library shelves year after year without end. The Bible is right in its view that inquiry should not be thought of as purely secular because in itself it is open to all dimensions and depths including the infinite.

Wisdom literature is written in a mode that is appropriate to this view: as a riddle to invite questioning rather than as a teaching to end it. Certainly the book of Proverbs, apart from its constant exhortations to seek Wisdom (that is, to inquire about everything) is a collection of sayings rather than a collection of instructions. Most proverbs will be equally "true" if applied to any situation or realm of truth or social reality (family or community or state) and often equally "true" if reversed. (For example Prov 22:3, "the clever see danger and hide; but the simple go on, and suffer for it" is no truer than its inverse: "the clever see danger and pass through it; but the simple hide themselves, and suffer.") The proverb is not a true statement about a specific reality but rather a way of thinking that the reader should retain, absorb, and learn how to use appropriately. Thus "too many cooks spoil the broth" is no truer than "many hands make light work," and each can be applied to cooking, building a dam on the Mississippi, or negotiating a peace treaty. These are not instructions but models of inquiry.

It must be noted that even the form of biblical proverbs is often an invitation to puzzle, not only in cases where the main trick is unexpected metaphor or play on words, but also in many examples where the "parallel" stich of a proverb proves to be unparallel and the point of the proverb is seen by noting and thinking through this failure of correspondence. For example, Prov 10:7 reads "the memory of the righteous is a blessing, but the name of the wicked will rot." Memory, in the sense of recalling aloud, is a true parallel to "the name." But "will rot" is not a natural parallel to "blessing." Rather one would expect the second stich to read "but the name of the wicked is a curse." The biblical proverb chooses to reject the obvious parallel, with the result that the reader is drawn to puzzle a bit and to wonder if perhaps the wicked are too insubstantial to effect a curse—they merely rot. Similarly, the following proverb appropriately parallels "the wise of heart" with "babbling fools" but whereas the former do good deeds the latter are reduced to disappearing.

It may be noted that the LXX has from time to time been so distressed by this failure to write perfect parallels that it has taken upon itself to correct the verse. These "corrections" invariably reduce the proverb to trivial logic and even nonsense. For example the LXX translates Prov

14:17: "One who is quick-tempered acts foolishly, but one with discretion is patient." It is not easy to find that observation very enlightening. The original Hebrew reads: "One who is quick-tempered acts foolishly, and the schemer is hated." The Hebrew offers a poor parallel in that being hated is not parallel to acting foolishly, and the Greek translator has made a very clever shift of meaning so that the speed of the temper is understood as characterizing the foolishness as well, and then this speed is contrasted with the "patience" of the second stich. The resulting proverb is cleverly parallel but otherwise meaningless. The Hebrew text, far from making a banal statement, offers a tricky question: which is it better to be—a quick-tempered bungler or a shrewd pariah? The original Hebrew form of this proverb invites the reader to wonder and to puzzle. It is natural, but regrettable, that many modern translators and commentators make the same mistake as the LXX.

Puzzling seems to be the literary genre of all the books of Wisdom. Thus Qoheleth is a brilliant puzzle throughout, delighting most readers with its wit and inviting them to think everything anew. The Song of Songs presents women as supreme in the domain of love and carries a forceful message about the role of human love in awakening the love of God, but its literary form is not that of direct statement. Rather it proceeds indirectly, in a form so puzzling that readers for millennia have been both delighted by it and drawn to endless debate about what the poem is about. It too is a puzzle. So also the book of Job, which is an impassioned book certainly, is profoundly a puzzle. It is *not* an answer to the problem of evil. Commentators, when they come to discussing the theology or meaning of the book, will write the weakest part of their commentary if they attempt to show that God's speeches are an answer to the foregoing speeches of Job. The very brilliance that often goes into this attempt underlines the fact that God's response is something other than an answer to an argument. Rather the whole book is a passionate invitation to think deeply about the problem of evil and a passionate refusing of all simplistic answers. Wisdom of Solomon may be understood as teaching that the soul is immortal but its whole approach consists of complex reasoning in which Israel's traditions, and in particular biblical texts, are cleverly reinterpreted through the categories of Hellenistic philosophy. The book invites the reader to engage in complex thinking throughout, and the intended teaching is never directly formulated though it is cleverly suggested by the mention of ambrosia at the very end. Sirach is an exception in that it does offer a lot of straight teaching and its overall mode is more influenced by Torah than are the other Wisdom books.

Wisdom as Desired Consort of God

Our second question was about the transcendent object. What is the reality of this voice that calls us? In Prov 8:30-31 Wisdom is presented in the figure of a confidant whom God loves, and who in turn loves humans and finds all her delights among us. Is this purely a literary fiction? or does it correspond to a real object?

It has sometimes been thought that texts like this were to be understood as types in the sense of propaedeutical fictions, "preparations" for the real thing: they expressed a preparatory idea that would eventually be understood to refer to the Word of God, or to the Holy Spirit. The liturgy, on the other hand, has often referred these texts to Mary, the mother of God, assumed into heaven. Such typological approaches can serve rhetorical purposes, but if they are read to imply unreality in the meaning of the OT texts they are simply mistaken. If the "type" is not real, then why would the NT writers or Church Fathers go in search of it again and again and adduce such flimsy materials in connection with God? Far from strengthening their statements about the Lord, or about the Spirit, or about the mother of God, such references of a real and transcendent antitype back to a fictional type would not deepen understanding but rather would tend to introduce a frivolous and insubstantial distraction. It would weaken the sense of power, and the invitation to faith, in their discussion.

One answer is given in the OT itself. After the exile, when the Jews had a sophisticated codified Law that imposed a style of life whose difference from that of their neighbors was a matter of intimate experience for them, the Law was perceived as embodying a specific culture, a shared vision of how life's problems could be resolved. This was expressed in the notion that the Torah was Israel's Wisdom. Thus the post-exilic addition to Deuteronomy uses this notion to exhort obedience to the Law (Deut 4:6-8). Sirach 24:23 identifies the heavenly woman Wisdom as the Torah, and the same is found in Bar 3:9 and 4:1.

Wisdom, then, as transcendent object is understood by these texts to be that mysterious reality that is normative culture, in other words, the complex of beliefs and understandings commonly held by a society. And a normative culture is in turn a voice calling out to demand learning and search on the part of youth. This reading makes sense in a unified cultural context where the law of the land is understood as revealed by God. This reality is very close to the Greek *logos* (word, reason) that is so important in the NT.

For those who live in secular or mixed societies, however, this reading is not easily real. One might instead propose an alternative identification for the desirable woman Wisdom that would be both real and helpful in understanding these texts. We must turn to cognitive theory for the understanding of human knowledge that was elaborated in scholastic philosophy. In that analysis all inquiry into the nature or meaning of things implies a prior (implicit) affirmation that things are intelligible, and all affirmations about the nature or meaning of things imply affirmation that beings are real and intelligible, and ultimately that Being is real and intelligible.

Now inquiry about reality is unlimited, and it follows that its object, Being, is unlimited. At that point there arises the question about the relation between "real unlimited being" and God as revealed to us as a person in the Bible, or in Jesus, or in the Church, and one enters into the discussion of the relation between natural and supernatural. For present purposes that relationship can be left undefined. Unlimited Being, which scholastic philosophy described as "the proportional object" of the human intellect, is neither the Father, nor the Son, nor the Holy Spirit. It is, however, the object of the unlimited striving of humanity for the Good, the True, and the Beautiful, and it is as real as the striving is real and is unlimited. Surely that reality is precisely Wisdom as transcendent object: the spiritual woman who calls to humans at every turn and whose possession is the objective of all puzzling, inquiring, discussing, wondering, yearning. It is Wisdom that turns a person into a live and responsible being in response to Being. The exhortation to seek Wisdom is not an exhortation to knowledge but rather an exhortation to being spiritually alive, and ultimately to being open to faith.

The impact of Wisdom on the NT provides a bridge between the earliest belief in Christ as exalted to the belief that Christ preexisted with God prior to his life on earth. Outstanding examples of the influence of Wisdom occur in John 1:1-18; 1 Cor 8:5-6; Col 1:15-17; Heb 1:1-3a; and Matt 11:27-30 where Wisdom terminology from the OT as well as intertestamental literature is used. They are influenced by the idea of Wisdom's preexistence (Proverbs 8) but they are to be understood as asserting that Christ embodies the extraordinary role of Wisdom. The fullness of God's creative and saving activity resides in Christ. God's outreach to humankind ascribed to Wisdom is now manifested in Christ. This is the seed of the doctrine of the preexistence of Christ.

Wisdom and Skepticism

Before we conclude, a word must be added about what has often been called biblical skepticism regarding Wisdom. The word "skepticism," although it can mean no more than caution in thought, usually implies some denial of hope or possibility of knowledge. It is a word that is used most often in the discussion of Job and Qoheleth. It is important to recognize that what is called skepticism in these books is, in fact, not a negation of puzzling or a refusal of understanding. Rather it is an inquiry into Wisdom itself, a puzzling about this mode of thought. As such it is a superior Wisdom, best understood not as skepticism but as a critique of the abuse of Wisdom.

Just as it is possible (and therefore inevitable?) that religious people will abuse the biblical law codes by turning them into an instrument for controlling God, so that individuals are misled to believe that if they obey the Law they will have saved their own souls, so it is possible to misread many proverbs, turning them into simplistic doctrines and understanding them to reveal mechanisms of good behavior that assure wealth and happiness. Conversely, in this perverse reading of proverbs anyone who is struck by misfortune is immediately judged to be suffering the effects of her or his misdeeds.

The book of Job offers a profound struggle with such mechanistic theology and finally a refusal of such abuse of Wisdom. The "comforters" of Job are condemned by God for such false beliefs whereas Job's cry of complaint is declared to be justified (42:7). Of course God also accuses Job of lacking Wisdom in his wild discourse (38:2), but this may be understood to refer not to Job's cries of pain and bitter complaint (which are similar to those of Jesus on the cross: see Matt 27:45-50) but rather to those aspects of his discourse in which he becomes complicit in the mechanistic debate. Job 28 discusses Wisdom explicitly, pointing to human limitations in seeking it. It has been understood by some as indicating that humans should not aspire to Wisdom (vv. 23-24), but rather should turn to morality instead (v. 28). However, that reading is excluded if one understands Wisdom as this essay has attempted to portray it. Wisdom, as the object of desiring, is directly possessed only by God (vv. 21-22). Still, it remains as the good that humans should seek with all their energy. The "fear of YHWH" (28:28) to which one is instructed to turn is not an alternative to Wisdom but rather it is the central characteristic of Wisdom itself. "Fear" means what we might call faith, understood as trust in and hunger for infinite truth and love. Thus Job offers not skepticism, but rather a critique of the abuse of Wisdom, while it affirms and enjoins a superior Wisdom.

Qoheleth also has been discussed as a book that preaches skepticism rather than Wisdom. Like Job 28 it ends on the notion of the "fear of God," and that verse does, in fact, understand "fear" as an alternative to Wisdom. But, again like Job, the whole book is a consummate model of Wisdom writing, which spends much of its energy critiquing abusive interpretations of proverbs (see especially 6:10–9:6). Most modern translations have unfortunately followed the early Greek translation in giving the book's repeated theme a negative (skeptical) tone: "Vanity of vanities, all is vanity." The original Hebrew, however, read *hebel,* which is not an univocal abstraction such as "vanity" but rather a complex symbol: it means basically "a breath," a "puff of air," which can be symbols of evanescence and insubstantiality but also perhaps of a brief effort or burst of energy (see, for example, Prov 13:11). The word often refers to idols who are illusions, or to empty words. (A better translation in Qoheleth might be: "A huff and a puff, all is air.") If one then reads the opening hymn in a lighter vein it is not at all a world-weary report about meaningless repetition, but rather a joyous marveling at the tireless energy of creation. Thus v. 8 observes the remarkable fact that our eyes and ears are never tired of seeing or hearing new things, and its translation should begin: "All things are full of energy: more than one can express!" The hymn makes light of human striving and history, which are not remembered anyway; it does this not by portraying human effort as evil in any way but by extolling the wonders of nature. Similarly, the hymn in ch. 3 should not be read as portraying a meaningless periodicity but rather as an exuberant celebration of divine providence in creation. (The word chosen for "time" there, both in Greek and in Hebrew, does not mean a point on the clock or calendar but precisely a right time, a moment appointed by providence in the sense of Prov 15:23: "a word [or deed] in season, how good it is!") The author does show that Wisdom, even royal Wisdom, does not finally benefit the wise person (see Eccl 1:16-17; 2:12-17). Taken literally this is skepticism. But the whole conceiving of it is an exercise in superior Wisdom. The book is about bursting the simplistic balloons that humans often admire and dispelling illusions about false values, in this case the false value of competitive wisdom. For a workaholic culture such as ours in North America the author offers valuable insights into the inanity of much competitive striving. The Wisdom of the author is that happiness is not something achieved by human effort at all; rather it is a grace, a pure gift of God. This teaching is presented in the image of eating, drinking, and joyous labor. On our own we humans often find no joy in simple pleasures (and how easily we waste our life in petty bitterness), but with God's gift of joy our hearts are filled (Eccl 2:24-26; 5:18-20). Finally he says, as does Job 28, that we cannot understand everything, and he explains why this is so: God has put eternity as a surpassing mystery within things, and at that point our Wisdom must consist not of understanding but of joy in living and the fear of God (3:10-15). Thus Qoheleth too enjoins not skepticism, but faith-filled, superior Wisdom.

Conclusion

Qoheleth wrote that "wisdom excels folly as light excels darkness" (2:13), and also that Wisdom is much vexation since those who increase knowledge increase sorrow (1:18). This makes excellent sense in terms of the notion of Wisdom developed in the foregoing. If Wisdom as human activity is the unlimited desire to know and love, then surely it will be both "light" and enhanced "sorrow." Job is the perfect example, for it was precisely his faith (light) that made his suffering intolerable. Job was wiser than his comforters because he fully believed in unlimited truth and love as the destiny written into the basic aspiration of humans, and as this wisdom proved inadequate when faced with the equally human experience of meaningless suffering he increased his vexation and sorrow by refusing to abandon his wisdom.

The discoveries of modern experimental science have provided a content of knowledge far beyond that of Solomon. However, the horizon of modern experimental science has been led to exclude data that cannot be verified by the senses and duplicated again and again. This is a fruitful discipline but it excludes value and implies a functional but mechanistic and meaningless world. Wisdom, on the other hand, proposes an unlimited horizon for knowledge and her voice is transcendent: it invites science to explore all those forbidden open questions, respecting all "why?"s, which eventually link reason to faith. Biblical Wisdom demands the building of bridges from science to faith.

Job

Roland E. Murphy

Introduction

Not many who use this commentary will be reading the book of Job for the first time. We have all acquired certain presuppositions or assumptions from other sources (where did the idea of the "patience of Job" come from?), and from dipping into the book at various places or hearing it read (too infrequently) in the liturgy. Our treatment will be geared to two readings: first we will briefly test certain impressions and assumptions for reading the book, as it were for the first time. Then we shall give a second reading in greater depth, sharing with the reader our understanding of the text. It will rely on some of the insights achieved by commentators in the long history of the interpretation of the book. This demands a serious second reading on the part of the reader, giving close attention to the biblical text. Some difficulties will not be resolved—the text and language of the book are notoriously difficult—but the reader will be the richer for having wrestled with the text and then be in a position to agree or disagree with the conclusions offered in the second reading. Many commentators readily admit that there is no one necessarily correct understanding of the book. The second reading provided here is meant to challenge the reader, to allow for the thrill of interpreting one of the classic pieces in world literature.

The following observations are put forth as the assumptions of this writer, widely shared by biblical scholars, that may serve as starting points for the reader.

(1) The structure of the book. Fortunately the structure of the work is relatively uncomplicated. It can be divided thus:

Prologue: chapters 1 and 2
Dialogue: chapters 3 to 31, in which Job and his three friends have what can be called a debate
Elihu's appearance: chapters 32–37, four speeches by young Elihu
The Lord intervenes and speaks to Job and Job responds: chapters 38 to 42:6
Epilogue: 42:7-17

Further subdivisions are possible, but the above is the main framework. The dialogue is somewhat choppy in chs. 26–27, as we shall see, but this outline is a reliable guide.

(2) The author. We know nothing about the author or authors, neither names nor times. Majority opinion places the work in the post-exilic period but there are no compelling reasons for this; we have no reliable means of dating. The issue is further complicated by additions that are alleged to have been inserted in the book (e.g., ch. 28; the speeches of Elihu). But it is not very helpful to pursue such uncertainties. It is the book as a whole that remains for us to read and understand. This is its "canonical form," as it is called (the form in which the community of faith has received it), and it is not really profitable to reconstruct a merely hypothetical picture of the manner in which the book could have been put together.

If we do not know the author, do we know more about Job, the "hero" of the book? Job is mentioned in Ezek 14:14, 20, along with Noah and Dan[i]el as holy men. Even the presence of these three in Jerusalem would not save that city from the destruction that the Lord is going to bring upon it. Obviously it is around this time (about 600 B.C.E.) that the person of Job is honored as being righteous. It is important to note that none of the three is an Israelite. Job, as we learn from Job 1:1, is from the land of Uz, which is perhaps to be located south of Palestine. The three friends of Job are also described as non-Israelites, coming from areas in the general vicinity of Edom and the desert (Job 2:11). This all fits very well with the perspective of ancient Israelite wisdom, which was regarded as an international legacy shared with Egypt and Mesopotamia, the deposit of observations and lessons drawn from the experience of the folk. Thus there are no references to the sacred traditions, such as the promises to the Fathers, or to the Exodus, Sinai and the Law, etcetera.

The traditional "wisdom books" of the OT are Proverbs, Job, Qoheleth, and the two deuterocanonicals, Sirach and the Wisdom of Solomon. [See also the article "Wisdom: A Way of Thinking About God."] There also seems to be a fair amount of wisdom influence on other parts of the Bible (e.g., Psalm 37). Comparisons have been made between the wisdom writings of Egypt (e.g., the *Teaching of Amenemope* and Prov 22:17–23:11) and of Mesopotamia (e.g., for Job see the long poem *Ludlul,* or "I Will Praise the Lord of Wisdom" in *ANET,* 596–600). The reader who is interested in this broader cultural movement of wisdom can read and compare Job and the *Ludlul.* The similarity seems a bit remote. It is not surprising to find human beings, ancient and modern, complaining to God about divine justice. One may say that this kind of "complaint" literature was anticipated earlier than the book of Job, but the biblical work shows no immediate dependency upon the Mesopotamian work. It is noteworthy that the question of retribution—the justice or injustice that marks the life of human beings—is a problem peculiar to the wisdom literature. It is not absent from the rest of the Bible, but throughout the wisdom books it is at the forefront. Proverbs (e.g., 3:1-10; 10:2-3) is optimistic on the whole, while Job and Qoheleth (e.g., Qoh 3:16; 8:14) wrestle arduously with the problem, and it is treated at some length in both Sirach (15:11-20; 18:1-14) and Wisdom (3:1-14; 4:10–5:15).

We have seen that the person named Job was known as a non-Israelite and that his affliction was not a solitary one, but a perennial question that Israel and its neighbors addressed. More important is the manner in which the author has portrayed him. Job is a *literary* figure as described in the book. We are not to think that these several chapters are an historical resumé of a great debate that took place while Job was suffering in pain on a refuse heap. No, these speeches are works of consummate literary quality that could not simply be delivered in such trying circumstances. There was no reporter or tape recorder to capture all this. Rather we have a literary production of high art, carefully thought out and expressed, not a passing debate. One indication of this literary aspect is the use of irony that pervades the book, and that we will exemplify in the second reading. By irony we mean the double meaning that occurs so frequently in which another (often later) meaning negates or transcends the first meaning. For example, Eliphaz asks Job in 12:3 whether Shaddai, the Almighty, gains anything by Job's righteousness—a putdown of Job. The reader, however, knows from the prologue that Shaddai *will* gain, because the Satan will have lost and the LORD's belief in the trustworthiness of his servant Job will have been sustained. Eliphaz provides several opportunities for irony. In 5:1 he taunts Job, "Call now! . . . To whom among the holy ones will you appeal?" Indeed, the head of the "holy beings" or members of the heavenly court will eventually respond—no less than the LORD (38:1).

(3) We have been considering the general assumptions that can be affirmed about the book. But what about the assumptions of the reader? It does not matter how many presuppositions we have in approaching the work. Rather, how valid are they? For example, everyone has heard of the "patience" of Job and perhaps wondered about it. The term comes from the letter of James (5:11) in the NT, and it translates the Greek word *hypomonē,* which properly means steadfastness or endurance (and is so rendered in modern versions). Hence we need not torture our understanding of Job's character as "patience." He is not patient, but he proves himself ultimately steadfast in his adherence to the LORD.

Another frequent assumption concerns the figure of Satan in chs. 1 and 2. A common tendency is to equate this character with the devil, or *diabolos,* of the NT. This is a mistake. The Satan in Job is a kind of chief prosecutor who has a special function of patrolling the earth (cf.

Job 1:6-7; 2:2-3). Indeed, he is *among* the sons of God (1:6; 2:1) whom the LORD calls together, and he does only what the LORD tells him. One might say that he doesn't trust human beings; in fact one might argue that he does not want the LORD to be deceived by such a person as Job about whom he has serious doubts, and against whom he makes the serious charge in 1:10-11. He is merely a member of the heavenly court that is frequently referred to in the OT (cf. the question in Isa 6:8 or the scene in 1 Kings 22:19). The Lord did not dwell alone, but was attended by the "sons of El (or Elohim)" who served the divine purposes (e.g., Psalm 29). It is true that the figure of the Satan grows more and more hostile in the OT, and by the late period and in the NT is recognized as an evil power—but the process is a gradual one.

Another assumption: we tend to regard Job as the hero, the one who suffers unjustly. We must be careful about this. Job does suffer, as we would put it, unjustly, and hence we tend to shut off the speeches of his opponents, the three friends. But this is a shortsighted view. We have to realize that behind Job, the friends, and even the LORD, stands the (unknown) author of the book. He is not writing in order to exalt Job as a great debater. The three friends are not simply straw men for Job to knock down. The author has broader purposes. He wants to highlight the problem of the innocent sufferer and he rehearses various explanations and solutions that were current in his time. But he did not have the answer. Even the LORD does not give an "answer" to Job's problem, although the divine speeches are important. The point is that the author behind these characters is laying out all the theology that is available to him in an effort to throw light on a very difficult problem. Traditionally, Israelite theology recognized a connection between sin and suffering. The psalmists, for example, readily admit that their suffering is due to their wrongdoing (e.g., Psalms 32, 38, 39, 51). But there are also psalms in which they protest they are innocent and suffering unjustly (e.g., Psalms 7, 17, 26). Israel had no easy answer to suffering (which remains a mystery for Christians as well!), and several points of view were current. The author of Job gives all sides a hearing. At the same time it is clear that Job is his main mouthpiece, and that he is dissatisfied with the traditional orthodoxy of the friends. They argued backward from suffering to sin. Their arguments were elaborate and doubtless reflected the opinion of many, but they did not prevail. The application of human standards of "justice" to the relationship between God and humans is not a simple thing, but the author presented as complete a hearing as he was capable of. Other writers, too, struggled with this puzzle, as can be seen in Gen 18:22-32; Jer 12:1-5; Psalms 37 and 73 together.

FIRST READING

Perhaps one is reading the full text of Job for the first time. The point of a first reading is to acquire a personal grasp of the book as a whole, not to understand all the details. Still, every book of the Bible, and especially this one, calls for an aggressive, questioning reading, with pencil and paper. The actual reading might stop at critical junctures of the book in order to weigh the material that is covered: what are the significant lines in chs. 1–2? How do the speeches of Job and the friends match each other in chs. 4–14? What is the nature of Job's complaint in ch. 31? What translation is one using? And so on.

After reading the book as a whole, within which the parts can have meaning, the reader may read at leisure a second time, section by section, without allowing any pressure to limit the time to be given to feeling into the world of the text. The following pages concerning a "first reading" are meant as a guide to the undertaking. We will present a framework that is the background for all the speeches.

Prologue and Epilogue

The prologue describes the situation on two levels: what happens on earth and what happens in heaven. On earth a man named Job is described as saintly, "blameless and upright" (1:1), solicitous for the honor of God and the conduct of his family. In heaven the Satan questions Job's integrity and suggests a testing—that he be deprived of all he possesses. God accepts. The scene reverts to earth, and a wave of cataclysms wipes out all that Job has, including his children. His reaction? Those immortal words: "The Lord has given, and the Lord has taken away. Blessed be the name of the Lord" (1:21), and the author explicitly records that Job did not sin. But the Satan is not satisfied because Job's person has been spared. So a second affliction is agreed to by God: bodily disease. Job accepts with equanimity his wife's strong words: both evil and good are to be accepted from the Lord, and a second time the author declares that Job said nothing sinful. But his afflictions become known and three friends arrive to bring him some comfort. Silence—for seven days, no less—is their awe-filled reaction, as they cannot speak, but only offer their presence as a consolation.

It is at this point that Job begins the famous lament of ch. 3. It will ignite a series of debates in which even the voice of the LORD God will be heard (38:1–41:26).

The epilogue (42:7-16) is a kind of world turned upside down. It is Job, the LORD says, who has spoken rightly, not the friends who thought they were defending the divine honor. Indeed, the LORD consents to accept Job's intercession on their behalf. The fabulous "happy ending" continues as Job is blessed even more than before, and he dies "old and contented."

That is the story, the setting, into which all the speeches have been woven. Almost as if the speeches contained no problems of themselves, this (no doubt legendary) framework generates all kinds of questions for the reader. How do Job's riches, moral integrity, Satan's opposition, and the LORD's acquiescence to Satan's plan all fit together? What has really happened in the speeches that makes it possible for the LORD to proclaim Job the "winner," as it were, and to reward him in the old traditional way of blessing him with the things of this world? These questions will receive some sort of answer in the second reading, but they are among the most disturbing of the many questions that will arise on a first reading of this puzzling work.

The Dialogue

It makes little difference whether one begins the debate between Job and his friends at ch. 3 or ch. 4. It is true that Job is not speaking specifically to the three friends in ch. 3; this is rather a soliloquy, a bitter complaint (about God and himself, although God is mentioned only indirectly in 3:23). Job utters a beautiful curse upon the day he was born, and throws the eternal "why" at the heavens.

Of course this is enough to prompt the senior Eliphaz to remonstrate with Job in a conciliatory manner, in an effort to help him understand his plight. The main thrust of his speech is "Can anyone be righteous as against God?" (4:17). Starting at this high altitude, he thinks he is making it easy for Job to recognize what is happening to him, and he proclaims what apparently was a frequent theme among the sages: happy the one God reproves (5:17; cf. Prov 3:11-12; Elihu in Job 33:16-17, 29-30).

Job's reply in chs. 6–7 is longer than that of Eliphaz—in general Job out-talks the individual friends. The reader may not be distressed by the length, but it is somewhat unsettling to come to realize that in a sense Job and his friends talk past one another. There is no neat arrangement of points scored or points answered, as Western logic might expect. But this is not a cause for complaint! Rather let the reader enjoy it and yield to the many ramifications that the speeches give rise to. Another important observation should be made about the speeches: the friends deliver lectures to Job; Job replies to them, but in the first several speeches he inevitably ends up speaking or even praying to God. This is truly a remarkable feature that is particularly prominent in what is called the "first cycle" of the speeches. The cycles depend on a complete speech of Job and the three responses; the first ends with ch. 14. The second extends from 15:1 to 21:34. The third is not really a cycle: Zophar does not speak at all, and many think that the text has been disturbed here. What follows in chs. 28–31 is outside of the so-called cycles.

For a first reading of the speeches, a profile of each of the speakers can be offered. Eliphaz is not Zophar, and even Job is not consistent with himself. In the second reading one can follow in detail the several twists and turns of each character. Here we wish merely to set up the broad lines of discourse by describing each speaker.

Eliphaz. As already indicated (Job 4:1–5:27), this man seems well-disposed toward Job; he attempts to dissuade him from his reckless speech, and puts before him a description of a happy future (5:17-27). The increasing edginess and anger in the repartee is easily noticed. In 15:1-35 Eliphaz is sarcastic; he repeats himself (cf. 15:14-16 with 4:17-19) and concludes with a description of the fate of the wicked. In his third speech (22:1-30) Eliphaz accuses Job directly of wrongdoing, but he ends upon a happy note of deliverance *if* Job turns to God.

Bildad. He, too, holds out the prospect of divine blessing if only Job will turn to God (8:5-7, 20-22). A second time (18:1-21) he rebukes Job and provides a description of the fate of the wicked (cf. Eliphaz, 15:17-35). The very short (and suspect) third speech contrasts divine majesty with human corruption.

Zophar. In a scattershot approach (11:1-20) Zophar exalts divine majesty in contrast to human sinfulness. But a happy future awaits Job if he will repent. His second speech goes back to a favorite theme: the fate of the wicked. Mercifully, perhaps, there is no third speech, and the significance of this is debated.

Job. It is almost impossible to give a brief characterization of Job's speeches. His various arguments and varying moods constitute a charming aspect of the book. He uses the speeches of the friends as mere foils for his outbursts. He has nothing to prove, but only the reader knows that. He knows he is without fault and is suffering "without cause" (the phrase used in 1:9 and 2:3), but he cannot prove it. He can only maintain it (27:2-6). It is always God to whom Job is speaking, directly or indirectly. It is almost as if he bypasses the "arguments" of the three friends of whom he remarks that silence would be their (only) proof of wisdom (13:5)! The author pulls out all the stops: Job attacking God (9:22-24), proclaiming his despair and desire for respite in Sheol (9:16-19; 10:20-22) hoping against hope (13:15), entertaining the idea of some kind of arbiter (9:33; 16:19; 19:25-27—perhaps God against God?), making touching pleas (10:3-12), searching for God in the "dark night" (ch. 23), recalling the memory of former days (ch. 29) and ending his speeches with bravado (ch. 31). Job is a subtle character and not subject to our logical verdicts about his inconsistency.

The Speeches of Elihu

Elihu (32:1–37:24) has puzzled commentators. After his pompous introduction (ch. 32) he appears to be one of the first readers of the previous speeches, for he picks up several ideas from what has gone before and develops them (e.g., the medicinal aspect of suffering, 33:14-30), and he voices a remarkable hymn to the divine power. But he disappears as suddenly as he appeared in the beginning (ch. 32).

The Speeches of the Lord

By the time the reader reaches ch. 38 and the theophany of the LORD there is an expectancy: now a real answer will be given to Job! The striking and somehow beautiful irrelevance of the speeches of the LORD (38:1–41:34) constitute magnificent poetry. Moreover they are effective, to judge from Job's reaction in 40:2-5—which can be taken as the beginning of his transformation. The final surrender of Job to God is based on a *vision* of the Lord that chs. 38–41 articulate in words. There are many unanswered questions one would like to raise. But we are left only with a vision, an experience such as Job had (42:5).

SECOND READING

Prologue: Job 1–2

The opening verses (1:1-5) make the virtue of Job perfectly clear: he is blameless and upright. In line with typical biblical thought, he is blessed accordingly in a manner that suggests an ancient Semitic patriarch: immense possessions of sheep and camels, oxen and asses. His tender conscience is illustrated by his offering holocausts for his children, just in case they may have done wrong and "blasphemed" (lit., "blessed"—a euphemism for "curse" when this word is used with God as object; cf. 1:11; 2:5, 9).

The sudden change of scene to the heavenly court galvanizes the narrative. YHWH (only in the prologue and epilogue and in introducing God's speeches in 38:1 and 40:1 is the sacred name used) musters out the "sons of Elohim," the members of the heavenly court who do the divine bidding. Among them is "the Satan," whose function is revealed in the casual conversation the LORD initiates. His mission is to patrol the earth. In that case, what does he think of YHWH's servant Job? The latter's virtue is described by the LORD in the same words as those of v. 2. Then comes one of the most important questions in the Bible—and on the lips of the Satan: "Is it for nothing that Job fears God?" And the Satan presses on: "Have you not hedged about him and his family and all his possessions?" In other words, who would not be God-fearing under those conditions? This is a fundamental issue in life: what is the quality of one's love of God? Are there not degrees or limits, as Bernard of Clairvaux (*On the Love of God,* chs. 8–9) indicated?

According to him the first degree is when we love ourselves for our own sake, our own interest. This can be expanded by love of one's neighbor. Then there is disinterested love, not offered with a view to obtaining anything. Such is the third degree: love of God not for one's own sake, but for the sake of God. Where does Job fit in? So the Satan calls for a test: take away all that he has and he will curse (again the euphemism, "bless") the LORD to his face. The agreement or wager is struck, but Job's person is not to be touched.

What kind of a God is this? Is not the LORD omniscient (and thus unfairly entering into this agreement, since he knows the outcome)? Apparently this is not the supposition of the author. Moreover, on the supposition of divine omniscience the LORD would be little more than an unfeeling tyrant in causing the calamities that follow. So God does *not* know whether Job will pass the test. If one were to claim that God knew, and so could have refused the challenge of the Satan, then the reader can ask another question: Would it be because God feared that Job might be serving merely for personal gain? Would God be hesitant to trust creatures to show loyalty in the face of adversity? When one comes to think of it, just why does one love God? Is there any way of knowing that a love is genuine except by its being tested? In a sense, the author has put YHWH in a no-win situation: a tyrant because he says yes, uncertain and timorous if he says no. This is certainly not a naive scene in the heavenly court; it is fraught with implications for human living.

The narrative wastes no time in describing the tragic results for Job and his possessions. The four catastrophes are announced by messengers, one on the heels of the other, that raids, lightning, and storm have destroyed everything. Job's reaction is famous: his sorrow is great but his faith in God is greater. There is the deliberate notice that Job is without sin (1:22).

But the Satan is not yet finished, and we are treated to a kind of repetition of the heavenly court scene. The LORD taunts the Satan "for nothing (as in 1:9, "without cause") you have incited me against him." But the Satan calls for a second test. A direct affliction of Job's person is now put forth. The LORD grants this and Job is struck with a disease that we cannot identify with certainty except that he rubs himself with potsherds to obtain relief. Job's wife seems to have had enough and she offers the ambiguous words, "Curse (i.e., "bless") God and die." St. Augustine regarded her as the "helper of the devil" (and this is no help in understanding the scene). It is not clear if she is sarcastic (she repeats the words God uses in 2:3) or if she is proposing a way out for Job (if he cursed God, would he not be obliterated by God?). At any rate, Job holds no regard for her remark, and proclaims that one must accept both evil and good from God (since God is the cause of both in the OT view of things). Again the author notes Job's sinlessness (2:10). This is quite deliberate since for the purposes of this work the hero must be a saint. It would not be surprising if a reader asked whether Job is gutless. At this point one doesn't know; there are only the words of the author that Job is sincere. But it will be clear from the dialogue to follow that Job is far from gutless. And again the understanding of YHWH that is presupposed in both of the heavenly court scenes is bothersome to many readers of the Bible. It is not a solution to say that this is only the imaginative description of the author. It is that, but it also means that his conception of God did not exclude such actions. The situation is similar to the *Akedah,* the "binding" of Isaac (Genesis 22), when Abraham is told to sacrifice his son and the reality of the scene is taken for granted. The LORD is such a God, mysterious indeed.

Chapter 2 closes with the appearance of Job's three friends. Their reaction is appropriate (2:12-13); they display the customary signs of grief and show extreme sensitivity by their seven-day silence—so appalling is Job's condition. At this point we merely mention the hypothesis that the proper continuation in the "original" narrative was in 42:7-17, where Job's restoration is described. Thus a story with a happy ending was supposedly taken over by the author of the book of Job to give the framework for the dialogue that is to follow. All this is a matter of conjecture. What is not conjecture is the manner in which the author has already enlisted the sympathy of the reader for the innocent Job. At the same time it would be a mistake to think that the author is not fair to the three friends in the dialogue that follows. He makes no effort to caricature them, even though his intention to support Job, his mouthpiece, is clear. All the speakers (including Elihu and YHWH, who will eventually appear) are to be taken seriously. The fact of the matter is that the author had no "inside" information about the problem of human suffering.

One can maintain with confidence that the author did not agree with the reasoning of the friends, but their view was shared by many in Israel. God rewards the good and punishes the evil—on a social level (this is the view of the Deuteronomistic history) as well as on an individual level. When the principle is reversed and one concludes from suffering to sinfulness, then the problem appears in all its sharpness. That is the mistake of the three friends (and also it is clear in the question of the disciples in John 9:21). Some have argued that there existed in Israel a firm belief that there was a mechanical connection between an action and its result: a good act begot good results, and a bad act begot bad results. Inherently, punishment follows upon a bad action; when I dig a pit for an innocent person to fall into, I end up falling into it (cf. Prov 26:27; Ps 7:15-17, etcetera). It could not have taken long to see through this; retributive or "poetic" justice simply does not follow such a neat rule of thumb. It is often claimed that Job himself was of the same mentality until he experienced his personal suffering. But is Job's mentality that simple? When we analyze the speeches that he makes, we find that he is not grousing about the possessions he lost. All he can see is the divine indifference, indeed hostility, to him. He has no other way of judging his sad plight. If he is applying human standards of justice to God, he is of course mistaken, and he shares in the common tendency of human beings to do that. But he never seems to deal with God on a *quid pro quo* basis even when he argues with God. It is his personal relationship to the deity that has been destroyed. This he cannot understand.

Job: Job 3

The contrast between the Job of ch. 1 and the Job of ch. 3 is striking; there is a movement from resignation to cursing. Yet the tone and temper of ch. 3 are not as strong as that of many of the laments preserved in the psalter. True, Job curses the day he was born (Jer 20:14-18 is a similar curse), and the artistry and skill with which he develops his curse is of such a high order that one does not feel at first the power of his explosion. Perhaps the most striking line is v. 4: "let there be darkness"; this exactly negates the words of God at creation, "let there be light" (Gen 1:3). The question "why?" (vv. 11, 12, 20) is also characteristic of laments. But on the whole this outburst is mild; it cannot compare with the complaints Job will register against God in the dialogues to come. Indeed, God is mentioned only once, in v. 23 and in a somewhat indirect way. It is also an ironic mention because it speaks of God "hedging in" the way of one who is lost. This is the same word that the Satan uses in 1:10 to describe God's *favorable* treatment of Job: surrounding him with prosperity. It is only in vv. 24-26 that Job explicitly describes, in a very general way, his sufferings. For the rest the lament sounds a more universal note: "why is light given to the sufferer?" (v. 20). Job of course includes himself among those who are thus stricken, and he launches into a description of Sheol that makes it look very desirable. There everyone is equal, high and low alike, for death is the great leveler. But at least it would be some kind of respite from his present suffering. Sheol/Death is a motif to which he will have recourse again (cf. 7:15, 21; 10:21-22). The tone is subdued, but Job is only warming up for the debate.

Eliphaz: Job 4–5

In a similar way the reaction of Eliphaz is low-keyed: Job should derive some consolation from the counsel he has often given to people who were in a similar situation. Job's "fear" of God and his "blamelessness" (*tam,* the same word used in 1:1, 9) should be his source of strength. But v. 7 is not very promising; it assures Job that the innocent and upright will be preserved; it is the wicked who will be punished. Where does that leave Job? Then in a remarkable description of some kind of theophany Eliphaz describes an experience that issues in a platitude: mortals cannot be righteous before God who finds fault even in the angels—how much more true would this be in the case of lowly human beings (4:12-21)! Eliphaz hardly needed a special revelation to support the conclusion that the righteousness of God is unique!

He goes on to point out that Job has no hope for an intercessor among the holy ones of the heavenly court (the "sons of God" mentioned in 1:6). Without explicitly identifying Job as an immoral fool, he describes their fate and that of their progeny. Mortals are like that, "born for mischief." Hence they must have recourse to God who is all-powerful, saving the lowly and the poor (vv. 7-16). A still greater paradox: "Happy is the one whom God reproves." Eliphaz develops this view (vv. 17-27) from the sayings in Prov 3:11-12. Chastisement is a sign of God's love? If there was a warm tone to the beginning of Eliphaz's speech, a certain cold logic has now appeared. It is not directly accusatory. It is a lecture, but Job cannot mistake that he is the target of the lecture, and that his condition is somehow due to his sinfulness. If only he would turn to God he would be delivered. This mode of lecturing on the part of the friends will return again and again. It is striking that they never address God. In contrast, Job will give out a few lectures or answers of his own, but he will also address God directly (cf. chs. 3–14), and his appeal to God will be a delicate mixture of complaint and prayer. It should be noted that all parties refer to God as "El" or "Eloah" or "El Shaddai" (perhaps "the mountain one," rendered as "Almighty" in the LXX).

Job: Job 6–7

Job's reply is typical of the indirection that is employed in his argument; he goes on for thirteen verses without mentioning his friends. There is very little logic to the sequence of argument between them all; occasionally one will attempt a direct response to the words of another, but the reader gets the impression that the author is letting each speaker make his own point without particular concern for mutual answers. Job's opening words here are intensely emotional: no suffering can be compared to the "arrows of the Almighty" that have struck him. In two obscure sayings (vv. 5-6) he indicates that he has every reason to speak as he does. This is followed by a bold but confident statement that if God would do away with him, his consolation would be his fidelity to God (vv. 8-10). But he has no more strength left. As to the friends, they do not show the loyalty that should be expected; instead they are comparable to wadies that are full of water in the rainy season and dry the rest of the time, thus deceiving all wayfarers. His friends merely serve up words, not actions—ugly characters, as the insult of v. 27 indicates. He challenges them to show where he is wrong (v. 24), so firm is he in his own clean conscience (vv. 28-30).

In ch. 7 Job begins a description of the human condition that soon turns into a complaint about his own physical and mental condition: nights of physical suffering with no hope for any letup, only for death and Sheol. In vv. 7-8 there is an interesting development of the theme of vision. Job recognizes that he will never see happiness again, and that the *eye that beholds* him will not see him. Then, addressing God directly, he says "your eye will see me and I shall be gone" (to Sheol). It is clear from this and the whole tenor of the book that Job entertains no hope of a life with God after death; there is only the darkness of Sheol. A certain soft sadness attaches to these words about the divine gaze. But it is shattered by the violent tone of vv. 11-21. Actually God has placed a guard over him, as though he were *Yam,* the Sea, or the Dragon (the obstreperous powers of chaos; cf. 3:8; 26:12; 41:1; Isa 51:9-10). This torture is too much; his life is but a breath, so better that he die now (cf. 3:11-19). In vv. 17-21 he launches into another bitter attack upon God by making a parody of Psalm 8, which is filled with awe and admiration of the creation of human beings when seen against the whole panorama of God's creative activity (see also Ps 144:3). Now the divine solicitude is described as harsh and unrelenting in searching out human failings. God, the great watcher and spy, just will not let up! If God is so forgiving (Exod 34:6), one would think such mercy might be shown to Job. At least this should be expected (even if Job is not willing to admit any sin and is in fact blameless, as the reader knows from chs. 1–2). God is so distant from Job despite the close watch that any putative sin of Job is a nothing. His last words (v. 21) even imply that God might have some afterthoughts about the whole thing—God would look for Job (tenderly)—but Job would be gone (in Sheol).

Bildad: Job 8

Bildad is cast as a theological "heavy." He dismisses Job's words as "mighty wind" and ponderously asks the impossible: does the Almighty distort justice? He makes an indelicate reference to Job's children (v. 4) and assures Job of God's protection (and also future prosperity; he sounds like the Satan in a different key). He delivers his lecture in vv. 8-22 about the teaching that the stalwarts of past generations have handed down.

Verses 11-13 are a kind of parabolic proverb about plants (v. 8) that need water and care (as mortals need God). The godless will perish but God will care for the virtuous (vv. 14-19 are not clear).

Job: Job 9–10

In ch. 9 Job contemplates the possibility of a legal contest with God and legal language is prominent. From the outset he states that it is impossible for him to have a fair trial (vv. 2-4; 14-20). Why? No one can resist the divine power, and Job launches into a gripping portrayal of the manifestations of God's rule of the universe: heavens and earth and constellations. Before these wonders Job can only confess bewilderment: "If he passes by me, I cannot see him . . . Who can say to him, what are you doing?" (vv. 11-12). The legal situation is therefore utterly devastating: "Even though I were in the right, I could not answer him . . . I do not think he would listen to me" (vv. 15-16).

Unwittingly Job states that God wounds him "without cause" (the very word the LORD uses against the Satan in 2:3!—of course the author repeats this deliberately) and thus he speaks more truly than he knows. The reader gets the impression that Job is not really speaking to the friends but to himself—a soliloquy that closes with a bitter accusation against God who is irresponsible, destroying both "the innocent and the wicked" (v. 22). Or better, God *is* responsible! In OT thought God is the agent behind everything that occurs, good or evil (e.g., Isa 45:7). God is worse than wicked judges. In 9:25 Job begins a complaint addressed to God (vv. 28b, 31): his life is short; there is no hope for acquittal, and so forth. The first appearance of an arbiter or mediator occurs: in v. 23 Job laments the lack of such a person, but the idea will linger in his heart (cf. 16:19; 19:25).

One of the most moving complaints appears in ch. 10. Job still wishes to know the charge, and he plays cleverly on the attachment that the creator must necessarily feel for the creature, despite all appearances. It is almost as if the creator should get in touch with reality. Why despise "the work of your hands?" (10:3), or is there no sympathy in the creator, as though God were a fussy, narrow-minded mortal? Could it be that God is as shortsighted as humans, after all? Job's sarcasm is deft and almost gentle at this point, as if he refuses to believe that God can act thus. Why search for sin in me when you really cannot find any? He reminds God of the tender care that went into his formation (cf. Ps 139:14-15). But this almost loving recollection is destroyed by the ugly fact of that terrible "watch" (v. 14) to catch Job in sin. Then "if I should be guilty, woe is me; and even if innocent, I dare not lift up my head" (v. 15).

Job returns to the old question "why?" (cf. 3:11-16). Instead of obtaining respite, such as a transition from womb to grave would provide, he is given a short span of life (filled with suffering), and then off to Sheol, the place of deepest darkness. When we look back at chs. 9–10 we cannot but admire the twists and turns that the author gives to Job's arguments and complaints: fanatical charges against God on the one hand, and on the other a refusal to really give up on God—as it were appealing to God against God, from the God he knew to the God he cannot find (9:11). His statements of despair are colored with faith, and are never to be seen apart from his faith. This is the verisimilitude that characterizes the author, who is able to experience and express the extremes of despair and hope.

Zophar: Job 11

Zophar's opening words to Job are harsh, but he stumbles into unconscious irony in vv. 4-5 in wishing that God might speak to Job and reveal to him "the secrets of wisdom." His wish will be granted indeed, but not in the way that Zophar imagines! He has begun on a lofty tone (God's secrets) and he continues discoursing about the mystery of God in terms of its enormous majesty, higher than the heavens, deeper than Sheol, broader than earth and deeper than the sea. Basically, however, he shares the same blind view as his comrades. Job must obviously be at fault; he is urged to turn to God, and his life will be changed (vv. 13-20).

Job: Job 12–14

This is the last in what is usually called the first cycle of speeches between Job and the three friends. The tension can be seen to grow steadily. Job begins with the sarcastic gibe that wisdom shall die with them (12:2). He has as much "heart" (i.e., intelligence) as they. Indeed, wisdom is also found in the mere beasts of the earth, the fish and birds, for they all know that "the hand of the Lord has done this" (v. 9). Here Job seems to quote Isa 41:20 (this would explain the unique use of the sacred name here within one of the speeches). "Hand" in the Bible is an ambiguous organ; normally it means power, but it could mean loving care. The description in vv. 14-25 clearly indicates that power, and raw power at that, is meant. Wisdom does not belong to age and experience as tradition has it; it is the property of God (v. 13). What seems to start out as a hymn in honor of divine wisdom now turns into a savage description of the destructive power of God. Typical is the divine dealing with the waters: holding them back so that a drought results and letting them loose to destroy the land. There is this positive and negative rhythm to God's way with creation. The various classes of leaders are likewise subject to the divine whim: king, priests, elders, and princes. God calls up darkness (v. 22) and all of society is upset, only to end up in darkness (v. 25).

At the close of this rather rambling discourse Job claims to have seen and known all God's actions (13:1-2). His knowledge is as great as that of the friends (if not, by implication, greater). He would dismiss them since he wishes to argue with God (13:3), not with them. They are liars and lying for God is dangerous (here Job is defending the divine honor against these deceitful three!). Job trusts in his own honesty against their lies on behalf of the divinity; true wisdom for them would be silence.

Job calls imperiously to them to be quiet while he speaks, come what may. This bravado is continued in v. 14 in an obscure verse ("I take my flesh in my teeth," v. 14a), that must indicate some risk (cf. "my life in my hands," 14b). One of the famous quotations is the King James rendering of 13:15, "though he slay me, yet will I trust in him." But the Hebrew text is ambiguous. The reading *(Qere)* suggests "will trust in him" (I will hope), but the consonantal text *(Ketib)* reads a similar sounding word meaning "not" in place of "in him" (thus yielding the translation "I have no hope"). In any case Job is going to continue pressing his cause (lit., "his way," v. 15b). The author may be responsible for permitting the ambiguity in this verse, but he never in fact allows Job to give up hope. Indeed, v. 16 speaks of "salvation" or deliverance as a possibility because of his innocence: "no impious person can come before him." It is remarkable how Job alternates between despair and faith, faith in God as well as in himself and his integrity.

Indeed, Job seems reinvigorated. He calls upon his friends to witness the case he is to make (13:17-18) and then glides into direct address to God. It is the old question: what are my faults and my sins? Why this treatment of me? Although he speaks of the "faults of my youth" (13:26), this cannot be taken seriously. It appears to be a way of magnifying the horrendous suffering he is now undergoing, not a real admission of sin. The tenor of the argument that he is building up (14:1-6) is the sorry plight of the human condition—why is God so judgmental in the case of poor human beings, frail and limited in days of life? Let God look away so that humans like Job can have some respite.

At this point Job moves on to a remarkable comparison between trees and humans. He personifies a tree, as if it can have "hope"; i.e., a tree, like a human being, faces death. It is cut down but it has the "hope" of living again even after death. One can witness the rebirth of trees in the constant cycle of nature's life. But when human beings die? They will never again be roused from their sleep. Life disappears from them like the absence of water from what was a lake. In a bold leap of imagination in 14:14-17, Job then expresses the wish that God would "hide" him in Sheol, here conceived of as a shelter from the passing divine wrath. Then God would remember him—and divine remembrance is not merely a function of memory, but of re-presentation—a matter of re-establishing a former relationship of care and love. Ah, were mortals to live again! Job would endure anything ("all the days of my service I would wait" v. 14b) until that moment of rebirth. He describes the happy awakening: "You would call, and I would answer you; you would esteem the work of your hands" (v. 15). The current antagonistic relationship where God seems to be on the watch for Job's downfall would be all past, obliterated, as if his "sin were sealed up in a pouch" (v. 17) Again, Job is not admitting here to sin, but to the conduct that is conceived as deserving of the treatment Job has received—iniquities are not seen because they don't exist. But this is all impossible. "As waters wear away stone," God destroys human hope (in contrast to the "hope" of the tree, v. 7). Human beings perish forever, with no consolation that their children might have been successful or failures—without knowing anything except grief (vv. 18-22).

It seems almost impossible psychologically for Job to have entertained this unlikely prospect of living again only to relapse into despair. The comparison with the constant revival of nature is perhaps not an unusual one for the poet to think of. But the powerful emotional thrust that is given to this vision is almost unparalleled in the book. It is one of the deepest expressions of a desire for immortality that one can find in the OT. It captures succinctly a modern question: can/does one live again? The so-called first cycle of speeches has ended.

Eliphaz: Job 15

The second speech of Eliphaz is in striking contrast to the first. He attacks Job immediately, comparing his speech to the hot dry sirocco from the desert, as impious and sinful. He sarcastically rejects Job's claim to wisdom with the question of his age (ever the sign of wisdom among the sages): Was Job born before the Primal Man (a myth referred to in Ezek 28:11-19)? Has he listened in on the divine decision-making? One need only remember that it is personified wisdom who is described as being present before and during the creation of the world according to Prov 8:22-31. Eliphaz is making a rather erudite gibe at Job's arguments. He retains the image of an elder, and in the spirit of 4:6 he talks about the "consolations of God" that should have buoyed up the spirit of Job and kept him from his angry outbursts. The phrase of Ps 8:5, "what are human beings?" is repeated by Eliphaz (as if the parody on this psalm by Job in 7:17 had never been heard!) and he returns to the old theme of human sinfulness (cf. 4:17) and angelic guilt (5:1). This supposedly should make it easier for Job, a mere human, to admit his sinfulness. Eliphaz takes up the usual lecture mode, out of touch with reality as he describes the fate of the wicked (15:20-35): a list of catastrophes—robbery, darkness, the sword, the loss of everything.

Job: Job 16–17

Job can rightly reply that he has heard all this before from "the comforters of trouble," as he calls them (a kind of oxymoron: their comfort—such was their original purpose in 2:11—brings suffering; cf. 13:4). But talk is cheap, and Job turns his attention to a description of the attack that God has launched against him (vv. 7-17). The divine actions are violent, and the style of the description is similar to the laments of the psalter: tearing, mockery, blows, arrows, and so forth. These are conventional images. No one can live through such an assault; Job is in a piteous condition, weeping and praying (vv. 16-17).

Job calls upon the earth as though it were a person to cover not his blood—not only to let it be seen, but also to be heard. This idea is reflected in the old belief that the blood of one who has been unjustly put to death will live on to obtain vengeance from God (thus the blood of Abel in Gen 4:10). At least there will be a posthumous vindication for such a person. As a second measure he claims to have a spokesperson in heaven who will give testimony in his favor. With whom is this mediator to be identified? Several answers are given by commentators. Perhaps it is God (cf. 19:25-27), or perhaps the prayer of Job? Others think it is a member of the heavenly court (cf. 9:33) despite the denial of Eliphaz in 5:1. Whatever be the precise meaning, there will be a voice in his favor even though Job himself is practically in the grave. Time is running out.

Another possibility presents itself to Job's imagination. Is it possible that some one would go surety for him? The idea of pledge or going surety for another (who is, for example, in debt or in some distress) is mentioned frequently in the Bible. It may be a duty but it is not to be taken lightly in any case (the sages frequently warn against it; cf. Prov 6:1; 11:15, etcetera). Job rejects the idea himself because of the way he has been treated. He is visibly an outcast of society and no one with any sense would speak for him—unless it would be that ever-mysterious God? In vv. 11-16 he returns to the motif of Sheol, but this time it is not a place of respite; it is a place of corruption where hope (repeated twice in v. 15) is utterly extinguished.

Bildad: Job 18

In 16:9 Job accused God of tearing him to pieces. But no, says Bildad, that is what Job is doing to himself (18:4). Then he launches into a favorite *topos* of the three friends: the fate of the wicked person: plunged into darkness, caught by all kinds of traps, consumed by the "first-born of death" (i.e., disease), tent destroyed, progeny gone, no longer remembered by later generations except as a horror.

Job: Job 19

In this chapter Job never speaks to God (for the first time), but the chapter contains (v. 25) an act of faith made famous by Handel's *Messiah* ("I know that my redeemer liveth and that he shall stand at the latter day upon the earth . . ."). Job speaks directly to the friends, accusing them of unjust reproaches because God is to blame for his condition. He then describes the divine onslaught as if it were a battle with God's army pitched around his tent. Furthermore he is an outcast to all—friends, relatives, and servants—even to his wife (there is some exaggeration in this *typical* description; the author is not interested in historical information about Job's wife). In the face of such opposition Job calls out for pity, for "the hand of God has struck me" (cf. 12:9), and also appeals that his words may become a permanent record, etched in rock forever: "As for me, I know that my vindicator lives . . . ."

Unfortunately the text of 19:25-27 is very obscure, probably corrupt. But a few points are quite clear. This is an act of faith in a *goʾel* (vindicator, not "redeemer"), namely one who will come to his aid. The *goʾel* was a person next of kin who fulfilled certain obligations to a less fortunate relative: financial help, redeeming from slavery (as the Lord "redeemed" Israel from the Egyptians, Exod 6:6), etcetera. Who is the "vindicator?" Job has already pointed out in vv. 13-19 that he has no one upon whom he can rely. Previous to this he has wished for an arbiter or mediator (9:30; 16:19), but he has not identified this figure. Traditionally, the *goʾel* in v. 25 has been identified with God. This is not an easy solution. Job has been crying out against God as his enemy throughout the book. It is quite an assumption to think he means God here. What is clearly stated is that he will *see* this figure. This is emphasized by *threefold* repetition of seeing (God?) in vv. 26-27. When and how is this to occur? The text fails us at this point: One cannot be sure if this is before or after death (and does it anticipate the vision of the Lord in chs. 38–42?) In 42:5 there is great emphasis on Job's seeing God with the eye. But it must be admitted that the text of 19:26-27 is terribly ambiguous on the question of time and manner. A traditional translation, considerably influenced by the Vulgate rendition of St. Jerome, supported the idea of a resurrection for Job. This is not likely; the Hebrew text is, as we have claimed, quite obscure, and moreover the situation of Job would have been considerably different if he actually entertained a resurrection belief. The statements about Sheol and mortality throughout the book (e.g., 14:7-22) rule out such an expectation on the part of Job. But the passage (vv. 25-27) is a clear affirmation of faith in a vindicator, a *goʾel* (possibly to be identified with God) whom Job will certainly see with his own eyes (cf. 7:7-8, the eyes of God). In the circumstances of the dialogue thus far it is a remarkable faith statement in a deliverer. The chapter closes with a warning to the friends that their accusation of him should make them fear a sword-like judgment.

Zophar: Job 20

Zophar's opening words would suggest that he has found Job's last remarks upsetting, but he presses on with the usual lecture concerning the fate of the wicked. The triumph of the wicked is shortlived; they will disappear, and Zophar expresses this (vv. 4-11) in several ways (like a dream; people will ask, "where is he?"). Though such a person grow rich, prosperity will not endure (vv. 12-22). God will wage a war against him or her unto utter destruction (vv. 23-29). There is not much new here; the fate of the wicked has been described many times before by one or another of the friends (5:12-16; 15:17-35; 18:5-12).

Job: Job 21

Job concentrates on the friends. If only they would listen to him; that would be "consolation" (21:2). They could and should learn something just by contemplating his situation (vv. 2-6). Now Job will tell them what the fate of the wicked is really like (vv. 7-24). The prosperous and good life that the orthodox theory holds for the virtuous is in fact the lot of the wicked, despite their rejection of God (15-16). Job wants the divine wrath to be brought down upon them, not upon their children (as the traditional orthodoxy held out). How are tranquillity in life for one and suffering for another to be reconciled? Both end up in Sheol, and that is not justice. The friends are naive; anyone could overturn their arguments by pointing out that the wicked go down to Sheol in peace (v. 33, "sweet to them are the clods of the valley," i.e., where they are buried).

Eliphaz: Job 22

The speech of Eliphaz is generally considered as introducing the so-called third cycle that is judged by most commentators to be somehow mangled because Zophar does not make an appearance as in the first two "cycles." There is neat irony in Eliphaz's opening lines. Yes, Shaddai *does* gain if Job remains faithful—the Satan's judgment of Job will have been proved wrong; the LORD has reason to trust his servant for true love and sincerity. The friends do not so much accuse Job of specific sins as presume that he is a sinner; his suffering "proves" that. They are shocked by his passionate outbursts but reply only with generalizations about the fate of the wicked and the blessings of the just. Eliphaz has been considerate, but now he accuses Job of specific sins: social sins against neighbor (the most piteous, hungry, thirsty, widows, orphans, vv. 6-9). That is why he has been suffering. God is omniscient, sees all and judges all. Hence the denial of God offered by Job and the wicked will be punished. But Eliphaz holds out restoration for Job if he converts and returns to God who is the deliverer of the innocent (vv. 21-30).

Job: Job 23–24

Job's reply is a bitter lament over the absence of God in his life: he cannot find God (vv. 3, 8-9). It is true that behind this lies his old desire for due process. At the same time it helps us to see that the issue for Job is far deeper than any *quid pro quo* arrangement such as the Satan had suggested in the prologue. Job is upset because his relationship to God is apparently destroyed. Yet he retains confidence that his own upright character, i.e., his fidelity to God, would be recognized. In any kind of testing he "would emerge as gold" because of his loyalty. But Job can go no further. God does what God wishes to do, and that is the bottom line. That is why Job is terrified: God is so puzzling. Despite the divine justice, conditions on earth are outrageous and Job lists a series of wrongdoings that affect the poor especially (24:2-11). Darkness is the ideal time for the injustice that is perpetrated (vv. 12-17). The remaining verses (17-24) are obscure. Job can hardly be mouthing the traditional theory; these lines may be curses that he levels at the wicked. He closes with an air of bravado about the irrefutability of his statements.

Bildad: Job 25

Suspicions are cast on these six verses (the shortest chapter in the book), and many hypotheses have been put forward to account for them (e.g., Job interrupts in 26:1-4 and Bildad continues in 26:5-14). The few lines of Bildad are surprising in that they sustain a hymnic tone about the divine dominion and power.

Job: Job 26–27

After the usual antagonistic introduction Job presents a short hymn, almost as it were a continuation of what Bildad started to say in 25:2-3. This is not the first time for this topic (cf. 9:3-10; 12:9-25), but there is a strikingly admiring and reverent tone to what are called "the outlines of his ways," "the whisper of what we hear of him" (v. 14). All areas are included; the poem begins with Sheol and Abaddon (place of perishing; cf. 28:22), and ends with the Sea, Rahab, and the dragon, none of whom can escape the divine hand. The poem abounds in these mythological references. God even creates the North (Zaphon, the mountain of the divine assembly or heavenly court), and leaves the earth hanging out in space. Clouds, moon, horizon ("the boundary of light and darkness," v. 10) are all God's handiwork.

The hymn tone ends abruptly with ch. 27, where Job is introduced by a new phrase: he takes up a *mashal* (so also in 29:1), i.e., a "theme" or "discourse." He proceeds to make solemn oaths, "as God lives," in vv. 2-4; "far be it from me," in v. 5. The paradox in all this is his oath by the life of the God who *withholds* his right—on the life of that God he affirms his innocence! He asserts that God is unjust at the same time that he, Job, is innocent. "Far be it from me" means "let it be profane to me," i.e., it would be sacrilege for Job to act otherwise than he has done. He remains faithful to the avowal of innocence he has upheld throughout and that was originally acknowledged by the LORD (1:8; 2:3). How does the series of purificatory oaths in ch. 31 differ from these? There he wishes an evil upon himself that would be appropriate to the crime he denies he has committed, but here he defies God in the very words of the oath: "As God lives who withholds my right."

The rest of the chapter yields problems. Job speaks of an enemy in the singular whom the LORD will punish; perhaps this is an imprecation. In vv. 11-12 he seems to speak to the friends and promises them a lesson. The lesson that follows in 13-25 is one that they do not need. It describes the fate that the wicked receive from God. Is he promising them that such a future faces them, thus turning the tables on them? The description is typical of what the friends have said about the fate of the wicked: descendants are destroyed, fortune is lost, and the wicked person is swept away. Is Job making a parody of the typical lectures that they have delivered to him in the past?

A Poem on Wisdom: Job 28

Chapter 28 is famous for several reasons. It presents a personification of wisdom and thus resembles other such personifications (e.g., Proverbs 8; Sirach 24). It is not introduced as spoken by Job or the three; moreover, it seems to be out of character, if not irrelevant, in view of the debate thus far. Hence it has been judged to be a later insertion, although many try to integrate it into the book as an "interlude." The point of the poem on wisdom is found in the refrains in vv. 12 and 20, asking "where is wisdom to be found?" (see also Bar 3:9-44). The answer is deceptively simple. The poet begins with a description of how precious stones can be found by digging deep into the earth. Treasures are hidden there and no animals can find them, only humans. But the location of wisdom is a mystery, and the author develops the theme. Wisdom is far more precious than the gold and precious minerals that humans can find and it is hidden from everyone, even the Sea and the Abyss. Sheol has merely heard about wisdom. Finally (vv. 23-27) it is said that God knows the way to it. This might be expected since God *sees* the entire universe and set it up (vv. 24-26). But what did God do with wisdom? Verse 27 is quite vague: God numbered and measured and probed it. It is not said where God put it, but it appears to be somewhere in the world (see vv. 23-26). Then suddenly in 28:28 we read: "He said to humankind: 'Lo, the fear of the LORD is wisdom; to avoid evil is understanding.'" This seems to be a line added to the poem, telling the reader, after all the futility and vagueness of vv. 1-27, where wisdom is to be found. Obviously it interprets the poem in a traditional way, connecting it with the description of Job in 1:1. Fear of the LORD is a key idea in the wisdom literature (e.g., Prov 1:7; 9:10). Many would regard this line as an addition, but it is also interpretive, answering more clearly than the poem itself just where wisdom is to be found. In the context of the book is this the author suggesting another view concerning wisdom—informing the reader that ultimately wisdom is beyond us, that we cannot solve the problem that the book has raised? Then the only solution is the practical one of fear of God. We really cannot get beyond Job 1:1, 8, where (at least implicitly) wisdom is seen in terms of conduct, in contrast to 28:1-27, where precious wisdom seems to be the divine knowledge itself, utterly at God's disposal.

Let it not be thought that this ch. 28 is reductionistic, that it cancels the honesty that lies behind the exploration of divine governance. The author is simply putting up front all the considerations that can be brought to bear. Fear of the LORD and the very mystery of wisdom are involved. And this is still not the final word, since the speeches of the LORD remain to be heard.

Job: Job 29–31

The debate is over; we will not hear again from the three friends. But Job is far from finished. In these chapters he delivers a long harangue, and only at the end does he address God directly. The chapters can be divided thus: 29: Job's description of the good life he once enjoyed; 30: a lament over the change that has led to his present status; 31: a series of purificatory oaths that witness to his innocence, and a final bold word to God.

Contrasts to Job's present condition abound throughout this soliloquy: Light as opposed to darkness (29:3), the presence of God instead of absence (vv. 4-5). Publicly Job was at the height of his power and acknowledged by all, especially for his righteousness (v. 15): "eyes to the blind and feet to the lame." No wonder he thought he would end his days like the phoenix (a reference to the myth of the bird that ever renews its life). Job "lived like a king" and enjoyed the esteem of all in those good old days. But now he has been brought so low by the divine treatment that he is beneath the scum of society (30:1-9) who ridicule and even persecute him (vv. 12-14), and he is finishing his days in misery. He appeals to God (vv. 20-23), but without much real hope: "I cry out to you and you do not answer me; while I stand you look at me. You turn upon me mercilessly . . ." (20-21). Despite his care for others, he finds now only darkness and ostracism from society ("a brother of jackals"); in such suffering his music is to the tune of mourning and weeping.

Chapter 31 is famous as a series of imprecatory oaths that have been compared to the confessions of the Egyptian funerary texts. There is a regular formula: "If I have acted in such a manner (mention of the crime), let such and such (the punishment) be done to me"; cf. vv. 7-8, 9-10, 21-22, 38-40. The full formula is not always used; it is enough to mention the crime, and the punishment is then presumed without being mentioned (e.g., vv. 24-25, 31-32). Whatever be the exact number of oaths Job takes in this chapter, the setting is very solemn and more impressive than all his previous claims of integrity. The climax comes in vv. 35-37 when he challenges God: "Let Shaddai answer me: here is my *tau*" (the last letter in the Hebrew alphabet—Job's final statement). Should an accusation be written up, Job would wear it as a badge of innocence since it could in no way diminish him: "like a prince I would stand before him" (v. 37). The ending of v. 40 explicitly marks the last words of Job, but we shall see that he does make responses to the LORD in the final chapters.

Elihu: Job 32–37

Nearly all readers are surprised to find a new character introduced at this point. A certain suspense had been built up by the debate and by Job's final word and challenge. If ever there will be a reply from God, it should happen now. Instead, a newcomer appears—an angry young man as he is repeatedly described, who is irate because of Job's claims and the failure of the friends to refute him. To set things right he delivers four speeches: chs. 32–33; 34; 35; 36–37. These reflect close attention to the course of the dialogue, but their content leaves a lot to be desired. Elihu seems to repeat, sometimes to strengthen, the arguments of the friends. Hence many consider these chapters to be a later insertion, but we need not delay over this hypothesis.

The reader will be somewhat puzzled by the introduction given to Elihu. His anger is extraordinary; it is mentioned four times. His speech in 32:6-22 is quite bombastic. He had kept silent because, as convention had it, age should speak wisdom. But no, it is a spirit, "the breath of the Almighty" (v. 8), not age that matters. His patience is now exhausted, "my bosom is ready to burst" (v. 19). Even when he begins to address Job in a substantive manner in ch. 33 he is wordy and laying claim to the "spirit of God," "the breath of Shaddai" (33:4) and he dares Job to refute him. He attacks the innocence that Job claims (it is true that the author behind Elihu has intimate knowledge of the dialogue). Elihu maintains that God *does* answer the charges that human beings make. In dreams at night warning is given to turn sinners from their evil ways. Although this entails suffering, even close to death there is a way out. If they have an "angel" to intercede, they will be redeemed from the "pit" and restored (vv. 23-28). All will be sweetness and light; the sinner (Job should take the lesson) will acknowledge sinfulness and render thanksgiving to God for the deliverance. Thus by God's reaction to human acknowledgment of sin, deliverance from the pit is made possible.

The second speech opens with an address to the "wise men" (vv. 2, 10, 34) immediately after Elihu has delivered a warning to Job (33:31-33). He practically quotes Job against himself (34:5 and 27:2) that God has deprived him of his right. This man Job, he charges, maintains innocence while he consorts with evildoers. In return, Elihu maintains the righteousness of God the creator (see vv. 14-15). God is impartial to all, and none can escape the divine eyes (vv. 21-22), especially the wicked and powerful. But God hears the cry of the needy. Elihu urges Job to confess his wrongdoing; the decision is up to him.

In the third speech Elihu takes up the question of Job's conduct, just or sinful, before God. In either case Job loses: his wickedness affects humans; his virtue gives God nothing (35:1-8). When people cry out to God their case does not go unnoticed, but they should approach God with trembling (vv. 9-16). With his incredible boasting and confidence Elihu opens his fourth speech (36:1-4) presenting himself as "one perfect in knowledge." His teaching remains unchanged. God reacts to humans as they deserve, but (v. 10) corrects and exhorts them; the choice now is theirs to make, for good or evil. The afflicted can be delivered by their very affliction; this is the divine means of education (v. 15). The most impressive section of Elihu's four speeches is 36:22–37:24, which is almost entirely taken up with a description of God's "wonders" that Job is invited to contemplate (37:14). It forms a kind of prelude to the speeches of the LORD that begin in ch. 38. God teaches through creation. Elihu points to the rain and the clouds, the lightning and the thunder, the tempest, the cold, snow and frost—all this under a divine control that stupefies him (37:1). He taunts Job (37:14) about his ignorance and impotence in the face of the display of such power. The final verses capture the import of Elihu's speech: "Shaddai—we cannot find him; great is he in power and justice, abundant in righteousness; he need not give an answer. Hence he is revered by mortals; although none can see him, not even the wise" (37:23-24). There is a neat irony to the last verse because Job is about to see the LORD in the great theophany.

The LORD: Job 38–41

It is well for any reader to review his or her expectations in approaching the speeches of the LORD. It can safely be said that the LORD's words do not seem to be successful from the point of view of logic. Indeed, the LORD does not *answer* Job. Instead, one question after another is raised: Who is this? Where were you? What do you know? Can you? It would appear that Job's worst fears have been verified: "should one want to contend with him, he could not answer him once in a thousand times" (9:2). One has to ponder whether the speeches of the LORD are truly overwhelming in a sarcastic sense—or are they questions that really tell Job nothing new (e.g., cf. 12:10-25), but remind him in a gentle way of what they *both* know. In one sense they are no answers at all, and it is perhaps the modern impulse to have an answer at all costs that has raised the problem of "answer." Perhaps the most obvious first impression is that the LORD's speeches are irrelevant. Even if the speeches of the three friends were not correct, and failed to communicate the truth, at least they were centered on Job's condition. The LORD does not once refer to Job's plight. The LORD walks Job through creation and the powers of chaos (Behemoth and Leviathan) without ever referring to the bothersome question that the Satan raised (1:9, "is it for nothing . . .")—and the LORD does not answer this question either! Twice the LORD tells Job "I will ask you and you shall inform me" (38:3; 40:2).

The LORD's first speech ranges over the various feats involved in the work of creation. What does Job know about all this: the foundations of the earth, the joyous occasion (the singing of the morning stars) when the cornerstone was set, the taming and dressing of the Sea *(Yam)* in swaddling clothes at its birth, the work of shaking up the wicked and coloring the earth when the light of dawn arises, "the gates of death," the home of light and darkness (vv. 4-20)? It is only in v. 21 that sarcasm appears when the LORD implicitly compares Job to the privileged position of personified Wisdom who, unlike Job, *was* present at creation (Prov 8:22-31)! The tour of the cosmos continues as meteorological data are brought up: snow and hail, the weapons of the LORD; winds and storms; rain and ice (vv. 22-30). The LORD is not above singling out what might be judged as erratic behavior, such as sending rain where no one dwells. Divine authority rules the constellations and directs lightning and clouds (vv. 31-38). Job is powerless to provide for the needs of the animal world: food for lions and ravens; care for the delivery of the young of animals, even of mountain goats and hinds (38:39–39:4); freedom for the wild ass; strength for the powerful wild ox; balancing the stupidity of the ostrich with its speed (39:5-18). In 39:19-25 there is a lively description of the eagerness, speed, and bravery of the war horse who is personified as smelling the battle and snorting "Aha" at the sound of the trumpet. The tour concludes with soaring birds such as eagle and hawk, safe in unreachable perches and espying food. Has Job the wisdom to account for all this (vv. 26-30)? The ending of the first speech is as sudden and as perplexing as the beginning. The author does not seem to be concerned to pursue the dialogue and complaints that began back in ch. 3. Rather, the LORD is given an opportunity to revel in the LORD's own creation, even "showing off" to Job.

There is no anger, but a gentle, even underplayed, sarcasm.

Readers should note that the versification numbers in chs. 40–41 are different in various versions; we shall follow the Hebrew numbering. What is to be made of Job's reaction (40:1-50)? Job's reply is frankly ambiguous: "I am small." He admitted as much even while he argued in his complaints. This does not appear to be a strong reaction, but rather tentative, cautious, and ambiguous. He goes on to say that silence ("hand to mouth," cf. 29:9) is his choice; he has nothing more to say. Surely this is a surprising ending, but this author is full of surprises. He now introduces a second speech by the LORD, repeating the earlier challenge "Gird up your loins . . . I will ask and you shall inform me" (40:2; cf. 38:3).

In 40:8-14 the beautiful irrelevance of the first speech is set aside and the LORD directly accuses Job of impugning divine justice, of condemning God in order that he might be justified. Job certainly had done this; cf. 27:2-5. God challenges Job as to his power and ability to control the world, i.e., to humble the proud. Could Job do this, the LORD would praise him; "your own right hand saves you" (40:14). In other words God challenges Job to play God! After all the marvels displayed in chs. 38–39, does Job think he can do better? No opportunity to answer is given to him. One must regard what follows as the Lord answering his own question, for it is a description of the divine dominion over the powers of chaos, Behemoth and Leviathan. It is remarkable that the main issue of the debate does not appear in the speeches of the Lord. What is the meaning of this? The book must be read to the end before we can attempt an answer.

Commentators still dispute over the identity of Behemoth and Leviathan. Are these animals the crocodile and dragon? Or do they symbolize the destructive powers of chaos? Probably the latter. This does not mean that the author was not inspired by whatever he knew about the fierce animals of antiquity. His purpose was not to enlighten the reader about the anatomy of these creatures, but to reinforce the idea of the LORD's dominion in contrast to Job's impotence and inability to handle them. This is not to deny, however, the obvious delight the author takes in parading these powers before the reader.

The description of Behemoth (vv. 15-24) is not spectacular in any rhetorical way, except for the final question: can he be captured or pierced? Obviously Job had better not try. This mood is quite pronounced in the lengthy description of Leviathan (40:25–41:26 = 41:1-34). The introduction to this creature is peppered with sarcastic questions such as "Can you play with him like a bird? Can you put him on a leash for your young ladies?" The final words are quite fitting: he is described as "king over all proud beasts" (41:28).

Job's Final Words: 42:1-6

Job's reply in 42:2-6 contains several puzzles. His first statement (42:2) is recorded in two ways. If read one way (the *Qere*) Job's words are quite clear, but they tell us nothing new. He well knew that God was powerful enough to implement the divine plan. If we read the other way (the *Ketib*), Job tells God, "you know you can do all things." This seems more feisty, and it suggests that Job may be holding back. However, the generally submissive tone in vv. 2-6 would suggest that the *Qere* is the better reading. Verse 3a repeats (except for a negligible variation) 38:2. Why is this aggressive question of the LORD found again? Merely as a setting for Job's humble admission of ignorance in v. 3bc? A second repetition (or quotation of the lines of God) is found in v. 4b, repeating 38:3b and 40:7b. Verse 4a is not a repetition, although it is put in quotation marks as the words of the LORD in many translations. These repetitions have led to some overly subtle interpretations that we can omit here. What is clear is that Job seems to acknowledge the divine power and purpose, and also his own ignorance. He had been reaching for things beyond his ken. This notion is strengthened by the powerful v. 5, which can be taken as a summary statement of the effect that the theophany and speeches of God have had upon Job: hearsay has been replaced by a vision and experience of God that now enables him to forget the old questions, such as "why?" Eyes have replaced ears, and the vision suffices.

However, the difficulties in Job's response are not yet over. The translation and hence interpretation of v. 6 is not clear. The emphatic "therefore" would suggest that he does not deny v. 5, but probably introduces another note of submission to the LORD. He recants (or "rejects"), but no object is given for this verb. What follows cannot be reasonably translated as "repent in dust and ashes." Job does not repent (in the sense of repenting for sin, or for having been too bold in his language, or the like). The verdict of the LORD in v. 7 (that Job spoke rightly about God) rules out such "sorrow." "Repent" can often mean simply a "change of mind." This fits more exactly Job's attitude at this point. He has changed, as the experience he referred to in v. 5 indicates. The reference to "dust and ashes" is difficult; it may refer to his own humanity and limitations (cf. 30:19).

Epilogue: 42:7-17

The first item in the epilogue is the Lord's decision concerning Job and the three friends. Addressing Eliphaz, God tells them of the divine anger because they did not speak rightly about God as did God's servant Job. There is supreme irony here. They had been defending the orthodox belief, as they thought. Now they must ask the intercession of the person they vilified—his prayers the LORD will accept—and they are to offer a holocaust. The verdict is repeated: they did not speak rightly as Job did.

The restoration of Job (42:10) has been looked on askance by many, as if it were the denial of what the book is about, a remnant of the old legend about Job that has been unfortunately included. This is a short-sighted view, in addition to being based upon reconstruction. The restoration does not destroy the points scored in the book. As a matter of fact the LORD is arbitrary enough to reward those who are God-fearing and avoiding evil. The author would not wish to deny that possibility. Besides, what alternative was there? To leave Job sitting on the *mazbelah* and lamenting? There has to be some closure, some resolution to the situation YHWH created in the first place. This gives no support to the interpretation that claims a "happy ending" for the book. It is impossible to allow the last few verses to determine the meaning of the work. Rather one may claim that the author deliberately took over such a traditional and orthodox story in order to shoot it down, to prove how much of an oversimplification it was.

The author's hand is behind the twofold restoration that Job receives from the LORD. This is what is prescribed in Exod 22:4 in the case of theft! Verse 11 indicates that relatives and acquaintances visit to console and comfort him for the "evil" he had received from the LORD. The observation is puzzling; the visit of friends (unlike that of the original three, to be sure) after the fact is small consolation. But realism also demands that Job be recognized as having joined the human family after his ostracism (cf. 19:13-19). That YHWH was the agent of his suffering is quite clearly indicated. Among the gifts is the *qesitah,* a unit of exchange whose value is unknown. The meaning of the names of the daughters are "turtle dove," "cassia," and "horn of antimony." It is unusual that they would share the inheritance with their brothers. The ending describes the typical fortune of a deserving patriarch.

Afterthoughts

If ever a biblical book (or even a commentary on it) deserves a postscript, it is the work we have just been commenting on. There are so many questions that linger even after a careful reading. The book seems to have layers of possible meanings that a reader can explore.

What kind of a God is YHWH? At the outset this God orchestrates two tremendous trials of Job. It is small consolation that the actions of the Satan are delimited and controlled. Job actually prefers death and Sheol (ch. 3). One can say that calling the attention of the Satan to Job was a way of moving the tale along. Was it a setup? Was it boasting? The challenging question of the Satan (1:9) raised an issue that the Almighty could not back down from, at the expense of appearing to be careless and flighty and lacking in trust. It matters not that this description of the divinity occurs only here, or that it is merely a detail in setting up the dramatic dialogues. The rendering of YHWH does not seem to disturb the author or the intended reader, whether on a historical or conceptual level. God then disappears until the famous and tantalizing speeches of chs. 38–41, and we encounter another mysterious aspect of YHWH there.

It is often said that the theological "point" of the prologue is to be found in 1:9 (2:3), the question of the Satan, "Is it for nothing . . . ?" It is certainly the trigger for further development. This has been phrased as "disinterested piety." The rather abstract phrase should be understood in a broad sense: "How much self-love is involved in one's love of God?" Or, from the point of view of the Satan, "Can human beings be trusted to serve God except on a self-serving *quid pro quo* basis?" However, it is striking that this issue (or the Satan!) is never mentioned in the epilogue. It seems to be essential to the book. Even YHWH cannot answer convincingly to the Satan without submitting Job to the test. That testing is essential to knowing if Job is really "upright." Whether suffering is deserved or undeserved, whether God is "just," or the question of how one is to live with suffering—all such concerns are secondary (not unimportant) to the intention provided by the prologue.

The same question of identity can be put to Job. What kind of person is he? It is widely held that Job shared the same view as the friends concerning retribution, the orthodox doctrine that prosperity is the divine blessing upon the good and suffering is the punishment for the wicked. Where does Job manifest such a mentality? It is true that in ch. 29 he looks back longingly to his salad days when everything went so smoothly. But this is understandable, coming from a suffering Job. Nowhere does Job ask for restoration of what he lost. His questioning of God is at a deeper level: what has happened to the relationship that he once had with God? He can appeal for deliverance in the only way he knew: challenge God in the familiar way that must have always marked their relationship—even go beyond that and accuse God of injustice, as a wounded lover might. Obviously the author rendered the situation all the more acute by repeating again and again, "why?" Perhaps it can be said that Job mistakenly measured divine justice by human standards. Or, to borrow the phraseology of Gerhard von Rad, Job claimed that "God must." But no other possibility was open to him, or the author would not have had a story to tell. It is important always to keep in mind that the author is not describing an actual case, but rather the typical. Job is in a sense all of Israel (or all of us!) and the author is making Job his protagonist. This typical aspect of the situation is the reason why there are many digressions similar to the motifs of the laments in the psalter. The very language, with its exaggeration, is a sign of this. There is no need to be "historical"; Job can refer to youthful aberrations (7:21; 13:6; 14:17) and to members of his family and friends (19:13-19).

The three friends have received bad press, and there is no question that they deserve some blame; after all, the verdict of the LORD (41:7-8) is against them. It is easy to say that they are inflexible and rigid. However, it is also true that they represent a widespread mentality. The connection between sin and suffering runs through the Bible. The author has manipulated them; they seem to be automatons at the end, giving the same lecture over and over. They fail to focus on the situation of Job; instead they abound in generalizations, e.g., human frailty and sinfulness before God. This is a frequent OT theme; even Job can agree with it. But it is beside the point. Similarly with the medicinal quality of suffering: true, but don't kill the patient! Most difficult of all is the change in attitude from genuine mourners and consolers (2:12-13) to downright accusers. Finally, they have not been vouchsafed a knowledge of the arrangement between YHWH and the Satan. What would the dialogue have been like if they had shared what the reader knows? They seem to be so terribly closed-minded, yet Job is rigid in his own way, running God into the ground with his own almighty certainty, even though we sympathize with him and even urge him on in his fidelity.

The questions we raise about God and Job are bound to reflect modern concerns arising from *our* presuppositions about the relationship between God and human beings. The book itself does posit some questions for us to ponder. The silence of God is something Job struggles with throughout. How much of this can we tolerate? Are we confronted, as Job was, with a strange God, one known perhaps only one-sidedly from our tradition? Ultimately Job struggles for the God he knows and trusts. He fights for and against God at the same time. When God becomes an "enemy" he tries to restore an image of the God he knows (10:2-12). There are no limits to the boldness of his language. It may be that we support Job and urge him on. Why? Because we know how the encounter with the three friends is going to turn out and are influenced by the verdict of the LORD in 42:7-8? The three failed to "hear" Job, to be realistic instead of remaining with their inflexible God. They discussed his case as an abstraction and as problem-solvers. In passing by Job they passed by God.

There is general agreement that somehow God "answers" Job in the speeches of the theophany. As a result Job is transformed. The difficulty is that any analysis of these speeches is not commensurate with a rational "answer." The reply of God is too oblique, as it were. Job is left out of the magnificent panorama that God describes. But perhaps it should be urged that Job gave the answer to the question of the Satan (1:9) when he said that we should accept evil as well as good from God (2:10). This is not a gutless answer; it is going to be developed throughout the rest of the book. That is one of the goals of the author: to show that Job has what the author of the epistle to James (5:11) called *hypomonē,* "steadfastness."

Who won the wager? Obviously YHWH was the winner. Was it just a game, or did God truly gain something? God tested and learned in the *only way possible* of the loyalty of God's servant Job. One wonders how many bets have been laid down and collected through the course of history.

The reader will have perhaps noted the relative absence of references to the Fathers and commentators of the past. There are two reasons for this. I do not think the comment of anyone on a single verse is all that important. The book of Job is so constructed that the meaning lies in its whole. The importance of 1:9 might be an exception to this, or perhaps 28:28. Second, there is something to be said for an examination of the outstanding commentators over the centuries. These show us how trends developed, and also how they changed. Moreover, their presuppositions are instructive for us. We are forced to examine our own presuppositions, to contrast our insights with theirs, and thus perhaps to correct our own errors. In any case, they force us to look at the book differently.

Fortunately, a recent study provides us with a lively contrast of interpretations offered by significant figures in history: *Where Shall Wisdom be Found?* by Susan E. Schreiner (University of Chicago Press, 1994.) From her work I will draw two major figures to exemplify the afterlife of the book of Job, Gregory the Great and Thomas Aquinas.

Gregory wrote his *Moralia in Job* as abbot of a Benedictine monastery at the end of the sixth century. He treats the text of Job literally as well as typologically (here Job becomes a type of Christ in his suffering). He finds in Job a turning inward, brought about by suffering that enables an ascent toward God. Tranquillity in life is judged to be fatal, dangerous, enslaving one to this world, whereas suffering reveals and purifies, bringing about a new perception. Gregory turns Job upside down: the values of the biblical Job are seen as temptations by Gregory's Job. Job suffers (he was not sinless, but his debates were free from sin) and thus makes known God's deliverance and also increases the merit of suffering. The friends fail to understand all this. From one point of view they represent heretics, but from another point of view Gregory discounts them as narrow even if they see a medicinal aspect in suffering. It is also clear that Gregory identifies the Satan with the devil.

The *Expositio* of Thomas Aquinas (*A Literal Exposition on Job: A Scriptural Commentary Concerning Providence,* translated by Anthony Damico with interpretive essay and notes by Martin D. Yaffe [Atlanta: Scholars Press, 1989]) was written between 1261 and 1264. Thomas reads Job as a historical work and follows the debate more exactly. Both sides agree that there is a providence, but disagree on the afterlife (affirmed by Job, denied by the friends). Aquinas recognizes a connection between suffering and sin but this did not always obtain here, whereas it functioned for the afterlife. Job was not sinless (there were venial sins), but he was tested (as Gregory maintained) by suffering "without cause" (Job 1:9) that was apparent to this world. Aquinas does not adopt the ascetic approach of Gregory. His concern is to seek a providence that enveloped suffering in light of the doctrine of a future life. Obviously Thomas was influenced by the Vulgate translation of Job 19:25-26 that clearly enunciates such a belief. The divine theophany in chs. 38–41 shows the ignorance and lack of power in humans, and Job recognizes this—even his pride is attacked.

Schreiner presents brief analyses of representative modern commentators and literateurs. She finds that the remoteness of God is a primary emphasis. God becomes more and more distant, and along the way that the biblical Job or the modern Job travel there is little of positive value. Carl Jung's *Answer to Job* (1971) starts from the point of view that there is evil in God (shown by Satan in the book). H. G. Wells (*Undying Fire,* 1919), Archibald MacLeish (*J.B.,* 1956), Elie Wiesel (*Trial of God,* 1979), and Franz Kafka (*The Trial,* 1914) are opposed to the traditional answers of theology. The transcendence of God is not presupposed, and the divinity is inaccessible. Indeed, there is a tendency to apotheosize a human being, as in *J.B.* The world has no meaning, and God is absent, indeed silent. Wiesel's *Trial of God* is also a kind of apotheosis—of the Jew who has survived the Holocaust (earlier Wiesel had written an essay, "Job: Our Contemporary"). Kafka does not deal with Job directly, but *The Trial* has been described as a kind of "midrash" on the book of Job. God is absent from the story and Joseph K., the hero, who has been accused of a crime that remains mysterious and unknown, searches in vain for justice. A judge never appears, a crime is never specified, and in the end K. is simply executed. In a sense the book of Job has disappeared among modern literatures. There is only meaninglessness, not a struggle for meaning.

BIBLIOGRAPHY

Alonso Schökel, Luis, and J. L. Sicre Diaz. *Job.* Nueva biblia española. Madrid: Editiones Cristiandad, 1983.

Andersen, Francis I. *Job.* Tyndale OT Commentaries. Leicester: InterVarsity Press, 1976.

Clines, David J. A. *Job 1-20.* WBC 17. Dallas: Word Books, 1989.

Green, Barbara. "Recasting a Classic: A Reconsideration of Meaning in the Book of Job," *New Blackfriars* 74 (1993) 213–222.

Habel, Norman C. *The Book of Job.* OTL. Philadelphia: Westminster, 1985.

Janzen, J. Gerald. *Job.* Interpretation. Atlanta: John Knox, 1985.

Newsom, Carol A. "Considering Job," *Currents in Research: Biblical Studies* 1. Sheffield: JSOT, 1993.

____. "Cultural Politics and the Reading of Job," *Biblical Interpretation* 1.2 (1993) 119–138.

Pope, Marvin H. *Job.* AB 15. Garden City, N.Y.: Doubleday, 1973.

Schreiner, Susan E. *Where Shall Wisdom be Found?* Chicago: University of Chicago Press, 1994.

Simundson, Daniel J. *The Message of Job: A Theological Commentary.* Minneapolis: Augsburg, 1986.

Psalms 1–41

Hans-Winfried Jüngling

FIRST READING

The psalms are the *official prayer* of the Church. They provide the basic framework for the Liturgy of the Hours and the prayer of monastic orders in choir. In the Liturgy of the Word during Mass the responsorial psalm always follows the first reading, and the Church also prays the psalms when celebrating the other sacraments.

In its great appreciation of the psalms the Church stands within a tradition that can be observed even in the New Testament. The many references to and quotations of the psalter show that it was the favorite Old Testament book of the NT authors. In one passage (Luke 24:27) the gospel of Luke refers to the third part of the OT as "the writings" or "the books," as did the Jews, but elsewhere (Luke 24:44) it calls that part "the psalms." This terminological shift in the Lukan gospel indicates that Psalms was seen as the most important book among the "writings."

Use of psalms in the liturgy became more and more extensive from the middle of the fourth century onward. Christian hymns, which began to appear near the end of the first century and developed strongly in the second and third centuries, were suppressed. The Synod of Laodicea (ca. 360 C.E.) ruled that only psalms were to be sung during the official liturgy (canon 59). Ambrose, the Bishop of Milan (d. 397), although he himself wrote hymns that were introduced into the Church's liturgy, energetically advocated the use of the psalms in the Church's public prayer. In his interpretation of Psalm 1 he characterized the whole psalter in this way:

> A psalm is the prayer of praise of the people of God, the exaltation of the Lord, the joyful song of the congregation, the cry of all humanity, the applause of the universe, the voice of the Church, the sweet-sounding confession of faith, entire surrender to [divine] power, blessed freedom, a cry of happiness, an echo of joy. A psalm softens wrath, relieves care, and lightens sorrow. It is a weapon at night, teaching in the day, a shield in fear, a festival celebration in holiness, an image of quietness, the pledge of peace and harmony. The psalm arises at day's beginning and is still sounding at day's end (Ambrose, *Explanatio Psalmi* 1, CSEL 64.7).

The psalter acquired such importance in the early Church because it had an undisputed place within the canon of Sacred Scripture that was gradually taking shape. It is a part of the Bible that possesses even today a special dignity.

But the psalter not only has an important function in the Church's public liturgy. There are very early testimonies in the ancient Church pointing to a *personal, "private" use.* The solid anchoring of the psalms in the Church's public prayer may in fact be traceable in part to the high value placed on the psalms by individual believers and their intensive use of them both in their own prayer and in the circle of their family. Reading of the psalter was recommended to lay people as well as monks, to women and men, young and old. Jerome attests that women learned Hebrew in order to better understand and pray the psalms. The manifold praise of the ancient Church was summarized by Athanasius of Alexandria in his letter to Marcellinus. Four ideas from this classic document deserve special emphasis:

1. The psalter is a Bible in miniature. In it those who believe in Christ find the essentials of all that is found in the Bible as a whole.
2. A human person can be utterly at home in the psalter. There he or she finds expression for all types of human experience.
3. The psalter is used by all who believe in Christ. Thus those who pray the psalms do so in the community of the saints.
4. The psalter is a pure mirror of Christianity. It leads us to self-recognition, to God and all creatures (MPG 27.11–46).

Athanasius's characterization of the psalms is paralleled in the preface Martin Luther attached to his translation of the psalms in 1528; it was retained in his last edition of 1545. Praise for the psalms as prayers and liturgical texts of the first order has not fallen silent from the time of the ancient Church and that of Martin Luther to today.

The words "psalms" and "psalter," drawn from the Greek, are Christian names for 150 poetic prayer texts collected into a single book of the Bible. The Jewish name for them is *tehillim.* These three names are all very old and need explanation. The word "psalms" is the title of the collection in one of the major manuscripts of the Greek Bible (the fourth-century Codex Vaticanus). The same manuscript ends with the notation, "Book of the 150 Psalms." A "psalm" is a song accompanied by a musical instrument. The noun occurs 42 times as an exact translation of the Hebrew word *mizmor,* which in turn functions 57 times as a designation for an individual text within the collection. The name "psalter" is also found as a title in the text tradition of the Greek Bible (in the fifth-century Codex Alexandrinus). In secular Greek this word means "stringed instrument," and in the Greek Bible it is used to translate the Hebrew word for "lyre." But as a title the word "psalter" can only mean a collection of songs to be sung to instrumental accompaniment. In the Jewish tradition the collection is called *(sefer) tehillim,* as Jerome noted. This name means "the book of praises." The word *tehillim* is striking in the context of biblical Hebrew because it is the masculine plural of a noun that is otherwise found in the Hebrew Bible only as feminine, namely *tehillah,* the regular plural of which is *tehillot.* However, the masculine plural is found in the Qumran texts from as early as the middle of the second century B.C.E. (4Q 504 Fr 2v, c. 7.10), and the Qumran psalm roll from the middle of the first century C.E. contains a prose note on David's poetry indicating that David wrote 3,600 *tehillim* (that is, psalms: 11Q 05, c. 227.4-5). Although the collection contains more laments and pleas than prayers of praise, so that the Hebrew title "praises" does not seem quite appropriate, it does point to an essential quality of the psalter: even human laments are sustained by praise of God.

Modern biblical scholarship has most recently placed renewed emphasis on the interpretation of the text as a whole and on understanding the final form of the text as means of access to this book that has been so important to the lives of many in the course of history. In this way scholarship is approaching the manner in which, so far as we can determine, the ancient Church and early Judaism viewed the psalter; at that time the whole book was appropriated meditatively, learned by heart, and recited over and over again privately and in "associations" or "guilds." By this approach modern scholarship supplements the form-critical investigation of the psalms, which was introduced by Hermann Gunkel in 1926 and since that time has steadily established itself as the only valid way of interpretation.

The Book of Psalms acquired the form we know today in the second century B.C.E. Here we find the psalms as separate entities, but at the same time the sequence of the individual texts given in the book is important for their understanding. The *independence* of the individual texts, coupled with the *importance of their contextual position in the book,* is evident from the *titles and subtitles* that mark their arrangement. For 116 of the psalms a *title* emphasizes the text's independence, and even for the remaining 34 psalms without titles it can usually be shown that they are to be regarded as independent entities. Only four psalms (10, 114, 115, and 116) are particularly problematic. The Greek translation, followed by the Latin, documents the problem by the fact that it counts the psalms differently than does the Hebrew text. Probably correctly it combines Psalm 10 with Psalm 9. Given the title-less Hebrew sequence of Psalms 114, 115, and 116, the Greek combines Psalms 114 and 115 (H) into a single psalm (Psalm 113 G) and divides Psalm 116:1-9 (H), 10-19 (H) into two psalms (Psalms 114 and 115 G). Psalm 147 (H) is regarded by the Greek Bible as two psalms. Thus we have the following numbering scheme for the psalms in the Hebrew and Greek (and Latin) Bibles respectively:

Hebrew Numbering	Greek/Latin Numbering
Psalms 1–8	Psalms 1–8
Psalms 9–10	Psalm 9
Psalms 11–113	Psalms 10–112
Psalms 114–115	Psalm 113
Psalm 116:1-9	Psalm 114
Psalm 116:10-19	Psalm 115
Psalms 117–145	Psalms 116–145
Psalm 147:1-11	Psalm 146
Psalm 147:12-20	Psalm 147
Psalms 148–150	Psalms 148–150

The titles of the 116 individual texts contain some genre designations that are difficult to interpret. The most frequent and clear-cut is *mizmor* (= psalm), which occurs 57 times. The titles of 15 psalms (Psalms 120–134) include the description "pilgrim song." They constitute a cohesive group. In five cases the genre name is coupled with a personal name. Four in this group are associated with David (Psalms 122, 124, 131, 133), one with Solomon (Psalm 126). Thus these five psalms from the sequence of pilgrim songs also belong to another group containing a total of 101 texts in whose titles the names of historical persons are included. In the conception of the final redaction of the psalter these names indicate the authorship. Thus seventy-three psalms are ascribed to David, two to Solomon (Psalms 72 and 126), twelve to Asaph, eleven to the sons of Korah, and one each to Moses (Psalm 90), Heman (Psalm 88), and Ethan (Psalm 89). The psalms of David are distributed throughout the book in a traceable external and internal/content-related system. In Psalms 3–32; 34–41 Davidic psalms follow one another in sequence. Within the scope of Psalms 42–89 a nearly symmetrical ordering is discernible:

Psalms of the Sons of Korah: Pss 42–49
  Psalm of Asaph: Ps 50
    Psalms of David: Pss 51–65, 68–70, 86
  Psalms of Asaph: Pss 73–83
Psalms of the Sons of Korah: Pss 84, 85, 87, 88

After this sequence, in which David-psalms have a double framing, only the following texts are assigned to David: Psalms 101, 103, 108–110, 122, 124, 131, 133, and the grouping 138–145. Here also the Davidic psalms 108–110 and 138–145 constitute a frame around Psalms 107–145. With Psalm 146 the final "hallel" of the psalter begins. Psalms 146–150 begin and end with the shout of "alleluia." The ten "alleluias" in Psalms 146–150 correspond to the 10 + 1 appearances of the verb "praise, acclaim" in the internal text of Psalm 150. The arrangement of the psalms ascribed to David underscores the movement represented by the whole Book of Psalms. It invites the praying people to perform in an audible recitation that same movement: from prayer in great distress to praise, from lament to acclaiming God. Psalms 3–89 are designated as Davidic laments twice by their titles (Pss 17:1 and 86:1) and once by a subscript (Ps 72:20). The prayers of lament must be spoken if we are to arrive at the full-voiced final alleluia (Psalms 146–150). This begins with David's acclaiming God (Ps 145:1). The psalms of David and their ordering within the psalter justify in a special way the Hebrew title of the book, "praises."

The arrangement of the psalms with names in the superscript titles is confirmed by an ancient division of the psalter into five books. Jerome mentions and discusses this division but rejects it, referring to the authority of the Hebrews and the apostles. A Qumran fragment (1Q 30 fr. 1) contains the word "fivefold." The fragment does not prove that the division of the psalter into five books was known in Qumran because the word "fivefold," if it refers at all to something "written," could be describing the Pentateuch.

The arrangement of the psalter in five books rests on *doxologies* in Pss 41:14; 72:18-19; 89:53; and 106:48. These doxologies mark stopping places in the continuum of the sequence of psalms, for they are in themselves independent of the psalms they conclude. They are really *subscripts*. The first and last of these doxologies are very similar and constitute an inclusion. The second doxology (Ps 72:18-19) is broadly developed in a soteriological and creation-theological sense. There is no doxology after Psalm 150 that directly corresponds to the others, but the psalter as a whole seems to be ordered toward the concluding "hallel" in Psalms 146–150. This full-voiced ending takes up motifs from the proemium of the psalter (Psalms 1–2): the rulers and judges of the earth are summoned to the service of YHWH. Service of YHWH is praise of YHWH. If the peoples and nations, kings and rulers fail to obey this summons they will be destroyed and will be unable to stand before the judgment (cf. Pss 148:11 with 2:10; 149:7 with 2:1; 149:8 with 2:8; 149:9 with 1:5). The "open" ending of the psalter thus closes the link back to its beginning. In this way it invites the reader to start over again. The division of the psalter into books is as follows:

Proemium: Pss 1–2
I. Pss 3–41; concluding doxology in 41:13
II. Pss 42–72; concluding doxology in 72:18-19
III. Pss 73–89; concluding doxology in 89:52
IV. Pss 90–106; concluding doxology in 106:48
V. Pss 107–145
Final "hallel" for the whole psalter: Pss 146–150

The second and third books of the psalms (42–89), like the first, contain psalms of David. Although the doxology in Ps 72:18-19 is so broadly constructed in its theology and thus indicates a strong caesura, the ordering of the psalms according to authorship and the perceptible tendency to substitute the general substantive "God" *(elohim)* for the divine name, YHWH, forges a close connection between books 2 and 3 (the "elohistic psalter"). The fourth book of psalms is the "Mosaic" book. Moses appears at the beginning (Psalm 90, title), in the middle (Pss 99:6; 103:7), and at the end (Ps 106:16, 23, 32). Psalms 90–106 celebrate what God did for Israel through Moses.

The division of the psalter into five books, something not entirely undisputed among Jews and Christians in antiquity, was in any case done by way of analogy to the five books of Moses. A preamble to the Psalms, known to us under the name of Hippolytus, spells out this analogy unequivocally, and the midrash on Psalm 1 formulates it in this way: "As Moses gave the Israelites the five books of the *torah,* so David gave them the five books of Psalms."

Form- and genre-critics do not find any internal content ordering in the psalter; there seems to be no clear structure. In the psalter texts of the same or similar genre are ordinarily not found together. For genre critics the titles and doxologies given in the book furnish only very superficial structural signals to the actual content. In addition these critics posit that the book was organized in this way only in its final stage of composition (at the earliest, in the second century B.C.E.). Correspondences or relationships of opposition between successive psalms as well as common key words are of only minor significance for genre critics. Their interest lies in describing the characteristics of form and content that appear in a number of individual texts, defining text types (genres), and seeking the original life settings of the genres thus discovered. Of these three areas of research within genre criticism the determination of the original life setting poses the most problems. In this field we can expect at best hypothetical results. The description and analysis of the genres necessarily has two disadvantages: in the first place the current canonical ordering of the psalms is disrupted, and in the second place the concrete, individual character of a text must be neglected if it is to be clearly assigned to a particular genre.

In spite of these deficiencies genre criticism's description of the principal genres represented in the psalter is an indispensable aid in reading the psalms. These principal genres are: hymn, individual song of lament, individual song of thanksgiving, national lament, and national thanksgiving. The *hymn,* typified most prominently by the Song of Miriam (Exod 15:21), consists of a call to praise God (introduction) and the reasons for it (body). The "reasons" for the praise are often expressed in the act of praise. The hymn may have a special ending that refers back to the beginning (examples are Psalms 117; 33; 113; 8).

The *individual song of lament* (whose "I" should not be misread individualistically) is the most common genre in the psalter. It begins by calling on the name of God and begging for help; this may be intensified by varied repetition and augmentation with expressions of confidence (introduction). The body of the song of lament consists of a description of the particular distress, a plea for divine action, a listing of reasons why God should act, and the vow of the one who prays. A conclusion filled with hope and confidence, often expressed in terms of certainty of being heard, is characteristic of the songs of lament. Only Psalm 88 ends in absolute darkness. (Examples include Psalms 3; 5; 6; 7; 13.) The motif of confidence in the songs of lament are sometimes collected into a psalm of their own, a *"song of confidence,"* such as Psalms 16 and 23.

The *individual song of thanksgiving* corresponds to the song of lament. It begins with a declaration of the desire to give thanks. The formula of thanksgiving may be expanded by other hymnic elements. A statement of the place and purpose of giving thanks is part of the body of the song of thanksgiving: one gives thanks in the assembly of the faithful. This assembly is witness to the divine act of salvation and should acknowledge the God who saves. The one giving thanks narrates the experience of distress and rescue (a recalling of the past). The song ends with a vow to praise, and the praise offered by the individual praying is to be incorporated in that of the whole assembly. (Examples include Pss 22:22-26; 30; 40:1-11.)

A *national song of lament* begins by calling on the name of God; this is sometimes given a hymnic expansion. The body consists of a description of the distress (lament) that affects the whole people; it is thus frequently political in nature. The lament ends with a plea that this misfortune be altered. This plea is made urgent through a recalling of the history of Israel with its God. Here again the end expresses confidence of being heard. (Examples include Psalms 44; 60; 74; 79; 80.)

There are only a few clear examples of the corresponding *national song of thanksgiving;* hence the existence of this genre is somewhat controversial. From Psalms 65, 66, 67, 68, and 124 we can derive the following typical elements: at the beginning there is a call to give thanks followed by an appeal to declare God's saving actions (introduction). The body again represents a recalling of the past, with the narration of political distress, and God's coming to the rescue of the people.

The time of origin of the individual psalms can only be very vaguely indicated in most cases. Many may have originated during the exile or in the post-exilic period. A very few of the texts that were composed during that period were used in the liturgy of the restored Temple. The psalter is neither the hymn book of the Second Temple nor that of the early Jewish synagogue.

However, more important than the time of origin is the fact that the psalter is a collection of poetic texts. *Parallelism,* the pairing of phrases, is the sign of biblical poetry. Two phrases or sentences placed in parallel augment each other in that the second repeats the thought of the first in different words or poses an antithesis to the first. This poetic medium is an invitation to see and appreciate God, the human being, and the world in their manifold richness. It is at the same time an invitation to meditation. The psalms themselves are this kind of invitation to *meditation and recitation.* It is important to read them as independent poetic works. Their unalterable individual character is to be grasped through patient reading and re-reading. The next step is to recognize the relationship between several texts that make up a single type and mutually illuminate one another. The fact that in the psalter not all the hymns, songs of lament, or songs of confidence are grouped together in one place, but that instead the genres are mixed together, makes it an image of human life with all its unexpected shifts and changes. All human distress, despair, and disappointment in God and humanity is repeatedly interpenetrated by praise and thanksgiving. The dynamic of the psalter as a unit has for its goal a movement from the multiplicity of the human world to the one thing necessary, the full-throated praise of the one God. The psalter invites us into this movement. From the beginning and then from one psalm to the next it steadily leads us toward its end and from the end back to the beginning. Repetition is the method the psalter itself suggests for dealing with it. Through repetition the psalter will become our book of life.

SECOND READING

The commentary on the individual psalms will focus first on the linking of the psalms within their canonical sequence (the *context*) and then on the *structure* of each psalm.

Arrangement of the first Book of Psalms: Psalms 1 and 2 are the programmatic preface to the psalter. With Psalm 3 begins the series of Davidic psalms (all, except for Psalms 10 and 33, have "David" in the title). The first Book of Psalms (Psalms 3–41) shows an internal arrangement including the following groups: Psalms 3–14; 15–24; 25–34; 35–41. The two "liturgies of entrance into the Temple" in Psalms 15 and 24 and the alphabetic Psalms 35 and 40 mark caesuras in the sequence of the psalms. Psalms 35 and 40 display parallels in the corresponding sections on the contempt and ridicule heaped by enemies on the one who prays (Ps 35:25-26 //

Ps 40:14-16). However the caesuras in the text are not such as to halt the flow of the psalm sequence. There are always relationships to the psalms immediately before and after: for example, the boundary between Psalms 14 and 15 is "permeable." At this particular point in the first Book of Psalms the context very clearly extends itself across the marked limits of the individual psalms.

The first book concludes with the doxology in Ps 41:13, but the end of the first Book of Psalms corresponds to the end of the second book not only because of the similar doxology in Ps 72:18-19. The similarities between the final parts of the first two books of Psalms are still greater: the lament and plea in Psalm 69 are preceded by Psalm 40 as the narrative of rescue from sinking in the bog (Ps 40:2 // Ps 69:2, 14). Moreover Ps 40:13-17 reappears as Ps 70. The first two books of Psalms conclude with similar-sounding final chords.

Psalm 1

Context

This psalm is an independent entity but is also closely connected to the one following. These two taken together constitute the programmatic beginning of the psalter. The theme of "the law of the Lord" (v. 2) is taken up again in Pss 19:7 and 119:1 where it is developed at length.

The key words "happy" (1:1; 2:12 // 40:4; 41:1), "*torah*" (1:2 // 40:8; cf. 37:31), "delight/desire" (1:2 // 40:6, 8, 14; 41:11), "stand/rise" (1:5 // 40:2; 41:8, 10) create links between the beginning and end of the first Book of Psalms.

Structure

The psalm consists of two parts (vv. 1-3 and 4-5). Verse 6 is the conclusion. The thematic words of vv. 5 and 6 are ordered chaistically: God knows the way of the righteous. God is attentive to the righteous. The way of the wicked will perish; that is, the wicked bring ruin on themselves. The two parts of the psalm are related chiastically as statement/image (vv. 1-2 and 3) and image/statement (v. 4 and v. 5).

The beatitude pronounced in Psalm 1 applies to individuals who stand up against the pull of the many wicked, sinners, and scoffers (vv. 1-3). Such an individual's devotion to the Lord's *torah* means a life of fulfillment (vv. 3, 6a). The person whose joy is in the Law of the Lord is contrasted to the many wicked (vv. 4-5, 6b). In spite of their apparently successful lives the judgment on their existence can only be that their way leads to ruin. The reflection on the life of the wicked brings certainty that people who live religious lives seriously in accord with the Lord's *torah* are not alone: the community of the righteous is a reality (vv. 5b, 6a).

Psalm 2

Context

This psalm is tied to the previous one by a number of key words and phrases: the meditation on the Law of the Lord in 1:2 is contrasted with the vain and empty plotting in 2:1b. Psalm 2, like Psalm 1, ends with the words "will perish" and "way." The rebellious kings and rulers of the earth perish in the way (2:12a; cf. 1:6b). The blessing of the individual in 1:1 has a significant corresponding term in 2:12b, where the individual has become many. Structurally the two psalms mirror one another: Psalm 1 begins with a person who resists the pull of the majority (vv. 1-3) and then speaks of the many wicked (vv. 4-5, 6b). Psalm 2 introduces many peoples and nations and their rulers who set themselves up against God and God's anointed. The many rebel against individuals. First the nations and kings speak (v. 3); then God (v. 6) and God's anointed (vv. 7-9, 10-12) speak. The direct speeches make this short text a kind of drama. This dramatic character is emphasized by the question that opens the psalm (v. 1). In this way the description of the situation becomes part of a speech, although it is unclear who is speaking.

The concluding "hallel" of the psalter (Psalms 146–150) calls on the "kings of the earth," the "peoples," the "princes," and "all rulers of the earth" to praise God (Ps 148:11). Thus the end of the psalter turns back to its proemium in Psalms 1–2 (cf. Ps 2:2, 10 // 149:7-8, as well as the "iron" in Ps 2:9 // 149:8 and "judgment" in Ps 1:5 // 149:9).

Structure

Three parts are discernible: (1) The tumult and plotting of the nations and their rulers against God and God's anointed in vv. 1-3; (2) the reaction and speech of God in vv. 4-6; and (3) the speech of the anointed one in vv. 7-9. The appeal to the kings and rulers of the earth to turn from resisting God and God's anointed to serve God (vv. 10-12) can easily be understood as a speech by the messianic king. The conclusion (vv. 10-12) takes up key words from v. 2 ("kings," "earth") and v. 5 ("wrath"). Regarding the correspondence between vv. 3 and 11, cf. Jer 2:20.

Both these initial psalms in the psalter invite the readers to a decision for God that leads to a successful human life. Psalm 1 does this in a rational and cool manner, while Psalm 2 presents us with a drama. Psalm 1 directs its attention to people in Israel, while Psalm 2 turns to those charged with responsibility for other nations. Special weight is laid on the invitation to follow YHWH's *torah* and serve YHWH by the fact that the speaker of this invitation is the anointed of YHWH (i.e., David) who presents himself as a person entirely shaped by God's *torah*.

These two psalms resist any categorization by genre, although individual elements in them follow a particular text type—for example, the macarisms in both psalms and the royal crowning ritual in Psalm 2. These psalms are not prayers in the strict sense. Neither has a direct address to God, which is a sign of the language of prayer.

Psalm 3

This is the first psalm attributed to David.

Context

The anointed one established on the Lord's holy mountain (2:6) receives a response from the Lord spoken from God's holy hill (3:4). The anointed under attack (= David: 2:2) speaks and laments that he is surrounded by many foes. He begs for rescue from the Lord. This psalm, in contrast to the proemium, introduces the new vocabulary of the individual lament into the psalter.

Structure

After the superscription there follows, in proper style, an appeal to God by name (v. 1: the divine name is the first word after the superscription), a lament (vv. 1-2), an expression of confidence (vv. 3-6), and a plea that develops into assurance of being heard (v. 7). The concluding sentence moves beyond individuals and expands to include the whole people of God, which is secure in the salvation and blessing of God (v. 8). The parts of the psalm are connected by the repetition of key words: lament and petition are intimately linked by the words "rise" (vv. 1, 7) and "help" or "deliver" (v. 2 // v. 7). "Deliverance" in v. 8 takes up the same word from v. 2. The lament is set in contrasting parallel to the expression of confidence (v. 1 // v. 6). The combination of "deliverance" and "your people" constitutes the frame around Psalms 3–14 (3:8 // 14:7).

Psalm 4

Context

Psalm 3 is a morning prayer (3:5), while Psalm 4 is an evening prayer (4:8). Psalm 4 has motifs and words in common with Psalm 3: "call" and "answer" (4:1 // 3:4), "my honor" or "my glory" (4:2 // 3:3), "many say" (4:6 // 3:2), "abound" (4:7b // 3:1), and "lie down and sleep" (4:8 // 3:5). The key word "vain" (4:2) links this psalm with Ps 2:1.

Structure

Psalm 4 is a psalm of confidence. Petition, acknowledgment of the experience of divine rescue (vv. 1, 7), and an expression of trust (v. 8) are set as a frame around instruction directed at the "children of humanity" (cf. Pss 49:2; 62:9; Lam 3:33): do not love what is vain (v. 2); trust in the Lord (v. 5). The instruction is organized by recurrent references to the personal experience of an individual (v. 3) and the prayer of many (v. 6). The psalm is well structured: "call" and "answer" are found in vv. 1 and 3b, so that the first part of the frame is linked with the first part of the teaching. "Heart," "bed" or "lie down," "be safe" and "in safety" connect vv. 4-6 with vv. 7-8 (in other words, they tie the second part of the instruction to the second half of the frame). "Right" (4:1, 5) connects the first part of the frame with the second part of the instruction.

Psalm 5

This psalm belongs to the genre of individual songs of lament. Stylistically it takes its own course and introduces new formulations in the plea to be heard.

Context

The psalm speaks of morning rituals (5:3) and thus is complementary to the evening prayer of Psalm 4 and parallel to Psalm 3. This psalm is linked to the one before it: the verb "pray" (5:2b) refers to 4:1b ("prayer"), while the verb "hear" (5:3a) refers to 4:1b, 3b, and the noun "lies" (5:6a) to 4:2b. The verb "hate" with God as subject (5:5b) corresponds to the verb "love" with human beings as subject in 4:2a. The verb "bless" (5:12) refers to 3:8 ("blessing"), and the expression "all who take refuge in you" (5:11a) to 2:11b.

Structure

The sections that are typical for the genre (calling on the divine name, plea for hearing, motif of confidence, description of the need and petition) are edited into two major sections: vv. 1-7 and 8-12. This two-part division is emphasized by the contrast between v. 7b and v. 10b. The first part contains intensive pleas for hearing (vv. 1, 2a, 3a) and descriptions of the psalmist's worship: he not only prays (v. 2b), but prepares the morning offering and watches for God (v. 3b). He enters the Temple and throws himself down before the sanctuary (v. 7). The pleas and descriptions of the actions form a frame around a section praising God because God despises injustice and evil, which are concretely seen as the boastful, evildoers, liars, the bloodthirsty and deceitful (vv. 4-6). The expanded first section is the basis for the petition to be led in God's way in the sight of the enemies (v. 8). The personal address ends at this point. It is followed by a characterization of the enemies (= lament), whose relationship to the psalmist is no longer expressly described: they think and speak injustice. Their thoughts and their speech destroy human community (v. 9). The sins of thought are also present in the plea presented to God that the enemies may expiate their wrongs (v. 10). The further petitions have to do with the joy of those who take refuge in God and love God's name (v. 11). Verse 12 speaks in the singular of the just person who receives God's blessing.

Psalm 6

This is the first of the seven ecclesial penitential psalms (Psalms 6, 32, 38, 51, 102, 130, and 143). It belongs to the genre of individual songs of lament.

Context

The psalm is connected to its predecessors in a number of ways: "be gracious" (6:2a) points to the same phrase in 4:1; "save" (6:4) connects to 3:7, "your steadfast love" (6:4b) to 5:7, and "all you workers of evil" (6:8a) to 5:5. The word group "hear/voice/prayer" (6:8b-9) extends back via 5:2-3 to 4:1. "My enemies" (6:10) points back to 3:7 (cf. 5:8), but with the noun "foes" (v. 7b) a word is introduced that will be used again in 7:4. Psalm 6 describes what the one praying does at night (v. 6). We find the sequence "morning" (Psalm 5) and "night" (Psalm 6), similar to that in Psalm 3 (morning) and Psalm 4 (evening).

Structure

The psalm divides into three parts: there is a twofold progression through the elements of the song of lament (plea and lament) in vv. 1-3 and 4-7, followed by a concluding section with the assurance of being heard (vv. 8-10). The first and third parts are closely connected by recurring words: "terror" (vv. 2, 3, and 10), "be gracious" (v. 2a), "supplication" (v. 9a).

The text speaks of a sick person (v. 2) whose urgent prayers ask for healing. A motif is introduced to induce God to intervene: a dead person cannot remember God and give God thanks. In the reversal at the conclusion it can be said that praise of God means life. The psalm speaks clearly both of sickness (6:2) and of the enemies of the one who prays (6:7b, 8a, 11). In this short lament we find an example of how the psalms resist a clear categorization in mutually incompatible genres (for example: prayers of a sick person versus the prayers of a person attacked by enemies). The "open situation" allows the texts to be prayed in many different types of distress.

Psalm 7

Context

This psalm stands in dialectical relationship to Psalm 6. Whereas Psalm 6 begs that God's wrath be turned away from the one praying (6:1), the petition is now that God intervene wrathfully on this person's behalf against the fury of the enemies (7:6). The plea "save me" (7:1) is identical to that in Ps 6:4. In its content Psalm 7 continues the theme introduced in Ps 4:1 ("my right") and Ps 5:8 ("your righteousness"), i.e., justice or righteousness (Ps 7:8, 17). "You are not a God who delights in wickedness" (5:4) corresponds to "God is a righteous judge, and a God who has indignation every day" (7:11). The key phrase "my honor" or "my glory" is found in 7:5 as in 3:3 and 4:2. The psalm begins with a personal expression of confidence (7:1a). Psalms 2:12 and 5:11 make fundamental statements about the blessedness and joy of trusting in God.

Structure

The psalm divides into two major sections: the first (vv. 1-10, framed by "save") is marked by the sustained address to God, the use of the divine name, and the first-person discourse of the psalmist. The second part (vv. 11-16) speaks about God (v. 11), and especially about violent people who destroy themselves through their violence (vv. 12-16). The psalm ends with a promise to give thanks for God's righteousness and to sing to the name of the Lord (v. 17). These two parts are closely knit together. In the first section the elements typical of the genre of the individual lament are visible: vv. 1-2 and 6-10 are chiastically arranged: motif of confidence (v. 1a), petition (vv. 1b-2) // petition (vv. 6-9), and motif of confidence (v. 10). The section thus framed (vv. 3-5) contains a conditional self-surrender to the enemy that functions as a protestation of innocence. The petitions, besides "save me" (7:1; cf. 3:7; 6:4), employ the important words "deliver me" (i.e., take me away) in 7:1 and "judge me according to my righteousness" (i.e., do justice for me) in 7:8. These appear here for the first time in the psalter. In the second part of the psalm the personal dimension is abandoned. The human violence that was already alluded to in vv. 2 and 5 is now uncovered. But the violent are subject to the power of the God who judges (v. 11). Moreover, human violence turns on those who perpetrate it (vv. 12-16).

An innocent person who has been accused seeks justification from the righteous God who tests minds and hearts (7:9). God, who does right, judges justly (v. 6), and brings about justice (v. 17) in the sight of people and nations (vv. 7-8a) proves to be a righteous judge also for an individual who has been unjustly accused. Therefore God is to be praised, and one should sing to the name of the Lord most high (v. 17). This promise to praise and sing to God recurs in Ps 9:1-2. Between these two announcements of divine praise stands Psalm 8 as the accomplishment of that praise: the name of the Lord is majestic.

Psalm 8

Context

The name of God was introduced as a theme in the corresponding Psalms 5 and 7 (5:11; 7:17), and the same theme will be taken up in Ps 9:2, 10. Psalm 8 confesses the glory of the divine name (vv. 1, 9). It formulates a theological anthropology that is highly important for the sequence of psalms from 9 to 14: as soon as a human being acknowledges God as Lord he or she achieves full humanity. To be fully human is to be little less than God (Ps 8:4-5). As a consequence of this anthropology Psalms 9–14 develop the counter-thesis that human beings degenerate when they no longer allow God to be Lord (cf. Ps 12:4b). The designations for "human being" introduced in Ps 8:4 are repeated: "human being" in 8:4a is found in Pss 9:20 and 10:18, "child of humanity" or "humankind" *(ben ʾadam)* in Pss 11:4; 12:1, 8; 14:2. The description of human wickedness in the lament sections becomes ever more intensive until it reaches its climax in Psalm 14. In the midst of this steadily intensifying sequence of human degradation comes, in Psalm 13, the dramatic cry: "How long?"

Structure

The psalm is framed by a group confession ("O LORD our Sovereign," vv. 1a, 9) and divides into two parts: the first (vv. 1-2) concentrates entirely on God's greatness and glory, which cause God's children to give praise and God's enemies to fall silent. The second part (vv. 3-8) celebrates the greatness of the human being who, as God's creature, gives thanks to God. Only that person is truly and genuinely human who abandons all egoism and acknowledges God as his or her creator and Lord. Although it lacks the typical marks of this genre, Psalm 8 must be called a hymn.

Psalm 9/10

Beginning with this psalm the numbering in the Hebrew and Greek/Latin Bibles differs, for the Hebrew Bible read this psalm as two separate texts while the Greek (and Latin) translations correctly understood it as a single psalm.

Context

After the praise of the divine name in Psalm 8 this psalm again takes up the promise to give thanks and praise expressed in Ps 7:17. The psalm speaks of God's name in vv. 2 and 10. Psalm 9/10 has in common with Psalm 7 (cf. 7:6-8) the theme of God's role as judge, expressed with great urgency in 9:4, 7, 8: God is the defender of the individual (9:4) and the judge of the nations (9:8). The comparison of the persecutor (or the wicked person) with a lion is another feature common to both psalms (Pss 7:2 and 10:9). Psalms 7 and 9 describe the self-destructive actions of the wicked: they fall into the pit they have dug (7:15-16 // 9:15-16). The key theological word "mortal" for the human being in Ps 8:4a is taken up in Pss 9:19, 20 and 10:18. The expressions for "foe" and "enemy" from Ps 8:2 reappear in Ps 10:5 (cf. Pss 6:7; 7:4) and Ps 9:3, 6 (cf. Ps 3:7; 6:10; 7:5).

Structure

The psalm is alphabetically arranged: that is, the initial letters of every second verse follow the sequence of the Hebrew alphabet (yielding an alphabetic acrostic). However, the manner of construction is only partly discernible. In spite of this formal structure the text is rigidly constructed. It divides into two major sections: the first (Ps 9:1-14) is shaped by the first person discourse of the one who prays. The second section contains 9:15–10:18. In both major sections we can discern subsections: in the first of these the one praying calls himself or herself to praise, confession, and rejoicing because his or her enemies are retreating (9:1-3). In the next part (9:4-10) the one praying proclaims that God has accomplished justice for him or her (v. 4), rebuked the nations, and destroyed the wicked (vv. 5-6). This part closes with praise for God as the righteous judge (vv. 7-8). God has not abandoned those who seek God (v. 10b). That is the reason for hope that God will be a stronghold for the oppressed (v. 9) and that those who know God's name can trust in God (v. 10a). The third subsection (9:11-14: framed by "Zion") calls for songs of praise to God who bears the title "the one enthroned in Zion." God's judgment on the bloodthirsty and engagement on behalf of the poor (v. 12) demands praise for God. The one praying implores to be rescued from the threats to his or her life so that he or she can recite God's mighty deeds as he or she has intended to do from the beginning (vv. 13-14). The mood of the text sketches a downward curve: at the beginning there is great confidence, but toward the end of this part the prayer is increasingly despondent. It concludes with a plea for personal rescue from the realm of death.

In the second major section of the psalm (9:15–10:18) personal discourse is dropped. This part is distinguished from the other by the absence of the first person speech of an individual. It is framed by 9:15-20 and 10:12-18. The assertion in 9:18 that God will not forget the needy corresponds to the prayer in 10:12. The first part of the frame asserts that the nations and the wicked will be destroyed by their own deeds (9:15, 16). Despite this assurance it issues in urgent pleas that the wicked and the nations, who are unmindful of God, will not retain the upper hand (9:17-20). In the latter part of the frame there are also prayers (10:12, 15, 17b) interspersed with acknowledgments that God has seen (10:14) and heard (10:17a) and that God is the helper of orphans (10:14b). Both parts of the frame contain the cry, "rise up, O LORD!" (9:19; 10:12; cf. Pss 3:7; 7:6). The central section (10:1-11) consists of a description of the deeds of the wicked (10:2, 3, 4). Their arrogant talk is portrayed at length (10:1-7), whether it be inward meditation (10:1-6) or speech to others (10:7). Then their violent deeds are described (10:8-10). The description ends with the content of the thoughts of their hearts (10:11), thus turning back to the beginning and emphasizing godlessness as the essence and origin of the actions of the wicked that destroy their neighbors (10:3b, 4 // 10:11).

The psalm begins with the formal characteristics of an individual song of thanksgiving (9:1-4) and then uses characteristic forms of the hymn (9:5-8, 11-12). At the end of the first major section there is a personally formulated plea, characteristic of individual songs of lament. Other elements of these latter songs are found scattered throughout the second major section of the psalm: pleas (9:19-20; 10:12, 15), accusing questions (10:1, 13), and the description of the distress of the poor caused by the speech and actions of the wicked (10:1-11). The psalm ends with a hymn to God as king. The divine king helps the poor, the oppressed, and the orphans to obtain justice (10:16-18). The psalm unfolds a theology of God's reign. It begins with a confession of God as the righteous judge and consequently leads to a confession of God's eternal reign (9:4, 8, 19; 10:18; cf. 9:7). God, the king and righteous judge, is a refuge for the oppressed (9:9). The rare word "oppressed" occurs at the beginning and end of terminology for the poor that is used throughout the psalm (9:9 and 10:18). Expressions for the semantic field "poor" are found in 9:12, (13), 18; 10:2, 8, 9, 10, 12, 14, 17, 18. The theology of the poor emerges here for the first time in the psalter. God's engagement on behalf of the poor is contrasted to the energy with which the wicked do violence to them. The wicked sin against the innocent and the poor (10:2, 8, 9, 10). It is obvious that we have here a theological anthropology within which the brutal, inhuman actions of the wicked against the poor are explained by the fact that they have renounced and taken their leave of God (10:3b, 4, 11; cf. 10:13).

Psalm 11

Context

This psalm has linguistic ties to Psalms 7 and 5: "I take refuge" (11:1a // 7:1a), God tests (11:4b, 5a // 7:9b), God is righteous (11:5, 7 // 7:9, 11), "the upright in heart" (11:2b // 7:10b), "violence" (11:5 and 7:16). Especially important is the Hebrew verb "to do," which establishes a firm connection between Psalms 11 and 7 (11:3 and 7:13; cf. also "arrows" in 11:2 and 7:13). Beyond these two psalms, however, that same verb shapes the series of Psalms 5–7 and 11, 14–15 (5:5; 6:8; 7:13, 15; 11:3; 14:3; 15:2). The dialectic of love and hate is found in 11:5b, 7a and in 5:4, 5b. We read of God's "eyes" in 11:4 and 5:5, while "holy temple" is found in 5:7 and 11:4. The word "wicked," used in the plural in Pss 1:1, 4, 5, 6; 3:7; 7:9, was elaborated at length in Psalm 9/10 (9:5, 16, 17; 10:2, 4, 13, 15) and is taken up again in Ps 11:2, 5, 6. In this way Psalm 11 is firmly tied to Psalms 5 and 7, which are themselves interconnected in their content. With the expression "humankind" [literally "children of humanity"] Ps 11:4 takes up one of the key ideas of the theological anthropology of Ps 8:4b. Like Psalm 9/10 it contributes something to the developing theological anthropology of the psalms. Psalm 11 is also tied to Psalm 9/10 by the verb "to say," which introduces direct speech (11:1); in Psalm 9/10 it introduces the internal speech of the wicked (10:6, 11, 13). The verb "to say" begins the series 9/10–14; 11:1; 12:4, 5; 13:4; 14:1.

Structure

This psalm has two parts: vv. 1-3 and 4-7. The first word in each part is the divine name. Each part discusses the difference between "the wicked" and "the righteous" (vv. 2-3 and 5-6). The verb "look" constitutes an *inclusio* in the second part (vv. 4b, 7b). In Hebrew the verbs "take refuge" (11:1a) and "look" (11:4b, 7b) sound very similar. The first-person speech at the beginning (v. 1) is not continued through the psalm. The praying person's "I" retreats in favor of objective instruction. It is difficult to understand the first part of the psalm because it is not clear how far the quotation from the praying person's speech extends beyond v. 1. However, the violent actions of the wicked against the group of the "upright in heart" are perfectly obvious. The wicked are not only violent; they also act under cover of darkness. Even though there are no direct verbal links the deeds of the wicked are described similarly in 10:2a, 8-10 (cf. 7:13). The shaking of the foundations is attributable to the deeds of the wicked. Before them a righteous person is powerless (vv. 2-3). Is this righteous one a human being, or is the power of the righteous God being called into question here (cf. Ps 7:9, 11)? The second part is clear: from the Lord who is present in the Temple and enthroned in heaven, who loves righteousness and is righteous but hates those who love violence, no human deed remains hidden. God destroys the wicked (v. 6), while the "upright" person (v. 7; cf. v. 2) beholds the face of the Lord.

Psalm 12

Context

This psalm adds a new aspect to the description of the person who declares independence from God, a description begun in Psalms 9/10 and 11: the destruction of human relationships by the misuse of language. There are verbal links to the neighboring psalms: the words for "poor" and "needy" in 12:5 are also in 9:18. The cry "rise up" (9:19; 10:12; cf. 3:7; 7:6) corresponds to God's saying "I will now rise up" in 12:5. The verbs "help" and "disappear" (12:1) are a tie to 7:1, 9. The expression "humankind" at the beginning and end of the psalm (12:1, 8) is also found in 11:4 and represents a continuation from 8:3. The direct contradiction in 12:5 against 8:1, 9 gives a key to understanding the psalm: people do not recognize any sovereign power and by their arrogant behavior destroy every kind of verbal communication among human beings.

Structure

The psalm is symmetrically constructed. After the urgent plea for help in v. 1 the community-destroying talk of humankind is described (v. 2). This is followed by a petition: may God destroy the boasters (v. 3). The first part culminates in the quotation of the kind of arrogant speech uttered by humankind (v. 4). This is followed by a quotation of divine speech as God arises to help the poor (v. 5). The description of the words of God, which in contrast to those of humanity are "pure" and "refined," functions as an expression of confidence. The contrast between human and divine speech is not only asserted in terms of content but made clear in formal terms by the fact that the corresponding parts (vv. 3-5 and 6-7) have no words in common other than the verb "say" and the divine name YHWH. There are petitions at the beginning of the psalm (vv. 1a, 3) and it concludes with petitions (vv. 7-8): human beings are wicked persons who assert themselves with words that destroy community. God is asked to shelter from these deeds the poor who confess God's "pure" word. Elements typical of the genre of the individual lament are inserted throughout the symmetrical structure of the psalm:

A Prayer language (petition and lament); "humankind": v. 1
B "Lips," "heart," "tongue" (lament and petition): vv. 2-3
C "Tongue," "lips" (quotation of human speech): v. 4
C' "I will now rise up . . . place them in safety" (quotation of divine speech): v. 5
B' God's word (motif of confidence): v. 6
A' Prayer language; "humankind": vv. 7-8

Psalm 13

Context

This strictly-composed text stands at an important point within the series of Psalms 9/10–12 from a compositional point of view: The complaint to God in 13:2 refers to the speech of the godless wicked in Ps 10:11. The godless assert that God has forgotten, has hidden the divine face and has not seen what is happening. Psalm 9/10 already contradicted this godless and unbelieving opinion (9:12, 18; 10:14, 17), but the experience of the power of the violent wicked is so great that nothing remains but to utter an urgent plea that God will not forget (10:12). The descriptions of enemies in Pss 11:2-3 and 12:2-3 yield a desolate picture. The godless who undermine the bases of human mutual existence even to the point of perverting language have overwhelming superiority. Even though God promises to rise up "now" and save (Ps 12:5) we find in Psalm 13 the dramatic appeal to know when God will finally remember and arise to intervene on behalf of the poor. The expression of confidence in 13:5 takes up the words of 9:14—a further point of connection to Psalm 9/10. There are other important verbal relationships with psalms other than 9/10, including ties to 12:1, 5 by way of the root "save"/"salvation" (13:5) and to 12:8 through the verb "rise up" (13:2).

Structure

This psalm is the classic example of an individual song of lament. In the fourfold question "how long?" the psalmist laments God's absence (v. 1), his or her personal distress (v. 2a), and the aggression of the enemy (v. 2b). However the suffering caused by God, oneself, and the enemy is not explored at length. There is no "narrative of suffering." In a series corresponding to the sequence of lament-questions the psalmist prays for God's response (v. 3a), the removal of personal suffering, and rescue from the enemy (vv. 3b, 4). The psalm closes with an acknowledgment of trust (v. 5) and the promise of praise and thanksgiving (v. 6). With this promise to praise the direction changes: the one praying now speaks about God rather than to God as was the case up to this point in the psalm.

The psalm is classically brief and pure in form. Hence genre critics regard it as ancient, i.e., preexilic. Such a prime example of an individual song of lament can help us see how difficult it is to discern the concrete distress out of which the psalm arose or the kind of suffering it has in view and is prepared to confront, for complaints about God, about one's own miserable life, and about hostility from other people represent a summary of all the areas that can ever create problems and be burdensome to human beings.

Psalm 14

Context

With Psalm 14 the series Psalms 9/10–14 reaches absolute bottom. Psalms 9–12 have spoken in such absolutely negative terms of "human beings" (Psalm 9/10) and "humankind" (Pss 11:2; 12:1, 8)—a theme already introduced in Ps 8:4—that the fourfold question "how long?" in Psalm 13 was unavoidable. In Psalm 14 "humankind" is again at the center and under God's scrutiny (14:2). The connection with the immediately preceding Psalm 13 is wrought by the verb "rejoice" (Ps 14:7 and 13:4, 5), which also points farther back to Ps 9:14. In Pss 9:14 and 13:5 the verb is combined with the noun "salvation," which in turn is found also in Ps 14:7. Thus there is a thread connecting Psalms 9/10–14. Other elements constitutive of the connection between Psalms 9/10 and 14 are the name "Zion" (9:11, 14 // 14:7), the introduction of an internal dialogue (10:6, 11, 13 // 14:1), and the statement "There is no God" (10:4 // 14:1). Added to this are the verbs "be glad" (9:2 // 14:7) and "seek" (9:10, 12; 10:4, 13, 15 // 14:2). In Ps 14:5-6 the words "righteous" and "poor" connect back to Pss 11:2 and 9/10 (cf. 9:12). The word "humankind" in 14:2 ties it to 11:3, where is found not only the same expression but the same idea: God is enthroned in heaven and tests humankind. These striking connections enable us to see a deliberate composition in the series Psalms 9/10–14, with 9/10 and 14 marking the beginning and end of the series respectively. In addition, the linking of the nouns "salvation" and "people" in 14:7 and 3:8 form a frame for the first major section of the first Book of Psalms.

Although the caesura in the sequence after Psalm 14 is very clear we cannot speak of an absolute end point in Psalm 14. Not only does the formulation of the last verse (14:7) point forward to the following psalms; Psalm 15 projects the counter-image of the series in Psalms 9/10–14. "Zion" in Ps 14:7 becomes the "holy hill" in Ps 15:1. For the parallelism of these two expressions cf. Ps 2:6. Psalm 15 takes up a number of expressions from Psalm 14; the following are especially impressive:

> "say in their hearts" (14:1) // "speak the truth from their heart" (15:2)
> "there is no one who does good" (14:1b, 3b) // "do no evil to their friends" (15:3a); "who do these things" (15:5)
> "evildoers" (14:4) // "who do what is right" (15:2a).

Structure

The form of Psalm 14, which is exactly paralleled in Psalm 53, is unfortunately not very easy to comprehend because the psalm, especially in vv. 4-6, is very poorly preserved. Nevertheless we can discern the following sections:

1. The "fool": vv. 1-3
2. God's (or a prophet's? the psalmist's?) question: v. 4
3. The "righteous" and the "poor": vv. 5-6
4. The salvation of Israel: v. 7

After the superscription begins a section whose crucial word is "non-being." It occurs four times in vv. 1-3 (twice in v. 1 and twice in v. 3b). Contrasting with this Hebrew word is the word "existence" in v. 2b. Although the words "all" and the negative statement "they do not call upon the LORD" preserve the ties to vv. 1-3 the noun "my people" in v. 4 indicates a new direction. Moreover the mention of "*my* people" in v. 4 narrows the perspective from the universal (vv. 1-3) to Israel (v. 4). The clear conclusion in v. 3 indicates that v. 4 is a new beginning and stands independently. Therefore it is not clear who utters the question and how far it extends. Is the expression "my people" (14:4a) an indication of divine speech, or of the speech of a prophet or the psalmist? In v. 4b God is again referred to in the third person.

In vv. 5-6 the two half-verses 5a and 6a can scarcely be interpreted at all, but the two clauses introduced by "for" are clear: "for God is with the company of the righteous" (v. 5b) and "but the LORD is their refuge" (v. 6b). In spite of the poor state of the psalm's preservation the sense of this part is probably that the evildoers (v. 4a) are terrified (v. 5a) and their plan against the "poor" will not succeed (v. 6a).

The expression "restore the fortunes" in v. 7 is exilic and post-exilic language. This verse is frequently regarded as an exilic postscript to a prophetic text composed before the exile and used in worship. However the repeated word "people" creates a connection to v. 4 and vouches for the original character of the verse. It is questionable whether Psalm 14 belongs to the late pre-exilic period or was used in worship. Since this psalm uses characteristic wisdom expressions such as "fool" and "wise" (vv. 1, 2) it may well be a reflective poem from the time of the exile, so that v. 7 can be understood as an integral part of it.

Psalm 15

Context

Psalm 14:7 expects the salvation of Israel to come from Zion. Psalm 15:1 speaks of the "holy hill," which is Zion. Thus Ps 14:7 prepares for Psalm 15. Psalm 14 stands at the end of a downward-tending series that spoke with increasing pessimism about humanity. It reached its low point in Ps 14:1b, 3b:

> There is no one who does good (14:1b)
> There is no one who does good, no, not one (14:3b).

In Psalm 15, then, we find the counter-description of

> Those who walk blamelessly . . . and do no evil to their friends (15:2ab).

The contrast and correspondence of the two psalms must evidently be explained in this way: Psalm 14 makes urgently clear what is wrong with a person who abandons God and therefore is unable any longer to do what is good. Psalm 15 on the other hand makes it clear that only those who do good can live in the presence of God. Probably we can also say that human beings are only empowered for this good, humanly worthy way of acting when they remain in the presence of God. In any case the content of Psalms 14 and 15 is in clear opposition.

Psalm 15 has close connections to Psalm 12. Psalm 12:2-3 concentrates entirely on what happens within the human heart and what people say. The three words "lips," "heart," and "tongue," with the three uses of the verb "speak" give these two verses a decisive "speech" flavor. The words from Psalm 12 reappear in Psalm 15: "speak" and "heart" (v. 2b), "tongue" (v. 3a). Again the contrast between the two psalms is very clear. The verb "speak" and the noun "heart" also play a part in Ps 14:1a. Another important point of connection between Psalms 12 and 15 is the concept of the "neighbor" (Ps 12:2 // Ps 15:3ab). The connections to Psalm 15 extend beyond the sequence of Psalms 11–14 back to Ps 5:4-5. Psalm 15 is not absolutely disconnected from the sequence in Psalms 9/10–14, but it stands in clear opposition to the preceding psalms and from that point of view constitutes a new beginning within the first Book of Psalms. Psalm 15 is regarded as a classic example of a so-called entrance liturgy (entrance *torah,* portal liturgy). It is closely related to Psalm 24. Hence these two parallel texts, Psalms 15 and 24, can be regarded as caesuras in the sequence of the first Book of Psalms. Another example of an entrance liturgy is Isa 33:13-16.

Structure

The structure of Psalm 15 still reveals the traits of a worship service. Those visiting the Temple inquire of those standing guard before the gates of the sanctuary to learn the conditions of entrance (v. 1). A priest gives the information requested (vv. 2-5). Other phases of the ritual that are discernible include the confession of innocence on the part of those seeking access (cf. Pss 5:4-7; 26:3-8) and the response of the priest permitting them entrance. The prayer language in 15:1 (differing from the parallels in Ps 24:3 and Isa 33:14b), however, gives only an indirect glimpse of the worship service. The sequence of conditions for entrance, which are eleven distinct concepts, contains a set of fundamental social-ethical demands that have their parallels both in the law codes of the Pentateuch and in the wisdom literature. They can be summarized in the great commandment, "love your neighbor as yourself" (cf. Lev 19:18).

On the Sequence of Psalms 15–24

Psalms 15–24 are symmetrically arranged, with Psalm 19 at the center surrounded by a series of frames:

Entrance liturgy: Psalm 15
  Song of confidence: Psalm 16
    Song of lament: Psalm 17
      Royal psalm: Psalm 18
        Hymn to God's glory and *torah:* Psalm 19
      Royal psalms: Psalms 20 and 21
    Song of lament: Psalm 22
  Song of confidence: Psalm 23
Entrance liturgy: Psalm 24

Beyond this, within the sequence Psalms 17–18 and 20–21 reveal the corresponding prayers of the king and the people: the king's prayer of lament (Psalm 17) and prayer of thanksgiving (Psalm 18) correspond to the people's petition (Psalm 20) and prayer of thanksgiving (Psalm 21) for the king. The verbs "fall down" (20:8) and "meet/confront" (21:3), found in the petition in Ps 17:13 furnish a further connection between the psalms, which exceeds their thematic relationship (under the heading "God and God's anointed king").

Psalm 16

Context

If Psalm 15 relates to Ps 14:1b, 3 by presenting the person who does no harm to his or her neighbor in contrast to utterly corrupt humanity, Psalm 16 now offers a counter-statement to Ps 14:1a. To the one who says "there is no God" it contrasts the person who says to the Lord "You are my LORD; I have no good apart from you" (16:2). Psalm 16 develops genuine humanity as a life created and given by God. A human being is such only because God is his or her portion and inheritance. Psalms 15 and 16 correspond not only because they develop the ideas of "dwelling" (15:1; 16:9) and "not being moved" (15:5; 16:8) but also because Psalm 15 comments on the behavior of righteous people toward their neighbors while Psalm 16 (which has a theological orientation) develops the commandment of love of God even though the word "love" is not used. Psalm 16, together with Psalm 15, stands as a contrast to the portrait of the wicked developed up to Psalm 14. The paired "rejoice" and "be glad" in Ps 14:7 are taken up in reverse order in Ps 16:9 and are a further indication of this contrast. In addition the group of Psalms 15–24 is doubly bracketed: Psalm 15 has a parallel in Psalm 24 and Psalm 16 finds its counterpart in Psalm 23. The key word "good/goodness" (16:2) that marks the sequence of Psalms 14, 15, and 16 both in corresponding and contrasting forms carries over Ps 21:3 to Ps 23:6 (cf. also the noun "cup" in 16:5 and 23:5; the contrast to 16:5 is 11:6). "Goodness" is here always related to the one praying. Psalms 25 (v. 13) and 34 (vv. 12, 14, 16) also use the adjective "good." But these usages with reference to human beings are supplemented by the statement: God is good (25:8; 34:8).

Structure

The one praying speaks always of himself or herself, in the first person. Divisions are visible primarily through changes in the direction of the discourse. The first-person speech is shaped, in vv. 1, 2, and 5, as direct address to God, and this returns at the end of the psalm in vv. 10-11. Verses 6-9 speak about God. Thus there are three sections: a petition, founded on the assertion that one has taken refuge in God, introduces the prayer. The content of the first part (vv. 1-5) is confession of God as the sole good. This confession (vv. 2, 5) frames the turning away from "the holy ones," from other gods (vv. 3-4: here the text is quite opaque). The world of imagery introduced by the words "portion" and "lot" (v. 5) is developed in the part that speaks about God (vv. 6-9) in terms of "boundary lines" and "heritage." This part seems to reveal a double sequence of "experience of God—praise as a consequence" (vv. 6-7, 8-9). The one praying experiences God as a counselor (v. 7a). In the presence of God she or he is glad (vv. 8a, 9). The last part (vv. 10-11) addresses God and expresses confidence that, in the face of death, one will not be abandoned by God. In vv. 10-11 God's presence is protection and help against the advancing powers of death this side of death's boundary. However, the wording of the verse also indicates that God's presence is a stronghold for human beings at the moment of death and beyond.

This psalm is a song of confidence; as such it develops an important element of the individual song of lament into an entire psalm.

Psalm 17

Context

Psalm 17 is an individual song of lament. It has striking verbal connections with the preceding psalm: "heart" (17:3 // 16:9), "night" (17:3 // 16:7), "hold fast" (17:5 // 16:5), "be moved" (17:5 // 16:8), "God" (17:6 // 16:1), "seek refuge" (17:7 // 16:1), "right hand" (17:7 // 16:8, 11), "protect/guard" (17:8 // 16:1), "my life" (17:13 // 16:10), "portion" (17:14 // 16:11), "be filled" (17:14, 15 // 16:11), "you [God's] face" (17:15 // 16:11). But since the motifs of confidence that customarily appear in the course of an individual song of lament (vv. 7, 8, 15) are subordinated to the defining sections ("petition" and "declaration of innocence") this psalm, in spite of these numerous verbal echoes, has a very different feeling from the other song of confidence found in Psalm 16. The word for "human being" (17:4) connects Psalm 17 with the sequence in Psalms 8, 11–14. The comparison of the wicked to lions (17:12) creates a connection to Pss 7:2; 10:9; 22:13, while the declaration of innocence in 17:3-5 connects with Pss 5:4-7; 7:3-5.

Structure

The text of Psalm 17 can scarcely be translated at some points (vv. 3-5, 10a, 11, 14) but we can still detect the structure of the psalm as a whole. The three intensively-constructed series of petitions form the overall structure vv. 1-2, 6-8, 13-14. The three parts thus created can be characterized as follows: petitions and declaration of innocence (vv. 1-5), petitions and description of the suffering caused by the wicked and the enemies (vv. 6-12), and petitions and declaration of confidence and innocence (vv. 13-15). Although all three parts of the psalm are connected (vv. 1 and 6) there are closer ties between the first and third parts (divine name, righteousness, seeing, night/waking). The crisis for the one who prays cannot be precisely determined. It has its source in human beings who are this person's enemies and surround him or her. Experiencing other people as one's enemies, something repeatedly mentioned in the psalm, is nothing to be put off by. This type of prayer against enemies is realistic and, by praying God to save one from the enemy, serves to decrease the rage and tendency toward violence in the one who prays it. In vv. 8 and 15 there may be references to the Temple. The psalm may be placed in the period before the exile.

Psalm 18

Context

Psalm 18 has a very precise parallel in 2 Sam 22:1-51. In 2 Samuel "the song" is appropriately located at the end of the David traditions. Psalm 18 is (after Psalms 119 and 78) the third-longest text in the psalter. The comprehensive prayer includes such genres as song of thanksgiving, hymn, description of a theophany, and instructive discourse, and masterfully combines them into a single whole. It is attributed to David, who bears the honorific title "servant of the Lord" (title), "the Lord's king," and "the Lord's anointed" (v. 50). David is presented as the prime example of one who prays. The song of thanksgiving by David, the servant of YHWH, is a grandiose twin to David's prayer of lament in Psalm 17. Characteristic words from the song of lament are repeated in the song of thanksgiving: "enemy" (17:9 // 18:title, 3, 17, 37, 40, 48), "save" (17:13 // 18:2, 43, 48), "take refuge" (17:7 // 18:2, 30), "rise" (17:7, 13 // 18:38, 39, 48), "confront" (17:13 // 18:5, 18), "God hears" (17:1, 6 // 18:6), "bow down" (17:13 // 18:39), "righteousness" (17:1, 15 // 18:20, 25), "test/prove/refine" (17:3 // 18:30; cf. Ps 12:6). The petitions expressed in Psalm 17 ("hear," vv. 1, 6; "save," v. 13; "overthrow," v. 13) have been fulfilled in Psalm 18 (v. 6; vv. 2, 43, 48; v. 39). The same correspondence between petition and answer is found with regard to the word "steadfast love" (17:7 and 18:50). The common vocabulary points to the common themes of the two psalms: the problem of enemies, salvation by God, and the righteousness of the one who prays. What was addressed in a classically abbreviated form in the song of lament (Psalm 17) is dressed out richly, with a kind of baroque fullness, in the song of thanksgiving. Connections are established between Psalms 18 and 19 by the use of the word "perfect" or "blameless" (18:23, 25, 30, 33 // 19:7, 13). The whole sequence of Psalms 17–21 shows how the servant of YHWH, the anointed king, petitions (Psalm 17) and gives thanks (Psalm 18), acknowledging God as the creator and allowing himself to be formed by

YHWH's *torah* (Psalm 19). The people prays (Psalm 20) and gives thanks (Psalm 21) for such a king who has placed himself totally in the hands of God.

Structure

Although the psalm frequently shifts direction, from address to God to discourse about God and back to address, and although it makes use of a variety of forms and thus produces a somewhat discordant impression, its structural plan can be read in the repetition of certain striking words and sequences of words. The extensive superscription corresponds to an equally extensive subscript (v. 50). Taken together these give David's full title: he is YHWH's servant, king, and anointed. The opening line in v. 1 corresponds to the closing line in v. 49. The series of solemn divine titles in v. 2 corresponds to the resumé of titles with personal attribution in vv. 46-48 ("my rock," "the God of my salvation," "my deliverer"). But vv. 46-48 have a further function: they constitute the conclusion of the section comprising vv. 30-48. The beginning of that section (vv. 30, 31) also refers back to v. 2 ("shield," "take refuge," "rock"). The body of the psalm consists of two narratives of rescue (vv. 3-19 and 30-48). The middle (vv. 20-29) is connected to the first rescue narrative (vv. 27-28 // vv. 3, 11, 12) as well as to the second (vv. 23, 25 // vv. 30, 32, and v. 27 // v. 48). It develops the concluding statement of the first rescue narrative: God has rescued because God delights in the one who prays (v. 19b). God's delight rests on people who pray if they are righteous and pure. Righteousness and purity mean fidelity to YHWH's ways and commandments.

The first rescue narrative, expanded by a description of a theophany (vv. 7-15), is connected to the second by the words "deliver," "enemies," and "those who hate" (v. 17 // vv. 37, 40, 48) and by the idea that God has created a "broad place" for the one who prays (v. 19 // v. 36). It speaks of the crisis that presses hard on the one praying. This person's enemies are death and the underworld (vv. 3-5, 16). YHWH has led this person from that "fenced-in" situation into a broad space (vv. 6, 19). The second rescue narrative scarcely speaks of the crisis directly. The enemies (vv. 37, 40, 38) and those who stand up against the one who prays (vv. 39, 48) are handed over entirely to the royal speaker by God's help (vv. 30, 35).

In the present structure, which cannot be literarily dissected, we can still recognize the different tradition history of certain parts: at the beginning there was probably a royal song giving thanks to God for a fullness of power over his enemies in war (vv. 30-48). This song was combined with a song of thanksgiving that gave much more emphasis to the crisis situation (vv. 3-19). The middle of the psalm (vv. 20-29) formulates the teaching that God saves the righteous. The teaching itself is transcended by the idea that God creates salvation for a humble people and casts down the eyes of the proud (v. 27). For a moment the focus shifts from the king to the people, who confess the LORD as the one and only God (v. 31). The royal song of victory and thanksgiving could go back to the early pre-exilic period. The individual song of thanksgiving (vv. 3-19), which need not be spoken only by the king, mentions the Temple (v. 6) and therefore can also be dated to the pre-exilic era. The composition as a whole should probably be located after the exile. The theology of the poor at the center of the instruction (v. 27 within the framework of vv. 20-29) and the community's confession of God's uniqueness (v. 31) are indications of that later period.

Psalm 19

Context

This psalm does not fall into two unrelated sequential texts, an ancient Canaanite creation hymn (vv. 1-6) and a newer, post-exilic psalm on the Law (vv. 7-14), nor does the psalm as a whole stand in isolation within the series of Psalms 18–21. The relationships between Ps 18:20-32 and Ps 19:7-13 are especially striking: "perfect" (18:23, 25, 30, 32 // 19:7), "be blameless" (18:25 // 19:13), "purity" and "pure" (18:20, 24, 26 // 19:8b-9a), "enlighten" (18:28 // 19:8), "law" (18:22 // 19:9), "righteousness" and "be righteous" (18:20, 24 // 19:9), "keep/observe" (18:23 // 19:11). The connection of the two psalms is rendered still more firm by the following words: "servant" (18:title // 19:11, 13), "rock" (18:2, 31, 46 // 19:14), "heavens" (18:9, 13 // 19:1, 6), "God" (18:2, 30, 32, 47 // 19:1), "voice" (18:13 // 19:3), "earth" (18:15 //

19:4), "run" (18:29 // 19:5). The divine hurler of thunderbolts is certainly to be understood as a warrior (18:14). The perfect devout/pious man (18:25) topples ramparts and leaps over walls (18:29), thus proving himself an experienced warrior (18:34). The sun is compared both to a bridegroom and to a warrior (19:5). Psalm 18 ends with the hymnic participles "[giving] great triumphs to his king and [showing] steadfast love to his anointed [= Messiah]." The verb "to work" is taken up immediately in Ps 19:1 as a noun: "handiwork." The psalm concludes with a promise to sing to the name of YHWH (18:49), and the glorification of God follows in Psalm 19. There the heavens and the firmament, day and night begin the song.

Structure

The psalm has the following arrangement:

The glory of El: vv. 1-6
  The narrative of the heavens: vv. 1-4ab
  The arising of the sun: vv. 4c-6c
The integrity of the Lord's commandments and of the speaker: vv. 7-14
  The integrity of the Lord's commandments: vv. 7-10
  The integrity of the speaker: vv. 11-14

Psalm 19 is a unit, but its parts are so clearly marked, both stylistically and thematically, that it is common to speak of it as two psalms. The first part (vv. 1-6) is carefully divided into two smaller sections (vv. 1-4a and 4b-6). The first of these introduces heaven and the firmament, day and night as proclaimers of the glory of God. They themselves are works from God's hand and speak wordlessly to the whole universe of God the creator's power and the beauty of creation. In v. 4a the text comes to a pause: "heavens" at the beginning (v. 1) and "earth" (v. 4a) constitute a whole. The section beginning with v. 4b is devoted to the sun. "Sun" (v. 4b) and "heaven" (vv. 1, 6) are alliterative nouns in Hebrew. As the psalm began with "heavens," so again the noun "heavens" stands at the end of the first part. The sun, likened to a bridegroom and a warrior, is the universal herald of the divine glory. Although nights may also declare to one another the power of God (v. 2b), the second section gives precedence to the message about God proclaimed by the day (vv. 2a, 4b-6).

The second part of the psalm (vv. 7-14) has YHWH's *torah* for its theme. Like the first part it consists of two carefully formed and closely connected sections: vv. 7-10 and 11-14. The sections are differentiated by the shift in the address. Verses 7-10 speak about God, while vv. 11-14 address God. Characteristic of this whole part is the sevenfold use of the divine name YHWH. In the first section (vv. 7-10) it is related to two groups of three genitive attributes. These groups of three attribute two feminine substantives in the singular and one masculine substantive in the plural to the divine name (vv. 7-8a and 8b-9). The seventh use of the divine name is found in the emphatic final position as a vocative (v. 14). The sevenfold use of the divine name, which is entirely absent from the first part of the psalm, indicates a deliberate ordering of the text; similarly the use of the word "perfect," or "blameless" (vv. 7, 13) points to the intended concern of the psalm. The first section praises YHWH's expressed will. YHWH's *torah* sustains the life of the human being. The praises of the Lord's commandments culminate in a comparison: gold is not more desirable than YHWH's righteous ordinances, nor is honey sweeter than they are (v. 10). The second section personalizes the praise. The one who prays has personally experienced the beneficial effects of the divine *torah* (v. 11) and yet YHWH's *torah* is transcended: the psalmist prays YHWH directly for innocence and the ability to stand fast against the arrogance of the wicked (vv. 12-13).

In addition to a series of unique characteristics of style the following matter points particularly to the internal relationship of the two parts of the psalm: The *torah,* which in the hymn in vv. 7-10 is brought into direct relationship to "Lady Wisdom," is presented as a bride to whom is owed all human devotion (cf. Song 6:9-10). This yields a correspondence to vv. 1-6, where the sun is directly compared to a bridegroom.

Psalm 20

Context

This psalm has very few connections to the one that immediately precedes it. The theme of "day" reveals the contrast between the two: Psalm 20 speaks of the "day of trouble" (v. 1) and the "[day] when we call" (v. 9). These are not the same days as those that Psalm 19 sang about as the proclaimers of God's glory (v. 2). On the other hand the statements in Ps 19:8 and Ps 20:4 ("heart") are complementary. "Heaven" is found in Pss 20:6 and 19:1, 6. "Mighty" in Ps 20:6 is related to the "hero" with whom the sun was compared.

There are many connections to Psalm 18: "day" (20:1, 9 // 18:title, 18), "answer" (20:1, 6, 9 // 18:41), "name [of God]" (20:1, 5, 7 // 18:49), "send [help]" (20:2 // 18:16), "support" (20:2 // 18:35), "give" (20:4 // 18:13, 32, 35, 40, 47), "salvation"/"save" (20:5, 6, 9 // 18:2, 3, 27, 35, 41, 46, 50), "anointed" (20:6 // 18:50), "heaven" (20:6 // 18:9, 13), "the right hand of God" (20:6 // 18:35), "fall," (20:8 // 18:39), "rise" (20:8 // 18:38, 39, 48), and "king" (20:9 // 18:50).

Structure

The structure of the psalm is evident from two phenomena, namely the shift in the direction of address and the repetition of words. (1) With regard to the change in direction of address the psalm divides into two sections, vv. 1-4 and 5-9. In vv. 1-4 we find a strictly maintained rhetorical situation: God is spoken of in the third person. Petitions to God are expressed on behalf of a person who is addressed directly. The speaker could be a priest (cf., for example, Num 6:24-26). Verses 5-9 represent the speech of a group. This section is marked by "we" expressions (vv. 5a, 7, 8, 9b). In v. 5 the group is still addressing the subject from the previous section. The address to a single individual is then dropped and returns only in v. 9a, but there it is YHWH who is addressed directly. An "I" interrupts the speech of the group in v. 6. It speaks of the past and present/future actions of YHWH for YHWH's anointed.

(2) The division of the psalm occasioned by the shift in the direction of address is confirmed by the repetition of words important to the psalms. "Salvation"/"save" forms an inclusion around vv. 5-9 and also appears twice in v. 6. Other repeated sequences of words like "answer" (vv. 1, 6, 9) and "the name of the God of Jacob," "the name of our God," "the name of YHWH our God" (vv. 1, 5, 7) support the unity of the psalm. Cf. also the root "remember" in vv. 3 and 7.

In outline form, the structure of the psalm may be represented as follows:

1. Prayer (of the priest) for the king: vv. 1-4
2. Confession and prayer of the community: vv. 5-9
   - Confession of the group ("we"): v. 5a
     - Prayer for the king: v. 5b
       - Confession of the "I": v. 6
   - Confession of the group ("we"): vv. 7-8
     - Prayer for the king and the group: v. 9

The voices audible in the psalm permit us to recognize a liturgical action but it cannot be more precisely identified as, for example, a service at the king's ascent of the throne. As for the identity of the person for whom the first part of the psalm prays and who is continually addressed, there is no clarity at the beginning. The content of the prayer insinuates that this "you" is not just anyone. Only at the end of the psalm does the word "king" appear (v. 9), but we cannot tell with certainty from the wording whether this means the human or the divine king. The prayer of the priest is followed by the prayer of the group (vv. 5, 7-9). It is interrupted by the confession of an "I" who can best be understood as the anointed one, that is, the king. The repeated passages in vv. 5-9 involve shifts in meaning (the earthly sanctuary of Zion in v. 2 is contrasted to the heavenly sanctuary in v. 6; cf. Ps 11:4), but they do not justify any literary-critical division of the psalm. Shifts of accent can also be detected in the various phases of the prayer. In the priestly prayer God is the active subject, but the benefits of God's action are solely for the king. The prayer emphasizes the king's prominent position. When the group begins to speak (v. 5a) it does confirm salvation by the king as a reason for rejoicing and it takes up the priestly prayer, but at the same time it refers to "the name of our God." In God's name the group raises its banner; it withdraws from any glorification of the king. Not through the means of military power, but through the name of God does this group find security (vv. 7-8, 9). The king in his own confession (v. 7) takes up the references to his dependence on the saving power of God. The expression "his anointed" describes both the dignity of the king and the limits of his power. If he does not turn to YHWH he is nothing, for YHWH alone has saved (v. 6). The psalm, as a prayer for the king, shows complete loyalty to the king who knows himself dependent on YHWH and acknowledges that dependence. At the same time the psalm problematizes royalty. There is a threefold tension between God, king, and people that must be brought into a state of equilibrium. The poles are named at the beginning and end: may God answer the king (v. 1a), and may God answer the people (v. 9b).

Psalm 21

Context

This psalm begins where Psalm 20 ended: "king" and "save"/"salvation" are the closest spatial connectors (20:9 and 21:2). The close association of these psalms both in content and language is unmistakable. The petition in 20:4 is fulfilled in 21:2: "may God grant"/"you have given." The close relationship between these two royal psalms has always been recognized. For both of them a common setting in a liturgical celebration related to the royal institution was postulated: the prayer service on going to war (Psalm 20) and the liturgy of thanksgiving after return from victorious battle (Psalm 21); alternatively two phases in the coronation celebration or within the framework of the celebration of the anniversary of the king's accession. It is true that the concept of a royal institution aware of its own power as expressed in Ps 21:2-6, 8-12 is not so fully developed in Psalm 20, where it is evident only in vv. 2-4, 5b. On the other hand, while the elements in Ps 20:5a, 6, 7-9 that relativize the position of the king find less emphasis in Psalm 21, they are not absent (vv. 1, 7, 13). Ultimately they furnish the conceptual framework for the whole psalm. In v. 7 "steadfast love" refers back to Pss 17:7 and 18:50 and forward to Ps 23:6. The verb "trust" (v. 7) points to Ps 22:4, 5, 9. In Psalms 20 and 21 there is an underlying pre-exilic stratum that bears the clear features of an ancient oriental ideology of kingship (20:1-4; 21:1-6, 8-12). These parts may have had their historical basis in a ritual for the king (cf. also Ps 18:29-48). In Psalms 20 and 21 these bits of royal ideology have been defused. The king is placed within the community of those who revere YHWH, and the king's allegiance to YHWH justifies his existence and activity. This reinterpretation within the psalms probably occurred only in the period of the exile or thereafter.

Structure

The psalm is constructed in a clear and artful manner. Two sections (vv. 1-6; 8-13) are formulated in second person singular address and are separated by the objective speech in v. 7. The formulation at the beginning (v. 1) is resumed in an altered form at the end (v. 13). In v. 13 the group that speaks of itself as "we" takes the floor and has the last word. Thus there is a tension between the beginning and end of the psalm: the king should rejoice in the power of YHWH (v. 1); the group, the nation, will sing of the power of YHWH (v. 13b). This connection of the king to the people is found also in Psalm 20 (vv. 1a, 9b). An overview of the structure of the psalm is as follows:

1. Direct address to YHWH: YHWH's gifts and ordinances for a king: vv. 1-6
   a. v. 1-3 // b. vv. 4-6
2. Discourse on YHWH and the king: v. 7
3. Direct address to the king: royal intentions toward enemies (vv. 8-12)
4. Petition of the community: v. 13

The psalm praises the greatness and glory YHWH has given to the king (vv. 1-6) and represents the king as a victorious warrior against his enemies (vv. 8-12). He is thus the warrior against evil (v. 11). However, at the same time the psalm states the conditions for the king's actions: the king trusts in YHWH and only through the grace of the Most High does he stand fast (v. 7). When the community celebrates the power of YHWH and trusts in YHWH it acquires royal features of its own (v. 13).

Psalm 22

This psalm, according to the gospels of Matthew and Mark, is Jesus' dying prayer (Matt 27:46; Mark 15:34).

Context

This lament stands as a profound contrast to Psalm 21. The key word "help" common to both psalms (21:1 // 22:1) starkly illuminates the contrast. The king rejoices in YHWH's help; now one who is no longer even a human being experiences the distance of God; hence for this person there is no help. Other important words that link these two psalms are "trust" (21:7 // 22:4, 5, 9) and "offspring" who will experience a contrary fate (21:10 // 22:23, 30). With the acknowledgment of YHWH's rule and dominion over the nations (22:28) another contrasting relationship to Psalm 21 is set up. The image of the "ravening lion" for human enemies (17:12 // 22:13, 21) and the uncommon verb "encircle" (17:9 // 22:16) link Psalm 22 to Psalm 17. The threefold framing of the royal psalms (18, 20, 21) by Psalms 15 // 24; 16 // 23; and 17 // 22 is confirmed by these links.

Structure

The text of this psalm, which is great by any measure, has a clear structure that appears in outline as follows:

I. The Lament: vv. 1-21
   1. First series, "lament and petition," vv. 1-11
   2. Second series, "lament and petition," vv. 12-21

II. Song of Thanksgiving: vv. 22-26

III. Hymn: vv. 27-31

The individual song of lament in vv. 1-21 is framed by the words "distance" and "help/rescue" (v. 1), nouns that are echoed by the corresponding verbs in the concluding petition (vv. 19a, 21). The verb "answer" (v. 2) is resumed, in the MT, at the end of the petition and marks the transition to the song of thanksgiving (v. 21). The plea in v. 11 that God be not far away divides this extensive lament into two sections whose structure is shaped respectively by the narrative of crisis (lament) and petition (vv. 1-11 and 12-21).

In the first series of "lament and petition" there are other elements typical of the genre of the individual lament. The lament itself is framed by the motif of trust expressed by "my God" (vv. 1, 10b). The fundamental lament at the experience of being abandoned by God (vv. 1-2) is contrasted with the petitioner's memory of the holy God who is far away, enthroned on the praises of Israel (v. 3). Yet it is precisely in this holy God that the ancestors placed their trust, and they were rescued (vv. 4-5). The emphatic address to the holy God (v. 3) corresponds to the emphasis with which the petitioner introduces him- or herself: "But I am a worm, and not human!" (v. 6). The lament of this destroyed person concentrates, then, on the behavior of the people who despise and mock her or him (vv. 7-8). The quotation of the mockers' speech dramatizes the text. In v. 9 the petitioner turns to God, recalls his or her own experience with God, and expresses a confession of trust. This also functions as a motivation for God to intervene on behalf of the petitioner (vv. 9-10). The lament concludes properly with a petition that employs the dialectic of "far and near" (v. 11). The divine name YHWH has thus far appeared in the psalm only in the speech of the people who mock the petitioner.

The second series of lament (vv. 12-18) and petition (vv. 19-21) concentrates on the behavior of the people round about. The "company of evildoers" (v. 16) is compared to bulls, lions, and dogs (vv. 12-13, 16a, 17b, 18). The accusation against the enemies forms the framework on which to hang the personal lament (vv. 14, 15a, 17a) and the lament addressed to God (v. 15b). The lament to God, which is formulated as briefly as possible, is at the center of the narrative of crisis:

Accusation against the enemies: vv. 12-13
    Personal lament: vv. 14-15a
        Lament to God: v. 15b
Accusation against the enemies: v. 16
    Personal lament: v. 17a
Accusation against the enemies: vv. 17b, 18

The petition (vv. 19-21) is strictly oriented to the preceding description of the overwhelming distress. In a chiastic sequence recapitulating the lament there is a mention of the "dog," the "lion," and the "wild oxen/bulls."

This song of lament, so elaborately developed, is intended to express the distress and fears of a human being. In this description of human suffering that exceeds the possible or actual experience of any individual, a great many people will or can discover themselves and their own anguish. The words of the psalm make available words for all human suffering. The lament in Psalm 22 demonstrates, as is also evident from the book of Job, that suffering does not preclude formally perfect discourse.

The last word in v. 21 (according to the MT), "you have answered me," forms the transition to the individual song of thanksgiving that follows in vv. 22-26. There is discussion about whether this word should be regarded as an indication of the existence of a priestly oracle of salvation. The liturgical action in which, after a petitioner has sung a song of lament, a priest gives him or her a response in the name of God ("fear not, I am with you") is often adduced as an explanation for the "change of mood" that regularly appears in individual songs of lament.

The individual song of thanksgiving can only be found in v. 22 as a kind of summary. This song of thanksgiving would be sung in the midst of the extended family. In vv. 23-26 it is expanded into a song not merely of an individual but of the community of those who fear YHWH. The community praises God's concern for the misery of those who suffer. In spite of this expansion the order of the text as a whole is such that the confession of YHWH who does not despise the anguish of the sufferers is placed at the center. Verses 22-23 and 25-26 frame v. 24:

I-declaration; direct address to God ("congregation," "praise");
Speech about God; call to praise: vv. 22-23
    Reason: God has not despised: v. 24
I-declaration; direct address ("great congregation," "praise");
Speech about God; call to praise: vv. 25-26

In the final section (vv. 27-31) the group of people who praise God is again expanded in both space and time. First all the ends of the earth and all the families of the nations are called to remember, repent, and worship. This call is founded on the assertion of the rule of YHWH over all nations (vv. 27-28). Universal adoration of God is also to be practiced by all generations, those who have already lived and those now living (vv. 29-31). The generations yet to come must be told of the Almighty. This call to adore and to tell the story is founded on the action of God, who is called the LORD (v. 30). That the dead also adore God is a sign that the final expansion of the text, with its broadening in space and time, must be located at a very late period. But it does not neglect to retain the connection to the older, individual song of thanksgiving (v. 22) by use of the verb "tell" in v. 30.

Psalm 23

Context

This psalm has numerous connections to its surrounding context. First of all, in the overall structure of Psalms 15–24 it is a song of confidence corresponding to Psalm 16. Striking words in both psalms underscore this relationship "my cup" (16:5 // 23:5); "goodness" (16:2 // 23:6). The noun "mercy/steadfast love" (23:6) creates a connection to Ps 17:7 via Ps 18:50 to Ps 21:7. The word combination "goodness and mercy/ steadfast love" (23:6) ties it to Psalm 21 (vv. 3, 7). This psalm also adds another to the series of metaphors for God in relation to one who prays (Pss 16:2, 5; 18:1, 2, 46; 19:14; 22:9, 10, 19); this time "my shepherd." The metaphor of the shepherd is joined in Psalm 23 with that of the host. Both of these were introduced in Psalm 22 in reverse order: 22:26 speaks of the banquet of the poor while 22:28 speaks of YHWH's reign. In ancient oriental and biblical discourse the king is a shepherd.

The plea for God's nearness and help, so urgently formulated in Ps 22:19-20, the plea for the rescue of one's life, has been heard: the shepherd restores life (23:3a). Psalm 23 is the fulfillment of the telling of the name of YHWH (23:3b) promised in Ps 22:22. The motif of trust from Psalm 22 that appealed to God's readiness to help (22:9, 10, 19) is taken up with these new metaphors and further developed. The lament to God (God's distance in 22:1; God's placing the one who prays in the dust of death, 22:15b) is replaced in Psalm 23 by the confession that God leads one in green pastures (23:2a) and abides with the one praying (23:4). In Psalm 23 God is the shepherd of an "individual." This is a derived use of the metaphor. Originally it referred to Israel (Ps 80:1; Ezekiel 34). In Ps 22:28 the metaphor was prepared for with the royal title that was the foundation of all the remembering, repenting, and adoring of the nations of the earth. The final expansion of Psalm 22 establishes further word connections to Psalm 23: "fat ones"/ "anoint with oil" (22:29 // 23:5) and "righteousness" (22:31 // 23:3).

Structure

The structure of the psalm is marked by two compositional schemata that reinforce one another but also are layered upon each other to create an artistically designed tension: the ordering of the text according to the metaphors of "shepherd" and "host" does not match the order created by the shift in the direction of address.

YHWH is shepherd: vv. 1-4
    Speech about God; I-discourse: vv. 1-3

Speech to God; I-discourse: v. 4
YHWH is host: vv. 5-6
Speech to God; I-discourse: v. 5
Speech about God; I-discourse: v. 6

The psalm begins and ends with the name of God (vv. 1, 6b). For the sake of the divine name (23:3) YHWH is self-revealed as shepherd and host to individual devout people (cf. 22:22), to the community of those who fear God and regard themselves as the poor (cf. 22:23, 26), and even to the nations who turn to YHWH (cf. 22:27-28). The psalm is to be understood, in its present context, on all three levels.

God's care for the one praying, expressed by both metaphors, is emphasized by parallels at the level of content: YHWH, as shepherd, leads into green pastures and beside still waters—that is, YHWH provides food and drink (v. 2); as a host YHWH spreads the table and fills the cup (v. 5). As a shepherd YHWH comforts with rod and staff (v. 4); as host YHWH gives goodness and mercy (v. 6). The two metaphors are mutually supportive: the shepherd's protection accompanies the wandering herd; the host takes care that the guests are content and that they remain. The parallel construction of the text, oriented to the metaphors, that in turn leads to parallel and mutually expanding statements of content, is crossed by the shifting direction of speech within the psalm. The parts in direct address (vv. 4 and 5) oriented to the two metaphors have the same thought pattern insofar as both of them speak of the danger threatening the one who prays: "the darkest valley" (v. 4a) corresponds to "in the presence of my enemies" (v. 5).

Psalm 24

Context

The psalm begins with a formulation analogous to that in Ps 22:28. The earth belongs to YHWH (24:1; cf. 3:8). These two statements enhance each other and are referred to one another. The hymnic conclusion of Psalm 22 presents the theme of "dominion" (22:28) and "righteousness" (22:31), both of which are taken up in Ps 23:1, 3 and developed in Psalm 24. Psalm 24:3-5 develops the theme of "righteousness" and vv. 7-10 the theme of the "king of glory." The expression "those who seek YHWH" establishes a connection between Ps 22:26 and Ps 24:6. In regard to the immediately preceding psalm there is first of all a contrast between the individual who dwells in the house of YHWH (23:6, a corrupted text) and those who dwell on earth, but similarity in the depiction of the Temple (23:6) and the mountain of YHWH with its sanctuary and its gates (24:3, 7, 9).

The words "earth" and "world" (24:1) and the depiction of the "strong and mighty" Lord in 24:8 establish connections to Ps 19:5, 6. Similarity of structure (double question with "who" and answer) and a common vocabulary ("hill," "holy place," "clean," "heart," "lift up," "swear," "righteousness") link Ps 24:3-6 to Psalm 15. The psalms that are similar in genre and language thus mark off segments within the sequential continuity of the psalms. They indicate stopping points but not an absolute end. Thus the rare expression "lift up the soul" (24:4 // 25:1), the expression "God of their/my salvation" (24:5 // 25:5) and the noun "heart" (24:4 // 25:17) are links between Psalms 24 and 25. The contacts between Psalms 24 and 26 are still stronger: "clean hands" // "innocence of hands" (24:4 // 26:6), "pure heart" // "tested heart" (24:4 // 26:2), "holy place" // "the place where your glory abides" (24:3 // 26:8) "blessing" // "bless" = praise (24:5 // 26:12).

Structure

The psalm has four parts:

1. Hymn to the one who founded the world, to whom the world belongs: vv. 1-2
2. Liturgy for ascent of the mountain of YHWH ("*torah* of entrance"): vv. 3-5
3. Confirmation of identity: v. 6
4. Liturgy for the entry of YHWH into the Temple: vv. 7-10

The name of God frames the psalm as a whole (vv. 1a, 10). The emphatic introduction of YHWH in vv. 1-2 has its flanking wings (insertion of the personal pronoun in vv. 2 and 10) in the liturgy for YHWH's entry into the Temple. The name of God seems to mark the boundaries of the various sections of the psalm: the liturgy for people's ascent to the mountain of the Lord is framed by the name of YHWH (vv. 3a, 5a). The responses in the liturgy for YHWH's entry into the Temple again make emphatic use of the divine name (v. 8, twice; v. 10). In addition both liturgies are given their character by the double question "who" (vv. 3a, b and vv. 8, 10) and the respective answers (vv. 4-5 and 8, 10). Common to both liturgies is the verb "lift up" (vv. 4, 5, 7, 9). Verse 6 seems isolated within the fabric as a whole. Its function is to establish identity. The parallel between those who seek YHWH and those "who seek the face of Jacob" is unusual, but the verse not only makes parallel those who seek YHWH with those who seek Jacob; it equates them. Concretely this means that the verse plays on the theme of the pilgrimage of the nations to Zion. While in Psalm 22 the poor who seek YHWH and the tribes of the nations who turn and adore YHWH are still different groups (vv. 26, 27), they are united in Ps 24:6. The late post-exilic theology of the pilgrimage of the nations reveals this verse as a posterior interpretation of a pre-exilic Temple theology. The attempt to give a detailed reconstruction of the two liturgies in this psalm, with their complementarity of content and mutual interplay, places too many demands on the text as we have it. The psalm is more a literary summary of pre-exilic theology than a concrete and up-to-date textbook with chapter headings.

YHWH is hymnically introduced as the proprietor of the earth, the owner as founder. It is YHWH who mastered the waters of chaos and was thus shown to be the creator God; it is as creator that YHWH is celebrated, for YHWH is constantly needed and constantly at work in holding the world together, preserving it against the waters of chaos that are continually trying to overcome it. YHWH has founded the earth and is still establishing it (vv. 1-2). The liturgy for the people's ascent of the mountain of YHWH (24:3-5) is similar to its analogous images in Psalm 15 and Isa 33:14-16, but it has its own profile. In contrast to Psalm 15 the exclusion of the neighbors in Ps 24:4 is remarkable. The formulation of the conditions for entry into the holy place is here concentrated on cultic purity and steadfast devotion toward YHWH. Those who are admitted to the sanctuary will take away from it blessing and righteousness—that is, fullness of life—from YHWH, the God of salvation. Because human beings do not lift up their lives to what is false, that is, to other gods, they obtain fullness and life from YHWH. The people's ascent of the mountain of YHWH (vv. 3-5) corresponds to YHWH's entry into the sanctuary (vv. 7-10). YHWH does not dwell on Zion as a god enclosed within a sanctuary. The creator and owner of the world comes to the sanctuary to encounter human beings. The liturgy acknowledges YHWH as the king of glory, an expression that is repeated five times. Human beings live from their encounter with YHWH, the king of glory. YHWH as warrior against chaos (v. 2) and one mighty in battle (v. 8) provides protection in every danger.

Psalms 25–34

The alphabetical psalms 25 and 34 frame the next complex of psalms. Directly related to the character of these two psalms as alphabetic acrostics are some additional common features: each psalm lacks a *waw* line. Both run through the Hebrew alphabet (except for *waw*) and then add a *pe* line with the same verb ("redeem"). The *mem, ayin,* and *pe* lines have similar beginnings in each case. Beyond these very formal common features are the thematic connections of the two psalms in which the word "good" plays an especially important role. It is found in both psalms as a predicate of God (25:8 // 34:8). At the same time Psalm 34 announces the theme of "doing good" in the human sphere, which will be treated in Psalms 35–41 (34:10, 12, 14; 35:12; 36:3, 4; 37:3, 16, 27; 38:20; 39:2).

The theme of divine "grace" is also important in delimiting the section of psalms encompassing 25 through 34. The confession "your mercy . . . and . . . your steadfast love . . . have been from of old" (25:6) is followed by a corresponding statement in Ps 33:5, "the earth is full of the steadfast love of the LORD." Between these fundamental statements about divine grace are the following instances of the concept of "grace" or "steadfast love": 25:7, 10; 26:3; 31:7, 16, 21; 32:10; 33:18, 22. Although Psalm 25 contains a plethora of theological concepts the important nouns "blessing" and "righteousness" from Ps 24:5 are not incorporated. This omission seems again to emphasize the function of Psalm 25 as a new beginning within the sequence of the psalms.

Psalm 25

Context

This psalm is connected to the one immediately before it by the very unusual expression "lift up my soul" (24:4 // 25:1). Precisely the same expression as in 25:1 is found in Pss 86:4 and 143:8. The verb "lift up" plays an important role throughout these two psalms (24:4, 5, 7, 9 // 25:1, 18). Other connective elements in Psalms 24 and 25 are the "who" questions in 24:8 (cf. vv. 3, 10) and 25:12, and the expression "God of salvation" (24:5 // 25:5). The question of access to the sanctuary is answered in Psalm 24 by reference to one's personal dedication to YHWH. Psalm 25 asks with constantly varied pleas for a conduct of life according to the ways of God.

Psalm 25 introduces a new vocabulary within the psalter that in turn creates new relationships. New to the psalter at this point is the verb "hope," also translated "wait for" (Ps 25:3, 5, 21). It is taken up again in Ps 27:14 and appears within the first book of psalms also in 37:34; 39:7; 40:1 (and later in Pss 52:8; 69:20; 130:5). Also new to the psalter at this point is the pairing of "way" and "path" (25:4), which is used again in Ps 27:11. The same is true of the verb "teach" in Ps 25:8, 12 and Ps 27:11. For the first time in the psalter this psalm speaks of the "covenant" (25:10, 14) and "mercy" (25:6); the latter is paralleled with God's "steadfast love." "Steadfast love" itself (25:6, 7) follows the noun "truth" or "faithfulness" (25:5); the two are paired in 25:10 and the same pairing follows immediately in 26:3. The connection between "steadfast love and faithfulness" on the one hand and "mercy" on the other is also found in Ps 40:10-11 where (in vv. 9-10) it is augmented by the theme of "righteousness." In Ps 33:5 "righteousness and justice" are closely connected with "steadfast love." The notes first sounded in Psalm 25 combine in Ps 40:9-11 to form the closing chord of the first book of psalms.

Structure

In spite of the formal restrictions of the acrostic we can observe a meaningful sequence and intentional structure in this psalm. In outline the structure appears as follows:

- A Prayer: confidence, hope, shaming, enemies: vv. 1-3 (// vv. 19-21)
- B Prayer: God's ways, forgiveness of sin: vv. 4-7 (// vv. 16-18)
- C About God: God's goodness and that of God's ways, covenant: vv. 8-10 (// vv. 12-15)
- D Prayer: forgiveness of sins (v. 11)
- C' About God: God knows the way and leads out of trouble, covenant: vv. 12-15 (// vv. 8-10)
- B' Prayer: rescue and forgiveness of sins: vv. 16-18 (// vv. 4-7)
- A' Prayer: enemies, shaming, hope: vv. 19-21 (// vv. 1-3)
- E Prayer: for Israel's redemption (v. 22)

Components of prayer emerge very clearly in vv. 1-7, 11, 16-22. In vv. 8-10 and 12-15 the psalmist speaks about God. Repetitions of words indicate additional movements within the structure. The sections are thematically arranged. Most obvious is the framing at the beginning and end of the psalm: the motifs of "hope," "shaming," and "enemies," together with the language of prayer frame the sections in vv. 1-3 and 19-21. Verses 4-7 and 16-18, also formulated as prayers, show thematic concentration on the theme of divine mercy and forgiveness of sins. Verse 11 belongs with them, forming the center of the psalm as a whole. The two corresponding pieces that speak about God (vv. 8-10 // 12-15) are characterized by their emphasis on the important themes of "God's ways," "God's teaching," and "God's covenant." The individual sections, although well delimited, are still connected one to another. This is especially true of the main section in vv. 4-18. The theme of "God's ways" is introduced in prayer (vv. 4-5) and developed in reflections about God (vv. 8-10, 12-15). The theme of "sin," which is worked out in prayer (vv. 7, 11, 18) remains present also in the section represented by vv. 8-10 (v. 8). The repetition of the verb "bring out" from v. 15 in v. 17 makes it clear that the theme of "being led on God's ways" is not dropped in the prayer section in vv. 16-18. In addition the "I" who characteristically speaks in vv. 1-7, 11, 16-21 also appears in v. 15; this is another indication of the connections among the parts of the psalm. Even the last verse of the psalm (v. 22), which transforms the individual prayer to a petition on behalf of Israel (and was certainly added at a later time) preserves the relationship to the text as a whole by repeating the word "troubles" from v. 17. The verb "redeem" in v. 22 points to Pss 26:11 and 31:5, but especially to 34:22. Striking here is the address "God" as opposed to "my God" in v. 2 and especially "YHWH" in vv. 1, 4, 6, 7, and 11.

At the beginning and end of the psalm are petitions for rescue from the accusations of the enemy. These pleas, intensified by assertions of confidence in God, are characteristic of the individual song of lament. The principal part of the psalm, however, does not match that genre, nor are there any indications of liturgical actions. The psalm is a high theological composition, probably from the late post-exilic period. It introduces wisdom motifs ("ways and paths") and connects them with many of the deeds and characteristics of God depicted in the book of Exodus. The psalm is an exercise of memory on the part of the one who prays it, with an appeal to God's ability to remember as well. God is the God of salvation because God can remember God's gracious ways and mercy. God is good, and God's ways are steadfast love and faithfulness. God teaches; that is, God gives the *torah* (vv. 8, 12) and makes the divine covenant known (v. 14). It is important that human beings keep that covenant (v. 10). God forgives human sins (vv. 11, 18). The psalm is first of all the prayer of an individual who depicts herself or himself as alone and poor, but the point of view expands from that of one who fears God (v. 12) to that of all those who fear God (v. 14), from the individual poor person (v. 16) to the group of the poor (v. 9). In connection with the universalism of Ps 24:6, where those who seek YHWH are identified with those who seek Jacob, and with the key-word links between Pss 24:4 and 25:1, Psalm 25 acquires an additional element beyond the meaning established in v. 22 (a prayer for Israel): that is, Psalm 25 is the prayer of the nations that turn to YHWH and acknowledge YHWH as God.

Psalm 26

Context

This psalm is connected to Psalm 25 by the following elements: "right"/"vindicate" (25:9 // 26:1), "integrity" (25:21 // 26:1, 11), "trust" (25:2 // 26:1), "heart" (25:17 // 26:2), "steadfast love and faithfulness" (25:10 // 26:3), "my eyes" (25:15 // 26:3), "hate" (25:19 // 26:5), "sinners" (25:8 // 26:9), "my soul" (25:1, 20 // 26:9), "my feet" (25:15 // 26:12), "redeem" (25:22 // 26:11), "be gracious" (25:16 // 26:11).

The content bears close relationship to Psalm 24: the sanctuary and cult play an important part in both psalms. In addition there are important and striking connections at the level of vocabulary: "hypocrisy" (24:4 // 26:4), "place" for sanctuary (24:3 // 26:8), "clean hands," "wash hands" (24:4 // 26:6), "glory" (24:7-10 // 26:8), "blessing"/"bless" (= praise) (24:5 // 26:12). The relationship between Psalm 26 and Psalm 24 should probably be explained as follows: Psalm 26 is to be understood as the response to the teaching on cultic participation in Ps 24:4-5. The conditions for ascending the mountain of the Lord and standing in the holy place (24:4) have been fulfilled by the one who speaks Psalm 26 (26:4, 6).

The relationship between Psalms 25 and 26 is one of partial opposition. In the beginning of Psalm 26 someone speaks with full consciousness of his or her own integrity, while Psalm 25 speaks with a low voice and with reserve. In Psalm 25 the human being is aware of his or her sin. Integrity or innocence is not her or his firm possession, something that can never be lost. This person prays for integrity and innocence (25:20). But the end of Psalm 26 has also lost much of its initial force. At the conclusion we find a declaration of intent to walk in integrity before God and a petition for redemption and grace. The progression from the attitude the one at prayer has maintained in the past and that proposed to be maintained in the future, as these appear at the beginning and end of the psalm, is also especially evident in 26:4a and 5b: "I do not sit . . . and will not sit." The look back into the past immediately connected with an intention toward the future, moreover, shapes the entire section in which the psalmist speaks of his or her attitudes and behavior (vv. 4-8).

Psalms 25 and 26 are also connected by the theme of "hatred." In Ps 25:19 the speaker laments over the powerful hatred of the enemies. In Ps 26:5 the psalmist speaks of his or her hatred of the company of evildoers. There is an exchange of roles here.

Structure

The structure of Psalm 26 is both clear and complex. Petitions (vv. 1-2 and 9-11) frame the confession of hatred toward evildoers and love for YHWH's sanctuary (vv. 3-8). This confession constitutes the major portion of the psalm, which is thoroughly imbued with prayer language (vv. 1-11). However, the last verse does not maintain the direction of the previous address; it speaks about God (v. 12). In overview, the structure is as follows:

Petition and self-depiction (prayer language: "I/thou"; "innocence"; "walking"): v. 1a (// v. 11)
  Petitions and self-depiction: vv. 2-3 (// vv. 9-10)
    Confession of hatred and love: vv. 3-8
  Petition and depiction of sinners: vv. 9-10 (// vv. 3-4)
Self-obligation and petition (prayer language: "I/thou"; "innocence"; "walking"): v. 11 (// v. 1a)
Confidence and promise to praise God: v. 12

The petition for vindication (v. 1) and the petition for grace (v. 11) frame the principal section of the psalm. Verses 1a and 11 correspond also in their use of vocabulary. The verses are chiastically constructed:

Petition—confession of walking in innocence (v. 1) //
Promise to walk in innocence—petition (v. 11)

Despite these correspondences the two verses are different. The assurance of having lived an innocent life (v. 1) is replaced by the intention to live innocently. At the end the issue is no longer vindication, but grace. The petitions in vv. 2 and 9 reveal no common vocabulary. Beyond the formal factor that both are "petitions," however, there are connections between the content of vv. 2-3 and 9-10. The petitions in vv. 2 and 9 and the depiction of self and other in vv. 4 and 10 stand in mutual relationship to one another: in v. 2 the speaker asks to be tested by God. This thorough and profound testing corresponds to the petition in v. 9 that YHWH may not "sweep away" the petitioner's "soul" and life with sinners and the bloodthirsty. The content of vv. 3 and 10 sets them in antithesis to one another: the one who prays is entirely surrounded by the steadfast love and fidelity of YHWH, while the hands of the sinners are full of evil devices and bribes.

The confession speaks of hatred and love (vv. 5, 8). It consists first of all in the rejection of all community with evil people; the latter are described in a series of four expressions. None of these is univocal: "the worthless" or "people of falsehood" and similar expressions (= idolaters in Pss 24:4; 31:6; for this expression cf. Job 11:11—or is the idea here one of social injustice: cf. 12:2; 41:6; 144:8, 11?); "hypocrites"; "evildoers"; "the wicked." These the psalmist hates (vv. 4-5). Then the psalmist speaks of herself or himself: she or he has innocent hands. In this innocence the psalmist will walk around the altar in YHWH's sanctuary and in doing so will utter praise of YHWH and tell YHWH's wondrous deeds (vv. 6-7). The speaker has loved the sanctuary of YHWH and still does so (v. 8).

This psalm names many parts of the human body: heart and mind (v. 2), eyes (v. 3), hands (v. 6), "soul" or life (v. 9), hands and right hands (v. 10), foot (v. 12). It mentions the Temple and cultic actions. Still it is not easy to concretize the information of the psalm. It cannot be simply interpreted in connection with entrance liturgies (like Psalms 15 and 24) because the situation of entry into the sanctuary is not clear. However, the psalm can also not be understood directly as the prayer of a priest or Levite uttered before entry into his office because the past and future behavior of the one praying is not exclusively priestly; instead it applies to every individual in Israel. The psalm is the prayer of someone aware of his or her integrity before God. This consciousness is maintained in the confession that this integrity before God must be preserved. For that preservation the individual is dependent on YHWH's grace and redemption. To human integrity before God belongs not only turning away from the company of evildoers and toward YHWH's sanctuary, but loud thanksgiving, the proclamation of YHWH's marvels, and praise of YHWH in the circle of those who call one to the assembly.

The references to the Temple and its liturgy point to a pre-exilic time of origin for this psalm.

Psalm 27

Context

This psalm has numerous words in common with Psalm 26: "my life" (26:9 // 27:1, 4, 13), "evildoers" (26:5 // 27:2), "heart" (26:2 // 27:3, 8, 14), "trust" (26:1 // 27:3), "dwell" (26:4, 5 // 27:4), "your house"/"house of YHWH" (26:8 // 27:4), "aloud" (26:7 // 27:7), "be gracious" (26:11 // 27:7), "take up"/"sweep away" (26:9 // 27:10), "level" (26:12 // 27:11). "My flesh"

(27:2) continues the series of nouns representing members and organs of the human body begun in Psalm 26.

Structure

The psalm consists of two parts, clearly discernible from the shift in the direction of address: vv. 1-6 speak about God, and vv. 7-12 (except for v. 10) to God. Verses 13-14 return to speaking about God. The transition from confessional language to direct address to God, the thematic shift from the threats of enemies and military power (vv. 1-3) to threats from false witnesses (v. 12), and the different genres developed in the two sections (vv. 1-6: song of confidence with vow of thanksgiving; vv. 7-12: song of lament with motifs of confidence) have led to the plausible thesis that the psalm once consisted of two independent prayers that were only later put together to form a unit. The fusion into a single psalm seemed to be obvious because the independent texts have a common vocabulary: "salvation" and "God of my salvation" (v. 1 // v. 9), "adversaries" (v. 2 // v. 12), "my heart" (v. 3 // v. 8; cf. v. 14), "rise up" (v. 3 // v. 12), "seek" (v. 4 // v. 8), "hide" (v. 5 // v. 9). Added to this is the common orientation to the Temple although this is expressed in differing linguistic forms (vv. 4-5 // v. 8). The urgent plea to behold the beauty of God in the Temple in the first part (v. 4) corresponds to the certain belief in seeing God's goodness in the land of the living in the second part (v. 13).

The structure of the psalm looks this way in outline:

I. Song of confidence with vow of thanksgiving: vv. 1-6
   1. Confession of trust: vv. 1-3
   2. Petition to see God in the Temple: vv. 4-5
   3. Confidence of being heard and vow of thanksgiving: v. 6

II. Song of lament with motifs of confidence: vv. 7-13
   1. Plea to be heard, and for grace, response, and God's presence: vv. 7-9
   2. Confession of trust (before the community): v. 10
   3. Petition for divine guidance and rescue from enemies and lying tongues: vv. 11-12
   4. Confession of assurance of seeing God: v. 13

Concluding admonition (to those who hear or read the psalm): v. 14

The song of confidence confesses, in the face of the most extreme dangers, the human assurance of security in God. Cannibalism (cf. Num 23:24; Mic 3:3; Ps 14:4; Jer 2:3; Isa 9:19 as something practiced in war!) and warfare as the extremes of human brutality cannot frighten the one who prays because he or she feels safe in YHWH. The predications of/about/for YHWH (v. 1; cf. Ps 18:3) and the danger of war here presupposed could be indications that vv. 1-6 are a royal prayer. With the vow of thanksgiving (v. 6) the song of confidence comes to its stylistically correct conclusion. The mention of the Temple and sacrificial worship are indications that this part originated before the exile.

The song of lament (vv. 7-13) employs the expression "seek the face of YHWH" as a way of referring to the presence of God in the Temple; however, the orientation to the Temple is not as strongly developed as in the first part of the psalm. In the face of false witnesses and violent people the psalmist takes refuge in YHWH, whose help he or she has already experienced and whom he or she can therefore call "God of my salvation" (v. 9). A developed Temple liturgy is replaced by the circle of the extended family as the locus of prayer: YHWH takes the place of father and mother. In contrast to the servant's prayer that YHWH's anger be turned away (v. 9) the confession of YHWH whose presence and love are more lasting than those of father and mother expresses immense love for and intimacy with God (v. 10). The human being is the child of God. The assurance of the one who prays rests on the confidence of seeing YHWH's goodness in the land of the living, rather than in the Temple (v. 13; cf. v. 4). The song of lament appears estranged from the Temple and therefore is probably to be dated later than vv. 1-6.

Psalm 28

Context

This psalm is connected to its predecessor by the following words: "call" (27:7 // 28:1), "rock" (27:5 // 28:1), "hear" (27:7 // 28:2, 6), "trust" (27:3 // 28:7), "my heart" (27:3, 8 // 28:7), "my help"/"I am helped" (27:9 // 28:7), "sing"/ "song" (27:6 // 28:7), "stronghold"/"saving refuge" (27:1 // 28:8), "salvation" (27:1, 9 // 28:8, 9). The psalm begins chiastically to Ps 27:7: the sequence "hear" and "answer" in Ps 27:7 is ordered chiastically to "not be silent" and "hear" in 28:1-2. The petition that God not hide God's face from the one who prays (27:9) corresponds structurally to the petition that God not be silent (28:1). Both psalms speak of the Temple (28:2 // 27:4; cf. 26:6, 8). The formulation in Ps 28:2 is unusual and does not appear elsewhere in the psalter. Contrasted are the living (27:13) and those who go down to the Pit (28:1).

Structure

The following parts of the psalm may be distinguished on the basis of the shifts between address to God and discourse about God:

1. Petition to be heard (address to God): vv. 1-2
2. Petition regarding the wicked (address to God): vv. 3-4
3. Reason for the petitions (discourse about God): v. 5
4. Assurance of being heard (discourse about God): vv. 6-7
5. Confession of YHWH as strength for the people and for YHWH's anointed (discourse about God): v. 8
6. Petition for YHWH's people (address to God): v. 9

The psalm is an individual song of lament in which the element of petition, typical of the genre, is fully developed. The "description of suffering" characteristic of the song of lament is incorporated in and subordinated to the petitions. The pleas in vv. 1-4 are divided between petitions to be heard by God (vv. 1-2) and those that refer to wicked people (vv. 3-4). The reason for the petitions (v. 5) refers specifically to these latter (cf. v. 4). Although the address to God is dropped in giving these reasons the key word "work" creates a connection among vv. 3-5. The assurance of being heard (vv. 6-7) directly resumes the petition to be heard (v. 6 // v. 2): God has heard and the one who prays will receive help. The petitioner's heart has rejoiced and he or she is now ready to thank God in song. The assurance of being heard issues in a promise of thanksgiving. This concludes the individual song of lament. The expansion of the prayer to encompass the nation and the king in v. 8 repeats the predication of YHWH from v. 7: the strength of the one who prays (v. 7) is also strength for the nation and saving refuge for the king ("anointed": v. 8). The concluding petition is again directed to YHWH and refers entirely to the nation (v. 9). The image of God as shepherd implied in the verbs "pasture" and "carry" (cf. Isa 40:11) emphasizes the subordination of the human king (the messiah) to YHWH.

The situation presumed by the individual song of lament cannot be clearly determined. Danger of death caused by illness (vv. 1b, 3a) could as easily be the occasion as persecution by people who conceal their evil intentions behind peaceful words.

Psalm 29

Context

The important lexemes "strength" (28:7, 8 // 29:1, 11), "people" (28:[8], 9 // 29:11), and "bless" (28:9 // 29:11), as well as "holy" (28:2 // 29:2), and "peace" (28:3 // 29:11) link Psalm 29 to Psalm 28. The "voice of supplication" or "sound of pleading" (28:2, 6) corresponds to the "voice of YHWH" (29:3, 4, 5, 7, 8, 9). The end of Psalm 28 spoke of YHWH's anointed, the human king in Israel (28:8). In Psalm 29 YHWH is king (29:10). The word "forever" (28:9; 29:10) also joins the two psalms together: in both it refers to YHWH as king. YHWH the royal shepherd is asked to pasture and carry the sheep (28:9). As the king enthroned forever YHWH is petitioned to give strength to the people and bless them with peace (29:10-11). Both psalms speak, though in a different vocabulary, of the sanctuary (28:2 // 29:9).

Structure

The psalm gains its specific character from the numerous repetitions of words. Those most frequently reiterated are the divine name (18x) and the word "voice" (7x). These two words also give the decisive indication regarding the structure of the psalm. Three parts may be distinguished:

I. "To the Lord": vv. 1-2
II. "The voice of the Lord": vv. 3-9
III. "The Lord": vv. 10-11

The first part is a call to give praise "to the Lord," the second speaks of the "voice of the Lord," and in the third "the Lord" is the direct subject of the action. In the second part as well, YHWH or "the voice of YHWH" is the subject of the action (vv. 3b, 5b, 8b). There is an interesting relationship among the uses of the divine name YHWH: four times "to YHWH" (vv. 1-2), seven times "the voice of YHWH" (vv. 3a, 4a,b, 5a, 7, 8a, 9a), and seven times "YHWH" (vv. 3b, 5b, 8b, 10a,b, 11a,b). Characteristic of the structure of the psalm is that the words "glory"/ "honor" and "strength" in the call to praise YHWH (v. 1) announce the content of the body of the psalm to follow. "Glory" frames the section that tells of the "voice of YHWH" (vv. 3, 9b), while "strength" from v. 1 returns in v. 11 and thus constitutes the theme of the third part of the psalm.

Stylistically (through the climactic parallelism in vv. 1-2) and in its motifs (the god "El" and the divine beings surrounding El, "glory" and "holiness" in vv. 1-2; realm of the god Baal in vv. 3-10) this psalm has parallels in Ugaritic texts. It re-coins the extra-biblical religious ideas in applying them to YHWH and confesses YHWH as the God who unites the kingship of El and Baal. The psalm with its concentration on glory, holiness, and the kingship of YHWH manifested in the natural concert and drama of the thunderstorm is an example of the praise of YHWH in the pre-exilic Temple. Theologically and terminologically it is close to Isa 6:1-4. The transcendent God can be experienced in nature while being sovereign over its powers. From this God the people can expect strength, blessing, and peace.

The words "glory" (vv. 1, 2, 3, 9) and "peace" (v. 11) are the basic elements of the angelic hymn in the gospel of Luke as the angels respond to the annunciation to the shepherds of the birth of Christ (Luke 2:14).

Psalm 30

Context

The two words "strength" (v. 7) and "glory" (v. 12) join Psalm 30 to Psalm 29 ("strength": 29:1, 11; "glory": 29:1, 2, 3, 9). The word "forever" appears in both psalms: the quotation of the arrogant assertion of the one praying that he or she will never waver (v. 6b) is contrasted to the confession of YHWH's reigning as king forever (29:10). At the end the one who prays promises to praise God forever (30:12), as is owing to God who reigns forever. A further linguistic contact between the two psalms is found in certain parallel expressions: "holy splendor" (29:2) and "holy name" (30:4), and the resumption of the verb "whirl" (29:8, 9) in the word "dancing" (30:11).

The following words typical of the genres of individual songs of lament and thanksgiving also link Psalm 30 with Psalm 28: "call" (28:1 // 30:8), "call for help" (28:2 // 30:3), "voice of supplication" (28:2, 6) // "make supplication" and "be gracious" (30:8, 10), "help"/"helper" (28:7 // 30:10), "thank" (28:7 // 30:4, 9, 12), and "hear" (28:2, 6 // 30:10). Striking because it appears so seldom in the Psalms is the expression "they who go down to the Pit" for the dying and the dead (28:1 // 30:3; cf. Pss 88:4; 143:7).

Structure

I. Narrative and thanksgiving: vv. 1-5
   1. Call (addressed to the self) to exalt YHWH, with a report in the first person addressed to YHWH as reason: vv. 1-3
   2. Call to the devotees of YHWH to sing and give thanks, with confession of YHWH as reason: vv. 4-5

II. Narrative and thanksgiving: vv. 6-12
   1. Report in the first person addressed to YHWH about danger and rescue: vv. 6-11
   2. Impersonal call to give praise and call to oneself to give thanks: v. 12

The psalm divides into two parts distinguished by the genre-typical elements of the individual song of thanksgiving (vv. 1-5 and 6-12). Each part emphasizes a different moment in the past experience. In the first part the call to oneself to exalt YHWH is followed by reasoning in the form of a personal report addressed to YHWH. The one praying tells of the danger from which YHWH has rescued him or her. From the wording this must be a life-threatening illness (vv. 1-3). In vv. 4-5 the direction of address shifts. The community of the devotees of YHWH are called to sing and give thanks because YHWH's graciousness is lifelong. The second part of the psalm begins immediately with the narrative of danger and rescue by YHWH (vv. 6-11) and ends in a final sentence formulated with an impersonal subject, stating as goal the never-ending glorification of God (v. 12a), and calling on oneself to give thanks forever (v. 12b). The verbs "sing" and "thank" from v. 4 are repeated here. The appeals to oneself (v. 1) and others (v. 4) to praise God that frame the first part are drawn together in v. 13 to form a final chord.

There are some minor shifts in meaning between the two parts of the psalm and even within a single part: the enemies of the one who prays (v. 1) do not appear in the second part. In both parts the one praying first depicts himself or herself as a person doomed to die, one over whom a dirge will be sung (vv. 3, 9). But according to v. 11 it is the speaker who has raised the dirge (for someone else). The "I" has shifted from object to subject of the dirge. In spite of the shifts in meaning this text is not a basic psalm (vv. 1-5) with vv. 6-12 "added on." At the same time those shifts do not allow us to see the *Sitz im Leben* exclusively in a thanksgiving service in the Temple following a recovery of health. The danger from which the one praying has been rescued is very broadly interpreted in the psalm. The statement in v. 5 is important theologically: God's grace is far greater than God's wrath (cf. Isa 54:7-8). It rescues human beings from threats to their lives and bestows a joyous, dancing life. That is why life itself is praise of God. The psalm is probably pre-exilic even though there are no precise indications of its date. The title documents that at a very late period the psalm was prayed at the festival of the dedication of the Temple (cf. *bSoferim* 18.2). The feast of dedication was celebrated to recall the re-consecration of the Temple in the year 164 B.C.E. after it had been desecrated by Antiochus IV Epiphanes (1 Macc 4:36-61; 2 Macc 10:1-8). In the Christian liturgy this psalm has its fixed place in the liturgy of the Easter Vigil as a response to the fourth reading (Isa 54:4a, 5-14).

Psalm 31

Context

This psalm is Jesus' dying prayer according to Luke's gospel (Luke 23:43-46). Stephen follows his Master's model in dying with the same psalm on his lips (Acts 7:59-60). There appears to be a further allusion to Psalm 31 in Titus 3:4 (cf. Ps 31:19). The NT appropriation of the psalm has resulted in its appearance in the central festivals of the Church year: the hymn in Titus 3:4-7 is used as the second reading at the second Mass for Christmas, the so-called "shepherds' Mass" in the early morning. On the feast of Stephen (December 26) Psalm 31 is the responsorial psalm following the reading from Acts 6:8-10; 7:54-59.

The numerous connections between Psalms 31 and 30 result from the fact that both psalms incorporate the features of the genres of individual songs of lament and thanksgiving. The two psalms speak, not exclusively but predominantly, of the crisis of a life-threatening illness (30:2, 3 // 31:9, 10). The common vocabulary of the two psalms includes the following words and phrases: "forever" (30:6, 12 // 31:1), "be for me" (30:10 // 31:2), "refuge" (30:7 // 31:2, 4), God's "faithfulness" (30:9 // 31:5), "rejoice"/"joy" (30:1, 11 // 31:7), "my soul"/"my life" (30:3 // 31:7, 9, 13), "enemy" (30:1 // 31:8, 15), "establish" (30:7 // 31:8), "be gracious"/"make supplication [for graciousness]" (30:10 // 31:9, 22), "life" (30:5 // 31:10), "hear" (30:10 // 31:13, 22), "I said/thought" (30:6 // 31:14, 22), "my God" (30:2, 12 // 31:14), God's "face" (30:7 // 31:16, 20), "call" (30:8 // 31:17), "be silent" (30:12 // 31:18), "Sheol" (30:3 // 31:17), "hide" (30:7 // 31:20), "call for help" (30:2 // 31:22), the "faithful" (30:4 // 31:23).

There are numerous links to Psalm 32 as well: compare the complex in 31:6b-7a with Ps 32:10b-11a ("trust in YHWH," "exult," "rejoice"). The description of the physical weakness of the one who prays and the connection with guilt, only hinted in 31:10, are taken up and fully developed in Ps 32:3-5, using the key phrase "hand [of God]" (31:5, 15 // 32:4). In Ps 31:21-22 there are links to Ps 28:2, 6, and in 31:24 to Ps 27:14.

Structure

The layering of a number of compositional efforts shapes this psalm. The poet is completely in control of the elements typical of the genre of the individual song of lament, with the result that a fully individual text is presented. Together with a great number of words and phrases that appear frequently in the psalter we find an imposing list of expressions found only here: for example the predication "YHWH, faithful God" in 31:5.

From the point of view of the direction of address the psalm can be divided into two parts of differing length. In vv. 1-20 YHWH is addressed (except in v. 6). In v. 21 the psalm begins to speak about God; then in v. 22 there is an address to YHWH in a quotation of the thoughts of the one praying. The discourse about God has a confessional character. It issues in the invitation to love God addressed to the faithful (vv. 23-24). The address section (vv. 1-20) is shaped in such a way that two sections, thematically oriented to the word "hand" and furnished with motifs of petition and confidence (vv. 1-8 and 14-20) are placed before and after a central portion with a petition and extensive description of the danger at hand. The ring composition that thus seems to appear (A – B – A' + C) is not fully satisfactory as regards the psalm in its entirety. Instead the psalm is shaped by the double application of the form of the individual song of lament. Chiastically repeated elements structure the psalm into a completed whole. In outline it appears as follows:

- I. Petition with motif of confidence: "in your hand," vv. 1-8
  1. Petition and motifs of confidence with reduced lament: vv. 1-4 (// vv. 15b-19)
  2. Assurance of rescue and self-addressed encouragement to rejoice in God's graciousness: vv. 5-8 (// vv. 14-15a, 21-24)
- II. Song of lament with motif of confidence: "in your hand," vv. 10-25
  1. Petition with lament, "cornered," vv. 9-13
  2. Motif of confidence with petition: "in your hand," vv. 14-20 (// vv. 1-6)
  3. Assurance of being heard and encouragement to the faithful to praise YHWH because of the wonders of divine graciousness: vv. 21-24 (// vv. 5-8)

The sequence of the elements of the individual song of lament is followed through twice in the psalm with differing accents each time. In the first passage (vv. 1-8) the elements of petition and the motif of confidence are strongly developed. In the second passage as well there is a fully developed section with petitions that are intensified by confessions of trust in YHWH to motivate God to intervene (vv. 14-20). This part is preceded by the description of the danger. The lament, so briefly uttered in the first passage and there revealing the danger as "hidden nets" (placed by other people) in v. 4a and attacks by "idolaters" in v. 6a, is developed after a single petition for graciousness (vv. 9-13). Here sickness is defined as the danger, an illness that destroys the integrity of the human person (vv. 9-10) and brings him or her to the threshold of death (v. 12). Added to this is danger from the immediate neighbors who are disgusted by the illness as well as danger from enemies who aggressively seek the life of the one who prays (vv. 11, 13). The section containing the petitions reveals a further danger of false accusations from lying lips during a legal proceeding (vv. 18, 20). The final section (vv. 21-24) speaks about God and thus stands out from what precedes it. Structurally, however, it corresponds to the element of assurance of being heard, with vow of praise, the final section of an individual song of lament. Despite the change in the direction of the address it parallels vv. 5-8.

This psalm is an exercise in trusting the God who is faithful and gracious. The human being endangered from every side brings his or her danger before God. This person is driven into a corner by illness and the aggressive attacks of enemies. Such emergencies can and must be brought before God. Describing one's need to God is already evidence of trust. God sees and hears, and brings the petitioner out of troubled straits into freedom. God gives good things to those who fear God (v. 19) while the wicked collapse and fall silent in Sheol (v. 17). The call to love God addressed to the faithful is founded on the thesis that YHWH preserves the faithful but repays beyond measure those who "act haughtily." There is a striking variation in the distribution of plurals and singulars within the psalm. In vv. 1-18 the enemies, opponents, and wicked are a large group (vv. 4, 6, 11, 13, 15, 17); they are many (v. 13) in contrast to the singular just person (v. 18). In v. 19 those who fear YHWH constitute a group in contrast to the children of humanity in general ("everyone"). At the end, however, in the address to the faithful of YHWH the faithful are opposed by a single villain who acts haughtily (v. 23). This offers encouragement. The faithful of YHWH, those who are true and wait on YHWH, will have the upper hand.

This psalm is so artfully constructed that it should probably be regarded as a literary work. It belongs to the period of the exile or thereafter.

Psalm 32

Context

Psalm 32 is the second (after Psalm 6) of the seven ecclesial penitential psalms. (The others are Psalms 38, 51, 102, 130, and 143).

This psalm has abundant connections to Psalm 31: "people, human beings" (32:2 // 31:19), "iniquity" (32:2, 5 // 31:10), "spirit" (32:2 // 31:5), "my bones" (32:3 // 31:10), "hand" (32:4 // 31:5, 15), "I said" (32:5 // 31:14, 22), "all the faithful" (32:6 // 31:23), "time" (32:6 // 31:15), "great"/"many" (32:6, 10 // 31:13, 19), "hiding place"/"shelter" (32:7 // 31:20), "trouble"/"affliction" (32:7 // 31:7, 9; cf. v. 11), "preserve" (32:7 // 31:23), "deliver" (32:7 // 31:1), "surround"/"all around" (32:7 // 31:13), "my eye upon you"/"far from your sight" (32:8 // 31:22), the verb "to be" with comparisons (32:9 // 31:12), "the wicked" (32:10 // 31:17), "the righteous" (32:11 // 31:18), "heart" (32:11 // 31:12, 24), and the whole complex of words including "trust in YHWH," "rejoice," "be glad," and "steadfast love" in 32:10b-11a and 31:6b-7a.

In the context of Psalm 31 there was reference only in passing to the connection between suffering and guilt (31:10b). Psalm 32 elevates this relationship to its main theme. Psalm 31:5a, 15a uses the key phrase "in your hand" to emphasize certain parts within the psalm. We could indicate the connection between Psalms 31 and 32 preserved by their common vocabulary by calling Psalm 32 "Under YHWH's Hand" (32:4).

Structure

The structural plan of this psalm is not easily discernible. We may suggest the following provisional outline oriented to the different directions of discourse:

I. Acknowledgment of God who forgives sins and protects: vv. 1-8
   1. Forgiveness of sins: vv. 1-5 (// vv. 6-7)
   2. Protection: vv. 6-7 (// vv. 1-5)
   3. Word of God: v. 8

II. Appeal to those nearby: vv. 9-11

The first part (vv. 1-8) is shaped by first-person discourse and address (vv. 3-5, 7-8), but it also contains speech about God and human beings (vv. 1-2); it is said of the pious person's prayers that they should be offered "to you" (v. 6). Since the crucial key words from vv. 1-2 are repeated in v. 5 the first part of the psalm contains a clearly defined unit in vv. 1-5. It begins with a double blessing of those whose sins God forgives (vv. 1-2). This general statement receives a personal application through confession of the speaker's own experience of being forgiven. In vv. 1-5 the contrasts between "keeping silence" (v. 3) and "saying" (v. 5) mark off a sub-section in vv. 3-5. It contains a personal confession of wrestling with sin. The sequence of an "impersonal/general statement" and "personal confession" is repeated in a shortened form in vv. 6-7. "Those" in v. 2 correspond to "all who are faithful" in v. 6. The statement about the prayer of the faithful is followed by a personal confession of YHWH as protector (v. 7). Although it is not clearly introduced as divine speech, v. 8 can easily be understood as such (cf. Pss 25:8, 12; 143:8). In this way the confessions of the speakers receive a divine response: God promises to be teacher and counselor to those who pray. The promise that "my eye" will be "upon you" (v. 8b) contrasts with the earlier experience of the speaker at the time before he or she acknowledged these sins and YHWH's hand lay heavy upon her or him (v. 4).

The second part of the psalm (vv. 9-11) is addressed to a group that is at first anonymous and calls on them to achieve insight (v. 9). These challenges are further directed to the righteous and those with upright hearts: they should rejoice in YHWH and shout for joy because of their God (v. 11). It is important to obtain insight into the fact that the torments of the wicked are many while people who trust in YHWH are wrapped in divine protection (v. 10). The appeals and instructional statement correspond closely to the preceding main part of the psalm and can therefore not be separated from the body of the poem.

As long as the speaker concealed his or her sin that person's physical and spiritual existence were destroyed and God's hand was felt as a heavy burden (vv. 3-4a). But that experience of God was dissolved by another: that of the God who bears the guilt of our sins (v. 5b). This insinuates a closeness of God that does not burden human beings, but protects them from everything that "hems them in" and makes them happy in the fulfillment of their being (v. 7). God does not force people, but lets them first come to God and gives them a "jubilant" existence. The eye of

God on human beings is not that of an inspector (cf. Job 7:18-20), but represents the presence of God that liberates people to be themselves.

The appeal to the group of the righteous in vv. 9-11 is drawn out of that experience and thus invites them to seek God in joy. It invites to a rational, significant existence that trusts in YHWH and therefore experiences life as shaped by YHWH's steadfast love.

On the basis of the speaker's "narrative" (vv. 3-5) and the appeal to the righteous to joy and praise of YHWH, Psalm 32 can be classified as an individual song of thanksgiving. However, Wisdom terminology intrudes so strongly into this text (vv. 1-2, 8, 9) that it can also be understood (in line with its title) as a "Wisdom song." Reserve toward everything cultic is characteristic of Wisdom texts. Thus the silence about such things as sacrifice for sins and other rituals of reconciliation need not in itself point to a late period, during or after the exile; however this late date seems most appropriate for the composition of this psalm.

Psalm 33

Context

Psalm 33, like Psalms 1 and 2, has no title. In this it is unique within the first Book of Psalms (Psalms 3–41). It begins where Psalm 32 leaves off. Moreover, both at the beginning and at the end Psalm 33 has strong connections to Ps 32:10-11.

In Ps 33:1 we find four elements from Ps 32:11: the verb "rejoice," the group of "the righteous," the divine name YHWH, and the adjective "upright," also used to designate a group. The word "heart" (32:11) is repeated three times in Psalm 33 (vv. 11, 15, 21). "Our heart" at the end of Psalm 33 is only one of the elements from the conclusion of Psalm 32: in addition we find the verbs "rejoice" (33:21 // 32:11) and "trust" (33:21 // 32:10) and the noun "steadfast love" (33:22 // 32:10). Further points of contact between Psalms 33 and 32 draw us to the center of the two psalms: the discourse about YHWH's "counsel" and "eye" in Ps 33:11, 18 refers back to the divine speech in Ps 32:8.

Psalm 33 concentrates on the theme of "YHWH's steadfast love" as developed in the two preceding psalms. The statements about YHWH's steadfast love become more and more universal from psalm to psalm. Psalm 31 speaks about that love with strict attention to the one who prays: YHWH's steadfast love is the reason for the speaker's joy (31:8); the petitioner calls on that love when asking YHWH for help (31:15); YHWH's steadfast love is a miracle for the one who prays (31:22). In Ps 32:10 we find an additional statement that considers not merely the individual but everyone who trusts in God (32:10). Psalm 33 goes still farther: the earth is full of the steadfast love of the Lord (33:5). That is the high point. This statement expresses the spatial limitlessness of YHWH's love. It is a complement to Ps 25:6, which spoke of its endurance from earliest time. Complementary to Ps 33:5 in another way is the statement in Ps 36:5: YHWH's steadfast love extends to the heavens. The sequence of Psalms 25, 31, 33, 36, in each of which the expression "steadfast love" appears three times, reveals a thematic direction: in Ps 25:6 YHWH's "steadfast love" is paralleled with YHWH's "mercy." The complementary statement in Ps 33:5 connects "YHWH's steadfast love" with the theme of "righteousness and justice" developed in Ps 36:5-7. In Ps 33:18 the steadfast love of the Lord is the object of hope, and in 33:22 of prayer.

Structure

Psalm 33, which has twenty-two verses corresponding to the number of letters in the Hebrew alphabet, is regarded as the prime example of an extended OT hymn. The three parts—introductory song (call to praise), development (justification) of praise, and closing song—are clearly discernible by the change in the direction of address. The structure in outline is as follows:

I. Call to praise directed to the righteous and upright: vv. 1-3 (address to the community: you plural)

II. Body of the psalm: development (justification) of praise: YHWH's upright and faithful work: vv. 4-19 (discourse about God: HE)
  1. Basic premise: word and work: vv. 4-5
  2. Creation of heaven and earth; God's power over the nations; the election of Israel: vv. 6-12
  3. God's power over human beings: vv. 13-19

III. Closing song: community confession of YHWH: vv. 20-22 (we-discourse)

The object of the praise is YHWH's word and work. Law and justice are bound up in God. God desires a righteous order of life in creation. YHWH's graciousness fills the earth and is to be imitated by human beings in bringing about justice and righteousness (vv. 4-5). The hymn praises God's creative power. God has created heaven and earth through the divine word, holds sovereign control over the fate of the nations, and chooses Israel as God's own portion. Because of that election this nation is to be called blessed (vv. 6-12). Human beings are also subject to God's creative power. The king, who is especially exposed to the danger of overestimating himself, is shown his limitations. Those who fear God, who are particularly subject to the danger of despair beyond measure, are reminded of YHWH's care, which belongs especially to them (vv. 13-19).

The introductory song alludes to the use of musical instruments and the community's performance of praise. This psalm could therefore have been sung and prayed in the Temple before the exile. On the other hand the principal part of the hymn contains so many developed theological themes that were taken up primarily at a later period that it suggests composition during or after the exile.

Psalm 34

Context

This psalm has close connections to Psalm 33 (and to Psalms 31–32), as well as to Psalms 35 and 25. As regards the relationship to Psalm 33 we note that the call to sing praise (33:1) is answered by an individual in Ps 34:1. The statement that YHWH's eyes are on those who fear God (33:18) is repeated in 34:15. Other vocabulary common to Psalms 33 and 34 includes "righteous" (33:1 // 34:15, 19, 21), "happy" (33:12 // 34:8), "deliver" (33:16, 19 // 34:4, 17, 19), "name" (33:21 // 34:3), "look" (33:13 // 34:5). The themes of "fear of God" (33:8, 18 // 34:7, 9, 11) and "hunger" (33:19 // 34:10) are common to both psalms. "Save" appears in 33:16 and 34:6, 18.

Psalms 32:10 and 34:19 are set in opposition to each other: the "torments for the wicked" are contrasted with the "afflictions of the righteous." The theme of the "eyes of the Lord" is addressed repeatedly in Psalms 31–34 (31:22; 32:8; 33:13, 14, 18; 34:15).

The adjective "good" appears four times in Psalm 34 (vv. 8, 10, 12, 14) and is used each time to introduce a new theme. Applied to the actions of human beings (34:14), it is a constant theme in Psalms 35–39 (35:12; 36:3, 4; 37:3, 16, 27; 38:20; 39:2). The introduction of this theme corresponds to that of "righteousness (and justice)" in Ps 33:5 (cf. 35:[23], 24, 28; 36:6; 37:6; 40:9, 10). The adjective "good" as predicate for God (34:8) is also a reference back to Ps 25:8. Beyond this theme of the kindness of God, Psalms 25 and 34 are very closely related both in form and content. Both are alphabetic psalms, each lacking a *waw*-line, and each concludes with an additional *pe*-line commencing with the same verb. Thus Psalms 25 and 34 are a frame for Psalms 26–33. With Psalm 34 there is a caesura in the sequence but the connections between Psalms 34 and 35 again show that the pause indicated by Psalm 34 is not absolute. Instead the themes addressed in Psalm 34 extend beyond the given text to the sequence of Psalms 35–41.

Structure

In spite of the externally evident formal schema of an alphabetic acrostic we can discern a concentric order in the psalm:

Call to praise: vv. 1-3
- Narrative of rescue: delivery from all: vv. 4-6
  - Presence of YHWH's angel: v. 7
    - "Goodness" as gift and task: vv. 8-14
  - Presence of YHWH: vv. 15-16
- Narrative of rescue: delivery from all: vv. 17-19

Concluding contrast: vv. 20-21, 22

The central section (vv. 8-14) is also concentric:

Imperative (with the element "good"): v. 8
- Imperative: v. 9
  - Statement of fact (with the element "all good things"): v. 10
    - Imperative: "Come . . . fear of YHWH": v. 11
  - Question: "which of you?" (with the element "enjoy good"): v. 12
- Imperative: v. 13

Imperative (with the element "good"): v. 14

Strikingly, in contrast to the counterpart Psalm 25 there is no address to God. The psalm speaks *about* God! The call to praise and glorify Yhwh (vv. 1-3) is founded in the central portion of the psalm by means of a narrative (vv. 4-6, 17-19) and by teaching (vv. 8-14). The narrative attests the personal experience of rescue by YHWH, but it also points to many other stories of rescue by the close, present, hearing and seeing God. The experience of a God who saves leads to a teaching directed to "children." It is teaching about the goodness of God and the fear of God. Attachment to God through "fear of Yhwh" means a fulfilled life. The natural and necessary consequence of experience of the good God is the doing of good.

In spite of the formal constraints of the acrostic the psalm employs the genres of the individual song of thanksgiving and the Wisdom hymn. In the absence of direct prayer language, the Wisdom element dominates. Psalm 34 probably originated in the exile or in the post-exilic period.

Psalm 35

Context

Psalm 35 is an individual song of lament. As such it is in tension with the song of thanksgiving realized, at least incipiently, in Psalm 34. The contrasts between the two psalms are underscored by their common vocabulary: the life ordered and rescued by God in Psalm 34 is contrasted to the life threatened by enemies and pursuers in Psalm 35. The things for which Psalm 34 gives thanks and offers teaching are not personally experienced realities in Psalm 35. That YHWH saves (34:4, 17, 19) and that YHWH's help is for the poor (34:6; cf. v. 2) is acknowledged by the one who prays Psalm 35, of course. This one praises YHWH's incomparability, because YHWH rescues the poor (35:10). But the experienced presence of the angel of YHWH that inspires to praise (v. 7) and the nearness of YHWH (vv. 18, 15) in Psalm 34 are, for the one who prays Psalm 35, objects of petition (35:5, 6, 22). If Psalm 34 sketches an ethics of solidarity (34:14), Psalm 35 laments unsolidary people who reward good with evil (35:12) and destroy peace (35:20).

The common vocabulary includes "pursue" (35:3, 6 // 34:14), "my soul" or "my life" (35:3, 4, 7, 9, 12, 13, 17 // 34:2), "seek" (35:4 // 34:14), "salvation," "save" (35:3, 9 // 34:6, 18), "be ashamed" (35:4, 26 // 34:5), "my dishonor," "my calamity" (35:4, 26 // 34:21), "all my/their bones" (35:10 // 34:20), "deliver" (35:10 // 34:4, 17, 19), "poor" (35:10 // 34:6), "evil/good" (35:12 // 34:14), "rejoice" (35:15, 19, 24, 27 // 34:2), "young lions" (35:17 // 34:10), "those who hate" (35:19 // 34:21), "peace" (35:20 // 34:14), "speaking deceit" (35:20 // 34:13), "their mouth"/"my mouth" (35:21: 34:1), "our eyes"/ "eyes of the Lord" (35:21 // 34:15), "exalt"/ "magnify" (35:26, 27 // 34:3), "delight" (35:27 // 34:12), "always" (35:27 // 34:1), "praise" (35:28 // 34:1). In particular, vv. 27-28 of Psalm 35 crowd together a great many words from Psalms 32–34, and the key word "bones" (35:10) connects with Pss 31:10; 32:3; 34:20.

At the end the psalm returns to its beginning: a plea that the enemies of the petitioner be shamed is found in vv. 4 and 26. However, this petition frames not only Psalm 35 but also the group of Psalms 35–40, for 35:26-27 has a close parallel in 40:14-16. In spite of the many connections between Psalm 35 and the preceding texts, Psalms 35 and 40 can be regarded as the framing psalms for the fourth part of the first Book of Psalms.

Structure

The structure of the psalm is evident from its use of the common stylistic device of inclusion. We find the following divisions:

I. Petitions for help against enemies and pursuers: vv. 1-10 (// vv. 23-28)
  II. Description of the crisis and petitions: vv. 11-22
    1. Depiction of the crisis: vv. 11-16
    2. Petitions for rescue, with reasons: vv. 17-22
III. Petitions for help in a legal dispute: vv. 23-28 (// vv. 1-10)

The first part of the psalm consists of developed petitions and a very brief description of the crisis; the extensive middle section contains a detailed narrative of the need/affliction and petitions corresponding to the lament. Thus there is a twofold sequence of petition and lament (vv. 1-10) and lament and petition (vv. 11-22). After the second passage the petitions are developed into a separate section of their own that runs generally parallel to the first sequence of petition and lament (vv. 23-28).

The first sequence of petition and lament is revealed by an inclusion. The petition "say to my soul, 'I am your salvation'" (v. 3b) corresponds to the same elements in the confession of trust in vv. 9-10. The resumption of the verb "be strong" (v. 2a) in the adjective "strong" (v. 10) is also to be regarded as an element of inclusion. With the exception of v. 7, vv. 1-8 are petitions against those who seek the life of the speaker. The crisis is mentioned explicitly only in v. 7. The metaphorical formulation is difficult to interpret in concrete terms. The dangers indirectly indicated in the petitions are war (vv. 1-3, 5-6) as well as more general dangers from people who seek the life of the petitioner and desire his or her misfortune (v. 4).

The major central section of the psalm (vv. 11-22) consists of an extensive description of the crisis (vv. 11-16) and corresponding petitions (vv. 17-22). The petitions are in turn framed (v. 17 // v. 22). Their foundation on the basis of a reference to the false, peace-destroying speech of the enemies and those who hate the petitioner takes up motifs of the lament (vv. 19-21 // vv. 11-12, 15). The petitions beginning in v. 22 after a brief acknowledgment of assurance of being heard ("you have seen, O Lord") are expanded with more intensity in vv. 23-27, which run parallel to vv. 1-10 and culminate in the promise to continually meditate aloud on God's righteousness and give praise (v. 28).

The formulations in this psalm are so open that the emergency lamented is never absolutely clear. The crisis of war is addressed, so that the king could be considered as the petitioner (vv. 1-3). But then there are statements about malicious witnesses (v. 11); in that light the speaker would be an innocent accused person (cf. vv. 23-24, 27). We cannot go beyond the classification of the psalm as an individual song of lament. In the crisis caused by warlike, violent, unsolidary people the speaker calls to YHWH for help. Three times he or she begins to praise the incomparable God (vv. 9-10, 18, 28). God's incomparability is demonstrated in the divine initiative on behalf of the poor (v. 10). The speaker is, on the one hand, alone in the face of enemies and persecutors (v. 12), but on the other hand is also one of those who are "quiet in the land" (v. 20) and knows of people who rejoice in his or her righteousness. The psalm never makes reference to the Temple and its cultic observances. It may be an exilic or post-exilic composition. The opposition between the groups of those who rejoice in the misfortune of the petitioner and those who rejoice in his or her righteousness (vv. 26, 27) is appropriate to that time period.

Psalm 36

Context

This psalm falls within the horizon of the themes of "doing good" (34:14) and "steadfast love, justice, and righteousness" (33:5) already proclaimed. Following on the lament over the wicked enemies in Psalm 35, it gives a thorough analysis of the character of the godless and offers hymnic praise of the righteousness of YHWH to which appeal was made in Psalm 35. There are important verbal links to Psalm 35: "servant" (title // 35:27), "heart" (36:1, 10 // 35:25), "eyes" (36:1, 2 // 35:19, 21), "slippery" (36:2 // 35:6), "hate" (36:2 // 35:19), "speak" (36:3 // 35:20), "mouth" (36:3 // 35:21), "deceit" (36:3 // 35:20), "do good" (36:3 // 35:12), "devise, conceive" (36:4 // 35:4, 20), "not good/evil" (36:4 // 35:12), "righteousness" (36:6, 10 // 35:24, 27, 28), "judgment, cause" (36:6 // 35:23), "fall" (36:12 // 35:8), "drive, thrust" (36:12 // 35:5), "rise" (36:12 // 35:2, 11).

Structure

The psalm has a clear structure, with different directions of discourse marking out three parts:

I. Analysis of the character of the godless: vv. 1-4
II. Hymnic depiction of YHWH's steadfast love, righteousness, and just judgments: vv. 5-9
III. Petition for YHWH's steadfast love and righteousness, and assertion of the sinners' fall: vv. 10-12

The first part of the psalm is an analytic description (with a dramatizing self-quotation by the wicked in v. 1?). This section speaks objectively about God and the wicked. The second part is shaped by direct address to YHWH. This hymn issues in a communal confession: "in your light we see light" (v. 9). The conclusion is made up of petitions for those who know YHWH (v. 10) and for an individual just person (v. 11: "me").

The last verse brings the assertion of the fall of those who do evil (v. 12). The petitions in vv. 4 and 5 are thus fulfilled.

The analysis of the character of the wicked establishes the absence of "fear of God" as *the* source of all sin. A necessary consequence of godlessness is inability to do good. This analysis has structural and content parallels in Ps 14:1-3, 5. The hymn, the first word of which (in the title) is the divine name YHWH, leads outward into universal breadth: it praises the steadfast love, faithfulness, righteousness, and righteous judgments of YHWH, which fill heaven and earth. God saves human beings and animals. God's care, as in heaven, is experienced by human beings in the shelter of the sanctuary. God's very self is life and light for the community. Petitions for steadfast love and righteousness for the group of those who know YHWH, and the personal petition for preservation from arrogant overestimation of oneself precede the assertion of the collapse of the evildoers.

This psalm is a composition *sui generis*. The combination of reflection, hymn, petition, and judgment, together with the vocabulary, place it in the realm of Wisdom literature. In spite of the Wisdom-style reserve with respect to cultic matters it speaks positively of the Temple. It can therefore be dated to a period before the exile.

Psalm 37

Context

The complementary themes of "doing good" (vv. 3, 27) and "justice and righteousness" (vv. 6, 28, 30) mark the alphabetic Psalm 37. The theme of "justice and righteousness" was first introduced in Ps 33:5. Psalm 36:6 took it up and developed it. This psalm has much in common with the announcement of the theme of "doing good" (Ps 34:14) and its development in Psalms 35 and 36. Among the common vocabulary shared by Psalms 36 and 37 are the words "do good" (37:3, 27 // 36:3, 4; cf. 35:12; 34:14), "good" (37:16 // 36:4), "bad, evil" (37:27 // 36:4), especially the contrasting of the verbs "do evil" (37:8; cf. vv. 1, 9) and "do good" (36:3), "faithfulness" (37:3 // 36:5), "hearts" (37:4, 15, 31 // 36:1 // 35:25), "way" (37:5, 7, 14, 23, 34 // 36:4), "light" (37:6 // 36:9), "see" (37:35, 25, 34, 35, 37 // 36:9 // 35:17, 21, 22), "upright" (37:14, 37 // 36:10), "know" (37:18 // 36:10), "precious" (37:20 // 36:7), "transgressors"/"transgression" (37:38 // 36:1), "take refuge" (37:40 // 36:7). In the same semantic field are "delight, joy" (37:4, 11 // 36:8).

The vocabulary common to Psalms 37 and 35 includes "peace" (37:11 // 35:20, 27), "gnash teeth" (37:12 // 35:16), "Lord of all" (37:13 // 35:17, 22, 23), "trap," "cause to stumble" (37:14, 24 // 35:8), "poor and needy" (37:14 // 35:10), "be put to shame" (37:19 // 35:4, 26), "seek" (37:25, 32, 36 // 35:4), "be judged"/"judge" (37:33 // 35:24). The noun "the wicked, evildoers" appears 13x in Psalm 37 (vv. 10, 12, 14, 16, 17, 20, 21, 28, 32, 34, 35, 38, 40). It is used twice in Psalm 36 (vv. 1, 11). The counterterm "the righteous" is used 9x in Psalm 37 (vv. 12, 16, 17, 21, 25, 29, 30, 32, 39); it appears also in 31:18; 32:10; and 34:15, 21 following a long absence (since Ps 14:4).

Structure

The most striking structural element in the psalm is the acrostic. The initial letters of (roughly) every second verse represent the sequence of the Hebrew alphabet. In contrast to Psalms 25 and 34 in which every verse begins with the next letter of the alphabet, the acrostic in Psalm 37 marks off sections of three to six half verses. Despite the formal constraints of the sequence of verses oriented to the alphabet the psalm reveals an order marked by formal and content signals. The different speech acts are decisive. The shifts in the direction of address reveal the following major sections:

I. Address: admonitions and rationale: vv. 1-11
II. Exposition: vv. 12-26
III. Address: admonitions with extensive rationale: vv. 27-40

These sections themselves reveal a carefully shaped internal order, while at the same time they are strongly connected one to another. To mention some details: the divine name YHWH appears 15x in the psalm, with five instances in each of the three sections (vv. 3, 4, 5, 7, 9; 17, 18, 20, 23, 24; 28, 33, 34, 39, 40). Five times the fate of the righteous is described as inheritance of the land (vv. 9, 11, 22, 29, 34; that is, these are chiastically distributed throughout the sections in the pattern of 2:1:2). Five times the wicked are threatened with being rooted out (vv. 9, 22, 28, 34, 38; these are not so symmetrically distributed).

Psalm 36 prays for rescue from the wicked. The petition presumes the power of those wicked persons; however, the psalm is calm in the certainty that "there," that is, in the sanctuary, the people who create evil have already fallen. They are so crushed that they will never rise again (36:12). In Psalm 37 a teacher seeks to convey that certainty to someone who is outraged at the successful lives of the wicked. In order to calm that outrage the teacher presents an entire repertoire of theology and rhetoric. The first section (vv. 1-11) speaks urgently to "fretful" people (vv. 1, 7, 8), urging them not to be enraged at the happy lives of bad people. In fact the success of the wicked is only for a short time (vv. 2, 9, 10). The poor and those who hope in YHWH will possess the land (vv. 9b, 11a). However the teacher not only introduces the action/result connection but speaks also of personal human connection with God. The teacher pleads for trust in God (vv. 3, 5) and describes the tenderness of the experience of God (v. 4), which resembles that of a great peace in the inherited land (v. 11). The second part of the psalm (vv. 12-26) is pure exposition concluding with a personal account of experience (vv. 25-26). The Lord of all things laughs at the actions of the wicked who plot against the righteous (cf. Pss 2:4; 59:8). The sword and the bow that the wicked lift up against the poor and those whose ways are straight turn back on themselves (vv. 12-15). The righteous and the wicked are directly contrasted and their ways of life evaluated (vv. 16-24). The righteous learn that God upholds them (vv. 17, 24). Not only the bows of the wicked (v. 15), but also their arms are broken (vv. 15, 17). The wicked are YHWH's enemies. Like the glory of the pastures, their lives vanish. So says the central verse of the psalm (v. 20), varying the comparison used at the beginning (v. 2). As the Lord of all has seen the day of the wicked (v. 13), so the Lord also knows the days of the blameless, whose inheritance will last a long time (v. 18). The psalm also speaks of the descendants of the righteous (vv. 25, 26). That is: the teacher's description incorporates prophetic-eschatological features. These are reinforced in the third section, which returns to the form of individual address (vv. 27-40). Verses 27 and 29 add to the parallel statements in vv. 3, 11, 22 that the dwelling of the righteous will last forever. The descendants of the wicked will be rooted out (v. 28).

Because God loves justice (v. 28) human beings must allow themselves to be shaped by justice and preserve it in what they do. Wisdom, justice, and *torah* (vv. 30-31) constitute a trio. God will decide the direct confrontation between the wicked and the righteous in favor of the latter (vv. 32, 33; cf. v. 12). In a struggle over justice YHWH will not leave the righteous in the lurch. The last part of the third section (vv. 34-40) recommends to the addressees that they place their hope in the Lord. The promise of the land is directed very personally to the conversation partner (v. 34). Such a person will have his or her own experience of the collapse of the wicked, just as the teacher in turn can point to such an experience (vv. 34, 35, 36 // vv. 25-26 // vv. 10-11). After a renewed admonition to preserve integrity and uprightness because the peaceable have a future (v. 37) the psalm concludes with a negation of the future for the wicked and a promise that YHWH will save the righteous (vv. 38-39). The liberation and aid extended by YHWH is already a matter of experience, and that experience is the basis for the hope that YHWH will deliver from the wicked and save, thus giving a future (v. 40).

This artistically formed psalm draws together theological lines from Wisdom, the Pentateuch, and the prophets. Wisdom themes include the connection between deeds and results as well as personal piety; themes from the Pentateuch narratives are taking possession of the land and receiving blessing (vv. 22, 26). The theme of "justice and righteousness" constitutes the bridge between Wisdom and prophecy. Hope and future are prophetic-eschatological themes. This psalm, which according to its genre represents the principal part of a Wisdom teaching discourse (cf. Prov 3:5-12; 24:1-22) was probably composed in the exilic or post-exilic period.

Psalm 38

Context

Psalm 38 follows Psalms 6 and 32 as the third ecclesial penitential song. It is linked to Psalm 6 by the almost identical beginning (6:1 // 38:1) and to Psalm 32 by the lament over the hand of YHWH that rests heavy on the speaker (32:4 // 38:2) and the speaker's bodily distress (32:3 // 38:3; key word "my bones"). The confession of sins is also common to these two psalms (32:5 // 38:3, 4, 18), and the words "be heavy" (38:4 // 32:4), "groan" (38:8 // 32:3), and roots underlying words meaning "be silent" and "deaf" (32:3 // 38:13) build a bridge between the two.

There are also important connections between Psalms 38 and 35: in both the mourning rituals are formulated similarly (35:14 // 38:6) and both psalms speak of the rewarding of good with evil (35:12 // 38:20). The parallelism "my foes . . . those who hate me" in conjunction with "lies" (35:19 // 38:19), the rejoicing of the foes (35:15, 19, 24 // 38:16), speaking falsehoods (35:20 // 38:12), the rare word for "stumbling" or "falling" (35:15 // 38:17), and the petition to YHWH not to remain far off (35:22 // 38:21) are common to both psalms.

In addition there is a connection to the content of the preceding psalm through a partial contrast: the righteous receive salvation or rescue from YHWH (37:39) and YHWH has helped them and will help them. Because the speaker of Psalm 38 confesses his or her sin, and therefore is not righteous, the psalm ends with a plea for help strengthened by the motif of confidence that the almighty Lord is the salvation of sinful human beings (38:22). Poor people and all who trust in YHWH enjoy the fullness of peace (37:11). The one who prays Psalm 38 laments the absence of peace (38:3). This person is not "peaceable" (cf. 37:37). The "nonexistence" attributed to the wicked in Psalm 37 (vv. 10, 36) also marks the one who confesses his or her sins (38:3, 7, 10, 14).

Psalm 38 is also connected to Psalm 37 by certain words and phrases: "wrath" (38:1 // 37:8), YHWH's "arrows" (38:2) corresponding to the "bows" of the wicked (37:14), "YHWH's hand" and "the hand of the righteous" (38:2 // 37:24), "nonexistence" (38:3, 7, 10, 14 // 37:10, 36), "peace" (38:3 // 37:11, 37; various translations in English), "pass by," "go over" (38:4 // 37:36), "heart" (38:8, 11 // 37:4, 15, 31), "Lord of all" (38:9, 15, 22 // 37:13), "forsake" (38:10, 21 // 37:8, 25, 28, 33), "light" (38:10 // 37:6), "seek my life," "seek to kill" (38:12 // 37:32; cf. vv. 25, 36), "evil," "ruin" (38:12, 20 // 37:19), "man" (38:14 // 37:7, 37), "pay back" (38:20 // 37:21), "good" (38:20 // 37:3, 16, 27), "help" (38:2 // 37:40), "salvation" (38:22 // 37:39).

Structure

Those parts of the psalm that address YHWH build a structural framework for the lament. In outline the structure is as follows:

- Address to God (petition and lament to God): vv. 1-2
  - Description of the danger (destruction of the person, sin): vv. 3-8
- Address to God (acknowledgment that God hears one's desires and prayers): v. 9
  - Description of the danger (sickness and alienation from friends): vv. 10-14
- Address to God (confession of confidence): v. 15
  - Description of the danger (slipping, falling, pain; foes and those who hate): vv. 16-20
- Address to God (petition for YHWH's presence and help, with motif of confidence): vv. 21-22

The use of divine titles in each address to God is more and more intensified toward the end of the psalm: "YHWH" (v. 1), "Lord of all" (v. 9), "YHWH"/"Lord of all"/"my God" (v. 15), "YHWH"/"my God"/"Lord of all"/"my salvation" (vv. 21-22). The sections that address God are petitions at both beginning and end (vv. 1, 21, 22) and confessions in the middle of the psalm (vv. 9, 15). The petitions imply fundamentally different experiences of God: the initial pleas that divine wrath be turned away presuppose the nearness of God experienced as pain and burden (vv. 1-2). In the final petitions that nearness is help and salvation (vv. 21-22). The three lament sections extend successively outward: at the beginning the speaker laments an existence destroyed by illness, a state that is also affected by sin. The speaker concentrates solely on self and God (vv. 3-8). In the second part being abandoned by friends, companions, and neighbors is the object of the lament. Others seek aggressively to snuff out the life of the defenseless speaker (vv. 10-14). In the third lament passage the view broadens to include foes and those who hate, who would repay with evil one who desired only good (vv. 16-20). The assertions of personal sinfulness (vv. 3, 4, 18) and personal innocence (v. 20b) are not contradictory; rather they are part of the vitality of religious language.

This psalm is a song of lament. We cannot say with certainty whether it is also the lament of a sick person rooted in institutional cultic practice. There are no direct indications of cultic activity. The conceptual proximity to the Job poems (e.g., in the evaluation of divine nearness!) appears to point to an origin in the exilic or post-exilic period.

Psalm 39

Context

This psalm is linked both thematically and in detail with Psalm 38. Both speak of the pain and distress (38:17 // 39:2) connected with the speaker's sin (38:4, 18 // 39:1, 11). Both psalms discuss God's corrections and punishments (38:1-2 // 39:10-11). In both psalms the speaker alludes to being silent (38:13-14 // 39:1-2, 9). The theme of silence connects these two psalms also to Ps 37:7-8. The thematic and detailed connection between Psalms 38 and 39 is underscored by a rich common vocabulary: the introduction of a conversation with oneself by the use of the word "say" (39:1 // 38:16), "sin" as verb and noun (39:1 // 38:3, 18), "mouth" (39:1, 9 // 38:13), the preposition "before" in the sense of "with" (39:1, 5 // 38:9, 11, 17), "silent," "be silent" (39:2, 9 // 38:13), "happiness"/"good" (39:2 // 38:20), "pain, distress" (39:2 // 38:17), "my heart" (39:3 // 38:10), "muse"/"meditate" (39:3 // 38:12), "nothing"/"nothingness" (39:5, 13 // 38:3, 7, 10, 14), "man" (39:6, 11 // 38:14), "Lord of all" (39:7 // 38:9, 15, 22), "hope," "I hope/wait for" (39:7 // 38:15), "not open [the mouth]" (39:9 // 38:13), "stroke" (39:10 // 38:11), "the hand of YHWH" (39:10 // 38:2), "punishments"/"retorts" (39:11 // 38:14), "sin/guilt" (39:11 // 38:4, 18), "punish" (39:11 // 38:1).

Structure

The structure of the psalm is easily discernible from the shifts in the direction of address. The psalmist's address to himself or herself (vv. 1-3) is followed by a lament addressed to God (vv. 4-13):

1. Report of the attempt to quiet oneself: vv. 1-3
2. Song of lament: vv. 4-13
   a. Plea for insight into the vulnerability of one's own life: v. 4. Lament over the shortness of life and the weakness of human beings: vv. 5-6
   b. Plea for liberation from sins and the divine stroke: vv. 7-10. Lament over God's punishments and the weakness of human beings: v. 11
   c. Plea to be heard and receive an answer from God: v. 12. Plea that God may look away, and lament over the fleetingness of life: v. 13

The speaker first offers a narrative of having encouraged himself or herself to keep silent, but silence in the face of the wicked—that is, in light of the successes of the wicked—was not easy. Although abandoned by all happiness and in inner turmoil (distress, heat, fire), the speaker kept silence toward the wicked. But finally he or she did speak (vv. 1-3). The object of this account of experience is the citation of the prayer that follows (vv. 4-13). The three divine names, "YHWH" (v. 4), "Lord of all" (v. 7), "YHWH" (v. 12) mark subsections of the lament. The first sequence of petition and lament concentrates entirely on the weakness of one's own life and the nothingness of human beings in general (vv. 4-6). In the second passage, which begins in argumentative fashion ("and now") the psalmist asks where hope is to be placed (v. 7). That hope belongs to the God who forgives sins. The mortality of one's personal existence and that of human beings as a group is brought into close association with God's punishment (vv. 10-11). In the final petitions (vv. 12-13), as in Psalm 38 (vv. 1-2, 21) the ambivalence of the divine presence is expressed: the psalmist begs that God will hear and respond as a guarantee of the divine presence (v. 12), and yet God's gaze appears destructive. The psalmist asks God to look away (v. 13).

This psalm raises the problem of individual life in view of the happy existence of the wicked. Its thinking approaches the questions raised in the book of Job. It was probably composed in the exilic or post-exilic period.

Psalm 40

Context

Psalm 40 begins with words and phrases found in Psalm 39: "I waited" (40:1 // 39:7), "he heard"/"hear" (40:1 // 39:12), "my cry" (40:1 // 39:12). Psalm 40:1-4 is a song of thanksgiving corresponding to the song of lament in 39:4-13. The use of the nouns "praise" (40:3) and "prayer" (39:12) focuses the relationship between Pss 40:1-4 and 39:4-13 on those concepts. In both psalms the speaker makes personal speech a theme (40:5 // 39:3). At the same time this theme marks a relationship of contrast between the two psalms: Psalm 40 emphasizes the desire to speak (40:5) and having spoken (40:9-10), while Psalm 39 speaks of the desire to keep silent (39:2) and having been silent (39:2, 9). There are further connections between the two psalms at the level of vocabulary: "my mouth" (40:3 // 39:1, 9), "you made/you did" (40:5 // 39:9), "nonexistence" (40:5, 12 // 39:5, 13), "tell, speak" (40:5 // 39:3), "say" (40:7, 10 // 39:1), "know" (40:9 // 39:4, 6), "my heart" (40:10, 12 // 39:3), "sin, iniquity" (40:12 // 39:11), "deliver" (40:13 // 39:8).

Psalm 40 has the following words and phrases in common with the immediately succeeding Psalm 41: "happy" (40:4 // 41:1), "hurt, trouble" (40:14 // 41:1, 7), "deliver" (40:17, cf. 41:1), "thought"/"take thought, imagine" (40:5, 17 // 41:7). Worthy of special mention is the verb "establish"/"raise up" that appears in both psalms (40:2 // 41:8, 10).

However, Psalm 40 is closely connected not only to the other psalms in its immediate neighborhood. There is an especially close relationship between 40:9-17 and Psalms 35–38:

Psalms 40 and 35: Verses 14 and 15 of Psalm 40 generally correspond to 35:26, 27. In addition, 40:15 is related to 35:25a. This forms an inclusion for the fourth sub-section in the first Book of Psalms. Both psalms speak of the great congregation in which the speakers raise their voices to praise God (40:9, 10 // 35:18).

Psalms 40, 36, and 37: The close association of righteousness (40:9, 10a), fidelity (40:10), steadfast love and faithfulness (40:10, 11) finds corresponding echoes in Pss 36:5, 6, 10, 37:3, 6, and 33:4-5.

Psalms 40 and 38: The idea that sins grow head-high or are more numerous than the hairs of one's head unite Pss 38:4 and 40:12. There is correspondence between 38:10 and 40:12: the speaker has lost strength or "heart." We also find in both the petition "make haste to help me" (38:22 // 40:13).

The paired words "poor and needy" connect Psalms 35 (v. 10), 37 (v. 14), and 40 (v. 17). The noun "salvation" joins Pss 33:17; 37:39; 38:22; 40:10, 16.

This vocabulary shows that the psalms in the fourth part of the first Book of Psalms are closely interwoven, yet Psalm 40 reveals a larger context as well. The connections to the preceding Psalm 39 in vv. 1-13a are enriched in v. 3 with other links to Ps 33:3 (as well as Pss 96:1; 98:1; 144:9; 149:1). The combination of "steadfast love and faithfulness" with "mercy" in 40:11 is also found in Ps 25:5-6, 10. This forges a connection to the third part of the first Book of Psalms (Psalms 25–34).

In addition Psalm 40 has connections to the end of the second Book of Psalms: the correspondence of 40:2 to 69:2, 14 appears especially important. The lament and petition in Psalm 69 is anticipated by the narrative of rescue from sinking in the mire in Psalm 40. Then Ps 40:13-17 appears as a separate psalm (Psalm 70). There are also close relationships between Psalms 40 and 71: both speak of hope and trust (40:3, 4 // 71:5); in both one's mouth is full of the praise of YHWH (40:3 // 71:8); in both the speaker proclaims the righteousness and salvation of YHWH (40:9, 10 // 71:15) and tells of YHWH's wondrous deeds (40:5 // 71:17).

Structure

The structure of the psalm is evident from the shifts in the direction of address:

1. Narrative of God's salvation ending with a beatitude: vv. 1-4
2. Address to God about God's deeds and those of the speaker: vv. 5-12
3. Address to God as petition and lament: vv. 13-17

The psalm begins with a narrative of experience of being saved by YHWH. The danger from which God has saved the speaker recalls the torments to which the prophet Jeremiah was exposed (Jer 38:6; cf. Ps 69:2, 14-15). The speaker makes the personal experience of not being disappointed by YHWH in one's hope (vv. 1-3a) a fruitful experience for the congregation, since many should be drawn by this experience to trust in YHWH (v. 3b). Only they are happy who turn away from idols and toward YHWH (v. 4).

The second part of the psalm addresses God (vv. 5-12) and is set apart from the third section by an inclusion. Verse 11 with its emphatic "you, O Lord" and v. 12 with its verb "be strong, powerful" lead back to v. 5. YHWH's wonders and thoughts are too numerous and mighty for a human being to be able to tell them, and yet the speaker desires to communicate them (v. 5). YHWH does not desire sacrifices (v. 6); the speaker desires to do the will of YHWH, for YHWH's *torah* is within his or her heart. The contrasting formula in vv. 6-8 takes up ideas from Ezek 3:3; 36:26-27; Jer 31:33. YHWH has accomplished many things and therefore the speaker has given testimony before many, in the "great congregation" to God's righteousness, faithfulness, steadfast love, and trustworthiness (vv. 9-10). Because the speaker has not held back in testifying to YHWH's righteousness he or she is also certain that YHWH in turn will not hold back the divine mercy and that YHWH's steadfast love and faithfulness will endure.

The third part of the psalm (vv. 13-17) is also marked by inclusion ("my help," vv. 13b, 17). It contains an urgent plea for deliverance (v. 13) as well as a petition for the shaming of those who seek the speaker's life, desire his or her hurt, and give free rein to their cynical pleasure in it (vv. 14-15). This section, however, also contains a petition for joy in God for those who seek God and love God's salvation (v. 16). In contrast to the parallel passage in 35:27 that prays for those who rejoice in the speaker's righteousness, a consistent theological orientation appears in this verse (40:16) as also in Ps 70:4. Only in the last verse does the speaker return to his or her own concerns. The lament speaks of God (v. 17a), while the urgent plea is again an address to God (v. 17b).

Psalm 41

Context

This psalm is connected to its predecessor by a series of characteristic words: "happy" (41:1 // 40:4), "trouble"/"hurt" (41:1, 7 // 40:14), "give" (41:2 // 40:3), "[wicked] desire"/"life" (41:2, 4 // 40:14), the introductory phrase "I said" (41:4 // 40:7), "to see" (41:6 // 40:12; cf. 40:3), "tell" (41:6 // 40:5), "their hearts"/"my heart" (41:6 // 40:10, 12), "think" (41:7 // 40:17, cf. 40:5), "trust" (41:9 // 40:3, 4), "be great"/"boast" (41:9 // 40:16), "raise up"/"set in place" (41:10 // 40:2), "I know"/"you know" (41:11 // 40:9), "be pleased" (41:11 // 40:6, 8, 14). The theme with which Psalm 40 ended, the evaluation of oneself as poor (40:17) is taken up in the beatitude of Ps 41:1 with a different word and making a different point. The verb "deliver" and the participle "deliverer" do not have the same root but they correspond nevertheless (41:1 and 40:17). The same is true of the theme of "sin" that takes an important part in both psalms, but in different words: "sin"/"iniquity" (41:4 // 40:12). At the end of Psalm 41 the words "set [in place]" (v. 12) and "be pleased" (v. 11) take up motifs from Ps 40:2 and 40:6, 8 respectively.

Besides those to the immediately preceding psalm, there are important links among Psalms 41, 35, and 38: first, the talk about "my enemies" and "those who hate me" (41:5, 7 // 35:19 // 38:19). In addition, the scandalous behavior of the speaker's closest human companions is described very similarly in the three psalms (35:12, 15, 20, 21 // 38:11-12, 16 // 41:5-9). All three contain the verb "repay [good with evil]" (35:12 // 38:20 // 41:10) and the noun "peace," not always used in the same sense (35:20 // 38:3 // 41:9). The expression "the man of my peace" ["my bosom friend"], 41:9) constitutes a link to Ps 37:37 ("peaceable"), and the "boasting" of the unfaithful trusted one, or the foes, over the speaker is such a link to Psalm 38 (41:9 // 38:16).

Psalms 38–41 are joined by the introduction to speech, "I said" (38:16 // 39:1 // 40:7 // 41:4) and the theme of "sin" (38:3, 5, 18 // 39:1, 8, 11 // 40:12 // 41:4). The same elements link Psalms 30–32 ("I said," 30:6 // 31:14, 22 // 32:5; "sin," 30:5a, 6a // 31:10 // 32:1-5).

Structure

The structural plan of this psalm is not entirely transparent. On the basis of the shifts in the direction of address we may discern the following sections:

1. Blessing of those who consider the poor;
   Speech about God: vv. 1-3
2. Plea for healing and lament over the enemies and those who hate;
   Speech to God: vv. 4-10
3. Assurance of being heard;
   Speech to God: vv. 11-12

4. Doxology to conclude the first Book of Psalms:
   Speech about God: v. 13.

Those who consider the poor are called blessed. God saves and preserves them and keeps them alive. The beatitude is remarkable insofar as it refers to the intellectual initiative of a human being in favor of the poor. The verb used here certainly also has a connotation of solidary praxis with the poor, but it emphasizes rational effort on their behalf. There seems to be no thought of blessing someone who sees the poor as personal examples and considers them as people who are especially preferred by God. The section feels unbalanced because of the two sudden shifts from speech *about* God to address *to* God (vv. 2a/2b and 4a/4b). Verse 3 speaks of divine help in sickness. The prayer language (vv. 2b, 3b) prepares, both in content and form, for the quotation of the song of lament in vv. 4-10. The latter begins with a petition for grace and healing, thus continuing the content of v. 3. The description of the danger (vv. 5-9) concentrates entirely on the malicious and cynical behavior and attitudes of the enemies and those who hate the speaker, indeed, his or her bosom friend. The petition that closes the song of lament (v. 10) returns to its beginning (v. 4) and is explicitly directed against an expectation of the enemies (v. 8). The plea to be able to exercise personal vengeance is striking (v. 10b). In many psalms retribution is explicitly left to God (cf. Ps 31:23; 62:12).

The conclusion of the psalm constitutes a section in which the speaker expressed confidence in having been found pleasing to God, being perceptibly upheld by God, and being placed in God's presence (vv. 11-12). The experience of being rescued by God is already in the past. The speaker can point to it. The consciousness of one's own guilt (v. 4) and moral integrity (v. 12) are complementary contrasts in the complete course of the prayer. It is not appropriate to draw from this contrast any literary conclusions regarding the unity of the psalm.

Verse 14 is the praise offered to the God of Israel at the end of the first Book of Psalms (cf. 72:18-19; 89:52; 106:48).

Psalm 41 can be understood, with its various sections, as a liturgy: the blessing and instruction are spoken by the priest to the person asking for healing in order to establish the preconditions for being heard by God (vv. 1-3). Then follows the prayer of the sick (vv. 4-10). The assurance of having found favor with YHWH is given to the petitioner through the priestly oracle. The priest proclaims in the name of God that God has heard the petitioner. Of course, this is simply a reconstruction of the different sections in terms of a ritual for cases of illness. In particular the existence of a "priestly oracle" is an exegetically problematic notion. The awareness of being heard and accepted by God can also be elicited through the process of prayer. As the text of a ritual for the sick the psalm may be pre-exilic.

BIBLIOGRAPHY

See page 859.

Psalms 42–89

Kathleen Farmer

FIRST READING

The traditional division of the psalter into five "books" is somewhat artificial. These divisions may reflect the existence of a series of earlier sub-collections that were later brought together in the final collection we now know as the canonical psalter. But the so-called "books" themselves are not always internally coherent. The division between Book 2 (Psalms 42–72) and Book 3 (Psalms 73–89) is marked both by a doxology in 72:18-19 and a final note in 72:20 that calls the reader's attention to the end of the second of the two "Davidic" collections in the psalter. But this Davidic collection does not comprise the whole of Book 2. Other psalms in Book 2 are attributed to the Temple singers known as "the sons of Korah" (Psalms 42–49) and "Asaph" (Psalm 50). These Temple singers also have groups of psalms attributed to them in Book 3.

Thus the headings of the psalms in Books 2 and 3 imply that three distinguishable sub-collections have been gathered together in this section of the psalter. But the boundaries of these sub-collections do not coincide with the traditional division of the psalter into books. There may once have been earlier collections known as the "Korahite" psalms or the "Asaphite" psalms. The different guilds of Temple singers may once have included the psalms that bear their names in their repertoires or these psalms may have some other qualities that set them apart. But these earlier collections have not been kept altogether as discrete units in the present form of the psalter. Nevertheless, the psalms that have been grouped together into Books 2 and 3 do have a number of formal, linguistic, and stylistic characteristics in common, and the features they share are often peculiarities that set them apart from the rest of the psalter.

(1) The psalmists who speak in Books 2 and 3 prefer to address their prayers to "God" (using the Hebrew word *ʾelohim* and its variants) rather than to "the LORD" (using the Hebrew word *yhwh*). In other sections of the psalter *yhwh* (LORD) is used about ninety percent of the time, but the speakers in Book Two use *ʾelohim* more than eighty percent of the time while the references to *yhwh* and *ʾelohim* are about evenly divided in Book 3.

A dramatic illustration of the Elohistic bent of these psalms can be found by comparing Psalm 53 with Psalm 14. The two psalms are very similar except for the names they use for God. Psalm 53 seems to be an Elohistic reworking of Psalm 14. In Psalm 53 the divine name is changed from *yhwh* to *ʾelohim* in three out of four references (see commentary on Psalm 53).

(2) Some technical (poetic, cultic, or musical) terms occur more frequently in Books 2 and 3 than in other parts of the psalter. The term *maskil* occurs seven times in Book 2 (in Psalms 42, 44, 45, 52, 53, 54, 55) and four times in Book 3 (in Psalms 74, 78, 88, 89) but only twice in all of the rest of the psalter (in Psalms 32 and 142). The term probably means a "clever" psalm in which a certain kind of name-play is used (for example, a pun on the name of the person to whom or

about whom it is sung). However, the term could refer either to the type or content of the psalm or to a typical musical setting or musical accompaniment.

The term *selah* is used in only thirty-nine psalms, and twenty-nine of these are psalms included in Books 2 and 3. The LXX understands the term to mean an instrumental interlude but it might also be used to designate appropriate places for the choir or the congregation to sing or respond, to bow down and pray or lift up their voices and shout, etcetera.

In the psalter as a whole the majority of psalms are confessional in character. Most are addressed either to God or to the worshiping community. Only a few psalms contain oracles (where God is said to speak) within them. But the majority of these oracular psalms are found in Books 2 and 3 of the psalter (see commentaries on Psalms 46, 50, 75, 81, 82).

It has long been noted that the psalms can be subdivided into groups according to recognizable patterns of thought, speech, imagery, and intentionality. Those who speak from peaceful, prosperous settings in life often have different things to say to God and different ways to say them than do those who are caught in the midst of a crisis that threatens their physical, emotional, or spiritual well-being. Psalms that gratefully celebrate the various gifts and blessings the singers have received from God are sometimes called "hymns" or "psalms of confidence" or "thanksgiving psalms." Formalized cries for help addressed to God by individuals or communities who have been caught up in situations of crisis, oppression, distress, pain, or grief are sometimes called "psalms of lament" or "psalms of disorientation" (Brueggemann). In the psalter as a whole about a third of the psalms can be said to be psalms of lament. But in Books 2 and 3 more than half of the psalms are laments, either of the individual or of the community.

Thus it seems that in many ways Psalms 42–89 can be better understood as one larger subunit rather than as two separate entities within the psalter. However the reader would still be wise to remember that these "books" are more like anthologies than essays. In other words these "books" are collections of mostly separate (and often apparently unrelated) prayers and songs that have been sung and said by a wide variety of individuals and groups in a wide variety of social and historical situations. Even if the psalms found in "Books 2 and 3" have many characteristics in common they were probably never meant to be read continuously at a single sitting or in a single devotional setting.

There are some adjacent psalms that can be meaningfully read together or in conjunction with each other (e.g., Psalms 42–43, 70–71, and 88–89). But for the most part each psalm deserves to be read and studied as an entity in its own right. However, it might be helpful for the reader to begin by reading similar psalms together in order to get a feel for the ways in which similar patterns of speech reflect similar "seasons" of the human heart.

An initial reading of the psalms in Books 2 and 3 might be done in this order:

(1) First read the psalms that celebrate the sovereignty, graciousness, and saving acts of God: Psalms 47, 48, 63, 65, 66, 67, 68, 70, 71, 76, 78, 84.

(2) Then read the psalms in which God speaks to the worshiping community in the form of a prophetic oracle: Psalms 46, 50, 75, 81, 82 and the psalms that contain statements of confidence or assurance addressed to the community rather than to God: Psalms 49, 52, 53, 58, and 62.

(3) Next read the psalms of lament (which are by far the most common type) subdivided as follows:

- (a) those in which the speakers feel abandoned or rejected by God: Psalms 42, 43, 44, 60, 74, 77, 85, 88, 89;
- (b) those in which the speakers cry out to God for help in desperate situations: Psalms 54, 55, 56, 57, 59, 61, 64, 69, 79, 80, 83, 86.

(4) Finally, read the psalms that are more singular in type:

- (a) royal psalms (sung on behalf of the king): Psalms 45, 72
- (b) a psalm dealing with questions of justice and retribution: Psalm 58
- (c) a song of Zion, praising the city of God: Psalm 87
- (d) a penitential prayer: Psalm 51.

General Contexts for Interpretation

Original Historical Contexts

For the most part the psalmists use vividly poetic but historically non-specific language to describe their joys and sorrows, their hopes, doubts, fears, faith, and despair. The confessional way in which the psalmists address themselves to God enables succeeding generations of worshipers to use the psalms as their own prayers. But the confessional mode does not lend itself to precise historical reconstruction. Few of these psalms can be directly tied to known periods or events in the history of Israel.

While a number of the "Davidic" psalms in Book 2 have headings that link them with specific incidents in the life of David there is good reason to believe that these headings were added long after the psalms themselves were composed. David's remorse after committing adultery with Bathsheba is connected to the penitential language of Psalm 51; the persecution David suffered under Saul is said to provide the occasions for Psalms 52, 56, 57, and 59; David's military campaign against Edom is mentioned in the heading to Psalm 60; his flight from Absalom is said to have provided the setting for Psalm 63. However, a close look at the contents of the psalms themselves often indicates a high degree of disparity between the situations described in the bodies of the psalms and those described in the headings. It might be safest to say that the headings tell us more about the ways the psalms were understood or used by later communities of worship than they tell us about the period of time in which the psalms originated.

Occasional references to the geography, politics, and traditions of the northern kingdom of Israel lend weight to the supposition that some of the Elohistic psalms originated in the north, around the shrine of Dan (see commentary on Psalm 42). In addition to preferring the divine name Elohim, the Korahite and Asaphite psalms seem to be interested in northern kingdom affairs and Psalms 77, 80, 81 all mention Joseph (whose sons were said to be the ancestors of the chief northern tribes of Ephraim and Manasseh).

Some of the psalms that contain northern references may have been brought to Jerusalem in the time of Hezekiah, after the fall of Israel to Assyria (see 2 Chr 30:10). Psalms that had once been associated with the cultic center at Dan may have been accepted and adapted at that time to become a part of the Jerusalem psalter. But once they had been incorporated into the southern tradition they gradually lost most if not all of their (hypothetical) northern aspects.

The Sub-Collections in Books 2 and 3

The Psalms of the Sons of Korah

There are eleven psalms in Books 2 and 3 that mention the "sons of Korah" in their headings: 42–49 (with the exception of 43) and 84–88 (with the exception of 86). Psalm 43 is similar in many ways to Psalm 42 and may once have been considered the twelfth psalm of the sons of Korah. In the historical narratives Korah is said to be one of the descendants of Levi through Levi's son Kohath (Exod 6:16-24). According to Numbers 16 Korah was one of the leaders of a rebellion against Moses and Aaron in the period of the wilderness wanderings. Korah seems to have perished as a consequence of his attempt to seek priestly equality with the descendants of Aaron (Num 16:31-35) but the "sons of Korah" apparently survived (Num 26:11). The Chronicler describes the singing of the sons of Korah as a crucial element in leading the armies of Israel to victory in a much later period (2 Chr 20:18-22). Heman (who is mentioned in the heading of Psalm 88) is also said to be a son of Korah in 1 Chr 6:33.

The Psalms of Asaph

There are a total of twelve psalms in the psalter that specify Asaph in their headings. The first Psalm of Asaph is found in Book 2 (Psalm 50) and the other eleven Psalms of Asaph are found in Book 3 (Psalms 73–83). According to 1 Chr 6:33-47 Asaph was descended from Levi's son Gershom. In 1 Chr 15:16-22, 16:4-6 Asaph is described as a Levite musician who played a leading cultic role during David's time. Ezra 3:10 indicates Asaph's descendants carried on their ancestor's musical functions and Ezra 2:41 (Neh 7:44) names the Asaphites as the only levitical singers who returned from the Babylonian exile.

The Elohistic Davidic Collection

Psalms 51–70, with the exception of 66 and 67, all contain the name David in their headings. In addition it seems that Psalms 71 and 72 should be included in this Davidic collection even though their headings do not specifically mention his name. Psalm 71 is often understood to be the completion of the prayer begun in Psalm 70, and Psalm 72 (which has "of/to Solomon" in its heading) is usually received as a speech addressed to Solomon by David. At the end of Psalm 72, after the doxology that marks the end of the second book, is the line "The prayers of David son of Jesse are ended," which strengthens the argument for including all of Psalms 51–72 in this Elohistic Davidic collection.

Canonical Contexts

The authors of the NT used citations from these psalms in a variety of ways. Sometimes they understood Jesus Christ to be the speaker of various phrases in the psalms (Ps 69:9 // John 2:17, Rom 15:3). Other psalmic expressions that originally referred to God or to an Israelite king were seen through the eyes of faith to apply descriptively to Christ (Heb 1:8-9 // Ps 45:6-7). Still other phrases in the psalms were received as predictions of events in NT times (see, e.g., Acts 1:20 // Ps 69:25 or Matt 13:35 // Ps 78:2). Sometimes the NT community identified the suffering of the innocent in the psalms with their own suffering (Rom 8:36 // Ps 44:22) and sometimes they equated the "enemies" of the psalmists with those who refused to accept the gospel in their own age (Rom 11:9-10 // Ps 69:22-23). According to John 10:34-36 Jesus used Ps 82:6 to argue that it was not blasphemy for him to call himself the Son of God.

Church Usage

Athanasius of Alexandria's description of the Psalms as "a mirror in which you contemplate yourself and the movements of your soul" ("Letter to Marcellinus: On the Interpretation of the Psalms" 12, Bright translation pp. 63–64) is typical of the way in which the psalms have been understood and used in the Church. From biblical times to the present age the psalms have nourished the prayer lives of the faithful in both public and private worship. As Athanasius says, "the Psalms teach us what words to say when we are giving thanks . . . what words the fugitive should cry out, and what words are appropriate to offer up to God while you are persecuted and after being rescued" ("Letter to Marcellinus" 10, Bright translation p. 62).

With a few exceptions Christians throughout the ages have prayed most of the psalms as their own prayers. As Athanasius says, "in the words expressed by others of themselves, each person sings what has been written as about himself or herself, not at all as if receiving and reciting what was intended for someone else; they take it as their own, as if the words were theirs, and offer it to God as though they had composed the words themselves" ("Letter to Marcellinus" 11, Bright translation p. 63).

However it is this very same personalizing aspect of psalms usage that leads some Christians to censor the psalms when they use them in worship by omitting phrases and verses that seem inappropriate for Christian piety. The psalms represent the full range of human emotions in conversation with God, but some forms of Christian piety find the psalmists' candid and graphic portrayal of rage, pain, and despair unpalatable.

Very few of the psalms in Books 2 and 3 have been appointed for use in the Sunday Eucharist. None is used in its entirety in the *Ordo Lectionum Missae* of 1969 and those that are used have been censored, so that most of the vindictive petitions (which form an integral part of the original prayers) are eliminated. Psalms 58 and 83 have been completely left out of the Liturgy of the Hours while seven other psalms from Books 2 and 3 have had between one and nine verses removed from their original texts (54:5; 55:15; 56:6b-7; 59:5-8, 11-15; 63:9-10; 69:22-28; 79:6-7, 12). It is particularly interesting to note how frequently the NT quotes the very sections in Psalm 69 that modern Christians tend to avoid. (See Rom 11:9-10 and Acts 1:20.)

Instead of ignoring the so-called problem verses I recommend reading each psalm in its entirety, all the while remembering that these prayers describe the way real people in real situations have felt in the past and may still feel today. We do not need to approve of what the psalmists have said. We do not need to imitate or emulate their wishes, but neither should we pretend that these angry, bitter, and vindictive thoughts have now been banished from the realm of human existence. Rather than imitating the psalmists' attitudes toward their enemies we should learn to imitate their willingness to articulate feelings of anger and pain as well as joy in the presence of God.

Holding firmly to our ideals (believing that we ought to love our enemies and do good to those who persecute us) does not automatically wipe all angry or vindictive feelings from our hearts and minds. Such thoughts and feelings do occur even to the most faithful of us, in spite of our best efforts to the contrary. The psalmists advise us to be "honest to God," to acknowledge the presence of anger, pain, and despair as openly as we acknowledge the presence of peace, hope, and joy in our lives and to hand all of these things over to God in prayer.

SECOND READING

Psalms 42 and 43

Psalms 42 and 43 should be read together as two parts of a single poetic unit. For the terms *maskil* and Korahites in the title see the introduction (above).

When our enemies oppress us we may feel abandoned by God. This seems to be the case in Psalms 42–43. Oppression convinces the speaker in this double psalm that he or she has been forgotten (42:9) or cast off (43:2) by God. In order to have hope for a release from this feeling of abandonment the psalmist recalls a previous occasion when God had seemed particularly close and present during a joyful communal celebration in the "house of God" (42:4).

The geographical references to Jordan and Hermon in 42:6 and to the cataracts in 42:7 imply that the "house of God" the speaker remembers is the one at Dan (in the northern kingdom of Israel) rather than the Temple in Jerusalem. The sanctuary at Dan stood near the place where the life-giving waters of the Jordan burst out of the side of Mount Hermon in a thunderous stream.

The word which the NRSV translates "soul" (Hebrew *nephesh*) in 42:1, 2, 4, 5, 6, 11, and 43:5, refers to the whole person. The speaker's *nephesh* cannot be separated from the speaker's body in Hebrew thought. The *nephesh* includes the body, the mind, and the spirit of a living being.

The word translated "hope" in the refrain (42:5, 11, 43:5) more precisely means "to wait confidently for." This "hope" is not something that is merely wished for; rather this "hope" is something that is confidently expected to come. Thus it seems that this person in pain only feels abandoned by God for the moment. The psalmist has experienced the presence of God in the midst of a worshiping congregation in the past (42:4), and recalling the past enables the speaker to wait confidently for the "light" of God's presence (43:3) to turn the present painful situation around.

Psalm 44

This psalm begins on a deceptively positive note. The first section (marked off from the rest of the psalm by *selah* in 44:8) contains only praise for God's role in the triumphs of the past, but there is a radical change of tone between 44:8 and 44:9.

In 44:9-16 we discover that a disaster of immense proportions has recently occurred in this community. They have had reason to boast of God's help in the past, but the current situation is far different. Now their armies have been defeated, their citizens have been slaughtered or sold into slavery, and they have become an object of scorn among the nations.

The speakers (both the "we" who speak in the majority of verses and the "I" who speaks in 44:4, 6, and 15) assume that God has been an active agent in causing (or allowing) all of these things to happen. Their reasoning goes like this: If God's presence spelled victory in the past (44:4-7) their current defeat must mean that God has "rejected" them (44:9). They conclude that it must have been God who "scattered" them (44:11), "sold" them (44:12) and made them a "laughingstock" among their neighbors (44:13-16). Nevertheless the speakers insist that they have done nothing to deserve such rejection (44:17-22). If they had been disloyal to God or to God's covenant they might have expected such disasters to happen (44:17). But in fact, they argue in 44:22, it is their very loyalty to God that brings about their destruction (see Rom 8:36). Thus they conclude that God is the one who is at fault in the present situation. The final section (44:23-26) is a statement of protest against a God who seems to have repaid their loyalty with affliction.

How can they account for God's failure to notice what is happening to them? Must they assume God has been sleeping while they "sink down to the dust?" If so, they are determined to wake their Lord up with their cries of pain (44:23-25). The people's confidence in the strength of God's love allows them to use the boldest of language in their prayers. As the community worships together (remembering what God has done for them in the past) they gain enough confidence in God's "steadfast love" to make radical demands on their Lord and Savior (44:26).

Psalm 45

The heading calls this "a love song" *(shir yedidot)*. We might say more precisely that it is a wedding song celebrating a royal marriage. The singer describes the luxurious trappings of the bride and her attendants in the wedding procession (45:8-9, 13-15) and offers the bride a bit of advice on how she should behave toward her husband (45:10-12).

In 45:7 the king whose wedding is celebrated here is said to have been "anointed" by God. The Hebrew word for "messiah" and the Greek word for "Christ" originally meant simply "the anointed one." In ancient Israel the title "messiah" or "anointed one" was applied to a variety of different people (such as Cyrus, the Persian ruler who freed the people of Judah from exile, in Isa 45:1). But since the Church recognizes only one true Messiah Christians have often identified the king mentioned here with Christ.

The LXX (an early Greek translation of the OT) facilitated the messianic reception of this psalm. The Greek translation seems to imply that the king himself was divine ("Your throne, O God, endures forever and ever"). However, the Hebrew phrase may just as easily be translated "Your throne is a throne of God, enduring forever," implying that the ruler who is getting married here has God's support and approval (see the parallel in 1 Chr 29:23). It is the LXX version of Ps 45:6-7 that is quoted in Heb 1:8-9 and provides the basis for the messianic reading favored by the early Church.

Psalm 46

Where can security and stability be found in troublesome times? The singers in Psalm 46 say that God is their most dependable source of strength in times of trouble. Whether it is the chaotic forces of nature (46:2-3) or the hostile forces of humankind (46:6) that disturb us it is the presence of God in our midst that casts out fear (46:7).

The heading seems to indicate that this song was meant to be sung by young women (Hebrew *ʿalamoth*), or perhaps by soprano voices. It has sometimes been called a "song of Zion" and the city mentioned in 46:4-5 often has been assumed to be Jerusalem. However neither Zion nor Jerusalem is explicitly named in the text.

The "sea" and the "waters" in 46:2-3 have a cosmic as well as a natural dimension. Ancient Near Eastern peoples associated the "waters" with those cosmic forces of chaos and evil that have periodically threatened to overturn God's created order. "Be still" in 46:10 means "relax" or "be calm." In times of crisis the faithful need not feel compelled to engage in frenetic activity. The LORD is capable of calming both the "waters" and the warring nations that threaten us with death and destruction.

Psalm 47

This psalm celebrates the sovereignty of the LORD over "all the earth" (47:2, 7). The speaker calls upon "all peoples" to praise the One who reigns supreme over all the "nations" (47:8). Verse 3 interrupts the overall tone of the psalm, inserting a nationalistic note (from an Israelite perspective) into what is otherwise a universally oriented statement. Verse 3 momentarily shifts the emphasis of the speaker from God's universal sovereignty over the world to the benefits Israel has accrued because of that sovereignty.

In the last two verses the psalmist envisions God sitting on "his holy throne" while the leaders of the nations pledge their loyalty to God. To claim that the "shields" of the earth belong to God is to say that all the military powers owe their allegiance to the one Great King.

Psalm 48

Unlike Psalm 46 this song explicitly attaches the name Zion to the "city of our God," (48:1, 8). Zion (Jerusalem) is said to be the city "which God establishes forever" (48:8). The phrase the NRSV translates "in the far north" (48:2) would be better understood to refer to Zaphon, the mythological mountain where the Canaanites thought their high gods lived. In later times the word *zaphon* came to mean "north" in Hebrew, but in this psalm the speaker seems to claim that Zion is the true "Zaphon," the true dwelling of the true high God.

The temple of the LORD was built on mount Zion, within the fortified city of Jerusalem. The towers, ramparts, and citadels of Zion are impressive and may symbolize the presence of God for the worshiper (48:12-14), but the enemy kings who fled in panic (48:4-8) are not simply astounded by the fortifications of Jerusalem. Rather they flee from the awesome presence of God within (48:3). The psalmists know that it is God's Self and not the city walls that protect them as they live and worship in this location (48:3).

Psalm 49

An overwhelming majority of the psalms are either addressed to God or call upon worshipers to praise God. But God neither speaks nor is spoken to in Psalm 49. Instead the speaker seems to be a wisdom teacher who calls upon "all inhabitants of the world" (49:1) to hear what "wisdom" has to say about the relationship between life and death (49:3).

The wisdom teacher's message speaks primarily to those who stand in awe of the rich or to those who feel that the rich have some overwhelming advantages when it comes to matters of life and death. Like Qoheleth, Psalm 49 reminds us that all human beings, no matter how rich and powerful or well-educated they may be in this life, will eventually die. And when they do they will lose all their trappings of wealth, power, or education. We are all equal in death. No amount of wealth, no amount of wisdom, can save us from "the pit" or the grave. See Eccl 2:14-16, 3:19-20; Job 21:7-15; Luke 16:25.

It is unclear whether Ps 49:15 should be taken as the psalmist's opinion (that is, "they will go down to Sheol but I will not") or whether the psalmist is quoting what the foolhardy say. Only the foolhardy would think that they could purchase eternal life for themselves.

Psalm 50

The heading or title of Psalm 50 links it with the other "psalms of Asaph" found in Psalms 73–83 (see the introduction above). It is sometimes called a "prophetic psalm" because it presents us with words of God addressed to humankind (50:5, 7-15, 16b-23) and because its outlook with regard to animal sacrifice and hypocritical worship is a common theme in other prophetic texts (see Amos 5:21-22; Hos 6:6; Isa 1:11-13, 16; Jer 6:20, 7:22).

The LORD appears in the midst of a storm (50:3) and calls on the heavens and the earth to witness the imposition of judgment both on the insecurity of the upright and on the hypocrisy of the wicked. The psalm implies that both the upright and the wicked have misunderstood the purpose or function of making sacrifices. On the one hand the upright (those who have faithfully kept the provisions of the covenant) have mistakenly assumed that sacrifices had to be made before God would respond to their cries for help. On the contrary, says the LORD, all the faithful need to do is "call on me in the day of trouble; I will deliver you" (50:15). All God asks in return is that they be thankful (50:14, 23).

On the other hand the wicked (those who give nothing more than lip service to the ethical provisions of the covenant, 50:16-17) have also misunderstood the nature and purposes of the sacrificial system. The wicked have mistakenly assumed that offering sacrifices to God will make God overlook the way they treat their fellow human beings (50:18-21). In the early Church 50:16-23 was read as a cautionary word addressed directly to Christians by God (*1 Clem.* 35:7-12).

Psalm 51

Psalmists who ask God to help them out of their difficulties often claim that they are innocent of sin and free of guilt, but Psalm 51 assumes that the sufferer has indeed sinned and deserves to be punished. In Psalm 51 the speaker's guilt is readily acknowledged, though not in specific terms (51:3-5).

The psalm is concerned with the depth of the psalmist's own sin. There is no attempt to blame anyone else for the pervasiveness of sin in the psalmist's life. Thus 51:5 should be understood as a confession that the psalmist has been inclined toward sin since the moment of conception. Although this statement has sometimes been a source of misunderstanding in Christian circles it is clear in the context of this psalm that the emphasis is on the sin of the speaker, not on the speaker's mother or on the act of conception itself.

It is particularly noteworthy that this psalmist asks not only for forgiveness but for transformation. It is one thing to ask God to "blot out" or wash away the results of previous sins (51:1, 2,

7, 9) and quite another to ask for a transformation of one's heart and spirit (51:10). This penitent psalmist asks to be delivered not merely from the consequences of sin but from all future inclination toward sinfulness. This potential for making a completely new beginning seems to be what is meant by the words translated "broken spirit" or "broken and contrite heart" in 51:17. The sacrifice acceptable to God is the willingness to be transformed, to accept a new personhood free from the inclination to sin.

The attitude expressed in 51:15-17 toward animal sacrifice is similar to that found in the previous psalm and its prophetic parallels, but at some later date an interpreter from the time of the exile or later seems to have added a postscript (51:18-19) that moderates the prophetic statement. The early Christian Letter of Barnabas (written about 130 C.E.) uses 51:17 to argue that the Jewish sacrificial system was no longer acceptable to God.

Psalm 52

The heading attached to the beginning of this psalm attempts to explain the speaker's bitter and accusatory tone by connecting it with an incident related in 1 Sam 21:1-8 and 22:6-19. Like Psalm 49, Psalm 52 is neither addressed to God nor does it call on others to address God. Instead the speaker heaps verbal abuse on someone who is characterized as a mischief-maker, a "worker of treachery," and a liar (52:2-3). The speaker confidently asserts that those who "trust in the steadfast love of God" will thrive like healthy olive trees (52:8) while those who trust in the power of wealth more than in the power of God will be "uprooted" (52:5-7).

Psalm 53

Psalms 53:1-4 and 53:6 are nearly identical with Ps 14:1-4 and 14:7. However, the speaker in Psalm 53 prefers to use the Hebrew word *ʾelohim* for God, rather than the divine name *yhwh* (which is translated LORD). YHWH occurs in vv. 2, 4, 6, and 7 of Psalm 14 but not at all in Psalm 53. The first line in 53:5 is the same as the first line in 14:5, but the rest of the verse is different. Psalm 14 adds a sixth verse that has no parallel in Psalm 53.

The term Mahalath in the title does not occur in Psalm 14. It may be the name of a tune or a musical setting. Neither Psalm 14 nor Psalm 53 is addressed to God. In both psalms the speaker berates those who foolishly think and act as if God neither exists nor cares what humankind does on earth.

Since the Hebrew of 53:5 refers to "the one who encamps against you" it seems that the psalmist equates the fools who disregard the reality of God with the political enemies of Israel. Paul uses a version of vv. 1-3 to describe both Jews and Greeks who are under the power of sin (Rom 3:10-12).

Psalm 54

The title links this psalm with the narrative in 1 Sam 23:19. As a prayer for deliverance from enemies (54:3) it is addressed directly to God (54:1-2), who is called "my helper" (in 54:4). The mood shifts within the psalm (as is often the case in a psalm of lament) from a petition begging God for help (in 54:1-3) to a statement of confidence that God's help certainly will be forthcoming (54:6-7). In the recitation of the Liturgy of the Hours the psalmist's claim that God will "repay my enemies for their evil" (54:5) is omitted.

Psalm 55

The agitated, somewhat disjointed speech of the psalm reflects the speaker's emotional distress (55:2-5). Like many urban dwellers today this speaker would like to flee from the city, which seems so full of violence and strife (55:9-11), to seek peace and shelter in the wilderness (55:6-8), but it is clear that flight from the city will not heal the deepest source of the speaker's anguish. The real problem is that the psalmist's present worst enemy is a former close friend (55:12-14, 20-21). The psalmist feels betrayed as well as angry and afraid.

This psalm acknowledges the reality of vindictive feelings (55:15) as a natural human reaction to the pain of treachery or betrayal, but it does not encourage the sufferer to act upon such feelings. Instead of fleeing from the situation, instead of seeking to punish the treacherous friend, the troubled one is urged by a third party to cast the "burden" of this painful situation upon the

LORD (55:22). The vindictive wish in 55:15 has been left out of the Liturgy of the Hours.

Psalm 56

When your enemies are out to "get you" who can you turn to, who can you trust? The speaker in this psalm says reliance on God chases away fear (56:3, 4, 11). Trust in "the Most High" reminds us that a human opponent is nothing more than a frail reed (mere "flesh," 56:4; "a mere mortal," 56:11) in contrast to the power and permanence of God (cf. Rom 8:31). The heading suggests that the situation referred to here is the one reported in 1 Samuel 21:10-15.

This psalmist is confident that God keeps track of human suffering and pain (56:8) and causes the enemies of the faithful to retreat when the faithful ask for help (56:9). The mood of the psalmist shifts in 56:12 from pleading to thanksgiving. The psalmist gives thanks to God in the final verse for having been rescued from the life-threatening situation described in the preceding verses. Again the retributive wishes in 56:6b-7 have been removed from the current form of the Liturgy of the Hours.

Psalm 57

Psalms 56 and 57 begin with identical pleas for mercy in Hebrew (even though the NRSV obscures this similarity). The traditional "Lord have mercy" in the eucharistic liturgy comes from the Greek (LXX) translation of this plea.

The term "Do Not Destroy" that occurs in the heading of this psalm (and is used again in the headings of the next two psalms) is found only in Book 2 of the Psalms. It may be the name of a tune or a musical setting.

The dangerous situation from which this psalmist begs to be delivered is described in picturesque, figurative terms: being blown away in a storm (57:1), being trampled to death (57:3), being eaten by hungry lions (57:4), and being trapped in a pit or a net (57:6). The heading suggests that this psalm describes how David may have felt "when he fled from Saul, in the cave" (see 1 Samuel 22). But whatever the actual nature of the problem the psalmist knows that God's "steadfast love" and "faithfulness" are "sky-high" (57:10) and can be relied upon to come to the aid of those who cry out to God Most High (57:2).

Psalm 58

This psalm may seem more foreign and more shocking to the average Christian reader than any other passage in the psalter. It is not used either in the Liturgy of the Hours or in the Lectionary for Mass. In order for us to read it with some degree of understanding we must try to enter into the thought world of the speaker. The psalmist lives in a community of faith that teaches its members to believe that the God they worship will reward the righteous and punish the wicked on earth (in this life as we now know it), but this belief can easily be challenged when those whom the psalmist thinks of as wicked appear to escape punishment for their sins (58:3-5). The extremely bitter, vindictive requests made of God in 58:6-9 must be seen in the light of the psalm's concluding statement. The psalmist wants to believe (and convince others) that there really is a God (with a capital G) who punishes the wicked and rewards the righteous on earth. All the vengeful wishes expressed here grow out of the psalmist's need to see proof of the community's faith claim made manifest "on earth" (58:11).

The ambiguity of the original Hebrew makes it difficult to decide who is being accused of perverting justice in 58:1. The idea that there might be a heavenly court or a divine council over which God presides may very well have been a part of the psalmist's thought world. A heavenly court staffed by various divine functionaries is also mentioned in Psalm 82; Job 1:6-12; 1 Kings 22:19-23, but a number of versions (including NAB) assume that the psalmist's words are addressed in a sarcastic manner to human rulers who dispense judgment as if they were gods.

In either case we can conclude that the psalmist is asking the LORD God to take over the task of judging people's actions on earth instead of leaving it to (either divine or human) functionaries who have habitually "dealt out violence on earth" rather than justice.

Psalm 59

The first four verses of this psalm would fit in very well with the story referred to in the heading (as reported in 1 Sam 19:11-17) but the analogy begins to break down in 59:5 with the reference to the plotting of "nations," and in 59:7, 11-13 the speaker seems more concerned about the threat to his reputation than about any threat to his life. He is wounded by the lies his enemies tell (59:7, 12). He is hounded by slanderers who are likened to packs of dogs foraging in the city streets at night (59:6, 14). But even in the midst of his distress, the psalmist thinks of God as a fortress in which the persecuted can hide and gain strength (59:8, 16-17).

As in Psalm 58 the wish that these enemies might be "consumed" by God's wrath is motivated by the psalmist's hope that the destruction of the wicked will prove that God does indeed rule over Israel (59:13). Large portions of this psalm (59:5-8, 11-15) have been omitted from the Liturgy of the Hours, including all the derogatory references to "the nations" and to God's derision or punishment of them.

Psalm 60

The heading seems to refer to an incident reported in 2 Sam 8:13-14, except that in 2 Samuel it is David (rather than Joab) who is said to have killed 18,000 (rather than 12,000) Edomites in the Valley of Salt. Since the psalm itself reflects an experience of defeat rather than victory (60:10) we might envision this psalm being prayed before David's armies encountered the Edomites.

The speakers in the psalm complain that God's anger has torn their community apart as an earthquake tears open the land (60:1-2) and they plead for God to give them a victory so that those "whom God loves" can be rescued (60:5). The words in Ps 60:5-12 are duplicated in Ps 108:6-13.

In 60:6-8 the singers picture God speaking from the national sanctuary. In their minds they can see God putting the tribes of Israel in a place of honor and rejecting the nations who opposed Israel's expansion in the land of Canaan. Since psalmists usually assume that the enemies of Israel are the enemies of God the singers here are able to envision God making disparaging remarks about their enemies (Moab, Edom, and Philistia). This verse is used in the Liturgy of the Hours but is omitted from the Lectionary for Mass.

The last two verses of the psalm can be made into an appropriate prayer for any age or generation. Only God's help is ultimately effective against the ultimate foe. (See Psalm 62 for a similar theme).

Psalm 61

Even when we think we are as far away from God as we can get, we can still call out to God for help. The phrase "from the end of the earth" can be understood literally (meaning the speaker is physically far from the Temple of the LORD, as in exile) or figuratively (implying that the speaker feels spiritually remote from God) (61:2). In either case the first half of the psalm asks for the distance between God and the speaker to be removed. God's "tent" and God's "wings" are both metaphors for the protective presence of God that the psalmist seeks (61:4).

The second half of the psalm refers to the life and reign of an unnamed king. The psalmist may be speaking about himself in the third person, but in the LXX (and in later Christian tradition) this psalm was read as a messianic prayer. As such it hopes for the coming of a future king whose reign will be supported by "steadfast love and faithfulness," an ideal attained by few, if any, historical kings (61:7).

Psalm 62

When you are being verbally assaulted by those whose only goal is to bring you down, remember that "power belongs to God" (62:11). Whether they hold high office or not (62:9), whether they resort to hypocrisy, lies, or bribes (62:10) human beings can exert no more force than "a breath" or a puff of air (62:9) over against the rock-hard protection of God. Furthermore, the psalmist assures us, God's power is combined with "steadfast love," which tells us that we will be "repaid" according to our deeds (62:12, see Matt 16:27).

Psalm 63

Extreme thirst is used here as a metaphor for the psalmist's desire to be in communion with God (though the metaphor may have been prompted by an actual experience in the wilderness, as the heading assumes). The psalmist knows that God's presence with us is as necessary as food and water for the sustenance of life.

Being away from the presence of God is as life-threatening as being persecuted by one's enemies (63:9-11). Praising God and meditating on the steadfast love of God is "a rich feast" that satisfies the spiritual hunger of the faithful (63:5).

Athanasius (bishop of Alexandria from 328 to 373 C.E.) advised a friend: "If in being persecuted you flee to the desert, do not fear being alone in that place, because God is there. So arise early in the morning and sing Psalm 63" ("Letter to Marcellinus" 20, Bright translation p. 69). However all references to the cause of the speaker's trouble (63:9-11) have been removed from the 1969 Lectionary for Mass.

Psalm 64

Slander and false testimony can be as deadly as weapons of war. *The Jerusalem Bible* captures the metaphorical sense of the language used in this psalm by translating 64:3b as "shooting bitter words like arrows." The psalmist has been wounded by the sharp-edged tongue of slander and hopes that God will "shoot" a similar type of "arrow" back at these enemies (64:7).

Even those who believe in "turning the other cheek" may identify (on some occasions) with this psalmist who hopes that God will turn the wickedness of the wicked back upon them. The psalmist assumes that God will use the liars' own lies to bring them down (64:8a), causing everyone else to think twice about following in their footsteps (64:8b-9).

Psalm 65

Praise is due to God, sings the community in Zion, because the God we worship is the one who answers prayers (65:2) whether they are prayers for forgiveness (65:3) or prayers for deliverance from various kinds of danger (65:5). The deliverance for which the singers most specifically give thanks in this psalm is from the threat of drought. The rains have been plentiful (perhaps in answer to their previous prayers), the harvest will be bountiful (65:9-11), and the land itself sings for joy (65:12-13) along with the community of faith.

Psalm 66

"All the earth" (66:1, 4) is called upon to "come and see" what the God of Israel has done on Israel's behalf (66:5). In this psalm the recipients of God's grace bear witness to the rest of the world.

The first testimony comes from the community as a whole. The people of Israel remember that their God enabled them to escape from bondage by "turning the sea into dry land" (66:6a) and that their God enabled them to cross the Jordan and enter into the promised land (66:6b). Seen from the perspective of the promised land the trials they have previously suffered appear to have been little more than tests (66:10-12).

The second testimony comes from an individual who has experienced God's grace on a personal level (66:16-19). The God of Israel is worthy to be praised both because this God acts on behalf of the whole community (66:6-12) and because this God also acts on behalf of individuals within the community (66:13-20).

Psalm 67

In this song a prayer for a plentiful harvest is combined with (or disguised as) a call to praise. The praise-wish begins with a modified version of the blessing formula used by the priests descended from Aaron (Num 6:24-25). The community asks to be "blessed" not for selfish reasons (they say), but because their blessedness will lead the rest of the world to acknowledge God's "saving power" (67:2). If other nations are to be impressed by God's blessing of Israel, these other nations will need to see some concrete evidence that God's blessing makes a difference in the lives of those who are blessed. A plentiful harvest (67:6) will both supply tangible evidence that Israel has been blessed and provide an occasion for all the earth to praise the Provider.

Psalm 68

This psalm seems to be a medley composed of nine shorter songs or portions of songs revolving around the theology of the kingship of the LORD. In theory an ancient Near Eastern king was supposed to protect, defend, and promote the welfare of everyone over whom he exercised dominion (see comment on Psalm 72). By analogy God as king would be expected to act in similar ways. Thus three sections of this psalm refer to

God's "scattering" of any outside enemies who threaten the safety of God's people (68:1-3, 11-14, 28-31). Three other parts of the medley (68:4-6, 7-10, 19-23) call upon the community of faith to name and celebrate the ways in which their King acts within the community to promote the well-being of all his subjects. God as King of Israel defends the marginalized, frees those who are in bondage, provides the homeless with a home (68:4-6) and gives "rain in abundance" to those who need it (68:7-10). Furthermore, as King, God both "daily bears us up" (68:19a) and rescues us (68:19b), bringing us back from the faraway points to which we have been driven by our enemies (68:22).

The final three song segments (68:15-18, 24-27, 32-35) suggest ways in which God's kingship was celebrated liturgically within the community of Israel. In 68:15-18 a singer commemorates the building of the Temple of the LORD on Mount Zion by imagining (1) the jealousy that one high mountain might have felt when the LORD chose to reside on another mountain and (2) what the scene might have looked like if the LORD had actually marched from Sinai to Zion in a formal procession (68:17-18). In 68:24-27 we find a more realistic picture of the worshiping community as it celebrates the kingship of the LORD in a formal procession; 68:32-35 calls upon the kingdoms of the earth to celebrate the heavenly kingship of the God of Israel.

Psalm 69

We might say that the speaker in this psalm is "up to the neck in trouble." Flood waters, mud, and mire are used in 69:1-2 and 69:13-15 as vivid images for the dangerous situation that threatens to pull the petitioner down into death. Although it is possible to read this prayer as the lament of an individual there may be reason to believe that the "I" who speaks here is a representative figure. Like the "Suffering Servant" in Isaiah 53 this servant of the LORD (69:17) may personify the righteous remnant within the exilic community of Israel.

Those who were innocent of the sins that caused the downfall of Judah were nevertheless caught up in the devastation of the Babylonian exile. Though righteous they were "wounded" and "hurt" (69:26) when God allowed the Babylonians to destroy Judah and Jerusalem. In this psalm they complain that they did their best to no avail. Their "zeal" for God's house, their weeping and fasting in the face of impending destruction, gained them nothing but scorn (69:7-12) from their fellow Judeans. They wish to be rescued (69:13-15) themselves, but they also wish for the guilty (those who scorned their efforts on Judah's behalf) to be thoroughly punished (69:22-28). In the end, however, they are confident that the LORD will hear them as they cry out from their captivity (69:29-33). They faithfully expect God to rebuild the cities of Judah and to settle them and their children there (69:35-36).

Psalm 69 is frequently quoted in the NT. According to the gospel of John the way Jesus cleansed the temple reminded the disciples of Psalm 69:9a (John 2:17). Paul refers to the second half of the same verse in Rom 15:3 and to 69:22-23 in Rom 11:9-10. In John 15:25 Jesus seems to be quoting from Psalm 69:4 and in Acts 1:20 Peter describes the death of Judas as the "fulfillment" of one of the vindictive wishes made against the "enemies" in Psalm 69:25. Nevertheless, the vengeful wishes in Ps 69:22-28 were thought inappropriate for Christian prayer and have been left out of the Liturgy of the Hours.

Psalm 70

Do you feel secure enough in your relationship to God to say "Hurry up and help me, O LORD!" as this psalmist does (twice in both 70:1 and 70:5)? This petitioner feels free to speak openly and frankly with God, knowing that God will not abandon the "poor and needy" (70:5) either because of their lowly condition or because of their boldness of speech. Psalm 70 is often read as the introduction to Psalm 71 because of the apparent incompleteness of Psalm 70 and because of the similarity of vocabulary and subject matter in the two psalms. When they are read together the Davidic heading of Psalm 70 is then understood to apply to Psalm 71 as well.

Psalm 71

"Cast me not off in the time of my old age" is this psalmist's poignant (and very modern-sounding) prayer (71:9). Many of us today live in societies that equate usefulness with youthfulness. The structures of power in the world sometimes act as if they (like the psalmist's enemies) think that the elderly are god-forsaken (71:10-11), but the psalmist reminds us that those who are gray with age have some distinct advantages over the young. The older the recipients of God's grace get, the better they can testify to the continuing faithfulness and righteousness of God (71:8, 14-18, 22-24).

The "righteousness" of God is a key theme in this particular psalmist's praise. When the term righteousness is applied to God in Ps 71:2, 15, 16, 19, 24 it refers to God's determination to reverse injustices, to make things "right." As an aging person who is failing in physical strength (71:9b) this petitioner for God's protection draws hope for the future based on a lifetime full of previous experiences with the saving righteousness of God (71: 5-8, 17, 20-21).

Psalm 72

In theory a human king was supposed to supervise the ways in which the "righteousness" of God was carried out on earth. Thus an ideal king would be one who carried out God's will for order and fairness in every part of his kingdom (see commentary on Psalm 68). The word *shalom* (which the NRSV translates "prosperity" in 72:3 and 7) refers to the well-being, health, and wholeness of the land and its people. It is the king's duty to bring *shalom* (peace, prosperity, wholeness) to the land, but *shalom* can only be attained when the poor and the needy are treated fairly, with "righteousness" and compassion (72:2-4, 12-14).

A king who functioned not just in theory but in reality as God's channel for justice, equity, and compassion (72:12-14) would be the recipient of many prayers for the length of his life and his rule (72:5-11, 15, 17).

The "doxology" in 72:18-19 and the postscript ("The prayers of David son of Jesse are ended") in 72:20 bring both the second Book of Psalms and the second Davidic collection of Psalms to an end. Both the postscript and the heading of Psalm 72 ("Of Solomon") lend strength to the theory that this is the prayer of an elderly or dying David on behalf of his son and successor Solomon. But since it was clear that no human king in Israel's history ever lived up to these ideals Psalm 72 was received in the early Church as an expression of messianic expectations. Both Origen and Jerome saw references to Christ in the psalm. However, Theodore of Mopsuestia firmly defended its traditional reading as an expression of David's hopes for the reign of Solomon.

Psalm 73

Book 3 opens with the second of the twelve Psalms of Asaph (the first was Psalm 50; the other ten follow in Psalms 74–83). The psalmist raises a very modern-sounding question: what do you do when the things you have been told are true about God are not "in synch" with your experience?

There is an apparent discrepancy between the ideals of Israelite faith and the reality of life. The tradition says that "God is good to the upright" (73:1) but the psalmist has seen how the wicked apparently prosper and feel "no pain" even as they defy God (73:3-9). As the psalmist says, it is easy to be tempted to follow in the footsteps of the wicked (73:2-3) when it seems that piety and upright living bring trouble rather than riches or fame (73:13-14).

However a moment of revelation comes to reassure this speaker. Going "into the sanctuary of God" (73:17) leads the psalmist to the conclusion that those who are far from God have no real future (73:18-20), but those who claim God as their inheritance (or "portion") can with confidence put themselves and their futures in God's hands (73:23-26).

Psalm 74

Generation after generation of faithful worshipers believed that the LORD had chosen to dwell in the Temple built by Solomon on Mount Zion in Jerusalem. The Temple was a hub of religious activity, a focus of piety, and a symbol of stability in Judah. When the Temple was mutilated and burned (74:4-7) during the Babylonian conquest of Judah the survivors were shocked and disoriented by God's failure to protect either the sanctuary or the "congregation" who had worshiped in it (74:2). It seemed that God had "cast them off forever" (74:1). Nevertheless they continued to direct their anguished prayers to God, reminding themselves that the one who had created both their world and their nation

(74:12-17) was capable of turning the chaos of their present situation around.

The psalmist uses images drawn from ancient Near Eastern mythology to describe how God had "worked salvation in the earth" from the oldest times on. The sea, the dragons, and Leviathan (74:13-14) were known to the Canaanites as chaos monsters who had to be subdued before creation could begin. The congregation of Israel merged the old myths with their own story so that the reference to the conquest of the sea in 74:13 also hints at the Exodus experience and the crushing of Leviathan in 74:14 reminds Israel of their time in the wilderness on the way to the promised land. The first half of 74:15 refers to God's activity in the creation of the world while the second half of the verse hints at the miraculous way in which the Israelites were able to cross the Jordan into Canaan (see Josh 3:14-17).

The prayer in 74:18-23 seems to appeal to God's pride. God has a well-earned reputation for keeping promises and rescuing the poor and oppressed, but the psalmists imply that God's reputation will suffer if God does not keep the covenant (74:20), if those who have destroyed Judah are allowed to abuse God's name (74:18, 22), if God lets the downtrodden be put to shame.

Psalm 75

It is important to notice that this psalm changes back and forth between human speech and divine speech. A community speaks collectively to God in 75:1, God addresses the community in 75:2-5, an individual (perhaps someone representing the community) speaks about God in 75:6-9, and God makes a final declaration in 75:10. Such a format suggests the psalm might once have been used as a liturgy in a worship setting.

The image of having the accused people drink from a cup of some sort may reflect an ancient custom intended to separate the innocent from the guilty. The cup might prove to be a "cup of salvation" (as in Ps 116:13) or a cup of wrath (as here and in Isa 51:17, Jer 25:15; 49:12, and elsewhere; see also Pss 11:6, 60:3). The word "horn" is used as a figure for power or prominence (75:4-5, 10). Those who "lift up" their own "horns" are those who boast of their own powers or engage in self-exaltation.

The term translated "lift up" is used as an organizing image for describing both human action and divine reaction. The psalm echoes a common biblical theme: when God executes judgment (in God's own good time, 75:2) those who have exalted themselves will be brought low and those who have been humbled will be lifted up (75:4-7,10).

Psalm 76

Like Isa 2:2-4 and Mic 4:1-3 this psalm links the reality of God's opposition to human warfare with "Salem," or Jerusalem, whose very name invokes peace/*shalom* (76:2). The psalmist says that the God who has chosen to dwell in Salem (in Peace) has broken and will continue to break the instruments of war, the symbols of human arrogance (76:3).

The psalmist looks both backward and forward in time. The remembrance of God's victories in the past on behalf of Israel and Judah (76:5-6) melts into the anticipation of God's victory in the future over all human "wrath" (76:10). The comparatively feeble "wrath" of humankind serves only to emphasize ("praise") the infinitely greater power of God (76:10). The fact that God has inspired and will continue to inspire fear in the hearts of earthly rulers is ample reason for us to "bring gifts to the one who is awesome" (76:11-12).

Psalm 77

This psalm seems to fall naturally into two parts, a lament or complaint in 77:1-9 or 77:1-10 and a hymn of praise in 77:10-20 or 77:11-20. The two parts of the whole are linked through the uses of the word "meditate" in vv. 3, 6, and 12. The lament is a meditation on the sufferer's current circumstances. The hymn is a meditation on previous wonders performed by God.

Agony and suffering prompt the questions in 77:7-9. God's favor, steadfast love, grace and compassion are usually the subject of hymns of praise. Steadfast love *(ḥesed)* is the one characteristic that all witnesses affirm is an essential part of God's nature (see Exod 34:6), but the psalmist's misery leads him or her to conclude that God is not acting like God in the current situation. God seems to have forgotten God's most characteristic feature!

However, there is still hope! The traditions of the creation (77:16) and the Exodus (77:19-20) remind the speaker that God has acted before without leaving any "footprints" (77:19). Thus the psalmist has reason to hope that God is invisibly at work in the current situation as well.

Psalm 78

This psalm begins like a wisdom instruction similar to those found in Proverbs 1–9. The wisdom teacher's purpose is stated in 78:4-8: he or she intends to hand the traditions received from the previous generation on to the next generation in order that children not yet born might avoid making the same mistakes their ancestors had made. The handing on of the tradition will be done here in the form of a "parable" or in riddles (Matt 13:35 quotes from the LXX translation of Psalm 78:2). The "parable" of the psalm consists of a synopsis of Israel's early history that emphasizes the people's lack of faith and gratitude for God's many gracious acts on their behalf. The implied "riddle" of the psalm seems to ask why God would continue to put up with Israel's recalcitrance.

Flashbacks from the Exodus (78:12-14 and 43-53), the wilderness (78:15-41), and the premonarchical traditions (78:54-64) are used by the psalmist to illustrate the remarkable restraint God has shown in dealing with constant provocation from previous generations of the chosen people (vv. 38-39). The psalmist mentions (almost as an aside) that some of the guilty have perished because of their sins, but the essential point the psalmist wants to make is this: God continues to be gracious even when the chosen people fail to respond to God in an appropriate manner.

The climax of this recital (78:65-72) implies that the choice of Zion as the location for YHWH's dwelling and the choice of David to be a "shepherd" over Israel is the most recent and the most important of all God's gracious actions on behalf of the chosen people. The psalmist's unspoken implication is that Judah had better learn from its ancestors' mistakes. Judah must respond this time with appropriate gratitude to God for the gift of the Davidic line of kings!

Psalm 79

Once again a psalmist speaking on behalf of the whole community describes the destruction of God's sanctuary in Jerusalem in graphic detail (compare 74:3-7 with 79:1-3). Once again the community wonders if the present heat of God's anger will last "forever" (79:5 and 74:1; see also 77:7-9). The speaker in Psalm 79 complains that the bodies of the dead have been left unburied and exposed to scavengers, adding further insult to the sting of defeat (79:2-3). This psalmist also appeals to God's pride (79:9-12) as did the speaker in 74:10, providing God with a motive for action against those who have "devoured Jacob" (79:7): God's reputation will suffer if those who have shed the blood of God's own servants are not punished (79:10).

The psalmist wants God to take revenge against "the nations" who have afflicted Israel, reasoning that the enemies who taunt Israel are also the enemies of God. These vindictive pleas in 79:6-7 and 79:12 have been omitted from the Liturgy of the Hours. While these verses contain wishes we may consider inappropriate for our own prayers we should note that they do not advocate taking revenge into one's own hands. The psalmist is clearly convinced that whatever retribution the despoilers deserve should be carried out by God, not by humankind.

Psalm 80

In the ancient Near East rulers were frequently called the "shepherds" of their people. In Psalms 78, 79, and 80 the metaphor of shepherd is also applied to the divine ruler. Israel's God is said to be both shepherd and king of Israel. In Psalm 78 God was said to have guided Israel like a flock of sheep in the wilderness (78:52). In Psalm 79 the people declare themselves to be the sheep of God's pasture, under God's protection (79:13). Here again in Psalm 80 God is addressed as the "shepherd of Israel" and the "guide of the flock of Joseph" (80:1).

To the metaphor of shepherd in Psalm 80 is added the metaphor of God as the gardener or vine dresser (80:9-12). Israel is compared to a grapevine that God once carefully planted and cultivated (see also Isa 5:1-7). The people complain that the God who once tended them like a cherished planting now allows passersby to steal their fruit and predators to trample them down (80:12-15).

However, the people who complain have no doubt that their caretaker is capable of defending them. The one they call "Shepherd of Israel" is also known to them as the commander of the hosts of heaven. The refrain in 80:3, 7, and 19 connects the caretaking activities of the shepherd and the vine dresser with the warrior imagery of the "LORD of Hosts." The petitioners ask the LORD who commands the hosts of heaven to restore his "sheep" and his "vines" to their previously secure positions.

Like the psalmists, we too may experience the actions of God in our lives in a variety of ways. This psalm encourages us to use a variety of metaphors to describe the reality of God's relationships with us.

Psalm 81

Imagine the celebration of a harvest festival as the setting for the recitation of this psalm (probably the Feast of Booths or Tabernacles—known in Hebrew as Sukkoth—as described in Numbers 29). The time of the ingathering of the fruits of the land is a time to rejoice (81:1-3) but it is also a time to recall God's saving actions in the Exodus (81:6) and in the wilderness (81:7), as well as a time to recall the expectations God placed upon the people of Israel in the giving of the covenant at Sinai (81:8-10).

In 81:6-16 God speaks (through the voice of the psalmist) to the congregation gathered to celebrate the feast. God's speech reminds Israel of their failure to live up to God's expectations in the past (81:11-12). This reminder is not meant to induce guilt but to motivate reform. God offers the worshipers a new opportunity to respond appropriately in the new year (81:13-16).

Psalm 82

Monotheism (the belief that only one God could and does exist) developed relatively late in the history of Israel's religious thinking. Like Job 1:6-12 and 1 Kings 22:19-23 this psalm reflects the more ancient idea that Israel's God ruled over a heavenly court or council composed of lesser deities. (See also the commentary on Psalm 58).

While the psalmist can conceive of the existence of other gods he or she is convinced that the supreme God is a God of justice who upholds the rights of those who are marginalized in human societies (82:3-4). The psalmist implies that all the lesser gods (that is, those who show partiality to the wicked, 82:2) are doomed to die because of their failure to support the purposes of Justice (82:5-7).

Psalm 83

The speaker in this final "Psalm of Asaph" assumes that those who plot to wipe out the nation of Israel must surely be the enemies of God (83:2-5). The stories told in Judges 4–8 provide the psalmist with a model (83:9-12) for expecting God to fight on Israel's side in the current crisis. We may not approve of the things the psalmist asks God to do to Israel's enemies (83:13-17) but we should at least note the rationale given: shaming the enemy or putting the enemy to rout should function as an instrument of conversion (83:16b, 18).

Psalm 84

The second set of Korahite psalms begins here (the first set was found in Psalms 42–49). The speaker in this psalm, like the speaker in Psalm 42, "longs" to be in the presence of "the living God" (compare 42:1-2 with 84:2) and expects to find communion with God in the sanctuary, which is understood to be the "dwelling place" of the LORD of hosts (84:1).

A pilgrimage scene is envisioned in 84:5-7, leading us to suspect that the person who thirsts for the presence of God is a pilgrim on the way to Jerusalem to celebrate one of the three annual pilgrimage feasts. The pilgrims are pictured as blessing the barren places with their presence as they pass through the dry wadis on their way to "see" God in Zion (84:7). When they arrive at the Temple they offer up prayers for themselves (84:8) and for their anointed king (84:9).

Those who have to come long distances to meet the LORD "at home" in the Temple may envy both the birds who make their nests right in the Temple precincts (84:3-4) and the "sons of Korah" who are said to be the hereditary gatekeepers of the Temple (see 1 Chr 9:19; 26:1, 19). As this psalm affirms, guarding the doors of the LORD's dwelling is an office worthy of respect, an honor rather than a burden (84:10).

Psalm 85

Once again we see how a worshiping community bases its hopes for salvation (85:4-9) on the remembrance of what God has done in the past (85:1-3). This congregation's prayer involves a play on words. A single Hebrew root word is used in its various forms to mean "restore" (85:1,4), "turn" (85:3, 8) and "again" (85:6). The same Hebrew root (*swb* or *shubh*), which has the basic sense of "turn" or "return," can be used to connote repentance (turning away from sin) as well as restoration. Thus the psalmists recognize that the "turning" of Israel's fortune (from defeat to victory, 85:4a) depends on the "turning" of God (away from wrath toward mercy, 85:4b) and that the turning of God's anger depends on Israel's turning away from sin (85:8). The final stanza (85:10-13) pictures what it would be like to have true repentance/restoration in the land.

The current (1969) Lectionary for Mass eliminates the first six or seven verses from the reading of Psalm 85, effectively changing this community lament into an oracle of salvation that has no context either in the past or in the present. As a result "we lose a model for lamenting over our own nation in hope of insight about how we might turn to God and find consolation" (Kaufman, "Undercut by Joy," 74).

Psalm 86

An individual who wants to pray for help in a situation of distress would do well to use this psalm as a model. Complaints and supplications in 86:1-4, 6-7, 14, 16-17 are interspersed with and supported by statements of faith in 86:5, 8-13, 15. Belief in God's "steadfast love" (86:5, 13, 15) gives the petitioner a reason to hope, to anticipate giving thanks to God for a narrow escape from death (86:12-13). The psalmist claims to be "devoted" to God, a "servant" who trusts in God (86:2, 4, 16). Like the penitent who spoke in Psalm 51 this psalmist also prays for transformation, requesting "an undivided heart" with which to worship the LORD (see Jas 4:8).

Psalm 87

This song celebrates the glory of Zion, the city of God (87:3). Zion is extolled as the spiritual birthplace of all who "know" the LORD. The foreign nations listed in 87:4 include many places where displaced Israelites settled after the destruction of the Temple. "Rahab" in 87:4 is used elsewhere to designate Egypt (Isa 30:7). The word translated "Ethiopia" in the NRSV could refer either to regions around the southern part of the Nile or to the mountainous regions east of Babylon (as in Gen 2:13 and 10:8). Thus the psalmist assures the Jews of the Diaspora that even those who were born in exile could refer to "the city of God" as their true place of origin. The early Church received these Zion traditions as applicable to "the heavenly Jerusalem" (Heb 12:22) and concluded that true "citizenship" for the people of God is in heaven (Phil 3:20).

Psalm 88

In modern terms the person who speaks in this psalm might be said to suffer from "clinical depression." Terminally ill, on the brink of death, the psalmist complains of being treated like one who is already dead (88:4-5). Even worse than the physical pain is the mental anguish the speaker suffers because he or she feels abandoned or shunned by friends, by acquaintances, and by God (88:8, 13-14, 18). The psalmist assumes that both the sickness and the pain of abandonment by friends are caused by God (vv. 6-8, 15-18), yet this person of faith still addresses the LORD as the "God of my salvation" (88:1).

Psalms of lament typically contain both statements of complaint and statements of confidence in God's positive response, but Psalm 88 begins, proceeds, and ends in darkness and despair. The NAB captures the most complete sense of the final line: "my only friend is darkness." There is no resolution of the psalmist's dilemma. God does not speak or respond in the text of this psalm. But the silence of God does not silence the psalmist. The psalmist continues to cry out to God daily (88:9, 13), even when no word of hope or assurance of deliverance penetrates the gloom in which the sufferer is immersed.

Those who composed, edited, and handed the psalms down to us were content to let this psalm stand as it is in the canon, complete without a happy ending. The presence of this psalm in the canon reminds us that not every crisis in human life is susceptible to an immediate solution. Even the faithful can be bogged down in the depths of despair or caught up in what the mystics called the "dark night of the soul."

Psalm 89

The final psalm in Book 3, like the final psalm in Book 2 (Psalm 72) is concerned with the succession of the Davidic line of kings. However, Psalm 72 refers to the reign of the first of David's successors (Solomon), while Psalm 89 refers to the end of the house of David's rule over the kingdom of Judah. The promise made to David in 2 Samuel 7 (89:3, 19-37) provides the basis for the psalmist to lament the destruction that has overtaken the kingdom of Judah in the psalmist's own time (89:38-45). The poignant cry "How long, O LORD? Will you hide yourself forever?" (89:46) calls attention to the stark contrast between the memory the psalmist holds of God's covenant promises (89:3-4, 19-37) and the present reality in which the psalmist lives (89:38-45). The psalmist does not think that God is unable to keep these promises. After all, the psalmist knows that the LORD is the mightiest of all gods (89:6-8); the LORD is the one who crushed the forces of chaos in the process of creating the heavens and the earth (89:9-11). Thus the psalmist boldly calls God to account for what seems to be God's neglect to keep the promises given to David (89:49-51).

Commentator Marvin Tate suggests that Psalms 73–74 and 88–89 function like matching "bookends" to frame the rest of the psalms in Book 3 of the psalter. "[A]t both ends of Book III there is a psalm which deals with the theological distress of an individual followed by a psalm which expresses the distress in terms of the nation. In fact, Book III seems to deal over and over with the bafflement of believers who are struggling with the gap between promise and reality" (Tate, *Psalms 51–100,* 429).

The speaker in Psalm 89 finds no satisfactory way to account for the apparent disparity between the community of Israel's understanding of the Davidic covenant and the reality of the Babylonian exile. The NT community bridged this gap for themselves by proclaiming Jesus the offspring of David through whom the promises of God were fulfilled (see Acts 13:23).

The doxology in 89:52 is not a part of the psalm itself but marks the traditional end of Book 3 in the psalter.

BIBLIOGRAPHY

See page 859.

Psalms 90–150

Gianfranco Ravasi

FOURTH BOOK OF THE PSALTER: PSALMS 90–106

FIRST READING

The fourth book of the Psalter does not contain many psalms but its poetic and theological quality is notable. The collection, which is characterized by the use of the name YHWH, contains five psalms on the divine kingship (93; 96–99), which make it the richest collection of texts in this literary genre (see Psalm 47). Erich Zenger regards these as the key to the entire book. There is also a pair of "Hallel" psalms (105–106) that are part of a collection whose other members will appear in the following book. There are texts of high literary quality such as Psalm 90, a moving song of human frailty; Psalm 103, a fervent celebration of the love of God; Psalm 104, a splendid canticle of creatures, and the diptych of contrasting pictures in the historical Psalms 105 and 106.

The hypothesis has been offered (by Michael Goulder) that this book was organized in the post-exilic period as a liturgical text for the autumn feast of Booths, with each psalm referring directly or indirectly to events of Israel's Exodus experience. In fact, however, the most that can be said is that the Hebrew title of Psalm 92, the LXX titles of Psalms 93–94, and the content of Psalm 95 show some relationship with the liturgy of Israel, while the psalms concerning YHWH as royal sovereign were used in the synagogue liturgy and perhaps reflected aspects of its ritual. With regard to the titles, the reliability of many of which is still debated, a good ten psalms are "orphans," that is, they lack any attribution; two are attributed to David (101 and 103); Psalm 90 is attributed to Moses and Psalm 102 to an anonymous afflicted person "when faint and pleading before the LORD."

In my opinion the heterogeneity of the contents and even of the literary genres obscures any clear plan of organization for the present collection of psalms. On the other hand, two pointers of a general kind do permit a more organic and continuous reading. First and foremost, the series of psalms about YHWH as king, with their distinctive acclamation, *YHWH mālāk,* stands out in a special way. Even though the first example of such psalms is Psalm 47 there is no doubt, as I note above, that the majority of these psalms are found in the fourth book of the Psalter (Psalms 93; 96–99).

Discussion of their origin has yielded different hypotheses: they are texts with a mythological origin intended for a New Year's feast modeled on a similar Babylonian solemnity and dealing with the cyclical return to the *Urzeit* or primordial time (Hugo Gressmann); they are texts of cultic origin that speak, again on New Year's, of the reactivation of creation by the divinity (the "myth and ritual" school and Sigmund Mowinckel); they are eschatological texts, intended to outline the perfect age "in which God will mount the throne of the universe to become king of all the earth" (Hermann Gunkel). These are only three of the explanations that have been offered.

In point of fact, what is certain about this group of psalms is that they are meant to extol YHWH's two roles as Lord of creation and Lord of history, which YHWH is determined to lead to salvation according to a plan marked by both justice and grace. It is not accidental that these psalms are surrounded by other compositions dealing either with the history of salvation (examples are Psalms 95; 104–106) or with the cosmos (Psalm 104).

The second guideline for a more systematic reading of the fourth book is perhaps to be sought in the two dominant figures we encounter in it. On the one hand these psalms give a portrait of God as a just and holy ruler (Psalms 96–99; see 94), as transcendent Lord (Psalm 93) yet active in the history of Israel (Psalms 95; 100; 105–106), protector and father of the faithful follower (Psalms 91; 103), and majestic Creator (Psalm 104). On the other hand there is humanity, described in its creaturely weakness and its trials (Psalms 90; 102), in its prosperous fidelity (Psalms 92; 101; 105) and in its sinfulness (Psalms 95; 106). God and human beings are closely linked by a bond of love and justice (Psalm 103).

SECOND READING

Psalm 90

The fourth book begins with a sapiential meditation, but one that also has the element of supplication due to the transience of human existence. The contrast between human time and God's eternity, between human frailty and God's perfection is emphasized in the two movements of the psalm: the sapiential elegy of vv. 1-10 and the supplication in vv. 11-17. The statement in v. 4 sums up the entire first section: "a thousand years in your sight are like yesterday when it is past, or like a watch in the night." At the divine command human beings return to the dust from which they were taken (v. 3; see Gen 2:7; 3:19; Ps 104:29; Qoh 3:20; 12:7).

Human beings are swept away as by a tempest; life is but a dream that shatters at daybreak; human life has the insubstantiality of grass that by evening has already withered (vv. 5-6; see Job 14:1-2; Isa 40:6-8). The entire course of life's seventy or eighty years is "toil and trouble" (v. 10). The theme of Psalm 90 is one dear to the literature of every age (think only of the Greek poet Mimnermus or the philosopher Pascal, or Dante who alludes to this psalm in his *Divine Comedy, Purgatory* XI, 115–117) and to the ascetical tradition, but the psalm also leads one to hope: through divine grace God can give solidity, value, and power to the work of human beings, and joy to their days (vv. 15-17).

Psalm 91

This psalm, which Satan cites during the temptations of Jesus (vv. 11-12 in Matt 4:6 and Luke 4:10-11), is a sapiential exhortation that has trust in God as its theme and is sealed by a concluding oracle uttered by God (vv. 14-16). The context may therefore be cultic, as is suggested by the symbolism the psalmist uses: refuge, fortress, shield, buckler, and, above all, the shadow and wings of the Most High (vv. 1-4), this last being a clear reference to the cherubim on the ark and therefore to the protection provided by the Temple on Zion.

From without, nocturnal terrors rage against the psalmist, as do malignant spirits, the monstrous symbols of evil (lions, vipers, dragons), epidemics, the fiery arrow of the sun or of plagues, and enemies. All this is the classic typology of the evil that is overcome by YHWH, who places God's faithful ones in the refuge of the Temple (see Mark 16:18; Luke 10:19). To repeat Bernard of Clairvaux's question: "Of all the psalms is there any more suited to encouraging the fearful, admonishing the negligent, and instructing those who are far from the perfection of faith?" (*Sermon* 12, 3).

Psalm 92

As the title indicates ("A Song for the Sabbath Day"), Jewish custom reserved this psalm for the Sabbath. It is a hymn to the divine justice that rewards good and punishes evil according to the traditional norms set down in the thesis on retribution that Job will reject. After mention of the joy that comes from praising God (vv. 1-4) the hymn goes on to celebrate the justice of the Lord who is "on high forever" (vv. 5-12) and ends with a celebration of the righteous in some sapiential images drawn from the plant world: the palm and the cedar when these are rooted in the earth of the Temple, this last being a symbol of union with the God who insures a long life like that of the patriarchs (vv. 13-16).

Greek Christian tradition took advantage of the double meaning of the Greek word *phoinix,* which is both "palm" and "phoenix" (the bird of immortality), in order to turn the psalm into a song about the immortality of the just. But the Mishna had already said that "on the Sabbath day is sung the *song for the Sabbath day* [that is, Psalm 92], a canticle for the time to come, for the day that will be totally Sabbath and rest in everlasting life" *(m. Tamid).* In fact, the psalm as it stands is an assertion of the blessing on the righteous and the curse on the wicked, who "sprout like grass" that has no substance (v. 7), unlike the solidity of the palm and the cedar, which symbolize the faithful.

Psalm 93

After Psalm 47, and prior to the series Psalms 96–99, this psalm is a hymn to YHWH the sovereign, as can be seen from the opening exclamation, *YHWH mālāk,* "the Lord is king!" This formula is typical of these compositions, which many scholars connect with the pre-exilic Jerusalem liturgy (a ritual procession of the ark in the Temple?). But Psalms 96–98 show clearly that they are of post-exilic origin. The conception of the divine "reign" is dynamic: it expresses the action of the Lord who is determined to carry out the divine plan within creation and history.

The central point of this short psalm is conveyed through the image of the "mighty waters" *(mayim rabbīm)* or the "floods" or the rebellious waves of the sea. In biblical cosmology the earth is seen as a platform set upon the primordial ocean, which symbolizes the chaos and nothingness that threaten creation. In vain do the "mighty waters" of the ocean issue their challenge to God: the heavenly king is mightier than their thunder and revolt (vv. 3-4). From the transcendent divine throne on high God overcomes all dark and disintegrative forces and keeps the world firmly established (vv. 1-2, 5).

Psalm 94

Communal lament and prophetic protest with elements of judgment, thanksgiving, and sapiential reflection are fused in this psalm that calls for judgment from the "God of vengeance . . . judge of the earth" (vv. 1-2) in face of the scandalous success of the wicked, the perversion and corruption of earthly tribunals, and the humiliation of the poor. The song is divided into two appeals arranged as an *inclusio* (vv. 1-2 and 22-23), two lamentations (vv. 3-7 and 16-21) that protest against the wicked who oppress the weak and blaspheme God, and two sapiential lessons that are respectively an invective against the unjust (vv. 8-11) and a beatitude for the just (vv. 12-15).

The psalm is dear to Paul, who cites it both directly and by allusion (1 Cor 3:20 for v. 11, and Rom 11:1-2 for v. 14; see 2 Thess 4:6 for v. 2, and 2 Cor 1:5 for v. 19). Its dominant note is hope in God "the avenger," that is, the defender of justice for the victims of power and deceit: "the LORD is a God of recompense, he will repay in full" (Jer 51:56). Consequently, while being an utterance of trust Psalm 94 is also an "apology" for the apparent silence of God, which the wicked regard as proof of God's indifference and powerlessness within history.

Psalm 95

In the "today" of the liturgy (v. 7) there is set before Israel the great choice it must make between fidelity and infidelity as it recalls the sad events at Massah and Meribah in the wilderness (Exod 17:1-7; Num 20:2-13). The psalm therefore supposes a liturgical context and begins with two short hymnic texts (vv. 1-5 and 6-7c), each based on a profession of faith ("the LORD is a great God," v. 3; "he is our God," v. 7a) and on celebration of the activity of God in the cosmos (vv. 4-5) and in history (v. 7bc).

These mini-hymns are followed by a cultic oracle (vv. 7c-11) that calls upon the worshipers not to have a "hardened" (v. 8) and "straying" heart (v. 10) like the generation in the wilderness. Because of this call and because of the liturgical setting Psalm 95 has become one of the prayers of Judaism for the "entrance" into the Sabbath, and is also used as an "invitatory" preceding the Catholic Liturgy of the Hours. On the other hand the letter to the Hebrews (chs. 3–4) gives an eschatological interpretation of this song: the entrance is no longer into the promised land and its "rest" but into the "eternal rest" of the heavenly country and temple, from which we must not exclude ourselves through infidelity.

Psalm 96

This psalm begins the short collection of psalms about YHWH the King (but see also Psalms 47 and 93). The typical acclamation: "The LORD is king!" appears in v. 10 and dominates this anthology-psalm, made up of references to other psalms and to Second and Third Isaiah (Isaiah 40–66) that show it to be surely a late composition (fourth century B.C.E.?). This "new song" ("new" in the biblical sense of "perfect" and eschatological) consists of two main acts: the first (vv. 1-9) is a profession of faith in the first commandment, which prohibits idolatry (vv. 4-6); the second (vv. 10-13) extols the divine sovereignty.

This sovereignty is expressed in the Hebrew verb *špt,* which means "to govern and judge": YHWH "is coming to judge/govern the earth. He will judge/govern the world with righteousness, and the peoples with his truth" (v. 13). At this entrance of the divine sovereign into history the world bursts into a cosmic chorus and dance that involve its three vertical (heavens, earth, sea-Sheol) and two horizontal elements, that is, the two regions described in their relation to human beings: the cultivated countryside and the wild forests. The psalm is a hymn of jubilation arising from all that is to the Creator, Ruler, and supreme Judge. Psalm 96 is cited, with some slight variations, in 1 Chr 16:23-33.

Psalm 97

The opening acclamation *YHWH mālāk,* "the Lord reigns!" immediately reveals the genre of the psalm, which is comparable to the preceding and two following psalms. The references to other psalms and to Second Isaiah, as well as the universalist perspective (the "coastlands" of v. 1 signify the far ends of the earth), place the composition in the late post-exilic period. The song is linear in its structure.

The text begins with a theophany (vv. 1-6) in which the great king appears with his "attendants," both cosmic (clouds, darkness, fire, lightning) and historical (judgment, righteousness, glory). This epiphany elicits two reactions: that of idolaters and their idols (vv. 7-9), who fall to the ground in frightened adoration, and the joyous and luminous response of the faithful (vv. 10-12).

Psalm 98

A perfect example of the psalms about YHWH the sovereign ruler, this "new song"—which like the preceding two psalms is a post-exilic anthology—emphasizes the connection between the present action of God in history (vv. 1-3) and God's definitive and perfect, that is, eschatological, action (v. 9), which as before is expressed in the verb *špt,* "judge/govern." To this certain connection the believing community responds with its most impassioned praise (vv. 4-8), in which the entire cosmos is called to participate.

Considerable use is made of the symbolism of the number seven, which signifies perfection. The name of God is mentioned seven times (YHWH six times and *ʾelohēnū,* "our God" once, in v. 3); there are seven divine actions (has made, has gotten victory, has made known, has revealed, has remembered, is coming, and judges/governs); seven divine attributes (victory, vindication, steadfast love, faithfulness, justice, righteousness, wonders); seven verbs of praise (sing, make a joyful noise, break into joyful song, sing praises, roar, clap hands, sing together). The harmony among all that exists under the divine government is thus expressed even at the lexical level.

Psalm 99

Psalm 99, which opens with the acclamation typical of the literary genre, *YHWH mālāk,* "the Lord is king!" is the last in the series of songs dedicated to the divine sovereignty; the series began with Psalm 47, included Psalm 93, and continued with Psalms 96–98. Unlike the preceding three this psalm is not anthological and may be pre-exilic (there are no citations from or allusions to Second Isaiah). The song is divided into sections by three solemn assertions of the holiness, that is, the transcendence of God: *qādōsh hūʾ,* "holy is he," in vv. 3, 5, and 9.

In vv. 1-4 the Lord is described as reigning in Zion, in Jacob, and over all the peoples, and having seven attributes (great, exalted, great, awesome, holy, mighty, and just). In vv. 5-9 the covenant dialogue between the Lord and Israel is described as mediated by Moses the lawgiver, Aaron the priest, and Samuel the prophet. At the center, however, is the solemn figure of the Holy One, the King, who appears above "his footstool" (v. 5), that is, the cover of the ark, the *kapporet,* the seat of God's presence in the Temple.

Psalm 100

Psalm 100, which is entitled "A psalm for the *tōdāh,*" that is, the thanksgiving to the Lord, is a short hymn of praise (make a joyful noise, worship, come, know, praise, bless). Augustine commented: "Let praise become your food. By praising you will acquire new strength, and the one you praise will become sweeter to you" (MPL 37:1281). At the center of the hymn is a profession of faith in the Lord: YHWH is God, our creator, who established the covenant with Israel ("we are his people"), YHWH's love is everlasting, the divine faithfulness for all generations (vv. 3, 5).

Psalm 101

This psalm has traditionally been called "the mirror of princes" and in the past was dear to "Christian" kings. Athanasius described it as an examination of conscience for the faithful. In a first section it lays out the gifts connected with personal moral life or "the way that is blameless" (vv. 1-4): an upright political figure must be far removed from any idolatry and wickedness. Next come the social virtues (vv. 5-8): rejection of slander, delation, false testimony, arrogance; the defense of the faithful; a careful choice of courtiers, advisers, and ministers.

At the end (v. 8) the speaker promises a radical extirpation of evildoers, but does so in imprecatory language that causes some perplexity to Christian readers, so much so that Augustine applied the verse to God's final judgment. In fact the strong language is meant simply to underscore the just king's firm and radical commitment to getting rid of the evil and injustice that constantly lurk in society.

Psalm 102

This psalm is one of the series known to Christian tradition as the "penitential psalms" (together with Psalms 6; 32; 38; 51; 130; 143); because of its intriguing title ("A prayer of one afflicted, when faint and pleading before the LORD") Augustine interpreted it as a prayer of the suffering Christ during his passion. The psalm is a lamentation that moves from personal to national supplication and back again. The personal plea (in vv. 1-11 and 23-28) uses strong images to describe the bodily decline and loneliness of the person praying: the cries of the owl and little owl, waste places, darkness, the song of the lonely sparrow, a table laid with bitter food, the ashes of mourning, tears as drink.

The psalm then moves from the praying person's body in decay to a city in ruins: Jerusalem (vv. 12-22) that, despite everything, elicits a declaration of love: "your servants hold its stones dear, and have pity on its dust" (v. 14). Against the backdrop of destroyed Zion (the psalm is post-exilic) the psalmist sings a song of hope and national resurrection, entrusting it to a written oracle (vv. 18-22) for all to see.

Psalm 103

Regarded as one of the gems of the Psalter and, by Christian readers, as an ideal prelude to the "God is love" of 1 John 4:8, this hymn is a blessing of praise and gratitude but also contains sapiential elements. It has two movements. In the first (vv. 1-9) the love and forgiveness of God are extolled in a series of hymnic participles (God is the one who forgives, heals, redeems, crowns, satisfies), various nouns (vindication, justice, making known, acts, mercy, graciousness, steadfast love), and statements about the divine, forgiving mercy.

In the second movement (vv. 10-18) God's everlasting love is set side by side with human frailty. The vertical and horizontal dimensions of space and the psychological dimension of the depth of the Father's love are likened to divine "compassion": the word used here is *rḥm* and suggests the maternal womb, even while the comparison is to a father. Thus masculine and feminine elements are combined in the representation of God. Human weakness, on the other hand, is described in the classic image of dust shaped by a potter (Gen 2:7; Jer 18:1-12) and in the image of flower and grass, which we have already seen in Ps 90:5-6. The poet exhorts us to rely on God in faith, move out of our transience, and share in the everlasting permanence.

Psalm 104

This majestic "canticle of creatures" is undoubtedly one of the masterpieces of the Psalter; French writer François Auguste René de Chateaubriand thought it superior to some lyrics of

Horace and Pindar. Two questions are much debated by exegetes. The first has to do with the connection between Psalm 104 and the texts on creation in Genesis 1–2, the other biblical hymns to the Creator, and, above all, the Egyptian hymn to Aton. We know, in fact, that Pharaoh Amenophis IV Akhnaton in the fourteenth century B.C.E. effected a "monotheistic" religious reform that was focused on Aton, the solar disk and a divinity celebrated in a magnificent hymn. It is difficult to disentangle this web of connections: in relation to the hymn to Aton, which seems to show through here and there in the psalm, we may think of Canaanite mediations or indirect influences since the poet of the psalm is firm in the belief that the sun is only a splendid creature and not a divine being.

The second question has to do with the literary structure of the hymn, which is variously defined. In my view we may identify a set of seven concentric strophes; here I shall simply outline their themes and leave it to the reader to taste directly the vivid picture given in each description. The first strophe (vv. 1-4) presents a heavenly theophany of the Creator; in the second (vv. 5-9) creation is described as a divine victory over the waters of chaos, while the third strophe (vv. 10-18) is inspired by the life of the earth with its springs, trees, fruits, and animals. In the fourth strophe (vv. 19-24) the rhythm of time and daily life is established by the sun and the moon; the fifth (vv. 25-26) describes the sea with its population of ships and living beings. The sixth strophe (vv. 27-30) is more theological, telling how all creatures are dependent on the Creator for their life; the final strophe (vv. 31-35) again describes a cosmic theophany as creatures sing their song to the Creator and evil is banished.

Psalms 105 and 106

These two historical psalms are to be read as a contrasting pair: the first is full of light and divine grace while the second is dark and marked by sin. In Psalm 105 the liturgical acclamation *hallelujāh,* "praise the Lord," appears for the first time in the Psalter. It is part of a meditation, in hymnic form, on the history of salvation (see Psalm 78): the covenant with the patriarchs (vv. 8-15); the story of Joseph (vv. 16-22); the "plagues" of Egypt, which number eight scourges (vv. 23-26) as compared with the ten in the Exodus story and the seven of Ps 78:44-51; the Exodus from Egypt (vv. 37-43); finally, the arrival in the promised land (vv. 44-45). The perspective adopted is that of the divine salvific actions, "the wonderful works, the miracles, the judgments" of the Lord (v. 5). Note, too, that vv. 1-15 of this psalm are cited in 1 Chr 8:22, while Ps 106:11, 47-48 appears in 1 Chr 16:34-36.

In Psalm 106 the same history is reread from the viewpoint of the infidelity of the people. It begins with a rebellion while the people are still at the Sea of Reeds (vv. 6-12; see Exod 14:10-12); it moves on to the wilderness, the complaint about hunger, and the consequent divine gift of the manna and quail (vv. 13-15), the rebellion of Dathan and Abiram (vv. 16-18; cf. Numbers 16), and the worship of the golden calf at Horeb (vv. 19-23). Next is described the "grumbling" of Israel, which sums up all the infidelities of the time in the wilderness (vv. 24-27), but special mention is made of the idolatry at the sanctuary of the Baal of Peor (vv. 28-31; see Numbers 25). The lack of faith at the waters of Meribah (vv. 32-33) and the idolatry in the promised land (vv. 34-36) crown this history of human sins and divine punishments, which then turns into a call for conversion in order to win forgiveness.

Verse 48 contains a blessing, which editors added as a doxology marking the end of the fourth book of the Psalter whose seventeen psalms we have been reading. The fifth and final book of the Psalter now lies before us.

FIFTH BOOK OF THE PSALTER: PSALMS 107–150

FIRST READING

The fifth is the most extensive of the five books into which the Psalter has traditionally been divided. Some groups within the book are easily identified because they bear specific titles. We may think of the set of fifteen "Songs of Ascents" (Psalms 120–134), the so-called "Passover or Egyptian Hallel" (Psalms 113–118), or the "final Hallel" (Psalms 146–150). These sets are evidently liturgical in kind and show the use made of the Psalter in post-exilic and synagogal worship. The first composition, the "thanksgiving" of Psalm 107, also seems to be liturgical.

Given the large number of texts gathered in this last book (at least forty-four psalms according to the arrangement in the MT; the same number in the LXX, but with different divisions: Psalms 114 and 115 of the MT become Psalm 113 in the LXX, while Psalm 116 of the MT is divided into Psalms 114 and 115 of the LXX, and the single Psalm 147 of the MT is divided into Psalms 146 and 147 in the LXX) it is not easy to suggest a scheme for a continuous reading. At the redactional level some major collections immediately stand out; these are the two mentioned above, the "Songs of Ascents" (fifteen psalms) and the "Hallelujah" psalms (in the MT, Psalms 111; 112; 113; 117; 135; 146; 147; 148; 149; 150 have the explicit title *hallelujāh*).

Within these two sets, however, a variety of themes can be distinguished that are not always consonant with the basic tonality of the "ascent" to Jerusalem (I shall speak further on of the significance of this term) or of the praise proper to the "Hallelujah" psalms. We might also add a series of "Davidic" psalms, relying on the title given to these (Psalms 108; 109; 110; 122; 123; 124; 131; 133; 138; 139; 140; 141; 142; 143; 144; 145), a title often accompanied by other instructions that are also found elsewhere in the Psalter, such as *mīzmōr,* "psalm," *lamenaṣeaḥ,* "to the director of the choir," *maskīl,* etcetera. But in this series, too, it is difficult to identify a clear guiding thread.

We can, therefore, proceed only by following themes or noting clearly marked units. The two collections mentioned: the "Songs of Ascents" and the "Hallelujah" psalms, as well as traces in other compositions (for example, 107; 110; 135; 136), place us explicitly in a liturgical setting. Israel's worship provides the horizon within which the people of the covenant not only find their spiritual roots but also bring together their history and their daily lives. It therefore becomes possible to identify, in this setting of praise and liturgy, a series of events and constant factors in both human existence and divine salvation, even amid the diversity of the historical and literary coordinates proper to the various psalms.

First and foremost, God is shown to be present in the history of salvation, in fundamental events recalled by various psalms (114; 117; 126; 135; 136), in the Davidic dynasty and in the reinterpretation along messianic lines of the psalms that exalt the dynasty (110; 132), in the sacred space of the Jerusalem Temple (122; 134) and its worship (100; 118; 150), but also in the spaces of the cosmos (148; 150). The face of God that is reflected in this section of the Psalter is the one shown to us on so many other pages of the Bible: God is Creator, Savior, Deliverer, provident and everywhere present (111; 113; 116; 121; 124; 125; 127; 138; 139; 144; 145; 146; 147), and radically different from lifeless and ineffective idols (115).

In contrast, another face appears: that of human beings with all their sufferings and their personal and collective perils (Psalms 107; 108; 116; 123; 129; 137; 138), with their longing for justice in the midst of a world marked by harsh injustice (109; 120; 137:7-8; 139:19-24; 140; 141; 142; 149), with their sinfulness and need of forgiveness (130; 143), but also with their uprightness and love (112; 133), their fidelity to the word of God (119), their joy and family prosperity (127; 128), and, above all, the praise they offer in the hymns and trustful prayers, filled with a pure and unqualified faith (131), that predominate in this last book of the Psalter.

SECOND READING

Psalm 107

This spacious hymn of thanksgiving, which begins with an invitation to praise of a liturgical kind (vv. 1-3), develops by describing four situations that call for votive offerings. The first (vv. 4-9) describes the scattering and rescue of a caravan in the desert. The second (vv. 10-16) depicts prisoners set free by the Lord, while the third picture (vv. 17-22) shows sick persons who have been freed of their suffering and sin. The final scene is the most picturesque and represents the experience of some sailors who have been rescued from a terrifying storm (vv. 23-32). Oswald Loretz has even imagined that this scene at sea was modeled on an old song of thanksgiving to Baal by Phoenician mariners.

Each of the four scenes follows a fixed pattern and involves the entire assembly in thankful praise. At the end a choral hymn (vv. 33-43) recalls the Exodus and seems to apply the preceding song to all of Israel, since it draws from it a lesson concerning a life of fidelity to the Lord (v. 43). Gregory of Nyssa in ch. 8 of his first treatise on the Psalms interpreted this hymn as a spiritual biography of the believer who is set free from all the miseries of life.

Psalm 108

From the viewpoint of content this psalm arises from the juxtaposition of two parts of other psalms (57:7-11; 60:5-12), to which I refer the reader. It is difficult to determine the value of this collage; it does, however, show how Israel reinterpreted its literary and religious heritage and reused it in new and different contexts. Perhaps the intention was to apply an ancient promise to a new and dangerous situation. The hymnic praise of the first fragment would terminate in a divine oracle in which YHWH declares lordship over the entire promised land that was perhaps being invaded at the time, and then opens Israel's field of vision to light and hope (the second fragment). Oddly enough, in the sixteenth century Cardinal Robert Bellarmine thought that Psalm 108 was composed solely in order to make the psalms number one hundred fifty!

Psalm 109

Along with Psalm 58, this is the "imprecatory" psalm *par excellence* and was excluded from use in Catholic worship by Vatican II precisely because the curse at the center of the composition (vv. 7-19) is so violent. The curse is uttered by an innocent believer who has been slandered and who perhaps thinks of his or her action as a denunciation at the supreme tribunal of God. The hyperboles used in the twenty curses of the psalm reflect Near Eastern and Eastern styles, while they also give voice to the passionate response of the one praying to the violation of justice, the restoration of which is entrusted to God, the just judge.

The psalm bears witness to the way in which the word of God is "enfleshed" in the particularity of a culture and an age and human feelings. It can be understood and repeated as a prayer for justice, a prayer marked by contempt for corruption and the illegitimate use of power (see Matthew 25). Justice is restored, however, only by the intervention of God, who condemns and punishes human injustice.

Psalm 110

This royal hymn contains only sixty-three Hebrew words (including particles) but it has given rise to an immense bibliography and has elicited profound veneration, especially in Christianity, where it has been reread as messianic and christological. The NT repeatedly cites vv. 1 and 4 (of the LXX version): v. 1 in Mark 12:36 par.; Acts 2:34-35; 1 Cor 15:22-23; Eph 1:20-23; Heb 1:13; 10:12-13 (to give only the more important references); v. 4 plays a very important role in the letter to the Hebrews, especially in ch. 7. The use of the psalm in the liturgy of Evening Prayer, especially on Sundays and feastdays, has led to its being accompanied by a very great number of musical settings (by Monteverdi, Händel, Vivaldi, Mozart, and others). There is disagreement on the dating of the psalm, which may, however, have referred initially to the current Davidic monarchy and have been reinterpreted after the exile as a messianic song. (The solution also depends on the connection with the Melchizedek tradition of Genesis 14.)

In the first part of the psalm (vv. 1-3) YHWH addresses an oracle to the psalmist's "lord," that is, the king, proclaiming the latter's enthronement at "my right hand" (reference to a rite of royal investiture as king near the ark? or to the locating of the royal palace near the Temple? or a symbolic statement of the Hebrew king's role as God's representative?). In the Hebrew text v. 3 is obscure and seems to refer to a military parade in the king's honor, with the participation of "the dew of your youth," that is, the flower of the people and the army. But the LXX and the Vg gave a free reading of the verse along the lines of Ps 2:7 and made it assert the divine sonship of the Davidic sovereign: "With you is supremacy on the day of your strength, among the splendors of your saints; from the womb, before the morning star, I begot you."

The second part (vv. 4-7) contains another divine oracle that ensures the Davidic sovereign a dignity that is also priestly; it refers to the ancient priest-king of Salem (Jerusalem), Melchizedek (Genesis 14), whom Abraham met. The psalm is perhaps seeking a way of conferring on the king a priestly rank that is different from the Levitic and Aaronic or Zadokite priesthood. After this further investiture the king makes a victorious triumphal march, drawing strength as he goes from a stream (v. 7); this last is perhaps a reference to the sacred spring of Gihon in Jerusalem (1 Kings 1:32-40), or is symbolic of the divine blessing. Still fundamental, however, is the messianic interpretation (known at Qumran) and the christological interpretation that was to prevail in the history of the Christian tradition, especially along the line of the priesthood of Christ as celebrated in the letter to the Hebrews (which relies also on Ps 2:7).

Psalms 111–112

Both psalms are acrostic/alphabetical (like Psalms 25; 34; 37; 119) and Hallelujah psalms; they have been regarded as "twins" (Walther Zimmerli). In the first the principal figure is the Lord and his "works" in the history of salvation; we find here the entire vocabulary of the covenant (justice, truth, right, uprightness, redemption, mercy, tender love, remembrance, wonderful deeds, covenant). As Jerome would later say in commenting on v. 9, God is revealed as "holy to the holy, terrible to sinners," kindly toward the righteous, implacable toward the rebellious.

In the second psalm, on the other hand, the principal figures are the righteous and the wicked, but they are obviously given unequal space: nine verses for the faithful, one for the wicked. The most extolled moral quality is "social": generosity toward the poor (vv. 5 and 9). In its Latin version *(Beatus vir)* Psalm 112 found a place in the Catholic liturgy of Evening Prayer and, like Psalm 110, became the subject of countless musical scores.

Psalm 113

Psalms 113–118 are a collection of Hallelujah psalms and are usually known as the "Egyptian or Passover Hallel," both because of the Exodus theme (Psalm 114) and because of their use in the Jewish Passover liturgy (but also on other solemnities and celebrations). The first of these psalms has been called the "Magnificat" of the Psalter because of the use of vv. 7-8 in the canticle of Mary; it has become part of the Catholic psalmody for Evening Prayer. In three strophes of great thematic clarity it celebrates the transcendence of the God of Israel (vv. 1-3 and 4-6), but also God's active presence in history, where God supports the poor and the wretched (vv. 7-8).

Psalm 114

This psalm is dear to the Jewish tradition, but also to the Christian (Dante in his *Divine Comedy* makes it the song of those in purgatory: *Purgatorio* II, 46–48); it has been set to music a number of times (by Mendelssohn, Bruckner, Kodàly, in spirituals, etcetera). The LXX and Vg erroneously combine it with Psalm 115 (making it Psalm 113). The psalm evokes the Exodus event in a lively way by having nature participate in it. The sea looks and draws back to let Israel pass through; in the presence of the theophany the mountains of the Sinai move like skipping lambs; the Jordan turns back in its course to make a passage for Israel; the earth trembles like a woman giving birth (v. 7). In astonishment, the person praying asks why all this is happening, and God answers by referring to the Exodus gesture when God made water spring from the rock (v. 8) as a sign of divine love for this people in whom God's presence dwells (v. 2). The song is clearly a poetic "Passover" meditation.

Psalm 115

This work of criticism of idolatry (see Isaiah 44; Wisdom 13–15) can be seen as having a liturgical setting in two acts. The first gives the praying assembly an instruction on the true God (vv. 1-3), who is the Creator and Redeemer of Israel, and on idols (vv. 4-8), which possess seven useless organs (mouth, eyes, ears, nose, hands, feet, throat) that are a sign of nothing but death and helplessness. The second liturgical action is a summons and a blessing that have for their object "the house of Israel," that is, the people, "the house of Aaron," that is, the priests, and "those who fear the LORD," that is, proselytes (if this phrase is understood in the special meaning it has in post-exilic usage) or, in a broader sense, the more authentic believers of Israel (vv. 9-18). With the divine blessing is associated the blessing (that is, praise) of the faithful who have professed their faith in the true "God of Abraham, Isaac, and Jacob, the God not of the dead but of the living" (Matt 22:32).

Psalm 116

A hymn of thanksgiving (vv. 2, 7, 8, 12), into which are woven a plea (vv. 1, 2, 4, 10-11) and protests of trust (vv. 5, 10). The psalm proceeds in two movements. The first (vv. 1-13) tells, in several stages, the story of serious suffering endured, of a real deadly snare. But God stepped in, and in a soliloquy (vv. 7-13) the one praying describes his or her deliverance in deeply felt sentiments and images. The second movement (vv. 14-19) describes a liturgical thanksgiving *(tōdāh),* during which the one praying makes three statements: God is not indifferent to the death of God's faithful ones (this is the meaning of v. 15 as read in the perspective of immortality); the just are members of the household of God ("your servant, the child of your serving girl," v. 16ab); the Lord breaks the chains of death (v. 16c).

This, then, is a song of profound trust in the power of God over physical death and evil. Because of v. 13 ("I will lift up the cup of salvation . . .") the song became part of the Jewish Passover liturgy in connection with the rite of the third cup of wine. Paul cites v. 10 (according to the LXX) in 2 Cor 4:13: "just as we have the same spirit of faith that is in accordance with scripture—'I believed, and so I spoke'—we also believe, and so we speak." The apostle also cites v. 11—"Everyone is a liar"—in Rom 3:4.

Psalm 117

This, the shortest of the psalms, is like a short invocation. It was set to splendid music by Mozart in his *Solemn Vespers for a Confessor* (K 339) and has been used repeatedly in the Catholic liturgy. It is a short hymn that celebrates the covenant between YHWH and Israel by recalling the two divine virtues that mark it: *ḥesed,* steadfast love, and *ʾemet,* enduring faithfulness.

Psalm 118

The "Passover Hallel" (Psalms 113–118) of the Jewish liturgy ends with this difficult but impressive psalm. In the view of many, however, the song was originally connected with the feast of Booths. Let me attempt an interpretation of a liturgical kind that will allow us to follow its very complex course, one that has been variously reconstructed and explained. A solemn call to praise (vv. 1-4) introduces the three categories of participants in worship whom we met earlier in Psalm 115: Israel, "the house of Aaron," that is, the priests, and "those who fear the LORD," that is, perhaps proselytes or the more faithful Jews. Then begins a first hymn of thanksgiving (vv. 5-18), sung "in the tents of the righteous," that is, in the city of Jerusalem, where the procession winds along with the soloist (vv. 5-7, 10-13, 14, 17-18) and the chorus (vv. 8-9, 15-16) alternating. The theme is clear: in distress we must have a lively trust in the God who leads us to complete and triumphant victory.

When the procession reaches "the gates of righteousness," that is, the Temple, a second hymn of thanksgiving begins (vv. 19-29) that includes several ritual elements. There is the dialogue between priests and faithful as the latter ask admission to the Temple (vv. 19-20; see Psalms 15 and 24); there is the acclamation addressed to the unyielding "stone" of the Temple, which symbolizes YHWH, the rock of safety (vv. 21-25); there is the priestly blessing (vv. 26-27); there is the sacred dance and the procession around the altar with leafy branches (this suggests the Jewish ritual for the feast of Booths); there is the final hymn for soloist and chorus (vv. 28-29). We may recall that vv. 22-23, concerning the stone of the Temple, were taken over into the gospels beginning with the parable of the murderous vineyard workers (Matt 21:42) and applied to Christ (see also Acts 4:11 and 1 Pet 2:7), while vv. 25-26 were applied to the triumphal entrance of Christ into Jerusalem (Matt 21:9); also that the acclamation *hoshīʿa naʾ* ("Oh, save us!"), became the "hosannna" of the Christian tradition.

Psalm 119

This enormous sapiential psalm consisting of 1064 Hebrew words is the longest in the Psalter, yet it was a psalm that Blaise Pascal recited daily. It is structured according to a complex acrostic, or alphabetical, and lexical system. The successive letters of the Hebrew alphabet begin the first word in each of the eight verses of the twenty-two eight-line strophes that make up the psalm; for example, the first stanza begins with *ʾaleph,* the first Hebrew letter, and so does the first word of each of the eight verses of the stanza. Furthermore, almost every verse contains one of the eight terms with which the Law/word of God is described and praised: Law *(tōrāh),* word *(dābār),* testimony *(ʿēdūt),* judgment *(mīšpāt),* saying *(ʾīmrāh),* decree *(ḥoq),* precepts *(pīqqūdīm),* and commandment *(mīṣwāh).*

The Torah of which the psalm sings is not only the biblical law but also the word of God: this word "is a lamp to [the] feet and light to [the] path" of life (v. 105); it is food sweeter than honey (v. 103), a treasure more priceless than gold (v. 127), a wellspring of joy and light (vv. 47, 130, 135). The song is a true and proper alphabet of surrender to God, a mirror for the faithful, a ceaseless movement of praise. It resembles a Near Eastern melody in which the resonant phrases wind along in a spiral so that though the verses move in parallel circles they also open ever new vistas. Repetition leads to assimilation and deeper understanding. Dietrich Bonhoeffer rightly remarked that "Ps 119 is doubtless burdensome by reason of its length and monotony, but we should really move from word to word, phrase to phrase, very slowly, calmly, patiently. We will then find that what seem to be repetitions are in fact new aspects of one and the same reality: love for God's word."

The Songs of Ascents: Psalms 120–134

Psalms 120–134 are usually called "Songs of Ascents." What does the word *ma'alōt,* "ascents," mean? Some regard it as a purely literary quality: by repeating some words these fifteen psalms create a crescendo that moves to a thematic climax. According to others (the LXX and Jerome) they are psalms that were to be sung on the fifteen steps leading into the Temple (whence the term "gradual songs"). For still others they were the songs sung by the repatriates from Babylon as they returned to Zion, while others think of the symbolic value of prayers that "rise up" to heaven from the community. Finally, it is likely that the name was given to a set of psalms used for the "pilgrimage" to Zion at the three feasts of Passover, Pentecost, and Booths; the term "ascents" was used because people were literally climbing up toward Jerusalem (the holy city was eight hundred meters above sea level), while at the same time they were rising spiritually toward God.

Psalm 120

The first of the "Songs of Ascents" is this trust-filled lament that begins with *'ēl YHWH,* "to the LORD." In a first strophe (vv. 1-4) the psalmist protests against the lying tongue that hurls arrows and burning coals, that is, false words that are dangerous, especially in an oral culture such as the Semitic. The second strophe (vv. 5-7) describes the state of war in which the person praying feels involved, as if he were in the midst of barbarians (Meshech, a tribe near the Caspian Sea, and Kedar, an Arabian tribe). At the end, in the phrase *'anī-šālōm,* "I (am) peace," there is an allusion to "Jerusalem," which was popularly interpreted as meaning "city of peace."

Psalm 121

This delightful song of the divine "sentinel" (the verb *šmr,* "keep," is heard six times) is a pilgrimage hymn in honor of the "guardian of Israel." God is a shadow that protects against the desert sun, the defender who stands at the right hand of the protegé, the defense at night against the glow of the moon, which was thought to blind or make mad. The "hills" of v. 1 are either a symbol of Zion, "from where help will come," or of the "hills" on which were erected the idolatrous sanctuaries from which no help can come.

Psalm 122

In the first strophe (vv. 1-2) the author of this fervent song of Zion brings together the present moment in which he is crossing the threshold of the holy city, and the day, now distant, when he told his village of his decision to "go to the house of the LORD." In the second strophe (vv. 3-5) he launches into his praise of Zion, "built as a city that is bound firmly together," a center of unity for the twelve tribes, the only place of legitimate worship (Deut 12:13-14; 16:16), seat of the Davidic dynasty and of "the thrones for judgment," that is, the highest court of justice.

The song closes in the third strophe (vv. 6-9) with a wish based on the Hebrew greeting *šalōm,* "peace," in conjunction with the popular etymology of the name "Jerusalem," that is, "city of peace" (Ps 120:7). The fervent wish of "peace and prosperity" in vv. 7-9 gave rise to the same Franciscan greeting. In Jerome and especially in Augustine the psalm becomes a hymn to the heavenly Jerusalem: "The stones of this city have been cut in the hills by the hands of preachers of the truth; they have been squared in order to be placed in the body of an everlasting dwelling" (MPL 37:1619).

Psalm 123

A prayer of personal (vv. 1-2a) and communal (vv. 2b-4) petition, marked by great simplicity and tenderness, this psalm plays throughout on the word "eyes." In fact the controlling symbol in this short text is one characteristic of the world of Eastern courts: that of the eyes of servants who attentively watch the hands of their masters in order to catch even the slightest sign of their will and favor. This image is applied to the hope of the poor person whose "eyes are ever toward the LORD, for he will pluck my feet out of the net" (Ps 25:15; see 69:4).

The expectation is intense because the life of the person praying is sated with scorn and humiliation from the "proud." In Hebrew this last term *(ligʾēōnīm)* can also be divided into two *(ligʾē yōnīm),* meaning "proud Greeks," and thus be an allusion to oppression by the Syro-Hellenistic Seleucids (2nd c. B.C.E.). It is thus possible that the psalm was subsequently turned into a nationalistic ritual.

Psalm 124

A communal thanksgiving with a liturgical background (suggested by the interpolation, "let Israel now say"), the psalm speaks of a nightmare that has tormented Israel and from which the Lord has delivered it. The images of monsters that swallow up, of waters that overwhelm, of the snare that like a running knot squeezes the neck of the victim belong to the repertory of images used in petitions and hymns of thanksgiving to signify the danger that has been avoided. It is therefore difficult to determine the historical coordinates of the danger and deliverance that Israel has experienced and to which the psalm refers.

Psalm 125

Given faith in the permanence of Israel, which in turn is due to the unshakable solidity of the Temple (vv. 1-2), it is possible to face even the risks that a serious danger, external and internal, brings to the Jewish people. Verse 3 refers to the "scepter of wickedness" (Antiochus IV Epiphanes, Syro-Hellenistic oppressor of Israel in the 2nd c. B.C.E.?), but also to the danger that "the righteous [may] stretch out their hands to do wrong" (see also v. 5). The hope—the only hope—however, is the goodness of the Lord who defends "the good and upright of heart" (v. 4) and condemns both "evildoers" and those who turn aside from the path of justice and associate with them.

Psalm 126

Regarded by many as a hymn of those who have returned from the Babylonian exile (recall the pages of Second Isaiah), this psalm wonderfully combines joyous gratitude and a plea for the future whose horizon is not yet empty of fears. Verses 1 and 4 can, however, be understood not only as praise of God who "brings back the prisoners to Zion" but also as praise of the God who "restores the fortunes of Zion." Then the song would be a more general celebration of the rebirth of Jerusalem.

The agricultural image at the end (vv. 5-6) is a powerful one: sowing is the period of expectation; the dry watercourses of the Negeb desert symbolize thirst; the harvest sheaves signify prosperity and joy; the swollen streams make the steppe bloom. The images thus represent the two stages of oppression and deliverance; the patristic tradition saw these as imaging the pedagogy of the Lord, who purifies by chastisement and then offers an even greater gift (thus, for example, Augustine and Bernard of Clairvaux in his sermon on Saint Benedict).

Psalm 127

In Psalm 126 national happiness was said to have its origin in the divine blessing; here it is personal and family happiness that depend on the Lord. The model followed in the development is the classical one of retribution that rewards the just with a numerous and vital posterity. The psalm plays on the assonance, in Hebrew, between *bnh,* "build," and *ben,* "son." The one who has received from God strong sons, born of youthful vigor, can face the future with tranquillity, like a strong warrior armed with sharp arrows. Pursuing the image, the psalm says that with a quiver filled with arrows (sons), the just one will be able to face internal and external enemies at the city gate. The final scene, which is set precisely at the gate, the civic center of ancient Near Eastern cities, thus describes a "sheikh" surrounded by a vigorous and numerous offspring, and feared and respected even by enemies.

Psalm 128

This short poem, which is a sapiential continuation in ideal terms of the theme of the preceding psalm, speaks of familial fruitfulness and tranquillity as a sign of God's blessing. It is for this reason that Psalm 128 has become a classic element in the nuptial liturgy, both Jewish and Christian. In vv. 1-3 there is a beatitude, expressed through the plant symbolism of the vine and the olive tree. The vine represents the wife, a fruitful mother, surrounded by olive branches that are her children who, like the tree, are full of vitality. The little picture is one of prosperity and peace; also present in it is the father who is satisfied with the fruits of his labor. In the second part (vv. 4-6) the beatitude is succeeded by a blessing that takes a wider view of the future of this family but also of the destiny of all Israel, to whom the poet wishes *šalōm,* "peace," in keeping with the wordplay, already noted in the "Songs of Ascents," that alludes to Jerusalem, "the city of peace."

Psalm 129

Although it is spoken by an "I" Psalm 129 seems to be a national supplication in which Israel is described as subject to oppression "from [its] youth" (enslavement by the Pharaohs, or the destruction of Jerusalem in 596 B.C.E.?). Two agricultural images describe the suffering of the people in symbolic terms. The first (v. 3) is plowing: the soil harrowed by the plow becomes an image for the human back that is scourged, but it also represents a devastated city. The second image (vv. 6-7) is used in curses against oppressors: may they be like the grass that grows on the roofs of houses in the East, made as these are of beaten earth on a framework of reeds and wood. This naturally growing grass is unable to flourish or to provide a reaper with much hay. Such are the enemies of Israel: a handful of grass that withers even before growing.

Psalm 130

The *De profundis,* like the *Miserere,* is one of the best-known and best-loved of the penitential psalms, especially in the Christian tradition. Luther called it a "Pauline psalm" because of its theme; Augustine applied it to himself in his autobiography; Gregory the Great reflected on it in his *In septem Psalmos poenitentiales expositio;* such writers as Oscar Wilde and Charles Baudelaire have made imaginative use of it. It is a supplication that arises from the vortex of death and evil (vv. 1-2) and develops the theme of guilt and forgiveness. In the first strophe (vv. 3-4) there is an interesting link established between forgiveness and fear: rather than the anger of the Lord it is divine goodness that should give rise in us to a fear of offending God.

In the second strophe (vv. 5-6) expectation of forgiveness is interwoven with the liberating word of God. There is the very poetic image of "watchers"—sentinels, or the priests serving in the Temple—who wait for the first light of dawn that they may escape from nocturnal fears. In the third and final strophe (vv. 7-8) the succession of events in the individual sinner's life is extended to Israel as a whole, which must look to the Lord for redemption from all its sins. Although some of the Fathers (for example, Hilary, Chrysostom, and Theodoret) saw in this national "redemption" the deliverance from the Babylonian exile, the text is first of all a deeply spiritual hymn: God's forgiveness of sins is a gift that brings with it every other gift.

Psalm 131

As an ideal representation of the believer this jewel with its few verses represents trust in the image of the "weaned child"; this is therefore not a blind, ignorant trust, but rather supposes a relationship of spontaneous, yet informed intimacy. There is the charming though implicit image of God as mother and the hint of a "spiritual childhood," which Jesus will make his own (Matt 18:1-5), as will the Christian mystical traditions (I need only mention Thérèse of Lisieux and Charles de Foucauld). Opposed to this attitude is the proud person who has not "calmed and quieted [one's] soul" (v. 2) but aims at "things too great and too marvelous" (v. 1) and does not trust in God. A final antiphon applies the psalm to Israel as a whole.

Psalm 132

This solemn royal and liturgical psalm is difficult to interpret; it refers in ideal terms to the transfer of the ark from the "fields of Jaar" (perhaps Kiriath-Jearim in the story as told in 1 Samuel 6) to David's new capital, Jerusalem. Some scholars think that the psalm is based directly on the hymn sung at that transfer. The text is certainly liturgical (choir, faithful, priests), but it seems perhaps to fit a rite or procession commemorative of the event to be celebrated in the Temple on Zion. The text receives its structure from two oaths.

The first oath (vv. 1-10) is that of David, who vows not to set foot in his house in Jerusalem or to sleep there until the ark of the Lord has a permanent dwelling in the city. A royal acclamation, subsequently interpreted as messianic, closes this first section (v. 10). The second oath (vv. 11-18), on the other hand, is uttered by YHWH who promises permanence to the Davidic dynasty in the oracle of the prophet Nathan that is described in 2 Samuel 7.

The permanence, however, depends on a condition: the "keeping of the covenant" by David's descendants. Hope nonetheless pervades the whole ending. God will enlighten the "messiah" king, that is, God's anointed one, with a lamp that is the sign of life within a house. The images of the "sprout," which will be dear to the subsequent Davidic-messianic tradition (Isa 11:1; Jer 23:5; Zech 3:8; 6:12), and of the gleaming crown are meant to extol the life, fruitfulness, and continuity of the Davidic dynasty. Because of the presence in it of the ark later Christian tradition applied the psalm to Mary, *Foederis arca,* "ark of the covenant."

Psalm 133

Resembling a miniature, like Psalm 131, this song of (spiritual) kinship, so dear to the Christian monastic tradition (Augustine already claimed that it "has given birth to monasteries" and been "the trumpet that calls Christians to perfection": MPL 37:1729), develops around two symbols. The first is the oil of priestly consecration typified in Aaron, the ancestor of the biblical priesthood: kinship is like a sacred force that permeates the physical (beard) and spiritual (garment, symbol of dignity) vigor of a community. The other image is the dew: the psalmist dreams that the rich dew on Hermon, the northern mountain of Palestine, will spread wonderfully throughout the land of Israel and reach the distant southern mountains of Zion. Kinship must permeate the entire holy people.

Psalm 134

The fifteenth and last "Song of Ascents" is a simple, short composition that has been used as an evening and night prayer in the Christian tradition. The faithful who are leaving the Temple turn again to the Levites and those who will keep watch in the Temple at night (vv. 1-2). The priests, "servants of the LORD" who "stand by night in the house of the LORD" with hands lifted in prayer, give the faithful their blessing (v. 3). It is an ideal leavetaking of Zion and its liturgy, an ideal seal on the section of "Songs of Ascent."

Psalm 135

An anthological hymn (that is, containing citations from and allusions to other biblical texts), this song to the Lord of the universe and history was combined (from v. 4 on) in the Jewish tradition with Psalm 136 to form the "Great Hallel," the solemn Passover praise of the synagogal liturgy. The hymn begins with an extensive invitation to praise (vv. 1-4) and then turns into a profession of faith ("For I know . . .") that runs from v. 5 to v. 18. It sings first of God as creator of clouds, thunder, rain, and winds (vv. 5-7) but then goes on to celebrate the Creator as, above all, the historical Redeemer who acted in the events of the Exodus from Egypt (vv. 8-14). These various activities allow the psalmist to exalt the living God in contrast to the dead and ineffective idols that cannot save (vv. 15-18; see Ps 115:4-8). A liturgical benediction uttered by Israel, by the priests ("house of Aaron"), the Levites ("house of Levi"), and those who "fear the LORD," referring perhaps to Jewish proselytes, ends (vv. 19-21) this psalm that anticipates the solemn profession of faith in Psalm 136.

Psalm 136

This hymn for soloist and chorus, that (with Psalm 135) forms the "Great Hallel," that is, the praise *par excellence,* is given its pattern by the repeated antiphon *kī lᵉʿōlām ḥasdō,* "for his steadfast love endures forever." In twenty-two couplets (vv. 4-25) the soloist proclaims three basic articles of faith in a "historical creed." The first article of faith is original here as compared with other examples of comparable professions of faith (see Deut 26:5-9 and Josh 24:1-13), since it exalts not the revelation to the patriarchs but creation (vv. 4-9), which is seen as the first divine intervention in history (the theme is a favorite of post-exilic theology, for example, Second Isaiah).

Verses 10-20 turn to the second fundamental divine action, the Exodus from Egypt and the ensuing laborious journey in the wilderness. God, described here as a warrior, conquers the sea and the historical enemies of God's people: the Pharaoh and the kings of the wilderness. The third and final divine act is the gift of the land of Canaan (vv. 21-25). The two revelations of the Lord, the cosmic and the historical, are brought together in a single action of praise, a single profession of faith in the *ḥesed* of YHWH, that is, God's steadfast love.

Psalm 137

The *Super flumina Babylonis,* as it has been called since the Latin Vulgate made its appearance, is justly famous in the history of literature and music. It is a song of the Hebrew exiles in Babylon. They are unwilling to accept the order of their jailers that they should sing the sacred songs of Israel. Their song is, above all, a kind of self-curse: the right hand is indispensable for a cithara player, but it is better that it "forget me" (that is, become paralyzed, or wither) if "I forget" Zion; the tongue is indispensable for the singer, but it is better that it cling to the roof of the mouth if I do not remember the holy city (vv. 1-6).

The ending of the psalm contains a famous and furious curse upon the enemies of Israel (vv. 7-9) that has been excluded from use in the Catholic liturgy after Vatican Council II. The curse is aimed first at the Edomites, who joined the Babylonians in the siege and destruction of Jerusalem (586 B.C.E.). On the other hand, a cruel beatitude is reserved for anyone who will avenge Israel by striking at Babylon and smashing its little ones against a rock, following a gruesome practice in war in the ancient East. This embittered and rhetorical cry that ends the psalm is, however, an appeal to the divine judgment and should be interpreted in the light of the other "imprecatory" psalms, such as 58 and 109. It is a manifestation of the tragedy and despair of an oppressed people but also of the enfleshment of God's word in the emotions and historical experiences of humanity.

Psalm 138

This song of thanksgiving, which is somewhat stereotyped in its expression, begins a series of eight psalms that bear the later title "of David." In fact these are post-exilic compositions that use psalmic and biblical materials already familiar. The one praying in Psalm 138, who faces "toward your holy temple" (perhaps an indication that the believer is living in the Diaspora), draws into this grateful praise "all the kings of the earth" (v. 4) in a universal hymn that signals a new and different sensibility in regard to other peoples, one typical of some post-exilic prophecies. For this reason Athanasius described this song as "the psalm of the universal call to salvation."

Psalm 139

This is another masterpiece of the Psalter even though the text as it has come down to us is not transparent. The theme is immediately clear: God is omniscient and omnipotent, and human beings cannot escape either divine love or divine judgment. To put the thought into the language of Paul in his address on the Areopagus in which he uses for it a citation from the Greek poets Aratus and Cleanthus: "In him we live and move and have our being" (Acts 17:28). The first strophe (vv. 1-6) of this sapiential psalm celebrates the divine omniscience. God knows me "when I sit down and when I rise up," knows "my path" and "my lying down": these contrary actions of life, which sum up all the others, do not escape God's gaze, just as God knows our thoughts and our words even before they are formed.

The second strophe (vv. 7-12) is devoted to the divine omnipotence. It describes a human being's attempt to escape God by traversing all of space, vertically from heaven to Sheol (the lower world) and horizontally from east to west (from the dawn to the Mediterranean Sea). All time, too, with its sequence of night and day, is likewise patrolled by God, whom neither death nor darkness can resist. The powerful third strophe (vv. 13-18) focuses on the human being and its existential vicissitudes. Using the "plastic" symbol of the potter and the "textile" symbol of the weaver, the poet describes God's action within the womb of the pregnant mother, which is compared to the womb of Mother Earth. The womb is penetrated by the creative gaze of God, who participates in the making of this "wonder" that the human creature is even in its embryonic state (*golmī,* "unformed substance," v. 16), and who already anticipates all the days and events of each creature's existence.

The final strophe (vv. 19-24) is marked by strong language, as it brings on the scene the divine judgment on evil, from which the one praying sees himself or herself to be separate. The petitioner even takes the field against God's enemies—the idolatrous and the bloodthirsty (vv. 19-20)—and "hate[s] them with a perfect hatred" (v. 22), walking the very path of God, which is an "everlasting way" (v. 24), a phrase that some have interpreted as suggesting immortality. The medieval Jewish commentator, Ibn Ezra (twelfth century), claimed that "no psalm can be compared with this for the grandeur of its sentiments, the variety of its images, and the depth of its thought."

Psalm 140

Psalm 140 is a personal supplication, sustained by confidence in God's just judgment, which is a source of liberation for the oppressed and a light in the darkness of trial. It unfolds in two movements, the first contained in vv. 1-5, the second in vv. 6-13, and it leads to a final profession of faith: "I know that the LORD maintains the cause of the needy, and executes justice for the poor" (vv. 12-13). The trial to which the just one is being subjected is calumny, as indicated in v. 3 where the psalmist denounces the viper's tongue (the other image, of a trap, in v. 5, is more stereotypical and common in psalms of supplication).

In v. 7, however, God is represented as the one who protects the psalmist's head, as though in a battle; as a result the arrows of calumny will rebound upon the petitioner's adversaries and strike their own heads (v. 9; see Ps 11:6 and Rom 12:20). Jerome uses the psalm as a weapon against sins of the tongue; Augustine sees in the persecuted one of the psalm the features of the suffering Christ, who is accused by false witnesses (see Mark 26:61).

Psalm 141

The text is especially obscure in vv. 4-7, which have been variously reconstructed and interpreted. The psalm is a song of entreaty and in the early Christian tradition became an evening song because of v. 2: "Let my prayer be counted as incense before you, and the lifting up of my hands as an evening sacrifice." The theme of this verse is prophetic: prayer itself is already a sacrifice offered to God, comparable to the sacrifice offered in the evening in the Temple on Zion. The verse manifests the process, begun by the prophets, of the spiritualization of worship. The remainder of the supplication simply repeats two fundamental sentiments: the unshakable faith of the praying person that he or she will be rewarded by God and that the ungodliness of the wicked will be punished by justice meted out in this life (the traps the wicked have set for the just one will become a snare for their feet). These two sentiments also govern vv. 4-7, the details of which cannot be reconstructed except by a patient, and not rarely hypothetical, work of criticism.

Psalm 142

According to the testimony of Thomas of Celano and Bonaventure this sorrowful but also deeply trustful supplication was the last prayer recited by Francis of Assisi before his death on the evening of October 3, 1226. The fervent dialogue with the divine "You" reveals an intense spirituality. God "knows" the steps and destiny of the faithful one who is, however, plunged into emptiness and desolation. It is for this reason that the one praying allows himself or herself to say to the Lord: "Look . . . and see," "I cry to you," "Give heed" (vv. 4, 5, 6). The petitioner also says that he or she has no one at the right hand to take care of him or her (v. 4); the right hand was the place where a defender stood, whether a favorable witness in a trial or a bodyguard in war.

There is, then, a clear call to God to take the side of the just one who expresses trust in God, "my refuge, my portion in the land of the living" (v. 5). This expression is part of the vocabulary of the promised land and is therefore a profession of faith in the Lord, who does not abandon the chosen one but continues to give life. This expression and the reference to the prison in v. 7

have been given a paschal interpretation in the Christian tradition.

Psalm 143

This is the last of the seven penitential psalms of the Christian tradition (the others are Psalms 6; 32; 38; 51; 102; and 130). It has become a penitential psalm because of v. 2: "no one living is righteous before you"; this statement of the universal sinfulness of the human race was taken up by Paul in his reflection on sin and grace (Gal 2:16; Rom 3:20). Despite the title "of David," the supplication is post-exilic in its vocabulary and theology; it has two phases. In the first (vv. 1-6), the one praying is in mortal danger, prostrated and trampled down; the petitioner lifts prayer and hands to the God who is faithful to the promises. The image of the *nefeš* ("throat" and "soul") as parched earth that awaits the fructifying water of God's word (v. 6) is a powerful one.

In the second section (vv. 7-12) the psalmist feels life slipping away. Only God can draw him or her out of the pit, but he or she is sure that "in the morning" (the classical time for God to give ear, after a night of prayer and suffering) the Lord will appear as Savior and lead the faithful one onto "a level path" that is easy and full of blessings, a path some understand as alluding to immortality. On the other hand God must also wipe out evil, represented by those who have trodden down the Lord's "servant."

Psalm 144

Marked as it is by allusions and references to Psalm 18 and other psalms (8:5; 39:6-7; 33:2-3), this song seems to be a composite work. The first fragment (vv. 1-11) is a song for the king's victory, to which the Lord has contributed by a theophany in the form of volcanic eruptions, lightning, and the "aliens," that is, oppressors of Israel, who are subjected to judgment (note the introduction of the theme of enemies in vv. 7-8 and 11). This liberating irruption of God is accompanied by the thanksgiving of the psalmist who on the ten-stringed harp extols YHWH, who gives victory to the Davidic king. A messianic application seems easy, especially in light of the post-exilic origin of the passage.

The second fragment develops the no less messianic theme of *šalōm,* "peace," which is described in three charming little pictures. The first depicts a family with vigorous sons who are like flourishing trees and daughters like "corner pillars," that is, ornamental, elegant columns of a palace (v. 12). The psalmist moves then from the family to the countryside with its flocks, its full barns, and its well-fled cattle (vv. 13-14a). The final picture is of the city, which no longer need fear *pereṣ,* that is, "breaches," made by invaders, *yōṣēʾt,* that is, "exile," or *ṣewāḥāh,* the "cry" of the injured, the orphan, or victims (v. 14bc). Later commentators, both Jewish and Christian, have seen in this city a sketch of the future messianic Jerusalem, the city of peace and perfect joy (see Rev 21:3-4).

Psalm 145

Entitled "*tehīllāh* of David" (we glimpse here the root *hll,* "praise," that will appear again in the Hallelujahs of subsequent psalms), this acrostic, alphabetic psalm was described by Origen as "the supreme canticle of thanksgiving" and by Augustine as "the perfect praise of Christ, a prayer for all the circumstances and events of life"; both writers were engaging in a characteristic christological rereading. Augustine also begins his *Confessions* by citing v. 3 of the psalm, a hymn that has its literary and theological center in vv. 11-13, which celebrate God's *malkūt,* that is, supreme divine sovereignty (see Psalms 47; 93; 96-99).

God's sovereignty includes creation and providence; it extends to every being; it is without beginning or end (v. 13); it is everlasting and manifested in the divine majesty (vv. 3-5); it is righteousness and goodness (vv. 6-7), mercy and love (vv. 8-9), faithfulness and protection (vv. 13-14), generosity (vv. 15-16), and parental tenderness (vv. 17-20). The royal face of YHWH as sketched in this psalm resembles much more the face of a loving parent than that of an emperor. God is certainly a transcendent sovereign, but is also sensitive to the hunger of creatures (vv. 15-16).

Psalm 146

This post-exilic psalm begins the "Final Hallel"; in fact, the last five psalms have Hallelujahs running throughout. As in the preceding hymn, so in this one the heart of the song is the proclamation of the divine sovereignty: "The

LORD will reign forever" (v. 10). This climax is reached by way of a litany of divine attributes that are listed so as to make the perfect number twelve (nine participles, three imperfects): creator of heaven and earth, faithful to the covenant with God's people, executing justice for the oppressed and giving food to the hungry, liberator of prisoners, opening the eyes of the blind, lifting up the fallen, loving the righteous, protecting the stranger, supporting the orphan and the widow, turning the life of the wicked upside down, and reigning forever. Human beings are confronted with a choice: either to "trust in mortals," that is, in beings who are weak, or to "hope in the LORD," the eternal and faithful God. Verse 4b is cited in 1 Macc 2:63.

Psalm 147

The LXX, followed by the Vg, breaks this single Hallelujah hymn into two psalms (146–147) thereby effecting a return to the same numbering in MT and LXX. The second (vv. 12-20) has often been used in the Christian liturgy and become the subject of musical settings such as the *Lauda Jerusalem.* The canticle, which can be dated to the post-exilic period because of the combining of creation and history (a typical motif in Second Isaiah), can be broken down into three movements that, after an invitation to praise (vv. 1, 7, 12), celebrate God's action in history and in the universe (vv. 1-6, 7-11, 12-20) in different ways.

The psalm has a very lofty poetic and spiritual quality. God commands the army of the stars, but also stoops to the hungry young of the raven; God guides the peoples, but also bends down to bandage the wounds of the poor. The song is marked by a close attention to nature: the snow is like white wool, the frost like ashes, the hail like breadcrumbs; the cold strikes fear, the rain makes grass grow on the hills, and so on. But God is great especially when gathering "the outcasts of Israel" in Jerusalem, where God is personally at work strengthening the city's defenses and setting an abundant table for its children (vv. 13-16). The psalm is thus a wonderful song of God's cosmic and historical revelation.

Psalm 148

In a magnificently choreographed cosmic procession all creatures pass before the Creator. In heaven (vv. 1-6) there are the astral singers: angels, sun, moon, shining stars, heavenly spaces, and the waters above the heavens, that is, the rains. Their praise has for its theme creation and the laws imposed on it by God. On earth (vv. 7-14) there are twenty-three singers (some reduce the number to twenty-two, the number of letters in the Hebrew alphabet, by reading v. 7 as "sea monsters *in* all deeps," instead of "sea monsters *and* all deeps," the result being a kind of alphabet of being). Monsters, deeps, fire, hail, snow, frost, wind, mountains, hills, fruit trees, cedars, wild beasts, domestic animals, reptiles, birds, kings, peoples, princes, rulers, young men, young women, old people, and children are summoned to praise the Lord for the sublime divine transcendence (v. 13) and God's closeness to God's people (v. 14).

This immense chorale, which indulges in the liking for lists that is characteristic of ancient Near Eastern wisdom, aims at exalting the whole of reality as a harmony willed by God; all of reality responds to God in praise (see Psalm 104). The psalm thus belongs to the genre of "canticles of creatures" that will have an impressive parallel in Francis of Assisi's "Canticle of Brother Sun."

Psalm 149

Some critics consider this psalm one of the most recent, dating it to the Maccabean period (second century B.C.E.); in their view it would be a kind of battle hymn of the group known as the *hasīdīm* or Hasids (vv. 1, 5, 9), that is, the movement for faithful observance (the Hebrew word means "faithful, devout") that joined the Maccabees in resisting the politico-religious oppression of the Syro-Hellenistic king, Antiochus IV Epiphanes. In 1 Macc 2:42 we read, in fact, that "then there united with them [the Maccabees] a company of Hasideans, mighty warriors of Israel, all who offered themselves willingly for the law." In the psalm they are depicted as taking part in a "holy war."

Their praise is continual and rings out even "on their couches" (v. 5), that is, during the nights of waiting before battles. At dawn, there they are with the songs of Israel in their mouths and with hands grasping "the two-edged swords" (v. 6). They throw themselves into the fray without ever drawing back, executing reprisals and binding kings and generals, for they are convinced that they are carrying out "the judgment decreed" by God (vv. 7-9). It is evident that this psalm would have been reread in an eschatological perspective in the later Jewish and Christian tradition.

Psalm 150

The final psalm is a joyful musical doxology in which the Hallelujahs never die out. The last word of the psalter is a word of pure praise, adoration, poetry, and music. The purpose of the hymn is in fact to mark the end not only of the Hallel in Psalms 146–150 or of the fifth book of the Psalter (Psalms 107–150), but of the entire collection of psalms. The theological thread that runs through the one hundred fifty psalms, even amid the lamentations, the tears, the pictures of everyday life, is always the unrestrained and trustful celebration of God. To this celebration the last psalm summons the Temple orchestra with its seven instruments: horn *(shōfār),* harp *(nēbel),* cithara or upright lyre *(kīnnōr),* tambourine *(tōp),* various stringed instruments *(mīnnīm),* pipe *('ugāb),* cymbals *(ṣelṣlīm).*

But also called to this celebration is "everything that breathes" (v. 6), especially human beings, who give a voice to the entire cosmos in their cascading hymn of the text's ten Hallelujahs. Psalm 150 inevitably became a classic piece of religious music, from Franck to Bruckner, from Stravinski to Britten. It is the joyful farewell of the prayer of the psalms because, as Augustine used to say, *magnum opus hominis laudare Deum,* "praise of God in the great work of humanity."

BIBLIOGRAPHY (PSALMS)

Bright, Pamela, trans. "Athanasius of Alexandria: On the Interpretation of the Psalms," in Charles Kannengiesser, ed., *Early Christian Spirituality.* Philadelphia: Fortress, 1986.

Broyles, Craig C. *The Conflict of Faith and Experience in the Psalms: A Form-Critical and Theological Study.* JSOT.S 52. Sheffield: Sheffield Academic Press, 1989.

Brueggemann, Walter. *The Message of the Psalms: A Theological Commentary.* Augsburg Old Testament Studies. Minneapolis: Augsburg Publishing House, 1984.

Craven, Toni. *The Book of Psalms.* Message of Biblical Spirituality 6. Collegeville: The Liturgical Press, 1992.

Gerstenberger, Erhard S. *Psalms. Part I with an Introduction to Cultic Poetry.* FOTL 14. Grand Rapids: Eerdmans, 1988.

Goulder, Michael D. "The Fourth Book of the Psalter." *JThS* 26 (1975) 269–289.

Gunkel, Hermann. *Die Psalmen.* Göttingen: Vandenhoeck & Ruprecht, 1926 (1968).

Holladay, William L. *The Psalms Through Three Thousand Years: Prayerbook of a Cloud of Witnesses.* Minneapolis: Fortress, 1993.

Kaufman, Ivan T. "Undercut by Joy: The Sunday Lectionaries and the Psalms of Lament," in Jack C. Knight and Lawrence A. Sinclair, eds., *The Psalms and Other Studies on the Old Testament.* Nashotah, Wis.: Nashotah House Seminary, 1990.

Mays, James Luther. *Psalms.* Interpretation. Louisville: John Knox Press, 1994.

Mowinckel, Sigmund. *The Psalms in Israel's Worship.* 2 vols. Translated by D. R. Ap-Thomas. Nashville: Abingdon, 1962.

Rust, Renee. *Making the Psalms Your Prayer.* Cincinnati, Ohio: St. Anthony Messenger Press, 1988.

Sabourin, Leopold. *The Psalms. Their Origin and Meaning.* New York: Alba House, 1974.

Shepherd, Massey H. *The Psalms in Christian Worship: A Practical Guide.* Minneapolis: Augsburg, 1976.

Tate, Marvin. *Psalms 51–100.* WBC 20. Waco, Tex.: Word Books, 1990.

Westermann, Claus. "The Role of the Lament in the Theology of the Old Testament," *Interp.* 28 (1974) 20–38.

Wilson, Gerald Henry. *The Editing of the Hebrew Psalter.* SBL.DS 76. Chico: Scholars Press, 1985.

Zenger, Erich. *A God of Vengeance? Understanding the Psalms of Divine Wrath.* Translated by Linda M. Maloney. Louisville: Westminster/John Knox, 1996.

_____. "Das Weltkönigtum des Gottes Israels (Ps 90–106)" in Norbert Lohfink and Erich Zenger. *Der Gott Israel und die Völker.* SBS 154. Stuttgart: Katholisches Bibelwerk, 1994, 151–178. English translation forthcoming from The Liturgical Press, 1999.

Zimmerli, Walther. "Zwillingspsalmen" in Josef Schreiner, ed., *Wort, Lied und Gottesspruch. Beiträge zu Psalmen und Propheten. Festschrift für Joseph Ziegler.* FzB 1, 2. Würzburg: Echter Verlag; Stuttgart: Katholisches Bibelwerk, 1972, 2.105–113.

Proverbs

Gilberto Gorgulho and Ana Flora Anderson

FIRST READING

The book of Proverbs has thirty-one chapters full of all sorts of comparisons, containing everything from proverbs to long analogies, from pithy sayings to rhymes. In our present text they are all placed in five collections that take popular sayings and narratives and unite them in a powerful whole. Is it possible to identify the central theological and spiritual teaching in the midst of such diversity? We think that the editors of these different texts united them to show us the meaning of active wisdom as discernment (Prov 1:2-7). The people of God believe that YHWH is the center of their lives (Proverbs 16) and the redeemer (*gōʾel,* Prov 23:11) of the poor and oppressed. If they are to walk in the ways of justice they must learn as a people to discern what is just (what pleases YHWH) and leads to life. All injustice is a path to death.

The first word and the title of the book of Proverbs in Hebrew are *mishlē shelomōh,* usually translated as the proverbs of Solomon. The word *mishlē,* however, has a more comprehensive meaning than the English word proverbs. It refers to many types of comparisons and analogies including proverbs. The longer analogies occur at the beginning and end of the book, forming a framework for the three collections of proverbs in the middle.

All proverbs originally come from a contextually limited situation. For this reason some seem to be contradictory. Archaic proverbs must be read dialectically. The ancients were fascinated by truths that seemed to be contradictory because they were seen in a different light in different circumstances. For them the heart of the contradiction reveals the deepest truth. An example of a proverb whose meaning depends on its context comes from Brazil: every monkey on his own branch. This can affirm a certain truth if used in a context that means one should not pretend to be what one is not, but it is an ideological straitjacket if it is understood as a defense of the status quo without any change or reform.

When these proverbs were being collected, no one proverb could be used as proof of what the people thought in that period. When the proverbs were joined together in collections a literary effort was made to give them a certain unity. As to chronology, most commentators agree that the Hebrew Bible took on its present form in the post-exilic period. Others think that most of the Hebrew Bible was written in this period. It was at that moment that the post-exilic editors gave literary and theological unity to the book of Proverbs. This is important for our reading of Proverbs. Its many references to the tree of life (Prov 3:18; 11:30; 13:12; 15:4) remind us that Genesis 1–11 was written about the same time. Its vision of Woman Wisdom going out to the marketplace, seeking, finding, and inviting those she meets to enter her home remind us of the Shulammite in the Song of Songs who is the same type of liberated woman who brings the one she loves to her mother's house.

The book of Proverbs is a fascinating one for us to read today. Its main themes are very important for us. The whole book revolves around the search for life, the quality of life, the fullness of life. The frame of the book (Proverbs 1–9; 30–31) and its very center present different types of women and their influence on society. A third theme of the book is discernment. Remembering that proverbs must be read dialectically and contextually we recognize that a certain way of acting is not always the right way to act in a different situation. Discernment becomes the mark of the wise, the mature.

The Sages, like us, lived in a violent society and they try to understand the meaning of violence, especially as a trap that leads to death and deprives us of the much-desired fullness of life. Discernment is seen as liberation from violence and for the building up of a just society. We would like to develop these five themes, so important for pastoral ministry in our times.

Life

The book of Proverbs speaks of life and living over thirty times. It takes for granted that the deepest human desire is to have fullness of life. The great gift of Wisdom is that she is a path to life (Prov 5:6; 6:23; 10:17; 15:24) and especially that she is a tree of life (3:18). Those who find Wisdom find life (8:35). The teaching of the wise and the just (10:11; 13:14), the fear of the Lord (14:27), and good sense (16:22) are a fountain of life. Those who pursue justice and kindness will find life (21:21) and a tranquil mind will give life to the body (14:30). Both those who hate bribes and those who stop being gullible will have fuller lives (15:27; 9:6). In conclusion Proverbs promises years of life to those who listen to and follow Wisdom (3:2; 4:10; 9:11; 10:2).

Women

What is surprising about the book of Proverbs is that the symbol that determines the meaning of the whole book is Woman. We are presented with five different women, all symbols that unite and give meaning to the whole. In Proverbs 1-9 we meet Woman Wisdom and Woman Folly. In Proverbs 31 we have Lemuel's mother and the strong, capable woman. It would be interesting before we go farther to read these chapters and discover the many facets they illustrate. The fifth woman, also found especially in Proverbs 1-9, is difficult to define. In Hebrew she is *zārāh* and sometimes *nokriyāh* (Prov 5:20). As Athalya Brenner has shown, *zārāh* can mean foreign, strange, liminal, outsider, or simply other. *Nokriyāh* usually means foreigner but can mean outsider. It is very likely that in the long history of these analogies and proverbs these terms have meant all of the above at one moment or another.

The rest of the text will develop these symbolic figures, but we would like to conclude by saying that we agree with all those who point out the sociological importance of these texts. Women must have been of importance socially if they were to become such important figures in post-exilic literature. A symbol not based on reality would not be accepted by the reader. Both Woman Wisdom and the Other *(zārāh)* go to the streets, the marketplace, the gates of the city. They invite those they seek to their home. The Strong Woman of Proverbs 31 oversees a large household. She buys and sells, produces food and clothing, cares for the poor and the needy; her teaching *(tōrah)* leads to solidarity *(hesed)* which in Proverbs is the essence of Wisdom. She is worthy of the fruit of her hands. There is no doubt that she is a symbol, but she is also part of the reality of women's lives in the post-exilic period.

Discernment

The center of moral theology is discernment: to do the right thing at the right time. The book of Proverbs uses a half dozen terms to try to explain what this entails. Discernment is insight; it is intuition, understanding, subtlety, prudence (Prov 1:2-3). It can also be described as a path. To follow the good path means to do what is right and just and fair (2:9). Proverbs believes that the path of the righteous becomes clearer to them as they travel down it (4:12-13, 18). Proverbs presents the paths to good and evil as generally clear-cut. Later in the post-exilic period Ecclesiastes (Qoheleth) will object to this. Proverbs itself agrees with Ecclesiastes that we can never know ahead of time what the next day will bring (27:1) but thinks we should plan ahead (14:15) and try to foresee the consequences of what we plan (21:5). If we believe that we can make choices that have no consequences we are choosing the path of death (2:18). We should instead choose the path of life (10:17; 9:6, 11).

Discernment means listening to the counsel of others. Individuals can only conjecture what is just and fair. The community that discerns together is on the path to life. This third theme is the greatest contribution of Proverbs to the Christian tradition. The center of Paul's ethics is discernment in a faith community. The Jesuits have been among those who keep alive this tradition in the Church today. The book of Proverbs teaches that the gift of Wisdom is discernment (cf. Prov 3:1-12).

Violence

The path to life is a path of love. Human relations and community building depend on love. Violence is the contrary of love. It is mutual aggression that appears on all levels of existence. In Proverbs 1:10-19 we have a perfect description of violence. It is unprovoked, sets traps for the honest and the innocent, and is often used for personal gain. It would be opportune to read this text now.

Violence, in the end, is a trap that leads to death. Those who hate Wisdom love death (8:36).

Wisdom and discernment make us slow to anger (4:17; 15:18; 19:11), while every fool is quick to start a quarrel (20:3). The wicked perpetrate violence (21:7); it is concealed in their mouths (10:11). Proverbs 10:12 says that hatred stirs up disputes, but love covers all offenses. The NT repeats this proverb in 1 Cor 13:4-7; 1 Pet 4:8; Jas 5:20. It is used as an example of Jesus' teaching against violence. Those who do not discern, who follow the path of evil, will drink the wine of violence (4:17), but discernment frees us from reciprocal violence. We follow the path of justice, which is like a shining light that grows in brilliance (4:18). Our desire should not be with the evil and the violent (24:1-2). Our house (life) should be built by wisdom, understanding, and knowledge (24:3-4). The wise are more powerful than the strong (24:5) and they have no need of violence.

Justice

Justice *(ṣedāqāh)* is a basic category of the book of Proverbs. Once again it is closely related to life. The recompense of the just leads to life (10:16). The wicked do not acknowledge the rights of the poor (29:7). They understand nothing of justice (28:5). They increase their wealth by oppressing the poor (22:16). They trust in riches (11:7, 28) and imagine that their wealth protects them from all harm (18:11).

The wicked use the Law to devour the poor (13:23). They make fortunes by their lying tongues (21:6) and by charging too much interest on loans to the poor (28:8). Proverbs, however, thinks a good name is more desirable than riches (22:1). It is also better to be poor than to be shamed or to look foolish (12:9; 19:1, 22). In truth it is better to eat only herbs where there is love than to eat luxuriously where there is hatred (15:17).

The Strong Woman cares for the poor and the needy (31:20). Wisdom will not let us shut our ears to the cry of the poor (21:13). We will be blessed if we give to the poor (22:9) and we ourselves will not know want (28:27). The Lord guards the house of the widow (15:25) and defends the cause of the poor and the needy (22:22-23). The Lord is the redeemer *(gōʾel)* of the orphans whose fields are invaded by the rich.

Lemuel's mother (31:8-9) advises him that a king (government) should defend the rights of the destitute and those who have no voice in society. He should promote just laws and defend the needy and the poor. God, who is just, guarantees justice for all people (29:26). When a nation is governed by the just, the people rejoice (29:2). In the post-exilic period the Sages, like their forebears, searched for a form of government that would minimize injustice and guarantee the rights of the poor and freedom from oppression. Once again this is a process of discernment in community. Those who pursue justice and kindness will find honor and life (21:21).

General Contexts for Interpretation

Theological and Literary Structure

The content of the book of Proverbs has a long history, but in its present form, coming to us from the Sages of the post-exilic period, it is made up of five collections:

I. The Prologue: Wisdom and Life: 1–9
II. The First Collection of the Proverbs of Solomon: 10:1–22:16
III. The Sayings of the Wise: God, the Redeemer *(gōʾel):* 22:17–24:34

IV. The Second Collection of the Proverbs of Solomon: 25–29
V. The Epilogue: Wisdom and Life: 30–31

Original Historical Context

Each of the above collections has its roots in a different historical context that will be further detailed in the Second Reading. The oldest is the Second Collection of the Proverbs of Solomon (Proverbs 25–29). It is dated from the time of King Hezekiah (eighth century B.C.E.). The first part of the collection (Proverbs 25–27) comes from the northern kingdom (Israel) to be "transmitted" in the southern kingdom of Judah after the fall of Samaria (Prov 25:1). This collection structures the life of the population around the king and the commandment to love one's neighbor (Prov 25:1-7, 21-22). Social life revolves around the concept of honor (God's, the king's, the just one's).

Proverbs 28–29 probably comes from the time of King Manasseh (seventh century B.C.E.). It originates with the resistance groups who opposed the king's politics of syncretism and oppression. It reflects the hopeful view of those who prepared the deuteronomistic reform in the time of King Josiah. It is a defense of the poor and the needy and an expression of the desire to again have a king who would defend the cause of the poor (Prov 29:1-4, 7, 14).

The Sayings of the Wise compose the center of the book of Proverbs. Wisdom presents God as the redeemer *(gōʾel)*. These sayings have been compared to ancient Egyptian wisdom (the Teachings of Amen-em-ope) especially in the first part (Prov 22:17–23:11). Today more emphasis is placed on the three units that make up the collection:

Prov 22:17–23:11: God/*gōʾel* defends the poor and the needy;
Prov 23:12–24:22: five instructions about discipline passed on by parents to their son;
Prov 24:23-31: a small collection about the function of wisdom.

The environment of these units is that of the elders active in King Josiah's reform (Deut 21:18-19; Prov 23:21).

The First Collection of the Proverbs of Solomon is dated from the end of the monarchy after the death of Josiah and in the violent context of occupation by the neo-Babylonian army. The Sages of Jerusalem present the just one who will live by faithfulness (Hab 2:4). Wisdom is the discernment that frees us from death and opens the path of justice and poverty (Prov 12:28; 15:33; 18:12; 22:4). Wisdom reveals to us the difference between the just and the wicked.

Proverbs 30–31 is the Epilogue of the whole book. It contains a series of enigmas about the meaning of wisdom. There are two basic models that give unity to the text:

> Agur represents the Sage who seeks divine wisdom. He is related to the Sage in Psalms 49:3-6 and 73:5, 7 and in the book of Job.
>
> The figures of two women close the book of Proverbs. The first is a foreign queen speaking to her son Lemuel. The text makes it clear that the counsel of his mother transcends that of the king. The second figure is that of the Strong Woman. Some think this text is the teaching of a mother given to her daughter so that she will understand what it means to be a woman in a patriarchal society. Others think the Strong Woman is personified Wisdom who is practical (she maintains her household) and whose teaching leads to solidarity (31:26).

This epilogue together with the prologue are from the post-exilic period.

Proverbs 1–9 is the Prologue of the book. It introduces us to all the themes we will meet in the other collections. Its center is Wisdom, the Woman who leads us to the tree of life.

Canonical Context

Sirach 47:18[17] speaks of the proverbs and sayings that made the figure of Solomon the wonder of the world. Thus our first reference to the book of Proverbs appears in a text written in Jerusalem around 190–180 B.C.E. Proverbs is also mentioned by Flavius Josephus in *Contra Apion* 1.8. He regards the collection as precepts for the conduct of a human life. Even though Proverbs has been traditionally accepted as a holy book of the Jewish people, the authors of the Talmud were wary of the contradictions in it and were tempted to hide this book from the public. Christians received the book of Proverbs in the Greek Bible and have always considered it canonical. It is interesting to see how Proverbs is referred to in the NT. In Paul, Luke, and James, Proverbs is quoted to stress the importance of justice, love, and humility. In 1 Peter the moral context of Proverbs is more pivotal to the text.

The Fathers of the Church follow this latter development and use Proverbs more for its ethical than its theological and social content. Among the most interesting texts from the Fathers are the fragments we have received from Hippolytus. He begins his commentary on Proverbs by making a theologically important leap in thought. The proverbs are attributed to Solomon whose name means the peacemaker. But the true peacemaker, as all Christians know, is Jesus, our redeemer. The term "redeemer" is a translation of the Hebrew word *gōʾel* so important in the book of Proverbs (23:11). YHWH is the savior *(gōʾel)* of the poor and the oppressed. In the New Covenant, Jesus is the true peacemaker and redeemer. Again the process of discernment that is so important to us today is emphasized when Hippolytus speaks of true judgments. They are only possible when our thoughts are free of passion and not in a state of excitement due to external appearances.

Also to be able to discern we must understand that desire is a fire, a tyrant. This is an important point in Proverbs and should be studied in the perspective of desire and the destructive power of violence as has been done by anthropologists such as René Girard. For Hippolytus the tree of life, so important to the Sages, is Christ himself. Saint Augustine and the Venerable Bede also have commentaries on Proverbs, but the book achieved greater recognition in the Middle Ages when the scholastic theologians, beginning with Albert the Great, became interested in its teaching.

Church Usage

The New Testament and especially the gospel of John have presented Jesus as Wisdom. This is especially important in Proverbs where woman Wisdom presents the Law *(tōrah)* as love and solidarity *(hesed),* Prov 31:26. The liturgy has always seen Mary as an incarnation of Woman Wisdom. Christian tradition has the special hermeneutic that comes from the faith of God's people. Christian reading of the Hebrew Bible illuminates ancient texts at the same time that it illuminates Christian texts and traditions.

The book of Proverbs is used once a year in each liturgical cycle. In Year A it is read on the Thirty-third Sunday in Ordinary Time. Proverbs 31:10-13, 19-20, 30-31 is used to complement Matt 25:14-30 where the householder leaves his servants responsible for his properties. In Year B, Prov 9:1-6 is read on the Twentieth Sunday in Ordinary Time together with John 6:51-58. As Jesus prepared a meal for the hungry crowds, Wisdom also has spread her table with food and drink for those who want to advance in the way of understanding. In Year C, Prov 8:22-31 is read on Trinity Sunday together with John 16:12-15. John emphasizes the role of the Spirit of truth who reveals God the Father and the Son to us. Proverbs 8 is a hymn to personified Wisdom that has always been used by Christians to understand the Word of God, the firstborn of God's ways.

In the daily cycle for Year II, Proverbs is read during the twenty-fifth week. On Monday the reading is from Prov 3:27-34. It is a commentary on how we should treat our neighbor. It is read together with Luke 8:16-18 about the light of witness that should not be hidden under a bed. On Tuesday, Prov 21:1-6, 10-13 is read together with Luke 8:19-21. In Luke, Jesus distinguishes between blood relatives and those who belong to him because they listen to God's word and do his will. Proverbs says that it is the Lord who proves hearts and sees what is right and just. On Wednesday the Church reads Prov 30:5-9 together with Luke 9:1-6. These texts are an interesting combination. Luke narrates the mission of the Twelve. They must set out to preach the reign of God without taking material comforts with them. The speaker in Proverbs asks to be neither rich nor poor. Those who are rich and well-nourished are led to doubt that God exists. Those who are too poor and have nothing to eat are led to steal and profane God's name.

SECOND READING

This commentary will be more useful if it is read together with the biblical text of Proverbs.

I. Prologue: Wisdom and Life

Proverbs 1–9 forms an introduction to the whole of the book of Proverbs. It presents Wisdom as the revelation of God, the fountain of life. Wisdom gives us the discernment that frees us from death and leads us to life. The themes of the general prologue can be divided into three parts:

Wisdom and the Fear of the Lord (Prov 1:7-9, 20-23; 2; 3:1-12; 4:8-9).
The Strange (Other) Woman (Proverbs 5–7)
The fusion of the above mentioned themes (Prov 2:16-19; 7:1-5; 9).

The Prologue is a synthesis of the teaching of Deuteronomy and Jeremiah. There is a strong relation between Proverbs 2:20–7:3 and Deuteronomy 11,18–22. Proverbs makes relevant the prophetic teaching of Deut 4:6 and its source, Jer 31:31-34.

Proverbs demythologizes Wisdom. She is not a goddess like those of the ancient fertility religions (Prov 3:16; 8:22). She is the revelation and the presence of YHWH, the God of life. We become wise through discernment that comes from the fear of the Lord (Prov 1:7; 9:10). Wisdom is the word of the living God who pours out the divine Spirit (1:23). Those who respond to Wisdom's call will possess the tree of life (3:16-18) and participate in the messianic banquet (9:1-6).

Title and Purpose

1:1-7: The first verse is the title and attributes the whole of the book to Solomon, famous for his wisdom (1 Kings 5:9-14). In the post-exilic period that wise king was the symbol of the ruler who receives the gift of Wisdom from God so that he can unite the people around the Jerusalem Temple (2 Chr 11:7-13; Sir 47:15-17). *Verses 1-4:* the counsel that Wisdom offers is especially meant for the gullible and the young. Wisdom herself speaks to them (1:22; 8:5; 9:4) as does Folly (9:13). *Verses 5-6:* The wise will be enriched by proverbs and parables. These will add to their understanding (21:11) and deepen their personal discernment. Wisdom in this sense is received by instruction and acquired by experience. *Verse 7:* Ancient wisdom is at the same time mental ability and daily practice. It is an ethical discernment that controls acts of aggression or rivalry. In Israel this form of discernment was seen as explicitly religious. The fear of God is the highest expression of this concept of Wisdom (1:7; 9:10; 14:26-27; 15:33) that communicates the spirit of solidarity (1:20-23).

Fools (10:8) are the chief opponents of the wise because they reject wisdom. Dullards are the hardheaded and the thick-skulled (26:4) who despise learning and wisdom. The mockers are the cynical who scoff at all that is serious (1:22) and are insolent to the just (21:24). More generically, the rivals of the just are the wicked (25:27).

Proverbs 1:8–9:18 is divided into ten sayings that can be called "the ten words of wisdom":

The Appeal to Conversion, 1:8-33

This saying shows the three parts of the act of conversion: *Verses 8-19:* The path of violence must be abandoned. The first step on the path to life is to clearly perceive how wide the net of violence extends. *Verses 20-27:* The essential step on this path is to hear and receive the Spirit that comes through Wisdom. Wisdom here acts as a prophet, announcing a definitive judgment. Its appeal is to liberty and the spirit of solidarity. *Verses 28-33:* The third step on the path to conversion is the high point of our text and the principal idea of the book of Proverbs. Retribution is the fruit of our own acts. The just receive the fruits of their good acts and the wicked wallow in unhappiness, the fruit of their evil acts. Conversion gives them access to the tree of life (13:12).

The Process of Liberation, 2:1-22

The second saying shows the dynamism of liberation:

it begins with a gift given to the human heart;
it leads to acts of intelligence, here and now;
its content is based on the discernment of what is right and just and fair;
it frees us from the evil path and the Strange/Other Woman;
it reveals the path of justice.

Verses 1-4: This inner nature of wisdom reflects the deuteronomistic perspective and that of Jeremiah when he speaks of the heart as the inner force of the new life in the Covenant (Deut 4:6; Jer 31:31-34). *Verses 5-8:* Only an intelligent heart is capable of discerning in accordance with the word of God and the spirit of love. *Verses 9-11:* The content of wisdom is the knowledge of God (Hos 4:1-4) and the prophetic values of the Covenant such as justice and righteousness (Hos 2:18-20; Amos 5:24). *Verses 12-15:* The way of the wicked is that of mutual violence. Wisdom frees us from this relationship and makes communion possible. *Verses 16-19:* Discernment is a concrete and existential act. In these verses it reflects a post-exilic problem: the Strange/Other Woman is seen as a danger to religious and social life (v. 18). Discernment is central to Proverbs 1–9, especially in chs. 5 and 7. *Verses 20-22:* Proverbs 2 ends with a description of the path of the just. They will live in the land that is being restored after the exile (Prov 3:33-35).

The New Covenant, 3:1-12

Proverbs 3 is a synthesis of Wisdom spirituality. The first part is inspired by Deut 4:6 and 6:5-7. *Verses 1-4:* The new covenant germinates in hearts touched by the word of God. It gives birth to solidarity and fidelity, characteristics of the living and merciful God (Exod 34:6). *Verses 5-6:* God's gift illuminates and strengthens the weakness of the human heart. The spirit of poverty leads to enlightenment and compassion (15:33) and makes straight the path that leads to the fullness of life (v. 6). *Verses 7-8:* A life of wisdom consists in renouncing self-sufficiency and evil and in fearing and honoring God with all our being. *Verses 9-12:* YHWH gives us every blessing, especially that of life. Wisdom is thus an act of praise to the God of life. The Lord chastises the beloved to help them grow in wisdom.

The Tree of Life, 3:13-35

This second part of the synthesis is a hymn to Wisdom's divine transcendence. *Verses 13-21:* This is the most important part of the hymn. Many see here an influence of the Egyptian goddess Maat and other goddesses of fertility, but even though the authors knew of these myths they present Wisdom as a gift of God. Proverbs 3:16 and 8:22-31 could possibly refer to the Egyptian myth of Maat as the personification of the order that rules the universe. She is the dear daughter of the great god Re, creator of the world (8:22). The goddesses of fertility are the source of life that comes from the god of fertility (Hos 14:9-10 writes in the style of Wisdom literature when demythologizing the Canaanite goddesses).

Woman in these texts is a symbol of life. Through her Wisdom is revealed as a messianic gift. Woman is the symbol of God's gift acting in creation and in history. She is the tree of life itself: the gift of God that makes possible and sustains all righteousness. *Verses 21-35:* The synthesis ends with an invitation to live in union with Wisdom and on the same path as the community of the *anawim,* the poor of YHWH. Wisdom frees us from the paths of violence and leads us to the path of communion.

Access to Honor, 4:1-9

It is through Wisdom that we acquire honor. *Verses 1-4:* Both mother and father teach wisdom in its many forms: advice, knowledge, and words that penetrate our very hearts. *Verses 5-7:* Wisdom is a personal act. The authors convey this through the verb used for procreation in Gen 4:1 and in Prov 8:22. Wisdom engenders intelligence, which is an active discernment. For the wise this is the most perfect aspect of life (Prov 23:23). *Verses 8-9:* Active discernment involves the whole person and brings fulfillment through honor which is the totality of human life. Honor is the identity and the complete integration of a person in the community, as in the case of Job (Job 19:9; 29:20; 31:36).

The Two Paths, 4:10-27

Wisdom indicates the difference between the two paths in their existential aspects. *Verses 10-13:* It is through Wisdom that we choose and direct our way of life. Wisdom is the life of those who engender and possess her. *Verses 14-17:* Wisdom prevents us from walking in the way of the wicked and drinking the wine of violence. This is essential to discernment. Eating and drinking express the human desire for love (Prov 13:12). The bread and wine symbolize human desire to choose either violence or life (Prov 9:5). *Verses 18-19:* The path of the just is like a light that always tends toward the dawn but the way of the wicked is darkness and shadows. *Verses 20-27:* Those who have Wisdom in their hearts walk in the path of life and distance themselves from the way of wickedness.

The Conflict to be Faced, 5:1-23 + (6:1-19)

These verses form a single unit that is presented as a discernment of the problems of the post-exilic period. As we have seen in the section on women in the First Reading, the Hebrew Bible uses two terms to describe some women of that epoch and these terms are not easily translated. The group that returned from exile was much more conservative than the people who remained in Judah. The laws about marriage can refer to foreign women or any other Jewish woman who is considered different or strange. The leaders of the people were worried about the consequences of marriage outside of their own group. Since wives could inherit at this time a family's portion could fall into the hands of the widow's family. Also some women brought with them foreign gods which they established in their homes beside YHWH. The themes of the foreign or strange woman and of adultery sometimes take on the symbolic meaning of unfaithfulness to the covenant and of even of lack of faith in YHWH. Discernment in face of this conflict is presented in six sayings. They are warnings:

about foreign or strange women: 5:1-14, 20-23;
about loving one's wife with all one's heart: 5:15-20;
about contracts and false economic security: 6:1-5
about work, or the sluggard and the ant: 6:6-11;
about evil (similar to the agent of evil in Job 4:8): 6:12-15;
about anti-social behavior: 6:16-19.

Proverbs 6:1-19 may be a later addition.

A Warning About Illicit Sex, 6:20-35 + 7:1-27

In this saying the parents exhort the son to discern here and now that:

6:20-35: Illicit sex is a threat.
7:1-5: The Other/Strange Woman and the foreigner (outsider) are threats to youth.
7:6-23: This text may be an apocalyptic midrash as in Dan 14:15-21. The woman seen through the window is said to be dressed as a prostitute. In the Hebrew Bible this term often refers to idolatry.
7:24-27: This exhortation may be against marriage to foreign women or only to those different from the norms of the post-exilic community. In either case the parents are sure that if the youth follows this path he is headed for the grave (Mal 2:14-16).

Messianic Wisdom, 8:1-33

Wisdom fulfills the promises made by the prophets (Isa 11:2). This unit has three parts:

THE USE OF PROVERBS 8 AND OTHER LADY WISDOM TEXTS IN CHRISTIAN LITURGY

Wisdom is frequently presented as a woman in the OT. The identity (reality) of this woman is discussed in the general article on "Wisdom" but Christian piety has frequently seen Wisdom as a figure of Mary, God's mother. What is the basis of this notion?

It is important to understand that the origin of Marian devotions is found in teachings about Christ. Preliturgical devotion to Mary in the second century, for example, thought of her as prefigured in Eve just as Jesus was thought of as prefigured in Adam (Rom 5:12-21). The flourishing of Marian liturgies dates to fifth-century developments in christology and is associated with the title given her of *theotokos* (God-Bearer, i.e., Mother of God). This title was formally attributed to Mary by the Council of Ephesus in 431 C.E. The council was concerned to honor Mary but primarily to affirm something about Christ, namely that he is one, not two persons. Thus Mary was mother of the one divine person.

Prior to the proclamation of *theotokos* at Ephesus liturgical expressions of Marian piety were minimal. The public scenes of excitement accompanying the declaration of *theotokos* resulted in a multiplication of liturgical feasts to Mary. At this point Wisdom texts began to be used in this context. Initially Wisdom texts were used in Marian liturgies to celebrate Mary's virginity. For example, Sir 24:3-16 was used in this way as it had earlier been used in Roman liturgies to celebrate the virginity of Saints Agnes and Agatha.

In the sixth century Prov 8:22-35 was adopted by the liturgy for the first time in the Mass of the Nativity of Mary (September 8). There is no record of this text being used earlier for any other saint. As in so much early Marian piety this was a christological reading: "The Lord created me at the beginning of his work" (Prov 8:22) refers to the historical Christ ("me") in the thought of God from eternity, but Mary is immediately involved in that eternal thought as mother of Christ. Hence the Church found it appropriate to read that text on her birthday, the day commemorating her own origin, for she too was present in the thought of God "at the beginning of God's work."

Prov 8:22-31 and Sir 24:1, 3-4, 8-12, 19-21 are found in our present lectionary in the Common of the Blessed Virgin as an inheritance from the Christian community of the sixth century. These texts can be understood as evoking Lady Wisdom as created and as an intimate of God. In this sense they are a fitting expression of Mary's relationship to her son. —*Camilla Burns*

Verses 1-11: Wisdom as revelation. Wisdom, as a prophet, goes to the crossroads and the gates of the city. She preaches to all she meets, declaring that her words are truth and worthy of belief. She is worth more than any human treasure. *Verses 12-21:* Messianic Wisdom. Wisdom's dignity comes from her closeness to prudence (discernment), her knowledge, and her discretion. She has counsel and good judgment, understanding and power. She is the fulfillment of the messianic gifts promised in Isa 11:2 (Jer 10:6-12; Job 12:13). Wisdom reveals herself as the source of prosperity with honor for those who walk with her on the path of justice. The goal of this path and of all messianic gifts is love (Deut 6:5-15; 10:12; 11:1, 13, 22). *Verses 22-36:* Wisdom as savior. The third part of this unit is Wisdom's justification of herself. Her origin is in God and she is God's collaborator in the work of creation. She existed before all things were made.

Proverbs 8:22 uses the verb *qānānī,* which can mean "acquire" or "possess" (Vulgate). The LXX and Peshitta translate *qānānī* as "created" (Gen 4:1; 14:19). To harmonize this term with others in the following verses (bear, give birth), perhaps it could be best translated as "the Lord gave me being." The interpretation of this term played an important role in the christological debates of the fourth century. In Arian circles Prov 8:22 was used to argue for the creaturehood of the Word, since Wisdom was one of the great christological titles. Athanasius of Alexandria argues against the Arian exegesis, showing that in Wisdom literature *qānānī* can have different meanings and that in relation to Christ it can refer to the Incarnation.

In v. 23 Wisdom states that she was poured forth at the first, before the earth (Sir 1:4). This term is used in the installation of kings, as in Ps 2:6-7. Once again in v. 30 we have a controversial term, *amon/oman/amun/omen.* The different forms of this Hebrew root can mean architect or artist (Song 7:2), to bind together, or even nursling. Wisdom 7:21 says that Wisdom, the architect of all, teaches (Wis 14:2). These two Wisdom texts are similar to Prov 8:30 and clarify its meaning.

Verses 32-33 form an inclusion with Prov 1:8: children should listen to their parents' teaching so that they will find Wisdom and in finding her will have life.

The Messianic Banquet, 9:1-18

The last saying in our Prologue is a decisive call to conversion. It is presented in an allegory about Woman Wisdom's banquet contrasted to the banquet of Woman Folly. *Verses 1-6:* In Wisdom's banquet everything has a symbolic meaning. Her house with its seven columns evokes the image of the Temple with its atrium. The Banquet is presented as a sacred, liturgical meal that is a foretaste of the messianic banquet (Isa 55:1-3, 5; 65:11-13; 25:6). Her maidservants are sent forth with a prophetic message to the city (Jer 7:25: 25:4; 26:5). The heights around the city recall Jerusalem (Ps 125:2). The maidservants call out to the simple and those who lack understanding, inviting them to eat and drink of Wisdom's food so that they might live (Prov 4:17). *Verses 7-12:* This text is a later addition that returns to the traditional theme of the just and the wicked. *Verses 13-18:* Folly's banquet is a caricature of that of Wisdom (Prov 5:15-16). She too calls out to the passersby to divert them with false promises. The only gift she really has to give is death.

II. The First Collection of the Proverbs of Solomon

This collection has two parts (chs. 10–15; 16–22:16) bound together by deuteronomistic teachings (14:26–16:15). It is dated from the end of the monarchy, after the death of Josiah. The neo-Babylonian army has surrounded the people with violence and threats to their lives (Hab 1:1-4). In the midst of this crisis a group of Sages organized a series of moral and legislative sayings to show that the just will be saved from violence and death and that they will live in faithfulness (Hab 2:4). Wisdom calls the people to conversion: they must seek justice and poverty as the prophet Zephaniah taught. This is the central thought of the collection. Wisdom frees the people from violence and directs their desire to mutual love and solidarity. This freedom from violence must characterize their work within the tributary mode of production (Prov 10:4-5; 12:24).

On the literary level our collection is structured in five chapters:

1. The Life of the Just One: 10–12
2. Desire: Fulfillment and Socialization: 13:1

3. The Role of Wisdom: 15:20
4. Wisdom is Liberation: 17:25
5. The Fruit of Justice and Poverty: 19:27

1. The Life of the Just One (Proverbs 10–12)

A. The Figure of the Just One, 10:1-30

The just person is presented in this unit as a worker (v. 5). *Verses 1-7:* Once again this section opens with a reference to the instruction given by the mother and father to their son. It presents the fundamental characteristics of the just son:

—justice satisfies his righteous desires and saves him from death (vv. 2-3);
—work enriches him and does him credit (vv. 4-5);
—God gives blessing (divine power) to the Just One, whose memory and name will live on (vv. 6-7).

Verses 8-13: All of life is carried out in conflict. The fool (mentioned nineteen times in Proverbs) is the antithesis of the wise. The term comes from Egyptian wisdom and refers to someone who talks much with little content. The Hebrew root means to be first or strong, but during the monarchy it was used ironically to describe all babblers, whether pretentious or naïve (Isa 19:11; Prov 10:14, 21; 14:17; 16:22). The babbler is always a servant of the wise (Prov 11:29). Such a one is irresponsible (Prov 22:15) and spurns a father's advice (Prov 15:5). Even beatings will not stop this kind of person from being foolish (Prov 27:22).

Verses 14-21: The just choose what is fair and righteous and this leads to an ever richer life. They are especially careful of what they say and thus their words nourish those who hear them. *Verses 22-26:* The Lord's blessing is again seen as the strength of the just. God grants the desires of the just and makes them secure and firm. *Verses 27-30:* Because the just fear the Lord they live longer. God makes them secure in the land.

B. The Rectitude of Justice: The Lives of the Just are Shaped by Their Deep Desire for Justice, 10:31–11:28

Verses 10:31–11:2: Wisdom is a gift that comes from within; its source is humility (Mic 6:8). Wisdom frees the just from pride and leads them on to please the Lord. *Verses 11:3-8:* Justice is a straight path, but the wicked walk where they will fall into intrigue and trouble. *Verses 11:9-15:* This text shows the effects of justice on the city and the people of a nation. A country that accepts guidance will be secure. *Verses 11:16-22:* This text underlines the importance of honor in ancient societies. It begins by presenting the kindhearted woman and ends with those who have no discretion. Honor is kindheartedness (vv. 16-17) and righteousness (vv. 18-21). When there is also solidarity with others the just achieve fulfillment. *Verses 11:23-28:* Life is like a tree. It can produce good fruit and bad. Those who seek good find good will, but those who go looking for trouble find it instead.

C. The Context of Freedom: It is Through Work That One Learns to be Free, 11:29–12:28

Verses 11:29–12:7: The context of life is the household where the extended family of the ancient world lived and worked. It is here that the tree of life is found. *Verses 12:8-14:* This text describes work as it was at that time: caring for animals, producing food, and working with the hands. Through this work the righteous escape trouble and flourish. *Verses 12:15-21:* Freedom is the fruit of correct discernment. Understanding and counsel orient a path to justice. Truth is the fruit of justice and peace. Those who do not work will be given into forced labor (1 Kings 4:21; 12:18). *Verses 12:22-24:* The practice of truth is the fulfilling of the will of God. Forced labor is a denial of God's gift of freedom. *Verses 12:25-28:* The path of justice leads to life but the gullible insist on taking the path to death. Verse 28 (the path of the gullible leads to death) was corrected at the time of the Maccabees to emphasize the resurrection of the just (the way of the just does not lead to death).

2. Desire: Fulfillment and Socialization (13:1–15:19)

The tree of life is central in this text. Desire fulfilled is the tree of life (13:12) as is the soothing tongue (15:4).

A. Desire Fulfilled, 13:1-25

These sayings have been collected as an instruction about human desire. Eating is used symbolically to suggest the direction of desire for good things or for violence (vv. 2, 4, 19, 25). *Verses 1-4:* The text begins by saying that desire must be disciplined. When desire is negative it leads to violence and the downfall of the undisciplined. They desire in vain. The positive dynamism of desire leads to good things, life, and satisfaction. *Verses 5-9:* Justice points desire in the right direction and leads to integrity. The righteous are like a light shining bright. *Verses 10-13:* A society is put in crisis and divided by pride. Pride is the most destructive fruit of desire, but those who are willing to hear others and take advice can create a society with mutual understanding. In this context human desire is fulfilled and all can eat of the tree of life.

Verses 14-19: This text also treats the theme of life. Those who listen to the teachings of the wise have already found the tree of life. Those who accept discipline will find honor. When desire is fulfilled, how sweet it is!

Verses 20-25: Here we have a new subjective dimension in the transmission of wisdom. Living in a community of Sages is more important than instruction. The just prosper and leave an inheritance for their children. As much as the Sages want to promote the ideal of hard work on the land they know it is useless if justice does not exist. Children who are loved are disciplined because their parents know that unrestrained desires lead to ruin.

B. The Socialization of Desire, 14:1-35

This is a process of mutual exchange between the household (14:1-27) and the rest of the population (14:28-35). *Verses 1-3:* The wisest of women *(hokmōt nāshim)* or women Sages build up the household. Once again women are personified Wisdom: she socializes (promotes solidarity) because she builds on justice and the fear of the Lord. *Verses 4-5:* On the practical level this means the household must have work and find justice at the city gates. *Verses 6-7:* The cynic, who is not wise or discerning, destroys the household (family, society).

Verses 8-14: These verses show how a household can be built up or destroyed. The wicked of v.11 are the opposite of the wise in v.1. They destroy a household while the workers in the field (living in tents) flourish. *Verses 15-18:* These verses are a contrast between gullible, quick-tempered fools and the wise who are prudent, knowledgeable, and fear the Lord.

Verses 19-24: Here we find traces of paronomasia. Evil and good (vv. 19, 22); poor and rich, poverty and wealth (vv. 20, 21, 23, 24) are compared to the values of the covenant (the love and faithfulness found in Hos 2:18-24; Exod 34:6). The text ends by emphasizing once again that a household is built up by hard work. *Verses 25-27:* The household is secure if its inhabitants fear the Lord. Their faith is a fountain of life.

Proverbs 14:26-27 begins the deuteronomistic section that units this part of the collection. *Verses 28-35:* The king is presented as the catalyst of the new social life the population is seeking. The axis of this new society is the peaceful heart that repels violence and cares for the poor. The role of the King in deuteronomistic thought will be referred to again in Prov 16:10-15; 20:28; 21:1.

C. The Sages, Mediators of Communication, 15:1-19

The wise intercourse that exists among the Sages frees them from violence and nourishes fellowship. The role of the Sages in dialogue and communication unites the following sayings.

Verses 1-7: The tongue of the wise repels violence. God guarantees communication because God's eyes are everywhere watching the good and the evil. Verse 3 has been influenced by the Greek term *sophia* (wisdom) that is used here as a verb, *ṣofet* (watching over). This presence is an attribute of God's Wisdom. The text now returns to the soothing, serene tongue of the wise. It wards off violence and guarantees community life: it is a tree of life. Life in the extended family is possible and a tree of life if there exists the protection of YHWH, a soothing tongue, and discipline.

Verses 8-11: This text is important theologically. It is developed through three stages of thought:

religion as observance (prayer and sacrifice);
life in general (a path with discipline and justice);
God's judgment.

God's eyes see all (v. 3) and God's judgment decides all: it is God who weighs the human heart.

Verses 12-19: There are two ways to communicate: from a happy, discerning, cheerful heart that leads to knowledge and community, or from a cynical, foolish, angry heart that leads to heartache, oppression, and violence.

3. The Role of Wisdom (15:20–17:24)

Wisdom is a discernment whose source is poverty. This theological reflection owes much to the prophet Zephaniah. Poverty is the way of the wise before their God.

A. The Discipline of Poverty, 15:20-33

Verses 20-24: This section once again contrasts the wise and the foolish son. Wisdom comes from discerning in a community that leads one to an adequate ethical response. And understanding keeps one on the straight path. *Verse 25:* The Lord tears down the house of the proud but protects the land belonging to the widow (Prov 22:28; 23:10-11; Deut 19:14; Luke 1:51-54). *Verses 26-28:* God is revealed as the judge of our thoughts: the heart of the just is pleasing to God, who detests the wicked and the greedy. *Verses 29-32:* God is here mentioned for the third time. God is present in the prayers of the just and distant from the wicked. God's presence brings joy and health. Discipline, rebuke, and correction help educate our desire and lead us to understanding. *Verse 33:* Wisdom is defined as a discipline whose source is poverty and whose end is honor (Zeph 2:3).

B. The Role of Wisdom, 16:1-33

Wisdom can be described as a light that comes from the power of God and directs human liberty in the discernment of what is good and what leads to the fullness of life. *Verses 1-5:* The Lord directs all human acts and projects. The image of God weighing our motives comes from Egypt: God is the source of our discernment. *Verses 6-9:* The role of Wisdom in the human heart is to lead us to the values of the covenant (love and faithfulness) and to help us understand that true discernment is not only a process of human intelligence but depends on God's gift to us. *Verses 10-15:* This section on the just king could be a memory of the much respected King Josiah. The people of the post-exilic age also longed for a just king to help them build a new society.

Verses 16-20: Wisdom generates intelligence and poverty brings us the discernment that frees us from destruction. *Verses 21-24:* The wise heart is discerning and is a fountain of understanding. Fools, however, long for folly; they are negative and destructive. *Verses 25-31:* The path to death is made up of quarrels and violence, but the good work hard and have a long life. *Verses 32-33:* The text ends by concluding that the patient and serene do more to build up cities than do warriors. The ancients cast lots to know the future but the wise know that it is in the hands of God.

C. Overcoming Conflict, 17:1-20

This text speaks of the role of religious sacrifice in the midst of social violence. Sacrifice overcomes violence and makes social and community life possible. *Verses 1-8:* When religious sacrifice is in crisis, violence dominates society and destroys the identity of people and of groups. *Verses 9-13:* Violence destroys friendships. The only way to overcome it is to do good to those who do evil to you. *Verses 14-18:* God's will is love. Violence is the negation of love. Those who love at all times and are united in adversity destroy dissension and violence. *Verses 19-20:* Those who continue on the way of violence invite destruction and ruin.

4. Wisdom is Liberation (17:21–19:26)

Wisdom prepares us for a life of honor in solidarity because it frees us from violence and destruction.

A. The Just are Different from the Wicked, 17:21–18:3

Verses 17:21–18:3: A household disintegrates when it no longer distinguishes among wisdom, ignorance, and injustice. The unfriendly look out for their own interests; they deny wisdom and pervert justice. They lead the household to shame and disgrace. Wise children of serene spirit build a household with intelligence and restraint.

B. The Free Act, 18:4-21

When we are free our desire repels violence and builds community. *Verses 4-5:* Deep waters refer to an unending source of discernment that comes from within human beings (Jer 2:13; 17:8-10). *Verses 6-9:* Evil words and acts reveal a person's inner being. *Verses 10-11:* A contrast is drawn between the security of those who trust in the name of the Lord and that of the wealthy who trust in riches. The prophet Habakkuk speaks of the strong tower that saves us from violence (Hab 2:8, 12, 17; 3:13).

Verses 12-14: Verse 12 is the center of this narrative. Zephaniah insists that only the poor will be free (Zeph 1:18). *Verses 15-21:* This text returns to the discerning heart and its power to discipline desire. This heart leads us to do what is good. Once again eating refers to the act that liberates desire in the right direction.

C. Doing the Will of God, 18:22–19:26

This text gives us seven concrete examples of doing God's will:

18:22: A wife is a sign of God's will and when there is love the household will flourish.

18:23–19:4: The poor may be despised by society but they are loved by God. The Sages follow deuteronomistic theology. For them the treatment given to the poor is the heart of discernment.

19:5-8: This text condemns false witness (which destroys the concept of justice) and continues to speak of how society treats the poor.

19:9-12: False witness is again criticized because of its importance for local justice. It is placed in relation to the king because in God's name he is the defender of justice, especially for the poor.

19:13-17: The foolish son, the quarrelsome wife, and the sluggard bring down a household. But a prudent wife is a gift from God.

19:18-23: Human beings long for unfailing love. Faith in the Lord will bring them love and life. This is the heart of God's will.

19:24-26: The sluggard and the cynical deny God's will. They cause shame, destruction, and dishonor.

5. The Fruit of Justice and Poverty (19:27–22:16)

Wisdom frees us so that we may know the fruits of justice and poverty because she gives us access to life and honor.

A. 19:27–20:1

These verses show us how wisdom is rejected. The words directed to "my son" interrupt the unit about the cynic. This is taken up again in v. 28. The cynic mocks justice and can be compared to the corrupt Belial of Deuteronomy (10:17-18; 17:2). The wine of the cynic leads astray (Hab 2:5); it is a denial of wisdom. The wicked gulp down evil and desire violence.

B. The King as the Measure of Human Action, 20:2-9

The negative part of this measure comes from those who anger the king, who are quick to quarrel and lazy. The positive side is presented by the king who winnows out evil, making discernment possible for the just. They walk in integrity. All human beings face the tension in v. 9: who can say "I have made my heart clean; I am pure from my sin"?

C. YHWH Inclines Human Action Toward Justice, 20:10-19

God's will judges and gives meaning to integrity in commerce (vv. 10-12); at work (v. 13); in fraud (vv. 14-17); in counsel (v. 18); in secrecy (v. 19).

D. The Lamp of the Lord, 20:20–21:1

The Lord searches our spirit and determines our action in cursing our parents (v. 20); in longing for inheritance (v. 21); in vengeance (v. 22); in commerce (v. 23); in all human acts (vv. 24-25). Since human acts are illuminated by the light of the Lord's presence no one can discern correctly without God (v. 24).

Verses 20:26–21:4: The wise king screens out evil among his subjects and punishes the wicked (Isa 28:27-28). Human motivation, however, is judged by YHWH. The closer the king keeps to the spirit of the covenant (love and faithfulness) the more secure are his nation and his throne. Young kings have strength and old ones have experience. Proverbs 21:1 returns to Prov 16:1-15. The heart of the king is in God's hand and is directed by God.

E. God Weighs Our Hearts, 21:2-11

God directs our actions on a path that is right and just and leads to uprightness. The way of the guilty is devious, but vv. 2, 3, 5 show the positive influence of God in human life. We must be converted to justice and poverty (Zeph 2:1-3). Conversion is a liberation from violence to discernment.

F. God is Just and Justifies Human Action, 21:12-21

God judges the wicked and causes the downfall of their house. Justice frees us from death.

The household is built up with actions that assuage anger, give joy to the righteous, present the family with a choice of foods and life, prosperity, and honor. Those who live in this household are fulfilled.

G. The Fruit of Justice, 21:22-31

This is the main theme of this unit that ends by presenting again the ways of the wise and the wicked. The wise reach integration in their lives. The wicked disintegrate because they cannot accept the wisdom of the Lord.

H. The Conclusion, 22:1-16

The text ends by presenting four sayings about YHWH (vv. 2, 4, 12, 14), six about wealth and poverty (vv. 1, 2, 4, 7, 9, 16), two about the education of children (vv. 6, 15) and one about the importance of knowledge (v. 12). The focal point at the beginning and end is wealth/poverty. The fruit of human action is judged in the light of poverty (Zeph 2:3).

Verses 1-4: Integrity is found in a good name. It comes from poverty and the fear of God and leads to prosperity, honor, and life. Verse 4 is the vision of the rural population at the end of the monarchy. They lived lives of poverty with deep faith in God. For them their future was guaranteed by their way of living. *Verses 5-8:* Once again we read a description of the path of the wicked. *Verses 9-11:* When our lives are blessed we are generous in word and in act. *Verses 12-14:* The effectiveness of God's action: the eyes of God are above all other authority. The sluggard and the Other Woman are presented as examples of lives that lead to no good. The mention of these two figures comes from the editor who wants to tie this section in with the Prologue (Prov 6:9-11, 26; 7:5). *Verses 15-16:* The collection ends with two of its themes: children must be disciplined; the rich cannot oppress the poor.

III. The Sayings of the Wise

This collection is composed of three units: one is an instruction that can be compared with texts of Egyptian wisdom, especially those of Amen-em-ope (22:17–23:11). Another collection is similar to the Assyrian teachings on Ahiqar (23:12–24:22) The third synthesizes the social role of wisdom (24:23-34). This booklet originated among the Sages linked to the deuteronomistic reform and to Jeremiah (8:8; 18:18; 36:10). It seems to be a manual of discipline used by the elders to guarantee justice at the gates of the city and in the daily life of the householders (Jer 26:17; Deut 21:2, 19). Wisdom protects the people, beginning in the rural households (Prov 24:3-6) against those who plot violence. God is the liberator/redeemer of the poor (Prov 23:11). The figure of God/*gō᾿el* is the center of this booklet, and in the present edition of the book of Proverbs it is the center of the whole book. It relates God to the theology of Exod 6:1-7 and Job 19:25-29.

1. Introduction (22:17-21)

For a long time the term thirty was read into v. 20 and interpreted as dependence on the Teachings of Amen-em-ope which are divided into thirty sayings. Today few accept so direct an influence on our text. Verse 21 indicates the social function of this collection in a society structured on obedience to God and the king (Prov 24:21). Wisdom's teaching is true and forms the basis for the justice the poor seek at the gates of the city (Jer 22:16-17; Deut 19:12, 18; 21:19).

2. Ten Commandments of the Wise (22:22–23:11)

These ten commandments are oriented to God/*gō᾿el* (Prov 23:11), the redeemer of the poor and the needy (Zeph 3:12-14). Its themes are a guide to the spirit of the deuteronomistic reform: the oppression of the poor; association with the violent; security for debts; changing ancient land boundaries; slavery; meals with the stingy; conversation with fools; encroaching on the fields of orphans.

3. Parental Discipline (23:12-36)

In the second unit (23:12–24:22) there are five well-defined sayings (23:12-18; 23:19; 23:22-26; 24:3-4; 24:13-14) distributed through the next three parts (nos. 3, 4, and 5).

Verses 12-18: The first saying is typical of instruction given to a son. *Verses 19-21:* He must fear the Lord, avoid wine (Jeremiah 35, the Rechabites), and not be a glutton (Deut 21:18-21). *Verses 22-26:* By discipline the son's heart is transformed and he is led to live in the spirit of truth in the covenant. *Verses 27-28:* The son should avoid the prostitute and the foreigner/outsider. In the context of the covenant this could be a saying against idolatry and a defense of the patrimony of the household (Deut 22:21-30; Prov 29:3). *Verses 29-36:* Another saying against wine in the style of the Rechabites (Jer 35:2, 5). The description of a drunken state is very ironic but written with great poetic art.

4. The Power of Wisdom (24:1-12)

The fourth saying presents Wisdom as a power that saves the lives of the people. *Verses 1-2:* This is an appeal to avoid the violent. *Verses 3-4:* Wisdom maintains the household (Prov 14:1). *Verses 5-6:* Again deuteronomistic thought appears in this popular advice (Prov 12:15; 13:10) and in the hope of a people's war whose ideology the deuteronomist restored (Deut 20:1-5). *Verses 7-12:* The text concludes with a word about the excellence of Wisdom. God weighs our hearts, guards our lives, and repays each person according to what he or she has done.

5. A Project for the Future (24:13-22)

This fifth saying teaches the path to a happy future. *Verses 13-22:* Correct discernment, resistance to the wicked, mercy for a fallen enemy, and having God's justice as our reference are the guarantees of a happy future. The last two verses of this saying are deuteronomistic: YHWH and the king are the center of the nation (Jer 22:16-17). The LXX translates Prov 24:21: Do not revolt against one or the other.

6. A Synthesis (24:23-34)

Verse 23 indicates that this is an independent saying. We find here a series of anonymous sentences that form a synthesis about the social function of Wisdom. *Verses 23-25:* Wisdom is discernment between innocence and guilt. *Verses 26-27:* This is a delightful analogy of truth: it is like a kiss on the lips! Once again Wisdom praises the outdoor life: take care of your fields and build your own house. *Verses 28-29:* Words against false witness and the retribution of evil. *Verses 30-34:* The sluggard (Prov 6:6-11) is the last figure in the synthesis, the one who causes the destruction of the household and serves as a lesson to the wise.

IV. The Second Collection of the Proverbs of Solomon

This collection has as its principal themes justice (Proverbs 25–27) and poverty (Proverbs 28–29). Proverbs 25–27 originated in the court of King Hezekiah. After the fall of Samaria collections of sayings and comparisons were brought from the northern kingdom and applied to the kingdom of Judah. The collection is made up of commandments (positive and negative) and of comparisons interspersed with paronomasia (that is, assonance, alliteration, rhyme and wordplay, including verbal repetition). Society is judged from the perspective of the king's court and has as its center the concept of honor: God's, the king's, and the just one's (Prov 25:2-3, 26-27). Proverbs 25 seems to be an independent literary unit in the style of Egyptian Wisdom. It begins (vv. 2-3) and ends (v. 27b) with the concept of honor.

1. God and the King (25:1-3)

The text begins with two antitheses that are the basis of society. God is sovereign and implements the divine designs in history (Isa 29:14). It is the role of the king and the Sages to discern God's designs (Isa 5:20-21; 31:1-3). God's authority is absolute. That of the king is always relative and dependent. *Verse 3:* The king seems to be as inaccessible as the heavens but his role is to investigate and then explain his decisions and acts. This contrasting vision of God and the king prepares the way for the deuteronomistic theology (Deut 17:18, 20).

2. Justice and the Throne (25:4-8)

This text begins with demands and explanations intertwined. These commandments and prohibitions are directed toward human behavior. *Verses 4-5:* The silversmith can only work well with silver that has no impurities. Politics must follow this principle of art. Justice is the creative source of society. A king must purify his court of all wickedness. The stability of the government is based on this principle.

Verses 6-7: These verses are based on very ancient proverbs that warn not to praise oneself in the presence of the king or occupy the places reserved for the mighty. In its present form this saying is similar to that of Jesus in Luke 14:7-

11: if you occupy the lowest places at the banquet you will be invited to sit nearer to your host! *Verse 8:* In the same line one should not take haste in broadcasting others' faults and then be shamed oneself.

3. The Attitude of the Sage (25:9-15)

This text presents five points to promote communication: *Verses 9-11:* All true converse is based on justice. We must argue our case without betraying the confidences of others. Betrayal puts an end to communication. The last verse underlines the power of the spoken word. To say the right word at the right moment is like apples of gold in a setting of silver. *Verse 12:* Among the wise a reprimand that brings one back to the path of justice deepens communication. *Verse 13:* Here the role of the messenger is given importance. In this monarchical society the large property owners send messengers to the peasants working on their lands. Their delight is to find a faithful messenger. *Verse 14:* Boasting is another obstacle to communication. No one believes in a person who promises much and delivers little. *Verse 15:* The text ends with a theme dear to the Sages. A patient and serene tongue persuades rulers and is powerful enough to break bones!

4. Love Your Enemy (25:16-22)

This unit presents the high point of relationship to the neighbor. *Verses 16-17:* These are two typical examples of popular proverbs with parallel terms. To eat a little honey and make few visits to your neighbor's house creates an equilibrium. Too much honey makes you sick and too much of you leaves your neighbor ill! *Verses 18-19:* To give false witness is a denial of justice that destroys relationships. In a crisis to have a traitor by your side is a catastrophe. *Verses 20-22:* For the Sages these verses are the heart of ethical action. The first verse shows the destructive side of relationships, but vv. 21-22 present the essence of the love commandment. Love transforms relationships and pleases God. This text is quoted by Paul in Rom 12:10. It is also cited in Matt 5:44.

5. The Resistance of the Just (25:23-28)

The just person searches for the type of honor that will make community life possible. *Verses 23-24:* Once again we begin with the negative. A backbiting tongue and a quarrelsome woman destroy family and community life. Verse 24 repeats Prov 21:9. *Verses 25-26:* The ancient proverb that gave origin to v. 25 seems to have been "Like cold water in a dry throat is good news from abroad." Once again as in v. 13 this is an affirmation that things can change and life can be renewed. The comparison in v. 26 shows how the just must be strong so as not to be overcome by the wicked. *Verses 27-28:* Verse 27 returns to the theme of honey (v. 16). In the Hebrew text this verse ends with the phrase: researching their honor brings honor. Verse 28 affirms that people without self control are like a city whose walls are broken down and that has no defenses (Isa 1:7).

Proverbs 26

The Sages analyze society from the perspective of three antithetical models. None of the three has honor, which is essential for a wise life.

1. The Dullard is Always Coarse (26:1–12)

The Hebrew root for dullard suggests a person whose spirit is thick and impermeable. Its origin is ancient and comes from rural areas. The city, however, preferred the term fool (vv. 2, 4-5, 11-12), which is most frequently contrasted with the ideal of the wise.

Proverbs 26 presents seven aspects of the dullard:

- v. 1: Honor is as incompatible with the life of the dullard as snow in the summertime.
- v. 3: The dullard acts only when forced to do so and must be pushed on to act as if he or she were an animal.
- v. 6: Whoever uses a dullard as a messenger will see the dullard cause violence and will suffer it oneself.
- v. 7: The dullard is incapable of understanding the comparison made in a proverb.
- v. 8: Attributing honor to a dullard is like entangling a stone in your sling.
- v. 9: Dullards are so thick that the beauty of a comparison is lost on them.
- v. 10: Dullards will cause violence wherever they work.
- vv. 11-12: This synthesis speaks of the dullard, the fool, and the sage.

2. The Sluggard (26:13-16)

This text is a collection of humorous sayings about the sluggard interrupted by two sayings repeated from other chapters. *Verse 13:* Repeats Prov 22:13. The sluggard is treated with irony. *Verse 14:* The sluggard has no initiative. Like a door swinging on its hinges, the sluggard accomplishes nothing. *Verse 15* is a repetition of Prov 19:24. *Verse 16:* The sluggard presents a real danger for the community. Such people imagine they are more intelligent than the wise. The Sages know that a society cannot be built without intelligence and work. The sluggard wants to escape reality by dreaming in bed.

3. The Malicious (26:17-28)

Verses 17-28 are a collection of sayings about people who destroy community and society especially by means of a malicious tongue. The first part of the text speaks of the evil of quarreling (vv. 17-21) and the second part (vv. 22-26) concentrates on pernicious gossiping. The third part is a conclusion (vv. 27-28) for these sayings and for the chapter as a whole. *Verse 17:* True justice is the result of discernment by the community (at the gates of the city). The malicious meddle in other people's quarrels intending to cause more trouble. *Verses 18-21:* The malicious are destructive and evil-minded. They speak with venom to destroy the confidence that is necessary for solidarity and concord. They create suspicion, despair, and alienation. They light the flame of dissension (v. 21). They are bitter, rancorous, and at times vicious. They are incapable of living in society. *Verses 22-26:* The really evil cover their malice with soft words. Verse 25 warns not to be fooled by charming words. Eventually all this evil will be exposed in the assembly. *Verses 27-28:* In these cases what is retribution? It is self-destruction. The traps that are laid for others will end by trapping the trappers, whose lying tongue is a sign of the hatred that fills their being.

Proverbs 27

Love is the heart of discernment in the present and in the future.

1. Friendship (27:1-4)

Wisdom leads us to friendship. It is the fulfillment of our desire for reciprocal love in the present moment. The text begins by emphasizing the importance of the present moment (v. 1) and the necessity of depending on the judgment of others. Provocation by fools, anger, and jealousy destroy friendships.

2. The Context of Friendship (27:5-10)

Human fulfillment is found in friendship. The sayings on friendship in vv. 5, 6, 9 are related to Prov 17:17 and 18:24. The text begins with a wisdom theme: it is better to rebuke a friend than to make believe you do not like him or her. A friend can hurt us and still care for us, but false affection from an enemy is dangerous. Verse 7 returns to the theme of honey, but in this context it refers to human need. When we are deprived, even what is bitter tastes sweet. The saying in v. 8 develops the sense of need in v. 7. Everyone needs a circle of friendship, a source of life and security for the future. This unit ends by saying that human beings cannot live in isolation. The counsel of our friends and the help of our neighbors bring us happiness and strength.

3. The Sage's Attitude (27:11-17)

This unit is a collection of parental instructions. *Verses 11-12:* The Sage is astute but the young are often gullible (Prov 1:1-7). The astute and the gullible are two types we meet in daily life. The term prudent *(ʿārūm)* in v. 12 is a paronomasia with the term for depositing a pledge *(ʿārab)* in v. 13.

Verses 13-17: These verses are warnings about what should be avoided in post-exilic society: depositing a pledge for a foreigner, especially a foreign woman (Prov 6:1-5; 20:16); hypocrisy (Prov 26:23-26); a quarrelsome wife (Prov 18:22).

4. Honor and Fulfillment (27:18-22)

These verses are about the perfection of honor that comes to human beings and society through the value of work that is well done. *Verses 18-22:* This unit begins with one of the most quoted proverbs in the collection. The first part of v. 18 is an ancient rural proverb that insists on the peasant's right to the fruits of his or her own production. In such a society the workers are honored. The second part of the verse was written in the royal court and presents a society of forced labor where the fruits of production belong in the first place to the rulers of that society. Verse 19 reflects the thought in v. 17: it is an allusion to the imitative tendency of human desire (Prov 30:15-16). The interaction of our human desires either destroys us or fulfills us. The eyes of v. 20 are also an expression of never-ending human desire (Qoh 2:10; 4:8). The last two verses of this unit contrast the attitude of the person who is transformed like gold in a furnace with fools who, no matter what they pass through, are committed to their folly.

5. True Security Comes from Work and Production (27:23-27)

This last paragraph is a picture of the agricultural life in Judah in the eighth century B.C.E. *Verses 23-27:* A rural household depends on its production. The process is presented from the perspective of the court and the taxes that will maintain the crown economically. The court is interested in stable production. Herds of cattle existed in Judah, but this text speaks of the peasant who only raises sheep and goats and the hay they need to survive. This description is close to other biblical texts that date from or analyze this era and its society (Isa 5:8-24; Mic 2:1-3; Prov 25:1).

Proverbs 28

The second part of this collection (Proverbs 28–29) was edited in the post-exilic period. This is made clear by certain indications in the text. The division of Scripture into three parts: the Law, the Prophets, and the Writings (Prov 29:18-19) comes from the post-exilic period. There is also a mention of the custom of reading the Law in the synagogues. The theme of the strong opposition between the just and the wicked (found also in Psalm 1) is also from this later date. Another later theme is that of confidence in a future guaranteed by the Davidic throne (Prov 29:1-4, 7, 14). These indications make it clear that there was a post-exilic rereading of the text, but it is also possible to see intermingled in it a more ancient text written in a time of oppression and hope.

The description of the oppression of God's poor people places the text near to the teaching of the prophet Zephaniah (Zeph 2:1-3; 3:12-14). The context of the booklet suggests a crisis in the rule of Manasseh (2 Kings 21:16). The Sages who reflect on this crisis have the mentality and ideology that existed in the era of Hezekiah and Josiah and in the writings of Jeremiah (Jer 8:8-9; 36:12). Wisdom begins to be identified with the Law. The rural poor, suffering under the heavy taxes of Manasseh (Prov 29:4, 7, 14), have hope for political and social changes. They criticize the state that is destroying farm life and rural households (Prov 28:24). They long to be free (Prov 28:1, 18) and to receive God's judgment in favor of themselves and against their proud oppressors (Prov 29:1-7, 23, 26).

1. The Hope of Liberation (28:1-5)

The term "revolt" *(pēshaᶜ)* is used seven times in these chapters. It appears for the first time in 28:2 and gives unity to this second part of the collection. *Verse 1:* The wicked flee even when no one chases them. The just, who trust in God, are as bold as lions. *Verse 2:* Here an unstable political situation is described. The term "revolt" appears and gives the tone to the rest of the text. *Verse 3:* When a rich person becomes poor and then begins to oppress those who are even poorer he or she becomes a destructive force. *Verse 4:* This verse describes the group that supports the wicked: they are those who ignore the Law and want no changes in the oppressive situation. They are opposed by those who keep the Law and struggle against all that is evil. These terms are typical of the deuteronomistic theology: ignoring the Law (Deut 28:20; Hos 4:10; Jer 9:13; 16:11; 17:13; 22:9) and keeping the Law (Deut 4:6; 5:1, 29; 6:3; 7:11-12). *Verse 5:* The conclusion contrasts the wicked and the just. The evil will never understand justice, but those who seek it diligently will understand it completely.

2. The Basic Conflict (28:6-11)

The basic conflict is between the rich and the poor. In this case the rich are wicked and the poor are just. *Verse 6:* Poverty with integrity is compared with an empty life lived in wealth. *Verse 7:* Parental instruction is important, but that of YHWH gives us an illuminating wisdom. *Verse 8:* Wealth is not necessarily evil. It is not incompatible with generosity and compassion.

This proverb, however, implies that great fortunes can come from exorbitant interest on loans. Only the next generation has the possibility of living justly with the poor. *Verses 9-10:* Many see in this text a reference to the reading of the Law in the synagogues. What is the place of the Law in the scale of religious values? If one does not intend to obey God's will it is foolish to pretend to pray. *Verse 10* presents the destiny of the just and the wicked. *Verse 11:* This whole chapter contrasts the great difference between rich and poor (vv. 6, 8, 11, 20, 22, 25, 27). Discernment here is the search for YHWH. The wicked are now defined as being self-sufficient and not submitting themselves to either God or the divine Law. The poor have a spiritual penetration that permits them to see through the self-sufficiency of the rich and leave them secure.

3. The Center of Oppression (28:12-18)

The term revolt *(pēshaᶜ)* now appears again to indicate the center of oppression. The text suggests the reign of King Manasseh and the oppression of the poorest peasants (vv. 15-18; Zeph 3:12-14).

Verse 12: This unit begins as an antithesis between the just and the wicked. The effect on the population is remarkable. They rejoice when the just are in power and go into hiding when the wicked triumph. *Verse 13:* This is the only verse in Proverbs that refers to the confession of sins (cf. Ps 32:5). It is a prophetic saying that expresses the milieu of religious resistance in the reign of Manasseh. *Verse 14:* The fear of the Lord is a blessing, but those who harden their hearts against the poor do not fear the Lord.

Verse 15: The four verses that begin here are a description of an evil ruler and his court (Prov 29:26). He treats his people as if he were a roaring lion or a charging bear. Very different is this from the hope of the just that makes them as strong as lions (28:1). *Verse 16:* An oppressor loses judgment. Abuse of power is a form of stupidity. Sooner or later this power is destroyed. *Verse 17:* Murderers are judged by YHWH. They will be fugitives on earth until they die. *Verse 18:* Once again we are confronted with the path of justice and the way of the wicked. The two choices express the radical motivation that is within the human person. We become what our decisions make of us.

4. Hope and Disintegration (28:19-23)

In this unit we have the third repetition of the term revolt *(pēshaᶜ)*. It expresses the depth of disintegration that has marked the lives of the peasants (vv. 19-20). *Verse 19:* This verse is almost identical to Prov 12:11. It is a description of rural life and the situation of the poor in the tributary system (high taxes to maintain royalty). The just take this up as their cause and their hope for the future. They are convinced that the future lies with the land and that the people should not risk their futures in commerce and other financial transactions. *Verse 20:* This is an appeal for social responsibility. To be wealthy and at the same time to have integrity, to be able to live in solidarity with the poor: this is the ideal of the Sages.

Verse 21: This verse refers to justice at the gates of the city. Justice is destroyed by partiality and by tempting poor witnesses with food. *Verse 22:* Those with an evil eye are so eager to get rich that they cannot see that poverty will also strike them. *Verse 23:* This verse is similar to Prov 27:5, 14. Truth in friendship will always win out.

5. Oppression and Hope (28:24-28)

Revolt *(pēshaᶜ)* is now used for the fourth time to describe the climax of the situation of oppression. *Verse 24:* The consequences of oppression reach within the peasant household, turning the children against their parents. *Verses 25-26:* These verses express confidence in YHWH who will keep the just safe and prosperous in the midst of greed and dissension. *Verse 27:* Deuteronomist theology influences this verse. Give to those who have become poor (Prov 28:3, 6) or you will be cursed (Deut 27:16; 28:16). *Verse 28:* This conclusion is a refrain from Prov 28:12. For the just to be able to thrive, the oppressors must perish.

Proverbs 29

The hope of the people is in a Davidic king who will defend the rights of the poor and bring prosperity to the land (Prov 29:4, 7, 14).

1. Hope for the Davidic King (29:1-5)

From the depths of oppression the population longs for a king who will establish justice and liberate the poor (Isa 11:4-5). *Verse 1:* This verse compares a stiff-necked person who accepts no correction to the kingdom of Judah. Obstinate people do not change their ways because they are rebuked. Judah also will only change its ways when it faces destruction and there is no other remedy. The word used here for destruction *(shēbēr)* is typical of Zeph 1:18; Isa 1:27-28; 30:13; Jer 4:6, 20; 6:1). *Verse 2:* This is the same refrain found in Prov 28:12, 28. Under oppression the people groan, but when the just resist transgression and struggle to free the population from injustice the people will rejoice. *Verse 3:* The situation in Judah is compared to a son who wastes the patrimony of the household in running after prostitutes (Isa 1:21; Prov 23:27). *Verse 4:* The defense of justice and of human rights is the cornerstone of the new society the Sages hope to build. This verse echoes the prophecy of Nathan (2 Sam 7:8-14). The figure of the Davidic king represents the population's desire for peace and prosperity. *Verse 5:* Here is one more allusion to the oppression in the reign of Manasseh (Prov 28:15). The comparison between flattery and a trap is a description of the court and the general spread of misanthropy.

2. The Great Conflict (29:6-10)

Our key word "revolt" *(pēshaᶜ)* is now used for the fifth time. The group of the wicked direct their action against the city of Jerusalem (Isa 28:14, 17). *Verses 6-7:* These first two sayings present the action of the just in the prophetic language of Jer 22:15-17 and Isa 10:1-2. The just act like the ideal prophetic king who cares about justice for the poor. *Verses 8-10:* This is the heart of the conflict in the city of Jerusalem. The groups that want to destroy the city are described through three figures: the mocker, the fool, and the bloodthirsty. Hope for the future of the city depends on the action of the wise: they must turn away anger, judge the fools in the court, and struggle against the bloodthirsty, defending the lives of the just.

3. The Climax of Hope (29:11-14)

YHWH is revealed in the struggle between the poor and the oppressors (v. 13). The throne of YHWH's king will be built on justice. *Verse 11:* Giving vent to anger is the sign of a fool. The wise, given time, calm anger. Fools are slaves of their impulses. The wise work to control violence by enlightening the population and helping to solve social problems. *Verse 12:* This is an allusion to the wicked ruler (Prov 28:15-16; 29:26). The climate of the court is one of deceit and falsehood (Jer 8:8; 18:18). *Verse 13:* The rich and the poor have the same rights because they have the same Creator (Prov 22:2; 14:31; Job 31:15). *Verse 14:* A king secures his throne with justice (Isa 11:1-5; 16:1-4; Prov 16:12; 20:28; 25:4-5). The Sages know that real hope is based on justice (Jer 23:1-4).

4. The Means for Change (29:15-21)

Verses 15-17: For the Sages the principal means for change is discipline (Prov 24:13-14; 19:18). The other means is in the group of the just who must multiply because they are the hope of the people. For the sixth time revolt *(pēshaᶜ)* is used in relation to the wicked who are multiplying. *Verses 18-21:* In this unit the instruments for change are prophecy, the Law, and the sayings of the wise (Jer 18:18). The Sages at this moment are beginning to see the unity of revelation. They are already treating the Law and prophecy as a unit (Hos 12:11; Ezek 7:26; Lam 2:9). In the deuteronomistic period the sayings of the wise will also be included as revelation.

When prophecy is lacking in a nation the people have lost their spiritual guides. They must fall back on the written Law, a permanent witness of the divine will. The words of the wise are not enough to bring about change. There must be discipline. For the Sages, pampering makes fools even of the most intelligent.

5. God's Judgment (29:22-27)

Verse 22: Revolt *(pēshaᶜ)* is used for the seventh and last time to describe the action of the angry and the hot-tempered. Uncontrolled wrath is the source of revolt. *Verse 23:* Pride leads to humiliation, but the humble obtain honor (Isa 2:6-17). Honor is an important theme of the collection in Proverbs 25–29. God's judgment reveals that before we can obtain honor, we must become poor (Prov 15:33; Zeph 3:12-14).

Verses 24-26: These three sayings are united by the alternative they present: we can trust in thieves and kings or in YHWH who frees us from injustice and leads us to safety (Prov 28:1, 25). *Verse 27:* In this conclusion of the Second Collection of the Proverbs of Solomon we return to the choice of the two ways of life: either justice or evil.

V. Epilogue: Wisdom and Life

The Obedient Sage (Proverbs 30)

The Latin Vulgate translates Agur as the one who unites, understanding the phrase to refer to Solomon. He is the son of Jakeh, the one who disperses, understood to refer to David. This intuition that Agur should be understood symbolically has led interpreters to read The Sayings of Agur as a mashal (comparison) of the figure of the Sage, who is presented as being very similar to Job (Job 17:6; Pss 49:4; 120:5; 15:1).

This chapter is symmetrical: it includes a confession (vv. 1-3) and a final prayer (vv. 7-9). These two texts are a frame for two enigmas. The first is the recognition of human frailty and ignorance (v. 4) and the second is a concern for the proper acknowledgment of God (vv. 5-6). Verses 10-14 form a practical conclusion.

1. Agur's Prayer, 30:1-3

The most likely Hebrew root for Jakeh means to be pious or obedient. The modifier "son of Jakeh" presents Agur as an obedient man offering the following collection of sayings. In the first verse Agur presents an oracle and an announcement. These two terms come from the prophetic vocabulary *(masā'; na'um).* They are also found in Num 24:3, 15; 2 Sam 23:1). The translation of this verse is controversial. In Hebrew it is very close to the beginning of Jer 20:9 and Ps 73:22 (I was stupid and ignorant; I was like a brute beast toward you). As a prophetic prayer this verse is understood by many to say "I am weary, O God, I am weary, O God. How can I prevail? Surely I am too stupid to be human; I do not have human understanding. I have not learned wisdom, nor have I knowledge of the [Holy One]." This proposed translation fits well with vv. 2-3 and is a reflection of a theme common in wisdom literature: all human beings and their intelligence are limited in relation to God's great wisdom (Job 11:8-9; Prov 3: 5-7). *Verse 2:* This verse also reflects the book of Job with its constant search for the true meaning of wisdom and of the name of God (Job 38). *Verse 3:* When the word "holy" is used in the plural (Prov 9:10) it refers to God, the source, the measure, and the end of all wisdom. For Agur wisdom is a partial answer but he longs for knowledge of the Holy One.

2. The Unfathomable Enigma, 30:4

Verse 4: These six questions surround the mystery of God and God's holy name. According to 2 Sam 22:31, what human investigation could not understand has been revealed by God.

3. The Word of God, 30:5-6

Verses 5-6: This text is a composite of David's victory song in 2 Sam 22:31 and Moses' discourse in Deuteronomy 4:2. The word of God is flawless; it is a shield for all who seek God's protection. Verse 6 answers Job's challenge in Job 24:25 (Deut 4:2; 12:32). Agur goes beyond this text ("do not add to these words") and warns that in that event God will reprove those who do and show them to be liars.

4. The Prayer of the Sage, 30:7-9

Verses 7-9: This prayer reflects Agur's sense of defenselessness and susceptibility. When God tests us we can only trust in the divine word. The prayer touches on two dangers: that of wealth and self-sufficiency and that of such extreme poverty that one is led to blasphemy.

5. Curses and Blessings, 30:10-14

Verses 10-14: The Sages are marked by their attitude to the poor (Prov 15:33). God hears the curse of badly treated servants and of all the poor when they are cruelly taken advantage of (vv. 10, 14). The Sage perceives that in the conflict of generations people curse their parents (v. 11); there are people whose piety turns them into hypocrites (v. 12) and there are people so proud they become overbearing (v. 13).

6. The Sages' Enigmas, 30:15-33

In this unit the literary device of numerical proverbs is used to synthesize the content of wisdom and the function of the Sages. It is worth noting here that Prov 31:10-31 uses the device of the alphabet to present a series of wisdom sayings. These literary forms were often used to teach children popular wisdom while they were learning their numbers and the alphabet.

Verses 15-16: Using the numbers two, three, and four, the mystery of Sheol (the afterlife) is presented as insatiable. *Verses 18-19:* These verses present the mystery of procreation and conception. *Verses 21-23:* Here we find four inversions of the values of the epoch that the author feels will lead to such arrogance that even the earth will not be able to tolerate it. *Verses 24-28:* The Sage points out the wisdom of nature and of animal life. *Verses 29-31:* Examples are given of four impressive figures: the king only comes after the lion, the strutting cock, and the he-goat! *Verses 17, 20* do not fit into any numerical pattern and are probably later additions. *Verses 32-33* present us with suggestions for leading a wise and tranquil life: be modest and do not stir up anger.

Proverbs 31

The book of Proverbs closes with the figure of Woman Wisdom in two scenes. The first is that of the mother and counselor of kings and the second that of the capable woman who administers and maintains a household and all those who dwell in it.

The Mother-Counselor and the King, 31:1-9.

Wisdom literature delights in paradoxes. A paradox, like its literary relation, the parable, makes people stop and think. From its very first chapters the book of Proverbs has warned against foreign/strange women, yet it concludes the whole collection by giving the next to last word to a foreign queen! The queen is the mother of King Lemuel (this is a foreign name that might mean "Lim is god"). She speaks to the son of her womb (v. 2) in an oracle that reflects the universal wisdom image of the ideal king (vv. 8-9). The king accepts her counsel because he respects her wisdom. He is king but she is part of the more powerful and transcendent concept of Woman as Wisdom personified.

Her counsels are typical. The king is not told to avoid women, but he is not to spend his strength on them. In the same vein he is told that as king he should not crave strong drink because it may make him forget his main function in ancient societies: to speak up for those who cannot speak for themselves, for the rights of all who are destitute. He is adjured to speak up and judge fairly, to defend the rights of the poor and the needy (vv. 8-9). It is interesting to note that the queen thinks the sick and the destitute may take strong drink to help them forget their problems, but this is not possible for a king.

The Strong Woman and Her Household, 31:10-31

The concluding unit of the book of Proverbs is an acrostic poem, that is, one that uses the letters of the Hebrew alphabet in succession at the beginning of each line. It presents Wisdom as the Strong Woman who is a fountain of life and stability for all her household. Several commentators have seen in this poem the instruction of a mother given to her daughter. The young woman learns the alphabet and at the same time is taught how to be indispensable in a patriarchal society.

This woman is presented in v. 10 as being *ḥayil,* a word our Bibles translate as virtuous, worthy, noble, perfect, or valiant. The same term is translated in v. 3 as strong and in v. 29 as admirable (cf. Ruth 3:11). In the rest of the Hebrew Bible the term is used almost always to refer to power and strength. We are speaking of a strong woman in a patriarchal society. In this world a woman is defined by society as the daughter, wife, or mother of men. On another level, however, Woman as Wisdom presents this housewife of post-exilic Judah as an ideal for all human beings. She is free, capable, wise, loving. She is the axis and the security of a large household. Her administration of this household is a projection of what post-exilic Judah could and should be. In this same text we have the traces of a socially limited woman and of a strong, fulfilled figure who is a model for humankind.

In Prov 9:1 Woman Wisdom builds her house. She offers many promises of a fulfilled way of living. In 31:10-31 Wisdom's household is established with happiness and success. This Woman, who fears the Lord, has built her life on wisdom (Prov 31:30; 1:7; 15:33). She is called a strong woman (vv. 10, 29) and is praised as Wisdom herself.

This text is one of the most interesting about life during that period. The large household that the Strong Woman administers is rural and includes an extended family and servants. She buys fields and plants vineyards. She manufactures and sells garments. She makes clothes out of the wool she herself has produced. Her family and servants are fed and clothed as the result of her organization. It is recognized that she deserves the fruits of her work (31:31). But above all this she is a person of strength and dignity (v. 25). She speaks with wisdom and teaches the Law *(tōrah)* of love and solidarity *(hesed)* (v. 26). She is universally admired. The elders praise her at the city gates (v. 31) and her husband and children bless her (v. 28).

The great themes of the book of Proverbs (see above) are fulfilled in this Woman:
She is a fountain and a sustainer of life;
She is the culmination of all the other Women/Wisdom figures;
She is an example of discernment in everyday life and in teaching love to her extended family;
She opens her arms to the poor and the needy;
Her teaching of love frees her family from mutual violence and firmly installs solidarity in her household (v. 26).

The book of Proverbs ends by presenting Woman Wisdom in much the same way as the Song of Songs presents the Shulammite (Song 6:9 = Prov 31:28). The Strong Woman and the woman full of peace (Shulammite/Shalom) both are the incarnation of Wisdom. As v. 29 states, "Many women have done excellently, but [Woman Wisdom] surpass[es] them all."

BIBLIOGRAPHY

Brenner, Athalya, and Fokkelien van Dijk-Hemmes. *On Gendering Texts.* BIS 1. Leiden: E. J. Brill, 1993.

Brenner, Athalya, ed. *A Feminist Companion to Wisdom Literature.* Sheffield: Sheffield Academic Press, 1995.

Camp, Claudia V. *Wisdom and the Feminine in the Book of Proverbs.* BLS 11. Sheffield: JSOT, 1985.

Crenshaw, James L. "The Sage in Proverbs," in John G. Gammie and Leo G. Perdue, eds., *The Sage in Israel and the Ancient Near East.* Winona Lake, Ind.: Eisenbrauns, 1990.

Farmer, Kathleen. *Proverbs and Ecclesiastes.* Grand Rapids: Eerdmans, 1991.

McKane, William. *Proverbs.* Philadelphia: Westminster, 1970.

Murphy, Roland E. *The Tree of Life.* ABRL. New York: Doubleday, 1990.

Newsom, Carol A. "Woman and the Discourse of Patriarchal Wisdom," in Peggy L. Day, ed., *Gender and Difference in Ancient Israel.* Minneapolis: Fortress, 1989.

Scott, R.B.Y. *Proverbs, Ecclesiastes.* AB 18. Garden City, N.Y.: Doubleday, 1965.

Washington, Harold C. "The Strange Woman of Proverbs 1–9 and Post-Exilic Judean Society," in Tamara C. Eskenazi and Kent H. Richards, eds., *Second Temple Studies 2. Temple and Community in the Persian Period.* JSOT.S 175. Sheffield: JSOT Press, 1994.

Westermann, Claus. *Roots of Wisdom: The Oldest Proverbs of Israel and Other Peoples.* Translated by J. Daryl Charles. Louisville: Westminster/John Knox, 1995.

Whybray, R. N. *Proverbs.* Grand Rapids: Eerdmans, 1994.

____. *The Composition of the Book of Proverbs.* JSOT.S 99. Sheffield: JSOT, 1994.

____. *Wealth and Poverty in the Book of Proverbs.* JSOT.S 99. Sheffield: JSOT, 1994.

Ecclesiastes

Antoon Schoors

FIRST READING

Getting Started

A reader who wishes to understand the following comments will find it most helpful, not to say necessary, to first read the book of Ecclesiastes itself. It is a rather short book that can easily be read in less than half an hour, but that would be too fast. An attentive reader needs some forty-five minutes to see the peculiar ideas and to sense the typical concise style of the book. If the reader does not have that much time he or she can get an idea of what Ecclesiastes is all about by reading chs. 1–2, but precisely this reader should read the whole book, which will teach him or her the relativity of many things, such as lack of time.

The Book as a Whole

Ecclesiastes—Qoheleth in Hebrew—is a short, difficult but fascinating book. Readers of the Bible who are used to the prophets or psalms cannot easily integrate this book into their idea of the Bible: it is so different that one can hardly believe it is part of the Bible.

Ecclesiastes is a wisdom book, comparable in form and content to Proverbs and Sirach. It was written in the Hellenistic Period (third to second centuries B.C.E.) and is one of the latest books in the OT. Although the term of address "my son" does not occur in the book proper as it does in Proverbs and Sirach, Qoheleth seems to have been a wisdom teacher who more than once addresses his pupil in the second person singular (5:1-9; 7:9-10, 13-22; 8:2-3; 9:7-10; 10:4, 20; 11:1-6) and Eccl 11:9–12:7 is directed to a "young man." Only the epilogist addresses the reader as "my son" (12:12).

In spite of much scholarly ingenuity it is not possible to detect a clear literary structure in the book, but there is no doubt that it has a thematic unity: the author is in search of an answer to the problem he poses in 1:3, "What do people gain from all the toil at which they toil under the sun?" The answer is: "None." Therefore Ecclesiastes begins and ends his book with a statement that everything is absurd (1:2 and 12:8). He does not try to explain away this reality but, as we shall see farther on, he presents enjoyment of life as the best though not the perfect solution.

Exegetes are not unanimous in characterizing Qoheleth's philosophy of life: he has been called an atheist, a pessimist, a skeptic, an Epicurean, but also an optimist, a believing or godfearing man. He is certainly a nonconformist and the best characterization of him is that he is a skeptic or even an agnostic in the etymological sense of the word: someone who confesses human ignorance of a number of ultimates and undermines all sorts of certainties (not a freethinker or an atheist). He is at the edge of faith but remains a searching believer; he asks many questions but gives few answers. But all this is meant for the best: he speaks honestly with a feeling of compassion for tormented humankind. His book often sounds very modern.

The thesis or, in other words, the anticipated conclusion of the book is presented in 1:2: "All is absurdity," which is traditionally rendered "All is vanity" (RSV, NRSV). The author does not "prove" his thesis in a logical exposition but instead offers various musings that reveal that absurdity. Therefore it is not necessary to read the whole book in the order of its final composition. It is advisable to read chs. 1–2 first because they set the stage for understanding the whole book. [For a different view see the article "Wisdom: A Way of Thinking About God."] The following pericopes can be read in a more or less arbitrary order except for 12:9-14, which is a double epilogue that seems to be from a different hand.

At first sight the book is full of contradictions or at least paradoxes, but this is due to the fact that Qoheleth quotes traditional wisdom in the form of proverbs that he then contests with other proverbs or with objections of his own making. This way he shows that any truth wisdom can attain has only a relative value; there is always a pro and a con and this again illustrates the absurdity of life.

His teaching can be summarized as follows: A human being lives only once, today; there is no morrow. Life is fixed in the laws of the world, in the inevitable, it is impossible to speak about future or hope. Therefore his practical advice is to enjoy life, for that joy is the gift of God.

Original Historical Contexts

Qoheleth wrote in the Hellenistic period (third to second centuries B.C.E.), an era of important change and progress in Judea's living conditions. The Jews came into contact with a world where doctrine was not in the hands of priests and prophets but of philosophers. These philosophers were mainly interested in right moral conduct: some found it in behavior according to a fixed world order (the Stoics); others taught that good and evil are not absolute but based on an agreement in society and therefore people should accept the prevailing opinion. Qoheleth himself is not a prophet but a "thinker"; he is not a preacher although since Luther his name has sometimes been so translated, but a teacher who like the Greek philosophers offers guidance to the public. He remains a Jew, of course, but the new conditions of life reveal their influence: he relativizes the growing prosperity and technical prowess; he pays attention to the individual and to the world in its totality, not only to the Jewish community, as is illustrated by the fact that he never uses the name of Israel's God, YHWH; he is critical of traditional ideas but of new ones as well.

Canonical Intertextuality

In spite of his originality Qoheleth is rooted in biblical tradition. He knows the Pentateuch: Eccl 5:3-5 is related to Deut 23:22-24; Eccl 12:7 refers to Gen 2:7; 3:19. He knows, of course, the traditional wisdom in the form of proverbs but he is critical of that approach. Ben Sirach manifestly knew and used the book about 180 B.C.E.

History of Reception

The rather negative approach to life in this book explains why there has been discussion in rabbinic Judaism about its canonicity. From the Mishna, the Jewish legal traditions codified about 200 C.E., we learn that the rabbis were divided as to whether or not the book of Ecclesiastes "makes the hands unclean," i.e., belongs to the sacred books (*Yadayim* iii.5). The Mishna decides positively, that Ecclesiastes makes the hands unclean, but it also reports rather extensively the dissension in certain rabbinic circles. The two great schools of Shammai and Hillel were divided on the subject, but the reason why the book is sometimes considered non-canonical is not always the same. Ecclesiastes does not make the hands unclean because it contains only the wisdom of Solomon (*Tosephta Yad* ii). In the Talmud we read "Solomon, where is your wisdom, where is your understanding? Not only do your words contradict the words of your father David, but they also contradict one another" (*Shabbat* 30a). The contradiction alluded to is between Eccl 4:2, "I thought the dead, who have already died, more fortunate than the living," and 9:4, "a living dog is better than a dead lion." Farther on in the same talmudic tractate it is said: "The sages wanted to 'hide' (i.e., to declare apocryphal) the book of Ecclesiastes, because its words contradicted each other. Why did they not 'hide' it? Because it begins with words of the Torah and it ends with words of the Torah." It begins with "What do people gain from all the toil at which they toil under the sun?" (1:3), and it ends with "Fear God, and keep his commandments" (12:13). This proves that the editorial finale has been a factor in the rehabilitation of Ecclesiastes. Even in later times we find echoes of this discussion, for example in the rabbinic commentary on Ecclesiastes, *Qoheleth Rabba:* "The sages wanted to 'hide' the book of Ecclesiastes, because they found in it words that incline to heresy." We find these discussions reflected in Jerome's commentary on 12:13: "The Hebrews say that, among other writings of Solomon which are obsolete and forgotten, this book ought to be obliterated, because it asserts that all the creatures of God are vain, and regards the whole as nothing, and prefers eating and drinking and transient pleasures before all things. From this one paragraph [12:13-14] it deserves the dignity that it should be placed among the number of the divine volumes, in which it condenses the whole of its discussion, summing up the whole enumeration, as it were, and says that the end of its discourse is very easily heard, having nothing difficult in it, namely, that we should fear God and keep his commandments." (Translation by C. D. Ginsburg, *Coheleth,* London 1861, p. 15.)

As for the Christian canon, objections against the sacred character of Ecclesiastes surfaced in a work by Theodore of Mopsuestia (fifth century), but Ecclesiastes kept its canonical status in Judaism and in the Church. Together with the other wisdom books, Proverbs and Job, it belongs to the third section of the Jewish canon, the Writings (Kethubim), but it has a special place since it is one of the five Scrolls (Megilloth). These form a separate collection because they are the liturgical readings proper to the important feasts: Ecclesiastes is read on the third day of the feast of Booths.

Except for the work by Theodore of Mopsuestia alluded to above we do not find traces of similar dissensions in the ancient Church., but it is striking that Ecclesiastes is not quoted in the NT and that in comparison with other biblical books it inspired relatively few commentaries by Church Fathers that have come to us. The oldest Christian commentary we have in full, by Gregory Thaumaturgus (third century), already sets the beacons for the traditional Christian interpretation: "The design of Ecclesiastes is to show that all the affairs and pursuits of man which are undertaken in human things are vain and useless, in order to lead us to the contemplation of heavenly things" (translation by Ginsburg, *Coheleth* 99; older commentaries by Hippolytus, Origen, and Dionysius of Alexandria are preserved only in fragments). In his homilies Gregory of Nyssa (fourth century) follows the same line: "The design of the book is to elevate the mind above every material object, and to quiet it, so that it may soar above all which seems great and sublime in this world, to that which the perceptions of the senses cannot reach, and to excite in it a longing after the super-sensible" (Ginsburg, *Coheleth* 100). According to his Latin contemporary Jerome, the design is "to show the utter vanity of every sublunary enjoyment, and hence the necessity of betaking oneself to an ascetic life, devoted entirely to the service of God" (Ginsburg, *Coheleth* 102). He seeks to defend Ecclesiastes from charges of Epicureanism. One of the best patristic commentaries is the one by Gregory of Agrigento (sixth century; *PG* 98.741–1182) who favors the literal interpretation, which allows him to play down the importance of the so-called Epicurean passages and interpret them as an acceptable invitation to moderate use of earthly goods in accordance with the divine plan. Apart from commentaries Ecclesiastes was widely cited in the works of the Fathers, especially the opening verses on the vanity of all things and 3:1-8 where in their view the importance of discerning the times and seasons was emphasized.

In the liturgy Ecclesiastes plays a minor role. For only one Sunday in three years is a lesson taken from this book (18th Sunday of Year C: 1:2; 2:21-23); another three lessons are used on weekdays in the 25th week of Year 2 (1:2-11; 3:1-11; and 11:2–12:8) and in the Liturgy of Hours pericopes from Ecclesiastes are read with responsorial psalms during the 20th week of the year.

Present Significance

Since a careful reading of Ecclesiastes makes a very negative impression one can wonder whether it would not be preferable to forget the book altogether, to stop reading it as a sacred book, as at least some rabbis have suggested. This would be a too hasty and wrong conclusion. Ecclesiastes is part of our Bible as it has been accepted by Jewish-Christian tradition. Therefore it has something to tell us for the good. In a certain sense it shows us the darker side of human life. What Ecclesiastes expresses is something real: the struggle with the meaning of our existence and the feeling of not mastering the problem, or at least not mastering it very well. If we had only the work of prophets and priests and sages who believe and hope enthusiastically, who know exactly what it is all about, sages who give the impression of having everything under control, then the Bible would not be really human. It would almost seem to be a message that does not have its feet on the ground, that does not know or that disregards a portion of the human world. Ecclesiastes can produce a sobering effect; it can help us to take seriously the problems of humanity.

On the other hand this book is not the only one in the Bible. One should read the whole Bible: the history of God with God's people, the prophets who condemn what is wrong and proclaim salvation, the story of Jesus and the community of his disciples in the NT. The Bible can help us find answers to the questions asked by Qoheleth. We can confront his image of the distant God in 5:1 with Isa 55:8-11, "my thoughts are not your thoughts, nor are your ways my ways . . . my word . . . shall not return to me empty, but it shall accomplish that which I purpose, and succeed in the thing for which I sent it." Here God's transcendence has a salvific meaning.

But there is more. We can profit much from some sayings of the book. A good deal of Qoheleth's advice is to the point: for instance the idea that the attempt to plan too carefully for the future can prevent action (11:4, 6). In 7:1-10 we find a fine series of advisory proverbs ending with the idea that it is not wise to ask, "Why were the former days better than these?" Moreover, we should not underestimate his advice to enjoy the good things of life: in fact we should enjoy God's good creation in contrast with some rather pagan traditions of contempt of the world that have pervaded Christianity (cf. 1 Tim 4:3-5, but that text is more inspired by Genesis 1). Another teaching of Qoheleth is that against exaggeration in 7:16-18. More examples will be treated in the second section of this article.

Ecclesiastes also teaches us to live with unsolved or unsolvable problems: in spite of all his negative experiences he goes on living; he does not commit suicide. On the contrary, he gives practical advice: you should work in this manner; with rulers you should behave like this; you should communicate with other people; you should enjoy the good things in life, and so on.

Even with regard to our image of God and our attitude toward God Qoheleth has something to say. He offers perhaps a corrective to our Christian image of God, for "God as a father" can be misunderstood: God is merciful and forgives our sins but is not "a good fellow"; we do not have God in our pocket, at our disposal. God always remains the wholly other, a mysterious Being. We should not imagine that we see through God and therefore we should avoid speaking in the name of God. "God is in heaven, and you upon earth" (5:2). Of course from the NT we know that God also "dwells in you" (cf. 1 Cor 3:16; 2 Cor 6:16), and this is an important corrective for the image of God offered by Qoheleth.

Qoheleth's conception of life after death also needs a corrective. For him there is no hope; death is a desolate end. This idea needs to be corrected on the basis of Jesus' resurrection: we are called to eternal life with God. On the other hand Ecclesiastes may help us not to see afterlife too much as a reward: we should do what is right because it is right and not in order to merit heaven. In the end Ecclesiastes falls short of solving any problem and from Jesus we have to draw answers to his cry of despair: God is near and does not abandon us. But Ecclesiastes shows us the relativity of many things in this life "under the sun," and in a number of instances he shows some sense of humor, which is a good remedy against deadly earnest, especially for committed people. God has the last word and Ecclesiastes would tend to see this as a problem, while we would say "that is for the best."

SECOND READING

Superscription: 1:1

Like other wisdom books (Proverbs, Wisdom) Ecclesiastes is ascribed to Solomon, but this is a traditional approach with no historical value.

Thesis: 1:2

There has been much discussion on the exact meaning of the Hebrew word *hebel,* which occurs thirty-eight times in the book. The literal meaning is "breath, breeze, vapor." In the Bible it is almost always used in a transferred sense: "ephemerality, inefficacy, deceit." Therefore it is sometimes used to characterize the false gods.

But these meanings are incongruous in most of the contexts of Ecclesiastes. Ecclesiastes 11:10 is an instance where "ephemeral" can be a good rendering of the word: "for youth and the dawn of life are vanity." But the rendering "vanity" in the sense of triviality or futility certainly is insufficient and has a moralizing ring that is absent from Ecclesiastes. The best translation for the word in practically all of Ecclesiastes is "absurdity," not in the mere logical sense but in an existential sense as it has been understood by the existentialist philosophers. "The essence of the absurd is a disparity between two phenomena that are supposed to be joined by a link of harmony or causality but are actually disjunct or even conflicting. . . . Absurdity arises from a logical contradiction between two undeniable realities" (Fox, *Qoheleth and his Contradictions,* 31). What is absurd for Ecclesiastes is not merely incongruous or ironic; it is oppressive, an injustice: "it is the confrontation of the irrational in life with the passionate desire of lucidity whose appeal resounds in the depths of man" (Albert Camus, *Le mythe de Sisyphe.* [Paris: Gallimard, 1948] 37.).

Solomon's Confession: 1:3–2:26

The first pericope (1:3-11) sets the trend: since nothing new happens in nature all efforts of humanity are futile; their toil can achieve nothing that would not have occurred anyway. The same thesis is demonstrated by the so-called royal fiction in 1:12–2:26. Here Ecclesiastes takes the guise of King Solomon and therefore the book has traditionally been ascribed to that king (see 1:1). Under the guise of the wise and wealthy king he "search[es] out by wisdom all that is done under heaven" (1:13). He seeks to amass wisdom and test it (1:16-18; 2:12-17); he tries it with pleasure (2:1-11); he examines his toil for wealth (2:18-23). All his explorations again and again lead to the conclusion that "all is absurdity and vexation (NRSV: "all is vanity and a chasing after wind)." This absurdity is particularly apparent in the futility of trying to find any order in the world by the acquisition of wisdom (1:16-17). In any case the wise person and the fool are equal in their death (2:14-16). Here the author has in mind a form of afterlife that was known by the ancient Israelites, that is, remembrance. With respect to this Qoheleth opposes traditional wisdom in which the righteous, that is, the really wise person, faces a future different from that of the wicked: "The memory of the righteous is a blessing, but the name of the wicked will rot" (Prov 10:7). Ecclesiastes does not know of this hope and therefore he hates life (2:17).

In sum the balance of life is rather negative. How should one behave then? Qoheleth is a teacher of wisdom: he must indicate a direction to his disciples, a way of coping with this life. In face of the total failure of life he has but one practical answer: enjoy the few good things that life offers, for these too are in the plan of God (so it is not simple hedonism; 2:24-25). Seven times he expresses this recommendation of enjoyment: here and in 3:12-13, 22; 5:18-20; 8:15; 9:7-9; 11:8. For the most part he speaks of eating and drinking and enjoyment in general, but in 5:18-20 he also mentions wealth and property as objects of enjoyment. This shows that Qoheleth does not mean "joy" or "enjoyment" in the sense of "happiness," but "pleasure." Here he stands in an ancient Near Eastern tradition that was already present in the old Mesopotamian Epic of Gilgamesh (ANET 90):

> Gilgamesh, whither do you rove?
> The life you pursue you shall not find.
> When the gods created mankind,
> Death for mankind they set aside,
> Life in their own hands retaining.
> You, Gilgamesh, let full be your belly,
> Make merry by day and by night.
> Of each day make a feast of rejoicing,
> Day and night dance and play!
> Let your garments be sparkling fresh,
> Your head be washed; bathe in water.
> Pay heed to the little one that holds on to your hand,
> Let your spouse delight in your bosom!
> For this is the task of [humankind].

Human Beings Under the Law of Time: 3:1-15

All people carry their past with them while the future is a sealed book and the present is volatile and ambiguous: in sum, they are stuck in time with its incomprehensible whims. Ecclesiastes 3:1-9 illustrates this problem with a fine piece of poetry on the law of time. That the intention is to represent all the vicissitudes of a human life is indicated by some literary devices: the number of items is twenty-eight, or fourteen pairs, a multiple of seven, the number indicating totality; they are arranged as pairs of opposites, a device that also stands for totality (merism); the first pair, birth and death, marks the limits of human existence itself (Whybray, *Ecclesiastes,* 68). The lesson of this poem is not, as is often suggested, that everything has its opportune time that should govern our action, but that everything happens at its fixed time. This appears from the first pair, life and death, which lie beyond human control. We do not hold our life in our hands; it is one big adventure in which we experience a great number of experiences but we cannot control our life; nobody can change anything about these fixed times. In the following vv. 10-11 Qoheleth shows that he is not an unbeliever: God has ordered these fixed times and God also gave humankind the desire to grasp this process; they would like to gain insight into the divine foundation of creation but they cannot. It remains completely opaque and they cannot do anything about it (3:14-15; cf. 1:15; 7:13; 6:10). Here again the author's practical advice is to enjoy the good things in life as a gift from God (3:12-13).

Life in Society: 3:16–4:16

Another area where Ecclesiastes experiences absurdity is society, for there he sees much injustice and many things that are not right (3:16; cf. 5:7). In his opinion there is no satisfactory solution to this problem, for in death the just and the evildoers, the wise and the fools are equal. He develops this idea in a gripping way in 3:16-21 although there are some problems with the text. In v. 16 he expresses his observation of injustice in this world. In reaction to it he finds a solution to this bad state of affairs, telling himself that God will judge the wicked as is commonly accepted in traditional faith and wisdom. This is reasonable, for inasmuch as everything has a time divine judgment must also come to pass (the law of time: v. 17). But ultimately this possible judgment does not make the difference since all must die and there is no after-life: "the fate of humans and the fate of animals is the same; as one dies, so dies the other. . . . All go to one place; all are from the dust, and all turn to dust again. Who knows whether the human spirit goes upward and the spirit of animals goes downward to the earth?" (vv. 19-21). "Individual existence is absurd, because all distinctions in life, even the difference between humans and other creatures, are obliterated" (Fox, *Qoheleth,* 197). Therefore enjoyment is again the practical solution (v. 22).

In 4:1-3 Qoheleth clearly shows his compassion for the oppressed and he is troubled by the lack of humane response to their suffering. These verses produce an effect of emotional intensity that is rare in Ecclesiastes: he is not just a cool observer. In 4:4-6 he criticizes in a very compact form the traditional view of work and sloth. Work, he says, comes from one person's envy of another. Then applying his favorite method he quotes a traditional saying in favor of work and against sloth, "Fools fold their hands and consume their own flesh" (v. 5; cf. Prov 6:9-11). But immediately he adds his own opinion that shows the relativity of that wisdom: "Better is a handful with quiet than two handfuls with toil, and a chasing after wind." This pericope on work as a fruit of rivalry deals with a topic for our time. Many people are enslaved to their work whereas we should relativize it and not subordinate everything to work and results, not only in the industrial and commercial realm but also in less economic tasks. Although it is good to work hard we cannot change everything and we must not do everything ourselves either.

In 4:7-12 Qoheleth continues with some sayings that show the importance of life in community, perhaps a sound warning against isolation and individualism. "In a world of oppression, of injustice, and of striving, to face life without companionship and support is decidedly painful. Death may indeed be preferable. However, a different perspective is possible if there are others willing and able to share our burden and to participate with us in confronting this enigmatic world, to minimize its frustrations and pain. Commitment to and with the poor and oppressed is the concrete shape of the 'good news'" (Ogden, *Qoheleth,* 70).

Another set of unreliable though much desired values is the mix of popularity, political success, and power: even the youth who got out of prison to sit on the throne will be replaced by someone else. This hazard of power is exposed in the difficult pericope Eccl 4:13-16, which Michael V. Fox has aptly paraphrased as follows:

(13) A poor youth who is shrewd is better off than an old king who is puerile and no longer has the sense to take precautions. (14) For it happened that one such youth in spite of having been born in poverty in the old king's kingdom went from prison to power. (15) Nevertheless I could foresee that all the living who go about on earth would join the following of whatever young man would take over next. (16) Limitless masses would follow the successor and what's more, even later generations would not appreciate that first shrewd youth. Surely this injustice is a vexatious absurdity (Fox, *Qoheleth,* 209).

Advantage of Silence over Inconsiderate Words: 5:1-9

This pericope consists of five exhortations that have a similar structure, namely a command or prohibition followed by two explicative clauses: 5:1, 2-3, 4-5, 6-7, 8-9. The advantage of silence over inconsiderate words, particularly in our behavior toward God, is the explicit subject of the three central exhortations and it is implicit in vv. 1 (to listen is better) and 8 (it is no use to protest against such a situation).

About Wealth: 5:10–6:9

The values people toil for are unstable, as incalculable as the course of time. This is true of wealth as we already know from 2:4-11 (Solomon); 2:18-23. In opposition to traditional Israelite wisdom and to the deuteronomistic ideology where wealth is a reward for piety (e.g., Ps 128:1-4; Job 42:10-17; Deuteronomy 28–30) Qoheleth exposes its unreliability and the concerns it carries: it creates a restless desire to acquire more; it attracts others who swallow it up; it brings only worries; it can be lost again; and finally, at death the possessors "shall take nothing for their toil, which they may carry away with their hands" (5:15). Here Ecclesiastes can be a helpful medicine against preachers who mislead their congregations by simply presenting wealth as a guaranteed result of piety. In 5:20 Qoheleth praises pleasure for keeping one's mind off the brevity of life or its frustrations. The unreliability of wealth is such a frustration, rendering life bitter: the stillborn is better off than such a wealthy person (6:1-6).

The ideas of Ecclesiastes on wealth or success are of contemporary interest: success and wealth are the idols of our time (and no doubt of all times); they enslave humanity and in the end are unreliable. Following Jesus we would add that there are many more important things in life.

What is Good for Human Beings? 6:10–7:14

Nobody can tell: whereas God knows in advance whatever happens, human beings have no knowledge of events before they happen (6:10-12). There are only things that are relatively better than their opposite (7:1-8), just as wisdom is better and more helpful than wealth (7:11-12).

Righteousness and Wickedness: 7:15-22

Many readers, Jewish as well as Christian, have been scandalized by Eccl 7:16-18: "Do not be too righteous, and do not act too wise; why should you destroy yourself? Do not be too wicked, and do not be a fool; why should you die before your time? It is good that you should take hold of the one, without letting go of the other; for the one who fears God shall succeed with both." It seems unthinkable that Ecclesiastes would recommend here some degree of unrighteousness or immorality, but many commentators are of the opinion that he preaches the famous *via media,* the golden mean. Jerome was one of them. A number of modern commentators reject this idea and find here a warning against self-righteousness and pretensions to wisdom, especially when carried to extremes. Some even speak of an anti-pharisaic bent, and this would seem possible since there are other indications that Qoheleth was of a Sadducean tendency, for example his conservative view of afterlife which we will discuss when commenting on Eccl 9:1-10; 12:7. In any case this anti-pharisaic leaning implies some sort of golden mean: one should not be a rigorist but rather enjoy life; on the other hand one should not give full rein to pleasure like a fool who through levity does not care for law and discipline. It is well known that exaggerated striving after perfection often leads to scrupulosity.

The Dangerous Woman: 7:23-29

Is Qoheleth a misogynist, a woman-hater? From 7:26 it could be inferred that he is: "I found more bitter than death the woman who is a trap, whose heart is snares and nets, whose hands are fetters." However here Qoheleth again uses his favored method of discussing traditional sayings that he quotes. We must read the verse in the context of 7:23-29. Since traditional wisdom was of no help to him in solving his problems Qoheleth tries wisdom derived from research (lit. "wisdom and calculation"). In his research he often finds the saying of v. 26. In v. 27 he introduces the result of his own research but he interrupts this with a parenthesis in v. 28 dealing with another pessimistic and misogynic traditional proverb: "What I further have searched heart and soul and did not find [confirmed] is [the saying]: One [good] person I found in a thousand, but a [good] woman I did not find in these" (my translation). Finally he expresses his own result in v. 29: against the negative saying about women Qoheleth states that humankind in its totality is no good, not because God made them wrong ("not straightforward") but because they misuse their intellectual power, their ingenuity ("they have devised many schemes"). It must be admitted, however, that according to some exegetes this passage remains irreparably misogynistic. In their opinion Ecclesiastes is saying in v. 26: "see where my painstaking search led me: to the knowledge that woman is a menace!" (Fox, *Qoheleth,* 242). But with such an interpretation it is hard to see the coherence of the whole pericope. The discovery that the seductress is more bitter than death and that lucky people (those who please God) escape her breaks no new ground: it is a traditional topic in biblical wisdom literature (Prov 5; 6:20-35; 7; 22:14; 23:26-28; Sir 9:1-9; 26:9-12). But Qoheleth is ordinarily very critical of traditional wisdom. Therefore it should be no surprise that he also rejects or at least greatly relativizes the traditional stand that women are particularly dangerous.

Authority: 8:1-9

This section offers some practical directives on how to behave toward the king (vv. 2-6). However even the person in authority has no control over the life-spirit or the day of death (vv. 7-8).

The Problem of Retribution: 8:10-17

Qoheleth points out that the unjust situation of the wicked not being properly punished induces humankind to do evil. In his typical paradoxical way he then invokes the traditional view that "it will be well with those who fear God . . . but it will not be well with the wicked," but this "dogma" is immediately rejected by the experience that "there are righteous people who are treated according to the conduct of the wicked, and there are wicked people who are treated according to the conduct of the righteous." This is one of the absurdities of life. This the wise cannot explain: they cannot understand the work of God (vv. 16-17). This is Qoheleth's fundamental critique of wisdom: although it can be of some practical help (see under 9:13–10:1) final insight is unattainable. His complaint is not that he lacks a certain degree of wisdom but that human wisdom itself does not reach as far as he would like; his view is quite the opposite of the confident attitude of Proverbs 8 (see also 7:23-24).

The Problem of Death: 9:1-10

This is not the only place where Qoheleth confesses that he does not believe in a worthwhile afterlife. We have already met his idea that the wise person and the fool are equal in their deaths (2:14-16). The idea that the same fate overtakes everybody is expressed in a more emphatic way here in 9:1-3, and in the following vv. 4-6 he again underlines the emptiness of death: "The living know that they will die, but the dead know nothing; they have no more reward, and even the memory of them is lost." Qoheleth does know that the human spirit returns to God, as may appear from 12:7. This is a traditional view that we find in Ps 104:29; Job 34:14-15 and Sir 40:11: the spirit that God has blown into the human being (Gen 2:7) returns to God at the hour of death. However, this does not mean individual survival but a return to the source: just as dust returns to the earth (Gen 3:19), so the spirit returns to God. Dying consists precisely in the fact that God takes back the life-spirit and from this point of view humans and animals are equal. Thus the doubtful question of Eccl 3:21 is not turned against tradition but rather against new ideas of his time about the individual immortality of the human soul. That Qoheleth defends the traditional biblical conception of life after death is very obvious here in 9:10: "Whatever your hand finds to do, do with your might; for there is no work or thought or knowledge or wisdom in Sheol, to which you are going." In Sheol, the netherworld, people lead a vacuous existence; they are aware of nothing (see Job 14:21; Pss 88:11-13; 115:17); there is neither reward nor punishment to be received nor any joy to be found (see Sir 14:16). "Qohelet saw no basis for optimism about the next life, either in its Hebraic expression, the resurrection of the body, or in its Greek expression, the immortality of the soul. For Qohelet, Sheol (the realm of the dead) was a place of nonbeing" (Crenshaw, *Ecclesiastes,* 163). The only practical solution is again to enjoy the good things of life. Next to bread and wine, in 9:7-9 the enjoyment also includes white garments and oil and a beloved woman: "Enjoy life with the wife whom you love, all the days of your vain life that are given you under the sun, because that is your portion in life and in your toil at which you toil under the sun."

Proverbs on Chance: 9:11-12

The vagaries of chance may prevent the gain from falling to the one who deserves it.

Wisdom is Powerful but Not Immune from Folly: 9:13–10:1

Wisdom itself is fickle. Qoheleth is a wisdom teacher himself, standing in a long tradition of sages whose teachings are often preserved in proverbs. For the public he is a wise man, somebody who can cope with life and who helps others to that end. A sage teaches people how to succeed in life through right behavior in the family, in their contact with others, in business, in their attitude toward authorities, and so on. Wisdom is even a gift of God. However, Qoheleth is critical of wisdom. Being a sage himself he ascribes a certain value to wisdom, but in the end it is not much use in his eyes. In 7:11-12, 19 and 8:1 he is positive about wisdom: it is better than wealth and it can be helpful, particularly for solving practical problems such as defending a city (9:15), as entrepreneurial cleverness (10:10) or wisdom of life (2:14). But the final balance is quite negative because one cannot find any order in the world. "Wisdom is better than weapons of war, but one bungler destroys much good. . . . a little folly outweighs wisdom and honor" (9:18–10:1). Even as practical cleverness wisdom is always vulnerable. This appears from the short story on the wise in the besieged city.

Proverbs: 10:2-20

The following proverbs deal alternately with the advantage of wisdom over folly (vv. 2-3 and 12-15) and with rulers and subjects (vv. 4-7 and 16-17). In between is a collection of proverbs on the risks of any action (vv. 8-11) and at the end a few that have been added by association of catchwords (eating and drinking, sloth, king: vv. 18-20).

Risks are to be Taken if One Wants to Realize Something, Because Nobody Knows in Advance What Will Happen: 11:1-6

Enjoy the Light as Long as You Can: 11:7–12:7

This is a somewhat longer composition, the theme of which is set in 11:8: "Even those who live many years should rejoice in them all; yet let them remember that the days of darkness will be many." Therefore enjoy your youth (11:9-10) and remember the age of darkness and death (12:1-7) before the days of unpleasantness come (v. 1b), before the winter of life comes (vv. 2-5), before death comes (vv. 6-7). In 12:2-7 we have the so-called allegory of old age, though not all exegetes agree that this text is allegorical. There are so many philological problems with this poem that no interpretation is entirely satisfactory. Defenders of the allegorical interpretation have tried in different ways to decode the objects mentioned in the poem as parts of the body: after the storm as a general picture of old age in v. 2 follows the description of the keepers of the house (hands, legs), the strong men (bones, arms), the grinders (teeth), those that look through the windows (eyes), the doors (mouth, ears). From verse 4b on the allegory is abandoned for a more realistic description of aging: the elderly person does not hear very well, rises early in the morning and is afraid of heights and even of walking on the road (5a). Verse 5b again is often understood as part of the allegory: the blossoming almond tree represents the white hair; the grasshopper dragging itself could suggest the painfulness of bodily movement; and the failing desire (or caper?) would refer to lack of appetite. But from vv. 5c-7 it appears that the subject of the passage undoubtedly is death. Therefore it is more appropriate to abandon the idea of an allegory of the declining body altogether and to consider vv. 3-5b as the description of mourning over death. Such a funerary interpretation seems preferable but not all details appear to accomodate themselves to it. In any case it is a gripping poem, the imagery of which "creates an atmosphere of pain, contortion, and constriction" (Fox, *Qoheleth,* 289). Verse 7 clearly alludes to Gen 2:7; 3:19.

Inclusion: 12:8

This verse repeats the motto of 1:2.

Epilogue: 12:9-14

In the end Qoheleth does not see any lasting gain (Hebrew *yitron*) in human life, but only a limited portion (Hebrew *heleq*) of the pleasures of life. The results of his meditation on human life are quite negative. This was felt from the beginning, for example by the final editor, who concluded the work with 12:12-14: "Of anything beyond these, my child, beware. Of making many books there is no end, and much study is a weariness of the flesh. The end of the matter; all has been heard. Fear God, and keep his commandments; for that is the whole duty of everyone. For God will bring every deed into judgment, including every secret thing, whether good or evil." Fox has very well summarized the essential function of the epilogue as "to mediate Qohelet's words to the reader in a way that makes them more plausible and more tolerable" (*Qoheleth,* 316). The epilogue testifies to the reality of Qoheleth; it projects an attitude of respect toward him (12:9-10); it identifies the book as a whole with an indisputably orthodox attitude (vv. 13-14). The epilogist sets a certain distance between himself and the words of Qoheleth (v. 12) and he places his words in a broader literary and religious context, "the sayings of the wise" (v. 11).

BIBLIOGRAPHY

Crenshaw, James L. *Ecclesiastes. A Commentary.* OTL. Philadelphia: Westminster, 1987.

Eaton, Michael A. *Ecclesiastes. An Introduction and Commentary.* TOTC. Leicester, England, and Downers Grove, Ill.: Inter-Varsity Press, 1983.

Fox, Michael V. *Qoheleth and His Contradictions.* BLS 18. Sheffield: Almond Press, 1989.

Ginsburg, Christian D. *Coheleth.* London: Longman, Green, Longman, and Roberts, 1861; repr. New York: Ktav Publishing House, 1970.

Loader, J. A. *Ecclesiastes. A Practical Commentary.* Translated by J. Vriend. Text and Interpretation. Grand Rapids: Eerdmans, 1986.

Ogden, Graham. *Qoheleth.* Readings—A New Biblical Commentary. Sheffield: JSOT Press, 1987.

Seow, Choon-Leong. *Ecclesiastes.* AB 18C. New York: Doubleday, 1997.

Whybray, Roger N. *Ecclesiastes.* NCBC. Grand Rapids: Eerdmans, 1989.

Song of Songs

M. Timothea Elliott

FIRST READING

A. Getting Started

Why is a book of poetry that celebrates human physical love included in the Bible? Why would anyone want to read and reflect upon a book that appears to have no "religious" orientation whatsoever? None of the great biblical themes and concerns are found in it; not election, covenant, prophecy, salvation, or the Law. There is no apparent moral teaching and there is only one explicit mention of God's name (8:6)!

How does this book communicate "God's word"? What divine revelation may be discovered through the medium of ardent love dialogues and intense sensual images? What might be gained by way of personal insight and faith enrichment? What can it bring to ministry? This article will attempt to answer these questions.

The Song of Songs is among the briefest books of the Old Testament. It consists of a mere one hundred seventeen verses divided into eight short chapters. However, as the title itself suggests, it is esteemed as one of the most unusual and beautiful books of the Bible.

"Song of Songs," like "vanity of vanities," is the Hebrew way of expressing the superlative, and commentators throughout the ages have tended to use superlatives when speaking of this book. Rabbi Akiba, for example, toward the end of the first century remarked, " All the world is not worth the day that the Song of Songs was given to Israel. All the writings are holy, but the Song of Songs is the holy of holies" (*m. Yad.* 3.5). Another rabbi of this period commented, "If God had not given the Torah to Israel, the Song of Songs would be sufficient to govern the Universe."

The unifying theme of the book is love, the highest and fullest expression of the human heart. The setting is springtime, and the season itself becomes a unifying metaphor for the unfolding love of a young couple.

The reader will notice immediately that the Song is written in lyric poetry and in the form of dialogues. The principal participants in the dialogues are the young man (Lover or Bridegroom) the young woman (Beloved or Bride) and the Daughters of Jerusalem.

The young woman (Beloved or Bride) is the focus of this lyrical dialogue. Hers are the first and last words. The book begins *in medias res* with her passionate invitation, "Let him kiss me with the kisses of his mouth!" (1:2) and ends with an equally ardent imperative, "Haste away—be off!" (8:14). While the Lover or Bridegroom is frequently absent (1:7-8; 3:1-3; 5:6-8; 6:1), *she* is present to every scene, and the narration of events, thoughts, and feelings comes from her point of view. Of the total number of verses all but eight are spoken by her, to her, or about her.

While the *Revised Standard Version* is the most literal English translation, it is perhaps not the best to use for a first reading of the Song. The *Jerusalem Bible,* the *New American Bible,* or the *New English Bible* present more "poetic" translations that are more harmonious with the subject matter. They have the added advantage of dividing the text according to the elements of dialogue and clearly labeling the speaker(s).

Repetition is one of the most notable characteristics of the Song of Songs. The lovers delight in naming one another and savoring these names by pronouncing them over and over. He is "my love" (1:13-16; 2:3, 8-17 and *passim*) "the one whom my soul loves" (1:7; 3:1-4), "king" (1:4, 12; 7:5), and "friend" (5:16); she is "the most beautiful among women" (1:8; 2:10), "my beloved" (1:9, 15; 2:1 and *passim*), "my dove" (2:14; 5:2; 6:9), "bride" (4:8, 11) "sister bride" (4:9–5:1), "my perfect one" (6:9), "garden dweller" (8:13).

There are a number of motifs that are repeated with endless variations: presence and absence, seeking and finding, desire and mutual possession, the voice of the loved one, sleeping and waking, eating and drinking, and the uniqueness of the loved one. The motifs are developed through vibrant images that appeal to all the senses: sight (4:1), hearing (2:8), taste (4:11), smell (4:11), and touch (1:2).

B. The Book as a Unit

Until the rise of modern critical methodologies the Song of Songs was viewed as a single unified work and attributed to Solomon as the title, "Solomon's most excellent song" (1:1), suggests. From the end of the first century C.E. when the Song was incorporated into the Hebrew canon, it was regarded as a sacred allegory depicting the love between God and Israel.

In the nineteenth century the allegorical interpretation of the Song was supplanted by the position that the Song of Songs was, in fact, a drama. Proponents of the dramatic theory cited as authority the ancient Greek versions, Codex Sinaiticus (fourth century C.E.) and Codex Alexandrinus (fifth century C.E.), both of which provided marginal notes assigning parts to various speakers.

The latter half of the twentieth century witnessed the abandonment of the dramatic theory. The Song was seen to have insufficient narrative content, plot, or character development to qualify as a drama. Despite the presence of certain elements such as monologues and dialogues and the occasional interjection of a chorus, the text itself simply does not conform to a dramatic structure. Besides, the dramatic form itself was unknown in ancient Hebrew literature. Among Jews dramatic performances were held in horror, regarded as heathen, irreligious, and contrary to tradition until the sixteenth century. The Song of Songs was unlikely to have been accepted among the sacred writings in this form.

Form-critical studies of the twentieth century have come to the consensus that the Song of Songs is lyric poetry. However, there is an unresolved debate among contemporary scholars with respect to the issue of poetic unity. This has serious implications in the area of hermeneutics. Many claim it is an anthology, and they recognize anywhere from fifteen to fifty-two individual love poems coming from the hands of as many authors, assembled without any particular organization in mind. Others affirm a basic poetic unity that is the work of a single author or redactor, and a structure of five or six parts.

The position adopted in this commentary is that the Song of Songs is a textual unity that is the work of a single poet.

C. Formal Structure

Verbal repetitions are the most important criteria for discerning the poetic units in Hebrew verse. In the Song there are four types of repetitions to be considered: (1) words exactly repeated in close proximity to one another (4:8; 5:9; 6:13); (2) word pairs, usually epithets ("the one whom my soul loves," 1:7; 3:1, 2, 3, 4; "most beautiful among women," 1:8; 5:9; 6:1); (3) phrases or half verses that reappear in different contexts ("grazing among the lilies," 2:16; 4:5; 6:3; "sick with love," 2:5; 5:8) and (4) whole lines or entire verses that are repeated ("his left hand under my head and his right hand embracing me," 2:6 and 8:3; "I adjuree you, O daughters of Jerusalem, by the gazelles or the wild does: do not stir up or awaken love until it is ready" 2:7; 3:5; 8:4). The first two forms of repetition create a particular effect and are elements of style. The last two are refrains and indicators of the Song's formal structure.

These two lengthy refrains, one of embrace and one of adjuration, occur together and in the same order near the beginning and end of the Song (2:6-7 and 8:3-4). In both instances a cluster of similar motifs converges. First of all there is mention of bringing the loved one into a house (the verb *bw'*); second there is a reference to feasting and/or drinking wine and finally the embrace of the lovers is succeeded by sleep. The combination of these elements has the effect of setting off the initial and final sections (1:2–2:5 and 8:5-14) from the rest of the text. The poet appears to employ this strategy to create a type of introduction and conclusion to the total work, which in fact functions as a Prologue and Epilogue to the entire poem.

The adjuration refrain occurs alone at 3:5 in a similar cluster of motifs. There is reference to bringing the loved one into the house (the verb *bwʾ* in 3:4d), and embrace (3:4c) is succeeded by sleep (3:5). The adjuration refrain thus serves as an inclusion that establishes 2:7 to 3:5 as Part One of the Song.

The next major break occurs after 5:1. Even though there is no refrain at this point it is a well recognized division where the text naturally separates into two almost equal halves. The same coincidence of motifs occurs. The verb *bwʾ* is present; there is feasting and wine; the embrace of the lovers is followed by sleep (5:2). Part Two, therefore, extends from 3:6 to 5:1.

The only place between 5:2 and 8:3 where the text is marked by a full line of refrain is at 6:3. The portion of the text that lies between 5:2 and 6:3 is a closely unified dialogue. The second half of the Song thus falls into two parts: Part Three, 5:2 to 6:3 and Part Four, 6:4 to 8:2.

The poet has thus structured the text of the Song of Songs in six parts:

Prologue: 1:2–2:5
- Part One: 2:8–3:4
- Part Two: 3:6–5:1
- Part Three: 5:2–6:2
- Part Four: 6:4–8:2

Epilogue: 8:5-14

The refrains located at 2:6-7; 3:5; 6:3; and 8:3-4 function as transitions in the text. Each of the six parts begins with a situation in which the young lovers are separated from one another in some sense. Each part ends with a renewed union. The concluding refrains accent these moments of union and repose.

In a first reading of the Song of Songs it is important to focus on the obvious and immediate sense of the text as a song that celebrates the love of a young man and woman. Assuming the position that it is a single song, one recognizes the celebration of a single, exclusive, and faithful relationship against the background of Jewish social life and marriage practices.

D. Original Historical Contexts

Scholars do not agree on the actual date of composition for the Song of Songs. Parts of it appear to be quite early, suggesting the time of Solomon himself (3:6-11), yet the presence of Persian (*pardēs* = park in 4:13) and Greek (*ʾappiryon* = litter in 3:9) vocabulary point to a much later period. At the present time there is a fairly broad consensus that the Song in its finished form dates from the post-exilic period and may be as late as the third century B.C.E.

The title (1:1) attributes this book to Solomon, in keeping with the tradition that credits him with the composition of a thousand and five songs and three thousand proverbs (1 Kings 5:12). He is said to have had seven hundred wives and three thousand concubines (1 Kings 11:3), making him an expert on the topic of love.

Traditional claims of Solomonic authorship find little support in the work itself. Solomon is not among the speakers, all of whom are anonymous. References to him are in the third person (1:5; 3:7, 9, 11; 8:11-12). Those in chs. 1 and 8 are figurative allusions to Solomon's wealth and not claims of authorship. There are three passages that identify the Lover as "king" (1:4, 12; 7:4), but no identification is made. The three references in ch. 3 depict Solomon as the Bridegroom and the entire pericope (3:6-11) stands in sharp contrast to the rustic setting found elsewhere in the Song. These facts suggest that it is a song composed for the occasion of one of Solomon's marriages to a foreign princess (cf. Psalm 45) that had been conserved and placed here.

The purpose of the Solomonic ascription is hermeneutical. Solomon stands as the icon of wisdom as Moses does for the Law. In the concluding verses of the Song we find a strong imprint of the wisdom tradition and methodology in the form of a *mashal* (proverbial saying) in 8:6-7, and some parables (8:8-10, 11-12) all of which serve as a reflection on the mystery of love. Thus both beginning and end inform the reader that the intended authoritative context for interpreting the Song of Songs is the Wisdom tradition. [See also the article "Wisdom: A Way of Thinking About God."]

The prophet Jeremiah suggests a setting for the type of love poetry found in the Song of Songs: "there shall once more be heard the voice of mirth and the voice of gladness, the voice of the bridegroom and the voice of the bride" (Jer 33:10-11; cf. Jer 7:34; 16:9; 25:10). After the Babylonian exile and the giving of a "new covenant" written on their hearts (31:31-33) the love songs of bride and groom, sung during the week-long festivities, become tangible reminders of the nuptial relationship between God and God's people.

An anonymous poet collected love songs that had been passed down orally for centuries, and with great creativity composed some new ones and carefully wove them into a well-unified whole for a new era of Israel's history. It was a period of restoration, of high hopes and bitter realities. Widespread divorce threatened marriages (Mal 2:13-16) and thus it was a period when a book such as the Song of Songs was a necessary reminder of "how things were at the beginning" (Matt 19:1-4).

E. Canonical Intertextuality

The nuptial mystery, whether in the human or divine dimension, pervades the entirety of Sacred Scripture. The first word attributed to a man at the dawn of time is a love song: "This at last is bone of my bones and flesh of my flesh; this one shall be called Woman, for out of Man this one was taken" (Gen 2:23). The last word is also a love song; "The Spirit and the bride say, 'Come'" (Rev 22:17).

The Song of Songs cannot be fully appreciated in isolation from the cultural patterns of the ancient Near East or apart from the entirety of the Old and New Testament canon. Genesis presents us with the first love story in the Garden of Eden. This was an innocent and perfect love between equals, and between the original couple and God. The whole of creation, fresh from the hand of God and declared "good," served love. Then sin changed everything.

The OT books present us with image after image of human love gone wrong, of domination instead of mutual donation (Gen 3:16), of deception (Gen 38:12-26), unfruitful unions (Gen 29:31), infidelity and violence (2 Sam 11:1-27). Similar, painful patterns enter into the relationship between God and humanity whose covenant bond is presented as spousal (Hosea 3). Yet within this drama of brokenness we find the Song of Songs echoing with the language of Eden and containing the promise of love redeemed.

It should not surprise us, then, to discover that the NT takes up the nuptial theme to disclose the reality of our salvation. Jesus appears as the Messiah-Spouse as he opens his public ministry (John 1:26-27). John the Baptist is the "friend of the bridegroom" who rejoices to hear his voice (John 3:29). It is at a wedding feast that Jesus first reveals himself, giving joy and an abundance of wine (John 2:1-11). He meets, satisfies the thirst, and makes a disciple of a Samaritan woman beside a well (John 4), the site of historic courtships and marriage proposals (Gen 29:9-14; Exod 15:2-21). In order to explain the mysteries of the reign of God, Jesus resorts to parables that speak of wedding feasts (Matt 22:1-14; Luke 14:16-24). Finally, after his passion and death, Jesus "sleeps" in a garden tomb (John 19:41-42). On the third day Mary Magdalene rises when it is still dark and goes searching for him. She knows the divine lover and clings to him when he calls her by name (John 20:1, 11-18 and Song 3:1-4).

The Pauline correspondence frequently dwells on the nuptial mystery. The apostle, writing to the church of Corinth, reminds them: "I promised you in marriage to one husband, to present you as a chaste virgin to Christ" (2 Cor 11:2), and the letter "to the Ephesians" admonishes husbands to love their wives as Christ loved the Church and gave himself for it (Eph 5:25).

F. History of Reception

The Song of Songs was received into the Hebrew canon along with Proverbs and Qoheleth toward the end of the first century C.E. The Hebrew canon places the Song among the five scrolls or *Megilloth,* after Ruth and before Qoheleth. Both the Septuagint and Vulgate maintain the order Proverbs, Ecclesiastes, Song of Songs, and place all three with the other writings that compose the Wisdom literature.

Once it had been incorporated into the canon the interpretation of the Song was influenced by the older and stronger traditions found in the Law and the Prophets. The decalogue required absolute fidelity on the part of Israel to one God. The one human relationship that required such absolute fidelity was that of a woman to her husband. The prophets, particularly Hosea, Jeremiah, and Isaiah expressed the relationship of Israel to its God in spousal terms and gave it a new intensity. By the end of the first century B.C.E., then, it appears that the Song was interpreted in an allegorical manner reflecting the influence of these older traditions. This interpretation, found in the Targum and *Midrash Rabbah,* saw in it Israel's history from the Exodus until the coming of the Messiah. The liturgical reading of the book belonged to the season of Passover.

The Wisdom tradition appears to have been totally eclipsed. Rabbi Akiba is no doubt responsible for the impetus given to the allegorical tradition of interpreting the Song. He said, "he who trills his voice in the chanting of the Song of Songs in the banquet halls and makes it a secular song has no share in the world to come" (*t. Sanh.* 12:10). The dichotomy sacred/secular is alien both to the Song itself and to the Wisdom tradition.

When the allegorical interpretation passed over into early Christian commentary the figures underwent an accommodation. The Bridegroom was Christ; the Church became the Bride. This was a natural development in light of key NT passages (Matt 9:15; 25:1-13; John 3:29; 2 Cor 11:2; Eph 5:22-33; Rev 19:6-8; 21:9-11; 22:17). Origen developed the Christ/Church allegory in an influential commentary. The Song was a favorite text of the early Church Fathers in their development of ecclesiology. It portrayed fresh, young love against the background of a new creation, a generous and faithful spousal love that was completely reciprocal. Origen also admitted the possibility of seeing an individual soul in the figure of the Bride. The latter interpretation was taken up by Gregory of Nyssa, and Ambrose applied it to Mary. The Middle Ages saw the greatest flowering of commentaries on the Song of Songs. Over one hundred serious studies were completed during this period. Bernard of Clairvaux wrote eighty-six sermons on it, interpreting it as a dialogue between Christ and the soul. The Cistercian tradition favored this mystical interpretation of the Song, while Hugh of St. Victor and many others applied it to Mary.

The history of Christian spirituality has drawn much of its inspiration from the Song. Treatises on prayer quote from it extensively. Teresa of Avila, John of the Cross, and Luis de León wrote spiritual commentaries on it, and others like Francis de Sales and Thérèse of Lisieux commented on it extensively in their writings.

In its liturgy the Church has selected readings from the Song of Songs for feasts of the Blessed Virgin Mary from the earliest times and used these liturgical reflections in the development of mariology. At the present time only three passages from the Song are used in the liturgical cycles. On December 21, during the days of immediate preparation for the feast of Christmas, Song 2:8-14 appears in conjunction with Luke 1:39-45, and on July 22, the feast of Mary Magdalene, Song 3:1-4 occurs with John 20:1-2, 11-18. The Common of Virgins offers Song 8:6-7 as an alternate reading.

SECOND READING

Title: 1:1

Two concepts are expressed in the initial verse. The first is the title, "The Song of Songs." As already noted, this is a superlative form and signifies "the most beautiful song" or "the most excellent song." The singular form of the noun indicates that the work is to be read as a unit, not an anthology. The Hebrew term *sīr* denotes a song that is joyous and full of enthusiasm.

Second, the expression *līsəlomoh* may be understood in one of three ways. Most often it is translated as attributing the authorship to Solomon, that is, "Solomon's Song of Songs." However, it may also mean "dedicated to Solomon" or "in the style of Solomon" (cf. 1 Kings 5:12).

Prologue: 1:2–2:7

A prologue to a poetic or dramatic work serves the purpose of introduction. It describes the characters, establishes the setting in which they find themselves, and gives a hint of the themes to be developed. The prologue of the Song of Songs resembles the overture to a musical masterpiece in many ways. Major themes come briefly to the ear, enter one's consciousness, and pass. One melody blends easily into another; nothing is developed in depth. The mood is set and the audience prepared to better hear all that is to come.

1:2-4: The Prologue opens with the Beloved's cry of desire. The three verses switch rapidly back and forth from third to second person. This characteristic of Hebrew poetry (cf. Psalm 23) and love poetry in particular need not be disconcerting. The lovers frequently address one another in the third person in the Song, and often switch easily back and forth from third to second person (cf. 1:12; 2:1-3; 4:6; 6:9; 7:10).

The Beloved is alone at the opening; her Lover is at a distance. She expresses her longing for his kiss and likens that kiss to a draught of sweet wine (cf. 8:2b). The imagery moves from the sense of taste to that of scent. The very name of the Lover is like a released perfume. She calls him "king," underscoring his desirability and perfection. The Daughters of Jerusalem enter the dialogue by praising the Lover. We may think of them as companions or bridesmaids (see Judg 11:34-38; Matt 25:1).

1:5-6: Addressing the Daughters, the Beloved describes herself as black and beautiful. Two metaphors fill out the description: black goatskin tents (*qēdār* means black) and Solomon's curtains (a symbol of colorful beauty and luxury). The Beloved charges the Daughters not to stare at her and explains that her brothers are responsible for her darkness. In their anger they have set her to work in the vineyard. These few verses establish a connection with the end of the Song (cf. 8:8-9 and 8:11-12) and introduce the Beloved's mother who is mentioned several times (3:4; 6:9; 8:2). It is significant that the Beloved refers to herself as a vineyard. The fruits of the vineyard are what she bestows on her Lover throughout the Song.

1:7-8: Initially the Lover was called "king"; here he is a shepherd and addressed as "the one whom my soul loves" (cf. 3:1-4). The Beloved insists on knowing how to find him, where he will have his flocks at noon so that she can join him. The double question, "where" . . . "where" introduces the search motif into the Prologue, and the epithet "the one whom my soul loves" underscores the intensity of the Beloved's feelings. The companions of the Lover are mentioned only here and in 8:13. They are comparable to the Daughters except that they do not speak in any of the dialogues.

The Daughters' response contains a bit of irony. The Hebrew ethical dative is used twice, paralleling the Beloved's twofold question. This form directs the emphasis toward the will of the Beloved herself, implying that there may be something willful about her ignorance. If she loves her shepherd so totally she should know, her instincts should tell her where to find him. If she does not know, let her go out in the manner she has already suggested. The epithet "O fairest among women" is the Daughters' unique way of addressing her (cf. 5:9 and 6:1).

1:9-11: Thus far the Prologue, through the voice of the Beloved, has created an atmosphere of yearning, of ardent desire for union. When the Lover speaks for the first time he creates the impression that at last they are together. Hereafter the lovers gaze at one another and exchange words of admiration. Each of the four parts of the Song (2:8–3:5; 3:6–5:1; 5:2–6:3; 6:4–8:4) undergoes this transition from desire to union, often from absence to presence.

Today's woman would not appreciate the Lover's choice of words to praise her, nor would she consider them a compliment. In the context of ancient love poetry the Lover expresses both his admiration and the effect that his Beloved has on him. (Verse 9 contains the only use of the feminine term "mare" in the Bible. Only stallions were used to draw the chariots of Pharaoh. A single mare among the stallions would throw an advancing army into complete confusion.) References to animals abound in descriptions of both Lover and Beloved throughout the Song. Seeing her beauty, he desires to adorn her with every sort of precious ornament. The expression "we" may refer to his companions or may be a plural of majesty appropriate for the kingly figure.

1:12-14: The Beloved responds to the Lover's praise by returning to scent imagery. These verses are intimately linked to 1:2-4. There love or caresses were equated with perfume and the Lover's name identified with perfumed oil. Here the name "king" is resumed and the Beloved also calls him "my Love." Moreover, she identifies him with the names of three perfumes as if they were quasi-epithets. In the remainder of the Song nard, myrrh, and henna will be associated with the Beloved.

1:15-17: The couple gaze upon one another and praise one another, using almost identical expressions. They describe their woodland trysting place. The singular possessives ("my beloved," "my love") shift to the plural "our couch," "our house" and are spoken in unison.

2:1-5: Although the Lover has declared her to be beautiful (1:15) the Beloved observes that her beauty is of a rather humble variety. She describes herself in terms of two common field flowers. The Lover takes up the term "lily" and turns it into an affirmation of superlative beauty by way of contrast with thorns. The Beloved listens and then imitates the form of the compliment, likening him to an apple tree among all the common trees. Then, selecting two aspects of the apple tree, its shade and its fruit, she extends the metaphor. The Lover's shade represents his covering protection while the fruit that is sweet to her palate is his love or kisses (cf. 5:16; 7:9).

An analogous thought is expressed in verse 4. The vertical tree has its counterpart in the banner raised over the Beloved. Being brought into the "house of wine" or banqueting hall corresponds to tasting the Lover's fruit since wine has already been used as a metaphor for love and for kisses (1:2). Finally the Beloved declares that she is "faint with love" and asks for those fruits that have already been metaphorically identified with her Lover.

2:6-7: The Prologue comes to a conclusion with two refrains, one of embrace and one of adjuration. Where the name of a deity should come in the adjuration refrain the expression "by the gazelles or the wild does" occurs. The Hebrew expression is a circumlocution for two divine names, "YHWH Sabaoth" and "El Shaddai." Absence has resolved in presence and desire in union.

Part One: 2:8–3:5

The adjuration refrain occurs at the beginning and end of Part One. The poetic unit has two phases: 2:8-15 occurs by day and 3:1-4 by night.

2:8-14: The approach of the Lover reminds the Beloved of a gazelle or a young stag. His movements are agile, swift, and graceful. The sound of his voice is full of desire as he calls her to rise up and come forth. Springtime has arrived and assaults the senses with beauty: a profusion of flowers, singing, the turtledove's cooing, the fig tree's blossoming. As the Lover arrives at her house and tries to gain sight of her through the protective lattices he compares the Beloved to a dove hiding in the recesses of the cliffs and expresses his desire to see her and hear her voice.

2:15: The Beloved responds by singing a lilting song about the little foxes in the vineyard. The animal imagery introduced in 2:8 continues to the end. The Beloved is the vineyard (1:6) and is in blossom.

2:16: The refrain speaks of mutual donation and possession. It occurs again at 6:3 and 7:10 with some modification. The Lover "grazes" or "pastures his flock" among the lilies (cf. 1:7): the Beloved is a lily (2:1).

2:17: The second refrain marks the passing of day to evening (cf. 8:14) and ends on a note of union and repose.

3:1-4: The Lover has come and gone. Presence has given way to absence; day has become night and the search motif is resumed. The epithet "the one whom my soul loves" occurs only in this passage and in 1:7. Conveying both love and desire, it becomes especially poignant in its fourfold repetition, once in each verse.

The passage has three phases: (1) the Beloved searches unsuccessfully for her Lover; (2) the Beloved is found by the watchmen and questions them about her Lover; (3) the Beloved finds her Lover, grasps him, and brings him to the intimacy of her mother's house. "House of the mother" appears only three times in the Bible (Song 3:4; 8:2; Ruth 1:8) and in each case in the context of marriage arrangements. "House of the father" often included more than one wife, concubines, numerous relatives, servants and slaves. Marriage contracts were arranged in this smaller, more intimate unit.

3:5: The adjuration refrain brings all the movement to repose and sleep again. In this case the caution not to awaken love before its time interacts with the epithet "the one whom my soul loves."

Part Two: 3:5–5:1

The second major part of the Song is best characterized by its unifying wedding motif. It opens with a description of the wedding cortège, includes a song praising the beauty of the bride, and concludes with references to the consummation of conjugal union.

3:6-11: The refrain "Who is that coming up from the wilderness?" is both an exclamation and a question. The moment of quiet union achieved at the conclusion of 3:1-5 abruptly gives way to a scene filled with excited activity. It is the bride who approaches, carried within the litter of Solomon. At a symbolic level the litter stands for the bride herself. As has already been noted in the Prologue, "Solomon," "king," or "King Solomon" are taken to mean the Lover throughout the Song. (See 1 Macc 9:39 for another description of a wedding procession.)

The emphasis in vv. 7 and 8 is on the sixty warriors. The fact that they are named three times underscores their importance. Attention is first drawn to the impressive number of this guard, then to its excellence. The poet describes them as a unified body of men trained in warfare and then turns to the individuals, each equipped with a sword at his side. A tone of dread and night concludes the section.

Such an emphasis given to the guard suggests a further relationship with the litter of Solomon. Just as the litter belongs to an unfolding paradigm of enclosed images representing the Beloved, so also the warriors belong to a corresponding paradigm of "protection" with respect to those images. The vineyard (Beloved) is protected by "keepers" (1:6; 8:11) and the litter by warriors. The keepers of the vineyard catch the foxes that ravish the vines (2:14) and the warriors surround the litter, grasping swords against the terrors of the night.

Corresponding to the six elements describing the mighty warriors surrounding Solomon's litter are six elements pertaining to its magnificent adornment. These are related in an order that progresses from the exterior to the interior. The last item in the description is, "its interior . . . inlaid with love." The term *ʾahabāh* contains homonyms, one meaning "love" and the other "leather." In a listing of precious materials "leather" is the expected word, but "love" is the principal theme of the Song.

Within this brief passage the Bride approaches the waiting Groom in the wedding procession (3:6-10) and he goes forth to receive her (3:11). Night gives way to day, the wilderness to the city, terror to joy. The sixty gallant warriors who protect the arriving cortège are balanced by the Daughters of Jerusalem surrounding the king. Attention focused on the mother of the bride (3:4) shifts to the mother of the groom (3:11).

4:1-7: This passage represents the contemplation of the bride and is a song in which the Lover praises all the aspects of her beauty. The descriptive song has a vertical viewpoint, moving slowly downwards; eyes, hair, teeth, lips, cheeks, neck, and breasts. A multitude of similes identifies the body of the Beloved with the flora, fauna, and geography of the land. Summing up his admiration, he proclaims, "You are altogether beautiful, my love; there is no flaw in you" (4:7).

4:6: Contemplation leads to desire. Thus the Lover announces his intention to go to the Beloved. He describes her as a mountain of myrrh and a hill of incense (cf. 3:6). He uses the names of perfumes that she previously employed in describing him (cf. 1:12-14). This creates a type of "mirror-effect." Throughout the Song identical images are attributed first to one and later to the other of the young lovers; or it may be that the images are analogous: the Lover is compared to an apple tree and the Beloved to a palm tree. Both trees have desirable fruit. Sometimes as motifs are repeated the personal focus reverses: the Lover beckons the Beloved to come out in 2:8-14; the Beloved beckons him in 7:11-12.

These repetitions of image and motif are more than mere echoes or parallels. The poet uses this device to suggest the transforming power of love whereby one changes and begins to resemble the person loved, to assume similar values, desires, feelings, and in time even physical characteristics. Subtly the device affirms their growing communion.

4:8–5:1: The verb *bwʾ* (come) establishes an inclusion that sets off this poetic unit. It begins and ends with imperatives, and the epithets "bride" and "sister bride" appear exclusively in this part of the Song.

Repetitive parallelism is used with such liberality in 4:8-11 that it occurs in practically every line. The "sound" effect produced by such an accumulation of poetic repetitions is similar to stuttering and stumbling over words, repeating oneself almost incoherently. It perfectly exemplifies the Lover's state of being as contemplation leads to ardent desire.

In 4:6 the Lover announced his intention to go to her, this "mountain of myrrh." But now it is not enough that he should go to her; she must also come to him. His desire to posses her is so great that he repeatedly cries out, "Come!" Although she is quite near, close enough to hear his praise (4:1-5), she is not close enough to meet his desire. Thus she seems to be as distant and inaccessible as the peaks of Lebanon, Amana, Senir, and Hermon, all located in the extreme north of Israel.

4:9: Contemporary western love poetry attributes an emotional and affective role to the heart, while for the ancient Hebrew the heart was more frequently associated with the mind or discerning faculty. Thus the meaning of "you have ravished my heart" is one of agitation and mental confusion or the deprivation of the capacity to think. The Lover claims that his Beloved has caused this confusion with one of her eyes, one jewel of her necklace. Her eyes, frequently described as "doves" (1:15; 4:1) or "pools" (7:4), nevertheless have a disturbing quality.

4:10-11: Focusing on the sensual delights of the Beloved, these two verses bear a striking resemblance to 1:2-3 and are another example of the "mirror-effect." She has described his love, his kisses "better than wine," and his very name (person) as "perfume poured out." Here, he describes her expressions of love as "better than wine," her kisses as "nectar," "honey and milk"; the scent of her oils is better than any spice and her fragrance like that of Lebanon. Exchanges of love are described in terms of eating and drinking, of breathing deeply of the loved one, of union by bringing the loved one within oneself.

4:12-15: The metaphor of the Bride as a garden occurs in the center of the Song and it holds the most intense expression of the lovers' spousal union. The Bride is presented as a closed garden. The descriptive terms accent the sense of her belonging exclusively to her Lover. She is locked or bolted from the inside as well as sealed from the outside. She is also a fountain sealed from within, a statement of her chaste fidelity. The epithets "my sister, my bride" along with all the possessive pronouns heighten awareness of mutual donation and possession.

Only superlatives appear adequate to describe the Bride. She is simply not in the same category as a common garden; she is a "paradise." The term is a Persian loan-word signifying an elegant enclosed park or orchard more typical of the wonders of Babylon than an Israelite garden. She produces only the most choice fruits and spices.

The final verse (4:15) completes the description of the Beloved as a garden-delight, "O fountain of gardens! O well of living waters! O flowing streams of Lebanon!" The three images of water complement those in 4:12-13. In the first case the aspect of enclosure, collecting, and sealing up dominated. In 4:15 the emphasis is on the inner vitality of the water, its renewability, and its outward-flowing movement. Between vv. 12 and 15 lies a picture of the garden's fertile abundance.

4:16: Accepting the compliment, the Beloved assumes the identity of the garden as she replies. Calling to the polar extremities of the earth, she summons the winds with urgent imperatives, asking them to cause her garden to breathe so that its spices may flow out. The Bride surrenders "her garden" as she invites her Beloved to come into "his garden" and eat.

5:1: The self-donation of the Bride is accepted by her Lover. He takes possession of her through the images of eating and drinking. At this point there is silence on the part of both Lover and Beloved. Instead, the poet steps forward and offers a toast to the couple: "Eat, friends, drink, and be drunk with love!" This salutation occurs at the very center of the Song of Songs. In the manner of the title (1:1) and the conclusion (8:6-14) it carries the stamp of the Wisdom tradition. It is the poet's appreciation of the goodness of what God has created and similar to the admonition offered by Qoheleth, "Enjoy life with the wife whom you love, all the days of your . . . life" (9:9).

Part Three: 5:2–6:3

Elements of dialogue unify the third part of the Song. In 5:2-8 the Beloved describes herself as sleeping but with heart awake when the voice of the Lover presses upon her consciousness. The threefold repetition of the verb "open" significantly contrasts with the threefold emphasis on closure in 4:12. The Lover's imperative "Open to me!" is not an imperious command but an exigency of love. Four epithets (my sister, my love, my dove, my perfect one) establish his exclusive claim to entrance.

The urgent call of the Lover evokes a strange response in his Beloved. Rather than immediately opening to him, she begins to question. Awakened by his voice, she becomes aware of her own situation, and in a state of confusion she first sees only the practical problems in answering his request. Twice she makes a statement and twice she asks a question. These confused remarks momentarily delay the movement.

5:4-6: The ardor of the Lover's desire, first spoken, is now signed by an impatient effort to gain entrance. It stirs the emotions of the Beloved and impels her to act. Just as the voice of the Lover found a response in the voice of the Beloved, so also the action of the Lover's hand finds a corresponding reaction in the hands of the Beloved.

The paradigm of enclosed images representing the Beloved continues. She is both a locked house and the owner who dwells within, just as in Part Two she is both the litter of Solomon and its occupant (3:6-11) and the locked garden and its owner (4:12–5:1).

5:7: The Bride's discovery that her Lover had departed once she rose to open to him leads to a new development of the search motif. The search itself is presented briefly, but her encounter with the city guards is considerably lengthened (cf. 3:3) and their behavior is difficult to comprehend. They find her, beat and wound her, and take off her shawl. A clue to meaning may be found in v. 7 where the guards are called "sentinels of the walls," which suggests a connection with the metaphor of the Beloved as a locked house. The role of the guards then seems to parallel that of the warriors in 3:7. Just as the locked house forms part of the paradigm of enclosed images symbolic of the Bride, so too the guards belong to the parallel paradigm of protection.

5:8: Hindered from going out in search, the Beloved turns to a third party , the Daughters of Jerusalem, to continue her search, and she exacts a promise from them under oath. Should they find her Lover they must tell him that she is faint with love.

5:9: Such a solemn charge provokes the Daughters of Jerusalem to question her. First they ask what he looks like. How can they recognize him? Then they require an explanation in terms of quality. How is he so different or more than anyone else that the Beloved would take the extreme measure of imposing an obligation on them by oath? Their questions require the answer the Beloved makes in 5:10-16.

5:10-16: The Beloved's response is a song of descriptive praise that follows a pattern similar to 4:1-7 where the Lover sang her praises. The opening verse declares an overall beauty and thereafter the description proceeds to the particulars, following a downward movement from head to feet. The radiant quality of his total aspect as well as the extraordinary value she places upon his person are reflected in the vocabulary. The head, as representative of the entire body, is described first: "His head is the finest gold." The intention is not to imply that he is blond, but that he is precious in her eyes and that she is dazzled by him.

While visual imagery (brilliance, color, movement of doves) is appropriately used to describe the head and eyes of the Lover, images of fragrance surround his cheeks and lips. The choice of these particular images is significant; they are key to understanding this unit of the poem as it moves gradually toward the surprising conclusion in 6:2-3.

The Beloved describes the Lover's eyes as "doves" (5:12), but he has first described hers as such (1:15; 4:1); in fact he has already named her "my dove" (2:14; 5:2). The Beloved is saying that she sees herself reflected in his eyes; they mirror her presence. She likens his cheeks to beds of spices, "towers of aromatic herbs!" Again the Beloved uses a comparison first applied to herself (4:10; 5:1). She says his lips are lilies, but she has first called herself a lily. He associates her breasts with lilies (4:5) and she says that he grazes among the lilies (2:16). His lips drip myrrh and her fingers and hands do also (5:5); in fact the Lover links her person to myrrh throughout Part Two (3:6; 4:6; 5:1). Thus through these poetic images of fragrance in 5:13 the Beloved again achieves a suggestion of union, of intermingled presences. She herself, her hands, fingers, breasts, and the very scent of her person are on his cheeks and drawn to his lips by these associations.

5:14-16: After prolonged consideration of her Lover's head, the Beloved's song moves more quickly in describing his arms, torso, and legs. Each part of his body is described in terms of a precious substance. There is a parallel between 5:15b and 5:10a since both deal with general appearance and the impression of towering splendor. The imagery again is a bond between the Lover and the Beloved. He has praised her appearance (2:14), likened the fragrance of her garments to that of Lebanon (4:13), and called her a stream flowing from Lebanon (4:15).

6:1: The Daughters display greater interest in participating in the Beloved's search. They respond with questions parallel in form to those of 5:9. In asking where the Lover has gone they seek to know the direction he has taken so that they may search for him.

6:2: The Beloved's answer seems to indicate that her Lover has not gone away after all. She speaks of the garden and repeats the refrain of mutual possession. The Lover is not absent, but present in his garden; their union is not interrupted. As the Beloved sings her Lover's praise she discovers his presence within herself and her presence in him. In this way a moment of physical absence leads to the awareness that love's union is all-embracing and cannot be easily broken.

Part Four: 6:4–8:4

The fourth part of the Song is established by the refrains of 6:3 and 8:3-4. Internally the text is composed of two long descriptive songs in praise of the Beloved (6:4-10 and 7:1-9) and finally a passage that resumes both the garden and search motifs.

6:4-10: Part Three concluded with the refrain of mutual possession (6:3). The refrain is not a simple repetition, for it comes at a point in the Song where a deeper level of union has been realized than when it was first used (2:16). Something similar may be said of the song of praise that opens Part Four. It appears to be a repetition of 4:1-7 but it has original elements that make it a new song, the result of renewed contemplation of the Beloved.

The two songs begin in the same way (at 4:1 and 6:4), but the first song moves downwards with a vertical description of the Beloved. The second (6:4) tends to be a still portrait. It captures a sense of the awe and wonder the Beloved inspires while allowing our gaze to linger primarily upon her head and face.

6:4: The Beloved is compared to the two capital cities of Israel and Judah. The comparison introduces another enclosed image for the Beloved. Along with the aspect of beauty (Tirzah means "pleasant") the poet introduces a note of awe and terror.

6:8-9: From a singularly focused contemplation of the Beloved's face and head the Lover's gaze turns in a broad encompassing circle. He sees her now in comparison with others and uses more spectacular images to express her extraordinary beauty. The second person direct address shifts to third person without losing the personal immediacy of the song being sung to her.

The numerical sequence—sixty, eighty, innumerable—sets up a pattern of intensification that deepens awareness of the superlative beauty of the Beloved. This multitude of women, commonly assumed to be remarkably beautiful, is collectively referred to by the single pronoun "they" (6:8). By way of contrast with this host there is a second numerical sequence with regard to the Beloved (6:9). Instead of a steady progression of large numbers there is an insistent repetition of the number "one." In this way the poet repeats the pattern of intensification used in 6:8, but uses it to underscore the Beloved's uniqueness. The overall result is a testimony that mirrors 5:10 where the Beloved proclaims her Lover to be "distinguished among ten thousand."

6:10: The unparalleled and awesome beauty of the Beloved finds further emphasis in the series of comparisons: the dawn, the moon, the sun, and bannered hosts.

6:11-12: Contrary to the notation in the Greek version it is the Lover who speaks in these verses. Throughout the Song he is always the subject of any verb indicating motion toward or entrance into the garden (cf. 4:16; 5:1; 6:2). The Beloved is identified with the garden itself. By using the verb "see" three times the poet accents repose in the Beloved by means of contemplation.

6:12: Often designated the most difficult verse in the entire Canticle, 6:12 makes no sense whatever as it stands in the Hebrew text. Literally the line reads, "I do/did not know my soul (it) set me chariots of my princely people." If the phrase is translated as an idiom the result is "I was delirious (out of my senses); I found myself in the chariot with a prince."

6:13: The rhythmic style of the Chorus's intervention at 6:13 seems to imitate the dance itself. Used four times, the imperative "turn" resounds like an accompanying chant. The Beloved is referred to as "Shulamite," the feminine counterpart of Solomon. The meaning of the root on which these names are constructed has the sense of "peace" or "wholeness." Hence the delightful woman is the one who brings peace. The Bride responds by asking what they will see in the Shulamite and they respond "a dance before two armies" or "the dance of the two camps." This particular dance originated as a way of joyously celebrating a military victory. It was a whirling dance performed by women, frequently accompanied by musical instruments and sometimes antiphonal chanting (cf. Exod 15:20; Judg 11:34; 1 Sam 18:6; 21:12; 29:5).

7:1-9: The end of the lengthy song of praise that follows is marked by the refrain that occurs at 7:10. The song has two movements: one of contemplation (7:1-5) and one of expressed desire (7:6-9). These two movements are clearly indicated in the text not only by the content but also by the repetition of a cry of appreciation ("How fair!") coupled with an epithet ("O queenly maiden" (7:1) and "O delectable maiden" (7:6).

7:1-5: This last song of praise begins at the feet and moves upward to the head. As with the Beloved's song in 5:10-16 that proceeds in the opposite direction (high to low) there is a complete vertical movement. The anatomical references in each line create a sort of inner column or "trunk" to which descriptive words or phrases are attached. There is an interplay of verticality and roundness in the song itself suggesting a tree, and that is the metaphor the Lover takes up explicitly (7:7-8) in the second movement.

There are an unusual number of geographic references in vv. 4-5. It has already been noted how the body of the Beloved is identified with the flora and fauna of the land (cf. 4:1-6 and 6:4-7). There is an even greater emphasis in this song. Mount Gilead alone was mentioned in the earlier passages; here there are also Lebanon and Carmel. The names of three cities—Heshbon, Bath-rabbim, and Damascus—extend the woman-city metaphor established in 6:4.

7:6-9: Having gazed upon his Beloved in the dance, allowing his gaze to travel from feet to head, the Lover compliments his Beloved by introducing the image of a tree. In the Lover's comparison of his Beloved to a palm tree we may see another instance of the "mirroring effect." She has already likened him to the apple tree (2:3) and the cedar of Lebanon (5:15). The clusters to which her breasts are compared are the clusters of dates found on the date palm.

Contemplation gives way completely to desire for possession. In a state of heightened emotion the Lover freely associates a number of images: dates, grape clusters, apples, and wine. The Lover's desire for union, represented as longing to grasp and eat and to bring in fragrance culminates in the final image of drink in 7:9. The Beloved breaks into her Lover's excited effusion of praise and pleading with a response of acquiescence. Taking up his image of wine, she continues the sequence of associations and brings them to a conclusion.

7:10: On a note of repose the Beloved begins the familiar refrain "I am my beloved's" (or: "My beloved is mine") and concludes it with an unusual variation, "and his desire is for me." The formula of mutual possession appears three times and each time there is a modification determined by the context (cf. 2:16; 6:3). The variation "his desire is for me" introduces an unmistakable reference to Gen 3:16 where we find "your desire shall be for your husband, and he shall rule over you." In the Song of Songs the subjects are reversed. He desires her and she is wholly given to him. This phrase, so suggestive of Genesis, makes us aware that the refrain falls between a unit in which the primary image is the "tree" (7:6-9) and one in which the image is "garden" (7:11-13). The refrain in this context thus functions as a statement of balanced desires, lack of domination, and mutual invitation and response. It suggests the power of love to redeem the curse of Gen 3:16.

7:11–8:2: The final unit of Part Four is delimited by the single refrain of 7:10 and the double refrains of 8:3-4. The Beloved's response begins with two verbs denoting motion outwards ("come," "let us go out") and concludes with two verbs indicating motion inwards ("I would lead you," "I would bring you in," 8:2). Four plural cohortative forms follow in rapid succession: "let us go out," "let us spend the night," "let us rise early," and "let us see." The verb forms themselves strongly bespeak the lovers' union, their movement together. The enclosed image of the city lies behind the call to go out. The "field" signifies an open cultivated area outside a walled city where there are vineyards, grain fields, orchards, and gardens of other food crops (cf. Gen 37:7; Ruth 2:2; 2 Kings 4:39).

The Beloved's invitation to "come out" and observe the signs of spring mirror 2:10-13 to some extent. However, the sense conveyed by 7:11-12 is beyond that of 2:10-13. In the earlier passage (2:10-13) the description of nature's spring awakening forms the background for love's timid awakening. In the latter passage (7:11-12) it is the budding and blossoming taking place in the field and vineyards that have moved to the foreground and become the very image of their own love that has been awakened.

7:13: The Beloved promises to give her caresses and kisses to her Lover (7:12); in 7:13 it is the mandrakes that give off their scent. The phrase is very expressive not only because mandrakes *(dudāi)* so resemble love *(dodai)* in 7:12, but also because of the many explicit associations between giving expressions of love and giving scent (1:2-3; 1:12-14; 4:10; 4:15; 5:5). The imagery moves quickly from scent to food.

8:1-2: It is not a sibling relationship that the Beloved is seeking, nor does the title "brother" signify a spousal epithet as "sister" does in 4:9-10; 5:1-2. The reason she wishes he were her brother is that then she would have freedom to express her affection spontaneously in public as children do, without risking social censorship. The sequence of verbs reveals a steady progression of intimacy and movement inwards: "meet," "kiss," "lead," "bring you in," and "give you to drink." The spiced wine the Beloved would give her Lover to drink is made of pomegranate. Pomegranates refer to herself (4:3, 13; 6:7); therefore to give their wine is to give herself.

8:3-4: The concluding refrains of embrace (8:3) and adjuration (8:4) fittingly bring Part Four to a close on a note of union and repose.

Epilogue: 8:5-14

An epilogue is a short poem or speech spoken after the conclusion and serving to complete the plan of the work. It usually recapitulates the principal themes. Often the epilogue draws a practical application from the work and delivers a strong emotional appeal to the audience.

8:5-7: In contrast to 8:3-4 with its accent on union and repose, 8:5 initiates a new movement. Like a spotlight suddenly illuminating a still and darkened stage the question "Who is that?" concentrates interest on the Beloved. It is her person that unifies and dominates the Epilogue. This cry of wonder, expressed by the Daughters of Jerusalem or an anonymous chorus (cf. 3:6) announces her arrival to speak the final, all-important message of the Song.

The Beloved's words about awakening her Love under the apple tree are a puzzle, and one wonders what they have to do with the powerful verses that follow. Why should they be the first words of an epilogue that seeks to clarify and interpret the entire Song? The adjuration refrain has been seen as one of the most important structuring devices of the Song. The Daughters are admonished three times not to awaken love (2:7; 3:5; 8:4). The precise meaning of the refrain has remained elusive. It could refer to "love" in the abstract sense or it could signify a person, and refer to either the Beloved or the Lover. Here in the epilogue the Beloved declares that she has "awakened" her Lover. In what sense has she awakened him?

The clues are in the text. In the Prologue the Lover is identified as the apple tree, a place where the Beloved rested and feasted, and the apple tree was also the place of embracing (2:5-6). In 8:5 "there" corresponds to "under the apple tree." There are further correspondences between the subjects "I" and "your mother" and the predicates "to be in labor," "to bear," and "to bring forth a child." The implication is that the Beloved who "awakened" her Lover corresponds in some way to his mother who was in labor and brought him forth into the world. The sense of 8:5 is an awakening to new life. In the embrace of love she has given him a new birth. This is the power of the love in the Song. Hence the adjuration takes on a new weight of meaning. Its entreaty not to "stir up or awaken love until it is ready" is more than a caution not to disturb a loved one's sleep. It is a warning not to trivialize a powerful force that gives rise to a new creation.

8:6-7: Often quoted and referred to as the "summa" of the Song, 8:6-7 is a statement on the mystery of love that is appropriate only here. In the Song itself Lover and Beloved speak "in" love to and about one another. They are shown interacting: speaking and listening, calling and responding, discovering and praising, acting and reacting. By the time the Beloved utters her quasi-covenantal profession, "I am my beloved's and my beloved is mine" (6:3) the attentive observer has already realized that a confluence of souls is taking place. Particularly in the songs of praise one perceives a deep union expressed by a type of "mirroring" of one another. Mutual discovery has also been a discovery of the created world. The loved one is seen in all of creation, and all of creation is disclosed in the loved one. Lest the audience fail to realize the measure of this love and mistake it for something less than it is, the Epilogue offers a final word "about" love, about the nature of love to which the Song witnesses.

The image of the "seal" is suggested by the refrain of 8:3. Supported by his arm and held against his heart, the Beloved desires to remain there but in an even more profound way. She asks to become like the personal seal he wears on a cord around his neck that rests on his heart, or like one he binds to his arm. By becoming this seal she would identify who he is and authenticate all he does. She would become a type of enclosure for him, for all his thoughts, affections, and deeds.

The next four phrases give the reason for the Beloved's imperative, "Set me as a seal." Using the terse, vivid style characteristic of the *mashal* in Wisdom literature she expresses another dimension of this love. Just as it is creative of new life, so it also contends with the destructive powers of death and the nether world. The definite article that appears with the noun "death," along with the attribution of strength and cruelty, indicates that "death" and "Sheol" are personified and matched in combat against "love" and "jealousy," attributes of God. The next phrase, "Its flashes are flashes of fire; a flame of Yah!" *(šalhebetyāh),* clearly identifies the nature of this love as an opening to the transcendent experience of YHWH.

Much more is suggested by 8:7 than the simple idea that love is a fire that many waters cannot extinguish. The primary reference for "many waters" is YHWH's struggle against the sea dragon Rahab or Leviathan, God's subduing of the chaotic waters prior to creation and continuous domination of the sea. In other words love's triumph over the mighty waters and rivers that originate in the deeps is a victory over cosmic evil. By extension "many waters" signify all kinds of disasters, obstacles, and experiences of struggle with evil and oppression. Love is stronger than they are; it cannot be suffocated by them.

The scope of vision offered by these three verses (8:5-7) is immense. A very particular love relationship is defined as a creative force (8:5) requiring an unbreakable bond of mutual commitment (8:6). Thus sealed, its power can only be compared to the unleashed primordial elements of fire and water. It fills the expanse of the cosmos, reaches downward to the nether world and breaks its hold; it soars upwards like a flame to the transcendent experience of God who is Love.

8:8-10: The Beloved's brothers, those whom she calls "my mother's sons" in 1:6, are probably the speakers in 8:8-9. The role of a girl's brother in protecting her and making marriage arrangements is well attested (Gen 24:50-51; 35:6-18). In the brothers' opinion their sister is not yet developed. They contemplate means of protecting her until she is of marriageable age. Meanwhile the Beloved claims that she has matured and has found peace in the eyes of her Lover. The presence of the word "peace" at the end of 8:10 is important. It brings the exchange between the brothers and the Beloved to a point of resolution. An earlier incident (1:6) was marked by tension, anger, and disfavor. The initial act of the brothers had been to protect their sister; here it is to enhance and beautify her.

8:11-12: This is a parable set in the indefinite past. Solomon initially appears as a historical-legendary figure. The location of his vineyard in Baal-hamon is more symbolic than geographic. The name means "husband of a multitude." As the parable progresses it suddenly shifts from the distant past to the present. The Beloved directly addresses Solomon: "My vineyard, my very own, is for myself; you, O Solomon, may have the thousand (silver pieces), and the keepers of the fruit two hundred!" One is aware that both Solomon and the vineyard operate at a literal and figurative level. This phenomenon occurs also in the Prologue where Solomon at one moment is the Solomon of history, symbol of wealth and luxury (1:5) and at another her Lover, the "king" who leads her into his chambers (1:4) and reclines at her breast (1:12). The vineyards are those the Beloved tends (1:6) where she is darkened by the sun, and also a symbol of herself (1:6; 2:15; 6:11; 7:12).

Paradoxically, the experience of love has given the Beloved self-possession. Thus she tells Solomon (her Lover) to keep his wealth, or give some to the keepers of his vineyards' fruit (the brothers). Her vineyard is "gift" and not to be bought at any price (8:7).

8:13-14: The conclusion of the Song is unexpected. In a brief exchange of dialogue the Lover addresses his Beloved by a new epithet, "O you who dwell in the garden." He tells her that his companions are waiting for her voice. The Beloved's response to his plea is a surprising: "Flee away, my Love." The verb in this case does not mean simply "hurry" or "make haste." It means to leave in a hurry. However the final phrase, "upon the mountains of spices" (cf. 4:6) seems to be an invitation to come to herself rather than a separation. There is a tension between the two parts of her final words: hurry away and come.

The Beloved tells him to go off quickly but implies that his going is a way of coming again, that absence is a way of presence, that their love is never static and meant to linger long in one embrace. It is dynamic and continuously developing. The Song of Songs ends just as it began, *in medias res.*

BIBLIOGRAPHY

Arminjon, Blaise. *The Cantata of Love.* Translated by Nelly Marans. San Francisco: Ignatius Press, 1988.

Elliott, M. Timothea. *The Literary Unity of the Canticle.* Frankfurt and New York: Peter Lang, 1989.

Fox, Michael V. *The Song of Songs and the Ancient Egyptian Love Songs.* Madison: University of Wisconsin Press, 1988.

Lys, Daniel. *Le plus beau chant de la creation: Commentaire du Cantiques des Cantiques.* LeDiv 51. Paris: Cerf, 1968.

Murphy, Roland E. *The Song of Songs.* Hermeneia. Minneapolis: Fortress, 1990.

Origen. *The Song of Songs: Commentary and Homilies.* Translated by R. P. Lawson. ACW 26. Westminster, Md.: Newman Press, 1957.

Pope, Marvin H. *Song of Songs.* AB 7C. Garden City, N.Y.: Doubleday, 1977.

Wisdom

José Vílchez

FIRST READING

As is often the case in the books of Sacred Scripture, the title of the book of Wisdom does not belong to the text but rather to the written tradition that preserved this word, *Sophia,* as a common term.

The text of the book has been preserved either in whole or in part within five manuscripts written in uncial script or capital letters: A, the Codex Alexandrinus from the fifth century C.E.; B, the Codex Vaticanus of the fourth century; א, the Codex Sinaiticus of the fourth century; U, the Venetian codex of the ninth century, and C, a palimpsest of the thirteenth century called Ephraemi Rescriptus (a text of Ephraim the Syrian written over an original fifth-century codex) in which the book of Wisdom is partially preserved. We will rely on a good critical edition of the original Greek text prepared by Joseph Ziegler, *Sapientia Salomonis* (Göttingen: Vandenhoeck & Ruprecht, 1962).

Of the ancient versions the most authoritative is the Vetus Latina (VL or La), which Jerome left intact; it probably dates from the second half of the second century and is of African origin. There are also other ancient versions of lesser importance: Coptic, Syriac, Ethiopic, Arabic, and Armenian versions.

Who is the author of the book of Wisdom? Wisdom 9:7-18 refers to Solomon without naming him, though the title of the book (*Sophia Salōmōnos,* "Wisdom of Solomon") uses his name. Some Fathers of the Church, Jewish and Christian writers of the first centuries and of the Middle Ages, as well as some later writers also attribute the authorship of the book of Wisdom to Solomon. But for weighty reasons we are obliged to deny that Solomon was the literary author of Wisdom. The style of the book, the teachings that are presented there, the cultural and historical ambience reflected in the book—none of these reflect the times of Solomon. In addition, among the Fathers and ancient writers there are some highly credible authors such as Jerome and Augustine who also deny the supposed authorship of Solomon.

If, then, Solomon is not the author of the book of Wisdom, who is? We can affirm with assurance that the author was an Alexandrian Jew of Greek language and culture.

With reference to the date of the composition of the book of Wisdom, there are two extreme opinions: one relies on the Greek text of the Bible (placing it at the beginning or end of the third century B.C.E.) and the other attributes it to the period of Philo of Alexandria (ca. 20 B.C.E. to 40 C.E.). Our proposal is that the book of Wisdom was probably written during the reign of Augustus Caesar: between 30 B.C.E. and 14 C.E., based on an analysis of the book itself which includes probable allusions to historical situations at the time of the author, philosophical and literary sources, vocabulary, etcetera.

Concerning the unity of the book of Wisdom there were no disputes until the mid-eighteenth century, but those interminable sterile discussions were generally resolved and the unity of the composition was affirmed.

The book of Wisdom belongs to the laudatory genre in its general and basic lines, but it is a model unto itself. Nevertheless, we also find in Wisdom lesser literary genres such as exhortations, hymns, prayers, speeches, historical reflections, etcetera. In the first part the sapiential gnomic genre predominates together with eschatological and apocalyptic elements; in the second part the eulogy prevails, and in the third the midrash and syncrisis or comparison.

As audience the Jewish author of Wisdom always has before his eyes the Egyptian Jewish community of his time. With his words he tries to strengthen and console his fellow worshipers in the faith, but also to extend his work to the non-Jewish environment. He is realistic enough to know that the book of Wisdom could fall into the hands of any cultured person, including those high dignitaries in Alexandria who were such avid seekers of culture.

As for the sources of influence that appear in the book of Wisdom, some come from the external Hellenistic milieu in which the author lived; others, the majority, derive from Judaism itself (especially the Hebrew Scriptures).

Can one discover vestiges of Wisdom in the NT (the Christian Scriptures)? We must be open to the possibility that some NT authors knew the book of Wisdom since the Bible they used was principally the Greek one that came from Egypt (Alexandria). At least it is probable that a relationship of dependence exists between Rom 5:12 and Wis 2:24; Heb 1:3 and Wis 7:25; Matt 27:39-43 and Wis 2:18. Likewise, the gospel of John is very close to Wisdom because of their common themes from the Exodus.

Wisdom, a Canonical and Ecclesial Book

Originally written in Greek, Wisdom was never included in the canon of sacred Palestinian books but rather in the Alexandrian canon. As time passed, the book of Wisdom was used more and more in the Christian churches. There was a growing appreciation and esteem for this book even by those who did not consider it sacred. The book was known and cited explicitly from early times in the Church: by Clement of Rome, Irenaeus, Tertullian, Clement of Alexandria, Cyprian, Origen (despite some reservations), the Cappadocians, the Antiochene writers (except Theodore of Mopsuestia); in the West, Hilary and Ambrose used Wisdom and the other sacred books indiscriminately. Jerome, firmly holding to the Hebrew canon, did not consider it a sacred book. Augustine, however, tirelessly defended the presence of the book of Wisdom in the canon. After the Council of Trent in 1546 Catholics no longer discussed its canonicity. Because of having been so controversial, the book of Wisdom is among the deutero-canonical books; Jews and Protestants, however, consider it apocryphal.

There is frequent use of the book of Wisdom in the liturgy, in the missal as well as in the breviary. The missal includes in Cycle A: Sundays in Ordinary Time 16 and 32; Cycle B: Sundays in Ordinary Time 13, 25, and 28; Cycle C: Sundays in Ordinary Time 19, 23, and 31, and in the ferial lectionary Friday of the fourth week in Lent; the lectionary for Ordinary Time in uneven years uses it in Week 32, and it is used in the Common of martyrs, where it is the fifth suggested reading from the First Testament. It is also suggested for funeral rites for adults (second and third readings from the First Testament); the Common of doctors (second reading from the First Testament); and for the votive Mass of the Holy Cross outside paschal time.

In the Breviary, Wisdom appears in the Office of Readings for the thirty-third week in Ordinary Time; Week I of the Psalter; the first reading of the Common of several martyrs, the Common of doctors, and the Common of male saints. In the Liturgy of the Hours its canticles are used for Lauds for Saturday of the third week; Canticles II and III of the Common of apostles; Canticles I, II, and III of the Common of martyrs; Canticle III of the Feast of the Corpus Christi.

SECOND READING

The book of Wisdom is a re-reading of the First Testament (Hebrew Scriptures) made by a Jew of the Diaspora at the dawn of the Christian era. In this *second reading* we shall try to follow the author step by step on his journey. Since his work is a sacred text, we will accept his message as the message of God.

God promises final eschatological victory to individuals (Part One) and to whole peoples (Part Three) although some of these may have to suffer partial defeats that might seem definitive to profane eyes. Those who desire to discover and do God's will must know Wisdom. She transforms them into just and holy friends of God, prophets and kings (Part Two). Those who forget God and follow their own criteria are transformed into offenders against God and humankind.

Part One: 1:1–6:21

The life and experience of each day show us a cruel reality: the wicked boast of their power and triumph while those who are governed by the norms of justice are the objects of mockery, derision, and even physical violence. The wise person, passionate lover of justice (1:1-15) and of Wisdom (6:1-21), reflects on this reality and gives a very positive response from the point of view of his or her personal and eschatological faith. This perspective is not their own creation; they accept it as the living tradition in Israel over the past century and a half.

The Exhortation to Love Justice (1:1-15)

This first pericope serves as introduction to the entire book. Wisdom 1:1-5 demonstrates the kind of justice the powerful of the earth ought to love and what their relationships with God ought to be. The great themes of justice, wisdom, and the Holy Spirit appear here. Wisdom 1:6-11 seems to be a little treatise on the sins of the tongue. Wisdom 1:7 is a well known text chosen for the liturgy of Pentecost. It is a traditional teaching on the doctrine of the omnipresence of God (see Jer 23:24; 1 Kings 8:27; Ps 139:7; Gregory the Great, *Moral.* 2.12.20: MPL 75.565). In Wis 1:12-15 the author typically develops through contrasts the theme of death and immortality, the central theme of the first part.

The Face-to-Face Encounter Between the Wicked and the Just (1:16–2:24)

The pericope is presented in an artistic form customary for an academic work at that time. The antithesis between the wicked and the just is the hinge on which hangs the first part of Wisdom. There is an *introduction* in which the wicked are presented as the protagonists (1:16–2:1a). There follows a long *discourse* that the author puts into the mouth of the impious; these expound on their understanding of life and their condemnation of the just (2:1b-20). We are dealing with a completely materialistic view of human existence, one that denies any kind of life after death and admits no divine intervention in human life. Death is the absolute and only horizon in life. The victims of this kind of worldview will be the weak and the just. Who is this innocent poor or just one? In Christian tradition the *just one* prefigures Jesus on the cross. However, we cannot argue or clearly demonstrate that Wisdom 2:12-20 is a messianic text. The just one is not some specific person, but rather a typical figure. Naturally, then, the text can be applied to Jesus, the Just One *par excellence.*

The discourse is a masterly piece of rhetoric that can be divided into four stanzas. Their titles could be the following: (1) Life is short (2:1b-5); (2) Let us enjoy life (2:6-9); (3) Let us eliminate the weak and all those who consider themselves just (2:10-16); (4) Let us prove who is right, they or we (2:17-20).

Having finished his discourse on the wicked, the author shows once again his disagreement with and rejection of their way of thinking (2:21-22). He expresses his own belief in the transcendent destiny of human beings according to the magnificent plan of God and human response to this plan (2:23-24). In Wis 2:23 the author affirms the positive doctrine and fundamental pillar upon which rests his own eschatological hope and that of all the just ones to whom he explicitly refers (3:1-9), that is, that the human person is not a being hurled out into the emptiness of existence in order to return to nothingness; this creature of God is endowed with a destiny worthy of its Creator, namely a happy eternity with God. The whole person, an indivisible reality, is an image of God and the privileged place of visible creation where God is manifested. Revelation in Christ has carried this theme of the icon of God to its utmost limits in Jesus Christ who is the image of God *par excellence* (see 2 Cor 4:4; Col 1:15).

Following this luminous picture of a happy immortal life with God (2:23) we read the dark contrast of 2:24: the entry of the kingdom of death, presided over by Satan, enemy and adversary of the human race. The author no doubt refers to the account in Gen 3:1-23 and sees behind the tempter serpent the tempter devil. Wisdom 2:24a ("death entered the world") is a prelude to Rom 5:12a. Paul depended on Wisdom for a formulation of his own doctrine even though he does not acknowledge the author of Wisdom as his source. Wisdom 2:24 does not contain *ex professo* the doctrine of original sin but neither does it deny it. Paul reads Genesis through Wisdom or through a vision like that of Wisdom.

A Revelation Concerning the Paradoxes of This Life (Wisdom 3–4)

This section gives the central focus to the first part of the book. A succession of four diptychs presents in alternating passages both the just and the unjust:

Just	**Unjust**
3:1-9	3:10-12
3:13-15	3:16-19
4:1-2	4:3-6
4:7-16	4:17-20

Under a new light that radiates faith in personal immortality the author goes on giving answers to the enigmas and paradoxes life presents. Three such paradoxes particularly attract attention: suffering, sterility, and the premature death of the just.

The Trials of the Just; the Punishment of the Wicked, 3:1-12

The Wisdom writer responds to the enduring question that arises to challenge one's faith in God, namely the evident contradiction life presents: the failure of the just and the triumph of the wicked (see Eccl 4:1; 7:15; 8:14; Psalm 73 and the resistant attitude of Job who rebels against God because of the unexplained destruction of his life).

In Wis 3:1-9 the author confronts the scandal of persecution and suffering of the just; this, he says, does not happen without reason. On dying, the just one arrives at the place of peace or blessedness with God (3:1-3). Suffering in this present life is the test to which God puts the just in order to purify them (3:4-6). Faith in eternal life (which is the resurrection for us) gives meaning to existence. Finally, 3:7-9 (parallel to 3:1-3) moves us to a place beyond this life: the glorious manifestation of the prize attained by the just.

Following this luminous picture of the future happiness of the just (3:1-9) there is a dark description of the future of the wicked in 3:10-12. The author takes it upon himself to sketch the strong contrast by means of repeated antitheses and references where all is negative concerning even those things that might be considered of greatest value: work, family, and the fruits of one's work. The contrast is complete: light/darkness; plenitude/emptiness; life/death. The author sees this bleak future as remote, and so presents it in the present time as an irreversible and final state.

Sterility and Fecundity, 3:13–4:6

The author responds with total assurance and authority to another of the enigmas for the Israelites. According to their tradition, children are the most precious blessing from God (see Lev 26:9; Deut 7:14; 28:4, 11; Ps 128:1-4); they are a gift of God, as Joseph confessed to his father Jacob in Gen 48:9. The same message is expressed in the various narratives of sterile mothers who conceived and gave birth to children because they had asked it of the Lord: Sarah (Genesis 17), the mother of Samson (Judges 13), Hannah, the mother of Samuel (1 Samuel 1). In their children the name and memory of the parent survives (see Sir 40:18; Ruth 4:14). With the loss of children even the possibility of remembrance is jeopardized (see Job 18:17-19).

On the other hand the festive image of the house of the impious person is a stumbling block for the Israelite. In the face of this reality one might ask: is fruitfulness always the sign of God's blessing? Of what is sterility a sign? Of condemnation? For the just it is a hard test (see 1 Sam 1:5-6) and for women it is a source of humiliation and the permanent cause of bitterness and despair (see 1 Sam 1:9-18). The author tackles this age-old problem from the new viewpoint of faith in personal immortality.

The Fecund Sterility of the Just (3:13-15)

Continuing with the author's pattern of alternating terms, now the just have their turn; these are represented by a sterile woman and a eunuch. A motif rarely addressed in former times is here proclaimed by the book of Wisdom: Happy are the sterile. The faithful eunuch, like the barren woman, ought to be called fortunate. In Israel the Law excluded eunuchs from the assembly of the Lord (Deut 23:2) and from offering sacrifices on the altar (Lev 21:20); however, Isa 56:4-5 states: "To the eunuchs who keep my sabbaths, who choose the things that please me and hold fast to my covenant, I will give, in my house and within my walls, a monument and a name better than sons and daughters; I will give them an everlasting name." Our author's Greek shows many similarities with the Greek translation of Isaiah, and on this point he has inherited the prophet's doctrine.

The Sterile Fruitfulness of the Wicked (3:16-19)

The author here opposes the fruitful sterility of the just with the sterile fecundity or useless value of the wicked people's offspring. Since not all lack of posterity is lamentable (3:13-15), neither is all posterity a sign of blessing (3:16-19). Beginning with Wis 3:16 the center of attention changes: the parents are not considered the culpable ones as might be expected, but rather it is the children or descendants who receive blame. Underlying the entire verse is the ancient concept among the Israelites of the strict, legal solidarity among members of a family (see 2 Samuel 21; Exod 20:5; Jer 31:29; Ezek 18:2).

Blessed Childlessness and Useless Fecundity (4:1-6)

This diptych contains another antithesis: lack of children (4:1-2)/numerous progeny (4:3-6), which does not correspond exactly to the sterility/fecundity antithesis (3:13-19), at least not in its first part. In 3:13-19 the author is interested in emphasizing the positive value of the sterility of the just and the negative aspect of the fecundity of the wicked through viewing their fruits or the concrete results of their sterility or fecundity. It's a matter, therefore, of rightly appreciating—in the light of faith in one's personal immortality—some human contradictory situations that always seem to offend the just. Then, in 4:1-6, the author is concerned with the theme itself, that is, the lack of children among the just (4:1-2) as well as the numerous offspring of the impious as a concrete phenomenon, capable of being analyzed and evaluated in itself (4:3-6).

The Premature Death of the Just and the Tragic End of the Wicked, 4:7-20

We have come to the fourth antithesis of this central section of the first part of the book, where the author deals with what has been an enigma for the wise of all times. The death of the young is doubly enigmatic even for those who consider life to be a gift from God. The enigma becomes an unsolvable mystery if, in addition to being young, the person who has died is also just and God-fearing. At the same time the author makes older people reflect seriously, but not so much on the themes of wisdom and prudence. This pericope likewise consists of a diptych or two successive descriptions.

The Death of the Just Person Who is Young (4:7-16)

Wisdom 4:7 briefly formulates the author's thesis. The just person about whom he speaks is a model person according to the will and plan of God (4:10, 14a), a person who has arrived at human maturity according to divine measures and norms that are not always commensurate with human ones. The premature death of the just had always been a stumbling block for the devout faithful, accustomed as they were to reading in the Scriptures the promises of a long life and prosperity for those who observe the Law (see Exod 20:12; Deut 5:16; 30:20; Pss 21:4; 23:6; 91:16; Prov 3:1-2, etcetera). Nevertheless, at the dawn of the NT era the hope of the just penetrates beyond the frontiers of death. No longer is there so much fear of death: the just will enjoy repose, eternal rest, in the words of the Christian liturgy (Wis 3:3; Isa 57:1-2), since they will be forever in the hands of God (Wis 3:1).

On the other hand, the correct measurement of a life is not its number of years but its virtue (see Prov 16:31; Sir 25:4-6); virtue is the patrimony of the just although they be young, and not that of the wicked who may have countless years (Wis 3:17; 4:16). The sapiential tradition of Greece and Rome as well as the Fathers of the Church have left us precious testimonies of this teaching. The authors see in the young person taken before his or her time (4:10) a clear allusion to the mysterious figure of Enoch (see Gen 5:22, 24; Sir 44:16; also Heb 11:5).

The Tragic End of the Wicked (4:17-20)

The antithesis between the wicked and the just continues in this pericope; however, it is the wise rather than the just person who appears in 4:17a. At the end there is a description of the state to which the wicked will be reduced after their deaths. Their death is the consequence of God's laughter but this must be interpreted as satire since 4:19 takes its inspiration from Isaiah where the prophet speaks against the king of Babylon (Isa 14:4-20).

The Just and the Unjust in an Eschatological Judgment (5:1-23)

The author, through a literary invention, transports us to the end of history in order to present a judgment scene in which the final sentence is pronounced, a massive destruction favoring the just and destroying the unjust. The Wisdom text, like that of Matt 25:31-46, is a literary fiction that corresponds to reality.

The Confidence of the Just; the Terror of the Wicked, 5:1-3

The scene seems to develop outside of time; it is a replica of the one already presented in 2:10-20. The just person of 5:1 makes reference to the just one of 2:10. This is not the Messiah (see 5:5); because of its exemplary and paradigmatic value this passage takes on collective meaning (see 5:15; 3:1-9, and Vg).

The strong contrast between the attitude of the just and that of the unjust particularly attracts attention. To the steadfastness and quiet confidence of the just the author opposes the bewilderment and dread of the unjust. This dramatic form gives substance to a teaching that will always be difficult for mortal ears, namely that the definitive destiny of the persecutor will never be the same as that of the innocent victim, or the eternal fate of the impious the same as that of the just.

Treatise on the Impious, 5:4-13

This impassioned discourse on the wicked responds along general lines to Wis 2:1-20; the situation, however, has changed radically. In 2:1-20 the wicked have not yet died and they reflect upon their present life as well as future death; in 5:4-13 their time has already passed, and with it earthly life. All that develops seems to be in the hereafter.

In their first discourse the wicked wanted to see if the just were right (2:17); in the second they see that it is effectively so (5:2, 4-8) and that they themselves have been mistaken (5:6). Only in one area have they not erred: in their judgment about the transitoriness and brevity of life (cf. 2:1, 4-5 with 5:9-13); but now they recognize that they had badly interpreted its meaning (5:6-13). The author must surely be thinking of Psalm 49.

The Author's Reflections, 5:14-23

Shadows and light alternate in this final scene in which there appear again the wicked and the just, not as actors, but each receiving his or her merited reward from God. The only protagonist is God. We can divide the pericope into four stanzas: the diverse fortune of the wicked and the just (5:14-16); preparation for divine activity (5:17-20); creation as an ally to God's action (5:21-23b) and the final desolation (5:23c, d). The author raises to a universal level the wicked about whom he had spoken in the entire first part. Since wickedness leaves no space untouched in all of creation or the cosmos, the struggle against evil is also universal (5:23). Within that universal struggle creation also must intervene, the creation that is good (see Wis 1:14; Genesis 1) and is on God's side (see Rom 8:19-22).

Exhortation to the Rulers (6:1-21)

Wisdom 6:1-21 presents in an explicit form the doctrine about political power common in all Semitic areas. There is only one source of power: the Lord (1 Chr 28:9; Prov 8:15-16; Dan 2:21, 37; 5:18). Neither king nor kingdom is recognized independently of God. Kings, governors, and the like are only ministers of the kingdom of the Lord (Rom 13:1-4). If the rulers are not the source of power, neither are they the source of law or justice. They also are subject to the law and ought to judge rightly and justly since they, in turn, will be judged.

To the Rulers, 6:1-11

The persons addressed in 6:1-2 are the same as those in 1:1, the kings, the governors, those who have royal power over the people. It should not surprise us that a Jewish writer would address kings, princes, or governors who are not Jewish. The sapiential writings, from their very beginnings, customarily count among their audience every person endowed with authority.

Wisdom Guides the Kingdom, 6:12-21

Something new begins here that serves as introduction and transition to the second part of the book or praise of Wisdom; Sophia is already the center of attention, forming an inclusive circle (6:12-21b). Before going more deeply into the mystery of the origin and nature of Wisdom in 6:22-25 the cantor presents her to us as easily accessible and worthy of being sought and loved (see Proverbs 8). With desire alone she can be had, and the possession of Wisdom leads to the kingdom. The author speaks to the rulers who govern the kingdoms of the earth that can be either exalted or overthrown; he invites them to participate in the heavenly reign that will never end.

Part Two: In Praise of Wisdom: 6:22–9:18

This second part is dedicated entirely to Wisdom. It is the central part of the book and the source of the title. Through literary invention the author is transformed into a king wise beyond comparison, namely Solomon (see 9:7). Thus his words acquire more authority, allowing him to plainly direct his teaching to kings and governors.

Solomon's Discourse on Wisdom (6:22–8:21)

The author is transformed into Solomon. No one in Israelite antiquity could speak of Wisdom with more authority than Solomon (see 1 Kings 3–10); both canonical and non-canonical literature is attributed to Solomon. He was able to demand quality performances from his addressees, the sovereign rulers of nations, as well as possessing depth of material.

The discourse begins with a short introduction (6:22-25) that is then followed by seven parts or sections. The first section (7:1-6) and the last (8:17-21) possess a certain correlation and likeness: they deal with the weakness and mortality of Solomon; both sections conjure up facts about his birth. The second section (7:7-12) and the sixth (8:10-16) praise the value of Wisdom, superior to all good gifts. The third (7:13-22a) and fifth sections (8:2-9) laud Wisdom, greater than all cultural and moral goods. The most important part of the discourse is that which discusses the characteristics and nature of Wisdom (7:22b–8:1).

Introduction to the Discourse of Solomon, 6:22-25

Solomon promises to uncover all the mysteries of Wisdom and to seek truth in everything. As is the author's custom, he devotes a few verses to the closure of the section and also announces what is to come.

Solomon is Like All Mortals, 7:1-6

Here we find a simulated self-presentation of Solomon. It remains very clearly established that if Solomon has anything to communicate to us —and indeed he has—it is not because he has a superhuman nature, but rather because what he has he has freely received. Without entering into a direct polemic the author firmly establishes this fundamental truth: all people without exception, kings as well as subjects, are equals in the human condition.

Wisdom is Superior to All Other Goods, 7:7-12

Here the praise of Wisdom itself begins. She exceeds the most esteemed gifts on earth: power, riches, health, and beauty. This Wisdom does not belong to human nature nor is it the property of kings or rulers. Solomon has to ask for it in order to receive it. The passage refers to the dream of Solomon in the high place at Gibeon (see 1 Kings 3:4-15 and 2 Chr 1: 6-12).

Wisdom is Superior to Moral and Cultural Goods, 7:13-22a

In this new stanza the pseudo-Solomon continues praising Wisdom for herself: inexhaustible treasure because of her intimate union with God. Thus the author identifies Wisdom and God. What is attributed to God—being of divine origin and the source of all good—is also predicated of Wisdom as the artificer of all.

The Nature and Characteristics of Wisdom, 7:22b–8:1

This is the central stanza of the second part and the most important section of the praise of Wisdom. It is outstanding for its rhetorical style and philosophical, religious terminology more closely related to Greek genius than to the Semitic. Wisdom 7:22b-23 deals with the kind of spirit to be found in Sophia, to whom are ascribed twenty-one distinct attributes.

The activity of Wisdom in the cosmos and among people is the central idea brought forth in this section (7:24–8:1). Verses 24-26 of ch. 7 stand out as the first subsection of this composition whose theme is the divine origin of Wisdom. Apparently Wis 7:25-26 has influenced NT christology: Hebrews 1:3 uses the metaphor of reflection or reverberation and links it to glory. This metaphor, applied to Christ, is common in the Pauline writings (see 2 Cor 3:18; 4:4; Col

1:15). This doctrine of divine Wisdom leads to the revelation about the person of the Word once it has been revealed to us in Christ; in turn, the darkness concerning Wisdom and her relationship with God are illumined by Christ, "the wisdom of God" (1 Cor 1:24).

Wisdom 7:27–8:1 moves us through all of creation and history in order to illuminate in them the action and presence of Wisdom. Structurally, Wis 7:27 is at the exact center of the entire pericope. The greatness of Wisdom is manifested in her works: creation or the universe as a whole and the human being as its privileged creature. In Jesus Christ we have been shown the love of God: God loves us before we love God and in spite of our sins (1 John 4: 9-10; Rom 5:8; John 15:12-15).

Wisdom has All Desirable Goods, 8:2-9

The relationship of the wise person to Wisdom is like that of bridegroom to bride. The author develops this comparison with great detail, beginning with courtship and proceeding to conjugal life. This pericope corresponds in general structure to the stanza in Wis 7:13-22a. The difference is that the author refers to divine Wisdom in this particular eulogy. He has already pointed to divine Wisdom in 7:22b–8:1; it is only to God that such words apply.

Wisdom is the Best Companion for the Just and Wise One, 8:10-16

The interior discourse of Solomon begins here (see 8:17a) and all of it is oriented toward the future. The stanza sings of the advantages Solomon obtains because of his having espoused Wisdom, especially worldly fame and imperishable glory after death. Wisdom 8:13 is rightly designated the central verse of this section; seven verses precede it and seven follow. Likewise, the just transcends future time since the remembrance of the wise will be immortal.

Wisdom is a Pure Gift of God, 8:17-21

This short unit summarizes what went before and introduces the following section. Wisdom continues to be the center of attention. Solomon is dedicated to her above all. "Immortality" can mean imperishable fame as in 8:13, but it also means personal life beyond death as is clear from the reference in 8:3 and by virtue of our free participation in Wisdom, the very nature of which presupposes a kind of intimate parenting relationship. Wisdom is always the central theme and in no way can it be merited; it is a true gift of God.

Solomon's Prayer for Wisdom (9:1-18)

This beautiful prayer is a worthy colophon of the song to Wisdom. It is inspired by the prayer of Solomon in 1 Kings 3:6-9 and 2 Chr 1:8-10, but it is enriched with contributions from sapiential literature. We can divide it into three stanzas, each intimately related to the others, yet each autonomous. The central theme of the entire prayer, as well as of each stanza, is Wisdom as a divine gift.

Without Wisdom a Person is Nothing, 9:1-6

This section touches fundamental themes: the God of Israel, creator of the universe (9:1b) and of the human race; the creative function of Wisdom with relationship to humanity (9:2a); the calling and destiny of human beings to be good stewards over all creation (9:2b-3); the destiny and vocation of Solomon, which he will not be able to realize without the Wisdom of God (9:4-6) since, as a human, he is totally weak and impotent (9:5-6). It is, therefore, of vital necessity that God give him Wisdom (9:4a); with her all is possible; without her nothing will succeed (9:6b).

Wisdom from on High, 9:7-12

This whole section refers to Solomon, chosen for a mission he will not be able to accomplish if God does not give him Wisdom. The structure is concentric. One obvious inclusion that marks the beginning and end of the stanza is *ho laos sou,* your people (9:7a and 9:12b). Wisdom 9:7-8, which depicts Solomon as king, judge, and builder, corresponds to 9:12 wherein Solomon acts as judge and king. In the same manner Wis 9:9 is replicated in 9:10c-11. In the center of the circle Solomon asks for divine Wisdom with genuine insistence (9:10a, b).

Wisdom and the Designs of God, 9:13-18

A change to the third person by means of the interrogative pronoun introduces us to a generic theme couched in the terms of a philosophical and theological reflection. In the last section of the prayer it is not Solomon who is the center of the scene but humanity in which Solomon is presented as a mere part of the whole (see Wis 9:14b and 16a, b). Human beings cannot know, much less understand, the designs of God without Wisdom. The chapter ends with the reassurance that salvation has already been realized in past history, thanks to Wisdom (9:18). This becomes a magnificent argument for trust both in the present and in the future.

As it is used here the verb *sōzein,* "save" does not carry the full meaning it will acquire much later in the NT, namely liberation from spiritual dangers and death and the gift of new life in Christ. It means only what is ordinarily understood in the OT: liberation and protection from any natural danger that may be imminent. Nevertheless, Wis 9:18 could be the cause of a more spiritual interpretation of the action of Wisdom in the world. In fact, by Wisdom God creates humanity (9:2a) and through her saves them (9:18c). The same God who creates the world (9:1a) saves it through the wisdom of the wise (see 6:24a).

Part Three: The Justice of God in History: 10:1–19:22

The author reflects on the past actions about which the tradition of his people speaks and uncovers the divine action doing works of justice in history, first through the mediation of Wisdom (10:1–11:1) and then through God's direct action (11:2–19:22). The dominant literary genre is the midrash or free commentary on the canonical Scriptures.

From Adam to Moses: Salvation by Wisdom (10:1–11:1)

The special transitional character of this pericope should be recognized. The author tries to integrate, in broad strokes, the action of Wisdom during a period extending from Adam to Moses. In doing so he presents a series of just persons or types of just persons who through Wisdom have succeeded in overcoming the most diverse trials coming from enemies or impious oppressors. No single name is cited but all are easily identifiable.

From Adam to Noah, 10:1-4

The protective action of Wisdom covers the prehistory of humanity, from Adam to Noah. In Wisdom 10 there is a substitution: rather than YHWH or the angel of YHWH as protector of the patriarchs and the chosen people of Genesis and Exodus, it is now Wisdom. Her protection extends to all kinds of external dangers. In this first section Wisdom shows herself to be the savior of the world and, twice, savior of humankind, that is, in Adam and in Noah.

Abraham and Lot, 10:5-9

The author makes rapid progress in time. He is only interested in underlining some aspects or moments already known to his addressees and those most often treated in non-canonical writings. He makes Abraham (Gen 12:1-9) the contemporary of the episodes surrounding the tower of Babel narrated in Gen 11:1-9. The action of Wisdom is manifested also in the liberation of Lot and the punishment sent upon the cities of the Pentapolis. For this section the author avails himself of non-biblical sources in addition to Genesis 19.

Jacob and Joseph, 10:10-14

First Jacob confronts his brother, Esau; second, his uncle and brother-in-law, Laban; finally, in a very different sense but no less daring, Jacob challenges God. Afterwards Joseph, the just man sold by his brothers, is mentioned. The schema of the story of Joseph, the just man persecuted and glorified, is used elsewhere in the Hebrew Scriptures (Job, Tobit).

Israel and Moses, 10:15–11:1

Earlier, the author praised Wisdom as the protector and liberator of parents; from here on the action of Wisdom is extended to the entire chosen people. Moses fulfills the function of mediator. The epic journey of Exodus is the work of Wisdom. In this section the three central figures of the third part are now present: Israel, Egypt (the enemy), Wisdom (God, the savior).

The Judgment of God upon History (11:2–19:21)

Wisdom 11–19 (if we exclude the two digressions) is a haggadic midrash whose central theme is the confrontation of Israel and Egypt during the Exodus event. Israel appears idealized as the people of God and Egypt is designated the wicked nation, the enemy of Israel. In order to reestablish justice within history, God who is just (12:15) defends and protects the oppressed people and pursues and punishes the oppressor.

In Wisdom 11–19 the author uses both the rabbinic method of midrash and the Hellenistic technique of syncrisis or development through comparisons. He begins with a narrative that briefly summarizes the presence of the people in the desert and the assistance of God in their need (11:2-4). He then proposes a thesis summarizing the theme of the homily (11:5) and proceeds with an explanation and illustration of the theme in seven diptychs, according to the syncretic method (11:6–19:9). There follow some reflections of the author (19:10-21) and the final doxology (19:22). The development into seven diptychs is quite artificial and not always linear or homogeneous since it contains two digressions: one on divine mercy and omnipotence (11:15–12:27) and the other on idolatry (chs. 13–15).

Introductory Narrative, 11:2-4

These three verses summarize the history narrated in Exod 12:37–17:7. This straightforward and simplified history is the subject of Wis 11:1 whose protagonist is Moses, the holy prophet. The episodes in the desert serve as historical introduction to the doctrinal theme of the third part. The grammatical subject is always the same: the people of Israel.

Theme of the Homily, 11:5

The author proposes the theme of his homily in apodictic form: God uses the same means to punish some and benefit others. This principle is repeated in different ways throughout the development of the homily (see 11:13; 16:2, 24; 18:8). It is a synthesis of the theological vision the author has of this particular period as a decisive one in the history of Israel.

Water from the Rock; Bloodied Waters from the Nile, 11:6-14

The first illustration of the general theme was inspired by Exod 7:17-25: the plague involved the waters of the Nile being turned into blood. The theme of this section is the water (11:6-7), the instrument of chastisement for the Egyptians and blessing for the Israelites. Thirst (11:8-14) is another theme, illustrative of the diversity of punishments meted out to various people.

The Two Digressions (11:15–15:19)

The second diptych, the plague of the animals and the provision of quail, is not presented until 16:1-4. Before that the author introduces two important digressions: 11:15–12:27 and 13–15. The thematic and formal unity of the two digressions is resumed in ch. 15:18-19 which closes the cycle of the digressions like pincers.

The Omnipotent God is Merciful to Egypt and Canaan, 11:15–12:27

The vision of the things that befall the Israelites in Egypt, in the desert, and in Canaan—as narrated in the Pentateuch—is clearly theological.

The Lord's Mercy and Compassionate Treatment of the Egyptians (11:15–12:2)

The memory of the plague of irrational animals and reptiles, of vile and despicable vermin, is countered by the memory of divine omnipotence. God did not punish the Egyptians as these insignificant animals had been punished lest his power be dwarfed. Instead God, who always hopes for the conversion of the sinner, acted out of mercy and compassion.

After some introductory verses (11:15-16) the author argues, using negative phraseology, about the divine omnipotence (11:17-20a, b, c) and formulates, in positive style, the principle of balance arranged by God throughout creation, the center and hinge of this entire digression on God's mercy (11:21–12:1). Finally he synthesizes some of the themes and sends us back to the introductory verses, thus forming an inclusion (12:2). The structural form is concentric.

God's Compassion Toward the Canaanites (12:3-18)

Here we find a response to an implied objection: "Why are the Canaanites punished?" The author feels obligated to justify their possession of the Promised Land and yet their annihilation as a people. For that reason he presents a historical act that is then converted into a theological reason: that even while punishing, God reveals divine mercy. The theme of pardon, compassion, and kindness runs through the entire pericope, which is divided into two parts: the Canaanites and their abominable practices (12:3-7) and the moderate and exemplary punishment of the Canaanites on God's part (12:8-18). The author combines the theme of moderation with the theme of justice and injustice.

Double Conclusion to the Theme of the Lord's Mercy and Moderation (12:19-27)

The last part of the first digression consists of a double conclusion to the discourse on the Lord's moderation. The first (12:19-22) teaches the just to be kind, good, and compassionate toward their own enemies, given the example of God's having been compassionate, merciful, and hopeful in pardoning their errors. The second conclusion (12:23-27) is also a teaching: one ought to take advantage of the example of the Egyptians who were punished and corrected because of their idolatry by the very animals they considered gods.

A Criticism of Pagan Religion, 13:1–15:19

The theme of the second digression, worship of false gods, is well known in the Scriptures. Together with Baruch 6 these chapters are the place where the question is treated most fully and systematically. In Wisdom 13–15 the most authentic voices of Israelite tradition and of the philosophic tradition of the Greco-Hellenistic culture come together and are harmonized. The author's plan as proposed in Wisdom 13–15 is obviously apologetic. Together with the destructive criticism he makes of the worship of false gods he reaffirms faithful Jews or strengthens vacillating believers in the true faith. At the same time he intends to help non-Jews of good will who have not yet found the one, true God. For this reason he makes reference continually to the Scriptures as well as using aids from Hellenistic culture.

The Worship of Nature (13:1-9)

This first part of the second digression forms a thematic unity: the worship of God's works, that is, of nature. The principal motif of Wis 13:1-9, accentuated by the stylistic technique of the inclusion in 13:1b and 13:9a, is that nature can be the starting point for acquiring true knowledge of God.

Criticism of the pagan religions begins with the rejection of the most elevated forms of idol worship: the divinization of cosmic elements, of the forces of nature and of the astral world. Starting with Wis 13:10 our author will address the theme of idolatry in its literal meaning, that is, the adoration of things fabricated by human hands.

The pericope found in Wis 13:1-9 is one of the most significant in the book. In it the Judeo-Hellenistic background of the author is perfectly reflected. Present is the world of ideas and religious convictions about the divine found in the pagan cultural milieu in which he lived. There is, as well, the unbreakable faith in God, the creator of the universe, as believed and lived by the Israelites. Augustine has written some valuable reflections on Wis 13:1-9 in his *Confessions,* 10.6.9 and 10.27.38.

The Worship of Idols, its Origin and Consequences (13:10–15:13)

In the previous section the author had in mind the world of the philosophers and wise people; in the present one he directs his teaching rather to the masses. The tone is simple, less polished. In 13:1-9 human beings have a divinized nature, the work of God; in 13:10-19 they divinize the works of their own hands, a greater degradation that carries with it more unfortunate consequences.

The Carpenter and Wooden Idols (13:10-19)

After the introduction (13:10) the author confronts the theme of the making of idols. He develops it ironically, not because it is not important but because he adapts himself to the literary genre of humiliation. He ridicules the idols (13:11-15) as well as those who adore them (13:16-19). The sources of inspiration for the author are biblical (see Isa 44:13-19), but not exclusively so.

Invocation and Transition (14:1-10)

The beginning of this passage is marked by a new theme: that of navigation and ships (14:1-6). We are reminded of Israel's passage, dry-shod, through the Reed Sea and of Noah's ark. The blessing of the wood and what follows, the curse of the idols and their builder (14:7-10), flow from the same theme and serve as transition to the central pericope. Some fathers and doctors of the Church have applied Wis 14:7 to the cross of Christ. In my opinion this is merely the application of a text, different in its original sense, to a new context.

The Origin and Consequences of Idolatry (14:11-31)

The author pauses to reflect upon the phenomenon of idolatry itself, its causes and effects.

He tries to give a reasonable explanation of its origins and dares to predict its future, that is, its disappearance. The protagonist throughout this entire process is the human being, whose responsibility remains evident since it is humans who initiate, promote and reap the fruits of their historic idolatrous actions. God's creation, which is good, is converted into a scenario where the human drama unfolds. God remains hidden and in the background, but it is God, the Lord of creation and of history, who has the last word.

14:11-14: Introduction

Before v. 11 "idol" was spoken of in the singular; with this verse idols are treated in the plural. Wisdom 14:12 partially announces 14:22-31, and 14:14a introduces 14:15-21.

In the strict sense, Christianity dealt a mortal blow to idolatry in the western world, although there still exists the idolatry about which the prophets and Jesus spoke, which will never end precisely because of human injustice.

14:15-21: The Origins and Roots of Idolatry

In this passage the author explains to the overlords the origin of familial and private false worship (14:15) as well as public worship (14:16-20); at the end he draws a penetrating conclusion (14:21). The author appears to be acquainted with the explanation of the origin of faith in popular gods according to *Euhemeros* (the deification of heroes) and he takes advantage of this reasoning to attack idolatry in all its forms. In Ptolemaic Egypt it was part of royal protocol to divinize the highest authorities.

The moral consequences of idolatry (14:22-31). This section portrays the sad, dark state to which idolatry leads: the corruption to which pagan society had, in fact, already come. An inclusion underlines the first and fundamental cause of this corruption: erring in their knowledge of God (14:22a) and thinking ill of God (14:30b).

Wisdom 14:22-26 is the portrayal of a darkened world without direction, a world that does not know the God who has a name and who gives life, a world that puts its trust in manufactured gods and in dead, nameless beings. The judgment is very severe but not unjust. The principal focus of this passage is a list of the evils that afflict a society that has lost its sense of the divine. Similarly, Paul presents impressive pictures of moral corruption in Rom 1:24-28, 1 Cor 6:9, Gal 5:19, and elsewhere.

An Invocation to God and a Transition (15:1-6)

This pericope offers a strong contrast to the preceding text. It is like coming to a life-giving oasis in the desert after having walked through a wasteland. Structurally it corresponds to Wis 14:10. Wisdom 15:1-3 and 14:3-6 are the only prayers directed to God in these three chapters.

The Potter and Clay Idols (15:7-13)

This verse constitutes a new unit determined by its theme—the potter and the clay idols—as well as by the two inclusions: earth (15:7a and 13b) and vessels (15:7d and 13b). It matches the pericope of the carpenter (13:10-19) to which it repeatedly makes reference and from which it is clearly distinguished: the carpenter makes a wooden idol in order to satisfy a particular devotion. The potter, on the other hand, is cynical and ambitious, making clay idols not because compelled to do so out of personal devotion but because of a desire to make money (15:7-13). In 13:10-19 the author scarcely notices the person of the carpenter; his attention is centered on the idol. In this case the center of attention is the potter who tries to be a demi-god.

The Universal Idolatry and Animal Worship of the Egyptians (15:14-19)

A very severe judgment is pronounced against the Egyptians in these verses because they have accepted all the Gentile idols (15:15a) and have worshiped living and worthless animals (15:18-19). This last theme, animal worship, serves as a literary turning point for the digressions that continue from 11:15 to 15:19 and give way to the continuation of the midrash at 16:1.

The Animal Plague and the Quail, 16:1-4

The second diptych or comparative picture of the homiletic midrash is of small animals that torture the Egyptians while the quail satisfy the hunger of the Israelites in the desert. The brief pericope is made up of elements from a true diptych, that is, a negative aspect with relation to the Egyptians, oppressors of the chosen people, and a positive aspect in favor of Israel, the oppressed nation. An inclusion intentionally marks its limits: they were tormented (16:1b and 4b).

The Serpent Bites and the Plague of Insects, 16:5-14

The author relates the story of the serpents in the desert (Num 21:6-9) to the plagues of grasshoppers and other insects in Egypt (Exod 8:12, 17-20; 10:12-17). He likewise discovers a new contrast that constitutes the third diptych of this third part: the serpent bites give occasion for God to exercise mercy toward the people (16:5-7, 10-12) while the grasshopper and fly bites cause the extermination of the Egyptian people (16:9). The medium is the same: the bites of these animals are the cause of ruin (16:9) for some and of salvation for others (16:10).

The author avoids the mediation of Moses, thus more clearly manifesting the salvific action of God. The causality of God does not supplant that of creatures but affirms the fact that an act of a transcendental order will always be required to explain the order of nature. The gospel of Jesus Christ reflects this clearly in John 5:17.

The Plague of Storms; Manna, the Gift of Heaven, 16:15-29

This section is a particular example of haggadic midrash. It is not a case of narrating historical deeds but of interpreting data from Scripture and Jewish tradition in the light of faith and through the screen of the current cosmological understanding. This pericope occupies a central place in the third part. The theme, of great theological significance, is not new in the course of the book but is a thematic variation that throws light on the thesis of Wis 11:5. What is unique here is its application of the physical law of contrasts, as currently understood, to some of the actions narrated in Exod 9:16 and Numbers 11. The author freely meditates on the plagues of Exodus without being limited by any historical perspective. Thus from a purely subjective stance the author allows himself to make a connection between the plagues and the episode of the manna in the desert.

Most surprising of all is that two elements such as water and fire that under normal circumstances would mutually and naturally destroy one another actually enhance each other's power. The author finds a solution to this cosmological enigma in the theological interpretation of reality. Nature is not an absolutely autonomous being; it is at the service of its Creator. This fundamental theological principle is fulfilled in a marvelous way in the paradoxes found in the narratives of Exodus and Numbers. The cohesiveness of this doctrine throughout the book is perfect (see Wis 1:14; 5:17-20; 16:17-25; 19:6, 18-21). To this theological vision, so deeply rooted in the tradition of the Hebrew Scriptures, the author is able to adapt the principally stoic, physical theories about the transformation of elements. The will of the Lord rules over the forces and the elements of nature in order to realize his plan of punishment or salvation.

The second part of the diptych (16:20-29) reminds us of God's goodness to the people in giving them manna in the desert. To the plagues caused by atmospheric complexities that beat down the Egyptians corresponds the great blessing of manna for God's people. God had sent from heaven punishment to the Egyptians and blessing to the Israelites. The author disregards the content of the Exodus story to concentrate only on the significance of the act of God who mercifully ministers to the people during their forty years in the desert (Exod 16:35) by giving them unfailingly tasty bread, tirelessly and effortlessly. The traditions preserved in the Pentateuch do not recognize the variety of flavors present in the manna (Exod 16:31; Num 11:4-9). Nevertheless, there were rabbinic traditions that sang of the excellent qualities of the manna, the diverse flavors suited to the tastes of those who ate it. The author rightfully takes advantage of these extra-biblical traditions to illustrate the doctrine that nature is at the service of the just (16:17).

The biblical theme of the bread from heaven culminates in John 6:31-58: Jesus is the bread come down from heaven, the true bread of life. John is certainly inspired by Exod 16:4-8, but it is also probable that he was at least acquainted with the tradition reflected in the text of the book of Wisdom. The Latin liturgy has reunited all these Scriptural texts in the context of the feast of Corpus Christi.

The Plague of Darkness and the Column of Light, 17:1–18:4

After a brief introduction (17:1) the fifth diptych or contrast begins: darkness and light. The author is faithful to the method of midrashic amplification used in the former diptychs. The principal account is the story of the Exodus (Exod 10:21-23). The contrast of darkness and light reminds us of the contrast between the impious and the just that serves as the backdrop for the entire book of Wisdom.

The division of this diptych into two sections is a logical one: darkness for the Egyptians (17:1-21) and light for Israel (18:1-4). The darkness acquires a transcendent meaning and serves the Lord as an instrument of punishment. Later the metaphor of darkness will express, in eschatological and apocalyptic style, the reality of the definitive separation from God after death (Matt 8:12; 22:13; *1 Enoch* 46:6; 63:6; 103:8; 108:14, and elsewhere).

Opposite the long discourse on darkness in ch. 17 there appears the tiny passage on light in 18:1-4. These four verses constitute the second part of the fifth diptych with which the author illustrates the thesis of his instruction (11:5).

The Death of the Firstborn of Egypt and the Liberation of Israel from Egypt, 18:5-25

The sixth contrast or antithetical diptych consists of two parts, clearly separated by the theme and inclusions: the death of the firstborn sons of Egypt and the Hebrew people's having been spared the same death.

The Death of the Firstborn Among the Egyptians (18:5-19)

This section recalls the memorable events of that night, disastrous for Egypt, happy for Israel (Exodus 11–12). The author combines two calamities: the terrible punishment of death among the Egyptian firstborn and the catastrophe suffered by the Egyptians at the Red Sea. After the introduction of the new theme (18:5) the development unfolds in two phases: the night of salvation for Israel (18:6-9) and the night of extermination for the Egyptians (18:10-19). In 18:14-16 the author raises the poetic tone of the moment: the profound calm of the midnight hour is about to be torn to pieces by the unexpected appearance of death. The author bases his account principally on Exod 12:29, but he has discovered that a profoundly poetic expression of the facts would harmonize the theological speculations about the meaning of that Passover night and the omnipotent power of the word of YHWH.

The Liberation of Israel (18:20-25)

The author makes connections between very different historical periods and confronts a difficulty: although Israel also was tested by the plague of death in the desert it was not equal to that of Egypt. The trial of death that the Israelites suffered in the desert (Num 17:6-15) was solely a test of the anger of God, an anger that was easily placated through the intercession of Aaron, their mediator, and through the reminder of oaths and promises spoken in favor of the Israelites. We discover certain parallels between the first comparison in Wis 11:6-14 (water from the rock/bloody water of the Nile) and this seventh comparison. Water is the common element, a vital element that is converted into an instrument of death and extermination. To such a state of perversion has human folly developed!

Final Reflections, 19:10-21

After the development of the theme proposed in Wis 11:5 with its six comparisons (11:6-14 and 16:1–19:9), the author adds some closing general reflections. First, calling the Israelites to remember their having freely passed through the Red Sea (19:10-12) serves as a confirmation of the theological principle that runs through the entire book and is magnificently formulated in 16:24. There is a double action in nature; according to how it is applied, it either punishes the unjust or benefits the faithful ones of the Lord. Second, Wis 19:13-17 relates the blindness of the inhabitants of Sodom to the plague of darkness in Egypt (Exod 10:21-23; Wis 17:1–18:4). The author works consistently within the preestablished scheme, that is, the order of Genesis 1 (cf. 19:7a with Gen 1:2; 19:7b with Gen 1:9-10; 19:7c with Gen 1:11-12; 19:10 with Gen 1:20-25). The theme of light and darkness (Gen 1:3-5, 14-19) was overlooked but in Wis 19:17 the darkness reappears.

Finally, there is a reflection on the metamorphosis of creation in Wis 19:18-21. In this section themes addressed in the fourth and seventh diptychs are revisited. Wisdom 19:18 poses a kind of theological, philosophical principle previously suggested in 19:6. Wisdom 19:19-20 confirms it with the happenings at the Reed Sea (19:7-9); and 19:21 confirms it with the clusters from the fourth diptych: 16:15-29 (see 19:10-12).

At the end of his discourse the author returns to the theme of supernatural food, which he calls "heavenly food" (19:21c) because it gives immortality or at least is suitable for immortal beings. It does not seem to be pure chance that the midrash ends with words relating to ambrosia. Likewise God ends the sixth day of creation by giving food to humans and all the animals (Gen 1:29-30). Let us also recall that the account of Paradise in the Yahwist version ends with the "tree of life" (Gen 3:24). In the new creation, therefore, there exists a food given by God that offers us the possibility of immortality. The author implies this since he refers directly to the time of the Exodus, but its finality is parenthetical, for which reason his thought is applicable to either present or future time.

Conclusion: A Hymn in Praise of God (19:22)

The author closes his midrash in dialogue with the Lord in a prayerful, hymn-like style. According to the author Israel's entire past history could be converted into a hymn of praise to the Lord, its God. Whatever Israel is or has been is a gift, as its stories narrate. The third part of the book has magnificently demonstrated this praise of God.

The author writes to the Israelites of the Diaspora, perhaps at a moment of testing. The lessons gleaned from history both for the present and for the future are lessons of hope: God is faithful to Godself; what God has done in times past with God's people, God will continue doing in the future. This affirmation of hope in God as savior is valuable for Israel in all times and for all peoples who recognize the merciful sovereignty of the Lord. It is true for the new Israel of God (Gal 6:16) since Jesus himself has promised his help until the end of time: "remember, I am with you always, to the end of the age" (Matt 28:20).

BIBLIOGRAPHY

Reese, James M. *The Book of Wisdom, Song of Songs.* Wilmington, Del.: Michael Glazier, 1983.

____. *Hellenistic Influence on the Book of Wisdom and its Consequences.* AnBib. Rome: Biblical Institute Press, 1970.

Reider, Joseph. *The Book of Wisdom.* New York: Harper, 1957.

Winston, David. *The Wisdom of Solomon.* AB 43. Garden City, N.Y.: Doubleday, 1979.

Sirach

Daniel J. Harrington

FIRST READING

The title "Sirach" derives from the author's name, "Jesus son of Eleazar son of Sirach" (50:27). It is customary to refer to the author as "Ben Sira" ("son of Sirach"). In the Latin tradition the book is known as "Ecclesiasticus" ("church book"). It is regarded as canonical by Catholics and Orthodox but not by Jews and Protestants (though it is used in the latter traditions).

The book of Sirach was composed about 180 B.C.E. in Hebrew. It was translated into Greek by the author's grandson in Egypt about 117 B.C.E. The Greek version became the primary (canonical) text and the source of the Latin and other texts. In 1896 and thereafter substantial parts of the Hebrew text were recovered from the Cairo Geniza, and in 1964 several chapters of the Hebrew text were found at Masada. Both the Greek and Hebrew textual traditions have short and long recensions, thus creating many textual complexities. The Hebrew fragments are regarded as generally authentic, though there is some evidence of retranslation from the Syriac version.

According to the grandson-translator there is "no small difference" between the Hebrew and the Greek. Most modern translations take the Greek version as the base text (since it is the most complete and has functioned as the Church's text through the centuries) and distinguish between the short and long recensions by different sizes of type or by footnotes. Some translations (NAB, NRSV) use the Hebrew to correct corruptions in the Greek tradition or to represent more accurately what the grandfather-author wrote. The complexity of the textual transmission has also resulted in confusion regarding the numbering of chapters and verses. All the Greek manuscripts show a textual displacement whereby 30:25–33:13a and 33:13b–36:16a have changed places. Recent translations follow the numbering system in Joseph Ziegler's 1965 edition. I have followed the New Revised Standard Version because it embodies recent scholarship and is widely circulated, though its effort at gender inclusiveness sometimes distorts the text.

Sirach is a wisdom book. [See also the article "Wisdom: A Way of Thinking About God."] It assumes a situation in which Ben Sira, the experienced sage and teacher, is instructing a younger man ("my son") who wishes to become wise. The prospective sage is male, someone who has financial resources and will become head of a household. The young man is being trained as a scribe—someone not only able to read and write but also prepared to exercise public leadership (see 38:24–39:11). Ben Sira conducted a school in Jerusalem, perhaps near the Temple, for such young men (see 51:23-30). There he showed his students how to join the wisdom traditions of the ancient Near East with their Jewish religious traditions. For autobiographical notices, see 24:30-34; 33:16-19; 34:9-13; 39:12-13; and 50:27.

Ben Sira's basic mode of communication is short sayings of two members in either synonymous (same ideas) or antithetical (opposite ideas) parallelism. His major contribution to the Hebrew wisdom tradition consisted in joining together individual sayings by common words or themes, and using small units to develop logically a theme or argument in paragraph form. Within this general literary framework he used the devices typical of the wisdom movement: numerical sayings ("I take pleasure in three things . . ."), beatitudes ("happy are those who . . ."), warnings ("do not . . ."), questions, comparisons, and so on. He also employed poetic devices (assonance, alliteration, rhyme), inclusions (beginning and ending a unit in the same way), chiasms (A–B–A' patterns), and acrostics (51:13-30). The book reaches its climax with a hymn about God's glory made manifest in nature (42:15–43:33) and a poetic retelling of Israel's history (chs. 44–50).

It is not easy to discern a clear outline for the book, especially in the material up to 42:15. Many commentators take the series of wisdom poems (1:1-10; 4:11-19; 6:18-37; 14:20–15:10; 24:1-33; 38:24–39:11) as structurally significant and so divide the book into parts on that basis. Some parts contain blocks that treat the same or related topics: speech in chs. 18–20, and sin in chs. 16–23. But for the most part the book gives the impression of being an anthology of teachings with a loose general structure.

A first reading can be disconcerting. It is sometimes hard to know where one unit ends and another begins, and the succession of apparently unrelated topics can easily lead to distraction. The basic insight of the book is clear: True wisdom is found in the Torah and is expressed in the attitude of "fear of the LORD." Ben Sira's theological genius was to unite the secular wisdom tradition based on practical insight and experience with the particular revelation of the God of Israel in nature, the Law (or Torah), and history.

In approaching Sirach for the first time one might want to read the book straight through. That is the way Ben Sira wrote it and the way it has come down to us. Another approach is to focus on topics treated at several places in the text. The following list can facilitate a topical reading and also indicates the most important subjects in the book:

Autobiography: 24:30-34; 33:16-19; 34:9-13; 39:12-13; 50:27; 51:13-30.
Creation: 16:24–17:24; 18:1-14; 33:7-15; 39:12-35; 42:15–43:33.
Death: 38:16-23; 41:1-13.
Fear of the Lord: 1:11-20; 2:1-18; 34:14-20.
Friendship: 6:5-17; 9:10-16; 19:13-17; 22:19-26; 27:16-21; 36:23–37:15.
Happiness: 25:1-11; 30:14-25; 40:1-30.
Honor and Shame: 4:20–6:4; 10:9–11:6; 41:14–42:8.
Humility and Pride: 3:17-29; 10:6-18.
Manners and Moderation: 31:12–32:13; 37:27-31.
Money Matters: 3:30–4:10; 29:1-20; 29:21-28.
Parents and Children: 3:1-16; 7:23-25; 16:1-4; 30:1-13; 41:5-10; 42:9-14.
People of God: 36:1-22; 44:1–50:24.
Prayers: 22:27–23:6; 36:1-22; 39:12-35; 50:22-24; 51:1-12; 51:12ff.
Rulers: 9:17–10:5.
Sacrifice: 34:21–35:26; 50:5-21.
Sickness and Doctors: 38:1-15.
Sin: 7:1-17; 15:11-20; 16:1-23; 16:24–17:24; 17:25-31; 18:30–19:3; 21:1-10; 22:27–23:6; 23:7-15; 23:16-27; 26:28–27:29; 27:30–28:7.
Social Justice: 4:1-10; 34:21-27; 35:14-26.
Social Relations: 7:18-36; 8:1-19; 11:29–12:18; 33:20-33.
Speech: 5:9-15; 18:15-18; 18:19-29; 19:4-17; 20:1-31; 23:7-15; 27:4-7; 27:11-15; 28:8-26.
Wealth: 11:7-28; 13:1-24; 13:25–14:19; 31:1-11.
Wisdom: 1:1-10; 4:11-19; 6:18-37; 14:20–15:10; 19:20-30; 21:11-28; 22:1-18; 24:1-34; 32:14–33:6; 34:1-20; 37:16-31; 38:24–39:11; 51:13-30.
Women: 9:1-9; 23:22-26; 25:13–26:27; 36:26-31; 42:9-14.

General Contexts for Interpretation

Original Historical Contexts

More is known about the historical circumstances of Sirach than of most other biblical books. It was written in Jerusalem by a teacher named Jesus (50:27) around 180 B.C.E. On the one hand the high priest Simon (50:1-24) who died in 196 B.C.E. seems to have been a figure of the past. On the other hand there is no mention of the events put in motion by the Seleucid King Antiochus IV Epiphanes in 175 B.C.E. that issued in the Maccabean revolt, and the translator-grandson had come to Egypt (presumably as an adult) in 132 B.C.E. The Hebrew fragments give access to large parts of the original text as it came from the author. A date of about 180 B.C.E.

places Ben Sira in Israel, first under Egyptian/Ptolemaic control and then from 198 B.C.E. under Syrian/Seleucid control with Antiochus III (223–187 B.C.E.) and Seleucus IV (187–175 B.C.E.). Yet Ben Sira does not refer directly to these turbulent times, preferring instead to dispense timeless wisdom apparently applicable in all circumstances. Though often described as a traditionalist or conservative, Ben Sira was a theological pioneer in integrating biblical and secular sapiential traditions. There are striking parallels with the Greek elegaic poet Theognis and the Demotic Egyptian "Instruction" of Papyrus Insinger that suggest some literary dependence or, at least, participation in the international wisdom movement.

The historical context of the translator-grandson is also important. By rendering his grandfather's Hebrew composition into Greek he made it available to a new audience (diaspora Jews) in a different language and with a different conceptuality. In the prologue he reflects on the difficulty of translating the work and notes that there is "no small difference" between the Hebrew and Greek. Where the Hebrew is available it is possible to see that in comparison with most books in the LXX the grandson's version is relatively free with regard to word order, vocabulary, and number of words. His text—the Greek translation made in Egypt about 117 B.C.E.—has determined how his grandfather's work has been understood by most readers for over 2,000 years.

Canonical Contexts

Sirach provides important evidence regarding the history of the OT canon. In his prologue the grandson claims that Ben Sira devoted himself to reading "the Law and the Prophets and the other books of our ancestors," thus suggesting that the threefold division of the Hebrew Scriptures was known in Egypt in the late second century B.C.E. Throughout the work there are numerous indications that Ben Sira knew and used Proverbs, the Torah, and many other biblical books. The catalogue of Israel's heroes in chs. 44–50 shows a thorough familiarity with the historical books and the prophets.

The Hebrew text of Sirach was not entirely lost after the Greek translation. It continued to be used at Qumran and Masada (where the earliest fragments were found), served as the basis of the Syriac version, and was copied at least up to the time of the medieval (eleventh–twelfth century) manuscripts. But (probably because it was regarded as having been composed too late) it did not become part of the Hebrew canon, which in turn served as the basis for the Protestant OT. Nevertheless, Sirach was frequently quoted in the Talmud and other rabbinic works.

The grandson's Greek version became part of the larger canon followed by the Catholic and Orthodox churches today. It was part of the LXX and the Christian OT from earliest times. Its presence in the Christian canon along with the Wisdom of Solomon expands substantially the corpus of biblical wisdom literature.

Ben Sira's extensive use of other OT texts makes it a good example of intra-biblical dialogue. His style is often described as "anthological" in the sense that he used the OT books as a source for vocabulary and expressions that he then used in new combinations and fresh ways. The book is thoroughly "biblical" in thought and expression.

Sirach is not quoted directly in the NT. The strongest parallel is Matt 11:28-29 (see Sir 6:24-25; 51:26-27). But even there it may be a matter of common terminology and conceptuality. Yet Sirach is a precious resource for understanding the presuppositions of Judaism in the late Second Temple period and for discerning what was or was not innovative about Jesus and early Christianity. Thus it is important for students of the NT even though there is no direct quotation of it.

Church Usage

The earliest patristic evidence for Sirach occurs in *Didache* 4.5 and *Barnabas* 19.9. Both texts appear to cite Sirach 4:31 without attribution and in quite a different Greek form as one of many pieces of good advice. Sirach, along with other biblical books, was translated into Latin, Coptic, Syriac, Ethiopic, Armenian, and Arabic, thus promoting a wide circulation. Many Greek (Clement of Alexandria, Origen, John Chrysostom, Cyril of Jerusalem) and Latin (Tertullian, Cyprian, Jerome, Augustine) writers quoted or used material from Sirach in their own presentations. In his *Stromateis,* written in the late second century, Clement of Alexandria quoted Sirach 1:1 ("all wisdom is from the LORD") to justify the inclusion of Greek wisdom (1.4.27) and

Sirach 25:9 ("happy . . . is the one who speaks to attentive listeners") to highlight receptivity toward the gift of the Wisdom of God (2.4.15). Clement even went so far as to suggest that Sirach (attributed to Solomon) inspired the pre-Socratic philosopher Heraclitus (2.5.17, 24).

Gregory the Great, bishop of Rome in the second half of the sixth century, quoted Sirach so profusely that after his death his immediate disciple, Paterius, a notary of the Roman church, decided to arrange Gregory's writings on Sirach into an almost continuous commentary. A complete commentary on Sirach was finally produced by the ninth-century Benedictine Rhabanus Maurus, then abbot of Fulda. This followed the attempt at such a commentary by Bede a century earlier. Rhabanus, a disciple of Alcuin, produced a remarkable synthesis. With clear exposition and an entertaining style he communicated a knowledge of Sirach adjusted to the society and Christian mind-set of his time. His commentary witnesses to his deep knowledge of the traditional Christian sources in his quotation of Origen, Jerome, and Gregory the Great ("whose interpretations I followed often in my present work," *PL* 109.829). At the same time, as a Carolingian humanist he quotes Cicero, Virgil, and Ovid. The continuous stream of commentary on Sirach quoted in small sections shifts constantly from one level of interpretation to another, giving a valuable witness to the historical, allegorical, and moral levels of interpretation of this wisdom book during the first millennium of Christianity.

In the *Lectionary for Mass* prepared in response to Vatican II the first reading for Holy Family Sunday (between Christmas and New Year's Day) is always from Sirach 3:1-16 (on parents and children). The first reading for the Second Sunday after Christmas is Sirach 24:1-4, 8-12 (Wisdom's praise of herself); in many countries, however, this is superseded by the transfer of Epiphany. In Year A of the Sunday cycle two texts from Sirach are read with excerpts from Matthew: the Sixth Sunday (Sir 15:15-20 and Matt 5:17-37—on choosing to keep the commandments), and the Twenty-fourth Sunday (Sir 27:30–28:7 and Matt 18:21-35—on willingness to forgive others). In Year C three texts from Sirach are paired with texts from Luke: the Eighth Sunday (Sir 27:4-7 and Luke 6:39-45—on speech revealing the heart), the Thirteenth Sunday (Sir 35:12-14, 16-18 and Luke 18:9-14—on prayer), and the Twenty-second Sunday (Sir 3:17-28 and Luke 14:7-14—on humility). The seventh and eighth weeks of Year I in the daily cycle feature a continuous reading of twelve texts from Sirach, but these passages frequently get lost in the transition into Lent and from the Easter season. In Year II the passages about David (47:2-11) and Elijah (48:1-14) are used to summarize and round off long series from the OT historical books.

Present Significance

In its own right Sirach is an entertaining and (mostly) edifying book. Much of it is solid advice on the level of practical human experience. The variety of literary devices gives it a freshness lacking in other wisdom books. Moreover, the breadth of its subject matter offers a window into the agenda of Jewish religious life and thought in the early second century B.C.E. Its beautiful reflections on the search for wisdom and the personification of Wisdom provide inspiration for serious religious thinkers. The texts on the value of the "name" and the catalogue of Israel's heroes can teach people today what it means to stand in a religious tradition.

There are, however, some negatives. Ben Sira's statements on women are notorious today in some circles. In his defense one must take account of the patriarchal society in which he lived and his position as an instructor of young men seeking to become scribes and sages, which provides the narrative setting implied in the book. Equally outrageous are his sayings on how to treat slaves (33:25-30), which not only assume the existence of slavery as an institution but recommend very harsh discipline for slaves. Less obvious, but nevertheless troublesome, are his obsession with honor and shame, his excessive caution in social relations, and his quickness to dismiss many other persons as "fools."

The NT book closest to Sirach in topics, literary form, and spirit is the letter of James, which is long on practical experience and short on distinctively Christian theology. Familiarity with Sirach can also help toward appreciating Jesus as a wisdom teacher in his choice of topics and modes of teaching according to the synoptic gospels. But Jesus' emphases on loving enemies and on the coming reign of God set him apart from Ben Sira. The personification of Wisdom, especially in Sirach 24, along with Proverbs 8 and Wisdom 7, contributes to appreciation of the early Christian hymns (John 1:1-18; Col 1:15-20; Heb 1:1-2) that celebrate Jesus as the Wisdom/Word of God. These themes were decisive in shaping the idea of Jesus as the revelation of God (the center of Johannine theology) and in the recognition of Jesus as preexistent and present at creation in trinitarian theology.

SECOND READING

The exposition of individual passages that follows seeks to open up the book of Sirach on the literary, historical, and theological levels. It is not a substitute for reading and reflecting on the text. Rather, it seeks to enrich and stimulate that reading and reflection. On the literary level it calls attention to the narrative situation (Ben Sira instructing his student), the literary and rhetorical devices, the striking images and expressions, and the progress of thought or logical structure. On the historical level it points out social or cultural assumptions (about women, slavery, the household, etcetera) that are needed for a fair, if not sympathetic, reading. Since Ben Sira's comments about contemporary events around 180 B.C.E. in Jerusalem are at best allusive, little effort will be given to trying to make them explicit. On the theological level it tries to indicate where Ben Sira stood on particular issues. It gives special attention to the sources and parallels in the OT and suggests similarities and differences with various parts of the NT.

Prologue

The foreword or preface to a book usually explains the purpose and provides information about the work's genesis. Written in elegant Greek (as Luke 1:1-4 is), the prologue to the Greek translation of Sirach tells in three long sentences about the original author and his purpose, the problems facing the translator, and the circumstances of the translation. The book was written in Hebrew by a certain Jesus (son of Eleazar, son of Sirach, of Jerusalem; see 50:27) on the basis of the Jewish Scriptures to help other Jews make progress "in living according to the Law." Note that the wisdom elements so prominent in the work are subordinated to the Torah. The audience for the translation are Greek-speaking Jews, who are asked for indulgence in approaching a Greek version from a native of Israel. Yet this version is not a mechanical reproduction of the Hebrew but rather an effort to express the author's thoughts in good Greek. Just as the books of the Old Greek "differ not a little" from their Hebrew originals, so the Greek of Sirach differs (even a little more) from the Hebrew. The translator is the author's grandson who came to Egypt in 132 B.C.E. (the thirty-eighth year of Ptolemy VII Psychon Euergetes II) and completed his translation about 117 B.C.E. His purpose was to achieve for diaspora Jews what his grandfather sought for Palestinian Jews: to help them gain learning and make progress in living according to the Law.

The Origin and Nature of Wisdom: 1:1-30

Where does wisdom come from? What is it? How does one get it? The initial poem (1:1-10) deals with those issues first by making statements and asking questions (1:1-3, 4-6) and then by developing the theme of God as the origin of wisdom (1:8-10). The truly wise One created all wisdom and gives it to those who love him. Wisdom appears as a female creature as in Proverbs 8:22-31; she is later identified with the Torah (see 24:23). Such ideas are in the background of John's hymn about Jesus as the Word of God (John 1:1-18), though Jesus surpasses Wisdom in dignity ("the Word was God").

The proper response to God's gift of Wisdom (1:11-20) involves "fear of the Lord"—the respect, gratitude, and reverent behavior that are owed to the Creator of all wisdom. The poem celebrating fear of the Lord first reflects on the good results of fearing the Lord (1:11-13) and then praises fear of the Lord as the beginning (1:14-15), fullness (1:16-17), crown (1:18-19), and root (1:20) of wisdom. The portrayal of Wisdom as a female personal figure is continued, and so is the emphasis on wisdom as a gift from God. Though Ben Sira probably did not believe in life after death, his comment in 1:13 about the sage being blessed on the day of his death at least prepares for such a belief.

The section contrasting unjustified anger and patience (1:22-24) operates on the level of practical wisdom and gives particular attention to the consequences of such behaviors. The second section (1:25-27) brings together Ben Sira's major theological interests: the connection between wisdom, fear of the Lord, discipline, and keeping the commandments. Thus he links the secular wisdom tradition exemplified in 1:22-24 and Israel's religious tradition, especially the Torah. The third section (1:28-30) joins practical wisdom teachings regarding integrity vis-à-vis God and humans with a warning that God will surely expose and bring shame upon the hypocrite. An analogous procedure occurs in the NT "ethical" teachings where much received wisdom appears in a framework shaped by the central significance of Jesus' death and resurrection.

Fear of the Lord: 2:1-18

The six short units in the chapter explore various facets of fear of the Lord or "faith" in the sense of fidelity toward God. Fear of the Lord is Ben Sira's integrating theme; it brings together faith and works, knowledge of God and behavior, love of God and love of neighbor, and so forth. The center of the chapter is the affirmation that "the Lord is compassionate and merciful; he forgives sins and saves in time of distress" (2:11). Because God is merciful, one should be respectful and faithful. The concluding confession (absent in the Greek but present in other texts), "equal to his name are his works," assumes that God's name is "the merciful one" *(raḥūm)*. Biblical "fear" and "faith" are based upon the character and experience of God the compassionate one.

The first unit (2:1-6) warns one who would try to be faithful to God to expect "testing" (a powerful biblical theme), and to remain trusting and hopeful despite temporary or apparent humiliations. It explains suffering as a discipline: "For gold is tested in the fire, and those found acceptable in the furnace of humiliation" (2:5; see Prov 3:11-12; 17:3; 27:21; Wis 3:6; Jas 1:12; 1 Pet 1:7). The second unit (2:7-9) addresses "you who fear the Lord" and echoes the first unit (see 2:6) with commands to "trust" (believe) in God and "hope" for good things. The questions in the third unit (2:10-11) are based on Pss 22:4-5 and 37:25, though the book of Job calls into question the easy "yes" answers that Ben Sira expects. For the Lord as "compassionate and merciful" see Exod 34:6, and as "forgiving" sins and "saving" see Pss 37:39-40; 103:3; 145:18-19. By way of contrast, the fourth unit (2:12-14) features three "woes" (warnings or threats) against the timid and sinners. The Lord's "reckoning" mentioned in 2:14 most likely refers in Sirach to events within the person's lifetime, though other Jewish and Christian texts use the same vocabulary to describe the Last Judgment. Taking up the language of 2:7-9, the fifth unit (2:15-17) describes the characteristics of "those who fear the Lord." The final verse (2:18) prefers the lordship of God to that of human beings because God is the merciful one. The first two chapters, with their reflections on the origin and nature of Wisdom and on the faithful service of God ("fear of the Lord"), provide a theological framework for the rest of the book.

Parents and Children: 3:1-16

How fear of the Lord expresses itself in family relationships is illustrated by the precept "Honor your father and your mother" (Exod 20:12; Deut 5:16). Addressing adult children ("my sons") rather than youngsters, Ben Sira uses wisdom traditions to explain the reasons for as well as the results and advantages that follow upon honoring one's parents. His teachings expand upon the biblical promises "so that your days may be long and that it may go well for you" (Deut 5:16). The fundamental reason why children should honor both parents is the social order decreed by God that places parents in authority over their children (3:1-2). A series of participial phrases ("those who . . . ," 3:3-7) describes the spiritual blessings that come from honoring parents: atonement for sins, spiritual treasure, long and happy life, and so on. The two instructions associate respect for and from parents with honor and shame (3:8-11), and promise that caring for parents in their old age will be rewarded by God ("credited to you against your sins," 3:12-15). The poem ends (3:16) by returning to 3:2, and warns that neglect of father and mother is blasphemy. In the NT family obligation is sometimes subordinated to the reign of God (see Mark 3:31-35; Luke 8:19-21; 9:57-62; 12:49-53).

Humility: 3:17-29

The first section (3:17-20) concerns humility (or "meekness") in action, and the remaining two units (3:21-24; 3:25-29) warn against intellectual pride. Those who act humbly will be loved by others (who loves an arrogant person?) and by God (since wise persons recognize their own limits and thus also the unlimited glory of God). The warnings against intellectual pride are often read against the background of Ben Sira's own conflict with Hellenistic philosophy and culture around 200 B.C.E. But they apply to people of any age and are presented here as general statements. The true sources of wisdom are "what you have been commanded" (3:22; see Qoh 12:13) and the wisdom tradition (3:29). Those who neglect the Torah and wisdom to meddle in things beyond them go astray; they thus display a "hard heart" that ends in destruction. The humble attitude toward God and others is the basis for Jesus' beatitudes on the "poor in spirit" and the "meek" in Matthew 5:3, 5.

Almsgiving: 3:30–4:10

Though giving to the poor was not a part of Greek wisdom, it was an important element in the Jewish tradition (see Tobit). These instructions presuppose that the sage has wealth and so is in a position to play the role of benefactor. For the ideal sage as benefactor, see Job's self-portrait in Job 29. The first unit (3:30-31) gives reasons for almsgiving: atonement for sins and widening one's circle of friends. The second unit (4:1-6) lists ten things not to do when giving alms and adds a reason for avoiding these actions (God will heed the curse of the rejected beggar). The third unit (4:7-10) contains general teachings about how the sage should behave in society and especially about his obligations to the poor, oppressed, and orphaned and widowed. The instruction ends with a promise that the charitable person will be "like a son of the Most High" and especially loved by God (more than by his mother!). These teachings find echoes in the NT: charity as a way of making friends (Luke 16:9), giving to beggars without hesitation (Matt 5:42/Luke 6:30), and true religion as caring for orphans and widows (Jas 1:27).

The Benefits of Wisdom: 4:11-19

As in ch. 1, Wisdom appears as a personal figure, an intermediary between God and humans. The first unit (4:11-14) lists the benefits of seeking wisdom: instruction and help, life, joy, glory, and blessing from God. See Luke 7:35 ("wisdom is vindicated by all her children") for a parallel to 4:11. In the Greek text there is an alternation between singular and plural participles: "whoever loves her . . . those who seek her." The Hebrew text of the second (4:15-16) and third (4:17-19) units presents wisdom as the speaker ("those who obey me . . . I will hand them over"). The rewards listed in 4:15-16 probably pertain to this world, not to the fullness of God's realm or life after death (cf. Wis 3:8; 1 Cor 6:2). Despite its many rewards, the way of wisdom involves testing (see 2:1) and discipline (4:17-19). Those who persevere on wisdom's way will find joy and knowledge; those who do not will end in destruction. Underlying all these rewards is the conviction that serving wisdom is the same as serving the Holy One (see Matt 10:40-41; Mark 9:37; Luke 9:48; 10:16; John 13:20 where the same dynamic applies to Jesus).

Honor and Shame: 4:20–6:4

The five units display an interlocking or concentric outline: A–the need for self-restraint (4:20-21); B–truthful speech (4:22-31); C–avoiding presumption (5:1-8); B'–truthful speech (5:9–6:1); A'–the need for self-restraint (6:2-4). The first unit (4:20-21) places the instructions in the framework of honor and shame. The key word is "self" or "soul" *(psychē),* and the sage is told to exercise restraint and discernment in which fear of shame can play a salutary role. The second unit (4:22-31) consists mainly of "do not" clauses concerned with speech as a major element in social relations ("wisdom becomes known through speech," 4:24), along with instructions about not showing partiality (4:22, 27), fighting for the truth (4:28), and generosity (4:31; see Acts 20:35). The central unit (5:1-8) is framed by sayings about not relying on wealth (5:1-2, 8) and focuses on presumptuous attitudes toward God (5:3-7). These attitudes include denying God's power over oneself, presuming God's forbearance and mercy, and putting off repentance. These postures reflect the excuses commonly put forward by sinners, though there may also be a criticism of Greek philosophical schools or even Qoheleth. The theme of truthful speech is taken up again in the fourth unit (5:9–6:1) where the key word is "double-tongued" *(diglōssos,* 5:9, 14; 6:1) or "slanderer." The saying about being quick to hear and slow to answer is found also in Jas 1:19. In the second part (5:13–6:1) honor and shame appear as motives for avoiding "double-tongued" behavior. The final unit (6:2-4) takes up the key word of the first unit, "self" or "soul" *(psychē).* Ben Sira's anthropology is not exactly the same as those of the ancient Greeks or of people today. For him, the soul is the life-principle (Hebrew *nepesh*). An evil soul destroys its possessor and brings shame. The sage who follows all these instructions will stay out of trouble with respect to others and to God.

Friendship: 6:5-17

Ben Sira provides the most extensive treatment of friendship in the Bible (see also 9:10-16; 19:13-17; 22:19-26; 27:16-21; 37:1-6). His approach is not theoretical, nor is he much concerned with the definition of friendship or why people need friends. Rather he offers practical advice about making friends and warns against fair-weather friends. After holding up pleasant speech as a way of attracting friends (6:5), he counsels a cautious attitude (6:6-7, 13) toward friends and gives a series of examples about false friends (6:8-12) who quickly fall away in times of trouble and testing. On the other hand, true friends (6:14-17) are like a shelter, treasure, and life-saving medicine; they are to be found especially among those "who fear the Lord." This latter theme prepares for the NT idea of those who do God's will as true family of Jesus (Mark 3:35; Luke 9:21) and his friends (John 15:15).

Discipline as the Way to Wisdom: 6:18-37

The three units in this section (6:18-22, 23-31, 32-37) begin with "my child" and advise the young sage to accept "discipline" *(mūsar)*—the kind of intellectual and moral formation that produces wisdom and its rewards. The first unit (6:18-22) contrasts those who accept discipline (like farmers who work and then enjoy a rich harvest) and those who reject it (for them it is like a heavy stone). Discipline is "like her name" (6:22) in that fools "cast it aside" (a play on *mūsar* meaning "discipline" and the Hebrew verb *sūr* meaning "turn aside").

After a call to pay attention (6:23), the second unit develops the image of discipline as a "yoke" that binds the whole body (6:24-25), moves to images of searching and hunting (6:26-28), and shows how the yoke is then transformed into glorious apparel (6:29-31). What discipline gives is wisdom—which results in "rest" and "joy" (6:28). The imagery and the content are the same in Matt 11:29-30: "Take my yoke upon you . . . and you will find rest for your souls. For my yoke is easy, and my burden light" (see 51:27-28).

The third unit (6:32-37) directs the young sage to spend time with wise elders and to listen to their discourse and proverbs as the way of becoming wise. This kind of intellectual discipline would be typical of ancient Near Eastern wisdom writings. Ben Sira's distinctively Jewish approach to discipline and wisdom emerges in 6:37: The prospective sage must attend to the commandments of God and recognize God as the source of wisdom. For Jews "discipline" includes not only tested human wisdom but also (and especially) the Torah. For Christians Jesus' teaching and example provide the true discipline (which includes natural wisdom and the Torah).

Avoiding Evil: 7:1-17

This passage (with what follows) represents the practical advice expressed in "godly discourse" and "wise proverbs" that constitute the discipline of the sage. Each of the sixteen units except the last (7:17) begins with a negative command: "Do not . . . ." The topics include avoiding evil and injustice (7:1-3), ambition for high offices and public recognition (7:4-7), presuming on God's patience and mercy (7:8-9), carelessness in speech (7:10-14), and other matters (7:15-17). The pieces of advice are sometimes accompanied by theological motives about the sovereignty of God (7:11), the evil effects of injustice (7:3) and lying (7:13), and the threat of punishment (7:17). In the Hebrew text the punishment is simply "the worm" (= death), while in the Greek it is "fire and worms" (perhaps an indication of the grandson's belief in punishments after death). There are some echoes in the NT: counting the cost of becoming Jesus' disciple (7:6; see Luke 14:28-32), not repeating oneself in prayer (7:14; see Matt 6:7), and "fire and worms" (7:17; see Mark 9:48).

Social Relations: 7:18-36

These instructions are directed specifically to the male head of a household—one that includes slaves (7:20-21), cattle (7:22), children (7:23-25), a wife or wives (7:19, 26), and parents (7:27-28). The man of means and power also has obligations to friends (7:18), the priests of God (7:29-31), and the needy (7:32-35). The instructions assume that slaves can gain their freedom (Exod 21:2; Lev 25:39-43; Deut 15:12-15), that marriages of daughters are arranged by their fathers (7:25), that only the husband can initiate divorce (7:19, 26; see Deut 24:1-4), and that priests deserve their portion (7:29-31; see Num 18:9-20). The motivations for acting in the "right" way range from self-interest (harmony, avoiding trouble, good reputation) to obligations imposed from outside (parents, God). The instructions prepare for the NT household codes (Col 3:18–4:1; Eph 5:21–6:9), though in the NT there is more emphasis on mutual responsibilities and a certain "equality" before the Lord. For works of mercy toward the needy (7:32-35) see the great judgment scene in Matt 25:31-46. The admonition to "remember the end of your life" as a way to avoid sin (7:36) can be taken as another hint at judgment after death and afterlife, though it may refer only to a good reputation here.

Caution in Social Relations: 8:1-19

The form in which the advice about persons and situations the sage should avoid is given as a command ("do not . . .") and a reason why the person or situation is to be avoided. The reasons are mainly pragmatic (avoiding harm or disgrace), though the motive clauses in 8:5-7 are more spiritual or philosophical. At the center of the text is the command to attend to the discourse of the sages (8:8) and the elders (8:9), thus stressing the traditional character of this wisdom based on human experience. The kinds of persons to be avoided—powerful, rich, loudmouths, ill-bred, sinners, the insolent, and so on—have the power to work harm to the sage. Even those who seem powerless—repentant sinners, the old, the dead—can be the occasion for disgrace unless the sage acts cautiously. For the sage whose social status and personal identity are closely intertwined, the attitude of prudent calculation in dealing with others—especially those who can cause harm—is most appropriate. One element in protecting one's social position is the avoidance of self-revelation to fools and strangers (8:17-19). The relation between social and personal identity is a major concern among the sages.

Relations with Women: 9:1-9

The addressee here (as everywhere in Sirach) is the young man who wants to become a sage. The advice to him about women follows the form (command plus reason) and the tone (calculating caution) of the preceding passage. Whereas in Proverbs 1–9 "loose women" tend to represent Dame Folly, here the advice concerns various types of real women who can bring harm and disgrace to the prospective sage: a jealous wife, a dominating woman, a loose woman, a songstress, a virgin, a prostitute, a beauty, and another man's wife. The OT penalties for seducing a virgin (9:5) involved a financial payment to her father and marriage (Exod 22:16-17; Deut 22:29), and for adultery with another man's wife (9:9) death (Lev 20:10; Deut 22:22). The calculating caution recommended to the sage contrasts sharply with Jesus' willingness to deal compassionately with sinful women (Luke 7:36-50; Jn 7:53–8:11) and to converse freely with the Samaritan woman (John 4).

Friendships: 9:10-16

This section begins with a word of caution (9:10) regarding new friends expressed in a chiastic pattern: A–old friends, B–new friends, B'–new wine, A'–old wine. Then it lists (9:11-13) three kinds of persons to be avoided as friends—sinners, the ungodly, and those who have the power to kill—along with reasons why they should be avoided. Those who are to be pursued as friends (9:14-16)—the wise, intelligent, and righteous—share the sage's concern for the Law of the Most High and fear of the Lord. True friendship is found "in the LORD"—where friends share common spiritual ideals (see 6:5-17).

Wise Rulers: 9:17–10:5

The good ruler is the wise ruler. The unit begins (9:17) and ends (10:5) with images of "hands"—those of the artisans and of the Lord. It identifies wise words as the "tools" of the good ruler (9:17-18), reflects on the positive effects that a wise ruler has on the city's inhabitants (10:1-3), and traces the ruler's wisdom and success back to "the hand of the Lord" (10:4-5). If the good ruler is wise, the one most competent to rule is the sage (who knows wisdom). Ben Sira trained sages to take an active role in the affairs of state (see 38:32-34). The model of wise rulers governing for the common good and having their authority from God is echoed by Paul in Romans 13:1-7 (but see Revelation 13, 17–18).

Pride: 10:6-18

The sage should avoid pride and the insolent behavior that flows from it because pride is hateful to God and other humans and because it has disastrous effects (10:6-8). The development of these ideas is related to the preceding section on rulers (see 10:8, 10, 13b-17). Death is the great equalizer among humans and the ultimate source of humiliation, since all human arrogance and pride end in corruption (10:9-11). The third section (10:12-18) begins by tracing the origin of pride to a deliberate turning away from God (= sin) in 10:12-13a and ends by denying that God or nature is the source of pride in 10:18. In between (10:13b-17), it reflects on how God puts down the proud and powerful and raises up the humble and lowly. The language echoes the Song of Hannah (1 Sam 2:1-10), which is in turn taken up in Mary's Magnificat (Luke 1:46-55). Because pride means turning from God, God is not on the side of the proud and such persons can expect disastrous results.

Honor and Shame: 10:19–11:6

In Ben Sira's world, honor and shame derived from one's social standing and what other people thought of one. Those who had wealth and power were regarded as the most important; those who had neither could easily be despised. This reflection on true glory follows neatly from the preceding section on pride. The basic principle appears in 10:19: Those who fear the Lord are worthy of honor; those who transgress the Lord's commandments deserve dishonor. Various aspects of this principle are developed in short units: fear of the Lord and wisdom as the sources of true glory (10:20-25), avoiding boasting (10:26-27), humility (10:28-29), honor for the wise and the rich (10:30-31), wisdom as the source of honor (11:1), not judging by appearances (11:2-3), not boasting about fine clothes (11:4), and the reversals that befall kings (11:5-6). The reflection redefines what brings glory to a person. Instead of wealth and power, the sources of true honor and glory are knowledge, wisdom, fear of the Lord, and keeping the commandments—a combination of practical human wisdom and Jewish theology. Compare Jas 2:1-7 for a NT meditation on this theme.

True Wealth: 11:7-28

The section begins with a brief unit (11:7-9) about discretion in dealing with others; it may be taken either as an introduction to what follows or simply an independent piece. The remaining short units all concern God as the real source of wealth and warn against the false security of earthly riches (11:10-13, 14-19, 20-21, 22-24, 25-28). There are repeated warnings about presuming on one's efforts to amass wealth and thereby to guarantee security (11:10-11, 18-19, 20-21a, 23-24) along with reminders that God retains power over wealth and security (11:12, 14, 17, 21b, 22). Two wise observations stand out: the attitude of the "rich fool" whose security is robbed by death (11:19; see Qoh 2:21; 4:8; 5:12-14; Luke 12:16-21!), and our selective memories regarding prosperity and adversity (11:25). Over all human efforts at acquiring wealth there lies the shadow of death (11:19, 26-28). Since true wealth is wisdom and fear of the Lord, true character becomes manifest only at the time of death ("call no one happy before his death"). Though Christians instinctively read these texts as referring to life after death, Ben Sira may have been referring only to the person's reputation and physical descendants.

Caution in Social Relations: 11:29–12:18

Those persons pose danger to the sage who have the power to make his life miserable. Therefore the sage should exercise great caution in letting strangers into his household (11:29-34), in acts of kindness and beneficence (12:1-

7), and in dealing with enemies (12:8-18). The three sections assume that social relations are full of danger even (and especially) for those who approach them with good will. The first section assumes that the sage is head of the household and warns that a scoundrel can ruin the sage's reputation and turn his own household against him. The second section urges caution in almsgiving and restricts the recipients to the good, devout, and humble on the grounds that "the Most High hates sinners" (12:6). The third section suggests that nearly everyone be treated as a potential enemy (12:8) and reflects on how the enemy will behave in the sage's adversity. Therefore the sage should always be on guard, even if the enemy seems to be friendly: "Who pities a snake charmer when he is bitten?" (12:13). The calculating caution proposed in this unit contrasts with Near Eastern ideals of hospitality and almsgiving and with the NT ideal of loving enemies (Matt 5:43-48; Luke 6:27-36; Rom 12:14-21). The viewpoint is pragmatic and experiential.

Rich and Poor: 13:1-24

In a context in which wealth was pursued and riches were regarded as a divine blessing Ben Sira urges caution in cultivating the rich. His basic principle is that wisdom and fear of the Lord are far more important than economic status. The first section (13:1-7) reflects on the dangers of trying to befriend the rich, for they will exploit and discard you. Two memorable images appear in 13:1-2: "Whoever touches pitch gets dirty. . . . How can the clay pot associate with the iron kettle?" The second section (13:8-13) begins and ends with calls to caution, and gives advice about dealing with a "powerful" person in a reserved and guarded manner. The third section (13:15-20) considers the fundamental incompatibility of rich and poor with the help of images from the animal kingdom (wolf/lamb, hyena/dog, wild asses/lions). The fourth section (13:21-23) compares the favorable treatment given to the rich and the unfavorable treatment of the poor: People support and make excuses for the rich, but criticize and dismiss the poor (see Jas 2:1-4). Though Ben Sira was no social revolutionary, he described sharply the dangers posed by riches to those who seek wisdom and fear of the Lord.

Using Money: 13:25–14:19

The first section (13:25–14:2) reflects on the relation between the "heart" (in the Bible the place of psychic activity involving thinking and feeling) and the person's external appearance (13:25-26) and happiness (14:1-2). This may simply be an independent unit, or it may introduce the following poems on internal dispositions regarding the use of money. The poem in 14:3-10 begins and ends with mentions of the "miser" who, though his whole life is devoted to money, never enjoys it and so leads the most miserable of human existences. The miser does harm to himself (14:5-6, 9) and does no conscious good to others (14:7-8). Yet in the end the miser works not for himself but for others, since when he dies his heirs will get the enjoyment of his money (14:4). The theme of death as the proper context for reflecting on the use of money (see Luke 12:13-21) is developed at length in 14:11-19. Now is the time to use your money to serve God (14:11), to help others (14:13), and to enjoy yourself (14:11, 14) because you cannot do so after death when your estate will be taken over by others (see Luke 16:19-31). The section ends with a beautiful meditation on death and the changing of generations (14:17-19).

Seeking and Finding Wisdom: 14:20–15:10

The two sections concern the search for wisdom (14:20-27) and the benefits of wisdom (15:1-10). The first poem begins with a beatitude (14:20-21) that declares happy or blessed the wise person in terms based on Proverbs 3:13, 17. The search for wisdom is portrayed with three patterns of imagery: the hunt (14:22), the house (14:23-25), and the shady tree (14:26-27). The "house of wisdom" image appears also in Proverbs 8:32-35; in this context it may allude to Ben Sira's wisdom school (see 51:23-28).

The second poem begins (15:1) by linking fear of the Lord, the Law, and wisdom—the essential elements of Ben Sira's theology. Wisdom portrayed as a female figure (15:2-6) will shower benefits on the wise, including the "bread of learning" and the "water of wisdom" (see John 6:35-51 and 4:20-25!) as well as "an everlasting name" (the immortality of memory). On the other hand, wisdom has nothing to do with fools and sinners (15:7-8). Only the wise can praise God properly (15:9-10); sinners cannot do so.

Free Will and Sin: 15:11-20

Though some OT texts suggest that God makes people sin (see Exod 11:10; 2 Sam 24:1), Ben Sira vigorously denies it at the beginning (15:11-13) and end (15:18-20) of the passage. There is a fundamental incompatibility between the wise God and human sin. In one of the most important parts of his book Ben Sira emphasizes human freedom in the face of good and evil (15:14-17). The freedom in which God created humankind (Genesis 1–2) remains the privilege of all human beings. Ben Sira pays no attention here to "original sin"—whether it be Adam's sin (Gen 3:1-24; Rom 5:12-21) or that of the "sons of God" (Gen 6:1-4; 1 Enoch 1–36). Instead, he focuses on the human "inclination" or *yeṣer*—the disposition internal to the person that may incline toward good or evil. For Ben Sira, free will can overcome all moral obstacles: "If you choose, you can keep the commandments" (15:15). The extremes—fire and water, life and death (see Deut 30:15-20)—are matters of human choice, and so is everything in between. Ben Sira's rejection of God's role in sin and his stress on the *yeṣer* as the seat of sin are nicely paralleled in Jas 1:13-16. Paul (see Rom 1:18-32) attributes more power to "sin," which he conceived in personal terms.

Human Responsibility and the Effects of Sin: 16:1-23

Having insisted that keeping the commandments and sin are matters of individual free will, Ben Sira, in four loosely related sections, takes up issues of collective and individual responsibility for sin. Whereas in biblical times many children were regarded as a divine blessing, Ben Sira in 16:1-4 insists on quality ("one can do better than a thousand") that depends on "fear of the LORD." This reflection leads into a meditation (16:5-10) on groups of sinners—the ancient giants (Gen 6:1-4), Lot's neighbors (Gen 18:16–19:29), the Canaanites, the 600,000 Israelite soldiers in the wilderness (Exod 12:37; Num 11:21)—whose evil ends came as the result of their sinfulness and stubbornness. Ben Sira's insistence on free will and individual responsibility is clearly stated in 16:11-14: "He judges a person according to his deeds." Thus he implies that each member of these collectives was a sinner (see Ezekiel 18). This principle, based on Ps 62:12, is taken up by Paul in Rom 2:6, though Paul places more emphasis on the effects of Adam's sin and the Law on human freedom (Rom 7:1-25).

Perhaps in response to Greek philosophers or even to ideas expressed in Qoheleth and Job, Ben Sira concludes in 16:17-23 with a parody on those who claim that God is distant and has no concern for individual persons and their moral responsibility. He uses the form of a monologue in which the speaker reasons that the creator and sustainer of the universe could hardly care about one individual ("what am I in a boundless creation?"). The monologue is prefaced by the formula "Do not say" and concluded with a judgment on the folly of one who speaks such thoughts.

Creation and Responsibility for Sin: 16:24–17:24

In view of the vastness of God's creation, how can an individual be held accountable for sin? Taking up the challenge of the monologue in 16:17-22, this unit contends that God has put an order into creation (16:26–17:4) that is discernible through human reason (17:6-10) and the Law (17:11-14), and that God knows and judges the actions of every person (17:15-24).

After a call to pay attention (16:24-25), the first section (16:26–17:4) uses ideas and phrases from Genesis 1–3 to describe the creation of the universe, the earth, and human beings. The emphasis is on God's order and care for creation ("in an eternal order . . . they never disobey his word"). Human beings made "in his own image" (17:3) exercise dominion over the earth.

The orderliness of God's creation should be recognized and celebrated by human beings through their senses, their reasoning powers, and, most of all, the "fear of him" that God has placed in the human heart. The proper human response to God's creation is to praise the creator (17:6-10). Moreover, the "Law of life . . . an eternal covenant" (17:11-14) adds encouragement to praise God and warning to beware of evil deeds. The Law is God's special gift to Israel—part of God's special relationship ("Israel is the Lord's own portion"). Ben Sira's view of the human condition is more optimistic than that of Paul (before and apart from Christ). Compare Rom 1:18-32 where idolatry has clouded the natural knowledge of God, and Rom 7:7-25 where the Law enters into an alliance with sin and further enslaves sinful humankind.

The monologue of 16:17-22 denied that God could be concerned with one person. In 17:15-23, Ben Sira affirms that every person's works are known to God and that "all their sins are before the LORD" (17:20). Thus the reflections on creation, human nature, and the Law converge on the conclusion that God does care about our actions and will hold us responsible for them (17:23). However, God's justice can be delayed or tempered by almsgiving (17:22) or repentance (17:24). The final mention of repentance prepares in turn for a call to repent in 17:25-32.

Call to Repentance: 17:25-32

The fundamental reason for repentance is the mercy of God: "How great is the mercy of the Lord, and his forgiveness for those who return to him!" (17:29). The initial call to repent (17:25-26) contains the elements of genuine repentance: turning from sin to the Lord, prayer, and hating sin. The idea that the dead in Sheol (a shadowy afterlife) cannot praise God (17:27-28; see Pss 6:5; 30:9; 88:10-12; 115:17-18; Isa 38:18) is used as a motive to repent *now* and praise God while you are alive (see Luke 16:19-31). Though Ben Sira's vision of the human condition is positive, he recognizes the reality of sin that flows from human weakness and mortality (17:30, 32). If the sun can "fail" by way of an eclipse, how much more can the "inclination" and frail humanity ("dust and ashes") be expected to fail! The reality of sin, the dynamics of repentance, and the merciful forgiveness of God appear in narrative form in the NT parable of the prodigal son (Luke 15:11-32).

God's Majesty and Mercy: 18:1-14

Flowing from the meditation on God's gift of creation in 16:24–17:4, the first part (18:1-7) of this unit proclaims God as the creator and only just one, asks rhetorical questions to establish the inability of humans to express God's mighty deeds, and says that humans can hardly begin to understand God's wonders. Why then is the Lord patient and merciful toward them? Precisely because they are so weak and mortal (18:8-12). God takes pity on them and grants them forgiveness. The reflection ends (18:13-14) by contrasting the recipients of human mercy ("their neighbors") and divine mercy ("every living thing"). The merciful God is like a shepherd with his flock—a powerful image for God in the OT (see Pss 23:1-4; 80:1; Isa 40:11; Ezek 34:11-16) and for God and Jesus in the NT (Matt 18:10-14; Luke 15:3-7; John 10:11-18; 1 Pet 2:25; Heb 13:20; Rev 7:17). God shows compassion especially to the wise—those who accept his discipline and precepts (not only the traditional wisdom of the schools but also the commandments of the Torah). Therefore those who seek to become wise will be more likely to experience God's mercy.

Words and Gifts: 18:15-18

Over the next few chapters Ben Sira presents wisdom sayings on various topics and gives relatively little attention to distinctively biblical themes. Moreover, the units are more anthological than logical in their literary development. The unit about words and gifts (18:15-18) introduces a major theme of the following chapters: speech (see 19:4-17; 20:1-8, 18-23, 24-31). Each of the four verses refers to words and gifts. The frame verses (18:15, 18) depict negative cases in which a good gift can be spoiled by bad words, and the center verses (18:16-17) insist that a good word is better than a gift and that the best person offers both.

Reflection and Action: 18:19-29

This unit begins (18:19a) and ends (18:29) with references to words. But the topic is more general than "before you speak, learn." The unit, on the whole, counsels the need for foresight or reflection before, during, and after action. The sage is "cautious in everything" (18:27)—before things happen (18:19-21) and in times of plenty (18:25-26), fully aware that "all things move swiftly before the Lord." Particular attention is given to foresight in making and fulfilling vows (18:22-23)—an example of giving thought before acting. Compare the tragic story of Jephthah's vow in Judg 11:29-40.

Self-Control: 18:30–19:3

Failure to exercise self-control brings disastrous results. The title of the unit, "self-control," appears in Greek and Latin manuscripts. What need control are the "base desires" and "appetites" related to money and sex. The focus of these reflections is the bad effect of giving in to these instincts: becoming a laughingstock to your enemies (18:31), becoming poor (18:32–19:1), being led astray by wine and loose women (19:2), and death (19:3, "decay and worms will take possession of him"). The behavior of the younger son in Luke 15:12-14, 30 is a narrative illustration of such behavior and its results.

Gossip: 19:4-17

Whereas a good word is better than a gift (18:16-17), loose talk is destructive not only to its subject but also to its purveyors. In 19:4-12, the prospective sage is warned against too quickly accepting slanderous tales about others (19:4-6) and against the evils of spreading gossip (19:7-9) except where it might be sinful to remain silent. Whereas the sage is admonished "Be brave, it will not make you burst" (19:10), the gossip is compared to a woman about to give birth and to someone with an arrow stuck in his thigh (19:11-12).

When a friend or neighbor is the topic of gossip, Ben Sira, in 19:13-17, recommends a direct approach. By means of a personal confrontation one may discover either that the story is false or that the friend's indiscretion is real but may serve as the occasion for correction and reform. The reference to letting the Law of the Most High take its course in 19:17 is probably from Lev 19:17-18—the source of the NT teaching, "you shall love your neighbor as yourself" (see Matt 5:43; 19:19; 22:39; Mark 12:31; Luke 10:27; Rom 13:9; Gal 5:14; Jas 2:8).

Wisdom and Cleverness: 19:20-30

What is the difference between wisdom and cleverness? Ben Sira's definition of true wisdom is fearing the Lord and fulfilling the Law (19:20). Without this religious foundation what may look like wisdom is, in fact, "a cleverness that is detestable" (19:23). In 19:25-28 he presents the characteristics of those whose cleverness is really guile and deceit: exact but unjust, only externally compassionate, and pretending not to notice but only waiting for an opportunity. How then can you discern between a wise person and a hypocrite? Ben Sira, in 19:29-30, suggests that a person's appearance (clothing, laughter, carriage) can provide some guidance. Though Ben Sira was a wisdom teacher, passages like this one indicate that the religious framework ("fear of the Lord") in which wisdom is learned and practiced was his criterion for distinguishing true wisdom from mere cleverness. This distinction underlies Jesus' prayer: "I thank you, Father, Lord of heaven and earth, because you have hidden these things from the wise and intelligent and have revealed them to infants" (Matt 11:25).

Speech: 20:1-31

The chapter consists of small collections of sayings mainly concerned with speech. The sayings for the most part are related topically or by catchwords rather than by logical progression. The sayings about admonition or rebuke (20:1-3) begin with a reminder that sometimes it is wise to be silent. The idea behind 20:4 ("like a eunuch lusting to violate a girl") is apparently that a sinner cannot be forced to do what is right; it is only vaguely related to 20:3. The second unit (20:5-8) reflects on the relative merits of speech and silence in specific situations. The paradox about the silence of the wise (20:7) leads into a series of paradoxes generally concerned with gifts and money (20:9-12).

The motifs of gifts and money, as well as the theme of speech and silence, are developed in 20:13-17 with particular attention to the gifts and words of the "fool." The "fool" in the wisdom tradition is deficient not only intellectually but also morally. The next unit (20:18-20) deals with types of inappropriate speech: slips of the tongue, coarse stories, and untimely proverbs from a fool. The unit on shame (20:21-23) ends with a reference to a foolish and unnecessary promise that only makes an enemy.

The following unit concerns the evil of the lie and the liar (20:24-26). Though most of the chapter treats the dangers or evils related to speech, the final section (20:27-31) expresses the positive ideal of the sage who influences "the great" by articulate words (20:27-28), warns the sage against being prevented by gifts from speaking the truth (20:29), and urges the sage to speak out and not to hide wisdom (20:30-31).

The chapter is noteworthy not only for its organization by catchwords (a device used in the Synoptic discourses, James, and Hebrews) but also for its "natural" reasoning. There is no appeal to fear of the Lord and the commandments. Rather, the appeal is to human experience as the source of practical wisdom.

The Destructive Power of Sin: 21:1-10

Why avoid sin? Because it can destroy you. The address "my son" begins a new unit here and elsewhere in the book. The sage's basic advice is to stop sinning and ask for forgiveness (21:1; see John 8:11). In the midst of the sage's warning about sin is the idea that God has a special openness to the prayers of the poor and will vindicate them (21:5). The bulk of the unit concerns the destructiveness of sin. Sin is compared (21:2-3) to a snake (see Gen 3:1-5), a lion's teeth, and a two-edged sword. Several examples (21:4, 6-8) show what happens when people build their lives on sins such as pride, arrogance, and greed. The destructive effects of sin are illustrated by two memorable figures of speech (21:9-10): An assembly of sinners is like combustible material ("a bundle of tow") that ends in a blazing fire, and the way of sinners is smooth but ends in Sheol (the abode of the dead). Though readers familiar with Jewish apocalyptic and early Christian texts may read 21:9-10 as referring to "hell," Ben Sira may simply have been commenting on the self-destructiveness of sinners and death as their "end."

The Sage and the Fool: 21:11-28

The difference between the sage and the fool is developed by a series of short units (21:11-12, 13-14, 15, 16-17, 18-21, 22-24, 25-26, 27-28). Apart from 21:11, the appeal is to practical human experience, and the content can be accepted by all kinds of people. With the opening verse, however, Ben Sira equates true wisdom with keeping the Law and fear of the Lord, and thus gives the standard sapiential teachings a distinctively Jewish religious framework. It is paired with a warning that mere cleverness is not enough (21:12; see 19:24-25). The contrast between the sage and the fool is captured by the images of the lifegiving spring and the broken jar (21:13-14). The contrast is especially manifest in speech (21:16-17, 25-26) and in openness to learning (21:15, 19, 21). Whereas to the fool education is like a fetter or a manacle, to the sage it is a "golden ornament" and a bracelet. They differ also in behavior, shown in their different ways of approaching a house (21:22-24). The unit ends (21:27-28) by describing two kinds of fools—one who curses another, and the slanderer—who bring even more misfortune upon themselves. Thus the fool is everything that the sage does not want to be, and the essence of Ben Sira's wisdom involves keeping the Law and fearing God.

Dealing with Fools: 22:1-18

Ben Sira's basic advice about fools is avoidance. One type of fool—the idler or lazy person—is like a "filthy rock" (i.e., a stone used for wiping after bowel movements) and balls of dung (22:1-2). It is especially painful when one's own children are fools (22:3-6), particularly in the case of a daughter. The uselessness of trying to deal directly with fools (22:9-10) is brought out by various images: trying to put back together a broken pot, rousing a sleeper, and telling a story to one who is drowsy. Since being dead is better than being a fool (22:11-12), the fool is even more to be pitied and mourned. The best strategy for the sage is to avoid all contact with fools (22:13), lest one suffer intellectual and moral contamination "when he shakes himself off." The burdensome character of fools is expressed in a series of comparisons (22:14-15): heavier than lead, and harder to bear than sand, salt, and iron. The unit ends by contrasting the hearts/minds of the sage (22:16-17) and the fool (22:18).

Friendship: 22:19-26

The main part of this section (22:19-22, 24) concerns ways in which friendships are destroyed—especially by "reviling, arrogance, disclosure of secrets, or a treacherous blow" (22:22). But a faithful friend (22:23, 25-26) stands by even, and especially, in hard times—whether it means sharing in the friend's subsequent prosperity (22:23) or suffering harm because of the friend (22:25-26). Avoiding harsh words and keeping confidences are the best ways to preserve a friendship.

Prayer and Sin: 22:27–23:6

Prayers are unusual in a wisdom book in which the teacher instructs the prospective sage. This prayer (see also 36:1-22; 51:1-12) serves to introduce the following units on sins related to speech (23:7-15) and sexuality (23:16-27). Its presence reminds us of the distinctively Jewish stamp that Ben Sira places on common-stock wisdom teachings. The two parts of the prayer follow the same outline: a question (22:27; 23:2-3) and a petition addressed to God as "Father" that effectively answers the question (23:1; 23:4-6). The first part (22:27–23:1) concerns sins of the tongue (see Jas 3:1-12), and the second part (23:2-6) deals with sins of the flesh arising from a disordered inclination *(yeṣer)*. An important motive for avoiding sin is shame before one's adversaries (23:3b). With this prayer Ben Sira acknowledges the need for God's help in avoiding sin and its consequences. The sage by himself is not fully capable of doing so. The prayer at least remotely prepares for the dynamic of redemption outlined by Paul in Romans (see Rom 8:31-39).

Sins of Speech: 23:7-15

The unit begins (23:7-8) with a call to listen to "instruction concerning the mouth" and a warning about the disastrous consequences of sins of the tongue. Then it focuses on oaths uttered in connection with God's name (23:9-11) and the special scrutiny they merit from God. In 23:11 there is a listing of ways one can sin through swearing oaths: too many oaths, oaths sworn in error, oaths that are disregarded, and false oaths. Ben Sira's caution about oaths prepares for Jesus' blanket condemnation of oaths (see Matt 5:33-37; Jas 5:12). The final part (23:12-15) singles out some other sins of speech: blasphemy (23:12), coarse language (23:13-14), and abusive speech (23:15). The penalty for blasphemy was death (see Lev 24:16; Matt 26:65-66; John 10:33). Remembering one's parents (23:14) in the midst of a social situation can restrain one from acting like a fool and thereby incurring shame. For discipline of the tongue as the key to discipline of the whole body (23:15) see Jas 3:2: "Anyone who makes no mistakes in speaking is perfect, able to keep the whole body in check with a bridle."

Sins of the Flesh: 23:16-27

The unit begins (23:16-17) with a numerical proverb listing three kinds of sexual sins (hot passion, incest, and fornication) and warning about their destructive effects. Then it focuses on adultery—first by the husband (23:18-21) and then by the wife (23:22-26). The psychology of the adulterer is beautifully sketched in 23:18: He only fears getting caught by human beings, whereas the One to whom he is ultimately responsible is God (23:19-20). The adulteress who bears a child by another man is guilty of offending both God and her husband (see Exod 20:14; Deut 5:18). She will suffer a public punishment (see John 7:53–8:11), and her children will not be accepted among the people of Israel. In these cases Ben Sira assumes that sin is always punished (23:21, 24-26). The punishments of the adulterer and the adulteress underscore the central message of the entire book: "nothing is better than fear of the Lord, and nothing sweeter than to heed the commandments of the Lord" (23:27).

Praise of Wisdom: 24:1-34

The approximate physical center of the book is marked by one of its most important and famous passages consisting of personified Wisdom's praise of herself (24:1-22) and Ben Sira's comments (24:23-34). Wisdom dwells in Jerusalem, and Wisdom is the Torah. [See also the excursus "The Use of Proverbs 8 and Other Wisdom Texts in Christian Liturgy" in the commentary on Proverbs.]

Wisdom's praise of herself (24:1-22) takes as its literary model Prov 8:22-31, which depicts Wisdom as a female figure who existed before creation and takes part in God's work of creation. Ben Sira's creative contribution lay in assigning Wisdom a home in the Jerusalem Temple (24:8-12). The narrative introduction (24:1-2) describes Wisdom in female personal terms as praising herself in both earth and heaven. The female characterization may simply be grammatical, since the Hebrew *(ḥokhmāh)* and Greek *(sophia)* words for "wisdom" are feminine nouns. Or perhaps there is an influence of a pagan female deity (Isis).

The first stanza (24:3-7) in Wisdom's poem concerns the origin and activity of Wisdom.

Wisdom is clearly a creature of God ("I came forth from the mouth of the Most High"). As she travels through heaven and earth, she seeks for a lasting dwelling place; compare *1 Enoch* 42:1-3 where Wisdom finds no earthly dwelling and so returns to heaven. In the second stanza (24:8-12), Wisdom recounts how God assigned her a dwelling place in Israel at the Jerusalem Temple. Thus Ben Sira brings together the wisdom, cultic, and legal strands of Israelite piety. The comparisons of Wisdom to the various trees and bushes (24:13-17) emphasize her attractiveness and life-giving power. The final stanza (24:19-22) is an invitation to eat from Wisdom's fruits, with the observation that those who eat and drink from them will seek even more (compare John 6:35).

When early Christians celebrated the person of Jesus they took over elements from this personified Wisdom tradition of Proverbs 8 and Sirach 24. The most prominent examples are the hymns in Col 1:15-20 and John 1:1-18 (see also Heb 1:1-2). Of course in the NT the figure of Wisdom is masculine (Jesus). But the ideas of Wisdom's pre-existence, sharing in the work of creation, and seeking a home (see John 1:10-11) are affirmed with regard to Jesus. Basic to this development is the idea of Jesus as the "Word" of God (a wisdom concept) whose very being reveals his heavenly Father: Jesus is Wisdom incarnate.

Ben Sira's comments (24:23-34) are introduced by his momentous equation of Wisdom and the Torah: "All this is the book of the covenant of the Most High God, the Law that Moses commanded us as an inheritance for the congregations of Jacob" (24:23; see Deut 33:4). Then he compares Wisdom to six mighty rivers (24:25-27). Note the neat literary pattern of verbs ("overflows . . . runs over . . . pours forth"), nouns ("wisdom . . . understanding . . . instruction"), and seasons ("first fruits . . . harvest . . . vintage"). So great is Wisdom that she transcends human understanding and the bounds of nature (24:28-29). In the final stanza (24:30-34) Ben Sira defines his own role as a wisdom teacher ("As for me"). He develops first the river imagery ("like a canal . . . like a water channel") and then images of light ("I will again make instruction shine forth like the dawn") and prophecy ("pour out teaching"). Ben Sira the wisdom teacher is conscious of his social function of handing on the wisdom tradition to "all future generations" of those who seek wisdom (24:33b-34). See 33:16-19 for more autobiographical reflection.

Happiness: 25:1-11

What kinds of people are happy? Of the three sections, two (25:1-2 and 25:7-11) are numerical proverbs. The three pleasant sights (25:1) involve harmony among people, while the three loathsome sights (25:2) concern people who do what is neither necessary nor appropriate. The reference to the old fool who commits adultery leads into an ideal picture of old age (25:3-6) marked by wisdom and fear of the Lord. The list of ten happy thoughts (25:7-11) culminates also in wisdom and fear of the Lord (25:10-11). These are the sources of genuine happiness and will bring about the other items on the list. The list in 25:8-9 features the "beatitude" form found also in the NT (see Matt 5:3-12; Luke 6:20-23) but here in a sapiential rather than eschatological context.

The Bad Wife and the Good Wife: 25:13–26:27

Ben Sira's comments on women are notorious in many circles today. To appreciate them demands a clear grasp of the literary setting (the experienced male teacher is instructing the young male pupil) and the cultural setting (the ideal is patriarchy, where the husband exercises oversight of the household). There are five major sections alternating between the bad wife (25:13-26; 26:5-12) and the good wife (26:1-4; 26:13-18) and concluding with basic advice to the young sage (26:19-21) and with contrasts between bad and good women (26:22-27).

The first section (25:13-26) laments the bad effects of living with an evil and angry woman ("I would rather live with a lion and a dragon"). The patriarchal assumptions include shame over living off the wife's money (25:22), the idea that woman is the origin of sin (25:24; see Gen 3:6, 12-13; 2 Cor 11:3; 1 Tim 2:14), and the husband's prerogative in divorce (25:26; Deut 24:1-4; Mark 10:2, 10; Matt 19:3, 9). The contrasting section on the good wife (26:1-4) uses the beatitude form ("Happy is the husband of a good wife") and portrays the good wife as the source of long life, joy, and peace for her husband.

The second description of the evil wife (26:5-12) consists of a numerical proverb (25:5-6), three sayings on bad wives (25:7-9), and advice to the sage to keep strict sexual control over a rebellious daughter (25:10-12; see 42:9-14). The language ("tent peg . . . quiver") is very graphic. The contrasting section on the good wife (26:13-18) praises the virtues (charm, silence, modesty) and physical beauty of the good wife.

The ideal for the sage is to marry a wife from the daughters of Israel and raise up many children from her (26:19-21; see Prov 5:7-23). The concluding contrasts between evil and good women (26:22-27) help us to understand Ben Sira's ideal woman: pious, modest, honoring her husband, and quiet. Though present only in some Greek manuscripts and in the Syriac version, 26:19-27 was very likely part of the original text.

Sin and Related Topics: 26:28–27:29

The eight short units in this section concern three depressing sights (26:28), business and temptation to sin (26:29–27:3), speech as the criterion of the person (27:4-7), pursuing justice and truth (27:8-10), the speech of the godly and the fool (27:11-15), betraying confidences as the death of friendship (27:16-21), the hypocrite (27:22-24), and retribution (27:25-29). These topics are often treated with colorful and memorable rhetorical devices: the numerical proverb culminating in grief over the righteous person turning back to sin (26:28), the image of sin wedged like a stake between selling and buying (27:2), the scatological images (27:4), the idea of "doing the truth" (27:9—a favorite Johannine phrase), checking the time with fools but lingering with the wise (27:12), the inclusion about one who betrays confidences losing hope (27:16, 21), the vehement hatred for the hypocrite (27:24), and the comical images of retribution—how people destroy themselves with their own evil devices (27:25-29).

Forgiveness of Sins: 27:30–28:7

Two basic attributes of God in the Bible are justice and mercy. Those who seek vengeance on others (27:30–28:1) will have to face the justice of God. For the same dynamic see the parable of the unjust steward in Matthew 18:23-35. Those who seek God's mercy must be willing to show mercy to others (28:2-5)—a point made in five slightly different ways. For this dynamic see Matthew 6:12, 14-15. As further motivation for forgiveness the sage is urged to "remember" death and the commandments of God's covenant (28:6-7). Only those who deal mercifully with others can expect mercy from God. Otherwise prepare for strict justice from God.

Destructive Speech: 28:8-26

The four sections approach destructive speech from various perspectives. The root of strife, discord, and bloodshed (28:8-12) is the mouth—which can either ignite the flame or put it out (28:12). The unit on slander (28:13-16) focuses on its effects in destroying peace (28:13, 16) and in ruining men (28:14) and women (28:15), who are then driven from their homes (by divorce) and left without means. The destructive power of the tongue (28:17-23) is illustrated by a series of comparisons: worse than the whip, sword, yoke and fetters, death and Hades (= Sheol), flames, and lion and leopard. The final section (28:24-26) is direct advice to the wise about being cautious in speech. Various images are employed: fence of thorns, door and bolt, lock, balances and scales, and the prospect of ambush. For a similar exhortation about the destructive power of the tongue see Jas 3:1-12.

Money Matters: 29:1-20

The section on loans (29:1-7) first states general principles: Be willing to make loans as the Torah dictates (Exod 22:25; Lev 25:35-37; Deut 15:7-11; 23:19-20; 24:10-13) without taking interest from a fellow Israelite, and be scrupulous in paying back what you have borrowed. Then it reflects on the dangers of making loans in 29:4-7: You may not get paid back and may make an enemy for your trouble. The section on almsgiving (29:8-13) assumes that this is a good deed in accord with the Torah (see Deut 15:7) and focuses on the positive effects that are sure to come from such generosity with the image of a "treasure" (see Matt 6:19-21; 19:21; Luke 12:33; 16:9). Though Proverbs recommends against providing surety or collateral for another (see Prov 6:1-5; 11:15; 17:18; 20:16; 22:26-27; 27:13), Ben Sira, in 29:14-20, is favorably disposed toward the practice ("a good person will be surety for his neighbor") but also aware of the dangers and negative effects. His basic principle in standing surety and in all these money matters is expressed in 29:20: "Assist your neighbor to the best of your ability, but be careful not to fall yourself."

Depending on Others: 29:21-28

The situation presupposed by the instruction is sketched in Lev 25:35: "If any of your kin fall into difficulty and become dependent on you, you shall support them; they shall live with you as though resident aliens." Whereas the Torah looks at the situation from the side of the dispenser of charity, Ben Sira views it from the perspective of the recipient. In 29:21-22 he counts one's own home among the necessities of life, however humble that home may be. That modicum of independence contrasts with the shame of depending on the kindness of others who may treat you like a servant (29:25-26) and throw you out (29:27). The concluding comment about "the insults of the moneylender" (29:28) may allude to the cause of the dependency and so relate the passage to what preceded it.

Fathers and Sons: 30:1-13

A father should discipline his son because it will benefit the son in the long run and increase the father's reputation before others. Ben Sira's theories about raising children sound very dubious today, but they were hardly unique in antiquity (see Prov 13:24; 19:18; 22:15; 23:13-14). The first section (30:1-6) reflects on the positive effects of disciplining the son, and the second section (30:7-12) considers the negative effects of forgoing discipline. The final verse (30:13) summarizes the teaching: "Discipline your son and make his yoke heavy, so that you may not be offended by his shamelessness." The cultural ideal of the father is stern, distant (see 30:9-10), and deserving of respect. This passage is important for understanding the context of Jesus' idea of God as Father. We must avoid projecting modern, Western concepts of fatherhood ("Daddy") onto the NT texts that call God "Father."

Happiness: 30:14-25

Three important elements in happiness are good physical health (30:14-17), good food (30:18-20), and a good disposition (30:21-25). Whereas good health is more valuable than gold or silver, death is preferable to bad health. The section on food (30:18-20) is somewhat obscure in its imagery. The idea seems to be that for one who is sick and unable to eat (understood as a punishment from God; see 30:19), good food is as useless as what is set out by a grave or sacrificed to an idol and as fruitless as a girl embraced by a eunuch. The positive effects of a good disposition include a longer life (30:22; see Matt 6:27) and good digestion (30:25).

Riches: 31:1-11

Does wealth bring happiness and righteousness? The question is answered negatively in four small units. The first (31:1-2) establishes concern over money as a major cause of sleeplessness. The second (31:3-4) contrasts the leisure of the rich and of the poor: For the poor to take time off only increases their need. Far from bringing about righteousness, the pursuit of riches leads to ruin and destruction (31:5-7). The final unit (31:8-11) is a beatitude that praises the rich person who is blameless and not greedy. The Hebrew text of 31:8 uses the term "Mammon" (see Luke 16:9, 13) for wealth. The four units are summarized in Jesus' comment on how hard it is for a rich person to enter the kingdom of God (Mark 10:25).

Manners and Moderation: 31:12–32:13

How should one behave when invited to a banquet? The four units form a chiastic structure: A–table manners (31:12-18); B–moderation with food (31:19-24); B'–moderation with wine (31:25-31); A'–table manners (32:1-13). All four units assume an "upper class" culture in which public behavior is important in establishing and maintaining status.

The first instruction on table manners (31:12-18) is a list of "do's and don't's" to be observed when seated at the banquet table. The goal is to avoid drawing negative attention to oneself. The positive criterion ("judge your neighbor's feelings by your own") is a version of the NT Golden

Rule (Matt 7:12; Luke 6:31). The first instruction about moderation (31:19-24) compares the results of moderate and immoderate eating and proposes the rule: "In everything you do be moderate, and no sickness will overtake you" (31:22). The last two verses (31:23-24) take up a different but loosely related topic by contrasting public responses to generous and stingy hosts.

The second instruction on moderation compares the bad effects of drinking too much wine (31:25-26, 29-30) with the good effects of the moderate use of wine (31:27-28). The unit ends by advising the sage not to try to reason with a drunk (31:31). The final instruction on manners (32:1-13) first (32:1-2) counsels one who has been chosen to serve as "master of the feast" (see John 2:8-10) to do his duty in an inconspicuous manner—which ironically will increase his good reputation. The elder (32:3-6) is urged to speak in a restrained and accurate way and warned not to interfere with the precious musical entertainment. The younger man (32:7-10) is also urged to speak sparingly but at the same time to maintain modesty and diffidence—the kind of behavior that wins general approval. The unit ends in 32:11-13 with advice on going home in good time and on saying "grace" after the meal ("above all bless your Maker, who fills you with his good gifts"). These banquet instructions provide important background for many of Jesus' teachings (Luke 7:36-50; 14:7-24; 21:14-38; 24:28-31, 36-49).

Wisdom, Torah, and Fear of the Lord: 32:14–33:6

Ben Sira's ideal sage combines practical wisdom, keeping the commandments, and fear of the Lord. The individual sections in this unit reflect on the relation of the three entities in various ways. The term "Law" here refers specifically to the Torah—the divine Law revealed to Israel as the pattern for its relationship with God. The first section (32:14-17) contrasts the sage who seeks the Law and fears God with the hypocrite and sinner who avoid correction and the statutes of the Law. The second section (32:18-24) begins as a mere call to cautious behavior but then links such behavior to "the keeping of the commandments" and to fear of the Lord. The third section (33:1-3) again links wisdom, the Law, and fear of the Lord, and promises happiness and safety to those who act according to them. The final section (33:4-6) contrasts the thoughtful preparation of the wise before speaking with the mindless behavior of the fool. This text (and other such passages) goes to the heart of Ben Sira's intellectual program of fusing the common Near Eastern wisdom tradition with the distinctively Jewish experience of God and approach to life.

The Pairs: 33:7-15

Throughout his work Ben Sira has distinguished sages and fools, good and bad, life and death, without ever explaining how an all-good and all-powerful God could allow the existence of evil (the question of theodicy). Finally he approaches this issue with his doctrine of the "pairs," which is articulated most clearly in 33:14-15: Within God's plan for creation there is a certain dualism (good versus evil, life versus death, godly versus sinners). Ben Sira leads up to this teaching by reflecting on the Jewish calendar (33:7-9) in which some days are important (Passover, Sabbaths, etcetera) and other days only get a number (day one, day two, etcetera). Then he applies this duality to God's creation of human beings (33:10-13) and dealings with them ("like clay in the hand of the potter"). Ben Sira proposes a modified dualism in which everything (good and evil) remains under God's sovereignty (see Isa 45:7) and appeals somewhat vaguely to the divine plan working itself out in the "nature of things." He does not present a strong Satan figure (as in the Dead Sea scrolls and the NT) who leads the children of darkness to do the deeds of darkness.

Autobiographical Note: 33:16-19

Unlike most biblical books, Sirach is neither anonymous nor pseudonymous. The author identifies himself by name (50:27) and sprinkles his book with autobiographical comments (24:30-34; 33:16-19; 34:9-13; 39:12-13; 50:27; 51:13-30). By comparing himself first to a gleaner and then to a skilled grape picker, he suggests that his long study and appropriation of the biblical and wisdom traditions have yielded rich results (33:16-17). Then he affirms that his study and teaching are not for himself but rather for the general public (33:18-19). The wisdom teacher has a public vocation and benefits others.

Master of the Household: 33:20-33

Ben Sira addresses the head of the household—a male with financial resources and slaves. He first (33:20-24) urges the householder to preserve his independence ("do not let anyone take your place") and not to distribute his property until the hour of death (see Luke 15:11-32). In Ben Sira's day, human slavery was a socially and religiously sanctioned institution. Persons became slaves by being taken captive in war or by financial reverses. Ben Sira's initial advice (33:25-30a), however pragmatic and effective, is very harsh ("bread and discipline and work for a slave"); it is tempered somewhat by an appeal for justice in 33:30b. The advice ends (33:31-33) with the case of a householder who has only one slave and whose self-interest demands good treatment of the slave. See Jesus' servant parables in Luke 12:35-48 and Matt 24:45-51; 25:14-30.

Sources of Wisdom and Happiness: 34:1-20

The first section (34:1-8) is strong critique of the value of dreams. In antiquity dreams were regarded as giving knowledge about the future (unlike the modern psychoanalytic use of dreams as indicators of the past). With sharp insight Ben Sira calls dreams a mere reflection of the self (34:3). He makes an exception for dreams "sent by invention from the Most High" (34:6; see Gen 28:12-16; 31:10-13, 24; 37:5-10; 40:8-19; 41:1-32; Dan 2:1-19, 27-45; Matthew 1–2). But how does one know? Instead of relying on dreams it is preferable to fulfill the Law and thus exercise perfect wisdom.

The second section (34:9-13) praises the value of experience gained through travel, and includes Ben Sira's autobiographical testimony (34:12-13; see 33:16-19) about how experience saved him from the dangers of travel (see Paul's comment in 2 Cor 11:25-27).

The third section (34:14-20) reflects on the positive ideal of fear of the Lord: "Happy is the soul who fears the Lord." With a series of striking images ("a shelter from scorching wind and a shade from noonday sun . . . he lifts up the soul and makes the eyes sparkle"), Ben Sira describes the blessings that accompany one who fears the Lord, which is true wisdom.

True Religion and Social Justice: 34:21–35:26

The three sections in this unit are reminiscent of the language and ideas of Isaiah 56–66. Ben Sira, who was positively disposed toward, and even enthusiastic for, Temple worship (see 50:1-21), insists that religious practices be accompanied and animated by a concern for justice.

The first section (34:21-31) makes that point in a series of short units (vv. 21-23, 24-27, 28-29, 30-31). God will not accept the sacrifices of those who have exploited the poor (see Jas 5:1-6). The most striking images appear in 34:30-31, which alludes to the fast of the Day of Atonement (see Lev 23:27-32). Unless the fast is accompanied by a resolve not to sin again, God will not hear prayers for forgiveness of sins. Such presumption is compared to someone who incurs ritual defilement by touching a corpse (see Num 19:11-13), goes through the process of ritual cleansing, and touches the corpse again.

The second section (35:1-13) begins with a short poem (35:1-5) that equates observing the commandments, doing acts of kindness, and avoiding sin with various elements in the Temple cult (see Isaiah 58). Yet good deeds do not substitute for Temple worship, nor do they stand in opposition to it. The second poem (35:6-13) is an enthusiastic endorsement of offering sacrifices at the Temple during the pilgrimage festivals ("Do not appear before the Lord empty-handed") and a plea for generosity in first fruits and tithes ("With every gift show a cheerful face," see 2 Cor 9:7). The theological dynamic of sacrifice is *do ut des* ("I give that you may give") on the assumption that God "will repay you sevenfold" (35:13).

The third section (35:14-26) focuses on the justice of God. As the just judge God cannot be bribed by dishonest sacrifices (35:14-15). God will attend to the complaints of orphans and widows (35:16-19; see Luke 18:1-8) and to the prayers of humble and righteous people (35:20-22a, "the prayer of the humble pierces the clouds"). The concluding description of God as a delivering warrior (35:22b-26) features four "until" clauses and concludes with a beautiful image of God's mercy being as welcome "as clouds of rain in time of drought." The language of 35:22b-26 is reminiscent of the prophets and very much at home in Jewish apocalypticism (destruction of the unrighteous, judgment according to deeds, vindication and happiness for God's people).

Prayer for God's People: 36:1-22

This lament urging God's intervention on Israel's behalf follows from the description of the Lord as warrior in 35:22b-25. The first part (36:1-12) addresses the "God of all" and contrasts "no God but you" (36:5) with enemy rulers who say "There is no one but ourselves" (36:12). Though Ben Sira may have had in mind the Seleucid king Antiochus III, the language is so biblical and traditional that one cannot identify a specific occasion. The appeal is expressed in the language associated with the Exodus ("new signs . . . other wonders . . . make your hand and right arm glorious"). What is at stake is not so much Israel's reputation but God's reputation: "As you have used us to show your holiness to them, so use them to show your glory to us" (36:4). Whereas the first part urges God's intervention against the Gentiles, the second part (36:13-22) prays for the ingathering of all Israel and God's blessing on the Jerusalem Temple. Again (as is frequent in the Psalms), the appeal is to God's own self-interest: God's people and Temple should be glorious, God's prophecies should be fulfilled, and all peoples should know "that you are the Lord, the God of the ages" (36:22).

Friends and Associates: 36:23–37:15

The three main instructions are prefaced by a short unit on discernment or discretion (36:23-25) that evokes by way of comparison the ability of the tongue and stomach to tell one food from another. The section on choosing a wife (36:26-31) compares the happiness of a man married to a beautiful and modest woman (36:27-29) with the rootlessness and aimlessness of the unmarried man (36:30-31; see Gen 4:12, 14). Ben Sira's cultural assumptions come out in his comment that "a woman will accept any man as a husband" (marriages were arranged, and the woman had no choice) and in his remark that he who acquires a wife gets "his best possession."

In choosing a friend (37:1-6), one should be aware of "friends only in name," friends who become enemies, and "fair weather" friends (37:1, 2, 4). Failures in friendship are traced to the "inclination to evil" (37:3), an important concept in Ben Sira's approach to the human condition. But friends who prove faithful in times of testing ("during the battle") should be rewarded (37:5-6).

In choosing a counselor (37:7-15), one should find out the counselor's own agenda and interests lest the counselor work only to his advantage (37:7-9). This basic principle is followed by a list of inappropriate counselors (37:10-11), including a woman about her rival (as a second wife?) and a lazy servant about a big task. The best sources of good advice (37:12-15) are those who keep the commandments, one's own heart and mind, and God in prayer.

Wisdom and Moderation: 37:16-31

The first unit (37:16-18) explores the relation between words, plans, and actions (and their results). It calls the word "the beginning of every work" and the tongue a ruler. The second unit (37:19-26) contrasts clever people who lack wisdom (37:19-21) and the truly wise person who benefits both himself and his people (37:22-26). The several references to the "people" may account for the saying about the days of Israel being "without number" (37:25). Moderation in eating (37:27-31; see 31:19-31) is characteristic of a wise person. One must approach food with discretion and restraint lest one grow sick and die (see Num 11:18-20). The principle "not everything is good for everyone" (37:28) is evoked in different contexts by Paul in 1 Cor 6:12 and 10:23. The references to sickness prepare for the following advice about physicians.

Sickness and Doctors: 38:1-15

The sage is urged first to be respectful and cooperative with physicians (38:1-3) and to look upon medicines as gifts from God (38:4-8). Ben Sira emphasizes that both physicians and medicines have been created by God and work their healing as instruments of God. The allusion in "water made sweet with a tree" (38:5) is to the Marah incident in Exod 15:23-25. The sage, when sick, is instructed first to attend to the spiritual duties of prayer, repentance, and sacrifice (38:9-11), and then to cooperate fully with the physician (38:12-15). Again, there is an emphasis on God's action: Physicians too should pray that they may make the correct diagnosis and be successful in healing (38:14). This ideal situation contrasts with that of King Asa (2 Chr 16:12) who did not seek the Lord but sought help only from physicians (38:15). In his advice Ben Sira blends reliance on God and on doctors and their medicines.

Mourning: 38:16-23

When a loved one dies, grief should be intense but circumscribed. The first section (38:16-17) describes the rituals associated with mourning and urges serious compliance with them "for one day, or two" (38:16-17). But Ben Sira is more concerned with the harmful effects of excessive grief (38:18-20) and concludes with a meditation on the inevitability and finality of death (38:21-23). Though there is no explicit denial of life after death, neither is there much affirmation of it ("the dead is at rest"). Ben Sira's real interest is facing the fact of physical death and its value in placing grief over the death of a loved one in proper perspective.

Tradesmen and the Scribe: 38:24–39:11

For Ben Sira scribes were far more than those who copied documents. They not only could read and write but also were public figures, intellectuals, and rightful leaders. Such persons were trained at Ben Sira's school (see 51:23-28). The first part (38:24-34a) contrasts the leisure of the scribe (38:24) with the preoccupations of the farmer (38:25-26), artisan (38:27), smith (38:28), and potter (38:29-30). The scribe has the "leisure" (Greek *scholē,* from which derive "school," "scholar," "scholastic," etcetera) that befits the "free" person (Latin *liber,* from which derives our idea of a "liberal" education), and so has the opportunity to learn and develop the necessary intellectual and rhetorical skills. The passage is often compared to the Egyptian satire on the trades (in "The Instruction of Khety, Son of Duauf"). Ben Sira, far from denigrating the tradesmen (see 38:31-32a, 34a), acknowledges their positive and necessary contributions to society. Yet they cannot do what the scribe does: exercise political and legal leadership (38:32b-33).

Ben Sira's description of the scribal ideal first lists the components of a proper scribal education (38:34b–39:4), which includes the Law of the Most High and other elements of Israel's religious tradition, the ancient wisdom collections (proverbs and parables), service among the great, and travel (see 34:9-13). This learning must be accompanied by prayer and the wisdom of the Torah, because God is the ultimate source of wisdom (39:5-8). The reward of such scribal discipline is public recognition and fame, as well as a "name" that lives on after the scribe's death (39:9-11). Immortality through memory is the fitting tribute to the faithful scribe.

God's Creation and Evil: 39:12-35

The most difficult question facing any scribe/intellectual is the problem of evil. After a call to listen and to praise God (39:12-15), Ben Sira affirms the goodness of creation and the absolute sovereignty of God over it (39:16-21). With an allusion to Gen 1:9-10 ("at his word the waters stood in a heap"), Ben Sira places special emphasis on God's purpose in creation ("everything has been created for its own purpose"). The author's solution to the dilemma (39:22-31) affirms that God created good things for good people, but for evil people these can become bad (39:25). Thus the ten necessities of human life ("water and fire and iron and salt . . ." 39:26) can turn into evil for sinners. And things that have bad effects ("winds . . . fire and hail and famine and pestilence," 39:28-30) can serve to punish the wicked. While preserving the sovereignty of God and tracing evil to the perverted will of the wicked, Ben Sira leaves untouched the problem of innocent suffering explored in Job. In his epilogue (39:32-35), Ben Sira reaffirms that "all the works of the Lord are good" and "everything proves good in its appointed time." See his earlier reflection on "the pairs" in 33:7-15.

Misery and Joy: 40:1-30

The topics are treated in four loosely connected units on the misery associated with the human condition (40:1-10), the triumph of righteousness (40:11-17), the joys of life (40:18-27), and the misery of begging (40:28-30). The first unit (40:1-10) traces the fears and anxieties that all humans face to the "heavy yoke . . . laid on the children of Adam"—surely a reference to Genesis 3 but probably not yet a doctrine of "original sin" as in Romans 5. The description of restless sleep and bad dreams in 40:5b-7 is especially vivid and true to life. The issue of innocent suffering is broached in 40:8-10 where all are said to share in the punishments intended for the wicked (who suffer sevenfold). These somber thoughts are balanced by a confidence (40:11-17) that wickedness and the wicked will be swept away and what will abide are good faith, kindness, and almsgiving. Though Ben Sira probably expected this triumph within the normal course of history, the content fits well with the apocalyptic language of Daniel and some NT passages.

The third unit (40:18-27) is a numerical proverb of an unusual kind. Each of the ten sections (nine in Greek) names two good things and asserts that a third thing is even better. Thus wealth and a salary are good, but finding a treasure is even better. The list climaxes in the declaration that fear of the Lord is best of all (40:26-27). The worst misery that befalls human beings is to be reduced to begging (40:28-30): "It is better to die than to beg." Again Ben Sira shows keen psychological insight by calling attention to the loss of self-respect and the internal hostility that accompany begging.

Death and Reputation: 41:1-13

An important mode of immortality is the "name"—the reputation and memory one leaves behind. The opening reflection on death (41:1-4) provides the framework for what follows: death is unwelcome to the prosperous and welcome to the wretched; it is nonetheless "the Lord's decree for all flesh" and so inevitable. Through their "abominable children" (41:5-10), sinners suffer perpetual disgrace, for their children not only endure the disgrace of their parents but also replicate their behavior. This bleak picture is punctuated by a warning: "Woe to you, the ungodly, who have forsaken the Law of the Most High" (41:8). This helps to define the sinful behavior that Ben Sira had in mind. The positive side (41:11-13) is developed in three verses about how a good and virtuous "name" lives forever. This teaching prepares for the catalogue of Israel's heroes in Sirach 44–50.

Shame: 41:14–42:8

After a brief comment on the public character of wisdom (41:14-15 = 20:30-31) Ben Sira distinguishes things of which one should be ashamed and not ashamed (41:16). The list of shameful things (41:17–42:1a) includes both actions that bring shame and persons before whom one would be ashamed to do them. The first and most important thing in the list of things not to be ashamed of (42:1b-8) is "the Law of the Most High and his covenant" (42:2). The two lists provide interesting mixes of actions and persons. Knowing how to discern between what does and does not bring shame leads to a good "name" for the sage (42:1a, 8).

Fathers and Daughters: 42:9-14

As was the case in the advice about disciplining one's son (30:1-13), the major concern is the father's reputation before others. The assumption is that daughters in "good" families live protected lives as they are prepared for arranged marriages. The passage consists of a list of a father's worries about his daughter (42:9-10) and a stern warning to supervise her closely (42:11-13). If he does not, the father runs the risk of becoming a public "laughingstock . . . byword . . . shame." The low point in Ben Sira's misogynism comes in 42:14a: "Better is the wickedness of a man than a woman who does good."

God's Glory in Creation: 42:15–43:33

Ben Sira's understanding of wisdom (fear of the Lord and keeping the commandments) takes as its horizon or background the glory of God made manifest in creation (42:15–43:33) and in Israel's history (44:1–50:24). At this point the book puts aside the practical advice so characteristic of the wisdom movement and offers a historical and theological framework in which the practical advice gains meaning and depth.

The introductory poem (42:15-25) praises God's creation as "full of his glory," and reflects on the omniscience of God and God's purpose in creation. That all creation is made "by the word of the Lord" (42:15) recalls Genesis 1 but also alludes to the praise of Wisdom in Sirach 24 and forward to 43:26 ("by his word all things hold together"). These ideas and images underlie the christological hymns in John 1:1-18; Col 1:15-20; and Heb 1:1-2. Ben Sira also reasserts his modified dualism in 42:24 ("all things come in pairs"); see 33:7-15; 39:12-35; 40:8-10.

The second poem (43:1-12) celebrates God's glory made manifest in heavenly bodies: sun (43:2-5), moon (43:6-8), stars (43:9-10), and rainbow (43:11-12). It gives special attention to the moon's role in fixing Israel's calendar ("the sign for festal days"), thus suggesting the use of a lunar calendar at the Jerusalem Temple (the Qumran community followed a solar calendar). For the rainbow in the Noah story see Gen 9:12-17.

The third section (43:13-26) echoes the ancient "storm" poem in Psalm 29 and celebrates God's glory in the elements of nature: snow, lightning, clouds, hailstones, and so on. The imagery is quite striking and violent, but the assumption is that everything in nature fulfills God's purpose (see 43:26). Compare the climactic poem in Job 38–39, where the emphasis is on the human inability to grasp God's purpose.

The fourth section (43:27-33) proclaims that God is "the all"—not in a pantheistic sense but rather in the biblical sense of Creator and Lord. The proper response to the manifestation of God's glory in nature is praise: "you cannot praise him enough" (43:30). The final verses (43:32-33) acknowledge the limits of human understanding ("I have seen but a few of his works," see 42:15) and affirm that God is the source of wisdom for persons of piety.

God's Glory in Israel: 44:1-15

How God's glory has been made manifest in Israel's history (see Wisdom 10–19) is the theme of chs. 44–50 ("Now let us praise famous men"). Ben Sira presents these great figures of Israel's past as manifestations of God's glory. The introductory poem (44:1-15) makes this point in the invocation (44:1-2): "The Lord apportioned to them great glory." The reflection is introduced by a list of twelve types of famous men (44:3-6). The persons celebrated in these chapters deserve the immortality by name and memory so praised by Ben Sira in 41:11-13. How 44:9 fits in the context of 44:7-15 is debated: It can be taken as a simple acknowledgment that some people are forgotten. Or it can more likely refer to oblivion as the fate of the wicked (see 41:5-10). For similar catalogues of Israel's heroes see 1 Macc 2:51-64 and Hebrews 11. The climax of Ben Sira's catalogue is Simon the high priest around 200 B.C.E. (see 50:1-24). These seven chapters can be regarded as an encomium of Simon. Much of what Ben Sira chooses to emphasize (glory, covenant, priesthood, Temple, building projects, etcetera) has been chosen to lead up to Simon's portrait.

The Patriarchs: 44:16-23

Because of his mysterious transfer to heaven (Gen 5:24), Enoch (44:16) evoked great interest as a revealer of heavenly secrets and thus was a fitting character to begin and end (49:14) the list of heroes. Why he was hailed as an "example of repentance" is not clear (see Wis 4:10-12). Noah (44:17-18) is described as "perfect" (Gen 6:9) and "righteous" (Gen 7:1), and as the vehicle for "everlasting covenants" (Gen 9:8-17). Abraham (44:19-21) is the "great father of a multitude of nations" (Gen 17:4-5). What Ben Sira regarded as most important about Abraham is that "he kept the Law of the Most High" (long before the Law was given to Moses on Sinai!) and that he entered into the covenant of circumcision (see Gen 17). Thus Abraham's fatherhood of many nations is through the distinctive elements of Israel's tradition—the Law and circumcision. Compare Paul's treatment of Abraham in Galatians 3 and Romans 4. God's promise to Abraham is carried on through Isaac (44:22a), and Jacob and his twelve sons (44:22b-23).

Moses, Aaron, and Phinehas: 45:1-26

With the short but enthusiastic description of Moses (45:1-5) as a miracle worker and teacher Ben Sira continues his motif of God's glory (45:2, 3) by allusions to Exodus 33–34 (see 2 Cor 3:12-18). As the one to whom God revealed the commandments (45:3, 5), Moses was empowered to "teach Jacob the covenant" (45:5)—an important link between the covenant and the Torah in the unfolding of Israel's history. The disproportionately large space given to Aaron (45:6-22) prepares for the climax of chs. 44–50 with the praise of Simon in 50:1-24. God made an "everlasting covenant" with Aaron (45:7) and "added glory" to him (45:20). The detailed descriptions of the high priest's vestments in 45:8-13 (based on Exodus 28, 39) and his functions of offering sacrifice and rendering judgments for the people in 45:14-17 foreshadow the description of Simon in 50:5-21. The episode of Korah, Dathan, and Abiram (Numbers 16) illustrates God's protection of Aaron (45:18-19), which is indicative of the special status of the priesthood (45:20-22; see Num 18:20; Deut 12:12). The section on Aaron's grandson Phinehas (45:23-26; see Num 25:7-13) carries on the motifs of glory (45:23, 26) and covenant (45:24, 25), and reinforces the importance of the priesthood with a short prayer (45:26).

Joshua and Caleb, Judges, Samuel: 46:1-20

Joshua and Caleb (46:1-10) move forward the history of the covenant by defeating Israel's enemies and leading Israel into "the land flowing with milk and honey." For Joshua's military exploits see Joshua 1–11, and for the mission of Joshua and Caleb see Num 14:6-10 and Josh 14:6-11. Ben Sira suggests that God used them to teach lessons to the Gentiles ("he was fighting in the sight of the LORD," 46:6) and to Israel ("how good it is to follow the LORD," 46:10). Only those judges (46:11-12) who did not fall into idolatry (compare Gideon in Judg 8:22-35) are blessed; for bones sending forth life see 2 Kings 13:21. The primary role attributed to Samuel (46:13-20) is prophet. But he is also a judge (46:14) and a priest (46:16; see 1 Sam 7:9). As the prophet of the Lord, Samuel functioned as a kind of "elder statesman" who established the monarchy and anointed Saul and David as kings. His integrity was beyond doubt (46:19; see 1 Sam 12:1-5), and even after death he prophesied on Israel's behalf (46:20; see 1 Samuel 28).

Early Kings: 47:1-25

Nathan (47:1; see 2 Samuel 7 and 12) provides continuity with Samuel the prophet in the time of David. The treatment of David (47:2-11) highlights his election by God (47:2-3), his exploits as a warrior (47:4-7), and his initiatives in public worship at Jerusalem (47:8-10). The motif of glory is again prominent (47:6 [twice], 8, 11), and the references to worship prepare for the description of Simon in 50:5-21. The summary evaluation (47:11) presents David as a forgiven sinner to whom God gave "a covenant of kingship and a glorious throne in Israel." Solomon (47:12-22) was chosen by God to reign in a time of peace and to build the Jerusalem Temple—where Simon would preside some eight hundred years later (47:12-13). Using the device of direct address Ben Sira divides his treatment of Solomon into a celebration of his wisdom (47:14-17) and a somber reflection on his greed and lust (see Deut 17:17) that resulted in division between Israel and Judah (47:18-21). Solomon stained his own "glory/honor" and made himself an example of folly (47:20). Yet the covenant with David continued (47:22) despite the split caused by Rehoboam and Jeroboam (47:23; see 1 Kings 12) and the subsequent history of sin and exile (47:24-25). The affirmation of God's fidelity to the covenant with David is a rare "messianic" passage in Sirach and is especially poignant in the context of sin and exile.

Prophets and Kings: 48:1–49:16

Ben Sira gives a fairly full summary of the exploits of the great prophet of the northern kingdom of Israel, Elijah (48:1-11; see 1 Kings 17–19 and 2 Kings 1–2), and a shorter summary about Elisha (48:12-14; see 2 Kings 2–13). Both stood up to wicked kings (48:6, 8, 12). With regard to Elijah, Ben Sira again uses the device of direct address in 48:4-11 ("How glorious you were, Elijah, in your wondrous deeds!"). He also alludes to the prophecy of Elijah's return (48:10; see Malachi 3–4), which is prominent in the NT (Matt 11:10, 14; 17:10-13; Mark 1:2; 9:11-13; Luke 1:17, 76; 7:27; John 1:21). He gives disproportionate attention to the lifegiving power of Elisha's bones (48:13-14; see also 46:12 and 49:10). Yet, according to 48:15a, the prophets could not overcome the people's sinfulness, which led to the defeat and exile of Israel in 722 B.C.E.

The fortunes of the southern kingdom of Judah are described with reference to its prophets and kings (48:15b–49:13). The only good kings of Judah (as in 1–2 Kings) were Hezekiah (48:17-22) and Josiah (49:1-3). Ben Sira praises Hezekiah's building projects (48:17; see 50:1-4 for Simon's building projects) and his leadership with Isaiah's help during the invasion by Sennacherib (48:18-21; see 2 Kings 18–19; Isaiah 36–37; 2 Chronicles 32). Isaiah (48:22-25) advised Hezekiah and even prolonged his life (see 2 Kings 20:8-11; Isa 38:7-8). The references to Isaiah's comforting "the mourners in Zion" and revealing "what was to occur to the end of time" (48:24-25) indicate that Ben Sira regarded the entire book of Isaiah as coming from the pre-exilic prophet.

The name of Josiah (49:1-3; see 2 Kings 22–23) is honored because he removed "the wicked abominations," whereas through the wickedness of the other kings of Judah (49:4-6) the "glory" of God's people was given over to a foreign nation despite the prophecies of Jeremiah (49:7; see Jer 1:10). Mention (49:8-10) is also made of Ezekiel ("who saw the vision of glory," see Ezekiel 1), Job (but the text is not certain), and the Twelve Prophets (see the "new life from the dead" motif also in 46:12; 48:14). As the catalogue moves toward Simon it praises the memories of Zerubbabel and Joshua (48:11-12; see Haggai) who rebuilt the Jerusalem Temple, and Nehemiah (48:13; see Neh 6:15) who rebuilt the city walls (see 50:1-4). The omission of Ezra is surprising.

The final unit (49:14-16) moves backward to Adam by way of Enoch (see Gen 5:24), Joseph (see Gen 50:25-26; Exod 13:19), and Shem (Gen 11:10) and Seth (Gen 5:3-8). The high importance ascribed to Adam ("glorified above every living creature") is unparalleled in the OT; see, however, the Adam–Christ comparison developed by Paul.

Simon the High Priest: 50:1-24

The climactic figure in Ben Sira's parade of Israel's heroes is Simon (or Simeon) II, son of Onias (Yohanan), who served as high priest from 219 to 196 B.C.E. He probably had died a few years before Ben Sira wrote his book. The public works projects (50:1-4) that Simon organized served to strengthen the Temple and the city (as Solomon, Hezekiah, Zerubbabel and Joshua, and Nehemiah had done). A high point of the book is Ben Sira's description of Simon presiding at a Temple liturgy (either the daily offering or the Day of Atonement) in 50:5-21. Simon's entrance before the people is called "glorious" (50:5, 11), and the impression is heightened by a series of eleven similes in 50:6-10 ("like the morning star . . ."). Mention of the high priest's robe (a topic of symbolic significance for Philo, Josephus, and the Fathers) reminds the reader of the elaborate description of Aaron's vestments (45:6-13). What follows is the order of the ritual: offering the parts of the sacrificial animals (50:12-14), pouring out wine as a libation (50:15), sounding of trumpets and prostration of the people (50:16-17), song and prayer (50:18-19), and the high priestly blessing (50:20-21; see Num 6:24-26). In response to this glorious scene Ben Sira calls Israel to bless the "God of all" and to ask for happiness, peace, mercy, and deliverance (50:22-24).

Postscript and Epilogue: 50:25-29

The numerical proverb in 50:25-26 has no relation to what precedes or follows it; it sounds like a postscript or a stray note. The three hated nations—Seir (Edom or Idumea), Philistia (the "Sea Peoples" of old, perhaps the Greeks of Ben Sira's day), and Samaria—all had done great harm to Judah, at least in the eyes of Judeans like Ben Sira.

The final unit (50:27-29) consists of a "signature" by the author and a beatitude on those who take seriously his book and act upon it. The work ends as it began—with a testimony to the importance of "fear of the Lord."

Three Appendixes: 51:1-30

The first appendix (51:1-12) is a thanksgiving hymn embodying many of the conventions of the biblical genre and those in the Qumran *Hodayot*. Nothing in it demands that it was composed by Ben Sira. After the customary thanksgiving formula (51:1) it describes the many dangers (mostly slander and false accusation) from which the speaker has been rescued (51:2-6a) and how, in the extremity of danger, he turned to God in prayer (51:6b-10). It concludes with the customary formula of thanks (51:11-12) but without mention of offering sacrifices.

The second appendix (51:12ff.) is not part of the Greek or Syriac version but appears only in a medieval Hebrew manuscript. It is modeled on

Psalm 136 ("for his mercy endures forever"). The epithets applied to God are mostly biblical phrases, and there are important parallels to the Jewish Eighteen Benedictions, especially regarding the messianic hopes and the patriarchs. Nothing in the text demands that Ben Sira was the author.

The third appendix (51:13-30) is an autobiographical poem on the search for wisdom. If Ben Sira did not write it, he should have; its ideas and hopes capture the spirit of the whole book. Discovery of a large part of the Hebrew text in the Qumran Cave 11 Psalms Scroll indicates that it was originally an acrostic, each unit beginning with a new letter of the Hebrew alphabet. It first describes Ben Sira's search for and discovery of wisdom (51:13-17) and his effort at living by wisdom (51:18-22). The search involved prayer and Temple worship (51:13-14, 19), and ended with Ben Sira's praise of God (51:22). The second part of the poem (51:23-30) is Ben Sira's invitation for students to join his school. Though there is no set fee (51:25), this kind of schooling will result in acquiring silver and gold (51:28). Ben Sira's call to "put your neck under her yoke" (51:26; see 6:23-31) and his testimony "I have labored but little and found for myself much serenity" (51:27) are parallel to, if not the sources of, Jesus' invitation to discipleship in Matt 11:28-30.

BIBLIOGRAPHY

DiLella, Alexander A. *The Hebrew Text of Sirach: A Text-Critical and Historical Study.* The Hague: Mouton, 1966.

Haspecker, Josef. *Gottesfurcht bei Jesus Sirach.* AnBib 30. Rome: Pontifical Biblical Institute, 1967.

Lee, Thomas R. *Studies in the Form of Sirach 44–50.* SBL.DS 75. Atlanta: Scholars, 1986.

Mack, Burton L. *Wisdom and the Hebrew Epic: Ben Sira's Hymn in Praise of the Fathers.* Chicago and London: University of Chicago Press, 1985.

Marböck, Johann. *Weisheit im Wandel: Untersuchungen zur Weisheitstheologie bei Ben Sira.* Bonn: Hanstein, 1971.

Middendorp, Theophil. *Die Stellung Jesu Ben Siras zwischen Judentum und Hellenismus.* Leiden: Brill, 1973.

Prato, Gian Luigi. *Il problema della teodicea in Ben Sira.* AnBib 65. Rome: Pontifical Biblical Institute, 1975.

Sanders, Jack T. *Ben Sira and Demotic Wisdom.* SBL.MS 28. Chico: Scholars, 1983.

Skehan, Patrick W., and Alexander A. DiLella. *The Wisdom of Ben Sira.* AB 39. New York: Doubleday, 1987.

Trenchard, Warren C. *Ben Sira's View of Women: A Literary Analysis.* BJS 38. Chico: Scholars, 1982.

Wright, Benjamin G. *No Small Difference. Sirach's Relationship to Its Hebrew Parent Text.* Atlanta: Scholars, 1989.

Yadin, Yigael. *The Ben Sira Scroll from Masada.* Jerusalem: Israel Exploration Society, 1965.

Ziegler, Joseph, ed. *Sapientia Iesu Filii Sirach.* Septuaginta: Vetus Testamentum Graecum 12:1. Göttingen: Vandenhoeck & Ruprecht, 1965.

Prophetism and Prophets

Joseph Blenkinsopp

The Many Forms of Prophecy

"Prophecy" is one of those slippery words that have a remarkably broad and ill-defined range of meaning. It is commonly understood as the ability to predict the future, but it can also refer to the founding of a religion (by Moses, Jesus, or Mohammed, for example), to vital, emotional preaching like that of Oral Roberts or Billy Graham, to the leadership of a cult or sect (with reference to someone like David Koresh), to social activism like that of Oscar Romero or Martin Luther King, Jr., and no doubt to other categories and phenomena. There is also a widely accepted understanding that the prophet is essentially an opposition figure at odds with the political or religious establishment. While this was often the case in ancient Israel and in the history of the Church, as also in the modern world, the biblical prophet could play a supportive as well as a destabilizing role in his or her society. Early Christian prophecy, in fact, was primarily of the sustaining and supportive kind, serving, according to 1 Cor 14:3, for edification, encouragement, and consolation.

According to the traditional Christian view from NT times to the early modern period, the primary role of the OT prophets was taken to be that of predicting the new reality in Christ and the Church. Prophetic foreshadowing served therefore to bind together past and future in one uninterrupted history of salvation. In Judaism, on the other hand, the emphasis remained firmly on the Law (Torah) as the basis for the life of individual and religious community, and the prophetic role was consequently defined as that of preaching and passing on to posterity the original Mosaic revelation.

Since the early modern period critical biblical scholarship has felt the need to investigate the

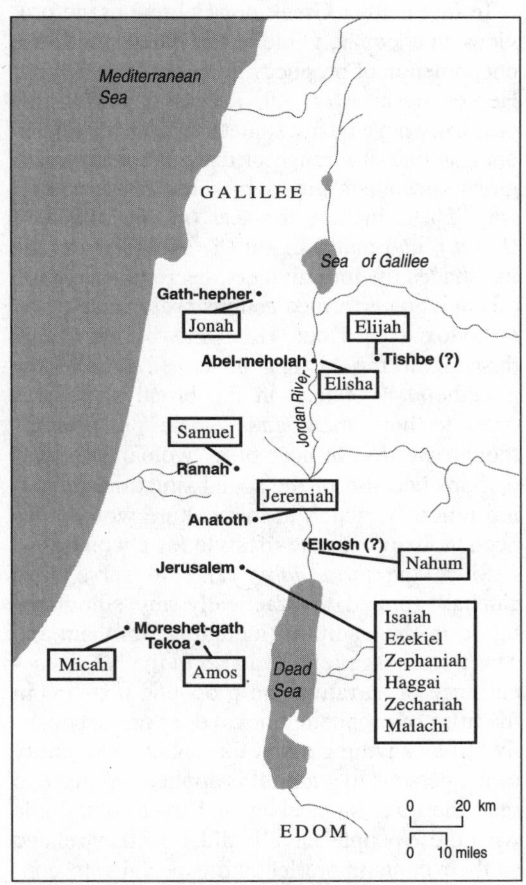

THE PROPHETS OF ISRAEL AND JUDAH

prophetic phenomenon without reference to these dogmatic presuppositions. Scholars were therefore led to ask what the designation "prophet" implied in its original linguistic, literary, and social context. The English word derives from the Greek *prophētēs,* referring to one who speaks on behalf of another, generally a deity. The task of the Delphic *prophētēs,* for example, was to interpret the unintelligible, ecstatic utterances of the Pythian priestess, mouthpiece of Apollo, but there were also prophets like Cassandra who proclaimed doom, and in fact anyone thought to be inspired by a god could be called a prophet. It is worth noting that in order to stress the more declarative and rational aspects of prophecy as they understood it the Greek translators of the Hebrew Scriptures used the word *prophētēs* and the corresponding verb rather than *mantis* and its related verb (the latter meaning an ecstatic or mantic person and ecstatic behavior respectively).

In fact neither Greek nor Hebrew usage provides an adequate guide to the actual multiform phenomenon of prophecy in Israel. The standard Hebrew term *nābiʾ* (pl. *nebîʾîm*), which may originally have meant something like "the called one," is one of a range of designations for religious specialists gifted in some extraordinary way. These include the seer *(roʾeh),* visionary *(ḥōzeh),* and man of God *(ʾîs ʾelohîm),* and the list shades off into diviners, necromancers, and others who performed actions proscribed by the orthodox (see Deut 18:10-11) but practiced throughout the history of Israel. Unlike the priesthood, prophecy in the broad sense was open to both male and female practitioners though we do not hear of a "woman of God," perhaps because of the social situation, including itineracy, which in that culture would have been an inappropriate lifestyle for a woman.

Since the term *nābiʾ* came to serve as a catchall applied to practically any significant figure in the tradition (including Abraham and Moses), a usage reflected also in the NT, its occurrence in narrative and prophetic texts (as in the titles of prophetic books) does not necessarily tell us anything about the status and identity of the persons to whom it is applied. We have to read the texts themselves and try to determine what these people actually did, how they related to their contemporaries and especially to contemporary institutions, on what basis they staked a claim to speak and be heard, and how they understood their mission. Given the nature of the biblical sources this goal is never easy and in some cases impossible to attain.

Sources

For our knowledge of Israelite prophecy we are indebted almost exclusively to the relevant biblical texts. Two or three inscribed potsherds *(ostraca)* written shortly before the destruction of Jerusalem in 586 B.C.E., discovered at Tell ed-Duweir (Lachish) in the 1930s, allude to one or more prophets serving as messengers who were obviously involved, as was Jeremiah during the same epoch, in political matters. An inscription written in ink on plaster discovered in 1967 during the excavation of Deir ʾAlla east of the Jordan features Balaam the seer (see Numbers 22–24) who, however, was not Israelite and about whom biblical and Jewish tradition is not unambiguously favorable. The Palestinian winter and spring rains have seen to it that, so far, no other writings relevant to prophecy have survived from the biblical period.

Valuable comparative data are available from other ancient Near Eastern regions, all of which made use of intermediaries who in ecstatic trance or through dreams, visions, or divinatory techniques passed on communications, generally of a supportive nature, to those who consulted them; in the first place these were rulers. The most interesting material derives from the Kingdom of Mari in Upper Mesopotamia from the eighteenth century B.C.E. Ecstatics and oracle-givers, some employed in a temple and others private individuals, some male and others female, passed on messages to Zimrilim, last ruler of Mari, from different deities in a form similar to standard forms of speech used by Israelite prophets. "Prophetic" phenomena of more recent date (as among the Nuer of the Sudan or the Plains Indians) are sometimes introduced into the discussion, but comparison is of limited value because of the profoundly different nature of the societies in which these phenomena occur.

The principal biblical sources are (1) the historiographical work known to critical scholarship as the Deuteronomistic History (hereafter Dtr) comprising Joshua, Judges, 1–2 Samuel, 1–2 Kings, in which prophets play an important role; (2) the collection of fifteen "books" attributed to prophetic authors, the three long ones (Isaiah, Jeremiah, Ezekiel) and the twelve short ones that fit on a scroll roughly equal in length to each of the three long ones; (3) allusions to prophets and prophecy in the Pentateuch (especially Deut 13:1-5; 18:9-22; 34:10-12) that, however, derive from later reflection on prophecy rather than referring directly to the phenomenon itself; finally (4) 1–2 Chronicles, composed in the fourth or third century B.C.E., reflecting a very late stage of development in which prophecy is primarily a cultic phenomenon.

The Formation of the Prophetic Books

Together with the historical books from Joshua to 2 Kings the fifteen prophetic books form the midsection of the tripartite Hebrew canon known as the Prophets *(Nebi'im)*. In early Judaism the conviction developed that historiography was a prophetic activity since, as Josephus put it, "the prophets alone had this privilege [of writing history], obtaining their knowledge of the most remote and ancient history through the inspiration they owed to God" (*Ap.* 1.37-38). About four centuries earlier the author of Chronicles mentions so many prophets among his sources as to leave little doubt that he shared the same conviction. In the Old Greek or Septuagint version the Prophets are placed at the end rather than in the middle, perhaps to indicate an orientation to the future that was to dominate in certain segments of Judaism and in early Christianity. The order of the individual books is also slightly different. Daniel is listed with Prophets rather than Writings, and there are numerous textual variations: for example, Jeremiah is one eighth shorter than the Masoretic (Hebrew) text and the chapters are arranged differently.

It seems that the compilation of the fifteen prophetic books was in place, more or less as we have it, by the second century B.C.E. Ben Sira (Ecclesiasticus), writing about 180 B.C.E., lists Isaiah, Jeremiah, Ezekiel, and the Twelve in that order (Sir 48:22-25; 49:6-10), and a little later we begin to hear allusions to "the Law and the Prophets" (for example, in 2 Macc 15:9), an expression familiar to readers of the NT. From the first cave at Qumran we have the complete Isaiah scroll dated on epigraphical grounds to about the middle of the second century B.C.E. (1QIsa[a]), and the earliest known commentaries on prophetic books (specifically Isaiah, Hosea, Micah, Nahum, Habakkuk), known as *pešarim,* were also discovered at Qumran.

We speak of a prophetic "book," but the use of this term will mislead if we conclude that it resembles a modern book in the sense that all of its contents derive from the prophet whose name is on the title page. Prophetic utterances were not copyrighted; they were expanded, edited, and recycled to meet the needs of later situations. Amos's total condemnation of contemporary society would hardly have been preserved and read by later generations if it had not been edited and expanded to hold out the hope of a new beginning *after* judgment (see especially Amos 9:11-15). The attentive reader will find numerous other illustrations of this ongoing process of expansion and reinterpretation. Isaiah 15:1–16:11, to take a different example, is a verse oracle against Moab that is followed by a comment added at a later time: "this is the word that YHWH spoke concerning Moab in the past; but now YHWH says . . ."—and another oracle follows (Isa 16:13-14). This should not be theologically problematic since there seems to be no good reason to deny inspiration to a plurality of authors, most of them anonymous.

In many, perhaps most cases oracles would have been delivered orally and committed to memory by members of the prophet's support group. Others may have circulated more widely. Note, for example, how a timely quotation of an oracle of Micah, originally delivered more than a century earlier, saved Jeremiah from death during his trial for sedition in 609 B.C.E. (Jer 26:17-19; Mic 3:12). Sayings delivered over a period of time may have been put together into small collections quite early, as seems to have been the case with oracles of cultic prophets in Assyria. We are told that Baruch wrote at Jeremiah's dictation sayings delivered over more than two decades and that after the scroll was destroyed by king Jehoiakim he produced a second and expanded edition of the same oracles (Jeremiah 36). Writing prophetic sayings seems, however, to have been mainly a response to special circumstances or to crisis situations. Jeremiah, for example, committed his sayings to writing only after being barred from speaking in the Temple precincts (Jer 36:5). The oracles of Amos and Hosea were first committed to writing as a Judean response to the fall of Samaria in 722

B.C.E. It is no coincidence that the appearance of the first prophetic "books" coincides with the overwhelming military and political menace of Assyria in the eighth century B.C.E. Finally, it is not difficult to understand why (as seems likely) a major compilation of prophetic material was put together in the decades following the fall of Jerusalem in 586 B.C.E. Not all would have accepted the prophetic explanation of the massive disasters of that time (see, for example, Jer 44:15-19), but for those who did the prophecies of impending judgment had been fulfilled and God's purposes for Israel had been vindicated.

The Prophetic Profile Reflected in the Literature

According to the opinion of most contemporary scholars the first of the prophets to whom "books" are attributed was Amos, active around the middle of the eighth century B.C.E. Dtr, however, attests that by then prophecy had been a familiar phenomenon in Israel for about three centuries. In keeping with the general deuteronomic understanding of prophecy as continuing the mission of Moses (Deut 18:15-22), the historian presents a series of "his servants the prophets" who preach law observance and warn, ineffectively as it happened, of the disastrous consequences of nonobservance (e.g., 2 Kings 17:13).

During the period prior to Amos prophetic activity was concentrated in the Northern Kingdom (later the kingdom of Samaria), though the court prophets Nathan and Gad played a significant role at the side of David. Dtr focuses on a few influential figures, beginning with Samuel's call to a prophetic career in the Shiloh sanctuary (1 Sam 3:1-18). The historian has also incorporated extensive excerpts from old traditions, oral or written or perhaps both, about Elijah and his disciple Elisha (1 Kings 17–2 Kings 13), their miraculous activity (especially that of Elisha), and their involvement in the political and military affairs of that time, that is, the high period of the kingdom of Samaria under the Omri and Jehu dynasties (roughly the second half of the ninth century B.C.E.).

The reader may well get the impression that these are solitary figures who suddenly appear on the scene and eventually disappear, generally under mysterious and, in the case of Elijah, spectacular circumstances (2 Kings 2). A closer reading will, however, reveal their links to those prophetic-ecstatic conventicles referred to as "sons of the prophets" *(benē hannebîʾîm)* or simply "prophets" *(nebîʾîm).* These were groups of dervish-like YHWH-enthusiasts settled in or near religious sanctuaries in the central hill country of Palestine and in the Jordan valley, for example, at Bethel and Gilgal. They were recruited from the poorest and socially most marginalized strata of Israelite society, lived some form of common life though not celibate (see, for example, 2 Kings 4:1-7), were sometimes ridiculed as crazy but were also feared, engaged in religious and ecstatic exercises under a sheik or (anachronistically) abbot or "father," a title used with reference to Samuel (1 Sam 10:12), Elijah (2 Kings 2:12), and Elisha (2 Kings 13:14), who presided over such coenobitic groups. Dtr's account of the two centuries of the Northern Kingdom's history shows how these YHWH-enthusiasts, either communally or singly, played an important role in the rise and fall of successive dynasties and the course of warfare with Syria to the north and Judah to the south. We may perhaps also see these conventicles as from time to time bringing forth powerful prophetic figures (Samuel, Elijah, Elisha) who go their own way without severing their ties with the group and in so doing prepare the ground for the explosion of prophetic activity in both Israel and Judah in the eighth century B.C.E.

One or two concluding observations are in order regarding this early stage of communal, ecstatic prophecy. First, the members of these conventicles illustrate the possibility of prophecy being displayed not just in what is said but in the adoption of a certain lifestyle. In this respect the "sons of the prophets" anticipate the well-known sects of the Greco-Roman period and religious orders throughout the history of the Church. Second, even during the time of the "writing" or "classical" prophets, limiting prophetic activity to speaking became progressively more problematic. We detect a tendency to have recourse to the performance of expressive and symbolic actions (for example, Isaiah walking naked, or nearly naked, through Jerusalem, Isa 20:1-6; Jeremiah picketing the Temple, Jer 7:1–8:3; Ezekiel engaged in a kind of street theater, Ezek 4:1–5:12). In other words the prophetic call was evolving from a specific commission to say certain things or confront certain people to a kind of life-investment. In due course this would lead to a rudimentary type of prophetic biography exemplified in the narrative traditions about Moses, Jeremiah, and the Isaian Servant. The cardinal points in this prophetic life story are the call, opposition and persecution, the vindication of the mission in the face of opposition, and often martyrdom. Elements of this prophetic biography have no doubt contributed to the formation of the gospel tradition about Jesus, especially as presented in Luke's gospel.

The High Tide of Protest Prophecy in the Eighth Century B.C.E.

By the middle decades of the eighth century taxation, the expropriation of patrimonial domain by the state, indentured service, and military conscription were beginning to break down the traditional form of society in both kingdoms based on kinship and ownership of a small plot of land. At the same time both Israel and Judah came under heavy and, in the case of Israel, terminal pressure from the advance of the Assyrian armies. It is this situation of crisis, internal and external, that helps to explain the intensity of prophetic activity at that time. Amos and Hosea in the Northern Kingdom, Micah and Isaiah in Judah were all active during the middle decades of the century. Although prophets do not explicitly refer to or quote each other it can be shown that they were familiar with the sayings of their prophetic colleagues past and contemporary to the extent of collaborating in the formation of a prophetic tradition of political, religious, and social protest. Needless to say that tradition is still an immensely important factor in the formation of the social conscience of Christian and Jewish communities.

Since the time of Augustine it has been common practice to represent Amos as a kind of inspired yokel, a rustic Piers Plowman rising up to denounce a basically corrupt society. But however we interpret the descriptions and self-descriptions in the book (Amos 1:1; 7:14-15), the sophisticated use of literary forms, the broad historical perspective, and the knowledge of contemporary affairs evinced by Amos and the other great prophetic figures of that time leave no doubt that they took up the cause of the marginal and dispossessed from a relatively elevated social and cultural position. We must also ask in what sense, if any, they saw themselves as belonging to the ranks of the prophets *(nebîʾîm).* None of the four identifies himself as a *nābiʾ* or is identified as such by others. Amos defends his right to a hearing while dissociating himself from the office of *nābiʾ* (Amos 7:14-15), Micah defines his status in contrast to contemporary prophets (Mic 3:5-8), and the frequent critique of these prophets as inauthentic and fraudulent (for example, in Hos 4:4-6; Isa 3:2; Mic 2:6-11) leaves us wondering whether Amos and his colleagues would have wished to be known by that designation. It seems, at any rate, to have been important for them to distance themselves from the *prophetic profession* as it was then practiced in Temple and royal court.

The need for critical and balanced appraisal is especially important in examining the substance of prophetic protest. We will find exaggerations, a lack of constructive criticism, utopianism (especially in Hosea), and a certain culture hostility (especially in Amos). All of these criticisms, however, are far outweighed by the positive and enduring aspects of prophetic preaching. The prophets of Israel reject idolatry in any of its forms, whether religious in the sense of cult offered to other deities, socioeconomic in the sense of giving absolute priority to material well-being and prosperity, or political in the sense of refusal to confer absolute validity on any form of political organization. By speaking of "a remnant" they implied that Israel would indeed survive even though its existing political form (a state, a kingdom) would be swept away in the destructive flow of historical events. We note too their adamant insistence on the creation and maintenance of a just society. This ideal is not, however, proclaimed in generalities. On the contrary these prophets *itemize* and direct their criticism at specific targets. They condemn the forcible expropriation and enclosure of land essential for the agrarian household, the emergence of a kind of rent capitalism, taxation and rates of interest of a confiscatory nature, and the corruption of the judicial system, the only recourse for the poor oppressed by the wealthy. What may in this context surprise the religiously observant reader today is the fierce condemnation of religious practice by the prophets in their own day (Amos 5:21-24; Hos 4:4-6; Mic 3:5-12; Isa 1:10-17). The reason may be that they were more keenly aware than we are that religion can be used to justify or simply cover over a basically immoral way of life. Prophets like Amos or Micah seem to be saying that a society that neglects justice and righteousness, *even one in which religion flourishes,* does not deserve to survive.

Later Developments

It is hardly surprising that the message of the eighth-century prophets had a limited impact on their contemporaries. It did, however, achieve a degree of official recognition by influencing in a variety of ways the deuteronomic program (Deuteronomy 12–26), a first edition of which was composed and perhaps promulgated during the reign of Josiah (640-609 B.C.E.). The tradition of challenging current social and religious arrangements was also continued by other prophets, conspicuously Jeremiah and Ezekiel, both from priestly circles. Another form of prophecy represented by Nahum and Habakkuk, probably of cultic origin, commented on international affairs during the interim between the collapse of the Assyrian and the consolidation of the Neo-Babylonian empire.

The Babylonian conquest, the fall of Jerusalem in 587/586 B.C.E., and subsequent deportations and exile precipitated a massive crisis of faith in the reality, power, and ethical character of the God of traditional religion, comparable in some important respects to the ongoing, agonized attempt to come to terms with the Holocaust. The crisis necessarily affected attitudes to prophecy, both because prophets served as the emissaries of that God and also because they were thought either to have contributed to the disaster by predicting it or to have failed to prevent it by refusing to intercede—intercession being an important aspect of the prophetic role (see, for example, Jer 14:11-12). It is therefore not entirely surprising to hear the deportees in Egypt, among whom women are mentioned explicitly, *after* the disaster rejecting Jeremiah's explanation of what had happened (Jer 44:15-19). The basic problem with prophecy, then as now, was the difficulty of coming up with verifiable criteria for distinguishing between the true and the false prophet. Failure to resolve this problem led not to the end of prophecy after the exile, as is sometimes affirmed, but to the emergence of quite different kinds of prophetic speech and prophetic activity, exemplified by Haggai, Zechariah 1–8, Malachi, Joel, and Isaiah 56–66 from the early post-exilic period.

Contemporary biblical exegesis tends to emphasize indeterminacy, ambiguity, and plurality of meanings depending on the terms of reference with which the interpreter approaches the texts and the interpreting community to which he or she belongs. The Christian interpreter of prophetic texts will therefore presumably read them with Christian presuppositions and as part of the Christian Bible inclusive of early Christian writings that draw so often upon the prophetic books. But a Christian reading can and should also be a *critical* reading, one that is informed by the results of critical, scholarly inquiry into the prophetic writings over the last two centuries.

BIBLIOGRAPHY

Blenkinsopp, Joseph. *A History of Prophecy in Israel.* 2nd ed. Louisville: Westminster/John Knox, 1996.

Brueggemann, Walter. *The Prophetic Imagination.* Philadelphia: Fortress, 1978.

Mays, James Luther, and Paul J. Achtemeier, eds. *Interpreting the Prophets.* Philadelphia: Fortress, 1987.

Petersen, David L., ed. *Prophecy in Israel.* Philadelphia: Fortress, and London: SPCK, 1987.

Isaiah

Anne-Marie Pelletier

FIRST READING

I. Beginning to Read

If they are even slightly familiar with the New Testament, readers of Isaiah know from the outset that this prophetic book has an especially close relationship with the confession of the Christian faith. Indeed, it is a passage from Isaiah—an excerpt from the fourth oracle of the Suffering Servant, chs. 52 and 53—that the eunuch of the Candace, the queen of the Ethiopians, is reading when, according to the account in Acts 8:26-40, the disciple Philip catches up with him on the road from Jerusalem to Gaza; and it is the interpretation of this text, in the light of the resurrection, that opens for him the way to faith in Jesus and leads him to ask for baptism. Besides, stored in the memory of any Christian are many texts from Isaiah quoted in the liturgy throughout the year. Israel's heart beats in this book in which all the violence of history rises like a tide, in which the vicissitudes of the covenant are expressed in often agonizing questions. The heart of the Church also beats here since these texts reveal the nascent hope that points to the incarnation. As a preliminary to a systematic reading, a good way of approaching the book may be to simply experience the compelling strength and beauty of its words, which are among the most magnificent and poetic in the whole Bible. For instance, one may read anew passages rendered familiar by the liturgy, hear anew the words that, in Advent, announce the salvation that is at hand: "The people who walked in darkness have seen a great light" (9:2), or those that, during Lent, tell of Israel's distress and anguish and its sighs of longing for God: "O that you would tear open the heavens and come down!" (64:1), or those that express the return of the exiles who "come to Zion with singing; everlasting joy shall be upon their heads" (35:10), or the oracles of Zion, which are an invitation to Jerusalem to wonder and rejoice because of the salvation that is coming (49:14-23 and ch. 54).

Having thus sampled the book and tasted its flavor, readers will be able to begin to explore it in a more systematic manner. One way to get initiated may be to read first a series of passages in which the prophet describes the state of affairs, as it were, by fathoming individuals' hearts and peoples' projects. In this vein it will be helpful to read 1:21-24; 5:8-25; or 57:1-13 addressed to Jerusalem; 13:1-20 and 47:1-15, which concern Babylon, the prototype of an idolatrous and proud city.

As a consequence one will see that the proclamation of judgment occupies an important place. However, the judgment of evil humans by the holy God of Israel is not the ultimate burden of the book of Isaiah. Alongside this message of judgment the book enunciates the eternal thought of God whom nothing can discourage. God wants to save Israel, the chosen people, and humanity, the work of God's hands, to snatch humans from their sins and clothe them with divine righteousness. It will be good to read ch. 35 in connection with 43:16-21, where the perspective of a new Exodus is discernible; and also 40:1-11; 41:8-20; and 43:1-7, full of the proclamation that God is going to "comfort" God's people; along the same lines the beautiful address to Jerusalem in 54:1-10 may also be read.

But this plan of God employs a veritable strategy, vast as God's thoughts, which are beyond human thoughts, and that the text evokes more or less explicitly, depending on what God begins to reveal about this strategy at the time the text is written down. Examples of this are the announcement that God is going to humble every sort of pride (2:11-22) and begin the divine work with a lowly "remnant" (10:10-23); the birth of a "Prince of Peace," heralded in the oracle of 9:1-6, to which one can join 11:1-9; or else the coming of a Servant, proclaimed for instance in the oracles of 42:1-7 and 52:13–53:12, a Servant who will establish justice and save sinners.

Finally, it will be helpful to read some of the oracles that give a glimpse of this work of salvation, first in Israel (4:2-6 and ch. 60), then beyond the chosen people, when salvation will, through Israel, reach all the nations of the earth (2:1-5; 56:1-8; 66:18-21).

II. The Book as a Whole

Whatever has been said above, the book of Isaiah is not a mine of selected excerpts. It is meant to be read as an organic whole and therefore in its entirety. It is imperative to undertake a continuous reading. At this point difficulties arise that may lead to discouragement. The first has to do with the *length* of the book: with its sixty-six chapters, Isaiah is the most voluminous among the prophetic texts. Besides, various *literary genres* coexist side by side. Several stories have a biographical tone: ch. 6 reports the vision granted to the prophet in the Temple and the mission he receives; 8:1-4 speaks of the birth of a son to Isaiah; chs. 36–39 narrate the invasion by the Assyrian Sennacherib and the ministry of Isaiah to King Hezekiah in these perilous times. Here and there we find psalms (for instance, 12:1-6; 25:1-5, and also Hezekiah's prayer to be cured of a deadly disease in 38:9-20), lamentations (47:1-15), hymns of thanksgiving (for example, 12:25; 26:7-19; 38:10-20; 42:10-17; 61:10-11). Several sections are real theological discussions (41:26-29; 43:9-12). Besides great cosmic visions, certain verses express Isaiah's trust, distress, and compassion when calamity befalls the people (for example, 21:1-4; 22:4).

Of course the oracles occupy the largest place and they are very diverse. They may be negative, evoking the judgment of God and the ruin of the wicked; they often begin with the apostrophe "Ah" (*hōy,* a cry of mourning that gives a tone of funereal lamentation, for example, to chs. 5; 10:1-11; 28; 29; 30; 33). Conversely, other oracles announce God's help, the deliverance or the conversion of Israel (10:20-21; 14:1-2; 27:12-13; 41:1-20; 44:1-5). They take the form of a lawsuit in 1:18-20 and also in chs. 13–15. Several purport to describe a mysterious personage called the "servant" (42:1-9; 49:1-9; 50:4-9; 52:13–53:12). Who is speaking to whom is not always easy to know. In certain oracles the prophet invites the people to listen to God (28:14). In others God directly addresses either the people or the leaders of the people or else the powerful rulers of the nations. The same oracle can be directed to one addressee and then, without transition, to another. Finally, symbolic language holds an important place in this book, with numerous comparisons (1:8; 29:8, 11; 31:4, and so on), parables (songs of the vineyard in 5:1-7; 27:2-5; parable of the farmer in 28:23-29).

However, what is most disconcerting is the arrangement of these oracles. A first reading easily produces the impression of a random, not to say incoherent sequence. At every turn condemnation and salvation, distress and restoration, waywardness and fidelity, upheaval and peace succeed one another. In 5:25 and following God's wrath allows the Assyrian army to overwhelm God's people, but in 10:24 God comforts the people and urges them not to fear Ashur. One oracle speaks of a time when Israel "will sanctify the Holy One of Jacob" (29:22-24). The next oracle denounces the "rebellious children . . . adding sin to sin" (30:1-5). The prophecy of the unexpected recovery of King Hezekiah, which gives a new future to Israel, is immediately followed by the announcement that nevertheless Babylon will sweep everything away and will reduce the king's descendants to the condition of eunuchs in the palace of the king of Babylon (chs. 38 and 39). Nevertheless, the dividing line is not drawn between Israel and the nations; Israel and the nations are by turns shown in the grip of blindness, delivered to the distress of punishment, and promised restoration in justice and peace.

Besides these technical difficulties encountered in the reading, another aspect of the book strikes readers. This text, which contains so many beautiful passages and speaks eloquently of comfort, is at the same time constantly in the throes of drama. Thus, from the first chapters on, images of war, of destroyed cities, of ravaged fields, of men and women fleeing before enemies are piled up and, besides, are heightened by predictions of more days of trials and terror. In ch. 1 the charge brought against the people is made clear: God upbraids the people and reproaches them with their unfaithfulness. This image of the lawsuit will be found all through the book, as well as under the form of the action that, here and there, Israel or the nations bring against God. Isaiah 2:10 introduces the theme of the wrath of God who is going to arise in order to terrify the earth, and in 5:14 "Sheol has enlarged its appetite" in order to engulf impious humans. In fact, the two themes of judgment and salvation are interwoven all through the pages of the book with now one, now the other dominating. Up to ch. 39 Isaiah is full of visions of extreme violence. It is true that ch. 30, for an instant, tells of grace and healing, but it is not before ch. 40 that consolation gains the upper hand so that now the themes of healing, awakening, and glory are stressed in the oracles. Even here the dominance is not absolute because for all that, violence does not disappear. Side by side with cries of exultation and joy, utterances of judgment continue to be heard. Despite the future exaltation of Holy Zion, Israel remains cast as a blind servant; the servant of 50:6 is shown covered with "insult and spitting," and words of distress and abandonment still echo in ch. 65. Although God declares eternal tenderness toward Israel and solicitude toward the nations, God continues to pronounce words of judgment and to take the form of a warrior ready to confound the bloodthirsty so the righteous may be liberated. Besides, the book concludes with the vision of the corpses of humans who rebelled against God given as prey to the eternal fire.

Thus the book of Isaiah shows Israel in history, confronted by history. At a more superficial level the problem for God's people is to survive the assaults of rapacious neighbors who move boundaries and populations according to their political whims. At a deeper level the task at hand is to persevere in hope, assured that God does not forget God's people in spite of appearances to the contrary and in spite of the deepening experience of the inability to forswear unfaithfulness in order to, at last, live according to the covenant. The drama is also what is expressed here in the themes of blindness and lack of understanding. Again, from the first verse of the book the problem is clearly shown: Israel does not comprehend, Israel does not know God. It does not recognize God's work in its life and history. "The ox knows its owner, and the donkey its master's crib; but Israel does not know, my people do not understand" (1:3). Chapter 6, which records Isaiah's mission, brings back this motif with maximum brutality since the prophet is commanded to declare, "Keep listening, but do not comprehend; keep looking, but do not understand" (6:9). The theme of Israel's hardening marks the beginning of the book. The supreme drama is that God's word meets with humankind's refusal, humankind that, besides, is without memory, forgetting the testimonies of power and faithfulness given by God to the ancestors. As a consequence, humanity stands before the events of history as before an immense and painful enigma. If Israel had any memory it would know where its foundations are, where its strength is; it would escape its enemies and bondage. How will Israel know? Thus, instead of celebrating God who, in spite of its unfaithfulness, has saved Jerusalem from the Assyrians' grip, people find nothing else to say but, "Let us eat and drink, for tomorrow we die" (22:13). Who will overcome this lack of understanding? In many a passage of Isaiah the question tragically remains unanswered.

Readers cannot be uninvolved spectators of this history: first of all because they will easily recognize the adversities that continue to befall humanity. There is an impressive similarity between the violence in many of Isaiah's oracles and the extremes of cruelty characterizing our modern times. Streets strewn with corpses as if they were refuse (5:25) are, in today's world, a common sight. Human faces disfigured by torture (53:3) haunt modern history. Thus this text does not speak only of the terror spread abroad by the great empires of the first millennium before our era.

In this respect Isaiah forcefully implicates its readers and overall is harrowing to read. One must endure through the series of oracles that again and again bring back the spectacle of distress, as Israel must have endured in hope, and as humankind must do in its turn. Besides, the question asked of Israel's understanding concerns readers themselves. Are they going to understand? or are they going, in their turn, to walk like blind persons through this sequence of chapters that blow hot and cold? Will they have a better memory as they read on so that they may perceive the coherence of the story told them? Will they have enough patience and trust to believe that in the anarchic series of disappointments and restorations the covenant is on its way toward its fulfillment?

Indeed, the understanding of Isaiah is not a matter only of information and intellectual knowledge. This book highlights, perhaps better than any other in the Bible, the obstacles standing between humanity and God, even though the human heart has already been prepared—as is Israel's case—by God's long and patient pedagogy. At one moment or another this book leads readers to experience for themselves the awesome obscurity of divine revelation. We must remember that this difficulty involves two facts: (1) The first is that sinful humans have a clouded vision and impaired hearing; they see and hear what God does but do not understand, at least as long as they have not owned their blindness and deafness which only God can cure (this is the theme of the hardening of hearts). (2) The second is that God's thoughts are beyond human thoughts (40:13; 55:8-9) and that there are of necessity delays—both in listening and remembering—before humans can begin to understand who God is and what God does.

Let us add that one of the effects of this book is also to test the images of God that humanity harbors in itself. At times it does so in a very bold and brutal way. For instance, God is compared to a barber using the king of Ashur as a razor to bring devastation (7:20); God is described as "a trap and a snare for the inhabitants of Jerusalem" (8:14); God is shown as a warrior covered with the blood of those God has trampled (63:2-4) and as one releasing the invaders' chariots against God's own people (5:26-30). In a world dominated by the violence of sin, God has the terrible countenance of the judge who strikes down wicked humanity. However, just beneath the surface of the harshest oracles one glimpses the features of the God whose glory is ultimately to grant reprieve, to heal, to gather Israel and all nations in an eschatological banquet at which all the tears of history will be wiped away (25:6-9). Thus the book contains the most deeply moving expressions of God's tenderness and love for Israel and, beyond Israel, all mortals (51:12-16; 54). The right sort of reading is therefore one that will have the patience to let the features of that face within the text gradually appear and that will recognize in them the expression—unequaled in clarity in the rest of the OT—of the love of God, culminating in the one of whom it is said that "he did not open his mouth," that "he was wounded for the crimes of his people," (53:7-8) and whose image one day will coincide with the accused whom Pilate will point to, saying, "Here is the man" (John 19:5).

Indeed, it is *history* that is at the heart of this book, by turns as its raw material, as the milieu of its redaction spanning a long duration, and finally as what is here the object of an ample and grave meditation.

(1) First of all, like the other prophetic books, the book of Isaiah is written in immediate contact with history. Throughout, there surface references to events in the life of Israel and of the great empires surrounding it, between the eighth and sixth centuries B.C.E. One reads in succession the names of the kings of the southern kingdom (Uzziah, Ahaz, Hezekiah), the references to the Assyrians with Sennacherib, then the Babylonians, the Persians with Cyrus, each successively having dominion over the region. Because of this it is indispensable to constantly shed light on the text by recalling the historic events that are its background.

(2) But the book of Isaiah is not just the recitation of a long history of struggles, disappointments, and hopes. Its very writing took place over a long period of time, as the Jewish exegetes of the Middle Ages had sensed. Modern exegetical research enables us to discern diverse strata of redaction stretching from the eighth century to probably the fifth. The book we read today is indeed the end product of a long and complex meditation, covering several generations, on an initial text. It demonstrates that in Israel the prophetic utterances were transmitted in a living and active way, constantly enriched by the fresh understanding gained through the course of centuries and the flow of events. Thus a complex writing process and numerous redactional steps are concealed under the name of Isaiah.

Three large divisions, themselves complex in structure, can be distinguished: chs. 1–39;

40–55; 56–66. Today commentators agree in regarding Isaiah, who was writing in the eighth century, as the author, at least partially, of chs. 1–39 only. Around this remarkable spiritual personality there seems to have arisen a group of disciples who, after his death, continued his meditation and preaching. In the sixth century, at the time of the Babylonian exile, an anonymous prophet, heir to this tradition, composed the whole of chs. 40–55, designated "Deutero-Isaiah." The remaining chapters belong to a later period, clearly post-exilic. Sometimes the expression "Third Isaiah" is used, but the diversity of style in the oracles that compose this section suggests that it is rather the work of a final redactor. The task of this person would have been twofold: (1) to add a new series of oracles to the existing corpus, and (2) to review and rework the whole, including the texts of the eighth century, in order to make it into a definitive synthesis. So in the initial and properly Isaian part—which had already undergone much previous editing—incontestably more recent chapters were inserted. Actually the inspired theologian who became the final redactor of the book could see that these chapters answered ancient oracles and contributed to sketching an outline of the history of salvation beginning to be more clearly discernible.

(3) However, the function of these oracles was not limited to recording historical events, or even to decoding events lived day by day. On the basis of these the oracles propose a true meditation on history. This book attests to Israel's conviction, which is also the Church's, that "God speaks of God in history" (see the Constitution on Divine Revelation, *Dei Verbum,* of Vatican II). It is also the most complete expression of the meditation in which Israel was constantly engaged, a meditation on what the history lived by humankind means, on the way God intervenes in that history, and on its goal and end.

For there is an enigma of history. One can sense it in the contradictory and paradoxical mixture of events that constitutes the political history of the time. It is a fact that bloodthirsty people succeed and thrive; likewise, the great empires that worship false gods (for example, Babylon and its deities) live either from violence (Ashur) or from a purely human wisdom (Egypt). True, the book of Isaiah shows the precariousness of the reign of tyrants one could have believed to be unshakable. An oracle of ch. 33 addresses the one who spreads devastation with apparent impunity: "When you have ceased to destroy, you will be destroyed; and when you have stopped dealing treacherously, you will be dealt with treacherously" (33:1). In harsh and solemn oracles the great, proud cities that terrify Israel and appear impregnable are shown as brought down, reduced to nothing, changed into pastures for animals (10:5-19). Babylon, that for a moment is used as an instrument of God's vengeance against unfaithful and corrupt Israel, is described under God's judgment as a ruined, deserted city from which life has fled (24:10-12). However, when in 539 the Babylonian capital falls it will be taken by surprise, without destruction, in a way that runs counter to the oracles. Only in the 480s will Xerxes effectively destroy the walls and sanctuaries of the city.

However, the enigma of history is also made up of the paradoxes and disturbing reversals the history of Israel contains. Thus King Hezekiah's politics, despite his probity and faithfulness to God, end in a national failure; by contrast the land thrives under the reign of Manasseh, his impious successor. Similarly, King Josiah, the promoter of the great religious reform with which certain oracles of Isaiah are contemporaneous, dies tragically at Megiddo. The story of Eliakim in ch. 22 is also very troubling. In place of Shebna, the dishonest steward of the royal palace, YHWH God calls Eliakim, God's "servant," and gives him as a "father to the inhabitants of Jerusalem and to the house of Judah," a trustworthy support for the people. Nevertheless, the same oracle concludes with the laconic and chilling announcement that "the peg that was fastened in a secure place will . . . be cut down and fall," dragging to ruin those who had relied on it (22:15-25).

There is, as it were, an apparent chaos in history that is reflected in the manner in which the oracles succeed one another, evoking by turns darkness and light without the latter always overcoming the former. Oracles follow oracles in enigmatic sequences. After the ruin of an enemy has been solemnly proclaimed, a new oracle anxiously asks again, as if nothing had been said, when the peril will come to an end. An example of this is Edom, the very symbol of Israel's enemy nations, which is shown as delivered to the "eternal fire" in ch. 34, but which reappears in ch. 63 with the description of the terrifying figure of the divine victor returning from Edom after having exterminated wicked people. In ch. 24 the text that depicts the joy of deliverance on the occasion of the fall of the "city of nothingness" (vv. 14-15) ends with the mysterious and frightening mention of the "treacherousness" that continues to be rampant in God's people. The prophet can only speak of his bewilderment: the mystery of history that his seer's eyes uncover.

Another aspect of the enigma of history is that of the delays and tardiness in the fulfillment of God's promises. From the prophet's question "How long?" addressed to God who threatens to punish (6:11) to the end of the book the questions accumulate: questions from God who wants to bring Israel to the truthful evaluation of its spiritual condition; questions also from Israel asking: Why does salvation tarry? Why do we not find the justice that was announced? Why darkness when light was expected? Could it be that God's arm is too short to save us? (cf. 59:9-11).

The problem is to discern the coherence of history and the manner of God's intervention in it, to decipher what is still veiled and hidden in God's secret. Thus at certain moments the eye sees farther and encompasses the whole sequence of time, for the mystery of history is on the scale of the totality of ages and one cannot begin to comprehend this mystery without this amplitude of vision and understanding. Therefore the text recapitulates the creation that already contains God's intentions and projects, and reaches as far as the perspectives of eschatology and of what is several times called "God's day." [See also below, the excursus "The Day of YHWH" in the commentary on Joel.]

All the while the prophet's mandate is to uncover, beyond the restless and chaotic surface of events, the presence of another history in which reside the real stakes that determine the history we see. In a vocabulary whose connotations are sometimes mythical (evocation of a primordial combat underlying the conflicts of the political powers of this world, for instance, in 24:10, which mentions the "city of chaos," *tohū,* cf. 27:1) we find expressed the conviction that there exists a depth of history that exceeds what we spontaneously perceive and what is described by historians. History is not only the story of the events by which the life of empires and the suffering of the people are conditioned. More fundamentally it is that of the relationship of humankind with God and, in the first place, the relationship of Israel, the chosen people, with God. Ultimately history is not only that of alliances and military tactics but that of the covenant between God and Israel, preceded by the "eternal covenant" concluded between God and the people in the days of Noah (Gen 9:9-16).

The book of Isaiah therefore appears as a vast meditation that, with the events of the eighth century as a point of departure, scrutinizes time, aiming at its extreme reach, that is to say salvation, which faith acknowledges to have been accomplished in the person of Jesus. The point of departure is the avowal—also present in other eighth century prophets—of a world wasted by violence and injustice. Lies and depravity are conspicuous in the city, while in the outside world the great empires dream only of conquests and annexations.

But as the book progresses the diagnosis of the nature of the disease becomes more thorough. It is formulated in particular by the metaphor of the "suit" that God institutes against God's people. The most obvious evils—which, however, they refuse to look at—are that blood is poured, the weak are not respected, good is called evil and evil is called good (5:20), religious acts are used as screens to hide crime (1:11-17). From this state of affairs arises the sickness that wastes away not only human society, but also the world and nature (24:4-5).

The initial evil at the root of these perversions is, according to Isaiah's words, forgetting God, which leads people to indulge in lies and violence and, correlatively, idolatry and pride (see for instance chs. 1 and 5). In many passages of Isaiah and under diverse forms pride is shown as the root of evil: through pride, leaders become tyrants who lead their subjects to death (14:3-21); through pride, humans make themselves God's rivals and usurp God's place, thwarting their own identity by disregarding God's. Each of the different pagan kingdoms spoken of in the book illustrates in its own way this distortion of the relationship between God and humanity. Even in the land of Israel it is pride that leads people astray from the covenant, prompts decisions concerning what is good and what is bad, entrusts to human means the defense of the people to whom God promised to give life.

Then God's justice is the response to the contempt for justice in the city and the world. First, God's justice is expressed by what the text calls God's "wrath" (5:25; 9:11, 16, 18, 20; 10:4, 5, and so on) manifested by punishments that are as many judgments pronounced against human wickedness. This is how the calamities that strike the people are interpreted, whether they are invasion (for instance, that in which the northern kingdom disappeared in 721), or exiles and deportations, as happened in the sixth century. However, Isaiah also contains this observation, formulated in the opening verses (1:5-6), that punishments destroy the body but do not touch the heart. Indeed, everything seems lost past remedy when the book opens. Thus a divine strategy begins to be established: it begins with this extremely paradoxical reality, the "hardening." God imprisons sinners in the sin they have chosen in order that they may experience its deadly effects. Nevertheless, the "plan of God" (10:12; 28:21; 60:21) is not only that the wicked be confounded and judged, but also that justice and righteousness enter the hearts of humans once they consent to acknowledge their sin. The text tells of the healing God wants to bestow, is going to bestow (19:22; 57:18, 19) on those who will have agreed to leave the heights of pride and walk on the low paths of humility: healing of the body of the people injured by adversity, healing of the heart that remembers the covenant. Thus in the book's final form, from one end to the other, judgment and salvation are conjoined. Here we find a fundamental structure, already attested in the episode of the flood in Genesis: sin calls for God's judgment, but judgment does not mean that God repeals the plan existing from the creation. The plan of salvation advances, transmitted through the narrow channel of a few persons or even one single person. In Isaiah this plan finds expression in the notion of a "remnant" (4:3; 10:20-22; 11:4, 16; 24:6; 28:5; 37:4, 32; 46:3). It is at the end of a mighty pruning that will have done away with all dead branches that Israel will be saved. Even the messianic oracles, which confirm that the Davidic dynasty will last in spite of all upheavals, are stamped by this theme of remnant when they evoke the "stump . . . the holy seed" (6:13). It is the "shoot" from the "stump of Jesse," upon which the "spirit of God" rests, that will bring "understanding" and justice.

The Exodus of the thirteenth century serves as a prefiguration sketching, as a first drawing still uncertain, this salvation of the future and the promise of "comfort" that God's plan intends. Simultaneously going forward in time and in its text, Isaiah focuses its interest and its gaze on the mediations of this salvation. Then the figure of a mysterious mediator-servant appears, a "sharpened arrow" in God's hands (49:2), set apart (42:6), possessor of the spirit for the salvation of the people (42:1), delivering them from every blindness and darkness. This servant is at the heart of the mystery of history set down in Isaiah under the form of a series of oracles that feature him. He is a very mysterious figure in whom are joined election, disfigurement, suffering, and in all likelihood resurrection in the text of 52:13–53:12. In addition, these oracles of the servant are accompanied by another series that in its turn concerns the female figure of Zion, suddenly appearing in an unprecedented transcendence and perfection (see 49:21; 54:4-5). This holy Zion is described as giving birth to a new people (49:21; 54:1; 66:7-9). This is another aspect of the mystery of history, the more so as now the newness of salvation entails the joining of the nations with Israel. This book, which fulminates terrible judgments against the proud and idolatrous nations, also penetrates the vision of the gathering of the nations around Zion. Against all hope the act of pure grace that forgives Israel's sin reaches the pagan nations themselves that lived far from Israel's faith (45:14; 56:1-8; 66:18-21). On the horizon of the present, eschatological time continues to maintain the perspective of judgment for rebellious and evil persons who make history a nightmare, but also, and in equal measure, that of universal jubilation for all those redeemed by God and invited to the "feast of rich food, . . . of well-aged wines" that God will give on Mount Zion (25:6).

This sequence of narratives and oracles that ponder the mystery of history is the opposite of a synthesis or a deductive discourse in which every event would find its place and explanation. In contrast to the great philosophical systems that seek to enunciate the meaning of history, Isaiah, despite the force of its words, leaves an impression of obscurity and enigma. The authors of these pages obviously respect the opacity of reality. They do not want to rush the interpretation of what is before their eyes, even though the readers' anguish might be alleviated and their hope strengthened if they perceived more coherence in the text. It is clear that the writers experience the same distress due to the vicissitudes of the times as those whom they are addressing; they share the same trials and the same questions. They submit to the rhythm of the revelation of God who chooses now to hide, now to be seen, according to a pedagogy that greatly disconcerts human thinking. The final redactor, who reviews with keen insight the three centuries that elapsed before his time, remains caught in the struggle with history. This is perhaps most strikingly illustrated by the oracles of the servant placed at intervals throughout Deutero-Isaiah. From one oracle to the next the outlines gain in precision, the servant's identity seems to grow more distinct. Yet it is the opposite that in fact happens because each new description reinforces the mystery of the servant.

This is why, contrary to every systematic method, this text is written by mode of juxtaposition. It is a sort of puzzle that is offered to readers. Like a mosaic, the book remains difficult to decipher at close range. It is only by hindsight that this text, totally focused on the future, will reveal the meaning of what it speaks. At any rate, for five centuries it would continue to be pondered until the day of Christ when the apostles and disciples would discover in its oracles the prophecy of what they were living. Even then it was only after the resurrection and the gift of the Spirit that the meaning would well up (see Acts 13:27-41, showing how people "did not recognize him or understand the words of the prophets that are read every sabbath" and so "fulfilled those words by condemning him").

In their turn readers must respect this characteristic of the text and refrain from erasing the questions and exclamations in the book; they are so many indications of a revelation that goes beyond human thought and desire. Besides, even though the veil is partially lifted for Christian readers the oracles of Isaiah deal with events some of which have not yet been accomplished. The end time, as time of the Church, is certainly evoked in several passages, but this time itself has a duration and a denseness; it still contains much that is unfulfilled. Readers are therefore invited to a discernment that will lead them to recognize what, in the words they read, still retains the status of prophecy. Like Israel in its own time they are urged to ply the understanding of memory, the endurance of faith, and the perseverance of hope. Twice (21:11-12 and 62:6) Isaiah mentions the figure of the sentinel. "Sentinel, what of the night?" the oracle of ch. 21 asks, and the response comes, "Morning comes, and also the night. If you will inquire, inquire; come back again." At the hour of Christ, Simeon, the watcher who waits for "the consolation of Israel"—a locution of Isaiah's—can declare, "Master, now you are dismissing your servant in peace, according to your word" (Luke 2:29). Watchfulness, however, continues to be the duty of Christ's disciples who, for a time, are still experiencing the darkness of history in the expectation of the full revelation of God's glory.

III. Historical Context

Behind the book of Isaiah lies a long and complex history extending from the eighth to the fifth centuries B.C.E. This history is that of political events, often of international import, that are alluded to throughout the text. It is also that of the spiritual evolution, considerable and decisive, that happened in Israel's faith during those centuries. Last, it is a history of the rereadings and rewritings that progressively resulted, over three and a half centuries, in the book we read today. [See also the article "Prophetism and Prophets."] Three main periods must be distinguished.

(a) The first part of the book (most of chs. 1–39) places us in the kingdom of Judah in the eighth century B.C.E. during the reigns of Uzziah, Jotham, and especially Ahaz (735–726) and Hezekiah (716–700). This period is dominated by the history of the expansion of the Assyrian empire, which became particularly aggressive when Tiglath-pileser came to power in 745 B.C.E. The armies of this king add conquest to conquest, move deep into the West, conquer and reduce to submission entire territories whose only options are vassalage or annihilation. The practice of systematic deportation of the conquered populations results in the suppression of any attempt at revolt.

From 734 B.C.E. onward, during the reign of Ahaz, the Assyrian threat bore directly on the small states of the west coast. They decided to join forces to resist the invader. The kingdom of Aram (with Damascus as its capital) and Israel (with Samaria as its capital) formed a coalition and also sought to secure the protection of

Egypt, which responded the more favorably as it saw here a way to recapture territories that had formerly been its colonies. Urged to enter this coalition, the kingdom of Judah refused, choosing to play the Assyrian card. The members of the coalition regarded this strategy as treachery; they responded by marching against Jerusalem in order to depose the king and forcibly associate the southern kingdom with the resistance against Assyria (Isa 7:1). The expedition failed, but the "Syro-Ephraimite" war would be a dislocation both in the political order and the spiritual. The northern kingdom and the southern kingdom were confronting one another; the ancient messianic promises relative to the throne of David were imperiled. Shortly afterward Assyria moved against the northern kingdom: within a few years it was dismantled and its capital, Samaria, taken in 722 B.C.E. From then on the northern kingdom became nothing but an Assyrian province whose population was made up for the most part of transplanted foreigners. The event had great repercussions in the South. King Hezekiah, who has effectively been in power since 716, apparently learned from these dramatic events. He broke the vassalage treaty concluded by Ahaz with Assyria; however, he did not hesitate to enter into an alliance with Egypt. The Assyrian menace was felt again in 701 at the time of the Palestinian campaign of Sennacherib, who swept away all resistance in the region and threatened Jerusalem. The city seemed lost when suddenly the enemy army broke camp and returned eastward, sparing Jerusalem and preserving the future of its dynasty. Later, the historian Flavius Josephus attributed the withdrawal of the Assyrians to an epidemic of plague in the army.

The prophet Isaiah is associated with this history, as he is the author of a large number of the oracles appearing in chs. 1–39. He might have belonged to the aristocracy of Jerusalem. He was consulted by Kings Ahaz and Hezekiah, who listened more or less obediently to his counsel. The text mentions the symbolic names of his two children Shear-jashub ("a remnant will come back") and Maher-shalal-hash-baz ("loot in haste"). One detects behind his writing an exceptional personality endowed with intelligence and faith, at the service of the prophetic mission he received in 740 B.C.E. and would exercise for half a century. Isaiah meditates anew on the words preserved by the southern tradition. He lets them speak within the circumstances of the time, adding to them the visions and revelations he receives. Some passages of his book show that he was familiar also with the Wisdom tradition.

He is first seen intervening during the Syro-Ephraimite war. King Ahaz and the people fall prey to panic. According to the story recorded in 2 Kings 16 the king goes so far as to sacrifice his son to Moloch. Isaiah, as God's spokesman, urges him to let go of fear. He declares that the "two smoldering stumps of firebrands" (7:4), the kings of Damascus and Samaria, will be defeated. Ephraim will "be shattered, no longer a people" (7:8). Judah will escape and the promises made to the dynasty of David will be fulfilled. The condition is that the king should renounce the deceptive support of human alliances and at last lean on God, and God alone.

Afterward Isaiah's activity seems to weaken until Hezekiah comes to power. Chapters 36–39 —which in fact are a later addition dating from the time of the exile and borrowed from 2 Kings, written at that time—speak of a new phase of Isaiah's ministry under that king. Again Isaiah condemns the politics of alliances, this time with Egypt, a nation whose political actions have often proved to be opportunistic and deceitful (hence the denunciation of 30:12, "you . . . put your trust in oppression and deceit, and rely on them"). In any event this enterprise leads to disaster by unleashing Sennacherib's campaign of 701 that ravages Judea, sparing only Jerusalem. But then Isaiah is charged by God to reassure Hezekiah, "I will defend this city to save it, for my own sake and for the sake of my servant David" (37:35). The foretelling of the event probably strengthened the prophet's authority, but obviously the political leaders of Judah cared little about a man who opposed to their short-sighted but realistic strategies the appeal to rely on God alone. When Hezekiah is stricken with a deadly disease it is again Isaiah who is commanded to announce that the king's life will be prolonged and Jerusalem protected, but not without predicting, in a last message, that David's city will be destroyed and the king's sons enslaved (39:5-7).

Let us add that Isaiah's role was certainly decisive in the politico-religious awareness that developed at that time, at least for some, in the land of Judah. In meditating on the bitter lessons of the events at the end of the eighth century people began to ask themselves questions about the spiritual unfaithfulness that had preceded the ruin of the northern kingdom, and they had to admit that the situation of injustice and infidelity, diagnosed as the cause of the calamities of the North, had an undeniable relevance to the southern kingdom, even though up to then it had been miraculously spared. The consequence was a first spiritual reform under King Hezekiah, mentioned also in 2 Kings (18:1-8); a few decades later there was a second reform, more extensive and decisive, under King Josiah after the reign of Manasseh, during which syncretism had come back with a vengeance.

In any case Isaiah died in a land where neither rulers nor people were willing to open their eyes to the meaning of the tragedies they had just experienced and that the prophet's words had interpreted for them. "Do not prophesy to us what is right; speak to us smooth things, prophesy illusions." These words, attributed to the people in Isaiah 30:10, give an idea of what sort of reception the prophet's preaching must have encountered. Besides, Isaiah mysteriously declares in 8:16-18 that he buries his message and seals its revelation in the heart of his disciples. He himself had to modify his oracles in the course of his life when he perceived that obviously the hope placed in the dynasty of Judah was not going to be fulfilled by the kings who reigned at that time. Faced with the painful eclipse of "God's face hiding itself from the house of Jacob," Isaiah turns with hope toward the future he will not see; he is confident that the hour of darkness will one day come to an end, that the message preserved by his disciples will at long last be heard.

Indeed, this entombment of the message lasted for a time, probably accompanied by assiduous meditation on the oracles entrusted to a group of disciples sometimes called the "Isaian School." In any event, the text was the object of meditation in the seventh century during the reign of Josiah (640–609 B.C.E.), in particular at the time of the fall of Nineveh, the hated symbol of Assyrian domination, overcome in 612 by the Babylonians who, in their turn, became a hegemonic and threatening power. At that time the corpus of oracles left by Isaiah was submitted to modifications and additions. Oracles against Babylon (chs. 13 and 14:3-33), which are seen as an echo of what had been experienced a century earlier, were inserted into the eighth-century text because from then on it was Babylon that was at the center of current events; there are allusions to Passover (for example in 30:29) that seem to belong to the time of Josiah when the importance of this feast greatly increased.

(b) Events of the sixth century are in the background of the second part of the book of Isaiah (chs. 40–55). This part opens with the announcement that the exile of Israel is soon to come to an end: the Babylonian power is about to collapse; soon the deported will return. Jerusalem will be restored after its great humiliation. These events are the denouement of a historical period that began at the beginning of the century with the unstoppable dismembering of the kingdom of Judah, culminating in the capture of Jerusalem in 587 B.C.E. by the troops of Nebuchadnezzar. The elites were deported to Babylon; the lower classes remained under the surveillance of a collaborator, Gedaliah, who himself would be assassinated. Against every expectation, when it seemed that the exile would continue, a strange piece of news shook the Near East in 539 B.C.E.: the Persian Cyrus, who since 549 has won fame in several campaigns, especially that in which he defeated the Lydian Cresus (see Isa 41:25, "he shall trample on rulers as on mortar, as the potter treads clay") took Babylon without encountering any resistance. The great, the invincible city, disabled by the defection of King Nabonidus, fell, and with it the Babylonian hegemony. Moreover, as early as 538 Cyrus had promulgated an edict declaring all peoples enslaved by the Babylonian empire free to return to their lands and take their gods with them. In Isa 45:1 it is this personage, a pagan of course, who is designated as God's "anointed," accomplishing God's will.

The oracle that gives Cyrus this title, as well as the others that surround it, emanated from the prophet called Deutero-Isaiah. Anonymous, with his identity carefully concealed, this man is completely subordinated to his message. He is a "voice," "the messenger of the good news." Readers do not escape the extraordinary power of his words and visions, which are among the most beautiful pages in Isaiah. This prophet meditates on the text of First Isaiah. He announces an unheard-of work that God is going to do; he proclaims the restoration of Israel that is soon to come. Jerusalem becomes "Holy Zion" adorned with beauty and justice by God and in subsequent oracles is made the magnetic center of peace toward which all the peoples of the earth converge. From the opening of ch. 40 the mission of the anonymous prophet is presented as a ministry of "consolation" after the trial of the exile (hence the title given to this part of Isaiah, "the book of the consolation of Israel").

In this period of the middle decades of the sixth century B.C.E. Israel was experiencing the immense trauma caused by the Babylonian victory and exile in a foreign land. The book of Lamentations is the echo of the material and spiritual distress the people felt because of the humiliation of Jerusalem and the destruction of God's Temple. This was a time of darkness and violence, of extreme abandonment when Israel might have believed its history ended forever, submerged in the crucible of the great pagan empires. The land was lost, the people dispersed, the language vanishing and replaced by the Aramaic of the Chaldeans; the Temple was destroyed, and worship discontinued. A great pagan culture displayed its splendor to the Israelites' eyes while magnificently celebrating its gods in the temples of Babylon. To withstand these allurements Israel had only its memory, itself in danger of remaining entrapped in disappointment and nostalgia. The majority, to be sure, lived these trials in a state of inner revolt, accusing God of unfaithfulness and helplessness

But this time was also, at least for some for whom the message of our anonymous prophet had a vital importance, the time when a spiritual awareness unprecedented in Israel arose and developed. Through the oracles of Deutero-Isaiah it becomes clear that at this time some in Israel looked squarely at the state of affairs in all its radical starkness, and discovered in it the drama of Israel's history and life. The exile was not merely one episode, more tragic than the others, in the political history of the little kingdom of Israel. More exactly, we might say that the spiritual dimension of this history suddenly became clear: the reason the covenant with God seemed void was that Israel, not God, had for a long time spurned it, trampled it underfoot, and finally broken it. Israel's sin and unfaithfulness were the cause of its faltering before the Babylonian armies. The exile was the obverse of this breaking of the covenant. It was ultimate punishment. From there, looking back on the past, one could see that this same spiritual problem had since the people's origin been part and parcel of the history of Israel. (The same conclusion was reached by Ezekiel; see for instance his ch. 20, in which he rereads this history and shows that from the time of their enslavement in Egypt the people had been unfaithful and given to idolatry). Therefore the issue was not simply one of being delivered from physical bondage to Babylonia, but from another exile, deeper and more difficult to overcome, the bondage to the darkness of ignorance, spiritual blindness, the congenital infidelity that surfaced again and again throughout the ancestors' history down to the present.

Thus the sixth century B.C.E. was in Israel the century of memory: memory willing to acknowledge the long chain of sin, rebellion, and contempt of God; memory that, reviewing the history of Israel's unfaithfulness, knows also how to discern in it the witness of God's indefectible faithfulness. The theology of the Deuteronomist school, which took shape at this time, insists on these themes. [For further discussion see "Introduction to the Deuteronomistic History" above.] It is in this same spirit that a fresh reading of the oracles of First Isaiah is undertaken. This analysis of Israel's spiritual condition equally undergirds the oracles of salvation that burst forth in Deutero-Isaiah, for—and this is the core of the message—God is about to do something new. For the first time the word "gospel" appears, meaning "good news of salvation by God." By a free decision of grace God is going to bring the exile to an end and restore the divine presence. God is going to renew the prodigies of the Exodus, but much beyond what the events of the thirteenth century had been. One must therefore both forget the travails of the past (43:18) and remember that God has never forgotten this people (44:21). And so the eschatological rereading of past history begins. Through this exercise of memory Israel will be able to glimpse something of the salvation that is in the process of germinating (42:9). By using the vocabulary of germination and birth the text suggests that what is coming will be a prolongation of the past and yet new and unheard of. The newness is that the Spirit will be given. But Deutero-Isaiah is first of all interested in the mediator of this salvation, that is to say, the Servant, accompanied by the feminine figure of Zion.

As a consequence, one characteristic trait of the exilic period is the establishment of a new relationship with time and, singularly, with the past. Up to then one kept the memory of a legacy on which individual and collective life relied in order to continue. Now one discovers the past as a word bearing on the present and the future. The past is prophecy of the future. The meaning of the past goes far beyond the understanding the ancestors had of the events they were living; far beyond also whatever had been understood about these events. It is therefore imperative to read afresh the old texts with the insight gained in this time of trial. In this "typological reading" persons as well as historico-geographical facts become theological figures for the end of time. The Exodus, among all memories of the past, acquires the highest status: what God worked at the Exodus is going to happen again, but in a mode that will transcend the still narrow limits of the event of Moses' time.

(c) Everything seemed to be completed or about to be completed with ch. 55, but again a state of painful expectation prevails at the opening of the third part of the book of Isaiah, written in the fifth century B.C.E. and, in all likelihood, still later. In the meantime the return from exile had taken place, but the disappointments had been plentiful. This return had nothing in common with the magnificent event evoked in the oracles of Deutero-Isaiah. Only a small number of the exiled had returned while many remained in Babylonia and became assimilated. Those who did return had the bitter experience of seeing Jerusalem ravaged and the countryside given to idolatry. The reconstruction of the Temple met with obstacles. Above all, despite the spiritual lessons brought by the trial they had suffered, it seems that very few hearts underwent conversion. Frauds, injustices, vile actions again were rampant in the city; idolatry reigned (see 57:1-13; 59:15, which are very close to the words of First Isaiah denouncing a "rebellious people" who are also treacherous). In a word, evil was in full sway.

The moral crisis at the return from exile was compounded by a spiritual crisis: the fulfillment of the divine promises is delayed; apparently nothing had changed. The pain caused by these circumstances disturbed the remnant of the Israelites who had remained faithful; they confess their sin and implore a salvation they know is undeserved (see the psalm in 63:7-19, which must date from the beginning of the return from exile). A turn has been taken: it must be understood that the act of facing the truth, a humble confession of sin, is the preliminary condition for the future of the people, but few were those who effectively acquiesced in this spiritual conversion.

In response to this situation the text develops oracles strongly eschatological in tone. They announce God's final judgment. God is about to come in person, on the day of vengeance, to destroy the wicked and deliver the weak and innocent. Other oracles speak of the Messiah, "the anointed of the Lord," bearer of the Spirit, who is coming to announce, along with the day of vengeance, a "the year of the LORD's favor" (61:2). Then the messianic people will be able to arise and gather into the covenant both Israel and the pagans (that is, the peoples who do not share the faith and hope of Israel). Here universalism reaches its fullest extent.

This vast synthesis took shape after the exile at a key moment in biblical history, when many applied themselves to rereading and rewriting the ancient texts. During the same period the Pentateuch received its definitive form and several of the prophetic texts were submitted to a final revision. The Bible was taking shape in its two main parts, the Law and the Prophets. It was neither a question of salvaging in a desperate gesture what remained nor of inventing a future for a hope that had been disappointed. Rather, one wrote and rewrote because of the awareness that from now on God's design was beginning to be more clearly deciphered. To persons "contrite and humble" (57:15) God was revealing the meaning of the history that had been veiled in obscurity when it was lived in the past.

The debate concerning the identity of the author or authors of the last eleven chapters of the book continues; these chapters are at once different from and in agreement with Deutero-Isaiah. A plausible hypothesis is that a final redactor gathered and synthesized the oracles from the eighth century, written by Deutero-Isaiah and anonymous and more recent prophets, in order to produce the present text. In any case one has to advert to the fact that the entire work was placed under the name of one single eighth-century prophet. This expressed the determination to affirm the continuity and theological unity of this text, apparently discontinuous and disjointed; the determination to say that one and the same movement carries the revelation of one and the same plan of God throughout the sixty-six chapters. What remained to be done was to hear the message. Four centuries elapsed before the incarnation, four centuries to practice and perfect the art of listening.

IV. Canonical Intertextuality

In the Hebrew Scriptures

It is not impossible that First Isaiah here and there adopted older oracles taken up and reused in the eighth century (see ch. 7). Besides, we have seen that this section borrowed whole blocks from 2 Kings (chs. 36–39). Likewise one can interpret several passages of the Song of Songs, a later writing, in connection with some of the book of Isaiah's oracles (for example, the theme of the "awakening" of the chosen people in Isa 60:62; 63:7–64:11; 26:12-19; also in Song 5:2 this theme is associated with that of the dew as it is in Isa 26:19). Similarly, one finds an echo of the destiny of the Servant described in 52:13–53:12 in Psalm 22 regarding the just one delivered to death ("My God, my God, why have you forsaken me?"). Chapter 2 of the book of Wisdom speaks of the same situation as does Isaiah, but this time from the perspective of the impious who hound the just one ("Let us condemn him to a shameful death, for, according to what he says, he will be protected"). This just one, like the Suffering Servant, can be identified with a collective figure (persecuted Israel) or an individual (the interpretation adopted by the Christian reading of the text). For his part, Zechariah in ch. 12 contemplates a mysterious personage "pierced" who will be, like the Servant, the salvation of Jerusalem. [See also the article "Interpretation of the Bible Within the Bible Itself."]

In any event, when the codex of the scrolls of the Hebrew Scriptures was organized the book of Isaiah was set in the first place among the prophets and was thereby designated as the great prophetic book offering a synthesis of the whole history, in parallel with the Pentateuch, whose final redaction dates from the same period.

In the Christian Scriptures

Whether explicit or simply allusive, the quotations from the book of Isaiah are exceptionally numerous in the NT. In the gospels they have the peculiarity of being introduced with the mention of Isaiah's name, which gives them a particular weight in comparison to other prophetic words quoted (for instance Matt 3:3; 4:14; 8:17; 12:17; Mark 12:2; 7:6; Luke 3:4; John 1:23; 12:38, 39). [See also the commentary on the Gospel of Matthew where this use of Second Isaiah is extensively illuminated.] From the annunciation to the resurrection Jesus is shown as the one who fulfills in an eminent way Isaiah's prophecies. Thus the "annunciation" to Joseph (Matt 1:22-23) and that to Mary (Luke 1:30-37) refer to Isaiah's text. This surfaces again in the Magnificat (Luke 1:46-55), in the canticle of Zechariah (Luke 1:67-69, taking up Isa 40:3; 11:6; and 9:1), in that of Simeon waiting for the "consolation of Israel" (Luke 2:29-32, echoing Isa 42:6; 49:6; 52:10). The teaching of John the Baptist is commented upon by Isa 40:3 in Matthew 3:3 and parallel texts, whereas in John 1:23 the same John the Baptist is designated as the voice of Isa 40:3. Jesus' baptism in its turn is written with allusions to Isa 42:1 in Matt 3:17 and to Isa 63:19 in Mark 1:10, mentioning the skies that are rent. Jesus' ministry in Galilee in Matthew's gospel (4:15) is commented upon by the prophecy from Isa 8:23–9:1, which speaks of the "Galilee of the nations" over which a great light arises. When speaking in parables Jesus refers to the hardening of hearts spoken of in Isa 6:9-10 according to the three synoptic gospels as well as John in 12:39. The same words, pronounced by Paul, are found again at the conclusion of Acts. In the debates with some of the Pharisees on hypocrisy (Matt 1:7-9 and parallel texts) Isa 29:13 is quoted. The mention of the keys in Isa 22:22 concerning Eliakim, who receives the power to open and close in an authoritative manner, recurs when Peter receives the keys of the kingdom in Matt 16:19 (cf. Rev 3:7). The parable of the "murderous tenants" (Matt 21:33-46; Mark 12:1-12) is in continuity with the song of the vineyard in Isa 5:2. In the background of the works of justice enumerated in Matt 25:35-39 are verses from Isaiah 58. In Jesus the healer Matt 8:17 recognizes the Servant of Isa 53:4. In the synagogue of Nazareth (Luke 4:18) Jesus reads the text of Isa 61:1-2 and declares that this word is fulfilled that very day. The conversation with the Samaritan woman (John 4:7-26) and the discourse in the synagogue of Capernaum (John 6:25-40) also contain allusions to Isaiah. These references culminate in the accounts of the passion. Moreover, it is to these texts that Jesus refers when speaking with his disciples on the road to Emmaus, "Was it not necessary that the Messiah should suffer these things and then enter into his glory?" (Luke 24:26). Finally, the last words of the gospel of Matthew in 28:20 ("I am with you always, to the end of the age") resonate with the name of the Immanuel.

The theology of the history of salvation developed by St. Paul, especially in the letter to the Romans (cf. Rom 11:32: "God has imprisoned all in disobedience so that he may be merciful to all"), is directly based on Isaiah. Jesus is acknowledged there, in the image of the servant of Deutero-Isaiah, as the one through whom the multitude is justified (Rom 5:19, echoing Isa 53:11). Chapters 9–11 of the letter, meditating on the "time of the Gentiles" and the final conversion of the people chosen by God, pivot around the notions of "hardening" and "remnant." Paul's central conviction is couched in the words of Isaiah, "Out of Zion will come the Deliverer" (Isa 59:20, quoted in Rom 11:26). In the letter to the Ephesians the same mystery of the reconciliation of Jews and Gentiles again attracts quotations from Isaiah (Eph 2:17-18, quoting Isa 57:19). The christological hymn from the letter to the Philippians (2:6-11) is in its turn akin to the fourth song of the Servant.

Finally, the book of Revelation uses many texts from Isaiah: in particular the vision of the divine throne in ch. 4, which reflects Isa 6:1-5; the sign of the woman in ch. 12, which echoes Isa 7:10, 14; the judgment of the great whore in chs. 17–18, reusing the oracles against Babylon; but also the final visions of Jerusalem in which many references to the last part of the book of Isaiah are woven (especially Isa 54:11-12 and 60:1-4, quoted in Revelation 21 and 22). Let us note, finally, the expression "Lamb of God," which often designates Jesus in Revelation but is already present in John 1:29 and 36; one of its sources is Isa 53:7.

V. History of Reception

Commentary on the Text

Among the manuscripts discovered in Qumran there are nineteen copies of the book of Isaiah. The most complete is also the oldest. It dates to the end of the second century B.C.E. and accords remarkably, on the whole, with the text of the LXX. Frequently quoted in the Essenes' writings, the book holds a central place in the spirituality of the community of Qumran whose messianic hope it fashioned and sustained. Jewish commentary on the text of Isaiah continued throughout the Middle Ages, when Ibn Ezra and Rashi restricted the historical scope of the book to Jewish history.

As early as Hippolytus of Rome and throughout the patristic era Isaiah was often commented upon by Christians. For the school of Antioch most of the prophecies were realized within Jewish history. The school of Alexandria highlighted much more strongly the christological significance of the text. But it was the controversy with Judaism that gave the book an all-important place. The Justin's *Apologies* and *Dialogue with Trypho* as well as Irenaeus's *Demonstration of the Apostolic Preaching* and *Adversus Haereses* (4.33) attest to the way in which the book of Isaiah is at the center of the "prophetic demonstration" that proclaims that Jesus is the Messiah fulfilling the hope of the OT. The polemics are particularly acute when it comes to oracles such as Isa 7:14-16.

For Christian readers this passage is a capital text. It sheds a great light on the mystery of salvation and gives hints of the paradoxes of God's work. In Ahaz's time and in an infinitely more radical manner at the time of the incarnation God displayed the divine power to save in a way that is the direct contrary of power. The splendor of God's strength expresses itself in the vulnerability of a newborn carried by its mother. The Word of God speaks through the gift of a child still unable to speak. The repeated reference in the first chapters of the gospel of Matthew to "the child and his mother" (Matt 2:11, 13, 14, 20, 21) could be linked to this oracle from Isaiah 7 announcing salvation through the woman who gives birth at the royal court.

It should be noted that this Christian interpretation argues from the Greek translation in the LXX that reinterprets the prophecy of the Immanuel within the ancient Jewish tradition by translating the Hebrew *ʿalmāh* ("young woman") with *parthenos* ("virgin"). Christianity thus sees the virginal conception of Jesus prophesied in this oracle. In response to this, Jewish translations of the first century C.E. restore the Greek word *neanis* ("young woman") in opposition to the Christian interpretation.

Besides the exegesis of Isa 7:14-16, the controversy with Judaism also revolved around the oracles of the Servant in Deutero-Isaiah, in particular the fourth (52:13–53:12). Judaism sees the Servant as a collective figure, the symbol of Israel, exposed to persecution through all its history and playing a vicarious role with regard to the nations. Christianity, for its part, finds in him the basis for its recognition of Jesus as Messiah and its confession of faith. Jesus identified himself with this servant and the first Christian community did likewise (see Acts 4:27, "your holy servant Jesus, whom you anointed"). However, it is worth noting that contemporary Judaism did not extend its traditional interpretation of the text to the Shoah as one could have expected. Indeed, how can one recognize in the Servant who offers his life in sacrifice the figure of Israel delivered, without any possible initiative, to the Nazi terror? Similarly, how can one compare the destruction of the Jewish people to a "sacrifice," that is to say, according to the first meaning of the word, a homage rendered to God?

More anecdotally, the tradition of the ox and donkey at the manger has its origin in early commentaries on Isa 1:3. As to the martyrdom of Isaiah, who was supposed to have been sawed to pieces on King Manasseh's order, it is found in an apocryphal source dating from the end of the first century C.E., the Ascension of Isaiah. The legend attests that in both the Jewish and Christian traditions Isaiah is an eminent figure of the endurance of faith not shrinking from martyrdom.

Christian Liturgical Usage

The book of Isaiah is the central reference for the time of Advent. In proposing it for reading the liturgy invites believers to pray, to prepare God's way, to recognize the one who comes to fulfill the messianic hope. At the end of this vigil the words of the aged Simeon are recalled by the Church, taking up the word spoken by Israel in its Scriptures. For four Sundays, in correspondence with the gospel texts, themselves replete with allusions to Isaiah, readings taken from the same book succeed one another (first Sunday in years A and B: Isa 2:1-5; 63:16-17; 64:1, 3, 8; second Sunday in years A and B: Isa 11:1-10; 40:1-5, 9-11; third Sunday in years A and B: Isa 35:1-6a; 61:1-2a, 10, 11; fourth Sunday in year A: Isa 7:10-14). Fifteen out of the twenty-four weekly readings are also excerpted from Isaiah during that time, as is the totality of the biblical readings at the Liturgy of the Hours. From day to day the expectation of the Church becomes more clearly focused on the act of power and salvation of God who is coming in person to visit God's people, as many passages of Isaiah describe; at Christmas the Church will understand that the Christ, who was expected to appear in grandeur, is in fact present in the extreme smallness of the child of Bethlehem. God's power is not in the human mode; it is that of a love that agrees to enter into the limits of our lives and our words in order to join us where we are. The four Christmas Masses, that of the vigil, the night, the dawn, and the day, all take their first readings from Isaiah (62:1-5; 9:1-6; 62:11-12; 52:7-10). The same happens at Epiphany (60:1-6) and the Baptism of the Lord (42:1-4, 6-7).

During Lent Isaiah's text is less present, but nevertheless not absent (in particular on the fifth Sunday of cycle C, 43:16-21). From Palm Sunday (50:4-7) on, it returns with great importance during Holy Week (42:1-7; 49:1-6; 50:4-9). The fourth oracle of the Servant (52:13–53:12) is read on Good Friday; in the unique person and destiny of the Servant, who bears the sin of the wicked and saves them through the suffering he endures from them, the work of God who gave the only Son of God and "for our sake made him to be sin" in order that "in him we might become the righteousness of God" (2 Cor 5:21) is revealed in a light beyond compare. Among the readings of the Paschal Vigil, two are taken from Isaiah: 54:5-14, where the new Jerusalem is invited to exult with joy because of the children who come to her, and 55:1-11, which announces the free gift of water (Spirit) and bread (Word) bestowed by the Servant accredited by God. Over its three cycles Ordinary Time contains some twenty excerpts from Isaiah. The oracle of Isa 7:10-14 is read on the feast of the Annunciation. For the burial service the Lectionary offers the eschatological oracle of Isa 35:6-10 proclaiming that God will abolish death forever.

SECOND READING

Overall Plan of the Book of Isaiah

First Isaiah (1–39)

1. Judgment of Israel and perspectives for salvation (1–12)

2. Oracles against the nations; perspectives for conversion and salvation (13–23)
3. Cosmic judgment and universal hope (24–35)
4. Rereading of history: punishment of Ashur's pride, salvation of Jerusalem and Hezekiah (36–39)

Deutero-Isaiah (40–55)
1. God's suit before the nations and announcement of God's justice that is to come (40–46)
2. Announcement of a new phase of salvation history (47–48)
3. Three oracles of the Servant, three oracles of Zion (49–55).

Final Chapters (56–66)
1. Delay of salvation because of sin; continuation of the divine promise (56:1–59:21)
2. Nearness of salvation; revelation of the priestly people in Zion toward which the nations converge (60–66)

I. First Isaiah (Eighth Century and Later Additions): Isaiah 1–39

Theological Structure of the Text

1. 1–12: Judgment of Israel (covenant suit) and perspective for salvation: "little remnant," messianic hope connected with the birth of Immanuel.
2. 13–23: Judgment of the nations; loss, conversion, and salvation. First paradoxical reversal of the situation.
3. 24–35: "Mystery" of the cosmic judgment and universal hope connected with the Temple; reign, resurrection/hell. Judgment and salvation associated with an eschatological perspective.
4. 36–39: Condemnation of the pride of the king of Ashur. Salvation of Jerusalem and King Hezekiah. This amounts to a second reversal of situations.

1. Judgment of Israel and Perspective of Salvation (Isaiah 1–12)

A. Sins of Zion That Will Nevertheless be the Place of Salvation, Isaiah 1–5

i. The Suit (Isaiah 1)

The book opens with the word "vision." It is the meaning of history and its events, revealed to Isaiah, that is to be the object of the oracles. God convokes the whole creation that it may be witness to the revolt and treason of God's people. Despite the severity of the punishments already inflicted by God (vv. 5-6) Israel goes deeper into infidelity and ignorance (v. 3). As a consequence, the land lies desolate (vv. 7-8); the description of Jerusalem as "a booth in a vineyard" aptly evokes the condition in which the city finds itself after Sennacherib's Judean campaign in 701.

Then comes a new oracle (reference to Sodom and Gomorrah, symbols of depraved cities) denouncing the sort of worship one uses as a screen in order to commit evil with greater ease. God proclaims weariness with this false worship (not worship in general). However, the text continues with a word of hope: YHWH intends and desires to forgive. Verse 18 even suggests a mysterious act of power on God's part. Let humans present themselves at the trial; let there be discussion, and God will transform the scarlet crime into innocence. The contract is again spelled out: God will insure the people's life if they promise to obey, that is to say, live according to the righteousness and justice God requires of them (vv. 19-20). At the time the book was written, in the southern kingdom, the notion of law was certainly not yet as elaborate as that of the Ten Commandments was to be, but still the heart of the question is undoubtedly the choice of good and righteousness against that of evil.

The same theme is repeated in the following oracle denouncing the prostitution of Zion, now in the hands of profiteers and assassins. The same movement is repeated: judgment is announced, but with it a perspective of conversion that will make Zion the "city of righteousness" (v. 26). The insistence on the motif of fire (vv. 7, 25, 31) could be an echo of the experience lived at the time when Assyria ravaged Judah, an experience repeated at the hands of the Babylonians.

ii. Judgment and Salvation on the "Day of YHWH" (2:1–4:6)

This section is made up of a central part developing the suit against idolatry (2:6–4:1) framed between two evocations of Mount Zion toward which "in days to come" (2:2), "on that day" (4:2) the nations will go up and where the survivors of Israel will gather. The themes of judgment and salvation seen previously are found again, but here salvation occupies a larger place than before.

The trial denounces both idolatry and pride as sources of violence and injustice. Idolatry, rampant in the land, is vigorously connected with pride. It appears here for the first time in First Isaiah. Using a highly structured mode of composition with a play of parallels (2:10 parallel to 2:19 and 2:11 parallel to 2:17) flanking the mention of the "day of YHWH against all that is proud and lofty" (cf. 2:12) the text declares that God will humble all forms of pride. It is noteworthy that at this point in Isaiah only the destruction, and not the conversion of the proud is mentioned. Verse 22 introduces a theme that will reappear in numerous passages: one must cease to place one's trust in humans rather than in God. Isaiah 3:1–4:1 describes the state of anarchy prevailing in Jerusalem, perhaps at a period when power was in the hands of a regent (3:4), and the way in which women's pride will be crushed. The text of the beginning and end of this section (2:1-5 and 4:2-6), with its eschatological connotations, is made up of later additions. It reveals the final intention of the redactor and, as a consequence, of the final text itself. It describes the future Temple with new and remarkable characteristics. In 2:1-4 we see the nations flocking to it, exhorting one another to ascend to the Temple of YHWH and practice the Law. A figure of the "judge of the nations" appears and a beautiful eschatological image shows the peace that will be established (4:2-4). In order to shed light on this passage we must remember that in Israel's hope the eschatological era is not understood as the end of the world, but as the end of adversity. The very structure of the text urges us to associate this end with the end of pride. Moreover, in echo to 2:1-4 the post-exilic 4:1-4 completes the vision by introducing elements suggesting a very mysterious reality. Mount Zion is far from being a mere geographical entity. The "survivors of Israel" gather there, a holy remnant after the destruction (4:2). The material building is no longer mentioned, but the cloud, a sign of God's presence, which rests over the *sukkāh* ("booth" or "pavilion"), the word used for the city of Jerusalem in 1:8. It is the people, grown more numerous by the inclusion of the nations (2:2-3), that seems from that point on to be the true Temple. Its glory is in the "branch of YHWH" (4:2). However, in this unheard-of vision, decidedly universalistic, it is noteworthy that Israel remains first and central (2:3c). Finally, the text says that the "branch of YHWH" will be "the pride and glory" of the survivors of Israel. The presence of the word "branch" or "shoot" *(ṣemaḥ),* the technical word for the Messiah in Zechariah and Jeremiah, confirms the post-exilic nature of the text. This messianic connotation could have been projected back on 2:4 because of the correspondence that exists between the two parts of the text framing the central portion (and also because of the resonances perceptible between 2:4, 4:2, 9:3-6 and 55:4).

iii. Crimes of Israel and Announcement of Its Punishment (Isaiah 5)

The song of the vineyard (5:1-7) makes use of a traditional designation of Israel in order to again proclaim judgment and announce the punishment of the unfruitful vine. Verses 8-24 are arranged around a center (v. 15) that foretells (as previously 2:11-18) the destruction of pride together with the exaltation of YHWH whose judgment and justice will be recognized. The themes correspond concentrically: injustice of the life of the city (vv. 8-9 and vv. 23-24), drunkenness (vv. 11-12 and vv. 21-22), lack of knowledge (v. 13 and v. 19). God will judge those who call "evil good and good evil" (v. 20) and defy God's work (v. 19). God's anger is shown as working in two steps. The first (v. 25) seems to speak of an earthquake, but the punishment will continue under the form of an invasion (vv. 26-30) difficult to identify historically (734? 722? 701?).

B. The Book of Immanuel, 6:1–12:6

i. Vision in the Temple and Mission of Isaiah (6:1-13)

The scene could have taken place in 740 B.C.E. In the *hekāl* of the Temple the prophet receives a vision of the solemn heavenly liturgy in which the "seraphs" (*serāphīm,* meaning "the burning ones") acclaim God's holiness. Confronted by this august theophany, Isaiah is afraid because of his uncleanness. A seraph touches his lips with a burning coal. What follows is not a story of vocation in the strict sense as in the case of Jeremiah or Amos. God is seeking someone for a mission that will mark a new step in Israel's history. This mission has a terrifying and paradoxical object: to harden the people, to make their hearts heavy and stonelike, incapable of hearing and understanding the signs and the Word God is about to give. Of course this in no way means the holy God obliges humans to sin. This disconcerting command must be understood as a judgment of God on sin. God imprisons human beings in the sin they have chosen in order that they may taste its bitter fruits and at last come to recognize it as evil. At the heart of the drama the book of Isaiah records is human blindness, the refusal to identify good and evil for what they are. Only the experience of what evil produces will perhaps be able to open the sinners' eyes.

We must note that this blindness is described as a temporary trial (6:11-13). It will last for a time, the time necessary to effect the devastation it entails, to empty the land of its inhabitants until only a "stump" is left. However, a hint of hope accompanies this vision of calamity: the "stump" *(maṣevet),* for its part, will be a "holy seed" *(zeraʿ).* The judgment is therefore not the announcement of utter ruin for the sinful people, but of its rebirth, on the very brink of its downfall, when all the dead elements have been eliminated. In v. 13 the notion of "remnant" is glimpsed, a notion central to the theology of Isaiah's book.

ii. Immanuel (7:1–9:1a)

What follows sheds light on the nature of the sin that is condemned as hardening of the heart, for the episode of the Syro-Ephraimite war (735 B.C.E.) poses a serious question: What sort of help should one seek when faced with the Assyrian threat? As Ahaz is trembling at the approach of the troops of Aram and Samaria, Isaiah speaks to him of the promises made by God to David; God will protect and save, provided total trust be present and merely human strategies be rejected. The question at the heart of the episode is the opposition of faith to fear. Without faith one will not "stand firm" (the verb in v. 9b has the same root in Hebrew as the verb "believe" and the noun "faith," *emunāh*). At any rate, the faith required of Ahaz is almost superhuman and could be nothing but suicidal fanaticism. This is why God is ready to uphold this faith by giving a sign to the king, as striking as the king might want (7:11). Ahaz piously objects that he does not want to put God to the test. In fact this is sheer evasion because the point is not to test God but to accept what is offered. But by accepting the sign the king could be constrained to enter the faith that God asks and in which he, the king, has no desire to get involved because it would entail the renunciation of human securities. His refusal makes explicit the thoughts of his heart. It is indeed the logic of hardening.

Therefore God alone will choose a sign that takes its full meaning in the context of the moment. The Syro-Ephraimite war imperils David's dynasty and, as a consequence, the promise attached to it since Nathan's prophecy (2 Sam 7:1-17). Now the oracle of 7:14-16 foretells the birth of a boy at the royal court. A little later this oracle will be completed by that of 9:5-6, and again, probably at the end of Isaiah's life, by that of 11:1-10.

These verses are the object of numerous discussions among exegetes. One such discussion bears upon the word that designates the "woman" who will give birth. *ʿAlmāh,* says the Hebrew, using a word that means "young girl" or "young woman" without specifying whether a virgin or not. The LXX translates this as *parthenos,* which means "virgin," probably because the Greek did not have the equivalent of the Hebrew *ʿalmāh.* It is this word *parthenos* that will support the Christian interpretation when it refers to Isaiah's text in the recounting of Jesus' birth, including the affirmation of Mary's virginity. This does not imply that at its origin the oracle was in the least intended as the prediction of a miraculous birth of this sort. However, it is possible to conceive of a subsequent rereading of the oracle in an eschatological sense, influenced by the figure of Zion that ch. 66 will present.

Another divergence of opinions exists concerning the identification of the woman and child mentioned in 7:14. The hypotheses are many and disparate: the woman is given either a collective or an individual interpretation, the child is identified as a son of Isaiah or as a son of the king, and so on. Similarly, the "sign" must be more clearly defined. It seems that—within the strict limits of the events of the eighth century—the great announcement to Ahaz was that the young woman, that is, the queen, was to give birth to a male child. This is news of considerable importance at a time when the throne of David is threatened by the Syro-Ephraimite coalition. The dynasty will continue. Moreover, the kings of Damascus and Samaria will be defeated in the near future, "before the child knows how to refuse the evil and choose the good" (v. 16), that is, before he reaches the age of reason. We have indeed the sign, expressed by the name Immanuel, that "God is with us." The child to be born will be the living proof of the solicitude

God continues to have for the house of David, and the sign of the salvation God will offer.

But the oracle, as we read it, does not concern only this happy event. Its text, obscure in several points anyway, is more complex. Enigmatic verses (particularly vv. 17-20) that promise happiness while evoking trial and misfortune demonstrate this complexity. This is also shown by a series of grammatical incoherences showing that the text was rewritten, apparently by Isaiah himself. At first the onset of a period of messianic prosperity is mentioned, related to the birth of the child (vv. 15-16). The themes of food and good and evil are consonant with the vocabulary of the Yahwist text of Genesis 2–3. The child will be fed with "curds and honey," the classic products of the Promised Land in the Bible, but also the supernatural food of the gods according to ancient pagan traditions that see in it the pledge of the gods' immortality. Thanks to this food the child will know how to "refuse the evil and choose the good." (There is no doubt that the words of v. 15b must be read as *"in order to* know how to choose between good and evil"). The entire country will be renewed by this food, more precious than the tree of knowledge of good and evil since it will confer the spiritual judgment necessary to overcome original sin. Thus the oracle ends with the prophecy of a new condition of the earth inaugurated by Immanuel in the person of Ahaz's heir.

However, the perspective of paradisiacal happiness presented by the oracle interweaves positive and negative details. Verses 18-19 and 21-22 paint with a pastoral vocabulary an era of prosperity that will extend to Israel's two enemies, Egypt and Assyria. On the positive side we have the bees for which God will whistle; by settling on fields previously barren they will become a source of prosperity. As to the flies, called back from the delta of the Nile, they could be interpreted in connection with the Canaanite traditions that associate them with the god Baal and the fecundity of the herds (they were supposed to excite cows and make them receptive to fertilization!). There is a logical sequence then in vv. 21 and 22: the fecundity of the cattle will be such "on that day" that it will be sufficient to raise one cow and two ewes to live in plenty. For the harsh condition established in ch. 3 of Genesis, ("by the sweat of your face you will eat bread") the text therefore substitutes the vision of the miraculous fertility of the Promised Land. But on the negative side, the announcement of a disaster is added to this initial glimpse of a final "day" of paradisiacal prosperity. Verse 20 alludes to a deportation following a military defeat (the custom was to shave the heads of prisoners). Verses 23-25 describe the devastation of the earth: where vineyards used to thrive only brambles and thorns will grow, the signs of its curse in Genesis 3; the plowed fields will return to mere pastures. These last words could concern the events that occurred at the end of the eighth century when Assyria swept through the land several times. Thus the prophecy oscillates between the announcement of a calamity that will destroy the land and that of a regime of bucolic peace and abundance. Besides, the reestablishment of Eden that is suggested will be delayed by terrible days (v. 17) so that the "curds and honey" will be tasted only by those who will be "left in the land" (v. 22). Again the theme of the "remnant" appears, which obliges one to conclude that the selection of the survivors will have been made through tragic events.

The complexity of the text leads us to surmise that Isaiah himself reworked his text at the end of his life. Probably he would have become convinced that the message to Ahaz meant more than the birth of Hezekiah: the Messiah was to be expected beyond the immediate future and person of the present king.

It is noteworthy that several centuries later the gospel of Matthew, when reporting the dream of Joseph and the announcement of Jesus' birth by an angel (Matt 1:18-25) will quote Isa 7:14. Exactly what was the evangelist's intention? Not simply, it seems, to uphold faith in the virgin birth. It is the name of Immanuel that is certainly the key of the quotation: the evangelist's aim is to affirm that Jesus fulfills the ancient oracle of Isaiah by himself being the presence of God among the people, that is "God with us." (In passing, we note that Matthew slightly modified the text of the LXX: instead of "[she] shall name him Immanuel," he wrote "they shall name him Emmanuel," suggesting that this time a large number of people will apply this title to Jesus.) Finally, the same gospel of Matthew ends with Jesus' word, "I am with you always, to the end of the age." We have here a vast *inclusio* that makes of the whole of the events reported in the gospel, between these two mentions of Emmanuel, the fulfillment of Isaiah's prophecy.

The theme of hardening continues in 8:1–9:1a. First comes the announcement of the birth of a son to Isaiah. He will bear a daunting symbolic name, "Maher-shalal-hash-baz" ("Quick, the booty! the looting!"), a presage of a time of darkness in spite of the provisional protection of Assyria. Another oracle (vv. 5-8) foretells the ruin of Judah for having despised the "waters of Shiloah" (an allusion to the spring in Jerusalem that symbolizes God's protection); the result will be that Judah will be submerged under the mighty waters of the Assyrian Euphrates. A third oracle (8:9-10) evokes the destruction of the nations that have no staying power before Judah, whose strength is that of the presence of God in its midst, "God with us." Verses 8:11-9:1a return to the theme of hardening. It renders one blind to the signs given by the prophet and deaf to his word, which repeats that only YHWH must be feared. The distraught people have recourse to necromancers. Thus the One who is the rock of Israel is going to become its stumbling block. As for Isaiah, he remains hopeful even when God's face is hidden, and he seals his revelation, which nobody wants to listen to, in the hearts of his disciples.

iii. Salvation of the Remnant of Israel and the Root of Jesse (9:1b–12:6)

The passage from 9:1b to 10:19 announces the salvation that will follow Israel's crimes. The section begins with a new messianic oracle. Verse 1b is its heading: it declares that the lands subjugated by Assyria in 732 will be liberated. The text alludes to events set in motion by the Syro-Ephraimite war: rejecting God's backing, Ahaz appeals to Assyria against the coalition. Most happy with this request, Assyria rushes to crush Aram and enslave a part of northern Israel which becomes the "district" *(gālīl)* of the nations or Gentiles (hence the appellation "Galilee of the nations"). A part of the Promised Land is from that point on condemned to live in the darkness of pagan occupation. In 721 Samaria fell in its turn. These territories are precisely those about which an oracle of deliverance is pronounced—a strange utterance as well, since it proclaims not only liberation from the pagan yoke but the utter destruction of every warlike power and the establishment of a reign of peace (vv. 5, 7). This announcement is connected with the mention of the birth of a child (v. 6), which brings us back to ch. 7. This child receives royal insignia and four most exalted titles. These could allude to the Egyptian practice of the crowning of the Pharaoh, a practice that was adopted by Jerusalem in David's time. The Pharaoh received, besides his own name, five prestigious titles. In that case we would have here an allusion no longer to the birth of Hezekiah, but to his coronation that might have taken place (there are problems with Hezekiah's chronology) when he was still a child. As it is formulated the oracle obviously looks far beyond the young king's birth. It tells of the institution of cosmic peace by a child coming from Jerusalem. Of necessity a long purification will still be required before the oracle is fulfilled because in the immediate future there is the blindness denounced at the end of ch. 8.

Then comes a fresh series of oracles directed at the pride of the kingdom of Israel (9:8–10:4). A terrifying refrain broadcasts God's anger which does not succeed in producing conversion and, as a consequence, is going to continue: "For all this his anger has not turned away; his hand is stretched out still" (9:12b, 17c, 21b; 10:4b). God lets the people be burned since they are arrogant and unjust. The next section concerns the judgment of Assyria. Oracles from different periods are here gathered to announce the ruin of the nation that was an untoward ally under Ahaz and became an overt enemy under Hezekiah. When God will have "finished all his work on Mount Zion" will come Assyria's punishment for having abused the mandate it had received, plundered and exterminated numerous nations. From Assyria's haughty pride there will be left, after God's fire has done its work, only a pitiable "remnant" (10:18-19).

The section in 10:20–12:6 depicts the paradoxical reversals that are about to befall David's dynasty. First of all, the theme of the "remnant" reappears in 10:20, but in a completely different light. It pertains now to the remnant of Israel that will come back after the crushing of the oppression, described here in the terms of a new exodus (v. 26b). God then will brandish a rod, not of threat but of deliverance, as in the days of the coming out of Egypt.

Another oracle (10:27b-34) describes an invasion from the north headed for Jerusalem. With this God will "lop the boughs with terrifying power" (10:33). A radical judgment seems to be announced, linked to the prophecy of the "remnant," and corresponding to what was already suggested in 6:12. Only a stump will remain.

As a logical sequence, then, we have 11:1-16 with the "shoot" coming out from the stump of Jesse. From the desiccated stump to which Jesse's family will be reduced life will spring up again in a "shoot" *(neṣer)*. The Hebrew word derives from the verb *nṣr,* which means "keep in store," "preserve." This shoot is given the features of an anonymous individual who exercises the royal power by restoring justice. He receives "the spirit of YHWH" formerly promised to Israel's judges and kings. With this spirit he receives wisdom, understanding, counsel, might, but also the "knowledge . . . of YHWH" that he will impart to the people, thus making possible what v. 9 describes ("the earth will be full of the knowledge of the LORD as the waters cover the sea"). He also will be filled with the "fear of YHWH," according to an expression current in wisdom circles, designating the contrary of the pride that had corrupted and ruined the royal family. Verses 3-5 describe this person as a new Solomon, clad in righteousness and fidelity, rendering justice to the lowly, and destroying the wicked. Verses 6-8 evoke the extension beyond the people of this newly recaptured righteousness to the cosmic order. Peace and harmony will return among animals; the nursling will play near the cobra without danger. In this text depicting a new Eden it is quite plausible that the mention of the snake is an allusion to the serpent in Genesis 3. As of now the perspective is eschatological: through the "shoot" God is about to inaugurate a new world order in which the Promised Land becomes the extension of the "holy mountain" (11:9) where God is present in the Temple. But the prophecy takes an unexpected turn in v. 10 with the strange vision of the "root of Jesse" standing erect "as a signal." What was hidden in the earth is going to become the glorious standard of reunion. This oracle, certainly from a much later period, speaks in terms painting the new exodus of the return from exile (11:15-16), and not only the return of the exiles but the reconciliation of the enemy siblings, northern Israel and Judah (11:13). Therefore the reunion is announced in connection with the messianic figure of the shoot of Jesse. Verse 14, though sounding vengeful, designates only the reconquest of the territories that from the beginning were part of the Promised Land.

This whole section concludes with a psalm-like text (12:1-6), a later addition. At a time when God is exalted and fear has fled Zion's inhabitants draw water from the sources of salvation; after the evocation of the return from exile (11:15-16) this thanksgiving borrows the words of the song in Exodus 15 celebrating the liberation from Egypt, "the Lord is my strength and my might" (Exod 15:2; Isa 12:2).

2. Oracles Against the Nations; Perspectives for Conversion and Salvation (Isaiah 13–23)

A. General Characteristics

This section is made up of a series of oracles concerning the nations. Generally designated *massāʾ* (meaning "charge," "grievance," "reproach"), these oracles are also attested in Amos, Jeremiah, and Ezekiel. Addressed to Israel, they announce God's verdict on the peoples that surround it, first of all Egypt and Assyro-Babylonia and in second place the other populations involved in the political game of the region.

The oracles concerning Babylon are an unexpected beginning and end in a text that belongs to the eighth century, for Babylon would become a powerful and redoubtable empire only later (625–539 B.C.E.). Besides, the mention of the Medes in 13:17 probably refers to the alliance that was concluded between them and the Babylonians in order to crush Nineveh at the end of the seventh century. The universalistic tenor of several passages (18:7; 19:21-22) clearly belongs to the post-exilic period; finally, elements of the Deuteronomists' theology are found in other verses. The present state of the text proves that a long and complex work of modification and rewriting took place from the eighth century down to the post-exilic period.

What theological affirmations and intentions are revealed by the text in the form in which it was finally fixed? God, the sovereign ruler of Israel and the nations, is at the heart of history. On the one hand God uses the nations as a rod of anger (see 10:5) in order to punish the unfaithfulness of the people; on the other hand God also punishes these nations, swelled with pride, who insult God's glory and abuse God's mandate (this is similar to 10:5-19 concerning Assyria). The warlike figure of YHWH Sabaoth holds the first place here. However, once human pride has been humbled and destroyed the nations will be converted, and in Israel's sight will come in their turn to glorify God. The insistent references to Babylon, anachronistic in a text dating from the eighth century, prove that here Babylon becomes a symbolic figure of the pride of any power that, usurping God's place, generates only violence and tyranny. Looking toward the "day of the LORD," the text has an eschatological tonality. In the last analysis these oracles ultimately have a positive content: they both let us glimpse the end of the exile and show us the impossible, that is, the conversion of idolatrous nations. Through a totally free act of divine power not only will pride and idolatry be cast down, but humans who do not know God will turn to glorifying God. These passages witness to an unheard-of universalism of the covenant; it will join Israel and the nations into a common praise.

Thus despite the disconcerting intermixing of historical and geographical references that abound in the text this section has a real unity and inserts itself in a very coherent way into its context. The thanksgiving in ch. 12 just before this section can be considered a true heading for it: that passage celebrates, in anticipation, the conversion and salvation spoken of afterward in the oracles concerning the nations. Israel remains present in the background of these oracles: subjected to the violence of the nations, it is also a witness for them, and the prospect of their conversion is an incentive for God's people to be converted as well.

B. Structure and Commentary

Judgment of Babylon and Its Divinized King (13:1–14:23:)

This whole passage, focusing on Babylon, can be dated for the most part in the sixth and fifth centuries B.C.E. Appearing as a warrior surrounded by valiant men (13:3), God speaks in the first person and initiates the judgment about to strike the pride of Babylon (13:11, 19). Isaiah 13:14 evokes the liberation caused by this downfall that the other peoples are going to celebrate, but the text of 14:1-2 goes even farther: to the prospect of Jacob's return is added that of a reversal of the situation in which the nations will join Israel as the oppressors of yesterday become the slaves of God's people, perhaps by a voluntary submission to those whose God they recognize as superior (cf. Zech 2:15). The allusion in 13:10 to the stars divinized by idolaters is picked up in the satire aimed at the king of Babylon in 14:3-22. He who styled himself "Day Star, son of Dawn" (14:12), the persecutor of peoples, is shown as reduced to the putrefaction of a corpse (vv. 11, 19) and even as dishonored by being cast out of his grave (vv. 18-20). At the center of this text are two correlated problems, the classic problem of idolatry and that of the political power that divinizes itself in order to better impose its tyranny. The trial of the leader whose pride destroys his people is magnificently conducted against him who wanted to "ascend to the tops of the clouds" to be the equal of God (v. 14). There is here an echo of Gen 3:5 and also of the story of the tower of Babel (Genesis 11). Verse 21, "prepare slaughter for his sons," an expression of shocking brutality, indicates that the tyrant will be deprived of descendants, but more deeply it also could be connected with the meditation of the Yahwist tradition that in the creation story deals with the beginning of sin from the viewpoint of its transmission and the solidarity of the generations. (This is in particular the function of the maternal figure portrayed in Genesis 3; the woman in the account of the temptation is shown first of all as a mother). On the contrary, the prophetic text announces that the race of the wicked will come to an end (cf. likewise 14:22) so that a new series of generations of righteous people may arise.

Oracles Concerning Assyria, Philistia, Moab, Damascus, and Samaria (14:24–17:14)

This whole section is composed of texts from the eighth century (14:24-27 refers to the Assyrian invasion; 14:28-32 refers to the Philistines; 17:1-6 speaks of the Syro-Ephraimite war; 17:12-14 could allude to Sennacherib's invasion) to which other, later oracles were associated. A first oracle foretells the collapse of Assyria (probably an allusion to Sennacherib's invasion in 701) and goes on to say that all nations will be submitted to God's judgment (14:24-27). At the end of this section, in 17:12-14, the same theme reoccurs with the impressive depiction of the nations God rejects or disperses. This is a vision of primordial combat in which the comparison with the "mighty waters" brings back the memory of the Exodus. The vocabulary of 17:14b ("fate," "lot") shows that these events are part of God's plan.

The following oracle is directed against Philistia (14:28-32) and denounces the glee that it showed at the death of Ahaz, the king who had aroused against it the wrath of Assyria in 734 at the time of the Syro-Ephraimite war. It mysteriously prophesies the coming of a successor who will be a much more serious threat to Philistia than Ahaz. Although nothing must remain of Philistia, God nevertheless promises that there will be a refuge in Zion for the "needy" and the "poor" among its people (14:30, 32); these two words certainly have here a spiritual connotation.

The oracle concerning Moab (15:1–16:14) opens with the lamentation that rises from the land of Moab, ravaged and humiliated (see v. 2, "on every head is baldness, every beard is shorn"). Even the survivors are not safe from a "lion" that here may be the symbol of the punishment God continues to inflict on them. At this point the Moabites seek the protection of Judah (16:1-5). They are ready to give the symbolic offering of a lamb (16:1). They even invoke in their favor the promises made to the Davidic dynasty (16:5). But the answer is negative: proud Moab can only lament over its useless riches such as vineyards and maritime commerce (16:8) and the futility of its worship (16:12). At the very end of the prophecy a new punishment is even announced after which only a feeble little remnant will be left (16:14).

"An oracle concerning Damascus" (17:1) brings us back to the period of the Syro-Ephraimite war. It announces both the destruction of Damascus and that of the towns of Ephraim that forgot its God and did not remember its Rock, Zion, the true city of refuge (17:10a). A day will come when people *(hāʾādām)* will renounce their illusory cultic practices to turn toward their Maker and look to the Holy One of Israel (17:7), but as long as people put faith in the puny rites of the cult of Adonis, hinted at in vv. 10 and 11 (a possible reference to the practice of the "gardens of Adonis"), the land will languish and its disease will be incurable.

The Destinies of Egypt and Assyria Linked with One Another; Final Conversion (18:1–20:6)

Several passages pertain to Isaiah's time (18:1-6; 19:1-5; 20:1-6). The first oracle concerns Cush, that is, Nubia. It is possible that this oracle alludes to the memory of an embassy that had made a strong impression in Jerusalem, but this magnificence will not prevent God's judgment on Cush. After a message of misfortune directed against Cush (18:1-2), the oracle takes on a universal dimension by addressing the "inhabitants of the world" (18:3). Approaching is a major pruning of humankind that God contemplates from God's dwelling. The name designating God ("cloud of dew") will recur in 27:19 to indicate God's beneficent and healing presence, but for the moment the spectacle is terrifying since we are shown heaps of corpses so high that a summer and winter will be necessary for the wild beasts to completely rid the earth of them. With v. 7 the vision and tone radically change since now we see Cush converted to YHWH and offering a sacrifice in the Temple on Mount Zion.

There follows a new oracle concerning Egypt (19:1-15). It begins by showing Egyptian wisdom in disarray (vv. 1-4); God judges Egypt by plunging into confusion those who trust oracles pronounced by idols and have recourse to necromancers; the political wisdom of Egypt collapses. Verses 5-10 enumerate the natural catastrophes that are about to strike the land. Verses 11-15 return to the indictment of the wisdom of Egypt: smitten by God with a spirit of bewilderment, the counselors of Pharaoh go astray and cause the land to stagger like a drunkard. They are utterly incapable of perceiving and revealing what the design of YHWH is (v. 12). The figure with which the oracle concludes is the exact opposite of that described in 11:2-6.

A prose passage begins in 19:16. First comes the dramatic description of the panic that overwhelms Egypt when it discovers that God desires expiation for the wrongs done to Judah. Nevertheless, Egypt will be converted and healed by YHWH (vv. 18-22). It will have an altar at which it will serve and a stele that will be a "sign" and a "witness" (some have seen here an allusion to the Jewish colony of Elephantine in upper Egypt or else to the freedom gained in the Persian period to celebrate the worship of YHWH on Egyptian soil). God will listen to Egypt when it cries for help and will send the savior who will defend and deliver it. The "knowledge" YHWH accused Israel of lacking will be given to Egypt. What is more, from v. 23 on the perspective widens to the point of depicting the reconciliation of the two rivals, Egypt and Assyria, coming to join with Israel. The stunning blessing in 19:25 sounds like a formula of covenant that joins with Israel both Egypt and Assyria. However, among the nations thus convoked Israel remains the "heritage" of YHWH.

The Prophet, Sign and Presage (20:1-6)

The text refers to the year in which Ashdod was taken by Sargon the Second (711). After King Ahaz's death some choose to trust Cush in order to withstand Assyria. At this point Isaiah is commanded to walk about naked in order to give Jerusalem an image of the shameful nudity of the captives; such will be the fate of the two powers on whose help they are relying. The oracle ends on the mention of the despair of Philistia's coastland now deprived of any support against the threat of Assyria (v. 6).

Fall of Babylon and
All Human Glories (21:1–23:18)

Now follow more oracles concerning the powerful nations to the east (the "wilderness of the sea," that is, Babylon, in 21:1-12, then Arabia in 21:13-17) and to the west (Tyre and Sidon in ch. 23). These two series frame ch. 22, devoted to Judah and Jerusalem.

The downfall of Babylon, which opens the section, brings back motifs already present in ch. 13. In a frightening vision Medes and Elamites launch an assault against Babylon, where people are feasting. This last detail does not fit in with what is known of the event in which, in 739, the city was besieged by surprise in the absence of King Nabonidus, who for several years had resided in Tema. A watcher-seer broadcasts the news of the hated city's collapse (v. 9). To Seir (= Edom), which asks him about the time of night, the watcher responds in v. 12 by speaking of a respite (the "morning" with the deliverance by the Persians) that will last but a moment since night will come back. Only a return, that is, a conversion on Edom's part could give rise to the hope of an end to the darkness. Another oracle announces the end, within a year, of Kedar, a nation in the Arabian desert.

Matching these oracles, those of ch. 23 concern the cities along the Phoenician coast. To everyone's stupefaction, the ruin of Tyre, the great commercial city proud of all its riches, is announced (23:1, repeated in 23:14). More powerful than the powerful of this earth, YHWH's arm has been stretched out over the sea (v. 11) as in the days of the Exodus. God has ordered the destruction of the cities of Canaan. An epilogue in prose may be interpreted as a mysterious allusion to Israel's future history. For seventy years (the symbolic duration of the Babylonian domination, corresponding to the length of the exile) Tyre will be forgotten; then God will visit it on the occasion of a change in rule (a circumstance similar to the conduct of Cyrus toward Israel at the end of the exile); Tyre will again prostitute itself without restraint, but its profits will in the end serve the well-being of God's people.

Chapter 22 is set between these oracles concerning the nations; it is devoted to Judah under the strange title of "the oracle concerning the valley of vision." Its fate will not be any different from that reserved for the pagans' pride. The text probably refers to the episode in 701 when Jerusalem was spared at the end of a campaign horribly destructive for the territory of Judah. Isaiah cannot repress his distress (v. 4) at the thought of the rout of Judah (here called by the expression dear to Jeremiah, the "daughter of my people" parallel to the "daughter of Zion") that could do nothing but flee before the Assyrian troops (22:2b-3). The surrounding region having been ravaged and occupied, Jerusalem in its turn is in danger of falling, despite the extensive works that have been undertaken for its protection. After having been miraculously spared by the intervention of YHWH the people will still not know how to turn to God and make peace by acknowledging the sins that have brought the disaster so close to them. Under these conditions the ruin of the people is unavoidable. The episode of Shebna and Eliakim, masters of the royal household under David, is a confirmation of this (vv. 15-25). The first, Shebna, a social climber, an official whose existence is documented outside the OT, a man proud of his weapons and his pro-Assyrian politics (v. 18b), swollen with self-conceit even in death (v. 16), will be stricken by YHWH. The second, on the contrary, Eliakim (meaning "God has established"), is called by God "my servant" and destined to be a "father to the inhabitants of Jerusalem," and he receives the keys of power. Fixed in a solid spot, he will however fall in his turn when, once again, people will place in him their hopes and reliance instead of trusting YHWH. The very same drama is thus replayed in Israel, as well as in pagan lands, every time out of pride, which substitutes human glory and security for confidence in the one who is the sole master of history.

3. Cosmic Judgment and Universal Hope (Isaiah 24–35)

A. Eschatological Oracles, 24:1–27:13

These three chapters from a much later period introduce us to a resolutely eschatological view of events. They speak of both the cosmic judgment that God will pronounce over all the peoples and the salvation God will bring, inviting all to the eschatological banquet on Mount Zion. The question of death reoccurs several times in this section

24:1-23: A first series of oracles describes the cosmic judgment that is going to be passed on humankind that has broken the "everlasting covenant" sealed at the time of Noah (24:5). God disperses "the inhabitants of the earth" (24:6; cf. Genesis 11) and allows the universe to waste away. The "city of chaos" (24:10) is thrown down. The songs of acclamation and joy on the part of the islands orchestrate the ruin of that city, whose identification poses problems. Is it one of the cities of Moab or one of the other cities that, ultimately, will find their symbolic expression in Babylon, the city of evil? Coming from the sea, that is, out of a new exodus, a whole people acclaims God, but the salvation is still only provisional because the mystery of iniquity will produce traitors within this people (v. 16). Hence there is a new era of darkness and cataclysms spoken of in apocalyptic terms. Hence too the pained exclamation of the prophet in vv. 17 and 18. Then, as in the time of the flood—the first great figure of judgment—the sluices of heaven will open, the earth will be torn asunder, and all the false powers in heaven and on earth will be punished and shackled. Only then will God reign on Mount Zion in Jerusalem. Only then will God's glory be manifested in the eyes of the elders of the heavenly court (v. 23).

25:1–26:6: This part is centered around the eschatological feast described in 25:6-10a. God will offer a banquet to the peoples of the earth and will destroy death forever. One recognizes in this description the characteristic traits of a sacrifice of communion, *šelamīm*, because of the foods that are mentioned (fat/oil, strong wine, marrow). But here God will share among humans the fat that is normally reserved for God in this type of sacrifice. Thus death will be vanquished thanks to a communion with divine life, thanks to the sharing in a food that belongs to God.

Two developments, echoing one another, surround this feast (25:1-5 and 25:10b–26:6). They evoke the destruction of the "city of pride." Again the historical identification is difficult: Moab is mentioned in 25:10b, but it may also be Babylon. In any case one must not lose sight of the fact that from now on it is the mystery of history that is meant, beyond references to particular human cities. The promise is that God will make an end of tyrants' pride and will offer a safe place in the "fortified city" built by YHWH in response to the hope of the "poor" (25:4–26:1). The words of 25:5-6 prove that what is meant is spiritual poverty opposed to pride.

26:7-19: This passage, which is in the form of a prayer, contains elements that decisively make of it the continuation of the eschatological banquet of ch. 25. The humble confession of the "poor in spirit," this text first tells of the desire for God and the trust in God's plan of salvation in the midst of the sinful world. It is also the confession of faith welling up in Israel's heart when it acknowledges its failure to fulfill the mission it had been entrusted with (vv. 17-18). But the one speaking is the God of Israel having power over death. With restraint and a certain aura of mystery two verses express two viewpoints on death. Verse 14 reminds us that the dead do not come back to life; it has a polemical allusion since it uses the word *rephāʾim* which designates the spirits of the ancestors supposed to be—according to old Canaanite beliefs—active after death. Verse 19 on the contrary declares that the dead of YHWH will live again. Of course salvation first bears on the end of sin, but if we perceive the extreme implications of the covenant it also includes the end of death. The mysterious locution "dew of light" echoes Hosea's words in 14:5, in which God says, "I will be like the dew for Israel." God is going to model bodies as in Genesis 2, but this time the dew from heaven will be mixed with the dust. The true *rephāʾim* will be those whom the power of YHWH will have raised.

26:20–27:13: These last verses return to the theme of the wrath of the last days and the slaughtering of Leviathan, the ancient serpent that is an incarnation of evil. We remember that 24:22 mentioned an imprisonment of the powers of evil subjugated by God and their definitive defeat "after many days." Therefore there are delays. In the meantime God will give refuge to the people (26:20; cf. Exod 12:22-27). Israel, the vineyard, formerly punished (Isa 5:1-10), will become again a choice vineyard. This section ends with the announcement of the reunion in Zion of the children of Israel, brought back from the lands of exile, "gathered one by one" by the divine solicitude. However, vv. 10 and 11 insert into this announcement of salvation the vision of the "fortified city . . . like the wilderness." There is here the reminder that the dry branches and the city offering a deceptive refuge will pass through fire. This could be an allusion to Jerusalem falling back into its perversions after the return from the exile.

B. The Twofold Mystery of the Hardening of Hearts and God's Plan, 28:1–29:14

Indeed, the continuation of the text is a clear description of the resistance met by the revelation of the plan of salvation God is preparing. Thus the motif of the hardening of hearts recurs in force (28:7-13 and 29:9-11). In the beginning of ch. 28 oracles dating from Ahaz's time (the Syro-Ephraimite war) are the background of this meditation. The fate of Ephraim, who is going to fall like a fig, is first described and contrasted with that of the "remnant": the "proud garland of the drunkards of Ephraim" (28:1, 3) will be trampled under foot, but YHWH will be a "garland of glory" (28:5) for the survivors of the people, with whom God will share the divine spirit (28:6). From then on the spirit will become the possession of the entire people.

Verses 7-13, with their image of Judah staggering like a drunkard, describe the implementation of the mission of the hardening of hearts already announced in 6:9-13, because "they would not hear" (28:12). Therefore God will speak in an incomprehensible language.

What follows sheds light on the "work" God will do (28:21), a deed "strange" and "alien" according to a "plan" exhibiting the same wisdom as that of the farmer who acts in an orderly manner until the harvest (28:23-29): plowing and threshing are only steps. Likewise God unfolds a plan in history for preparing the harvest; thus God will send a destructive scourge over those who trust in lies and have made a pact with death (28:15, perhaps an allusion to child sacrifices reintroduced under Ahaz and Manasseh in the valley of Gehenna). But God will not crush the good grain. Moreover, God will place in Zion a "stone" that is both foundation stone and standard of the righteousness and justice (28:17) that will reign in this new building.

In 29:1-8, an oracle certainly connected with the events of 701 recurs and is used to stress anew the work of the judgment of YHWH on Jerusalem: condemning its unfaithfulness, God abandons it to the enemies that encircle it. The city is here called by the symbolic name "Ariel," which means "lion of God"; it is painted in its initial state, pre-Israelite, such as it was when David encamped against it to seize it. But the same YHWH promises that Ariel's enemies will be annihilated as a nightmare vanishes. It remains that for the present hearts are hardened and prevented from hearing Isaiah's words (29:9-11). The message is sealed without recourse. Verse 13 brings a complement to the diagnosis of the hypocrisy of the heart previously made: one honors God with words but carefully stops at the threshold of faith ("their hearts are far from me"). According to the paradoxical logic of the hardening of hearts God will continue to be manifested through signs that are so many enigmas for human wisdom (29:14).

C. Unveiling of God's Plan, 29:15–31:9

29:15–30:17: The deceitful inversions of mendacious people (29:15) will be turned around by the paradoxical work of God who will produce still greater inversions. Indeed, the text foretells the end of the hardening (29:18, 24: the deaf hear, the blind see, the erring become wise; the whole process is expressed by the images of Lebanon, orchard, and forest). In passing v. 23 mentions in a rather mysterious way new children being born to Jacob from the very self of God (we shall find this idea again in Deutero-Isaiah and the texts of chs. 56–66).

Chapter 30 opens with new oracles again denouncing futile alliances with Egypt, a "people that cannot profit them" (30:5). At this point Isaiah receives the order to write in a book words that will remain as a witness to the divine word rejected by a rebellious people. A deeper level of the thoughts of the hearts is uncovered: in order not to have to be converted to trust in God and the righteousness God demands, the people requests, "Do not prophesy to us what is right . . ." (30:10-11). This deliberate choice of untruth will be paid for by a headlong flight before the enemy until only a lone flagstaff is left on the hill of Zion (30:17).

In strong contrast to the above, the following section (30:18-26) centers on the announcement that God will forgive those who will place their hope in God and that their hearts will be changed. Then, in a quasi-rhapsodical mode, the prior motifs recur: prediction of God's wrath, which will harry the nations and chastise Assyria (30:27-33); warning against the false security given by the Egyptian alliance (31:1-3). God will come to Mount Zion to rout Assyria and save Jerusalem.

D. Establishment of God's Eschatological Reign in Zion, 32:1–35:10

Chapter 32 introduces the figure of a righteous king, a noble ruler, a refuge for the people (curiously, the text repeats what was said of God in 25:4). The ruler is also associated with the end of the hardening (vv. 3-7). But between now and then, "in little more than a year," indifferent and unfaithful Jerusalem will have been destroyed (32:9-14). Then the time of the great reversals previously promised will arrive (32:15 parallel to 29:17) when the spirit will be poured out (32:15).

Chapter 33 opens by saying that the destroyer will be destroyed. But a voice now is raised saying, "we wait for you" (v. 2) and proclaiming God exalted in the city in which at last reign righteousness, justice, faith, wisdom, fear, and knowledge of God (vv. 5-6). Then the divine voice is heard, "Now I will arise. . . . Now I will lift myself up" (v. 10). God will no longer tolerate the enfeeblement of the earth caused by the breaking of the covenant (vv. 7-8). In Zion even sinners are in anguish. Who will survive? The answer is in the portrait of the righteous person who follows the way of YHWH (v. 15). Then follows an invitation to contemplate what is not yet called the great "newness" but already opens onto the mystery of salvation into which Deutero-Isaiah will probe. The proud having been humbled, people will contemplate "the king in his beauty" and Jerusalem in peaceful safety, "a land that stretches far away" (v. 17), but altogether different from the proud commercial powers that are known to all (v. 21). YHWH shines there, being called "king," "judge," "lawgiver," and "savior." Thus a chain is formed linking the king of 32:1 and 32:3, that of 33:17, and the figure of YHWH who here reign over a people "forgiven their iniquity" (v. 24b). Discreet and mysterious brush strokes are in the process of painting an unexpected figure of the Messiah.

Last comes the section 34:1–35:10, which pertains to the post-exilic period. In the form of a diptych the final fate of Edom, here become the symbol of evil, and that of the holy people gathered in Zion by God at the end of time are described in contrast to one another. After having punished the heavenly armies and the nations God's anger falls upon Edom, the people of the false brothers of Bozrah, descended from Esau (see Num 20:14-21, where Edom refuses to allow Israel to pass through their land during their march to the Promised Land). The divine punishment is frightful: as an antithesis to the life-giving sacrifice of 25:6-8 God describes a hecatomb of peoples (34:6-7). A figure of hell is given here: eternal fire (cf. Sodom and Gomorrah), chaos, solitude, dispersion, empty fortresses haunted by demons and birds of prey (see in vv. 16-17 the strange development on the buzzards whose work is written in God's book).

But the punishment of hell is only the other side of the salvation brought by Zion's defender. Already looking to Deutero-Isaiah, ch. 35 is an invitation to exultation because of the eternal happiness of the redeemed (that is, those liberated from slavery), a people born of the new exodus. For water will spring forth in the desert, the hardening of hearts will come to an end, God in person will come to save (v. 4b). Similar to the sacred way of the temple of Marduk in Babylon, adorned with lions and dragons, but in contrast to it, a "Holy Way" will be open to the holy people headed for Zion (v. 8). The passages of the NT speaking of Jesus as the "way" will echo these solemn verses.

4. Rereading of History: Punishment of the Pride of Assyria, Salvation of Jerusalem and Hezekiah (Isaiah 36–39)

These four chapters are composed of fragments from 2 Kings (chs. 8–20) and 2 Chronicles (ch. 32) inserted at the time of the exile. They are the rereading, two centuries after the actual events, of stories concerning King Hezekiah and the prophet Isaiah. These chapters record how, as Sennacherib was campaigning and seizing the fortified cities of Judah, he twice defied King Hezekiah (36:1-20; 37:9b-13) and through him the God of Israel. The scene is set at the exact place where Isaiah had already spoken to Ahaz at the time of the Syro-Ephraimite war (cf. 36:2b and 7:3). The Assyrian king's cupbearer contests the reliance of Hezekiah on his alliance with Egypt (vv. 4-6). Worse, he derides the faith the king places in the power of YHWH, alluding to the reform by which Hezekiah had suppressed all local shrines. Using the language already found in the prophet's mouth, the foreigner even dares to claim that he is acting on the orders of the God of Israel. Then, addressing the people, he seeks to have them turn away from their king by perfidiously appropriating the speech of the God and King of the covenant (vv. 16-17). Hezekiah goes into mourning and turns to God (37:1); he goes to the Temple and consults Isaiah. God, through Isaiah, urges the "servants of King Hezekiah" not to lose confidence when hearing the blasphemies of the "servants of the king of Assyria." The sending of a mysterious "spirit'" is announced as well as a twofold punishment (retreat and death of the king of Assyria).

A second time Sennacherib defies Hezekiah by means of a letter in which he states that when faced with the king of Assyria national gods are powerless, and YHWH among them (37:10-13). Going up to the Temple, Hezekiah responds with a prayer that demonstrates his genuine faith: his entreaty is that the glory of the One who is the sole ruler of nations be manifested in the eyes of all (37:16-20). God answers through Isaiah by uttering against Assyria an oracle couched in the terms of a subtle dialectic of enslavement: the one who subjugated the earth and whose pride has insulted the Holy One of Israel will find himself with a ring in his nostril, enslaved in his turn (37:22-29). Jerusalem will be saved and YHWH will show faithfulness to David. Verses 36-39 report the realization of the verdict in the immediate future. Sennacherib will lift the siege of Jerusalem, and later he will be assassinated by his sons.

Chapters 38 and 39 return to the drama: King Hezekiah is stricken with a deadly disease. Through Isaiah as intermediary the "God of David" promises to grant a reprieve to Hezekiah and gives him a sign. Hezekiah's canticle that follows (38:9-20) attests to the faith of the king who knows how to give thanks for the work of God who can bring back from death, who heals, and who remits sin. The divine cure granted to Hezekiah clearly appears in continuity with the sign of the child to be born (ch. 7) and as a guarantee of the future of the Davidic dynasty. But the king asks for another sign, showing thereby the limits of his faith (v. 22 mentioning the ascent of the king to the Temple finds a more explicit interpretation in the account of 2 Kings where the very possibility of going up to the Temple is part of God's promise to Hezekiah: see 2 Kings 20:5). The rest of the story confirms the ambiguity of the king's character. Receiving a foreign embassy, he displays his riches in order to secure a merely human alliance (39:1-4), and he is incapable of looking further than his own death (39:8). Isaiah prophesies that everything on which he based his security will cave in.

The notion that takes form here is that already with Hezekiah the exile appears ineluctable. A profound solidarity connects all these events throughout the centuries, for the logic inherent in them is spiritual in nature, and spiritual problems stretch across the spans of successive reigns and individual lives. Thus this last part of First Isaiah is far from being an accessory appendix; rather it is a final meditation on the contents of this first part of the book that, at the same time, directs readers toward the times to come. These times will bring new trials but also the glimmer of the promise that "from Jerusalem a remnant shall go out, and from Mount Zion a band of survivors" according to the prophecy received by Hezekiah in 37:32. At the time of the exile the memories of the eighth century, testifying to Hezekiah's cure from a deadly disease and Jerusalem's escape from the Assyrian danger, will have the function of inviting people to believe that God can still wrest from the claws of death.

II. Deutero-Isaiah (Sixth Century and Later Additions): Isaiah 40–55

Theological Structure of the Text

1. Isaiah 40–46: Suit of God against the nations and announcement of God's "justice" that is coming.
2. Isaiah 47–48: Word of God to fallen Babylon and to Israel. God declares that a new phase of the history of salvation is opening.

3. Isaiah 49–55: The salvation, whose mediator the Servant is, brings restoration to Zion. God creates a new people in Zion.

1. Suit of God Against the Nations and Announcement of God's Justice That is Coming (Isaiah 40–46)

A. Consolation of Israel; the Sovereign "Justice" of God Will be Manifested in the Person God has Sent, Isaiah 40–41

i. By Any Chance was God Unjust Toward Israel? (Isaiah 40)

Deutero-Isaiah opens with a mysterious display of utterances in 40:1-11. Someone whose identity is not specified declares that God wants to console the people, whose term has been served. Israel has been engaged in a travail that is now coming to an end (vv. 1-2). The voice commands, "Speak tenderly to Jerusalem," thus (in biblical language) announcing an appeal not only to the feelings but to the intelligence and will of the hearers. Then, in vv. 3-5, an equally anonymous voice entrusts to a collectivity the mission of lowering the mountains (cf. the mountains of pride of First Isaiah) in order to open the road of humility on which YHWH will walk. This is a very mysterious text because we know from what has been said before that bringing pride down is a superhuman work needing forces beyond those of the mere good will of humans. Who then is going to be in charge of this undertaking? In v. 6 the voice addresses the prophet, enjoining upon him the task of reminding people of the steadfastness of the word of the Lord who is coming (v. 8). This coming is that of the Almighty (v. 10) who, however, is presented as a shepherd full of attentiveness and tenderness (v. 11).

Anticipating the divine answer to the accusations Israel makes against YHWH in v. 27, Isaiah invites the people to meditate on the wisdom-filled power that God displays in creation and also in history. Magnificent images depict God's sovereignty and "justice." This last word will often recur in what follows. It is a major element of the lengthy "lawsuit" that is in progress in Deutero-Isaiah. On the one hand the "justice" of God totally exceeds that of humans and can only be, in them, a gift of God; but on the other hand this divine "justice" seems constantly belied by the reality of evil, the violence that reigns in the world, and above all by the suffering of the innocent. God is therefore put in the position of presenting a defense, first before Israel, which is saying "my right is disregarded by my God" (v. 27). God must clearly prove the divine "justice." However, the prophet reminds Israel that it should have known (vv. 21 and 28a revolve around the expressions "not know," "not understand"). Verses 28b-31 conclude by saying that not only does God not tire of laboring for humankind, but those who hope in God receive in their turn the gift of swiftly and tirelessly running on their way.

ii. Trial of God Before the Nations

The word of God is addressed successively to the nations (41:1-7), to Israel (41:8-20), and again to the nations (41:21-29). The nations are invited to be present at the trial that God is initiating and to present their witnesses. In fact, symbolized by the "coastlands" (image of the farthest abode of humanity), they have no more consistency and credibility than the idols they serve. God alone is the master of history, summoning from the east an invader who causes the ends of the earth to tremble (41:5). This is an allusion to Cyrus who conquered Lydia and advanced as far as the Ionian islands in 546. But he is not named in either 41:2-3 or 41:25. No one among the nations had foreseen the rise of this dispenser of justice armed by God's own hand; in Israel, however, he had been announced long since. Faced with him, the coastlands are seized with fear and take refuge in the making of their idols.

By contrast, Israel is called to recognize the deliverance that is coming. Verses 8-20 describe at length the personal bond of tenderness binding God and God's servant Israel: chosen, it cannot be rejected; it is grasped by the powerful hand of God and therefore must not be afraid (the word is used three times). YHWH is its redeemer (v. 14c; the word alludes to the condition of spiritual bondage from which Israel must be redeemed. Probably the word also alludes—in this text where Israel is identified with a feminine figure—to the betrothal of the daughter of Zion to God according to the practice of the levirate). The innocent suffering of the needy and poor is the object of vv. 17-20; for them God will work the miracle of the water that quenches every thirst.

B. God Ceases to be Silent: God's Servant-Response; God Opens the Witnesses' Mouths, 42:1–43:15

i. God Ceases to be Silent (42:1-17)

At the beginning of ch. 42 God introduces the "Servant" (vv. 1-7). This text, in fact made up of two oracles, is the first presentation in Deutero-Isaiah of the figure of the Servant. He has been chosen, kept in reserve, and "called in righteousness." He is the bearer of the spirit and will "bring forth justice" in a way that is in strong contrast with the figure of the conqueror shown in the preceding chapter: his word will not exert any violence. He will be, for Israel and the nations, the one who cures the blind and liberates the captives. In vv. 8 and 9 God comments on this great new thing, the first one, which prepares other things. Verses 10-12 enhance this prophecy by a song of praise, stamped with newness also since it joins together Israel and the islands in one and the same acclamation. This "going forth" of God out of God's eternal mystery (v. 14) is in fact a painful birthing that will entail both judgment and deliverance. The figure of the Exodus is suggested by the march of the blind healed and led by God.

ii. But God Will Also Cause the Witnesses to End Their Silence (42:18–43:15)

In contrast to the Servant just described, the people are shown as blind and deaf. They are also a people deported and humiliated (42:22) whose sight can only cause the nations to blaspheme the name of God. What a strange and paradoxical "witness" God selects by choosing them! One understands why in this suit used by Deutero-Isaiah as a setting God has to speak in person to present a defense. However, God is not reluctant to bring "witnesses" forward (the word "witness" recurs three times, in 43:9, 10, and 12). Besides, a beginning of the confession of sin is formulated in 42:24, an incipient conversion. The oracle that opens ch. 43 foretells in its turn the "redemption" of Israel/Jacob by none other than God; images from the time of the Exodus appear: the water that does not submerge and the fire that does not consume (an echo of Isa 1:25 in which YHWH announces purification through the crucible of adversity). The "ransom" of Israel, the people of "sons" and "daughters," will be paid by Egypt, as is suggested in 43:3. This is a prophetic allusion to the way Egypt will be conquered, not by Cyrus but by Cambyses in 529. Finally, the Servant receives the order to "bring forth" this servant-people (43:8), blind and deaf although they have eyes and ears. It is another mysterious "going forth" after those of the Servant in 42:1b and of God in 42:13. Afterward, the fall of Babylon is announced in 43:14.

C. The Good Exercise of Memory; Salvation and Ruin, 43:16–44:23

This section repeats the preceding themes (do not fear; Israel as witness; God is sovereign whereas idols are nothing; Israel redeemed by YHWH), but the motif of "remembrance" is introduced through a subtle dialectic. On the one hand God asks that one "not remember" (43:18) the misfortunes of yesterday because a new thing already is "springing forth" (43:19). This last phrase echoes the oracle in 4:2 where a messianic figure is evoked by the mention of the "branch of YHWH" that will "be beautiful and glorious" for Israel. On the other hand this whole passage is an invitation to remember: let the people of Israel remember that they did not labor for God, but God labored for them; that they were not enslaved by God, but by a strange reversal they did enslave God; that beginning with their first ancestor, Jacob, they have lived in sin and rebellion. But the appeal to memory concerns also the time of the Exodus which becomes the key reference needed to decipher what God is about to do: open a road through the desert—in order to bring the people back from a captivity that is clearly more radical than those from Egypt and Babylon—pour the water, the spirit, that will change their hearts (see 43:20 and 44:3, echoing 41:17-19). Thus is revealed the mystery of salvation hidden in God "from eternity" (44:7) and shared with Israel, the elect and the beloved. In opposition to this stands the blindness of those who pitiably trust the idols they make with their own hands. The amplitude of the development of this last theme (44:9-20) is an important part of the argument for the defense in favor of God against Israel. One senses how powerful the temptation to idolatry must have been in Israel at the time of the exile to Babylon. In fact it is a counter-figure of salvation that is presented in these "ash-eaters" who will never consent to acknowledge their blindness (44:20).

D. God's Concern for the People Triggers the Action of God's Servant, Cyrus, 44:24–46:13

The speech for the defense continues with a series of statements regarding the work God is engaged in. The discourse is punctuated by the repeated affirmation "I am the LORD, and there is no other" (45:5, 7, 14, 18, 22; 46:9). The initial focus of the argumentation is on Cyrus and the unexpected and providential mission entrusted to this idolatrous foreigner. Although he does not even know God (45:4, 5) he is established as the "anointed" (45:1) destined to save Israel, for it is a true investiture of this most paradoxical servant that we witness in 45:1-6, a passage where the expressions found in the first oracle of the Servant (42:6) are used again. This plan of God is indeed a mystery profound enough to disconcert the sages, but we are forcefully reminded that God is the creator, the master of all things, the source of light and darkness, of peace and woe (45: 7), equally capable of drying up the ocean and making Cyrus the "shepherd" who will obey God's orders (44:27-28). The text of 45:9-11 is a direct answer to Israel's wonderment because the people is forgetting that the creator's thoughts are deeper than the creatures'. Verse 11 suggests a birthing and a labor of God in the world surpassing human thoughts, like the newness already mentioned several times previously.

From 45:14 to the end of ch. 46 the theme of the judgment of the nations recurs. Israel's foes are about to be confounded and they will confess that YHWH is without equal and the only savior (45:15). The vocabulary is that of war (45:14b), but the context makes it clear that the conflict is a spiritual one: what is meant is not that peoples should be made subject to another people, but that lying and idolatry should be reduced to servitude to the truth of the unique sovereignty of God. For it is salvation that is in question here (as shown by the insistence on the theme in 45:15, 17, 20, 21, 22; 46:2, 7, 13). Who in truth is the savior? the idols? or YHWH? The answer is given in the grand vision of the rout of the false gods Bel (that is, Baal) and Nebo, son of Bel, whose idols are loaded on beasts of burden. This is a prodigious reversal: the gods, supposed to carry their people, are reduced to being pathetic pieces of luggage heavy on the shoulders (46:1, 2). Again, by another reversal, the God of Israel carries the people like a mother (46:3, 4) and grants them an imminent salvation, represented by the recurrence of Cyrus's figure, a raptor obeying the orders of YHWH (46:11). We must note the important place given from now on to the maternal images of God. Already in 42:14 the image of the woman in labor was found, curiously joined with the image of the warrior shouting the war cry. In 44:2, 24, Israel was said to have been formed by God "in the womb." The very same terms occur in 46:3 to depict the bond that ties Israel and YHWH. It is therefore a bond identical with that existing between mother and child, within a context that, besides, speaks of a new, paradoxical work of generation in which Israel, enfeebled by the exile, will be given a numerous and unexpected progeny.

2. Announcement of a New Phase in the History of Salvation (Isaiah 47–48)

These two chapters mark a turning point in Deutero-Isaiah: the end of the Babylonian exile (48:20) and the time of the newness at hand (48:6b) are intimated. Chapter 47 is an utterance addressed to Babylon, depicted as a female figure. The God of Israel announces to it its ruin and the humiliation of its pride. Instrument of the punishment inflicted on unfaithful Israel, the Babylonian power has in its pride taken advantage of the mission entrusted to it (see "I am, and there is no one besides me" repeated twice in 47:8 and 10). It is true that in 539 B.C.E. Babylon was taken without being harmed, but the oracle declares that one day it will be set aflame. Neither recourse to sorcery nor the wisdom of its sages of whom it is so proud (v. 10) will be able to save it. It will find itself widowed and childless (47:9). Chapter 48, in turn, is an utterance addressed to the house of Israel, which God reminds of the strategy observed up to then: the advanced revelation of events that was meant to enable Israel to discern between the idols and the One who can truthfully say "I am He" (48:12), because God is the "I am" (48:17). "From this time forward" (48:6) God creates an absolute newness that vv. 20 and 21 suggest by using the prophetic past tense: Israel is redeemed by a new exodus in which God cleaves the rock from which waters spring up, the symbol of the spirit, God's vital power. Judaism will see in the rock a figure of the Messiah, and Paul will identify Jesus with the "spiritual rock" that Exodus 17 mentioned in figure

(1 Cor 10:4). Finally, who is designated as bearer of the spirit in 48:16c? Zerubbabel, who led back a caravan of exiles sometime between 538 and 522? the people itself? or the "Servant" about whom much will be said in what follows?

3. Three Oracles About the Servant; Three Oracles About Zion (Isaiah 49–55)

This new part furthers the announcement of the great newness we have just read about. Its characteristics distinguish it from what precedes: we do not find here either any explicit mention of Cyrus or the long polemic tirades against idols, but the figure of Zion clothed in righteousness and holiness, a trait totally unheard of up to now, is spoken of with increasing insistence. In the text sections focusing on the male figure of the Servant alternate with sections focusing on the female figure of Zion, according to the following plan:

—49:1-13, Servant (second oracle)
—49:14–50:3, Zion
—50:4-11, Servant (third oracle)
—51:17–52:2, Zion
—52:13–53:12, Servant (fourth oracle)
—54, Zion

The oracles concerning the Servant in particular challenge interpreters with numerous and difficult problems. In 49:1-8 the Servant first speaks in his own name, then God presents him. The Servant begins by addressing the "coastlands"; he appears as predestined by God from his mother's womb in order to accomplish God's plan (vv. 1-3). Without a doubt he reminds us of the prophets (Jeremiah, for instance); however, what is said about him goes farther than what is ordinarily said about prophets. His words are like a "sharp sword" (v. 2), which brings to mind the shoot from the root of Jesse exercising a function of judgment. Hidden in the shadow of the divine hand, he is reserved for the hour God has chosen to put God's plan into effect (this is confirmed by v. 8). Strangely, this elect one whom God glorifies (v. 5) gives vent to his weariness and discouragement, like a laborer who has worked in vain. Even more strangely, he is shown as a suffering and humiliated being; he is a righteous person whose righteousness is not recognized, except by God. Verse 7 poses formidable problems of interpretation. In particular, what is this "nation," specified by the word *(goy)* that is customarily reserved for the Gentiles, and in a most unusual way is written in the singular (though consistently translated as plural in English)? Is it possible that this term designates the people of Israel, who in the presence of the Servant are in a position similar to that of Gentiles, the latter being in their turn represented by the "rulers" or "tyrants" in the same verse? One thing that is certain is that in God's presentation of the Servant two expressions are borrowed from the first oracle in ch. 42, "light to the nations" and "covenant to the people" (49:6, 8).

Can we identify this mysterious figure more precisely? The locution "my servant Israel" (v. 3) leads us to see in him an incarnation of the people (corporate personality). However, this same person receives the mandate to bring back Jacob and gather Israel, which makes it difficult to sustain the collective interpretation. Moreover, it is difficult to see to what historical person of the past the text might allude: no one ever addressed the coastlands, even at the time of the return from the exile. All these questions must be kept in mind as we progress in the text to the next oracles about the Servant.

Isaiah 49:9-13 contains an oracle concerning the new exodus connected with the Servant: God will lead those gathered from the different directions by watching over their lives and opening a road that, again, will level the mountains.

The next section (49:14–50:3) concerns Zion. In a way reminiscent of the words of the Servant in ch. 49, Zion expresses fear of being abandoned by God (v. 14). This is answered by momentous words of consolation in which God, like a mother, proclaims indefectible divine faithfulness to God's child, Israel. Verse 18 continues, now with the image of Zion as a bride and a mother, gifted with an unexpected progeny, receiving foster fathers and nurses through new ties with the nations. Zion is here the reverse of Babylon that, in ch. 47, was described as widowed and childless. The text underlines the mystery of this fecundity that gives Zion sons and daughters about whom it inquires, "Who has borne me these?" (v. 21). The mention of the signal in v. 22 shows that the oracle is not independent of the meditation in ch. 11. Last, 49:24–50:3 can be read as a commentary inspired by this magnificent vision of Zion's fecundity. God will overcome the adversaries (49:21-26) and forgive the unfaithful wife put away for a while. This is a gesture of power to which the unbelievers are wrong to object: the miracles of the Exodus are the language in which God's sovereignty is proclaimed anew (50:2b-3).

The recurrence of certain themes (the Servant's spontaneous listening in 50:4; invitations to listening in 50:10; 51:1, 4, 7; the wearing out of creation in contrast with the eternal stability of God's salvation and justice) enable us to delineate a new section (50:4–51:8). This opens with an oracle concerning the Servant, who begins to speak. He declares himself a disciple of the Lord God from whom he receives the words to sustain the weary, as described in 50:10. The Servant is shown as a man full of confidence (in contrast with the rebellious ones denounced in preceding oracles), and yet he is persecuted, insulted, tried; it is in this situation that he declares that YHWH comes to his aid. Again he is a mysterious figure who reminds us of the one in ch. 49. Verse 10, where an anonymous voice (the prophet's?) urges people to listen to God's Servant, prevents us from identifying the latter simply with the writer of Deutero-Isaiah. The invitation to listen is multiplied in the beginning of ch. 51 with its successive exhortations. It is noteworthy that the heretofore frequent mention of Jacob/Israel is absent; from now on spiritual categories are used: those who "pursue righteousness" (51:1), those who "know righteousness" (51:7), the "people who have my teaching in their hearts" (51:7). This people is urged to remember the faith of Abraham and Sarah from whom they are descendants, all of them cut from the same quarry. They also are invited to recognize God's justice which is eternal, whereas the heavens, the earth, and its inhabitants are destined, like the Servant's enemies (50:8-9), to wear out and end up in tatters like a garment.

The following section (51:9–52:12) is characterized by calls for the awakening of the "arm of YHWH," and then the awakening of Jerusalem. This section is symmetrically structured around a central part (51:17–52:2) which is a poem of Zion. The arm of YHWH is first entreated to renew the prodigies of the Exodus, but the events of the thirteenth century now acquire a new and infinitely ampler stature. The vocabulary of creation (the verb "cut in pieces," the noun "abyss," and so on), the mention of the forces of evil designated by the mythological figures of Rahab and the dragon, transpose the old memories of the past to the realm of all-encompassing history. The question now is to speak of God's great salvific act that, in history, will conquer the powers of evil, of which humanity is both the accomplice and the victim. This text, which recalls the beginnings in order to announce the liberation, seems in v. 16 to return to the Servant (cf. 50:4 and 49:2) while adding this new detail that his being placed in reserve is contemporary with the creation (this is a key text for the Jewish tradition of the preexistent Messiah).

Verses 51:17 and following incite Jerusalem to wake up. It has drunk the cup of the divine wrath that devastated it and struck all its children, but YHWH remains its lord and defender. From now on named "holy city," Jerusalem receives from God the promise of victory since the uncircumcised and the unclean will no longer enter it (52:1). The captivity only served to have God's Name blasphemed among the nations by giving them the spectacle of a humiliated people whose sole testimony seemed to be to God's powerlessness (52:5). But now, God announces, "my people shall know my name," and therefore will be redeemed. The text of 52:7-10 confirms God's return to Zion (v. 8), announced by the messenger of peace who is, in the strict sense, bearer of the "gospel," that is, the good news of victory. From the historical point of view v. 11 alludes to the restitution of the sacred vessels to the Temple of Jerusalem after the decree of Cyrus in 538 B.C.E. This new exodus confirms in the eyes of all the salvation the people receives from God. At this new exodus people will come out with their heads high (52:12), as the Elohist tradition reports the coming out of Egypt, and not in haste, as the Yahwist tradition of the Passover has it.

The fourth oracle of the Servant, which follows (52:13–53:12), is a key text of Deutero-Isaiah. It is complex in both its structure and its language. The latter has provoked many debates, demonstrating the importance of what is at stake theologically when it comes to this figure of the Servant. A narrative part, introduced by a "we" given without any further explanation, runs from 53:1 to 11b. It is framed by two declarations made by an anonymous voice—manifestly God's—that comments on what happens to the Servant.

The first of these two statements announces in advance the denouement of the narrative that follows. The Servant will succeed ("prosper," "be exalted and lifted up") at the end of a strenuous travail that, as the two previous songs (49:1-9 and 50:4-9) had already hinted, was to be the Servant's own task. Against all expectations the Servant will be glorified after having been disfigured beyond all human appearance. He will be recognized by multitudes. It will be an unheard-of event. However, nothing has yet been said about what actually happened to the Servant.

The account of these happenings (53:1-10) opens with the expression of the astonishment and bewilderment provoked by the Servant's destiny. Then comes the recounting of the events intimated in the first oracle and interrupted here by a commentary-confession. Called a "shoot" or "young plant" (cf. 11:1, 10), the Servant is represented in the narrative part as a man of suffering from whom people avert their gaze (53:2-3). Then he is described as humiliated, arrested, subjected to an unjust judgment to which he submits like a lamb led to the slaughter. Through all these trials he remains silent. He accepts without revolt the fate that is dealt him and that leads him to death (vv. 7-9). These are the events that vv. 4-6 and 10-11 comment on. Who speaks here by saying "we"? The pagan kings or peoples previously mentioned? Israel taken as a collectivity? perhaps both, joining their voices, as the "all we" of 53:6 could suggest? Be this as it may, this voice speaks in the tone of a meditation trying to decipher the paradoxical history of the Servant. Thus we learn that the despised and condemned man was manifesting not his own sin but that of those who prosecuted him, for YHWH has made him the victim of his torturers' crimes, but he did not rebel. After having been mistaken on his account, believing that he was punished by God, those who witness his suffering see their own sin in the affliction that befalls the "just": "he was wounded (a variant reads 'he was treated like an evildoer') for our transgressions, crushed for our iniquities" (53:5).

In a still more astonishing way the vision of sin heaped on the Servant becomes, for those who look on him, the vision of their healing and justification, "upon him was the punishment that made us whole, and by his bruises we are healed" (v. 5). In the last analysis the text speaks of a twofold rehabilitation, that of a condemned person and that of those who condemned him.

Verse 10, which is the object of much debate, adds to the mystery: the text seems to affirm that it is God in person who has willed this suffering of the Servant ("it was the will of the LORD to crush him with pain"); it is God's plan that is fulfilled in him. At the same time the Servant is not deprived of all initiative. It is he who humbles himself (v. 7), who offers his life to atone for sin according to a possible reading of v. 10, who takes upon himself the sin of evildoers (v. 11), who "poured himself out to death" and "made intercession for the transgressors" (v. 12). Therefore he is described both as included in a divine plan and as a voluntary actor in this plan. Through his suffering, accepted and consented to, he accomplishes a mysterious "work" in and for humankind. Besides, the vocabulary of sacrifice is used in v. 10, "an offering for sin" (*ʾāšām* in Hebrew). Again the passage is much discussed, some interpreters reading that it is God who makes a sacrifice of the Servant's life while for others it is the Servant himself who makes this sacrifice. Finally, looking to the future the text announces that this same Servant "will see his offspring, and shall prolong his days." Although we do not have here the technical terminology of the resurrection (which will appear only in later writings), this verse suggests a raising up of the Servant beyond death.

This interpretation, which may be deemed to overstep what the text explicitly says, agrees nevertheless with the commentary that calls what happens to the Servant "unheard of," for the condemnation to death of an innocent person cannot be called an unheard-of fact but the restoration of that person beyond death is rightly commented in reference to the "arm of YHWH" (53:1). This expression of divine power was associated by Isaiah in 51:9-10 with the work of creation ("Was it not you who cut Rahab in pieces, who pierced the dragon?") and that of the Exodus ("Was it not you who dried up the sea, the waters of the great deep, who made the depths of the sea a way?").

Finally, this part of the oracle ends with the affirmation that the Servant "shall see" and "shall find satisfaction through his knowledge"; the motif of "knowledge" in v. 11 is also an object of debate. Perhaps it is an echo of a previous text of Isaiah, where an oracle in 11:9 prophesies that "the earth will be full of the knowledge of the LORD as the waters cover the sea."

The conclusion (vv. 11b-12) summarizes again the Servant's life "numbered with the transgressors; yet he bore the sin of many." The same voice that spoke in the beginning utters words of victory and triumph and proclaims the fecundity of the trial undergone by the one whom it again calls "my Servant" (v. 11).

It remains for us to attempt an identification of the mysterious figure of the intercessor that this fourth oracle sketches. Although details concerning his history are accumulated throughout the text we are unable to penetrate his anonymity or solve the questions it entails. Does the text speak of one and the same person or of several in succession? Is the Servant to be understood as an individual or as a collectivity? The biblical tradition is familiar with the notion of "collective personality" whereby an individual symbolizes and represents the whole of the collectivity. We saw that the expression "my servant Israel" in 49:3 would support this hypothesis; similarly, the parallelism between the designations of "my servant" and "my witnesses" in 43:10. But other verses have an eminently personal quality that precludes the unconditional adoption of the preceding interpretation. Finally, one can ask whether any historical figure corresponds to the description of the Servant. Sometimes Zerubbabel is selected; he was a prince from David's line who in the second half of the fourth century B.C.E. began the rebuilding of the Temple. Another person named is Josiah, who tragically perished at Meggido in 609; he reminds us of certain traits of the Servant. In any case there is something in this text that, exceeding our efforts at interpretation, carries it forward and gives it a prophetic dimension. These verses have an explicit relation with the "unheard-of" deed announced from the beginning of Deutero-Isaiah. Everything in the redaction of this text suggests that the redactors themselves describe a person who is far beyond what they can know of him and are the first to be faced with this enigma. This passage from Isaiah remains difficult (as proved by the variants in the manuscripts) and fundamental—difficult perhaps *because* fundamental.

One can ascribe these multiple interpretations to the difficulties of the language. One can also think that the enigmatic character of the figure on whom the prophet focuses is at the root of the additions and rewritings of a text that was certainly much pondered before being definitively fixed. These verses, which are one of the summits of this book, are, as such, deeply implicated in the Judeo-Christian controversy. On the Jewish side their scope and career tended to be limited. However, the oracle was the object of rereadings with a collective bent in which the Servant's tribulations were seen as a figure of the trials lived by Israel in exile among the nations. As a corollary of this the sufferings of righteous persons were believed to have a salutary role for the community. The Middle Ages (with Rashi and Ibn Ezra) will even interpret this text as speaking of Israel: like the Servant, Israel is the righteous people created by God in order to carry the sin of the world and allow it to continue in existence. On the Christian side the same oracle is found, from the beginning, at the center of the confession of faith; it is understood to apply to an individual since it is exclusively read in the light of Jesus' passion and resurrection, which in their turn receive from it their interpretation. The mystery of innocent suffering had been pondered by Israel for a long time, and since the book of Job it was known that God unfolds within history a plan in which the suffering of the righteous finds its place. But this was still a dimly perceived certitude on which Isaiah shed some light by describing a righteous man undergoing an unjust death and saving his tormentors. The Christian reading it sees the hour of Christ as the moment when the light suddenly shines, when Jesus fulfills the prophecy in his flesh, giving a vivid demonstration of how God saves sinners by delivering to them the only Just One, God's Son. Similarly, the enigmatic ambiguity of Isaiah's text, suggesting an interpretation of the Servant now as individual, now as collective, becomes clear with the revelation of the "total Christ" in which the head, Jesus, receives his body in the community of the Church.

In counterpoint to the figure of the Servant, that of Zion reoccurs in ch. 54. Therefore Zion's fecundity is linked with the Servant's work that has just been reported. Freed from its sterility, Zion will give birth to children more numerous than before the exile. This people will be born of God's very self, creator and spouse of Zion loved with "an eternal love." After having abandoned Zion because of its sin, God establishes with it a definitive covenant of peace (v. 10). God will rebuild its ramparts with precious stones and for its foundation will give it the righteousness that God in person will teach Zion's children. Thus, all weapons having been laid down, Zion will know the peace that is based on justice. As can be seen, the reality named Zion in this passage amply transcends the limits of merely human experience. Zion is the holy people endowed with divine fecundity (54:1-3), the bride loved with an "everlasting love" (54:8). These are as many ways of prefiguring the Church understood in its deep identity that is spiritual and mystical, therefore not reducible to the individuals that compose it and who remain sinners (which is well expressed in the prayer of the eucharistic liturgy, "Lord, look not on my sins but on the faith of your Church").

Chapter 55 serves as an epilogue to Deutero-Isaiah; it echoes ch. 40 that served as a prologue (the same themes recur: the sovereign power of YHWH, the efficacy of the word, the new exodus). This text is a call to decision ("seek the Lord," "call upon him" in v. 6, "return" in v. 7); it is addressed to those who are coming back to Jerusalem at the time when God freely gives water to those who are thirsty and forgives the sinners.

The opening lines are sapiential in tone: they are an invitation to the banquet of the "everlasting covenant," which is consonant with the promises made to David (v. 3b). Afterward, in vv. 4 and 5, there is mention of the one who is called "witness to the peoples," "leader and commander for the peoples." In fact this is a new word concerning the Servant, who will gather a new Israel made up of persons who did not know him. This passage recalls and confirms the oracle found in 49:21-23, which mentions the "signal" raised for the nations bringing to Zion a numerous posterity.

The call to conversion "while [the LORD] may be found" is subsequently linked with the act of faith that agrees not to judge the plan of salvation according to purely human thoughts (vv. 6-9). Already the fourth oracle of the Servant in chs. 52–53 showed a way of salvation that strongly disconcerted human logic. The "pardon" turning sinners into righteous persons that is mentioned in v. 7 (with a word that appears only once in Isaiah) might well, along with the figure of the suffering and glorified Servant, be part of these unprecedented realities that Deutero-Isaiah announces. The following development on the efficacy of the word "that goes out from [God's] mouth" and does not return without having produced its result (vv. 10-11) subtly echoes the proclamation of the Servant's success in 53:13. This paves the way for the revelation of the savior as incarnate Word. Finally, this passage focuses on the vision of an ultimate "going out" (exodus) preceded, as throughout Deutero-Isaiah, by a long series of references to going out. These were appeals to the people to come out (43:8; 48:20; 49:9; 52:11, 12), and also assertions of a going out of God, of righteousness, of justice (42:13; 45:23; 48:3; 51:4, 5; 55:11).

The comparison of the beginning (ch. 40) and the end (ch. 55) of Deutero-Isaiah allows us to measure the distance covered. In both cases God's solicitude and consolation and a new exodus are stressed, but at the end the prophet's words center rather on the conversion of sinful humans and the forgiveness of God. The power of God the creator is shown to be at the service of the conversion and the life of thirsty humans who turn to God at the hour of grace. Finally, between the prologue and the epilogue of the book of the consolation of Israel the figure of the Servant occupies an all-important place and is the great newness being revealed. This newness is more awesome and disconcerting than what the prophet is able to sense at the time of his writing, although even he sees God standing by the side of this Servant and strangely declaring to Israel, "you have burdened me [or: 'made me your servant'] with your sins" (43:24). The incarnation will unveil the depths of this mysterious word by showing the Son of God in person "taking the form of a slave" (Phil 2:7) and fulfilling the mission of the Servant depicted in Isaiah for the salvation of sinners.

III. Final Chapters (Return from Babylon and Post-exilic Period): Isaiah 56–66

Theological Structure of the Text

(1) Isaiah 56:1–59:21: Delay of the announced salvation because of the sin that stands against the divine grace (the hardening of hearts continues). But God steadfastly maintains the promises of the Covenant and confirms anew the gift of the spirit and the word.

(2) Isaiah 60:1–63:6: Announcement of the dawn that is nevertheless breaking. Two poems of Zion (60:1-22 and 62:1-12) frame an oracle concerning the Servant (61:1-11). In counterpoint to the promises made again to Zion, vision of the Avenger who destroys the pride of Edom (63:1-6).

(3) Isaiah 63:7–66:24: In response to Israel's humble and trustful meditation on God's fatherhood, announcement of new heavens and a new earth. Zion/Eve will give birth to a holy people, whereas the unquenchable fire of the judgment will burn for those who chose evil.

1. Delay of Salvation Because of Sin, but God Maintains the Divine Promises and Gifts (56:1–59:21)

Chapter 56 opens with a text that dates from the return from the exile but continues themes of Deutero-Isaiah. It announces the imminent coming of salvation and the revelation of God's justice (v. 1). A beatitude proclaims "happy" every human being (see *ben-ʾādām,* "mortal," in v. 2) who becomes a servant of God by observing the Sabbath and avoiding evil. The universality of salvation is expressed in a solemn manner by the twofold reference to the foreigner, excluded from the covenant, and the eunuch, traditionally barred from worship and priesthood. Both are now invited to be part of the holy people provided they live as befits servants of God. They receive the promise that they will be led to the "holy mountain" and the Temple, which from now on will be called a "house of prayer for all peoples" (v. 7). This passage—which certainly reflects the debates occurring at the return from exile on the subject of foreigners—concludes with the mention of "gathering," which is one of the important themes of this final section of the book of Isaiah.

However, without any transition the text turns to the contrast between the righteous, servants of God, and the evil rulers of the people, drunkards without any understanding. Because of the latter "the righteous perish" (57:1) although they are the future of the people. The tone of this passage recalls that of First Isaiah when he denounced the injustices rampant in the city (chs. 1–5). As before, idolatry and its practices are inveighed against along with injustice: child sacrifices (57:5), cults with sexual rites (57:8) through which unfaithfulness to YHWH becomes, more than ever, prostitution. The hardening of hearts, which one could have believed overcome at the end of Deutero-Isaiah, is still present. The actual return from the land of exile has not been accompanied for all by a spiritual return. As a consequence the words of judgment recur also: let humans who trust in idols for their salvation be abandoned to these idols that the wind will carry away (57:13). This sequence, written in the mode of the suit of the covenant, nevertheless ends with a mention of the "holy mountain," already named in 56:7 when speaking of the foreigners and the eunuchs. This holy mountain will be the portion of the righteous persons God gathers.

Indeed, the following passage speaks of the "way" God will open up to the Temple: a way of justice contrasting with that of the impious spoken of in 56:11 and 57:13. The God who inhabits the heights is revealed at the same time as dwelling with the contrite and humble persons whose life God guarantees. This had already been said about the Servant in ch. 53. Besides, the salvation/consolation is from now on, and twice here, couched in terms of "healing" (57:18-19). We remember that the same word was used in the fourth oracle concerning the Servant, "by his bruises we are healed" (53:5). We witness here the discreet but strong coherence of the text from Deutero-Isaiah to its final section. This salvation leads now to the "fruit of the lips" (57:18), that is to say, the thanksgiving that is the true sacrifice pleasing to God (cf. Hos 14:3 and Psalm 51). Finally, peace is announced to those near and to those far off (v. 19), while the violence of the evildoers is abandoned to itself like a stormy sea.

Chapters 58 and 59 continue along the same lines: persistence of sin; return of darkness; judgment of the wrongdoers. They also describe God's strategy when confronted with inveterate unfaithfulness: God will not hear a hypocritical prayer. God will only, through the intermediary of a messenger, give the word that uncovers sin before coming back for the avenging judgment that will save those who turned to God. The text is made up of a series of addresses.

First the messenger is addressed by God (58:1) and receives the mission of exposing the sin that hides in Jacob. This command is followed by a lengthy divine invective denouncing the hypocrisy of a false fast and contempt for the

Sabbath (58:2-14). People complain of not being heard by God (v. 3), but the genuine fast is the liberation and service of the oppressed. This is the indispensable condition to satisfy if people want God to be close and not hidden and silent. Here God identifies with the poor and oppressed to the point of saying, "Here I am" to anyone who welcomes them (v. 9). Similarly, respect for the Sabbath is a privileged way of manifesting that one belongs to the covenant, especially at a period when many identifying marks have been lost, when the Temple has been destroyed. The Sabbath is also a way of renouncing pride by remembering that God's work takes precedence over human works. The promises attendant on this faithfulness are reiterated: God will be guide, protection, "delight" to the righteous, and they will find in God the strength to rebuild the walls of Jerusalem (a task still in the future in the second half of the fifth century).

Then comes a discourse from the messenger who answers those who are scandalized by the delay of salvation now that people have actually returned from exile. The reason why God does not answer prayer is that people continue to live in violence leading to bloodshed (59:3, 7), in lies (59:3), and in bondage to nothingness (59:4). God certainly has said "peace" to humanity, but they have not said "peace" to other people. As a result they "beget iniquity" (v. 4) with which they reproach God.

These accusatory words provoke a response from the people, a response that is a beginning of confession of sin (59:9-14). A degree of awareness is dawning, expressed by the repetition in the first person plural of the prophet's words. This acknowledgment of the infidelity of sin in which one lives even expresses itself in a direct address to God in v. 12, "our transgressions before you are many." But there is a return to more impersonal statements in vv. 13-14. The interplay of personal pronouns is an avowal of the distance that human beings have established between themselves and a God who is ready to say, "Here I am" as soon as righteousness is chosen over delinquency.

Faced with this unfaithfulness, whose price is the suffering of the innocent ("whoever turns from evil is despoiled," says v. 15), God arises and puts on the garments of salvation and vengeance (v. 17). This warlike figure, described in terms that might suggest Cyrus, is the counterpart of the holiness of God who can no longer tolerate bloodthirsty people in power at the expense of the weak and the righteous. The anger and the judgment of God are also redemption (v. 20) for the humble who turn to God.

In 59:21 God again speaks to reaffirm in a solemn way the eternal covenant through the gift of the spirit and of a word that cannot fail ("my words that I have put in your mouth, shall not depart out of your mouth"). This assurance is given against every intimidation that would want to silence the speaker. To whom are these last words directed? To a "you" that certainly designates the prophet but also, beyond him, the people ("your children . . . your children's children"); and we know from Deutero-Isaiah that this people will include more than Israel according to the flesh.

2. Salvation is Near; Revelation of the Priestly People in Zion, Where the Nations Converge

The core of this final part of Isaiah is made up of 60:1–63:6, themselves containing two oracles of Zion surrounding an oracle concerning the Servant. In a magnificent and radiant text describing how the nations of the world and all their riches converge toward the Temple, Jerusalem is invited to exult before the glory of God that is arising and covers it with splendor. The great gathering begins that will make the city "a light to the nations" (cf. 60:3) according to the expression used with regard to the Servant in 49:6. In a style akin to that of Deutero-Isaiah, at the end of the sixth century Jerusalem is shown glorified by God while still bearing the marks of the tragedy it has lived through, for if the altar has been reestablished, the Temple and the walls have not yet been rebuilt. However, those who will stream toward it will call it "the city of YHWH, the Zion of the Holy One of Israel" (60:14). It will be beautiful not because of material goods, in which human cities pride themselves, but because of the very goods of God and, what is more, of God's very self dwelling in it, "your God will be your glory" (v. 19). Indeed the city will be governed by Peace and Righteousness (v. 17), its ramparts will be Salvation and Praise (v. 18), gold and frankincense will come in abundance toward it, and all will sing the praises of YHWH (v. 6). It will be the city of the righteous receiving the promise to "possess the land forever" (v. 21). This text speaks of something vastly different from a dream of human power, the revenge of a wounded and humiliated city; it is a meditation on the real transfiguration the city of YHWH will experience at the hour when God will gather the righteous of God's people and the nations.

Chapter 61 begins with the words of a prophetic voice that repeats, but this time in the first person singular, the terms of the first oracle concerning the Servant in ch. 42, "the spirit of the Lord GOD is upon me." The one who says "I" has received the anointing that qualifies him as the "anointed" (that is, the Messiah). Moreover, he no longer addresses Israel and the nations but, selectively, "those who mourn in Zion" to whom he is to announce the good news of God (that is, the gospel). This consists in a year during which they will receive the grace of the Lord, but this year will be accompanied by the day of vengeance (this will be made explicit in 63:1-6).

The messenger speaks to "afflicted" persons who here cannot be simply the victims of the captivity in Babylon because they have been exposed to "shame" (61:7) like the Servant (49:7; 50:5-7; 53:2-9). To them is announced that they will become God's priestly people (v. 6) and that they will be recognized among the nations as "a people whom the LORD has blessed" (v. 9). To them also is made the promise of the "everlasting covenant." Verses 10-11 depict the nuptial joy of Zion clothed with salvation and righteousness and becoming a holy "shoot" before all the nations.

The section 62:1–63:6 contains first of all a long celebration of Jerusalem, in continuity with ch. 60 and also with ch. 54 in which it was already said, "your maker is your husband" (54:5). A voice is raised interceding for the beloved, abandoned for a time, but who now, having put on the garments of justice and salvation, will again be God's joy (v. 5). It will receive a "new name," the echoes of which are found in vv. 4 and 12. Sentinels are to be posted on its walls, unceasingly asking God to hasten salvation and the hour of the wedding, suggested by the mention of the reapers who will "drink . . . in my holy courts" (v. 9). The "going out" spoken of in v. 10 refers this time to a people invited to pass through the gates in order to lift the "ensign" of the gathering of nations. Now the prophet's voice is heard to the ends of the earth: it announces to Zion the coming of its savior.

Indeed, it is the arrival of God that is announced in 63:1, but a strange arrival it is, one that fills with astonishment the very person who utters the oracle (shown by the two questions that follow one another in this verse). With brutal realism the text speaks of vengeance, wrath, fury. Blood nearly splashes on the reader. Who is meant here? This is a king, harvester-and-judge of nations who comes from Bozrah, the capital of Edom, the people of enemy-relatives, of criminals (cf. 59:16-20). He is at once the *go'ēl,* the redeemer, the avenger of blood who comes to ransom his people, and the one who has just completed "the day of vengeance" already mentioned in 61:2. (The year of grace and the day of vengeance are announced in both 61:2 and 63:4, but in reverse order). His garment is royal purple but stained by the blood of the enemies that has splashed from the wine press where he trod on them. Besides, he has trodden all by himself since no one from among his people has come to his aid in the strenuous toil of the struggle against evil. This vision is extremely violent and may appear the more shocking as the Christian tradition has seen in it a prophecy of Jesus' passion. We may be the more scandalized as we tend to have a very abstract conception of the passion. We forget that the depths of redeeming love revealed by the passion cannot be dissociated from a supreme struggle (this is the root meaning of the word "agony") and also from a judgment (see for instance John 9:39, "I came into this world for judgment"). The passion is a travail in the strongest sense of the word in which, like the vintager Isaiah depicts, Jesus confronts the sin of humankind, and in this toil he too finds himself alone, abandoned by all. [See also the article "Violence and Evil in the Bible."]

3. New Heavens and New Earth; Zion Gives Birth to a Holy People; Pagans Become Priests of YHWH

Having arrived almost at the end of Isaiah readers encounter, in the psalm-confession of 63:7–64:12, one of the most sublime expressions of the humble and filial sentiments that developed in Israel, in the heart of the remnant, through several centuries of the history of the covenant. The mystery of salvation history begins to be revealed to those who accept conversion. Thus the prayerful memory of the devout becomes accustomed to recognizing in the covenant and the Exodus the attentive faithfulness of God to God's children (63:8); they are saved because God *in person* came to their aid. Such is the meaning of 63:9: "It was no messenger or angel but his presence that saved them." The text will again return with insistence to the theme of "face" or "presence" (64:1, 7; cf. 63:19, "name") as an expression of the closeness and commitment of YHWH to the people. The same small remnant also discovers more clearly than ever God's presence powerfully acting in the person of Moses, servant and shepherd of the people; God twice had Moses go through the waters of death by saving him from the Nile and having him cross the Reed Sea; God also placed the divine spirit in him. A new light is cast on these old memories during the decades following the return from exile; these decades are difficult ones because of the persistence of the hardening of hearts that necessitates that God act anew, more radically than ever. Where is today the one who formerly displayed divine power in favor of Israel? Why does YHWH not put an end to this time of darkness when Jerusalem is deserted and the holy Temple of God lies in ruins (64:9-11)? A new Moses would be needed, a Messiah who in the power of the Spirit would safely lead the people through the deadly waters of sin. The presence of God in person would be needed, coming to save those who have strayed away for so long (63:19) and whom even the patriarchs do not recognize as their own (63:16). The text juxtaposes the two hoped-for figures of salvation without synthesizing them any further. The mystery of the incarnation is very close to this text, but at the time of this writing the prophet can say no more.

It remains that this prayer of the poor and sinners (64:5-7) knows that it has no claim on God since the breaking of the covenant. Its sole support is the fatherhood of YHWH. Three times this fatherhood is recalled (63:16 [2x]; 64:8) and it is mentioned in the covenant formula, which comes again to the lips of the repentant people, "you are our Father . . . we are your people" (64:8-9). The prayer reflects the humble certitude that the paternal heart of God cannot remain unmoved by the suffering of God's children. The hope for a new Sinai rests on this sole certitude that God in person would come to snatch the people from the power of evil (64:1). This is a completely unprecedented perspective opening to the people's hope a newness that surpasses everything that was ever revealed (cf. 64:4).

In ch. 65 God answers. First of all, the paradoxes of the mutual search of God and humankind are enunciated: God is found by those who did not seek (v. 1). By contrast, those to whom God came with insistence by saying "Here I am" preferred the mendacious cults of the sacred groves and the tombs, accomplices of death (vv. 3-4). God will not let this iniquity go unpunished; God will chastise the unworthy people. However, vv. 8-16 indicate that there are limits and restraints to the punishment: God will spare the "wine" found in the vineyard of Israel. The theme of the remnant recurs here, centered on the references to the "descendants" born of Jacob and a messianic heir whose identity is not specified any more precisely. Then the blessings and curses of the new covenant are reiterated. Those who have not responded to the call and have set the table for the gods of Canaan (v. 11) will be killed by the sword. For the faithful people, on the contrary, the desolate tracts of Sharon and the cursed Valley of Achor will become fertile pastures. This people will bear a new name and "the God of Amen" (that is, faithfulness, steadfastness) will be honored.

But it appears that this salvation, when the adversities of the past will not be remembered, can only come about by the creation of a new cosmos, "new heavens and a new earth" (v. 17), the creation of Jerusalem as a joy (v. 18). For the innocent, suffering will have disappeared from this world (v. 23) and God will answer human prayers before they are even verbalized (v. 24). In v. 25 this new world of eschatological times is described in terms similar to those of 11:6-9, but it is specified here that the "serpent—its food shall be dust" (65:25), an allusion to Gen 3:14; the curse of the original serpent is confirmed, which gives the assurance that "they shall not hurt or destroy on all my holy mountain."

A short passage (66:1-5), an echo of the debates arising at the return from exile about the reconstruction of the Temple, adds to the preceding verses on the new creation the perspective—new also—of a temple not made by human hands. Beyond the mendacious worship against which the text inveighs once more (66:3-4) one glimpses the image of a temple that is no longer a material reality but a community of persons with poor and humble hearts, gathered by God. From the Holy of Holies comes the frightening voice of God who is coming in flames of fire for eternal judgment and eternal salvation (66:6-24).

One last song of Zion in 66:7-14 brings the announcement of the virginal messianic birth, the ultimate flowering of the hope progressively fashioned throughout the book. All the passages that from Deutero-Isaiah on spoke of the unheard-of newness of the work God was about to accomplish converge in the vision of Zion giving birth. It is really a figure of the new Eve that is proposed here: she gives birth without having to suffer the sentence of Gen 3:16 ("before she was in labor she gave birth," 66:7). Moreover, she gives birth to a son who is immediately identified as the corporate personality of the people. The oracle speaks of the birth of a "nation" and this nation is mysteriously begotten by God in person (it is God who opens the womb, v. 9). Confronted with these prodigious perspectives the author of the text finds again the tone of Deutero-Isaiah, full of questions and interjections (vv. 8-9). It is also in connection with these verses from the end of the book that one day the ancient oracle concerning Immanuel in 7:14 will be reread and that it will be possible to reinterpret its promises as a prophecy of the virginal birth that is glimpsed here. The translation of the LXX, speaking of a "virgin" instead of a "young woman," might find here its original explanation. The following verses (10-14) reinforce the maternal figure of Zion and invite all those who love her to rejoice. The theme of consolation finds here its crowning moment: God consoles as a mother consoles. Jerusalem will be consolation. Verse 14 concludes with the joy of God's servants that will be the vision of the grace born in Zion.

This salvation implies that evil be eradicated through the definitive judgment by fire of evil and idolatrous persons (vv. 15-17 and then v. 24, which conclude the book with the vision of the corpses delivered for eternity to the fire of Gehenna). Nevertheless, this time will simultaneously be that of God's great gathering "all nations and tongues" in Jerusalem, on the holy mountain. This means that God will bring to an end the dispersion of Babel (see Genesis 11). Finally, from among these persons from the nations God will choose some delegates who will be witnesses to the divine glory (vv. 18-19). They will bring back, in a cortege of varied mounts and conveyances, the "kindred" of Israel, converted pagans who will be an offering to YHWH. By making some of them priests God will institute a prolongation of the levitical priesthood, associating with Israel persons chosen from the nations. Thus the "name" and the "descendants" of Israel will remain firm. These are the last words of the book: salvation does not gloss over the dramatic reality of evil, but hope opens onto the mystery of God's involvement in history and onto a universalism that associates the nations with the highest praise of the God of Israel.

BIBLIOGRAPHY

Brueggmann, Walter. *Using God's Resources Wisely: Isaiah and Urban Possibility.* Louisville: Westminster/John Knox, 1993.

Clifford, Richard J. *Fair Spoken and Persuading: An Interpretation of Second Isaiah.* New York: Paulist, 1984.

Hanson, Paul D. *Isaiah 40–66: A Bible Commentary for Teaching and Preaching.* Louisville: John Knox, 1995.

Hayes, John A., and Stuart A. Irvine. *Isaiah, The Eighth-Century Prophet: His Times and His Preaching.* Nashville: Abingdon, 1987.

Melugin, Roy F., and Marvin A. Sweeney, eds. *New Visions of Isaiah.* JSOT.S 214. Sheffield: Sheffield Academic Press, 1996.

Sawyer, John F. A. *The Fifth Gospel: Isaiah in the History of Christianity.* Cambridge: Cambridge University Press, 1995

Scullion, John. *Isaiah 40–66.* Wilmington, Del.: Michael Glazier, 1982.

Seitz, Christopher R. *Isaiah 1–39.* Louisville: John Knox, 1993.

Stuhlmueller, Carroll. *Creative Redemption in Deutero-Isaiah.* AnBib 43. Rome: Biblical Institute Press, 1970.

Ward, James M. *The Message of the Prophets.* Nashville: Abingdon, 1991.

____. *Preaching from the Prophets.* Nashville: Abingdon, 1995.

Westermann, Claus. *Isaiah 40–66.* Philadelphia: Westminster, 1969.

Whybray, R. N. *The Second Isaiah.* Sheffield: Sheffield Academic Press, 1983.

Jeremiah

Barbara Bozak

FIRST READING

The book of Jeremiah fascinates the reader with its striking images, its presentation of a God who is both free to transform reality and bound to the covenant, its portrait of a prophet who suffers because of his fidelity. Even a cursory examination draws the reader into the complexity of this captivating work which is probably best known for two seemingly contradictory elements: the heart-rending laments of the prophet (which have given us the word "jeremiad"), and the hope-filled promise of a new covenant written on the heart. Furthermore, this is the only biblical book that gives some insight into the prophetic *persona* and the all-consuming nature of the prophetic vocation. [See also the article "Prophetism and Prophets."]

Despite its ability to engage the reader this book can frustrate initial attempts to find a logical structure. Most scholars consider the book as a whole incomprehensible—a hodge-podge of writings, an anthology of anthologies. It is written from at least two different points of view: that of Jeremiah who both announces God's word to the people and reflects on his own life, and that of Jeremiah's biographer, who narrates episodes of the prophet's career. Some oracles address a pre-exilic Israel while others, with their promise of return, speak to Israel already in exile. This intertwining of pre-exilic with exilic oracles and a general disregard for chronological order, even in those pericopes that have a clear historical referent, evidence the manifestly ahistorical bias of the book. Yet read in light of the Babylonian Exile, to which it makes explicit reference, the book of Jeremiah reflects the fears and hopes of a people who are first threatened with destruction (pre-exilic oracles) and then, in the darkness of a lost national identity, receive a muted word of assurance that they will return to their land (exilic oracles).

The book's complexity mirrors the intricate web of relationships among Israel, Jeremiah, and YHWH. The book offers insights into (a) what it means for Israel to be the covenant people of God; (b) the implications for Jeremiah of being called to stand for God over against the community of which he is part; and (c) the transformative pathos of YHWH who, bound by the covenant stipulations, grants genuine freedom to the people.

The Israelites are blind to what it means to be the people of YHWH. They turn from the covenant requirements and choose death over life. They embrace deception and reject truth. Jeremiah challenges them to ponder their origins, to recognize who they are, and to turn back to the God who has brought them to life. YHWH's action alone can overcome their inability, rooted deep in their being, to keep covenant. Without divine intervention there is no hope for the change of heart they need to live as the people of God.

The prophet Jeremiah is a paradoxical figure. He cares deeply for his people, identifies with their suffering, and repeatedly calls them to repentance. However, he also rails against their sin and issues threats of destruction. His relationship with God has a similar tone. As much as he faithfully obeys what he understands to be

God's commands to him, he also complains to God when he feels God is deceiving him or the people.

YHWH appears in the guise of both creator and destroyer. God has cared for the people over the centuries (from the Exodus until the Exile), bringing them to freedom, giving them the land, promising them a future. This same God who has loved the people into life, gifted and encouraged them, is now rejected by them. In their failure to recognize that YHWH was the one who gave them food and freedom they have embraced their independence to the point of seeking freedom even from their God. YHWH accepts the people's choice with its consequences. The covenant that is binding on God as well as on Israel is ended. The resulting punishment, however, is not the last word. God promises to transform the people by a new creation leading to a new covenant.

Division of the Book

Despite the difficulties of the text, a careful reader—the commentary that ensues will be all the more profitable if the reader has the book of Jeremiah in hand—can discern several major divisions in the book, differentiated by a change in style (from poetry to prose or vice versa) and/or theme:

Introduction: Call of Jeremiah (poetry)—1:1-19

Part 1: Inescapable Destruction Announced (poetry)—2:1–10:25

Part 2: The Suffering Prophet (poetry with some prose)—11:1–20:18

Part 3: Sinful Kings and False Prophets (prose with some poetry)—21:1–29:32

Part 4: Hope for the Future (first poetry, then prose)—30:1–33:25

Part 5: Final Years of Judah (prose)—34:1–45:5

Part 6: Oracles Against the Nations (poetry)—46:1–51:64

Historical Conclusion: Jerusalem Destroyed (prose)—52:1-34

1:1-19: The brief introduction contextualizes the book historically and offers a thumbnail sketch of the whole, both content and style. It locates Jeremiah's influence in the era of the three kings who ruled Judah just before the exile. While accenting YHWH's abiding presence it recognizes the coming disaster and points to Jeremiah's role in the work of God, both destructive and salvific. A mixture of poetry and prose, it indicates that the rest of the book uses both literary forms. Here the word of God is revealed both in oracular speech and in ordinary events, a phenomenon repeated frequently in subsequent chapters. Furthermore, YHWH's presence to save as well as to punish is the final word in this chapter, as it will be for Jeremiah's vision of the future.

2:1–10:25: Part 1 is composed almost entirely of poetic oracles addressed to Judah/Israel that intertwine accusations of sin and threats of destruction. Although the prophet's voice dominates, Jeremiah himself is all but invisible in these chapters. He is little more than God's mouthpiece. In a variety of images drawn from nature the oracles conjure up a return to pre-creation chaos and set a tone of unrelieved darkness.

The people's offense, their rejection of YHWH, is played out against the backdrop of God's continuing care. Israel has been faithless (5:11), and turned away from God (5:7). By practicing injustice toward the needy (5:26-28) the leaders act in opposition to their official role (5:30-31). All these transgressions, which contradict Israel's very identity as the people of God, cry out for retribution. In the Temple Sermon (7:1-34), the major prose section of this part, Jeremiah underscores the people's self-deception that is perhaps their greatest sin. He likens the people to animals out of control (2:23-24; 5:8; 8:6) and people who have turned their back on a relationship, yet somewhat surprisingly, he still keeps alive the hope for a change of heart (3:12-13, 19, 22; 4:1, 14; 6:16; 7:3-7). This hope coupled with YHWH's ongoing care offers some basis for closing with an intercession that YHWH mitigate the inevitable punishment (10:23-25).

11:1–20:18: This part's free intermingling of prose and poetry as well as Jeremiah's palpable presence mark a major shift in emphasis. The prophet not only proclaims the coming destruction but actually experiences it in his own life. Both his laments to YHWH (11:18–12:6; 15:10-21; 17:14-18; 18:18-23; 20:7-18) and his own reports of what YHWH demands of him (16:1-9; 17:1-12; 19:1-15) reflect Jeremiah's deep personal suffering. In these chapters the prophet's life mirrors both YHWH's anguish at being rejected by the people and the people's distress in the face of inevitable destruction. The text is replete with death imagery. Already at work in Jeremiah's life, death casts its pall in the announced disaster and the desolation of the land as well as in the threat of exile. The God who loves Israel is unable to halt the evil the people have unleashed by their sin (13:10-11; 18:15-16).

21:1–29:32: Historical and biographical narratives about Jeremiah and other persons dominate Part Three, although poetic oracles still occur. Because the oracles recounted here are directed to particular kings they anchor the book firmly in a defined historical context. Specific transgressions of the leaders, and no longer the general sins of idolatry and apostasy, dominate Jeremiah's speech. Dashing any hope for YHWH's protection (21:3-10) Jeremiah denounces both sinful rulers and false prophets and proclaims them responsible for the inescapable doom (21:11–22:30; 23:9-40; 27:1–28:17). As a result Jeremiah faces real threats to his life, but the threats do not deter him from proclaiming the word of God to his contemporaries.

Although settling down in exile might appear to be a breach of covenant faith—such a life meant acceptance of foreign rule and the loss of national identity—Jeremiah writes to the exiles (29:1-32), and encourages them to embrace life where they are. Building a future, even in a foreign land, hints at the possibility of a new beginning. The text has already suggested what the newness would entail: new shepherds who will execute justice (23:3-6), a new name for YHWH (23:7-8), a return to the land (24:4-7; 29:10-14), foreign nations brought under the power of YHWH (25:15-29), the final fall of Babylon (27:6-8), restoration of the Temple vessels to Jerusalem (27:22). The encouragement to life even in exile that concludes 21:1–29:32 offers a logical link with the oracles of salvation found in the next part.

30:1–33:25: Part Four, often entitled "The Little Book of Consolation," focuses on hope in the midst of desolation. The light shining through these chapters dissipates the black cloud of unavoidable destruction set out in chs. 2–29. A series of poetic oracles of salvation proclaimed by Jeremiah (30:1–31:40) and a biographical prose narrative (32:1–33:26) declare that God will restore the fortunes of Israel, reverse the punishment, heal their wounds and bring them to new life in the land. This short section, placed in the midst of texts that point to disaster and are permeated by an undertone of assured destruction, holds out hope against hope. This is exemplified in Jeremiah's prayer asking YHWH to explain why, now that the city is under attack and he is in prison, he should purchase a field from his cousin (32:16–25). By doing this apparently illogical deed Jeremiah demonstrates to the people that they must trust in God's promise to bring them not only restoration but radical newness.

34:1–45:5: Part Five continues the narrative account of Jeremiah's life and relates his struggles to make God's word known during the final years of Judah. The persistent threats to the prophet's life undergird these concluding chapters and exemplify the threat of destruction the people face. In a series of oracles spoken by Jeremiah and in biographical narratives that describe his plight, the text moves beyond national destruction to focus on personal death: for the kings, the people, and even Jeremiah himself.

Beginning with the first incident that occurs during the siege of Jerusalem (34:1-22), this part has strong historical ties that link personal experience to world events and national tragedy. The complete rejection of God's word is physically exemplified in 36:1-32 when the king burns the scroll on which Jeremiah's oracles were written. Repudiation of the prophet's word then becomes rejection of the prophet himself. The incidents from Jeremiah's life reported in 37:1–38:28 show the Israelites to be their own worst enemy, their own actions precipitating their devastation. The prophet's oracles of doom have come to pass. Life comes to a grinding halt with the fall of Jerusalem (39:1-10). But the bleakness of such overwhelming destruction is softened by the concluding verses that offer hope to one person: Baruch (45:1-5).

46:1–51:64: This series of nine poetic oracles pronounced by Jeremiah announces death and destruction to those nations that had threatened Israel at some point in its history. The whole is framed by oracles against the two major powers of the time, Egypt and Babylon. Not only were they important for the role they played in world politics but both had a profound impact on Israel's self-understanding as a covenant people: the exodus from Egypt and the return from exile in Babylon were crucial moments in Israel's experience of God's salvific presence.

The oracles against the nations are filled with images of a fast-approaching enemy (46:9-16; 47:3-6; 50:35-42; 51:27-32): horses and chariots, the devouring sword, the fallen warrior. By using imagery similar to that earlier applied to Israel (the suffering from an incurable wound; disparagement by other nations; life given over to mourning rites; terror experienced on all sides) these oracles imply that Israel is no different from the other nations. It is not surprising that it has been brought down.

One by one Babylon destroys Israel's enemies until finally Babylon itself succumbs to YHWH's might. With all of Israel's enemies brought down, there is space for the new creation previously announced in 30:1–33:25. By proclaiming the demise of Judah's historical enemies the prophet alludes to a future for the people of YHWH.

Yet the final word declares that the power of YHWH will not only deal a deathblow to Babylon (50:17-18) but will also transform Israel by pardoning its sin and removing its guilt (50:19-20). This alone can effect a true "return." The bright spark of salvation shines through the dark cloud of destruction that alone will make a new creation possible.

52:1-34: The narrative prose of the historical conclusion first gives a detailed description of Jerusalem's destruction, then recounts the fate of the exiled King Jehoiachin. As though the book could not end with Babylon's demise, it returns to the people of God and their capital city, Jerusalem. All is lost. The Temple has been destroyed; the last king is in exile. Every sign of God's presence with the people has been taken from them. Yet by aiming the final spotlight on the honor accorded Jehoiachin in exile the author once again, in a veiled manner, hints that even in what appears to be total destruction hope is not irrevocably lost. Just as the salvation oracles are virtually lost in a sea of judgment oracles, so God lies hidden in the midst of the people.

Contexts for Interpretation

A. Original Historical Context

The book of Jeremiah, like all biblical prophetic works, combines narratives about the prophet with oracles first proclaimed by him and later set down in writing. Since the prophetic word is a response to an actual historical situation the events contemporaneous with the preaching, writing, and editing of the work, as well as Israel's self-understanding at the time, form the background against which the book must be read.

Jeremiah lived through the tumultuous years that saw the Assyrian empire collapse only to be replaced by Babylon. Active during the reign of three Judahite kings (Josiah, Jehoiachim and Zedekiah) and one governor (Gedeliah), he preached in response to various political changes, from Israel's relative autonomy under Josiah (640–609) to the rise of Babylon and the destruction of Israel (587). Since politics and religion were intimately linked in the Ancient Near East—a ruling nation imposed the worship of its gods on conquered peoples—Israel could practice its religion without hindrance only when free from the domination of other powers. The power vacuum created by Assyria's decline (626–612) therefore gave Judah, during Josiah's reign, not merely political independence but an opportunity for religious reform.

Ostensibly desirous of strengthening social and political as well as religious unity, Josiah undertook a renewal of cultic practices. During repairs to the Temple ca. 621, the law book of Deuteronomy (probably Deut 12:1–26:15) was discovered. Declared to be truly the word of God by the female prophet Huldah, it fed the reform that was underway. The deuteronomic credo that obedience to Torah was a requirement for possession of the land rendered all the more urgent the task of purging the territory of other gods and of centering worship in Jerusalem.

Beginning with the Sinai covenant, Israel understood itself to be constituted as a people by YHWH's presence, first in the Ark of the Covenant and later in the land and the Temple. For over five hundred years this was the source of confidence in face of all threats. In 722 B.C.E. Assyria invaded and destroyed the northern kingdom (Israel/Samaria) and besieged Jerusalem, the capital city of the southern kingdom of Judah. Just when destruction appeared inevitable the enemy suddenly withdrew. Many believed that God had miraculously spared Jerusalem (2 Kings 19:35; Isa 37:36), the city which housed YHWH's Temple. Thus by the time of Jeremiah the people's expectation that YHWH's presence in their midst would protect them from their enemies had a precedent. Such unexamined confidence in the Jerusalem Temple would prove their downfall.

Jeremiah entered the scene during the reign of Josiah, in 626 B.C.E. This was either the year of his birth or the year he was called to be a prophet, depending on how one interprets Jer 1:3-5. If Jeremiah began preaching in 626, his early words would probably have been addressed to the remnant of the northern kingdom (Israel/Samaria), possibly in support of the Josianic reform. If he was born in 626 he would have begun preaching no earlier than the time of Josiah's death in 609 when the stability of Judah was just beginning to be challenged. In either case it seems that Jeremiah initiated his prophetic career during a time when Judah enjoyed relative peace and a corresponding self-complacency.

Jeremiah's prophetic message attempted to make sense of a constantly changing situation. After Assyria's power had crumbled and Babylon had grown stronger, Jeremiah, recognizing the futility of an alliance with Egypt, preached confidence in YHWH. Using both the spoken and the written word he addressed the people at home as well as those in exile. He warned them of the coming destruction which he, like Deuteronomy, interpreted as punishment for their sins. Eventually he came to realize that this apparent end to the nation was not the last word. To those who faced destruction and exile Jeremiah preached a new beginning, a new creation, a new covenant.

Since the several oracles collected in the text originally addressed different audiences it should not be surprising to find Jeremiah taking apparently contradictory approaches toward the same issue. Although he had a good relationship with Zedekiah, at times Jeremiah appears to be against kingship. In one breath he calls Babylon the servant of YHWH, while in another Babylon is the enemy who destroys Zion. He clearly proclaims that foreign powers are not to be sought out for protection yet announces that life will be found in submitting to Babylon.

Most scholars would say that the best way to understand these oracles is to interpret them in light of their original audience. But there are no simple or certain criteria to determine from what period a given oracle has come. What we do know is that the book of Jeremiah is the product of several hands at work over a long period of time, perhaps as much as one hundred years.

To simplify its composition history to the extreme one can say that the book of Jeremiah has three authors, each responsible for a given speech genre. For the most part the poetic oracles are considered to contain the authentic words of Jeremiah addressed to pre-exilic Judah and/or Israel (627–587). The narrative prose accounts, a later reflection on the prophet's life, were composed by Baruch or another contemporary of Jeremiah. Both the sermonic prose and the material reflecting the Deuteronomic concerns of obedience to the Law and possession of the land are attributed to the Deuteronomist's exilic additions (587–537). Modern readers must recognize that a given pericope may date from as early as 626 (Josianic reform), be as late as the exilic period, or be the product of one or more redactions.

The long and complicated history of the development and transmission of Jeremiah is reflected in the discrepancies between the LXX and Masoretic versions. The LXX Greek version of Jeremiah is not only considerably shorter but also has a different arrangement than the Hebrew Masoretic. The oracles against the nations (46:1–51:57 in the Masoretic) provide a striking illustration. Besides the fact that the LXX places these oracles between 25:14 and 25:15 of our Masoretic text, the order in which the nations are addressed is different in the two versions. This problem raises the issue of which version is the earlier. Although the Masoretic is likely the later redaction, it is the text used by the twentieth-century Western Church and so the one we follow here.

B. Canonical (Scriptural) Context

Composed by persons who were steeped in their own religious heritage, the book of Jeremiah reflects its place in a continuum of sacred writings. It not only takes up language and ideas of earlier works but it is used in turn by subsequent ones. No one contests the influence of Deuteronomy or the psalms of individual lament on Jeremiah. Deuteronomy's role in the Josianic reform would have given it prominence in the life of the prophet, while the lament psalms provide Jeremiah with a language to articulate his own suffering. Living in a political climate similar to that of Isaiah and Hosea, both of whom preached in response to the Assyrian threat about 100 years earlier, Jeremiah had the images and ideas of the earlier prophets to inspire his own oracles.

Hosea

The many striking similarities between the imagery of Jer and that of Hos indicate a literary dependence, with Jer probably borrowing expressions from some written version of the earlier prophet. Hosea's metaphorical description of Israel as an unfaithful wife (Hos 1:2–3:5) apparently inspired Jer who repeated it several times in the opening chapters (Jeremiah 2–4).

Hosea 1:2–3:5 links God's experience of Israel with the prophet's own experience of a wife who turned away from him. Whether or not he actually took a prostitute as wife at the command of YHWH, as the book declares, Hosea did speak of YHWH as the loving but rejected husband: "Go, love a woman who has a lover and is an adulteress, just as the LORD loves the people of Israel, though they turn to other gods and love raisin cakes" (Hos 3:1). Like Hosea, Jeremiah remembers Israel as the beloved and once-loving bride (Jer 2:2-3) who has now turned away from her husband to seek freedom with other lovers. Her whoring (Jer 2:20; 3:1-3, 6, 8) is but a manifestation of her real sin. She turns away from the one who loves her: ". . . as a faithless wife leaves her husband, so you have been faithless to me, O house of Israel" (Jer 3:20, see also 2:25, 33; 3:13; 4:30).

Hosea 2:9 offers the husband's response to his wife's rejection: "I will take back my grain in its time, and my wine in its season; and I will take away my wool and my flax." Like the prophet from the north, Jeremiah preaches that Israel's refusal to accept YHWH as the source of these gifts (Jer 3:3; 23:10) would result in its being deprived of the food, clothing, and protection that according to Exod 21:10 a husband was required to guarantee his wife. The wife's rejection of her husband relieves him of any responsibilities in her regard.

The end to a mutual commitment, portrayed in the broken marriage metaphor, must be read against the images of a caring relationship. Both Hosea and Jeremiah recall an earlier time when Israel was the loving bride of YHWH (Hos 2:15b; Jer 2:2-3). Describing the bond between God and Israel/Judah as that of parent and child, Jeremiah, like Hosea, alludes to the unreserved and undeserved care Israel had earlier received. Hosea 11:1-9 depicts God's care for Ephraim as that of a loving mother: "When Israel was a child, I loved him . . . it was I who taught Ephraim to walk . . . I bent down to them and fed them . . . my compassion grows warm and tender . . . ." Jeremiah 31:9b, 18-20 uses similar imagery to portray YHWH as the loving father who addresses his son with tender words.

Jeremiah uses the same nature images as Hosea to portray the relationship between YHWH and Israel, but in a manner diametrically opposed to that found in Hosea. What conveys order and a good rapport in Hosea is reversed in Jeremiah to communicate the chaos engendered by Israel's sin. A luxuriant vine in Hos 10:1a, Israel is a vine gone wild in Jer 2:21. An olive tree dear to YHWH in Hos 14:7, it is one that should be destroyed in Jer 11:16.

Hosea's description of the coming devastation as anti-creation is expanded in Jeremiah. The creatures who inhabit the world according to Gen 1:20-27 are brought to death in Hos 4:3: "the land mourns, and all who live in it languish; together with the wild animals and the birds of the air, even the fish of the sea are perishing." Jeremiah 4:23-26 extends the anti-creation beyond living beings to embrace the extinction of light and the annihilation of the world. A similar, though less developed, scene of the universe brought to an end is presented in Jer 9:9.

Even the major Jeremianic theme of repentance, which echoes throughout the book with the frequent repetition of *swb* ("turn"), has its roots in Hosea. The single root *swb* with its various meanings (turn away, turn back, turn aside, return, turn around . . .) is used by Hosea to accuse the people of sin (they turned away from God, Hos 11:5, 7) and to call them to repentance (turn back to God, Hos 14:1-2). Jeremiah expands on the Hosean usage, stretching the same root in word-plays frequently lost in translation: "Return, O faithless (turning away) children, I will heal your faithlessness (turning away)" (3:22). Similarly, Jer 15:19 says: "If you turn back, I will take you back (make you turn) . . . it is they who will turn to you (in dependence), not you who will turn to them."

It is clear that Jer uses Hosean images to convey the broken relationship between YHWH and the people: the forsaken marriage, nature gone wild or in distress. Jeremiah not only repeats but also manipulates the imagery and language of Hosea (expanding ideas, moving them in the opposite direction) to convey its particular message.

Isaiah

In a similar way, Jeremiah is indebted to Isaiah of Jerusalem whose images for the people's sinfulness it repeats. As in Isa (3:14; 5:8; 10:2) so also in Jer (5:27; 22:13-14) those who accumulate wealth at the expense of the poor are condemned. Their sin of worshiping "the work of their hands," introduced by Isa 2:8, becomes a refrain in Jer (1:16; 10:3; 25:6-7; 32:30; 44:8). Isaiah 37:19 describes the idols worshiped by Israel as "no gods," an accurate description used by Jer 2:11 and 5:7.

Isaiah's song of the vineyard (Isa 5:1-7) laments the vine that, despite all the owner's efforts, produces only wild grapes. As though giving a précis of this well-known hymn, Jer 2:21 refers to Israel as YHWH's well-tended vine gone wild. Isaiah's description of Israel as silver turned to dross and needing purification (Isa 1:22-25) is taken one step further by Jeremiah's comment that refining is in vain and Israel is nothing more than refuse silver (Jer 6:27-30). Both Isa 30:15 and Jer 30:10 describe salvation as return and rest, which Isa declares will not occur, while Jer holds it out as a promise for the future.

Deuteronomy

The textual links between Jeremiah and the law book of Deuteronomy (Deuteronomy 12–26), discovered and promulgated as word of God under Josiah, have long been acknowledged. Deuteronomy 1:1–2:2 calls for the destruction of all the places of pagan worship "on the hills and under every leafy tree." Jeremiah adopts this same expression to articulate the sin of the people (Jer 2:20; 3:6, 13; 17:2) as well as to justify Josiah's centralization of the cult in Jerusalem. The divorce law of Deut 24:4 appears in Jeremiah to explain why there is no turning back the coming judgment (Jer 3:1), while Jer 13:11 bases YHWH's rejection of the people on their failure to be what they were meant to be: a name, glory, and honor to YHWH (Deut 26:19).

There are striking parallels between the Song of Moses (Deuteronomy 32) and Jeremiah that have been variously interpreted. Some scholars interpret the similarities to indicate Jeremiah's use of Deuteronomy 32 while others would date both at the Exile. In a way reminiscent of Jeremiah's use of Hosea, Jeremiah gives a negative twist to an idea used positively by Deuteronomy. The statement of Deut 32:4 that YHWH is without deceit is turned on its head by Jer 2:5 with its accusation that Israel's ancestors acted as if there were deceit in God. Similarly, Jer 2:27 charges Israel with considering a rock (a stone idol) the source of its being while rejecting YHWH, quite the opposite of Deut 32:18 which calls God the rock that gave birth to Israel.

Both Jeremiah and Deuteronomy 32 foresee a time when the people will suffer the consequences of their sin. While Deut 32:37-38 announces a time when the people will be left to the protection of the (pagan) gods they have worshiped, Jeremiah repeats the idea (Jer 2:27b-28; 11:12) but also carries it further. For Jeremiah the ultimate punishment of Israel's infidelity was that the people of God would be sent into exile to serve other peoples and their gods in foreign lands (5:19b; 15:14; 16:13; 17:4).

Psalms

There is a remarkable similarity in tone between the psalms of individual lament and the confessions of Jeremiah. Both the psalmist and the prophet cry out against those who mock his trust in a God who does not save (Jer 15:15b-16; 20:7b-8; Ps 22:7). Both articulate a complaint against YHWH who has forsaken them (Jer 15:18; 20:7; Pss 10:1; 22:1; 77:7-9). Jeremiah's prayer that YHWH destroy his enemies (Jer 11:20; 15:15a; 18:21-23; 20:12) echoes similar prayers in the lament psalms (Pss 35:1-6; 64:7-8).

In prayers concerning YHWH's dealings with Israel, Jeremiah also quotes or expands on some psalms. In an attempt to redirect God's wrath toward the enemies of Israel, Jer 10:25 quotes Ps 79:6-7. Jeremiah 10:24, on the other hand, expands on Ps 6:2 or 38:2. The prophet accepts YHWH's chastisement but asks that it not be administered in anger. According to Jer 33:11 the praise due YHWH for the return from exile can best be expressed with the words of Ps 136:1, a prayer of thanks for God's steadfast love.

Later Uses of Jeremiah

Ezekiel

Like Jeremiah, which adopted and elaborated on ideas to which it was heir, so the later prophetic writings of Ezekiel and Deutero-Isaiah expanded Jeremiah's insights. The lengthy allegory of Ezekiel 23 in which Samaria and Jerusalem are the sisters Oholah and Oholibah appears to be inspired by the metaphor of Jer 3:6-13 which describes Israel and Judah as two sisters, one of whom did not learn from the experience of the other. Ezek 34:1-16 takes up the declaration in Jer 23:1-4 that YHWH will give the people new shepherds to replace those who have scattered the sheep, and modifies the ending. The new shepherds will not be earthly kings; YHWH alone will shepherd the flock. Similarly, Ezek 18:1-10 elaborates at great length on Jer 31:29-30. The assertion that every person will suffer the consequences of his or her own sin negates the proverb that children will suffer for their parents' deeds.

Deutero-Isaiah

Deutero-Isaiah in its description of the Suffering Servant twice uses language which reflects that of Jer. "The LORD called me before I was born, while I was in my mother's womb he named me" (Isa 49:1) is almost a verbatim repetition of Jer 1:5. The description of the Servant as "a lamb that was led to the slaughter . . . [who] did not open his mouth. . . . For he was cut off from the land of the living" (Is 53:7-8) echoes the lament of Jer 11:19.

Much as Jer had done, the two major exilic prophets used the existing traditions and the corpus of writings available, repeating some ideas, changing and developing others.

Jeremiah in the New Testament

The NT rarely cites Jer, yet the few references it does make, found mostly in Paul, Hebrews, and Matthew, are well known and much quoted. In fact "new covenant," the OT expression which has not only influenced theology but also given us the term "New Testament," (Greek *diathēkē* is translated both "testament" and "covenant") is taken from Jer 31:31.

Paul

Paul shows his indebtedness to Jer particularly in 1 Cor 11:25; 2 Cor 3:4-5; Gal 1:15. While the earliest institution narratives identified the cup of wine with the covenant, Paul, clearly inspired by Jeremiah, is the first written witness to add the qualifier "new"—found in the gospels only in the longer Lukan tradition (Luke 22:17-20). Jeremiah, who coined the phrase, uses it to announce a new relationship with YHWH that will assure the continued existence of the Jewish people. Paul, in 1 Cor 11:25 ("This cup is the new covenant in my blood"), uses the expression to convey that Jesus' death fulfilled the eschatological expectation of a new community between God and the people. Echoing the words of Jeremiah, Paul makes explicit what was only implicit in the tradition he received: that Christ's blood ratified a new covenant to replace the (old) Sinai covenant. In 2 Cor 3:5-6 the expression "new covenant" appears in another context. This time Paul takes up Jeremiah's understanding of the new covenant as one written on the heart rather than on stone to explain his ministry of proclaiming the gospel.

In 1 Cor 1:31 and 2 Cor 10:17 Paul insists that the people are called to be members of the new covenant not because of their wisdom or power but because of the saving power of the Christ. He creates a link between life in Christ and life according to the Sinai covenant by abbreviating and giving a new twist to Jer 9:24. Instead of "let those who boast, boast in this, that they understand and know me, that I am the LORD," Paul writes "Let the one who boasts, boast in the Lord."

Finally, seeing himself in the line of the prophets, Paul describes his call in Gal 1:15 with words taken from Jer 1:5.

Hebrews

Hebrews 8:8-12, the NT citation of Jer that has had by far the greatest impact on the development of Christian theology, quotes in its entirety Jer 31:31-34, while Heb 10:16-17 recalls the same text. In his comparison of the old (levitical) priesthood and the priesthood established in Jesus, the author of Hebrews repeats Jer's notion of two covenants: the old one written on tablets of stone and leading to sin, the new one written on hearts and bringing forgiveness of sin. While for Jer the new covenant was to be established in Israel, for Hebrews the new covenant is fulfilled in Jesus' death which, more than a single act of sacrifice, is the consummation of all God's action.

Gospels

Matthew is the only evangelist who makes explicit mention of Jeremiah. In Rachel weeping for her children who "are no more" because they are in exile (Jer 31:15), he finds Herod's slaughter of the innocents foreshadowed (Matt 2:17-18). According to Matt 16:14 Jeremiah can be compared with John the Baptist and Elijah as a prophet whose return would prepare the way for the Messiah. The basis for his inclusion with the other two is difficult to discern, though it may be because Jesus, like Jeremiah, was rejected by many. Matthew 27:9-10 considers the purchase of the potter's field with the silver acquired by the betrayal of Jesus to fulfill a Jeremianic prophecy. In reality the "quotation" is a pastiche taken from three texts and two books: Zech 11:12-13; Jer 18:1-3; 32:6-25.

All three synoptics (Matt 21:13; Mark 11:17; Luke 19:46) have Jesus justify the cleansing of the Temple by citing Jer 7:11 ("Has this house become a den of robbers?") and Isa 56:7 ("My house shall be called a house of prayer"). The evangelists may have thought that Jesus, like Jeremiah, proclaimed these words against a people who deceived themselves into thinking that proper sacrifice and worship would assure their safety even when they failed to live the covenant in their daily lives.

Since Jer is more concerned with false prophets than are other OT books, it is not surprising that the gospels have found their inspiration on this subject there. In Luke 6:23, 26 Jesus recalls the fact, reflected in the life of Jeremiah, that true prophets were defamed by the people of their generation while false prophets were accepted. Similarly in Matt 7:22 Jesus announces that those who prophesied falsely in the name of God, a theme of Jeremiah, will not have access to the kingdom.

These NT citations and allusions attest to the fact that Jer was part of an ongoing tradition that shaped existing material to respond to the contemporary situation and was, in turn, reshaped by others. At times ideas are simply repeated or developed along the same line. Sometimes, as in the case of the new covenant text of Jer, they are reinterpreted with an entirely new meaning.

C. Fathers of the Church

In his *Dialogue with Trypho the Jew* (15.5) Justin Martyr cites Jeremiah as part of his argument designed to convince Trypho of the truth of Christianity. Posing the question "And have those same Scriptures also predicted that God had announced a new covenant, other than that which he made at Mount Horeb?" (ch. 67), he implies that the new covenant of Jeremiah is brought to fulfillment only in Christ. Yet Justin also appears to admit the continuing validity of the first covenant. In *Homily* 9.2 he states: "These people did not believe in Moses but we, in believing Christ, believe in the covenant made by the intermediary of Moses." Taking what could easily appear to be an anti-Jewish stance Justin, in the *Dialogue with Trypho,* quotes the LXX version of Jer 11:19 "they devised counsels against me, saying: Come let us put wood on his bread, and cut him off from the land of the living, and let his name be remembered no more" as proof "that the Jews planned to crucify Christ" (ch. 72). This statement is hard for contemporary readers to reconcile with Justin's actual effort to convince non-believers, including Jews, of the truth of Christianity.

For Origen (died ca. 254), Jeremiah's life foreshadowed Christ's. In *Homily 1 on Jeremiah* (6.25-28) he elucidates Jer 1:4-10, saying: "These words, if one refers them to the Saviour, do not present a problem for the exegete for Jeremiah is here a figure of the Saviour." In *Homily* 10.4 he applies Jer 11:19-23, in which the men of Anathoth seek to kill the prophet, to Jesus: "The obedience of God . . . was also realized in this word which refers . . . not to the life of Jeremiah . . . but it is said of Christ." In *Homily* 14 which links Jeremiah and Jesus in suffering, Origen meditates on Jer 15:10-16, a lament to God articulating the prophet's distress. Giving an exposition of Jer 15:15, Origen says: "The prophet himself could well say this, since he was persecuted by the people who reproached him, hated by those who did not welcome the truth; for he had become an enemy to his listeners in speaking the truth to them. But our Saviour could also say this for he was also persecuted by this people."

Despite his acceptance of the Jewish Jeremiah as a type of the Jewish Jesus, Origen cited Jeremiah in ways that fueled the anti-Jewish polemic. In a series of Lenten homilies on Jeremiah 1–20, besides noting the similarities between Jeremiah and Jesus he indicates that the loss of their Temple, their prophets, and their land (4.2) proves that the Jews have been rejected by God. Commenting on Jer 3:8 he remarks that, "effectively, God repudiated this people and gave them a bill of divorce" (4.3). Since these homilies seem to be directed toward those preparing for baptism, this may have been a way for him to accent the need for accepting the new covenant in Jesus.

While the struggle to develop a Christian identify different from Judaism may have led, in the early Christian centuries, to some statements that were manifestly anti-Jewish, such comments can be properly interpreted only in light of the issues and debates of the time. Whatever the original intent of these assertions the post-Vatican II Church, with its more refined social and historical consciousness, underlines that the authority of such interpretations must remain confined to their original contexts.

D. Liturgical Context

The eucharistic liturgy, the major locus where the Church hears Scripture proclaimed, gives some insight into how Jeremiah is understood in the Christian context. Whether in ordinary time or in the festal seasons, the readings taken from Jeremiah consider this prophetic work to foreshadow two aspects of the Messiah: his suffering and the fullness of life he brings. Jeremiah's suffering looks forward to that of Jesus, the one who will face death because of his faithfulness to the Father. An extension of the same idea, the prophet's distress at being separated from the community and rejected by his own people, anticipates Jesus' experience. But the newness preached by Jeremiah was also an essential part of the message. The Christian community understood Jesus' death and resurrection as inaugurating the new creation and establishing the new covenant announced by Jeremiah.

In any given year at least a small part of Jeremiah is heard on Sundays during both ordinary time and the festal seasons: two readings in year A; three in year B; four in year C. The three-year lectionary cycle for Sundays in Ordinary Time includes seven readings from Jer (two in year A, two in year B, three in year C) while that of the festal seasons has two (one in Lent in year B, one in Advent, year C). The weekday eucharistic lectionary uses Jer five times during Lent (2nd, 3rd, 4th, and 5th weeks), once in Advent (December 18) while the weekdays of Ordinary Time include an eight-passage semi-continuous reading of Jer in Year 2. (The latter does little more than reflect the story of the book as a whole.)

Three of the readings from Jeremiah heard on the Sundays in Ordinary Time highlight the suffering of Jeremiah as presaging Jesus' rejection (Jer 1:4-5, 17-19 with Luke 4:21-30—4th Sunday, Year C), and the suffering that will come to the followers of Jesus (Jer 20:7-9 with Matt 16:21-27—22nd Sunday, Year A; Jer 38:4-6, 8-10 with Luke 12:49-53—20th week, Year C). Jeremiah's suffering also provides encouragement to follow God whatever the consequences (Jer 20:10-13 with Matt 10:26-33—12th Sunday, Year A). Two of the Jer readings look to a time when life will be renewed and justice will be the rule for all. In healing the blind Bar-Timaeus Jesus signifies that the fullness of life Jeremiah offered as hope for the future has arrived (Jer 31:7-9 with Mark 10:46-52—30th Sunday, Year B). Furthermore, Jeremiah's promise of a good shepherd who would lead the people in justice comes to pass in the person of Jesus (Jer 23:1-6 with Mark 6:3-34—16th Sunday, Year B).

The Jer readings found in the Lenten lectionary focus either on attentiveness to God's word or on the prophet's suffering. Two Lenten weekday readings (Thursday of the 2nd week: Jer 17:5-10; Thursday of the 3rd week: Jer 7:23-28) reiterate the prophet's insistence that the people heed the word of the Lord. The three other Lenten weekday readings taken from Jeremiah (Wednesday of the 2nd week: Jer 18:18-20; Saturday of the 4th week: Jer 11:18-20; Friday of the 5th week: Jer 20:10-13) present Jeremiah's suffering as foreshadowing that of Jesus. The Jer passage for the 5th Sunday of Lent in Year B (Jer 31:31-34) announces new life in the new covenant and so introduces John's account of Jesus' impending death (John 12:20-23) as the first step in the eschatological fulfillment of Jeremiah's promised salvation.

The two readings from Jer heard in Advent (1st Sunday, Year C: Jer 33:14-16; Dec. 18: Jer 23:5-8) herald the coming of a righteous branch from the Davidic line to rule the land with justice.

The Christian church has understood Jesus to be the fulfillment of this promise.

Clearly the contemporary liturgical use of the book of Jeremiah points to the prophetic presence as a herald of the Christ event.

SECOND READING

Introduction: 1:1-19

Historical Introduction (1:1-3)

The opening verses declare that the book of Jeremiah is both word of the Lord and the "word of Jeremiah" spoken in a precise historical context. Jeremiah's prophecies, bridging the reigns of several kings, address a variety of situations: the relative peace with its concomitant religious reform enjoyed under Josiah; the unrealistic hope during Jehoiakim's reign that Judah would escape the threat at its portal; the exile imposed during the time of Zedekiah. While Jeremiah's priestly origins indicate his familiarity with cultic activity, his link with Anathoth rather than Jerusalem implies that he stood outside the corridors of power, at a distance from the royal court, and was thus able to consider the political situation with some objectivity.

Call of Jeremiah (1:4-19)

The call of the prophet, composed of a dialogue with YHWH (1:4-10) and two visions (1:11-19), sets the stage for all that follows. The opening dialogue introduces the prophet as a person whose whole life is directed by YHWH, the God who promises to be with Jeremiah, to guide his words and deeds. With its emphasis on the deeds of destruction to which Jeremiah is called (pluck up, break down, destroy, overthrow), the final verse of the dialogue (v.10) presages the many oracles of judgment Jeremiah pronounces and their negative consequences in his life. Nonetheless the same verse, by auguring new life in the fact that he will also "build" and "plant," keeps alive a spark of hope that will glimmer through the overwhelming darkness.

Despite their very different content both visions allude to the ordinary as the locus of God's revelation: words or events. The first vision (1:11-12), using a word-play (the Hebrew words for "almond rod" and "watching" have the same sound), points to words or language, while the second vision (1:13-16) by its symbolic interpretation of a boiling pot points to an object or event. With an utterance that at first glance seems assuring, God reiterates the prophet's task of proclaiming a word of judgment to Judah (1:16,18). While reinforcing the teaching that sinful Judah will be punished, the text hints that the traditional wisdom that assures blessing to the obedient may not always be true. The prophet of YHWH is not promised a comfortable life, for the promise of YHWH's support is undergirded by the fact that the prophet as "fortified city," "iron pillar," and "bronze walls" will stand alone, outside the community in which he finds life (1:18-19).

Part 1: Inescapable Destruction Announced: 2:1–10:25

Judah's Many Gods (2:1-32)

This first section consists of three parts (2:1-13, 14-27, 28-32). Each contains a series of accusations addressed to Judah, followed by YHWH's reflection on the situation. In all three the accusations are the word of God communicated by Jeremiah to the people in language that alternates metaphoric expressions and factual description.

The whole of the first part (2:1-13) develops a sense of distance between YHWH and Israel/Judah. It opens with a recollection of Israel's early days as the people of God (2:2-3). To recall the time when Israel reciprocated YHWH's love and care is to hold it up as a point of comparison with its subsequent history and present attitude toward God. In light of this Israel's sins become all the more damning. Even the language of this accusation's closing words (2:11), by shifting from second person ("you") to third person ("my people"), conveys the distance that has come between YHWH and Israel. Yet by glancing back at their ancestors, who from the time of the Exodus turned from God (2:5-7), the text implies that this sinfulness is in the people's blood.

YHWH's reflection, addressed to the heavens (2:12-13), introduces the image of fresh water (2:13), especially meaningful in semiarid Palestine, as a fitting metaphor for the lifegiving presence of God that, like fresh running water, cannot be controlled or guaranteed. The shocking reality is that Israel has refused this life.

The second part (2:14-27) first reflects on Israel in ruins (2:14-16), then places the blame for the devastation on its shoulders (2:17-27). Israel's fundamental sin is that it distances itself and turns from God (2:5, 8, 13, 17), a sin magnified by its self-deception (2:23, 27). Its sinfulness is conveyed in a series of metaphors, each metaphor revealing an aspect of Israel's being. Like the already dead prey of a roaring lion (2:14-15), Israel cannot escape destruction. Like a vine that turns from its intended purpose and becomes useless to the vinegrower (2:21), Israel has lost its raison d'être. Like a young camel or a she-ass in heat (2:23-24), Israel is out of control in its life and activity.

Through metaphor the text also describes Judah's real historical situation. The question of 2:14 points to a basic tension in the existence of Israel who has been freed from slavery yet remains a servant: of either YHWH or other nations. Israel's quest for water from the Nile and the Euphrates is a metaphor for how it sought the political and military assistance of Egypt and Assyria (2:18). In an attempt to determine its own future even if that meant compromising its relationship with YHWH (2:20) Israel sought help from powerful neighboring nations. While the service of other nations is bondage from which YHWH alone can free them (witness the Exodus event), service of YHWH is a source of freedom for Israel that according to 2:20 it has rejected.

The brief third part (2:28-32) addresses Judah directly, accusing the nation of embracing other gods. With a rhetorical question (2:31) that refers ironically to YHWH's care for Israel during the Exodus the prophet suggests that Israel has failed to understand or remember the care shown it by God. It should it be as unlikely that Israel, whose very identity comes from being the people of YHWH, should forget God as it is that a maiden fail to put on the ornaments or a bride the attire (2:32) that conveys her status in the community and suggests the potential for life she bears.

The movement from image or metaphor to factual information and back again conveys the ambiguity and confusion that permeate the relationship between YHWH and Israel at this moment in history. These accusations are all the more damning since they follow the remembrance of Israel's earliest days as the people of God, when the first blush of love colored their life together (2:2-3). Love has turned into rejection. Israel not only accepts but expects the gifts of God while rejecting the gift-giver just as their forebears had done.

Love Gone Awry (2:33–3:5)

The few verses that make up this section are accusations addressed to Judah, organized around the single theme of sexual promiscuity, and closely linked to 2:1-32. Undergirding the whole is the idea of intimacy refused. This is expressed in the consistent use of feminine singular address with its allusion to the covenant-spousal relationship that Israel/Judah formerly enjoyed with YHWH. Marriage, employed in 2:1-3 to describe the covenant between YHWH and Israel, is again used to portray the present situation (3:1). But in a shift from the positive imagery of 2:1-3, these verses describe a marriage gone sour. Like a divorced woman who goes to another man (3:1), Judah cannot expect to return to its former situation. Like one who takes the life of the innocent (2:34-35), Judah's denial of guilt will not save it from the inevitable punishment, either future (2:36-37) or present (3:3). This is reiterated by the closing verses (3:4-5) that, showing the inconsistency between Judah's words and its actions, imply that words alone are meaningless. As the shift from metaphor to fact attests, not only is the present drought an inescapable reality but the coming shame is unavoidable.

A Call to Return (3:6–4:4)

This call to repentance opens with an allegory in which YHWH describes for Jeremiah the sinfulness of Judah (3:6-10). After several summons to "return" (3:12-14, 22a) and a promise of future blessing (3:15-18) the people respond to YHWH's words (3:22b-25). God in turn reiterates their need to return and become again the covenant people (4:1-4).

Poetic accusations without a specific historical context, allegorical prose situated during the reign of Josiah, and the sixteen-fold repetition of the root *swb* (turn away, turn back), communicate the change that must permeate the heart of those called to repent in 3:6–4:4. The call to turn back, repeated four times (3:12, 14, 22; 4:3-4), is grounded in an understanding of YHWH as a merciful God (3:12, 22) who not only calls to repentance but plays a role in the change of heart (3:22). Even the unexpected turn of the opening allegory's conclusion (3:11) portrays the largesse of YHWH's spirit that does not condemn but calls Israel to return. The requirement that the sinful nation acknowledge its guilt is simply a reminder that covenant is a two-sided relationship that requires the commitment of both parties. Thus the sound of weeping (3:21) and the admission of sin (3:23-25) raise hope for the future.

In the midst of glances back to past infidelity (3:6-10, 13, 20-21, 25) and calls to turn again to YHWH (3:12-14, 22; 4:1-4) is an amazing promise of restoration (3:14-18) that looks to an idealized and glorious future. The promise made to bring the Israelites back to Zion is a call to believe in God's power to do wonders. This is clear when the book is read from the point of view of those in Exile, for whom only a promise such as this could offer hope in what looked like a hopeless situation.

In his description of the miraculous return the prophet alludes to a transformation in the manner in which God will be present to the nation. Not only will the throne of God, localized for generations in the Ark of the Covenant, now encompass the whole city of Jerusalem (a first indication of a more profound change toward the Temple to be developed in chs. 7 and 26), but the way in which Jerusalem gathers all the nations to itself looks forward to the time when YHWH will be ruler of all the earth. Change in the future does not, however, negate the covenant made in the past. Marked in the flesh by circumcision, covenant commitment must touch the depth of the person and permeate their every thought and choice. The people must either live the covenant with their entire being or face destruction from YHWH (4:4). The choice is theirs. YHWH leaves them free.

All-Encompassing Destruction (4:5-31)

This judgment speech involves the audience in a series of highly charged images that, in contrast to the call to repentance in 3:6–4:4, create an atmosphere of deep darkness. It opens with a command to proclaim coming destruction (4:5-18), apparently given by God to Jeremiah as their dialogue in 4:9-10 suggests. The text leaves ambiguous whether the personal distress expressed in 4:19-22 and the vision conveyed in 4:23-31 are Jeremiah's or YHWH's.

The hope held out at the beginning that salvation might be found in fortified cities (4:5-6) soon gives way to hopelessness (4:7-8). Death is everywhere. The prophet uses figures of the devastation brought by war (4:5-22), the apocalyptic return to pre-creation chaos (4:23-26), and the agony of birthing a first child (4:31) to announce unavoidable doom. The bleakness is pierced by a single spark of light: the desolation will not be complete (4:27).

Although the devastation will be wrought by a real historical enemy it is YHWH's hand that threatens them. The textual intertwining of the two sources of destruction affirms their mutual interdependence. Even if Babylon, the threat from the north, is already on Israel's doorstep in Dan, its northernmost city (4:15), or besieging impregnable Jerusalem in the south, the prophet reiterates that YHWH alone controls what happens to the covenant people (4:6b). Because YHWH acts in response to their actions (4:14, 17, 18), the God who controls history is, at the same time, controlled by Israel's deeds.

Into this bleak picture the prophet inserts a shocking remark. He accuses YHWH of deception (4:10), and blames God for holding out hope when there is none. This is the same accusation YHWH later makes against the prophets. Although it may be an exilic addition, this accusation, which raises the question of who God is and how God acts, hints that the ways of Israel's God are so complex that understanding them eluded even the YHWH prophet.

The ambiguous role of the prophet comes to the fore in the cry of anguish (4:19) which shows that the punishment of the people, announced by Jeremiah himself, has touched the very core of his being (seen in the repetition of *mʿy,* "viscera" though translated "anguish"). By not clearly distinguishing the words of YHWH (4:22) from those of the prophet (4:19-21) the author identifies the two and suggests that the God who punishes also agonizes over the people's suffering.

With apocalyptic imagery the prophet describes the destructive potential of human sin, whose effects reach beyond the life and habitation of the sinner to touch the entire universe. In language suggesting the undoing of the first act of creation and a return to pre-creation chaos the text describes a universe without light. Other signs of the desolation are mountains that are no longer a sign of stability and the actual disappearance of life (birds and humans) or that which promises life (arable land). The prophetic vision is a terrifying portrayal of the end to all created reality.

Against this backdrop of destruction Israel's self-deception becomes ever more apparent. It is demonstrated in the image of a woman setting out to attract those who want only to destroy her. Still, all hope is not lost, for this judgment on Israel closes with a metaphor that, though it prolongs the threat of destruction, alludes to life in the future: despite the pain, helplessness, and threat to her own life, a woman gives birth to her first child.

A Faithless Nation (5:1-19)

This threat of destruction opens with a dialogue between YHWH and Jeremiah (5:1-5a). Jeremiah's personal reflections on the situation (5:5b-6) move imperceptibly into God's judgment speech addressed to the people (5:7-9). Then YHWH's attention reverts to Jeremiah (5:10-17) before returning again to the people (5:18-19). The hope held out in ch. 4 continues to shine through the declarations of destruction while Jeremiah, in 5:3-6, tends to justify the coming evil. The words of YHWH, both those directed to Jeremiah and those directed to the people, reflect a desire to mitigate the coming devastation.

In a scene reminiscent of Genesis 18 where Abraham haggles to keep YHWH from destroying Sodom if ten just persons can be found, Jer 5:1 portrays YHWH as ready to pardon the nation for one person who seeks the truth. The question that opens 5:7 communicates this same desire to pardon, while in 5:10, 18-19 the expected pardon changes to chastisement in the hope of repentance. A certain vacillation in YHWH's relationship to Israel becomes clear in the shift of attitude between 5:7 where God's overriding concern is the good of the people and 5:9 where God's apparent concern is self-vindication.

Jeremiah's ambivalence in his role as one who announces judgment is felt in 5:4-5. Torn between the people of which he is part and the God who called him to speak, the prophet struggles to accept the announced destruction as inevitable. He cannot escape the reality that not even the wealthy with the leisure to study, learn, and live the law of God have accepted its constraints. The images of a broken yoke and bonds thrown off (5:4-5) suggest the people's desire for freedom and their perception of service to YHWH as subservience they seek to escape by taking control of their own lives. The same situation is described quite differently in YHWH's words: in their desire for freedom the people are like animals controlled by their sex drive. But in a surprising switch from earlier accusations the sin of the people is imaged not as harlotry but as adultery. The fact that the sinner is male rather than female implies that God plays the role of the rejected wife. Furthermore, the accusation of male sexual promiscuity directed against Israel hints at the position of power that Israel had in its relationship with YHWH.

Despite the damning accusations against Israel, YHWH's words hold salvation in tension with the coming destruction. While rejection of God's word will unleash the destructive force of an all-consuming fire (5:12-14) and the approaching enemy is described in terms that conjure up the spectre of inescapable death (5:15-17), a remnant will remain. The vine image, used in 2:21 against Israel, becomes a symbol of hope, for the possibility of renewal remains in the stock that endures despite the pruning of the branches. In the closing words of this pericope, however, the prophet holds out a hope that is akin to hopelessness for the Judahites. The future, he suggests, lies with the people in exile and the covenant with YHWH, which was tied to the promise of land, will be abrogated. For the people of God whose very identity presupposed national existence, survival in exile is hardly salvation, yet this will be their future.

A Foolish People (5:20-31)

These few verses spoken by YHWH alone reveal the overwhelming and all-encompassing evil unleashed by the people's sin. Using terms that highlight the stupidity of the Judahites, YHWH gives Jeremiah messages both for himself (5:23-24, 26-31) and for the people (5:21-22, 25), who are characterized as both blind and deaf (5:21). Language used elsewhere to depict idols accents their lack of reflection on their own deeds. The people's foolishness is all the more striking when contrasted with the immediately following description of God as the one who holds sway over the powers of chaos (5:22).

Underlying all the people's sin is deceitfulness, portrayed by the image of a trapper (5:26) who by profession ensnares the unsuspecting prey. The worst indictment against the people, who are initially described as foolish and incapable of recognizing the reality before their eyes, is their injustice toward the defenseless (5:28). This flies in the face of their covenant with YHWH, the one who guarantees the rights of all in the community, especially the marginalized and the dispossessed. Since spurning the covenant was spurning the covenant partner who is none other than the God of creation and life it is not surprising that this sin provokes a drought. Thus the text portrays the interconnectedness of all life.

The image of God in this pericope is two-sided: the one who controls chaos and blesses the earth apparently contemplates evening the score (5:29). Blatant rejection of the covenant calls forth a response in kind. The selective hearing and vision the people practice can be dangerous to them.

Zion Beyond Refining (6:1-30)

With threat leading to accusation and accusation to threat, ch. 6 calls into question the future of Zion and implicates the prophet in the process. The word of YHWH addressed to Judah (6:1-8, 11b-23) and to Jeremiah (6:9, 27-30) dominates this chapter. In very brief interludes Jeremiah engages in a soliloquy (6:10-11a) and calls the people to repentance (6:26). We also hear the people's terrified response to the overwhelming destruction (6:24-25). The text shifts from hope of life to mourning over death in oracles that gradually change from metaphorical to factual description of the future. Central to the whole is the sin of the people: injustice, deceit, and self-deception (6:13-15). The last is the worst since it renders repentance and return to YHWH impossible.

The first oracle, a call to leave the city whose existence had been guaranteed by the presence of YHWH, implies that God has withdrawn, leaving the people without defense and without a future. The ostensibly idyllic image of shepherds in Jerusalem conveys the opposite reality since "shepherd" is a metaphor for a foreign ruler and the city turned to pasture land presupposes total ruin. Although the city knows the menace of an advancing army, the actual threat to its existence, the real source of the violence, comes from within (6:7). Much as illness and wounds slowly destroy a healthy body, so the violence and wickedness of the people will bring about their demise. The sins of which they are accused eat away at the fibre of their own community.

By moving from simple metaphors to language imbued with covenant overtones ("uncircumcised ears," 6:10), and by using the covenant curses of Deuteronomy 28 (house, field, wife taken by another) the text conveys the undisputed end to Israel's relationship with YHWH (6:9-12). While none escape guilt (6:13), none admit it (6:15). From this follows the people's unwillingness or inability to hear and heed the call to return. YHWH's refusal of cultic offerings is a response to the people's refusal to take seriously their common social obligations (6:19-20). Since covenant is two-sided by nature, one party's (Israel's) rejection of the agreement frees the other (YHWH) from any covenant obligation.

The prophet's use of a female figure to portray in visual and aural images (6:22-23) the enemy's cruel power makes the description all the more horrific (6:24-26). A woman's vulnerability and loss is greater than a man's. Not only does she suffer helplessness and terror but she is called to lament her only son, the sole guarantee of a future for an Israelite. Death permeates the entire scene. The horror deepens with each succeeding image in the text, only to be reiterated in the final words to Jeremiah (6:27-30). The refining process to which the prophet has been called produces unexpected results: the precious metal to be purified (Israel) is so mixed with dross that nothing is salvageable. God has rejected God's own people!

False Worship (7:1–8:3)

This collection of oracles on false worship constitutes a long prose interruption of the poetic oracles stretching from ch. 2 through ch. 10. It includes YHWH's message to the people which Jeremiah pronounced at the Temple gate (7:3-15, 21-26), and God's words addressed to the prophet in the form of command (7:16, 27-29) and description (7:17-20; 7:30–8:3). Although the refutation of the people's naive faith in the Temple as the guarantee of God's protection has given Jeremiah the name of one who preached against the cult, the gist of this speech (introduced in 6:20) is not the inherent evil of cultic activity but the gap between the deeds of the Israelites and their acts of worship (7:8-10).

In 7:12 Jeremiah uses Shiloh, the cultic centre of the northern kingdom from the time of Joshua (Josh 18:1; Judg 21:19) as a point of comparison. He makes it clear that just as the sanctuary at Shiloh was not able to save Israel from the Assyrian invaders who destroyed it in 722, so also the Jerusalem Temple cannot guarantee that Judah will be protected from its enemies. In the midst of this polemic against Israel the reader comes face to face with the prophet's personal involvement in the life of his people. YHWH demands that the prophet, a member of the community he addresses and thus a participant in their fate, refrain from the single act that might bring hope: he may not intercede with God on their behalf. This is the first indication of a separation from the community that will eventually lead to Jeremiah's isolation and intense personal suffering (chs. 11–20).

Judah's false worship is two-sided: the worship of false gods and false worship of the one God, the latter including misplaced confidence in cultic activity. In startlingly sarcastic words the prophet makes it clear that God is not interested in sacrifice alone. Unless they live lives of justice as the covenant people (7:5-11), as far as God is concerned they might as well eat the "burnt offering," that part of the sacrifice reserved to YHWH (7:21). This and other remarks are buttressed by direct references and allusions to Israel's history and its repeated desire to act independently of God's commands (7:22-26).

The command that the people cut off their hair (7:29) is a call to lament their own demise with a visible and enduring sign. Disaster will reach them even in the realm of death since lack of a proper burial (7:33), which was considered essential to a person's finding lasting peace, is worse than death. Worse still is disturbing the peace of those long buried by opening their tombs (8:1-2). Every vestige of hope disappears. This people for whom death was the end will be driven to make the unthinkable choice (8:3).

From Deception to Destruction (8:4–9:16)

The poetic oracle of Jer 8:4–9:16 focuses on the deception of self and others that permeates Judah's existence and keeps it from repentance. Except for 8:14-15 which convey the people's response to the coming disaster, the rest of this section can be construed as God's word to the people (8:4-13, 16-17; 9:4-6), to Jeremiah (9:7-16), or YHWH's musings (8:18–9:3), although it is not clear whether 8:18–9:2 are God's words or the prophet's. This ambiguity echoes the obscurity of whether Judah is the addressee as well as the subject of the discourse in 8:5-13. By giving Judah a more objective view of its own reality and thus diminishing its sense of being threatened the prophet might more easily engage the nation to consider what has happened.

Using birds' instinctual knowledge as a point of comparison (8:7), YHWH indicates that Judah's stance is contrary to its nature as the people of God. The repetition of 6:13-15 in 8:10-12 links the two chapters and reiterates the essential sin of the people: not only greed but self-deception and the inability to feel guilt for their sin. The imagery conveys a twofold destruction that none can escape: one that is seen, heard, and feared (8:16); one that is unannounced and unexpected (8:17). It appears that in the midst of the terror and death that surround them the people can do little more than fall back on familiar formulas for hope and protection (8:19). Yet the prophet raises the question of their honesty by two rhetorical questions that challenge them to consider their own attitudes: where has their trust in the assistance of other nations gotten them (8:22)? Although the balm and physicians of Gilead were renowned for their ability to heal, reliance on other nations' products, wisdom, and gods will not bring Israel wholeness.

The intensity of the horror is reflected in the rather ambiguous words of the prophet. On the one hand he mourns for the people while on the other he wants to separate himself from them and their sinful deeds (8:23–9:2). The sudden change of speaker from Jeremiah to God (9:3), while confusing the issue of which words are in whose mouth, serves to closely identify the prophet with God and hints that his suffering reflects the suffering of God. Furthermore it introduces the close and at times indistinguishable roles that the two will play in the rest of the book.

The deception that permeates the life of Israel courses in its very lifeblood. The Hebrew text uses a play on words to trace Israel's history of deceit back to Jacob, their ancestor. Jacob, the father of the twelve sons from whom originated the twelve tribes of Israel (Gen 49:1-28), deceived his father and stole the birthright of his brother Esau (Genesis 27). Since deceit is the heritage of Israel, community, which by its nature is built on mutual trust, is no more. The curses of Deuteronomy 28 have become reality. The repeated disobedience of God's people, textually suggested by the repetition of their sin, will lead to their exile.

Coming of the Grim Reaper (9:17-26)

This short section, with its call to mourning, affirms the pervasive presence of death. Apparently Jeremiah addresses the people as a whole (9:17-19) before turning his attention to the women mourners (9:20-22). At the end it seems that YHWH speaks to the prophet, giving him both a command (9:23-24) and information about the future (9:25-26).

Insofar as the call to mourning indicates that the nation is in ruin it is a first step toward the admission of guilt and the hoped-for repentance. The words addressed to "skilled women" who celebrated in song both joy and sorrow, life and death for the people of Israel announce that death is everywhere. None can escape the grim reaper who is already gathering rich and poor, young and old (9:23-24).

The concluding words, a call to true wisdom, to know who the Lord is, imply that the people are responsible for their fate since they trust themselves instead of their God. Second in a list of nations that practice circumcision (all included in the oracles in chs. 46–51), Judah is equated with others who, despite the mark in their flesh, have no relationship with YHWH. Thus the final verses point beyond the physical act of covenant belonging to insist upon the involvement of the heart—i.e., the total person.

YHWH's Power to Create or Punish (10:1-25)

Without denying the coming destruction this final section of the first part of Jeremiah raises the hope that YHWH will act, if not directly in favor of Israel, at least indirectly by bringing down its enemies. Although this section opens with the LORD's word to Israel (10:1-5) and Israel's response (10:6-10), the remainder of the chapter is the word of Jeremiah first to Israel (10:11-22) and then to YHWH (10:23-25). In his speech to Israel Jeremiah includes a brief word of YHWH (10:18).

The lengthy description of how idols are made gives them their place in the scheme of things (10:3-5, 8-9, 14). By focusing on the power of Israel's intangible God and the powerlessness of the beautiful idols of other nations the text points to the foolishness of those who reject YHWH and the certainty that YHWH will act. The appealing description of the idols leads the audience to understand their power to deceive. Israel, whose life has been presented as one of deception, is thus identified with the idols which are stupid (10:8) and perish in their time (10:15). Even the verb (*qlʿ*, "tear away") used to convey that, like the idols with which it identified, Israel will meet destruction, is replete with a sense of power and violence (10:18). By insisting that both the people (10:20b) and all dwelling places (10:22) will come to an end the text leaves no doubt that the devastation is all-pervasive.

The closing lines are a cry for mercy. Despite the command that he not intercede (7:16), the prophet who has already tried to cajole YHWH into a change of heart tries again (10:23-25). This attitude implies that God is perceived as compassionate. Although the promised destruction has been justified the prophet mitigates the people's responsibility by accenting their lack of control, thus attempting to convince God to temper their punishment. If YHWH's wrath has already been unleashed, perhaps it can be redirected against Israel's enemies. The one who was told not to intercede uses all his powers of persuasion to save the people from the wrath they deserve. If the earlier identification of Jeremiah with YHWH has an influence on these words, the compassion of the prophet alludes to God's continual desire to forgive.

Part 2: The Suffering Prophet: 11:1–20:15

Covenant Broken (11:1-17)

The covenant theme permeates this short passage with its repetition of the word *berit* (covenant) five times in the first ten verses and its use of the "covenant formula" in 11:4. The words

Jeremiah is called to pronounce to the people (11:2-8) remind them that covenant is more than a simple promise of protection on the part of YHWH. It is a two-sided agreement, made clear by the covenant formula: "You shall be my people and I will be your God" (11:4b). Thus this pericope reflects on the relationship once established between God and Israel and on how it has shaped their life over the generations.

YHWH is portrayed as the God whose care for the people became enfleshed in the act of leading them out of (*yṣʾ,* 11:4) and up from (*ʿlh,* 11:7) Egypt. The use of two verbs to describe YHWH's active engagement on behalf of the people suggests the double activity of freeing them from slavery (out of the iron furnace or "iron smelter," with its allusion to a time of refining and cleansing) and of bringing them into the land. For the Israel of Jeremiah's generation their possession of the land signaled the ongoing covenant with its assurance of YHWH's protection, while from the viewpoint of Israel in exile their loss of the land signified God's absence and the end of the covenant.

In an intriguing interplay of parties to the conversation, the author shifts from the words spoken by YHWH to Jeremiah for Israel (11:2-8, 13, 15b-17) to the words addressed to Jeremiah about Israel (11:9-12, 14-15a). This in some way identifies the prophet with the people of whom he is part. Thus the prohibition against Jeremiah's interceding for the people is grounded in his own identification with them and suggests that the words he addressed against them came not from himself but were truly the words of YHWH. Furthermore the prohibition against intercession also alludes to a God whose hand might be stayed, who might finally forgive. The ambiguity in YHWH's attitude toward Israel is clear in 11:15 where God can still call Israel/Judah "my beloved." This tension between a caring, forgiving love and the need to punish a people who do not respect the covenant foreshadows the tension in a salvation that comes only through exile.

Innocence Does Not Guarantee Blessing (11:18–12:6)

In this first of Jeremiah's six personal laments (traditionally called "confessions") the prophet cries out to God, seeking to understand why the one who is faithful to YHWH should suffer. Unique in the prophetic corpus, these confessions, whatever their historical origin, offer a glimpse of the OT understanding of the prophet's inner life.

Composed of two dialogues between YHWH and Jeremiah (11:18-23; 12:1-6), this lament reaches to the heart of the prophet's suffering: rejection even by his family. The first dialogue introduces the threat to the prophet in his own words (11:18-20) and gives YHWH's response (11:21-23). YHWH's affirmative response to Jeremiah's call for vengeance against those who seek his life may seem shocking to contemporary ears. In its own context where "an eye for an eye" was a way of stemming the escalation of blood feuds God's response is not so surprising, especially when one considers that "men of Anathoth" refers to Jeremiah's own flesh and blood (see 1:1). Furthermore their prohibition of his prophesying reveals that they have rejected the word of the LORD, which they recognize as powerful.

For the Hebrews, to speak is to set in motion the events described in words. To speak of destruction, as Jeremiah had done, was to unleash the evil itself. Having been rejected by the people, the prophet is separated from the society to which he belongs. YHWH's response, which does not promise protection but simply gives an assurance that his enemies will be destroyed, hints at the final chapters of the book, which focus not on salvation for Israel but on the destruction of its enemies.

The second dialogue gradually erodes any sense of hope. Using questions typical of lament psalms (Why? How long?), Jeremiah presents himself as distanced from the people (12:1-2), at one with nature (12:4) and questioning his own knowledge of God. According to the received wisdom the good enjoy prosperity and God's blessing while the evil suffer poverty and deprivation. Jeremiah's experience of threats to his life contradicts what he has been taught concerning God and leads to questions about how God deals with good people and evildoers. His second cry for vengeance (12:3) receives an unexpected and rather startling response. Not only is there no assurance that the evildoers will be punished, but YHWH, using images taken from nature (12:5), warns Jeremiah that what he has experienced thus far is only the beginning. Instead of promising protection YHWH simply warns the prophet to take care of himself.

This first sketch of the prophet's personal experience indicates that the prophetic existence was under the sole guidance of YHWH. Torn from even his family, the prophet was called to rely totally on God whose presence did not take the expected and traditional forms. The solitude of the prophet introduced here undergoes further development in later chapters.

YHWH's Heritage Turned to Desolation (12:7-17)

In this judgment oracle the prophetic presence disappears, leaving YHWH alone to speak in what appears to be a soliloquy. The first part of the oracle is in poetry (12:7-13), and conveys what has already happened to Israel. The second (12:14-17), in prose, looks toward the future of foreign nations. This self-reflective speech in which God refers to Israel as "my beloved" and yet hands the nation over to destruction manifests God's ambivalence in its regard. The motif of heritage/inheritance, repeated nine times in 12:7-15 (*nḥl* 7x; *ḥlq* 2x), creates a strong link between the two oracles, the first concerned with the heritage of YHWH, the second with that of the people. As the "heritage" over which YHWH exercises control Israel should enjoy the protection of YHWH, but its enemies have been allowed to destroy it.

In a surprising transformation the second oracle holds out a promise to the foreign nations who have devastated Israel. Furthermore the mercy *(rḥm)* YHWH will show these nations is not, according to the text, dependent on the people's initial turning to God (12:15). The text hints at the total gratuitousness of YHWH's salvation but still insists on the need to respond in daily life to God's initiative ("if they will diligently learn the ways of my people," 12:16).

Linen Waistcloth Spoiled (13:1-14)

This is the first of several reports of symbolic actions performed by Jeremiah at the command of YHWH. As "outer visions" they express the Israelite belief that God's revelation most often occurs in the ordinary events of life. The two parts contain (1) a series of actions performed by and for the benefit of Jeremiah, with their interpretation by YHWH (13:1-11), and (2) a parable-like saying for the people (13:12-14). Although very different, they interpret one another and so must be read together. The symbolic action suggests that the prophet must experience in his own body a situation analogous to YHWH's experience with Israel. There is no doubt that symbolically the linen waistcloth represents Israel. But since this same garment is part of the "holy" clothing of the high priest the waistcloth appears to symbolize Israel as a priestly people, as the holy people of YHWH. Knowledge of geography makes it clear that it would have been virtually impossible for Jeremiah, who was living in Israel, to go back and forth from Israel to the Euphrates (in Babylon/Assyria) to fulfill one command after the other as the text suggests. The exclusion of a literal interpretation suggests that the image is metaphorical, that the Euphrates refers to the hope for life and protection Israel sought from Assyria or Babylon (see 2:18).

The storytelling technique is brilliant. YHWH gives a command and the prophet fulfills it without any idea of what will come next. By repeating the command of God in the same words when describing the action of the prophet the author gives time for each successive action to make an impression. All leads to the prophet's final reaction (13:7), which is the catalyst for his receiving the word of God (13:8-11). Just as the waters of Babylon/Assyria have made of the waistcloth something to be thrown away, so the "life" they offer Israel will result in the people's being cast off.

The saying of 13:12-14 could be construed as the prophet's communication of his experience to the people. Jeremiah, in terms that apparently have no connection with the symbolic action, first engages their attention and evokes their agreement with his words (13:12). Then, using a technique common in parables, the prophet jars the consciousness of the audience by a slight shift of the image. Since the vessels here mentioned were used as containers for any liquid (water, milk, oil, or wine) and since wine symbolized the joy of God's rule, to say that "every wine-jar should be filled with wine" was to look forward to a time of peace, prosperity and joy. In a statement that frequently loses its punch in translation ("drunkenness" follows the list of people in the Hebrew), the prophet foresees not the joy of God's rule but the destruction that comes from loss of control. The verb used in the Hebrew text of 13:14a to express YHWH's action against the people has a double meaning: to shatter an earthen vessel (the wine jars) and to scatter a people (Israel in exile).

The closing line disturbs the reader much as the prophet's words would have troubled his audience. The compassion *(rḥm)* God was willing to show foreign nations in 12:15 is denied to YHWH's own people (13:14).

The Flock in Captivity (13:15-27)

Using images a modern audience finds rather shocking, the oracles of 13:15-27 teeter between hope and hopelessness. The earlier scenes of a military machine wreaking havoc yield to descriptions that portray violence from a different, more personal perspective: rulers lose their crowns (13:18), women are shamed (13:22, 26). Jeremiah first addresses Judah directly (13:15-17), then with YHWH's words for its rulers (13:18-23). Finally YHWH's unmediated word is directed to Jerusalem, metonymy for the people of Judah (12:24-27).

Underlying this oracle is a sense of hopelessness conveyed in the repeated mention of exile, presented as if it were already underway (e.g., the perfect tense used in 13:18-19). Still the words of the prophet offer a glimmer of hope, for initially they see the darkness as a future, rather than a present reality that can therefore be held at bay (13:16). While elsewhere the people sinned by looking to other nations and their gods for help, here their sin is pride (13:15, 17). The summons to glorify YHWH (13:16) is an indirect accusation of their failure to recognize their own God, made explicit in 13:25 which links it with self-deceit, one of the themes of chs. 5–9.

The announcement of exile to the king and the queen mother (13:18-19) begins the accusation. Although the text almost certainly refers to Jehoiakin and his exile in Babylon the larger context is indefinite enough to make these lines a general indictment of those rulers of Israel who led the nation toward disaster. So in the habit of acting in wickedness, they cannot change their ways any more than a leopard can change her spots.

The accusation (13:27) expressed by the image of sexual transgressions, both male (adultery, neighing, see 5:7-8) and female (harlotry, see 2:20; 3:6), looms as the reason for exile. Since the penalty for sin is frequently related to the offense it is not surprising that the punishment is also described in terms that suggest sexual shame. Twice in the accusation YHWH threatens to "lift up the skirts" of Judah/Jerusalem. The issue here is not rape, as commonly assumed, but nakedness and the shame it causes. Although such violence against the female figure offends contemporary sensibilities this imagery, like the utter destruction of the city, serves to horrify the listeners. Using the image of such outrageous ill-treatment, the prophet might shock Israel into reforming its ways.

Despite the emphasis on coming punishment this oracle presents YHWH as compassionate, suffering with the people. The text conveys this by leaving the speaker ambiguous in 13:17. It is clear that the prophet speaks in 13:15-16 and YHWH in 13:18-27. While 13:17 appears at first glance to be in Jeremiah's mouth it is not impossible that these words are YHWH's. This is yet another instance of the identification of YHWH and the YHWH prophet, suggesting that the God of Israel, like Jeremiah, suffers with and for the people. YHWH not only makes repeated attempts to bring them back but also suffers at their refusal to acknowledge their God.

Israel's Plea for YHWH's Intervention (14:1–15:4)

This plea for help is composed of three parts (14:1-10; 14:11-16; 14:17–15:4), each of which presents a situation, a corresponding prayer to God and YHWH's response. The first and third parts, mainly poetry, each offer a description of death (14:1-6, 17-18) followed by the people's plea that God come to their aid (14:7-9, 19-22) and YHWH's response (14:10; 15:1-4). They enclose a prose dialogue between Jeremiah and YHWH (14:11-16). While the prophetic prayer and YHWH's response both condemn false prophecy, the prayer that Israel addresses to YHWH, with its acknowledgment of guilt, raises the hope that repentance will lead to salvation. But YHWH's responses in 14:10 and 15:1-4 belie this hope.

From the very beginning all the imagery evokes the spectre of death, setting the stage for the people's repentance. The description of Judah and Jerusalem (the place standing for the people) in 14:2 contrasts their physical stance which is downward (*ʾbl,* walk with one's head down; *ʾml,* droop or hang down the head; *qdr,* be dark like the earth) with their voice that rises heavenward. This contrast reflects the innate contradiction in their being. They turn away from the covenant by their actions yet call upon God to continue protecting them. The images move farther from life and closer to death: no water, no food, no air, no life. All living beings are affected: nobles and their servants, farmers, domestic and wild animals.

For the first time in the book, following the description of devastation, the people raise a prayer to their God (14:7-9), attempting to move YHWH to action. They would expect YHWH to respond with mercy to their admission of guilt (14:7) or at least to the reminder that it would not be right to let God's name lose esteem in the eyes of the nations (14:8-9). They appear to try shaming God into acting for Israel by their characterization of YHWH in 14:8-9 that turns the image of God around from one who has saved in the past to one who cannot save. In an almost imperceptible shift God is compared first to a resident alien who is not attached to the people (14:8a), then to a traveler who is still less involved (14:8b), and finally to a strong young man who, despite physical prowess, is unable to "save" (14:9).

YHWH's rejection of their prayer (14:10) is a startling turn of events. The repeated accusations of Jeremiah 1–13 have raised the hope that repentance would bring salvation. But here that hope is dashed. Still the prophet appears to understand God as one with whom dialogue is still possible (14:11-13). Immediately after God tells him that intercession is useless Jeremiah attempts to excuse the people's deed by showing their obedience to their leaders, the prophets. Although it is unsuccessful, Jeremiah's appeal implies that hope is not completely lost.

The pattern of death described, a plea for mercy and YHWH's refusal encountered in 14:1-10 returns in 14:17–15:4. The prophet's suffering at the destruction he sees conveys a pessimism for the future (14:17-18). The people approach YHWH once again, appealing to the pride of God who deserves to be honored by others and merits continued recognition by Israel (14:19-22). God's response is unexpected: not even Moses, who kept YHWH from destroying the Israelites after the golden calf incident (Exod 32:11-14), would be able to stay the hand of destruction (15:1-4). This seems to prove the accuracy of Jeremiah's earlier accusation that God has deceived the people.

Glory Turned to Shame (15:5-9)

This entire poetic oracle is placed in the mouth of YHWH. It initially reflects direct contact with Judah by the use of second person address (15:5-6), then creates a certain distance by moving to third person speech (15:7-9) as if to imply that only increased non-involvement will permit YHWH to carry out the threatened destruction. The three opening questions bring Jerusalem, a metaphor for the people and their leaders, to realize how alone the city is. Not only does no one act favorably toward it (15:5a), no one even cares about its fate (15:5b). The sense of the city's forsakenness is intensified by the images of women who lost husbands and sons in battle. Jerusalem is like the woman who, having borne yet lost seven sons, finds herself without support or defense. The source of her glory, now lost, is the source of her shame.

Although the overarching theme of the oracle is the destructive power and potential of YHWH, the Hebrew text of 15:6 leaves no doubt that Israel has brought this on itself, as the emphatic use of "you" indicates: "You, [you are the one who has] rejected me." Until now YHWH's attitude has been one of forgiveness (15:6c) and educative punishment (15:7a), but to no avail. Hence the destruction is justified.

Jeremiah Laments His Existence (15:10-21)

This second lament, like the first, is composed of two exchanges between the prophet and God (15:10-14; 15:15-21). In the first part Jeremiah addresses his words not to YHWH but to himself or to his mother (15:10), yet YHWH responds to him (15:11-14). In the second part of this lament Jeremiah directs his words to God (15:15-18) whose answer is less than reassuring (15:19-21).

With an opening cry of pain akin to despair the prophet laments his birth in terms echoing the previous oracle that describes a mother lamenting the loss of her sons. The difficult Hebrew text of 15:11-14 beginning with "The LORD said" is YHWH's reaction to the prophet's lament. Assuming that v. 11 might be translated: "Have I not set you free *(šrh)* for good? Have I not met *(pgʿ)* with you at a time of difficulty and at a time when you were in straits with the enemy?," YHWH's response to Jeremiah lacks compassion. Reminding the prophet of a former time God helped him, YHWH gives Jeremiah no more than an implicit assurance for the future. In an almost imperceptible shift (from the second person singular to the second person plural) the text slips from addressing Jeremiah (15:11) to addressing the people (15:14) and thus suggests, with the second person singular of 15:13, that the prophet and the people are one. As becomes clearer in the following dialogue and in subsequent texts his being part of them is a source of his suffering, both because he suffers with them and because he must be separated from them.

The dialogue of 15:15-21 portrays a disillusioned prophet addressing a God who first challenges, then reassures. The prophet's words move from a standard prayer that YHWH avenge Jeremiah (15:15), through a description of joy in YHWH (15:16), then to indignation (15:17-18a), and end with a shocking accusation that God has been double-dealing (15:18b). Since obedience to the one who should be the source of peace and happiness has isolated him from society and caused him an anguish beyond telling, the prophet is justified in referring to God as "waters that fail." That which promised life suddenly proves a sham. YHWH has acted out of character and contrary to expectations.

YHWH throws the ball into Jeremiah's court (15:19). The two conditional clauses ("If you turn back . . . If you utter what is precious . . .") imply that it is Jeremiah who needs to take a first step toward reestablishing his relationship with God. Using a root-play ("if you turn . . . I will cause you to turn"), the text both indicates the importance of the prophet's initiative and intimates that human deeds can influence divine action. Introducing God's promise to save (15:20b-21) is YHWH's declaration that Jeremiah will continue to stand in opposition to the people (15:20). This attenuates the final promise of deliverance. God's presence is both positive and negative, the source of the prophet's life as well as of his suffering. The promise of presence does not guarantee future ease.

No Life in the Land (16:1–17:4)

This pericope weaves the words YHWH addresses to the prophet (16:1-9, 14-18, 21) with those addressed to the people (16:11-13; 17:1-4), adding a new dimension to both the growing threat and the portrait of God. Opening with a renewed promise of death and ending with the assurance of neverending exile, it presents an amazing contrast between an absolute end and a new beginning. The people's response to their fate belies their self-deceit (16:10). The prophet's prayer reflects his confidence in God (16:19-20).

YHWH's opening demand that the prophet not marry (16:1-4) is nothing less than an injunction that he experience in his flesh the dissolution of all hope, that his life presage the nation's demise. In Israelite society where progeny was considered the only way to assure life beyond death, the celibacy YHWH demands of Jeremiah would be considered the equivalent of suicide. Furthermore, he is to endure this affliction without the support of the community (16:5-9), the only means to make his isolation bearable. Jeremiah, as presented here, is a man of sorrows. The source of his suffering is not society or his family, as the earlier confessions have maintained, but the God in whom he trusts. YHWH's image changes from source of life to bringer of death, even to the good.

The threat of exile, till now only mentioned in passing (5:19; 9:15; 10:18), looms as an incontrovertible fact, for the death that hovers over even the prophet of YHWH overruns "this land" (five times in 16:2-9). In the midst of repeated threats the profiles of sinful Israel and an uncompassionate God come into sharper focus. The depth of Israel's sin is indicated in two ways. The present generation not only worships others gods, but has made itself its own idol (16:12). Even the foreign nations to which Israel was compared in 2:11, recognize the worthlessness of their gods (16:19b-20), leaving them open to know YHWH (16:21). The people of YHWH, however, embrace what the others nations reject. Affecting both their ability to choose (heart) and their worship (altar), Israel's sin, like an engraving made with tools of iron and diamond (17:1), is everlasting.

The most extraordinary aspect of this passage is the ray of hope in the midst of the growing darkness. Immediately after YHWH denies compassion to the people (16:13) the text reveals a change in the way YHWH will be perceived and known. Up to now Israel's God has been understood as the one who saved them from slavery in Egypt. Now the primary salvific moment will be shifted to return from exile. With YHWH newly identified as the God who brings the people back to the land from exile the text points to what appears to be an utter devastation as the starting point for a new life, looking forward to the promise of salvation in chs. 30–33. And although up to this point in the book YHWH's action for Israel has awaited their initial return to God, here God's action for them appears totally gratuitous. The God whom they think they know acts in previously unthinkable ways. YHWH demands a living death of the good prophet and promises life to a people who show no sign of changing their sinful ways.

Water Alone Gives Life (17:5-13)

This short poetic piece contains a proverb (17:5-8), a declaration (17:9-10) and a simile (17:11), all spoken by YHWH, and words of the people (17:12-13) showing they have finally understood. Its overriding negativity is tempered by the closing words that acknowledge that YHWH is the fountain of life, as stated at the very beginning of the book (2:13). Since lack of water and the search for water are two threads that have run through the text from the start, the proverb, which compares people to plants either in the desert or by a stream (see also Psalm 1), is apt.

The statement that YHWH recompenses people according to their deeds (17:10) justifies the destruction Israel suffers but raises some serious questions about God. If the human heart cannot change from its evil ways, is punishment of those who cannot choose justified? And if life reflects a person's deeds, how explain the suffering of the prophet? Once again hope shines through despair but the character of YHWH's justice becomes less clear.

The Suffering Prophet (17:14-18)

Jeremiah's third lament reflects deep confidence in a God who has not treated the prophet as justice would prescribe. With a cry that articulates a suffering so intense and ineluctable that it racks the prophet's body as well as his spirit (17:14) Jeremiah brings his pain before God whom he holds responsible. Despite the earlier repeated statements that YHWH rewards persons in conformity with their actions, the prophet's experience belies the received wisdom. According to the unemended Hebrew text of 17:16a ("I did not withdraw from being a shepherd [leader] after you"), the prophet's life has been totally dedicated to God's service, which should lead to blessing. But Jeremiah has come to learn that the same God who comforts and rescues can be a source of terror (17:17). So he prays for the protection God promised at his call, asking that his persecutors suffer the shame and terror they have imposed on him (17:18). Such a prayer, strange to ears trained in the Christian message of "love your enemy; do good to those who persecute you," is little more in its own context than a request that God keep God's word and protect the faithful prophet.

To Keep the Sabbath (17:19-27)

Sent by YHWH to the Benjamin Gate where people gathered to conduct business and settle disputes, Jeremiah proclaims an oracle to all who pass by, leaders and common folk alike. He does not enact his message as he does at other times. His only role in this scene is to be the mouthpiece of God, conveying to the people YHWH's words of both accusation and promise, recorded in the form of a covenant speech. Once again the text identifies past with present generations. Like their ancestors, the people fail to keep the Torah prescription concerning the Sabbath (17:21-23).

This short prose speech promising a future comparable to the Solomonic era when Jerusalem was a powerful city (17:25-26) suggests that despite all the announcements of destruction, hope is not lost. The people will determine the fate of their capital city (and their nation) by the way they keep the covenant. Thus the statement of 17:10 that God recompenses people according to their deeds becomes concretized (17:24, 27). By limiting his discourse to non-cultic Sabbath regulations the prophet alludes to the fact that life's day to day activities affect the people's relationship with God. But in his detailed description of how the people fail to keep the Sabbath, Jeremiah attenuates the very hope he proffers.

YHWH the Potter (18:1-12)

This brief narrative describing an event in Jeremiah's life exemplifies how the word of God is revealed to the prophet not in visions or other extraordinary ways but in the ordinary events of daily life. Seeing a potter at work, Jeremiah realizes that just as the artisan must work with the clay and shape it until the form respects the material, so does YHWH act with Judah. The God of Israel recognizes the people's freedom to choose good or evil. The creator, human or divine, is limited by the properties of the raw material.

Neither Jeremiah nor YHWH addresses Judah directly here. Rather an indirect approach in which Judah listens to how YHWH acts in general might bring the people, freed from any stance of self-defense, to consider and change their ways. As a potter works and reworks the clay until a useful (and good) vessel is shaped, the text suggests that the same may be true of Judah. Yet the people's shocking response destroys any optimism that God's compassion or the call to repentance (18:11) may have raised. Their explicit refusal to turn from their own ways leaves no room for God to act with mercy. YHWH leaves the people free even when their choice is self-destructive.

From Idolatry to Desolation (18:13-17)

In a poetic soliloquy (all references to Israel are in the third person) YHWH responds to Judah's stubbornness by confirming the decision to destroy. The two rhetorical questions at the beginning of this poetic musing (18:14) by using universally held knowledge imply that Israel's actions are contrary to its existence as the people of YHWH. The specific accusation is twofold. If 18:15a is understood to mean ". . . they burn incense in vain" then Israel is reminded in words that recall the Temple sermon (ch. 7) that cultic offering does not eliminate the need to live the covenant in ordinary life (18:15). Furthermore, the choice of the footpaths over the paved road is a wonderful image of Israel's refusal to follow the Torah in daily life (18:15b). The people have preferred a familiar way, worn by use but constantly changed by the seasons, the rain and the wind, to a way that is built up, paved, proven, and lasting. The nation's own choices have led to its demise, expressed first by YHWH's absence (which results in its becoming a horror) and then by YHWH's active decimation of the nation through exile (18:16-17).

The nature imagery throughout this poetic reflection is a metaphorical means to communicate the senselessness of Israel's choices. Indeed, the presence of twenty-four sibilants in the Hebrew of these few lines of poetry evokes the whistling that was a common reaction to destruction. The final line leaves uncertain the source of Israel's tragedy: YHWH? Israel? foreign nations? Underlying the conclusion, however, is the fact that YHWH refuses to intervene in Israel's favor.

Fourth Lament: Prayer for Revenge (18:18-23)

In another personal lament the prophet cries out to an apparently absent God. Jeremiah's opponents ("they" of 18:18) trust in the very people the YHWH prophet has condemned as deceitful: the priests, the sages, the prophets. The contrast between the Israelites' acceptance of the other prophets and their rejection of Jeremiah betrays their non-acceptance of his prophetic role.

For all its gloominess and pessimism Jeremiah's prayer is not hopeless, for he offers concrete suggestions of how YHWH might act. Still the prophet raises the unavoidable issue of why the good suffer. According to 18:20a which can be read: "Will evil, instead of good, be rewarded (with *shalom*)?" Jeremiah contests YHWH's apparent blessing of his foes. He prays that God keep the promise made in 6:11-12 to destroy the whole population, that God's anger be redirected toward those who deserve it. If his prayer for their forgiveness results in his suffering, perhaps his prayer for their punishment will bring him peace.

These words reflect the psychic pain of the prophet who is besieged on all sides. His attempts to follow YHWH's words have brought only pain and death threats. This is not the God Jeremiah thought he knew, the God who rewards the just and punishes the wicked.

A Sign at the Potsherd Gate (19:1-15)

This unit of prophetic biography is composed of three parts, each one shorter than the preceding: Jeremiah's proclamation at the Potsherd Gate—the very name presages his action—(19:1-9), his breaking an earthen flask (19:10-13), and his words in the Temple court (19:14-15). The earthen flask that was used in 18:1-11 as a sign of hope now becomes the symbol of hope shattered beyond repair.

Death's pall, like a suffocating wave of darkness, progressively overtakes Judah and Jerusalem. It moves from outside the city (19:3-7) to its very heart (19:14-15). Hinted at in 19:1-2 with its reference to the Potsherd Gate, it becomes explicit in 19:11, 13, 15. Death stalks the land. Unburied bodies suggest that the dead will never find peace (19:3-9). Destruction permeates the city YHWH should protect (19:12-15). The horror is heightened by cannibalism which reveals a situation of unimaginable desperation.

Since the religious leaders are to accompany Jeremiah from the city to the Potsherd Gate (19:1) and witness the breaking of the flask (19:10), implicitly they shoulder the blame for the coming devastation. The sin of deception that brings destruction permeates even the cult. Pashhur, whose future exile symbolizes the nation's fate, is a priest. Just as a crushed flask cannot be mended, neither can Israel.

Those who have failed to respect their covenant obligations with YHWH will face pitiless suffering (19:7-9). Not even the YHWH prophet, who fulfills the obligations God has imposed on him, can avoid it. None can escape the power of God's word, neither those who embrace it nor those who deny it or fail to heed it.

The Desperate Prophet (20:7-18)

This long poetic lament, the last in the book of Jeremiah, reflects intense pain bordering on despair. It portrays Jeremiah confessing to God, whom he deems responsible, that he has reached the limit of his endurance. Although 20:7-12 contains two complaints, one against YHWH (20:7-9) and one against the prophet's enemies (20:10-12), together they form a single unit that gives expression to his pain. The short hymn of 20:13 is typical of the lament psalms while 20:14-18, in the form of a curse, conveys the despair Jeremiah feels when he considers the unending suffering in his own life.

The lament opens with an address to YHWH that over the centuries has shocked more than one commentator. Using a word that has been translated "seduce" (Exod 22:15), "allure" (Hos 2:16) or "trick" (Judg 14:15; 16:5), all of which include an element of treachery, the first accusation addresses a God who apparently cannot be trusted. The word of the LORD that should be a source of strength and peace has become a source of tension and self-doubt. The prophet feels himself pulled between needing to and fearing to proclaim the word that unleashes a destructive force in him. YHWH, Jeremiah's protector, is no better than his friends who betray him. The accusation against YHWH may have been one way of getting YHWH's attention and calling to action the God who, according to the traditional understanding, protects the innocent and punishes the guilty.

The short hymn of 20:13 expresses Jeremiah's confidence that God can change the course of events and punish the prophet's enemies. A brief song of praise in the midst of hopelessness, it lifts this lament from total darkness and shows a residual hope in the God of Israel. Is it Jeremiah's way of thanking God in advance for intervening or an effort to make sure that God acts on his behalf? Perhaps it is little more than an attempt to escape despair by focusing on what his faith has taught him to be true.

Rejected by his own family and friends and, what is worse, abandoned by YHWH, the prophet senses the futility of his own life and questions the value of his existence. He articulates his pain in a curse that is more a statement of fact than a wish projected into the past. Since the Hebrew language rarely uses the simple copulative verb, one could translate 20:14-16 "Cursed *is* the day on which I was born; . . . cursed *is* the man . . . that man *is*/will be like . . . ; he *will* hear . . ." His final words, "Why, ever, was I born?" create a sense of hopelessness, much as Israel must have felt in the exile. Despite the glimmer of light in 20:13 the gloom of death suffuses the atmosphere.

Part 3: Sinful Kings and False Prophets: 21:1–29:32

Life Through Surrender (21:1-10)

In ch. 21 the text begins to shift to a more explicitly historical setting. For the first time there is a reference to a datable event: the immediate pre-exilic period of ca. 588 and Nebuchadrezzar's siege of Jerusalem that was repulsed by an Egyptian invasion. Set against the memory of an earlier miraculous intervention by YHWH when Sennacherib suddenly lifted his siege of Jerusalem ca. 700 (see Isaiah 36; 2 Kings 18), Zedekiah asks for a word from God in the hope that YHWH will again act to save them. The unexpected response gives a startling portrayal of YHWH: the Protector of Jerusalem will take up the fight against it until all life has been destroyed.

Addressing the people in the name of YHWH, Jeremiah offers them the choice between life and death (see Deut 30:15, 19). In contrast with Deuteronomy where "life" meant possession of the land and its blessings while "death" meant loss of the land, here life is found in exile and death in remaining in the city of God. This reversal of a long-held belief intimates other, more striking changes in the relationship with YHWH whose presence is no longer in the city, the seat of both political power and religious leadership.

This introduction to the third part of the book, in which narrative and history play a growing role, offers a future to those who can accept what appears to be an about-face in YHWH's promise: Leave the land if you wish to live.

Responsibilities of Kingship (21:11–22:30)

The explicit mention of a particular king (Zedekiah) in 21:1-10 has set the stage for this series of oracles against the royalty of Judah. Up to this point those held responsible for the coming destruction were the deceitful prophets and priests and the people who sought protection and assistance from foreign nations rather than from God. Now the focus shifts to the kings because they have failed to discharge their royal duty of protecting the weak and powerless. The resulting devastation extends beyond the city consumed by fire, as threatened at the end of the previous section (21:10), to embrace death for all the inhabitants (22:6-7), the nation's exile, and the end of the dynasty (22:5, 11, 26-27).

This section is composed of five oracles, two directed to the kings of Judah in general (21:11-14; 22:1-9) and one addressed to each of three kings: Shallum, whose throne name was Jehoahaz, meaning "YHWH has seized" (22:10-12); Jehoiakim (22:13-23); and Coniah, also known by his throne name Jehoiachin, meaning "YHWH establishes" (22:24-30). In all five Jeremiah confronts the kings with their desire for personal aggrandizement. What they seek is contrary to their duties of defending the life and guaranteeing the rights of the poor and the unprotected. Because of such blatant neglect of the covenant (see 2 Kings 23:3) it is not surprising that although the immediate source of the coming devastation will be Judah's enemy, Babylon, (21:7, 10) its real source will be Judah's covenant partner, YHWH (21:4-6, 8, 10).

The first oracle (21:11-14), although explicitly calling on the "House of David" to act with justice, accuses the people, personified by the city (seen in the feminine singular address and the plural "you" in 22:13-14), of arrogance, of considering themselves protected by their location on a height. Using the image of an uncontrollable and all-consuming fire the LORD, speaking through Jeremiah, threatens the self-sufficiency of unbreachable Zion.

The second oracle (22:1-9) gives a clear reason for such destruction: lack of justice on the part of those meant to guarantee it. The lack of justice is presented implicitly in the need that those who go to (not through) the city gate, the place of all legal decisions, must be attuned to God's word (22:2). It is also stated explicitly in the call to act justly (22:3), implying that not even the minimum, the avoiding of violence, could be expected. The rulers' blatant disregard for the covenant prescriptions releases God from the promise that David would have an everlasting dynasty. In the comparison he makes between Israel and two important centers of the Ancient Near East, Gilead and Lebanon, Jeremiah expresses the ambivalence of YHWH's relationship with the Davidic dynasty. Even if the house of the king of Judah is like Gilead—a wealthy territory protected by its location on a great height and famous for its healing balm or Lebanon, forested with cedars like those used to build the palace and Temple—it will still face ruin. Israel has often reminded YHWH that through its power other nations are brought to recognize God. YHWH changes the terms of discourse, implying that God does become known through Israel but not always in the expected way. God's power will be recognized now by virtue of Israel's destruction, rooted in its rejection of its God. The image of God continues to change and challenge.

The three oracles against Shallum, Jehoiakim and Coniah that follow the oracle to Zedekiah (although his reign succeeded theirs) not only link injustice with exile, but also clearly signal that chronology was not a major concern of the author/redactor. The very brief oracle of 22:10-12 directed against Shallum (Jehoahaz), reflects his short tenure as king before being taken captive to Babylon. It highlights the horror of exile as worse than death.

The oracle against Jehoiakim (22:13-19) opens and closes on a note of lament. With no more than an implicit reference to the coming exile (22:18) it contrasts the visible honor he enjoys, gained by injustice, with the disdain he will experience in death. His wealth in itself is not sinful, for his father who enjoyed the perquisites of kingship is praised as a good ruler who acted with justice and righteousness (cf. Exod 22:21-24), fulfilling his obligation to protect the poor and the needy. As stated in 21:14, Jehoiakim will enjoy the fruits of his own deeds. The violence with which he treated the people will return to him, at least in death (22:18-19). In some way this gives an initial, if inadequate, response to the issue raised by Jeremiah of why the evil prosper. Wickedness brings its own reward.

Before turning to Coniah the text inserts an oracle that uses feminine singular address (22:20-23), probably directed to Jerusalem, a symbol of the people. Their lament on the surrounding heights of Lebanon, Bashan, and Abarim conveys the distress of one abandoned, having neither foreign allies (lovers) nor national leaders (shepherds) to care for her. Injustice suffered at the hands of their leaders does not lessen the responsibility of the people who have turned their back on God. The image of a pregnant woman who cannot avoid the pain of childbirth and must suffer it alone aptly expresses the inevitability of the coming destruction.

Finally the text turns to Coniah/Jehoiakin (22:24-30) who becomes a personification of the nation's devastation. In likening him to a clay pot broken beyond repair the prophet's description betrays the violence of the event. The total destruction predicated of Jerusalem in ch. 18 takes on the face of one man destined to be childless, with no hope for the future. In thus declaring an end to the Davidic dynasty and the Davidic covenant (see 2 Sam 7:13-15) Jeremiah raises the nagging question of how faithfully God keeps promises.

Righteousness Restored (23:1-8)

With a surprising shift the text briefly offers a breath of hope in the oppressive atmosphere of despair. It begins with a cry of woe against the rulers (23:1) and reiterates their destruction (23:2-3), but then opens the door to a new and promising future by presenting rulers who will act in conformity to the nature of their office (23:4-6). The coming change involves three groups or individuals (the people, the rulers, YHWH) and points to three significant moments in the history of Israel. The fact that the people will "be fruitful and multiply" (23:3) recalls creation and the patriarchal era. The "righteous branch" of David (23:5) offers hope for the dawn of a new era in Israel filled with the glory of the first years of the monarchy. Both intimate a renewal of past hope and splendor. These actions of YHWH together with the return from exile (20:8) suggest a new beginning for the nation. Israel's identity will henceforth be tied not so much to God's liberating them from slavery in Egypt as to YHWH's rescuing them from captivity in Babylon. God's restoring the people to their land will reconstitute them as the people of YHWH and reveal to them a new understanding of God.

The Sins of the Prophets (23:9-40)

This lengthy section portrays those prophets who, unlike Jeremiah, are not attentive to the word of the LORD but announce what pleases the people. Although it falls into six parts (23:9-10, 11-15, 16-17, 18-20, 21-32, 33-40) identified by changes in speaker (Jeremiah or YHWH) and audience (the people or Jeremiah), it forms a unit around a single theme: the sin of the prophets and its consequences for themselves, for the people, and for the land.

In the opening lines (23:9-10) Jeremiah bemoans his own pain and brokenness. Unlike his personal laments that situate the source of his suffering in the people's rejection of him, this soliloquy communicates his agony over the death that fills the land. While here, as in the confessions, the word of the LORD is at the root of Jeremiah's pain (23:9c), the prophet's speech connects the devastation of creation with the sin of the false prophets simply by introducing his dirge with the words "concerning the prophets."

In 23:11-15 YHWH explains to Jeremiah why the situation is what it is. The blame for the crisis is placed squarely on the shoulders of the prophets. Using a variety of images the text portrays the extent of the evil (23:11, 14), its inevitable outcome (23:12, 15), and the fact that it is worse than that of the past (23:13-14). YHWH's words point to the sin as all-pervasive. Even the Temple is a repository of evil and those whose lives are dedicated entirely to God, priest and prophet alike, have not kept the covenant. The slippery path in the darkness is a perfect image to convey the actual, irreversible situation. Like those unable to stay on their feet or control their movements and unable to find a foothold or a handhold in the dark, the prophets find the evil they do overtakes them and leads to their demise. A comparison of the Jerusalem prophets with those of Samaria, such as made here, would have shocked Jeremiah's contemporaries. While YHWH appears to agree with the Judeans that the Samaritans had deserved the destruction they suffered in 722 (when the northern kingdom was defeated and irreversibly subjugated to the Assyrians) because of their worship of false gods, God condemns the Jerusalem prophets as much worse than their northern counterparts. The words chosen to express their respective sins strongly conveys the difference: the Samaritans engaged in what was merely "foolishness" while the Judeans' actions were "horrible" (a word whose Hebrew root suggests calculated evil). Thus YHWH's threat of destruction is not surprising.

With few words YHWH invests the people with responsibility for their own deeds (23:16-17). While elsewhere Jeremiah has tried to stay God's hand by placing the blame for the people's sin on their leaders, here YHWH makes it clear that the people are to judge for themselves and must themselves distinguish between true and false prophets, between those who announce the word of the LORD and those who preach pleasing words. What the Judahites like to hear does not necessarily reflect the truth. To this Jeremiah adds his own insight: YHWH's decisions stand and, once set in motion, will come to fruition whatever the response of the prophets or the people (23:18-20). To work against this will only bring destruction.

Using a series containing rhetorical questions, similes, and a wordplay, YHWH's words to Jeremiah address the issue of false prophets, finally calling them to responsibility for their words and actions. After bringing the listener/reader to an acute awareness of the inescapable presence of YHWH through a series of rhetorical questions (23:23-24) the text uses several similes to contrast the lifegiving and powerful word of God with the lies and useless dreams of the prophets (23:25-32). The language itself attests to YHWH's irrefutable presence with the tenfold repetition of "says the LORD" or "oracle of the LORD" (Heb.: *nʾm yhwh)* in 23:23-24, 28-32, in contrast to the more ethereal "dream" (found five times in 23:25-28). In a subtle linguistic tour de force based on a wordplay YHWH tells these prophets that they who congratulate themselves on speaking the "oracle of the LORD" are instead the "burden of the LORD" (23:33-40). The root *nsʾ* ("lift up"), translated "burden," could as easily mean "oracle" since what is "lifted up" may be a material reality (a burden) or a word (an oracle). Thus the prophets who, claiming to speak in the name of YHWH, say "the oracle *(msʾ)* of the LORD" (23:33, 34, 36, 38 [3x]), are, because of their disobedience, the burden of the LORD (*msʾ*, 23:33) to be lifted up (*nsʾ*, 23:39) and rejected.

Recalling the "lie" and "deceit" earlier shown to be the sin of the people, these words against the prophets reiterate the importance of openness to the word of the LORD and the danger of self-reliance that easily becomes self-deception. Just as all must assume responsibility for their deeds, all suffer the consequences of sin with its ripple effect down through nature itself. None can escape, not even the YHWH prophet.

A Vision of Figs (24:1-9)

This vision clarifies for Jeremiah the meaning both of the exile imposed by Nebuchadrezzar and of the truth of the oracle recorded in 21:1-10. By the opening words (in the Hebrew) "The LORD showed me . . ." the audience is invited to contemplate with the prophet two baskets of figs. This allegorical vision, which twice mentions the quality of the figs, leaves the audience to determine its own reaction. It thus justifies the disconcerting action of YHWH who, by promising life to those who leave the land but death to those who remain there under Babylonian domination, turns their expectations and worldview upside down.

With its repetition of the question "What do you see?" (24:3) which harks back to the first visions of Jeremiah's prophetic career (1:11-16) the text recalls what had been proclaimed from the beginning and thus eliminates any surprise from the announcement of exile. What is surprising is YHWH's promise to reestablish the covenant and give the people a new heart (24:7), ideas to be developed later in the salvation oracles of 30:1–31:40. Just as the good figs portend a pleasant and desirable future (24:4-7) so the rotten figs augur ruin and rejection (24:8-10). The accumulation of images assures the prophet that life will turn to death for those who comply with Babylon and stay in the promised land. While those finally driven out will experience spiritual and emotional death, be despised and considered a curse (24:9), those who remain will be physically destroyed by nature if not by the enemy (24:10).

Although hope is held out, its terms bring traditional understanding into question. The prophets, priests, and leaders cannot be trusted. Those who preach peace will, because of their deceitfulness, provoke destruction, while the one who preaches destruction may (eventually) turn out to be the source of hope.

Seventy-Year Exile (25:1-14)

By its specific reference to the exile Nebuchadrezzar will impose, this oracle of judgment confronts the reader with the effectiveness of the word of the LORD. The text's repetition of "you have not listened" (25:3, 4, 7, 8) echoes the people's recurring failure to heed the word, developed in 25:1-7. Similar repetition, but now looking toward the future (25:9-11), hammers home the message of devastation and desolation as the inevitable result of the people's rejection of the word and their refusal to change. Four words portray the frightfulness and desperation of the coming situation: exterminate, waste, hissing, desolation (25:9). Day to day life, depicted in three pairs of expressions, will cease (25:10). Ruin and waste (25:11) describe the hopelessness reiterated by the threat of seventy years under the yoke of Babylon. The apparently simple imagery of 25:10 creates a deathly, ghostly silence that undermines the possibility of ordinary existence. All the sounds and signs of life will disappear: celebrating voices; marriage with its promise of life continuing; the singing mill whose grinding marks the beginning of the day, and the shining lamp that marks its end.

The seventy-year limit to the exile (25:12) harbors a tacit promise of restoration, albeit not for this generation. Like the Exodus generation who died before crossing the Jordan into the land of Canaan, the generation who left the promised land for exile would die in foreign territory. This implicit comparison of the two groups offers an unspoken hope for a new beginning, expressed obliquely in the last word of the oracle foretelling Babylon's destruction. Death outside the promised land does not mean an end to the promise.

The Cup of Wrath (25:15-38)

There are two parts to this new condemnation of all leaders, those of Israel as well as those of the nearby lands. The first presents a metaphorical vision of the cup of wrath (25:15-29); the second describes their ruin as all-pervasive chaos (25:30-38). Both the noise of a drunken gathering that underlies the imagery of 25:15-29 and the roar and wails voiced in eight different expressions (25:30-38) put an end to the deathly silence of 25:10.

The cup of wrath that Jeremiah must give to the kings and nations listed represents an anti-banquet in which wine, generally a symbol of joy and gladness in the OT, becomes a symbol of sickness and drunkenness. The references to lack of control (25:16) with resultant inability to stand (25:27) and finally destruction by the sword (25:29) leave no doubt about the outcome of drinking the cup.

The poetic oracles of 25:30-38 portray YHWH as a lion who threatens not the sheep but the shepherd. Found in parallel with the clamor of those treading grapes to make wine, the roaring (a lion roars not before killing its prey but before eating it), twice predicated of God in 25:30, reaffirms the negative tenor given wine here and the reversal of images that fills this text. Wine becomes the source of death and YHWH is the enemy. The power of destruction has been unleashed and, like a lion on the prowl, it will attack when the prey is least suspecting it.

Jeremiah on Trial (26:1-24)

With this pericope the book begins to turn its attention more directly and consistently to the life of Jeremiah and how his preaching the word of the LORD made him the object of repeated death threats. If the historical reference in 26:1 is correct, the trial recounted here occurred at the beginning of Jehoiakim's reign, that is, *before* Jeremiah pronounced the oracle recorded in ch. 25. Thus there is a conflict between the literary presentation of events and the historical sequence. From a strictly literary standpoint Jeremiah's trial and condemnation (26:8-12) appear to be the result of his preaching the wrath of God (25:1-38). Yet the historical note in 26:1 leads the reader to consider the events in their chronological order, and to recognize that Jeremiah continued to proclaim the word of the LORD even after his preaching evoked reactions that imperiled his own life.

Following a summary of the Temple sermon (26:4-6, see 7:1-15), the text depicts the YHWH prophet threatened by the religious leaders but supported by the princes and people who recognized in Jeremiah's words the word of God. The accounts of what happened to two other prophets, Micah and Uriah, one long dead, the other a contemporary, builds narrative tension around the fate of Jeremiah. Will he find himself in the good graces of the king or will he meet with disaster? By presenting both scenarios through the stories of Micah and Uriah the text implies that either outcome is possible. For those who have ears to hear, a comparison of the two stories makes it clear that the source of disaster was not the message of the prophet (all three preached the destruction of Jerusalem) but his desire to escape the king's wrath (26:21-23).

In some way the fate of Uriah and Jeremiah, neither of whom fled to protect their own lives, foreshadows the fate of the Judahites when the Babylonians take over the land. Those who, like Jeremiah at the trial, will give themselves into the hands of the enemy will save their lives; those who, like Uriah, try to save their lives by fleeing will lose them.

The Yoke of Babylon (27:1-22)

This chapter, which opens with a symbolic action of Jeremiah and closes with a sign of YHWH's absence from Judah, is composed of three oracles directed in turn to the leaders of other nations (27:1-11), to King Zedekiah of Judah (27:12-15), and to the priests and people (27:16-22). These words betray a tension between the people's desire to remain in the land and the warning that YHWH will no longer be there in their midst. Yet the reader knows that, since the one addressed is the last king of Judah, the text alludes to the imminent end of the nation.

First the prophet addresses the rulers of surrounding nations (27:2-11) as they sent delegates to Jerusalem in the hope of establishing a military coalition against a Babylon that was still in process of consolidating its power. By wearing a yoke, a symbol of subjugation throughout the ancient Near East, Jeremiah announces that YHWH, the God of all the earth, has granted Babylon power over the all these nations for a lengthy but limited time. They, like Judah, must choose between subjugation to another power or destruction at the hand of God.

Addressing Zedekiah with the same words used for the other nations (27:12-15), the prophet implies that the covenant is at an end, that Judah no longer enjoys "favored nation" status in the eyes of YHWH, that salvation lies in accepting slavery.

The third oracle (27:16-22) makes an indirect reference to the exile and implies that the process has been set in motion. The plundering of the Temple furnishings symbolizes an end to YHWH's presence in Jerusalem and to the covenant whose cultic expression was linked to the temple. Israel cannot escape the fate the false prophets deny. Even in the midst of desolation the final words, with their promise of eventual restoration, remind the people of YHWH's care. All is lost, but not forever.

Prophets in Conflict (28:1-17)

This pericope, recalling earlier accusations (e.g., 14:14-15), is a detailed example of the prophets prophesying lies in the name of YHWH. The face-to-face confrontation between Jeremiah (a true prophet) and Hananiah (a false prophet) shows the YHWH prophet coming out on top for the first time in the book. While it never offers criteria for determining who is a false prophet, the text implies that one who preaches what the people want to hear must be judged with cautious suspicion. The example here given is a case in point. The prophet Hananiah, who was probably aware of some cracks in Babylon's armor, preached that the return from exile would occur within two years. He may well have understood the first deportation (598) to be the punishment announced by Jeremiah, and therefore holds out hope that the king and all the exiles will soon return. He breaks the yoke to assure his announcement.

Before giving his full response to Hananiah (28:12-16), Jeremiah first reacts to the issue of true or false prophecy (28:8-9). Thus the text accents the fact that Jeremiah speaks not his own word but that of YHWH. He replaces the wooden yoke with an iron one as a symbolic illustration of what he spoke in 27:7—that the exile will last several generations and not merely two years. Jeremiah's words are verified by Hananiah's death as predicted. For the first time it appears that God will indeed punish the lying prophets.

Letters to the Exiles (29:1-32)

These two letters that Jeremiah sent to the exiles in Babylon not only attest that he continues his struggle to make the word of God heard and understood but also show that his life is still threatened. Shemaiah's reaction (29:26-28), his refusal to accept the exile with equanimity, indicates that Jeremiah's preaching continues to shock the Israelites. A modern reader would say that Nebuchadrezzar took the Israelites to Babylon; Jeremiah asserts that YHWH has sent them into exile (29:4). It makes sense therefore that the word of God would encourage them to settle down and make a life in the place where YHWH has brought them, even if this idea seems blasphemous to the generations whose identity as the people of God had been linked to life in the promised land. Despite appearances the prophet does not preach despair, for he holds out hope of return in the future (29:10-14). (This hope, contingent on the people's change of heart, is developed at length in chs. 30–33.) Rather than speak of their return to the ancestral land with its links to the Abrahamic promises and to the Exodus the prophet, in a surprising change of idiom, proclaims a return "to the place from which I sent you into exile" (29:14b). This indicates yet again that the return from exile emerges as a new Exodus. In an attempt to convince the people to heed the word of the LORD, Jeremiah uses two specific examples: the fate of those who remained in Jerusalem instead of going into exile (29:16-19), and that of those who, having gone into exile, still failed to obey the word of YHWH (29:21-23).

This pericope, which takes up many ideas and expressions previously used, presents the prophet as one who suffers on account of God's word that the people fail to heed. As a whole therefore ch. 29, stressing as it does the written word (in the letters) points to the ongoing validity of the word of God beyond the generation who hear it.

In these letters God is portrayed as one who makes constant demands on the people. God not only sends them into exile but also tells them how to live there. They must come to understand that the only way to life is through obedience to the word of YHWH even when it does not fit their expectations.

Part 4: Hope for the Future: 30:1–33:25

Life Anew (30:1–31:40)

Jeremiah 30–31, a lengthy poetic interlude in the midst of the biographical narrative, offers hope to a people in exile. It is part of the "Little Book of Consolation," so called because it contains the most developed oracles of salvation in Jeremiah. Since these oracles are not contextualized in space, time, or the prophet's life they are out of place in this part of the book that is concerned with historical events. Nevertheless, because they proclaim life beyond exile these oracles follow well on the heels of ch. 29 which is about life in exile.

Jeremiah 30–31 deals essentially with the promise of restoration of Israel and the return to the land. Throughout the oracles there is an interplay between judgment and salvation, with salvation gradually becoming more and more important. Although the theme of punishment is not absent (see, e.g., 30:11, 14; 31:18) these two chapters gradually develop, with ever greater insistence, the understanding that God is not merely reviving the past, but is establishing something new.

The hint of newness begins in 30:17 where YHWH promises to heal the people's incurable wound (their sinfulness). Although 30:18-22 and 31:2-6 focus on renewal of past glory and joy ("again" is repeated three times in 31:4-5) the recognition of a new life begins to develop in 31:8-9. Here the returnees include the weak and those excluded from public worship. YHWH's presence will assure them that, unlike what they did in the past, they will follow the right way without stumbling.

The newness becomes explicit in 31:22: "the LORD has created a new thing on the earth: a woman encompasses a man." This verse, one of the most discussed texts of Jeremiah, seems to indicate that finally the people (the woman) will take the initiative in the relationship with God (the man). The newness is a post-exilic ideal. Besides the new covenant (Jer 31:31 being the only time this expression is used in the OT) that reiterates the fact of the law written on their hearts, the repeated "no longer" (31:29, 34, 39) further accentuates the change. Children will no longer suffer for their parents' sins, with the result that the sins of the previous generations will no longer be the operative world for the Israelites. Knowledge of God, the intimate reciprocal relationship guaranteeing covenant, will be innate and no longer need to be learned. [See also the excursus "Covenant" in the commentary on Exodus 19–24.] The most astounding change is expressed metaphorically in 31:38-40 with its statement that the valley of the dead will become a holy place. That which once represented distance from God will become the place of God's presence! YHWH's intervention, much more than a return to an idealized past, will transform life and create a new existence for Israel.

Jeremiah Purchases a Field (32:1-44)

The oracles and event recounted in Jeremiah 32–33 give a more prosaic expression to the hope held out by the poetry of salvation in Jeremiah 30–31. The center of focus is initially the prophet Jeremiah, whose imprisonment is juxtaposed with his purchase of his uncle's field as if to concretize in a single life the incongruity between the present situation of life brought to a halt and a promise-filled future. The very fact that Jeremiah is imprisoned because he announces that the king will be taken into exile is a reminder that speech, word, and deed are considered effective as prophetic actions that guarantee the outcome. Since biblical law stipulated that property was to remain, as far as possible, in the family, Jeremiah's purchase of the field roots the event in history and bespeaks a real, not idealized, continuity of life. Jeremiah's having the deeds of sale placed in an earthenware vessel which will preserve them from deterioration shows that this public act proffers a hope not for the immediate but for some distant future. Although he obeys what he understands to be God's will, Jeremiah's prayer to YHWH reflects both faith and disbelief. In it Jeremiah recognizes God's former deeds for Israel but also wonders why he should perform such an apparently senseless action.

YHWH's response details Israel's disobedience referred to in Jeremiah's prayer: their turning from YHWH to other gods. As surprising as the call to purchase land of ambiguous ownership (does it belong to the occupying enemy or to the original owners?) is YHWH's about-face concerning Israel. The same God who assured destruction at the hands of the enemy now assures a new beginning in the land.

Throughout ch. 32 the land retains its importance. Land purchased, land granted, land lost, land regained accents how closely Israel's belonging to God was linked with possession of the land. Although these oracles have a historical locus they intimate the much deeper reality of belonging. They also reflect the tension between holding God responsible for all that happens, including the people's hardness of heart, and recognizing Judah's responsibility for its own plight. These verses give the impression that the evil the nation suffers is its fault while the good it experiences is a gift of God.

Covenant Guaranteed by Creation (33:1-26)

The final word of salvation is more striking because it is juxtaposed with images of death and destruction: healing will replace death (33:4-9); joyful expressions of life will fill once empty streets (33:10-11); deserted fields will know the presence of flocks and shepherds (33:12-13). The oracles of ch. 16 will be reversed. The presence of king and priest (33:17-18) reflect the importance of a tangible, visible power by which all nations may recognize YHWH's might and authority. Once again the prophet looks back to an idealized past as a way to move toward hope and the future.

Although the present bleakness undergirds the whole, a variety of images, many of which were used negatively earlier in the book, hold out hope. The purchase of fields and the restoration of the Davidic kings allude to a renewed national existence. Healing recalls the need to overcome sinfulness; the reinstating of celebrations indicates ongoing life. Life will be renewed at all levels and in all places. It will be guaranteed by the stability of creation (33:19-24) and the life-giving care of the creator God.

Part 5: Final Years of Judah: 34:1–45:5

Covenant Broken (34:1-22)

Following the brief interlude of hope in Jeremiah 30–33 the darkness of judgment descends again in this chapter which is framed by an assurance of Jerusalem's destruction (34:2, 22). Arranged around the positive images of covenant kept and freedom granted, the two oracles of Jeremiah 34 are a study in contrasts. While YHWH's word to Zedekiah in 34:1-5 fosters hope in hopelessness, the words addressed to the people in 34:12-22 declare that their confidence in YHWH's protection as God's favorable response to their momentary obedience (34:8-11) has been misplaced. Thus keeping covenant and turning from it, both of which have been developed in highly metaphorical language up to this point, find concrete expression.

By holding out hope, however limited, for the king alone (34:1-5), the text underscores the importance of keeping covenant, especially in those areas that regulate rights in society. The basic distinction between Zedekiah who kept the covenant and the people who did not is their ultimate end. While all face death at the hands of the enemy, one is assured that his body will be buried and remembered (34:5) while the others will be eaten by animals and forgotten (34:20), a not insignificant difference for a people who understood peace in the afterlife to be determined by how one's body was treated after death.

The striking imagery found in the description of a covenant ceremony (34:18), the most graphic of the entire Hebrew bible (the only other one is in Gen 15:9-18), suggests the efficacy of the event. Those who fail to keep their side of the covenant will have no more future than do the animals between whose halves the covenant partners pass. Since the Israelites failed to keep the covenant, destruction is inevitable. Underlying the whole is the notion of choice. With a play on words YHWH's message to the people underscores the importance of freedom (34:17). Having used their freedom to keep others from being free, the people will be given a new freedom—for their own undoing and death.

Like covenant, freedom can be positive or negative. Lived in conformity to YHWH's intention, they are sources of life; lived in ways that diminish the rights of others, they assure death.

The Example of the Rechabites (35:1-19)

Suddenly there is a surprising shift of focus from the Israelites to the Rechabites. In fact, with its drawn out introduction and lengthy description of this group the text lightens the oppressiveness of the unrelieved threat against Israel. It allows the space to compare and contrast the two groups, first implicitly, then explicitly. The Rechabites' unswerving obedience to the commands of their ancestor is markedly divergent from the Israelites' repeated refusals to obey their God. While for both groups the commands concern self-identity the Rechabites alone have taken them seriously. The explicit comparison of the attitudes of the two groups (35:12-16) results in the announcement of contrasting outcomes. Those who are faithful to their origins will have a future while those who refuse to live in accordance with their founding principles will know evil. The tension may be momentarily relieved but Israel's future still remains bleak.

The Scroll Destroyed and Rewritten (36:1-32)

This finely crafted narrative with its detailed presentation of the word given to Jeremiah builds the expectation that perhaps repentance will hold the announced destruction at bay. It presents the power of the word that remains alive and active despite all attempts to destroy it. The word given to Jeremiah, its lasting validity attested to by the fact that it was written and could thus be pronounced on numerous occasions, endeavored by its threats to lead the people to repentance (36:3, 7). Not only the three successive readings of the scroll as recounted in the text but also the fear this word engendered and the resultant need to protect Jeremiah from the king's wrath (36:19, 26) all reflect that it was taken seriously. Yet the rejection of the word of God, referred to many times over in Jeremiah, attains concrete expression in the action of King Jehoiakim who seeks to eradicate it definitively (36:22-24). By destroying the scroll containing Jeremiah's oracles the king symbolically rejects the word of God in all its manifestations and justifies the judgment of God on Israel. The rewriting of the scroll demonstrates that the word of the LORD endures despite all efforts to stifle it.

Because he is regarded as a threat to the king the YHWH prophet is forced into hiding and removed from the scene. Thus the word of the LORD takes precedence over the prophetic presence, with Jeremiah becoming ever more passive as the book moves toward its conclusion. The prophet is dispensable; the word endures.

Word of the Lord for Zedekiah (37:1-21)

The hope held out through ch. 36 comes to a swift end in ch. 37, with Jeremiah's personal experience reflecting the plight of the nation. Jeremiah's words deflate any reassurance Israel may have felt when the Chaldeans (Babylonians) withdrew before the approaching Egyptians (37:10). Any such hope is nothing more than another instance of the self-deception Israel was so often accused of in earlier chapters. Rather than belittling Israelite strength, which at first glance he appears to do, Jeremiah accents YHWH's ability to intervene and change the apparently inevitable outcome. The Babylonian withdrawal is only temporary (37:8-10). The text reiterates that all one can expect is the unexpected, whether it be the re-established power of Babylon or Jeremiah's imprisonment due to a false accusation (37:11-16). The devastation he announced for the city and the king has fallen on his own head.

Although he is willing to suffer the consequences of fidelity to his vocation of proclaiming God's word the YHWH prophet rails against the threat to his own life that he feels in prison (37:18-21). Defending himself to the king he wins not freedom, but more humane treatment. Jeremiah's life becomes a metaphor for the life of God's word: treated with both contempt and respect, simultaneously threatened and protected. Destruction crouches at the gates of Jerusalem and Jeremiah, who announced it, is under attack. No one can escape, not even the YHWH prophet.

Jeremiah and Zedekiah (38:1-28)

In many respects Jeremiah 38 should be considered part of the unit Jeremiah 37–38. Both chapters are concerned with the prophet's imprisonment; both present the relationship between Jeremiah and Zedekiah; both deal with surrender to the Chaldeans; both conclude on the same note. Despite the correspondences each chapter has its own particular emphasis. Jeremiah 38 offers a parallel between the prophet and the king as if to emphasize the similar end to all authority in Israel, religious or political. Jeremiah's life is threatened by his own people who imprison him in a cistern (38:4-6), while a foreigner saves him (38:7-13). In analogous fashion the king who feels himself caught between a rock and a hard place, between reprisals from the Judeans who have already surrendered to Babylon (38:19) and death in Jerusalem (38:18), is told that life will be found at the hands of foreigners, the enemy of Israel (38:17). Israel's breaking the covenant and refusing to live by the rules of the game turns upside down everything that was known and expected.

The cistern, an image of the broken covenant and thus a threat to the well-being of Israel earlier in the book, now reappears as a material object and a threat to the prophet's life (38:6-13). Furthermore a dry cistern is a useless cistern, lacking its raison d'être. Empty of that which supports life, it signals a threat to the people who rely on it. It serves here as a figure for Israel's embracing other gods and turning away from YHWH, suggesting that Jeremiah has been rejected because of Israel's inability to live the covenant. Once again Jeremiah's life is inseparably intertwined with that of his people, for ill rather than for good.

Whether or not Zedekiah takes Jeremiah's warning seriously is left to the next chapter. For the moment the reader is left contemplating the destruction that will come if the king refuses to surrender (38:17-23). Zedekiah has nowhere to turn. No matter what he does he faces disaster. Jeremiah on the other hand, in spite of the continual threats, is safe. The YHWH prophet finally begins to experience the protection God had promised him.

The Fall of Jerusalem (39:1-18)

In recounting the Babylonians' capturing Jerusalem the author spotlights the fate of three persons: the king, the prophet, the foreigner. The latter two, who trusted in the word of YHWH, were saved, while the king, afraid to meet the enemy as God instructed, was spared to endure a fate worse than death. He is blinded after witnessing the death of his sons.

The threats that Jeremiah proclaimed are finally actualized although somewhat differently than he had announced. The poor who stay in the land survive, while the officials fleeing from Babylon's final siege of Jerusalem are captured and slaughtered. Life is in surrender to the enemy, as the prophet who stayed in the captured city had proclaimed. The prophetic word is finally vindicated.

Life in the Land (40:1-12)

This pericope presents an extraordinary shift of tone between its beginning and end. It opens with what appears to be the end to hope: Jeremiah in chains as a captive of Babylon, the besieging army. It concludes on a note that should evoke rejoicing: the return of exiles and an abundant harvest. YHWH's action is hidden not in the Israelites' deeds but in those of the Babylonians who protect Jeremiah and set Gedaliah over those left in the land. Jeremiah draws a shocking contrast between the covenant people and the foreigners. A foreigner, the captain of the guard, recognizes YHWH as the powerful God of Israel (40:2-3) in striking contrast to Israel's attitude of repeatedly turning away from its God.

Jeremiah's choice to remain in the land with Gedaliah is tacit recognition that his leadership is blessed by God. Those exiled to other lands and the leaders of the "open country" gather around Gedaliah to begin life anew in Judah. The text gives the impression that the return has begun, that Hananiah had been right in foreseeing a very short period of Babylonian presence (ch. 28). The abundance of the land signifies YHWH's blessing and suggests the new beginning of which Jeremiah spoke. Yet, as the following section shows, the intimation that God has begun to bless the people is no more than the spark of a dying ember that kindles a false hope.

Violence in the Land (40:13–41:18)

The threat to Gedeliah's life, which suggests that the unity of the people who had gathered around him is also threatened (40:15), dashes the hope found in 40:1-12 almost as soon as it is raised. In fact the slaughter of Gedaliah and those with him at Mizpah (41:1-3) is immediately followed by the massacre of seventy men from the north (41:4-7). This first act of murder unleashed such a wave of violence that bodies filled the great cistern constructed by King Asa (41:9). The earlier statement that the Israelites keep fresh their wickedness as a cistern keeps water fresh appears to be true. Now a cistern is filled with the results of their evil deeds. This tale of violence (a real account?) fulfills Jeremiah's warning that death would come to those who stayed in the land.

Ishmael's deed of violence sets off a chain of evil: Israelite acts against Israelite (14:11) and the protecting foreigner becomes the feared enemy (41:16-18). Once again safety is sought in Egypt and the land is left empty as Jeremiah had warned.

Refuge Sought in Egypt (42:1–43:13)

This scene centers almost entirely on the word of God: the word requested (42:1-6), given (42:9-22), refused (43:2-7). The prophet is little more than an instrument of the word, as the simple statement that he had to wait ten days before receiving it (42:7) attests. His passivity in this situation is yet another assurance that the power at work is exclusively that of YHWH.

Initially it appears that the Babylonian presence has brought about repentance, for those left in the land approach Jeremiah with a request for a word of the LORD. In light of the people's reaction to Jeremiah's message their admission that they need to obey the word whatever it may be becomes self-condemnatory. Against all human logic the people are challenged to trust that YHWH will somehow save them from the enemy who has caused them to suffer. If they choose security and peace in Egypt they will experience destruction. Furthermore, this word calling for the people to remain in the land is the opposite of what Jeremiah preached earlier. Yet in both instances the prophet insists that life is to be found in acceptance of Babylonian rule. Before the fall of Jerusalem that meant surrender to the enemy and probable exile. After the fall it simply means accepting the power of Babylon over the land.

As happened over and over again, the people refuse to obey the word of God. The covenant people act as if the covenant does not exist. They have yet to learn that they can become an object of horror and ridicule as readily in Egypt as in Israel (42:18). The prophet himself is once again identified with the people to the extent that, contrary to the word of YHWH, he is taken down to Egypt to suffer with them the consequences of their sin.

In Egypt Jeremiah performs one final symbolic action that, reiterating the Babylonian threat to Egypt, effectively seals the fate of the Israelites who had sought refuge there. No security can be found for those who reject the word of the LORD.

Idolatry in Egypt (44:1-30)

The final, lengthy word of the LORD for the Judahites in Egypt falls into two parts: (1) a description of Judah's destruction to serve as an example to the people in Egypt (44:1-14); (2) the punishment that flows from goddess worship (44:15-30). Both parts announce total annihilation yet both temper the absoluteness of the announcement by concluding on the note that a tiny remnant will survive (44:14, 28).

Repeating the phrase "evil deeds," 44:9 underscores the extent of the people's evil and injurious activity without detailing its content. A similar technique in 44:12-13 (repetition of "sword," "famine," "be consumed," "punish") drives home the all-consuming destruction. The people's past experience of Jerusalem's devastation points to the seriousness of the present threat.

The people's reaction shows that they take the threat lightly. They counter Jeremiah's words with their own reading of the past and note the prosperity they enjoyed when worshiping the queen of heaven (44:17-18). This is by far the boldest (and least metaphorical) presentation of how the Judahites turned their back on the covenant, acknowledging and embracing other deities. The story of Jeremiah concludes on this note that, like the opening, grounds YHWH's rejection of covenant in the people's refusal to live their part of the agreement.

This narrative section of Jeremiah leaves no doubt as to the finality of judgment. It points to irreversible devastation—an end not only to the Temple and the holy city, not only to the nation, but to the people and thus to the covenant itself, since without a covenant people there cannot be a covenant. The unthinkable has occurred.

One Person Saved (45:1-5)

The closing oracle, clearly received some time before the fall of Jerusalem, is placed here to offer a spark of light in the darkness. Despite the decimation of the people at least one individual will survive, much as indicated in 44:14, 27-28. The nation may have come to an end, the covenant may lie in ruins, but there is at least one just person whose life offers hope.

Part 6: Oracles Against the Nations: 46:1–51:64

Oracle Against Egypt (46:1-28)

This first of the oracles against the foreign nations is directed against Egypt, which was both one of Judah's major foes and the place where many of the Judahites sought refuge in their flight from the invading Babylonians. The introduction to the first part (46:2) recalls the campaign of 605: Babylon defeated Egypt and established its hegemony over Palestine. The introduction to the second part (46:13), like the oracles themselves, has no clear chronological referent. Both describe Egypt being vanquished by a foe but leave the identification of the enemy to the prose introductions (46:2, 13) and conclusion (46:26).

After graphically describing the summons to war, the first poem pictures the terrified soldiers fleeing before an unnamed enemy. Such vagueness effectively suggests that the real foe is YHWH, whose role is made explicit only in 46:10. The common, positive image of the Nile inundating the land to bring life is turned on its head because here Egypt rises up not for life but for death (46:7-8). This suggests that what till now has been a source of good may very well become the source of evil.

These oracles, which follow close upon Jeremiah's announcement that the Judahites should not seek safety in Egypt, reinforce his earlier words. If Egypt has been defeated and will fall into the hands of Babylon salvation will not be found there. Those who fled to Egypt will not be spared as they had hoped. Memphis and Tahpanhes, the Egyptian cities in which Israel trusted, will be destroyed (46:14, 19).

In a surprising shift the text moves from describing the destruction of Egypt to offering hope to both Egypt and Israel. While Egypt will return to its former life (46:26b), Israel will be gathered from exile (46:27-28). The text then cites the promise of 30:1-11, recalling for the reader chs. 30–31 with their promise of a new creation and a new covenant. Destruction may be unavoidable but it is not the last word.

Oracles Against Seven Different Groups (47:1–49:39)

Between the oracles against Egypt and Babylon are seven oracles of widely differing length addressed to various nations and groups: the Philistines (47:1-7), Moab (48:1-47), the Ammonites (49:1-6), Edom (49:7-22), Damascus (49:23-27), Kedar and Hazor (49:28-33), and Elam (49:34-39). The accusations leveled against these nations echo Israel's sin in a ploy to bring Israel to recognize its own situation.

The oracle against the Philistines (47:1-7) conveys the all-enveloping nature of the coming devastation with the simple device of alluding to Egypt (to the south) by speaking of Pharaoh while describing the event as an inundation from the north. Since the sea lay to the west and an impassable desert stretched to the east, their fate is inescapable. The pathetic image of parents unable to save their own children suggests the futility of any attempted flight while all-pervasive death is visible in the physical manifestations of lament—the baldness and self-inflicted cuts of those fleeing.

The oracle against Moab (48:1-47) is surprisingly long—longer, in fact, than all the other prophetic oracles against Moab (from whatever biblical book) taken together. Given the scarcity of historical information available on Moab it is difficult to explain why this small country bordering on Judah should be the subject of such a lengthy oracle unless Moab is simply an example of expectations overturned.

Using vocabulary and imagery earlier applied to Israel, this oracle portrays a land so totally devastated that the only possible response is a summons to lament (48:17, 20, 31-32, 37-39). Not even the gods remain; Chemosh himself will go into exile. Total destruction is the fate of Moab, much as it was the fate of Israel; no town shall be spared. The reason for all this is Moab's arrogance and trust in its own power (48:7, 26, 30, 42). Surprisingly, at the very end YHWH promises to restore the fortunes of Moab.

Since no enemy is named in the oracle against the Ammonites (49:1-6) it is clear that their destroyer must be YHWH. Ammon, a territory east of the Jordan, is similar to Moab in several ways. Both nations sin through arrogance (48:14) and so receive a summons to replace their boasting with lamentation. Like Moab, Ammon will suffer both desolation of the land and exile but also receive from YHWH a promise of restoration.

The oracle against Edom (49:7-22) has the unique feature (for this series) of twice referring to the Genesis story. Edom's identification with Esau, whose loss of his birthright to his brother Jacob was a source of lasting animosity, alludes not only to Edom's loss of all property but also to the longstanding enmity between Edom and Judah. Unlike thieves or those who harvest the vine and leave something behind, YHWH will strip Edom bare leaving no progeny, no kinfolk, no life in the future and no support in the present (49:10). The comparison of Edom to Sodom and Gomorrah (49:18) evokes an image of total devastation with no renewal of life, no future settlement. Edom, priding itself on its impregnable location on the heights (49:16), must, like the other nations, learn that YHWH alone directs history and decides the fate of all peoples.

The oracle against Damascus (49:23-27), the shortest oracle in the collection, is one of three pieces that speak of territories not in close proximity to the borders of Israel. These few lines, using the image of a woman in labor, focus on the overpowering fear that takes hold of the city and renders its warriors ineffective (49:26). YHWH's final word for Damascus is not salvation but total annihilation by fire.

The oracle against Kedar and Hazor (49:28-33), directed against Bedouin settlements in the Arabian desert, suggests the extent of the destruction that will spread beyond the cities and settlements to embrace even the nomadic tent-dwellers. None will survive.

By describing the annihilation of Elam as a scattering to the four winds, this oracle (49:34-

39) evokes the wide dispersion of the people. The king deposed points to a new beginning: in the future YHWH alone will rule. Since for Judah of Jeremiah's day Elam was on the edge of the known world, this oracle alludes to the universality of YHWH's power.

These several oracles effectively recapitulate the oracles delivered to Judah. The sins are the same: trusting in the works of their hand, arrogance, and self-reliance. The punishment, too, is similar: devastation at the hands of Babylon, cities burned, property taken. Yet all this leaves an opening for YHWH to act and to be the shepherd of the people.

Oracle Against Babylon (50:1–51:58)

The introductory verses set the theme of this long oracle that celebrates the defeat of Babylon and the triumph of YHWH. It proclaims a time when Babylon will be rendered helpless, its gods Bel and Merodach proven powerless (51:2). Babylon, the superpower, once the instrument of God, faces the same devastation it has brought on Israel and the surrounding nations.

The restoration of Israel through the defeat of Babylon is the central message of 50:4-20, which opens and closes with words of comfort to Judah. In a single breath it looks toward an everlasting covenant for Israel and proclaims that Babylon will be brought to its knees. The sword will reap the destroyers of Israel while Israel will be fed with the gifts of the LORD. The author gives an unexpected twist to the vision of the future. YHWH's wondrous deed for Israel will be a change of heart, the removal of guilt rather than the awaited return to the land.

The second part, 50:21-40, which opens with a call to battle taken up again in 50:29 and 50:35-38, focuses on the overwhelming devastation that Babylon will face. The text presents Babylon's enemy as none other than YHWH who will cause its wealth to be destroyed (50:26-27) and its habitations to be burned (50:32, 39-40). All of this is due to its sin of arrogance (50:24, 29, 31, 32). The devastation once predicated of Jerusalem is now directed against Babylon who will suffer the same fate it inflicted on others. The text leaves no doubt that all is controlled by a decision of YHWH alone (50:44-45).

The image of winnowing that leaves nothing behind (51:1-2) and a threshing floor trodden underfoot (51:33) by the power of YHWH are part of the harvesting motif that opens and closes 51:1-33. The nation that reflected YHWH's power to the world finally cedes its place to the power of YHWH who alone controls both creation and history (with its wars).

In 50:34-44 Israel cries to God for vengeance (vv. 34-35) and receives as response a promise to make Babylon a deserted land. Those who have survived in Babylon are encouraged to flee (51:45-46, 50) from the destruction that will befall this nation. The focus is now the end of Babylon, a power become powerless under the powerful hand of God.

Symbolic Act in Egypt (51:59-64)

The final word of Jeremiah is a symbolic action that the prophet entrusts to one of Zedekiah's entourage, with him in Babylon. To signify the ultimate and total end of Babylon, Seraiah is to sink a scroll in the Euphrates. The word once again will effect what it proclaims: final disaster, no hope of rising again.

Historical Conclusion: Jerusalem Destroyed: 52:1-34

The concluding chapter of Jeremiah gives another summary account of Jerusalem's capture and the deportation to Babylon. It is composed of four episodes (52:1-6, 17-23, 24-30, 31-34). The first two, the taking of Jerusalem (52:1-6) and the plundering of the Temple (52:17-13), have as bleak an outlook as does the parallel in 2 Kings 24:18–25:30. The third and fourth episodes mitigate the hopelessness by focusing on the survivors. After reporting how many Judahites were taken to Babylon in three waves of deportation (54:24-30), the text gives a glimpse of the Judahite king Jehoiakin, still in exile but honored by his captives (54:31-34). The future remains uncertain. Salvation is only a promise. But at least some Israelites survive. As hinted earlier in the text, Babylon may well be the new Egypt.

The book ends in exile. Suspended between a bleak past and an unpredictable future, the people of YHWH live in a present devoid of light. Their only source of guidance or hope is the word of God. Having a similar faith stance, contemporary readers, lured by the text to participate in the deportees' experience, are invited to wait and listen for the next word of the LORD wherever it appears—in speech, in action, in the text itself.

BIBLIOGRAPHY

Boadt, Lawrence. *Jeremiah.* 2 vols. OTMes. Wilmington, Del.: Michael Glazier, 1982.

Brueggemann, Walter. *To Pluck Up, To Tear Down. Jeremiah 1–25.* Grand Rapids: Eerdmans, 1988.

____. *To Build and To Plant. Jeremiah 26–52.* Grand Rapids: Eerdmans, 1991.

Carroll, Robert. *Jeremiah. A Commentary.* London: SCM Press, 1986.

____. *Jeremiah.* Old Testament Guides. Sheffield: JSOT Press, 1989.

Clements, Ronald E. *Jeremiah.* Interpretation. Atlanta: John Knox Press, 1988.

Holladay, William. *Jeremiah.* 2 vols. Hermeneia. Philadelphia: Fortress, 1986, 1990.

____. *Jeremiah: A Fresh Reading.* New York: Pilgrim Press, 1990.

King, Philip J. *Jeremiah: An Archaeological Companion.* Louisville: Westminster/John Knox, 1993.

Lamentations

Victor Manuel Fernandez

FIRST READING

Sorrow, disaster, failure, punishment: these words can describe the situation of the Jewish people in the early years of the exile (around 580 B.C.E.). Here, in exile, their way of conceiving their faith and their relationship with YHWH die; their traditional convictions and image of God change. The great crisis of the exile demanded a profound reawakening of Jewish belief, and allowed for the clarification of new truths within the Jewish faith. In order to help us understand how the people lived through so important an estrangement we are given a precious document, a direct and immediate witness to the existential repercussions of the tragedy, namely the book of Lamentations.

It is true that we rely on the historical accounts to tell us what happened (2 Kings 24–25; 2 Chronicles 36; Jeremiah 52), but so intense and dramatic an experience needs to be expressed poetically. Narration does not suffice for telling of a peak experience when sorrow is too great or almost unbearable. In such moments the mere narration of an event cannot begin to express what really happens; a shout, a dirge, or a complaint is necessary. For that reason we have Lamentations.

Lamentations does not deal with a "human problem" as does the book of Job, but rather with a terrible and unique historical moment, a collective drama that notably influenced Jewish history. The first four poems are written in the form of an acrostic, each verse beginning with a letter of the Hebrew alphabet and following the sequence of Hebrew letters. The fifth poem has twenty-two verses, corresponding to the number of letters in the Hebrew alphabet.

It is unusual that such dramatic poems written under the impact of recent happenings should have been composed with this very careful, artificial structure. The basic motive is not so much to facilitate memorization but to produce a specific impression: to give a sensation of totality and to make one feel that an experience of immense sorrow is being described, including every possible suffering from "A" to "Z"; it is as if the people's capacity for suffering had been completely exhausted and not even one further sorrow could be borne. This can be confirmed with some similar data from Jewish and other Oriental traditions: texts affirming that a people or an individual fulfilled or violated the Law "from aleph to tau," lists of sins in alphabetical order, enumeration of all the syllables to frighten away a devil, etcetera.

The poems have a peculiar rhythm, the result of the *qinah* construction: one line with three accented syllables and another shorter line with two. The second hemistich seems to be a sorrowful echo of the first, thus producing a sensation of desolation and lament. There are, however, some variations that avoid excessive monotony. [See also the article "Truth Told in the Bible: Biblical Poetics and the Question of Truth."]

Lamentations is a mixture of community and individual laments, mournful chants, pleadings, etcetera. One can identify here the writer's intention of using distinct modes of expression so that, in conjunction with the unusual variety of images and their multiple descriptions, the vivid sorrow of the people may be clearly shown. We can say that the third lament is principally that of an individual, the fourth that of a group, while the other three are mournful national chants.

The contribution that Lamentations makes to theology and spirituality can be summarized in the following themes: confidence in God in the midst of failure and sorrow; the invitation to give sincere expression to one's bitterness and deepest questions in heartfelt prayer; the primacy of the divine plans and their free initiative that transcends all that can be humanly explained or understood; a humble attitude before God, recognizing the imperfection of one's own life; the social sensitivity that allows one to transcend one's own sorrow in order to live the communal drama and to "weep with those who weep" (Rom 12:15); the underlying idea of a God who has to deal with human life, who acts in history and who will continue acting. It is worth pointing out some texts of profound beauty that express an intense spiritual experience, such as 3:20-33 and 5:15-22.

The contemporaneity of this book is indisputable since today similar situations continue to repeat themselves in countries scourged by hunger, war, and other group calamities. The prayerful reading of Lamentations unites us to the sorrow of the peoples who suffer and can be transformed into an impassioned prayer and a profound expression of love that receives as its own the pain of others.

General Contexts for Interpretation

1. General Historical Context

The five Lamentations were written during the period of the exile and denote a similar historical ambience although there are variations due to the distinct moments in which each Lamentation was written. It seems that the first Lamentation refers to a first deportation, in 598 B.C.E., when Jerusalem was sacked and some inhabitants were deported, those who because of their ministry or work could be useful in Babylonia (2 Kings 24:10-17). The second and fourth Lamentations, on the other hand, probably refer to a second attack on Jerusalem, when the Temple was destroyed and there was a massive deportation of persons from the entire kingdom of Judah: the great deportation of 587 B.C.E. (2 Kings 25:8-21; Jeremiah 52). The first Lamentation, therefore, speaks of the sack and profanation but not the destruction of the Temple (1:10). This also explains why the second and fourth describe very cruel scenes and seem to let die the hope that was still alive when the first Lamentation was written. The third and fifth Lamentations, more quiet and reflective, are the last ones written, several years after 587.

All the Lamentations were composed in Judah by a poet linked to the spiritual movement of the prophet Jeremiah, one of the group that remained in Jerusalem (Neh 1:2). There is the possibility that they are the work of several writers, though finally edited by a single redactor since one cannot deny the theological, spiritual, and literary unity of the five poems.

The details that in other times led scholars to attribute this work to Jeremiah only indicate that the author wanted to situate himself within the Jeremiah tradition and to identify with the prophet who was the paradigm of suffering and lament. In 2 Chr 35:25 we read of an elegy referring to the death of King Josiah but there is no evidence that this refers to Lamentations since the book does not contain references to that monarch. On the other hand, there are some unusual differences (Lam 2:9 and Jer 42:4-22; Lam 5:7 and Jer 31:30; Lam 4:20 and Jer 22:13-19). It is likewise difficult to think that so spontaneous a spirit should be subjected to an artificial construction such as an acrostic.

2. Canonical Context

In the Hebrew Bible Lamentations belongs among the *ketubim* ("writings") and, together with the books of Ruth, Song of Songs, Ecclesiastes, and Esther is part of the Megilloth (scrolls that are read on feast days). The Greek version of the LXX and the Latin Vulgate place the book within the collection of the prophets, between Baruch and the letter of Jeremiah (LXX) or after the book of Jeremiah (Vg).

Lamentations is not mentioned in the canons of the third Council of Carthage nor of Trent. That is understandable, however, since traditionally Lamentations was considered a prolongation of the book of Jeremiah and the work of the same prophet. In fact, in the ancient canon of the *Decretum Damasi* (in the Roman Council of 382) it was called "Jeremiah, with his lamentations."

Besides the obvious similarities to the book of Jeremiah, we also observe some contact with the book of Amos. Reading Amos 2:4-5; 5:1-2, 16; 7:17; 8:10-14 we are left with the impression that Lamentations strives to show that the proclamations and threats of Amos have also been fulfilled for the southern kingdom as a consequence of its sin. It is also worth noting the similarities present in some of the Psalms (Pss 74; 79; 80; 88). It is difficult to be precise as to whether or not there has been some direct influence of Lamentations on Second Isaiah, but we cannot ignore the similarities to the Servant Songs (Isaiah 42–53).

In Lamentations we find the idea of a free God who cannot be enclosed in human schemes and plans, an idea that will appear later in the poetic section of the book of Job and in Ecclesiastes. The freedom to pour out sorrow before God, as seen in Jeremiah and in Lamentations, opens up a way for the honest expression of other bitter laments such as the one in Job 10:1-3.

3. Use Throughout History

Although Lamentations is seldom cited today it has been abundantly used throughout history, especially to illustrate situations of profound sorrow or of terrible and unusual sufferings, many times with a christological meaning related to the Passion. In Lam 4:20, which refers to the king, the "LORD's anointed, the breath of life" for the people, the Fathers see a reference to Christ as spiritual food (Ambrose, *De Mysteriis* 58: *Exp. Evang. sec. Lucam* I, 27; VII, 38, 120; Origen, *Second Homily on the Song of Songs;* Theodotus, *Extractos,* sec. A, 18,2). Thus the desires, the admiration, and the fervor that the Jews in the south felt for their king, the "anointed one" who protected them and was central to their identity, are now applied to Christ.

There is another text often cited for the meaning of its imagery: "the children beg for food, but no one gives them anything" (Lam 4:4). Many times this text is used with reference to the Word and to the Eucharist, particularly when there is a need to explain to the faithful the mysteries of their faith. (Cf. Gregory the Great, *Moralia in Job* I, 29; Council of Trent, Session 22, ch. 8).

Also among the Scholastics we find abundant references to Lamentations. In the works of Bonaventure, for example, there are more than two hundred and thirty explicit quotes, particularly related to the need for the grace and the mercy of God for doing good, and to the value of accepting suffering humbly.

Of special theological importance is the use of Lam 5:21 by the Council of Trent which cites it in order to say that "we are full of the grace of God" (Session 6, ch. 5). The *Catechism of the Catholic Church* cites it when it asserts that conversion is primarily the work of grace (1.432). With respect to what is just and good about groaning and lamenting before God, it is worth remembering the words of Augustine: "The more holy and full of good desires a person is, so much the more will their prayer be full of tears" (*Civ. D.* 20.17).

4. Use in the Liturgy

A considerable part of Lamentations is read in the Liturgy of the Hours, in the Office of Readings for Holy Week (even years) when reference is made to the sufferings of Christ. This book also appears in other situations of great suffering: in the lectionary for funerals of children, in Masses at times of earthquake or hurricane, and in the Liturgy of the Hours when commemorating the Holy Innocents.

SECOND READING

The First Lamentation

Let us ponder particularly this first lamentation since it gives us a general view of the content. Then we will refer more briefly to the other four, indicating the specific contributions and peculiarities of each one.

1:1-6: Jerusalem appears as a disconsolate and solitary widow. One is not to imagine here the "death" of YHWH as spouse, but the city no longer populated by a people full of life. The refrain in v. 2 will be repeated in vv. 16, 17, and 21: "she has no one to comfort her." It indicates a situation of deep sorrow where there are no human supports that could make the suffering more bearable. Finally a new motive for sorrow is added: treason and disillusionment. Friends who ought to be at her side in this tragedy have "become her enemies." These enemies are the neighboring peoples in whom Judah had placed its confidence, especially Egypt (Jer 2:36-37). Verse 3 refers to the desert experience which she still cannot accept serenely since she remembers the terrible anguish that the people have just lived through when they tried to escape but were surrounded by enemies. Verse 4 returns to the deplorable state of Jerusalem where the beauty and joy of celebration no longer exist. The priests groan instead of praising; the virgins, instead of singing happily, are submerged in bitter grief. In vv. 5 and 6 children and nobles, symbols of hope and of power and splendor respectively, are added to the list of sufferers. Verse 5 adds noteworthy theological content; it states that it is the Lord who has caused this affliction because of "the multitude of [Jerusalem's] transgressions."

1:7-11: Verse 7 is like a parenthesis that summarizes the lived experience. Verses 8 through 11 again emphasize the painful aspect: the state in which Jerusalem found herself and the fact that the people were without strength and nourishment. It also recalls the anguished prayer of the people: "O LORD, look at my affliction!" Even though it did not enter their minds to think that YHWH would cause so much sorrow to the chosen people, the Jews did recognize that the deepest cause of all this was the sin and impurity of Jerusalem.

1:12-16: The new description of the situation in which Jerusalem finds herself underlines even more her internal suffering and invites all others to "look" upon her great affliction. The poet feels the pressing need to exteriorize and share the bitterness of his soul: having identified with his people, he can no longer hold within him the bitterness he feels. Even more important is the basic conviction accented here: that all this has been provoked "directly" by YHWH, and this is perhaps what most disturbed the Jewish soul. Overturned now is the false security of Jerusalem who had firmly believed in the traditions of election and stable institutions; she had believed in a God who served those traditions. Now Jerusalem must accept the fact that God transcends everything; that God is the only absolute; that God cannot be enclosed in human schemes and plans, not even within the holy institutions God loved. The reflection of v. 10 is interesting: the same God who forbade the profanation of the sanctuary is the one who allowed it to be profaned by the pagan invader. In reality, more than "allowing" this desecration, the author seems to indicate that YHWH chose this action: "He sent fire . . . spread a net . . . crush[ed] my young men . . . trod [me down] . . . proclaimed a time against me." This historical crisis is part of God's plan for the good of God's people. YHWH is a God who acts with a "strong arm" in the midst of the chosen people while looking to repair the relationship that had forged the alliance. Here we must keep in mind the line of prophets from the south who undoubtedly influenced the thinking behind Lamentations. They denounced a showy religiosity that would view YHWH as merely a beautiful tradition: "those who say in their hearts, 'The LORD will not do good, nor will he do harm'" (Zeph 1:12) "and have said, 'He will do nothing'" (Jer 5:12).

We could conclude that the geographic and sociopolitical situation of Judah would make the domination of Babylonia inevitable unless God intervened to avoid it. But God denies this help in order to awaken in the people a true opening of their hearts, thus ending their false security. So when we say that God is the one who ruined Jerusalem, we are affirming the exact opposite of what the people expressed when they said "He will do nothing." In an obvious paradox this very affirmation is what awakens hope and motivates the prayer: if God had to bring about the destruction, God will also be able to intervene in reconstructing Jerusalem. YHWH is a God both alive and active in the history of God's people.

1:17-19: Verse 17 is a new parenthesis similar to the one in v. 7. It synthesizes the situation, in agreement with the writings of Jeremiah (Jer 25:9; 27:6) and Isaiah (Isa 10:5; 13:5), that now the foreign power has been transformed into an instrument of YHWH. Verse 18 states how, due to the proximity of the happenings, the poet wavers constantly between bitter complaint and the submissive acknowledgment of God's justice.

1:20-22: The wavering continues, but now prayer blossoms with greater strength as an expression of a renewed confidence. The people pray because they trust in a God who has intervened and can intervene again.

The Second Lamentation

This lamentation, together with the fourth, repeats the themes of the first but explains them better and uses more elaborate and expressive images. Here hope seems weaker than in the first lamentation. In fact, in 2:13 we read: "who can heal you?" and in 4:16 there is no trace of hope:

"the LORD himself has scattered them, he will regard them no more."

With respect to this second lamentation it should be emphasized that here we are to consider how God has treated "without mercy" (2:2, 17, 21), "like an enemy" (2:4, 5; cf. Jer 30:14), "in his anger" (2:1, 6, 21-22) precisely the people God had chosen, and the city that was God's "footstool" (2:1) and the "perfection of beauty" (2:15). For that reason, with all the spontaneity that pours out of sorrow and dismay the people say to YHWH: "Look, O LORD, and consider! To whom have you done this?" (2:20).

Another peculiarity of the second lamentation is its reference to false prophets (2:14) who could have avoided the ruin of their city if they had confronted it with its sin instead of awakening false hopes (Jer 14:13-16; 23:30-40). This possibility of the prophetic intervention changing the destiny of the city is beautifully expressed in Jonah 3:1–4:2. In Lamentations 2:17 we see how the true word of YHWH announced by the faithful prophets is fulfilled even in the city's ruin. Verses 20-21 are the most merciless, but in no part of the poem does the author stop to describe all the details in a masochistic way; rather he passes quickly from one detail to another. In vv. 18-19 he invites an open expression of sorrow "before the presence of the LORD," standing firm and crying out to God, no longer with empty words but "with the heart." This authentic petition and honest groaning in God's presence become the expression of an interior conversion to YHWH, the new attitude that the Lord wanted to arouse in the heart of God's people.

The Third Lamentation

The third and fifth lamentations form the last echo of the crisis: the two manifest the state of "interior exhaustion" in which the Jewish people found themselves after the deportation. This third poem does not describe the exterior disaster as much as it provides a quiet reflection on a typical case of the so-called "corporate personality": one who at that moment seems to be a prophet like Jeremiah and in other verses seems to be the people or the city of Jerusalem, or in still others seems to be the symbol of every suffering human being. In some verses the poet identifies with Jeremiah in order to symbolize the suffering of the people (for example, compare Lam 3:14, 53-55, 58 with Jer 20:7, 12; 38:6). For that reason we find within the text an oscillation between the individual complaint and the collective lament. Although this alternating movement between lament and hope is sustained, here a renewed hope predominates.

3:1-18: In these verses the individual lament is accented: "I am the one who has seen affliction." The most penetrating sorrows are remembered. They are described for YHWH, the author of the ruin, in a variety of images: persecutor, lion, hunter, torturer, thief, etcetera. In that situation all hope seems dead (3:18) and even prayer appear useless (3:44). To live thus is the same as having died (3:5) because to have God as enemy was to live without any possibility of peace or happiness (3:17).

3:19-33: These very beautiful verses express the strongest hope found anywhere in Lamentations, and are perhaps some of the most beautiful confessions of faith and hope to be found in the entire Bible. The poet makes the point that what he has said until now is what he feels when he recalls what he had lived in the past (3:19-20), but that when he takes his focus off those memories and places it again on the true God whose compassion is never exhausted, his heart is filled with hope (3:21-22). What the Lord wants is that the faithful ones simply hope in God and search for God (3:25). It is always good to hope but this hope has to be humble: it will not impose upon God what is to be done; it submits to God's unfathomable plans. That is why the poet uses the word "perhaps" (3:29; cf. Amos 5:15; Joel 2:14). The Church has always taught that we can have a "very firm hope," albeit not certain knowledge of our salvation (Council of Trent, session 6, ch. 13).

Humility, after all, does not darken a conviction that is always borne in a faithful soul: "the LORD will not reject forever" (3:31). Finally it is worth pointing out that included here is an affirmation that illuminates all of the lamentations: "he does not willingly afflict or grieve anyone" (3:33). So it is clear that God does not directly will human suffering but accepts it to the extent that it is necessary for a good or as part of a good that God has prepared for God's people.

3:34-54: In vv. 34 to 38 we see a confession of faith in a God who is committed to human life, one who is near to those who suffer and intervenes in history. In vv. 39-42 the poet invites a remembrance of individual sin as a possible preparation for a better future, but in Lamentations we find elements that seem to break the rigidity of the chain that links sin and punishment. On the one hand there is recollection of the ruin that followed the laudable religious reform of Josiah, a worthy king and one zealous for the Law. Likewise the prophet Jeremiah, who appears in this lamentation as a symbol of the suffering person, was not precisely a model of the sinner who merited punishment. We see hinted at here the questions that will reach their high point in the book of Job (Job 31:2-37) and will cast aside the traditional belief in a mechanical kind of recompense. Instead a greater consciousness of the absolutely free initiative of God is opened here. In vv. 42-54 we again remember the moment of great sorrow when God seemed to have parted definitively with the people God had previously rejected.

3:55-66: Here a confident hope is reborn: God has begun to hear their prayer and will act even more favorably on behalf of God's chosen ones. Everything is subject to the dominion of God.

The Fourth Lamentation

Together with the second lamentation this fourth one reflects the moment of greatest confusion and bitterness. Some images (4:4-5) are unusually impressive, especially those used to express how certain values were lost: how, because of their despair, mothers no longer worry about their children and even abandon them as ostriches abandon their eggs (4:3) and how, in desperation, they come even to eat their own offspring (4:10). Neither are priests or old people respected (4:16).

All this happened because the people trusted in false political hopes, forgetting YHWH (4:17), and allowed themselves to be deceived by their prophets and priests (4:13). This document close to the traditions of the south also incorporates a lament about the fate of the king, the "LORD's anointed" (4:20). Finally, as in Obad 10-15, the Edomites who rejoiced over the ruin of their neighbors (4:21-22) are shamefully rejected. Here, as in the rest of the book, we can notice the need to turn from the evil path that Jewish society was taking. For that reason Lamentations does not describe the end of *the* world, but the end of *a* world that would open the way for something new and better. God, who has the right to claim the lives of the faithful, also has the right to withdraw any of the divine gifts for a higher and more noble purpose. In fact, the exilic and postexilic periods were characterized by a greater consciousness of the transcendent power of God, of God's inscrutable plans and of incomprehensible mystery. On the other hand the unjust and powerful (4:13) were those who lost most in the catastrophe. The exhortations of Jeremiah to prosper in Babylonia (Jer 29:4-7) make one think that the people lived relatively well during the exile. In fact, many words of encouragement were needed in order that at least a part of the exiled would decide to return to Judah.

The Fifth Lamentation

The poet asks the Lord to look upon the sad state of the people. This attitude of placing everything in the sight of the Lord is an expression of confidence: YHWH's glance is not one of indifference but of mercy. Once the disaster is over, the deepest sorrow for the people is the memory of their own sin, a fact that becomes very evident to them (5:16-17).

Verses 3-18 recall anew the most difficult moment during the siege of Jerusalem, when the people were mocked and tortured by the servants of the emperor (5:8), but in vv. 19-22 there is a final chant of hope that recognizes the reign of God in history (5:19). It is equally clear that the restoration of Jerusalem will depend on divine initiative: "Restore us to yourself, O LORD, that we may be restored" (5:21). This implies being healed of sin, and, as a consequence, the end of Babylonian rule as well as the reconstruction of Jerusalem. Jewish mentality would not understand these happenings in a purely spiritual way or, on the other hand, as separate from a change of hearts, as Jeremiah had already announced (Jer 31:31-34). In this sense we find here a foreshadowing of the Christian doctrine of grace (Rom 9:16).

Baruch

Luis Heriberto Rivas

FIRST READING

General Character of the Book

The Septuagint has compiled an "anthology" of texts dealing with the Babylonian captivity:

1. An introduction in two parts
   a. Historical setting (Bar 1:1-9)
   b. Letter to the inhabitants of Jerusalem (Bar 1:10-14)
2. A prayer in two parts
   a. Confession of sins (Bar 1:15–2:10)
   b. Penitential entreaty (Bar 2:11–3:8)
3. Two poems
   a. Praise of the Law as wisdom (Bar 3:9–4:4)
   b. A poem in five parts referring to the captivity and the hope of return (Bar 4:5-9a; 4:9b-16; 4:17-29; 4:30–5:4; 5:5-9)

This anthology, known as "Baruch," has been placed after Jeremiah and is completed in turn by the book of Lamentations and the Letter of Jeremiah. These several works, distinct from each other in character, have a common theme: the thoughts and feelings of the Jewish people at the destruction of Jerusalem and the subsequent captivity.

We have Baruch only in Greek, but it seems to be a translation of a Hebrew original. The book is divided, in accordance with a logical plan, into two parts of equal length; the division must be respected in its interpretation:

I. Liturgical (1:1–3:8)
II. Prophetic (3:9–5:9)

Each part can be read as a unit, but without losing sight of the book as a whole. Part I contains a confession of the sins that led to the exile in Babylon. Part II begins with an acknowledgment of sins and moves from there to the joy produced by the prediction of a future return from captivity.

General Context for Interpretation

1. Original Historical Context

The texts, which may have been edited during the exile while under the impression left by the destruction of Jerusalem, were later combined for the use of believers living in the Diaspora. The people suffering exile far from their native land were consoled by the promise of a restoration.

2. Canonical Context

The Jewish communities of the Diaspora and, later, Christians accepted Baruch as an appendix to the book of Jeremiah. The latter provides the context and appears to be a necessary point of reference for a correct understanding of Baruch.

3. Canonical Intertextuality

The constant explicit and implicit references to Deuteronomy and Jeremiah in the first (liturgical) part, and to Second Isaiah in the second (prophetic) part show that Baruch cannot be fully understood unless these other documents have been read first.

SECOND READING

I. Liturgy: 1:1–3:8

Introduction 1: Historical Setting (1:1-9)

The author is not concerned to give a faithful picture of events in the time of Baruch, but rather to provide readers with a model of the sentiments and attitudes that ought to be present during the penitential liturgy commemorating the destruction of Jerusalem (vv. 14-15): lamentation, fasting, prayer, and almsgiving. All classes and groups of the people are represented.

Introduction 2: Letter to the Inhabitants of Jerusalem (1:10-14)

A description is given, in letter form, of the order to be followed in a liturgical penitential celebration; this is a model for every celebration: offering of sacrifices (1:10), prayer for the authorities (1:11-12), penitential prayer for the exiles (1:13), public reading from the Bible (1:14).

Prayer, Part 1: Confession of Sins, 1:15–2:10

The letter does not contain the prayer for the authorities, but only a model for a penitential prayer. This is a moving prayer in which the people acknowledge their responsibility for the catastrophe and deportation they have experienced and are experiencing. The same themes and the identical expressions found in Deut 9:4b-19 and 1 Kings 8:46-51 make their appearance here, while ideas and vocabulary are also taken from Jeremiah and Deuteronomy along with citations of the text of both books.

Those praying acknowledge their guilt for not having listened to the word of God. The universality of the guilt is emphasized: all groups within the people are guilty (1:15b-16; as in Jer 32:32 and Dan 9:7b); the rebelliousness has been there throughout Israel's history (with expressions from Jer 7:25-26; see Deut 9:7).

Various contrasts should be noted: justice for God but shame for the people (1:15 and 2:6); God set them free, but they are disobedient (1:19); what God offered them and what they have received (1:20). God does as God says (1:20; 2:1, 7), but the people do not listen ("listen" occurs fourteen times in the prayer, but only three times outside of it).

As in Deuteronomy there is a connection between the lack of obedience to the commandments and the evils the people suffer in their captivity. Deuteronomy makes it clear that God has chosen Israel as God's personal possession (7:6; 14:2; see 4:20, 34), and that for this reason it will enjoy all kinds of blessings as long as it remains united to God. When the people abandon YHWH and instead serve kings and foreign gods they must suffer the loss of these blessings and endure the hard hand of foreigners (Deut 28:47-48).

YHWH delivered the people from slavery (1:19), but they preferred to be slaves of other masters (1:22). God respected their decision by making them "subject to all the kingdoms around us" (2:4). God has not acted unjustly, having done no more than carry out what was promised (Deut 28:15-68; 29:24-27; see Lev 26:14-39; Dan 9:11).

Prayer, Part 2: Plea for Forgiveness, 2:11–3:8

The acknowledgment of sins is followed by a plea for forgiveness. Those praying address God as "God of Israel"; they recall what God has done for "[God's] people" at the Exodus, and they ask that God's anger turn away from them. This "anger" is identified with the tragic consequences of their actions.

God is asked to "incline your ear . . . open your eyes and see" those who pray (2:16b-17). The image used to describe the deportees (v. 18) recalls the mission of the prophet in Isa 42:7; 49:8-10.

Baruch 2:19-26 is out of harmony with the rest of the prayer. It ceases to ask for forgiveness and returns to the confession of sins, with numerous allusions to the book of Jeremiah. It does not speak of all the sins of disobedience, but of one in particular: the sin of King Zedekiah, who did not listen to the word of the Lord that ordered him to submit to King Nebuchadnezzar (Jer 27:12). Baruch expands the passage in Jer 27:1-15 by adding other texts of the same prophet. The threats are taken from Jer 7:34 and 34:22, which in their original context referred to other situations; the threat in Jer 27:8 is amplified by introducing Jer 8:1 and 36:30. The passage ends by recalling the situation seen in the Temple, due to "the wickedness of the house of Israel and the house of Judah," as in Jer 32:32.

In vv. 27-35 the tone of the prayer changes: along with frequent references to Jeremiah numerous allusions to Deuteronomy also make their appearance. The theme of God's justice in carrying out threats is left aside, and the theme of forbearance and mercy is introduced. God manifested kindness in making threats and promises in advance through Moses (Deut 4:27; 31:9; 28:62, and elsewhere).

The prophecies of punishment in Deuteronomy included the promise of future conversion and forgiveness (30:2-3). This conversion will begin in the heart, as in Deut 30:1-2; Jer 3:10; 29:13 (see 1 Kings 8:47-48). When the people are converted God will give them a new heart and new ears (see Deut 29:3). The new heart is a recurring theme in the literature of the exilic period (Jer 24:7; 32:39; Ezek 11:19; 36:26; Ps 51:12). As a result of this change of heart and ears they will praise YHWH in the place of their exile (see Bar 3:6-7; Tob 13:6; the opposite view is found in Ps 137:4).

When they "turn" from their wicked ways God "will bring them again into the land that I swore to give to their ancestors" (formula from Deut 1:8; 6:10; 6:18; 8:1, and *passim;* see 1 Kings 8:48). But this time they will enter the land in order to "rule over it," and not to be ruled.

This part of the prayer ends with the promise of a multitudinous people, using the same formula as in Jer 30:19 (see Deut 6:3; 7:13; 8:1). The promise is parallel and antithetical to the threat of reduction to a few with which this part of the prayer began (see 2:29). Verse 35 predicts an everlasting covenant (Jer 32:40; "new covenant" in Jer 31:31) and a commitment not to repeat the exile. "The land that I have given them": as in Deuteronomy the land is a gift from God, and possession of it depends on God's will.

The last part of the prayer (3:1-8) begins with new titles for God: "Lord Almighty" *(kyrios pantocratōr)* and "God of Israel" (3:1). The first represents the Hebrew expression "YHWH of hosts," while the second is a name God has by reason of the covenant. Those praying appeal to the divine commitment to the covenant and the divine omnipotence in their plea for forgiveness and the end of the exile. This last section of the second part of the prayer forms an *inclusio* with its beginning (2:11), which likewise spoke of the power of God manifested in the Exodus and of the name that God has in virtue of that deliverance.

Baruch 3:1-4 contrasts the omnipotence of God with the condition of Judah in exile: God reigns "forever," while "we are perishing forever"; those who come before the almighty Lord are "dead" (that is, in exile). Verse 7 returns to the theme of 2:32: praise of the name of God. In order that the people might be able to invoke this name, God has put the fear of God into their hearts (expression from Jer 32:40). Like the psalmist of the exile they recognize that if they are to be able to praise God, YHWH must change their hearts and purify their lips (see Ps 51:12, 16-17). The final words (3:8) no longer ask for anything, but describe the pitiful situation of the people: for this the words of 2:4 are used again, with the addition of "punishment" (*ophlēsis*, a word used only here in the Bible).

The people plead with God in the anguish of exile. They are poor folk who cry out because they lack freedom, have been despoiled of their land, and see all their religious and political values (the Temple and Jerusalem) in ruins. Like the poor of the psalms, they too ask that justice be done them even while acknowledging that this situation has not come about without fault on their part. It is God's will that they be a people who are God's possession and that they live in freedom under divine protection, but by a wrong choice they have subjected themselves to the control of those who now harass and despoil them.

II. Prophecy: 3:9–5:9

First Poem: The Law as Wisdom (3:9–4:4)

This poem, which begins with the words of Deut 6:4: "Hear, O Israel," is addressed to the people in exile with the intention of making them aware that they have fallen into this plight because they had abandoned the Law, which is identified with wisdom. The commandments are described as parallel with "prudence" *(phronēsis),* a term that here represents the Hebrew words meaning "wisdom" and "understanding." The passage begins by asking Israel about its situation; the question has four parts that describe this situation in increasingly extreme terms. There is but one answer: Israel has abandoned the commandments, the source of wisdom.

An objection arises: no one can lay hold of wisdom (see Job 28), and those who have sought it have been unable to find it. Baruch 3:16-23 describes several groups of persons who were seemingly powerful and were commonly thought to possess great wisdom. But they did not in fact attain to wisdom; all of them, and their descendants after them, have vanished and left no remembrance of themselves. Neither did the peoples of the East, renowned for their wisdom (1 Kings 5:10), in fact achieve wisdom, nor did the mighty giants (a reference to Gen 6:4; Num 13:33; Deut 1:28; 2:10-11, 20-21; 3:11) because despite their strength they did not find wisdom but perished because of their folly (Sir 16:7; Wis 14:6; the apocrypha). The only one who possesses wisdom is God, and God has revealed it only to Israel, God's "servant" and "beloved," by giving it the Law. (Compare Bar 2:29-31 with Deut 30:11-14.) As a result wisdom, which has its dwelling in heaven (Wis 9:4), has been sent by God and has come to Israel (Wis 9:9-10; Sir 24:8), and now resides in the midst of humanity.

According to 3:37 wisdom "appeared on earth and lived with humankind." Post-exilic texts tend to give wisdom personal traits (Prov 1:20-33; 3:16-19; 8–9; Wisdom 9; Sir 24:1-23, and elsewhere). All these passages were reread in the NT and form the background of the prologue of the Fourth Gospel, which uses this literary figure to expound the mystery of Christ's pre-existence: Wisdom, identified with the Word of God and with the Law, was already united to God from all eternity and was present with God in the work of creation; it manifested itself in various ways in the history of the Israelite people and finally took flesh in Jesus Christ.

When Christian antiquity reread Bar 3:37 in light of the prologue of John's gospel it saw in it the revelation of the incarnation of the Son of God: "Our Lord Jesus Christ can be seen, in his divinity, with the heart's eyes when these are pure, perfect, full of God; but he was also seen in his body, as is written: 'Afterward she appeared on earth and lived with humankind'" (Augustine, *Sermo* 277, 16; MPL 38:1266). "These words clearly manifest to us the incarnation of the Only Son" (Theodoret of Cyrus, *Commentary on Baruch* 3:38; MPG 81:773–774B).

The poem ends with an exhortation to Jacob (Israel) to embrace wisdom, which is identified with the Law. Wisdom has a special connection with life and light, themes extensively developed in the gospel of John. The final verse (4:4) is a beatitude that refers to those who have been blessed with the revelation of the Law.

Second Poem: Consolation for the Exiles. Part 1 (4:5-9a)

The prophet addresses a message of consolation to Israel in exile: their present situation is not final. The imperative "Take courage!" is uttered at the beginning and will be repeated three times (4:21, 27, 30). The words are typical of eschatological or messianic pronouncements by the prophets in the LXX (Joel 2:21-22; Zeph 3:16; Hag 2:5; Zech 8:13, 15), where they translate the formula "Fear not!" The people are called those "who perpetuate Israel's name" (v. 5): the only thing that remains of Israel is what memory preserves. The description of the people's sins (vv. 7-8) is inspired by Deut 32:15-17, but the reproaches serve only to highlight the inconceivable message: God will not destroy them.

Second Poem: Consolation for the Exiles. Part 2 (4:9b-16)

Jerusalem speaks to the neighboring cities as though she were a desolate widow. Her discourse has two parts (4:9b-12a and 14-16) that frame a description of the sins of her sons and daughters (vv. 12b-13). In the first part of the discourse she exhorts the neighboring cities not to rejoice at her suffering, and she acknowledges that the sins of her children have led to her desolation. In the second part the same cities are called upon to share her sorrow at the captivity of her children. The foreign invasion is remembered in words from Deut 28:49-50 (see Jer 5:15).

Second Poem: Consolation for the Exiles. Part 3 (4:17-29)

Jerusalem now turns to her children. To them she speaks not of tears but of consolation because of the salvation she awaits. There is barely a reference to guilt (v. 28a); the emphasis is on the joy of the return. The entire passage is framed by vv. 18 and 29, which repeat the same ideas. The city tries to help her children (v. 17) by urging them to cry out to God for salvation (vv. 21 and 27), as she herself does while clad in robes of mourning (v. 20). The same God who brought evils upon them (vv. 18, 25, 29, 30) will bring salvation.

Second Poem: Consolation for the Exiles. Part 4 (4:30–5:4)

Using expressions from Isaiah, the prophet addresses Jerusalem and urges her to gaze joyfully on her sons and daughters as they return from captivity. In this part of the poem attention is directed to the change the happy return effects in Jerusalem. The section in framed by the new name God gives to Jerusalem (4:30 and 5:4), as in Isa 62:2-4, 12b. In 4:30-35 Jerusalem is consoled by the prediction of the punishment that will come upon the nation that has enslaved her children (see Isa 13:21; 34:9-10, 14).

In 4:36–5:4 Jerusalem is urged to exchange her garments of mourning (see Bar 4:20; Isa 60:20; 61:3) for the robes of glory and justice that come from God (Isa 52:1; 61:10) and to look eastward and see her children (Isa 49:18-23; 60:4) as they are gathered together and brought home by "the Holy One" (the divine name used most often in Second Isaiah).

Second Poem: Consolation for the Exiles. Part 5 (5:5-9)

The prophet again addresses Jerusalem and bids her contemplate with joy the return of her children, but here attention is focused on those returning from captivity. As in the fourth part, expressions are taken from Isaiah. Jerusalem is urged to arise (Isa 51:17) and gaze from the height on her children as they come from east and west, drawn by the voice of God (see 4:37; Isa 49:18-23; 60:4). Note the contrast between their going out on foot, led by the enemy, and their glorious return, carried on thrones by God. The Lord orders that the rough ways be made smooth (see Isa 40:3-5; 49:11), bids the trees provide shade and fragrance (see Isa 41:19; 55:12-13), and he personally serves as guide (see Isa 49:10; 52:12).

The organization of the parts of the book of Baruch has brought the reader from mourning over sin and oppression by enemies to an exultation caused by the proclamation of future salvation. Following the line traced by Jeremiah and Second Isaiah, the book proclaims the eschatological renewal of a suffering people. The signs of liberation that can be seen in history provide a glimpse of the future that God is preparing for God's people. For Christians, the book of Baruch thus leads toward the revelation of the new life that begins with the resurrection of Jesus Christ.

Letter of Jeremiah

Luis Heriberto Rivas

FIRST READING

General Character of the Book

The Letter of Jeremiah is an independent book in the LXX but in the Vulgate was combined with the book of Baruch. When the biblical text was divided into chapters the letter became ch. 6 of Baruch and appears in this form in many modern Bibles.

This work may have been written originally in Hebrew but it has come down to us only in Greek. It is an apologetic work attacking the worship of idols. A sentence that is repeated with some variations (vv. 14, 22, 28, 39, 44, 51, 56, 64, 68—all verse numbers as in the Greek text) divides the work into sections of unequal length and focuses the reader's attention on a single idea: we must neither fear idols nor place our trust in them since they are not gods. The opening verse, which imitates Jer 29:1-3, identifies the addressees.

General Context for Interpretation

During the exilic and post-exilic periods the Jews living in the Diaspora would have been impressed by the magnificence and wealth of the pagan temples and might have felt drawn to the worship of idols. As a result there arose an extensive apologetic literature that is represented in the Bible chiefly by Jer 10:1-16; Isa 44:9-20; the story of Bel and the Dragon (ch. 14 of Daniel LXX); and chs. 13–15 of the book of Wisdom. The Letter of Jeremiah belongs to this genre.

SECOND READING

Verses 1-2: Jeremiah 25:11-12 and 29:10 indicate that the exile was to last for seventy years. The Letter of Jeremiah, like Dan 9:24, extends this period to seven generations because it wants to make the Jews living in the Diaspora understand that they too are still living in captivity.

Verses 3-6: The first warning is against the fear these Jews may feel when they see the images of the Babylonian gods being carried on people's shoulders. The reference may be to the stately New Year's procession in which the brilliant statues of the gods were carried on platforms. The author ridicules this cult in order to arouse laughter instead of fear and so keep the Jews from feeling a desire to imitate the pagans.

Verses 33-39: The idols and their worship are described by comparing them with the God of Israel: they can do nothing by themselves (see vv. 45-57, 69-72) and need others to move them (see vv. 23-26). Confined as they are to their temples, they are like criminals shut up in jails. Since they are utterly incapable of acting they are unable to do the good works that God does: repay both good and evil (see Ps 18:20), bestow wealth (2 Sam 2:7), demand the fulfillment of vows (Deut 23:22), deliver from death (2 Sam 2:6; Ps 30:3), rescue the weak from the hand of the strong (Ps 18:17), give sight to the blind (Ps 146:8), take pity on the orphan and the widow (Pss 68:5; 146:9).

The worship of idols permits reprehensible acts such as temple prostitution (see vv. 42-44), which is prohibited in Israel (Deut 23:18). The presentation of the offerings by women, the touching of the idols by unchaste women, or the mourning of priests in the temples are activities unacceptable to Jews and not allowed in Israel (Lev 12:1-4; 15:19; 21:5-6).

Israel's religion was set apart by the fact that no images were allowed in its worship, as strictly ordered by the second commandment: "You shall not make for yourself an idol" (Exod 20:4; Deut 5:8-10). Care was taken that no creature should be an object of worship since such worship was regarded as proper to pagans. The representations found in the Jerusalem Temple, as later in some synagogues, were purely decorative.

The Christians of the first five centuries adopted the same practice, and the representations of Christ and some saints, along with scenes from the Old and New Testaments such as can still be seen in the catacombs were decorative. There is no evidence that they were venerated. In addition some local councils prohibited these representations, and some of the Fathers proceeded to destroy them:

> I asked what place this was, and when they answered that it was a church I entered it in order to pray. It happened that a curtain hung in front of the doors of the church; this was dyed and on it was painted a representation of Christ or of some saint. I do not recall whose image it was. On seeing that, contrary to the authority of the scriptures, they had hung an image of a human being in the church of Christ, I tore down the curtain and told the guardians of the place that they might better use it to wrap the corpse of some poor man and carry it out for burial (Epiphanius, in the letters of Jerome, *Letter* 51.9; MPL 22:526).

Beginning in the fifth century people began to appreciate the didactic aspect of images but they did not allow any veneration of them. Some Fathers of the Church recommended them as a way of setting scenes from the Bible and the lives of the saints before the people, who could not read and therefore had no access to books. In 600 Gregory the Great wrote to a bishop of Marseilles: "We praise you for prohibiting the veneration of images, but we blame you for destroying them. . . . It is one thing to venerate images, another to learn from paintings what it is that is to be venerated. . . . Paintings give to the uneducated what reading gives to readers" (Gregory the Great, *Letters,* 11.13; MPL 77:1128).

The first testimonies to the veneration of images of the Lord appear in the seventh century as a result of theological discussions and councils dealing with the humanity of Christ, but the practice was soon hindered by the iconoclasts for reasons that were at times more political than theological. The veneration of images was finally approved by the Second Council of Nicea (787 C.E.; *DS* 600–603).

The Reformers again raised the question of the legitimacy of the veneration of images in light of the OT prohibition. The Council of Trent in 1563 resolved the apparent contradiction between the OT prohibition and Christian practice by pointing out that gestures of veneration are addressed to those whom the images represent (*DS* 1823–1825).

The belief that some power or divinity resides in the images or that prayer can be addressed to the images as such or that confidence can be placed in them is something the Council says is proper to pagans (as the Letter of Jeremiah shows) and must not be imitated by Christians. In paganism worship is addressed to idols in themselves; in Christianity veneration is paid to a reality distinct from the image, namely to the person represented.

Ezekiel

Jesús Asurmendi Ruiz

FIRST READING

The book of Ezekiel has never been very fashionable. Its effect on readers is a mixture of fascination and rejection. A whole series of diseases and mental disturbances have been suggested to explain the prophet's personality. His lengthy chapters written in a very strange language, his bizarre symbolic actions, his fantastic visions are at once attractive and repellent. In fact, the book itself is quite "binary." Its message is stretched between two extreme poles: the implacable judgment of Jerusalem and Judah and the announcement of an unbounded hope. Never were the history and reality of Israel painted in such dark colors, with such a total and negative radicalism. Yet at the same time, never were such unexpected prospects offered to a people crushed and emptied of all hope (33:10-11; 37:11). One of the essential characteristics of biblical prophets is exemplified in Ezekiel's case: their message runs counter to the current fashion. The more optimistic, blind, and unconcerned the people (13; 33:30-33), the more Ezekiel denounces the reality of sin and injustice that of necessity calls for judgment. When this judgment happens in the fall of Jerusalem (33:21-22), despair seizes Israel and then the prophet preaches faith and hope (chs. 33–37). As in the history of Israel, there is in Ezekiel a "before" and "after" the fall of Jerusalem.

This message of the book of Ezekiel, made up of contrasts, literally sticks to the prophet's skin. His personal life is permeated by it: he must remain impassive at his wife's death and refrain from carrying out the mourning ritual as a sign of a much greater misfortune: the disappearance of "the delight of your eyes, and your heart's desire" (24:21), Jerusalem and its Temple. This also exemplifies another essential characteristic of biblical prophetism: the message of the prophets is of a piece with their lives (for instance Hosea's marriage, Jeremiah's celibacy, Isaiah's children). The very personality of Ezekiel shares this twofold aspect of his mission. Not only he is at once passionate and cold in his ministry—the length, the details, the relentlessness of his descriptions show it (see 16:1-34; 23)—but he is at the same time priest and prophet. A priest because a priest's son (1:3), he is well versed in the teaching *(torāh),* in the distinction between clean and unclean, sacred and profane (22:26; 44:23); he possesses a knowledge of the sanctuary he has received from tradition, the Temple workers, and the priests who preceded him. This traditional teaching seeks to be equally pertinent and precise in its application to various cases, yet it runs the risk of falling into aridity and casuistry. But through the Lord's call Ezekiel becomes a prophet in a foreign, unclean land. This is a first shock: he is now a prophet in a time of acute crisis, dealing with the new, the unexpected, the present circumstances. It is not that he disregards or despises tradition (after all, he is a priest); but rather than repeating it, he adapts it (as a prophet) to foster the relations of God and God's people in the present circumstances.

The very contents of Ezekiel's book witness to this bipolarity of his message and personality, for chs. 1–24 contain, after the impressive overture narrating the call (1:1–3:15), a series of oracles and denunciations of the sin of Judah and Jerusalem and predictions of their imminent punishment. Chapters 25–32 present what are commonly called "oracles against the nations," often held to be a measure of Ezekiel's originality. Chapters 33–48 are devoted to the proclamation of hope for Israel and the description of some of the elements of that hope. This division of the book into three large blocks does not mean that in the present state of the book there are no texts built on the punishment-hope model (see for instance, chs. 8–11 [11:14-21]; 16 [16:59-63]; 20 [20:32-44]). However, one cannot forget that the whole of the book is built on the three great visions that form its skeleton: 1:1–3:15, the appearance of the glory and the call of the prophet; 8–11, chastisement of Jerusalem and departure of the divine glory; 40–48, return of the glory of YHWH into the new Temple.

There is also the problem of the origin and authenticity of Ezekiel's book. The hypotheses are many. Moshe Greenberg upholds Ezekiel's authorship for the ensemble of oracles and the organization of the book but does not claim that it is the exact expression of the prophet's actual words. He questions, often with good reason, the criteria used by biblical exegesis; these are often uncertain and result from unjustified *a priori* assumptions. At the other extreme, Joachim Becker considers the book of Ezekiel a pseudo-writing of the fourth and third centuries B.C.E. Karl-Friedrich Pohlmann gives up the attempt to rediscover the portrait of the prophet who becomes a figure only from the time of the composition of the book as we have it now—after the exile—according to the scheme "announcement-fulfillment." The most reasonable hypothesis, however, attributes to Ezekiel not only a recognizable historical existence but also the substance of his book. This does not mean that his oracles in particular have not been rewritten and enlarged by more or less direct disciples, to the point that the text sometimes becomes incomprehensible (especially 1:1–3:15). Ezekiel is too striking a figure to be only a vague literary and theological product whose connection with history would be untraceable. [See also the article "Prophetism and Prophets."]

This understanding of an ancient text requires a special effort because of the cultural distance to be overcome. Ezekiel's book contains a whole series of particularities. It freely uses a few formulas. The first of these is "son of humanity," that is, "mortal" (*ben ʾādām*). The locution is typically Hebraic. Ezekiel employs it (ninety-three times) with a clear intention: to show the contrast between the glory of God, the Lord who speaks to him, and the smallness of the prophet who is merely a human being. Another formula recurs with variations: "you (plural you, they) will know that I am the LORD." It appears fifty-four times throughout the book, most often at the conclusion of an oracle. Every time it intends to show the link between YHWH's action and divine knowledge. The knowledge of God in Ezekiel is revealed in and by God's action.

Juridical, even casuistic language is another characteristic of the book of Ezekiel, appearing chiefly in chs. 18 and 33. It is also true that the prophet loves controversies; at any rate he takes the opportunity offered by the words of the people to deliver his message (12:21-27; 18:1-4; 20:32; 28:2; 33:11, 17, 20, 23; 37:11). Parables and allegories are also to Ezekiel's liking (chs. 15; 16; 17; 19; 23; 29; 31).

Symbolic actions have pride of place in Ezekiel's language and message. Of course the prophet is mainly the bearer of words, but miming can be a help in delivering the message by analogy: hence the public dimension of the prophetic ministry. Mime also is useful for emphasizing the efficacy of the prediction. Several symbolic actions are found in chs. 4–5 and in 12:1-16; 24:1-14, 15-27; 37:15-28.

Ezekiel also uses mythology to express the word he has received. Thus the myth of the first human being and the paradisiacal garden are clearly visible in ch. 28, and in ch. 21 the prophet uses the myth of Erra (the magic sword) to announce the arrival of the Babylonian troops.

The images and metaphors of the book of Ezekiel are numerous. Borrowing the image of the woman-partner used by prophets that preceded him to express the relation between Israel and its God, he uses it in several different ways in chs. 16 and 23. But it is water that appears with unparalleled force and in the extreme polyvalence of its symbolism. First it is the water of agriculture, simple and indispensable (ch. 19), that takes on mythical overtones (ch. 31). The absence of water—thirst—serves to express the precariousness of life (4:9-17). The sound of water is used to signify the grandeur of the advent of the glory of God (43:2). There are the waters of purification (36:25) that bring blessing (34:26). Finally, there is the water of life in its fullness, water of inexhaustible fecundity (ch. 47).

It is no easy thing to enter into Ezekiel's book. Taking account of the foregoing remarks, readers can attempt a first reading of certain key texts that can show the essential features of the book and the personality of its author; these can serve as a framework for a second and complete reading.

The story of the call (1:1–3:15), a difficult text, gives the program of the first part of the book and legitimizes the prophet's mission. The manifestation of the glory of God on foreign soil shows the bonds God has with a people, not with a land or a temple. In contrast to other similar narratives it offers no reasons for hope. But the very mission of the prophet is a source of hope. The second great vision (chs. 8–11) contains a fair number of the essential themes of the book's message: the role of the prophet as pillar and counselor in the community, description of the idolatry and punishment of Jerusalem, estrangement of God from the Temple, affirmation that a remnant will survive. The third vision (20:1-31) is that of the history of the people as seen by Ezekiel. Chapter 18 attempts an answer to the Israelites' contesting of the traditional theology of retribution and responsibility; the pastoral dimension of the prophet's mission appears clearly here. Chapter 17 is a good example of the perception Ezekiel has of politics and the criteria he uses in judging. A passage that shows the commitment of the prophet to be of one piece with his personal life and becomes "symbolic action" is 24:15-27. The second part of his ministry, which is also the second section of his message, appears clearly in texts such as ch. 37: Israel will live, thanks to the divine breath. The landscape of the new life that flows from the dwelling of the God of Israel is depicted in 47:1-12.

General Context

1. Historical Setting

The book of Ezekiel supplies us with an important number of dates that allow us to situate the prophet's activity and oracles in history. The dates refer to the first deportation to Babylon in 598–597 B.C.E. The "thirtieth year" of 1:1 is questionable; it probably refers to Ezekiel's age at the time of his calling. It corresponds to the fifth year of the deportation, 593. The last dated text is in 29:17, the oracle against Egypt given to Nebuchadnezzar as a reward; it corresponds to the year 571. For over twenty years Ezekiel has proclaimed the word of the Lord, and in a tragic period.

In 612 the capital of the Assyrian empire fell into the hands of the Babylonians and the Medes. The whole Near East was in turmoil. Within the nascent political realignment Egypt pretended to defend Assyria in order to prevent an excessive development of Babylon as a great power. To achieve this Pharaoh Neco went to Megiddo where he encountered Josiah, king of Judah, who wanted to thwart any help for Assyria. The king of Jerusalem was killed; his son was deported to Egypt when the Pharaoh returned and Jehoiakim was installed in his place. Nebuchadnezzar ascended the throne of Babylon in 606 and effectively became the master of the whole region. However, the struggles with Egypt continued. In 601 there was a confrontation with no decisive results. Jehoiakim of Jerusalem interpreted this as an expression of the Babylonians' powerlessness and refused to pay tribute. Nebuchadnezzar moved into the region and laid siege to Jerusalem at the end of 598. Jehoiakim died during the siege. His son Jehoiachin took his place and capitulated. He was deported to Babylon with the elite of the land, among whom was Ezekiel. The Babylonians installed a new king in Jerusalem, Zedekiah. The Israelite community was therefore cut in two: one part in exile and the other in Judah. Jeremiah was among the latter. The exiles as well as those who remained had but one dream: to see the return of the deported and the end of submission to Babylon.

It is for the most part possible to follow the events of the period on the basis of the dates given by Ezekiel. In 594–593, the year of Ezekiel's call to prophesy (1:2, the fifth year of the deportation), a plot was hatched in Jerusalem, a plot in which Judah and the neighboring regions participated. The plot came to nothing and Zedekiah had to go to Babylon in order to give a pledge of his loyalty. The prophet's ministry attempted to arouse the people and incite them to conversion (8:1, the sixth year, 592–591). The very somber description of the history of Israel (ch. 20) dates from the following year, 591–590; it has the same purpose as chs. 8–11 and the same lack of success. The pro-Egyptian party at the Jerusalem court was continually intriguing to provoke a rebellion against Nebuchadnezzar (29:1-7, the tenth year, 588–587). The tribute ceased. The Babylonian army arrived before the ramparts of Jerusalem on January 15, 588 (24:1-2). The Egyptians gave some help but the fate of the city was already sealed. Zedekiah tried to flee but was caught and led to Nebuchadnezzar. The Babylonians blinded him and led him to Babylon, where he died. Jerusalem was taken. The city and the Temple were put to the torch on August 25, 587. The majority of the oracles that bear a date go back to this year (26:1; 30:20; 31:1; 32:1; 33:21). There was a new deportation; what had remained of the elite of the people now joined those deported in 597. The Babylonians installed a governor, Gedaliah, of the Shaphan family, protectors and friends of Jeremiah. But he was assassinated by the last Judean resisters, who took flight. There would be still another deportation to Babylon a few years later, probably as a consequence of a last rebellion.

Little is known of the life led by those deported to Babylonia. Settled in abandoned villages for the purpose of bringing them back to life, they enjoyed a certain amount of freedom. This regrouping of the exiled probably resulted in their regaining control of their lives and creating the social and religious conditions favorable to the restoration of the people on the basis of the former theological traditions. All institutions had disappeared. Ezekiel's role and influence in this work, as vital as it was strenuous, were probably of prime importance.

2. Ezekiel's Abiding Influence

Ben Sirach cites Ezekiel among the prophets after Jeremiah (Sir 8:10). Apocalyptic literature (whether biblical or not) borrows a great number of images and scenarios from Ezekiel while clearly keeping its distance from his message. Among the biblical texts discovered at Qumran there are fragments of six copies of Ezekiel's book, but it is not possible to reconstruct a complete scroll. His book is, however, explicitly regarded as Scripture in these fragments because he is quoted with the introductory formula "as it is written."

In the NT the gospels do not quote Ezekiel directly. Nevertheless, it is evident that the image of the vine (John 15:1-10, especially v. 6) is an echo of Ezek 15:1-8. Similarly, the image of the good shepherd (John 10:11-18) is an echo of Ezek 34:11-16 with elements drawn from Zech 11:4-17. It is also possible to see a similarity between John 7:37-39 and Ezek 47:1-12. In addition, one can consider Ezek 37:1-14, among the traditional texts on the resurrection of the dead, as the background of Matt 28:51-53. But it is particularly Revelation, attributed to John, that liberally borrows from the book of Ezekiel, although this is not its only source. Even the trajectory of the two books is similar. The symbolic action of the prophet swallowing the book is used in Rev 5:1 and also in 10:1-11. The fountainhead in Ezek 47:1-12 explicitly reappears in Rev 22:1-3 along with other OT texts. Several elements of Ezekiel's description of the new temple and the new Jerusalem are found also in Rev 11:1 and 21:10, and there are other less explicit, but quite numerous, allusions (Rev 4:2-11, cf. Ezek 1:4-28; Rev 6:8, cf. Ezek 14:21; Rev 11:1, cf. Ezek 40:3).

In rabbinic literature two different problems arose. On the one hand, there is the difficulty of matching the legislative data of Ezekiel's book with the Torah (for example, Ezekiel 18 and Exod 20:5; Ezek 20:25 and Lev 18:5; Ezek 44:22 and Lev 21:14; Ezek 46:13 and Num 28:4). The question was so thorny that withdrawing Ezekiel's book was considered, but the intense work of Rabbi Hananiah ben Hezekiah, who "took three hundred jars of oil, settled in the attic, and remained there until he succeeded in explaining everything," saved the book *(b. Menaḥ).* In fact, this policy of establishing agreement between the Law and Ezekiel was the solution used in most cases. Whenever agreement could not be discovered, scholars put off the hope to see the light until Elijah's return at the beginning of the messianic era. There was also the danger that the prophet's visions could be used as a justification for mystical and/or esoteric speculations that were not always to the orthodox rabbis' liking. The reading of Ezekiel's book was prohibited, although this interdict was not always faithfully observed. Traces of this kind of speculation are found in Qumran, where one of the fragments speaks of the angels "who praise the model of the throne of glory." The doctrine of the *merkābāh* (the divine chariot of visions) takes its point of departure from

Ezekiel's visions. It was already one of the three characteristics of Ezekiel according to Sir 49:8: "It was Ezekiel who saw the vision of glory, which God showed him above the chariot of the cherubim." Certain elements of these mystical-esoteric doctrines are sometimes met with in rabbinic literature, but the first substantial documents centered around the *merkābāh* appear at the end of the fourth century C.E. in different mystical groups. The Kabbala, which will take shape at the end of the Middle Ages, is rooted in this doctrine, but Maimonides did not like Ezekiel because of the danger he represented.

The Fathers of the Church did not exert much effort in interpreting the book of Ezekiel. He is the prophet least quoted by the Apostolic Fathers. Clement of Rome cites the book four times. Only Origen among the Alexandrians writes a complete commentary on Ezekiel, but only a few fragments survive. Jerome has also transmitted to us fourteen homilies on Ezekiel by Origen; the passages used are 1:1-16; 13:2-17, 24; 28:11-14; 44:2. Needless to say, Ezekiel's text lends itself to Alexandrian allegory.

In a completely different mode we have the commentary on the book of Ezekiel by Theodoret of Cyrus, who belonged to the school of Antioch. Without disregarding a certain typological dimension of the writing the commentator sticks to the meaning of the text in its proper context (Ezekiel speaks of the freedom of God bringing the people back from exile) and the visions are seen only as attempts at expressing the inexpressible. The third great commentary is Jerome's. As is often the case, Origen is in the background of his work. Finally, we must cite the twenty-two homilies of Gregory the Great. His purpose is not to comment on the prophetic text but to write spiritual discourses based on Ezekiel.

However, very early certain texts from Ezekiel's book were liberally exploited, and first of all ch. 37. It appears in what is called *Testimonia,* a sort of anthology of passages treating a given subject that function as "scriptural proof." Texts of the OT, inspired by God, serve to prove theological statements drawn from the NT. This practice of using *Testimonia* clearly shows how the Fathers of the Church, especially the Alexandrians, read the Scriptures. At the same time, the Antiochians had a way of interpreting Scripture closer to that in use now.

Within this framework, and the larger one of the writings of the Fathers in general, Ezek 37:1-14 received several interpretations. A first interpretation was inspired by millenarianism, rooted in Judaism: it foretold the resurrection of the righteous and their gathering in Jerusalem during the thousand years of the messianic kingdom.

A second interpretation, already present in the NT (see Matt 27:51-53), holds that the prediction of Ezekiel is realized in the resurrection of Christ. The use of this text in the liturgy of the paschal vigil as early as the fourth century attests to the existence of this interpretation. Along the same lines, Paul and some Fathers of the Church, like Jerome, believe Ezekiel's oracle to be definitively fulfilled in the new Israel, the Church, of which the resurrection of Christ is the firstfruits.

The last interpretation, which will become the most widespread, sees in Ezekiel's text the announcement of the resurrection of the righteous at the last judgment.

Ezekiel 47:1-12 is one of the rare texts that have been abundantly used. The *Letter of Barnabas* quotes it among the prophecies proclaimed during the ceremony of baptism: the wondrous trees of life of the prophetic text are identified with the baptized who, having entered the water laden with sins, come out laden with fruits. The literary genre of the *Letter of Barnabas* is that of a Jewish midrash, frequently met with in the NT literature. This text of Ezekiel is presented, along with other passages of the OT (Zech 14:8, which depends on Ezekiel; Jer 2:12-13; Isa 16:1; 33:16), according to the method of the *Testimonia* and allowed for the elaboration of a whole theology of baptism. Other texts of early Christian literature follow the same theological route, which in its turn will influence artistic representations as well as the Roman liturgy.

This review of the traditional readings of Scripture raises the problem of the interpretation of the OT by Christians, whether in the patristic era or in our own times. On the one hand we must be acutely aware of the limitations of any interpretation, always dependent on the underlying anthropology and mentality of the period. On the other hand, it is obvious that the absolute criterion of the Christian reading of Scripture is none other than Jesus Christ, his work, his death, and his resurrection. On the foundation of their adhesion to the person of Christ the Savior, Son of God, Christians read the OT as a testimony to the hope that is realized in and by Christ. Christ is the one who sheds light on the ancient texts, allowing us to place them in proper perspective and connect them to the current of definitive liberation and salvation that he brings to humankind. From this viewpoint it is perfectly legitimate to read Ezek 37:1-14 as a justification of the hope in the resurrection fulfilled by Christ. Likewise, the use of Ezek 47:1-12 in the context of baptism is quite inescapable.

All that precedes must not obscure the necessity of respecting the OT writings for what they are, in their context of origin, and with regard to the intentions of the authors and the needs of their original addressees. The reason for this is simple: Christians have not yet arrived at the fullness of the realization of salvation that at present is completed only in Christ. Christians are stretched between the way of hope of the people of the OT and the certainty of their faith that gives them the assurance that the realization has already begun in Christ. Every text of the OT has these two facets.

Christians will of necessity find these texts relevant and make them their own in different ways according to their individual mindsets, but within a specific believing community animated by the life of the Church. In any event, the book of Ezekiel offers a great wealth of insights to today's people. [See also the article "How to Interpret the Bible."]

Fear is at the very core of human beings. In our day, often with good reason, this fear takes the form of a deadly despair. The strength of Ezekiel's hope, in circumstances as tragic as those of today, can prove a powerful encouragement for today's Christians. Ezekiel's hope is not a mere product of his fervid imagination, but a manifestation of the spirit of God. This sort of hope presupposes a vivid and clear vision and an awareness of the real state of affairs that must be addressed. Ezekiel is not about fighting reality with an imaginary construct, tragic circumstances with an illusory flight. In the book's basic structure and in the different manifestations of his ministry Ezekiel can be read by today's Christians for who he was: one who truly and closely observed both reality and hope.

Another interesting subject is the lasting influence the book of Ezekiel has had on artistic representations. It is well known that the Jewish religion prohibited the making of images. However, this rule was not always rigorously followed, the classic example being the synagogue of Dura-Europos, a city on the banks of the Euphrates. The walls of this community house, built about 224 C.E., were adorned with frescoes. Among the best known events of the OT—Abraham's sacrifice, Moses and the departure from Egypt, and so on—the scenes from Ezekiel 34 hold a place of honor, covering one whole wall of the building. The first scenes represent the different moments of Ezek 37:1-14, giving an eschatological perspective to the last images, which show the return of the lost ten tribes of Israel. The last two scenes depict Ezekiel's martyrdom, inspired by popular Jewish traditions—as is the case for certain details in the preceding scenes. However, certain typically Hellenistic features are recognizable in these frescoes, for example, the strongly stressed separation of body and soul. It is equally noticeable that nothing in these paintings alludes either to the visions of the glory and throne of God or even less to the mystical speculations of the *merkābāh.* The scene of the miracle of Moses' causing water to well up in the desert is treated in relation to Ezekiel 47, as was already the case in some rabbinic texts.

As far as Christian iconography is concerned, it can be divided into two classes. First is a series of representations of those symbolic actions of the prophet that were striking by their strangeness: for instance, the eating of the scroll (2:8-9). The second class is more important. The vision of the chariot is represented many times in frescoes, carvings, and illuminations. The vision of the closed gate (44:1-4) also appears a few times. But it is Ezek 37:1-11 that is most often chosen as a subject in frescoes, sarcophagi, miniatures, paintings. Without doubt we have here texts whose theological content is weightier and the last of these is an intimate part of the nucleus of the Christian message, the resurrection of Christ.

This same passage has inspired musical compositions. Let it suffice to mention Liszt's work, *Ossa arida,* some works by Israeli composers, and several African-American spirituals.

Finally, we must speak of the influence the book of Ezekiel has had on the liturgy. The use of Ezekiel's text in synagogue worship poses a problem. Whether Ezekiel's writings qualified as *haftarot* (prophetic reading in synagogal worship) was a controversial question for a long time, even within Pharisaic circles. This is true especially of ch. 1, because of the risk of encouraging mystical aberrations, and ch. 16, because of the denunciation of the sins of Jerusalem and Judah. Despite all this, the reading of ch. 1 was accepted, along with Exodus 19 and 24, in a well-defined theophanic ensemble. This grouping, which is also present in Rev 4:1-6, is appropriate. Indeed, not only is the theophanic dimension clear, but it is used in the service of the Torah, a classical approach. In addition, bringing in ch. 1 gives the texts of Exodus a particular coloring. The Torah is thus linked with the very place of divine presence, the throne, a powerful symbol of the presence and might of God. And because it takes place in Babylonia, land of exile, Ezekiel's theophany, tied as it is to the Torah, opens the horizons of the Torah to the circumstances of the people of the Diaspora. The geographical confines burst open and become universal. The resulting interplay of texts manifests one of the dimensions of Scripture: texts shed light on one another, answer one another, are torn open and outpaced by other texts. The same theological device is found in Sirach 24.

The readings assigned for the Sabbath of paschal week are Exod 13:17, the departure of Israel from Egypt; Deut 14:22, the regulations concerning tithes; and Ezekiel 37. The reason for this choice of readings is evident: old and new Exodus exist harmoniously side by side. The way these texts are brought together shows that the deep dynamism of the faith of Israel is based on the "permanent Exodus."

Other passages from Ezekiel find their place in synagogal worship. Even though they do not occupy by any means a place as important as those drawn from Isaiah, their place is not negligible and their position next to the Torah is theologically fruitful.

In the Roman lectionary assembled after Vatican II, Ezekiel occupies a modest but significant place. In the lectionary for Sundays and feasts, the paschal vigil offers for all three years of the liturgical cycle Ezek 36:16-28, together with the other traditional texts. One could have expected Ezekiel 37, but this is reserved for the vigil of Pentecost. The choice of Ezek 36:16-28 is easily understood: the gathering of the people and the purification by pure water, gift of a new heart and spirit, are fully befitting the perspectives of the Christian Pasch.

This same passage is read again on the fifth Sunday in Lent in Year A, together with John 11:1-45, the resurrection of Lazarus. This juxtaposition appears immediate and legitimate, even though there is a real risk of limiting the meaning of the text to individual resurrection, thereby overlooking other essential dimensions of the prophetic text.

In general the selection of texts from Ezekiel to accompany the Sunday or weekday gospels is felicitous and the relationship between Old and New Testaments fruitful. The last three of the nineteenth week (even years) are a more problematic choice.

SECOND READING

Title and Introduction: 1:1-3

These three verses contain two different elements: information on the date and place of the vision to follow (1-2, 3b) in the first person singular and the general title of the book (3a) in the third person singular and in the style of other prophetic books (Hos 1:1; Mic 1:1, for example). The chronological data are not clear. The fifth year of the deportation of King Jehoiachin corresponds to the year 593. As to the thirtieth year, it is often thought to be Ezekiel's age at the time. The scene is in Babylonia, the land of the Chaldeans, by one of the many irrigation canals, the "river" Kebar *(naru kabari),* known through some texts of the Persian period. A colony of Judeans is settled there as a consequence of the deportation of 597. Being the son of the priest Buzi, Ezekiel is also a priest. His age at the time of the deportation leads us to think that he did not yet exercise his profession. However, he has been prepared for this ministry, and the rest of the book shows to what extent he is imbued with the priestly turn of mind.

Ezekiel's Call: 1:4–3:15

The purpose of the call story is simple and clear: to theologically legitimate the mission of the one sent. The reception of the book by the believing community shows its legitimacy. The call story is a sort of summary of the whole book as far as its goal and contents are concerned.

The structure of the narrative belongs to the literary genre of the call story (see Isaiah 6; Jer

1:4-19; cf. Exod 3:1–4:17). The essential elements are present: the theophany (1:4-28), the sending on mission (2:1-5, 7; 3:4-7, 10-11), the objections of the elect—Ezekiel does not react like Jeremiah, but God forewarns him not to be rebellious like those to whom he is sent (2:6, 8a)—and finally, the sign given by God as a guarantee (2:8b–3:3).

Ezekiel is not called by his name. He is addressed as "son of humanity," which simply means "human being," "mortal." The distance separating him from the one speaking to him is thus obvious, which does not detract from the intimacy of the dialogue.

The spirit also appears (3:12, 14; cf. 8:3; 11:1, 24; 37:1; 43:5). It is rarely present in other prophets. In Ezekiel its role is that of an instrument of the divinity that enables the prophet to fulfill his ministry. The expression "the hand of the Lord" (2:9; 3:14, 22; 37:1; 40:1) has a meaning similar to that of "spirit."

Ezekiel's Vision (1:4-28)

The book of Ezekiel was a legacy to a community of disciples and believers who did not regard it as a work definitively closed and not to be altered. The particularities of the theophany contemplated by Ezekiel offered easy opportunities for additions. Ezekiel uses a great number of terms of comparison, a proof, were one needed, that he does not claim to describe the ineffable or the material vision of any object or person, but simply to share an experience. To achieve this he employs the literary form of "vision." With the passage of time other details and complements came to be added to the text that make it often difficult to understand. There is no need to seek to discern a teaching in every individual element of the description; these elements, whether earlier or later, aim only at emphasizing the attributes of the divinity.

Some themes of the vision are classic, others less so. The *wind* of the storm is infrequent, appearing as an accompaniment to theophanies in 1 Kings 19:11 and Ps 50:3. On the other hand, *fire* is a classic feature (1:13; 1:27, "something like fire"; 10:2). In the theophany of Sinai (Exod 19:18) we read, "Now Mount Sinai was wrapped in smoke, because the Lord had descended upon it in fire" (cf. Exod 24:17; see also Lev 9:24). In 1 Kings 18:24, 38, fire is the criterion of God's presence and power. But fire can also be the sign of God's punitive action (Num 16:35). *Light* also is a feature of theophanies, as in Isa 9:2 and even more in Isa 60:1-3. The *four living creatures,* a symbol of totality, with variations, belong to the iconography of the ancient Near East. According to v. 22 they uphold what seems like a dome that, in antiquity, was a sort of cupola above which rested the upper waters and the abode of the gods.

All these images accompany and prepare the mention of "something like a throne" upon which was "something that seemed like a human form . . . this was the appearance of the likeness of the glory of the LORD." We are thus at the end of the theophanic description. The glory of God, very prominent in the priestly tradition, is important also in Ezekiel. Later its departure from Jerusalem (chs. 8–11) and its return (ch. 43) will be described. What we see here is a way of speaking of the personal presence of God. It is manifested in Babylonia, a foreign, unclean land. This affirmation could only shock the exiles, and still more those who had remained in Judea. How is it possible for the God of Israel to reveal the divine self with such majesty outside of God's temple and land? The God of Ezekiel is not the God of a temple or a land, but the God of a people.

The stage is set. God's presence with the exiles is confirmed. This vision has fascinated readers throughout the whole of history. The throne has even become one of the favorite subjects of Christian iconography: one finds it repeatedly in frescoes, carvings, and illuminations. But it is above all the point of departure for the very important *merkābāh* current of Jewish mysticism.

Ezekiel's Mission (2:1-3, 15)

Ezekiel is prostrate; he hears a voice speaking to him: "I am sending you to the people of Israel." Here are the key elements: God, who sends; Israel, who receives; Ezekiel, the messenger, the bridge between the two. Therefore it is God who takes the initiative of sending the divine word to the people. The scroll the prophet must swallow has a threefold meaning. In the first place, by this gesture God establishes Ezekiel as prophet. In the second place, it means that the message and the messenger are identified; the prophet is of one piece with the message. In the third place, what is written on the scroll is explicit: moans, lamentations, and wailing; Ezekiel appears as a messenger of judgment and punishment. But he is also the sign of the God who speaks to God's people even in exile; God is always present to the people even though, for the time being, that presence is manifested through the punishment itself. The third actor in the scene of Ezekiel's sending on mission, the people, is called "a rebellious house" four times in this passage for emphasis' sake, the more so as Ezekiel is warned not to be like that rebellious house (2:8). All through his book Ezekiel paints this rebellious people in the darkest colors: "a nation of rebels who have rebelled against me; they and their ancestors . . . to this very day" (2:3). This inveterate revolt has hardened their hearts and faces (2:4). Here the problem lies. It is not a failure in communication, a question of language; it is a matter of stubborn hearts and hardened foreheads (3:4-7).

It is therefore indispensable that in view of his legitimate fear Ezekiel be sustained by God and present to the people a face as hard as their faces and a forehead as hard as their foreheads (2:7; 3:8). Thus he will be able to bear the message of God that he has made his own, whether they listen or not. The people will not be able to deny the prophet's presence, and the responsibility for what happens will be entirely theirs (2:5; 3:10-11).

The encounter is over; Ezekiel, reeling from the experience, returns to his people, impelled by the spirit. Now he can begin his mission.

The story of Ezekiel's call has given rise to various mystical speculations based on the very vague description of the glory of God and the divine throne. The interest of this passage does not lie there, but in the affirmation of God's presence in the midst of the people, wherever they are, and in the dialogue initiated by God. In spite of the tragic tone of the text the message of hope is evident. It is not farfetched to connect this flamboyant passage with the gospel of John. In John 1:14 we read, "And the Word became flesh and pitched its tent among us." This is the realized image, the hope fulfilled by and in Christ. The sacred place is the gathering of those who welcome the Word. There is no longer any temple, any sacred space. It is the community of believers welcoming their Lord that is God's place. This is the hour when people will not worship the Father in this temple or that chapel, but "in spirit and truth" (John 4:23).

The scroll full of words of lamentation that God gives Ezekiel to eat so that it will be part of his very being may perhaps prefigure symbolically the word of God that Christians are invited to eat in order to live by it. And if the sighs of the scroll in the prophet's mouth are "as sweet as honey," the ultimate Word will, *a fortiori,* be sweet also. (This does not mean that the mission and responsibility that result from it are less difficult than Ezekiel's.) Christian iconography, which sometimes represents Ezekiel eating his scroll, has not adverted to this connection.

The Sentinel of Israel: 3:16-21

This brief unit seems out of place in this chapter, especially since there is a long development on the same theme in 33:1-20, where it fits better with the context. At that point it opens the second phase of Ezekiel's activity, or the second part of the book, which collects all the oracles of hope. It is another way of describing the prophet's mission. He is responsible for the conversion of the people by delivering the words of God exactly as they come to him. The difficulties of the mission are obvious. It is probable that the last redaction added this passage here in order to present an overview of Ezekiel's mission.

The Mute Prophet: 3:22-27

The logic and the coherence of this passage in relation to the context are problematic. Even before he has opened his mouth Ezekiel is silenced and ordered to remain bound with ropes in his house. This silence could be connected with his wife's death (24:15-27) and with the prediction of the fall of Jerusalem (33:22).

The Siege of Jerusalem: Ezekiel 4–5

Ezekiel's ministry begins with three symbolic actions. Although prophets are primarily wordbearers, many among them use symbolic actions as a means of expressing their message. This peculiar method is essentially pedagogic. One can describe the symbolic action as a mime representing the prophetic message by analogy. Hosea marrying a whore (1:2-9; 3:1-5), Isaiah walking naked through the streets of Jerusalem

(20:1-6), Jeremiah going to the Jerusalem court with a yoke on his neck (27:1-12) are some of the most famous symbolic actions. Ezekiel is especially fond of this mode of expression. In these two chapters, as is usual in the book of Ezekiel, we are presented with his symbolic actions and various rereadings and additions.

The Siege (4:1-3, 9-17; 5:1-4)

The first action described here is simple; its purpose is simple as well: it is a sign for the house of Israel. The plot of the action is minimal because the miming is so clear. But the performance itself attracts attention. If we take into account that the "Jerusalem" of the first verse is an addition that nullifies the suspense the action would have been even more powerful because the original readers would not have known what city was meant and, deep down, hoped that it was Babylon.

The second symbolic action concerns the food of the besieged (4:9-17). Stress is placed first (vv. 9-11) on the precariousness and scarcity of the foods and on the fact that they are mixed (contrary to the Law) and second on the conditions of uncleanness in which the food is consumed. Ezekiel's reaction—an additional dramatization—underlines the priest's horror in the face of such unclean conditions.

There are similar intimations in the gospels. At the time of Christ, worrying about purity had become an obsession in certain devout circles (Mark 7:1-23). What is only a relative and limited aspect of faith too often becomes the very content of a faith gone astray. This danger is still lurking today.

The third symbolic action concerns Ezekiel's beard (5:1-2). Again the meaning is clear. It is not surprising that this image has inspired some Christian iconographic representations. The explanation comes in vv. 5-12, and the opening sentence is like a bolt of lightning: the city is Jerusalem. The psychological effect is achieved; all that is left to do is to draw the consequences of the above progression in symbolic actions: siege, living conditions during the siege, final dispersion. This is why the explanation directly introduces the prediction of the catastrophe, the punishment for the sins of Jerusalem.

The rebellion that was spoken of in the call story as characteristic of Israel is expanded upon here: the people have rebelled against the ordinances and laws that God had given them. Ezekiel will come back to this point at length in ch. 20.

The text insists on the particular responsibility of Jerusalem: situated in the midst of nations and peoples, it had a special role to play. As Ezekiel often emphasizes, it was responsible, by its behavior, for the honor of God among the peoples (cf. 36:20, 22). Its sin is therefore double.

In 5:7-17 a series of "because" clauses (vv. 7, 8, 11) announces the punishment while giving fresh reasons to justify it. In v. 13 we encounter for the first time the well-known expression dear to Ezekiel "they [you] shall know that I [am] YHWH." With slight variations, it appears fifty-four times in the book. In the majority of cases it is the conclusion of an oracle or a symbolic action. The formula strongly shows Ezekiel's will to link the knowledge of the God of Israel to God's way of acting. One knows YHWH in the divine action, and such knowledge concerns YHWH's relation with humankind. It necessitates dialogue.

Ezekiel 4:4-8 is a difficult passage. It is obvious that it interrupts the series of symbolic actions concerning the siege, even though it attempts a connection to it (vv. 7, 8). The meaning of the dates is uncertain. The number forty has an evident symbolic meaning, but the other number—which differs between the Greek and Hebrew texts—is not clear; it probably alludes to the whole of Israel's history. An important idea appears in this passage: Ezekiel is made to "bear" the sins of the house of Israel. However, it is difficult to see here a sort of substitution as is the case, in a certain way, in Isa 52:13–53:12, for it is the people who will be punished. Is it only a matter of showing by the number of days/years the extent of the sin of Israel and Judah? The scene has been represented a few times in Christian iconography.

In 5:3-4 another idea appears: a remnant will be saved, but it too will have to be purified. It is not difficult to see here an addition by someone eager to make every point clear.

Idolatry and Punishment: Ezekiel 6

This chapter has four parts. *6:1-7* is centered on idolatry practiced on the high places. Because of this Ezekiel calls to the mountains and hills of Israel where the places of worship were situated. This passage supposes and takes for granted the centralization of worship in Jerusalem, established in connection with the deuteronomic reform. From that time on all sanctuaries, whether on high places or elsewhere, had become idolatrous. However, in the history of Israel sanctuaries other than that of Jerusalem (*a fortiori* when the one in Jerusalem did not exist) had been normally accepted, even commended (Exod 20:24-26). Ezekiel reproaches the mountains only because of the places of worship set up on them; the center of the oracle is in v. 3, "I, I myself will bring a sword upon you, and I will destroy your high places."

6:8-10 is a new little oracle, one of hope this time; for those who escape the predicted disasters, the remnant spared by the Lord, there is hope: they will remember the Lord who will purify their wanton hearts. Recognition of the Lord and of the fairness of the punishment as well as repentance will follow. We must note that in this oracle the essential initiative is God's: it is God who leaves a remnant and destroys the source of sin, that is, the wanton heart. This last expression was already classic with the prophets since Hosea (see Hosea 1–3). It refers to Israel's "idolatrous heart."

6:11-14 is slightly different in tone. The Lord invites Ezekiel to make gestures that seem to be a manifestation of joy but accompany a word of judgment: the three classic instruments of punishment are on their way: sword, famine, and plague.

The End and the Day: Ezekiel 7

The text of this chapter is difficult. The Greek of the LXX is shorter and seems to correspond to a Hebrew document anterior to and less altered than the Masoretic text of today. [See also the article "How Reliable is the Text of the Bible?"] The first oracle, following the introductory formula of v. 1, is in 7:2-4, whose key word is "the end." Already Amos had had a vision concerning the end. Ezekiel takes up the image and its symbolic meaning. The coming of the end involves the entire land. The cause of the end is obvious: the abominations and behavior of the people. The first of these two terms has the cultic connotation of impurity. Ezekiel often uses it and broadens its meaning to include other, profane domains. The behavior, the "ways" relate to daily life and to relationships between persons. Once more there is the divine declaration: God will have no pity.

7:5-9 forms a new unit that blends three terms: the end, the day, and the "doom"—a word difficult to interpret. In fact, we have here a repetition of the first oracle and of the following one on the Day of YHWH. The use of the word "doom" introduces an apocalyptic dimension that reveals the hand of a late writer influenced by the book of Daniel.

7:10-27 deals with the Day of YHWH, even though the complete expression is not used here. [See the excursus "The Day of YHWH" in the commentary on Joel, p. 1128.] Its description is similar to other descriptions of the same genre in which the two terms are found together. Once again it is Amos who gives us the first precise use of the locution. It is he who, for the first time, mentions it while giving it a meaning different from what it had before. Amos sets his audience straight: the Day of YHWH will not be a day of victory and salvation accomplished by YHWH in favor of Israel; it will be the day of judgment. A few years before Ezekiel, Zephaniah composed a splendid poem of the Day of YHWH (1:7, 14-18); Ezekiel quotes from it in 7:19b. In this poem, which will subsequently undergo many changes, Ezekiel makes use of themes become classic in the description of the Day of YHWH. We must add that the reason for the coming of this terrible day is made explicit: pride, violence, and wickedness blossom and thrive (vv. 10-11). The punishment seems terrible; clearly Ezekiel is thinking of the destruction of Jerusalem and the kingdom of Judah. For him the Day of YHWH is a very concrete historical event, which does not obviate the fact that through successive accretions the text has taken on a different, eschatological tonality. This is the normal evolution of the expression, as can be seen, for example, in the book of Joel.

Punishment of Jerusalem, Departure of the Glory of God: Ezekiel 8–11

The second part of the book of Ezekiel begins here with this majestic vision into which blend various components. One easily perceives the correspondence between the beginning, 8:1-3 (setting the stage), and the end, 11:24-25 (return to the point of departure and conclusion of the narrative). Similarly, there is a certain parallelism in the description of the sins of Israel, idolatry (8:4-18)—against the background of the Jerusalem Temple—and the lack of justice and kindness in human relationships (11:1-21). Chapter 9 and part of ch. 10 depict the command for the punishment to be meted out by God to Jerusalem and its execution. We must say at once that vv. 1-17 of ch. 10, minus a few fragments, are developments that break into the description of the punishment and the departure of the glory of God (10:18-22; 11:22-23); they are probably the fruit of later ruminations.

8:1-3a: A year has elapsed since the call story. Ezekiel is at home. The community leaders come to him, probably to consult the Lord through the prophet (cf. 14:1; 20:1). Is there a word of hope for Israel? Seized by God, Ezekiel is led to Jerusalem through divine visions.

8:3b-18: A guided tour of the Temple is going to show Ezekiel Israel's true situation. The tour is in four steps, each more horrible than the former: "you will see still greater abominations" (8:6, 13, 15). The first step brings Ezekiel to the north gate of the sanctuary (vv. 3b-6). There, at the entrance, is an idol of jealousy, and north of the gate is its altar. This idol was probably a protecting divinity, according to the custom in the ancient Near East of placing such statues before the doors of temples and palaces.

The second step (vv. 7-13) is more important, even though its locale is not clear. Ezekiel observes how, on the sly, all the leaders of the people give themselves up to idolatrous practices, offering incense to representations of animals portrayed on walls. It is interesting to note that the one person who is named belongs to the family of Shaphan, defenders of Jeremiah and serious worshipers of Israel's God. The sentence placed in their mouths is significant: "YHWH does not see us; YHWH has forsaken the land" (v. 12). According to the leaders of the people, YHWH does not count any more, as the deportation of 597 shows. It is better to seek help elsewhere.

The third step (8:14-15) leads Ezekiel to the entrance of the Temple proper. There women are performing rituals in honor of Tammuz. This ancient divinity of love and fertility took many forms in the ancient Near East. Rather than Tammuz, the Bible calls the god of the fertility cults "Baal" (cf. Hosea).

The fourth step (8:16-18) shows the worst of abominations. The setting is the inside of the Temple proper, where, among other cultic objects, are the altar of holocausts and the altar of incense, in front of the entrance to the Holy of Holies. Twenty-five men are prostrate toward the Mount of Olives, toward the east, toward the rising sun. They thus have their backs turned to the dwelling of the God of Israel. This says it all. Not only do they indulge in idolatrous worship, but they do so within the very precincts of the Temple. Their bodily posture reveals their state of mind. The consequence is swift in coming: "Therefore I will act in wrath" (v. 18), says YHWH.

9:1–10:17: The punishment of Jerusalem is about to begin. Chapter 9 and some parts of ch. 10 describe it. YHWH calls the executioners, seven ministers, one to mark the foreheads of those who will be saved and six to kill. The punitive expedition follows in reverse order that observed during Ezekiel's tour of the Temple. It starts where the sin is most grievous: "Defile the house . . ." (9:7). One can only shudder when hearing God in person giving the order to God's ministers to defile God's own house. How great must the sin of the people be! What kind of god must the God of Israel be, who is not attached to institutions that are supposed to serve God, worship God, be God's own institutions!

The massacre begun in the sanctuary ends with fire from the sanctuary. This fire, supposed to burn the offerings representing the communion of Israel with their God, the Entirely Other, becomes the instrument of punishment and of the disappearance of the people: a just reward!

Ezekiel intercedes (9:8), like Amos during his first two visions (Amos 7:1-16). God's answer underlines the perversity of the people. However, those who are marked will be saved. Ezekiel, again like Amos, insists on the enormity of the sin and its logical consequence, that is to say, a total and definitive destruction. But then the very mission of the prophet would be meaningless. Moreover, the faithful love of the God of Israel for God's people is beyond logic and the retribution justly deserved by Israel's sin.

10:16-22; 11:22-23: After the slaughtering of the idolaters and the destruction of the city, the glory of the Lord can depart. The depiction of the departure is spare. The route it takes, in four stages, corresponds to the logic of the text. Just as the tour of the Temple had been in four stages—showing the massiveness of the sin—

the glory leaves the Temple and the ravaged and destroyed city in four steps. There is no possible doubt about its departure. Of course, the text does not say where it goes, but the call story has clearly shown its new dwelling: it will be with the deportees.

11:24-25: Ezekiel is brought back home among the exiles. This great vision shows two essential characteristics of Ezekiel. On the one hand he is horrified by Israel's idolatry. More than any other prophet he incessantly speaks about it and chooses it as the main target of his censure. In this he shows that he is a priest to the core. At the same time, he describes with such power the departure of the glory of God from "God's own" temple—an unthinkable idea for a priest—that at this point the priest is left behind by the prophet. Now the priest becomes a prophet. Now the spirit's impulse is evident.

11:1-21: Two units form this block. Its place in the overall description of the vision poses a problem. The first unit (vv. 1-13) is easily discernible, even though it is overloaded. As noted already, Ezekiel is speaking here of the community leaders who, after the first deportation, feel secure in Jerusalem and therefore oppress the people. The prophetic oracle reminds them that the pot, that is, the city, is full of the corpses of those they have oppressed and that those responsible for this tyranny will not be protected by the pot, but on the contrary will be taken out of it to undergo their punishment.

The episode in v. 13 is rather surprising. It must have been written to support the preceding oracle, as a proof of the validity of the prophetic utterance. Nothing is known about the persons named in this verse.

The following passage (vv. 14-21) is in a completely different mode. We are presented with two groups of Judeans: those who remain in Jerusalem between the two deportations in 597 and 587 (unless what is meant are those of the period following 587) and the exiles. The former feel secure in Jerusalem. The latter are carrying the full weight of the sin; they are paying for all. This reading of the situation, which can appear simplistic, corresponds well enough to the popular mentality, but the Lord's oracle takes a completely different turn. After the departure of the glory from Jerusalem—which is an obvious announcement of the destruction of those who have remained—Ezekiel explains the meaning of this departure: the Lord is going to be "for a little while" the sanctuary of the exiles. The material location of the sacred place has no part in the relationship of God with God's people. This was something difficult to imagine for the people of that time. The events will help them to understand.

Besides this surprising statement we find, for the first time in Ezekiel, the well-known promise of a loyal heart, a heart of flesh, and a new spirit (vv. 19-20). This promise will reappear in 36:26, but already here hope is dawning; there is a future. Moreover, to complete the picture the return to the land of Israel is predicted in the second person plural (vv. 17-18).

An Exile's Baggage. The Value and Appropriateness of Prophecies: Ezekiel 12

Two brief symbolic actions open this new section that will conclude with ch. 24, when Ezekiel must again perform a particularly painful symbolic action: renunciation of mourning for the death of his wife. In both passages Ezekiel is a sign for the house of Israel (12:6, 11; 24:24).

12:1-16 presents the first action. Once again the text has been altered in order to add some of the known details of the flight of King Zedekiah at the time of the fall of Jerusalem (cf. Jer 52:6-11; 2 Kings 25:3-7). The symbolic action is simple: Ezekiel must gather what he can hand-carry and, with face covered, go out in front of those deported with him. Verse 7 laconically states that the command is obeyed. God wants to know whether the spectators have reacted to the action and explains its meaning. Verse 11 summarizes the whole: Ezekiel's action is a sign of what will befall those who are not yet exiled.

The function of the symbolic action, called a "sign" in the text, is to help the people understand. As a consequence, the prophet who performs the action becomes a sign. This sign is necessary because the people neither want to see or hear (v. 2): not so much to see nor hear the prophet as to see nor hear God (3:7). Isaiah also had met with the blindness and deafness of the people (Isaiah 6). However, the sign, which is a part of the prophetic message, contains a glimmer of hope: "perhaps they will understand, though they are a rebellious house" (12:3).

The meaning of the symbolic action is not as clear as it appears at first sight, for the prophet's behavior could be understood as the prediction of the return of the deported. But this direction is not the one the message takes. To the contrary: those who are not yet in exile are going to experience it.

12:17-20 tells of a second symbolic action: Ezekiel must eat his bread with quaking and drink his water with trembling. The meaning of this action is clear and the reason given for it is the violence of the inhabitants of the land.

With 12:21-25 a section begins that continues to the end of ch. 13; it deals with the problem faced by all prophets. As is often the case with Ezekiel, the oracle is a response to an objection placed in the mouths of the people: "The days are prolonged, and every vision comes to nothing." The other little oracle, 12:26-27, follows the same pattern and is a variation of the one preceding it. In both cases the topic is the incredulity of Ezekiel's hearers concerning the validity, and therefore the appropriateness of the prophetic ministry. They are ready to accept the validity of the oracles, but for other people and other times.

However, a prophet's function is not to predict future events or to guess at the course of history. It is to read the present in relation to the faith and past of Israel in order to open its future. Prophets are readers of what happens today for the benefit of their contemporaries. God seems hurt to the quick by the cynical reaction of the Israelites and promises immediate action. God's word is necessarily effective. The punishment will be meted out unless conversion occurs. Conversion is the goal of all prophetic words and actions.

False Prophets and Magic: Ezekiel 13

The problem of the discernment of true and false prophets is a constant theme in the Scriptures. Try as one may, one cannot isolate a clear and precise set of criteria that could be mechanically applied to make such a discernment possible. Similar quarrels with other prophets occupy an even greater place in the book of Jeremiah. The political and religious difficulties of the time render the confrontation more acute.

The return to the land of Israel (v. 9) supposes the exile, but one cannot say whether the date is before or after 587. Thanks to the multiple formulas present in this chapter it can be divided into two major parts: vv. 1-16 and vv. 17-23. Each of these is composed of two oracles: vv. 1-9, 10-14 and vv. 17-21, 22-23. All four oracles are built on the pattern of oracles of judgment with their accusations and sentences. The first and third are also oracles of misfortune; hence their negative charge is reinforced. They are further rendered more forceful by vv. 15-16, which are probably an addition of the same kind as other comments within the oracles themselves (cf. vv. 4, 11-12); but whether their text is original or reworked, these two verses do not deflect the thrust of the oracles.

The first oracle, 13:1-9, attacks the prophets who follow their own way, the easy path. Their messages are as worthless as those who utter them. The prophet's role is to watch intently for what happens to the people. Now the punishment is imminent because of the sins of the people, which the prophet must denounce. The punishment, in the literal as well as the figurative sense, is the destruction and dismantling of the city and the people. The false prophets do nothing to stabilize and improve the situation. They do not lead the people to conversion, the only thing that could obtain God's pardon. Instead of the truth that saves but is painful because it demands a change, they have preached the illusion that lulls to sleep. The punishment is severe; it is exclusion from YHWH's people. The false prophets will be absent from the council of the people (cf. Amos 3:7; see also 1 Kings 22:1-29; Isaiah 6; Jer 23:18-22). They will not be enrolled in the register of the house of Israel; they will not enter the land of Israel.

The second oracle, 13:10-14, gives more precise information on the illusion preached by the lying prophets. Like those against whom Jeremiah struggles (Jer 6:14; 14:11-16; 23:16-17) they preach peace (13:10), whereas war and disaster are at the door. By doing so they smear with whitewash the wall that was ill-constructed and poorly finished by the people. This can only make the catastrophe worse. We find here the same accusation as in the first oracle, but with another image. The false prophets' words are not in accordance with the reality of the people's circumstances and, as a consequence, not in accordance with the will of God. God's action will uncover illusions and appearances.

The third oracle, 13:17-21, is addressed to the female prophets. Even though they do not appear often in the Scriptures, there are a few: Miriam (Exod 15:20); Deborah (Judg 4:4); Huldah (2 Kings 22:14; Noadiah (Neh 6:14). Like their male colleagues, these women prophets denounced by Ezekiel follow their own inspiration. What is worse, they practice magic—although it is not possible for us to know exactly what is alluded to here. Magic is an attempt to manipulate God for one's own benefit. If in addition it is a question of life and death, whose sole master is God, the accusation is the graver.

The fourth oracle, 13:22-23, is limited to making a little more explicit the third oracle by mentioning the effect of the women prophets' magic on the people whose conversion they discourage.

The violence of the accusations Ezekiel hurls at other prophets shows both how acute is the problem and how difficult the discerning between chaff and grain when it comes to prophetism. One thing is certain: the believing community played a decisive role in this discernment. It was, for the greater part, the acceptance of some prophets and the rejection of some others that decided this arduous question. But on what basis did such acceptance rest? No one knows this with certainty. We do notice the convergence of theological lines found in the different prophetic books of the Scriptures: the call to ongoing conversion, that is, in the concrete, the fierce defense of the rights of human persons and of the practice of justice among them, and the recognition that the life of the people comes entirely from the God of Israel who acted in history in favor of the chosen people. All this necessarily gives grounds for hope. The prophets' political stands, their positions on the institutions in existence may be different, if not opposed, but the fundamental themes are present in all of them.

The outcome is that in concrete cases the Israelites did not have one measure, one yardstick to routinely employ. But they were not without landmarks either, and as always in matters of faith, material security and mathematical precision do not apply. Risk is an integral part of faith.

The discernment of prophecy and prophets continues to be as difficult today as it was in Ezekiel's time. Of course, the institutional Church is there to insure such discernment. However, because an essential element of prophetism is its irreducibility to institutions, the prophets' conflicts with the institutional dimension of the Church will often be unavoidable.

The Lord and the Idols: 14:1-11

The plan of this passage is simple enough. The first verse gives the exact setting of Ezekiel's oracle: the first part is in vv. 2-5 and it ends with an exhortation in v. 6. Verses 7-10 contain two related elements: the Lord's reaction to the idolatrous Israelites who come to consult the prophet and the Lord's response to the prophet himself. Verse 11 is an additional explanation.

One easily deduces from the first three verses that the leaders of the exiled community who come to consult YHWH through the prophet expect a word of consolation. The Lord's reaction is clear: it is impossible to consult God when in the inquirer's heart there is a major obstacle, idolatry. Consultation, communication presuppose communion. One cannot commune with idols and consult YHWH. From the individual case the text moves to the house of Israel (v. 5). Then vv. 7-8 explicitly return to the individual case and vv. 9-10 to that of the prophet who, despite the petitioner's inner conflict, pronounces a word. All are equally guilty: "the punishment of the inquirer and the punishment of the prophet shall be the same" (v. 10). All will be cut off from the midst of the people.

Here we again find Ezekiel the priest. He uses the classic priestly formulas; first comes the statement of the case, "any of those who . . ." or "if someone . . ."; then comes the conclusion/sentence, "I will . . . cut them off from the midst of my people" (v. 8). This formula is found elsewhere only in chs. 17 and 20 of Leviticus, texts typically priestly. Indeed, the priest is the person who declares what is right, gives instruction concerning clean and unclean, the sacred and profane (cf. Jer 18:18; Ezek 22:26). But side by side with this priestly "mentality" we find a clearly prophetic perspective in vv. 6 and 11: exhortation to conversion (v. 6) and unveiling of God's desire to be in intimate relation with God's people (v. 11). In the book of Ezekiel the worlds of the priest and the prophet meet as they do nowhere else.

Judgment, Intercession, and Salvation: 14:12-23

In the same juridical style as that of the preceding episodes the word of YHWH announces four kinds of punishment and the fate of each person in 14:12-20. The point of departure is the sin of the land. God reacts by sending the four classic disasters: famine, wild animals, sword, and pestilence. In this land there are three just persons: Noah, Daniel, and Job. Their righteousness will not serve to save the land. They themselves will be saved because they are righteous. The solidarity of generations does not obtain any more; it is each one for himself or herself. The sentence is unmistakable and emphasized three times by the divine oath "as I live" (vv. 16, 18, 20). Curiously, the three "exemplary" persons are not Israelites. These examples demonstrate Ezekiel's knowledge. Furthermore, the manner in which Ezekiel darkens history aims at stressing the magnitude of the sin: there are no longer any exemplary figures in Israel.

However, vv. 21-23 deliver another message. Difficult as these verses are, it is evident that the idea of a remnant to be saved is present as it already was in 9:4, 6, 11. This remnant of the "saved" comes to the exiles of the first deportation. Their presence even justifies the punishment sent by God. But in what way can this console the exiles? Simply in the sense that God's justice, which has just been shown in the punishment, also has another aspect, that of salvation.

The Vine and the Fire: Ezekiel 15

The symbol of the vine is often used in the OT. The best known and most compelling example is Isaiah's poem (Isa 5:1-7), but Hosea (Hos 9:10; 10:1) and Jeremiah (Jer 2:21; 6:9; 8:13) also use it to designate Israel and Jeremiah applies it to Moab (Jer 48:32). The image will recur in chs. 17 and 19 of Ezekiel. After the introduction of v. 1, the description of the vine and the questions concerning it are in vv. 2-5. The unveiling of the meaning takes place in vv. 6-8.

In the texts from the other prophets referred to above, the terms of comparison are the fruit of the vine and the care this chosen plant receives. In Ezekiel 15 there is no mention of fruit or election. The reader's imagination registers surprise. The interest of the vine is not in its wood. Besides, what is a vine doing "among the trees of the forest?" One more nonsensical detail! Yet it is in this sort of thing that Ezekiel's literary and theological art resides. He twists the image and, in the process, upends its meaning as well as the commonly received theology. There is no longer a question of yield; the horizon is far vaster: the vine in the forest, Israel/Jerusalem among the nations. Once more Ezekiel purposefully darkens the scene. Not only has Israel ceased to be the chosen vine, but it is of less value than the other sorts of wood, the other peoples. It is of no value at all.

The twofold setting of the torch is probably an allusion to the double exile.

The symbol of the vine will have a famed sequel in John 15:1-10, a passage in which the perspective changes further. In his work Jesus assumes all the lines of thought in the OT. Moreover, by identifying himself with the vine he becomes the source of good fruit.

History of Jerusalem: Ezekiel 16

This chapter is one of the most characteristic in the whole book. We have here the denunciation of the sins the prophet must publicize, "Mortal, make known to Jerusalem her abominations" (v. 2). This public denunciation leads to a suit whose verdict is pronounced at the end (vv. 35-41a). The image of the relationship between man and woman to speak of that of God with God's people is nothing new in the Bible. It was initiated by Hosea (Hosea 1–3), who uses it with an unparalleled force. Jeremiah also has the same image (Jer 2:2; 3:6-11). But again Ezekiel gives the metaphor a twist all his own. Besides, this symbolic narrative is going to develop in different directions in order to end in a complex ensemble.

The basic story in 16:1-15, 21, 24-25, 35, 37, 39-41a contains several scenes. The first, vv. 1-7a, narrates the rescue of the newborn. In the second, vv. 7b-13, the young girl becomes a woman and marries her savior. The third, vv. 15, 21, 24-25, deals with the woman's unfaithfulness. The fourth, vv. 35, 37, 39-41a, concerns the woman's punishment. A certain number of verbs, strategically located, indicate the logical structure of the text, for example the verb "pass by" or "pass through" *(ʿbr)*. In vv. 6 and 8, it is the Lord who passes by: it is life; it is love. In vv. 15, 21, 25, the subjects are different: in v. 21 the woman delivers her children to fire, that is, has her children pass through fire, as a sacrifice; in vv. 15 and 25 it is the woman who offers herself to any passerby. It would be impossible to find a stronger contrast between the "passings" of God and those of the woman. The verb "see" *(rʾh)* is also important. In vv. 6 and 8 it is God who sees the newborn and the young girl. Then it is life; it is love. In v. 37 the lovers see the woman in her nakedness. Then it is punishment. The verb "grow," "increase" *(rbh)* underscores the contrast once again. YHWH caused the young girl to grow. In v. 25 the woman causes her whoring to increase. In v. 41a the punishment will take place before a multitude of women. The same play of relation and contrast can be observed in the verbs "give" and "take."

What we are speaking of here appears clearly in this passage. This is a case of misappropriation: of the life and gifts the passerby-savior had lavished on the woman who in her turn, by giving herself to any passersby, offers them what she had received from her savior.

The peculiarities of Ezekiel's text are of several kinds: first of all in the origins he attributes to Jerusalem, which are very probably historically correct. But Ezekiel is unique not only because he is more faithful to history but especially because he gives it to be understood that from its beginning to its end Jerusalem is an abominable pagan. From this point of view and with consistency (cf. ch. 20) Ezekiel never alludes to a golden age at the onset of the relationship between God and God's people, in contrast to the texts of Hosea and Jeremiah mentioned above. In spite of the gifts received, the true nature of Jerusalem has prevailed: she is unfaithful and devious, a prostitute.

This is the more painful since the gifts received are absolutely free. Jerusalem, Israel, was created out of nothing; its destiny was death. It is only because God passed by and looked that Jerusalem was given life and a reason for living: love. The misappropriation committed by the woman calls for an inescapable punishment.

The additions that this history of Jerusalem has received manifest the fecundity of the prophetic word. It is not impossible that Ezekiel himself modified and enlarged his text. As in ch. 23, vv. 26-30 look at the woman's misconduct in the light of the political alliances of Judah in the last years of its existence. Exploiting the image of the prostitute, vv. 32-35 show the absurdity of the situation: a prostitute who pays to prostitute herself! Verses 44-58 compare the behavior of Jerusalem to that of Sodom and Samaria. We must admit that the comparison is daring. It is no wonder that this chapter was not read in the synagogues, that Christians made use of it in their polemics against the Jewish people, and that rabbis were faced with many problems on its account. There is a strong contrast between this passage and Isaiah's poems on Jerusalem (Isaiah 40–66). Verses 59-63 introduce the hope of an everlasting covenant. The expression is Ezekiel's own but is found in priestly documents, along with "remembering the covenant" (Gen 9:15, 16) or "establishing the covenant." The verb is *qūm* in Hebrew. The contents of the covenant are much weightier than what we had in v. 8 and, as in the priestly texts, mean in fact God's total gift that humankind can only receive. One breathes here the same air as in the famous passage of Jeremiah (Jer 31:31-34) where the expression "new covenant" is found. In both cases it is the perfect and definitive relationship of God with God's people. [See also the excursus "Covenant" in the commentary on Exodus 19–24.]

Political Alliances: Ezekiel 17

Whether a riddle, an allegory, or a parable, vv. 1-10 are a picturesque story from which Ezekiel derives a precise teaching in vv. 11-15. This literary genre was highly regarded in antiquity (Judg 9:7-20; 14:10-20). Verses 16-17 give a brief description of the historical events. Verses 19-21 are an oracle of direct judgment against Zedekiah. From the historical point of view we must clarify that the king of Judah was judged in Riblah, where Nebuchadnezzar had installed his headquarters, and not in Babylon.

However, the way Ezekiel presents the story is awkward. The intent, at least, is transparent: Does Ezekiel mean to tell his hearers to what extent they are blind when faced with such an obvious state of affairs? He refers to King Jehoiachin, taken prisoner at the time of the first deportation in 597. The vine planted by the great eagle is, of course, the last king of Jerusalem, Zedekiah. Therefore the interest of this text is not in the riddle or parable but in the interpretation Ezekiel gives it. God takes on Zedekiah and announces that he is going to "wither" like the vine that sent its roots toward a spring other than the one that had given it life. Indeed, we can say that God does not delight in seeing people look for strength (cf. v. 21) elsewhere than in God (cf. Isa 30:1-5; 31:1-3). But there is more. Political alliances entailed oaths of loyalty and appeals to the divinities of the contracting parties. YHWH therefore is called as a witness to Zedekiah's loyalty. The breaking of the covenant whose guarantor was God obliges the Lord to chastise the perjurer. Prophets perceive God's action in history and God's participation in human lives—therefore in politics—in a way completely different from our own. They see in the political and military events of their time the direct and immediate action of the Lord. We must take this conception into account when we interpret these texts today.

Verses 22-23 take up the allegory of the great tree in order to draw from it a different teaching. God is precisely the master of history. God intervenes directly in order to bring life or death according to the divine will. This idea is directly applied to Israel. What was the allegory of the cedar has become an oracle of salvation.

To "bring low the high tree, and make high the low tree" is a prophetic leitmotiv that shows the true place of humans before God. There are unmistakable echoes of this key theological concept in the NT, especially in the Magnificat (Luke 1:46-55; cf. also Matt 11:25-27).

Whose Fault is It? Ezekiel 18

The reason for the discussion that follows is presented in v. 2 which cites—in order to refute it—a popular saying based on a proverb about children paying for their parents' misdeeds. This debate forms the warp of the chapter and is found again in vv. 19, 25, 29 and also, indirectly, in v. 23. Therefore Ezekiel answers the hotly discussed questions of his people. Indeed, faced with the disasters that follow in close succession, plus those that are in store according to the prophet himself, the question arises: "Whose fault is it?" Besides, the disasters are of such magnitude that they cannot be caused only by the sins of one generation.

The debate is at the very heart of Ezekiel's book. It will recur several more times. Questions arise in the minds of Ezekiel's hearers, unceasingly buffeted by his ominous preaching. Those hearers ask questions molded by their own mentality, the "corporate personality," which could also be termed "collective responsibility." This notion informs the relationships between individual and community, and vice versa. It extends to all aspects of the life of the group, in the present, the past, and the future: "As for me, I am establishing my covenant with you and your descendants after you" (Gen 9:9).

In his answer Ezekiel uses the juridical language of the priesthood. First the case is presented (vv. 5, 10-11a, 14); then comes the justification for bringing it through the description of the accused's behavior (vv. 6-9a, 11b-13a, 15-17a); finally comes the declaration of guilt or innocence. Leviticus (cf. ch. 13, among others) reflects this priestly way of proceeding.

In vv. 1-4 God answers the complaint of the people by declaring that God is the master of life and by stating the basic principle, repeated in v. 20, "it is only the person who sins that shall die." Verses 5-9 present the case of the righteous person: the verdict comes; the person will live; v. 10-13 that of the unrighteous son who will die for his sins; vv. 14-17 that of the grandson who does not follow the bad example of his father: he shall live. Each time, with variations, the description of the right way consists in an enumeration of deeds and overall attitudes that define righteousness or unrighteousness. We must note that besides sins of idolatry the lists emphasize particularly the domain of human relationships summarized in the expression "[do] what is lawful and right" (v. 5).

In vv. 19-20 people do not accept that the righteous son should not suffer the consequences of the father's sin. Ezekiel reminds them of the principle of v. 4 and explains the rule: each one is responsible for his or her acts; he will develop this later in vv. 21-29. Conversely, no one is marked in an indelible manner by his or her actions, good or bad. Both conversion and apostasy are always possible.

Verses 30-32 are the summit and goal of the chapter as shown by the "therefore" of v. 30. We arrive at the all-important exhortation: "Repent and turn from all your transgressions. . . . get yourselves a new heart and a new spirit." The lengthy explanations in the purest priestly style end with the most classic prophetic appeal: repent; be converted. And there is a decisive argument for this appeal, "I have no pleasure in the death of anyone, says the LORD God"; and the conclusion follows naturally, "Turn, then, and live."

Commentators have often accused Ezekiel of substituting for the principle of collective responsibility a ferocious individualism worthy of the worst "accountants of the confessional," that is, those confessors that demand exact numbers and precise details. Of course he strongly underscores individual responsibility, but he never forgets the communal dimension because individuals are part of their people, Israel. Chapters 36, 37, and 40–48 amply demonstrate this. He does not conceive the restoration and the future of the people in any other way. However, if one looks at ch. 18 from the viewpoint of "retribution" one can seriously misunderstand it. The book of Job shows Job's friends falling into this sort of misunderstanding by ignoring the balance of individual and collective responsibility.

We must also understand what Ezekiel means by "live" and "die." This is not life and death in the physical sense, but communion with God, the giver of life, or separation from God, which can only bring death.

Lament for the Monarchy: Ezekiel 19

Verses 1 and 4 set the tone. We have here an elegy, a funeral lament. This passage is easily divided into two parts, vv. 1-9 and 10-14. The first part is made up of two episodes concerning one of the cubs of the lioness. Verses 4 and 9 show that the young lions represent the last kings of Judah. The first of these last kings seems clearly identified: it is Jehoahaz, deported by Neco, king of Egypt. The second is more difficult to identify with certainty. He could be Jehoiakim or the very last king of Jerusalem, Zedekiah. If the lioness is the queen, mother of both Jehoahaz and Zedekiah, the matter is settled. But if the lioness represents the whole of Judah, everything is possible.

Verses 10-14 take up the image of the vine already used in chs. 15 and 17. The vine may well represent Judah and/or its dynasty. The two laments are a funeral song for the last kings of Judah. However, it seems that Ezekiel still believes in the dynasty as such, personified in Jehoiachin, who is, like himself, exiled in Babylon.

The History of Israel: Nothing but Sin: 20:1-31

Here Ezekiel summarizes the history of Israel in a few stages. The scene is set in vv. 1 to 4. As has happened already in 8:1 and 14:1, the leaders of the exiles come to consult the prophet. God gives a first, curt answer, "I will not be consulted by you" (v. 3). The same expression recurs in v. 31, thus enclosing the unit. Instead the leaders are treated to a review of the history of the people they are part of, a totally dark history in which there is nothing but sin.

This history is divided more or less rigorously into three parts structured in the same way: (a) sin: "but the house of Israel rebelled against me" (vv. 13a, 21a); (b) God's reaction: "then I thought I would pour out my wrath upon them" (vv. 8c, 13c, 21c); (c) counter-reaction on God's part: "but I acted for the sake of my name, that it should not be profaned in the sight of the nations" (vv. 9, 14, 22). Of course, there are other formulas that recur also, but the pattern just mentioned is sufficient to help readers see how the text functions. The first stage, vv. 5-9, shows Israel in Egypt, the first generation. The second stage, vv. 10-17, treats of the behavior of the same generation, but in the desert where they experienced both the liberation from Egypt and the gift of the Law. Verses 18-26 refer, with a certain vagueness, to the generation that witnessed the result of its parents' rebellion. However, the same thing—disobedience—follows. At this point, curiously, the history is interrupted and this generation is dispersed by God because God does not repent from the threat of v. 23 (as had happened in preceding stages). Here is the judgment announced by Ezekiel in v. 4. Verses 30-31 connect the sins of the ancestors with those of the people now living: they are all the same. The present punishment is richly deserved.

The history of Israel as told by Ezekiel offers a fair number of peculiarities. First of all, vv. 27-29 do not belong to this story, according to the majority of scholars; they contradict vv. 23-26. In Ezekiel's eyes the history of the people is a chain of disobediences. It is true that none of the prophets are tender when speaking to their people. But no other prophet has portrayed the history of Israel as a chain of unrelenting sinning (cf. Jer 2:1-3). For Ezekiel this sin began in Egypt and it was there the Lord nearly destroyed the people (v. 8). Nowhere else in Scripture is there anything like it. Second, the traditions concerning the second generation are varied, but nowhere is it said that this second generation was prevented from entering the Promised Land, that it was scattered before ever entering it. One of the characteristics of the prophetic ministry—

noticeable in all prophets, and most radically in Ezekiel—is to take the received theological traditions and transform them in such a way that they serve the needs of the moment. It is obvious that Ezekiel knew perfectly well that the second generation entered the land of Canaan; he himself was exiled from there. But for him Israel never truly entered the Promised Land because the people were always unworthy and sinful. All this means that Ezekiel is never content with parroting the accepted theological traditions. He wants them alive and applicable to the present. Tradition is not worth anything if it is not a fountainhead of newness and of response to the problems of today.

Verses 25-26 have been the subject of much discussion. How can the Lord promulgate laws by which the people cannot live? It is clear that throughout its history Israel knew practices that, with time, proved to be negative. But in their minds there was one sole cause: God. Therefore one could interpret any trying event as coming from God as a punishment. This, it seems, is the least unsatisfactory explanation.

Several times (vv. 9, 14, 22) the Lord gives the reason for repenting: "for the sake of my name." In v. 5 the people are reminded that God had revealed to them both the divine self and the divine name. The reason for God's mercy is God's name. This seems strange to us. We get the impression that God acts for God's self, for God's glory, for God's honor, and that the people are only an occasion for God's action even though they might benefit by it. However, we must know that to reveal one's name to someone means to give oneself to someone, to bond one's existence so completely to the other that the two destinies are indissolubly linked. So when God is said to act "for the sake of God's name," God is acting for the people whose destiny is so to speak "under God's skin." And conversely, the behavior of Israel unavoidably involves God.

Hope in Spite of All: 20:32-44

Another controversy: the words of the people in v. 32 reflect the catastrophic circumstances in which they find themselves, at least after the first deportation. The temptation is understandable: to melt into the mainstream of the conquerors' culture and so have a chance to live. Obviously the experience of punishment did not teach them anything. But God has made a commitment with this people by revealing the divine name. Their destinies are linked forever. God cannot not react to the dissolution of the very people God has chosen. This is what "I shall act (I acted) for the sake of my name" means. God must save the people in spite of themselves. A new exodus appears on the horizon. In the "wilderness of the peoples" there will be a judgment, a sorting, and a covenant, and the Lord will reign over them.

The Fire and the Sword of Judgment: 20:45–21:32

The first part, 20:45–21:7, is made up of three distinct units: 20:45-48; 21:1-5; 21:6-7. The first two are connected by the mention of the Negeb and the prediction of judgment. Ezekiel's reactions in 20:45 and 21:7-8 serve as a bridge to introduce what follows. The omnipresent motif of the sword dominates the body of this passage while the motif of the fire frames it in the beginning (20:45-48) and end (21:31-32). The two oracles of 20:45-48 and 21:3-7 have in common the affirmation that a judgment without appeal is coming. Both images are classic: fire and sword. The Negeb (south) and the north of the first oracle are meant to express the totality of the judgment. We must note the reactions of Ezekiel, who speaks of himself as a prophet: he appears as a marginalized person for whom people have no use, except perhaps for a laugh (cf. 33:30-33). But one of the functions of prophets is precisely to be a witness, a sign and a proof for later when, the predicted events having taken place, the people will be obliged to recognize the pertinence and divine origin of their message: "Whether they hear or refuse to hear . . . they shall know that there has been a prophet among them" (2:5; cf. Isa 8:16-18; 30:8). The symbolic action of 21:6-7 dramatizes the message.

Verses 8-17 are another double oracle. Verses 8-12 present a poem on the sword (vv. 9b-11 and its application/explanation. Verses 14-17 contain a mixture of symbolic action, "strike hand to hand," explanation of the action of the sword, and address to the sword (v. 16). The theatrical character of the whole is obvious. The sword appears personalized, which is not uncommon in surrounding cultures. The Mesopotamian epic of Erra is a good parallel. The executioner's identity is not revealed; the intended victims are: "my people" and "all Israel's princes." The sword is presented as God's weapon for the benefit of the people (Josh 5:13-15; Isa 31:8). But once more Ezekiel turns the image upside down and makes of it the expression of YHWH's judgment upon Israel. The sword of victory becomes the sword of judgment. In v. 17 the sword appears as the instrument of God's fury.

Verses 18-27 unveil the executioner's identity with a luxury of detail that reflects the circumstances. He is Nebuchadnezzar, king of Babylon. Both Ezekiel and Jeremiah see in him the instrument of YHWH judgment on this people (see Jeremiah 27). The prince of Israel, the last king of Jerusalem, is subjected to a radical condemnation without appeal. Chapter 15 and still more ch. 17 have given the deep reasons for such a condemnation.

In vv. 29-32 the poem of the sword is resumed and this time is applied to Ammon, who was one of the possible targets of Nebuchadnezzar's campaign (v. 21). The concern for parallelism in the punishment of the two peoples is perhaps the reason for this oracle. False visions and lies would fit Jerusalem better than Ammon (see ch. 13). We have here one more passage, dramatic, detailed, and spirited, on Israel's punishment. The emphasis is not on the reasons for the punishment, but it remains true that the predicament of Israel could not be more serious.

Jerusalem, the Bloody City: Ezekiel 22

With this composite ensemble we are advancing toward the end of the oracles of judgment in the book of Ezekiel. The color of this chapter is red, red as blood, red as fire: the blood of sin, the fire of punishment.

Verses 1-16 make up the first section, although its structure is not very coherent. Verses 1-5, following the usual introductory formulas, state the accusation and punishment. The shedding of blood—referring to both social and religious misconduct—is one of the two counts of accusation; the other is idolatry. No other particulars are given. The whole of the Jerusalem scene is termed an "abomination." Usually this word has cultic connotations. For Ezekiel, the priest, and his disciples, the social and religious sins are the two faces of one transgression rooted in revolt against YHWH. The punishment, disgrace, and mockery (vv. 4-5) and dispersion (vv. 15-16) have an international dimension, as has the sin. But vv. 6-12 give details about the shedding of blood. All instances refer to social life, to relationships between human beings. The oracle is insistent, using eleven times (with one variation) the words "in you." One cannot escape the feeling of a certain similarity with the Ten Commandments, even though we do not have here a list of concrete cases but rather counts of guilt (cf. Hos 4:2). Verse 15 comes back to the punishment.

Verses 17-22 are a new unit dominated by the image of metal smelting. It is possible that texts like Isa 1:21-26 and Jer 6:27-30 are the background of this passage. When the operation is completed there is not even one gram of usable metal. As is Ezekiel's custom, he gives scant hope in this oracle.

Verses 23-31 establish once more the counts of the preceding indictment in a rather classic enumeration. The officials assuming responsibility for the functioning of the social and religious institutions are accused of not discharging their duties. Isaiah 1:21-26 and Zeph 3:1-5 are good parallels. It is notable that the entire people is accused of oppression and injustice in its human relationships. No one escapes; no one is righteous enough to save others through his or her righteousness or even to save himself or herself. Once again the tone of the oracle is disconsolate.

The Two Sisters: Ezekiel 23

Once again Ezekiel presents the history of his people by using images. In contrast to ch. 16 in which the allegory man/woman was used, here we have two sisters with the same husband. It seems that not only Hosea (Hosea 1–3) but Jeremiah also (Jer 3:6-13) are in the background of this allegory.

The first main block of this chapter, vv. 1-27, goes over the history of Israel and Judah. The description is violent and unsparing in its details. Ezekiel's mind is fertile in finding ways to open the eyes of his people to harsh reality. As in ch. 20 the perversion of the two sisters begins in Egypt. The perversion has "always" been there. The image is exploited in its political dimension. All the examples of the unfaithfulness of the two sisters are cast in that political light, along with the unavoidable consequence that any alliance with other powers entails: idolatry. As in ch. 15

and especially in ch. 17, the punishment is sure to come, and the comparison between political and conjugal unfaithfulness is pertinent.

We must note that v. 27 offers a glimmer of hope because it says that God will put an end to the "whoring brought from the land of Egypt." This time there is a ray of light in the darkness. Verses 28-31 add nothing new, but vv. 31-34 bring a new image: the cup of destiny one must drain. This is a logical sequence to the preceding text.

The rest of the chapter, vv. 35-49, is a replaying of the allegory, but in another key. Here the unfaithfulness is no longer in the political order and becomes the example not to be followed in the moral order. This is a considerable weakening in the discourse of Ezekiel.

The End: Ezekiel 24

With this chapter we reach the last of Ezekiel's utterances on the fall of Jerusalem (if we except the oracles against the nations). Verses 1-2 give a date, 5 January 587, the beginning of the siege of Jerusalem. Contrary to the other dates in the book, which refer to Jehoiakim's reign, this date refers to Zedekiah's. The pot, already seen in 11:1-13, is the basis of two allegories. The first (vv. 3-5) and its explanation (vv. 9-10) dwell on the contents of the pot, the meat, as a symbolic object. As in 11:3 the symbol represents the inhabitants of Jerusalem who are going to be cooked and recooked. Nothing good will come of this; the outlook is not optimistic; the judgment appears definitive.

The second allegory (vv. 6-8) and its explanation (vv. 11-14) concentrate on the rust of the pot, the image of the bloody city. The red color might be again the connecting link: the red of blood—the red of rust. Whereas the preceding allegory was speaking of punishment, this one speaks of purification. Verse 13 suggests that there is a possible future when "I have satisfied my fury upon you."

The second part of our passage, vv. 15-27, deals with Ezekiel's life and the fall of Jerusalem. Verses 15-23 depict a symbolic action that this time is not "acted" but lived. The brutal death of Ezekiel's wife gives him the opportunity to behave in such a way as to cause people to wonder, and thereby makes it possible for him to deliver his message. The death of his wife, "the delight of your eyes," symbolizes the death of the city. The abstention from mourning on the part of Ezekiel foreshadows what Judeans will have to go through at the time of the fall of the capital. One must not fool oneself; at that time it will be of no use to wail, but only to acknowledge one's sins. As in the case of Hosea's marriage we have here an example of the radical personal involvement of prophets with their message. Prophets bear the word they receive with their whole bodies, their whole beings, as women carry their children in the depths of their bodies. Verse 24 makes this clear, although we had understood it already.

Verses 25-27, while placed in the same framework, are in another mode and are to be read after the passage in which Ezekiel is rendered speechless by the Lord (3:24-26). They announce when and why he will be able to speak again. Later, the end of Ezekiel's muteness is mentioned in 33:21-22. This sequence makes sense. When the siege of Jerusalem begins, all is finished. There is room for neither repentance nor prophetic preaching. This is not yet the time to preach hope. Ezekiel remains mute. After the fall of Jerusalem a new period begins—and a different message.

Oracles Against the Nations: Ezekiel 25–32

The oracles of judgment against Israel being completed, we arrive at those directed against the nations. Afterward will come the oracles of hope. This "theological" order of the oracles in prophetic books is logical. Ezekiel says this clearly in 28:24-26: after all have received their due it is possible to envision the future. Other prophetic books contain similar oracles, for instance Amos 1–2; Isaiah 13–23; Jeremiah 46–51; Zeph 2:4-14. The surrounding civilizations also employ texts and oracles of the same kind. Most often they are condemnations of other peoples. Prophets, seers appear as the spokespersons of the national gods who defend "their" people against foreigners. In political and military conflicts these oracles can play the role of magical and efficacious guarantees.

We find oracles of the same kind in the prophetic books of the Bible, for instance those of Ezekiel 25. We have there a patent example showing how deeply Ezekiel is rooted in the culture and religious mentality of his time. But although the biblical prophets share in this mentality, they are not limited by it because their horizon is far vaster, even in the domain of the oracles against the nations. Other oracles, for instance those of chs. 26–32, have a much greater literary and theological richness. Finally, there are also oracles of salvation directed at foreign nations, for example Isa 19:18-25; Zeph 3:9-10. These oracles against the nations are not often used in the liturgy and do not enjoy a high regard in the theologies of the OT, but they make an important contribution to the understanding and evaluation of the ministry of the prophets who are rooted in a social and political culture both concrete and limited and, at the same time, often go far beyond that culture.

Against the Neighbors of Judah (Ezekiel 25)

The series begins with five oracles against the close neighbors east and west of Judah, four of which are Ammon, Moab, Edom, and Philistia. All four had frequent and tumultuous relations with Judah and Israel throughout their history. The first two have particular connections with Israel, as Gen 19:30-38 shows. Edom is even more, a brother (Deut 23:7) as the cycle of Jacob (Genesis 27–33) shows. As to Israel's relations with the Philistines, they were antagonistic most of the time, even though David worked for them and enrolled some of them in his army (1 Samuel 27; 2 Sam 8:15-18).

The accusations are well enough known. In vv. 6, 7, 15-17 Ammon and Moab are reproached for their glee over and profit from the disaster striking Judah and Jerusalem. The Lord appears as the avenger of God's people. The first oracle against Ammon contains another accusation (vv. 2-5). Ammon mocked the sanctuary, the land, and the house of Judah in their calamity. Verses 8-11 censure Moab for regarding the house of Judah as no different from any other people and, therefore, YHWH as not above any other god. The punishments are varied, but each time the reversal of situations is paramount.

Against Tyre and Sidon (Ezekiel 26–28)

Readers of these three chapters inevitably feel crushed under these ponderous oracles. Indeed, it is difficult to retrieve Ezekiel's texts from the midst of added commentaries. The whole thing comprises diverse oracles of judgment against Tyre (26:1-6, 7-14, 15-18, 19-21, 28:1-10) and two lamentations (27:1-36; 28:11-19), these last following in the main the rules of this literary genre. In 28:20-23 we have a generic oracle against the ancient city of Sidon. The last three verses (24-26) serve as a conclusion to chs. 25–28.

Tyre was built on an island very near the coast. At the time of Ezekiel it had become the center and symbol of Phoenician economic power. In the political turmoil of the time Tyre was part of the anti-Babylonian coalition whose ambassadors convened in Jerusalem order to organize the revolt (Jer 27:1-11). Tyre's power was a major asset for the kingdom of Judah. But the Babylonians kept the city under siege for thirteen years. It emerged considerably weakened but it was neither destroyed nor pillaged, contrary to what Ezekiel's oracles state in chs. 26–28 (see especially 26:21; 27:36; 28:19). Ezekiel's utterances aim at removing every illusion the Judeans might have concerning the help they can expect from Tyre. Certain oracles going back to the time after the fall of Jerusalem show that far from coming to the aid of Jerusalem, Tyre profited by its fall (26:2).

Another theme found in these oracles is the condemnation of the pride of the Phoenician city. This pride was the fruit of its commercial success, a consequence of its "wisdom." Wisdom is manifested equally in the conduct of politics and in business acumen but, causing the inebriation of triumph, it ends in pride. This aspect of Tyre's pride takes on a special color in the lament of ch. 27 and the oracle and lament of 28:1-19. The mythological themes of the primordial human beings who take themselves for gods are explicitly recalled, especially in this last chapter. The themes of original happiness and perfection, fall, and expulsion from the dwelling and the company of the gods are liberally used. We are reminded of Genesis 2–3, even though in that book the themes are treated in a somewhat different way. The greater the pride and original eminence, the deeper the fall. We will meet Tyre again in a rather surprising context in 29:17-20.

Verses 24-26 are the literary and theological conclusion of the ensemble of chs. 25–28. Everyone has been judged, Israel as well as the neighboring nations, guilty of their conduct toward the people of God. The block of oracles against Egypt ought to have been placed before these last verses so that the oracles of hope for Israel might begin.

Against Egypt (Ezekiel 29–32)

This is the last block of oracles against the nations. It can be divided on the basis of the formulas of introduction and conclusion, which does not mean that there are not subdivisions like 29:1-16, 17-21; 30; 31; 32:1-16 (a text presented as a lament although it is no such thing); 32:17-32. These chapters are strewn with mythical or quasi-mythical images and it is not easy in this overgrown thicket to distinguish Ezekiel's words from those of his commentators.

Egypt always had a special place in the history of Israel and Judah. Ezekiel sets in Egypt the birth of his people as well as the beginning of their rebellion against the Lord (ch. 20), and he is well acquainted with the particular political relations and the attraction that Judah never ceased to feel toward the kingdom of the Pharaohs (chs. 17; 19; 23). In these oracles concluding the series of proclamations against the nations Ezekiel condemns the ignorance, grandeur, and power of Egypt, not in themselves but because of the harmful effects they had on Judah. Egypt is the snare and the illusion *par excellence.* Taking up the image already used in Isa 36:6, the broken reed that wounds the one who leans on it, he clearly delivers his message—hence the avalanche of invectives and images he uses to describe Egypt's defects.

The contrast between the tone of the oracles against Egypt and that of the oracles against Babylon as well as the manner in which Ezekiel conceives their relationship must be noted. Although often called by Ezekiel the most tyrannical of all nations (30:11; 32:12), Babylon plays a positive role in the plans of the God of Israel. On this point 29:17-21 is a singular text. It is the last of the entire book if we believe the date given in 29:17. Ezekiel's oracle on the fate of Tyre, delivered to Nebuchadnezzar (27:1-6, explained in 27:6-14), was not realized. Tyre was not plundered or destroyed by Nebuchadnezzar. According to 29:17-21 Egypt was delivered to the Babylonian king to compensate for what he had not gained from the siege of Tyre because Egypt "shall be the wages for his army. I have given him the land of Egypt as his payment for which he labored, because they worked for me, says the Lord GOD." It is evident that the criterion of the realization of a prophecy was not retained when it came to discerning which biblical prophets' writings were part of Scripture. Ezekiel's case is not the only one (see Amos 7:7-9). This is important to remember in order to correctly understand the true nature of biblical prophets. They are not diviners. They are readers of events and of the life of the people, whose deep meaning they present or uncover, always in the light of the faith of Israel. It is obvious that Egypt has been a trap for Judah at the time when the salvation of Judah lay in submission to the Babylonians, but it is even more obvious that Ezekiel strives to convince the people to place their trust solely in the Lord. He struggles to avoid the idolatry of force and power that political alliances with great powers entailed. However, the prophetic conception of God as directly causing the twists and turns of history, a conception at the very root of the prophets' preaching, is not a component of the Christian faith.

Another surprise in this whole passage concerning Egypt is the oracle in 29:13-16. After having undergone the same fate as Israel, that is, dispersion, Egypt will again be reunited by God. True, it will no longer be a great power but only a modest kingdom. This promise is not as generous as that recorded in Isa 19:18-25, but there will be a restoration.

Reactions of the People to the Fall of Jerusalem. New Mission of Ezekiel: Ezekiel 33

The first part of the book of Ezekiel (chs. 1–24) is built around the oracles of judgment against Judah and Israel. The second (chs. 25–32) is made up of the oracles against the nations. The third is devoted to the oracles of hope. Chapter 33 opens the whole of Ezekiel's preaching in its second phase, after the disaster that overtook Judah. This chapter contains several units: the parable of the sentry as applied to the prophet (vv. 1-9), the reaction of the exiles to their condition (vv. 10-11), God's response through Ezekiel (vv. 12-20), a historical account of the fall of Jerusalem (vv. 21-22), the reaction of the inhabitants of Judah and the answer of God (vv. 23-29), a divine word on the attitude of Ezekiel's audience and on God's reaction to it (vv. 30-33).

The historical account (vv. 21-22) specifies the moment at which someone who escaped Jerusalem arrives and Ezekiel's speech is restored as well as his movements (see 3:25-26a; 24:26-27). Ezekiel fell silent when the siege of the city began. By finding his voice again he becomes a sign of the utmost clarity for the exiles. His authority is confirmed.

Ezekiel's mission is confirmed and renewed at the outset of this new and decisive stage in Israel's history, but in the same way Ezekiel had been the prophet of the most doleful judgment in the first part, from now on he becomes the prophet of the most unbounded and unreasonable hope. The image of the sentry had already been used by other prophets to define their role (see Hos 5:8; Jer 6:17; Hab 2:1). To describe the prophetic ministry few images are more felicitous than that of the sentinel for the event and the anticipation of God's word. Prophets are the decipherers of the event in order to announce the word of God, ready to illuminate it and unveil its meaning within God's plan. Prophets watch for the event and the word. This image shows an essential aspect of the prophetic mission: the urgency of the situation. Prophets appear in the most troublesome times. What is more necessary at the time of the fall of Jerusalem than a voice that proclaims its meaning and the way to follow? Moreover, the image points to another essential aspect of the prophetic mission: if the watch that the prophets assume is to be meaningful it is because the circumstances can change as a result of their labor; the danger can be averted. Hence the key word of the whole chapter, even though it is not always spelled out, is "conversion." Change, life made possible in the face of mortal danger reside in the opportunity offered that demands conversion as a response: "I have no pleasure in the death of the wicked, but that the wicked turn from their ways and live; turn back, turn back from your evil ways; for why will you die, O house of Israel?" (33:11).

Ezekiel often speaks of death and life in his oracles. The present moment is particularly concerned with these two realities. The exiled people's concern bears precisely on this point: "how then can we live?" (33:10). This query is bitter, full of despair. For the first time the people acknowledge their revolt, but in this cry there is no hint of conversion. What is more, in v. 17 the quarrel between God and Israel continues, with the people contending that the way of the Lord is not just. Ezekiel answers that God is not only just but also generous in offering life, provided there be a response to God's proposal. Verses 12-20 are akin to ch. 18. Ezekiel, it is obvious, considers the future of Israel as a community, as a people; chs. 36, 37, and 40–48 are proof of it. But in ch. 18 and 33:12-20 (as well as in vv. 1-9, but in another way) he places the emphasis on personal responsibility, using the juridical, even casuistic method and style customary with priests. By their very function they were aware of the personal dimension of the believers' conduct. Besides, after the collapse of social and religious institutions it was urgent to pay attention to the conduct of individuals. As a result, Ezekiel runs the risk of describing a harsh state of affairs, in contradiction with reality: Individuals are responsible for everyone of their actions. When there is a reversal in behavior, accumulated acts of righteousness offer no guarantee of life and accumulated acts of unrighteousness do not necessarily end in death; only the relationship and communion with the Lord on the one hand or, on the other, the distance and estrangement from the Lord, source of life, are of any account.

The second reaction of the exiles (vv. 30-33) when listening to Ezekiel's new preaching is the same as before; it is one of condescending irony. Here we see another characteristic of prophetic preaching: it is always going against the prevailing ethos. When the people are carefree, not seeing they are on the brink of suicide, prophets threaten punishment and call for conversion. After the punishment, when the people are in despair, they proclaim hope against all hope. The proof that prophets are necessary resides in the fact that their lot is either mockery or persecution.

The reaction varies with the circumstances with which each person is faced. The Judeans who remained in Jerusalem and its surroundings have a completely different view of reality (vv. 23-29). Since they have not been "punished" by exile and have remained in the land they claim for themselves the old promises, especially vital in Deuteronomy (Deut 1:8; 6:10; 9:5; 30:20; 34:4). Events have served no purpose. There is no more conversion among them than among their exiled compatriots.

Shepherds and Sheep; YHWH the Good Shepherd: Ezekiel 34

This chapter occupies an important place in the book of Ezekiel and also in the NT and Christian tradition. Verses 1-16 are its first part; vv. 17-22 form a second unit followed by a short oracle, in 23-24, on David, shepherd and prince. Verses 25-30 offer hope in the form of a relation of peace (a "covenant" of peace). Verse 31 concludes the whole with a general principle.

In vv. 1-16, the image of the shepherd is applied to leaders without specification. The image was already used in Jer 23:1-2. The two texts are very close, even in vocabulary, although this does not necessarily prove a direct literary dependence on Ezekiel's part. The borrowing of the theme is sufficient to account for the similarity. The image is widely used in the ancient Near East to designate gods and kings. The latter share in the pastoral duties of the former whose lieutenants they are. Isaiah uses it to speak of Cyrus (44:28), and in the tradition describing the ascent of David to the throne David is shown as a shepherd. God too is called a shepherd, especially in the psalms (Pss 23, 28, 78, 80), but also in Gen 49:24.

In vv. 17-22 the relationships of sheep with sheep serve to illustrate those of the Judeans among themselves. The leaders are not the only persons addressed.

The accusations in vv. 1-16 are clear and close to those found in Jeremiah: the rulers of Israel are responsible for the exile in Babylonia. The shepherds have sought their personal profit instead of that of the sheep, abandoning the flock and leaving it unprotected from destruction. The political and religious catastrophes are proof of this neglect. The accusations in vv. 17-22 concern the people as a whole: the strong oppress the weak; the rich exploit the poor.

After the punishment has happened, the Lord's action against the shepherds and the judgment between sheep manifest, of course, an attitude that is the reverse of that of the accused. To the scattering caused by the bad shepherds the good shepherd opposes the gathering of the flock. Against the injustice of the fat sheep the Lord commends the protection of the weak and the justice that saves them. The text envisions a possible and happy future for the people. Verses 11-13 and, in part, 27-28 use the language of Exodus. YHWH's action is conceived as the cause of a new exodus. Isaiah 40–55 thoroughly exploits this parallelism. A happy future is possible thanks to the good shepherd's activity. It is not that the new David will play a role of first importance; he is called simply "prince," although in 37:15-28 his task, as described, is more clearly in conformity with traditional descriptions of the monarchy. The relationship of peace ("covenant" of peace) of vv. 25-30 simply expresses the new state of well-being (in the deepest sense) and of communion that YHWH is going to establish with the people. We are here in the same perspectives as those of the famed texts of Jeremiah (especially 24; 31:31-34). For both prophets the relationship of YHWH with the chosen people after the disaster supposes a sort of new creation of humankind. Ezekiel 36:16-38 and 37:1-14 develop this theme.

That the image of the shepherd was applied to the Christ of the NT was to be expected; the contrary would have been surprising. This image is found everywhere except in the Pauline corpus: Matt 9:36; 18:12-14; Luke 15:1-7; Mark 14:27; John 10:1-30; 21:15-17 (where Peter is entrusted with the feeding of the flock of the Risen Christ); 1 Pet 5:1-4; Rev 7:17. The application of the image to Christ is uncomplicated: he is the true shepherd, he brings salvation by giving his life so that his sheep may live. The good shepherd has been a beloved theme in Christian iconography. For a vast number of urban Christian communities this image does not make much sense today, but a simple hermeneutics can easily restore its dynamism for the benefit of believers. At any rate, in the present state of affairs when there is a painful lack of leaders—and those who happen on the scene are charlatans and cheaters, exploiting the credulity of people who are adrift—the message of the good shepherd will find acceptance. The passage also gives a criterion allowing us to evaluate the "shepherds": the well-being and thriving of the sheep.

The Mountains of Edom and Israel, Punishment and Hope: 35:1–36:15

As we saw in ch. 6, the mountains represent the peoples who live on them. In this unit the mountain of Seir symbolizes Edom and the mountains of Israel the people of God.

35:1-15 constitute a block of oracles against Edom. After the introductory formulas, vv. 1-4 contain a proclamation of condemnation without explicit motive. The balance of ch. 35 is made up of three oracles of condemnation with motives: vv. 5-9, 10-12a, 12b-15. Edom profited by the calamity that struck Judah and Jerusalem and greedily fell upon those who were left and despoiled them. The animosity toward Edom is omnipresent in the Scriptures and is symbolically represented by the conflicts between Jacob and Esau (see these stories in Genesis). Other texts speak of this enmity with the same virulence, for example, Isaiah 34; 63:1-6; Jer 49:7-22; Obadiah; Lam 4:21. When committing this evil, Edom misunderstood what was really at stake. Deeming the political situation to be the outcome of a mere play of forces, Edom forgot YHWH (35:13). In fact, the disaster overtaking Judah is the work of God within the framework of God's relationship with the chosen people. Although deserted, the mountains of Israel are not for the first comer's taking. This would mean that Israel had no future, that it was all over.

36:1-15, an oracle addressed to the mountains, show that God has plans for these mountains. This text is made up of several components, as is clear from the different formulas of introduction and conclusion, but the central nucleus is unmistakable. It is a companion piece to ch. 6, an oracle of judgment against the mountains of Israel, and the reverse of the oracle against the mountain of Edom (35:1-15). These ancient mountains will not be the possession of other peoples (v. 2); they will be inhabited again, and fertile for "my people Israel" (vv. 8-10).

The New Heart and the Spirit of God: 36:16-38

This passage is one of the best known in Ezekiel. It is true that it represents one of the summits of the OT. As usual, from the literary point of view the text is rather overloaded. Verses 33-36 and 37-38 are two independent oracles, clearly distinct. The movement of the rest of the text will be easy to perceive if we remember that it has three parts.

36:17-20 is the first part, coming after the introduction of v. 16. Ezekiel has already spoken of the history of his people (chs. 16; 20; 23). Here he presents it succinctly, terming it a defilement, a word with cultic connotations. However, this word includes all the sins of Israel. The result is well known: deportation and dispersion among the nations (vv. 19-20).

36:21-22 is the second part and gives the reasons for YHWH's reaction that is about to be shown. The scattering of God's sinful people among the nations can cause a misunderstanding. Indeed, at first sight YHWH appears as a god unable to protect the god's own people. The punishment meted out to Israel can be seen as weakness on YHWH's part. Therefore YHWH must react to save the divine honor and rank. This is a classical argument in the OT (see Exod 32:12; Num 14:16). It is used at times to put pressure on God in order to obtain God's renunciation of the decision to punish and to seek divine forgiveness. The same theme also occurs frequently in the psalms, for example in Pss 6:4-5; 35:22-26; 71:9-11; 109:21-29; 143:11-12.

Verse 22 often shocks readers, as is also the case with 20:1-31 (see above, ad loc). But we have already seen that God's action "for the sake of my name" also means "because of Israel" to whom God has revealed the divine name; their destinies are intimately connected.

36:23-38 form the third part, which focuses on the future now that the reasons why God acted have been made clear. First of all, there is the liberation of Israel from dispersion among the nations and the return "into your own land" (v. 24). Then comes the purification of the people with clean water (v. 25); here Ezekiel's priestly background shows clearly. Finally, there is the climax of divine action: the radical newness, the complete transformation of the people. A heart of flesh replaces the heart of stone. God places the divine spirit in the innermost depths of the people. The heart and the spirit symbolize the whole of the person. There is no hesitating in declaring that we have here a new creation, a re-created Israel.

In this connection we must remember the passage in 11:19-20, which is a parallel, with a few variants, of our present text, but above all we must remember ch. 18:30b-32, which concludes the long discussion on personal responsibility. In that text God invites the people to conversion, to total interior renewal: "get yourselves a new heart and a new spirit" (18:31). Human beings themselves must be the artisans of their conversion. At the time ch. 18 was written, it was judged possible that humans could do so. But here (vv. 26-28) things have changed. It is God in person who re-makes humans, re-makes Israel, "A new heart I will give you, and a new spirit I will put within you." The initiative, as well as the completion of the task, are the work of God. We cannot ignore the parallel with Jeremiah, for whom the situation of Israel is desperate: "Can Ethiopians change their skin or leopards their spots? Then also you can do good who are accustomed to evil" (Jer 13:23). And further, "The sin of Judah is written with an iron pen; with a diamond point it is engraved on the tablet of their hearts, and on the horns of their altars" (Jer 17:1). This is why "in the days to come" the commandments and the laws will be engraved "on their hearts" (Jer 31:31-34). Some commentators have accused Jeremiah of a pessimistic view of human nature. Rightly so. But the same can be said also of Ezekiel. Both arrive at the conclusion that by themselves human beings are incapable of following the ways God enjoins on them—"my laws and my ordinances"—incapable of responding to God's invitation to live in communion with God, and therefore of being converted. Hosea already had used the same theme, "I will heal their disloyalty" (Hos 14:4). We must recognize this obvious truth: for the prophets, conversion itself is the work of God; hence the prayer of Israel, "bring me back, let me come back" (Jer 31:18; cf. Ps 80:3).

The consequences of this reversal are evident. First of all, "the nations shall know that I am the LORD" (vv. 23, 35, 36). The goal has been reached. In the second place, the people of Israel will, at long last, observe the laws and statutes of the Lord (v. 27). At this point we encounter the expression of this relation of God and God's people, summarized in the famed formula of mutual belonging, "you shall be my people, and I will be your God." What follows is the logical consequence of this mutual belonging: the cities will be populated, the land fertile; everything will be the reflection of the communion of God with God's people.

The Resurrection of Israel: 37:1-14

This is another important and famous text. Its structure is simple. Verses 1-3 give the introduction and the setting of the whole passage, presenting the persons involved in and the elements of the vision. Afterwards, the question God asks Ezekiel, "Mortal, can these bones live?" poses the essential problem. The prophet's evasive answer leaves the door open to YHWH's initiative. Verses 4-10 form the second part, the symbolic action, itself made up of two parallel and corresponding members, vv. 4-8 and 9-10. There are two commands to prophesy given by the Lord to Ezekiel; there are two narratives to tell the result of these prophecies. At the end, the goal is reached when the bones revive and stand up. Verses 11-14 form the third part and contain two different components. Verse 11a gives the meaning of the vision of the dry bones; vv. 11b-14, starting with a complaint of the people, are a new oracle in the same mode (life-death) but with a different image.

This whole passage is structured as a unit since the three parts are closely linked together. Besides, the formulas of introduction and conclusion, while separating the text from what precedes and what follows, enclose the whole. There is no doubt that the hinge of this passage is the lamentation of the people in v. 11b. This lamentation supplies Ezekiel not only with the theological opportunity to make his prophecy but also with the image on which the vision is built. The dry bones as an expression of despair are found in Ps 31:10. According to his custom, Ezekiel takes into consideration the state of mind of his people and their words in order to take a contrary stand and deliver his message. In this second phase of Ezekiel's activity there is another identical case, which we have already seen, in 33:10—a text very close to 20:32. With variants the three verses betray the same state of mind: "Our bones are dried up/our sins weigh upon us, and our hope is lost; we are cut off completely"—all that is left for us is to disappear as the people of Israel by becoming part of the nations. Each time, Ezekiel forcefully reacts.

In our passage the reaction is impressive, the vision spectacular. We cannot help but think that we have here (as already in 36:26-28) a new creation. And with good reason: the similarities with Genesis 2 are many. The vocabulary is intentionally chosen to suggest this comparison to the readers, as are the references to Israel's theological traditions.

The verb "know," "be cognizant" appears at strategic points in this unit. First of all, in v. 3 when Ezekiel answers that God, not he, Ezekiel, knows whether the bones can possibly revive. At the end, when the images and their meanings have been completely explained, "you shall know that I, the LORD, have spoken and will act" (v. 14). In between, vv. 6 and 13 use the verb in the same expression as does v. 14, an expression dear to Ezekiel. In this way the unity of the whole passage is ensured.

The text also plays with another verb that is very significant in the biblical tradition: "enter," "come." In v. 5 this verb states the aim of divine action, "I will cause breath to enter you, and you shall live." It is found again, logically, in vv. 9 and 10, and finally in v. 12, where the return to the land of Israel is announced.

The verb "mount," "ascend" also plays a twofold role. It is used to describe the "mounting" of flesh over the bones, but especially, in the second image, it is used to describe Israel coming out of death, ascending from the grave. The Hebrew verb *(ʿlh)* is one of those that biblical tradition uses to speak of the "coming out of Egypt" and it is used here intentionally. The situation of the exiles in Babylon resembles in many respects that of Israel in Egypt. In view of the theological importance the tradition of the Exodus had assumed in Israel it is not surprising that Ezekiel sees the plight of his people in the light of the first exodus.

Another reality of great import in this text is, without doubt, that of the *spirit.* The Hebrew word *(rūaḥ)* has several meanings that are all found in this text of Ezekiel. In vv. 5, 6, 8 one can translate it by "breath of life." It is this breath that revives the dry bones. In v. 9 it is accompanied by the article, in contradistinction to the preceding verses, and seems already more personalized. Afterward, in Ezekiel's prophetic utterance, we find "Come from the four winds, O breath, and breathe upon these slain, that they may live." This expression is equivalent to the "four cardinal points," designated by the four winds in the ancient Near East. *Rūaḥ* also serves to speak of the wind. Finally, there is the spirit of YHWH in v. 14. We must underline that the text is framed at the beginning and end by the mention of the spirit of YHWH that is the very soul of this passage and of the future of the people.

Even though the images and development of the text are not identical with those of 36:16-38, the perspectives and the message are the same: the re-creation of Israel. Certainly in our present text the image is much clearer and more to the point. At the same time there is a doubt hovering over the promise: Is it possible? For the people, as the lamentation of v. 11b shows, it is not possible; the die is cast. God in person asks the question. Ezekiel answers that only God knows, but in thus affirming the divine knowledge he also affirms the divine power. We have here one of the essential tenets of Israel's faith: the people has existed and can exist only by the action and grace of God. It was so for its birth; it will be so for its rebirth. This confirms what was said in the preceding chapter on the subject of conversion. Israel is unable to be converted, to turn back. Only the Lord has the power of bringing Israel back to life, to its own self, to its own land. Both the origin and the future of Israel are found only in its God.

It is needless to recall that this text has been read and reread in both the Jewish and Christian traditions as a prediction of the resurrection of the dead, as a clear prophecy of life after death. Nevertheless we must be clear also about its originally intended meaning: it referred only to the historical renewal of Israel after the Babylonian exile, its historical resurrection as the people of God. It did not for a moment envision the possibility of individual resurrection after death. This correct understanding of the text did not prevent its being read as a prediction of the individual resurrection, whether in the frescoes of Dura-Europos or in the writings of many Fathers of the Church. The meaning of scriptural writings is not one and univocal. This sort of reading is legitimate inasmuch as one uses the text with its splendid forcefulness to express the Jewish or Christian faith developed later on. In doing so one should not forget the primary meaning of the text and should remain aware of the distance between the two readings and of the theological act that allows the later interpretation.

The evocative power of Ezekiel's words in our passage also influenced Western art, even in the middle of the twentieth century. It is evident that the historical, social, and religious conditions are not the same today as at the time of the exile. However, many of our contemporaries could make their own the words of Ezekiel in 37:11b. The disillusionment over the state of the world is one of the most inexorable facts in the closing years of this century. Suicide, whether individual or collective, haunts the minds of many men and women, in particular the young. The absence of a future and the lack of any goal on the horizon are the daily experience of many human beings and very often of whole societies. Churches and especially individual Christians cannot be content with repeating by rote the message of faith, "Christ is risen." To be credible, the message must be audible; to be audible, it must answer the questions and anxieties of today's hearers. In the same way as Ezekiel's message on the resurrection of Israel played a vital role in the rebirth of Israel as a people after the exile, the evocative power of his vision can be placed at the service of Christian faith in order to revive the hope and life of our contemporaries.

Political and Religious Restoration: 37:15-28

This last section of ch. 37, containing three parts, logically follows the vision of the dry bones. Verses 15-19, 22, the first part, present the description and explanation of a symbolic action, both simple once one has understood what the "sticks" mean, and this meaning is self-evident. Curiously, Ezekiel shows great interest in the northern kingdom and the problem created by the political division between the tribes of Israel. As long as the northern kingdom existed it followed its own way, as did the southern kingdom. Amos and Hosea never dream of a reunification of the two political entities. Isaiah, on the contrary, speaks of it, and in Jeremiah's time the question becomes urgent again on account of the collapse of the Assyrian empire and the possibility that Josiah might recover the territory of the defunct northern kingdom. The circumstances of the exile, when the people is about to be re-created, lead the people to recall the beginnings and imagine the future on the same pattern. What is envisaged is indeed the social and political refounding of the people headed again by a king, symbolized by David. In the same way as the unity of the tribes into one single political entity belongs to an ideal, so does David. What is meant is not that David will return, but that a king whose ideal model is David will be installed.

The second part, vv. 21, 23-25, is an oracle on the return from exile and the one king. Another essential theme appears also, the cleansing of the land. Already in 36:26-28 purification had been emphasized. Here also there is insistence, even though there is no mention of the rites of purification. The high point of these verses is the formula of mutual belonging. Israel, dwelling in a cleansed land, will put into practice God's laws and ordinances.

The last part, vv. 26-28, is a condensed reiteration of the hope expressed by Ezekiel and summarizes ch. 37 and the whole of the second phase of Ezekiel's ministry. A promise of a permanent and peaceful relation between God and God's people sums up the whole passage. Peace, of course, means much more than the absence of war; it is a state of global and profound well-being. Here we reach the last element of this promise of restoration: God's dwelling will be among the people. This presence of God in the sanctuary in the midst of the people will also be for the nations a sign of the reality and supreme dignity of the God of Israel. We recognize here Ezekiel the priest and his school. The future, the hope are dressed in cultic garments. The restoration of the people is couched in liturgical terms: the sanctuary of YHWH in the midst of YHWH's people. Other prophets have imagined hope in different guises not explicitly connected with worship. Ezekiel the prophet, conditioned, as is normal, by his origins and his formation, shows himself once more in this text, as in other passages of his book, to be a priest. Every person has his or her roots and limits.

Just the same, in these last two oracles from 38:15-28 one is struck by the frequency of the expression "forever." It recurs with each of the promises: return to the land that had been promised to the ancestors, practice of laws and ordinances, David prince and king of all the children of Israel, and above all the peaceful relationship of God's people with God residing among them in the sanctuary. All this is "forever" *(lʿolām).* The eschatological dimension (future, definitive, and salvific manifestation in favor of God's people) is unmistakable, as are also the limits of such a vision; for the eschatological hope at the root of eschatological texts is one thing, the representations, images, and figures used to express it are another. The thrust of hope is truly permanent in the Jewish and Christian Scriptures, but the various figures used to express it are transient. There is an undeniable distance between the promise of a David-like king at the head of the risen and restored people and the Son of David whom Christians recognize in Jesus of Nazareth. It is a long way between the sanctuary in the midst of the people of which vv. 26, 27, and 28 speak and the Word made flesh who sets up his tent among humans. Figures of speech and institutions are always as necessary as they are limited in order to give body to hope, faith, and mission. It is not fruitless to observe and comprehend this on the basis of this beautiful text of Ezekiel.

Eschatological War Against the Nations: Ezekiel 38–39

Among the strange texts of Ezekiel's book these two chapters occupy an eminent place. We must set apart the last portion of these chapters (39:23-29) which is a summary of Ezekiel's themes of hope. These verses are a bridge between chs. 38:1–39:22 and chs. 40–46; they also recall chs. 33–37. The different formulas allow for the delimitation of the several units, which are not necessarily homogeneous: 38:1-9, 10-13, 14-23; 39:1-5, 6-16, 17-20, 21-22.

In spite of numerous attempts to identify Gog we must be content with seeing in Gog a symbolic name for all the enemies of Israel; hence the mention of the various countries that represent the totality of the foes. The central theme is the decisive battle between Israel's adversaries and Israel's God. The return will take place (38:8), the final act of salvation, future and definitive. The motif of the assembly of the nations against the people (the city, the anointed) is a classic one in the OT (Isa 5:26-30; 8:9-10; Pss 2; 48). It can represent a historical, concrete people (Isa 10:5-15). In Jeremiah it becomes "the enemy from the north" (Jeremiah 4–6). In other texts it takes on an eschatological coloring (see especially Joel 3). The depiction of the God of Israel as a warrior god is a throwback to ancient texts (Exod 14:14, 24-25). The banquet offered to birds and wild beasts fits in well with the eschatological setting. The whole creation (see the earthquake in 38:19) takes part in the final battle, but it is God who directs the action, although Gog and his cohorts are the ones who are busy moving about. Gog becomes the instrument and the object of God's plan to bring about the definitive salvation of the people. The idea is not new (see Isa 10:5-15) but here it is in an eschatological context. The description of the cleansing of the land, heavy and oversimplified, betrays a thoroughly priestly preoccupation.

This sort of passage cannot be read or understood in a faith perspective except within a wider setting. The striking images are at the service of the central idea: God saves the people definitively. However, we must not forget that in the Scriptures the representations of this salvation are not univocal, especially when it comes to the salvation or destruction of other peoples. Ezekiel 38–39 and Joel 3 propose a nationalistic eschatology that excludes other peoples from salvation. But other trends of thought, other representations, are also at work (see especially Isa 56:1-8; 66:18-23). There is not one eschatology in the OT, but several; they do not necessarily agree.

A New Land, a New City, a New Temple: Ezekiel 40–48

One cannot pretend that the reading of these chapters is pleasant. However, taken together they are an important element of the book. We have here a third great vision reported by the prophet (cf. chs. 1–3; 8–11). These three visions are the skeleton of the whole work and hold it together. The logical connection between them is obvious: the first establishes Ezekiel's mission; the second justifies and "realizes" the judgment of Jerusalem and the departure of the glory of God from the Temple. The last, with the return of the glory, does not mean simply the restoration of the land, the people, and the presence of the glory of God. It also means—as a continuation of chs. 33–37—the concrete implementation of this new creation promised and announced by Ezekiel.

This does not imply that these chapters form a homogeneous whole: far from it. Commentators are not unanimous, but the minimalist hypothesis attributes three blocks to Ezekiel himself: 40:1-2; 43:4-7a; 47:1, 2b, 8, 9b, 12. In all likelihood this hypothesis is closest to the truth. The rest of the text is not without value, but its value is of a different order.

Fourteen years after the fall of the city, Ezekiel, "in visions of God," is led to the land of Israel and set on a high mountain from which he sees to the south "a structure like a city." Thence he contemplates the arrival of the glory of God and the word that designates the temple as the place of God's throne (43:4-7). With the vision of the spring welling up from the temple and growing into a life-giving stream the scene is complete: God is among the people and prosperity reigns; the people will live. The two cardinal themes of the message of hope delivered by Ezekiel, presence of God and life for Israel, are joined in this last vision.

The nucleus of this text has been heavily complemented. Ezekiel and his disciples share a central preoccupation, to erase all that can have been the cause of Israel's sins and has led to the catastrophe, in order to stress the real communion between Israel and YHWH: hence the last word of the book. When everything has been realized, the sought-after goal will be reached: YHWH is there. But whereas Ezekiel is content with sketching the main traits of this radiant future (return of the glory of God and life-giving source), his disciples add particulars on the places and persons as well as on the norms that regulate their relationship with the source of life, the sacred, the temple. The descriptions abound in minutiae concerning the exact dimensions of the territory (along with its apportioning), the buildings, the kitchens, the doors. Strict norms are given for the roles of the different members of the temple personnel—with polemical jabs at the Levites in order to enhance the power of certain groups against others—the marriage of priests, the presents for princes. Perfection in the proportion 2:1 is sought in the way space is structured. Besides, the more one advances into the sacred space the more one ascends. The obvious intention is to suggest the distance and separation between the sacred and profane. We easily notice that the vision of Ezekiel runs out of breath. By overdoing the refinement of the means one loses sight of the spirit and end. This risk is a permanent fact of human experience.

The New Temple (Ezekiel 40–42)

If one examines these difficult texts closely one can find not only a good deal of information but also theological trends and facts of great interest. After the theophany of the introduction in 40:1-2 comes a long development on the new temple, 40:3-42. A strange personage comes upon the scene: "a man . . . whose appearance shone like bronze, with a linen cord and a measuring reed in his hand." This man is going to guide Ezekiel and act as an intermediary between the divinity and the prophet to transmit the information and commands relative to the measures and arrangement of the new temple. From 44:5 on, it is the Lord in person who speaks to Ezekiel; the man ceases to play a relevant role. Later this personage, the intermediary/guide, will become the "interpreting angel" of apocalyptic writings, but there is nothing apocalyptic about the book of Ezekiel.

The description of the temple is a plan, not a series of cross sections; this plan is clear enough. We must visualize a large square—the symbol of perfection—of some 350 feet (100 meters) on each side. Three gates in the center of three sides of the square, the north, south, and east, give access to the great court. Backed against the walls, inside, is a series of rooms with kitchens placed in the four angles of the square. In the middle of the great court thus delineated there is another square, about 175 feet (50 meters) on each side, surrounded by a wall; this square also has three gates. If one enters the inner court formed by this square through the east gate facing the Mount of Olives, one finds the altar; continuing in the same direction, toward the west, one sees a door opening onto a vestibule that adjoins the room called "the Holy," behind which, still in the same direction, is "the Holy of Holies."

The gates of the outer and inner courts are alike and resemble the typical gates of cities of the ancient Near East, whose openings were narrower than the passages into which they led. These passages were flanked by two or three rooms where guards were posted to watch over the entrance. In the description of Ezekiel's temple these gates are built toward the inside as far as the external encircling wall is concerned; this was the case for typical city gates. Conversely, as far as the inner court and its entrances are concerned, the narrow entrance is built toward the outside. Moreover, each level of the edifice is built about three feet (one meter) higher than the preceding: the whole of the temple is about three feet (one meter) higher than the profane surroundings; the inner court about three feet above the outer court. Behind the Holy of Holies there is a large rectangular space for the needs of the priests.

The meticulous description of the sanctuary is guided by two very precise principles. First, there is the concern for symmetry and proportion, always regarded as a manifestation of perfection and, as a consequence, an attribute of God. Second, by comparison with what we know of the first Temple, the reinforcement of the control (for instance, the "military" gates) of the entrances to the sanctuary shows the pains taken to avoid by all possible means the profanations that Ezekiel himself never ceased to denounce in the course of his ministry (see chs. 8–11). One would have expected the description of the altar at the end of ch. 42, but this is located, in fact, after the depiction of the return of the glory in 43:1-12, in which one finds again the full power of Ezekiel's inspiration.

Return of the Glory of God (43:1-12)

Verse 3 explains that this vision, this experience, is of the same kind as the two preceding theophanies at the time of the destruction of the city and at the time of Ezekiel's call. The arrival of the glory of God is sparely described. There are few theophanic elements: the noise of the mighty waters and the radiance. The glory follows the same road, but in reverse, as its departure in 10:19; 11:23. The glory of God fills the house. This can have two meanings: either the building containing the Holy of Holies or, in a wider sense, the whole of the Temple precincts. Here it seems that the Holy of Holies is meant. It is there that God speaks to the prophet to designate this dwelling as God's own. An all-important detail is added: *forever.* This is the nucleus of God's discourse.

Foreigners, Priests, and Levites (Ezekiel 44)

Verses 1-3 offer some interesting information: first, the fact that the prince sits down at the east gate of the inner court to take his food after the sacrifices of communion; then the fact that this gate remains always closed. The gate is closed because the glory of God came back through it into the temple; it has been sanctified in a particular way. The closed gate has been one of the themes rarely encountered in Christian iconography inspired by Ezekiel.

The closed gate has been interpreted by certain theologians as a symbol of the Virgin Mary and her virginity. Despite the birth of Jesus the gate remained closed, and at the same time it became in a certain way the *janua coeli* (gate of heaven). Popular devotion has thus acclaimed her in the litany of the Virgin, but the connection with Ezekiel is certainly now unrecognized.

The closed gate is probably at the root of another popular tradition. In what remains of the Temple of the time of Christ, enlarged and embellished by Herod the Great, the gate in the enclosing wall of the Temple called the "golden gate" is always closed in the expectation of the Messiah.

Verses 4-31 are concerned with other serious problems. On the one hand, there is the question of foreigners and their access to the sanctuary. Without circumcision, men could not enter the sanctuary. Of course, circumcision existed before Ezekiel and the exile, but it was at that time that it took on its religious dimension. Then it became the sign of a male's belonging to the people of Israel, the sign of God's promise to God's people. Verse 9 uses two significant expressions: circumcision of heart and flesh. Jeremiah especially gave a poignant force to circumcision of the heart (Jer 4:3-4; 9:24-25), but Ezekiel's text became a sort of motto of Judaism, and at the time of Christ there was posted at the entrance of the Temple an inscription forbidding entrance into the Temple to every pagan, which came down to saying every uncircumcised male. To receive circumcision was proof that a man's conversion to Judaism was genuine and total. It is not surprising that there were more women "proselytes" than men. The difficulties caused by the question of circumcision in the early Christian community are well known: must a man be a Jew, that is, be circumcised, in order to be a Christian?

Then there are the quarrels with the Levites. The origin, differences, and distinctions between Levites, priests, and levitical priests, that is, descendants of Zadok, are not all that clear. What seems certain is that Ezekiel takes the side of the Jerusalem priesthood against the priesthood of other sanctuaries, left unemployed as a consequence of the deuteronomic reform and centralization of worship (see 2 Kings 23:8-9), but he disapproves of the levitical priests of Deuteronomy (Deut 18:1-8). These priests probably served idols in sanctuaries other than that of Jerusalem. However, besides the fact that until the deuteronomic reform these sanctuaries were perfectly Yahwist, and no more defiled than the Temple in Jerusalem (see Ezekiel 8–10), it was only the centralization of worship in Jerusalem that disqualified them. The "Levites" are therefore relegated to subordinate positions whereas the priests who are descendants of Zadok retain the true priestly power. It goes without saying that the persons who altered these texts of Ezekiel are part of this group, like Ezekiel himself. That there was strife between the different priestly circles is evident. The last part of the chapter is devoted to precise norms concerning priestly life.

Division of the Territory, Place and Role of the Prince (Ezekiel 45–46)

To begin with, we must notice that the text no longer speaks of a king; the experience of the monarchy seems to have so baneful that even the word is avoided (see ch. 34). Here the term used is *nāsîʾ* ("chief," "prince"). This person plays a restricted role. A series of norms regulate his place in worship and society: he is firmly hemmed in by limitations. The setting of limits on royal authority was a trend already present in Deuteronomy (17:14-20). The prince is no longer the cornerstone of Israelite society; he is subject to the Law. In Ezekiel the prince is *de facto* in a position of dependence on the priests who have direct access to the inner sanctuary, the source of the people's life. The religious and political institutions exchange place and role. Before the exile the priest was only a delegate of the king. After the return from Babylon the prince is subordinated to the priest. These quarrels between the different institutions of the OT may seem childish to us. However, a quick perusal of the history of Christianity proves to what extent such quarrels have influenced the relationship between the "temporal" and "spiritual," even within Reformed churches. How many times has appeal been made to the OT, and Ezekiel in particular, to gain the advantage in the innumerable conflicts between civil and religious power! There is need for a serious hermeneutics in the reading and use of biblical texts when it comes to the relationship between politics and religion. In this domain, the quoting of proof texts is never to the point.

The Paradisiacal Fountainhead (Ezekiel 47)

We arrive at one of the high points in Ezekiel's book: the source of life-giving water flowing from the Temple. Even though the text is somewhat disfigured by additions, it still retains great power. Water appears fourteen times in this unit, twice seven, the symbol of plenitude multiplied by two—abundance and plenitude. It would be difficult to find a better image to describe the new life flowing from the presence of God "forever" in the midst of God's people. The image of the fountainhead has a before and an after. The water welling up from the Temple flows to the south, approximately the direction of the torrent Kidron, normally fed by the spring Gihon. Jerusalem lives by this spring and in its history there have been high moments: for instance, the anointing of Solomon as king (1 Kings 1:32-40). But now the spring wells up from Jerusalem, and it fills two functions: to cleanse the Dead Sea and to enliven the desert along its banks with Edenic life. The increasing quantity and depth of the water as it gets farther and farther from the Temple symbolizes its greater and greater efficacy. One hardly escapes being reminded of ch. 37 where life takes on other but equally powerful images and forms.

Of course, like fire, water is ambivalent, in religions in general and in the OT in particular. The Flood is the water of punishment; the water of the Reed Sea is death for the Egyptians, life for the Israelites. Anthropologically every culture and every civilization gives water a primordial place. Ancient cosmogonies often make water the source of life—the primordial Ocean, the Original Water; even in Genesis "a wind from God swept over the face of the waters" (1:2) before creation. Water is indispensable to humankind. "Bread and water," this is life's minimum and necessary requirement, what is given even in the recesses of a prison, what is consumed unless one engages in a complete fast. Mastery over water gave rise to the civilizations of Egypt and Mesopotamia. Today the control of the water supply gives power to states that are fortunate enough to have such a supply. Access to water is the cause of interminable conflicts. Aqueducts will soon be as numerous as oil pipelines. A vital force, water is a major concern of today's civilizations: polluted water, treated water, disputed water. Water—yesterday, today, and tomorrow.

There is nothing surprising in the fact that the NT confers on water the life-giving force of definitive salvation, especially in the Fourth Gospel, not only in the episode of the conversation with the Samaritan woman (John 4) but also in John 7:37-39 where Jesus at the Feast of

Booths invites all to come to him so that streams of living water may flow from believers. Furthermore, these two passages must be read in connection with John 2:13-22 where the new temple is Christ himself. Ezekiel's image: temple—presence of God—source of living water is seen as perfectly realized in the work and person of Christ. Is it excessively farfetched to read in this perspective the text of John 19:31-37, the water and the blood that flow from the side of the Crucified One? Would it have been possible not to make water an essential element of the sacrament of Christian initiation? What is surprising about the key celebration of the Christian faith, the paschal vigil, being centered on water and fire? And what shall we say concerning the blessing of water during this vigil, gloriously unfolding the "salvific history of water?" How can one not endorse the liturgical practice of the *Asperges* or the *Vidi aquam* at the beginning of the Eucharist?

The words of Ezek 47:1-12 sink their roots deep into the immeasurable waters of the human soul and at the same time serve as a bridge between human desire—the hope of Israel—and the new life brought by Christ whose crucified and glorious body becomes the spring welling up for all.

The New Boundaries of the Land (47:13–48:35a)

Coming down from these heights, the text returns to simpler realities: boundaries of the land, apportioning of the territory, everything that had begun in ch. 45. We must wait for the last sentence of the book to hear, as a closing, one of the central themes of Ezekiel's message: when all of this has taken place, the name of the city will be "YHWH is there."

BIBLIOGRAPHY

Cody, Aelred. *Ezekiel.* Wilmington, Del.: Michael Glazier, 1984.

Davis, Ellen F. *Swallowing the Scroll. Textuality and the Dynamics of Discourse in Ezechiel's Prophecy.* JSOT.S 78. Sheffield: Almond, 1989.

Greenberg, Moshe. *Ezekiel. A New Translation with Introduction and Commentary.* 2 vols. AB 22. Garden City, N.Y.: Doubleday, 1982–1983.

Joyce, Paul. *Divine Initiative and Human Response in Ezechiel.* JSOT.S 51. Sheffield: JSOT, 1989.

Lust, Johan, ed. *Ezekiel and His Book. Textual and Literary Criticism and Their Interrelation.* Leuven: Leuven University Press, 1986.

Zimmerli, Walther. *Ezechiel. A Commentary on the Book of Ezechiel.* Translated by Ronald Clements. 2 vols. Hermeneia. Philadelphia: Fortress, 1979.

Daniel

André LaCocque

FIRST READING

General Introduction

Because they speak of the end-time, providing keys to discerning the signs of the End in general and more specifically the end of contemporary "empires of evil," Daniel and Revelation are considered by some of their readers the most important books of the Bible. It is of particular interest that modern totalitarian governments, such as World War II Japan, for example, prohibited the reading of Daniel and Revelation in occupied territories. The belief that such books are subversive is historically grounded. Already in the first two centuries of our era in Palestine the cultivation of apocalyptic literature led to repeated bloody insurrections against Rome by Jewish parties convinced that the enormous military superiority of the Roman legions would be crushed under angelic armies. This had catastrophic effects. Jerusalem was razed to the ground and rebuilt as a "Jew-free" city. Palestine ceased for centuries to be the Jewish homeland it had always been since King David (tenth century B.C.E.). Thus what had been intended as subversive to the foreign powers became fraught with peril for the readers themselves.

The book is of a uniquely mixed character: it is bi-generic (narrative and apocalyptic), bi-lingual (Aramaic and Hebrew), bi-temporal (sixth century and second century B.C.E.). It tells the story of a great sage inspired by God (as were the prophets) and able to interpret the signs of the time as no one before (even surpassing the patriarch Joseph). In short, the book that we are about to read is very unusual; it is a strange book. Its form and style are unexpected; its diction is at times forbidding or at least mysterious. (For further comment on this topic, see the commentary on the book of Revelation, "First Reading.") It is fraught with dangers of misinterpretation. "Daniel A" (chs. 1–6) offers stories that can be easily dismissed as "childish," that is, poor in content and stretching credibility. "Daniel B" (chs. 7–12) presents predictions so fantastic and expressed in phraseology so contorted as to be suspect of disguising a lack of depth. No wonder that in the recent past apocalyptists were judged severely by scholars, who called them *epigones* (pale imitators) of classic prophets. Their visions were deemed artificial, even fabricated, prophecies *post eventum* (i.e., in retrospect). Nowadays, however, such scholarly condemnations have been all but abandoned. Daniel's visions are recognized as genuine spiritual experiences. The book is judged on its own terms without trying to measure it against the writings of other inspired people or other literary genres and without forcing it into the preconceived mold of classic wisdom or prophecy. The acknowledgment that the stories in "Daniel A" are not naive, but engage the political powers of second-century tyrants such as Antiochus IV, called Epiphanes, has opened up their symbolism and shown how powerfully effective they are as "good news" to the oppressed. As to "Daniel B," it claims to reveal the deepest secrets of the universe and of universal history. They are about the ultimate meaning of creation, the ultimate purpose of all that exists. The apocalyptist is convinced of arriving at the end of time and of being endowed with the charisma of understanding. Before his or her awestruck eyes the veil that covered the divine secrets is torn in two from top to bottom (cf. Matt 27:51).

Character of the Book

The book of Daniel represents a complex process of composition. One half of the book is made up of short stories with Daniel as a wise Jewish courtier in Babylon (Daniel A) and the other half is an apocalypse with Daniel as the visionary (Daniel B). The respective dates of origin of A and B are vastly different, the tales being much older than the apocalyptic part. The latter can be dated prior to 160 B.C.E., give or take a few years.

Daniel B is the first full-fledged apocalypse in the Bible. A second is found in the NT with the book of Revelation. In the Greek text of Theodotion for Dan 2:28, 29, 47 God is said to be *"apokaluptōn mysteria,"* (revealing mysteries). The best definition of the genre is proposed by John Collins: Within a narrative framework it is a revelation "mediated by an otherworldly being to a human recipient, disclosing a transcendent reality which is both temporal, insofar as it envisages eschatological salvation, and spatial as it involves another, supernatural world" (*Semeia* 14 [1979] 9). The apocalyptic genre is already present in Isaiah 24–27; Ezekiel 38–39; Zechariah; Joel 3; it has been used widely since that time. One finds apocalypses originating from Iran, Israel, and all lands that Christianity penetrated; they date from the second century B.C.E. onward. The Jewish and Christian apocalyptic literature knew its heyday from then until the second century C.E. Most of it is found in the so-called intertestamental literature such as 1 Enoch, 2 Baruch, 4 Esdras, etcetera. Their formative milieus vary, but not their subversive message announcing the end of an era with its politically oppressive regimes as well as of history and of the world. They present no hope that things will get better, for the succession of kingdoms goes downhill until it reaches its nadir, that is, pure evil. The world would then revert to nothingness were it not for God's inauguration of God's reign, an everlasting rule wiping out all historical regimes. At its head is God, or God's delegate who in Daniel is called "Son of Man" ("one like a human being").

One recognizes here the prophetic concern for history. But while the prophets emphasized historical change in Israel (return; conversion; restoration of fortune), apocalyptic eschatology has all but abandoned hope that a restoration event will occur in Israel. Rather for the apocalypse history contains within itself the key to divine secrets, the truth about its end in failure and the transcendence of its finality in the reign of God. The apocalypse contains a hero characterized by mantic (divinatory) wisdom. Daniel is such an ideal figure. He is able to read signs, interpret dreams, exegete texts, decipher strange writings, etcetera. In short, Daniel understands the secret message of God enshrined in creation and especially in the course of events (cf. 12:9).

Daniel displays an unprecedented synopsis of history, which may be seen as divided into four successive periods of decline, a vision that is surprisingly close to myth. Such universal consideration goes so far as to obliterate the very concept of *"Heilsgeschichte"* (salvation history), a most striking fact that, although not unique in the Hebrew Bible, is still unexpected in a genre whose special interest lies in eschatology (doctrine of the end-time). The eschatology here is cosmic and because of that it is paradoxically trans-historical, as the End comes not within history but after it. It is thus understandable that apocalypses were written and read as political manifestoes promising to oppressed people a divinely inaugurated realm that will bring both judgment and annihilation to wicked powers and blessing and triumph to the persecuted.

As a consequence history in the book of Daniel, while real, has a mythical face. So for instance the human empires in succession are described by Daniel 7 as four monstrous and hybrid animals emerging from the waters of the (primordial) ocean and representing the original chaos; they are ravaging the earth and are increasingly imposing evil that even reaches heaven itself and throws stars down from on high (8:10). God puts an end to this debauch of brutality by setting up a tribunal and delegating judgment and power to the "one like a human being (= Son of Man)" who comes to the scene among the clouds of heaven, thus recapitulating what was said of the god Baal in Canaanite (Ugaritic) literature. One may wonder about the re-adoption of myth that had been so adamantly condemned by the prophets of Israel. The reason for its resurgence is that the apocalyptists were conscious of evil as an absolute. If it is to be defeated more than flesh is required, "for our struggle is not against enemies of blood and flesh, but against . . . the cosmic powers of this present darkness, against the spiritual forces of evil in the heavenly places" (Eph 6:12; cf. Dan 10:20–11:1).

Like other biblical genres the apocalypse views history as having a beginning and an end. So also is human existence a finite life without reincarnation or "karma" renewal. In the world and in human life the events are always unique and non-repetitive; existence on this earth is finite; this world is only for a while.

The book of Daniel in its present form comes from the crucible of the first historical religious persecution ever, initiated by a man, Antiochus, whom many pious Jews (or "Hasidim") considered the last and ultimate incarnation of evil. From this perspective it is clear that the visions of Daniel are not abstract speculations, nor are they about events to come some twenty-two centuries later. They do not speak directly of Hitler, Stalin, Ghadafi, or Pol Pot. They speak specifically about the events of 167 to 164 B.C.E. when all Jewish religious practice was prohibited by the regime, when to circumcise a boy was to mark him for slaughter, when indeed people of all ages died as martyrs, honoring God rather than "Caesar."

Thus the readers of Daniel were not confused by names like Nebuchadnezzar, Belshazzar, Darius, or by the mythological figures of monsters or hybrid animals. They understood these as ciphers for specific powers of the second century B.C.E. The more the tyrants rage, the closer is the time of salvation. When Antiochus-the-Monster comes "into the beautiful land" (Israel) and accumulates victories and triumphs, when he goes out "with great fury to bring ruin and complete destruction to many . . . he shall come to his end, with no one to help him" (Dan 11:41-45).

One oppression strikingly resembles another. Suffering is uncannily uniform. Evil has a dramatically limited range of invention. In the sixth century B.C.E. under Nebuchadnezzar, in the second century under Antiochus, or in the twentieth century under a fascism, a communism, or a capitalism gone berserk, it is always a matter of erecting an idol representing the megalomania of some deranged individual or system and demanding a unanimous devotion. The statue is golden but its belly is a crematorium ready to consume all dissenters, all independent souls unwilling to disappear in the mass (see Daniel 3).

The claim of tyranny is that it will last forever. Nazism, Communism, Fascism thought that they would be there for another thousand years, and the ideological machines' victims themselves cannot foresee the end of their misery. In response the visionary proclaims the end as near, the reign of God as close at hand.

Formative Milieu of the Book

In view of what has been said it becomes possible to decipher the *Sitz im Leben* (setting in life) of the book of Daniel. It was written in reaction

a. to Antiochus Epiphanes's persecution;
b. to the Hellenization of the Middle East (with its conquest by Alexander the Great);
c. to the non-fulfillment of earlier prophecies of hope (according to which the destruction of Jerusalem by the Babylonians and the Judean exile were a last judgment that was to be followed by a glorious restoration).

The phenomenon of "Hellenization," a process through which a "Western" culture and way of life swept the Middle East, deserves reflection. New cities were founded on the model of the Greek *polis.* Their highly popular athletic competitions (in the nude), public baths, religious institutions with sacred prostitutes of both sexes, orgiastic festivals, etcetera, were to the pious Jew nothing short of abominable. In the public sphere those who resisted their attraction appeared backward and boorish. In Jerusalem the "elite" or the upper classes were open to Hellenism and the onus of responsibility rested on them when the persecution was unleashed. They requested the intervention of Antiochus IV against their fellow Jews in 167.

Daniel saw the Antiochian persecution as the last surge of evil in history and Hellenization as the ultimate test of the righteous ones. He saw the non-fulfillment of prophecy as the sign of the end of this era and the advent of a transhistorical/angelic dispensation.

General Contexts for Interpretation

Original Historical Contexts

The dating of Daniel's final composition is more precise than in the case of other biblical books. This is due to the fact that it is indirectly indicated within the text itself. In Daniel 11 the author reviews the events that led to the contemporary Antiochian persecution using slightly veiled language but with very specific reference to historical facts. Then, in vv. 40-45, he forecasts the end of the tyrant in a style sharply contrasting with what precedes. As long as the "prophecy" was *post eventum* (retrospective, presenting past historical events as if still to happen) the information was historically correct. When the text really does turn to the future, however, it ceases to be accurate. The death of the tyrant is described on the model of the enemy "falling upon the mountains of Israel" (Ezek 39:4; cf. Isa 10:5-11; 31:8-9; Ezekiel 38–39; see also Zech 14:2; Joel 3:2; Isa 14:25). We thus know for certain that Daniel 11 was written toward the end of the time of persecution and before the death of Antiochus, namely in 164.

Authorship

Daniel is a pseudepigraph (a work ascribed to an author other than the real one). The pseudepigraphic genre became most popular during the Second Temple period at a time that coincided with the rejection of contemporary prophecy (cf. Zechariah 13). The prophets' successors supported their claim to revelation by attributing their work to well-known spiritual leaders of ancient times.

The issue of the unity of authorship hinges on the striking difference of ethos in the two halves of the book. The difficulty is due not only to the difference of genres, and hence of styles, but also of atmosphere: While Daniel A presents the foreign courts as generally willing to promote Judeans to the highest positions and even as open to repentance when confronted with their injustices and shortcomings, Daniel B presents the reader with much more threatening displays of power on the part of foreign kingdoms, indeed with a catastrophic view of all sovereignty in history. Daniel A was certainly in existence long before the composition of the apocalyptic part. Those stories belonged to a traditional cycle of Daniel (or Danel) that can be traced back to Canaanite folklore. Its existence has been proven in recent times by the discovery among the Dead Sea scrolls of the so-called Prayer of Nabonidus (4QPrNab) and of the apocalypse of pseudo-Daniel (4QpsDan). These latter documents date from the first century B.C.E. but reflect older traditions. To these must be added the Greek Additions to Daniel, which in part will be dealt with below, and whose composition also comes from the same period. Against such background Daniel's author has reworked the material into its present shape to accommodate allusions to problems specific to the second century B.C.E., for instance the dietary laws (or *kashruth*) in 1:5-8; the king's (self-)deification in 6:6-10; the death of martyrs in 3:19-21; 6:17-23.

Canonical Contexts

The book of Daniel sheds light on the canonical process in the Bible. It belongs to the third part or *ketubim* (miscellaneous writings) of the Hebrew Bible, but to the second part or *nebiim* (prophets) in the Greek translation (Septuagint). This difference of attribution probably reflects Pharisaic suspicion vis-à-vis the apocalyptic genre. Furthermore one could argue that Daniel's inspiration is indirect because he cites his predecessors: for instance ch. 9 is based on Jeremiah 25 and 29; elsewhere he cites Habakkuk and Second Isaiah. Of interest is the judgment of a Talmudic text such as *b.Sanh* 94a that Daniel was both inferior and superior to (the last prophets) Haggai, Zechariah, and Malachi "for they were prophets and he was not. But he was their superior in that he saw the vision which they did not see." Incidentally, one will notice that Daniel is not compared here with prophets of the Exile in spite of its ostensible setting in sixth-century Babylon, but only with post-exilic prophets!

Daniel is, however, to be considered not only within the context of (mantic) wisdom, but also of the late (Second Temple) prophetic tradition. The modifications brought to the latter in Daniel deserve notice. Thus in mentioning Daniel 7 above we saw the reemergence of myth. With (post-)exilic prophecy of salvation, as a matter of fact, there occurred an eschatologization (a projection into the remotest future) of the Zion–David cultic tradition and the re-use of the motif of the fight against chaos, so omnipresent in myth (see, in the second part of the book of Isaiah, 43:16-18; 51:9-11; cf. 8:7-8; 28:15). In pre-exilic conceptions an enemy had been regarded as a scourge to punish Israel, but not so in Daniel. The foe of the community is also the enemy of God, a theme already found in Isaiah 10, for example, but now becoming an apocalyptic trademark: cf. Ezekiel 38–39; Zechariah 12–14; (Judith 1–3).

In a similar vein the motif of a pagan ruler going up to the heavens to set his throne above the stars, supreme expression of his hubris (see Daniel 7) is already extant in Isaiah 14 (vv. 3-15), a dirge deeply influenced by mythology. Furthermore, on the model of Ezekiel 1 and 43 the cultic (and mythic) "visibility" of God reappears in Dan 7:13. God is the king of kings, and Daniel attributes to the quasi-hypostasis sitting at the right of the Ancient of Days the role of supreme judge, on the model of the evocation of an angel with similar functions in Ezekiel 8–11 and 43. Indeed the parallels with Ezekiel 8 are impressive (as they are for the same reasons with Psalm 110). The angelic anthropomorphic personage found in Ezekiel, and then in Daniel's "Son of Man," is a bridge between two worlds, the celestial and the terrestrial. This is a fundamental concept in the apocalypse genre.

Synagogue and Church Usage

An important milestone on the road to Daniel's canonization is found in 1 Macc 2:59-60 (about the end of the second century B.C.E.) where Mattathias exhorts his sons to remember the martyrdom in the furnace of Hananiah, Azariah, and Mishael, and of Daniel in the lion-pit (see also 3 Macc 6:6-7, first century). On the other hand Daniel is inscribed within an evolving line that started with so-called pre-apocalyptic texts (such as Ezekiel 38–39; Third Isaiah [55–66]; Joel; Zechariah) as well as apocalyptic parts of the intertestamental document called 1 Enoch (some parts of which are of the third century B.C.E.).

As to the gospels, the most striking feature that reveals the deep influence of Daniel is of course the expression "Son of Man" in Jesus' mouth. As is well known, it is at times difficult to decide whether it is a simple way of speaking of himself, equivalent to the first person singular, or if it is a generic term for humanity in general, or again a titular designation of a heavenly and eschatological figure (cf. especially Mark 13:26 and Matthew 24). Jesus does speak in some places of that "Son of Man" (of Daniel 7–8).

Excursus I: The Influence of Daniel on the Gospels and the Book of Revelation

The ambiguity of the expression "Son of Man" served the Markan theme of Jesus' "messianic secret" well: as a human Jesus was to suffer and die (Mark 8:31; 9:31); as the one expected with the clouds of heaven he was to come again in his glory (Mark 8:38; 13:26; 14:62). The same dialectical conception is present throughout the Gospel of John. There the emphasis is on the preexistence of Jesus and his eschatological judgment that, paradoxically, is effected during his ministry (see especially John 3 and 5). In Matthew, where the notion of kingdom is central, the Son of Man is described as the royal judge on the model of Daniel 7 (Matthew 13; 16; 24; 25). The Son of Man to whom belongs the last judgment is also a theme present in Mark 8:38; 14:62; Rev 1:7; 14:14. In those texts "coming on the clouds" is a movement down from heaven to earth and the scene is eschatological. At times, however, the movement is understood as going from earth to heaven, and then the allusion is to the ascension of Christ (see Matt 26:64; Luke 22:69; Acts 7:56).

The book of Revelation deserves special mention. Here the "one like a son of man" is an angelic figure, thus retrieving a meaning that may be aboriginal (see below at Daniel 7). Through some kind of conflation, however, both the figures of "the Ancient of Days" and "one like a son of man" designate in Revelation the Christ exalted.

Naturally several features of the NT use of Daniel are found again in patristic literature where there are four applications of Daniel's visions to the person and ministry of Christ: (1) his human nature; (2) his celestial origin; (3) his ascension; (4) his second coming.

As for Christian liturgy, it uses the book of Daniel on the Feast of Christ the King (every year). Daniel 12:1-3 (on the resurrection) is read in conjunction with Mark 13:24-32 (the "Son of Man" sends his angels to gather his elect from the ends of the earth). On the preceding Sunday, once every three years, Dan 7:13-14 (the enthronement of the "Son of Man") is read with John 18:33-37 ("my kingdom is not of this world . . ."). Moreover, every second year the

Church prepares for this feast by meditating on Luke 21 (signs of the end of time) in the context of Daniel (chs. 1; 2; 5; 6; 7).

Present Significance

Within the two parts of Daniel history is seen as a whole and as universal, a notion that had to wait until the European eighteenth century to triumph! Moreover history is non-repetitive: events occur once for all and along a line that has a beginning and an end. Each "empire" in succession is worse than its predecessor until the absolute evil comes "incarnated" in a tyrant the like of which the world never experienced before. Antiochus IV Epiphanes in the second century B.C.E. was seen as the head of the "fourth empire" (or the "fourth beast") that dwarfed all previous manifestations of arrogance and cruelty and brought about in Israel the "ultimate" crisis, even winning the favor of some Israelites through deception; his evil power went so far as to be able to sweep some stars down from heaven (8:10). Such a vision does not look unfamiliar in our own days, but the apocalypse comes with its indefectible trust that God will triumph, if not in human history, then beyond history, after the end of the world.

There is here a vibrant affirmation that death (individual as well as collective) is not the last word of God. Daniel 12 is the first Biblical text expressing faith in the resurrection of the just, those whose fidelity to their religion led to martyrdom (see 1 Macc 1:49-64; 2 Maccabees 6–7), later called in Hebrew *"qiddush ha-Shem,"* the sanctification of the divine Name.

The resurrection follows a universal divine judgment. In Daniel 7 heavenly thrones are being set for the final trial of the earth. This remarkable notion, as well as all the other elements of Daniel 7, knew an immediate and lasting success. Most impressive is the pairing of "the Ancient of Days" with a heavenly figure appearing to the seer as "one like a son of man" (like a human being). This apocalyptic breakthrough changed for ever the nature of messianic expectations in Israel. Jesus' mission is a fulfillment of that expectation.

Today the resilience of apocalypticism is obvious in the ongoing existence of Christian apocalyptic sects who often seriously misunderstand the direct meaning of these texts. The sects calculate the date of the *parousia* despite Mark 13:22, and they have successively identified the Fourth Beast (see also Rev 13:18) with every tyrant of the twentieth century. This literalist interpretation not only proves fallacious time after time but is an obstacle to authentic understanding of the apocalypse. The message is one of hope in the midst of despair. Such a message is in no need of being reduced to fantastic speculations.

SECOND READING

Daniel A: Daniel 1–6

Daniel 1

Daniel and His Companions are Introduced, 1:1-21

This is a kind of prologue. Already at this point it becomes clear that a narrative cycle of Daniel has been reworked, reshaping the hero and his historical setting to fit the circumstances and problems of the second century B.C.E. Thus for instance the issue of *kashruth* (dietary laws) comes to the fore (1:5-8).

From the outset there is emphasis on politics. The captives are trained to become reliable courtiers at the foreign seat of power. Even their regimen is a means to make them accept another identity, which consequently entails their renaming. Thus simultaneously the young Jews are promoted and demoted; they earn a new status by losing their former one. The stories in Daniel 1–6 are to be read against that background. The problem is to know whether Daniel and companions will fail as servants of a King more powerful than Nebuchadnezzar. That is why their request not to eat and drink the royal diet alerts the reader to a coming confrontation with the powerful of "Babylon." So the book opens on a negative and ominous note and it will end on the evocation of the final cataclysm (12:9-13).

The situation of the Judeans recalls the "royal pages (boys)" of the Hellenistic courts. The training of Daniel and his companions before their introduction to the king is characteristic of that of the ideal scribe in the ancient Near East. Furthermore Hellenistic education *(paideia)* could transform a "barbarian" into a Hellene in the eyes of the contemporary Greeks. In such a milieu the question of *kashruth* in particular would find all its urgency (see 1 Macc 1:63; 2 Macc 5:27; Est 14:17; etcetera, and especially *Jubilees* 2:16).

"Good looks" are often ascribed to kings (cf. 1 Sam 9:2; 10:23; 16:6, 12, 18; Ps 45:2), and the mention that they are "without blemish" recalls 2 Sam 14:25 describing Absalom son of David. It is a cultic expression describing the priests or their offerings (Lev 21:17-23; 22:17-25). Note that Daniel, according to 1:3, is of Davidic descent. In short, the sage Daniel at the royal court is in a familiar environment; his rank enables him to talk to the king face to face.

It is a sign of the times that Daniel has two names, one "pagan" and the other Jewish: Belteshazzar (cf. 1:7) and Daniel (cf. also Ezek 14:14, 20; 28:3; see *1 Enoch* 6; 7; 69:2; on the basis of an ancient Canaanite hero by the name of Danel). A parallel is provided by Esther whose Jewish name was Hadassah. He lives in two worlds (cf. chs. 1 and 6), has two occupations (courtier and visionary), speaks two languages (Chaldean and Aramaic, cf. 2:4), and lives, so to speak, in two different epochs, the sixth century (the time of the Babylonian exile) and the second century (the generation for which he has visions).

The change of names (v. 6) is an important process of transformation (cf. Gen 41:45, Joseph's Egyptian "naturalization"). The four names' derivations are complex but it is clear that they are, as usual in the ancient world, invocations of divinities. From start to finish Daniel is set by the author within a highly religious environment and his dealings will definitely be religious. The confrontation between YHWH and the pagan gods has started. The polite refusal of the royal regimen went much beyond expediency and in contrast to Esther the foreign names given to the Judeans will not "stick," so to speak. Daniel remains forever in the tradition "Daniel," not Belteshazzar!

The main point of the chapter is paradoxical: the Judeans' wisdom and usefulness to the crown surpasses by far any corresponding virtue of those whose allegiance to Nebuchadnezzar is unconditional! Such paradox is, of course, fundamental for the Jewish Diaspora (see the story of Joseph or of Esther) and is indeed normative for the Jewish people or for the Church "in the world." Here the four Judeans' wisdom is characterized by their capacity to interpret dreams. Dreams, in fact, play an important part in the whole book. Clearly Daniel is here put on a par with the patriarch Joseph: both are at a foreign court and both see the dreams of their non-Israelite masters as prophetic (cf. Gen 20:3-7; 31:24; Jdg 7:13-15; Matt 2:12; 27:19). Daniel 1 is a self-portrait of Daniel's authorship, that of someone convinced of being privy to the secrets of God (cf. also 4:6; 5:11-12).

Daniel 2

Nebuchadnezzar's Dream
About the Statue, 2:1-49

This important chapter gives the tone to Daniel A as a whole. Made up of four different parts, it may originally date from the fourth century but there have been evident second-century revisions.

2:1-12: The irony present in ch. 1 continues. There is something demented in the king demanding that his dream be retold by others, a feat that is unique in ancient annals. In the power game the more irrational the demand, the greater the power of the demander. In reality Nebuchadnezzar shows himself a pathological megalomaniac (cf. v. 11, "no one . . . except the gods"). Note that his "sages" do not acquit themselves much better. They have so far manipulated their king; now that the moment of truth has come they are in total disarray. This gives the author the opportunity to denounce the inanity of human wisdom as well as magic, for God alone is sovereign over history and can reveal its secrets. The parallel with the story of Joseph is clear. Indeed, our chapter in Daniel is close to Gen 41:8, 16, 24.

Verse 1 presents an impossible chronological "precision" that contradicts 1:5, 18. This lack of consistency is a sure sign that these stories of the Daniel cycle had an independent existence before being re-used in the extant composition.

Verse 4: "in Aramaic"! The word may be original here or a marginal note that was later integrated in the text by mistake. However that may be, at this point the language of the tales in Daniel A changes from Hebrew to Aramaic. It will finally revert to Hebrew with the beginning of ch. 8 (apart from the Greek Additions, of course). Aramaic became the diplomatic language from the seventh century on (cf. 2 Kings 18:26); thus its mention here is not anachronistic.

2:13-16: The potentate's decision to destroy the wisdom cadres of his empire belongs to the same equation of power with insanity. What is decided amounts to self-destruction, of which the twentieth century is particularly rich in examples (one thinks of Cambodia, the USSR, North Korea, Bosnia, Rwanda, etcetera).

Popular lore places sage courtiers among the magicians and sorcerers at foreign courts. This was already true of the earlier stories with Moses and Aaron in Exodus 3–11. Thus when God's people triumph it is on the very terrain of their pagan competitors. At first Daniel and his companions are conspicuously absent from the stage, as if Daniel was unknown and then "discovered," as in the story of Susanna (see below). He and his companions learn about the exorbitant demand of the king and know that they will be under threat if the demand of the king is not satisfied. Nebuchadnezzar pretends that he does not remember his night vision. Jewish postbiblical tradition sees that oblivion as real and a kind of psychological blockage. The sages of Babylon tell the king: no one who is not divine (v. 11) is able to "reveal it to the king." Thus in the latter part of this chapter Nebuchadnezzar bows before Daniel as before a divinity. Such a demonstration of allegiance has been anticipated and prepared from the start.

2:17-28: What the king has dreamed is revealed by God to Daniel in a vision that, in conformity with apocalyptic conception, comes after due preparation and prayer (cf. Daniel 9). The suspense relaxes but will be woven again, for the dream is ominous and its retelling to the king will be fraught with extreme danger. Daniel, however, praises God for breaking the stalemate. He trusts that the One who is unveiling the secret is also the One who will protect. There is here a sort of epistemological reflection on revelation, where it comes from, to whom it is given, and for what purpose. In this particular instance God has found a worthy recipient in Daniel, a just and saintly man. The human mediation is indispensable, for God has chosen to remain, as it were, behind the scene. The function of the Israelite at the court is one of interpretation. The "signs" are everywhere to be read, but all the experts in divination of Babylon need Daniel to tell their meaning.

Daniel's superior spirit does not come from his own skills but from "the God of heaven" (v. 19). This divine title given currency by the Persian overlords is already present in Gen 24:7. Daniel's prayer for illumination ends in v. 23. It gives us some idea of the Jewish liturgies in Aramaic and of the influence upon them of deuteronomistic theology (see especially Daniel 9, below).

Daniel had affirmed that "[God] changes times and seasons" (v. 21; see 7:12), a polemical thrust against Babylonian astrology (and also against Hellenistic "fate"). From that perspective the visionary announces to Nebuchadnezzar the coming of the "end of days" (v. 28): time is not cyclical; it is not a wheel spinning around its axis and bringing with regularity the "eternal return" of the same. With this meaning of the term "end," however, we are still close to classical understanding: the king has foreseen the end of his empire as well as of all empires, but the "eschaton" is deferred, a sign that our text stands between the decline of prophecy and the rise of apocalypticism.

2:29-45 constitute the third part of the development. Daniel has gone before the king confident that the truth is self-demonstrating, undeniable, and liberating. Like Moses returning to confront Pharaoh, Daniel does a courageous thing. The accent of the story, however, is not on the messenger's intrinsic qualities but on God's fidelity toward God's servants. The content of the dream is exposed (vv. 31-35). The king saw a huge colossus of composite materials. There actually were immense statues that Daniel's author might have seen or heard about, for instance in Thebes, Rhodes, or Babylon (cf. Herodotus, *Histories* 1.183). Here the statue is divided into four parts according to a now familiar schema that divides history into four empires that dominated the ancient Near East from the sixth to the second century B.C.E.: Babylon, Media, Persia, and Macedonia/Greece, with the latter being divided after Alexander's death; the Seleucids received Syria and the Ptolemies Egypt. This fourfold schema is old; it is found in Hesiod (eighth–seventh centuries B.C.E), *Works and Days* 109–201; Polybius (202–120 B.C.E.), *History* 38.22; Ovid (43 B.C.E.–28 C.E.), *Metamorphoses* 1.89-150. In the Bible itself see Gen 4:17-18; Zech 1:18-21; 2:6, and elsewhere. In Daniel these terrible empires will be followed by the extra-historical reign of God (not a fifth empire).

According to an old list Assyria comes first; Daniel, however, begins with Babylon, the power that destroyed the Temple and exiled Daniel and his people, thereby displacing forward the envisaged chronology. The "head of gold" is the Babylonian Nebuchadnezzar (2:37-38). He is "king of kings" (a Persian title) and reigns even over "the wild animals of the field, and the birds of the air" (v. 38) in accordance with the myth of the primal human (see Ezekiel 28). Babylonian kings reenacted it by keeping wild animals in menageries as a symbol of their universal domination (see Jer 27:6 and 18:14). The human empires are initiated by Nebuchadnezzar and continue till the end of times as a single undertaking doomed to destruction. They are four reigns rolled up into one and they are sweepingly condemned as idolatry.

After Babylon comes Media (2:39). Then comes Persia, and the fourth empire/reign is Greek. It is stronger than the preceding ones it smashes, but its unprecedented extension will have fragile foundations. Its feet are partly iron, the representative metal of that kingdom, and in part "potter's clay." The unity of Alexander's conquests was in fact ephemeral. The Seleucids in Syria and the Ptolemies in Egypt, among others, disputed its spoils.

As the colossus's feet are partly in ceramic a little stone is all it takes to overthrow the edifice. By contrast the stone is indestructible. Of utmost importance is that the stone is "cut out not by human hands" (v. 34; in rabbinic literature the stone is the Messiah; so also in some of the patristic works). In Daniel, God acts independently of human politics. The little stone becomes a mountain, fills the earth, and crushes under itself all the empires (vv. 44-45). In fact, according to v. 35 the stone becomes a great boulder, a term that in Scripture is regularly associated with the divine presence; cf. Num 20:8; Deut 32:4-18; Isa 8:14; 51:1.

2:46-49, the fourth part, shows Nebuchadnezzar prostrating himself before Daniel who, unexpectedly, does not protest. The text is consistent with biblical prophecy: the nations must some time fall down before Israel and lick the dust (cf. Isa 4:23; 45:11-24). There is here, besides, a possible allusion to a legend according to which Alexander the Great did prostrate himself before the high priest Simon, saying: "It is not him I am worshiping, but the God who honored him with the office of high priesthood" (Josephus, *Ant.* 11.8.5). The great conqueror also shocked his liberal generals in accepting that his Oriental subjects prostrate before him. This opened the door to his successors' self-deification. Daniel 2:46 "demythologizes" this practice in having an alleged god, Nebuchadnezzar, worshiping a man, Daniel.

Verses 48-49 are about the promotion of Daniel and his companions. The parallel with Joseph in Egypt is again clear; one thinks also of Mordecai in the book of Esther (8:1-2). The last note of the chapter about the division of tasks between Daniel and his three companions is in preparation for the following chapter from which, most surprisingly, Daniel is absent.

Daniel 3

Nebuchadnezzar Sets up a Golden Statue, 3:1-18

Daniel does not appear in this new confrontation with pagan powers. The LXX adds a date: the eighteenth year of Nebuchadnezzar (587). Thus the erection of the statue by the Babylonian commemorates the ruin of Jerusalem. One can recognize Antiochus's persecution in the background. Although the statue is not called an idol the response demanded from the populace is one of worship (a technical term appears in the original). The regime's stability seems to be made visible in the monolithic aspect of one huge statue, but it is shown for what it actually is: a crematorium. Death is the great equalizer; the symbol of the empire is an ash-urn; its national anthem is nothing but an endlessly repeated slogan whose force of conviction resides entirely in its reiteration (cf. vv. 5, 7, 15).

The exorbitant royal demand that all nations worship his statue and the threat to dismember any opponent is anachronistic during the Babylonian regime or at any time before the era of Antiochus's religious and cultural madness (cf. 1 Macc 1:41-53). (For a discussion of the cult of the emperors that started during Hellenistic times from the fourth century B.C.E. onward, see the commentary on the book of Revelation "First Reading.")

Chapter 3 is an exhortation to martyrdom (cf. 1 Macc 1:57-63; 2 Maccabees 6–7). Perhaps the young men's miraculous salvation foreshadows the resurrection of the just in ch. 12; it is so interpreted in early Christian art and Jewish literary tradition.

By contrast with chs. 1 and 2, Daniel 3 presents a very different royal state of mind. If the stele (rather than statue) is not the king himself it is all the same a manifestation of grotesque hubris. Some conservative scholars have suggested that the king here wants to give shape to his dream in ch. 2. It is simpler to think of a previous independent existence of the tale in oral tradition. In its present form the incorporation of Persian and Greek terms betrays its later reworking. Noticeable are the Greek words *"psaltērion"* and *"symphonia,"* which Polybius associates with Antiochus's taste for the bagpipe or double flute. The *"kitharis"* and the *"sambuke"* are also Greek.

3:1-12: We find here a story of passive resistance. The young Jews who shunned the royal diet in ch. 1 now do not obey a kingly order they find to be in contradiction with their primary allegiance to God. True, they do not wield a power to match that of the tyrant, but at least they can refuse to be contaminated by his insanity. They do not plot a revolution, but still this apparently inoffensive resistance is deemed intolerable because it questions the very totalitarian ideology that suffers no dissidence lest it die.

3:13-18: The action had started in v. 8: the "Chaldeans" or Babylonian sages denounce the Jews' reluctance to worship the statue; this in turn provokes the king's fury (v. 13; a familiar theme in popular lore). But in spite of his terrible threats, affirming as a fact that no one can save from the absolute potentate, not even a god (v. 15), the young men remain firm in their position and will not compromise with idolatry. In a declaration that constitutes one of the biblical jewels they say that whether or not God is able/willing to save them this will not alter their fidelity to God. They expect no reward (cf. Job 1:9; 13:15, which according to one tradition reads: "Behold He may slay me; Him will I trust."). Thus the King is utterly defeated; the love of God has surpassed the fear of dying.

The Youths in the Fiery Furnace, 3:19-30

The story moves from the royal threat to its execution. Nebuchadnezzar is miming his own erected image! The king's face is distorted and the furnace is overheated: the one is prolongation of the other. This is a shocking reversal of Gen 1:28 where it is said that the human is the image of God. Hubris has changed human glory (cf. Psalm 8) into a grimacing idol, rigid, lifeless, horrible. Death is already stamped on his face and those he controls are zombies whose purposeless death means nothing.

The "furnace of blazing fire," veritable dramatic focus of the tale, recalls Deut 4:20: the Exodus was salvation from the furnace (see also Jer 1:13-19; 29:21-22). Nebuchadnezzar gives orders to tie up the youths (vv. 20-21) and we are reminded of the famous "binding" of Isaac (Genesis 22). Also, here as there, a substitution for the intended victim occurs at the last minute (v. 22). As an angel appeared to Abraham, so here the king sees in the furnace a divine/human epiphany. The figure looks "like a son of God/gods," a parallel expression to Daniel 7's simile, "like a son of man." Although conspicuously absent here, Daniel comes to mind: he too is filled with the spirit of God/gods (cf. 4:5, 6, 15; 5:12; 6:4) and he also is called a "son of man" (= mortal) in 8:17. This probably explains why Theodotion (codex Chisianus) calls the angel "the vigilant watcher angel Daniel," In this interpretation Daniel is not as absent from this chapter as it first seemed.

Right after v. 23 in the Greek version come the beautiful Prayer of Azariah and The Song of the Three Young Men. They are later additions and had originally nothing to do with their present context. This is no reason for disregarding those prayers that have enriched the Church's liturgy. They were inserted at this place in Daniel because it was felt inappropriate that martyrs would go to their death without uttering a prayer to God.

Strikingly, the deliverance occurs within the furnace, not from it (vv. 24-27). This trait of the story is most compelling because it corresponds to a concept of the saving God as participating in the suffering of God's children. The king rejected the thought of a god capable of delivering from his hand but he could not fathom that the God of his victims would be going into hell with them to protect them there, thus vindicating their martyrdom by being co-victim with them. As Elie Wiesel reports in his classic work "Night," someone witnessing the torture of a young lad in an extermination camp asked "and now, where is God?"—to which was responded, "He is there hanging on the gallows."

The angelic presence in the furnace unsettles completely the set of events programmed by the sick mind of the tyrant. Its appearance is "of a god" while it is counted as a fourth man in the fire (vv. 24-25). The Fathers of the Church saw there a close parallel with the "someone like a son of man" in Daniel 7. He is sitting in heaven at the right hand of God and is therefore, he also, "someone like a son of God!" Such is the divine response to a man who was playing God and making a fool of himself. Furthermore another major doctrine of Daniel B is adumbrated, namely the resurrection of the just. The dust and ashes into which the king thought of reducing the faithful is, as it were, once again the material for the creation of humanity.

3:28-30: The chapter ends with the royal verification of the miracle and with a striking royal confession of respect for the Jewish God followed by a decree that reverses the initial ordinance term for term. The reversal is also indicated by the fact that, following a folktale logic (cf. Esther), those who attacked God's people pay for their temerity with their lives. They undergo the fate they intended for others (cf. Deut 19:18). It is an illustration of the irresistibility of truth. Even Nebuchadnezzar must confess as much. The book presents us with other spectacular confessions of faith from an illustrious pagan as an indication that the times are ripe for an astonishing dénouement of history. Signs are accumulating in heaven and on earth: the end is at hand.

The young Jews' promotion brings the end of ch. 3 back to the point we left with the conclusion of ch. 2, as if those two tales had run parallel to one another.

Daniel 4

Nebuchadnezzar's Dream About the Cosmic Tree, 4:1-37

Daniel 4 is the result of different interwoven (oral?) traditions. This is reflected in the two versions of the story as found in the Masoretic (Hebrew) text and in the LXX (Greek). The latter is considerably longer than the Semitic text; the former betrays a linkage with and perhaps an imitation of other chapters of Daniel (e.g., the doxologies in 3:33 and 4:34-35 and those in 2:20-23 and 6:27-28). Strangely, in the Greek text the destroyed tree is changed into a beast. In both versions Nebuchadnezzar sees a cosmic tree that, here and in Ezekiel 3, symbolizes the union between gods and human beings, bridging the two worlds along an *axis mundi.* The tree recalls the statue of ch. 3, and indeed in both tales the hubris of the king is evident and causes his downfall. On that score although no literary element can be traced directly to the second century the contemporary reader had no difficulty in distinguishing the one who by derision was called Antiochus "Epimanes," the madman.

Within the Dead Sea manuscripts 4QPrNab (The Prayer of Nabonidus) does preserve more primitive features of the same tale. It presents the Babylonian king Nabonidus as seriously ill "for seven years in Teima(n)." A Jewish exorcist exhorts him to repent. After complying and being healed Nabonidus thanks the true God and renounces the false ones. There are possibly some remnants of history in this legend, for according to a Babylonian text Nabonidus left the regency to his son Belshazzar (different from Belteshazzar, the Babylonian name of Daniel in ch. 1). Daniel 5 mentions Belshazzar, who therefore is given a historical confirmation. As Nabonidus is never mentioned in the Bible, Daniel understandably substituted the name of Nebuchadnezzar, the pagan king *par excellence* who destroyed Jerusalem and the Temple.

Prefacing the story the Greek text provides a date, "the eighteenth year of Nebuchadnezzar" (as in 3:1 LXX; see above)—that is, again the date of the destruction of Jerusalem (cf. Jer 52:29)! By contrast with that profanation the king in v. 8 recognizes in Daniel the presence of "a spirit of the holy gods" (cf. Gen 41:38). As in Daniel 2 this charisma enables Daniel to explain the vision of the huge tree.

4:1-18: Nebuchadnezzar now speaks in the first person singular, and the narrative's movement is from end to beginning. The king again had a dream that proved premonitory. He actually saw an *axis mundi* joining heavens and earth; according to Daniel's interpretation the tree represents the dreamer himself. Thus in the king's eyes Babylonian power amounts to a cosmic force, a claim supported by the very name of Babylon which means "gate of the divine" in the image of the "Tower of Babel" in Genesis 11 (cf. here v. 22). As the latter story shows, hubris leads to catastrophe and the king should know it by now. His dream is a divine warning, as in ch. 2. Once again, the message is "always already there" but in need of being interpreted by a mediator, and once again, when the unveiling (apocalypse) has occurred, the truth of the message is obvious.

4:19-27: Daniel is overwhelmed by the enormity of the revelation. His wish that the dream be different is understandable, if only through deference for the king. Nebuchadnezzar's future is dismal. Although it is a cosmic tree it does not endure (in contrast with the righteous person who is also compared with a tree in Pss 1:3; 92:13-15). In imitation of Ezek 31:10-14 and Isa 6:13 Nebuchadnezzar's tree is cut down, hardly a stump remaining as a promise of regeneration (? v. 15). The iron and bronze bands around the amputated trunk are seen by Jerome as a strait-jacket, but for the medieval Jewish commentator Rashi they assure the stability of the throne (see v. 26). In light of a parallel text like Amos 3:12 survival is improbable but not impossible.

The point is elaborated by Daniel who advises the king how to change the course of events, which after all are not determined: i.e., v. 27 "break off your sins" through the practice of charity or almsgiving. Strikingly, Daniel uses the term "perhaps!" (v. 27) and we are reminded of Jonah 3:9, for example. It is in the perspective of that "perhaps" that Daniel selects in the royal dream the parts he wants to decipher and that may lead to the defeat of determinism. Surprisingly, we learn that history and the king's soul are in an uncanny correspondence. If Nebuchadnezzar practices righteousness and comes to the rescue of the oppressed not only his destiny but history in its universal dimension will be changed accordingly.

4:25-33: Daniel's advice remains unheeded and every detail of the king's dream comes true. This happens after a delay of twelve months, in parallel with the false prophet Hananiah's death two months after Jeremiah's prediction (Jer 28:1, 17). This is a time for reflection, pregnant with possibilities to acknowledge that "Heaven is sovereign" (v. 26). This is an important motif since Ezekiel, who insists on human recognizance as the ground for many a divine action. The same applies to the reprieve granted to Adam and Eve, who do not die on the spot after eating the forbidden fruit in spite of Gen 2:17. (Human hubris is far from absent from the Genesis narrative). Like Adam losing his glory, Nebuchadnezzar loses his kingship; in both cases animals play an important role, serving as reference to both demotions.

Within the discourse of Daniel one will notice the deft and dramatic shifting of the second person singular ("it is you, O king!" v. 22) to the third person ("the king saw . . ." v. 23) before reverting again to the second person (v. 25). Thus the discourse fits perfectly the alienation of the king who at some point becomes an "it" rather than a "thou"; he is totally dismissed as a decision-maker.

The King's malady recalls lycanthropy, which is the basis of the superstition about werewolves. This horrible sickness would spell the king's extinction were it not for the time limit, "seven times" (seven years, vv. 23, 25, 32, cf. 34; the historical Nabonidus may have spent ten years in Teima).

4:34-37: As also foretold by Daniel, the king repents and confesses that the God of Israel is sovereign over kings and empires (4:34-35). This restorative dénouement is appropriately in the first person (v. 34). Significantly, the confession is also a return to reason. As hubris was insanity, sanity is praising God; this is emphasized by v. 36, "at that time," or "at that very moment." As in the epilogue of the book of Job, the king having come to his senses is restored to his power, which is even increased in the aftermath of his confession. There are, however, ominous clues in the royal discourse, with an unexpected insistence on his person, "my reason . . . to me . . . my kingdom . . . my glory" etcetera. This closely resembles the boasting words that unleashed his recent chastisement.

Before we turn to ch. 5 some reflections are appropriate on the credit granted by Daniel to pagan rulers and their insights. The striking praises put in the mouths of Nebuchadnezzar (3:28-29; 4:34-37) or Darius (6:26-27) are such that they could have been placed on the tongue of the psalmists. It is most remarkable how characters escape their stereotypes. Nebuchadnezzar is not just the brutal destroyer of Jerusalem and Darius is genuinely attracted to the person of Daniel. In the same line Second Isaiah hailed king Cyrus as the Anointed of YHWH (see 45:1-17) and 1 Maccabees even describes the dying archvillain Antiochus as repenting of his crimes (see 6:12-13).

Clearly, with the exile in Babylon there was an Israelite "discovery" of the nations and a new appreciation for some of their achievements. Conceivably God could appoint Cyrus the Persian and call him God's messenger and "Messiah." Moreover Daniel's author and the party he represents in Judea are convinced of the worldwide irresistibility of the truth. Even the diehard idolaters on the throne of Babylon must bow to it, and this is itself an irrefutable sign of the coming of the end. There is a subtle shift of temporality from the prophetic "now, for it is not too late," to the apocalyptic "now or never."

Daniel 5

The Inscription on the Wall, 5:1-30

The atmosphere between Belshazzar and Daniel is friendly, but the king surpasses Nebuchadnezzar, his father (actually his grandfather) in profaning Jerusalem's sacred utensils (v. 2). History, as we saw, confirms Belshazzar's existence (as regent rather than as king). It also confirms the reports of Herodotus and Xenophon about the city's capture "without battle" by Cyrus during an orgy at the royal palace. The date was October 11, 539.

5:1-9: The great rulers of the past appear to later Israelite literary imagination as continually feasting (cf. Esther 1 and elsewhere). The presence of low-status women at those parties leaves no doubt about their orgiastic nature (cf. 2 Macc 6:4: Antiochus IV introduced sacred prostitutes in the personnel of the Temple). The blasphemy of using Jerusalem's spoils is compounded by the toasting to other gods or idols in v. 4. The vases consecrated to the glorification of God now serve the vulgar satisfaction of the lowest instincts. Moral affront shifts to religious outrage.

The orgiastic feast is suddenly interrupted by a detached hand writing on the plaster of the wall, but its text remains cryptic to the sages as were the earlier dreams and visions (v. 5). This verse introduces the drama in almost the same words as 4:36 "at that very moment," or "immediately," a supplementary link with the previous chapter that had ended on the note of human hubris. The lesson of the father is not learned by the son, a fact that is highlighted here by the king's (allegedly?) not knowing who Daniel is.

The scene in the banquet hall is haunting; it may be compared with 1 Samuel 28, the evocation by the Endor medium of Samuel's ghost. Appropriately the revelers are now replaced by sorcerers, diviners, conjurers, and the like. The stage is ready for another confrontation of God's people with the pillars of paganism (cf. Moses and Aaron, Joseph, Daniel in both canonical and extracanonical [Greek] traditions). Not surprisingly, the Babylonian sages are incapable, as they were in chs. 2 (v. 11) or 4 (v. 7). The parallel with ch. 2 is striking. Here also the inscription must first be read before it can be interpreted (v. 8). The king and his nobles are all the more baffled (v. 9).

5:10-16: On the intervention of the "queen" —Nebuchadnezzar's widow—who seems to remember Daniel (Joseph also had to be remembered in his prison), Daniel is introduced into the royal palace (v. 13). He is again recognized as endowed with special powers, with an extraordinary spirit (cf. 2:22; 4:5-8; Susanna 45). Again here a pagan is credited with insight; the only mistake of the queen is to believe that help will come from her own gods. At any rate the reader is warned that the nature of the inscription is extraordinary, yet the key to the enigma is very close, in the next room of the palace! It is at hand, but the king must want to receive it. Instead he shuns the simplicity of the solution; the Bible is full of such examples of people bypassing the obvious and looking for outlandish sham solutions.

Here the king addresses Daniel as an unknown (vv. 13-14), but he betrays himself by calling him an exile from Judah, which he did not hear from his mother. It is thus appropriate that Daniel would remind Belshazzar of his father and indirectly of how the latter, himself not immune from arrogance (v. 20), promoted him to a high rank. What happened to "the head of gold" (2:38) may happen *a fortiori* to lesser limbs. This indirectly exemplifies the deterioration of history from one reign to the next, a good preparation of the reader for Daniel B (chs. 7–12).

The new blasphemy has obviously incensed Daniel; the episode is particularly informed by the defilement of the Temple by Antiochus IV with the "abomination of desolation." To be sure, Daniel's anger is not assuaged by the ambiguous reward that the king offers "if [Daniel is] able to read . . . and [to interpret] . . ." (v. 16). As is well known, the biblical narrative shies away from analyzing the psychology of its characters. The reader learns about their moods and the tone of their discourse through their actual effects. For example we learn about the crooked nature of the king's offer by the refusal of Daniel (v. 17). The king entertains the illusion that he can influence the oracle and deflect a vision intuited as fatal.

5:17-28: Daniel reads the inscription (v. 25). It consists of four words with the first one said twice. It seems that the original sequence of three alluded to decreasing units of weight or monetary values. In other words Belshazzar cannot be compared with his "father" in glory *(mene = mina),* and the empire is about to be conquered by Medes and Persians *(tekel = shekel; parsin).* That latter combination explains the plural *parsin* (the word *parsin* is in alliteration with *parsi,* Persian). The first unit, the *mina* was later duplicated to have four terms corresponding to the four empires in chs. 2 and 7. Thus the following succession obtains: Babylon (a *mina*), Media (a *mina*), Persia (a *shekel* = one fifth of a *mina*), Alexander's divided empire (*parsin:* some half-minas, or two half-minas if the Ptolemies and the Seleucids are intended). Let us note that the present disproportion between Medes and Persians corresponds to the views expressed by Isa 13:17; 21:2; 2 Kings 17:6; Jer 51:11. The prophecy of Isaiah is also at the basis of the astonishing "Darius the Mede" in Dan 6:1 and 9:1, preceding "Cyrus, king of Persia" in 10:1.

"That very night," the King was killed (5:30). Of this murder we have no reliable historical confirmation.

Daniel 6

The Lion Pit, 6:1-30

The faithful are miraculously saved while their persecutors are devoured by their evildoing (cf. Dan 3). Early Christian art used this chapter as figurative of Christ's resurrection and of the victory of life over death. In contrast to chs. 3 and 5, however, ch. 6 passes from public to private observances, with similar intrusion and oppression (cf. 1 Macc 1:42; 2 Macc 6:6). But "Darius the Mede" (v. 1) is an enormous historical blunder. There has probably been a confusion with Cyrus who captured Babylon in 539 (Cyrus was 62 in 538 B.C.E.). In the background is the division of the Persian empire into satrapies carried out by Darius I (522–486). (Cf. Dan 5:2; Est 1:1; *1 Esd* 3:2.) The parallel with Esther and Joseph is also evident. Here as there the enemies resort to devious methods (6:5) and there is a clash between two "laws." Daniel's (or God's) is lifegiving but the "immutable, irrevocable, and unchangeable" law of the Medes and Persians (vv. 9, 15; cf. Esther) brings with it the recalcitrant's death in the lion pit (cf. Ezek 19:2-9). Assyrians and Persians kept caged lions, so verisimilitude obtains. Lions, however, represent chaos, as is attested by Ps 91:13 or by the Qumran text 1QH 5.6-7. Symbolically Daniel is forced into the nether world.

The story in this chapter is stunning. Jewish religion serves as a pretext for entrapping Daniel, object of the jealousy of his peers. Analogously with another familiar situation of the Jewish Diaspora in the book of Esther the officials mobilize the whole of the empire's legal system in targeting one man. They affect to flatter Darius, ostensibly deifying him while manipulating him into publishing an edict that this supposedly "supreme god" (cf. v. 7) regrets immediately but cannot alter (cf. Esther) because it escapes his control and becomes as it were automatic. Thus no one will really soil his hands with innocent blood; the state machine will blindly do the job.

The machine in the time of king Darius is a lion pit, and its efficiency matches modern technology. It is programmed to devour Daniel on the pretext of his lack of devotion to the crown, a veritable true-to-life portrait of any totalitarian regime. In a non-mechanized civilization the author thinks of wild beasts or dragons (see Dan 7:1-28) whose only performance is destruction.

The obscenity of the state's oppression is compounded by the absence of guilt on the part of the victim. Daniel has merely prayed in the privacy of his room, turning his gaze toward Jerusalem as was the custom in post-exilic Judaism (cf. *m. Berakhot* 4.1; *b.Ber.* 31a, etcetera; Acts 3:1; 10:9). In order to accuse him of impropriety spies must barge into his abode and pry into his most personal affairs. They make of Daniel before anything else a "non-person." They demand that his innermost thoughts conform with the official doctrine. The state-robot admits only citizen-robots.

At that point nothing can save Daniel, not even the royal friendship. Verse 12 reveals the irony of the Persian "immutable" law. The king is caught in his own trap (cf. Esther). He must now test Daniel while knowing that he is testing God! (see vv. 17, 20). If the rescue of Daniel would imply God's triumph (vv. 27-28) his death would imply God's death. The king seems to be sincere in his regret, however, which mitigates his culpability (vv. 19-25). He even uses the significant title "living God," and eventually fulfills Deut 19:18 (cf. ch. 3 above). Addressing Daniel, he says (in stark contrast with Nebuchadnezzar's discourse in ch. 3), "May your God, whom you faithfully serve, deliver you," meaning something like "at this point only God could do something for you." The reader, however, who can re-read the text and knows the dénouement of the story cannot but see in the kingly words a prophecy. As in ch. 3 where a mysterious personage entered the crematorium with the three martyrs, here too an angel accompanies Daniel in the pit and shuts the mouths of the lions.

Verse 23 subtly combines the motifs of the lions and of the furnace (see Daniel 3; cf. Heb 11:33-34) and associates Daniel and his companions with the Maccabean martyrs, intimating that God is with them in the pit (v. 22) as formerly in the furnace. The King is "overjoyed about Daniel" (v. 24) and puts to death the slanderers with their wives and children according to Persian law (v. 25). The parallel between 6:26-29 and 3:29-31 softens the shock. Thus those who actually fall are those who ensnared Daniel; the pattern is also found in Esther where the punishment is also extended to the culprits' wives and children. The motif stresses several points. First the "friends" of autocracts are sometimes no better off than their enemies (this was to be verified dramatically with Antiochus's capricious moods; cf. below on 8:23-25). It is also a warning for the Jews in the Diaspora who constantly skirt danger, even when the powers are for a while favorably inclined toward the minorities. Third, Darius's cruelty exemplifies the vengeance of the weakling who realizes that he has been connived against. Fourth, in a popular tale like this the audience is no doubt relieved when the wicked and their seed are eradicated for good. After all, if Daniel had a family the latter would have been included in the ordeal among the lions.

6:25-28: The story reaches its culmination with an edict acknowledging the divine ability of God to save and deliver God's servants and to change death into life, the very message of Jewish apocalyptic! The motif is once again the unexpected repentance of the despots and their acknowledgment that Daniel's God is the true lord of heaven and earth. We are at the end of times; the ancient message of Israel reaches now the confines of the earth.

Daniel A closes on the mention of "Cyrus the Persian" with which it started in 1:21, thus forming an *inclusio* of the first six chapters of the book. The fact of Daniel's prosperity is assuredly not due to the successive kings' benevolence, but to God's protection.

Bel and the Dragon

In the Greek Bible an addition called "Bel and the Dragon/Serpent" shows Daniel deriding Cyrus's idol "whose name was Bel." Daniel exposes its priests' deception and the king puts the priests and their families to death. The story continues with Daniel causing a serpent, also worshiped by the Persians, to burst. The angered populace compels the king to punish Daniel who is thrown into a lions' den. As in Daniel 6, however, Daniel remains unscathed, even being fed by the prophet Habakkuk who is dispatched by God from Palestine for that purpose. The king must confess the uniqueness of Daniel's God; he throws the conspirators in the den and they are readily devoured. Habakkuk's flight recalls similar phenomena in the time of Elijah and Elisha (1 Kings 18:12; 2 Kings 5:26). Very little is added to Daniel 6 by this tale, probably from the first century B.C.E. Bel is an epithet of Marduk, the chief Babylonian god (cf. Jer 50:2). The destruction by Xerxes I (486–465) of the temple of Bel is probably in the background. But zoolatry is documented in Egypt rather than in Babylon. Clearly the tale wanted to include animate as well as inanimate pagan idols and show their impotence. For prophetic sarcasm regarding idolatry see Isaiah 44–46. On holy iconoclasm, see *Jubilees* 12.

Daniel B: Daniel 7–12

Daniel 7

The Four Beasts and the Son of Man, 7:1-28

With this vision the apocalyptic part or Daniel B opens.

7:1-8: First we are presented with the primordial chaos from which emerge monsters representing four empires (cf. ch. 2). The first empire is Babylon; the second is Media the bear, well known for its cruelty (cf. Isa 13:17-18; 21:2-10; Hos 13:8); the third is Persia, whose four wings and four heads might represent the four Persian kings known to Scripture: Cyrus, Artaxerxes, Xerxes, and Darius III Codomannus (who was defeated by Alexander the Great). When the fourth beast comes the author is at a loss to describe it (v. 7; it recalls the mixed nature of Mesopotamian bestiary figures). It symbolizes Macedonia. This fourth empire, of Alexander the Great, differs from the others in coming from the west;

its conquests are without parallel in ancient history. The outgrowth of one of its horns (vv. 7-8) is Antiochus IV Epiphanes whose arrogant eyes are also mentioned in 8:23, cf. Isa 2:11. Regarding his immodest mouth (v. 25) see 11:36 and Ps 12:3, 1 Macc 1:24-25, 2 Macc 5:17; Rev 13:5. There is no fifth avatar of wickedness because Antiochus is evil incarnate. Thus history comes tragically to its end.

The present form of this chapter seems to date from 168, that is, from the midst of persecutions and the Temple's profanation. The high priest Onias III is replaced by Jason, whose investiture is a new humiliation to the faithful. As a response to this parody of crowning Daniel 7 substitutes another enthronement. The chapter takes its readers to a place that combines heaven and earth, that is, the transcendent abode of God (vv. 9-10) and court of judgment (v. 14). We see the enthronement of "one like a human being [= son of man]," a celestial high priest/king, or at least someone who has his entry in heaven. As such he is given an everlasting "dominion and glory and kingship" over all nations (7:14).

7:9-14: The description of the thrones (v. 9) is heavily dependent on the vision of the "chariot" in Ezekiel 1 and 10. Fire is the dominant motif, a reminder of Temple theophany (cf., for example, Exodus 19; Isaiah 6; but especially Ezek 8:1–11:25 showing God's presence in the Temple). The setting of the enthronement festival is Sukkoth (Tabernacles, in September–October: see Lev 23:34-36; Deut 16:13-17). It culminates with the *teruᶜah*/acclamation acknowledging God (and God's appointed lieutenant) as Creator/Judge/Savior/King (cf. Psalm 47). Daniel 7 gives that feast an eschatological (end-time) interpretation (cf. John 7:2, 8). Because of the festival's connection with creation and re-creation it was fitting to introduce on the side of God someone "like a human being," that is, the human *par excellence*. The "man" re-enacts the *Urzeit* (primordial time) in the (celestial) Temple at the *Endzeit* (end-time). In the terms of Ps 72:8, 17 he reigns from one ocean to the other. Remarkable here is the shift from the Jerusalem king to a transcendent "(son of) man" (v. 13). The terms used in the context of v. 14 illustrate elsewhere the sovereignty of God (cf. 3:33; 6:27); for example, the "man" is "served" in v. 14, a term used for divine service. This daring development in Daniel 7 is of utmost importance in understanding the NT formulation "Christ (= Messiah) is the Lord (= YHWH)."

The transition in Israel's messianic expectation is best understood against the backdrop of the failure of kingship. The apocalyptic condemnation of the "powers" includes Israel's as well. Hence the eschatological hope is "democratized," the "messiah" being the corporate personality of God's people. The messiah is thus "bi-dimensional," collective and individual.

7:15-28: Consequently in the third section the "man" is identified with the "saints" (in v. 27 we should understand the eschatological Israel already present in history in the persons of the faithful). In other words Daniel has seen, sitting side by side with God, Israel's transcendence, a complex figure, not only the human *par excellence* but also the angelic supreme personified in the archangel Michael. The model for that conflation of the human and the angelic is provided by Ezekiel 8–11, 43. Such glorification of Israel coincides with the destruction of "the last enemy," as the NT will say. This enemy is identified with Antiochus, whose persecution lasted from 168 to 165, a time computed in v. 25 as "a time, two times, and half a time," that is, three and a half years (cf. 4:13; 9:27; 12:7; the formula is stereotyped in Luke 4:25; Jas 5:17).

The "man" is collective: he is royal/messianic Israel, a dimension merged here with the individual (cf. Revelation 12). His kingship is emphasized in the aspect of judgment/victory over the nations and ultimate exaltation.

Daniel 8

The Vision of the Ram and the He-Goat, 8:1-27

(Without warning the text shifts back to Hebrew until the end of the book.) As in the preceding chapter there is a little horn; it arises from a bigger one and grows in an extraordinary manner. The parallels with Daniel 7 are numerous but the mood is gloomier.

8:1-12: The visionary is transported to the river Ulai in Susa of Elam (cf. Habakkuk's transfer to Babylon in "Bel and the Dragon" above). There once again Daniel sees animals representing empires: a ram and a male goat in which we readily recognize Persia and Macedonia/Greece. The two unequal horns of the ram are Persia and Media; the first prevails over the second, for the Persian military secured successes in all directions in the sixth and fifth centuries (Asia Minor, Syria, Palestine, Babylon, Egypt). In 480 Xerxes of Persia sacked Athens (cf. Dan 11:2), but he met a formidable obstacle in Alexander the Great, symbolized here by a unicorned he-goat. Xerxes was defeated at Issus in 333 (v. 7), then decisively at Arbela in 331. Daniel 11:3-4 alludes to these events.

However, Alexander died suddenly in Babylon in 323 and his empire was divided between four "Diadochs" (v. 8): Ptolemy (Egypt), Philip (Macedonia), Seleucus (Syria), and Antigonus (Asia Minor). The vision of the little horn focuses our attention on Syria and its contemporary representative, the perverse Antiochus IV Epiphanes (v. 9). The latter had indeed campaigned "toward the south and toward the east" against Egyptians, Persians, Parthians, as well as against Palestine, "the beautiful land." At this point, in parallel with Daniel 7, the scene shifts from earth to heaven, indeed to the transcendent dimension of Israel, that is, "the host of heaven" (v. 10) that Antiochus "tramples" under foot by profaning the Temple (v. 11) and by dealing arrogantly with the "prince of the host," that is, the high priest Onias III (assassinated in 171). He casts down "truth," an expression that we understand in the light of Mal 2:6 for which the truth is the *torah.* We remember that Antiochus burned all the sacred books he could find (1 Macc 1:54-57) and prohibited the practice of Jewish religion in general. For Jerome, Antiochus is himself both the Antichrist and also the type of the Antichrist.

8:13-14: In v. 13 the seer poses the apocalyptic question *par excellence:* "for how long?" Daniel hears one of the "holy ones" from the "host" of 8:12 speak to another holy one, the one in communication with Daniel, who reveals that the Temple will remain defiled for about three and a half years (1,150 days). During that period the "transgression that makes desolate" will stay; the allusion is to an idol installed in the Temple in December 167 by Antiochus. See also 9:27; 11:31; 12:11; cf. 1 Macc 1:54. The computation given here is four months shorter than in 7:25, as ch. 8 was composed after ch. 7, probably four months later. The central message in these verses is that God has set a limit to the profanation and the suffering of the saints. It must not be construed as permission to calculate the time of the End.

8:15-25: Verse 15 is a close cognate of Dan 7:13 in its evocation of someone "having the appearance of a man." Now, however, *geber* (man, hero) is used rather than *ʾadam* (human), in assonance with the name given to this personage in 8:16 "Gabri-el." For the first time in the Bible an angel is designated by name; Gabriel became the traditional messenger of the heavenly world. Later in the book Michael is also named: see 9:21; 10:13, 21; 12:1. In ch. 8 as in ch. 7 the comparability of the human and the divine is stressed. It is with "a human voice" that another angel speaks to Gabriel in v. 16. In the next verse Daniel himself is called "son of man (= mortal)"! The effect on Daniel is dramatic. He falls into a sort of seizure, somewhat in parallel to the reaction of Belshazzar in ch. 5. But Daniel is surrounded by guardian angels who help him overcome his panic.

Deuteronomy 32:8-9 presented us with patron deities of nations; other texts spoke of a divine court around YHWH (cf. 1 Kings 22:19-24; Isa 6:1-9; Job 1–2). Psalm 82 is witness of an evolution: all the gods have been stripped of their powers. Now, with apocalyptic, the gods are reinterpreted as angels and they are patrons not only of nations, but of individuals.

What is revealed to Daniel is that the events of the vision are definitely eschatological: they bring history to its acme. That is why vv. 23-25 resort to poetry to express one of the main apocalyptic motifs: salvation erupts at the paroxysm (8:23) of the transgression (8:25b). Such redemption is purely divine and cannot be attributed to human force or skill, "not by human hands" (8:25). Meanwhile, however, the success of the transgressor by means of force and deception is amazing (8:24-25a). "In a time of peace" (or "without warning") signals one more element of the royal cunning illustrated by 1 Macc 1:30. The event occurred in the spring of 167 and has prompted the composition of Daniel 8: Antiochus tricked Jews into trusting him, then fell upon the city of Jerusalem and "dealt it a severe blow." Put in Daniel's terms: the king "shall even rise up against the Prince of princes" (8:25, i.e., either God or God's representative), but he will fail.

8:26-27: In v. 26 Daniel receives the order to "seal up the vision" (cf. 12:10). The rationale for this order is threefold: to explain how it could be that such a revelation, ostensibly made in the sixth century, was hidden until the second; to show how trustworthy is that vision given so long before the actual events; and to signal that when the seal is broken and the contents are known the end will come (a frequent motif in the book of Revelation). The last words of the chapter (in v. 27) are ambiguous; they mean either that Daniel could not comprehend the message received, or that no one can.

Daniel 9

The Seventy Weeks of Years, 9:1-27

Chapter 9 begins with a literary genre that is unique in Daniel, no longer a dream or a vision but a meditation on a (pre-canonical) text of Jeremiah (25:11-14 and 29:10).

9:1-2: Both Jeremiah's oracles foretold the end of the exile after seventy years or ten sabbatical cycles (cf. Lev 25:2-7; see also 26:34-39). Jeremiah expected the restoration to be an eschatological second Exodus surpassing the first, but the delay in the accomplishment of that prophetic promise became a major embarrassment for the returnees to Zion in the sixth century. Down to the time of Daniel there were speculations as to the reason why the restoration had not come, and with it the paradisiacal era. Remarkable in Daniel is the shift of blame, which the prophets used to level squarely at Israel, onto Antiochus, a foreigner who is evil incarnate. There is still a place for Israel's confession of sin but penance has acquired the unusual character of being preparatory to the reception of divine secrets.

The insistence on the date (v. 2) as right after the return from exile when Jeremiah's prophecies should have come to their realization emphasizes the necessity to reopen the "books" (revered as Scriptures for the first time here and in Sirach, Prologue) and see what they really mean. There must be a hidden truth that needs to be uncovered. Daniel 9 finds it concealed in a prophetic text as previously it was hidden in a vision or a dream. The understanding of the secret will demand an ascetic preparation (cf. Exod 34:28; Dan 10:3). That is why Daniel's prayer is at home in a liturgy for the Day of Atonement and resembles other prayers of its kind (cf. 1 Kings 8; Ezra 9:6-15; Neh 9:6-37).

9:3-19: Daniel intones a beautiful prayer of confession. Its date of composition is moot. It is a mosaic of quotations from Deuteronomy and Jeremiah but it has been updated by the author.

9:11-14: The Temple's destruction by the Babylonians in 587 (for the second-century readers its profanation by the Syrians in 167) was an unprecedented catastrophe but it has been permitted by God and was even written down in advance in the *torah* of Moses (cf., for example, Deuteronomy 28). Note the newly coined expression "as it is written," that will become so widely used in the NT and in Jewish tradition.

The author at this point forgets about the book's fictional setting and adopts the current Jerusalemite point of view when giving vent to his deep resentment of the sarcasm of nations, "all our neighbors" (v. 16; cf. Ezek 21:28-32; 25:4-7).

Strikingly the speaker begs God to have pity for God's own sake (v. 17) and forgive Israel. Only a profound sentiment of love could dictate such accents. This verse has been called the *Kyrie eleison* of Jewish Scriptures.

9:20-27: The chapter's second part starts with v. 20. Daniel turns toward Jerusalem (cf. 9:3) at the hour of the evening offering in the Temple. The language of v. 20b is ambiguous: does he pray on behalf of the mountain or is Daniel on the holy mountain (liturgically or spiritually speaking)? If the latter, the message to the second-century audience is clear: there is a Temple not built with human hands that is universal and that no one can defile. Then comes the angel-interpreter (encountered in ch. 8); his name is Gabriel or "the man." He flies to Daniel (v. 21; cf. Isa 6:2, 6; Ezek 1:6, 14) and brings him a divine message. As usual in the apocalypse, faith is linked to the understanding of "mysteries," of the meaning of God's work in history. It demands a spirit of humility, expressed here precisely by the prayer of repentance.

Prayers need not pile up words; from the beginning Daniel has been heard (v. 23) and God has decided to reveal to Daniel the hidden sense of Jer 29:10. The seventy years of Jeremiah's texts are seventy weeks of years (v. 24), that is, ten times seven sabbaths of years, or 490 years. This ultimate jubilee is near at hand. In effect the computation takes us to the time of the Maccabees. (In later readings of Daniel it was felt necessary to re-compute the time of the fulfillment, for instance to the end of the Roman empire or to the days of Jesus [Matt 25:15 = Mark 13:14; 2 Thess 2:4].) At the time of the end, says

Dan 9:24, vision and prophet will be "sealed together," that is, there will be no hiatus between the announced and the announcer, but sheer coincidence in time (contemporaneity) and message (the spirit is the letter).

The Temple of Jerusalem is to be rededicated soon. From the beginning of the exile (here 564) to the enthronement of the high priest Joshua (515), seven weeks have passed (cf. Hag 1:1, 14; Zech 3:1-5. Sixty-two more weeks (434 years) is either a "miscalculation" (Montgomery) or a "round number" (Collins) between 515 and 171, the year of the murder of the second "anointed one," Onias III. Of the last week half will elapse between Onias's murder and Antiochus's persecution. After the remaining half week (168–165) "the decreed end [will be] poured out upon the desolator." The theme of devastation appears five times (9:18, 26, 27). In v. 27 the apex is reached when the "abomination that desolates," an expression already encountered, is set up in the Temple.

How must we understand the declaration that "a most holy place/thing/one" will be anointed (v. 24; cf. Exod 30:26; 40:9)? What or who is this "most holy place/thing/one"? In 1 Chron 23:13, for example, the expression (there translated "most holy things") may designate Aaron; the community of the Dead Sea scrolls considers itself to be the sanctuary (see the Temple Scroll; cf. also 1 Macc 1:46). This personification led the Peshitta (the Syriac version of the Bible) to translate the "most holy" here by "messiah" (and later Hippolytus referred here to "the son of God"). In fact it must be said that the structure of the text points in that direction. The "seventy weeks" are divided, in vv. 25-27, into three parts, each of which mentions an event concerning a "messiah": v. 25 "until the time of an anointed prince [= messiah] there shall be seven weeks" (the high priest Joshua in Zechariah); v. 26 "after the sixty-two weeks, an anointed one [= messiah] shall be cut off" (Onias III [and the beginning of the persecutions that lasted three and a half years; cf. Dan 11:22]); v. 24 (really the conclusion of this pericope) "Seventy weeks are decreed . . . to anoint a most holy place/thing /one" (an eschatological high priest to come).

The countdown to the end of time continues in v. 27. Even "many" in Jerusalem will fall for Antiochus's demagogy. All sacrifices will be replaced by an idol installed "on the wing," that is, after the "horns" of YHWH's altar have been leveled (cf. Jdt 9:8). The expression "abomination that desolates" mixes the plural and the singular (something like "abominations that desolates" [sic]). This anti-grammatical construction alludes to the plural form of the noun *Elohim* (God) that governs a singular verb or predicate. Antiochus's idol pretends to be the God of the Jews while being only an abomination. In the image of its author it desolates the "desolator."

Daniel 10–12

The Great Final Vision, Daniel 10–12

These final chapters constitute a literary unit. The inspirational texts are now Second Isaiah's songs on the Servant of the Lord. "[I]t concerned a great conflict" (v. 1) is unclear as are several elements of the chapter. The scene in ch. 10 is indeed very complex. It takes a long preparation before Daniel is told the meaning of the vision by the angel who looks like "a man," but his understanding is incomplete without the intervention of Gabriel. A fourth personage, the angel Michael, battles principalities and powers (cf. Eph 6:12) in 10:13, for the turmoil on earth is a replica of celestial events.

10:1-14: The purported date of the vision, "the third year of King Cyrus" (v. 1) is 538, that is, the time of the restoration so eagerly expected (Isa 41:14; 43:1, 14; 44:6, 22-24; 53:1-5). It marks the end of the "slavery" (same word for the same reality in Isa 40:2). Verse 10:1b is closely akin to 9:23 and that kinship reveals the identity of the angel as Gabriel in 10:16-21. There is also on the part of Daniel a similar ascetic preparation (10:2) appropriate for a Day of Atonement as in ch. 9 (cf. 9:3).

The first angel (vv. 5-9) wears a priestly vestment (cf. Lev 16:4, 23) and is called "a man" with the same ambiguity as in 7:13. One recognizes again Ezekiel 1; 8-12 in the background. The angel speaks with Daniel, who is once more the only one to hear the voice (vv. 7-8; cf. Daniel 5 where only Daniel can read the inscription). The effect on him (v. 9) recalls again what was said in ch. 9, but here too the prayer has been heard from the beginning and its response delayed (vv. 12-13) only because of the opposition by the angel of Persia. Gabriel ("the man") fought against him but had to be helped by Michael (that is, the "son of man" of ch. 7, the guardian angel of Israel). "Do not fear," says the angel (here and in v. 19): this revelation formula introduces a salvation oracle and is specifically used by priests in response to an individual lament (cf. Lam 3:57).

The main part begins in v. 10 with a detailed historical survey from Persian days down to Antiochus's period. Verse 14 is a citation of Hab 2:2-3. Daniel is to be privileged with the interpretation of that mysterious prophetic text regarding the "end of days." Note Daniel's kinship with Habakkuk, which we saw expressed above in the apocryphal "Bel and the Dragon."

10:15-21: Verse 15 begins a second development on the model of (pre-) apocalyptic texts like Ezekiel 38–39; Isaiah 24–27. Daniel feels unworthy of the forthcoming revelation and the angel must touch his lips, as was the case with the prophet Isaiah (Isa 6:7). The details of the revelation are given, beginning with 10:20. The battle is—strikingly in the image of myth—a *Götterkampf* (struggle between gods) before it is a *Völkerkampf* (struggle between nations).

Daniel 11: The course of events that culminated in the defilement of the Temple of Jerusalem—the first pogrom in history—and stirred Jewish resistance under the Maccabees, is as follows. At his death in 323 Alexander the Great left an immense empire that his generals, called *diadochi* (successors), immediately set to disputing. Egypt fell to the lot of Ptolemy, while Syria, which included a vast territory embracing Babylonia and Persia, was governed by the Seleucids (after the name of Seleucus I). Palestine, a buffer between the two rivals, was hotly disputed and passed from the Ptolemies to the Seleucids in 198.

In Jerusalem the high priest exercised authority by proxy; he was vested with both religious and political powers. This led to profound rivalries between leading families with most regrettable consequences such as the bidding for position by individuals of questionable morality. Thus Jason, brother of the high priest Onias III, promised huge sums of money to Antiochus IV Epiphanes, successor of Seleucus IV Philopator. With him the Hellenizing party came to power in Zion (174–171). In 172 one Menelaus stripped Jason of his position by promising even more money to Antiochus.

Daniel 11 reviews the events between the fourth and second centuries. The Persian period is marked by four kings. The fourth, defeated by Alexander (v. 3) is Darius III Codomannus, and therefore the four must be Cyrus, Xerxes, Artaxerxes, and Darius. Persia was conquered in 334–330, but the Alexandrian empire was short-lived. It was divided among the *diadochi* (v. 4; cf. 8:8 for the image). The allusions in 11:5 are to Ptolemy I, king of Egypt [the South] (323–285); he was supplanted by Seleucus I in Babylon, but Palestine remained under the Egyptian Ptolemies until 198. The text designates the Seleucids as kings of the North although their empire lay to the east of Palestine. A politically arranged marriage in 250 between Antiochus II and Berenice, daughter of Ptolemy II, ended tragically with their death by poison (v. 6). Their heir, Ptolemy III, succeeded in invading the Syrian Seleucid empire, going as far as Babylon. From there he carried off a great deal of booty, including idols (11:7-8).

Starting with v. 10 the focus is on the Seleucids, particularly Antiochus III the Great who conquered Palestine in 198 but not without resistance from the Egyptians, who inflicted heavy losses on him in Raphia (217). Verse 12 describes Ptolemy IV Philopator's exaltation after Raphia, but this was short-lived. In 205 Antiochus came back in force (11:13). He routed Philopator's son, Ptolemy V, in 198 at Panion and was received as a liberator by the Jerusalemites (11:14; cf. Josephus, *Ant.* 12.3.3). They even helped him to take Sidon (11:15). But Antiochus calculatingly offered his daughter Cleopatra as wife to Ptolemy V (also called Epiphanes) the better to destroy him (11:17). "It shall not succeed," says our text, for Cleopatra unexpectedly adopted the Egyptian cause and called on Rome for help against her father who meanwhile had sent a fleet against the Egyptian-controlled coastland of Asia Minor (11:18). The Roman Lucius Scipio (called here "a commander") defeated the Seleucid in Magnesia, then at Thermopylae (cf. Livy, *History* 37.39-44). Antiochus III died by the hands of Elamites whose temple of Bel he was pillaging (11:19). His son, Seleucus IV, inheriting a gravely depleted war chest, sent Heliodorus to steal the Jerusalem Temple's treasure, but the attempt failed (11:20; cf. 2 Maccabees 3).

At this point and until the end of the chapter (11:21-45) the text focuses on the wicked Seleucid usurper Antiochus IV Epiphanes (175–164). His wicked actions are "prophesied" in fairly accurate detail but the forecast of his eventual destruction is historically incorrect. This "contemptible person" (v. 21) ousted his brother's son Demetrius, the legitimate dynastic heir, and seized the throne. He defeated the Egyptians and had the priest Onias III ("the prince of the covenant" in 11:22; cf. 9:25) assassinated in Jerusalem (in 171), probably for collaboration with the enemy. Some in Jerusalem supported him (11:23) although he was religiously detestable to Jews and even to his own people (11:36-39). Antiochus conquered Egypt (described as "strongholds" in 11:24; cf. 1 Macc 1:19). Though "large and powerful means" were concentrated there (11:25) Ptolemy VI was betrayed by his generals in 170. He and Antiochus held political talks, qualified as lies by Dan 11:27. All this fulfills the divine design, as Hab 2:3 already said (cf. 8:17, 26; 10:14).

Meanwhile Antiochus's death was falsely announced and the former high priest Jason proclaimed himself ruler in Jerusalem. Antiochus, on his way back from Egypt, punished the city (11:28). He organized a second campaign against Egypt but Popilius Laenas, delegate of the Roman Senate (designated here by its Mediterranean fleet, the "ships of Kittim"), forced him to withdraw. Epiphanes vented his rage by attacking Jerusalem, most probably encouraged by the Hellenists in the city (he "shall . . . pay heed to those who forsake the holy covenant," 11:30 and 32; cf. 1 Macc 1:11-15). He massacred 40,000 persons and sold as many again as slaves. He subsequently initiated a religious persecution, forbidding the practice of circumcision, of dietary regimen, of keeping the Sabbath, and of reading sacred texts. Daniel 11:29-39 retraces the several stages of the catastrophe. These verses should be read alongside 1 Maccabees 1 and 2 Maccabees 5. Daniel 11:32 speaks of dissension among the Jews. Opposition elements crystallized and were at the origin of the Hasidim (and later of the Pharisees) in their strife against the establishment (later Sadducees).

The author of Daniel doubtless belonged to the Hasidim, or at the very least to a splinter branch of those pious people mentioned by 1 Maccabees (cf. 2:42; 7:12). They are, says Dan 11:33, not only wise but they "give understanding to many." They also are the martyrs 12:1-3 will speak about. They receive "a little help" from the Maccabees (11:34) but the only propitiation is their martyrdom (11:35; cf. Isaiah 53; Rev 3:18). They are the real winners although not by resorting to military means. Their adversaries are described in 11:32 as "those who violate the covenant," an expression also found in the Dead Sea scrolls (1 QM 1:2; see also CD 20:26); these are the Hellenists. "Those who acknowledge him" Antiochus "shall make more wealthy" (11:39; cf. 1 Macc 1:52). The summit of blasphemy is reached in the king's self-deification as he utters "horrendous things against the God of gods" (11:36), for evil must crest before God's wrath is complete. Even the king's abandonment of the customary Near Eastern deities for the sake of adopting a western pantheon appears outrageous to the author. Antiochus is said to have left Adonis/Tammuz, "beloved by women," for Zeus, "god of fortresses" (vv. 36-38; cf. 1 Macc 1:50; 2 Macc 5:7-10; Dan 7:8, 20). The Temple of Jerusalem was renamed the Temple of Zeus Olympios and its main altar was flattened (the four "horns" broken) so as to elevate its level for the sacrifice of non-kosher animals, including swine, to foreign divinities. This, for Daniel, constitutes "the abomination that makes desolate" (Dan 9:27; 11:31; 12:11; see 1 Macc 1:54, 59; Josephus, *Ant.* 12.253).

The events predicted in 11:40-45 did not materialize, especially the prophesied third (victorious) campaign against Egypt with the conquest of Libya and Ethiopia (11:43). In actuality Antiochus died in November/December 164 in Persia, not "between the [Mediterranean] sea and the beautiful holy mountain [of Zion]" (v. 45), which is a visionary scene of the end of times inspired by Ezek 39:4. By contrast the Maccabees' successes, their purification of the Temple (Hanukkah), and other events are not mentioned. Writing before those occurrences, the author believes that the end-time has arrived. The Qumran scroll 1QM is an elaboration on these eschatological verses.

Daniel 12: The vision that opened in ch. 10 reaches its peak in Daniel 12. The author of Daniel was called to lead the "many" on wise paths (11:33). That is why he writes his book in the first place (12:3). He is himself one of the many scribes who fill the ranks of the Hasidim (1 Macc 7:12) as they later would in the Dead Sea community. Significantly the author insists upon (levitical) purity (1:1-17; 6:11; 10:3), for the Antiochian persecution is here as much a matter of spiritual deceit as of brutality (contrast 11:31-32 with 33-35); besides, sword, flame, captivity, and plunder have the effect on the spiritual level of refining, purifying, and cleansing for the time of the end (11:35).

The persecution (from December 7, 168, till between November 20 and December 19, 164, the date of Antiochus's death at Tabae in Persia) included the profanation of the Jerusalem shrine, which the Seleucid propaganda "justified" by spreading defamatory ideas about the Jewish people. It was then that the accusation of ritual murder was made against the Jews for the first time.

12:1-4: The first verses are very dense. Jeremiah 30 (the restoration of Israel) serves as a source of inspiration: the time of anxiety is about to end. The Jeremian text was evidently read in the second century as a promise of individual resurrection when the end comes with the paroxysm of evil, at the time of death (collective and individual). As there is no revivification until after death it is shown to Daniel that suffering is part of salvation. The greater the distress, the more imminent the victory. Every saintly life is inscribed in the book (v. 1); the righteous will "wake up from the dust." Many a writing of the Apocrypha reflects this far-reaching insight (cf. *Ass. Mos.* 10:2; *1 Enoch* 20:5; 103:4) and the NT expresses it in motifs of awakening of the dead, eternal life, transfiguration, and glorification.

Because resurrection imagery had been part of Baal mythology there was a long-lasting Israelite resistance to adopting a doctrine of an after-death destiny. When that imagery appears in Hos 13:14 it parodies Canaanite beliefs. The text was, however, later interpreted in a positive sense (see the early translations into Greek and Latin, and also 1 Cor 15:55). The imagery is again present in the "Isaianic apocalypse" (Isaiah 26–27) which Daniel reinterprets as referring literally to life after death (see Isa 26:19). Such literal and concrete interpretation of figurative or abstract expressions can be found, for example, in 2 Kings 6:17, where Elisha prays God to literally "open the eyes" of his servant!

Typical of the apocalypse, the hope for transcendence of death and the ultimate transfiguration of the faithful into bright stars finds its parade expression here. As stars follow strict "rules," so the just have always followed their appointed ways and thus they will join the stars and shine. This association with the stars in Dan 12:3 recalls again Isaiah's oracles on the Servant (52:13); like him also the righteous of Daniel's vision are healed (Isa 53:10-11) and justify multitudes (53:11). After the announcement of the faithful ones' "trans-mortality" (vv. 1b-3) Daniel himself will be beneficiary of the resurrection (v. 13), but the sixth-century Daniel is to keep this revelation secret as its message is for another generation (12:4, 9; cf. above on 8:26).

Excursus II: The Resurrection in Daniel

In the Bible death is a sign of the fundamental weakness of the human creature before God. Human finitude is our common share as "there is no righteous, not even one" before divine justice. That is why YHWH is absent from Sheol, the place of the dead, unlike the agrarian divinities whose kingdom includes the abode of the dead. Israel therefore was not disposed to speculate about the God of life intervening in the realm of death and bringing the deceased back to life as if they were subject to a cyclical "eternal return" of the same.

This disposition, however, was radically questioned in the second century B.C.E. The untimely death of martyrs "for the sake of heaven" was in contradiction to the definition of death as a deserved punishment or as a sign of human fallibility (cf. Ps 90:10). Martyrdom was of the innocent, the beloved of God. Instead of "saving their lives" they were "losing their lives!" Such a death required a divine response, different from the negative judgment as found for example in Genesis 3. This response, according to Daniel 12, is the resurrection of the just to eternal life.

12:5-13: The epilogue of the book begins in 12:5. Gabriel asks Michael (see v. 6 and compare with 10:5) when these ultimate events would occur. The response is: three and a half times (years?) as in 9:27. This would amount to 1,260 days (if each month has thirty days; cf. Rev 11:2-3), but in 12:11-13 there are two successive glosses prolonging the delay from the 1,150 days in 8:14 to 1,290, and the 1,290 days (the extra month may represent the period of composition of chs. 10–12) to 1,335 days (the extra one and one half months for the whole book's editing?). Verse 13 applies to Daniel (and to his readers) the promise of Isa 26:19: "you shall rise for your reward at the end of the days."

Susanna and the Elders

The Greek versions have an additional tale, Susanna and the Elders, that introduces Daniel as a child endowed with an extraordinary wisdom and insight. According to its ostensible chronology this story should constitute the first chapter of the whole book. The composition (in its two versions) dates from Hellenistic times. It tells us about Susanna, a Judean exile in Babylon, who is falsely accused by community elders of being adulterous.

Susanna includes no miracle and unlike Esther or the other stories in Daniel the confrontation is internecine between Jews. At issue is personal morality, a theme very popular in Hellenistic times. Its literary genre resembles that of the Joseph story, except that the present tale is about a woman and that Susanna is not a (dream-)interpreter as was Joseph. Common to both stories, however, are a deep skepticism regarding human nature and also the absence of religious jargon.

The chastity and modesty of the heroine is emphasized; it is protected by the sealing of the garden where she bathes (vv. 17-18). By contrast the elders are crude; they hiss, "give your consent, and lie with us" (v. 20; cf. Gen 39:24-26). Susanna feels "trapped" but she emphatically refuses to "sin in the sight of the Lord" (vv. 22-23). Slandered, she is condemned (v. 41) and entrusts her fate to God (vv. 42-43). Her prayer is heard (v. 44) and Daniel confounds the elders with his wisdom (vv. 48-61; cf. Luke 2:42-47). The epilogue of the story parallels Daniel A or Esther: the accusers are punished with the fate they meant for their victims (cf. Deut 19:19).

The earliest citation of Susanna is found under Irenaeus's pen (second century). The unswerving chastity of the heroine provided a moral exemplar for Christian teaching.

BIBLIOGRAPHY

Collins, John J. *Daniel. A Commentary on the Book of Daniel.* Hermeneia. Minneapolis: Fortress, 1993.

DiLella, Alexander A. *A Book for Troubling Times.* Hyde Park, N.Y.: New City Press, 1997.

Hartman, Louis F., and Alexander A. DiLella. *The Book of Daniel.* AB 23. Garden City, N.Y.: Doubleday, 1978.

LaCocque, André. *Daniel in His Time.* Columbia: University of South Carolina Press, 1988.

Seitz, Christopher R., ed. *Reading and Preaching the Book of Daniel.* Philadelphia: Fortress, 1988.

Towner, Sibley W. *Daniel.* Interpretation. Atlanta: John Knox, 1984.

The Minor Prophets

Horacio Simian-Yofre

The "twelve prophets" are treated as a single book in Sir 49:10. The calculation of the sacred books made by 2 Esdras 14 and Josephus, *Ap.* 1.40 also assumes that the twelve minor prophets constitute a unit. The Babylonian Talmud (*B. Bat.* 13b-15a) dictates that only three lines should separate the minor prophets from each other (instead of four, as with the other canonical books), and it collectively cites them as the Book of the Twelve Prophets. Jerome asserts that "the book of the twelve prophets is one" *(unum librum esse).*

It is thus possible that the Book of the Twelve Prophets is the final result of a long redactional process based on the prophecies of Hosea, Amos, Micah, and Zephaniah. These texts had been edited in deuteronomistic circles, after the fall of Samaria but before their insertion in the Book of the Twelve Prophets, to emphasize the promises of salvation. The existence of this corpus would explain, for example, the similar superscriptions of these four prophets, different from those in Haggai and Zechariah and absent from the other six, the adoption by Mic 1:7 of the prostitution theme (cf. Hosea 1–3), and the incorporation of the refrain of Amos 1:4, 7, 10, 12 (14); 2:2, 5 in Hos 8:14b.

This corpus, together with the other formed by Haggai and Zechariah, and a thoroughly edited group of short texts ("prophetic sayings" and liturgical texts found in Nahum, Habakkuk, and Malachi) is the basis of the Book of the Twelve. Joel and Obadiah, which have a somewhat anthological character, were edited to join the Book of the Twelve together. The contrast between Hos 14:6-8 and Joel 1:10-12 belongs at this redactional level. The last texts included in the Twelve were Jonah and Zechariah 9–14. Zechariah 13:9b recapitulates Hos 2:23. Some contacts with the book of Isaiah reflect the last written work common to both *corpora.*

Hosea

Horacio Simian-Yofre

FIRST READING

General Character of the Book

The book of Hosea, through successive editions, has reached a clear literary unity and organization, but it has preserved some tensions of religious thought that make reading it a particularly fascinating task.

1. The Organization and Content of the Book

The book can be divided into four large sections preceded by an editorial superscription situating the text within the history of Judah and Israel (1:1) and closed by a conclusion in the tradition of sapiential literature (14:10). The "theological biography of Hosea" (Hosea 1–3) relates the personal history of the prophet, theologically elaborated on the basis of some important themes of the book.

The prophet receives from God the order to marry a prostitute (Gomer), accepting as his own and giving specific names to her children (ch. 1). Abandoned by the woman, the prophet swears he will punish her (ch. 2), but he receives a new order from YHWH to look for her and bring her to his house (ch. 3). Into this personal story are woven theological reflections: Hos 1:7; 2:1-3; 2:16-25; 3:4-5.

Chapters 4–13 tie together the prophet's utterances, which are arranged in a thematic manner. Chapters 4–7 have as their principal hearers the Yahwist priests of northern Israel whose center of worship was Bethel. Each textual unit refers to one particular aspect of the actions of the priests, which the prophet bitterly criticizes.

After a general utterance (4:1-3)—which perhaps served as introduction to the entire book before the incorporation of chs. 1–3—vv. 4-15 denounce the abuse of the priests in manipulating public worship; ch. 5 excoriates their interference at court and the negative influence they exert on the political life of the country; and ch. 6 describes the negative consequences of their activity for the religious life of the people. Chapter 7 includes an allegory about the relationship of the priests and the royal house and a renewed criticism of the negative effects of the priests' activity. Chapters 8–10, on the other hand, concentrate on the existing complex relationships between the legitimate worship of YHWH and the illegitimate worship of the Baals and calves, the internal situation of the country (ch. 8), and the contacts with Assyria and Egypt (9:1-9), alternately allies and traditional enemies of Israel.

Beginning with 9:10 there follow four descriptions of the actual situation of Ephraim/Israel, three of which are also related in the ancient history of Israel (the treason in Baal-peor, 9:10-14; the wicked deeds committed in Gilgal, 9:15-17; and the war of Gibeah, 10:9-15). Hosea 10:1-8 foreshadows the disappearance of the altars of worship and of the monarchy.

The last section (Hos 11:1–14:1) is of a meditative tone and is concerned for the personal relationship of YHWH with Ephraim. YHWH, as actor or speaker, appears at decisive moments, while appeals are hardly ever made to Ephraim.

Hosea 11:1-9 reflects on the election of Israel in Egypt and the people's education in the desert. Chapter 12 is a long comparison between the behavior of Israel and that of their ancestor, Jacob. Finally, Hos 13:1–14:1 is integrated by heterogenous elements and sounds: YHWH is lamenting over the broken relationship with Israel. Hosea 14:2-9 includes the prophet's exhortation to the people (vv. 2-4) and a generous promise from YHWH (vv. 5-9) that contradicts the end of the previous section (13:14). The sapiential conclusion (14:10) reflects on the content of the entire book.

2. Structural Elements

There are three structural elements that unify the book. The first is a strong experience of personal relationship and the suffering caused by separation. This experience of suffering, together with the breaking of the relationship, defined God's way of relating to this people. The second structural element is the knowledge of the problems affecting the country: political problems such as the incapacity of the kings to lead the people according to the plans of YHWH, and political-religious problems including the negative influence of the priests on the life of the country. Finally there are strictly religious factors like the confusion of the people in the face of corrupt or idolatrous cults.

The third structural element contributing to the unity of the book is the reference to the traditional history of the people. The prophet interprets the present situation and extracts opportune consequences beginning with the national history and including popular traditions. These three elements give the book its unity, a unity that is perhaps more rigorous than that of other prophetic books since the activity of the prophet covers fewer years and is condensed within a relatively brief text.

3. Characteristics of Style

As in other prophetic books, here also in some passages of the book of Hosea YHWH speaks in the first person. Elsewhere others speak of YHWH in the third person; but more clearly and frequently than in other prophetic texts the word of the prophet is seen as different from the word of YHWH when, in the first person, he exhorts, warns, threatens or condemns the individual hearer, a group, or the entire people. In a few (autobiographical) texts Hosea speaks of himself in the first person. The lack of an explicit addressee obliges one to consider some texts of Hosea as soliloquies, meditations, or lamentations in which God or the prophet refers to the people in the third person.

The variety expressed in the person addressing as well as in the ones addressed, together with the richness of images, make this a particularly lively and attractive text. The vocabulary used is inspired by nature and includes the steppe, dawn and nightfall, the dew, rain and wind of the desert, grain, unfermented grape juice, oil and wine, flax and linen, silver and gold, the hawthorn, blackberry, and stinging nettle, the fig tree and the olive, the oak and the cypress, the poplar and terebinth, cattle and sheep, the lion and the panther, bear and lion cubs, birds and doves. With unadorned precision Hosea describes orgiastic cults, court feasts, or the horrors of war; he alludes to the techniques of the hunter and the peasant, the baker and the thief; he evokes the rancor of the man abandoned by his wife and the tenderness, perplexity, and anger of YHWH; finally, he is capable of concentrating, in a single proverbial sentence, the entire content of a discourse.

4. The Composition of the Text

The text of Hosea can be read as a single unit that proceeds almost in its entirety from the author, traditionally considered "the prophet Hosea." The words of the prophet, pronounced publicly during a relatively short period of time, were probably gathered for the hearers, fixed into written form, and organized into chs. 4 to 13 with criteria that were more thematic than chronological.

In the first three chapters it is necessary to distinguish levels of reading—biographical, historical, and religious/theological—that are superimposed and integrated until they become the actual text, although this does not necessarily presuppose diverse authors. We may include the task of a final editor who put a certain order into the totality of the text. The use of formulae (inconsistent with the style of Hosea, such as "the oracle of YHWH" or "on that day") help one recognize in Hos 2:16-23 an elaboration edited for the purpose of incorporating these texts into the whole, but the thought, the vocabulary, and the images are strictly coherent with the content of the prophecy.

We are inclined to believe that the text in Hosea 14:1-9 may be the work of a faithful disciple of the prophet Hosea. There is a certain repetitiveness of thought, development of terms used before, and the expression of thoughts in such general terms that it is difficult to imagine the concrete situation of the text.

Hosea mentions Judah when it is necessary to put in relief the similar origins of Judah and Ephraim (11:12), or their personal relationship with YHWH (6:4), their common responsibilities (10:11), their infidelity as well as YHWH's reaction to that faithlessness (5:10-14), and when he speaks of his hope for an improved common destiny (1:11). From this we may conclude that of the fifteen references to Judah, unusual in a text focused on Samaria and the northern kingdom of Israel, eight belong to the original text of Hosea (1:11; 5:10, 12, 13, 14; 6:4; 10:11; 11:12) and seven to a final editing probably made in Jerusalem after the fall of Samaria (1:1, 7; 4:15; 5:5; 6:11a; 8:14; 12:2). This minor editing with references to "Judah" occurs when the text permits a reflection on the actual situation in the southern kingdom, for example when the faults of that nation are compared with those of Ephraim (5:5; 8:14), or when the prophet is exhorting the people to a different kind of behavior (4:15); when he is predicting punishment (6:11) or expressing hope in God's mercy (1:7), or, finally, when he acknowledges Judah, as well as Ephraim, as descendants of an ambiguous figure named Jacob (12:2).

It is probable that the reference to King David in 3:5 does not belong to Hosea either. Other lines are difficult to integrate into the textual unity (cf. 4:16-19 and 11:10-11), nor does Hosea 14:1-9 belong to Hosea. Though it is a true epilogue and repeats the favorite expressions of Hosea it is not in the spirit of Hosea; instead it converts his hard message into an unconditional promise of restoration.

General Context of Interpretation

1. Historical and Cultural Context

The Crisis of the Monarchy

One of the structural elements of the prophecy of Hosea is its knowledge of the crisis that threatens the monarchy in Israel in the second half of the eighth century.

Hosea does not condemn the monarchy. Some texts predict the disappearance of the king based on his deeds (1:4; 3:4) or verify it either in imagination or really (7:7; 10:7, 15). Others describe the submission of the nobility to the powerful (7:3; 8:4), and the disillusionment that generates in the people. Hosea 5:1 exhorts the court to protect itself against such threats. Hosea 13:10, 11 affirms the right of YHWH to establish or to abolish the king.

The relationship of Hosea to the monarchy can be easily understood during the turbulent period following the forty years of economic and political expansion in the reign of Jeroboam II and his death (in the years 747–746 or 746–745). Within a few months he was succeeded by his son Zechariah who reigned for six months. Zechariah was the last descendent of Jehu and was assassinated by the usurper of the throne, Shallum, who in turn was eliminated one month later by Menahem. Menahem restored stability to the kingdom for a period of ten years. The assurance with which Hosea speaks of the end of the monarchy (1:4) suggests that the reign of Menahem in fact did not yet enjoy much stability. The "house of Jehu" (1:4) included the actual reigning house as well as the usurpers acting in the name of the founder of the dynasty. The end of the monarchy is presented as the consequence of a military defeat in the valley of Jezreel (1:5).

The Cult of the Baals

The use of the singular as well as the article with Baal in Hosea 2:8; 13:1 presupposes, behind the multiplicity, the tempting and specific figure of Baal as the divinity antagonistic to YHWH. The cult of Baal and his consorts appears in the first contacts of Israel with the land of Canaan (Num 25:1-5) and it continues during the period of the judges (Judg 6:25) and into the times of the prophet Elijah (1 Kings 18:17-40). In spite of the efforts to root it out in Israel (2 Kings 10:18-28) and in Judah (2 Kings 11:18)

BAAL

Baal *(baʿlu)* is a common noun in Akkadian, Ugaritic, Phoenician, Aramaic and Hebrew. Originally it meant "lord," "husband," "owner," or one who possessed a special quality. There is evidence that the term was used as an epithet for various gods in Mesopotamia from early times (*"baal* [lord] of such and such a place") and was later converted into the proper name of a divinity worshiped in different places under particular representations.

Baal, son of *ʾEl,* the creator, and also of Dagon, the wheat, was the god of time, of rain, of vegetable and human fertility, and also a war god.

According to Ugaritic texts the cult of Baal included the feast of the new year, the grape harvest, and the unfermented grapes (September–October). It was celebrated with pergolas constructed on the roof of the temple, sacred banquets, and perhaps with the recitation of the myth of *Baal* or the hierogamy of *ʾEl, Atirat,* and *Rhmj,* represented by the king, the queen, and a priestess. Less clearly identifiable are the feast of the consecration of the temple in the Spring equinox, the mourning for the death of Baal, and the celebration of his victory over Mot, death, in June.

"Baal" in the Hebrew Scriptures, whether used singularly or plurally, expresses the diversity of places, forms, and times of his cult (cf. *Baal Peʿor,* Num 25:3, 5; Deut 4:3; Hos 9:10; Ps 106:28; *Baal Berit,* Judg 8:33; 9:4; *Baal Zebub,* 2 Kings 1:2, 6, 16). Hos 2:13, 17 and 11:2 suggest a collective and indeterminate meaning.

Similarly, the names of the companions of Baal are not used in a homogeneous manner in the Hebrew Scriptures. *Atirat,* spouse of *ʾEl* and mother of the gods in Ugarit, appears in the Hebrew Scriptures as "Asherah," companion to Baal (cf. 1 Kings 18:19; 2 Kings 23:4; Judg 3:7). Asherah can also signify the cultic representation in wood of the divinity (1 Kings 14:15; Deut 16:21).

Likewise Astarte is a companion of Baal (Judg 2:13; 10:6), whose cult would have been introduced by the foreign wives of Solomon (1 Kings 11:1-8). Texts such as 2 Kings 21:3; 23:13-15 and 2 Chr 33:3 exhibit a certain confusion between Asherah and Astarte.

Anath, also the spouse of Baal, does not appear as a divinity in the Hebrew Scriptures but only in the names of places (Josh 19:38; Judg 1:33) and persons (Judg 3:31; 5:6). *—Horacio Simian-Yofre*

the cult is present in the eighth century in the time of Hosea, is supported by Manasseh in Judah in the seventh century (2 Kings 21:1-9), and becomes the occasion for the radical religious reform of Josiah at the end of the same century (2 Kings 23:4-20).

Deuteronomist theology (2 Kings 17:7-18) interprets the fall of Samaria as a consequence of the idolatrous cult. The cult of Baal included altars and sacred pillars (Judg 6:25; 2 Kings 17:16), priests and prophets (1 Kings 10 and 18), offerings and sacrificial banquets with special ornaments and perhaps, though on extraordinary occasions, human sacrifice (Jer 19:5; Hos 13:2?). There may have been the practice of sacred prostitution as well (Judg 8:33; Num 25:1).

The Worship of the Calf

Different from Baal, the calf was probably not an idol or an object of worship replacing YHWH, but rather a "symbolic support" to the presence of YHWH and its placement was an act to authenticate the sanctuary of Bethel just as the ark, carried from Shiloh to Jerusalem, had legitimized an ancient Jebusite sanctuary. The calf, which had been an epithet and emblem of El in Ugarit, would have been associated also with YHWH in Israel (cf. Num 23:22; 24:8). In Deut 33:17 the clan of Joseph, "owners" of the sanctuary of Bethel where the bull was kept, was consequently associated with the bull. (Cf. also Gen 49:24, "the bull of Jacob.") Jacob appears intimately related with Bethel (Gen 28:10-22; 31:13; 35:7). The title "Bull of Jacob" is spiritualized in Ps 132:2 as well as in Isa 49:26 and 60:16.

Aaron would have been the eponymous figure of a sacerdotal group linked to the cult of YHWH in Bethel (cf. Judg 20:26-28), bearing the image of the bull as its symbol. This group may have been antagonistic to the Zadokite priesthood of Jerusalem, the only official priesthood left after the suppression of the priesthood of Abiathar by Solomon. The calf of the temple of Bethel would have tried to legitimate the priesthood of northern Israel by associating it with Aaron and his descendants, a legitimacy guaranteed by the presence of Aaron together with Moses in the tradition of the Exodus.

Hosea probably wants to use the bulls to point out the totality of Yahwist worship as it was practiced in Bethel and perhaps in Samaria. Hosea 8:5 and 10:5 indicate that this Yahwist practice, although it did not imply a formal idolatry, had become useless for Samaria and was now close to disappearing entirely. The absence of a reference to the bull or to idols in Hos 10:15, "Thus has Bethel done for you" [author's translation] confirms the impression that the object of the accusation and condemnation is the cult itself as realized in Bethel, not its possible idolatrous contaminations or influences.

2. Canonical Context

Hosea appears in all the traditional texts as the first book of the twelve "minor prophets," including the traditions of the LXX that present, besides the order of the Masoretic Text, another that modifies the sequence of the first six books (Hosea, Amos, Micah, Joel, Obadiah, Jonah). The manuscripts of Qumran witness to this order as well, thus giving evidence of the distinctive textual connections existing among the twelve minor prophets. The most recent studies confirm the testimony of tradition since they also illuminate the diverse textual connections existing among the twelve minor prophets.

3. Intertextuality

The prophecy of Hosea has used different traditions from the history of Israel, in particular those about the patriarch Jacob (Hosea 12; cf. Genesis 25–33), the infidelity of Moab (Hos 5:1-7; cf. Num 25:1-5), the fratricidal war against Benjamin in Gibeah (Hos 5:8-15; cf. 9:9; 10:9; Judges 20–21) and an obscure happening in Gilgal (Hos 9:15-17). Also there is reference to the theme of the desert, vaguely related to the Exodus from Egypt and presented in a different manner.

The influence of the prophecies of Hosea on the other books of the Hebrew Scriptures can be felt in their use of images and theological motifs. The image of the city-prostitute (Isa 1:21) may be independent of Hosea. On the other hand, his influence is evident in the origins of the matrimonial metaphor of YHWH as spouse of his people and of Israel as unfaithful bride appearing in Jer 2:2, 20, 25; 3:1-2, 6-10, with some variations but, nevertheless, articulating the same motifs (love of youth, gifts of the earth, infidelity and separation) and expressed with a similar vocabulary. Ezekiel 16 and 23 develop the metaphor with baroque richness. The metaphor reappears in a sober context in Deutero-Isaiah (Isa 50:1; 54:6-8).

Other influences of Hosea are felt in Jeremiah, including his insistence on the theme of "generosity" (*ḥesed,* Jer 2:2; 9:23; 16:5; 31:3; 33:11); the lack of knowledge of YHWH on the part of the priests (Jer 2:8) and of the entire people (Jer 4:22); the sonship of Israel (Jer 3:19, 22) and conversion (Jer 3:22-25); and the remembrance of the traditions of Rachel (Jer 31:15-22; cf. Hos 12:13).

The Deuteronomist has probably assumed the theology of Hosea in the theme of YHWH's love for the people *(ʾhb),* and also the motif of the search for YHWH, *drš* (to search, Hos 10:12). More important is the influence of Hosea (and the other prophets of the eighth century) on the deuteronomic laws for judges (Deut 16:18-20) and prophets (Deut 18:9-22). The conception of the monarchy differs in Hosea and in Deut 17:14-20.

One particular similarity of motifs and images can be found in Hos 14:1-8 and the Song of Songs, although it is difficult to establish a relationship of dependence.

The text of Hosea is scarcely ever used in the Christian Scriptures. Among the few references one finds Hos 11:1 (Matt 2:15); 6:6 ("I desire steadfast love and not sacrifice," Matt 9:13; 12:7; cf. also Mark 12:33); and 2:1, 25 (Rom 9:25-26, the election of the Gentiles). Literary allusions appear in Acts 13:10 (Hos 14:9), 1 Cor 15:55 (Hos 13:14) and Rev 6:16; 10:3, the image of the roaring lion (Hos 11:10) and the invocation to the mountains (10:8). But it is especially in the great theological metaphors that the influence of Hosea is found: God as the farmer who cares for the land (Hos 10:1; cf. Matt 15:13), the allegory of the great prostitute (Revelation 17; cf. Hosea 2), and in this context the reference to Jezebel (Rev 2:20; cf. Hosea 1) and the story of Naboth.

4. The Interpretation of the Classical Authors

Four Fathers of the Church wrote commentaries on the minor prophets: in 406 Jerome completed a commentary that included Hosea and four other prophets, a study which he had begun many years before. Other patristic commentators were Theodore of Mopsuestia (d. ca. 428), Cyril of Alexandria (ca. 444), and Theodoret of Cyrus (ca. 466). Jerome's commentary on the minor prophets hesitates between his literal fidelity to the Hebrew text and his messianic interpretation.

Particular interest arose among the classical authors concerning the interpretation of Hosea 1–3, and especially whether or not it deals with an authentic episode in the life of the prophet. There is also a question about how to explain the morality of the divine order received and accepted: or is it a theological allegory in which each term ought to be interpreted figuratively? Augustine (*De Doctrina Christiana* 3.33) affirms that "It is necessary to recognize as figurative that which in a divine discourse cannot refer in its literal meaning to the honesty of the customs or to the truth of the faith." In Jerome also (*Commentariorum in Osee prophetam libri tres ad Pammacium,* CCSL 76.1) there is tension between a literal interpretation—in part rejected and in part interpreted positively—and an allegorical reading that considers Hosea 1 as a prophetic discourse whose meaning is found in the names of the sons interpreted historically and typologically.

In the following centuries authors always opted for the allegorical interpretation. One such was Rupert of Deutz (d. ca. 1130), *Commentariorum in duodecim prophetas minores libri XXXI* (MPL 168. 9ff.). Other medieval Christian readers try to confront the literary and theological problem. Andrew of St. Victor (d. 1175) closely follows the interpretation of Jerome almost to the point of offering a summary of Jerome's work. The interpretation of Stephen Langton, teacher of theology in Paris and archbishop of Canterbury (d. 1228) affirms the historicity of the narrated happenings, establishes a clear relationship between chs. 1 and 3, and derives a spiritual interpretation from the deeds themselves. Israel has prostituted herself spiritually and bodily but she ought still to be consoled since God, symbolized by the prophet, has decided to espouse her.

Abraham ben Meir Ibn Ezra, (1092–1167) and Moises Maimonides (d. 1204) *Guía de descarriados,* Book II, chs. 32–46 interpret the story of Hosea as a vision. The prophetic images seen or realized in the vision are not real actions perceived by the senses.

In the thirteenth century Hosea 1–3 gave rise to bitter theological disputes over the essence of ethical conduct. While John Duns Scotus (d. 1308) defends the fact that God can dispense from the natural law in a broad sense, Thomas Aquinas (d. 1274), to the contrary, affirms that God can only demand that which by its nature is good. The case of Hosea is explained as a *dispensatio improprie dicta,* an exception from the commandments possible in some particular cases (*ST* I IIae, q. 100, art. VIII).

Martin Luther (d. 1546) defends an intermediary exegetical position, a less frequent stance among scholars. Hosea would have been legitimately married, he holds, and would have had legitimate children, but the prophet is speaking "spiritually, of spiritual prostitution, i.e., of the idolatry of the people" ("Vorrede bei dem Propheten Hosea," 1532, *WADB* 11/2, 182).

In his *Comentaria in Duodecim Prophetas Minores* (Antwerp 1625), Cornelius Lapide (Van den Steen, d. 1625) rejects the interpretation of Hosea 1 and 3 as a vision and interprets those chapters as historical fact, though read in a favorable light. Much like Aquinas, Lapide suggests that Hosea would have received the order to build a stable marriage with Gomer in order to denounce in that way the idolatrous behavior of the people of Israel.

Hermann von der Hardt (d. 1746), *Hoseas historiae et antiquitati redditus libris XXIX pro nativa interpretandi virtute, cum dissertationibus in Raschium* (Helmstadt 1712, pp. 67ff.; 90-91) introduced an interpretation that has appeal in our day. The story of Hosea is also a story of the love of the prophet for a woman whom he had believed to be honest, and who opened for him an understanding of YHWH's love for a people whom God had chosen to be faithful. His biography would then consist of seven successive episodes (four in Hosea 1, one in Hosea 2:2-3, and two in Hosea 3) that correspond to the seven consecutive moments in the real life history of the prophet.

5. Liturgical Use

The Roman Catholic liturgy presents six different pericopes of Hosea on eleven different days. Hosea 2:14-22 is used on the feast of St. Cecilia and the Eighth Sunday of Cycle B; 6:1-6 in Lent and on the Tenth Sunday of Cycle A; 11:1-9 on the feast of the Sacred Heart, Cycle B; 14:2-10 during Lent. The same texts, with the exception of Hos 6:1-6 and adding 8:4-13 and 10:1-12, are read in the continuous daily readings of the fourteenth week in even years.

SECOND READING

1:1

The editorial title of the book mentions four kings of Judah and only one from Israel, Jeroboam. The author is probably an inhabitant of the kingdom of Judah where the book of Hosea receives its definitive editing.

1:2–3:5

This section constitutes a complex and tightly knit unity; it relates the story of Hosea and Gomer. In reading these chapters it is necessary to respect three complementary levels, one biographical and theological, another historical, and a third, religious. (The verses in these chapters are numbered differently in Hebrew and in some modern translations, including English. Hebrew 2:1–25 corresponds to English 1:10–2:23. The verse numbering given below is for the English text.)

1:2-9

This short section relates the story of Hosea, Gomer, and their children. By order of YHWH Hosea "takes for himself" a "wife of whoredom" (cf. Hos 2:2, 4; 4:12; 5:4) and assigns special names to their children. "Jezreel," "Jehu," and the mention of "whoredom" appear in close relationship with the history of the rebellion of Jehu, anointed by the prophet Elisha (2 Kings 9–10; cf. 2 Kings 9:22) for the punishment of Joram and the sin of Ahab, his father. The latter had given in to the initiative of his wife, Jezebel, and permitted the assassination of Naboth of Jezreel in order to gain possession of his vineyard (1 Kings 21). "The blood of Jezreel" means the crimes committed in Jezreel for which "the house of Jehu," whose last king is contemporary with Hosea, are responsible. The punishment announced ("to break the bow" indicates a military defeat; cf. Hos 2:20; Jer 49:35; 1 Sam 2:4; Zech 9:10) also falls on the "house of Israel" (1:4b, 6b), which within the context of dynastic problems means it falls on the people who are the guarantors of legitimate authority. The "valley of Jezreel" had been the proverbial battle camp of Israel (Judg 6:33-35; 1 Sam 29:1-11). "Not pitied" alludes to the contrast between Israel and Judah (Hos 1:6-7). "Not my people" evokes the formula of the covenant, "I will be your God and you will be my people." The people will suffer the consequences of the king's actions and of their own inertia, and will become the "non-people" of YHWH.

1:10–2:1

This section interrupts the continuity of argumentation between 1:2-9 and 2:2-13 and elaborates theologically on the names of Gomer's children, giving them new meanings. The prophet anticipates the growth of the population, threatened at the moment by wars and deportations. (The presence of Tiglath-pileser III in Israelite territory as a consequence of the Syro-Ephraimic war against Judah would give sufficient reason for that concern.) He also looks forward to the conversion of "not-my-people" into "children of the living God" and the reunification of Israel and Judah under a single authority. The plant metaphor "to grow from the earth" and the name "Jezreel" ("God sows") confirm this promise.

The reunification came to be a permanent political and religious preoccupation of many Israelites. The mention of a "head" in place of a "king" (1:11; cf. Num 14:4; Judg 11:8) expresses the disillusionment they experienced in the face of the contemporary kings and the monarchy (cf. Hos 8:4; 10:3, 15). The "place" where this occurs underlines the existing relationship between the place of the crime and that of the punishment (1 Kings 21:19).

2:2-13

After the interruption, this section continues the personal story of Hosea and Gomer, with hidden allusions to the relationship between YHWH and Israel. The text is the monologue of a person, the prophet, who speaks directly to his children in v. 2 and then speaks about them in v. 4. The prophet declares that he is not the husband of the woman (cf. 1:9) or the father of her children; he imagines three short interventions with her, at times using the word "she" (2:5, 7, 12), and he adds her reactions (2:2, 5, 7, 13). He speaks of her lovers in the third person (2:5, 7, 10, 12, 13) and judges the relationship between the woman and her lovers and the cult of the Baals practiced by these lovers (2:8). The interlacing theological motifs direct the attention of the reader at times toward Hosea who is remembering Gomer fleeing from the house with a lover and at other times to YHWH who decides what punishment to level against an apostate people and a land contaminated by their infidelity.

The sadness over the disappearance of "festivals, new moons, sabbaths, and . . . festivals" (2:11) is a personal sentiment expressed by the woman (cf. Isa 32:9-14) but also by the entire people. An account will be exacted of both of them for "the festival days of the Baals" (2:13) in which they actively participated. The images and expressions are applied as much to the people as to the nation, the land, or an individual person. The story of a man and a woman as symbol of the story of humanity with God is used to advantage also by Genesis 2–3; Jer 3:6-9; the Song of Songs; texts of Ezekiel and of "second" and "third" Isaiah.

2:14-22

These verses have in common with 1:10–2:1 a preoccupation with the future (1:10, 2:16, 21), for example, the mention of a "day" on which promises will be fulfilled (1:11, 2:16, 18, 21). Its interest for etymological connotations of Jezreel ("God sows" 1:11, 22, 23) and the use of "land/earth" without further precision (1:11, 18, 21, 22) is another unifying facet. The text is a word of YHWH that takes up the motifs of the Canaanite world (the wilderness, 2:14-15, the cult of the Baals, 2:17, the topic of fertility, 2:21-22, and the nuptials, 2:16, 19-20) and elaborates on them theologically, together with the proper understandings from Israelite theology (covenant and the abolition of war, 2:18) in order to express the new relationships being established between YHWH and the people (cf. 1:11b). The names of the children are repeated in 2:23. From the free-flowing ambiguity of vv. 2-13 between Gomer, the people, and the land we move to a homogeneous text that refers to the people; there are allusions to the land and the place where they live. The theological language of the covenant (2:18), of the divine attributes (2:19-20) and of the renewal of nature (2:21-22) replaces the language of the passions (2:2-13).

Hosea 2:14-22 shows the gratuitous aspect of YHWH's love, indeed, a love that does not expect any change in the attitude of the people. YHWH leads this people to the desert in order to give them divine gifts. Words like "allure" and "convince" situate us in an ambience of offense and reconciliation. The wilderness, in this instance, is not a synonym for punishment and parched land (2:3), nor is it the place of YHWH's election (9:10) or the place of privileged knowledge of God (13:5; cf. 13:4). This reference to wilderness is not to the place of the Exodus (9:10; 13:5), the hypothetical golden age of relationships between YHWH and the people, nor is it a literary and pastoral motif (cf. Song 3:6; 8:5) but a paradigmatic place far from the urban cult of the Baals. It is the dwelling place of YHWH, and for that reason an apt image of a definitive salvation not linked to the past history of the chosen people.

Verses 19 and 20 are set up as contrast to the price paid by Hosea in order to recover his wife (3:2-3). Here YHWH espouses his bride with generous gifts: justice, right, tenderness, fidelity. These gifts can be summarized as "magnanimity," which describes both human and divine attributes and implies the disposition and capacity to act positively in service of one's own life and the lives of others (cf. 2:19; 4:1; 6:4, 6; 10:12; 12:7).

Hosea has expressed the relationship of God with the people in personalist categories. YHWH is father and spouse of the people, one who holds close a relationship founded on respect for the rights of the other person. For that reason the attitude Hosea shows toward the cult is one of profound distrust. The claim to seek YHWH with sacrifices is condemned to failure (5:6; 6:6; 8:13); Israel's altars serve only for sinning (8:11), and for that reason they will be destroyed (10:2) or buried under thorns and thistles (10:8; 12:12).

3:1-3

This section continues quite naturally the story of Hosea in 2:2-13. Its autobiographical style puts into sharp relief the drama of the story's ending, the betrothal of Hosea. The order that Hosea receives to again look for an adulterous woman, now the property of another man, suggests that this woman is none other than Gomer.

The wide range of meaning for "adulteress" includes adultery in its proper sense (Hos 4:2; 7:4; cf. Lev 20:10) or that which was linked to sacred rituals (Hos 4:13-14), idolatry (Jer 3:9), or the wickedness of the people in general (Jer 9:1-2). All these possible meanings permit a comparison with the Israelites who "are turning to other gods" as an unfaithful wife turns to other men (cf. Deut 29:17; 30:17; 31:18).

These actions, presumably biographical, receive in Hos 3:4-5 an interpretation that is historical and theological. It takes the form of a discourse by YHWH predicting the future relationship of Israel with YHWH (a similar process to that observed in 1:10–2:1 with respect to 1:2-9 and in 2:14-23 with respect to 2:2-13). The text suggests the imminent disappearance of the monarchy, the authorities, the legitimate sacrifices and of other less acceptable elements of worship: the cultic pillar, sign also of the Baals, and the instruments for consulting the divinity *(ephod)* as well as the small idols representing the household gods *(teraphim)*.

Hosea 4

This chapter is framed by two exhortations to listen (4:1; 5:1). Verses 1-3 of ch. 4 encourage the Israelites to be conscious of the indictment YHWH has issued against the nation (4:1b) because of the evils that grieve God, evils expressed both negatively (4:1b) and positively (4:2). Verse 3 alludes to the consequences of the situation for the entire country including nature. The text uses several expressions already present in 2:2–3:5: "accuse," "judgment"; the triple repetition of "there is no . . . without" (4:1b; 3:4); the concepts of "magnanimity, faithfulness, knowledge" (4:1b; 2:19-20); the verb "to commit adultery" (4:2a; 3:1); the mention of the beasts of the fields and the birds of the air (4:3a; 2:18); the triple repetition of "land, earth" (4:1, 3; 2:18, 21, 22).

Verses 4-14 present an accusation against the priests as the ones who are responsible for the sins of the people (4:4, 6, 9; cf. 4:5, 7, 8, 10). The relationship between YHWH and the priests (4:7-10) is dominated by the vocabulary of transgression: "sin," "shame," "iniquity," and of retribution: "punish" and "repay." While vv. 11-14 denounce cultic prostitution, v. 14 summarizes the situation as follows: the women of Israel have prostituted themselves in the sacred worship but an account of their actions will not be asked of them; rather it is the priests who are the truly responsible ones ("they," v. 14a).

Verses 15-19 complete the description of the situation in which the country finds itself and denounces the priests as the responsible agents. Though there is no precise function for the partial repetition of vocabulary such as "play the whore," "guilt," "lewdness," this repetition—together with the allusions to "idols," drunkenness, altars, and the lack of any development in the thought—suggests that these verses are at least partially for the purpose of academic precision.

5:1-7

This short section is delimited by the three imperatives of v. 1, three further imperatives in v. 8, the different geographical names mentioned, and the persons addressed in each text. In Shittim, as in Mizpah and Tabor, places of sanctuaries, the action of the priests is the occasion for corruption of the people. The "house of Israel" and the court of the king ought to be conscious of that. Two motifs with variations, whoredom (5:3b, 4b, 7a) and the uselessness of the cult (5:4a, 6a, 7b) are woven around the central affirmation of v. 5a: the Pride of Israel (YHWH) bears witness against the priests.

The prophet addresses the priests and speaks systematically of YHWH in the third person. Ephraim and Israel are not the ones addressed, but they also become characters spoken of in the third person.

5:8-15a

These verses are unified by the presence of YHWH in the first person and by the pronounced presence of those addressed: "you." "Blow the horn" and "blow the trumpet" suggest that the ones addressed are the priests to whom is reserved the function of calling together the community for a cultic gathering (Num 10:4, 7) to break camp (Num 10:5-6) or go on a defensive war (Num 10:9).

"Judah" (5:10, 12, 13, and 14) unquestionably belongs to this text that condemns Judah's attitude, just as it does Ephraim's. Both tribes of

Israel have transgressed the boundaries of justice. Ephraim and Judah are equally culpable (5:10, 11), responsible (5:13) and deserving of punishment (5:12, 14).

It is probable that in a situation of conflict with Judah over boundaries the priests would have found it an urgent need to seek the help of Assyria in order to shatter the enemy/brother people. Perhaps it is for that reason that Hosea alludes to the war against Benjamin described in Judges 20. Hosea also condemns as crimes against YHWH the attitude of favoring unjust and bloody solutions.

5:15b–6:7

The linking of 5:15b with 6:1 allows the same subject to act in the whole text, and favors the hypothesis of textual unity. The text is not an exhortation to conversion on the part of the prophet nor is it an authentic declaration of the desires and intentions of Ephraim and Judah; rather it is a presumed discourse of the people pronounced by the prophet in the name of YHWH who exposes the pretended and therefore deceitful conversion of the people. In 6:1-3 the people apply to themselves in a positive way the threat hidden in the discourse of YHWH (5:13-15a). YHWH moves away, let us then follow after him; YHWH crushes but also heals; YHWH will wait until the people seek God, the people are disposed to live in God's presence ("before him"); YHWH hopes that they will look for God, and the people suppose that YHWH's coming will be as sure as the dawn.

But YHWH again takes up the response of the people (6:4-6) in order to denounce this illusory conversion. God's will, indeed, will be manifest as the dawn; YHWH will not come as the rains of winter or spring because the fidelity of Israel is like a morning cloud that promises rain and then dissipates. The knowledge of YHWH will not water the earth because the fidelity of Israel is as tenuous as the dew that disappears before the morning sun. The contrast is resumed in 6:6. "For I desire steadfast love and not sacrifice, the knowledge of God rather than burnt offerings."

The text continues to hold in ambiguity the person or persons addressed until 6:8-9. The powerful group being accused is Gilead, an influential part of the "house of Israel" (6:10) in which priests also participated. The text is a soliloquy of YHWH in the face of the inconsistent fidelity of the people and the power of its leading group.

6:8–7:16

This text is made up of four sections, each marked by a negative expression that reflects the distortion of reality between YHWH and the people and the inadequate reaction of those addressed by the text: "they do not consider that I remember all their wickedness" (7:2); "none of them calls upon me" (7:7); "they do not seek [God]" (7:10); "they do not cry to me from the heart" (7:14).

The text begins with a violent denunciation by the prophet, including concrete names (6:8-11a). This is followed by a reflection on the part of YHWH who wants to "heal" Israel (7:1) and who "remembers" their wickedness (7:2a). Hosea 6:8–7:2 is related to 7:3-7 because of the repetition of the terms "wickedness" and "crime" (7:1, 2, 3). The group being accused is referred to as "the people of Gilead." The text could be referring to the conspiracy of Pekah against King Pekahiah and his assassination about 735, a plot in which fifty men from Gilead participated (2 Kings 15:25), but also it could refer to a prior conspiracy of the Gileadean party—to which the conspirators Shallum and Menahem and probably some priests belonged—a plot against King Zechariah, son of Jeroboam II, assassinated by Shallum in Ibleam, "en route to Shechem." It is not likely that the prophet would speak of assassinations as more or less private crimes. Hosea 7:3-7 uncovers the strategy of the group denounced through the allegory of the baker (the king) who is careless about the ovens (the groups in power) and thus lets the dough (the situation) deteriorate. Verses 8-12 describe the situation of Ephraim itself. The two comparisons (vv. 8 and 11) with their respective applications (vv. 9 and 12) articulated through a denunciation (v. 10) express the consequences that will fall upon the people because of the action of the accused group.

The text concludes with a lamentation (7:13-16) that is joined to the previous section by the mention of Egypt (7:11, 16). A second unifying feature is the tension between YHWH who tries to trap the people and unite them to God again (v. 12), and the theme of Ephraim who "has not returned" (vv. 10b, 16a), who "goes" toward another destination (v. 11b), who "strays" (v. 13a), and who "rebels" (vv. 13b, 14b). These relationships suggest that we should consider vv. 13 to 16 of ch. 7 an integral part of the unit composed of vv. 8-16 and distinct from vv. 3-7 which do not directly refer to Ephraim.

8:1-14

This chapter is a treatment of the situation of the country delimited by two imperatives (8:1; 9:1) and organized into two major sections connected by v. 7. YHWH directs the prophet to sound the trumpet and to speak "as a herald" against the temple of YHWH (vv. 1-3), actually the ancient temple at Bethel. YHWH orders him to denounce the violation of the covenant by the priests (cf. Hos 6:7; Josh 7:11, 15; 23:6; Judg 2:20; 2 Kings 18:20) and their ignorance of the will of YHWH. Verses 4 to 6 specify the transgression and establish a close relationship between the evils that afflict Israel, the sins into which they have fallen, and the presence of the bull within the cult. The word "they" can scarcely be made to refer to the people as a whole; rather the accused are those who "made kings [and] . . . set up princes" without the authority of YHWH, the ones who fabricated idols of silver and gold (v. 4). The accused are the leaders, the authorities or priests who dispose of power and have the necessary means for carrying that action to its end. Verse 7a is a metaphor taken from agricultural life. One gathers, qualitatively and quantitatively, what has been sowed (Hos 10:12; Prov 22:8; Job 4:8). The metaphor articulates the two sections of the text (8:1-6 and 8:8-14) because both contain the two elements: the fluidity of the wind and the violence of the whirlwind. Wind is the claim to know YHWH (8:2), to be able to make princes and fabricate idols (8:4). The hurricane will be the enemy (v. 3) and the destruction of those idols (v. 6b). Vain are the efforts made to gain the good will of the oppressor (vv. 9, 10, 11); violent will be the dispersal into foreign territory (v. 8), submission (v. 10), exile (v. 13) and destruction (v. 14). Verses 8-13 anticipate the consequences that will fall on the city because of the attitudes described in vv. 4 to 6; they recall the transgression (8:11-13a) and announce the punishment. Verse 14b can be found almost literally in Amos 1:4, 7, 10, 12; 2:2.

The text is not an oracle directed toward the guilty but the reflection of the prophet expressed as the word of YHWH and directed to him about the situation, perhaps at the time of Menahem, who brought to a close the internal political crisis subsequent to the death of Jeroboam II but who should have confronted the external political and military crisis and paid the tribute of 1000 talents of silver to Tiglath-pileser (cf. 2 Kings 15:19). This text could be conceived or rightly spoken by the prophet when a delegation from Israel went to Assyria to pay the annual tribute (see 8:8, 9, 10). Hosea speaks of the responsibility of the leaders, authorities, and priests in the third person because, in fact, they are not present, but neither are the people completely innocent since they have permitted such a situation to exist or have excused themselves from taking the initiative to change the situation. For that reason Hosea can also speak of their guilt and punishment (8:11-13).

9:1-17

Chapter 9 maintains a thematic continuity with ch. 8. Hosea 9:3b ("Ephraim shall return to Egypt") picks up 8:13b. The prophet had already spoken of sacrifices (9:4) in 8:11-23, and the "gathering" as part of the punishment (9:6a) is also found in 8:10. Finally, 9:9b is a literal repetition of 8:13b. However, the discourse about Israel/Ephraim from 8:8-14 is changed into an interpellation aimed directly at Israel in 9:1, 5, and interest centers not on the relation of religion to politics as in Hosea 8 but on worship and the prophets.

Hosea 9 is divided into two principal sections framed by the inclusion "peoples"/"nations" (9:1, 17) and related to one another through the mention of the wine vat, libations (vv. 2 and 4), and grapes (v. 10). The allusion to Baal-peor (v. 10) may relate to the idolatry mentioned in v. 1a. Verses 1 to 9 describe a situation of threat and punishment and are closely linked by the repetition of some expressions. In vv. 1-5 a cultic vocabulary prevails: "rejoice . . . exult" (9:1; cf. Lev 23:40; Deut 16:11, 14, 15), "threshing floor" and "wine vat" (9:1, 2; cf. Deut 16:13); "eat unclean food" (vv. 3, 4); "house of YHWH/house of God" (vv. 4, 8); "day of appointed festival // festival of YHWH" (v. 5). Verses 6-9 are characterized by the vocabulary of punishment, both present and future: "days of punishment" // "days of recompense" (v. 7); "days of Gibeah" (v. 9); "hostility" (vv. 7, 8); "visit," "iniquity" (vv. 7, 9). There are others: devastation, bury, trap, corruption, sins. The prophet speaks of YHWH in the third person (9:1, 3, 4, 5, 8) while questioning Israel directly (vv. 1, 5) or refers to it in other verses.

"Israel" could refer to the people as a whole (9:1, read in the light of v. 3), but the importance of the threshing floor and the wine vat in the legislation about the retribution of the Levites (Num 18:25-32 and particularly vv. 27 and 30) suggests that it is a particular reference to those in charge of worship. Verse 1 does not refer to the technical impurities of the sacrifices about which the prophet speaks beginning with v. 34, but rather refers to the celebration itself. Hosea criticizes the totality of the present cult to which the celebration on foreign soil will add only a legal impurity.

Hosea also criticizes Israel for its abuse of prophecy, turning it into either ecstasy or charlatanism. Interest is concentrated on the perplexity created in the minds of those hearing the rhetorical question "What will you do?" (9:5) if the people in the Assyrian exile are not able to offer an acceptable worship, a worship in which you had placed all your hope. The only possible answer—that "a sentinel for my God" be able to orient the people—is seen as thwarted by the snares lying in wait along the path (9:8).

Hosea 9:10-17 is composed of two sections (9:10b-14 and 9:15-17) preceded by an introduction (v. 10a) that determines that they are a discourse of YHWH and correspond closely to each other. Each section begins with the mention of a geographical place (Baal-peor, Gilgal), describes the deception of YHWH because of the treason of Israel/Ephraim in those two places and important moments of their history, and, finally, announces different punishments.

The prophet speaks in the name of YHWH in vv. 10-13 and 15-16 and in his own name in vv. 14 and 17, whether he is interceding ambiguously for the people or upholding the decisions of YHWH. "My God" (v. 17) stands over and against an implicit God of "your ancestors" (v. 10), which identifies the addressees. The same vocabulary is repeated in both sections: Ephraim, love (9:11, 15), birth, womb (vv. 11, 16), dry breasts, dry roots (vv. 14, 16), miscarrying womb, unproductive of fruit (vv. 14, 16), emphatic "even if" (vv. 12, 16). Verses 10a and 16a contain contrasting vegetation metaphors.

YHWH has found Israel in the desert accidentally, and not as the result of a long-prepared search; YHWH is happy, but very soon is disappointed in that joy. The denunciation of the people's faults is implied in the two historical allusions, to Baal-peor, synonym for religious and idolatrous transgressions, and to Gilgal, a probable reference to political faults. In both sections punishment, which is expressed in terms of a progression (9:11, 12, 13) falls on the descendants of Israel. There is the image of a sterile tree and reference to children who are dying (v. 16).

The second section also introduces the thought of the desert (9:15) and the dispersion (9:17b). The accused are "your ancestors," those responsible for the deeds of Baal-peor (v. 10) and "their officials" (v. 15), but the people must also bear the consequences of belonging to this nation. The prophet tries to minimize their suffering and uphold the idea that "his God" is ultimately not the same as "the God of those others."

10:1-8

This section is arranged concentrically. Verses 1-2 present the two extremes of the process the people are living: altars multiply as the consequence of economic well-being but this fact has corrupted their hearts. Expiation requires destruction, but before this can occur the people must experience the events presented in vv. 3-8, recognizing the incapacity and absence of their king while injustice rules over the country, the useless veneration of the calf and grief over having lost it, the general state of confusion, and the definitive disappearance of the king. Verse 8a returns to the final situation anticipated in v. 2: thorn and thistle take possession of these places of worship recently destroyed.

In 10:2 all the elements of the pericope are concentrated and represented by the comparison and contrast of two verbs: "be inconstant, be divided" on the one hand, and "pay, expiate" on the other. Israel is inconstant in its political attitudes (that is, its relationship with the king), in its religious attitudes (syncretism), and in its political-religious attitudes (the establishment of alliances sealed with religious insignia). Because of a lack of principles Ephraim must pay according to the dictum expressed in 8:7: with the loss of a king there is also the loss of religious signs and the destruction of the symbols of its alliance.

Hosea 10:9-15 weaves into the former text through v. 15b which emphasizes and amplifies the affirmation of v. 7a concerning the disappearance of the king. Verses 9-10 probably allude to the war of the tribes of Israel against the Benjaminites in Gibeah (Judges 20; cf. Hos 5:8; 9:9). Hosea denounces the conviction of Israel that since that time any war would be as easy for them as the operation of Gibeah. They had not experienced that event in their own flesh. The defeat of Benjamin had been not only a punishment for it, but also a sin on the part of Ephraim.

The violent fratricidal struggle, with the risk of complete annihilation of a tribe (Judges 21) constituted a paradigmatic moment for Hosea and those who reflect on the ancient and long-lasting animosity existing between the "tribes of Israel." At the moment when Israel/Ephraim try to ally themselves with the powerful (Assyria) by means of submission and treaties, it is likely that Hosea foresees a repetition of the ancient experience of powerful coalitions bent upon destroying Judah or any other lesser kingdom.

11:1-11

Chapter 11 is composed of two unequal sections. In vv. 1-9 YHWH recalls three successive moments in the divine relationship with Israel/Ephraim: first, YHWH's love for a son, Israel, expressed in images of paternal and maternal tenderness (vv. 1-4); second, the inevitable suffering of Israel because of its own decisions (vv. 5-7); and finally, the divine anguish that carries on a debate between justice and tenderness and finally opts for mercy (vv. 8-9). Verses 10-11 speak of YHWH in the third person, inverting the theme from the exile to Egypt and Assyria (v. 5) and concluding with the formula "oracle of YHWH" (cf. Hos 2:15, 23).

The call of Israel, as son, out of Egypt (11:1) alludes to the Exodus (cf. Exod 4:21-22). To this call is contrasted that of the "others" (11:2, "Baals" and "idols"), who are attracting the attention of Israel and to whom Israel is offering sacrifice and incense. YHWH teaches this people how to walk; he takes them in arms to care for them and heal them (11:3, cf. Hos 5:13; 7:1; Jer 7:14). YHWH bends down toward this people in order to feed them (11:4; cf. Ps 40:2), lifts them up to kiss them. But Ephraim does not recognize the attitude of YHWH ("they did not know that I healed them," 11:3; cf. 2:10; 4:6; 7:9).

YHWH attracts the people "with cords of human kindness, with bands of love" (11:4a), not with the chains of authority. The anticipated exile is situated on the historical level (Assyria) and also on the theological level (Egypt). It is caused by the "plans" made for Israel (cf. Hos 10:6; Ps 5:11) because these are tied to their apostasy.

YHWH's internal deliberation (11:8-9) is situated within the perplexing question of 6:4 and witnesses to the process of doubt and regret prior to decision. YHWH is the parent who ought to judge a beloved and rebellious son (cf. Deut 29:22-23). Verses 10 and 11 are anticlimactic: the didactic repetitions, the ambiguity of "they shall come trembling," and the geographic impreciseness (out of the sea, from the west) suggest that at least v. 10b may be a poorly conceived interpretative gloss. The image of YHWH as a roaring lion (cf. Hos 5:14; 13:7; Amos 1:2; 3:4, 8) who precedes a group of the exiles returning like migratory birds suggests at least an editor familiar with the strongly imaginative style of Hosea. The final formula, "oracle of YHWH" (cf. 2:15, 18, 23) supports the hypothesis of an editorial elaboration.

Hosea 12

(There is a displacement between the Hebrew text and translations: Hebrew ch. 12 begins with 11:12 of the translation.) The story of the patriarch Jacob is interwoven with that of Ephraim. Jacob's story is presented not only with explicit references but also by means of allusions. The explicit references include the episodes of the birth of Jacob (Hos 12:3; cf. Gen 25:26; 27:36), his struggle with the mysterious person in Penuel (Hos 12:4a; cf. Gen 32:23-32), and the encounter with YHWH in Bethel (Hos 12:4b; cf. Gen 28:10-22a). The flight of Jacob to Aram and his work as a keeper of the flock "for a wife" (12:12) is an obvious reference to Gen 27:43 (flight) and 29:15, 20 (service).

The allusions to Jacob begin with the flight to Aram (12:1: Ephraim "herds the wind" and "pursues the east wind all day long"; cf. Gen 30:31; 31:23). Verses 5-6 apply the story of Bethel to the situation of Israel. "YHWH is his name" corresponds to the presentation "YHWH, the God of Abraham your father and the God of Isaac" from Gen 28:13 (also see Exod 3:15 for the association of "name" and "title"). "Return to your God" recalls the promise of YHWH to Jacob (Gen 28:15) and the exhortation given Ephraim to "hold fast to love and justice" (Hos 12:6b) and to "wait continually for your God" evoke the promise of YHWH to protect Jacob (Gen 28:15).

Verses 7-8 criticize an Ephraim that takes advantage of its neighbors and is satisfied at having become as rich as Jacob did in the service of Laban (Gen 30:43). Hosea 12:11 alludes to the covenant between Jacob and Laban in Galeed (Gen 31:44-54; cf. the mention of the heap of stones [vv. 46, 51, 52] and the etymological explanation of Galeed as "a mound of testimony," [vv. 47, 48]).

Hosea 12 is a rigorous literary unity. The identity established between Ephraim and Israel in v. 1 is confirmed in v. 14 which associates Ephraim with the house of Israel. The prophet wants to include Judah in his criticism of Ephraim. YHWH now mentions the divine name and rights as the God of Israel from the land of Egypt (12:9a) in order to assure the people that the imminent punishment (made known through the numerous visions given the prophets [12:10] as in the time of the "festival" in the desert [12:9b]) is included in a total plan of YHWH who punishes in order to correct.

The story of Jacob/Ephraim denounces lying, deceit, and falsehood which each has manifested in dealing with brothers, in lack of confidence in YHWH, in economic relationships, and in the ambiguity of pacts. Jacob has sinned by deceit and Ephraim will be punished by the prophets who will publish their visions in the midst of the people (cf. Hos 4:2; 7:3; 9:2; 10:13; 11:12). Jacob sought his salvation in flight to Aram, Ephraim in his relationships with the east. This will be Ephraim's punishment, but as with Jacob, perhaps the beginning of his conversion as well. But before that he has to serve his sentence (Hos 12:14): the "his Lord will bring his crimes down on him," and before allowing him to return to his land will "pay him back for his insults" that Ephraim has first given to God (cf. v. 2).

13:1–14:1

This section is framed by the mention of the culpability of Ephraim (13:1) and of Samaria (14:1); it is structured as a word of YHWH (13:4-14) and is framed by two reflections that can be conveniently attributed to the prophet himself. The text uses expressions, images, and motifs from the prophecy of Hosea but does not reflect a precise situation. The emphasis on the material cult of the Baals (13:1-2), the recourse to Hosea's vocabulary but with an inversion of meaning in some of the images (v. 3), the introduction of the theme of the king as opposed to YHWH as savior, and the careful concentric composition all suggest that this text was planned as the conclusion to the book. It introduces a precision foreign to the core of Hosea's thought but especially picks up again and deepens reflections about the relationship of Ephraim and YHWH.

One can distinguish four sections. In the first (13:1-3) Ephraim is accused of idolatry. The second section (vv. 4-9) describes the past actions of YHWH in favor of the people; it also describes present and future action against them. Stylistically vv. 4-9 correspond to vv. 1-3. This is particularly true with vv. 3 and 7 ("they shall be"/"I will become"). Each verb is then followed by four comparisons.

The third section (13:10-14) underlines the king's incapacity to act in favor of his people and the tragic future that awaits Ephraim for having put its confidence in such a king. The question "where?" (13:10 and 14b), preceded in v. 14a by another double question, frames the section.

The fourth section (13:15-16) announces the definitive punishment and corresponds to the denunciation of the crimes committed (13:1-3). In both sections the discourse is pronounced by the prophet in his own name and refers as much to Ephraim/Samaria as to YHWH; all the actors are referred to in the third person.

Hosea 11:8-9 seemed to explain the interior process of YHWH who opted for a unilateral generosity and pardon, but this pardon had not been desired nor required. Prepared by 12:15, then, ch. 13 marks YHWH's moment of judgment. Following an explanation of faults (13:2, 6) and punishment (13:3, 9, 11) there is a parenthesis of commiseration (v. 13). However, v. 14

is decisive. YHWH's question, "Shall I ransom them . . . Shall I redeem them . . . ?" waits for those addressed to express interest in their own destiny. But they are absent (the question uses the third person) and the verse concludes with a sad affirmation (13:14b) that v. 15 will develop meditatively and v. 16 will seal with a condemnatory sentence.

Attempts have been made to explain the disconnectedness between chs. 11 and 13 by appealing to the historical tradition of the text of Hosea or to its composition, but in either case we must accept the obvious disconnectedness of the final text.

14:2-9

This text includes two different sections. In vv. 2-4 the prophet exhorts the people to be converted and includes the very "words" the people ought to speak in presenting themselves before YHWH. The proclamation of the mercy of YHWH who pardons every fault (14:2b) and who has compassion on the orphan, the prototype of the helpless (14:3b) provides the setting for the implicit recognition of faults and the promise of the people (14:2b-3a). The "fruit of our lips" (14:2b) expresses a decision to change the course of action and can be accepted as satisfactory compensation by YHWH.

The people recognize the grave faults (14:3) that Hosea has denounced in his prophecy, namely putting confidence in the help of military or foreign powers and abandoning themselves to the worship of idols (cf. 13:2). The new attitude of YHWH toward the people, now that the divine anger has been placated (14:4-8), is felt in the language, which now uses and corrects expressions and metaphors taken from Hosea 1–13 and introduces others of a bucolic nature. The dew, image of inconstancy and the fickleness of the people (Hos 6:4; 13:3) means now the living strength of YHWH who makes Israel flower like lilies. The forests of Lebanon suggest a deep rooting (Ps 104:16), vigor and greatness (Isa 2:13; Ps 92:13), beauty and happiness (Song 4:8); the text is enfleshed with images of fecundity: the new growth and the olive tree (14:6a; cf. 13:15). The shade of the trees on the renewed earth replaces the shadow that protected the corrupt cults (4:13). The grain (cf. 7:14) will now be "revived" (cf. 6:2). Israel, "bitter grapes" (9:10) and "flattened vineyard" (10:1), is now a flourishing vine and the wine (element of corruption in 7:3-7) is part of the renown (cf. 12:5) of the nation.

The question of 14:8 (cf. 6:4; 11:8; 13:14) suggests an apology to the people for having confused YHWH with their idols. Hosea 14:4-8 seems to express, notwithstanding 13:15 and the lack of any sign whatsoever of a change of attitude on the part of the people, that a compassionate Yahwist experiences nostalgia. After the destruction of Samaria and the deportations that accompanied it (2 Kings 18:11) he looks at his people with understanding and to God with unshakable trust.

Hosea 14:9 is a concluding sapiential reflection that has perceived the importance of the theme of "knowing" within the prophecy of Hosea (cf. 2:8; 4:14; 5:3, 4; 6:3; 7:9; 8:2, 4; 9:7; 11:3; 13:4, 5). The conclusion in 14:9b contrasts the straight paths of YHWH (a unique expression in the Hebrew Scriptures) along which the upright walk with the twisted paths denounced by the prophecy of Hosea (2:6; 4:9; 9:8; 10:13; 12:2) as the places of "stumbling" (4:5; 5:5; 14:2) for transgressors. But the difficult point for the wise person to understand must be the disconnectedness between the culpable and recalcitrant behavior of Ephraim and the frequent severe words pronounced by Hosea, on the one hand, and the exuberant promises of 14:4-8 on the other. The wise person does not want to deny a possible solution, though it be extreme in mercy. The promises are comprehensible only in the mystery of the divine decisions: human persons must deal with the fact that only the just walk in the paths of YHWH while traitors stumble along the way.

BIBLIOGRAPHY

Andersen, Francis I., and David Noel Freedman. *Hosea.* AB 24. New York: Doubleday, 1990.

Limburg, James. *Hosea–Micah.* Atlanta: John Knox, 1988.

Macintosh, Andrew A. *A Critical and Exegetical Commentary on Hosea.* Edinburgh: T & T Clark, 1997.

Wolff, Hans-Walter. *Hosea.* Translated by Gary Stansell. Edited by Paul D. Hanson. Hermeneia. Philadelphia: Fortress, 1974.

Joel

Ana Flora Anderson and Gilberto Gorgulho

FIRST READING

Getting Started

The book of Joel has a special significance for today's reader. In many parts of the world, in both hemispheres, there is more unemployment, hunger, devastation, and a general feeling of living in a period of crisis than has been felt since the world wars. This experience of devastation and crisis is the center of the prophecy of Joel (Joel 2:1-11).

The prophet also speaks of ecological wasting and the destruction of the ecological balance: once again, a problem that is almost universal in today's world. Joel questions the devastation of nature: Does humanity have complete dominion over nature? Or has it not lived up to its deep ecological responsibilities?

All over the world we hear a cry: Where is God? Who is God? Can anyone help us escape from what seems to be an almost universal destruction? Joel tries to answer these questions within the historical context of his time (Joel 1:15; 2:12-14). For the first time the call to assembly and to decision is universal: the elderly, the young men and women, adolescents, children and slaves are united in Zion to face the future and to receive the promise of the gift of the Spirit.

The book of Joel has four chapters in Hebrew, but only three in the Greek translation (LXX). Most English-language Bibles follow the Greek text. The Hebrew text of Joel 1–2 = 1:1–2:27 in our Bibles. Joel 3–4 = 2:28–3:21 in our translations. In this commentary we will use the enumeration found in most English-language Bibles. It would be good now to open our Bibles and follow the structure of Joel's theological context, including the heart of his prophecy:

(1) The prophecy is framed with references to the *generations* who will hear and respond to it (1:3; 2:2; 3:20).

(2) The spiritual context of the prophecy is the *House of YHWH,* threatened by devastation and dis-grace and at the same time an instrument of salvation or grace (1:9, 13, 14, 16; 3:18).

(3) The *Day of YHWH* is a call to sanctity and to conversion before God who comes to judge the people and the nations (1:15; 2:1, 11; 3:14).

(4) The heart of Joel's theology is found in 2:13-29. In these verses we have the determining pivot of his text. It is because God is *who God is* that the prophet can promise that from dis-grace there will come grace.

Joel presents us with his revelation of God's very being (2:13). Our God is *gracious (ḥanun), compassionate (raḥum), slow to anger, and full of love (ḥesed).* This verse echoing Exod 34:6 is the basis of Joel's theological vision: this generation will pass from dis-grace to grace because of YHWH's identity. The one who is compassionate and has an abundance of love will give us the greatest gift.

(5) This gift is the outpouring of the Spirit on all the community, women and men, young and old (2:28-32). This is the salvation that comes with the Day of YHWH.

The Book as a Whole

There are many theories about the unity of the book of Joel. Joel 1:2–2:17 is seen as a series of repetitive liturgical laments in which the people emphasize the dimensions of the national crisis. Judah is presented as a young woman (*betūlāh,* 1:8), dressed in sackcloth and mourning her husband.

Joel 2:18 is a turning point in the text. The community is called to face the future: for them it will be grace and blessing, symbolized by the abundance of wine and grain and oil. The people should not fear, but rejoice and be glad (2:21-23) because by YHWH's wish prosperity has returned to the land. The prophecy ends with four oracles against foreign nations. In the Valley of Jehoshaphat (= YHWH judges) they are called to retaliation (3:1-8), that is, to pay back for what they have done to Judah.

Today most commentaries stress the unity of Joel because the five theological points we mentioned above (cf. Getting Started) are repeated through the four chapters of the prophecy. Joel 1–3 has a well-defined literary structure:

—it begins and ends with the generations (five times) and the House of YHWH (five times);
—the Day of YHWH unites the whole text from 1:15 to 3:14 (five times);
—the heart of the text unites the two parts: the very being and identity of YHWH (2:13) is the source of YHWH's most important gift to the community, the outpouring of the Spirit (2:28-32).

The first part (1:2–2:27) is seen as a description of the nation's disgrace and the second part (2:28–3:21) as God's response which is grace and salvation (2:31-32).

Original Historical Context

The text of Joel permits us to situate the prophecy in Jerusalem after the reforms of Nehemiah and Ezra (398 B.C.E.). At that time Judah was becoming a theocracy led by priests and the doctors of the Law. In the midst of this hierarchical society there are prophetic groups looking for equality and solidarity. [See also the article "Prophetism and Prophets."] They propose a liturgy that celebrates:

—the coming of YHWH;
—the Day;
—the outpouring of the Spirit;
—a covenant of God's prophetic people foreseen by Moses (Num 11:26-30).

Post-Exilic Institutions

The prophecy of Joel contains several indications that point to a post-exilic origin. The community that worships in the Temple is led by elders and priests. The priests are called ministers of YHWH or ministers of the altar (Joel 1:9, 13; 2:14). The sacrifice called *tāmīd* is a post-exilic liturgical institution. Other historical allusions support the chronology suggested by the cult:

—the destruction of Jerusalem is past history (3:1-3);
—the Temple has been rebuilt (1:9, 14, 16; 2:17; 3:18);
—the walls around the city have been reconstructed (2:7, 9);
—Joel 3:4-8 may refer to the destruction of Sidon by Artaxerxes III Ochus in 343 B.C.E.

This indicates that the prophecy has its origin after the reforms of Nehemiah and Ezra. The reform of Ezra (398 B.C.E.) was fundamental for the new organization of the community led by a hierarchy of priests responsible for the Temple sacrifices and obedience to the Law.

The post-exilic reform period with its liturgical reorganization tempted the faithful to believe history had come to an end. Joel calls the community to conversion in a singular way: he convokes the people for a day of penance and preaches oracles based on ancient prophecies (Isaiah 13; Ezekiel 36; 47). This is a prominent feature of Joel's oracles and narrative, which are a web of over twenty citations from ancient texts.

Canonical Intertextuality

The Babylonian Talmud mentions the canon of the twelve prophets, whose edition is attributed to the great men of the synagogue. 2 Maccabees 2:13-15 states that Nehemiah collected the books about the kings, the writings of the prophets and of David. In 190 B.C.E., Jesus ben Sira (Sir 49:10) praises the twelve prophets who gave new strength to Jacob. Thus by the beginning of the second century B.C.E. the twelve minor prophecies were a fixed unit contained in one manuscript.

The canon, according to Jerome in his commentary on Joel, places Hosea and Joel at the head of the list of the twelve minor prophets. In the etymology of Jerome, Joel means "the one who begins." Jerome thinks the meaning of the names of the prophets influences the content of their books. Hosea writes for Ephraim, that is, Israel and Samaria. Joel writes for Jerusalem and Judah. In the eyes of Jerome these two prophets are an introduction to all the prophecy addressed through the ages to the North and the South. Later exegetes also see a theological content in Hosea and Joel that is an introduction to the understanding of the other minor prophets. The center of Hosea's prophecy is the merciful God and God's covenant with God's people. Joel presents the same merciful God who reveals God's love and justice on the Day of YHWH, the outpouring of the divine Spirit and the presence of God in the midst of God's people. Joel also quotes the prophet Amos (Amos 1:2; 9:13) in relation to the Day of YHWH, the judgment of the nations and the prospect of restoration.

By its position in the canon Joel influences our understanding of the eschatology of the prophets who come after him: Obadiah, Jonah, Micah, Nahum, Zephaniah, Zechariah, and Malachi.

Passages Used in the New Testament

The book of Joel had a deep influence on the early Church. Acts 2:17-21 quotes Joel 2:28-32. Acts uses this text to show that the prophecy of the outpouring of the Spirit on all humanity has been fulfilled. For Luke this is the true meaning of Pentecost. Romans 10:13 uses Joel 2:32 in the famous quotation "everyone who calls on the name of the Lord shall be saved." The universalism of the Spirit in Joel 2:28-32 clarifies Paul's new creature in Christ (Gal 3:27-28; 6:15). Revelation 9:7-9 has a locust plague that is described in the same language as Joel 1:6 and 2:4-5. The locusts are like horses armored for battle, as strong and dangerous as lions. According to Jerome, the Jews interpreted the four locust plagues historically. They are the invading armies of the Assyrians, the Persians, the Greeks, and the Romans. Mark 4:29 ends the parable of the seed that grows of itself with a quote from Joel 3:13. It is an example of realized eschatology. The use of Joel in John's gospel is more suggestive than direct. John 4:14 speaks of the living water and the well (= Joel 3:18) in such a way that the water is seen as God's wisdom and Spirit (cf. John 7:37-39). In his theology of the Day of YHWH Joel stresses the darkness (2:2). John's gospel, from the Prologue (1:5) to 8:12 and 20:1, stresses the theological meaning of darkness as the hostile world of evil that cannot overcome Christ, the Light of the world.

History of Reception

Joel was quoted by and commented on by many Fathers of the Church, among whom are Justin, Clement, Origen, Tertullian, Ambrose, Jerome, Augustine, and Athanasius. As we have seen above (cf. Canonical Intertextuality) Jerome interprets the onslaught of locusts allegorically. They can represent the four great ancient empires or the four causes of perturbation or mental agitation in the soul. He sees Pentecost as the fulfillment of the prophecy on the universal gift of the Spirit.

The use of Joel in the liturgy is a commentary on the way the Church community understands the message of the book. Joel is read in the liturgy of the Vigil of Pentecost (2:28-32) and in the sacrament of Confirmation. In both cases the Church emphasizes Joel's teaching on the Spirit of God present in the world. Joel 2:12-18 is read on Ash Wednesday and during the special liturgy for the pardon of sins. Joel's call to penance is read every year to open the Lenten season.

In rural areas all over the world the thanksgiving liturgy for a good harvest has as a first reading Joel 2:21-27. Joel's theology of God's judgment on the nations is used in the liturgies of Friday and Saturday of the twenty-seventh week of the common year (during the uneven years). These liturgies of the end of the liturgical year are always strongly eschatological, calling the community to penance because God's judgment is near.

SECOND READING

I. A Day of Desolation: 1:1–2:11

In this first section of the prophecy Joel's focal point is that the decisive Day of YHWH is near (v. 15). His lamentation presents five aspects that help us understand this dreadful moment.

1. An Onslaught of Locusts (1:1-4)

Joel 1:1-4 is an introduction that was written to parallel Joel 2:25 and form an inclusion for the first part of the prophecy. The locust plague destroyed the agricultural life of the country. It threatened the fertility of the land and the very life of the people who had placed their security in the Temple and its sacrifices. They have to find the meaning of this onslaught for their life as a nation. All inhabitants (1:12), all fields and produce (1:10-12), all flocks and herds (1:18-20) are affected. Joel 1:4 echoes Exod 10:4-6 with its locust plague and Deut 28:38-40 with its imprecations against those who do not listen to God's word.

2. A Call to Mourn the Devastation (1:5-14)

The prophet now calls three groups to mourn with him:

—those who drink wine (1:5-9);
—those who produce wine (1:11-12);
—the priests who use wine in the cult (1:13-14).

The drinkers of wine must wake up and understand that the destruction of the land is a worse enemy than wild animals. The loss of the land is compared to a young bride whose husband dies and leaves her without children (v. 9). At that time a woman without a husband and without children had no security. Just like Judah at this moment, she is without a future. The people cannot even offer sacrifices of bread and wine in the Temple because the grain and the grapes are no more. The vinedressers and farmers must also grieve and face despair (vv. 10-12). The land is their living and it has been ruined. The joy of the harvest (Deut 16:13-14) no longer will be heard.

Joel 1:12 repeats three times a very strong verb that is usually translated as dried up or withered *(havaš)*. At this moment, in the same way, the vine, the fruit trees and those of the field and human joy have all withered away. Joel 1:13-14 is directed to the priests. They must be the first to do penance and to call the people to a special assembly and a holy fast. In the midst of *dis-grace* the people will find *grace* in the power of God.

3. The Day of the Almighty (1:15-18)

The third and central part of the lamentation describes the Day of YHWH: the day that comes "as destruction from the Almighty" (v. 15, cf. Isa 13:6). This phrase is a play on words in Hebrew: destruction = *šod* and Almighty = *šaddai* (one of the most ancient names for God, also used in Gen 17:1; Ruth 1:20-21; Job 5:17).

The prophet begins this text (v. 15) by using symbolic language to reveal the power of God to judge and to save the people. He continues (vv. 16-18) with another revelation: God's people are weak and totally dependent on God. The destruction of the land by the locust plague (a natural event) becomes a call to conversion. Every aspect of their lives—economic, cultural, religious—has been halted by one act of destruction. Surrounded by ruin and drought, in the midst of a virtual desert, God's people will find salvation (in its fullest sense of a rich, fulfilled life) by turning to God.

4. A Prayer for Salvation (1:19-20)

In the midst of desolation, this lamentation psalm reverts to the collective "I" of the psalter, recognizing that only God's coming will free them from a deadly situation.

5. That Dreadful Day (2:1-11)

This text presents the central truth of the prophecy. It is a *judgment* in which God communicates the divine presence and reveals Godself in the midst of the people, as in the theophany on Mount Sinai (Deut 4:11; Exod 19:16-18). The fifth part of this lament is based on a poetic use of parallel language:

—the coming of the Day of YHWH (vv. 1, 11);
—darkness and black clouds (v. 2) come together with the sun, moon, and stars that no longer shine (v. 10);
—the horses and chariots (vv. 4-5) prepare us for the attack of the army (vv. 7-9);
—in the center of the parallels is v. 6 that describes humanity in the face of this terrible crisis.

As we read 2:1-11 we see that vv. 1-2 announce the coming of the Day of YHWH based on the text of Zeph 1:15. Here we have the principal symbols of the theophany:

—symbols of the holy war: trumpet, alarm, gloom;
—symbols of a theophany: darkness, shadows, and especially the cloud, the symbol of the

THE DAY OF YHWH

I. The Texts

Three groups of texts refer to the Day of YHWH. First, sixteen texts mention *yôm yhwh* (the Day of YHWH): Amos 5:18 (2x), 20; Isa 13:6, 9; Zeph 1:7, 14 (2x); Ezek 13:5; Obadiah 15; Mal 3:23; Joel 1:15; 2:1, 11; 3:4; 4:14. Three texts have *yôm lyhwh* (a day for YHWH): Isa 2:12; Ezek 30:3; Zech 14:1.

Second, several texts employ another formula to express the same idea: "the day of Y's wrath" (Zeph 1:18 [following "the day of Y" in 1:14]; Ezek 7:19); "the day of Y's anger" (Zeph 2:2, 3 [in the context of "the day of Y"]; Lam 2:22; cf. 1:12; 2:1, 21); "the day of Y's slaughter feast" (Zeph 1:8 [following "the day of Y" in 1:7]); "a day of Y's vengeance" (Isa 34:8; cf. 61:2; 63:4; Jer 46:10), "My Lord YHWH Sabaoth has a day of panic, rout, and confusion" (Isa 22:5).

Finally, many texts refer to the day without qualification, frequently in the context of the preceding formulas (e.g., "a day for YHWH" [Zech 14:1] followed by "that day" v. 4; "on that day" vv. 6, 8, 9, 13, 20, 21). Over two hundred texts have "on that day." Expressions like "behold, the days are coming" and "in the latter days" might be added.

II. What Happens on That Day?

All (except Lamentations) are prophetic texts and refer to a day on which YHWH acts. It is never called "the day of Elohim (God)," but always "of YHWH," Israel's savior. The day, therefore, is connected with salvation history.

The first reference to "the day of YHWH" is in Amos (5:18-20). Did Amos use a familiar expression or did he invent what later became a technical term? He contradicts people's expectation. They believed the day would be light; he predicts it will be darkness. Amos spoke about "the day of battle" when YHWH would punish Ammon (Amos 1:14). In the oracles against the nations "the day of YHWH" often refers to the day when YHWH will judge Israel's enemies (Joel 3:4; 4:14) like Babylon (Isa 13:6), Egypt (Jer 46:10; Ezek 30:3, 9) or Edom (Isa 34:8; Obadiah 15). This is indeed light for Israel. But Amos, rejecting the belief that YHWH was unconditionally with Israel (5:14; 9:10), calls it a day of darkness, the end of Israel (2:16; 3:14; 6:3). "The day of YHWH" often refers to the judgment against Israel (e.g., Amos 5:18-20; Zeph 1:7, 14; Joel 1:15; 2:1, 11). All texts of the first and second group, and many of the third, are in oracles of doom. The day is a theophany of YHWH crushing enemies, the nations, or unfaithful Israel. But prophets know that YHWH's final word is hope. Zechariah describes "the day for YHWH" as judgment (1:1) first of Jerusalem (1:2), then of the nations (1:3), but says that "on that day" Jerusalem will regain its splendor (1:6-21). About sixty oracles predict the restoration of Israel (Hos 2:18, 20, 23), or of the nations (Isa 2:2-4) "on that day." The day of YHWH is YHWH's judgment: punishment for sinners and salvation for the just.

III. When is That Day?

The "day" is more a temporal, *historical* event than a fixed time span. The day in a few texts refers to a past disaster: Sennacherib's invasion in 701 B.C.E. (Isa 22:5), Egypt's defeat at Carchemish in 605 B.C.E. (Jer 46:10), or the conquest of Jerusalem in 587 B.C.E. (Ezek 13:5; Lam 2:22). Generally the day is in the future, "the day of YHWH is coming" (Isa 13:9; Joel 2:1), or imminent, "the day of YHWH is near" (Isa 13:6; Zeph 1:7, 14; Ezek 30:3; Obadiah 15; Joel 1:15; 2:1; 4:14). Each of these days of YHWH constitutes the end of a period for Israel or for the nations (Ezek 30:3) (= limited historical eschatology). In some late-exilic, more apocalyptic texts "the day of YHWH" has an *eschatological* meaning (= absolute cosmic eschatology). It is The Day, the decisive universal cosmic judgment, the end of this world order and the beginning of a new creation (Joel 3–4; Zechariah 14).

IV. The Origin

The secondary question of its origin dominates research. The discussion flows from the different images used to describe the day of YHWH as warrior, king, and judge. Hugo Gressmann, following Hermann Gunkel, believed that because of its cosmic images the day expresses a pre-prophetic eschatology borrowed from Babylonian eschatology. On that day the creator who conquered chaos in the beginning enjoys final victory over it. Sigmund Mowinckel and John Gray propose a cultic origin: YHWH's enthronement at the New Year festival. Gerhard von Rad sees the origin in the Holy War because of the war images. It is the day of YHWH's victory over enemies. Frank M. Cross combines the cultic and war theories. F. J. Héléwa and F. C. Fensham propose the covenant as its origin. The day brings curses through war and cosmic changes to Israel, but the curses against the nations imply blessing for Israel. M. Weiss and C. Carniti suggest that Amos coined the expression. Yair Hoffmann proposes Zephaniah. Hans M. Barstad also thinks the term originated with the prophets. During public lamentations in times of crisis the prophet proclaims in the oracles against the nations that God will judge them on that day. —*Walter Vogels* presence of God who is coming! For the prophet the Day of YHWH is unequaled in history—it is the day in which God communicates the divine presence (v. 2).

The imagery of the invading army is used in vv. 3-9. This image also expresses the very act of God's judgment. Joel makes use here of the classical imagery taken from Nah 2:11 and Isa 13:8. The locusts advance irresistibly over the country as did the army that destroyed Nineveh (Nah 2:4-7; 3:2-3, 15-17). In this same way the Day of YHWH will come as an irresistible force.

This unit concludes (vv. 10-11) by using again the eloquent language of Sinai (Exod 19:16-18). The allusion to the voice of God is the center of the theophany. It is the manifestation of God who has come to judge. This voice that leads the army reveals that the locust plague is a sign of God's judgment being fulfilled. It is the end of the old era of injustice and the beginning of a new world based on God's mercy!

II. Conversion to a Compassionate God: 2:12-27

Conversion is the only possible response to a compassionate God who comes to the people offering hope and the promise of salvation (2:12-14, 18-27).

1. The Call to Conversion (2:12-14)

Conversion is an urgent invitation to return and to encounter the living God of the Exodus (v. 12; Exod 34:6-7). It is an experience of YHWH who is gracious, compassionate, slow to anger, full of love. As seen in v. 13, conversion has an outward expression of fasting, weeping, and mourning which are only signs of a deeper reality that consists in returning to God with all our heart. Here Joel takes up the constant appeal of the prophetic tradition found in Hos 6:6; Jer 4:4; Isa 58:5-7; Zech 1:3. The call to conversion ends with an expression of hope (v. 14): "Who knows? The Lord your God may turn, have pity, and leave behind a blessing" (cf. Jonah 3:9).

2. The Plea for Salvation (2:15-17)

Using a series of imperatives (blow the trumpet; declare a fast; call an assembly; gather the elders and the children; let the priests weep) the prophet calls once again for a liturgical assembly (Joel 2:1). This assembly will be much more egalitarian than in the past. The prayer in v. 17 expresses at the same time the crisis and the hope of Joel's community. They are God's heritage (Deut 4:20; 9:26, 29), and they will not be an object of shame or a byword among the nations. We find this same situation in Mal 2:17 and Ps 79:8-10.

3. The Liberation of God's People (2:18-20)

Once again the third point of the unit is focal for the prophet. God answers the cry of the people, blessing the land and freeing them from plagues. Verse 18 is a reminder of the theology of the jealous God of Ezek 36:23; 39:25, 27-28. During the exile and now in Judah God will not let God's people be shamed among the nations. YHWH will take pity on them. It is this love that God has for God's people that will be the root of their renovation (Isa 63:15; Zech 8:2).

The text continues by showing that God's blessing on the land is complete (vv. 19-20). Traditionally, the enemies of the people came from the North (Jer 1:13-15; 4:6; 6:1). God will first free the people from oppression and destruction to prepare them to receive all blessings.

4. The Liberating Act of God (2:21-24)

The joy of the people is expressed in a psalm of praise and thanksgiving (cf. Ps 111:2, 6). The prophet invites others to join him in this song:

—the land *(ʾadāmāh)* itself (v. 21);
—the beasts of the field (v. 22);
—the people of Zion who cultivate the soil (vv. 23-24).

The autumn rains will come with justice and permit future harvests (v. 23). Jerome sees here a messianic prophecy about the Lord Jesus who will come in justice with the fullness of salvation. But for the peasants of Judah the promise of grain, wine, and oil was the threshold to freedom (v. 24; cf. Ps 84:7).

5. Salvation and Union with God (2:25-27)

The conclusion of this unit reveals a God who constantly repeats the wonders of the Exodus

(v. 26; cf. Exod 15:11). This God deserves our psalms of praise for this God is always in our midst, has done wonderful things and has no equal!

III. The Day of Salvation: (2:28–3:21)

Joel again speaks of the Day of YHWH in an eschatological perspective. Judah and Jerusalem are restored by the coming of the Spirit and the nations are judged according to the law of talion.

1. The Outpouring of the Spirit: (2:28-29)

Joel formulates his vision of this new community as one that fulfills the desire of Moses: "If only the whole people of YHWH were prophets, and YHWH gave the divine Spirit to them all" (Num 11:29). This gift of the Spirit is the new covenant (Ezek 39:29; Isa 59:21). The Spirit gives the community the gift of prophecy through dreams and visions (Num 12:6; cf. Dan 1:17; 2:19, 28).

2. The Coming of the Day of YHWH (2:30-32)

The Day of YHWH arrives with wonders: fire, darkness, and blood. These are reminders of the wonders and the plagues of the first Exodus from Egypt (Exod 7:14-24; 10:21-27). Joel gives them a new cosmic meaning. The prophet quotes Obadiah 17 to show that salvation is found in the name of the Lord. Those who call on the name of the Lord are YHWH's people and they will be saved.

3. The Judgment of the Nations (3:1-8)

In eschatological language, Joel presents the restoration of Judah and Jerusalem that historically have been so badly treated by the pagans. He increases the tension by using the language of ancient justice. Whatever has been done to Judah and Jerusalem by the pagan nations, YHWH must do to them.

Verses 4-5 are a clear indication of Greek activity on the coast of Palestine at that time. Judeans and Jerusalemites were sold to Greeks in the slave trade that flourished especially in the fourth century. For this reason, the Phoenicians and Philistines will be judged by God. They began the spiral of violence that goes from the theft of the Temple treasury to the selling of Jewish war prisoners as slaves. God will apply the law of talion so that Judah's enemies will have done unto them what they did to others!

4. The Power of the Day of YHWH (3:9-17)

In these verses the language of the holy war expresses the struggle between the power of God and the power of the nations. All the arms of the world cannot destroy YHWH. Ironically, Joel misquotes the paradisal prophecies of Isa 2:4; 11:6; Mic 4:3 to suggest that even if the pagan nations were to transform all their agricultural implements into weapons they still could not overcome the power of YHWH!

Joel's vision reaches its high point with the presence of God in the midst of the people (vv. 15-17). Joel suggests that Zion will be a new Sinai. God will reveal Godself in a great theophany in which God's powerful voice will sound out like thunder. In the language of Amos he shows us YHWH roaring like a lion (Amos 1:2) and in the language of Psalm 46 he presents God's presence as protection for God's people.

5. God's Gift of Abundant Fertility (3:18-21)

The conclusion of the prophecy is divided into three parts and begins with "on that day" (v. 18), an ancient prophetic phrase that points to a new and wondrous act of God. The drought is over and the wine, milk, and water are flowing in abundance (v. 18). A fountain will flow from the Temple to the Valley of the Acacias, a symbolic term. Acacia wood was used in the confection of sacred materials such as the tent and the altar of holocausts (Exod 26:15; 27:1). Joel uses the term to express his confidence that in the future the entire region around the Temple will also be consecrated. The water that flows from the Temple, as in Ezekiel 47, indicates that this new abundance is a gift from God.

Those who oppressed Judah will be punished. Egypt and Edom are examples of traditional enemies of God's people (v. 19). The prophecy ends with a divine guarantee:

—Judah and Jerusalem will always be inhabited;

—their guilt will be forgiven;
—YHWH will dwell with the people in Zion.

BIBLIOGRAPHY

Crenshaw, James L. *Joel.* AB 24C. New York: Doubleday, 1995.

Glazier-McDonald, Beth. "Joel," in Carol A. Newsom and Sharon H. Ringe, eds., *The Women's Bible Commentary.* Louisville: Westminster/John Knox, 1992, 203–204.

Ogden, G. S. *A Promise of Hope, a Call to Obedience: A Commentary on the Books of Joel and Malachi.* Grand Rapids: Eerdmans, 1987.

Prinsloo, W. S. "The Unity of the Book of Joel," *ZAW* 104 (1992) 66–81.

Redditt, P. L. "The Book of Joel and Peripheral Prophecy," *CBQ* 48 (1986) 225–240.

Wolff, Hans-Walter. *Joel and Amos.* Hermeneia. Philadelphia: Fortress, 1977.

Amos

Rui de Menezes

FIRST READING

General Character of the Book

Why Read the Book?

Two questions arise in the mind of a present-day Christian who is invited to read the book of Amos. First, why should I read the oracles of an Israelite prophet of bygone days who prophesied the destruction of the northern kingdom of Israel long after that prophecy was fulfilled? Second, why should a Christian who believes that "God is love" go back to this firebrand among the prophets who seems to offer nothing more than threats and woes in the name of YHWH? Even post-exilic generations of Israelite believers were confronted with the first question. They realized that precisely because the words of Amos had come true in the shattering experience of the exile they still had a very contemporary relevance for them. As regards the second question, as we shall see, Amos had himself interceded on behalf of Israel when YHWH had threatened to make an end of the nation (cf. 7:2, 5). Amos had also exhorted and pleaded with Israel to "seek YHWH" not in the false security of cult but in a change of lifestyle so that Israel might live, that is, survive the impending catastrophe (cf. 5:4-6, 14-15). Finally Amos had also promised hope to the "remnant of Joseph" (5:15). Keeping all this in mind an inspired redactor reinterpreted the message of Amos for the people who had survived the catastrophe of the Babylonian exile (9:1-14). Further, what Amos says about religion and cult, what he says about international and intranational justice have a tremendous relevance for our present times.

John's "God is Love" (1 John 4:8) can be understood naively, which is of course to misinterpret it, for justice is the basis of love. God remains a mystery who not only threatens us human beings with the consequences of our life's decisions but who also offers us unconditional love! In fact the words of Amos have a tremendous relevance for us today who think we can attain progress and prosperity at the expense of the poorer members of our society.

The Book and Its Authors

One could very profitably begin reading this small book (with its nine chapters or 146 verses) with the biographical section that tells of the confrontation between Amos the prophet of YHWH and Amaziah the official priest of Jeroboam II in the royal sanctuary of Bethel (7:10-17). This section gives us an insight into the prophet whose "words" and "visions" this book contains (1:1). It brings out very forcefully the tension that exists between divine authority under which the prophet Amos stands and human authority under which the cultic official Amaziah stands. The prophet is God's spokesperson. "Thus says YHWH!" is the messenger formula he uses whereas Amaziah refers to Amos's words as "Thus says Amos!" (7:11, 17). In NT times too the apostles, who are the NT prophets, will refuse to submit to the authority of the Sanhedrin when it conflicts with divine authority: "Whether it is right in God's sight to listen to you rather than to God, you must judge" (Acts 4:19). The silencing of God's prophets by human authority (Amos 2:12) continues in our times and will go on to the end of time.

With the appearance of Amos at Bethel a new era dawns in the history of Israelite religion. Amos is the first of the so-called "writing prophets," that is, prophets whose oracles we have in writing. Up to the time of Amos the oracles of Israelite prophets could only be heard. From Amos's time on their oracles can be read. [See also the article "Prophetism and Prophets."]

The book of Amos, who lived in the second half of the eighth century B.C.E. around 750, was most probably composed in various stages. His disciples might have collected their master's oracles and put them down in writing by giving them, for example, a suitable introduction. There are also clear hints at a post-exilic redaction especially in the last section of the book (9:11-14). The polemics against the altars of Bethel (3:14) could point to a deuteronomistic edition after Josiah's reform. At any rate the doxologies that are placed at strategic positions in the book (4:13; 5:8-9; 9:5-6) point to the fact that very early "the book of Amos" was read in liturgical celebrations. Thus this book is a fine example of how the faith community of Israel and not merely a lone individual was instrumental in transmitting God's message to us.

Background of Amos

We are not sure whether "Amos" was his real name, possibly a contraction of Amasiah meaning "YHWH has loaded" (i.e., with benefits) or a nickname meaning the "loader" because he loads "burdens" (i.e., oracles of woe) on Israel's head.

The superscription of the book calls Amos a "shepherd," which corresponds to the rare Hebrew word *noqed.* However the usual word for "shepherd" in Hebrew is *roʿeh* (1:2; 3:12). In Ugaritic the corresponding term refers to some type of priest or temple official. In the Hebrew Bible the term is used of Mesha, the king of Moab who was a "sheep breeder" who used to pay a tribute of one hundred thousand lambs and the wool of one hundred thousand lambs to the king of Israel (2 Kings 3:4). Amos, however, speaks of himself as a "cattle rancher" (7:14). But the text goes on to say that YHWH took him "from following the flock." Whether this is to be taken literally or is simply a theological cliché as we find it in the case of David's election (2 Sam 7:8) is an open question. On reading the book one does not get the impression that Amos was an illiterate shepherd at all but rather a man with a tremendous political acumen and breadth of vision. He is aware of the political and social situation of the countries neighboring Israel (1:3–2:5) as well as that of Israel and Judah (3:9-10; 6:1-7, 13). He is at home in the cultic traditions of Israel (4:4; 5:21). He is acquainted with the wisdom traditions as we can gather from his exhortations (5:4-6, 14-15; 4:4) as well as from the numerical patterns (1:3–2:6). He is also well versed in the area of Israel's theological concepts such as election (3:1), the Exodus (9:7) and the "day of YHWH" (5:18-20).

Amos himself denies having ever belonged to any prophetic guild. That seems to be the meaning of the phrase "son of a prophet" (7:14). What is more problematic is his denial that he is a *nabiʾ,* that is, a prophet. Either he denies that he is an ecstatic or mantic prophet (one who goes in a trance and then utters oracles) or that he charges a fee for delivering oracles. Such prophets usually flattered the people (cf. Mic 3:5). And as we are well aware there is not a trace of flattery in the oracles of Amos! When Amaziah tells him to go to Judah and earn his bread there Amos seems to be refuting precisely this (7:12). On the contrary Amos says that he was a normal individual going about his business as a cattle rancher and a dresser of sycamore trees (7:14). Sycamores grow in the *shephelah* (lowlands) to an altitude of one thousand feet and so one could object that in Tekoa, which is about 2,700 feet above sea level, Amos could not have pursued this profession. But of course Amos does not tell us that he dressed sycamores in Tekoa. What is important to note is that Amos had a normal profession from which YHWH called him to deliver his message: "Go, prophesy to my people!" (7:15). This he did most courageously.

Literary Style and Characteristics

The style of Amos is forceful, vivid, and picturesque (6:1-7). He captures the attention of his hearers by means of questions (2:11; 3:3-6; 5:18-20, etcetera). He has recourse to sarcasm (4:4-6) and word play, apparent of course only in the Hebrew, e.g., *gilgal galoh yigleh,* "Gilgal shall surely go into exile" (5:5). He has a fondness for the number five. Thus we have the series of five warnings that YHWH gave to Israel culminating in the phrase also repeated five times, "yet you did not return to me" (4:4-11). Then we have the five visions of the coming end (7:1–8:3; 9:1-4). Amos also mentions the five regions to which YHWH's dominion extends: the underworld, heaven, Carmel's peak, the sea bed and the country of exile (9:2-4). He also uses the number seven. Thus we have the seven questions in the disputation oracle (3:3-6) and the seven units of the Israelite army identified by Shalom Paul (2:13-16).

Structure

A very basic structure can be discovered in the book of Amos as follows:

Superscription (1:1)
Introduction (1:2)
Oracles against the nations (1:3–2:16)
Crimes of Israel in detail (3:1–9:10)
Conclusion (9:11-15)

However, when one begins to analyze the main section of the book dealing with Israel one realizes that there is no proper subdivision of the oracles. There is a good deal of repetition and cyclic movement. The same theme is treated more than once, for example that of social justice (3:9-10; 4:1-7; 6:4-8) and the oppression of the poor (1:6; 4:2; 5:11-12; 8:4-6). Thus also the theme of formalism in religion or the hollowness of Israel's cult appears more than once (4:4-5; 5:4-5; 5:21-24). Nevertheless the overall effect of Amos' message is powerful.

Historical Context of Amos's Message

Amos, the prophet who hailed from Tekoa at the edge of the Negeb desert in the southern kingdom of Judah prophesied for a short time in Bethel and probably also in Samaria during the reign of Jeroboam II of Israel (783–743) rather toward the end than at the beginning of the king's reign. Uzziah (Zechariah) was Jeroboam's contemporary in Judah (781–740). Both kings lived at peace with each other and so Jeroboam in particular was able to attain a second Golden Age in Israel. An important factor was that the superpower of Assyria was dormant at that time. However, toward the end of Jeroboam's reign Assyria had just begun to awaken from its sleep. Jeroboam regained a good deal of territory in Transjordan that had been lost to Damascus (6:13). Success in war and prosperity at home were attributed by the people to the lavish worship that was practiced in Israel's sanctuaries, especially at Bethel. The petty neighboring nations, free from the interference of a superpower, were exploiting one another. In Israel itself the richer classes were oppressing the poorer masses. Religion had become an alibi for a life that was devoid of all morality or experience of God. These are the evils against which Amos will fume in the name of his God whom he compares to a roaring lion (1:3; 3:18). If Israel does not listen to YHWH the punishment is inevitable: exile from its own land. The agent of the exile is nowhere mentioned by name in the book but one can take for granted that the prophet is referring to Assyria (though harassment by Damascus cannot be ruled out: cf. 3:11 where the Hebrew refers to an adversary that is already surrounding the land) and not a future adversary as the versions have it.

Canonical Context and Intra-biblical Dialogue

The book of Amos is third among the so-called Twelve Minor Prophets in the Hebrew Bible but second in the Septuagint or Greek Bible. The original Hebrew text is in relatively good shape and there are no major discrepancies between the Hebrew text and the early Greek, Latin, and Syriac versions. The final redaction of the book has placed the oracles against the nations at the beginning of the book though in the rest of the prophetic books these come after the oracles against Israel. The book of Zephaniah, however, has first an introduction on the day of YHWH followed by oracles against the nations and finally oracles against Jerusalem.

Examples of intra-biblical dialogue can be seen from the influence Amos exerted on Joel and Jeremiah. Joel has exactly the same oracle on YHWH roaring from Zion (compare Amos 1:2 and Joel 4:16). Jeremiah, however, has a slightly different version (Jer 25:30).

The vision of post-exilic hope for Israel in Amos (9:11-14) is strikingly similar to the conclusion of the book of Joel (4:18-21). Both mention the flow of new wine on the mountains and both make an allusion to the revenge on Edom. The theme of the "day of the LORD" that appears for the first time in Amos has been taken up by Zephaniah and Joel in particular. The former emphasizes more the anger of YHWH (Zeph 1:18

and 2:2-3) whereas Joel stresses rather the aspect of darkness and has a more eschatological and cosmic slant (Joel 2:28-31; 2:2).

The largest number of similarities are to be found in the book of Hosea. Both Amos and Hosea mention "false balances" (Amos 8:5; Hos 12:7). The "pride of Jacob" in Amos (6:8) corresponds to the "pride of Israel" in Hosea (5:5). The idea of justice becoming poison is found in both (Amos 6:12 and Hos 10:4). Polemics against the cult at Bethel and Gilgal is common to both (Hos 4:15; 5:8; 6:10 and Amos 4:4; 5:5). Bethel (house of God) is called Beth-aven (house of nothingness) in both (Hos 4:5 and Amos 5:5). Both allude to YHWH hurling fire on a nation in order to burn its strongholds (Amos 1:4, 7, 10, 12, 14; 2:2 and Hos 8:14). In both is found a reference to YHWH restoring the fortunes of the people (Amos 9:14 and Hos 6:11). In quite a number of these instances, in particular regarding future hope, it is possible that the material was neither in Amos nor in Hosea but that later redactors have introduced it into both.

The deuterocanonical book of Tobit (2:6) has an explicit quotation from the book of Amos (8:10) which says that YHWH would change Israel's songs into lamentation. It looks like a casual quotation but it seems more probable that the author is stressing the message of Amos that in our festivities we should not forget the poor. In fact the senior Tobit does tell his son Tobias to invite some poor Israelite to the dinner prepared for him (cf. Tob 2:1-2).

Finally we have two references in the NT, both in the Acts of the Apostles. The first is in the context of the speech of Stephen that refers to the idols made by Israel (Acts 7:42-43; cf. Amos 5:25-27). In Acts there is an explicit allusion to idolatry that in Amos is implicit. The text of Acts has "the images that you made to worship" (7:43). Note that these words are absent both in the LXX and in the Hebrew text of Amos. The Hebrew text has "your images, your star-god, which you made for yourselves" (Amos 5:26). Luke seems to say that the refusal to accept Jesus and his message is tantamount to idolatry. One could also speculate whether the exile "beyond Damascus" in Amos that is changed to "beyond Babylon" in Acts is a reinterpretation in favor of Rome as is the case in Revelation and 1 Peter where "Babylon" is a cryptic name for "Rome" (Rev 14:8; 17:5; 1 Pet 5:13).

The other reference to Amos is in Acts 15:16-17. Luke quotes from the LXX: "I will rebuild the dwelling of David, which has fallen; from its ruins I will rebuild it, and I will set it up, so that all other peoples may seek the Lord—even all the Gentiles over whom my name has been called." The book of Amos had referred to Judah inheriting the "remnant of Edom and all the nations who are called by my name" (Amos 9:12). The particularism of the passage in the Hebrew book of Amos has been reinterpreted by the LXX in keeping with the thought of Amos who had taken away all privileges from Israel. Luke, however, takes this over and now applies it to the universalism of salvation in the name of Jesus.

Close resemblances to Amos are to be found in the letter of James in his castigation of the rich (Jas 2:1-9; 5:1-6) as well as in the woes against the rich in the gospel of Luke (Luke 6:24-25) and the parables of the rich fool (Luke 12:13-21) and the rich man and Lazarus (Luke 16:19-31).

Patristic Usage

Two Fathers of the Church, Cyril of Alexandria and Jerome, wrote commentaries on Amos. Jerome does not have any regard for Amos's *sermo* or "eloquence" but only for his *scientia* or "learning." But even a hurried reading of Amos reveals that both eloquence and learning are to be found in the book. Chrysostom who in the spirit of Amos had always fought for the interests and rights of the poor has a section on Amos in his *Synopsis of the Old and New Testaments.* Epiphanius in his *Life of the Prophets* tells us that Tecue (Tekoa) is in Zebulun (the northern kingdom) an idea that will be taken up again by later authors. Hilary of Poitiers in his sermon on Ps 51 (Ps 52 of the Hebrew Bible) interprets Amos's "booth of David" (cf. Amos 9:11) as the temple of the body of Christ that was raised after death. Referring to the same text Jerome says that what had fallen in the synagogues would be raised in the churches, and in line with the LXX version of Amos 9:11 we quoted above Jerome tells us that all the nations that had forgotten the Lord would be converted.

Liturgical Usage

Given the importance and relevance of the message of Amos the Church has made sure that believers are given an opportunity to hear the main passages from the book. Thus during the thirteenth week of Year II readings from all the chapters except the sixth are included, and that chapter is incorporated in the reading for the twenty-sixth Sunday of Cycle C. Besides that selections from chs. 7 and 8 are included again in the readings for the fifteenth and twenty-fifth Sundays of Cycle C. Thus Christians are reminded of the main thrust of the message of Amos, that ritual worship cannot be a substitute for life and that belief in God must go hand in hand with concern for the poor.

Role of the Book in the Life of the Church

Down the centuries the book of Amos has been a source of inspiration for all those working for the uplifting of the poor, beginning from John Chrysostom. In recent times Amos has been a pillar of strength and a beacon of light for all those involved in the theory and praxis of liberation theology, particularly in so-called developing countries.

SECOND READING

Introduction

There is bound to be an element of subjectivity in the identification and selection of individual passages or themes; however, it must not be forgotten that the aim of our exposition is not merely literary but theological or, better, kerygmatic. For this reason we shall explain the given passage in its historical context wherever needed. We shall steer a safe middle path between the Scylla of a subjective assessment of the authenticity of so-called original Amos oracles and the Charybdis of irrational fundamentalism that unquestioningly ascribes everything in the book to Amos. Our exposition will pursue an ongoing dialogue not with the historical Amos (which is not possible) but with the present canonical text, thus seeking to discover its relevance for our present situation.

Superscription: 1:1

The superscription with its two subordinate relative clauses is loaded and does not flow smoothly. We are told that we have here the "words" of Amos "which he saw," obviously a mixed metaphor. We have the identical mixed metaphor in the superscription of ch. 2 of Isaiah (Isa 2:1), but it must be remembered that *dabar* in Hebrew can mean "word" or "vision" as well as "event." In the book of Jeremiah too the superscription of the book reports "the words of Jeremiah" (Jer 1:1). In most other prophetic books we are given "the words of the LORD" (cf. Ezek 1:3; Hos 1:1; Joel 1:1; Jonah 1:1; Mic 1:1; Zeph 1:1; Zech 1:1; Mal 1:1), and in fact the prophets are given a vision of future events by God which they then proclaim to God's people (cf. Mic 3:5-7). The formulation "words of Amos" is puzzling, but this is the paradox of our Scriptures: that they are God's words in the words of humans.

The mention of Uzziah king of Judah before Jeroboam II king of Israel points to the fact that the editing took place in Judah. Both these kings, as we have seen, contributed much to the material welfare of their kingdoms (cf. 2 Chr 26:1-15 and 2 Kings 14:25). We are told that Amos prophesied precisely two years before "the earthquake." Apparently this earthquake was engraved in the memory of the people and it left behind an indelible mark on the geography of the land by causing the rift between Mount Scopus and the Mount of Olives. Even the prophet Zechariah recalls it centuries later (Zech 14:5). Josephus too in his *Antiquities of the Jews* weaves a legend around it of how during this earthquake King Uzziah was struck with leprosy.

Introduction: 1:2

The oracle reflects the style of Amos but it seems to have been placed here by a redactor who thought that it summarized the whole message of Amos as a warning to Israel from YHWH who is boldly compared to a roaring lion. Total destruction is proclaimed, from the low-lying pastures to the heights of Carmel.

International Justice: Oracles Against the Nations: 1:3–2:16

The present book of Amos contains oracles against eight nations including Judah and Israel. It is unique in all the prophetic literature that the "chosen people" should be lined up with the so-called "nations." Israel always thought of itself as "a people living alone, and not reckoning itself among the nations" (Num 23:9). For Amos, as centuries later for Paul, all have sinned and are in need of God's grace (Rom 3:23). In fact Israel's crimes are more than those of any other nation whose charge sheet is recorded. While the other nations' crimes are mentioned in two or three verses, those of Israel require a full eleven. The phrase "for three transgressions . . . and for four . . ." is a stereotyped phrase that is found in wisdom literature (cf. Prov 30:15-24; Sir 26:5) and should not be taken literally. At most three but usually only one or two crimes of each nation are mentioned except, of course, in the case of Israel. A similar gradation from seven to eight is found in the prophet Micah (Mic 5:5). Rather than the number, what is stressed is the intensity of the crimes. The Hebrew word for "transgression" is *pesha*ᶜ, which denotes an act of rebellion.

The question naturally arises in our minds: why has Amos left out the superpowers Egypt and Assyria? Is it because they were dormant at that time and so did not have actual relevance? What Amos insists on is that the nations by harassing one another are violating an accepted *jus gentium* or international law; they are rebelling against YHWH who is the lord of history. Indeed, the crimes that are listed are cruelty in war (1:3), lack of humanity toward women and other civilians (1:13), breach of international treaties (1:9), civil war (1:11), and slave trade (1:6, 9). We see that Amos does not conceive of YHWH as a tribal god or as a local divinity but as one who holds sway over the nations. To YHWH all nations are accountable. One could even speak here of an implicit monotheism. As we shall see further on, Amos conceives of YHWH both as lord of history and as lord of nature (cf. 4:6-12; 9:2-4). When we look at the oracle on Judah we see that it lacks the punch of Amos and that the theme is more religious and cultic whereas in the other oracles it is either international or social justice. It is quite possible that this oracle was appended in post-exilic times when the northern kingdom no longer existed but only Judah. Thus the message of Amos was shown to be still relevant in a changed context.

Let us now see the structure of these oracles. Even though Amos does not slavishly adhere to a structure the following elements stand out:

Introduction: Thus says YHWH!
Name of transgressor
YHWH's inexorable decision to punish
Statement of crime
Punishment for crime
Conclusion: Says YHWH!

In most oracles the ones accused are those guiding the destinies of nations, for example the king and his officials (1:15), the ruler and his officials (2:3) and finally "the one who holds the scepter" (1:5, 8). The parallel to "the one who holds a scepter" in these two oracles is rendered by some English versions as "inhabitants" (pl.). However the Hebrew has the singular *yosheb* which should be translated as "ruler" or literally "one sitting on the throne" (cf. Ps 2:2). It is also interesting that all the oracles mention that the punishment will be the destruction of the "strongholds," that is, the well-guarded palaces of kings (1:4, 7, 10, 12, 14; 2:2, 5). In the case of Israel the plundering of the strongholds is mentioned later (cf. 3:11). The oracles against Tyre (1:9-10) and Edom (1:11-12) do not have the abovementioned structure. They also omit the reference to the rulers. The oracle against Tyre repeats almost verbatim the charge against Gaza regarding slave trade. We know that Tyre engaged in the deportation of slaves from Judah to Greece in much later times (cf. Ezek 27:13 and Joel 4:6). The charge against Edom makes sense only after the sack of Jerusalem by the Neo-Babylonian forces. The Edomites betrayed a total lack of humanity when they made a clean sweep of Jerusalem after the departure of the invaders. For these reasons once more it is possible that these oracles were added later to show the relevance of Amos's message in later times.

The oracle against Israel (2:6-11) contains a summary of the charges that will be expanded in the main section of the book (3:1–9:10): oppression of the poor (2:6-7) and the hollowness and hypocrisy of Israel's worship (2:8) combined with the refusal to follow YHWH's directives as given through the prophets (2:11-12). Israel is portrayed not only as a sinner but as the greatest of them all. Its punishment will be total paralysis in a war that enemies will wage against Israel (2:13-16). Amos describes YHWH's benevolence toward Israel, in particular the Exodus from the slavery of Egypt and the entry into the land of the powerful Amorites, and the raising up of prophets and nazirites. This last item is something peculiar to Amos who considers this a part of salvation history. The nazirites could well be those warriors consecrated to YHWH, that is, the "judges" like Samson raised up by God to save the people (Judges 13). This has nothing to do with the vow of a nazirite that a person freely undertook; such vows are mentioned in the later priestly legislation of the book of Numbers (Numbers 6). All this Amos contrasts with Israel's ingratitude as shown in its crimes, chief among which is the exploitation of the poor. Amos gives four synonyms for poor: "righteous" (better "innocent"), "needy," "poor" (better "the common people"), and "afflicted" (3:6-7). The clause "push the afflicted out of the way" (2:7) should be translated "twist the rights of the afflicted" (cf. Deut 16:19). That such a great cattle rancher and sheep breeder came to have such an intense concern for the rights of the poor is remarkable. Normally the rich are not sensitive to the lot of the poor and forget about their rights. Did Amos himself undergo a conversion after receiving his call to be YHWH's prophet?

Intranational Justice: 3:1–9:10

Amos now passes on to what is happening within the borders of Israel. How are the rulers treating their subjects? What is the attitude of the richer classes toward the poor? The basis of Amos's concept of social justice is the covenant that is never mentioned by Amos but is implicit.

Sounding the Alarm in Samaria (3:1-15)

Amos relativizes the privilege of Israel whereby it thinks of itself as the chosen people of YHWH. Amos says that election entails only greater responsibility and a harsher punishment. The seven rhetorical questions in the disputation oracle (3:2-7) prove that nothing happens by chance but only through a decision of YHWH. The crimes of Samaria, a total breakdown of law and order and a violent oppression of the poor, with its incumbent punishment, the plundering of its spoils well stored in the guarded palaces, are to be broadcast in nearby Ashdod as well as in faraway Egypt. The magnificent mansions of the rich and the ruling classes, with winter apartments on one side and summer apartments on the other (cf. Jer 36:22) will be brought to ruin by knocking one side against the other (3:15). The cult in Bethel will not be of any avail to ward off the coming punishment (3:14).

Graded Warnings and Final Summons (4:1-13)

The introductory verses of this chapter treat of the "cows of Bashan," the opulent women from the ruling classes who oppress the poor (4:1-4). They are threatened with dire consequences that cannot be averted by the sacrifices and offerings in the cult sanctuaries of Bethel and Gilgal. Now Amos reminds his hearers of the various warnings YHWH had given them in the recent past such as famine (4:6), drought (4:7-8), crop failure (4:9), war and captivity (4:10), and earthquake (4:11). All these went unheeded. Israel failed to retrace its steps toward YHWH, and so YHWH has no choice but to summon Israel to meet its God (4:12) whom a later redactor describes in this doxology as a creator God (4:13).

Ruling out of False Security (5:1-27)

This is the central chapter and the longest of the nine. It contains practically all the important ideas of the book. Themes already mentioned before reappear once more, including the oppression of the poor and the needy (5:11-12), insistence on justice and righteousness (5:7, 15, 24) and YHWH's rejection of Israel's cult (5:20-24). An idea that is new in the book and new in the whole of biblical literature is the theological concept of the "day of the LORD" (5:18-20). Israel was looking forward to this great day of rejoicing when YHWH would destroy its enemies and bring victory to the chosen people. Amos turns the idea upside down. The day of the LORD will be a day of defeat, gloom, and sadness (5:18, 20), of mourning in the city streets and lamentation in the vineyards (5:16-17). False security in the day of the LORD as well as in a hollow cult (5:21-24) are ruled out. [See also the excursus "Day of YHWH" in the commentary on Joel.] Important in this chapter are also the exhortations Amos makes in the name of YHWH. "Seek me and live" (5:4), "Seek the LORD and live" (5:6), "Seek good and not evil, that you may live" (5:14). The verb "live" should be rendered as "survive" (the impending catastrophe). The correlate of all this is that Israel should not seek the cult at Bethel, Gilgal, or Beersheba (5:5). Again, Israel should "hate evil" (5:15). If Israel changes its lifestyle, if justice and righteousness flow like a never-ending stream, then and only then there might be some hope for the "remnant of Joseph" (5:15). This last idea of remnant, which will become popular in later times, we meet for the first time in Amos.

Almost at the end of this section we find a verse that has baffled translators both ancient and modern. It runs, "You shall take up Sakkuth your king, and Kaiwan your star-god, your images, which you made for yourselves" (5:26). It is to be kept in mind that this translation is made possible only by changing the vowels of the Hebrew consonantal text. Thus *sikkut* has been changed to Sakkut and *kiyyun* to Kaiwan. Both Sakkut and Kaiwan are Babylonian astral divinities. The problem is that astral deities were imposed on Israel only in the time of the Assyrian domination, and so their presence in Israel in the time of Amos is a historical anachronism. Two solutions are possible. One is to say that this text comes from a later redactor. The other is to vocalize *sikkut* as *sukkat,* which could mean "booth" or "palanquin." The next word, *kiyyun,* could be left as it is since it has the meaning of "pedestal." The Hebrew word *kokab* translated as "star-god" could be rendered as "star symbol of your god." Thus one could translate "You shall carry the palanquin of your king (referring to a god), the pedestal of your idol and the star-symbol of your god." The Hebrew has a threefold genitive form (of your king, of your idol, of your god) that is absent in the versions. This could well go back to Amos himself. The idea is similar to that found in Hosea, who tells us "The thing itself [the calf of Beth-aven] shall be carried to Assyria as tribute to the great king" (Hos 10:6). But the sarcasm is much stronger in Amos. YHWH, Israel's God, had carried Israel out of Egypt (Exod 19:4) but Israel's idols will be carried by Israel into exile. It is worth noting that the carrying of the palanquin *(palkhi)* of the God Vitthoba is an annual feature in the cult of the Warkaris in Maharashtra, India.

Consequences of the "Ruin of Joseph" (6:1-14)

Once again the rich and the ruling classes both at Zion and in Samaria (6:1) are threatened by YHWH for their gross luxury combined with a total unconcern for the "ruin of Joseph" (6:6). The notables of the "first of the nations" (6:1) who anoint themselves with the "finest" oils (6:6; in Hebrew "first") will be the "first" to go into exile (6:7). One is reminded of the parable of the rich man and Lazarus in Luke's gospel (Luke 12:16-21). No sins of the rich are mentioned, only their unconcern for the poor or for the ruin of the country. What matters to them is their food, their wine, their comfort, and their amusement (6:1-6).

Inexorability of the Coming End: Five Visions (7:1–9:6)

In this section we find five visions, three of them described one after another (7:1-9) while the next two are set apart from these as well as from each other. Now the question arises: what kind of visions are these? When we compare them to the visions in the books of Ezekiel and First Zechariah (Zechariah 1–8) as well as to the visions that are described in later apocalyptic literature the following observations could be made. One has the impression that the visions of Ezekiel, in particular that of the glory of God and God's chariot (Ezekiel 1), are the result of some mystical experience. When we compare his visions to those of Amos it looks as if the latter's visions are of a different type. It is possible that the vision of the locusts (Amos 7:1-3) and that of the basket of summer fruit (Amos 8:1-3) could have been physical visions that Amos under God's inspiration interprets for the benefit of Israel. When we come to the vision of the "fire" that consumes the "great deep," that is, the cosmic ocean (7:4-6) and that of YHWH giving orders for the destruction of the altar (9:1-4) we find that these two look like mystical visions. All the same when we compare the visions of Amos with one another we see that the first two visions have an almost identical structure, as does the second pair. It could well be that Amos or some later redactor has given us what we could call a "vision report." When we come to the visions of First Zechariah and the later apocalyptists we get the impression that they are literary compositions. Let us now have a closer look at the visions of Amos by placing the two pairs of visions in parallel (see next page).

In the first pair of visions, of locusts and fire, the destruction threatened is total. The prophet's

First Vision

This is what the LORD GOD showed me:
he was forming locusts at the time the latter growth began to sprout . . .
When they had finished eating the grass of the land,
I said,
"O Lord God, forgive, I beg you!
How can Jacob stand?
He is so small!"
The LORD relented concerning this;
"It shall not be," said the LORD.
(Amos 7:1-3)

Second Vision

This is what the LORD GOD showed me:
The LORD GOD was calling for a shower of fire,
and it devoured the great deep and was eating up the land.
Then I said,
"O LORD GOD, cease, I beg you!
How can Jacob stand?
He is so small!"
The LORD relented concerning this;
"This also shall not be," said the LORD GOD.
(Amos 7:4-6)

Third Vision

This is what he showed me:
The LORD was standing beside a wall built with a plumb line . . .
And the LORD said to me,
"Amos, what do you see?"
And I said, "A plumb line."
Then the LORD said,
"See, I am setting a plumb line in the midst of my people Israel;
I will never again pass them by;
the high places of Isaac shall be made desolate,
and the sanctuaries of Israel shall be laid waste,
and I will rise against the house of Jeroboam with the sword."
(Amos 7:7-9)

Fourth Vision

This is what the LORD GOD showed me—
a basket of summer fruit.
He said,
"Amos, what do you see?"
And I said, "A basket of summer fruit."
Then the LORD said to me,
"The end has come upon my people Israel;
I will never again pass them by.
The songs of the temple shall become wailings
in that day," says the LORD GOD.
(Amos 8:1-3)

---

mediating function comes to the fore. Amos pleads on behalf of Israel and YHWH relents. This is quite a contrast with the inexorability of YHWH in the oracles against the nations (1:3–2:16)

In the second pair of visions too, of plumb line and summer fruit, the destruction implied is definitive. YHWH gives the prophet no chance to mediate, but immediately asks him a question. Finally YHWH alone interprets the visions as signifying the end for Israel. To make doubly sure YHWH says that from now on the people will no longer be spared.

The final vision (Amos 9:1-4), that of YHWH supervising the destruction of the sanctuary so that most of the worshipers are smashed under the debris and whoever escapes is put to the sword, stands quite apart both in content and in form from all the previous ones. First of all Amos does not even tell us that the Lord showed him the vision but rather that he himself saw the Lord bringing about the total disaster. Amos tells us that no person and no place is exempt from YHWH's jurisdiction (9:2-4). It is in keeping with the thought of Amos that the final and complete destruction takes place in a sanctuary where the worshiping community is gathered. The irony of it all is that the God who is being worshiped is the one who brings about the destruction of the worshipers. Amos wants to stress that Israel's God cannot be appeased or blackmailed by cult. What interests YHWH is a change of our lifestyle. The section is fittingly brought to a close by the redactor who places here the last doxology to the creator God (9:5-6)

No Privileges Before YHWH (9:7-8)

This section is one of the texts of Amos that is very often quoted. Amos assures us that we cannot claim security and protection by relying on the God of the Exodus who had chosen Israel as God's special people. YHWH has no favorites. Whether they be Ethiopians, Philistines, or Arameans, YHWH is behind the exodus of each of these peoples. There is nothing special about Israel's Exodus from Egypt. Amos is anticipating Paul of Tarsus by centuries: "There is no longer Jew or Greek, there is no longer slave or free" (Gal 3:28; cf. Rom 10:12), and again "God shows no partiality" (Rom 2:11). All peoples are equal before God irrespective of their color, their creed, or their cult. This is a timely warning for all those involved in interreligious dialogue, which should respect members of all religious faiths as equal partners speaking from the same platform because they are children of the same

Father. Whichever nation is sinful will be punished by God (9:8). This had been stressed already in the section of oracles against the nations (1:3–2:16).

Element of Hope in the Message of Amos (9:9-10)

A hotly debated question in the interpretation of Amos is: does Amos reserve hope for Israel? We have seen that both implicitly and explicitly Amos did give the people of Israel hope, implicitly because of the very fact that Amos is inviting the people to be converted, but explicitly also, as will be shown immediately. We have seen how Amos pleads with the people in his three exhortations (5:4-6, 14-15). On the other hand it is true that in the visions of the final disaster YHWH relented after Amos had pleaded on behalf of Israel in the first two visions (7:1-6), but in the last three (7:7-9; 8:1-3; 9:1-4) all hope has been ruled out. All the same the idea of the "remnant of Joseph" (5:15) clearly implies hope, and now at the end of the book Amos makes it more than clear that when YHWH sends the people into exile only the sinners among them shall die by the sword (9:10-11). Amos also reassures the people that YHWH "will not utterly destroy the house of Jacob" (9:8).

Conclusion: Hope for Post-Exilic Israel: 9:11-15

Verses 8-10 of the last chapter of Amos were a fitting conclusion to the prophet's message, but now suddenly in v. 11 a new beginning seems to appear with the phrase "on that day," which has an eschatological ring. The historical situation reflected in vv. 11-14 points to the fall of the city of David, that is, Jerusalem, the breaches in whose walls YHWH now promises to rebuild (cf. Isa 49:16; 44:28). The "remnant of Edom" the Jews will inherit refers to the promise that Judah would inherit whatever would remain after Edom had been sacked by the Babylonians. We know that Edom was sacked some years after the fall of Jerusalem, which fell in 586 B.C.E. Again, as v. 15 shows, YHWH is going to plant the people firmly in the land from which they had been uprooted. All this presupposes the exile and points to times that are separated by centuries from Amos.

When we compare vv. 11-15 with the rest of the book of Amos we see that although in the proclamation of Amos there is no doubt a glimpse of hope the overall message is that the doom that is awaiting Israel is inexorable. In contrast the last three verses of the book offer post-exilic Israel a superabundance of hope. The one who plows will overtake the reaper and the treader of grapes will overtake the sower. The mountains and the hills will flow with sweet wine (cf. Joel 3:18). What is therefore important for the interpretation of the book of Amos is that the post-exilic faith community found it profitable to meditate on the words of Amos that had already come true. The proclamation of Amos and the other prophets was a constant reminder to Israel that its sins had brought about the destruction of Jerusalem and had flung Israel into exile, but Israel also realized that God had not definitively abandoned or utterly destroyed it (9:8). YHWH was always ready to forgive and to make a new beginning. Later generations would make the following confession: "To us belong shame and confusion, but to you, O Lord, glory and grace!" (cf. Dan 9:7-10). It is in this spirit that a post-exilic redactor of the book of Amos reinterpreted his message.

BIBLIOGRAPHY

Coote, Robert B. *Amos Among the Prophets: Composition and Theology.* Philadelphia: Fortress, 1981.

Doorly, W. J. *Prophet of Justice. Understanding the Book of Amos.* New York: Paulist, 1989.

King, Philip J. *Amos, Hosea, Micah—An Archaeological Commentary.* Philadelphia: Westminster, 1988.

Soggin, J. Alberto. *The Prophet Amos.* London: SCM, 1987.

Wolff, Hans-Walter. *Amos the Prophet: The Man and His Background.* Philadelphia: Fortress, 1973.

____. *Joel and Amos.* Hermeneia. Philadelphia: Fortress, 1977.

Obadiah

Victor Salanga

Obadiah is one of the least known of the prophetic books, because of its length (only twenty-one verses) or because of its content (seething anger!) or because of its language (marked by excess!).

FIRST READING

The literary genre of the book presents no problem; it is prophecy. But unlike other prophetic books it begins, as it were, in the middle of things: No mention of reigning kings when the prophet lived; no mention of the place where he preached. It briefly identifies whose vision it is and launches into a series of oracles introduced by "Thus says the LORD God."

Attempts to link the prophet with other biblical persons bearing the same name have been unsatisfactory. It is almost impossible to determine the identity of Obadiah, the place where he preached, and to whom he preached. What is clear is that the angry oracles were against Edom, made by God on behalf of Israel.

Who was Edom, and why such anger? The beginning of Jacob's story (Gen 25:18-34) explains Edom's roots. There Isaac's wife, Rebecca, learns from the LORD that the twins in her womb represent two nations: "One nation will be stronger than the other; the older will serve the younger" (Gen 18:23). The older, Esau, is born "red," (Heb. *ʾadom*) and his body hairy (Heb. *seʿir*). So the nation Esau represents is called "Edom," and at times "Seir." Meanwhile the younger, Jacob, buys the birthright of the famished Esau in exchange for "red, red stew." This is another pun to associate the color "red" with Esau. Later Jacob steals Esau's blessing as firstborn. Esau, deceived a second time, plots to kill Jacob. Thus the enmity between the twin brothers, Jacob and Esau, earlier announced by the LORD, was actualized. Jacob's name was subsequently changed to Israel—the nation he represents. The enmity between the brother nations, Israel and Edom, smoldered.

The intense degree of anger between the brother nations seems to require further explanation. But before all else it is important to get acquainted with the text, reading it unit by unit. There are three such units:

1. Edom's arrogance before God (1-7)
2. Edom's hostility against Israel (8-15)
3. Edom's destruction, Israel's restoration, God's triumph (16-21).

Original Historical Context

Obadiah's historical context is understood to be the time when the Babylonians punished Judah for its rebellion in 587 B.C.E. There is a notion that Edom actually pillaged Jerusalem, even murdered fleeing refugees. Not only did Edom abandon Judah, it became an ally of Babylon.

Another possible context is the migration of Edomites after the fall of Jerusalem, seizing and annexing much of the Negeb desert area of Judah. Again, hostility and deep hurt abide because a nation has taken advantage of a sibling's misfortune. To adapt the psalmist's complaint: If an enemy had done this I could have borne it, but it was you, a brother, a sister who did it (Ps 55:12).

Obadiah then has to do with the experience of anger and resentment against a brother/sister or brother/sister nation who becomes an enemy, an experience not unlike the experience of Filipinos during the Japanese occupation of the Philippines. At that time the word "collaborator" referred to a Filipino who, instead of helping a brother or sister Filipino, cooperated with the enemy, the Japanese. It sparked intense animosity among Filipinos, bringing pain and anguish to them. Or, to bring our example up to date, there was a much-commented picture in a Manila newspaper of an untidy and disheveled woman in a squatter area, weeping and screaming against the leader of the demolition team. The police officer was her own brother-in-law! It is this experience that the book of Obadiah addresses.

To return now to the text, the two events described above, the fall of Jerusalem and the occupation of Judean territory, are believed to have sparked the production of texts in which the understanding of "Edom" evolved. The frustration felt by Judah in 587 was included in worship in the form of a condemnation of Edom. "Edom" became a cultic theme, and later a prophetic, literary theme. "Edom" is not only a particular enemy of Judah; it evolves in literature into a type or symbol to represent all enemy nations of Judah!

Obadiah 1-14, 15b (21) with the addition of 15a, 16-18 reflects this evolution. The author appears to have taken the original oracle against Edom, the typical enemy of Israel, in Jer 49:7-22 and transformed it in the style of Ezekiel 25–26, 35–36, i.e., judgment based on specific deeds. Jeremiah's view of the arrogance of Edom ending in utter shame is combined with Ezekiel's emphasis on specific crimes of Edom, the representative of the nations, on the day of Israel's ruin. For comparison, read the passages from Jeremiah and Ezekiel.

The remaining verses, 19-20, stem from the redaction of the collection of Minor Prophets, known as the "Book of the Twelve." The proposed date for the present form of the text is the end of the exilic period.

Canonical Context

In the Psalms, the poems are divided into five books—the result of editing to align them with the five books of Moses. This editorial activity was meant to show that the Psalms were as central as the Pentateuch. Something similar is found in the Book of the Twelve. Not the numbers, but the content and positioning of the twelve books closely echo the subject matter of the major prophetic books of Isaiah, Jeremiah and Ezekiel. The Twelve taken as a unit also discuss the same prophetic themes of sin, judgment, and renewal. The first six—Hosea, Joel, Amos, Obadiah, Jonah, and Micah—highlight covenant and cosmic sin as their main issue without denying that each touches on judgment and renewal too. The next three—Nahum, Habakkuk, and Zephaniah—focus on covenant and the cosmic nature of punishment as their principal interest. The last three—Haggai, Zechariah, and Malachi—have covenant and cosmic restoration as their central concern.

The "sin" section unfolds in this sequence: Hosea declares Israel's infidelity. Joel repeats the theme and discusses the sin of the nations. Amos adds more details to the sin of the nations. At the end of that book, in 9:12, Amos promises that Israel "will possess the remnant of Edom." Obadiah picks up this idea and denounces Edom, the representative of the nations. In Jonah, the prophet is like the Edomites who stood aloof, desired the destruction of a neighbor, and displayed no compassion; so did the prophet sin and, if the prophet is taken to represent the nation, Israel also sinned. Micah summarizes the previous points and provides the transition to punishment and repentance. In the final redaction of the Book of the Twelve the individual books mesh together as one voice announcing the basic themes of prophecy—the same themes as those of the great prophets Isaiah, Jeremiah, and Ezekiel. [See also the article "Prophetism and Prophets."]

Patristic Interpretation

The Greek Fathers Theodore of Mopsuestia (350?–428), Cyril of Alexandria (ca. 350–444) and Theodoret of Cyrus (393–466) wrote commentaries on Obadiah while Hesychius (d. 450) merely listed topics *(capita).* The three commentators trace Israel's anger against Edom to the Esau–Jacob sibling rivalry. Theodoret says that the rivalry degenerated into a sort of "congenital hatred" (Latin *"insitum odium"*; Greek *"oikeian dusmeneian"* (*PG* 81.1710). But Hesychius does not mention Edom at all. He refers to him as the devil and speaks of what "he and those in error and wickedness under him will suffer from the apostles" (*PG* 93.1351-54).

This reading using "Esau" as the backdrop for interpretation and "Edom" as the devil personified seems to be in continuity with the development pointed out earlier. "Edom" becomes not only a type or symbol of an enemy, but the devil personified. There seems to be a remarkable intuition that Edom represents any error or wickedness or evil and that such evil is unacceptable. Similarly the anger described in the text reveals the force and vehemence with which one should oppose such evil.

The Latin fathers Jerome (345–420) and Augustine (354–430) lived when the Church had emerged as a sort of state religion of the Roman empire. Jerome points first to those who scoff at the true Church, then to fleshly desires that dominate the soul as Edomites in his day. Thus he extends the meaning to the realm of theology and spirituality. Whatever be the case, Edom is seen as evil and righteous anger as the appropriate response.

Augustine (*City of God* 18.31) also describes the Idumeans as evildoers. ("Idumea" is Greek for "Edom"; Herod the Great was an Idumean.) Augustine understands the Idumeans to represent the nations in need of saving. While saving evildoers is not the spirit of the text of Obadiah, this is not a bad evolution: one annihilates one's enemy by making him or her one's friend.

Liturgical Reading

It is most telling that Obadiah is not read or heard at all in the Roman liturgy. Could its absence indicate some fear on the part of the community of bringing before God the angry feelings and resentments that plague individuals and groups? Could its absence indicate some fear of facing squarely before God the evil that triggers such negativity? Obadiah offers a way of expressing indignant anger against an evil deed within the purview of prayer and worship. It can be done and *is* done—precisely because it is within the context of a relationship with God. Handling anger and resentment need not be limited to therapy rooms, nor combating evil only to the halls of Congress. They, too, can be confronted honestly in prayer and worship. Moreover, prayer and worship often become one of the few viable and meaningful ways left to denounce the injustice in dictatorial regimes, as was done in the Philippines during the Marcos regime.

Present Significance

The text of Obadiah and its patristic interpretations point to a very interesting development regarding Edom: Edom is first a brother/brother nation who has become an enemy; then in the context of worship and of literary editing it becomes a type or symbol of all the enemy nations of Judah. Later, among the Greek Fathers, Edom becomes the devil personified.

If Obadiah portrays so much of Judah's anger and hurt, accompanied by vengeful condemnations and threats of annihilation, what the texts reveal is the immensity of wrong and evil that human beings, especially among those who are related by blood and race, are capable of doing. The ongoing conflicts between North and South Korea come to mind; so do the past bloody wars of North and South Vietnam and many similar cases in our modern world! Correspondingly the texts also reveal the frustrating anger and just opposition of those who painfully experience such evil as well as those who come to know about it. That this may be so with regard to Judah is further reinforced by the realization that it was in no position to "annihilate" any enemy. From 598 until the formation of the present state of Israel it has had no army and no political power whatever. Obadiah invites us to hate evil (whoever the perpetrator may be, blood relation or otherwise) and—no matter how frustrating it may be in the midst of suffering—to trust that God through Christ's own opposition to evil for which he too suffered will restore well-being and bring salvation. This is an apt way to end the section, for in the survey of interpretations ending with Augustine we found it to be his concern that evildoers eventually be saved. For further reading, see the article on "Violence in the Bible."

SECOND READING

Edom's Pride Before YHWH: Obadiah 1–7

3–4: References to "height": living in clefts of the rock (Heb. *selaʿ*), dwelling high, soaring like an eagle, nesting among stars may point to an actual description of Sela, an Edomite city in the Petra complex in present day Jordan, a rock mass of red sandstone that rises to a dizzying height of 3,700 ft above sea level. But beyond geography is the symbolic use of "height" to express pride. Notice the upward and downward movement, reminiscent of the Tower of Babel story in Gen 11:1-9; the taunts against the king of Babylon (Isa 14:12-15) and against the Prince of Tyre (Ezek 28:2-9; 31:1-4). It is not the human who goes up; it is God who comes down. If at all, it is at the invitation of God that the human being goes up: see Exod 3:7-8; 19:11, 18, 20; Num 11:17, 25; 2 Sam 22:10; Isa 31:4; 63:19; Pss 18:10; 144:5; Neh 9:13.

5–7: The reference to Edom's allies and confederates means the Babylonians. There is irony here: little does Edom realize ("no understanding in it," 7d) that the nation whom they support against Judah is the same nation that destroys them. The Babylonian Nabonidus probably brought Edom's end in 552 B.C.E.

Edom's Hostility Against Israel: Obadiah 8-15

"That day" of 8 and "the day of the LORD" of 15 form an inclusion. The *Leitwort* of the whole unit is "day," repeated 12 times. The repetition underlines the reciprocal action of the law of revenge exactingly carried out on the Day of the LORD. In this judgment oracle, "Day of the LORD" states metaphorically that this is the "day" YHWH has appointed for intervening, where what is promised will occur, and from which no one can escape.

8-9: The link with the previous unit is "understanding," 7d and 8c; Teman is a place name in Edom, regarded as a seat of wisdom.

10: To the prophets, "violence" (Heb. *ḥamas*) is one of the major sins of Israel and her neighbors: Ezek 28:16; Isa 53:9; 60:18; Jer 6:7; 20:8; 22:3; Ezek 7:23; 45:9; Joel 4:19; Amos 3:10; Mic 6:12.

11-14: The preferred translation is "do not + verb" to portray immediacy, a vivid imagining of Jerusalem's fall, rather than "you should not have + verb," suggesting that Edom *had* behaved in the way it did. These verses are not to be taken as history but more as a poet's description. This warning to Edom is reminiscent of OT wisdom tradition: "Do not rejoice when your enemy falls, and let not your heart be glad when he stumbles" (Prov 24:17).

15b: Contrast also the law of revenge with Jesus' teaching in Matthew 5 and Paul's in Romans 12.

Israel's Restoration: Obadiah 16-21

16: Drunkenness, figuratively pictured as men reeling and staggering from much intoxication, refers to those who suffer disaster from God's punishing anger: cf. Ps 107:27; Lam 4:21; Isa 19:14; 29:9; 51:21; Jer 13:13; 23:9; 25:27; Ezek 23:33; Nah 3:11; Rev 17:2.

17-18: The idea that "Mount Zion" (Jerusalem) shall win out even after its ruin stems from the twin convictions of Jerusalem theology: that YHWH had chosen Zion as a home forever (Ps 132:13-14; 1 Kings 8:30-35; Ps 48:2-3) and had chosen David's family to establish a line of kings to reign forever (2 Sam 7:4-16; 23:5). The most common designation of Edom in Obadiah is "Mount Esau": see 8, 9, 19, 21.

19: The grammar of this verse is contorted but the intent is that the three southern regions (Negeb, Shephelah, and Benjamin) are taken into possession by the exiles of the former Southern Kingdom and the three northern regions (Ephraim, Samaria, and Gilead) by the exiles of the "house of Joseph," the former Northern Kingdom.

20: "Halah" is a region in Mesopotamia, probably Nineveh, where Tiglath-pileser II exiled some of the Israelites in 734. "Zarephath" is a city name in Phoenicia (see 1 Kings 17:9-10). "Sepharad" is another place to which the people of Jerusalem were exiled—probably Sardis in Asia Minor or a region of Media. We may note that the lands recovered by the former Northern and Southern Kingdoms are beyond their former boundaries.

21: Crucial here are the words "savior" or "deliverer" (Heb. *mošiaᶜ*) and "to judge" (Heb. *špt*) rather than RSV's "to rule." The usual action of a deliverer is to judge: cf. Judg 3:9-10, 15; Isa 19:20; 2 Kings 13:5. Because the verb "to judge" rather than "to rule" is used, this seems to be more an application of the judgment or fulfillment of what has been predicted than something more positive, an eschatological event. The consequence of the deliverer's judgment (following the text literally) is that "she will be the kingdom to the LORD"—i.e., after its punishment, the kingdom (of Edom) shall be the LORD's.

BIBLIOGRAPHY

Bartlett, John R. *Edom and Edomites.* JSOT.S 77. Sheffield: JSOT Press, 1989.

Coggins, Richard J., and S. Paul Re'emi. *Israel Among the Nations: A Commentary on the Books of Nahum and Obadiah.* ITC. Grand Rapids: Eerdmans, 1985.

Dicou, Bert. *Edom, Israel's Brother and Antagonist. The Role of Edom in Biblical Prophecy and Story.* JSOT.S 169. Sheffield: JSOT Press, 1994.

Wolff, Hans Walter. *Obadiah and Jonah. A Commentary.* Minneapolis: Augsburg, 1986.

Jonah

Erik Eynikel

The book of Jonah is unique in prophetic literature. No other book in the prophetic canon contains so much prophetic narrative and so little prophetic speech (only five words!). Jonah's audience (the Ninevites) is also unique. There are prophets, like Jeremiah, who preached against the Gentiles, but only in Jonah are the Gentiles not just condemned but given a choice to convert. The reason why Jonah is included in the Prophets (and not, for example, in the Wisdom literature) is because it essentially speaks about reconciliation (cf. the Jewish liturgy where the book is read on Yom Kippur).

FIRST READING

To understand the book of Jonah it is essential to take into account the reference to this prophet in 2 Kings 14:25-27. There it is said that Jonah proclaimed a message of redemption to Jeroboam II (787–747) not because this king was righteous (on the contrary: "He did what was evil in the sight of the Lord"), but because God had mercy on Israel ("The Lord saw the distress of Israel"). At the same time Jonah is a prophet of doom for Israel's enemy because the territory recovered by Jeroboam is a loss for the Arameans. In this sense the Jonah mentioned in 2 Kings 14:25 is truly one of the pre-literary prophets, comparable to Samuel, Nathan, Gad, and Elijah, a major feature of whose prophecies was that they are unconditional and irrevocable. For them conversion changes nothing: the verdict can be delayed but not canceled (e.g., 1 Kings 21:27-29).

We may expect from our reading of 2 Kings 14:25 that the Jonah of the book of Jonah will act as the Jonah in 2 Kings did, but he does not. In his book Jonah is not a glorious prophet proclaiming salvation for Israel but a stubborn man trying to escape from his prophetic mission. However, we should take into account that the historical Jonah of 2 Kings 14 is a different reality than the Jonah of the book of Jonah. The relationship with the Jonah of 2 Kings 14:25 is *literary,* not historical. The book of Jonah was written long after the time of Jeroboam II. This is shown by the historical inconsistencies in the book. In this book Nineveh was already a legendary name, whereas in the time of Jeroboam II Nineveh was not yet the capital of the Assyrians. Moreover, historically the king of Ashur was never called the "king of Nineveh" (3:6) but always "king of Ashur" even when he resided in Nineveh. Again, the diameter of Nineveh was never more than five kilometers on the longest side and not "a three days' walk" (3:3). Furthermore, the language, which gives evidence of the time of composition, contains Aramaisms: expressions such as "the God of heaven" (1:9), or "the nobles" to indicate royal officials. These influences occurred during the Persian period after the exile. This was the time of the reconstruction of the second Temple and the revitalization of Judean religion under Ezra and Nehemiah. They took measures to purify religion from syncretic influence. This particularism went very far: mixed marriages had to be annulled (Ezra 9–10; Nehemiah 8–10) and the neighboring people, especially the Samaritans, were not allowed to cooperate in rebuilding the temple (Ezra 4:2-3). No wonder this policy led to opposition and protest literature: Ruth and Jonah against the particularism, Job and later Qoheleth against the rigid interpretation of wisdom teaching at that time. All this protest literature was published pseudonymously. But by choosing to name his protagonist after the salvation prophet of 2 Kings 14:25 the author of the book of Jonah leads the reader to ask: what salvation message will Jonah offer to Israel here?

The book of Jonah consists of two major parts, each containing a story (chs. 1 and 3) and a commentary (chs. 2 and 4).

If we consider Jonah to be the leading character in the book (and he really is) we may describe the formation of the book in two series of three scenes:

1–1	Jonah is sent to the Gentiles but he is willfully disobedient (1:1-3)	2–1	Jonah is sent to the Gentiles and he performs (3:1-3)
1–2	The Gentiles confront Jonah: the sailors convert (1:4-16)	2–2	The Gentiles confront Jonah: the Ninevites convert (3:4-10)
1–3	Jonah confronts God; he utters a lament (2:1-6) passing into praise (2:7-9) that ends in his salvation (2:10)	2–3	Jonah confronts God; he utters a lament (4:1-3) passing into a further lament (4:8) that ends in a rebuke (4:11)

There is much debate among exegetes about the literary genre of the book of Jonah. The best proposal is to call it a parable. It is true that it is unusually long compared with NT parables, but Jonah never had an oral phase as the other parables in the Bible had. The best parallel to Jonah is the parable of the Prodigal Son in Luke 15:11-31 because the question "do you accept your converted brother?" is also at stake in Jonah. This will be developed further in *The Subject Matter of Jonah.*

SECOND READING

I. Jonah is Willfully Disobedient

1.1 Jonah is Sent to the Gentiles (1:1-3)

The Lord calls Jonah to go to Nineveh. This call is comparable with the call of other prophets: Hosea, Joel, Micah, and Zephaniah; but it is even more closely related to the formula with which Elijah receives his divine messages (1 Kings 17:8; 18:1; 19:9; 21:17, 28). However, this call formula is used only after Elijah had been introduced to the readers. In Jonah 1:1 the prophet has not yet been introduced to the readers, so that we must interpret this formula as a reference to 2 Kings 14:25.

Jonah's name is also programmatic for the whole book: "Jonah son of Ammitai," meaning Jonah, son of "trustworthy." As we will see, Jonah struggles with God's veracity versus his own notion of what God's veracity should be. The word Jonah means "dove"; Israel is compared to "a dove, silly and without sense" in Hos 7:11 (compare Hos 11:11; Ps 74:18-19). Jonah represents Israel's miserable side. This dove is sent by the Lord with a message having two possible meanings: either "proclaim against Nineveh *that* their wickedness has gone up to me" or "proclaim . . . *because* their wickedness . . . ." In the first meaning, v. 2b refers to *what* Jonah has to proclaim in Nineveh; in the second meaning, *why* he has to proclaim against Nineveh. Since ambiguity is a characteristic feature in the book, we may assume that both are meaningful for our reading. Jonah, the "dove" (a symbol for peace) is sent with this message to Nineveh, which is called "the city of bloodshed" in Nah 3:1 and to the Assyrian king whose name is "King Warlike" (Hos 5:13). No wonder Jonah flees—to Tarshish, exactly the opposite direction. A return trip to Tarshish by ship could take three years (1 Kings 10:22); Jonah did not plan to go to Nineveh very soon! We read in Isaiah that the Lord says of Tarshish that it is among the nations "that have not heard of my fame or seen my glory" (66:19). Fleeing to Tarshish instead of going to Nineveh does not seem to be such an excellent choice after all, except of course that Assyria and Nineveh were *the* symbols of evil (Hos 9:1-6; 11:1-5; Isa 7:17-20; Jer 50:17). Jonah, however, is not fleeing from the Ninevites, but from his God (cf. v. 3b).

1.2 The Gentiles Confront Jonah (1:4-16)

1:4-6: The sailors very soon see that Jonah is fleeing from his God: "the Lord hurled a great wind upon the sea . . . [so] that the ship threatened to break up." The sailors, Gentiles, each of whom prays to his own god, are, however, forbearing. They have no preconception against the stranger Jonah (contra sailors' reputation: cf. Ezek 27:9, 27, 29); on the contrary they respect Jonah, or better Jonah's god. There is even a noticeable growth in faith. First they fear the storm but then they become more godfearing, fearing Jonah's god. They even convert to the Lord, pray that this god would not make them guilty of innocent blood (they do not condemn Jonah) and at the end offer a sacrifice and vows to the Lord. The sailors act as the Ninevites will do later. The captain parallels the king of Nineveh. He summons everybody (including Jonah) "to call on his god" using words resembling those of the Lord when calling on Jonah to go to Nineveh. The captain takes over the role of the prophet. The ship is Nineveh in miniature.

1:7-16: Jonah, who went to sleep (cf. Mark 4:35-41), however, reacts fatalistically when the captain summons him to pray. In reply to the captain's question in v. 8 he utters his credo: the Lord is "the God of heaven, who made the sea and the dry land"—so where should he hide anyway—and "throw me into the sea." It is only in the belly of the great fish (the chaos monster of the primeval sea, the symbol of the underworld, as we know it from Isa 27:1 and extra-biblical myths) that Jonah comes to his senses.

1.3 Jonah Confronts God (2:1-10)

Jonah is in that despairing situation for three days and three nights. The figure three indicates completeness in the Bible and when related to suffering (Exod 15:22; 1 Sam 30:12) and death (Luke 24:12; John 11:17) "three days" means until the bitter end. So when Jesus recovers from the grave after three days, this is only possible because of God (Matt 12:10; compare Hos 6:1-2).

The Church Fathers refer many times to Jonah in their writings. Almost all references are to the passage in the belly of the fish, e.g., Augustine, *Civ. Dei* 18.13: "Jonah . . . by his own passion so to speak prophesied of Christ's death and resurrection. For why was he taken into the whale's belly . . . except to prefigure Christ who was to return . . . on the third day?" Many exegetes therefore equate "the sign of Jonah" in Matt 12:40 (quoting Jonah 1:17) and 16:4 with Jesus' resurrection. It is also possible that the sign of Jonah refers to the act of repentance, because in Luke 11:30 the sign of Jonah refers to Jonah's (and Jesus') entire preaching.

Jonah is indeed at the bitter end. Only when he is in the deepest misery does he lament to God. It is typical for a lamentation in the Psalter that the cry for help be followed by thanksgiving, as if the situation has been remedied during the praying (implying an oracle and an act of faith; Psalm 22 is the most familiar example). This sudden change from lament to praise is best explained by the supposition that the suppliants, after expressing the situation, crying for help, and expressing confidence, suddenly start thanking because they are sure that God will not leave them in misery (compare John 11:42: Jesus thanks God *before* calling Lazarus out of his grave). More problematic is the fact that the content of the psalm does not fit in well with Jonah's situation. The vocabulary is very different from the context, so is the style (poetry) and Jonah's attitude (submissive). The reference to the holy temple is out of place in the belly of the fish. This encourages some commentators to dismiss vv. 2-9 as a later addition. This is, however, not necessary. Perhaps the psalm existed already and the author of the book of Jonah may have used it, tolerating the imperfections of the psalm that we just mentioned because it expresses Jonah's partial change of mind. He will no longer run away from God; he will seek God and make vows to God. What these vows are is not clear; maybe going down to Nineveh: at least that is what he does immediately after his release from the fish. Yet in another way, Jonah has not changed. He contrasts himself in the psalm with "those who worship vain idols and forsake their true loyalty." His opinion about the Gentiles has not changed. This will become clearer in the second part of the story.

II. Jonah Performs

2.1 Jonah is Sent to the Gentiles (3:1-3)

The story recommences with the same wordings as in ch. 1. Nineveh is an exceedingly large city (literally "large for God"). Large cities have a bad reputation in the Bible: the cities built by Nimrod (including Nineveh, Gen 10:12), Babel (Gen 11:4), Sodom and Gomorrah (Gen 13:10). According to Jonah, Nineveh is the largest of all: "a three days' walk," which must refer to its diameter. In Nineveh corruption must have reached its summit. Jonah enters the city but does not go to the city center. He proceeds only a day's walk and there he acts for the first and last time as a prophet: "Forty days more, and Nineveh shall be turned over." In Hebrew it is no more than five words but they are very ambivalent. It can mean: forty more days and Nineveh will be destroyed. The word for "turn over" is used in this sense for Sodom and Gomorrah (Gen 19:21, 25, 29). But it is used in the sense of "reform" in other passages (Exod 14:5; 1 Sam 10:9). The figure forty with a period of time is also very ambiguous in the Bible: it often has a negative connotation (Goliath challenges the Israelites for forty days in 1 Sam 17:16; the rain lasted for forty days during the great flood in Gen 7:4, etcetera) but many other examples show it as a transitional period to better times. In Deut 9:18-19 Moses prostrated before the Lord forty days, fasting and praying for the people because he feared God would destroy them. The Ninevites understand Jonah's message as a call to repentance and reformation. But Jonah has other ideas. Although he finally fulfills his prophetic mission he does it in a minimal way: he did not penetrate the city farther than its suburbs; he proclaimed his message only once and he limited it to the very minimum. Nothing is said about "their wickedness has come up before [the LORD]" (1:1); God is not even mentioned in Jonah's words, only doom. It is clear that Jonah hopes that his words will have no effect, that the Ninevites will continue with their wicked actions and burn up like the inhabitants of Sodom. What a miscalculation!

2.2 The Gentiles Confront Jonah (3:4-10)

The Ninevites perceived immediately that Jonah proclaimed a divine message, although they did not know which god threatened them (for the Ninevites as for the sailors "the LORD" is never used, only God, "Elohim"). Like the sailors, the Ninevites also possess a prophet: their king. He assumes Jonah's role and proclaims fasting and repentance for the whole city, including the animals. It is not that they were so sure that God would reconsider the decision to destroy Nineveh. Not at all, but they did everything they could, even the absurd (clothing the animals in sackcloth), to change God's mind. Jonah, however, did know that there was salvation for the Ninevites if they would convert (cf. 4:2-3), but Jonah withholds that information in his prophecy because he absolutely did not want the Ninevites to do so. He wanted them to be punished.

The words that the king and the Ninevites use are almost literally the same as Joel's (Joel 2:12-14). Joel is a prophet of the post-exilic time, when the book of Jonah was written. It seems that the Ninevites understood the aim of prophecy better than Jonah, who adheres to the irrevocability of the pre-classical prophecy of doom.

2.3 Jonah Confronts God (4:1-11)

4:1-3: Jonah begins lamenting again when God's mind changes. He explains why he fled to Tarshish. He knew that when the Ninevites were aware of their fate they would reform and be saved. Very ironic of course is that Jonah in his lament sums up five qualities of God for which God is praised in Exod 34:6-7 and that are used in a call for mercy in Joel 2:13. Jonah has his own ideas of what God's qualities accomplish. He can as well die now since his prophecy will not materialize: he is a false prophet (Deut 18:21-22). His attitude is grotesque in light of the death-fear he went through in the belly of the fish. Jeremiah (32:16-25) and Elijah (1 Kings 19:4) also wished to die when they could not cope any more with their prophetic task. When compared to them, Jonah overreacts, and he has a very different motive. Jeremiah and Elijah complained that their prophetic activity was unsuccessful because the Israelites were disobedient to their words. Jonah wants to die because his mission *is* successful, and because of God.

4:3-5: But God is not vengeful toward Jonah. God is merciful (4:2) as ever: the Lord gently asks Jonah if he has reason to be so angry. But Jonah does not want to reply. Stubborn, he leaves Nineveh and waits under a booth for what would happen with the city. Many commentators relocate 4:5-9 before 3:10, since there is no point in waiting outside anymore. If we remember, however, that Jonah is literarily connected to the pre-classical prophets we can understand Jonah's attitude as clinging to that tradition, even when he knows that God has left it. Jonah is prepared to wait for forty days because prophecy is prophecy.

4:6-9: God is a good pedagogue. If words don't work, actions may do so. The Lord appointed a castor oil plant to shelter Jonah from the sun and to deliver him from his anger. The last goal follows from the first. Jonah is delighted with the shade from the plant; his anger is turned into happiness. Nineveh seems totally out of his mind. This is not enough for the Lord, who does not want Jonah to forget Nineveh but to accept it. God appoints a worm that kills the plant, even adding a sultry wind (a symbol of God's anger in Exod 10:13; Isa 27:8, and Jonah 1:4, 13). Jonah is back where he was at the beginning of this chapter: full of anger, not because of the Ninevites but from self-pity. This is obvious from his reaction to God's question in v. 9. Earlier Jonah did not reply to that question (v. 3). Now he cannot restrain himself. He explodes: "Yes, angry enough to die."

4:10-11: But God's patience is never-ending. The event with the plant becomes a parable. God is concerned with the Ninevites as Jonah was with the plant. The word "concerned" is used elsewhere to indicate a subject's (God's or an individual's) sympathy toward humans of lesser status, or else a subject's anxiety about possessions (Gen 45:20). Jonah considered the plant his possession although it was given to him. Should not God then take care of the Ninevites, who, as the text signals, are not only God's creation but are more like the Israelites than Jonah thinks? The city contains "more than twelve times ten thousand people" (*adam,* "humankind" is used here, providing a link to creation); and the Hebrew text does not use the simple numeric system to say "a hundred and twenty thousand," but rather a convoluted formula as if the writer wants to say "twelve tribes" (like Israel) of ten thousand (the highest figure in Hebrew). "Right side" is connected with "good" and "left side" with "bad" in Qoh 10:2. If the Ninevites do not know the difference between good and bad, can they be held responsible for their wickedness (1:1) when nobody tells them? Who other than the prophet should tell them? God asks Jonah to reflect on these questions. But the story is open-ended. These answers must come from the reader.

THE SUBJECT MATTER OF JONAH

The leading character of the book is not Nineveh but Jonah, representing Israel. Is Israel going to accept the Gentiles or will it give in to prejudice? That this change presupposes a new insight into the prophetic role is made evident in several ways: the most humorous are the way the sailors behave in contrast with Jonah and the way the animals and plant fulfill their task immediately while Jonah is not willing to accept the message of God until the end. The reference to Elijah (especially 1 Kings 19), is also instructive for this matter.

1 Kings 19: There are many thematic similarities between Jonah and 1 Kings 19: fleeing away, the death-wish, the dialogue with the Lord, the plant/bush, a day's walk, forty days. But the most important element differs: it is not from the Lord that Elijah flees, but from Jezebel to save his life. Jonah, on the other hand, flees from the Lord, and because of this his life is in danger! Elijah, strengthened by the angel and revitalized by the experience at Horeb, continues his task. Jonah also experienced the Lord; how will he react? This is left open.

Exodus 14: A comparison with Exodus 14:12 where the Israelites are complaining against Moses is enlightening. "Is this not what we have said in Egypt?" (compare Jonah 4:2); "better for us to serve the Egyptians than to die in the wilderness" (parallels Jonah 4:3); "a strong east wind" (Exod 14:21) to save the Israelites parallels Jonah 1:4, 13; 4:8. Israel in Exodus 14 and Jonah (Israel!) are tested. Israel would rather live in Egypt than die in the wilderness; Jonah would rather die in the wilderness than live with such a God. Israel's attitude in the wilderness can still be explained as a psychological breakdown. Jonah, however, is revolting against a basic concept of Israel's faith.

Luke 15:11-30: To conclude, we must consider the intertextual relationship of Jonah 3–4 with the parable of the Prodigal Son. Both parables are about the triangle: God—the righteous—the converted. Both have many intrinsic similarities: the converted take the risk although they have no certainty that they will receive forgiveness; the converted were not unjust toward the righteous but toward God; the righteous adopt a "legal attitude" but the personal relationship of the converted with God transcends any legal claim of punishment; God offers a soft rebuke, and finally there is the open ending. Both parables invite the reader to live compassionately instead of with juridical harshness. What is our choice?

BIBLIOGRAPHY

Bolin, Thomas M. *Freedom Beyond Forgiveness. The Book of Jonah Re-Examined.* JSOT.S 236; Copenhagen International Seminar 3. Sheffield: Sheffield Academic Press, 1997.

Fretheim, Terence E. *The Message of Jonah.* Minneapolis: Augsburg, 1977.

Gunn, David M., and Dana N. Fewell. *Narrative in the Hebrew Bible.* The Oxford Bible. Oxford: Oxford University Press, 1993.

Limburg, James. *Jonah: A Commentary.* Louisville: Westminster/John Knox, 1994.

Magonet, Jonathan. *Form and Meaning: Studies in Literary Techniques in the Book of Jonah.* Sheffield: Almond Press, 1983.

Sasson, Jack M. *Jonah.* AB 24B. Garden City, N.Y.: Doubleday, 1990.

Wesselius, J. S. "The Message of the Book of Jonah." *Studies in Biblical Narrative Texts* (Amsterdam, 1989) 21–39.

Micah

Jan Holman

FIRST READING

I. The Prophet Micah

The name *mikaya(hû)* "Who is like YHWH" occurs eleven times in the OT. The best known bearer of this name is the prophet Micah, born around 750 B.C.E., from Moresheth-Gath *(tell el gudede),* a Philistine town in the present day Gaza strip. Micah is known in history as a farmers' prophet. He stands up for the rural population against the elite of the city of Jerusalem. This ruling class enslaves peasants when they are no longer able to pay their debts. In rough, bold language Micah gives the exploiters a piece of his mind. According to Micah they are those "who tear the skin from off my people, and their flesh from their bones; who eat the flesh of my people, and flay their skin from off them, and break their bones in pieces, and chop them up like meat in a kettle, like flesh in a caldron" (Mic 3:2-3). But Micah is more than just another critic of the society of his days. His primary duty is to point out the sin of his people (Mic 3:8). Micah is in a difficult position. His adversaries are formidably powerful and above all they are theologically well-informed. Still, Micah's preaching must have been impressive. King Hezekiah (727–698/97 B.C.E.) also is moved by the preaching of Micah (Jer 26:18-19). Even a century after Micah's appearance, people in Jerusalem remember his message. The rest of Micah's life is a mystery.

II. Micah's Time

Micah 1:13-16, the climax of the first chapter, seems to endorse the opinion that Micah starts his career as a prophet in Lachish *(tell edduweir)* a few years before the fall of Samaria (722 B.C.E.). Lachish was a strategically important stronghold of the kings of Judah on the road to Egypt in the Shephela (the lowland). About ten years later Micah clashes with the leading citizens of Jerusalem. The period of Micah's activity coincides with the Assyrian expansionist policy. Tiglath Pileser III (745–727 B.C.E.) has the intention of subduing the whole West Semitic world. Conquered peoples become puppet states. In case of rebellion these vassals are reduced to the status of a mini-kingdom under a ruler kindly disposed toward Assyria. Parts taken from the realm in question become Assyrian provinces. The ruling class is deported to other regions of Assyria. If in spite of all these measures a tenant-ruler dares to rebel again, the whole mini-kingdom is finally annexed to Assyria. It all reminds us of what Asia, Africa, and Europe had to endure from Japan, Fascist Italy, and Nazi Germany during World War II.

III. The Book of Micah

1. A Division

Nowadays a division of the book of Micah into chs. 1–5 and 6–7 is widely accepted. Chapters 6–7 are supposed to originate not with Micah from Moresheth, but with a namesake of his in the north of Israel (A.S. van der Woude), or are considered to be an editorial mosaic of texts from post-exilic times (538 B.C.E.) (B. Renaud). In exegesis this led to the distinction between a proto- (first) and deutero- (second) Micah. So there are two separate historical contexts for the prophetic preaching handed down to us by the present book of Micah. We should add to this a third one, namely that of the final editing of the book of Micah. The advantage of establishing such a division is not merely academic. It may sharpen our eye for the presence of individual theological profiles and other specific differences of the message in each part of the book of Micah that otherwise may escape us. For a concrete, nuanced theological specification see the synthesis of the theology of the book of Micah further on, where we exploit the two historical contexts of the prophetic preaching presented in the book. The context of the final editing of the book of Micah may become obvious in the Second Reading, where we will point out, e.g., omissions of location so as to make the book of Micah meaningful for readers anywhere, at any time in the future.

There are, in fact, several good reasons for assuming the present division. The most obvious are the following:

(a) In the book of Micah there are intertextual links both with the book of Isaiah originating from the south (Judah) and with the book of Hosea which comes from the north (Israel). These similarities are nicely distributed over Micah 1–5 regarding its links with Isaiah, and over Micah 6–7 concerning its agreement with Hosea.

(b) With respect to the geographical references there appears again an interesting twofold distribution over Micah 1–5 and 6–7. Jerusalem (7x) and Mount Zion (9x) occur only in Micah 1–5. Northern places such as Gilgal (Mic 6:5), Basan, Gilead (7:14), and Carmel we find in Micah 6–7.

(c) The first verse of the book of Micah seems to imply a division represented by the two parallel relative sentences: "The word of YHWH (a) that came to Micah of Moresheth . . . (b) that he saw concerning Samaria and Jerusalem." For more details see the Second Reading at 1:1.

2. The Main Thrust of the Message of the Book of Micah

The principal difference between Micah and his opponents lies in the way they appropriate the YHWH traditions. Strictly speaking Micah's adversaries are not unorthodox nor do they deny any religious truth. It is more the way they deal with the religious inheritance of Israel that parts them from Micah. Micah's antagonists made God's revealed truth a static, impersonal, a-historical ideology, a kind of instant religion applicable in their own favor in any way, at any time, and anywhere. Micah, however, is convinced that the word of God has its own time and place. For instance, the opponents of Micah quote Ps 46:7, "The Lord of hosts is with us; the God of Jacob is our refuge," in Mic 3:11: "Is not the Lord in the midst of us?" According to Micah the selfish rulers of Jerusalem are not entitled to use such texts to cover up their immoral behavior.

3. Synthesis of the Theology of the Book of Micah on the Basis of Keywords

This compendium follows the order of the chapters of Micah. I recommend a first cursory reading of the book of Micah in conjunction with the following thematic treatment. It may be practical to photocopy the outline given later on under the heading "Literary Structure of the Book of Micah." Clip it to one page for a better overview and use it as a guideline to get acquainted with the book of Micah as a whole. You may mark during your reading the main divisions of the outline in your own Bible.

a. Theophany, Mic 1:2-5

Micah is acquainted with the old Israelite tradition of theophany. It consists of three elements: (1) God's coming; (2) cosmic reactions to this coming; (3) God's salvific intervention. But Micah changes this traditional pattern of theophany by replacing the salvific element by the execution of divine judgment.

b. Social Criticism, Mic 2:1-5, 8-9

Micah's social criticism is primarily aimed at the abuse of power for money by rulers, especially with respect to the expropriation of peasants' land and houses. "Justice" *(mishpat)* is the central notion in this context. Micah restricts himself to words of accusation and judgment. He does not make room for admonitions to practice justice or for an appeal to repentance. The sins of the leaders bring total destruction on Jerusalem. Micah's vision of the future implies that the peasants of Judah ("my people") will recover their expropriated land.

c. The Law of Retaliation or Talion
(Ius talionis), *Mic 2:1-5; 3:5-7*

According to the law of retaliation or "talion," good and bad acts carry their own reward or punishment. The evil deed recoils banefully upon the agent, the good one beneficially. Chickens come home to roost. Do well and be well. Psalm 7:17 conveys this principle as follows: "His mischief returns upon his own head, and on his own pate his violence descends." Micah shares the traditional belief that there is a recognizable connection between what one does and what happens to one. A crime only comes to rest when retribution has overtaken the perpetrator. This retribution is not a new act coming from somewhere else: rather, it is a fruit of sin itself.

d. True and False Prophets, Micah 3

Micah stands in sharp contrast to the prophets connected with the priesthood and the ruling class. The preaching of these false prophets was based on the Zion tradition that in their opinion automatically guaranteed the safety of Jerusalem and its inhabitants. It is precisely this religious automatism, inspired by supernatural selfishness, that makes them false prophets. They reject Micah's prophecy of doom over Jerusalem as a nefarious act denying one of their dearest religious convictions.

e. Zion Tradition, Mic 3:12 and Chapter 4

Micah is interested in the city of Jerusalem and its religious tradition of Zion. The name Zion is in the Bible a synonym for Jerusalem as the divine dwelling place. Zion is the city YHWH has chosen as a dwelling. There YHWH has put the divine *Name* (Deut 12:5), an OT predecessor of the Catholic "real presence" in the Eucharist. What is shocking to his contemporaries is Micah's conviction that Jerusalem will not only fall into enemy hands but will also be destroyed. The reason for this is its corrupt leadership. There is no hope of survival for the Holy City. Any form of seeking refuge in Zion because of the divine presence there is ruled out by Micah. Zion is not invulnerable. Any reliance on the Zion dogma without moral behavior is an exercise in religious futility.

f. Messianism, Mic 5:2-6

Christians often erroneously assume that the Messiah (i.e., the Anointed One, *mashiach* in Hebrew, *Christos* in Greek) holds a central position in the OT. But there are several relativizing factors with respect to "the Messiah." First, the OT does not know "the Messiah" as a pure and simple concept. The term "Messiah" is always accompanied by an apposition. Best known is the combination "the Anointed of the Lord." Moreover, such a messianic figure is of secondary importance in the salvific expectations of Israel as we know them from the OT. Its interest is much more directed toward a salvific *period of time* than to a salvific *individual.* Israel hopes for an era of prosperity that will be inaugurated by YHWH really ruling as sovereign. In other words, Israel looks forward to the coming of the reign of God. If Israel expects a messianic figure, it is a particular instance of Israelite eschatology. Third, another relativizing factor is the expectation of not just one but sometimes two Messiahs, one royal and one priestly (Zech 4:14 and Qumran). Thus there is a pluriformity of messianic expectations in Israel. We will not list all the possible meanings of Messiah in the OT here, but before the Babylonian exile (587–537 B.C.E.) "Messiah" signifies an actually ruling king from the house of David. The Deuteronomic history (i.e., the complex of books from Joshua through 2 Kings) uses Messiah in connection with any past, present, and future Davidic king. This observation is of some relevance here since the book of Micah is supposed to have gone through a process of deuteronomic edition. OT messianic expectation in its original form goes back to the reaction of prophets like Isaiah and Micah against the unfaithfulness to YHWH of the kings of the house of David. On the one hand these prophets stuck to the belief in the divine promise to the house of David as voiced by Nathan (2 Sam 7:16); on the other hand they were convinced of the downfall of the failing Davidic dynasty. Micah expects doomsday for the royal rulers of Judah, but at the same time he believes that YHWH will keep the promise. Micah's messianic expectation is not the result of his disappointment with the kingship in Jerusalem but the fruit of his steadfast faith in YHWH's fidelity to the divine promise made to the dynasty of David. The present house of David will vanish from Jerusalem but via Bethlehem, the home town of King David, YHWH will make a fresh start. "But you, O Bethlehem of Ephrathah, who are one of the little clans of Judah, from you

shall come forth for me one who is to rule in Israel, whose origin is from of old, from ancient days" (Mic 5:2).

In general we may hold that OT texts that the NT presents as predictions of Jesus as the Messiah are in fact Christian re-readings (*relectures;* see our comments on Mic 5:2-4; 6:9; 7:11) according to an exegetical method generally accepted by Jews and Christians alike in the early days of Christianity and known from the Qumran community (ca. 100 B.C.E.) as the *pesher* method. It consists in applying the OT texts to the actual situation of the reader. This interpretation can be quite different from the original intention of the author in his or her own day. Theologically speaking there is nothing wrong with a re-reading of OT and NT as one book by a community of believers considering Jesus Christ as the final editor in a metaphorical sense.

g. Theology of Deutero-Micah, Micah 6 and 7

In the theological connections of Deutero-Micah (chs. 6–7) with Proto-Micah (chs. 1–5) there is similarity, but also difference. Some call Deutero-Micah a rhapsody on themes of Proto-Micah. Thus the social criticism of Mic 2:1-5, 8-9 and Mic 3:1-5, 10-12, for instance, has its counterpart in Mic 6:10-12 and 7:2-6. But in Deutero-Micah we miss the lying and the injustice of specific groups such as priests and prophets known from Proto-Micah. The scope of Deutero-Micah's reproof seems to be wider: "They *all* lie in wait for blood, and they hunt *each other* with nets" (Mic 7:2). The law of retaliation appears in Mic 6:13-16. The darkness of Mic 3:6 is also present in Mic 7:8 but "the Lord will be a light to me." In the end, the law of retaliation is broken by God's steadfast love and mercy (Mic 7:18-19).

Themes such as theophany, the discussion of true and false prophets, messianism, and Zion tradition are no longer focused upon. On the other hand Deutero-Micah has a theological face of its own within the book of Micah because it introduces a few new items. Chapters 6–7 remind us of the deuteronomic theology of northern Israelite provenance. This theology that the book of Micah shares with the contemporary prophet Hosea is known for its interest in the covenant and, in this covenantal context, its polemics against idolatry (Mic 6:16), its focus on salvation history (Mic 6:3-5; 7:15), e.g., exodus, occupation of the land, and the appeal to live according to the stipulations of the covenant (Mic 6:8). The reference to the people's guilt and YHWH's steadfast love and mercy at the end of ch. 7 is also characteristic of Deuteronomy's theology. The southern Israelite theology of Zion, or kindred ideas preceding it, so typical of the book of Isaiah, is the basis of religious life in Proto-Micah (chs. 1–5). The covenantal community of life with YHWH accompanied by a vivid remembrance of a variety of old Israelite traditions, as presented by Deuteronomy, appears to be characteristic for Deutero-Micah (chs. 6–7). So this twofold spiritual orientation coincides with the main division of the book of Micah and supports it.

4. Micah and Its Canonical Context

The similarity between Isaiah and Micah is a well known fact. Both of them use the formula "in that day" as a major editorial device (Mic 4:6; 5:9; 7:12 and Isa 7:18-25; 22:8-25). They have typical expressions in common such as "from now and ever more" (Mic 4:7; Isa 9:6; 59:21), "for the mouth of YHWH has spoken" (Mic 4:4; Isa 1:20; 40:5; 58:14), "[YHWH] will reign in Mount Zion" (Mic 4:7; Isa 23:23, unique for the OT). Also the contents of Isaiah and Micah show close connections. Micah's social critique, for example, bears a considerable amount of resemblance to that of Isaiah. Compare the texts on the expropriation of the land in Mic 2:1-5 and Isa 5:8-10. Isaiah is assumed to be slightly prior to Micah. There is, however, no evidence to claim a "teacher-disciple" relationship between them. Rather, similarities seem to point in the direction of a more or less common existential situation of the two prophets with common religious traditions. Some even claim that the same editor redacted the book of Isaiah and the book of Micah.

It is precisely for this reason that it is interesting and useful to pay attention to the differences between the two. Whereas theophany in Isaiah is salvific, according to Micah it brings doom. As for Zion, Isaiah foresees its downfall because of the sins of the people; Micah prophesies its total destruction due to its corrupt leadership. Both Isaiah and Micah oppose prophets in Jerusalem. But Isaiah makes a distinction between "prophets" *(nebiʾim)* and "seers" *(ḥōzim),* regarding himself as one of the latter. Isaiah includes the prophets in the people. Micah sees the prophets as a separate body. Isaiah's opponents do not reject his message of doom but his offer of salvation through trust. Micah met with opposition for his message of divine judgment. Micah does not call for repentance as Isaiah does. Micah presents his social critique in stronger words of accusation and judgment than Isaiah does. Finally, Micah's view of the future concerns not Jerusalem but the land as a whole.

The dissimilarity of Isaiah and Micah also becomes apparent in their heirs. Jeremiah seems to follow Micah in a number of respects, whereas Jeremiah's opponent Hananiah stands more in the tradition of Isaiah, especially as far as the future of Zion is concerned. Like Micah, Jeremiah prophesied the destruction of Jerusalem (Jer 9:11). Micah described the preaching of the false prophets as telling lies, and so does Jeremiah (Jer 6:14; 8:11; 14:13-16; 23:23). The false religious security of Micah's opponents is taken up by Jeremiah as an important theme in his preaching (Jer 5:12-13; 8:19).

IV. Micah and the New Testament

We come across at least four texts of Micah in the NT, two of them in citations and two in allusions. Matthew 2:6 quotes Mic 5:2: "And you, Bethlehem, in the land of Judah, are by no means least among the rulers of Judah; for from you shall come a ruler who will govern my people Israel." God does not work according to our norms and calculations. Being in power is no guarantee for security. The unassuming and humble have God's preference. The use of Mic 5:2 by Matt 2:6 can allow us to see that, because of his divine mission, the tricky and lascivious king David and his successors down to Hezekiah led a life the meaning of which was far beyond anything they grasped. Conversely it may make us understand that the mission of Jesus is to lead a people to greatness and finally to universal prosperity in a resurrected bodily sense. Matt 10:21, 35-36 [Mark 13:12; Luke 12:53] echoes Mic 7:6: "For the son treats the father with contempt, the daughter rises up against her mother, the daughter-in-law against her mother-in-law; your enemies are the members of your own household." Note the difference between the meaning of this text in Micah and the allusion in the gospels. Micah has in mind a backlash from the infidelity of the people of God to YHWH. The evangelists point out that living by the word of God may make you hated and lonely. It is "the cost of discipleship" (Bonhoeffer). Matt 23:23 echoes Mic 6:8: "He has showed you, O mortal, what is good; and what does the Lord require of you but to do justice, and to love kindness, and to walk humbly with your God?" This is the Sermon on the Mount in a nutshell, showing where the main stress in our lives should lie. The Magnificat (Luke 1:55, 72-73) and Rom 15:8 point to Mic 7:20: "You will show faithfulness to Jacob and steadfast love to Abraham, as you have sworn to our ancestors from the days of old." An assurance of God's faithfulness and steadfast love are the final words of Micah and the first words of the NT. God is consistent. Besides these texts there are about fifteen less conspicuous hints of the book of Micah in the NT.

V. The Book of Micah in the Ecumenical Lectionary

In the ecumenical lectionary and in the liturgical texts for eucharistic celebrations revised following Vatican II the following seven pericopes from Micah function as readings. They are ranged according to the order of chapters of the book of Micah.

Micah 2:1-5 is read on Saturday of the fifteenth week during Year 2. The liturgy "For Time of War and Civil Disturbances" uses Mic 4:1-4. These two readings have a literal meaning that is the same for the hearers of the prophet Micah and for those hearing them in a liturgical celebration nowadays. As for Mic 5:2-5, which we hear on the fourth Sunday of Advent, cycle C, on the feast of the Birth of the Blessed Virgin Mary (September 8), and as one of the common texts of the Blessed Virgin Mary outside Eastertide, the situation is quite different. Micah is still looking forward in hope to a coming ideal ruler he cannot pinpoint in history, whereas our Christian liturgy looks back in gratitude and reads this text with the knowledge of faith that Jesus of Nazareth, the Son of God and the son of Mary, "she who was in travail and has brought forth her child" (Mic 5:2), has fulfilled the expectations of Micah and more than that, of all humankind. We listen to Mic 6:1-4, 6-8 on Monday of the sixteenth week of Year 2. No

reinterpretation is necessary here. The text with its appeal to moral behavior as a response to divine goodness, for which cultic observance cannot substitute, is just as meaningful today as it was in the time it was spoken by a prophet. The same holds true for Mic 6:6-8 which is read in the common texts for holy men and women, number 17. The final texts, Mic 7:7-9 for an optional reading for the fourth week in Lent and Mic 7:7-14, 18-20 for Saturday of the second week in Lent and for Tuesday of the sixteenth week of Year 2 are as timely for us today as they were at the time they were spoken and written. The unifying thread running through these readings seems to be the eternal truth: "in God we trust" in spite of human shortcomings.

Special mention should be made of the famous *Improperia* in the liturgy of Good Friday, sung during the veneration of the cross ("My people, what have I done to you? How have I offended you? Answer me!"). Mic 6:3-5 appears there in connection with Isa 5:2-9 and the Trishagion ("Holy, holy, holy . . ."). Throughout the history of Christian liturgy till now the people of God have kept alive an awareness of their ungrateful offenses against the divine lovingkindness by chanting God's complaints in the wording of Micah. We are asked to ponder on the tragedy of Israel's continuous ingratitude and perversity in order to understand our own lives as including that horror and above all that need of conversion.

VI. Literary Structure of the Book of Micah

We present an outline of the book of Micah based on literary indices such as repetition of words (e.g., the imperative plural "listen" in 1:2; 3:1; 3:9; 6:1-2; 6:9) and the tenor of the individual chapters. The Achilles' heel of this reading hypothesis is Mic 2:12-13. This verse sounds very positive, but it may well be a sardonic raillery at the reassuring preaching by the false prophets. With this reservation in mind we offer the following diptych, in which doom and salvation alternate.

Part I. Chapters 1–5: God appears (theophany), punishes and heals.

- A. Message of doom for the present situation: chapters 1–3
  1. Chapter 1: theophany, its cause and consequences
     - —superscription: v. 1
     - —appeal to the nations: v. 2
     - —the Lord descends: v. 3
     - —creation reacts: v. 4
     - —cause of theophany: sin of Samaria and Jerusalem: v. 5
     - —consequences for Samaria: vv. 6-7
     - —consequences for Judah: vv. 8-16
  2. Chapter 2: accusation with discussion
     - —accusation against landowners: vv. 1-5
     - —accusation against false prophets: vv. 6-13
  3. Chapter 3: accusation with discussion
     - —accusation against the leaders of the people: vv. 1-4
     - —accusation against the false prophets: vv. 5-8
     - —accusation against the leaders, priests, and prophets: vv. 9-11
- B. Message of salvation in the guise of a utopia: chapters 4–5
  1. Chapter 4: realm of peace in spite of actual distress
     - —vision of peace: vv. 1-5
     - —Jerusalem in distress destined for redemption: vv. 6-14
  2. Chapter 5: the Messiah and his kingdom
     - —not from Jerusalem (cf. 4:8) but from Bethlehem: vv. 1-3
     - —not corrupt (cf. ch. 3) but bearer of well-being: vv. 4-8
     - —but thorough purification of the people is required: vv. 9-14

Part II. Chapters 6–7: God carries out a lawsuit.

- A. Message of doom for the present situation: chapters 6–7:6
  1. Chapter 6: accusation and condemnation
     - —indictment: vv. 1-2
     - —accusation of ingratitude: vv. 3-5
     - —cultic practices do not help; justice does: vv. 6-8
     - —accusation of fraud: vv. 9-12
     - —judgment of God: vv. 13-16
  2. Chapter 7:1-6: injustice and punishment
     - —complaint: vv. 1-4a
     - —day of visitation by YHWH: v. 4b
     - —do not rely on people: vv. 5-6
- B. Message of salvation in the guise of a utopia: chapter 7:7-20
  1. Chapter 7:7-13: a positive vision of the future

—faith in the future: vv. 7-8
—confession of sins and act of hope: v. 9
—enemy humiliated: v. 10
—fate of enemy: vv. 11-13

2. Chapter 7:14-20: final hymn
—supplication full of confidence: vv. 14-17
—hymn on God's forgiveness and fidelity: vv. 18-20

SECOND READING

1:1. Superscription

The first verse of Micah seems to presuppose a division of the book signaled by the two parallel relative clauses: "The word of YHWH (a) which came to Micah of Moresheth . . . (b) which he saw concerning Samaria and Jerusalem." This construction is unique for the beginning of a book of a biblical prophet. Admittedly the book of Amos also has two relative clauses in its opening, but they are not put in parallelism. There is general agreement that the events of Micah 1–5 take place during the reign of king Hezekiah (727–698 B.C.E.). The mention of the preceding kings Jotham (739–733 B.C.E.) and Ahaz (733–727 B.C.E.) in the first verse of the book of Micah could well stem from the final editor. He gives himself away as deuteronomistic by the expression: "The word of YHWH." The reason why he introduces Jotham and Ahaz may be that the unknown namesake of Micah of Moresheth who worked in the northern kingdom and is responsible for Micah 6–7 preached during the period when Jotham and Ahaz ruled in the South (A.S. van der Woude). That time coincides roughly with the rule in the North of kings Pekahiah (742–740 B.C.E.) and Pekah (740–731 B.C.E.). Thus the final editor of our present book of Micah may have translated the period of the northern kings Pekahiah and Pekah into the chronology of the kings of the South, Jotham and Ahaz. This is why we read in our Bible that Micah of Moresheth also worked as a prophet during the time of Jotham and Ahaz, whereas historically speaking this is true only for his unknown colleague in the northern kingdom. We do not have irrefutable evidence for such a development in the text, but this theory presents a plausible coherent explanation for the striking and unique superscription of the book of Micah.

1:2-7: Micah uses two traditional literary forms. In the context of a typical *prophecy against the foreign peoples* Micah describes the coming of YHWH with its cosmic repercussions *(theophany).* Like Amos 1:2, Mic 1:3 describes a theophany at the beginning of a prophecy against the nations. The literary genre of such a prophecy ending in a judgment of Judah and Israel produces an element of surprise. This is a trick to captivate the audience. While everybody is nodding assent to the words of the prophet he directs the arrows of his criticism all of a sudden at his very listeners. The theophany, usually applied to announce a salvific divine intervention, conveys here an element of surprise as well. It introduces God's coming not to save but to punish the people.

1:8-16: This is a very enigmatic passage because of its many puns, the point of which escapes us. Its first part (vv. 8-12) is a lament phrased in characteristic terminology, addressed to "you" in the plural. The second half (vv. 13-16) is an announcement of doom to a singular "you." The names of the places and their whereabouts the text plays upon are mostly unknown to us except for the villages in the neighborhood of Lachish mentioned in vv. 13-16. The mention of Jerusalem in vv. 9 and 12 may imply that the obscure place names of vv. 10-11 refer to hamlets around Jerusalem. As for the outcome of Micah's prophecy, Samaria fell in 722 B.C.E. but the Assyrians did not continue their advance to capture Jerusalem. The downfall of Jerusalem came only more than a century after Micah's preaching. So Micah was correct in seeing a connection between the sinfulness of the ruling class of the Holy City and its destruction. But he was mistaken concerning the time.

2:1-5: The section offers a classic prophetic announcement of doom because of social injustice by pointing out (a) the situation (v. 2), (b) the word of YHWH (v. 3) and (c) the prediction of punishment (v. 4). Verse 4 is a clear instance of the law of retaliation. The ruthless landowners are precisely robbed of what they had stolen from the poor peasants: the ownership of the land. That was not just a means of support. Landownership, however small the plot might be, was a title of civil and religious rights in the community of Israel. The corrupt elite will lose its right to partake in the assembly of the people of God. The allotment of land, referred to here, reminds them that the real owner of the land is God alone.

2:6-13: In this pericope Micah quotes the reaction he received from his opponents (2:6-7a) to his social criticism (cf. 2:1-5). But divine promises, Micah retorts, do not work automatically, irrespective of human behavior. Micah's words are beneficent to those who live according to God's commandments (v. 7). In fact, Micah's opponents do not do that. They trample on the God-given rights of the weaker members of Israel's community (women and children). Micah appeals to them to leave the Holy Land they defile by their immoral behavior (v. 10). Like Luther, Micah says "Here I stand, I cannot (do) otherwise" (v. 11). Then Micah presents his mockery of the prophecy of salvation "this (despicable) people," i.e., the followers of his opponents, would like to hear (vv. 12-13). These two verses sound like good tidings, but they lull the hearers in a misleading way.

3:1-12: This chapter is a literarily well-knit unit. As a clearly demarcated text it is very helpful in detecting a structure in the book of Micah. (See the outline.) In all its terseness it contains fundamental criticism of different ruling groups in Jerusalem and Judah. Three clear subunits (vv. 1-4; 5-8; 9-12) can be distinguished in which we see a continuity of theme, a consistency of metaphors, a parallelism in development of thought, a repetition of vocabulary. They speak of the leading class in general (vv. 1-4), specifically of the false prophets (vv. 5-8), and then the heads of the people, priests and prophets as one body (vv. 9-12). This is understandable since the official prophets and priests functioned as public relations officers and spokesmen of the corrupt rulers. Micah opposes here his own prophecy of doom ("But I say . . .") to their prophecy of salvation, which we just have heard at the end of ch. 2. In contrast to that deceptive "good news" Micah maintains that the immorality of its leaders will cause the downfall of Jerusalem. The big difference between the false prophets and Micah is that they prophesy moved by self-interest, whereas Micah is driven by the spirit of YHWH. This may also serve as a useful criterion to distinguish true prophets from false in other parts of the Bible and even nowadays. The announcement of the destruction of Jerusalem (v. 12) must have sounded as a downright blasphemy in the ears of Micah's opponents. More than the preceding social criticism (2:1-5), this message of Micah triggered a fierce discussion with the official servants of religion in the following chapter.

A difficult problem in chs. 4–5, however, will be to tell with certainty who is speaking: Micah or his opponents. A simple way to answer this question is to see whether a text is favorably disposed toward Jerusalem (the opponents) or not (Micah). But an objection against this solution could be the fact that his critical attitude does not prevent Micah in advance from saying anything positive on the items under debate. A modern analysis of the so-called narrative syntax suggests that Mic 4:1-9 is spoken by the opponents of Micah; Mic 4:10 would be the responsibility of Micah, whereas vv. 11-13 are supposed to be the opponents'. Micah 4:14–5:3 are the words of Micah. In vv. 4-5 the opponents are speaking, v. 6 would be Micah's, vv. 7-8 again give the opinion of the opponents and, finally, vv. 9-14 are from the mouth of Micah.

Chapter 4: The present text opens the discussion on three themes: (1) the future of the Temple in Jerusalem (4:1-5; 9-13), (2) the future of the people of God (4:4-5), (3) the reunion of the divided kingdom under one Davidic ruler (4:6-8). The predominantly positive oracles are intermingled with prophecies of doom on the downfall of Jerusalem (4:10) and the humiliation of the Davidic king (4:14). In contrast to his opponents Micah maintains that the people of God will have to go through the depths of utter misery before reaching salvation.

4:1-5: This is a parallel text to Isa 2:2-4 on the pilgrimage of the nations to Zion. It is still unclear who borrowed from whom or whether both editors took this pericope from a common source. Obvious is that for the establishment of international peace human effort and dedication are indispensable, but ultimately it remains a gift from God. Noteworthy for Christians busily engaged in laudable, outgoing, centrifugal mission work is that here we witness a centripetal movement of the nations toward Israel by attraction. This raises the question whether we as Christians are aware of the importance of being attractive enough to cause a similar centripetal movement toward the Christian message among outsiders.

4:6–5:1: The pericope starts out by describing a similar centripetal movement of a return to Zion among the people of God as an echo of the pilgrimage of the nations (vv. 6-8). After an announcement of doom implying exile and finally deliverance (vv. 9-10), the well-known biblical theme of the inviolability of Zion is expressed in the context of hostile nations. If the Assyrians are gathered against Jerusalem it is YHWH who assembled them on purpose in order to let them meet their annihilation. But before this can come about Israel has to suffer humiliation by the shameful fate of its king (v. 14).

5:2-5: God will make a fresh start by appointing Bethlehem again as the birthplace of a future king. Like David, the coming ruler will stem from the insignificant town of Bethlehem. God prefers the humble and lowly as a starting point for the realization of the divine salvific plan. We do not know whether Micah was referring to a specific descendant of David. Micah's basic attitude of hope during his night of spiritual darkness is still inspiring for us. But to Christians this particular text is more meaningful if understood of Jesus from Nazareth. They consider OT and NT as *one* sourcebook for their faith and read the whole Bible in the light of the Easter candle, symbol of the risen Lord Jesus Christ. On this basis they feel entitled to fill the OT texts with an interpretation pointing directly to Jesus. For this NT messianic re-reading *(relecture),* see our sections on "Messianism" and "Micah and the New Testament" in the First Reading above and our comments below on Mic 6:9 and 7:11. YHWH will extradite them, i.e., the inhabitants of Jerusalem, to the Assyrians, who will deport them till the time the mother of the coming king has given birth to him (v. 2). His brothers and sisters, the good exiles, will return home to live as reunited people under the guidance of the new king.

5:5-9: The coming anointed ruler will bring about peace by forming a coalition of an indefinite number ("seven . . . and eight" is a so called "staircase number") of partners against the intruders. The people of Jacob, i.e., the whole of the chosen people, will be a blessing for the world. Just as dew descends from above on an arid country, so that blessing for the nations will ultimately not originate from human resources but from God in whom the people confide.

5:10-15: The people of God will have to learn to live without any reliance on their own military and religious means of survival. Offensive weapons (horses, chariots) as well as defensive armor (fortified cities, ramparts) will be of no avail. As for the elusive hostile spiritual powers, it will be useless to resort to magic practices such as sorcery and the worship of idols and phallic symbols ("pillars") in order to have them under control. The Lord will wipe them out during a process of thorough purification which God's people has to undergo as a necessary condition for salvation.

6:1-8: Deutero-Micah starts with a dialogue between God and the people. The rhetorical form used here is based on the structure of international treaties in the ancient Near East. Those treaties between overlord and vassals had a typical structure. After the overlord makes a self-presentation with full titles in an *introduction,* a brief survey of the lord's relationship with the vassal in the past is presented, the so-called *historical prologue,* listing the benefits of the overlord and the instances of disloyalty of the vassal. Then follows the *basic declaration of fidelity* to the overlord binding the vassal under all circumstances. Hereafter come the *specific stipulations* of the treaty. An *appeal to witnesses,* usually the gods of both partners of the covenant, is added. A presentation of *curses* to be realized in case of a breach of the treaty and *blessings* to be expected in case of observance of the covenant concludes the formal structure of a covenant. Structural elements of this type of vassal treaty may here be recognized as the call upon witnesses, the enumeration of God's benefits toward the people in history, and moral behavior as a grateful response to God's goodness. The element of curses will follow in the next pericope (6:9-16). This reminds us of the deuteronomistic preaching known from the book of Deuteronomy and the Deuteronomistic History (Joshua, Judges, 1–2 Samuel, 1–2 Kings).

In the style of an indictment the prophet calls mountains to witness God's judgment (vv. 1-2). This witness is not meant to provide information as in a criminal court case but to add solemnity as, e.g., in the celebration of matrimony. Then God defies the people to answer the question whether God has done anything wrong to them in order to create the opportunity to contrast herewith the good things God did for them in history (v. 3). This famous question God asks the people lives on in the Christian liturgy from the very beginning till now. It is known as the *Improperia* (contumelies) of Good Friday. YHWH lists the founding facts of salvation history during the Exodus and the occupation of the Holy Land (vv. 4-5). In its reaction the people asks what its primary duty toward God should be after all these benefits. Cultic practices appear not so important in comparison with correct moral behavior expressed in justice and fidelity (vv. 6-8). See also the theological comments on the *Improperia* above under the heading "The Book of Micah in the Ecumenical Lectionary" in our First Reading.

6:9-16: This difficult pericope is best understood in connection with the preceding covenantal elements (vv. 1-8) as a unit consisting of curses and their motivation. Verses 9-12 describe God's reasons for the curses expressed in vv. 13-16. The city mentioned in v. 9 is originally not Jerusalem but rather Samaria. This is suggested by 6:16 where the northern kings Omri and Ahab are mentioned, both of whom reigned in the city of Samaria. The name of the city may have been left out on purpose to create room for a *relecture,* i.e., to make the text applicable to later generations of readers in a similar situation. Everybody can fill in the name of his or her own place. Verses 13-16 present the curses as "futility curses" (vv. 14-15), well known from covenantal allusions in Deut 28:30-33 and Hos 4:10; 8:7; 9:12-16. Utter frustration will be the punishment.

7:1-6: This unit is a lament functioning as a dark backdrop for the following shining message of salvation in the guise of a utopia as presented by 7:7-20. In vv. 1-4a the prophet—as we have seen, this is not necessarily Micah of Moresheth—utters a complaint because of his loneliness, reminding us of Jeremiah (Jer 5:1-6; 9:1-8). Verse 2 introduces the theme of "spying, lying in wait" that recurs in v. 4 as a retaliation for v. 2. The wicked in Israel lie in wait to destroy their neighbors (v. 2). But the enemies of the people also spy upon it for its downfall (v. 4). That will be the day of YHWH's visitation of the people in a negative sense. The corrupt leaders are rightly compared with a prickling fence and a bramble bush. If you contact them, they will hurt you. The conclusion is obvious: it can happen to you that by way of retaliation for your own infidelity you cannot trust your neighbor, not even your closest relatives (v. 6) any longer. Jesus refers to this in Matt 10:35-36, Luke 12:53. But there is a difference. The gospels have in mind not a retaliatory punishment for a lack of faithfulness to God as Micah has, but the possible consequences of a radical following of Jesus. You may have to sacrifice your natural bonds for the imitation of Christ. This could well be "the cost of discipleship" (Bonhoeffer).

7:7-13: To the preceding dark background without perspective (7:1-6) the following section (vv. 7-20), in which the prophet is also "spying," i.e., looking for God in full confidence, is set off in a striking contrast (cf. the negative spying, lying in wait in vv. 2 and 4). The present utopia is conspicuous by its admixture of negative elements of life that give this vision of the future a realistic ring, quite recognizable for most of us. Undiluted happiness is rare in this world. The prophet seems still impressed by a recent disaster. Verse 8 mentions an anonymous female enemy. She recurs in v. 10 where she is humiliated. Verse 12 reveals that she is Assyria. In v. 11 we come across a reference to an anonymous place the walls of which will be rebuilt. The text does not necessarily imply a city. These walls can be of a vineyard or any other private property. But a city cannot be excluded categorically here either. The names of Bashan and Gilead in v. 14 suggest we have to think of a place (region, city) in the north of Israel, or perhaps they are just a reminder of the days of old. Originally vv. 11-13 pointed rather to the enemy of v. 8, i.e., Assyria, which in retaliation will undergo the same fate Israel had to suffer from Assyria. It should be kept in mind here that Assyria had annexed parts of the northern kingdom of Israel. Only Ephraim was left. Thus vv. 11-13 work out the humiliation of the enemy predicted in v. 10. After the present text of Deutero-Micah was edited in combination with Proto-Micah (chs. 1–5) as the present book of Micah with its stress on Jerusalem, the interpretation that the anonymous place in v. 11 is Jerusalem became possible. This illustrates how a *relecture* (re-reading, see 6:9) can take place within the Bible itself.

7:14-20: This is a beautiful closing psalm consisting of a prayer for the restoration of the good days of old on behalf of God's people (vv. 14-17) and a hymn about God's characteristic mercy and faithfulness (vv. 18-20). Both parts play with a *chiaroscuro* technique of opposing positive and negative elements. As for the prayer (vv. 14-17), the wellbeing of God's people (vv. 14-15) brings with it as a matter of course the confusion and humiliation of God's enemies (vv.

16-17). They are as two sides of one coin. The hymn (vv. 18-20) puts the divine passing over our transgressions and the treading our iniquities under foot (vv. 18a and 19) alongside the delight God takes in steadfast love and compassion (vv. 18b and 19). Again we have one coin with two sides. This final appeal to God's incomparability because of God's typical features ("Who is a God like you," *mī-ʾēl kamōkā,* v. 18) functions on the one hand as a manipulative motivation for the hearing of the prayer (vv. 14-17) and on the other hand as a signature of the prophet Micah (*mī-kā-yāhū,* "Who is like YHWH") under the whole book of Micah. Finally (v. 20) the prophet links his motivation for the prayer (God's mercy and faithfulness) with a reference to the covenantal promises God made to the patriarchs Abraham and Jacob "from the days of old," adroitly echoing by way of an inclusion the beginning of the psalm ("as in the days of old," v. 14). In Hosea, Deuteronomy, and in deuteronomistic literature (Joshua–2 Kings) God's mercy and steadfast love are intimately connected with the covenant concluded with the patriarchs. Again Deutero-Micah shows the basis of his spirituality: he is a member of the covenantal community of life with YHWH. The promises of a land and of a numerous posterity played an important role in that covenant. They were very timely in the days the territory of God's people was threatened with annexation by Assyria and the people itself could disappear in exile. They are also timely for us as the people of God who find our religious community threatened by tensions and uncertainties within and by animosity from without. The final word of the book of Micah to us is: "In God we trust."

BIBLIOGRAPHY

Hagstrom, David. *The Coherence of the Book of Micah.* SBL.DS 89. Atlanta: Scholars, 1988.

King, Philip J. *Amos, Hosea, Micah—An Archaeological Commentary.* Philadelphia: Westminster, 1988.

Wolff, Hans-Walter. *Micah the Prophet.* Philadelphia: Fortress, 1981.

Nahum

Santiago Ausín

FIRST READING

The title of the book of Nahum is unusual: "An oracle concerning Nineveh. The book of the vision of Nahum of Elkosh." It lacks mention of "the word" or "the words of the LORD directed to . . ." as is the case in the titles of the prophetic books preceding it. Instead, the key words are:

(1) *Vision:* the poetic, detailed, and vivid description of the fall of Nineveh, capital of Assyria since the reign of Sennacherib, together with its eschatological coloring, prefigures the definitive judgment of God against God's enemies.

(2) *Book of visions:* a written text that not only could not have been previously proclaimed but also that, as occurs in the book of Jeremiah (cf. Jer 30:2; 32:16), guarantees its own faithful fulfillment.

(3) *Oracle (massa')* against Nineveh, similar to other oracles against nations. A *massa'* emphasizes the fact that the power of the LORD extends to all peoples and that the ruin of the pagans is a lesson for Israel as well, viz., that Israel also must pay for its sins.

Original Historical Context

The canonical book begins with a very elaborate hymn that sings of the sovereign power and justice of God (1:2-8). Over the past century scholars have been able to establish the date of composition of this hymn from two factors: first on the basis of literary conventions, since Nah 1:2-8 is an alphabetic psalm (the poet arranges the letters of the Hebrew alphabet vertically and makes each verse begin with the appropriate letter); second through the content, which reflects a theology that gives meaning to the rest of the book.

It seems clear that the other oracles had been written in the seventh century, some time after the year 662 when the Egyptian city of Thebes (*No-amon* in 3:8) was destroyed, and before 612 when Nineveh disappeared at the hands of the Neobabylonian empire. The vivid descriptions of the assault (2:1-11) and the cruelty of the invaders (3:1-3) reflect the fact that the author is not very distant from the action; but given the lack of any concrete details about the city one suspects that these are not oracles that happened after the event. Moreover, three years after the fall of Nineveh, when King Josiah died at the hands of the Egyptians, the great enemy was Babylon; and there was no longer a special reason for celebrating the fall of Nineveh. Therefore it seems reasonable to think that the book was written a little before the year 612, probably at the time when the death of Asurbanipal (632 B.C.E.) inflamed national sentiment among the Jews. These oracles would come to be an important contribution to the religious and political reform movement to be implemented about the year 622 B.C.E.

If the introductory psalm had been composed two centuries later we would have to suppose that a Deuteronomist writer had updated the old oracles against Nineveh, interpreting them as if they were directed against Babylon, the colossal oppressor of the time. The alphabetical hymn from 1:2-8 would give Nahum's words a more universal significance, easily applicable to any circumstance of political oppression. Although this explanation is evocative, it is difficult to accept since the vocabulary as well as the style of the initial psalm are similar to the rest of the book. This unity and coherence can better be explained if we suppose that the entire book was the work of the same author and of a given epoch.

The originality of the title (1:1), as noted above, indicates that Nahum, like Habakkuk, is not one of the traditional prophetic books but one that used a specific literary genre, i.e., prophetic/sapiential, sometimes called "prophetic controversy." It consists of a sacred author's attempt to dissipate doubts or objections about a concrete theme. In this case the sovereign power of God is placed in doubt as much by the Jews who are unable to reconcile it with the splendor of Nineveh as by the Ninevites themselves who by their crimes seem to mock God with impunity. The response is as forceful as it is poetic: the imminent destruction of the great capital is a work of the LORD who, acting justly, annihilates Nineveh while saving the chosen people.

The initial outline of the book probably had the three parts that are easily detected today. Only the title (1:1) was added later:

I. Hymn and theophany exalting the power of God over God's enemies: 1:2-10.
II. Explanation directed to Judah who, after experiencing the fall of Nineveh, should recognize that it was God's exclusive act and should, then, celebrate the gift of election: 1:11-15.
III. Explanation directed to the Ninevites who, when their capital was to be assaulted and destroyed, might recognize that action as well to be the unique work of the LORD: 2:1–3:19.

Canonical Context

The book of Nahum holds seventh place among the codex of minor prophets in the Hebrew as well as Greek manuscripts (in the latter, the order of the first six varies somewhat). The fact that it always appears in the same place is a very ancient tradition that at least reflects the fact that with Nahum begin the latest books, those that undertake a different theme, underscoring the judgment of God and revealing eschatological influence.

There is an obvious relationship between Nah 2:1 and Isa 52:1, 7 but Nahum is the older: the infrequent or unusual expressions of the verse more closely correspond to a seventh-century author than to Deutero-Isaiah. The description of the messenger is much more restrained in Nahum, and in ch. 52 of the Deutero-Isaian text Assyria is mentioned as the oppressor of the people together with Egypt and Babylon (cf. Isa 52:4), so that the messenger of peace is already a commonplace figure evoked in the three classic situations of oppression. For that reason we conclude that the Isaiah text relies on the text of Nahum and is consequently the first updating of the salvific message of Nahum within the exilic circumstances during the Babylonian captivity. On the other hand, Rom 10:15 and Mark 16:15-16 are references to Isa 52:7 and not to Nahum.

The allusion to the locusts in Joel 1:4 and its subsequent explanation (Joel 2:4-9) could have some point of contact with Nahum 3:15. There is an even clearer influence of Nahum on the book of Tobit (Tob 14:12-15) which recalls with elation the ruin of Nineveh as fulfillment of a prophecy. It is the first nationalistic interpretation given to Nahum. The same nationalistic joy bursts from the *Jewish Antiquities* (9.2.3) of Flavius Josephus who comments with irony: "All the predictions about Nineveh were fulfilled after 150 years." (Josephus dates Nahum in the eighth century during the reign of Jotham, son of Uzziah).

Some fragments of a commentary that updates the prophetic book have appeared at Qumran *(4QpNah)*. This *pesher* has great historical interest because it mentions Demetrius III Eukairos in his struggle with Alexander Janneus about the year 88 B.C.E. This nationalistic reading has been a constant among the Jews, and even for the great medieval authors like David Kimchi (d. 1235).

In the NT there is no citation of the book of Nahum, perhaps because of the nationalistic interpretation of the period. Neither is it used in the Christian liturgy. Among the patristic writings it is the least cited work, next to Haggai and Obadiah. The patristic commentaries emphasize the power and justice of God. Jerome comments on the message of the prophet as one of consolation ("Nahum can be interpreted as comforter") because the divine justice reaches everyone ("Let it be known, however, that whatever is now said against Nineveh will be proclaimed figuratively about the whole world" [*PL* 25.1231]). A later commentary by Julian, bishop of Toledo (seventh century) separates out the four medieval meanings since this prophecy speaks "historically of Nineveh; allegorically of the desolation of the world; mystically of the reparation of the human race by Christ; and morally of the restoration to pristine dignity" (*PL* 96.706). Among the Greeks one has to wait until Theophilactus (eleventh century) who wrote an *Expositio* on Nahum. Its central theme is the universality of divine justice: "It teaches all mortals that, since God is just, there is nothing outside [God's] providence, but that punishment is imposed upon each one as deserved" (*PG* 126.969).

SECOND READING

Title: 1:1

The heading presents the oracles as a unit: "a *massa*ʾ, a book, a vision" are the three aspects of a unique literary piece.

It is difficult to identify Elkosh, the homeland of Nahum, with accuracy. Among the villages of the north not one has been found that could coincide with Elkosh either by name or etymology, nor does it seem probable that Nahum would belong to the groups of Israelites who were deported by Sennacherib. It seems more likely that the prophet was from Judah, although that cannot be completely verified. Neither does the title mention Nahum's occupation or the circumstances surrounding his oracles.

I. Hymn and Theophany: 1:2-10

The alphabetic poem (vv. 2-8) contains characters proper to a hymn or psalm of praise: the participles (v. 2a) qualify the person of the LORD, and the imperfect verbs indicate YHWH's specific action (3b-4). Descriptive praise is complemented with narrative praise.

There are three somewhat concentric sections: the first (vv. 2-3a) present the LORD as "jealous and avenging." The theme of the "wrath of God" reoccurs frequently in the OT (cf. Exod 20:1; Pss 2:12; 60:3; 79:11, etcetera) as an expression of the sovereign power of God and of divine transcendent justice. The second section (vv. 3b-6) describes the theophany: God is manifested amid extraordinary phenomena: storm, hurricane, and thunder (vv. 3b-4; cf. Exod 19:16-25; Isa 6:1-10); before the divine presence inanimate beings are moved to respond and inhabitants ask rhetorically what their attitude must be before God (v. 6). The last section (vv. 7-8), like the beginning, describes the divine attributes and, on this occasion, God's goodness, protection, and mercy, although in the end the power of God is emphasized, the power that is capable of destroying enemies.

The hymn closes with a sapiential reflection (vv. 9-10) in the style of a challenge or controversy. The rhetorical question "Why do you plot against the LORD?" and the subsequent explanation presuppose the doubt that Judah and Nineveh have about the sovereignty of God: the divine inactivity could be interpreted as impotence. These verses in the second person plural are thus directed to the general audience, Jews and Ninevites, and in a later reading to all those who may pose the same objections.

II. Sapiential Explanation Directed to Judah: 1:11-15

The one addressed in this section is designated with the feminine singular pronoun (vv. 11, 12, 13); hence it is Judah or Nineveh. However, the prophet does not seem to address Nineveh at one time (e.g., 1:11, 14; 2:1c-2; 2:3b) and Judah at other times (e.g., 1:12-13; 2:1ab; 2:3a) because it is difficult to suppose such artifice in a prophet of the seventh century. It is even less probable that the salvific oracles of vv. 12 and 13 and the promise of a messenger of peace (2:1ab) are directed to Nineveh. It would seem, therefore, that all these oracles are addressed to Judah.

The difficulty of v. 11 can be resolved if it is understood to be, like v. 9, an appeal to the nonbelieving Jews: perhaps the prophet remembers the attack of Sennacherib that did not, in fact, reach as far as Jerusalem, as told in 2 Kings 18–19; and he reproaches his hearers for their lack of faith, conjuring up the fact that "from you (Jerusalem) one has come out (God caused to come forth) who plots evil against the LORD (Sennacherib), who counsels villainy (Assyria)."

Judah is also the one addressed in v. 14, which announces the death of the king of Assyria, commemorated with a lamentation at the end of the book (3:18-19). By its grammatical form in the second person masculine the oracle is directed to the Assyrian king. Nevertheless it might well be a rhetorical means of giving greater strength to the message of salvation. The prophet remembers, by means of a literal reference, the divine decision to make the Assyrian monarch disappear.

In summary, this section is a salvific oracle directed to Judah to strengthen its faith in the divine power because God who, on one occasion, made the enemy Sennacherib flee (v. 11) will definitively break the chains of Assyria (vv. 12-13). Everyone knows well the divine decision to annihilate the Assyrian king and his descendants (v. 14). At the end a messenger of peace will invite all of Judah to celebrate the festive rituals (v. 15).

III. Explanation Directed to Nineveh: 2:1–3:19

Maintaining the style of challenge or dispute, the prophet appeals now to the Ninevites. He begins with a sapiential denunciation of Nineveh's lack of faith in the power of God: God alone permits the Babylonian invader to rise (v. 2) because YHWH alone will restore God's vineyard, Israel (v. 3). In this way the experience of siege and defeat will be able to serve Nineveh as a lesson since it will recognize that God was the author of that disgrace.

The description of the fall of Nineveh is great poetry; it is not a descriptive, cold literary piece, for each brush-stroke is loaded with feeling. The author expresses disciplined joy, surprise, and delight at detailing each one of the moments of siege and the destruction of the city:

(a) *The siege* (2:3-13) is described with nervous and graphic strokes summarized in the sequence "devastation, desolation, and destruction" (2:10).

(b) *The denunciation of the crimes of Nineveh* (3:1-7) has its climax in the divine judgment: "I am against you" (v. 5). The image of a woman exposed to the mockery of her compatriots is of great poetic effectiveness.

(c) *The comparison with Thebes* (3:8-15a) is illustrative: if the strategic situation of that city served for no good, neither will the strongholds of Nineveh serve her. That the conqueror (Nineveh) should have the same fate as the conquered (Thebes) is an irony that the prophet underlines with special emphasis.

(d) *The innumerable army of the Assyrians* (3:15b-17): their numerous and apparently well-organized officials are like locusts and insects that before the least setback disappear and flee "no one knows where" (v. 17).

(e) *The lamentation for the death of the monarch of Nineveh* (vv. 18-19) is a poetic satire of great impact. All who see or know the fact will feel relief because at the end the oppressor has been oppressed.

The reading of the book of Nahum leaves in the reader the certainty that God and God alone directs the course of history; no one can seriously oppose God's plans. Nahum is not an extreme nationalist nor a prophet of prosperity but a master who teaches with great poetic inspiration about the sovereignty of God, the inevitable divine judgment and definitive salvation.

BIBLIOGRAPHY

Achtemeier, Elizabeth R. *Nahum—Malachi.* Atlanta: John Knox, 1986.

Coggins, Richard J., and S. Paul Re'emi. *Israel Among the Nations: A Commentary on the Books of Nahum and Obadiah.* ITC. Grand Rapids: Eerdmans, 1985.

Haldar, Alfred O. *Studies in the Book of Nahum.* Uppsala: Almqvist & Wiksell, 1947.

Habakkuk

José María Abrego

General Characteristics of the Book

Habakkuk wears the halo of mystery that surrounds the unknown: an odd name, undefined personal features, ambiguous text, a book not regularly used. Yet it is worth our trouble to attempt a reading of it: its themes are still of interest since their focus is the incomprehensible silence of God before the suffering of the innocent and international injustice. The shortness of the book is also a help.

The Hebrew root *hbq* signifies "to embrace," but the etymology of the name suggests rather the Akkadian name of a plant. The Greeks had difficulty in pronouncing it or else were following an older morphology: they said *Ambakum.* We do not know the author's family name or place of birth. There is no sufficient critical reason for identifying him with the Habakkuk mentioned by a Greek manuscript (*syr* 88) in the title of the apocryphal legend of Bel and the Dragon: "From the Prophecies of Habakkuk, son of Joshua, of the tribe of Levi" (the text parallels Daniel 14 in our Bibles). The Jewish legend that identifies Habakkuk with the son of the Shunammite (2 Kings 4:8-37) is based on the fact that this woman "embraced" her son; it lacks any critical value.

The word *māssāʾ,* with which the book opens, is a technical term often used for an oracle against a foreign people. The book of Nahum begins in the same way, as later that of Malachi; the book of Zechariah uses the term in the title of two strategically located sections: in the middle (ch. 9) and at the end (ch. 12). Nahum and Habakkuk are always placed together. This association is perhaps the reason for the discussion of a possible cultic origin of Habakkuk's prophecy. Was Habakkuk a cultic official? Details suggesting this are not lacking. The clearest argument is the psalm in ch. 3, by reason both of its genre (a hymn) and the several musical instructions inserted into the text (3:3, 9, 13) or at its end (3:19). Some commentators think that the first two chapters also give the text of a liturgy for a day of repentance. Lamentation, prayer, direct divine address through the mouth of a cult official are common elements in the ancient liturgy of Israel. The problem, as in the case of Nahum, is to know whether these elements have become independent of the liturgy and been reorganized in prophetic form or whether some prophetic oracles have been reshaped for use in worship. In any case fundamental doubts about authenticity have been raised in the case of Nahum because his book contains exclusively oracles of salvation for Judah.

The title *nābīʾ* in Hab 1:1 does not provide an argument for the cultic origin of Habakkuk, even though it does not appear in the titles of the books of prophets who may have been his contemporaries (those whose activity is located between the time of Josiah and the events connected with the fall of the kingdom of Judah). The term does not, in fact, appear in the titles of Zephaniah, Nahum, or Jeremiah, even though the last-named is regularly described as a *nābīʾ.* [See also the article "Prophetism and Prophets."]

The book of Habakkuk has given rise to various debates about its interpretation, but in a first reading it is easy to identify two parts: Habakkuk 1–2 and Habakkuk 3. Exegetes usually divide the first part into a dialogue between the prophet and God (1:2–2:5) and a series of five "woes" (2:6b-20). In a second and more detailed reading we shall maintain this basic division but assess its dynamics and meaning on the basis of its literary reality. What does the book say? How does its message unfold?

FIRST READING

Part One: Habakkuk 1–2

Opening Dialogue (1:2–2:5)

The text of the first two chapters is usually understood as a dialogue between the prophet and YHWH. It consists of two statements of the prophet (1:2-4, 12-17) and two replies by YHWH (1:5-11; 2:1-5). The order of the text as we have it creates a tension between the problem raised by Habakkuk and the content of the two replies of YHWH.

The prophet begins by raising the problem of justice (the guilty not punished, the innocent oppressed), in the form of a lament (1:2-4). He complains that YHWH remains impassive in the presence of injustice. "How long?" (1:1) is a juridical complaint filled with a sense of heartbreak. The theme and tone call to mind the confessions of Jeremiah and the book of Job. YHWH's reply raises the problem to the international order: YHWH is going to raise up a people whose "justice and dignity proceed from themselves" (1:7). The text identifies the punisher with the Babylonians (1:6). This people escapes the hands of YHWH; they claim excessive powers and distort their mission: their "own might is their god" (1:11).

The excesses of their rule seem to be the reason for the prophet's second intervention (1:12-17): he regards the purity, holiness, and eternity of YHWH as incompatible with the insatiable greed of the oppressor. But the suspicion remains that this reading is due to the location of the verses: if they did not come after YHWH's first reply they could be applied without hesitation to a king such as Jehoiachin (see 2:12 and Jer 22:13).

Finally comes YHWH's second reply (2:1-5), which raises more problems. It takes the form of an account of a vision; the content of the latter is debated, nor is it certain that 2:5 belongs where it is. Nevertheless, there is agreement on the basic interpretation: YHWH does not immediately answer, and the prophet must remain on watch; therefore he records the content of the vision on a tablet in the hope that it will be fulfilled. The passage thus introduces the theme of the time between reception and fulfillment of the divine word: YHWH does not always appear when it seems appropriate, nor is YHWH's word always immediately fulfilled. The mission of vigilance places the prophet on a watchtower, the place *par excellence* of watchfulness for the fulfillment of God's word in history (the Jehovah's Witnesses use this symbol as the name of their publication, but with reference to its apocalyptic meaning). The prophetic message covers the time between the announcement and the fulfillment and fills it with hope. This passage again locates the theme at the international level: God's patience will allow ages of history to elapse despite the oppressions they bring with them; certainty about the ultimate fulfillment of God's plan is reserved to the faithful who firmly hope and believe.

The Woes (2:6-20)

The series of five "woes" (2:6-20) is attached to the preceding section like a satirical song that all the nations will chant against the insatiable ambition of the oppressor. The text in its present form allows us to trace signs of a structure:

Woe! (Alas!)	vv.	6	9	12	15	19
Will not? Has not? (= *halo*ʾ)		7		13		18
Because (= *kî*)		8	11	14	17	

Each of the woes contains a thematic tension between the personal referent of the opening statement and the international application of its explanation. The satire is one of universal application in which the greedy person, the thief, the despot, the lustful, or the idolater may be taken as concrete persons who typify social strata or personify empires. The successive explanations speak of plundering nations (v. 8), destroying them (v. 10), of people whose labor is only fuel for the fire (v. 13), and violence in lands, cities, and peoples (v. 17). In other words the objective referent of the song remains ambiguous: it is either a person or an empire. This consistently maintained ambiguity gives the text as we have it its wealth of reference, even if this was historically produced by the work of editors or by chance.

The final woe (vv. 18-20) shows peculiarities of language and content. The theme of idolatry is expressed here in typically post-exilic formulations (emptiness, work of human beings, etcetera). The mention of mute idols is contrasted with the solemn plea contained in the universal silence before the true God (v. 20).

The unity of the first two chapters is thus framed by a semantic transformation: the initial complaint at the silence of God in the face of injustice is changed at the end into a demand for a sacred silence before YHWH in the Temple. Within this framework both the words uttered by YHWH and the attentive and watchful waiting of the prophet who describes the vision take on heightened meaning.

Part Two: Habakkuk 3

Closing Psalm

The most easily identified unit in the book of Habakkuk is the psalm of ch. 3, by reason of its musical notations (the intermediate pauses) as well as the introduction and final notation. The commentary on Habakkuk that was discovered at Qumran (1QpHab) lacks this chapter. This proves little, since it would not be unusual for the end of the work to have suffered the greatest deterioration. In any case the chapter is not without meaning in the book. The psalm sings of God's intervention on behalf of God's people. In the context of the book as a single whole the reference is to the definitive intervention of God that has been announced in the preceding vision (2:2-25). The upheaval described serves as a setting for the theophany of the warrior God who comes "to save your people, to save your anointed" (3:13). The praise and confidence expressed at the end correspond to the opening invocation.

Basic Data for an Interpretation

Original Historical Context

We have no certainty about the date of Habakkuk's activity. The book speaks of a "fierce and impetuous nation, who march through the breadth of the earth" (1:6); the text identifies this people with the Babylonians (1:6) but this may be a gloss. The description fits well with the historical memory that invader left behind. On the other hand the mention of a period in which justice is lacking makes it possible to locate Habakkuk in the time of Jehoiachin (609–597 B.C.E.). (Marvin Sweeney connects the period with the interruption of the Josian reform.) No hypothesis is more than probable; various critics have identified the invading people with each of the successive historical empires: Assyrians, Egyptians, Arabs, Persians, Greeks, and Seleucids. An eschatological reading of the prophet blurs the historical features of any people and turns it into the vague shape of a mythical enemy. Although efforts to situate Habakkuk's message in a historical period are praiseworthy, the problem of evil, even at the international level, transcends particular historical moments. The text of Habakkuk allows this variety of references.

Context in the Canon

Echoes of the book of the prophet Habakkuk are fairly frequent in both testaments and in Jewish literature, primarily as a result of an eschatological reading. The prophet is mentioned in the additions to the book of Daniel ("Now the prophet Habakkuk was in Judea . . .": Dan 14:33-39) in a story that tells of Daniel being miraculously fed in the den of lions. (See the remark on "Bel and the Dragon" above, the title commonly given to this midrash.)

The book of Habakkuk has deep roots in the OT. The first thing to be mentioned is the citations of other prophetic books in Habakkuk: Hab 2:13-14 reproduces almost verbatim Jer 51:58 and Isa 11:9. Various commentaries single out the use of the "complaint" genre (especially in Hab 1:2-4) or the similarity between Habakkuk and some psalms, as well as the use of the same vocabulary or images as are found in other prophets. Deserving of special mention is the double use the LXX makes of Habakkuk 3, since it includes it also among the *Odes of Solomon* (Ode 3). Despite all this the major influence of the book of Habakkuk must be seen in later eschatological thought. Proof of this is the mention of the prophet in the book of Daniel, the commentary found at Qumran, and the importance given to this prophetic book in the targums.

In the NT the book of Habakkuk is rather frequently cited, but the references are limited basically to Hab 2:3-4. We find this passage cited in Rom 1:17; Gal 3:11, and Heb 10:37-38 (according to the Greek translation). Paul uses it in his argument for the saving value of faith as opposed to fidelity to the Law; this distinction is alien to Habakkuk. The argumentative force that the Reformers give to the text is to be attributed to Paul rather than to Habakkuk. According to Acts 13:41 Paul cites Hab 1:5 in his homily at Antioch as a warning to accept the seemingly incredible resurrection. Readers of Habakkuk will find echoes of his message in 2 Thess 2:1-12 and in 2 Pet 3:8-9. Nor can we help hearing an echo of Hab 2:11 in Luke 19:40. In the patristic age attention must be called to the mention of Habakkuk in the *1 Clement* and the commentary of Jerome on this book.

Liturgical Use

The prophet Habakkuk did not receive much attention from the postconciliar liturgical commission: passages of the book are read on only two occasions and the focus of interest then is on Hab 2:4 and the classical interpretation of "the righteous live by their faith." On Saturday of the eighteenth week of Ordinary Time (even years) 1:12–2:4 is read. The first reading for the twenty-seventh Sunday of Ordinary Time (Cycle C) is made up of Hab 1:2-3 and 2:2-4. In the first instance what strikes us is how sparingly this book is read: since we are dealing with a *lectio continua* we can say that these verses represent the entire liturgical reading from Habakkuk. In the second instance the selection of the passage is motivated by its correspondence with the gospel passages (Luke 17:5-10): "If you had faith the size of . . . ." There is little interest in this book for its own sake.

Contemporary Meaning

The problem of evil is the *bête noire* of monotheistic faith. [See also the article "Violence and Evil in the Bible."] Polytheism has the advantage of being able to attribute evil to a negative divinity. In an ethical and not merely cultic religion injustice, whether social or international, sullies God personally. How can God permit the suffering of the innocent? To profess that God is master of history seems normal to believers, but if we reflect even a little we will see how bold such a profession is. Does God govern the history of our day? under what kind of law? If we add that God usually singles out the poor and the oppressed we will see that our profession of faith is not something to be taken for granted. When we become aware of the weakness of our position we should find a place for Habakkuk.

Some ways of handling the problem that are part of everyday language ("God writes straight with crooked lines"; "There is no good that does not come through evil") are serviceable in resolving little anomalies, but the great historical contradictions remain. Sometimes we bring in "time" in order to postpone the problem: we leave the resolution to the "end." Habakkuk seems to hint at this solution, but without being naïve; he leaves aside any attempt to give a logical justification and simply notes how certain his conviction is.

The prophet has to overcome a series of obstacles in his confession of faith. First, he finds a situation of injustice in which the "wicked" swallow up the "righteous." This is contrary to his faith, and he appeals to God. God tells him that a foreign people will dictate what is to be legal. The problem shifts from the individual or social level to the historical level of international politics, but it is still unresolved: God remains silent. The vision in 2:3-4 claims to provide an answer: we must simply wait with faith for the historical intervention of God on behalf of God's people. Logic is of no use; the only help is found in the historical hints that support hope. The cross of Christ is the supreme example of the problem and the crux of the solution.

SECOND READING

It is impossible to resolve all the problems that exegetes of the book of Habakkuk have raised in the course of history. I do not claim to settle the history of the book's redaction. The critics offer many hypotheses but no certainty. Eckhart Otto's article on the subject is very complete, although open to objection.

There is no clarity on the original historical point of reference either, since we cannot identify with certainty either the "righteous" or the "wicked" (1:4, 13) nor interpret the opposition between the proud and the innocent (2:4). Still uncertain is the interpretation of some expressions, such as "the law becomes slack" or "the Torah is falling into disuse" (1:4). The content of the "tablets" (2:2) is debated. It is not possible to decide whether in the mind of Habakkuk the political failure the Jews suffered historically under the Babylonians is to be interpreted as a divine punishment or whether international changes led to a social breakdown of the people that professed to be chosen. Let us leave as unattainable answers that we cannot provide, and be content with some established facts. The book of the prophet Habakkuk as it exists today was received by the believing community (both Jewish and Christian) as revealed, that is, as the basis for a real experience of salvation.

As we make an effort to read Habakkuk with greater care, the grammatical and syntactic particulars of the text will serve as pointers to the understanding of his themes and the structure of his message.

The Prophet's Complaint: 1:2-4

The verbs and first-person pronouns identify the prophet as the subject. The legal background is obvious. Habakkuk complains to God, the supreme judge, out of his weakness. His cry for help receives no answer. The deterioration of the prophet's world is summed up in an abundance of terms: injustice, wrong, destruction, violence, strife, conflict, and the resulting corruption of justice (vv. 3-4). The "righteous" are oppressed by the "wicked"; thus justice is trampled under foot, the Torah is paralyzed. As for the syntax, note the opening question, the description of the situation, and the result of the situation (*ʿal-ken,* v. 4).

God's Answer: 1:5-11

The plural imperative points to a change of subject: God is now speaking. The addressees (plural) remain anonymous; we may suppose that the answer is directed at Habakkuk and those he represents. The connection with the preceding section is shown by various points: the verb "look" (vv. 3, 5), the expression "establish justice" (affirmed in v. 7, twice denied in v. 4), the references to violence (vv. 3, 9).

YHWH bids the prophet lift his gaze to the international level and wonder at the incredible historical action of YHWH who is going to raise up a conquering people that will impose its law by means of violence. YHWH does not say that this is a punishment for the situation earlier described, but only that this people will carry out oppression. Comparisons with animals emphasize this people's swiftness (v. 8); their resoluteness is seen in their forward gaze (v. 9). Their deification of their own might is expressed in lapidary form (v. 11).

The Prophet's Rejoinder: 1:12-17

A new question (linked to a pronoun) opens the section. The addressee is clearly YHWH (v. 12); we can suppose that the singular subject is the prophet. There are many points of agreement with the first section that rouse admiration for the literary inclusion found in this chapter: a similar syntactic structure (question, description of situation, explanation of the consequences of the situation: a double or triple *ʿal-ken*); sameness of vocabulary ("look," evil, mention of YHWH at the beginning: vv. 2, 12), power of the guilty over the innocent. Given so many similarities it is not surprising that there have been attempts to bring the two sections together and to explain the section between them as an editorial interpolation, but the text as we have it suggests that we identify the wicked oppressor with the invading people whom YHWH has raised up. It is also possible to read the singular as referring to the king, whose function corresponds to that described in v. 12; hence the hypothesis that the subject may be King Jehoiachin.

The incompatibility between God and injustice is due to God's holiness and eternity. The expression "we will not die" in v. 12 should be read as "you shall not die" or "immortal." This is one of the *tiqqunê soferîm* or corrections deliberately made by the scribes in order to avoid any blasphemous doubt about a divine attribute.

When ch. 1 is read as a unit the description of injustices and numerous forms of oppression provides the setting for the action of a violent people (vv. 7, 11) whom YHWH has raised up (as a punishment? simply as a stage in history?).

Account of the Vision: 2:1-5

The first-person pronouns identify Habakkuk as the subject who awaits the divine answer. At the end of the section a new question, connected with a pronoun (v. 6), indicates the beginning of the following section. In a parallelism with the first part of ch. 1 the opposition between the innocent and their enemy is repeated (vv. 4-5), although this time the former will come out better. The prophet again comes into the presence of YHWH; this time, however, he does not complain but awaits YHWH's response. The delay does not lessen his certainty.

In this section two semantic fields intersect. One is temporal: urgency, haste, delay, waiting. The other has to do with stability: certainty in the face of disaster. If time presses and it becomes necessary to read readily and quickly the vision is delayed and the prophet waits. With time doubt can arise, but it is not mentioned. Its place is taken by greed and ambition, as opposed to certainty about the fulfillment. The vision opposes the patient just person to the arrogant (v. 4). Unexpectedly, all the peoples and nations join against the irrepressible ambition of the enemy (v. 5).

The Series of Woes: 2:6-20

Verse 6 maintains the narrative perspective. The alliance of peoples, which in v. 5 could be foreseen as geared to war, is changed into a satirical chorus. The pronouns with which each of the woes begins refer back to v. 5 (the arrogant and the greedy). I prescind for the moment from vv. 18-20, because they are clearly different from the others in structure and theme (idolatry instead of injustice). I have already pointed out the basic compositional structure: "Alas!" plus a participle and reason for the punishment *(kî);* at the end the action of the wicked is raised to the international level. The repetition of "because of human bloodshed . . . all who live in them" in vv. 8 and 17 forms an inclusion for the first four woes.

In addition to the express citations of Jer 51:58 and Isa 11:9 in vv. 13 and 14 respectively there are many echoes of other prophetic texts in this section. Luke 19:40 seems to use the idea in v. 11, but with a different meaning. The message is not a difficult one to grasp: the pride of the thief destroys his own house; anyone who flaunts power through violence is struggling against the knowledge of God's glory; the lustful will eat their fill of disgrace. Each reader can formulate his or her own beatitudes.

In vv. 18-20 the structure changes and the theme of idolatry is introduced. If we read these verses thoughtfully we will recall that many other prophetic texts treat injustice as a form of idolatry that has its gods, its worship, its faithful. "Idolater" is a name that sums up the ambitious person thus far described. The presence of YHWH, who from the Temple will impose justice on the earth, urges us to a sacred silence proper to the end time. This silence contrasts with the opening cry (1:2) and makes something positive out of the prophetic waiting with which this chapter began. In ch. 2 the watchtower of the prophet and the Temple of the Lord are structures that endure, as compared with the nests raised on high without support, the stones and the woodwork that cry out for justice, or the cities soaked in blood. When these two chapters are taken together the seeming lack of a divine response to injustice becomes a religious silence as God's judgment is carried out.

The Psalm of Habakkuk: Habakkuk 3

The new title (v. 1) makes clear the new literary form; the note to the director signals its end. The unity of the whole is shown by the twofold invocation of the name of YHWH that frames the entire psalm (vv. 2, 18-19). The triple reference to a liturgical pause (*Selah,* vv. 3, 9, 13) suggests a tripartite structure, but the location of the pauses does not appear to be relevant to the meaning. (Perhaps it was for the singing).

It seems significant that the single use of the word "God" (v. 3) begins a description, in the third person, of God's coming in theophany; a further mention of the name "YHWH" (v. 8) begins a direct invocation (in the second person); the verbs and pronouns in the first person beginning with v. 16 again focus the text on the reaction of the prophet. I offer, therefore, the following literary division: invocation (v. 2); description of a theophany (vv. 3-7); upheaval accompanying the theophany (vv. 8-15); reaction of the prophet (vv. 16-19). The first and fourth of these sections have to do with the relation between God and the prophet; the middle two with the relation between God and the earth (*ʾereṣ* occurs five times). The entire composition is placed in the mouth of the prophet, who invokes YHWH, describes, appeals to YHWH, and reacts.

Invocation (v. 2): The prophet is impressed: he has heard the message and seen the work of God. In his fear he asks for mercy. "In our own time" locates the action in history, but in a history whose events are interpreted eschatologically.

Theophany (vv. 3-7): YHWH's manifestation is described as a procession with a cosmic retinue: light and plague, glory and pestilence are its two extremes. In the vertical dimension the light flashes from YHWH's hands (the heavens), and pestilence is at YHWH's feet. YHWH's standing still causes a universal shudder and the collapse of all power (nations, mountains, Midian).

Upheaval (vv. 8-15): The theophany turns into a colossal upheaval of water, lightning, and thunder. The great luminaries are dimmed by such brightness. But the terror is meant solely for the enemies; only the wicked house is destroyed in the whirlwind. For the chosen people and the anointed YHWH's presence brings salvation. The essential salvation at the Exodus is echoed in v. 15.

Prophet's Reaction (vv. 16-19): The vision causes the prophet to tremble from top to toe (lips, bones, steps). What is unexpected is the motive for the fear: the distress that overtakes the oppressor. Verse 17 may be an addition relating to an agricultural celebration, but it reinforces the prophet's hope. History bears out YHWH. Nature may fail, but the prophet remains unmoved in his gladness.

After his initial outcry the prophet has learned to hope. Ultimate salvation is the reason for his joy. From a literary point of view the short book of Habakkuk contains some expressive and powerful verses. Theologically it urges us to abandon religious individualism and adopt a historical and international outlook in our religious ethic.

BIBLIOGRAPHY

Copeland, Paul E. "The Midst of the Years" in Robert P. Carroll, ed., *Text as pretext: essays in honour of Robert Davidson* (= JSOT.S 138) Sheffield: JSOT Press, 1992, 91–105.

Johnson, M. D. "The Paralysis of the Torah in Habakkuk 1, 4," *VT* 35 (1985) 257–266.

Otto, Eckart. "Die Theologie des Buches Habakuk," *VT* 35 (1985) 274–295.

Sweeney, Marvin A. "Structure, Genre, and Intent in the Book of Habakkuk," *VT* 41 (1991) 63–83.

Zephaniah

Walter Vogels

FIRST READING

I. General Character of the Book

Some people cannot wait to finish a book. After reading the beginning they flip to the end to see how things turn out. Zephaniah lends itself to such reading. The first words, "The word of the Lord" (1:1) and the last, "says the Lord" (3:20), form a single inclusion. The whole book is presented as God's word. The beginning speaks of a terrible destruction (1:2-4): "sweep away" (vv. 2-3 [3x]); "destroy" (vv. 3, 4 [2x]); "lead astray" (v. 3), but the end describes a beautiful restoration (3:18-20): "remove disaster" (v. 18); "save" (v. 19); "gather" (vv. 19, 20); "bring home" (v. 20); "restore your fortunes" (v. 20). This contrast is even stronger in the Hebrew text. In the beginning God "gathers" *(ʾsp)* to punish (1:2), at the end God "gathers" *(ʾsp)* to save (3:18). The punishment affects the whole "face of the earth" (1:2, 3) but also Jerusalem (1:4), and so does salvation: Israel will be praised "in all the earth" (3:19), "among all the peoples of the earth" (3:20). Zephaniah combines universalism and election.

God's punishment responds to people's behavior. Zephaniah describes the sins of the nations and Judah and leads us into their hearts by quoting their words. The Jerusalemites say: "Neither good nor evil will the Lord do" (1:12). The book shows their error. God can and does destroy and save. Assyria, one of the nations, says: "There is no other than I" (2:15). The book also shows the nations' error. God humbles human pride. The possibility of restoration after destruction is based upon Zephaniah's belief in a "remnant" whose qualities he describes. Disaster and salvation will happen on "the day of the Lord," which is near.

One beautiful aspect of the book is the repetition of words or expressions and the way Zephaniah stresses a point by a variety of words or images. He likes fourfold descriptions (1:3, 4-6; 3:3-4), since four symbolizes totality.

II. General Contexts for Interpretation

1. Original Historical Contexts

Zephaniah prophesied under king Josiah of Judah (640–609 B.C.E.) (1:1). He breaks the three quarters of a century of prophetic silence after Isaiah and Micah (end of eighth c.). Jeremiah, Nahum, and Habakkuk followed soon after. Josiah's reform of 622 B.C.E. (2 Kings 22–23) reacted against syncretism common under Manasseh and Amon, his predecessors (2 Kings 21). Since Zephaniah condemns the idolatry in Jerusalem, he preached before this reform and perhaps promoted it. Zephaniah started his ministry around 630 B.C.E. in Jerusalem which he knows well (1:10-11).

This period was also turbulent on the international scene. Assyria, which dominated the ancient Near East for over a century and destroyed the Northern Kingdom in 721 B.C.E., had been in decline since 625 and collapsed with the fall of Nineveh in 612 (2:13). Babylon took its place as a world power.

Zephaniah witnessed a profound religious reform in Judah and drastic international changes. This explains why he combines universalism and election.

2. Canonical Contexts

In all versions of the OT Zephaniah is ninth in the collection of the twelve minor prophets, after Habakkuk and before Haggai. The book contains the common prophetic themes of human sin, divine judgment, and God's compassion demonstrated in a restoration. [See also the article "Prophetism and Prophets."]

3. Canonical Intertextuality

Zephaniah is rooted in prophets who preceded him. The similarities with Amos are striking, e.g., "the day of the Lord" is a day of "darkness" (1:14-18, cf. Amos 5:18-20). Like Isaiah, Zephaniah believes that this day is near (1:7, 14; cf. Isa 13:6).

Zephaniah inspired some of his successors. Joel quotes part of Zephaniah's description of the day of the Lord (1:15; cf. Joel 2:2). A few NT passages quote or recall Zephaniah. The darkness of the day of the Lord reappears at Jesus' death (Matt 27:45; Mark 15:33). The NT writers retained Zephaniah's preaching of God's universal judgment and applied it to the eschatological judgment when the humble will be saved (Matt 5:3).

4. Patristic Interpretation

The NT and patristic literature rarely quote Zephaniah. He enters into Christian discourse through Origen of Alexandria's *Commentary on Romans* (early third c. C.E.) which highlights the great day of the Lord's wrath. At the time of Origen (mid-third century C.E.) and in the early fourth century C.E. two African apologists, Arnobius and Lactantius, focused on Zephaniah's theme of God's wrath. Lactantius wrote a treatise against the Epicurean theory of a deity without emotions.

5. Liturgical Use

Although Zephaniah played no important role in Judaism or in the early Church the passage on the day of the Lord (1:14-18) deeply influenced Christianity. A Franciscan (possibly Thomas of Celano [1255]) composed a poem based on the Vulgate: *Dies irae, dies illa,* which served as the sequence in Requiem Masses from the fourteenth c. C.E. until 1969. The song for the final commendation at funeral Masses, *Libera me, Domine,* was also inspired by Zephaniah's passage. Now that the severe notion of the day of the Lord is no longer popular, other texts, mainly chosen from Zeph 3:9-20, which contains Zephaniah's promises of salvation, are used in the lectionary, especially during Advent.

6. Use Through History

The call to conversion which "perhaps" leads to salvation (2:3) is the basis of Luther's *sola gratia* and *desperatio fiducialis* doctrine.

SECOND READING

Superscription: 1:1

The superscription, containing three elements, is similar to that in Hosea and Micah, and partly to that in Joel. (1) The *message* is "the word of the Lord." (2) *Information about the prophet* provides his name, "Zephaniah," a common name (cf. Jer 29:29; 52:24; Zech 6:10, 14) meaning "YHWH protects, hides, or treasures," or "Zaphon (a Canaanite deity) is YHWH." As always his genealogy is added, but it is unusual to give four generations. Since he is the "son of Cushi," his father was perhaps a Cushite, an Ethiopian. The other names, all typical Hebrew names, were probably added to prove that Zephaniah was a real Israelite. The last name, "Hezekiah," was the name of a king of Judah (716–687 B.C.E.). Whatever Zephaniah's precise origin, the reader connects him with foreigners and royalty. His message indeed speaks of universalism and election centered around Jerusalem where the Lord is king. (3) The *historical context* is "in the days of Josiah." Josiah was remembered as the perfect king because of his reform, but he is "the son of Amon," a less perfect king who tolerated idolatry. The three elements of the superscription define the prophet as mediator.

I. Chaos on the Day of the Lord: 1:2-18

(A) *Universal destruction (1:2-3).* Zephaniah stresses the terrible destruction: "sweep away" (3x), "destroy," "all things," "from the face of the earth *(ʾadamah)*" (2x, as inclusion). God's decision recalls the flood, when God swept everything "from the face of the earth" (Gen 6:7; 7:4; 8:8), though God then promised "never again" (Gen 8:21). As human wickedness caused the flood (Gen 6:5), so now the cause is "the wicked," which is parallel to and synonymous with "humankind *(ʾadam)*." The destruction reverses the sequence of creation (Gen 1:20-28) by starting with "the human being" *(ʾadam)* who loses authority over the world, moving on to the "beasts," who share the land with humans, "the birds of the sky" and, finally, "the fishes of the sea." All living creatures and all places are destroyed in a return to chaos. Creation took seven days, the destruction on "the day of the Lord" only one.

(B) *Destruction of Judah (1:4-6).* Because Noah, the just, survived the flood (Gen 6:8-9) and God would have spared the just in Sodom (Gen 18:23) the chosen people may think they will survive now. Wrong! "Judah" and "all the inhabitants of Jerusalem" will know the fate of the rest of humanity: God will "destroy" (the same verb). Their sin is idolatry (vv. 4-5), syncretism (v. 5) and indifference toward the Lord (v. 6). Four gods of four nations illustrating four aspects of the divinity are listed: "Baal," Canaan's god of fecundity; "the host of heaven," Mesopotamia's astral religion; "the Lord," Israel's God of Exodus and Covenant; "Milcom" (*mlk* = king), Ammon's god of political life. God cannot be divided: the Lord covers all these aspects.

(C) *Silence for the day (1:7).* Who is called to respectful silence, the inhabitants of Jerusalem (vv. 4-6) and/or the whole of humanity (vv. 2-3)? Two reasons are given for the command. There must be silence before God's power in his judgment: "for *(ki)* near is the day," and there must be similar liturgical silence during a sacrifice: "for *(ki)* the Lord has prepared a slaughter feast . . . ." We wonder, as did Isaac (Gen 22:7-8), where the sacrificial animal is. The text says later that Judah will be sacrificed. The guests are "consecrated," set apart and cleansed. Are they the nations who will witness Judah's judgment?

What follows develops the two reasons for the silence: first the sacrifice of Judah and then the nearness of the day that extends to the universe. This gives Part I (1:2-18) a chiastic structure with v. 7 in the middle:

- A. world (2-3)
  - B. Judah (4-6)
    - C. SILENCE (7)
  - B'. Judah (8-13)
- A'. world (14-18)

(B') *The day for Jerusalem (1:8-13).* In the three subdivisions of this section describing the slaughter feast (cf. v. 7b) the criticism of Jerusalem concentrates on three groups. The verb, "I will visit," obviously to punish, dominates (vv. 8, 9, 12).

"On the day of the Lord . . ." (vv. 8-9): the first group is officialdom, the political leaders (the king himself is omitted). They adopt foreign dress and customs to be "modern" and to adjust to this world. Some "leap over the threshold," which may mean that as followers of foreign religions they jump over it for fear of evil spirits (1 Sam 5:5) or that, as perpetrators of social injustice, they penetrate the houses of the poor. Others fill the royal palace with violence and deceit, which always leads to self-destruction.

"On that day . . ." (vv. 10-11): the second group are the merchants of different sections of Jerusalem who have economic power. Their "cry," their "wail" (2x) and "loud crashing" (note the crescendo) will be clearly heard in the silence of that day.

"At that time . . ." (vv. 12-13): the third group are those who are satisfied with themselves and unable to change. What they say God cannot do contrasts with what God says: "I will explore . . . I will visit (punish)." They will not enjoy the houses and vineyards, the symbols of the good life (Deut 28:30, 39) that they consider the guarantee of their security.

(A') *The day for the universe (1:14-18).* The text resembles a hymn announcing that the "great" day is "near" (v. 14, cf. v. 7a). It describes this terrible day (vv. 15-16a), the anguish we will *feel,* the total destruction, desolation and darkness we will *see,* and the noise of war we will *hear* in the silence (v. 7). This day is a reversal of creation, a return to chaos and darkness (Gen 1:2). The word "day" is repeated seven times as though the work of the seven days of creation will be undone in one day. The text specifies what God will do to humanity *(ʾadam)* on that day when neither "silver" nor "gold," so powerful in our world (cf. vv. 11, 13) will be able to save them (vv. 16b-18a). The hymn concludes with "the end" (v. 18b) of "all the earth" and "all who live on the earth."

Exhortation 1: Seek the Lord: 2:1-3

Zephaniah addresses an urgent *demand* (v. 1) to "a nation without shame" (or "who do not long [for the Lord]") to "gather together" (2x). The universal perspective from the preceding verse (1:18) is delimited. One nation, no longer "all who live," has to gather in one restricted area instead of "all the earth." The *reason* (v. 2): they must do it quickly "before" (3x) "the day of God's anger" (2x) that is coming soon (1:7, 14). *What to do* (v. 3): That nation, specified as "all you humble of the earth," is asked to do what Judah failed to do (1:6), namely "to seek (3x) the Lord," which means "to seek justice and humility." "Humility" (2x) is important, since this "perhaps" leads to being sheltered on "the day of the Lord's anger" (third time).

The exhortation forms a bridge. It concludes Part I, which speaks of total destruction (1:2-8), and introduces Part II, where the reader expects to discover whether this "perhaps" becomes fact.

II. Judgment and Hope on the Day of the Lord: 2:4–3:7

Zephaniah returns to the universal judgment on the day of the Lord. Like Isaiah, Jeremiah, Ezekiel, and Amos, he utters oracles against a few nations and ends, as does Amos 1–2, with an oracle against Judah.

(A) *Oracle against the Philistines (2:4-7)* covering the West. The description of the destruction of the cities and the inhabitants (vv. 4-5) is full of assonances lost in translation. Zephaniah suggests that these cities will undergo what their names mean. The verbs rise to a crescendo. R. Gordis renders it as follows: "Indeed, Gaza shall be deserted (like a betrothed woman), and Ashkelon will be desolate (like a deserted woman), Ashdod will be driven out in broad daylight (like a divorced woman), and Ekron will be uprooted (like a barren woman)." No reason is given for the judgment, but "I will humble you" suggests that the Philistines lacked the humility needed (cf. 2:3) to escape the day. Their territory will be given to "the remnant of the house of Judah" (vv. 6-7). So there is a remnant, not only "perhaps," but certainly. The peaceful images of pasturing the flock contrast to the war images of the day. There is a remnant "for the Lord their God shall visit them," not to punish Judah as on the previous visit (1:8, 9, 12), but "to bring about their restoration" or "to restore their fortune." There is reason to seek the Lord (2:1-3), "for *(ki)*" there is judgment (v. 4), but also hope "for *(ki)*" (v. 7b).

(B) *Oracle against Moab and Ammon (2:8-10)* covering the East. Ironically, the two nations resulting from the incest of Lot and his two daughters who escaped the destruction of Sodom and Gomorrah (Gen 19:30-38) will become like those two cities (Gen 19:24-25). Their sin is pride, which bring them to insult God's people and thus God. Their territory also will be given to the remnant of God's people.

Intermezzo (2:11) in the middle of the oracles against the nations. It applies to all. God's purpose in humbling them is not their total destruction because, as with Judah (2:7, 9), there is hope. They will consent "to adore" the Lord.

(C) *Oracle against the Cushites (2:12)* or the Ethiopians, covering the South.

(D) *Oracle against Assyria (2:13-15)* covering the North, which is the most feared direction (Jer 1:15) because Assyria is the real enemy. The Lord "will stretch out a hand" as against Judah (1:4). Assyria's destruction is the worst. It is not turned into pasture (cf. 2:6-7) but into a desert where wild animals shall live "in her midst." The reason is Assyria's pride, its self-security and self-worship in believing itself to be God (like Babylon later: Isa 47:8, 10). Assyria will be totally despised (cf. 1 Kings 9:8). Pride is the sin of all these nations (cf. Gen 11:1-9).

(E) *Oracle against Judah (3:1-7).* After the oracles against the nations proclaiming a universal judgment Zephaniah turns to Judah, as he did in Part I. While Assyria is called "the exultant city" (2:15), "the city" Jerusalem has three characteristics (v. 1) that are developed in detail (vv. 3-4). She is no longer the Lord's spouse but "rebellious" (cf. v. 4a), no longer consecrated but "polluted" (cf. v. 4b), no longer a place where justice is respected but "oppressive" (cf. v. 3). She refuses four things: she does not listen, accept, trust, or "draw 'near' to God" (= worship God) (v. 2; cf. 1:6, 12) even though the day of the Lord is "near" (1:7, 14). The princes "in her midst" (the same root as "near"), judges, prophets, and priests, the four groups of leaders responsible for political, judicial, and religious life, do the opposite of what their function demands (v. 4). Despite this corruption, the Lord has not abandoned the city. YHWH is "in her midst," "just" and faithful as the daily sunrise (cf. Gen 8:22) (v. 5, which lists four activities of God). The Lord used many ways to "visit" Judah (cf. 1:8, 9, 12; 2:7): God's word through prophets (vv. 2, 4), the Law (v. 4), the daily sunrise of nature (v. 5), and history (v. 6). Therefore, God hoped, "Surely now you will fear me . . . accept correction." It is all in vain, because people still think that God does not act and is absent (1:12). The sin of Judah is worse.

Exhortation 2: Wait for the Lord: 3:8-9

Exhortation 1 above (2:1-3) is a turning point between Parts I and II. Exhortation 2 has a similar function. After recounting God's useless efforts to convert Judah, the text moves on to "therefore . . . ," which normally introduces a punishment. But surprisingly the passage is an ambiguous mixture of destruction and salvation. People are invited "to wait" for the Lord on the day of the Lord—this verb is often synonymous with "to hope" (Isa 8:17; Ps 33:20). As in the first exhortation one nation is invited "to gather" (2:1), so here God will "gather the nations." The verb "to gather" is ambiguous; it may mean destroy (1:2) or save (3:19-20). Here God gathers the nations to pour out "blazing anger" on them, as previously prophesied for one nation (2:2). The day is thus a day of destruction, "for *(ki)*" (v. 8 [2x]). Verse 8 ends by repeating the conclusion of Part I (1:18), "For in the fire of my jealousy shall all the earth be consumed." However, the first time the statement went on to say that it would be "the end," but this time the text moves unexpectedly into another "for *(ki)*" (v. 9) that speaks of salvation.

III. Salvation on the Day of the Lord: 3:9-20

Part III develops the salvation, anticipated in Part II, of Jerusalem (2:7 = 3:13, 20) and the nations (2:11 = 3:9).

(A) *First promise of salvation (3:9-13).* The sudden change in the text shows God's real intention. God brings salvation through destruction, first to the nations, "for *(ki)* then (= at that time) . . ." (vv. 9-10), then to Jerusalem, "for *(ki)* then . . ." (vv. 11-13). The two sections are linked together by a reference in the middle to "on that day" (v. 11). The paragraph moves from the universal to Judah, as Zephaniah did when he described the judgment on the day of the Lord. The purification of the nations reverses the story of Babel (Gen 11:1-9). The nations, called "the daughter of my dispersed (scattered) ones," since they were "scattered" (Gen 11:4, 8, 9) will speak the same "language" (= lips) after their "lips" are purified (Isa 6:5-7). They will no longer speak their own name but call upon the Lord's "name," and no longer be scattered but act "with one accord." Next comes the purification of Jerusalem. She need no longer be "ashamed" (Gen 2:25). The Lord will remove "on that day" (cf. 3:8) "from your midst" all pride, which is the real sin (v. 11). A humble (2:3) "remnant" (2:7, 9) that, like the nations, will trust in the "name" of the Lord (Gen 4:26; 12:8), will be left "in your midst" (v. 12). Like the Lord, who always remained "in her midst" (3:5) as the only just one, this new people will do no wrong. They will act in a manner totally opposed to how the people of Jerusalem are living now (3:1-4). This lifestyle, summarized in three things they will not do, will assure them the three basic human needs: nourishment, tranquility, and security (v. 13).

(B) *Invitation to rejoice (3:14-15).* There are four imperatives to rejoice (v. 14) for four reasons (v. 15). One is that Jerusalem will have no enemies to fear. God will destroy the internal enemies who caused her destruction (first promise of salvation, 3:11-13) and the external enemies who took people into exile (second promise, 3:19-20).

(B') *Invitation to trust (3:16-18a).* The invitations to rejoice and to trust are both addressed to Jerusalem, called "the daughter of Zion" and "the daughter of Jerusalem," as the nations were called "the daughter of my dispersed ones" (3:10). The two invitations have a chiastic structure and are linked together, like the preceding section (v. 11), by "on that day" right in the middle (v. 16).

a. *Shout for joy . . . sing joyfully* (v. 14)
  b. The Lord . . . has *turned away your enemies* (v. 15a, b)
    c. The Lord is *in your midst* (v. 15c)
      d. you have nothing further to *fear* (v. 15d)
        e. ON THAT DAY (v. 16a)
      d'. *Fear* not (v. 16b)
    c'. The Lord is *in your midst* (v. 17a)
  b'. a mighty *savior* (v. 17b)
a'. The Lord will *rejoice* over you . . . *sing joyfully* (vv. 17c-18a)

Zephaniah invites Jerusalem to rejoice and describes how the Lord, called "King" (v. 15) and "your God" (v. 17), rejoices over Jerusalem. The covenant is restored. "[God] will be silent (LXX 'renew you') in [God's] love" (v. 17). God finds no words to express the depth of the divine love. This silence "on that day" contrasts with the war cry on the same day (1:16).

(A') *Second promise of salvation (3:18b-20).* The first promise of salvation says that Jerusalem's *shame will be removed* "on that day" (v. 11a), and that Jerusalem will be purified and *populated* by a remnant (vv. 11b-13). The second promise contains two similar elements. "At that time" (3x) the Lord will destroy Jerusalem's enemies; the "mighty savior" (3:17) will "save" the outcasts. God will "restore their fortunes" (cf. 2:7) and *populate* Jerusalem with the people whom the Assyrians took into exile after conquering the Northern Kingdom. Zephaniah expresses Josiah's hope that his reform will reunite North and South. And so Jerusalem's *shame will be removed,* even reversed; the Lord will give her "renown and praise among all the peoples of the earth" (2x; cf. Gen 12:2; Exod 19:5). The text moves once more from Jerusalem to a universal perspective.

BIBLIOGRAPHY

Ball, I. J. *A Rhetorical Study of Zephaniah.* Berkeley: Bibal Press, 1988.

Ben Zvi, Ehud. *A Historical-Critical Study of the Book of Zephaniah.* Berlin and New York: Walter de Gruyter, 1991.

House, Paul R. *Zephaniah: A Prophetic Drama.* Sheffield: Almond Press, 1988.

Haggai

José Loza Vera

Introduction

The book of Haggai, the tenth of the minor prophets, is short and almost monothematic; in it the prophet expresses the urgent necessity for Judah and Jerusalem to reconstruct the Temple of YHWH. After the edict from Cyrus of Persia (538 B.C.E.) part of the population of Judah, exiled by Nebuchadnezzar, were able to return to their own land. When Haggai began his prophetic activity the altar of sacrifices had scarcely been restored. The delay was due partially to the opposition of their neighbors (cf. Ezra 1–6).

We know very little of Haggai and what we know is almost solely from his book although the book of Ezra confirms the role he played at the beginning of the return to Jerusalem and the function he performed, together with Zechariah, in the reconstruction of the Temple (cf. Ezra 5:1). He is the only person in the Bible who bears the name *"haggai,"* which means "my delight."

Haggai announced the word of YHWH in a specific time and place. His use of prophetic formulae is abundant. Some such utterances are found in the introduction, e.g., "the word of the LORD came . . ." (1:1, 3; 2:1, 10, 20). The word of God constitutes a punctual happening presented through a specific person and in a determinate moment. Even before listening to his words we already know who moved him to preach. Other formulae are found in the same oracles such as "thus says the LORD of hosts" or "says the LORD" (1:2, 5, 7, 8; 2:6, 7, 11) and "the voice of the LORD" ["of hosts"] (1:9, 13; 2:4 [3x], 8, 9 [2x], 14, 17, 23 [2x]). These formulae offer an adequate perspective for understanding the predictions of Haggai. The proclaimed word does not proceed at his initiative; it is the word of YHWH spoken at a precise moment for the inhabitants of Judah and Jerusalem. If it is the voice of YHWH it is understandable why he should urge the people to listen. In the words of Haggai they hear the voice of God, for God has commissioned Haggai to speak in God's name (1:12).

Haggai speaks to the governors of Judah and the population in general. Initially the message is directed to the governor, Zerubbabel, and to the high priest, Joshua (1:1), but it is entirely fitting to suppose that the "remnant of the people" also forms a part of his audience (v. 12). Governor, high priest, and people are being addressed by the prophet in 2:1-9 (see v. 2), and the consultation in 2:10-14 is probably with the priests on matters of religious legislation. At any rate the content is not a private matter; the prophet takes from the answer received a message or lesson for all (2:15-19). The last section (2:20-23) is an oracle for the governor, Zerubbabel.

The book of Haggai is an edited unity: the oracles are introduced by a person speaking in the third person and introducing Haggai, the prophet of YHWH. There is a duality between the words of the prophet and the one who introduces them, indicating that the word of YHWH came to Haggai in a determinate moment. The day is located in the second year of the reign of Darius. Besides there being a duality between the word of the prophet and introductory elements, sometimes there are indications of re-reading or the actualization of the words of the prophet in subsequent circumstances within the life of the people of God and in response to other needs.

The chronology of the book in the introduction to each action of Haggai indicates that his prophetic mission lasted little more than three months, i.e., from the first day of the sixth month to the eighteenth day of the ninth month of the second year of Darius of Persia. Those dates, if expressed in terms of absolute chronology, would point to the fact that the preaching of Haggai extends from August 29 to December 18 of the year 520 B.C.E., although according to a different calculation it may have been some months prior to those mentioned.

Patristic and Medieval Commentaries on Haggai

Since the prophets of the Hebrew Scriptures were read within the liturgical assembly as early as the second century C.E. (see, e.g., the testimony of Justin, *Apology 1,* 67) homilies have preceded explicit commentaries. The use of prophetic texts to demonstrate the unity of the divine economy (i.e., the continuity between the Hebrew and Christian Scriptures) is also found already in the Apologists, especially Irenaeus. Origen, however, was the first we know to have composed explicit commentaries on the twelve minor prophets (see Eusebius, *HE* 6.32.2) but these have not been preserved.

The first fully extant commentary on Haggai is that of Theodore of Mopsuestia (ca. 350–428) on all the minor prophets (*PG* 66.124–632); his method is strictly "Antiochene," adhering to the literal and historical sense and avoiding any messianic application. Cyril of Alexandria (d. 444) on the contrary, in his commentary on the minor prophets (*PG* 71.9–72.364) uses the typological method extensively and interprets the majority of the prophecies in a christological sense. Theodoret of Cyr (ca. 393–466), though not of the Antiochian school, in his commentary on the minor prophets (*PG* 81.1545–1988) attends not only to the literal sense but also uses the allegorical and typological methods and recognizes the messianic interpretation of many prophecies.

In Latin, Jerome (ca. 342–420) commented briefly, probably in 393 (when he was beginning to translate from Hebrew) on Haggai (after Nahum, Micah, Habakkuk, and Zephaniah), but he completed his commentary on all the minor prophets only in 406 (*PL* 25.815–1578; see the critical edition in CCL 73–76 [1963–1970]). Jerome gave in his commentaries a translation from the Hebrew and from the Greek of the LXX, but after discussing the problems of the text he based his spiritual interpretation on the LXX, following Greek patristic predecessors (especially Origen).

From among several medieval commentators on the minor prophets, including Haggai, one could mention Albert the Great (ca. 1200–1280) and later Dionysius the Carthusian (Denis van Leeuwen or Denis Ryckel, 1402–1471).

Commentary

The Time of Building (1:1-14)

The introduction (v. 1) to the first intervention of Haggai, as always in this book, shows that the word of YHWH is presented as a timely happening. It is a mediated word; it comes to the ones addressed through a prophet. The introduction mentions only the governor, Zerubbabel, and his priest, Joshua, but v. 12 (cf. v. 2) offers the clarification that Haggai spoke to the entire people and made his announcement publicly. The expression "to all the remnant of the people" indicates that, having lived through the catastrophe of the Babylonian exile, the Israelites experienced a growing consciousness of being the "remnant" promised particularly in the oracles of Isaiah and his school. The mention of the governor and the high priest is important. Although they held a subordinate power (Judah was subject to the Persians) they nevertheless exercised authority and its impact was decisive for the success of the empire. If the high priest were to be particularly involved in the reconstruction of the Temple, that would hold specific promise for the governor, Zerubbabel (2:20-23).

The point of departure for the oracle is what the people say about the Temple of YHWH: that the time for the reconstruction of the edifice has not yet arrived (v. 2). The words of the prophet are intended to pull the people out of their lethargy. He does not detail the external reasons that could influence them; he simply asserts that the delay is unjustified and culpable. While the people dwell in "paneled houses" the "LORD's house" is a heap of ruins (v. 4; cf. v. 9). In pondering the difference between their houses and this one we ought to remember that in spite of the prophetic criticism of worship or texts such as 1 Kings 8:27 the Hebrew Scriptures constantly affirm that God has chosen the Temple as the dwelling place of the divine name. There God finds delight and from this Temple manifests the divine glory and blesses God's people (cf. especially Ps 132:13-16). That is what v. 8 so succinctly proclaims: the Temple is to be reconstructed so that there "'I may take pleasure in it and be honored,' says the LORD."

We can better understand the text of Haggai in light of Psalm 132. The prophet calls for attention and reflection: "Consider how you have fared" (vv. 5, 7). He levels a challenge and suggests actions to meet it. The actions form two series (vv. 6 and 9). The enumeration is in this form, and is interrupted by two verses, in order to make one hear the concluding terms of each statement; that is, the people must look for materials and begin immediately to rebuild the Temple.

What relationship is there between the material needs expressed and the order to build? The poor harvests have not been the fruit of bad luck, but have been poor because of YHWH's intervention. The "I" of YHWH's active will sounds forth repeatedly: "I blew it away" (v. 9); "I have called for a drought" (v. 11). The word of the prophet is an invitation to look for the deeper reason, the "why" (v. 9) of the evils afflicting Judah. The answer to the question is "because my house lies in ruins" (v. 9). If the blessing of YHWH does not accompany the people it is because the Temple is in ruins; but things will change if it is rebuilt.

The reaction of Zerubbabel, Joshua, and the people is positive: a reverential fear before YHWH inundates their souls (v. 12). Haggai encourages them to act with the security that YHWH will accompany them: "I am with you" (v. 13). The reconstruction will soon begin (v. 14). There is an underlying question connected with this proposal. Does one have to read v. 15 as the chronological beginning of the work, which would then have occurred on the twenty-fourth day of the sixth month, or is that verse out of place and meant to introduce another task?

Commentators frequently opt for the second possibility and believe that the date should be related to vv. 15-19 of ch. 2, which were wrongly placed. From the perspective of the final text it can only be the conclusion of 1:1-14. Haggai spoke, and although he may have convinced the authorities and the people of the urgency of God's message the decision to rebuild and the plan of the work could only have happened after the passage of some amount of time.

The Temple and the Glory of YHWH (1:15b–2:9)

A critical problem exists between 2:5 and the remaining content of ch. 2. If the "promise" is the supporting feature to the "deeds" of the prior verse, we have an exhortation to practice the Law given by YHWH, but a thematic relationship with the message of the book is not evident. It seems preferable therefore to consider that at least the beginning of v. 5 was added to the text. Verse 5 does not seem to be consonant with v. 4 nor with the entire section, which contains words of relief and encouragement relative to the work of rebuilding the Temple.

This reading does not give the impression that we are advancing; it insists, rather, on going back to what had already been expressed. Thematically the impression is a correct one, but why all the insistence? Some older people had remained in Judah and had seen the glory of Solomon's Temple, now destroyed by the Babylonians. Since memory usually idealizes the past their comparison of the present with that past glory would of course favor the past. The words of these older people (v. 3: "who is left among you that saw this house in its former glory?") could be sowing discouragement among the builders.

Thus it is not an easy task for Haggai to intervene, inviting the people to compare the glory of Solomon's Temple with the present one (v. 3). For his word of comfort to be effective it is essential that the judgment be unfavorable to the Temple currently being built. Indeed the glory of the post-exilic Temple was nothing compared to the glory of Solomon's Temple. However, the prophet can transmit the divine promise of a welcome change: YHWH will fill the new Temple with the divine glory (v. 7), but even more, "'the latter splendor of this house shall be greater than the former,' says the LORD of hosts" (v. 9).

The term "splendor" is central and is repeated three times. In vv. 3 and 9 a comparison between the Temple of Solomon and the present one is pervasive; however, a change in the relative importance of the latter is affirmed. The intermediate passage (v. 7) gives the reason for the change: YHWH will fill the new Temple with the divine glory, not only because God will make the riches of the nations flow—although that may seem to be the most obvious reason—but also because God will dwell in it. The Temple is the dwelling place of YHWH's glory (cf. Exod 40:34-35; 1 Kings 8:11).

The change announced in v. 4 is the reason for following through on the work. The prophet reiterates the same word of encouragement to Zerubbabel, to Joshua, and to the people. There must be no room for discouragement since YHWH will accompany them. In addition there is a mysterious equivalence between "I am with you" and the presence of the "spirit of YHWH" that some later prophet will consider the gift *par excellence* of the time of definitive restoration (Joel 3:1-2) and that Luke will see realized on Pentecost (Acts 2:17-21 cites Joel 3:1-5).

The primary sign of this change in favor of Judah will be an exceptional divine intervention. It is described as a serious cosmic cataclysm: "I will shake the heavens and the earth and the sea and the dry land" (v. 6). This is akin to the apocalyptic language that would develop in the future to describe the signs announcing the end of the world. The nations will also experience the powerful intervention of YHWH and will go to Jerusalem with their treasures (vv. 6-7), an idea expressed many times in the Hebrew Scriptures (cf. Ps 72:10-11). But the ascent to Jerusalem is also affirmed in a more universalist perspective (Isaiah 2–4; Mic 4:1-3; Isa 56:6-8; Zech 8:20-23).

Beginning with 2:5 someone thought it opportune to underscore another aspect. Instead of encouragement that will make the people able to work (v. 4), what is needed is the putting into practice of the demands of the pact made by YHWH with Israel at the time of the Exodus. It is one thing to encourage people to work and another to demand fidelity to the Law. The second has no immediate relationship to the theme that concerns Haggai.

Consultation, Answer, and Consequence (2:10-14)

Here we witness not a discussion among participants but rather the account of a consultation Haggai made, by divine order, with the priests of the people (v. 11). (The consultation may have been at a time prior to this public announcement, as evidenced in v. 14.) Why might Haggai have consulted the priests? He would have done so because they were the depositories of the *torah* that, in addition to being the "Law," was the book of "instructions" concerning matters related to the worship of the Temple and religious practices (cf. Jer 18:18). Haggai proposes two questions relative to the consequences of contact with what was consecrated (is food consecrated by being part of a peace sacrifice, or by contact with what is consecrated?) as well as with impurity, especially in virtue of contact with a corpse (cf. Lev 22:4). The answers establish a difference: contact with what is consecrated does not sanctify anything else, but contact with the impure makes anything that touches it also impure (vv. 12-13). We are not really given the reasons for such a difference. The important thing is the consequence, which Haggai explains in v. 14: YHWH declares impure whatever the people present as an offering (the term "this nation" in v. 14 has a pejorative meaning, as is often the case in the Hebrew Scriptures). Why? Because it has been in contact with the people, itself impure. The impurity of the offerer is communicated to the offering.

The Promised Blessing (1:15a; 2:15-19)

Many critics believe that the beginning of 1:15, which is incomplete, was originally part of the oracle of 2:15-19, so that the twenty-fourth day of the sixth month would be the date of the second intervention by Haggai. Verse 17 may have been added to this pericope; it essentially repeats the message of Amos 4:8, though with some textual problems that are difficult to resolve. The reference, if it had been placed after v. 14, would have given the reason for the impurity of the people's offerings. If it followed v. 14 there would be an unfolding of information, i.e., if Judah did not find itself under the sign of divine blessing the reason would be profoundly different: not having had a legitimate Temple, or the sin of the people.

Thematically the passage is very close to the first intervention; it develops the consequences of the absence of divine blessing in the life of the people and repeatedly echoes the call to be attentive (vv. 15 and 18; cf. 1:5, 7). In both passages it is clear that the harvest is unsatisfactory and that hope is seen as a fraud. But the point of view is different. No longer is it a matter of finding the cause for what is happening. The important fact is the certainty of a radical change: divine blessing will accompany Judah. There is such certainty in the prophet's announcement that the date for beginning work on the reconstruction of the Temple can be pointed out with definite perimeters. There is a "before" (vv. 15-16) and an "after" or, to put it more accurately, "from this day on" (vv. 18-19).

The Promise to Zerubbabel (2:20-23)

As in 2:10-14 the oracle to Zerubbabel is dated the twenty-fourth of the ninth month. The initial part of the announcement uses expressions similar to or complementary to those of 2:6-7. The formulation, briefer with reference to the cosmic cataclysm (v. 21), develops in greater detail the annihilation of the power of the kingdoms (v. 22). YHWH destroys the military power, turning some who brandish arms against the others. We are far from a mutual agreement to renounce arms entirely (cf. Isa 2:4; Mic 4:3).

This is the preliminary stage and the means for the future restoration ("that day") of the chosen people, though the message is more implied than enunciated. What is said refers to Zerubbabel. Although many are called "servant of YHWH," the phrase "my servant" denotes intimacy. A comparison with Deutero-Isaiah arises spontaneously; there the expression is applied to the mysterious "servant of YHWH" (Isa 42:1; 49:3; 52:13; 53:11) or to Israel as a whole (Isa 41:8, 9; 42:19; 44:1, 2, 21; 45:4). Certain passages about Israel relate the expression to the election of a people (Isa 41:8; 44:1-2) as occurs in Haggai, but here it deals with the election of one person. Hence we conclude that the election carries with it the mission that person will have to serve the people of God (cf. Jer 1:5 although this reference does not speak explicitly of election).

The comparison of a person to a seal, even though it be the seal of YHWH, seems less clear. A seal authenticates documents; it is a signature (cf. 1 Kings 21:8). It is tied around the neck with a cord (cf. Gen 38:18) or worn as a ring (cf. Jer 22:24). The passage in Jeremiah is illuminating although there are differing aspects: there the reference is to a signet ring that is removed in order to be thrown away; Zerubbabel, on the other hand, is chosen and destined to be like a signet ring. Will this be the announcement of the restoration of the Davidic dynasty in the person of Zerubbabel? It is strange that there is no mention of his condition as a Davidic prince. The important aspect is the power of YHWH, not that of a monarch or a dynasty. Whether the restoration of the monarch is affirmed or not, one thing is without question: the role of Zerubbabel is a dependent one. He will be only a sign of the absolute and universal power of YHWH.

Given the growth of revelation, we Christians have learned to see some things in a different way. Our acceptance of the living God and our son- and daughtership "in spirit and in truth" (John 4:24) are no longer conditioned by a determinate place or by the Temple built there (cf. John 4:21). Because the Word was made flesh and dwelt among us (cf. John 1:14) it is our profound conviction that the Father has blessed us definitively in Christ, but also that God's blessing is something better than good crops or success in our plans and projects. The blessing is a spiritual one. "Blessed be the God and Father of our Lord Jesus Christ, who has blessed us in Christ with every spiritual blessing in the heavenly places" (Eph 1:3). It is not a matter of God's being absent from what is happening here and now. It is simply that, since Christ's coming, we can no longer consider what happens to us as reward or punishment, an unequivocal sign of divine blessing or absence. "If for this life only we have hoped in Christ, we are of all people most to be pitied" (1 Cor 15:19).

BIBLIOGRAPHY

Wolff, Hans-Walter. *Haggai, A Commentary.* Minneapolis: Augsburg, 1988.

Zechariah

Pablo R. Andiñach

FIRST READING

Characteristics of the Book

In the book of the prophet Zechariah we can distinguish two sections that suggest two different epochs and two distinct authors. Chapters 1–8 contain a cycle of eight visions and some interpolated oracles. The style of the utterances reminds one of the prophecies of Ezekiel who was so enamored of filling his texts with images, metaphors, and symbols. During the night Zechariah receives visions in which he is accompanied by an angel who walks with him explaining the meaning of these visions by means of rhetorical questions and in the form of dialogue. This angel has a special relationship with the heavenly spheres and is presented as the one who mediates between the prophet and the reality of God. The priest Joshua and the figure of Zerubbabel are praised in various ways and under a variety of symbols. The reconstruction of the Temple is the relevant historical fact underlying the entire prophetic production of these chapters. Because of literary characteristics and some historical facts present in these eight chapters it is clear that they are more ancient than the following ones. We can surmise that they were probably proclaimed and written down by the prophet Zechariah himself.

Chapters 9–14 are a collection of texts in which one can distinguish a variety of oracles and sayings. They are in a style totally different from that of the first section. In chs. 9–14 Zechariah is not mentioned; there are no visions, nor do we find the figure of the angel. There is no mention of the date on which the message was proclaimed and, what is perhaps the most significant, the reconstruction of the Temple is not mentioned, nor are Joshua and Zerubbabel who were central figures in the initial chapters. At the same time this section is subdivided into two parts (chs. 9–11 and 12–14) signaled by the text itself in its introductory titles at 9:1 and 12:1. Each of these parts develops the message of the previous one, bears new elements for reflection, and offers its own theological overtones.

Chapters 9–14 (sometimes called "second Zechariah") are historically posterior to the former chapters and were perhaps produced by more than a single author. We do not have any information on them; they remain unknown to us and at the moment it is impossible to reconstruct either the lives or the works of these authors. It is probably for that reason that the final editing of the book attributed chs. 9–14 to the first Zechariah and organized the material into the two parts already mentioned. An attentive reading of the final work allows us to see that these sections are a re-reading of the older texts in chs. 1–8. This re-reading modifies the meaning of those chapters and relocates them so that they may be more relevant to the new social and religious context. On the other hand there are certain themes present in both parts of the book that manifest a certain semantic continuity. We find that in both parts there is the proclamation that Jerusalem will be a place where all nations can worship YHWH (1:12-16; 9:8-12); the call to a universal kingdom open to all peoples (8:20-23; 14:16-19) is another common theme, as is the purifying action of God in the community (5:1-11; 13:1-2).

The time is long overdue for restoration and the joy of again dwelling in the land. Feasts for the reestablishment of worship and sacrifices on Mount Zion need to be celebrated. The generation of those who have returned from exile has died and now there are other challenges and problems confronting the community in need of a prophetic word. In addition to these challenges and needs the faith of Israel seeks new theological horizons that would allow it to understand the reality and action of its God. The book of Zechariah, with its dense language and somewhat enigmatic images, is a response to that search.

Historical and Literary Context

The Historical Situation and Epoch

Zechariah, whose name means "YHWH remembered," proclaimed his message between the years 520 and 518 B.C.E. (cf. 1:1, 7; 7:1). It is probable that the time of his prophetic activity had already ended by the time of the inauguration of the Second Temple in the year 515 B.C.E. (cf. Ezra 6:15) since he is not mentioned in connection with that event. But the preaching and the message are contextually appropriate to the reconstruction of the Temple and the rededication of the people's life. Our prophet is mentioned in Ezra 5:1 and 6:14; in both cases he is in close relationship with his companion-prophet, Haggai, and with the reconstruction of the house of God. In Neh 12:16 there is also mention of a priest named Zechariah from the house of Iddo, but it is more difficult to ascertain whether or not it is a reference to the same prophet although zeal for the Temple and for the judgment of God are consonant with being a prophet-priest and thus strengthens the possible linkage.

It is not difficult to point out the general context of chs. 1–8, but situating the second part of the book is more complex. For the first part we must bear in mind that when the Persians under the leadership of Cyrus conquered the neo-Babylonian empire in 539 B.C.E. they established a new policy with respect to conquered peoples. Cyrus would concede them the possibility of returning to their land and reestablishing their religious authorities and local cults. In general his attitude was one of tolerance toward the captured peoples and in this way he was able to create a unified sector amenable to his policies and government among the societies of conquered peoples. This becomes clear in texts such as Ezra 1:2; 5:13; 6:14. Due to the burdensome task of receiving the returnees to the community Cyrus will even provide funds for the reconstruction and restitution of Temple utensils sacked by Nebuchadnezzar (2 Kings 25:13-17). But time passes and in the wake of a series of problems—principally the opposition of the Samaritans (Ezra 4:1-5)—the first euphoria of return and the expectations of an immediate political restitution grow cold. This is reflected in the delays surrounding the reconstruction of the Temple as well as in a certain anxiety among the people that this goal would never be accomplished. The joy of return is soon filled with dark storm clouds in the face of a harsh reality to be lived. The people dwell in the land but are not able to enjoy its fruits; they harvest the produce but it is collected for the Persian royalty; they may offer worship to their God but their bodies and possessions are enslaved. Texts such as Neh 9:36 give sufficient testimony to this situation. Depression and lack of a clear future begin to dominate the lives of the people. The political situation tends to be perpetuated and there are no signs on the horizon of a possible change or restoration of well-being and justice. It is in this social and theological context that the preaching of Zech 1:8 is situated. His preferred themes, like those of the prophet Haggai, are the reconstruction of the Temple and the announcement of hope in the definitive action of God when God will do justice and rescue the people.

Chapters 9–14 offer us some principal historical references that help locate them in time. The mention of the Greeks (9:13) seems to indicate an epoch later than the military expeditions of Alexander the Great (332 B.C.E.) although we cannot affirm this date with absolute certainty. On the other hand in Zech 10:10-11 Egypt and Assyria are named as places where the people had been held captive, a fact that would establish the date in the eighth and seventh centuries B.C.E. when Assyria still existed as a political entity. However we must bear in mind that common practice often used these names to refer to the Hellenic governors of the third century, governors whose political thrones were established as much in Mesopotamia as in the Nile delta.

Another perspective presents itself to the observer of certain theological and literary facts. (1) The material of chs. 9–14 does not possess a solid literary or thematic structure. It has meaning when it is read as a continuation of chs. 1–8. (2) Under literary analysis the material appears more like a collection of sayings and oracles from different authors than a homogeneous work. (3) The strong theological emphasis on eschatology and on the day of YHWH as a battle God will fight on behalf of Israel is a recurring theme in the prophetic books following the Exile. This emphasis locates the material and links it with the apocalyptic literature that will develop at the beginning of the third century B.C.E. On the basis of this information we can affirm that the epoch described in chs. 9–14 lasts from the end of the fourth century and extends to the end of the third century B.C.E. This period in Judah is characterized by a lengthy political stability under the dominion of the Lagid family in Egypt. A second characteristic is a certain theological tranquility during which the voices of the prophets become silent while Messianic expectations and apocalyptic language become the form of expression of a new social and theological reality.

Its Place in the Canon

Zechariah is part of the book of twelve prophets, sometimes called "minor prophets" to distinguish them from the "major prophets." This distinction merely reflects the length of the books and ought not to be considered a judgment of the value of their content. The book of Zechariah is placed before that of the prophet Malachi, the last in the list of prophetic books, although again the placement in the listing does not correspond to the chronological order of the prophetic utterances. If indeed the ministry of Zechariah developed in a later epoch it is likewise true that the books of Obadiah, Joel, and Jonah were without doubt written after Zechariah 1–8. The book of Daniel is even later than Zechariah 9–14.

It is interesting to observe that Zech 9:1 and 12:1 begin with the same words as Mal 1:1 ("An oracle. Word of YHWH . . .") in conformity with the series of three units, each with certain thematic connections. This makes one think that Malachi may originally have been the final part of Zechariah 1–8 and that at a later time chs. 9–14 could have been interpolated. That process would have ended when it was separated from the principal body of the work of Zechariah in order to create a collection of twelve books, a number particularly appreciated by the Jewish system of symbols. Nevertheless at the present we have no textual witness to confirm this possibility. [See also the article "Prophetism and Prophets."]

Zechariah in the Hebrew and Christian Scriptures

There is a remembrance of the "former prophets" at the beginning of the book (1:4-6; see also 7:7). Zechariah is interested in explaining that his message is in line with that of the classical prophets within the faith of Israel. This linkage is clear in numerous texts. Zechariah invites the people to flee from Babylon (2:10; cf. Isa 48:20; Jer 50:8; 51:6). In a vision our prophet sees a man measuring the city in order to rebuild it (2:5-6); cf. Ezekiel 40–42; Jer 31:38-39). In another text he announces the coming of a servant called "the Branch" (3:8; 6:12; cf. Jer 23:5). Like Joel he announces the eschatological battle in which all nations will be gathered together and destroyed by YHWH (14:2a; cf. Joel 3:2, 12). A fountain will pour out water with which the people are to purify themselves (13:1; cf. Ezekiel 47). There are also numerous references to the Law (3:7 reminds one of Deuteronomy 6); the promise of rain is remembered in Zechariah 10:1 (cf. Deuteronomy 11:14). Nor are the psalms far from Zechariah's mind (9:10; cf. Ps 72:8). He refers also to the book of Job (3:1-2; cf. Job 1:6a). All of these references are part of Zechariah's program of reconstruction. Alongside his use of the Temple theme the prophet considers it necessary to find himself again within the faith and historical memory of the people.

Writers of the Christian Scriptures found inspiration in various passages of our prophet, but it is the author of Revelation who, more than the others, used the material of Zechariah. We find the recurring use of the image of horses (1:8; 6:2-3; cf. Rev 6:2-4; 19:11). The measurement of the city is present in both texts (2:5; cf. Rev 11:1). The enemy who puts Joshua to the test (3:1) is also found in Revelation (12:10). Zechariah 4:11 presents olive trees and lampstand that appear again in Rev 11:4. Light and water are other referents in both texts (14:7-8; cf. Rev 21:25; 22:1, 5). Other allusions are less clear and perhaps merely the consequence of the fact that both texts share the same linguistic and literary universe from which they extract their images.

Zechariah is cited in the gospels as well, in parts central to the life of Jesus. In the description of Jesus' entry into Jerusalem, Matt 21:5 and John 12:5 literally cite Zechariah 9:9, locating Jesus' ministry within the context of an idea of a peaceful and nonviolent messiah. On the occasion of the purchase of a field for thirty pieces of silver Matt 27:9 cites Zech 11:12-13. However, the evangelist is mistaken—probably because he was citing from memory—and gives credit to Jeremiah (32:6-15) as the author of the citation. At the time of Jesus' death on the cross, when a soldier drove a lance into his side, John 19:37 cites Zech 12:10 to recall the prophetic image of piercing. In addition to these, Eph 4:25 cites Zech 8:16 ("speak the truth to one another . . .") in the context of an exhortation as to how a new person in Christ is to act. Finally Zech 14:5 is mentioned in 1 Thess 3:13.

Zechariah in the Apostolic Fathers

Zechariah is a work cited by the Apostolic Fathers although during this period there are no significant helps to understanding the book. We find the earliest mention of Zechariah in the final exhortation of the *Didache* (26.7) where there is a quotation from Zech 14:5 alluding to the saved who will accompany the Lord on the final day. This same text is cited in the Christian Scriptures (1 Thess 3:13). In the *Letter of Barnabas* 5.12 (the intention is to carry on a dispute with second-century rabbinic Judaism) the image of the sheep who wounds the shepherd (Zech 13:6-7) is used to point to the Jewish people who rejected Christ. In *Barn.* 2.8 a free rendition of Zech 8:17 is used within the framework of an admonition to go beyond the ritual sacrifices proper to Judaism and to live an upright life rejecting evil and lying. Allusions can be found in the *Shepherd of Hermas* although these are fragmentary (cf. the use of colors in *Herm. Vis.* 1.10 and Zech 1:8; 6:2).

Use in the Christian Liturgy

In contrast to the appreciation the Christian Scriptures show toward the text of Zechariah one gets the impression that actual Christian liturgy scarcely reads this prophet. In the ecumenical lectionary there are three Sundays on which texts from Zechariah are used. For Palm Sunday and the seventh Sunday of the Church year there is a reading from Zech 9:9-10. On the fifth Sunday, Zech 12:7-10 is read, alluding to the protection God gives to the people. It is evident that only the messianic text has been retained and that the Sunday liturgy seems to favor simply a general knowledge of the book's message.

The Message of Zechariah

The book of Zechariah in its actual form bears a message that upon attentive reading reveals a clear and direct statement. Basically it says to us that if humanity should lose hope in its ability to build a better and more just world it ought to remember that the word and action of God will be there to create new hope and new visions for the future, visions that will make justice and peace possible.

To the optimistic euphoria of chs. 1–8 based on the reconstruction of the Temple and the installation of new leadership within the community chs. 9–14 are now added and reveal a different spirit. These chapters severely criticize the leadership of Jerusalem as one that cannot be trusted and should be destroyed (11:8). Historical experience no longer allows the support of the prestigious descendants of Joshua and Zerubbabel who govern from the Temple. Now useless shepherds are called forth (10:3; 11:3, 17). But the message is not only one of disaster and criticism; there will come a messiah, humble and poor, not to govern as did the wicked shepherds but to rule with justice and proclaim peace (9:9-10). Chapters 9–11 have updated the text and made it relevant to the current situation.

Chapters 12–14 advance the message of Zechariah even more. The people have been unfaithful once again. There is idolatry and despair within the heart of the community (13:2). There are prophets who have lied to the people (13:3-6). The message must therefore deal with the purification and reconsecration of the people. At the end the Day of YHWH is announced (ch. 14). On that day all will be gathered together and God alone will be the one who saves and rescues the faithful ones. The injustice and oppression to which they have been subjected is not the last word of God for God's own people nor for humanity. In unified and comprehensible language Zechariah invites us to trust that justice will have the final victory.

SECOND READING

1:1-6

These verses serve as introduction to 1:7–8:23. We are told that it was in the second year of the reign of Darius (518 B.C.E.) that the word of YHWH was directed to Zechariah. The prophet begins by reminding the people of the rebellion of their parents. Although the ancient prophets had called them to conversion their parents would not listen to the voice of the prophets. Three elements particularly stand out in these lines: (1) Zechariah urges the people not to reject the word of God as had their ancestors. (2) The prophet positions himself firmly within the tradition of the great spokespersons of YHWH. His message takes up again the message and spirit of those pre-exilic prophets who sought to correct the people. (3) It becomes clear that the tragedy of the exile is that it is the product of the attitude of the people who would not hear God's message (v. 6).

The Visions

From 1:7 to 6:15 there follows a series of eight visions and some interpolated oracles. These are scenes seen during the night in which the distinct elements receive symbolic value. The intervention of YHWH is always mediated through angels, one of whom speaks with Zechariah to create times of personal contact, guide him, and explain to him the distinct situation in which the prophet is involved. The fourth vision (3:1-7) has a literary structure distinct from the rest, making one suppose that it did not form part of the original group of visions. Letting that one rest for the moment, we see that the remaining seven are organized concentrically: visions 1 and 2 (1:7–2:4) as well as 6 and 7 (5:5–6:8) declare punishment for the foreigners and condemn idolatry. Visions 3 (2:5-9) and 5 (5:1-4) proclaim the reconstruction and purification of the people. Finally the central vision (4:1-10) situates the lampstand and the two anointed ones (Zerubbabel and Joshua) as the craftsmen of that reconstruction. To this plan we immediately add the fourth vision of the apparel of Joshua (3:1-10) so as to emphasize his presence and exalt the priestly role in both the present and the future of Israel. It is probable that 6:11 may have been modified in the excitement of the moment (see below).

The Horsemen (1:7-17)

After a distinctive introduction making one think that 1:1-6 could have been incorporated into this text in a second editing we find the first vision of the series. It presents the horsemen who traverse the earth as emissaries of God to observe and indicate that all is at peace. They refer to the tranquility the empire enjoys at the time of Darius. But Jerusalem and Judah continue to be humiliated since, as the author points out, YHWH has been irritated with this people for the past seventy years. This time covers the period since the destruction of the Temple (587 B.C.E.) during which there was no possibility of reestablishing sacrifices or worshiping YHWH as had been done during the time of the First Temple. The mention of those seventy years places us in the year 517 B.C.E., two years before the reinauguration of the Second Temple in Jerusalem. The angel who acts as interlocutor cries out to YHWH for compassion toward the city and the land, and the response of God is unexpected: beginning at that moment God will again have pity on the people. God's irritation against Jerusalem is changed into irritation toward those neighboring nations of Judah who probably have not suffered the total destruction of their places of worship. The vision closes with an announcement that the Temple will be rebuilt and Jerusalem will again be YHWH's chosen city. God has not forgotten God's people.

The Horns (1:18-21)

The following vision presents four horns. Horns are a symbol of power in all cultures of the ancient East: a political power that rises above the people and subjugates them. In the case of Judah, Israel, and Jerusalem the horns specifically refer to those nations that dispersed them (such as the Chaldeans of the sixth century B.C.E. who deported the chosen people to Babylon) or they refer to the Persians or the Greeks who used the policy of transplanting whole sectors of the subjugated population to avert uprisings against themselves (Joel 3:2, 6). The horns have a second meaning: the four points of the altar where sacrifices of foreign nations were burnt were also called "horns." These were sculpted and the corners were raised so that they created the sensation of representing the horns of a calf, a popular god in all the cultures of the ancient biblical world. The mention of "horns" can be applied as much to the nations that dispersed Israel as to the idolatry the parents practiced that made them lose their way as a chosen nation (1:4-5). In both cases the task of the four blacksmiths is to destroy those who humiliated Israel.

The Measurer (2:1-5)

The third vision consists of a man with a measuring tape (Ezekiel 40–42). He measures the city in order to rebuild it. It is a vision of blessing and hope announcing that the tasks are already being realized and that soon the city will again be inhabited as it was before. It will overflow with people and cattle and this time YHWH will be like a wall of fire that will defend it from all danger.

The Summons to Return (2:6-13)

This oracle is a call to return to the land of Judah. It is directed to the Jews who live in Babylon who for one reason or another have not returned from exile. It is established that they are there because YHWH has scattered them throughout the earth. This theological mode of understanding exile interprets it as the result of the people's sins. However this does not seem to contradict the necessary condemnation of injustice and aggression of the nations who conquered the Israelites and stripped them of their land. Now that the time has come for them to be reunited it is YHWH who calls them to return to the land of their ancestors.

It is highly probable that some Jews lacked confidence that the city and the Temple would be rebuilt or that worship and community would again be established in Judah. The situation of the first returnees was not good economically and perhaps not from the political point of view either. For many Jews already established on the banks of the Euphrates for over two generations it was more secure to remain in exile than to return to the insecurity of a land that now had new rulers and in which there was much work to be done. The announcement of the universality of the power of YHWH ("many nations shall join themselves to the LORD," 2:11) necessarily points to the devaluing of the power of the Babylonian gods who competed with the God of the Jews for the dominion of the universe. The Babylonian religion had within its pantheon gods and heroes of greater prestige than had the Israelites and it is probable that many Jews felt seduced by the ideological strength of the religion of the empire. Once again therefore the power and exclusive choice of Jerusalem as their place of residency and worship needed to be affirmed.

Joshua the Priest (3:1-7)

The purpose of this vision is exalt the figure of the priest Joshua. Its literary and linguistic structure is different from the rest of the visions, a fact that makes one believe that it was not an integral part of the original text but was added later. In this vision Joshua presents himself before an angel of the Lord who represents the heavenly tribunal. Next to Joshua is the adversary who accuses him, Satan (Job 1:6). But the angel of YHWH curbs Satan, not allowing him to continue accusing Joshua and announcing once more the chosen status of Jerusalem. This indicates that the accusation probably had to do with the role of Jerusalem in the new Israel. Perhaps there were groups that, since Babylon, had questioned the city's status as a holy place or the true seat of the Temple. Satan would be representing those who doubted the possibility of the reconstruction and, on the theological level, the validity of YHWH's choice.

The time of judgment has ended for Israel and a new time of prosperity was being unveiled. This change can be seen in the apparel of the priest: it is said that Joshua dressed in dirty clothes representing the disgraces of the past and judgment on the people. Now those clothes are changed for festive robes that symbolize the beginning of this new time. Likewise Joshua places a tiara on his head symbolizing the high priesthood for which he has been chosen. Finally it is affirmed that Joshua will be the one who rules the Temple; i.e., he will be the high priest. If in the first verses we witness a dispute among those who believed in the reconstruction and those who doubted it, now we see a mounting tension among distinct local sectors who in the face of the imminent reconstruction of the Temple and the initiation of sacrifices as well as the celebration of religious feasts begin to evaluate even the possibility of inheriting priestly succession.

The Servant Named "Branch" (3:8-10)

After showing support to Joshua as high priest the prophet announces there is the intent to involve a servant named "Branch" (cf. 6:12). In Jer 23:5-6 he is referred to as a descendant of David who will reign with justice and protect Israel and Judah. We find the same suggestions in Isa 4:2. The name is symbolic in the sense that although the dynasty of David had been uprooted it will now again sprout forth as a special envoy from God. The name "Branch" may also conceal a criticism of a certain spurious leadership that was proposing to be the power during the new period of reconstruction. In that sense supporting "Branch" established the continuity of the dynasty of David as the only genuine lineage. This is confirmed later in 6:12-13 when there is a parallel drawn with Solomon whose building of the Temple demonstrated royal power.

It is difficult to identify "Branch" as a person. It may be a name applied to Zerubbabel that for some reason or other—perhaps his death—never came into effect. Doubtless the semantic linkage was more direct when the message was first proclaimed, but his being mentioned reinforces the idea that YHWH must provide a king who will rebuild the Temple and govern justly. Although at first we do not know whether "Branch" was a specific person or an ideal model it does become evident that in the development of the faith of Israel "Branch" became the image of the awaited messiah.

The oracle continues the comparison of the reconstructed Temple to a rock. This rock possesses eight eyes. Eyes have always been symbols of the justice of God since through them YHWH sees and knows all and therefore judges rightly. Although disputes arose in the heart of Judaism throughout the diaspora as well as in Judah itself, the recognition of the justice and equity of YHWH helps to establish a criterion for the resolution of such conflicts. And although we can imagine a theological application of the term "will of God" we must recognize that the survival of Jewish identity depended on the ability to define clearly a leadership and a place in which to establish a Temple.

The Lampstand and the Olives (4:1-14)

This vision has as its goal to strengthen the image of Joshua and Zerubbabel. The lampstand with seven lights is flanked by two olive trees. The same text explains that the seven lamps represent the eyes of YHWH that scan the earth leaving nothing outside their scope, thus making it possible for God to work justly. The olive trees represent the two anointed ones: Joshua by reason of being the high priest and Zerubbabel who bears the royal anointing of political power. Their placement next to God grants them the highest standing and central role in the new Jewish community.

There are three references to Zerubbabel within the vision. On the one hand it is said that YHWH speaks directly to him without the mediation of the prophet. It is the promise of the Spirit of God that will give strength to Zerubbabel to carry forward the divine plan. Then there is an enigmatic reference to a mountain that will be leveled and made smooth before Zerubbabel. This may refer to Mount Gerizim which rose up as a threat of idolatry from Samaria. One might also think of the debris left from the building of the Temple under the direction of Zerubbabel. Finally the word may be directed to Zechariah who was announcing that just as the work of the Temple was begun by Zerubbabel's laying of the cement blocks, so it would be Zerubbabel who would direct the work to its finish.

The Flying Scroll (5:2-4)

The scroll is of enormous dimensions, almost as large as the facade of the Temple (1 Kings 6:3). It is the symbol of the Law of God that goes out in search of the thief and the blasphemer to punish them. It is a manner of purifying the people on the eve of the inauguration of the Temple. In this vision the denunciation of the sins of the people is attached to God's will to reconstitute a healthy community.

The Woman and Evil (5:5-11)

This vision continues the theme of the purification of the community. It is an opportunity to confront the theme of idolatry. The prophet sees a bushel basket (the measuring barrel) within which there is a woman called "wickedness," which in Hebrew is also a word for idolatry. Then there appear two winged women who lift the bushel container into the air and take it to Shinar (Babylon) where it will be deposited. There are two symbols here: first that idolatry is returned to Babylon, its place of origin. The returnees to Jerusalem probably brought some of Babylon's idolatrous or syncretic forms of worship with them. The new community must terminate this seduction from Babylonian cults and leave behind all non-Yahwist practices of religiosity. It is pointed out that in Babylon a temple will be built and this woman will be deposited there. In the context of their own construction of a Temple in Jerusalem the post-exilic community states that all idolatry will be returned to the place of its origin and no religious form contrary to the faith of Israel will be allowed to remain in Jerusalem.

Second, it is significant that wickedness is represented by a woman. This may be consonant with the reference to the condemnation of some particular Babylonian goddess or simply of foreign women who came with the exiled to live in Jerusalem. In both cases the woman who is in the basket represents the threat of loss of the Jewish people's cultural and religious identity. It is well known that the leaders of the post-exilic community had an aversion toward foreign women, considering them the font of deviations and evil (Mal 2:11-12; Ezra 9–10). The linkage of evil with the feminine in itself does not seem to be the intention of the text, given the fact that it is women who return her to Babylon. Their being winged is a symbol of their holiness.

The Chariots (6:1-8)

This vision is parallel to the first (1:7-17). In this case the chariots come forth to punish the nations, but here only one nation is mentioned, the country to the north. This alludes to Babylon, newly identified with evil and idolatry as in the former vision (Jer 3:18; 4:6; 6:1, 22; Ezek 38:6, 15; Joel 2:20). Such has been its influence in the exiled community that every symbol of punishment is concentrated on that city. We must remember that even during the time of the restoration a Jewish community survived in Babylon. It was this community that was repeatedly invited to return to Jerusalem, but the apparent failure of the invitation is probably due to the fact that the community was established in Babylon and that Jerusalem itself was not enjoying the expected stability and prosperity.

The Coronation of Joshua (6:9-15)

The cycle of visions (1:7–6:8) closes with this oracle in which the priest Joshua is crowned (6:11). The text is confusing. It gives the impression that the coronation was really destined for Zerubbabel but that, on second thought, the name of the beneficiary of the royal sign was changed for that of the high priest. This happened for two probable reasons: first because the priesthood of Jerusalem grew stronger and took power at the second stage of the restoration, and second because Zerubbabel, who had been the great hero of the reconstruction of the Temple, mysteriously disappeared from history, nor was any explanation of this happening ever offered. His name could have been replaced in order to deflect attention from his memory and focus it on the new leader.

The actual text says that a crown ought to be made with the gold and silver donated by certain people about whom we have no further information, nor are their names to be found in the rest of the Hebrew Scriptures. That crown must be used to crown Joshua and announce to him that God would send a man named "Branch" who would be responsible for the rebuilding of the Temple (3:8). There is also a call to those still far away in Babylon to return to Jerusalem. All these events will be a sign that YHWH is still interested in the people and sends them messages through the prophets.

The Fast (7:1-3)

This text describes what happened two years after the visions, in the fourth year of Darius (520 B.C.E.). A question arises as to whether or not it was necessary to keep such a fast since the reconstruction of the Temple was so imminent. The fast of the fifth month recalled for the people the destruction of the Temple (2 Kings 25:8). The answer will be found in the discussion of 8:18-19 in relation to the other feasts of lamentation that were converted into celebrations of joy.

Sins of the Past (7:4-14)

The text continues with the theme of the fast. Now the fast of the seventh month recalling the death of Gedaliah, governor during the time of the exile, is added to the other fasts (2 Kings 25:25). The seventy years refer to the time from the destruction of the Temple by Nebuchadnezzar to the present. Zechariah declares that the fast they proclaim is an infringement since it has not been done in agreement with God's demand for justice, God's claims on the people. Then he reverts to the memory of the ancient prophets who preached to the parents of the present Israelites the need for justice and love. The reference to doing justice to the widow, the orphan, the alien, and the poor seems to indicate that in the new post-exilic Israel there already were practices of injustice and intolerance toward those sectors of society.

Salvation for Jerusalem (8:1-17)

This extensive oracle balances the accusations of the previous one. If in that oracle sins and the punishment YHWH had inflicted on the people were recalled, now in this oracle the central aim is to announce the blessing of God for that same people. It proclaims that Jerusalem will again become a faithful city and the mountain will be a holy place where YHWH dwells. In contrast to the desolation of the abandoned and semi-destroyed city Zechariah announces that it will again be inhabited and that in its plazas there will again be old people and children. Verse 7 announces the return to Jerusalem of those who were still dwelling in Babylon. On this occasion the return will not be the gift of the Persian kings but rather the direct fruit of the action of YHWH. It is God alone who is the bestower of such a blessing and the return is interpreted as an act of YHWH that saves those who are in exile. The return from exile has not been fulfilled in its entirety and the prophet announces the will of YHWH to reunite the whole people around the Temple, but this reunion is not only an act of historical restoration: it is a way of actualizing an ancient pact. Verse 8 recalls the pact at Shechem (Joshua 24) in which the people freely chose to be the people of YHWH in exchange for being faithful to God's words and laws.

From v. 9 the text continues in prose. The blessing now is centered on the Temple itself. Its reconstruction has concentrated all life's meaning on that point and we catch a glimpse of a glorious era ahead. It is announced that just as at the beginning of the reconstruction there had been very hard times for the people, now YHWH is promoting peace upon Israel. The imposing presence of the Temple inaugurates a new era. There follow special images of a time of prosperity: the flowering of the vines, the rain. The change of fortune from curse to blessing is a reality already visible. Indeed, salvation is near at hand. Verses 14-15 declare it to be so. The end of the oracle again insists on the ethical demands for being the people of God. Truth and justice are the basis of a correct relationship with God.

The Answer Concerning the Fast (8:18-19)

This brief oracle responds to the question posed in 7:3 about expanding the number of fasts to the four that recall the disgraces of the destruction of Jerusalem and the beginning of the exile. The fast of the tenth month commemorated the beginning of the siege of the city while the fast of the fourth month remembered the opening of a breach in the wall that would occasion the defeat of the king and his sons (2 Kings 1–4). The reconstruction of the Temple supposes a change of attitude in the people. No longer will it be necessary to fast for the disgraces of the past; rather this is a time of joy in which to celebrate the action of God who today blesses and restores God's people. Toward the end of the oracle there is a return to the ethical theme: truth and peace will be the signs that identify the new community founded around the Second Temple.

The Salvation That is Near at Hand (8:20-23)

Zechariah 1–8, called "First Zechariah," ends with this oracle. It is a word of salvation that accents the supranational character of the God of Israel. It announces that other nations will discover the value of YHWH-God and they will want to come to Jerusalem in order to worship YHWH and be part of the chosen people. Perhaps we ought to deduce from this that they will come to Jerusalem to ask pardon for their sins and faults, especially those against the Israelites. No longer will there be disdain or mockery; to the contrary, strangers will want to integrate with the people of

God. They will be from all nations and tongues, and the actualization of such a community will be a judgment on the happenings at the tower of Babel (Gen 11:1-9). If there the nations were scattered on the basis of their languages, here they will be called together by YHWH into God's new Temple.

"First Zechariah" concludes its message by announcing that God has a plan for all nations. Israel will be the people summoning others to come and the Temple will be the place to which people will come from all parts of the world. The dirge of destruction has been changed into a word of hope.

An Oracle Against the Nations (9:1-10)

A new title ("An Oracle. Word of YHWH . . .") marks the initiation of the second part of this book. We are in a different era and in the presence of a different author (see above). This part begins with an oracle directed against the nations that surround Israel. They will be destroyed and will suffer tragedy while YHWH will take possession of the Temple to protect it. This mention of the protection of the Temple and the restraints on the oppressors (v. 8) reveals the fact that the nations now being judged have already worked against Israel, perhaps forming an alliance with the foreign armies in the time of the occupation. It is necessary to observe, however, that Israel never conquered its neighbors in the violent way the text suggests. This makes one think that the oracle is reflecting upon the imminent action of a foreign army—perhaps the invasion of Alexander in the year 333 B.C.E.—that left the nations in ruins and now is being interpreted by the prophet as an act of divine justice to compensate for the injustices received from them.

The Humble Messiah (9:9-10)

After announcing the defeat of the foreign nations that at various times assaulted Israel the text goes on to declare a time of glory for Zion and Jerusalem. In an era when the monarchy had disappeared and the priestly institution had monopolized the little sphere of political power still remaining to the community in the Hellenistic period the proclamation of a monarch could be understood as a criticism of those sectors that held control of the Temple or controlled political relationships with the centralized power. This becomes increasingly true if we look at the character of the approaching king as described in the text: justice and peace will be the outstanding signs of his personality and mission. His arrival will be marked by a climate of humility and austerity that were not common among the ancient kings or perhaps among the religious leaders as well. This contrasts with the historical monarchy in which pageantry and excess were part of the demonstration of power (1 Kings 10:14-29; Jer 17:25; 22:4). The king who comes is described as one mounted on an ass, an allusion to an ancient custom also present in the anointing of Solomon (1 Kings 1:33, 38), a way in which kings expressed their humility before the people (Judg 10:4).

This king who is to come has to restore a kingdom of peace, signified by the eradication of the horns of Ephraim (a symbol of power and idolatry) and the horses of Jerusalem (military power). The armaments of war will be destroyed and thus the nations will enjoy a perpetual peace. In describing the kingdom the prophecy presupposes some ideal borders that might cover a territory extending from the Mediterranean to the Dead Sea and from the Euphrates to the southern desert. Not in any part of its history, however, has Israel ever possessed such a territory.

In this oracle the messianic perspective flows throughout the text. Those who hear it long for the promised peace; they hope for the justice this king is going to bring. It gives a word of hope in a time when there is no real possibility of reinstating the Davidic monarchy and when the former euphoria of the return and the reconstruction of the Temple are already far from memory. In one sense the new Temple has been transformed into a new center of power foreign to the interests of the people, and for that reason it attracts the attention of the prophet and his community of hearers. In this setting it is difficult to determine if the text is referring to one person in particular or if it was in principle understood as messianic. We can assert that as we approach the second and first centuries B.C.E. it was interpreted in the messianic sense.

The Call of the Captives (9:11-17)

This text does not seem to acknowledge the contradiction between the former oracle dealing with a peaceful Messiah and these words inciting to war and vengeance. The proclamation develops in two phases. On the one hand it is a call to prisoners. The cistern used as a prison cannot be merely a metaphor since we know that it was not unusual to use cisterns in this way. Because of this general use of the cistern it is difficult to determine which nation is being referred to here. It is probable that we are in the presence of a captivity produced by some incident with the Lagids who held the throne in Egypt and who from the time of the dissolution of the empire of Alexander the Great (319 B.C.E.) governed Israel as well (i.e., until 200 B.C.E.).

On the other hand this oracle also bears an invitation to the war against Javan (v. 13), a way of referring to Greece. The relationship with Greece was always to the disadvantage of Israel, and longstanding wounds were often recalled and coupled with the desire for revenge (Joel 3:7). Greece was known for its commerce in slaves (Ezek 27:13) and for the alliance it made with enemies of Israel. But even supposing some type of bellicose capacity on the part of Judah a war of such magnitude surpassed all real possibility.

The Fortunetellers (10:1-2)

This passage criticizes those who practice fortunetelling or lie to the people. This practice had often been condemned (Lev 19:31; 20:6; 1 Sam 15:23; Mal 3:5), and it was considered an activity foreign to the Yahwist tradition (Ezek 21:26). The theme of the sheep without a shepherd presages the criticism in 11:4a. To oppose having recourse to the diviners the prophet speaks of confidence in God.

Against the Shepherds (10:3–11:3)

There is sharp criticism of the shepherds in this oracle, a way of addressing the leaders of the community. The text announces the return of those who are in Egypt and Assyria, the classical names designating the territories of the Lagids and Seleucids. The crossing of the Red Sea recalls the Exodus story; now the emptying of the Nile is an added dimension. As on the first occasion, here also glorious acts are described that will laud the action of YHWH toward the people. The oracle closes with a new denunciation against the shepherds, proclaiming that they will be replaced. This opens the way to the following passage.

The Two Staffs (11:4-17)

This oracle bitterly criticizes the leaders of the community. These are probably the priests, although the image of a shepherd in ancient literature is more often linked to kings (Jer 23:1-3; Ezekiel 34). With the exception of David (Ps 78:70-72) and curiously enough of a foreign king like Cyrus (Isa 44:28) the image of a shepherd in the Hebrew Scriptures is used only to criticize the actions of kings (Jer 2:8; 10:21). YHWH alone is the true shepherd (Psalm 23; Isa 40:11). Nevertheless we are encouraged by the positive image that announces new shepherds who will be designated by God to replace those who have betrayed God's commands (Jer 3:15; Ezek 34:23).

The text uses the image of sheep to denounce the sale of slaves by the leaders of the people. This business is done with such impunity that they even thank God for the wealth obtained thereby. The prophet is also denouncing the spurious and inhuman origin of the wealth of the ruling class. He speaks of three shepherds whose prestige has fallen to such depths that they have been easily eliminated. We do not know to whom he refers although they are doubtless religious leaders and those made rich because of their involvement in the commerce of slaves.

The narrative presents several symbolic acts. The staffs have a particular meaning. They bear the names "Favor" and "Unity." The staff is the instrument the shepherd uses to guide the sheep. The breaking of the staff named "Favor" indicates the rupture of a relationship between Israel and the adjacent nations. These relationships were supported theologically by the universal love of the God of Israel but that love was exploited to justify commerce in slaves. To break with the religious legitimacy of these relationships clearly revealed the cruel character of the business carried on by the leaders. Then the prophet presents his second symbolic gesture: demanding his salary. Thirty shekels of silver are offered as the equivalent of the value of a slave (Exod 21:32). If the value is also that of one of the youths sold to a foreigner the symbol has an even more bitter meaning: they want to pay the prophet of YHWH with money coming from the marketing of slaves. The meager pay and the suspicious origin of that money give clear evidence of the bad will of the leaders and their rejection of the word of God expressed by God's prophet.

Then there follows the story of the broken staff named "Unity." We are perhaps witnessing the definitive separation between Judah and Samaria, but the effects of the broken message manifest the internal division hidden deep within the community of Israel. It is probable that Samaria was linked to the commerce in slaves or that it was a crossroads for other nations engaged in that commerce. The announcement of the division between Judah and Samaria reveals, in the mind of the prophet, that unity cannot be sustained on the bases of injustice and cruelty.

The oracle ends with the pronouncement of a last act of condemnation and punishment for the leaders who have not known how to protect the people. YHWH will designate a shepherd, but not for blessing; rather this shepherd will bring about the ruin of their businesses and their lives.

The Purification of Jerusalem (12:1–13)

As in ch. 9:1 the inclusion of a new title ("An Oracle. Word of YHWH . . .") signals the beginning of a new section that will then end the book. This section is more eschatological in nature and uses a mode of speech that is distant from the more direct, historical approach. The intent is always to speak about what will happen "on that day . . . ," a formula that is used seventeen times and with which the book ends (14:21b).

This first part ought to be understood as an oracle spoken in the context of a situation of social and political immobility. Israel is convinced that there is nothing that can possibly change its fortune. In some sense these texts are the product of the despair into which the people had fallen. Out of that context an announcement is made that there will be a battle in which YHWH will personally save and deliver Israel from oppression. The direct action of God will be focused on defending Judah and Jerusalem which, in this period, had been transformed into the only recognizable political entity in existence.

The mention of "the one whom they have pierced" (12:10) is enigmatic and difficult to resolve. The text supposes the death of a beloved person at the hands of unknown assassins. The lamentation will be great and compared to that for a firstborn child. Verse 11 alludes to the plains of Megiddo, which makes one think of the death of King Josiah (2 Kings 23:29). That king had carried on a purifying religious reform in Jerusalem, doing away with idols and disallowing the pagan altars (2 Kings 22–23). Nevertheless the reference in Zechariah is without doubt to a contemporary person, probably some leader who had intended a reform in the style of the one initiated by Josiah. Given the fact that this situation of idolatry was repeated in the time of our prophet it is possible that both histories were linked to each other. The fact that the allusion to this death ends with the proclamation of the opening of a fountain in Jerusalem for the purpose of purification from sin and uncleanness indicates that perhaps this person's death—or his life—was understood by his people only after a time, and after he had been killed. We cannot speculate any further on this but it is certain that this material served the evangelist John (19:37) in linking this image to that of Christ on the cross, pierced as he was by the Roman lance.

This section closes with a hard word directed toward the prophets. During those times prophecy had fallen into discredit for three reasons: first because many no longer believed in the prophecies since they saw that the promises of prosperity and freedom spoken through the classical prophets had not been fulfilled; second because the leadership (the shepherds of 11:4-17) were doubtless closely linked to the prophetic institution and such was their repute that parents would rather kill their sons who intended to prophesy than allow them to join the ranks of the prophets (13:3); finally the same text (13:2) warns us about the relationship between the prophets and idolatry. It is probable that the influence of Hellenistic culture that would be so strong in the centuries to come was already infiltrating the ranks of the prophets who, according to the Greek style, were interpreting oracles coming from gods foreign to the Yahwist faith. This condemnation and near prohibition of prophecy will have its counterpart within prophetic literature in the words of Joel 2:28-32 when he announces a time in which there will again be those who prophesy through the action of the Spirit of God, thus breaking the limits of traditional prophecy.

A New Oracle Against the Shepherd (13:7-9)

The criticism of the leaders of the community continues (see 10:3; 11:3, 8, 17). On this occasion there is mention of "the man who is my associate" (v. 7), probably the high priest or the principal political figure of the moment. All the weight of the accusation and the sword are left to fall upon these two persons, the shepherd and the political figure, but this time the punishment is set in an eschatological framework and is a call to a judgment in which only a third part of the people will be saved and recognize YHWH as their God while the remaining two-thirds will die. It supposes, then, a time when idolatry and misery abound in the midst of the community and when the leaders count on the support of an important part of the population. Within that context the oracle tries to exalt the value of the rescued third part since they will be the faithful remnant from that moment on. Those who survive will be tested like gold and silver and, when purified in this way, will come to be the new representatives of the people of God.

The End of Time (14:1-21)

The final chapter is the most eschatological of the entire book. It is a succession of images and symbols we are not always able to identify but that indicate that the prophet's closing message might establish the manner in which YHWH will do the final work. In vv. 1-5 the nations are called together to fight against Jerusalem, take it and destroy it. Not only is the destruction of houses announced but also violence toward women and the capturing of half of the population as a superlative form of aggression. But it is a misleading summons: in Jerusalem they will be annihilated by the action of YHWH in person. We have already found this in Ezekiel 38–39 and Joel 3:9-14. A judgment will fall upon the Jews, but not all will die. YHWH, it will be announced, will take a stand on the Mount of Olives—that is, opposite the Temple—and from there will receive the half who will be rescued. In a description full of symbolic images we are told that the Mount of Olives will be divided in two and the saved will flee through that valley forming a column of the holy ones of YHWH. There follows a description of a fountain of living water (water from the spring that was used for purification rites) that, gushing forth from the Temple, will cover the earth. All of this will happen on an ultimate day when the distinction between day and night will have disappeared and the hills will be leveled. Only God knows those sets of happenings, and when God acts tranquility will dwell in Jerusalem. Three oracles have combined a word of punishment for those who have abandoned themselves to idols with a word of exaltation and hope for the faithful.

In vv. 12-21 the first announcement is of the destruction of the enemies of Jerusalem, followed by the worship of those who survive. They are the Jews of the diaspora who will not be destroyed together with the villages they inhabit and who, from that moment, will have the possibility of returning freely to Jerusalem. Verses 17-19 warn about the calamities those will suffer who, having had the opportunity of worshiping in Jerusalem, decided not to do so. They will carry off the wealth of the nations and will grow fat on the splendor of the city, a subtle though concrete allusion to the wealth that was historically taken from the work of the people for the succeeding foreign governors. At first terror will run rampant among the nations and even the animals will suffer from the plagues and from death. But once this time of war has passed the survivors of the diaspora will be returned to YHWH and will go up to worship on the feast of Booths. This was the most popular of the feasts of pilgrimage to Jerusalem and celebrated the enthronement of YHWH in the Temple. This proclamation presupposes a criticism of certain sectors of the diaspora who had probably fallen into syncretism or idolatry. Worship on the feast of Booths is linked to recognition of the exclusive nature of the sanctuary in Jerusalem and of its God. The final message is that YHWH did not forget the people and gathers them together in order to save them and give them peace and well-being.

BIBLIOGRAPHY

Petersen, David L. *Haggai and Zechariah 1–8: A Commentary.* Philadelphia: Westminster, 1984.

____. *Zechariah 9–14 and Malachi: A Commentary.* Louisville: Westminster/John Knox, 1995.

Redditt, Paul L. *Haggai, Zechariah and Malachi.* Grand Rapids: Eerdmans, 1995.

Malachi

Adrian Graffy

FIRST READING

General Character of the Book

The most striking feature of the book of Malachi is its use of a unique literary form, often called the "disputation." After the title in 1:1 six disputations follow, and the book ends with two appendices in 3:22-24 (4:4-6). Each disputation begins with a statement of YHWH or of the prophet. The people then ask for clarification of this statement. The clarification is provided. Into this didactic structure the prophet inserts words of reproof and judgment due to current abuses, or words of encouragement, even love.

Contexts for Interpretation

Original Historical Context

The material in the book of Malachi quite clearly dates from after the rebuilding of the Second Temple in 515 B.C.E. Initial enthusiasm has waned; abuses have crept in. The term used for "governor" in 1:8 *(pehah)* also points to the Persian period (cf. Hag 1:1). The same abuses reprimanded by Malachi are tackled later by Nehemiah. Priests are neglectful of their duties of offering sacrifice and instructing the people (1:6–2:9). Nehemiah 13:28-31 shows awareness of priestly abuses. Marriages to pagan wives are denounced in Mal 2:10-16 and also in Neh 13:23-27. Malachi 3:6-12 makes it clear that tithes are not being paid. A similar situation is apparent in Neh 13:10-13. A further indication of a date in the middle of the fifth century B.C.E. may be seen in the reference to the devastation of Edom in 1:4. The Edomites were under pressure from Arab tribes at this time. The initial enthusiasm of the return from exile and the rebuilding has given way to an atmosphere of tiredness and boredom. Is it really worth the effort to follow the ways of the Lord? (3:14).

Use in the New Testament

Both Paul in the letter to the Romans and the three synoptic evangelists place texts from Malachi in new contexts. In Romans 9 Paul writes about God's free choice of Israel, a choice not due to human merit. It is in this context that in Rom 9:13 he quotes Mal 1:2-3, "I have loved Jacob, but I have hated Esau." Paul demonstrates that just as God is not constrained by Esau's being the firstborn to make him heir to the promise, likewise God is not bound to limit salvation to the descendants of Abraham. God's freedom is demonstrated in the NT by the offer of salvation to both Jew and Gentile. Paul relocates Malachi's statement about divine freedom in the context of the offer of salvation in Christ.

Texts from Malachi concerning the coming messenger are used by the synoptic evangelists in reference to John the Baptist. Mark 1:2 quotes Mal 3:1 and Isa 40:3 to describe the mission of John. Matthew (3:3) and Luke (3:4) omit the Malachi text, quoting from Isaiah 40 alone. Mark transposes the prophet's reference to one who prepares for the day of the Lord to John's mission of preparation for the messiah. The prophetic longing is fulfilled in an unexpected way. Mark in quoting from Malachi points to the eschatological dimension of Jesus' coming to proclaim God's reign.

Matthew and Luke use Mal 3:1 later in their gospels. After the messengers from the imprisoned John the Baptist have left him Jesus speaks warmly to the people about John as the messenger who prepares the way (Matt 11:10 and Luke 7:27). These two evangelists have Jesus himself acknowledge John's eschatological mission.

The apparent identification of the messenger as Elijah in Mal 3:23 allows Jesus in Matt 11:14 to describe John as the returning Elijah. Once again the messenger of God becomes the forerunner of the messiah. Similarly when the disciples question Jesus after his transfiguration about the return of Elijah before the end Jesus affirms that Elijah has come and "they did to him whatever they pleased" (Mark 9:13 and Matt 17:12).

Though Luke omits the disciples' question after the transfiguration he too identifies John the Baptist as the one who is to come before the day of the Lord in fulfillment of Mal 3:23. In Luke 1:17 the words attributed to Gabriel state that John will go before the Lord "with the spirit and power of Elijah . . . to turn the hearts of parents to their children." Luke points to the vital nature of the mission of John before the end comes. Words in the Benedictus echo the same idea (Luke 1:76). Each evangelist thus sees the words of Malachi as fulfilled in the crucial contribution of John the Baptist in preparing for the coming of the messiah.

In Mal 3:2 the Lord comes to the Temple to bring judgment and purification. It is worth considering whether this text has influenced the traditions of the cleansing of the Temple by Jesus found in Mark 11:15-19 par. and John 2:13-22.

Use in the Patristic Writings

The Didache (ch. 14) concludes its words on the Eucharist with an adaptation of Mal 1:11 and 14: "'to offer me a clean sacrifice in every place and time, because I am a great king,' says the Lord, 'and my name is held in wonder among the nations.'" The writer makes it clear that the pure sacrifice is the Eucharist. The unacceptable sacrifices and pure offerings in Mal 1:11-12 are identified by Justin (*Dialogue with Trypho* chs. 28 and 41) with Jewish worship and the Christian Eucharist. For Justin the text refers to the rejection of Judaism and heralds the Christian Eucharist. Irenaeus (*Adv. Haer.* 4.17.5-6) takes a similar line in his use of Mal 1:10-11. For Irenaeus too the end of Jewish sacrifices is foreseen in this text. Cyril of Jerusalem (*Catechesis* 18.25) uses Mal 1:10-11 to speak of the rejection of the "church" of Judea and its replacement by the "catholic" Church.

A further significant example of Christian interpretation of Malachi can be seen in patristic commentaries on 3:1. For Jerome (*In Mal.* 3) the messenger of v. 1a is John the Baptist and the Lord coming to the Temple is the Savior. Cyril of Jerusalem (*Catechesis* 15.2) saw in the same verse references to the two comings of Christ. "The Lord" entering his Temple is a reference to the first coming while the arrival of the "messenger of the covenant" is considered to refer to the second coming, due probably to the mention of judgment in 3:3 and 5.

Use in the Liturgy

Texts from the prophet Malachi are used as readings at Mass on two Sundays. Malachi 1:14–2:2, 8-10 is read on the 31st Sunday of Year A. It is unfortunate that the structure of the disputation has been disregarded. On the 33rd Sunday of Year C 3:19-20, a small fragment of the sixth disputation, is read. Malachi 3:13-20 is read on the Thursday of week 37 in Year 1. Division of the text in the Office of Readings in the Liturgy of the Hours (Friday of week 28) also disregards the structure of Malachi. Malachi 3:1-4 is the first reading on the feast of the Presentation of the Lord and vv. 23-24 are added to this for the first reading on December 23.

In the pre-Vatican II liturgy there was more scope for using prophetic texts in the sung parts of the Mass. Malachi 1:11 appeared in the Tract of the Votive Mass of the Blessed Sacrament. Malachi 2:6 was used in the Introit for the feast of St. Irenaeus (June 28). Traces of such use are still found in the reformed liturgy. The entrance antiphon at Mass on the Solemnity of the Epiphany and the invitatory antiphon for the Liturgy of the Hours on the feast of the Presentation owe something to Mal 3:1. The second responsory for the Office of Readings on the feast of St. Dominic (August 8) uses Mal 2:6.

The most prominent use of a text of Malachi (1:11) now comes in the third Eucharistic Prayer:

"From age to age you gather a people to yourself, so that from east to west a perfect offering may be made to the glory of your name."

Use Through History

Malachi 1:11 was used extensively at the Council of Trent in reference to the Eucharist (*Doctrine on the Most Holy Sacrifice of the Mass,* ch. 1). The same verse is quoted by Vatican II (*Lumen Gentium* 17) in the context of the missionary activity of the Church. The building up of the Church is brought about above all by the Eucharist. In its *Decree on Priestly Ministry* Vatican II uses Mal 2:7 in a footnote to speak of the priest's role in communicating the message of God (*Presbyterorum Ordinis* 4). The *Catechism of the Catholic Church* (2643) refers to the Eucharist in words taken from Mal 1:11.

One significant and well-known use of Malachi is in Handel's oratorio, *The Messiah.* In Part One the recitative "Thus saith the Lord" combines words from Hag 2:6-7 with part of Mal 3:1. There follows the aria "But who may abide the day of his coming?" which uses Mal 3:2 with the exception of the words "like fullers' soap." Finally the chorus "And he shall purify" uses part of the text of Mal 3:3.

SECOND READING

Title: 1:1

The book of Malachi begins in a rather abrupt, "staccato" fashion. The opening words are similar to Zech 9:1 and 12:1, which introduce sections of the book of Zechariah. Here, however, they introduce something new, the disputations of Malachi. The people now dwelling in Judah are addressed as "Israel," for they are the remnant of the people of God. *Malʾaki* has been treated as a personal name in Jewish and Christian usage but the sense of the word is simply "my messenger." It is interesting to note that the prophet Haggai is called *malʾak* ("messenger") in Hag 1:13. The name of our prophet is not known.

First Disputation: I Love You: 1:2-5

The opening statement of YHWH in this first disputation is "I love you." Although it is frequently translated in the past tense, the usual meaning of the perfect tense of verbs such as *ʾahab* is present. Other declarations of God's present love can be found in Jer 31:3 and Isa 43:4, in both cases reassuring the exiles. The words here are trumpeted out, breaking God's silence. The people then ask for clarification: "How do you love us?" The answer delivered by the prophet is that God chose to love Jacob and to hate Esau. Israel's hatred for the Edomites, the traditional descendants of Esau, is justified by the complaint that Edom took advantage of the destruction of Judah. (Read Ps 137:7; Ezek 35:5, and Obadiah 10-11.) Our text focuses on what seems like a recent devastation of Edom seen as proof of God's hatred. The language echoes the threats against Edom in Isa 34:13 and Ezek 35:3. The eerie image of jackals among ruins occurs again in Jer 9:11; 10:22, and 49:33. The prophet goes on to assert that God will frustrate any attempt by Edom to rebuild (v. 4). New names for Edom emphasize God's anger at Edom's fratricidal wickedness. What happens to Edom will enlighten Israel. As often in Ezekiel, historical processes allow people to know God. The people will exclaim: "God is great over Israel." The Hebrew expression *meʿal le* means "over" or "above," as in Gen 1:7 and Ezek 1:25. It is God's love for Jacob/Israel that is stressed here, not God's power beyond Israel.

Second Disputation: You, O Priests, Despise My Name: 1:6–2:9

It is the priests who are arraigned in this extended disputation. Once again YHWH delivers an opening statement. Instead of giving the honor and fear due to God as "father" and "master" the priests "despise my name." YHWH will intervene to rehabilitate the divine name. (Compare Ezek 36:22.) The priests ask twice for clarification (vv. 6-7) and attention centers on sacrificial worship. Prophets of earlier times had found fault with the people's sacrifices because they neglected their social responsibilities (cf. Isa 1:11-17). This prophet finds fault because the priests have come to treat the rules of worship with disdain, offering unacceptable animals, the blind, the lame, and the sick. (Compare Lev 22:17-30.) Such animals would never be offered to the Persian governor (v. 8). The prophet's voice intrudes briefly in v. 9 as he encourages repentance, and YHWH expresses frustration, urging that the doors of the Temple be closed to prevent such worship (v. 10). Prophets had often proclaimed God's displeasure at sacrifices (Amos 5:22 and Jer 14:12) but hope had been expressed that God would find them acceptable once Jerusalem and its Temple had been rebuilt (Ezek 20:40-41, 43:27). Such hopes, it seems, were illusory.

In Mal 1:11 the horizon is dramatically broadened. "From the rising of the sun to its setting" may have both the temporal sense of "all day long" and the spatial sense "from east to west." Similarly expansive is the same expression in Ps 113:3. But what is the prophet's meaning? Does he have in mind the worship of the Diaspora Jews living in far-off Babylon and Egypt? Or does he here express the audacious idea that the true God receives worship from pagans and that they, unlike the priests, honor God's name? Do we have here something even more amazing than the book of Jonah's tale of God's acceptance of the repentance of the Assyrians? Or does the prophet's concern for the purity of Jewish ritual make such an idea unlikely?

Verses 12-13 repeat the accusations against the priests, stressing the contrast between what happens "among the nations" and what is done at the heart of Judaism where the priests consider sacrificial worship a chore. Verse 14 ridicules the hypocrisy of the person vowing such an offering, the "cheat" who keeps the healthy males of the flock back and offers a blemished victim. Finally, respect for the name of God among the nations is again mentioned. YHWH declares: "I am a great king." (Compare Isa 43:15 and 44:6.) While Ps 99:3 invites the nations to revere the name of YHWH our prophet seems to declare that they do so already: it is outside Israel that the name is revered.

A further accusation is brought against the priests in Mal 2:1-9: their instruction of the people has led many astray (v. 8). YHWH echoes the first injunction, that glory should be given to the divine name. (Compare 2:2 with 1:6. NSRV's "glory" and "honor" are both *kabod* in Hebrew.) YHWH threatens to curse the priests and their blessings. The blessings the priests impart, such as the priestly blessing of Aaron in Num 6:22-27, become curses. Since priests do not respect YHWH's instruction, YHWH renders their benedictions useless. Since they belittle their priesthood, their priesthood is belittled. The rebuke is extended to the whole priestly line. (It is unnecessary to change *zera*ʿ [line] to *zero*ʿ [arm].) The prophet declares that God will defile the priests with the dung of the offerings. (Compare Ezekiel's concern for purity in Ezek 4:12-15.)

The priests have become useless both in bringing blessing and making offerings. YHWH concludes: "I will put you out of my presence." The "covenant with Levi" is then recalled. Both the priests and the Levites, generally presented as subordinate to the priests, would seem to be included here but the prophet does not speak explicitly of "Levites." In Num 25:12-13 God promises a "covenant of peace" to the priest Phinehas. Here too the focus is on the ancient, worthy beginnings of priesthood. In similar vein to Malachi, Nehemiah on his reforming mission in Jerusalem laments the defilement of the priesthood and of the "covenant of the priests and the Levites" (Neh 13:29). Priesthood according to the covenant called for fear and awe. There is here another echo of YHWH's initial complaint that no honor or fear was being shown by the priests (1:6). Malachi 2:6-7 presents the ideal of priestly teaching. With the *torah* of truth on his lips the priest should instruct in the ways of goodness, bringing many back from evil. The priest, indeed, is the messenger (*malʾak* again) of the Lord of hosts. Despite their high vocation these priests have made their *torah* a stumbling block and corrupted the covenant. Like the priests addressed centuries before by Hosea they have rejected knowledge and forgotten the *torah* of God (Hos 4:6). As they brought down others, they too shall be brought down (v. 9). The descendants of Levi, entrusted with teaching and offering sacrifice (Deut 33:10), have been found wanting in both tasks.

Third Disputation: Judah has Acted Treacherously by Marrying the Daughter of a Foreign God: 2:10-16

The third disputation begins with an extended opening statement from the prophet (vv. 10-13). The people's request for clarification comes only in v. 14. The prophet makes the point by rhetorical questions that God is father of all the people and that there should be trust among them. Another covenant has been profaned, "the covenant of our ancestors." Judah has committed abominations: the sanctuary has been profaned and the "daughters of foreign gods" have been taken as wives. It is implied that the taking of pagan wives has defiled the holy city, just as for Ezek 44:7 the presence of uncircumcised foreigners had profaned the sanctuary. While Abraham, Moses, and David may have had foreign wives Deut 7:3-4 forbids marriages with pagans due to the danger of worship of other gods. (Recall Solomon in 1 Kings 11:1-13.) Nehemiah and Ezra will campaign against mixed marriages and confirm our prophet's stance. (See Neh 13:23-27 and Ezra 9–10.) The prophet continues: "May the LORD cut off from the tents of Jacob anyone who does this—any to witness or answer, or to bring an offering to the LORD of hosts." The man who rejects his wife to marry a foreign woman will be deprived of the support of the community. A second accusation from the prophet highlights the hypocrisy of such men who come in tears to the Temple and bewail God's disfavor (v. 13). The people's request for clarification allows the prophet to spell out the fundamental charge: YHWH is witness (Gen 31:50) that you have dealt treacherously with the wife of your youth. (Contrast Prov 5:18.) The crucial point is the ill-treatment of the woman who was "your companion" (Hebrew "bound to you"), your "wife by covenant." While God's covenant love remains (1:2-5), both priests (2:8) and husbands (2:10 and 14) have broken God-given covenants.

Verse 15 defies satisfactory translation and most versions emend the Hebrew text. A literal translation of the unemended Hebrew might give the best sense: "No one has done this who has a trace of the spirit. And what does this one seek?—godly offspring." Verse 16 also has its problems. The statement "I hate divorce" found in many translations relies on a correction of the Hebrew text but it fits the context, unlike the ancient LXX and Vulgate translations that seem to sanction divorce. The text is clearly opposed to the dismissal of the "wife of your youth." This is finally described as "covering one's garment with violence," "parading one's violence." (Compare Ps 73:6.) Such action is clearly declared to be an act of violence against women. Divorce is not only a betrayal of trust.

Fourth Disputation: You have Wearied the LORD with Your Words: 2:17–3:5

The fourth disputation, like the third, begins with an opening statement from the prophet that echoes Isa 43:24 ("you have wearied me with your iniquities"). The request for clarification follows and the prophet replies with words, or thoughts, of the people. "Why do the wicked prosper?" The same issue is treated at length in Psalms 37 and 73. Goodness does not seem to bring any reward. The people call on the God of justice to intervene. God's response is first to send a messenger *(malʾak).* This messenger, like *malʾaki* the prophet, is unnamed, and this one is even more mysterious. God promised in Exod 23:20 to send a messenger before the Israelites to guard them on their way. This messenger is to "prepare the way before me," to prepare the way for YHWH's coming. His role is like that of the prophet in Isa 40:3 who prepares the way before the liberating intervention of God at the end of the exile. It is tempting to consider this *malʾak* as identical with the prophet Malachi. But as with the servant in Second Isaiah it is better not to identify and limit what the prophet has left open.

The Lord's coming is to be sudden. Like the God who returns to the rebuilt Temple in Ezek 43:1-9, the Lord comes to purify. The Lord is further described as *malʾak berit* (messenger of the covenant). This possibly is a reference to the "covenant with Levi" (2:4-5), for the Lord is about to purify the sons of Levi (3:3). But it could refer to the covenant between God and Israel, renewed as the Lord comes to purify the Temple. Malachi would thus take up one of the great themes of restoration prophecy. (Compare Jer 31:31-34; Ezek 37:26; and Isa 54:10.)

Use of *malʾak* in Malachi:

1:1 The word of the Lord to Israel by Malachi
2:7 he (the priest) is the messenger of the Lord of hosts
3:1a See, I am sending my messenger . . .
3:1b The messenger of the covenant . . . is coming

The longed-for coming presents an unexpected challenge (v. 2). Two images of purification are used now as illustrations. The Lord will be like a "refiner's fire." The image of refining metal is used commonly of God's judgment. (See Jer 9:7; Isa 48:10; and Zech 13:9.) The Lord is also "like fullers' soap." In the work of cleansing the Lord will imitate the fuller who treads and beats the cloth to clean and soften it. The purification Israel could not achieve by washing itself (Jer 2:22) will be achieved by the coming Lord. This arrival is dramatic, but the Lord comes to purify, not to destroy.

Verse 3 gives prominence to the priestly ideal of "purification" found frequently in Leviticus (e.g., 13:6 and 16:19). It is the "descendants of Levi," all those involved in priestly and levitical duties, who will be purified. Once purified they will make offerings "in righteousness." The shameful disregard for cultic laws described in 1:6-14 will come to an end. The offerings of Judah and Jerusalem will now please YHWH.

The final verse of this disputation satisfies the lament of the people in 2:17 fully, for YHWH comes in judgment against all kinds of evildoers. Sorcery had been outlawed in both the Covenant Code (Exod 22:18) and the Deuteronomic Code (Deut 18:10). The judgment against adulterers reaffirms the prophet's defense of faithfulness between husband and wife (2:11, 14). The Holiness Code in Leviticus contains a prohibition against swearing in YHWH's name in order to deceive (Lev 19:12). In his great speech against the Temple Jeremiah includes some of these misdemeanors (Jer 7:9). The final groups of wrongdoers reflect the social legislation of the Deuteronomic Code. (See Deuteronomy 24, especially vv. 14, 17.) Those who oppress the hired worker, the widows, the orphans and the foreigners are to be judged. All these, like the priests (1:6), show no fear of the Lord.

Fifth Disputation: Return to Me and I Will Return to You: 3:6-12

Like the first and second disputations, the fifth also begins with words of YHWH. God has not changed toward God's people. This brings to mind God's first words in Malachi: God still loves this people. Despite their inadequacies the people have survived. Like Jeremiah (2:5; 7:25-26; 11:7-8; 16:11) Malachi recalls a long history of sin. Zechariah too refers to the sins of the ancestors and has an identical appeal to repentance (Zech 1:2-3). The expected request for clarification comes and the prophet makes the accusation specific. The people are cheating God. How?—in the matter of tithes and offerings. The Pentateuch's legislation regarding tithes is complex. (See Leviticus 27, Numbers 18, Deuteronomy 14.) A tenth of produce and income was to be paid by the Israelites for the support of the priests and Levites. This was to be considered an offering to the Lord. That tithing was not properly observed is confirmed by the reforming efforts of Nehemiah. (Read Neh 10:36-39; 12:44; 13:10-12.) The people are under God's curse for they cheat God of tithes and offerings.

The solution God promises is to bring the whole tithe to God's own storehouse. The book of Nehemiah also mentions the storehouse for tithes and offerings (especially 10:38). God invites the people to impose this kind of test to see if God will not shower gifts upon them. In Haggai 1 blessings on land and produce are promised if the Temple is rebuilt. In similar fashion on delivery of the tithes God promises to open the windows of heaven to pour down abundant blessing. These "windows" are described as opening for the torrential rain of the flood in Gen 7:11 and to end the drought in 2 Kings 7:2, 19. YHWH will rebuke "the devourer," presumably the locust. (Joel 1:2-12 describes an invasion of locusts and in v. 4 provides a classification of them according to their methods of devastation.) At such transformation surrounding nations will see the people of Judah as blessed by God. Delight replaces despair as in the Zion poem in Isaiah 62 (especially v. 4). Ezekiel's vision of the land as a new Eden to the amazement of the nations becomes a reality. (See Ezek 36:29-30, 35-36.)

Sixth Disputation: Your Words Against Me have Grown Harsh: 3:13–4:3

The final disputation also begins with an opening statement from YHWH. The God who began by saying "I love you" now expresses hurt at the people's harsh accusations. This is similar to the prophet's opening statement in the third disputation (2:17): "you have wearied the LORD with your words." The request for clarification follows as usual. Like the psalmist in Ps 73:13 the people consider it useless to serve God. What is the point, they ask, of keeping God's commands? The fulfillment of such commands, Deuteronomy promised, would lead to prosperity. (See the repeated promises in Deuteronomy 11.) These people have their doubts. Why should they walk "as mourners" before the Lord? The expression suggests darkness and loss, and is used of misery (Job 30:28), illness (Ps 38:6), and persecution (Pss 42:9 and 43:2). These individuals consider keeping the Law a similarly mournful duty. They are envious of the wicked who prosper. (Read Ps 73:3 and Jer 12:1.)

Verse 16 makes clear that those who revered the Lord were concerned at such sayings. (The LXX by contrast has: "this is what those who feared the Lord said.") A tender concern is shown by God, who heeds and understands. God is presented as recognizing the problem people have at seeing the prosperity of the wicked. God is intent on caring for God's own and punishing the wicked. A book of remembrance is written to record those who fear God. In Ps 69:28 the psalmist prays that his enemies be blotted out from the book of life. The same image of God's book had appeared in Exod 32:32-33, and in Dan 7:10 the books are opened in Daniel's vision of the coming judgment. (See also Rev 20:12.) The emphasis in Malachi at this point is less on judgment and more on God's care for those who fear God. They will be God's "possession," an expression used often of God's choice of the covenant people (Exod 19:5; Deut 7:6; 14:2; 26:18; Ps 135:4). On the day God is making (an expression that reappears in Ps 118:24 in a tone of rejoicing) those who fear God will be treated with compassion as God's children. Psalm 103:13 makes a similar point. A father knows that "children who serve" need understanding. (Compare Matt 21:28-30.) Such treatment will allow people to see how God really behaves and refute the false notions of vv. 14-15.

The fate of the wicked and the virtuous becomes clearer in 3:19-21 (which the Septuagint, Vulgate, and English translations give as 4:1-3). The tone changes abruptly to speak of the burning up of the wicked. Punishment by fire is threatened by other prophets, as seen in Zeph 1:18 and Obadiah 18, but Malachi uses the more specific image of the (baker's) oven found again in the destruction of the enemies in Ps 21:9. The arrogant and the evildoers, those who had been thought to prosper (v. 15), become stubble for the fire (cf. Isa 5:24.). By contrast, for those who fear YHWH's name the sun of justice rises. Psalm 84:11 speaks of YHWH as sun and shield for the virtuous, but this description of the sun with healing in its rays (or wings) is unique to Malachi (through reminiscent of the images of the sun-god in surrounding cultures). The tenderness of the caring God appears again and jubilation is evident in the virtuous leaping like calves from the stall. The healing of God produced a similar effect on the lame in Isa 35:6. The final note of this disputation is the trampling of the wicked. Like the haughty king of Tyre punished in Ezek 28:18, they too are trampled underfoot.

Appendices: 4:4-6

The last verses contain two additions concerning Moses and Elijah. A later legalist focuses attention on the *torah,* not that of the priests but the *torah* of Moses. With language clearly reminiscent of Deuteronomy, v. 22 urges remembrance of all the statutes and ordinances. Verses 23-24 in their turn recall Elijah. These verses give an answer to the question of the identity of the *mal'ak* who precedes the Lord in 3:1a. This is the earliest text to witness to speculation about Elijah's return before the end, also found in Sir 48:10. The second part of v. 23 is identical with Joel 2:31. One has the impression that the final editor of the Twelve Prophets has a hand here. Elijah's role is to bring reconciliation between fathers and children "so that I will not come and strike the land with a curse." There is an eschatological urgency as Malachi, and the Twelve Prophets, come to an end.

BIBLIOGRAPHY

Coggins, Richard J. *Haggai, Zechariah, Malachi.* Old Testament Guides. Sheffield: JSOT Press, 1987.

Mitchell, Hinckley G., John M. P. Smith, and Julius A. Bewer. *Haggai, Zechariah, Malachi and Jonah.* ICC. Edinburgh: T & T Clark, 1912.

Petersen, David L. *Zechariah 9–14 and Malachi: A Commentary.* OTL. London: SCM Press, 1995.

The Intertestamental Period and the Rise of Apocalyptic

Paul D. Hanson

Introduction

This article will trace the history of the period from the end of the Davidic monarchy in 586 B.C.E. to the birth of Christianity in the Roman Period. The perspective from which it is written is theological, and more specifically Christian. While honoring the integrity of the OT in its own right as witness to God's revelation and the authenticity of the Jewish faith, both before the era of Christ and later in the form of rabbinic Judaism, the author will emphasize themes that are particularly important as background for understanding Christian origins.

Since the NT goes to great lengths to relate the life of Jesus to biblical prophecy we shall follow the development of prophetic tradition and the various ways in which it was interpreted, some more historical in orientation, some more apocalyptic. Similarly, since the title Messiah played a central role in early efforts to explain the significance of Jesus' life we shall pay attention to the ways in which the Jewish concept of God's anointed one *(māshīaḥ)* was applied by various communities during the period covered. Because general concepts like "messiah" and "kingdom of God" and specific terms like "Servant of the Lord" and "Son of Man" did not develop in a vacuum we shall explain the social, political, and historical conditions within which the faith of Israel developed.

The result of our survey will be this: When we come to the NT we shall possess sufficient background knowledge to grasp the theological significance of the early Church's claim that Jesus Christ fulfilled the Law and the prophets and inaugurated the long-awaited reign of God. We will be able to notice lines of continuity, points of revision, cases of choice between distinct alternatives, and new departures. Our enhanced understanding of the long, often intriguing history leading up to the life of our Lord will magnify the miracle of the event occurring in the "fullness of time," the appearance of Immanuel, God with us, dwelling among humans not as one "to be served, but to serve," even dying for those he loved with the obedience and faithfulness of the righteous Servant of the Lord.

A Critical Turning Point: The Exile

The exile, the period of time from 586 to 538 B.C.E. in which the leadership of the Jewish community and a substantial part of the general population were held captive in Babylon, represents a critical threshold in biblical history. After this period nothing was quite the same in the ways Jews viewed the world, expressed their faith, organized their institutions, and cultivated their values and customs.

The impact of the events of this time were of such magnitude as to force change. The Temple had been robbed and destroyed by the armies of a foreign pantheon. How could claims to YHWH's special status be upheld? The land of Israel, promised to the ancestors and then given to the Hebrews, had been occupied by the Babylonians. What did this imply for the notion of God's election of a chosen people? The Davidic king had been humiliated and dragged off as a prisoner. Could the notion of God's eternal covenant with David be salvaged?

The foundation-shaking trauma inflicted by the Babylonian conquest was followed by more subtle, long-range, and hence wearing influences. The people were forced to "sing the Lord's song in a foreign land" (Psalm 137). They had to intone their hymns to God's superior power and infinite grace in the shadows of the majestic pagan temples and under the din of the processions of the pagan gods who were the patrons of the victorious armies. No doubt large numbers were tempted to follow the course of those who drew the rather logical conclusion that events had overtaken and left YHWH behind. Turn to Tammuz (Ezek 8:14), reach out to the Queen of Heaven (Jer 44:17), join the procession of Bel or Nebo (Isa 46:1); victory belongs to the gods of the new imperial power!

Because of the historical orientation of biblical faith, events, even disastrous events, could not be ignored; sense had to be made of them in relation to divine will. In the case of the Babylonian conquest the faithful came to recognize not YHWH's defeat but the downfall of a false conception of God. Perhaps the simplest way to describe the impact of the exile on biblical faith is to say that it wielded a death blow to Israel's flirtation with imperial religion.

Imperial religion equates deity with the power and interests of the throne. It ties religion to the cause of the elite. It justifies the exploitation of common folk on the basis of claims of a special relationship between deity and powerful rulers grounded in the order of creation. In the period leading up to the crisis the Jewish community was being pulled by the opposing forces of imperial religion and traditional religious beliefs and values preserved from the tribal period by the prophets. On the one side were the "ways of the king" (1 Sam 8:11), enforcing the claims of the king over the lives of his subjects, on the other the "laws of Moses," embodying God's compassion in evenhanded administration of justice on behalf of all people.

What was destroyed in the fires of the Babylonian destruction? The answer depended on one's perspective. From the point of view of ancient Near Eastern royal ideology it could be concluded that YHWH, the divine patron of the House of David, had been discredited. From the point of view of Temple ideology it could be argued that YHWH, whose House had been destroyed, was proven weaker than Marduk. On the other hand, from the point of view of the ancestral Yahwistic faith preserved by the prophets, what had been discredited was an idolatrous perversion of belief that had substituted false security resting on human institutions for true security resting on trust in God. Over a century earlier Isaiah had announced (Isa 30:15-16):

> For thus said the LORD GOD, the Holy one of Israel:
> In returning and rest you shall be saved;
> in quietness and in trust shall be your strength.
> But you refused and said,
> "No! We will flee upon horses"—
> therefore you shall flee!
> and, "We will ride upon swift steeds"—
> therefore your pursuers shall be swift!

From the perspective of the relativization of all institutions before the only Reality worthy of trust, Second Isaiah interpreted the recent calamity as a chastening event (Isa 42:24):

> Who gave up Jacob to the spoiler,
> and Israel to the robbers?
> Was it not the LORD, against whom we have sinned,
> in whose ways they would not walk,
> and whose law they would not obey?

Second Isaiah stands squarely in the tradition of classical prophecy in this interpretation. From one vantage point alone could sense be made out of human experience, whether on the personal or national level: namely from the vantage point of faith in the one God before whom all other claimants are declared idols. The changes that entered biblical faith during the Second Temple Period (515 B.C.E.–70 C.E.) cannot be understood apart from the exilic community's reaffirmation of this first-commandment principle.

Already in the message of Second Isaiah one can recognize the chastening effects of the rigorous scrutiny of prophetic faith within the context of the ambiguities of human experience. Those aspects of tradition that pass the test of faith are commended ("remember the former things," 46:9; cf. 44:21), whereas traditions and institutions that have raised what is penultimate to a level attracting attention away from the "new thing" being enacted by the true God are to be forgotten:

> Do not remember the former things,
> or consider the things of old.
> I am about to do a new thing;
> now it springs forth, do you not perceive it?
> (Isa 43:18-19)

The theological process of discernment outlined by Second Isaiah is fraught with peril. License to sift through religious tradition to determine what is worthy of remembering and what can be forgotten raises the spectre of a highly arbitrary process producing a Scripture merely replicating human desires. Indeed, such subjectivism has ravaged religious communities and misled the faithful of all ages. On the other hand, without such a process of discernment religion becomes weighted down with a legacy of interpretation that can obscure its essential truths. So what safeguards the process of theological discernment from human perversion? Only the faithfulness of the prophet and the prophetic community to the one Reality, Immanuel, the God both known to them through the testimony of their ancestors and still in their midst guiding them and instructing them in the way of mercy and justice.

The judgment of the disciples who preserved Second Isaiah's words was corroborated by the savants who included his words in Scripture as a part of the book of Isaiah: He belonged among the prophets as a revealer of God's will and as one qualified to distinguish between what is eternal and what is passing. What follows are some of Second Isaiah's judgments that were handed down to enrich God's people of all subsequent ages:

(1) Regarding God's covenant with the House of David, now seemingly discredited by the Babylonian conquest:

> I will make with you an everlasting covenant,
> my steadfast, sure love for David (Isa 55:3b).

God's covenant with a people gathered from the nations of the earth to serve God's gracious purpose is not annulled; it is clarified. David was chosen as a shepherd of this people, not as one set apart to enjoy special exceptions and privileges. The distortion of the covenant that was introduced by kings who defined their office in terms of special entitlement was banished by Second Isaiah when he reaffirmed God's everlasting covenant with the entire people. [See commentary on the Gospel of Matthew: "people-covenant," *inter alia.*]

(2) Regarding the continuing validity of the office of messiah (anointed one): Second Isaiah restored it to its proper function by removing it from the mythic trappings of absolute kingship and returning it to its historical context: "Thus says the LORD to his anointed *(māshīaḥ),* to Cyrus . . ." (Isa 45:1a). Worthiness to bear the title of the Lord's messiah is not secured by lineage, but by faithfulness to God's purpose. God's freedom to designate anointed servants is not circumscribed by human institutions like royal dynasties. Second Isaiah dramatically reaffirms God's freedom by announcing that God has appointed a foreigner to the function formerly held by the descendants of David and Zadok. God has called the Persian Cyrus to restore the exiled people to their land.

(3) Regarding the one who will guide the chastened Jewish community back to faithfulness, Second Isaiah introduced the figure of the Servant of the Lord (42:1):

> Here is my servant, whom I uphold,
> my chosen, in whom my soul delights;
> I have put my spirit upon him;
> he will bring forth justice to the nations.

As in the past God had chosen kings and priests and prophets to govern, to lead, and to admonish, God was now choosing one called the Servant. The description of the Servant is multifaceted, no doubt intentionally. As one called to restore Israel to faithfulness, to bear witness to God's will to the nations, and to suffer and die to atone for the sin of the people, the Servant does more than provide a biographical sketch of a specific person or group. The Servant redirects attention to the nature of the agents God uses to help perform God's saving purpose on the earth. They humbly stand in solidarity with common people; they rely on God for their strength and direction; they are obedient even to death. The Servant image picks up where Second Isaiah's critique of idolatrous institutions left off, by renewing a clear picture of the essential meaning of being God's people.

Second Isaiah was not alone in courageously drawing from recent experiences of divine chastisement a sense of clarified direction. Jeremiah too drew attention away from human edifices and pretensions, redirecting it to the human heart as the staging ground of God's saving new action (Jer 31:31-34). Ezekiel attacked Israel's fatal idolatry and described the purging holiness of God as the source of the destruction (Ezekiel 8–11). Faithful priests redoubled their efforts to clarify the heart of the Law in love of one's neighbor (Deut 6:5 and Lev 19:18) and in care for the poor and the alien (Leviticus 25), and to provide for the indispensable human need of divine atonement for sin (Leviticus 16–17). Job stressed the importance of honest questioning as a part of genuine faith, even when it touched some of the central tenets of ancestral tradition, and etched into the collective consciousness the mysterious being of God as the only enduring Reality amid life's uncertainties.

The probing and questioning in response to unprecedented experiences that characterized the exilic period created the climate for the significant theological growth and change that occurred in the following centuries. It provided profound insights and powerful images for those who sought to apply the traditional faith to a dramatically different world. In that application, though, a new ingredient was added. Whereas the exiles lived within the context of political, social, and economic structures provided by their foreign hosts, the returnees needed to translate faith into the concrete institutions of a society autonomous in matters of religion, ethnic customs, and local governance but bound by the international policy of the new, imperial overlords, the Persians. In that translation differences emerged between groups with rival interpretations, a phenomenon that demands the attention of anyone seeking to understand the Second Temple period. For what occurred was a shaping of traditions that would continue to influence groups throughout the Persian and Hellenistic periods and all the way down to the time of the early rabbis and the early Christians.

The Jewish Community Engages in the Task of Restoration: The Persian Period

The fall of the dreaded neo-Babylonian empire was as rapid as its rise. Second Isaiah, from the vantage point of Yahwistic faith, interpreted Cyrus's defeat of the Babylonians and his edict allowing Jews to return to their homeland as the fulfillment of divine purpose. Subsequently the size of the population of Judah mushroomed between the years 538 and 520 B.C.E. The pressure this placed on community leaders to restore religious, political, and economic organization was enormous.

Predictably, those who had held the reigns of power before the national disaster seized the initiative, basing their efforts on plans that had begun to take shape in Babylon. Preeminently this involved the Zadokites, among whom the authority of the prophet Ezekiel loomed large. Even as he had attributed the fall of the nation to idolatrous repudiation of God's holiness, so too he prescribed structures of reorganization that would secure sanctity within the land, enabling the return of God's glory. As a central focus this meant a rebuilt Temple (see Ezekiel 40–48) with Zadokite priests overseeing the holy rituals. Levites were strictly subsumed as minor clergy. Though the twin brother to the Zadokite priesthood, the prince after the pattern of David, was given a place in Ezekiel's plan, it was a secondary place conscientiously removed from the center.

It is not difficult to imagine the enormity of the challenge facing these leaders. Devastation was widespread. The economic infrastructure of the land had been destroyed. Morale was low. First efforts to rebuild the institution combining vital economic, political, and religious functions, namely the Temple, failed. The book of Haggai describes the situation persisting in 520: famine, lack of basic commodities, economic depression combined with runaway inflation. Only the combined effort of the three main offices within Jewish culture—priesthood, monarchy, and prophecy—was able to break the impasse and complete construction of a modest Temple.

The lack of physical splendor was compensated for by the theological interpretation Haggai and Zechariah gave to the most recent turn of events:

> For thus says the LORD of hosts: Once again, in a little while, I will shake the heavens and the earth and the sea and the dry land; and I will shake all the nations, so that the treasure of all nations shall come, and I will fill this house with splendor (Hag 2:6-7). . . . On that day, says the LORD of hosts, I will take you, O Zerubbabel my servant, son of Shealtiel, . . . and make you like a signet ring; for I have chosen you (Hag 2:23).

The angelic interpreter in one of Zechariah's night visions explains that the two branches flanking the bowl of the golden lampstand are "the two anointed ones who stand by the LORD of the whole earth," that is, Zerubbabel and Joshua (see Zech 4:14).

The accomplishments of the team effort were considerable, given the obstacles that had to be overcome. Traditional structures were again in place to secure the Jewish community in its new existence as a subject people under the Persians. Worship of Israel's God resumed, the Torah was reestablished as the moral guide for the people, and efforts got underway to restore economic stability. But the social edifice, built to the specifications of Ezekiel's plan, proved to be a fragile structure.

In the eyes of some the Zadokite/Davidic restoration omitted certain important ingredients. Another planner had pictured a restoration in which "your people shall all be righteous, . . . you shall be called priests of the Lord" (Isa 60:21; 61:6). This picture, inspired, it would seem, by Second Isaiah's reenvisioning of Israel as a Servant nation and harking back to a very ancient ideal (Exod 19:5-6), holds to a broadly inclusive ideal of peoplehood. Negatively it perhaps addresses lingering memory of abuses of exclusion and special privilege that plagued the institutions of Israel's past and contributed to hubris, decline, and fall.

A conflict emerged—that would be repeated in similar form in future generations—between a dominant inside group and dissidents forced to the periphery. The program of the dominant group had a long antecedent history with roots reaching to the Davidic age and revolving around notions of a vast empire centered at the Temple in Jerusalem and a diarchic form of leadership consisting of Davidic king and Zadokite priest, both enjoying the support of loyal prophets. The split of the nation into rival kingdoms was a setback that reformer kings like Hezekiah and Josiah had already addressed. One nation, one Temple had been the clear, albeit illusive goal of the royal program. John Hyrcanus I returned to the task in the late second century B.C.E. It seems safe to surmise that Zerubbabel was already guided by the same plan in the last third of the sixth century.

However, the goal of a reconstituted Davidic empire reaching from the Euphrates to the River of Egypt was to elude Zerubbabel as it had Hezekiah and Josiah. We can only speculate on the reasons, basing our reflections on tantalizing bits of evidence. Passages in so-called Third Isaiah indicate clearly that the Temple rebuilding efforts of the Zadokite-Davidide coalition encountered strenuous opposition (Isa 66:1-5). Within the divided community the brilliant visions of the Isaiah and Ezekiel schools were frustrated. The Temple was rebuilt, but in the eyes of critics the officiating Zadokite priests were more intent on personal gain and pleasure than preserving the sanctity that could assure divine pleasure and presence (Malachi 1–2). As for the king, his Davidic pretensions seemed to arouse Persian concerns that a subject people was overstepping its proper limits—or at least this seems to be a reasonable way to interpret the disappearance of Zerubbabel from the tradition (and even from the text; cf. Zech 6:9-15).

The fifth century found the Jewish community struggling to preserve its religious identity within a vast pagan empire and with a domestic situation that was far from ideal. Gone, at least for the time being, were the universal visions of Israel as light to nations (Isa 49:6), and nations bringing their offerings to worship YHWH in Jerusalem (Isa 18:7). The present reality was an Israel threatened from within by intermarriages and obliged to maintain good relations with Persia on Persian terms (cf. Neh 10:28-31). It was a situation that was to be repeated many times in subsequent Jewish history, and it became the legacy of Ezra and Nehemiah to equip a people for survival under such adverse conditions.

Central to the equipment they bequeathed was the final, definitive version of the Torah of Moses. In effect the first five books of the Bible became under Ezra's leadership the charter of the Jewish community and the cornerstone of Judaism for all subsequent ages. Ezra as scribe introduced to the Jewish people the office that would outlive that of High Priest and King and, by the Roman period, become the guardian of Jewish tradition and the guide into the ever-changing future. In taking the Torah and extending it through interpretation to cover new situations (Neh 8:7-8), Ezra defined one of the most important functions of the scribe and his successor, the rabbi, for it was from these roots in the Persian period that the Pharisees cultivated a tradition of oral law that, in the form codified in the Mishnah and

Talmud, came to be acknowledged alongside the Torah as the normative rule of Judaism.

But as dissident voices in the sixth century had called attention to the fact that there was more to the spiritual legacy of Israel than even the reform program of Zerubbabel and Joshua could exhaust, so too voices arose in the fifth and fourth centuries calling attention to prophetic themes that developed more universal and eschatological aspects of the ancestral faith. The tone was set by the last prophetic voice heard in the OT (Mal 1:11):

> For from the rising of the sun to its setting my name is great among the nations, and in every place incense is offered to my name and a pure offering; for my name is great among the nations, says the LORD of hosts.

It also found expression in an idyllic romance that traced David's ancestry to a Moabite (Ruth 4:17-22), in the tale of a grouchy prophet who sought in vain to hinder God's merciful intention of saving the pagan Ninevites from destruction (Jonah), and in the words of a seer who foretold a time when God would pour out the divine spirit on all flesh (Joel 2:28).

The presence of diverse traditions in biblical writings originating in the Persian period has led some scholars to posit two distinct religious streams, one characterized by an eschatological orientation, another by focus on the Law. This rigid division cannot be sustained by detailed study of the materials in question. The picture that emerges is rather one of considerable diversity and the presence of perspectives and motifs that are available for reapplication by subsequent groups that find them meaningful and useful. It is in a looser sense of continuity, therefore, that one can see, for example, certain eschatological and messianic motifs that arose in the sixth century taken up and applied to a new setting in the second century. Similarly, certain features of the reform program of Ezra become hallmarks of Pharisaic Judaism in the Roman period, and early followers of Jesus drew upon motifs like the Servant of YHWH and God's initiative on behalf of the Gentiles in interpreting the life and message of their teacher. While not being reducible to a simple dualistic understanding of the Second Temple period, the diversity of traditions provides an important key to understanding the rich interpretive possibilities that were present in late biblical and early post-biblical religion, possibilities that became building blocks of the communities, both Jewish and Christian, that grew from roots in Hebrew Scripture.

The Jewish Community Struggles to Preserve Its Identity: The Hellenistic Period

The bitter struggle between the Greeks and the Persians for control of the eastern Mediterranean was decided in favor of the former by the lightning conquests of Alexander the Great in 332–322 B.C.E. The Hellenistic culture that this turn of events introduced proved to be quite different from the Persian culture under which the Jews had lived for nearly two centuries. While the Persians generally had been content to permit the Jews to live according to their own religious and social customs, the Hellenistic rulers were motivated, with varying degrees of zeal, by a desire to spread what in their minds was a superior culture destined to become the basis for a new world order. From the side of the conquered peoples there was commonly an openness to Hellenization as a means of personal advancement through careers in civil administration, commerce, and the military. The starting point was mastery of the Greek language, followed at times by the adoption of aspects of the religion and lifestyle of the Macedonian masters.

The Jews of Palestine and in the diaspora were not immune to this influence. Throughout the third century, during which Palestine was under the control of the Ptolemies based in Egypt, Jews both in their homeland and in Egypt were allowed to live in conformity with their Torah as they had under the Persians. Indeed, the Macedonians often showed respect for the laws and customs of Abraham and Moses, and for their part Jewish apologists seldom lost an opportunity to make connections between their ancestors and the heroes of the Greeks and to point out the superiority of Mosaic monotheism over pagan polytheistic religion. In part because relations were often benign, Hellenistic influences made considerable inroads into the thinking of the Jews. In Egypt, where the Jewish members of the population left behind more records than in most other parts of the diaspora, we find Jews adopting Greek names, pursuing the classical education of their overlords, and rising to important positions in trade and government.

Though there are cases of Jews forsaking their ancestral tradition entirely for the new manner of life, far more common were efforts to adapt Mosaic religion to Greek ways. It is out of this milieu that the Septuagint (LXX), the translation of the Hebrew Bible into Greek, arose in the third century B.C.E., alongside pious tales and historical writings developing Jewish themes in the Greek style. Especially in Alexandria there flourished a prosperous Jewish elite that cultivated a Jewish-Hellenistic tradition culminating in the works of Philo in the first century of the Common Era.

A notable case of a Jewish family that rose to prominence in the service of the Ptolemies is of the family of Tobias, the commander of Ammanitis east of the Jordan River. In an archive of correspondence belonging to an official named Zenon who served the Alexandrian finance minister Apolonius we find Tobias writing not only to the finance minister but to the king himself. Within a regime that sought to exercise strict control over the commerce of all of the lands under its control Tobias performed the valued service of maintaining security through his command of a military garrison in the strategic area adjacent to the Nabatean kingdom. From this outpost Tobias also maintained influential ties with Jerusalem, first through marriage to the sister of the high priest Onias II and then through his son Joseph and grandson Hyrcanus, who carried on the family tradition of serving the Hellenist overlords in return for a generous share of the tax revenue they collected (Josephus, *Ant.* 12.4).

Though Jerusalem itself was not of particular importance to the Hellenistic rulers, it maintained its role of leadership within the scattered Jewish world community. From all points in the diaspora the faithful sent their contributions to the Temple, and to Jerusalem they looked for legal decisions. Though the Hellenistic reform movement had strong adherents in Jerusalem, especially within pro-Ptolemaic circles, there were also groups adhering to a more traditional understanding of Judaism that resolutely resisted accommodation to the foreign rulers. This was demonstrated in the mid-third century when the high priest Onias II refused to send the designated tribute to Ptolemy, evidently as a gesture of opposition to the hellenizing influences coming from Egypt. As a proof of their loyalty the pro-Ptolemaic faction represented by Joseph, the son of Tobias, hastily sent the full tribute to Egypt.

Given Jerusalem's strategic importance in the lives of Jews in all countries and the presence there of both traditional and hellenizing factions, it was inevitable that the Holy City would find itself at the eye of the storm once the forces contending for the devotion of the Jews came to the conflagration point. The struggle involved nothing less than the definition of the essentials of Jewish faith and is far too complex to dismiss by simply identifying traditionalists as true Jews and hellenizers as apostates. Progressive elements within the Jewish population in Jerusalem, as in Egypt, took pride in the translation of their native traditions into the world idiom of Hellenism and apparently experienced no sense of betrayal in this rapprochement of Moses and the Greek muses. The book of Ecclesiastes illustrates from a considerably earlier period how foreign concepts could be blended with native themes and yet find acceptance in the community. More illuminating still is the book of Sirach, written around 190 B.C.E. in Hebrew in the Jewish homeland and reflecting considerable Greek influence, then translated into Greek by the author's grandson to serve the intellectually keen Egyptian Jewish community, and through the entire process preserving profound respect for Mosaic Torah, for the long chain of religious leadership in Israel's history, for the authoritative role of the high priest, and for the importance of the new teachers of wisdom (later to be named rabbis).

Among the Jews who learned Greek and became steeped in Hellenistic literature and philosophy were progressives who sought to demonstrate that the religion of Moses was not in conflict with Greek thought, but epitomized what was most noble in it and pointed both to its source and its ultimate intention, but equally sincere were leaders like the high priests Onias II, Simon the Just, and Onias III, who feared that the new Greek fashions were attacking the very heart of the ancestral faith.

The tragic conflict that ripped through the Jewish community in the second century B.C.E. thus had deep roots in that community itself, but the immediate causes had more to do with the world politics of the time. In the period around the turn to the second century the people of Jerusalem were caught up in the to-and-fro struggle for control of Palestine between the Seleucids and the Ptolemies, that is, the Syrian and Egyptian parts of the empire left behind by Alexander. In the last decades of the third-century Palestine stood in the balance as the Ptolemies struggled to maintain control in the face of the aggressive moves of Antiochus III ("the Great"). Since the most avid of the supporters of the Ptolemies were those who benefited most from the blending of Jewish and Hellenistic interests, as illustrated by the family history of the Tobiads, it was quite natural that those seeking to safeguard the tradition from assimilation to Hellenistic values saw their best interests as lying with the Seleucids. For them Antiochus III was a deliverer and his defeat of Ptolemy V's general Scopas in the Battle of Paneas in 200–199 B.C.E. was a godsend. Indeed, Antiochus showed his appreciation for the support of the high priest, Simon the Just, and the other members of the pro-Seleucid group by contributing to the Temple and reaffirming the amicable policy set during the time of Ezra by the Persian emperor and continued by Alexander and the Ptolemies in the third century, namely the policy of granting the Jews special permission to live according to "the laws of their ancestors," the Mosaic Torah.

Though Antiochus the Great's successor, Seleucus IV, at first followed his father's policy, things soon took a bitter turn. The king, deeply in debt to the Romans as a result of the treaty of Apamea (188 B.C.E.), initiated the practice of raiding the Temple that was to become a pattern in the next two decades. Matters got worse with the rise to the throne in 175 of Antiochus IV Epiphanes. Increasing numbers in Jerusalem began to awaken to the irony that the world power that had promised to enhance the security of the Jewish community was positioning itself to deliver the most serious assault on the Jewish faith since the Babylonian conquest. The disintegration of the situation in Judea was abetted by factors both domestic and international. At home opportunistic hellenizing groups refocused their attention on the new king as the best hope for advancing their interests and convinced him to repeal the long-standing policy of granting observant Jews the right to adhere to the ordinances of the Torah. Jason, whose Greek name accurately reflects his cultural orientation, purchased the office of high priest from the Seleucid king, thus displacing his brother Onias III. Under his leadership the status of Jerusalem was transformed from that of a Jewish city to a Greek *polis* named Antiochia, which was at once a resounding victory for the extreme hellenizers and a stinging humiliation for traditional Jews (2 Macc 4:7-17). Jerusalem thus took its place in the world empire alongside Alexandria and Antioch! This was a huge step forward for those seeking full assimilation to Hellenistic culture in all its aspects, including gymnasium, state cult, and the standard curriculum of Greek philosophy and literature for Jewish youth, the financing of which was to come from the Temple treasury.

As if sufficient evidence were not in hand to prove to all but the most strident hellenizers that the ancestral faith was under attack, a rash of new developments occurred that raised the crisis to new heights. In 171 B.C.E. Menelaus, a radical hellenizer without hereditary ties to the high-priestly family, out-maneuvered Jason and purchased the high priesthood at a price that forced him to seize Temple assets and sharply increase the taxes imposed on the Jewish population. Adding to the shame and humiliation, Antiochus himself, on his way back from battle in Egypt, entered the Temple and carried away vast amounts of gold and silver, including the sacrificial instruments. The flash point of revolt occurred in 167 when the walls of Jerusalem were leveled to the ground and the transformation of the city into a Greek *polis* was completed with the construction of the Akra, a citadel where the leaders of the hellenizing party dwelt together with their foreign allies. This was followed by a decree from Antiochus abolishing observation of Sabbath and the Jewish festivals, banning circumcision, and ordering the burning of the Torah scrolls. In place of the holy sacrifices a pig was offered upon the altar and the Temple was dedicated to Zeus Olympius, whose statue was set up to greet worshipers (2 Macc 6:1-6).

It is hard to imagine a more vicious attack on the heart of Jewish faith. We have emphasized the rich diversity of tradition that characterized the Persian and Hellenistic periods, with the theme of strictly defined Jewish identity found alongside the theme of God's universal sovereignty, with careful elucidation of Mosaic Torah alongside translations of Jewish thought into Greek concepts, with longings for a return to Davidic rule alongside movements of popular piety, with praise for the Temple high priests alongside the growing stature of the wise teachers.

What is remarkable about the policy and actions of Antiochus IV and his supporters is that they frontally attacked all of these traditions, producing a powerful bonding of otherwise disparate segments of the Jewish community into a fiercely determined resistance movement.

Common to nearly all Jewish religious groups of the time was deep respect for the Torah. In spite of differences in details of interpretation and in attitudes toward apologetics relating to Greek philosophy, the Torah was honored as God's unique gift to Israel. Jewish identity was tied to Mosaic Law, and whatever else changed in the world of rising and falling powers one truth remained, that Israel was related to the one true God on the basis of obedience to the Torah. Whatever rights foreign sovereigns might exercise over a vassal Jewish nation, therefore, annulment of the Jewish right to obey God's Law could not be included among them.

The jewel in the crown of the Torah was the command to worship no God but YHWH. Around this command the Temple cult had developed, with the understanding that Israel's security rested upon God's invisible presence in that holy sanctuary. Now the altar upon which proper sacrifices were offered to God bore the sacrilege of abomination, and where the holy God was to abide the idol of a pagan deity stood tall. The guardian of proper worship, the Zadokite high priest, had been replaced by one lacking both priestly lineage and the moral courage to stand up against the pillaging of the Temple.

Similarly violated were traditions emphasizing God's universal reign of peace and justice. From Jerusalem/Zion, according to these ancient traditions, God would teach the nations with the blessed result that "nation shall not lift up sword against nation, neither shall they learn war any more" (Isa 2:2-4). Led by their shepherd David, the nation would enjoy a covenant of peace with both the animals of the land and the nations around them (Ezek 34:23-31; cf. Jer 33:14-26 and Isa 65:17-25). Those yearning for the dawn of the blessed age in which Israel would dwell securely under the righteous leadership of its king were confronted instead with an apostate priest and a ruthless pagan ruler. This drew attention to a motif connected both with royal tradition and late prophetic eschatology, namely that preceding the dawn of the blessed age the righteous would experience terrible suffering at the hands of both foreign nations and apostates within Israel (for example, Psalm 2, Ezekiel 38–39, Zechariah 12). This motif was combined with one associated especially with Jeremiah, that God had placed Israel for a set time of seventy years under a foreign conqueror as punishment for its sin (Jer 25:11-12; 29:10). Together these two motifs created a mood of urgent questioning among those suffering under Antiochus. Had the time of punishment reached its culmination? Was divine deliverance at hand? If so, would God intervene directly? or would God act through an intermediary? Would the agent of God's deliverance arise from the House of David? Would the faithful be summoned to join the fray?

The revolt initiated by the Maccabees (Mattathias and his sons: see 1 Maccabees 2) gave an answer to these questions that consolidated the diverse streams of interpretation into one oppositional force. The widespread conclusion was that God had raised up a defender of the faith, and all those who feared God and were obedient to the Torah were called to join in the holy war. The story of the Maccabean revolt and the astonishing success with which it led to the cleansing of the Temple in 164 B.C.E. and the restoration of conditions in which the Torah could be honored and obeyed can be pieced together on the basis of evidence from the latter half of the book of Daniel, parts of *1 Enoch* and the *Testament of Moses,* and especially 1 and 2 Maccabees, which stem from authors with opposing points of view and thus pose a particular challenge for anyone trying to give a historical account of the revolt. Here we shall need to limit ourselves to observations bearing on the themes of apocalyptic and messianism.

Chapters 7–12 of the book of Daniel reflect the period of crisis in the three years between the desecration of the Temple and its rededication. They illustrate how sense was made of the persecution and how support for the initial Maccabean effort was built on the basis of prophetic tradition. For example, the "seventy years" of Jer 25:12 was interpreted to signify that the present time was the point of transition from the divinely set time of punishment to the inauguration of the righteous kingdom (Daniel 9). Themes from the Bible were enriched with motifs stemming from neighboring cultures, such as the picture of the heavenly coregency of the

Ancient One and the Son of Man (7:9-14) and the notion of a sequence of four world kingdoms (7:17). The resulting projection of the apocalyptic denouement is highly creative, mysterious in its ambiguity, and pregnant with suggestiveness for future theological reflection. It is most likely that the interpretation of contemporary events found in Daniel 7–12 is the product of the circle of pious defenders of the Torah called Hasideans by the Maccabean writers. By viewing the conflict against Antiochus and his hellenizing supporters in terms of holy war they justified military defense on the Sabbath as a necessary part of their full participation in the military campaigns of Judas. For them the present conflict was more than a historical conflict between Jews and Syrians; it was an eschatological battle between the hosts of light and the hosts of darkness. The battlefield was the one described earlier in Zech 14:5: "Then the Lord my God will come, and all the holy ones with him." Or as they described the dreadful final horn of the fourth beast:

> . . . this horn made war with the holy ones and was prevailing over them, until the Ancient One came; then judgment was given for the holy ones of the Most High, and the time arrived when the holy ones gained possession of the kingdom (Dan 7:21-22).

The strategy of the Maccabees was initially successful. The professional armies of the Seleucids were defeated in a rapid succession of stunning victories; control over the city of Jerusalem was regained; the Temple was cleansed and rededicated late in 164 B.C.E. (exactly three years after its profanation), an event celebrated ever since in the festival of Hanukkah.

The eschatological backdrop against which these events were being viewed guaranteed that the Maccabean victory would raise serious questions for those seeking to understand human history in relation to divine will. Was the outcome of the recent wars indication that God's long-awaited vindication of humiliated Israel had finally come? Had the Maccabean victory against huge odds proven that God had invested in the sons of Mattathias the royal prerogatives long associated with the House of David, even though they were not direct descendants of David? Were those who had remained faithful to the Torah through the tribulations of the past now to receive their reward in the kingdom of everlasting peace earlier described by the prophets? Was this to be a transcendent kingdom reserved for the faithful martyrs (Dan 12:1-4)? or was it to be an earthly kingdom in which the territorial claims of David would be regained?

Judas's brothers, Jonathan and Simon, in their succession as heads of state, apparently became willing supporters of the view that interpreted the recent events as signs that under their leadership the historical kingdom of David was being restored and that God's promises to Israel were thereby being fulfilled. In keeping with this political/realistic eschatology they accepted the ascription to themselves of sacerdotal and royal attributes that gave a this-worldly spin to messianic traditions. Jonathan, in 152, assumed the title of high priest. Simon carried the interpretation a step farther by wedding high priestly and political authority in his own person, as described in 1 Macc 14:41-45. Though a hint of futuristic eschatology is indicated with a mysterious phrase, "until a trustworthy prophet should arise," it is clear that for the present Simon was regarded as God's agent in the restoration of Israel to its former glory under David and Solomon.

Under John Hyrcanus, Aristobulus, and Alexander Jannaeus, policies of conquest and strategic alliances with the Seleucids and Romans were pursued vigorously, no doubt still in search of the golden era of David and Solomon. The coins minted and the titles assumed by these kings of Judea leave no doubts about their imperialistic aims, but the worldly pleasures (and debauchery) that escalated along with their conquests raised a serious question in the minds of many: Did the interpretive trajectory of the Hasmoneans and their supporters (including the author of 1 Maccabees), the one unequivocally associating the successes of the descendants of the Maccabees with divine will, offer an accurate guide to Jewish history? or did it represent a lying witness that threatened to blind the people to their true vocation as God's people and to the true character of God's kingdom as a reign not of imperial conquest and earthly luxury but of justice, mercy, faithful witness on behalf of God's Torah to the nations, and even willingness to suffer for the sake of righteousness?

A blunt repudiation of the Hasmonean claims arose already during the time of Jonathan and Simon among some of the pious ones *(ḥasidim)* who, just a decade or so earlier, had joined the armies of Judas after becoming convinced that the sacrilegious atrocities of Antiochus IV constituted nothing less than a call to holy war. Increasingly the secularizing tendencies of the Hasmoneans alienated those who abhorred the idea of a Jewish nation emulating the ways of the pagan world. Deeply offensive to some was the claim to the title of high priest initiated by Jonathan and implemented by Simon. Simon added royal presumptions beyond this.

The pious ones were moving in the direction of breaking ranks with the new Jerusalem regime when they received renewed encouragement and guidance from a number of Zadokite priests recently forced from office by the Hasmonean takeover. One of these priests, designated in the Dead Sea Scrolls as "the teacher of righteousness," became the leader of a determined group of dissidents from Jerusalem in a wilderness refuge on the eastern edge of the Judean wilderness (Qumran). There they cultivated an alternative vision of God's plan for Israel within an assembly assiduously dedicated to remaining obedient to the Torah in every detail and thus preserving the holiness that provided the necessary condition for God's presence. Having repudiated the priestly and royal claims of the Hasmoneans, they awaited God's act of restoring Temple leadership to the legitimate priestly family of Zadok and royal authority to God's chosen Messiah in the day of vindication. The messianism that grew out of this expectation received formulaic expression in the phrase, "the Anointed Priest and the Anointed of Israel" (1QSa 2.17-22). It is a concept dependent on the designation given in the late sixth century B.C.E. by the prophet Zechariah to the Davidic prince Zerubbabel and the Zadokite priest Jeshua, "the two anointed ones" (literally, "the two sons of oil," Zech 4:14). In contrast to what they perceived as corrupt and self-serving leaders in Jerusalem, their community awaited the coming of an anointed king and an anointed priest whose twin reign would put a definitive end to the false regime in Jerusalem, restore the faithful to their city with its new Temple replacing the one defiled by false sacrifice, and lead them in celebration of the eschatological banquet. Another Qumran text, drawing on a tradition found in Jer 33:14-15, Zech 3:8, and Zech 6:12, makes explicit the connection between the awaited king and the House of David: ". . . in the end of days a shoot *(ṣemaḥ)* of David will arise" (4QFlor 1.11). Until the messianic age arrived, however, it was the vocation of the faithful, organized sacrally in their wilderness as earlier the camps of Israel had been organized under Moses, to maintain themselves, as it were, as an undefiled, holy temple and to preserve a community order adumbrating the kingdom of Israel to come.

Though it is difficult to arrange the sectarian writings of Qumran in a chronological sequence it seems likely that the increased belligerency of the Jerusalem leadership, combined with its pro-Roman policy and deepening moral depravity, led to an increasingly pessimistic outlook. Frustration was no doubt heightened also by the delay of the expected arrival of the royal and priestly messiahs. A rigid dualism came to characterize the thinking of the pious ones. A temporal framework was provided by a historiographical tradition that had been cultivated among kindred groups at a somewhat earlier time, as evidenced by the Animal Apocalypse and the Apocalypse of Weeks in *1 Enoch* and the book of *Jubilees.* According to this tradition the second Temple from its very beginning was defiled and under divine judgment. The Hasmonean kings, when interpreted within the framework of this tradition, in spite of their military conquests and control over the Temple ritual were emphatically not carrying forth the Davidic legacy but were bringing to culmination an era of wrath that would end when God would destroy the defiled Temple and its sinful city in an act of cleansing that would introduce the final era of holiness. When the day of wrath arrived, they were to be prepared to join in the fray. Cultivating holiness through obedience and ritual observance took on the added archaic function of maintaining the purity requisite for holy war, according to the rules of which strict ritual holiness, including adherence to the practice of celibacy that some believe became a permanent feature of the Qumran community, was required of those preparing to fight alongside angels. Battle readiness was also maintained by preparation of an arsenal of sanctified weapons and by cultivation of a perfect hatred toward all of the enemies of God. This strategy of holy war, replete with dualism and heightened apocalyptic worldview, was detailed in the tractate "The War of the Sons of Light against the Sons of Darkness." Only after the assault of the hosts of Darkness and the armies of the nations and terrible suffering would God finally vindicate the elect, who would then live in their blessed kingdom under the twin messiahs.

The attempt to understand the exact nature of the messianism and eschatology of Qumran is bedeviled by a high degree of diversity of traditions, an obscure language intended to be comprehensible only to the initiated, much archaism, and rich metaphor. The description of the final battle, drawing on Ezekiel 38–39, is charged with mythological motifs that seem to suggest that restoration is envisioned on a plane transcending this world. Similarly, depictions of the messianic banquet contain elements suggesting a heavenly location. Nevertheless, the overall impression given by the sectarian writings is of a community that seeks to regain control over the historical Jerusalem. The blessed kingdom, ruled by a king and priest, seems to be a kingdom arising on an earth purified of all evil and inhabited only by the elect members of the covenant community. This is not to deny many themes that point to a more otherworldly orientation akin to that found in the final chapter of Daniel. Indeed, one looks in vain in the Jewish literature of the last two centuries B.C.E. for a consistent vision of the future. Rather characteristic is a broad diversity of eschatological, apocalyptic, and messianic outlooks. Generally speaking, however, the this-worldly undercurrent we detected underlying the various eschatological motifs at Qumran predominated within the thinking of most Jewish groups. This is certainly true of the eschatology of the rabbinical writings of the following centuries, where the model of the world to come is not an otherworldly heaven, but an obedient nation living under its Davidic king, much in the manner described in 1 Kings 4–5.

From the above it seems fair to conclude that most Jewish groups of the Hellenistic period would agree with the historical orientation of the Hasmonean interpretation of Jewish tradition. That God would administer divine rule over Israel through an anointed king was assumed. That sacrifice would be offered in the Jerusalem Temple under the leadership of anointed priests was taken for granted. Where dissidents parted company with the Hasmoneans was over the question of the pedigree of king and priests, over the nature of their relationship to the powers of this world, and over the moral character of their reign, judged against the standards of the Torah.

As the example of the community of Qumran illustrates, critique, even condemnation, of the Hasmoneans extends back nearly to the beginning of that dynasty. For those looking for proof that the Hasmoneans' priestly claims and royal pretensions were both illegitimate, the final scions of that line could not have been more compliant. The rival claims of Hyrcanus and Aristobulus and the bloody civil war that ensued in 67–64 B.C.E., combined with the history of drunken debauchery and careless international diplomacy that had become a well-established part of the Hasmonean court, led the Roman general and future emperor Pompey to view the chaotic conditions in Judea as a threat to Roman security in the area. Roman patience had run out. Pompey led his armies into Judea in 63 B.C.E., dismantled the Jewish kingdom built up by the Hasmoneans, and made the Jewish nation even more a tributary of Rome.

For the Jewish people, the fulfillment of prophetic promises of a restored Israel seemed more remote than they had been since the time of the Babylonian conquest of Jerusalem. The questions facing those exiles of an earlier era resurfaced for the Jews of the early Roman Period. Had God abandoned Israel? Was God helpless before greater powers? Or was there a third explanation?

Written in the wake of Pompey's conquest, the *Psalms of Solomon* offer a third explanation, and thereby afford us an important insight into at least one Jewish group's eschatological outlook in the period immediately preceding the birth of Jesus of Nazareth. Far from being evidence of God's abandoning Israel or forsaking the promises, the defeat of the nation was directly attributable to the arrogance and faithlessness of the Hasmoneans. Since the time of Aristobulus (104–103 B.C.E.) they had designated themselves as kings and, as we have seen, had laid claim to the high priestly title since the time of Simon. Herein lay the cause of the humiliating defeat of the nation by the armies of Pompey:

> With pomp they set up a monarchy because of their arrogance;
> they despoiled the throne of David with arrogant shouting.
> But you, O God, overthrew them, and uprooted their descendants from the earth,

> For there rose up against them a man alien to our race (*Ps Sol* 17:6-7).

The pattern adopted to interpret the calamity conforms to the one used by the classical prophets. The people of Jerusalem are in bondage to sin, from the king to the common citizens:

> For there was no one among them
> who practiced righteousness or justice:
> From their leader to the commonest of the people,
> (they were) in every kind of sin:
> The king was a criminal
> and the judge disobedient;
> (and) the people sinners (*Ps Sol* 17:19b-20).

It was accordingly in response to Israel's sin that God acted in righteous judgment using the well-precedented means of a foreign power as the agent of wrath. But after the judgment, upon what could Israel base hope for the future?

The reply of the *Psalms of Solomon* comes straight out of the Davidic covenant:

> See, Lord, and raise up for them their king,
> the son of David, to rule over your servant Israel
> in the time known to you, O God (*Ps Sol* 17:21).

The Davidic king, to whom is ascribed in v. 32 the title "Lord Messiah," will reestablish righteousness in the land and set Israel in a place of honor among the nations, all to God's glory. Evidently with the intention of clearly distinguishing between the ruthless tactics of the Hasmoneans and the just rule of the future Messiah King, the weapon that he will use is described as "the word of his mouth" (17:24). The *Psalms of Solomon* shed important light on the question of the background of eschatological and messianic thought to the ministry of Jesus and the development of earliest Christianity, since they offer the earliest unambiguous formulation of Davidic messianic thought while at the same time betraying deep roots in biblical prophecy and a likely relationship to themes more obliquely expressed at Qumran.

The second important witness to messianic thought in the period following Pompey's conquest is found in the "Similitudes of Enoch," consisting of chs. 37–71 of *1 Enoch,* which is the only section of this pseudepigraphical work not attested at Qumran. On the basis of both textual and thematic evidence these chapters can be dated to the early years of the first century C.E. Considerable scholarship has been devoted to the Similitudes because of their elaborate development of the theme of the Son of Man, a figure also referred to as the Elect One, and in two cases as the Lord's Messiah. The political background is that of the Jews living as subjects under foreign domination. The Elect Son of Man is portrayed as existing in the company of the Lord of the Spirits since before creation. The fact that he has been "concealed in the presence of the Lord" (48:6) indicates that at the end of time he will be revealed. Indeed, his functions in the eschatological events are described quite extensively. To him will fall the responsibility to judge Azazel (one of the fallen angels who, according to *1 Enoch* 8–10, seduced and oppressed humans) and the host of fallen angels (ch. 55) as well as the "kings, the governors, the high officials, and the landlords" whom he will deliver to the angels for punishment (ch. 62). An interesting connection with ch. 17 of the *Psalms of Solomon* is the reference to his instrument of judgment: "The word of his mouth will do the sinners in . . ." (62:2). A further interesting motif is that he (referred to both as "the Elect One" and "his Messiah"), as the one who holds authority over the metal-bearing mountains, will cause all of the iron, bronze, tin, and lead used for weapons to vanish (ch. 52). Though the nations, in a final desperate act, will attack the elect ones and inflict much suffering, they, in keeping with an ancient mythic pattern incorporated in Psalm 2 and Zechariah 12, will be thrown into a panic as they approach Jerusalem (56:5-8). When the judgment has been completed the elect will live forever in the blessedness of the Lord of the Spirits and with the Son of Man (62:13-16).

The portrait of the Elect Son of Man/Messiah in the Similitudes is influenced by traditions as diverse as the canonical psalms, biblical prophecy, Daniel 7, and *1 Enoch* 14–17. It is not surprising, therefore, that the resulting picture is less than consistent. For example, whereas in 47:3 and 60:2 it is the Lord who is enthroned as judge, in 61:8 (and probably in 62:2, though a textual problem obscures the passage) the Lord "placed the Elect One on the throne of glory; and he shall judge all the works of the holy ones in heaven above . . . ." Finally, in 71:14, a surprising identification is drawn between Enoch and the Elect One.

Though written at about the same time as the Similitudes of Enoch, *Biblical Antiquities,* a retelling of biblical history from Adam to Saul's death by Pseudo-Philo, reflects a different eschatology. To Jews living under the domination of the Romans Pseudo-Philo teaches, by way of retelling the story of an earlier era, "Now we know that the Lord has decided to save his people; he does not need a great number but only holiness" (*Bib. Ant.* 27:14). In keeping with an eschatology that has no room for a political messiah he focuses on what happens after death and what occurs during and after God's visitation. His eschatological vision resembles Daniel 12 in depicting the righteous living forever "like the stars of heaven" (*Bib. Ant.* 33:5).

The Jewish historian Josephus adds important information concerning the diverse eschatological/messianic views of the early first century C.E. that can be summarized as follows. The Sadducees, due to their rejection of any Scripture save the five books of Moses, placed no credence in eschatological teachings. The Pharisees, much like Josephus himself, generally were skeptical of the political activism of groups calling for rebellion against Rome and often rallying behind purported messiahs like Judas son of Hezekiah, Simon, and Athronges. To be sure, Pharisaism was a broad movement covering a wide range of eschatological interpretations and changing in response to particular historical and political circumstances, as illustrated by Rabbi Akiba's endorsement of Simon bar Kosiba (bar Kokhba) as Messiah in the Second Jewish Revolt (132–135 C.E.). Such wide diversity within a single party is not surprising when one recalls the common roots of the Pharisees and the Essenes reaching back to the tumultuous events of the early second century B.C.E.

Josephus had no sympathy for the political extremists of his time, the Zealots and the Sicarii. Their calls for reconquest of the land for the Jews and the acts of violence to which they resorted were, in his judgment, points along the path to the calamitous events that finally engulfed the Jewish community in unspeakable suffering. Historically, the Zealots and Sicarii can be understood as adherents of the kind of political messianism that believed that God was calling the Jewish people to militant action in order to restore the autonomy and prosperity of the Davidic era. Josephus, no doubt sharing the attitude of the majority of the Pharisees, looked upon their efforts as suicidal. The position opposing political messianism that became normative among the rabbis solidified after the failed attempt of Bar Kosiba (bar Kokhba) and his supporters to gain freedom from Rome in the Second Jewish Revolt of 132–135 C.E. (the rabbinic writings commonly rewrite his name bar Koziba, that is, "son of a lie").

Eschatological and Messianic Ideas in the Ministry of Jesus

Excluding the Sadducees, it seems clear that within some Jewish circles of Jesus' time there was hope that God would act through the Messiah to restore Israel. Four key elements fostered this hope: (1) memory of the Davidic era, especially in the idealized form found in 1 Kings 4–5; (2) the tradition of God's covenant with the House of David, as expressed, for example, in 2 Samuel 7 and Psalm 89; (3) prophetic promises, both those relating explicitly to David *redivivus* (Jer 23:5-6; 33:14-26; Ezek 34:23-24; 37:15-28) and those more generally developing the idea of the eschatological era of peace (Isa 2:2-4); (4) the humiliation and hardship that were an everyday part of life under the Romans.

Concretely it was a period of intense political ferment, with various eschatological and messianic visions being discussed and enacted. There can be little question that a preacher proclaiming the eschatological theme of the nearness of God's reign, as Jesus appears to have done, would catch the attention of potential supporters and critics alike. By virtue of the tense political situation there was openness especially to a militant messianic leader who could crystallize the Jewish resistance to Rome and mobilize it in defiant action with an appeal to God for support.

Very significant, therefore, is the probability arising from a critical reading of the gospels that Jesus sought to place distance between his movement and militant messianic groups. Though the account of the feeding of the five thousand in John 6:1-15 already reflects considerable theological interpretation, its conclusion draws out a theme that seems to be implied in the synoptic version of the story (Matt 14:21 // Mark 6:44) and fits the situation of Jesus feeding the hungry and thereby awakening traditional images of the messianic banquet: "When Jesus realized that they were about to come and take him by force to make him king, he withdrew again to the mountain by himself" (John 6:15). How very natural for the politically agitated people of Galilee to respond thus to a prophet/teacher who interpreted their Scriptures authoritatively, possessed healing powers, and satisfied both their spiritual and their physical hunger. The interpretative tradition, well aware of the political climate within which Jesus lived, was in a position to realize how the crowds that gathered around him sought to acclaim him as their Messiah, meaning by that title the one sent by the God of Israel to lead them in their struggle against the oppressive foreign occupier. It seems very plausible that a disciple like Peter who had accompanied him in his mission of mercy, listened to his teaching about God's reign, and observed his acts of healing could be brought to the confession, "You are the Messiah," and that Jesus, fearing the misunderstanding this confession could raise among the restive crowds, would order him to tell no one (Matt 16:13-20 // Mark 8:27-30 // Luke 9:18-20). The same high degree of verisimilitude is claimed by the account of John the Baptist's sending disciples to Jesus asking, "Are you the one who is to come [that is, the Messiah] or are we to wait for another?" (Matt 11:3; Luke 7:19). It seems entirely possible that the gospel writers and the sources they used were anticipated by the original disciples when they inferred from Jesus' words and acts distinct messianic traits.

It is hard to imagine the extent of the following Jesus could have mustered had he come out and publicly announced, "I am indeed the long-awaited Messiah, and I have come to lead you in your struggle against Rome." The absence of such a direct declaration in the synoptic tradition is a reliable indication that Jesus avoided such an explicit identification, for surely, had he ever claimed the title, it would have been amplified and elaborated many times over by subsequent interpreters. As it is, the only direct messianic claim attributed to Jesus comes in the latest and most theologically interpretive gospel, namely in John 4:26 ("I am he"). It is probable that the closest he was willing to come to an affirmative answer to the question of whether he was the Messiah was in his tantalizingly ambiguous answer to Pilate, "You say so" (Matt 27:11 // Mark 15:2 // Luke 23:3; see also Matt 26:64 // Mark 14:62).

The fact that the charge leading to his execution was the one inscribed on his cross, "The King of the Jews," and the mode of execution (crucifixion) indicate that the Romans recognized in Jesus a threat taking shape along the lines of political messianism. This raises a question: What motivated Jesus to engage in activities that awakened in the minds of followers and enemies alike associations with the Messiah of the Jews and yet to stop short of giving assent to and thereby exploiting that identification?

To simply say that Jesus was restrained by fear of the violence this might cause seems inadequate. He was not one to shy away from confrontation, even when it led to execution. Our answer is more complex. It necessitates careful consideration of the tradition that most directly provided the shape and direction of his ministry, namely the prophetic tradition, especially as it had been applied by Second Isaiah to the situation of the Jews living under Babylonian rule. While preserving the concept of God's sovereignty, Second Isaiah modified and enlarged the vision of God's plan for Israel in light of the Babylonian destruction of the Davidic kingdom. God would "bring forth justice to the nations" (Isa 42:1) so that God's "salvation may reach to the end of the earth" (49:6). Not just the historical entity, Israel, but all of creation would experience God's healing power. As for the human agency used by God to accomplish these purposes, royalty would play its part inasmuch as Cyrus the Persian would effect Israel's release from political bondage (44:25–45:7). But much more central in this eschatological vision was the agency of the Servant, construed both collectively as the faithful in Israel and individually as a leader patiently and obediently carrying forth God's purpose. Through the Servant, God would accomplish the restoration of health to people and land in keeping with the promises associated in the Torah tradition with obedience and summarized in the description of the jubilee year (Leviticus 25). Release of those in bondage, healing of the sick, hope for those afflicted with poverty, and forgiveness to those suffering under the burden of sin were all aspects of the mending of the cosmos to which the Servant was called, a vocation that in Judaism to this day is called *tikkun ʿolam,* that is, "the repairing of the world" (see Luke 4:16-30).

Second Isaiah's singular focus on God's purpose resulted in the relativization of popular traditions and institutions that in the minds of many had come to be identified with divine reality, preeminent among which was the now severely discredited institution of messianic kingship. God's covenant made with David and the steadfast promises associated with it were now extended to the faithful community. Not an exalted, dazzling king but a humble, obedient Servant was thereby commissioned by God and empowered with God's spirit to "bring forth justice to the nations" (Isa 42:1) and to usher in the reign of justice and peace awaited by the prophets (e.g., Amos 9:11-15; Isa 2:2-4). This Servant was anointed by the Lord to bring good tidings to the poor (Isa 61:1). The Servant as the "anointed one" was by definition the "Messiah" *par excellence* (the Hebrew verbal root *mashaḥ* is translated "to anoint with oil"). [In the late Aramaic Targums of Isaiah, the Servant is explicitly referred to as "Messiah," in portions of the text of the Targums that may go back to a pre-70 C.E. period. *—Ed.*]

Jesus' ministry stands in continuity with this prophetic vision of restoration. Like the vision of Second Isaiah, it transcends the nationalism of political messianism. Yet Jesus' refusal to allow his movement to merge with the military revolutionaries was not driven by spiritualization in the sense of a dismissal of the importance of social structures and political realities. God's reign transcended the boundaries erected by humans, and therefore Jesus extended the same invitation to Judean, Samaritan, Galilean, Roman centurion, tax collector, fisherman, leper, Pharisee, and prostitute: "Come to the banquet" (cf. Matt 22:1-10 // Luke 14:16-24 with Isa 55:1-2). Wide as creation, it brought release to the possessed, wholeness to the infirm, sight to the blind, freedom to those in bondage, forgiveness to sinners. The breadth of Jesus' eschatological vision is seen in this: his words and activities go beyond the limits of any specific political agenda or social program. He accepted any committed to the righteousness of God's reign (Luke 9:49-50 // Mark 9:38-40). The mission, though, called not upon angelic warriors (Matt 26:53), not even human warriors; the compassionate Servant gathered fellow servants as meek agents of the heavenly Sovereign. They went out as he did to mend and to heal, and the profound significance of their ministry becomes apparent in his response to their report of success: "I watched Satan fall from heaven like a flash of lightning" (Luke 10:18). Wherever Jesus and his disciples moved, the evil that tears away at creation retreated as harmony was restored, whether through word, touch, sign, or acts of self-sacrifice. The intimate plea that he raised to his Heavenly Father was thus being answered: "Thy Kingdom come, thy will be done, on earth as it is in heaven" (Matt 6:10).

True to the prophetic tradition, Jesus' ministry embodied an eschatological vision. It was propelled by a steadfast belief in God's purpose to restore creation to its intended beauty and harmony, and it recognized the opposition of evil that could overwhelm humans and make them helpless prisoners. To combat the power of evil human resources were insufficient. Only God's power could exorcise demons, banish sickness, and forgive sins, and it was that power that Jesus believed God had given him to pass on to his disciples as God's agents of healing. Luke's version of the mission of the disciples makes explicit the connection between their work and God's reign: "Whenever you enter a town and its people welcome you, eat what is set before you; cure the sick who are there, and say to them, 'The kingdom of God has come near to you'" (Luke 10:8-9).

The kingdom of God is creation restored to the harmony and beauty intended by God. This was the eschatological vision to which Jesus was committed. Its roots were as old as the release of slaves from Egypt, for there God was actively at work to gather together "a treasured possession," a "priestly kingdom and a holy nation" (Exod 19:5-6). Its roots reached back to the Torah that guided God's servant people to the righteousness that would enable them to be witnesses to divine mercy and justice in the world. It was nourished by the glimpse of restoration expressed in the jubilee year and given direction by the tireless efforts of Israel's prophets to renew the covenant of blessing through repentance and obedience. Finally the vision was formulated for the reader in a summary description of the Servant's mission stemming from the circle of

Second Isaiah and fittingly placed in the mouth of Jesus by the evangelist Luke (Luke 4:16-21). That description, found in Isa 61:1-3, reads in part:

> The spirit of the Lord GOD is upon me,
> because the LORD has anointed me;
> he has sent me to bring good news to the oppressed,
> to bind up the brokenhearted,
> to proclaim liberty to the captives,
> and release to the prisoners;
> to proclaim the year of the LORD's favor,
> and the day of vengeance of our God;
> to comfort all who mourn . . .

The circle of Second Isaiah, out of the suffering and humiliation of life under a pagan regime, caught a glimpse of God's Messiah (that is, "anointed one") not in terms of the elite splendor of political monarchy but in the image of one anointed and empowered by God to serve faithfully in the healing of a broken creation. This, it seems, was the eschatological and messianic tradition upon which Jesus drew in his proclamation and enactment of God's reign. His rejection of the political messianism of his day therefore was not just a negative response to a strategy he feared would lead to disaster; it stemmed from his adherence to an alternative vision of how God's reign of peace and justice would be established. At the center of that vision was the figure of the Servant, understood by tradition both as the steadfast community and the faithful leader, anointed by God, endowed with God's spirit, and prepared to suffer to bring back the lost to God's realm of peace and harmony. The version of the Beatitudes preserved by Luke formulates the alternative eschatological vision embraced by Jesus with beautiful simplicity:

> Blessed are you who are poor, for yours is the kingdom of God.
> Blessed are you who are hungry now, for you will be filled.
> Blessed are you who weep now, for you will laugh (Luke 6:20-21).

The eschatology embedded in these simple blessings reaches all the way back to the Song of Hannah (1 Sam 2:2-8) and embraces all living creatures, including the humblest peasant. Its impact on society is potentially more transformative than any political ideology, for it accepts no partisan limitations and addresses human existence on its most basic level (cf. Matt 25:31-46), and it extends to every corner of the world, since its agents are not kings and emperors but ordinary human beings, responsible to God. It is an eschatology that can elicit the opposition of world regimes such as that of ancient Rome due to its refusal to offer ultimate allegiance to any earthly ruler (as in the book of Revelation). And because of the blindness of world rulers to the alternative values of God's reign, the mission of one anointed to proclaim the good news of the reign of God was easily mistaken for a threat to their earthly dominion. Within the context of Roman politics it is entirely understandable that Jesus was executed as a political enemy of Rome.

Moreover, blindness to the realities of God's reign was not limited to the Romans. Jesus faced an agonizing dilemma vis-à-vis his Jewish audience. As our survey of their traditions makes clear, many were looking for a Messiah in the tradition of King David, that is to say, a Messiah who would restore the political independence of Israel through the defeat of Rome. However, Jesus understood his anointing (that is, messiahship) as an empowerment of the spirit of healing and reconciliation, not the empowerment of military might. He had been anointed as the Servant of the Lord, not as a leader who relied on the sword. Through acts of compassion God's creation would be delivered from bondage to sin and the brokenness of sickness and poverty and despair. To be sure, meekness and patience ran against the grain of the rage of the general populace against the Roman oppressor. How was Jesus to reeducate such a restive audience so as to prevent them from confusing his mission with that of the popular political messiahs? The evangelists Matthew, Mark, and Luke give a plausible answer to this question in portraying Jesus as one who went about doing the restorative work of God's reign and accompanying his merciful acts with lessons to those closest to him explaining the "secret(s) of the kingdom of heaven" (Mark 4:10-12 // Matt 13:10-11 // Luke 8:9-10), that is, the important ways in which it differs from the kingdoms of this earth, including the Davidic kingdom envisioned by many of their compatriots.

The evangelists develop their portraits of Jesus around the profound irony that is already at the heart of Second Isaiah's Servant of the Lord: God has chosen an agent through whom the long-awaited restoration will occur, but that agent is not the popularly expected militant king but a humble Servant through whose faithful service even in the face of suffering God's reign will be established. This irony is developed through several subthemes: Jesus is empowered by God's spirit, but is abused by those holding human authority. Jesus has the authority to forgive sins, and yet dies at the hands of sinners. Jesus is God's Messiah, yet dies the death of the accursed. Though the nature of the messianism and eschatology that guided the life of Jesus and the interpretation developed by the early disciples must be drawn primarily from NT sources, the above survey should show how the presence within Jewish tradition of an alternative messianism and eschatology derived from prophetic tradition (see also Jer 31:31) deepens our understanding of the irony of the crucified Messiah and the mystery of God's redemptive purpose.

Eschatological and Messianic Ideas in Earliest Christianity

Even as Jesus drew upon the eschatological and messianic traditions that were current in his time, so too his own life contributed profoundly to the reshaping of tradition that occurred within the early Church. As the disciples sought to explain the meaning of his life, death, and resurrection, they continued the pattern of continuity and change that is characteristic of biblical faith in all ages. Within the gospels, to be sure, the words of Jesus and the layers of interpretation of those words are so intertwined as to make definitive disentanglement impossible. As in the above section words like "likely" and "probably" abounded, so too will they be present in this section as we seek to discern the impact that Jesus' post-crucifixion appearances had on the eschatological and messianic ideas of the first generations of Christians.

We have suggested that Jesus viewed his own ministry against the background of the prophetic tradition that produced the exilic image of the Servant of the Lord. We have also observed how his viewing the restoration to come in terms of the reign of God led to an engagement with notions surrounding the title of Messiah and the accompanying need to distinguish his understanding of God's kingdom from popular political notions. Also present at his time in eschatological speculation was the term "Son of Man," as we have seen above in our discussion of the Similitudes in *1 Enoch* 37–71. Did this title also figure into Jesus' reflections on the future?

This is one of the most complex questions in NT scholarship. The term appears frequently in the gospels, always in words attributed to Jesus. Though frequently the connection is made between Jesus and the Son of Man, in some cases the identity of the Son of Man is left ambiguous (Luke 12:39-40 *par;* Luke 17:22-37 *par*). The association of the Son of Man in the NT with the judgment on the wicked that will appear suddenly resulting in the vindication of the righteous is in harmony with the picture in *1 Enoch.* As in the case of the application of the term Messiah in the gospels, so here too an irony is developed: The one who is to come in glory to exercise universal judgment is the very one who was afflicted by the world's powers and forced to suffer and finally die on a cross. There is no way to determine whether Jesus drew this imagery explicitly into his teaching about his own mission (though the term Son of Man almost always appears on the lips of Jesus). What is clear is that the themes connected in tradition with the Son of Man were found useful by the disciples as they struggled to understand the ironies implicit in the story of their Lord.

The questions surrounding the image of the Son of Man also pertain to the image of the suffering Servant. While it is virtually certain that Jesus, from his prophetic perspective, would have seen his ministry connected to the mission of universal healing and restoration formulated in the book of Isaiah, and that he would have reflected on the inevitability of his obedience to God's reign leading to suffering and perhaps a violent death, it is difficult to be certain how far and in what detail the role of the Servant in Isaiah formed his understanding of servanthood. Did Jesus see himself giving his life as "a ransom for many" (Isa 53:12; cf. Matt 20:28 // Mark 10:45)? His words to the disciples on the night he was offered up as preserved in the Church's gospels: "this is my blood of the covenant, which is poured out for many for the forgiveness of sins" (Matt 26:28; cf. Mark 14:24) indicate that Jesus did see his forthcoming death as atoning in accordance with God's will revealed in Isaiah. In any case, for the disciples after the resurrection the connection was obvious. Their Lord's suffering and death were not simply the tragic tale of a brave individual; they were essential parts of a divine plan for redemption. It is unlikely that Jesus would have missed the essential point in this plan, that is, that innocent suffering is redemptive.

In the resurrection God had made plain that Jesus' obedience had not been in vain, and Paul, for one, found that this event significantly revised his understanding of his Jewish religious heritage (Gal 1:23). Indeed, he was willing to stake the credibility of his entire ministry on this belief: ". . . if Christ has not been raised, then our proclamation has been in vain and your faith has been in vain" (1 Cor 15:14). The one announced by prophecy as the one "wounded for our transgression," "the righteous one, my servant, [who] shall make many righteous" (Isa 53:6, 11), had come and completed the task of reconciliation that opened up a new era for humanity. Through faith in what God had accomplished in Jesus believers received as a gift the righteousness that Abraham had received, that is, the righteousness through which God restores wholeness to the children of God (Rom 4:23-25). The eschatological vision of universal redemption glimpsed by Second Isaiah and embodied by Jesus in his extending the good news of God's grace to all, whether Jew, Samaritan, or Roman, was formulated explicitly by Paul as he worked out the implications of the gospel for the mission program of the young Church. For Paul it was no longer to be kept a secret that Jesus was the Christ, the Messiah of God. At the same time Paul preserved, and if anything heightened the irony implicit in Jesus' life as recorded by the gospel writers of the Church, namely that *this* Messiah was not the militant victor of political messianism, but the suffering Messiah of the universal reign born of God's wisdom as an alternative to the destructive kingdoms of this world (see 1 Corinthians 1–4).

A Christian eschatology and messianism shaped around the idea of a Servant of the Lord obedient to suffering and death thus became a central theme in the Church's proclamation (1 Cor 1:17-25). Luke points to Isaiah 53 as the passage through which Philip was able to explain the "good news about Jesus" to an official of the Ethiopian court (Acts 8:27-39), and by the time of the author of 1 Peter the image of the obedient suffering Servant could be assumed as an effective basis for practical exhortation (1 Pet 2:21-25).

The prophetic tradition was thus useful not only to Jesus but to the early Church as a means of shaping its eschatology in a way that rejected political messianism, yet avoided the world-renouncing message of Gnosticism. The restoration that God was at work to accomplish through Jesus was not detached from life in this world, but neither was it a political agenda in the manner of human regimes. It was far more encompassing in time and space, being both universal and eternal, and the power at its disposal was not the conventional power of armies but the (foolish in the eyes of the world) alternative power of patient and meaningful suffering love.

Biblical Eschatological and Messianic Themes and the Contemporary Church

The challenge facing the contemporary Church as it seeks self-understanding and struggles to define its mission in the world in the light of the eschatological and messianic themes of Scripture is similar to the challenge presented by any recourse to Scripture in any area of human endeavor: The Bible presents a wide variety of images, reflections, and motifs on any given subject. In the area of eschatology and messianism we have encountered a vast repertoire, ranging from pictures of a reconstituted Davidic state to the advent of a supernatural Judge to the image of a Servant through whose suffering God accomplishes the goals of the universal divine reign of mercy and justice. If the Bible and its subsequent interpretive traditions are treated abstractly as inventories of images available for free adoption on the basis of human preference, the individual or group turning to the Bible can find whatever image or motif suits the occasion. Is one seeking biblical justification of a party's nationalistic agenda? The image of the political Messiah can suit the purpose well. Is one seeking justification for a counter-cultural program of social reform? The image of the wrathful eschatological Judge appearing as the Son of Man can meet the need.

For Christians, however, the Bible need not be such an unordered storehouse of images. It is rather the record of God's creative, redemptive activity within specific settings and always guided according to a faithful divine plan. The various eschatological and messianic themes, like all other themes, are handed down to the Church through the mediation of One who embodied God's creative, redemptive purpose and thus clarified authoritatively the manner in which traditional themes and images contribute to our understanding of the Church's vocation as a continuation of Christ's vocation as God's chosen anointed Servant. A faithful application of an eschatological theme or image is one that stands in continuity with Christ's ministry of healing and redemption. An improper application is one that contradicts that ministry. The Church in many ages has taken from Scripture eschatological images that have furthered worldly goals at the expense of God's plan of restoring creation to its intended wholeness. In the name of a victorious Christ, nationalistic claims have been advanced. In the name of the Son of Man, the rights of the weak have been violated. Armies have conquered in the name of the Messiah, yet the conquests have not redounded to God's glory but to the glory of human magistrates. There is only one guide to the proper use of the eschatological and messianic themes of the Bible, and that guide is the One who was born not in a palace but in poverty (Luke 2), who associated not with kings and princes but with ordinary people, who explained, "I have come to call not the righteous but sinners" (Matt 9:13 // Mark 2:17 // Luke 5:32).

New Testament

The Meaning of the Term "Gospel"

Philip L. Shuler

The Greek word for "gospel" is *to euangelion* and it means *good tidings,* or *good news. Euangelizomai* is the verb form, which means "proclaim or preach the gospel." The term "gospel" originally referred to the "reward" given to a messenger who brought the news, and it soon became identified with the news itself. In texts of the Greco-Roman world including the LXX the noun appears mostly in the plural form and evidence indicates it was used in cultic rituals with reference to thank-offerings for good tidings. It also appears in Hellenistic texts related to the imperial cult. Here the emperor is deified and his birth celebrated as an *euangelion* that is the first of more good tidings (plural form) still to come. A new era has dawned and the world itself has taken on a new meaning. Whereas such usage would make the term gospel both familiar and meaningful within a Greco-Roman context, of equal significance to the early Christian communities is the use of "proclaiming good tidings" as it appears, for example, in Isa 52:7 or 61:1 (LXX) in which the good news is related to news of salvation and directed to those in need. It is therefore not surprising that early Christianity began to use both the noun and verb forms with reference to the announcement of the good news that Christians presented with increasing success to the Greco-Roman world: namely the proclaimed testimony that, in the death and resurrection of Jesus Christ, God has acted decisively to bring salvation to every person, Jew and Gentile alike.

Paul's letters are the earliest NT writings in which *euangelion* directly refers to God's saving act in Christ. Paul uses the term in an absolute sense: that is, the gospel is complete, requiring neither embellishment nor qualitative description. It is one and there can be no other (Gal 1:7). It originated with God and was revealed to Paul by God (not by a human agent). Paul's authority as an apostle is grounded in the gospel he understands to be the gospel of God and of "his son," Jesus Christ (Rom 1:1-5). This gospel to which Paul has responded and by which he now functions is the story of Jesus Christ (Phil 2:6-11) including his sufferings, death, and resurrection (glorification). The content of the gospel finds striking affinity with the prophetic oracle of the suffering servant in Isaiah 53. This gospel is totally sufficient for salvation and is freely given by God's grace to be received by faith, the faith that finds full expression in the actions of all who believe. Paul the apostle has been set apart to proclaim the gospel of Jesus Christ to the Gentiles (all nations). It is also, therefore, the gospel for the uncircumcised (Gal 2:7). That both Jew and Gentile can participate in the joy of salvation through faith in Jesus Christ constitutes the good news of the gospel.

According to the Church the term gospel takes on a literary character with the first four books of the NT canon: the "gospels" according to Matthew, Mark, Luke, and John. (See article on the Church's Gospel Canon, infra.) In these books the good news is presented in the form of the story of Jesus Christ including an account of his birth (or other traditions preparing the reader for what follows), ministry, death, and resurrection. Although Mark is the only author who specifically refers to his narrative of Jesus as a gospel (Mark 1:1) the term became the accepted canonical title for all four of the NT accounts of Jesus along with the several other noncanonical works that present traditions related to Jesus (for example, *The Gospel of Thomas, The Gospel of Truth, The Gospel of Peter*). Gospel therefore refers to the good news of salvation through Jesus Christ as in the Pauline letters; it also refers to a type of literature revered in various Christian communities. This literature may contain a presentation of the story of Jesus Christ as set forth in a narrative "biography" form (for example, the canonical gospels: see article on "Genre(s) of the Gospels," infra), it may take the form of traditions presented as Jesus' sayings (as in *The Gospel of Thomas* and *The Gospel of Truth:* see article on the books found at Nag Hammadi, infra), or it may present material topically organized around specific events in Jesus' life (for example, *The Infancy Gospel of Thomas*). Clearly the dynamic concept of the gospel of Jesus Christ as proclaimed by Paul and the other early Christian evangelists provided the conditions in which the term gospel became the literary designator for those books containing the story or traditions related to the story of Jesus Christ.

BIBLIOGRAPHY

Stuhlmacher, Peter, ed. *The Gospel and the Gospels*. Grand Rapids: Eerdmans, 1991. See especially Otto Betz, "Jesus' Gospel of the Kingdom," 53–74.

The Synoptic Problem: How Did We Get Our Gospels?

David L. Dungan and John S. Kloppenborg

Why Were the Gospels Written?

As far as we know Jesus did not write anything. The four gospels we have are the products of later Christian writers and reflect the efforts of these writers to set down an account of Jesus' life and teachings that would speak meaningfully to particular ecclesial communities in the first century. After Jesus' death and resurrection some of his followers preached the gospel in and around Jerusalem while others traveled to foreign lands. As time passed, under varying circumstances, some Christians put into written form what they had taught of all that Jesus had said and done, and thus Jesus' words and actions became part of a large corpus of interpreted tradition, known as "the gospel: good news" (see above on "The Meaning of the Term 'Gospel'").

The gospel of Matthew is a compact collection of the Lord's teachings and actions arranged in a broadly biographical framework. A noteworthy feature is the group of more than sixty references to the Hebrew Scriptures designed to prove that Jesus of Nazareth had indeed fulfilled a carefully chosen number of prophecies regarding the long-awaited Messiah, the Son of David.

Mark wrote a gospel that is similar in outline to Matthew's, though much shorter. Mark presents Jesus not so much as a speaker of long sermons but as a healer, exorcist, and wonder-worker. Curiously, Mark's Jesus is misunderstood even by his disciples, who abandon him prior to his death. Only after the resurrection are the disciples predicted to be reunited with him (although Mark does not actually narrate this reunion).

The gospel of Luke is the first part of a two-part narrative describing the life and ministry of the Savior, followed by a history of the spread and development of the Church outside Palestine. This gospel may have been written in part as a response to the recent execution of the apostle Paul in Rome (traditionally dated during the reign of Nero). However, it also seems to have been written in response to the terrible destruction of Jerusalem in 70 C.E. This event was understood by the author of the gospel of Luke to have been clearly predicted by the Lord Jesus.

John's gospel differs substantially from the first three (synoptic) gospels, not only in its selection and arrangement of stories but in its overall tone. The Johannine Jesus speaks in lofty, deliberately symbolic or allegorical speech, and most of John's message is focused on the identity of Jesus as God's Son sent from heaven rather than on ethical teachings or instructions for Church life or mission.

These records of Christ's testimony to God took the form of four biographical narratives. They are similar in the most important aspects, yet each preserves a striking originality and uniqueness as well. Each is inspired by the living presence of Christ in a particular community of faith; each is conscious of standing in historical continuity with Jesus himself. In this way the Church received four narratives of the gospel of Jesus Christ. [See "The Church's Gospel Canon: Why Four and No More?" below.]

The late second-century Church Father Origen gave this beautiful explanation of the writing of these gospels.

> Let it be supposed that certain men [viz. the apostles] by the Holy Spirit see God [in Jesus Christ] and his holy words and his appearance, which he prepared for them, to be revealed at chosen times for their progress, who are several in number and in different places. . . . They are not blessed by wholly similar visions and benefits [but] each one, in his own way, announces what he sees in the spirit concerning God [in Jesus Christ] and his words, concerning his appearances to his saints. Thus [the first Gospel author] announces certain things said . . . and done by God [in Jesus Christ] at a certain time and place, but to another [Gospel author] he reveals other things concerning oracles and divine fulfillments. Then there is a third man [who] wants to teach us other things than what has just been said concerning the two just mentioned. And let there also be a fourth doing something analogously to the three [just mentioned]. But let these four agree with each other concerning certain [basic] things revealed to them by the Spirit and let them disagree a little concerning other things (*Commentary on John* 10.3).

In this way the Church received not one but four portraits of the Lord Jesus Christ. "So Jesus is many things, in the sense of different [external] impressions. Concerning which it seems probable that the gospel writers, receiving differing conceptions, while still agreeing with each other in some [things], recorded the gospels" (*Commentary on John* 10.4).

But Why Four Gospels? Why Not Just One?

From earliest times the discrepancies between the Church's gospels made them the object of ridicule by those outside. This led to a situation in which these gospels became a source of confusion within the Church itself. Opponents of Christianity used such discrepancies as proof that the gospels are based on rumor and hearsay. One favorite target was Christ's genealogy in Matthew, which is very different from the one in Luke. It was not unusual for early Christian scholars to use harmonizations of the gospels in their polemical writings against outside critics to minimize the differences. Tatian's *Diatessaron,* which was probably based on an earlier Greek harmony prepared by his teacher Justin Martyr while he was teaching in Rome (mid-second century), is the most famous example in the early Christian Church, but harmonies were commonly constructed in the late medieval and early modern periods and can be found in the missionary literature of early Anglo-Saxon Christianity, medieval Persian Christianity, and modern Chinese Christianity.

The explanations given by the second- and third-century Church Fathers as to why God would bring about the writing and canonization of *four* authoritative gospels are instructive. The earliest is that of Irenaeus of Lyon (ca. 130–ca. 200):

> It is not possible that the gospels can be either more or fewer in number than they are. For since there are four zones of the world in which we live, and four principal winds, while the Church is scattered throughout all the world, . . . it is fitting that she should have four pillars breathing out immortality on every side and vivifying people afresh (*Adv. haer.* 3.9).

Putting this into our language we might say that because the people of God would need to be upbuilded in many different cultural contexts on the earth God gave the Church four *culturally diverse portraits* of our Savior at the very beginning. Matthew is a profoundly Hebrew account while Luke is filled with those literary touches that would delight a Greek audience. Mark focused on the power of Jesus to heal, forgive, and teach, and on his courage in the face of death in order to provide a model for those who wanted to learn of him. The gospel of John, perhaps composed in Ephesus or Antioch, addresses a Jewish-Christian community that has found itself in profound conflict with other Jews over the identity and significance of Jesus of Nazareth.

Viewed in this way the gospels offer a lesson in multicultural harmony, enshrined at the very beginning of our New Testament, a beacon light to guide Christians of all generations.

The Church Father Augustine suggested another reason why God would want the Church to have four gospels. He noticed how different the gospels were with respect to their central "image" or portrait of Christ. Matthew, he says, undertook to "construct the record of the incarnation of the Lord according to the royal lineage" of Christ (*De cons. evang.* 1.2.3). Mark played the role of a king's courtier in the sense that he "follows [Matthew] closely and looks like his attendant and summarizer, for in his narrative . . . he has a very large number of passages in concord with Matthew" (ibid). "Luke, on the other hand, seems to have occupied himself rather with the priestly lineage and character of the Lord" (ibid). Mark was sometimes understood as having united the kingly role of Jesus in Matthew with his priestly role in Luke (so Augustine, *On the Harmony of the Evangelists.* 4.10.11). The portraits in Matthew, Mark, and Luke in general are more similar to each other than they are to John, who is in a class by himself. The reason for this, says Augustine, is that they sought to portray Christ after the flesh, that is, in temporal terms. John, in his turn,

> had in view that true divinity of the Lord in which He is the Father's equal, and directed his efforts above all to the setting forth of Christ's divine nature in his gospel. . . . Therefore he is borne to loftier heights, in which he leaves the other three far behind, [passing] beyond the cloud in which the whole earth is wrapped and reaching to liquid heaven from which, with clearest and steadiest mental eye, he is able to look upon God the word, who was in the beginning with God, and by whom all things were made (*On the Harmony of the Evangelists* 1.4.7).

To these considerations we may add one final thought, often mentioned by theologians both ancient and modern. With four different accounts we are given a more reliable historical and theological base for our faith than if we had just one gospel. Four different yet similar accounts make room for each Christian to learn in her or his own way how to respond to Christ personally. Each gospel writer expressed the common tradition in one distinct way so as to communicate most fully to the particular intended audience. The diversity that one observes within the gospels does not undermine the "truth" of the gospel. On the contrary, it shows how the message of Jesus was capable of faith-filled adaptation to a variety of historical and cultural circumstances, just as it continues to be adapted today.

The Similarities are Understandable; What Should We Do About the Differences?

Given the powerful conviction from earliest times that the gospels all spoke the one, holy truth about Jesus Christ, the most frequent method Christians have adopted for handling the many differences among the gospel narratives has been to harmonize them. Many early Church Fathers (exceptions are Origen and his student Eusebius) sought to minimize the divergence among the four gospels by harmonizing their different details. The two most famous examples of this approach are the *Diatessaron* of Tatian the Syrian (late second century), and Augustine's *On the Harmony of the Evangelists* (written around 405), in which he painstakingly recreated what he took to be the original, full chronology of Christ's life and ministry. Augustine's approach set a precedent within orthodox western Christianity, both Roman Catholic and Protestant, that remains widely followed to this day.

At the opposite extreme is the approach of taking one of the gospels as the guide and disregarding the others where they disagree with it. Although this approach is rarely defended explicitly there are some even today who in practice base nearly everything on the gospel of John or that of Mark, disregarding the others.

There is a better way. After the Reformation, Christians both Roman Catholic and Protestant became convinced that a historical understanding of when and by whom the gospels were written would be a great help in interpreting them appropriately. In particular if we knew the original order of composition and saw correctly how each gospel author used or departed from the traditions contained in the gospels written by his predecessor(s) we would gain valuable insights into how that author understood the gospel tradition himself. This would be an invaluable aid to our understanding of the development of the gospel tradition. If Christians can learn something about the actual life-setting and situation of each biblical writer they will begin to see how the early Christian Church grew and developed, what obstacles it faced and overcame, and how it encountered many diverse cultures and found ways to inculturate itself without losing the core and essence of God's saving word. [For further discussion see "The Church's Gospel Canon: Why Four and No More?" below.]

What are the Main Ways Scholars View the Writing of the Gospels Today?

To inquire into the composition and authorship of the gospels is to ask fundamentally historical questions of them in the conviction that the more is known of the concrete circumstances of composition the more responsibly we can understand and interpret the gospels. It is of course true that much of the genius and artistry of a gospel is still evident irrespective of whether one is able to identify its author or its original intentions, in much the same way as works of art or literature or music retain their value even if the artist remains unknown. Nevertheless, from a theological point of view the character of Christianity as a historical faith with its fundamental conviction that God has acted and continues to act in history by means of historically situated human agents underscores the importance of situating its foundational documents historically. John Paul II has stated: "The Church of Christ takes the realism of the incarnation seriously, and this is why she attaches great importance to the 'historico-critical' study of the Bible. Far from condemning it, as those who support 'mystical' exegesis would want, my Predecessors vigorously approved" (John Paul II, "Address on the Interpretation of the Bible in the Church").

The frank acknowledgment of the historical character of the gospels has important consequences when approaching the issues of their composition and authorship, for it implies on the one hand that the composition and transmission of the gospels are complex, having many dimensions (historical, social, cultural, psychological, technical) and are therefore not subject to simplistic or unidimensional explanations. On the other hand this implies that, as in all historical endeavors, the historical investigation of the gospels is limited by the nature of the evidence itself. Although it may be desirable to know with certainty the identity of biblical authors and the exact scope and circumstances of their activities this is rarely possible, given the general dearth of data.

Following the mainstream of twentieth-century biblical scholarship, the Pontifical Biblical Commission has, in its efforts to provide a model for understanding the Jesus tradition, proposed a three-stage development *(Instructio de historica Evangeliorum veritate).* This is a heuristic model and is not intended to be used woodenly, but it is nonetheless useful. Throughout, the Commission stresses that all of the discourse in the gospels must be viewed in the context of the habits of speech and expectations of the various early audiences addressed in the gospels. Thus at the first level, that of Jesus and his immediate disciples in early Roman Palestine, Jesus employed "the modes of reasoning and of exposition which were in vogue at the time" (§15 VII). For their part the disciples after Easter employed sayings and stories of Jesus in accordance with the immediate needs of preaching and other pastoral praxis, adapting them to the needs and mentalities of their audiences in a variety of locations in the Mediterranean world. At the third stage, that of the evangelists, the Jesus tradition continued to be selected, arranged, and adapted in accordance with the particular ecclesial situations addressed by the evangelists.

This organic view of the development of the Jesus tradition, insists the Commission, does not compromise its ultimate truth or value; on the contrary, insofar as the gospels (and the Scriptures generally) are the expressions of faith of various ecclesial communities, and their reception as Scripture a matter of the consensus of ecclesial communities, the varying ecclesial "re-readings" of the Jesus tradition are integral parts of the gospels as Scripture.

In order to describe in concrete terms the development and history of "re-readings" of the Jesus tradition that the Commission discusses in general terms it is necessary to articulate the relationship among the gospels.

The strong consensus of synoptic scholars of all stripes is that a literary relationship exists among the synoptic gospels. This conclusion is based on the striking agreements that exist among the three synoptics, both in the wording of various pericopes and in the sequence in which these pericopes are reported. For example, all three gospels agree in reporting the healing of a paralytic (Matt 9:1-8; Mark 2:1-12; Luke 5:17-26), the call of Levi/Matthew (Matt 9:9-13; Mark 2:13-16; Luke 5:27-32) and the question about fasting (Matt 9:1-8; Mark 2:18-22; Luke 5:33-39), even though there is no obvious connection among them or necessity that they be related in this order. Similarly, there is often near-verbatim agreement in the reproduction of sayings (for example, Matt 3:7-10 // Luke 3:7-9; Matt 12:41-

42 // Luke 11:31-32), agreement that can hardly be explained by appeal to oral tradition.

The Basic Data to be Explained

At this point the consensus weakens, for there are several fundamentally different ways of understanding the literary relationship among the gospels, and in particular the direction of dependence of one gospel on another. Nonetheless, solutions to the Synoptic Problem, the problem of the literary relationship among the gospels, begin with the following data:

The synoptic gospels exhibit a particular configuration of agreements and disagreements in the sayings and stories they relate.

(a) There are a significant number of details in which all three are in agreement, both in regard to the wording of the pericopes and the relative order in which they appear.

(b) When two of the gospels are in agreement a distinctive pattern emerges: there are a large number of instances where Matthew and Mark agree in wording and/or in their relative positioning of pericopes where Luke has a slightly differing wording; and in other instances Mark and Luke agree (in wording and/or sequence) against Matthew. But there are significantly fewer instances of Matthew and Luke agreeing in wording against Mark, and no unambiguous instance of Matthew and Luke having a pericope that also occurs in Mark in the same relative position, in disagreement with Mark's position.

In the nineteenth century three different theories came to be widely discussed. The first said that the gospels were the product of a complex process of oral tradition involving considerable "cross-pollination" as the four gospels evolved over the early decades. A second view said that Matthew was the first gospel to be written. This view also said that Luke was a revision of the Jewish Matthew for use in Paul's Gentile churches. Mark was produced by Mark, the follower of St. Peter, as a sort of bridge between Matthew (the Gospel for the Circumcision) and Luke (the Gospel for the Uncircumcision). This view is known today as the Two Gospel Hypothesis.

A third view said Mark was the first gospel to be written, appearing some time in the late 60s C.E. Matthew and Luke were independent revisions of Mark, adding considerable sayings material taken from a now lost source, called "Q" (from the German word for "source", *Quelle*). This view is now known as the Two Document Hypothesis or the Two Source Hypothesis.

A description of the Two Document Theory will be given below. It must be stated that *all* of the ways of accounting for the composition of the gospels are *hypotheses*—that is, heuristic models that allow us to imagine the compositional process. None of the currently viable hypotheses is "proved" beyond a reasonable doubt and each admits of strengths and weaknesses. Let us consider the main reasons for thinking that the Two Gospel Hypothesis is correct.

The Two Gospel Hypothesis

The name Two Gospel Hypothesis is derived from the claim that the gospel of Mark is based on the two earlier gospels, Matthew and Luke. To begin with, this hypothesis says that the most Jewish gospel—Matthew—was the earliest written gospel, putting into writing the "good news" preached by the Jerusalem apostles. One of its purposes was to show the fulfillment of the Law and the Prophets in the ministry of Jesus.

This hypothesis says the gospel of Luke was the second gospel to be written, because the gospel of Matthew was very difficult to understand in the wider international missionary area where Paul's churches were located. It appears that Luke, quite likely a co-worker of the apostle Paul, undertook to prepare a revision of the gospel of Matthew for use in Gentile churches, a revision that incorporated considerable new material (cf. Luke 1:1-4).

Mark, as the third gospel, functions to expedite the gospel of Jesus Christ by carrying forward the essential agreement between Paul and the "pillars of the Church" reached at the Jerusalem conference (Galatians 2). A historical confirmation of this "conciliar" view can be found in the situation of the Church after the death of Peter and Paul. During their life they led separate missions, Peter to the circumcised, Paul to the uncircumcised (Galatians 2). After their deaths there was a possibility of that separation widening. Against any such tendency Mark argues for holding together the two branches of Jewish and Gentile Christianity. Mark accomplished this by drawing on common material found in Matthew and Luke, adding little else.

Finally, the gospel of John was the latest of the gospels to be written and seems to be largely though not completely independent of the other three.

What are the Reasons for Supporting This View?

First of all, a careful study of the gospels reveals the fact that there is a very close correlation between content and order of stories in Matthew, Mark, and Luke, while there is very little correlation either of content or order of stories between these three and the gospel of John. This close similarity among most of the gospels should not be surprising, since it means that the evangelists responsible for each gospel tried to work in close cooperation with their predecessor(s), a picture of apostolic coordination that we can see reflected in Paul's report in Gal 2:1-10. The agreement in the relative order of the pericopes among the Synoptic Gospels is explained by the second writer having frequently preserved the pericope order of the first, and the third having followed the order common to his sources, i.e., where they agreed with one another, and having followed the order of either one or the other where they departed from one another. This was a perfectly intelligible compositional practice of writers in antiquity. See the preface to his account of "The Expedition of Alexander" given by the historian Flavius Arrian, a contemporary of the evangelists, translated in *Documents for the Study of the Gospels* by David R. Cartlidge and David L. Dungan (Cleveland, New York, and London: William Collins, 1980) 126.

Second, granting that the Jesus movement was Jewish in origin, it is both right and natural that the most Jewish of the gospels be recognized as foundational for the development of the Christian faith, knitting together both the Law and the Prophets with God's self-revelation in Jesus Christ. The Belgian scholar Eduard Massaux, in a comprehensive study of which gospels were quoted in Church writings of the first two hundred years, discovered that the gospel of Matthew was quoted far more often than any of the other gospels, with Luke coming in second, John third, and Mark, our shortest text, hardly at all. This pattern of quotations supports our view that Matthew was from the beginning regarded as the Church's foundational gospel.

Third, if we examine the Greek text of the gospels we discover many tell-tale signs of careful use by the later writers of the earlier gospels: phrases that are favorites of Matthew tend to reappear in Luke and Mark but not vice-versa. The same is true of Luke: Luke's favorite words and phrases tend to appear in Mark, but not in Matthew, consistent with his being in the second position. Finally, Mark's characteristic words and grammatical constructions are found in neither Matthew nor Luke, consistent with his having been written last of all. The gospel of John has only a handful of the stories found in the other three gospels, and John's language and diction are unique.

Fourth, the evidence from the Church Fathers bears out the hypothesis that Matthew and Luke were written first. For example, according to Eusebius (*Hist. eccl.* 614.5-7) Clement of Alexandria preserved a tradition in his *Hypotyposeis* from the primitive elders with regard to the order of the gospels as follows: "those were written first which include genealogies." Thus Matthew and Luke with genealogies would have been written before gospels without genealogies. This would presumably include not only abbreviated forms of these earlier gospls like Marcion's version of Luke, but also the canonical gospels of Mark and John.

Finally, there is a positive correlation between agreement in order and wording among the gospels indicating that Mark used both Matthew and Luke (Farmer, p. 217).

What is the Major Difficulty for the Two Gospel Hypothesis?

The apparent lack of sequential agreement between Matthew and Luke is the most serious difficulty for the Two Gospel Hypothesis. The 1996 book *Beyond the "Q" Impasse: Luke's Use of Matthew,* edited by Allan McNicol, deals with this difficulty. It serves to remove not only the major difficulty for this hypothesis but also a major reason for hypothecating "Q."

What are the Benefits of This Theory to Preaching and the Work of a Pastor?

First of all, in contrast to other speculative schemes this approach to the gospels sticks to the canonical writings themselves and attempts to understand them without recourse to hypothetical sources. This is very important, since it means scholar and pastor start from the same place. That situation is not helped when scholars, without providing their readers convincing reasons, take as their starting point for interpreting the gospels a complex and arcane theory that can only baffle most intelligent lay persons because it involves the use of hypothetical texts only the scholars themselves know anything about.

Second, in the task of reading the *whole* Bible as witness to the word of God each parish priest or minister should look for hints and signs where the biblical writers themselves have quoted earlier books and statements. The attentive reader will become aware of a real dialogue within the Holy Bible itself. The Two Gospel Hypothesis draws attention to this fact. Look at the OT on the one hand and at the gospel of Matthew on the other. Old Testament passages are explicitly quoted in the gospel of Matthew, sometimes by Jesus himself, more than sixty times. This gospel is, as it were, the great bridge between the Law and the Prophets and the good news of God in Jesus Christ. No other approach to the gospels brings this momentous fact out as sharply and distinctly.

Finally, the two great gospels of Matthew and Luke contain the most cherished passages dealing with God's preferential option for the poor and the divine concern for justice and well-being. On the Two Document Hypothesis the most powerful of these passages (for example, Matt 25:31-46; Luke 4:16-19) are missing from Mark and "Q."

The Two Document Hypothesis

The most commonly encountered solution to the Synoptic Problem is the Two Document Hypothesis. In brief compass this hypothesis suggests that Mark is the earliest of the three synoptic gospels and that Matthew and Luke have independently utilized Mark as the framework for their gospels. But since Matthew and Luke share some material that does not appear in Mark—much of the Sermon on the Mount and the "woes" against the Pharisees, for example—it is necessary to posit a second source from which Matthew and Luke obtained this material. This source, for lack of a better name, is called "Q," (German *Quelle* = "source").

The Two Document Hypothesis accounts for the basic data to be explained in the following manner.

(a) Since, on this hypothesis, Matthew and Luke employ Mark as their main narrative source they are in general guided by Mark's wording and sequence, and hence often agree with Mark.

(b) Since Matthew and Luke independently used Mark without having seen each other's gospel, there is little possibility of agreement when one (say, Matthew) altered Mark's sequencing of pericopes or wording. When both Matthew and Luke changed Mark's sequence or wording, they normally also disagree with each other. This holds completely in respect to the sequence of pericopes, but there are a number of verbal agreements of Matthew and Luke against Mark (the "minor agreements"). Many of these are probably coincidental agreements caused by both Matthew and Luke improving Mark's style, sometimes in the same way. There are a few instances of agreements that cannot be explained so easily, however. These represent the most serious difficulty for the Two Document Hypothesis.

The lack of agreement between Matthew and Luke in the material before Mark 1:1 and after Mark 16:8 is explained on the supposition that both used Mark as their principal narrative outline, but both also wished to include stories of Jesus' birth and of his appearances. But since Mark had neither, Matthew and Luke turned to other (oral and written) sources, presumably circulating in their respective communities.

An almost total lack of sequential agreement in the "double tradition" results from the fact that Matthew and Luke have independently combined Mark with Q; and since Matthew had not seen Luke's gospel he could not be influenced by Luke's combination of Mark and Q (and vice versa). Thus, for example, Matthew introduced the Sermon on the Mount (largely taken from Q) at a point parallel to Mark 1:21 (or perhaps 1:39, depending on how the two gospels are aligned), whereas Luke introduced his shorter Sermon on the Plain at Mark 3:19. Luke's woes against the Pharisees occur in the course of his "travel narrative" (Luke 9:51–18:14), which is inserted at Mark 10:1; Matthew's woes appear in the context of Mark 12:37b-40. Even though Matthew and Luke often agree closely in the wording of the double tradition (Q) material (since they were copying from a written document), they practically never agree in the way it was combined with Mark, which is precisely what one should expect if Matthew and Luke worked independently. On the other hand, because the "Q" material had a fixed order, with, for example, the story of the centurion's servant following Jesus' opening sermon, Matthew and Luke (influenced by the Q order), placed these materials in the same relative order even if they actually disagreed in the overall placement of the Sermon and the healing of the servant relative to Mark's order.

What is the Major Difficulty for the Two Document Hypothesis?

Since on the Two Document Hypothesis Matthew and Luke are independent of one another, in general they should not agree with one another against Mark. The verbal agreements of Matthew and Luke against Mark (the "minor agreements") are, therefore, considered to be the major difficulty for the Two Document Hypothesis. The basic work on the "minor agreements" is Frans Neirynck, *The Minor Agreements of Matthew and Luke against Mark: With Cumulative List*.

What are the Consequences of This Theory?

The consequences of the Two Document Hypothesis for understanding the development of the synoptic gospels are considerable.

(1) Mark is the earliest of the three synoptic gospels and the shortest. It has a rather rough style characterized by excessive use of certain adverbs ("immediately," "again"), redundancies, the use of the historic present, and a dramatic if not verbose narrative style. None of these is necessarily an indication of Mark's originality; but on the assumption of Markan priority it is not difficult to understand why Matthew and Luke variously eliminated or modified many of these features. Mark also contains a number of infelicitous expressions (Mark 6:5-6: "And [Jesus] *could* not do any miracles there, except that he laid his hands on a few sick people and healed them and he marveled because of their unbelief" [emphasis added]), and historical errors (Mark 2:26: "when Abiathar was high priest" [Ahimelek was actually the priest in the episode to which Mark refers]).

(2) Both Matthew and Luke rewrote Mark, improving Mark's style, omitting Markan elements that might be misunderstood or that were theologically objectionable, and correcting historical errors. For example, Matthew changes Mark 6:5-6 to "And [Jesus] *did not* do many miracles because of their unbelief" (Matt 13:58; emphasis added) and both Matthew and Luke omit entirely the reference to Abiathar.

(3) Both Matthew and Luke (independently) supplemented Mark's account by means of the common materials (mostly sayings) they had from Q and from other stories and sayings circulating within their respective churches. For Matthew this included improving the depiction of the disciples (who are criticized in Mark) and of Jesus' own family, emphasizing the majesty of Jesus (by means of further christological titles and confessions, and expressions of his foreknowledge), and stressing the roles of Jesus as an interpreter of the Torah, as one who was faithful to the Law and as one whose ministry was the fulfillment of eschatological hopes enshrined in the Hebrew Bible. Luke also stresses continuities between the ministry of Jesus and the Hebrew Bible (though citing different OT texts to supplement Mark's OT quotations), but also edits his account with a view to establishing continuities with the activities of the apostles and of Paul detailed in Acts.

The Two Document Hypothesis does not necessarily imply that all that was added by Matthew and Luke to Mark were secondary creations by the evangelists. On the contrary, it is normally assumed that many of the sayings (for example, Matt 10:5-6, 23; Luke 17:20-21) and stories (for example, Matt 20:1-15; Luke 15:11-32;16:1-8) are ancient, conceivably authentic materials that did not find their way into either Mark or Q but were nonetheless preserved by the Matthaean and Lukan communities. In accordance with the principles of redaction criticism those critics who adopt the Two Document Hypothesis normally assume that much of the variation that exists among the gospels is a reflection of the different ecclesial communities to which the gospels were originally addressed. Nonetheless, the Two Document Hypothesis also implies a measure of theological development, from Mark's rather unrefined christology

In addition to the Two Gospel and Two Document hypotheses there are four others being critically defended in contemporary scholarship.

First, the Multiple Source Hypothesis defended by Marie-Emile Boismard posits several earlier sources and provides for a proto-Mark combining earlier "Matthean" and "Lukan" hypothetical sources. In this way it can account for the evidence that otherwise supports the view that Mark is third and has combined the two earlier gospels, Matthew and Luke.

Second, there is the Austin Farrer hypothesis, defended today by Michael Goulder. This hypothesis posits the gospels being composed in the sequence Mark—Matthew—Luke, with Matthew copying Mark, and Luke combining the two earlier gospels. Like the Two Gospel Hypothesis, the Austin Farrer hypothesis regards the third gospel as based on two earlier gospels where the second has made use of the first. In principle this hypothesis has an equal right to be called a "two gospel" hypothesis, since it regards the third gospel as based on two earlier gospels rather than on sources that include the hypothetical "Q" document.

Third, there is the "Deutero-Markus" hypothesis, defended primarily by Albert Fuchs. According to this hypothesis canonical Mark was revised by an unknown author, whose revision of canonical Mark was copied independently by both Matthew and Luke, which would explain why Matthew and Luke sometimes agree against canonical Mark.

Finally, there is the traditional Augustinian hypothesis that posits a compositional sequence Matthew—Mark—Luke. Like the Two Gospel and Austin Farrer hypotheses, the Augustinian hypothesis recognizes that the second evangelist used the first gospel written and that the third evangelist used both earlier gospels. It too has an equal right to be called a "two gospel" hypothesis. *—Ed.*

in which Jesus is depicted largely as an unrecognized wonder worker executed by Pilate (in accordance with the divine plan), to a more complex christology that depicts Jesus as a Torah interpreter and teacher, a true shepherd of Israel and the founder/leader of the Church (Matthew) and from Mark's rather negative view of the disciples and Jesus' family to the construction of a salvation history beginning in the Hebrew Scriptures and compassing John the Baptist (and his parents), Jesus' parents, his disciples ("the apostles") and the post-Easter community, including Paul (as Luke has it).

BIBLIOGRAPHY

Bea, Augustin. *The Study of the Synoptic Gospels.* English version edited by Joseph A. Fitzmyer. New York: Harper & Row, 1965.

Bellinzoni, Arthur J., ed., with the assistance of Joseph B. Tyson and William O. Walker, Jr. *The Two Source Hypothesis: A Critical Appraisal.* Macon, Ga: Mercer University Press, 1985. A basic source book for classical essays aguing for and against Marcan priority and the existence of Q.

Dungan, David L., ed. *The Interrelations of the Gospels: A Symposium led by M-E. Boismard, W. R. Farmer, and F. Neirynck.* BEThL 95. Leuven: Leuven University Press, 1990. A comprehensive treatment of three of the major solutions for the Synoptic Problem.

____. *The History of the Synoptic Problem.* ABRL. Garden City, N.Y.: Doubleday, 1999.

Farmer, William R. *The Synoptic Problem: A Critical Analysis.* New York: Macmillan, 1964.

____. *The Gospel of Jesus: The Pastoral Relevance of the Synoptic Problem.* Louisville: Westminster/John Knox, 1994.

John Paul II, "Address on the Interpretation of the Bible in the Church" in Pontifical Biblical Commission, *The Interpretation of the Bible in the Church.* Vatican City: Libreria Editrice Vaticana, 1993, 13. "Mystical exegesis" was promoted in an anonymous pamphlet circulated in Italy in the early 1940s by persons vigorously opposed to the application of historical methods to the Bible. Such anti-historical pleadings were rejected in Pius XII's encyclical *Divino Afflante Spiritu* (1943) and again by the Pontifical Biblical Commission (*Instructio de historica Evangeliorum veritate,* 1964), parts of which also appeared in the Constitution on Divine Revelation of Vatican II (*Dei Verbum* 1513).

Kloppenborg, John S. *Making Difference: Basic Issues/ Disputed Questions on the Sayings Gospel Q.* Minneapolis: Fortress, 1999.

McNicol, Allan J., ed., with David L. Dungan and David B. Peabody. *Beyond the Q Impasse: Luke's Use of Matthew.* Valley Forge, Pa: Trinity Press International, 1996. The basic work seeking to demonstrate that Luke used Matthew.

Neirynck, Frans. *The Minor Agreements of Matthew and Luke against Mark: With a Cumulative List.* BEThL 37. Leuven: Leuven University Press, 1974. For a discussion of solutions to the minor agreements in the context of the Two Document Hypothesis see Frans Neirynck, "The Minor Agreements and the Two-Source Theory," *Evangelica II: 1982–1991. Collected Essays,* edited by Frans Van Segbroeck. BEThL 99. Leuven: Leuven University Press, 1991, 3–42; see further

Andreas Ennulat, *Die "Minor Agreements": Untersuchung zu einer offenen Frage des synoptischen Problems*. WUNT 2/62. Tübingen: Mohr/Siebeck, 1994. See further Georg Strecker, ed. *Minor Agreements, Symposium Göttingen 1991*. Göttingen: Vandenhoeck and Ruprecht, 1993, which contains Frans Neirynck, "The Minor Agreements and the Two-Source Theory," and William R. Farmer, "The Minor Agreements of Matthew and Luke Against Mark and the Two Gospel Hypothesis" among other essays on the Minor Agreements.

Sanders, E. P., and Margaret Davies. *Studying the Synoptic Gospels*. London: SCM Press; Philadelphia: Trinity Press International, 1989. An advanced textbook for study of the synoptic gospels with a critical evaluation of the four most widely discussed solutions to the Synoptic Problem.

The Nag Hammadi Corpus

Frederik Wisse

In December 1945 a farmer digging for topsoil some nine kilometers from the ruins of the monastery of St. Pachomius in upper Egypt discovered a large jar filled with thirteen papyrus codices in their leather covers. Eventually twelve of the codices—and eight leaves of a thirteenth that already in antiquity had been stuffed into the cover of Codex VI—found their way to antiquities dealers in Cairo. What is known today as Codex I was purchased as a gift for the famous psychiatrist C. G. Jung of Zurich, but it resides now with the other codices in the Coptic Museum in Cairo. They were named the Nag Hammadi codices after the district town nearest to the place of discovery.

Some of the codices, such as II and VII, are in an excellent state of preservation while others, namely codices IV, IX, X, and XII are very fragmentary. The codices contain from one to eight distinct texts each: parts of at least fifty-two tractates survive. If one takes into account the four duplicates and one triple attestation there are forty-six different texts, written in Coptic but all translated from Greek. More than half of the tractates are Gnostic but there are also a considerable number of heterodox Christian writings as well as some pagan texts. Apart from a garbled translation of Plato's *Republic* 588b–589b [VI.5] only *The Sentences of Sextus* [XII.1] and two of the three Hermetic tractates [VI.7 and 8] were previously known. Among the Oxyrhynchus papyri found in the late nineteenth century there are three fragments representing three different Greek manuscripts of *The Gospel of Thomas* and one Greek fragment of *The Sophia of Jesus Christ,* but their identity was not recognized until complete copies showed up in the Nag Hammadi find.

A facsimile edition of the codices has been published in twelve volumes (James M. Robinson et al., *The Facsimile Edition of the Nag Hammadi Codices* [Leiden: Brill, 1972–1984]). A fourteen-volume text edition that also includes the parallel texts in Codex Berolinensis 8501, with English translation, introduction, notes, and indices was completed in 1995 (*The Coptic Gnostic Library,* Nag Hammadi Studies, Leiden). The same team has published translations of all the tractates in one volume (James M. Robinson, ed., *The Nag Hammadi Library in English.* 3rd rev. ed. Leiden: Brill, and San Francisco: Harper & Row, 1988). For further bibliography see David M. Scholer, *Nag Hammadi Bibliography 1948–69.* Nag Hammadi Studies 1, Leiden 1971, and annually thereafter "Bibliographia Gnostica: Supplementum" in *Novum Testamentum.*

Most of the Nag Hammadi tractates defy categorization in terms of Christian orthodoxy and specific Gnostic sects. This is in part due to the fact that the dividing line between early Christianity and Gnosticism was not a clear one, nor was the line between Gnosticism and Middle Platonism. Furthermore it would appear that the great majority of the Nag Hammadi tractates were not written within doctrinally well-defined groups or sects, but rather are the creations of individuals writing in a syncretistic milieu. Apart from the excerpt from Plato's *Republic,* the three Hermetic (pagan Gnostic) texts (*The Discourse on the Eighth and Ninth* [VI.6], *The Prayer of Thanksgiving* [VI.7], and *Asclepius 21–29* [VI.8]), and an enigmatic pagan text (*The Thunder: Perfect Mind* [VI.2]) the following broad categories appear appropriate:

(1) Sixteen heterodox Christian texts written most likely before the establishment or outside the confines of Christian orthodoxy, and similar in form and content to the previously known Christian apocrypha and pseudepigrapha. They tend to be ascetic and esoteric in outlook, and Gnostic elements, if any, are inconspicuous or relatively minor: *The Prayer of the Apostle Paul* [I.1], *The Apocryphon of James* [I.2], *The Gospel of Truth* [I.3; XII.2], *The Treatise on the Resurrection* [I.4], *The Gospel of Thomas* [II.2], *The Exegesis on the Soul* [II.6], *The Book of Thomas the Contender* [II.7], *The Dialogue of the Savior* [III.5], *The Apocalypse of Paul* [V.2], *The (First) Apocalypse of James* [V.3], *The (Second) Apocalypse of James* [V.4], *The Act of Peter and the Twelve Apostles* [VI.1], *Authoritative Teaching* [VI.3], *The Teachings of Silvanus* [VII.4], *The Sentences of Sextus* [XII.1], and probably also *Fragments* [XII.3].

(2) Ten Christian Gnostic texts of which the following four appear to be Valentinian: *The Tripartite Tractate* [I.5], *The Gospel of Philip* [II.3], *The Interpretation of Knowledge* [XI.1], and *A Valentinian Exposition* [XI.2]. The other six texts cannot be linked to a specific Gnostic sect mentioned by the Church Fathers. Several of them explicitly take issue with the orthodox Christian position on various issues and they appear to have borrowed some elements from mythological Gnosticism: *The Concept of Our Great Power* [VI.4], *The Second Treatise of the Great Seth* [VII.2], *The Apocalypse of Peter* [VII.3], *The Letter of Peter to Philip* [VIII.2], *Melchizedek* [IX.1], and *The Testimony of Truth* [IX.3].

(3) Fifteen texts represent mythological Gnosticism. They range the full spectrum from those with significant Christian elements to others that are only marginally Christian and some that lack Christian themes and terminology. Though all appear to borrow from Middle or Neoplatonism this is most pronounced in the texts that lack Christian elements. Most prominent in the group are the five so-called Sethian-Gnostic texts that, though very diverse in content, share a distinct set of mythological figures and themes and generally present their teaching in a Christian framework: *The Apocryphon of John* [II.1; III.1; IV.1], the most important of this subgroup, *The Hypostasis of the Archons* [II.4], *The Gospel of the Egyptians* [III.2; IV.2], *The Sophia of Jesus Christ* [III.4] which is a Christianized and augmented version of *Eugnostos, the Blessed,* and *Trimorphic Protennoia* [XIII.1].

A second subgroup of ten writings shows no or only minor Christian influence, but makes eclectic use of Sethian-Gnostic, Jewish, Manichaean, magical, astrological, and especially Middle or Neoplatonist traditions: *On the Origin of the World* [II.5; XIII.2], *Eugnostos, the Blessed* [III.5; V.1], *The Apocalypse of Adam* [V.5], *The Paraphrase of Shem* [VII.1], *The Three Steles of Seth* [VII.5], *Zostrianos* [VIII.1], *The Thought of Norea* [IX.2], *Marsanes* [X.1], *Allogenes* [XI.3], and probably also the poorly preserved *Hypsiphrone* [XI.4].

As in the case of the Dead Sea Scrolls there were from the start high expectations about the significance of the Nag Hammadi tractates. Significance, however, is to a large degree in the eye of the beholder. The North American scholars who in the late 1960s became the main force in the publication and study of the Nag Hammadi codices were specialists in New Testament studies whose expectations tended to focus on the significance of the find for the understanding of Christian origins, or more specifically the role of Gnosticism in the development of earliest Christianity. This is, however, only one of several areas of potential significance and in fact the one that is the most remote, speculative, and influenced by modern ideological considerations. The significance of these documents is best assessed by distinguishing between four periods or phases proceeding from the last and most certain to the earlier and increasingly less certain phases.

The Coptic Monastic Phase

There are strong indications that the Nag Hammadi codices were produced and used not by a Gnostic sect, as was first assumed, but by monks in a Pachomian monastery located near the discovery site. Documents used as cartonnage to stiffen the leather cover of Codex VII include monastic letters among which is one from Pachomius to Paphnoute. These documents also include several dates from the middle of the fourth century that prove Codex VII was written after 348 C.E. The three scribal colophons that survive at the end of codices I, II, and VII conform to the pious scribbles found in monastic manuscripts. The Coptic dialect in which most of the tractates were written is standard Sahidic, the orthographic convention created in fourth-century monastic scriptoria. The generally ascetic outlook of this diverse collection of tractates also fits the monastic setting. Thus the most direct significance of the Nag Hammadi codices is the light they shed on early cenobitic monasticism in Upper Egypt.

The production and use of heterodox, Gnostic, and even some pagan writings by Pachomian monks during the early years of the cenobitic monastic movement is not altogether surprising. Pachomius's own documented involvement in language mysticism would indicate that interest in esoteric literature was the rule rather than the exception in the early decades of the movement. What unified the monks was a shared dedication to the ascetic life rather than to orthodoxy. It took quite some time before the orthodox hierarchy in Alexandria was able to exert some control over the rapidly growing monastic movement. We know of a purge of heretical books under abbot Theodore, the successor of Pachomius, in response to Athanasius's anti-heretical Paschal Letter of 367 C.E. This may well have been the occasion of the burial of the codices at some distance from the monastery, perhaps in the hope of recovering them at a later time. It is likely that the monks cherished these unorthodox books mainly for their ascetic and esoteric value.

The Translation Phase

The scribal mistakes in the Nag Hammadi tractates betray that they were copied from Coptic exemplars. Thus the translation from Greek to Coptic must have happened some time before the mid- to late fourth century date of the codices. Though we do not have direct evidence for the translation phase a probable case can be made that it took place in the late third and early fourth century among Greco-Egyptian ascetics. The most famous of these is St. Anthony but more likely candidates would be persons like Hierakas of Leontopolis who wrote in both Greek and Coptic and was known for his radical encratism and heterodox views. The earliest known biblical translations into various Coptic dialects appear to come from the same time and setting and they are similarly idiosyncratic and flawed as translations. These translations were most likely intended for private use by unilingual Copts who were joining the increasingly popular anchoritic monastic movement. These hermits would have brought their esoteric books into the cenobitic communities that some of them joined during the first half of the fourth century. The minority of Nag Hammadi tractates written in the Subachmimic dialect are probably closer to the translation phase than the Sahidic ones. If this reconstruction of the translation phase is correct it would indicate that third- and early fourth-century Christian ascetics in Egypt operated outside orthodox control and were attracted to Gnostic and other esoteric literature that reflected their ascetic outlook.

The Composition Phase

It is impossible to be specific or even generalized about the date, place, and circumstances of the composition of the individual tractates. This has not tempered the temptation to speculate on these matters. Several mistaken assumptions have guided the scholarly reconstruction of the composition phase. The first is the tendency to work on the basis of the earliest possible date of a text. In view of the age of the codices, however, and the translation phase some decades earlier, composition could have been as late as the early fourth century. Since the estimated date of composition often has far-reaching implications proper historical method demands that one start with the latest possible date and move to an earlier one only if there is sufficient internal or external evidence to warrant this. For none of the Nag Hammadi tractates are there compelling reasons to date them before the third century C.E., though it is certainly possible that some were composed earlier. Even in the case of *The Gospel of Thomas,* which some scholars date as early as the late first or early second century, the earliest external attestation in Hippolytus, *Refutatio* 5.7.20 and the earliest Greek fragments do not necessitate a date earlier than about 200 C.E. Nothing in the content of *The Gospel of Thomas* requires an earlier date. Some scholars have taken the absence of Christian elements in a tractate or the absence of the influence of the "great" second century Gnostic systems to be indicative of an early date, but there was no necessity for third century authors to include such elements.

A second mistaken assumption in much of Nag Hammadi scholarship is that the tractates were composed in and for distinct Gnostic sects. This was also the conjecture of the Christian heresiologists beginning with Irenaeus, who thought that the Gnostic writings known to them incorporated the teachings of distinct sects though they did not have direct evidence for this. They conceptualized the Gnostics behind the text as sectarians who, like orthodox Christians, defined themselves in terms of a set of doctrines. This, however, is highly unlikely, for the tractates look like the creations of visionaries who would rebel against the orthodoxy of any group and who were open to ideas from a variety of religious traditions as long as it served their ascetic and esoteric interests. Even the Valentinian tractates do not appear to adhere to any community "orthodoxy" though there is no doubt abut the existence of Valentinian communities in late antiquity.

The third questionable assumption is that the apostolic names assigned to some of the writings were not arbitrary but point to the specific community that produced these pseudepigrapha and assigned them to a particular apostle with whom they identified. Thus the writings assigned to the apostle Thomas are thought to originate in Edessa in northern Syria though their contents have little in common, and it is assumed that tractates attributed to the apostle James have a Jewish Christian connection. Unfortunately such speculations are beyond proof and disproof. As far as we know the apostles were revered in all areas and by all factions of the Church and the reason for choosing one name rather than another, if there was one, is in most cases obscure.

Even though the original setting of the tractates appears to be beyond recovery there is no doubt about their significance for our understanding of early Christianity and Gnosticism. They provide an important corrective to the questionable ways in which the diversity in early Christianity has been conceptualized. Diversity tends to be seen as a struggle between competing "orthodoxies," but a much more likely model is that of heterodoxy in which the lines between truth and falsehood were not yet defined and the structures were not in place to adjudicate between divergent teachings. The heterodox Christian writings indicate that tolerance for views later considered heretical continued throughout the third century in certain parts of the Church, and even into the late fourth century in the monastic movement.

The conceptualization of Gnosticism also needs correction in light of the Nag Hammadi discovery. If the Gnostic tractates are representative, and there is no reason to assume they are not, then we need to move away from the Church Fathers' assumption that these writings represented the teachings of different sects and see them more as the products of eccentric individuals, some in and others outside the Church. Also the modern idea that the Gnostics were intellectuals who rebelled against small-minded orthodox authority appears mistaken. Most of the tractates appear to be the work of dilettantes without much understanding of philosophical and theological matters, and preoccupied with esoteric knowledge. Finally the so-called great Gnostic systems look more impressive and cohesive in the Church Fathers' refutations than in the Gnostic texts themselves. Gnosticism as a major religious movement and world view appears to be a modern construct, far removed from the reality of the ancient writings that are our only direct witnesses. Apart from the Valentinian ones the Gnostic texts imply little more than a relatively vulgar and heterogeneous literary phenomenon on the fringes of Christianity and Platonism. Gnosticism appears to be a case where the whole is less than the sum of its parts.

The Pre-Composition Phase

Much of the interest in the Nag Hammadi texts, especially from the side of NT scholars, is in the earlier traditions that may have been incorporated in them. There can be no doubt that at least some of the tractates are based on earlier traditions and were subject to later redaction. For example *The Apocryphon of John* is extant in a shorter and longer version and its first part is based on a Gnostic document known to Irenaeus in about 180 C.E. while the longer version has interpolated a major section it claims to have taken from "The Book of Zoroaster." The same mythological themes appear in a number of writings and eclectic adaptation of material from other texts appears to be the rule rather than the exception. Attempts to isolate the sources and redactional material, however, are frustrated by the vulgar nature of most of the tractates. The authors appear to have made little effort to plan their treatises and thus the many unexpected shifts and anomalies are more probably weaknesses in the original composition than evidence of incorporation of sources or of later redaction.

This means that the modern claims about the use of early, independent traditions of the sayings of Jesus in such works as *The Apocryphon of James* and *The Dialogue of the Savior* lack sufficient basis, though it cannot be ruled out, and the same is true for the claims of the use of early Jewish Christian materials in, for example, the First and Second *Apocalypse of James*. Most of the scholarly attention, however, has been focused on *The Gospel of Thomas,* which is a collection of sayings of Jesus apparently selected for their enigmatic character and intended for private esoteric interpretation. It has a more serious claim to being an independent witness to early sayings sources but the attempts to prove that it is not dependent on the canonical gospels remain inconclusive. Since the potential relevance of at least some of the Nag Hammadi tractates for our understanding of Christian origins cannot be proven nor dismissed these texts will continue to expose the ideological fault line between traditional and revisionist views of Christian origins.

The Church's Gospel Canon: Why Four and No More?

William R. Farmer

In order to understand the history and importance of the fourfold gospel canon one needs to see its creation within the context of the history of the formation of the NT canon as a whole. A convenient survey of this development is provided in *The Formation of the New Testament Canon, An Ecumenical Approach,* 1983. This survey shows that the fourfold gospel canon was created to meet certain urgent needs of the Church in the mid-second century.

The canonical gospels, Matthew, Mark, Luke, and John, were all composed during the second half of the first century. The latest of the four, the gospel according to John, was probably composed around 90 C.E., about the same time that an effort was made to collect and publish a corpus of Paul's letters. A Christian reformer from Asia Minor named Marcion took this Pauline collection and edited it for his own purposes. He did likewise with the gospel of Luke. Marcion's reforms, whatever their aims, functioned to draw the Church away, if not sever it, from its scriptural roots in Judaism.

Marcion's gospel and his edited form of the Pauline corpus provided his Church with a streamlined and updated scriptural basis for its mission. Although Marcion's reforms were rejected by the Church at large and specifically by the elders of the church at Rome where Marcion had made a bid to gain influence, Marcionite churches grew in number and flourished long after his death. The popularity of Marcion's gospel, for which Marcion made special claims of reliability, was one factor that influenced the Church in its efforts to define which of the existing gospels could be authorized for use by the faithful.

How Did the Church Decide Which Gospels to Include in Its Canon?

The process of deciding which gospels were to be included in the Church's gospel canon was not, as some would suggest, the result of some plan made by a centralized ecclesiastical authority. The case of *The Gospel of Peter* provides some insight into how the selective process actually worked. This relatively short gospel was being used in some churches in Asia Minor when, late in the second century, a bishop named Serapion got wind of its troublesome character and took steps to inform the churches using it that not everything in it was in accordance with the "true teaching of the Savior" (Eusebius, *Hist. eccl.* 6.12.3-6). "True teaching" was to be established by some ecclesial norm to which the bishop could appeal. What was that norm?

The Rule of Faith

There was an ecclesial rule in early Christianity referred to by Irenaeus, Tertullian, Clement of Alexandria, and Origen as the "Rule of Faith." Its history can be traced back to the Scriptures read by Jesus, which are referred to collectively as the Law and the Prophets. The way Jesus read these Scriptures shaped him spiritually and normed his teaching and ministry. His disciples in turn received from Jesus this way of reading the Scriptures and after his death and resurrection they passed it on to those they made disciples. Clement of Alexandria summarized this Rule of Faith, which he sometimes called the "Rule of the Church," as "the concord and harmony between the Law and the Prophets and the covenant brought into being by Jesus Christ" (*Stromata* VI.15.125.3).

From the beginning, therefore, the Church had a knowledge of what is normative for Christian faith, and this norm or canon has always shaped everything authentically Christian. Christians today might call it the Spirit of Christ, but in the second and third centuries it was called the Rule of Faith, the Rule of Truth, or the Rule of the Church.

Jesus and the Rule of Faith (or the Rule of the Church)

Jesus identified himself to his disciples as the Son of Man who, fulfilling the role of the Suffering Servant, would give his life as a ransom for many and, like the Servant of the Lord in the book of Isaiah, would pour out his life for the forgiveness of sins. According to the prophet Isaiah that Servant would be born, would grow up, suffer, die, be buried, and then be vindicated and raised up. The evangelists Matthew, Mark, Luke, and John have not merely presented Jesus to their readers christologically in the role of the Suffering Servant in Isaiah. Their gospels are examples of the concord and harmony between the Law and the Prophets (in this case primarily Isaiah) and the covenant brought into being by Jesus Christ that Clement of Alexandria was accounting for in his definition of the Rule of Faith.

It is not clear whether Bishop Serapion, by referring to the "true teaching of the Savior" had in mind the Rule of Faith in the broadest sense or whether he is including the gospels handed down from the time of the apostles as normative expressions of that Rule of Faith. The two are so integrally related that we may assume that the expression "true teaching of the Savior" functioned for Bishop Serapion as shorthand for referring to a norm that was in accord with the Rule of Faith as it came to expression in the gospels that were known to have come from the time of the apostles.

The Problem of New Gospels

An increasingly important factor leading to the formation of the fourfold gospel canon was the ever-increasing number of new gospels. The adherents of these new gospels could always claim that their gospels were better suited than others to serve particular interests of certain Christian communities. In the case of *The Gospel of Peter,* Bishop Serapion identified its authors as *docetae,* that is, Christians who were charged with claiming that Jesus only "seemed" to do some of the things required by the Rule of Faith, and to which the earlier gospels witnessed. For example, Jesus as he hung on the cross "felt no pain" according to *The Gospel of Peter*. Thus though he may have seemed to suffer in his death, he did not actually suffer and hence did not fulfill the prophecies of Isaiah.

In ways like this bishops, who in their leadership roles were in a position to provide churches copies of the gospels, were able to assist the faithful in culling out later gospels that departed from the "true teaching of the Savior" that had been 'handed down" from the time of the apostles, that is, that formative sixty-odd year period of time following the death and resurrection of Jesus until the last of the Church's four gospels and some of the later letters were written. It should be noted that in the case of *The Gospel of Peter* what was decisive was not whether its composition was attributed to an apostle but whether what it taught was in accord with the "true teaching of the Savior." Since *The Gospel of Peter* was not in accord with this teaching it could not be accepted and used as an authentic work of someone sent by the Savior even though the name of someone sent by the Savior was attached to it.

Which Gospels were from the Time of the Apostles?

Which were the gospels that had been faithfully "handed down" from the time of the apostles? For an answer to this question we turn to the school of Justin Martyr and to the work of his student Tatian who combined the texts of the four gospels, Matthew, Mark, Luke, and John, into the text of a single gospel. This came to be known as the *Diatessaron* (= "through the four") because through use of four gospels it was possible to produce a single narrative unifying the whole.

Justin's school flourished in Rome in the period following Marcion's rejection and at the beginning of the great missionary effort to which Marcion devoted the remainder of his life. Marcion asserted that Christianity contradicted Jewish Scriptures; Justin maintained that it fulfilled them. According to Justin, Christians in Rome would gather on Sunday and listen to the reading of the memoirs of the apostles or the writings of the prophets. Justin does not specify the names of the apostles whose "memoirs" were being read in church but he knew that these texts were composed by "the apostles and those who followed them." This distinction suggests that Justin knew that Mark and Luke were not written by apostles but by disciples of apostles. At one point, however, Justin refers to a statement that is found only in our gospel according to Mark (3:16-17) and says with reference to this statement that it is recorded in Peter's memoirs (*Dial.* 106.3), indicating that Justin regarded the text we know as the gospel of Mark as a memoir of the apostle Peter. There is no reason to doubt that the other texts he referred to as "memoirs of the apostles" were our gospels according to Matthew, Luke, and John. Justin knows other gospel-like texts concerning Jesus but he appears to have used them sparingly.

The important point is this: at the same time that Marcionites were learning to read a single gospel based on what Marcion believed to be the most original form of the "gospel" that Paul had read, the churches that followed the lead of Christians in Rome read no single gospel. Justin uses the plural: "memoirs of the apostles."

The advantage enjoyed by the Marcionites in having a single "gospel" free of discrepancies and alleged "Judaistic" additions was very real. No doubt the whole problem was discussed in Justin's school in Rome. As has been mentioned, one of his students in Syria, after Justin's martyrdom (ca. 165), published a single unified gospel that basically drew together into a coherent whole the traditions contained in Matthew, Mark, Luke, and John.

The strong preference that was shown in Justin's school and in Tatian's *Diatessaron* for Matthew, Mark, Luke, and John over all competing gospel texts was, as far as we know, shared in all parts of the Church that rejected Marcion and the Gnostics. At one point, however, Marcion made a lasting contribution to the churches that rejected him. As did the apostle Paul, Marcion emphasized that there was only one gospel. This helps explain why the practice developed of referring to each separate apostolic "memoir" as "the gospel (singular) according to Matthew (. . . Mark, . . . Luke, . . . John)." In some such way as this the "Fourfold Gospel Canon" of the Church came into being and has come down to us equipped with this revealing set of separate titles for each of the four books.

Why Four and No More?

If we ask why the Church that formulated our biblical canon recognizes only these four gospels the answer is that these four writings are the only texts coming from "the time of the apostles" that tell the gospel story in a manner that is in accord with what Bishop Serapion and the churches that rejected "docetism" and Marcionism regarded as the "true teaching of the Savior." We can even say that these four writings are the only texts known to us that tell the story of the flesh and blood martyrdom of the Son of God. There may have been other such gospels circulating in the early Church, but if so we cannot know this to have been the case. They certainly have not survived, and so we cannot examine them to determine their true character.

The church at Rome that rejected Marcion and recognized Justin as a martyr was only one of the churches that rejected "docetism." These gospels would have functioned to sustain the faith of any of those martyrs of the Church who, like Jesus and the apostles Peter and Paul, were faithful unto death. Ignatius and Polycarp, who died as martyrs, were spiritually formed by these same gospels; this indicates that churches in Syria and Asia Minor following these Apostolic Fathers at the beginning of the second century were disposed to proceed as Bishop Serapion proceeded later in that century and as would the churches of Gaul in the time of Irenaeus. We are talking, therefore, of something that appears to have been rather widespread in the Church at this time.

To test this conjecture we return to the case of *The Gospel of Peter.* We should note that this text is largely restricted to an account of the Passion of the Savior. Based on the content of *The Gospel of Peter* it is clear that when Bishop Serapion discovered that there were parts of the gospel that were not in accordance with the "true teaching of the Savior" he was not referring to the "sayings" of Jesus, neither to his teaching in the Sermon on the Mount nor to his parables; rather he was referring to the Savior's teaching about his Passion.

We noted that *The Gospel of Peter* states that as Jesus hung on the cross he felt no pain. Such a statement is not in accord with the "true teaching of the Savior" who, as is clear both from the four canonical gospels and from the letters of Paul (see especially 1 Cor 15:1-3; Rom 10:16 citing Isa 53:1; and Rom 15:21 citing Isa 52:15; also Rom 4:25 echoing Isa 53:4-5; Rom 5:19 echoing Isa 53:11; Gal 1:4; 2:20 echoing Isa 53:8-9; Phil 2:7-8 echoing Isa 53:10-12; Phil 2:9 echoing Isa 53:13) grounded his teaching about his suffering and death in the "gospel" we know from the book of the prophet Isaiah. In Isaiah the *suffering* and death of the Servant Messiah are redemptive (Isaiah 53). In the gospel according to Matthew we read that during his final meal with his disciples Jesus "took a cup, and after giving thanks he gave it to them, saying, 'Drink from it, all of you; for this is my blood of the covenant, which is poured out for many for the forgiveness of sins'" (Matt 26:27-28; cf. Isa 53:12 "he bore the sins of many"). In his first letter to the church at Corinth the apostle Paul reminded his brethren of the terms in which he preached "the gospel" to them (1 Corinthians 15). Of first importance was that tradition he had received from those who were apostles before him, "that Christ died for our sins in accordance with the scriptures." The Scriptures referred to include Isa 52:13–53:12, which begins: "See, my servant . . ." and ends: "he bore the sins of many, and made intercession for the transgressors."

Only Matthew, Mark, Luke, and John tell this redemptive story of the flesh and blood martyrdom of the Son of God. In teaching that Jesus as he hung on the cross "felt no pain" *The Gospel of Peter* makes it clear that Jesus did not experience a flesh and blood martyrdom; that is, he did not suffer as we would have suffered and thus his death could not be redemptive for us. The failure of *The Gospel of Thomas* to make any reference to the passion of Jesus is important. None of the gospels left aside and neglected by the Church are true to the gospel preached by Paul or those apostles from whom he received the tradition he passes on in 1 Corinthians 15. By definition the rejected gospels introduce new understandings of the term "gospel," understandings that are not grounded in writings known as Scripture by Jesus or his disciples.

The book known as the gospel according to Mark opens with the words: "The beginning of the gospel of Jesus Christ, the Son of God." Here the noun "gospel" is used absolutely as in the letters of Paul. It is significant that the author associates this "gospel" with the book of the prophet Isaiah by immediately proceeding to say: "As it is written in the prophet Isaiah." The text he cites combines texts from other Scriptures besides Isaiah, but it is only Isaiah that he mentions. This is not a careless error on the part of the evangelist. Rather it indicates that Isaiah was normative for his reading of Moses and the Prophets. With Mark, for the first time, the Isaianic term "gospel" becomes associated with a narrative text featuring the life, teaching, and passion of Jesus. From this connection of "gospel" with a written narrative came the practice of referring to the books of Matthew, Mark, Luke, and John as "gospels." What is important to note is that according to this understanding of Church history the term "gospel" as related to written texts originally was normed by the book of the prophet Isaiah.

As long as these four books lived their separate and independent lives in various parts of the Church each could have been received and handed on as the main authoritative gospel account for its respective adherents. Under these circumstances it was possible for Christians to favor one gospel over all others, or in some cases to combine them. There is some evidence that Justin made use of texts of the sayings of Jesus that were the result of combining the texts of these sayings from parallel texts in the gospels of Matthew and Luke.

What Consequence Flowed from Choosing These Four?

The primary effect of bringing these four gospels together into a single fourfold canon was twofold. On one hand the separate authority of any one of these gospels tended to be restricted by the necessity to take account of the other three. At the same time the authority of these four, by comparison to that of all others, tended to be increased. One could clearly see from reading these four that by comparison all other written accounts, such as *The Gospel of Peter* or *The Gospel of Thomas,* lacked the kind of textual support for their teaching that could be easily adduced for much of the teaching in Matthew, Mark, Luke, and John. Much of the teaching in Matthew or in Mark or in Luke was confirmed by what one could find in one or both of the other two.

The gospel of John was another matter. But if one could regard John as the "spiritual" gospel that like an eagle soars above the others it could be read as enhancing the authority of the other three in comparison with all the newer "gospels" that continued to appear here and there in the Church. Like Matthew, Mark, and Luke, and unlike all other gospels, John also told the redemptive story of the flesh and blood martyrdom of the Isaianic Son of God as the Davidic Servant King Messiah. A final advantage of bringing John together with the other three was that it discouraged any tendency for John's Gnostic adherents to move farther and farther in a docetic or Gnostic direction. The fourfold gospel canon served to save John (with its especially high Son of God christology) for the contra-Marcionite, contra-Gnostic Church of the apostles. Without reading it in relation to the other three there was no effective way to check or limit the kind of Gnostic speculation that served to undermine "apostolic" faith. Central to the "apostolic discourse" of the Church that formed the fourfold gospel canon was the teaching requiring public witnessing (Matt 10:26-28) and the promise that those who are obedient unto death will be saved (vv. 17-22).

With the fourfold gospel canon in hand the Church had an effective jawbone with which the faithful could keep at bay misdirected Christians who wandered from that "truth of the gospel" (Gal 2:5) to which even the pillars of the Church in Jerusalem (Gal 2:9) were subject (Gal 2:14), and that found its *kanøn* in "the cross of our Lord Jesus Christ" (Gal 6:14-16).

Finally, to read Matthew in the light of John, Mark, and Luke helped enable the adherents of the First Gospel and thus of the Jerusalem and Antiochian churches to stay the course set by their leaders in the apostolic period (Gal 2:1-10) and avoid any post-apostolic temptation to abandon the mission to the Gentiles. At the same time saying "no" to Marcion required a compensating "yes" to the more Gentile gospels of Luke, Mark, and John to balance, supplement, and complement the extremely Jewish character of that gospel which, while it powerfully committed the disciples of Jesus to a unified mission to make disciples of all the nations (Matt 28:19-20), also preserved the troublesome doctrine that "not one letter, not one stroke of a letter, will pass from the law until all is accomplished" (Matt 5:18).

Trust in God's promise to save the nations, set forth in the book of Isaiah, is basic to Christian faith. The good news of the gospel is that God in the Church is prefiguring the fulfillment of this promise through faith in Jesus as the Christ. The Church as body of Christ is a sign of this gospel for both Jew and Gentile. This same Church has handed down to us the fourfold gospel canon and teaches Christians to honor it with their lives.

Genre(s) of the Gospels

Philip L. Shuler

To ask a question concerning the "genre(s) of the gospels" is to inquire into the nature of the literary character of gospel composition. That is, to what literary type or category does a gospel belong? The determination of the literary character of a gospel is one of the initial questions a reader asks, for the answer helps identify the kind of information one expects to gain from his or her reading. A reader, for example, who reads one of the canonical gospels with the conviction that a New Testament gospel belongs to the category of "biography" or "history" brings certain presuppositions to the interpretation task and asks questions that biographical or historical texts are expected to answer. In reading a "biography" one would expect to receive information concerning a subject's character, development, and growth by which the reader could more aptly appreciate the hero's or heroine's significant actions and contributions. From a "history" one could expect reliable chronological information and accurately described events from which the reader could discern the important details of the central character's life in the broader sphere of human activities. While the NT gospels do possess the appearance of a "life" of Jesus and do contain traditions from which the interpreter can gain significant biographical information about Jesus, attempts to reconstruct *the* biography of Jesus do not come close to yielding a definitive account that reflects equally the diverse traditions found within those gospels available for investigation. In other words the canonical gospels are not, strictly speaking, biographies or histories as these terms are currently understood. In fact, on the surface it is difficult to find *any* literature within the ancient world with which the gospels may be directly compared. For this reason prior to the 1970s the dominant conclusion ably expressed by Karl L. Schmidt was that the canonical gospels belong to no extant literary genre. They are the result of a natural, evolutionary process: they are unique, that is, *sui generis*.

Currently gospels are seen as falling into two groups: those that contain a *bios* or "life" format and those that present random collections of various sayings of Jesus or other traditions related to him. The NT gospels fall into the former category. The *sui generis* view of their origin offers the following explanation. The early evangelists used early faith statements (called *kerygma:* for example, Phil 2:6-11, speeches in Acts, or certain OT passages such as Isaiah 53), expanded them by inserting sayings and miracle traditions, and added an extended passion narrative. It is difficult not to view this explanation as source dependent because the resulting "gospel" looks very much like the Gospel of Mark. Such an explanation, while giving justifiable credit to the faith statements, OT prophetic traditions, and Jesus traditions, does not fully account for the *bios* form present in each of the canonical gospels. While some scholars explored the genres of aretalogy and dramatic history, more recent discussions by Talbert, Shuler, and Burridge (see bibliography) focus directly on ancient biographical writings as the explanation for the *bios* form within the NT gospels. These studies have reached the following conclusions:

(1) the NT gospels are the products of "authors" who intentionally wrote their works to share the "good news" of Jesus Christ with their readers; (2) they effectively communicated their contents to a Greco-Roman audience familiar with *bios* ways of writing; and (3) they do belong to the general literary category of ancient biographical works. Furthermore, while Shuler's work concerns itself with the more generic praise character of the gospel narratives as seen in the rhetorical rules for the encomium, Talbert has turned his attention to the different types of ancient biographies and the function of the individual works: thus John and Mark defend against misunderstanding, Luke–Acts recounts the life of Jesus and the story of his followers as does Diogenes Laertius, while Matthew presents Jesus as the hermeneutical key to his teachings. Burridge retraces the debate and further demonstrates that the NT gospels do indeed belong to the overall genre of *bioi*. The discussion of subgenres continues, but the case for viewing the NT gospels as examples of ancient biography is normative.

The second group of gospels consists of those containing the sayings of Jesus and other kinds of tradition related to Jesus. Into this group fall the sayings gospels, including the Gospel of Philip and the Gospel of Thomas (from the Nag Hammadi collection). These gospels contain no *bios* motif and give emphasis to the authority of the Gnostic redeemer. Other gospels such as the Infancy Gospel of Thomas seek to fill in gaps concerning Jesus' childhood or emphasize certain other aspects of Jesus' life and death: for example, the emphasis on the virgin birth of Jesus and the birth of Mary in the Gospel of James and the Gospel of Peter's focus on Jesus' passion. Recent scholarship has used the extant sayings gospels (especially the Gospel of Thomas) as a supportive model for the reconstruction of the illusive so-called gospel "Q" whose sole claim to existence rests on the observation that there are parallel passages in the gospels of Matthew and Luke that are not found in the gospel of Mark. The argument for Q is sometimes supported by appeal to quotations of Jesus recorded by some of the early Church Fathers. In extreme cases this work on the sayings gospels and so-called "Q" purports to discover a more original Jesus, the Gnostic redeemer, the account of whose ministry has been modified by canonical Mark.

Highly speculative conclusions deriving from a hypothetical "Q" gospel, for which there is no historical evidence, find little support among the majority of scholars. Indeed, recent research (McNicol) persuasively challenges the necessity of even positing the existence of "Q" by effectively demonstrating how Luke has in fact used Matthew's gospel as his major source. The basic historical validity of the portraits of Jesus as presented in the NT gospels continues to remain both foundational and reliable for the Church.

BIBLIOGRAPHY

Burridge, Richard A. *What are the Gospels?* Cambridge: Cambridge University Press, 1992.

Cartlidge, David R., and David L. Dungan. *Documents for the Study of the Gospels*. Minneapolis: Fortress, 1994.

McNicol, Allan. *Beyond the Q Impasse: Luke's Use of Matthew*. Valley Forge: Trinity Press International, 1996.

Shuler, Philip L. *A Genre for the Gospels: The Biographical Character of Matthew*. Philadelphia: Fortress, 1982.

Talbert, Charles H. *What Is a Gospel?: The Genre of the Canonical Gospels*. Philadelphia: Fortress, 1977.

Matthew

*Adrian Leske**

FIRST READING

A Hellenistic-Jewish Christian Gospel

A careful reading of this gospel will reveal its Jewish background and origins. It emphasizes the fulfillment of the Hebrew Scriptures, deals with concerns regarding Jewish understanding of the Law, Pharisaic traditions, and scribal interpretations, and focuses on the controversies with Jewish religious leaders. There is a strong concern to criticize Jewish rejection of Jesus. Jesus' Jewish roots are emphasized: he is "son of Abraham" and his messiahship is that of the "son of David." It confronts Jewish concern about the Law: the works of righteousness (ch. 6), Sabbath laws, Temple tax, and sacrificial rituals. The gospel contains many Semitisms, words and phrases in Hebrew idiom, and unexplained Jewish customs (thus presupposing Jewish readers who will understand these references without explanation). It makes clear that Jesus' mission was first to gather "the lost sheep of the house of Israel" into the reign of God to be a light to the nations. This emphasis on the "light to the nations," drawn from Isaiah, shows that the gospel of Matthew is thoroughly open to the Gentile mission. It ends with the universal mission of the Eleven to the whole world (28:19-20) as it begins with the arrival of the Magi to greet the newborn Messiah (ch. 2).

That the author is writing primarily to Jewish Christians is evident also in what he assumes of the readers. He takes it for granted that they are familiar with the Hebrew Scriptures, Law and Prophets alike. While the events of Jesus' ministry are as much contained in Matthew as in Mark, Matthew has a clear bent toward a doctrinal presentation: his gospel emphasizes Jesus' teaching more than any other. It would be difficult to believe that the author has simply "rejudaized" a gospel written from sources produced by a more Gentile Christianity; rather it presents a Hellenistic-Jewish Christian Church still firmly rooted in its Jewish origins but on its way to receiving all Gentiles among its ranks on the basis of the universalism it finds in Jewish Scriptures, both Hebrew and Greek. (For evidence that the evangelist is writing out of a Hellenistic-Jewish background note the discussion of "the crucifixion," 27:32-44, where attention is drawn to clear echoes of Wisdom of Solomon, a Hellenistic Jewish Scripture originally composed in Greek.)

Its Place in History

The gospel of Matthew was universally held by the Church Fathers to be the first gospel written. Some of them claimed that it was written originally in "Hebrew" (which may mean Aramaic). The only author proposed for this gospel was the apostle Matthew. Eusebius of Caesarea (ca. 260–340) reports Papias, bishop of Hierapolis (ca. 100–110), as recording that "Matthew arranged the Lord's oracles in order in the Hebrew language (or dialect) and each one translated (or "interpreted") them as he was able" (*Hist. eccl.* 3.39.16). Eusebius also reports that

**The author gratefully acknowledges the contributions to this commentary made by Denis Farkasfalvy and Rudolf Pesch, and the editorial assistance of John Norris.*

Pantaenus (ca. 150–215), teacher of Clement of Alexandria, went to India and found that people there were already acquainted with the gospel of Matthew, a copy in Hebrew having been taken there by the apostle Bartholomew (*Hist. eccl.* 5.10.3). Irenaeus, bishop of Lyons, writing around 180, also spoke of Matthew having written a gospel in Hebrew around the time that Peter and Paul were preaching and establishing the church in Rome (*Adv. Haer.* 3.1.1). These traditions continued to be expressed by other Church Fathers.

It was not until the second half of the nineteenth century that the Two Source Hypothesis became popular. This theory, which is still widely accepted, posits Matthew as a later gospel based on Mark, together with a sayings source "Q." It pays little attention to the external evidence from early Church Fathers and internal evidence from the Greek text of Matthew that witnesses convincingly to the Jewish origins of this gospel. The tendency of many NT scholars to interpret Matthew through the filter of Mark and Q often results in a distorted perspective: (1) interpreting the more Jewish Matthew from the point of view of Mark and Q (or Luke); (2) isolating individual pericopes from their Matthean context and overlooking the strong internal consistency of the gospel's structure; (3) not recognizing fully the Hellenistic-Jewish Christian perspective from which Matthew is written.

In recent years the Two Source Hypothesis has come under fire as many of its presuppositions have been questioned, with the result that confidence in the adequacy if not the reliability of that hypothesis has eroded. A growing number of scholars are now arguing for returning Matthew to its place as the first gospel followed by the other two synoptics, a theory known as the Two Gospel Hypothesis (see article on the Synoptic Problem).

Whichever hypothesis one follows, the best approach to the study of Matthew is to focus on the text of this gospel, paying close attention to its compositional structure. Most importantly, all scholars agree that Jewish Christianity as such is prior in time to Gentile Christianity. The beginning of wisdom in understanding our Hellenistic-Jewish Christian Matthew is to view it as having developed out of its original Jewish matrix into a gospel committed to the mission to the Gentiles rather than to reverse the order of historical development and view it as a later, judaized version of a more Gentile gospel.

Matthew and the Old Testament Heritage

A most prominent feature of this gospel is the frequent use of quotations and allusions to the Jewish Scriptures, many of which are found only in Matthew. Scholars have usually isolated ten so-called formula citations (1:22-23; 2:5-6; [2:15], 2:17-18; 2:23; 4:14-16; 8:17; 12:17-21; 13:35; 21:4-5; 27:9-10) that usually begin with "This was to fulfill what was spoken by the prophet . . . ." These quotations frame the narrative and form an integral part of its context, giving the narrative meaning and significance. They resemble the quotations spoken by Jesus in Matthew's gospel (examples are in 11:10; 13:14-15; 15:7-9; 21:16; 21:42). Besides these patterned quotations, other quotations and allusions to the OT are found in Matthew's narrative and on the lips of Jesus. Thoroughly familiar with the context of the prophetic quotations, Matthew expects his readers to read them with a similar frame of mind. He sometimes combines words from two different texts in one quotation in order to alert the reader to the context of both (e.g., 21:5 [Isa 62:11; Zech 9:9]; 27:9 [Jer 18:1-13; 19:1-12; Zech 11:12-13]; 11:10 [Exod 23:20; Mal 3:1]).

Matthew also uses OT Scriptures to transmit subliminal messages. For example, he uses words in Matt 3:4 to describe the Baptist's clothing that are almost identical with 2 Kings 1:8, a description of the garments worn by Elijah. In this way he alerts the reader to recognize John as the returning Elijah (cf. 11:14; 17:13). Similarly, in 27:41-43 he characterizes the chief priests, scribes, and elders by using words that describe the wicked in Ps 22:8 and Wis 2:10-20 in order to point out that these religious leaders of Jerusalem were the wicked who were persecutors of the righteous Servant described in Psalm 22 and Isaiah 53, who is thus identified with Jesus. All this indicates that Matthew saw Jesus and the new age he had inaugurated as the fulfillment of the Scriptures, not only in expected but also in unexpected ways.

Date of Writing

Scholars for the past century have generally argued for a date around 80–85 C.E. Ignatius shows evidence of use of Matthew in his writings. Many do not wish to put it earlier than 80–85 because of the presuppositions of the Two Source Hypothesis. Assuming that Mark was written around 65 C.E., after Peter's death, and that Matthew used Mark as a source, Matthew must have been written well after 65 C.E.

It has been argued that Matthew 22:7 and ch. 24 presuppose the destruction of Jerusalem in 70 C.E., but the language of 22:7 is based on Isa 5:24-25 and Mal 4:1, and ch. 24 is stated in general apocalyptic terms and shows no specific knowledge of what happened in 70 C.E. On the other hand the gospel seems to contain evidence of familiarity with an ongoing cultic life of the Temple, its worship, and collection of the Temple tax (5:23-24; 23:16-22; 17:24-27).

Similarly, the argument that the tone of the discussions of the Law and references to "their synagogues" in Matthew indicate the gospel was written after the so-called Council of Jamnia, when Christians were thought to have been barred from the synagogues, is inconclusive. Because of Pharisaic influence Jesus would necessarily have had to address the matter of the Law and his relation to it. We find an account of Jesus' relation to the law in Matthew's gospel, and this account and the oral tradition on which it is based would have continued to be of importance in any Jewish context. "Their synagogues" may be a term pointing to the Pharisaic control of these institutions rather than to the separation of Christian and Jewish communities after Jamnia. Finally, Matt 23:2-3 would make no sense if Matthew's community were barred from the synagogues.

If we study the gospel on its own ground as a gospel written initially in a predominantly Jewish-Christian context it is easy to see that the issues raised in the gospel represent well the time of Jesus and the apostolic generation. There is no need to perceive Matthew as composed in a post-Jamnia period. The issues Jesus had to address would have been of continuing importance to Jewish Christians as long as they maintained close ties with their Jewish heritage.

Place of Writing

Scholars who hold that the gospel was written for a Jewish Christian community have suggested places in Palestine or one of the Diaspora communities as the place of origin. Most have opted for Antioch in Syria because of the prominence of that city in the early Church (Acts 11:19-30; 14:24–15:35; Gal 2:11-14). If, as some Church Fathers contend, Matthew was originally written in Hebrew, there is a likelihood that it was written in a Palestinian setting. A likely place could have been Galilee. Even though in Acts Luke concentrated on those areas of the Jewish Diaspora that figured in Paul's mission, he did mention that the Church existed and continued to grow in Galilee and Samaria as well as in Judea (Acts 9:31). Galilean Jews were generally trilingual (Hebrew, Aramaic, Greek) because of the mixed population, and so both a Hebrew gospel and its Greek version could have originated in their midst. Patristic tradition certainly favors a Palestinian origin, and there are good reasons for locating it in Galilee: (1) The anti-Pharisaic tone of the gospel would suggest a place where the influence of the Pharisees was strong. (2) The theme of persecution of a prophetic minority by fellow Jews and the condemnation of some cities in the Galilean area that did not respond in faithfulness points to Galilee. (3) It is in Galilee that the faithfulness of the first Gentiles is proclaimed (8:5-13; 15:21-28). (4) The strong emphasis given to "Galilee of the Gentiles" with the quotation in 4:12-16 of Isa 9:1-2 begins the whole ministry of Jesus that continues until 19:1. (5) Matthew emphasizes that Jesus returns to Galilee after the resurrection (26:32; 28:7, 10, 16), and that is where the gospel ends. At the same time a provenance just to the north of Galilee in southern Syria, including a city as far north as Antioch, is still possible. In that case, from the perspective of Matthew's readers Galilee of the Gentiles (the mission base for the evangelization of Syrian Christian communities) would have lain just on the other side of Mount Hermon, which dominated the southern horizon. That is how close Christians in southern Syria could have felt they were to their religious and cultural roots.

The Author

The Church Fathers regarded the author of the First Gospel as being the apostle Matthew whose call they saw specifically described in 9:9. The majority of modern scholars have rejected that view. This rejection is in part based on the presupposed dependence of Matthew on Mark. While the gospel itself does not indicate who its author was, there are a number of indications within the gospel that could point to the apostle Matthew. First of all, there is the account of Matthew's call: apart from his, only the calling of the first four disciples is mentioned. The author emphasizes that Matthew was a tax collector who led other Jewish tax collectors to hear Jesus (cf. 9:9-11; 10:3), but he does not avoid references to tax collectors in a derogatory sense (cf. 5:46; 9:10, 11; 11:19; 18:17; 21:31, 32). A tax collector would have had to be well educated, fluent in both Hebrew/Aramaic and Greek as well as familiar with Latin. The author of this gospel gives evidence of such fluency. In other synoptic accounts of the call Matthew is referred to as Levi (Mark 2:13-14; Luke 5:27), which probably indicates that he was of Levitical descent. If so, that would explain his education and also the constant use of the term "chief priests" for the Zadokite priesthood in Jerusalem that had virtually replaced the Levitical priesthood after the exile. There is some suggestion that the author may also have functioned as a "scribe" because of his positive use of that term in 8:19; 13:52.

Genre and Structure

Taking a cue from the five formula sayings ending the five discourses ("When Jesus had finished saying these things . . ." 7:28; 11:1; 13:53; 19:1; 26:1) many have structured the gospel as five books, following a traditional Jewish arrangement like the Pentateuch. However, that appears somewhat arbitrary and breaks up 4:23–9:35 which the writer clearly wanted to keep together as indicated by repeating 4:23 again in 9:35 as an *inclusio.* The author's concern is to present the Good News as it unfolds, so he begins with the announcement of Jesus as Messiah and his preparation for his mission. Then comes Jesus' proclamation of the Good News of the kingdom in word and deed, the training of twelve apostles to carry on that mission, the response to the message with growing opposition by some and acceptance by others. As a consequence of the opposition Jesus is revealed as the Suffering Servant/Son of Man who will relive Israel's history by going the way of suffering, death, and resurrection, thus redeeming the faithful in order that as true Israel the faithful people of God may become a light to the nations. In this way the Good News of the reign of God will be proclaimed throughout the world and they will make disciples of all nations. The following brief outline is suggested:

I. Jesus' Origins: 1:1–2:23
II. Narrative: Preparation: 3:1–4:25
III. Sermon 1: The Proclamation of the Good News in Word: 5:1–7:29
IV. Narrative: The Proclamation of the Good News in Deed: 8:1–9:34
V. Sermon 2: The Mission of the Disciples: 9:35–11:1
VI. Narrative: Misunderstanding and Growing Opposition: 11:2–12:50
VII. Sermon 3: Speaking in Parables: 13:1-52
VIII. Narrative: Rejection and Acceptance: 13:53–16:12
IX. The Revelation of Who Jesus Is: 16:13–17:27
X. Sermon 4: Living in the Community: 18:1-35
XI. Narrative: On the Way to Jerusalem: 19:1–20:34
XII. Narrative: Jerusalem and its Religious Leaders: 21:1–22:14
XIII. Narrative: The Opposition Seeks to Entrap Jesus: 22:15–23:39
XIV. Sermon 5: The Future and the Final Judgment: 24:1–25:46
XV. Passion Narrative: Jesus' Way of Suffering: 26:1–27:66
XVI. The Resurrection of Jesus and the Future: 28:1-20

Some Major Themes in Matthew

Fulfillment

This is the central theme, providing a foundation for all that Matthew presents. Jesus' announcement in the Sermon on the Mount: "Do not think that I have come to abolish the law or the prophets; I have come not to abolish but to fulfill" (5:17) is really the basis of Jesus' whole message and mission. Jesus had undergone John's baptism because it was "proper to fulfill all righteousness" (3:15). Matthew adds to that the ten formula citations throughout the gospel that all go to show how an event "fulfills" the prophets. The importance of these fulfillment citations is indicated in the words of Jesus at the time of his arrest in Gethsemane: "how then would the scriptures be fulfilled, which say it must happen in this way? . . . All this has taken place, so that the scriptures of the prophets may be fulfilled" (26:54, 56). Matthew's emphasis on Jesus as the fulfillment of prophetic expectations in the context of the Jewish origin of this gospel argues for the proclamation of the messianic identity of Jesus as the Christ. This concept of fulfillment is inclusive, all-embracing. All Israel's history, hope, and purpose are coming to fulfillment through Jesus.

Much of that history, hope, and purpose had been summarized by a prophet near the end of the Babylonian exile whose writings have been incorporated in the book of Isaiah (primarily chs. 40–55) and whose message of hope was reaffirmed after the return (in chs. 60–62). These chapters particularly become the basis for Jesus' message and proclamation of the Good News of the reign of God and his mission to fulfill Israel's history in himself, to exemplify true Israel as the Servant of God, God's chosen one. The whole book of Isaiah plays a most important role in Jesus' teaching, and to a lesser degree so also do those prophetic writings that have been influenced by Isaiah, such as Malachi, Zechariah 9–14, Jonah, Daniel, Wisdom of Solomon, and the apocryphal Parables of Enoch (*1 Enoch* 37–71).

The Law and the Prophets

Jesus' relationship to the OT Law was important in a context strongly influenced by the scribes and Pharisees. According to rabbinic teaching there were 613 commandments to which were added the "acts of righteousness," almsgiving, prayer, and fasting. A person's life was to be governed by meticulous observance of these commandments. Many if not most Jews (including Mary, Joseph, Jesus, and his disciples) obeyed God's commandments joyfully. However, righteousness always can turn to self-righteousness and hypocrisy.

Matthew presents Jesus coming to fulfill the law in its true sense. *Torah,* law, means essentially the "teaching" of God, and that "teaching" was established in the covenant stipulations, the Ten Commandments. The teaching of God was essentially how to live in true relationship with God and with one another. The stipulations set down the parameters of these relationships, ties that were to be developed and generated by love as a fitting response to God's love and grace in gathering together a slave people and making them God's own. Love, Jesus taught, was the motivating force, the very essence of the Law and the prophets (22:34-40), not the legalistic casuistry against which Jesus cries out in his woes against the scribes and Pharisees. Matthew demonstrates that righteousness in Jesus' terms is not the meticulous and literal interpretation of casuistic or priestly laws (e.g., 5:17-48; 9:13; 12:7) but faithfulness to the covenant relationship. Jesus has the faithful depend on God's righteousness (5:6; 6:33) so they act in righteousness to God and one another in selfless love (5:10, 20; 6:1). This is because they "know righteousness, [the] people who have my teaching *(torah)* in [their] hearts" (Isa 51:7; cf. Jer 31:33). As such the faithful become "a covenant to the people" or a "people-covenant," "for a light to the nations" (Isa 42:6; 49:6, 8; 51:16) so that God's teaching and justice might go forth as "a light to the peoples" (Isa 51:4; cf. 45:22-23; 55:10-11). By his word, example, and inspiration, Matthew points out, Jesus not only fulfills the Law but also all righteousness.

Matthew demonstrates that Jesus has come to fulfill Isaiah and the prophets by proclaiming the good news of the reign of God, by teaching the true meaning of participating in that realm as God's chosen servant Israel. He fulfills the promises of Second Isaiah by gathering together the "lost sheep of the house of Israel" to be a "people-covenant" and a "light to the nations" and thus carry out their role as true Israel. This understanding of the prophets gives meaning to all Jesus does, leading up to his suffering, death, and resurrection.

The Kingdom of Heaven

By far the most all-pervading concept in the teaching of Jesus in Matthew's gospel is the concept of the kingdom of heaven (or "reign of God"). The term "kingdom of heaven" (*basileia tōn ouranōn,* used thirty-two times) is found only in Matthew in the NT and was used in typically pious Jewish fashion to avoid saying God's name, although Matthew does use the term "kingdom of God/reign of God *(basileia tou theou)*" a few times (12:28; 19:24; 21:43). The concept comes from the announcement of the good news in Isa 40:9 and 52:7 that "Your God reigns." This is the good news that Jesus has come to proclaim and demonstrate. The concept emphasizes the direct rule of God over God's people. God will reign over the people not through intermediaries such as the kings and priests of the past, or for that matter the scribes and Pharisees, but because God's teaching will be in their hearts (Isa 51:7). Jesus presents this kingdom in contrast to the nationalistic concept of a future political kingdom often espoused by the Jewish parties looking for independence from Rome. One need not wait for, or even seek, the overthrow of a foreign oppressor in order to participate in this kingdom. The kingdom belongs to all who seek to remain faithful to the covenant relationship with God (5:3, 10, 19, 20; 6:33). It is God's gracious gift, open to all who seek or knock (7:7-12). Jesus described the kingdom of heaven as a family, the children relating to God not as a stern judge but as their heavenly Father in trust, confidence, and love. Thus the kingdom of heaven exists wherever one relates to God in this familial way in the community gathered by Jesus—in this life and in the next.

Jesus described the kingdom to the faithful in a series of parables: how it quietly grows among his followers, always spreading forth its fruits, influencing the community and the world round about. Only at the end will the evil forces be weeded out and eliminated (ch. 13). It is a realm in which people show the same forgiving love as their Father (18:21-35), always witnessing to God in word and action and so proclaiming the good news of God's reign before all the nations of the world until the end (28:16-20; 24:14).

Christology

For the most part Matthew lets the progression of events reveal *who Jesus is* but in his first two chapters he sets down clearly and emphatically Jesus' origin and purpose. There Jesus is introduced as "Jesus the Messiah, the son of David, the son of Abraham" (1:1). Matthew wants to make the point to his detractors that Jesus *is* the Anointed One (= Christ, Messiah), he *is* the Son of David, the royal Messiah expected by the Pharisees and others, he *is* the descendant of Abraham through whom the nations of the earth will be blessed (Gen 22:18). Jesus is the fulfillment of messianic hopes.

However, Matthew was also conscious that Jesus used the term "Christ/Messiah" ("Anointed One") and understood his role as such in a different way. During the Babylonian exile Second Isaiah, with his strong emphasis on God's direct reign, had said that the everlasting covenant made with David (2 Sam 7:13-16) was actually transferred to the people, thus becoming a "covenant to the people" or a "people-covenant." They were now to be witnesses to God's power (Isa 55:3-5) as God's chosen Servant Israel. With this in mind Third Isaiah could speak of the role of the Servant as the "one anointed" by God to bring good news to the afflicted (61:1). The faithful were to carry out this role. In ch. 2 Matthew goes on to show that Jesus, born in Bethlehem as the royal son of David (2:5, quoting Mic 5:1-2), fulfills his messiahship by also fulfilling the role of God's Chosen One, Servant Israel as depicted in Isaiah 40–66. The gifts brought by representatives of foreign nations (2:11) are the gifts brought to Servant Israel in Isa 60:6. They are brought to Jesus because he is the "light to the nations" (Isa 42:6; 49:6). In 2:13-23 Matthew shows that Jesus relives the history of Israel: his flight into Egypt and return and consequent withdrawal to the district of Galilee is Israel's history in miniature.

In his opening chapter (1:23, quoting Isa 7:14) Matthew identifies the child Mary is to bring forth as "Emmanuel," and explains to his readers that this means "God with us." In what sense God is with the people in Jesus is revealed to his readers by Matthew as the story of Jesus as Suffering Servant unfolds in his gospel. Similarly in the second chapter (2:15, quoting Hos 11:1) Matthew designates Jesus as God's son, alerting the reader to a central christological theme of the evangelist. But in what sense Jesus is the "Son of God" only becomes clear to the reader as Jesus fulfills the role of Servant Israel in the rest of the gospel. In Jesus' baptism, which he undergoes "to fulfill all righteousness" (3:15) he is identified by God as the Servant of Isa 42:1. He undergoes testing in the wilderness (4:1-11) as Israel was tested, but whereas Israel in the past failed, Jesus as Servant Israel succeeds. Matthew 11:4-5 makes it clear that it is by proclaiming the good news in word and deed that Jesus fulfills the role of the Anointed One of Isa 61:1 as the Servant, and Matt 12:15-21 emphasizes with its quotation of Isa 42:1-4 that it is as

Servant Israel that Jesus always speaks and acts. However, the designation Jesus uses of himself is "Son of Man," a term deriving from Dan 7:13 and given emphasis in *1 Enoch* 37–71. It is in Matt 16:13-28 that the meaning of this term for Jesus is revealed. We see how it is transformed and fulfilled by Jesus in the role of Servant Israel. It is in this context (16:21) that Jesus reveals to his disciples that he must now bring the Servant's role to completion by fulfilling all of Israel's past history. The exile for Israel had been a suffering and death experience, but God had raised Israel up in order to fulfill the divine purpose of making many to be accounted righteous (Isa 53:11-12). However, Israel had failed to carry this out. Jesus, representing Israel, must therefore undergo suffering, death, and resurrection on behalf of the faithful and thus prepare them to be "a light to the Gentiles" that they may "make disciples of all nations" (Matt 28:19).

Thus it is through coming as the Servant and giving himself as a "ransom for many" (20:28) that Jesus makes it possible for the faithful to follow his example and become true Israel. The term "Son of God," originally used as an equivalent for Servant Israel, takes on deeper meaning in Jesus who fulfills all the law and the prophets, who fulfills both God's promises and Israel's purpose. For this reason all authority has been given to him in heaven and on earth (28:18) and all righteousness is thus fulfilled in him (3:15). The centurion's words at the cross, "Truly this man was God's Son" (27:54) become our utterance of faith.

Matthew's description of the origins of Christ not only proclaims his royal heritage, messianic fulfillment, and fulfillment of the role of the true Israel; it also tells of his divine Sonship by relating Christ's unique and miraculous conception.

SECOND READING

I. Jesus' Origins: 1:1–2:23

The Background of Jesus Messiah (1:1-17)

The word *genesis* can mean both "genealogy" and "origin" (cf. Gen 5:1; Matt 1:18a). The use of *Jesus Christ* as a name here is late (found elsewhere in the gospels only in Matt 1:18; Mark 1:1; John 1:17; 17:3) and is used apologetically to emphasize that Jesus fulfills *all* hopes for the long-awaited "Anointed One" or "Messiah." The order of the titles is also highly apologetic. Matthew is emphasizing that this Jesus who came from Galilee is both a descendant of David (mentioned first in order to focus on Jesus as the Davidic Messiah) and a true son of Abraham (cf. 3:9). He is also implying that God's covenants with both David (2 Sam 7:12-16) and Abraham (Gen 12:1-3; 18:18) were being fulfilled in Jesus. We note how these separate covenants converge and are combined in Matthew's gospel. Abraham was also portrayed as the father of all nations (Gen 17:5), and it is through Jesus that all the nations will be blessed. Matthew is heir to the "biblical" tradition of bringing things together, of "bringing forth out of his treasure what is new and what is old" (Matt 13:52).

The genealogy is presented in a pattern covering three periods of Israel's history. Verses 2-6a cover the premonarchic period from Abraham to David, the two ancestors just mentioned in v. 1, thus firmly linking Jesus to this formative period. David is explicitly referred to as "the king" because in him begins the dynastic principle from which the messianic hope emerged. In this first list of fourteen ancestors extracted from 1 Chr 1:34; 2:1-15 three women, Tamar, Rahab, and Ruth, are mentioned, a rare occurrence in genealogies. Only *Tamar* (v. 3) was mentioned in the source (1 Chr 2:4). She was actually the widowed daughter-in-law of Judah, who fathered her twin sons (Genesis 38)—certainly an irregular relationship! Yet Jewish tradition in regard to this incident spoke of the sinfulness of Judah, while Tamar was seen as having been led by the spirit of God to act in accordance with God's will. *Rahab* (v. 5) was a Canaanite prostitute in Jericho who hid the Israelite spies (Joshua 2) and because of her faith and action was spared in the destruction of Jericho (Josh 6:25; cf. Heb 11:31; Jas 2:25). Jewish tradition regarded Rahab as a hero who helped to fulfill God's purpose for Israel and played an important role in David's ancestry. *Ruth* was another non-Israelite woman, a Moabite, who became an ancestor of David by entering into marriage with Boaz by somewhat questionable means (Ruth 3). Jewish tradition held that all three women were proselytes who helped fulfill God's purpose through Israel. In a sense the promise to Abraham that he would be a blessing to all nations was already being fulfilled through these women.

The second period (1:6b-11) covers the monarchy from David to the Babylonian exile. Here a fourth woman is mentioned: *the wife of Uriah.* Bathsheba is so called in order to recall the words of 2 Sam 12:9-10 by which David was judged both for his adultery and his murder of Uriah the Hittite. In spite of this irregular relationship Bathsheba was held in high esteem as the one who was destined by God to continue the Davidic line. The number of ancestors listed in this second period is again fourteen if we do not count David a second time.

The third section (1:12-16) covers the period from after the exile to the birth of "Jesus who is called the Messiah." Perhaps Jehoiachin (Jechoniah) is to be counted also in this section since he was a transitional figure who was taken into exile in 597 B.C.E. and continued to live into the post-monarchic period. The last verse of this section (v. 16) brings the list of "begettings" to completion. In v. 16 the passive *egenēthē* is a so-called *passivum theologicum,* naming no man but pointing to God as the cause and origin of Jesus' conception. Verse 16 also gives us the fifth and final woman of the genealogy: *Mary.* Like the other women, Mary too is the instrument through whom the divine purpose is achieved through the working of the Holy Spirit. Once again this birth is by means of an irregular conception (vv. 18-25), one that is not tainted by sin but that will bring about deliverance from sin for the people (1:21). Those who would point a finger of suspicion at the circumstances of Jesus' birth should look at the whole history of the line of David. The fact that this genealogy gives Jesus' *legal* ancestry and not physical descent both distances Jesus from its imperfect story and legitimizes Jesus' messiahship. Matthew has made a masterful statement! With the inclusion of the four women in the genealogy Matthew has not only led up to Mary's irregular conception but has indicated that Gentiles are also included in God's purpose.

Matthew has arranged this genealogy into a pattern of three ages of fourteen generations each (v. 17). There may be two explanations for the use of the number fourteen: (1) The Hebrew letters of the name David add up to fourteen (ד = 4, ו = 6, ד = 4), and so Matthew may be emphasizing that Jesus is the Davidic Messiah and that the whole genealogy is messianic in form. (2) Matthew often has groups of seven, a number symbolizing fullness or completeness (for example, seven parables in chapter 13; seven woes in chapter 23; also 12:45). So Matthew may be pointing to the past as six sevens and Jesus as the one who inaugurates the seventh seven, the age of fulfillment. Jesus is the transitional figure bringing to an end the former age of Israel and inaugurating the final state, the longed-for messianic age. This symbolic pattern also emphasizes four focal points: (1) Abraham, whose covenantal promise to be a blessing to all nations is fulfilled in Jesus (Gen 22:18; cf. Matt 8:11); (2) David, to whom the promise of a messianic descendant is fulfilled in Jesus; (3) the Babylonian exile, the turning point and time of the promised restoration of the kingdom, which Jesus will inaugurate; (4) finally, Jesus himself, called the Messiah, who brings all things to fulfillment.

The Origin of Jesus Messiah (1:18-25)

Matthew's use of *genesis* (v. 18) as in v. 1 ties the account of Jesus' conception to his background as a true Israelite and son of David. The account of Jesus' conception is told in relation to Joseph who is identified as "son of David" (v. 20) and through whom Jesus legally becomes a descendant of David. Mary had been betrothed to Joseph. Betrothal was actually the binding contract for marriage negotiated between families usually a year or more before the actual wedding took place when the husband would take his bride into his house (cf. Matt 25:1-13) and the marriage would be consummated. Such a contract could only be terminated by divorce or death (cf. Deut 20:7; 22:23-28). It was before the marriage celebration took place that Mary was found to be pregnant by the Holy Spirit. This conception had been brought about by God in an unusual way in order to accomplish the divine plan for humankind.

When Mary's pregnancy became apparent to Joseph the only way open to him appeared to be to divorce her privately in order not to bring her to shame, but God's messenger communicated with Joseph through a dream, a common means of divine revelation to patriarchs and prophets in the OT (cf. Gen 20:3; 31:10-11; Num 12:6), addressing Joseph as "son of David" because that is the title he was to pass on to Mary's future son by taking Mary into his home and accepting the child as his own. "Do not be afraid" was always the word of comfort and assurance that what God planned for the people would be accomplished (e.g., Gen 15:1; Isa 35:4). That God is about to accomplish part of that plan is indicated by the name by which the child is to be called: Jesus or Jeshua (v. 21) meaning "salvation." Joseph was to give the child this name as a way of acknowledging that he was adopting him. Jewish law stated that if a man said "This is my son" the action was to be accepted legally (*m. B. Batra* 8.6). This giving of a significant name was in the true prophetic tradition (cf. Hos 1:4-10; 2:1; Isa 7:3, 14; 8:1-4, 18) as a sign of what was to come.

"Saving from sin" is a unique concept when considered against the OT background where the verb "to save" was used primarily of deliverance from one's enemy. During the exile it came to be used to express God's deliverance of the people from exile and their restoration to God's kingdom (cf. Isa 35:4; 43:11-12; 45:20-21). The exile was acknowledged as punishment for Israel's sin of breaking their covenant with God (cf. Isa 50:1; 59:2, 12), and near its end Second Isaiah's message of good news was that they had now paid the penalty and God would remember their sins no more (Isa 40:2; 43:25; 44:22). This forgiveness, however, was to be understood as the restoration of a proper relationship with God. Jesus' mission now was to restore that relationship for the people and so fulfill God's purpose. Following the prophetic understanding of Second Isaiah, Jesus in Matthew's gospel announces the forgiveness of sins (9:2-6; 12:31; 26:28).

Verses 22-23 give the first of Matthew's so-called formula citations, which he uses to pull together ideas already expressed, extend the imagery, and give a more encompassing picture. In its historical context the quotation from Isa 7:14 was a sign given by the prophet to King Ahaz who had been threatened by two kings of the north. The prophet warned the king to maintain his trust in YHWH and not to seek other alliances, for by the time a young woman conceived and bore a son she would be able to call him Immanuel, "God is with us," out of thankfulness that God had delivered Judah from this crisis. The name of the anonymous woman's child was a message of hope. Matthew's use of this quotation was apparently motivated by two concerns: (1) of lesser importance would be its possible use against any charge of illegitimacy; this depends on interpreting the LXX rendition *(parthenos)* of the Hebrew *ʿalmāh* of Isa 7:14 as "virgin" rather than "young woman," the normal translation (cf. Ps 68:25; Song 1:3; cf. Prov 30:19). [See the commentary on Isaiah in this book, both the "History of Reception" and the discussion of Isa 7:1–9:1a.] (2) More importantly, Matthew's purpose was to emphasize that through this birth Israel would be able to experience God's presence among them once again. The emphasis in the quotation is on "Emmanuel . . . God is with us"—that in Jesus God would overcome their present crisis and restore the relationship of God to the people promised in Isa 41:10; 43:5 and elsewhere. Then, recognizing that God is with God's people, the nations would come to Zion and be blessed (Isa 45:14; Zech 8:23). This account of the birth of Jesus alludes to Second Isaiah, who spoke of God's deliverance of Israel from exile as being like a divine birth (Isa 42:14) and of Israel as God's chosen servant whom God had created and formed from the womb, called by name, whom God had carried in arms from birth (Isa 42:1; 44:1-2; 46:3-4). As the next chapters will show, Matthew depicts Jesus as carrying out the role of Servant Israel. It is significant that in the quotation from Isa 7:14 Matthew has changed "she shall name" to "they shall name," that is, the people whom Jesus saves from their sins will recognize him as "God is with us." So Joseph did what the angel of the Lord advised him (vv. 24-25), took Mary as his wife, but did not have marital relations with her (literally "know" her) until (that is, "up to" or "before") the birth of the child. "To know" here normally has the meaning of "to know intimately, sexually."

THE PERPETUAL VIRGINITY OF MARY

The Greek expression translated "until" does not imply that Joseph had marital relations with Mary after the birth of the child. Catholic doctrine has taught from tradition that not only was Mary a virgin at the moment of the birth of the Savior, but she remained a virgin throughout her life. This Catholic teaching on the perpetual virginity of Mary in no way means to deny the goodness of marriage or sexuality; instead, following the tradition handed down about Mary in the Church, it affirms the unique character of Mary's role in the plan of salvation as the special instrument of the Incarnation. Through Mary's *fiat,* through her acceptance of the will of God, she became the Mother of God. It is possible that those passages that refer to Jesus' brothers and sisters reflect Semitic usage, by which these terms could refer to a wider range of family members and were not restricted to actual blood siblings (cf. Matt 12:46; 13:55; 27:56; and see 14:3, where Herod Philip is described as the "brother" of Herod Antipas, although the two were really half-brothers). —*Ed.*

Matthew sees this miraculous conception as another sign of Christ's fulfillment of the prophecy of Isaiah (Isa 7:14), another sign of Christ fulfilling the role of the Suffering Servant. Yet beyond this the virginal conception points to the divine nature of Jesus' Sonship, his unique relationship with God, so that when Jesus is seen as God's presence among the people of Israel the presence is that of God's beloved Son (Matt 3:17).

Matthew has thus shown that Jesus is to usher in the messianic age, and he is "God with us" by conception and son of David by adoption, but he is also son of Abraham (cf. Isa 41:8) who will lead his people to be a light to the nations and thus fulfill the promise to Abraham (Gen 12:3; 17:4). Jesus' mission is the central point of this account; the virginal conception is contributory to it.

The Recognition of the Birth of Jesus Messiah (2:1-12)

Tradition has it (Herodotus, *Hs.* 1.107–204) that magi, by their study of the stars, foretold the birth of Cyrus who was to become a great king and establish the Persian Empire. During the exile Second Isaiah prophesied Cyrus's coming as God's "Anointed One," the "shepherd" to restore the exiles to their homeland (Isa 44:28; 45:1). By 538 B.C.E. Cyrus had taken over Babylonia and permitted the exiles to return to Judah. Thus Cyrus was used as God's instrument to end the exile and begin the restoration of Israel. That restoration, as the reign of God, is now to be brought to fulfillment, and it is again the magi from the East who make the announcement of the "Anointed One" (Matt 2:4), the "shepherd" (2:6) of Israel who will accomplish this.

Bethlehem of Judea was the birthplace of David (1 Sam 17:12) and the place where he was anointed king (1 Sam 16:1-13). Matthew mentions "of Judea" to emphasize that Jesus as the promised Messiah did indeed come from Judea as foretold, even though he was a Galilean. In Matthew, Mary and Joseph are depicted as having resided in Bethlehem (cf. v. 11). Herod here is Herod the Great who died in the spring of 4 B.C.E. Thus Jesus was probably born between 6 and 5 B.C.E. The "magi" were a Persian priestly caste of the Zoroastrian religion who were renowned throughout the ancient world as astrologers and interpreters of dreams. They seek the king of the Judeans because they have seen "his star at its rising." A birth was often likened to the rising of a star. The mention of the "rising star" would have reminded Matthew's Jewish hearers of the promise to Abraham, often recalled, that his descendants would be as the stars of heaven (Gen 15:5; 22:17; Exod 32:13; 1 Chr 27:23; Neh 9:23). One of those descendants in particular was already understood messianically (Num 24:17: "A star shall come out of Jacob"), a reference Matthew must have had in mind. The magi "pay homage to" the child, the oriental way of showing honor and respect (cf. Matt 2:8, 11; 8:2; 9:18; 14:33).

News of the birth of the promised king would certainly have troubled Herod (vv. 3-4), who had already put two of his sons to death and was soon to execute his oldest, Antipater, for fear they wanted to take over his throne. Matthew uses the phrase "all Jerusalem" to include above all the corrupt Jewish leadership of the Zadokite (Sadducean) priesthood, elders, and Pharisaic leaders (see Matt 3:5, 7; cf. Zech 12:6-10) who later are responsible for Jesus' death.

In the quotation (vv. 5-6) Matthew again emphasizes that this is Bethlehem *of Judea* and that it is "in the land of Judah," a phrase added to the quotation from Mic 5:2 to identify the place of birth of the Messiah. But the reader familiar with the context of Micah 5 would have recognized its allusions to Isa 7:14 which Matthew had already quoted (1:23). In addition, the context speaks of this future ruler as one who will "stand and feed his flock in the strength of the Lord" (Mic 5:4). But instead of continuing the quote from Micah, Matthew has grafted on a saying from 2 Sam 5:2 (1 Chr 11:2) spoken to David ("It is you who shall be shepherd of my people Israel") to tie it in more specifically with David. Note that the saying in 2 Sam 5:2 comes from the words of the elders of the northern tribes who had come down to Hebron to anoint David, king of Judah, their king as well. Matthew is making a subtle point that this Messiah will not only be "king of the Judeans"(2:2) but also of God's people elsewhere. For that reason he also reverses the original of Mic 5:2: "who are one of the little clans of Judah" to read "You . . . are by no means least among the rulers of Judah." The original implication in Micah 5, that this leader will come from Bethlehem because the leadership in Jerusalem was corrupt, is still retained.

Herod secretly inquires of the magi the actual time of the appearance of the star in order to ascertain the age of this child (vv. 7-8). The renewed sight of the star and its identification of the location of the child cause the magi to be overcome with joy. Matthew uses a string of superlatives here because he sees the coming of the magi as the beginning of the fulfillment of prophecies from the time of the exile that nations would come to the light and kings to the brightness of the rising of faithful Israel (Isa 60:3), bringing gifts and eager to recognize the God of Israel because "God is with" them (Isa 45:14; cf. 49:7; Matt 1:23). Frankincense was used in making the holy incense (Exod 30:34) as well as for sanctifying offerings (Lev 2:1-2; 24:7). Myrrh was used for the oil of anointing (Exod 30:23). Both were used as perfume (Song 3:6; Sir 24:15). These are royal gifts as promised to faithful Israel (Isa 60:6; cf. Ps 72:10-11) who would become God's crown of beauty, God's royal diadem (Isa 62:3; cf. 28:5). Jesus here is thus identified as representing true Israel, while the magi represent the nations.

The Young Child is Identified as True Israel (2:13-23)

That this young child's mission was to represent true Israel is here made explicit. The mention of Bethlehem, Egypt, Ramah, and Galilee implies messiahship, the Exodus, exile, and mission to the Gentiles. In other words the young child relives Israel's history leading up to Israel's mission, and so becomes representative of Israel.

Once again Joseph is given a divine message in a dream, this time to flee to Egypt. "For Herod is about to search for the child, to destroy him" has its parallel in the story of Moses who fled to the land of Midian because Pharaoh sought to kill him (Exod 2:15); it also recalls Pharaoh's orders to slaughter the male children of the Israelites (Exod 1:15). Here Matthew continues his depiction of Christ not only as the true Israel but as a new Moses. The quotation in v. 15 from Hos 11:1 that reads in full "When Israel was a child, I loved him, and out of Egypt I called my son" emphasizes Jesus' role as representative of Israel. It also evokes the Exodus motif, suggesting the coming restoration of the kingdom as a new exodus, an implication often drawn by Second Isaiah (cf. Isa 43:1-3; 48:20-21). Israel was often referred to as God's "son" and "servant," synonymous terms for the vassal in a covenant relationship. So God's command to Pharaoh was "Let my son go that he may worship me" (Exod 4:22-23).

In vv. 16-20 the parallels with Israel's sojourn in Egypt continue. Just as Pharaoh had ordered that all male children be put to death, so Herod orders that all the male children two years old and under in Bethlehem and the surrounding area be killed. Such drastic action to destroy a potential messiah was quite in character with Herod. His atrocities are well documented (see Josephus, *Ant.* 16.392–394; 17.42–144, 167). The quotation in v. 18 from Jer 31:15 expresses the people's sorrow over the exile to Babylon in a context of hope for future return and reconciliation with God through a new covenant in which God's teaching would be written upon their hearts (cf. especially. vv. 31-34). In that chapter YHWH promises to be "a father to Israel" (v. 9) and Israel is YHWH's "firstborn" and "dear son" (vv. 19, 20). Matthew has quoted this verse here to draw the parallel between the massacre of the infants in Bethlehem and the slaughter and exile of the people in 587 B.C.E. Thus the early life of Jesus becomes one with the history of Israel and the implication is drawn that Jesus, as true Israel, will fulfill the covenant relationship as God's son. Ramah, a town about eight kilometers north of Jerusalem, was the place where those to be exiled were gathered for deportation to Babylon (Jer 40:1). First Samuel 10:2 places Rachel's tomb near there, but Gen 35:16-19 and 48:7 put it near Bethlehem, and this is what Matthew had in mind. "When Herod died" (v. 19) parallels the announcement of the death of the king of Egypt in the Exodus story (Exod 2:23) and the statement: "those who were seeking the child's life are dead" parallels the announcement to Moses in Exod 4:19-20.

So Joseph, Mary, and the young child returned to the land of Israel to find that Herod the Great had died and that his son Archelaus now ruled as ethnarch over Judea, Samaria, and Idumea. Archelaus had quickly gained a reputation for brutality that eventually led to his exile in 6 C.E. Being warned of this in another dream, Joseph did not return to Judea but took the family to Galilee, a district with a mixed population made up largely of Jews, Greeks, and Romans. The Jews made up about one third of the population and spoke both Greek and Aramaic. Nazareth (v. 23), not mentioned in the OT or early Jewish literature, was a small agricultural village with a Jewish population. "He will be called a Nazorean" is not a quotation from an individual prophet but a general statement incorporating a number of prophetic concepts. "Nazorean" does not refer specifically to an inhabitant of Nazareth. That term is "Nazarene" (cf. Mark 1:24; 10:47; 14:67; 16:6; Luke 4:34; 24:19). "Nazorean" derives from the Hebrew *nēṣer* meaning "shoot" or "branch" in Isa 11:1. Originally this passage spoke of an ideal future Davidic king, but during the exile the everlasting covenant made with David was transferred to faithful Israel who were to represent YHWH's rule to the nations (Isa 55:3-5). For that reason the people become the "shoot" of God's planting (Isa 60:21) to grow up into "oaks of righteousness, the planting of the LORD" (61:3) and function as God's "anointed" (Isa 61:1). Other royal terminology was also transferred to the faithful who will be God's "crown" and "royal diadem" (62:3). By the time of Jesus the term "Nazorean" would have identified a person who followed in this prophetic tradition and sought to fulfill the role of faithful Israel as that "shoot," thus referring to a movement rather than a place. Thus Jesus was often referred to as "Jesus the Nazorean" (Matt 26:71; Luke 18:37; John 18:5, 7; 19:19; Acts 2:22; 3:6; 4:10; 6:14; 22:8; 26:9; cf. 24:5). The name "Nazareth" may also come from the same word *nēṣer* and may have been established by a group who wished to live out that role in Galilee away from the Jerusalem priesthood. Up to now the life of the young child has been described as a microcosm of Israel's history. In this last verse the title of "Nazorean" indicates that it is through this man that Israel's purpose is to be achieved.

II. Preparation: 3:1–4:25

John the Baptist: Preparing the Way (3:1-12)

Unlike the other canonical gospels, Matthew does not introduce John the Baptist as unknown to the reader. Furthermore, he emphasizes the continuity between John and Jesus more than Jesus' superiority over his forerunner. In fact, John's teaching as presented by Matthew contains three statements later repeated verbatim as sayings of Jesus (3:2 = 4:17; 3:7 = 23:33; 3:10b = 7:19). In no other gospel is such a coincidence verified. Through both his teaching and destiny the Baptist anticipates the words and deeds of the Messiah. For this reason Matthew's eye is directed more toward their common features than to the contrasts between them.

Significantly, Jesus' mission begins with the activity of John the Baptist depicted as fulfilling Isa 40:3: the voice calling for people to prepare for the coming reign of God. The restoration and renewal are about to begin. Matthew tells of John the Baptist only what is relevant to his preparation for Jesus' mission. However, John's preaching of repentance, his call to undergo a ritual purification, and his warning of imminent judgment had a great impact on the Judean population, and his fame spread throughout Palestine. Luke tells us that he was the son of elderly parents, members of Levitical priestly families, and that "he was in the wilderness till the day he appeared publicly to Israel" (Luke 1:5-25, 57-80). It is possible that he was given a home by the celibate Essenes of Qumran, a priestly movement in opposition to the priesthood in Jerusalem. These Essenes had developed their own monastic community near the Dead Sea and saw their role as preparing for the coming Messiahs and the establishment of a future kingdom in terms of Isa 40:3 [1QS 8:13]. If John had been brought up by this group, he could have moved out to warn all the people of the impending judgment. "The wilderness of Judea" refers to the area in the Jordan rift at the northern end of the Dead Sea. John was probably active at the river crossings between Perea and Judea.

There is as well an ancient tradition about "the wilderness" with its theological meaning running through Israel's history. It signifies the place of God's initiatives for the sake of educating and converting the people. The desert of the

Sinai was the place of the Mosaic legislation. The wilderness is where God "speaks tenderly to" Israel (Hos 2:14). In Second Isaiah the desert is a place where the marvels of God are to be manifested again (Isa 42:11; 43:19-20).

John's call to repentance was a call to turn back to God in covenant faithfulness (cf. Jer 3:12ff.). Second Isaiah looked to the future restoration as being the direct rule of God in the hearts of the people (Isa 51:7). The quotation from Isa 40:3 (v. 3) bears the message: "prepare for the restoration of God's rule," just as the Qumran community regarded itself as doing. Here the Baptist is depicted as "the voice of one crying out in the wilderness" calling *all* the people of Israel to prepare themselves. The passage originally referred to preparing for deliverance from exile. John's message emphasizes the coming judgment before the reign of God can be established.

Matthew describes John's clothing (v. 4) almost exactly as the clothing of Elijah was described in 2 Kings 1:8 in order to give a subliminal message that the Baptist is the returning Elijah (Mal 4:5). A garment made of camel's hair was common dress for a prophet (cf. Zech 13:4). John's diet of locusts and wild honey was ritually clean food available in the wilderness. Locusts were one of the few insects Jews were permitted to eat (Lev 11:20-23). Thus John comes in the way of righteousness according to the Law.

The call to prepare for the coming kingdom (vv. 5-6) evoked a strong response from the people of Jerusalem and Judea and around the Jordan. People were looking for deliverance from Roman oppression and for renewal and so were willing to undergo this ritual of purification. The Essenes performed daily washings as a symbol of purification in preparation for the coming of the Messiahs, but John's ritual of cleansing was a once-for-all act recalling Zech 13:1 (cf. Isa 4:4; Ezek 36:25-27), calling for people to acknowledge their sins and be cleansed as a means of preparing themselves for the kingdom. The Pharisees were a non-priestly party who sought, by following both the written and oral Law in every detail, to become the righteous ones who would inherit the kingdom under the Davidic Messiah. It was their concern for the kingdom and opposition to foreign domination that made them popular among the people. The Sadducees, of Zadokite priestly background, were more elitist and had more political influence. Their actions were governed by priestly law and political expediency, and they were more concerned to maintain the Temple rituals and sacrificial rites in Jerusalem. Although there was no love lost between these two parties, both were hated by the Essenes of Qumran and generally despised by the prophetic movement. In calling them a brood of vipers John was accusing them of being deceitful and corrupt leaders, as the prophets had done in the past (Isa 59:5; also 1QH 5.27-28). Jesus later used this same phrase in Matt 12:34; 23:33. The wrath to come is described in Isa 59:17-18, but John also has in mind the brood of vipers seeking to escape from the burning stubble of Mal 4:1, the prophet's warning to the priesthood and their followers of the coming judgment (cf. also Amos 5:18-20; Isa 13:9; Zeph 1:15). A tree bearing good fruit (v. 8) is a common symbol for one who lives a life of faithfulness to God (Psalm 1; Jer 17:5-8). When one returns to a faithful relationship with God, the fruit of it will become evident.

"God is able from these stones to raise up children to Abraham" (v. 9). In Hebrew this is a play on words: *ʾăbānîm* ("stones") and *bānîm* ("sons"). It alludes to the comment in Isa 51:1-2 that Abraham and Sarah were like lifeless stones but God raised up descendants from them. It responds to an assumed objection claiming that salvation is guaranteed to every Israelite. That God can make children of Abraham "out of stones" insinuates that fleshly descent does not guarantee a share in the blessings promised to the descendants of Abraham. Only faithfulness to God would ensure participation in the kingdom.

Returning to the tree metaphor (v. 10), John warns that the fruitless ones will soon be cut down—an allusion to Isa 10:33-34, the reference to a judgment coming prior to a branch *(nēṣer)* growing out the roots of the stem of Jesse (Isa 11:l). John expected the fruitless would be utterly destroyed by fire, a common metaphor for the final judgment (Mal 4:1) before the promised kingdom could be established.

John's baptism (v. 11) was a ritual washing, but he sees the baptism of the one who comes after him as inaugurating God's judgment. The word *baptizein* refers to ablution by water. To this basic meaning the baptism of John added the act of repentance with a confession of sins.

"The one who is coming after me" may refer to the messenger of the Lord who will suddenly come to the Temple (cf. Mal 3:1), identified by Malachi as Elijah *redivivus* (Mal 4:5). This is certainly consistent with his role of "baptizing with Holy Spirit and fire," describing the judgment of the righteous and the wicked as we find it in Mal 4:1-3 (cf. Isa 4:4). But according to Matthew, when sending his disciples John shows a lack of assurance about Jesus' identity. In his inquiry (11:3) he raises exactly that question. At that point Jesus will identify himself as the servant of YHWH in terms of Isaiah 40–55 while pointing to John as Elijah *redivivus,* and in this sense the one who is to come. The judgment is imminent, for already "his winnowing fork is in his hand" (v. 12), the symbol used to express the judgment of exile on Judah (Jer 15:7) or on those who contend with God's people (Isa 41:15-16). The destruction of the wicked as a burning of the worthless chaff after the good grain has been gathered in draws on the image of burning off stubble (Mal 4:1). Jesus later used the same image to emphasize that the judgment will happen after the gathering in of the righteous into the kingdom (13:24-30, 36-43).

John and the Baptism of Jesus (3:13-17)

Many Galileans had the same disdain as John for the Judean leadership, the perpetrators of oppression through legal and ritual means, including taxes and tithes. Jesus also, by coming to John to be baptized, was thus identifying himself with John's message. John's question regarding Jesus' desire to be baptized presupposes prior conversation between the two and perhaps prior preaching activity by Jesus in Galilee. John evidently recognized in Jesus the spirit of Elijah. Matthew points out that John the Baptist only reluctantly received him. "I need to be baptized by you," he says. John here prophetically recognizes both the lack of sinfulness in Jesus and his superiority.

Speaking for the first time in Matthew's gospel, Jesus talks of their mission. The verb "fulfill" is most often used in Matthew for fulfilling prophecy (1:22; 2:15, 17, 23; 4:14), and that is the way it should be understood here. "To fulfill all righteousness" has reference to both divine and human righteousness in Isaiah 40–66. "Righteousness" is essentially acting in faithfulness to the covenant relationship. So in spite of Israel's stubbornness and lack of righteousness God will bring about divine righteousness by delivering the people (Isa 45:21-24) and reigning over them as sovereign (Isa 41:21; 43:15; 52:7). Israel will then respond with righteousness as God's witnesses (43:12; 44:8) so that in the restoration they will all be righteous, the shoot of God's planting (60:21), to grow into "oaks of righteousness" (61:3). In so doing Israel, the Righteous One, will cause many to be accounted righteous (53:11). Thus in undergoing baptism Jesus participates with John in initiating the whole plan of God's righteousness, the people's righteous response, and their consequent witness to all nations.

BAPTISM

Early Christian theology saw in Jesus' baptism an anticipation of Christian baptism not only as a ritual but also as a preview of Jesus' voluntary "descent" (humiliation) into his acceptance of the role of the "suffering servant" (Isaiah 42, 48, 53), his death, to be followed by his ascent (glorification: Isaiah 53) that reveals his divine sonship. The antithesis of descent/ascent is the image underlying the christological hymn in Phil 2:6-9 as well as the Johannine texts about the descent of the Son (John 6:33, 41, 50-51, 58; 13:13) so that he may be "lifted up" on the cross (John 8:28; 12:32-34; 13:14) and "ascend" to the Father (John 20:17). Furthermore, just as Jesus' baptism anticipates his death and resurrection, so too in baptism the individual Christian shares in the Lord's passion and glorification, an aspect of baptismal theology emphasized by Paul (Rom 6:4-6, 10; 7:4; 1 Cor 6:17). Because of its multiple rapports with christological doctrine and sacramental life Jesus' baptism assumed an important role in patristic teaching and liturgy and maintained a special preeminence among Eastern Christians. —*Ed.*

After being baptized Jesus immediately went up from the water (v. 16), just as the former "Joshua" had led the people up from the Jordan in haste (Josh 4:19), as a new crossing into the promised kingdom of God (cf. Isa 43:16-21). The Exodus motif was a common metaphor for the deliverance of Israel, as it was in Isa 63:10–64:8. It is this context that is alluded to in "suddenly the heavens were opened to him and he saw the Spirit of God descending like a dove and alighting on him." This is the response to the cry of the returned exiles waiting for the promised restoration: "O that you would tear open the heavens and come down" (Isa 64:1). In their plea they had acknowledged: "You, O LORD, are our father" (63:16; 64:8) in response to God's acknowledging them as God's own children (63:8). The "Spirit of God coming down" not only recalls this context (Isa 63:11) but also the promises of the divine spirit in Isa 44:3; 59:21; 61:1. "Like a dove" alludes to the Spirit's activity in creation and its renewal (Gen 1:2; 8:8-12). With this background in Isaiah the "voice from heaven" (v. 17) is God's response to the faithful who have said "Father." The use of this title had come as a result of faithful Israel being called God's servant whom God has created and formed as God's child from the womb (Isa 43:1, 6, 7; 49:1, 3, 5; 63:8). In the light of this it is understandable for the words of the Father to be: "This is my Son, the Beloved, with whom I am well pleased." This statement thus combined many of the descriptions of Israel as the Servant of YHWH into one summary title using Isa 42:1 as the basic quotation. The insertion of "the Beloved" in place of "my chosen" is made in order to include another frequent Servant title (cf. Isa 41:8; 43:1-4), but it also ties in with the reference to Israel (and consequently to Jesus) as God's "son" whom God "loves" in Hos 11:1, already quoted in relation to Jesus in 2:15. "My son" and "my servant" were interchangeable designations of a vassal in a covenant relationship in the OT (cf. 2 Samuel 7; 2 Kings 16:7; see also Wis 2:12-18). So for Jesus being named by God as "my son" means being identified as Servant Israel, the ideal representative of God's faithful people (cf. Matt 5:9).

Here, as at the transfiguration, Jesus alone is addressed as "the Beloved Son" pleasing to the Father. The gospel of Matthew ends with the universal mission of the disciples, sent to baptize with a trinitarian formula, and thus aims at announcing a world-wide communion with God. The "sonship" declared at Jesus' baptism inaugurates an era in which participation in that sonship is to be offered through preaching and baptism to all nations.

The Testing of God's Son (4:1-11)

As that ideal representative Jesus now undergoes tests similar to those undergone by Israel during the forty years in the wilderness. The Spirit of God now takes him into the wilderness to be tested according to Deut 8:2-5 which speaks of God testing Israel in the wilderness "as a parent disciplines a child." Jesus is put to the test by the devil who is the agent of the testing since he is the one whose power will be most threatened by Jesus' fulfilling Israel's role. The term "devil" is the LXX translation of the Hebrew *sātān,* the one who played the role of accuser and tester in God's heavenly court (Zech 3:1-3; Job 1:6-12) and later was depicted as the enticer to evil as a fallen angel (cf. Matt 13:39; 25:41). Fasting forty days and nights is analogous to Israel's being tested in the wilderness where God let them hunger, but it also connects with the forty-day fasts of the two great prophets of the past who established and reaffirmed the covenant of Israel with God at Sinai: Moses (Exod 34:28; Deut 9:9, 18) and Elijah (1 Kings 19:8). "Afterwards he was famished," as Israel was. The quotation of Deut 8:3 by Jesus needs to be put into the whole context of 8:1-3 that focuses on word as revelation: God has made Israel hunger in the wilderness, fed them with manna, and tested their heart so that they might learn what their ancestors did not know: "one does not live by bread alone, but by every word that comes from the mouth of the LORD." God's word on Horeb needs the hunger and the trials in the desert as preparation and context. In the Matthean context one can see a parallel: the trials prepare the "word" of the Sermon on the Mount.

The first test is the desire to satisfy that hunger, to see one's ultimate purpose as the satisfaction of one's own physical needs and to forget that God has a greater purpose for the Son: to be God's Servant (Isa 49:5-6). Jesus responds to the temptation by quoting the divine word from Deut 8:3, a word that Israel in the wilderness had failed to understand.

For the second test (vv. 5-6) the devil takes Jesus into the Holy City and sets him on the pinnacle or "little wing" of the Temple, some small projection of the Temple building. The term "wing" may have been used purposely as an allusion to Ps 91:4 ("under his wings you will find refuge"), because the devil soon quotes from this psalm (vv. 11, 12) in order to test Jesus. The temptation is to use God's promise of protection in a self-serving way and thus force God's hand. Jesus rejects the subtle temptation by quoting

Deut 6:16, again referring to the context of Israel in the wilderness when the people put YHWH to the test, forcing God to supply them water from a rock (Exod 17:1-7). Once again Jesus passed the test as God's son that Israel in the wilderness had failed.

The third test (vv. 8-9) is the ultimate temptation for power and wealth. That Satan could offer "all the kingdoms of the world and their splendor" was regarded as within his power (2 Cor 4:4; John 12:31; 14:30; 16:11), but the offer is an empty one because it would require Jesus to acknowledge the devil's power and authority. A blasphemy is already implied in the offer "all these I will give you," so clearly violating the Creator's rights as proclaimed in the faith of every Israelite: "The earth is the Lord's and its fullness." It is through his service to God and fulfilling God's purpose that all authority will become that of God's son (28:18-20; 10:1). Jesus' answer is to send Satan on his way with a quotation of the first commandment from Deut 6:13. In the wilderness Israel had broken that commandment by worshiping the golden calf (Exod 32:1-10).

Jesus had passed all the tests failed by Israel in the wilderness. Jesus will fulfill the role of the true Israel, just as the birth narrative had prepared the reader to understand. So as the angel ministered to the prophet Elijah, bringing food to strengthen him for his trip to meet with God on Mount Horeb (1 Kings 19:5-8), so angels come and minister to Jesus who is soon to go up on a mountain and proclaim: "Your God reigns!" (cf. Matt 5:1 and Isa 52:7).

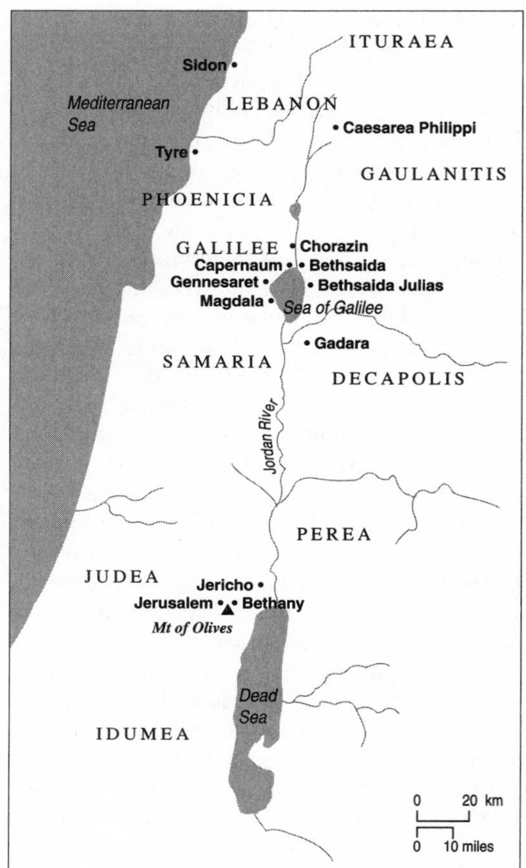

MATTHEW'S PALESTINE

The Mission Begins in Galilee (4:12-25)

The similarity of Jesus' initial message to that of John indicates that he stood in solidarity with the Baptist (cf. 3:2 with 4:17; 3:8, 10 with 7:17-20; 3:12 with 13:30, 41; cf. also John 3:22-4:3). It is in Galilee that he will begin his ministry. Matthew mentions that Jesus made his home in Capernaum, a busy town on the northwest corner of the Sea of Galilee (cf. 9:1; 17:24-25) on one of the trade routes between Damascus and the Mediterranean. Matthew accentuates Jesus' move to "Capernaum by the sea" with the quotation (vv. 14-16) from Isa 9:1-2, mentioning only the geographical locations leading up to "Galilee of the Gentiles." In its original context in Isaiah the passage spoke of those regions that saw the first deportation of Israelites by the Assyrians who then replaced them with people of other nations (2 Kings 15:29; 17:24-27). Isaiah had spoken of those being deported as finding hope in a future messianic leader who would bring about peace and promise for them (9:5-7). By the slight change to "the people who sit in darkness" (cf. Isa 42:7) Matthew has brought the text of Isaiah into closer relation to Jesus' mission, identified in 3:17, to represent Israel (Isa 42:1), given as a people-covenant, a light to the nations (42:6). What better place for Jesus to begin his mission, therefore, than the place that had first been given the promise of the light and had become known as "Galilee of the Gentiles." Such would be a strong response to any objections that the Messiah could not come from Galilee.

Settled in Capernaum, Jesus begins his ministry by proclaiming (v. 17) the same message as John the Baptist (3:2). However, by the reference to "Galilee of the Gentiles" the good news preached by Jesus, in distinction from that of John, obtains a universal dimension from the beginning. Contrary to the preaching of the Baptist, Jesus' invitation to repentance is not accompanied with the threat of "the wrath to come."

John the Baptist "had been arrested" (lit. "handed over") and incarcerated by Herod Antipas, leading to his execution. The verb "deliver" or "hand over" *(paradidōmi)* is used about Jesus' fate of betrayal, arrest, and violent death throughout the NT. Jesus' return to Galilee cannot be understood as motivated by caution to avoid a fate similar to that of John, for Jesus remained in Nazareth and Capernaum, towns also under the jurisdiction of Herod Antipas.

Jesus now begins recruiting his first disciples (v. 18), three of whom will become his inner circle (17:1; 26:37). The names of the two brothers indicate the mixed culture of Galilee. Simon is the Greek form of the Hebrew "Simeon" and his brother has a Greek name, Andrew. These brothers were originally from Bethsaida (John 1:44), just a few miles east of Capernaum. Andrew was originally a disciple of the Baptist (John 1:35-40). Contrary to the practice of a rabbi, Jesus chooses his disciples rather than the disciples choosing him. They follow not simply to listen and learn but to take an active part: to be fishers of people (cf. Jer 16:15-16). Just as they have gathered fish in their nets, so are they called to gather people into God's kingdom (Isa 49:5, 6). Their immediate response to Jesus' call indicates previous contact in which they had become familiar with Jesus' mission. James and John (vv. 21-22) are sometimes referred to simply as "the sons of Zebedee." This may indicate the father's backing of the mission, for it seems the whole family was committed to the cause (20:20; 27:56). The very brief and schematized narrative of the call of the first disciples focuses on their unreserved following of Jesus. This response is presented in the text as an example for Christian discipleship.

Verse 23 is an *inclusio* repeated in 9:35 to indicate that everything in between describes in detail what these verses say in summary. Jesus' mission was conducted throughout Galilee with a few forays into surrounding areas. He directs his message to those of the Jewish faith, for he teaches in "their synagogues" and heals "the people" of Israel in order for them to become a people-covenant and a light to the nations. Matthew often uses the phrase "their synagogues" (9:35; 10:17; 12:9; 13:54; 23:34) to identify them as the places in which the people of Israel gather to worship and hear the word. In this summary statement Jesus' ministry is described as involving teaching, proclaiming, and healing. In direct correlation to Moses, in Matthew's gospel *teaching* is the primary activity of Jesus. He teaches "as one having authority and not as their scribes" (7:29). Only after his resurrection does Jesus pass on this authority to the disciples (28:19-20). The teaching function was normally carried out by the scribes because of their familiarity with the Scriptures. For Jesus the purpose of teaching was to call the people to fulfill their purpose as servant Israel, as a witness to God's glory (Isa 43:10-12; 42:6, 21; 44:8; 55:4) and to have God's teaching in their hearts (Isa 51:7; Jer 31:31-34).

Proclaiming in Matthew always has as its object the kingdom of heaven (3:1; 4:17, 23; 9:35; 10:7, 27; 11:1; 24:14; 26:13). The term *euangelion* also is for Matthew the good news of the kingdom (4:23; 9:35; 24:14; 26:13). Both of these terms derive from the Isaianic expression of the announcement of deliverance from exile and the restoration of the reign of God over the people (Isa 40:9; 41:27; 52:7). In the restoration there is no mention of an earthly monarch or messiah; it is God alone who will rule and shepherd the people. The good news to be proclaimed to the afflicted is: "Your God reigns!"

The third expression, *healing,* has the general, more inclusive meaning of "being in attendance, caring for." "Healing" is also closely related to "proclaiming" in this gospel and is really part of proclamation. It has its origin in Jeremiah's promise of return and restoration as healing (Jer 30:12-17), a motif that was expanded in the Isaianic literature where it promises that "in that day" the deaf will hear, the blind will see, the afflicted and the poor will rejoice in the Lord (cf. Isa 29:18-21; 35:5-7; 61:1-3). The good news of the kingdom of God, therefore, is what brings restoration and healing (Isa 57:18-19), an integral part of the proclamation. "Every disease and every sickness among the people" relates to the description of suffering Israel in Isa 53:3-4. Jesus brings healing and restoration to suffering Israel so that they can carry out their God-given purpose (Matt 8:17). There is no real distinction between spiritual and physical healing. The "great crowds" (v. 25) come from different places and these are now about to hear the good news of the kingdom.

III. The Proclamation of the Good News in Word: 5:1–7:29

Introduction (5:1-2)

The Sermon on the Mount begins with the statement that Jesus "went up the mountain" (cf. 14:23; 15:29), often said of Moses when he received the covenant on Mount Sinai. When Second Isaiah heard the cry: "Get you up to a high mountain, O Zion, herald of good tidings," and was told to announce to the people, "Your God reigns!" (Isa 40:9; 52:7) it was a call for renewal of that covenant relationship. The proclamation Jesus is about to make is the fulfillment of these words. Jesus "sat down" as a sign that he was ready to teach, since teaching was normally done in a sitting position (cf. Matt 13:12; 15:29; 24:3; 26:55).

> The beatitudes have received unusual attention in the history of exegesis and, in spite of increasingly minimalist interpretations in the last two hundred years, are still widely regarded in catechesis and liturgy as a "summary" of what it means to be a true disciple of Christ. From as early as Clement of Alexandria and his disciple Origen they were read sequentially as the outline of a spiritual ascent. Major exegetes who expanded and transmitted this tradition until the end of the Middle Ages were Gregory of Nyssa, Augustine, Popes Leo the Great and Gregory the Great; medieval monastic thought on "conversion" popularized this tradition, elaborating on it with a great deal of psychological insight. From the eighth century until our own day the gospel passage for the feast of All Saints (November 1) has been taken from this particular passage, so that in a way the ideal of Christian perfection became "canonized" in terms of the beatitudes. With the monastic framework left aside, exegetes and pastors of the modern age have considered these teachings a call to perfection, while historians and critics have tried to regard them as a manifesto for a program by which Jesus obtained his initial success by gathering around himself the poor, the hungry, the meek, the oppressed, and the persecuted. —*Ed.*

The Beatitudes: Covenant Blessings (5:3-12)

The question has often been raised whether these blessings are law or gospel, ethical requirements or eschatological blessings. Much of the argument has focused on whether the word "blessed" is the translation of the Hebrew *'ashrē* or *bāruk*. The former is found predominantly in Wisdom literature; the latter comes out of a covenantal context. *Bāruk* sayings relate strongly to covenantal promises, and that is what we have in the beatitudes. The basic intent of the *bāruk* saying is the invocation of the covenant promises on the recipient (cf. Abraham, Gen 12:2, 3; 22:17, 18). In relation to the Sinai covenant, God's covenant faithfulness was seen as a blessing on the people (e.g., Deut 7:12-13; Isa 61:9). Thus the beatitudes become the proclamation of the fulfillment of all these promises, the blessings of the everlasting covenant pronounced on the faithful who keep the covenant.

"The poor in spirit" (v. 3) is a Semitic phrase (*'anawē ruaḥ*, also found in 1QH 14:3 and 1QM 14:7) and refers here to the good news announced to the afflicted (*'anāwīm*) in Isa 61:1. The "afflicted" are those who have been wrongfully treated and often reduced to wretchedness, powerlessness, and even poverty. So the "afflicted" cry out to YHWH, who upholds the cause of the righteous (cf. Amos 2:6-7; Isa 3:14-15; 10:1-2). During the exile the whole people of Israel had become the afflicted and oppressed (Isa 49:13; 41:17), stricken, smitten of God and afflicted (Isa 53:4, 7), but later the term came to be used only of the faithful (Isa 61:1). The phrase "poor in spirit" is synonymous with "brokenhearted" (Isa 61:1), "smitten" or "crushed in spirit" (Isa 66:2; 57:15), phrases that relate closely to Israel as the Suffering Servant (Isa 53:4, 5, 19). All express the dependent relationship of the faithful on God as they await God's deliverance (Isa 40:9). This is the proclamation of the good news: the reign of God has come and it is theirs! The blessing given is that the reign of God's love and justice has begun for them!

Jeremiah had spoken of the exile causing mourning (e.g., 14:2-4) that God would eventually turn to joy (31:13). Second Isaiah picked up that motif near the end of the exile and announced that God would now comfort the people (Isa 40:1-2; 52:9) by reestablishing God's reign in Zion (52:7). The faithful were assured of this restoration after the return from exile (Isa 61:1-2). The concept of the kingdom would be brought to its fullness and then those who mourn over Jerusalem would be comforted (66:7-11, 13). The second beatitude (v. 4) is saying that this time has come. The faithful who mourn over affliction and oppression will be comforted because the kingdom has come and it is theirs.

The third beatitude (v. 5) is a quotation from Ps 37:11; in its Hebrew text we find *ʿanāwīm* (afflicted) while the LXX [36:11] refers to the "meek" *(praeis).* This passage connects with Ps 37:22 where the psalm says "those blessed by the LORD shall inherit the land." The meaning of "meek" therefore is essentially the same as "poor in spirit." Possession of the land became a real concern for the returning exiles who hoped that they would be able to reclaim their ancestral home, but for many this remained only a pious hope (Isa 57:13; 60:21) of which Psalm 37 became the concise expression. The concept of inheriting the land in Jesus' teaching functions as a figure for experiencing God's just rule through inheriting the kingdom.

The fourth beatitude (v. 6) also parallels expressions of hope for the restoration of God's rule found in Isaiah, especially 49:10; cf. 41:17-20. In Isa 55:1-2 the celebration of the restoration of the reign of God is put in terms of an invitation to those who hunger and thirst to come to the celebration banquet at which time the "everlasting covenant" made with David is transferred to the people (Isa 55:3-5). Those "hungering and thirsting for righteousness" are those waiting for God's righteousness, the fulfillment of God's promises to restore the people to freedom and prosperity (Isa 45:13; 42:6, 21). Those who seek the Lord's righteousness (51:1) are assured that it is coming speedily (51:5), and God's faithful will be vindicated (59:16; 63:1). They will be satisfied.

These first four blessings all express the same dependence of the faithful on God's grace. The proclamation in each is the same: for those who have been looking for God's covenant righteousness, it is here: God reigns! The next four touch on aspects of human righteousness as response to God's. For this reason both sets end with the same word: righteousness.

The Hebrew word *ḥesed,* meaning "steadfast love" is the focal point of the fifth blessing. It was God's saving, redeeming steadfast love that was the basis of the hope for deliverance in Isaiah (55:3, 7; 54:7-10; 63:7). This love was to be reflected in God's people (cf. Hos 6:6; 10:12; Mic 6:8). The faithful who seek God's steadfast love in the kingdom are those who practice it (cf. Ps 37:28; Isa 57:1), and they will obtain it. The emphasis is on the proclamation.

The sixth beatitude (v. 8) draws on Ps 24:4-5: "Those who have clean hands and pure hearts . . . will receive blessing from the LORD." This summarizes references to the faithful in Isa 51:7; 57:15; 61:1; and 65:14. They are blessed because they shall "see the glory of YHWH" (Isa 35:2). The good news is announced to them, "Behold, your God! (40:9; 52:7, 8; cf. 66:14, 18). When Israel broke the covenant relationship it was commonly said that God's face was "hidden" from them (Isa 59:2), but with the relationship restored they would now "see" God. A pure heart is one that identifies with and follows "every word that comes from the mouth of God" (cf. Deut 8:3 quoted in Matt 4:4). Once again this passage summarizes the promises to those who are waiting for the kingdom: it is theirs.

The seventh beatitude (v. 9) draws on another aspect of the promise to live peaceably in the covenant relationship without conflict, oppression, or injustice. God bestows that peace but its continuance is dependent on people living together in covenant faithfulness as peacemakers (Isa 60:17; 54:10; 52:7). In light of the sense of *shālōm* as a comprehensive concept in the OT the peace spoken of in this verse is no mere ending of hostilities or reconciliation between enemies, but a promotion of God's rule on earth in a total sense. Promoting the rule of God, these peacemakers qualify as "children" of God. To be called children of God is to be acknowledged as members of the true Israel (Deut 14:1; Hos 1:10; 11:1), as faithful members of God's family (cf. Isa 63:16; 43:6; 49:1, 14-15; 64:8). Thus they will be "like angels" (Matt 22:30) who (often called "sons/children of God" in the OT) "continually see the face of my Father" (Matt 18:10). Being the "children of God" must therefore be considered parallel to the expression "see God" in the previous verse. Both express the same gift of the eschatological kingdom: belonging to God's house and family. All of this comes to fruition in God's reign that has now come.

Those who are persecuted for the sake of righteousness (v. 10) are those faithful to the covenant but taken advantage of by the wicked. The "persecuted" are the same as the "afflicted in spirit" of the first beatitude, and both receive the same pronouncement: "theirs is the kingdom of heaven." This *inclusio* brings all the blessings together as one. The only difference is that the last four beatitudes illustrate more the active stance of the faithful, while the first four show their dependent relationship on God. In each case, however, the emphasis is on the pronouncement because that is the good news. Because this beatitude is the one that will most immediately affect those who follow his teaching, Jesus addresses it to his audience (vv. 11-12) and thus reinforces that this proclamation is for them: "Blessed are you . . ." combining words from Isa 51:7 and 66:5. Just as those who first received the promises experienced slander and persecution from their own people after the return from exile, particularly from the priesthood (Isa 66:1-6), so the followers of Jesus should expect the same (cf. Matt 10:39; 16:25; 19:29).

"Rejoice and be glad" (v. 12) is a constant refrain found throughout Isaiah expressing the "joy and gladness" of living in covenant relationship under God's rule (e.g., 35:10; 51:3, 11). The word "reward," found often in Matthew, picks up the theme of "reward and recompense" in Isaiah that came to mean the largesse graciously measured out by the suzerain to servants. In Isaiah this largesse is salvation, redemption, the establishing of an everlasting covenant (61:8; 40:10; 49:4). It is part of the proclamation of the restoration, the culmination of the blessings of the kingdom announced in the beatitudes, the rule of God breaking into their lives here and now. "For in the same way they persecuted the prophets who were before you" indicates an emphasis on the prophetic heritage. The number of times (thirty-seven) prophets are mentioned in this gospel, the constant citations and allusions to their writings, references to their persecution (5:12; 13:57; 23:30-31, 37; 26:68) all indicate that Matthew's gospel comes out of the prophetic tradition.

Belonging to the Kingdom (5:13-16)

Jesus continues to address the audience as those to whom the kingdom belongs. In Isa 42:6; 49:1-8 the real purpose of Servant Israel was to be "a people-covenant, a light to the nations." With the restoration of the kingdom that purpose is to be brought to fruition. As "people who have [YHWH's] teaching in [their] hearts" (Isa 51:7) they are called to be a living covenant, a people who through demonstration of their covenant faithfulness will draw all peoples and nations into a bonded relationship with their only God and Father (Isa 45:20-22). After the exile it became a Temple ordinance that offerings presented to God were always to be sprinkled with salt (Ezek 43:24; Lev 2:13) to emphasize that the covenant they had with God was an "everlasting covenant" (cf. 2 Chr 13:5). Pure salt by its very nature does not lose its taste, but salt that is impure can lose its saltiness and consequently have no value whatever. So when disciples are told "you are the salt of the earth" (v. 13), they are to be that permanent living people-covenant that would draw others together into a living relationship with God.

"You are the light of the world" (v. 14) fulfills the other purpose stated in Isa 42:6; 49:6, to be "a light to the nations." The theme of bringing light to people who dwell in darkness recalls Isa 9:1-2; 42:6-7, 16; 49:6; 51:4; 48:8, 10; 59:9. All these sayings come to a climax in Isa 60:1-3 with its reassurance of the return to the people of God's brilliant presence that will be reflected in them (cf. 60:19-20; 62:2). "A city built on a hill cannot be hid." In Isaiah "Jerusalem" was often used figuratively for faithful Israel (40:2, 9; 51:17). The people of the kingdom will by their very nature reflect God's light to all as a corporate witness. Verse 15 emphasizes the individual's responsibility as a lamp that "gives light to all in the house." The interplay of the corporate and individual nature of the witness has always been important in the understanding of the covenant relationship. The purpose of the people's witness is to give glory to the heavenly Father (v. 16). Restored Israel was called to be the witness before the nations of God's power and glory (Isa 43:10, 12, and elsewhere). It is the Lord's brilliant presence that they are to reflect to the nations (Isa 60:1-3), to the far ends of the earth (Isa 66:18-22). So those belonging to the kingdom participate in the ongoing restoration by being a people-covenant, a light to the nations that God may be glorified through their faithfulness. "Your Father in heaven" is the title Jesus prefers for God (cf. Isa 63:16; 64:8).

Fulfilling the Law and the Prophets (5:17-48)

This section on the Law must be seen in the context of the proclamation of the restoration of the kingdom and Israel's ultimate purpose. From the outset the passage takes a polemical, even defensive tone: it defends the message of Jesus against the accusation that he came to abrogate "the law and the prophets," a phrase referring to the totality of God's word. The issue raised here is introductory to the casuistics of the rest of the sermon: the "righteousness" of the disciples must exceed the "righteousness" of the Pharisees. The statement appears radical, even exaggerated, since the Pharisees' observance of the Law was well known to be thorough and aimed at including the smallest of the commandments.

"Do not think that I have come" (v. 17) is a defensive statement. After Jesus has just announced to the people that the kingdom is theirs, those who had been taught by the scribes and Pharisees would have been wondering: What about all those 613 commandments and the acts of righteousness required for entry into the kingdom according to their scribes? "To abolish the law or the prophets": the same verb is used in the claim made against Jesus that he said he would destroy the Temple (24:2; 26:61; 27:40). Rejection of Temple and Torah was the accusation often made against Jesus and his followers. In speaking of the Torah Jesus was not using this term in the same way as the scribes and Pharisees to refer to the legal tradition, that is, the accumulation of case laws and priestly traditions. Jesus' proclamation was firmly based in the prophetic tradition that understood Torah as "teaching" rather than "law" in the forensic sense. Hence rather than "rabbi" Jesus was called "teacher" (5:2; 7:28-29). For the prophets Torah, as teaching from God, referred primarily to the relationship expressed in the basic stipulations of the Sinai covenant (cf. Hos 4:1-6). It was faithfulness to this covenant relationship—to God and one another—that was always the concern of the prophets. This was the real Torah, the teaching of God (Amos 2:4; Jer 16:11-12; 26:4-5; Isa 30:9). Because that teaching had been made into a lie by "the false pen of the scribes" (Jer 8:8), Jeremiah promised that God would make a new covenant in which God would write this teaching *(tōrāh)* on the hearts of the people (31:31-34; cf. Isa 51:7). It is this Torah that Servant Israel is to proclaim to the nations (Isa 42:6; 50:4). Consequently Jesus has not come to abolish or destroy, but to fulfill it. The verb used here almost always has the meaning in Matthew of fulfilling prophecy, and so is appropriate here.

In this light v. 18 becomes comprehensible. It is really a summary of the message in Isaiah 51 where God gives assurance to the "people who have my teaching in your hearts" (v. 7) that even though the heavens "vanish like smoke" and the earth "wears out like a garment," yet God's salvation, God's righteousness would never end (v. 6). That Torah that will go forth from YHWH as a light to the peoples (51:4) is the whole message of the true covenant relationship with God that will accomplish God's purposes (Isa 55:11). So, as Jesus puts it, not a *yōd* or a *wāw,* two insignificant Hebrew letters that are sometimes omitted from words, will be dropped from this teaching until all is accomplished. Thus it is not the legal codes that are the focus but the whole teaching of God in regard to covenant, kingdom, and God's purpose for Israel and the nations (cf. 28:18-20). Verse 20 brings to a climax what Jesus has been saying about the Law and the prophets and acts as a transition to vv. 21-48 in which Jesus shows how one should understand the covenant law over against the popular teaching of the scribes and Pharisees. Jesus is not calling for a stricter and more meticulous observance of the Law, but a different attitude. Righteousness is a relational term and in this context means loving faithfulness to God and neighbor in accordance with God's covenant teaching. It is on this basis, not by some legalistic approach, that one understands the law of God. Examples of this are now given:

On Murder, 5:21-26

One breaks the covenant law, "you shall not murder" (Exod 20:13; Deut 5:17) not only with the actual deed but also in thought and word. The commandment is broken whenever one does harm to another, whether it be physical, mental, or spiritual. "You have heard" (v. 21) preceding "that it was said" implies that an interpretation has been put on what God had said. "To those of ancient times" refers to the ancients who received the covenant law. "Shall be liable to judgment": the judgment was death as this commandment was interpreted in Lev 24:17;

Exod 21:12-14. "But *I* say to you" (v. 22) is in contrast to what people have been taught that God has said. "If you are angry with a brother or sister" recalls Lev 19:17-18 and Gen 4:3-8. "You will be liable to judgment" repeats the phrase of the previous sentence in order to emphasize that evil thoughts or attitudes are just as bad as evil deeds (cf. 15:19). To call someone *Raka* (an Aramaic term) was to say "empty-head," "worthless fellow" (cf. Judg 9:4; 11:3; 2 Sam 6:20; 2 Chr 13:7). "Council" here means the divine council (cf. 1 Kings 22:19-23; Zech 3:1-5). To say "you fool", another term of contempt, would be to call a person ungodly and evil (cf. Pss 14:1; 53:1; Isa 32:5-6; Matt 23:17), another expression of hating instead of loving. To be liable to "the Gehenna of fire" (a term derived from the "valley of the son of Hinnom" on the south side of Jerusalem, where that man was condemned because of idolatrous practices, later used for burning garbage [cf. Jer 7:31-32]) also means to be liable to ultimate judgment. Judgment, council, Gehenna of fire are just three different ways of describing the final divine judgment to which the one who breaks the covenant relationship in thought, word, or deed is liable.

The covenant involves an inseparable two-way relationship with God and neighbor, so offering a sin or guilt offering to God (vv. 23-24) is of no avail if one has not first sought reconciliation with the neighbor wronged. The prophets had long argued that sacrificial rituals were meaningless if the worshiper did not seek justice and righteousness and show steadfast love (e.g., Isa 1:10-17). The illustration used in vv. 25-26 is that of being taken to the debtor's court and being imprisoned until one has paid the last *quadrans,* the smallest Roman coin. The terms used here suggest court procedures. We have every reason, indeed, to consider these two verses as a condensed, even compressed, parable about two people in dispute on their way to court. The storyteller points out the advantage of settling out of court for the sake of avoiding a fine to be paid and being thrown into jail if one cannot come up with the money. The urgent message is: make amends now before one is overtaken by the final judgment (cf. Matt 18:23-35).

Adultery and Divorce, 5:27-32

Another basic commandment that defines human relationships is taken up. Once again it is not just the act of adultery that breaks the Law, but thoughts and desires that lead to it. The basic law on adultery is in Exod 20:14; Deut 5:18, but Jesus also incorporates Exod 20:17; Deut 5:21. Coveting a neighbor's wife is implicitly adultery and not just a desire to have someone's property. Except when both were caught in the act of adultery (Lev 20:10, but cf. Deut 22:22-27) there was a tendency in the legal traditions to relate the commandment regarding adultery particularly to women (e.g., Gen 38:12-26). In order to address that imbalance Jesus directs his statement particularly to men, referring to one opinion reflected in the rabbinic school of Hillel, later expressed by R. Akiba (*m. Giṭ* 9:10), that if a man saw another woman more beautiful than his wife that was reason enough to divorce her. Jesus uses hyperbole (5:29-30) to illustrate that just as physical amputation, particularly abhorrent to the priestly law (Lev 21:17-23), was a drastic measure to prevent the spread of disease to the whole body, so spiritual surgery is even more necessary to prevent the destruction of the whole person in the final judgment. "Causes you to sin" means to put a barrier or "stumbling block" in the way (Isa 8:14; Jer 6:21; Ezek 3:20; 44:12). The "eye" was seen as expressing the thoughts of the heart (cf. Deut 15:9; Prov 22:9; Sir 14:8-10; Matt 6:22-23) and the hand as carrying out the action. The right eye and hand are mentioned here to emphasize the severity of the surgery (cf. 1 Sam 11:2; Zech 11:17). The "whole body go[ing] into Gehenna" was the lot of one executed for a capital offense. That is where an attitude of self-gratification will ultimately lead.

The discussion about divorce is a sub-theme on adultery. The quotation here is from Deut 24:1, part of a casuistic law that dealt with remarriage after divorce. The appropriateness of this quotation following the saying about cutting off the hand is lost in translation, for in the Hebrew "certificate of divorce" meant literally "certificate of cutting off." Deuteronomy 24:1 states that if a man's wife "does not please him because he finds something objectionable about her" he may write her a bill of divorce. While the rabbinic school of Shammai argued that "something objectionable" meant divorce should be permitted only on the basis of marital unfaithfulness the more liberal school of Hillel argued that a man could divorce his wife for being "objectionable" in anything, even spoiling his dinner or appearing less comely in comparison to another woman (*m. Giṭ* 9:10). A woman, however, could not divorce her husband on any account, although in extreme circumstances she could ask the courts to compel her husband to divorce her (*m. Ketub.* 7:10). Jesus points out that these interpretations and this practice of divorce were really legalized adultery. The law on adultery was established to protect and uphold a faithful relationship between husband and wife, the basis of all family and community relationships (Gen 1:27; 2:24; cf. Mal 2:14-16; see also Matt 19:3). A divorced woman was under pressure to remarry in order to survive unless she was able to return to her father's house. That is why a man who divorces his wife "except on the ground of *porneia*" makes her to be adulterous, and the man who marries her becomes guilty of adultery too. Of course the man who divorced her and then remarries becomes guilty of adultery himself (19:9). What, however, is the meaning of *porneia?* A number of points must be considered: (1) The etymological root of *porneia* is "prostitution, harlotry" and the word itself is related to "harlot" (*pornē:* 21:31-32; Luke 15:30; 1 Cor 6:15-16; Heb 11:31; Jas 2:25) and "to act as a harlot" (*porneuō:* 1 Cor 6:18; 10:8). (2) The word is to be distinguished from "adultery" since both words are mentioned side by side in Matt 15:19. (3) It is used in the context of marital relationships. On the basis of this, *porneia* should be understood as "persistent unfaithfulness," such as prostitution, which breaks the covenant of the marriage bond irreparably. Jesus was not setting up new rules here but was explaining the essential meaning and purpose of the covenant stipulation over against what was allowed by some teachers of the Law.

On Oaths, 5:33-37

The quotation (v. 33) is a summary of a number of laws on oaths and vows, incorporating Lev 19:12; Num 30:2; Deut 23:21-23. The practice of making oaths or vows had become so commonplace by the time of Jesus that the rabbis spent much time discussing valid and invalid forms. Originally oaths were made before the altar in the presence of God when the truth of a matter could not be substantiated by witnesses or documents. Included in such an oath was the invoking of a curse if the oath was false (cf. Zech 5:1-4; Deut 29:19-21). Later, in order not to take the name of God in vain it became the practice to use circumlocutions for God's name, and even beyond that, in popular practice, to swear by anything of value. The rabbis discussed at great length which of these different types of oaths and vows were valid (cf. *m. Šeb.* 4:13; *m. Ned.* 1:3; *m. Sanh.* 3:2). Jesus points out that no matter how one words the oath, it is still an oath before God. Heaven is God's throne and the earth God's footstool (Isa 66:1), Jerusalem is the city of the great king (Ps 48:2), and the value of a person's head is the value God puts on it. Those who belong to the kingdom will speak in sincerity and faithfulness so their simple "yes" and "no" can be accepted as trustworthy before God and people (v. 37). While oathtaking today may be required by courts and other institutions the essential point here is speaking with utter honesty and sincerity. This passage was not forgotten in Christian teaching. James 5:12 may be the oldest quotation from our passage, while Justin's *First Apology* certainly quotes the gospel text and considers it a practical rule for Christian living.

On Retaliation, 5:38-42

These laws found in all three law codes (Exod 21:22-25; Lev 24:17-22; Deut 19:21) were regarded as putting a limit on revenge. Rabbis of Jesus' time allowed fines instead of acts of revenge in some cases among their own people, but this law was taken seriously. "Do not resist an evildoer" (v. 39) is not an invitation to commit suicide or let injustice go unchecked, but a call to counter evil with good, hatred with love, and so to transform human relationships. To strike someone on the right cheek was more insult than injury since it was done with the back of the hand (cf. *m. B. Kamma* 8:6). Turning the other cheek is hyperbolic to emphasize that reacting to evil with evil only begets more evil. Love, though vulnerable, is the only power that can overcome evil. To illustrate, Jesus uses a common picture of a poor day-laborer being dragged off to court by a creditor who would take his inner garment or tunic (v. 40). According to legal tradition (Exod 22:26-27) a creditor could not take a person's outer garment as pledge for more than a day in payment of a debt, so the way around that law was to demand the inner garment. Jesus advises: Let him have your outer garment as well to the shame of the creditor! The point is made: Return evil with good.

It must be made clear that this passage does not fully agree with what today is called a "nonviolence" stance, frequent in political movements. First, there is no political goal or ideology at stake; second, Jesus invites the individual to prefer the attacker's well-being to his or her own but does not abolish the obligation of defending others (especially the ones a person is responsible for) if they are violently attacked.

The background of v. 41 is the hated Roman practice of *angareia,* a rule by which Roman soldiers were permitted to press into service anyone passing by and make them carry their equipment for no more than one mile (for example, Simon of Cyrene in 27:32). Generally this practice only increased the mutual enmity, but to respond by volunteering to carry the load twice the distance would dissipate the hostility and allow friendship to develop. Lending to a person who may never be able to pay (v. 42) was already in the legal tradition (Exod 22:25; Lev 25:35-38). Jesus reaffirms this as an act of compassion to one who is in real need.

On Loving, 5:43-48

This section expresses what Jesus has been leading up to: reaching out to people in love and concern is the way of fulfilling the Law and the prophets (v. 17) and showing better righteousness (v. 20). Jesus' teaching was not entirely new, for passages like Lev 19:34 (cf. Exod 23:4, 5; Prov 25:21-22) taught consideration for foreigners. However, what was often popularly taught was to love one's own and hate those who are outsiders. In times of occupation one could find commands like Exod 34:12; Deut 7:2; 20:16; 23:3, 6 and psalms in the liturgy (e.g., Pss 137:7-9; 139:19-24) that seemed to teach "hate your enemy." Jesus' response, however, is: "love your enemies and pray for those who persecute you" (v. 44). There are no distinctions to be made between neighbors and enemies, for all are the recipients of God's love and consequently are to be recipients of one's own love. This love is always to be shown in an earnest desire for the good of the other and for their membership in the family of God. "So that you may be children of your Father in heaven" (v. 45) recalls v. 9: the peacemakers will be called "children of God."

Throughout this Sermon Jesus has been directing his hearers to the ideal of the kingdom: that all peoples and nations will eventually be part of God's universal family acknowledging God as Father. Just as God cares for the evil as well as the good, the unrighteous as well as the righteous, so God's children acting as Servant seek to make many righteous (Isa 53:11) through reflecting their Father's glory (Matt 5:16), even when there seems to be no response. Love restricted to friends is hardly more than a counterpart of what the law of retaliation entails, for "an eye for an eye" means "tit for tat" and thus "a good deed for a good deed." To illustrate that loving one's neighbor as oneself means going beyond simply loving or greeting one's own Jesus points to two groups generally despised, toll-collectors and Gentiles. Jews who purchased the toll-collecting concessions from the Romans were usually put in the same category as murderers and robbers by the rabbis (*m. Ned.* 3:4; *m. B. Kamma* 10:1, 2; *m. Ṭohar.* 7:6) and were often denied Jewish civil rights (*m. Sanh.* 3:3; *b. B. Kamma* 94b). Jesus set the example in extending fellowship to them (9:10-11). For "reward," see above at 5:12.

"Be perfect, therefore, as your heavenly Father is perfect" (v. 48) means seeking to live in God's image and likeness once again (Gen 1:27), reflecting God's nondiscriminating love. The word "perfect" often means "blameless," a synonym for "righteous" (Ps 18:21-30), but in this context God's love is perfect in the sense that it is complete, that is, it includes not only those who love God, but God's enemies as well.

Doing the Acts of Righteousness (6:1-21)

Jesus now turns to the traditional acts of righteousness: almsgiving, prayer, and fasting (cf. Tob 12:8-9; *m. ʾAbot* 1:2). It was taught that the keeping of the 613 commandments plus these three deeds together constituted total "righteousness." So Jesus warns: "Beware of practicing your piety before others to be seen by them." This continues the discussion of the Law and righteousness begun in 5:17-20. Nowhere in 6:1-18 does the word "Pharisee" occur, and therefore one would be wrong in interpreting this section as an attack against a specific group as opposed to an attitude that may be found in any person. Specifically, however, it is directed against those who are wrongly motivated in their strict compliance with the Law, and in this regard it is correct to say that it is directed against some of the religious leadership of the Jews in Jesus' time. Just as Jesus had done with the Law, so here he puts these acts of piety into the proper perspective: they are meaningless unless they are motivated by a sincere and faithful relationship with God and one's fellow human beings.

Almsgiving was enjoined in the Law (Deut 15:7-11) and recognized as a means of sharing the gifts of God with one another in covenant relationship (Isa 58:7; Ps 112:9; Tob 1:16-17). "Hypocrite" is a Greek word that originally meant "actor," "performer." The persons here criticized are performing to an audience in making a show of their almsgiving in the synagogues and in the streets. They do it that they may be glorified by the people and thus seek the glory that should be given to God (5:16; 9:8; 15:31). With the applause given these actors their reward is paid in full, but there is no reward from God. The child of God gives alms without fanfare, so spontaneously and unassumingly that even one's left hand does not know what the right hand is doing, but God knows and blesses.

Prayer (v. 5) also can become a performance instead of personal communion with God. Those hoping to be seen by the greatest number of people have their reward in full: they are seen by people. The child of God, however, enters into a quiet place in order to converse with the heavenly Father without disturbance or distraction. The "room" is actually an inner storeroom, a secret place (cf. Isa 26:20). When God's children turn to God in sincerity and purity of heart, they are always heard.

The importance of prayer calls for further comment. The kind of ritual prayers used by the Romans that had to be said in the right formula in order to be valid and to gain the material blessings sought is probably what is being referred to here (cf. also Isa 8:19). They also prayed much and at great length. From this one logically deduces that brevity would be a main feature of the type of prayer that Jesus teaches. "Your Father knows what you need before you ask him" recalls part of the divine response to the faithful in Isa 65:24. In fact the prayer of the faithful in that context, which extends from Isa 63:7 to 64:12, and God's response in Isa 65:1-25 form much of the background to the prayer now presented as a model.

The Lord's Prayer (vv. 9-13) is an example of how to pray and the kind of petitions a child of God will share with the heavenly Father. Following the preceding commentary, the Lord's Prayer excels in its brief and pregnant formulas. "Our Father in heaven" expresses the intimate relationship between the faithful and their God (Isa 63:16; 64:8). "Hallowed be your name": God's name is to be sanctified before the nations by the faithful witness of God's people (Isa 29:22-23; 49:3). As they witness to their God through their covenant faithfulness God's name will be glorified (5:16), God's name made holy. There is also a deeper meaning of what is happening when believers sanctify the Name: they form here on earth a community of worship that joins the heavenly court in crying out "holy, holy, holy" in unceasing liturgical worship (cf. Isa 6:2). This petition, therefore, implores that the people of God may be gathered from all over the earth into the unity of the heavenly liturgy.

"Your kingdom come": Jesus had already proclaimed that the kingdom has come and that it belongs to the faithful (5:3-12), but this petition requests that the reign of God will continue to come with its consequent blessings to all those who seek it. The kingdom belongs to the poor in spirit (5:3) and thus their crying out for its coming is not an invocation frustrated by its repeatedly extended delay. The praying person focuses on an actual participation in this kingdom while enkindling the desire for its full arrival. The reference to heaven and earth is not to be understood as temporal parallelism. "Heaven" means the realm in which God's will reigns, while the earth refers to this realm in which sin and Satan still abide.

"Your will be done" really repeats the sentiment of the previous petition but focuses on the fact that God has a purpose for God's people to fulfill: to gather all God's people together, to be a witness, a light to the nations (Isa 42:1-4). Second Isaiah had constantly reminded the exiles that the God who has planned all this is the one who created the heavens and the earth (40:21-22; 42:5). While the heavens and their host respond to God's call (48:13; 40:26), the earthly creation seems to question the divine purpose. So this petition calls for God's earthly creation to respond to God's purpose also.

"Give us this day our daily bread": The word that has been the focus of much discussion is an original Greek word, *epiousion,* here translated as "daily." In the inaugural celebration of the kingdom in Isa 55:1-2 the bread refers to the spiritual blessings of being in God's kingdom. The restoration had been spoken of in terms of satisfying hunger and thirst (Isa 49:9-10), and in God's response to the prayer of the faithful they are assured that they will eat and drink and rejoice (Isa 65:13-14). So this petition can be seen as a request for the spiritual food of the kingdom, experiencing God's blessings now.

Church Fathers who faced the problem of explaining and translating the word *epiousion* (such as Origen in the East and Jerome in the West) remain in basic agreement with the liturgical tradition by translating it as "bread of sustenance." This does not prevent them and the whole patristic and medieval tradition from seeing here, on another level of spiritual sustenance, that is, the eucharistic bread. This latter interpretation reveals, however, the influence of the eucharistic discourse in John 6 as well as the liturgical custom of praying the Lord's Prayer before communion, attested already in the *Didache* (late first or early second century). *—Ed.*

"Forgive us our debts" is the request to be released from the indebtedness of past failures in order to live in full and open relationship in the kingdom. The restoration of the kingdom was often described as pardon from sin, sweeping away transgression, God's remembering Israel's sin no more (Isa 40:2; 43:25; 65:16-19). Jesus is emphasizing that forgiveness is an essential part of living in the kingdom, but he adds "as we also have forgiven our debtors" as a constant reminder that a faithful and true relationship with God is always inextricably bound up with a faithful relationship with one's neighbor (cf. 22:34-40). The priority of our forgiving makes reference to something already achieved, an idea in agreement with Matt 5:24 that says: "first be reconciled to your brother or sister," for only afterward can one approach God. Verses 14-15 further explain the significance of this petition and emphasize the interrelational nature of the family of God in the kingdom.

Temptation, as in 4:1-11, means being put to the test as Israel was in the wilderness (Exod 16:4; Deut 8:2). Persecution and oppression were seen as being tested in the "furnace of affliction" to refine them like silver (Isa 48:10; Mal 3:3). The expression "do not bring us to" does not assume that God positively causes temptation (God does not tempt us) but that God allows temptations to take place and might lead our destiny in such a way that trials (which include temptations) might take place. The godly life is always being put to the test for the purpose of being refined, but what is being asked for here is the strength to resist evil. God's response to the faithful seeking deliverance from evil is always the assurance that God will care for them and that the forces of evil will not prevail.

Quite early, as we see in the *Didache,* a doxology was attached to the prayer: "For yours is the power and glory forevermore." Although this addition compromises the brevity of the prayer, its return to the "you" of the first lines after the "us" of the last lines provides a means of inclusion, a sense of completeness that a text used in isolation must possess.

Fasting was a common practice in Jewish life, particularly on the Day of Atonement and as a sign of mourning (e.g., Ps 35:13; cf. Zech 7:1-14; 8:18-19). Stricter Pharisees fasted at least twice a week to commemorate Moses' ascent and descent on receiving the Law on Sinai. In warning the people not to be like the hypocrites who make their faces unrecognizable (v. 16), an allusion to the practice of covering one's head and smearing ashes on one's face, Jesus shows the irony of their action: they make their faces unrecognizable so that their fasting may be recognized by people. Their reward is that they are recognized for what they are. Anointing one's head with oil as on festive occasions and washing one's face would allow one's fasting to be a sincere sharing of one's sorrow with the heavenly Father. According to Isa 58:1-11, to put on sackcloth and ashes and to mortify oneself by fasting was meaningless unless one sought to satisfy the needs of the afflicted, to relieve the anguish of the hungry and the homeless.

"Treasures on earth" (vv. 19-21) are these so-called acts of righteousness, often referred to as treasures (Tob 4:9; 12:8; Sir 29:11-12). When people put their trust in the praise and recognition of others rather than in God they have put their trust in earthly treasures that soon disintegrate. The phrase "where moth and rust consume" is borrowed from Isa 50:9; 51:7-8. In contrast, "treasures in heaven" are the blessings of a sincere relationship with God and humankind, which come to those in whose heart is

God's teaching (Isa 51:7). "For where your treasure is, there your heart will be also." In Hebrew thought the "heart" is the organ of thinking.

Evidence like this suggests that close reading, reflection upon, and inward digesting of the books of the prophets, especially Isaiah, were especially important in Jesus' spiritual formation. On the other hand, biblical phraseology may have laced the speech of Joseph and Mary so that, even before he could read, the influence of Isaiah was already at work on Jesus in his home. After all, Jesus' family memories would have reached back to the time of the exile, and the text of Isaiah could have been a life-giving book among his relatives from that time forward. *—Ed.*

Jesus concludes (vv. 22-23) this discussion on Law and the acts of righteousness by focusing on the need for a true perspective. In the ancient world the eye was seen as expressing a person's attitude (e.g., Deut 15:9; Ps 18:27; Prov 22:9). Thus to say that "the eye is the lamp of the body" is to say that one's attitude controls what one does or says. "Body" in this case refers to the whole person, the self. When the psalmist prays: "It is you who light my lamp; the LORD, my God, lights up my darkness" (Ps 18:28) he expresses that God's word defines all his attitudes and actions for good (cf. Ps 119:105). So if the eye is healthy, that is, if one's attitude is sincere and open to God's guidance, then one's life will have meaning, understanding, and fulfillment. But if the eye is evil, blind to God's will, then one's life becomes meaningless and destructive; one is "grop[ing] like the blind along a wall" (cf. Isa 59:9-10). The mission of Jesus is for "the people who sat in darkness" to see "a great light" (Matt 4:16; Isa 9:2) and that the eyes of the blind might see (Isa 29:18; 35:5).

About Earthly Concerns (6:24-34)

Verse 24 forms a transition to speaking about attitudes toward material needs and possessions in vv. 25-34. One cannot put God first and at the same time have material needs as one's prime concern. "Hate" and "love" are not always seen as strict opposites in Hebrew thinking but often in a comparative sense (e.g., Gen 29:30, 33; Mal 1:2-3), the way they should be understood here. "Mammon" is a late Semitic term meaning "property, money, possessions" (cf. *m. ʾAbot* 2:12; 1QS 6:2; CD 14:20). To serve wealth (mammon) as well as God is to break the first commandment. Life in Galilee at the time of Jesus with tolls and taxes, tribute and tithes would have been much concerned with security and survival. It is in this situation that the question "Which master are you going to serve, God or mammon?" is very real. Jesus' advice is really a commentary on a number of scriptural passages, particularly Psalms 103:15-17; 104; 147:7-11 and Isa 40:6-8. These texts not only see God as the supplier of the physical needs of all creation, but also contrast the impermanent nature of these things with the permanence of God's steadfast love (Ps 103:17) and God's word that stands forever (Isa 40:8). Jesus is not saying that one need not work, but that one need not worry (v. 26). If God supplies the necessities of life for the birds of the air, surely they will not be lacking for God's children. Worry does not help to prolong life, but shortens it (v. 27). Only God can prolong the life of the faithful (1 Kings 3:14). God provides for the beautiful flowers in spite of their short life (v. 28; cf. Ps 103:15; Isa 40:6) yet no adornment is as beautiful in color, design, and variety as are the wild flowers that appear without cultivation or fertilization. Surely God will take care of God's own people! "You of little faith" (v. 30) is always addressed to disciples (8:26; 14:31; 16:8) and Jesus is calling them to put trust in God first in their lives (v. 33). Seeking God's kingdom is seeking God's reign now and forever in one's heart (Isa 51:7; 52:7). God's righteousness is the fulfillment of all the covenant promises. Putting God first means that the necessities of a person's life will all fall into place in a proper balance. Anxiety is always a matter of focusing on the negative (v. 34). The point is that seeking God's kingdom and righteousness in hope and trust is focusing on the positive and gives one the opportunity to see in the light (v. 22) and to have a vision for the future. This section fights both the mentality of the Gentiles (v. 32) and of those who lack confidence in divine providence (v. 30). It may well be that both verses target the same pagan idea that depicts the deity as both distant from and indifferent to human needs. The God of Jesus Christ is a Father with a parental attitude that also includes the wayward children.

On Passing Judgment (7:1-6)

To those who would pass judgment on others and deny them entry to the kingdom Jesus responds that the basis on which they want to judge others is the basis by which they also will be judged (cf. Ezek 7:27). If they use false measures, they themselves will be measured by those same scales (cf. Lev 19:35-36). Participants in the kingdom are to leave the judgment to the final judge. Like their master, they are to be involved in healing and restoration. The mutuality seen above in the Lord's Prayer is represented here again, as we are to be judged on the basis of our own attitudes. The outlook of the sermon is such that it cautions rather than prescribes.

The point is further illustrated with a carpenter's hyperbole (vv. 3-5): the picture of a person with a rafter-beam in the eye trying to remove a speck of saw-dust from the eye of a neighbor! The eye, as in 6:22-23, represents one's attitude and understanding. The saying illustrates the hypocritical failure of a judgmental attitude, a failure to see one's own faults. Fraternal correction of a wrong is not being condemned here, but rather the spirit in which the correction is being done (cf. 18:15-35). The motivation is always loving one's neighbor as oneself.

When a disciple is confronted by such a person who rejects the good news and seeks only to pass judgment Jesus now advises: do not get into a dispute with them, for they lack understanding and will only use what you say to attack you. Jesus takes the adversarial language of those passing judgment and turns it back on them. "The holy thing" ("what is holy") was that portion of a consecrated offering that was given to the priests and their families. No stranger or outsider was to eat of this because it was a holy thing (Exod 29:33; 22:10-16). Dogs were regarded as unclean because they ate the flesh of animals whether clean or unclean (Exod 22:31) and of human corpses (e.g., 1 Kings 14:11). Hence "dogs" was often a term used in Israel for Gentiles, enemies, fools, and male prostitutes (Pss 22:16-20; Prov 26:11; Deut 23:18). Swine were unclean according to Jewish law (Lev 11:7; cf. *m. B. Kamma* 7:7); the term was also used derogatorily. Jesus turns the saying around to say that the kingdom and its way of life are holy, the pearl of great price (13:45-46), and they cannot be forced on anyone who resists them because they come by grace (cf. 10:11-14; 12:14-16).

The Kingdom is for the Asking (7:7-12)

These verses are about receiving the kingdom of God and God's righteousness (6:33). Over against the entrance requirements established by the Pharisees, Jesus is saying the kingdom is everyone's for the asking. The invitation has been there: "Seek the Lord while he may be found, call upon him while he is near" (Isa 55:6). The indictment on those rejected by God is that they did not ask, did not seek God even though God was saying all the time: "Here I am" (Isa 65:1; cf. Jer 29:10-14). If earthly parents can respond to the requests of their children, how much more so can the heavenly Father (vv. 9-10). The requests for "bread" or "fish" are for the basic food items. The references to the "stone" and the "serpent" may have been chosen because they are similar in form: a round stone like a round loaf, and a serpent similar to an eel-like fish; or they may be based on similarities in sound of the Aramaic words for bread/stone and fish/serpent. The point is that even if the human parents do not see or hear well, they still give what they know is good for their child. Being "evil" (v. 11) should be understood in the sense of "one who has human failings," in contrast to God, the only "one who is good" (19:17). The heavenly Father is always ready to give the blessings of the kingdom to those who simply seek God. Verse 12 acts then as a summary of what Jesus has been saying about living in relationship with one another as God's people. "In everything do to others as you would have them do to you": similar sayings have been found in negative form in Tob 4:15 and uttered by Hillel the Elder. By putting it into the positive Jesus has transformed a wisdom saying into an action of love instead of self-protection. In this context it becomes the equivalent of the love commandment on which depend "all the law and the prophets" (22:34-40). That is what the kingdom is all about (cf. Isa 58:6-11).

Final Warnings and Exhortations (7:13-27)

Just as the Sinai covenant concluded with warnings and exhortations, so Jesus finishes this Sermon with a series of antitheses. All of these describe approaches to the kingdom that, despite external similarities, have vastly different results: life or death. The section begins with this moral dualism: there are only two ways. The text does not recognize the possibility of being on a "neutral" or "undecided" course in life in which the issue of salvation would be dormant or suspended. In the text that follows the issue is not a statistics of salvation but the danger in which most people exist with regard to their eternal future. A consideration of the harshness of this view and its reappearance or modification in later chapters of the gospel are essential to the commentary as a whole.

Enter Through the Narrow Gate, 7:13-14

This is an exhortation to become part of the faithful and not simply to follow the crowd or give in to social pressure and thus become lost. Jesus is setting before his hearers the two ways expressed in the Sinai covenant and throughout the OT (Deut 30:15-20; Jer 21:8; Psalm 1). He gives essentially the same exhortation as Deut 30:19-20. The hard road (v. 14) is a way "full of affliction" and refers to the persecution that comes with going the way of the kingdom (5:10-12; 10:17-25; 13:21; 24:9-31). That is why there are few who find it in spite of the open invitation (7:7).

Beware of False Prophets, 7:15-20

Those who would lead people through the wide gate and on the spacious way to destruction are the false prophets. In the OT false prophets were those who said what people wanted to hear and were motivated by self-interest (cf. 1 Kings 22; Ezekiel 13). The term "false prophets" is used here to refer to any who falsely claim to be the spiritual leaders of the people, including even some of the most scrupulous of God's people. The metaphors of shepherd and sheep are common in the OT. God is the Shepherd of Israel (Pss 23; 78:52; 100:3; Ezekiel 34). The kings and leaders of Israel often took that representative title, but as the classical prophets pointed out, the ones the people trusted as shepherds often turned out to be rapacious wolves (Zeph 3:3-4; Ezek 22:27-28; Matt 10:16). For Jesus true prophets were to be identified not only by whether their prophecies came true (Deut 18:15-22) but also by how they lived, whether they bore good fruit (v. 16). Thorns and thistles were symbols of the fall into sin and the desolation it brings (Gen 3:18; Hos 10:8; Isa 7:23-25).

Beware of False Discipleship, 7:21-23

False leadership can emerge from within as well as without. There will be those claiming all kinds of powers in Jesus' name for their own aggrandizement. Since only those who do the will of the heavenly Father (cf. 6:10) will enter the kingdom their claims to do many mighty works in Jesus' name do not fit into that category and so are false. "On that day" refers to the final day of judgment, as elsewhere in Matthew (24:19, 22-29, 36, 38; 26:29). The picture is of Jesus as the Son of Man presiding as the judge on that day (16:28; 19:28; 24:30-31; 25:31). "Did we not prophesy in your name?" recalls Jer 14:14 and 27:15. Claims to cast out demons and do many mighty works would identify these people as false disciples since it was to his disciples that Jesus later gave authority to do these things (10:1, 8). "I will declare to them" is the language of the court making a solemn and binding declaration. "I never knew you" is the declaration affirming that the claimants were not part of Jesus' disciples. This standard formula of rejection appears especially harsh if we realize that the sermon immediately follows the passages about the calling of the disciples, setting up a relationship of close intimacy between Jesus and them. "Go away from me, you evildoers" is a quotation from Ps 6:8, the cry of the righteous sufferer whom God vindicates before enemies.

The True Foundation, 7:24-27

Just as the deuteronomic sermon on the covenant finished with a warning of the two ways ("life and prosperity, death and adversity," Deut 30:15-18), so Jesus' sermon does the same. The phrase "everyone . . . who hears these words of mine and acts on them" is similar to the frequent exhortations to hear the words of the covenant and do them found in Deuteronomy (e.g., 5:1; 6:3). The sermon is thus identified as the new covenant, one that renews the original intent of the covenant at Sinai but is to be written in the hearts of people (Jer 31:31-34; Isa 51:7). To build one's house on a rock would have readily been understood by the audience to mean "to build one's life on God," since God was often referred to as "the Rock" (Deut 32:4-31; Ps 62:6; Isa 26:4). A life built on this covenant relationship with God cannot fall, no matter how strong the forces against it. The images of the false and firm foundations recall Isa 28:14-18 and Ezek 13:10-16. The danger of false leadership is very much in mind in this final exhortation to faithfulness.

Concluding Comments (7:28-29)

"Now when Jesus had finished saying these things" is repeated in almost the same words at the end of all the major discourses in Matthew (11:1; 13:53; 19:1; 26:1) as a formula for ending the teaching and beginning a new section. The "crowds were astounded" at both his teaching and his manner of teaching. His teaching of the kingdom was radically and refreshingly different, not hedged around by regulations and requirements as interpreted by the scribes and Pharisees. Instead of being a quasi-political institution the kingdom was described as the gift of a loving, gracious heavenly Father. This kingdom brings about a covenant relationship with God and with one another—something that reached beyond the boundaries of gender, status, or nation. Second, whereas the scribal method was to quote various authorities before giving their synthetic interpretation Jesus went straight to the heart of the matter with "but I say to you." His authoritative statements demonstrated a command of Scripture that no scribe could match and an authority that came from his unique relationship with the heavenly Father.

IV. The Proclamation of the Good News in Deed: 8:1–9:34

Between the two long discourses, the one on the mountain and the one beginning in 9:35, Matthew presents the healing ministry of Jesus in a sequence of miracles. Events of similar content are lined up between two blocks of teaching. This section of the gospel functions as a compositional unit. Nevertheless, the narrative flow is still assured not so much by a chronological framework but by indicators of the geographic setting and Jesus' movement within this setting that allow the reader to visualize the sequence of events. The evangelist then makes the events point to theological themes and conclusions that they cumulatively support: primarily that of 9:9-17 where the power of Jesus to perform miracles is shown to be a sign of his power and his mission to forgive sins. Quite appropriately, the mingling of Jesus with sinners is placed here and is followed by a controversy in which on the one hand his participation in a lavish dinner prepared by sinners is attacked, and on the other hand he announces the coming of tribulation when his disciples, deprived of his presence, will fast and lament.

By weaving miracle and discipleship stories together in these chapters Matthew relates the restoration of Israel and establishment of the kingdom to the new kind of discipleship that is necessary. The prophets had often spoken of the restoration of God's people as the healing of their wounds (Hos 6:1; Jer 8:11, 22; 30:17; Isa 30:26). In Isaiah this restoration was depicted as healing the deaf, blind, afflicted, weak, lame, dumb, and broken-hearted. Israel, the one despised and rejected (Isa 53:3), would be restored to health in order that through it the will of the Lord might prosper (Isa 53:10). By carrying out these healings Jesus was both announcing that restoration and bringing it about.

The Healing of the Leper (8:1-4)

Leprosy was regarded as contagious and anyone having this disease was strictly quarantined (cf. 2 Chr 26:19-21) and was required to warn any person approaching (Lev 13:45). Because of the seriousness with which this disease was held there were detailed regulations concerning it (Leviticus 13–14). Approaching Jesus and kneeling before him instead of crying "unclean" was evidence of the leper's conviction that Jesus could heal him. The leper addresses Jesus as "Lord," "master," as one who teaches "with authority" (7:29). Jesus responds to this faith by touching him, even though such contact was regarded as defiling (Lev 5:3), and the man is immediately cleansed of leprosy.

According to the Law the leper was first to get official recognition of his being cleansed from a priest, and until that pronouncement had been made he was still officially unclean. Jesus advises that he do what the regulations stipulate (Lev 14:4, 10) as a witness to the people before he speaks to them. For Matthew this statement means more than showing proof of being whole, as his quotation of Isa 53:4 at the end of this first set of miracles would indicate (v. 17). The cleansing of the leper is a prime illustration of the restoration to wholeness of God's people; one who was "despised and rejected by others" is made new (Isa 53:3). That Isaiah 53 was sometimes seen as a description of a leper is indicated in the Babylonian Talmud (*b. Sanh.* 98b).

The Healing of the Centurion's Servant (8:5-13)

The "centurion" was probably an officer in charge of a hundred foot-soldiers who maintained a Roman presence in Capernaum. Matthew gives little detail; the real issue for him is that a Gentile can be included in the kingdom. "Lord" (v. 6) means no more than "sir," "master," but in address to Jesus it came to express that "authority" of 7:29. The servant's paralysis has caused him to be in great pain, and the centurion is acting out of deep concern. According to rabbinic tradition, to enter the house of a Gentile would be to defile oneself (*m. Ohol.* 18:7). The centurion's response, "only speak the word, and my servant will be healed" (v. 8) may have taken that into account. It is by a word that God heals (e.g., Ps 107:20; Wis 16:12) and will accomplish the redemption of all nations (Isa 45:23; 55:11).

> Catholic tradition has connected the recitation of the words of the centurion with the reception of the Eucharist. These words framed in such a context not only remind one that the Eucharist "heals the soul" (according to Ignatius of Antioch it is a "medicine of immortality"), but also exhort one to receive the sacramental presence of Christ with faith comparable to that of the centurion. *—Ed.*

Jesus "was amazed" and told the crowds "in no one in Israel have I found such faith" because the centurion's faith was one of sincere single-mindedness and total reliance on Jesus' authority and power to heal. "Many will come from east and west" (v. 11) repeats the promise that part of the restoration would be that nations would come to the brightness of Israel's rising and celebrate in acknowledgment that God is the only Lord (Isa 49:12; 60:3-7; 66:18-23; Zech 8:20-23). This coming of the Gentiles has been anticipated already in Matthew in the journey of the Magi. "Eat" or "sit at table" means to celebrate the restoration of the kingdom of God with Israel in a messianic banquet (cf. Isa 25:6; 55:2). The heirs of the kingdom (v. 12) here are those who were expecting to inherit it as descendants of Abraham, Isaac and Jacob. This is a rejection of those who claim membership by race rather than by faith. The evangelist might be anticipating here the banquet of tax collectors in the following chapter. "Outer darkness, where there will be weeping and gnashing of teeth" is the rejection at the final judgment: being totally apart from the brilliant presence of God. This is a favorite saying in Matthew (13:42, 50; 22:13; 24:51; 25:30), referring to the action of the wicked grinding their teeth in malice toward the righteous (Pss 35:16; 112:10; Lam 2:16; Job 16:9).

The Healing of Peter's Mother-in-law and Others (8:14-17)

As a married man Peter has his own house in Capernaum. His mother-in-law is in bed burning up with fever. Jesus touches her hand as he had touched the leper (v. 3) and others in healing (9:29; 20:34), and with the touch Peter's mother-in-law is completely restored to health. Significantly, the word for her "getting up" is the word used primarily in the NT to refer to being raised from the dead. Being restored to fullness of life, she immediately responds with acts of service. Demon possession (v. 16) covered any recurring involuntary psychic or physical reactions believed to be caused by spiritual forces other than God. These spirits are cast out with a word, recalling the centurion's statement of faith and the Isaian references to God's saving "word" that accomplishes what God purposes (see v. 8). The quotation from Isa 53:4 refers to all the miracles mentioned so far. Jesus, as the true representative of Servant Israel, is bringing healing and restoration to Israel. The implication is that Jesus as the true Servant is fulfilling Israel's vocation as God's Servant in the kingdom.

On Discipleship (8:18-22)

These two stories illustrate that discipleship in the kingdom calls for a commitment above and beyond the demands of anything else. As Jesus prepares to depart to the other side of the Sea of Galilee a certain scribe expresses his desire to follow Jesus. "Scribe" here is a neutral term denoting one who, because of his knowledge, was looked to as a teacher and interpreter of the Scriptures (cf. 13:52; 23:34). The scribe addresses Jesus as "teacher," quite appropriate for a scribe who wants to join him as a disciple. This scribe's statement is nothing less than an enthusiastic response to Jesus' invitation to the kingdom (7:7-11) and to what he has witnessed. Jesus answers that the invitation to the kingdom does not promise the political and economic security that many long for, but discipleship is total commitment to the mission of the kingdom. Jesus' words are a call to display that commitment by following his example. The poetry of this verse is similar to that of Matt 6:26-30, the "birds of the air" and "lilies of the field." A romantic self-pity must not be read into the verse. Against the background of the sections against worrying about physical sustenance one must see the uncertainties of the disciples' life with Jesus as a constant practice of reliance on the heavenly Father. Verse 21 ("another of his disciples") hints that the call was heeded. Jesus refers to himself here as the "Son of Man" for the first time, a title he continues to use throughout the gospel.

In the second lesson (vv. 21-22), since it was the son's responsibility to give his parents proper burial (Gen 50:5; Tob 4:3) the disciple requests leave to stay behind and take care of family obligations first before getting involved in the work of the kingdom (cf. 1 Kings 19:19-21). Jesus' response, which appears shocking, is really no more than the requirement for one who has taken a Nazirite vow (Num 6:6-7) or for a chief priest (Lev 21:11). Jesus is saying that the urgency of the kingdom takes precedence over family traditions (10:35-39; 12:46-50; 19:29) and so it becomes the prime commitment. The dead who bury their own dead are those not spiritually alive to the urgency of the kingdom, non-disciples.

Calming the Storm (8:23-27)

This nature miracle emphasizes the dependence and faith necessary for discipleship. There is also a subtle reminder of the Jonah story (Jonah 1:1-16) which was an indictment of Israel's failure to witness and be a light to the nations. Jonah represented Israel seeking to flee from that task and having to be turned around by God to carry it out. Jesus, on the other hand, is representing ideal Israel and is carrying out

THE SON OF MAN

Near the end of the exile Second Isaiah spoke of the people of Israel as God's Servant, God's Chosen One on whom God had poured out the divine Spirit to be a witness, a people-covenant and a light to the nations (Isa 42:1-7; 43:10, 12; 49:1-8). The trauma of the exile had been for Servant Israel a process of being refined "in the furnace of adversity" (Isa 48:10). Despised and rejected by the nations, the Servant would rise up from this death to a renewed life to fulfill the divine purpose as God's Righteous One, making many to be accounted righteous (Isa 53:11). The everlasting covenant made with David is now transferred to Servant Israel as God's representative to the nations (55:3-5). This theme is continued in Isaiah 56–66 but with the emphasis that this collective term refers only to the faithful of Israel (Isa 60–62; 65:9, 13-16).

In Zechariah 9–14 that corporate group of the faithful is referred to as "Judah," who in spite of persecution from the leaders in Jerusalem will represent God's rule and lead to the restoration of all (cf. Zech 9:9; 10:3, 6; 12:4-7; 13:1). Later, in Daniel, the corporate term for the faithful Servant becomes "one like a son of man" [= "one like a human being"] to whom is given "dominion and glory and kingship" (Dan 7:13). He represents "the holy ones of the Most High" who "receive the kingdom" (Dan 7:18, 22, 27). These are the wise "who lead many to righteousness" (Dan 12:3).

All these various ideas are drawn together in the Parables of Enoch (*1 Enoch* 37–71) where the one called the Son of Man (46:2-4; 48:2; 60:10; etcetera) is also referred to as the Righteous One (38:2-5; 53:6), the Chosen One (39:6; 40:5; 45:3-4; etcetera) and as the Anointed One (48:10; 52:4; cf. Isa 61:1). These collective terms are used of an individual to whom God gives authority and a throne and who will vindicate all the righteous and chosen and bring judgment on "the kings and the mighty ones" who oppress the righteous. These parables, written around 4 B.C.E., drew heavily on Isaiah 40–66 and Daniel but place more emphasis on judgment and vindication.

Jesus has drawn on this development, and transformed the concept incorporating both Servant Israel's mission and the vindication/judgment theme into the representative title "Son of Man," while at the same time calling all Israel to fulfill the Servant role in its witness to the nations.

God's purpose willingly; so he can act with God's power and authority, for "something greater than Jonah is here" (12:39-41). The boat was being covered by the waves but Jesus, like Jonah (1:5), was asleep (v. 24). Jesus rebuked the winds and the sea as God had done for the children of Israel to escape across the Reed Sea (Ps 106:9). This demonstrates that God has given authority to the Son of Man to carry out salvation and judgment (cf. Dan 7:14; *1 Enoch* 46:4-6). What we may today call a "nature miracle" is for the ancient reader a sign of power over a mysterious realm of existence: the wind and the sea, a realm particularly important for fisherfolk. The wind and storm belong to the realm of the air dominated by spiritual beings according to the cosmology of the time. The question of Jesus' identity is aligned to the progression in revelation of Jesus' nature; first he taught with unprecedented authority, afterwards he healed people, first by touch and then from a distance, and here he shows power over the higher realms of storm, wind, and sky.

The Healing of the Demoniacs (8:28-34)

Coming to the other side of the Sea of Galilee brings Jesus and his disciples into the neighborhood of Gadara, one of those cities populated by Greeks and so placed by the Romans under the control of the province of Syria (Josephus, *Ant.* 17.11.4). The city itself lay about ten kilometers southeast of the Sea of Galilee. Matthew gives only the briefest description of the demoniacs as fierce and dangerous to passersby, for his focus is on the authority of Jesus. "What have you to do with us?" (v. 29) is really a Semitic statement of rejection (e.g., 1 Kings 17:18; 2 Kings 3:13). The demonic spirits within the men recognize Jesus as Son of God. The full significance of that title will become clear in the resurrection. But in their next question, "Have you come here to torment us before the time?" they also acknowledge that he is the one who will be their judge in the final judgment as the Son of Man (cf. 25:41; *1 Enoch* 67). Knowing they will be cast out, the demons plead for another place of habitation, the unclean herd of swine (v. 31). Their wish is granted (v. 32), but with unexpected results. The herd of swine rushing down the steep bank into the waters actually brings about the final judgment on these evil spirits (cf. *1 Enoch* 67:13). It is over these waters that Jesus has just exercised his authority (vv. 23-27), and now he has shown his authority in judgment over the demons. The response of the Gadarenes is really no better than that of the demons Jesus had destroyed; they are more concerned about the loss of the herd of swine than about the inbreaking of the reign of God. So there is a warning here: Jesus as the Son of Man who has exercised final judgment over the supernatural powers will be the same one who exercises judgment over the nations (cf. 25:31-32).

The Healing of the Paralytic (9:1-8)

Jesus as the Son of Man also has authority to forgive sins. In this miracle it is the faith in Jesus' authority of the people bringing the paralytic that moves Jesus to heal. Jesus addresses the paralytic as "son," a term of endearment. "Your sins are forgiven": Jesus is declaring God's forgiveness by the authority given him as another sign of the restoration of the reign of God. Forgiveness was part of the announcement of the good news (see above at 1:21). Because they see the forgiveness of sins as granted only by God on the Day of Atonement some of the scribes (v. 3) understand Jesus' words as blasphemy.

The Calling of Matthew (9:9-13)

Matthew was probably a name Jesus conferred on Levi (cf. Luke 5:27) when he became an apostle, just as he had called Simon "Peter." That he was also known as Levi would indicate that he was of the priestly tribe of Levi. Matthew functioned as a customs official collecting duty on goods being brought into or leaving the territory of Herod Antipas. He may also have been responsible for the collection of Roman taxes. On both counts Matthew would have been regarded as a collaborator with the forces of oppression and would have been under suspicion of using his office to enrich himself. The rabbis classified tax collectors with murderers, robbers, and the unclean and approved of lying to them in order to escape taxation (*m. Ned.* 3:4; *m. Ṭohar.* 7:6). Such persons were regarded as incapable of belonging to the messianic kingdom and were often associated with "sinners" and "Gentiles" (cf. Matt 5:46-47; 9:11; 18:17). But Jesus offers Matthew the simple invitation: "Follow me," to which he responds immediately with joy. This was not just a call to discipleship but an invitation to enter the kingdom. As Jesus reclined at table (v. 10), the practice at festive gatherings, many joined him, responding to the open invitation to become part of God's kingdom after having been excluded for so long by the traditional teachings of the scribes and Pharisees. Following Matthew's invitation to the kingdom this scene has overtones of the banquet celebrating the kingdom described in Isa 55:1-2. The Pharisees are appalled that a teacher should eat with such people, who were regarded as a lost cause (v. 11). Jesus responds with three points: (1) The sick are the ones who need a physician: Jesus has come to heal Israel (Isa 53:3). (2) For the readers, a Christian community composed of Jews and Gentiles, the story demonstrates a relativization of the legal prescription: if Jesus can eat food with "sinners," the Jewish Christians can share meals with non-Jewish fellow Christians. Jesus uses a typical rabbinic expression to introduce a significant scriptural quotation: "Go and learn what this means." His quotation from Hos 6:6 (repeated in 12:7): "I desire mercy, not sacrifice" also takes into consideration its context which speaks of God healing the people (Hos 6:1; 7:1) and calls for an intimate faithful relationship with God (cf. Hos 2:19-20). (3) "For I have come to call not the righteous, but sinners" is ironic in that the Pharisees were regarded as righteous, while Jesus' mission is to the lost sheep (9:36; 10:6; 15:24), those still looking for the kingdom.

The Question of Feasting and Fasting (9:14-17)

Jesus' open invitation to sinners and celebration of their acceptance of him has clearly moved beyond John the Baptist's warnings of judgment, and John's disciples are bewildered. Their questioning Jesus about not fasting is an indication of a growing rift that culminated in John's question to Jesus in 11:2. John's disciples fast because of impending judgment and the need for repentance, but instead Jesus rejoices when people turn to God. The readers of Matthew know that Jesus began his ministry with fasting and therefore cannot be opposed to fasting as such. The synoptic tradition is unanimous in telling us that he imposed no special discipline of fasting on his disciples. "The wedding guests cannot mourn as long as the bridegroom is with them, can they?" alludes to celebrating the restoration of the kingdom described in Isa 61:10; 62:5 (cf. Jer 33:11); *1 Enoch* 62:13-15. This restoration was not a time for fasting but for feasting (Isa 55:1-2; Zech 8:19). "When the bridegroom is taken away from them" is a reference to Isa 53:8: "by a perversion of justice he was taken away," which will be fulfilled in Jesus through growing opposition and lack of understanding of his mission.

By fasting, John's disciples and the Pharisees were only trying to patch up the old worn garment, and with disastrous results. The old would pass away and God would cause new things to spring forth (Isa 43:18-19; 48:6). Those who opposed the faithful and resisted the restoration of God's rule would wear out like a garment (Isa 50:9; 51:7-8). Goatskins with the openings sewn up were often used for aging new wine. Old wineskins that had lost their resiliency could not be used for this purpose. Likewise the old traditions and customs of Israel had lost their ability to change, and so there needed to be a new beginning.

The Ruler's Daughter and the Woman with a Hemorrhage (9:18-26)

Two stories wedged together make up the first of the third triad of miracle stories. They illustrate saving faith; this faith that is the required response to the ushering in of the kingdom demands a new way of looking at things. While Jesus is still reclining at table a synagogue official enters and kneels before him. His faith is such that he believes Jesus can bring his daughter back to life by putting his hand on her. Disregarding Jewish law that touching a dead person would render him unclean for seven days and require a ritual of purification (Num 19:11-13; *m. Ohol.* passim), Jesus leaves the banquet immediately and follows the official. Meanwhile the woman suffering from a hemorrhage, having lived in a state of uncleanness for twelve years (Lev 15:19-30; *m. Zabim* 5:1, 6), approaches Jesus from behind and touches the tassel of his garment. The tassels on the corner of the garment symbolized the covenant relationship Israel had with God (Num 15:38-39; Deut 22:12; cf. Zech 8:23). Her action expressed her dependence on that relationship and faith that she would be delivered from the uncleanness that had prevented her from living a normal life or having hope for the coming kingdom. Jesus' response (v. 22) acknowledges her as a child of God, and healing comes immediately as a direct result of Jesus' word.

Arriving at the ruler's house (v. 23), Jesus finds that flute players and professional mourners hired for funerals were already there. (Cf. *m. Ketub.:* "R. Judah says: Even the poorest in Israel should hire not less than two flutes and one wailing woman." Cf. Jer 9:17-22; Amos 5:16; 2 Chr 35:25). The noisy professional wailers laugh in ridicule at Jesus' statement that the girl is not dead but sleeping. Jesus indicates that her death is not permanent, but that she will awaken as from sleep (cf. Dan 12:2). In faith the ruler dismisses the crowd and Jesus takes the girl's hand and restores her to life. Both actions are life-giving signs of the incoming reign of God, and this report spreads throughout all the land.

The Healing of Two Blind Men (9:27-31)

Jesus returns now to Capernaum and is followed by the two blind men. The restoration of the kingdom was often described as the blind receiving their sight, the ears of the deaf being unstopped, the tongues of the dumb singing for joy (Isa 29:18; 35:5-6). These signs are now illustrated in miraculous healings in the next two stories. The cry of two blind men, "Have mercy on us," is the common cry of the afflicted in the Davidic psalms (e.g., 6:2; 9:13). The blind were often rejected from normal society since blindness was seen as a curse that had come on an individual because of sin (cf. Gen 19:11; Deut 28:28-29; John 9:1-34). In calling Jesus "Son of David" the men are hoping that Jesus is the promised Davidic Messiah who will bring justice and righteousness for them as well (cf. Psalm 72). The title had been made popular by the Pharisees, and while others used it of Jesus (12:23; 15:22; 20:30-31; 21:9, 15) neither Jesus nor his disciples did. The term "Son of David" was often interpreted in a political and nationalist sense, one that Jesus would certainly wish to avoid. The title may have been used here as well as in Matt 20:29-34 in order to represent the specific character of the blindness of those who misunderstand the role of the Messiah. As on other occasions, Jesus heals them "according to their faith" (cf. 8:13; 9:22; 15:28) so that their eyes are opened (cf. Isa 35:5; 42:7). As the Isaiah passages indicate, these physical healings always imply healings of spiritual blindness so that those healed "see God" (5:8). Jesus' stern charge to them, "See that no one knows of this" relates to their understanding of his messiahship.

The Healing of the Deaf and Dumb Man (9:32-34)

The Greek word means both "deaf" and "dumb" since both afflictions were commonly linked together (e.g. Isa 35:5-6). The afflictions, here and in 12:22, are attributed to demonic influence that Jesus must exorcise. The amazement the people express at Jesus' power is a fitting climax to the whole account of the messianic deeds, just as was their astonishment to the account of the messianic words (7:28-29). In contrast, the Pharisees claim that Jesus is deceiving them with his own demonic power, a claim picked up again in 12:22-32.

V. The Mission of the Disciples: 9:35–10:42

The Mission of Jesus Makes Preparation for the Mission of the Twelve (9:35-38)

Verse 35 repeats 4:23 almost identically as an *inclusio* statement to bring closure to the description of Jesus' mission in word and deed, emphasizing once again the restoring of Israel as "a [person] of suffering and acquainted with infirmity" (Isa 53:3). Jesus' compassion for the crowds expresses concern for the lack of spiritual guidance given by self-serving leaders. The motif of the sheep scattered and lost upon the hills and the need to gather them into the reign of God grew out of the experience of the exile and is prominent in Jesus' mission to Israel (cf. Jer 23:4; Isa 40:10-11; Zech 10:2; Matt 10:6; 15:24; 18:10-14). They are "harassed and helpless," a phrase that implies being ravaged and abused and left to die. The harvest is often a metaphor for judgment (Joel 3:13; Isa 18:4; Matt 3:12; 13:30, 39-40), but also, as here, for gathering the faithful into the kingdom (Isa 27:12; Matt 13:41-43). The time is ripe to send out workers to assist in this gathering because the kingdom has come. This passage, joining two traditional metaphors used for pastoral activity, offers a foundation for the purpose and timeliness of the calling of the disciples in the next chapter.

The Calling of the Twelve to Mission (10:1-4)

Twelve disciples are chosen to represent Israel gathering together the twelve tribes to be a light to the nations (Isa 49:6). The authority they are given is to demonstrate the restorative power of the reign of God, just as Jesus has exercised this authority in word (7:29) and deed (9:6, 8; 21:23-27). It is the authority to heal and proclaim (vv. 7, 8) the good news of the kingdom. They are not given authority to teach, which comes only at the end of their training (28:18-20). The term "unclean spirits" is an allusion to the promise in Zech 13:2 that at the time of the restoration the unclean spirit would be removed from the land, as Jesus has already been doing (9:33). This is the only time Matthew uses the term apostles ("sent ones"), relating to Jesus' "sending them out" (v. 5), just as he had been sent "to bind up the brokenhearted, to proclaim liberty to the captives," (cf. v. 40; Isa 61:1). Matthew simply lists the Twelve in pairs (cf. Mark 6:7; Luke 10:2) with little explanation; some of them are not mentioned again. First, Simon called Peter is distinguished from Simon the Cananaean (Aramaic for "the zealous one"); then Matthew is identified as the tax collector (9:9), and Judas as the betrayer. The first mentioned are the original four disciples, Peter, Andrew, James, and John, called in 4:18-21, and with Jesus from the beginning. Matthew shows no interest in giving further details about the apostles. Jesus and his proclamation of the kingdom are always the focal point.

The Sending out of the Twelve (10:5-15)

The Twelve are sent out with the explicit charge to go only to the lost sheep of the house of Israel, Jesus' immediate purpose. His mission so far has been to announce the good news of the kingdom and to gather faithful Israel together to carry out its purpose to be a people-covenant and a light to the nations. The Twelve are now to participate in that proclamation and gathering, so at this stage they are told: "Go nowhere among the Gentiles, and enter no town of the Samaritans." Israel is first to be gathered in order to fulfill its purpose of being a witness to others. "The lost sheep of the house of Israel" refers to the common people of Israel as a whole: the crowds who are "harassed and helpless" (see above at 9:36). The Twelve are to be like their teacher (vv. 7-8) and go through the towns and villages of Israel as heralds, announcing and demonstrating the kingdom (bringing about the restoration of communion with God) in preparation for the coming of the Son of Man (10:23). Since they have been redeemed "without money" (Isa 52:3) and invited into the kingdom "without money and without price" (Isa 55:1), so they are also to share the good news of the kingdom freely. There is a sense of urgency to their proclamation, so they are simply to go without first procuring money and supplies (vv. 9-10); God will see that they are provided for (cf. 6:31-34). Jesus forbids any "commercial" use of the authority he confers on the Twelve. There is no need to take a bag (used for carrying bread and other food) or two tunics as extra clothing, or sandals, or a staff—the normal equipment for a journey (cf. Exod 12:11). The prohibitions emphasize the immediacy and spontaneity of the mission and signify that in carrying out that mission the disciples put themselves totally into the hands of God to supply their needs.

On entering the house of one regarded as worthy the apostles were to "greet it," meaning that they should seek the peace and welfare of the residents (cf. Gen 43:27; Judg 18:15). With the coming of the kingdom that greeting takes on special significance. The Twelve are conveyers of the messianic peace that restores relationship with God (cf. Isa 52:7). If the people there reject the message of the kingdom, then that peace is to be taken back. There is no peace for the wicked (Isa 48:22; 57:21). The disciples are not to stay and argue with those who will not accept the proclamation (v. 14), but are to leave. "Shake off the dust from off your feet" describes a common gesture of repudiation, a sign that those repudiated were still unregenerate (cf. Acts 13:51) and liable to the judgment (13:24-31). That judgment will be worse than the one delivered to the land of Sodom and Gomorrah, the traditional symbol of iniquity and punishment (cf. Gen 19:15-29; Isa 1:9; 13:19).

Expect Persecution (10:16-25)

Two proverbial expressions are dovetailed together as a warning to the disciples to be prepared for rejection and persecution. "I am sending you out like sheep into the midst of wolves": the apostles are in solidarity with the crowds who are sheep without a shepherd (9:36), and so they will certainly arouse the attention of those who are regarded as shepherds but are wolves "in sheep's clothing" (7:15; cf. Ezek 34:3; Zech 10:2-3; 11:4-17). "So be wise as serpents and innocent as doves." The first part of this phrase takes its vocabulary from Gen 3:1 where the serpent is described as "more crafty than any other wild animal" God had created. The Greek word behind "innocent" means literally "unmixed," having a single-minded devotion to the cause.

The disciples should expect nothing better than the prophets who had proclaimed God's message in the past (5:10-12). They are warned that they will be handed over to the disciplinary councils of local synagogues and flogged as punishment for breaking the legal traditions or encouraging others to do so (cf. Deut 25:1-3; Matt 23:34; Acts 5:40-41; 22:19; 2 Cor 11:24). Their proclamation that the kingdom is open to all who seek it would have been seen by Pharisees and scribes as breaking down the discipline of the Law. Like their master, the apostles would be living out the role of faithful Israel (Isa 53:4-5). The mention of governors and kings refers in safe, general terms to the official authorities of that time. The passage foresees disruptions on all levels of society, including the family. This situation is quite conceivable at the first mission of the Twelve but reflects even more the plight of the Church facing families divided by belief after the resurrection. The disciples will be hated "on account of me" to the point of being ostracized, arrested, imprisoned, and eventually put to death. Such a view presupposes that Jesus has also been treated in this way. In ancient societies a household usually meant much more than a nuclear family. The gospel is seen here as disrupting this larger family by setting believers against nonbelievers in the same household and fomenting enmities among kin.

Through their faithfulness the disciples would be God's witnesses (Isa 43:10, 12; 55:4) and a light to the nations (Isa 42:6; 49:6). They will be given the power to speak because being in faithful relationship with their heavenly Father leads to the divine Spirit working in and through them as had been promised (Isa 42:1; 44:3, 8; 51:16; 61:1) and witnessed in Jesus' baptism (3:17). Since the direct attribution to the Spirit of the words spoken by the disciples belongs to the vocabulary of prophetic inspiration, suffering becomes "witnessing" because it constitutes a source of divinely inspired speech. This concept was highly important in the context of martyrdom in the early Church, as witnessed by Ignatius's letters and the accounts of early martyrs such as Polycarp. Those who find their security in the laws, customs, and rituals will be threatened by the new ways of the kingdom (cf. 9:16-17). This verse echoes Mic 7:6 which is alluded to more explicitly in vv. 35-36, a passage that speaks of the breakdown of society when people put their trust in human institutions instead of God. They will be hated because of the unsettling situation brought about by resistance to the good news. However, "the one who endures to the end will be saved." The disciples' goal is to proclaim, to witness, but not to get involved in dispute (v. 23). They were to keep moving because of the urgency of their task, which they will not have completed before the Son of Man (see excursus at 8:20) comes to gather the faithful together. Since they are to proclaim the same message in word and action as Jesus does, they should not expect to get any better treatment than their master (vv. 24-25). Beelzebul (see 9:34; 12:24-27) was originally the Canaanite god Baal, the lord of fertility. Foreign gods came to be called "demons" in Jewish thinking from the time of the exile. The saying indirectly reflects the closeness of Jesus' relationship with the Twelve: they belong to a common household.

Fear Not! (10:26-33)

This section recalls the words of encouragement given to Servant Israel in the "fear not" sayings in Isaiah (35:3-4; 41:9-10). In spite of opposition the disciples are to remember that God has called them to proclaim God's message and so will help them. They are to lift up their voices with strength and fear not (Isa 40:9). For those "new things, hidden things" (Isa 48:6-8; cf. 42:9), the good news of the kingdom not previously known, are now to be revealed. "What I say to you in the dark, tell in the light" further alludes to the Isaianic motif of bringing the good news to Israel (Isa 42:16). What Jesus has taught his disciples privately they are now to proclaim with boldness, even upon the flat housetops that form an ideal platform for proclamation to a crowd. For the faithful, physical death is limited, for they shall rise and shine like the stars forever (cf. Dan 12:2; Mal 4:1-2). The disciples can be assured that their heavenly Father who watches over even the sparrows (v. 29) is watching over and taking care of them, for everything that happens in this world is under God's control. Surely God will especially value those whom God has called to be messengers. The cry of the faithful of Israel had been: "You are our father" (Isa 63:16). With this in mind Jesus reminds his disciples of their solidarity with him and with God as their Father (cf. "your Father," v. 29 and "my Father," vv. 32, 33). Here Jesus reveals more of his mission as the Son of Man, referring to his role in judgment before the Father, a role that accentuates the importance of Jesus as Lord. To acknowledge their unity with him is to be acknowledged before the Father, but to deny him is ultimately to be denied before God.

Conflict and Recompense (10:34-42)

"I have not come to bring peace, but a sword" is a very strong statement. Of course the Christ does bring peace (Isa 52:7; 57:19) that comes to those who enter into the restored relationship with God, but there is no peace for those who reject the invitation (Isa 48:22; 57:20-21). God's message, then, brings both salvation and judgment, and thus acts as a two-edged sword (cf. Hos 6:5; Eph 6:17; Heb 4:12). As the word of God's witness, Servant Israel's preaching is "like a sharp sword" (Isa 49:2). The mention of Jesus' "coming" also refers back again to the image of the Son of Man and the image of judgment that occurs in the preceding verse (cf. excursus at 8:20). The social disruption prophesied in Mic 7:6 (cf. vv. 35-36) comes as a result of Jesus' mission. The divine word causes division in families as some accept and others reject (cf. vv. 21-22), for discipleship is a total commitment that places Jesus and his mission above family ties. Love for parents, relatives, or neighbor is not to take precedence over love for God and God's purpose. This verse is the only synoptic passage in which the disciples' relation to Jesus is described as love, although such a love relationship has been implied all along. "Taking up the cross" is the symbol of total willingness to suffer for the cause, a saying that took on new meaning in Christ's crucifixion. The paradoxical statement in v. 39 further emphasizes the need for total commitment in order to find real life in relationship to God. Similarly, those who receive the Twelve into their homes are receiving Jesus himself and his message and, consequently, the heavenly Father who is the original Sender (v. 40), for the one who receives those coming out of the prophetic movement will receive the reward and recompense promised by the prophets (Isa 40:10; 62:11-12), and anyone who receives a representative of Servant Israel, the Righteous One, will receive the reward of being accounted righteous before God (Isa 53:11; *1 Enoch* 38:2; 53:6). (See above at 5:12.) The prophets and the righteous are paired again in 13:17 and 23:29.

"One of these little ones" (v. 42) refers to the disciples as children of the heavenly Father (cf. Matt 18:1-10; Zech 13:7; cf. also Matt 11:25). Giving "a cup of cold water" was the simplest act of hospitality, and even that will be rewarded (cf. 25:31-46). So the Twelve will find rejection but there will nevertheless be those who receive them gladly. Those will be the recipients of the blessings of the kingdom. The formula saying (cf. 7:28; 13:53; 19:1; 26:1) concludes the discourse on the disciples' mission and leads into narrative indicating the lack of understanding of some who have been confronted by the message.

VI. Misunderstanding and Growing Opposition: 11:2–12:50

The episodes presented here exhibit an increasingly polarized response to Jesus in which initial faith and simmering hostility are juxtaposed. This polarization is a fulfillment of what has been said in the previous chapter about the divisiveness of Jesus' message. The narrative framework of John's imprisonment also links the reader naturally to the martyrdom and persecution prophesied by Jesus to the disciples. Here again, as earlier (see Matt 3:1-12), Matthew tends to portray the parallel courses of John and Jesus, leading the reader through John's life and death to the death and resurrection of Jesus. Thus John fulfills his role as herald even within the narrative structure of Matthew's gospel.

Failure to Understand: John the Baptist (11:2-15)

Since John's arrest (4:12) he has been hearing of the works of the Anointed One. This is the first time in the ministry of Jesus that Matthew uses the term *christos,* and it clearly relates to Jesus' role as Servant Israel (Isa 61:1). In this way Matthew continues the process of continual revelation of Jesus as the Messiah, the Anointed One, within the context of the Son of Man viewed in the light of the Servant of Isaiah 40–55. The "works" (NRSV: "what the Messiah was doing") refer to all Jesus' words and deeds recorded in 4:23–9:35. John's concern is that Jesus is not fulfilling the role he had expected. "Are you the one who is to come?" relates to John's expectation, expressed in 3:11-12, for the return of Elijah mentioned in Mal 3:1-2; 4:1-6, the prophet who would come announcing judgment. Instead, Jesus and his disciples were reaching out to the lost and demonstrating the restoration of God's reign. Jesus' response that John's disciples should go and tell him what they "hear and see" (v. 4) is a subtle warning to them not to be afflicted with the spiritual deafness and blindness that so often had afflicted Israel (e.g., Isa 42:18-20; cf. Matt 13:13-17). The restoration of the kingdom is demonstrated in the fact that the "blind receive their sight" and "the deaf hear" (v. 5). Jesus refers back to his "works" of proclaiming the good news and healing as signs of the restoration of the kingdom promised in Isa 26:19; 29:18; 35:5-6; 61:1-3. Each "work" mentioned also refers back to what Matthew has already recorded in chs. 5–9. In all this Jesus clearly demonstrates that his mission is to restore the reign of God according to the promises of Isaiah and not merely to announce warning and judgment as John expected.

As the disciples of John leave, Jesus addresses the ever-present crowds concerning John's place in God's plan. John's preaching had certainly caught the popular imagination initially, and great numbers had gone to be baptized by him (3:5-7), but they were not looking for someone unstable and untrustworthy (cf. Ezek 29:6-9; Wis 4:4) or for a political leader from among the oppressive rulers who lived in royal palaces, but for a prophet from God. John, in fact, is more: he is really the "Coming One" himself. The quotation from Mal 3:1 is combined with Exod 23:20 because the messenger who went before Moses was to lead the people into the promised land, while Elijah would prepare the way into the promised kingdom. By applying these texts to John, Jesus was implying that John himself is carrying out the role of the returning Elijah and has been preparing the way for Jesus.

Among humanity in general there is no one greater than John. Yet "the least in the kingdom of heaven" is greater. The word translated "least" *(mikroteros)* is the comparative form of "little one," the term used in 10:42 and 18:6, 10, 14 for "disciple." Even the most insignificant disciple, then, is greater than John because he or she has accepted the good news of the heavenly Father's restoring love and has entered into that healing relationship. John, expecting judgment, has not yet understood that message. He followed the common belief that judgment would come first, and only then could the kingdom come into being. Since the Baptist had begun proclaiming the coming of the kingdom and calling for repentance there had been an intensification of political activism among religious and nationalist groups in the belief that force and violence against foreign domination was the path of righteousness. This response was just the opposite of what Jesus had proclaimed in Matt 5:38-48. The kingdom of heaven comes about by God's grace and reflected love, and to try to bring it about by force is to violate it. Such attitudes had led to violence against John and now were building up against Jesus himself.

"All the prophets and the Law prophesied until John came" (v. 13) emphasizes the prophetic nature of Scripture (see 5:17). John is included among the prophets who have prophesied the coming of the kingdom, but Jesus now says explicitly what he had implied in v. 10: John is Elijah (Mal 4:5), the Coming One, even though many including John himself did not know it (cf. 17:12-13; John 1:21). Of course this is to be understood figuratively. Those who have the ears of faith will understand (cf. v. 4).

Failure to Understand: "This Generation" (11:16-19)

"This generation" refers specifically to the religious leaders (cf. v. 19 with 9:10-15) who act like self-willed children wanting others to play their game. When the Baptist came calling everyone to repentance before the coming judgment they said he was demon-possessed and complained that he did not rejoice. When Jesus came rejoicing, proclaiming the good news of the kingdom, they complained he did not fast, and accused him of gluttony and drunkardness. In their "wisdom" they rejected both John and Jesus; but "wisdom," says Jesus, "is vindicated by her works" (NAB). The works of the Anointed One have already been referred to in 11:2-5 and demonstrated in chs. 8–9. This is to say that "wisdom" is not with those who claim it, but with Jesus.

Failure to Understand: Woe to Those Unrepentant Cities (11:20-24)

There is no excuse for those towns that witnessed many of these works and did not repent. Chorazin and Bethsaida were towns not far from Capernaum, the center of Jesus' ministry. "Woe to you" is an expression of a covenant curse (cf. Deut 27:11-26) in contrast to the covenant blessings (5:3-12). Verse 20 makes it clear that the reason for the "woes" is the lack of repentance. In this way the passage can be applied to those towns' lack of response to either John or Jesus, since the call to repentance was a common theme of their preaching. The indifference of the residents of these towns is compared to that of Tyre and Sidon, Phoenician cities renowned in earlier times for their arrogance and indifference to God's will (e.g., in Isaiah 23). Even these cities would have repented in sackcloth and ashes, like Nineveh in Jonah 3:5-10, if they had witnessed these works of healing. The day of judgment will be harsher on those who saw these works and yet remained indifferent. Jesus' mission has been to gather Israel to be faithful witnesses to these foreign nations. The comparison is a clear anticipation that eventually the kingdom will be announced and accepted among the nations, in spite of those of Israel who do not repent.

The greatest rebuke is kept for Capernaum, Jesus' "own city" (9:1) where most of the healings took place. To this city is ascribed the supreme arrogance of the king of Babylon, quoting from Isa 14:13-15, who had exalted himself to sit above the stars of God only to be brought down to the depths of Sheol, the realm of the dead. Even the city of Sodom, the ancient symbol of ultimate judgment, would have responded better than Capernaum had they witnessed these signs of the kingdom (cf. 10:15).

Gratitude for the Faithful Who Understand, and an Invitation (11:25-30)

The balancing of grim pictures of conflict and condemnation with bright promise and praise is characteristic of Matthew's gospel. Thus the sweeping statements against "this generation" are paired off by the exaltation of those who are responsive to Jesus and listen to him. In response to this indifference and rejection Jesus now thanks God for those who have received the good news. The unique address "Father, Lord of heaven and earth" recalls the urging of Second Isaiah for Israel in exile to know that their God is YHWH, the creator of heaven and earth, who redeems them (Isa 40:12-31; 42:5) and calls them forth to be God's witnesses before the nations (43:8-13). That God has "hidden these things from the wise and the intelligent" recalls the words of Isa 29:13-14 referring to false leaders and hypocrites who do not listen to God but claim to have done so, a passage Jesus later quotes against Pharisees and scribes from Jerusalem (15:8). That these things have been revealed "to infants" alludes to Isa 28:9. The infants are the disciples who have truly heard the message Jesus has revealed, the ones who become like little children (18:1-4; cf. 10:42; 11:11). "For such was your gracious will" (v. 26) reflects Isa 42:1, quoted in 12:18 and used in the divine pronouncements at Jesus' baptism (3:17) and transfiguration (17:5). In these pronouncements the Father acknowledged his relationship with Jesus as his Son/Servant. It is as that faithful Servant-Son of God that Jesus addresses God as Father (cf. Isa 63:16), saying "we are the clay, and you are our potter" (Isa 64:8), unlike the "wise and intelligent" who reverse that saying (see Isa 29:16). The crucial word in v. 27, and indeed for this whole section, is the word "know" used in its Semitic sense meaning "to be in relationship with" (Hos 2:20; 4:1, 6). Servant Israel is called to know God (Isa 40:21-23, 28; 43:10) so that "by his knowledge" the righteous Servant "shall make many righteous" (Isa 53:11). It is in this context that "no one knows the Son except the Father," an allusion to the cry of the faithful in Isa 63:16. At the same time the reciprocal relationship between Father and Son in their knowledge of each other is remarkable. That only the Father knows the Son becomes important in Matt 16:17 where it helps to explain why it was not flesh and blood but rather the Father who revealed to Peter who Jesus is.

> The equal dignity of Father and Son revealed in the reciprocal relationship between Father and Son played an important role in the development of christology. This is one of the scriptural seeds leading to the insight that the Father and Son are equal on the level of being. *–Ed.*

"No one knows the Father except the Son and anyone to whom the Son chooses to reveal him" refers to the role of Servant Israel who is to gather all the scattered of Israel to be a light to the nations so that salvation may reach to the ends of the earth (Isa 49:1-6). In this context the term "Son" refers to Jesus' fulfilling the role of the Servant. The idea that God would reveal the hidden things through God's Servant is implied in Isa 42:9; 48:6-8; 53:1, 11. According to the Parables of Enoch it is this Righteous One as the Son of Man who reveals the secrets to the chosen ones and judges the wicked (*1 Enoch* 38:3; 51:3; 58; 60:1; 61:13). In this passage we have the only synoptic description of Jesus' private prayer to the Father, a passage that parallels similar passages in the gospel of John.

The invitation now offered (v. 28) is thus the call of Jesus as Servant Israel, the herald of good news, to the faint and weary of Isa 40:28-31. Unlike the false leaders who do not heed the call to "give rest to the weary" (Isa 28:12), Jesus promises: "I will give you rest"—that peace and security that come through a right relationship with God. Those who "are weary and are carrying heavy burdens" are those who have been laden with the Pharisees' many requirements for admission to the kingdom. If they respond to Jesus' good news they will find the rest they are seeking. The rabbis spoke of the "yoke of the Torah" (e.g., *m. ʾAbot* 3:5; *m. Berakot* 2:2), but the Pharisees with their oral traditions had made that yoke heavy on others with their legalistic demands (see ch. 23). Jesus' yoke, in contrast, is suited to their needs and his burden, a faithful relationship with God, is light. For he himself is afflicted and lowly in heart, a phrase that summarizes the description of the Servant (Isa 41:17; 54:11; 61:1). Jesus thus expresses solidarity with the faithful (5:3, 5). "You will find rest for your souls" picks up a phrase from Jer 6:16. The invitation given here seems to echo the invitation of wisdom in Sir 51:23-30; 24:19-34, and this is deliberately done to show that words are not enough: true wisdom is vindicated by her deeds (11:19). Jesus here offers his rendition of the invitation in Isa 55:3 to enter into that faithful relationship with God in the kingdom.

Growing Opposition from the Pharisees (12:1-14)

The failure of the Pharisees to understand Jesus' mission is illustrated in their rigidity in regard to the Sabbath. It was permissible by law to pluck heads of grain from the borders of someone's grainfield (Lev 19:9-10; Deut 23:25), but the issue for the Pharisees was that Jesus permitted his disciples to do this on the Sabbath. The basic Sabbath law in the Sinai covenant was established in order for the people to remember and reflect on their special covenant relationship with God who had delivered them from slavery and given them rest (the meaning of "sabbath"). However, the Pharisees had hedged that Sabbath law around with all kinds of prohibitions. According to the Mishnah (*m. Šabb.* 7:2) there were thirty-nine classes of work that were prohibited on the Sabbath, one of these being "reaping." The Pharisees obviously regarded the plucking of heads of grain to eat as reaping. Matthew emphasizes that the disciples were hungry, and the appeasement of hunger was a sign of the restoration of the kingdom (Isa 65:13). Only a fool would let the hungry go unsatisfied (Isa 32:6; cf. 58:6-7, 10), but for the Pharisees the only legitimate reason for breaking their Sabbath laws was the danger of death. As the one "anointed" (11:2) to bring this good news to the afflicted Jesus confronts the Pharisees with the action of another "anointed one" dear to them, King David (vv. 3-4). When he and his companions were hungry they had eaten five loaves of the old showbread on the Sabbath, the day fresh loaves were set out. The old loaves were normally eaten by the priests (Lev 24:5-9; 1 Sam 21:1-6). If hunger took precedence over the Law in David's case, then surely it should also at this time when the kingdom was being restored. That Jesus has the restoration of the kingdom in mind is brought out even more by this second illustration. The priests were expected to do "Temple" work on the Sabbath such as changing the showbread (Lev 24:8), conducting the Sabbath sacrifices (Num 28:9-10), and other duties that were seen as overriding the Sabbath law (*m. ʿErub.* 10:11-15; *m. Pesaḥ* 6:1-2). They could "work" on the Sabbath and yet be guiltless because it was work sanctified by the Temple. Jesus points out that the kingdom of God into which all God's people are to enter is "something greater than the temple" and now supersedes it. Those who have God's law in their hearts (Isa 51:7) know how to act in compassion even on the Sabbath (cf. Isa 56:1-2). By appealing once again to Hos 6:6 Jesus was calling for steadfast love rather than ritualism. "Son of Man" (v. 8) refers to Jesus, exemplifying God's Servant chosen to proclaim the kingdom in word and deed with authority (cf. 7:29). One recalls here Matt 9:6 that has already depicted the Son of Man as having authority.

By entering "their synagogue" (cf. 4:23; 9:35) Jesus has entered the Pharisees' sphere of influence. They now seek to entrap him in an indictable offense. According to the Law "everyone who profanes [the Sabbath] shall be put to death" (Exod 31:14). Because of Jesus' reputation for healing and his statement about mercy the Pharisees bring to him a man with a withered hand and put the question to him: "Is it lawful to heal on the sabbath?" (RSV). For them the answer is clearly in the negative. The man's life is in no immediate danger (*m. Yoma* 8:6), and his affliction was commonly regarded as the result of a divine curse (cf. Zech 11:17; 1 Kings 13:1-6). Jesus first points to the inconsistencies of his questioners' own practice (vv. 11-12). They can be concerned about their own property but not about another human being. Appropriately, Jesus uses the example of rescuing a sheep on the Sabbath since he saw his immediate task as gathering together the lost sheep of the house of Israel. It is lawful to do good on the Sabbath because steadfast love is the fulfilling of the Law (Hos 6:6; Matt 22:34-40). Jesus' act of healing is another sign of restoration for God's people, but the Pharisees are blind and have not understood the sign. Jesus' action provides the evidence they wanted and now they plot how to exact the penalty.

Jesus as Servant Israel (12:15-21)

Jesus' understanding of his mission and destiny is displayed here. He avoids promoting confrontation by departing, yet on the other hand Matthew shows that the time of Jesus' death remains in suspense and does not depend on the plotting of his enemies. Jesus' response to the Pharisees' opposition and plotting leads Matthew once again to remind the reader that Jesus is carrying out the role of Servant Israel. (See 8:17.) This is Matthew's longest quotation (Isa 42:1-4), and every verse has relevance for Jesus' mission in contrast to the attitude of the Pharisees. It is an expansion of the identification made of Jesus at his baptism (3:17) and later at his transfiguration (17:5). Jesus withdrew from the synagogue to avoid further needless confrontation, just as he had advised his disciples to do (7:6; 10:13-14). In contrast to the attitude of the Pharisees many follow him in faith, and he heals them all and once again orders that they are not to make him known (cf. 8:4; 9:30; 16:20; 17:9). As Isa 42:1-4 points out, God's Chosen One is to be revealed to the faithful (cf. 11:25-27) and eventually to the nations. Matthew makes slight changes to the quotation to emphasize various aspects of Jesus' mission as Servant. "He will proclaim justice to the Gentiles" is part of the Servant's goal to be a "light to the nations" (Isa 42:6). That "he will not break a bruised reed or quench a smoldering wick" has already been exemplified by Jesus' compassion on those seeking healing, particularly and most recently the man with a withered hand (vv. 9-13). In Jesus' mission as Servant the oppressed are being liberated and justice is made victorious.

Further Pharisaic Opposition (12:22-37)

This account of the Pharisaic accusation that Jesus casts out demons by the prince of demons corresponds to the healing of the dumb demoniac in 9:32-34 and the healing of the blind men in 9:27-31. The continued blindness of the Pharisees is in stark contrast to Jesus, as Servant Israel, opening "the eyes of the blind" (Isa 42:7). The Pharisees had often spoken of the future Messiah as the Son of David who would come to liberate Israel. While they saw this liberation as gaining independence from foreign domination "all the crowds" in their amazement at the healing of the demoniac and with their question, "Can this be the Son of David?" give witness to a different kind of liberation (cf. Isa 61:2). It is not so much the act of healing as it is the liberation from the covenant curses (cf. Deut 28:28-29; Isa 59:10) and from the forces of evil that are recognized by those who appeal to Jesus as Son of David (cf. 9:27; 20:30-31; 15:22; 21:9, 15). The Pharisees, however, see such a response as disgraceful, since one who breaks the Sabbath laws can only do his deeds by the power of Beelzebul (see 10:25) or Satan, the ruler of the forces of evil. The rabbis listed both profaning the Sabbath and sorcery as offenses deserving of death by stoning (*m. Sanh.* 7:4). Once again the power of Jesus is portrayed in his knowledge of the thoughts of his enemies. Jesus responds by pointing out the inconsistency of their logic; besides, how do they explain how members of their own party (lit. "your sons") carry out exorcisms (cf. Acts 19:13; Josephus, *Ant.* 8.46-48).

Jesus casts out demons "by the Spirit of God" (v. 28) as the faithful Servant upon whom the Spirit has been poured (Isa 42:1; 61:1). Here the Pharisees have come face to face with the kingdom. This is a call to them to open their eyes to the reality of Jesus' mission and to work with him rather than against him. To emphasize this Jesus alludes to Isa 49:22-25, where the Lord brings back to the restored kingdom the children of Israel who had been scattered among the nations. When the question is raised in that context whether the mighty nations will let them go, YHWH's response is: "Even the captives of the mighty shall be taken, and the prey of the tyrant be rescued; for I will contend with those who contend with you, and I will save your children." Through his healings Jesus has been binding the strong man and setting the captives free so that he might gather Israel into the kingdom. If the Pharisees work against Jesus they are contending with God. Part of the Servant's purpose was to gather scattered Israel together (Isa 49:5). Jesus is doing just that: gathering the lost sheep of the house of Israel (10:5; 15:24). The Pharisees, by working against Jesus, have aligned themselves with the tyrants and oppressors of the past and thus are working against the Spirit of God. This is the blasphemy against the Spirit that will not be forgiven (vv. 31-32). The Pharisees were well aware that blasphemy was also one of those grave offenses that called for death by stoning (Lev 24:16), but even such offenses against God and the people can be forgiven. Blasphemy against the Spirit—that is, deliberately resisting the working of God's Spirit and refusing to acknowledge the Spirit's power—is unforgivable. To say "a word against the Son of Man" is forgivable. Once again the representative title "Son of Man" is used as an alternative for the representative title "Servant of Yahweh" (cf. *1 Enoch* 46:4). One may fail to recognize that Jesus is God's Servant, but deliberately to reject the working of the Spirit is to put oneself irrevocably outside the kingdom. For the image of the tree and its fruit (vv. 33-35) see 7:15-20; 3:8, 10, and for good treasure see 6:19-21. These two verses, with no parallels in the other gospels, provide self-contained teaching about the connection of our words and the judgment to which we will be subjected. One will be justified or condemned by one's words, a position strongly consistent with scriptural teaching of old that every word uttered is of significance since it either manifests what is good or is pronounced in the service of evil.

This Evil Generation (12:38-45)

Scribes now join the Pharisees in confronting Jesus. They want a sign they can use to verify whether Jesus fits their criteria for the Son of David (cf. v. 23), but Jesus has already identified his messiahship as the Anointed Servant with many signs (11:2-5) and again with these recent healings (12:9-14, 22). "An evil and adulterous generation" (cf. 16:4; 17:17; 11:16) draws on common OT sayings (cf. Deut 1:35; 32:5). Faithlessness was depicted as adultery because the covenant was often described as a marriage relationship between YHWH and Israel (cf. Hos 2:16-20; Isa 1:21). Jesus offers "the sign of the prophet Jonah" because Jonah, symbolizing Israel, had tried to escape from the task God had given him because of intense dislike for Nineveh. Nineveh, the capital of the hated Assyrians, represents those foreigners most hated by the Israelites of old, and Jonah's reluctance illustrates Israel's failure to be a light to the nations; yet God intervened and through a traumatic experience for Jonah sent him to his task so that all Nineveh repented. So Israel's purpose would be carried out in spite of this faithless generation, and anyone hindering it would be judged by those nations. Nineveh thus serves for Matthew the double purpose of reminding the hearers of the mission to sinners and outsiders as well as foretelling the post-resurrection mission to the Gentiles.

Just as Jonah went through a death and resurrection experience, so the Son of Man, representing Israel, must do the same (v. 40; cf. Isa 53:8-11) in order to bring Israel to recognize and fulfill its purpose of witnessing to the nations. In this prediction of the death of the Son of Man we see once again that in looking for a sign in their search for the Messiah the Pharisees have not yet understood the heart of Jesus' messianic character, which is not that of the triumphant political figure of the Son of David, but here that of the Servant (depicted by Jonah) who undergoes suffering, death, and resurrection—all this more explicitly revealed by Jesus in Matt 16:21. "The heart of the earth" refers to the place of death, the grave (Jonah 1:17; 2:2; cf. Isa 53:9).

So the failure of this generation will be condemned by the nations (vv. 41-42) that repent and come to faith, typified by the people of Nineveh (Jonah 3:5-10) and the queen of Sheba (1 Kings 10:1-10). The "something" greater than Jonah and Solomon is Jesus proclaiming that the reign of God is at hand and calling for Israel to repent. The proclamation by Jesus in word and deed superseded the work of the Temple and its priesthood (12:6), and now supersedes that of the era of the prophets and kings.

The parable (vv. 43-45), seen against the background of vv. 22-29, is a warning to the one healed of demon-possession not to be misled by the scribes and Pharisees. This section is addressed to the same persons who first accused Jesus of sorcery. It is meant to bring Jesus' reply to a logical close: his accusers are under satanic influence. That the unclean spirit seeks rest but finds none is in the nature of the wicked (cf. Isa 48:22; 57:20; *1 Enoch* 63:6). Where there is no relationship with God, one is left open and unprotected to all kinds of destructive relationships.

Jesus' True Family (12:46-50)

Considering the growing opposition and hostility to Jesus' ministry, Jesus' mother and brethren have become rather concerned for his security and perhaps wish to encourage him to give up his mission. Jesus' commitment, however, is first to the reign of God (6:33; 10:34-39), so his response is to point to his disciples as his true family; those who in faith know God as their Father are brother and sister and mother to Jesus.

VII. Speaking in Parables: 13:1-52

The overriding issue pervading all these parables is the variety of responses to Jesus' preaching. For this reason they are at a most logical place in the gospel for they follow arguments, accusations, and condemnations—a variety of reactions against Jesus. Within the context of the narrative as a whole, opposition and hostility lead to a change of strategy. Jesus now begins to speak in parables.

A parable is always based on a simple picture, event, or relationship taken from daily life with an arresting feature by which the listener is challenged to enter into an active search for discovering deeper spiritual meaning in the simpler realities described. The disciple in this context as listener and believer is not expected to be a passive recipient of teaching but has the task of investigating its meaning on various levels, finding a new relevance or application amid the changing facets of human life. Therefore although it is plausible to assume that the parables have their origin in Jesus' original preaching, by their very nature they cannot be expected to be preserved and again delivered without being enriched in the course of oral transmission. With regard to every parable one must have open ears and eyes to see these same metaphors or similes applied to doctrinal and moral and personal questions in free and creative ways.

Parable of the Sowing of the Seed (13:1-9)

The introductory verse states that Jesus went out to the seashore and presented this parable to the large crowd that had gathered. That the boat makes a natural pulpit and the waterfront provides good acoustics are easily recognized. Jesus' sitting in relation to the crowd standing symbolizes a posture of teaching authority. The first parable describes the distribution of seeds by the sower falling in four different kinds of places with consequent results, explained in vv.

18-23. "Let anyone with ears listen" (cf. 11:15; 13:43) echoes the *shemaᶜ Israel* and the constant call in Isaiah for spiritual hearing (Isa 32:3; 43:8; 50:4, 5; 55:3). The incredible success of this crop, up to a hundredfold yield, manifests the eventual triumph of the kingdom even amidst the opposition that Jesus and the disciples have begun to experience. The image of the growth of a crop will be repeated again in the next two parables as a means of attempting to explain the nature and character of the kingdom, especially in light of the state of the kingdom during Jesus' preaching.

The Purpose of the Parables (13:10-17)

The disciples ask Jesus why he now speaks in parables to the crowds. "The secrets of the kingdom of heaven" (v. 11) are those "hidden things" that are to be revealed by the Servant (see above at 10:26; 11:27) and can only be understood by faith. Once again the Isaianic theme of spiritual blindness and deafness is emphatically raised with a quotation from Isa 6:9-10 (see above at 11:4). The technique of an anticipatory quotation is used for the sake of emphasis. As in Isaiah's text, Matthew treats the result or the bad consequence allowed by God as if it were divinely intended. If one sees in this a literally deliberate desire on God's part to confuse and condemn one raises doctrinal problems by imposing a perspective foreign to the prophet and the evangelist. It is the growing hostility and the deliberate refusal to understand Jesus' message that leads to this condemnation and rejection. The disciples are blessed (vv. 16-17) because they are able to witness and participate in the gathering of the faithful into God's kingdom, something that had been awaited by prophets and the righteous since the exile (see 10:41).

Interpretation of the Parable of the Sowing of the Seed (13:18-23)

The seed is described as "the word of the kingdom," synonymous with "good news of the kingdom" (4:23). Jesus, identified as the Son of Man in 13:37, is the sower, although in this parable the emphasis is on the seed and the soil, that is, the word and its reception by the hearers. The background to this is the spreading of the word in Isa 55:10-11, coming as it does after the invitation to the celebration of God's reign and the installation of the faithful as God's witness to the nations (Isa 55:1-5). So the seed on the path that is devoured by birds is the word that falls on the ears of the spiritually deaf and is soon snatched away by the evil one (cf. 12:43-45). The seed on rocky ground that soon withers and dies is the word that is received with initial enthusiasm at seeing the messianic works and hearing the good news, but as soon as there is opposition these hearers wither like grass in the heat of the day (cf. Isa 40:6-8, 24). The seed among thorns is the word that is understood initially by the hearer but is soon choked out by a selfish lifestyle. "Thorns" are a symbol for an unproductive, godless life (e.g., Isa 34:13; Jer 12:13). The seed that falls on good soil is the word that bears fruit in the lives of its hearers who receive it in faith and are transformed accordingly to be fruitful according to the different levels of their ability. All four types of hearers have been evident in the crowds who have come to hear Jesus. In the face of the growing opposition Jesus wants to assure the faithful that the word of God that stands forever will not return empty but will indeed accomplish God's purpose (Isa 55:11).

Three Parables and an Explanation (13:24-43)

Parable of the Weeds in the Wheat, 13:24-30

"The kingdom of heaven may be compared to . . ." describes some aspect of the kingdom without defining and thus limiting it. The parable is a response to the common belief that the messianic kingdom would only be established after the destruction of the wicked. It illustrates that the kingdom is already present with the germination of the seed that has fallen on good soil, that the kingdom is open to all, just as God sends rain and sunshine on good and evil (5:45), so all have opportunity to germinate and bear good fruit. "Weeds" in this parable probably refers to bearded darnel, a poisonous weed that looks very much like wheat until the ears form. In order to prevent contamination of the wheat in the winnowing process these weeds would have to be gathered first at the time of harvest. Only at the end of the harvest, that is, when all have had the opportunity to respond to the word, will the judgment take place (v. 30).

Parable of the Mustard Seed, 13:31-32

The smallness of the mustard seed was proverbial (cf. 17:20; *m. Nid.* 5:2) and is used here to contrast the small beginning of the kingdom with its ultimate growth. With all the hostility the beginning may seem small but the end result will inevitably be great. The mustard seed grows quickly to a full-grown shrub about three meters high. The "tree" with birds nesting in its branches is symbolic for a great kingdom (cf. Ezek 31:3-9; Dan 4:10-12, 20-22), particularly for the messianic kingdom (Ezek 17:22-24). According to Isa 60:21 and 61:3 God's faithful people are a "shoot" (cf. Isa 4:2; 11:1) of God's planting that would grow into "oaks of righteousness." Birds of the air that nest in its branches symbolize the openness of the kingdom to all, offering security and protection (cf. Ps 104:10-12, 16-17).

Parable of the Leaven, 13:33

This parable also describes how the kingdom will become great but adds to the picture the quiet and unassuming nature of its growth. Leaven quietly causes the dough to rise, so Jesus uses it as an illustration of the quiet growth of the kingdom going on within the hearts and lives of people. Three measures of wheat flour is an enormous quantity (about fifty pounds), enough for a large feast (cf. Gen 18:6) and once again emphasizes the enormous ecclesiastical growth from the word of God. To disciples witnessing growing opposition these were comforting parables.

Use of Parables, 13:34-35

As Jesus finishes addressing the crowds Matthew reiterates that Jesus uses parables so that his message is only revealed to those who seek it. In the quotation Matthew combines prophetic sayings with Ps 78:2. "What has been hidden" (cf. Isa 48:6-8) are revelations not previously known, the good news of God's restored kingdom. "From the foundation of the world" refers to the beginning of creation (cf. 2 Sam 22:16; Ps 18:16) and alludes specifically to the use of the phrase in Isa 40:21.

Explanation of the Weeds in the Wheat, 13:36-43

Returning to his house, Jesus now addresses only his disciples. "The one who sows the good seed is the Son of Man" who is also described as a chief representative of God's kingdom and divine judgment (v. 40), and as lord of the harvest (v. 41). He is the Righteous One who reveals the good news of the kingdom to those accounted righteous (Isa 53:11; *1 Enoch* 38:1-3). The "good seed" are those who have been influenced by the "word" (vv. 18-23) and bear good fruit. "The weeds are the children of the evil one" who opposes God's plan of salvation, those described in v. 19 (cf. 12:43-45). "The end of the age," a common phrase in Matthew (13:39, 40, 49; 24:3; 28:20) refers to the judgment as the end of the period of growth before the final consummation of the kingdom.

Much of the description of the judgment on the wicked (vv. 40-43, 50) has been colored by Mal 4:1-3 and Dan 3:6; *1 Enoch* 41:2; 54:1, 6. Here we read of the reign of the Son of Man, for "dominion and glory and kingship" are given to him (Dan 7:14) as he represents the heavenly Father's rule and judgment (cf. *1 Enoch* 62:2-7; Matt 16:27-28; 25:31-46). For this reason it is also referred to as "the kingdom of their Father" (v. 43). "The righteous will shine like the sun" (v. 43) picks up the imagery of God's brilliant presence coming upon the righteous (Isa 60:1-3, 19-21; cf. also Dan 12:3; *1 Enoch* 58:3, 6).

Three More Parables and a Conclusion (13:44-52)

The Hidden Treasure, 13:44

Finding such a treasure is everyone's fantasy but was not beyond the realm of possibility in Palestine. When people from Judah were sent into exile in 587 B.C.E. some would have buried their treasures in the hope of returning, but many never did. Discovering what has been "hidden" (see v. 35), that is, the kingdom that is now revealed, can change one's whole life and give it ultimate meaning. Once one discovers what the good news is all about and understands the word (v. 23) one is ready to give up everything else in order to have it and to participate in Jesus' discipleship and community.

The Pearl of Great Price, 13:45-46

Pearls were rarer in the ancient world and valued more highly than today. The discovery of the very finest pearl that superseded all others would be irresistible to a merchant. So also a person searching for the ultimate answers in life would give up all other ways in order to embrace the reign of God.

The Dragnet, 13:47-50

The dragnet with its floats on the top and weights on the bottom could be dropped by two boats and gradually dragged into shore, bringing with it all the fish of the enclosed area. Some of the catch would be inedible and some unclean (according to Lev 11:9-12), and these would have to be thrown back while the good, edible fish would be put into containers. The main point here is the same as that in the parable of the weeds in the wheat: the separation between the evil and the righteous takes place after the catch has been brought ashore, not before. The kingdom is open to the good and the evil. It is left to God on the day of judgment to separate the good from the evil.

Conclusion

The Scribe of the kingdom, 13:51-52. Jesus now asks his disciples a very significant question: "Have you understood all this?" This is significant because the whole chapter has dealt with understanding the word (vv. 13, 14, 15, 19, 23), what has been hidden but now is revealed. The disciples' answer is an emphatic "Yes," and so the word does not return empty but accomplishes its purpose (cf. Isa 55:11). "Scribe" is used here for one who studies the word, in this case the disciples. They bring out the "new things" that have now been declared (Isa 42:9; 48:6-8). The message of the kingdom now takes precedence over the old and gives it new meaning.

VIII. Rejection and Acceptance: 3:53–16:12

Failure to understand on the part of some has led to a growing polarization even among Jesus' own people.

Rejection at Nazareth (13:53-58)

Because of hardening resistance this is the last time Matthew mentions Jesus preaching in a synagogue. The people marvel at Jesus' preaching and healing as demonstration of the kingdom. They recognize him as the son of Joseph the carpenter and Mary and identify his brothers as James, Joseph, Simon, and Judas (cf. 12:46-49; John 2:12; Acts 1:14; 1 Cor 9:5), and his sisters as living among them. (For traditional Catholic teaching on whether Jesus had blood brothers and sisters, see above at 1:25.) James later became leader of the congregation in Jerusalem (Acts 12:17; 15:13; 21:18; 1 Cor 15:7; Jas 1:1) and is referred to as "the Lord's brother" by Paul (Gal 1:19; 2:9, 12). Judas may be identified with "Jude" the "brother of James" (Jude 1). John 7:5 tells us that the brothers of Jesus did not believe until after the resurrection, but they later took part in the early mission (1 Cor 9:5). Closing out any recognition of Jesus' works, the townspeople placed their own obstruction in their way to God (cf. Isa 57:14). Thus Jesus as God's prophet experiences rejection even in Nazareth (cf. Jer 11:21; 12:6).

Death of John the Baptist (14:1-12)

Herod the tetrarch is Herod Antipas, ruler over Galilee and Perea from 4 B.C.E. to 39 C.E. Hearing reports of Jesus' mighty works and that he was regarded as a prophet (13:57; 21:46), as John was (v. 5), Herod feared that Jesus was John raised from the dead. He had put John to death at the urging of his wife Herodias, who according to Matthew was formerly his brother Philip's wife. Josephus tells us that Herod had John imprisoned because of his great influence over the populace. Matthew gives the religious reason: John's criticism of Herod's breaking of the law by marrying his half-brother Philip's wife (cf. Lev 18:6; 20:21). Herodias had used Roman law to divorce Philip, an act not valid in Jewish law. Antipas had divorced his first wife, the daughter of the Nabatean King Aretas, to marry Herodias, his own niece. Herod's reluctance to kill John may represent a parallel to Pilate's reluctance to hand Jesus over to death. "The daughter of Herodias" (v. 6) was still in her teens when she asked for the head of John the Baptist. Making a foolish oath in front of his guests put Herod in a position where he felt he had to fulfill the bizarre request (v. 9). John was beheaded without trial.

Feeding of the Five Thousand (14:13-21)

The news of John's death leads Jesus to withdraw from the crowds and seek a private place for prayer and reflection, but while Jesus goes by boat, the crowds follow by land. In spite of the growing danger from both religious and political leaders the work of the kingdom continues. "He had compassion on them, and healed their sick" (RSV) recalls the promise of the restoration in Isa 49:13, just as feeding the hungry fulfills Isa 49:10 (cf. also 58:10). Jesus is not simply satisfying need here but celebrating the kingdom coming to the powerless and afflicted. Acting as host, Jesus orders the people to recline as they would at a banquet. He then takes the food and looking up to heaven (Ps 123:1) blesses God, breaks the bread, and gives it to the disciples for distribution to the crowd. There are strong similarities here with the last supper Jesus later celebrated with his disciples (26:26-29). Both are anticipations of the messianic banquet, feasts celebrating the reign of God (Isa 55:1-2). "All ate and were filled" recalls the feeding of the children of Israel in the wilderness (Exod 16:4-12) as this is also a "deserted place" (vv. 13, 15). The phrase itself is a common one symbolizing covenant blessing (Deut 8:10; 11:15; cf. Matt 5:6). The twelve disciples filled the bags they had carried with them, indicating the abundance of blessing given in the invitation to the celebration of the kingdom (Isa 55:1-3). "Five thousand men, besides women and children" was a typical style of counting Israel in the wilderness (cf. Exod 12:37; Num 11:21). This feeding miracle thus is the celebration of the restoration of the reign of God in the lives of God's people.

Walking on the Water (14:22-33)

This account underscores the authority of Jesus in calming the storm (8:23-27) with the added feature of walking on the water. After having urged the disciples to get into their boat and return to the other side, Jesus dismissed the crowd and finally had time alone to ascend the mountain and speak to his heavenly Father during the night. Later, "early in the morning" (literally "during the fourth watch of the night" [3 A.M. to 6 A.M.]) Jesus came to the storm-tossed disciples walking on the sea. The early hour of the morning appears in the Psalms as the time of God's favor (cf. Pss 90:14; 143:8; 92:2; 5:3; 88:13). As God has control over the sea and calms its waters (Pss 89:10-11; 107:23-32) and rescues God's people by making "a path through the mighty waters" (Ps 77:16-20; Isa 43:16; 51:10), Jesus bears witness to possessing God's saving power here (cf. Isa 43:10,12). The disciples, thinking Jesus is an apparition, cry out in fear (cf. Ps 107:28). Jesus' response is, literally, "I am. Do not be afraid," recalling those divine assurances to a people of little faith in Second Isaiah: "Do not fear, for I am with you, do not be afraid, for I am your God . . . . It is I who say to you, 'Do not fear, I will help you'" (Isa 41:10, 13, 14).

Recognizing Jesus, Peter responds in faith with initial excitement at Jesus' presence and power. Jesus' call and Peter's walk on the sea show him, as the representative of the Twelve, participating in Jesus' mysterious power and might while on his way. When distracted by the wind he begins to sink. This episode of faltering is symbolic of Peter's denial of Jesus in the Passion story (Matt 26:69-75); at the same time it represents any Christian's way of walking to Christ amidst a storm: we are supported by the Lord's power and sink on account of our own shaken faith. The reader is expected to identify with Peter, crying out: "Lord, save me!" (8:25; Ps 69:1-3). Jesus, reaching out and taking him by the hand, saves him. "You of little faith" is a common phrase in Matthew (6:30-33; 8:26; 16:8; 17:20) that Jesus uses of his disciples who have not yet learned to trust implicitly in the power of God's reign and in the presence of that power in Jesus. "Doubt," a word found only here and in 28:17, means "hesitate." The emphasis is on the need for an unwavering faith in the Lord's power to save. The disciples show their adoration and wonder with the exclamation: "Truly you are the Son of God," thus acknowledging not only that Jesus is that true Servant and witness of God announced at his baptism (3:17) and even acknowledged by the demonic powers (4:3, 6; 8:29), but also deepening their vision of the divine character of this Son who has authority even over the sea and the wind.

Healings in Gennesaret (14:34-36)

People of Gennesaret, a region on the western shore south of Capernaum, aware of Jesus' healing power, gather all their sick and beg "that they might touch even the fringe of his cloak," like the woman with the hemorrhage (see above at 9:20). In spite of opposition and impending danger from the religious and political leaders, the common people still show faith in God's power and seek the kingdom.

Tradition of the Elders and True Purity (15:1-20)

Jesus' reputation has also reached Jerusalem where religious leaders have become concerned. Pharisees and scribes come as an official delegation to inquire why Jesus does not follow their understanding of the Law. The delegation attacks Jesus' disciples as a way of getting at him. "The tradition of the elders" refers to those oral traditions, later written down in the Mishnah, that were the scribal interpretations of OT laws, setting down elaborate rules that often went beyond those laws. The accusation that the disciples did not wash their hands before eating was based on ritual purity laws required of the priesthood (Exod 30:17-21) that the Pharisees had imposed on everyone. Jesus accuses the Pharisees of putting their tradition above the commandment of God, transgressing one of the basic covenant stipulations (Exod 20:12; Deut 5:16), which required the death penalty (Exod 21:17; Lev 20:9). They were using their traditions to negate obligations to parents. The "gift" or "offering" refers to a specific legal tradition discussed at length in the Mishnah *(Nedarim)* referred to as *qorbān*. It refers to the practice of making a vow declaring one's goods or property as dedicated to God while continuing to use it. Such a vow was regarded as binding (Num 30:2; Deut 23:21-23) and as such could have been used as a means for evading financial obligations to parents. To do so was to place another tradition above the basic covenant law. Consequently, Jesus describes those who do so as hypocrites (v. 7; see above at 6:2) and quotes Isa 29:13, alluded to before (11:25-30). Then, turning to the crowds, he calls upon them to "listen and understand"—significant words since what Jesus has to say is hidden from the "wise and the intelligent" (11:25; Isa 29:14; cf. 6:9-10). In the eyes of God real impurity comes from within a person, not from the outside (v. 11).

The disciples express concern that the delegation from Jerusalem has taken offense at what Jesus has said, but Jesus, alluding to the parable of the weeds among the wheat (13:24-30, 36-44), points out that these "leaders" are not of God's planting (Isa 60:21; 61:3). They are still spiritually blind like the leaders in Isa 56:10-12, and those who follow them will share in their fate. Peter did not understand what Jesus had said in v. 11 and requests an explanation, so Jesus answers with frankness and clarity: "Do you not see that whatever goes into the mouth enters the stomach, and goes out into the sewer? But what comes out of the mouth proceeds from the heart, and this is what defiles" (vv. 17-18). A person is defiled by the evil in his or her own heart and not by omission of purification rites. All human regulations become subordinate to love for God and for one's neighbor as oneself (22:34-40).

The Canaanite Woman (15:21-28)

Going into the district of Tyre and Sidon, Jesus is confronted by a Gentile woman whose persistent faith is in stark contrast to the blindness of the Jerusalem leaders. Following upon the story of the petty insistence upon dietary laws by the scribes and Pharisees, this story affirms the possibility of a mission to the Gentiles that is consistent with Jesus' own message of divine salvation. "Canaanite" is a term that appears anachronistic, since Canaanites were the original inhabitants of this land but had long since disappeared. However, Greek traders had taken up residence in this part of the world; they were generally despised by Jews because of unethical trade practices (cf. Joel 3:4-8; Zech 9:13) and so were called "Canaanites" (cf. the Hebrew of Zech 11:7, 11; 14:21). Matthew uses this derogatory term to heighten the contrast between the "pious" religious leaders and this foreign woman. "Have mercy on me, Lord, Son of David" is virtually the same cry as that of the blind men in 9:27 and in 20:30-31 (see on 9:27 and 12:23). The Greek woman, knowing of Jesus' fame as a healer and having heard speculation about his being the Messiah, believes that Jesus can heal her demon-possessed daughter. After this striking confession, that "he did not answer her at all" is even more striking. This is a test of faith, but the disciples are embarrassed by her persistent cries and plead with Jesus to dismiss her (cf. 14:15). Jesus' response to the disciples, "I was sent only to the lost sheep of the house of Israel" (see 10:6), emphasizes that Jesus' primary mission is to gather all the faithful together into God's kingdom so that they might become a people-covenant and light to the nations (cf. Isa 49:1-6). Jesus is much more willing to listen to the woman than the disciples, who are ready to reject her without a hearing. Said in the hearing of the woman, Jesus' response is a test of her faith. She continues to plead for help. Jesus now uses a derogatory stereotype used by Jews of Gentiles, but using the diminutive form, "pups," to tone down the harshness of the prejudicial term. The "children" are the children of Israel. The woman shows no resentment and extends Jesus' metaphor into a Gentile context, saying that even the pups get the crumbs that fall from their masters' table. With such a response the woman has passed every test. Jesus praises her great faith, and her daughter is healed from that hour (cf. 8:13). Here a woman successfully ignores the stigma put on her and her people to claim a place in the household of God. The healing of her daughter is a sign that the reign of God belongs not to those with ethnic or social status, but to those of great faith.

Feeding of the Four Thousand (15:29-39)

There are many similarities here to the feeding of the five thousand (14:13-21) but the differences intensify the sense of a messianic celebration of God's reign. Returning to the north shore of the Sea of Galilee, Jesus goes up on the mountain and sits down, just as he had done for his initial proclamation of the kingdom in 5:1-2. As in that instance, this action has definite allusions to Isa 40:9-11 and 52:7, for now "he will feed his flock like a shepherd" (Isa 40:11) as a celebration of the kingdom (Isa 55:1-2). Prophetic tradition had spoken about the gathering of scattered Israel to God's holy mount, Zion, and God caring for and feeding them there (cf. Ezek 34:11-16, 25-31; Isa 25:6-10). Matthew sees this now taking place in Galilee rather than Judea. To disabilities previously mentioned, "lame" is added. This is done to draw into the picture the promise in Ezekiel that God will gather the scattered sheep, the lost, the strayed, the injured, and the weak. Then, as in Ezekiel, God will heal and feed them (Ezek 34:13-16). Witnessing all these healings, the crowds "praised the God of Israel," a divine title common in the OT (cf. particularly Isa 29:23; 45:3, 15; 48:1-2). The fact that the people have been with Jesus "for three days" is evidence of their zeal for the kingdom. Once again Jesus' compassion on them echoes Isa 49:13 (cf. Matt 9:36; 14:14). Again (cf. 14:19) the organization of a meal is followed by the triple actions of blessing, breaking, and giving paralleled later in the Last Supper. The seven "baskets" are different from the wicker baskets in 14:20 and the term may refer to larger, more flexible containers. While the numbers of baskets and people differ from the previous feeding story, the message remains the same: Jesus has begun the celebration of the kingdom in the hearts and lives of the people. The repetition serves to underscore and heighten the message.

Leaven of the Pharisees and Sadducees (16:1-12)

Now even the Sadducees, the priestly party of Jerusalem, make common cause with Pharisees to put Jesus to the test by asking for a sign from heaven (cf. 12:38-42). These two groups are rarely depicted together in the NT, for good reason. In Jesus' time they represented opposing positions in Israel's political and religious life. Opponents of the Pharisees, the Sadducees more readily collaborated with the Romans. Doctrinally they rejected the resurrection, a belief of importance to Pharisees. The joint resistance of such unlikely "bedfellows" to Jesus' teaching and signs is the issue on which the gospel focuses here. They seek to entrap him. Verses 2-3 are an indictment of those who claim to foretell the weather but cannot read the barometer of their own lives and see the warning signs in their own society. Again the only sign they are given is the sign of Jonah, emphasizing their need to make a complete turnaround in order to become what they are called to be, a witness and light to the nations. Like Jonah, they are heading in the opposite direction.

IX. The Revelation of Who Jesus Is: 16:13–17:27

Revealing the Identity of the Son of Man (16:13-20)

At Caesarea Philippi, a town at the foot of Mount Hermon and once the northernmost point of the land of Israel, Jesus puts the question to his disciples: "Who do people say that the Son of Man is?" Because Jesus has been using this title as a self-designation (8:20; 9:6; 10:23; 11:19; 12:8, 32, 40; 13:37, 41) it is now time for his disciples to know who Jesus really is.

The title "Son of Man" functions here, as elsewhere in Matthew, as Jesus' peculiar self-designation. Nevertheless, it was an enigmatic title that probably was perplexing to Jesus' hearers. Some may have related it to Daniel 7 and perhaps even to the Parables of Enoch (*1 Enoch* 37-71) where the Son of Man is described as the one who will remove kings and mighty ones from their thrones (46:1-5).

The answer to the first question ("Who do people say . . .") is somewhat ambivalent. Popular opinion identified Jesus with some revered prophets of the past. Elijah was greatly venerated by the people, and having been taken up to God in a miraculous way (cf. 2 Kings 2:11) he was expected to return as precursor of the Messiah (cf. Mal 4:5-6). According to Matt 14:2, Herod Antipas took Jesus for John the Baptist risen from the dead. Matthew includes, with the Jewish tradition (cf. *Paralip. Jer.*), the name of Jeremiah, the suffering prophet *par excellence,* who was assumed into heaven, pointing forward to the first prediction of the Passion (v. 21).

When Jesus asks his disciples, "Who do you say that I am?" Simon Peter answers: "You are the Messiah (= Anointed One), the Son of the living God." It is Peter who speaks, but all the disciples are addressed by Jesus and this highlights Peter's role as the spokesperson or representative for the disciples (cf. 19:27; 26:35, 40). Peter identifies the Son of Man mentioned in Jesus' question with both "the Messiah" and "the Son of the living God." This confession does not change the meaning of the expression "Son of Man" but affirms that Jesus, the one who so designates himself, is to be regarded as Messiah and Son of God.

The term Anointed One ("Christ" or "Messiah"), apart from the infancy narrative, has been mentioned by Matthew only in 11:1-6, where it clearly refers to the Servant who brings good news to the afflicted (11:5; Isa 61:1). Peter is affirming that Jesus as the Son of Man is carrying out that role not as the "Son of David" but as the "Son of the living God." This title is given to the faithful of Israel in Hos 1:10, but in this context it will take on a new meaning. As Son of Man Jesus is Son of God/Servant Israel come to gather the faithful into the kingdom so that they may carry out God's purpose to save the nations.

Verses 17-19 form a neat unit. The words of Jesus form three strophes (one for each verse) and each strophe contains three lines. The first line of each strophe expresses a new theme ("Blessed are you . . . ," "And I tell you . . . ," "I will give you the keys . . ."), and the second and third lines develop the theme in antithetic propositions. Now Jesus no longer asks questions, but makes a series of statements. In regard to subject matter there are actually three different themes: God's revelation, Peter as the "rock," and the keys to God's kingdom.

(1) Simon Peter has confessed Jesus to be the Christ, the Son of God. Now Jesus takes up Peter's confession and shows its implications. Jesus begins with a beatitude ("Blessed are you . . .") because full knowledge of the dignity of Jesus and of the mystery of his person does not come from below, but from above. The reason is given in Matt 11:27: no one but the Son knows the Father, and no one but the Father knows the Son; therefore only the Father could have made known to Peter the full measure of Jesus' divine sonship. This explains why the Son of God cannot be revealed to Peter by "flesh and blood" but only by the Father who is in heaven (Gal 1:12, 16; *1 Enoch* 62:7). In this way the text makes clear that Jesus set Peter aside to function as "rock" on the basis of his correct answer to Jesus' question, an answer that was supplied to Peter by the Father.

(2) As response to Peter's answer Jesus says: "you are Peter *(Petros)* and on this rock *(petra)* I will build my church *(ekklēsia).*" In Matt 16:13-20 many phrases reflect an Aramaic background, and the play on Simon's title becomes clearer in Aramaic. Jesus calls Simon *"Petros",* the Greek translation of the Aramaic word for "rock," *kēphāʾ,* the name given to Simon by Jesus. Paul refers to Peter by name as "Cephas" (Gal 2:11). "Rock" is often a designation for God as the only foundation for one's life (Isa 17:10; 44:8; but cf. Isa 51:1-2 where "rock" refers to Abraham). As the conveyor of divine revelation Peter himself, insofar as he is the one who bears witness to Jesus' true identity, is the rock on which Jesus will now build the community of the faithful. The image of Peter as the "rock" is best understood in light of

the parable of the wise man who "built his house on rock" (7:24). The word *ekklēsia,* used only here and in 18:17, is the equivalent of the Hebrew *qāhāl,* used for the whole assembly of the faithful (cf. Gal 1:13). According to *1 Enoch* 62:8, after the Son of Man has been revealed to the holy and chosen ones "the congregation of the holy ones shall be planted [cf. Isa 60:21] and all the chosen ones shall stand before him" (cf. *1 Enoch* 38). Jesus will now build up this restored community of the faithful (Isa 57:14-15; 61:4; cf. *1 Enoch* 53:6). "And the gates of Hades [death] will not prevail against it," picking up the imagery of Isa 28:15-19 and 38:10, emphasizes that it will stand forever against all the forces of death and evil because God has made with the members of this restored community an everlasting covenant (Isa 55:3) and they will remain with the Son of Man forever (cf. Jer 15:19-21; *1 Enoch* 62:13-16).

(3) "I will give you the keys of the kingdom" uses the image of responsibility pictured in Isa 22:15-25. As in that passage, Peter is given the responsibility of a servant who will look after the master's household in tune with the master's wishes, but also with a responsibility and freedom of personal discernment. The image of binding and loosing should be understood first of all as belonging to the semantic field of legal obligations. Thus Peter receives the role of imposing and canceling obligations. These are not specified further, but include all we "owe" to God and one another. This is why in 18:18 the same image applies to the specific issue of forgiving sins. The image may also be thought of in terms of proclaiming good news of the kingdom which was often expressed in terms of "loosing the bonds of injustice," "proclaiming liberty to the captives and the release to the prisoners" (cf. Isa 42:7; 49:9; 58:6; 61:1). However, it also involved binding those without a wedding garment (Matt 22:11-14; cf. Isa 61:10). In other words, like the steward of Isa 22:22, Peter (and the faithful in 18:18) has the responsibility of opening the door of the kingdom to those who sincerely seek it but closing it to those who would destroy or abuse the bonds of community. What Peter "binds" and "looses" now on earth will be ratified by God ("in heaven"). The Church is therefore not identified with the future kingdom, but in Matthew the relationship becomes very close. It is significant that the keys of the kingdom are not mentioned in 18:18, where the power of binding and loosing is extended to all the apostles.

The identity of the Son of Man as the Anointed One of Isa 61:1 has been revealed to the disciples (Matt 11:1-5), but because the term is so easily misunderstood the disciples are not to tell anyone that Jesus is "the Anointed One."

Implications of the Identity of the Son of Man (16:21-28)

Now that his purpose and mission have been revealed, Jesus can speak about the shadow side of the Servant role: his impending suffering, death, and resurrection. The passion prediction lays emphasis on the necessity of this death and resurrection. Israel had suffered and died as a nation in the exile but had never really fulfilled the resurrection of Isa 53:10-11 (cf. Ezek 37:1-14) or its purpose as Servant Israel in saving the nations.

"The elders and chief priests and scribes" in Jerusalem made up the membership of the Sanhedrin, the powerful advisory council that influenced many of the actions and attitudes in Jerusalem. Jesus must suffer and "on the third day be raised" just as Jonah was delivered after being in the "belly of Sheol" for three days (Jonah 1:17; 2:2; cf. Matt 12:40) and Israel was to be raised on the third day to be children of the living God (Hos 1:10; 6:2-3). Not understanding, Peter begins to chide Jesus. He can see the victory ahead but cannot comprehend the requisite suffering and death that would lead to it. Jesus' response is decisive. "Get behind me, Satan!" was a sharp reminder that by not considering what was God's plan Peter was playing the role of tempter. As such he had become a stumbling block in front of Jesus instead of an obedient disciple behind. Peter, again representing the disciples, revolts against this vision of the Son of Man and thus anticipates his own failure after the arrest of Jesus. The evangelist appears to have intentionally created a contrast about Peter for the reader to keep in sight by exposing the apostle's utter failure to understand the necessity for Jesus' suffering and death.

To be a follower of Jesus means to surrender oneself totally to God and be ready to follow Jesus in every aspect of the Servant role, even to carrying a cross. The teaching of this section has been anticipated in the words about martyrdom in 10:38-39. There can be no renewal without a dying to the old ways of thinking. True discipleship is lived in the light of the coming judgment where those who have lost their lives for Jesus' sake will find them amid the blessings that accompany the abundance of life with the Father in the kingdom (v. 27). Jesus as the Son of Man will be placed on the throne of glory to carry out judgment in God's name (cf. Dan 7:13, 14, 27; *1 Enoch* 45:3; 55:4). That some of the disciples standing there will see him coming in his kingdom (cf. Dan 7:13-14) during their lifetime is a prediction that they will witness Jesus' vindication in the resurrection and his coming as the triumphant Son of Man when he gives his enthronement speech in 28:18-20. The judgment that is soon to come upon Jerusalem is the beginning of the judgment of the Son of Man (cf. 24:1-8).

The Transfiguration of Jesus (17:1-13)

The transfiguration draws on many OT allusions to portray Jesus as the Servant/Son of Man who will now be revealed to be Son of God, superseding Moses and Elijah. The precise time, "six days later," connects the scene to the revelation of Jesus as the Servant/Son of Man in the previous chapter and is an allusion to Moses, who was on Mount Sinai for six days before God called to him out of the cloud (Exod 24:16). Matthew thus alerts the reader to the coming divine revelation of Jesus as God's beloved Son (17:5). That "his face shone like the sun," as well as the brightness of his garments, shows that Jesus is in the presence of God and is reflecting that brilliance as promised in Isa 60:1-3, 19-20, just as Moses had reflected the brilliance of God at Mount Sinai (Exod 34:29-35). Moses and Elijah both had come into God's presence on Mount Sinai, were messengers of divine revelation, and were regarded as the great religious leaders of Israel (cf. Mal 4:4-6). Moreover, both had been taken up to heaven. Peter excitedly speaks about building three booths, the temporary shelters for the feast of Booths, symbols of celebration and rejoicing before God (Deut 16:13-15). In post-exilic times the feast of Booths became associated with looking forward in hope to the restoration of the kingdom (cf. Isa 62:8-12; Zech 14:16-21). Peter wants to build three booths to honor Jesus, Moses, and Elijah equally. Before Peter is finished speaking the divine voice speaks from the cloud to correct Peter's assertion by repeating exactly the divine declaration made at Jesus' baptism (see 3:17) with the addition of the words "listen to him!" These words, taken from Deut 18:15, point to Jesus as the prophet who supersedes Moses. In the past Elijah was sometimes regarded as that prophet. Now Jesus supersedes both as the Servant *par excellence.* The bright cloud symbolizes the brilliant presence of God (cf. Exod 13:22; 24:15-17) as God comes bringing light and brightness in the kingdom (Isa 4:5-6). As they descend the mountain Jesus commands the disciples to tell no one of the vision "until after the Son of Man has been raised from the dead." It is only after the resurrection that people will be able to understand the full import of the vision when they "see the Son of Man coming in his kingdom" (16:28). The scribes had taught that Elijah would come to restore the covenant and herald the day of judgment (Mal 4:5-6; Sir 48:10). Jesus acknowledges that the scribes were right to expect Elijah, but they did not recognize him when he came in the person of John the Baptist. Jesus could expect no better from them, for already their opposition had made it evident that the Son of Man would suffer at their hands.

The Power of Faith (17:14-20)

Coming to the crowd and the rest of the disciples, Jesus is confronted by a man with a deep concern for his epileptic son who is self-destructive. The disciples had not been able to do anything for him in spite of the fact that they had been sent out earlier to preach and heal (10:1, 8). There is a contrast here between the exhilarating experience on the top of the mountain and this lack of faith below it. Moses had also experienced Israel's lack of faith when he came down from the theophany on Sinai (Exodus 32). Jesus expresses his exasperation at this lack of faith by using phrases Moses had used to describe the faithlessness of Israel (Deut 32:5, 20); then he expels the demon and the boy is healed. Later, when the disciples are alone with Jesus, they ask him why they were unable to expel the demon. Jesus' response is: "Because of your little faith," a phrase he has used before (6:30; 8:26; 14:31). "Faith" is both receptive and active because it expresses a relationship with God that is reflected in relationships with others. This is why Jesus draws on the proverbial statement in Isa 54:10 when he says that if they have faith the size of a mustard seed (see 13:31) they will be able to move mountains.

Jesus Again Speaks of His Impending Death and Resurrection (17:22-23)

"As they were gathering in Galilee" suggests a coming together of a larger group to plan the pilgrimage to Jerusalem for the Passover. Ever since the transfiguration the flow of events has pointed to the final days in Jerusalem. Another aspect is also increasingly gaining the central position, namely Jesus' full identity as Son of God. So once again (see 16:21) Jesus alerts his followers to what is going to happen there. While he must suffer and die, the emphasis is again on the resurrection, for this is the vindication of the Servant/Son of Man (Isa 52:13; 53:10). The disciples are greatly distressed because they still have not understood why Jesus must suffer and because they are not sure what part they will play in it (cf. 16:24-26).

Paying the Temple Tax (17:24-27)

The half-shekel Temple tax, collected in Galilee prior to Passover, was an annual tax taken of all Jewish males over twenty years of age (*m. Seqal.* 1:1-3; 2:1) to pay for the regular public and festival-day sacrifices. The amount was based on Exod 30:11-16 and was more than ample. Since all were expected to pay this half-shekel it became a way of identifying oneself as a member of the Jewish community. Consequently most Jewish males paid it, even if they were not concerned about the sacrificial cultus or the Temple in Jerusalem. "Does your teacher not pay the temple tax?" may have been asked of Peter because there was some question whether priests and rabbis were expected to pay. Since they will be going to Jerusalem for the Passover, Peter expects that Jesus will pay. When Jesus arrives he raises the question with Peter as to the validity of the tax. In secular kingdoms rulers do not charge family members customs duty or poll-taxes. Peter, who confessed that Jesus was Son of God, must now reflect on a dilemma: if Jesus is the Son of God he must not be expected to pay for his Father's house. That the sons are free constitutes the principle that implies that the Son of God is free from the Temple tax. The implication goes beyond Jesus' relationship to the Father; Christians, especially within the context of Matthew's Jewish Christian community, should be free from obligations to the Temple. The whole Temple sacrificial cultus is brought into question once again (cf. Hos 6:6). However, in order not to cause anyone to stumble through lack of understanding Jesus complies with the custom, and Peter is told to cast a hook into the sea and find the money for the tax for both of them in the first fish he catches.

X. Living in the Messianic Community: 18:1-35

Greatness of the Little Ones (18:1-20)

Receiving the kingdom means entering into an intimate relationship with the heavenly Father, each person being equally precious to God. So when the disciples ask about status and rank, the kind of hierarchy common in the secular world, Jesus' response is to put a young child into their midst as an object lesson: those who belong to the kingdom see themselves as children of the heavenly Father (cf. Isa 63:16; 64:8), for only as such can one enter the kingdom. The only status one has is the status given by the heavenly Father to all his children.

True greatness comes through being in a dependent and trusting relationship in solidarity with Jesus as God's Son through whom God is revealed (cf. 25:31-46). For this reason, to cause one such disciple to stumble is a very serious matter. Disciples are once again referred to as little ones (10:42; 18:10, 14; 25:40, 45; cf. 11:25), for it is when they are the least that they are, paradoxically, the greatest (cf. Jer 31:34; Isa 60:22). To cause someone to stumble is to cause that relationship with God to be severed and the person lost, the greatest evil incurring the greatest punishment (cf. Isa 57:14). The millstone, a large heavy stone worked by donkey-power, tied to someone's neck and cast into the sea graphically depicts the seriousness of the situation for the evildoer as well (cf. Jer 51:63-64).

Stumbling blocks (v. 7) may be necessary to test and refine the faithfulness of the righteous (cf. Mal 3:3-4) but this does not excuse the action of one who causes another to stumble (cf. 26:24). Using hyperbole (see 5:29-30) Jesus emphasizes as a matter of life and death the need for the disciple to overcome stumbling blocks and avoid those who cause them. One needs to be on constant watch to get rid of those obstructions one finds within oneself. In contrast to the priestly law (Lev 21:16-24) Jesus points out that what is important is to be spiritually whole, to enter into life with God in God's kingdom.

All disciples are children of God no matter how little (v. 10) they may be. Even the most insignificant are not to be despised because they come under God's special protection and care. The parable of the lost sheep (vv. 12-13) summarizes Jesus' mission to seek after the lost sheep of the house of Israel (10:6; 15:24) and gather them into the kingdom. The exile had been described as God's people being like lost sheep, scattered on the mountain, afflicted and oppressed by their leaders (Jer 50:6; Ezek 34:1-10). The promise given by the prophets was that God would seek out the lost, bring back those who had strayed, and gently lead them (Jer 23:1-4; 31:10; Ezek 34:11-24; Isa 40:11; Zech 10:2-3). The will of God is that no one from the people should be lost, and God's children are to have the same loving concern toward those who stray, to restore them to a full relationship in God's community. Traditional doctrine about guardian angels has been attached to Matt 18:10 for centuries. This text implies that, in solidarity with the whole created world, God is committed to every human being's rescue; that is, the divine will for salvation neglects no human being. In the context of the verse this means in particular that by allowing sinners to be lost the Church community would fail to embrace an intention held in unison by the whole heavenly world; this attitude would clearly be in conflict with discipleship.

The next verses (15-18) speak of how someone who belongs to the kingdom deals with the sin of a brother or sister in the light of the Father's concern that not one should perish. The goal is to win back one's brother or sister lest he or she stumble or cause others to stumble. Consequently, motivated by love and concern, one speaks between oneself and the other alone (cf. Lev 19:17-18). If the brother or sister still persists in the sin, then the aid of "one or two others" should be enlisted, not as witnesses in a trial (cf. Deut 17:6; 19:15), but in order to urge him or her to return to faithfulness. If the brother or sister still will not listen, the disciple must tell it "to the church," the community of those who belong to the kingdom. The whole purpose of this action is to remove every stumbling block, to bring back the strayed into fellowship with the whole community. If that fails, however, "let such a one be to you as a Gentile and a tax-collector"—a common proverbial phrase indicating those outside the kingdom (cf. 5:46-47). The purpose of this action is still to win back the one who has strayed. This is how God's children carry out the responsibility of the keys of the kingdom. The words addressed to Peter in 16:19, "whatever you bind on earth will be bound in heaven, and whatever you loose on earth will be loosed in heaven," are now addressed to the Church, the whole community called by Jesus (v. 18). It spells out the divine authority backing up certain actions taken by the community through its leaders as they "exclude" and "include", impose and cancel obligations, state guilt and forgiveness. These are no mere human acts, for divine acts (taken "in heaven") will authorize and validate them. The emphasis nevertheless remains on bringing the good news to the lost rather than on any disciplinary action. In light of the above, vv. 19-20 should be interpreted as the divine affirmation of the action of God's servants acting in concert with Jesus, the Servant *par excellence.* Jesus' presence among his people to lead and guide provides divine assurance that the concerns on which two agree are motivated by the will of their heavenly Father (v. 14; cf. Mal 3:16-18).

Belonging to the Kingdom: In Forgiveness (18:21-35)

The concern over another's sin in vv. 15-17 was motivated by a desire to remove any stumbling block from the person and the community. There is no place for personal retaliation because one always lives in the forgiving love of the Father (Isa 40:2; 43:25) and so reflects that forgiving love to others. Peter's offer to forgive "seven times" is in response to Jesus' teaching and in contrast with the sevenfold vengeance for Cain (Gen 4:15; cf. Lev 26:21). Jesus' answer of forgiving "seventy-seven times" is in contrast to the vengeance for Lamech (Gen 4:24). Seven and its multiples are symbolic for fullness. In the kingdom unlimited forgiveness is to take the place of retaliation.

The parable of the unforgiving servant illustrates that living in the kingdom means experiencing the immeasurable forgiveness of God and that those who belong to the kingdom reflect that forgiving nature in their relationships with others. Throughout the parable sin is compared metaphorically to debt, the language already used in the Lord's Prayer. Ten thousand was the highest Greek numeral, and a talent was the highest unit of currency. The servant owed the king an absurdly high amount and there was no possibility of his paying it back in spite of his promise to do so. Being sold into slavery because of debt was not uncommon in the ancient Near East but was more commonly used for punishment than for payment of debts. The king, however, hears the plea and forgives. When that forgiving nature is not reflected in the servant's attitude toward another, even for a debt that could easily be repaid, his failure to show mercy where he had received mercy leads to the king's mercy being rescinded, and the unforgiving servant is now handed over to the torturers (v. 34) until he should pay the impossible debt. The social structure of the parable assumes that human beings are "fellow servants" living in comparable relationship to God and having various amounts of debt, yet all of them indebted. Acting in forgiveness is the way of the kingdom. To refuse to forgive puts one outside the kingdom and, consequently, outside the realm of God's forgiving love. The parable masterfully harmonizes two points of Jesus' teaching that are easily taken as contradictory: the mercy of God is unlimited; nevertheless there is divine rejection and condemnation with appropriate punishment. The synthetic thought is that the sovereignty of God demands that divine mercy be the measure of forgiveness in our relationships with each other.

XI. On the Way to Jerusalem: 19:1–20:34

So far all Jesus' ministry has been in and around Galilee. Now he and his disciples join other pilgrims for the journey to Jerusalem for the Passover. The pilgrims normally crossed the Jordan and traveled down through Perea in order to avoid Samaria. Once again many crowds follow him and he heals along the way. From here the narrative moves with increasing intensity to the final showdown at "a place called Golgotha" (27:33).

Marriage and Divorce (19:3-12)

Pharisees among the pilgrims, familiar with Jesus' teaching on adultery and divorce (see 5:27-32), seek an opportunity to expose Jesus in front of the crowds as being lax in regard to the Law. The fact that John the Baptist was imprisoned and martyred for speaking out against Herod's breaking the law on marriage may explain the basis for the question: a provocation to force Jesus to speak out on a politically sensitive issue. When they ask the question: "Is it lawful for a man to divorce his wife for any cause?" they have in mind Deut 24:1 where Moses allowed divorce if a man "finds something objectionable" in his wife. Jesus points them to Scripture, which refers to God's purpose for humankind, to the creation accounts (Gen 1:27; 2:24) to show that it is God's will that when two become one in marriage they have entered into a covenant relationship that is never to be broken. It is not for human beings to destroy what God has intended. Ignoring Jesus' scriptural pronouncement, the Pharisees now bring in the "law" of Deut 24:1: "Why then did Moses command . . . ?" Jesus then points out that this is not the law of God but something Moses allowed because of their rebellious nature (cf. Isa 48:8). Such an accommodation is never to be regarded as divine law. Faithfulness to the covenant relationship supersedes the legal tradition. As in 5:32 the only permissible reason given for divorce is *porneia,* "persistent unfaithfulness" (see above at 5:31-32). To divorce one's wife for any other reason and marry another constitutes adultery. The traditional interpretation of the text admits divorce in the case of adultery as a right of the betrayed marriage partner without allowing a second marriage. This interpretation reflects a pastoral praxis as early as the second century but may not render correctly the meaning of the interjected exception in the text.

Speaking from the context of these loose divorce practices, the disciples question whether it is then advantageous to marry (v. 10). Jesus' response asserts that such a permanent relationship in marriage can only be comprehended in the context of what constitutes a faithful relationship in the kingdom of God. Such understanding is given by God as one comes to know the love of the Father who constantly seeks to take Israel back as his bride in spite of her unfaithfulness (cf. Isa 54:1-8). Children of the kingdom are to imitate their Father (5:48). There are exceptions to the divine purpose: eunuchs who have been so from birth, eunuchs who have been made so by others (that is, those who have been emasculated for service in royal households, a common practice in the ancient Near East; cf. Jer 29:2; 38:7; Isa 56:3-5), and eunuchs who have made themselves such for the sake of the kingdom (that is, those who have abstained from marriage in order to carry out the proclamation of the kingdom, as Jesus himself had done).

Blessing the Little Children (19:13-15)

This little interlude is deliberately placed here before the story of the rich young man as a reminder that one can only enter the kingdom of God as God's child dependent on God for all things. The pilgrims, having witnessed Jesus' healings, want him to bless their children, but the disciples seem to have forgotten the lesson Jesus had given them before about greatness in the kingdom (18:1-4).

The Rich Young Man (19:16-30)

This account and the parable of the laborers in the vineyard (20:1-16) belong together and deal with the whole question of belonging to the kingdom : does one achieve it on the basis of human goodness or God's goodness? The relation of wealth to discipleship is secondary. The young man thinks he can achieve what is basically a self-centered desire for eternal life by his own goodness. Jesus' response is to direct him to the "one who is good," God alone (cf. 20:15), an allusion to the *Shema* recited regularly (Deut 6:4, 5), a reminder that every action is to be motivated by love for God. It is in that light that Jesus speaks of keeping the commandments, which set out the basis of relationship with God and neighbor. Jesus cites the second table of the covenant stipulations (Exod 20:12-16; Deut 5:16-20) and ends with the quotation from Lev 19:18 as a summary of those commandments. Love for neighbor comes as a result of love for God. That the young man has not understood is evident in his claim that he has kept all the commandments. Jesus calls the young man to demonstrate that claim by giving his wealth to the needy and finding "treasure in heaven" (see above at 6:19-21) as a disciple. This is the real test of putting the kingdom first (6:33) and giving it the highest value (cf. 13:44-46), but the pull of earthly riches proves too strong.

In the Christian spiritual tradition a distinction between the ten commandments and the "evangelical counsels" is based mostly on this pericope. The so-called evangelical counsels are a special and privileged route to the special challenge of Christian love. For the intended readers of the gospel of Matthew a point being emphasized in this pericope is that this young man has failed to see that both this life and life eternal are the gracious gifts of the God who is good.

Jesus uses humor to make his point (vv. 23-24). A loaded camel would find it difficult enough entering the gate of the city, the "Eye of the Needle" being a name for a narrow gate into the city. In order to enter the kingdom one needs to be relieved of the burdens of earthly treasures. The disciples are astonished at Jesus' saying. Their question, "then who can be saved?" expresses some of the same bewilderment experienced by the young man. If one who has kept the commandments cannot enter the kingdom, then who can? With his gaze fixed on them Jesus answers that salvation is possible only with God. It is impossible for people to earn their own way into the kingdom.

Peter's statement is the focus of the passage. As spokesman for the disciples he points out that they have carried out what the rich man refused to do. Those who have given up everything to follow will in the renewal of all things (the unusual word *palingenesia* means "re-creation": cf. Isa 65:17; 66:22), when the Son of Man sits on the throne to carry out God's judgment (cf. Dan 7:13-14; *1 Enoch* 45:2; 62:5-7), participate in that judgment and rule as the "holy ones of the Most High" (Dan 7:18, 22, 27). So the disciples, representing the twelve tribes of Israel, will participate in judging those who have rejected the good news of the kingdom. Thus the world's values are turned upside down in the kingdom, where the powerful and rich become powerless, and the powerless are lifted up to become powerful by the act of God's goodness (v. 30). This is illustrated further in the following parable of the kingdom, which is tied into this verse by 20:16.

Workers in the Vineyard (20:1-16)

The point of this parable is that in the kingdom the blessings and rewards are received out of the goodness and love of God and not on the basis of merit or length of service. In the kingdom there is no room for envy or greed. The owner of the vineyard represents God in the kingdom (Isa 5:1-7). The early hour of hiring day-workers would have been around 6 A.M., the beginning of the twelve-hour summer work day. The other times represent roughly 9 A.M., midday, 3 P.M., and 5 P.M. The denarius was the standard daily wage for a day laborer. The owner sees people who are without work and consequently without income and calls them to work in his vineyard.

At about 6 P.M. the owner calls his steward to pay the workers their wages according to law (Lev 19:13; Deut 24:15), but he is to do so beginning with the last and ending with the first to make the point that even though the last ones have only worked one hour their sustenance will be provided, just as it is for those who have worked through the heat of the day. Similarly, those who come into the kingdom at the last hour will receive the same blessings of eternal life as those who have been there longer. (Cf. Ezek 18:21-23.) God's goodness cannot be a point of dispute. Those who mutter are reminded that they received what had been agreed upon. No injustice has been done, but all have received according to God's goodness (v. 15).

Third Passion Prediction (20:17-19)

As they draw nearer to Jerusalem, Jesus feels the need to share once again, privately, with the Twelve exactly what the significance of this journey is for them: it is for him to go through a death and resurrection experience as Servant Israel in order to lead many to righteousness (Isaiah 53). He now gives more explicit details so they will be prepared. Jesus' being "handed over" is a passive form that denotes divine action. God will permit that the shameful suffering of Jesus take place, that he be crucified, but the (Suffering Servant) Son of Man will triumph and be raised on the third day.

The Sons of Zebedee and the Kingdom of the Son of Man (20:20-28)

The idea that Jesus is soon to enter his kingdom leads "the mother of the sons of Zebedee" to request that her sons James and John sit on the thrones of greater authority next to Jesus in his kingdom, thrones that the Twelve have heard will belong to them (19:28). James, John, and their mother still held some traditional views of the nature of the kingdom. Perhaps there is an intended irony in the fact that those who end up on the right and left side of Jesus are crucified (27:38). The cup the brothers claim in ignorance they are ready to drink is the cup of suffering mentioned in 26:39. The Babylonian exile was called the "cup of God's wrath" (Jer 25:15-31; Ezek 23:31-33) which at the end of the exile was to be put it into the hands of their tormentors (Isa 51:17-20). However, because of Israel's failure to carry out its purpose and the opposition to his message Jesus sees that as the Servant he must still drink that cup. The brothers will share in his suffering, but the kingdom belongs to the Father. The indignation of the other disciples leads Jesus to call them all together to explain that the kingdom is not like the kingdoms of the Gentiles where leaders seek to dominate by having power over others, but just the opposite: it means serving in love, helping others to achieve their potential. True leadership means service, following the example of the Son of Man. The Son of Man is to give his life as a ransom for many. He will drink the cup for Israel's failures for "he shall bear their iniquities" as well as those of the nations to which Israel was to be a light (Isa 53:10-12). The "ransom" implies that Jesus is to give his life to bring about Israel's redemption, and through Israel's faithful witness also the redemption of the nations. The word "ransom" means "redemption," the verbal form of which is frequently used in Isaiah 40–66 to describe God's "buying back" Israel from exile as next of kin (cf. Lev 25:47-55). Thus Jesus is saying that part of his role as Servant/Son of Man is to give his life to bring about redemption for "the many." In Isa 53:11-12 it is the Servant who will "make many righteous" for "he bore the sin of many." Thus the statement "to give his life as a ransom for many" combines two ideas: that of Servant Israel's death in exile as a guilt offering (Isa 53:10), and that of God's redeeming of Israel to live in righteousness. Jesus' death and resurrection will thus release many from their guilt so that they may respond to the good news of the kingdom and live in covenant faithfulness.

Two Blind Men (20:29-34)

This account of the healing of two blind men is similar to 9:27-31. The story is significant on three counts: (1) It is a subtle reminder that the sons of Zebedee need to see again with the eyes of faith; (2) it shows that the Son of Man even as he enters Jerusalem is ready to serve those despised and rejected; (3) the cry to Jesus as "Son of David" sets the stage for the crowds hailing him as Son of David (21:9). The blind men sit by the roadside seeking alms from pilgrims coming for Passover, but hearing that the prophet from Galilee is coming they instead call out to him for mercy and healing. They address him as Son of David, the one who can bring justice for them. The crowd, eager to get to Jerusalem, tell them to be silent, but Jesus has compassion and heals them. Their lives are touched by Jesus and they follow as disciples.

XII. Jerusalem and Its Religious Leaders: 21:1–22:14

Jesus' Entry into Jerusalem (21:1-11)

Many of the people in the crowds are pilgrims from Galilee who see Jesus as the hope for renewal and cleansing from corruption in both political and religious spheres. Two disciples are sent into Bethphage to get a donkey and its colt for which prior arrangements have been made. The password is simply: "The Lord needs them," and they are released immediately. Two animals are mentioned rather than the one referred to in Zech 9:9. This may have been because it was necessary for a young colt, never ridden before, to be accompanied by its mother in the noisy crowds. With Zech 9:9 Matthew has combined Isa 62:11. Both come from the context of the harvest thanksgiving, the feast of Booths (cf. 17:4). In that context Isa 62:11 celebrates God's deliverance in which the people will be called

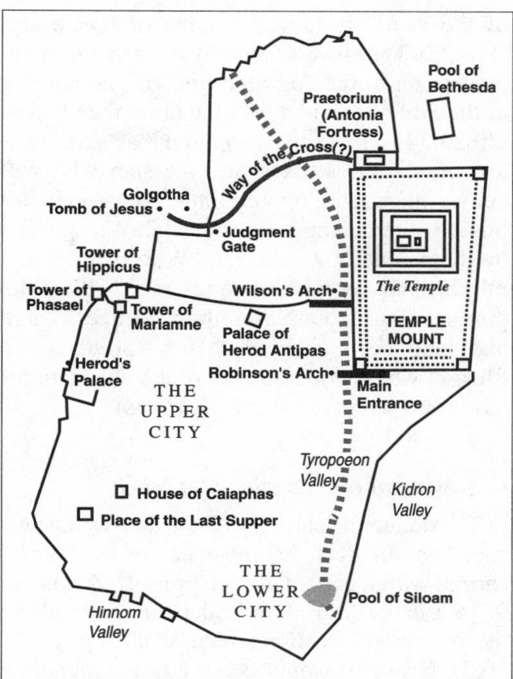

JERUSALEM IN THE TIME OF JESUS

"The Holy People, the Redeemed of the Lord" (62:12). In Zech 9:9 the prophet describes a king entering Jerusalem as Judah of old entered Shiloh for the feast of Booths (Gen 49:10-12). God's flock, the house of Judah (Zech 10:3), is here depicted as representing God's reign as a king of peace since in Isa 55:3-5 the everlasting covenant made with David had been transferred to them. Matthew recalls all these prophecies in this combined summarizing quotation.

Jesus is about to ride into Jerusalem as the one who represents the role of faithful Israel, as the Servant King who brings about the restoration of God's kingdom. When the crowds see Jesus riding on the colt they immediately make the connection and spread their garments on the road before him as a royal carpet (cf. 2 Kings 9:13). Others cut down branches as required for the feast of Booths (cf. Lev 23:39-43; Neh 8:13-18; 2 Macc 10:6-8) and spread them on the road. The excitement grows as the pilgrims, using the last of the Hallel psalms (Psalms 113–118) sung at major festivals, continually cry out in joyous acclamation of Jesus in the role of the messianic king. "Hosanna" is the Greek rendering of a Hebrew phrase meaning "Save us" (Ps 118:25), and "Blessed is the one who comes in the name of the Lord" is the next verse of that psalm (118:26). The crowds naturally connect this royal procession to the common hope in the coming of the Son of David as did the blind men before (20:29-34). The festive reception they give Jesus identifies him as a Davidic messiah who will deliver them from oppression. This issue is politically charged and controversial. When asked by the people of Jerusalem, "Who is this?" the pilgrims answer with some reserve, "This is the prophet Jesus from Nazareth in Galilee." There had long been a belief that a "prophet like Moses" would come to restore the covenant relationship with God (Deut 18:15-18).

Cleansing of the Temple (21:12-17)

The deliberate entry into Jerusalem as the Servant King of Zech 9:9 representing the faithful carried with it certain expectations. In Zechariah 9–14 it is the Jerusalem leadership, particularly the priesthood, who are seen as corrupt (Zech 10:3), but there would come a time when they would no longer oppress the people, when the Lord would suddenly come to his temple (Mal 3:1). The pilgrims, reenacting some of the joyous rites of the feast of Booths, remembered that when the Maccabees cleansed and rededicated the Temple in 165 B.C.E. they celebrated the feast of Booths although it was well after the harvest season (2 Macc 10:6-8). There had developed a popular belief that Jerusalem and the Temple would be cleansed with the coming of the Messiah (cf. *Ps Sol* 17:30). Coming into the Court of the Gentiles, Jesus and the pilgrims would have been confronted by the sheer commercialism that had developed around the Temple and its religious rituals. The lambs for the Passover had to be without blemish (Exod 12:5) and approved by the priests. It was much simpler to buy such a lamb from the priesthood who would also have to carry out the ritual slaughter for the people. The priesthood had a monopoly on such transactions, and prices were often inflated (cf. *m. Ker.* 1:7). Besides, Roman currency had to be exchanged for Tyrian coinage for use in the Temple. The whole sacrificial system had become big business and had corrupted the spirit of worship. Jesus' action was a rejection, like that of the prophets of old (cf. Isa 1:10-17; Jer 6:20; Hos 6:6; Amos 5:21-25), of what the whole sacrificial system and its priesthood had become. Driving out the traders from the Temple (cf. Zech 14:21), Jesus combines quotations from Isa 56:7 and Jer 7:11, both prophetic rebukes of Temple abuse. Jeremiah had predicted that the Temple would be destroyed because it had "become a den of robbers" (Jer 7:1-15). The implication of Jesus' use of this phrase is that the hypocritical use of the Temple will soon lead to its destruction.

Anticipating a new era, the blind and the lame come to Jesus in the Temple and are healed. An old tradition had prohibited them from entering the Temple (2 Sam 5:8), and that had been affirmed by the Pharisees by imposing the priestly law on all (cf. Lev 21:16-24; *m. Ḥag.* 1:1). Jesus heals them as a sign of the restoration of the kingdom. As a sign of Jesus' popularity even the children have joined in the pilgrim chorus singing "Hosanna to the Son of David" in the Temple, much to the indignation of the chief priests and scribes who now see Jesus as having violated both Temple and Torah.

Cursing of the Fig Tree (21:18-22)

The cursing of the fruitless fig tree is a deliberate symbolic act, a parable of action. Returning early next morning to Jerusalem, Jesus is struck by the lack of faithfulness and holiness of the "holy city." His hunger is really hunger for the fruits of righteousness (cf. 5:6; Isa 61:3). A fig tree by the wayside becomes a lesson in kind. It has leaves giving signs of life, but no fruit. Normally early figs come forth before the leaves and afterward the larger summer fruit develop. Jerusalem is a city that shows signs of life but has no fruit. The curse is on the faithless leaders of Jerusalem and has the finality of the final judgment. The disciples express amazement at how quickly the fig tree has withered. Jesus' response is to encourage them to faithfulness. It is this kind of faithfulness, never wavering, by which the disciples will experience God's power in their lives. Once again drawing on Isa 54:10, expressing the immovability of the steadfast love of God, Jesus says that such faithfulness can cause "this mountain" to be removed and cast into the sea.

Jesus' Authority is Questioned (21:23-27)

Returning to the Temple to teach, Jesus is confronted by the powerful chief priests and elders. Their blunt questions to Jesus imply that they regard themselves as the authorities on religious matters, and that Jesus has usurped that authority and humiliated them. By responding with a counter-question about the baptism of John, Jesus is throwing the question of authority back in their laps. The baptism and preaching of John had had a great impact on the people (cf. 3:5-6; 11:12) and could not be ignored by the religious leaders. They had held John to be an impostor, but the people had seen him as a prophet of God (cf. 11:9; 14:5). The fact that they are afraid to answer in front of the crowds is an indication of the popularity of both John and Jesus among the common people. By answering "We do not know" they negate their own authority and leave Jesus' authority as a prophet intact. It is with this authority that Jesus then addresses those present with the following parables.

Parable of the Two Sons (21:28-32)

Jesus uses this story of how two sons respond to their father's bidding to show that obedience to God is only evident in action, not confession. He points out to the leaders that tax collectors and prostitutes, those they regard as hopelessly excluded from the reign of God, are the ones who will enter it before them. The leaders' rejection of John's baptism puts them into the category of the second son. In calling people to repent John was acting by God's authority in the way of righteousness, yet the religious leaders still rejected his message. If they had accepted the authority by which John had acted they would have understood that Jesus is acting on the same authority.

Parable of the Tenants of the Vineyard (21:33-46)

This is an updated version of the Song of the Vineyard in Isa 5:1-7, where the owner is God and the vineyard is Israel that, in spite of care and cultivation by the owner, produces only wild grapes. In this version tenants are added who are to care for the vineyard and are responsible for producing the fruits for the owner. These tenants are the religious leaders whose responsibility is to nurture spiritual growth and fruitfulness among the people. This is the fruit the owner's servants the prophets are sent to collect. The mistreatment of the prophets of the past by beating, killing, and stoning is well attested (Jer 20:2; 26:21-23; 2 Chr 24:19-21) and was often referred to by Jesus (5:12; 22:6; 23:30-37). Now God has sent God's son, Jesus. As the tenants sought to get rid of the son and heir, so the chief priests and elders were wanting to get rid of God's Son. The Jerusalem leaders miss the point of the parable, which is that God will get rid of the false leaders and hand over the responsibility to those who will teach and inspire covenant faithfulness.

"Have you never read in the scriptures . . ." Jesus asks the chief priests and elders, quoting again from Ps 118:22-23, with which they would have been thoroughly familiar. Earlier in the psalm the one who had become the "stone" had said: "I shall not die, but I shall live, and recount the deeds of the LORD" (v. 17). Thus the implication of the quotation becomes clear: it points to the vindication of the Son in his imminent resurrection. This resurrection of the one whom they will cast out and kill will be the turning point that will lead to the kingdom being taken from these religious leaders and given to a people producing the fruits of it. The responsibility of the kingdom will be transferred to the faithful as promised in Isa 55:3-5. The chief priests and Pharisees begin to realize what Jesus has been saying and see him as dangerous; however, Jesus' popularity among the crowds is such that they can do nothing at this stage.

Parable of the Wedding Banquet (22:1-14)

Joyful wedding celebrations were often the imagery used by Jeremiah to describe the future messianic kingdom (Jer 33:11, 14-16; cf. 16:9). The return from exile was to be such a celebration with the faithful soon to be clothed with "the garments of salvation," the "robe of righteousness" as God's bride (Isa 61:10; cf. 62:1-5). Jesus has come inaugurating that time of the kingdom but many of those who had previously been invited to participate in this celebration have rejected the invitation. Here the king is God who offers the celebration of the kingdom to those invited, the people of Israel. Servants sent to call the invited represent the prophets since the exile who have called the people to return to God in order to carry out their God-given purpose. Israel, however, has not listened to the prophets. Other prophets were sent to call the invited, expressing greater urgency for "everything is ready," but again those invited proved to be more interested in their own pursuits. Others insulted the prophets and killed them (cf. v. 35). The destruction of the faithless by the king's armies and the burning of their city is a repetition of Israel's situation before Jerusalem was destroyed by God's "servant" Nebuchadnezzar (Jer 25:8-9). The message to the Jerusalem leaders is that their rejection of the invitation will soon lead to a renewal of that destruction.

Nevertheless the celebration will go on, and this time God's servants, prophets, apostles, evangelists, will invite not only the lost sheep of the house of Israel but also tax collectors, sinners, and Gentiles to participate (cf. 28:19). However, not all respond with sincerity of faith. A man who has no wedding garment is one who is not willing to change. He has come for what benefits he can gain for himself but is not a true child of God (cf. Isa 61:10; *1 Enoch* 62:15). Those invited to the celebration must give evidence of their commitment, and so the judgment (v. 13) is the same as that visited on all those who lack faithfulness (cf. 8:12; 13:50; 24:51; 25:30; Ps 112:10). The people of Israel had always regarded themselves as God's chosen, but Jesus points out that it is only those who respond in faithfulness to the call who are "chosen" (cf. Isa 41:9; 42:1; see also Matt 24:22, 24, 31).

XIII. The Opposition Seeks to Entrap Jesus: 22:15–23:39

Paying Taxes to Caesar (22:15-22)

Jesus is here confronted with the united front of his opposition. First the Pharisees seek to entrap Jesus. Being sympathetic to the popular resentment of the hated poll tax that was levied on all Jews regardless of income, the Pharisees collaborate with those of opposite view, the Herodians, who had a vested interest in supporting Herod Antipas and Rome as agents of stability for trade and commerce in the region. The question they put to Jesus after their flattering comments thus confronts him with the double dilemma: say yes to paying the annual head tax and lose the respect and backing of the crowds who regard him as a prophet, or say no and be accused before Roman authorities of inciting insurrection. Jesus immediately confronts them with their hypocrisy and asks them to show him the denarius used to pay the tax. While an ordinary denarius used in Palestine bore no image out of consideration for pious Jews (Exod 20:4), the coin used for the poll tax had to be the Roman coin with the emperor's image and inscription. So Jesus' response, "Give therefore to the emperor the things that are the emperor's," was an appropriate way of avoiding the trap of the Pharisees. Jesus' reply does not merely skirt the issue; it delivers a teaching about accepting the temporal order as long as it respects its relationship to God's sovereignty. Jesus keeps his distance from revolutionary movements yet exhibits no enthusiastic support for the empire. What makes Jesus' reply particularly clever was the fact that a Pharisee must have considered a Roman coin contrary to the Law because of the image of Caesar on it. His additional response: "and [give] to God the things that are God's" implies that just as the coin carries the emperor's image the human being carries God's and therefore belongs to God.

Belief in the Resurrection (22:23-33)

The Sadducees now take their turn by posing a riddle regarding the performance of levirate marriage and the resurrection. The Sadducees held only the five books of Moses as their scriptural authority and consequently ruled out any belief in the resurrection (cf. Acts 23:8; Josephus, *Ant.* 18.1.4). Referring to the law of levirate marriage (Deut 25:5-6; cf. Gen 38:8), they quote a case of seven brothers marrying the same woman without bearing offspring (cf. Tob 3:8-15) in order to raise doubts about the feasibility of the resurrection in such a case. Showing their understanding of resurrection to be inadequate, Jesus points to a wholly new kind of life with God where spiritual relationships take precedence. While Isa 26:19 and Dan 12:2-3 are explicit references to the resurrection, Jesus is limited to Scriptures the Sadducees accept. So drawing his argument from Exod 3:6, 15-16 in which context God tells Moses that God is the eternal "I am," he argues that the use of the present tense means that the patriarchs exist in a permanent relationship with God that is beyond earthly existence (cf. 8:11). Jesus once again leaves his opponents speechless.

The Great Commandment (22:34-40)

The Pharisees make a third attempt to snare Jesus. This time they use a legal expert to engage Jesus in a common rabbinic dispute over the "greatest commandment" although every commandment was equally binding. They seek to lead him into making a statement on the basis of which they can accuse him of abolishing the Law (cf. 5:17). Jesus answers first from the *Shema* (Deut 6:4-9) to which he adds Lev 19:18 as being like the first. The two commandments are inseparable, for one cannot love God without loving every person as a child of God. These two commandments focus on a loving relationship as the basis for interpreting all law and the prophets (cf. 7:12).

The Anointed One: Whose Son is He? (22:41-46)

Jesus now puts a vital question to the Pharisees that touches on a major difference in understanding between them regarding the Messiah. In order to understand the reason for this question, the following should be noted: (1) The Pharisees were strong proponents of the coming messianic age in which the Messiah would be the son of David according to the Scriptures (2 Sam 7:12-16; Ps 89:3-4; Jer 23:5) who would establish his kingdom bringing national, political, and religious freedom and power. (2) In the prophetic tradition the covenant with David was understood as having been transferred to the people (Isa 55:3-5). (3) The term "Anointed One" in Matt 11:2 and 16:16 was used to refer to Jesus as the Servant of Isa 61:1. (4) Later, when asked by the high priest whether he is "the Anointed One, the Son of God," Jesus responds by referring to himself as the "Son of Man seated at the right hand of Power," a reference to Ps 110:1. (5) Jesus has been called "Son of David" as a popular messianic title (9:27; 12:23; 15:22; 20:30-31; 21:9, 15). Jesus questions the Pharisaic belief on the basis of Ps 110:1, regarded by them as both Davidic and messianic (v. 44). "The Lord" is the translation of "YHWH" and "my lord" translates the Hebrew *ʾadonī,* a respectful form of address, meaning "my master." This is not the way a Jewish father would speak of his son, although a son may use that form of address for his father (cf. 21:30). Jesus is questioning the Pharisaic answer that the Anointed One is the Son of David, even though he has been called such himself. What Jesus implied was that the Anointed One is the Son of Man, the true representative Servant Israel to whom the everlasting covenant made with David has been transferred (Isa 55:3-5; 61:1). As that Anointed One Jesus could still be called "Son of David" but in a quite different sense than the Pharisaic understanding. It was for that reason that Jesus had earlier charged his disciples not to reveal that he was the Anointed One (16:20).

Failure of the Religious Leaders (23:1-39)

Jesus now turns from the Pharisees to speak to the crowds concerning these leaders who have been influential over them. He warns them and his disciples to beware of the ways of these leaders, then follows with an outright condemnation in the strongest terms given in the form of prophetic woes (as in Isa 5:8-23), dire warnings akin to covenant curses.

Warning Against the Scribes and Pharisees, 23:1-12

The scribes and Pharisees sit on Moses' seat since they had virtually taken over the priestly function of instructing the people regarding covenant law. Therefore, because they are conveyers of the covenant law Jesus instructs his listeners to do . . . and follow (cf. Deut 4:6; 7:12; Isa 56:1) everything they say. Jesus is referring to the basic covenant stipulations and is certainly not condoning here the ways in which the scribes and Pharisees interpreted the laws in their oral tradition (cf. 12:1-14; 15:1-20; 16:5-12; 19:3-9). "Do not do as they do" includes also their interpretations of the Law (see 15:1-20). For the common people the only access to hearing the Scriptures was in the synagogues dominated by Pharisees and scribes. The "heavy burdens, hard to bear" they place on people's shoulders are their interpretations of the Law and the imposition of these interpretations on others. Jesus taught a different attitude toward the Law, where his yoke was pleasant and his burden light (Matt 11:30). The flaw in the concept of righteousness under attack by Jesus (6:1-18) is that

ANTI-JUDAISM AND THE GOSPEL OF MATTHEW

Accusations against Matthew's so-called "anti-Judaism" are based to a large extent upon this chapter, which has been interpreted often enough as the summary of Christian polemics against Judaism as such. This perspective becomes even more slanted and vicious if we assume that this text expresses a confrontation between the Christian Church of a Gentile identity and the Jewish people taken at once as an ethnic and religious entity, considered in separation and isolation from the Christians. Regardless of how distinct or even separated from Judaism is the community addressed here by Matthew, the passionate hostility of the evangelist's words and the bitter invectives contained in Jesus' words are not directed at the ethnic and religious entity of Judaism, but rather at those Pharisees who in their leadership role opposed Jesus and rejected him as Israel's true Messiah. Jesus follows the tradition of the deuteronomistic school and of the ancient prophets, especially Jeremiah, when he accuses Jerusalem as the murderer of the prophets and the just ones sent by God. In this vision Jesus is seen as linked with the destiny of all people who have ever been innocently persecuted and killed, yet this comprehensiveness is placed only on the side of the victims, not the victimizers. Neither are all Jews subsumed under a formula of collective guilt nor does the text intend to generate hatred against "Jews." In the context of the gospel there remains no doubt that those standing on Jesus' side (the disciples, friends, and supportive members of the family) are all entirely Jewish. Matthew is vehemently opposed to the Pharisees, not because of their Jewishness but because of their perceived leadership role in rejecting Jesus. Of course, as with all other sayings of Jesus, these statements against Pharisaic Judaism took on new significance in the eyes of Christians: first when the Christian message about Jesus as crucified and risen Messiah was rejected by the majority of Jews, and later when the tragedy of the Jewish people unfolded with the Jewish revolt and the destruction of Jerusalem.

That there has been a misguided and wicked use of these texts by Christians to justify anti-Jewish attitudes and practices within the Church should not be denied. The danger of such denial is ever present and a matter of gravest pastoral concern. The Church's public repentance for the sin of anti-Judaism provides the pastor with an essential ecclesial presupposition for Christian reflection on this text. (See "Anti-Semitism in the Bible and After".) —*Ed.*

these particular leaders did their acts for show (the meaning of "hypocrite"). Jesus gives as examples: (1) using wider and more noticeable straps to tie on their phylacteries, those small leather boxes containing excerpts of the Law that were strapped to the forehead and left arm as a quite literal rendering of Exod 13:9 and Deut 6:8; (2) making their tassels, attached to the corners of a garment worn as reminders of the covenant, extra long to gain attention; (3) seeking the place of honor at banquets next to the host, and the front seats in the synagogue reserved for elders and teachers. "Rabbi," can generally be understood as "teacher." However, in this context it helps to know that the title literally means "my great one."

Jesus reminds his disciples (vv. 8-10) that in the reign of God there is only one teacher and Father, and that is God (cf. Jer 63:16; 54:13-17; 31:33-34), and with God's teaching in their hearts all are equal; none can claim positions of authority and control over others. The disciples are not even to use the title "instructor" to elevate themselves above others, for there is one instructor to show them the Father, the Anointed One (cf. 11:25-27). In contrast to the scribes and Pharisees and the kingdoms of this world, those who would be greatest in the kingdom will humble themselves and be servants to others (cf. 18:4; 20:26-27).

Denunciation of the Scribes and Pharisees, 23:13-36

The first woe condemns the teaching and practices of the scribes and Pharisees that make it virtually impossible for their followers to enter into a faithful relationship with God since they are taught to depend on their own scrupulous actions instead of God's grace. The second woe refers to their practice of traveling to Jewish communities throughout the Diaspora to encourage them to maintain the traditions. They would seek to proselytize Gentile "God-fearers" in these communities by converting them to their understanding of the Law and thus instilling in them a zeal for the Law that would close them out of the kingdom. In the third woe they are referred to as blind guides (vv. 16, 24; cf. 15:14) and blind fools (vv. 17, 19; cf. v. 26; 5:22). They need guidance themselves rather than giving it. Here Jesus expands on a subject he has spoken of before (see above at 5:33-37), the practice of making legalistic distinctions in oaths. There is no room for such foolishness in the kingdom, for ultimately any oath involves God as the one who is invoked. In God's reign even such oaths are unnecessary (5:37).

The fourth woe shows the extent to which scrupulosity in matters of law can go. While the law of giving one tenth of one's crop to God (Lev 27:30-32; Deut 14:22-23) referred to field grain and fruits, the scribes and Pharisees extended that to herbs grown in the back garden (although a few herbs were exempt; cf. *m. Šheb.* 9:1). By concerning themselves with such minutiae they were neglecting to do what really counted: justice, steadfast love, and faithfulness. These virtues summarized the essential meaning of the covenant relationship (cf. Mic 6:8) as the proper response to God's steadfast love and faithfulness (cf. Hos 2:19-20; Isa 56:1). "Without neglecting the others" refers to the other stipulations of the covenant and does not condone their legal scrupulosity: they strain out a small insect from their drink because it is unclean (Lev 11:20-23) while they swallow a camel which is also unclean (Lev 11:4)! This witty saying is even more humorous in Aramaic where there is a pun on the words *qāmla,* "gnat" and *gāmla,* "camel."

The fifth woe addresses the concern to impose on everyone the ritual purity (cf. 15:1-20) meant only for the priesthood. Concern for what constituted purification of cups and dishes was especially irrelevant when compared to the need to cleanse their own hearts of rapacity and self-indulgence. The sixth woe expresses that same concern through the image of whitewashed tombs. Daubing with whitewash was a way of making something shoddy look good (cf. Ezek 13:8-16). It was also the practice at the time of festivals, particularly prior to the Passover, to whitewash tombs so that the throngs of pilgrims would be warned not to touch them (*m. Šhek.* 1:1) lest they incur defilement for seven days (Num 19:16). The false piety of the scribes and Pharisees was similar: outwardly righteous, inwardly hypocritical. The final woe really gets at the crucial difference between the scribes and Pharisees and Jesus. The scribes and Pharisees hypocritically profess to honor the prophets and the righteous of the past by building tombs and monuments to them, but in their traditions they have totally ignored the prophets' divine messages. The prophets and the righteous (cf. 10:41; 13:17) are those who proclaimed and lived faithfully in spite of persecution and oppression (cf. Isa 57:1; Dan 12:3; Mal 3:18). By acknowledging as their ancestors those who had killed these prophets and righteous ones the scribes and Pharisees were indicting themselves.

"Prophets, sages, and scribes" are the disciples Jesus will send out to continue his proclamation of the good news of the kingdom and carry it to all nations (10:16, 40-41; 24:9-14; 28:19). They are the new messengers of God, the wise who will shine like the brightness of the firmament and turn many to righteousness (Dan 12:3; Isa 53:11), the new scribes who will be the faithful conveyers of the covenant relationship. These will replace the present religious leaders who will do to the disciples what they will do to Jesus (10:16-25). Because they perpetuate the same faithless attitude as their ancestors (cf. Jer 7:25-26) the guilt of the blood of all the righteous will now be on this generation (v. 36; cf. *1 Enoch* 47). From Abel, the first innocent martyr recorded (Gen 4:10) to the last mentioned in the Hebrew scriptures, Zechariah (2 Chr 24:20-22), the blood of all will be on them. Zechariah was actually the son of the priest Jehoiada, a prophet who was stoned to death in the court of the Temple. Jewish tradition often confused this Zechariah with the prophet of Zech 1:1 whose father was Barachiah.

Lament over Jerusalem, 23:37-39

These are words of judgment on Jerusalem and its Temple. Jerusalem generally was the place where the prophets were killed. Jesus had longed for Jerusalem to repent, but once again they had refused the divine message. As God's Son, Jesus uses language of love and protection always attributed to God. "As a hen gathers her brood under her wings" is the OT image of God's protection of the people (Pss 17:8; 91:4; Isa 31:5). Now because of faithlessness the Temple is left deserted by God, as the prophets had warned (cf. 1 Kings 9:6-9; Jer 22:5; Isa 64:10-11). They will not see Jesus from now on until they are able to greet him with the words of Ps 118:26 as the pilgrims did when he entered Jerusalem (21:9). From now on they will only see him when they can accept him as God's Anointed One, the Son of Man coming into his kingdom (16:28).

XIV. The Future and the Final Judgment: 24:1–25:46

Jesus now begins to prepare his disciples privately for what is to come. The imminent destruction of Jerusalem and its Temple becomes a metaphor for the final judgment at the close of the age, a warning and encouragement to the disciples to be constantly in a state of preparedness for the coming of the Son of Man.

Prophecy of the Destruction of the Temple (24:1-2)

As Jesus departs the Temple grounds the disciples, taken with the magnificence of the buildings, comment on them in the light of Jesus' rejection. Herod the Great had begun the building of this temple in 20 B.C.E. and it was still in the process of final construction, yet because of the faithlessness evident in its leaders the Temple would soon suffer the same fate as Solomon's Temple when Jerusalem became a heap of ruins, as Micah (3:12) and Jeremiah (7:11-15) had predicted.

Trials and Tribulations Before the End (24:3-14)

The disciples come with two questions, one regarding the destruction of the Temple and the other regarding the *parousia* and the end of the age. The coming of the Son of Man in glory and the end of the age are understood by the disciples as essentially one event, with the destruction of the Temple being the beginning of the end of the age. However, as Jesus had pointed out in the parable of the weeds in the wheat (13:24-30, 36-43), there is a distinction to be made between the Son of Man coming in his kingdom and his coming at the end of the age in judgment. The disciples will have their part to play between these two events. *Parousia* (a Greek word meaning "coming"), used here four times (vv. 3, 27, 37, 39), refers to Jesus' final coming. "The end of the age" in apocalyptic literature meant the end of this present era when the great judgment would take place. "In my name" in this context means claiming to be who Jesus truly is, the Anointed One. There were such claimants right up to the time of the destruction of Jerusalem in 70 C.E. (cf. Acts 5:36-37).

Wars between nations and kingdoms, people fighting against one another are signs of human wickedness and godless confusion (cf. Isa 19:2; Hag 2:21-22), and famines and earthquakes are signs of consequent divine punishment (cf. Isa 29:6; Jer 10:10; Ezek 38:18-23; Zech 14:5). These will happen because of human sinfulness but they do not herald the end. They are but "the beginning of the birthpangs," a metaphor of the suffering that would suddenly come upon the wicked (cf. Isa 13:8; Mic 4:9-10; Jer 13:21), particularly as this led up to the coming of the Son of Man (cf. *1 Enoch* 62:4-5). This metaphor was also used to refer to the act of divine restoration leading to the new age (cf. Isa 42:14; 66:7-8). These events are the beginning of change, but they are not the end. They will bring many trials and afflictions and even death on the disciples as they proclaim the good news of the kingdom to all the nations, a responsibility given them after the resurrection (v. 14; cf. 28:19). "Then many will stumble" (v. 10) because of the trials, and this will lead to betrayal and hatred even among the disciples. Out of this situation come false prophets motivated by their own self-interest (see above at 7:15-20). With the growth of wickedness the majority of disciples will withdraw their love for neighbor because of treachery, deceit, and fear of being taken advantage of. Only those whose love endures will be saved from these tribulations (10:22b) and find rest at the end of days (Dan 12:13). After his resurrection Jesus will commission the faithful to go and make disciples of all nations. That purpose must be completed before the end will come.

Flee Jerusalem, Flee Falsehood (24:15-28)

While the next verses (15-22) refer more specifically to the destruction of Jerusalem, the point is to encourage the disciples to learn from this desolation and beware of premature claims of the coming of the Son of Man. "The desolating sacrilege" is derived from Dan 11:31; 12:11; cf. Dan 9:27; 1 Macc 1:54, where it referred to the statue of Zeus by which Antiochus Epiphanes desecrated the Jerusalem temple in 167 B.C.E. The "sacrilege" there now is of a different stripe. Jesus has already declared the Temple "desolate" (23:38), desecrated by false priests, elders, scribes, and Pharisees, soon to be destroyed. "Let the reader understand," recalling

Dan 12:10, is a call to the faithful (Dan 12:3; Isa 60:1-3) to keep themselves pure from the abomination in the holy place.

The urgency of fleeing from marauding armies without stopping even to pick up one's coat, a person relaxing on the flat roof of the house suddenly leaving without picking up any belongings, a worker in a field rapidly running off, Judeans everywhere suddenly fleeing into the hills—these give a heightened impression of the unexpectedness of the eventual destruction of Jerusalem. The real message behind these images is that the final judgment can come just as suddenly and unexpectedly to a person. The picture is made more graphic and the horror intensified by reference to pregnant women and nursing mothers having to flee in this situation or the difficulty of trying to escape in winter, traveling on the muddy Palestinian roads, or fleeing on the Sabbath when the city gates are closed. Borrowing language from Dan 12:1 and Joel 2:2, Jesus paints a picture of terrible suffering and devastation. The time of evil is shortened, however, because the fullness of time belongs to God and God's holy ones, "the elect" (22:14; cf. Dan 7:21-22, 25-27), a parallel term for Servant Israel (Isa 41:8, 9; 42:1).

During a national crisis it is easy for people to be duped by the claims of a messiah like the one Pharisees had promised, but the faithful are forewarned and will not be led astray. The end is not yet here; the coming of the Son of Man will be made known not by human claimants but by divine proclamation. "The lightning" that suddenly illumines up the world was a sign of God's powerful presence (Pss 77:17-18; 97:4), and when accompanied by a loud trumpet blast (cf. v. 31) it was to declare God's covenant action (Exod 19:6; Zech 9:14). When God finally announces the coming of the Son of Man the world will be ripe for judgment. The image is one Jeremiah often used as a symbol of judgment on Jerusalem prior to its destruction in 587 B.C.E. (Jer 7:33; 15:3).

Coming of the Son of Man (24:29-35)

"Immediately" emphasizes the suddenness and unexpectedness with which the Son of Man will appear. "After the suffering of those days" refers to all the affliction God's faithful will undergo until the end time. Jesus uses figurative language drawn particularly from Isa 13:10, 13 and 34:4 (cf. also Joel 2:10; 3:15; Amos 8:9) to indicate that the appearance of the Son of Man will mean judgment. A constant tension between the judgment on Jerusalem and the final judgment is deliberately maintained. "The sign of the Son of Man . . . in heaven" is the signal for the gathering of the faithful (cf. Isa 11:10-12). "All the tribes of the earth will mourn" draws on Zech 12:10-14 which speaks about the families of the land, the political and religious leaders of Jerusalem, who mourn in repentance over what they have done to "the one whom they have pierced." The language of Dan 7:13-14 is used to describe the Son of Man "coming . . . with power and great glory." Jesus has been gathering the faithful to fulfill their purpose in the world, and in his coming as the Son of Man they, Israelite and Gentile alike, will be gathered into the presence of God. The highly figurative language is used in these verses to convey the truth that imminent judgment and vindication are to be carried out on God's behalf by the Son of Man. This generation will see the judgment brought on Jerusalem just as every generation will experience the judgment of the Son of Man, for God's righteousness and salvation will ultimately be fulfilled (Isa 40:8; 54:10).

Need to be in Constant Readiness (24:36-51)

Jesus has been deliberately vague in answering the questions of the disciples (v. 3), and his use of apocalyptic symbolism has lifted the questions out of human time into God's time. This has left the disciples with a feeling of impending crisis and uncertainty as to when these things will happen. All this has been leading up to Jesus' instruction on how they are to live until the close of the age. The coming of the Son of Man as judge at that time now becomes the focus of instruction. Only the Father (cf. 11:27) knows of the day and hour of that coming (cf. Zech 14:7). The flood at the time of Noah (Genesis 6–8) was always a picture of judgment on the faithless and deliverance for the faithful (e.g. Isa 54:9; *1 Enoch* 54:7-10; 66; 67). So the disciples, leaving the time of judgment in God's hands, live righteously in constant readiness for the coming of the Son of Man. At the end of the age there will be a sudden and final separation of the righteous from the unrighteous, illustrated with two graphic pictures. Those "taken" represent the gathering of the elect (v. 31). The example of a thief breaking into a house (literally, "digging through" the mud walls) emphasizes that one never knows when the *parousia* will happen, so constant readiness is essential. The parable in vv. 45-51 contrasts a faithful and prudent servant with a wicked one. To be "put in charge of [the] household" to manage the owner's affairs is to be given the responsibility of being faithful to one's participation in the kingdom, representing the Father in showing care and compassion to others. The Son of Man may come earlier than expected, but the faithful, living as the children of the heavenly Father, will always be ready.

Parable of the Ten Virgins (25:1-13)

The ten virgins all belong to the kingdom. Five of them were foolish enough not to be prepared. The processional lamps used here symbolize people belonging to the kingdom living their lives in a way to give light to others. The bridegroom represents the Son of Man, as in 22:1-14 and 9:15. The marriage feast is, again, the celebration of the kingdom: this time its consummation. The idea of delay is emphasized also in 24:48 and 25:19 as a correction of the disciples because they were expecting an imminent return. When the bridegroom finally is announced at midnight the foolish maidens are not prepared (cf. Prov 13:9; Job 18:5). Their request to use the oil of the wise ones who brought an extra supply is strongly rebuffed, for no one can rely on another's faithfulness. The bridegroom takes in with him those who are there fulfilling their purpose and the door is shut, giving a real sense of finality. The return of the foolish comes too late; their cry "Lord, lord," and the response "I do not know you" are reminiscent of 7:21-23. The response of the bridegroom indicates that the foolish maidens represent those who are in the community of the faithful but lack any real commitment and so are unprepared. "Keep awake therefore" is a warning to remain constantly faithful and committed to one's relationship with the Father in the kingdom.

Parable of the Talents (25:14-30)

This parable shows that being prepared is to be understood as making good use of what God has given. The Son of Man will soon be going away and leaving his disciples in charge to carry out the mission he had begun. Each one is given responsibility according to ability. A talent was a very large sum of money, the equivalent of six thousand denarii (one denarius was a day's wages for a common laborer). The greater the ability, the greater the responsibility. The first two both double what they had received but the third only hides his talent to keep it for the master's return. All are given sufficient time to make good use of the resources entrusted to them. On the day of reckoning the first two servants, even though they had been given different amounts according to their abilities, receive equal commendation and are given greater responsibility and honor. Both enter into the loving presence of their Lord. The third servant excuses his lack of action by complaining that the master expects too much. The master responds with the explanation that the simple act of investing the talent with bankers would have earned interest. The servant was irresponsible, so what he had is taken away and given to another, and he is cast out (cf. 8:12).

Judgment of the Nations (25:31-46)

Here the theme of final judgment reaches its climax as the basis on which that judgment is made is revealed. The talents given to the servants are identified here as love and compassion, living according to the double commandment (22:34-40) on the basis of the infinite love and grace received from the Father. In the Parables of Enoch the Son of Man is seen primarily as coming to judge sinners and dwell with the righteous and the elect. As such he is usually depicted as "sitting on the throne of his glory" (*1 Enoch* 45:3; 55:4; 61:8; 62:5; 69:29), placed there by God to carry out judgment on God's behalf (cf. 61:8; 62:2-6). The background to all these images is Dan 7:13-14 and Isa 53:7-11. The final judgment comes only after the good news of the kingdom has been proclaimed to all the nations (24:14; 28:19; cf. Isa 42:6; 49:6). It will be on the basis of their response to the good news that people will be judged. In the OT "goats" was used as a term for oppressive leaders who harmed the sheep, God's people (Ezek 34:17-19).

The Son of Man is king (v. 34) because God has seated him on his glorious throne as God's representative over the nations (cf. 13:41; 16:28; 21:5 [= Zech 9:9]). "Blessed by my Father" acknowledges that it is the reign of God into which people have been called. The acts of love and compassion mentioned, recalling the advice of Isa 58:6-11, are the natural response of the righteous to the Father's love. The physical and spiritual realities are never really separated. The question of the righteous only emphasizes the spontaneity of their actions, which they do quite naturally as the children of the heavenly Father (5:43-48). The acts of compassion mentioned four times as ultimate examples of covenant faithfulness are done without discrimination. However, to have done them for "one of the least of these who are members of my family," that is, for a fellow child of God, is to do it for Jesus himself (cf. 12:48-50). Still, the widest scope should be given to the recipients of this compassion, since one is to imitate the heavenly Father who sends rain and sunshine on both the righteous and the unrighteous (5:43-48). It is only by acts of kindness that one gives witness to the kingdom and leads the unrighteous to respond to the love of the Father. The accursed go into "the eternal fire prepared for the devil and his angels" (cf. 5:22; 13:42, 50; 18:8, 9), for they have failed to be servants and to minister to others (20:26-28; cf. Isa 61:6).

XV. Jesus' Way of Suffering: 26:1–27:66

Jesus has come to Jerusalem for the Passover to suffer and die on behalf of Israel as Servant/Son of Man in order to bring about through redemption and expiation a new Israel to be a people-covenant and a light to the nations. The passion story is a remarkable account of Jesus' determination to fulfill Israel's history and thus draw the faithful into a resurrection experience, a new beginning, thereby fulfilling the purpose God has for them.

The Plot to Kill Jesus (26:1-5)

Jesus now reminds his disciples that he has come to the major task set before him: he will be "handed over to be crucified" during the Passover. Once again the passive character of this action indicates the providential will of God in this plan that will bring about salvation through the suffering of the cross (cf. Matt 28:5). Jesus had alerted them repeatedly to the fact that he would fulfill the role of the Servant in accordance with Isaiah 53 (Matt 16:21; 17:22-23; 20:18-19). The Passover began on the 14th Nisan with the slaughter of the lambs around 3 P.M., and the Passover meal was held that evening, the beginning of 15th Nisan (the Jewish day begins at sunset), the Jewish Friday (see Exod 12:1-27). "The chief priests and the elders of the people" representing the Jerusalem leadership meet in an enclosed courtyard at the residence of the high priest Caiaphas, the ruling high priest from 18–36 C.E., to discuss ways of arresting Jesus "by stealth" in order to kill him. Particularly during the Passover with so many pilgrims in the city believing Jesus to be a prophet (21:46) it was not a good time to draw attention to what they were doing. Any kind of riot would only give the Roman soldiers, brought into the city for the festival, reason to use violence.

Anointing at Bethany for Burial (26:6-13)

After the intrigue of the Jerusalem leaders, the contrasting story of anointing brings Jesus' coming death into real perspective. It happens at the house of "Simon the leper" who had probably been healed by Jesus (cf. 8:1-4). Anointing one's head was common for festive occasions, but this unnamed woman had acquired expensive, highly perfumed oil to anoint Jesus. This was certainly an act of love and generosity, but it may have been more. A few days earlier Jesus had ridden into Jerusalem as the king of Zech 9:9 and had been hailed as Son of David (21:5, 9, 15). This woman had taken the initiative to hail Jesus as the Anointed One in her own way, as her act of devotion. One can imagine her surprise at the response she received from the disciples who regarded her expensive gift as "waste" when she could have used that money for "the poor." Jesus chides the disciples because the woman "has performed a good service for me" (cf. 5:16). She has actually fulfilled the command of Deut 15:11, for Jesus is the poor man *par excellence* as Servant Israel going the way of one stricken, smitten by God and afflicted (Isa 53:4, 7; see above at 5:3, 5; 11:29-30). In the light of these prophecies Jesus interprets the woman's action as preparing him for burial by changing Isaiah's phrase, "on his head" (v. 7), to "on my body" (v.

12). The woman's act of true righteousness will be remembered throughout the world because she has acted out her sincere faith.

Offer of Betrayal (26:14-16)

Immediately after the disciples' expression of concern about money "one of the twelve" goes out and makes a deal with the chief priests to betray Jesus. Judas Iscariot's reasons for being willing to betray Jesus may have been his love for money, or greed, or envy, or disillusionment. However, he accepts a rather modest sum of thirty silver shekels. This was the compensation price of a slave (Exod 21:32; cf. Zech 11:12). The chief priests needed to arrest Jesus somewhere away from the crowds, in a quiet place at the right time. Only an insider could supply that information. The faithfulness of the woman in Simon's house is set in stark contrast to the faithlessness of one of the Twelve.

The Last Supper (26:17-30)

Matthew sees the Last Supper as a Passover meal that took place at the beginning of the 15th Nisan. The first day of Unleavened Bread was probably 14th Nisan, the day on which all leaven would be removed from the house and destroyed (*m. Pesaḥ.* 1:1-3). This day, not really part of the seven-day celebration (Exod 12:14-20), had been added to the Passover feast and was popularly referred to as the "first day." The disciples need to prepare for the Passover meal, but for reasons of security Jesus has so far not told them where in the city they would eat it. Arrangements had to be made earlier to reserve a room in someone's house, since the meal was to be eaten in Jerusalem. Jesus directs them to a certain person in the city, probably a Jerusalem disciple, with the prearranged password: "The Teacher says, My time is near." The Greek word used here for "time" is *kairos* which has the specific meaning of "time of fulfillment." The preparation for the Passover involved acquiring the foods and their preparation in a way that retained the symbolism of the deliverance from Egypt.

After sundown Jesus and his disciples celebrate the Passover meal as planned. In Matthew's account Jesus' following at this point has been narrowed down to the Twelve, one of whom is to betray him. In these Twelve the remnant of Israel, Jesus' new family, are represented (cf. "The Eucharist in the New Testament"). As at all special meals they recline on cushions at the low table. When Jesus announces that one of them will betray him the disciples are "greatly distressed," and fearing their own vulnerability under pressure they ask: "Surely not I, Lord?" Since all will have dipped their bread into the common bowls of food Jesus' answer only emphasizes that it is one of them who has shared in this fellowship meal with him. "The Son of Man goes as it is written of him" refers to Jesus' predictions of his suffering, death, and resurrection experiences as found in Isaiah 53 and Jonah 1:17–2:10. These prophecies, however, do not exonerate those responsible for his suffering and death. Judas asks the same question as the others except that he calls Jesus "Rabbi," revealing his lack of understanding of Jesus' role. Jesus' answer, "You have said so," puts the emphasis on "you" and thus places the responsibility for the answer on the questioner.

During the meal, and as part of it, Jesus takes bread, blesses God, and breaks the bread and gives it to his disciples—all actions that fit well with the order of the Passover but also recall the feeding miracles in 14:19 and 15:36 with their strong allusions to the messianic banquet (Isa 25:6-9; 55:1-3). The breaking of bread itself is an expression of the bond of community. Against the background of the traditional story of deliverance from Egypt, Jesus says: "Take, eat; this is my body." The disciples are not only bonded in covenant community with him but incorporate him into themselves. The background of the sacrificial lamb lends weight to the idea that Jesus is giving himself as a sacrifice for others. "Drink from it, all of you" passes no judgment; no one is excluded, not even the disciple who is about to betray him. The language of v. 28 draws heavily on Isa 53:12, for Jesus is that Servant who will pour out his soul to death and bear the sin of humankind. "This is my blood of the covenant" recalls the words used by Moses as he threw the blood over the people as a sealing of their covenant with God (Exod 24:8; cf. Zech 9:11). The reading of that covenant was always an important part of the three major festivals. However, on the basis of Jer 31:31-34 (cf. Isa 51:7) Second Isaiah had spoken of the Servant as a "people-covenant" (Isa

42:6; 49:8). Thus Jesus as the Servant who in his very life and action gives witness to the love of the Father is the living covenant of which the disciples are now to partake and share in an everlasting bond as they take on the role of Servant (28:18-20). "The forgiveness of sins" is the basis of the restoration of the kingdom (see above at 1:21), and in Isaiah 53 the Servant's suffering, death, and resurrection are seen as the means for extending that kingdom to all. "Fruit of the vine" is the phrase used for "wine" in the order of the Passover meal (see *m. Ber.* 6:1). Jesus will not drink wine from now on until he drinks it new with the disciples in the celebration of the reign of God (Isa 55:1-2).

In this Last Supper meal Matthew presents the supper within the light of his understanding of the events of the crucifixion and the resurrection, but also within the perspective of the celebration of the Eucharist within his own community, a perspective that would be shared by everyone in his audience. Building on the eucharistic images already found in the multiplication of the loaves (for example, the terms "giving thanks" and "breaking of the bread" became liturgical terms used for the Eucharist), Matthew integrates a vision of the Last Supper as a figure of the messianic banquet with an understanding of the expiative and redemptive suffering and death of Jesus on the cross. This integration comes not only from the experience of Matthew's community but is rooted in the words and actions of Jesus himself, though expanded upon, like the parables, through the growing understanding of the post-resurrection Church. In Matthew especially the importance of Jesus' blood lies in the redemptive power of that blood to atone for the sins of God's people, Israel. The understanding of Jesus' ministry through the prophecies of the Servant of Israel in Second Isaiah climaxes in Jesus' self-understanding of the suffering and death of the Son of Man within the context of Isa 53:11-12, that he will bear the sins of many. In the Last Supper, Jesus constitutes this vision as a new type of Passover experience, which Paul and Luke link more closely to its predecessor by their addition of Jesus' request to celebrate this meal in his memory (1 Cor 11:24; Luke 22:19). This redemption will be extended to all peoples, in agreement with the vision of Isaiah (cf. "The Eucharist in the New Testament").

Jesus Predicts the Disciples Will Fall Away (26:31-35)

The disciples "will all become deserters" because of what will happen to Jesus. The quotation from Zech 13:7 speaks of the good shepherd who represents God's rule but is rejected by the religious leaders (Zech 11:4-17). The little poem (Zech 13:7-9) speaks of God's sword striking the shepherd, scattering the sheep, God's hand turned even against the "little ones," the lambs of the flock (cf. Isa 40:11; Matt 10:42; 18:6, 10, 14). These will all go through a devastating experience; a portion will emerge through the refining fires of affliction as tested and faithful. On a positive note Jesus adds that after he has been raised up he will meet them in Galilee. Peter, once again representing the disciples, denies that he himself would ever desert, but his protestation (and that of the other disciples), echoing the words of Jesus about true discipleship (10:38-39; 16:24-25), is met with the simple allegation that before the early dawn he would have thrice denied his Lord.

Prayer of Anguish in Gethsemane (26:36-46)

Jesus takes his disciples to Gethsemane (the name possibly meaning "oil press"), a garden on the slope of the Mount of Olives. Although he had spent the previous nights in Bethany (21:17; 26:6), for the night of the Passover the pilgrims were supposed to stay within the city limits, which for the feast were extended to include the western slopes of the Mount of Olives. Having been present at the Last Supper, Judas would have known where to find them. The three disciples who had expressed willingness to stand by Jesus, Peter (v. 35) and the sons of Zebedee (20:22), are taken farther by Jesus who asks them to watch with him, for they are to be witnesses once again of the divine purpose they are to proclaim after the resurrection (cf. 17:9). Jesus, feeling anguish and distress as the time of betrayal and death draws closer, expresses himself in words similar to the cry of the righteous sufferer in Pss 42:5, 11; 43:5. However, Jesus' prayer is one of total submission to the Father's will, even as he had taught his disciples (6:10). The cup he must drink is the cup of wrath (cf. 20:22) that was to be taken from Israel and given to the oppressors (Isa 51:17-23), but that he sees he must now drink in order to fulfill the "will of the Lord" (Isa 53:10) to bring the kingdom of God to the nations. Meanwhile the three disciples have fallen asleep. Matthew explicitly mentions Jesus praying three times and finding the disciples sleeping three times. This is not only to express Jesus' continuing anguish but also, in contrast, the failure of the three. Jesus, however, knows that the time has come and so he arouses his sleeping disciples to be witnesses to his betrayal and arrest.

Betrayal and Arrest (26:47-56)

After his prayerful struggle Jesus is in complete control of the situation. "A large crowd" probably would have consisted of Jewish Temple guards, members of the high priest's household, and a few others alerted by the chief priests and elders at this late hour. They come "with swords and clubs." Judas greets Jesus with a kiss, a normal way of greeting a friend in Palestine, but here the ironic signal of Judas's treachery. Jesus addresses Judas with "Friend," a term (see 20:13; 22:12) that puts some distance between the speaker and addressee. His next words probably are meant as a command: "do what you are here to do," rather than a question. The sign has been given, and Jesus is arrested. "One of those with Jesus" uses his sword to prevent Jesus' arrest, but Jesus' response is that violence only begets more violence (cf. Gen 9:6), consistent with what he has taught before (5:39-46). Jesus knows that he could be rescued from this situation by God's protecting angels (Ps 91:11), but "the Scriptures" of the prophets (v. 56) had already shown what must be accomplished (see Hos 6:1-6; Isaiah 53; Jonah 1:17–3:3; Zechariah 9–14; Daniel 7–12). There is irony in Jesus' question why they had come out with swords and clubs "as though I were a bandit [or: robber]," for Jesus had accused the priests of having turned the house of God into "a den of robbers" (21:13).

Jesus Before the Council (26:57-68)

Jesus is taken to a meeting of the Sanhedrin in the middle of the night, to those who had initiated the arrest: Caiaphas, his chief priests and elders, together with the scribes as legal experts. Peter, having more courage than the rest, follows and gains access to the courtyard of the high priest's palace in order to await the outcome. The Sanhedrin was made up of seventy-one members. Probably not all would have been present at that hour. False testimony was being sought against Jesus to find sufficient evidence to justify the death penalty. Many false witnesses are heard but nothing is substantial enough to make a death penalty stick until two witnesses come forward with the same testimony—necessary according to the Law (Deut 17:6). The accusation that Jesus said he was "able to destroy the Temple of God" was based on half truths. Jesus had been critical of the Temple and its sacrificial cult like the prophets before him; he had driven out the traders, much to the indignation of the leaders (21:12, 13), and he had also predicted the destruction of the Temple (23:38; 24:2). The high priest calls on Jesus to answer these allegations in the hope that he will say something that can be used against him, but Jesus remains silent in fulfillment of Isa 53:7 (cf. Ps 38:12-14; see also Matt 27:12, 14). This silence leads Caiaphas to force him to respond by putting him under oath. "I put you under oath before the living God" (1 Kings 22:16) as an oath forces Jesus to respond to the statement: "Tell us if you are the Anointed One, the Son of God." Both terms in popular understanding were titles for the hoped-for Messiah who would destroy the enemies of Israel and establish the kingdom. Caiaphas pressed Jesus to affirm this so that he might report to Pilate that Jesus was planning an insurrection, but Jesus' response is "you have said so," forcing the accuser to take responsibility for the answer without incriminating himself. While Jesus is the Anointed One, the Son of God as revealed in 16:16 (see above), he is not so in the political sense implied by the high priest. He is the Servant/Son of Man who will return as judge. So by his statement to the high priest, "From now on you will see the Son of Man . . ." is both a reference to his vindication and enthronement in the resurrection and a warning of the final judgment that Jesus had spoken of in relation to the Temple (24:30; 25:31; cf. 16:27-28). "Seated at the right hand of Power" refers to Ps 110:1 and *1 Enoch* 62:5 and interprets the Son of Man rather than the Son of David as sitting at the

Lord's right hand (see 22:41-46). Being seated in that position is the sign of bearing delegated authority; this begins with the triumph of the resurrection (cf. 28:18). "Power" is another pious circumlocution for "God" (cf. *1 Enoch* 62:7). "Coming on the clouds of heaven" refers to the coming of the Son of Man in Dan 7:13.

Jesus' answer has given Caiaphas a new cause for condemning him: "He has blasphemed," which carried the death penalty (by stoning: Lev 24:10-23). As an expression of the heinousness of this crime Caiaphas tears his clothes, an act that was forbidden to the high priest (cf. Lev 21:10; 10:6). Jesus had not taken God's name in vain, but Caiaphas attributed blasphemy to Jesus because he had arrogated to himself the authority of God. So they decided he should die, a penalty they could not carry out themselves. The religious leaders now ridicule and humiliate Jesus just as the Servant was humiliated (Isa 50:6; 53:3, 5).

Peter's Denial (26:69-75)

Meanwhile Peter, previously bold in his confidence of his faithfulness to Jesus, now succumbs to fearful denial. He makes his first denial "before all of them" within hearing in the courtyard by expressing incomprehension: "I do not know what you are talking about." In the second instance Peter denies "with an oath," claiming ignorance: "I do not know the man." The third time Peter repeats his claim of ignorance with greater vehemence. At the height of his denial the cock crows and Peter remembers the words of Jesus.

Jesus is Handed over to Pilate (27:1-2)

The Sanhedrin had condemned Jesus to death for blasphemy during the night. Now that it was morning it was "legal" for the Sanhedrin to meet, so they ratified their earlier decision that Jesus should be put to death. Since only the Roman governor could approve the death penalty they handed Jesus over to Pontius Pilate (governor of Judea from 26–36 C.E.) who was in Jerusalem to maintain order during the festival. Of course their charge of blasphemy would not do. They would have to manufacture another charge.

The Death of Judas (27:3-10)

Judas's reaction to the Sanhedrin's decision is immediate. He had not expected anything like the death penalty to be brought against Jesus, and realizing the enormity of his betrayal he regrets what he has done and seeks to amend his action by returning the money. "I have sinned by betraying innocent blood" acknowledges both his guilt and Jesus' innocence. The religious leaders, callously ignoring their own guilt, dissociate themselves from Judas with the remark: "See to it yourself." "Throwing down the pieces of silver in the temple" recalls Zech 11:13 in which the rejected shepherd had been paid off by the religious leaders with thirty shekels of silver which he took and cast into the Temple. Judas does likewise with the blood money, throwing it into the inner sanctuary that only the priests may enter. Then in his despair he hangs himself. The chief priests acknowledge that it is "blood money," and so it would not be lawful to put it into the Temple treasury. Against the enormity of their own guilt this concern for what is "lawful" is ironic (cf. 23:24). "The potter's field," which became known as the Field of Blood because it was bought with blood money, is traditionally situated in the southwestern corner of the Valley of Hinnom (see Jer 19:1-13).

Matthew has mentioned all of this because there are allusions in those events to prophetic images of judgment on the chief priests and elders of Jerusalem. These he now draws together into one formula quotation under the name of the prophet Jeremiah, even though the basic quotation comes from Zech 11:12-13. In the Hebrew of Zechariah the shepherd was told by God to cast the thirty shekels of silver "to the potter in the house of the LORD." The "potter" points back to Jeremiah's "parable of the potter" in Jer 18:1-12, where the potter is God who can make or break what has been created (cf. Isa 64:8). In that context (19:1-13) Jeremiah is then instructed to buy a potter's ceramic jar, take with him some of the chief priests and elders, and go to the valley of the son of Hinnom (which the leaders had filled with the blood of innocents, 19:4). There he was to smash the jar into pieces with the message that in this way God would "break this people and this city . . . so that it can never be mended" (19:11). Buying that potter's field was just one more step toward the chief priests' own destruction.

Trial Before Pilate (27:11-31)

This was hardly a trial. Although the Sanhedrin had condemned Jesus for blasphemy and thus "legitimized" his death the high priest had made the accusation that Jesus had claimed to be king and so was an insurrectionist. Hence Pilate's question: "Are you the King of the Jews?" Jesus' response, "You say so," hands the responsibility for the answer back to Pilate without affirming it (cf. 26:25, 64-65), but the chief priests and elders are there in full force to make sure that their judgment is carried out. Jesus remains silent even to further questions from the governor (Isa 53:7). It is obvious to Pilate that this person is hardly to be regarded as a revolutionary and that he is simply being used by the Jewish leaders to condemn someone to death. Nevertheless, without any real trial he makes the offer to release either Barabbas (probably a brigand well known to the leaders) or "Jesus who is called the Messiah," using the description given him by the accusers. Only Matthew mentions Pilate's wife seeking to influence her husband to prevent a death sentence. She sees Jesus as an "innocent man," indicating some knowledge of Jesus as a teacher, but her entreaty is of no avail: the process has begun. The religious leaders are bent on getting rid of Jesus and so incite the crowds to seek release of Barabbas and death for Jesus. The crowds do the leaders' bidding without knowing what evil Jesus has done (v. 23). So Barabbas is released and Jesus is to be crucified. Pilate could see that the crowd was breaking into a tumult and so he gave in to them. Washing his hands was a symbolic ritual to declare before the crowd that he was not responsible for Jesus' crucifixion, a ritual act Jews would readily have understood (cf. Deut 21:6-9; Pss 26:6; 73:13). "See to it yourselves" is passing over the responsibility to them, as the chief priests and elders had done to Judas (v. 4). The people standing by readily accept it with their cry: "His blood [is] on us and on our children!" To express acceptance of responsibility in this way was common in the OT (e.g., Deut 19:10-13; Jer 26:15). In the context of the gospel of Matthew this response may refer back to the salvation in Jesus' blood promised in Jesus' name and offered to the many in the Last Supper. In this case, rather than a blanket acceptance of guilt by the Jewish people at the time (and *not ever* to be understood as an acceptance of personal guilt by later generations of Jews as Christ-killers), this passage instead indicates metaphorically the offer of redemption present in the shedding of Jesus' blood (cf. "The Eucharist in the New Testament"). Pilate released Barabbas and handed Jesus over to be scourged, a brutal beating to hasten death on the cross, and then to be crucified. Now racked with pain from the scourging, Jesus is taken by Roman soldiers to the praetorium, the governor's Jerusalem residence, for further humiliation; he is mocked as "King of the Jews" and then beaten before being taken out to be crucified (cf. Isa 50:6; 53:4-6).

The Crucifixion (27:32-44)

Jesus being in no shape to carry the heavy crossbeam after the scourgings, the soldiers carry out their prerogative of pressing into service a passerby to carry it for him (cf. 5:41). This man was Simon from Cyrene, whose name is given, indicating that he later became well known among the disciples (cf. Mark 15:21). Cyrene on the north coast of Africa had a strong Jewish community. Golgotha was the Aramaic name for "Place of a Skull," a prominent public place just outside the city wall where crucifixions would be well displayed as a warning to others. "Wine . . . mixed with gall" (cf. Ps 69:21) would have been offered as a drug to deaden the pain as one was being nailed to the crossbeam. Jesus refuses to drink it, determined to remain fully conscious to the end. He had told his disciples he would not drink wine again until he drank it new with them in the kingdom (26:29).

Matthew does not focus on the graphic details of crucifixion but proceeds to the matter of the soldiers casting lots for Jesus' garments, a reference to the treatment of the righteous sufferer in Ps 22:18. "This is Jesus, the King of the Jews" is the inscription nailed on the cross to document the charge that incurs crucifixion. As part of the execution it needs an interpretation from a Roman point of view, namely: this man was a pretender to the throne and as such he has committed treason. On the other hand, the expression is the royal title of God, in whose name and on whose behalf David and his dynasty exercised power. In the context of Matthew's gospel Jesus was sought for execution even as an infant by King Herod, a usurper of the title. The two robbers crucified with Jesus were probably brigands, political rebels who often robbed traveling merchants; they may have been companions of Barabbas who was released. So Jesus "was numbered with the transgressors" (Isa 53:12).

The crucified Jesus receives the same derision from passersby as the righteous sufferer in Pss 22:7 and 109:25. The members of the Sanhedrin had made sure their propaganda had its effect among the people. Even "the chief priests, . . . along with the scribes and elders" come to deride Jesus. Their mocking remarks are an echo of the derisive sayings of the wicked in Ps 22:8 and Wis 2:10-20. In the latter their derision was directed toward the "righteous one" who "professes to have knowledge of God" and calls himself a "servant of the Lord" (Wis 2:12, 13)—a description based on Isaiah 53—and who "boasts that God is his father" (Wis 2:16). The religious leaders are clearly depicted as the enemies of the righteous.

The Death of Jesus (27:45-56)

Matthew does not describe the actual suffering and death of Jesus but focuses on the events that happen around Jesus, with many subtle biblical allusions to guide the reader to the significance of those events. From midday to around 3 P.M. there is "darkness . . . over the whole land." Whatever the physical cause of the darkness, it is in fact to be seen as a sign of God's judgment. Jesus had spoken in apocalyptic language of the sun being darkened and the moon not giving light as a portent of the coming of the Son of Man in power and glory (24:29). These words were already being fulfilled. At the end of the period of darkness Jesus exclaims with a loud voice the opening words of Psalm 22, the cry of agony of the righteous one who later receives divine vindication and praises God (vv. 22-31). Jesus' exclamation does not then express despair or a lack of faith but instead confirms his understanding of the role of the suffering servant who will triumph in his death by accomplishing the forgiveness of sins. Hearing Jesus saying the Hebrew *Eli* ("My God"), the bystanders mockingly conclude that he is calling for Elijah (= "My God is YHWH") who was expected to come to prepare for the messianic age (see 17:3, 10-13). The "sour wine" was mixed with bitter herbs and was probably offered with good intentions to alleviate suffering (cf. Ps 69:21).

Before yielding up his spirit to God, Jesus cries the cry of the righteous sufferer (Ps 22:5, 24). Apart from the splitting of the curtain of the Temple, only Matthew of the evangelists tells about the instantaneous effects of the death of Jesus in vv. 51-53. He does not explain their significance but hints at their theological meaning. Zechariah 14:4-5 gives a description of God coming upon Jerusalem with power with "all the holy ones" just prior to establishing divine rule; when the Mount of Olives shall be split in two, the people shall flee as from an earthquake. There is a similar pattern here: the curtain of the Temple is split in two from top to bottom, the earth is shaken as if by an earthquake (v. 54), and the holy ones are raised and enter the holy city. This is the only time Matthew uses the term "saints" (= "holy ones"), a term originating in Isa 62:12 and repeated in Dan 7:18-27 and *1 Enoch* 51:2-4. The belief in the resurrection as expressed in Isa 26:19 and Dan 12:2 was often associated with the coming of the Messiah when all the righteous would be vindicated. Matthew is thus pointing the reader to the resurrection when the Son of Man will be seated on his throne of glory. The climax comes with the confession given by Gentiles: "Truly this man was God's Son!" (v. 54) spoken by the centurion and his soldiers. They, as outside observers, make this statement simply on the basis of what they have witnessed, just as the disciples had done (cf. 14:33). The cumulative effect of the wonders surrounding the death of Jesus, pointing to his coming resurrection, is a fulfillment of the preceding revelations that Matthew has recorded at the baptism and the transfiguration (Matt 3:17; Matt 17:5), leading to a profession of faith by a Gentile, signifying that in the death of Jesus the mission of God is accomplished and the reign of God is at hand.

"Many women . . . from Galilee" were also there as witnesses to these events. They too were disciples and served Jesus just as he had come to serve (20:28). Three of these women are mentioned specially: "Mary Magdalene" has not previously been named by Matthew, but Luke (8:2) says that Jesus had healed her of evil spirits. "Mary the mother of James and Joseph" could be the Mary referred to in 13:55. In 27:61 and 28:1 she is referred to as "the other Mary."

The fact that these two Marys are mentioned as the only ones who follow to see where the body is taken and go back to the tomb on Sunday morning indicates a special relationship to Jesus. The third woman, "the mother of the sons of Zebedee," has been mentioned once before (20:20).

The Burial of Jesus (27:57-61)

The Deuteronomic law (Deut 21:22-23) required that a hanged man be buried before night. Joseph, "a rich man from Arimathea," asks for the body of Jesus to give it a decent burial. Joseph is described as a "disciple of Jesus"; elsewhere (Mark 15:43; Luke 23:50) he is said to be a member of the Sanhedrin who had not agreed to the decision recorded in Matt 27:1. Pilate readily complies, convinced as he is of Jesus' innocence, so Joseph reverently wraps the body in a clean linen shroud and places it "in his own new tomb." It was common for those who could afford it to have a tomb cut out of the limestone close to Jerusalem and to be buried there to await the resurrection at the coming of the Messiah. The "great stone" was usually a heavy round slab of limestone that could be rolled in front of the tomb entrance to seal it off. The two Marys watch all that has been going on so that they know where Jesus has been buried.

Setting a Guard at the Tomb (27:62-66)

Only Matthew mentions the setting of a guard. His concern is to counter the claims disseminated by the Jewish leaders that the disciples had stolen the body of Jesus and faked the resurrection. The chief priests and Pharisees, opponents on most matters but in agreement on the death of Jesus (cf. 21:45), go to Pilate on the Sabbath. They are concerned that Jesus had said he would rise again in three days, the sign of Jonah, and they wanted to make sure the disciples did not work some deceit to claim that Jesus had risen. Their request is that Pilate do something about it. Pilate gives them a detachment of his soldiers to guard the tomb but passes the responsibility for sealing the tomb back to them. So on the Sabbath they go and seal the tomb with official seals and set their guard over it.

XVI. The Resurrection of Jesus and the Future: 28:1-20

The Resurrection of Jesus (28:1-10)

Since the Sabbath ended at sunset, the first day of the week followed immediately. It was thus during twilight that the two Marys returned "to see the tomb" and to observe what would happen, for Jesus had said that he would be raised on the third day. The anointing had already taken place in Bethany (26:6-13), so these women were here to observe (cf. Mark 16:1; Luke 24:1). They first experience an earthquake, not unknown in that area. The "angel of the Lord descending from heaven" is seen as the cause of this tremor as he rolls away the heavy stone from the tomb to show that Jesus is risen. The angel's appearance "was like lightning" because of being in the brilliant presence of God (cf. 13:43; 17:2; Dan 7:9; 10:6; cf. also *1 Enoch* 51:4). This brilliance is too much for the soldiers, who are overcome with fear and faint (cf. Dan 10:7-9; *1 Enoch* 60:3). Now the angel addresses the women with "Do not be afraid; . . . he has been raised," the divine passive emphasizing God's action. The women had seen the body of Jesus placed in this tomb and so the angel invites them to "see the place where he lay" in order to establish the veracity of their witness. "He is going ahead of you to Galilee" is what Jesus had earlier told his disciples he would do (26:32).

Throwing all circumspection to the wind the women run to tell the disciples but are met by Jesus, who greets them very much alive with the common salute, "Greetings". Their spontaneous reaction is to take "hold of his feet" in joyful adoration and relief. Like the angel's, Jesus' opening words to them are "Do not be afraid," the comforting words of divine assurance; he reiterates the message that the disciples are to go to Galilee where he will meet them. Because Jesus sent these women to tell his disciples the news of the resurrection they became known as "apostles to the apostles" in later Church tradition. In this sense they were Jesus' first apostles.

The Bribery of the Guards (28:11-15)

Before his grand finale Matthew gives us one last glimpse of the depths to which the religious leaders are ready to go, desperately making one last attempt to stop something that is unstoppable because it is the will of God. Because the guarding of the tomb had been assigned by the chief priests, the soldiers report to them "everything that had happened." This would have shaken the chief priests and elders considerably and necessitated the calling of a special meeting of the Sanhedrin to decide what to do. Their decision was simple: the soldiers will easily accept a bribe if they are offered "a large sum of money." The promise to the soldiers that there would be no repercussion from the governor for their failure to stay awake while on guard implies that the Jewish leaders were in a position of influence with the governor as well. The soldiers take the bribe and a concocted rumor is spread.

The Great Commission (28:16-20)

These traumatic events have shown the eleven their vulnerabilities but have also radically changed their lives. Only the Eleven are mentioned as coming to meet Jesus because they have been chosen as the representatives of Israel, and so the commission is to be addressed to them. This restriction does not rule out the presence of others. With Mount Zion in Jerusalem under judgment it is only appropriate that they should return to the place where Jesus began his ministry, to "Galilee of the Gentiles (= nations)" (4:15-16) where Jesus now gives the commission to "go . . . and make disciples of all nations."

"When they saw" Jesus they gave him homage as soon as they recognized him, but some hesitated since they were meeting someone who had been raised from the dead. Jesus came to them in response to their hesitation. "All authority in heaven and on earth has been given to me": The passive verb emphasizes that this authority has been given by God. Jesus' saying that the Son of Man would be seated "at the right hand of Power" (26:64) has now been fulfilled. While Jesus had given evidence of his authority before, now all authority has been given him (cf. Dan 7:13-14). The power and authority of Jesus as the Son of God have been revealed in his resurrection. Jesus' authority has been a topic masterfully developed in the body of the gospel. His ministry in Galilee manifested authority, as did his teaching (7:29), healing (8:9), acts of forgiving (9:6, 8), expulsion of demons (10:1). In the Temple his prophetic action provoked a dispute about his authority (21:23, 24, 27). Now he claims authority on a universal scale: the risen Lord, the Son of Man in glory, passes on to his disciples their mission and purpose. Jesus had been concerned to gather "the lost sheep of the house of Israel" together to carry out what Israel had been chosen to do: to be a people-covenant and a light to the nations (Isa 42:6; 49:6, 8; see Matt 5:13-16). Now the disciples, representing faithful Israel, are to "go . . . and make disciples of all nations." Living as children of the heavenly Father they would draw others in Israel and in all nations into covenant with God. They would be a light to which all nations would be drawn (Isa 60:1-7). To fulfill this universal mission of Israel announced in Isaiah 40–66 had been Jesus' goal from the beginning and would now be carried out through his disciples.

"Baptizing" has only been mentioned previously in regard to John's baptism (3:1-17; 21:25), but now that symbol of purification and renewal, of regeneration as a child of God will become an act of commitment for all. This baptism signifies entering into a life of renewed relationship with the Father revealed through the Son and to be filled with the Holy Spirit (cf. 11:25-27; 12:28-32). Now that the disciples have been taught, they are prepared to teach all nations how to live as people belonging to the kingdom. "And remember, I am with you always, to the end of the age." That bond of communion expressed before (18:20) and sealed in the celebration of the Lord's Supper (26:26-29) is now made universal as a constant comfort and assurance to all disciples until the end of the age (cf. 24:3).

The last sentence concludes the gospel without bringing the story to an end. The ongoing presence of Jesus with the disciples is the ultimate meaning of the resurrection. Not only does it fulfill Isaiah's prophecy about Immanuel (Isa 7:14) quoted in Matt 1:23, but also the promise made to the community in 18:20. Jesus' presence among those gathered in his name is now extended in the bond of community sealed at the supper (26:26-29) over the rest of history until the close of the age (cf. 24:3). We see now the fullness of the sense in which his words retain their effectiveness and validity, just as he had promised (24:35), and one can understand that the Church is guaranteed to prevail over the forces of death (16:18) because its mission is based on the Lord's continued ministry reaching all people of all times.

BIBLIOGRAPHY

Anderson, Janice Capel. *Matthew's Narrative Web: Over, and Over, and Over Again.* JSNT.S 91. Sheffield: Sheffield Academic Press, 1994.

Bauer, David R. *The Structure of Matthew's Gospel: A Study in Literary Design.* JSNT.S 31. Bible and Literature Series 15. General editor David M. Gunn. Sheffield: Almond Press, 1988.

Buchanan, George Wesley. *The Gospel of Matthew.* The Mellen Biblical Commentary. Lewiston, N.Y.: Mellen Biblical Press, 1996.

Carter, Warren. *Matthew: Storyteller, Interpreter, Evangelist.* Peabody, Mass.: Hendrickson, 1996.

Davies, Margaret. *Matthew.* Readings: A New Bible Commentary. Sheffield: Sheffield Academic Press, 1993.

Edwards, Richard A. *Matthew's Narrative Portrait of Disciples: How the Text-Connoted Reader is Informed.* Harrisburg: Trinity Press International, 1997.

Ellis, Peter F. *Matthew: His Mind and His Message.* Collegeville: The Liturgical Press, 1974.

France, R. T. *Matthew: Evangelist and Teacher.* Grand Rapids: Zondervan, 1989.

Hagner, Donald A. *Matthew 1–13.* WBC 33A. Dallas: Word Books, 1993.

____. *Matthew 14–28.* WBC 33B. Dallas: Word Books, 1995.

Harrington, Daniel J. *The Gospel of Matthew.* SP 1. Collegeville: The Liturgical Press, 1991.

Howell, David B. *Matthew's Inclusive Story: A Study in the Narrative Rhetoric of the First Gospel.* JSNT.S 42. Sheffield: JSOT Press, 1990.

Jones, Ivor H. *The Gospel of Matthew.* Epworth Commentaries. London: Epworth Press, 1994.

Kealy, Seán P. *Matthew's Gospel and the History of Biblical Interpretation.* Book I. Mellen Biblical Press Series 55a. Lewiston, N.Y.: Mellen Biblical Press, 1997.

Kingsbury, Jack Dean. *Matthew as Story.* 2nd revised and enlarged ed. Philadelphia: Fortress, 1988.

Levine, Amy-Jill. *The Social and Ethnic Dimensions of Matthean Social History: "Go nowhere among the Gentiles . . ." (Matt 10:5b).* Studies in the Bible and Early Christianity 4. Lewiston, N.Y.: Edwin Mellen, 1988.

Luz, Ulrich. *Das Evangelium nach Matthäus.* EKK 1/1, 1/2 [etc.] 2nd ed. Zürich: Benziger, and Neukirchen-Vluyn: Neukirchener Verlag, 1989–. First volume available in English: *Matthew 1–7, A Commentary.* Translated by Wilhelm C. Linss. Minneapolis: Augsburg, 1989.

____. *The Theology of the Gospel of Matthew.* Translated by J. Bradford Robinson. New York: Cambridge University Press, 1995.

Meier, John P. *The Mission of Christ and His Church: Studies on Christology and Ecclesiology.* Good News Studies. Wilmington, Del.: Michael Glazier, 1990.

Wainwright, Elaine M. *Toward a Feminist Critical Reading of the Gospel According to Matthew.* Berlin and New York: Walter de Gruyter, 1991.

Mark

Virgil Howard and David B. Peabody

FIRST READING

Some Approaches to Reading

Mark designates what he is writing as "the beginning of the good news of Jesus Christ, the Son of God" and while it is unclear precisely what he wants included in this superscription it does afford the reader important clues. For one thing, it is clear that Mark is writing for persons who are already familiar with and committed to "the gospel." The way he uses the word shows that by the time he wrote it has become a commonly accepted word for the saving kerygma at the heart of Christian faith ("the gospel" in 1:15; 8:35; 10:29; 14:9; cf. similar usage already by Paul in Rom 1:9, 16; 10:16; 1 Cor 4:15; 9:14, 18; 15:1; Gal 1:11; 2:2; Phil 1:5, 7, 12, 27; 1 Thess 2:4, 8, 9; Phlm 13). But he is writing about "the beginning" of that gospel. Beginnings are crucial for subsequent interpretation and appropriation and if readers are asked to return to *"the beginning"* it can only mean that fundamental assumptions and formative experiences are being presented with the aim of facilitating a deeper level of comprehension and commitment. Thus whatever we may ask of Mark's gospel, already it asks of the readers a posture of openness and a willingness to be challenged and deepened in faith. The telling of the story of the gospel becomes gospel.

Mark's story, briefest of all the canonical gospels and no longer than a modern short story, is at once dramatic and complex. One could be guided by the geographical movement in the story. Following formative experiences with John the Baptist, God, and Satan in the Judean wilderness (1:1-13) Jesus returns to Galilee and begins to proclaim the good news that the Reign

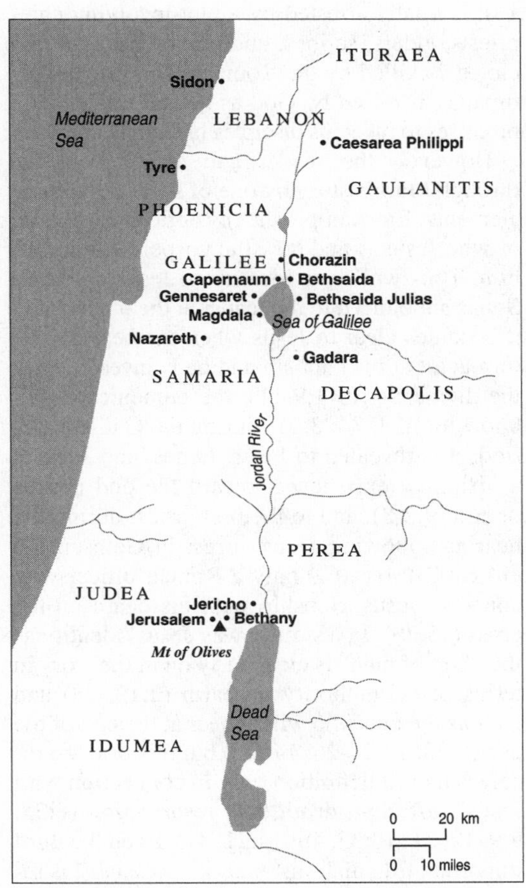

MARK'S PALESTINE

of God has drawn so near that human beings are now called to orient their lives exclusively in relationship to it (1:14-15). This public ministry (1:16–8:26) takes place largely in Galilee and adjoining areas and includes not only teaching (1:21-22, 39; 2:1-2, 13; 4:1-33; 6:1-2, 34) but also exorcisms (1:21-28, 32-34, 39; 3:11-12, 22-30; 5:1-20; 9:14-29) and healings of various kinds (1:29-31, 32-34, 40-45; 2:1-12; 3:1-6, 7-10; 5:21-43; 6:53-56; 7:24-30, 31-37; 8:22-26; 10:46-52) as well as miraculous feedings (6:30-44; 8:1-10) and a few miracles associated with nature (4:35-41; 6:47-52; 11:12-14 and 20-24). Jesus then moves toward Jerusalem (8:27–10:52) and concentrates on teaching the Twelve that it is God's will for him to go to Jerusalem, die a violent death at the hands of the Jewish and Roman authorities, and then be raised from the dead by God. In Jerusalem (11:1–16:8) Jesus continues to debate with religious authorities and teach his disciples about what lies ahead (ch. 13), is finally arrested by a plot involving chief priests, elders, scribes, and one of his own disciples, is killed by the Romans (ch. 15), and ultimately is raised by God as he had trusted, and promises to meet his disciples in Galilee (16:1-8).

However, the reader can also be guided through Mark's story by one of several thematic elements, for example the mysterious revelation of who Jesus is and how the gospel begins with him. Thus while the identity of Jesus as God's Son is announced to the reader at the outset (1:1) it becomes clear to Jesus when the heavens are torn apart at his baptism and he is invested with the divine Spirit (1:9-11); the demonic powers know it (1:24, 34; 3:11) during the Galilean period; it is revealed to Peter, James, and John in a visionary experience toward the end of this period (9:2-8), and to the high priest during the hearing following Jesus' arrest in Gethsemane (14:61-63); but it is only a Roman officer who connects Jesus' Sonship with his death on the cross (15:39). In a similar way Jesus' identity as the "Son of man" is clear early on in the story in terms of his authority on earth (2:10, 28) and later as the one who will appear at the end of the age (8:38; 13:24-26; 14:62), but this title too receives its full definition only in connection with Jesus' suffering, death, and resurrection (8:33; 9:9, 12, 31; 10:33, 45; 14:21, 41). Even the third important title of Jesus, that of "Messiah," is revealed at key points throughout the gospel (1:1; 8:29; 9:41; 12:35; 13:21; 14:61) but like the others is ultimately defined by the cross (15:32).

Finally, a reading of Mark's story could be guided by observing the responses to Jesus by various characters. The early ministry brings overwhelmingly positive responses on the part of crowds of people to the exorcisms and healings Jesus performs (see above) as well as to his teaching (1:22, 27; 2:1-2, 13; 4:1; 6:34; 8:34; 10:1). The positive reaction of "sinners and tax collectors" is especially noted (2:15). The favorable response to Jesus culminates in a demonstration of support for Jesus as he approaches Jerusalem when he is celebrated as "the one who comes in the name of the Lord" (11:1-10). Crowds are not portrayed as being hostile to Jesus until provoked by the chief priests in the hearing before Pilate (15:6-15). Representatives of the scribes and Pharisees, on the other hand, are consistently hostile toward Jesus and their conduct ranges from opposition to him in debates about practices that seem to transgress Torah, sometimes to the point of blasphemy (2:7, 15-17, 18-20, 23-28; 3:22; 7:1-5; 8:11-12) to the formation of alliances with Herodians (3:6; 8:15; 12:13) and chief priests and elders (11:18; 12:12; 14:1) for the purpose of destroying Jesus. Sadducees appear as debating opponents only once (12:18). The Romans, including Pilate, are pictured as being manipulated by the chief priests and elders without any personal reactions to Jesus (15:1-24).

Of all the varied responses to Jesus those of his followers are the most complex. They obey at once when called to follow him (1:16-20; 2:13-14) and all accept appointment as "apostles" to be with him, and to be "sent out" (3:14-19). Several accept new nicknames from him (3:16, 17). Even when they are puzzled about him (4:41) or are criticized by him (4:40; 8:17-21, 33; 9:19, 42) or fail to comprehend what he is saying (9:32; 10:32) they nonetheless follow him to Jerusalem. He gives them private explanations (4:33-34; 7:17-23; 9:28-29, 33; 10:10-12, 32; 13:3) and entrusts them with the same "authority" as his own (3:14-15). On the other hand, Peter opposes Jesus directly (8:32) and the incomprehension of the Twelve on the way to Jerusalem gives way to betrayal (14:10-11; 15:43-45), denial (14:66-72), and abandonment (14:50). Women followers are portrayed in a more positive way in the story as those who prepare Jesus for his death (14:3-9), are present at his death (15:40-41, 47) and dare to come to the tomb on the first day of the week (16:1-2).

Just how important the issue of responses to Jesus was for Mark is evidenced by his inclusion of the allegorical interpretation of the parable of the sower (4:3-9, 13-20). Inevitably the reader is led to ask about her or his own response to Jesus and the gospel he embodies.

Some Characteristic Features

Even in English translation Mark's style is not elegant: the non-literary, common Greek *(koinē)* shines through in places, for example in incomplete (1:1) or awkward sentences (2:10), in the connection of sentences and incidents by a simple "and" without further transition, in the overuse of the adverb "immediately" that while it may lend a sense of urgency also lends a sense of tedium, in the use of the "historical present" in the middle of a story (that is, the Greek present that reports an event in the past and can be used to suggest that the writer was an eyewitness: "he says," "he walks over"). The Evangelist translates Aramaic words for the reader (3:17; 5:41; 7:11; 15:22, 34) but not Latin ones (5:9; 6:37; 12:14-15; 15:15-16, 39).

Alongside evidence of an unpolished style, however, there are some skillful rhetorical devices. For example, repetition focuses attention on certain events such as miracles on the sea (4:35-41 and 6:45-52), healings of blind persons (8:22-26 and 10:46-52), and feeding miracles (6:34-44 and 8:14-21). The pattern can also be threefold as in calls to discipleship (1:16-20; 3:13-14; 6:7-13), passion predictions (8:31; 9:31; 10:33), prayers of Jesus and failures of disciples to stay awake in Gethsemane (14:32-42), Peter's denials of Jesus (14:66-72). Events portend others still to come: the conflict between Jesus and Simon is foreshadowed already in 1:35-39; the charge of blasphemy against Jesus by the high priest (14:61-63) is raised already in 2:6-7; Jesus' violent death is anticipated in 2:20 and 3:6. Various responses to Jesus and the gospel are already outlined in 4:13-20. And along with the overuse of "immediately" that seems to rush the narrative forward there is a little-noticed phenomenon that points the reader backward as well. In fifteen places Mark employs the word "again" retrospectively, uniting two or more separate literary units in order to establish patterns and interconnectedness. For example in 2:1 the evangelist reminds the reader that Jesus has already been in Capernaum (1:21) and in 3:1 does the same thing except that now the point is to establish the fact that Jesus frequented the synagogue (cf. 2:1, 13; 3:1, 20; 4:1-2; 5:21; 7:14, 31; 8:1, 13; 10:1 [2x], 10, 24; 11:27).

An even more sophisticated literary technique is Mark's "intercalation" of incidents in such a way that they cast interpretive light on each other. This can be done by splitting the narration of an incident into two parts and inserting another incident between the two halves. This has happened with a healing story in 2:1-12 where a debate concerning forgiveness of sins (2:5b-10) placed between the two parts of the healing story leads the reader to ask what the real miracle is—a physical cure or the eschatological forgiveness of sins. The story of a woman suffering from long-term hemorrhaging (5:24b-34) now appears in the context of the story of a little girl who is raised from the dead by Jesus (5:21-24a and 35-43), leading the reader to suspect that in being restored to "cleanness" the woman has also experienced resurrection from death. In 6:6b-13 Jesus sends his disciples on a preaching and healing mission and their return is noted in 6:30. In between Mark has placed the story of the violent death of John the Baptist at the whim of political powers (6:14-29), raising the question of the fate of disciples. The story of Jesus' temporary disruption of activity in the Temple (11:15-19) is framed by the story of his cursing of a fig tree that is unfruitful because it is the wrong time for it to bear (11:12-14, 20-24) and thus becomes a story not of a "cleansing" of the Temple but of a prophetic "cursing" of it. The same effect can be achieved by placing a given incident between two other incidents and asking the readers to reflect on the significance of the connection. The saying about new and old (2:21-22) is preceded by two conflict stories dealing with table guests (2:15-17) and fasting (2:18-20) and followed by two conflict stories about Sabbath observance (2:23-28 and 3:1-6). Statements about the attitudes of Jesus' family toward him in 3:20-21, 31-35 form the frame for a conflict story centering on attitudes of the scribes toward Jesus (3:22-30) and incite the readers to compare the two sets of attitudes. Stories of deceitful preparation for the death of Jesus (14:1-2, 10-11) frame a story about loving preparations for his death (14:3-9), and Peter's denial of Jesus (14:53-54, 66-72) is in stark contrast to the enclosed story of Jesus' own courageous confession and echoes the unbelief of the high priest (14:55-65). The same thing can be achieved with key words as in 1:21-28 where the teaching authority of Jesus (1:21-22, 27) frames the story of an exorcism, and it is at least possible that the very same technique has guided Mark's overall structuring of the gospel with the Galilean period (1:16–8:26) and the Jerusalem period (11:1–16:8) framing the center, namely Jesus' instruction of the Twelve about God's will for him and the implications of his death and resurrection for their own discipleship (8:27–10:52).

The literary style as well as the thought of the gospel are strongly influenced by Jewish apocalypticism. This is especially apparent in ch. 13, the so-called "synoptic apocalypse," that includes major elements of apocalyptic thought and writing: concern about the end of this present age and the full realization of God's new age (13:4b, 26-27, 29, 31), social and cosmic upheavals (13:5-8, 14-25), persecution of the faithful (13:9-13) and their vindication by God (13:27), and the appearance of the Son of man in power (13:26, 29; cf. Dan 7:13; *1 Enoch*, especially ch. 46). Apocalyptic imagery appears elsewhere in the gospel as well: for example, the idea of being tried or tested by Satan (1:12-13), the Reign of God (1:14-15), resurrection of the dead (8:31; 9:9, 31; 10:34; 12:18-27), cosmic darkness (15:33), and perhaps the symbolic destruction of the Temple (15:38).

Mark's story is full of references to the Hebrew Bible, usually in its Greek translation (LXX). These may be explicit quotations introduced by an introductory formula: 1:2-3 (attributed to Isaiah); 7:6-7 (Isa 29:13); 7:10 (Exod 20:12; Deut 5:16); 10:6-8 (Gen 2:24); 11:17 (Isa 56:7; Jer 7:11); 12:10-11 (Ps 118:22); 12:19 (Gen 38:8); 12:26 (Exod 3:1, 6, 15); 12:29-30 (Deut 6:5; Lev 19:18); 12:36 (Ps 110:1); 14:27 (Zech 13:7). In other cases there is no explicit attribution, but the allusion is clear: 14:62 (Dan 7:13; Ps 110:1); 15:24 (Ps 22:18[19]); 15:29 (Ps 22:7[8]); 15:34 (Ps 22:1[2]); 15:36 (Ps 69:21[22]).

Mark and the Other Gospels

There can be no doubt that the gospels of Matthew, Mark, and Luke stand in some form of literary relationship to each other. Although today's canonical order was established early, no later than the time of Origen (c. 185–c. 254), the order of composition was believed to be Matthew–Luke–Mark–John at least as early as Eusebius of Caesarea (c. 260–c. 340) who quotes Clement of Alexandria (c. 150–c.215); he in turn claims to quote "the primitive elders" before him to the effect that the gospels with genealogies (Matthew and Luke) were written before those without genealogies, presumably at least Mark and John and perhaps others (Eusebius, *Eccl. Hs.* 6.14.5). Into the ninth century in some parts of the Church such as Egypt (Clement of Alexandria), North Africa and Rome (Augustine), Spain (Isidore of Seville), and Ireland (Sedulius Scottus) the critical view that the gospels were composed in the order Matthew–Luke–Mark–John and/or that Mark had combined elements of the earlier gospels, Matthew and Luke, was still current in the tradition. By the time of the medieval schoolmen such as Thomas Aquinas (thirteenth century), the Reformers (sixteenth century), and the early Enlightenment (eighteenth century) this view seems to have been lost until Henry Owen in England (in a publication dated 1764) and Johann Jacob Griesbach in Germany (1745–1812) (re)discovered it. Following their work this view again became the reigning critical view during the first half of the nineteenth century, at which time the novel idea of Markan priority began to eclipse it and to become the dominant position regarding synoptic relationships. Since the middle of the twentieth century a growing number of scholars have demonstrated the viability of the earlier view. (For a fuller discussion, see the article "The Synoptic Problem" and the bibliography provided.) The present commentary is not primarily focused on literary issues and will thus not be dependent upon any literary theory of synoptic relationships. Comparisons between Mark and the other gospels will be made for purposes of seeing how traditions about Jesus could be remembered and formulated in different ways.

Authorship and Audience

Any internal evidence regarding the authorship and original setting of the gospel is indirect and implicit. The author's name is not mentioned in the gospel, but this was not unusual in the ancient world and is not different from the other canonical gospels. In none of the slightly differing lists of the names of the Twelve disciples or apostles now contained in the NT does the name "Mark" appear (cf. Matt 10:1-4; Luke 6:12-16; Mark 3:13-19; also the list of the eleven in Acts 1:13). The name does appear, however, in other NT writings: Acts 12:12, 25; 15:37, 39; Col 4:10; 2 Tim 4:11; Phlm 24; 1 Pet 5:13. While attempts have been made to combine all of these references into one historical figure, Mark, the author of the gospel that bears his name, such attempts are dependent on material all of which is external to the gospel itself, and they fail to deal with several critical questions including the dating and authorship of the NT documents utilized in such a reconstruction (Black, *Mark* 1994). At least since the time of Papias (c. 60–155 C.E.) Mark has been associated with Peter as his "interpreter" or "recorder" (Eusebius, *Eccl. Hs.* 3.39.14-17). However, in light of serious questions that have been raised about the sources and meaning of Papias' statement, it is best to leave open for further discussion not only the question of the historical identity of the author of the gospel of Mark, but the question of his historical relationship to Peter as well.

Tradition has affirmed that the gospel was written in Italy *(Anti-Marcionite Prologue, Manichean Prologue to Luke and Mark)*. In fact the tradition is usually more specific, citing Rome as the site of composition (Clement of Alexandria, *Outline to 1 Peter*). Later traditions associate Mark with the city of Alexandria where he was claimed as the first bishop (Eusebius, *Eccl. Hs.* 2.16.1; Jerome, *Lives of Illustrious Men* 8 and *Prologue to the Four Gospels;* cf. John Chrysostom, *Homily on Matthew 17,* 1.7). Others have suggested Syria. What we learn about Mark's intended audience from the document itself is that it consists of both Jewish and Gentile Christians who appear to be undergoing persecution or the threat of it and have become uncertain because the Jesus whom they have trusted to save them from the time of trial has not appeared.

Questions for the Way

In light of what has been said thus far it might be well to focus on some important issues to keep in mind during a closer reader of Mark's gospel. The reader may already have her or his own list, but the following need attention and response if the engagement with Mark is to be genuine. (1) What does it mean for Mark and his faith community to live in the Reign of God, to celebrate and be formed by its presence and to anticipate its imminent culmination in power? What, precisely, is the relationship between the gospel of God's Reign and the man Jesus of Nazareth? (2) Who is Jesus really? What does it mean to call him Christ, Son of God, Son of man? Why does Mark shroud the story of Jesus in mystery, combining great and open popularity with commands to be secretive about who Jesus is and what he is doing? (3) Inseparable from questions of christology are always questions of discipleship. Why is Mark so severely critical of the Twelve, especially Peter? What is the essence of discipleship that he and the others fail to grasp? (4) Mark's story moves inevitably to the cross and Jesus' shameful death and the final announcement that God has raised him from the dead and will soon reunite him with his disciples. What is the significance of Jesus' death and resurrection for the Markan community? (5) Finally, what is the "word" of Mark's gospel for the Church of the twenty-first century, a Church existing in a world of injustice and violence and loss of meaningful traditions? What is Mark's "word" for the one who reads and seeks to interpret the gospel for the Church?

SECOND READING

Prologue: 1:1-13

The opening superscription (v. 1) sounds formal and celebratory; it is filled with words that anticipate the narrative about to unfold and it makes clear to the reader the significance of what is being narrated. Writer and reader stand at the very beginning of momentous events that have to do with God and God's saving relationship to the world. It is difficult to imagine that a first-century reader who was at all familiar with the Hebrew Bible could fail to hear echoes of other "beginnings"—of creation (Gen 1:1), of wisdom and the fear of the Lord (Prov 1:7), or of the prophetic word (Hos 1:2), and thus be already here alerted to the divine source of the good news (cf. John 1:1 for a similar strategy).

The word "beginning" is richly suggestive in another way as well. Is Mark suggesting that the good news begins with the people of God, here represented by the quotation attributed to Isaiah? Or does the quotation merely serve to introduce John the Baptist whose fulfillment of the prophetic word and heralding of Jesus is the real "beginning" of the good news (1:1-8)? Does the good news begin with Jesus' experience with God (1:9-11) and Satan (1:12-13)? Perhaps all of these events prepare for the "beginning" of the good news in the first actual proclamation of it by Jesus himself (1:14-15). Finally, it is conceivable that Mark intends the entire account of the ministry, death, and resurrection of Jesus (1:1–16:8) to be understood as the "beginning" of the gospel that has been entrusted to the Church to proclaim in the whole world (13:10; 14:9).

Important as the word "gospel" *(euangelion)* is for Mark (cf. 1:14, 15; 8:35; 10:29; 13:10; 14:9), it is not his creation. The word has a long and complex history not only in religious but in political thought as well. In connection with the Roman imperial cult, for example, the word is used in the sense of "joyful tidings" on the birthday of the emperor or his accession to the throne. Thus a calendar inscription from approximately 9 B.C.E. calls the birthday of Augustus "the beginning of joyful tidings" (*Inscrip. Priene* 105, 40). Of particular interest in connection with Mark's usage is the verbal form in Isaiah (LXX) where it is associated with the joyous return of the exiles to Zion (40:9) and YHWH's care for the flock, with the announcement of peace, salvation, and the reign of YHWH (52:7), with the glory of YHWH and the coming of the nations to participate in salvation (60:6), and with YHWH's commitment to the poor and oppressed (61:1). Thus in political as well as religious contexts "gospel" conveys the sense of joyous news of some decisive benefit to the world or to a specific community and it is such eschatological and salvific nuances that are constitutive for the Christian use of the word. Already by the time Mark writes, "gospel" is a Christian code word signifying the "good," that is, the "saving" news by which the community of faith orders its life and that it proclaims to the world. Thus in Paul's writings the word can be used without further explication (cf. for example, Rom 1:16; 10:16; 11:28; 1 Cor 4:15; 9:14; 2 Cor 8:18; Gal 1:1; 2:2, 5, 7, 14; Phil 1:5, 7; 4:3, 15; 1 Thess 2:4; Phlm 13). Apart from the qualifiers "of Jesus Christ" in 1:1 and "of God" in 1:14 Mark always uses this word absolutely, a usage found neither in Matthew nor in Luke. Thus what Mark announces as the subject of his writing is nothing less than the living heart of Christian faith.

But as already noted Mark here qualifies "the gospel" as "the gospel of Jesus Christ." Both the singularity of this particular phrase in the NT and its use in the formal superscription make it likely that "Christ" is not being used here as part of a name, but in the titular sense of "Messiah." The good news is that of Messiah. But is the gospel of Messiah the gospel that Jesus Messiah *proclaims* or is it the gospel that *proclaims* Jesus Messiah? These two possibilities—gospel preached by Jesus or gospel preaching Jesus—are by the time of Mark no longer alternatives. "Gospel" embraces both. Moreover, when Mark parallels "gospel of Jesus Christ" (1:1) and "gospel of God" (1:14) it may be that we are intended to hear that the gospel's authority rests in Jesus Messiah, and that means in God. Messiah is not only bringer and content of the good news by which the community of faith lives, but the guarantor of its truth as well.

The final phrase of the superscription is textually uncertain but is used frequently enough throughout the gospel that its appearance here is not surprising (cf. 1:24; 3:11; 5:7; 8:38; 9:7; 12:6; 13:32; 14:36, 61; 15:39). It is a key expression of Jesus' identity and it makes sense that Mark would use it in this opening and definitive statement of the nature of the gospel.

Mark chooses to open his narrative with a quotation from Hebrew Scripture that consists of words from Mal 3.1 (and perhaps Exod 23:20 [LXX]) and Isa 40:3. Either Mark is using an already conflated text (from a collection of *testamonia*?), he himself has conflated the OT sources, or he has conflated the text from Matthew and Luke (compare the Malachi sentence with Matt 11:10 *par.* Luke 7:27 and the one from Isaiah with Matt 3:3 *par.* Luke 3:4-6). In any case Mark attributes the whole of this conflated quotation to Isaiah, suggesting the great importance of this prophet in the mind of the evangelist for understanding the origin of the gospel. The function of the citation, introduced by the formula "as it is written," is to show that the appearance of John and his heralding of Jesus ("the Lord") is the fulfillment of the promises of God to Israel. The good news that Messiah brings and embodies is part of the one history of God with God's people. Just as YHWH led Israel through the terrible wilderness on the way to the mountain of God and the Law (Exod 23:20) and brought Israel back through the wilderness to Zion following the exile in Babylon (Isa 40:3), so the same God is now acting in the wilderness (1:4 but also 1:12) for the benefit of humankind. Irenaeus was one of the early Fathers of the Church who sensed the significance of this soaring prophetic beginning of Mark's gospel and used it to justify assigning to Mark the symbol of the eagle from the list in Rev 4:7 (*Anti-Marcionite Prologue to Mark,* Recension 2 [longer text], in Eusebius, *Eccl. Hs.* 2.16.1).

In this place, then, of threat and promise—the wilderness—John the Baptist appears. The description of his activity is so thoroughly governed by the preceding prophetic word that it is characterized as "proclamation" (1:4) and this in a twofold form: John *proclaims* "a baptism of repentance for the forgiveness of sins" and he *proclaims* the one who comes after him (1:7-8). Whatever precedents John may have drawn upon for his baptism (provision in the OT and at Qumran for washings aimed at ritual purity? proselyte baptism?) he has adapted them to form what is now a one-time washing symbolizing repentance for the purpose of receiving forgiveness of one's offenses against God. Important as this activity may have been, however, John's real function as messenger is to proclaim the coming of Jesus, "the Lord" (1:3), and it is this preparatory function of John that seems to have been the one constant in early Christian memories of him. Memories differ on other aspects of the relationship. Thus while his appearance, described in 1:6, is probably intended to recall Elijah (2 Kings 1:8), as is the quotation of Mal 3:1, that explicit identification is not made anywhere in Mark.

How is Jesus' baptism by John to be understood? As Jesus' submission to a rite of repentance and forgiveness as Mark seems to suggest? or as the fulfillment of God's will, that is, obedience to the command of Jesus, as Matthew indicates (Matt 3:13-15)? as an act of identification with "all the people," as Luke suggests (Luke 3:21)? or as the moment of Jesus' being revealed to Israel, as John testifies (John 1:31)? Much about the Baptizer remains shrouded in mystery. What all the gospels agree on is that this mysterious, prophetic figure unites in himself Israel's past experience with God and the anticipation of a new and decisive encounter with God in the person of Jesus. With all that he is and does John points people to that now imminent encounter.

A final image of Jesus' superiority over John is that of their respective baptisms, John's being with water and Jesus' being with the Holy Spirit (1:8). But Jesus does not baptize in the gospel of Mark, nor does Mark connect the baptism by means of the Holy Spirit with an eschatological judgment (contra Matt 3:11-12). Thus in its present form the reference to baptism by the Holy Spirit serves as a vivid if not completely logical bridge to the account of Jesus' own baptism and experience of the Spirit.

It is with the story of Jesus' baptism and experience of the Spirit in 1:9-11 that we come to the very heart of the prologue to the gospel. The coming one, anticipated by OT prophets and announced by prophet John, is now named—Jesus, who *comes from* Nazareth of Galilee to the Judean wilderness and is baptized in the Jordan. There is no indication of any special understanding of the baptism and the simplest reading of the narrative is that he is baptized for the same reason that all others are baptized, problematic as that appeared to other Christian writers. Jesus *comes up out* of the water and "at once" (a favorite Markan word) sees the heavens being *torn apart*. Mark's language here is vivid to the point of being violent (cf. the more sedate "were opened" in Matt 3:16 and Luke 3:21, both of whom are linguistically nearer to the frequently cited Isa 64:1). Moreover, Jesus sees the Spirit coming down in the manner (not the "form": cf. Luke 3:22) of a dove into him. The visionary experience includes hearing the divine voice address him as "my son, the Beloved." It is true that others can be spoken of in similar language. Israel's king could be spoken of as God's adopted son (Pss 2:7; 89:26[27]); the righteous person can be called "a child of the LORD (Wis 2:13; 5:5); Israel itself could be referred to as YHWH's son (Exod 4:22-23; Deut 1:31; Hos 11:1). All these nuances may be gathered up into Jesus' designation as "Son," but he is not simply the sum total of such references. "Son" here unquestionably singles Jesus out as the only one whose relationship with God is so distinctive that what was foreshadowed in others now becomes reality in Jesus, a reality that can only properly be communicated by a shattering of the boundary between God and the world, by the "ripping open" of the heavens. In coming to Jesus God crosses boundaries, including the fundamental one between heaven and earth. So it is no wonder that the ministry of the Beloved will also be one of crossing and thus challenging boundaries. To some this will be healing, to some offensive, but to all profoundly provocative, calling *all* boundaries into question, relativizing all definitions human beings apply to themselves and each other. Even the most treasured of religious symbols lose their privileged status (cf. 15:32 where the same verb is used). But for now all of this is known only to Jesus—and to the readers.

What Jesus and the readers also know "at once" is that the status of Jesus as "Son" does not insulate him from suffering. The one who experiences God most immediately and profoundly also experiences evil with the same intensity. The very Spirit that has entered into Jesus now throws him out (cf. the more sedate "led" in Matt 4:1 *par.* Luke 4:1) into the wilderness. The verb Mark uses here is usually reserved for exorcisms (1:34, 39; 3:15, 22, 23; 6:13; 7:26; 9:18, 28, 38) or acts of physical violence (9:47; 11:15; 12:8; cf. 1:43; 5:40). Much of the imagery in 1:12-13 is reminiscent of Israel's experience: the wilderness is mentioned twice, the symbolic number forty (Exod 16:35; Deut 1:3; 2:7; 8:2, 4; 29:5[4]; Amos 2:10; Neh 9:21; as a time for punishment cf. Gen 6:5–8:22; as a time of fasting *Apoc. Abr.* 12:1; *T. Isaac* 4:7), wild beasts as symbols of danger (cf. Num 21:6-9; Deut 8:15; Isa 34:9-15; Jer 9:10-11; Zeph 2:14-15; Ezek 34:5, 25), and the angels representing the divine presence and feeding (*diakoneo* implies table service). The influence of apocalyptic thought appears in the figure of Satan and the verb "to test" in the sense of Satan's final onslaught and attempt to destroy the faith of the believer (cf. Dan 12:10; *1 Enoch* 94:5; 96:2-3. The same sense appears in the context of the Lord's Prayer in Matt 6:13 *par.* Luke 11:4). The apocalyptic language makes it clear that this experience of Jesus is not merely a private test of his resolve to be faithful to God or act as God's special agent. Rather this confrontation has cosmic dimensions and implications. Moreover, the scene is a summary and foreshadowing of the passion of Jesus: in him Spirit confronts Satan and suffers the full force of cosmic evil, and that Jesus emerges victorious from this conflict is evidenced in his proclamation of the gospel as the Spirit's triumph over evil.

Jesus Enacts the Good News: The Public Ministry: 1:14–8:26

The first major movement in the drama of the gospel centers around Jesus' public enactment, in word and deed, of the good news in Galilee. It may be helpful to note some of the recurring characteristics of the section.

(1) For one thing, geographical references are frequent. The Sea of Galilee figures prominently (1:16-20; 2:13; 3:7; 4:1, 35-41; 5:1, 21; 6:45-52; 8:13-21); the wilderness motif is continued in several places (1:35, 45; 6:31, 32, 35; 8:4); Jesus is sometimes "at home" or in a house (1:29-31; 2:1-2; 2:15; 3:20) or a synagogue (1:21; 3:1); he withdraws to the mountain (3:13) or goes from village to village (1:38; 6:6b); he spends time in the cities of Capernaum (1:21; 2:1; 6:1), Gennesaret (6:53), and Bethsaida (8:22), and in territory adjoining Israel such as "the country of the Gerasenes" (5:1), "the region of Tyre" (7:24), and "the region of the Decapolis" (7:31).

(2) Material is grouped into what appear to be several "collections": healing miracles (1:40–2:12; 5:1-43), debates (2:1–3:6; 7:1-23), and parables (4:1-33).

(3) A number of passages deal with the formation of the community around Jesus and its nature. In the first instance there is the group of the Twelve (1:16-20; 2:13-22; 3:13-19a; 6:6b-13) but the community is not limited to them (3:35).

(4) The question of Jesus' identity is woven throughout this section (1:24-25; 3:11-12; 4:41; 6:1-6a, 47-52) and will remain a crucial question to the very end. Frequently Jesus enjoins silence on those who know who he is, that is, the demons (1:25, 34b; 3:12) or those who experience healing from contact with him (1:43-44; 5:43; 7:36; 8:26; the command in 5:8 is somewhat ambiguous).

(5) Against the background of overwhelmingly positive response to Jesus on the part of

the crowds (1:28, 32-33, 45; 2:2, 12b, 13; 3:7-10, 20, 32; 4:1; 5:21, 24a; 6:34, 54-56; 7:14; 8:1) and tax collectors and sinners (2:15), Mark begins to develop the theme of conflict with and rejection by certain groups (2:6-9; 3:6, 21-35; 6:1-6a, 14-29), a theme that also runs throughout the entire gospel and will increase in intensity and scope.

The Good News in Galilee: Faith and Conflict (1:14–3:6)

The proclamation of "good news" occurs only after John's arrest and Jesus' return to Galilee. There he announces that *the* time (the *kairos*) is fully present, that moment toward which all time and history, all human and divine longing have been directed (1:15). The kairotic moment is present because the Reign of God has come near, so decisively near that it now is the one reality in which human beings are called to live and by which their lives are to be guided and determined. The word "repentance" here has its full biblical force of reorientation to a new existence. The remainder of Mark's gospel will deal with Jesus' continued announcement of this new existence, evil's continuing resistance to it, and the crisis into which that places those who hear the good news. *Now—it has begun.*

After the programmatic summary of Jesus' proclamation of the "good news" Mark places two series of stories, roughly parallel in arrangement and centering around statements regarding the purpose of Jesus' ministry.

1:16–2:12	**2:13–3:6**
Call of disciples (1:16-20)	Call of disciple (2:13-14)
Stories of healing (1:21-34)	Stories of conflict (2:15-20)
Purpose of Jesus' ministry (1:35-39)	Nature of Jesus' ministry (2:21-22)
Stories of healing (1:40–2:12)	Stories of conflict (2:23–3:6)

Jesus begins to form a community (1:16-20) by enlisting four men who will become the core of the apostolic group: they will always be listed first (Mark 3:16-19a; Matt 10:1-4; Luke 6:12-16), receive nicknames (3:16-17), and frequently accompany Jesus without the larger group (1:29; 9:2; 13:3; 14:33). In exemplary fashion they respond "immediately" to the call of Jesus (vv. 18, 20), abandoning family, friends, and livelihood in order to follow Jesus. In the gospel discipleship consists of "following" Jesus wherever the way of Jesus may lead. From the outset Mark makes it clear that the gospel is entrusted to the people of God and that the story of the gospel, the Messiah, and the people of God is *one* story.

Given what we know thus far, the content of Jesus' initial sermon in the synagogue in Capernaum must have been the Reign of God (cf. Matthew 5–7; Luke 4:16-30), but what seems to impress the hearers is that Jesus, in contrast to the scribes, appeals to no external standards such as Scripture and tradition but teaches on his own "authority" (*exousia* means literally "out of one's being"). The same words are used in v. 27b to describe the reaction of the onlookers to the exorcism they have just witnessed. This *inclusio* shows that Mark sees the exorcism as a testimony to the authority of Jesus to announce God's Reign. Unclean spirits recognize Jesus and his intent and cry out in an attempt at self defense. Jesus "rebukes" them (a favorite word in connection with demons; Mark 4:39, cf. Matt 8:26 *par.* Luke 8:24; Mark 8:32-33, cf. Matt 16:22; Mark 9:25, cf. Matt 17:18 *par.* Luke 9:42) and commands silence, a command that appears also in 1:25, 34b; 3:12 in connection with demons, and in 1:43-44; 5:43; 7:36; 8:26 in connection with other healings. At one level the command to silence can be understood as a defensive technique of the exorcist against the power that the demons have by virtue of knowing and pronouncing his name, but 1:34 makes clear that more is involved (see below).

The narrative in 1:21-28 can also serve as an illustration for the typical form of a healing miracle. Certain elements recur in greater or lesser detail: the encounter between the person in need and the healer (1:23; cf. 1:29-30, 40; 2:3-4; 3:1; 5:1-2, 22-23, 27; 7:25; 8:22; 9:14-18; 10:46-49), the naming and/or description of the disorder, frequently stressing the severity and thus the accomplishment of the healer (1:23; cf. 1:30; 2:3; 3:1; 5:2-5, 9, 23, 25-26, 35-40a; 7:25; 9:17-18), the action of the healer that can be an effective word/command (1:25, 41; 2:11; 5:13, 41; 9:25), the use of a substance such as spittle (8:23), a touch (1:31, 41; 5:41; 8:23, 25), or the announcement of the cure (5:34; 7:29; 10:52), some indication that a cure has actually taken place (1:26, 31b, 42; 2:12a; 3:5b; 5:15, 29, 42; 8:25b; 9:26-27; 10:52b), and, finally, a reaction, usually of amazement, from those who have witnessed the healing (1:27; 2:12b; 5:15-17, 42b). Most of these features are present in the account of Jesus' "raising" of Simon's mother-in-law (cf. the use of the same verb in 5:41-42; 9:26-27; 16:6), the story of a nameless woman described in traditional terms of her relationship to a man but who is empowered to "wait on" Jesus as the angels did (1:13).

The day in Capernaum begins and ends with exorcisms (cf. the summary in 1:32-34) and exorcisms continue to characterize the ministry of Jesus (1:39; 3:11, 22, 30; 5:1-20; 8:33; 9:14-29) as well as that of his followers (6:7, 13; 9:14-29; 9:38-41). Special note is made of Jesus' refusal to allow demons to speak, not simply because they know his name and thus possess a measure of power, but because they know *him,* that is, his identity as God's Son. At least since the time of Wilhelm Wrede (1859–1906) these commands to silence by Jesus have been understood as a part of a network of motifs in Mark that constitute a "messianic secret" and include such things as the theory of parables outlined in 4:10-12, the distinctively Markan motif of Jesus' withdrawal into a house where he instructs his questioning disciples on some elements of an earlier public teaching (see Mark 7:17-18a within the context of 7:14-23; Mark 9:28-29 within the context of 9:14-29; Mark 10:10-11a within the context of 10:1-12; and Mark 4:10-11a within the context of Mark 3:20-4:34), and the inability of the disciple to comprehend what Jesus is saying and doing (cf., for example, 8:17-21).

Whether one reads the exorcisms at a more literal level, as some cultures and sub-cultures do, or at a more psychological or symbolic level as structures of oppression or injustice, they speak about a very real human experience of bondage to powers that enslave and destroy the ability to make free and responsible decisions about things that matter. The demons here demonstrate remarkable insight when they sense that Jesus has indeed come to destroy them (1:24). The Reign of God is the ultimate threat to the reign of evil and this form of the "good news" has radical implications for every aspect of the Church's life.

Jesus' retreat to the wilderness to pray (cf. 1:12-13) is in stark contrast to the crowds and work of the previous day. Mark shares with Luke the stress on the importance of prayer for Jesus (cf. Luke 5:16; also Mark 6:46 with Luke 9:18; Mark 14:32, 35, 38 with Luke 22:41, 44-45). Simon represents expectations that are contrary to the intentions of Jesus who here announces that his priority is to *preach* in other towns because that is why he came out (cf. the clearer statement in Luke 4:38). The incident foreshadows stronger clashes between Peter and Jesus to come (8:31-33) and establishes in Jesus' own ministry the pattern for that of his followers (Mark 6:12-13).

Mark's version of the healing of a man with leprosy (1:40-45) reads more like an exorcism than Matthew's (8:2-4) or Luke's (5:12-16). "Leprosy" can denote a variety of skin disorders but here indicates an illness that is incurable and subject to Levitical ordinances (Lev 13:1–14:32). This leper chooses to ignore the barriers established by the Levitical code by approaching Jesus and kneeling before him (doing obeisance but also blocking the way?), confident that Jesus can help him. Even more amazingly, Jesus chooses to participate in the man's challenging of the boundaries between clean and unclean by reaching out and touching him. "Cleanness" restores him to the human community as shown in 1:45 and thus the community is healed as well. Certification of the man's cleanness by the priest is here put into the service of the person's resocialization. Ignoring Jesus' command to silence, the man instead becomes a missionary by putting his own story at the service of "the word" (mission language in Acts 8:4-5; 9:20; 10:42; 2 Tim 4:2).

The healing of a man unable to walk (2:1-5a, 11-12) becomes the vehicle for a debate about forgiveness of sins and thus serves as a transition from the collection of healing miracles in 1:21–2:12 to the collection of conflict stories in 2:15–3:6. The association of healing and forgiveness draws on OT tradition (2 Chr 7:14; Pss 41:3-4[4-5]; 103:3; Isa 19:22; 38:16-17; 57:17-18; Jer 3:22; Hos 14:4). Scribes, introduced here for the first time (2:6), accuse Jesus of blasphemy, the charge that will lead to his condemnation in 14:53-65; at the same time they give hostile witness that Jesus does in fact speak for God in announcing the eschatological forgiveness of sins. Using for himself the ambiguous title "Son of man" and thus suggesting his humanity (Ps 8:4), his prophetic obedience (Ezek

2:1), his role as apocalyptic agent (Dan 7:13), and his suffering and death (8:31; 9:31; 10:33) Jesus claims for himself the authority "on earth," that is, in the present, to forgive all sins (2:10). Thus Jesus embodies the Reign of God in his teaching, his healing, and his liberation of human beings from bondage to sin.

Persons who themselves live with disabilities or chronic illnesses have much to teach the Church about its reading of healing miracles. This is important since that reading has often been harmful instead of healing. They have made us aware that persons are not reducible to their disability or illness (thus "a man unable to walk" is more than "a paralytic"; cf. the good examples in the NRSV at 3:1; 5:2, 25). They show us that such persons are not passive objects subject only to the decisions and action of others (note how often the persons with illnesses take the initiative: 1:40; 5:2, 27; 10:50-52; in 2:1-12 the man unable to walk has mobilized friends to help him). They teach us that the often presumed, sometimes articulated causal connection between sin and disability must be challenged (do all "sinners" live with physical disabilities?), as well as that "faith" means trust and is not a sufficient precondition for being cured, and that in the gospel it is precisely those with disabilities who are said to have "faith" (2:5; 5:34; 9:24; 10:52). They make us aware that the healing miracles of the NT are understood to be "signs" intended to help others—presumably the "healthy"—to faith, that the "healing" of a person and a community involves more than the "cure" of a particular illness, and that the real "miracle" in all these stories is Jesus' refusal to respect definitions and boundaries imposed on persons by religion or society and his "touching" the marginalized back to their rightful place in the human family.

A second series of stories illustrating the nature of Jesus' enactment of the good news (2:13–3:6) is introduced by now-familiar Markan ideas—the sea, a crowd, Jesus teaching (2:13). The call of a fifth man to accompany Jesus is again recounted in stylized form (2:14). While the tradition is somewhat confused about his name (here it is Levi, son of Alphaeus, but cf. 3:18 and Matt 10:3, Luke 6:15; also Matt 9:9 where the man's name is "Matthew") it is clear enough about his occupation: tax collector, a despised underling of Roman tax officials or Jewish toll collectors, regarded as a collaborator with foreigners and a "robber" of the people. Levi's call to discipleship is the occasion for a dinner party at which Jesus seems to be the host—many "tax collectors and sinners" (mentioned three times in the story) are reclining "with Jesus and his disciples" (2:15). Religious officials—scribes and (for the first time) Pharisees continue to ask for an explanation ("why" at 2:7, 16, 18, 24) for Jesus' behavior, in this case his eating and drinking with people who do not observe Torah as prescribed by Pharisaic piety (cf. *Ps Sol* 2:37-41; 3:3-15; 12:7). Again Jesus has transgressed boundaries of clean/unclean. Moreover, the proverb of the physician makes clear that what the guardians of such boundaries regard as disrespect for God's will is, in fact, a sign of God's own presence under the familiar image of the banquet (cf. Matt 8:11; Matt 22:1-10; Luke 14:15-24, esp. v. 15; Matt 26:29; Luke 22:16, 18; Mark 14:25; Luke 22:18-20; Rev 19:9). Nothing in the story implies repentance as precondition or goal of eating and drinking with Jesus; rather he shares his table with the despised and thus announces that they belong to the family of God (cf. Matt 9:10; Luke 7:33-35; 15:1).

The image of banqueting is also at the heart of the second incident (2:18-20). Here the focus seems to shift from Jesus' behavior to that of his disciples, namely their nonobservance of fasting practices. The story may reflect debates over this issue in the early Church but it may have focused on Jesus himself. For one thing, practices of disciples are understood to reflect those of the teacher. Moreover, vv. 19-20 seem to soften the radicality of Jesus' reply in 19a, first by introducing the idea of the bridegroom's being "taken away," a veiled foreshadowing of Jesus' passion, and second by envisioning a time when fasting would once more be appropriate (cf. the parallel accounts in Matt 9:14-17; Luke 5:33-39; but also Matt 6:16-18; Acts 13:2-3; the variant reading at Mark 14:25). To the question regarding fasting Jesus responds that it is simply out of place in the midst of a party; it is "out of time" in the now fulfilled time of God's Reign.

The radicality of Jesus' statement is underscored by the twin parables of cloth and wineskins that constitute the center of the series of stories (2:21-22): the new, that is, the Reign of God being enacted in his own ministry, is not adaptable to the old forms and practices (cf. the rather different interpretation of Matt 9:17b).

Two more examples of the incompatibility of the new and the old have to do with proper observance of the Sabbath though in the first (2:23-28) the theme of eating is still present (clearer in Matt 12:1-8; cf. Luke 6:1-5). The seemingly omnipresent Pharisees ask Jesus again for an explanation of his disciples' behavior on the Sabbath. Whether they are referring to the disciples' "making a path" through the grain fields, their "plucking" (Sabbath reaping is prohibited in Exod 34:21), or whether Mark is assuming something like Luke's "rubbed them in their hands" is unclear. What is clear is that Jesus is moved to defend the actions of his disciples by arguing in good rabbinic fashion from an OT text (1 Sam 21:1-6), erroneously dated to the high priesthood of Abiathar instead of his father Ahimelech (cf. 1 Sam 22:20), from a theological proverb regarding the purpose of the Sabbath (2:27) and, if it is not part of the proverb, from a dominical saying regarding the authority of Jesus, Son of man (2:28).

The second Sabbath controversy occurs in a synagogue ("again" points back to 1:21) where Jesus encounters a man with a withered hand. Calling the man into their midst (from the fringes reserved for those with "defects"?) Jesus now poses the terms of the debate in sharp form: the issue is not doing or refraining from doing certain acts on the Sabbath; confronted by human need the alternatives are to do good or harm, to save life or kill. Acts of mercy and the saving of life were permitted on the Sabbath, as many later Jewish texts make clear (cf. *Mekilta,* tr. *Shabbetha* I, tr. *Nezikin; m. Yoma VIII.* 6; but cf. also Luke 13:14) and so Jesus' question is a rhetorical attempt to engage his opponents in a halakhic discussion, an invitation they refuse by remaining silent. But Jesus' question also points to his programmatic reinterpretation of the Sabbath: the presence of God's Reign makes all time the right time for doing good and saving life (cf. 1:21-34 where an entire Sabbath is spent in healing the sick). "Hardness of heart" grieves and angers Jesus wherever it is found (cf. 6:52; 8:17).

By providing examples of Jesus' behavior that bring him into conflict with the religious establishment Mark makes it clear that the decision of the Pharisees to eliminate Jesus is not a hasty one but the result of repeated instances of Jesus' failure to respect religious boundaries and customs (cf. 1:21-28, 29-31, 41; 2:5b-10a, 13-14, 15-17, 23-28; 3:1-6; 5:1-20; 5:25-34, 41; 7:1-23, 24-30, 31-36). The passion of Jesus begins with an alliance between religious and political powers (cf. 8:15; 12:13) committed to the "old," the status quo.

The Good News in Galilee: Confronting Evil Powers (3:7–6:6a)

Mark has arranged two sets of stories that deal in one way or another with Jesus' confrontation with powers of evil and death, one set (3:7-35) preceding and one (4:35–5:43) following a collection of parables that proclaims the certainty of the manifestation of God's Reign (4:1-34). The structure of the section thus testifies to the reality of Jesus' proclamation of good news in the midst of all sorts of destructive powers.

In response to the threat to his life posed by his opponents (3:6) Jesus "withdraws" to (toward) the sea only to have his life threatened by the crowds as well (3:7-12, esp. v. 9). These now come not only from his native Galilee but also from Judea and the border regions to the south (Idumea), east (Transjordan), and north (Tyre and Sidon). They flock to Jesus in an attempt to touch him and be healed (cf. 5:27-28; 6:56). Unclean spirits shout out his identity but are silenced to preserve the secrecy surrounding the Sonship of Jesus.

Without transition Mark has Jesus ascend "the mountain" and there appoint twelve men who are designated as "apostles" (3:13-19a) for the purpose of "being with him" and being "sent out" (3:14). Only in 6:30 is this group called "apostles"; otherwise Mark's favorite designation for them is "the Twelve" (4:10; 6:7; 9:35; 10:32; 11:11; 14:10, 17, 20, 43), a number almost certainly reflecting an understanding of the intimates of Jesus as representing a new form of the people of God. Their mission is to "be with" Jesus and when they are not accompanying him to continue his ministry by preaching the message of God's Reign and casting out demonic powers. They now share Jesus' "authority" to subdue evil powers (v. 15). Mark's list of apostles in 3:16-19 differs slightly from the other lists in the NT (Matt 10:2-4; Luke 6:14-16; Acts 1:13). Note should be made of "the mountain" that is mentioned here for the first time. The reference is geographically vague but its real significance is theological. It is not only a place of retreat from crowds (3:13; 6:46) but also a place of divine revelation (9:2 and possibly 13:3) and thus belongs in the same category as "the wilderness" (1:1-13, 35, 45; 6:31, 32, 35; 8:4) and "the sea" (2:13; 3:7; 4:1, 35-41; 6:45-50). Here, and even more so in 9:2-8, the mountain recalls the experience of Moses at Sinai (Exod 19–34; cf. Matt 5:1-2; 17:1; 28:16-20).

What has been mentioned in 3:7-12, 13-19a becomes the explicit subject in 3:19b-35. A third place of retreat from the crowds is "a house," whether Jesus' own or Simon's is unclear, but here also the crowds assemble and Jesus performs healings, especially exorcisms as is clear from what follows. He has no time even to eat (cf. 6:31). Such intense preoccupation with the sick is interpreted by Jesus' relatives (literally "those with him") as madness ("ecstasy"; cf. 2 Cor 5:13 where Paul contrasts it with being in one's right mind) and attempt to "arrest" him (3:21). Scribes who are apparently on a "fact-finding mission" from Jerusalem accuse Jesus both of being possessed by Beelzebub and casting out demons by colluding with "the prince of demons." The name Beelzebub is not found outside the NT and may be a local Palestinian variant of Baalzebub, the god of Ekron (2 Kings 1:2, 3, 6). The charge of demon possession and collusion appears in the other gospels (Matt 12:22-29; Luke 11:14-23; John 10:20), in Tannaitic texts (*b. Sanh.* 43a [Baraitha], 107b [Baraitha]; cf. *Sotah* 47a) and in early patristic texts (Justin Martyr, *Dialogue with Trypho* 69; Origen, *Contra Celsum* 1.6; 8.9.39; Tertullian, *Contra Marcionem* 2.6). Jesus' response to the accusation is "in parables" about a house divided against itself (vv. 23b-26) and the plundering of the strong man (v. 27), and in a direct accusation of blasphemy (vv. 28-30): to say that the Spirit that empowers Jesus (the "Holy Spirit"; cf. 1:10) is "unclean" is an unforgivable offense. No sooner has this judgment been spoken than Mark returns to the family of Jesus (from 3:21) who are "outside" and calling Jesus to come out to them. By framing the dispute with the scribes with the stories about Jesus' family Mark brings charges of madness and demon-possession under a common condemnation and in 3:33-35 replaces his biological family with the larger family of God, that is, those who (contrary to scribes and biological family) do the will of God (cf. 10:28-31). The sacred boundary of the family has been redefined in a radical way. It, like all other human institutions, is revalued in light of the Reign of God (cf. 1 Corinthians 7 where Paul does a similar revaluation in light of his eschatological expectation; also 2 Cor 5:16).

Though Jesus' teaching and preaching have been mentioned several times (1:14-15, 21, 39; 2:2, 13) little of the actual content has been reported apart from the programmatic statement in 1:14-15. In what is by now a familiar scene—the sea, large crowd, and Jesus teaching (4:1)—Mark reports a sample of Jesus' teaching, here "in parables" (cf. 3:23). It has long been recognized that this seems to have been the most characteristic form of Jesus' teaching. Frequently, however, the category of "parable" is defined more narrowly than it would have been in Jesus' own day. In the LXX the Greek "parable" translates the Hebrew word *mashal,* a term that can include riddles and proverbs, in fact any sort of similitude or figurative saying. Several sayings in Mark are clearly designated as parables: the sayings in 3:24-25 and 3:27 are called "parables" (3:23); the sayings in 4:3-8, 21-32 are called "parables" (4:2, 10, 30, 33); the saying regarding defilement (7:14-15) is a "parable" (7:17); and the story of the vineyard (12:1b-9) is called a "parable" (12:1a). But there are many other parabolic sayings in Mark's gospel: 1:17; 2:17; 6:4; 7:27; 8:15; 9:42, 43-48, 49; 10:25, 38-40; 11:23; 13:34.

Parables are "lively" forms of speech, not easily controlled. They can signify different things to different people, depending to no small degree on the social location of the hearer. There may be layers of meaning and allegorical details may introduce sub-themes. Nevertheless one does well to listen for a single, dominant point or concern in each parable or parabolic statement. Even allegories tend to have a major, focal interest.

Mark seems to understand the parable of the sower (4:3-8) as in some sense representative of all the parables: Jesus taught "many things" on this occasion but only this parable is reported; "in his teaching," that is, as part of his teaching (v. 2) he tells this parable; it represents "the parables" about which the Twelve and others ask him when the crowds are gone (v. 10). Moreover, this parable is of special significance: attentive listening is called for at the beginning (v. 3a) and the end (v. 9) and it is the key for understanding "all the parables" (v. 13).

Like all parables the story invites the reader into an imaginary though familiar world and leads her or him to ponder the spiritual implications of the known in such a way as to be led to new insights into what is unknown or partially known. Thus everyone "knows" about sowing seed and getting a harvest. When seed is sown it is inevitable that some is lost: some falls (not sown!) so near to the path (a boundary of the field) that it cannot be plowed under without destroying the path; some falls in places where the layer of topsoil is thin but the underlying limestone is nonetheless not visible; some falls among thorns, that is, in non-arable parts of the field and is lost among the weeds. But as is also well known, the majority of the seeds fall where they are intended to fall, on the good soil where they produce a harvest. The yield might have surprised the hearers of the parable even if the numbers report the number of grains from individual seeds rather than the overall yield of the crop. The parable could be used to make or underscore any number of points that concern beginnings and conclusions, but Mark has provided the reader with clear clues regarding the theme of Jesus' teaching (1:14-15; 4:11) and so the connection between "harvest" and Reign of God is not difficult to make: As surely as harvest comes after planting, just as certain is the culmination and manifestation of God's Reign that is being initiated (planted) in the words and deeds of Jesus (see "harvest" imagery in Joel 3:13; Matt 3:12 *par.* Luke 3:17; Matt 13:28-30; Luke 21:29-31; Mark 4:26-29; 13:28-29; Gal 6:7-9; Rev 14:15; in connection with the Christian mission see Matt 9:37-38 *par.* Luke 10:2; John 4:35-36).

The same point is reiterated in all the parables and parable-like sayings in this collection. A lamp brought into a room produces light in the room (4:21). Things hidden (not discarded) appear again at an appropriate time, and secrets invariably become known (4:22). The way of the wise person leads to the acquisition of greater wisdom and that of the fool leads to the loss of whatever was there to start with (4:24-25). Scattered seed leads mysteriously to the harvest (4:26-29), and planting a tiny mustard seed will always produce the pesky and oversized bush (4:30-32). As sure as any of these results is the now and future Reign of God.

Even the allegorical explanation of the parable of the sower (4:13-20) makes this same point in its own way. The imagery of the parable itself has become somewhat garbled. For example, what is sown is "the word" (v. 14) but also "the ones" that are sown and experience different fates. Sower, seeds, and soil are allegorized, perhaps reflecting the experience of the early Church after the time of Jesus' ministry. Even if this is the case it is remarkable how much the parable reflects its context in the gospel. A "first reading" of the gospel revealed how much attention is devoted in Mark to various reactions to Jesus and the message. Satan continues to oppose Jesus (the mention of Satan in this representative parable is especially striking given the location of the parable collection between two series of incidents involving Jesus' encounter with Satan); trouble and persecution cause even the Twelve to "fall away"; a rich man cannot bring himself to commit himself to Jesus (10:17-22). Moreover, in spite of the allegorical treatment of the various soils they have not become the focus of the interpretation nor is any injunction to be "good soil" implied. The focus remains "the word" and its final vindication in the world. Finally, the "harvest" is still the "end" of the story both in its certainty and its glorious character. Whoever is responsible for the allegorical explanation it is a marvelous homiletical model, scoring the point of the original parable in terms of the Church's own experience with "the word."

Between the parable (vv. 3-8) and the explanation (vv. 13-20) Mark reports a discussion about the parables between Jesus and a group of followers (fewer than a crowd but more than the Twelve) that is difficult in a number of respects. The literary relationship to the parallels in Matt 13:10-17 and Luke 8:9-10 is complicated. The words of Jesus divide hearers into two categories: insiders and outsiders. Those around Jesus are *insiders* because God has given them (God is the subject of the passive construction; cf. 8:17b) the "secret" *(mysterion)* of the Reign of God. The eschatological secret (the same understanding of "mystery" appears in Rom 16:25; 1 Cor 2:1, 7; 4:1; 13:2; 14:2; also in Eph 3:9; 6:19; Col 1:26) can hardly be knowledge of the imminence of God's Reign since that is the content of Jesus' public preaching. Nor can it refer to Jesus himself since his ministry is public, that is, given to everyone. What is "given" to those around Jesus is comprehension of and hence faith in the proclamation of Jesus (Matt 13:11 and Luke 8:10: "to *know* the secrets"). The *outsiders* are those who in the incomplete quotation from Isa 6:9-10 do not perceive or understand and hence are not forgiven. But does Jesus speak to them in parables *in order to* veil the truth, to prevent them from becoming insiders, as those who regard these words as an element in Mark's "messianic secret" think? That kind of determinism does not fit very well with the active, public ministry of Jesus to which crowds respond so positively. It is better to read "in order that" as an incomplete formula introducing the Isaiah quotation: "in order that the words of Isaiah might be fulfilled." The unbelief and opposition that Jesus experiences *fulfill* Isaiah's description of an unbelieving people of God and the parables of Jesus may be his attempt to overcome the incomprehension and unbelief. The parables of Jesus, then, are another form of his proclamation of God's Reign and they, like his exorcisms, healing, and teaching call forth different responses from different people as illustrated in the preceding parable and the following explanation.

The story of the storm on the sea (4:35-41) is the first of four accounts that pick up again from 3:7-35 the theme of Jesus' encounter with the power of evil. As in the story of the man with leprosy (1:40-45) Mark uses language that indicates that Jesus is dealing with demonic powers that are causing the storm and thus threatening the lives of those in the boat. Jesus "rebukes" the storm and "silences" the sea (cf. 1:25-26; 3:12; 9:25; but also 8:32-33). A recurring image of the sovereignty of God in the OT is God's control of the sea. God places the waters in their boundaries at creation (Gen 1:2, 6-9), opens the sea for Israel in its exodus from slavery (Exodus 14–15), and is praised as the One who rules sea and winds (Pss 33:7; 65:7; 77:16; 89:9; 107:23-32; 147:18; Prov 30:4; Job 12:15; 28:25; Isa 51:9-10; Amos 4:13; Nahum 1:3-4; cf. also 2 Macc 9:8). The same is true in the NT (Acts 4:24; 14:15), and one decisive apocalyptic sign of God's final vindication is that the sea is quieted (Rev 4:6), even eliminated (21:1; cf. also 7:1; 10:6). One obvious answer to the amazed question about who it is that wind and sea obey is *God.* Jesus, the bearer of God's spirit, does the works of God in overcoming life-threatening powers. Fear in the face of such powers is understood as an expression of unbelief (same word combination in 5:36) in the reality of God's Reign. Lack of faith and uncertainty regarding the identity of Jesus are two expressions of the same attitude.

Jesus' exorcism of the unclean spirit on the other side of the sea (5:1-20) is more detailed than most accounts. In a region inhabited primarily by Gentiles Jesus encounters a man "living" in a state of death; he dwells among the tombs, the place of death, and "on the mountains" (like the wilderness and the sea, the location of desolation, loneliness, and danger); his strength is superhuman but also inhuman and purposeless, freeing him only to further harm himself. In an attempt at self-defense the demon screams out the name of Jesus and begs not to be tormented by the Son of God. The full statement of Jesus' identity is not rebuked nor does Jesus enjoin silence. Rather he inquires about the demon's name. The name "Legion" may indicate the severity of the man's possession—like being possessed by an army (literally six thousand foot soldiers plus horsemen and some technical personnel) but may also suggest political critique of Roman occupation of Palestine. The size of the herd of pigs (two thousand) might indicate a Roman garrison nearby. The demons do not want to leave the country and propose the swine as an alternative dwelling. Once transferred into the swine, however, they do in fact leave the country by being plunged into that other dwelling place of demons—the sea. As a result Jesus himself is asked to leave the area (v. 17). Jesus does not allow the man to become a disciple (to "be with him," cf. 3:14), but encourages him to share the news with his friends. Again as in the case of the man healed of leprosy, this man's story becomes "good news."

A third "resurrection" story is the account of the twelve-year-old girl (5:22-24a, 35-43) whose father, in utter faith in Jesus as the healer, must beg Jesus "repeatedly" (another parent, in 7:24-30, has a similar experience though for clearly stated reasons) to come and lay hands on her (a common thaumaturgical technique; cf. also Mark 6:5; 7:32; 8:23, 25) and thus heal her.

As Jesus agrees and goes with Jairus he is interrupted by a woman suffering from a hemorrhage for twelve years (5:25). Her situation is desperate. She is "unclean" and to be treated as such, having no access to the holy place (Lev 15:25-31), and everything with which she comes into contact is unclean. All the more courageous does her faith appear as she deliberately violates the boundaries prescribed for her and decides to touch the clothes Jesus is wearing (5:27; cf. 6:56). "Immediately" her body tells her that she has been healed. Just as "immediately" Jesus turns to see who has touched him since in almost magical fashion he senses power leaving him. In a moving scene one boundary-crosser confesses to another; her healing is confirmed and she is blessed and sent on her way, a model of daring faith.

The little girl's story resumes with the news that she has died (v. 35). Ignoring the report, Jesus interrupts the formal mourners and announces that the girl has not died but is sleeping. Mark normally uses the verb to mean literal sleep (4:27, 38; 13:36; 14:37, 40, 41). Paul uses it figuratively for death (1 Thess 5:10). If Mark is using "sleep" figuratively here, Jesus is saying that the little girl has not succumbed to death in any final sense. As in 1 Thess 5:10 the verb already implies that she will be raised from the dead. In a similar way Jesus could be distinguishing between death and a deathlike, comatose state. Finally, it is possible that Jesus is speaking literally to the mourners: they are mistaken; she is not dead, but just asleep. The saying would then be a preparation for the command to silence in v. 43. Taking her hand (if she is dead Jesus is defiling himself by touching a corpse), Jesus commands her to "rise" (same verb as in 1:31; 9:26-27; 16:6) which she "immediately" does. Her walking about and eating confirm the return to life.

Mark has enveloped the story of the woman with the twelve-year hemorrhage within the story of the twelve-year-old girl, leading the reader to reflect on the miracle of a woman's movement from physical, emotional, and social isolation and death as a form of resurrection from the dead in the same way that rescue from the sea (4:35-41) and release from the prison of the cemetery (5:1-20) are resurrection experiences. The Spirit of God, having set aside the boundary between heaven and earth, clean and unclean, between Jewish territory and Gentile, between the Reign of Satan and the divine Reign, is the God of resurrection and life. In the midst of still active evil (3:7-35 and 4:35-5:43) the Reign of God moves toward its sure culmination (4:1-34).

This section (3:7–6:6) closes (6:1-6a) as did the collection of miracles and disputes (1:21–3:6) with Jesus experiencing misunderstanding and rejection, this time not from the religious-political establishment (3:6) and not from his family (3:21, 31-34), but from the people in his home town, presumably Nazareth (1:9). Astonished at his teaching (cf. 1:22 in Capernaum), they inquire about the source of his "wisdom" (illustrated in 4:1-34) and his mighty deeds (illustrated in 4:35-5:43), especially since they know him to be a craftsman who worked in wood and a member of a local family. It is his commonness that is at issue in their calling Jesus a carpenter rather than a dogmatic interest in protecting the idea of the virginal conception of Jesus by not mentioning Joseph as his father (6:3). There may be an implied insult here since naming a man by mention of his mother was at least not usual. In a wonderful irony the claim of the home town people to know Jesus demonstrates the profundity of their ignorance, ignorance that can be described as a form of unfaith (v. 6a). Those who know him best are scandalized by his pedestrian "roots" whereas the crowds who follow him are amazed and never inquire about his origins. The popular proverb Jesus quotes identifies him as a prophet and thus subject to the treatment of all prophets, namely rejection by their co-citizens (cf. Luke 4:24, illustrated by the fate of the prophets Elijah and Elisha [4:25-27]; also John 4:44). Though he cites the proverb Jesus is nonetheless affected by and amazed at the power of their unbelief.

The Good News in Galilee—And Beyond (6:6b–8:26)

Following the sending out of the twelve (6:6b-13) and their return (6:30), with the account of John's death sandwiched in between (6:14-29), Mark presents a cycle of stories about a miraculous feeding (6:31-44), a sea incident (6:45-52), and a summary of healings (6:53-56), another version of which appears in 8:1-21: a feeding story (8:1-13), a sea crossing

(8:14-21), and a healing miracle (8:22-26). Between the two cycles are a major debate with Pharisees and scribes (7:1-23) and two healings that occur in Gentile territory (7:24-37).

The call of four disciples (1:16-20) preceded a collection of miracle stories and debates in 1:21–3:6. The selection and appointment of the Twelve as apostles (3:13-19a) comes early in the section dealing with the Reign of God and the conflict with evil and death (3:19b-6:6a). Similarly the description of the first mission of the Twelve (6:6b-13) opens the present section.

Having scandalized the people in his own home town, Jesus leaves there and embarks on a third tour of the towns and villages. In the midst of this tour the Twelve assume their full "apostolic" identity and thus fulfill what was anticipated in 3:14-15: they are "called" and "sent out" by Jesus; they are "authorized" by Jesus, invested with his own authority (cf. 1:22, 27; 2:10, 28); they are an extension of Jesus himself in their preaching, exorcising of demons, and healing of the sick; and they report back to him upon completion of their mission (6:30). All of this reflects the OT (2 Chr 17:7-10) and rabbinic (*Ber.* 5:5; cf. Billerbeck 3:2) traditions of the *shaliach* that "the one sent by a man is as the man himself" (the same tradition is behind sayings such as Mark 9:37, 41; Matt 25:31-46). In their ministry the apostles make Jesus present. They are to depend wholly on those to whom they are sent for their livelihood, taking no food, no (begging) bag, no "small change," and no extra clothing. They are not to be itinerant beggars going from house to house but are to stay in one place. If the apostles are refused hospitality and a hearing (similar to Jesus himself in 6:1-6a) they are to leave and perform a symbolic act indicating that the inhabitants are now responsible for their own fate (cf. Luke 9:5; the note of judgment is stronger in Matt 10:14-15; cf. also Acts 13:51; 18:6 where the same symbolic act is mentioned also with varying nuances in meaning.) Apostleship here is not a matter of office but of authorization to continue the ministry of Jesus in the world.

Between the sending out of the twelve and their return (6:30) Mark places a note about various perceptions of Jesus (6:14-16). Opinions vary, but all agree that extraordinary "powers" are at work in him. No suggestion is made that they are evil powers (contra 3:19b-35). The various estimates of his real identity underline the mystery that surrounds this question. Herod's certainty that Jesus is John raised from the dead leads to a folktale-like account of John's death at the hands of the tetrarch (6:17-29; in addition to the synoptic parallels Matt 14:1-2 and Luke 9:7-9, cf. Josephus, *Ant.* 18.5.1-2). The role of Herodias brings to mind Elijah's conflict with the weak Ahab and the determined Jezebel (cf. esp. 1 Kings 18–19). Josephus's account stresses the political significance of John's denunciation of Herod. As it now stands the story makes clear that John dies as a result of several factors: his criticism of political figures who put themselves above the law, the weakness and vacillation of a man with power, and the whims of powerful people trying to impress others. Moreover, Mark's placement of the story between the sending out and return of Jesus' disciples may be intended as a foreshadowing of the fate of their own leader (note especially v. 29).

The stories of a miraculous feeding in the wilderness were among the most popular in the Jesus tradition judging from their six appearances in the gospels, most of which are combined with a sea story (Matt 14:13-21, 22-33 *par.* Mark 6:30-44, 45-52 *par.* Luke 9:10-17; Matt 15:32-39; 16:5 *par.* Mark 8:1-10, 13-21; John 6:1-14, 16-21). The location in "the wilderness" recalls not only Mark's emphasis (cf. 1:13, 4, 12-13, 35, 45) but also a major part of Israel's experience with God (Exod 16:14-35; Neh 9:15; Ps 78:17-29). Jesus begins teaching the crowd because they resemble "sheep without a shepherd" (Num 27:17; Ezek 34:5). The "compassion" of Jesus is frequently noted in the gospels (Matt 14:14; 9:36; 15:32 *par.* Mark 8:2; Matt 18:27; 20:34; Luke 7:13; 10:33; 15:20; Mark 1:41; 9:22 [in a request]). The disciples view the wilderness in its dangerous aspect: isolation (cf. 6:35-36), the late hour (v. 35), the paltry resources (v. 37b). Jesus embodies the divine presence in the same wilderness: hungry people are not to be sent away to fend for themselves (v. 37); there are resources available if one takes the pains to look for them (v. 38); the hungry are invited to God's banquet (vv. 39-40; cf. Isa 25:6-8); feeding the hungry is a form of Eucharist (v. 41; cf. 14:22); everyone has enough to eat (v. 42), and nothing is wasted (v. 43: each apostle/tribe has a small basket of leftovers). Thus shepherd Jesus feeds God's people, demonstrating that a person does not live only by every word that comes from the mouth of God but by bread (Deut 8:3; Matt 4:4 *par.* Luke 4:4).

No explanation is given for Jesus' "immediate" and urgent sending away of his disciples, his dismissal of the crowd and retreat to the mountain for the purpose of prayer (cf. Jesus' withdrawal for prayer in 1:35 and 14:32-42; his retreat to "the mountain" in 3:13). The concentration of places representing isolation and threat on the one hand and divine presence on the other (wilderness, mountain, sea), is striking.

The second sea story (6:47-52; cf. 4:35-41) in Mark follows the general pattern for miracle stories: the disciples are in distress, Jesus comes to them on the water, quiets their fears, calms the contrary wind, and the disciples are astonished. But there are also several puzzling elements. The phrase, "He intended to pass them by" (v. 48b) makes it sound as though Jesus' intent was not primarily to relieve the distress of the disciples but to provide them with a demonstration of his miraculous powers, making the story more of an epiphany than a calming of the sea. The phrase occurs in neither the Matthean nor the Johannine versions. If it is not a remnant from a different sea story, an epiphany that Mark has combined with the calming of the storm in something like its Matthean form, and if it is not an explanatory comment ("because he wanted to come where they were"), then it may be that Mark was using the OT motif of God "passing by" (Exod 33:19, 22; 1 Kings 19:11) to underscore the divine quality of Jesus' act in walking on the sea when coming to the service of his own.

In v. 52 the astonishment of the disciples at the miraculous appearance of Jesus and the calming of the wind is linked to their lack of comprehension "about the loaves" (cf. 8:17-21): as Jesus manifests the power of God against the threat posed by the wilderness, so he manifests these same powers in confronting the threat posed by the sea, but the Twelve do not grasp this because "their hearts were hardened." The passive construction can be read as a "divine passive," that is, God is the unspoken subject. This would imply that it is God's will that the disciples not comprehend who Jesus really is, a theme that appears in the Exodus story in connection with Pharaoh (Exod 9:12; 10:1, 20, 27; 11:10; 14:8; cf. also Deut 2:30; John 12:40; Rom 9:18; 11:7, 25). But alongside the notion that it is God who "hardens" Pharaoh's heart there are texts that portray the hardening as an act of will (Exod 8:15, 32; 9:34; cf. 1 Sam 6:6) and a whole series of passages in which responsibility—divine or human—is ambiguous (Exod 7:13, 14, 22; 8:19; 9:7, 35; cf. Mark 8:17; 2 Cor 3:14). What is clear in 6:52 is that the disciples are being criticized for their lack of comprehension, for an unfaithful astonishment at the appearance of Jesus on behalf of his followers. The incomprehension of the disciples stands in marked contrast to the clarity of people who bring crowds of sick people to him for healing (6:53-56).

The discussion centering around the issue of ritual washing (7:1-23) affords a glimpse of the evangelist engaged not only in reporting what Jesus said but attempting to spell out the significance of the teaching of Jesus for the early Church. A comparison with Matthew's version (15:1-20) helps to make this even clearer. Jesus is under intense scrutiny by a delegation of scribes and Pharisees who have come to Galilee from Jerusalem (Mark 7:1). That only "some of his disciples" are observed eating with unwashed hands (Mark 7:2, cf. Matt 15:2) indicates Mark's awareness of the composite character of the Church by the time he writes. The washing customs observed by Pharisees and, in Mark's view, all the Jews, and traceable to the "traditions of the elders," are explained for the benefit of Gentile believers (7:3-5). Another "why" question is directed to Jesus, but rather than responding directly Jesus turns the attack back on the religious leaders, appealing to Isa 29:13 (LXX) and thus setting the commandment of God (Scripture) over against "tradition" or the oral law of Pharisaic piety. It is unusual for Mark to have Jesus call the Pharisees "hypocrites" (only here, but cf. Matt 6:2, 5, 16; 7:5; 15:7; 22:18; 23:13, 15, 23, 25, 27, 29). In his example of the way he sees Scripture being voided by tradition (Exod 20:12a, 21:16) Jesus explains for Mark's readers the Aramaic term "corban" ("offering," hence not available for use in any other way). "Many things" are like that in Pharisaic piety, Mark generalizes. Jesus calls the crowd to special attentiveness at this point (v. 14b; some manuscripts add the "floating" injunction: "Let anyone with ears to hear listen" after v. 15; cf. 4:3a, 9) and tells them the parable about defilement (v. 15). In the privacy of a house (cf. 9:28, 33; 10:10) his disciples inquire about the meaning of the parable (cf. 4:10). Amazed that they apparently have no more insight than the scribes and Pharisees (v. 18a), Jesus nonetheless explains the parable to them (cf. 4:133-20), arguing that the only organ that can be involved in defilement is the heart, that is, the seat of human will and character (vv. 18b-23). In his parenthetical comment in v. 19b Mark makes a huge generalization by: (a) introducing a new subject: what began as a discussion of ritual washings ends as a discussion about "all foods" (literally "meats"), and (b) drawing a conclusion from v. 15 that is not necessary: the parabolic saying may mean that "what comes out of a person's heart is what really matters," and say nothing about food laws.

No reason is given for Jesus' movement to the northwest, to the "region of Tyre" (7:24), an area with a mixed population, except for his desire to withdraw from the public. As often happens the attempt is frustrated by people seeking his aid (1:35-37; 3:7; 6:30-34). In this case (7:25-30) it is a mother seeking help for her daughter who is possessed by a demon (parents bring children to Jesus also in 5:22-23; 9:14-29; 10:13-16). She is portrayed as an unusually strong woman: she does not happen to see Jesus, but hears about him and seeks him out; she disregards his desire for privacy and enters a (presumably) Jewish house; she also disregards the Gentile–Jew difference between herself and Jesus as well as the fact that she has no male sponsor. She is strong enough to plead with Jesus on her daughter's behalf and when rebuffed with a parable about what belongs to children of the household and what belongs to household pets she uses the parable against Jesus' objections to helping her. So impressed is Jesus by her counter-parable that he gives in and assures her of her daughter's healing. Daring to trust the word of Jesus without any physical signs of confirmation she goes home and finds that Jesus' word is true—her little daughter is lying peacefully on the bed.

The route Jesus takes from the area around Tyre back to Galilee suggests a longer period of time spent in areas of significant Gentile population (7:31) during which he performed miraculous cures, illustrated by 7:32-37. Jesus' attempt to remain out of public view continues (vv. 33a, 36) but is frustrated by the enthusiasm of those who are healed or witness miraculous cures. The healing of the man with a hearing and speech disability leads to a generalized proclamation about Jesus that may see in the miracles a fulfillment of passages such as Isa 29:18-19; 35:5-6; 61:1; cf. Matt 11:2-6 *par.* Luke 7:18-23).

Mark connects the second feeding miracle (8:1-10) to the time in Gentile territory ("in those days," v. 1) and to the first feeding (there is "again" a great crowd without anything to eat [v. 1; cf. 6:35-36], Jesus has "compassion" [v. 2; cf. 6:34], it takes place "in the wilderness" [v. 4; cf. 6:31, 32, 35 and contrast Matthew's location of the story on a mountain in Galilee in 15:29]). Moreover, the sequence of events in 8:1-26 is similar to that in 6:30-56 (feeding in 6:30-46 and 8:1-10; crossing the sea in 6:45-52 and 8:10, 13-21; healings in 6:53-56 and 8:22-26). Finally Mark expressly links the two stories in 8:19-20. On the other hand several linguistic changes from 6:30-46 may be intended to place stress on Gentiles in the present story (the emphasis on distance in 8:3, cf. 6:36; the change in the verbs from "bless" in 6:41 to "give thanks" in 8:6; the change from "small woven baskets" in 6:43 to rope or cord baskets in 8:8, and perhaps the change from "twelve" in 6:43 to "seven" [the number of completeness] in 8:8). As God's shepherd cares for the people of God—Israel—in the wilderness, so also for the people of God—the nations. Abruptly Jesus leaves the scene of the feeding miracle by sea (Mark 8:10).

Between two boat trips (8:10 and 8:13) Mark reports a brief encounter between Jesus and the Pharisees who ask him to provide them with a "sign" from God that will authenticate what he is doing. It is not a request for a miracle; they do not contest that Jesus is a miracle worker but miracles in and of themselves are ambiguous and can be performed by the power of God or, as they suspect in the case of Jesus, by that of Satan (3:22). Indignantly Jesus refuses the request for a sign (cf. Matt 16:1-4; 12:38-39; Luke 11:16, 29; 12:54-56) and leaves them standing as he departs by boat to the other side of the sea.

The conversation between Jesus and his disciples in the boat (8:14-21) brings into the open Jesus' growing frustration with the failure of the Twelve to comprehend in more than a superficial way the significance of what is actually happening in Jesus' ministry. Having forgotten to bring sufficient bread (loaves) with them, when Jesus warns them about the yeast of the Pharisees and Herodians (Matt 16:6: "Pharisees and Sadducees") they, rather surprisingly for the reader, think that Jesus is referring to their failure to bring bread for the journey. "Leaven" is used here in its negative connotation of bad influence or corruption (*b. Berakhoth* 17a; 1 Cor 5:6-8; Gal 5:9; positive use of the term in Matt 13:33 *par.* Luke 13:20-21) and in connection with the Pharisees and Herodians. The reference to the Pharisees comes from the conversation in 8:11-12 where their request for a sign to legitimate the miracles of Jesus stems from their conviction that Jesus is empowered by Satan. The Pharisees and Herodians appear together at 3:6 and 12:13, both times conniving against Jesus because they do not recognize in Jesus God's Spirit at work. The same question is now raised in connection with the Twelve. The series of questions that Jesus puts to them in vv. 17-21 seems to underscore the fact that if in the presence of Jesus they can argue over bread they have not seen or understood any more than the declared enemies of Jesus. As they failed to make the connection between the shepherd who cares for Israel in the wilderness and their trouble on the sea (6:52), so now they fail as do the Pharisees to make the connection between the one who provides more than enough bread in the wilderness and their own need. The answer to Jesus' question in v. 21 is: *no*.

Jesus' talk about not seeing and comprehending is dramatic preparation for the miraculous healing of the man who cannot see in 8:22-26. The story serves as a transition from the Galilean period of Jesus' ministry to the account of his way to Jerusalem (8:27–10:52) just as another story of the healing of a blind person (10:46-52) serves as a transition from the middle section of the gospel to the final section dealing with Jesus in Jerusalem (11:1–16:8). The healing of the man in Bethsaida is the only miracle story in the NT in which a second act of Jesus is required. The man brought into contact with Jesus sees only unclearly, much like the Twelve who have continued to follow Jesus and have "seen" things without really seeing them. A second, further effort is required of Jesus if the man, and the disciples, are to "see everything clearly" (v. 25).

Jesus and "The Way": 8:27–10:52

In the great middle section of the gospel "the way" of Jesus can be described in geographical terms: overall, it is "the way" from the northernmost area of Galilee to Jerusalem, the place of crisis, of death and resurrection. More specifically it is the way from the villages of Caesarea Philippi (8:27) through Galilee (9:30) with a stop in Capernaum (9:33), then on into Judea (10:1) with a further journey (10:17) up to Jerusalem (10:32) via Jericho (10:46). Jesus arrives at the Mount of Olives in 11:1 and in Jerusalem itself in 11:11. No more time is spent in the wilderness or on the sea. The movement is steady and inexorable. "On the way" is a common phrase in this part of the gospel (8:27; 9:33, 34; 10:32; 10:52).

More important than geography, however, is christology and, inseparable from it, discipleship. And so the way to Jerusalem is the way on which Jesus shifts his focus from the crowds to the Twelve (8:31; 9:31; 10:32). The crowds are still present (8:34; 9:14; 10:1) and Jesus teaches and responds to requests for healing (9:14-29; 10:46-52) and blessing (10:13), but the primary focus is on the Twelve. Moreover the focus of his teaching shifts from the Reign of God to the issue of his own identity and fate and—the most dramatic shift of all—while deeds of power that characterized the Galilean ministry are not absent, the stress is now on the powerlessness, suffering, death, and resurrection of Jesus, the inability of the Twelve to comprehend this redefinition of messiahship, and the implication of Jesus' death and resurrection for a true understanding of discipleship. The section is structured around a threefold proclamation of Jesus' imminent death and resurrection. Following the first passion prediction (8:26-31) there is opposition from the Twelve, especially Peter (8:32-33) that leads Jesus to talk about the nature of discipleship (8:34–9:1). The cycle continues with the transfiguration story (9:2-8), a conversation about the role of Elijah (9:9-13), and an exorcism (9:14-29). The second passion prediction (9:30-31) is followed by incomprehension on the part of the Twelve (9:32-34) that leads Jesus to again speak about the nature of true discipleship (9:35-37) and the Christian community: a strange exorcist (9:38-41), self-discipline (9:42-50), divorce and remarriage (10:1-12), the blessing of children (10:13-16), and the story of a rich man (10:17-31). The third passion prediction (10:32-34) is followed by a question demonstrating the failure of the Twelve to understand Jesus (10:35-41), prompting Jesus to describe once more what it means to be his disciple (10:42-45). The transitional story of Bartimaeus (10:46-52) closes the third cycle of stories.

On the Way: Messiah Jesus Announces His Death and Resurrection (8:27–9:29)

As if to illustrate the truth to which the healing story in 8:22-26 pointed, namely the need for and possibility of clearer (in)sight, Mark reports the crucial conversation between Jesus and his disciples during a tour of the northernmost villages of Israel (8:27-33). "On the way" (v. 27) Jesus inquires of the disciples what people are saying about him and hears from them the popular opinions (cf. 6:14-15). Then Jesus asks them the question they have already asked themselves (4:41; cf. 6:51-52). Representing the Twelve, Peter speaks clearly and confidently: "You are the Messiah" (8:29). The fact that the reader knows this from the beginning and that by the time Mark was writing the ascription of the title "Christ" to Jesus was self-understood almost to the point of its sounding like a proper name should not obscure the enormity of this moment in Mark's narrative. Thus far no one has used the word; the idea has not occurred to anyone. So here from the lips of Peter comes the revelation of one of Mark's key titles for Jesus (1:1). Between the series of questions Jesus put to the disciples in the boat a short time ago (8:17-21) and his question in the region of Caesarea Philippi, Peter and the Twelve have progressed in their insight to the point that they now recognize Jesus as the fulfillment of Israel's hopes for the time of God's Reign and the time of *shalom*.

The title "Messiah" (Hebrew *mashiach,* Greek *christos*), the "one who has been anointed" is familiar in the OT, referring primarily to Israel's kings: Saul (1 Sam 9:16; 10:1; 15:1, 17), David (1 Sam 16:3, 12-13; 2 Sam 2:4, 7; Ps 89:20), Solomon (1 Kings 1:34, 39, 45; 1 Chr 29:22), and others. Even a foreign king, Cyrus, can be called God's "anointed" (Isa 45:1). Priests are also anointed (Exod 28:41; 30:30; Lev 7:36; Num 3:3). There may even be evidence of the anointing of prophets (1 Kings 19:16; Ps 105:15. Isaiah 61:1, however, uses the idea figuratively and is of a different character than the preceding instance.). Hopes for a future ideal king were associated with David (2 Sam 7:16; Isa 55:3-5; Jer 23:5) and became the basis for one form of "messianic" expectation in post-OT Judaism. In the Mishnah the figure of Messiah plays no role at all and is mentioned only twice (*Ber.* 1.5; *Sot.* 9:15), but for early Christianity, including Mark, Peter's "confession" of Jesus as Messiah gathers into itself all of the religious and political yearnings and hopes of the people of God and claims that they are being realized in the words and deeds of Jesus.

If all of this is true, however, it is surprising to read that Jesus "rebukes" Peter and commands the disciples to tell no one about him. Is Jesus rejecting Peter's confession? Mark has used the word "rebuke" when describing Jesus' confrontation with demons who cry out that he is the "Son of God" (cf. 1:25; 3:12) but that in no way implies that "Son of God" is an inappropriate title for Jesus. Moreover, Jesus himself accepts the title from the lips of the high priest (14:61-62) and Mark has told us that it is a key way of talking about Jesus (1:1). Thus the reaction casts a shroud of mystery on what sounds like a clear and unambiguous confession. Could it be Jesus' own restrictions of the disciples that keep them from an open and enthusiastic proclamation of who Jesus is? Will there come a time when the shroud of mystery is lifted?

If the disciples' insight that Jesus is Israel's Messiah represents a critical moment in the narrative the subsequent announcement of Jesus in v. 31 is a shattering one. While there have been veiled references to Jesus' violent death (2:20; 3:6; 6:17-29), Jesus now says without parable or riddle that it is God's will that he should be killed and after a short time be raised from the dead. (The verb *dei,* "must," conveys divine necessity [Dan 2:28-29; Mark 9:11; 13:7, 10; John 3:14; Acts 1:17; 3:21; 4:12; Rom 1:27; 1 Cor 15:53; Rev 1:1; 4:1; 22:6; *2 Clem.* 2:5].) "Son of man" is used here as a circumlocution for "I," though by the time Mark writes all the nuances of the word are undoubtedly present as well: his humanity (Ps 8:4), his prophetic obedience (Ezek 2:1 *passim*), his role as apocalyptic agent of God (Dan 7:13), and his suffering (Mark 8:31; 9:31; 10:33). From this point on, the cross and resurrection of Jesus dominate the story in Mark.

Yet it is precisely this emphasis on suffering and death that the Twelve seem unable to grasp.

The same insight that led Peter and the others to confess Jesus as the Messiah now leads to vehement resistance to the idea of his violent death. The language of the encounter between Jesus and Peter is strong. In a private conversation Peter "rebukes" Jesus and is in turn "rebuked" by Jesus (8:32-33). The language suggests that just as Peter regards Jesus' talk of a violent death as "madness," so Jesus regards Peter's resistance to it as demonic ("Get behind me [that is, 'out of my sight'], Satan/Peter!"). As far as Peter is concerned Jesus has confused his categories, blurred boundaries, and brought the notion of suffering and death into the very heart of theological reflection. The mystery surrounding Jesus deepens even more.

Including the crowd in the conversation, Jesus then proceeds to redefine discipleship in light of his radical redefinition of messiahship (8:34–9:1). If Messiah must deny self and embrace suffering and death, then the disciple cannot avoid a similar fate. If Mark's original readers were undergoing persecution by the Romans the reference to martyrdom by crucifixion would have been far from theoretical speculation. If Messiah must suffer violence and rejection before being raised by God, the follower must also be prepared to stop grasping her or his existence and let it go for the sake of Messiah and the Church's proclamation of Messiah (on "the gospel" see 1:1 above).

All the sayings on discipleship (vv. 34-38) speak about relationship to Jesus Messiah not in terms of an interiorized or privatized realm but as a way of being in the world. These sayings may be especially difficult for persons and churches who have tended to view Christian faith as a means of guaranteeing approval, power, security, favored status in society. Words that may have meant comfort to persecuted Christians may be a call to repentance to those who have seemed to "gain the whole world." The seriousness of commitment to *this* Messiah and *this* understanding of belonging to him is underscored by two apocalyptic sayings that emphasize the certainty (8:38) and imminence (9:1) of the consummation of God's Reign and the crisis of judgment that it brings.

The disciples' vision of Jesus transfigured (9:2-8) is connected to the preceding events by a relatively precise chronological statement stressing the relationship between them (cf. Matt 17:1; different Luke 9:28). Several traits in the story are drawn from the OT: "six days" and the "high mountain" (Exod 24:16-17; cf. also 1 Kings 19 for another mountain of revelation), dazzling garments (Dan 7:9; Rev 3:5; 4:4; 7:9; *1 Enoch* 62:15-16; *2 Enoch* 22:8), the figures of Elijah and Moses, the mention of tents (as in "booth" in Lev 23:42 -43 or "tent of meeting" in Exod 27:21), the cloud and voice (Exod 16:10-12; 19:9, 16). Some elements remind one of a resurrection appearance: the mountain (Matt 28:16-20), the "metamorphosis" of Jesus (the word is used of the resurrection body in Phil 3:21 and 2 Cor 3:18; cf. 1 Cor 15:51), Elijah and Moses, figures who like Jesus have already been taken into the presence of God (Rev. 11:16; cf. 2 Macc 2:1-2; 15:13; 4 Ezra 14:9; 4 Macc 7:19; 16:25), and the vision that is not to be shared until after the resurrection (9:9). Although Peter's suggestion to build tents for each of the heavenly figures may be empty talk (v. 6) it may also indicate that Peter thinks they have seen the Reign of God arriving with power (9:1) and proposes setting up tents of meeting for the new age. As the voice from the cloud makes clear, such "realized eschatology" is not the point of the vision. The point is rather Jesus himself and the revelation of him now to human beings for the first time as God's Son. What readers know (1:1), what demons shout out (1:24; 3:11), the inner core of disciples now knows. Both of Mark's key titles for Jesus—"Messiah" and "Son" (1:1)—are now known by the disciples, but the accompanying command, "listen to him," is equally important, referring back as it does to what Jesus has said in 8:31–9:1. The divine voice confirms that the glorified Son is none other than the suffering, murdered one whom God has raised from the dead. Peter's desire to protect Messiah from suffering is demonic. Messiah *is* the Suffering Son.

In the conversation on the way down from the mountain (9:9-13) Jesus redefines still another tradition. When Jesus orders them not to share their vision until after he has risen from the dead they ponder what the resurrection means, not in general but in connection with Jesus, and realize that they have just heard another veiled reference to his violent death. To dissuade Jesus from what they still take to be his unnecessary preoccupation with death, and having just seen Elijah in a vision, they ask Jesus about the purpose of Elijah's appearance prior to that of Messiah. Elijah's coming to "restore all things" does not obviate the need for Jesus Messiah to suffer, and to make his point Jesus now interprets even Elijah in light of the teachings in 8:34-37. Referring to the violent death of John the Baptist, Jesus says that Elijah's preparations for the Son of Man consisted in his undergoing precisely the same fate. The Elijah tradition does not save Jesus from the cross. Everyone and every tradition is reinterpreted in its light.

The revelation of the glorified Jesus is situated between Jesus' redefinition of messiahship and discipleship (8:27–9:1) and Jesus' continuing conflict with demonic powers (9:14-29). In this third instance of a parent's entreating Jesus on behalf of a sick child (5:22-24a, 35-43; 7:24-30) Mark's version is much longer and more detailed than either Matthew's (Matt 17:14-21) or Luke's (Luke 9:37-42). The faith of the father in bringing the child (v. 17), his trust that Jesus could help (v. 22b), and his marvelous confidence that Jesus will make up what his faith lacks (v. 24) stand in stark contrast to the ineffectiveness of Jesus' disciples resulting from their own faithlessness (v. 19). When Jesus has taken over and banished the unclean spirit (forever!) he takes the boy by the hand (a frequent practice of Jesus: 1:31; 5:41; 8:23) and "raises him up" from this deathlike state (Jesus "raises" the sick: 1:31; 5:41, and is himself "raised" from the dead: 16:6). In the typical Markan "house scene" afterward Jesus explains that the only thing effective against this type of demon is prayer (v. 29). Some manuscripts move the practice of exorcism in the direction of a ritual by adding "and fasting," but for Mark the issue is faith, expressed in the absence of Jesus by prayer, that is, conversation with God rather than with critics (v. 14).

On the Way: Second Announcement of Messiah's Death and Resurrection (9:30–10:31)

The next cycle of stories and sayings (9:30–10:31) opens with the second formal prediction of his death by Jesus as he and his disciples are passing through Galilee. That this is in obedience to the will of God is indicated by the Greek verb that can mean "to betray" and "to hand over." It has the former meaning in all passion texts that mention Judas (3:19; 14:10; 11, 18, 21, 41 and *parr.*; cf. also 1 Cor 11:23). In the latter sense it is used when Jesus is "handed over to" the Gentiles by the chief priests and scribes (Mark 10:33), when he is "handed over" to Pilate (15:1) and when Pilate "hands him over" to the soldiers for crucifixion (15:15). But here the Son of man is given over to human hands. God is the acting subject (contrast 10:33 where specific groups are mentioned).

In a house in Capernaum Jesus learns how far the disciples still are from comprehending the way he must go when they report their argument on the way about which of them is the chief apostle (v. 34). Jesus' response this time takes the form of a saying that reverses all socially acceptable thinking about greatness (v. 35) and then the acting out of the saying: he picks up a child and says that to be a "servant of all" means serving the weakest, most vulnerable members of society, the children. To serve "the least" (in terms of power) is to serve God (cf. Matt 25:31-46). Competitiveness has no place in the Christian community. The same thing is true of the relationship of the community to those who do not belong to it in any declared or formal way (9:38-41). Anyone who does the will of God belongs to the family of Jesus (cf. 3:35). Members of the Church must pay special attention not to cause "little ones" to stumble in their faith. "Little ones" reminds one of the children from 9:36-37 but can also refer to all believers, perhaps even someone working outside the bounds of the Christian community (9:38-41). "Little ones" as a designation for believers is a favorite Matthean expression (Matt 10:42 *par.* Mark 9:41; Matt 18:6 *par.* Mark 9:42; Matt 18:10, 14; 25:40, 45). Death (9:42) or mutilation (9:43, 45, 47) are preferable to causing "scandal" among the faithful. It may be the mention of "fire" in 9:43-48 that provided a "catchword" association with v. 49 where fire in connection with salt symbolizes not judgment but an offering to God (Exod 30:35; Lev 2:13; Ezra 6:9; Ezek 43:24), a reference perhaps to persecution that believers are enduring (cf. 10:30, "with persecutions"). The positive image of salt as that which preserves (v. 50) is a nice counterbalance to the salt of sacrifice (v. 49). The command to "be at peace with one another" is Jesus' final word in response to the "argument" about greatness (9:34) and leaves no room for competition in the Church.

On his way from Capernaum (9:33) into Judea and the Jordan valley Jesus adheres to his custom of teaching the crowds that continue to flock to him and engaging the Pharisees in debates, for example on the question of divorce (10:2-9), an issue of critical importance to both first-century Judaism and the early Church (see Matt. 19:3-9 *par.* Mark 10:2-9; Matt 5:32 *par.* Mark 10:11-12 and Luke 16:18; 1 Cor 7:10-16). Already the form in which the Pharisees pose the question shows Mark adapting the issue to his Gentile Christian context. For Pharisaic Judaism the question was not whether divorce was permissible at all, as Mark's question implies, but rather, given the permission granted by Deut 24:1-4, under what conditions is it lawful (so correctly Matt 19:3). Letting Scripture critique Scripture, Jesus moves the discussion from what even he acknowledges to be a "commandment" (albeit a concession to "your," that is, Judaism's hardness of heart) to the larger context of creation where the question is no longer: "what is lawful?" but rather: "what is God's will for creation?" The shift is decisive because it allows the real question to surface: what is marriage? The answer, based on a combination of Gen 1:27 and 2:24, is that marriage is an expression of God's will for the union and perfection of man and woman and that such union ought not to be broken apart by human beings (on the use of Gen 2:24 see *Jub* 3:6; Sir 25:26). Moreover to reframe the discussion as Jesus does moves it from the realm of male prerogatives into that of male–female mutuality in blessing and responsibility.

In the following typical Markan house-scene (10:10-12) Jesus instructs his disciples further in the matter and again Mark's application of the question to his own cultural context, namely Hellenistic/Roman, is clear at several points. (1) A monogamous understanding of marriage is presupposed. If a man divorces his wife in order to marry another woman he is guilty of adultery. (2) The violation of the marriage is now understood not as an offense against another man, but as an offense "against her," the abandoned woman. (3) A woman is understood to have the right not only to sue for divorce but actually to divorce her husband which, of course, means that she is equally liable to the charge of adultery. The complex and painful nature of divorce that prompted heated debates in Judaism and early Christianity has persisted into the modern period and whether or not one comes to the same conclusions as Mark did it is comforting to modern-day pastoral care providers to have him as a companion in the task of translating Jesus' message into a different cultural context.

As women receive a new status in 10:12, so children experience the same thing in 10:13-16. No other group of people is mentioned in the entire gospel as being scolded by the apostles and hindered in their access to Jesus: not crowds, not ritually unclean persons, not even potentially dangerous persons (as in 5:1-20)—only the little children. No reason for the disciples' misguided action is given but surely it has to do with their "littleness" that is mistaken for insignificance. Such action provokes Jesus' indignation (10:14; cf. 10:41; 14:4), his command to stop hindering their coming to him (cf. 9:34a), and his announcement that far from being insignificant the children are the heirs of God's Reign. Mark reinforces this point by adding to the scene a saying of Jesus from another context (cf. Matt 19:13-15) that holds children up as models for those who would receive God's Reign, a saying analogous to sayings such as Matt 5:3 and 11:25-26). The detailed (three verbs!) description of Jesus' gentle treatment of the children (v. 16) is in stark contrast to their treatment at the hands of the "big folks" (v. 13), and guarantees for children a central place in the community of faith.

The final issue to be dealt with in this second cycle is that of possessions (10:17-31). The passage consists of the story of a rich man (vv. 17-22), sayings of Jesus about possessions and the Reign of God (vv. 23-37), and a saying of Jesus about those who have made sacrifices in order to be his disciples (vv. 28-31). This last section makes clear that this was a question of great interest in the early Church.

The man's question about "eternal life" (note the *inclusio* formed by the phrase in vv. 17 and 30) is another form of the question about the greatest commandment (12:28) and Jesus' insistence that only God is "good," the source and provider of every good thing, including eternal life (cf. 1 Chr 16:34; 2 Chr 5:13; Ps 118:1), may be a reference to the Shema (12:29-30). Unable to go beyond obedience to the commandments by surrendering his possessions for the sake of a heavenly reward (cf. Matt 6:19-21; 19:21; Luke 12:33-34; 16:9; Jas 5:3; 2 Esd 7:77) and for the sake of Jesus, he leaves the encounter in shock and grief. He is a dramatic illustration, Jesus says, of the truth that attachment to material possessions makes participation in the Reign of God impossible; it is like trying to put the biggest creature through the tiniest opening. It cannot happen . . . unless *God* frees a person from enchantment with possessions for life in God (10:23-27). Peter recognizes that this is precisely what has happened in the case of the disciples (cf. 1:16-20; 2:13-14) and the words of Jesus include them as well as everyone else who has left home and family for the sake of Jesus and the gospel. Christians are those who have received other houses (for example, those where Jesus instructs them as in 7:17; 9:28, etcetera?) and a larger family, the family of God (3:31-35), the Church. But all of this stands under the sign of the cross; it is only "with persecutions" that the Church of Mark's day lives. Only in the "age to come" when the "kingdom of God has come with power" (9:1) will life under the cross give way to "eternal life" (10:17, 30).

On the Way: Third Announcement of Messiah's Death and Resurrection (10:32-52)

The third announcement of the passion (10:32-34) occurs on the way up to Jerusalem and is the most detailed of all the predictions. It has almost certainly been formulated by the early Church and its Markan form reads like an outline of the passion story of chs. 14–16. Following the pattern of the first two passion sayings disciples, here James and John, act as though they had not heard what Jesus has just said. He speaks about death and (only then) resurrection but they speak only of resurrection "glory" (8:38; 13:26) and their desire to share places of honor at Jesus' enthronement (Matt 19:28; 25:31; Rev 20:4). Employing two OT images of suffering, the cup (Pss 11:6; 75:8[9]; Jer 25:15; 40:12; 51:7; Lam 4:21; Isa 51:17, 22; Hab 2:16; Ezek 23:31-33) and baptism (to be covered by waters: Job 22:11; Pss 18:16[17]; 32:6; 42:7[8]; 69:1-3, 14-15[16]; 124:4, 5; 144:7; Isa 8:7, 8; 43:2), Jesus brings the focus back to his suffering and death and asks whether they are able to share in that part of his fate. By the time Mark wrote the tradition knew that James had, in fact, shared this cup and baptism with Jesus, having been executed by Herod Agrippa in 44 C.E. (Acts 12:2). There is no reliable evidence for the martyrdom of John during the same early period, but the point of the conversation is not to glorify James and John as early Christian martyrs or to detract from their significance to the Church, but rather to make clear, as v. 40 does, that to share the martyr fate of Jesus does not bring any special prerogatives since all Christians are called to be willing to take martyrdom upon themselves (8:34-37; 9:49; 10:30b).

The competitive spirit breaks out again in the anger of the ten (v. 41) and prompts Jesus once again to stress the radical difference between the members of the Christian community and other, human institutions such as political rulers. In contrast to all hierarchical thinking the Church is called to be a community of equals. The primary question is not about positions of privilege and power (10:35-41) but about mutual service (10:42-44; cf. 9:35-50).

In one sense Mark 10:45 concludes the series of Jesus' sayings in connection with the third passion prediction (10:33-34). In another sense it serves to conclude the teaching of Jesus in the entire middle section of the gospel (8:27–10:52). It is a succinct summary of the three sayings about the fate of the Son of man (8:31; 9:31; 10:33-34). Like these sayings it radically redefines expectations connected with the apocalyptic figure of the Son of man (for example, in Dan 7:13). The Son of man (contrary to expectations) does *not* come to be served, but rather to serve, and for this reason can call followers to a life *not* (as might be expected) of privilege and power, but rather of self-giving service to others (8:34-37; 9:35-37; 10:42-44). The words of Jesus in 10:45 serve as a key source for understanding Christian discipleship as *imitatio Christi* (cf. Phil 2:5-11). The second half of the statement has also been enormously influential in the Church's understanding of the death of Jesus in terms of a vicarious atonement for sin in the sense of Isa 52:13–53:12. The Isaiah passage may lie behind Mark 10:45, but if so then only in a general way rather than on the basis of specific literary similarities. It is also possible that the saying has been formulated under the influence of eucharistic words such as 14:22-24. What is indisputable is the affirmation that the way in which Jesus as the Son of man decided to live and die was of eschatological benefit to humankind and that those who bear his name are called to make that very same decision about their own life and death.

As the cure of the man who could not see in 8:22-26 served as a transition to the middle section of the gospel, so the story of Bartimaeus (10:46-52) functions as a bridge from the middle section to the period of Jesus in Jerusalem (11:1–16:8). The departure of Jesus, his disciples, and a large crowd from Jericho sounds like a large group of pilgrims on the way to Jerusalem for the Passover. Crying out to Jesus and using the title "Son of David" for the first time in Mark's narrative (the man's use of the title anticipates the crowd's use of it in 11:10; cf. also 12:35-37), Bartimaeus asks for "mercy" (Pss 6:2; 9:13; 40:5, 11) and receives it though no cure is described, only the assurance that faith has cured him. Now able to see, the one who "was sitting by the roadside [or 'the way']" (10:46) now follows Jesus "on the way." The "following" is more than Bartimaeus's ability now to join the pilgrims on the way to the festival. "Following" is nearly always used either of crowds who are well-disposed to Jesus (2:15; 3:7; 5:24; 11:9) or, most frequently, in connection with disciples and discipleship (1:18; 2:14; 6:1; 8:34; 9:38; 10:21, 28, 32; 15:41). Given the positioning of the two stories at the beginning and at the conclusion of the section dealing with discipleship, Bartimaeus is intended to serve as an example of a person with "sight" and such a person follows Jesus into his passion.

Jesus in Jerusalem: 11:1–16:8

The Jerusalem period of Jesus' ministry is framed by incidents that emphasize his sovereignty: the triumphal approach to the city (11:1-10) and the resurrection announcement (16:1-8). Between them the story is a mixture of sovereignty and suffering. Several motifs continue from the earlier portions and some new ones appear.

(1) The Temple plays a major role in this section. When Jesus enters the city he goes straight to the Temple (11:11). The following day is devoted to his symbolic disruption of the Temple cult and its interpretation (11:12-25). It is the Temple incident that leads to discussions of "authority" (11:27–12:12). Jesus teaches in the Temple (11:27–13:1; cf. 14:49). He predicts the destruction of the Temple and uses that as the starting point for a long speech about the coming of the Son of man at the end of the age (13:1-37). At the hearing before the religious authorities he is accused of threatening to destroy the Temple (14:57-58) and at his death the Temple is symbolically destroyed (15:38). Moreover, from the time of his disruption of the Temple activity officials associated with the Temple—chief priests, high priest and elders—take over the initiative in his persecution.

(2) The conflict that began already in 2:1-12 and 3:6 continues and grows in intensity. It is interesting that there are no more stories of conflict with Satanic powers; now they are with the powers of religion and politics. The plot to destroy him reaches even into his circle of disciples (14:10-11, 43-45). Even the crowds become hostile (15:8-15). Betrayal, denial (14:53-55, 66-72), and abandonment (14:50) now characterize the relationship with his male disciples. Mark's critique of the Twelve reaches its high point.

(3) Apocalyptic thought plays a much more obvious role in this section, especially ch. 13, but also in Jesus' statement that the high priest will witness the appearance of the Son of man (14:62) and in the signs accompanying the death of Jesus, the darkness (15:33), and the ripping of the Temple curtain (15:38).

Jesus in Jerusalem: Conflict in the Capital (11:1–12:44)

Jesus' approach to Jerusalem (11:1-10) is much more detailed and dramatic than the actual entry into the city itself (11:11); if anything is "triumphal," it is this arrival at the gates of the city and not the entry. As important as the symbolism *within* the story is, its larger importance lies in the way in which it puts into proper christological perspective the events about to take place in Jerusalem: whatever happens to Jesus happens to the messianic king. As he has given radical new interpretations to the titles "Son of God" and "Son of man," so now as he prepares to enter the royal city he will replace current expectations of the "Son of David" with radical new content.

The scene is filled with OT images that came to be understood as having messianic significance. The location of the scene near the Mount of Olives recalls Zech 14:1-5, but whereas God is there portrayed as the Great Warrior who will lead Israel in the eschatological battle against all the nations from the Mount of Olives, the one who now stands there is anything but a warrior. Zechariah 9:9 (sometimes combined with Gen 49:11) already speaks of the triumphant but "humble" king who "comes" riding on a young donkey. The spreading of clothes and branches and the singing of one of the Hallel Psalms (Pss 113–118, here 118:26) framed by shouts of "Hosanna!" ("May God grant help and success!" Pss 12:1[2]; 20:9[10]; 28:9; 60:5[7]; 108:6[7]) celebrate the "coming kingdom" of David, but the kingdom that Jesus brings is far greater than a restored Israel. Thus in spite of familiar images and the public character of the scene something of the mystery that surrounded Jesus during his entire public ministry is retained here, the mystery occasioned at least in part by his thoroughgoing reinterpretation of messianic categories in light of his impending death and resurrection.

Jesus' approach to Jerusalem is portrayed as an intentionally symbolic act on the part of Jesus. So is the story of Jesus in the Temple (11:11-25). Both the story of Jesus' cursing of a fig tree (11:12-14 and 20-25) and the story of his outburst in the Temple (11:15-19) have been difficult to understand, especially for those who insist on a literal interpretation. Arrangement provides important clues. Matthew has a much briefer account of the Temple incident (21:12-13) and only after healings and debates in the Temple does he introduce the story of the fig tree (21:18-22). Luke also has a brief account of the Temple incident (19:45-46) and does not include the fig tree story at all (see his alternative version at 13:6-9). Mark has both stories, but splits them both into two parts and intertwines them so that they now comprise four movements in a single story.

(a) Jesus enters the city, goes to the Temple and looks around before departing for Bethany for the night (11:11).

(b) The next day (11:12-14) Jesus, on the way into Jerusalem and hungry, sees a fig tree (already) in leaf and goes to see if there is fruit. Finding only leaves because it was not (yet) the season for ripe fruit, Jesus "curses" the fig tree. The word Mark uses for "season" *(kairos)* can refer to seasons, but given its theological import (1:15; 12:2; 13:33) it may also suggest the sense of the fateful and decisive point of divine ordination (cf. Luke 12:56; Matt 16:3). The startling reaction of Jesus also suggests that more is involved in the scene than agricultural seasons. The fig tree is used to symbolize Israel's relationship to God (of special interest in Jer 8:13; but cf. also 29:17; Hos 2:12; 9:10, 16; Isa 34:4; Mic 7:1-6).

(c) Jesus enters the Temple (11:15-19) and disrupts activity in what could only have been the court of the Gentiles, justifying his actions by appealing to OT prophets (Isa 56:7 and Jer 7:1-15, especially v. 11; 26:1-15). His blocking of the carrying of "vessels" implies that he disrupts *all* sacrificial activity; in other words he has halted the whole Temple cultus.

(d) The next day (11:20-25) Peter calls attention to the withered fig tree. Jesus responds by calling the disciples and the early Church to faith, by which they can say to "*this* mountain," that is, the Temple mount: "Be gone!" Christian prayer, including proper preparation (11:25; cf. Matt 6:14-15 but also Matt 5:23-24) is superior to Temple worship.

Mark's weaving together of the two stories makes it clear that Jesus is not attempting a reform of Temple worship, for example by securing a place for Gentile worshipers, nor "cleansing" the Temple of corrupting commercialism. His action is more radical than that. Jesus, in Mark's view, pronounces the Temple dead, literally "out of date" in view of the now fulfilled time of God's Reign (1:15; 2:10, 19; 3:27) and replaced by the Christian Church. This is Mark's *theological* explanation for the *historical* fact that by the time he wrote the Temple had been destroyed by Titus (cf. Luke 19:41-44, esp. 44b).

Passages such as this call for great caution and sensitivity on the part of Christian interpreters. Early Christian struggles to understand their relationship to Jesus' religious heritage led them to conclusions similar to Mark's. The fate of Jerusalem and the Temple was divinely willed as retribution for Israel's rejection of Jesus as its Messiah. Such ideas, whatever their justification in the first century, have played a horrific role in the formation of Christian attitudes and behavior toward Jewish brothers and sisters. To be faithful to Mark at this point may mean joining in the enterprise of trying to discover, historically and theologically, the relationship of the Church to its parent faith, even if that means rejecting the answers to which Mark and other early Christians came. Perhaps the narrative can remind us that *all* religious institutions, including the Christian Church, stand under God's judgment.

In 11:27–12:44 Mark presents Jesus' teaching in the Temple. The remark in 14:49 suggests that his teaching there extended over a longer period of time than the three days suggested by Mark's compressed narrative. The first two units (11:27-33 and 12:1-12) deal with the issue of Jesus' authority. When he is again in the city and in the Temple the chief priests and scribes, who are already seeking a way to kill him (11:18) and are joined now by "the elders," inquire about the "authority" by which he is doing "these things," presumably a reference to his disruption of activity in the Temple (11:28). In his counter-question Jesus asks their opinion of the authorization—divine or human—for what John did. It is not clear whether Jesus' question assumes equality in the cases of John and Jesus as prophets of God ("as John's authority . . . so mine") or whether it represents an argument from a lesser case to a greater ("if John's authority . . . how much more mine"). In any case the questioners refuse (on tactical, not theological grounds) to answer and Jesus also refuses to answer their question.

The parable of the unfaithful tenants (12:1-11) represents what early Christianity understood to be the answer of the Jewish leaders to the question of Jesus' authority. Again the parable seems to be representative ("in parables," 12:1; cf. 4:2-10). A story that begins the way this one does would immediately remind Jewish and Christian hearers of Isa 5:1-10 with its story of "the vineyard of the Lord . . . the house of Israel" (cf. Ps 80:8-13; Jer 2:21). In Mark the point of the parable is not the barrenness of the vineyard but the refusal of those charged with the care of the vineyard to respect the authority of those who represent the owner, even and most especially the authority of the son. But as the owner of the vineyard vindicates the son by destroying the tenants, so according to the interpretive quotation from Ps 118:22-23 does God vindicate the Son Jesus. As in the case of the Temple, so here: God's vengeance is not directed at Israel but at Israel's religious leadership, a point that the leaders perceive (12:12).

In the four questions and discussions of 12:13-37 the teaching authority of Jesus (cf. 1:22) is demonstrated. The first question is posed to Jesus with hostile intent by a group of Pharisees and Herodians (3:6; 8:15) and asks Jesus' opinion on the lawfulness of Jewish payment of taxes to a foreign power, the emperor. Though both the Pharisees and the Herodians consented to the tax, the former as a concession, the latter on principle, the question places Jesus himself in a dilemma: a negative answer would leave him open to charges of rebellion (cf. the example of Judas the Galilean: Josephus, *Ant.* 18.1.1; Acts 5:37) and a positive response would endanger his standing with the populace. The question is not whether one ought to pay the tax but whether or not it violates Jewish Law. Noting that Roman coinage bears the picture and inscription of Caesar, Jesus counsels to give it (that is, the tax) to the owner, but only that: the tax. A strict limit is set on what Caesar has a right to claim, for the second part of Jesus' reply is the decisive one. Caesar has no right to claim what belongs to God, things like ultimate loyalty and love and obedience. It was precisely such questions that concerned many early Christians (Rom 13:1-7; 1 Tim 2:1-6; Titus 3:1-2; 1 Pet 2:13-17; and in a different context the book of Revelation).

Another question (12:18-27) concerns the resurrection of the dead. In their only appearance in Mark's gospel Sadducees, known primarily for their aristocratic origins, their acceptance only of the Pentateuch as Scripture, and their rejection of the idea of a resurrection of the dead (cf. Acts 23:6-8; Josephus *Ant.* 18.1-4), present Jesus with a story based on the provision for levirate marriage (*levir* means "a husband's brother") in Deut 25:5-10 and designed to demonstrate how ridiculous belief in resurrection of the dead is: after a woman has belonged to seven men on earth, whose will she be in the resurrection life? The first part of Jesus' response is that she will not be anyone's property but will be like an angel (*1 Enoch* 104:4; *2 Bar* 51:10). As for the question of resurrection itself, the Scripture (the Pentateuch) proves it. In rabbinic fashion Jesus points to the present tense employed in Exod 3:6 to show that the patriarchs were alive at the time of Moses, thus proving the truth of the resurrection of the dead.

In response to a scribe's apparently genuine question as to which is the first commandment (12:28-34) Jesus does not seek to prioritize among the six hundred thirteen acknowledged commandments. Instead he goes again to a more fundamental level, to the commandment on which all other commandments are based, the Shema (Deut 6:4-5), the prayer spoken daily by Jews (vv. 29-30). Unbidden, he adds the second, again quoting Scripture, this time from Lev 19:18b, and concludes that no commandment is greater than the commands to love God and love the neighbor, a sentiment not unknown in Judaism (cf. *b.Sukk.* 49b; *b.Ber.* 55a; *Deut. Rabb.* 5.201d). Though he seems to distinguish the commandments differently from Jesus (first commandment in v. 32, second in v. 33) the scribe affirms what Jesus has said, even adding his own scriptural affirmation (Hos 6:6; cf. also 1 Sam 15:22; Mic 6:6-8). The nearness of this scribe to the Reign of God with this understanding of the Law signals a form of Judaism in which Gentile Christians could easily see the roots of their own faith.

Following Jesus' statement of the two great commandments no one dares to pose further questions, and so in 12:35-37 Jesus himself raises the question about the scribes' use of "Son of David" as a messianic title. The question does not challenge the general conviction of early Christianity about Jesus' Davidic lineage (Matt 1:1, 6, 17, 20; 12:23; Luke 1:27, 32; 2:4; 3:31; John 7:42; Rom 1:3; 2 Tim 2:8; Rev 5:5; 22:16) nor does Mark reject the title outright (10:46-52; 11:9-10). What is at issue is whether the title is a *sufficient* one fully describing Messiah, as the scribes are saying. Using Ps 110:1, David's inspired words, Jesus makes clear that Messiah is not (merely) David's son, but his "Lord." While not wrong, the title as defined by the scribes is an inadequate one. Gentile theological interests are apparent.

As part of his teaching Jesus cautions his hearers to guard themselves against the scribes (12:38-40) who are described in terms of what they *seek* and acquire: distinctive clothing, respect, the best seats at worship and in social life, hospitality of which they take advantage, and admiration for their long public prayers (cf. Matt 6:5, 7-8; 23:1-7).

By way of contrast to those scribes Jesus calls the attention of his disciples to a "poverty-stricken widow" (12:41-44) who is described in terms of what she *gives,* two coins worth a penny, more than anyone else, everything she had, her entire living (literally her "life," her physical existence). The teaching of Jesus in the Temple concludes in Mark's gospel with Jesus drawing a contrast between people who want to save their life, to gain the whole world, but who will end up by forfeiting it (12:40b), and a woman who is willing to deny herself, to give up her "life" (Mark 8:34-37).

Hope and Steadiness in a Critical Time (13:1-37)

The setting for Jesus' final teaching of his disciples (13:1-4) reflects his relationship to the Temple as it has been described since 11:11: he "came out" of it for the final time; he predicts its destruction and sits on the Mount of Olives (see on 11:1-10 above) "opposite the temple." The so-called "apocalyptic discourse" (13:5-37) is his response to the question of the four intimates about the time and the sign "that all these things are about to be accomplished" (v. 4). The speech is Jesus' longest in the gospel and of great significance not only because it concludes his teaching ministry but because it deals with the issue with which the Church of the first century—and every succeeding century—has struggled. The question is especially acute for Christians for whom some form of apocalyptic worldview is still normative.

Several important clues are helpful in following the line of thought.

(1) In v. 4 the disciples ask when "this" will be and what the sign will be when "all these things" are about to be accomplished, and in v. 23 Jesus says that he has now told them "all things." This seems to suggest that the answer to the disciples' question is given in vv. 5-23. It is after *that* suffering that the Son of man will appear (vv. 24-27). In vv. 28-37 what has been said in vv. 5-27 is applied to the Christian community. Verse 29 picks up again the words "these things" and places the hearer between v. 23 and v. 24, looking back as it were to "these things" as described in vv. 5-23 and forward to the appearance of the Son of man. Indeed, "all these things" (v. 30), that is, the historical events described in vv. 5-23, will happen before the present generation of disciples has passed away. Between vv. 23 and 24 is precisely where the Church stands. When the events of vv. 24-27 will occur only God knows (v. 32).

(2) Twice in the speech Jesus uses the word "must": in v. 7 apocalyptic events "must" take place, and in v. 10 the gospel "must" be preached to all the nations. The word indicates divine necessity. The community is not abandoned to fate or accident. God is behind what happens.

(3) The discourse is full of imperatives: "beware" or "be alert" in vv. 5, 9, 23, 33; "do not be alarmed" in v. 7; "do not worry" in v. 11; "endure" (indirect imperative) in v. 13; "pray" in v. 18; "do not believe" in v. 21; "learn" in v. 28; "know" in v. 29; "keep alert" in v. 33; "keep awake" in vv. 35 and 37. This list of imperatives reads like a glossary of terms used in the pastoral care of a persecuted community!

(4) Another word scattered throughout the speech is "for" introducing a clause or sentence that explains a preceding imperative (vv. 8, 11b, 19, 22, 33b, 35b). Apocalyptic imagery is used in the service of pastoral care.

(5) The statements that "the end is still to come" in v. 7 and that false messiahs and apocalyptic catastrophes are "but the beginning of the birth pangs" in v. 8 are warnings against a temptation of all apocalyptic communities, namely to interpret events happening at the moment as "signs" of the end. Jesus here counsels patience and endurance.

These observations taken together indicate that the primary intention of the discourse, whether from Jesus himself or from the pre-Markan tradition, was not to speculate on the end of the age and signs that might aid in calculating its arrival, but rather to encourage believers to live faithfully in the time between the resurrection of Jesus and the coming of the Son of man.

Verses 5-8: Persons claiming the name of "messiah" and forming bands of loyalists were common enough in the first century (cf. Acts 5:21-39; Josephus *Ant.* 20.5.1; 20.8.5-6, 10; *Bell.* 2.13.3; 2.17.8-9; 6.5.2; 7.8.1; 7.11.1) as were wars in Palestine and North Africa and civil war in Rome itself in 68 C.E. These historical circumstances may have suggested other typical OT and apocalyptic themes: wars (Isa 13:1-9; Jer 4:13-26), earthquakes (Pss 18:7-15; 77:18), and famine (Jer 15:2; Ezek 5:17). Twice in this section readers are warned not to jump to the conclusion that these events signal the end; indeed they are the very beginning of the pains that accompany the end of the age (vv. 7c, 8c).

Verses 9-13: Addressing the Christian community in particular ("yourselves" in v. 9) Jesus announces that his followers will face external persecution from both Jews ("councils" and "synagogues") and Gentiles ("governors" and "kings") as well as internal conflict (vv. 12-13; cf. Tacitus *Annals* 15.44.2-8). In spite of the promise of persecution, however, the community knows that its suffering serves the proclamation of the gospel to all the nations; believers are confident that the Holy Spirit will give them words when they are brought to trial and that their own suffering is a faithful witness to the suffering of their Lord (cf. 8:31; 9:31; 10:33-45).

Verses 14-23: Opinions differ greatly on what is meant by "the desolating sacrilege" of v. 14, a phrase from Dan 11:31; 12:11; cf. 9:7 (cf. 1 Macc 1:54) and symbolizing something that Mark's readers are supposed to understand. Whereas in Daniel it causes the people of God to abandon the Temple, Jesus' hearers are to flee Judea. In contrast to Matthew who describes the sacrilege by means of a neuter participle (Matt 24:15 "it" is standing), Mark has a masculine form ("he" is standing). Mark probably intends the readers to think of the Roman general Titus who, according to Josephus (*Bell.* 6.4.7; 6.6.1) entered the Holy of Holies in 70 C.E. near the end of the Jewish-Roman war. Thus the conquest and destruction of the Temple is a signal to Christians to flee Judea, but in spite of "false" messiahs and prophets Christians are not to be deceived into thinking that the destruction of the Temple is "the end," either of this age or of their suffering.

Verses 24-27: It is only (some time) *after* this terrible suffering that the Son of man will appear accompanied by cosmic signs (cf. Joel 2:10; 3:15; Isa 13:10; 34:4; Ezek 32:7-8; Amos 8:9; Acts 2:20; Rev 6:12-14; 8:12; 9:2) and coming in the clouds, with power and glory (cf. 8:38; 14:62b; Matt 10:23; 1 Thess 4:13-18; Dan 7:13).

Verses 28-37: The reader is drawn back to the present and asked to bring the two parts of the discourse together. Comparable to the short time between the flowering of the fig tree and the appearance of fruit, approximately one month, is the short time between the historical events of vv. 5-23, culminating in the destruction of the Temple, and the event of vv. 24-27, the appearance of the Son of man. The Church lives between 13:23 and 13:24, the time of advent (Mark

13:24-37 is the gospel lection for the first Sunday of Advent in Year A) as well as the time of Easter and Pentecost. Since no one, not the angels and not even Jesus himself, knows the precise time of the coming of the Son of man the community is called to a life of constant wakefulness (vv. 33, 35), not in the sense of a faithless seeking for "signs" so as not to be caught off guard, but in the sense of a faithful anticipation of Christ's appearing. Moreover, Mark reminds his readers, what was true for the first generation of believers is true for every generation (v. 37).

Death of the Messiah (14:1–15:47)

In chs. 14–15 Mark comes to that part of the story of Jesus as the embodiment of the good news that has been anticipated so frequently in chs. 1–13 in open passion and resurrection predictions (8:31; 9:31; 10:33-34; 9:12) and in the passion narrative itself (14:3-9, 21, 27, 41), in sayings that interpret Jesus' death in terms of its salvific significance (10:45; 14:22-24), and in more veiled references to the passion (2:20; 10:38-39; 12:1-11). In addition the narrative itself has foreshadowed the passion (2:7; 3:6; 6:17-29; 8:15; 11:18; 12:1-11). While it does not do justice to Mark's gospel to call it a "passion story with a preface," nonetheless there can be no doubt that the story of the gospel and Jesus' proclamation of it is thoroughly governed by the passion narrative in chs. 14–15 and the resurrection in ch. 16. Scholars have wondered whether there was a pre-Markan passion story that Mark then edited and adapted to his gospel. For those who are convinced that Mark was using Matthew and Luke as sources the answer is clear. For those who regard Mark as a source for the other two gospels the answer is not as clear. Some elements of the passion story were preserved in pre-Pauline traditions: for example, Jesus' death, burial, resurrection, and appearance to witnesses were remembered in the kerygmatic summary in 1 Cor 15:3-5, and the betrayal and supper in 1 Cor 11:23-26. Other theories range from Mark's use of a minimal collection of events connected with the death and resurrection of Jesus to his supposed editing of a full-blown passion gospel. Of course, as in the rest of the gospel, the OT has provided major images and motifs, especially Pss 22 and 69 and perhaps the "other" passion story, Isa 52:13–53:12. Whatever sources Mark may have had, it is clear that he has employed them in such a way that his own theological and christological convictions come to expression.

The passion story opens with three units dealing with "preparations" for the death of Jesus. They capture nicely the dynamics of the story about to unfold. In the midst of hostile preparations from the outside—by the chief priests and scribes (14:1-2), and hostile preparations from the inside—by Judas, "one of the twelve" (14:10-11) an unnamed woman performs a loving act that Jesus interprets as an act of preparation for his death and burial. All three—the representatives of the religious establishment, Judas, and the woman—anticipate similar actions by others in the story.

The action of the woman takes place outside Jerusalem, in the home of a leper (nothing is said about his having been cured). The story assumes the certainty of Jesus' death and the fact that there will be no salving of his body before he is laid in a tomb (narratively because there was not time [15:42], theologically because the resurrection renders it senseless, historically because Jesus was executed as a criminal). Jesus praises her act of kindness because "she has done what she could." She cannot save him from death; what is possible is a loving gesture to help him face it. It was appropriate for the specific moment and that is why it is wrong to misunderstand Jesus as justifying the fact that some people live in poverty. As this act of love was appropriate at this moment, so acts of love toward the poor are always appropriate. Though some commentators see the "anointing" as a form of messianic anointing the verb Mark uses is not the one used in the OT (LXX) to refer to the anointing of kings, priests, and prophets. The "play on words" works only in translation! The act of love confronting openly the approaching death of Jesus is so singular that Jesus links the woman and her act to the proclamation of the gospel itself.

On Thursday, then, two of the disciples make final preparations for the Passover meal (14:12-16) at the house of a man who acknowledges Jesus as "the teacher" and has a guest room waiting for him ("*my* guest room"). It is clear throughout the report of the meal that Jesus is the host.

The meal itself is described in two scenes. In the first (14:17-21) Jesus solemnly announces ("amen," "truly") that one of those eating with him will "hand him over/betray him." The thought of v. 18 is repeated in v. 20. In both cases the language stresses the nearness and intimacy that the traitor shares with Jesus ("one of you/one of the twelve"; "eating with me/dipping bread into the bowl with me" (cf. Ps 41:9). "The bowl" probably refers to the bowl of stewed fruit eaten before the main course itself (*m. Pesah*\ X). The traitor is not identified (cf. John 13:21-30) and each of the disciples is allowed to make his profession of innocence. Wherever Judas is mentioned he is linked with betrayal (3:19; 14:10, 43) which is part of the terrible results of his deed for, as v. 21 makes clear, though the Son of man goes to death in accordance with the will of God his betrayer will bear the full consequences of his act. Of him it could also be said that "wherever the good news is proclaimed in the whole world, what he has done will be told in remembrance of him" (14:9).

In the second scene at the table (14:22-25) Christians from the very beginning experienced profoundest mystery and brightest revelation (cf. Matt 26:26-29; Luke 22:17-19a [shorter text]; Luke 22:17-20 [longer text]; 1 Cor 11:23-26; 10:16-17). For one thing it reminds the Church that for all of his tensions and conflicts with Torah and its official interpreters Jesus lived and died a Jew. Moreover, the shared final meal echoes the certainty of a table community for the followers of Jesus (2:15-17; cf. especially Matt 11:16-19 *par.* Luke 7:31-35) as an anticipation of the eschatological meal with God. Above all the earliest Christians heard and saw in this scene the meaning of the life and death of Jesus Messiah. Now the Church can understand "about the loaves" (6:52; 8:14-21). Ultimately the bread that feeds the people of God is Jesus himself ("my body" = my *self,* all that I am), a thought that receives its fullest expression in the Fourth Gospel (John 6:33, 35, 48). The ultimate commitment of God to the world ("covenant") is Jesus himself ("my blood" = my existence"; cf. Exod 24:8). Equally important for Mark is that Jesus offers himself precisely as *broken* body and *poured out* cup, that is, under the mysterious sign of the cross. This all is done "for many" (for all: Mark 10:45 and Isa 52:14, 15; 53:11b, 12b). Finally the vow of abstinence in v. 25 places the whole meal and its symbolism in the context of the Reign of God. While Mark records neither a command of Jesus to repeat his actions nor that he be remembered by such action the Church decided very early that both repetition and remembrance were faithful ways of living *in* the Reign of God *toward* the Reign of God (see the liturgically fuller statements in 1 Cor 11:23-26 and the longer Lukan form in 22:19b-20).

After the final hymn (one of the Hallel Psalms? Ps 118?) and on the way to the Mount of Olives (14:26-31) Jesus once more announces his death and resurrection but now adds a new dimension to his passion, his abandonment by all of his disciples, an abandonment that will be overcome only after he has been raised from the dead and has gathered them again in Galilee (16:7). It is interesting that Peter no longer attempts to argue him out of his way to the cross but is now concerned only with asserting his loyalty (as in 14:19 also). This he does "vehemently" (other times of "vehemence" are 8:32 and 14:71). As they approach Gethsemane "all of them" swear unfailing allegiance to him and at the close of the Gethsemane scene "all of them" desert him.

Jesus' time in Gethsemane is the third time Mark mentions Jesus at prayer (1:35; 6:46). The importance of the incident is underscored by the repeated use of "threes": three intimates are asked to be especially close to him, the prayer itself is said three times, Jesus comes to his own three times, and three times they fail to "keep awake" (14:34, 38; cf. 13:33, 35, 37). Jesus' emotional state is emphasized by using three different words to describe it (14:33-34 *par.* Matt 26:37-38; differently Luke 22:39-46; cf. John 12:27; Heb 5:7). Only in Mark does Jesus address God with the intimate "Abba," a term used also in early Christian worship (Rom 8:15; Gal 4:6). The cup image recalls the conversation with the sons of Zebedee (see above on 10:35-40) as well as Jesus' words at the supper (14:23-24). His threefold acceptance of the cup of suffering is contrasted with the threefold failure of the disciples to "keep awake." His relinquishment of his own will is a dramatic illustration of "denying" self (8:34-37). Even as Jesus announces his final acceptance of the cup and "the hour" (v. 41) Judas arrives (v. 43).

Mark calls those sent by the chief priests, scribes, and elders to arrest Jesus a "crowd," the first time in the gospel that a crowd does not relate to Jesus in a positive way, a fact recalled in

v. 49. The turning of the crowd accentuates the growing abandonment of Jesus in the face of suffering and death. The normal greeting—"Rabbi"—and the kiss (cf. Luke 7:45; 1 Cor 16:20) further magnify Judas's treachery. When a bystander attacks the slave of the high priest Jesus does not chastise that person but rather the ridiculous show of force on the part of the authorities that has the effect of making him appear to be a criminal and provoking violence in a crowd. At the outbreak of violence all of his disciples abandon him and flee, dramatically fulfilling both the Scripture (Zech 13:7) and Jesus' own prediction (14:26-27). With the simple sentence in 14:50 the Twelve disappear from the passion of Jesus, a point to which the narrative has been building (4:41; 6:51-52; 8:14-21, 32-33; 9:9-13, 32-34, 38-41; 10:13-14, 32b, 35-41; 14:10-11, 17-21, 26-31, 32-42). Those whom Jesus appointed to "be with him" (3:14) are not. The desperation of both disciples and bystanders to flee the scene is illustrated by the case of a wealthy young man who is determined to escape even if it means losing his fine linen garment and going home naked (14:51-52). Nothing in the text hints at his being a baptismal candidate/symbol or a (frightened!) angel, nor does anything support the theory of some of the Church fathers that the man was Mark (Acts 12:12), the author of the gospel. Nonetheless the plausibility of the idea that the evangelist might have "signed" his narrative in this way captures the imagination of many.

The stories of Jesus and Peter are intermingled in 14:53-72. Verses 53-54 present the main characters and their respective contexts in such a way as to make clear that the stories are happening at the very same time. Thus while Jesus is tried before the "supreme court" of Israel (14:55-65) Peter is "tried" by guards and servants (14:66-72). Three attempts are made to put together a case against Jesus that would justify a death sentence ("many" in v. 56, "some" in v. 57, and the high priest himself in vv. 60-65) and three times Peter is questioned about his relationship to Jesus (vv. 67, 69, 70). Jesus answers clearly that he is "Messiah, the Son of the Blessed" and that all those present will see him as the enthroned and coming Son of man (v. 62; the quotation combines Dan 7:13 and Ps 110:1; cf. Mark 8:38–9:1; 13:24-27). Peter answers with equal clarity three times, vehemently, and under oath that he does not even know Jesus (especially v. 71). The high priest pronounces Jesus guilty of "blasphemy" for claiming to be the Messiah, Son of God, Son of man (cf. 2:7) and a formal death sentence is proclaimed (v. 64). A crowing cock and Peter's own memory of Jesus' words (14:27-30) condemn Peter as an apostate (v. 72). Jesus is abused (v. 65). Peter weeps (v. 72). Christians experiencing persecution might well have read their own story in that of Peter and searched their own souls; they would have been encouraged by the good news that Messiah's faithfulness was greater than Peter's failure (see 16:7 where he is reinstated as a disciple of Jesus).

Some scholars have questioned whether what Mark reports in 14:53, 55-65 would have qualified as a "trial" by Jewish legal standards. The problem is difficult because documentation of Jewish legal customs is much later than the events Mark is narrating. The problem is also important because of the danger of caricature of Jewish religious leaders and feeding of anti-Jewish prejudice. While some aspects of the trial are framed in legal-sounding language (for example, the hearing of witnesses and the insistence that testimony be consistent, the formal charge of blasphemy, and the pronouncement of the death sentence) other aspects sound more as if they belong to a more informal "hearing" (for example, the date: Passover eve and at night, the location: the house of the high priest, the intention: not a trial but making a case against Jesus, and the absence of adequate witnesses against him). Theological interests on the part of the tradition seem to have exerted more influence on the narrative of the proceedings than Jewish legal customs: Jesus was condemned to death by Jewish authorities because he claimed to be—and was—the Messiah, Son of God, Son of man. Roman authorities play an instrumental role in his death. One of the special tasks of Christian interpretation in cases such as this is to free the Christian confession of Jesus from any anti-Jewish undercurrent.

If the "trial" of Jesus before the Jewish authorities raises questions, so does the "trial" before Pilate, narrated in an extraordinarily compressed form in 15:1-15. The "consultation" early Friday morning must have revolved around the question of what to do with someone who has been condemned to death when one does not have the right to carry out a death sentence, which was precisely the predicament. The decision is made to turn the whole matter over to the Roman authorities, namely Pilate *"[praef]ectus Iud[aea]e"* (so the Pilate inscription from Caesarea discovered in 1961). As Judas has "handed over" Jesus to the Jewish authorities they now "hand him over" to Pilate (15:1) who in turn will "hand him over" to be crucified (15:15; cf. especially 9:31; 10:33; Isa 53:12 [LXX]). Pilate's hearing of accused and accusers is summarized in 15:2-5. The Jewish title "Messiah" has been translated into "King of the Jews" for the Roman's sake (the correct form from the Jewish perspective was "King of Israel," as in 15:32). In other situations Jesus has redefined titles proffered to him in terms of the "Son of man" ("Messiah" in 8:29-31; "Messiah" and "Son of the Blessed" in 14:61-62), but for some reason he does not do it with the title "king." Pilate is amazed by Jesus' lack of responsiveness (cf. "You say so" in 15:2b with "I am" in 14:62). It is possible that here again Isaiah (53:7 [LXX]) has been influential in the formulation of the scene. In 15:6-15 Pilate is pictured as being totally susceptible to the wishes of the crowd that in turn is the mouthpiece of the chief priests. First comes their demand to have the rebel Barabbas released according to custom at the feast (a custom not attested outside the NT). Though Barabbas was a common name, the irony of the crowd asking for him (Bar-Abba = son of the father) and rejecting Jesus (cf. 14:36) would not have escaped Mark's readers. Mark's portrait of Pilate is that of the insecure and opportunistic politician pandering to a mob even at the price of justice. A further irony in the scene is that the one who is accused of being Israel's king is now to be executed in a manner reserved for criminals and slaves (the connection between "slave" and "death on a cross" in Phil 2:6-11 is historically as well as theologically significant). Barabbas is released. Jesus is flogged and "handed over" to be crucified. Crucifixion was normally preceded by a flogging designed to weaken the condemned person and begin bleeding, though it could also be used as a means of execution itself (Jos. *Bell.* 2.21.5; 6.5.3). As Jesus was abused by Jewish leaders and their servants after their announcement of the death sentence (14:65), so he is now abused by the whole assembled company of soldiers (probably not an entire "cohort" of six hundred) who mock him as "king of the Jews," thus bearing unwitting witness to him (15:18; cf. 15:32).

In 15:21-41 Mark's readers accompany Jesus in the final hours before his death and see some major themes in the narrative coming into ever sharper focus. After a very brief account of the crucifixion itself (15:21-24) major attention is given to the taunting of Jesus by various persons (15:25-32), the final minutes (15:33-39), and friendly observers (15:40-41).

Mark 15:21-24 reads like a statement of the "facts" of the death of Jesus: (1) The condemned person carried the plank that formed the transverse beam to the place of crucifixion, probably symbolizing the status of being a condemned person. As a result of the scourging Jesus was too weak to do this and help was enlisted. (2) The execution site was outside the city limits but easily accessible since crucifixion was to serve as an example and, in some cases, as entertainment (Philo, *Flacc.* 72.84-85). Whether the name of the place, Golgotha, comes from its shape or from the fact that skeletal remains littered the execution site is not clear. (3) Jesus refused a drink that might have served as a narcotic to lessen his awareness of pain. Jewish documents from a later period suggest that this practice was initiated by Jews in response to Prov 31:6-7 (*b. Sanh.* 43a; cf. also Ps 69:21). (4) In the simplest possible way Mark reports the event toward which the entire story of Jesus has been moving, the event that has cast its shadow over every incident and saying of Jesus: "And they crucified him." Mark's sparse statement may simply mean that there was no need to elaborate, for the horrors of this typical Roman form of execution were well known to many writers of the period and to persecuted Christians. The reticence may also result from the fact that for Mark as for Paul and other early Christians the historical fact of Jesus' crucifixion was of fundamental importance, but of even greater importance was its meaning for faith. (5) Victims were, as a rule, crucified naked and soldiers were entitled to take smaller possessions for themselves. As in Ps 22:18 the distribution of his clothes signals that Jesus is now so powerless that decisions are made for and about him over which he has absolutely no control.

The taunting of Jesus (15:25-32) comes from several sources and the amount of attention given to it corresponds to the central place of mockery in psalms that describe the suffering of the innocent, righteous person (cf. Pss 22:6-8, 16-17; 69:4, 6-12, 19-21; 109:25; but cf. also Isa 53:3). Derision comes from the Romans in the form of the sarcastic inscription (15:26; cf. 15:2, 12, 18) proclaiming the crucified one as "king." Passersby recall in a distorted form his prediction about the Temple (v. 29; cf. 13:2; 14:57-58). Chief priests and scribes see the contradiction between the one who cast out demons and healed the sick and the one who hangs now powerless to do anything for himself, and the contradiction between the titles "Messiah" and "king" and the dying one. Even the bandits who were crucified with him taunt him. The enemies and opponents of Jesus now challenge him to overcome the cross and thus enable faith, which is what the Twelve in their own way have been doing as well.

The taunts of 15:25-32 are replaced in 15:33-39 by darkness and death itself. Darkness at the death of important persons is well known (cf., for example, Philo, *Prov.* 2.50; Jos. *Ant.* 14.309; 17.167; Virgil, *Georgics* I, 466 –467). It is also a familiar symbol in OT (Amos 8:9-10; cf. Jer 15:9) and apocalyptic (Rev 9:2) thought. It may here be intended to remind the reader of Mark 13:24-27.

Jesus' cry (his only words from the cross) in the words of Ps 22:1 summarizes and radicalizes the theme of conflict and abandonment that has been so important in Mark's story. There has been the hostility of the religious leaders from the beginning (2:6-7; 3:6, 22 early on and increasing in intensity throughout) but also misunderstanding and rejection by his family (3:21, 31-35) and hometown acquaintances (6:1-6a). Crowds, friendly during the Galilean ministry, finally turn hostile (14:43; 15:6-15). Above all his disciples, unable to comprehend and accept his vision of his end, finally betray (14:10-11; 43-46), abandon (14:50), and deny (14:66-72) him. At the crucifixion they are conspicuous by their absence. Now, at the moment of his death, Jesus asks in the words of the Psalmist why (even) *God* has abandoned him (to death and ridicule). The fact that the cry is in the form of a quotation should not be allowed to lessen the impact: Jesus prays in the same spirit as the Psalmist, that is, as the faithful person who inexplicably suffers to the point of feeling that God has abandoned her or him, but who in the face of abandonment can only pray to that very God by whom she or he feels abandoned—a dramatic paradigm for faith, especially for those who may be entertaining similar thoughts in the face of their own experience of persecution. The misunderstanding of Jesus' prayer by some bystanders leads to an attempt to keep him alive in hopes of perhaps witnessing a miraculous rescue by Elijah (a misunderstanding harder to recognize in Mark's Aramaic form "Eloi" than in Matthew's Hebrew form "Eli," Matt 27:46), something the reader knows cannot happen since "Elijah" has already suffered a similar fate (9:9-13).

At the moment when Jesus screams for the last time and dies the Temple is symbolically destroyed at its very heart, the Holy of Holies, thus fulfilling Jesus' anti-Temple sayings and actions (11:12-25; 13:2).

Witnessing his death, the Roman officer in charge of the crucifixion detail who has stood "facing him," that is, gazing at him, says: "Truly this man was God's Son!" (v. 39). God has proclaimed Jesus "my Son" (1:11; 9:7). Demons have addressed him as "Son" (3:11; 5:7; cf. 1:24). The chief priest has confronted Jesus with the title in his charge of blasphemy (14:61). Now at last a human being, a non-Jew, a non-disciple with nothing to go on except the crucified and dead Jesus, says "in truth" what Christian faith itself comes to confess (cf. 1:11). Here is the narrative climax of Mark's theology of the cross, and in characteristic Markan fashion it proves to be a moment of both revelation and mystery. Jesus is God's Son, the Messiah, the Son of man, the Son of David, the King of Israel—all that has become clear and yet it is clear only in the figure of the powerless, abandoned, mocked, crucified one. It is the mystery of a suffering servant (Isa 52:13–53:12), of the embodied Spirit of God (1:10) ripping open heaven and challenging the power of evil in the world. It is the mystery of the divine Reign, present in the world as seed and secret (4:3-12, 26-29, 30-32) and promise (9:1).

Not until this point does the reader learn of a significant group of women who made it a practice to "follow" Jesus and provide for him during his Galilean ministry (Matt 27:55-56; cf. Luke 8:1-3). Mark has included a good number of women in his story and most of them are portrayed in a positive way: Simon's mother-in-law

(1:29-34), the woman in the crowd (5:24b-34), the foreign woman (7:24-30), a poor widow (12:41-44), the woman who anoints Jesus in Bethany (14:3-9). Thus it is no surprise that some would have performed the service described in 15:40-41: unable to follow or provide, they now watch.

At this point in the gospel another group of persons becomes conspicuous by its absence. Since Jesus replaced his own biological family with his new family composed of those who do the will of God (3:31-35; cf. 10:28-31) the mother, brothers, and sisters of Jesus (6:3) have not reappeared. They normally would have been the ones to appeal to Pilate for permission to claim the body and bury Jesus, but they do not come forward. With no family or disciples to bury the body the honor is done by a respected member of the council, Joseph from the village of Ramathaim-Zophim, twenty miles northwest of Jerusalem. Whether he was a pious Jew or a secret disciple of Jesus is difficult to tell on the basis of his longing for God's Reign (v. 43). Pilate grants Joseph the right to bury Jesus, not a self-evident concession since the denial of burial was a common form of continued humiliation (cf. Tacitus, *Ann.* VI, 29). Joseph cares for the body of Jesus. Mary Magdalene and Mary, the mother of Joses, watch.

The Beginning of the Good News (16:1-8)

The announcement of the resurrection of Jesus (16:1-8) is as brief as the announcement of his crucifixion (15:24) and death (15:39): "He has been raised." At a very early stage attempts were made to provide an ending to the gospel that would, like those of the other canonical gospels, include at least an appearance of Jesus to Peter and the Twelve (cf. Matt 28:16-20; Luke 24:34, 36-49; John 21; 1 Cor 15:5), to Magdalene or other women (Matt 28:9-10; John 20:1, 11-18), or to other people (Luke 24:13-35). Most translations of the NT print at least two such attempts. As it stands ch. 16, concluding with v. 8, does seem truncated not only by the absence of resurrection appearances but by the disobedience of the women who came to the tomb and were informed of Jesus' resurrection. Yet there are good reasons to think that it forms an appropriate conclusion to Mark's gospel. Affirmations are made that are constitutive for Christian faith. (1) God has raised Jesus from the dead (v. 6), a confession without which Christian faith is empty (1 Cor 15:12-19). (2) The risen Christ is none other than the crucified Jesus. The resurrection does not negate the crucifixion. Given Mark's focus on the cross as the locus of revelation he may have elected not to include resurrection appearances so as not to blur the final image the reader has of Jesus, namely as the crucified one. (3) The risen Christ revives the apostolic and apostate band of the Twelve, even the one who under oath has broken with Jesus and is no longer regarded as one of the disciples. (4) The risen Christ will manifest himself in human history in specific times and places. In 14:28 he promised his disciples that he would meet them in Galilee after he had been raised (and after they had abandoned him!) and that promise is renewed in 16:7. Whether Mark intends that meeting to be the coming of the Son of man is not clear, but that he will meet them in the place where his ministry was lived out, where they received their call and continued the ministry of Jesus, is evident.

And the flight and terror and amazement and silence and fear of the faithful women? It may be that their response is an appropriate one to a God who rips open the heavens and abolishes the boundary between sacred and secular and who rips open the tomb and abolishes that final human boundary between death and life. How, then, will the gospel be preached in the world? It is not Mark's project to answer that question. His purpose was to tell the story of "the beginning of the good news of Jesus Christ, the Son of God" (1:1). The gospel has begun and can now be preached to all the nations. That is the project of the Church.

BIBLIOGRAPHY

Anderson, Janice Capel, and Stephen D. Moore. *Mark and Method.* New Approaches in Biblical Studies. Minneapolis: Fortress, 1992.

Black, Clifton. *Mark: Images of an Apostolic Interpreter.* Columbia: University of South Carolina Press, 1994.

Hengel, Martin. *Crucifixion.* Philadelphia: Fortress, 1977.

Hooker, Morna D. *The Gospel According to Saint Mark.* Black's New Testament Commentaries. Peabody, Mass.: Hendrickson, 1993.

Kermode, Frank. *The Genesis of Secrecy. On the Interpretation of Narrative.* Cambridge: Harvard University Press, 1979.

Kingsbury, Jack Dean. *The Christology of Mark's Gospel*. Philadelphia: Fortress, 1983.

Lane, William L. *The Gospel of Mark*. NIC.NT. Grand Rapids: Eerdmans, 1974.

Orchard, Bernard, and Harold Riley. *The Order of the Synoptics*. Part 2: "The Historical Tradition," by Bernard Orchard. Macon, Ga.: Mercer University Press, 1987.

Pesch, Rudolf. *Das Markusevangelium*. HThKNT. 2 vols. 3rd ed. Freiburg im Breisgau: Herder, 1980.

Taylor, Vincent. *The Gospel According to St. Mark*. 2nd ed. London: Macmillan; New York: St Martin's Press, 1966.

Tolbert, Mary Ann. "Mark" in *The Women's Bible Commentary,* Carol A. Newsom and Sharon H. Ringe, eds. Louisville: Westminster/John Knox, 1992, 263–274.

Waetjen, Herman C. *A Reordering of Power. A Socio-Political Reading of Mark's Gospel*. Minneapolis: Fortress, 1989.

Luke

Samuel Oyin Abogunrin

FIRST READING

Luke is a Special Gospel

Luke is the only gospel with a sequel: the Acts of the Apostles. In these two books we are privileged to have a "seamless" narrative describing the whole story of the life of the founder of Christianity straight through the reaction of his disciples to his death, resurrection, appearance to them, and ascension to heaven. At that point, according to the second chapter of Acts, the Holy Spirit descended a second time (the first was at the baptism of Jesus in Luke 3:22) and gave the gathered disciples the power to speak in all foreign tongues so that they would be able to go forth, east and west and north and south, to spread the gospel of Jesus Christ.

The earliest traditions about the gospel of Luke tell us that it was written specifically for churches outside Palestine. It therefore represents the earliest conscious attempt to re-enculturate the gospel in terms and concepts Christians living in the wider ecumenical mission could understand and respond to. The gospel of Matthew was the account of Jesus' life, death, and resurrection written for Jewish Christians. It sought to prove from repeated quotations of Scripture that Jesus was the Messiah just as we see Paul doing in Acts 28:23: "After they had set a day to meet with him, they came to him at his lodging in great numbers. From morning until evening he explained the matter to them, testifying to the kingdom of God and trying to convince them about Jesus both from the law of Moses and from the prophets." The gospel of Luke is the attempt to take this original message and recast it in language and thought-patterns familiar to more hellenized Jewish, as well as "god fearing" Gentile readers.

What Do We Know About the Author?

There is nothing in the gospel of Luke that a Gentile could not grasp and understand. The Greek of Luke is the best in any of the four gospels and it is most likely that Greek was the native tongue of the evangelist. The gospel of Luke is lacking in Hebrew words, local Palestinian coloring, and direct OT quotations. Luke's audience, unlike Matthew's, was composed of predominantly non-Jewish listeners, foreigners who for various reasons had converted to Christianity as a result of the preaching of Paul or Peter or one of the other traveling evangelists such as Apollos. Naturally an urgent question would have been: "How can we be certain that we were told the truth about the Lord Jesus?"

The earliest Church tradition identifies Luke as the author of the gospel. The gospel itself is anonymous. A coworker of Paul named Luke is mentioned three times in the NT. In Phlm 24 he is referred to as Paul's fellow worker who sends greetings along with other companions of Paul. In Col 4:14 he is called "beloved physician" and sends greetings to Colossae. In 2 Tim 4:11 he is named as Paul's sole companion in Rome at that moment. The first writer to attribute Luke/Acts to "Luke" was Irenaeus.

The Cultural and Historical Setting Reflected in Luke and Acts

J. Massyngberde Ford has described the time Jesus was born as "one of the most turbulent and belligerent centuries of Jewish history" (*My Enemy is My Guest,* 1). In the fourth century B.C.E. Alexander the Great occupied Palestine. His successors introduced Greek culture into the holy land. When he died Palestine was subject to the Egyptians and then to the Syrians (322–142 B.C.E.) until Jewish nationalists arose, fought for, and secured independence (142–63 B.C.E.). But in 63 B.C.E. Pompey captured Palestine for the Romans. By 37 B.C.E. Herod the Great was appointed king of the Jews. Herod was hated by the Jews because he was an Idumean and because of the oppressive taxation that accompanied the introduction of Roman rule. There was relative peace in the empire and Roman rule did bring some benefits, but those representing the Roman authorities were guilty of violence, sacrilege, robbery, devastation, rape, and selling people into slavery. Though there was no open rebellion during the period of Herod the Great his reign was one of terror. He made efforts to wipe out all the Jewish nationalists and their followers, labeling them bandits.

There were many causes of unrest in Palestine. The occupation by the Greek and Roman armies had effects on the economy as well as on social and religious life. A moving army was usually accompanied by wives, concubines, children, servants, slaves, merchants, moneylenders, traffickers in booty, veterinarians, physicians, and others. The military factor is important because Palestine was occupied at least seven times after Alexander the Great. The presence of foreign troops created havoc since the local populace had to provide for the various needs of the "moving city." Women and children were captured. Such women were vulnerable to rape. This created a special problem for Jewish women because even if a Jewish woman had only been in danger of being raped a pious Jew could not sleep with her because she might have been defiled.

Land was confiscated by the Romans and Herodians for various reasons, but most especially for unpaid taxes or debts. The loss of small holdings increased unemployment. Here the parable of the workers in the vineyard comes to mind. Famine and drought also made the peasants lose their small holdings or fall into the hands of moneylenders. Again this reminds us of the parable of the two debtors as well as the message of John the Baptist in Luke. This was why the revolutionaries burned the public archives in 66 C.E. to destroy the records of debts. The Jewish aristocracy including the Sadducees, the Herodians, and the high priests collaborated with Rome and enriched themselves. The immense luxury of the high priest was a cause of great indignation to the masses. The high priestly family was corrupt. There was class war between the city priests and peasant priests in the country. Consequently the peasant priests hated the Romans. This hatred intensified when Temple authorities decided to accept sacrifices brought by foreigners, including representatives of the emperor. This was one of the immediate causes of the last Jewish war which began in 66 C.E. Banditry became epidemic under Roman rule. Religious zeal at this time occasionally developed into fanaticism and terrorism. Many zealots believed in the "holy war" or acts of violence perpetrated to ensure the observance of the Torah and religious duty. The killing of the godless was seen as a religious duty. The zealots quite often directed their ardor not against the Gentiles but against fellow Jews whom they regarded as "unorthodox." However, sometimes they fought against Romans and their protégés such as Herod and the Herodians.

When Herod the Great died in 4 B.C.E. much of his land went into Roman hands or was auctioned off. The indigenous farmers fared badly. Even where they retained their lands they were expected to give a considerable amount of produce to their landlords in addition to paying taxes and tithes. Drought quite often intensified the hardship. The peasant farmers then became a source of recruits for the revolutionaries. The Romans punished the Jews for the turbulence and revolts that followed Herod's death. Three thousand Jews were slaughtered in the Temple courts, four hundred talents were looted from the sacred treasury, two thousand insurgents were crucified. The chief centers of unrest were the royal agricultural estates where tension existed between tenants and landlords. This brings to mind the parable of the wicked tenants.

Added to this was the problem of religious division among the Jews. The situation gave birth to many religious sects. Among the major ones were the Essenes who withdrew to the wilderness of Judea. The Herodians were not a religious sect but Jews who supported Herod and Roman rule. They constituted the rich class and benefited from Roman rule. The majority of them belonged to the priestly class. Thus the whole religious system was corrupted by the rich and the priestly class as is the case in may parts of the world today.

The Message of the Gospel of Luke for the Church Today

The life and ministry of Jesus established the model for the Church to follow. In addition to preaching the message of the kingdom Jesus went about doing good: healing the sick, giving sight to the blind, making the deaf hear and the dumb speak, curing the crippled, and cleansing lepers. He was revolutionary in many of his actions. He did not allow the religious and racial prejudices known to some Jews to hinder him from free movement among various classes of people. He gave hope and confidence to men and women alike, to the outcasts and those declared religiously and ritually unclean; he gave equal attention to people of all races who needed his help. He denounced the religious and social structures that abetted the oppression of the poor. Although he had final control over his destiny he did not refuse crucifixion. His life that he gave on the cross and his resurrection became the source of life and hope for humankind. Jesus knew that poverty, prejudice, oppression, human wretchedness, tragedy, war, and death were due to the malignancy in the human heart that required his own sacrifice on the cross. Jesus' purpose in history therefore transcends all ideas and systems and utopias of men and women. The Church is the custodian of this royal message of redemption, which has become its greatest heritage. If the Church preaches, acts, and lives by this message it will always remain relevant. The challenge therefore comes to us in the following ways today.

1. On Earth Peace

In spite of the relative peace brought about by the reign of Caesar Augustus the Roman Empire was a world filled with fear, injustice, violence, and crime. The large majority of humankind suffering under various yokes of oppression were looking for liberation. It was to this world that the angel said "I am bringing you good news of great joy for all the people," and to which a multitude of angels sang "Glory to God in the highest heaven, and on earth peace among those whom he favors." The Church is to preach the gospel that is the powerful agency of God for the salvation and liberation of humankind. In spite of the end of the Cold War the world has yet to know peace. The dismantling of the Soviet Union has resulted in conflicts yet to be resolved. Resolutions to the wars in the Horn of Africa, the Sudan, and elsewhere in Africa are not yet in sight. For nearly fifty years various kinds of wars and violent political conflicts have occurred in the Middle East, the Far East, and Latin America. Most of these hostilities are exacerbated by rivalry among world powers. Today forty percent of the total budgets of African states are spent on arms, not for fighting outside enemies but for oppressing, maiming, and killing those who criticize their governments. Half of the total refugees in the world are in Africa. Now Islamic fundamentalism, especially in Asia and Africa, poses a danger to world peace.

The growth of the Christian Church in Africa is notable. According to the figures released by the Center for World Evangelization, by 1980 the number of Christians in Africa had reached 203 million with at least a four percent annual increase, that is, 6,200,000 per year made up of 1,500,000 by conversion and 4,700,000 by birth. It is estimated that by the year 2000 the number of Christians in Africa will be much higher. In spite of the astronomical growth of the Christian church in Africa its impact needs to be felt more as a message of peace, life, and hope. What we say for Africa is what we say for all the regions of the world. The Church must always challenge all structures of power that prevent people from enjoying the full benefits of what God did for humanity in Christ Jesus. If Jesus is the life of the world, it follows that he is life for people of all races regardless of where they live.

2. Jesus the Hope of the Hopeless

Luke presents Jesus as the hope of the hopeless. The Magnificat states this clearly: God fights on behalf of the poor and raises up the downtrodden. The stories of the pardon of the woman of the city, the healing of the woman with the issue of blood, the raising of Jairus's daughter and the only son of the widow at Nain, the ten lepers cured, Zacchaeus and Levi, the parables of the Good Samaritan, the Prodigal Son, and the Pharisee and the Toll Collector are all reminders of the mission of the Church in a world that is burdened with disease and both racial and religious prejudice.

The stable was the place where the Savior and Lord of all was born. What his parents brought to the Temple at the dedication of Jesus and the purification of Mary on the fortieth day was a poor family's offering. Roman society was generally heartless toward the poor who crowded its cities. Charity and care of the poor are urged in the Jewish Scriptures. Some, however, who practiced piety did so in order to receive human praise. Jesus condemned such hypocrisy.

Of course wherever the Church has gone with the gospel it has gone with enlightenment, compassion, and healing. The Church has led in giving the world schools and colleges, hospitals, orphanages, welfare centers, and progressive agricultural methods. Like rivers of compassion the Church has flowed into the valleys of need in all the continents of the world from age to age. The Church is busy daily binding the wounds of those terribly bruised and mending broken hearts. But the situation in Africa, Asia, parts of South America, certain parts of Europe and North America show clearly that the Church has not done enough. Most churches in the Third World do not have adequate programs for the poor masses. This may be due to the fact that the vast majority of Christians in these areas are still living in abject poverty. While Christians in rich nations have tried to alleviate the sufferings of Christians and non-Christians in other lands these efforts are like drops in the ocean. The poor in these rich nations are also crying for help. Mercy lays claim on the Church wherever there is human suffering. To have mercy is to bear other people's burdens in fraternal love, making their problems our own problems, and if possible like our Master to die in the service of others. In fact this is the supreme purpose of Calvary.

3. The Status of Women

Luke more than any other gospel gives various accounts of the unique roles that women played in the life and ministry of Jesus. It begins with the story of Elizabeth. In Luke it was Mary who directly received the announcement of the birth of Jesus from the angel Gabriel. The role of Anna the prophet is mentioned. Luke talks about the public woman, Mary of Magdala, Mary and Martha, the mother of James and John, the ministering women from Galilee, the women in the various parables, the weeping women in Jerusalem who were following Jesus after he was condemned to death and the women at the cross and at the tomb. These accounts are significant in light of the prevailing prejudices about women among the Jews and throughout the rest of the then known world. Jesus talked publicly with women; he even allowed the sinful and the unclean among them to touch him. They received equal attention with men. It is true that women are not listed among the Twelve but it is probable that some were included among the seventy-two. Women were among the one hundred twenty people upon whom the Holy Spirit descended on the day of Pentecost. The Church universal is still debating the issue of women and their role in the Church. There is need for the Church to reexamine the role of women in leadership roles in the churches of Paul. We need to consider the unique roles played by women as missionaries to most continents of the world during the last two centuries, particularly in Africa, Asia, and South America, as well as many islands of the world. Luke shows that God does not design for women a role that is inferior to that of men in the Church.

What is the Church doing about the areas of the world where women have taken to prostitution in order to survive and support aged parents? What is the Church saying about women in the Muslim world? What of poor women who produce babies without any means of housing, feeding, clothing, and educating them? What about those areas of the world where by custom women are the breadwinners who labor on the farms to feed their lazy husbands, many of whom are alcoholics? What is the Church doing about the need for and the right of all women to education? How much has the Church done in the area of theological education for women? What about single parents and what about polygamy? While the issue of ordination for women in the Church is important, the above issues are even more urgent and call for immediate action. There is need for a thorough reevaluation of the Church's approach to the question of the rights of women. At present some efforts toward solving these issues are misdirected and this is why their impact is not felt. Even societies that claim to have equality for men and women in reality do not. The solution after all may not be found in rewriting the Bible in inclusive language or in the attempt to change things that God in infinite divine wisdom has through nature differently bequeathed to men and women for the purpose of an orderly human society, but until the Church's efforts lead to the solution of the above problems our efforts would appear to be misdirected. The problem is deep-seated in the human heart and solutions must begin from there.

4. Proclaiming the Year of the Lord's Favor

In the Roman world about three quarters of the population was made up of slaves and freed persons with limited rights. Jesus in his sermon at Nazareth in Galilee proclaimed a new Exodus and year of Jubilee for all. This is the message that the Church must proclaim, live, and act in every generation in order to be relevant. How can the Church remain relevant in the midst of political and religious oppression in nations where it exists and thrives? How can the Church remain relevant when it does not address the issues of hunger and poverty? How can the Church remain relevant in its silence against various human atrocities and heinous crimes against humanity? Why has the Church, activated by the Holy Spirit, somehow remained silent or forgotten its prophetic voice? Humankind everywhere is looking to the Church for leadership and guidance. The Church ought to be the vanguard of freedom since Jesus came for all, died for all, and rose for all. Jesus displayed deep compassion for depraved people in the hope of winning them for a better life. A Christianity that does not proclaim the year of the Lord's favor to all and act on behalf of the poor and oppressed is not related to Jesus Christ as portrayed in the gospel of Luke.

SECOND READING

Introduction: 1:1-4

Luke begins with an introduction similar to what one would find in the work of a contemporary secular historian or biographer (for example, Philo's *Life of Moses* or Flavius Josephus's *Antiquities of the Jews*). Of course the value of the Preface does not lie in its beauty but in its testimony to the credibility of the history contained in the gospel. From this introduction we learn the following things:

(1) Many *(polloi),* the author admits, have written accounts of the ministry of Jesus before him. Luke does not reject these as inaccurate but finds them inadequate in the light of facts in his possession. One of these accounts would most likely have been the gospel of Matthew, a gospel with which Luke shares many things in common. Apart from the gospel of Matthew there must also be some other written source material, probably in the form of tracts. Luke was well traveled; he would have had the opportunity to gather material from far and wide.

(2) Luke says he received much of his material from eyewitnesses and "ministers of the word," that is, those whose task it was to treasure and preserve the sayings and doings of the Lord. Some of these would have been disciples of Jesus including members of the seventy-two, personal friends of Jesus and members of his family, such as Jesus' father's brother Cleopas, about whom we shall hear more later.

(3) Luke has thoroughly checked his information and will present it accurately, for example, with due attention to chronological order.

(4) The gospel is dedicated to someone addressed as "most excellent Theophilus." He may have been a high-ranking Roman official and probably was interested in Christianity. Luke may have wanted to present the new religion in the fullest and clearest terms so as to win his protection and support. The name "*theo-philus*" means "lover of God" and may have symbolized persons all over the world who were intelligent seekers after the truth whether Christian or not. Christianity was on trial and competing with other religions for a hearing in the marketplaces of the world, just as it is in Africa and Asia today.

The Birth Narrative: 1:5–2:52

This section has been called the "infancy gospel." The title is apt, for these stories serve as a prologue to the life and ministry of Jesus, showing how the Son of God was born and destined to bring universal salvation to the whole world. The major events are interwoven: the birth of John the Baptist (the forerunner) and the birth of Jesus the Messiah. In Luke's view, with these two events began a new and decisive epoch in human history. This is the beginning of a saving process that will be consummated in the creation of a new heaven and earth in which righteousness dwells (Isa 65:17; 2 Pet 3:13; Rev 21:1). There is much in these two chapters that may be hard for us to believe. The shepherds, surprised by the angel's announcement, could in disbelief have turned away from their message, regarding it as an idle tale. Instead they said to one another, "Let us go now to Bethlehem and see this thing that has taken place." With the shepherds, therefore, let us go with open minds and the eyes of faith to Luke's gospel as he unfolds the divine mysteries of salvation.

The Birth of John the Baptist Foretold (1:5-25)

Luke opens with "In the days of King Herod of Judea" (1:5). Herod reigned from 37–4 B.C.E. Though the exact date of Jesus' birth is unknown, he was born several years before 1 C.E. This discrepancy came about through a mistake in the revising of the Christian calendar in the sixth century. It is generally believed that Jesus was born sometime between 6 and 4 B.C.E. Both Matthew and Luke agree that Jesus was born when Herod was king of Judea (Matt 2:1-23). Jesus must have been born before Herod died in 4 B.C.E. He was not a Jew but an Idumean, a descendent of Esau, whose territory was directly across the Jordan in Edom, at that time a vassal state of mighty Rome just as Judea was. Nevertheless Herod built for the Jews a magnificent Temple and avoided religious persecution. Of course tyrants and emperors can build temples for the Church, as has happened recently in the Central African Republic.

Who was Zechariah? He was a member of one of the families of priests descended from the original high priest, Aaron, brother of Moses. There were numerous descendants in twenty-four divisions (1 Chronicles 24). Each division was in charge of the Temple for one week twice each year. At only three major festivals were all of the priests needed in Jerusalem to officiate: Passover, Pentecost, and Tabernacles.

Since Zechariah was a priest he could only marry a full-blooded daughter of a priestly family. In this case he had married a daughter from Aaron's own family. Both he and his wife were "righteous" and lived "blamelessly," yet godliness is no guarantee against suffering and the disappointment of human hopes. The two had no child and they were getting old. Childlessness was widely thought to be a sign of divine displeasure among the Jews. It was even a ground for divorce. Conversely, many children was a sign of God's blessing (cf. Ps 127:3-6). In most African communities childlessness is regarded as a tragedy and a curse. Unfortunately, quite often the woman receives the blame. For example, among the Yoruba of West Africa when a barren woman died in the old days she was not buried in the home but in the groves in order to distance her curse from the family. A wooden baby called an Omolangidi was tied to her back before she was buried to assuage the evil spirits.

Since there were many priests it was an important day for Zechariah when the lot fell on him to lead the prayers. As the smoke of the sweet incense rose up to heaven an angel appeared near Zechariah. Apparently his silently spoken plea before God had been heard. The angel Gabriel, whose name means "warrior of God," spoke: "your wife Elizabeth will bear you a son, and you will name him John," which means "YHWH is gracious." But Zechariah could not believe it. "Give me a sign," he stammered in fear. Gabriel replied, "I am Gabriel. I stand in the presence of God." Zechariah was struck dumb and remained speechless until the baby was born.

The Birth of Jesus Foretold (1:26-38)

Luke's account of the annunciation of the birth of Jesus parallels that of John at every point, but the prediction to Mary is presented with marked dignity and reverence. Luke sees the annunciation of Jesus' birth as the crown of all prophecies. It reveals the supreme mystery of the Christian faith and the nature of the promised Savior who is both human and divine.

The same angel who announced the birth of John comes to Mary to announce the birth of Jesus. In John's case Zechariah, the father, was the focus of attention. In the case of Jesus attention is focused on Mary, the mother. Mary was a humble young woman betrothed to Joseph, a carpenter, at the remote village of Nazareth in Galilee. Betrothal was quite as binding as marriage among the Jews. Should the man to whom a woman was betrothed die, according to the Torah his brother had to provide her with an heir (cf. Luke 20:28).

In some traditional cultures in Africa betrothal takes place as early as the age of eight. In some other cultures three to six years may elapse before marriage. In some cases where major social concerns are at stake interest in the infant girl of one family will be shown by another family from the time she is born. Here also betrothal is as binding as marriage. Once the two families agree according to the prescribed customs dissolution can only be by a formal divorce. If the man should die before the formal marriage the girl is regarded as a widow and passed on to the nearest kinsman for inheritance. However, this custom is changing fast as a result of the introduction of Christianity along with western culture into Africa. Surprisingly, most of the marriages contracted under the native law and custom lasted until death but unfortunately a large percentage of those contracted in the Church do not last. This experience is not unique to Africa. Homes are no longer stable today and this is where Satan's attack on the Church appears fiercest. Homes that can truly be described as Christian today are on the decline. The Church everywhere has to take this up as a challenge. There is need for rethinking the concept of the Christian home and marriage based on the Scriptures and things that are of value in the God-given cultures of the various nations of the world.

Gabriel salutes Mary: "Greetings, favored one! The Lord is with you." While she is perplexed about this strange salutation, she is told not to be afraid. She will conceive and give birth to a child to be called *Jesus,* which is a Greek form of the Hebrew name *Joshua (Yehoshua),* which means "Yah is Savior." The child will be called the Son of the Most High God.

Mary expresses astonishment but not unbelief like Zechariah. "How can this be, since I am a virgin?" This confirms the fact that Mary is still a virgin. There is no doubt that, like Matthew, Luke has Isa 7:14 and 9:6-7 in mind here (cf. Matt 1:20-25). The angel tells Mary that in a mysterious way she will become like the Temple upon which the *Shekinah,* the glory of God rested (cf. Exod 33:9-11; 1 Kings 8:10-11). Afterward, unlike John, Jesus will be divine and God's Messiah. Gabriel also tells Mary that her elderly barren relative, Elizabeth, has been pregnant already for six months. This was to prove that nothing was impossible with the almighty God. Mary's response is full of trust and humility. In spite of her faith there is no doubt that she was aware that the fulfillment of the promise might result in suspicion, shame, divorce, reproach, and even a death sentence. But she did not allow the thought of these terrors to deter her from humbly submitting herself to the will of God. Thus Mary is an inspiration for all Christians as the symbol of faith.

Mary Visits Elizabeth (1:39-56)

Mary hastens to visit her cousin Elizabeth upon hearing news of her pregnancy. She wonders why the Lord has miraculously visited her—for what purpose? When Elizabeth hears Mary's voice at the door the baby John leaps in her womb and suddenly the Holy Spirit enters Elizabeth. Inspired, she exclaims the famous words, "Blessed are you among women, and blessed is the fruit of your womb." It was a profound experience for both women, each carrying a very special baby. Mary responds with a song of praise that has come to be known as the "Magnificat." Her words echo the beautiful and poignant Song of Hannah in the OT when she was enabled by the Lord to give birth to the prophet Samuel (1 Sam 2:1-10). Mary's song beautifully expresses how the Lord remembers the poor and downtrodden to save them. She contrasts the blessedness of God-fearing people to the misery of the unbelieving, proud and rebellious, who will be scattered like chaff. God's promise to the patriarch Abraham will finally find its "yes" in her Son Jesus.

The Births of John and Jesus (1:57–2:20)

The prediction of the angel comes true at the end of nine months. We can see that John's birth was a stirring event. Among most ethnic groups in Africa the naming ceremony is a great affair, an occasion for singing, dancing, cooking, eating, and making merry. The baby's names must reflect the family history and status. When Elizabeth tells the neighbors that her child's name will be "John" ("YHWH is gracious") they object (1:60-61). They think he should have Zechariah's name, but Zechariah takes a writing tablet and writes "John"—and suddenly his tongue is loosed and he blesses God. His great and beautiful song ranks with the most exalted psalms in the entire Bible, bringing together into a few lines many of the most powerful themes in Israel's prophetic heritage.

Not long afterward the most momentous single event in the history of the world, the hinge on which the story of humankind hangs swung from the old order into the new. Luke reports that Joseph and Mary traveled the eighty miles from their obscure country village of Nazareth to return to his ancestral town of Bethlehem because of the census of Caesar. To most Africans where a person is born or lives may not necessarily determine his or her native home. One's home is one's ancestral town or village where one hopes to be buried when one dies. According to Luke this was also the period when Quirinius was the Roman governor of the province of Syria. Such censuses were taken periodically for the double purpose of taxation and military conscription. Obediently Joseph and Mary, then very pregnant, set off for Bethlehem. Conditions could not have been worse for this poor couple. When they arrived in Bethlehem they could find no place to stay. But when we think things are at their worst sometimes they are the best from God's perspective. Angels suddenly announce to shepherds that they will see their Savior, Christ the Lord, born nearby in Bethlehem. They would not find him in the most beautiful home in Bethlehem, but in a stable. A world Savior born according to the plan of God like a poor shepherd! Amazed, they go to see and sure enough, there is the baby as the angel had said. So they pay homage to the Deliverer. The poor after all will benefit from the hope of Israel.

The song of the angels in Luke 2:14 is variously translated. Some read: ". . . peace among those whom [God] favors," while others read, ". . . . peace, good will among all people." Recently discovered Dead Sea scrolls contain parallels that favor ". . . peace among those with whom God is pleased" or "whom God favors." There can be no dogmatic conclusion.

Like any young mother who gazes for hours at her sweet baby and wonders what the future holds in store, Mary kept all these strange events in her heart, pondering what they could mean.

Jesus is Dedicated in the Temple (2:21-40)

In this passage Luke describes ceremonies every Jewish boy is expected to undergo. The first is circumcision on the eighth day. Circumcision was given to Abraham as a seal of the covenant to mark out his descendants as God's special people (Gen 17:10-13). In the process the son is named. Another is the purification of the mother after childbirth (Lev 12:1-8). The offering was supposed to be a year-old lamb, but if the parents were poor two pigeons or turtledoves could be substituted. This was officially called "the offering of the poor." That this is what Joseph and Mary offered indicates that the Savior was born into a home where there were no luxuries, a home where members knew what it was to lack the essential, basic things of life, a home where every cent counts. When we as parents worry about the various needs of our children and how we will make ends meet we can remember poor Joseph and Mary who had a home like ours.

Luke describes two persons who met the young couple and their child at these ceremonies, a man and a woman (Luke likes to tell of pairs in this fashion, as we shall see). Simeon had been specifically told that he would not die until he set his eyes on the Messiah of Israel. Luke also speaks of Anna the prophet, who had spent eighty-four years of her widowhood in prayers and meditation mostly in the Temple. Quickened by the Holy Spirit they both come to the dedication ceremony. The songs of both prophets speak of Jesus' future in glowing terms, one of how Jesus will bring blessing to all nations and the other of the suffering and rejection Jesus will encounter.

Issues Arising from Luke's Birth Narrative

Questions sometimes arise in people's minds because the birth narratives in Matthew and Luke are so different. Actually there is more contact between Matthew and Luke than might appear at first glance. Consider the following parallels:

Parallels Between Matthew 1–2 and Luke 1–2

Matthew	*Luke*
1. Mary and Joseph will be Jesus' parents (1:16, 18-20, 24; 2:11, 13, 19)	1. Mary and Joseph will be Jesus' parents (1:27-56; 2:1-5, 16, 19, 34)
2. Joseph is betrothed to Mary (1:18)	2. Joseph is betrothed to Mary (1:27; 2:5; cf. 1:34-35)
3. Virginity of Mary (1:18, 23)	3. Virginity of Mary (1:27, 34)
4. Conception by Holy Spirit (1:18, 20)	4. Conception by Holy Spirit (1:35)
5. Jesus' family is from the line of David (1:1, 6, 17, 20)	5. Jesus' family is from the line of David (1:27, 32, 69; 2:4, 11)
6. Angelic annunciation (1:20)	6. Angelic annunciation (1:30)
7. Child's name given (1:21)	7. Child's name given (1:13, 31; 2:21)
8. Jesus as Savior (1:21)	8. Jesus as Savior (2:11)
9. Child visited (2:11)	9. Child visited (2:16)
10. Visitors worship (2:2, 11)	10. Visitors worship (cf. 2:20)
11. Jesus is born in Bethlehem (2:1, 5, 6)	11. Jesus is born in Bethlehem (2:4, 15)
12. Herod is King (2:1)	12. Herod is King (1:5)
13. There is "great joy" (2:10)	13. There is "great joy" (1:14; 2:10)
14. Use of "righteous" (1:19)	14. Use of "righteous" (1:6; 2:25)
15. "Fear" (1:20; 2:22)	15. "Fear" (1:12, 13, 29-30, 65; 2:9)
16. Abraham (1:1-2, 17)	16. Abraham (1:55, 73)
17. Family's home town is Nazareth (2:23)	17. Family's home town is Nazareth (1:26; 2:4, 39, 51)
18. Genealogy (1:1-17)	18. Genealogy (3:23-38)

On the other hand, despite these numerous points of contact we must not forget that Luke was writing for a completely different audience than did Matthew. He was facing an entirely different challenge: how to express the gospel of Jesus the Christ to non-Jewish Christians who lived far away from Palestine and had little or no knowledge of Jewish customs or language. Besides their local dialects Greek was the international language, and Greek customs and laws, mixed with local customs and laws, were what they lived by. It is the same in our African churches today where we struggle daily to hold together our Christian faith with the best of our God-given African customs and values.

Luke felt called to do something different from what Matthew had done in another sense. He wanted to write a two-part history of the Christian Church. The first part was a biography of the founder of the faith, Jesus of Nazareth, and the second part was to be the first history of the early Church. He wanted to tell about the principal apostles, especially Peter and Paul, who had brought the word of truth to the towns and cities in Asia Minor and Syria, Achaia, and even Italy. Why did he want to do that? Because the question uppermost in the minds of Luke's readers would have been: is the wonderful story about salvation in Jesus Christ really true? Did all the things the apostles Paul and Peter told us actually happen? Luke wanted to make certain that Christians living in the *oikoumenē,* the household of the nations, would be confident that they could trust the gospel of the Jewish Savior Jesus.

We should therefore expect that the beginning of Luke's narrative would be different from Matthew's. In Jewish culture the proper place to begin is with the family genealogy, which is what Matthew did. But in Greek culture a writer is supposed to begin with a preface to the readers assuring them of the veracity of the account. Next Luke tells the story of God's activity in such a way that the respective roles of John the Baptist and Jesus are more clearly explained than they were in Matthew. John and Jesus are introduced as agents of salvation in alternating passages: parallel accounts of birth, circumcision, naming, and announcement of the future missions of John and Jesus (Luke 1:57–2:39). At the same time Luke clearly raises Jesus above John as the central figure of his gospel story. John is a prophet of the Most High (Luke 1:76), but Jesus is the Son of the Most High (Luke 1:32). Jesus visits his Father's house (Luke 2:41-52); there is no similar development with John. John goes forth in the spirit and power of Elijah (Luke 1:17); Jesus will be taken up into heaven like Elijah (Luke 9:31, 51; 24:50-51). Above all Jesus is the Christ, the Chosen Son of God (Luke 9:20, 35; 24:26, 46). Luke appears to remain faithful to the essence of the account as we find it in Matthew while modifying it in significant ways.

Second, questions about the virgin birth have abounded since the beginning. Indeed, Matthew's gospel is the place where ugly suspicions are first mentioned (cf. Matt 1:19). But if we approach this account with a mood of suspicion we will certainly miss the point. We cannot hear the word of God if we say suspiciously, "Prove it and then I'll believe it!" The word of life is not about proof but faith. Christians walk by faith, not by sight. It is the world that walks by sight, not by faith; that is why it is in such terrible trouble. The voice of faith says: "God has visited us in human form in the man Jesus Christ, and his mother was given the promise in advance that this would be so." Therefore we cherish this abiding mystery as one of the most precious truths of the whole Christian faith: that an angel of God came to a humble woman and announced to her that she was to bear the Son of God for our salvation.

Jesus in the Temple at the Age of Twelve (2:41-52)

In Jesus' day every male adult Jew who lived within a day's journey of Jerusalem was expected to attend the annual feasts of Passover, Pentecost (first fruits), and Tabernacles (harvest). Those who lived far away were expected to struggle to attend these feasts at least once in a lifetime. A Hebrew boy becomes a man at twelve and is inducted into the covenant with other males in a ceremony now known as a Bar Mitzvah, which means "son of the commandment." It is the time when Jewish boys begin formal education in the Torah and reading of the Hebrew Scriptures so that they may fulfill all the ritual duties of an adult male Jew.

Luke describes this scene in part. Passover has taken place and Jesus' parents have left Jerusalem while he is still in the Temple speaking with the teachers. It is doubtful that Jesus' parents missed him through carelessness. Usually the women in caravans start much earlier than men because they travel more slowly than men. Joseph apparently thought Jesus was with Mary in the female party, while Mary must have thought Jesus was behind in the male party. In this case when the men caught up with the women in the evening it would have been discovered that Jesus was in neither of the two parties. In any case when at the end of the day's journey Joseph and Mary could not find Jesus they returned to Jerusalem to look for their son. After three days' search they found him in the Temple, "sitting among the teachers, listening to them and asking them questions" (2:46). To Mary's "Child, why have you treated us like this?" Jesus asks her in turn how she could fail to know where he would be, namely in his Father's house. He was not being rude; he simply spoke out of his consciousness of a unique relationship to God. Nevertheless he obediently got up and went with his parents to Nazareth. We see here an important lesson: being a Christian does not necessarily destroy earthly ties, particularly for Christians in pluralistic regions of the world. Christians should be good examples, discharging their human duties with unimpeachable fidelity (note Paul's advice in 1 Cor. 7:13-16).

The Preaching of John; The Baptism and Temptation of Jesus: 3:1–4:13

The Preaching of John the Baptist (3:1-20)

The Baptist was an inspired prophet who broke the long silence of centuries since the days of the prophet Malachi. Just as Malachi 4 ends with a reference to the coming of Elijah who will warn Israel of the day of judgment, so the NT era opens with John's voice calling out this warning as if he were Elijah: "Prepare the way of the Lord . . . and all flesh shall see the salvation of God" (Luke 3:4-6).

The momentous significance of this event is signaled in Luke 3:1-2 with an unusual "triple" calendar dating. First Luke gives the Roman dates. Since the whole Mediterranean world counted years according to Rome's rulers we

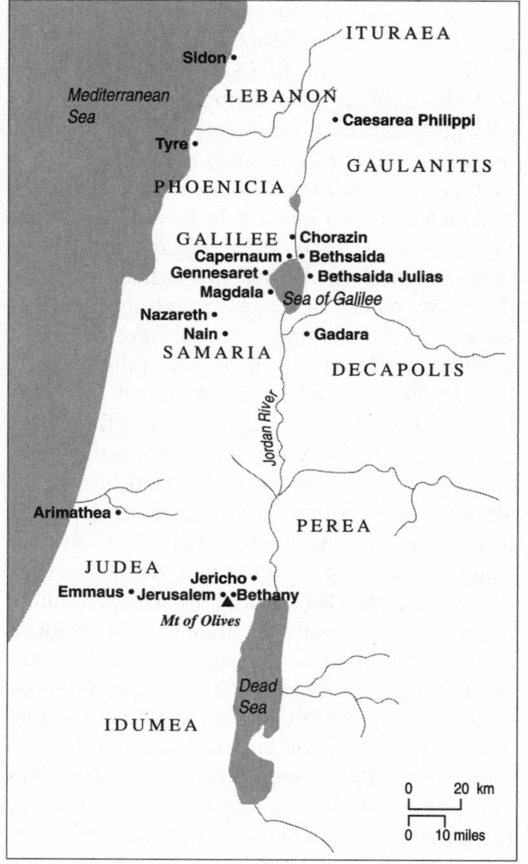

LUKE'S PALESTINE

learn that this was "the fifteenth year of the reign of Tiberius Caesar." Since Tiberius replaced Caesar Augustus in the year 14 C.E. (according to the Christian calendar) this would work out to 29 C.E. as the year when John began preaching. Luke goes on to mention the chief regional Roman official, Pontius Pilate, who was governor of Judea from 26 to 36 C.E. Then come the regional indigenous rulers of the places in which most of Jesus' ministry took place. Luke mentions two sons of Herod the Great: Herod Antipas, "tetrarch" (from *tetra archē,* "ruler of one fourth of a domain") of Galilee, and Philip, tetrarch across the Jordan River in the mountainous regions of Iturea and Trachonitis. Finally Luke mentions Annas and Caiaphas, leaders among the Jerusalem priesthood, by whose reigns pious Jews would have counted years. By this unusual three-tier calendar dating the author apparently wants to make triply sure that everyone will know when these great events began.

John describes the nature of his ministry in the words of Isa 40:3-5: "the voice of one out crying in the wilderness: 'Prepare the way of the Lord, make his path straight.'' The description employs oriental imagery: before a monarch made an official journey a servant was sent ahead to prepare the way and clear the road of all crowds (as well as flocks and other hindrances) because it would not be seemly for a royal person to have to detour around mere commoners. Warning his listeners about the coming day of judgment, John urges them to repent and return to the Lord. Calling those who come out to him a "brood of vipers," he in effect excommunicates the whole nation. He tells them they cannot trust in their physical descent from Father Abraham. God has no more regard for their physical descent than for desert stones. Nor will their being baptized amount to anything if they do not change their lives. He tells those who have two coats to give one to those who have none and otherwise to do what they can for the poor. He also has a word for the soldiers: they are to serve faithfully and be content with their pay. Today nearly half of the governments of the Third World are headed by soldiers, mainly as a result of the shortcomings of the political class. The countries under their rule have fared poorly, becoming breeding grounds for multimillionaires who become generals in their thirties. Meanwhile the poor pick garbage in order to survive.

Luke concludes on a grim note by mentioning John's imprisonment by Herod Antipas (the tetrarch). Josephus adds further details, noting that Herod had snatched Herodias from his stepbrother Philip (whom he killed), for which John castigated Antipas. Herod in turn imprisoned John in the prison fortress of Machaerus near the Dead Sea. John was eventually beheaded (cf. Josephus, *Ant.* 17.5.2). Today in Nigeria and elsewhere many fearless preachers like John are either in jail or have been killed by the tyrannical rulers of their countries. What is the responsibility of the Church in such situations?

Baptism of Jesus (3:21-22)

Luke is careful to emphasize that it is the Holy Spirit, not John, who baptizes Jesus. Matthew's account, with the dialogue between John and Jesus about who should baptize whom, might have been confusing to Luke's readers. In any case Luke focuses on what he regards as the real significance of the event: baptism by the Holy Spirit followed by the proclamation from heaven: "You are my Son, the Beloved; [today I have begotten you]" (cf. Ps 2:7). This was indeed the day Jesus began to act as God's Son, but not as a royal king would. Jesus sought to bring the earth into subjection to God as the Suffering Servant (cf. Isa 42:1-4; 53:1-12). From the time of his baptism Jesus was bound for the cross. He accepted the role of the Suffering Servant who humbled himself and became obedient unto death, even death on the cross (Phil 2:8).

The Holy Spirit came upon Jesus in a special way. Here we move near the twilight of a divine mystery and in the neighborhood of the Trinity. The activity of the entire Godhead is here made manifest. The Father speaks and the Holy Spirit descends from heaven. The beloved Son is the recipient of the Father's voice and of the Holy Spirit. The relationship henceforth depends on this manifestation and declaration from heaven. Having been baptized and empowered by the Holy Spirit, Jesus is ready to embark on his mission, to bear the sins of many and reveal the open door to the Father's love and forgiveness.

The Ancestors of Jesus (3:23-38)

Genealogy is very important in many African cultures. The list of ancestors is kept for the purpose of knowing blood relations and the list may date back several centuries. It helps to distinguish the true descendant of a great ancestor from the descendants of slaves and strangers who in the course of history also become part of one's family line. In relating the list of ancestors the elders tell the heroic achievements of many of them as well as the failures of others, including their physical appearance, nature of work, when and how they died. Genealogies also help one to know who is entitled to be chief or king. No matter how powerful or rich one is, he or she cannot acquire what is not his or her right by birth. For example, among the Yoruba the list of ancestors is related in family eulogies in poetic forms or songs similar to what Jacob said about each of his sons (cf. Genesis 49). Similarly the Yoruba preserve not only authentic lists of ancestors but their history as well. Thus family members who live far apart can still maintain their family identities. It is sometimes said of a man who does not know his family song, "he has lost his father's house."

Luke and Matthew give the genealogy of Jesus because of its importance, but it is not surprising that each does it differently. Matthew stresses Jesus' royal lineage while Luke emphasizes Jesus' universal sonship by going all the way back to Adam, "son of God." In this way Luke is saying with Paul that we have a new Adam who incorporates a new humanity in himself (cf. Rom 5:15-18).

The Temptation of Jesus (4:1-13)

The temptation is not just part of the preparation for ministry; it is the first desperate attempt by Satan to change the course of Jesus' mission, which Satan knew was bound to affect his grip and reign over the world. In the Fourth Gospel Jesus calls Satan a murderer, liar, and ruler of this world (John 8:44; 12:31). Paul calls him the god of this world and the prince of the power of the air (2 Cor 4:4; Eph 2:2). Many have questioned the existence of Satan or a personal devil, regarding it as a symbolic expression for the depravity of humankind. It is clear that Jesus believed in the reality of Satan. Both the OT and NT confirm the reality of a personal Satan (cf. 1 Chr 21:1-8; Job 1:6-12; Zech 3:1-2; Matt 4:1-11; Acts 5:3; 1 Cor 5:5; 1 Pet 5:8; 1 John 3:8; Rev 12:9). Events in our world today clearly show that satanic power is very real. The evils that fill the world cannot be merely the result of human stupidity and perversity. If evil is real in the world, the force behind it must be real. If we repeat the words of Jesus, "For where two or three are gathered in my name, I am there among them," (Matt 18:20) we may also say that where two or three are gathered together in the name of evil, the Evil One is in their midst.

Certainly African and Asian cultures are permeated by belief in the reality and existence of spirits who exercise some measure of control over people and the physical world of nature. In Africa belief in witchcraft, sorcery, and spirits inhabiting groves, streams, forests, hills, the air, and rivers is very common. The Yoruba think one can obtain riches through witchcraft. It is called *owogbona*—the money that burns. The "juju priest" who prepares the concoctions to obtain this "magic money" always tells the clients for how many years they will enjoy this wealth (it always ranges from one to ten years) and that they will burn in torments afterward.

Jesus was exposed to such temptations himself. The first temptation sought to divert Jesus from the path of suffering into becoming a "bread king" (cf. John 6:15, 25-27), a Messiah who would improve the economic conditions of people by supplying their material needs. Such a Messiah would be more popular than one hanged on the cross, Satan suggests to Jesus. By using his power to turn stones into bread he would gain the people's allegiance and conquer the whole world. But Jesus as the leader of the new exodus cannot do this. He knows that becoming enslaved to one's appetites is just a new slavery. True human freedom is living "by every word that comes from the mouth of the LORD" (Deut 8:3). The world is full of greedy political leaders and rulers who bribe some citizens with material gifts in order to stay in office. The world everywhere is in dire need of spirit-filled men and women who will not bribe either to get into or remain in office, who will provide the people with honest leadership.

Thwarted in his first attempt, Satan changes the scene. He and Jesus stand on a tall mountain where they can see all the great empires of the world. "Take them! They are yours if you will but acknowledge me as your Lord!" This time Satan challenges Jesus to become a political Messiah. Satan tells Jesus that he has the whole world in his grip and he will hand it over to Jesus if he will compromise a little and acknowledge his lordship by paying him homage. But there can be no compromise in the war with evil and Satan. If Jesus had succumbed to this temptation he could not have established the Reign of God for all space and time. Jesus saw that people's needs were much deeper than political deliverance. The whole universe needs deliverance from the tempter, Satan. Through his suffering on the cross Jesus would put all his enemies (Satan and his host) under his feet (1 Cor 15:25; cf. Rom 16:20; Col 2:15). In reply Jesus tells Satan that God alone deserves worship (Deut 5:7-10).

Knowing what Jesus' mission will be, Satan presses in for one last attack. Flying Jesus through the air to the great Temple in Jerusalem he lands on the uppermost pinnacle and says, "If you jump off the angels will protect you, won't they?" Here he strikes at the tenderest place in Jesus' heart, where he trusts in God's care and protection from all suffering and danger. Think ahead to Jesus' prayer in the garden of Gethsemane where he asks God to remove the cup of suffering. This time Satan tempts Jesus to become a miracle-working Messiah, to win the allegiance of people by astonishing feats of magic. Human beings are by nature addicted to signs and wonders. Everywhere in the world those who perform wonders always have a large following. Jesus is urged to announce his messiahship by dramatically jumping four hundred feet from the top of the Temple to the ground and landing unhurt.

Jesus replies: "It is said, 'Do not put the Lord your God to the test'," quoting Deut 6:16. The KJV had: "thou shalt not tempt God!" This answer may be a bit hard to understand because it involves some knowledge of Israel's history. If we look up the passage in Deut 6:16 we will find, in the New Revised Standard Version, "Do not put the LORD your God to the test, as you tested him at Massah." What happened at Massah? To find the answer to this we must turn back even farther to the story in Num 20:2-13, where we learn that the Israelites were wandering in the desert and grumbling because they had no water to drink. "Moses, did you bring us out here in the desert to die? We want water!" Even Moses and Aaron became frightened, so they complained to God that the people of Israel had no water and were about to perish—as if God did not already know what was happening and was not in control of events. Now read the text very carefully and notice what the LORD God does. First he instructs Moses to take Aaron's rod (which he used to part the Red Sea) and, in full view of all the elders so they will see what is happening and realize God is doing what they demand, go to a certain huge rock (that obviously had no water in it) and strike the rock twice. Water poured out and all the people drank as did their cattle. Notice what happened. The people and Moses and Aaron had dared to command God to do something. As a result God said to Moses and Aaron: "Because you did not trust in me, to show my holiness before the eyes of the Israelites, therefore you shall not bring this assembly into the land that I have given them" (Num 20:12). This terrible punishment of the great leaders themselves became a stern warning to Israel forever after: never put God to the test again as you did at Massah.

Of course we should pray to God for help when we are in deep trouble and suffering, but this does not mean we will thereby escape it. Look at Jesus' own example. Let us pray his prayer as well: "not my will but yours be done." With David we must pray for deliverance from the sin of presumption (Ps 19:13). Here is an illustration of that sin: not many years ago a prophet appeared in Ibadan, Nigeria, who said he could prove that he had the power to stop the mouth of lions as Daniel did of old. On the appointed day he went into a lion's cage shouting "Yah! Yah!" (for YHWH). The lion ate him in minutes.

Jesus' Public Ministry in Galilee: 4:14–9:36

Jesus Begins His Public Ministry (4:14-30)

In Jesus' day Galilee was under the control of Roman foreigners. Galilee is about fifty miles long and twenty miles wide, taking its name from the Hebrew *galil,* "circle" or "district." Its full name was *galil goyim*—"Galilee of the Gentiles" (cf. Isa 9:1; Matt 4:15) because there were so many Gentile foreigners living there, especially in the port city of Tiberias and the imperial city of Sepphoris (recently excavated) in the center, a morning's walk north of Nazareth.

Nazareth was one of the larger, more prosperous villages in Galilee and Jesus' father would have belonged to the free laboring class living in Nazareth. Anyone standing on the hilltop above Nazareth has a panoramic view of the whole area. The history of Israel stretches out before one's eyes. To the southwest is the plain of Esdraelon where Deborah and Barak fought the mighty army of Sisera and won (Judges 4), where Gideon had won his victories, where King Saul crashed to disaster and King Josiah was unexpectedly killed in battle (2 Kings 23), where Jehu slaughtered Jezebel in Naboth's vineyard (2 Kings 9:30-37). To the westward, on the coast, just barely visible in the distance, one can see the snow-covered tops of Carmel where Elijah fought the memorable battle with the prophets of Baal (1 Kings 18). Beyond it is the blue Mediterranean and the isles of the Great Sea (as it was then called).

Nazareth lay near three highways: the major interior north-south route from Damascus to Jerusalem through Samaria, the coastal route known as the "Way of the Sea" from Egypt north to the Lebanon, and the mountainous eastern route on the other side of the Jordan valley. The great coast road had been used since time immemorial by armies, merchant caravans, and pilgrims. The eastern route carried caravans from Asia as well as Roman legionnaires patrolling the borders with Persia and the Bedouin tribes. In short it is wrong to think that Jesus was brought up in a hitherto unknown, obscure village. He was raised up in a town and an area uniquely important in the history of Israel with the traffic of the ancient world at its doorstep. As a young man he almost certainly walked the short distance to the new Roman city of Sepphoris that was then being constructed about eight kilometers north of Nazareth. There he would have rubbed shoulders with Greeks and Syrians, Romans and Jews, being exposed to all their dialects and customs.

Luke notes that Jesus preached in synagogues on his way back from the area of temptation as he began his Spirit-led activity (4:14-15). A synagogue would have been the natural place for Jesus to address the Jewish people in a community. The male head of every household was supposed to assemble with his peers in the local synagogue at dawn for prayers before going to work. The synagogue was the community center and meeting-place. No sacrifices were offered there; that was done only at the Temple in Jerusalem. But every Jewish town and village had at least one synagogue. Indeed, wherever there were ten men, called a *minyan,* there was a synagogue (building or no building), and the God of Israel was in their midst.

Jesus came back to his home town and a very uncertain reception. He had already preached elsewhere and his reputation was growing by leaps and bounds. He went to the synagogue on Friday evening and by Jewish custom it was packed with men and women. Jesus' family and relatives and friends were undoubtedly present. As a mark of honor he was asked to read the lesson. It was from Isaiah. After reading he sat down as would a rabbi to give a short interpretation. Every eye was fixed on him expecting something wonderful to demonstrate what had suddenly made him famous elsewhere.

The passage in Isaiah pictures the joy of the Israelites at their deliverance from the Babylonian exile in language drawn from Day of the

Lord imagery in Isa 61:1-2, but Isaiah's prophecies of national renewal had not come true. Centuries after the return from exile the people of Israel were still under foreign oppression: first from the Persians, then the Greeks, and now the Romans. By the time of Jesus they were still a conquered, oppressed, and broken people. Jesus astonished everyone when he read Isaiah's words and announced the dawn of the Day of the Lord: "*Today* this scripture has been fulfilled in your hearing." How could he say this?—because he knew himself to be the bearer and bringer of God's kingdom. "The Spirit of the Lord is upon me . . . to bring good news to the poor . . . to let the oppressed go free." Jesus meant for these words of Isaiah to specify his program of salvation.

Some of Jesus' hearers were deeply impressed but others said, "Who does he think he is—the Messiah?" This they could not accept, especially without any miraculous proof. How could Jesus the son of Joseph the carpenter, whose mother and brothers and sisters were right there in the synagogue, claim to be the Messiah? Within minutes they became enraged and tried to kill him. This confirms what is written in the gospel of John, "he came to what was his own, and his own people did not accept him. But to all who received him, who believed in his name, he gave power to become children of God" (John 1:11-12).

General Discussion of Jesus' Miracles

The NT frequently uses the idiom *sēmeia kai terata,* "signs and wonders," to refer to miracles. Another Greek word often used with *sēmeia kai terata* is *dynamis,* "power." This refers to the power of God, Jesus Christ, or the Holy Spirit. Sometimes the Greek word *ergon,* "work," is used. We therefore have four words: "sign," "wonder," "power," and "work" that are translated by the single English word "miracle." Today many people, especially in industrialized countries, regard the miracles of Jesus as little more than parables to teach moral lessons. They believe that the world is controlled by universal laws of science that are unalterable. Such laws are said to be like mathematical descriptions of chains of causality that are expressed in all the processes of nature. Since miracles are a violation of these laws, they cannot happen.

God never changes. God's favors are not limited to a particular age and time. What God did three or two thousand years ago, God still does today. Miracles are real and will be present in churches and Christian lives until Christ returns. God still speaks in visions and dreams to people today. Of course all visions and dreams that are contrary to the teaching of the Scriptures and the traditions of the Church must be considered satanic in origin. God has spoken the final word in Jesus Christ and true revelation can only confirm what is already revealed in Jesus Christ. "Jesus Christ is the same yesterday and today and forever" (Heb 13:8; cf. 1:1-4).

Most of the African Indigenous Churches, the majority of which arose as a result of the shortcomings of the mission churches and the depression that followed the First World War as well as the colonial experience in some localities, are charismatic and believe in miracles. Many of their miracles are genuine. In fact the number of Christians, which has grown more than three hundred percent in the last fifty years, is due largely to their evangelistic work. The greatest fallacy is to say "it is not true because I have not experienced it," or "for it to be true everybody must experience what I experience." If evil men perform wonders today before our naked eyes in Africa, some of which make certain Christians panic, are we saying that the God of the ends of the earth is so limited or at a certain time in the past decreed to set limits on intervening in human affairs so that God no longer performs miracles today? While millions of Christians in the so-called advanced nations no longer believe in miracles, millions of Christians in Africa and elsewhere in the world will rise up to say they still believe in miracles and that they experience them daily.

Similarly the belief in demons and spirits was prominent in Judaism at the time of Jesus as well as in Babylon, Persia, Egypt, and in the Hellenistic world. It is also clear that this belief is still common to Africa and the whole of the East. Rituals and sacrifices are still offered to these spirits daily. Africans and peoples of the Asian nations (such as China, Korea, and Japan) believe that some of these spirits can torment or possess men and women. The belief in various forms of witchcraft is also common all over the world. It is one of the things that is dreaded the most.

In whatever way we as pastors and ministers of the word of grace may understand these things individually, our common task must be to preach the gospel with emphasis on the power of Jesus that has destroyed Satan and his host. In Jesus victory over the forces of the spirit world is sure. Of course we do not want to encourage superstitious beliefs within ourselves or among our congregations, and we will from time to time find ourselves caught up in situations that are terrifying or wonderful, strange beyond our experience. These are not limited to the "Third World." We live in a mysterious universe and God has much to teach us about it. The more we discover about it the more our ignorance and limited knowledge is revealed. After centuries and millennia of ceaseless probings we are far from fully comprehending the mystery of our own nature as human beings. Let us therefore keep an open mind and learn. As for our study of Luke, while the approach will be critical and make use of all critical apparatus we shall assume the reality of Jesus' miracles as signs of the dawn of the Messianic Age.

NOTE: You may want to look at the general article on "The Bible and Prayer in Africa," especially the section on Prayer in African Tradition and Contemporary Christianity. It develops these ideas further and gives a broader treatment of the African perspective.

—*The Editors*

Healings in Capernaum Fulfill Jesus' Claim (4:31-44)

Immediately after the disaster in Nazareth Jesus went to the neighboring city of Capernaum where he was treated very differently. Jesus went "down" to Capernaum, for Capernaum lies literally "down" from the higher elevation of Nazareth and is situated on the northern shore of the Sea of Galilee. In ancient times a major road from east to west went past the town, giving it a thriving market. This was the Capernaum in which Jesus preached, again on a Friday evening in a synagogue, but unlike the inhabitants of Nazareth the people of Capernaum reacted with amazement at his authoritative manner. There was a demon inhabiting one of the listeners who also sensed Jesus' authority. "What have you to do with us, Jesus of Nazareth? Have you come to destroy us? I know who you are, the Holy One of God" (4:34).

In Luke's account it is obvious that spirits, being on the spiritual plane, always know immediately who Jesus is while ordinary humans do not. What kind of demon was this? Ancient peoples believed that spirits were everywhere, always seeking to possess and take control of people. The Egyptians believed that there were thirty-six parts of the human body and any of them could be possessed and controlled by evil spirits. There were spirits of insanity, deafness, dumbness, epilepsy, fever, etcetera. Also there were spirits of lying, deceit, and uncleanness. It is true that many people in the modern world no longer think in terms of evil spirits as the cause of human sickness, just as they do not believe that natural calamities are caused by the particular sinfulness of the people affected. Nevertheless it is also well known that medical science is far from explaining completely how the spiritual side of the human body functions, for good or ill, just as it is clear that we can bring down all sorts of environmental disasters upon ourselves by our greed and hate.

In the story before us, note that Jesus' method of dealing with the demon does not include magic incantations or spells common to certain kinds of sorcery. Jesus approaches it frontally and the demon knows it faces "the Holy One of God." Jesus orders it to be gone. Maliciously causing one last convulsion in the poor man, the demon flees. The crowd reacts in astonishment at Jesus' power and instead of becoming fearful or angry at him as did the people of Nazareth, passes the report of his miraculous power far and wide.

As soon as this is finished Jesus goes to Simon's house. Modern archaeology, led by the Franciscan Order in Palestine, has probably identified which house in first-century Capernaum was said in the early Christian centuries to be Simon Peter's. It lay directly across the street from a first-century synagogue. A magnificent fifth-century synagogue is built over this earlier synagogue. Today its remains are a favorite place for tourists and pilgrims, who then inspect the earlier remains of Peter's house. Originally this house had an outer wall composed of undressed stones stacked about two meters high within which were a number of small rooms for cooking, sleeping, storage, and work. The living quarters were probably covered by a tiled roof and the courtyard and walkways were left open. The whole structure was about ten meters on each side with enough room for an extended family of fourteen to sixteen people. In general it was not unlike walled compounds housing extended families still found in African villages back in the bush.

Jesus was obviously invited by Peter to come over for a meal following the synagogue service, only to find that his mother-in-law had suddenly come down with a high fever and was unable to play her central role as the hostess. It could have been a very embarrassing situation, but Jesus proceeded to banish the spirit of high fever from her and she got up immediately and served her guests. Luke goes on to say that many came that night to be healed, some no doubt having walked for miles. It is a wonderful scene Luke paints, of Jesus tenderly going from individual to individual. For Jesus, individuals are never lost in the crowd.

Some Greek manuscripts of Luke conclude this account by saying that Jesus preached in the synagogues of "Judea" (4:44). Other ancient Greek texts of Luke have "Galilee." Experts on text criticism suggest that if "Judea" is the original reading someone with a better knowledge of geography later corrected the text to read "Galilee," whereas if "Galilee" is the original reading someone in the interest of widening the area of Jesus' preaching later substituted "Judea." Such changes were intended to improve the text but they sometimes unintentionally corrupted the text. Luke probably wrote "Galilee."

Jesus Calls His First Disciples (5:1-11)

This scene takes place by the lake, which is no more than a stone's throw from the lakeside wall of the house identified as Peter's. Today there is a row of eucalyptus trees between the house and the shore that serves as a sort of windbreak, but the house could not be more conveniently situated for the family business, which was fishing. It is clear from the size of the house and its prominent location in Capernaum that the family that owned it was not poor. The fish they caught could have been bartered for grain, cloth, vegetables, fruit, and other staples. A few chickens probably lived in the family compound providing eggs.

The famous sea of Galilee is known by three names: the Sea of Galilee, the Sea of Tiberias (for the port city of that name on the southern shore), and the Lake of Gennesaret, which means "Lake of the Garden of Riches"—an allusion to the beautiful plain lying south of Capernaum. The lake is about thirteen miles long and eight miles wide, lying in a deep place in the earth's surface about six hundred eighty feet below sea level. There were nine major towns clustered around it, each with sizable populations.

Luke explains that Jesus borrowed Peter's boat as an impromptu pulpit because the crowd was so large. When he was finished he asked Peter to take him onto the lake to do some fishing. Peter was dismayed. He had been up all night and caught nothing—how could they get any fish by daylight? "Put out into the deep water," Jesus commanded. In spite of his doubts Peter did as he was told. The results were amazing, so much so that Peter knew this was the man he wanted to follow the rest of his life, wherever he led. In valiant Peter's case it led to death on a cross outside Rome and a name known all over the world as that of the foremost of the Lord's disciples.

Today Jesus is still calling men and women to become "fishers" of the lost and lonely. We must listen to the Lord's call, not worry about our abilities or our past experience. We may have caught very little heretofore, but with Christ as our guide and helper we will discover that nothing is impossible. The Lord as never before needs us to go with our hooks and nets into our villages, towns, and cities, into prisons and hospitals, welfare centers and businesses, into government positions and universities—all the areas of the world where darkness reigns.

Jesus Cures a Leper (5:12-16)

There are various types of leprosy. One type usually appears in the form of a serious skin disease, but there is another kind that begins as a small spot and eats away the flesh until it has destroyed the sufferer who at last will be left with only the stumps of hands and legs, nose and jaw. Any part of the body where the leprosy develops becomes dead and gangrenous. In Jesus' time the Jewish people looked to Leviticus 13 and 14 for guidance on all aspects of dealing with leprosy. These regulations had been considerably amplified by the Pharisees in their laws dealing with personal cleanliness, many of which can be found codified in the Mishnah. Lepers were barred from society (cf. the famous lepers described in Num 12:9-12 and 2 Kings 5:1-14). They had to go live in the bush, wearing a covering over their mouth. They were supposed to give warnings of their approach by shouting: "(I am) unclean! Unclean! Stay away!" In some African societies lepers are exiled as soon as the disease is detected. Some will even take their own lives in order to save themselves and their families the shame and agony this will bring, although the disease is innocently acquired like most other contagious diseases. Lepers in such communities cannot be buried at home or in the community cemetery. In families where leprosy has struck a parent nobody in the community will want to marry their sons or daughters for this would amount to marrying descendants of a leper. The stigma usually remains for generations. Things are of course gradually changing with the introduction of leprosariums by many missions, but even today most of these people are too ashamed to return to their families and instead go and settle elsewhere.

This leper must have heard about Jesus and decided to break the law in the hope of being cured. In faith he cast himself before the Lord, begging to be healed. Jesus did not fly into a rage and order the people to pick up stones and drive the disfigured one from their midst. Instead he reached out his hand and touched the untouchable. "Be made clean," he said. Instantly the man was cured. By this act Jesus shows that no one is cut off from God's healing mercy. Countless brave Christian nuns, priests, and ministers, Christian doctors and nurses have ventured into leper colonies all over the world, in Africa, in India, in China and even—many years ago—in Europe, bringing healing and human contact. Leprosy, this loathsome, destructive, isolating, and pervasive disease that defiles both religiously and physically, presents us with a vivid parable of the working of sin in a person's life, but the story is equally powerful in telling of Jesus' mighty power to save and to heal, to forgive and to cleanse the very root of sin out of our lives.

Jesus Heals a Man with Paralysis (5:17-26)

The scene described in this account is full of drama. Jesus is traveling from village to village. On this day it is mid-morning and all kinds of people are packed into someone's house, eager to hear what he will say. In particular some religious experts who have heard of Jesus' doings are present. They are very suspicious; they have heard of his kind before, but they are blind to the power of God and so they do not recognize it in Jesus. Suddenly there is a commotion above them on the roof. Some men have got a stretcher up there with a sick person and they are taking the roof tiles off so as to let the bed down directly in front of Jesus. We can imagine the shouting and protests that burst out from the listeners at this rude interruption. Jesus, however, is delighted. "Friend, your sins are forgiven you," he says to the sick man. The religious experts are shocked to hear what they think is blasphemy. "What are you saying?" they shout at Jesus. "That is blasphemy!" These Pharisees are convinced that only the God of Israel could forgive a person's sins after appropriate sacrifices and penitential acts. They may even have thought that Jesus was meddling in a punishment God had justly laid on this man.

Sensing that they would not have gotten angry if he had simply healed the man, Jesus asks them: "Which is easier, to say, 'Your sins are forgiven you,' or to say, 'Stand up and walk'?" Of course neither is "easier"; both require divine power, but these experts were so blind they could not see that Jesus' power to heal came from the same God as his power to forgive. The crowd went home amazed, which means they really did not understand what had just happened.

The Call of Levi, the Tax Collector (5:27-32)

The most hated and feared people in Palestine were the tax collectors. The taxation system under Roman rule lent itself to abuse. Roman authorities normally sold the responsibility for collection of taxes and tolls to the highest bidder. That way they got local inhabitants to do their dirty work for them. Native citizens can always be found willing to sell their kinspeople for a price. The Romans sold the right to collect taxes in a district to the highest bidder for five years. As long as the tax collector could turn over the amount bid at the end of the year he could keep whatever else he could extract from the people.

There were several types of taxes: the poll or capitation tax, the ground tax consisting of one tenth of the grain harvest and one fifth of the wine and oil, and the tax on income. In addition there were all kinds of tolls imposed on people for using the main roads and markets. Farmers paid duties on their carts and the animals that pulled them. There were purchase taxes on luxury items as well as import and export duties. If someone hesitated to pay these taxes (and who has not resented paying taxes?) the tax collector could call on the local Roman soldiers and enforce payment. Tax collectors could stop people on the road and order them to unpack their bundles for assessment. There was little defense against excessive charges. If one could not pay the tax collector could offer to lend money at a high rate of interest and thereby further complicate a person's problems.

Most people mistrusted Jewish tax collectors and regarded them as traitors and enemies of the God of Israel. They often barred them from giving testimony in Jewish courts. Thus we can understand why in the gospels tax collectors are classified with habitual sinners (such as prostitutes), murderers, and robbers. It must have been a shock when Jesus called one of these men, Levi, to be his disciple! Why did he do it? Did Jesus see something in Levi's character? He must have known that Levi wanted to be more than a money-grubber. When the Master said to him, "Follow me," Levi was overcome with joy. He could not believe that such a beautiful and righteous person as Jesus would call him. His response was instantaneous and complete (5:27-28). Levi realized that if Jesus could welcome him he would not turn his back on his outcast friends, so he invited Jesus to his home for a feast in celebration of his new-found calling. At the feast Levi introduced his friends and fellow tax collectors to the Lord. This was a transforming event that shook the established world of Jewish piety to its foundation.

Some of the religious leaders who had been seeking every opportunity to amass evidence against Jesus were there at the feast, probably uninvited. In Oriental countries and in most parts of Africa uninvited guests often stand around the edges either as mere spectators or as poor people who might benefit from the leftovers (guests always leave some food uneaten for this purpose). Also in the East and in Africa table fellowship is a sign of full acceptance. Jesus' sharing at table with Levi and his fellow tax collectors meant that Jesus, far from shunning these outcasts, wanted to express before everyone that he considered them worthy of his companionship. The Pharisees were shocked that Jesus, who was thought to be a prophet, had welcomed table fellowship with such sinners. They grumbled to Jesus' disciples: "Why do you eat and drink with tax collectors and sinners?" (5:30). Overhearing what they said, Jesus responded, "Those who are well have no need of a physician, but those who are sick. I have come to call not the righteous but sinners to repentance" (5:31-32). From this point forward the die was cast. The religious authorities in Galilee were beside themselves in their consternation over what one of their own, a truly righteous man, was doing. Jesus appeared to be undermining the very basis of their religious authority on which they believed rested the salvation of the people of God. If they did not stop him the people would perish in their sins.

Why Do Your Disciples Not Fast? (5:33-39)

The Pharisees, not pleased with Jesus' answer, respond, "John's disciples, like the disciples of the Pharisees, frequently fast and pray, but your disciples eat and drink" (5:33). The Pharisees have a point. Fasting and prayer were the well-known marks of the pious man or woman. They want to know, if Jesus is such a great prophet, why his disciples do not act the part and fast and pray as John the Baptist's disciples do.

Jesus' answer must have gone right over their heads. He tells them a parable about how his disciples are like guests at a wedding party, about how joyful Peter and the others feel just being near him. We know this to be true from our own experience. A person who has just found Christ is full of "joy in the Lord." This is why it is so important for more mature Christians to work hard on bringing new converts into the Church where they may share their joy of discovery with them. It helps to remind us of our own earliest days when the love of God was an unbelievable gift setting our hearts on fire.

As Jesus went on to say to the Pharisees, "Can't you see why my disciples are rejoicing? They are with the bridegroom!" (cf. 5:34). This was no time for fasting or for half-measures. When the Messianic Age comes it does so in a radical way, giving one a new spirit and a new hope. Everything must be new so that God's power and grace can make a new path out of the old swamp of sin and despair. This is a time for deep soul-searching giving rise to a new lifestyle, given birth out of sheer joy in the Lord's blessing. The Psalmist said, "O sing to the Lord a new song, for he has done marvelous things. His right hand and his holy arm have gotten him victory" (Ps 98:1). Isaiah also was filled with this joy when he said, "See, the former things have come to pass, and new things I now declare; before they spring forth, I tell you of them" (Isa 42:9) and in a particularly moving passage he cries, "I am about to create new heavens and a new earth [says the LORD]; the former things shall not be remembered or come to mind" (Isa 65:17).

The Son of Man is Lord of the Sabbath (6:1-11)

By now Jesus had aroused the anger and suspicion of the Pharisees. If we look backward and forward in this context we can see that we are in the midst of a series of four stories in which the Pharisees, the religious experts in Galilee, become more and more critical of everything Jesus does. Jesus well knows he is being closely watched by them. He even seems to be deliberately challenging religious traditions that were obstructions to the freedom and love God originally meant God's children to have. In this account the Pharisees accuse Jesus' disciples of profaning the Sabbath.

The Sabbath—Hebrew *shabbat*—is the seventh day, the day of rest. According to Jewish tradition, it is to be kept holy, that is, unlike any other day since God had *rested* after creating the world (cf. Gen 2:2-3; Exod 20:10-11). In order to make sure no one did any work during the day of rest (Friday evening until Saturday evening), the rabbis later added numerous additional regulations so that scrupulous people could be sure they obeyed the Torah rule properly. In the process they focused on doing the right thing and making sure others did the right thing; as often happens in such cases, some people lost sight of the true meaning of the Sabbath. In this case the Pharisees accused Jesus' disciples of several kinds of wrongdoing. Eating the grain (wheat or barley) out of someone else's field was not a crime. That was permissible. This is similar to an old custom in many parts of Africa. Any hungry traveler can pluck a ripe fruit or grain but it must be eaten there on the farm and the husks left behind. One cannot take anything away: that would be robbery.

It was the other actions to which the Pharisees objected. Plucking meant the disciples had "reaped" the grain, which was forbidden on the Sabbath, and rubbing the kernels to remove the husks was "winnowing," another form of work that was also forbidden. Jesus defended his disciples by appealing to an action of the king, in this case David. The king's actions were always important to the people as a guide and example. In this case Jesus asked the Pharisees if what his disciples had done was wrong, what about the astonishing act of King David described in 1 Sam 21:1-6? The Pharisees could not condemn David, so they had to remain speechless. But Jesus went on to speak in coded language: "The Son of Man is lord of the sabbath" (6:5). This the Pharisees could not have understood, but Luke's hearers certainly did: Jesus was referring to himself as one certainly greater than David. Jesus as the "Son of Man" was ushering in the Messianic Age, the new dawn of redemption—even on the Sabbath! (cf. John 5:15-17).

Jesus Heals the Man with a Crippled Hand (6:6-11)

"On another sabbath . . ." Jesus again upsets the Pharisees. In the previous stories they became offended at things that happened elsewhere. In this account Jesus is in the middle of a Sabbath sermon when he suddenly stops. The Pharisees grow tense, wondering what he is up to. Aware of their hostility, he tells a man in the audience, "Come and stand here." Then, looking directly at his critics, he asks them, "The Sabbath regulations command us to do no work on that day. But what if someone has an accident? Do we just leave them in agony until the Sabbath is over?" (cf. 6:9). The Pharisees do not answer. "Stretch out your hand," Jesus says to the man, and the lame hand is instantly made whole. Furious at being unable to answer Jesus, the Pharisees begin to plot ways of getting rid of him. His bold statements and actions are calling into question their whole way of life. This can happen when a man or woman has the spirit of God. They begin to see too clearly. They discover guilty secrets and hidden evil. The lives of such men and women of God can come into serious danger. If as pastors we pray for the guidance of the Holy Spirit we must be prepared to take the consequences.

Jesus Chooses Twelve Apostles (6:12-16)

Luke introduces by name the small circle of men personally chosen by Jesus to be his "inner cabinet," his "school of disciples." This group went everywhere he went, ate when he did, slept where he slept, and learned everything they could about Jesus by attempting to do exactly what he did. The bond between master and apprentice was very close in the ancient world as it still is in many parts of Africa and elsewhere. Among the Yoruba in southern Nigeria when a young man was selected to be instructed in the great Yoruba oral tradition of wisdom, laws, customs, medical remedies, myths, and stories (known as the *Ifa Corpus*) it took years of memorization and observation with the young student always living in close proximity to his master.

It was the disciples' duty not to overlook anything Jesus said or did. Not that they were all outstanding men: in fact it is surprising how heterogeneous this group was, being composed of fishermen, a tax collector, a freedom fighter (Simon the Zealot), and a traitor. Nor did they learn what Jesus taught quickly and easily: on the contrary they seem to have made every mistake possible. Luke occasionally describes Jesus' closest associates in less than flattering terms, and yet, by the end of the gospel and in the book of Acts we shall see the power of the Holy Spirit making astonishing changes in the lives of these men, particularly Simon Peter. That should give every parish priest and minister hope. No matter how obstinate and blind and confused we feel we must always remember that it is the Holy Spirit guiding us. Nor are we alone, for the Lord Jesus is with us; he is in control and working for his purposes.

Luke concludes the list on an ominous note: "and Judas Iscariot, who became a traitor" (6:16). The Greek word here is *prodotēs*. It is a very powerful, negative word meaning "someone who betrays his parents, a blasphemer or apostate." Why did Jesus choose someone like this? In the garden of Gethsemane when Judas came up and kissed him why did he not say "Judas! Stop what you are doing!" To understand you must read Luke's account very closely for yourself. We will do our best in this commentary to point out key places that will throw light on the mystery of Jesus and Judas.

Jesus' First Sermon to His New Disciples (6:17-49)

Before Jesus chose his twelve apostles Luke describes him going up onto a nearby mountain where he could be alone as he spent an entire night in prayer and supplication to God. When the morning light came Jesus was full of the Holy Spirit and in quick succession chose twelve close associates whom he called *apostoloi* (or in modern terms "missionaries"), and then proceeded to describe in simple, eloquent terms the way of life expected of these new disciples.

Many scholars have noticed that the teachings in Luke 6:17-49 bear a close resemblance to Matthew's Sermon on the Mount (Matthew 5–7). Moreover, many teachings of Jesus in Matthew 5–7 that are not in this sermon of Jesus are found elsewhere in Luke. Luke carefully selected just those teachings that would be appropriate in Jesus' first sermon to his new disciples, explaining in the simplest terms what is the heart of Christian discipleship for those brand new to it. Luke's purpose behind this careful selection was to give his readers a priceless example of what the Lord Jesus himself would say to new converts.

Traditionally known as "the sermon on the plain" to distinguish it from Matthew's "sermon on the mount," Jesus' discourse has four parts: an opening recalling the announcement given back in Nazareth of salvation to the poor, oppressed, and grief-stricken peoples of the world (Luke 4:16-30), the body of the sermon concerning first non-retaliation and then non-condemnation, and the conclusion. We will consider these in order.

The Beatitudes, 6:20-26

As pastoral workers teaching new converts and catechumens, what do we single out when we want to tell them about the Reign of God? In the gospel according to Luke the choice is clear from the beginning: it is the beautiful passage from Isa 61:1-2:

> The Lord has anointed me . . . to bring good
> news to the oppressed,
> to bind up the brokenhearted,
> to proclaim liberty to the captives, . . .
> to proclaim the year of the LORD's favor.

The first thing Jesus says to his new disciples is that he has come to remind them of God's preferential option for the poor, disinherited, and excluded people of the world. In contrast to Matthew's wording, "Blessed are the poor in spirit" (Matt 5:3), in Luke Jesus directly calls blessed "you poor," and "you who hunger now," and "you who weep now" (Luke 6:20-21). The dramatic directness and almost physical element in his words has been noticed by theologians and Christian reformers from the times of Benedict and Francis down to Mahatma Gandhi and Martin Luther King, Jr. Luke's version applies directly to my continent of Africa where more than ninety percent live in abject poverty and malnutrition, where large numbers are almost slaves of the giant businesses run by the wealthy few, where millions are hungry and homeless. But even in Europe and North America thousands of homeless people sleep under bridges, on streets, and in bus and train stations. Meanwhile the government authorities as well as the Church appear or pretend not to be aware of all this suffering. As a result gangs spring up and crime and drug addiction run rampant because life has become meaningless and filled with pain.

In Luke's version of the beatitudes Jesus goes beyond blessings to a series of parallel woes. "Woe to you who are rich, you who have full stomachs, who laugh now" (cf. 6:24-25). Christ is not pronouncing curses on riches, possessions, laughter, and social acceptance in themselves. As we can see from other passages in Luke, wealth symbolizes those who are alienated from God. These are people who have gotten their wealth by unrighteous methods, squeezing the poor and pocketing everything for themselves (cf. below at 16:13). This kind of person will certainly experience the full weight of God's wrath (cf. Jesus' story of the rich man and the poor beggar at 16:19-31), but it must be understood that poverty, hunger, and sorrow are of no benefit in themselves unless they are accompanied by repentance, trust in God, and patience. If shame and evildoing are endured for the sake of the Lord Jesus Christ will they issue in eternal blessedness and reward? Riches are God's blessing as long as they do not lead to greed and selfishness. They are the means to help the poor. It is how we use God's blessings that will determine our standing before God.

Non-retaliation, 6:27-36

Since the beginning of the sermon echoes Isa 61:1-2 the next subject might be far from obvious. Why would Jesus—having announced God's special concern for the poor and oppressed—choose non-retaliation to place at the forefront of the Christian lifestyle? There is a very good reason that can be detected if we look at the course taken by Luke's gospel up to this point. In ch. 4 Jesus began his public ministry in Nazareth, where he had no sooner finished than his townspeople sought to kill him. Then he went to Capernaum where, despite a series of miraculous healings that amazed the people, the religious leaders got angrier and angrier. Everyone including the disciples must have wondered why Jesus did not react to their hostile attitude toward him. If he was the Son of God why did he not punish them? Here, Jesus gives his answer. "Be merciful, just as your Father is merciful" (6:36). As the Son of God Jesus revealed to humankind a vision of God long known in Israel but in no other religious tradition among the nations of the world: a God-image involving the centrality of forgiveness.

A classic passage in the Hebrew prophets says "I will not execute my fierce anger; I will not again destroy Ephraim; for I am God and no mortal, the Holy One in your midst, and I will not come in wrath" (Hos 11:9). Israel's God desired repentance and renewal of life, not punishment and death. Psalm 103 is filled with the message of the tender mercy of the God of Israel toward those who love God but who may not always abide by God's laws. "He does not deal with us according to our sins, nor repay us according to our iniquities" (Ps 103:10; cf. Mic 7:19). Just as God is merciful, so those of us who call ourselves followers of Christ ought to act mercifully toward those around us. This is the heart of the Christian life: giving of ourselves to the betterment of others.

The world does not live this way, nor does Satan's kingdom exhibit mercy. But those who belong to the Reign of God strive to live by Christ's teaching, "I give you a new commandment, that you love one another. Just as I have loved you, you also should love one another" (John 13:34). It must be remembered that God's forgiveness is accepted only by those who feel true remorse for their sins, make amends for their wickedness, and cease sinning (cf. the example of Zacchaeus in Luke 19:1-10). It is not accepted by those who do nothing to change their ways. As Paul warned: "Should we continue to sin in order that grace may abound? By no means!" (Rom 6:1-2). All who have not fully accepted God's forgiveness are in danger of God's wrath, for God hates evil. So also those who love God hate what is evil (Rom 12:9; cf. Amos 5:15; Ps 97:10: "The LORD loves those who hate evil"). Christ does not call us to love evil or forgive the evil person or business or nation that does evil repeatedly. The God of Jesus Christ is the same God of the Law and the Prophets, the creator of the world who chose Israel to be a witness among the nations, a beacon light showing them what genuine human community is like (Exod 19:5-6; cf. 1 Pet 2:9). There can be no genuine community without the justice and forgiveness necessary to reestablish community, but forgiveness must never function as an excuse to hide the absence of justice.

Thus the first new commandment the Lord Jesus gave new disciples is to let go of the world's blaming and bitterness and hatred. The new disciple is a new creation: "So if anyone is in Christ, there is a new creation: everything old has passed away; see, everything has become new!" (2 Cor 5:17). Neither nationality, nor socio-economic distinctions, nor even gender distinction is of primary importance any longer, "for all of you are one in Christ Jesus" (Gal 3:28).

Non-condemnation, 6:37-42

First Jesus stressed the centrality of the forgiveness of God that leads us to be forgiving toward all. Jesus' next teaching follows logically: if the love of God dwells in us we are inclined to be kinder in our judgments toward our fellow human beings. New disciples need to hear this since they are liable to be very judgmental and "holier-than-thou." Jesus wisely warned his new followers to remember that God alone is the ultimate judge.

This passage has sometimes been misinterpreted to say that Christians should not judge at all. That is incorrect. The Greek term here is *katadikazō,* a very strong word that means to condemn or denounce someone. It is like the parent who flies into a rage when he finds a child playing in the mud in its new shoes. What Jesus said meant: "do not intemperately condemn each other! Try to be more lenient in your judgments! After all, you yourself are human too!" Observe carefully how Jesus expressed himself at this point in his talk. These examples are curiously exaggerated; consequently we may be sure that Jesus' words were intended to be comical examples, themselves gentle reminders rather than harsh demands.

At the same time Christ calls pastors, priests, and lay people to exercise judgment concerning the world they live in. "See, I am sending you out like sheep into the midst of wolves; so be wise as serpents and innocent as doves" (Matt 10:16). Christians must constantly be on guard regarding what is happening in the cities where they live, in the nation, and in the world. Christians do not focus merely on "religious" matters. The Church must also exercise judgment in cases of misconduct within the Church (cf. 1 Cor 6:1-11; Matt 18:15-20). Actions count, not just words (Luke 6:43-49). Finally, Jesus warns his new disciples that they must show by their actions that they really are his followers in deed, not just in word. The picture-story told by way of illustration would have been familiar to most of Luke's readers. In the summer the earth dries and the soil becomes hard. A careless builder might erect a stone and wattle house without digging a foundation down to rock. When the rains come in the winter the earth suddenly produces creeks and streams that break against the house, which without a foundation falls to the ground. "Why do you call me 'Lord, Lord,' and do not do what I tell you to?" asks Jesus. God will not be mocked by such hypocrisy. This is why, at the end of Jesus' story, the ruin is "great."

Such was the sermon Jesus spoke to his new disciples and the new circle of the twelve apostles. He touched on the most important beginning elements of our faith. In later speeches and sermons in Luke Jesus will go into deeper matters.

Jesus Heals the Centurion's Servant (7:1-10)

The place where local tradition says Jesus gave this sermon is only a kilometer or so from the village of Capernaum. Thus Luke says,

"After Jesus had finished all his sayings . . . he entered Capernaum" since it was near by. There was a Roman officer living in Capernaum. His title was centurion, which is a Latin military term for the commanding officer in charge of a "century," or one hundred foot soldiers. In the Roman army there would be sixty centurions in a legion of six thousand men. At the time Jesus lived in Galilee there were two Roman legions stationed in Palestine with the military headquarters located in Damascus to the north. This centurion's soldiers would have been bivouacked in an army camp nearby.

The strength and backbone of the Roman legions depended on the quality of their centurions. They were not expected to be daring or bold, but tough and dependable under the fiercest attack. They were well paid and often served in a number of different legions. Centurions were frequently rotated and promoted, even from one legion to another, gaining experience and leadership training in the process. Moving around prevented them from becoming too attached to a particular group of men. Many centurions possessed considerable personal wealth and could maintain sizable households with servants and a personal bodyguard wherever they were stationed. In the case of this centurion Luke relates that he provided the funds to build Capernaum's synagogue, a most unusual indication of his wealth and close ties to the whole community. (Luke often "matched" scenes or themes in the gospel and Acts to show parallels between the work of Jesus and its continuation in the Church. Compare the treatment of the centurion here with the presentation of the centurion Cornelius in Acts 10.)

This centurion wants Jesus to heal an ailing servant of his but he goes about it circumspectly. Being a foreigner and officer in the occupying army he does not come directly to Jesus. Instead he sends local city officials to Jesus with his plea. Then after learning that Jesus has agreed to come he hurriedly sends "friends" (either of Jesus or of himself) to meet Jesus in the street with the statement that he is not "worthy" to have Jesus come under his roof, asking instead that he heal the servant from where he is. There were several reasons he might feel embarrassed to have Jesus enter his compound. For one thing, it is undoubtedly decorated with Roman military images; second, Jesus could accidentally come in contact with something that would make him unclean under Jewish purity laws. Jesus is deeply impressed by this foreigner's faith and considerateness. The story of this centurion's request is the first mention in the gospel of Luke of a foreign person responding to Jesus in faith. It reminds us of another Roman centurion who, according to Matthew, stood at the cross and said "this man was God's Son!" (Matt 27:54).

The story is a beautiful illustration of the way in which God sometimes leads foreigners to set us a good example. In Nigeria we have countless schools, hospitals, and clinics founded by Christian brothers and sisters from other countries. They are funded by money sent from Europe and North America. In many ways these distant Christians are helping to heal our people in the name of Jesus Christ without setting foot in a single village. By the same token we share our understanding of the gospel with Christians in other countries, for God has given Nigerian Christians a strong faith, greatly needed for these difficult times in our nation.

Jesus Heals the Widow's Son (7:11-17)

Luke begins this account by saying that Jesus set out on a mission tour to preach and heal among Jewish communities in the wider area around Galilee. Nain was a sizable village about a day's walk to the south, lying on the approach toward Mount Tabor a dozen kilometers or so southeast of Nazareth, near the border with Samaria and Judea. So great had Jesus' reputation grown that a large crowd abandoned their everyday activities and went with him, including the Twelve. The people were undoubtedly fascinated by Jesus and wondered what he would do next.

In Jesus' time Nain was a prosperous village surrounded by thriving olive and fig orchards, thanks to an abundant spring. The modern village of Nain only has a few houses and a hundred or so inhabitants, but in Jesus' day it was much larger with a good-sized marketplace and a population of several hundred. During the Middle Ages the gravestones of the young man and his mother, the main figures in this story, were still pointed out to pilgrims in the cemetery above the village.

It is the story of a very poignant event. Death has just taken away with a wicked hand a young lad, the only son of a widow. The condition of widows in those days was pitiable. They had few rights and could not inherit the property of their deceased husbands. They were dependent on their sons or the relatives of their husbands for everything, and sometimes nothing would be forthcoming. Her son's cruel death has left this widow hopeless and defenseless, and she is weeping bitter tears. She has probably spent all the money she had left to hire professional mourners to shriek and wail properly, so that everyone would know that she had given her son a proper funeral. On the day of burial a great crowd of mourners is just going out through the village gate when they run into Jesus and the large crowd following him on the way in. There must have been great confusion, greetings, questions, and so forth. Meanwhile the mourners would have kept up their earsplitting wails. When Jesus saw the funeral bier, says Luke, he felt pity and compassion. His spontaneous impulse to help the poor mother sprang from his great tenderness and sympathy. "Do not weep," he tells her. He stops the procession and touches the bier. Everybody stops talking and shouting as expectant silence falls over the whole scene. "Young man, I say to you, rise!" Jesus orders. The dead man sits up and begins to speak. Then, Luke says, "Jesus gave him to his mother."

These are such tender words. Any mother whose young daughter or son has died would give anything to have the Lord Jesus bring their precious one back to them. There is no grief more piercing than that of a parent who has lost a young child. Those who have followed Jesus from Nazareth, as well as the crowd that came out from Nain, are amazed and shout, "A great prophet has risen among us! God has looked favorably on his people!"

Attempts have been made to spiritualize this story or explain it away. This is a mistake. The early Church did not create these stories in order to glorify Jesus. They already believed he was the Christ, the Lord of Glory, a belief based on their understanding of Jesus and what they had personally witnessed. Gospel accounts such as this one do not surprise Christians in Africa where we have ourselves witnessed Christian prophets who heal the sick and, in the name of the Lord Jesus Christ, even raise up those who have been taken away while still young by an accident or severe illness. We know that Jesus dries the tears of mourners, binds up the brokenhearted, and inspires the hopeless with eternal hope. He is the Lord of life and will one day wipe away all our tears.

John Sends a Question to Jesus (7:18-35)

This account has been a source of worry for some Christians because the question of John suggests a doubt in his mind as to whether Jesus is the Messiah. The question arises because Luke is not being read as a whole but in small bits. Notice how the story begins. "The disciples of John reported all these things to him" (7:18). All what things? obviously the things that had just happened at Nain, including the reaction of the crowd at the end: "a great prophet has risen among us." The crowd's response was prompted by the fact that Jesus did the same miracles the great prophets of old, including Elijah, had done (cf. 1 Kings 17:17-24), and they responded appropriately. Eventually they would learn that Jesus was far more than a prophet, but one has to start somewhere. Many of us come into the Christian faith thinking one thing about Jesus and then, after we learn more and deepen our faith, come to a better understanding.

Second, to understand this story correctly one must read forward in Luke's narrative and observe that this question of John is just the first in a series of stories in which the same question comes up again and again: who is this Jesus? In the next story the guests of a Pharisee ask it (7:49), then his disciples ask it (8:25), then Herod asks it (9:9), then Jesus asks his disciples who the crowds say he is (9:18), and so on. The question is repeated until the momentous answer comes directly from God in the transfiguration scene: "This is my Son, my Chosen" (9:35).

The series, then, starts here. Note how Luke describes John calling two of his disciples and asking them the question, and then a few lines later shows them repeating the question to Jesus (7:19-20). In this way the reader or hearer will hear this question twice in rapid succession, like a bell tolling. The question becomes lodged in the reader's mind: who is Jesus?

Once the question is addressed to Jesus observe the curiously roundabout way he answers it. He performs a number of healing miracles before the eyes of the messengers of John that unmistakably recall the prophecy of Isaiah

Jesus quoted in his inaugural sermon in Nazareth (Luke 4:18) and then tells them to go tell John what they have seen. Why did he do that? Why did he not simply answer John's question?

As we noted above, the prophecy in the inaugural sermon implied that the Day of the Lord and the Messiah had arrived in the person of Jesus. John certainly got the point, but it is also clear that Jesus did not think it appropriate to answer such a weighty question himself. The full disclosure of who he was had to come directly from God. As we shall see, that is precisely what happens later. So it is with us. There may be times in our ministry when we lose all track and trail of the Lord Jesus. The only remedy is to abide in prayer with trusted believers until God reveals who the Son is to us once again.

Having sent the answer to John, Jesus then launches into an unparalleled eulogy declaring John the greatest of all those born of women (7:28). According to Jesus, John's greatness did not lie in moral cowardice that bends before every breeze but on the contrary John was like a solid rock that no storm of life could move. Second, John's greatness did not lie in self-gratification and self-indulgence. Instead, in fulfilling the divine task John endured all hardships while consecrating himself totally to God. His greatness also lies in his mission as the forerunner of the Messiah, whose greatest assignment was that of turning the thoughts and hearts of God's people to Jesus, the Messiah.

At the end, the story-picture Jesus gives of children playing is actually very lifelike. Remember when we were young, lying around on a hot Saturday, uninterested in doing anything and waiting for someone else to come up with a good idea? But when someone said, "Let's play catch the thief!" the rest of us said, "Oh no, it's too hot!" Then someone else said, "Then let's play counting stones!" Everyone said, "How boring!" As a result nobody did anything. The religious leaders are like such lazy, spoiled children, says Jesus, in the way they first rejected John and then reject Jesus, satisfied with nothing.

Jesus Forgives a Sinful Woman (7:36-50)

Certain features of Luke's next story require some background explanation. First of all, as is true everywhere around the world, to invite an eminent person into one's home for a meal is an indication that one wishes to honor this person. Naturally every effort would be made in such a case to abide by the proper rules of etiquette. And yet the host, Simon the Pharisee, rudely ignores all the common courtesies normally extended to a respected guest. He should have met Jesus at the door, placed his hands on Jesus' shoulders, and kissed him. He should have ordered a household servant to rinse off Jesus' feet with cold water after he entered and then give him a small amount of fresh water to wash his face and hands before eating. This should have been followed by the offer of a few drops of sweet-smelling ointment for Jesus' hair to give him a pleasant scent.

As for the meal itself, in Palestine people never sat on chairs or used tables for eating when there were guests present. They reclined on beautiful rugs with cushions to prop them up. When they ate a meal they reclined on their left side, eating with the fingers of their right hand. The food was placed in the center of the group on a large platter or tray and all those present ate from it until they were full. The leftovers were taken out and given to the servants. Servants never ate until the master's family and guests had eaten.

As for the woman, who is she? She is called a "woman of the city" and the meaning is obvious. She is a prostitute. She must have met Jesus before and been deeply impressed by his preaching. Learning that he is still in the town, she comes to the house where he is. How she got past the entrance attendants we will never know. They should have kept a woman like her out in the street, but they did not. Perhaps a woman among the door attendants knew the poor woman and sympathized with her. In any case she comes straight into the room where all the guests were and, not saying a word, begins a scandalous series of actions at Jesus' feet. She takes out a small jar made of alabaster (a beautiful, soft white stone often carved into perfume vials, candlesticks, and the like), weeps tears onto Jesus' feet to clean them, wipes them dry with her hair—not with a kerchief or part of her robe—kisses his feet, and then rubs the soothing oil on them from the alabaster flask.

Naturally the host and guests are shocked, especially Simon the Pharisee. Observe what he says: "If this man *were* a prophet . . ." (7:39). Who said that Jesus was a prophet? the crowds who witnessed Jesus raise up the widow's young son (Luke 7:16). So Simon the Pharisee also heard this report and decided to examine Jesus more closely for himself—and in a not very friendly way so far, even though he did invite him for dinner.

Of course the Lord well knows what evil thoughts are going through Simon's mind and challenges him. "Teacher," says Simon, "speak." Jesus tells him a little story, in the course of which he mentions a coin called a denarius. It was about equivalent to a day's wage for a field worker (cf. Matt 20:2). Simon listens to Jesus' story and with no difficulty give the right answers, but in doing so he speaks judgment on himself, which is Jesus' intent. Jesus takes Simon's answer, turns to the woman, and compares how she has treated him with the way Simon treated Jesus from the moment he set foot in his house. Jesus explains why their behavior toward him is so different: "the one to whom little is forgiven, loves little." It is not that Simon should become a great sinner so that he could be greatly forgiven; rather he should have asked God's forgiveness for hard-heartedly refusing to see who was in front of him while the poor sinful woman did recognize and love Jesus with all her heart.

Now it is the turn of the rest of the guests to become upset. When Jesus turns to the woman and says "Your sins are forgiven" they all draw back and exclaim: "Who is this who even forgives sins?" Notice that this is the second story in a row in which the question has come up: "Who is this . . .". The guests have no idea who it is with whom they are dining. Neither they nor Simon know that this humble, poor Galilean prophet is much more than a prophet. He is the Messiah of God, the expected Redeemer, the Savior of the world. How often we fail to note the presence of God and God's loving hand in the ordinary events of life!

The Ministering Women (8:1-3)

After these events, Jesus leaves that place and continues on "through cities and villages, proclaiming and bringing the good news of the kingdom of God." He is clearly continuing to put into effect the statement made at his inaugural sermon in Nazareth: "The Spirit of the Lord is upon me . . . to bring good news to the poor." (4:18).

Luke continues with the theme of women who responded to Jesus out of gratitude for the blessing they received from him. Several of them were well-to-do women who ministered to Jesus out of their material substance. The Lord himself was poor and without material possessions. He tells a would-be disciple, "Foxes have holes, and the birds of the air have nests; but the Son of Man has nowhere to lay his head" (9:58). Although he performed miracles to feed the hungry he never used his divine power to provide for his personal needs. Instead he humbled himself and had his needs met at the hands of a small band of women whom he had helped.

Bible records and the history of the Church show that it is common for godly women to help pastors, missionaries, evangelists, and others. It is therefore no surprise to read of this group of women who supported Jesus. The backbone of most modern missionary movements were women. Many young women forego marriage, wealth, and other privileges of their home countries to labor and die in the service of others in foreign lands. Women have remained secret prayer-warriors and financiers behind most of the successful Christian endeavors. Any Church that ignores the unique role of women and their ministry is spiritually blind and missing the blessings that have come to the Church through them. Many of the founders of indigenous churches in Africa are women prophets and men are serving under their leadership. There is need for the Church to reexamine its theology regarding women, but there is also need for advocates of the rights of women in the Church to reexamine whether equality is achieved only when men and women perform exactly the same roles and functions in the Church, or whether God and nature have assigned specific and sometimes different roles to both males and females in the building and spiritual development of the Church. Unbridled extremity on either side is sin.

Luke introduces these women here. They will come back to play a prominent role during Jesus' death, burial, and resurrection. Despite the danger involved they stood with Jesus at his crucifixion after his male disciples had fled (Luke 23:49); they helped prepare Jesus' body for burial regardless of official hostility toward Jesus (Luke 23:55); and they faithfully reported the angels' words to the eleven male apostles. However, these male leaders did not believe a word they said (Luke 24:9-11). Is Luke suggesting that there existed a sharp contrast between the courage and loyalty of these few women and those of the twelve apostles?

Those Who Do the Word of God (8:4-21)

Luke describes how the crowds around Jesus quickly grew so large that nobody could get anything done. People were curious to see what further miracles he would perform. Jesus decided it was time for a warning.

Why did Jesus speak in parables and stories? To someone living in a society saturated with newspapers, books, and television this seems a strange way to teach, but in Africa Jesus' approach seems natural. Parables, allegories, fables, and proverbs are common features of our daily life. They are often used to relate stories about legendary heroes and heroines of the past as well as about divinities, fairies, animals, trees, rivers, mountains, etcetera, performing human roles. Such stories are told by elders to young people in the evening while relaxing in the moonlight. Sometimes they are told while the elders are having a palaver, or settling an argument between two chiefs, or consoling the bereaved for the loss of a loved one. They often warn about the consequences of evil characters who break village taboos, causing a calamity for the whole village. Many African Christian preachers still draw many of their illustrations from such parables and fables to bring their message closer to home.

Like any good story or fable, Jesus' parable accurately reflects the living conditions of his native culture, but this means it might be hard to understand by those not familiar with farming practices in first-century Palestine. For instance, it might seem that the farmer was foolish to throw the seeds indiscriminately all over the ground, paying no attention to whether they fell on a path or among weeds or on rocks. What Jesus does not explain is the method of sowing seed used by dry land farmers. In countries that have plenty of rain the farmer usually plows the field first, then plants the seed, then tills it under. This repeated plowing and tilling of the soil releases much of the moisture in it, giving the seeds a chance to "breathe." Then the farmer waits for the rain to fall—nearly every day—and the seeds will germinate.

In Palestine the fields lie dormant after the harvest, soaking up the brief but fierce winter and spring rains. Grass and flowers and bushes sprout everywhere. People make shortcuts across the unused fields, forming beaten paths. When the time comes to plant again the farmer first goes out and scatters the seed over the whole field, over paths, plants, rocks, everything. Then the farmer plows the seeds into the ground and in the process also plows under the weeds, breaks up the path, and turns under rocks lying on the surface. This way of plowing is what Jesus' parable assumes.

Notice that Luke describes Jesus telling the parable to the crowds (8:4-8) but giving an explanation only to the twelve disciples (8:9-15). Why did Jesus pursue this two-pronged strategy?

The disciples ask Jesus why he speaks in parables, why he does not just state God's truth straight out? Jesus answers with a biblical allusion to the prophet Isaiah again. Matthew's version of this same scene gives the whole text of the Isaiah quotation (Isa 6:9-10), which explains a lot (Matt 13:10-15). Isaiah had tried to preach to the people and they did not listen. It is like the situation when you try to help someone and they don't want you to. When they hear your voice they close their eyes and plug up their ears with their hands. It is as if your voice makes them close their hearts. On the other hand, here are the disciples who have committed themselves wholeheartedly to Jesus. He knows they are very different from the mass of people crowding around out of curiosity and desire for something new.

Jesus says in Matt 7:6 "Do not give what is holy to dogs; and do not throw your pearls before swine, or they will trample them under foot and turn and maul you." Every pastor knows the importance of knowing what the listeners are ready to hear. There are times when the Holy Spirit has opened their hearts and they are joyfully receptive. At other times they will be like stones; nothing the pastor can say will have any effect. This is the reason for Jesus' reaction to the huge crowds in this account. He gives them the parable without interpretation. They would not understand it but they might begin to wonder. His disciples stay on and are given the interpretation, that is, "the secrets of the kingdom of God" (8:10). Jesus knows that he should give these only to those who have already taken the first big step of lifelong commitment to him. These are hungry for what Jesus will teach them; they are ready for the message of this parable.

What is the message? Luke 8:11-15 spells it out. Each type of soil is allegorically explained. A pastor knows each of these kinds of people all too well. In fact they could even correspond to the same person at different times in his or her life.

Following the interpretation Jesus adds a few additional examples about the proper placement of a lamp. This example describes behavior that is so ridiculous it must have been humorous when Jesus said it. Today we may not be struck by the ridiculousness of lighting a lamp and putting it under the bed but the conclusion Jesus draws is anything but comical. Still, we need to add a few words so that what Jesus said will be clearer: "Then pay attention to how you listen [to the Word of God] for [on the day of judgment] to those who have, more will be given; and from those who do not have, even what they seem to have will be taken away" (cf. 8:18).

No sooner has Jesus said this than someone comes running in with word that Jesus' mother and brothers are outside calling for him to come out because the crowd is too thick for them to get in. But Jesus does not go out; he has one last point to make. "My mother and my brothers are those who hear the word of God *and do it*." This is the deep message Jesus has saved for his disciples. In the last speech he has told them a few of the most important things the new disciple needs to hear. In this, his second speech, he lays it on the line: my disciple is the woman or man who acts on what I have said.

Some scholars say that all Jesus originally taught was the parable itself without the interpretation. They believe that the interpretation was added later, when the followers of Jesus had forgotten the original meaning of the parable and could not understand it any longer. They allegorized the details so that each part contained some lesson for the later Church. As recorded in Matthew the parable was originally intended to reassure the disciples that what was important was not how many people responded positively to their preaching, but whether in their preaching they had been faithful in sowing the seed of God's word to all without regard to who would most likely respond. God, not they, would bring in the harvest.

Jesus Calms the Storm (8:22-25)

After this important second speech Jesus sets sail with his disciples across the Sea of Galilee. If we may judge by a wooden boat discovered by archaeologists buried in the mud just off the shore of ancient Bethsaida, the boat was not very large and when a storm arose Jesus and the disciples were soon in danger of swamping. Luke tells this story with great economy of words. Exhausted from all he has been doing, the Son of God himself has to rest, surrendering to the claim of nature. This should be a lesson to all servants of the Master laboring in his vineyard that no matter how pressing the demands of our various callings we must find time to rest. In our sleep God not only refreshes us but occasionally speaks to us about the immediate problems and even distant ones. When we are in good health we can serve the Lord better and for a greater number of years.

The Sea of Galilee is notorious for its violent sudden squalls of wind. Situated more than six hundred feet below sea level, it is surrounded by hills and bluffs beyond which the great mountains rise to the north and south. Rivers have cut deep ravines through these bluffs, creating great funnels through which the north and west winds can sweep down onto the lake. It is one of these erratic winds that strikes the boat of Jesus. Naturally many of his disciples were experienced fishermen and quite familiar with that lake; they do everything to keep the boat headed into the wind so it would not capsize, but every effort to redeem the situation is in vain and the danger of drowning becomes real. Still Jesus remains fast asleep as if he were at home sleeping safely in his own bed. Finally the disciples can stand it no longer. "Master, Master" they shout, "we are perishing!" Jesus instantly wakes up, sees what is happening, and with a word calms the storm. The disciples are amazed. "Who then is this, that he commands even the winds and the water, and they obey him?"

Suddenly we recall the other people in the previous stories who asked the same question: "Who *is* this?" In each case Jesus did something outside the expectations of those with him, prompting their question. The definitive answer will come eventually, but a few more astonishing events have to take place first.

We can see in this story a perfect example of the difference between us and Jesus. We humans go by sight. We go by our senses. We decide what is happening by accepting the wisdom of what everybody else says is happening. Jesus goes by perfect faith and trust in God. In the midst of the most incredible storm he can sleep like a baby. When he wakes up his first words are: "Where is your faith [in me]?" That puts it in a nutshell. In the midst of the most devious plotting of the enemies of Jesus, despite all the terror of us humans who always trust our eyes instead of trusting God's word, let us have faith in Jesus! Jesus said, "In the world you face persecution. But take courage; I have conquered the world!" (John 16:33). Paul wrote "I am convinced that neither death, nor life, nor angels, nor rulers, nor things present, nor things to come, nor powers, nor height, nor depth, nor anything else in all creation, will be able to separate us from the love of God in Christ Jesus our Lord" (Rom 8:38-39). When we become terrified at the forces that surround us and threaten to sink our ship let us remember to stop looking with the physical eyes of sight and begin to see with our heart's eyes of faith, picturing our Lord Jesus sleeping soundly in the stern of our boat, and call on him to save us.

Jesus Drives out Legion (8:26-39)

The miracle of the calming of the storm at sea depicts salvation from the physical forces of nature potentially hostile to humans and over which they have no control. In this story we are told that there are spiritual forces that constantly seek our destruction. Such spiritual forces not only seek to destroy humans but quite often put the whole neighborhood of their operations in constant fear. The man in this story was violently insane, too dangerous to live within his own community. Consequently he had to live among the nearby tombs. The story is meant as an extreme example of how far satanic forces can destroy a human personality. All the symptoms have a note of authenticity: his living among the tombs, his abnormal strength, his nakedness, his insensitivity to pain, his hoarse shouting. When Jesus encountered him after arriving on the other side the demon-possessed man rushed to him and fell at his feet, instantly proving Jesus' greater power.

Jesus' first act is to ask his name. In most cultures of the world and particularly in traditional African societies to know a person's real name is to have power over the person and his or her destiny. To exercise this control one must use the specific name given at birth. The Yoruba of West Africa also believe that each species was given some esoteric name at its creation by God. The pronouncement of that name in the hearing of the animal or person means instant death. The invocation goes thus: "Thou goat (or thou man/woman) on the day that Olodumare (the Almighty) created you he called you . . . ." The object will dry up immediately and die. Those who claim to possess this knowledge occasionally test its efficacy on animals. Of course it is believed that if a man, for example, killed a goat through this means he must not eat goat meat because he would die also. In most cultures outside the West it is believed that there are people who can exercise control over the forces of evil or engage their services in tormenting their enemies, in getting rich, or seeking their protection when attacked themselves.

By healing the afflicted man, therefore, Jesus delivered the man's personality and deranged mind from the dominion of evil spirits. When he heard that the demon's name was "legion" he was being told that six thousand spirits inhabited the poor soul. (A Roman legion usually had six thousand foot soldiers.) They begged Jesus not to cast them back into the "abyss" (8:30-31). The Greek word *abyssos* was used to translate the very powerful word for "unfathomable deep" *(tehom)* in Gen 1:2. In the NT it refers to the realm of the dead (Rom 10:7) and the terrifying abode of Satan, the evil beast (Rev 9:1-2, 11; 11:7-8) who will be imprisoned in it by Christ in the last days (Rev 20:1-3). This horrible place frightened even the demons who came from it, so they begged Christ not to cast them back into it but to let them go into a herd of unclean pigs grazing nearby. The presence of pigs in the story proves that Jesus was in non-Jewish territory. No Jew would raise pigs or eat pork.

We may wonder why Jesus agreed to their plea and caused the pigs' destruction. It may have been that this was a foreign area where Jesus was not called to any greater work. Immediately after this healing the foreign inhabitants of this region across the Sea of Galilee became terrified of Jesus' power and begged him to leave their region. Human beings in their fallen and unregenerate state quite often feel more at home with demons than with Jesus the conqueror of demons. The Son of God does not impose himself on any groups or individuals. He abides only in the hearts and places where he is willingly accepted.

The man wanted to follow Jesus and become his disciple. Note what the Lord tells him to do: "Return to your home, and declare how much God has done for you." Similarly in many countries of the world where Christian missionaries have been driven out or rejected during this century the good news of the Kingdom has spread beyond any human imagination through a negligible number of enlightened people who have tasted the heavenly gift and shared in the Holy Spirit, tasted the word of God and shared in the power of the coming age (Heb 6:4-5).

Jesus Does Two Miracles in Capernaum (8:40-56)

Luke says that when Jesus returned a huge crowd welcomed him. They may have seen the disciples and Jesus set off across the Sea of Galilee and run into the great storm and worried that Jesus and the Twelve had drowned. They must therefore have been very relieved to see them coming back. The two stories of Jesus' miraculous powers that are told next, the woman with the flow of blood (Luke 8:40-48) and the daughter of Jairus (Luke 8:49-56), happen quickly, one right after the other. There is a detectable quickening of the pace in Luke's narrative. Events are building to a climax of some kind. What could it be?

These two stories illustrate very different aspects of Jesus' power to heal and to raise those who seem to be dead. Before we discuss their meaning we need a little background information. No sooner did Jesus set foot on shore when a prominent person of the city of Capernaum, the president of the synagogue (this would be equivalent to the mayor of a city today) came up to him with the terrible news that his twelve-year-old daughter lay dying at that very moment. Jesus immediately set off to his house with him. Along the way, however, something extraordinary happened. A woman with an abnormally long period of menstrual flow touched the fringe of his cloak and was instantly healed. What was the situation here?

The woman's infirmity was one that caused her to be "unclean" under Jewish laws pertaining to defilement caused by chronic drainage from the body's private parts, male or female (see Leviticus 15). These laws had a very important role in preserving community sanitation so they were strictly enforced by powerful taboos. For this woman even to be out of her house meant that she was doing something extremely dangerous since her condition could have been contagious. In any case she had no business being in the packed crowd around Jesus. It was even worse for her to intentionally touch someone, let alone a male person who was not even a relative. Her act was simultaneously shocking and forbidden. She must have been desperate.

Luke says that she reached out and touched the *kraspedos* of Jesus' *himation*. What was that? The *kraspedoi* were the four short tassels religious Jewish men wore, then as today, at the four corners of the *himation,* an outer garment or cloak (cf. Num. 15:38-39, Deut 22:12; Matt 23:5). This detail tells us one very important thing about the woman. She was so painfully aware of her unhealthy condition that she did not attempt to touch any part of Jesus' skin, or his sleeve, or even any part of his outer cloak. She touched the end of one of the tassels hanging off the bottom of the cloak, where she would make the least possible contact with him and still touch something about him. Instantly, Luke says, Jesus felt that someone had touched him. Turning around, Jesus asks, "Who touched me?" Peter tries to object to Jesus' question but Jesus will not listen to him. "I noticed that power had gone out from me." Trembling from head to toe, the woman steps forth and admits that it was she. Does Jesus become enraged? reproach her for breaking the purity laws? censure her for endangering all the people in the crowd? Not at all. He blesses her!

Here we find the amazing lesson in this story. Jesus did not even mean to heal this woman and still she was healed. Note that Jesus was not at all angry; he just wanted to know who it was who had tapped into his God-given power to save. This is our clue to this whole story. We may be trapped in the crowd; we may be in a filthy, disgusting stage of sickness. We may feel that Jesus has gone by and left us behind, but we must reach out to him anyway in our desperation and God's power will come back to us through Jesus Christ our Savior. Even if we feel that he is looking the other way Christ is our touchstone of God's healing power. In Christ we have to do with a God who will save us and not ignore us. This woman was healed and Jesus did not even intend to do it!

No sooner does this happen when a servant comes from the synagogue president's house saying, "Your daughter is dead; do not trouble the teacher any longer." Jesus says, "Do not fear. Only believe, and she will be saved." The others are reacting in fear and using their physical eyes to ascertain the meaning of events. Jesus, the Son of God, instantly corrects them: "look with the eyes of faith, not mortal sight." Likewise when they arrive at Jairus's house the wailing and mourning have already begun. Everyone is walking by sight, not by faith. They are using their everyday eyes to determine what has happened. When Jesus says, "she is sleeping," they laugh at him. When we think as the world thinks, we are convinced it is the only way to think. It takes Christ to reach out and shake our misplaced confidence—as he does here. He takes the little girl's hand and says, "Child, get up!" and she wakes and gets off her bed. "Give her something to eat," Jesus says. Her parents are absolutely amazed at the turn of events and send the mourning people home.

Luke says that Jesus told the parents not to tell anyone what had happened. As far as the mourners were concerned, Jesus had told them, "she is only sleeping." They had thought she had died, but they were wrong. No doubt Jesus did not want thousands of curiosity-seekers to descend on him again, which they certainly would if anyone learned the truth. This tells us a very deep lesson about Christ. He did not want to be sought for his miracles even though the power of God was in him to do them. Instead he kept telling everyone to have faith in God, to live according to God's word.

The parents were prepared to begin the funeral. For someone as wealthy and important as Jairus this would have involved most of the city. Professional weepers and mourners would have been hired. They would have hung over the body of the little girl crying out her name and begging her to respond. Relatives and friends would have come and joined in the screaming and crying. The scene of mourning when death occurs in most situations in Africa is similar to that in Jesus' situation. The house becomes especially chaotic if the dead person did not reach a ripe old age. The news of such deaths causes loud wailing and weeping to break out, beating of the head, hastening to the scene by neighbors and relatives. The name of the dead person is called by the people; death is blamed for having decided to kill this poor innocent person before her time. Rituals and sacrifices are carried out to bid the dead person farewell. Messages are sent to other recently deceased relatives to watch for the newly dead person and to be especially vigilant to protect the still-living members of the family from further evil. If foul play is suspected, abuse and curses are rained down on the suspects.

Jesus Sends the Twelve on a Mission (9:1-6)

Luke then says that Jesus assembled the Twelve and instructed them to imitate what he had been doing thus far, that is, to go out two by two on their own missionary travels "to proclaim the kingdom of God and to heal." Before they leave Jesus empowers them with the spiritual weapons they need to conquer all the forces of evil. He tells them to take no provisions for the trip. Jesus clearly means for it to be a quick trip, since they are to preach once and, if the response is favorable, stay overnight; if not, they are to keep going. The Twelve set out and soon they are everywhere in the nearby villages, "bringing the good news and curing diseases" (9:6).

The Twelve are instructed to "shake the dust off your feet" when leaving a place that would not listen to them. This was meant to be a serious threat signifying: we want no part of you. In some cultures in Africa, after burying the dead the mourners wash their feet and faces on their return home so as not to transfer the dead person's calamity to their home. Likewise when visitors from other towns arrive at one's doorstep they wash their feet so as not to transfer the misfortunes they have encountered or witnessed on the way. In religiously pluralistic societies Muslim beggars wash the coins they have collected since some of them were given by infidels and are unclean. Handling them makes the Muslim's hands impure and unfit for use in prayer until they have been washed.

Herod Antipas Wonders Who Jesus is (9:7-9)

While the Twelve are on their missionary tours through Galilee Luke switches scenes and we learn something about Herod Antipas, one of the sons of Herod the Great. This son had been placed over Galilee by the Romans when his father died in 4 B.C.E. Of course his job was to keep things under control, and when report after report reached him about astonishing events in the city of Capernaum and round about he naturally became alarmed. He was especially dismayed when some reported to him that John the Baptist, whose head he had cut off for chastising him about his recent marriage to his brother's wife Herodias, had come back from the dead. One can easily imagine his terror at that thought! What would happen to him the second time John the Baptist appeared before the man who had been his executioner? On the other hand there were other reports saying it was not John the Baptist but some other prophet or wonder worker. In any case Herod was worried and felt compelled to get to the bottom of it.

Notice that Herod's fears did not lead him to repent of his violent treatment of John. Instead he continued to be worried for his own skin. He was like many powerful leaders whose conscience is so dead that they keep on doing terrible things until some greater power stops them. As such he resembles many tyrants in the world. Later, when he finally came face-to-face with this person Jesus (23:6-12) he still did not repent.

The Disciples Return (9:10)

When the disciples return they do little more than tell Jesus what they experienced during their missionary tours. Luke says that Jesus immediately left Capernaum for the little fishing village of Bethsaida, about an hour's walk.

Feeding of Five Thousand People (9:11-17)

This event is the only miracle of Jesus reported in all four gospels, so it must have made a deep impression on many participants who later related their memories of what happened. The way Jesus miraculously provided for the people recalls God's daily providence of manna for the Israelites while they were wandering in the desert. The great lesson here is God's concern for our physical well-being. Our God is not a bodiless entity who wants our bodiless worship! Luke says that when Jesus saw all the people following him he instantly sensed their hunger and anxiety. Matthew writes that "when [Jesus] saw the crowds, he had compassion for them, because they were harassed and helpless, like sheep without a shepherd" (Matt 9:36). Luke says that Jesus "welcomed them, and spoke to them about the kingdom of God, and healed those who needed to be cured" (Luke 9:11). Then, since it was evening, Jesus told his disciples to give the people something to eat, as if they were the hosts at a great picnic. When the disciples said they could not, Jesus blessed the few fish and pieces of bread they did have and soon everyone had plenty to eat with twelve baskets of leftovers.

If the Church will be true to its origins it must be the champion of the cause of the poor all over the world. Everywhere the poor are calling the Church back to clearly defined goals in Christian commitment to Jesus Christ. The poor in our midst are challenging the Christians in poor and rich countries alike to rediscover Christ's spirit manifested in the feeding of the five thousand. Jesus says, "Give them something to eat!" but if our Church leaders look at each other and say, "we cannot do it, we do not have enough food" they will be acting exactly like Jesus' disciples. Yet if these same Church leaders heed Christ's command and say, "here is all we have, Lord," then Christ will bless it and it will miraculously multiply so as to be enough for everyone—with plenty left over!

Jesus Asks Who the Crowds and His Disciples Think He is (9:18-22)

This occasion represents one of the most crucial moments in the life and ministry of Jesus. He has just shared a sacred miracle with five thousand people. "Who do the crowds say that I am?" he asks his disciples. Jesus has good reason to wonder. Large crowds never think clearly. Too many rumors get started; too may fears or wild hopes spring up like rabbits, running in all directions when their nest is found. As expected, the crowd has many different (but mistaken) reactions to Jesus. "John the Baptist," says one disciple. Everyone knew John had been executed by Herod Antipas. Maybe Jesus looked like John; he certainly spoke with prophetic power as had John. Another disciple says that some people think Jesus is Elijah come to warn people about the day of judgment according to the prophecy of Malachi:

> Lo, I will send you the prophet Elijah before the great and terrible day of the LORD comes. He will turn the hearts of parents to their children and the hearts of children to their parents, so that I will not come and strike the land with a curse (Mal 4:5-6).

Other disciples report that the people believe one of the other prophets, possibly Jeremiah or Amos, had risen from the dead and was now doing all these things.

Notice what Luke has told us. Every single one of these responses to Jesus is incorrect. All these people had seen Jesus in person, heard him speak, even been miraculously fed by him in person. Did this direct contact with Jesus make it possible for them to know who he was? Not at all: no member of the "crowds" knew who it was that did these things. All kinds of speculations circulated, not far from the truth, but still not the truth. Be wary of what "crowds" think!

Then Jesus turns to his own disciples, those to whom he has chosen to reveal the secrets of the kingdom of God. "But who do you say that I am?" Simon Peter instantly responds with the famous words: "[You are] the Messiah of God" (9:20). The gospel of Matthew preserves his answer in a slightly longer form: "You are the Messiah, the Son of the Living God" (Matt 16:16). To this Jesus responded, according to Matthew, "flesh and blood has not revealed this to you, but my Father in heaven" (Matt 16:17).

Here again we see something very important. Being with Jesus in person was not enough. Having the wisdom of the crowds was certainly not enough. Knowledge of Jesus' true identity must be revealed to each of us by God in heaven. Then and only then will we know with all our hearts and minds and souls who Jesus truly is. If the public has vague and contradictory ideas about Jesus Christ it is because the Holy Spirit has not revealed to them who Jesus Christ is.

Lest his disciples immediately begin to dream of a political messiah who would lead a military rebellion against Rome Jesus goes on to explain what his messiahship would mean: "the Son of Man must undergo great suffering" (Luke 9:22). The Lukan Jesus' conception of the Son of Man can be traced to the "suffering servant" of Isa 52:13–53:12. This lesson that Jesus the Messiah and Son of Man would be the suffering servant would prove to be the most bitter pill the disciples had to swallow. It is no easier for us pastors and preachers who would love to tell our people sweet stories about a nice God who will always pamper us and keep harm away, but that is not the God of Jesus Christ, the God of the Old and New Testaments, the God of cross and redemption.

Disciples of Jesus Face the Cross as Well (9:23-27)

Jesus goes on to explain to his disciples, who had to be listening to him in dismay and anxiety, "if any want to become my followers, let them deny themselves and take up their cross daily and follow me." Thomas Shepherd (1665–1739) expressed it well in his hymn, "Must Jesus Bear the Cross Alone?":

> Must Jesus bear the Cross alone?
> And all the world go free?
> No; there's a Cross for everyone,
> And there's a Cross for me.

Jesus' message contained the paradoxical demand that those who would be free must give up their craving for security, pleasure, and self-gratification, and live in service to others. Strange as it may seem a life of service, including sacrificial suffering for others, can be a life of deep joy and serenity. This is not a life we can embark upon unaided. We need to keep in constant touch with our Lord Jesus, with other faithful Christians, holding up his example and those of the great saints and martyrs of the Christian Church before our eyes. Then, with God's gracious help, we also will join the "great . . . cloud of witnesses, lay[ing] aside every weight and the sin that clings so closely, and [running] with perseverance the race that is set before us, looking to Jesus the pioneer and perfecter of our faith, who for the sake of the joy that was set before him endured the cross, disregarding its shame, and has taken his seat at the right hand of the throne of God" (Heb 12:1-2).

Jesus Christ is Proclaimed as Son of God (9:28-36)

Having built up our suspense through several stories by means of the repeated question: "Who is this who even forgives sins?" "Who is this who can even command the wind and the water?" Luke concludes with the amazing story in which heaven answers the question. "Then from the cloud came a voice that said, 'This is my Son, my Chosen; listen to him!'" (9:35). Once again we learn that Jesus' true identity can only be revealed from heaven. Scripture repeatedly tells us in many different ways that humans cannot perceive the deep things of God by themselves. As Isaiah wrote, "my thoughts are not your thoughts, nor are your ways my ways, says the LORD. For as the heavens are higher than the earth, so are my ways higher than your ways and my thoughts than your thoughts" (Isa 55:8-9). Paul was profoundly aware of the same truth: "To them God chose to make known how great among the Gentiles are the riches of the glory of this mystery, which is Christ in you, the hope of glory" (Col 1:27).

We may find the account of Jesus' transformation into pure light hard to understand. This is precisely what Luke is trying to get at. Our frail human minds cannot understand, no matter how hard we try. Look at Peter's seemingly foolish reaction to the sight of Elijah and Moses standing beside Jesus. He wanted to set up tents so everyone could stay a while. Can we blame him? But the full divine power and glory can never be visible to humans for long. The God of Jesus Christ, the God of the prophets and poets and evangelists and apostles, always works through disguises. God chose Deborah to do battle with Sisera. God chose Elijah to do battle with the priests of Baal. God chose Isaiah to warn the king of Jerusalem about Nebuchadnezzar. God's chosen messengers are God's hands and feet and voice. Our task as pastors and preachers is not to get into arguments about the way the stories in the gospels are told and whether they literally happened, it is rather to point to the profound mystery of the Christian faith, that the God of Israel, the God of Moses and the prophets, acted through God's chosen one, God's son Jesus, to give us as full a picture of the divine ways as we can grasp. We can see this intention here, for what follows in a few verses is the account of the long trek to Jerusalem where Jesus will "be seized by lawless men and crucified." On the way Jesus will teach his followers about all the most important aspects of the Christian life: how to pray, how not to give up hope, how to deal with wealth, and so on. Standing in the background through it all is this shining image of Christ the Son of God and the words ringing out: "This is My Son, My Chosen; listen to him."

Jesus' Journey Toward Jerusalem and the Cross: 9:37–19:28

The Lukan "journey to Jerusalem" (commonly known as the "Lukan travel narrative") does not properly begin until 9:51 and continues through 19:28. Its theological importance is derived from the fact that it is Luke's account of Jesus' climactic journey culminating in his death on the cross. The details of the journey cannot be reconstructed because Luke provides only vague references to create the sense of Jesus' final trip (such indicators are at 9:51; 10:38; 13:22, 33; 17:11; 18:35; 19:1, 28, 41). Obviously for Luke the journey to Jerusalem and the cross is of crucial significance: it is not just another "journey."

The journey to Jerusalem is so important that Luke carefully prepares for it by prefacing the announcement of its beginning (9:51) with four stories, each of which involves a disciple who does not grasp what discipleship really is (9:37-43a, 43b-45, 46-48, and 49-50). Following the announcement he relates four additional stories demonstrating similar weaknesses on the part of those who would be his disciples (9:52-56, 57-58, 59-60, 61-62). Apparently the need for instruction on discipleship has become one of the primary reasons for developing an extended, final journey to Jerusalem and the cross packed with Jesus' teachings on discipleship.

Jesus Heals a Boy with an Evil Spirit (9:37-43a)

When Jesus leaves the glory experienced at the mount of transfiguration he returns to the valleys of human need, the blindness and hypocrisy of religious leaders, and the ignorance of his disciples. He returns to minister to all those who experience the evil forces that for ages have been in control of human beings and their societies. The father's concern for his only son that leads him to beg for help is poignant. Jesus' frustration over the inability of his disciples to heal the boy is a precious reminder of his humanity. The story raises our concern for the greater parts of the world where people bear daily the yoke of disease and mysteries of life beyond their understanding, a yoke they find it impossible to bear. They need a Church of divine origin that responds in the name of Jesus to the call for divine assistance in the face of unjust suffering. The importuning parent, not Jesus, is the main hero in this story of how we achieve access to God's sovereign love for the helpless victims of circumstance.

Jesus' Predicts His Death; the Disciples Fail to Understand (9:43b-45)

The contrast between the disciples' ineptness and Jesus' majesty continues in the prediction of Jesus' suffering. The apparent victory of the moment brought about by Jesus' healing of the epileptic boy is short-lived, for Jesus says: "Let these words sink into your ears: The Son of Man is going to be betrayed into human hands" (9:44). Once more we are reminded of the wide gulf between Jesus' conception of his messiahship and the then popular understanding expressed by the disciples. They have come a long way. Peter recognized Jesus as the "Messiah of God" (9:20) and three of the disciples have seen the Messiah in glory (9:28-36). Still, true understanding continues to evade them. The union of suffering with messiahship is inconceivable to them: Jesus' throne is to be the cross and his crown, thorns. This is the key to the divine mystery: Jesus' death will become the center of God's redeeming act.

Who is the Greatest? (9:46-48)

At the very time when Jesus is straining to prepare his followers for his death and its meaning in God's plan they are quarreling over *their* status in God's reign: namely which of them would be the prime minister of the new messianic order and its "emperor." Self-centered focus tends to blind people to divine purpose and the real meaning of their experiences. Self-centered theological focus leads to spiritual intolerance that in turn gives rise to Church divisions and Christian denominationalism. Similarly, self-centered ambition by political and military oligarchies wherever they be found breeds intolerance, oppression, suppression, and persecution. In stark contrast to Jesus for whom leading is serving, they see leadership as power to be employed for purposes of control. Indeed, the Lord Jesus is the model of humility, self-sacrifice, and selfless service on behalf of others. To receive and care for a "child" is to receive Jesus; to receive Jesus in this manner is to stand affirmed in the presence of God.

The Religious Elite (9:49-50)

The disciples' concern for prestige and status produces an elitism that finds expression in their rejection of one who though not of their number is nevertheless healing in Jesus' name. Jesus explicitly rejects this form of religious elitism. Clearly this brief episode reflects the common belief that invoking a person's name produces powerful results. The practice of invoking names of past and living heroes and heroines, paying homage to them, and asking for their aid is common in some areas of Africa, especially among professional healers, herbalists, magicians, exorcists, drummers, and the like. For example my family was famous for the use of herbs for healing and my great-grandmother was from a family famous for taking care of fractures and dislocations. I remember that when I was young I was invited to touch the herbs that had been gathered and say: "I pay homage to Olayoda Abogunrin, my father. May I not be put to shame." When someone had a dislocation or a fracture in the leg or hand I was invited to pull it and apply medication saying: "I pay homage to Aina, my father's grandmother. May I not be put to shame." Common belief is that such invocations aid the effectiveness of the medicine and increase the speed of the healing process. Invoking a person's name is equally common in exorcisms. We will see that when the seventy-two who are commissioned and sent out return (10:17), they report: "Lord, in your name even the demons submit to us!"

The mistake made by the disciples was that they thought the "outsider" who was invoking Jesus' name was in competition with them. Jesus, however, felt otherwise. All of us know persons who, though not committed disciples of Jesus, do perform humanitarian deeds and acts of kindness, perhaps even in a Christian context. Such deeds and acts are not to be condemned; rather we recognize that the word of God truly proclaimed and lived is always accompanied by social service and action. It is also a mistake to assume a radical separation of clergy and laity in the proclaiming and the living out of the word. We, the community of faithful followers, must be willing to tolerate and accept as allies all who are working for God.

The Journey Begins (9:51)

With 9:51 we reach a turning point in the gospel as the journey proper begins. The previous section concentrated on Jesus' deeds; this section focuses primarily on his teaching. The first major section (4:14–9:50) climaxed with Jesus' interpretation of his messiahship in terms of the Suffering Servant (9:18-22). This next section (9:51–19:27) introduces Jesus' resolute departure for Jerusalem and the cross. His decision to go to Jerusalem is not a casual one but represents a deliberate decision. That "he sets his face resolutely towards Jerusalem" (9:51 NEB) emphasizes the deliberate resolve of Jesus to do the will of his Father. According to Luke the journey takes Jesus to his destiny as determined by God's loving plan of salvation. Jesus is fully aware of this destiny, for he has twice before spoken of its ominous implications (9:22, 44). Also, only Luke reports that both Moses and Elijah appeared to Jesus at the transfiguration to discuss with him his departure *(exodos),* namely his suffering death (9:30-31). Jesus is the eternal Son of God not in spite of the cross but precisely because of it. He saw it coming and went to meet it without either hesitation or compulsion. Jesus demonstrates a clear understanding of the Father's will and an obedient acceptance of that will.

Scholars have pointed to the artificial nature of the structure of this Lukan travel narrative. From the information given one strives in vain to reconstruct the steps of Jesus' journey, but Luke's account of the journey is both literal and metaphorical, geographical and spiritual. The real objective of the journey is not Jerusalem, but heaven via the cross. In view of such an event the specific geographical details are of little consequence. They fade as a higher purpose takes control of the narrative. The entire section embraces this goal of Jesus' journey to the cross. All of these important teachings are presented in the shadow of the cross.

Luke places within the framework of this journey most of the material he has not already used that parallels Matthew 1–18, especially the first three major discourses (Matthew 5–7; 10; 13:1-52). On the other hand much of the material in this section is found only in Luke. It is as though Luke, if he was following Matthew or a source parallel to Matthew, skillfully made a surgical cut into his source precisely at a place corresponding to Matt 18:5 (the community regulations) and inserted into the literary incision not only traditions found elsewhere in Matthew's gospel but others from a source or sources with which we are not otherwise familiar. One cannot overestimate the value to the Christian community of such precious gems as the parables of the Prodigal Son and the Good Samaritan. These stories and others within the travel narrative that are unique to Luke contribute beyond measure to the Church's understanding of Jesus' preaching concerning the nature of God's searching, forgiving love and the dignity that belongs intrinsically to every human being. Luke accomplishes all of these purposes without disrupting either the content of his sources or the essential order he shares with Matthew.

A Samaritan Village Rejects Jesus (9:51-56)

The most direct route from Galilee to Jerusalem passes through Samaria. For centuries, however, Jews had little to do with Samaritans (John 4:9). Hence the more direct route was also the most hazardous one for a Jew. For Jesus, who reaches out to all, the more direct road, while more perilous to him personally as a Jew, provided an opportunity to preach the gospel to Samaritans.

Samaritans, originally descendants of the northern tribes, were now of mixed blood. Their temple (a rival to that in Jerusalem) was on Mount Gerizim and the Samaritans claimed that all the patriarchs including Moses had worshiped there. They accepted the Pentateuch as their Scripture. To prepare for this portion of the journey Jesus sends some of his followers ahead to arrange for accommodations in one of the Samaritan villages. Hospitality is not forthcoming because the Samaritans reject Jesus' followers. The rejection is due to Jesus' destination, the rival Jerusalem. The people of Samaria do not know the real reason for Jesus' journey to Jerusalem, the cross. James and John are incensed at this rejection and seek retribution. While the disciples are unforgiving, Jesus once more practices tolerance. Christians are to avoid being vengeful and using violence against their opponents. Christ did not come to destroy but to redeem.

But what must Christians do when in certain situations in Africa and elsewhere churches are burned down, Christians killed and maimed without provocation, or when persons with selfish motives use institutions of government for purposes of suppression? Christians are to be patiently tolerant and magnanimous under provocation. They must be prepared to accept hostility without retaliation or desire for revenge. Nevertheless they do possess the right to defend themselves and must not allow themselves to be slaughtered *en masse*. But for the fact that opponents know that Christians will go all out to defend themselves, Christianity would have been wiped out in several places in Africa and in some parts of Asia.

Whereas four episodes preface the announcement of Jesus' journey to Jerusalem and the cross the present account is the first of four that will immediately follow the announcement of the journey's beginning. The first four illustrate inept discipleship while the latter four demonstrate potential stumbling blocks before true disciples: in this case the failure to forgive by being patiently tolerant. By so framing the announcement of the journey (9:51) with these two sets of discipleship episodes Luke demonstrates the crucial importance of Jesus' teaching that permeates the whole journey section.

Underestimating the Price (9:57-58)

In these sayings the essential meaning reflects the cost of discipleship that includes sharing the unsettled and insecure existence of the Son of Man who "has nowhere to lay his head" (9:58). While Matthew connects this encounter with Jesus crossing the region of the Gadarenes (Matt 8:19-22) Luke associates it with Jesus' final departure from Galilee in anticipation of the mission of the seventy. Those who are sent into mission must not underestimate the level of commitment required of them.

Luke depicts Jesus as one who was always on the move in order to fulfill his God-ordained mission. His homelessness was not due to poverty, but rather to his missionary work that involved him in sleeping in peoples houses and inns without any home base to which he could return. Joseph Fitzmyer poignantly writes of the would-be follower of Jesus that he "makes a spontaneous enthusiastic offer of unconditioned allegiance. Jesus' sobering answer drives home the gravity of discipleship. The Son of Man is en route; he lives the life of a homeless wanderer, having no shelter, no home, no family—none of the things that people usually consider requisite for ordinary life, 'nowhere to lay his head.' Even animals are better off" (*The Gospel According to Luke* 1.834).

Failing to Respond Unconditionally (9:59-60)

The most obvious difference between this would-be disciple and the previous one is that this one is not a volunteer; he is called to follow. The response does not necessarily imply that the father has actually died. It may mean that the father is very old and the person who is called must first fulfill his familial obligations. In any case, for this would-be disciple there are prior conditions that he must meet: his response is not an unconditional one.

In Africa one of the greatest desires of a person is to be survived by children who will give one a fitting burial. The most fortunate and wealthiest person is the one who is survived by responsible children who will perform all the necessary burial rites. It is a time of joyful celebration for the children who are able to fulfill this obligation, and the parents consider themselves most fortunate in death.

As in Africa, burial of dead relatives, particularly parents, was a binding religious duty among the Jews, taking precedence over all other religious duties including the study of the Law. The primary duty of filial piety for a Jew is the proper burial of a parent (Tob 4:3; 6:14). Sirach 38:16-23 gives details of what a child is expected to do for the dead. "My child, let your tears fall for the dead, . . . lay out the body with due ceremony, and do not neglect the burial" (Sir 38:16b). The Yoruba people of West Africa have a saying: "The burial ceremonies of a childless rich man are for seven months, those of a childless pauper last for six months, but the burial ceremonies of the man with children last forever."

The request to be allowed time to bury one's parent was in accord with God's command to "honor your father and mother." Jesus' response "let the dead bury their own dead" is one of the most radical of his teachings. Nothing he did or said could have more effectively marked him out as a prophetic revolutionary. To follow him on such terms as these obliged his disciples to be prepared to follow him through thick or thin.

Unconditional Response Reemphasized (9:61-62)

Jesus' agrarian analogy is beautifully presented and rich in meaning. Anyone who has plowed a field knows that the first furrow is always the crucial one. When the first one is straight the result is a work of art; row after row moves in parallel like arrows to the opposite end of the field, thereby producing a pattern worthy of artistic appreciation. If the first is not laid properly the resulting pattern can be disastrous both to the eye and for the yield. How does one plow a straight furrow? by focusing on a point at the opposite end of the field and keeping the eye on that point as one plows. Under no circumstances does one look back before completion of the first furrow if one wants a straight furrow. This story emphasizes the need for an uncompromising singleness of purpose on the part of those called to be disciples. One who fails to possess such singleness of focus finds the call to be a disciple impossible to fulfill.

The Mission of the Seventy-two (10:1-20)

Following on the heels of the above four examples is the account of the commissioning of seventy or seventy-two other disciples for mission. The joyful return of these and Jesus' rejoicing over their success in mission (10:17-20) demonstrate the validity of his lessons on discipleship. Luke is the only evangelist to record the mission of the seventy(-two). The language of the passage is strongly Lukan but the account is probably based on traditions he has carefully examined. The emphasis here appears to be on the significance of Jesus' instructions. Even though his instructions to the seventy-two appear to be expanded when compared to those given to the Twelve both sets are virtually identical in meaning (cf. 9:1-6; 10:1-12). Yet in spite of their similarities there are notable differences between the accounts of the two missions. The mission of the Twelve involved their appointment to the apostolate; it was to be missionary and evangelistic as well as to confirm and demonstrate the power and authority given to them by Christ. No power or authority is confirmed on the seventy(-two). The primary aim of the latter mission is to prepare the way for the coming of the Master in specific towns and villages (10:1).

There is confusion in the textual history of the gospel as to the precise number involved in this mission. The tradition of "seventy" probably stems from the fact that God ordered Moses to bring seventy elders forward to share his spirit. Later two other elders also received some of Moses' spirit (Num 11:24-30). The textual evidence seems to favor "seventy-two" over "seventy." Another consideration, however, lies in the difference between the Hebrew account of Genesis 10 and that of the LXX. The Hebrew text lists seventy names as symbolic of the nations of the world while the LXX includes seventy-two.

The success of the seventy(-two) points to the joyful results ahead for those who join in mission as true disciples. In this respect the mission of the seventy-two prefigures the mission to the Gentiles of the primitive Church. As John the Baptist had heralded the coming of the Messiah at the beginning of Jesus' ministry, so now the seventy-two, in teams of two, are sent ahead to announce the advent of the Messiah at the beginning of his journey to Jerusalem and the cross. Because of the urgency of their task they must avoid carrying even the simplest of traveling gear. They must waste no time with those who reject their message, but move on to the next town or village. The harvest is ripe and must be gathered into the barns of God's kingdom. They have come bringing the message of peace, pardon, and hope. The purpose of their mission, therefore, is to present the gospel, to prepare for Christ's entrance into people's lives. They are to proclaim "the kingdom of God has come near to you." The Messiah will soon arrive in their midst. Salvation is at hand.

For those who reject Jesus a judgment worse than the one that befell Sodom awaits. Three towns that have witnessed his miracles yet remain unrepentant are specifically identified: Chorazin, Bethsaida, and Capernaum. When judgment comes there will be more tolerance given the Gentile towns in Phoenicia, Tyre and Sidon, than will be extended to the three mentioned above (10:13-15). To reject Jesus is to opt for destruction in the end.

These instructions for disciples are applicable in mission work today with few exceptions. Today we are to travel lightly and proclaim the nearness of God's reign with the advent of Jesus' coming; however, some situations require additional services. Where there is hunger, disease, and deprivation, our mission must carry the equipment that addresses these human physical needs. Jesus continues to be the Savior of the body and the soul. The need is even more acute than two hundred years ago. Human problems have compounded everywhere one encounters the folly, avarice, greed, and selfishness of people and their governments.

The return of the seventy-two brings joyful celebration, for its success represents victory over those evil forces that hold humankind in bondage. This celebration does not represent the victory of a select few; rather it is a celebration of the many. All the disciples rejoice in the fact that they are now citizens of record in God's kingdom (10:20).

Blessed are Those Who See (10:21-24)

This is the only occasion in the NT where Jesus "rejoiced." This exultant utterance by Jesus is a succinct summary of his feelings at the success of the seventy-two and the future of the Church. The disciples are seeing and hearing the wonderful mysteries of God's eternal purpose for the kingdom. Truly many prophets and kings would have liked to see what the disciples now see and hear, but they have not been able to do so. What the disciples see and hear is the mystery of God in Jesus: the intimate interaction of God and Son that has been manifested to those chosen by the Son (10:22). This is the power that destroys Satan and brings down all manner of evil (10:18-19). One notes the christological importance of this passage to the whole of Luke's gospel and the pivotal role it continues to play in the mission of the Church.

The Good Samaritan (10:25-37)

The setting for the parable of the Good Samaritan consists of questions asked of Jesus by a lawyer who appears to be interrogating him. The initial question asked (in 10:25) is "what must I do to inherit eternal life?" Although not posed in the context of the Passion narrative (as in Matt 22:34-40) it is asked on Jesus' journey to the cross and it is asked a second time at Luke 18:18-30. Here Jesus responds by asking the lawyer what the Scriptures say. The lawyer responds appropriately with words from one of the most familiar and revered texts of the OT, namely the Shema: "Hear, O Israel: The LORD is our God, the LORD alone. You shall love the LORD your God with all your heart, and with all your soul, and with all your strength" (Deut 6:4-5), adding "and with all your mind; and your neighbor as yourself." Jesus affirms the answer but the lawyer presses further by asking the crucial question (recorded only in Luke 10:29), "And who is my neighbor?"

The parable that follows involves one who is traveling from Jerusalem to Jericho, a journey of about twelve miles that involves a descent from 2,300 feet above to 1,300 feet below sea level. The road is narrow, winding, rocky, and notoriously dangerous, with caves that easily provide shelter for would-be thieves. The characters have been carefully chosen. The one who is robbed and beaten is a Jew while the one who offers gracious assistance is a Samaritan. Intense racial animosity existed between these two groups. Ben Sirach describes Samaritans as the "foolish people" whom his "soul detests" (Sir 50:25-26). Jews were forbidden to say "amen" at the end of a prayer offered by a Samaritan. On the other hand Simon the son of Gamaliel felt they should be treated like Israelites (*y. Damai* 6.2; *y. Ber.* 7.1; *y. Keth.* 27a). In either case Samaritans were considered "outsiders." The point of the parable in its Lukan context is that it is precisely this "outsider," the Samaritan, who proves to be the neighbor.

Tragically, the Church down through the ages has not always been able to live up to the standards of this story. The Church, acting and speaking when it should not and not acting and speaking when it should, has struggled with its positions involving slavery, segregation, and apartheid. Atrocities have been committed in the name of Christ, accompanied by the deafening sounds of silence. A Samaritan is my neighbor! Jesus continues on his journey to the cross.

Jesus Visits Mary and Martha (10:38-42)

This episode is beautifully filled with humor. Mary finds "sitting at the feet of Jesus" much more meaningful than fulfilling the responsibilities of being a host (10:39). Martha works in the kitchen while Mary visits with the guest. Mary's action is freely chosen, Martha's performed out of feelings of social obligation. In fact both wanted to be with Jesus. Jesus' reply to Martha's criticism of her sister is designed to gain her undivided and focused attention. She, like those in the stories above, is being challenged to "see" and "hear." If this conversation were to take place in a Yoruba home in West Africa it would go like this:

> *Jesus:* "Martha! Martha!!"
> *Martha:* "Yes, my Lord."
> *Jesus:* "How many times did I call your name?"
> *Martha:* "Two times."
> *Jesus:* "How many ears have you?"
> *Martha:* "They are two."
> *Jesus:* "What do you do with them?"
> *Martha:* "I listen with them."
> *Jesus:* "Then keep what I want to tell you now in your left hand lest you eat with it."

The Yoruba eat mainly with the right hand, which is washed before and after meals. It is forbidden to eat with the left hand and it is an insult to hand something to another person with the left hand. If one must use the left hand the person offers an apology before he or she completes the action. Keeping the information in the left hand which is used less frequently is keeping it close to the heart and allowing nothing to invade it.

What Martha is to "see" is that Mary has chosen the good portion that is not to "be taken away from her"; she sits at the feet of her Master. Relax, Martha. Life's greatest moments are lived above the worries and anxieties experienced through self-imposed obligations. Join Mary at the Master's feet. This is a fitting story to follow the story of the Good Samaritan. There are times when, if doing one's duty leads to complaining about the behavior of another, one should be open to the possibility that the other may be responding to an even higher calling.

Teaching on Prayer (11:1-13)

Matthew includes the Lord's Prayer in the Sermon on the Mount at the beginning of Jesus' ministry (Matt 6:5-15). Fitzmyer correctly observes that the Lukan form of the prayer fits well within the context of Luke's gospel, coming shortly after Jesus' own prayer to the Father (Luke 10:21-22), and that the passage is the first of three episodes dealing with prayer (*Luke* 2.896).

In my opinion the Matthean version is probably the original form of Jesus' prayer. It fits closely the life situation of Jesus. The Lukan form was adapted to meet the interests of the Church. The Lukan form of the first "us" petition is a prayer that God "continue to give us bread day by day" (the expression "day by day" is characteristically Lukan), thereby pointing to God's continuing daily care for the needs of God's people. The second "us" petition is for forgiveness, a petition that first begins with the confession of sin and guilt by the one petitioning. To be forgiven is to practice forgiving. The third "us" petition echoes a warning to the disciples, a reminder that temptation is always a potential hazard for the disciple. The phrase "lead us not into temptation," is a petition that we not yield to temptation, not just that we not be tempted. The verbal construction carries the meaning that "we not succumb to temptation" so as to miss the goal or purpose of God's reign.

The parable that follows, peculiar to Luke, emphasizes the importance of persistent prayer. This parable of the Friend at Midnight (11:5-8) is parallel to the parable of the Unjust Judge (18:1-8); both teach the importance of persistence. People avoided traveling during the heat of the day. Frequently, therefore, travelers would arrive at their destinations late in the evening, even as late as midnight. Hospitality is a sacred duty no matter what the time of arrival, and food was offered even if it became necessary to borrow from a neighbor. In Africa and portions of the East hospitality is one of the most sacred duties. Knowing a person beforehand is not necessarily a requirement. Some visitors might be angels, divinities, or spirits in human garb who are capable of blessing or doing harm, depending on the attitude of the hosts. More than once I and members of my family have gone to places where we were not personally known. Each time we have been offered food and accommodations. In some parts of Africa food is placed near the road so wayfarers with money can easily purchase what they need and those without money may eat freely. The only restriction of the latter is that they not take food along with them. Also whenever a friend in need seeks our assistance we must oblige, even if the hour is late. Persistent knocking will produce the provisions needed. This parable fits beautifully in African and Eastern settings.

God does not need to be cajoled into giving what we need. The commands to "ask," "seek," and "knock" refer to the believer's trust in God who wills good things for all people and provides for their essential needs. These commands (11:9-13) are an expanded version of Matt 7:7-11. Even more importantly for Luke's account, God gives even more than "good things" (cf. Matt 7:11). To the one who asks, God gives the Holy Spirit, considered in the early Church to be among God's richest blessings.

Jesus and Beelzebul (11:14-28)

Luke appears to draw from two Matthean episodes by conflating Matt 9:32-34 and Matt 12:22-24. The opposition to Jesus appears to intensify as he continues on his journey to the cross. After Jesus "[casts] out a demon that was mute" so that the man now speaks the people marvel, but "some" accuse Jesus of having cast it out in the name of Beelzebul. "Beelzebul," by the time of Jesus, had become the popular name for the prince of demons. Jesus responds to the accusation in several ways. Satan is not foolish enough to allow infighting among his demons. A divided people, like a divided army, cannot prevail. It is the "finger of God" (cf. Exod 8:19; 31:18; Deut 9:10; Ps 8:3) that breaks the power of Satan's domain; hence it is only through God's power that healing has occurred, in contrast to the incantations and charms employed by others. Through God's power one is able to stand firmly in the decision made for discipleship. The "either-or" requirement offers no exceptions: "whoever is not with me is against me" (11:23).

Caught up in the emotion of the moment, a woman in the crowd extols Jesus by speaking of how proud his mother must be for having given him birth. Verses 27-28 are peculiar to Luke. The woman's words stand as a fulfillment of Mary's prophecy in Luke 1:48. Jesus transfers the focus from himself (and his mother) to a more central emphasis: namely that those who are truly blessed are those who "hear the word of God and obey it." Again one sees a concern for themes involving women and blessing.

The Sign of Jonah (11:29-32)

People were crowding to Jesus as a result of his healing activities. When Jesus speaks of their seeking a sign, exactly what the sign is to indicate is not made clear. Given the context the sign was probably requested to provide evidence that Jesus' miracles were due to the power of God, not that of Satan. The demand for a sign is a demand for tokens and confirmation of divine authority. This is necessary because supernatural power is not, by itself, always good. In Africa, parts of Asia, and Latin America, for example, the display of supernatural powers is a common phenomenon. It is regularly attributed to medicine men, men and women possessed by certain divinities, sorcerers, magicians, and the like. Some ancestors have been deified because they were believed to have possessed supernatural powers, but not all supernatural powers associated with ancestors and used in this manner are beneficial to the faithful. In fact it is believed that evil spirits and some divinities can be conjured up and sent on evil errands. Most of the African indigenous churches emphasize glossolalia, prophetic utterances, healings, exorcisms, and deliverance from evil powers. Likewise some of the members are believed to be in close contact with the spiritual world and actually possessed by evil spirits. The spiritual gifts of such persons are the result of evil spirits rather than God. In some of these churches sacrifices to spirits and rituals associated with African Traditional Religion are still prescribed.

According to Luke the spiritual and moral quality of Jesus' miracles was so self-evident as not to require a sign or further proof that God was the source Jesus' wondrous acts. The only sign that is to be given is the parallel between Jonah as a sign to the Ninevites and the "Son of Man" to this generation (11:30). For Luke the parallel lies in the fact that both were sent to announce God's imminent judgment that necessitates immediate repentance. Further, through Jonah God graciously extended forgiveness and salvation to a Gentile nation. He was a "prophet" sent to the Gentiles. Similarly, through the death, burial, and resurrection of the Messiah God extends forgiveness and salvation to all humankind without partiality.

The Light of the Body (11:33-36)

This small section provides a beautiful summary for the disciples. It both highlights the meaning of the message the disciples proclaim and serves as a further response to the demand for a sign. No normal person will light a lamp and put it in a cellar (*kryptē,* a hidden or dark place) or under a bushel (*modios,* a measuring vessel). That Jesus gives no sign does not mean that secret or hidden information is being kept from anyone. On the contrary, the word is elevated high on a stand for all to "see" (cf. 10:23). Even so, seeing requires insight and a sound or healthy eye. A sound eye, like a lamp, illuminates the body, but if the eye is not "sound" God's light cannot penetrate the body and it remains in the darkest of darkness.

Jesus Denounces the Pharisees and the Lawyers (11:37-54)

For Luke, moving from Jesus' words regarding a distorted eye to his somewhat aggressive contact with Pharisees and lawyers is a smooth and easy transition. They do not have a "sound" eye. The occasion for the contact is provided when Jesus once again accepts an invitation to dine in the home of a Pharisee. Some have argued that the ensuing polemic, largely in the form of relatively short sayings, reflects the controversy between Jews and Christians as well as between Jesus and Jewish leaders. This may be true. The denunciations by Jesus are couched in the form of six woes, three addressed to Pharisees and three to lawyers. Taking their minute attention to washing as a starting point Jesus aggressively questions the Pharisees' religious emphases on outward purity without greater attention to inner cleanliness. For Jesus, ritual washings (11:38), almsgiving (11:41), meticulous tithing (11:42a), justice rendered in a perverted manner (11:42b), prestige gained from favored positions in the synagogue (11:43), are actions none of which cuts to the heart of true piety. What happens deep within the person—in the private regions of the inner self—is what matters in religious devotion, for the inner being is the place of commitment (11:39b-40). Lacking this commitment from the inner being, these Pharisees have become like unmarked graves (11:44).

Jesus' word to the lawyers is no less harsh. They impose minute and burdensome regulations on people, that they themselves do not take seriously (11:46). They build the tombs of the prophets while consenting through their actions to the persecution inflicted on prophets by their ancestors (11:47-51). Consequently the lawyers have removed the key to knowledge by distorting the eye that illuminates the inner self so that they cannot see the light of God, nor can others enter God's kingdom through them (11:52). This episode concludes with the introduction of "scribes" into the unit and the note that they have joined the Pharisees in conspiring against Jesus.

Today African churches are similarly legalistic, sometimes to the point of the absurd. Nonessentials often receive great emphasis, OT ceremonial laws are carefully followed in some areas, and often loyalty to the institutional Church appears to rank higher than devotion to Christ, the Church's Lord.

Fearless Trust and Confessing Christ (12:1-12)

Verses 1-3 prepare for the introduction of the next part of Jesus' journey. Here Jesus warns against the evil influence (leaven) of the religious leaders. He uses the term "hypocrisy," which refers to "acting a part in a play." God prefers a repentant, truthfully blunt sinner to one who play-acts a holy person. One cannot hide anything from God.

It is appropriate that immediately following the "woes" and "warnings" Luke presents Jesus' urging that the disciples not fear those who wield earthly power over them (vv. 4-12). God who created continues to be in charge. If even the smallest creatures are the objects of God's care, how much more will this be the case for those who fear God (vv. 4-7). One can expect scrutiny and even persecution due to one's public confession of Christ. Then one must choose between two options: submission to the legal procedures of our society and to human opinion or to the heavenly court in the company of angels who daily render obedient service to God (vv. 8-9). The term, "Son of Man" in v. 10 forms a link with v. 8. Christians can expect to be subjected to and dragged before courts (cf. Luke 12:11 with Matt 10:17-18). When this happens the Holy Spirit will give them a voice. Those who in their folly blaspheme against the Holy Spirit and the testimony given through the Holy Spirit will not be forgiven (12:10; cf. 12:11-12).

Many Christians outside the West have had to submit to the legal systems of their respective cultures, suffering persecution and even death rather than deny the faith. While the second option may not often be apparent the Christian does hope for his or her "time in court" before the angels of God where the verdict truly will be a just one.

Parable of the Rich Fool (12:13-21)

The first portion of this text (12:13-15) provides the background for the parable. "Someone in the crowd" asks Jesus to instruct his brother to divide an inheritance with him. What motivates such a request is not clear. Both the parable of the Rich Fool and its introduction are unique to Luke and the parable reminds one of the relationship between the younger and older brothers in the parable of the Prodigal Son (Luke 15:11-32). Jesus first responds by denying any jurisdiction over the dividing of inheritances but then warns that priorities must be clear when dealing with such matters. Greed and selfish interests can easily complicate these emotionally charged issues (cf. Deut 21:17).

The parable of the Rich Fool speaks of one for whom the acquisition of material goods has become an obsessive end in itself. Failing to appreciate the transitory nature of human existence, the man tears down and builds new structures to hold all of his acquired goods. The problem with all this building and hoarding, of course, is that when God suddenly requires this man's soul, who then will enjoy all of these "things"? Greed often corrupts one's priorities. The actions of the Rich Fool are too often emulated in our world. The cause of the heinous crimes committed by political leaders in many areas of the world is greed, avarice, and the insatiable desire to accumulate wealth at the expense of those ordinary citizens who live in abject poverty and die daily for lack of the basic necessities of life. These leaders wherever they exist have become looters, not leaders, of their people and they plunder from the rich resources of the nations they govern. Most of the wealth they secretly store with other nations benefits no one after they die because of the privacy rules applied by foreign bankers. The Church, as the oracle of God and the voice of Jesus Christ, must lead in the crusade for repentance both on the part of such leaders and those banking institutions whose policies permit such actions.

Trusting in God's Providential Care (12:22-34)

If greed can create problems for the Christian, so can inordinate worrying and anxiety. For the background traditions Luke used to present these teachings of Jesus, cf. Matt 6:19-21, 25-34. The intervening passage, Matt 6:22-24, was used by Luke earlier at 11:33-36. A similar expression of confidence in God's care for Christians was recorded at 12:4-12 with respect to one's response in legal proceedings. Now trust in that care is offered as an antidote to the everyday fears that beset our daily living. Worrying is of no value since it cannot extend a person's life. It can, in fact, shorten it. A close look at the beauty of nature, typified by flowers, shows how beautiful our lives are when they radiate the glory of God. In the quest for daily necessities one must not become consumed by the gnawing fear and anxiety of fulfilling basic human needs. God cares for us if for anything at all, and God will provide. At the same time these words remind the more affluent of the partnership that may be formed in providing adequate provision for those pressed for daily sustenance. God's provisions may be and often are distributed through human agents who have been led to form such a divine-human partnership. In either case primary focus is to be on the reign of God: all the rest will be added (12:31). The inner sanctuary of the heart is where one finds the real treasure (12:34).

Parable of the Watchful Servant (12:35-53)

If greed and anxiety are not appropriate to the disciple, what is? If this question were to be asked, Jesus' response according to Luke would be: alert watchfulness. One must be spiritually ready at all times for the advent of the Son of Man. The mind that is spiritually alert is one not preoccupied with worldly concerns, defensiveness, and the physical accumulation of wealth. The focus is to be on preparation for the Lord's coming. The servant of the Master is ready, according to the parable, for his coming whatever "watch" may turn out to be the time of his arrival. Further, the most effective security for any household is watchful preparation. Such a house cannot be violated.

Luke's story at this point parallels Matthew 24–25. The parable of the Ten Bridesmaids (Matt 25:1-13) is given in abbreviated form, and a conflation of the material in Matt 24:13 with that in Matt 24:42 provides the transition to a passage paralleling Matt 24:42-51. The theme of Luke here is: watch, for no one knows the precise time of the Lord's coming. The benefit derived from rigorous watchfulness is strength in a time of extreme pain and divisiveness. Luke 12:49-53 refers to the forthcoming divisions among family members that will occur at the time of the crisis. Jesus' coming precipitates the pain one experiences when confronted by divisions within families.

The Crisis is Near (12:54-59)

Jesus now turns to the crowd and expresses disappointment at their being able to read the signs of the weather (the saying differs somewhat from Matt 16:2-3) but not the signs of impending judgment. The legal analogy of 12:57-59 further reinforces the weakness of the crowd's understanding and stresses that the times are serious. The certainty of God's righteous judgment at the end time ought to lead people to seek full reconciliation with God, the final judge.

Three Exhortations to Repentance (13:1-9)

Luke has taken this passage from some other source than Matthew. Two of the exhortations to repentance are based on recent occurrences and the third is a parable. The first two episodes are tragic in nature. The first involves the massacre of a group of protesters, at least some of whom were Galileans. Galilean zealots were notoriously turbulent and Pilate was ruthlessly cruel in dealing with each uprising. Though this specific episode is not mentioned by Josephus, similar events are related in *Ant.* 18.3.2; 4.1. The second event, mentioned only in Luke's gospel, refers to an accident involving the collapse of a tower near to or connected with the Siloam tunnel built by King Hezekiah. Eighteen persons were killed in the collapse. The questions in both cases are parallel. Are the ones who suffer more criminal in their offenses than those who do not suffer? Did these persons die as a result of divine judgment? Jesus dispels such popular notions by stressing the universal need for repentance. Accordingly unless all repent and respond positively to the gospel, all will suffer alienation from God.

Following these two stories that encourage repentance and parallel one another in meaning there appears the parable of the fig tree that after three years of producing no fruit is ordered cut down by the vineyard owner. The vinedresser, however, suggests that the owner wait one more year and then, if after further cultivation and fertilizing there is still no produce, cut it down. While the story appears to give the "tree" another chance at producing the fruit expected of it one cannot help but note that the length of time of the tree's fruitless activity parallels Jesus' three-year ministry during which time humankind was offered the opportunity for repentance. The parable reminds us of the long-suffering of God but it also implicitly warns that those who persist in their sinful refusal to repent will suffer and eventually be "cut down."

Sabbath Healing of a Woman; Parables of the Mustard Seed and the Leaven (13:10-21)

The story of the healing of the crippled woman on the Sabbath is unique to Luke and it is the last report of Jesus appearing and teaching in a synagogue. The text attributes the woman's condition to "a spirit that had crippled her," one that no doubt bears Satan's stamp and has resulted in her "bent over" posture. A more contemporary work (Geldenhuys, *Luke,* 375) offers the diagnosis of *spondyhitis deformans,* which causes the bones of the spine to fuse together into a rigid mass. The number "eighteen," the number of years this woman has suffered, serves to link this passage with the previous one involving the accident resulting in "eighteen" deaths. The hypocrisy of religious leadership becomes apparent when, after Jesus' compassionate healing of the woman, the ruler of the synagogue attacks Jesus on a technicality: Jesus violated the Law by healing on a Sabbath. Jesus responds by stating that if they can attend to Sabbath emergencies involving their domestic animals they should not frown at the healing of a suffering daughter of Abraham on the Sabbath. The religious leadership is shamed and the people rejoice in God's glory.

Certainly this healing is a small event when compared with the "straightening" of a whole people and their restoration to the state of producing fruit for the kingdom (as with the fig tree above). The two parables in Luke 13:18-21 serve to remind the reader that great events have humble beginnings. The parable of the Mustard Seed and the parable of the Leaven are parallel to each other in the text. Both are reign of God parables that Luke has used and modified, paralleling part of Matthew's Parables of the Kingdom chapter (Matt 13:31-33). The first involves a man and the second a woman, another example of Jesus making his point with illustrations taken from the lives of both men and women. The point is the same in both instances. Large results come from small beginnings. The two parables link up closely with the victory won over Satan in the healing of the woman with the bent posture. Though not recognized by Jesus' critics the release and restoration of the bent woman bound by Satan for eighteen years was like a tiny seed (or a little leaven in flour) that would in the future grow into a greater and more majestic tree (large mixture of dough for baking) of universal victory over all satanic forces. The rejoicing of the people over the healing of the crippled woman is really rejoicing over the glory of God's kingdom that inevitably grows through the activities of the Church's ministry (which at times may appear "small" and inconsequential) to the needs of humankind.

The Narrow Door (13:22-30)

Jesus continues his journey to Jerusalem and the cross, traveling through "one town and village after another, teaching" (13:22) in full confidence of the inevitable victory of God's kingdom. In this context someone asks Jesus, "will only a few be saved?" Jesus' response points to deliberate effort and focused devotion, for the door is indeed a narrow one. Few will enter! The term "strive" (*agōnizesthe)* is the word from which the English "agony" is derived. The struggle to enter must be so singularly motivated and focused as to be described as agony that involves the whole person: body, soul, and spirit. Many will try; few will be able to enter (13:24).

Christian life is a daily struggle to rise to a higher spiritual plain. It is wrong to sit back and relax after we have made a personal commitment to Christ. We cannot remain stagnant in our loyalty to God's kingdom; unless we move forward we shall move backward.

Jesus Laments over Jerusalem (13:31-35)

The tension is mounting as Jesus continues his journey to the cross. Warnings previously given to the disciples begin to become reality for Jesus when "Pharisees" bring word that Herod wants to kill him. It may seem strange that a Pharisee would warn Jesus; however, this warning could have come from a Jewish religious piety that did not want a popular Jewish prophet to die at the hands of a Roman agent. It is more likely, however, that Jesus had friends among the Pharisees.

Jesus refuses to flinch in the face of danger. He remains steady on the course of his divine mission (13:32). Once again the necessity and inevitability of what lies before him in Jerusalem comes to the forefront of the text, and Jesus must continue on this journey toward the cross. The reality of his destiny, however, does not abate his feeling for the heart of his people's religious heritage. The city of Jerusalem, established by David and carried by him to heights of power that have not been duplicated, also saw God's prophets perish at the hands of its inhabitants. This place—and its house, the Temple—will be forsaken. The lesson of triumph through agony and destruction will be the lesson learned when Jesus reaches the end of this journey, the cross.

The passage as a whole serves as a transition to the instructions to follow. Jesus' "lament" over Jerusalem (13:34-35), which Luke records while Jesus is en route to Jerusalem, parallels Matthew's account of Jesus' words in the Temple after he had entered the holy city (Matt 23:37-39).

Dining and Discourses in the Home of a Pharisee (14:1-24)

The following series of scenes takes place at table in the home of a Pharisee. Luke 14:1-6 sets the stage as Jesus goes on a Sabbath to dine with a "leader" of the Pharisees. The comment that "they were watching him closely" implies careful scrutiny of Jesus and perhaps even a plot to entrap him (*paratēreō,* "to watch someone closely, scrupulously, or insidiously" or even "to watch maliciously"). A very sick man shows up and Jesus immediately heals him in a manner reminiscent of his healing of the crippled woman on the Sabbath (13:10-17). Healing on the Sabbath gives those who are watching ample opportunity to malign Jesus, and he knows it. Here he does not await their comment; rather he immediately asks them a question: "Is it lawful to cure people on the Sabbath or not?" (14:3). They are unable to answer. Jesus becomes a model for the Christian; he never allowed the fact that he was under the constant and critical scrutiny of opponents to dissuade him from staying the course on his journey to the cross. The Christian Church must never succumb to pressure to obey the "law" at the expense of neglecting weightier obligations.

Luke 14:7-11 includes a parable that teaches a humble stance when one is invited to dine. If one starts at the lowest place at the table the only way is up. There is great honor in being invited by your host to "move up" the table, but great insult at being asked to "move down" in the seating arrangements.

It is appropriate here to call attention to Luke 20:46 where reference is made to the haughty actions of scribes and Pharisees. "Beware of the scribes, who like to walk around in long robes, and love to be greeted with respect in the marketplaces, and to have the best seats in the synagogues and places of honor at banquets" (cf. Matt 23:6-7). There must have been occasions when Jesus saw colleagues scrambling for the most desirable seats. With such intense feelings on the line it would have been truly humiliating to be asked to "move down."

Luke 14:12-14 continues with instructions for giving a feast. Jesus' position is that when one does give a banquet it should be for the poor, the lame, and the blind; blessings will accrue. This is true because these persons are unable to repay the one who has graciously served them. Invite your friends and you secure an obligation on their part to return the favor by inviting you to their table at a later time. A Christian, however, does not share food with others in order to secure a reciprocal obligation: the concern shown for those in need reflects God's concern.

Luke 14:15-24 contains a story told by Jesus about God's eschatological banquet. There is a similar account in Matt 22:1-10. Jesus' story begins with a statement that clearly connects it with God's messianic banquet. "Blessed is anyone who will eat bread in the kingdom of God!" (14:15). The story follows. A man once invited guests to a banquet. Those who were invited, however, made excuses as to why they could not attend. The householder became angry and sent his servant to the highways to invite the poor, the crippled, the blind, and the lame. He sends his servant out a second time because the banquet hall must be filled. Those originally invited, however, will never taste this banquet. The application of the parable is not difficult to see. God has extended invitations to the messianic banquet. Those initially invited, however, have made excuses and are not planning to come. This parable strikes at the heart of self-righteousness on the part of religious leaders who have become complacent because of their assurance in religious matters. As a result of their refusal to accept God's invitation, God has opened it to others whom no one would ever expect to be invited. The invitation is extended to the religiously ostracized, the social outcasts, tax collectors and sinners, even Gentiles. By this parable Jesus unambiguously proclaims the nondiscriminatory nature of the reign of God.

To attend, one must freely accept the invitation. The phrase "and compel people to come in" (14:23), however, has been used to justify actions that call into question the free acceptance of the invitation. Augustine used this text to justify religious persecution of non-Christians, encouraging the coercion of people into the Christian faith. It is horrifying to realize that this Scripture was misused by the Church in defense of the Inquisition, torture, destruction, imprisonment, and intimidation against "heretics" and those who rejected Christianity. Thank God, through the voice of Pope John Paul II the Church has repented of this sin! Today we have certain churches in Africa that obtain confessions from alleged witches and wizards by the use of severe torture and gradual mutilation of the body. In 1995 the police arrested a woman prophet in Nigeria for burning the hands of a girl, destroying her ten fingers because she refused to confess that she was a witch. Similar criminal acts against humanity are committed with impunity and defended in different places throughout the world by quoting scriptural texts like this one. Here, to the contrary, "compel" *(anankason)* is used in the sense of moral and logical constraint rather than in the context of violent coercion or compulsion. Its usage in no way justifies the use of any form of physical or psychological torture by any authority, be that authority civil or religious.

The literary pattern evident in this passage is striking. The structure consists of two short parallel units (14:7-11 and 14:12-14) followed by a longer narrative parable (14:15-24). We encountered a similar structure in ch. 13 (13:2-3 and 13:4-5 followed by 13:6-9). We will find it again in ch. 15 (15:3-7 and 15:8-10 followed by 15:11-32). However in this case all three sayings are in the form of narrative parables. This structure indicates how Luke's tradition has been carefully shaped for teaching and preaching purposes.

The Cost of Discipleship (14:25-35)

Both context and audience change abruptly with this passage. There is no reference to a banquet or feast and no further mention of being in a Pharisee's home. The passage is directed now to the crowds and the theme is the price one pays in order to be a follower of Jesus. One can only guess why "large crowds" have suddenly gathered. Perhaps the populace believes that Jesus is after all the Messiah of Israel and that his journey to Jerusalem is to be the victory march that will dislodge the Romans. Perhaps they want to see his enthronement and share in the glory of the coming kingdom. In any case Jesus confronts them directly with the real demands of "accompanying" him on his journey. They must renounce everything (be it family or their own lives) in order to be his disciples. Jesus is not literally demanding "hatred" of family and self. The Semitic mind, and the African as well, can only entertain two extremes: truth and falsehood, love and hate, light and darkness. The present passage likewise reflects no middle ground between the extremes of loving or hating one's family and oneself. Discipleship demands deliberate and total commitment.

This message of commitment is punctuated by the two parallel analogies that follow immediately. No one builds without planning carefully (14:28-30) and no one wages war without thoughtfully weighing the costs (14:31-33). Then follows a third metaphor (14:34-35) illustrating the result of a compromised discipleship that does not take into account the kind of commitment required. One cannot help noticing the slight variation in the structural pattern previously identified as consisting of two shorter parallel stories followed by a single more developed one. Here a message of utmost importance is strongly stated. Two stories, parallel in meaning, are then presented, the content of which further accents the significance of that message. These two parallel stories are then followed by a third in the form of a metaphor in which the value of an inept, compromised form of discipleship is portrayed by analogy. It is like salt that has lost its taste: it is fit for nothing.

Jesus Defends the Gospel (15:1-32)

As the crowds have gathered around Jesus, so now "outsiders" like tax collectors and sinners "draw near" to him (15:1-3). This is not pleasing to the religious leaders who are also present and Jesus' reception of these outsiders provides the controversy setting for the three parables that follow. Again one notices the organizational pattern by which these parables are presented: two short parables in synonymous parallelism followed by a longer parable that makes the same point. This type of structure is the creation of a highly effective communicator.

The parables of the lost sheep and the lost coin in 15:3-10 have the same objective. It should be noted that here again Jesus makes his point by drawing illustrations from the lives of both men and women. The search for the sheep and the coin denotes God's search for lost children. In the parable of the lost sheep (cf. Matt 18:10-14) Jesus appeals to custom. Should one sheep stray the shepherd leaves the ninety-nine secure in the fold and searches "diligently" for the one that is lost. Because of the value of every single sheep to the shepherd this is no token search. When the sheep is found there is much rejoicing. Just so, there is rejoicing in heaven over the repentant sinner. The same points are made in the parable of the lost coin: (1) a coin (*drachma,* equal to the wage paid a laborer for a day's work) of value to the woman is lost; (2) she makes a vigorous search in a windowless room (customary for that period and locale) with the aid of a lighted lamp; (3) she rejoices with neighbors when the coin is found, and (4) there is rejoicing in heaven over the repentant sinner.

The parable of the Two Lost Sons in 15:11-32 is more commonly called the parable of the Prodigal Son. The popular name, however, does not do justice to the parable. The father here does not have one lost son, but two. One of the two, however, does not know he is lost.

The prevailing custom among Jews at the time of Jesus was that a father could bequeath his possessions to his heirs by drawing up a will or he could give them out in the form of gifts while he was still alive. As a rule, though, the property still remained under the authority of the father until he died. In some cases he could actually hand over the allotted inheritance before his death. A similar method of dividing ancestral property is followed in India where after the youngest son is grown any of the sons can demand a share of the father's property. Among various ethnic groups in Africa traditions governing the bestowal of property are generally consistent with those of the Jews.

The first portion of the story (vv. 11-24) unfolds beautifully. The younger of two sons asks his father for his rightful share of the property. There is no indication that either the request or the granting of the request is unusual or improper. The father complies and the son travels to "a far country" where he squanders all he had received. After tumbling to the depths of human existence as evidenced by his eating from husks used to feed the swine he "came to himself" (v. 17), realizing that his father's hired hands were better off than he. He decides to return and ask his father for employment. His father, seeing his younger son from a distance, rushes to meet him, listens to his son's words, embraces him, kisses him, gives him the finest robe, ring, and shoes, and then orders that a party be given in honor of the younger son who was lost but is now found.

At this point the elder brother enters the narrative (15:25-32). On hearing noises from the celebration he inquires as to the reason. When the explanation is given him by one of the servants his response is anger (cf. 15:2) and he refuses to join in the celebration. His father "[comes] out" and invites him to the celebration. The elder son then makes his case. The father says: "Son, you are always with me, and all that is mine is yours. But we had to celebrate and rejoice, because this brother of yours . . . was lost and has been found" (vv. 31-32).

Clearly the younger brother has been lost (as were the sheep and coin in the two previous parables). There is rejoicing precisely because he has returned (also as in the two previous parables). The popular name "prodigal" son is based on this portion of the story. What is not so obvious is the lost state of the elder brother. It is indeed commendable that he stayed loyal to his father through thick and thin for many years. His case is an excellent one. He deserves the inheritance, and the father even admits as much. The problem is that his self-image has taken him farther into a distant country than his younger brother had traveled. The elder brother is the *good* one, and unfortunately he *knows* it! Regarding himself as the only truly loyal son, he has erected a barricade of self-righteousness that prevents him from recognizing the unconditional love of his father that is always freely extended to *both* sons equally. In fact it is this barricade that now separates him from both his father and his younger brother. Reconciliation with the latter is necessary for there to be a meaningful relationship with the former. One does not learn whether the elder brother finally joined in the celebration. In this sense the story is incomplete. But as with all of our lives we each must decide what the ending to our incompleteness will be!

This story, found only in Luke's gospel, has been and continues to be a classic in Christian circles. It was the subject of elaborate interpretation in the commentaries of the Church Fathers including Tertullian, Clement of Alexandria, Gregory Thaumaturgus, Ambrose, Jerome, and Augustine (to mention only a few). The insights these stories contain and reveal concerning the nature of God and God's unconditional love, the way in which God actively searches for the lost children, the acceptance and affirmation of repentant sinners, the impact of salvation on the relationship of persons to other persons (brother/sister to brother/sister), and the wholeness that unconditional love bestows on those who will receive it are nowhere found in as effectively compelling a form as in Luke 15.

Parable of the Dishonest Steward (16:1-13)

When Jesus has finished addressing the three parables to the Pharisees he turns and speaks to his disciples. The Pharisees remain close enough, however, to overhear Jesus telling the parable of the Dishonest Steward (16:14). The parallel between the younger son "squandering" his inheritance and the dishonest steward mismanaging the master's finances would certainly be recognized by these religious leaders. As the younger son was received by his father and the dishonest steward commended by the master for his actions, so too is the same "turn around" available to those who "come to themselves" and take an account of what lies ahead.

The difficulty of understanding this parable (16:1-9) is not surprising. Patristic commentators often could not understand its meaning or the sayings that follow it and turned to homiletic postulations about the different characters and details of the story (Fitzmyer, *Luke* 2.1095–1096). The problem is that through the commendation of the steward by the master Jesus appears to condone fraudulent activity. The steward, who has been caught in the act of mismanagement and is to be released from employment, begins to handle the master's accounts in such a way as to insure his future livelihood. He begins to settle outstanding debts for reduced payment, thereby gaining favor from those who owe the master. When the master finds out he does not reprimand the steward; rather he compliments him for the radically prudent way he is preparing for his impending dismissal.

The sayings that follow (16:10-13) continue the above teaching. The proper end to which the Christian looks is the reign of God. If dishonest persons can employ their ill-gained wealth to win friends and influence for evil ends, how much more can good come from Christian resources. Every opportunity is a test of character and the goal toward which one strives determines the outcome of the test. Christians should exercise appropriate stewardship with their money. One's allegiance must not be divided between two masters, God and wealth.

The Law and the Reign of God (16:14-18)

The Pharisees, now referred to as "lovers of money" (only in Luke), are present and hear all Jesus has said. They begin to scoff at him. What Jesus has said by parable and implication he now verbalizes directly. God knows their hearts, and their quest for wealth is an abomination before God (16:15). With Jesus a new era has been initiated, one that both follows and surpasses that of the Law and the prophets (16:16). Jesus' pronouncement on marriage should be seen in the light of this new era and the law that is being enacted through Jesus. Wherever there is rigidity and hardness the stability of the home and marriage is affected. God's intention from the beginning was that man and woman live in a lifelong partnership of love.

The Rich Man and Lazarus (16:19-31)

The references to wealth and to the Law and the prophets in the previous unit provide the connecting links to Luke's parable of the Rich Man and Lazarus. Some interpreters have pointed to the relationship between Abraham and his servant, Eliezer (Gen 15:2-6) as providing the point of origin for this story by Jesus. Lazarus is the Latin form of the Hebrew name Eleazer. Eliezer means "God is (my) help" while Eleazer (Lazarus) means "God has helped (me)." The similarities of names and circumstance may be coincidental.

The story itself is about a very rich man who enjoys his wealth while on earth and a very poor man who has been reduced to begging. The poor Lazarus eats crumbs from under the rich man's table and dogs lick his sores. When they both die the poor man is taken up by angels to Abraham's bosom while the rich man is transported to the torments of Hades. Seeing the poor man Lazarus, in Abraham's bosom the rich man asks that Lazarus come and bring a mere smidgen of comfort. Abraham responds by reminding the rich man of the sumptuous joys he experienced while on earth. The rich man then asks that Lazarus be sent back to earth to warn his five brothers. Abraham poignantly replies that they have Moses and the prophets, and if they fail to listen to them they will not repent at Lazarus's visit ("even if someone rises from the dead").

The problem with the rich man was not that he had riches but that he had become callous and selfish, blind and deaf to the needs and agonizing cries of the poor and destitute around him. In the afterlife a reversal of circumstances will take place, and those who were poor and destitute will be comforted.

The Christian Life and Duty (17:1-10)

The audience changes again with the beginning of ch. 17. Whereas the preceding chapters have involved those outside Jesus' immediate community such as the crowds, scribes, or Pharisees, Jesus now gives attention to his disciples. The sayings in vv. 1-6 focus on the responsibility of leaders within the community. "Little ones" in this passage refers to members of the community. Leaders must take care lest their actions in some way cause others in the community to stumble or lose their trust in God. Such leaders will be severely punished. An able leader will rebuke those who sin and will forgive unceasingly those who truly repent of sin regardless of the number of times. The use of the number "seven" (v. 4) does not set limits. (Among the Yoruba of West Africa one of the prayers offered for a woman on her marriage day by her parents is "May you bear seven children completely," which asks that she bear the number of children she is destined to bear.) How can anyone live up to such standards? The imperative is that we must "increase our faith." In order to avoid misleading others by bad example and be able to forgive the habitual offender without hesitation the disciples ask for greater faith. They may begin with a little faith and, like the grain of mustard seed and the leaven (13:18-21), that faith will enable those who are true leaders to rise to the occasion.

Remember Who You Are, 17:7-10

These verses warn against arrogance. Their content reminds us of Paul's admonition in Rom 12:3 that people ought not to think of themselves too highly. We perform our daily tasks as God's faithful servants. As such we have no claim to position, prestige, or even a "thank you." In our service to God the whole idea of merit must be abandoned. The clear conscience of having done our duty is reward enough.

The Healing of Ten Lepers (17:11-19)

Again we are reminded that Jesus is on his way to Jerusalem (v. 11). He has reached a village situated somewhere between Samaria and Galilee. Here he is approached by ten lepers, one of whom is later identified as a Samaritan (v. 16). Common need sometimes creates unusual associations. As was customary at that time the lepers all stand at a distance and ask Jesus for healing. Jesus responds by sending them to the priests. Since this command is usually done after the healing has been accomplished Luke may have omitted the actual act of healing, preferring instead to concentrate on the Samaritan who returned to give thanks. Ten were healed, but only one returned. For the ungrateful nine their healing was just another ordinary gift of God to God's creatures. For the Samaritan, however, it was a new life of personal commitment.

The reference to the Samaritan and his identification as a "foreigner" (17:18) is a striking reminder of the all-encompassing love implicit in Jesus' compassionate ministry. It brings to mind once again the outsider who was casting out demons in the name of Jesus (9:49-50), the parable of the Good Samaritan in which the "foreigner" is identified as the real "neighbor" (10:25-37), and the criticisms leveled at Jesus' reception of the tax collectors and sinners (15:1-2).

The Day of the Son of Man (17:20-37)

Once more the audience shifts, this time back to the Pharisee who asks when the kingdom of God is coming. There are several passages in which this or a similar question is asked. In John 10:24 Jesus is asked: "How long will you keep us in suspense? If you are the Messiah, tell us plainly." John the Baptist asks the same question while in prison: "Are you the one who is to come, or are we to look for another?" (Luke 7:19; Matt 11:3). The same question must have been asked by the disciples over and over again. Even after the resurrection the disciples ask: "Lord, is this the time when you will restore the kingdom to Israel?" (Acts 1:6). With one voice the gospels record Jesus as having to correct notions concerning the Messiah. That the Messiah was to be the king and liberator of Israel from foreign rule, the one who himself would establish a world empire centered in Jerusalem, was not a part of Jesus' message. His teaching on tolerance, love of enemies, and forgiveness, his reception of outcasts and sinners raised doubts in the minds of many who heard him.

In 17:22-37 there is another change in audience. Turning from those who fail to see the kingdom because of their blindness he once more addresses his disciples, warning them that many will seek signs in vain. There will be rumors of time and place but the disciples are not to be misled. When the day of the Son of Man does come it will bring with it irrevocable disaster for an unprepared generation. This faithless generation will give itself up to godlessness as occurred in the days of Noah and Lot. The day that brings salvation for believers will bring judgment and destruction on unbelievers. The Son of Man will bring the separation of believer and unbeliever that no bond can transcend. For Jesus the path to glory and communion is through rejection, humiliation, and suffering. His resurrection and exaltation will be his vindication and his return in glory will bring about the final triumph of God.

Hardly a century has passed that has not entertained notions of precise dates and places for the Son of Man to appear. Ours is no exception. Africa today is full of Messiahs. Within the last forty years no less than three Messiahs preached and died in Nigeria alone. They are the Jesus of Calabar, the Jesus of Benin, and the Jesus of Oyingbo. Now in Nigeria, we have Olumba who claims to be "god the holy spirit," and we have Guru Maharaja who claims to be god and Messiah on earth. All have large followings. The Church in every age must seriously heed the warnings of Jesus about false teaching and Messianic pretenders.

Parable of the Unjust Judge (18:1-8)

The purpose for which this parable is told is clearly stated in the first verse: it is to underscore the disciples' "need to pray always and not to lose heart." On the one hand this admonition is a continuation of previous teachings on the Son of Man. The disciple is to pray persistently and not despair. The Son of Man will return as promised. It will be remembered that Jesus taught persistent prayer to his disciples at an earlier point in his journey to Jerusalem and the cross (11:1-13). The prayer taught by Jesus at that time was a prayer for the kingdom's coming. Here Jesus tells a parable to demonstrate the results that are achieved by those who pray tenaciously.

The key characters in the parable are a judge and a widow. The perversion of justice is condemned again and again in the OT. Judges are to be impartial arbiters and champions of the helpless, poor, widows, orphans, foreigners, and the like (Exod 22:22; 23:6; Deut 10:18; 16:19; Ps 68:5; Eccl 5:8; Isa 1:17; 10:2; Jer 22:3). In this parable the judge appears not to uphold this standard. The widow is a figure of the oppressed and the defenseless who suffer at the hands of ruthless rulers and unjust judges. The poor widow who is deprived of her rights by one more powerful than she is in this parable asking only for justice. The judge stands in stark contrast to God who throughout the Bible is described as one who cannot condone evil (for example, Gen 18:25; Deut 32:36; Pss 50:4; 98:9; 135:14; Hab 1:13; Acts 17:31; 2 Tim 4:8; Heb 10:30). If an unjust judge will eventually hear the persistent pleas of a poor widow, how much more will a just God hear our cries for help if we will only be persistent in our appeals. Therefore we should never despair, but like the poor widow persist in hope.

Under tyrannical governments in different parts of the world, bringing forth the justice to be actualized fully with the coming of the Son of Man will require tenacious and obstinate prayer both by the mistreated and excluded and by those standing in solidarity with them.

The Pharisee and the Tax Collector (18:9-14)

Luke continues the theme of prayer with the parable of the Pharisee and the tax collector. Here the spirit in which one ought to pray is emphasized. The parable shows the contrast between the self-righteous religious person and the repentant sinner, an outcast who humbles himself or herself before God. The prayer of the Pharisee is directed to God but is centered on the one making the prayer, thanking God that he is not like the tax collector, whom he regards as a sinner. Rabbinic examples show parallel prayers that illustrate the picture Jesus is here portraying. We offer a few examples. "Blessed art thou, O Lord our God, King of the universe, who have not made me a slave. Blessed art thou, O Lord our God, King of the universe, who have not made me a woman." Similarly Rabbi Simeon ben Jokai reportedly said: "If there are only two righteous men in the world, I and my son are the two; if there is only one, I am he!" The tax collector, by contrast, prostrates himself before God, offering only a simple prayer: "God, be merciful to me, a sinner!" The tax collector clings to no merit but casts himself before God and asks for mercy. Jesus says: "this man went down to his home justified [that is, in a right relationship with God] rather than the other."

Jesus Blesses Infants (18:15-17)

Luke continues the theme of humility in this account of Jesus blessing infants, using the Greek word *brephē* (infants, babes) instead of the more common word for children, *paidia*. This choice of words conveys even more strongly the feeling of love and tenderness for those who find themselves dependent and helpless. The disciples are not to become "childish"; rather, little children more aptly display the real qualities of discipleship in their receptivity to life, utter dependence, complete trust, humility, openness, and readiness to accept gifts with joy.

The Rich Young Ruler (18:18-30)

This story is a continuation of the kingdom of God theme and an illustration of the uncompromising demands of discipleship, a characteristic of the Lukan narrative. The rich man is referred to as a "ruler" *(archōn),* which means he could have been a leader in the synagogue, or a magistrate, or a member of the Sanhedrin.

The rich man addresses Jesus as "Good Teacher," which Jesus sidesteps in the conversation. Jesus simply says: "Why do you call me good? No one is good but God alone." As the story unfolds it is clear that the ruler knows the traditionally accepted answer to his inquiry about entrance into eternal life. He observes all of the commandments. Jesus realizes that there is something missing so he commands the rich ruler to sell all he has and give the proceeds to the poor. The sadness attributed to this man implies that he was unwilling to do what was asked because he was "very rich" (18:23b). This leads Jesus to comment on the difficulty of a wealthy person entering the kingdom of God. Other listeners press Jesus by asking who is able to do what he asks (18:26). Jesus' reply is that with God the impossible is indeed possible. Peter then jumps into the conversation by saying "we did it; we left our homes and followed you." It is not clear that Peter fully understands the implication of Jesus' call to follow. What may be unclear, Jesus clarifies: those who have left family and home for his sake will not only receive eternal life but will find themselves even now caring for more friends, homes, and a bigger family than they ever imagined. They will be caring for humankind, including the excluded of a poverty-stricken humanity.

The last two centuries have witnessed an astronomical growth and spread of Christianity. The growth has become a most wonderful phenomenon in Africa, Asia, and South America. It is made possible through the sacrificial labor of thousands of young men and women who left the security and safety of their homes to serve as missionaries. For them the rich young man has been an object lesson. Many of these dedicated persons have poured out their lives on the mission fields of human life and some have followed Jesus' journey to the cross.

Another Prediction of Jesus' Death Meets the Blindness of the Disciples (18:31-34)

Luke, having referred to the continuation of Jesus' journey to Jerusalem (17:11-12), once more conveys what will happen upon his arrival. "See, we are going up to Jerusalem, and . . . the Son of Man . . . will be handed over to the Gentiles; and he will be mocked and insulted and spat upon. After they have flogged him, they will kill him, and on the third day he will rise again" (18:31-33; cf. 9:22; 22:66-71). As Peter failed to grasp fully the implications of the previous summons to self-sacrifice so now the Twelve fail to understand (18:34). The reference to Gentiles is obviously to the roles of Pilate and the Roman soldiers. The cross is going to be the fulfillment of the purposes of God for humankind as recorded in the Scriptures of Israel (cf. Psalms 22; 69; and especially Isaiah 53).

The Blind Man of Jericho (18:35-43)

One notices the striking contrast between the blindness of the disciples to the meaning of Jesus' impending suffering as just recorded by Luke and the persistent "seeing" on the part of a man who not only is blind but must cry out to Jesus over the rebukes of the crowd.

The blind man has placed himself beside the road in order to beg. As Jesus passes by he cries out but is rebuked by the multitude. Only with persistent calling does he attract Jesus' attention with his cries for mercy. After making sure of the nature of the blind man's request Jesus heals him by restoring his sight. Once more, Jesus has responded to the needs of the blind and the poor, the excluded of that community. Of real significance for Luke is what happens as a consequence of the blind man's persistence when he actually meets Jesus. As was the case with the persistent widow (18:1-8), things happen and God is glorified.

Jesus is a Guest in the House of Zacchaeus (19:1-10)

This story begins to prepare for Jesus' entrance into Jerusalem, the place of his destination since his journey began at 9:51. The main character in this story is Zacchaeus who was a chief tax collector. He too wanted to meet Jesus as did the blind man above, and he too could not because of the crowd. Zacchaeus exhibited his tenacity by climbing a tree in order see Jesus because he was small in stature and could not see over the crowd. Here again we see the importance of determination and persistence on the part of the faithful (cf. 18:1-8).

As chief tax collector Zacchaeus was not highly respected. People avoided and despised him because of his wealth, which they regarded as ill-gotten. He is generally portrayed as a lost sinner who because of his affluence could not gain entry into God's kingdom. He needed divine assistance, and that assistance comes through Jesus who practically invites himself to dine with Zacchaeus. Though the crowd grumbles, Jesus eats with this "sinner."

Actually, Zacchaeus has done everything needful! He displays persistence by climbing a tree to see Jesus, a compensating act that focuses attention on his smallness of stature. He "dines" with Jesus. He repents of his sinful acts and promises both to share with the poor and to pay back fourfold those from whom he has extorted money for alleged taxes. Furthermore, he does this in spite of opposition in the form of grumbling and verbal abuse. In fact Zacchaeus epitomizes the model response for which Jesus is looking throughout the whole of his journey. Zacchaeus can now live up to the meaning of his name, "the pure one." Jesus says without equivocation that salvation has come to the house of Zacchaeus on this day (19:9).

In several regions of the world the major cause of poverty, disease, hunger, and all that accompanies these maladies is the insatiable desire of the leaders to accumulate wealth at all costs. Today in several nations of the world that God endowed with uncountable natural resources over ninety percent of the populace wallow in abject poverty. Schools and hospitals have collapsed; hunger, homelessness, and joblessness abound, yet the looting and plundering of the national wealth continues unabated. Only repentance can save these regions of the world from the impending, imminent disaster and an upsurge of revolutions similar to the rise of communism in the early part of this century. The Church universal through its prophetic voice and practical example must save these peoples from this approaching but avoidable catastrophe.

Parable of the Ten Pounds (19:11-28)

This parable of the Ten Pounds is the last episode in Luke's travel narrative. Its importance is highlighted by the fact that Jesus "was near Jerusalem" (19:11). Though this story is similar in some ways to Matt 25:14-30 Luke's version is very different. The emphasis in Luke's account is not so much on the use of the money entrusted to the servants but on the rejection of the nobleman, who, having secured royal power, is not welcomed as king by his own people. The accounting that is given upon the nobleman's return is not that of a head of the household but something required by a nobleman who is now king. As king the former nobleman orders that those who rejected him be brought and killed before him (19:27).

The parable focuses on Jesus who will soon receive the credentials of king but will be rejected by those who are under his care. To be sure, those entrusted with gifts will be held accountable for the manner in which the gifts have been developed. The real meaning for Luke is the refusal of the people to accept Jesus' kingship. This rejection of the king, Jesus, will find expression in his suffering and rejection previously referenced (18:31-34). But on the king's return (at the *parousia*) those who rejected him will receive their just reward, death. The very next verse reads, "After he had said this, he went on ahead, going up to Jerusalem" (19:28). This parable foreshadows Jesus' arrival in Jerusalem and points toward the cross.

The Passion and Resurrection of Jesus: 19:29–24:53

The Triumphal Entry (19:29-48)

The event that introduces the final act of the divine drama of redemption must have been vividly remembered, told and retold in the early Church with varying details. The crowd that accompanied Jesus was unarmed. Nonetheless, granting the messianic expectations of the Jewish people whenever the city was filled with pilgrims his entry, however small-scale it was in military terms, would have been provocative to say the least. He deliberately entered Jerusalem in a manner that directly evoked symbolism recognizable among the Jews as that of a king coming in peace (Zech 9:9). His popularity with the people appears to have prevented any violent reaction by the authorities.

Jesus out of compassion wept over the city spread out before him because of the impending devastating destruction of which the Jews were unaware (19:41). In rejecting Jesus the religious leaders were rejecting his way that leads to salvation, peace, and freedom. The decisive nature of Jesus' mission is indicated by the words "on this day" (v. 42) and "the time of your visitation" (v. 44). Unfortunately the leaders were spiritually and politically blind: hence the barrenness of their response to God's final appeal. In contrast to the disciples' outburst of rejoicing at his coming, the heart of Jesus bled over the impending doom of the city.

In several parts of Africa a dance around the town with fresh leaves and singing is a sign of victory or great rejoicing to mark an event. The women usually spread clothes on the paths of monarchs or important dignitaries as a sign of respect, adoration, and acceptance. Similarly the people spread their garments on the ground as Jesus approaches the city of Jerusalem (19:36). His anticipation of his rejection by the leaders and the ultimate destruction of the city (19:41-44) will be resumed later in another discourse against the city (21:20-24). For Luke, Jesus stopped improper practices in the Temple in order to insure that it fulfilled its spiritual purpose and meaning. His action was not a mere protest against commercialism. In order to prevent the animals presented for sacrifice being rejected by the priests (Lev 1:3) worshipers usually bought from those already deemed worthy by the priests. Nevertheless the echoes of Isa 56:7 and Jer 7:11 reflect earlier criticism of the leaders of the Temple. The emphasis on it being a market more than a place of meditation and worship is unmistakable. Jesus' critique appears to have been a major challenge to Jewish authorities, one that could not go unpunished. In Luke, Jesus begins his ministry in the Temple and ends it there (2:41-51; 20:1–21:38). There he taught daily until his arrest.

Jesus' Authority Questioned (20:1-8)

Jesus had become a popular figure and a major source of difficulty that the religious leaders could not ignore. He entered Jerusalem imitating Zech 9:9, the lowly king coming to his city. The incident at the Temple was not only revolutionary but also a major challenge to the whole Jewish religious system and Temple worship. Following his entry Jesus daily dominated the Temple courts with his teachings, attracting large crowds. The Temple authorities were expected by the Roman rulers to maintain order. These authorities saw Jesus' activity as a challenge to their competence and thus to their position of authority. How dare Jesus act like this? The only person who had such a unique authority was the Messiah, but Jesus' messianic claims were to them dubious in the extreme. Their intention therefore was to drive Jesus into a tight corner in order to make him appear as a messianic pretender who recklessly took laws into his own hands. They thought that Jesus in his answers could not escape offending either the crowd or the Roman authorities.

As usual Jesus is master of the situation. He responds with a counter-question that put the adversaries instead of Jesus in a great dilemma: "Did the baptism of John come from heaven, or was it of human origin?" The adversaries know that if they deny the divine origin of John's mission they risk being belittled by their own people. If they acknowledge its divine origin, Jesus would then say that John not only claimed to be the forerunner of the Messiah but actually identified Jesus as the expected Messiah. Thus they say that they do not know. They are the ones who fall into the dilemma. It is no surprise that the religious leaders thereafter mount stiff opposition against Jesus' claims and message.

Parable of the Wicked Tenants in the Vineyard (20:9-19)

This parable is told for three reasons. First, here Jesus indirectly answers the question concerning the source of his authority. Second, it functions as one of the final warnings from the Son of God to the leaders of Jerusalem concerning the terrible consequences of rejecting their Messiah. Finally, it suggests that Jesus will not only be rejected but also killed by these leaders.

The story realistically reflects the kind of thing that could and did happen in first-century Palestine, which by this time was an occupied territory where there were many large estates owned by foreigners who leased them out to tenants for a proportion of annual produce. Economic depression coupled with a nationalistic spirit often led to withholding rent from the absentee landlords. This on occasion brought violence and sometimes murder. A similar situation exists in parts of Africa where absentee landlords hand over their farm plantations to tenants who pay agreed annual percentages or rent in cash or in kind. It is common practice that if one farms on land belonging to a different family one must pay the agreed annual rent, usually a proportion of the farm produce. In the past refusal to pay the customary agreed-upon tax on land led to inter-tribal wars in different parts of Africa. Such practices are a fundamental reality of life throughout history. Jesus uses an episode drawn from this reality as a vehicle for his message.

The meaning of the parable in the hands of the evangelist Luke is quite clear. The story made use of a well known OT metaphor from Isa 5:1-7 where Israel is referred to as the vineyard of the Lord (cf. Deut 32:32-33; Ps 80:8-18; Jer 2:21; Ezek 15:1-6; 19:10-14; Hos 10:1). The tenants are the rulers of Israel into whose hands the nation was entrusted. The messengers are the prophets who were disregarded, persecuted, and murdered. The son who is killed is Jesus himself. The religious authorities have tried to discredit Jesus in the presence of the enthusiastic audience listening to him by questioning the source of his authority. Jesus not only exposes their plan but tells this story in order to state exactly where his authority comes from. He as the Son and the culmination of the prophets has been sent by God to make the final appeal to Israel. By saying that at last the owner sends "[his] beloved son" Jesus is stressing with utmost clarity by what authority he does these things and who gave him this authority. Although the Son came preaching repentance like the prophets, as the owner's son he stands in a completely different relationship to the vineyard than either the prophets or the Jewish leaders. They are only servants but he is the heir and joint owner with the Father. Israel as the vineyard of God is therefore the Son's property and Jesus has a claim to their faith, love, obedience, and devotion, but according to the story, instead of accepting the son (Messiah), the tenants, that is, the religious leaders, kill him.

According to Luke's account the murder of the son must lead to the destruction of the wicked servants (20:16). The religious authorities may succeed in putting Jesus to death but his Father will vindicate him after his death by making him the cornerstone in the eternal spiritual temple of God in universal praise. The repudiation and rejection of that stone would lead to total brokenness and ruin (Ps 118:22). The giving of the vineyard to others (20:16) may refer to the rise and role of the Gentile churches. If so it is possible that the Lukan form of this parable reflects a later version developed in the interest of the Gentile Christian churches.

God and the Emperor (20:20-26)

The failure of the attempt by the religious leaders to call Jesus to account for the cleansing of the Temple and the strong warning contained in the parable of the tenants further fuels their rage against him. They plan to put a quick end to Jesus' activities. They send their spies to put to Jesus a double-edged question about paying taxes to Rome. Once again they attempt to catch him in a dilemma. To answer "no" to the question about whether to pay the tax would put Jesus in serious trouble with the Roman authorities. It could end in his being sentenced to death. But to answer "yes" would certainly discredit him before the large crowd and especially the Galileans from whom he draws his largest support. Such an answer could also result in his being stoned to death by some of the Zealots who came for the Passover feast.

The tribute paid to the emperor was one denarius per year by every man between 14 and 65 years of age and every woman between 12 and 65 years. Jewish opposition was not just to the burden of the tax; the Zealots claimed that they had no sovereign but God and that it was wrong to pay tribute to anyone other than God. The question is therefore a religious one. The emissaries think that Jesus cannot possibly escape falling into their trap whichever way he responds. In order to gain ground they resort to flattery. Eventually Jesus responds by asking them for a coin. In the ancient world the sign of sovereignty was the issuance of currency, and the one who had authority to issue currency had the authority to impose a tax on the users. We have examples of Roman coinage in circulation in Jesus' time. On one appears the image of Tiberius Caesar with the following superscription: TI(BERIVS) CAESAR DIVI AUGUSTI F(ILIVS) AUGVSTVS (Tiberius Caesar Augustus son of the divine Augustus). Jesus asks his interlocutors whose image and inscription are on the coin they show him. They reply that it is the emperor's. Jesus tells them to give to the emperor the things that belong to him and to God the things that belong to God.

The question intended to undermine Jesus' authority has backfired. Since the opponents know that they were created by God and indeed in God's image they knew that they belong to God and are thus, on Jesus' counsel, obliged to render themselves to God and certainly not to the image of Caesar. That would be idolatrous. In several parts of the world and particularly in Africa both the early missionaries and African Church leaders have quoted this passage to discourage Christians from participating in politics. This is a good example of how *not* to use a text from the Bible. It represents a sweeping misunderstanding of Jesus' teaching.

The Question About Resurrection from the Dead (20:27-40)

The Sadducees are mentioned for the first and last time here in Luke. They come with a mocking question intended to ridicule the teaching of Jesus, particularly on the resurrection (cf. Luke 14:14). They therefore cite a hypothetical story framed in terms of the customs of the period. The Law prescribed that if a man died childless the husband's brother would take the widow into his family (Deut 25:5-6). This is known as the levirate law (from *levir,* "husband's brother"). For the Sadducees the levirate law made belief in the resurrection ridiculous because if there is resurrection there would be struggles in heaven over women inherited by brothers.

We know very little about the Sadducees from original sources. The scanty information that we have about them comes from the writings of their opponents. According to these sources they were the conservative aristocratic party, mainly from the priestly class. An earlier priest in Israel named Zadok may be the basis for the name (1 Kings 1:8; 2:35). The Zadokites were a class of priests who had control of the priesthood through much of the Second Temple period. They accepted only the five books of Moses as Scripture and denied the doctrine of the afterlife, with its rewards and punishments beyond the grave, because they did not believe it was taught in the Torah (Josephus, *Ant.* 13.297; 18.16; *Bell.* 2.165).

Jesus in his reply says that the next existence, which has no place for death, makes marriage and remarriage irrelevant. The opponents of the resurrection have quoted the Torah to justify their case, but Jesus also quotes the Torah (Exod 3:6) to prove that death does not write *finis* to human existence. When God says: "I am the God of Abraham, the God of Isaac, and the God of Jacob" this implies that God's relationship with these patriarchs is everlasting and personal. Abraham was God's friend. While human beings may lose friends by death, God does not. It therefore follows that the dead are living and will one day share in the resurrection life that the Messiah will inaugurate. The main object of human existence is to live for God and God's glory. That is why the faithful must live on after the brief span of human life and this will be made possible through the resurrection.

In Africa belief in the existence of the world of the dead is common, though with variations here and there. In the past when kings died in some of these cultures huge graves were dug with rooms inside. Beloved wives, slaves, and servants were buried alive with these kings in the belief that they would continue to serve them in the next world as they did here. If the question put to Jesus were put to Africans in their own social contexts the answer would be that the woman belongs to the first husband. Though the woman was inherited by six men she still remains the wife of the first husband. On the day of death the departed husband or wife will be the one who will come to call and welcome the living to the heavenly home.

Christians who are not given in marriage in this life have the freedom, if they decide to make this their vocation, to model for the Church what life will be like in heaven where the resurrected will neither marry nor be given in marriage according to Luke 20:35.

The Question About the Son of David (20:41-44)

Having silenced his various opponents Jesus turns the tables and asks them an important question in relation to a popular belief about the Messiah as the son of David. Despite what some may wish to believe, Jesus was not denying his own descent from David, a matter which the NT overwhelmingly affirms (Matt 1:20; Luke 1:27; 2:4; Rom 1:3; Rev 5:5; 22:16). Nor does Jesus' statement mean that he regarded Davidic descent as totally irrelevant to the office of the Messiah. In fact the messianic hope has its origin in the promise of an eternal throne to David even though the actual Davidic dynasty came to an end in 586 B.C.E. The general belief was that the Messiah would be a king like David who would subdue nations through warfare as David did. Jesus' intention was to correct the popular notion of a warlike Messiah. The Messiah would be a far more exalted person whose eternal throne is not that of an earthly king like David but the very throne of God. The Messiah is lord of David and of the hearts and lives of all.

The Bad Example of the Scribes (20:45-47)

Luke has already recorded warnings on this subject in 11:37-54. The Savior's heart weeps over the spiritual and moral condition of the religious leaders. Specifically Jesus condemns them for using their position as teachers and interpreters of the Law to demand excessive honor and veneration from the general public. Their long prayers in public are mere camouflage to cover up their unscrupulous and hard-hearted extortion and trampling on the rights of widows. Their guilt rests on their pretended piety and false concern for the underprivileged whom they rob by inducing them to give large Temple offerings and contributions for public worship. Of course it must be emphasized that not all scribes and Pharisees were corrupt, but the fact remains that in Luke's view the majority of the religious leaders at the time of Jesus' ministry had become entangled in religious formalism that had lost its spiritual meaning. Their spiritual blindness did not allow them to recognize the dawn of a new era in the coming of Jesus.

The Poor Widow's Offering (21:1-4)

In contrast to the demeanor of the scribes and Pharisees is the example of the poor widow. In the Temple precincts were various collection boxes. Jesus is sitting nearby as various people drop in their offerings. The poor widow comes, possibly dropping a mite *(lepton)* each into two of the collection boxes. These were the least in value of all coins. The name *lepton* means "the thin one" and it is the only Jewish coin mentioned in the NT. It was less than a penny in value.

The contributions of the rich leave Jesus unmoved because they are giving from the abundance they possess and therefore no sacrifice is involved, but the widow in spite of her extreme poverty gives from the little she has to live on. As far as Jesus is concerned the giver of the smallest offering is on this occasion the biggest giver. Her gift is an outflow of a loving, willing heart that is fully surrendered to God. She goes home in faith, trusting in the faithfulness and goodness of the Lord who can supply her needs. It is not the amount that a giver gives that matters most to the Lord but the inner disposition revealed by the gift. When a person is rightly related to God in body, soul, and spirit the giving will be spontaneous and, when appropriate, sacrificial.

The Eschatological Discourse (21:5-36)

According to Luke as Jesus continues his teaching in the Temple he utters a long discourse about the fate of it as well as what is coming upon the world at the end of the age. There are different views on the origin of the discourse.

Some hold that the passage is a recollection of a lengthy discourse spoken by the Savior toward the end of his ministry about the fall of Jerusalem and the fate of the nation (see parallels in Matthew 24 and Mark 13). Another view is that it is a collection of isolated sayings of Jesus uttered at different times and fashioned into what looks like a long discourse (Fitzmyer, *Luke* 2.1323–1323). Some believe that Jesus could not have predicted the destruction of the Temple. Still others regard the discourse as an apocalyptic writing that circulated in Palestine in the first century C.E. and was taken over by the Church which represented it as being the actual words spoken by Jesus. I myself am not disposed to think well of arguments that are based merely on the presumption that any prediction ascribed to Jesus and corresponding with what actually took place later must be a *vaticinium ex eventu*.

A divination system is part of the fabric of indigenous religion and Islam. Predictions are common. While there are hundreds of fake diviners and prophets, genuine guidance is given and predictions of the future are made. Jesus and the gospels stand closer to this social world than to Western Enlightenment thought. Without question, in the mind of the gospel writers Jesus made judgments on the nation and the future (Luke 9:44-45; 12:35-48; 13:31-35; 17:20-37; 18:8; 19:11-27, 41-44; 20:9-18; cf. Matt 7:22; 10:23; 19:28; 21:44; 24:25; Mark 13). G. G. Montefiore, a Jew speaking on this issue, writes: "It is in accordance with his prophetic character that Jesus should predict the destruction of the temple. . . . It is also a mark of his originality and his elevation above the religious level of his age" (*The Synoptic Gospels,* 296).

Another issue regarding this passage is why Luke included here material similar to that in 12:35-48 and 17:20-37. The focus in Luke 21 is on the Temple. It was appropriate for Luke to wait until this point to address this issue since the Temple is in Jerusalem. However, we must return to the issue of sources. Luke is unique in some ways when compared with parallel passages in Matthew and Mark. Although Luke knew Matthew he had other sources. For Luke, Jesus' intention was not just to impart apocalyptic secrets to the disciples but to make them ready spiritually for what was ahead. As already noted, the focus is on the destruction of Jerusalem as a divine judgment rather than on specific signs of the fast-approaching end of the world. Given this focus the Lukan account forms a continuous and homogeneous prophecy of a succession of historical events, namely the persecution of the Church culminating in the destruction of Jerusalem; this last was a divine punishment that would be executed by Gentile armies (21:20-24). The presumption is that the city will be ruled by Gentiles until the overthrow of the Gentile imperial power and the final vindication of those who follow Christ. The Gentiles will be the agents of God's judgment on Jerusalem before they themselves undergo God's punishment for their wickedness. This is in accordance with the understanding of the great prophets of Israel. Luke more than Matthew or Mark tries to distinguish clearly the time of the crisis that Jesus predicted would occur within a generation (that is, his final rejection, crucifixion, and death, the persecution of the disciples, and the fall of Jerusalem) from an indeterminate period called "the times of the Gentiles." Only after the latter period would come the end and the consummation of all things (21:27-28).

The Fate of Jerusalem and the Temple, 21:5-24

It is a comment on the splendor of the Temple that leads to Jesus' prophecy of the impending destruction of Jerusalem and the Temple itself (21:5-6). Immediately afterward the disciples are warned against the advent of false messiahs (21:7-11). The warnings of 21:7-11 are as pertinent to the Church today as in the first century. A combination of famines, plagues, wars, earthquakes, and persecutions was to precede the destruction of Jerusalem. The destruction of Jerusalem must come after a period of time following the departure of Jesus. This is because God wishes to give the people the opportunity to repent through the witness of the early Church (cf. Acts 2:23, 36-38, 40). If the leaders of Jerusalem had been willing to accept their error in participating in crucifying the Son of God and acknowledged the gracious offer of forgiveness and reconciliation the nation and the Temple would have been saved. Nevertheless Christ also warns that many will not seize the opportunity to repent and the desolation that would mark the days of vengeance must come (21:20-24). Therefore as soon as the disciples notice the city being surrounded by the Gentile armies they must escape from the city. It is the day of God's judgment and they must not wait to resist it. A great disaster and suffering will befall the city and the survivors will be led away into captivity by the Gentiles; Jerusalem will remain under the control of the Gentiles until the time determined by God has passed. Since Jerusalem's leaders have become corrupt and are ready to see their Messiah executed by the hands of Gentiles, Jerusalem will be destroyed. Overrun and trodden down by the Gentiles, it will become a Gentile city and be administered according to Gentile values until their times are fulfilled.

An additional note on the Temple is necessary here. The Temple of Solomon was destroyed in 586 B.C.E. and was later rebuilt by Zerubbabel after the Babylonian captivity; but this was a relatively small and simple Temple. Herod the Great, a despot but a great lover of architecture, drew up a grand plan for the rebuilding of the Temple. Priests were trained as builders in order to avoid having the Temple built by unclean hands. The construction began in 19 B.C.E. and the final decorations were only completed in 64 C.E. under Herod Agrippa II and Albinus, but the structure was substantially completed by the time of Jesus' ministry. According to the gospel of John, when Jesus spoke around 27 C.E. construction on the Temple had lasted for forty-six years (John 2:20). The renovated Temple occupied a much larger area than Solomon's and presented a marvelous sight to pilgrims.

After months of desperate siege by the Roman armies in 70 C.E. Jerusalem fell. During the siege the inhabitants suffered terribly. Jesus says "Woe to those who are pregnant and to those who are nursing infants in those days" (21:23). The fall of Jerusalem brought an end to the Jewish nation for nearly two thousand years. In 132 C.E. an insurrection led by a messianic pretender called Bar Kokhba led to a devastating destruction of the city by the Romans. Emperor Hadrian then made it permanently a "pagan" city and renamed it Aelia Capitolina, a name combining his own name Aelius and Capitolinus, the title of Jupiter whose shrine he built on the Temple mount. From the time of Constantine the city came under the rule of Christians but was overrun by Muslims in 637 C.E. under Omar. Today the Muslim sanctuary, the Dome of the Rock, stands on the Temple mount. It was only in one of the wars of the late twentieth century that Jews regained control of the city. If Jesus indeed predicted the fall of the city the prediction was amazingly and totally fulfilled (cf. Josephus, *Bell.* 5.14; 6.9).

The Coming of the Son of Man, 21:25-36

The focus of the discourse now shifts from the fall of Jerusalem to the coming of the Son of Man. The scene of the last days is described in vivid apocalyptic language and imagery. What Jesus is certainly saying is that there will be sudden and violent changes in creation that will lead to the emergence of a new order. The strange occurrences will plunge humankind into panic, dread, commotion, and fear. People will realize that strange things are happening without really understanding what will soon befall the earth and humanity in general. Men and women will become desperate, filled with terror and anxiety as a result of the alarming convulsive changes (signs) in the stars, sun, and moon. In the midst of this distress the Son of Man will appear in glory, that is, in royal power and majesty. The command "stand up and raise your heads" is peculiar to Luke (21:28). Jesus tells his followers not to panic when they see these strange signs occurring; rather they should regard the signs as a prelude to the redemptive final consummation of the salvation worked by Christ on the cross.

These verses are closely linked with the OT and are related to the apocalyptic tradition found in the prophet Daniel and in the book of Revelation. For this reason some scholars question the authenticity of the passage as coming from the earthly Jesus. But a close study of the gospels reveals that Jesus must have spoken of the coming of the Son of Man in terms of Dan 7:13 and the apocalyptic literature of his day. Jesus appears to have regarded Himself as that Son of Man. The appearance of clouds often indicates divine presence (cf. Luke 9:34) but here, as in Daniel, it may refer to a means of heavenly transport for the coming Son of Man.

Parable of the Fig Tree (21:29-33)

Jesus then told the Parable of the Fig Tree to stress the certainty of the coming of the Son of Man. The parable can be found in a similar form in all the synoptic gospels. To the reference to the fig tree Luke adds "and all the trees." Just as the appearance of leaves on fig trees shows that summer is at hand, so also the occurrence of these signs is a pointer to the approach of the advent of the kingdom. Luke 21:32 has occasioned great difficulty as to the correct interpretation of the phrase "this generation." The word *genea* ("generation") can mean descendants of a common ancestor, a race, a stock, or people living at a particular period or born at the same time. Thus we see that this word has considerable flexibility of usage. If it is taken as a reference to the contemporaries of Jesus it would mean that the things spoken by Jesus would come to pass before the majority, or at least the last of his hearers had died. Clearly within a generation Jerusalem was destroyed (70 C.E.). If the reference is to a race this would mean that Israel as a race would survive as a people until the coming of the Son of Man or that the fall of Jerusalem would not be decisive and final for the Jewish people. The nation of Israel like new fig leaves would rise again and have a share in the final salvation and redemption of the children of God. Most scholars, however, take it as a reference to what Jesus had earlier said about the fall of Jerusalem

In 21:33 Jesus stresses the absolute certainty of his predictions. He does not speak merely as did the OT prophets who had temporary access to God's presence, but as one possessing absolute authority, like God. "Heaven and earth will pass away, but my words will not pass away" refers to the enduring validity of the words of Jesus now and in the coming ages. Jesus as the eternal Son of God is not just a foreteller of the course of history but its origin, purpose, meaning, and goal.

Exhortation to Watch (21:34-38)

In most parts of Africa today people flock to churches where prophetic oracles form a major part of worship. In the West interest in various oracular ways of determining one's fate remains popular despite widespread secularism. People want to know what will happen next in their lives. Jesus did not predict the end of Jerusalem and the triumph of the people of God in order to satisfy people's curiosity about God's program for the centuries to come. His aim was to challenge his followers to true repentance, vigilance, and holy living in readiness for the coming of the Son of Man. Unlike the fall of Jerusalem that affected only the Jewish state, the coming of the Son of Man will affect the whole earth and determine the eternal fate of every human. Therefore every follower of Jesus must be on guard against sin and worldly pleasures that may cause the heart to stray from the path of righteousness even in the face of the severe persecutions that Christ's disciples may suffer.

Luke 21:37-38 concludes Luke's account of Jesus' teachings during the last week in Jerusalem. Though the leaders of Jerusalem were strongly opposed to Jesus they dared not arrest him in the Temple because the ordinary people wanted to hear him. Until the moment of his arrest the people hear Jesus gladly.

The Major Betrayal (22:1-6)

The Passover feast and the feast of Unleavened Bread refer to the same festival lasting seven days, from the fifteenth to the twenty-first of Nisan (March/April). All the evangelists agree that the crucifixion took place during this feast. Since the Jewish authorities knew that Jesus would attend the feast it became an opportunity for them to plan how to eliminate Jesus as a messianic claimant. Some regard the story of the betrayal by Judas as legendary. It is probable, however, that Luke's account is based on an original story of Judas's treachery. The four gospels are unanimous in saying that Judas Iscariot betrayed Jesus.

In the plot against Jesus only the priests and scribes, two of the three groups that composed the Sanhedrin, are mentioned. The elders, a third group, are not mentioned but they do serve as accomplices in the arrest of Jesus in 22:52. By the time of Jesus Jerusalem usually hosted many pilgrims and the atmosphere at Passover was always explosive. This was why the Jerusalem authorities were seeking for a way of secretly arresting Jesus without provoking a riot. Judas's action provided the perfect opportunity for them to act. Judas was probably an enthusiastic disciple who had expected Jesus to assume kingship in Jerusalem by driving out all foreign rulers and their armies. Like most other disciples he had hoped to play a key role in the messianic kingdom. He became the treasurer for the group though in the gospel of John he is portrayed as dishonest (John 12:4-6). Was Judas a sincere follower or just an opportunist who became increasingly disappointed as Jesus persistently talked more about dying than taking action to set up a messianic kingdom as they approached Jerusalem? Luke's narrative account leaves us to draw our own conclusions. Luke's own answer to the question why Judas betrayed Jesus was that Satan entered him. The early Church could do nothing but see such a momentous event as Judas's betrayal and the subsequent crucifixion of Jesus as the decisive battle in a cosmic struggle. Satan had to be behind it.

Matthew's account of the fate of Judas (Matt 27:3-10) gives some insight into his character. After Jesus was condemned to death Judas felt ashamed, returned the blood money, and hanged himself. Luke gives a different version of the same incident in Acts 1:18-19. Here it was Judas who bought land with the blood money and presumably suffered death by some kind of punitive miracle. At any rate Judas's act and fate apparently make Luke's answer: "Satan entered into [him]" an appropriate response to the question of motive. Did Judas gradually make himself a ready vessel in the devil's hand by regularly taking money from the communal treasury (John 12:6)? An African adage says: "It is a willing hand that the devil tempts to perform evil acts."

The Institution of the Lord's Supper at Passover (22:7-23)

At the outset of this unit Luke begins with Jesus' detailed instructions to his disciples to prepare for the Passover (22:7-13). The instructions given by Jesus here are similar to those regarding the triumphal entry into Jerusalem. Luke tries to show that everything, down to the last detail, takes place according to God's plan as carried out by Jesus. If it is like what obtains in most parts of Africa today, a man carrying a large water jar would be conspicuous in a situation where such duties are assigned to women. Preparations for the Passover would include the purchase of the lamb for sacrifice, the unleavened bread, the bitter herbs, and the wine, as well as the slaughtering and roasting of the lamb. The borrowed upper room must have been made ready for the feast by the landlord. There in the presence of his close followers Jesus will have the last meal before his martyrdom.

Luke's account of the Last Supper has several puzzling features. The first major issue is textual. The vast majority of the ancient manuscripts have what is known as the longer text, 22:19b-20, but there are some important ancient manuscripts that omit this section of the passage. Still, the massive testimony of ancient manuscripts supporting the inclusion of vv. 19b-20 is very impressive. Also a number of words and phrases such as "do this in remembrance of me" and "after supper" are paralleled in Paul's account in 1 Corinthians 11. In point of time Paul's letter is our oldest written source for the institution of the Lord's Supper. Luke may have been a follower of Paul; in any case he probably received his information on this event from the same source as Paul, or a similar one.

Another objection that has been raised against the text of 22:19b-20 is that it speaks about the death of Jesus as an atoning sacrifice. It is alleged that this is not typical of Luke's theology. This, however, is not a decisive argument against accepting 22:19b-20 as the genuine text. Luke does use atonement terminology elsewhere with respect to the death of Jesus (cf. Acts 20:28). Luke tends to see the whole event of Jesus' death and resurrection as a saving event. As the Old Covenant was ratified by blood (Exod 24:1-8) the New Covenant was ratified by Jesus' own blood as an everlasting covenant that cannot be broken (Luke 22:20). The Messiah will inaugurate the New Covenant through his death. The whole meal echoes the old Exodus when God liberated the people of Israel from slavery and they became free people of God to enter into covenant relationship with God. The Last Supper therefore points to redemption from slavery to sin and death as well as the creation of a new community in which the reign of God is to be established pending its consummation at the coming of the Messiah.

The entire meal reminds us of the sanctity of oriental customs. When people break bread together in the East a solemn pledge of love, affection, and mutual concern is set up between the participants. This pledge cannot be broken or marred by forgetfulness, betrayal, or distance. In similar fashion covenant making is paramount in Africa. It is what keeps societies together and governs inter-personal relationships as well as international relations. Above all it governs the relationship between the human and the Creator. Every religious group in Africa is bound together by a covenant. Africans understand their existence and role in the community in terms of covenant relations. A covenant breaker does not bring divine wrath upon himself or herself alone but may bring down judgment on the whole community.

The new covenant in Jesus' blood inaugurates a community of redeemed children of God. The rites not only point to our present redemption but to the final consummation at the last day. The mention of two cups is not out of place. During the Passover meal wine is served several times. It is not clear at what times the words of institution were said during the meal. Could Jesus' comments belong to different periods during the meal? There was no doubt in the mind of all the synoptic evangelists that the Last Supper was a Passover meal and that Jesus' death as symbolized in the Last Supper was a perfect fulfillment of the Passover not only for Israel this time, but for the whole of humankind. "This cup that is poured out for you is the new covenant in my blood" emphasizes the significance of the death of Jesus. His death has become a means of liberation for humans from the misery of sin and separation from God and subsequent death. On the cross God achieved total liberation for humanity.

The Farewell Discourse (22:24-38)

Jesus teaches humility (22:21-30). While he has been making strenuous efforts to prepare his disciples' minds for his death and its meaning according to God's plan they are busy quarreling about how to share offices in the messianic kingdom they thought was about to be inaugurated. Their primary interest is in who will have the chief positions of power. Self-centered ambition always blinds humans to divine purpose. Self-seeking ambition always leads to spiritual presumption and intolerance. Selfishness and lust for power by politicians and tyrannical oligarchies the world over are responsible for political intolerance, persecution, oppression, and repression of opponents. This is symbolized in the attitude of the disciples as they tarry after the meal. Unlike Jesus they see leadership positions as a means of lording it over the rest of the citizens rather than as a means of serving the people loyally and sacrificially. This even happens in the Church. The two letters of Paul to the Corinthians and the letter to the Galatians reveal that there were power struggles in the primitive Church. The problem has remained with the Church until now.

Luke has framed Jesus' response to the arrogance of the disciples in the form of an after-dinner speech (22:24-38). It has a number of similarities in theme to the speech given at an earlier banquet in 14:7-35. This speech is immediately precipitated by quarreling that breaks out among the disciples after Jesus announces that he will be betrayed by one of them (22:21-24). It can only be resolved by the gift of God's humility (22:25-30). According to Jesus the kind of selfish ambition that confuses greatness with power and honor with recognition is worldly and "pagan" (22:25-26). What our world needs most is service and not arguments about precedence. Nevertheless whenever he establishes his reign the disciples will rule with him and they will judge the twelve tribes of Israel. Before then the greater among them must serve the least (22:26-27). This is the principle that distinguishes God's kingdom from that of the oligarchies of the age.

A Warning to Simon, 22:31-34

Jesus warns Simon: "Simon, Simon, listen! Satan has demanded to sift all of you like wheat." It is noteworthy that the Greek word for "you" in the phrase "Satan has demanded to sift . . . you" is plural, indicating that Jesus means that Satan demanded all the Twelve. When Jesus goes on to say "but I have prayed for you that your own faith may not fail; and you, when once you have turned back, strengthen your brothers" the Greek for "you" in both instances is in the singular. Thus Peter is clearly singled out from the rest of his brethren as the one for whom Jesus is praying that his faith will not fail, so that following his repentance he may be able to strengthen the rest of the disciples to resist Satan. The best way to understand this text is to assume that it presupposes that Peter will deny Jesus but that later Jesus' prayers for him will prevail and Peter will repent and will indeed strengthen the others. Peter's response to Jesus is pitifully overconfident: "Lord, I am ready to go with you to prison and to death!" The fall of the confident Peter remains a powerful warning to any of us who would arrogantly rely on our own strength in weathering the storms of temptation.

Why Jesus would entrust leadership to an overconfident disciple he knew would betray him three times before daybreak is a mystery. There must have been something in Peter's faith that Jesus recognized could be strengthened by prayer and that would in turn enable Peter to strengthen the faith of others. Presumably that was Peter's recognition that Jesus was the anointed servant of God (9:20). Only after Jesus' suffering, death, burial, and exaltation (cf. Isa 52:3–53:12) would the full power of this faith turn Peter around and convert the vacillating fisherman into the apostle he became.

The Purse, Bag, and Sword, 22:35-38

This section is peculiar to Luke. Jesus reminds the disciples of the previous mission when they in faith relied on a hospitable reception and were supplied (10:1-12). Now they should expect stiff opposition and will have to fend for themselves. Jesus uses the sword as an illustration of the difficult time ahead and the hostility that will soon reach a climax in the arrest and crucifixion of Jesus. In this social context it is only a situation of serious hardship that would force a man or woman to sell his or her outer garment (22:36), since this was one's primary source of warmth day and night when traveling.

This section accurately describes the critical situation in which Jesus found himself during the last night. The reference to the sword has been a source of controversy. Certainly Jesus did not expect his disciples to repel attackers by armed conflict or to spread the gospel by the use of force. This is the very antithesis of Jesus' ministry (cf. Luke 6:27; Matt 5:9). The saying also has nothing to do with armed resistance to injustice, though Jesus clearly taught that evil must be vigorously resisted. Instead of taking up weapons of war as the Zealots did, Jesus emphasized the development of perseverance that would make them willing to surrender their last possession rather than give up the struggle for the reign of God. It goes without saying that this statement does not grant the Church the right to exercise tyrannical secular and ecclesiastical authority over humankind. This would be a terrible misconstrual of the apostolic mission of servanthood to which the Church as body of Christ is called.

According to Luke this situation arose to fulfill the prediction of Isa 53:12 (Luke 22:37). Jesus is presented as the Servant of YHWH who will be counted among the lawless. This will be fulfilled when he is arrested as if he were a robber (22:52) and crucified with lawbreakers (23:32). Jesus' reply: "It is enough" reveals the total inadequacy of human resources in meeting the challenge of satanic forces. One needs a spiritual rearmament in order to face the foe.

The Prayer on the Mount of Olives (22:39-46)

Here Luke maintains the facts of an incident told by Matthew but we also notice the existence of a different source tradition. Luke's account of the struggle in the garden is brief, omitting much of what the other gospels tell. In spite of the fact that he is quite aware of the impending arrest, Jesus still goes to the Mount of Olives as is his custom, to pray. Here the garden is not named. Jesus knows quite well that Judas has gone to inform the Jewish authorities about where to find him and he goes exactly there. As they enter the garden Jesus asks the disciples to pray not to enter into temptation. Peter has assured Jesus of his loyalty and that he will fight even if it means dying but he needs to be armed with prayer, not a paltry two swords. The only weapon of sure defense and victory over the power of darkness is prayer. Jesus therefore withdraws about a stone's throw from the disciples to face all alone the final attack being launched by Satan. The verb used to describe this action means to "tear away." Jesus tore himself away from them. There is no mention of any special role played by the three disciples as we have it in Matthew and Mark and also there is no report of fear or distress on the part of the disciples. Only Luke describes Jesus as kneeling in prayer (22:41). The normal thing in the East is to stand while praying. However the OT reports a few occasions when people knelt or prostrated themselves in prayer (Josh 7:6-10; 1 Kings 8:54; 2 Chr 6:13; Ps 95:6; Dan 6:10; cf. Acts 7:60; 9:40; 20:36; 21:5; Phil 2:10; Rom 14:11).

Jesus prays that if God wills it the cup may be removed from him (22:42). A cup in the OT is a common figure of either blessing or cursing (Pss 11:6; 16:5; 23:5; 75:8; Jer 49:12). Although Jesus prays for a possible removal of the cup he yields in full obedience to the will of the Father. The most natural thing for a vigorous young man in his early thirties is to want to live. Here Satan makes the last desperate attempt to try to turn Jesus away from the path of the cross. The angel does not come to alleviate Jesus' agony but to enable him to go through it at an even deeper level. Assuming that 22:43-44 is part of the original text, the Greek word *agōnia* ("agony") is peculiar to Luke (v. 44). *Agōnia* refers to an interior concentration that characterizes athletes about to begin a race: they turn pale, tremble throughout their bodies, and perspire profusely. The word is used to describe the depth of Jesus' inner feeling and struggle. Jesus goes into Gethsemane in agony; he comes out with victory assured and with peace of heart because he has been strengthened by the Father through prayer. Alas! the disciples are asleep at this critical hour of need.

The Arrest of Jesus (22:47-53)

The way in which Judas concludes his wicked crime is in perfect keeping with its essential baseness. He leads a mob armed with swords and clubs to the garden where he knows very well that Jesus prays and betrays him with a kiss. Usually a kiss is a sign of friendship but Judas' action is a false semblance of deep affection and may even have been a prearranged signal of identification for those who seek to arrest Jesus. It is repulsive. Likewise today acts of disloyalty to the Savior are more distressing in sacred surroundings and especially among those who make protestations of love, commitment, and loyalty. Jesus refuses to be defended by the sword. For him the cross is the goal. There is no going back. According to Luke Jesus even heals the right ear of one of the attackers that was cut off by the rash and almost comical use of the sword by a disciple.

Jesus turns around to rebuke his enemies who had come against him under the cover of darkness with swords and clubs as if he were a robber or notorious criminal (22:52; cf. 22:37). He had taught openly and daily in the Temple for nearly a week, but arresting him in the dark shows the wickedness of human hearts and that his arrest could not be justified. Jesus says "this is your hour, and the power of darkness." The struggle of Satan against Christ and the clash of the two kingdoms are themes that are clearly present in Luke. In the account of the temptation only Luke reports that Satan left Jesus for a while to return later. Now the last hour has arrived when Satan is desperate to turn Jesus aside or find some way to stop him.

Peter's Denial of Jesus (22:54-62)

The four gospels contain four similar but variant accounts of Peter's denial of Jesus. The story is not complimentary to Peter. The gospels preserved it in order to show that when he needed his disciples most Jesus was left to face his fate alone, yet even in the face of betrayal by those who were closest to him Jesus remained faithful in his commitment to God.

In Matthew, Mark, and John the arrest of Jesus is followed by a nocturnal trial. In Luke the mocking of Jesus and the denial in the night are followed by an early morning trial before the Sanhedrin. There is also confusion as to whether some of the complaints are addressed directly to Peter or to the bystanders. Oral traditions and/or another source appear to have exercised some influence on Luke's account. The similarities and dissimilarities in the four accounts are an invitation to reflect on the similarities and dissimilarities in accounts we have heard or read concerning other events of importance to us. We cannot always explain why accounts of important events differ. In this respect the gospel accounts do not differ radically from life as we know it.

Since the story of Peter's denial, like all other gospel stories, circulated orally before it was written down at different Christian centers the possibility of differing accounts and versions from various perspectives is intrinsically present. Two viewers of a game or drama will never relate the story of what they have seen in exactly the same way and two hearers of a story will not relate the story to others in exactly the manner they heard the story told. It is helpful to know this about differing gospel accounts because it invites each of us to form our own opinion of what most likely happened. In this way we become excited for a good purpose. We receive encouragement to think clearly and open ourselves to creative involvement in the never-ending task of interpreting the Scriptures.

Jesus Before the Council of Elders (22:63-71)

The group of soldiers detailed to guard Jesus until a formal session of the Sanhedrin the next morning play a guessing game at his expense (22:63-65). They blindfold and hit Jesus in an attempt to provoke him to speak, since as a prophet he ought to know everything. The soldiers add insult to injury. In both Matthew and Mark the mockery, the guessing game, and the hitting are at the conclusion of the trial, just before the denial by Peter. Luke gives the most detailed of the Synoptic accounts of this incident, describing how those who captured and blindfolded Jesus taunted him because of his claim to be a prophet.

All the gospels agree that Jesus was subjected to some version of a hearing or trial by the religious authorities in Jerusalem. According to Luke this took place after Peter's denial, early in the morning. Luke designates the court as the "assembly of the elders of the people" (22:66). According to Josephus (*Ant.* 12.42) this assembly, the Sanhedrin, consisted of priests, elders, and scribes. Luke does not record any night hearing given to Jesus as reported by the other gospels but he seems to know that the betrayal and beating of Jesus took place at night. By way of contrast, in the light of day his hearing before the Sanhedrin shows Jesus to be innocent.

The hearing begins immediately with the crucial question, "If you are the Messiah, tell us," (22:67). Jesus declines to answer, presumably knowing the ambiguity of the term "Messiah" at this time. He also realizes that the council is not really interested in definitions but in his being found guilty. He then identifies himself and his mission with the enthronement of the Son of Man in Daniel 7. It is *this* Son of Man (Luke 22:69) who will soon receive authority from God to be the ruler and judge of all (Dan 7:13). From now on this council and the nation are on trial before the heavenly court headed by the Son of Man. Unlike the other synoptics Luke has Jesus' detractors then pose another question: "Are you, then, the Son of God?" Jesus again answers ambiguously: "You say that I am." This is taken to be an affirmative answer to the second question. It is all they need to condemn Jesus. By having the hearing in the day Luke's account casts a cloak of legitimacy over the proceedings.

In many regions of the world today we see ruling juntas and oppressive regimes that do not always carefully follow the laws promulgated even by themselves. In spite of the fact that there are courts set up by valid constitutional authority to try all types of cases either the courts themselves are subverted or special courts and tribunals are appointed to dispense justice in such a way as to insure the outcome of the trial. The government not only appoints the members of such tribunals, the state is the accuser and prosecutor; if found guilty the accused can only appeal to the government, which has the last say. The accused cannot appeal to a higher court even if he or she feels dissatisfied with the decision of the special court. There have even been situations where gallows or stakes for executions were made ready either before the special court made its decision known publicly or before the members of the junta have met to review the tribunal's verdict. The basic human rights to life, freedom, justice, and humane treatment are divine gifts to individuals. No one ought to deprive another fellow human being of these sacred rights. The Church in such societies has the responsibility of speaking out instead of remaining silent. Any civilized nation that claims to be governed by these principles must mobilize its efforts and resources to oppose such oppressive regimes in order to serve justice, freedom, and humane society on a global scale.

Jesus Before Roman Authorities (23:1-25)

Jesus is now handed over by the official decision of the Jerusalem authorities to the Romans. The distorted accusations leveled against Jesus before Pilate are: "We found this man perverting our nation, forbidding us to pay taxes to the emperor, and saying that he himself is the Messiah, a King." These specific charges are intended to rouse Pilate, the Roman prefect, to action. Pilate then turns to Jesus and asks: "Are you the king of the Jews?" (23:3). Jesus replies, "You say that I am."

It is alleged that Jesus was a revolutionary. In spite of the serious allegation amounting to a charge of treason Pilate is very wary (23:4). Subsequently Pilate will declare three times that he finds Jesus not guilty as charged (23:4, 14, 22). Luke and Acts function as apologetic historiography. If the representative of the Roman authority could thrice declare Jesus, the founder of the Christian movement, not guilty there was nothing politically subversive about Christianity.

Pilate's conclusions are not acceptable to the Jerusalem authorities. After Pilate has declared

Jesus innocent those authorities make desperate efforts to get Jesus convicted by bringing additional charges alleging that he is inflaming the people with his teaching, beginning in Galilee and now all over Judea (23:5). On hearing this Pilate refers the case to Herod Antipas who is in Jerusalem for the feast of Passover. Again Jesus refuses to answer all the questions put to him. Herod has been eager to see Jesus and witness some of his miracles (cf. 9:9). He has no jurisdiction in Judea but can be consulted because Jesus comes from Galilee and the offensive teaching is said to have begun there. Herod also makes no direct judgment of guilt against Jesus although he allows his soldiers to treat Jesus with contempt. Luke is telling us that legitimate Roman authority did not find Jesus guilty of treason. Nevertheless Pilate under pressure from Jerusalem authorities ultimately canes Jesus and hands him over to their will to be crucified (23:25).

Pilate was the fifth Roman prefect who ruled over Judea after the deposition of Archelaus in 6 C.E. His office lasted from 26 to 36 C.E. Pilate was notorious for cruelty and corruption, treating the people badly and executing them without proper trials. Eventually his wickedness went beyond all bounds and he was removed from office.

Crucifixion (23:26-49)

All the synoptic gospels report that Jesus was exhausted and that Simon from Cyrene in Africa, who was probably in the city for the Passover, was made to carry the cross. Only Luke relates Jesus' encounter with the wailing daughters of Jerusalem on the way to Calvary (23:27-31). They, with the people, were concerned about the cruel death sentence and seemed to be sympathetic toward the plight of Jesus. Jesus uses the occasion to remark that the true tragedy is not his fate but that of their city that is in danger of imminent destruction. This is another echo of 21:20-24.

Then Jesus was brought to Calvary (a latinization of the Hebrew Golgotha), meaning "skull" (23:33). According to legend the skull of Adam was found there. The Chapel of Adam in the Holy Sepulchre gets its name from this belief. According to the legend Christ's blood flowed on Adam's skull which is often represented at the foot of the cross. The blood of the new Adam cleanses the old Adam. The name Golgotha is a fitting anticipation of the importance of the cross for the Christian era.

Why did Jesus follow the path to Calvary? Why did he not seek to remain alive and devote himself to the elimination of all forms of wickedness and woe? Why did he submit to a cruel and shameful death? Such questions, which will always be raised by people of faith, are deepened when we see the level of mockery Jesus faced while on the cross. Luke describes Jesus being taunted three times. The Jerusalem leaders challenge him by saying: "He saved others; let him save himself if he is the Messiah of God, his chosen one!" (23:35). The soldiers who stand guard mock, saying: "If you are the King of the Jews save yourself!" (23:37). Even one of the two criminals crucified with him scornfully says "Are you not the Messiah? Save yourself and us!" (23:39). Such was the ignominy he faced. Ever since then, in every generation people have had contempt for the apparent weakness of Jesus. This has happened among leading scholars and political leaders, academics, and even some theologians. The criminal wrongly believed that the validity of Jesus' claim rested on a capacity to provide immediate personal relief, to prove that he was the Messiah. He effectively says, "conform to my demands and I will believe you" (cf. 23:39). The world has been laying down similar conditions ever since.

The first thief was not totally mistaken in thinking that the coming of Jesus entailed the realization of salvation. He was, however, wrong about how that salvation was to be achieved. It was only by Jesus' remaining on the cross and dying an ignominious death that the worst of criminals could be rescued from the consequences of sin. Today one never ceases to be amazed at the stubborn and perennial conspiracy (often nourished by some scholars) to eliminate the crucifixion from the Christian faith or at least to regard it as not an absolute necessity for human redemption. As far as they are concerned Jesus' death, if historical, was at best the supreme example of martyrdom for a noble goal. Perhaps they are unaware of the comfort these claims give to the opponents of Christianity in areas where it is not strong. Muhammad denied that Jesus died on the cross. According to Islam one of the disciples was crucified in error. While that disciple was dying Jesus was somewhere laughing at the executioners' ignorance. Islam accepts most things that the Bible says about Jesus but when it comes to claims for his divinity it stops short at the cross. This helps explain why it was possible for Muhammad to start a new religion. Once the cross, its purpose, meaning, and significance are explained away the Christian faith loses not only its vital center but also its saving power. The recurring effort on the part of some people within and outside the Church to deny the centrality of the cross and resurrection for Christian faith amounts to destroying the dynamism of that faith. According to Luke the purpose of God shown in Jesus' life transcends all human ideas, systems, and utopian schemes. The cross is God's own remedy for the human tragedy. At the final cry of Jesus on the cross the curtain of the Temple is rent from top to bottom. Through the cross the way to God is now open to all humankind. The tearing of the curtain is therefore a sign of the abrogation of the Temple rituals and its sacrifices as a means of reaching God (23:45). From now on, even though early Christian believers would continue to worship in the Temple (Acts 3:1) they believed it was only a matter of time before all this would come to an end. The tearing of the curtain was also the first indicator of the coming destruction.

Why did God demand the death of the Son as a ransom for many? This question is neither raised nor answered by Jesus. The Son is simply ready to bow to the Father's will and offer himself. Such amazing expressions of generosity as shown by Jesus toward his enemies (23:34) and the second of the two criminals (23:43) do not go unnoticed. The centurion glorifies God (23:47) and the people watching are moved to repentance (23:48). Instead of the wrenching cry of Godforsakenness that comes from Jesus' mouth in Matthew and Mark, here Jesus confidently commits his spirit to the Father (23:46).

Burial (23:50-56)

Joseph, a native of Arimathea, is a secret disciple of Jesus (Matt 27:57). He is a rich and distinguished member of the Sanhedrin. Like many pious Jews he has a family grave in the city. He did not agree with the decision to crucify Jesus. Therefore at personal risk he requests the release of Jesus' body in order to give him a decent burial. The body is wrapped with fine linen, placed in the sepulchre, and the tomb is sealed. The women disciples who had followed Jesus faithfully from Galilee and served loyally (23:49, 55; cf. 8:1-3) see the body to the grave and take notice of the tomb. Apparently they plan to return after the Sabbath to embalm the body with spices and ointment: that is, their plan is to leave in time to purchase these things before the Sabbath begins and return early on Sunday morning.

The Proclamation of the Resurrection (24:1-12)

Luke's resurrection account takes place within the span of one glorious day (24:1, 13, 29). It is marked by the appearance to the women, the Emmaus incident, the appearance of Jesus to the Twelve, and the mission charge. This unit begins with the visit of the women to the tomb carrying ointments for the embalming of Jesus' body. The names of the women are not the same in any two gospels. The three synoptics agree on Mary of Magdala and Mary the mother of James and John, but in John only Mary of Magdala is mentioned. In Mark a third woman named Salome is listed while a third woman in Luke is Joanna. At any rate the women enter the tomb on their own initiative and discover it empty. In Matthew and Mark they are invited by angels to see the empty tomb. In Luke it is after they have discovered the tomb empty that they encounter two men (that is, angels: cf. 9:30). The angels announce that Jesus is risen. Full of excitement, the women do not keep the news to themselves but make a full report to the male disciples. Luke 21:12 is missing from Codex Bezae and Old Latin manuscripts. Some scholars feel that it is an interpolation based on John 20:3-10, but there are notable differences in the language. The verse makes sense in context and is needed to explain Luke 24:34. Luke is faithful to the tradition that Jesus first appeared to Peter.

The Walk to Emmaus (24:13-35)

Jesus' appearance to the two disciples on the way to Emmaus is the longest single post-resurrection appearance narrative in the gospels. In many ways it functions as a kind of counterpoint to the appearance of Jesus to Mary of Magdala in John. There is a brief allusion to the same incident in the longer ending of Mark (16:12-13); nevertheless the account is unique to Luke. Alfred Plummer refers to it as "the most beautiful of the treasures which he alone has preserved for us." He believes that Luke received the tradition directly from an eyewitness account and that the narrator was probably Cleopas (Plummer, *Commentary,* 552). Late in the afternoon on the day of the resurrection Jesus mysteriously joins two disciples on the road to Emmaus, which is about eleven kilometers from Jerusalem. They take Jesus to be a pilgrim from Jerusalem who must have witnessed the events of recent days or at least heard about them. Jesus feigns ignorance about what they are discussing and asks them why they are sad. In turn they then narrate how the Jewish leaders killed Jesus by crucifixion. He was a prophet great in mighty works and preaching. The theme of Jesus as prophet, so strong in Luke, thus reemerges (cf. 4:14-30, 7:16). But the disciples are deflated. They had hoped that this would be the man who would redeem *(lutrousthai)* Israel. This hope has been shattered by his death. For many Jews the concept of redemption meant a conquering Messiah who would set up a world-empire kingdom dominated by the leaders of Israel. That had not come to pass. The disciples conclude their story by saying that they were astonished by the report of certain women who claimed that the tomb was empty in the early hours of the morning. Some disciples at once went to the tomb and confirmed the women's story although the two had not seen Jesus himself. The story sounded like an idle tale to them.

Jesus begins to expound the Scriptures to them. The point is very significant because all along Luke has striven to say that from the beginning Jesus fulfilled the (scriptural) expectations of the people of God (Luke 1:1). In short, in Jesus' life, death, and resurrection he has fulfilled the Jewish hopes for the Messiah. Luke 24:22-23 is reminiscent of Peter's speech on the day of Pentecost (Acts 2:22-23). Luke 24:27 also anticipates the OT apologetic of the early Church. On arrival at Emmaus the two disciples persuade their companion to prepare to spend the night with them. At the meal table the companion without explanation assumes the role of the head of the family. He takes bread, gives thanks, breaks it, and gives it to them. It is at this stage, after the Scriptures have been explained and bread broken, that the disciples realize that the companion is Jesus himself. Such stories of hospitality to supernatural beings unaware are common in the Bible (Gen 18:1-8; 19:1-3; Judg 13:8-20; Heb 13:2). Among several communities in Africa stories of departed people appearing to relations who are not yet aware of their death within the first few days after their actual dying are common. This is not exactly the same as the Emmaus story, but in many social contexts in Africa the strange appearance of Jesus on the way to Emmaus would appear perfectly intelligible.

Indeed, the belief that death does not write *finis* to one's life is universal. Yet as arresting as the form of the account may be the critical point that Luke makes should not be overlooked. To those who would listen Jesus explains the real message of the prophets (24:25). The essence of that message is that the Messiah must suffer and die before he enters glory (24:26). Thus the death of the Messiah was not an accident: it was fully in keeping with the purpose of God (24:27).

Final Appearance and Farewell (24:36-53)

This passage apparently reduces to one tradition what were several traditions in Johannine circles. It appears to be a combination of the appearances to the disciples without Thomas, another appearance to the disciples (including Thomas), and still another epiphany to the seven disciples at the sea of Galilee (John 20:19-29; 21). Perhaps Luke received these as a complete unit of tradition. The later tradition in John is set in Galilee. Luke, on the other hand, locates all the appearances in Jerusalem.

Luke 24:36-43 is distinguished by a tendency to show through the narrative that Jesus' resurrection existence is far more than an apparition. The passage has some highly apologetic coloring. The risen Christ invites his disciples to touch his body deliberately to convince them that he is not a ghost but a figure of "flesh and bones" (v. 39). This seems to stand in some tension with the earliest appearance account in 1 Cor 15:1-7 and Paul's concept of a *pneumatikon sōma* (1 Cor 15:44-46). The disciples are not only invited to touch but to watch the risen Lord eating a meal of fish.

There is no doubt that both Luke and John agree that the resurrected body of Jesus was no longer subject to physical limitations but they try to emphasize its solid corporeal nature (cf. Acts 10:36-43). Normally the wider Greco-Roman society thought of reality in abstract terms based on universal truths, but for the Jews reality is always particular and concrete. Therefore for the resurrection to be real the risen Jesus must walk, talk, and eat as he had done in the earthly life. Most traditional Africans would think of reality in this way. For the Jews a disembodied spirit could be nothing but a ghost or apparition. Materialistic imagery therefore had to be used in order to demonstrate the reality of the resurrection. The early Church was faced with the heresy of Docetism that denied the reality of the human life of Jesus and taught that "the Christ" came upon Jesus at baptism and departed just before the crucifixion. The threat of some early version of proto-Docetism seems to be behind Luke's concern to show that the humanity of Jesus Christ was genuine.

The final section of the gospel reveals Luke's understanding of salvation history (22:44-53). Again he sees the OT history of salvation coming to perfection in Christ. God not only vindicated the Messiah but through his resurrection is bringing salvation to humankind. Luke tries to reconcile the idea of a conquering Messiah and the Suffering Servant. Before Jesus could become an all-conquering Messiah he must fulfill the role of the Suffering Servant. The risen Lord now commissions the Church to proclaim that through the cross and resurrection God is extending the forgiveness of sins and salvation to all nations (v. 47) but the disciples must remain in Jerusalem for the descent of the Holy Spirit before the proclamation of the gospel begins. Unlike what we have in the other gospels, in Luke the proclamation of the gospel message is destined to commence in Jerusalem rather than Galilee.

Luke is unclear at what time the events of 24:50-53 took place. Acts 1:1-2 seems to intimate it was some time after Easter Sunday. Luke begins his gospel in the Temple (1:5) and ends it in the Temple (24:53). The Messiah has come and brought about the restoration of Israel. With this work complete the one who is both the new Elijah and greater than Elijah takes his place with the heavenly Father (24:51).

BIBLIOGRAPHY

Bock, Darrell. *Luke.* Grand Rapids: Zondervan, 1996.

Carddock, Fred. *Luke.* Louisville: John Knox, 1990.

Fitzmyer, Joseph A. *The Gospel According to Luke.* 2 vols. AB 28, 28A. Garden City, N.Y.: Doubleday, 1981.

Ford, J. Massyngberde. *My Enemy is My Guest: Jesus and Violence in Luke.* Maryknoll, N.Y.: Orbis, 1984.

Geldenhuys, Johannes Norval. *Commentary on the Gospel of Luke.* Foreword by F. F. Bruce. NIC.NT. Grand Rapids: Eerdmans, 1960.

Goulder, Michael D. *Luke: A New Paradigm.* 2 vols. JSNT.S 20. Sheffield: Sheffield Academic Press, 1989.

Johnson, Luke Timothy. *The Gospel of Luke.* SP 3. Collegeville: The Liturgical Press, 1991.

Marshall, I. Howard. *The Gospel of Luke.* Grand Rapids: Eerdmans, 1983.

McNicol, Allan J., ed., with David L. Dungan and David B. Peabody. *Beyond the Q Impasse: Luke's Use of Matthew.* Valley Forge, Pa.: Trinity Press International, 1996.

Montefiore, Claude G. *The Synoptic Gospels.* 2 vols. 2nd rev. ed. New York: Ktav, 1968.

O'Toole, Robert F. *The Unity of Luke's Theology: An Analysis of Luke–Acts.* Good News Studies. Wilmington, Del.: Michael Glazier, 1984.

Plummer, Alfred. *A Critical and Exegetical Commentary on the Gospel According to St. Luke.* ICC. 5th ed. Edinburgh: T & T Clark, 1969.

Ravens, David. *Luke and the Restoration of Israel.* JSNT.S 119. Sheffield: Sheffield Academic Press, 1995.

Talbert, Charles H. *Reading Luke: A Literary and Theological Commentary on the Third Gospel.* New York: Crossroad, 1982.

Tannehill, Robert C. *Luke.* Abingdon New Testament Commentaries. Nashville: Abingdon Press, 1996.

Tyson, Joseph B., ed. *Luke–Acts and the Jewish People: Eight Critical Perspectives.* Minneapolis: Augsburg, 1988.

John

Teresa Okure

Introduction

The New Testament (NT) canon has four gospels: Matthew, Mark, Luke, and John. Syllabi of theological institutions and seminaries focus more on the first three (synoptic) gospels than on the fourth. Most people read John only in the context of the liturgy. Sometimes the pastor dreads parts of this gospel when they appear in the liturgical cycle (for example, John 6, read on four consecutive Sundays [17 to 21] in Ordinary Time, Year B, and Friday of the Second Week of Easter to Saturday of the Third Week of Easter). While the synoptic gospels are full of stories, parables, anecdotes, cures, and memorable sayings of Jesus, John's gospel seems to delight in monotonous discourses and has comparatively few stories. Its language is boring, its vocabulary limited and repetitive. The Jesus of John's gospel talks mostly about himself as opposed to the Jesus of the synoptics who proclaims the reign of God. On the whole the Fourth Gospel seems to move in a world of its own, removed from the world of the rest of the NT, and removed even farther from the world of the contemporary reader.

On the other hand certain sayings in John are memorable and have become household words in the liturgy (1:29; 20:19c), in such prayers as the Angelus (1:14), the fifth eucharistic acclamation (20:28), and among Christians of the charismatic renewal (cf. 3:3, 5), in missionary consciousness (3:16-17; 10:16; 20:21), and in ecumenism (17:20-23). The gospel is also rich in vivid imagery and scenes that have inspired many artists: the wedding at Cana (2:1-11), the woman at the well (4:7-26), the anointing at Bethany (12:1-8), the washing of the feet (13:1-11), the vine and the branches (15:1-8), the Good Shepherd (10:7-18), and Jesus' resurrection encounter with Mary Magdalene (20:11-18).

In research circles scholars see John's gospel as an enigma. There are unresolved questions about its origin, authorship, layers of composition, intended audience, and relationship to the synoptic gospels and Johannine epistles.

Thus John's gospel appears to be the simplest of the four gospels, yet the most difficult to comprehend. Why is this so? This commentary does not provide the answers; rather it seeks to assist the pastoral reader to enter into the mystery of the gospel, not by attempting to resolve all its problems but by feeling at home in it and appropriating its life-giving message. The commentary provides guidelines for this purpose. It presupposes that the reader already has a loving personal contact with the gospel. It also presupposes that the reader will look up the references given in each section of the commentary and supplement them with references from other sources. The First Reading deals with general questions on the gospel; the Second Reading invites the reader to undertake a more in-depth study of the gospel itself.

FIRST READING

The Gospel Itself

1. The Purpose of the Gospel

John's gospel, like all NT books, was written to meet the pastoral needs of a given audience.

Its unique content, style, and language are inspired and shaped by the peculiar pastoral problems of the Johannine audience. We do not know today the exact identity of this audience and its social location, but John 20:30-31 states why the gospel was written. This passage, therefore, holds the master key for understanding the gospel and the dispositions it seeks to inculcate in the reader. It also invites one to perceive through an attentive reading the faith problems the Johannine audience would have had and to which the gospel seeks, in its declared evangelistic purpose, to bring a christological solution.

The reader is now invited to read this passage carefully, take possession of this key, keep and use it judiciously to unlock the rich treasures of the gospel. This entails listening to the voice of the evangelist addressing both the individual personally and his or her faith community in the "you" (plural) of v. 31, inviting and persuading the readership in every episode to let the gospel minister its own life-giving, faith-based knowledge of Jesus to each person and community.

From this key passage one may draw the following clues or guidelines for its comprehension:

(a) The gospel is consciously written as a "book" (20:30; 21:25), not simply communicated orally. Its unique literary features are, therefore, important for its meaning.

(b) The complete meaning of the gospel lies in the book as a whole, not in isolated passages. Therefore to get its full meaning one needs to read this "book" from cover to cover. Each new episode recalls the testimony of Jesus' previous interactions with his audience, adds to and strengthens the witness to him for a life-giving faith. This cumulative memory of the witnesses to Jesus constitutes a strong foundation on which the reader's faith is based.

(c) The events narrated in the gospel about Jesus are deliberately selective, not comprehensively told. The author assumes a fuller knowledge of the Jesus traditions on the part of the intended reader. Such knowledge is found today more in the synoptic gospels than in the rest of the NT and finally in the living tradition of the Church. The modern reader needs this knowledge for a fuller comprehension of the gospel.

(d) The events narrated are deliberately called "signs." A sign points to a reality other than itself (a road sign to a place is not the place itself), but one needs to know the significance of the sign and follow it if one is to arrive at the desired goal or destination. The "signs" Jesus works in the gospel have an intrinsic connection to his claims (for example, giving sight to the blind and being the light of the world); hence they serve as reliable pointers to be followed in faith if one is to arrive at true knowledge of him and his saving mission.

(e) The gospel was written by a believer for other believers, either to strengthen the faith of those who already believed or to inspire belief in new converts. Christians today also need faith to fully comprehend the gospel.

(f) The primary mode of the gospel is persuasive. The evangelist exhorts the reader to listen with the heart to the total witness (19:35; 21:24) given about Jesus in the gospel, in order to believe in and gain eternal life from him.

(g) All the events narrated in the gospel have this one purpose, to persuade the reader to believe and confess along with others that Jesus is God's Son and Christ, sent by God out of love for the world, to give enduring life to those who believe in him. Every episode in the gospel is an attempt to elaborate this thesis.

2. Literary Genre

John's "book" is classified as a "gospel." Though the term "gospel" exists outside Christian literature, its distinctive usage as a genre is uniquely Christian. It applies specifically to the account of Jesus' origin, both divine (1:1-2, 18) and human (1:14, 45), his Galilean and Judean ministry, his passion, death, and resurrection, and his commissioning of his Spirit-filled disciples to proclaim this good news to the whole world (20:21-23).

In ancient literature the Hebrew and Greek words translated "gospel" in English expressed fundamentally a message of deliverance and salvation for the recipients. Basically it meant the defeat of an attacking enemy, deliverance from oppression (as in a state of siege) and the consequent removal of the threat to life. Such news of victory was normally brought with great speed and joy by a messenger or town crier to an anxiously waiting citizenry. It gave rise to public, jubilant celebrations among such liberated citizens (cf. Isa 52:7-12).

In John's gospel the evangelist is the messenger or town crier who brings the good news of

Jesus and his "victory over the world" for humanity (16:33; 19:30). The evangelist invites the reader to welcome and celebrate this victory by believing in Jesus and his saving mission. It is through believing that the reader personally takes hold of this good news that is Jesus himself (20:31). In other words, faith in Jesus proclaimed in the gospel constitutes the reader's victory over the world (cf. 1 John 5:5), that is, over sin and death (cf. John 3:16-17; 5:24; 6:40, 47; 10:28; 11:25-26).

For John, Jesus is the Good News because he liberates people from all death-dealing forces that oppress humanity and constitute the real threat to true (eternal) life. The heart of this good news is found in such passages as 3:16; 10:10; and 11:52. Believers today are to make this gospel their own good news by identifying the death-dealing forces and their concrete manifestations in their own social locations and by applying their faith in Jesus to eradicate them (cf. 20:21).

In order to interact better with this commentary the reader is invited to reread the whole gospel prayerfully, if possible in one sitting. This reading gives one a first-hand acquaintance with the gospel. It will enable the reader to approach this commentary with his or her own set of questions and so be able to dialogue better, even critically with the commentary. In this reading it is advisable not to dwell on problematic passages. The point of the exercise is to familiarize oneself afresh with the gospel as a whole and personally to hear the voice of the evangelist proclaiming the good news of Jesus, "the Christ, the Son of God" (20:30-31).

3. Structure and Outline of the Gospel

To speak of the structure of the gospel is to speak of a map that helps one to become aware of the interrelationship of its parts or to identify how its different sections hold together to form one harmonious whole. As with a map, structures are useful depending on one's starting point and final destination. Any structure adopted at a given time enables one to go through the gospel by a different road and thus to see a different perspective each time.

Of the many suggestions made for defining the structure of the Fourth Gospel, the most popular is that of a "Book of Signs" (1:19–12:50) and a "Book of Glory" (13:1–20:31), with 1:1-18 as Prologue and 21:1-25 as Epilogue. But Jesus' alpha sign recorded in 2:1-11 also reveals his glory, and the resurrection itself is the omega sign given by Jesus himself (cf. 8:28; 20:8, 24-29). A related suggestion views chs. 1–12 as "revelation of glory to the world" (that is, to outsiders), and chs. 13–20 as "revelation of glory to disciples" (but cf. 2:11).

The classical rhetorical framework of the gospel can also serve as a basis for its structuring. In this proposal the parts would be: *exordium* or introduction (ch. 1), *narratio* or presentation of the facts about Jesus (chs. 2–12), *expositio* or detailed explanation of the significance of the facts presented (chs. 13–17), *probatio* or presentation of the final evidence in support of the claims made by and for Jesus (chs. 18–20), and *demonstratio* or illustration of the significance of these claims for the disciples or believing community (ch. 21).

Since structure is determined by one's hermeneutical approach, the reader may want to work out his or her own structure as a way of gaining a comprehensive yet interrelated grasp of the gospel. Such a structure could be based on the major feasts mentioned in the gospel (2:13; 5:1; 6:4; 7:2; 10:22; 13:1), on Jesus' different journeys to Jerusalem and Judea (2:13; 5:1; 7:10; 11:7), or the major geographical locations where he carries out his mission (Galilee, 1:19–2:12; Judea, 2:13–3:36; Samaria, 4:1-42; Galilee, 4:43-54; Judea, 5:1-47; Galilee, 6:1-71; Judea, 7:1–20:29; Galilee, 21:1-19). The reader may also find useful the outline given in the second part of this commentary. Studying the gospel by using a different structure each time could prove a most creative and fruitful way of getting to know and love the whole gospel with its inexhaustible treasures.

4. Literary Characteristics

In keeping with its declared literary character, John's gospel employs many literary devices to communicate his message. The most striking of these devices are listed here for the benefit of the reader.

a. Classical Rhetorical Features

Rhetoric in the ancient world dealt with the art of persuasion or arguing with an opponent as in a forensic (court) setting in order to win over an audience or refute the charges of an accuser. In his attempt to persuade the reader to believe in Jesus the evangelist uses some of these rhetorical features. Notable among them is disputation. Jesus is often projected arguing with his opponents and answering their charges against him. This feature is most prominent in chs. 5–10 where Jesus is constantly at loggerheads with the Jewish leaders, especially over his claim to be Son of God and thus equal to God (5:16-18), even going so far as to claim the divine name (8:58). This forensic background accounts for the dominant use in the gospel of many terms found in law court settings:

- witnesses to Jesus' claims (e.g., 5:31-40; 14:26-27). These witnesses corroborate the claims he makes of himself or that others make for him.
- the "signs" Jesus works (e.g., 2:11, 18, 23; 6:2, 14, 26, 30; 7:31; 9:16; 11:47; 12:18, 37; 20:20). These "signs," also called "works" (5:36; 7:21; 9:3; 10:25, 32, 37-38; 14:10-12; 15:24), constitute concrete, verifiable evidence of his claims to divine ontological sonship. Notably, the materials used for these signs leave no room for one to mistake their explicit sign character and divine origin (e.g., the water turned into wine is that used for purification, not for drinking, 2:6; the illness of the paralytic lasted thirty-eight years and proved impossible to cure even in a miraculous setting, 5:5, 7; the man given sight was born blind, 9:1 (something unheard of in the history of the world, 9:32); Lazarus, who was raised to life, had been dead and buried for four, not the normal three, days, 11:39). The most conclusive of the signs is the resurrection (cf. 2:18-22; 20:28-30).
- Other clusters of forensic features include the vocabulary of judging and judgment (cf. 3:17-19; 5:22, 24, 27, 30; 7:24, 51; 8:15, 16, 20, 50; 12:31, 47, 48; 16:8, 11), of accusation (cf. 5:45; 8:6; 18:29), and even of the Spirit as Advocate or Paraclete (14:16, 26; 15:26; 16;7). In these latter instances the forensic setting applies not only to Jesus but also to his disciples who after his departure will receive the same treatment from the world (chs. 14–16).
- In other settings (that is, when the encounters are not of the law court type) the evangelist employs persuasive rhetorical devices such as the deliberative and demonstrative types used mainly for teaching (e.g., 3:3-21; 4:31-38, 39-42; chs 13–17) and the philosophical type characterized by appeal and persuasion (e.g., 4:7-26). Other rhetorical features scattered through the gospel include the use of techniques of persuasive preaching, drama with its emotive, aesthetic, or artistic aspects (drama was a handmaid of rhetoric in Hellenistic schools), and the very selectivity of the gospel material itself (20:30).

b. Misunderstanding and Irony

These two features are closely related though one may be seen as the opposite of the other. In misunderstanding, Jesus uses a concept that has both a natural and a spiritual or figurative meaning. His dialogue partners understand the meaning exclusively in the natural or literal sense while Jesus intends the spiritual or figurative one (e.g., the Temple, 2:19-21; birth from above, 3:3-8; living water, 4:10-15; Jesus' food, 4:31-34; the bread from heaven, 6:32-34; the going away of Jesus, 7:33-35; slavery and freedom, 8:31-36; the sleep of Lazarus, 11:11-12; his resurrection 11:23-24; the way to the Father, 14:4-6). In each case the misunderstanding enables Jesus to explain further the spiritual or figurative meaning intended.

In instances of irony, on the other hand, Jesus' dialogue partners make a statement about him that they intend in a derogatory or sarcastic manner or that inadequately expresses his identity, but the reader knows that these statements are more true or more meaningful than the speaker intends or realizes (e.g., a teacher from God, 3:2; greater than Jacob, 4:12; greater than Abraham, 8:53, 57-58; dying for the nation, 11:49-51; the kingship of Jesus, 19:3, 14, 19, 21). Through the use of irony the evangelist takes the reader into confidence as an insider who possesses a knowledge of Jesus' true identity that Jesus' dialogue partner lacks.

c. Twofold Level of Meaning

Some concepts used in the gospel have a twofold level of meaning, the meaning that would have been understood by Jesus' audience (the primary historical level), and the meaning that would have been given to them by the evangelist's post-Easter Christian audience (the secondary historical level). This applies in particular to such concepts as birth from above, referring to baptism (3:3-8), the hour that is coming but now is (4:23; 5:25), the living water (4:10, 14; 7:38) explicitly interpreted as referring to the Spirit (7:39), and the bread of life that is the Eucharist (6:35-38).

Sometimes the evangelist uses a word that has two meanings in the original Hebrew or Greek, exploiting both meanings simultaneously by playing on the words (e.g., wind, Spirit, 3:8; being lifted up, 3:14; 8:28; 12:32, 34; judgment/condemnation, 3:17).

John's gospel is deliberately cast on two levels of meaning. The most important level is that of the post-Easter audience for whom the gospel was intended. This audience stood removed from events that took place at the level of Jesus and his audience (cf. 20:30-31) and was thus expected to see in them a deeper significance than Jesus' Jewish audience would have done.

To this must be added a third level, the meaning at the level of readers over the centuries up to today in their different sociocultural and historical contexts. Though the message of the gospel remains unchanged, its application and nuances of meaning vary according to the different contexts in which it is read. The gospel itself as we now have it was influenced and enriched by the context in which it was written. Contemporary readers in their different sociocultural locations and with their different hermeneutical problems have the task of enriching the meaning of the gospel for themselves and others.

d. Narrating Events Before Situating or Identifying Them

Often the evangelist gives a geographical detail or the context of an event after narrating it (cf. 1:28, 39c; 4:54; 5:9b; 6:59; 8:20; 10:22; 19:20b, 31). This has the effect of making the reader focus attention first on the universal significance of the events narrated rather than on their location. On the other hand, the detail coming last gives this universal message its historical and geographical moorings and in some instances helps to move the narrative forward.

e. Inclusion

In this literary feature a word or concept mentioned at the beginning of a passage or section is repeated at the end of the same passage or section for emphasis (cf. lamb of God, 1:29, 36; Cana of Galilee, 2:1, 11, 4:46; 21:2; the place of John's baptism, 1:28; 10:40; Jesus and his mother, 2:1, 4, 19:25, 26; nonarrival of the hour of Jesus, 2:4, 7:30; 8:20; its eventual coming, 12:23; 13:1; 17:1). Sometimes this tying together of ideas and motifs spans wide sections of the gospel (e.g., 1:28, 10:40; / 2:1, 21:2; / 2:4, 19:26). These links serve as lampposts to the readers as they peruse the gospel; they invite one to be alert to the cumulative meaning and interconnectedness of the events narrated (for example, in 6:11 and 21:13).

f. From Dialogue to Proclamation

A remarkable feature of the gospel is that Jesus often begins a conversation with individuals or a group, but as the conversation progresses the audience seems to fade into the background. This has given the impression that Jesus' dialogue partners are simply foils or an excuse for him or the evangelist to impart his teaching, meaning that the conversations are not real. The feature has been attributed to the work of an editor who combined originally independent speeches. But viewed theologically the technique could be inspired by the fact that the revelation brought by Jesus cannot be communicated fully or even solely by dialogue. There comes a point at which the ideas and concepts known to the human dialogue partner become inadequate as a medium of the revealed message. At that point the conversation moves from dialogue to proclamation. The hearer is left with the choice of accepting or rejecting the message, knowing well the personal consequences of the decision (cf. 3:1-8, 19-21; / 4:31, 32-38; / 5:10-16, 17-47; / 6:25-34, 35-40; / 6:41-42, 43-51; / 6:53, 54-58; / 9:41; 10:1-18). This feature is an integral part of the didactic nature of the gospel.

g. Repeated Speeches

Some speeches of Jesus in the gospel are duplicated, at times almost word for word or verse by verse (3:31-36; 5:26-30), at other times only by echoes (5:31-32, 37-38; 8:13-18). This feature is particularly noticeable in the long discourse on the Eucharist (ch. 6) and in the farewell discourses (chs. 13–17). Again the feature could be explained as due to editorial work. The editor, finding separate fragments of the same speech, tried to preserve both at appropriate places. But in most cases the words repeated have a different nuance of meaning in the different contexts. The reader will gain by paying attention to the specific contexts in which such verses, motifs, or echoes occur.

h. Aporias or Apparent Breaks in the Gospel

The attentive reader notices what appear to be abrupt breaks or lack of geographical and chronological sequence in certain parts of the gospel. The most notable is the sudden switch from "Jerusalem" in Judea where events in ch. 5 take place to "the other side of the Sea of Galilee" in 6:1, whereas 7:1 seems to refer to events in ch. 5. (See also 7:19 and 10:26-27.) In other cases information is cited before an event's actual occurrence in the gospel (cf. 1:15 and 1:29-26; 11:2 and 12:3).

Some scholars attribute these features to the problem of redaction and advocate a reordering of the materials on the grounds that the final editor made a mistake in assembling them. But the key to the gospel (20:30-31) reminds one that the evangelist intends to present the material schematically, hence without too much concern for chronological sequence. Moreover, the evangelist assumes a fuller knowledge of the traditions in the audience since information about Jesus was widely shared in the early Church through traveling teachers (cf. Acts 18:1-5, 24-28; 1 Cor 1:12; 3:6-9). Such abrupt breaks only invite the reader to pay closer attention to the inner logic of the gospel and to the possible theological sequence the evangelist may be interested in establishing.

Special Features

1. Theology of the Gospel

The central question the gospel asks and to which it provides an answer is: "Who is Jesus?" On this question depends the reader's desired response (cf. 20:31) to the mystery of Jesus and his lifegiving mission (cf. 4:10). John answers the question by declaring that Jesus is the Christ, the Son of God. "Christ" refers to the long-expected Jewish Messiah in whom all the promises made to Abraham and the Jewish people are fulfilled. Other NT texts state the same reality in their own way (cf. Acts 4:12 and Col 1:17-20), but John's gospel brings a unique insight into the issue by declaring that Jesus is the Christ only because he is the uniquely begotten (not adopted) Son of God (cf. 1:18) who is also God and equal to God (cf. 1:1-2; 5:18; 8:58; 10:33, 36; 19:7; 20:28).

This Son of God became a human being (1:14) in order to reveal God (1:18), give fullness of life (10:10), and gather together the scattered children of God (11:52) by his death on the cross (19:30). John's theology here rejoins that of Paul who declares that God was in Christ reconciling the world to God (2 Cor 5:18-19; cf. Col 1:19-20). All of Jesus' deeds and words are those of God (cf. 14:9-11) whom the gospel constantly refers to as the "the Father" to whom Jesus relates as "the Son" (a parent-child relationship, in modern parlance).

The disciple of Jesus gains this eternal life by knowing Jesus and remaining in him (17:3), that is, by having a lasting and fruitful personal relationship with him (15:1-17). This knowledge is acquired by believing in Jesus and welcoming him into one's life. Through this believing, Jesus enables one to become a child of God (1:12-13). Accepting Jesus also means sharing concretely in his life of love for people even unto death (13:34-35; 15:12-13). This love is rooted in and sustained by God's own free and unmerited love for the world (3:16). God's love is the cause of Jesus' becoming human to give enduring life to anyone who believes in him.

The first part of the gospel (chs. 1–12) deals mostly with the question of the divine messianic identity of Jesus. The farewell discourses (chs. 13–17) expound in detail the significance of his identity and mission and the place and role of the disciples in relation to this identity and mission. His passion, death, and resurrection, which the gospel views as his glorification (chs. 18–20), constitute the decisive event that proves the truth of his divine identity and makes available to believers the fruit of his lifegiving mission: the gift of the Holy Spirit who enables one to be born of God (3:3-8; cf. 20:17b) and to become a living witness to Jesus (14:26-27; 21).

2. Disputative Character of the Gospel

A dominant aspect of the gospel not readily visible in the synoptics is its disputative character.

This derives from the very nature of the problem the gospel tackles. Since the evangelist sets out to demonstrate that Jesus is the Christ, the Son of God, the implication is that this claim was either disputed by some or needed to be sustained with documentary evidence in order to persuade and convince the readers. The evangelist performs this task not by preaching to the readers as in a homily, but by presenting Jesus in person directly to them in his own life situation. As the Johannine audience watches Jesus defending his claims and arguing out his case with his Jewish opponents in a variety of situations, as we might watch a video on a screen, this audience is invited to act throughout the projection as the jury. After a thorough hearing of the case it is to draw its own conclusions based on the evidence seen and heard and to decide in favor of Jesus by believing in him. The situation is unlike a contemporary court case because the decision of this jury is not impersonal; it has life-consequences for the one who makes it (cf. 9:41; 5:22).

The argumentative character of the gospel begins right from the prologue (1:1-18) and reaches its climax in the trials before the High Priest and Pilate (ch. 18). Because Jesus is the Christ, all other possible messianic figures who could be confused with him are relativized, as are foundational figures of the Jewish people: John the Baptist (1:6-8, 15, 19-36; 5:33-36), Moses and the Law (1:17; 5:45-47; 9:28-33), Abraham (8:52-59), and even the chosen people who as a whole were regarded as gods (10:34; Ps 82:6). The resurrection proves that, though Jesus appears to have lost the case by being condemned to death, the decision only served to vindicate him in a way that was beyond dispute (cf. 20:8, 28).

Though this approach is dominant in the Fourth Gospel samples of it occur in the synoptics where, for instance, Jesus argues that the Christ cannot be David's son since David called him Lord (Matt 22:41-44 // Mark 12:35-36 // Luke 20:41-43). Peter, preaching in Acts (2:34-35), also argues that David could not have been referring to himself in praying Pss 16:8-11 and 110:1, but to Jesus whom God raised from the dead.

Behind these disputations is the evangelist's concern to persuade the reader to believe in Jesus. This concern also explains why, unlike in the synoptics, the Johannine Jesus appears to proclaim more about himself in the "I am" sayings (the bread of life, 6:35; the light of the world, 8:12; the door to the sheepfold, 10:7; the good shepherd, 10:11; the resurrection and the life, 11:25; the way, the truth, and the life, 14:6), than about the reign of God. Ultimately Jesus and the reign of God are inseparable realities, since he is the principal agent who definitively ushers in this kingdom or reign of God and embodies it.

3. A Spiritual or Interpretative Gospel

The selected material recorded in the gospel is narrated in a way that brings out its meaning. Because of its interpretative nature, the gospel has been tagged "a spiritual gospel" since the time of Clement of Alexandria (Eusebius, *Hist. Eccl.* 4.14.7), and in more modern times an "interpretative gospel" or "theological gospel." This does not mean that the gospel lacks historical facts. It does mean that more so than the synoptics it deliberately sets out to write a theological history. The evangelist is concerned that the readers obtain a deep spiritual, theological insight into the person and mission of Jesus and make this the basis of their lifelong commitment to him as the first disciples did (cf. 6:67-69). The gospel is spiritual because both its writing and the message it embodies were inspired by the Holy Spirit sent by Jesus to lead the disciples into the complete truth about him and his teaching (16:13). Both ancient and modern readers need the assistance of the same Holy Spirit to comprehend the message of the gospel.

The interpretative nature of the gospel is manifest in three ways:

(a) The evangelist gives a direct interpretation of certain Hebrew words used (cf. 1:38, 41, 42; 4:25; 20:16) and of the meaning of events and sayings (2:11; 4:9; 11:52).

(b) The evangelist invites the reader to pay attention to how Jesus and his hearers understand each other. The Johannine features of misunderstanding *(double-entendre),* and irony mentioned earlier belong here.

(c) Each narrative of one of Jesus' "signs" is followed by a protracted discourse that draws out the full significance of the sign (cf. chs. 5; 6; 9; 11). Similarly the gospel reports no commission of Jesus to his disciples to baptize (cf. Matt

28:19), nor does it give an account of the last supper (cf. Matt 26:17-35; Mark 14:12-31; Luke 22:7-38). Instead Jesus underscores the eschatological necessity of baptism for each individual who wishes to enter into the reign of God (3:5-8), and the imperative to eat his body and drink his blood as a condition for having eternal life (6:53). His farewell discourse in ch. 13 replaces the account of the institution of the Eucharist with an account of Jesus' demonstration of his ultimate love in service unto death for his followers (13:1-11). The followers of Jesus are called upon not only to receive the body and blood of Jesus but to become in turn bread of life for others (13:34-35). This is the fullest meaning of the Eucharist.

4. Prominence Given to Women

John's gospel, like that of Luke, gives a special prominence to women. This is all the more remarkable if, as scholars tend to agree, the gospel was written toward the end of the first century when the features of "early Catholicism" with its tendency to relegate women to the background in the Church came into play (cf. 1 Tim 2:11-15). Given the selective nature of the material presented in the gospel, it is impressive that key roles are given to women in 2:1-11; 4:1-42; 11; 12:1-8; 19:25-27; 20:1-18. To this list may be added 8:1-11, though modern scholarship sees this passage as not belonging originally to John's gospel. The importance of these roles will be discussed in the second part of this commentary.

5. Concern with Mission

John's gospel also has a marked concern with mission, though this appears to be set in the same polemical mode as the revelation of Jesus' identity. Mission as understood in the gospel refers preeminently to God's sending of Jesus into the world as a mark of the enduring divine love for humanity (3:16). This sending constitutes the fountainhead of all the blessings embodied in the gospel. Jesus is God's sole agent of salvation who has neither predecessors nor successors. All the OT messengers of God are portrayed as his witnesses or those who prepared the way before him, the last of whom is John the Baptist (5:33-35). Moses and the Law wrote of him (5:46), the Scriptures bear witness to him (5:39), Abraham rejoiced to see his day (8:56). He alone reveals God absolutely and imparts lifegiving knowledge of God (1:18; 17:1-3) through his passion, death, and resurrection (cf. 3:14-15) by which he draws all peoples to himself (12:32, 34). As Paul would say, he becomes the agent of God's reconciliation of the world to God (2 Cor 5:18-19).

In the vision of the gospel this mission has implications for the disciples themselves. Since Jesus alone does and completes the work of salvation, all his disciples are reapers of the fruit of this mission (4:34-38). Their very participation in the work of mission is seen as a gathering in, not as a sowing, and the exercise itself is a reward for them. Jesus can therefore never be replaced within the community of believers since he continues to enable and sustain such believers to bear lasting fruit in him (15:1-17; 21:1-14). Whatever functions any of the disciples perform within the community become a mark of love and gratitude for the salvation and nourishment they have personally received from Jesus, or a privilege given to them to share in his own life of love even unto death (cf. 21:15-19).

This vision of mission is unique to John's gospel. It may have been inspired by the attitude of some believers who thought that because they were now fully children of God (1:12-13) they no longer needed Jesus as their indispensable way to God, or who may have been tempted to glory in the part that they played in the mission as did some of those mentioned in Paul's letters (cf. 2 Cor 11:12-15; 12:11; Gal 2:6), or who may have become a law unto themselves within the community as did Diotrephes (3 John 9-10). In the Johannine concept of mission Jesus is the constitutive missionary and all others are the fruit of his mission. The heart of the mission is to give life to believers and gather together the scattered children of God (10:10; 11:52). The Church today rightly defines itself as mission or as existing for mission. Such a definition, viewed from the Johannine perspective of mission, has serious implications for all Christians.

Some Clarifications

Many features in John that would have been clear to his first-century readers, or at least not problematic, require explanation today.

1. The Jews

John's gospel frequently uses the term "the Jews" in a combative, polemical manner. Read against the background of anti-Semitism and the Holocaust this may give the impression that the gospel itself is anti-Jewish. The gospel has become problematic today in interfaith dialogue because of this. Many people have also used the gospel as support for their anti-Semitic attitudes. In reaction some well-meaning people have sought to play down the gospel for fear of whipping up anti-Semitic feelings or offending our Jewish brothers and sisters.

In dealing with these problems one needs to remember that the author of the gospel and its original audience did not live through the Holocaust. Some scholars believe that the attitude toward the Jews in the gospel reflects the antagonism between church and synagogue especially in the days after the destruction of Jerusalem in 70 C.E. This antagonism, if such it can be called, did not arise from an anti-Semitic spirit in the modern sense of the word. The allegedly anti-Jewish polemic in the gospel can be explained first in terms of forensic rhetorical style. When two opponents go to court they are not exactly civil to one another; rather they each argue their case in a way that shows up the foolishness of the other. The two opponents who go to court need not be from different nationalities. Most often they are of the same nationality; otherwise they would have to be judged by an international court. Similarly, the anti-Jewish polemic in John does not necessarily mean that a non-Jew is writing against the Jews. If the author of the gospel was John the son of Zebedee and Salome (cf. Mark 15:40; Matt 27:56), then the gospel was principally written by a Jew from around Bethsaida (cf. 1:44; 19:25; Mark 1:16-20). In any case, the internal evidence points to a Jewish author.

A close reading of the gospel reveals that the polemic is not directed against the Jews as a nation but against the leaders who were the most strongly opposed to Jesus and eventually brought about his condemnation and death. When Jesus speaks, for instance, of "your law," meaning the Jewish Law (10:34), this is to be understood in terms of the law they use or misuse to judge and condemn Jesus. From Jesus' point of view this same law bears witness to him as do the great figures in Jewish history (5:39, 46). Besides, Jesus himself and all the disciples, men and women, mentioned in the gospel are Jews, mostly from Galilee. The mother of Jesus is a Jew. So is Joseph (cf. 6:42).

This same gospel that is alleged to be anti-Semitic contains the most explicit statement in the NT (after Rom 9:4-5) that "salvation is from the Jews " (4:22). New Testament Christians, Jews and Gentiles alike, were accustomed to dissociating themselves nationally from their compatriots who rejected belief in Jesus in order to affirm concretely that in Christ they now belonged to one family of the new Israel of God. That is why, for instance, Paul in 1 Cor 1:22-24 speaks of "Jews," "Greeks," and "we" (believers who are both Jews and Greeks). In the same way the first Christians at Antioch felt it necessary to call themselves "Christians," a new name that would destroy the divisive, even offensive, categories of Jews and "Gentiles" in the NT era (cf. Acts 11:26). In short, when seen in its own literary and historical contexts John's gospel cannot justifiably be regarded as anti-Semitic in the modern sense. To use the gospel in support of any anti-Semitic feelings or to accuse it of anti-Semitism and hence to refuse to read and love it are both ways of misusing and abusing the gospel.

2. Johannine Eschatology

In current theology eschatology deals with the doctrine of the last things: death, judgment, hell or heaven. In NT thought, however, this notion would be linked with the *parousia,* the final return of the Lord. New Testament eschatology deals with God's fulfillment of the promises to the Israelites to send them a savior or a prophet like Moses or to pour out the divine Spirit on all humanity "in the last days" (*en tais eschatais hēmerais;* cf. Acts 2:17, citing Joel 2:28-32; Isa 2:2; 33:10). The word eschatology comes from the Greek word *eschatos* (last). New Testament authors identify this eschatology with the inauguration of the new creation brought about by Jesus' passion, death, and resurrection and the outpouring of the Holy Spirit. This new creation includes the reunification of all things in heaven and on earth in Christ (cf. Col 1:15-20; Eph 1:3-10).

In Johannine thought, however, this eschatology begins with the incarnation, or the very coming of Jesus into the world (1:5, 14) because this coming establishes a great divide between the world of life and that of sin, darkness, and death. In other words Johannine eschatology begins in the person of Jesus as the Son of God become a human being. The theology is rooted in God's promise to Eve in Gen 3:15 that he would put permanent enmity between her descendants (that is, humanity, since she was the mother of all the living, Gen 3:20) and Satan. The triumph of humanity over sin, Satan, and all the forces of wickedness and death started right from the moment of incarnation when Jesus, who consistently identifies himself as a "human being" (the term is traditionally translated "son of man") ushered in the process of the defeat of the devil in his person as a human being and completed it in his glorification. This victory establishes a brand new era in humanity's relationship with God such that believers can truly be called children of God (1:12-13), no longer simply God's creatures (Gen 1:26-27). This end-time has certain imperatives for Jesus himself (3:14, 30a), for John the Baptist, the last OT witness to him (3:30b), and for all those who want to enter into the reign of God or the new era (3:3, 7; 4:24).

In the gospel this eschatology is related to a number of concepts: "the work" of salvation that belongs to God and that Jesus alone does and completes (4:34; 17:4), "the hour" that is coming and now is (4:21, 23; 5:25), and "the harvest" (4:35-38). Briefly, Jesus' coming into the world marks the beginning of the work of salvation. This work has a sowing phase and a harvesting phase. The sowing phase is the period before Jesus' glorification; the harvesting phase is the period after his glorification when believers receive the fruit of his accomplished work (cf. 19:30) and the Spirit of sonship and daughtership of God (cf. 20:17, 22) and are sent into the world as Jesus himself was sent into the world to deal with sin or participate in his mission of reconciliation (20:21, 23; cf. 2 Cor 5:18-21).

"The hour" is related to this concept in that for the immediate audience of Jesus and to a certain extent for Jesus himself the hour both is (in his very presence and mission in the world), and yet is coming, as it looks to its complete fulfillment in his glorification. For John's audience and for readers throughout the ages the hour now is, since they belong to the harvest phase or the phase of Jesus' completed work of salvation, when believers actually reap the fruit of Jesus' accomplished mission.

3. Johannine Dualism

The dualism present in John's gospel is closely related to the author's understanding of eschatology, though in the past this has wrongly been linked with the ontological dualism found in Gnosticism or in Qumran. According to these latter bodies the world is divided into the good and the bad, those destined to be saved and those destined to be condemned. Gnosticism identifies the latter as those belonging to the flesh, and Qumran calls them the children of Belial. John does use language that is dualistic: light and darkness, those who belong to the world and those who do not belong to the world, those who have already passed over from death to life and so are not judged and those who are still alive but are already judged. But in contrast to Gnosticism and Qumran his sphere of reference is moral, not ontological. That is, what constitutes being in the light or being in the darkness, of the world or not of the world, is one's response to Jesus and one's acceptance of the fundamental demand of that response to live as a child of God by loving as God and Jesus love (cf. 13:34-35). This teaching is clearly set forth in the first letter of John (especially chs. 3–4).

The beginning of eschatology with Jesus' very entry into the world has implications for humanity. Those who accept him begin even now to pass over from death to life, from the dominion of death into that of life given by God in Christ. Conversely those who reject him begin even now to experience death or judgment. The "last day" understood as the day of final judgment only makes manifest and finalizes one's lived response to Jesus. One either passes definitively into life or one passes definitively into judgment. Meanwhile one either chooses to belong to the world, understood as the sphere of rejection of Jesus, not the created world loved by God even to sending the divine Son to redeem it from sin (3:16), or one chooses to come out of the world and darkness and belong to God (3:20-21; 17:14-16). Seen in this way Johannine dualism is an essential aspect of Johannine theology of the incarnation, that is, the new creation in Christ, and grows naturally out of it.

Contexts for Reading the Gospel

1. Historical Context: Audience, Author, Date

(a) Life-situation of the audience addressed. The marked concern in the gospel to prove that Jesus is the Christ, the Son of God, its disputative character and declared intention to persuade the reader to believe in the divine messiahship of Jesus lead one to inquire about the life situation addressed by the gospel. The internal evidence of the gospel corroborated by the Johannine epistles leads one to affirm that a great number of the audience addressed would have been Jewish or people familiar with Jewish religious traditions.

The evangelist draws copiously from Jewish traditions in the effort to prove the thesis of the gospel, using powerful OT imagery to speak about Jesus: the word of God, God's agent of creation and unfailing messenger (1:1-18; cf. Gen 1:1–2:3; Isa 55:10-11); the prophet who is filled with zeal for the proper worship of YHWH (2:14-17; cf. 1 Kings 18:1-40; 19:14; Ps 69:9 [10]); the end-time prophet who gives manna from heaven and miraculously multiplies loaves of bread (6:11-14; cf. Exod 16:4, 15; Ps 78:24; 2 Kings 4:42-44), promises living water/Holy Spirit (4:10-15; 7:37-39; cf. Ezek 47:1-12; Joel 4:18; Zech 14:8-11), gives sight to those born blind (9:1-7; cf. Isa 29:18), stands as the promised true shepherd of Israel (10:7-18; cf. Ezek 34:1-31), and raises the dead to life (11:38-44; cf. 1 Kings 17:17-24; 2 Kings 4:32-37). Like the true prophets of Israel, Jesus is rejected (12:37-43) and consigned to death (11:47-53). His farewell discourses resemble the deathbed discourse of Jacob/Israel who gave enduring advice to his descendants and pleaded with them to remain in unity (chs. 13–17; cf. Gen 49:1-33). The letter to the Hebrews also uses OT Jewish traditions to argue that in Jesus God has spoken in a definitive way to the presumably Jewish audience addressed, though the letter itself does not mention a Jewish audience.

While the identity of John's audience is disputed, it is generally agreed that this audience was facing a crisis of faith in Jesus as the Christ, Son of God. A number of suggestions are made concerning the nature of this crisis. The most widely accepted theory, based on John 9:22 and 16:2, is that the community addressed must have been facing the trauma of ejection from the synagogue. Another equally plausible suggestion supported by the Johannine epistles is that at least some in the community must have been severely tempted to lose faith in the divine messiahship of Jesus after their initial conversion, on the grounds that he did not meet their messianic expectations (cf. 1 John 2:19-29). Matt 11:6 (parallel Luke 7:23) is evidence that people who initially believed in Jesus as the Messiah later had problems about that belief. The problem in John centers on Jesus' divine identity. The temptation for believers to apostatize is also recorded in Heb (3:12; 12:25).

This situation would be familiar to many today. Many Christians in Africa and elsewhere are tempted to give up their faith in Jesus and return to their traditional religions or to embrace one of the New Age religions or even the occult. Some Christian preachers are like the Antichrists mentioned in 1 John 2:19; they go about the established churches, as those did to the Johannine community, "harvesting souls" for their new sects and promising them instant prosperity. Such Christians today are as pompous and contemptuous of others as was the Diotrephes mentioned in 3 John 9. To all these Christians John's gospel makes a special appeal not to give up on Jesus since true life and prosperity can be found only in him. They are also to remember that humility is the distinctive mark of a true Christian (13:1-17, especially vv. 12-17).

Other suggestions made concerning the occasion for writing the gospel include the mission to Samaria (cf. John 4:1-42), an anti-docetic polemic (that is, a polemic against those who denied the humanity of Christ and held that he only appeared to be human; cf. 1 John 4:2), and apologetic against sectarians and disciples of John the Baptist who claimed that he, not Jesus, was the Messiah (cf. John 1:6-8, 15, 19-34). Others believe that the gospel is a general appeal to all Christians to turn the experience of rejection by the wider society (which was common before Constantine made Christianity the state religion) into a positive commitment to Jesus, sustained by the Holy Spirit.

Within this range of theories on the situation of the Johannine community, readers may identify the one that best speaks to their situation today. There may be personal or community faith problems not included in the range of theories offered here. The challenge then is to identify one's concrete problems of faith in Jesus to which the gospel can bring a divinely revealed and lifegiving message.

(b) Identity of the author. The earliest manuscripts of the gospel dating from the second century bear the inscription *Kata Ioanēn* (according to John). The name John means "God is gracious." Within the gospel itself the author or declared witness behind the gospel is called "the disciple whom Jesus loved" (19:26, 35; 21:24; cf. 13:23; [20:3, 8?]; 21:7, 20). An early and longstanding tradition of the Church ascribed the gospel to John the son of Zebedee, one of the twelve apostles. This tradition dates back to Irenaeus of Lyons (ca. 140–177 C.E.), who claims to have received it from Polycarp whose disciple he was and who he says often spoke with John, the disciple of the Lord (*Adv. Haer.* 3.3.4).

But as early as the end of the second century and beginning of the third this identity of the author was disputed. The *Alogoi* (so named by Epiphanius) ascribed it to the Gnostic Cerinthus. The most important questions asked today are (1) whether the author of the gospel was really an "eyewitness" of the events narrated, as the gospel and early patristic tradition claim he was; (2) If he was an eyewitness, was his real name John? and (3) If so, was he John the son of Zebedee, one of the twelve, or was he another John (for example, John Mark [cf. Acts 12:12] or the Presbyter John [cf. 2 John 1; 3 John 1])? In other words, does apostolic witness lie behind the gospel or do we have here the work of some mystic who may or may not have known Christ personally? Who indeed is the Beloved Disciple mentioned in the gospel as its author (21:24)?

As with most Johannine problems, the issue has defied solution. The longstanding tradition of the Church and the common belief of the faithful is that the author of the gospel was John the son of Zebedee, one of the twelve who along with Peter and his brother James were given special privileges by Jesus (cf. Matt 17:1-8 // Mark 9:2-9 // Luke 9:28-36). This patristic evidence was never really challenged until the nineteenth century. Problematic as this solution may be, others are not less problematic. Arguments that the son of Zebedee who was a fisherman could not have known such high theology as is reflected in the gospel can be countered by the claim in the gospel that he and other disciples were taught by the Holy Spirit, led into the complete truth (cf. 14:26; 1 John 2:27), and empowered to bear witness to Jesus (15:26-27; cf. 1 John 5:7). Jesus himself, who "never studied" (7:15), was also taught by the Holy Spirit whom he possessed in full (1:32, 33).

Moreover, patristic tradition starting with the Muratorian Canon holds that what John wrote was the collective memoir of all the apostles that had been reflected upon for years; hence it was not simply his own ideas with copyright as happens in modern authorship. As was the practice in ancient times up to the Middle Ages and the time of Thomas Aquinas, he would have written down his "witness" through the help of a scribe. To hold that John the son of Zebedee was the author of the gospel, therefore, does not mean that all the ideas embodied in the gospel are exclusively his, nor does it mean that he wrote everything himself without scribal assistance, which includes possible editing of the work during his lifetime or after his death (cf. 21:24-25). The idea of authorship in the ancient world was very different from the modern one.

Whatever the case, the most important issue in the discussion on authorship of the gospel lies both in the name "John" given by tradition as the author and the title of "Beloved Disciple" (BD) mentioned by the gospel. Both draw attention not to the achievement of the author but to that of God and Jesus. The name John points to God's kindness and graciousness while the designation "the disciple whom Jesus loved" singles out Jesus' love for the individual concerned. These names leave no room for boasting of achievement on the part of the author concerned, which perhaps explains why he deliberately refrains from mentioning his own name. By this action he draws attention to the fact that the real author of the gospel is the Holy Spirit. This is in keeping with the spirit of the gospel itself, which advocates deep humility on the part of the disciple.

Every true disciple is a person whom Jesus loves (cf. 11:3; 15:9, 13-15). Since, as John Chrysostom maintained, Christ's love for John was the essential motive for his writing the gospel (*Chr.* 88.2), all are invited to respond equally to this love by allowing the Spirit to lead them into the complete truth about Jesus today in their own social locations. Then, having reflected upon, assimilated through prayer, and believed the testimony of the gospel as the BD did (cf. 20:8; 2:22), each community and individual will become another evangelist who will bear witness to what they have personally known and experienced about Jesus as the BD did. In short, each reader is called upon to become a "Beloved Disciple," author of the gospel in his or her own context, by meditating on all the traditions received about Jesus and proclaiming them to others by life, deed, and word.

2. Date and Place of Composition

(a) Date. One of the most teasing problems about John's gospel concerns its date and place of composition. This problem is related to that of authorship. On the one hand the gospel contains details about Jewish religious customs and practices that predate the destruction of Jerusalem by Titus in 70 C.E. Some geographical details given have been corroborated by archaeological evidence (for example, the Sheep Gate with a pool and five porticos in Jerusalem, 5:2). In some instances the Fourth Gospel gives a more accurate chronology (for example, concerning events in Passion week) than do the synoptic gospels. All this would point to a date before the destruction of Jerusalem in 70 and to an author who knew Palestine and Jewish religious customs first hand. Some of the geographical and other details given appear to add nothing to the meaning.

Nevertheless, the most recent studies date the final composition of the gospel between 98 C.E., in the time of Trajan (to which period Irenaeus dates the last days of John son of Zebedee), and 100 C.E., that is, after the Jewish council at Jamnia (90 C.E.), when it is alleged that the complete rupture between church and synagogue took place. This late dating is supported by the marked development in the theology and christology presented in the gospel, the testimony of patristic authors that John wrote the gospel at a very advanced age, the evidence of the explicit use of the gospel by ancient authors, and the dates of its extant manuscripts, the earliest of which ($\mathfrak{P}^{52}$, found in Egypt), dates to the second century. This late dating of the finished gospel does not deny that the original gospel was composed much earlier by an eyewitness disciple of Jesus; it only posits that the work of the final editor of the gospel as we now have it dated from this late period.

Again the issue of the date and composition of the gospel has not been and in a sense cannot be definitively resolved unless archaeology discovers indisputable evidence. This is one of the mysteries of the gospel that the reader is invited to live with. What matters most is the message of the gospel that constitutes the heart of the good news of Jesus and of the Church's self-understanding. Whether the gospel is of early or late origin, it is evident from its place in the canon and its influence on the life of the Church and of individual saints that the gospel as we now have it was inspired by the Spirit of truth who cannot deceive Christ's followers. If knowledge of the exact dating of the gospel were necessary for salvation the Holy Spirit would have insured that we possessed such a knowledge.

(b) Place of composition. Though this has also been disputed there is not sufficient evidence to challenge patristic witness that the gospel was written in Ephesus where John the son of Zebedee is believed to have lived and exercised his apostolic ministry. Most recent research corroborates this patristic evidence, and indirectly the tradition that the son of Zebedee is the primary author or witness behind the gospel.

3. Canonical Context

John's gospel is clearly one of the last, if not the last, of the four canonical gospels to be written. Its being placed last among the gospels in the NT canon also reflects its chronological status. All available patristic evidence testifies that John was the last gospel to be written, and this testimony has never been disputed. As the last to be written the gospel embodies a more developed theology of the life, mission, and glorification (Passion, death, and resurrection) of Jesus than do the synoptic gospels. Patristic evidence also maintains that John wrote to supplement, correct, or better explain (give the inner meaning of) the data given in the other three gospels. Origen of Alexandria held that John's gospel was the basis ("premise") of the gospels just as the gospels were the "premises" of the NT, and the NT of the Bible (*In Ioannem,* SC 120, 1.4.23). He located the greatest contribution of John's gospel in its clear statement about the incarnation and divinity of Jesus (1:1-2, 14, 18; 8:58; 20:28). This is because Origen, like all the Fathers of the Church, believed that the Holy Spirit was the one author of the Bible and that the whole Bible was about Christ.

Already by the time of Irenaeus's *Adversus haereses* (3.1) John is included in a fourfold gospel canon. This acceptance into the canon meant that the universal Church recognized and accepted that apostolic authority lay behind its content. Second, it meant that the Church rejected some of the early theories that attributed the gospel to some Gnostic author. Though the last to be admitted, John's gospel was regarded as canonical long before the current NT canon was finally established about 367 C.E.

4. Catechetical Context

Certain features of the gospel itself and of tradition indicate that the material in the gospel was elaborated over a long period of oral transmission. Catechesis was a crucial aspect of life in the early Church. Famous catechetical schools existed in Alexandria and Antioch. It was not simply a matter of teaching catechism to catechumens or preparing people for receiving the sacraments as tends to happen today; rather catechesis was necessary for adults since most converts were admitted first into the community of believers before they received solid instruction in the faith or the Way (cf. Acts 2:41-42). In addition, the danger of heresies made necessary the sustained instruction of the faithful who were a minority in the ancient world and could easily fall prey to traveling teachers of all types of religious cults.

Modern scholars believe in the existence of a Johannine (catechetical) school where the traditions embodied in the gospel would have been reflected upon, taught, and finally transmitted in writing to a wider body, some would say to members of the school who had scattered because of the crises of faith mentioned earlier. Indeed, some of the dialogues in the gospel read like questions and answers that would have been given in such a setting, but worded in a creative and dynamic manner. The closest modern equivalent to the catechetical school would be the recently established "School of Evangelization" that is spreading throughout the world as part of "Evangelization 2000."

5. Liturgical Context

In addition to catechesis, the material embodied in John's gospel would also have been used in the liturgy. Liturgical usage would have taken the form of readings followed by homilies as in Luke 4:16-21. The marked preference for feasts and the allusions to the sacraments, especially baptism and the Eucharist, in John are a good indication of this. The Johannine community would have seen in Jesus a fulfillment, some would say replacement, of Jewish feasts and institutions mentioned in the gospel. They would therefore have celebrated their own feasts accordingly. Worship was seen as one of the primary duties of the people of God (cf. Acts 2:46-47); Jesus declares that such worship is to be carried out in spirit and in truth (in one's entire life), not merely in set places (4:23-24).

In particular the gospel has a marked interest in the sacraments: baptism and the accompanying gift of the Holy Spirit (3:3-21; 7:37-39); the Eucharist (ch. 6; cf. 20:13) to which some would add the new wine (2:1-11); and the forgiving of sins (20:22-23). All these sacraments are the fruit of Jesus' glorification (19:34) where bread (his broken body), wine (his blood), and water from his pierced side become the material for these sacraments (cf. 4:14; 6:52). Worthy of mention, too, are the hymnic (1:1-18) and prayer passages (11:41-42; 12:27-28; 17), some of which continue to be used in the liturgy even today.

Finally John's gospel gives rich images of the Church itself as the body of Christ (15:1-8), the one flock he leads into unity (10:7-16), or the unbroken net he sustains with his love (21:11) and for which he appoints a visible leader to look after it even to death (21:15-19). It is not surprising that John's gospel has been a cornerstone in the liturgical life of the Church through the ages, the worship Christ and his members offer to God.

General Issues

1. Composition and Redaction

The discussion of authorship makes it evident that John's gospel used sources, especially if the work represents the collective memory of the apostles. Internal evidence in the gospel also leads to the conclusion that the work must have gone through a series of redactions (or reeditings) in different contexts before it reached its present canonical form. Again the theories on the Johannine composition and redaction are complex, at times quite far-fetched. Scholars discern layers of composition and redaction within individual chapters and within the gospel as a whole. They posit three levels of composition: a primitive source, the bulk of the current gospel composed by the evangelist, and the work of a final editor who gave the gospel its current canonical shape. Some hold that this final editor added the prologue (1:1-18) and epilogue (ch. 21) and made modifications in the gospel that toned down its high christology or emphasis on Jesus' equality with God (cf. 14:28) in order to bring the theology of the gospel more in line with that of the synoptics and thus make it more acceptable to the universal Church.

A majority of scholars would posit a primitive "Signs Source" (SQ) that would have contained mainly a record of the signs (supposedly seven in number) Jesus worked. Some hold that 20:30-31 was originally the conclusion to this SQ. This "gospel of Signs" is believed to have been written to elicit the faith of the reader in Jesus as Christ, Son of God, but when this did not work the evangelist then rewrote the gospel laying emphasis on the words of Jesus as the means to elicit the desired faith. In the process, it is alleged, the evangelist kept the record of the original signs source but treated the whole issue of faith based on signs pejoratively in the gospel. John 2:23-25; 4:48; and 20:29 are cited as evidence of the gospel's negative attitude toward faith based on signs.

Though this theory has gained wide acceptance from prominent scholars it conflicts with the fact that if the "signs" as the current gospel understands them are removed, very little if anything would be left of it. In its current canonical context the gospel uses signs positively as pointers to the reality that is Jesus. That his audience misunderstood these signs (cf. 6:26) does not invalidate their significance. Today a number of Christians in the charismatic and pentecostal movements are also prone to misuse the miracles of Jesus recorded in the gospels, but that does not render these miracles invalid since they are clearly acts of God done in Christ.

The fact is that whether the gospel is based on the signs or the words of Jesus, each reader would have had to depend on the written testimony given about Jesus since he or she would not have been there to witness the ministry of Jesus personally. The problem with most of the theories of composition and redaction is that the evidence cited in support of them can also be explained on other grounds, for instance by the selective, schematic nature of the gospel material and its manifestly polemic, dualistic, and argumentative character. Whatever the case, despite the undeniable disjunctures or lack of smooth transitions the gospel does manifest a unity of style and theology. That it had different levels of composition is positive proof that the gospel was a living word within the community of believers who felt it necessary to reedit it from time to time to reflect their growth in the understanding of the faith. The reader today will not rewrite the gospel but is called upon to interpret it creatively to address the needs of his or her faith community.

2. Relationship to Other Canonical Books

a. The Synoptic Gospels

From the earliest days the relationship between John's gospel and the synoptics has been a problem. While all four deal with the total life and ministry of Jesus, obvious discrepancies are found in the body of the gospels and in the accounts of the passion and resurrection narratives:

- different datings of the cleansing of the Temple (2:13-22; cf. Matt 21:12-17; Mark 11:15-19; Luke 19:45-48)
- different accounts of the call of the disciples and naming of Peter (1:35-51; cf. Matt 4:18-22; Mark 1:16-20; Luke 5:1-11)
- overlapping of the ministry of Jesus with that of the Baptist (3:22-23; 4:1-3; cf. Matt 4:12-17; Mark 1:14-15; Luke 4:14-15)
- differences in the general chronology and length of Jesus' Jerusalem/Judean ministry (2:13; 5:1; 7:10; 11:7; 12:12-16; cf. Luke 9:51; 19:28-38; Mark 11:1-10; Matt 21:1-9)
- differences in the chronology of the passion and resurrection events (13:1; 19:31; cf. Luke 22:1, 7; Matt 26:2, 20; Mark 14:1-2, 12)
- differences in the number of women who went to the tomb and to whom Jesus appeared first (20:1-10, 14; Matt 28:1-10; Luke 24:1-11; Mark 16:1-8).

There are also significant omissions in John: the temptation and agony in Gethsemane (but cf. 12:27-30); the institution of the Eucharist and the commission of the risen Lord to baptize his prospective followers, which John replaces with the commission to forgive sins (20:23). Here too, differently from Acts 2, John places the imparting of the Holy Spirit before Pentecost (20:22). Instead of the institution of the Eucharist and the commission to baptize, John gives lengthy discourses explaining the real significance of baptism (3:3-21) and the Eucharist (ch. 6).

On the other hand, John narrates episodes not found in the synoptic gospels: the wedding feast at Cana in Galilee (2:1-11), the dialogue with Nicodemus (3:1-21), with the Samaritan woman and the whole Samaritan mission (ch. 4), the cure at the pool of Bethzatha (5:1-9), the cure of the man born blind (ch. 9), the raising of Lazarus (ch. 11), the coming of the Gentiles (Greeks) to see Jesus (12:20-22), and the washing of the feet (13:1-11). Differently from the synoptic gospels, most of the miracles that John consistently calls "signs" are followed by long discourses that point out the divinity of Jesus and different aspects of his lifegiving mission.

These differences in particular make one wonder whether the author of John ever knew the synoptic gospels. If he did, why such divergences on important issues? Briefly, in reply to the first question it cannot be proved that John did not know of any of the synoptic gospels. Some hold that he may have known of Mark and that the final editor was probably familiar with Luke. John probably used an independent tradition not known to the synoptic writers, but he did this knowing well that his audience had access to the information given in these other gospels. It was in view of this that patristic witnesses believed that John wrote to supply information that was missing in the other three gospels. The particular orientation of his material even when the same material is narrated in the synoptic gospels was influenced and shaped by his desire to bring out their meaning in order to persuade his intended audience to believe in Jesus (20:30-31). Some heretics in the patristic era saw the differences between John and the synoptics as evidence that the gospel was not inspired. They simply missed the point of why John wrote the gospel.

What is most important is that the similarities and especially the differences between John and the synoptics remind the pastor that the same gospel material can be handled differently depending on the needs and situation of the audience addressed. It is not helpful to prepare one homily and use it for a universal audience regardless of the circumstance or social location of the audience. It should also be remembered that modern interest in "accuracy" in narrating historical facts may not have been the concern of the NT authors and their audiences. It is a mark of respect to them and their world not to import our world into theirs or judge and dismiss them by our own standards.

What matters is the message of salvation these gospels embody. Origen and the allegorical theologians viewed the differences as blessings in that they provided greater opportunity and posed a challenge to look deeper into the inner meaning of what is narrated. Finally, it is to be remembered that the early Christians did not have modern facilities for recording events. Information passed on orally tends to change *en route,* not because the bearers want it that way, but by the very nature of oral narrative. One and the same story of Jesus of Nazareth is told differently by John and the synoptic gospels. The Church has always appreciated their different contributions; all efforts in the early centuries to harmonize the gospels and produce one account, such as Tatian's *Diatessaron,* failed.

b. The Gospel and the Johannine Epistles

John's gospel and the Johannine epistles are closely related. There are similarities in writing style and vocabulary (cf. 1:1-5; 1 John 1:1-4), in the mixture of persuasive and argumentative tone, in the insistent affirmation that Jesus is the Christ, the Son of God (20:31; 1 John 5:1, 5; 4:15; 2 John 3), in the theology of the incarnation (cf. 1:14; 1 John 4:2; 2 John 7), of God's love for the world as the motive for sending the Son (3:16; 1 John 4:9), and of love for the brethren as the distinguishing mark of the true disciple of Jesus and child of God (cf. 13:34-35; 15:17; 1 John 3:11, 16, 23; 4:7, 11-12).

But unlike the gospel the epistles more directly address the situation of the community. The introductions of the gospel and 1 John are similar; 1 John focuses not on the preexistence of the Word but on the fact that the author and his companions personally saw and experienced this Word that they now proclaim to the intended audience. Unlike in the gospel there is more direct emphasis on the necessity of love for the brethren, on Christian morals, and on guarding against spiritual pride, specifically manifested by believing that because one has been born of God one can no longer sin. The situation in the epistles reminds one very much of the attitude of a number of Christians today in the charismatic movements who consider themselves holy and those allegedly not "born again" as sinners.

These similarities and differences make scholars wonder about the exact relationship of the gospel to the epistles. In general most scholars believe that some or all of these works were written by the same author to meet the faith needs of the audience. While the gospel tackles the problem by putting the disciples directly in touch with Jesus and reminding them of the consequences of unbelief at that level, the epistles directly address the problems of faith and morals within the community. In other words the epistles seek to apply the message of the gospel more directly to the situation of the audience addressed. Though the works are similar, the style and vocabulary of the epistles is less polished than that of the gospel. This is because what is recorded in the epistles has not undergone the same polishing that the material in the gospel enjoyed through a long period of oral transmission.

c. *Old Testament and Judaism*

The relationship between the OT and John's gospel hardly needs to be emphasized. It is not possible to conceive of John's gospel without the OT and Jewish institutions. John dialogues fundamentally with these institutions, the matrix out of which Christianity grew. There are innumerable explicit references to OT passages (cf. 1:23, 51; 12:13, 15, 38, 40; 13:18; 17:12; 19:24, 28, 36, 37). In the Jerusalem Bible and in most of the recent Bible versions quotations to the OT are set in italics so they can easily be identified. The OT references are given in the margin at appropriate places and can be readily located and profitably consulted.

In addition John shows how the major themes and hopes on which Israel based its life and relationship with God are realized in Jesus: the very idea of Jesus as "the Christ, Son of God," Jesus as the Good Shepherd (10:1-16; cf. Ezek 34); bread of life and manna from heaven (John 6; Exodus 16), living water (4:1-15; 7:37-39; Ezek 47:1-12), the true vine (15:1-8; Isa 5:1-7; Jer 2:21; Ps 80:8-19[9-20]), the Temple (2:19); the references to Jewish feasts, especially the Passover. Indeed, some authors believe that John has a special concern for projecting Jesus as the one who replaces OT feasts: the Sabbath (5:1-47), the Passover bread of life (6:1-71), Tabernacles (7:1–10:21), and Dedication (10:22-42). Others see the first week of Jesus' ministry (1:19–2:1) as a parallel to the first week of creation (Gen 1:1–2:5). In brief, John's gospel lives and breathes in the OT world as its most natural habitat.

3. Qumran and Other Ancient Sources

In the nineteenth century it was fashionable to believe that John's gospel drew its inspiration from the work of Gnostic scholars, especially for its revelation discourses, but later with the discovery of the manuscripts at Qumran it became evident that the vocabulary and frame of thought scholars had thought was foreign to Palestine of the first century C.E. did in fact exist there. However, even though the language of John's gospel and that of Qumran resemble each other, for instance in the dualism of light and darkness and of belonging or not belonging to the world, a closer look reveals that these contrasts in John's gospel do not refer to ontological or cosmic dualities but to spheres of human behavior determined by whether or not one accepts or rejects Jesus as the Christ and conducts one's entire life accordingly. Today very few scholars believe that John's gospel had any appreciable links with Gnosticism, a second-century religious phenomenon.

The discussion on the relationship of John's gospel to the synoptic gospels, Johannine epistles, OT, and possibly the Qumran worldview indicates that the gospel did not exist in a vacuum but related naturally to its own religious and sociocultural world. The contemporary reader has the task not only of seeing how the gospel related to its world in history but of making serious efforts to relate this gospel to the thought patterns and scriptures or oral traditions of his or her own people without betraying the message of the gospel. This is the task of inculturation, which has become a necessary aspect of proclaiming the gospel. [See also the article on "Inculturation of the Biblical Message."]

John's Gospel in the Church

John's gospel is by nature an ecclesial document. It originated in the Church, was destined for church usage, was received into the NT canon by the Church, and throughout the centuries has served as a key gospel on which the Church bases its self-understanding.

John's gospel was born of the Church in a special way. Early patristic evidence narrates that the gospel was written by the apostle John at the request of his friends and bishops, and that what he recorded was the collective memory and cumulative reflections of all the apostles on the life of Jesus. The internal evidence of the gospel also proves its ecclesial character. John gives the unique evidence of the pierced side of Jesus from which blood and water flowed out (19:34). Patristic authors and saints like Juliana of Norwich interpreted this blood and water as signifying the two great sacraments of the Church, baptism and the Eucharist, which respectively give birth to and nourish God's children. They believed, accordingly, that the Church was born from Christ's pierced side on the cross.

In addition the gospel embodies powerful images of the Church understood as the body of Christ who always remains its inseparable head, indispensable source of life, and abiding shepherd (cf. 10:1-17; 15:1-17), enabling it to carry out its mission and setting the conditions for it (21:1-19). Concern with the harvest (4:35-38) and with the necessity of gathering together the scattered children of God (11:52; 17:20-23) constitute an integral part of this Johannine ecclesiology.

Today the Church defined as the "family of God" by the African Synod (*Ecclesia in Africa* no. 63) and as the "people of God" by the Second Vatican Council (*Lumen Gentium* 2) finds a solid gospel basis in John's consistent designation of all believers as disciples rather than apostles and in a less hierarchical manner than do the synoptics. John, for instance, never uses the term apostle for the disciples except in the parabolic context of 13:16, though he recognizes the twelve once (6:70). This does not mean that John is not in favor of leadership within the Church, for true leadership is an essential aspect of Jesus' continued care and concern for his flock (cf. 21:15-19).

1. The Gospel in History

Versions and translations of the gospel in Latin, Syriac, and Coptic suggest its widespread use in liturgical contexts in the ancient Church. The papyri Egerton 2 and Rylands 457, both discovered in Egypt and dated about 150 C.E., together with other papyri testify to its wide and early circulation within the Church.

Among the Apostolic Fathers, Ignatius of Antioch (ca. 110 C.E.) probably knew the gospel or at least knew of its traditions (cf. *Mang.* 7:1 [John 5:19; 8:28]; *Mang.* 8:2 [John 1:1; 8:29; 7:28]; *Phld.* 7:1 [John 3.8; 16:8]). So, too, Justin Martyr (ca. 150 C.E.; cf. *Apol.* 1.61 [John 3:8, 5]; *Dial.* 63 [John 1:13]; *Dial.* 88 [John 1:20]; *Dial.* 91 [John 3:14; 12:7]); Melito of Sardis (ca. 160–170; *Hom.* 78 [John 11:39-44]; *Hom.* 95 [John 19:19]); and Theophilus of Antioch (ca. 180), the first orthodox writer to ascribe the gospel to "John" (*Ad Autolycum* 2.22 [John 1:1]). While Ignatius, Justin, and Melito give only possible references to the gospel, Theophilus gives a direct reference. It is worth noting that the prologue which deals with the divinity of Jesus and the dialogue with Nicodemus which deals with the need for Christian rebirth formed the most common points of reference in this early usage.

In these early centuries John was also used by heretics. The first known commentary on the gospel is that of Heracleon (ca. 170 C.E.) mentioned by Origen in *In Ioannem*. Others included Basilides, Valentinus, and Ptolemaeus. These heretics used the gospel positively to buttress their tenets. The *Alogoi,* who were not really a sect, ascribed the gospel to Cerinthus, but according to an inscription preserved in the Lateran Museum (ca. 222 C.E.) this was rejected by Hippolytus.

In the second to the fifth centuries C.E. John's gospel was used in north Africa by Tertullian (ca. 145–220), Origen (ca. 222–231), Cyril of Alexandria (before 428), and Augustine (converted in 387). Tertullian wrote tracts against the heretics until he himself fell victim to the Montanist heresy (ca. 199). Origen wrote thirty-two volumes of commentaries on the first thirteen chapters of John, of which only eight and one half have survived intact (SC 120, 157, 22, 290, 385). Augustine's homilies on John (ca. 416) were directed mostly against heretics, both Manichaeans and Arians; his pastoral aim was to protect the faithful against these heresies. His homilies were to inspire Thomas Aquinas in the Middle Ages.

In the Eastern Church, John Chrysostom also wrote homilies on John before 398 (that is, before the outbreak of Nestorianism). He was known as the most powerful of the Johannine preachers. His homilies contained material for a well-instructed congregation and were a thorough and careful exposition comparable to the commentaries. Theodore of Mopsuestia, an older contemporary of Cyril of Alexandria, also wrote commentaries that were later translated into Syriac and Latin. He believed that the task of the commentator was to make the text clear, not to elaborate on its details as in a homily; he dwelt on the more difficult texts and on those perverted by the heretics.

Aquinas and Bonaventure, to a certain extent, stand out as representatives of medieval theologians who commented copiously on John's gospel. In their commentaries they sought to address all the heresies of the Church known to them. Since they were "schoolmen" their approach was disputative and academic without ceasing to be deeply theological, but it was a contrast to patristic exegesis that was more pastoral, theological, and life-oriented both for themselves and for their flock. This approach gave birth to dogmatic exegesis against which the Enlightenment and the historical-critical method reacted.

2. The Gospel in Modern Times

The importance of John's gospel in the life of the Church is not only a matter of history. Prior to the liturgical reforms of the Second Vatican Council, John's prologue was read at the end of every Mass, though this, like the rest of the liturgy, was in Latin. Today John's account of the Passion of Jesus (18:1–19:42) is read every year on Good Friday. In the seasons of Christmas, Holy Week, and Easter, John's gospel and epistles figure prominently, perhaps because they expound more theologically the mystery of the incarnation in all its aspects.

In the Lectionary of the Roman Rite almost the whole of John's gospel is used annually in the regular three-year cycle of readings and various liturgies of the Church: feasts of certain saints (for example, Mary Magdalene, July 22 [20:1-2, 11-18]; John the apostle, December 27 [20:2-8]; Thomas the apostle, July 3 [20:24-29]), for the administration of the sacraments (Christian initiation of adults and children, anointing of the sick, funeral Masses, marriage, confirmation, Holy Orders), consecration to a life of virginity and religious profession, institution of acolytes, anniversaries of the dedication of a church, Christian unity, votive Masses of the Eucharist, Sacred Heart, and Exaltation of the Cross, the commons of the Blessed Virgin and of pastors, and a host of other liturgical celebrations too numerous to mention. The whole gospel is broken into some 151 units, for use on about 272 different occasions.

Solid grounding in the faith of the gospel and awareness of the importance it has had in the life of the Church throughout the ages helps the reader to see it as a book of life that gives life. As happened in the early Church, John's gospel can also help Christians today to identify and combat the many subtle christological heresies that are gradually eroding their faith in Jesus, the Christ, Son of God.

Ways of Reading the Gospel

The basic principle of interpretation that governs the gospel itself is that Jesus is the Christ, the Son of God. This approach belongs to the general NT hermeneutic that saw the life and mission of Christ in terms of promise and fulfillment. Patristic and medieval exegesis sought to discover the inner (allegorical and spiritual) meaning, and in the Middle Ages in particular to use this meaning to refute heresies and defend the doctrines of the Church. Their approach, tagged "dogmatic exegesis," gave rise to the historical-critical method as a reaction to it. Until the last few decades of this century the historical-critical method was the primary tool used by biblical scholars. This method concentrated its search on the actual historical circumstances that inspired the writing of the gospel, its different levels of composition and redaction, and the religious background of the author and audience. This approach, also termed diachronic (through time), presupposed the existence and use of sources and different editions of the gospel. Each edition was believed to have its own theology and knowledge of Jesus. The main aim of the method, then, was to get back to the meaning that would have obtained at each level. The majority of the commentaries on John in this century were influenced by this method. Though the sources and levels of composition identified were purely hypothetical the approach drew attention to the need to take seriously the reality of the human as the context out of which the gospel grew and to which it was addressed.

In the past few decades a number of approaches termed synchronic (unified in time, the opposite of diachronic) have been developed for reading the gospel. These approaches include rhetorical methods, the reader-response approach, the incultural approach, and feminist hermeneutics. These approaches do not deny that the gospel went through different levels of redaction, but they emphasize the meaning of the gospel in its current canonical form. They work on the assumption that this current canonical form must have had a meaning for the final author and his audience; otherwise this work of the final editor would not have been undertaken since nobody writes a second or third edition of a book unless there is genuine need to modify what was written in previous editions. Besides, what has been canonized by the Church is this final form.

The reader-response approach may be seen today as the modern version of the allegorical/spiritual approach used by Origen and the medieval theologians, but it lays emphasis on what the text says to a given reader rather than on possible inner meanings that are not dependent on the life-situation of the reader (as was the case with medieval exegesis), and without concern also for the meaning it might have had for the author and his audience. This approach is used in certain charismatic circles. There is a tendency to loose the text from its historical moorings and read selected verses out of context, at times in a very fundamentalistic fashion. The Pontifical Biblical Commission has recently assessed the merits of the methods of interpretation currently in use (*The Interpretation of the Bible in the Church,* Rome 1993); it views fundamentalistic reading as the most dangerous approach.

The danger of subjectivism is real in any reading of the gospel, but since this gospel is essentially a community document one will need to sustain one's personal interpretation with the interpretation of the community, the Church, guided by the Holy Spirit. Moreover, since nothing is certain about the gospel except what is written in it, all interpretations must take seriously the entire data given in the gospel, not in isolation, but comprehensively. The interpretation will vary according to one's cultural background, theological interests, social location, race, class, and gender, but no authentic interpretation can be arbitrary. The gospel itself remains the ultimate judge of all interpretations. This calls for respect for the meaning intended by the author which, according to the Second Vatican Council (*Dei Verbum* 12), is the inspired meaning.

The real challenge facing the modern reader is to be able to make this gospel one's own without changing its inspired meaning. The faith dimension of the gospel also leads one to believe that the same Holy Spirit who inspired the evangelist and his community will continue to inspire Christian communities today and lead them to the complete truth God intends for them in their own contexts.

The current commentary gives priority to the final canonical text of the gospel and invites the reader to discover the gospel for himself or herself. Since the aim of John is to evoke a lifegiving faith in the audience, the reader is invited to allow the text to minister to each one in the concrete situations of daily life, for this is the place where one begins to experience concretely that fullness of life promised by Jesus in the gospel (10:10).

SECOND READING

Outline of the Fourth Gospel

Recalling our earlier discussion on structure, we propose the following outline as an example of the creative approach that was encouraged. The reader is invited to read each section of the gospel again, guided by this outline. The comments offered in this section are only intended to supplement the reader's own personal insights.

Part I: Introducing the Word/God and His Mission (1:1–2:25).

Introduction

- of the Word and his mission by the evangelist (1:1-18)
- of the Word made flesh by John the Baptist (1:19-36)
- of the first disciples to Jesus and of Jesus to the disciples (1:37-51)

Inaugural Self-Revelation of Jesus

- to the disciples at the initiative of his mother (2:1-12)
- to the Jewish leaders in Jerusalem (2:13-25)

Part II: Proclaiming the Agent and His Mission (3:1–4:42)

Proclaiming in Jerusalem and Judea (3:1-36)
- dialogue with Nicodemus on the necessity to be born of God (3:1-21)
- supportive witness given by the Baptist (3:22-36)

Proclaiming in Sychar and Samaria (4:1-42)
- dialogue of "the Christ" with the Woman of Samaria on life-giving water (4:1-26)
- dialogue with the disciples on the Father's work and what Jesus wants with the woman (4:27, 31-38)
- the woman and the Samaritans tell each other about "the Christ" and "the Savior of the World" (4:28-30, 39-42)

Part III: Jesus on Trial for His Claims and Mission (5:1–12:50)

For working like God by restoring life on the Sabbath (5:1-47)
- charged with the offense of healing on the Sabbath (5:1-16)
- defending against the charges and the implied claim to equality with God (5:17-44)
- reversing the charges: double unbelief of the accusers (5:45-47)

For offering himself as the Bread of Life (6:1-71)
- double evidence that the offering is real (6:1-25)
- dialogical invitation to believe in the offer (6:26-59)
- final rejection of the offer, and one response of faith (6:60-71)

For offering the Holy Spirit/Living Water, as "the Christ" (7:1-52)
- initial rejection by his relatives (7:1-10)
- debate and division over his messianic identity (7:11-36)
- the offer of living water (Holy Spirit) (7:37-39)
- responses of belief, unbelief, and attempted arrest (7:40-52)

For claiming to be God (8:1-11, 12-59): the first intensive hearing of the case
- an excuse for bringing on the trial (8:1-11)?
- Jesus' self-defense: he is the light of the world and the truth that sets humans free from sin (8:12-38)
- his counterattack on his accusers, children of the devil (8:39-47)
- his ultimate claim and offense: "I am" (8:48-59)

For giving sight to the blind, as the Light of the World (9:1-41)
- the cure of the man born blind, a revelation of God's work (9:1-12)
- the man and his parents on trial in place of Jesus (9:13-34)
- the accusers are indeed the ones who are blind (9:35-41)

For claiming to be the Good Shepherd (10:1-42)
- statement of the claim, readiness to die for the sheep (10:1-19)
- claims rejected by his opponents (10:22-42)

For claiming to be the Resurrection and the Life (11:1-57)
- the death of Lazarus certified (11:1-16)
- the raising of Lazarus as evidence of the claim (11:17-44)
- the evidence serves as the last straw against him (11:45-57)

Preparation for the final trial, prediction of ultimate triumph (12:1-50)
- Mary of Bethany prepares his body for burial (12:1-8)
- his triumphal entry into Jerusalem: he is acclaimed by the people, sought by the Greeks, believed secretly by some leaders (12:12-36, 42-43)
- the last resort of the opponents, the prophetic judgment, and Jesus' final appeal to them (12:9-11, 37-41, 44-50)

Part IV: Preparing the Disciples for the Future (13–17)

Called to love and service even in the face of betrayals (ch. 13)

Love: identity card of the true disciple (13:34-35)

Jesus their life, truth, and way to God through the Spirit (ch. 14)

Called to abide in Jesus and face the hatred of the world (chs. 15–16)

Jesus' public accountability to God for his mission and disciples (ch. 17)

Part V: The Final Trial and Victory: the Completion of the Work (18–20)

Judas's betrayal, arrest by enemies, and Peter's denial (18:1-27)

Final trials and condemnation by Pilate (18:28–19:16)

Conclusive evidence: the victory and bestowal of the fruits of the accomplished work on disciples (20:1-31)

Part VI: Conclusion: Disciples Sent on Mission, Remain In and Under Jesus (21)

To act without Jesus is futile (21:1-3)

Jesus enables the mission of the disciples (21:4-8)

Jesus sustains their life and love in mission (21:9-25).

Reading the Text

I: Introducing the Word/God and His Mission (1:1–2:25)

Prologue, 1:1-18

The prologue gives in a nutshell the content of the gospel in relation to the evangelist's purpose of revealing the true identity and mission of Jesus to the audience. It may be likened to the infancy narratives in Matthew and Luke in that it deals with Jesus' origins and announces the nature of his mission. Its major parts are vv. 1-5, the Word before the incarnation; vv. 6-9, 15, preview of the testimony of John the Baptist; vv. 9-13, human responses to the Word incarnate in the world; vv. 14-18, the incarnate Word as the visible glory or presence and unique revelation of the unseen God.

The Word Before the Incarnation (1:1-5)

In this section the evangelist introduces the identity of the Word in four spheres: pre-existent outside time (1-2), agent of creation within time (3), life and source of life (4), and the invincible principle conquering darkness or the forces of evil (5).

(1) The Word existed before creation and outside time (v. 1a) and its natural orientation was toward God (v. 1b); more than that, it was actually God (v. 1c). Some would say it was "a god," thus arguing that the Word was divine but not equal to God. Such an interpretation is weakened by what is said of the Word become flesh in the rest of the gospel (cf. 20:28). A major concern of John is to profess and establish faith in the divinity of Jesus as God's unique and uniquely beloved Son (v. 18). This notion of sonship draws attention to equality in nature, since a child is as truly human as are the parents. Jesus has the genes of God, so to speak, and is truly God (cf. 10:33).

Importantly, the prologue speaks simply of "the Word"' not of "the word of God." The OT describes the Torah as "the ten words" (Exod 34:28). In the course of time these ten words, elaborated and enlarged, came to assume a personal character in the personifications of wisdom (cf. Prov 8:22-36; Sir 24:3-22), that according to Sir 24:23 is "the book of the covenant of the Most High God, the law that Moses commanded us." Even in human context word and wisdom go together; otherwise one only utters folly. The spoken word becomes nonsense if it is not buttressed by wisdom and sound reasoning. A person's word reveals a person's thoughts, wisdom, reasoning powers, and mind at a given moment, but God is not a being that is becoming moment by moment. God is fullness of being (the "I Am") and unfathomable wisdom (cf. Rom 11:33); hence God's thought, wisdom, or mind expressed as word also has the fullness of all that God is. Therefore the prologue can state quite simply "the Word was God." The Word as concept and principle of expressed thought, knowledge, wisdom is as fully God as life and light.

(2) In the temporal order the Word was the agent of creation. Here John's gospel rejoins Gen 1:1–2:5 where God simply spoke and creation in its manifold variety came into being (cf. Pss 147:15; 104). God's Word is a creative force that accomplishes what it was sent to do (Isa 55:9-13); equally the word of Jesus himself endures forever (Matt 24:35). To appreciate the creative power of the Word in this verse one may reflect on the power even of the human word. Human beings made in the image and likeness of God (Gen 1:26-27) are essentially a word people. No interpersonal transaction or communication is carried out without the medium of the word, spoken or written. A word derives its power and authority from the speaker. In truly democratic societies the word of a nation's constitution is more powerful than that of the president, that of the president more weighty than that of the ordinary citizen. In an oral society like those of Africa the word becomes almost equivalent to action, especially when uttered as blessing or curse. The human word derives its effectiveness from God's Word and serves only as a tiny reflection of that Word.

(3) As God, the Word is life and source of life; the life of the Word that dwells in each person and people becomes their "light" of life, enlightening their consciences to distinguish between good and evil (cf. Rom 1:18-25, where Paul speaks of this in terms of innate knowledge of God). Psalm 119 (especially v. 105) celebrates this character of God's word with reference to the Torah. In Genesis 1 light was the first of God's creatures, because the ancient world believed that light was the principle of life, which put to flight darkness or nonexistence. John 1:4 moves from creation into the sphere of the moral authority of the Word.

(4) Verse 5 speaks of the struggle between the light and the darkness, not in the cosmic sense but in the ethical sense. The light "shines" (present tense), but the darkness "did not overcome" it (past tense). This light that is God (cf. 1 John 1:5), the light of truth, may be ignored, even suppressed, but it can never be put out. Darkness is the absence of light; it ceases to exist when light appears. No matter how thick the darkness, once there is a glimmer of light, the light cannot but be seen. Hence the saying "it is better to light one candle than to curse the darkness." The victory of the light over darkness recalls Paul's injunction, "do not be overcome by evil, but overcome evil with good" (Rom 12:21). Believers are to serve as light in the world, not to be overcome by the darkness of sin and evil. In this way they too share in the victory of the Word/Light over the darkness. (See also Matt 5:14-16.)

Preview of the Baptist's Witness (1:6-8, 15)

John the Baptist (JnB) is introduced in the prologue between the introduction of the Word in creation (vv. 3-5) and the coming of the Word into the world through the incarnation (v. 9). The Baptist is the last of the OT prophets and the representative of the OT covenant. Biblically this covenant stands between creation and the incarnation. As the last OT prophet JnB sums up OT witness about the Messiah and serves as a bridge between the OT and Christ. His role in the gospel is to identify for everybody the one of whom Moses and the prophets, that is, the entire OT tradition wrote (cf. 1:29, 35-36, 41, 45; 3:27-30). He is introduced again in v. 15 to underscore the radical difference between the OT dispensation given through Moses (v. 16) and what has come into existence in Jesus (v. 17).

Human Responses to the Word in the World (1:9-13)

Verses 9-11 speak of the negative responses to the Word in the world and vv. 12-13 of the positive response. These verses are a preview of the rejection or acceptance of Jesus, the Word made flesh. He is unknown by the world he created; more tragic still is his rejection by his own people: they did not receive him. In an African context reception of one's kith and kin involves celebration, recognition, giving gifts to the person received, and citation with pride of his or her achievements. The Word through whom the world was created received no such treatment from his own creation and his own people. In the gospel, for instance, Jesus' close relatives have no faith in him (cf. 7:3-5); his nation and the leaders of his people reject him even to death on the cross (cf. 18:35, 40).

Conversely, Jesus gives gifts to those who receive him. Verses 12-13 describe in detail the new birth of those who receive, that is, believe in the Word. They are given "power to become children of God." The word used for "children" here designates blood relationship. Believers are as much children of God and brothers and sisters of one another as are siblings and children of the same human father and mother. Concretely this enabling power is the Holy Spirit, the principle of new birth in God (cf. 3:3-8; 7:37-39). The first letter of John 3:9 speaks of this birth in God in terms of God's "seed" dwelling in the person. Jesus won for us this enabling power to become the children of God and blood brothers and sisters of one another by his death and the shedding of his blood on the cross (cf. 19:30, 33-34). This is the heart of the Easter message that Jesus entrusted to Mary Magdalene (20:17).

Contemporary charismatic, pentecostal, and various fellowship groups recognize the necessity of the Holy Spirit in the life of the believer, but the declaration that believers are siblings and children of God (in the blood of Jesus) holds great challenges for all Christians in our divided, racist, tribalistic, and nationalistic world. The measure to which one meets these challenges determines whether or not one is truly a child of God (cf. 1 John 3:11-18). Christians may be tempted also to decry the rejection of Jesus by his own relatives and people, but today we Christians are the closest relatives and people of Jesus. Do we receive him in his manifold comings: in the poor, the least of his brothers and sisters, in one another as blood brothers and sisters, in the Eucharist, in his teaching on gospel values, and in caring for Nature?

The Word Made Flesh: The Glory and Revealer of God (1:14-18)

The Word had already revealed God in creation and in the light of truth inherent in human beings. This Word became a human being in the person of Jesus Christ. In his person God pitched a tent among humanity in bodily, visible form, just as in the OT God dwelt visibly among God's people through the tabernacle that was housed in the tent of meeting and served as the locus for consulting YHWH and discovering the divine will through God's servant Moses (Exod 33:7-11; 40:1-38; Num 8:1-22; 17:8-13). The glory of the divine presence over the "tent of meeting" (NRSV) or "tent of presence" (NEB) was temporary; the tabernacle itself and the tent were made by human hands (Exod 35:10–39:43) and all the people contributed (cf. Exod 35:20-29). In Jesus, God's glory abides permanently with human beings, in human form. To know God fully one needs to study, know, and imitate Jesus and savor the joy of communion fellowship with him. This is how the contemporary believer can "see [and proclaim] his glory" even as the evangelist and his community did in their time (cf. 1 John 1:1-4).

A person's word emanates from a person's heart (out of the abundance of the heart the mouth speaks), reveals a person's thoughts, attitude, values, and character, or what and who one is (cf. Matt 15:18-20 // Mark 7:20-23). As God's Word made flesh Jesus not only embodies the fullness of the divinity (cf. Col 1:19); he also reveals the reality of God as far as human beings are capable of grasping it.

The human word, expressed thought, loses something in the process of transmission, and is subject to misunderstanding. One hears the word according to one's limited capacity. But as God's Word made flesh Jesus reveals God immediately, without any intermediary; to see and know him is to see and know God (14:6-7). Hence the possibility of the revelation losing something in the process of transmission is ruled out. God speaks and acts through him as he abides permanently in God's bosom (v. 18). The inevitable misunderstanding arising from the limitations of the hearer is taken care of by the gift of the Holy Spirit who alone knows the mind of God and leads believers gradually into the complete truth (14:16, 26; 16:13).

Verses 16-18 underscore the difference between the revelation of God brought through the Mosaic covenant and that which has come in the person of Jesus. The former derives its essence from the Law, a series of do's and don'ts. It was exclusive in nature. The dispensation that has come in the person of Jesus is stamped and characterized by "grace and truth." Grace is a totally free, unmerited, and undeserved gift; truth here is that which is genuine, real, and dependable. The Law prescribed what one was to do but gave one no power to do it. Grace is a power from within that transforms and empowers one to live as a child of God. The letter to the Romans (especially 7:7–8:4) serves as the best commentary on this issue of the relative merits of grace and the Law. This gift of grace is not received independently of Jesus who is the Father's exegete or interpreter and the irreplaceable dispenser of divine blessings.

The prologue is read at the Third Mass of Christmas; on December 31, the Seventh Day of the Octave of Christmas; and in the liturgy for Christian initiation outside the Easter Vigil. In these contexts the reading not only reminds us of the Word who became flesh in the person of Jesus; it invites believers to become in turn the embodiment of God's word in the world so that God may continue to be revealed and known through us. The early Christians had a profound respect for the gospel, the preached word. Paul saw it as the "foolish thing," humanly speaking, that God used to save believers (cf. 1 Cor 1:21). Christians today are encouraged to show the same love for the Word and the gospel and to watch over their own human word to ensure that it gives life and is equally full of "grace and truth."

Introduction of the Word Made Flesh by John the Baptist, 1:19-36

The Baptist's testimony concretely illustrates what was said of his mission in 1:6-8, 15, namely, that he would bear witness to Jesus so that all might believe in him. Bearing witness or giving testimony is very important in the gospel. To qualify as a witness one needs to personally experience first hand the events to which one testifies, and not act from hearsay. The Baptist's

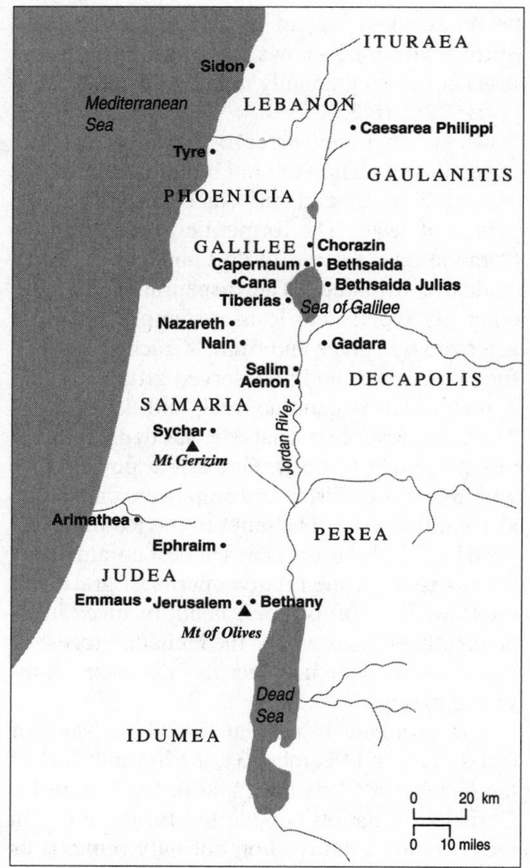

JOHN'S PALESTINE

testimony is given on three levels: to official Judaism (vv. 19-28), to the general public (vv. 29-34) and to his disciples (vv. 35-36). The manner of his bearing witness is as important as, if not more important than the actual content of his witness.

This manner is one of profound humility, already evinced in 1:15. The official delegation from Jerusalem (equivalent to the Congregation for the Doctrine of the Faith in the contemporary Roman Catholic Church) is sent to find out who John is. Implied in their question is "are you the Messiah?" The Baptist's answer is directed to this implied question. He emphatically disclaims being the Messiah or the other messianic figures expected in Judaism, Elijah (Mal 4:5 [3:23]) or the prophet like Moses (Deut 18:18). The verbs "confess" and "did not deny" (v. 20) register his total freedom and happiness in not wanting to be mistaken for the Messiah. Some scholars attribute this emphasis to the alleged anti-Baptist polemic in the gospel, but humility characterizes JnB's witness throughout the gospel (cf. 3:27-30) even as it characterizes Jesus' own witness to the Father (cf. 4:34; 5:29-30; 14:10); it should also characterize that of the Christian (13:15-17).

In the synoptic gospels Jesus identifies JnB as the Elijah whose task was to prepare the people for the coming of the Messiah by reconciling them to God and to one another (cf. Matt 17:10-12 // Mark 9:11-13). The Baptist's baptismal ministry in the synoptics serves this function of repentance and reconciliation (cf. Matt 3:1-3; Mark 1:2-4; Luke 3:1-6), but the Fourth Gospel focuses attention on JnB's mission as the one who points out the long-expected Messiah to the people. In the synoptics the Pharisees also went to John to be baptized along with the people. Here they come to ask questions. Though the synoptics do not say so, it is not unlikely that the leaders would have asked the Baptist questions similar to the ones recorded in John. The messianic identity of Jesus is not a matter for private, personal discovery. It can only be known through explicit revelation from God or Jesus himself (cf. 1:31; 4:25-26; Matt 16:17) and then communicated to others.

While JnB disclaims being the Messiah he identifies himself as the prophetic "voice" crying in the wilderness, spoken of by Isaiah (40:3). What matters about a voice (as that of a town crier or a radio or television newscaster) is what it says. The reference to the wilderness suggests that what JnB proclaims about Jesus will fall mostly on deaf ears (cf. 5:33). His testimony to official Judaism diverts attention from himself and arouses their curiosity to look for the Messiah who is in their midst, but is unknown to them.

This curiosity sets the scene for the identification of Jesus as the Messiah, lamb of God for the general public. Verses 29-34 recall the baptism of Jesus in the synoptics and presuppose it. This was the occasion on which JnB saw the Holy Spirit "descend and remain" on Jesus (v. 32). John's gospel interprets this event as God's promised personal revelation of the Messiah to JnB, who was commissioned to reveal him to the world. Having received and believed in God's own testimony, he is able to witness to Jesus before his people. His baptismal activity served as the place for discovering and proclaiming the Messiah just as each person's ministry should serve as the place for discovering and serving Jesus proclaimed in the gospel.

In JnB's testimony Jesus is "the one who baptizes with the Holy Spirit" (v. 33); some manuscripts add "with fire," perhaps under the influence of Acts 2:3-4. As mentioned in the discussion of 1:12-13, the Holy Spirit is the principle of our new life as children of God. Jesus' baptism is not one of external cleansing or purification as was the case with JnB's baptism. The Baptist does not hesitate to recognize the superiority of Jesus' ministry over his own (cf. 3:22-30).

He also identifies Jesus as the "lamb of God" and "Son of God." His own audience would have seen in these designations references to both the Jewish paschal lamb or the meek lamb metaphorically identified with the humble servant of God (Isa 53:7; Jer 11:19) and to the expected Davidic Messiah (some witnesses have "chosen one of God" instead of "Son of God"). The Johannine audience would have heard in them a reference to Jesus, the "uniquely begotten" Son of God and the Christian paschal lamb who was slain to take away the sin of the world (1 Pet 1:19; Rev 5:6, 12). The "sin of the world" here (singular) could be the sin of unbelief in God shown in the rejection of Jesus (cf. 3:19-20; 15:22) and consequently in the refusal to love all God's children. The Baptist's witness in this section reinforces that of the previous section and climaxes in his encouraging his own disciples to leave him and follow Jesus.

Introduction of Jesus to the First Disciples, 1:37-51

The process by which the disciples are called in John differs from that in the synoptics, where Jesus personally calls the first disciples (cf. Matt 4:18-22 // Mark 1:16-20). Here JnB first introduces two of his own disciples to Jesus. These in turn having discovered where Jesus lives, that is, having formed an intimate acquaintance with him, go in search of their friends to bring them to Jesus. John's account thus emphasizes the need for believers to lead others to Jesus. Today the charismatics speak of "sharing Jesus with others." This procedure is what would actually have happened in the Johannine community as it did in the early Church (cf. Acts 8:4-5; 11:19-20; 1 John 1:1-4). The same obtained in the missionary Church through the ages and needs to continue in our times.

Two other features of this call narrative are worth noting. One is the predominance of the verbs of seeing: vv. 29 (2x), 32, 33, 34, 36, 38, 39, 42, 46, 47, 48, 50 (2x), 51. The ability to "see" is an important aspect of discipleship and is regarded by Jesus as a beatitude along with the ability to hear (cf. Matt 13:16 // Luke 10:23-24). In this passage the ability to see goes with that of looking for and finding. Those who look for and find Jesus in this life in the company of other disciples will see him in his glory at the last day (cf. 1:51). As in the case of Jacob's ladder (Gen 28:12), cited in 1:51, one has only to look in one's own place of work and ministry to find Jesus (cf. Gen 28:16-17). Jesus depends on those who have seen him to proclaim him to others so that they too may "come and see" and remain with him for the rest of the day, or the rest of their lives (cf. v. 39).

The second striking aspect of the narrative is that both JnB and his disciples begin by proclaiming Jesus to their own kindred and closest companions. JnB introduced his own disciples to Jesus; Andrew, one of the first two to follow Jesus, found his own brother Simon to whom Jesus gave the name "Cephas" or "Rock" (Latin "Petrus," English "Peter"); Philip, the only one of this group called personally by Jesus, came from the same city as Andrew and Peter (v. 44). Nathanael is from Cana in Galilee (21:2) where Jesus will work his inaugural "sign" (2:1). He was most likely studying or teaching the Torah under the fig tree when Philip called him, something a true and perfect Israelite was expected to do (cf. v. 47). This narrative invites Christians today to proclaim or share Jesus with members of their families and with their closest friends and associates, for charity begins at home.

Inaugural Self-Revelation of Jesus, 2:1-25

Revelation to the Disciples at the Initiative of His Mother (2:1-12)

The episode of the wedding in Cana of Galilee brings one down to earth, to an ordinary human event in contrast to events at the end of ch. 1. This episode qualifies as a good short story: not a word is superfluous, yet it is packed with literal and symbolic meanings. The main characters are the mother of Jesus who "was there" and Jesus with his disciples who "were also invited." Is there any nuance in meaning between these two verbs? The wedding feast with its promise of new life provides the context or scenario for the drama.

The "third day" could be the seventh day of the first week of events in the gospel, beginning with 1:19. In this case the first week of the narrative would correspond to the first week of creation in Genesis (1:1–2:5). The wedding feast then would remind one of Gen 2:24 where in God's plan man and woman become one flesh. The seventh day of creation was a Sabbath. In John the seventh day becomes the first day of the new creation brought into existence by Jesus' mission. In this light the "third day" can be seen as a reference to the biblical third day when God intervenes in human life and situations to bring about salvation or judgment, hence a new order of reality and relationships.

The episode in Cana is John's account of Jesus' inaugural work or sign, comparable to Luke 4:18-21. Jesus begins his mission in earnest, a mission that consists in working "signs" to reveal his glory in order to evoke a lifegiving knowledge and faith in his audience. For the first time he reveals his glory, that is, he lets his disciples into the secret of God who dwells in him as at the transfiguration in the synoptic gospels. The "mother of Jesus" plays a decisive role in bringing about this inaugural sign. She serves as a midwife who helps a reluctant expectant mother to push and give birth. Her words in v. 3 are a most powerful prayer offered by way of information. (It reminds us of Jesus' teaching on prayer in Matt 6:7 and Mark 11:24.) Jesus objects on the ground that his hour has not yet come, but by her undaunted yet silent faith his mother initiates the event that foreshadows and leads to that hour. God, in this instance, upheld the rights of the mother over her son (cf. Sir 3:2b). On this hour, the decisive beginning of his mission, depended the hour of the completion of this mission, the hour of his "glorification" (cf. 13:1; 17:1).

The new wine Jesus provides functions on two levels. It is real wine for the wedding couple to save them from embarrassment—they were not even aware that they had no more wine. Symbolically it signifies the wine of true knowledge of Jesus that gives eternal life (cf. 2:11; 17:3). Jesus is the real bridegroom (3:29). He transforms the waters of our humdrum daily activities into pearls of grace. This event is an example of how the grace and truth that came with Jesus transcend the Law (here of Jewish purification) that was given through Moses. The ferment of the new wine is the blood of Jesus in the Eucharist and the gift of the Holy Spirit that in Acts 2:13 is associated with intoxicating "new wine."

This sign is called the "first," best translated "inaugural" or "foundational" sign (not the first in a series). It sets the purposeful pace for all signs and works of Jesus in the gospel, namely to reveal the presence and action of God in and through him (cf. 14:9-11). Jesus' mother is present at this inaugural sign as she will be at the last one. On both occasions Jesus calls her "woman" (2:4; 19:26). Some hold that Jesus is here rejecting the tradition that, especially in Africa, tends to evaluate the woman in terms of her ability to be the mother of somebody. Others see this designation as an example of Jesus' alleged contempt for his mother. The text points in a different direction. The term "woman," here used in the vocative, recalls the first good news for humanity in Gen 3:15, the promise that is fulfilled in John 19:30. Here Mary, the new Woman/Eve, becomes the mother of all the disciples whom Jesus loves (cf. Gen 3:20) and is taken into their homes (19:26-27) in the new order of creation that surpasses the first (cf. 2:10).

The problematic phrase in 2:4, variously translated as "Woman, what concern is that to you and to me?" (NRSV), or "Your concern, mother, is not mine" (NEB), or "Woman, why turn to me?" (JB)—(literally "what to me and to you?")—is also interpreted as indicating Jesus' rejection of his mother's interference in his mission. The expression is used in Mark 1:24 and 5:7 by demons who recognize that Jesus does indeed have something to do with them but are afraid of this action, his casting them out of the peoples whom they possess. For them it is a plea to be spared. Based on this analogy, Jesus' words are a covert recognition that his mother does have something to do with him, or that her concern is also his. Jesus seems reluctant to begin his work in earnest. His mother gives him no option, as it were, though what he does is up to him (v. 5). From this point onward Jesus begins his mission in earnest.

At the beginning of the story the mother of Jesus and Jesus with his disciples seem to be apart; the impression is given that they went to the feast independently of each other. As a result of the successful dialogue between them, a dialogue that happened because Jesus listened to her, they move away together as one family after the feast to Capernaum (v. 12), Jesus' home town. The omega sign of Jesus will bring together into a unity the scattered children of God (cf. 11:52). John 2:12 can be seen as foreshadowing this.

Revelation to the Jewish Leaders in Jerusalem (2:13-25)

In the synoptic gospels Jesus goes to Jerusalem only once, toward the end of his life, to face his passion and death, but in John most of his ministry takes place in Jerusalem and Judea. After the wedding feast in Cana of Galilee, Jesus goes to Jerusalem to celebrate his first Passover feast; the last Passover will be his own Passover from this world to the God who sent him (13:1). As in the synoptics, his first act in Jerusalem is the "cleansing" of the Temple. The Temple is supposed to serve as the center for worship and praise of God. What Jesus finds there is the very opposite.

The buying and selling would have taken place in the outer court of the Gentiles. Gentiles were already considered as unclean people. Polluting their court by the dubious trade that went on there added to contempt for them. Worse still, the animals sold and bought in this illegal trade were offered in sacrifice to God, something that benefited the leaders. The situation recalls that of contemporary drug trafficking where the drug barons stay at home and get the little people to do the dirty work for them.

By cleansing the Temple, Jesus transfers the concern for mere ritual purity (cf. the six stone jars used for purification in 2:6) to that for moral cleansing. The citation in v. 16 is from Zechariah 14:21, where God's house is seen as a house of prayer for all peoples, including the Gentiles. The leaders miss the symbolic value of Jesus' action and instead ask for a sign. The disciples who are ready to listen and learn by reflecting on Jesus' actions understand the meaning of the sign with the help of Ps 69:9[10]. Jesus gives the leaders the sign of his resurrection, as in the synoptics (the sign of Jonah). Again the leaders misunderstand, but the disciples, like Mary (Luke 2:51), keep his words in their hearts and ponder them. After the resurrection they remember and believe both the Scriptures and the word Jesus had spoken.

John 2:19-22 is read on feasts of the dedication of churches. Jesus referred to his body as a temple. The Holy Spirit dwells fully in that body (1:32). The body of the Christian is also a temple of the Holy Spirit (1 Cor 6:19). This passage invites us to reflect on what pollutes God's houses of prayer and the temples of human bodies today. Does illegal trafficking take place in the name of God and of religion? Do people proclaim the word in order to make money? Are ill-gotten goods and wealth offered to God? First Corinthians 5–6 serves as a good commentary on the "cleansing" that needs to be undertaken in human bodies dedicated to God so that we can celebrate God without "the yeast of malice and evil" but with that of "sincerity and truth" (1 Cor 5:8; cf. John 4:24).

Verses 23-25 are a summary passage recording that Jesus was not in the habit of being deceived by external show of faith in his "signs." In Jerusalem people "believed" in him because of the "signs" they saw, but their faith was not deep enough because it was not based on a true knowledge of Jesus and his mission. An example of such skin-deep faith is that of the people in 6:26-31: they saw the sign of the multiplication of the loaves and followed Jesus but failed to see the deep significance of that sign when Jesus explained it to them (cf. 6:60, 66). In the immediate context the passage is an introduction to the ensuing dialogue with Nicodemus in ch. 3.

II: Proclaiming the Agent and His Mission (3:1–4:42)

In Jerusalem and Judea, 3:1-36

Dialogue with Nicodemus on the Necessity of Being Born of God (3:1-21)

This dialogue has four sections: the introduction of Nicodemus (3:1-2), the teaching on the necessity of birth from God (3:2-8), the explanation of how this birth can happen, including an upbraiding of Nicodemus for his lack of understanding (3:9-17), and the consequences of this teaching for those who receive it (3:18-21).

Nicodemus, who has a Greek name, is introduced as a key figure among the Pharisees, who were known for their devotion to the interpretation and observance of the Law, and a leading elder among the people. He would have been a member of the Sanhedrin, the highest governing body in Judaism (cf. 7:50). In this double capacity he was "a teacher of Israel" (v. 10). He comes to Jesus at night, probably out of fear of his colleagues, given the previous confrontation between Jesus and the leaders during the cleansing of the Temple. Nicodemus is impressed with the signs Jesus worked during the feast of the Passover (2:23). He speaks for the people and the leaders ("we know") when he declares, on the basis of these signs, that Jesus must be "a teacher from God." His statement echoes that of the authorities in the synoptics when they go to question Jesus about paying tribute to Caesar (cf. Matt 22:16 // Mark 12:14 // Luke 20:21). Nicodemus admires Jesus, whom he regards as a teacher like himself, but he does not really know who Jesus is or what he wants from him. He typifies the imperfect believers mentioned in 2:23-25.

Jesus accepts Nicodemus's affirmation that he is a teacher from God, and proceeds to show him why he came from God as a teacher. The teaching is a solemn declaration on the necessity for human beings to be born from God ("anew" and "from above") if they are to enter or see the reign of God. Nicodemus misunderstands and thinks that "anew" means a second time, referring to natural birth. No one can be born physically a second time, whether one is young or old. Jesus takes great pains to explain to Nicodemus that he means birth from above, that is, from God, which birth is brought about through water and the Holy Spirit or baptism. As one becomes a human being by being born of earthly parents ("what is born of the flesh is flesh"), so one becomes a child of God by being born of God ("what is born of the Spirit is spirit"). Judaism spoke of its proselytes as people who experienced a new birth; hence Nicodemus as a teacher of Israel should have understood what Jesus meant. Instead he continues to ask incredulously how such a birth could happen.

Jesus first upbraids him for his incredulity and inability to grasp a teaching that is within earthly or human reach (things of earth), that is, that uses the analogy of physical birth to explain spiritual or ritual rebirth (vv. 10-12). Jesus also corrects Nicodemus's understanding of him as a teacher from God: he is from God in a unique way (v. 13), not simply as a charismatically endowed teacher among others (v. 2). Because Jesus is uniquely from God, he alone bears witness to things that he has seen in heaven; his testimony, though rejected, is therefore worthy of trust (v. 11).

Having drawn Nicodemus's attention to his own predicament, Jesus proceeds to teach him how and why the birth from above can happen. This birth will be made possible through his passion, death, and resurrection, or his being "lifted up" and "glorified" (v. 14), an act by which Jesus will draw all peoples to himself (12:32). The reference to the brazen serpent (Num 21:8-9) is a reminder that God used the very instrument of the people's punishment to save those who were willing to submit to God's saving action. By way of analogy Jesus, who is rejected, especially by the leaders, is God's unique agent of salvation for all humanity, and "they will look on the one whom they have pierced" (19:37).

The necessity to be born from God, if one is to become a child of the kingdom, is rooted in God's pure and unmerited love for the world (vv. 16-17). The depth of this love is measured by God's gift of the uniquely beloved divine Son, loved as no one else is loved. God could not have given anything more precious to prove how much God loves us. Romans 5:8-11; 8:31-39; 1 John 4:9-10 comment on this incredible love of God for the world. John emphasizes that God's action is to save, not to condemn or destroy. Jesus came to give life in its fullness to those who are willing to accept it (John 10:10). By loving unto death on the cross he concretized God's love for humanity in his own person (13:1; 15:13). God's love is the sole explanation for Jesus' mission of salvation.

A person's response to Jesus and his mission determines whether or not one is judged/condemned or whether one benefits from his saving mission (vv. 18-21). Jesus is God's light sent to the world to show human beings how they may walk in him, "the way, the truth, and the life" in order to reach God (14:6). Those who reject him choose to remain in darkness rather than face the challenge of changing their "evil" ways (vv. 19-20). By so doing they pronounce their own judgment and condemnation (v. 18b); conversely those who accept Jesus and walk with him or "come into the light" (v. 21) are not judged. They show by their deeds that they are indeed born of God. A concrete explanation of what it means to be "in the light" or "in darkness" is found in 1 John 2:7-11.

John 3:3-8 is a favorite passage among the charismatics who have merited the name "born-again Christians." The temptation is to play down baptism in favor of "Spirit baptism," as if the Spirit was not given at baptism. What is important in Jesus' teaching in this passage and in the passages from 1 John referred to above is that one who claims to be born again or born from God needs to show it by loving as God and Jesus loved humanity, even to the point of laying down their life for the brothers and sisters (13:34-35; 1 John 3:16). This love is the acid test of whether or not one is really born from God or is a born-again Christian. Experiencing charismatic gifts, though good, is not the real indication that one is a child of God. First Corinthians 13:1-3 makes this plain. The reading of John 3:1-21 during the Second Week of Easter reminds one that sharing in Christ's new life requires sharing concretely in his life of love.

Supportive Evidence Given by the Baptist (3:22-36)

This section records JnB's final testimony to Jesus. It has two parts: his acceptance of the implications for him personally of his witness to Jesus (vv. 22-30) and his final appeal to his audience to accept the teaching and claims Jesus makes in the dialogue with Nicodemus (vv. 31-36). The Baptist had previously confessed that he was not the Messiah and that Jesus was God's lamb who takes away the sin of the world. Taking him at his word, the people leave him to seek the baptism of Jesus. They must have believed the baptism of Jesus was more effective for purifying one from sins than that of John (cf. v. 25). Devoted disciples of John try to talk him into waking up to the fact that Jesus was taking the people away from him (v. 26).

The Baptist uses this opportunity to register once and for all his declaration that he is not the Christ. Jesus is here presented as taking over the baptismal activity of John (v. 22), or at least baptizing concurrently with him, though the synoptics do not record this. Instead of protesting, John sings his *Nunc Dimittis* and celebrates Jesus as the bridegroom who has finally come to claim his bride, an imagery heightened by the wedding feast in 2:1-11. He proclaims the eschatological imperative that Jesus must increase and he decrease. His final witness to Jesus consists in living out the implications of his mission.

The second part of his final witness (vv. 31-36) is a plea to all to listen to Jesus and accept his testimony. The appeal addresses in particular the themes of Jesus' dialogue with Nicodemus. (Compare 3:31-32 and 3:11-13; 3:36a and 3:16-17; 3:36b and 3:19-20a.) In addition this final witness underscores Jesus' unique relationship with God as the one whom God loves, to whom God has entrusted everything and who possesses the Spirit in full measure, which recalls 1:32. The Baptist is indeed one who has received God's testimony about Jesus and lived it to the full. From this point he disappears from the gospel, though his testimony lives on (cf. 5:33; 10:41).

The testimony of JnB challenges the contemporary pastor and Christian to examine their manner of bearing witness to Jesus. What does one do if a fellow Christian or pastor succeeds better than oneself in the ministry? Is the response one of rejoicing that people are led to Christ through such a ministry or is the temptation to act like the disciples of John the Baptist? Bearing witness to Jesus entails more than preaching. The most powerful witness is the testimony of one's life in Christ.

Proclaiming in Sychar and Samaria, 4:1-42

John 4:1-42 presents Jesus' mission in Sychar, probably modern Shechem, and Samaria in four sections: introduction (vv. 1-6), dialogue with the Samaritan woman (vv. 7-26), dialogue with the disciples (vv. [27], 31-38), and encounter with the Samaritans (vv. [28-30], 39-42). The reader may note the contrast between the response of the Samaritan woman and other Samaritans (strangers and enemies of the Jews) and that of Nicodemus, an orthodox and leading Jew.

Introduction (4:1-6)

Jesus' mission through Samaria appears to be occasioned by the growing hostility of the Pharisees but is in fact part of his mission of presenting himself and proclaiming his gospel to all nations, first the Jews, now the Samaritans, and finally the Greeks (representing the Gentiles: 12:20-26; but cf. 4:44-54 below).

The introductory scene in Samaria draws attention to the issue of gift (of the well by Jacob to his son Joseph), and the well itself. The verb used to describe Jesus' tiredness from the journey is used in the NT for missionary labor. The physical journey in the noonday heat, reinforced by the disciples' departure to look for food (v. 8), makes the request for a drink genuine. The ensuing dialogue with the woman has two parts: knowledge of the gift of God expressed as "living water" (vv. 7-15) and knowledge of who Jesus is (vv. 16-26). Verse 10, like the text for a homily, encapsulates these two themes. Knowledge of who Jesus is makes one ask him for "living water."

The Samaritan woman is an important character in the dialogue. The Jews regarded the Samaritans as people possessed by the devil (cf. 8:48). Sirach (50:25-26) despises them as a nation. Samaritan women not only shared this lot of their people, they were further regarded as menstruants from birth (*m. Nid.* 4.1), that is, ritually unclean by nature. Second Kings 17:5-21 gives the origins of the Samaritans, and Ezra 4 the background to the hostility between them and the Jews. The woman's moral record (v. 18), compounded with this general situation, would have made her a most unlikely dialogue partner with Jesus, a Jew.

The Gift of God (4:7-15)

In his dialogue with the woman Jesus uses the woman's daily experience as the medium of communicating the gospel: the fetching of water, the revered well that dates back to their ancestor Jacob. This ancestral heritage gave the Samaritans a biblical identity that transcended the contempt of their Jewish neighbors. The well was deep, fed by an underground stream, hence containing living (that is, running) water. The well was Jacob's gift to his most beloved son, Joseph.

In contrast Jesus is God's most beloved Son and gift to humanity. He is God's agent who gives God's gift of "living water," understood primarily as the Holy Spirit (7:37-39), and true knowledge of God and Jesus himself (17:3). This gift abides in the receiver, even as do Jesus himself, the Father, and the Holy Spirit (14:14, 23), sources of eternal life and love, unlike the well water which is external and needs buckets and strenuous efforts to reach (cf. vv. 11, 15).

Who Jesus is (4:16-26)

The woman is not impressed by Jesus' promise of living water until he, a stranger and a Jew, reveals to her that he knows about her private life (vv. 17-18). The five husbands of the woman have been interpreted symbolically as the five gods of the five foreign nations the Assyrians brought to inhabit Samaria (cf. 2 Kings 17:23-41), or the five books of Moses, the only part of the Jewish Scriptures the Samaritans acknowledged. These symbolic interpretations cannot rule out the literal one of five husbands, which is the way the woman understood it (v. 29a). Jesus' knowledge of her private life makes her open for the first time to his dialogue; it also moves the dialogue to its second theme, namely who Jesus is.

Recognizing that Jesus is a prophet because of his knowledge of her private life, the woman puts before him a problem that was dear to the prophets of Israel, namely true worship of God. Jesus' answer in vv. 21-24 would have greatly surprised the woman, since no "orthodox" Jew would have dared to relativize Jerusalem as a place of worship as Jesus did. The Jews believed that in the last times all nations would come to Jerusalem to worship (cf. Isa 2:1-3).

Jesus shifts the focus from the correct place to worship to the correct meaning of worship, and from what the ancestors did in the past to what the Father does now in true worshipers. God enables true worship in believers. Worship in spirit and truth means the orientation of one's entire life and being toward God. Jesus is the example of such a worshiper (v. 34). Jesus' words and manner must have led the woman to wonder whether he might not be the Messiah in the light of v. 10a; hence her statement of belief in v. 25 is not out of place. Jesus rewards this statement by openly revealing to her his identity as the Christ.

One may note in this passage the humble, patient, and respectful manner in which Jesus approaches the woman and leads her to knowledge of himself; yet respect for her ancestral and religious heritage does not hide the truth that God has something better to offer, nor that God's salvation to humanity came historically through the Jews as a point of departure (v. 22; Rom 9:4-5), not as origin or source. Salvation comes only from God. Once the woman is persuaded that Jesus is the Messiah she does not hesitate to run to the city to share the good news with her people and bring them to Jesus (vv. 28-30).

Dialogue with the Disciples (4:[27], 31-38)

Jesus' disciples play an important role in this episode. Verse 8 gives the impression that had they been present the dialogue with the woman would not have taken place. Their reaction in v. 27 confirms this. Their great surprise in seeing Jesus speaking with a woman arises from their religious and cultural upbringing whereby Jews were forbidden even to greet a woman in public (*b. Kid.* 70a), to say nothing of a Samaritan woman. They persuade Jesus to eat the food they had brought to him, possibly also as a way of forgetting "what Jesus wanted with a woman" (cf. v. 27).

Jesus uses their concern for food to instruct them about his commitment to God's work which includes his dialogue with the woman, even as he had used the woman's concern with water fetching to communicate with her in vv. 1-15. Jesus finds the reason for his existence and his sustenance in doing and completing God's work, namely the work of salvation (cf. 17:4). Either proverbially or at the time of the dialogue it was four months to the harvest (v. 35). The harvest is the NT imagery for the missionary work of the disciples (cf. Matt 9:37-38 // Luke 10:2), but God's scheme of salvation does not depend on human reckoning. The harvest is "ready" in the episode in the coming of the Samaritans to Jesus (v. 30).

God's work, which Jesus alone does and completes (4:34; 17:4), is the work of salvation. This completed work ushers in the harvest. All others, including the disciples and all future missionaries, benefit from this completed work (v. 38). Their very participation in the mission by leading others to Jesus is their own reward (4:36; cf. 1 John 1:4). God, Jesus, and the disciple-missionaries rejoice together since the harvest brings together God's scattered children into the one fold of Christ.

This teaching on the relative roles of God, Jesus, and the disciples in mission is illustrated in vv. 39-42. Having received the good news from Jesus, the woman proclaims it to her people. They invite Jesus to stay with them and he does so for two days, together with his disciples. In the process the Samaritans discover Jesus for themselves. The woman, their missionary, does not become an indispensable link between them and Jesus. Their personal contact with Jesus enables them to confess that Jesus is not only the Jewish or Samaritan Messiah but "the Savior of the World" (v. 42).

John 4:1-42 holds the key for understanding John's theology of and method in mission. Jesus' respectful attitude toward the woman and the Samaritans challenges all missionaries, that is, the entire Church, to learn from him the techniques of successful missionary undertaking. These include using the realities, traditions, and daily concerns of the people in proclaiming the gospel to them. True missionary work should break down age-old barriers of race, sex, and class between peoples. At the end of the endeavor the people evangelized should grow in stature as the woman did. She became an effective apostle to her people. Jesus depended on her to introduce him to the Samaritans just as he depended on John the Baptist to introduce him to the Jews; but as JnB faded out of the picture after he had done his work, so does the woman, and so should all true disciple-missionaries and witnesses to Jesus, so that Jesus and God may become all in all.

Back to Cana in Galilee (4:43-54)

The return to Cana in Galilee brings the first cycle of Jesus' missionary work (chs. 2–4) to a close. It began with a wedding feast in Cana of Galilee and ends here in the same Cana with the cure of the official's son. The official is most probably not a Jew, but a Roman official (cf. Matt 8:5-13 // Luke 7:1-10). If he is not a Jew, John has completed here the first cycle of friendly respondents to Jesus among the Jews, Samaritans, and Gentiles. Of interest in this section is the way in which the faith of the official moves from belief in Jesus' power to cure his son (v. 50) to belief in Jesus himself, together with his household (v. 53).

III: Jesus on Trial for His Claims and Mission (5:1–12:50)

John 5–12 is characterized by the disputative approach to Jesus' identity and mission. All the events (except those in ch. 6) take place in Jerusalem and Judea. The disputes are largely with the Jewish authorities. In the synoptics Jesus' ministry in Jerusalem or his encounters with the leaders are also marked by disputes, though these are not as fully developed as in John. The evidence from the synoptics indicates that John did not make up these disputes even though he may have given them their current literary, forensic rhetorical form. Two major themes run through this section: Jesus is the Messiah, the Son of God who is commissioned by God to give life to the world. Faith in him is all that is required of those who wish to gain this life.

On Trial for Restoring Life on the Sabbath, 5:1-47

The cure of the paralytic takes place on an unnamed feast day of the Jews (5:1) that also happens to be a Sabbath (5:9b), hence a double day of rest. The location of the episode, the pool of Bethzatha at the Sheep Gate in Jerusalem, has been discovered by archaeologists and fits the description given by John. It is believed to have been a pagan place of healing dedicated to Aesculapius, the god of health. This explains the presence of many sick people by the pool. Some of the witnesses add that at times an angel of the Lord descended into the pool and stirred up the water. The first to step in was cured, which also explains v. 7. The episode contains the cure itself (5:1-9), the attacks of the Jews on Jesus as sequel to the cure (5:10-18), Jesus' defense of his actions (5:19-44), and his reversal of the charges (5:38-47).

The Cure (5:1-9)

Jesus deliberately goes to this "pagan" place and takes the initiative in the cure. His question to the paralytic is important: "Do you want to be made well?" (v. 6). The answer of the paralytic, who had been ill for thirty-eight years, is equally intriguing (v. 7). Why had he no one to put him into the water? In the synoptics the friends of the paralytic were ready to destroy the roof of a house in order to bring their paralyzed friend to Jesus (cf. Mark 2:4 // Luke 5:18-19). As on that other occasion Jesus will associate the paralysis with personal sin (v. 14), something he does not do with other illnesses (cf. 9:3). Is there an intrinsic connection between physical paralysis (the Greek word for this means literally "being weakened, or drained of life") and sin? Is sin a paralysis of the soul that drains one of God's life? If so, the paralytic was right: he had nobody to help him except Jesus, the savior of the world, who takes away the sin of the world.

The paralytic evades Jesus' question but throws the blame on his lack of someone to help him. Jesus accepts this half answer and orders him to "rise" and take up his sleeping mat as a sign that he is well and willing to take up his responsibility for living. He is now to carry his mat for the rest of his life, instead of the mat carrying him for thirty-eight years. The Israelites spent thirty-eight of their forty years in the wilderness at Kadesh Barnea as a punishment for their lack of trust in God to bring them to the Promised Land (Numbers 14). The command to "rise" reminds one of what Jesus says to the dead daughter of Jairus (cf. Mark 5:41), though the command in that other passage is given in Aramaic. The Greek verb in John is the same as that used in v. 21 for raising the dead to life. The paralytic was as good as dead before Jesus found him out and restored him to life and wholeness of body and soul.

The Double Charge: Breaking the Sabbath and Claiming Equality with God (5:10-18)

That the man lay helpless for thirty-eight years attracted no attention. Now the religious authorities are concerned and rebuke him for breaking the Sabbath by carrying his sleeping mat. As previously (v. 7), the man throws the blame on his unknown healer. Once Jesus identifies himself to the paralytic and he reports this to the Jewish authorities they shift the attack, amounting to persecution, onto Jesus. The tense of the verbs in v. 16 is the imperfect; the idea is that Jesus was habitually persecuted because he was in the habit of curing on the Sabbath. John 6:2 indicates that he cured more than one person even on this particular occasion. Instead of apologizing for his action Jesus gives them yet another reason to persecute him: he claims to be God's Son, thus implying equality with God.

Defending Against the Charges (5:19-37)

Jesus grounds his defense on God's action. God's ceaseless work is to give and sustain life. As God's Son, Jesus cannot do otherwise. The Jews believed that though God rested on the Sabbath, God never rested from the work of giving life to creation since creation would have ceased to exist had God done so. In Jewish culture as in most traditional cultures male children were apprenticed to the trade of their fathers. As a human being, Jesus was a carpenter because Joseph his foster father was a carpenter; the sons of Zebedee were fishermen along with their father. Similarly, as God's Son, Jesus is apprenticed to his Father and does exactly what he sees his Father doing. This is expressed in the form of a parallelism:

Whatever the Father does, the Son does likewise (v. 19);
the Father raises the dead and gives them life;
so also the Son gives life to whomever he wishes (v. 21);
[as the Father is honored, so is the Son to be honored] (v. 23a);
anyone who does not honor the Son does not honor the Father (v. 23b);
the Father has life in himself; so he has granted the Son also to have life in himself (v. 26).

The relationship between Father and Son and the love that underlies it is expressed in v. 20. Jesus will later establish the same relationship between himself and his friends (15:15), including the doing of greater works (14:12).

Since like is judged by like, God leaves all judgment to the Son, who has become "a human being" (v. 27). Jesus gives life concretely by his word accepted in faith (v. 24). This faith guards one against experiencing judgment. Judgment is the equivalent of condemnation or second death (vv. 27, 29); the opposite is life, no condemnation or judgment. The judgment/condemnation language applies only to one who is under trial, not to those who are not; hence those who believe are not judged/condemned. The Johannine dualistic eschatology first mentioned in 3:20-21 is further explained here. To pass from death to life is to come out of darkness into light. Verses 28-29 extend this judgment/condemnation language into the *parousia,* what Rev 21:8 calls "the second death." Verse 30 returns to the theme of equality in v. 19 and rounds off Jesus' self-defense: his judgment itself is done according to God's will.

In 5:31-37 Jesus cites the witnesses to his claims: John the Baptist (vv. 31-35), Jesus' own works (v. 36), himself and God who enables him to do these works (v. 37) as Nicodemus recognized (3:2). The tense reporting the witness of the Baptist is in the perfect as in 1:34; either the Baptist is still alive or, what is more likely, his witness lives on.

Reversing the Charges (5:38-47)

Jesus now levels counter-charges against his opponents: Their rejection of him, God's envoy, shows that they do not know God (v. 38); they search the Scriptures for life but will not come to him who alone can give them life. Correct reading of the Scriptures would have led them to him (vv. 39-40); the obstacle to their believing is their self-seeking glory which they exercise in a kind of club; Jesus refuses to join this club (vv. 42-45). Ultimately Moses, on whom they claim to stand (in the Scriptures), will testify against them for their unbelief. The section ends with two rhetorical questions (vv. 44, 47). The first court hearing ends; the court adjourns until a further hearing.

John 5 gives one instance of an issue that is common in the synoptics, namely Jesus' habit of curing on the Sabbath. John here develops Jesus' claim in the synoptics that he is Lord even of the Sabbath. In the synoptics this claim is connected with giving life to his disciples who plucked ears of grain to eat. The passage gives us hope in knowing that God's primary concern to give and sustain our life takes precedence over legalistic religious observances. Giving us life includes liberating us from the age-old bondage of sin. As sinners we are unable to help ourselves. Jesus alone can heal us through the transforming power of the Holy Spirit. This work fills us with hope and joy, but also with a reminder not to go on sinning lest worst should befall us.

The last section of the episode can serve as a warning to scholars and Church leaders. It is possible to be so engrossed in defending traditional orthodoxy or in searching the Scriptures (thereby winning honor and prestige among colleagues) that one loses contact with Jesus and misses the life that only he can give. The episode challenges us to ensure that our defense of orthodoxy and assiduous biblical scholarship are rooted in a deep personal relationship with Jesus. The Fathers of the Church studied the Scriptures primarily in order to strengthen their own faith and then that of the people. Verses 39-40 may also serve as a warning to some modern-day charismatics who tend to play down the sacramental life of the Church, especially the Eucharist, in favor of the Bible. The Word/God, Jesus, is bigger than and gives full meaning and life to the word of God in the Scriptures.

On Trial for Claiming to be the Bread of Life, John 6

The geographical transition from ch. 5 to ch. 6 is problematic. Chapter 5 takes place in Judea and Jerusalem. Jesus could, therefore, not simply go over to "the other side of the sea of Galilee" which is in the northern part of Palestine. John 7:19-24 seems to follow logically after ch. 5; some commentaries even transfer this passage there before ch. 6. But we recall that John is not narrating events in their strict chronological order. The first court session ended in ch. 5. After court sessions people normally go home. Here Jesus goes to Galilee where he lives, as he did via Samaria in 4:1-4, 43. The events in ch. 6 thus take place in Galilee; Jesus returns to Jerusalem in ch. 7 for the feast of Tabernacles.

John 6 is one of the most important chapters of the gospel. It is by far the longest, and is read on some thirty-one occasions in the Church's liturgical year. It is also the chapter that causes the greatest despair to the pastor, especially when it is read consecutively from the Second to the Third Week of Easter and from the Seventeenth to the Twenty-first Sunday in Ordinary Time in Year B. The chapter appears to be very repetitive. "Bread from heaven" and "who has come down," for instance, are mentioned over seven times (see vv. 31-51, 58) for emphasis and fullness. It is likely that the author did not write the chapter in one sitting. The repetitions may also be the result of oral transmission; since people had no easy access to the written word, the text would have been read out and it would have been necessary to repeat important words and ideas for ease of recall.

The chapter contains John's version of the Eucharist and the first "I am" saying repeated four times (vv. 35, 41, 48, 51). It gives no account of the institution of the Eucharist, but rather a fully developed theology of its meaning. Jesus may not have given the discourse in its present form or on one occasion. The contents of the chapter are probably the fruit of the Church's reflection on the real meaning of the Eucharist and its indispensability for a full Christian life. The chapter combines Wisdom themes (the importance of Jesus' teaching, vv. 35-50) and sacramental themes (the importance of Jesus' body and blood as food, vv. 51-58). These are two inseparable carriers of lasting life for believers; the word of God and the bread of life provide a balanced diet.

The teaching on the Eucharist draws heavily on the people's Exodus and Passover traditions (v. 4). It is necessary for modern readers to digest the contents of this chapter against this OT background and against that of their own pertinent traditions so as to draw out its meaning and discover its relevance for our contemporary contexts. The different liturgical contexts in which the chapter is read also offer ample opportunities for a creative reading and fresh insights into its message.

The three main sections are: the signs of feeding (vv. 1-15), walking on the water and sudden arrival at the destination (vv. 16-21); the people's continued quest for Jesus and his response to this quest (vv. 22-59); reactions to Jesus' response by the crowd and the disciples (vv. 60-71).

The central thesis is that Jesus is "the Bread of Life" ("bread from heaven" or "living bread"); hence it is essential to eat this bread in order to have lasting life. Food and life go together as vital concepts. Unlike God and Jesus (5:26), we do not have life in ourselves but need food in order to live. Unless we eat physical food, we die. As physical food symbolized by bread sustains physical life that ends in death (vv. 27a, 49, 58b), so does the living bread give and sustain lasting life that triumphs over death (vv. 27b, 48, 50-51, 54-58a,c). It follows that if one wants to have this lasting life one must necessarily eat this bread of life.

The teaching is set in dialogical form where the main audience, the crowd, provides in typical Johannine fashion the key term of the dialogue: "bread from heaven" (v. 31). The sign of feeding and the double sign on the sea furnish concrete proofs that Jesus is able to accomplish what he promises in this teaching. The first sign is mostly for the crowd, the second for the disciples. At the end of the teaching both audience groups will have to make their own decision for or against Jesus.

The Signs (6:1-15, 16-21)

We note the zeal with which the people pursue Jesus tirelessly for material benefits all the way from Jerusalem (5:1; 6:2) to Tiberias (6:1), and to Capernaum (6:22-24). This contrasts sadly with their unbelief, "murmurings," and unteachability that climax in their complete rejection of him when he offers them lasting life (vv. 36, 41-46, 52, 60, 66). The miraculous feeding is reported in the synoptics (Matt 14:13-21 // Mark 6:32-44 // Luke 9:10b-17). John's gospel emphasizes Jesus' initiative in the feeding (vv. 5-6) and its "sign" character (vv. 14, 26). There is no real contradiction in these two verses: the people "see" only the miraculous character of the sign but fail to see its inner significance as authenticating Jesus' claims in the ensuing dialogue. They are prepared to do "the works of God" as demanded by the Law, but find it difficult to do that one basic work, "the work of God," which is believing in Jesus as God's envoy and agent of life (vv. 28-29).

The people's work has a corollary in the Father's work and in that of Jesus. The Father gives Jesus, the bread from heaven (v. 32), sends and commissions him to give lasting life to believers (v. 37), teaches people and draws or gives them to Jesus for him to look after, feed with living bread, give lasting life to, and ensure that none is lost (vv. 39, 44, 65). The work of Jesus is to do exactly as the Father has commissioned him (vv. 38). Only when the people do their one work of believing in Jesus as God's envoy can they benefit from the Father's and Jesus' joint work.

Philip and Andrew in the gospel are missionary figures. The material for the sign is provided by a little boy (v. 9), for nobody is insignificant or incapable of contributing to the proclamation of the gospel. The abundance and surplus (vv. 12-13) provided by the sign "on the mountain" (v. 3) recall the messianic banquet on God's mountain expected in Isa 2:2-3; 25:6. The "twelve baskets full" surplus is symbolic either for the twelve apostles who were doing the serving (a category not emphasized by John), or for the twelve tribes of Israel, who will never be in want. The desire of the crowd to make Jesus king shows that they connected this sign with the promised messianic banquet and so concluded that Jesus must be the expected Messiah or prophet (v. 14) but, as in 2:23-25, Jesus is not easily taken in by their enthusiasm which stops short of true faith in him (v. 15).

Some commentators see in the sign of walking on the sea a recalling of God's supremacy over nature (e.g., Job 9:8), or the crossing of the Red Sea (Exod 14:15-29). The crossing was followed by feeding with manna in the wilderness which sustained the Israelites till they reached the promised land (Exod 16:4, 15, 35; Ps 78:24). The motif of "murmuring" (cf. Exod 16:2-3) belongs to this tradition. On the human level the walking on water shows Jesus' real concern for his disciples. Since they were out at sea in the single boat available, the only way he could reach them physically to bring relief was to perform this sign. It strengthened the disciples' faith and shortened their laborious journey to the shore.

In our liturgical context baptism symbolizes the paschal event of our crossing over from slavery to new life in Christ (cf. Rom 6:1-14). This new life needs to be sustained with bread from heaven till we reach our own promised land: heaven. It also needs to be lightened by Jesus' companionship on the journey (cf. Matt 11:28).

The People's Quest and Jesus' Response (6:16-59)

The discourse on the bread of life is developed in three logically successive statements: (1) The real or true "bread from heaven" is not the manna once given by Moses, contrary to what the people believe (v. 31). It is literally the bread that has come down from heaven. God, not Moses, gives this bread (v. 32). (2) Jesus, who alone came down from heaven (vv. 38, 51a) as God's "gift" to the world (cf. 3:13, 16) is this bread (v. 35). This fact can only be known and accepted through believing, or through listening to and learning from God. "Doing the work of God" (v. 29) consists in this listening and learning (vv. 45-46). (3) This bread seen concretely is Jesus' own flesh (v. 51c). Here the theme of the Eucharist or thanksgiving first mentioned in vv. 11, 23 comes to the fore. In the synoptics Jesus speaks of his "body" (not flesh) and "blood." John's use of "flesh" emphasizes Jesus' humanity as the means of our nourishment (cf. 1:14). Moreover, the Exodus traditions spoke of eating flesh (quails) and of returning to the fleshpots of Egypt. By "flesh" John understands "flesh and blood," food and drink (vv. 53, 54). The flesh and blood of the Passover lamb played a key role in the Exodus (Exod 12:13). The communion sacrifice in Lev 7:18-27 speaks of eating "flesh." Hence the terminology of flesh was not entirely alien to Jesus' Jewish audience.

The people meet these assertions with two objections: (1) Jesus cannot be the bread from heaven because they know his human parents (vv. 41-42). Their assertion ironically confirms the fact of the humanity of Jesus. Jesus answers this objection in vv. 43-47. (2) Jesus cannot give them his flesh to eat (v. 52). Jesus answers this objection in vv. 53-58 by restating the necessity of eating his flesh and drinking his blood as the condition for having lasting life.

The issue here is not cannibalism but believing in God's and Jesus' power to give life by the means they choose (v. 63). This "believing" (note the dynamic form of the verb used throughout) is the master key that enables one to unlock and tap into God's life imparted by Jesus, his envoy, through word and sacrament. In the OT as in African traditions, "blood" is the bearer of life, which is sacred to God. This explains why the Jews were forbidden to eat "flesh with its blood in it" (Gen 9:4; Lev 7:26-27). A mother's blood sustains her baby's life in the womb and the milk from her breast nourishes the child after it is born. Today many occult groups believe in drinking human blood and even eating human flesh as a source of supernatural powers. They practice "black Mass" as a means of gaining access to the "blood of Jesus" which they believe to be most powerful. "Renewed" Christians believe in the power of the "blood of Jesus" and use it as a standard invocation for assured protection against all forces of evil. Jesus offers us his own body and blood as the natural food for the new life he came to give in abundance. Do we believe in its saving and nourishing power?

Reactions to the Claims and Offer (6:60-71)

The people's final reaction is rejection of Jesus' claims and offer. Belief in their traditions and natural reasoning powers constitutes the obstacle to believing in Jesus. Their earlier sustained quest for Jesus contrasts sadly with their being scandalized by the offer of living bread and definitively parting company with him, but Jesus refuses to water down his teaching to accommodate them. The disciples do not really understand either, but they affirm through their spokesperson Peter that they have no alternative to Jesus (vv. 68-69). This may be the Johannine version of Peter's confession (Matt 16:16 // Mark 8:29 // Luke 9:20). If so, Jesus' response here is not a bestowal of the keys of the kingdom of heaven; rather, in the context of the Last Supper, he recalls the betrayal of Judas (vv. 70-71).

The sustained emphasis in this chapter on the necessity of eating Jesus' flesh and drinking his blood suggests that the Johannine audience must have had some problems with the Eucharist. The same happened through the ages. Sadly, the doctrine of the Eucharist constitutes a point of division between Catholics and Protestants. What forms does unbelief in the Eucharist take in your particular contexts? Do Catholics really understand and appreciate the Eucharist today? or do they find better food and faith in other forms of prayer? How do you proclaim John 6 to those who today extol "the word of God" and miracles over the sacrament? The crowds were unable to transcend their traditions and believe in Jesus, yet Jesus used their traditions to teach them. What problems do our cultural and religious traditions pose to our proclamation and acceptance of the gospel? and how does Jesus' approach in John 6 help to resolve these problems?

On Trial for Offering the Holy Spirit, Living Water, John 7

Chapter 7 brings us back to Jerusalem where ch. 5 ended and to the important feast of Tabernacles (Sukkoth, Tents, or Booths). The rabbis called Sukkoth "the feast." The motifs of this feast span chapters 7 to 9: water, rain, and departure of the dead and of Jesus (ch. 7), light (of the world) and liberation from sin (ch. 8), and Jesus' demonstration that he is the light by curing the man born blind (ch. 9). The feast itself is rooted in the Exodus traditions.

In the Jewish liturgical context Sukkoth was celebrated for seven days and commemorated the period of the Israelites' dwelling in tents in the wilderness (Exod 23:16) and, according to Hosea, in complete dependence on God for water and all their needs (Hos 2:15[17]). It was marked by joy and happiness. Leviticus 23:42-43 gives the manner of its celebration. It was one of the three pilgrimage festivals (the other two being Passover and Pentecost) when a male Jew was obliged to go to the Temple in Jerusalem to make offerings for favors received from God. The eve of the second day was marked by an all-night colorful torchlight procession of the priests drawing water for purification with joy (cf. Isa 12:3) from the pool of Siloam. The eighth or closing day of the festival, "the last and greatest day of the feast" (John 7:37), was like a separate feast. It contained prayer for rain, a reflection on life and the uselessness of human strivings based on Qoheleth, and a commemoration of the departed. This background sheds light on the theme of Jesus' departure (vv. 33-36), his declarations in vv. 37-39, the need to be purified or freed from sin in ch. 8, and the reference to Siloam in 9:7.

The characters in this trial are Jesus' relatives, the ordinary people (including the Temple guards), and the leaders. The chapter can be read under three headings: (1) the unbelief of Jesus' relatives (vv. 1-10), (2) the debate by the people on Jesus' messianic identity and Jesus' own response to this (vv. 11-44), and (3) the attempt by the leaders to arrest Jesus (vv. 32, 45-52).

The Unbelief of Jesus' Relatives (7:1-10)

The "brothers" of Jesus need not to be taken as those of the same father and mother. As in the African context, they could be his extended family or even an entire village. Their rejection is probably the Johannine version of the rejection of Jesus by his own in Nazareth narrated in Luke 4:16-30. The unbelief of the relatives (most likely the male relatives, v. 5) is manifested in their cynical remark in vv. 3-4, which may mean "What kind of a Messiah are you?" At heart they do not think much of Jesus. They know that Jesus' life is threatened in Judea (v. 1), yet they want him to make a public appearance there as he would later in 12:12-19. The motive may have been personal and materialistic, especially since after the resurrection some of them at least became believers, though still legalistically, and occupied prominent positions in the community (cf. Acts 12:17; 15:13-21; Gal 2:9). If Jesus went as they desired, they would share in the reflected glory. This type of attitude exists often in families.

Jesus refuses to be pressured (v. 6). His opportune time has not yet come, though for evil the time seems always to be opportune. Later he goes to the feast in his own way, incognito (v. 10), not in the manner desired by his relatives. The motif of secrecy dominates the first part of this chapter. When he arrives in Jerusalem the people are whispering or discussing him secretly for fear of the leaders (v. 11-13).

The Debate on Jesus' Messianic Identity (7:14-44)

Jesus himself brings the debate on his identity into the open by his action in v. 14. The debate centers on the extraordinary knowledge revealed by his teaching, given that he was not a trained rabbi (v. 15; this verse does not mean that Jesus was illiterate [cf. Luke 4:16-19]), on his boldness in speaking publicly despite the known threat to his life (vv. 25-26), and on his audience's claimed knowledge of his origin, which in their interpretation of the tradition counts against him as Messiah (v. 27).

Jesus' first reply to these debaters (vv. 16-24) seems to refer more directly to events in ch. 5 (the cure of the paralytic, the Sabbath motif, and the dispute with the leaders over keeping or breaking the Law) than to the objections raised here by the people, but the link with this current context lies in the notion of a teaching that is from God and how that may be known (vv. 15, 16-17). A teaching that seeks the glory of the teacher cannot be from God; attunedness to God is the surest way of gaining true knowledge of God. In Jewish thought, knowledge of God meant intimate relationship with God, not abstract ideas. Since Jesus' teaching glorifies God, not himself, it serves as proof that he comes from God. The people's admission that the leaders seek to kill Jesus (v. 25) while the leaders deny this when Jesus confronts them with it (v. 20) is evidence that they too seek to please people and so lack true knowledge of God.

They are equally mistaken on the issue of Jesus' origin (vv. 40-44). Though he grew up in Galilee, Jesus was actually of David's lineage and from Bethlehem (cf. Matt 2:1-6; Luke 1:26-38; 2:1-11). As in many African cultures, one's place of origin is not where one was born or grew up, but where one's parents come from. The people's own position concerning the Messiah's place of origin is contradictory (compare v. 27 with vv. 41-42). Contradiction characterizes their interventions throughout. This can be explained by divided opinions among them where some hold one view and some another.

Against the Jewish liturgical context cited earlier, Jesus promises the Holy Spirit as a fountain of living water that the believer will receive from him (vv. 37-39). His own departure (death and resurrection or glorification) makes this gift possible. He appeals to the people to relate his own teaching and promises to the context of the feast they are celebrating. In the end some of them are persuaded and believe in him (v. 31), while others want to arrest him (v. 44). The entire scene is a good illustration of crowd psychology.

The Leaders' Attempt to Arrest Jesus (7:32, 45-53)

We notice how the leaders use themselves as the norm for accepting or rejecting Jesus, but the Temple guards sent in v. 32 are courageous enough to break from this grip; so too those in the crowd who believe in Jesus even though in the beginning they did defer to these leaders (vv. 13, 26). The guards have personally heard Jesus and are deeply impressed by him. Nicodemus (alleged to represent the crypto-Christians in John's community who feared to profess Jesus openly for fear of being ejected from the synagogue) finds courage in the action of the guards. He comes a little more into the light as Jesus had invited him in 3:21, and with some boldness challenges his colleagues to judge Jesus according to the dictates of their Law (v. 51). It is ironic that while the leaders accuse Jesus of breaking the Law they themselves discount the Law in dealing with him. This too happens in many ways in life among people in authority, in the family, the state and the Church.

Ultimately the leaders' rejection of Jesus has a racial and ethnic basis (v. 52). Jesus in John's gospel is rejected because of his family origins (from Nazareth,1:46; the son of Joseph, 6:42), his ethnicity (from Galilee, or a northern tribe), and his nationality ("King of the Jews," 19:3). He shares with Black Africa in particular rejection based on race and supposed low origins, though he has the choicest gifts to offer. Racism is a serious and blinding bondage to those who indulge in it. This chapter challenges us, among other things, to revise the criteria by which we judge and dismiss people and so deprive ourselves of the singular blessings God offers us through them.

On Trial for Claiming to be God, John 8

John 8 continues more directly the debate with the leaders started in ch. 5. At the end of ch. 7 the leaders go home nursing their grudges that the Temple guards did not arrest Jesus as directed and that Nicodemus challenged them to abide by the dictates of their Law in judging Jesus. Jesus himself goes to the Mount of Olives, to pray as his custom was (cf. Luke 21:37-38). In the morning he comes with the anointing of prayer to the Temple to teach the people who come to him of their own accord. Meanwhile the leaders are busy staging a comeback (7:53–8:6).

John 7:53–8:11 is missing in most manuscripts of the gospel and appears in other manuscripts in Luke's gospel. For this reason some Bibles and commentaries place this section in brackets. We read the story in its Johannine context to derive a meaning that is integral to its current setting.

Jesus is teaching in the treasury (8:20) where offerings made to God are kept. He is interrupted by the leaders who seek to trap him by asking him to pass judgment on the woman taken in adultery. If he declares that she should be stoned to death he will be in trouble with the Romans who forbade the Jews to administer capital punishment (cf. 18:31). If he lets her go free he will be breaking the Law of Moses. Jesus answers them as he does when in the synoptics they try to trap him with regard to paying tribute to Caesar (Luke 20:21-25). When they are obliged to pass judgment on themselves (vv. 7-9) instead of on Jesus or the woman, Jesus counsels the woman and sets her free. He now continues his teaching explicitly on his claim to be the light of the world (vv. 12-47), and addresses it directly to them. The dispute with his opponents finally leads him to declare himself God, which declaration results in the attempt to stone him for blasphemy (vv. 48-59). This is the first intensive hearing of the case against Jesus; the leaders declare war on him while he is quietly teaching the people in the Temple. No doubt they are further angered by this teaching, which they would have seen as a threat to them in their own territory.

An Excuse for Bringing on the Trial (8:3-11)

Commentaries on this episode focus on the testing of Jesus by the leaders and his brilliant way of dealing with them, recalling Solomon's method of dealing with the women who both claimed to be the mother of one child (1 Kings 3:24-28). Feminist interpreters stress that though the man and woman were caught in the act only the woman was brought to trial. This indeed was gross injustice. In this respect the woman is symbolic of Jesus who himself is here being unjustly tried. She reminds one of Susanna, whose story is read in Holy Week as a figure of Jesus. Susanna, of course, was innocent of the accusation leveled against her (Daniel 13). Like the accusers of Susanna, the men in this episode are guilty of sin. Their forced admission of sinfulness (v. 9) should lead to the admission that they are slaves to sin, but this is not so (vv. 32-38). Yet Jesus does not condemn them; he simply leads them to recognize their own sinfulness. Jesus does not condemn the woman either. But he himself who cannot be convicted of sin (v. 46) and who alone can set us free from sin (v. 36) will be condemned to death.

Jesus the Light of the World (8:12-47)

Jesus' claim to be the light of the world (v. 12; another "I am " saying, spoken to his opponents) is closely linked with the preceding event. This claim is refuted by his opponents (v. 13). Yet by forgiving the woman instead of judging or condemning her to death as his opponents would do (vv. 15-16) he gives proof of this claim and cites God's witness to him in support. Light is the principle of life, not of death (1:4). It is also the principle of the true knowledge of God and sets us free from the darkness of sin (3:20-21). Darkness can never overcome it (cf. 1:5). To reject Jesus and his teaching is to remain ignorant of God and of God's ways. True knowledge of God is enduring life (17:3).

The ensuing debate with its charges and countercharges sets forth antithetically (for example, in v. 23) this central divide: that Jesus is light and acts according to the principles of light, while his opponents are in the dark and act according to the principles of darkness. The argument runs as follows: Jesus is the light that leads to life (vv. 12-20). Only those who believe in him know this truth. Self-righteousness with its resulting spiritual blindness ("in your sins," vv. 21, 24) is a serious bondage that prevents one from recognizing one's sinfulness and therefore submitting oneself to be freed by the Son (vv. 31-47). Yet there is hope if only the opponents would recognize the opportune time given to them and turn to Jesus to save them before it is too late (vv. 21-30). Ironically, it is only when the opponents have gotten rid of Jesus (that is, lifted him up in crucifixion, v. 28) that they will recognize him to be the only one who can save them from sin. (This is the second passage on the theme of being lifted up, cf. 3:14; 12:32.) Jesus will be lifted up as Savior in 19:18. His glorification will thus serve as the definitive proof of his claim to be the light of the world, and by the same token prove the leaders wrong in their judgment of him.

Invitation to So-called Believers (8:31-38)

Some of Jesus' opponents are persuaded by his argument (v. 30), but only superficially as in 2:23-24. Jesus exhorts them to grow as his disciples (v. 31: that is, those who follow him and learn from him step by step the truth about Jesus as God's agent of salvation and about themselves as sinners in need of salvation), but the persisting contentious spirit of these so-called believers (v. 33) stands as a serious block to their discipleship. Jesus' statement in vv. 34-36 can be explained by reference to the Isaac-Ishmael story (Gen 21:8-21) or that of the prodigal son (Luke 15:11-32). When we sin we forfeit our identity as God's children. Only the Savior Son can set us free and reinstate us permanently in the home as did the father of the prodigal son.

Parentage of Jesus and of His Opponents (8:39-47)

The last stage of the debate deals with the issue of parentage. The opponents contend that they are descendants of Abraham (and belong to God) and so have never been slaves to anyone. According to Lev 25:39-53 every Israelite was considered as God's servant and so was never to be treated as a slave by anyone. Jesus points out that natural descent from Abraham does not make one his child (cf. Luke 3:8). Children speak the language of their parents. Since the opponents speak not the language of Abraham or of God, but of the devil (by telling lies, hating the truth, refusing to believe in Jesus, seeking to kill him) they are children of the devil. He on the contrary is God's child and proves this by judging no one, seeking only God's glory, declaring to the world only what he hears from God, speaking only on God's authority, and doing always what pleases God.

The Final Claim: "I Am" (8:48-59)

In their turn Jesus' opponents accuse him of being a Samaritan and having a demon (like Simon Magus in Acts 8:9-11). Jesus refutes this charge and goes on to declare solemnly that far from being in league with the devil (through whom death entered the world: Wis 2:24) he will give lasting life to those who keep his word. If even Abraham was not spared death, how can Jesus from Nazareth claim that those who keep his word will never die? The cynical reaction of his opponents to this declaration (v. 57) leads to his final solemn claim (v. 58). The idea of Abraham seeing his day may be a reference to the birth of Isaac, whom tradition sees as a figure of Jesus. This claim ("I am") evokes the divine name as in Exod 3:14 ("I AM has sent me to you"). It is a conclusive declaration by Jesus that he is indeed greater than Abraham and the prophets (v. 53). His opponents see this as blasphemy punishable by stoning (Lev 24:16), but Jesus escapes from them as he does in Luke 4:30.

The chapter started with Jesus sparing the woman caught in adultery from being stoned to death. It ends with attempts by the same people to stone him to death. This is quite a dramatic ending. How do we identify today with the different characters in the story: the woman caught in adultery, the leaders, and Jesus? What kinds of attitudes stand in the way of our true discipleship of Jesus?

On Trial for Giving Sight to the Man Born Blind, John 9

The trial of Jesus continues with the story of the man born blind. This time he is tried *in absentia,* through those who believe in him, notably the man born blind. We may contrast the attitude of this man when under interrogation with that of the paralytic in John 5. The chapter is concrete proof of Jesus' claim in 8:12 to be the light of the world (repeated in 9:5) and to lead true disciples to knowledge of the truth that sets free. It also confirms that the real blindness is spiritual blindness (v. 41). The liturgical context is still the feast of Tabernacles. Siloam (meaning "sent," v. 7) is a reference to him. In Luke 4:18 Jesus declares that he is sent to give sight to the blind. Those who immerse themselves in him are washed clean and healed by his blood. (One is here reminded of the traditional hymn: "Have you been to Jesus for the cleansing blood? Are you washed in the blood of the lamb?")

The cure of the man "born blind" (vv. 1-7) is the deed that occasions this trial. More characters are involved in this story than in previous ones: the disciples of Jesus (v. 2), the man himself, the crowd, the parents of the man and the leaders, specifically the Pharisees. Critics see in the parents of the blind man allusion to crypto-Christians of John's community who fear to be thrown out of the synagogue if they confess Jesus publicly. Jesus himself, the center of the debate, appears only at the beginning and end of the story. He passes the final judgment on this particular trial (vv. 39, 41).

An outstanding element of the "deed" is that this man is "blind from birth." Jesus takes the initiative to effect the cure and rejects the traditional belief that blindness, considered the worst type of punishment in Judaism, is the result of personal sin (vv. 2-3). As later in the raising of Lazarus, Jesus sees this case as an occasion to do God's work and give glory to God. Some manuscripts have "we must do" instead of "I must do" in v. 4, but the only one who does God's work here is Jesus himself, though critics interpret the "we" as a reference to the involvement of the Johannine community in this work of Jesus. His "crime" that brings about the trial is not the cure *per se* but his breaking the Sabbath (v. 14) by making clay out of spittle, spreading it on the man's eyes, and perhaps sending him to wash in the pool of Siloam.

Jesus Tried in Absentia (9:13-14)

The investigation of the deed begins with the reaction of the people. Verses 8-12 serve to establish beyond doubt that the man cured is the same as the one born blind. Unlike the paralytic in 5:13, the blind man knows exactly who cured him. The deed is certified; so are the doer and the means by which it was done (v. 11). The stage is now set for action. As later in the case of Lazarus the people bring this deed to the attention of the Pharisees (v. 13).

The manner of the cure is repeated three times for emphasis (vv. 7, 11, 15). The deed engenders division among the Pharisees. While some focus only on the breaking of the Sabbath, the evidence leads others to question their view of Jesus as a sinner. These latter recall Nicodemus in 7:51, but instead of changing their views on the basis of the evidence they resort to a series of subterfuges: seeking to know the man's verdict on Jesus (perhaps with the hope that out of fear he would say that he was a sinner because he broke the Sabbath) and sending for his parents to ascertain that he was really born blind. The parents refuse to be dragged into the issue for fear of being thrown out of the synagogue (this v. 22 serves as the classic case for the theory of the ejection of the Johannine community from the synagogue).

The leaders again try to force the man to pass an unjust judgment on Jesus, in the guise of asking him to glorify God (v. 24), but the man refuses to be bulldozed into doing what is wrong. His pragmatism in v. 25 baffles the Pharisees into wanting to know once more how he received his sight. The man's treatment of their question angers them yet more. They take refuge in their discipleship of Moses, set against Jesus, but even then the man does not allow them to get away with it. He cites their own theology (based on that same Moses whose disciples they claim to be) to show the fundamental contradiction and, ironically, the stupidity in their position (vv. 30-33). His conclusion in v. 33 is irrefutable. Throughout he gives the true interpretation of Jesus' deed or is alone able to read the meaning of this sign. Since God does not answer the prayers of sinners (cf. Ps 66:18; *b. Sanh.* 90a), and since Jesus has been able to cure a man born blind—something unheard of in human history—Jesus must be a prophet (v. 17b), God's committed worshiper and disciple (v. 31), and one sent and supported by God (v. 33). Effectively the man plays on behalf of Jesus a role similar to that of John the Baptist (cf. 3:31-36) in bearing witness to him and supporting his claims.

This episode has all the makings of a trial. The Pharisees separate the blind man from his parents when they interrogate the latter, to avoid any possibility of pressure from his mere presence. When they recall the man (v. 24) they repeat the same question in different ways and try to brainwash him into admitting that Jesus is a sinner. Finally, unable to beat him either theologically or on the grounds of common sense, they resort to physical force and throw him out of the synagogue rather than change their views about Jesus.

Jesus' Final Judgment on the Trial (9:35-41)

As Jesus found the paralytic in ch. 5 after his interrogations by the leaders, he now finds the man after he had been thrown out of the synagogue. His appearance shows that Jesus was present in the background throughout the trial. He now rewards the man for bearing witness to the truth at the cost of being rejected, by revealing himself to him as the Messiah even as he had done to the Samaritan woman (4:26). Though the man stood up for Jesus he did not yet know that he was the Messiah. The phrase "son of man" or "the human being" (v. 35) is Jesus' preferred self-designation as the Messiah (cf. 1:51). Employed eleven times in the gospel, the title emphasizes that this heavenly Messiah is yet a human being.

As a human being Jesus passes the final judgment on the significance of the entire trial (v. 41). As the man's blindness was not a result of sin, so his physical blindness is not the real blindness; rather the spiritual blindness of the Pharisees, their claim to see, constitutes the real blindness. If physical blindness was the worst type of punishment, spiritual blindness must be the worst type of spiritual illness. Jesus, the light of the world, reveals this truth. He gives both physical sight and spiritual insight to the man, while the leaders remain blind in their refusal to see (9:39 echoes 12:40).

The story of the man born blind lends itself most readily to dramatization as a creative way of bringing out its message in one's own context. Some patristic authors saw the man born blind as representing humanity whom Jesus enlightens. That the story is read during the Christian initiation rite supports this claim. Also read in its entirety during the Fourth Sunday and fourth week of Lent, the story invites all to conversion, especially with regard to not allowing prejudice to blind us to the goodness in others and refraining from manipulating evidence so that we may not have to change our attitudes and mentalities.

On Trial for Claiming to be the Good Shepherd, John 10

Jesus' claim to be the good shepherd gains in force when read against events in ch. 9. In contrast to the Pharisees, Jesus sought out the man both initially and after he had been rejected by his leaders, who there proved to be hirelings. Ezekiel 34; 36; Jeremiah 23; Psalm 23 constitute the OT background to this chapter. These passages could profitably be read as aid to understanding its message. In these OT contexts the conflict is not only between the shepherds and the sheep, but also between sheep and sheep, and between the shepherd and the Shepherd, God.

The contents are: a parable (vv. 1-6), its explanation as it applies to Jesus, the "Good Shepherd" (vv. 7-18), the objection to Jesus' claim and a restatement of the scriptural reasons for the claim (vv. 19-38).

The Parable (10:1-6)

A parable normally seeks to illustrate one truth at a time through the medium of a story. The OT sees God as the shepherd of God's people (cf. Ps 80:1). Israel's leaders (for example, David) exercised this ministry for God among the people. Because of their failure throughout history to really look after the sheep, God promised to come in person to look after the people, supply their needs, and administer true justice to them (cf. Ezek 34:11-31). In ancient times shepherds would bring their flocks for safety at night to one large fold guarded by a gatekeeper. In the morning individual shepherds would call out their flocks by name and lead them from the fold to pasture.

The immediate background in the Johannine community is probably the situation described in 1 John 2:18-19, 22-23, where members of the community who are disenchanted with Jesus' messiahship leave the fold and seek to draw others away with them. This happens frequently today in many Christian contexts where people leave one Church to establish another, often for personal and material reasons. In some African contexts these peoples call themselves "soul harvesters." They "harvest" mainly from the traditional churches. Others go on their own accord from one Church to another seeking the kind of Messiah ("a miracle-working God"; cf. the crowd in John 6) who would solve their immediate material problems in their own way.

The action and attitude of the Jewish leaders toward the ordinary people in 7:49 and their treatment of the man born blind serve as the contextual example in the gospel itself of shepherds who treat the flock with contempt. They, like the "soul harvesters" in the Johannine community (also called the "anti-Christ"), are literally those who come "before" Jesus (v. 8) in the sense of placing themselves above him or competing with his influence over the people and seeking to win their allegiance to themselves. A characteristic of "thieves and robbers" is selfishness, depriving others of what is theirs (often by force) for themselves. John the Baptist in the gospel serves as an outstanding contrast to them (cf. 1:15; 19-34; 3:25-36).

Explanation of the Parable (10:7-18)

Against these ancient and contemporary backgrounds Jesus declares himself twice in each case both as the "door [or gate] for the sheep (vv. 7, 9) and as "the good shepherd" (vv. 11, 14). "Good" (or "beautiful") here refers to the real, the true, and the genuine as opposed to what is symbolic or fake. As "door" Jesus is our gateway to possession of the full revelation of God and the blessings promised in the messianic age. The doorkeeper is God, who alone draws all believers to Jesus (6:44) as a gift for him to look after (6:39; 17:6). If in the OT God was the true shepherd of God's people, and if Jesus here claims this role for himself, it is because he and the Father are one (v. 30).

How concretely is Jesus the Good Shepherd? He exists to save the sheep, gives them free access to pasture (v. 9), supplies them with abundance or fullness of life (spiritually, morally, and materially; v. 10)—in contrast to the wolves that seek only to kill—and has an intimate, personal, and mutual relationship with them, comparable only to the relationship between him and the Father (v. 15), such that he is prepared even to die for the sheep (vv. 11, 15b). Not even death can separate him from the sheep (v. 18). In contrast to those who lead the sheep astray and scatter them into different folds, Jesus seeks to bring into one fold all his scattered sheep for more effective pasturing and union among the sheep themselves (v. 16; cf. 11:52; 17:20). Jesus' care for the sheep is not only in spiritual terms. It applies to all that the sheep need to have life in its fullness, life as God created it with all the real needs that go with it, including light, water, employment, adequate wages, means of transportation and communication, housing, and so forth.

Objection to the Claim and Its Defense (10:19-38)

As usual Jesus' claims generate a mixed response from the people, some of whom are still reflecting on the significance of the sign in John 9 (vv. 19-21). In the gospel's time scheme there is a gap (perhaps of some three months) between the first part of the chapter and vv. 22-38. The feast of Dedication or Hanukkah in which this last part is set (v. 22) commemorates the rededication of the Temple by the Maccabees in 165 B.C.E. after it had been desecrated by Antiochus Epiphanes (cf. 2 Maccabees 10). The feast took place some three months after Sukkoth (Tabernacles) and lasted the same eight days; it was a feast of great rejoicing (2 Macc 10:6). It would have been in the heart of winter. Hanukkah is essentially a feast of lights. This additional liturgical background highlights Jesus' claim to be the "Good Shepherd" in terms of one uniquely "consecrated" (dedicated) to and by God, even as the Jews dedicated the Temple. Some scholars see here John's declaration that Jesus, the real Temple (2:19-21), has also replaced this Jewish feast.

The Jewish leaders ask Jesus once more about his identity as Messiah, using the same tactics as with the blind man in John 9 (that is, hoping to hear a different response from him). This time they want to know it plainly (v. 24), not as in the figurative language of v. 6. Jesus, however, is not explicit with them, knowing very well that they are not really interested in believing as the blind man was, and to whom he had given a direct answer. Rather he draws their attention to their basic lack of the spirit of discipleship and redirects them to previous witnesses to his claims: his works (vv. 25, 32), which also serve as evidence of the oneness between him and the Father. As on previous occasions they attempt to stone him for blasphemy, for making himself "equal to God" (v. 33). Jesus in turn cites "their" Scriptures to show that they are wrong and unjust to accuse him of blasphemy: if mere human beings who received God's word could be called "gods" because they were taught by God, how much more the Word, God become flesh (1:1; 14)? He ends by appealing to their common sense in judging him, but instead of exercising it they seek to arrest him (v. 39).

The chapter ends with Jesus' withdrawal from Jerusalem back to Bethany beyond the Jordan from where he started his Jerusalem ministry (1:28). There in that "pagan" territory many came to believe in him on the double evidence of his "signs" and the witness of the Baptist. This chapter ends the cycle that started in 1:29 with the testimony of the Baptist. From now on Jesus will rely only on God's witness to him.

This chapter invites us to reflect on the implications of Jesus being the Good Shepherd today: to us as individuals and to the people whom we as pastors are graced to lead. The parable is particularly pertinent in the African and other Third World contexts where the question of good shepherds is being raised with regard to the activities of past missionaries and colonizers who in many ways despoiled peoples of their human dignity, cultural identity, and riches, leaving them greatly impoverished. Even today the first action of foreign nationals when trouble brews is evacuation.

It is also applicable on the level of selfish governments who treat whole nations as their private property. The people themselves often do not know their rights and so become easy prey to these governments, receiving token benefits from them with gratitude instead of demanding their full rights as citizens. It is applicable to the leaders in the churches who have a special mission to represent Jesus among the people. The current wave of fundamentalism that lacks a solid social program and yet claims to proclaim the gospel of Jesus and promises people quick and miraculous results needs to be revisited in the light of Jesus, the Good Shepherd. The chapter also challenges us to review our attitudes toward those sheep that are not of our own denominational or even local or national fold.

On Trial for Claiming to be the Resurrection and the Life, John 11

John 11 constitutes the climax of Jesus' signs and claims to divinity prior to the conclusive sign, his glorification (passion, death, and resurrection). He himself referred to this sign as one of the "greater works" God would show so that his opponents may marvel (5:20). Some scholars see it as the seventh and last element in the hypothetical "Signs Source" believed to be used by the evangelist. The chapter records one of the best known "I am" sayings of Jesus (v. 25). Liturgically, selections from the chapter are read in Masses for the Dead (vv. 17-27, 32-45), on the Fifth Sunday and in the fifth week of Lent (vv. 1-56), in Masses for Christian Unity and the spread of the gospel (vv. 45-52), and on the feast of St. Martha (July 29, vv. 19-27). These liturgical contexts offer opportunities for gaining new insights into the message of the chapter.

A noteworthy feature of chs. 11 and 12 is the prominence of Martha and Mary, the sisters of Lazarus (11:1-2; 12:2-3). The response of these two women to Jesus forms a striking contrast to the sustained rejection of him by the leaders and people in chs. 5–10. Verses 45-53 accentuate this contrast, especially as they are followed immediately by Mary's anointing (12:1-8). The rejection reaches its climax in chs. 18–19.

The chapter has three main units: the illness of Lazarus and his sisters' appeal to Jesus for help (vv. 1-3, 4-16), the raising of Lazarus to life (vv. 17-44), and the leaders' plot to kill Jesus as a consequence of the deed (vv. 45-57).

Illness of Lazarus and Appeal for Help (11:1-3, 4-16)

The illness of Lazarus (vv. 1-3) is the occasion for the sign. Emphasis is placed on Jesus' love for Lazarus and his sisters (vv. 3, 5, 36). This love gives Martha and Mary the courage to send for Jesus even though they know that his own life is in danger (10:39). Jesus seems deliberately to delay after receiving the message, perhaps in order to test the sisters' faith in his love (cf. vv. 21-22, 32b). His action is a mystery to the sisters, and even to the crowd (vv. 36-37), but the real reason for the delay is given in vv. 4, 15, 40.

Though the hostility of the leaders is mounting against him, Jesus, the light of the world, does not fear the powers of darkness. As light he cannot stumble in the dark or be overcome by darkness (cf. 1:5). Hence he deliberately emerges from his hiding to go to Jerusalem (vv. 11-14). Notice the features of Johannine misunderstanding in vv. 11-14. Thomas (from the Hebrew root for "twin") appears here for the first time as a pessimistic figure (cf. 14:5; 20:25). Though he speaks somewhat ironically (v. 16), some of the disciples will later die on account of Jesus (cf. 21:19). The early Church would have recalled the belief that in baptism we die with Jesus to sin so as to live for God (Rom 6:3-11).

The Raising of Lazarus (11:17-44)

As is typical of Johannine signs, Lazarus presents a case beyond remedy. In Jewish thought resurrection could occur "after three days," but Lazarus is four days dead and smelling. We notice, too, the contrast between the two sisters as depicted also in Luke 10:38-42. Martha is actively, pragmatically prayerful (vv. 20-28); Mary is contemplatively active (vv. 29-31). Mary feels deeply, draws sympathy from others (v. 31), and moves Jesus to tears (vv. 33-35). Her posture before Jesus is always one of reverence and that of a learning disciple ("at his feet," 11:32; 12:3; Luke 10:39). She must have been well known in the community as the woman who anointed Jesus for burial since she is identified by this role (v. 2) even before the action is narrated in 12:1-8.

Having reached Judea, Jesus appears to be in no hurry to act (v. 30), but he is moved to action by Mary's tears. In African cultures as in most others, men, unlike women, are not expected to weep, yet with deep emotion (troubled in spirit), "Jesus wept" publicly (v. 35, the shortest verse in the Bible), thereby showing his deep humanity and unashamed identification with women (cf. Luke 19:41).

Martha's confession (v. 27) resembles that of Peter (6:69; Matt 16:16 // Mark 8:29 // Luke 9:20). She stands next to JnB in the gospel in openly confessing Jesus as the Messiah who is coming into the world (cf. 1:29-30). Like that of Peter, this confession grew out of her constant and progressive but sustained contact with Jesus as his disciple and one loved by him. This is how we too come to know Jesus. In light of 6:69 her confession could be rendered "I have believed and have come to know that you are the Christ, the Son of God, who is coming into the world." It is to be noted that the most explicit confession of Jesus as Messiah in the formula "the Christ, the Son of God," which is the whole purpose for which the gospel was written (20:30-31), is made in the gospel only here by Martha. Her role in the gospel is by no means negligible. This points to the prominent role women like Martha played in the early Church and in the Johannine community in particular.

Martha's dialogue with Jesus raises the issue of realized and future eschatology. Martha believes in resurrection on the last day (v. 24: future eschatology). Jesus uses the occasion to underscore that believers transcend death even now and will be raised to life on the last day (v. 26). The exchange here is almost like a creed that Martha recites as happens on Holy Saturday night when Christians renew their baptismal promises. Martha does not actually express her faith in a realized eschatology, but in Jesus as the Messiah, Son of God. It is as though she were saying with Peter in 6:69: it is enough for me that you are the Messiah. With you everything is possible.

The Jews believed that at the last day an angel of God would come and open the tombs for the dead to come out. But Jesus is the Resurrection; this is a corollary to his being the Life. Because he is the Life, those who are in him are never really dead. They remain alive in him even now. Resurrection on the last day reveals that they were never really dead. In the case of Lazarus the issue is not a resurrection in the futuristic sense here discussed. He is simply brought back to this present natural life, not given a new life as in 1 Cor 15:42-50. Only when he dies again (cf. 12:10) will he look to this resurrection. Yet his resurrection here prefigures that of Jesus in 20:1-18.

We notice, too, Jesus' prayer of thanksgiving (vv. 41-42). Each time Jesus prays aloud, his prayer is almost always one of thanksgiving (cf. Matt 11:25-26 // Luke 10:21-22). Thanksgiving is regarded as the highest form of prayer. The implication of v. 42 is that Jesus often prays silently; his will and the Father's will are one. Here, as in the long prayer in ch 17, the purpose of his praying out loud is so that the disciples may hear and believe. Because his prayer is rooted in perfect faith in God he can simply call Lazarus once to "come forth" from the tomb. The mother of Jesus (2:3), Peter (Acts 3:6-8), and Paul (Acts 14:10; 16:18) show the same faith in their prayer. But today many miracle workers and those who conduct deliverances in the renewal movements often shout repeatedly before anything happens, and sometimes without anything happening. Is this indication of a lack of faith? (Cf. Matt 6:7).

Read symbolically, the illness and eventual death of Lazarus illustrates what sin does to us. If cure is not sought in time, the illness can lead to spiritual death. Like the sisters of Lazarus we need to love ourselves, our brothers and sisters, friends and relatives enough to seek help from Jesus before it is too late. Jesus is the remedy for sin (1:29; 8:34-36), the only savior of the world (4:42). An African pop song sings: "Jesus, the medicine you need." Do we believe that he loves us enough to be moved to tears by our tears as he was by Mary's?

The Plot to Kill Jesus (11:45-57)

One of the greatest ironies in John's gospel is that Jesus' raising of Lazarus from death to life becomes the decisive cause of his own death (vv. 45-53). We notice the role of some of the people who act as spies for the leaders. Such people exist today in the Church, in other institutions, and in government circles. They help to cause much suffering to those they report to the authorities. By their decision the leaders help to bring to fulfillment what Jesus himself had said in John 10:11. Caiaphas's statement, interpreted by John as prophetic, signifies more than he realizes. Jesus will die not to prevent the nation from being destroyed by the Romans as happened in 70 C.E. (first the Temple, then the nation), but rather to destroy all forces that divide and kill God's children (Jew and Gentile) such as racism, sexism, and ethnic hatred, and to reconcile us all to God and to one another (v. 52).

The leaders do not simply decide that Jesus must die; they begin to plot in earnest how to put him to death (v. 53). Again Jesus retires into hiding with his disciples, among them Judas his betrayer, in a town bordering the desert. His first battle with Satan took place in the desert (cf. Matt 4:1-11 // Mark 1:12-13 // Luke 4:1-13). This time the devil is among his very own disciples. How did Jesus feel with Judas there all the time? On the part of the people we notice the same curiosity about Jesus' attendance at the Passover feast (v. 56). The order issued by the leaders (v. 57) has an air of finality about it. Judas, one of the Twelve, will carry out this order.

The central NT message of gathering into one all God's scattered children is proclaimed differently by different authors (cf. Matt 27:50-51 [symbolically]; Eph 2:11–3:6; 1 Cor 12:13; Gal 3:26-28; Col 3:11; 1 John 2:2; Rev 5:9-10). The early Christian community understood this message well and tried to live it out, as described in Acts 2:43-47; 4:32-37. They struggled to overcome racism in the Gentile question and finally arrived at what we may call a constitutional solution in Acts 15:1-12. So important is this issue of unity and reconciliation that John presents it as Jesus' last will and testament for his followers. In the gospel itself the idea is expressed by harvest imagery (4:35-38), the one flock and one shepherd (10:16), the vine and branches (15:1-8), and the unbroken net (21:11). Traditionally Jesus' seamless garment that is not torn by the soldiers (19:23-24) is interpreted as signifying this unity.

Today in a world torn by racism, ethnic strife, and various kinds of divisions in families, Church, and state, the challenge of this central message of the gospel becomes even more imperative for us who believe in Christ. Each believer assumes a personal responsibility to identify the different forms in which these divisions operate in his or her heart and community and makes a personal commitment to cooperate with Jesus in gathering together God's children scattered by all these divisive forces. There is no neutrality here (Matt 12:30 // Luke 11:23).

Preparation for the Final Trial: Prediction of Ultimate Victory, John 12

John 12 brings to a close what some regard as "The Book of Signs" and begins "The Book of Glory." It also ends Jesus' interaction with the public in its forensic mode before the final trials in chs. 18–19. The chapter continues the focusing of attention on Jesus' disciples (Martha, Mary, Lazarus, Judas) that began in ch. 11 and climaxes in chs. 13–17. The following units are discernible: the anointing by Mary of Bethany (vv. 1-8), the plot to kill Lazarus (vv. 9-11), the triumphal entry into Jerusalem (vv. 12-19), the coming of the Greeks to Jesus (vv. 21-26), the necessity and reason for Jesus' being lifted up (vv. 27-36), the persistent unbelief of the Jews (vv. 37-43), the evangelist's comment on this persistent unbelief and Jesus' final appeal to his audience (vv. 44-50).

Events in this chapter are placed within the context of Passover, the greatest Jewish feast, which commemorated Israel's liberation from slavery in Egypt and the resulting Sinai Covenant, watershed of Israel's history (cf. Exod 12:1-20, 41-51; Lev 23:5-8; Num 28:16-26; Deut 16:1-8; 2 Kings 23:21-26). This Passover is the third and last for Jesus (cf. 2:13; 6:4). The anointing by Mary takes place six days before the feast (two days in Mark 14:1). Aspects of the Passover motifs in the chapter include the meal motif (Seder), preparation for Israel's/Jesus' departure, and triumphant crossing of the Red Sea/entry into Jerusalem. As people from other nations joined themselves to the Israelites on their journey, so here the Greeks come to see Jesus and he draws all peoples to himself (vv. 20-32).

The Anointing (12:1-8)

The "supper" for Jesus offered by Martha and Mary is in gratitude for his raising Lazarus, their brother, from death. Today people do public "thanksgiving" service to God for favors received, but this particular "thanksgiving" has an added significance in Mary's anointing, as noted by Jesus himself (v. 7). We notice the exuberance of love she shows. The ointment costs three hundred working days' or nine months' wages at the usual rate of a denarius a day (cf. Matt 20:2, 9). Hence Judas would be somewhat justified in his remark (v. 6) except that it is motivated by his love of money. Jesus forbids him to harass the woman. The anointing is the last act of charity done to him, and in Judaism burying the dead ranked above almsgiving as one of the greater works of charity. While there will always be opportunity to give alms to the poor, this act is done to Jesus once and for all (v. 8). This defense of Mary may be portrayed as the last straw that prompted Judas to betray Jesus.

Judas's attack is directed at both Jesus and Mary (notice the impersonal, passive voice in v. 6). Of all the four gospels, John's gives the most negative portrayal of Judas. He is called a "devil" in 6:70, a thief here, one into whom Satan enters in 13:2, and is described as one who leaves the company of Jesus, the light, to enter into companionship with the powers of darkness (13:30). Yet Jesus trusted him enough to make him the treasurer of the community (13:29). His deep hatred for Jesus is supernaturally engineered and contrasts sharply with Mary's tender and lavish love.

Contemplative Mary, like the BD, seems to have understood the inner mystery of Jesus from the heart and without words. Her silent anointing full of love and faith is the anointing of the king for the final victorious combat symbolized by the triumphal entry into Jerusalem. The anointing of the feet instead of the head (as in Matthew and Mark) is interpreted by Jesus as something done to his whole body (cf. 13:10). Mary's action is also a bold breaking with convention since decent Jewish women did not loosen their hair in public (cf. 1 Cor 11:6). In the synoptics Jesus shows his deep appreciation by asking that her deed be told wherever the gospel is preached in the whole world "in memory of her" (cf. Matt 26:13 // Mark 14:9). Origen saw the same meaning in the symbolism of the fragrance of the ointment filling the entire house (v. 3). Jesus' action in 13:4-20, which in many ways imitates her own, shows his further appreciation of her deed.

The Plot to Kill Lazarus and the Triumphal Entry (12:9-11, 12-19)

The plot against Lazarus registers the mounting vindictiveness of the leaders. It is yet another attempt, as in ch. 9, to destroy evidence in favor of Jesus. That they are prepared to go so far shows the depth of their hatred of him. Some of the people continue their quest for the sensational in the works of Jesus (v. 9), yet their curiosity is very natural.

All four gospels record Jesus' triumphant entry into Jerusalem (Matt 21:1-9 // Mark 11:1-10 // Luke 19:28-38 // John 12:12-15). Coming immediately after the plot to kill Lazarus on Jesus' account, this action shows Jesus to be the light whom darkness cannot overcome. In John 6:14-15 Jesus had fled to the mountain when he sensed that the people wanted "to make him king" by force. Now he willingly accepts their homage as "king of Israel," based on the sign of raising Lazarus, because he knows that his "hour" has come (cf. 13:1) and victory is assured. The action of the crowd is based on the witness of those who personally saw the raising of Lazarus from the tomb. The larger crowd heard this and believed, perhaps because most of them had gone in person to see Lazarus. In 20:29 Jesus counts as blessed "those who have not seen and yet believe." In 17:20 he prays for those who will believe in him because of the word of his disciples. Today many people who have not yet heard of Jesus can also believe based on our powerful testimony.

The triumphal entry recalls Israel's messianic hope (Zeph 3:14-15; Zech 9:9; Isa 35:4; 40:9). The evangelist recalls this hope although at the time it happened the disciples themselves did not understand what it was all about. It would seem that the people, pressed by their needs, were more ready to see Jesus as the Messiah than were his own disciples and the leaders. Today the people's christology is often much higher than that of the theologians who by profession should know Jesus better. The people's simple acceptance of the raising of Lazarus and their conclusion that Jesus is the Messiah drives the Pharisees to despair. Verse 19 may be an exaggeration based on this despair but the coming of the Greeks to see Jesus along with the believing Jews justifies their declaring that "the whole world" is coming after Jesus. Before now only the Baptist (1:19) and the Samaritans (4:42) have confessed Jesus as the universal Savior. Now the leaders do so although, in Johannine irony, they are not fully aware of the truth of their statement.

The Coming of the Greeks; Jesus Draws All to Himself (12:20-26, 27-36)

The coming of the Greeks (who are probably Gentiles) to see Jesus signifies the dawning of the "hour" Jesus had been waiting for, the hour of his glorification (cf. 7:30) when he will draw all peoples to himself. It is striking how in these last days of Jesus the ordinary people seem to be the agents of the events that announce the coming of the hour (the anointing by Mary, the welcome by the crowd to Jerusalem, now the coming of the Greeks). As Gentiles and strangers the Greeks seek associates of Jesus to introduce them to him; they regard him as "a big man." Philip is a Greek name, though he like Andrew and his brother Peter are from Bethsaida (1:40, 44). He and Andrew embody the missionary spirit of the community (cf. 1:41, 45; 6:7-9).

It is through and on the cross that Jesus draws all peoples to himself (v. 24). His thought in v. 27, which he rejects, might be John's version of the agony in the garden, a scene omitted from John's Gospel. Jesus accepts the "hour" as indispensable for the completion of his mission (cf. 3:14). He invites all true disciples (those who follow and learn from him step by step) to walk with him the way to victory through the cross (vv. 25-26). Mary of Bethany is one such disciple. She staked everything for Jesus: her reputation, wealth, common sense, and even "charity" as a manifestation of her love for Jesus. Mary Magdalene in ch. 20 is another such disciple.

A false theology today declares: "Jesus suffered for me some two thousand years ago, therefore I do not need to suffer any more." This theology is not from Jesus himself or from the NT. Readiness to suffer for the cause of Jesus is an essential part of Christian discipleship. This suffering is occasioned by the unbelieving world in which disciples live and by the sinfulness of us disciples ourselves. If one is prepared to love the unloved to perfection and declare for God in a self-seeking world, one must be prepared to suffer.

God's answer to Jesus (v. 28), like Jesus' own vocal prayer, is for the people to hear. It gives further evidence that Jesus' victory over the powers of darkness through the cross is assured (12:31; 14:3). We notice how the people seem to be at home with angels' voices, yet despite this supernatural intervention they are still incapable of listening and believing as they cling to their own traditions about the Messiah, a figure who was not to suffer or die. They equate the Messiah here with Daniel's "Son of Man" who is a heavenly figure, and whose throne is said to endure through the ages (cf. Dan 7:13), but Jesus warns them to grow out of this fixed attitude if they are to see the light of truth and life (vv. 35-36).

A supplementary section from the evangelist gives a global assessment of the people's response to Jesus, citing Isa 6:10 (John 12:40). The same passage is cited in Matt 13:14-15 and Mark 3:5 in relation to the unteachability of Jesus' audience. Because the people refuse to hear and respond, God's word has the effect of reinforcing their spiritual blindness, deafness, and hardness of heart. The frustration of God's agent had long since been noted by Isaiah, yet in the light of Isaiah 53 the toil is not in vain. Nevertheless many who see the truth, including people in authority, are still afraid to respond publicly (vv. 42-43). Nicodemus and Joseph of Arimathea may be among their number.

We notice the pathos in Jesus' last appeal to his people to believe in him. This pathos arises more out of concern that the people are rejecting God's authority, which Jesus always obeys, than from self-pity (vv. 49-50). Jesus and God never give up on us, no matter how bad we may be.

This passage with its many units is rich for the contemporary reader. It will be helpful to identify examples in one's own contexts of the different characters in this chapter and their different responses to Jesus. These responses need not be stereotyped. Sometimes we might be Judas, at others Mary of Bethany, at others the crowd or the leaders. At other times we might be courageous enough to suffer with Jesus in the cause of proclaiming the gospel. A prayerful and repeated reading of the passage with the help of the Holy Spirit will give fresh insights for application as they were given to the evangelist.

IV: Preparing the Disciples for the Future (John 13–17)

At Home with the Disciples, Called to Love and Service, John 13

John 13 introduces the Last Supper discourse which extends to ch. 17. These five chapters narrate Jesus' last and most intimate conversation with his disciples before his departure. Many if not all of the features of this Last Supper section are distinctive to John and are believed to come from traditions later than the synoptics. They are the mature fruit of the community's reflection on the meaning of Jesus and his mission and on the implications for them as disciples.

John 13 contains the washing of the disciples' feet and its interpretation (vv. 1-20), the prediction of Judas's betrayal (vv. 21-30), the new commandment of love (vv. 31-35), and the prediction of Peter's denial (vv. 36-38).

The Washing of Feet (13:1-20)

This episode forms a diptych with the anointing at Bethany. Both events take place within days of each other in the Passover week (12:1; 13:1). The similarities may be listed as follows:

- both take place during supper, with people reclining (12:2; 13:2)
- an action is done to the feet of another or others (12:3 [11:2]; 13:5)
- using part of own body (hair, 12:3; towel around waist, 13:4-5)
- both draw forth opposition from those present (Judas, 12:4-5; Peter, 13:6)
- Judas cites, and is linked with concern for, the poor as an excuse (12:5; 13:29)
- the action causes shock or dismay (12:4-5; 13:6-10)
- Jesus interprets the action with reference to himself (12:7-8; 13:7, 10-17)
- the action has a future scope (12:3c [Matt 26:13 // Mark 14:9]; 13:12-17)
- In the synoptics Jesus requires that the story be told "in memory of" the woman (even as in Luke 22:19 the Eucharist is to be done "in memory of" him). In John 13:14-15 Jesus counsels his disciples to imitate him by performing this humble service to one another.

These similarities make the washing of the disciples' feet form a diptych with the anointing of Jesus' feet. In this relay of perfect love that boldly breaks with all conventions (12:3; 13:4-5, 13) Mary, as it were, passes on the baton to Jesus, who with deep admiration passes it in turn to his disciples (vv. 14-15; 13:34-35). Seen as an expression of perfect love and readiness to serve and forgive others the washing of the feet forms an integral part of the celebration of the Eucharist. The Holy Thursday night liturgy highlights the aspect of humble service, but the other two aspects are equally important. Sacramentally, the washing of the feet symbolizes baptism (as happens during the Easter Vigil liturgy) by which we are cleansed, purified from sin, and given new life in the Spirit (3:3-8). Jesus also cleanses and renews us by his word (13:15; 15:3) and by his blood, the blood of the Paschal Lamb shed on the cross (John 1:29; 1 John 1:7).

Prediction of Judas's Betrayal (13:21-30)

This section stresses Jesus' foreknowledge of Judas's betrayal, which looms very large over the intimate gathering (vv. 2, 10c-11, 18-19). We notice the contrast between the peaceful mood in the previous section and this sudden troubling "in spirit" (v. 21). Jesus' perfect love for his own (13:1; 15:13) is accentuated by this shadow of hatred. The stronger the hatred grows, the deeper his love for his own. Judas's betrayal really pained Jesus. His gestures of love toward Judas only served to reinforce Judas's hatred. The Satan in him hates Jesus. The more Jesus displays what he is—love—the more Satan acts out what he is—hatred. But Jesus' love is stronger than death (15:13; cf. Song 8:6-7). By giving the morsel, Jesus seems to give Judas and the Satan in him permission to do their worst, knowing that the victory of love is assured.

Strikingly, the BD motif first appears in this context of deep, soul-disturbing betrayal of Jesus. His leaning on Jesus' breast is unconventional. Origen interpreted it as signifying the disciple's deeply personal and intimate knowledge of Jesus. He knows Jesus through a warm, heart-to-heart contact, just as Jesus knows the Father through abiding in his bosom (1:18). We notice also the pairing of Peter and the BD; this is developed later in ch. 21 and gives rise to the speculation that Peter and the BD were rivals in the community, but this view lacks supportive basis in the non-Johannine tradition. On the contrary, in the Lukan writings Peter and John are shown as working closely together (cf. Acts 3:1, 3, 11; 8:14) even as they were closely associated in Jesus' ministry.

The New Commandment (13:31-35)

The new commandment to love as Jesus loves (vv. 31-35) is sandwiched between the predictions of Judas's betrayal and of Peter's denial (vv. 21-30, 36-38). This implies that the disciples are to follow Jesus the whole way, learn from him how to love intensely in the face of hatred, serve one another humbly, and cleanse one another from sin (washing of the feet). As God's disciple, Jesus himself does the same: he listens to the Father, learns, and acts likewise. His love of his own to perfection (v. 1) is introduced against the background of Judas's betrayal (v. 2).

This commandment is the identity card of the true disciple (v. 35). It goes with the new covenant of love just as the Torah went with the covenant on Mount Sinai. It is new because the measure of love required is the measure by which Jesus loves us, not how we love ourselves. As with the OT law of love for YHWH (Deut 6:4-9), we disciples are to wear it on our bodies, write it in our hearts, in our lives, homes, and cities. Other passages such as 1 John 3:11-18 and 1 Corinthians 13 spell out in some detail what this love entails. Central to it is the readiness to serve and forgive one another even as Jesus served, forgave, and purified his disciples, knowing that they would soon abandon him and flee. We cannot really appreciate the challenge of this commandment unless we have a full grasp of the depths of Jesus' love for us.

Prediction of Peter's Denial (13:36-38)

As in the synoptics (Matt 26:33-35 // Mark 14:29-31 // Luke 22:31-34) Jesus warns Peter of his impending denial, but Peter, like Judas, pays no attention to the warning. Peter boasts of his readiness to die for Jesus yet lacks the courage to admit to a mere serving maid that he is one of Jesus' followers (18:17). The difference between him and Judas is that Peter loves Jesus. In the end Peter will learn from his actual denial not to count too much on his own love for Jesus but to depend more on Jesus' love for him. This awareness rules out boasting, teaches humility, and sustains a love that expresses itself in service of others (cf. 21:15-19). What is required of Peter is required of all true followers of Jesus today.

Jesus the Life, Truth, and Way to God, John 14

After Judas's departure Jesus instructs his disciples more intimately. This chapter repeats in a friendly and comforting manner the teaching Jesus gave the public in the first part of the gospel concerning his oneness with the Father and the need to believe this on the evidence of his works (vv. 9-11), the call to believe in him (vv. 1, 12) and to keep his commandments as a mark of love for him (vv. 15, 23), and his impending departure (vv. 2-4). It contains additional words of comfort for the disciples themselves: that though he is going away, he will never abandon them (v. 18), that they will do even greater works than himself if they believe in him (v. 11-12), and that he will send them the Holy Spirit as another Paraclete (vv. 17, 26). It is assumed that the disciples were with him when he was instructing the public and so should easily grasp this teaching as it applies to them.

The method employed is pedagogical. Jesus makes statements that move the disciples to ask questions to which he then provides answers: Thomas (vv. 4-7a), Philip (vv. 7b-13), Judas not Iscariot (vv. 21-22). The questioning actually starts with Peter in 13:36 as a response to Jesus' statement in 13:33. The opening section of ch. 14 is a direct reply to this question. Since these are the disciples' own questions, they should be ready to hear or learn the answers.

The central issue in the chapter is "what will happen to the disciples when Jesus departs from them?" The question is a real, not a hypothetical one. It is hard for us today to appreciate what Jesus' departure would have meant to the disciples, especially given the hostility of the leaders, their own hopes that he was the Messiah (understood as one who would "live forever," 12:34), and their unpreparedness to carry on Jesus' mission; after the resurrection, for instance, they returned to their old trade of fishing (21:1-14).

Jesus treats their fears as genuine and counsels against anxiety (vv. 1, 27). In his real concern for them he reassures them in three ways:

- Though he is going away he will always be with them, will return to them, and eventually will take them to be with him when the time comes (vv. 3, 18-19, 28). As the hour of departure approaches Jesus himself shows his own deep desire never to leave them physically, if it were possible (vv. 2-4), yet his departure is necessary for the completion of his mission and the maturity of the disciples themselves. Knowledge of this should be a source of joy for the disciples (v. 28).
- He will not leave them orphans (children bereft of parents, home, means of livelihood) but will send them the Holy Spirit as their abiding Paraclete (v. 26). "Paraclete" is a forensic term that signifies a lawyer, defense counsel, and legal adviser in the court of life and in the hostile world. Moreover, this Spirit will be in them (v. 17; hence the doctrine of the indwelling of the Spirit, which extends to the Trinity, v. 23) and will be their unfailing teacher (v. 26). The Spirit, as the Spirit of truth (Spirit of prophecy), will insure that they cannot be led astray by the falsehood of the unbelieving world (v. 17).
- He gives them a peace that no hostile forces (the world) can take away from them (v. 27), and foreknowledge of things to come so as to strengthen their faith and prevent them from being caught unaware (14:29; 13:19).

A most consoling message for the disciples is that they know the way to where Jesus is going (v. 6). Jesus is the way to God: they need to walk along it and have no fear of stumbling. He is the truth: they need to hold on to him and rely on him without fear of being failed by him. He is the life: they need to live it, live in him, and have no fear of death. This assurance is worthy of acceptance since Jesus and the Father are one, and since all he says and does in their midst are the words and works of God (vv. 8-11). Though one with the Father, Jesus is yet distinct from him (cf. vv. 1, 13, 23); as Son and human being he prays to the Father who is greater than he (vv. 16, 28c).

Attention needs to be paid to the strong trinitarian character of Jesus' comforting of the disciples in this section. The Father loves the disciples who love Jesus. They can ask him anything in Jesus' name and Jesus will grant it. The disciples will come to know that they themselves are in Jesus, even as Jesus is in the Father (v. 20). The Spirit's role is specifically to assist the disciples in knowing about Jesus and in standing firm against the world (vv. 17, 26). He appears here as closely linked with the peace that Jesus alone gives (wellbeing in mind, heart, and life), as is the case in 20:21-22.

The Spirit is introduced as in opposition to the world (v. 17). The world is everything that is opposed to Jesus, the truth, hence everything that is a lie. Truth and lie are radically opposed concepts; hence Jesus, the Truth, has nothing in common with the ruler of this world: Satan, the Father of lies. That is why the world can neither know nor receive the Spirit of truth. "The world" throughout this Last Supper discourse signifies this hostile unbelieving world that is opposed to God and Jesus, not the created world God loves so much (3:16). Jesus' answer to Judas not Iscariot in v. 23 makes this plain. Anyone who loves Jesus and keeps his word is a disciple and receives equal treatment from God and Jesus. Nobody is excluded from this discipleship. The spirit that underlies discipleship is radically opposed to that which underlies the world. Hence the world does not know the Spirit; the disciples do (v. 17). The world will not see Jesus; the disciples will (v. 19). The best commentary on this issue is probably Gal 5:16-26.

This chapter highlights Jesus' love for his disciples; it is warm and tender, not dry and heartless. This kind of love is often missing in methods in ministry today, yet it was very much present in the ministry of the early Church (cf. Acts 20:37-38; Phil 1:8; Rom 1:9) and needs to be revisited since it is an integral part of our humanity.

Invitation to Intimate Union, John 15

The theme of being with or remaining in Jesus mentioned repeatedly in John 14 is reemphasized and concretized in John 15 in the imagery of the vine and the branches. This imagery is one of the most cherished in John's gospel. Africans who do not have the vine can think of any fruit-bearing tree, like the orange tree, where only the branches bear fruit. The imagery draws attention to the inseparable union between the vine and the branches, the total dependency of the branches on the vine for staying alive and for fruitfulness.

In this passage the invitation to intimate union is expressed in the very concept of the vine and the branches, in the powerlessness of the vine to survive and bear fruit except through the vine, in the designation of the disciples as "friends" (those loved) to whom Jesus reveals all that he has heard from the Father (v. 15), in the declaration that the disciples are loved exactly as the Father loves Jesus (v. 9), that they are called and set up (propped up or sustained) to bear lasting fruit (v. 16), and that they will glorify God by their fruitfulness just as Jesus glorifies God by his entire life (v. 8). The imagery of "home" (15:4; cf. 14:17) encapsulates it well. A home is not simply a house or an apartment; it is a place where people feel they belong in a family context. Homes are "made" by the warmth of family members who work consciously to create an atmosphere of belonging where the needs of all are met. Homes are places of acceptance, relaxation, and freedom for all members. Jesus invites his followers to feel as much at home in his company and presence as he feels in theirs. John 10:9 registers the same sentiments.

Jesus the Vine, the Disciples the Branches (15:1-17)

The passage contains another "I am" saying, but this time it draws attention both to Jesus, "I am the vine," and to the disciples, "you are the branches." The "I am/you are" terminology emphasizes the living and inseparable relationship between Jesus and us his followers. Several OT passages see Israel both as the vineyard of God (for example, Isa 5:1-7) and as God's vine (for example, Ps 80:8-16). Here Jesus and his followers, the renewed Israel, are the vine. His most intimate union with the Father makes him a most fruitful vine, unlike Israel which often separated itself from God only to be "ravaged by the boar from the forest" (Ps 80:13[12]). The disciples get their identity from election by the vine to be its fruitful branches, just as Israel got its identity from its election by God to be God's people. Disciples are warned not to be unfaithful as Israel was lest they too become separated from Jesus and be totally destroyed as by fire (v. 6).

The passage focuses more on the fruitful branches (vv. 2b-5, 17) than on the unfruitful ones (vv. 2a, 6). As God planted and tended Israel as a choice vine, so God tends Jesus, the vine, and specifically in its branches, the disciples. God's activity is directed toward the disciples/branches, not the vine: God prunes the fruitful ones so that they can become even more fruitful. Pruning is an integral part of or necessary condition for greater fruitfulness. It is painful and personal. One cannot depend on the pruning of another or say "Jesus was pruned two thousand years ago; therefore I do not need to be pruned today." There can be no stunted disciples of Jesus. The more one is alive and vibrant in the vine the more one will need to be pruned.

This message would have had a special appeal to members of John's community. They would have been undergoing persecution from unbelievers or suffering from the trauma of division within the community caused by the anti-Christ departees or recovering from the trauma of the alleged ejection from the synagogue. The statement in v. 6 concerning the unfruitful branch recalls the letter to the angel of the church in Laodicea (Rev 3:14-22, especially vv. 15-16).

The disciples are pruned by Jesus' word (v. 3) that challenges them to grow and stand firm in face of these trials. Jesus' word of love (the gospel) is action, not merely information; it effects in the believer what it signifies. The disciple is required only to abide in Jesus and surrender to God's growth-enhancing activity. Jesus gives his possessions to the disciples, inside them, to insure this union: his words (15:7), his love (15:9-10), his joy (15:11), his Spirit (14:17), himself and the Father (14:23).

Intimate union between vine and branches results in and requires intimate union between the branches themselves (15:12-13, 17). Jesus' love for the disciples based on God's own love for him (15:9) requires this as a command (15:12, 17; cf. 13:34-35); it is a love that not even death can destroy (15:13). The disciples manifest that they have truly received this love from Jesus when they in turn love one another exactly as Jesus loves them (15:10). Each positive response from the disciples/branches carries a reward (see the "if" statements in 15:7, 10, 14).

Notably, Jesus' relationship with God constitutes the yardstick of his relationship with his disciples. He wishes for them all that he has or would wish for himself, humanly speaking. As he is with/in the Father by keeping the Father's commandments, so are the disciples to be with/in him by keeping his commandments (15:10). The disciples glorify God by their fruitfulness just as Jesus' does by doing God's will (15:8, 16); as Jesus remains in God and bears fruit (1:18; 10:30, 37-38; 14:10-11), so will the disciples by remaining in him (15:2); as people see God in seeing Jesus (1:18; 14:7-9), so should they see Jesus in seeing the disciples; as Jesus loves the disciples, so are the disciples to love one another (15:9, 12); as God loves Jesus and gives everything to him (3:35; cf. Matt 28:18), so does Jesus love the disciples and make everything known to them (15:15). The words and works of Jesus are those of God; so should the words and works of the disciple be those of Jesus (14:5-11). Jesus goes to God unto fullness of life; he sends the Holy Spirit to the disciples to dwell in them and inspire greater deeds in them.

How do we understand the imagery of the vine and the branches today? In an African context the child is the glory of its parents. Parents correct (or prune) their children to enable them to grow. An Ibibio (Nigerian) proverb states that a father gives bony meat only to the child that he loves. A child who runs away from home (that is, is cut off from the human source of its life) runs into serious trouble and may even endanger its life. God prunes us by sometimes allowing misfortunes to befall us. It was the injury received by Ignatius of Loyola during a military campaign that converted him into an ardent follower of Jesus and led to his founding the Society of Jesus which has given birth to many saints and has borne much fruit in the Church and the world. Childlessness, loss of one's employment, even the death of a dear relative, husband, wife, child might be the means God uses to prune us. Pruning is essential because of our finite and sinful nature that needs to be enlarged and purified till we are perfectly conformed to the image of God in Christ. Death constitutes the final pruning that transforms us fully into the image and likeness of God in Christ.

The reader is encouraged to explore how the insights gained in this section helps us to understand why the chapter is set in various liturgical contexts: baptism, religious consecration, funeral Mass, consecration of religious, and feasts of contemplatives like Teresa of Avila.

The "I am" saying in 15:5 is the last of these sayings in John's gospel. Its corollary is that we are the branches. Though these are not expressly stated, each previous "I am" saying has a corollary for us. Insight may be gained by revisiting these sayings and reflecting on the corollary each has for us, followers of Christ, in our own contexts.

Persecution, the Lot of True Disciples (15:18–16:4)

The basic question in this section is "what will happen to the disciples after Jesus is gone?" Jesus' warm-hearted concern for his disciples comes to the fore here as it did in chs. 13–14. Matthew 10:16-25 records the same concern but in a different context. Here it is strange that

Jesus should show this concern; as one about to die for the disciples, he should be receiving comfort. Instead, his knowledge that the disciples have not yet understood his teaching and mission and so lack firm faith in him (16:31-32) intensifies his concern for them.

John 15:18–16:4 warns the disciples against the world's hatred and persecution. Because of their intimate union with him they should be prepared to meet the same fate from the world of unbelievers as Jesus himself had met (15:25). This is set forth in a parallel in 15:18-20. As Jesus was hated and rejected because the people did not know God, so will his disciples be, because the people do not know Jesus.

In 16:33 Jesus seems to say, "I know fully well that you are not yet where I would want you to be with regard to your faith in me, but my love for you is stronger than your weak faith; that love will sustain you to the end. When you all run away through weakness you will remember that I knew about it all along, that I loved you deeply and unflinchingly in spite of it all and gave you my lasting peace. Remembering, you will take courage and return to me." This display of weakness happens in chs. 18–19, especially in Peter's denial (18:17-27). After the resurrection Jesus will seek them out, reassure them by word and deed, give them his peace and confer his Spirit on them, thus empowering them to stand firm in him till the end. Then they will be ready to be sent into the world as God sent Jesus himself (20:19-21). Meanwhile Jesus is concerned about the suffering that rejection and hatred from the unbelieving world will cause them. Sustained by the Spirit, the disciples will bear witness to him just as Jesus himself, filled with the Holy Spirit, bears witness to God unto death (14:31b). The disciples are saddened by these warnings (16:1, 6). They show it by their increasing silence compared to their ready interventions in ch. 14. Yet Jesus' departure is necessary for their own growth in faith (cf. 16:12), for the coming of the Holy Spirit, and for the Spirit's ministry and witness to Jesus in and through them.

The theory of ejection from the synagogue based on 16:2 (cf. Matt 10:16-27) is said to be a projection from the time of the disciples onto that of Jesus, but the exclusion of Christians from the synagogue need not be limited to the period after 90 C.E. Even in Jesus' time, disciples were persecuted along with Jesus. After Pentecost persecution started very early (cf. the fates of Peter and John in Acts 3–4; Acts 7–8; Gal 1:13-14) and on a large scale. After his conversion Paul himself would be thrown out not only from the synagogue but at times from the city (cf. Acts 13:50; 18:5-7; 19:9). In normal circumstances people who deviate from the tenets of a given religious group are dismissed early from the group before they do serious damage. Paul's activity against the Christians went beyond persecution and ejection from the synagogue to seeking total destruction of the young community. In our times many people have been persecuted and killed in God's name, not only by Muslim fundamentalists but also by Christian ones. Our Catholic Church has done the same in different forms through the ages.

The Role of the Spirit/Paraclete (15:26-27; 16:5-16)

A marked feature in the farewell discourses is the way in which the Holy Spirit, spoken of earlier in the gospel (cf. 1:32-33; 3:5-8; 6:63; 7:37-49), is progressively presented. In 14:16-17 s/he is the Spirit of truth who will comfort the disciples when Jesus is gone; in 14:26 the Spirit is the teacher (Spirit of prophecy) who will lead them into the complete truth, remind them of the teachings of Jesus, and give them insight into the meaning of events in Jesus' life (cf. 2:22; 12:16; 13:7; 20:9-10). John 15:26-27 highlights the role of the Spirit as the co-witness to Jesus with the disciples. The Spirit will bear witness to Jesus first by enabling the disciples themselves to understand and personally accept his meaning and mission, then by fortifying them to bear witness to the outside world to what they have understood.

John 16:5-16 emphasizes the indispensability of the Spirit's role in the spiritual maturity of the disciples (especially vv. 5-8). The Spirit will also vindicate Jesus and his claims before the world. Here the Spirit still serves both as advocate in court for the disciples and as their unfailing teacher even of things yet to come (vv. 12-13). More significantly, the Spirit will serve as a judge in court, deciding between Jesus who makes these claims and the unbelieving world that rejects them (vv. 6-11). Central to these claims is that he is "the Son of God." His return to the Father who sent him and the consequent sending of the Spirit will furnish the conclusive evidence that this claim was true; then the world will stand convicted of its refusal to believe in him (v. 9).

Jesus' return to the Father and the sending of the Spirit also spell the dethroning of the evil one in the lives of people. Jesus' death serves as the final judgment and condemnation of Satan, "the prince of this world" (v. 11). The Spirit is called "the holy Spirit" who indwells in believers. The implication is that there are unholy spirits who do not indwell but possess people. Spirit possession is a common experience in Africa and elsewhere. The cure for this is surrendering oneself to the indwelling of the Holy Spirit.

John 16:14-16 gives further insight into the Spirit's relationship with Jesus and the Father. This is one of the clearest passages in the gospel about God as Trinity in unity. As Jesus glorifies the Father in his life and is indeed the Father's very glory (cf. 1:14), so the Spirit dwelling in the disciples, guiding and teaching them, will enable them to become in turn Jesus' glory (cf. 17:10, 22-24). The persons in the Trinity exist joyfully and freely for each other. It should be the same among those who remain in Jesus (17:22-23).

The more Jesus unveils this mystery to his disciples, the more they become overwhelmed and say very little. Aware of this, Jesus tries to bring them into the conversation, even blaming them for not asking where he is going (16:5) despite 13:36. In 13:36 Peter was thinking, as did the Jews in 7:35-36, of Jesus' departure to another place, but as the farewell discourses progress the disciples understand that he is speaking of his departure in death and glorification (16:28). The disciples are now afraid to ask because their previous questions had revealed their poverty of understanding. Jesus has become more puzzling for them (vv. 16-19). They need the Holy Spirit to give them understanding. Like an alert and patient teacher Jesus comes to their rescue and answers their unasked questions for them (vv. 20-22).

The "little while" of his absence in death will give place to the "little while" of his presence among them after the resurrection (cf. 20:20). After that he will return finally to God who sent him. The pain of the separation in death is like the pangs a woman experiences in childbirth. The pangs are caused because the child does not want to be separated from the warmth of the mother's womb, yet this separation is necessary if the child is to get an independent life. Both the mother and the child experience the pain of coming to birth. Here Jesus is concerned only with the pain that the child (the disciples) will experience, not his own (but cf. 12:24). They will forget this pain in the joy of the resurrection.

The unbelieving world will rejoice at Jesus' death, which will cause great sorrow to the disciples, especially when compounded with their own inability to stand by him to the end (cf. 16:31b-33). One is struck by the gentle way in which Jesus reveals to the disciples that they will fail him in the end. His operative thought is that because he has conquered the unbelieving world the victory of the disciple is assured in his own victory. This operative thought is taken up confidently alongside others in the ensuing prayer (ch. 17).

This entire section on the relationship between Jesus, the disciples, and the unbelieving world has great significance for all today. The reader can make this message interact with his or her own social, political, and religious contexts. Are we among witnesses to Jesus or part of the unbelieving world, even though we profess faith in him? Like the disciples, are we afraid to ask Jesus for fear we might hear what we dread about having to suffer on his account? What forms do persecution and rejection because of our faith in Christ take in our different contexts? How much do we appreciate the gift of the Holy Spirit and open ourselves to the Spirit's guidance and inspiration? Any negative answers we may discover to these questions should not discourage us. Jesus' love for us triumphs not only over the world but also over our weaknesses, as it did over those of his first disciples. What matters is to remain in him; then God will continue to prune us to insure that we bear lasting fruit even as he pruned the evangelist to bear lasting fruit by his witness, which is this gospel.

Jesus' Public Accountability to God for His Mission, John 17

John 17 is generally described as Jesus' last will and testament. Traditionally in the liturgical context it is known as his "priestly prayer," especially for ordained priests; for this reason it is read at the Chrism Mass on Holy Thursday when priests renew their vows of ordination. In an ecumenical context it is called the prayer for

Christian unity. All these readings are valid, but within the context of the gospel itself the prayer stands as Jesus' last public accounting to God for his mission. As this mission was carried out before the disciples who were with him "from the beginning" (15:27; cf. 1:35-51), the accounting is made before them as witnesses. In this context the prayer compares well with such farewell discourses as that of Paul to the elders of Ephesus (Acts 20:17-35). This passage can shed great light on the prayer.

The prayer is made to God who always hears Jesus (11:42), but it is said aloud for the benefit of the disciples (17:13). With respect to God the prayer is intercessory; with respect to the disciples it is hortatory. The disciples are to be encouraged and strengthened by it in living out its content. As a public accounting to God the prayer is intended to persuade the disciples of the truthfulness of all that Jesus has been saying to them, especially in chs. 13–16. The prayer is largely for them; even the initial request that Jesus be given back his pre-existent glory has this persuasive goal in view. This prayer for glorification is necessitated by the reality of Jesus' humanity that now needs to be taken up inseparably into the glory of the pre-existent God/*logos* (1:1-2). Philippians 2:6-11 may shed light on this point. The plea for glorification is for the Word-become-flesh (1:14). The prayer sums up all that Jesus has been saying to the disciples in chs. 13–16 and presents the whole as a request to God to be granted to and for the disciples.

The following points deserve particular notice: The divine origin and relationship of Jesus with God is the basis of his mission (vv. 1-5), namely, to reveal God's name to the world and thereby impart life-giving knowledge of God. The disciples are the direct beneficiaries and witnesses of this mission (vv. 6-8). Based on these two facts (the divine origin and mission of Jesus and the witness to it by the disciples, God's gift to him), Jesus offers two key prayer points for his followers: that they be kept faithful to him and to God's revealed name, or put differently, that they be kept from contamination by the world (vv. 6-19); second, that they and believers yet to come may remain perfectly one in love, even as he and the Father are one. This oneness will be crowned by the inseparable union in heaven of Jesus and all his disciples (vv. 20-24).

Jesus' humanity, his perfect love for the disciples (13:1; 15:9), and his deep concern about their fate after his departure manifest themselves intensely in this prayer. He consecrates or sacrifices himself on their behalf and desires that they too be consecrated or confirmed in the truth, God's word given to them by Jesus (17:17-19; cf. 10:18). Thus consecrated, they too will be prepared to die in defense of the truth. Though Jesus will soon depart, he will continue his priestly /intercessory and prophetic/revelatory functions on their behalf in heaven (17:26; cf. Heb 7:25).

One senses Jesus' deep fear, humanly speaking, that the disciples may fail, so that he would have "labored in vain" (Isa 49:4). The divided situation within the Johannine community would have made this fear real for the evangelist. The united presence of the disciples in the world is a convincing sign that God sent Jesus (v. 23). Conversely, their division puts in question the divine origin of his mission. In this light the prayer, composed probably by the evangelist, is Jesus' last strong and agonizing appeal to this divided community to remain one in him. It is an aspect of his being the Good Shepherd who leads his flock into one fold under one Shepherd (10:16). In this concern Jesus shows a mother's sentiment for his followers as Paul does for the young churches, especially the church in Corinth that was rife with divisions (cf. 2 Cor 11:28-29; 1 Cor 1:10-12).

Jesus' pastoral concern for his disciples while alive consists in his teaching or nourishing them with God's word (17:8, 14), revealing God's name to them (in Semitic thought the name signified the inner reality of a person; to know a person's name was to have possession of the person), keeping them true to this revealed name, and watching over them (v. 12). These functions that Jesus performed on behalf of his disciples whom God entrusted to him (v. 6) he will later entrust to Peter, the leader of the group of disciples, to carry out for his sheep on his behalf (21:15-19).

We recall that "the world" throughout these farewell discourses (cf. 15:19; 16:8) refers to the unbelieving world that rejects Jesus (15:20-25) and will also reject the disciples (17:14), not the physical world created and loved by God to the point of sending Jesus as its Savior (3:16; 17:11, 13). Jesus does not pray for this unbelieving world, those who knew and yet rejected him, because refusal to believe confirms one in spiritual blindness. It ties God's hands from operating in one's life. God can be hindered by our unbelief (cf. Mark 6:5-6). Awareness of this places a serious responsibility on everyone to guard against the gradual invasion of unbelief and the subtle ways in which our faith is being undermined in today's world.

Overtones of the Lord's Prayer

Jesus' prayer in John 17 has clear overtones of the Lord's Prayer. There is emphasis from beginning to end on the glorification/revelation of God's name and faithfulness to it (17:11, 12, 26). The plea to glorify Jesus is a plea for God to glorify or make holy the divine name (17:1). Jesus did God's will by completing the work God gave him to do (17:4; 4:34), by giving life through death and revelation of God's name to those whom God entrusted to him. In him God's will is done on earth as it is in heaven (cf. 4:34; 17:4). For daily bread, Jesus prays for the daily needs of his disciples: that they be kept faithful to God's name and to their witness to Jesus. His prayer that they be kept from contamination by the world corresponds to the plea in the Lord's Prayer not to be led into temptation, but to be delivered from evil. Unity among the disciples is a mark of the coming of God's reign, which will receive its consummation in the inseparable union between Jesus and his disciples in heaven (17:26).

Our reflection on this prayer shows that it is a very important and rich prayer for Jesus' followers on many scores. It is necessary to reflect on it over and over again in the different contexts in which it is read. As pastors, teachers, parents, people in leadership positions, how do we identify with Jesus' sentiments expressed in this prayer, his last will and testament to his followers? How do we imitate his model of leadership and accountability so that it becomes a source of empowerment for those we are privileged to serve? Surely for us too, "the Hour" has come to glorify God in such a way that God may glorify us in Christ, especially as we prepare for the "Great Jubilee" 2000.

V: Final Trial and Victory (John 18–20)

All along we have been reading the gospel as portraying Jesus standing on trial for his claims about his identity and mission. Chapters 18–20 describe his final trial and victory in this protracted court case. Events in these chapters constitute what the evangelist terms Jesus' glorification. The word "glorification" refers to the conclusive manifestation to the world of Jesus' true nature as God incarnate. The evangelist's personal witness to this glorification, "full of grace and truth" (1:14), inspires the writing of this gospel. The reader will be most familiar with the events narrated in this last part of the gospel since they are read annually on Good Friday and during the Easter season. We are invited to accompany Jesus very closely in this, his long-awaited hour, and to pray for the grace to be able to understand these events as they invite us to become their witnesses in our own lives.

The Final Trial, John 18–19

John 18–19 narrate the events surrounding the final trial and condemnation of Jesus; looked at from Jesus' point of view the trial and condemnation usher in the long-awaited hour of his glorification seen as "being lifted up." The outcome of this trial proves beyond doubt that his claims in the gospel were true. Jesus is tried in the Jewish and Roman courts: before Annas and Caiaphas (18:12-27) and before Pilate (18:28–19:16); he is condemned to death as a result of the trial, though he is found innocent; the judgment against him is executed in 19:17-24. The last section (19:25-42) gives various responses to this trial by Jesus' mother and close disciples (19:25-27), and by more distant disciples, Joseph of Arimathea and Nicodemus (19:38-42); his death on the cross is the completion of his mission (19:28-37, especially v. 30).

The Arrest (18:1-11)

The Jewish/Roman coalition in the condemnation begins with the group that goes to arrest Jesus in the garden: the cohort is a detachment from the Roman garrison in Jerusalem while the guards are Temple police sent by the Jewish leaders (18:3). Tragically, this group is led to the arrest by Judas, one of Jesus' inner circle of followers (18:2).

John's account differs significantly from that of the synoptics. As in the account of the Last Supper, John presupposes the reader's familiarity with the events of the passion. This presumed knowledge accounts for notable omissions. The agony in the garden, for instance, was alluded to in 12:27 where Jesus, troubled in soul, rejected the possibility of asking God to save him from "this hour" since undergoing the hour was a necessary aspect of his mission (cf. 3:14).

The Johannine account is shot through from beginning to end with the majesty and glory of Jesus as one who is absolutely in charge of the situation. He lays down his life freely in order to take it up again; nobody takes it from him (cf. 10:18). One cannot grieve and lament over something one deliberately undertakes of one's free will. In this hour of suffering Jesus remains true to his word that the sheep for which he lays down his life cannot be devoured by wolves; he requests that his disciples be let go (18:8) while he gives his life to free them and all believers from sin. Verse 11 may be the Johannine version of Matt 16:21-23 // Mark 9:31-33, where Jesus rebukes Peter as an obstacle in his path.

Trial in the Jewish Court and Peter's Denial (18:12-27)

John does not describe the trial before Caiaphas, the High Priest, and the condemnation by the Sanhedrin, the Jewish supreme court, as do the synoptics (cf. Matt 26:57-68 // Mark 14:53-65 // Luke 22:63–23:1). The reason may be found in 11:45-54. In John, Jesus is sent to Annas who questions him about his disciples, after which he is sent bound to Caiaphas and later to Pilate (vv. 24, 28). A marked feature in the Johannine account is that while Annas is questioning Jesus about his teaching and his disciples (vv. 19-23) Peter in the background is busy denying knowledge of Jesus, despite his earlier protest (13:37). John may have intended this interplay as a warning to those disciples who were so self-confident in their power to stand firm that they did not heed the call to humility and acknowledgment of one's utter dependence on Jesus even for the grace to stand firm. Some charismatic people today have fallen into the same trap by denying certain orthodox practices of their Church and claiming a direct line to God.

Trial Before Pilate and Execution of Judgment (18:28–19:24)

The Jewish court, where Jesus was tried in absentia, has imposed the death penalty on him (11:53). That done, they now bring Jesus before Pilate to implement the death sentence for them. The statement of the Jewish leaders in 18:2 presupposes 11:53. In this earlier trial Jesus was not condemned for blasphemy as in the synoptics. Several times in the gospel the leaders had wanted to stone him for claiming to be the Son of God, even God (cf. 8:59; 10:31, 39). Their decision in 11:53 rested on their belief that if allowed to go on unstopped Jesus might endanger the life of the nation under Roman rule. Ironically they now ask these very Romans (represented by Pilate) to put him to death for them.

In 19:1 Pilate scourges Jesus for no apparent reason (unless Luke 22:22 furnishes an explanation). Scourging may have been intended by Pilate to placate the Jews in place of crucifixion; on the other hand, condemned people were often scourged in order to weaken them and thus hasten their death. Surprisingly, Jesus is accused vaguely before Pilate of being an "evildoer" (18:30). Such a crime should have been tried in the Jewish court by rules laid down in the Torah (cf. 18:31). In the Jewish court in the synoptics Jesus is condemned for claiming to be "the Christ, the Son of God" (Matt 26:63); "the Christ" and "Son of God" (Luke 22:67, 70), where the two terms are used synonymously; or "the Christ, the Son of the Blessed One" (Mark 14:61). It is striking that given the key importance of John 20:31 the title "the Christ, the Son of God" does not feature as a title in the condemnation of Jesus in the gospel. The plausible reason is that the claim embodied in this title had already been thoroughly made and defended in the earlier parts of the gospel.

The title "King of the Jews" is operative in the accusation before Pilate both in John and in the synoptics. In John, Pilate introduces the title (18:33) as though the accusation of being an "evildoer" (v. 30) were synonymous with being "king of the Jews" (18:33). In 12:13 the people had hailed Jesus as "the king of Israel." This title is synonymous with "Messiah" ("the Christ"). For Pilate who represented the colonial emperor, Caesar, this would not have been a harmless claim especially since, according to the Jewish historian Josephus, Palestine at this time was full of people claiming to be the Messiah and disturbing the peace. Even JnB had been mistaken for one (cf. 1:19-25).

The declaration by the leaders that Jesus has to die because he claims to be the "Son of God" comes after every other accusation has failed to convince Pilate that Jesus is guilty (19:7). This is the real reason why the leaders want Jesus to be put to death. The charge that he claims to be the king of the Jews, thus making himself Caesar's rival, is only a pretext for getting Pilate to condemn him. As soon as the leaders realize that their real charge does not produce the desired effect (v. 12a) because of Pilate's own impression of Jesus (vv. 8-11) they return to the charge of "king of the Jews." This claim would matter to Pilate, as Caesar's delegate. It is synonymous with being "Caesar's rival" (v. 12b). Pilate's career and loyalty to Caesar are at stake; even so he does not give in readily (vv. 13-14). As the leaders try to force him to condemn Jesus whom he twice declares to be innocent (18:38b; 19:4), he in turn forces them to betray their own conscience by denying God's kingship over them (19:15). In saying this they prove Jesus right when he told them that they were liars in their claim to know God and be God's children (8:55), and warned them that to reject and dishonor the Son was to reject and dishonor the Father (cf. 5:23; 1 John 2:22: to deny the Son is to deny the Father also).

In bringing charges against Jesus and condemning him to death, neither Pilate nor the leaders act truthfully; hence the irony in Pilate's question in 18:38. Jesus' debate with the leaders in 8:44-55 sheds light on this question, but Pilate has the last laugh in this game of mutual deceit. Though the leaders deny that Jesus is their king, Pilate nevertheless proclaims to the world in the three common languages of the time that "Jesus the Nazarene [is] the King of the Jews" (19:19-22). This little victory for Pilate tallies with Jesus' declaration in his favor in 19:11b.

There are many important points to note in the Johannine account of this trial. Structurally, scholars discern seven scenes that alternate between the interior of Pilate's palace where Jesus is a prisoner and outside where the leaders and people stand accusing him, refusing to go into the palace themselves for fear of contamination (18:28). The scenes are, starting alternatingly with the inside: 18:28-32; 18:33-38a; 18:38b-40; 19:1-3; 19:4-8; 19:9-12a; 19:12b-16. Pilate's shuttling from outside to inside between Jesus and his people reflects his own weak character. The leaders are simply using him.

In this scenic arrangement the mocking of Jesus as "King of the Jews" occupies the central place. In Johannine irony, while Jesus is thus being mocked he is in deed and in truth "the king," not only of the Jews but of the whole world, and of heaven and earth (cf. Matt 28:18; Phil 2:9-11), but his kingship is not of this world (18:36); it does not operate according to the norms of earthly kingdoms or use worldly means such as brute force to establish and maintain itself (18:11; Matt 26:51-54). Rather his is a "kingdom of truth and life, a kingdom of holiness and grace, a kingdom of justice, love, and peace" (Preface for the feast of Christ the King). We pray for the coming of this kingdom in the Lord's Prayer.

John's account emphasizes Jesus' rejection by his leaders and people, including Judas, one of his closest associates (cf. 1:10-11). The rejection begins with Judas handing Jesus over to his enemies among his people and is followed by those same people handing him over to a foreigner. It continues in their preferring Barabbas to Jesus and reaches its climax in their rejecting him as their king in preference to Caesar. But Jesus' love triumphs over all this. John's account does not include the curse the whole people bring upon themselves and their children as in Matt 27:25. Instead, it highlights Jesus' majestic and divine control from beginning to end.

Ironically, while his own people reject him the Roman soldiers (representing the Gentiles) hail Jesus as king, though mockingly, in 19:3. Pilate's inscription in 19:19 testifies to the truth of Jesus' claim to be king (18:37). This truth triumphs over all the lies that govern the trial. Ironically Jesus is crucified as a king with two bodyguards, so to speak (19:18). The synoptics describe them as bandits. Jesus dies among sinners to take away the sin of the world (cf. Isa 53:12), including that of the two bandits.

The Circle of Close Disciples; the Final Victory (19:25-42)

The rejection of Jesus by the leaders and generality of the people is countered by the faithful disciples who stand beneath his cross (v. 25). For the significance of calling his mother "woman" and committing his Beloved Disciple (BD) to her as son, see the comments on 2:4 above. It is significant that among the four or five faithful disciples who stand at the foot of the cross at least three, including Jesus' mother, are women. It is not clear whether "his mother's sister" is the same as "Mary the wife of Clopas"; it is doubtful, though not impossible, that two sisters would have the same name. The succession of ideas in vv. 25 and 26 would lead one to think that the "disciple whom he loved" would be one of the women named in v. 25. On the basis of this some have identified the BD as Mary Magdalene. The synoptic accounts also emphasize the faithfulness of the women disciples in this "hour" so long awaited by Jesus, and for which he came into the world in the first place. Women featured most prominently, at the very center, at the first real altar of sacrifice, Calvary or Golgotha (19:17).

Verses 28-30 show Jesus, though on the cross, completely in charge of the situation. He has completed once and for all the work the Father gave him to do (19:30; cf. 4:34; 17:4). Once completed, this work of salvation stays completed (cf. Heb 9:26-27; 10:10, 14). Verse 30b has a double meaning: Jesus dies and thereby releases the Spirit to believers. The blood and water that flow from his pierced side are traditionally interpreted as signifying the two great sacraments of initiation, Baptism and the Eucharist, by which Christ, through the Church, continues to give birth to believers and nourish them with his own body and blood.

The Passover motifs provide the background to vv. 31-37. In John's account Jesus is crucified as the Jews are preparing the Passover lamb for the festival, but his death, which occurs just before the feast begins at sundown (cf. v. 31), makes this slaughter of the paschal lamb obsolete. The real lamb who takes away the sin of the world (1:29) has already been sacrificed once and for all. The same haste that surrounded the eating of the Passover lamb in Exod 12:11 is captured in the hasty death and burial of Jesus (cf. vv. 31-33, 42). Verse 37 is best explained by 3:14; 8:28.

The trustworthy eyewitness in 19:35-36 is the BD (in the light of 21:20, 24). His (or hers?) is the witness of a believer who testifies to what he (or she?) saw, with a view to eliciting faith in the audience (cf. 20:30-31). This witness is the entire gospel; it is the witness of one whose entire life has been transformed through contact with Jesus. Others, for instance the soldiers, saw what happened but it meant nothing to them. Only believers can see the true significance of Jesus' death as glorification.

Joseph of Arimathea and Nicodemus, though disciples of Jesus in secret, now come forward to bury him. Jesus' death gives courage even to timid, fearful disciples. The garden motif in 19:41; 18:1; 20:15b recalls that of Eden (Genesis 2–3). As God used to walk in familiarity with Adam and Eve, so Jesus "often" met with his disciples in the garden where he was arrested. The arrest in the garden marks the beginning of the final combat over the sin brought upon humanity by the fall of our first parents. Jesus, the "offspring of the woman" (cf. Gen 3:15) surrenders himself to his arresters in the garden, is buried in the garden where he defeats the prince of this world (Satan) at his own game (death), and rises in the garden to restore the broken enmity between humans and God.

God went to meet Adam and Eve in the garden after the fall to drive them out lest they should eat of the tree of life and be confirmed forever in their state of sinfulness (Gen 3:22-24). Similarly Jesus goes to meet Mary Magdalene in the garden to assure her that henceforth there would be no more separation between him, his brothers and sisters, and God. The relationship broken by the Fall is permanently restored. Furthermore, humans are elevated from the state of being God's creatures to that of being God's children (20:17; 1:12-13). Such is the depth of God's love for us in Christ.

The Johannine account of the Passion is read every Good Friday because it is rich in theological and christological good news. The interaction between Jesus and the different characters in the trial and among the characters themselves offers rich food for thought. The reader is encouraged to read carefully this passage, visualize its contents as happening in real life, and identify contemporary situations in which the trial of Jesus continues in the same underhanded and unjust manner in the lives of God's children. Then one will learn a deeper appreciation of the reality of the trial and the depth of Jesus' love for us. One will also draw courage from the fidelity of the band of disciples who stood by Jesus. The presence and prominence of women at this crucial event in Jesus' life and mission invite the contemporary Church that acts *in persona Christi* to open its heart in imitation of Christ to the prominent roles women today can play in the Church's life.

Conclusive Evidence: The Victory, John 20

The resurrection marks the last stage in the protracted hour of Jesus' glorification. It is actually the manifestation of the victory he personally declared won in 19:30. The event is recorded in vv. 1-10. Witnesses to this victory are Mary Magdalene (vv. 11-18) and the other disciples (vv. 19-23, 24-29). Verses 30-31 inform the reader, deductively as it were, of the purpose for which the gospel was written.

The Resurrection (20:1-10)

Strikingly, while the events of the passion were described in detail with Jesus fully present, the account of the resurrection begins with the conspicuous absence of Jesus: the empty tomb (v. 2). This empty tomb announced to Mary Magdalene by the stone rolled away is the first evidence that something has taken place; but the tomb is not entirely empty: the linen cloths lying in the form in which Jesus' body lay (the head cloth in its own place apart from the body, vv. 6-7) give evidence of what has happened.

If Jesus' body had been stolen as Mary fears (v. 2), and as the guards in Matthew were paid to report (Matt 28:11-15), the linen cloths would have disappeared with the body. Instead, the presence of the cloths and their position indicate that the person who was wrapped in them has passed out of them. Jesus' body that was sown in death like a grain of wheat (12:24) germinates and is raised, transformed into a "spiritual body" (cf. 1 Cor 15:37, 42-44, especially v. 44), unlike that of Lazarus that was simply brought back to this life. Physical objects such as closed doors (vv. 19, 26) no longer affect his risen, spiritual body. This evidence of the resurrection is what the BD sees and believes (v. 8). One can say that unlike Thomas (v. 25) he believed what he had not yet seen. The "Scripture" in v. 9 that the disciples did not yet "know" could be a reference to Jesus' own predictions about his resurrection reported in the synoptics and the fulfillment of OT predictions in his life. These the disciples remembered after the resurrection (cf. 2:22; 12:16) with the aid of the Holy Spirit (14:26).

As in the Last Supper discourse and possibly after the arrest (cf. 18:16) Peter and the BD are closely linked. Mary, the first to discover the empty tomb "while it was still dark" (v. 1), runs to these two. In Johannine thought they represent Jesus' authority and charism of love within the Church. Traditionally believed to be the younger, the BD outruns Peter and reaches the tomb first. But Jesus' love for him is not a reckless love that flouts deference to authority as tends to happen among some fundamentalist charismatic groups today. The BD's deference for Peter is best explained by 1 Corinthians 13, read in the context of 1 Corinthians 12–14. Both the love and the authority are those of Jesus; properly understood and exercised, they can never be in conflict. This does not mean that Peter has no love or is not loved (cf. 21:15-19), nor that the BD has no authority, for his/hers is the authority behind this gospel (19:35; 21:24). Each disciple needs to recognize his or her gifts and use them for the building up of the Body of Christ, the Church (cf. Eph 4:9-16; 1 Cor 12:4-30). The alleged rivalry between the BD and Peter has very little, if any, NT textual support.

The Witness of Mary Magdalene (20:11-18)

All four gospels testify in different ways that Mary Magdalene was the first to see the risen Christ, either by herself as here in John or in company with other women (cf. Matt 28:1-8; Mark 16:1-8; Luke 24:1-9). Though the picture is not very clear in the synoptics, it would seem that the women went as a group to the tomb. Upon discovering the stone rolled away, Mary Magdalene must have left them and run to Peter and the BD, and in the process lost contact with the other women. Whatever the case, her unique witness to the resurrection in John's gospel gives her an unrivalled place in these resurrection narratives. This witness merited her the title of "Apostle to the Apostles" from the Fathers of the Church.

Mary is fearlessly driven to the tomb by her love as soon as the Sabbath is over and she has freedom of movement. As she was present at the foot of the cross (19:25), so is she present at the tomb. Her first mission of love begins with her message to the two disciples (v. 2). She is thus the human agent for the BD's believing without seeing. When the two disciples witness the empty tomb and linen cloths they simply return home, but Mary's love keeps her rooted to the spot. In African contexts women do not enter a tomb. Mary may not have had the opportunity of seeing the linen cloths as the BD and Peter did. We are not told that they communicated to her what they saw when they entered. It is still dark, and Mary cannot see clearly as she peers into the tomb; she is only aware that the body is not there. The two angels mark the length of the spot where Jesus' body would have lain (head and foot, v. 12). In her grief Mary is not even frightened by the sight of these two strange beings sitting in the tomb (cf. Luke 24:4).

The two angels ask her the same question that Jesus repeats word for word (vv. 13, 15). It would seem that her tears, like those of Mary of Bethany (11:33), brought the angels to the tomb and made Jesus interrupt his "ascension" to the Father in order to console her and wipe away every tear from her cheek (cf. Isa 25:6-12, especially v. 8; Rev 21:4). Traditional interpretations reinforced by art (for example, Fra Angelico's *Noli me tangere*) tend to play down or misrepresent the significance of the appearance to Mary Magdalene. Mary does not recognize Jesus immediately because his risen body looks different from what she knew (cf. 21:4), but like one of his sheep she recognizes him when he calls her by name. Verse 17a is read as though Jesus forbade her to touch him, for fear of being contaminated by her touch, she being a woman. But the tense of the verb in Greek shows that continuous touching, even holding tight, is the issue. Mary had feared that somebody had taken away Jesus, now that she has seen him she is not going to take any chances. Jesus reassures her that from now on he and his disciples are inseparable. Through his glorification they have become flesh and blood children of the one Father and God, begotten by his own blood shed on the cross (19:34; see the commentary on 1:12-13).

Most importantly, Jesus entrusts to Mary Magdalene the task of announcing to the brothers and sisters his central Easter message: that from now on he and his disciples belong together inseparably as members of the one family of God. She is not only the first to see the risen Christ, and be the Apostle of the Apostles, but is also the bearer of the message of the new creation (cf. 1 John 3:1-2). Jesus commissioned her though he was well aware that women's testimony did not count in first-century cultures. His glorification ushers in a new culture, the christological culture, which Paul sums up in Gal 3:25-28. This important role given to Mary, a woman, by the risen Lord merits emulation by the contemporary Church as a witness that God did indeed send Jesus (cf. 17:21).

The Witness of the Disciples (20:19-29)

Jesus appears to the disciples as a group twice in this section (vv. 19-23, 24-29). Two points deserve attention in the first appearance. Jesus has kept his promise to the disciples that a little while after his departure they would see him and their hearts would rejoice (v. 20; cf. 16:16). He gives them his "peace," freedom from fear and total wellbeing in body and mind, which the world cannot give (cf. 14:27). In this bestowal of peace Jesus does not raise a word about their having abandoned him in his hour of trial, as other human beings would have done. He shows them his wounded hands by which he will hold them fast and keep them from perishing (cf. 10:28; 17:12), and his side from which flowed and will continue to flow for them rivers of new life, which is the Spirit (7:37-39).

Second, Jesus bestows on them the Spirit he had promised as the necessary gift to them in his temporary departure (16:7). Endowed with and strengthened by the Spirit, they are now effectively (not just programmatically as in 17:18) sent into the world as God had sent Jesus into the world (20:21; 17:18). As Jesus was sent into the world to take away sin and bring into communion, so are the disciples. Verse 23 is at times interpreted as the scriptural basis for the current form of the sacrament of reconciliation in the Catholic Church, traditionally called "confession." In the Johannine context, however, the verse is more descriptive than prescriptive. If you forgive people their sins, the sins will be forgiven; if you refuse to forgive, or drop them, they will remain unforgiven.

This truth needs little elaboration. The Lord's Prayer invites us to forgive one another without limit and thus remain in communion, even as Jesus forgives us and brings us into communion with the Father and the Spirit (cf. 14:23). One of the works of the Spirit is to make us one in Christ (cf. 1 Cor 12:13). To retain the sins of others is to exclude them from communion. The fundamental meaning of sin in John lies here (cf. 1:29; 8:34-35). As disciples of Jesus we are called to bear witness to his risen life by breaking the barriers of sin and division in our hearts and communities. Indeed, the real "resurrection power" often extolled in pentecostal and charismatic circles lies here, not merely in the working of spectacular miracles, often without love in the heart (cf. 1 Corinthians 13; Rom 6:1-11).

The Purpose for Which the Gospel was Written (20:30-31)

The significance of this section was already offered in the first part of this commentary. Having prayerfully served as the jury in the trial of Jesus in the gospel, the reader is now invited by the evangelist to decide whether the evidence presented has succeeded in persuading him or her to believe that "Jesus is the Christ, the Son of God." This evidence is only a selection of "the signs Jesus did." This persuasion is not seeking an intellectual assent. It elicits from the reader that faith-response that will make one a partaker in the eternal life that Jesus, the Christ, the Son of God was commissioned by God to give (3:16; 17:2-3; etcetera). In short, the persuasive proclamation of Jesus' messiahship in the entire gospel has as its ultimate goal that the reader gains eternal life in Jesus. All that Jesus has claimed to be in the gospel is for this purpose. The "sign of signs," the resurrection, is the crowning event.

It may be difficult for us today to appreciate what the resurrection meant for the first disciples, but our efforts to rise from sin to new life and to help others to do the same will enable us to experience in our own lives the real meaning of the resurrection. May this resurrection power be fully ours through our openness to the Holy Spirit.

VI: Disciples Sent on Mission (John 21)

In the first section it was indicated that scholars regard John 21 as an addition to the gospel either by the disciples of the evangelist or by an ecclesiastical redactor. The purpose of this "addition," it is alleged, was to reinstate Peter's authority in the gospel and in the Johannine community (vv. 1-18) and thus make the gospel acceptable to the universal Church. Others believe it was to explain why, contrary to popular expectation, the BD was now dead (cf. vv. 21-23). But as was earlier pointed out there is no manuscript evidence that the gospel ever existed without ch. 21. Another explanation can be given for this last chapter of the gospel, which at first sight reads like an appendix.

In the forensic rhetorical framework used in this commentary John 21 serves as a *demonstratio* of the teaching Jesus gave to his disciples in chs. 13–17 concerning their dependence on him for their own personal life and missionary fruitfulness. The chapter illustrates this in two steps: to act without Jesus (as in the night-long fishing expedition) is futile; he alone enables the disciples' mission (vv. 1-8) and sustains their life and love in the mission (vv. 9-23).

Before the resurrection Jesus is the only one in the gospel who is sent by God. Only after the resurrection are the disciples sent, and they are dispatched on world mission, unlike in the synoptics (cf. Matthew 10; Luke 10:1-24). This Johannine arrangement brings out clearly the point made in 4:35-38 that all disciples are the fruit of Jesus' unique missionary labor; their participation in his mission belongs in the harvesting phase of the mission; the sowers are only the Father and Jesus. To be privileged to participate in this harvesting phase of the mission is itself a joyful privilege synonymous with receiving wages.

To Act Without Jesus is Futile (21:1-8)

The disciples have now left Jerusalem and returned to Galilee. The number seven represents fullness, hence all disciples are envisaged. Peter, appointed in the synoptics as their leader, decides to go fishing. The others follow suit. Some hold that Peter and the others were simply going back to their old fishing trade as reported in the synoptics before Jesus called them. There is no clear evidence for this. Besides, of the seven only Peter and the sons of Zebedee were reportedly fishermen. The episode focuses on the manner of Jesus' "third" (or conclusive?) appearance to the disciples (vv. 1, 14).

As in the account of the wedding feast of Cana the narrative is very cryptic; not a word is wasted. The course of the action is simple. The disciples decide on their own under Peter's leadership to go fishing. There is no mention of Jesus being in their company. The enterprise takes place at night (the normal fishing time for making the best catch). But in the missionary arena of Jesus this does not follow. Night represents darkness, which is opposed to Jesus, the Light. As dawn breaks Jesus goes to meet them and receives from them the confession that their nightlong efforts without him were fruitless. He then directs them to cast the net to the right side (i.e., to do it right this time). They obey and make such a catch that they cannot haul it into the boat. The BD recognizes from the miraculous catch that the person on the shore is the Lord. Peter again takes the lead in his characteristically impetuous style (v. 7), leaving the others to drag in the catch. The lesson is clear. Only in and through Jesus can disciples bear fruit, and in plenty (cf. 15:5).

Jesus Sustains the Disciples' Life and Mission (21:9-23)

When they come ashore the disciples find fish already cooking on the charcoal fire. This drives home the point made in 4:35-38 that the missionary fruitfulness of the disciples (here represented by the catch) is only part of the harvesting phase of Jesus' mission. The disciples eat of their own catch as their wages. The commentaries give various interpretations to the symbolism of the number 153. This number probably symbolizes the total number of churches at the time of the evangelist: 150 in the diaspora plus the three in Judea, Samaria, and Galilee. Whatever the case, this number in an unbroken net emphasizes abundance and unity.

The breakfast Jesus cooks and serves to the disciples has overtones of the Eucharist, though the phrase "giving thanks" is omitted in v. 13. The episode here reminds one of Luke 24:42 and has overtones of Jesus' encounter with the disciples on the way to Emmaus. There is, for instance, a note of purposelessness in the situation in which the disciples find themselves before they decide to go fishing. The unstated joy at the abundant catch recalls the heart burning with joy as Jesus explained the Scriptures to the two disciples. The giving of the bread registers the moment of recognition (cf. v. 12).

The Mission of Peter (and the BD) (21:15-25)

The significance of Peter's mission is best studied within the context of the metaphor of the Good Shepherd; its scope was mentioned briefly in the commentary on ch. 17. Here the following points are to be noted: Jesus first empowers Peter in the missionary enterprise and feeds him physically before giving him the charge of feeding and tending his sheep and lambs. Jesus' thrice-repeated question about love recalls Peter's boastful declaration in 13:37. His threefold denial of Jesus showed him incapable of keeping this boast (18:17, 25-27). Then he relied on his own strength. Now Jesus gives him the opportunity to learn that even to be able to love Jesus unto death is a gift. This gift is now given to him by Jesus, whose words (v. 18) effect what they signify. With this gift Peter is empowered to follow Jesus the whole way in the mission, even unto death. This he could not do before on his own strength (13:36, 38).

The episode brings to the fore the authority of Peter. This authority does not make Peter the owner of the sheep. Jesus owns the sheep: "tend my sheep," "feed my lambs/shearlings." Peter may be described as the manager of the household who is expected to give food to the members in due season. His role with respect to the sheep is that of tender loving care, modeled on that of the Good Shepherd. At each moment the sheep belong to Jesus and Peter has no authority to decide the fate of any sheep. This point is illustrated in v. 20. Jesus tells Peter to abandon his concern for the BD; what happens to the latter is Jesus' own concern.

Whether or not the statements in vv. 22-24 imply that the BD was dead at the time the gospel or this particular chapter was written is a matter for conjecture. In an African context a speaker can refer to himself or herself or the addressee in the third person. This cultural trait, which is a mark of respect, was not foreign to Jewish and other Semitic cultures (cf. Gen 44:6-10, 18-19). Significantly, the witness behind the gospel was an eyewitness of the events narrated; the narrative grew out of Jesus' personal love for that person.

Verse 25 reads like a poor, though conventional, duplicate of 20:30-31, yet it serves as a fitting conclusion to the entire gospel. It now embraces both the signs Jesus worked and the various aspects of the disciples' participation in his mission. In this chapter Peter and the BD serve as the embodiment of these various aspects of mission, especially that of feeding the sheep and proclaiming the lifegiving word. The BD does this most eminently through humility of witness to Jesus in the gospel. This disciple remains anonymous throughout. By this example the BD invites all readers to bear witness to Jesus by their lives of true and humble discipleship within the community of believers.

Looking Back and Looking Forward

As one comes to the end of the gospel one needs to go back to the "First Reading" to evaluate the issues raised in the light of a closer knowledge of the gospel. In what ways did this "Reading" shed light on certain features of the gospel? Are there aspects of the gospel that were not covered in that "First Reading"?

As readers accompanied Jesus through the gospel they were exhorted to establish a dialogue between the gospel and events in their own contexts. The readers would have paid close attention to Jesus' interaction with different individuals and groups. To what extent are these events happening at different levels and circles within one's own context? This contextual reading was aimed at enabling readers to see the gospel as a living word that gives life and energizes its hearers. The liturgical contexts in which different passages of the gospel are read offer one a rich opportunity to engage the gospel in dialogue with one's life and living context.

The approach adopted in this commentary has not exhausted the possibilities of reading the gospel. Another way of staying tuned to the gospel as a living word in one's context would be to become aware of the different ways in which the gospel is employed or appropriated by one's contemporaries. This can be done by keeping a collection or clippings of different works of art, paintings, stories, posters, hymns, and inscriptions on cars or doorposts based on and inspired by the Fourth Gospel.

This comprehensive attention to the gospel in context, in one's living context, and in history would enhance one's discovery of new ways of reading. Such a discovery, done in the context of faith and prayer, would equip the reader to serve as the contemporary Johannine author in his or her social location. Thus equipped, he or she may undertake to write a contextual commentary on the "signs Jesus worked," the gospel as lived by oneself and one's contemporaries.

BIBLIOGRAPHY

Brodie, Thomas L. *The Gospel According to John: A Literary and Theological Commentary.* Oxford and New York: Oxford University Press, 1993.

Brown, Raymond E. *The Gospel According to John.* 2 vols. AB 29, 29a. Garden City, N.Y.: Doubleday, 1966, 1970.

Brown, Raymond E. *The Gospel and Epistles of John: A Concise Commentary.* Collegeville: The Liturgical Press, 1988.

Burge, Gary M. *Interpreting the Gospel of John.* Guides to New Testament Exegesis. Grand Rapids: Baker Book House, 1992.

Flanagan, Neal M. *The Gospel according to John and the Johannine Epistles.* CBC NT 4. Collegeville: The Liturgical Press, 1989.

Lindars, Barnabas. *The Gospel of John.* NCeB. London: Oliphant, 1972.

McGann, Diarmund. *Journeying within Transcendence: The Gospel of John through a Jungian Perspective.* London: Collins Liturgical Publications, 1989.

McPolin, James. *John.* NTMes 6. Wilmington, Del.: Michael Glazier, 1984 (1979).

Okure, Teresa. *The Johannine Approach to Mission: A Contextual Study of John 4:1-42.* WUNT 2/31. Tübingen: J.C.B. Mohr (Paul Siebeck), 1988.

Quast, Kevin. *Reading the Gospel of John: An Introduction.* Rev. ed. New York, N.Y., and Mahwah, N.J.: Paulist, 1996.

Reinhartz, Adele. *The Word in the World: The Cosmological Tale in the Fourth Gospel.* SBL.MS 45. Atlanta, Ga.: Scholars, 1992.

Smalley, Stephen S. *John: Evangelist and Interpreter.* Nashville, Camden, N.J., and New York: Thomas Nelson Publishers, 1984 (1978).

Talbert, Charles H. *Reading John: A Literary and Theological Commentary on the Fourth Gospel and Johannine Epistles.* New York: Crossroad, 1992.

Luke: Portrait and Project

François Bovon

Luke, the only evangelist to write a prologue (an indication of his literary intention), announces his plan at the beginning of his first work: he intends to write a book concerning the events that have been fulfilled (Luke 1:1). With this clever and unusual formulation, by using the term "events" he points out that his message contains a historical dimension, the dimension of deeds that unfold in a defined space and time. However, the past participle "fulfilled" indicates that these events are not exclusively worldly. In them and through them what is outlined and realized is the will of God the creator and savior, the God of Israel who fulfills all the divine promises.

Moreover, at the beginning of the book of Acts Luke announces the content of his second work. In order to show that the Church—the form of Christianity he is defending—corresponds to the divine will he has Jesus state the plan of the book he is going to write: "You will be my witnesses in Jerusalem, in all Judea and Samaria, and to the ends of the earth" (Acts 1:8). Thus the book of Acts will relate the spreading of God's word by the witnesses of the Risen One from the center, Jerusalem, to the very ends of the world. Behind the Lukan formulation we sense the all-embracing hope of the OT, especially Isaiah's conviction (Isa 2:3) according to which the word and the Spirit of God will go forth in all directions from the holy mountain, from Zion.

Corresponding to the ascension in the gospel, in Acts we have the descent of the word on the endless variety of nations, human situations, and social structures. Jerusalem does not represent the center of the earth. It is the original center to which one is faithful by leaving it. In the same way the best reading of the text of the Law, according to Luke, will yield a gradual awareness of its christological and spiritual meaning. In other words, the Law is read as a promise of freedom.

The gospel and Acts correspond to each other. When it was establishing the canon the Church of the second century integrated Luke into the corpus of the gospels. In so doing it separated the two volets of the diptych and canceled its original symmetry. The binary structure of the work remains essential, but it is necessary to go farther back than the gospel.

Viewed together Luke–Acts form a unit corresponding to the Scripture of the time, the Bible of the early Christians or the OT. Luke's favorite books are the Psalms and the prophets. This is one sign among others of the prophetic meaning he assigns to Scripture. The entire OT has to be read from the perspective of the messianic time inaugurated by Jesus. Contrary to the interpretation of Hans Conzelmann, who divides the Lukan history of salvation into three periods, we must first grasp its symmetrical coherence. The Lukan Christ offers to his disciples, and through them to the readers, the hermeneutical key of Scripture: from Moses to the prophets and Psalms we should read the fate of the suffering and glorious Christ like a foreshadowing (Luke 24:25-27 and 24:49). Luke 16:16, whose exegesis has been bitterly debated during the past few years, probably implies one major break, rather than two, in history: before and after the irruption of salvation. After the ascension the Church did not fall back into a pre-messianic situation, a time from which the reality of salvation would have disappeared, as Conzelmann believed.

As the author has said and explicitly shown, the period of salvation inaugurated and brought forth by Jesus' ministry unfolds in two stages to which the two books correspond: Jesus' time during which the word became an event in Galilee and Judea (Acts 10:37) and the time of the Church, the time of the witnesses brought to the word by the Spirit.

Jesus' deeds are not exclusively the sum total of the miracles related in the gospel although these anticipatory signs of the Reign of God and the power of the Son should not be eliminated. Jesus' deeds involve the long journey of his life: the Galilean ministry that continues in Jerusalem. Luke summarizes it by the word *analēmpsis* (ascension) in Luke 9:51: going up to Jerusalem, being lifted up on the cross, rising from the tomb, and ascension to the Father. While Luke's gospel can be divided into three parts (the Galilean ministry, the journey, and the Jerusalem ministry), it is actually a single ascending movement.

The book of Acts narrates the spread of the word and the universal opening of the text of the Law whose first addressees persist in taking it literally. Acts 15 is the pivotal point of the book: at the Jerusalem meeting Gentiles are accepted into the Church. It is no longer necessary to impose circumcision on male Gentile converts. The remnant of Israel, rebuilt and reconstructed by Jesus the Messiah, the Christian community can spring up anywhere. Its distinctive mark is faith in Christ Jesus. After spreading to Jerusalem and in the Jewish milieu, the Good News, thanks mainly to Paul, progressively reaches the ends of the world. (Rome is obviously not situated at the end of the world, but being the political and cosmopolitan center of the empire it is the capital from which faraway places are reached.)

The mission of the Twelve is the evangelization of Palestine (besides, for Luke, these first disciples are seen as the guarantors of the truth of the gospel as well as the evangelizers of Judea). For their share the Hellenists, especially Paul, were given the evangelization of Greeks and Romans. Historically speaking this allocation corresponds to the decision of the Jerusalem Council (cf. Gal 2:1-10) but Luke is the one who highlights this decision in his work. To underscore the importance of that event in the history of early Christianity Luke designates Peter as the representative of the first period and Paul as the realizer of the second one.

Luke does know how to allocate and differentiate, but he is also a master at establishing transitions. John the Baptist is situated at the threshold of the two testaments; the ascension of Jesus marks the end of Jesus' life (Luke 24:50-53) and the origin of the Church (Acts 1:9-11); finally, Stephen appears at the shift from the mission in Judea to evangelization in Gentile territory (Acts 6:8).

These developments are not natural processes. Luke has triumphant notes but he also knows that God's life-giving will stumbles against people's violent reaction. John the Baptist was a murdered prophet, Jesus a suffering Messiah, and Stephen a martyred witness. Depending on the perspective in which we place ourselves the relationships of God and God's people are marked by antagonism or communion. What we perceive at the human level is that the people reject the messengers and kill them, but looking at these events through the eyes of faith we perceive that God sets these messengers back on their feet and saves them as well as their listeners.

Luke's theological orientation has been the focus of our attention so far; we will look at his personality at the end of this essay.

During the past few years exegetes have alternately stressed Luke's theological, pastoral, and historical qualities. It is a fact that the evangelist confers doctrinal consistency on his theological subject. It is also true that Luke is concerned about communities and wants to edify them by transmitting the message to them (we see that especially in his re-reading of various parables). Finally, it is evident that he does not invent or completely make up moving stories. He works like a historian of antiquity, on one hand respecting the past, on the other expressing his literary needs and doctrinal concerns (for example, contrary to a solid historial tradition, Luke wants to eliminate any appearance of the Risen Christ in Galilee).

Where are we to situate the evangelist? In the study of a wealthy scholar in one of those Roman villas won over to Christ, with one of its rooms set up as a meeting place? In the role of an *episkopos,* a minister of the Church in charge of leading a local community (in which case he would be both the author and the addressee of Paul's discourse to the elders of Ephesus gathered at Miletus in Acts 20:18-35)? In the office of a Christian teacher set up in one of the Pauline schools existing at the time in the great centers of Christianity?

Giving free rein to my imagination, I would rather envision an itinerant evangelist on a ship's deck or in a welcoming home. Exegetes have not sufficiently emphasized the fact that Luke is interested in the foundation of communities rather than in building them up. After the first converts are baptized Luke leaves them to their fate and focuses his attention on new conquests. His concern is neither that of a spiritual director nor that of a parish priest. Instead it is the concern of a missionary at the end of the first century. Tradition had the correct insight in viewing the evangelist as a traveling companion of Paul. Luke must been part of one of the evangelization teams that continued the task of the apostles after their deaths. Although itinerant, Luke is different from the prophets and evangelists who were busy crisscrossing the empire. Active in the Church, he is also able to withdraw—for a while—to present to his colleagues, to believers, and ultimately to an educated public a literary work that can stir up their inquisitiveness or strengthen their faith.

If Luke belongs to a group of itinerant evangelists we must not attempt to determine the place from which he writes. On the other hand it may be useful to wonder about his personal origin. An ancient tradition, verified by Eusebius and Jerome and confirmed by the western variant of Acts 11:28, situates his home in Antioch. One indication suggests placing his origin in the basin of the Aegean Sea, perhaps in Philippi. Several protagonists of Luke's work start their ministry in their own home towns: Jesus in Nazareth (Luke 4:16-30) and Paul in Tarsus (Acts 9:30). The "we," which is undoubtedly a literary subterfuge, appears first in the setting of Paul's journey from Troas to Philippi (Acts 16:10). Moreover, the evangelist is most familiar with Philippi and the municipal administration of that city.

Was Luke Jewish by birth? It is doubtful. His attitude to the Law of the OT as an unbearable yoke (Acts 15:10) cannot really be that of a circumcised man. It is more appropriate to situate our author in the Gentile fringes of the Jewish community. In fact, the "God-fearers" draw his attention (Luke 7:5; Acts 10:2, 35; 13:16, 26). Although they were attracted by Jewish discipline and monotheism these men and women hesitated to cross the barrier—to become real proselytes—because they felt they would be betraying their nation and changing their race. Their yearning to encounter a universal God stumbled against ritual precepts felt to be sectarian. These people became enthusiastic about one Jewish sect, Christianity, because it preserved the essence of the Jewish heritage at the same time as it was opened to the dimensions of the empire, if not the world.

Acts of the Apostles

Justin Taylor

FIRST READING

The story of Jesus' disciples after his resurrection is told in the Acts of the Apostles. It is a story that is continued in the history of the Church down to the present day. Besides telling us about the persons and events that shaped the Church in its infancy, this biblical book manages to convey what it was—and is—like to be a Spirit-filled follower of Christ.

The book of Acts stands in the middle of the NT. It forms a bridge between the four gospels, of which it is the continuation, and the Epistles of Paul, whose career is one of its chief subjects. Originally, the Third Gospel and the book of Acts were two parts of a single work that recounted not only the ministry, death and resurrection of Jesus, but also the first years of the Church that was formed by the Holy Spirit after the ascension of Jesus into heaven. The continuity between the two parts is shown by many links of style, vocabulary, and theological ideas, and quite specifically by the two prologues that introduce them (Luke 1:1-4 and Acts 1:1-2). They were separated when the Gospel of Luke was placed with the other three gospels and before that of John.

The Author of Acts

The author of both the Third Gospel and Acts is the same, and the tradition of the Church has been unanimous in identifying him as Luke (cf. the Muratorian Canon, the "Antimarcionite Prologue," Irenaeus, and Tertullian, all in the second century). He is generally taken to be the Luke who was at Paul's side during the apostle's imprisonment in Rome (Col 4:14; Phlm 24; 2 Tim 4:11). Paul implies that he was of Gentile origin, perhaps from Antioch in Syria. In any case he was thoroughly familiar with the Bible in its Greek translation, and some of the best Greek in the NT was written by him. Paul also refers to Luke as a doctor, and there may be traces of his medical training and interests in his writings.

Plan and Purpose of the Book

The theme and also the structure of Acts are announced in 1:8, in which the risen Christ tells his disciples: "You will receive power when the Holy Spirit has come upon you; and you will be my witnesses, in Jerusalem, in all Judea and Samaria, and to the ends of the earth." The *Holy Spirit* plays a central role in the book. Five times the Spirit comes in manifest power on groups of disciples (2:1-4; 4:31; 8:14-17; 10:44-48; 19:1-7). Miracles and other wonders worked by Christ's disciples are so many signs of this power (2:43; 5:12-16; 6:8; 8:6-8; 19:11-12). The Holy Spirit takes the initiative and directs the mission of the young Church at several important turning points (8:26, 29, 39; 10:19; 11:12; 13:2; 15:28; 16:6-9). Above all it is the Holy Spirit who is bringing the Church into being and drawing into unity many different individuals and communities. A corresponding atmosphere of excitement and wonder pervades the book.

The task of the disciples of Jesus is to be his witnesses. Throughout the story they will testify that he is risen from the dead, and that God has made him Lord and Christ, that is, Messiah (thus Peter: 2:14-36 and 3:12-26; Peter and the apostles: 5:29-32; Stephen: 7:54-60; Philip: 8:5, 35; Saul: 9:20; Peter: 10:34-43; Paul: 13:16-41, etcetera) The signs of the Spirit's power are God's testimony to the truth of what they proclaim. Beginning with Stephen they may have to seal their testimony with their own blood (the Greek word for "witness" is *martyr*).

Acts 1:8 also forecasts the plan of the book. In the first eight chapters everything takes place in Jerusalem. After the ascension of Jesus and the coming of the Holy Spirit at Pentecost we read of the life of the community in Jerusalem, of the witness given to Jesus by Peter and the apostles, of their first clashes with the authorities in charge of the Temple (chs. 1–5). The martyrdom of Stephen (chs. 6–7) and the resulting persecution cause many of the disciples to leave Jerusalem, but as they scatter they bring the Good News to the rest of Judea and to Samaria (8:1). That is the subject of chapters 8–12. In fact, the same movement out from Jerusalem under the impulsion of persecution carries the gospel as far as Phoenicia, Cyprus, and Antioch, the greatest city of the region (11:19). In 8:26-40 the first Gentile, an African, enters the Church. The Roman Cornelius is baptized in 10:48, and in 11:20 we read that the gospel was preached also to Gentiles at Antioch. However, it is with Paul that the gospel travels throughout Asia Minor, Macedonia, and Achaia (Greece), and is brought not only to the Jewish communities in those places but also to the Gentiles (from ch. 13 onward). The book ends rather abruptly when Paul arrives in Rome. Rome was not "the end of the earth" even in terms of the geographical knowledge of the time, but it was the capital of the Empire to which Judea was subject. The Good News of Jesus Christ was now being proclaimed "with all boldness and without hindrance" in the heart of that empire (28:31).

In the last analysis, although the book is entitled "Acts of the Apostles," it tells the stories not of all the apostles but principally of two, *Peter* and *Paul*. Peter dominates the first part of the book (chs. 1–12), which could be called the "Acts of Peter." He is not alone, however. John is at Peter's side in the early chapters, and Stephen and Philip are the heroes of chapters 6–8. Chapters 13–28 are the "Acts of Paul." We see Paul first as the missionary (chs. 13–20), then as the prisoner of the Romans in Jerusalem (chs. 21–23) and Caesarea (chs. 24–26), and finally on his way to Rome to an uncertain fate (chs. 27–28). Paul too has fellow workers and companions, principally Barnabas who was at first his sponsor and mentor, Silas, Timothy, Priscilla, and Aquila. The two parts of the book are not completely separated. Paul (under the name of Saul) is already introduced in the "Acts of Peter" with the account of his conversion (ch. 9), and Peter reappears in the "Acts of Paul" to take part in the Council of Jerusalem (ch. 15), which is the pivotal episode in the entire book. It is there that the issue of how to receive the Gentile believers is resolved in accordance with a solution put forward by James, who has become the leader of the Jerusalem community. Throughout the book Luke draws many parallels between his two heroes, whom he presents as complementing one another in a fundamental unity.

Acts and Ancient Historical Writing

At the beginning of his gospel (Luke 1:1-4), Luke writes that he had "investigat[ed] everything carefully from the very first." In order to write the book of Acts, Luke drew on a number of sources. Some of these can be traced more or less clearly. Underlying the first part of the book, the "Acts of Peter," there is probably an early document that told of the beginning of the church in Jerusalem, gathered around Peter, of the persecution of Stephen, and of the first expansion of the Church through the preaching of Philip and of Peter. For the "Acts of Paul," there seems to have been a similar document that told of Paul's conversion, missionary journeys, and captivity. Luke would have had the opportunity to check some of the information thus obtained or to supplement it from other sources. In his account of three journeys undertaken by Paul (16:10-17 from Troas to Philippi; 20:5–21:18 from Philippi to Jerusalem; 27:1–28:16 from Caesarea to Rome) Luke uses the "we" form of narration. Since Irenaeus, commentators have seen in these passages the proof that he accompanied Paul on his second and third missionary journeys and on his sea voyage to Rome. There is every reason to think that, at least in the majority of cases, the "we" passages are indeed drawn from the diary of a traveling companion of Paul who carefully noted places, distances, times, and many incidents of the voyage. On examination, however, they all seem to be related to a single voyage, namely the one Paul planned to make to Macedonia and Achaia in order to take up a collection for the benefit of the church in Jerusalem, then, with the collection, to Jerusalem, and finally to Rome (cf. 1 Cor 16:1-4; 2 Cor 8-9; Rom 15:25-29). Luke never mentions the collection in Acts (unless in 24:17), and he seems to have incorporated parts of the diary of the collection voyage at different places in Acts, where they now refer to different journeys undertaken at different times.

The book of Acts has come down to us in two principal text forms, the so-called "Western" Text and the "Alexandrian" Text. The differences between them can be significant, and some will be referred to in this commentary.

The Acts of the Apostles intends to be a history of the origins of the Church, but the type of history it relates differs throughout the book, depending on the source Luke makes use of at a particular point and also on the way he uses it. The accounts of Paul's missionary journeys reflect quite faithfully the world of the eastern Mediterranean in the first century: Roman administration, Greek cities, religious cults, roads and means of transport, political geography, and local topography. Here Luke is describing the world he knew at first hand, whether or not he was an eyewitness of events. By contrast, the earlier chapters are much less circumstantial and have the feeling of stories told of a past that to Luke himself now seems remote. A great part of the book is taken up with speeches. This is in accordance with the practice of ancient historians, who used speeches in order to reveal a person's thoughts or character, to analyze or reflect upon a situation, to present clearly the issues at stake. The historian would—or should—try to make these speeches resemble as closely as possible what was really said, or what could fittingly have been said, on the occasion.

Such a practice reminds us of the differences between ancient and modern ideas about what historical writing should be. There were ancient historians, such as Thucydides in the fifth century B.C.E., whose ideal of history came close to ours, namely to write down what really happened as accurately and impartially as possible. Most ancient historians, on the other hand, took liberties with their sources that we today would associate rather with the historical novel than with a work of history in the strict sense of the word. Even Thucydides did not mean to record the past for its own sake, but to serve as a lesson for future generations, and the ancients took it for granted that history should serve a purpose. By these standards Luke comes out well. Any liberties that Luke can be shown to have used with his sources, such as the travel diary, would have been allowed by his contemporaries, and if he had an obvious theological purpose in writing Acts—to show how the Holy Spirit came in power on Jesus' disciples, so that they became his witnesses throughout the world—he did not thereby disqualify himself as a historian in their eyes.

In two places, the conversion of Saul (ch. 9) and the Council of Jerusalem (ch. 15), Luke's account can be compared directly with that of Paul in Galatians 1 and 2. The comparison reveals a number of differences, some of which can be accounted for by the different perspectives and different literary projects of the two: Paul is writing a letter to a particular group of readers in order to state and defend his own case; Luke is writing a history intended for a wide readership. All the same, Luke seems to have used a freedom of composition resembling that of the painters of great historical scenes, who were more concerned to bring out the significance of the event than to reproduce it exactly. Once again, such a way of proceeding did not go beyond the bounds of what was permitted to ancient historians.

History of Interpretation

Throughout the ages the book of Acts has exercised a dynamic influence on the life of the Church and on Christian imagination and thinking. Its attractive portrait of the first community and its exciting accounts of Paul's missionary journeys have inspired countless individuals and groups. Many artists have tried to depict scenes such as the ascension, the coming of the Holy Spirit, the martyrdom of Stephen, and the conversion of Saul. Because of what it has to say about events and beliefs in the early Church this book has never ceased to be studied and debated.

A number of early Christian writers including Origen, Ephraem, Theodore of Mopsuestia, and Cyril of Alexandria commented on Acts, but for the most part only fragments of their works survive, often in anthologies or quotations by later writers. Important commentaries that have come down in their entirety from the Church of the first millennium are by John Chrysostom (d. 407) for the Greeks, Bede the Venerable (d. 735) for the Latins, and Ischo'dad of Merv (ninth century) for the Orientals. During the Middle Ages Peter Lombard, Stephen Langton, Alexander of Hales, and John Wycliffe were among those who wrote on Acts in the West, and Theophylact of Achrida and Dionysios bar Salibi in the East. The portrait of the primitive Church in Acts became central to the debates on the reform of the Church in the sixteenth century and the book attracted the attention of Erasmus, Cajetan, Calvin, Theodore Beza, and Bullinger.

In the nineteenth century Acts was once again the subject of scholarly controversy, this time over the history of Christian origins. In particular, commentators disputed the thesis of F. C. Baur of Tübingen that Luke was trying to heal the breach between followers of Paul and followers of Peter in the Church of his own time by presenting an irenic and idealized view of the past, and in particular of the relations between the two apostles. A little later, writers tried to find the sources used by Luke and to evaluate their historical worth, then, following the methods of "form criticism," to isolate the small units out of which Luke composed the larger sections. More recently attention has turned from "Luke the historian" to "Luke the theologian," but among the latest writings on Acts there is evident a renewed interest in Luke's historical purpose and method and in Acts as a source for the history of the early Church.

Acts in the Liturgy

The book of Acts occupies a significant place in the Church's liturgy. It is read continuously, and more or less in its entirety, at Mass in the weeks after Easter. Extracts from it are read in the Christmas vigil, on the great feasts of Easter, the Ascension and Pentecost, on certain other feasts (the Blessed Virgin Mary, saints, dedication of a church), and in the special Masses for the spread of the gospel, for persecuted Christians, for those suffering from hunger or famine, and for the sick. There are readings from Acts in the rite of Christian initiation outside the Paschal Vigil, in the rites for conferring the sacraments of confirmation and holy orders, in the blessing of abbots and abbesses and the consecration of virgins, and in visiting the sick.

Ideally a first reading of Acts would be of the entire book, at one sitting or at least with as few interruptions as possible, in order to get the flow and sweep of the story. If that is not possible the reader may like to read some of the key episodes in the order in which they occur, such as: the ascension of Christ (1:1-11); Pentecost (2:1-11); the martyrdom of Stephen (6:1-15 and 7:54-60); Philip and the Ethiopian (8:26-40); the conversion of Saul (9:1-19); Peter and Cornelius (10:1–11:18); the Council of Jerusalem (15:1-35); Paul in Athens (17:16-34); Paul's journey to Rome (27:1–28:31).

In the second reading of Acts we shall follow Luke's story step by step.

SECOND READING

> A brief prologue addressed to the unknown Theophilus (1:1-2; cf. Luke 1:1-4), recalls Luke's previous account of the deeds and teachings of Jesus from the beginning until his ascension. What follows, down to v. 14, duplicates Luke 24:46-53, but with significant differences. In chapter 2 Luke narrates the events of Pentecost and describes the way of life of the newborn Church.

The Last Instructions of the Risen Lord: 1:3-8

The risen Jesus continues to appear to his disciples for forty days, instructing them about the kingdom of God (cf. Exod 24:18). They are not to leave Jerusalem but must wait there for the promised baptism with the Holy Spirit (vv. 3-5).

Jesus' resurrection has demonstrated to his disciples that he is the Christ or Messiah, that is the "one anointed" by or on behalf of God, the king whom God designates to rule over Israel. Most of Jesus' contemporaries seem to have had nationalistic-political ideas of the Messiah and his kingdom, and many who came to believe in Jesus simply transferred these aspirations to him. In v. 6 the apostles voice these expectations: Jesus is the one through whom God is going to restore the kingdom to Israel. The only question is, when?

The Risen Lord first reminds his disciples that it is not for them to know times or dates fixed by

God (v. 7) and then proceeds to broaden their horizons (v. 8). They "will receive power when the Holy Spirit has come upon" them. The expression recalls Luke 1:35 and suggests a parallel between the conception of Jesus and that of the Church, and so a continuity between the life of Jesus, in which the Spirit was at work, and the life of the Church, in which the same Spirit is at work. There is a further parallel between the conception of Jesus and his baptism in the Jordan, when the Spirit came upon him (Luke 3:22). The coming of the Spirit on the disciples will thus be a baptism and also the beginning of a new life.

For Jesus, as for his disciples, the presence of the Spirit implies a manifestation of the power of God. This power is shown most characteristically in the healings and wonders worked by Jesus (cf. Luke 5:17; 6:19; Acts 10:38). So also the apostles, once they have received the power of the Spirit, will work wonders and heal the sick (4:29-31, 33: cf. 3:12; 4:7; 6:8). The power of the Spirit is the witness of God to support the preaching of the apostles. Furthermore, the healings worked by this power attack the powers of evil (10:38; also Luke 10:17-19).

The reign of Satan is coming to an end, and the reign of God and Christ begins (cf. Rev 12:9-10). The child born of Mary would inherit the throne of David and reign over the house of Jacob because he was conceived by the Holy Spirit (cf. Luke 1:31-35). The promise of 1:8, that the disciples will receive the power of the same Spirit, is the answer to their question in v. 6: when the Spirit comes upon the disciples the "kingdom will be restored to Israel." The meaning of that kingdom is thus transformed, for the kingdom of God is already there since it is founded on the power of the Spirit that has already been at work in Jesus and is going to be at work in the disciples after Pentecost (cf. Luke 17:20-21).

In v. 8b Jesus tells his disciples that they are to be his witnesses, to proclaim that he is the Messiah. An obvious objection could be made at the time to the proclamation "Jesus is the Christ:" he had been rejected by the leaders of the Jewish people and put to death as a criminal. On the other hand his followers proclaimed that God had raised Jesus from the dead, proving thereby that he is really the Messiah since the Scriptures foretold that the Messiah would be put to death and raised up again (cf. Zech 12:10-12; Hos 6:2; Isa 52:13 and 53:12; Ps 16:10-11, etcetera). The apostles, to whom Jesus appeared alive (Acts 1:3, etcetera), will have as their mission to be the witnesses of his resurrection (cf. Luke 24:48), his victory over death, and so over the Jewish authorities, which provides definitive proof that he had been sent by God and so is the Christ (see the speeches of Peter in Acts 2, 3, 5, 10).

The apostles will be witnesses to the Christ in Jerusalem, throughout Judea and Samaria, and even to the earth's remotest end. To show how that prediction is fulfilled is the theme of the book of Acts. The words of the risen Lord recall God's commission to his Servant in Isa 49:6: "I will give you as a light to the nations, so that my salvation may reach to the ends of the earth." Jesus' commission is therefore part of his reply to the disciples' question in v. 6. The design of God goes far beyond "restoring the kingdom to Israel." It is nothing less than to bring salvation to all peoples (also Luke 24:47). God no longer acts in favor only of one small nation considered as God's particular people, but offers salvation to the entire world.

The Ascension: 1:9-12

The narrative of Christ's ascension into heaven in Acts parallels that in Luke 24:50-51, but whereas the earlier account demonstrates that the risen Jesus is high priest and king (cf. Ps 110:1-4; Heb 8:1; 10:11-13), the later account has different emphases, seeking to show Jesus as the new Elijah and also as the Son of Man.

The ascension of Jesus into heaven inevitably recalls that of Elijah in 2 Kings 2:1-12. Indeed the exact words of 2 Kings 2:11 (LXX) are applied by the angels to Jesus in Acts 1:11. In Jewish thought Elijah was to return to prepare God's people for the Day of the Lord (Mal 3:23-24 [4:5-6]) and to restore the tribes of Jacob (cf. Sir 48:10). The angels also foretell the return of Jesus in the same way as the disciples have seen him go to heaven.

Also present is a reference to Dan 7:13-14, in which "one like a human being [Aramaic 'son of man']" comes on the clouds of heaven and is brought into the presence of God who confers on him a rule over all peoples that will never come to an end. This is the significance of the cloud that in v. 9 takes Jesus away from the sight of the apostles—and into the presence of God, where he receives royal power. The images of new Elijah and Son of Man fuse with one another since Jesus had already foretold that at the end people "will see 'the Son of Man coming in a cloud' with power and great glory" (Luke 21:27)—that is, in the same way as he has gone to heaven.

Waiting for the Spirit: 1:13-26

In vv. 13 and 14 we have the first of several summaries in which Luke affords his readers a glimpse of the life of the first believers (cf. Acts 2:42-47; 4:32-35; 5:12-16, 42; 6:7; 9:31; 12:24). As in the earlier account, the disciples after the ascension wait for the Spirit in continual prayer, but whereas in Luke 24:53 they are praising God in the Temple, in Acts 1:13 the place of prayer is "the room upstairs where they were staying" (cf. Luke 22:12; also 2 Kings 4:10-11). The narrative here may reflect the author's own time when the followers of Jesus no longer frequented the Temple but had their own places of worship in private houses.

Luke has already given a list of the Twelve in Luke 6:14-16. Obviously Judas is missing from the second list (Acts 1:13). John (not Andrew) is now mentioned next to Peter, a change that reflects the close association of Peter and John in Luke 8:51; 9:28; 22:8 (cf. Mark 14:13); Acts 3:1–4:23; 8:14.

The Eleven are present "together with certain women" who are probably the same as those mentioned in Luke 8:1-3; 23:49; 23:55-56; 24:1-10, 23: the silent witnesses of the central mystery of the faith. In another interpretation they are the wives of the apostles (one manuscript adds "and children"). In any case the women include "Mary the mother of Jesus." Mary is not expressly mentioned in the other texts referring to the women. Luke may wish here to reinforce the analogy between the birth of the Church and the birth of Jesus by the power of the Spirit. More surprising is the presence of "the brothers of Jesus." In the gospels the members of Jesus' family do not believe in him (cf. Mark 3:21; John 7:5) and are contrasted with his disciples (Matt 12:46-50; Mark 3:31-35, but not in Luke 8:19-21). Here they have joined the disciples, so they are now believers (cf. the appearance of the risen Christ to James in 1 Cor 15:7). Note the central position of Mary—the closest of Jesus' relations, but among the faithful women and, in Luke's perspective, the first believer and model disciple (Luke 1:38, 45).

The community numbers one hundred twenty: ten times twelve (v. 15). Its first care, even before the Holy Spirit comes in power, is to repair the loss to the Twelve caused by the defection of Judas. It is Peter who takes the initiative. In the first of many speeches in Acts (vv. 16-22) he reminds the group of the treachery of Judas and of his fate (compare Matt 27:3-10), pointing out that Scripture had already foretold both his fall from the ranks of the Twelve and his replacement (cf. Pss 69:25; 109:8). It is time now to choose someone who has been both a companion of Jesus during his ministry and a witness to his resurrection. The choice between two candidates is made, after prayer, by lot, a method of election frequently employed in ancient times that gave expression to the divine will (vv. 23-26). Matthias is counted with the Eleven.

The Descent of the Holy Spirit at Pentecost: 2:1-13

The disciples (probably not only the Twelve but all those previously mentioned) are assembled on the day of "Pentecost" (Greek for "fifty"), the name given in the LXX to the Jewish feast of "Shavuoth" (Hebrew for "weeks") celebrated seven weeks after the Passover (Exod 34:22; Lev 23:15-21; Num 28:26-31; Deut 16:9-12), originally a first-fruits festival. The account of the descent of the Holy Spirit on this occasion resembles other similar episodes in Acts (cf. 4:31; 10:44-46; 19:6-7). There is an outward sign of the coming of the Spirit (here, wind and fire); that the disciples have received the Spirit is shown by their speech (here, in v. 4, they "speak in different tongues," i.e., languages, or, according to the Western Text, simply "in tongues," a point to which we shall return).

The coming of the Spirit upon Jesus' disciples once again shows Jesus as the new Elijah: Jesus ascended into heaven sends his Spirit on his disciples as Elijah sent a double portion of his spirit on Elisha (2 Kings 2:9-15). The disciples at the ascension saw Jesus going up to heaven as Elisha saw Elijah and thus knew that he would indeed receive Elijah's spirit. In both cases others have a sign that the Spirit has been given.

The wind and fire that manifest the Spirit's coming recall the prophecy of John in Luke 3:16. The imagery of wind and fire there belongs to a wider imagery of God's judgment as a time of harvest when the wheat is separated from the chaff by the wind and the chaff is burnt. (The Greek word for wind in Acts 2:2, *pnoē,* is closely related to *pneuma,* which, like Hebrew *ruaḥ,* can mean both wind and spirit.)

The different readings of v. 4 may indicate that an earlier text in which the disciples speak "in tongues" (compare 10:46 and 19:6) has been transformed into our present narrative according to which the crowd, drawn from many nations, hears them speak "in different languages." For "speaking in tongues" (glossolalia) as a sign of the presence of God's Spirit, see its close connection with prophecy, which often involved ecstatic behavior (cf. 1 Sam 10:5-8 and 19:18-24; Isa 28:7-13, quoted by Paul in 1 Cor 14:21). Both are signs of being filled with the divine Spirit but might be interpreted as madness (or drunkenness, as in Acts 2:13; cf. 1 Cor 14:22-23). So when Jesus' followers speak in tongues it is a sign that the Spirit of God has taken possession of them. Jesus was a prophet (Luke 7:16; 24:19; Acts 3:22; cf. Matt 21:11, 46), and his prophetic spirit now rests on his disciples, as the spirit of Elijah rested on Elisha.

A transformation of speaking "in tongues" to speaking "in different languages" may reflect a reaction against the abuse of glossolalia in early Christian communities (cf. 1 Corinthians 14): the Spirit causes the apostles to speak in ways that are "not meaningless" (cf. 1 Cor 14:9-11), since they are understood by the multilingual audience. Here the gift of the Spirit is a remedy for the confusion of languages at Babel and the resulting dispersion of the human race (Gen 11:1-9). In the new age inaugurated by the coming of the Spirit, the good news proclaimed by the apostles can be understood and received by people of every nation on earth, who are consequently drawn into unity. The list of nations (vv. 9-11a) probably draws on a conventional list and is meant to represent "every nation under heaven" (v. 5) viewed from the perspective of Jerusalem, and so the universality of scope of the gospel message that is to go out from the holy city.

The Jewish feast of Pentecost eventually came to commemorate the giving of the Law on Sinai (Exodus 19). If it already had that significance when Acts was written Luke may intend us to see the giving of the Holy Spirit as the divine seal on the New Covenant and the Spirit as the new Law (cf. Jer 31:31-34; Ezek 36:25-27; Rom 5:5; 2 Cor 3:6). The account of the coming of the Spirit in Acts 2 has certain points in common with that of the theophany on Sinai in Exodus 19: "noise" and "fire."

Peter's Sermon at Pentecost: 2:14-36

Unsympathetic onlookers could laugh at the ecstatic speech of the disciples as the ravings of drunken men (v. 13). Peter defends his fellow believers (not without humor) by pointing out that it is only nine o'clock in the morning—too early to be drunk (v. 15). More seriously, he turns to the prophet Joel (3:1-5 [2:28-32]) to explain what has happened: "I shall pour out my Spirit on all humanity. Your sons and daughters shall prophesy" (vv. 17).

The heart of Peter's message to the crowd is expressed in vv. 22-24, 32: the Jewish authorities disowned Jesus and had him put to death by the Romans, but God raised him to life, "and of that we are all witnesses." So it is clear that "the Lord and Christ whom God has made is this Jesus whom you crucified" (v. 36). This was the constant theme of the preaching of the first disciples (compare Acts 3:13, 15). They were witnesses to the resurrection of Jesus by their prophetic speech which showed that they had received the Spirit of prophecy, and that in turn was the proof that the Jesus who had been crucified is now in glory at the right hand of God, whence he has sent the Spirit (v. 33).

Peter proclaims Jesus as king, Lord, and Christ. The resurrection of Jesus is the ultimate fulfillment of God's promise to David (2 Sam 7:12 LXX) to "raise up" one of his descendants to succeed him on his throne (vv. 30-32—note the play on the expression "raise up"). David's body corrupted in the grave, but his descendant, Jesus, was "not abandoned to the underworld," and his body "did not see corruption" (quoting Ps 16:9-10 LXX). Jesus is not a disembodied spirit (cf. Luke 24:39). He can return to earth in order to reign on behalf of God and establish God's kingdom.

The titles "Lord" and "Christ" in Peter's solemn conclusion put Jesus in relationship with all of humanity. They also reinforce the idea of the kingship of Jesus. Now that he has been raised up to the right hand of God, Jesus has received the name of Lord (compare Ps 110:1-3; Phil 2:6-11). Jesus is Christ, that is, Messiah or Anointed One. Here the background is Ps 2:1-6. Kings and princes have plotted against Jesus to put him to death, but God has thwarted their plans by raising him from the dead. Now all must return to their due obedience and recognize Jesus as "Christ," for he is the one who has received the royal anointing to rule the world (cf. Ps 2:8-9; Dan 7:13-14).

Peter's listeners were "cut to the heart" when they heard him speak and asked him and the other apostles, "Brothers, what should we do?" (v. 37). They realize that the world has entered a new age now that Jesus is king. People can no longer continue to live and behave as they have done. Peter tells them to repent and be baptized in the name of Jesus Christ. In that way they will receive the forgiveness of their sins and the gift of the Holy Spirit (v. 38). God's promise is for them and their children. But it is also for "those who are far away," that is, the Jews of the Diaspora and even non-Jews (v. 39; cf. Isa 57:19; Eph 2:17; Acts 22:21). Furthermore, salvation is the free gift of God, and God freely calls to it all those whom God wills. It no longer depends on belonging to one race or nation.

Peter's hearers "welcomed his message [and] were baptized, and that day about three thousand persons were added" (v. 41). The harvest has begun, and there is a rich crop waiting to be gathered.

Life in the Newborn Church: 2:42-47

The growth of the community is a constant theme in the early part of Acts, and it neatly frames this portrait of life in the Jerusalem church. We have just been told that "about three thousand persons were added" (v. 41). At the end (v. 47), we read "day by day the Lord added to their number those who were being saved." In its growth the Christian community resembles the community of Israel (compare Deut 1:11; see also Acts 4:4; 6:7).

In Acts 1:14 Luke wrote that the disciples "persevered in prayer." In 2:42 he expands this statement to write that "they devoted themselves to the apostles' teaching and fellowship, to the breaking of bread and the prayers." These four elements summarize the main features of life in the newborn Church. According to Acts 5:42 the apostles taught in the Temple, where they would have addressed other Jews, and also in private houses to instruct the new converts (compare the practice of Jesus, Mark 10:1, 10). In Acts 2:42 the "teaching of the apostles" is not their public proclamation of the good news but their private instruction to the other disciples in which they explained the Scriptures in the light of Christ and recalled the teaching of Jesus. Luke would have had in mind also the teaching of the leaders and the catechists in the Church of his own day.

The Greek word *koinōnia,* which here means "fellowship" or "community," is also used by St. Paul to mean the sharing of resources (Rom 12:12-13) and specifically the collection of money for the poor of Jerusalem (Rom 15:26). The two meanings are closely related, the financial contribution being the bond and proof of fellowship (cf. Acts 4:34-35). For "the breaking of bread," see Luke 24:35, where the expression seems to refer to the Eucharist (cf. also 1 Cor 10:16). The disciples were doing what their Master had done "on the night when he was betrayed" (1 Cor 11:23). By "the prayers" would be meant especially the singing of psalms, the great prayers of the Bible that Christianity has inherited from Judaism.

The instruction of the apostles, the fellowship and the collection for the poor that was its sign, the celebration of the Eucharist, the common prayers: these made up the inner life of the newborn Church. Another way of seeing these four elements is as the four parts of the early Christian liturgy, made up of what we would call the "liturgy of the Word," the collection for the poor, the "liturgy of the Eucharist," and prayers of thanksgiving. Thus the celebration of the liturgy is the image in miniature of the whole life of the community.

The first believers not only led their own lives. They had an impact on those around them: v. 43 tells us that "the apostles worked many signs and miracles." These "signs and miracles" were the visible proof that the Holy Spirit was at work in the apostles. They were a divine testimony backing up the witness that the apostles gave by their preaching. The "awe" of the bystanders was their reaction to this inbreaking of the power of God (cf. Acts 5:12-16).

Embedded in the first of these portraits of the Jerusalem community is a brief summary (vv. 44-45) that seems to go back well before Luke's own time and to describe the earliest days in the life of the newborn Church. That, at least, is the impression given by the Western text (the Alexandrian text seems to have been harmonized with the later portrait in Acts 4:32-37).

According to v. 44 "all who believed were together" (also 1:15; 2:1). Obviously they are much fewer in number than the three thousand given in 2:41—at most the 120 mentioned in 1:15. We are also told that they "had all things in common." Living together, the first Christians practiced absolute community of goods. Individuals possessed nothing of their own (cf. 3:6). The Western text of v. 45 tells us that "as many as had goods and possessions used to sell them and share them out to those who had need." The disciples were putting into practice the instructions of Jesus to give away one's possessions to the poor (Luke 12:33-34).

This way of life continues that of the disciples with Jesus during his ministry. They had formed a group about him that lived together, went about together, found lodging together wherever they could (Luke 9:57-58). They had left their possessions to follow Jesus (Luke 18:28), although some provision was made for their material needs (Luke 8:1-3). One of the group kept the common purse and was responsible for buying what they needed and for giving alms on behalf of all (John 12:6; 13:29). Once Jesus has left them to go to the Father the disciples continue at Jerusalem the same way of life. They live together, have a common purse, give alms out of the sale of anything they happen to possess.

How long did such a way of life last? How many adopted it? Probably there was a fairly fluid situation with the first disciples continuing to live as they had with Jesus, while newcomers were free to join them or to live a more normal life. In any case, even in the time of Jesus not all his disciples lived a wandering life with him, as we learn from the story of Martha and Mary (Luke 10:38-42). Growth of numbers would eventually have made it impossible for all to live in one place.

At the end of his gospel Luke shows us the disciples after the ascension "continually in the Temple blessing God" (24:53). In Acts 2:46 he picks up this brief statement and expands it: "Day by day, . . . they spent much time together in the Temple, . . . praising God and having the goodwill of all the people." Into this description of the first Christians taking part in the public worship of the Temple Luke now inserts a description of their own life of worship apart: they "broke bread at home and ate their food with glad and generous hearts." Along with the reference to the Eucharist ("the breaking of bread") Luke seems to have in mind the generous sharing of ordinary food. He probably means the "love feast" *("agape")* where the early Christians shared a meal in the course of which they celebrated the Eucharist (cf. 1 Cor 11:20-34). He implies that in Jerusalem, as in Corinth, there were several houses in which they gathered; from Acts 12:12 we know of one such house belonging to Mary, mother of John Mark.

In 3:1-10 Peter and John cure a lame man. There follows a series of incidents leading up to the descent of the Holy Spirit on the disciples as they pray for courage in proclaiming the good news of the resurrection of Jesus (4:31). Luke describes the unity and community of goods among the first believers, then goes on in chapter 5 to narrate the arrest of the apostles.

The Cure of a Lame Man: 3:1-10

Peter and John go up to the Temple for the afternoon celebration of prayer and sacrifice (Exod 29:38-42; 2 Chron 31:3; Luke 1:8-23). There they find a lame man being carried to the spot outside the Beautiful Gate of the Temple where he used to beg. Peter tells him: "Look at us" (v. 4). The lame man is to look to God for help, and God, working through the apostles, will restore his strength and raise him up (cf. Pss 25:15-16; 145:14-15).

Peter cures the man "in the name of Jesus Christ the Nazorean" (v. 6). This is the heart of the story (cf. 3:16; 4:7b, 10, 17b, 30). "Jesus" means "The Lord saves" (cf. 4:12). The cure of the lame man is the sign that a new age has begun in which God saves human beings through Jesus. This point is reinforced in what follows by frequent references to the name of Jesus and the saving action of God.

What does salvation mean? That is not expressly said, but it is implied in the symbols that occur in the story, which is about a "lame man" who eventually "walks and leaps and praises

God" (v. 8). These details recall Isa 35:6, "then the lame shall leap like a deer," and the rest of Acts 3 is full of references to Isaiah 35: to "joy," "God coming to save," and giving "strength to trembling knees" (compare Luke 7:22). Isaiah 35 is about the return of the Jews from exile in Babylon, which the prophet sees as a second Exodus: God is once again setting God's people free from oppression and bringing them back to their own land. Now Luke is showing that Isaiah was not only looking back to the Exodus but also forward to a liberation yet to come. The salvation brought by Jesus is a third and even greater Exodus, a deliverance and a return (compare 1 Pet 2:9-10, quoting Exod 19:5-6 and Isa 43:20-21).

In our story the lame man was laid down to beg at the gate of the Temple. According to the rules safeguarding the holiness of the Temple the blind and lame (and others with a physical handicap) were ritually impure and forbidden to go in (Lev 21:18; cf. 2 Sam 5:8). Once he is cured he can enter the Temple praising God with Peter and John. Thanks to the name of Jesus, the lame man is freed from (ritual) impurity and has access to the Temple, which is the house of God. This, too, is a symbol of the salvation brought by Jesus. Our Savior frees us from the moral impurity of sin and enables us to enter the house of God, that is, heaven, where he himself has already gone ahead of us. Jesus has given access to the Father.

There is a further symbolism in the gesture by which Peter took the lame man by the hand and helped him up. This recalls Mark 9:27, where Jesus after his transfiguration cures an epileptic boy, and it suggests a parallel between Peter and Jesus. (Cf. Mark 1:31, the healing of Peter's mother-in-law, with the same vocabulary.) In Mark the boy whom Jesus helped to his feet was thought by the bystanders to be dead. Furthermore the verb to "help up" in both Mark and Acts is one also used for raising up a person from the dead (compare Luke 7:14; 8:54). So the cure of the lame man, already a healing in its own right, symbolizes a further healing: the resurrection we are to have with Christ.

Peter's Speech to the Crowd: 3:11-26

Not surprisingly a crowd gathers, and Peter takes the opportunity to speak to the people. He makes it clear that the cure has been worked not in virtue of any power the apostles had, but in virtue of the name of Jesus. God has glorified God's servant Jesus. The people and their rulers accused "the Holy and Righteous One" but God raised him from the dead, and to that the apostles are witnesses (vv. 12-16).

By calling Jesus the servant of God (v. 13) Peter identifies him with the "servant of the Lord" who is the subject of several striking poems in the book of Isaiah. The servant was chosen by God to carry out a mission of deliverance (Isa 42:1-9 and cf. 35:1-10; 61:1). He was to set free the people of God who were held captive in Babylon, but his mission was to extend also to all peoples held captive in darkness (Isa 49:1-6). He would be humiliated and afflicted, but God would vindicate him (Isa 50:4-11). The first believers saw Jesus as fulfilling the mission and destiny of this mysterious figure in the OT. Above all, by his death and resurrection Jesus fulfilled the prediction that the servant would suffer and die on account of the sins of others, but God would raise him up and exalt him (Isa 52:13–53:12).

Jesus as the Holy One (v. 14) has been consecrated, that is, set apart by God for his mission, like the servant of the Lord (Isa 49:5) and the prophet Jeremiah (Jer 1:5; cf. John 10:36). Jesus the servant is the Holy One because he is the prophet, the one consecrated from the womb and sent into the world with the saving words of God.

Isaiah 53:11 joins together the titles of servant and Just or Righteous One. At the death of Jesus the centurion, according to Luke 23:47, declares: "Certainly this man was innocent (= righteous)," whereas according to Matt 27:54 and Mark 15:39 he calls him "son of God." The connection between the two titles is given in Wis 2:18, where the "upright man" is "God's child" in the sense of the one who enjoys God's special protection. The whole passage in Wis 2:12–3:9 takes on its full meaning in the light of the death and resurrection of Jesus—as Peter points out in Acts 3:14-15 (cf. Matt 27:43)—because it depicts the upright man who is put to death by the wicked but is vindicated by God.

So despite all that has happened, the Servant of God is alive—his disciples are witnesses to that—and Peter testifies to the resurrection of "the Just One" by restoring in his name the cripple at the Beautiful Gate of the Temple. Jesus is ready to fulfill the mission for which he was chosen and sanctified by God: to deliver all human beings from the powers of evil that dominate the world.

In the second part of his speech (vv. 17-26) Peter returns to themes that have already appeared in his sermon at Pentecost. He appeals to his listeners to repent and turn to God in order to obtain the forgiveness of their sins (vv. 19-20; cf. 2:38). The ancient prophets had exhorted the people to turn away from idolatry and back to God, promising that God would restore them in their own land (cf. Isa 43:25; Jer 16:14-15; 23:7-8; 24:5-7; 50:19-20; Hos 11:11). Jesus is being kept in heaven until the time comes for him to return as a new Elijah in order to bring about the "restoration of all things" (vv. 20-21; cf. 1:6-11; 2:33). He indeed is the Prophet whom Moses had foretold (vv. 22-3; cf. Deut 18:15-19). The passage concludes with a reference to the covenant of Abraham (vv. 25-26; cf. 7:2), to whose descendants in the first place the servant has been sent.

Peter and John Before the Sanhedrin: 4:1-22

The cure of the lame man and Peter's speech got the apostles into trouble with the priests and Sadducees. The religious authorities responsible for the Temple did not want the apostles to proclaim the resurrection of Jesus, which was God's negative judgment on them for refusing to listen to him, and the Sadducees were opposed to the doctrine of the resurrection from the dead (cf. Luke 20:27). The challenge to the apostles by the priests and Sadducees resembles that issued to Jesus by the chief priests, scribes, and elders in the Temple during the last week of his life (compare Acts 4:1-2, 7-8 and Luke 20:1-3). Other details of the present incident also recall debates that took place between Jesus and various opponents during that last week: compare Acts 4:11 and Luke 20:17-19; Acts 4:21 and Luke 20:19. Jesus' disciples are following in his footsteps (cf. John 15:20-21).

Peter and John, like Jesus himself, are put in prison overnight and must appear before the Sanhedrin as Jesus had foretold (vv. 3-7; cf. Matt 10:17; Luke 22:66). This seems to be a development of an earlier version of the story in which Peter and John debate with the Temple authorities on the spot (see vv. 10 and 14 in which the cured man is still at the side of the apostles, and v. 21 in which the crowd is still giving glory to God for what has happened). Peter once again proclaims that salvation is now given in the name of Jesus crucified and raised from the dead (vv. 8-12). The authorities are at a loss how to deal with the apostles (vv. 13-17; cf. Luke 20:5) and decide to warn Peter and John, who as laymen (v. 13) cannot be punished for a first religious offense, not to speak or preach in Jesus' name (v. 18). To that command Peter replies that it is impossible for the disciples not to proclaim that to which they are witnesses (vv. 19-20). Peter is being obedient to Jesus' teaching to his disciples (Matt 10:26-27; Luke 12:2-3). By hearing the word of God they learn what to say and do.

The Prayer of the Church and the Gift of the Spirit: 4:23-31

Peter and John go back to the community and tell them of the threats of the chief priests and elders (v. 23). The whole assembly then joins in a prayer (vv. 24-30) modeled on that of King Hezekiah when his country was threatened with the invasion of the Assyrian forces under Sennacherib (Isa 37:16-20).

The community of disciples remembers Ps 2:1-2, which had been fulfilled in the passion of Jesus when "kings" (Herod Antipas; cf. Luke 23:6-12; *Gos. Pet.* 1–2, 5c; *Didasc. Apost.* 5.19. 4-5) and "princes" (Pontius Pilate) had conspired with the Gentile "nations" and the Jewish "people" against the Lord and his holy servant Jesus whom he had anointed (cf. 3:13-14; the Greek word for "servant" here—*pais*—can also mean "child," and the title is used of Jesus in other early Christian prayers: *Did.* 9.2-3 and 10.2-3; *1 Clem.* 59.2-4; *Mart. Pol.* 14.1; 20.2; see also *Barn.* 6.1; 9.2). Now the disciples are faced with a similar plot against them. They pray, not for deliverance from danger, but to be enabled to proclaim God's message "with all boldness," as Peter had just done. They ask God to "stretch out your hand" to work signs and wonders (Exod 3:20). Such miracles will accredit the disciples as envoys of God (Exod 4:1-9; cf. Acts 7:25) and attest the truth of the witness they bear to the resurrection of Jesus.

Peter and John have already worked a cure by the power of God, like Jesus himself (cf. Acts 2:22; 10:38; also Isa 61:1). Then, "filled with the Holy Spirit," Peter was able to proclaim the resurrection of Jesus with an assurance even his opponents recognized, and they were incapable of contradicting him (cf. Luke 12:11-12; 21:15; also Isa 11:2). Now the disciples pray that all of them may be given the same power.

In reply to their prayer God sends them the divine Spirit, and they proclaim the word of God fearlessly (v. 31): again the presence of the Spirit is shown by a gift of speech, though not ecstatic. They also witness to the resurrection of Jesus "with great power," that is, by working "signs and wonders" (v. 33). The rest of the book of Acts will continue to show how their prayer has been answered.

As the Spirit came upon the disciples the place where they were gathered "was shaken." This is a sign that God has heard the prayer of the disciples in their hour of need and is going to come to their rescue by sending them the Spirit (cf. Ps 18:4-10).

The Unity of the Jerusalem Church: 4:32, 34–5:11

There follows a portrait of the Jerusalem church depicting its unity and the practice of community of goods that has attracted many Christians over the ages and inspired those who have tried to recapture the way of life of the first followers of Jesus, including the founders and foundresses of religious orders and the Anabaptists in the sixteenth century. Acts 4:32, 44-45 (we have read v. 33 with the previous passage) is clearly modeled on 2:44-45 but it evidently supposes a considerable growth in numbers and depicts social relationships and an organizational structure that have changed and developed with that growth. Now in 4:32 "the whole group of those who believed were of one heart and soul (or mind)." Here it is no longer a question of physical community, of living together: presumably the believers are now too numerous for that. Instead they cultivate a spiritual and psychological unity of "heart and soul," which is further emphasized in some early manuscripts with the phrase "and there was no division among them." For "heart and soul" together as the source of human conduct see Deut 6:5; for "one heart," translated into Greek as "one soul," as the expression of corporate unity see 1 Chr 12:38; for the promise of "one heart" as God renews God's people see Jer 32:39; Ezek 11:19. "One soul" also occurs in pagan Greek literature, especially with regard to friendship (e.g., Aristotle, *Nic. Eth.* 9.8, 1168b; Diogenes Laertius, *Life of Aristotle:* friends are "one soul living in two bodies"). Thus the believers are the renewed people of God foretold by the biblical prophets and also fulfill the Greek ideals of friendship.

Both 2:44 and 4:32 describe the way the Christians shared their material resources, and in almost identical terms: "[they] had all things in common" and "everything they owned was held in common." However, in the different situations presupposed by the two texts the same words in fact describe different ways of sharing goods. In the later situation what community of goods means is explained by the immediately preceding phrase, "no one claimed private ownership of any possessions." They remained the legal owners of their possessions, as is made clear in 5:4. But instead of treating their goods as their private property for their own exclusive use they put them at the disposition of all. Once again the expression that would be literally translated as "all things common" recalls well-known Greek proverbs about friendship (e.g., "for friends, all things are common" and even "the goods of friends are common"). Friends are expected to share everything and to be prepared to make their own property available to one another (see also Plato, *Rep.* 3, 416d; 5, 462c; Iamblichus, *Life of Plato,* 167–169).

The expression in 4:34, "there was not a needy person among them," recalls Deut 15:4, "there will . . . be no one in need among you." This command occurs in a passage that lays down the observance of the sabbatical year with its remission of debts owed by Israelites to one another, and it concludes (v. 11): "Open your hand to the poor and needy neighbor in your land." So the community of believers is shown as the people of God, keeping God's Law and enjoying the blessing that is promised to those who fulfill the divine commands. In Acts 4:34-35 Luke explains how it came about that "there was not a needy person among them": those who possessed lands or houses used to sell them and bring the price they got for them to the apostles and the proceeds were then distributed to any who might be in need.

If we compare this with Acts 2:45 we immediately see the difference. In the earlier passage the disciples were simply carrying out the command of Jesus to sell what they had and give to the poor, whoever they might be. Now everything takes place within the group itself. The distribution is organized for the benefit of the needy within the community (though presumably almsgiving to the poor outside the group has not totally ceased). To help the poor of the community there is now a fund to which the wealthier members contribute. This fund is administered by the apostles, who also supervise the distribution to the needy. Previously those who sold their possessions gave to the poor directly. Now they bring the price of the sale to the apostles. The growing community needs a more defined structure: the apostles take on a new ministry resembling that of the *episkopoi* (literally "overseers," whence our "bishops"; cf. 1 Tim 3:1-7) in the early Church, who looked after the goods of the community and saw to the needs of the widows and orphans.

Luke paints an idyllic picture. But how realistic is it? In fact he conveys by means of two contrary examples that the reality was less perfect. In 4:36-37 Barnabas carries out what has just been said about the group as a whole: "He owned a piece of land, and he sold it and brought the money and presented it to the apostles." Immediately afterward (5:1-11) Luke tells the story of Ananias and Sapphira, which lets us know that the utopian picture in the summary leaves out the imperfections of the community. This couple told a lie about the price they obtained for their property and secretly withheld part of it. From Peter's words to Ananias (5:4) it appears that there was no obligation on members of the community to sell their property and, even after the sale, no obligation to hand over all the money received. The sin of Ananias and Sapphira was their lie, presumably told in order to have the glory of handing over the whole sum while in fact keeping something for themselves. (For their punishment, compare 1 Cor 5:5.)

The Apostles Before the Sanhedrin: 5:12-42

A summary (vv. 12-16), essentially a development of 4:33, depicts in some detail the signs and wonders worked by the apostles and the reactions of the people. Moved by jealousy, the high priest and his supporters among the Sadducees put "the apostles" in prison, from which they were released during the night by an angel, who told them to go to the Temple and "tell the people the whole message about this life" (vv. 17-21). There follows a comic interlude (vv. 22-26) in which the apostles are found to be missing from the prison, then to be preaching in the Temple. They are brought before the Sanhedrin and reminded that they have already been warned not to preach in the name of Jesus (vv. 27-28; cf. 4:18, 21). This episode seems to be modeled on that in which Peter and John appear before the Sanhedrin.

The reply of Peter and the apostles (vv. 29-32) resumes the themes of 4:8-12 and 19-20. "We must obey God rather than any human authority (v. 29; cf. Luke 20:20-25; also Plato, *Apol.* 29d; Sophocles, *Antigone*). Jesus and his disciples are not opposed to lawful authorities in principle, but their ultimate loyalties lie elsewhere. Hence they are likely to come into conflict with those who wield power, whether religious or secular, who tend to demand total loyalty and absolute obedience. Peter repeats the kerygma (vv. 30-32): God has raised up Jesus "whom you had killed" to be leader and Savior, through whom repentance and forgiveness of sins will be given to Israel. "We are witnesses to these things, and so is the Holy Spirit."

This reply so infuriates the authorities that they want to put the apostles to death (v. 33). However, a leading Pharisee (Gamaliel I, said to be the teacher of St. Paul: cf. 22:3) persuades the Sanhedrin to wait and see whether this movement is of merely human origin, in which case it will fail like others in the past, or whether it is from God, in which case they would be fighting against God (vv. 34-39). The apostles are flogged and released with another warning and leave the Sanhedrin "rejoic[ing] that they were considered worthy to suffer dishonor for the sake of the name" (vv. 40-41).

This section of Acts closes with a summary recounting how the apostles proclaimed the good news of Christ Jesus in the Temple and taught in private houses (v. 42).

> Now, under the impulse of persecution, the Word goes forth from Jerusalem. Stephen was the first to witness to Christ by shedding his blood. He is introduced as one of the seven new ministers chosen by the early Christian community (6:1-6), and his martyrdom is recounted (6:8–7:60). Philip, another of the Seven, brings the gospel to Samaria and baptizes an Ethiopian (8:1-40).

Then the persecutor Saul is converted, to become the future apostle Paul (9:1-30).

The Choice of the Seven: 6:1-7

The occasion of the choice of new ministers was a dissension between the "Hellenists" and the "Hebrews." These were two groups of Jews who were distinguished above all by language and culture. The Hellenists spoke Greek and lived a way of life that was more influenced by Greek culture—many of them would have been Jews of the Diaspora who had settled in the holy city. The Hebrews were Palestinian Jews who spoke Hebrew or Aramaic and were less influenced by Greek culture. Our story concerns members of both groups who have joined the community of believers.

According to Acts the dissension between these groups was over the care of the widows. Luke thinks of the widows as forming a recognized group as in 1 Tim 5:3-16. Having no other means of support, they were looked after by the community and benefited from "the daily distribution" (cf. Acts 4:34-35). The Hellenists complained that their widows were being unfairly treated. It is easy to surmise that as numbers grew (v. 1) systems previously set in place no longer worked so well, and disputes would arise. Perhaps some were using the story of Martha and Mary (Luke 10:38-42) as an excuse for leaving "all the serving" *(diakonia)* to others. In addition, it seems, the Hebrews, no doubt the majority in the community, were neglecting the Hellenist minority.

A new ministry is instituted, that of the Seven, to "serve tables" (v. 2 *diakonein trapezais*). They were to relieve the Twelve of these material concerns, so that the Twelve could "devote [themselves] to prayer and to serving the word" *(diakonia tou logou)*. The relationship thus portrayed between the Twelve and the Seven resembles that later found between *episkopoi* and *diakonoi* (literally "servants" or "ministers," whence our "deacons"; cf. 1 Tim 3:8-13). Acts 6:1-6 offers a number of verbal contacts with Gen 41:33-45, where Pharaoh puts Joseph in charge of assuring the food supply of Egypt; also with Exod 18:21-26; Num 11:16-30; and Deut 1:10-18, where Moses chooses (seventy) elders whom he sets over the community in order to settle differences arising between members.

There are, however, some problems with this reading of 6:1-6. For one thing, the Seven all have Greek names (unlike the Twelve, most of whom have Semitic names) and one of them is described as a proselyte—a convert to Judaism—from Antioch: the inference is that they were appointed from among the Hellenists. In the rest of Acts the Seven are nowhere shown "serving tables." On the contrary, two—Stephen and Philip—are shown in "the service of the word," preaching "with power," that is, working miracles like the Twelve. The Hellenists of Acts turn out to be a very interesting group. We find that the earliest missionary contacts with non-Jews were carried out by Hellenists: Philip preaches in Samaria (8:5-13) and baptizes the Ethiopian (8:26-40); people from Cyprus and Cyrene go to Antioch, where they preach not only to Jews but also to "Greeks" (11:19-20).

These points suggest that the deepest reason for dissension between Hellenists and Hebrews was the question of a mission to non-Jews. At a certain point in Acts there is in fact a separation between "the apostles," who stay in Jerusalem after the martyrdom of Stephen (8:1), and others who go from place to place preaching the good news (8:4) as far as Samaria and even Antioch. In other words, while the Twelve restricted themselves to the evangelization of the Jews in the Holy Land, the Hellenists, and in particular the Seven, went to the Diaspora and proclaimed the word to Samaritans and even Gentiles. Such a division of missions is attested in Gal 2:7-9, and is symbolized in the double narratives of the multiplication of the loaves in Matt 14:20 // Mark 6:43 and Matt 15:34, 37 // Mark 8:5, 8. Matt 10:5-6 seems to reflect a controversy over the legitimacy of a non-Jewish mission.

According to this reading of our text the dispute over mission policy was resolved by the institution of the Seven, who proceeded to carry out the mission to the non-Jews demanded by the Hellenists, while the Twelve remained with the Hebrews and the Jewish mission (cf. Gal 2:9). Thus the Seven were to be for the Hellenists what the Twelve were for the Hebrews. It is therefore significant that there are contacts in theme and vocabulary between Acts 6:3-6 and Num 27:16-23, where Moses chooses Joshua to be, not his assistant, but his successor as leader of the community. The relations between the two missions, the respective missionaries, and the communities that sponsored them were to preoccupy Paul (Gal 2:2, 10; Rom 15:25-27, etcetera).

In v. 7 we read of the continued growth of "the word of God" and of the adherence of "many priests" to the faith.

The Martyrdom of Stephen: 6:8–7:60

The martyrdom of Stephen is the turning point or hinge in the story of the first twelve chapters of Acts. It is closely linked with the events of chapters 3–4: Peter and John were ultimately not punished because the priests and Sadducees were afraid of the people (4:21). Now by turning the people against Stephen his enemies are able to put him to death. The parallel with Jesus is clear and detailed.

There are inconsistencies in the story of the martyrdom of Stephen. It begins with a mass movement against him (6:12a) and ends with something that looks like a lynching (7:58). In between comes a trial before the Sanhedrin (6:12b), whose members are transformed from judges into a murderous mob (7:57). The speech that Stephen gives (7:1-56) is suitable neither for confronting an angry crowd nor for defending oneself before a court. It is possible that there was an original story (6:8-12a + 7:57-60) in which the people were turned against Stephen and stoned him to death. To this were added the trial before the Sanhedrin (another point of resemblance to Jesus) and the speech, which may once have served a quite different purpose.

Stephen's enemies are Hellenist Jews like himself who, however, have not become believers in Jesus. When they cannot best him in argument (6:10) they plot his death. Up till now the people have been favorable toward the followers of Jesus. Stephen's enemies turn the people against him by "procuring some men to say 'We heard him use blasphemous language against Moses and against God'" (6:11). Stephen is dragged outside the city and stoned (7:58). Compare the story of Naboth (1 Kings 21:1-16, especially vv. 11-13).

Before the Sanhedrin Stephen is accused of foretelling the destruction of the Temple (6:13), a charge brought also against Jesus (Matt 26:60-61 and Mark 14:57-59; compare John 2:19). A great part of his speech is taken up with convicting the Israelites of continual rebellion against God. The downfall of the Temple would be God's punishment on the people for not accepting the message sent to them through the prophet (cf. Jer 7:1-34).

Stephen takes up biblical history from Abraham (7:2; cf. 3:25), but retells it in ways that often seem to reflect non-biblical traditions rather than the text of Genesis and Exodus. Of old the Israelites had rejected Moses and so revolted against God (vv. 23-29 and 35-39). No sooner were they released from captivity in Egypt than they fell into idolatry with the golden calf (vv. 39-41). This set the pattern for their subsequent behavior. Stephen here resembles the prophet Ezekiel (Ezek 20:5-44), who had already detailed his people's long record of rebellion against God and interpreted the Exile in Babylon as God's punishment for their disobedience.

The Jewish people, Stephen implies, are now behaving like their ancestors. They too are "stiff-necked" (v. 51; cf. Exod 33:3, 5 and Deut 9:13 in reference to the golden calf) and have "uncircumcised hearts and ears" (cf. Jer 6:10; Bar 2:30-31). So the same judgment will be passed on them as on their forebears. Their city and Temple will be destroyed, and they will go into exile in a foreign land.

At the end of his speech Stephen has a vision of Jesus (vv. 55-56). It is essentially the same vision as the disciples had at the ascension (1:9-11). He can "see the heavens opened and the Son of Man standing at the right hand of God." Jesus, the new Elijah, is ready to return to earth. The day of judgment is at hand. It is this declaration that Jesus is the Messiah that provokes the murderous onslaught on Stephen (v. 57).

The murder of Stephen should not have surprised the disciples of Jesus. What happened to him was only what Jesus had told all who follow him to be prepared for (Luke 9:23-24; 21:12-19). Stephen continues to follow Jesus to the end. The story concludes with his twofold prayer: "Lord Jesus, receive my spirit" (v. 59) and "Lord, do not hold this sin against them" (v. 60), in which he imitates the dying Jesus (Luke 23:46 and 34). He kneels down, like Jesus in the agony (Luke 22:41). Then he "falls asleep." The death of a disciple of Jesus is not a destruction, but a sleep from which the disciple will wake one day (cf. 1 Thess 4:13-18 and 1 Cor 15:20). Stephen can rest in peace. God will give him back the spirit he committed to Jesus, as Jesus had committed his own spirit to his Father (cf.

Psalm 31:5; 2 Macc 7:23). The burial of Stephen is recorded in Acts 8:2.

The martyrdom of Stephen is a watershed in the Acts of the Apostles. Up till now everything takes place in Jerusalem, and the Church might have remained there. Then comes the death of Stephen, whereupon "a bitter persecution started against the church in Jerusalem, and everyone except the apostles scattered to the country districts of Judea and Samaria" (8:1). They took with them God's Good News of salvation in the name of Jesus (cf. 1:8). It was persecution that, like a violent wind, scattered the seed of the Word that until then had been clinging to the tree. This pattern will be repeated throughout the book of Acts, where so often persecution drives the missionary on to new fields.

Philip Evangelizes Samaria: 8:4-8

Philip, one of the Seven and a Hellenist, goes to "a Samaritan town" (v. 5). That he should do so shows that he and his group, at least, did not consider Matt 10:5-6 as determining for all time the missionary policy of the Church: the restriction to the "lost sheep of the house of Israel" is for the Twelve. On the other hand, vv. 6b-7 recall Luke 6:17b-18 and thus suggest that in preaching to non-Jews Philip is only continuing a mission already opened up by Jesus (cf. John 4:1-41).

This is the first time in Acts that the gospel is preached to people who are not Jews (the Samaritans were regarded by the Jews as heretics). Philip proclaims to them the Good News, which is guaranteed by the miracles he works. The people of the Samaritan town receive his words with joy (v. 8)—a note sounded frequently in Acts. It is in the first place the joy of the disciples in the resurrection and ascension of Jesus (compare Luke 24:41, 52). The new believers in Samaria now share in it.

Simon the Magician: 8:9-25

A certain Simon (who is known from other early literature) had already attracted a following in Samaria by wonders attributed to magic arts, and he was identified with "the power of God that is called Great" (vv. 9-11). Philip's preaching caused many to accept baptism, and even Simon became a believer, impressed as he was by the miracles worked by Philip (vv. 12-13).

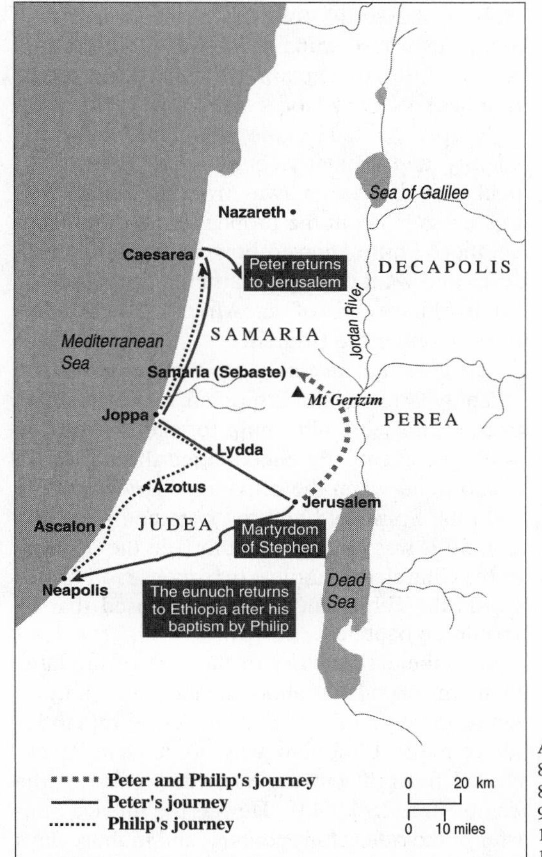

JOURNEYS OF PETER AND PHILIP

Acts 8:4-25; 8:26, 40; 9:32-36; 10:1, 23-24; 11:2

At this point Peter and John come from Jerusalem to see what is happening in Samaria. They lay hands on those who have been baptized so that they may receive the Holy Spirit (vv. 14-17). Simon offers money so that the apostles may give him too the power to confer the Holy Spirit—the origin of the sin of "simony"—but Peter rebukes him: money cannot buy what God gives for nothing (vv. 18-24). The apostles return to Jerusalem, "proclaiming the good news to many villages of the Samaritans" (v. 25).

Philip and the Ethiopian: 8:26-40

After leaving Samaria, Philip comes across the treasurer of the *Kandakē* or queen of Ethiopia, who has been on pilgrimage in Jerusalem. The Ethiopian was probably not a Jew but had leanings toward the Jewish religion. For Luke's Greek readers his country of origin, in Africa south of Egypt, would have represented "the ends of the earth" (cf. 1:8). As he was riding along he was reading the book of Isaiah and asked Philip to explain Isa 53:7-8. Here the prophet speaks of God's servant who was "like a sheep . . . led to the slaughter," suffering silently and patiently, humiliated, treated unjustly, his life "taken away from the earth." Was this passage about the prophet himself or about another? Philip showed how it was fulfilled in Jesus and went on to proclaim the "good news." So in the person of an African the Gentiles begin to enter the Church.

We note that in this story the initiatives are taken by God and the Ethiopian. It was an angel of the Lord who told Philip to take the road on which he eventually encountered the Ethiopian (v. 26), and when the official's chariot came in sight the Spirit told him to go up and join it (v. 29). So it was God who authorized the opening of the Church to Gentiles. In response to Philip's words the Ethiopian himself proposed that he should be baptized.

Like the earlier story of the cure of the lame man, this one also is about the inclusion of those who had previously been excluded. While in Jerusalem the Ethiopian was, as a Gentile, excluded from all but the outermost court of the Temple (cf. Ezek 44:9). He was the finance minister of the ruler of his country, and in those days it was common for court officials to be *castrati,* so common in fact that "eunuch" had become a synonym for "courtier," even if the person concerned had not undergone the operation. If the Ethiopian was in fact a eunuch, then on that ground too he was, according to Deut 23:1, excluded from the sacred assembly of Israel. But in announcing the last times Isaiah had declared that foreigners and eunuchs who were faithful to God's commandments would be acceptable to God (Isa 56:3-8; compare Wis 3:14). By baptizing the Ethiopian Philip proclaims that the new age has arrived, and all without exception can enter the community of Jesus' disciples.

In the background to our story is once again Isaiah 35 (cf. Acts 3:1-10) with its symbols of the desert, water in the desert, a road running across the desert, and the joy of those who travel on that road. The reception of the Ethiopian is a return from exile and a deliverance from captivity. The way the story is told—a journey in company with someone who explains the Scriptures, ending with a sacramental celebration—recalls the walk to Emmaus (Luke 24:13-35). The Ethiopian's baptism is described in terms that recall the baptism of Jesus himself (vv. 36-39; compare Matt 3:13-17 // Mark 1:9-11 // Luke 3:21-22). The composition of the narrative may well reflect the practice of the early Church of conferring baptism during the paschal vigil when the death and resurrection of Jesus are especially commemorated.

By showing Philip carried away (physically) by the Holy Spirit v. 39a likens him to OT prophets, and in particular to Elijah (cf. 1 Kings 18:12; 2 Kings 2:16). He goes on his way preaching in the cities of the coastal plain until he reaches Caesarea (v. 40; cf. Acts 21:8-9).

The Conversion of Saul: 9:1-30

Saul is introduced as a bystander who approved of the killing of Stephen (7:59; 8:1a) and then as a persecutor of the Church (8:3). The story of his conversion (9:1-30; cf. 22:1-21; 26:9-23) follows more or less what Paul himself tells us in Gal 1:11-24 about his persecution of the Church and his conversion. Luke does not, however, include all the information given by Paul and adds important details that are not in Galatians. In Gal 1:15-16 Paul attributes his conversion to a divine revelation but gives no details of it. In 1 Cor 9:1 he tells us that he "has seen the Lord," and in 1 Cor 15:8 that the risen Jesus "appeared to him too," but he does not associate either vision or apparition with his conversion. In Acts it is the risen Jesus who appears to Saul on the road to Damascus (9:5).

The detailed account of Saul's vision in 9:3-4, 6-9 is modeled on the visions of the prophet Ezekiel, who receives a divine mission to the people of Israel (Ezek 1:27-28; 3:22-23, 26). As God calls Jacob in Gen 46:2, the Lord calls Saul by name and identifies himself as "Jesus, whom you are persecuting" (v. 5). He tells him to go into the city of Damascus, where he will be told what to do (v. 6). Other OT precedents include the scales that fall from Saul's eyes (v. 18a), recalling the cure of Tobit (Tob 11:10-15).

It is clear from Acts that Saul's conversion is completed by his incorporation into a community and in particular through the ministry of Ananias (9:10-19). When Ananias lays his hands on Saul (vv. 12, 17) it is expressly to give him back his sight and to confer the Holy Spirit. The gesture has, however, another significance that is relevant here: to appoint for mission (cf. 6:6; 13:3). Saul's baptism after a three-day fast and his partaking of food (vv. 18b-19; cf. v. 9), may allude to the prebaptismal fast and postbaptismal Eucharist of the early Church (see the description written by Justin Martyr c. 150 in his *First Apology,* 61 and 65). His blindness and recovery of sight are an apt symbol of the effect of baptism, which was often referred to as "enlightenment."

In Gal 1:15-16 Paul speaks in one breath of his conversion and his mission to preach Christ: he receives both graces at the same time. Immediately after his conversion in Acts, Saul begins to preach in the synagogues, "[Jesus] is the Son of God" (v. 20). After a time the Jews at Damascus react against Paul's preaching and want to put him out of the way; the disciples help him escape (vv. 20-25; cf. 2 Cor 11:32-33). In Jerusalem the same sequence recurs and Paul goes to Tarsus (vv. 28-30). This sets up a pattern that is repeated continually in the second part of Acts: Paul enters a town, goes into the synagogue and begins to preach the gospel of Christ; at first he generally meets with some success, but then an opposition gathers strength and eventually drives him out of the town; he goes to the next place and begins again (cf. 13:14, 50; 14:1, 5, 6; 17:1-2, 5, 10a; 17:10b-11, 13-14). He thus fulfills Jesus' words in Matt 10:14 and Luke 9:5. In each place Paul leaves behind a small but faithful band of converts who are the nucleus of the church in that town.

> After a summary recording the peace and growth of the churches throughout Judea, Galilee, and Samaria (9:31), Luke brings us back to Peter. He has left Jerusalem and begun a tour of the towns along the coastal plain that brings him to Caesarea. There he receives into the Church the centurion Cornelius and his household (Acts 10), an action for which he is called to account on his return to Jerusalem (11:1-18). There follows an interlude briefly recounting the origins of the church at Antioch (11:19-30). This section of Acts concludes with Peter's release from prison and the death of his persecutor (Acts 12).

Peter on Mission: 9:32-43

Peter comes to Lydda (Lod), a town on the coastal plain northwest of Jerusalem, where he cures a man who has been bedridden for eight years (vv. 32-35). The cure of Aeneas recalls that of the lame man at the Beautiful Gate of the Temple (3:1-10): it is a new beginning for the ministry of Peter.

The brief story concludes with a reference to the Plain of Sharon where Lydda is situated, which recalls Isa 35:2. All the promises of salvation symbolized in the prophecy of Isaiah 35 had first been offered to the inhabitants of Jerusalem: the cure of the lame man at the Beautiful Gate was the sign. But they refused the grace that was offered them and stoned Stephen (cf. Luke 13:34-35). Peter now turns to the Jewish inhabitants of the plain of Sharon, who welcome the good news and see the glory of God of which the second cure was the sign. Peter's journey will lead him to Caesarea, to Antioch (cf. Gal 2:11) and, according to tradition, to Rome. For the first among the Twelve the command "not to go to Gentile territory" (Matt 10:5) was not permanently binding.

Meanwhile Peter is summoned to the town of Jaffa where a woman disciple named Tabitha has died. He restores her to life (vv. 36-42). The raising of Tabitha suggests a likeness between Peter and Elisha, who raised up the son of the Shunamite woman (2 Kings 4:18-37). It also suggests a likeness between Peter and Jesus himself, who raised up the son of the widow of Nain and the daughter of Jairus (Luke 7:11-17; 8:51-56). Thus Peter, the disciple of Jesus, continues the work of Jesus.

Peter and Cornelius: 10:1-48

While he was at Jaffa Peter was summoned to come to the city of Caesarea, the seat of Roman power in Judea, by a Roman army officer (centurion) who is a "godfearer," believing in God, praying and giving generously to Jewish causes. Seeing evidence of the presence of the Spirit with Cornelius and his household and friends, Peter orders them to be baptized, then stays some days with them. This action did not go unchallenged by those Jewish believers who could not see what place non-Jews might have in the Church.

In the earliest days the disciples of Jesus were far from separating themselves from Judaism. They could easily have settled for being a pious group of Jews with a special devotion to Jesus and a commitment to a way of life based on his teachings and example. Alternatively, they could have engaged in a mission, but exclusively to their fellow Jews, to win them to their view of the place of Jesus in the expectations of Israel (cf. Matt 10:6). Any mission to non-Jews would involve close social relationships with people who were considered impure. If individual Gentiles sought admission to the Church they would first have to accept conversion to Judaism.

As we have seen, these exclusive attitudes were challenged by the Hellenists, who wanted a large scale mission to non-Jews. The dissension between them and the Hebrews was resolved when new ministers, the Seven, were ordained from among the Hellenists. These embarked on a vigorous mission campaign in Samaria and farther afield. Meanwhile the Twelve remained in Jerusalem. Now comes a break in the fixed positions. Peter goes among Gentiles, receives them into the Church, then justifies his action to the community in Jerusalem. This new move—which has already been prepared in Acts (cf. 8:4-8; 8:26-40)—turned out to be decisive in the development of Christianity.

Peter does not take this step on his own initiative or because he has been won over by argument to another point of view. It is the Holy Spirit who cuts the Gordian knot that endless discussions would not have succeeded in untying. The Spirit, through an angel (vv. 30-32), prompts Cornelius to send for Peter (v. 20b). While Peter is at prayer the Spirit orders him to go with the messengers without making difficulties (20a). The Spirit comes upon the group around Cornelius (vv. 44, 46) in the same way as on the disciples of Jesus shortly after the ascension (2:4, 11; 4:31). Peter is only the docile instrument of the Spirit.

So the Holy Spirit resolves the problem about the Gentiles. They are to be admitted into the community because the Spirit has sent them to it. They are no longer to be considered as impure people, contact with whom renders impure, since the Spirit has commanded Peter to go with them and has even come personally to dwell within them. The second point—Gentiles are no longer impure—is underlined by the vision of clean and unclean animals that Peter is commanded to eat, with the revelatory word: "What God has made clean, you have no right to call profane" (v. 15; cf. Mark 7:19).

In this episode Peter undergoes a real conversion, a change of mind and heart. The Spirit has commanded him to go to the Gentiles. He draws the conclusion that he expresses to the people at Caesarea in vv. 34-35: there is no longer any distinction between Jews and Gentiles, but all are equal in the eyes of God if they live according to God's will. This doctrine is already in the Scriptures (cf. Deut 10:17; Isa 56:1-3, 6-7). Enlightened by the Holy Spirit, Peter understands that he must welcome Cornelius and his friends into the community as they are, without obliging them to undergo conversion to Judaism. God has no favorites, makes no distinctions between Jews and Gentiles, and gives the Holy Spirit to both (4:31 and 10:44). For someone to be pleasing to God it is necessary and sufficient to have an upright heart.

That Peter would undergo a conversion after which he would "strengthen" his brothers and sisters had been foretold by Jesus himself (Luke 22:31-32). As Peter progressively absorbs the truth that Christ is risen and living with the Church in his Holy Spirit he is able to throw off older habits of thinking and acting—even those with the most respectable authority behind them—and to encourage others as well to live in a new way.

At Caesarea, Peter gives a relatively long address (vv. 36-43) that is effectively the preparation of Cornelius and his companions for baptism. The core of this catechesis repeats the points of his speech before the Sanhedrin (5:30-32), which were the essentials of the primitive kerygma. At the outset Peter declares that Jesus has been "the messenger of peace" for Israel, but is the "Lord of all" (cf. Rom 10:12-13, quoting Joel 3:5 [2:32], as does Acts 2:21). Then he reminds his listeners about the ministry of Jesus in Galilee, Judea, and Jerusalem, beginning, like our four Gospels, with the baptism preached by John. God anointed Jesus "with the Holy Spirit and with power" (cf. Luke 1:17), and he went about curing all those who were oppressed by the devil (cf. Luke 4:17-21; Isa 61:1-4). The apostles are witnesses not only to the death and resurrection of Jesus, but also to his whole wonder-working activity, the sign of the coming of the kingdom into which the Gentiles too are invited to enter by belief in Jesus and the forgiveness of sins in his name.

Once Cornelius and his friends have received the Holy Spirit (v. 44) there is no reason why they should not be baptized. God evidently considers them as belonging to the kingdom. They receive the sign and seal of their belonging.

Peter Justifies His Action: 11:1-18

The "apostles and brothers in Judea" hear of the entry into the Church of Gentiles at Caesarea (11:1). On his return to Jerusalem, Peter is reproached with having visited the uncircumcised and eaten with them, thus contracting their impurity (v. 3).

To justify his conduct Peter reports everything that has happened in Caesarea, culminating in the coming of the Spirit on the Gentiles "in the same way as it came on us in the beginning" (v. 15). God has shown that there is no longer a barrier between Jews and non-Jews by giving the Gentiles "the same gift that he gave us when we believed in the Lord Jesus Christ." He concludes, with a touch of humor: "Who was I that I could hinder God?" (v. 17).

Those who had challenged Peter are satisfied and give glory to God, saying: "Then God has given even to the Gentiles the repentance that leads to life" (v. 18). The problem will, however, recur (Acts 15).

The Origins of the Church at Antioch: 11:19-30

Luke interrupts the "Acts of Peter" to insert a condensed account of the origins of the church at Antioch (which may have been his own place of birth). The coming of the Gospel to the third city of the Roman empire is attributed to Hellenistic believers who preached with success to the Jews and also to the "Greeks," i.e., Gentiles (vv. 19-20). Barnabas was sent from Jerusalem and went to fetch Saul from Tarsus; together they spent a year teaching at Antioch (vv. 21-25). Luke remarks that it was at Antioch that the disciples were first called "Christians" (v. 26).

Prophets also came from Jerusalem, and one Agabus predicted a universal famine that, Luke remarks, occurred during the reign of the emperor Claudius (41–54 C.E.), a period in which a series of famines affected wide areas of the empire. The new church at Antioch decided to send money to their brothers and sisters in Judea as a sign of solidarity as well as a practical help, and chose Barnabas and Saul to deliver it (vv. 27-30; cf. 12:25). It is the first example we have of "inter-Church aid."

Peter Freed from Prison: 12:1-25

In the year 43 (or perhaps 44) King Agrippa I decided to persecute the newborn Church as his grandfather Herod the Great had tried to do away with the newborn Jesus. He put James the brother of John to death and imprisoned Peter, intending to condemn him to death after the feast of Passover (12:1-4). During the night before he would have been executed Peter was freed from prison by an angel (vv. 6-11). He went to the house of Mary, the mother of John Mark, where a number of believers were assembled—in the meantime the whole Church had been praying for him (v. 5)—to show that he was alive and free. Then, after giving instructions to "tell James and the brothers," Peter "went to another place" (vv. 12-17).

This episode is, of course, a perfectly good story in its own right. There are many thrilling accounts of people who have been rescued from prison and certain death, and often there is a strong element of the providential, even the miraculous, in what happens. The way this story is told points out symbolic meanings in the incident as well.

For one thing the story of Peter's deliverance from prison calls to mind the deliverance of God's people from captivity in Egypt at the Exodus. This comparison is conveyed by several elements in the narrative. Peter is arrested "during the festival of Unleavened Bread" and is to be tried in public "after the Passover" (v. 4). He is therefore set free during the time of Passover, which commemorated the freeing of the Israelites (Exod 12:42). Other details in the story can now be seen to have a meaning connected with the Exodus. The light that fills Peter's cell (v. 7) recalls the light that shone among the Israelites while the rest of Egypt lay in darkness (Exod 10:23b; compare Wis 18:1-3). The angel tells Peter: "Fasten your belt and put on your sandals" (v. 8), as the Israelites were told to eat the Paschal meal with "your loins girded, your sandals on your feet, and your staff in your hand" (Exod 12:11). That the angel leads Peter out of prison reminds the reader how "the angel of the Lord" led the Israelites out of Egypt.

Peter "was sleeping" and the angel "woke him" (vv. 6, 7). These verbs have their normal sense in the story, but the fact remains that in the NT "being asleep" is said often of the sleep of death (Matt 27:52; John 11:11; Acts 7:60; 13:36; 1 Cor 7:39; 11:30; 15:6, 18, 20, 51; 1 Thess 4:13-15). Similarly, "to awaken" frequently means to raise from the dead (Acts 3:15; 4:10; 5:30; 10:40; 13:30, 37; 26:8 and other texts). The Passover is also Easter. These verbs in the story of Peter would have reminded Christian readers of the death and resurrection of Jesus. Also the chains that bind Peter and are supernaturally loosed symbolize the chains of death, as in Ps 18:5 (compare John 11:44).

There are also contacts between the second part of the story (vv. 12-17) and the appearance of the risen Jesus to his followers in Luke 24:36-48. In both, the disciples are gathered. At first they refuse to believe that it is really Jesus or Peter. Then they think it is a spirit or an angel. Joy makes them do the opposite of what they should do: the disciples of Jesus "were disbelieving and still wondering"; the servant girl doesn't open the door. In both accounts there is more than a touch of humor.

There are further contacts with the way John tells the passion and resurrection of the Lord. In Acts 12:13-14 a woman (Rhoda) recognizes Peter by his voice and is the first to believe that he has returned; in John 20:16 a woman (Mary Magdalene) recognizes Jesus when he speaks to her and is the first to believe in his resurrection. Peter asks those who see that he is alive to "tell this to James and to the believers [lit.: brothers]" (Acts 12:17) as Jesus tells Mary Magdalene to go and give his "brothers" the news of his resurrection (John 20:17-18). So Peter is delivered from prison as Jesus from the tomb. We can now understand the puzzling phrase in v. 17, "then he left and went to another place." Its very vagueness suggests some mysterious place that is none other than the place reserved for each one in "the Father's house" (John 14:2-3). Jesus has already gone there in his ascension, but he promised to come back and take us with him, so that we might be where he is.

It is easy to see the meaning of the story of Peter's deliverance from prison in the whole of what we might call the "Acts of Peter." The first story in the book of Acts is that of the appearance of the risen Christ and his exaltation to heaven. The last story in the first part of the book evokes the theme of the death and resurrection of Christ's disciples in the person of Peter. One of the most important episodes that we have seen is that of the cure of the lame man at the Beautiful Gate of the Temple (3:1-10). This story has a symbolic meaning in reference to Isa 35:1-10, announcing a new Exodus that frees human beings from every evil. The deliverance of Peter is a new announcement of this liberation of human beings in the name of Jesus ("the Lord saves"). Peter and other disciples may "fall asleep" in death, but God will "awaken" them as he "awoke" Jesus.

Luke adds an account of the death of Agrippa I (vv. 20-23), which can be compared with that given by the Jewish historian Flavius Josephus (*Ant.* 19.8.2). This first part of Acts ends with the last summary (v. 24) recording the spread of the word of God and the return of Barnabas and Saul to Antioch, bringing with them John Mark (v. 25).

We now take up again the story of Paul, or Saul as he is at first still called, with the account of his first missionary journey. Luke probably makes use here of an earlier narrative that he develops and amplifies.

Barnabas and Saul are sent out on mission from Antioch under the inspiration of the Holy Spirit (13:1-3). The missionaries go first to Cyprus, where they meet opposition from the "magi" but convert the Roman governor (13:4-12). Paul and his companions cross over to the southern coast of Asia Minor and penetrate into the interior as far as Antioch of Pisidia, where they first preach to the Jews, then turn to the Gentiles, but are driven out of the city (13:13-52). They next go to Iconium but again, after initial success, they are forced to flee to Lystra and Derbe, cities of Lycaonia (14:1-7). In Lystra, Paul cures a man crippled from birth. He and Barnabas are taken for gods and try to convert the local people to worship of the true God, but opponents arrive from Antioch and Iconium and turn the people against them (14:8-20). From Derbe the apostles retrace their steps, strengthening the new converts and appointing elders in each church. Back at Antioch in Syria, they report to the church (14:21-28).

Barnabas and Saul Sent on Mission: 13:1-3

Luke gives us a glimpse of life in the church of Antioch, where Barnabas and Saul and three other named persons are "prophets and teachers." These are engaged in worship and fasting when the Holy Spirit, presumably through one of the prophets, asks that Barnabas and Saul be set apart "for the work to which I have called them." This is done, after fasting and prayer, by the laying on of hands, and the missionaries are sent on their way. Antioch shows itself to be a church that has not only received the Gospel but is also playing its part in the spread of the gospel.

Competition and Conflict: 13:4-12

The newly designated missionaries set out from Seleucia, the port nearest Antioch, and sail to Cyprus, arriving first at Salamis at the eastern end of the island (vv. 4-5). The choice of Cyprus as the first goal of missionary endeavor on the part of the church of Antioch can easily be explained. It was in any case Barnabas' native country (cf. 4:36), but also people from Cyprus had been among those who brought the good news to Antioch and even communicated it to Gentiles there (cf. 11:20). The church of Antioch is now engaged in a "reverse mission" helping those through whom it had originally received the faith to continue the evangelization of their own country.

In fact, at least as far as we are told Barnabas and Saul, who were assisted by John (Mark), preached only in Jewish communities (v. 5), which were very numerous on the island. Their task was not easy. Not only did they have to persuade their fellow Jews that Jesus was the Messiah, but they had rivals in the form of the "magi."

The word *magos* (from which we get our words magic and magician) originally meant a priest of the ancient Persian religion known as Zoroastrianism, but at the period of the book of Acts it could mean any practitioner of Oriental religion mixed with science or pseudo-science such as astrology. Many "magi" were charlatans, although others would have had pretensions to be men of learning. Cyprus was one of their strongholds, but Jewish magi also had a high reputation. Barnabas and Saul meet one of them, called Bar-Jesus, when they arrive in the capital Paphos at the western end of the island (v. 6). Another, called Elymas (though the present text of Acts seems to identify the two magi) opposes the missionaries who have been summoned by the Roman governor (proconsul) Sergius Paulus who wanted to hear the word of God (vv. 7-8). Paul—the Roman name by which Saul is now called for the rest of Acts—rebukes the *magos* and strikes him with temporary blindness, thus demonstrating his superior power (vv. 9-11). The proconsul, we are told, "believed" (v. 12), though we hear nothing further about his conversion.

A Message for Jews and Gentiles: 13:13–14:6

From Paphos the party, of which Paul now appears to be the head, set sail for Pamphylia on the southern coast of what is now Turkey. At Perga, John left them and went back to Jerusalem (v. 13). In fact the missionaries were not interested in Pamphylia, at least at this stage, but pushed on through difficult, mountainous country until they reached another city with the name of Antioch (v. 14). This one was usually called Antioch "of Pisidia" to distinguish it from other towns of the same name. It was the chief of a series of veteran settlements and garrison towns with which the Romans kept a check on the wild highland tribes of Pisidia. Here and in other places of this remote region, including Iconium, Lystra, and Derbe, Paul spent his first missionary endeavors.

We may well ask why he went first to such towns, which had at most only local importance, instead of going immediately to the great cities on the Aegean coast of Asia Minor such as Ephesus, Smyrna, or Pergamum. Part of the answer may lie in Paul's encounter with the Roman governor of Cyprus. Although this Sergius Paulus has not yet been identified with complete certainty, his family is well known, both from Italy where they originated and from the city and region of Antioch of Pisidia where they had estates and were local notables. It is quite possible that the proconsul of Cyprus directed Paul to his kinsfolk there. But in any case these places were important in the system of roads that assured overland communications in Asia Minor. In particular Antioch of Pisidia was the most important town on the Via Sebaste, the military road the Romans had built to connect their strongholds in this part of Asia Minor, and travelers would naturally use this road that was relatively safe and easy. Paul could have seen the strategic role that Christian communities there could play in assuring communication between his base in Syrian Antioch and the places farther west that were his ultimate goal.

At Antioch of Pisidia Paul's first concern is for the Jewish community. He and his companions go to the synagogue on the Sabbath. After the reading of the Law and the Prophets, Paul is invited to give a "word of encouragement" (vv. 14-15). The address Paul gives (vv. 16-41) is the first of three great speeches he makes in the course of his missionary career as portrayed in Acts. It can no doubt be taken as typical of many others, in this case of his preaching to Jewish audiences. In fact, in the synagogue of Antioch of Pisidia Paul was heard not only by those born Jews ("Israelites," "descendants of Abraham's family") but also by others whom he calls "those who fear God" (vv. 16 and 26). These were Gentiles who were attracted to Judaism and followed many of its beliefs and practices but had not become full converts.

The speech falls into three parts. The first part (vv. 17-25) recalls the history of Israel from the Exodus to Samuel, Saul, and David, then moves forward to David's descendant Jesus, whose coming was prepared for by John the Baptist (vv. 24-25). The second part begins solemnly at v. 26 with the proclamation that the message of salvation is meant "for you" (or "for us" in some ancient manuscripts). This message of salvation concerns the death and resurrection of Jesus (vv. 27-31), for the resurrection of Jesus proves that he is the Messiah: this is the good news that the promise made to the ancestors has been fulfilled (vv. 32-37). In the third part of the speech (vv. 38-41) Paul draws the practical consequences for his hearers: forgiveness of sins comes through Jesus (vv. 38-39). At the same time Paul warns his hearers not to be among the "scoffers" who will reject what God is doing (vv. 40-41).

This speech of Paul has important links with earlier speeches in Acts. It carries forward a narrative of the history of Israel that began in Peter's speech after curing the lame man at the Beautiful Gate of the Temple (3:25-26), was continued in Stephen's speech before the Sanhedrin (7:1-53), and now reaches its climax in Paul's proclamation of Jesus the descendant of David. Paul's argument identifying the crucified and risen Jesus as the Messiah and urging his hearers to repentance echoes Peter in his address after Pentecost (2:22-36, 37-40) as well as in his address in the Temple (3:13-26).

The death and resurrection of Jesus occupy the central place in Paul's speech at Antioch of Pisidia as in Peter's speeches earlier in Acts. The facts are recounted (with interesting variations on the story as told in the gospels) in vv. 27-31. This section corresponds to the statement of the "tradition" received by Paul and handed on by him according to 1 Cor 15:3-5—Christ died, was buried, was raised from the dead—and also to the Apostles' Creed, especially in naming Pilate. The following verses, 32-37, argue that the resurrection of Jesus proves that he is the Messiah. This argument rests on the use of biblical texts. Ps 2:7—"You are my Son; today I have begotten you"—is interpreted by Paul (v. 33) as a prophecy of the resurrection of Jesus. In Ps 16:10 (read in the ancient Greek translation) God promised that God's "Holy One" would not see corruption, a promise that was not fulfilled for David personally, but has been fulfilled for his descendant Jesus, who is therefore the Holy One referred to in the psalm (cf. 2:31-32).

The concluding proclamation (v. 38) that forgiveness of sins comes through Jesus is developed into a statement of justification by faith: through Jesus everyone who believes is set free from those sins from which they could not be freed by the Law of Moses (v. 39). By implication salvation is offered not only to the Jewish people, but to all—including Gentiles—who believe. This declaration should be compared with Paul's statements in Gal 2:16; 3:6-7, and elsewhere.

The episode of Paul at Antioch of Pisidia ends with a series of events that recur in similar form several times in Acts. His preaching—to the Jews—meets with some success and wins some converts (here from "godfearers" as well as from Jews) but the majority of Jews refuse Paul's message that Jesus is the Messiah and mobilize a campaign of opposition in the city that leads to the expulsion of Paul and his companions (vv. 42-51). Since the Jews do not believe, the apostles turn to the Gentiles, who welcome the new teaching (vv. 46-49). Paul justifies this step with a quotation of Isa 49:6, which was already alluded to in Acts 1:8. In fact, by "turning to the Gentiles" Paul does not abandon his mission to the Jews. In Acts he invariably goes first to the synagogue and on two occasions in the future he will repeat his intention of "going to the Gentiles" (cf. 18:6; 28:28).

After being driven out of Antioch Paul and Barnabas went, no doubt by the "Via Sebaste," to Iconium (modern Konya). This ancient city to the east of Antioch was the cultural and religious heart of Phrygia. We are given few details of their ministry there, but "a great number of both Jews and Greeks became believers" (14:1). However the same pattern of events was repeated at Iconium as previously at Antioch, and the missionaries were driven out (vv. 2-6).

Mistaken for Gods: 14:7-20

From Iconium Paul and Barnabas went southeast to Lystra and Derbe. The distance was not very great, but a cultural and linguistic boundary was crossed, namely between Phrygia and Lycaonia (vv. 6-7). Lystra was a much smaller town than Antioch or Iconium but had a certain importance as a Roman garrison town and veteran settlement. It was the most easterly place on the "Via Sebaste." Derbe and neighboring Laranda gave access to roads leading to Tarsus and so eventually to Syrian Antioch. So Lystra and Derbe were probably not simply chance refuges for Paul and his companions, but places where they had planned all along to establish Christian communities.

By contrast to the brief and rather colorless account of the mission in Iconium, we have a vivid narrative of Paul and Barnabas at Lystra full of lively action and colorful detail. For once there is no mention of a synagogue or of Jews in the town, and we must suppose that the missionaries find themselves in an entirely Gentile environment. Nevertheless Paul speaks in public, and what he has to say makes a deep impression on a man sitting there who was crippled from birth. Paul sees that the man has the faith to be healed and orders him to stand up, at which the lame man springs to his feet and begins to walk (vv. 8-10).

This miracle recalls Peter's cure of the lame man at the Beautiful Gate of the Temple (3:1-10). Like that healing, this one provokes public astonishment that takes a turn not at all to the apostles' liking (vv. 11-13). The crowd begins to cry out in their Lycaonian language: "The gods have come down to us in human form!" They decide that Barnabas is Zeus and Paul Hermes—not the gods of Greece, but two gods who were worshiped in the region under the names of the Greek gods and who were probably regarded as givers of life and health. It is only when they see the preparations to offer sacrifice to them that the apostles realize what is afoot. They reject these divine honors by tearing their clothes and rushing into the middle of the crowd, insisting that they too are only mortals (vv. 14-15).

It is no doubt Paul who takes the opportunity to preach the "good news" to the crowd (vv. 15-18). They should turn away from "these worthless things" to the living God who made the heaven and the earth and the sea and all that is in them. Until now God has let the nations go their own way, but is not without a witness in the bounty of nature: rain, good harvests, food and the cheerful hearts that result, all point to the one who gives them. The implication is that the cure of the lame man is a sign of God's goodness, and that the people of Lystra should give glory not to human beings or to false gods, but to the one true God.

It is a simple message well adapted for simple country folk. Paul will develop some of its themes when speaking in Athens (17:22-31). The central message, to turn from false gods to serve a living and true God, was at the heart of Paul's preaching at Thessalonica (1 Thess 1:9). That God's eternal power and divine nature, though invisible, can be seen through the things that God has made is one of Paul's arguments in his letter to the Romans (Rom 1:20).

Even so the enthusiastic crowd can hardly be restrained from offering sacrifice (v. 18). But crowds are notoriously fickle, and this one was no exception. When Jewish opponents of Paul came from Antioch and Iconium they won over the people of Lystra, who stoned Paul. The next day he and Barnabas went on their way to Derbe (vv. 19-20).

Return to Base: 14:21-28

All we are told about the mission at Derbe is that the apostles "proclaimed the good news to that city . . . and made many disciples" (v. 21). As at Lystra there is no mention of Jews resident at Derbe, so presumably these converts were Gentiles. This time there is no opposition to the missionaries, who leave Derbe in their own good time.

Paul and his companions retrace their steps through Lystra, Iconium, and Antioch of Pisidia. In each place they have left communities of disciples whom they now strengthen and encourage.

Perhaps the new believers were dismayed at the ill treatment of the apostles or have even experienced persecution themselves. In any case the missionaries tell them that it is through many sufferings that we must enter the reign of God. They also see to the future pastoral care of these new churches by appointing in each one "elders" (or presbyters) on whom they lay hands. They take their leave after prayer and fasting, commending the new believers to the Lord (vv. 21-23).

From Antioch of Pisidia the apostles return to the southern coast of Asia Minor. They pass through Pisidia and Pamphylia, stopping this time to "speak the word" in Perga, until they reach the port of Attalia (modern Andalya) where they take ship (vv. 24-25). On arrival at Syrian Antioch, whence they had set out on this great missionary journey, they report to the church all that God has done through them, and how God has "opened a door of faith" for the Gentiles. The narrative concludes by informing us that they stayed at Antioch for some time (vv. 26-28).

> That God should have "opened a door of faith" for the Gentiles was not without its problems for Paul. Luke deals with them in his account of the "Council of Jerusalem" which takes up most of chapter 15 of the book of Acts. This is not the first time in Acts that we have heard of the questions posed by the reception of Gentiles into the Church. At the same time this is not the only place in the NT that tells how Paul met with the leaders of the church in Jerusalem to discuss some of these questions. In composing his narrative of the "Council of Jerusalem" Luke seems to make use both of an earlier account that continued the story of the aftermath of the conversion of Cornelius (cf. 11:1-18), and also of Paul's own recollections of his meeting in Jerusalem (cf. Gal 2:1-10).

Controversy at Antioch: 15:1-5

The previous episode ended with Paul and Barnabas once again at Antioch, where they remained for some time (cf. 14:28). We recall too that at Antioch the gospel had been preached to Gentiles (cf. 11:20). Now "some people" come to Antioch from Judea (i.e., from Jerusalem), and teach that the male Gentile believers must be circumcised, which stirred up no little controversy in the church of Antioch (vv. 1-2). Luke may be referring here to Gal 2:12, where Paul recalls the division caused in the church of Antioch when "some people" came from James (i.e., from Jerusalem) and apparently demanded that Jewish Christians should stop sharing meals—no doubt including the Eucharist—with Christians of Gentile origin, an act by which they were breaking the Jewish rules of ritual purity. One way of solving this problem was, of course, to circumcise all Christian males.

It was agreed that Paul and Barnabas and "some others" should go up to Jerusalem and discuss the question with the "apostles and elders" (v. 2). Luke probably has in mind Gal 2:1, where Paul writes that he went up to Jerusalem with Barnabas, and also Titus (who, however, is never mentioned in Acts). He was not greatly concerned by the fact that, according to Paul himself, this was only his second visit to Jerusalem since his conversion, whereas in Acts it is his third (cf. 9:26-30; 11:30).

The delegates from Antioch travel through Phoenicia and Samaria, telling as they go of the conversion of the Gentiles (whether at Antioch or in Asia Minor is not clear) to the great joy of all. On arrival in Jerusalem they are received by the church and by the apostles and elders, to whom they announce "what God has done with them" (vv. 3-4). All seems to be serene until some Pharisees who have become believers repeat the demand that male Gentiles be circumcised and the law of Moses observed (v. 5).

The "Council of Jerusalem": 15:6-12

At this the apostles and elders meet in what is portrayed by Luke as a solemn assembly that is frequently regarded as the first Church council (v. 6). Paul's recollection is rather of a meeting between the delegates from Antioch and what he calls the "pillars" of the Jerusalem church, James, Cephas (Peter), and John (cf. Gal 2:2, 9). They agreed that Paul and his companions should take responsibility for the mission to the Gentiles while the others saw to the mission to the Jews. This agreement founded the partnership between the apostles Peter and Paul, which was sealed in their blood. This partnership is central to the message Luke wishes to convey in Acts. It gave shape to Catholic-Apostolic Christianity, to the NT, and to the Church.

According to Luke's account of the Jerusalem assembly Peter rose to his feet and made a speech (vv. 7-11) in which the issue of circumcision of male Gentile believers is not mentioned but which, in the context, implies that it would place an unnecessary burden on them. His words silence the assembly (v. 12), and in fact circumcision is not mentioned again. Similarly, Paul tells us that his companion Titus, though a Gentile convert, was not compelled to be circumcised by the "pillars" of the Jerusalem church, but that he himself had to resist those who wished to "bring us into slavery" (Gal 2:3-4).

When we read the speech of Peter more closely we see that it really refers back to the episode of Cornelius and belongs to the controversy that greeted Peter's return in 11:1-18. Peter recalls (v. 7) that it was through him that, by God's choice, the Gentiles first heard the word of the gospel and believed (cf. 10:36-43). He also reminds his listeners (v. 8) how God had given the Spirit to the Gentiles "as to us" (cf. 10:44-45). He repeats (v. 9) his own earlier declaration that God makes no difference between Jews and Gentiles (cf. 10:34-35), and adds that God purified the Gentiles' hearts by faith. He concludes by declaring that it is "through the grace of Our Lord Jesus Christ that we (Jews) are saved as are they" (v. 11). Peter here speaks like Paul (cf. Gal 2:16). The reader is left in no doubt as to the unity of teaching between the two great apostles. The assembly then listened to Barnabas and Paul telling of the great things that God had done through them among the Gentiles (v. 12).

James' Proposal: 15:13-21

At this point James rose to speak. This was the "brother of the Lord" and the first of the "pillars" named by Paul (Gal 1:19; 2:9). He implicitly endorsed what Peter had said and quoted the prophet Amos (9:11-12) to prove that in the designs of God, once Israel had been restored, the rest of humanity would look for the Lord (vv. 13-16).

James too is opposed to "disturbing" those Gentiles who have turned to God (v. 19). On the other hand he is not in favor of letting them continue to live exactly as they had before. He proposes to write telling them to "abstain . . . from things polluted by idols and from fornication and from whatever has been strangled and from blood" (v. 20; the Western text omits the mention of meat that has been strangled). James' concluding reference to Moses (v. 21) shows the origin of his proposal.

The book of Leviticus includes a number of commandments that are to be observed not only by "the house of Israel" but also by foreigners resident among the Israelites in order to preserve the holiness of Israel. Chief among these is the commandment that sacrifice is to be offered only to YHWH and not to any false god (Lev 17:1-9). Next comes the commandment not to consume the blood of any creature, since life is in the blood and belongs exclusively to the Giver of life (Lev 17:10-14). Similarly both Israelites and foreigners will become unclean if they eat the flesh of an animal that has died a natural death or been savaged (Lev 17:15-16). As for "fornication," this term covers all the forms of unlawful sexual union that are prohibited in Leviticus 18 and are forbidden to Israelites and to foreigners alike.

These commandments and others like them were known to later Jewish tradition as the "Noahide commandments," regarded as given by God to the sons of Noah (cf. Gen 8:20; 9:4-5) and so binding on the whole human race. In imposing them on Gentile members of the Church James implicitly assigns to Gentile Christians the status of "resident aliens" who are not Israelites and not bound to observe the whole Law of Moses but are obliged to keep certain commandments—which are neither simply "moral" nor simply "ritual"—if they are to associate with the house of Israel. In particular by abstaining from sexual uncleanness and from unclean food Gentiles would avoid the principal sources of impurity with which they might contaminate Jews. Thus would be removed what, in Jewish eyes, was an obstacle to the sharing of meals, including the Eucharist, by Jews and Gentiles. The Gentiles would be required to conform to certain provisions of Jewish law, but not to undergo male circumcision.

The "Jerusalem Decree": 15:22-35

Then the apostles and elders "with the consent of the whole church" decided to choose delegates, Judas called Barsabbas and Silas, to send to Antioch with Paul and Barnabas bearing a letter (vv. 22-23). The letter (vv. 23-29) is addressed from "the brothers, both the apostles and the elders" to "the believers of Gentile origin in Antioch and Syria and Cilicia." The church of Jerusalem first disowns those who had disturbed the minds of people at Antioch: they had no mandate from Jerusalem. Then is recorded the meeting in Jerusalem with its decision to send Judas and Silas, along with Barnabas and Paul, to convey the message of the Jerusalem authorities. "For it has seemed good to the Holy Spirit and us to impose on you no further burden than these essentials: that you abstain from what has been sacrificed to idols and from blood and from what is strangled and from fornication" (vv. 28-29). If they keep these things they will do well.

The "Jerusalem decree" shows a complete confidence that the authorities of the Church have acted with the concurrence of the Holy Spirit (cf. Matt 18:18). The first prohibition—to abstain from food offered to idols—is more specific than the original proposal of James. The situation supposed by the decree was one of daily practicality: most meat sold in ancient cities had been killed in the temples as part of the ritual of sacrifice. The Jerusalem decree prohibits its consumption by Gentile Christians as involving participation in the idol worship. The Western text of v. 29 once again omits the mention of strangled meat but adds: "whatever you do not wish to be done to yourselves, do not do to others." This version interprets the decree in a moral rather than a ritual sense as prohibiting the three capital sins of idolatry, murder ("blood"), and adultery, and summing up "the Law and the Prophets" in the golden rule (cf. Matt 7:12).

On reflection we may find it surprising that according to Luke this decree was accepted by all who took part in the assembly, presumably including Paul, who is explicitly mentioned along with Barnabas (v. 22), and is also portrayed a little later as strengthening the churches in Syria and Cilicia along with Silas (16:4). The letter to the Ephesians (2:11-22) explicitly rejects any idea that Gentiles in the Church have the status of "resident aliens," as the decree implies, but insists that they are full citizens. Again, the implication that the Gentiles must take specific measures to avoid impurity does not go so well with Peter's statement (v. 9) that God had purified the Gentiles' hearts by faith, or with Paul's (Gal 2:16) that a person is not justified by "the works of the Law" but by faith in Jesus Christ. Again, in his own account of the meeting in Jerusalem, Paul makes no mention of the decree, and according to Gal 2:11-14 he protested vigorously against the attempt to make the Gentiles at Antioch "live like Jews."

On the other hand Paul had to concern himself with some of the issues dealt with by the Jerusalem decree. In his first letter to the Corinthians he is much occupied by the question of food offered to idols (1 Cor 8:1-13), and in the same letter the case of incest he denounces (1 Cor 5:1-13) is of a type specifically forbidden by the book of Leviticus (Lev 18:8). Some early Christian writings, including Rev 2:14 and 20, show that certain of the provisions contained in the Jerusalem decree were widely accepted and observed in the Church.

The delegates duly delivered the message of the "Council of Jerusalem" to the church of Antioch in solemn assembly. The letter was read out and found to be a source of encouragement and joy (vv. 30-31). Judas and Silas continued to exercise a prophetic ministry, strengthening and encouraging those at Antioch until the time came for Judas to return to Jerusalem, while Silas remained (vv. 32-33). In the meantime Paul and Barnabas with others were teaching and proclaiming the word of the Lord (v. 35).

> Paul's second missionary journey is recounted in Acts 15:36–18:22. At the outset Paul and Barnabas separate, and Paul leaves Antioch with Silas (15:36-40). Together they travel through Syria and Cilicia, then revisit the places in Asia Minor that Paul had evangelized with Barnabas in his previous journey (15:41–16:5). However, instead of continuing to preach the gospel in Asia Minor the missionaries are directed by the Holy Spirit to go to the coast and cross over to Macedonia (16:6-10). The greatest part of this section of Acts is taken up with Paul's missionary campaign in what is now Greece: Philippi (16:11-40), Thessalonica (17:1-9), Beroea (17:10-15), Athens (17:16-34), and Corinth (18:1-17). From Corinth Paul goes briefly to Ephesus in the course of his return journey to Antioch (18:18-22).

A New Journey: 15:36–16:10

After continuing the ministry at Antioch for a while Paul proposed to Barnabas that they should revisit the communities they had established on their previous missionary expedition. Barnabas agreed but wanted to take along John

Mark. Paul refused on the ground that John Mark had left them in Pamphylia (15:36-38; cf. 13:13). This difference of opinion became so sharp that the former colleagues decided to go their separate ways (a division that may echo the one mentioned by Paul in Gal 2:13). Barnabas returned to Cyprus, taking Mark, who was his cousin (cf. Col 4:10), while Paul set out with Silas who had previously come to Antioch from Jerusalem (vv. 39-40; cf. 15:22).

Paul and Silas went through Syria and neighboring Cilicia, strengthening the churches there and promulgating the decree of the "Council of Jerusalem" (15:41 in the "western text"). They went on to Derbe and Lystra where they came across Timothy, whose mother was Jewish and a believer in Jesus, but whose father was a Greek; he himself had a good reputation among the Christians of Lystra and Iconium (16:1-3). Paul decided that he was suitable to be a member of the missionary team, and since like his father Timothy was a Gentile, had him circumcised so that he would be acceptable to the Jewish communities in which they would be preaching the gospel (the current rule according to which the child of a Jewish mother is Jewish does not seem to have been in force at this period). On the other hand Paul resisted pressure to have Titus circumcised as a condition of belonging to the Church (cf. Gal 2:3-5). Once again, we read, the missionaries told the Christian communities, which were growing in faith and in numbers, to observe the Jerusalem decree (vv. 4-5), which Luke clearly regards as the basis of unity between Jews and Gentiles.

Paul and his companions passed through "the Phrygian and Galatian" region (v. 6a). This expression probably refers to such places as Iconium and Antioch of Pisidia, scenes of the earlier missionary effort, that belonged to the linguistic region of Phrygia but were part of the Roman province called Galatia. (Others think that it refers to an advance into Galatia proper, which was farther to the north.) In any case Paul no doubt intended to extend his evangelizing campaign to other parts of Asia Minor, and in particular to the most westerly part, historically called Asia, where the great cities of Ephesus, Pergamum, and Smyrna were to be found. The Holy Spirit, however, had other plans, and forbade Paul to speak the word of God in Asia (v. 6b). The missionaries turned north in the direction of Bithynia on the southern coast of the Black Sea, but again the Spirit of Jesus did not allow this course (v. 7). The only path open to Paul was westward through Mysia to the Aegean coast at Troas, a busy port at the hub of communications between Asia and Europe. There he had a vision that made it clear that God wanted him to preach the gospel in Macedonia (vv. 8-10).

A Happy Encounter: 16:11-15

At this point the story begins to be told in the first person plural ("we"), that is, it gives the impression that it is being related by someone who was a companion of Paul on this stage of his journey. The group sailed from Troas making for the landmark island of Samothrace, and in two days came to the port of Neapolis (now Kavalla). From there they continued by road to Philippi (vv. 11-12). Philippi is correctly described by the Western text of v. 12 as "a city of the first district of Macedonia and a (Roman) colony." It was not the capital of the province but had a certain status as a town settled by Roman citizens. More important, it held the key to land communications between Europe and the Aegean by way of the great road called the Via Egnatia, and in 42 B.C.E. it had been the scene of a decisive battle for mastery of the Roman world.

On the Sabbath Paul and his companions went to the Jewish place of prayer outside the city beside a watercourse where they found a group of women, including Lydia, a dealer in cloth dyed in purple who came from Thyatira, which was a center of the trade in Asia Minor. She was a "godfearer," and the Lord opened her heart to receive the message that Paul spoke. After being baptized along with all her household she offered hospitality to the missionaries (vv. 13-15).

An Exorcism and Its Consequences: 11:16-40

The missionaries' next encounter at Philippi led to trouble. They were accosted by a slave girl who was possessed by a spirit that could reveal secrets and foretell the future through the mouth of the girl, to the financial profit of the girl's owners. Paul drove out the spirit from the girl, an action that her owners, rather understandably, did not take kindly. They seized Paul and Silas—the "we" style quietly disappears at this point—

and dragged them to the forum before the magistrates, denouncing the missionaries as Jews who were trying to subvert the good old Roman ways of the town. The magistrates administered the usual summary punishment for those found to be disturbing the peace: Paul and Silas were beaten with rods and put in jail for the night (vv. 16-24).

Originally, it seems, the story continued immediately with vv. 35-40. Next morning the magistrates sent their officers ("lictors"), who had administered the beating, to release the troublemakers and order them to leave the city. Paul, however, had a surprise for them (and for the readers of Acts). He announced that he and Silas were Roman citizens. They had been beaten and imprisoned without due trial and sentence—an altogether improper mishandling of Roman citizens—and were not now going to slink away from Philippi in disgrace. Let the magistrates come in person and release them. On hearing that the prisoners were Roman citizens who might take their complaint to higher authorities the magistrates came, begged their pardon, but asked them—politely, it is true—to leave their city. Paul and Silas complied after returning briefly to the house of Lydia.

If that was the original narrative in Luke's source it would have been Luke who introduced the interlude (vv. 25-34) that takes place during the night Paul and Silas spend in the prison at Philippi. While the apostles are praying and singing hymns an earthquake shakes the foundation of the building, the doors open of their own accord, and the chains fall from all the prisoners. Similar things happen in other well-known stories, notably in a play, the *Bacchae,* by the ancient Greek dramatist Euripides, and like the deliverance of Peter from prison (cf. 12:6-19) this episode too recalls the resurrection of Jesus. The jailer supposes that his prisoners have escaped and prepares to commit suicide but is restrained by Paul who assures him that all are still there. The jailer is so impressed by the whole event that he takes Paul and Silas out of the prison and asks them what he must do to be saved, to which he is told, "believe in the Lord Jesus." The apostles take the opportunity to preach the word of the Lord to the jailer and all who are in his house. There and then, during the night, the jailer washes the missionaries' wounds, he and his household are baptized, and a table (the Eucharist?) is set. The night in prison has become a sort of Easter vigil.

Riot and Expulsions: 17:1-15

From Philippi, Paul and Silas proceed along the Via Egnatia through Amphipolis and Apollonia to Thessalonica, the capital of the Roman province of Macedonia. The city had a synagogue and for three consecutive Sabbaths Paul tried to persuade the Jews, by "opening" the Scriptures, that it was necessary for the Messiah to suffer and to rise from the dead, and that this Messiah was Jesus (vv. 1-3; cf. Luke 24:45-46). Some believed and joined Paul and Silas, as did a great number of Gentile "godfearers" and some women of the upper classes (v. 4).

Other Jews who oppose Paul rouse the rabble to create a public disturbance and go to the house of Jason, one of the new believers, where they suppose the missionaries to be. Not finding them there, they drag Jason and others before the city magistrates, who are correctly given the title of "politarchs" (city magistrates) (vv. 5-6). The missionaries are alleged to be revolutionaries ("turning the world [or the empire] upside down"), acting against the emperor by proclaiming another king, namely Jesus the Messiah (v. 7; cf. Luke 23:2).

These are extremely serious charges that, if substantiated, would carry the death penalty, but despite initial alarm the magistrates only make Jason give caution money for his guests' good behavior (vv. 8-9). Perhaps Luke has combined two stories, one about the denunciation of Paul as a revolutionary by some of his fellow Jews and the other about the persecution of his converts by their fellow citizens (cf. 1 Thess 2:14).

According to our narrative, Paul and Silas are smuggled out of Thessalonica by night. They go to Beroea, which was not on the Via Egnatia but was an important town, since it was the chief of the union of Greek cities in Macedonia. Once again they frequent the synagogue and this time meet with an excellent reception from the Jewish community, who eagerly receive the missionaries' message and search the Scriptures daily to verify it. Many believe, including Gentile women and men who were presumably "godfearers" (vv. 10-12).

It was too good to last. Jews from Thessalonica who heard that Paul was preaching at Beroea came and created a public disturbance (v. 13). His disciples spirited him out of the city in the direction of the coast, while Silas and Timothy remained (v. 14). Paul's escorts finally brought him—by sea, it seems—as far as Athens, then returned with the message that Silas and Timothy should join him as quickly as possible (v. 15).

An Appeal to Greek Philosophy: 17:16-34

The Athens Paul visited was living on the memory of past political and cultural glory. Luke, in recounting this episode, shows himself sensitive to the special associations of Athens and knowledgeable about places in the city. When Luke describes Athens as a city "full of statues of the gods" (v. 16), and the Athenians as always eager to hear something new (v. 21) and "very religious" because of their many altars to various divinities (v. 22) he is echoing other ancient authors. Much of the action can be located quite precisely in the great public area at the heart of the city known as the Agora, especially its northwestern corner where were to be found both the "painted stoa [or portico]," a favorite meeting place for philosophical discussion, and the "royal stoa" where the Council of the Areopagus held its regular meetings. On the other hand we have not so far found precise evidence of an altar bearing a dedication "to an unknown god" even though there were altars "of unknown gods" in and near Athens.

Paul is portrayed by Luke somewhat as a second Socrates, who taught and died at Athens in the fifth century B.C.E. Like Socrates, Paul engages in debate with all comers in the Agora as well as with Jews and "godfearers" in the synagogue (v. 17). He attracts the attention of philosophers who belonged to the two schools then dominant, the Epicureans and the Stoics, the latter taking their name from the "painted stoa." Some accuse him of picking up secondhand opinions while others say he is introducing new gods (Jesus and Anastasis or "Resurrection"), which was one of the charges brought against Socrates (v. 18). They bring him before the governing body of Athens, the council named after the Areopagus ("hill of Ares [or Mars]"), in order to find out more.

Paul takes the opportunity to expound his teaching to the philosophers and leading politicians of Athens (vv. 22-31). This is the second of his great speeches in Acts, this time to a Greek audience. The message he has to bring to the Greek world is that there is only one God and this God has raised Jesus from the dead and appointed him to judge the world, so that all should now turn from their old ways. The foolishness of nature worship or idol worship is a dominant theme in the book of Wisdom (e.g., chapter 13; cf. also Isa 44:9-20). Greek philosophy also had concluded that there can be only one truly divine being, so in this first part of his speech Paul was, as it were, preaching to the converted. A sharp reaction greets his reference to the resurrection of the dead, which Greek opinion could not admit. Some laugh out loud, others say "we will hear you again some time," and only a few believe, including Dionysius the Areopagite and a woman named Damaris (vv. 32-34).

Paul's speech is in fact well adapted to his audience and circumstances. Although it is relatively brief it is constructed according to the rules of Greek rhetoric. He first gets his audience on his side, suggesting that the God whom he preaches is not a new divinity but the one whom the Athenians have been unknowingly worshiping all along (vv. 22-23). He then sets out the facts his hearers are likely to admit (vv. 24-26): this God is the creator of the universe and of the human race, does not dwell in temples (cf. Isa 66:1-2; Acts 7:48-49), and has no need of sacrifices (cf. Ps 50:10-13). Next comes his central argument (vv. 27-28): it is for human beings to seek and find the God in whom we "live and move and have our being." Now follows the moral consequence (v. 29): we must give up the worship of idols. Finally comes the practical action Paul's hearers are exhorted to take (vv. 30-31): to "be converted." Paul cannot quote the Scriptures as an authority supporting his argument as he could with an audience of Jews and "godfearers," but he makes a comparable use of a quotation from the Greek poet Aratus: "For we too are his offspring" (v. 28). The speech shows an amazing openness to Paul's audience and a readiness to accept the best in their culture and philosophy as already a "preparation for the gospel."

Debates and Accusations: 18:1-17

From Athens Paul goes to Corinth, a great center of commerce with corresponding wealth and luxury, and capital of the province of Achaia. There he joins forces with a Jewish couple, Aquila and Priscilla, who had recently come from Italy. Luke connects their departure from Italy with the expulsion of "all the Jews" (in reality probably only some) from Rome under the Emperor Claudius, an event that can probably be dated to 41 (vv. 1-3).

Paul is shown debating in the synagogue, eventually with the assistance of Silas and Timothy who have come from Macedonia (vv. 4-5; cf. 17:15). He meets with vehement opposition and is moved to declare, with a gesture disclaiming further responsibility, that their blood is upon their own heads and he is clean of it (cf. Ezek 33:1-9). He says he will go to the Gentiles, whereupon he goes to live in the house of a "godfearer" (vv. 6-7). Despite the hostility of some in the synagogue we are told that Crispus, the leader of the Jewish community, became a believer together with all his household (cf. 1 Cor 1:14), and that many others believed and were baptized (v. 8). Paul is sustained by a vision and stays eighteen months at Corinth (vv. 9-11).

The only episode at Corinth of which we are informed in some detail took place "while Gallio was proconsul of Achaia" (vv. 12-17). Gallio is a well-known historical figure, brother of the philosopher Seneca, and was proconsul of Achaia in 51–52. Paul's opponents among the Jews denounce him on a vague charge of persuading people to worship God contrary to the law, which they hope that Gallio will consider as a crime or a misdemeanor. The proconsul, however, expressing an aristocratic Roman's contempt for the Jews (certainly including Paul) refuses to take notice of quarrels concerning "names and your own law" and drives them all away from the tribunal. At this Paul's accusers vent their frustration on the leader of the synagogue, Sosthenes.

Paul Returns to Antioch: 18:18-23

The time comes for Paul to leave Corinth for Syria and he sets sail, along with Priscilla and Aquila, from the port of Cenchreae on the Aegean, after first shaving his head in fulfillment of a vow (v. 18). On the way he calls at Ephesus where his discussions in the synagogue earn an invitation from the Jewish community to stay longer. Paul refuses but promises to return (vv. 19-21; the Western text specifies that Paul wants to be in Jerusalem for a forthcoming feast [Pentecost, cf. 20:16] and that Priscilla and Aquila stay on at Ephesus). From Ephesus he sails to Caesarea, goes up "to Jerusalem and greet[s] the church," then returns to Antioch (v. 22).

Acts 18:23–21:17 comprises what is generally known as Paul's third missionary journey. In fact it consists for the most part of an account of Paul's activities at Ephesus (19:1-40), one of the most important cities of the Roman East, where Paul spent a total of between two and three years (cf. 19:10 and 20:31). We have already seen that Paul had made a previous visit to Ephesus (cf. 18:19-21), and it is possible that in chapter 19 Luke includes material that originally related to several different periods.

Apollos: 18:23-28

In 18:23 and 19:1 we have an extremely compressed account of Paul's journey overland to Ephesus. These two verses serve to frame an interlude (18:24-28) concerning Apollos, who is mentioned several times in Paul's letters (1 Cor 3:4-6; 16:12; Titus 3:13). Apollos is introduced as a Jew from Alexandria who is learned and eloquent, "powerful" in the Scriptures, that is, able to interpret their true "spiritual" sense. He has been instructed in the word of the Lord, is "fervent in the Spirit," and can speak and teach accurately "the things concerning Jesus" he had learned from belonging to the movement of reform preached by John the Baptist ("the baptism of John"). On coming to Ephesus he speaks out boldly in the synagogue where he is heard by Priscilla and Aquila who take him aside and expound "the Way" to him more accurately (vv. 24-26). When Apollos later goes to Corinth he is able to demonstrate to the Jews through the Scriptures that the Messiah is Jesus (vv. 27-28). This was apparently the new element to which he was introduced by Priscilla and Aquila, and that transformed him from a follower of Jesus the teacher into a believer in, and preacher of, Jesus the Messiah. In a similar way the disciples on the road to Emmaus (Luke 24:13-35) had believed that Jesus was a "prophet" until they understood from the Scriptures that "the Messiah had to suffer these things and so enter into his glory."

Paul Returns to Ephesus: 19:1-20

At this point Paul returns to Ephesus (v. 1)—under the direction of the Spirit, according to the Western text. He asks "the disciples" (or, according to the Alexandrian text, "some disciples whom he finds") there whether they received the Spirit when they became believers. They reply that they did not even know there was a Holy Spirit—which does not mean they were ignorant of the existence of the Spirit of God, but that they did not know about the charismatic gifts of the Spirit (v. 2). In fact, like Apollos when he came to Ephesus they had received John's "baptism of repentance" (vv. 3-4a). Paul reminds them that John had told the people to believe in the one who was to come after him, namely Jesus. Presumably, since they are called "disciples" (and not "disciples of John") they already have some knowledge of Jesus. At any rate a further step is called for, and on hearing Paul's words they are baptized "in the name" of Jesus (vv. 4-5). Then Paul lays hands on them, and they receive the gifts of tongues and prophecy (v. 6). The resemblance to the first Pentecost is underlined by the remark that they were twelve in number (v. 7).

Once again Paul goes to the synagogue where for three months he debates about "the kingdom of God." Those who oppose him speak ill of "the Way" (cf. 18:26) to those outside the synagogue—that is, to Gentiles. Paul's response to this denunciation on the part of his fellow Jews is to take his disciples away from the synagogue to a public lecture hall known as "the hall of Tyrannus" where he held daily discussions—during the siesta hours, the Western text specifies. This was his activity for two years, we are told, and the word of the Lord spread throughout the region ("Asia") among both Jews and Gentiles (vv. 8-10).

Paul also gained a reputation as a wonder worker, and even cloths that had touched his body could work cures (vv. 11-12; cf. Acts 5:15; 14:3; 1 Cor 2:4). Exorcists drove out evil spirits "by the Jesus whom Paul proclaims" (v. 13), although one attempt to do so went badly awry (vv. 14-16).

These manifestations of divine power made a great impression on the inhabitants of Ephesus (v. 17). One result was the renunciation of magical practices and the burning of books of spells, for which Ephesus was famous (vv. 18-19). Once again, we are told, "the word of the LORD grew mightily and prevailed" (v. 20).

Paul's Plans: 19:21-22

Paul now proposed "in the Spirit" to cross over to Macedonia and Achaia, and from there to go to Jerusalem and on to Rome (v. 21). This itinerary corresponds to plans about which Paul wrote several times in his letters (Rom 15:22-32; 1 Cor 16:1-8). The occasion for this journey was the collection Paul asked the churches with which he was associated to make for the benefit of the church of Jerusalem (cf. 2 Cor 8–9). To prepare for it Paul sent Timothy and Erastus (cf. Rom 16:23) to Macedonia, while he remained in Asia (v. 22). It is one of the puzzles of Acts that despite Luke's obvious interest in everything that promotes the unity of the Church the collection is never mentioned, unless perhaps in 24:17.

The Silversmiths' Riot: 19:23-40

Meanwhile Luke gives us one of the great scenes in the Acts of the Apostles, which he introduces as "no little public disturbance [that] broke out concerning the Way" (v. 23). It was instigated by a certain Demetrius, a leading member of the guild of manufacturers of silver objects, which was an important trade at Ephesus. He himself made silver models of the temple of Artemis (Diana), who was the chief divinity of Ephesus, her temple being numbered among the seven wonders of the world. Paul's preaching against the worship of images was threatening not only his income and that of his fellow artisans, but the prestige of the temple of Artemis and the cult of the goddess, and so the prosperity of her city, which was a center of pilgrimage and for which the temple served also as a bank. Once again Luke implies a connection between false religion and financial profit (cf. 8:18-24; 16:16-21).

Demetrius easily stirs up his fellow members of the guild who raise the cry: "Great is Artemis of the Ephesians!" (vv. 24-28). The whole city is thrown into turmoil and the population begins to move toward the theater, which was the usual place of popular assembly, taking with them Gaius and Aristarchus from Macedonia, who were companions of Paul (v. 29).

Paul wanted to go to the assembly, no doubt to speak, but his followers would not allow it, and certain leading citizens of Ephesus (referred to by their title of "Asiarch") who had befriended him sent a message that on no account should he go to the theater (vv. 30-31). Meanwhile in the theater things were getting ever more confused. The Jews put forward a certain Alexander, who was about to address the assembly when he was recognized as a Jew, upon which the whole crowd took up the acclamation: "Great is Artemis of the Ephesians!" continuing for two hours (vv. 32-34). Finally the town clerk, who was in fact the chief magistrate of the city, quieted the crowd: Nobody, he said, doubted the privileges of Ephesus as custodian of the worship of the statue of Artemis "that fell from heaven" (perhaps a reference to a meteorite that was the original object of worship). There is no need for the people to be agitated. Gaius and Aristarchus are not guilty of sacrilege or blasphemy against the goddess, and if Demetrius and his fellow silversmiths have anything else against them they should bring it to the regular courts or to the Roman governor, the proconsul of Asia. Any other matter should be dealt with in a regular assembly. Disorderly gatherings like this one risk being regarded (by the Roman authorities) as seditious. With that he dismisses the assembly (vv. 35-40).

Paul in Macedonia and Greece: 20:1-4

After the "tumult" had died down Paul sent for the disciples and after encouraging them he embraced them and set out for Macedonia (v. 1). He passed through that province, speaking as he went, and came to "Greece" (v. 2). After he had spent three months there he decided to go back through Macedonia (v. 3—according to the Western text, at the prompting of the Spirit). Verse 4 gives the names of those who accompanied Paul on his journey, most of whom can be identified with greater or less probability with persons known from the Pauline correspondence. Some occur elsewhere in Acts. They are often taken to be representatives of communities that have contributed to the collection for Jerusalem.

Paul now begins his journey to Jerusalem. This journey—like that of Jesus in Luke's Gospel—occupies a large part of Acts (20:5–21:17). Again like that of Jesus, Paul's journey to Jerusalem is punctuated by prophecies of the sufferings that await him there. Nevertheless, like his Lord, Paul resolutely goes on his way.

At this point in the story the "we" style reappears—at Philippi (v. 6), where it previously left off (cf. 16:17). The narrative that follows, which is couched in the first person plural, may be taken as, at least in the main, the eyewitness account of a companion of Paul on, it seems, the journey with the collection from Macedonia and Achaia to Jerusalem. It appears to be taken from a shipboard diary or log that minutely records the stages of the journey, ports of call, distances, and some incidents on the way.

The Night at Troas: 20:5-12

According to vv. 5-6 the companions named in v. 4 waited at Troas for Paul and the diarist, who sailed from Philippi (i.e., from Neapolis) after the days of Unleavened Bread (Passover) and came in five days to Troas (the journey in the opposite direction had taken only two days: cf. 16:11). There they spent seven days.

At Troas the group passed the night of the first day of the week in vigil with the local Christian community, listening to Paul speaking. The assembly was interrupted by the fall of Eutychus from the third floor, but when he was found to be living Paul "broke bread" and continued speaking until dawn, when he departed (vv. 7-12). This story is told with clear overtones recalling the resurrection of Christ and associating it with the Eucharist. As Paul himself wrote, every time we eat "this bread" and drink "this cup" we proclaim the death of the Lord until he comes (1 Cor 11:26). It also gives us a certain insight into the liturgy as practiced by at least some of the first Christians.

Paul's Spiritual Testament: 20:13-38

From Troas the others embark for Assos, where Paul rejoins them. The vessel carries on to Mitylene, chief city of the island of Lesbos, then arrives the following day off the island of Chios. Two days later they touch at Samos, the large island that lies a little to the southeast of Ephesus. The following day the travelers arrive at Miletus. Paul had decided not to call at Ephesus as he was hurrying to arrive in Jerusalem for Pentecost (vv. 13-16).

From Miletus, Paul sent for the elders of the church at Ephesus to come to him (v. 17). There follows the long address of farewell Paul makes to them, the third of his important speeches in Acts. It serves as his spiritual testament (vv. 18-35). Paul is concerned for the welfare of the new Christian community after he himself has disappeared from the scene and wishes to give a last instruction to its pastors. The tone of the speech is deeply personal, a little somber, but full of affection and tenderness.

Paul first recalls his ministry at Ephesus during three years (vv. 18-21), then looks ahead to the completion of his journey to Jerusalem and more generally to an unknown future (vv. 22-24). He declares that he is innocent of the blood of those of his own people who have refused to accept his message (vv. 25-27; cf. Ezek 33:7-9). He charges the elders to watch over the flock the Holy Spirit has entrusted to their pastoral care (v. 28; cf. 1 Pet 5:1-2); he foresees that ravening wolves (i.e., teachers of error) will invade the flock (vv. 29-30; cf. Matt 7:15; 2 Tim 4:3-5), and bids the shepherds to be watchful and to bear in mind all that Paul himself has taught them (v. 31; cf. 1 Tim 1:3-7; 4:1-7). Finally the apostle commends the elders to God (v. 32) and declares his own freedom from self-interest in all his dealings with them (vv. 33-35; cf. 1 Sam 12:2-5; 1 Thess 4:11; 1 Cor 4:12). At the end Paul quotes an otherwise unknown saying of the Lord Jesus: "It is more blessed to give than to receive."

At this point Paul kneels and prays with them all (v. 36). His listeners are much moved, especially by his statement that they will not see him again (v. 25). It is with tears as well as embraces that the elders of Ephesus conduct Paul and his companions to their ship (vv. 37-38).

To Jerusalem: 21:1-17

The travelers leave Miletus and run before the prevailing northwesterly wind for the island of Cos in the Dodecanese. The following day they carry on to Rhodes, Patara (situated on the south coast of Lycia) and—according to the Western text—Myra, farther east along the same coast (v. 1). Each of these stages represents a day's journey by sea, and more or less the same route is indicated in other ancient travel stories. Paul and his companions change ship to a vessel bound for Phoenicia and set sail across the open sea to Tyre, a journey that would have taken five days (vv. 2-3). The only place that is mentioned on the way is the island of Cyprus, which is sighted but left on the port side: the ship was sailing south of it.

According to vv. 4-7 Paul and his companions find "disciples" at Tyre with whom they stay seven days and who warn Paul "through the Spirit" not to go to Jerusalem. After that they take their leave in a scene reminiscent of the farewells at Miletus and embark once more for Ptolemais (Acco). There they find "brethren" with whom they stay one day. On the following day the group leaves Ptolemais for Caesarea (v. 8), a journey that would also have taken more than one day. Caesarea has already been the scene of one of the most important episodes in Acts (cf. 10:1-48).

Paul and his companions, on arriving at Caesarea, go to the house of Philip the evangelist, who was one of the Seven. Philip had four daughters who used to prophesy (vv. 8-9; cf. 8:40). According to vv. 10-14 while Paul was at Caesarea the prophet Agabus came down from Judea (cf. 11:27-28), and foretold that at Jerusalem Paul would be bound and handed over to the Gentiles (cf. Luke 18:31-32). Paul's companions and the local Christians, dismayed by the prophecy of Agabus, beg Paul not to go up to Jerusalem (v. 12). He replies that he is willing not only to be bound but even to die there (v. 13). The others stop trying to persuade him and express their resignation to the divine will (v. 14).

The final leg of the journey, from Caesarea to Jerusalem, is recounted in vv. 15-17. The travelers stay over at the house of Mnason, a Cypriot and a disciple of long standing. In Jerusalem they are welcomed by the local community.

So Paul found himself at his first destination. If indeed, as we may suppose, he reached Jerusalem in time for Pentecost his journey from Philippi, which he left after Passover, would have taken between thirty and forty days.

> Shortly after Paul's arrival in Jerusalem he is attacked by an angry crowd in the precincts of the Temple and finds himself in the hands of the Roman army (21:18-40). An attempt to speak to the crowd is interrupted by renewed outcries and Paul is taken into the fortress Antonia (22:1-29). His appearance before the Sanhedrin also leads to an uproar (22:30–23:11).
>
> In the book of Acts the image of Paul the missionary is matched by that of Paul the prisoner,

to which roughly equal space is devoted. That shows the importance attached by Luke to this part of Paul's story in which he is called to be a witness ("martyr") to Christ before religious and civil authorities, both Jewish and Roman. It is a position in which at least some of Luke's readers have also found themselves down to the present day, and Luke intends them to draw courage and inspiration from the example of Paul. Luke may also want his readers to know that Paul meets the test of living in accord with the Apostolic Discourse (Matthew 10 with Lukan parallels) where it is foretold that Jesus' disciples will be dragged before magistrates and that if they remain faithful unto death they will be saved. This would serve to validate Paul's apostolic credentials in the eyes of the intended readers.

Paul and James: 21:18-26

The day following his arrival in Jerusalem Paul goes to see James, who is now the sole head of the church there (vv. 18-19). James explains that many zealous Jews have become believers. They have heard that Paul has been teaching Jews not to circumcise their sons and, James implies, they will cause trouble (vv. 20-22). There is no evidence that Paul ever said such a thing—and James professes not to believe it—but it is a possible conclusion from Paul's view that in Christ neither circumcision nor non-circumcision counts for anything (Gal 5:6). James proposes that Paul should demonstrate his fidelity to Jewish tradition by undergoing ritual purification and by paying the heavy expenses of four Nazirites (cf. Num 6:1-21) who are ending their period under vow and need to offer sacrifices in the Temple (vv. 23-24). As for Gentile converts, they have already been told to abstain from food offered to idols or improperly killed and from "fornication" (v. 25; cf. 15:20, 28-29). Paul follows James' advice (v. 26).

The Riot in the Temple: 21:27-36

In the Temple precincts Paul is set upon by a mob that has been stirred up by some Jews from Asia (i.e., Ephesus) who accuse him of speaking against the people, the Law, and "this place," that is the Temple (vv. 27-28a; cf. 6:11-13). They also charge that Paul has violated the Temple by bringing Gentiles into the sacred area (vv. 28b-29)—an offense for which, according to notices displayed in the Temple, the transgressor would pay with his life. The riot is eventually reported to the tribune, the officer commanding the Roman garrison in the Antonia fortress that adjoined the Temple on the north side. He and his guard rescue Paul from the mob, but at the same time place him under arrest as a presumed troublemaker (vv. 30-36). He remains a prisoner of the Romans for the rest of the book.

Paul Speaks to the Crowd: 21:37–22:22

While he is being taken up the steps leading into the Antonia fortress Paul asks the tribune if he may speak with him. The tribune, finding Paul in the midst of an excited crowd, at first supposes that he is an Egyptian agitator—known also from the Jewish historian Josephus—who recently led 4,000 assassins into the wilderness, but changes his mind when he hears Paul speaking Greek. Paul informs him that he is a Jew and a citizen of Tarsus and asks to speak to the crowd that has been clamoring for his blood (vv. 37-39). The tribune assents and Paul, standing on the steps, makes the customary gesture of the public speaker about to begin. He addresses the crowd in "Hebrew" (Aramaic?), thus gaining their attention (21:40–22:2).

Paul's speech to the crowd in the Temple (vv. 3-21) is essentially his autobiography. From the opening words—"I am a Jew"—Paul emphasizes his Jewish identity both in the past and in the present as the thing he has in common with his hostile audience. Using a formula common to ancient biographies to describe the early life of the subject, Paul states that he was born in Tarsus of Cilicia, brought up in "this city" (Jerusalem), and educated "at the feet of" Gamaliel in exact observance of the ancestral Law, "zealous for God, just as all of you are today" (v. 3).

Having thus done his best to get his audience on his side, Paul then recounts his early persecution of "the Way" and his conversion on the road to Damascus in a narrative that agrees broadly with the one already given by Luke (vv. 4-11; cf. 9:1-9). It is when Paul comes to talk about the part played by Ananias (vv. 12-16) that he presents things rather differently from the earlier account (cf. 9:10-19). Now Ananias is a Jew in good standing with local Jews rather than a "disciple," and he refers to the risen Jesus who appeared to Paul as "the Just One." It is Ananias who in this account delivered to Paul's fellow

Jews hints at Paul's mission to "all people." It was in the Temple at Jerusalem that Paul, as he now declares in the same Temple, received in a vision the mission to go to "the Gentiles far off" (vv. 17-21; cf. Isa 49:6; 57:19; Acts 9:15). At this point Paul's hearers interrupt him with renewed demands that he be put to death (v. 22).

Paul a Roman Citizen: 22:23-29

The tribune orders Paul to be taken inside the fortress and questioned under the lash, upon which Paul asks the centurion in charge whether it is lawful for him to scourge a Roman who has not been duly sentenced for punishment (vv. 24-25). The centurion alerts the tribune who expresses astonishment that the prisoner, who had a few moments before told him that he was a citizen of Tarsus (cf. 21:39), should now claim to be a Roman citizen. He himself had had to spend a large sum of money in order to become one, but Paul asserts that he has been a citizen from birth (vv. 26-28). This is the second time that Paul has made this claim and in similar circumstances (cf. 16:37). This time, however, the revelation is made before Paul is flogged with the scourge—a much more severe punishment than the beating with rods he received at Philippi. The effect on the Roman soldiers is the same as on the officials of Philippi, namely fear of the possible repercussions from subjecting a Roman citizen to such a punishment without due process of law (v. 29; cf. 16:38).

Paul Before the Sanhedrin: 22:30–23:11

The tribune realizes that he has a difficult case on his hands, but his first need is find out more about his prisoner. To that end he brings Paul next day before the Sanhedrin (22:30). Paul is living out the prediction of Jesus for his followers (Luke 21:12) and following in the footsteps of Jesus himself in his passion.

Paul's initial declaration of innocence is rewarded by the high priest's order that he be struck on the mouth (22:1-5; cf. John 18:19-23). Paul then takes advantage of the fact that the Sanhedrin consisted both of Pharisees, who accepted the doctrine of resurrection, and Sadducees, who did not. He cries out that he is a Pharisee, the son of Pharisees, and on trial for his hope in the resurrection of the dead. This causes a violent dissension in the council, with the Pharisees taking Paul's side (vv. 6-10). As the book of Acts goes on Paul will continue to claim common ground with the Pharisees on the resurrection of the dead—that Jesus is the "first fruits" of the general resurrection for which the Pharisees also hoped (cf. 1 Cor 15:20).

When the Roman commander learns of a plot to assassinate Paul he decides to send him to the governor at Caesarea (23:12-35). Paul duly appears before governor Felix who, however, keeps him in prison (24:1-27). A new governor, Porcius Festus, wishes to resolve the case of Paul and proposes to have him tried in Jerusalem, but Paul appeals to the emperor (25:1-12). Festus consults King Agrippa II (25:13-27) before whom Paul makes a final defense of his beliefs (26:1-32). Festus and Agrippa agree that Paul could be set free if it were not for his appeal.

Paul Transferred to Caesarea (23:11-35)

That night, still in custody in the fortress, Paul has a vision of the Lord who reassures him: Paul has borne witness concerning him in Jerusalem, and he must now do so also in Rome (v. 11).

It is when the tribune learns of a plot to ambush and assassinate Paul (vv. 12-22) that he decides to send his troublesome prisoner to the governor at Caesarea, where Paul will be both in safekeeping and off the tribune's hands. He arranges for a large military escort to leave that night (vv. 23-25) and writes an appropriate letter to the governor (vv. 26-30). The party sets out and eventually arrives at Antipatris, a meeting place of roads coming from the central hill country and the main north-south road along the coastal plain. They are now safely out of the dangerous mountains where an ambush was possible, and a smaller escort carries on to Caesarea where the tribune's letter and the prisoner are handed over to the governor.

The governor of Judea (whose official title at this time was "procurator") was Felix, a figure well known in history who owed his position to the fact that his brother Pallas was minister of finance to the emperor Claudius. In our story Felix, after learning that Paul is from Cilicia, agrees to give him a hearing when his accusers have arrived and orders him to be kept in Herod's palace (no doubt not in the royal apartments: vv. 31-35).

Paul and Felix: 24:1-27

Five days later Paul's accusers, the high priest Ananias and some elders, come down to Caesarea. They have engaged an advocate called Tertullus (vv. 1-2). The advocate, in a miniature example of a typical courtroom speech of the time (vv. 3-8), accuses Paul of being a "plague" who has incited violent dissensions among the Jews throughout the world (cf. 17:6) and the ringleader of the sect of the Nazoreans. He was caught attempting to violate the Temple and the Jewish authorities had been on the point of judging him according to their Law when the tribune Lysias seized him by force and told them to bring their complaints to the governor. Tertullus alleges that the governor can verify these charges, a claim that is supported by the other accusers (v. 9).

In reply (vv. 10-21) Paul asserts that he has only very recently come to Jerusalem, that he has not disputed or gathered a crowd around him in the Temple or elsewhere, and that his accusers cannot prove any of their charges. He himself serves God according to "the Way, which they call a sect," believing all that is written in the Law and the prophets, and having the same hope "as these people" in the future resurrection of the just and the wicked. After many years' absence he has come with alms for his people and offerings, and in the Temple he was in a state of purity and not causing any disturbance. His proper accusers are certain Jews of Asia who should be there before him. (Roman law took a dim view of people who brought charges but failed to turn up to face the accused.) The only thing that his present accusers can have against him is his claim before the Sanhedrin that he was on trial for the resurrection of the dead.

Felix put off making a decision until the tribune Lysias arrived (v. 22) but we never hear any more of the tribune. In the mean time Paul was to be kept in custody but in easy conditions and to be allowed visits from his friends (v. 23). A few days later, in an episode that recalls Herod Antipas and John the Baptist (cf. Mark 6:20), Felix and his wife Drusilla, who was the daughter of the Jewish king Agrippa I, summoned Paul and asked to hear more about his faith in Christ Jesus. Felix, however, did not like what he heard about justice and self-control and a future judgment, and dismissed Paul. He continued to have such conversations with Paul—hoping, writes Luke, to be given money, no doubt as a bribe to let Paul go (vv. 24-26). The result was that Paul was still in custody at Caesarea when Felix was recalled and replaced by Porcius Festus. Felix left Paul in prison—as a favor, comments Luke, to the Jews who in fact lodged complaints against Felix with the emperor.

Paul Appeals to the Emperor: 25:1-12

Festus made it a point to resolve the pending case concerning Paul without further delay and raised it with the Jewish authorities on his first visit to Jerusalem after taking up his post. They asked for Paul to be brought to Jerusalem, intending to ambush and kill him on the way (cf. 23:12-15), but Festus insisted that they should come down to Caesarea and accuse Paul there (vv. 1-5). Shortly afterward Festus took the case at Caesarea the Jewish authorities accused Paul of "many serious charges," and Paul replied that he has committed no crime against the Jewish Law, the Temple, or the emperor (vv. 6-8). Festus, to show favor to the Jews, asked Paul if he would be willing to go up to Jerusalem and be tried there. Paul demanded first to be heard by the governor at Caesarea, then appealed to the emperor. Festus agreed that he should go to the imperial court in Rome (vv. 9-12).

Paul and Agrippa II: 25:13-27

Jesus had foretold that his disciples would be brought before councils, governors, and kings (Luke 21:12). Paul has appeared before the Sanhedrin and two Roman governors. Now he comes before a king, Agrippa II, son of Agrippa I who had persecuted the leaders of the church in Jerusalem (cf. 12:1-3). The episode recalls that in the passion of Jesus according to Luke (23:6-12) Jesus was sent by Pilate to Herod Antipas, the great-uncle of Agrippa II.

This king, who ruled over certain areas in the north of the country, arrived in Caesarea to greet the new Roman governor, accompanied by his sister Berenice (their relationship was the subject of scandalized comment at the time). Since Agrippa was the secular head of the Jewish religion with power to appoint the high priest, Festus took the opportunity of consulting him about Paul. He briefly outlined the history of the case, admitting that no serious charge had been brought, but only "certain points of disagreement . . . about their own religion and about a certain Jesus, who had died, but whom Paul asserted to be alive." Since Paul has appealed to the emperor, Festus has ordered that he be sent to Rome (vv. 13-21). Agrippa tells Festus that he has long wanted to hear this man, and Festus assures him that he will soon have his chance to do so (v. 22; cf. Luke 23:8).

Next day there is a solemn audience at which Paul is brought before Festus, Agrippa, and Berenice. Festus once again recalls that the Jewish authorities have asked for Paul's death, but declares that he himself has not found anything in him worthy of capital punishment (cf. Luke 23:4, 14). He asks Agrippa to interrogate him to see if he can provide material for the report the governor must write for the emperor (vv. 23-27).

Paul's Last Speech: 26:1-32

Agrippa gives Paul the signal to speak (v. 1). After the usual introduction designed to win the favorable attention of his audience, here by appealing to Agrippa's knowledge of Judaism (vv. 2-3), Paul once again tells the story of his life and mission. As in the speech to the crowd in the Temple, here too Paul stresses that he is still a Jew. Christianity is presented here not as a different religion from Judaism but as its continuation and fulfillment. Paul was brought up as a Pharisee (vv. 4-5; cf. Phil 3:5). He is on trial now for his hope in the resurrection, which is nothing other than the fulfillment of God's promise to the twelve tribes of Israel (vv. 6-9). The reader of Acts has now the deferred answer to the question put to the risen Jesus by his disciples in Acts 1:6.

Once again Paul tells the story of his conversion from a persecutor to a believer in Jesus (vv. 9-15). This time he emphasizes that in the moment of his conversion he was told to go both to his own people and to the Gentiles (cf. Gal 1:16), so that—in terms that recall the liturgy of baptism—they might turn from darkness to light, from Satan to God (vv. 16-18; cf. Isa 42:6-7, 16). Paul has been faithful to that mission in Damascus, Jerusalem, Judea, and among the Gentiles, preaching repentance, conversion, and good deeds (vv. 19-20). For that reason he was attacked in the Temple (v. 21). In fact he has said only what Moses and all the prophets have said would take place, that the Messiah must suffer, and that, by being the first to rise from the dead, he would proclaim light for the people and for the Gentiles (vv. 22-23; cf. Isa 49:6).

Festus exclaims that Paul must be mad, but Paul asserts that he speaks the sober truth and appeals to Agrippa to support him. Agrippa remarks, no doubt ironically, that Paul almost persuades him to become a Christian (or, perhaps, "play the Christian"). Paul replies seriously but with a touch of humor that he would wish all his hearers to be like himself except for his chains (vv. 24-29). The audience is over and the great ones take their departure agreeing with one another that Paul has done nothing deserving death or imprisonment, and that he could be released if he had not appealed to the emperor (vv. 30-32). The stage is set for Paul's journey to Rome.

The last two chapters of Acts (27–28) tell how Paul achieved his ambition of coming to Rome (cf. 19:21; Rom 15:23). The great apostle realized the importance of preaching the gospel in the capital of the empire that included all the lands around the Mediterranean and a large part of Europe. Paul came, our story relates, as a prisoner, but still free to proclaim the good news (28:31).

In the narrative that follows some sections are written in the "we" style, which has already been associated with the travel diary that recorded Paul's collection journey. The same person who had accompanied Paul on that journey is seen going with him to Rome. These sections in the first person plural have been filled out by others written in the third person ("they").

Paul Sails for Rome: 27:1-12

Paul leaves for Rome in the company of other prisoners and some of his own friends under the guard of a centurion named Julius who turns out to be another of the "good centurions" we meet in the NT (vv. 1-3; cf. Luke 7:1-10; 23:47; Acts 10). The reader of Acts can easily follow with a map the progress of the ship around the western and northern coasts of Cyprus, westward along the southern coast of Asia Minor, then southwestward to the southern coast of Crete (vv. 4-8). We are told that this roundabout route was made necessary by adverse winds, evidently the nor'westers that prevail in the eastern Mediterranean during most of the summer.

On arrival at Fair Havens in Crete the travelers must decide whether to proceed any farther. The Jewish Day of Atonement ("the fast"), which falls in late September or October, had gone by, and with it the settled good weather and so the safe sailing season in the Mediterranean. It was not unusual on such occasions for everyone to express an opinion. Paul foresaw danger to human lives as well as to the vessel and its cargo, and warned against sailing, but the pilot and the ship's owner were anxious to move to a safer winter port and had in mind Phoenix farther along the Cretan coast. The centurion was no doubt eager to continue the journey if at all possible, and his view prevailed (vv. 9-12).

Storm at Sea and Shipwreck: 27:13-44

The onset of winter in the eastern Mediterranean is marked by sudden storms, and shipping off the southern coast of Crete can be hit by violent winds blowing from the north off the high mountains that lie just behind the shore. It was such a wind that blew the vessel off course as it was making its way, with an initially favorable breeze, from Fair Havens to Phoenix (vv. 13-15). The whole episode of the storm at sea is one of the most vivid passages in Acts, told with attention to precise details and exact nautical terminology, yet at the same time conveying a sense of drama and emergency (vv. 16-38).

At two points Paul plays a crucial part in events. In his first intervention (vv. 21-26) Paul makes an altogether pardonable reference to his own advice not to "set sail from Crete," but he does not simply point out that his predictions have been fulfilled. He encourages crew and passengers to keep in good heart. He knows now that only the ship will be lost, not their lives, as he has had a vision of an angel who assured him that he will yet stand before the emperor. They will run aground on some island.

In fact land seems to be near, and Paul foils an attempt by the sailors to abandon ship (vv. 27-32). Paul then advises the ship's company to take some food, and he himself takes bread, gives thanks for it to God, breaks it and eats. All (the number is variously given as seventy-six or two hundred seventy-six) follow his example (vv. 33-38). There are certainly eucharistic overtones in this meal and the ship itself seems for a moment to become a symbol of the Church tossed about on stormy waters but offering safety to those on board.

In the event the ship runs aground and begins to break up. The soldiers want to kill their prisoners in order to prevent their escape but the centurion forbids this in order to save Paul and organizes the operation by which all safely reach land (vv. 39-44).

Paul on Malta: 28:1-10

The ship had reached an island called Melite which is usually identified as Malta. The inhabitants treat the survivors kindly, which is not always the fate of those who suffer shipwreck (vv. 1–2). They are deeply impressed when Paul suffers no harm from a viper (vv. 3-6). Paul cures the father of Publius, the chief person of the island, and others who are ill (vv. 7-9; cf. Mark 16:18). When the time comes to leave the islanders supply Paul and his companions (we have lost sight of Julius, the soldiers, and other prisoners) with provisions for the journey (v. 10).

Paul Comes to Rome: 28:11-31

After winter is over Paul and his companions can sail to Sicily and then on to Puteoli south of Naples (vv. 11-13). There they find fellow Christians with whom they stay before continuing to Rome. The last stage of the journey resembles a royal progress as Christians from Rome meet them on the way and escort them into the city (vv. 14-15). Once Paul is at Rome we are reminded that he is, after all, a prisoner, but he is allowed to live privately with a soldier as guard (v. 16).

Paul's first concern is to get in touch with the leaders of the Jewish community at Rome, whom he invites to meet him. He explains that he has committed no offense against "our people or the customs of our ancestors." He had been handed over to the Romans (he does not say by whom), but the Romans wanted to set him free as being guilty of no capital crime. It was only when "the Jews" objected to his release that he was compelled to appeal to the emperor—and yet, he is anxious to make clear, he has no complaint against his own nation. He wants to meet the Jewish leaders of Rome because "it is for the sake of the hope of Israel that I am bound with this chain" (vv. 17-20). They reply that they have received no report about him but they would like to find out more concerning "this sect" that is everywhere spoken against (vv. 21-22).

On the day appointed the leaders of the Jewish community at Rome came again to Paul's lodging, and from morning to evening Paul spoke, "testifying to the kingdom of God and trying to convince them about Jesus both from the law of Moses and from the prophets" (v. 23). As so often in the past, some were convinced but others refused to believe (v. 24). As they left Paul quoted Isa 6:9-10 to explain their lack of understanding (cf. Matt 13:14; Mark 4:12; John 12:39-40) and announced that this salvation of God has been sent to the Gentiles, who will listen (vv. 23-28). This prediction, coming where it does, seems to envisage a Church that is increasingly composed of Gentiles, as was already apparent to Luke.

Acts ends with Paul still under house arrest in Rome. For two years he welcomes all who come to him and proclaims the kingdom of God and teaches about the Lord Jesus Christ (vv. 30-31). The last words of Acts—"with all boldness and without hindrance"—could be a program for all preachers of the gospel.

Luke breaks off his story unfinished—we do not even learn Paul's personal fate. He seems to imply that the story he tells, of the spread of the good news of Jesus Christ, could not be finished by himself. And indeed the story goes on until today and beyond as the Church tries to carry out the commission given by Jesus at his ascension to be "his witnesses to the ends of the earth."

BIBLIOGRAPHY

Recent commentaries on Acts that are widely read and are available in English include:

Bruce, Frederick F. *The Acts of the Apostles. The Greek Text with Introduction and Commentary.* 3rd revised and enlarged edition. Grand Rapids: Eerdmans, and Leicester: Apollos, 1990.

Conzelmann, Hans. *Acts of the Apostles.* English translation by James Limburg et al. Hermeneia. Philadelphia: Fortress, 1987.

Haenchen, Ernst. *The Acts of the Apostles. A Commentary.* English translation from 14th German edition by Bernard Noble and others. Philadelphia: Westminster, 1971.

This commentary owes much to:

Boismard, Marie-Émile, and Arnaud Lamouille. *Les Actes des deux Apôtres.* 3 vols. Études Bibliques n.s. 12-14. Paris: Gabalda, 1990.

Letters in the New Testament

John C. Hurd

I. The Ancient Letter

Letters are among the most ancient forms of written communication. Vital for NT study are the many private letters from the Hellenistic era, the period that followed Alexander's (d. 323 B.C.E.) conquests. Their importance lies in the light they shed (1) on the language of the NT as a whole and (2) on the letters and letter-like material found in the NT.

The NT was not written in the literary Greek of the first century. In fact until letters from this period began to be discovered in the late nineteenth century the peculiarities of NT language were often taken as evidence of its divine nature. These letters, however, make it clear that the NT was written in a style much closer to the language of ordinary life (which is one justification for modern, even colloquial, translations of the NT). This Greek is called *koinē* ("common") or Hellenistic Greek.

It is a surprising fact that except for the narrative books (the gospels and Acts) all the writings of the NT are either letters or have letter-like features. From Hellenistic letters we learn the style and conventions of letter writing: we learn how to read letters of this period. Thus the study of these letters is of major importance in understanding the letters of the NT.

Writing Materials

Generally letters in the Hellenistic period were written on papyrus, a tough, fibrous writing material made from thin strips cut from the papyrus reed. The strips were laid side by side in two layers, the back layer at right angles to the front layer, and the two layers glued together, pressed, and then polished. There was thus a good side (the *recto*) on which the writing ran with the grain of the papyrus and a bad side (the *verso*) on which the writer had to contend with the ridges of the vertical strips. These sheets could be purchased in various grades and sizes. Most letters of this period were written on the *recto* of a single sheet. The sheet was then rolled and the two ends folded to overlap at the center where the whole bundle was tied with string. The knot was sealed with a lump of clay and the addressee's name added. Philemon, 2 John, and 3 John could originally have had this form.

Longer documents required that single sheets be glued together to form scrolls. The writing then occupied columns at right angles to the long dimension of the scroll. The reader would allow the portion already read to roll up in the left hand while unrolling the scroll with the right hand to expose more text. As a result scrolls were generally left with the end on the outside. With time the outside of the scroll suffered from wear and occasionally the final sheet became unglued. Thus the closing portion of a text could be lost. This fact is important to the problem of the endings of Mark and of Romans (see the commentaries on these books).

Letters and Epistles

In common speech the terms "letter" and "epistle" are synonymous. In historical studies, however, there is an important distinction. A "letter" is a communication written by a real author to a known audience to deal with a specific set of problems at a particular point in time. It is part of an actual conversation between two parties. The relationship between writer and reader varies in intimacy from that between husband and wife, for example, to that between persons who have previously had no dealings with one another. But the life situation is always real and the writer makes himself or herself known to the reader(s).

An "epistle," however, is an essay given the appearance of a "letter" for reasons of style or custom. The author writes to a general readership, the nature of which he or she can only roughly predict. The readers in turn very probably do not know the author, if indeed the work bears the actual author's name at all.

The writer of a "letter" must not tell the readers matters they already know unless it is by accident or with some apology ("as you know . . ."). More precisely, the writer must not tell the readers things they know he knows they know. To do so, as in ordinary conversation, is condescending and puts a strain on the relationship between the two parties. This restriction is the key to identifying "letters." "Letters" provide priceless snapshots of moments in history, but they are often difficult to understand because so much shared information is omitted.

The writer of an "epistle," on the other hand, can presuppose no specific information on the part of the readers, and thus the main argument of an "epistle" must be self-contained. In giving the essay the appearance of a "letter" the author may refer to unexplained names and even events but the basic message must stand on its own. The study of letter conventions thus benefits the understanding of "epistles" only indirectly: we learn something of what the author of the text thinks a "letter" should look like although he or she is not actually writing a "letter" at the time.

Letter Structure

By convention Hellenistic letters began: A to B, "greeting." The names of the sender (A) and the recipient (B) were often supplemented by the name of their father or home town to avoid ambiguity. The usual salutation was the single word *chairein* ("greeting"). There often followed some polite wish for the good health or good fortune of the recipient. This opening section served to (re)establish personal relations between the two parties. The length of this section is a measure of how personal the letter was. Letters from a superior, for example, often plunged directly into the next part of the letter: the business section. The form of this section varied greatly depending on the business at hand; there were, however, a number of conventional elements. Then at the end of the letter the writer would express wishes or hopes for the future and perhaps add greetings to other persons. The letter would close with the word *errōso* ("goodbye," literally "be strong"), and often the date. There is therefore a general A–B–A' (personal–business–personal) structure presented in a past–present–future sequence in ancient letters.

II. The Pauline Letters

Among the various letters and letter-like documents within the NT there are a number of distinct groups: the Pauline corpus (Romans, 1 and 2 Corinthians, Galatians, Ephesians, Philippians, Colossians, 1 and 2 Thessalonians, Philemon), the "Pastoral" epistles (1 and 2 Timothy, Titus), and the "catholic" or "general" epistles (James, 1 and 2 Peter, the Johannine epistles, and Jude). Of these by far the most important group is the Pauline corpus, for Paul was the most notable letter writer of the early Church. In fact it was probably the importance of his letters that caused later NT authors to cast their message in letter form also; some later writings even invoke his name as author.

The Pauline Letter Corpus

The surviving letters of Paul were saved by the communities to which they were addressed and initially seem to have been known only locally. Then toward the end of the first century his letters were gathered into a single corpus and copies produced. The evidence for this assertion consists of the quotations of Paul's letters found in the earliest Church fathers. After decades in which the letters appear not to have been widely known Christian writers suddenly begin quoting the letters seemingly at random. First Clement (c. 96 C.E.) refers to Romans and 1 Corinthians; Ignatius (d. 108 C.E.) to Romans, 1 Corinthians, and Ephesians. (Cf. too the reference in 2 Pet

3:15-16 to "all the letters" of Paul and note the influence on Hebrews, 1 Peter, and Revelation described in III below.) Interest in Paul was certainly stimulated by the publication of the book of Acts, but whether the collection of the letters followed the appearance of Acts or whether the letters were known to the author of Acts is an unsolved problem.

Paul's letters seem to have been valued by their original recipients. There are only two references in the surviving letters to earlier letters that seem to be missing. The letter referred to in 1 Cor 5:9-11 (the "previous letter") is lost, although a fragment may be preserved as 2 Cor 6:14–7:1. In addition many scholars believe that the "severe letter" mentioned in 2 Cor 2:3-4; 7:8 is also lost (for understandable reasons), although others think that part of this letter survives as 2 Corinthians 10–13. There may have been "collection" letters sent to Philippi, Thessalonica, and perhaps Galatia (see 1 Cor 16:1) at the same time as the "previous letter." If so, Paul never referred to them in later correspondence. With these exceptions the letter sequence as it connects with Paul's career seems complete.

The earliest collection of Paul's letters contained seven, written respectively to the Romans, Corinthians, Galatians, Colossians, Philippians, Laodiceans, and Thessalonians. It is generally assumed that "Laodiceans" is the letter we call "Ephesians" (see commentary on 1:1) and that Philemon was combined with Colossians (note the linked closing greetings). Only at a later point were Corinthians and Thessalonians divided into two letters each. Also at a later point 1 and 2 Timothy and Titus (the "Pastoral epistles") appeared and were added to the collection. There was a variety of ancient orderings of Paul's letters. The various sequences reflect the practical problem of fitting the texts onto scrolls or into codex (that is, book) form; they have nothing to do with the order in which the letters were originally written. The present canonical arrangement is by decreasing order of length, first to congregations and then to individuals.

The Problems of Authorship

In order to understand Paul as a letter writer we must be clear about which letters he probably wrote. In general letters in the Pauline corpus have been denied to Paul on the basis of either their theological content or their vocabulary and style. In the late nineteenth century many German scholars considered that only Galatians, Romans, and the two Corinthian letters (the *Hauptbriefe* or "chief letters") were authentically Paul's (seventy-two percent of the original corpus). Modern scholarship, however, accepts Philemon, Philippians, and 1 Thessalonians also, and often Colossians as well (a total of ninety percent of the whole). Most doubt attaches to "Ephesians" (in part because of its similarity to Colossians) and 2 Thessalonians (in part because of its similarity to 1 Thessalonians).

Denial of authenticity on the basis of similarity, however, is a more difficult argument to sustain than is often recognized. Normally similarity between two texts is taken as evidence of common authorship. Paul in particular often repeated phrases and lines of thought from one letter to another.

The argument from difference is more serious and takes a number of forms. Some scholars of the past relied on their view of Paul as a systematic theologian, and they rejected letters that differed from the *Hauptbriefe.* Other scholars have tallied which words Paul used and in what sense. Letters with a vocabulary different from the established letters were disallowed to Paul. Features of style (such as word order or sentence length) are also counted. Nowadays computers allow detailed analyses of texts. This work has to be done with great care, however, both to avoid influencing the result by the way the questions are asked and because these texts are relatively short for statistical work. Thus far this analysis has not disqualified any members of the original Pauline corpus.

The "letter/epistle" distinction is another tool for answering the question of authenticity: it is hard to conceive of a situation in which a "letter" (as contrasted with an "epistle") would not be the actual work of its named author. Paul's letters range from those written to persons he knew well (e.g., Corinthians, Galatians, Philippians, Thessalonians, and Philemon) to those sent to congregations he had never visited (e.g., Romans) The former reflect real-life situations in Paul's career and are full of references to shared information not repeated (e.g., "Now concerning the matters about which you wrote," 1 Cor 7:1). The latter do not by their nature presuppose shared information, but they do connect to

Paul's life situation (e.g., Rom 15:22-32). Clearly 2 Thessalonians is a "letter" ("Do you not remember that I told you these things when I was still with you?" 2:5). Colossians, with its personal references (1:4, 9; 2:1; 4:7-8) and close relationship to the undoubtedly genuine Philemon (note the shared list of persons greeted, and the extra attention given to the duties of slaves in 3:22-25), is most probably a "letter" as well. "Ephesians" lacks the unique Philemon connection but it has the same personal notes as Colossians (1:15-16; 3:1-4, 7-8, 13; 4:1; 6:21-22) and is probably a "letter" also. If these last three are "letters" they were probably written by Paul. For more detail concerning individual letters see the commentaries on those letters.

Paul as Letter Writer

Paul used letters to make himself present to the congregations he founded or wished to visit at times when he was physically absent (cf. 1 Cor 5:3; Col 2:5). We tend to think of his letters as written texts, but for Paul they were oral. He dictated them to a scribe. (A dictation correction is found in 1 Cor 1:16; the name of a scribe in Rom 16:22.) They were delivered orally to the congregations to which they were addressed (1 Thess 5:27; silent reading was rare in the ancient world). The messengers were Paul's representatives and may have made supplementary statements (cf. Col 4:7-8; Eph 6:21-22). To authenticate his letters Paul added a line or two in his own hand as we would use a signature (e.g., 1 Cor 16:21-24; Gal 6:11-18; and 2 Thess 3:17-18, "This is the mark in every letter of mine; it is the way I write.").

The Sequence of Paul's Letters

Since Paul's letters reflect actual situations in his career it would be helpful if we knew the order in which they were written. The traditional method of ordering Paul's letters takes the narrative of Acts as the basic historical sequence. Each letter is then connected to some point in Acts. Thus the four "imprisonment" letters (Colossians, "Ephesians," Philippians, and Philemon) are usually dated from one of the pair of imprisonments at the close of the story (Rome, Acts 28; or Caesarea, Acts 24). Corinth is taken as the place of writing of 1 Thessalonians because of the reference in both sources to Timothy's arrival (1 Thess 3:6 = Acts 18:5). Paul was in Ephesus when he wrote 1 Corinthians (see 1 Cor 16:8), which is thus dated at Acts 19. He was in Macedonia when he wrote 2 Corinthians (at least chs. 1–9; see 2:13; 7:5), which is dated at Acts 20:1-2a. In Rom 15:25 Paul says that he is about to relinquish his current mission field to go to Jerusalem. Romans is therefore dated at Acts 20:2b. The Acts narrative does not allow an opportunity between the founding of the church in Thessalonica (Acts 17:1-9) and the writing of 1 Thessalonians (dated at 18:5) for 2 Thessalonians. Therefore the letter is usually placed just after 1 Thessalonians (unless it is denied to Paul entirely).

Galatians, which contains the most biographical information of any letter, poses the most serious problems for this method of dating. The basic problem concerns Paul's visits (1) to Jerusalem and (2) to Galatia. Paul swears (1:20) that he has visited Jerusalem only twice (1:18 and 2:1). In Acts his first visit is at 9:26-29 and his second at 11:27-30. Thus Galatians should be dated before his third visit, 15:4-29. (See, however, the manuscript problem at Acts 12:25, which may well refer to another visit.) However, Paul does not even reach Galatia until Acts 16:6. Moreover, the Greek of Gal 4:13 implies that Paul had already visited Galatia twice. Paul's second visit to Galatia occurs at Acts 18:23. Paul therefore must have written his letter before Acts 15:4 (or 12:25?) but not until after 18:23. Much ink has been spilled over this problem. One solution is to deny that "the Galatian region" of Acts 16:6 and 18:23 is the destination of Paul's letter. Paul is taken to be referring to Iconium, Lystra, and Derbe (Acts 14), which did in fact lie in the Roman province of Galatia although their inhabitants were not ethnically Gauls. This suggestion makes Galatians Paul's earliest surviving letter. Unfortunately this theory has serious difficulties—as have all other solutions to the problem when approached as above.

However, a different method is available. Recent appreciation of the theology of Acts ("redaction criticism") has made this chronological reliance on the overall sequence of Acts questionable. Clearly the sources out of which Acts was constructed contain much important information but the author has combined and expanded them so as to further his own purposes.

Moreover he seems not to have been entirely clear about the relationships among his sources. The links he adds to connect these sources are frequently vague in the extreme (e.g., "at that time," or "about that time," 11:27; 12:1; 19:23; "during those days," 6:1). The interval between Paul's conversion and his first visit to Jerusalem is specified by Paul as "three years" (Gal 1:18) but appears merely as "after some time" in Acts 9:23. Further, the frequent visits of Paul to Jerusalem in Acts may indicate that some of these sources overlapped. References to the same visit in two sources may appear in Acts as two successive visits. In sum, Acts is now considered secondary, that is, a second hand source for a knowledge of the events its author describes (although a primary source for a knowledge of his purposes). On the other hand Paul's letters are indisputably the primary historical source for our knowledge of Paul. Thus a number of scholars have been attempting to establish the sequence of the letters by observing the natural affinities of the letters and by reconstructing Paul's career from the letters alone.

There is surprising consensus among those scholars who have expressed opinions about the relationship of one letter to another based on their contents. When these opinions are collated the following sequence appears:

> 2 Thessalonians, 1 Thessalonians, 1 Corinthians, (2 Corinthians 10–13?), Philippians, 2 Corinthians 1–9, Galatians, Romans, (2 Corinthians 10–13?), Colossians + Philemon, "Ephesians"

Only over the position of 2 Corinthians 10–13 is opinion divided. Some scholars consider it to be part of the "severe letter" mentioned in 2 Cor 2:3-4; 7:8, but at least as many believe that the situation reflected in these chapters did not occur until after the writing of Romans. (Note that the letters whose authenticity is most often called into question lie at the ends of the above sequence.)

If we had only the letters of the original Pauline corpus we would suppose that Paul's life ran as follows: He visited Jerusalem three times (Gal 1:18; 2:1; and, by anticipation, Rom 15:25). He spent the time between the second and third visits trying to raise money for "the poor among the saints at Jerusalem" (Rom 15:26). This collection project was agreed upon by Paul and the Jerusalem apostles during the second visit ("they asked only one thing, that we remember the poor," Gal 2:10), announced to the Corinthians in the lost letter preceding 1 Corinthians (the "previous letter") mentioned again in 1 Cor 16:1-4, and, at a later stage, in 2 Corinthians 8 and 9. This project was the reason for Paul's last journey to Jerusalem, undertaken in spite of his premonitions (Rom 15:31) and his desire to journey westward to Rome and thence to Spain (Rom 15:24). During the period of the collection Paul experienced a crisis (imprisonment?) in which he despaired of his life (2 Cor 1:8). The letter to the Philippians fits this occasion nicely. In it we learn of Judaizing activity somewhere in his mission field. This activity reaches a crisis in Galatians and is reflected in Romans and 2 Corinthians 10–13.

It seems clear that the collection project presupposes an established group of churches. Paul's missionary work must have taken him from Syria and Cilicia (Gal 1:21) at least as far west as Corinth before the collection began, that is, before his second visit to Jerusalem. Into this period fall the letters to the Thessalonians. The remaining letters (Colossians, Philemon, and "Ephesians") were written during some final imprisonment. In sum: the biographical information in the letters fits well with the observations summarized above about the natural affinities of the letters.

Pauline Letter Structure

All the structural elements of the Hellenistic letter (as described above) are to be found in Paul's letters also. Paul expands each element, however, so that his letters (except Philemon) are many times as long as the usual personal communication. His letters open with his name and sometimes the names of one or more companions. These additional persons seem to serve as co-signers to the document; there is little likelihood that they actually participated in its composition. Paul modified his name with additional material that subtly emphasized that facet of his persona he believed to be relevant to the current letter (most notably in Rom 1:1-6). The designation of the addressees is similarly modified. Then instead of *chairein* ("greeting") he substituted the Christian term *charis* ("grace"—note the wordplay) and added the Jewish salutation "peace."

Paul next expanded the "health wish" of the common letter into a unique feature found in all his letters except Galatians (and 2 Corinthians 10–13?): the "Pauline thanksgiving." He established, or reestablished, personal relationship with his addressees by remembering before God (that is, in prayer) their virtues and past successes. Moreover he wove into these gracious introductions words that denote the main topics of the letter to follow. This section therefore looks not only at the past but also serves to introduce the matters now to be discussed. This habit of Paul's indicates how fully he had the contents of each letter in mind as he began to dictate. (In Galatians he substituted an "ironic rebuke" to set the tone of that angry letter.)

The "body" of the letter varies in structure depending on the complexity of the message to be communicated. Topics to be discussed are introduced by a "disclosure" formula such as "I do not want you to be unaware, brothers and sisters . . ." (Rom 1:13; 11:25; 1 Cor 10:1; 12:1; 2 Cor 1:8; 1 Thess 4:13) for new information, or "Do you not know that . . ." (Rom 6:16; 1 Cor 3:16; 5:6; 6:2, 3; 6:9, 15, 16, 19; 9:13, 24) to recall information already shared. Note also how Paul often used the vocative to signal a transition.

The closing section of the letter points to the future. It often begins with a "request" formula such as "I appeal to you, brothers and sisters, . . ." (Rom 12:1; 15:30; 16:17; 1 Cor 16:15; 1 Thess 4:10; 5:14). This section includes ethical material concerning the future behavior of Paul's addressees. Here (for the most part) we find the travel plans of Paul and his coworkers (Rom 15:22-32; 1 Cor 4:17-21; 16:1-11; 2 Cor 8:16-24; 9:5; 12:14–13:2; Eph 6:21-22; Phil 2:19-30; 4:15-18; Col 4:7-9; 1 Thess 2:17–3:6; Phlm 12, 22). Then follow greetings to (or from) individuals (Rom 16:1-23; 1 Cor 16:15-20a; Phil 4:21-22; Col 4:10-17), a peace benediction (Rom 16:20a; 2 Cor 13:11; Eph 6:23; 1 Thess 5:23-24; 2 Thess 3:16) and/or the kiss of peace (1 Cor 16:20b; 2 Cor 13:12; 1 Thess 5:26) and the autograph subscription noted above. Paul used this last feature to subtly underline the major concern of the whole letter (especially in Gal 6:11-17; note also the double reference to "love" in 1 Cor 16:21-23). Paul then ended with "grace" (Rom 16:20b; 1 Cor 16:23; 2 Cor 13:14; Gal 6:18; Eph 6:24; Phil 4:23; Col 4:18b; 1 Thess 5:28; 2 Thess 3:18; Phlm 25). Note how his letters begin "grace and peace" and end "peace" and "grace."

This last observation concerns the rhetorical pattern A–B/B'–A', or "chiasmus," a pattern often found in Paul's letters as any reader can verify even in translation. An example is the sequence "power–wisdom/foolishness–weakness" in 1 Cor 1:24b-25, and there are many others. Paul could also expand this pattern impressively: A–B–C–D . . ./. . . D'–C'–B'–A'. One example among many is 1 Thess 4:13-18; note how Paul ended where he began. The whole passage 1 Cor 1:18-25, which contains the example cited above, is itself highly structured; so too is 1 Cor 9:19-23. Further, Paul could balance whole blocks of text in patterns. Examples of Paul's "sonata" form, that is, A–B–A', are 1 Corinthians 8–9–10 and 12–13–14 where the third chapter in each case returns to the subject of the first after a related digression in the second. This type of organization benefited both Paul as he organized his thoughts and his hearers as they listened to his letters. The reader who looks for structure in reading Paul will gain a new level of understanding. (Often rearranging the text in sense lines brings out the structure.)

III. The Remaining Letter Material

About the remaining letter material there is less to say. For more detail than is given below, see the commentaries on individual books.

The Pastoral Epistles

First Timothy does not have the characteristics of a Pauline letter for it is almost entirely general, that is, an "epistle." The author has, however, used the names of Paul and Timothy and inserted in 1:3 a bit of local color. Second Timothy, by contrast, goes much farther in its likeness to Paul. The author has provided an opening thanksgiving and refers to a number of persons and events as though known to the readers. There are travel references near the end, closing greetings, and a final grace. On the other hand the main message (which is similar to 1 Timothy's) does not depend on the personal references. Titus also refers to unexplained persons and events but it has no thanksgiving and the closing is rudimentary. Most modern scholars consider these three writings to be post-Pauline on the basis of their theology and vocabulary. Letter study confirms this judgment: they are probably all "epistles" and not "letters."

The Catholic Epistles

James is explicitly a general work, being addressed to "the twelve tribes in the Dispersion." It has an epistolary opening that uses *chairein* as the greeting, but there are no further epistolary features.

First Peter is similarly addressed to "the exiles of the Dispersion" and thus is not a "letter." It has an epistolary opening and the author, like Paul, uses "grace and peace" in the greeting. Like 2 Corinthians it begins with a blessing (2 Cor 1:3a = 1 Pet 1:3a) but then all signs of letter structure disappear until the doxology in 5:11. There is, however, a subscription naming Silvanus and Mark, calling for "a kiss of love," and ending with a peace benediction.

Second Peter is addressed even more generally. The greeting seems based on 1 Peter's. There is no further attempt to produce the effect of a "letter" although in 3:1 the author speaks of himself as writing a letter (a sequel to 1 Peter) and he refers to "all" Paul's letters (3:15-16).

First John has no marks of a "letter"; its author casts himself in the role of a teacher ("I") writing to benefit persons ("children") in need of his message (2:1, 7, 12, 26; 5:13). Little 2 and 3 John, on the other hand, while theologically similar to 1 John, are very letter-like in their structure.

Jude has a stylized epistolary opening prefaced to a tract that appears also as 2 Pet 2:1-18. It ends with a liturgical doxology.

Other New Testament Material

Hebrews is a magnificent homiletic essay; it is clearly not a "letter." There is no epistolary opening. The author writes his "word of exhortation" (13:22) for a general audience. However, ch. 13 is made to look like the end of a Pauline letter with closing exhortations, recommendation of leaders, prayer request, benediction, and a subscription that even names Timothy and ends with the grace. The chapter is a clear indication of the influence of the Pauline corpus on later Christian authors.

Interestingly, the text of Revelation is placed in an epistolary frame (1:4; 22:21). This device and the seven messages to the seven churches in 1:4–3:22 may reflect the influence of the Pauline corpus. There is nothing else letter-like about the book.

Embedded letters are found in Acts 15:23-29 and 23:26-30. The greeting is *chairein* and the former ends with the secular "goodbye" (only here in the NT).

BIBLIOGRAPHY

Particularly helpful is William G. Doty, *Letters in Primitive Christianity.* Bible Guides: NT (Philadelphia: Fortress, 1973). More detailed are John L. White, *Light from Ancient Letters*. Foundations and Facets: NT (Philadelphia: Fortress, 1986), and Stanley K. Stowers, *Letter Writing in Greco-Roman Antiquity.* Library of Early Christianity (Philadelphia: Westminster, 1986). Both include a generous selection of contemporary letters. Concerned more particularly with Paul is White's *The Form and Function of the Body of the Greek Letter*. SBL.DS 2 (Missoula: Scholars, 1972). Useful for tracing similar phrases and structures in Paul's letters is Fred O. Francis and J. Paul Sampley, *Pauline Parallels*. Foundations and Facets: NT (2nd ed. Philadelphia: Fortress, 1984).

Romans

Jean-Noël Aletti

FIRST READING

The letter to the Romans (Rom) is justly regarded as one of the most significant writings from the apostolic period. For Luther it was, indeed, the supreme witness to the gospel of grace and salvation in Jesus Christ. In the centuries since Luther, Romans has undoubtedly been the NT book that has occasioned the most lively discussions and polemics between the churches because it strikes to the heart of their identity. Today the differences have been reduced, but the stakes are no doubt just as high because the very coherence of Paul's project—as regards the Mosaic Law, Israel and its historical role, justification with or without works, and so on—has been called into question, as we shall see. No presentation can any longer overlook these discussions, even if it is difficult to do them justice. Because a determination of the reasons amounts in reality to throwing into relief the rich but complex writings of the apostle Paul, it is no longer possible to read this letter without taking into consideration the many and varied literary techniques employed in its composition. In short, we must avoid plunging immediately into a theological reading lest we cause Paul to say the opposite of what he really says. Some precautions are indispensable if we are to appreciate the beauty of this writing, inspired though it is.

General Characteristics

1. Genre and Composition of Romans

Romans follows several compositional models. Like any letter it begins with an address (*praescriptum,* 1:1-7), ends with a farewell (*postscriptum,* 15:33), gives some items of news (15:17-32), extends greetings (ch. 16), and maintains a dialogical tone in expressing wishes, requests, and exhortations (chs. 12–15). But it also contains some rather long theoretical arguments belonging to the genre of discursive rhetoric. Each argumentative unit is, generally speaking, composed of a *propositio* (a proposition that Paul will attempt to define, explain, ground, or justify) and a *probatio* including one or more examples (7:1-4; 11:16-24), enthymemes (a type of syllogism: 6:5-10), principles (2:6, 11; 6:7, 10), scriptural references (3:4, 10-18; 9:6-29). The argumentative structure of Romans is also stratified because the argumentative units are grouped into sections and subsections that can be shown in tabular form as follows:

Section	Subsections	Small units
PROPOSITIO—PROBATIO	*(sub)propositio/ probatio*	*(sub)propositio/ probatio*
		(sub)propositio/ probatio
	(sub)propositio/ probatio	*(sub)propositio/ probatio*
		(sub)propositio/ probatio

If we want to know what Paul intends to demonstrate and how he does so we must examine the *propositiones* in each of the small argumentative units and sections. The principal *propositio* does not obviate the secondary theses or *propositiones* (called in Latin *subpropositiones*) that explicate it, in a sense applying the principle and permitting Pauline argumentation to define itself more precisely as it progresses and to develop in a series of stages that can be spotted rather easily. Romans also takes its overall format from discursive rhetoric: we note the presence of a prologue (or *exordium*) and an epilogue (or *peroratio*). Finally, Paul also uses another principle of composition, that of parallelism, which he combines with the epistolary and discursive genres both in the small units and the larger ones, so that at a number of levels the units are organized into a complex composition in the form ABA' (see below on the composition of Rom 5–8; 9–11; 9:6-29).

If we combine the different principles of composition the progression of Romans looks this way:

Address: 1:1-7
Exordium: 1:8-17
ending with a *propositio* in 1:16-17 (the main *propositio*)

	(A) 1:18–4:25	Jew and Greek justified by faith alone
PROBATIO	(B) 5–8	New life and the hope of the baptized
	(C) 9–11	Israel and the Gentiles: the future of Israel

Exhortations: 12:1–15:13
Peroration: 15:14-21
News and Final Greeting: 15:22-33 + 16:1-27

If Pauline argumentation develops in a unified fashion from Romans 1 to 8, chapters 9–11 appear to form a separate grouping not directly attached to what precedes and follows them. It will be necessary to examine their function within the argumentation.

Giving attention to the composition of the letter, especially the hierarchy of *propositiones* by means of which we can observe the progress and articulation of various arguments, enables us to determine whether or not there is a principal theme, and if so, what it is. Paul indeed speaks of the gospel, of divine justice, of justification by faith alone, of the impotence of the Mosaic Law, of the election of Israel, of its rejection of the gospel and its future salvation, but if we cannot see how these different themes fit together we will not be able to discern what Paul wants to demonstrate and how he does so.

2. Recommendations for a First Reading of Romans

(1) In accord with what we have just said about the letter's composition, the first concern of a reader of Romans should probably be to follow the apostle's argumentation in order to determine the respective functions of each unit—what does it intend to show, what arguments does it use, etcetera? For that purpose one may make use of the remarks on the composition provided below at the beginning of each section (Romans 1–4; 5–8; 9–11, and 12–15) as well as the subsections and different argumentative units.

(2) The major difficulty of Romans is the way in which the argumentation is begun in Rom 1:18–3:20. In order to make ourselves aware of the importance of this problem we can begin by reading the introduction to Romans 1–4. Why does Paul begin with such a long discussion of divine anger? Is the gospel of pure grace based on a proclamation of wrath and judgment? Moreover, in these first chapters there are a number of statements that seem to contradict Paul's usual doctrine of justification to the point that one could call them incoherent. But that opinion could only be advanced by commentators who are ignorant of the rhetorical devices the apostle used. Before asking whether Paul is coherent or not we need to take account of their origin and function because in Romans 1–3 Paul follows faithfully, step by step, the principles of the Judaism of his time. Before declaring peremptorily that the statements in these chapters are incompatible with those in other chapters of Romans and in other letters, we must first ask why Paul decided to begin his reflections with the pious Jew who ardently awaits the coming of divine vengeance on sinners. To put this recommendation in other terms: one must never isolate a single Pauline statement from the context within which it has a precise function.

(3) We will propose keys for reading each section and subsection of Romans, and we strongly recommend that the reader begin with them before venturing into the labyrinth of Paul's thought.

(4) The reader must not fail to note that Paul proceeds in each unit or subsection by precise and successive stages. He begins with strong statements *(propositiones)* that he explains and clarifies bit by bit (by means of a *ratio* and dif-

ferent kinds of arguments). The same is true of the major themes he develops in the course of the letter. It will be very useful for the reader to follow several of these lines of development, observing in each case how they gain progressively in richness and depth throughout the chapter. These are the principal themes:

- The gospel: its content, its effects, its aim, its addressees.
- Divine justice and its components: the connections between wrath and justice, justice and mercy, justice and election. (Cf. J.-N. Aletti, *Clefs pour interpréter l'épître aux Romains.*)
- The existence and actions of the believer, his or her righteousness: from justification to salvation; justification and morality; the believer and the commandments of the Mosaic Law.
- The Mosaic Law: its function, its relation to sin and salvation, Jesus Christ and the Law.

II. The Different Contexts for Interpretation

1. The Historical Context

Concerning the place and date of writing: Rom 15:26 mentions Macedonia and Achaia; Rom 16:1 speaks of Phoebe, deacon of the church at Cenchreae, the port of Corinth. Paul seems to be in Greece. Many people, by comparing these passages with the material in the book of Acts, have concluded that Romans was dictated at Corinth, but an exact dating is impossible: some time between 55 and 59 (perhaps during the winter of 57).

Any number of reasons might have caused Paul to write to the church at Rome, which he did not found, but for which he, as the apostle to the Gentiles, felt somehow responsible (cf. Rom 1:1-15; 15:15-16). That vocation even caused him to plan a trip to Rome in the future, with an intention to go on to evangelize Spain (Rom 15:24, 28). He may also have wanted to have contact with that community before carrying the collection to the churches in Judea, to present in more detail his ideas on justification by faith alone—the letter to the Galatians may have provoked an outcry among Christians of Jewish origin—and so on. Other reasons emanate from the community at Rome and its fame (because of its being founded by Peter and situated at the capital of the empire); no doubt the Jews and "god-fearers" who made up the community could have been troubled and agitated by his ideas on justification, the Law of Moses, and Israel. Friction between believers of Jewish origin and those of Gentile origin may also have led Paul to intervene by examining more profoundly the question of the relationship between Jew and non-Jew, and so on. But the particular reasons that occasioned the writing of Romans are insufficient to account for its content, which in turn, and uniquely, cannot be explained or interpreted by the conditions under which it was produced.

In terms of the development of Paul's thought, Romans very probably comes after 1–2 Corinthians and Galatians, in which the statements about justification are proposed with a good deal of vigor but without much development.

In addition to what it tells us about the primitive Church, Romans gives us precious information about Jewish exegesis and the literary models then in use; it demands that we take into account the rhetorical and exegetical methods, both Jewish and Hellenistic, that Paul used. Without awareness of them we will interpret erroneously. Through the window of Romans we can perceive as well a culturally and religiously varied world that presents itself for us to read and understand.

2. The Canonical Context

The Pauline letters in the NT are not classified in terms of theological or christological criteria, but in material terms: (1) whether the addressees are churches (from Romans to 2 Thessalonians) or individuals (from 1 Timothy to Philemon) and (2) in decreasing order of length, like the major and minor prophets in the OT. This seems to indicate the existence of a *codex*. While the topics treated by the different letters are complementary on the whole, and even overlapping, the letter closest to Romans is undoubtedly Galatians to the extent that the theme of justification by faith, outside the Mosaic Law, assumes a decisive place in both. A parallel and even synoptic reading of the two letters is not without interest.

With regard to the positions taken by Romans on justification by faith alone it is also necessary to read the letter of James (especially ch. 2) because the two writings seem to take contrary positions. See the comparison of their respective exegeses of Gen 15:6 ("Abraham believed . . . and the LORD reckoned it to him as righteousness") below (at Romans 4).

3. Interpretation Through the Ages

From the earliest centuries there have been commentaries on Romans. The most important patristic commentaries to which we can refer today are undoubtedly those of Origen and Augustine. Not that they were the only ones, but their influence was immense. We know how much Luther owed to Augustine! Of all the interpretations of Romans, that of Luther is the best known, and not only by Protestants, because for different reasons it has also left its mark on Catholics. Thirty years ago one of the best-known Catholic exegetes said to me: "The best commentary by far on Romans is that of Luther!" And yet this unanimous judgment has recently been called into question—by Protestants, who go so far as to say that Luther's reading of Paul, and especially of Romans, is completely wrong (cf. *infra*).

For the various commentaries on Romans from the patristic era to the nineteenth century, one should read the up-to-date account in J. A. Fitzmyer, *Romans,* 173–214.

III. Questions for Yesterday and Today

1. Romans and the Purity of the Gospel

For Lutheran interpretation in recent decades Romans presents the gospel of faith in all its purity. The true adversary of Paul was the pious Jew who made use of the Law for his or her own ends, for self-realization, boasting, and finally to achieve the illusion of being no longer dependent on God. For Paul the pursuit of the "righteousness of the Law" expressed, in typically Jewish accents, the desire of every human being to be recognized on the basis of what he or she has achieved. Hence Law and faith, Law and gospel, Judaism and Christianity are at extreme opposite positions. Paul perceived the radical novelty of Christianity, and Romans is the strongest exposition of that perception.

Other Lutheran exegetes see things differently. They do not question the desire that every faithful person has to fulfill the Law, to adhere to it with all his or her heart, but merely the possibility of realizing it: they no longer see this as pride or self-importance but as failure, even despair at never being able to observe and practice the Law of God, the divine will: poor Jew, who is incapable of doing anything and must recognize that he or she is unable to hear the voice of God. That interpretation, of course, can be combined with the preceding one: the disappointment and despair, the awareness of a real distance between what the Law demands and what I do, can alternate with pride and self-importance. Whether the so-called Pauline reading of Judaism is seen as qualitative or quantitative, we should simply note the consequences: justification by faith is the sole antidote to such dramatic situations.

Confessional readings, which are readings in faith, undoubtedly serve as a vehicle for rich and varied traditions, but they also run the risk of betraying the text, influenced as they are by ecclesial situations that have been in conflict for a very long time. We should simply recall the remarks of E. P. Sanders, with which most would agree today. According to him the readings of Pauline passages by the great exegetes of the last several decades, supposedly combating the fundamental legalism of Jewish religion, resulted only in "the retrojection of the Protestant-Catholic debate into ancient history, with Judaism taking the role of Catholicism and Christianity the role of Lutheranism" (*Paul and Palestinian Judaism,* 57). But the crisis of confessional interpretation (Lutheran or otherwise) also has its advantages: the reserves or suspicions it provokes have forced exegetes to embark on the longer but more secure route of historical and literary criticism.

2. Paul's Way of Presenting God in Romans is a Source of Difficulty

It is moving to present Paul's God as the true God who graciously justifies sinners—moving, but not very convincing if one does not take account of everything that in reality contradicts that justice. How can a God so overflowing with mercy and justice have hated so many people and hardened their hearts (Rom 9:13, 18; 11:7, 25) even before any negative response on their part (9:11-12)? Still worse, why imprison all humanity in disobedience in order the more to show them mercy: does God need the chronic weakness of human subjects in order to be able to manifest the divine glory, power, and goodness? The creatures Paul presents in Rom 9:19-23 seem, in fact, to be nothing but puppets, mute objects before a God ready to destroy them: could one really show the extent of divine justice and mercy at the same moment as one appears to suppress human freedom? Why does the apostle think himself obliged to emphasize that everything, without exception, is subject to divine wrath, when what he wants is to reveal the incredible truth of gracious justification? How does the election of one people not undermine the justice described in Rom 2:11, according to which God, completely impartial, shows no favoritism? But more than the internal coherence of Pauline discourse, it is his image of God and, consequently, of human beings, that raises questions.

3. Coherence of the Pauline Statements

If Paul is the faithful herald of the gospel, still the reader of Romans cannot fail to stumble over statements that are not completely compatible. It is difficult to reconcile the following two verses:

2:13 It is not the hearers of the Law who are righteous in God's sight, but the doers of the Law who will be justified.
3:20 No human being will be justified in [God's] sight by deeds prescribed by the Law.

Nevertheless, how can the Law, which is just and good (Rom 7:7-13) allow sin to abound and leave those who desire to obey it incapable of doing good (Rom 7:14-25)? Has God given to God's people a Law that is impossible to obey and practice, even though so many biblical statements affirm the contrary (Psalm 119; Deut 30:14, etcetera)? The most recent commentaries give an enormous amount of space to these questions, and my presentation will do them justice also, because what is at stake is the understanding of Romans.

SECOND READING

Justification by Faith Alone: Romans 1–4

The Starting Point and Its Difficulties

1. Questions

The first section, from Rom 1:18 to 4:25, is undoubtedly the one that produces the most difficulties and therefore deserves the closest attention. It is introduced by two series of questions, the first concerning the way in which Paul presents the gospel, the others on the sequence of his arguments.

a. The Way of Presenting the Gospel: The Power of God

If the gospel, the good news, is Christ, as the *exordium* of the letter says (Rom 1:3-9), why are the first four chapters not primarily christological in nature?

If the gospel is the best expression of divine graciousness, pardon, and compassion, can the first word of this gospel be divine wrath or vengeance against rebellious creatures (Rom 1:18-32)? Paul has just said that, through the gospel, divine justice is fully revealed, and he proceeds without transition to discourse on divine wrath. Does this mean that wrath is also the first word concerning divine justice?

Is it necessary to begin by impelling people to repent out of fear in order afterward to cause them to desire the mercy and forgiveness of God? Must human beings recognize their sin (Rom 1:18–3:21 would then be an attempt to convince them of it) before hearing the proclamation of the gospel (Rom 3:21-31)? And does God require the humiliation, fear, or repentance of creatures in order to demonstrate the greatness of divine mercy?

b. It is the Logic of the Section That Creates the Most Difficulty

To begin with (in 1:18–3:20) Paul does not question the role of the Mosaic Law; it enables him to formulate some of the principles on the basis of which he will underscore the components of divine justice. But beginning at 3:21 he clearly affirms the contrary: that this same divine justice has been manifested without the Law. Why would God have decided to manifest divine justice apart from a Law that had been given precisely for that purpose?

2. Some Answers

If the first section of Romans (especially 1:18–3:2) begins by developing the subject of divine wrath rather than universal mercy this is primarily in order to counter a prior objection coming from some of Paul's Jewish opponents. If Paul had begun with the statement that "all have sinned and . . . are now justified by [God's] grace as a gift," (cf. Rom 3:23-24) a religious Jew would certainly have subscribed to that, while adding that the gracious justification is nothing outside the Mosaic system, and is even inseparable from it. God's forgiveness and mercy do not dispense the faithful from the duty to do their best to fulfill the commandments of the Law. For the Jew a righteousness outside the Law of Moses—apart from its commandments, its processes for repentance and reparation for faults—is impossible. To the Pauline statement that "apart from Law, the righteousness of God has been disclosed" (Rom 3:21) the Jew would respond that that may possibly be the case for non-Jews who are not subject to the Law of Moses, but in any case the Jews can regard themselves as free with respect to a Law that God has commanded them to obey if they desire life (Lev 18:5, reflected in Rom 10:4). Paul himself is too familiar with Judaism not to know that works are inseparable from faith and are caused by it. He also indicates, in Romans 4, that the Jews are just as truly heirs and children of Abraham *as believers are* (cf. Rom 4:11-12). At the same time he acknowledges their precedence ("the Jew first") because their election can neither be denied nor forgotten. In thus affirming without reservation that the way of pardon and justification is the same *for all, Jews and non-Jews alike,* that faith alone in Jesus Christ is sufficient, Paul would have rendered his whole argument null and void for the very people to whom it was directed, pious Jews. First he had to show that justification would be the same for all without exception, that Jew and Greek are in the same situation in face of divine judgment and retribution. To begin with, why should God justify everyone in the same way, either by works of the Law or by faith? How could Paul show that justification would be the same for all, if not on the basis of the principles of those who could not accept it, his own co-religionists (cf. Romans 1–2)?

In Romans 1–3 Paul is thus not interested in awakening a somnolent humanity in order to show it the weight of its sin and bring it to shame and repentance, thus preparing it to receive the message of the gospel of mercy. Instead, he wants to show why justification should operate in the same manner for all, and he does so by beginning with a reprise of biblical and Jewish ideas on divine retributive justice.

Composition

This passage is divided into two blocks (1:18–3:20 and 3:21–4:25). In the first Paul reflects, together with Judaism, on the modalities of divine retribution; in the second he presents—this time using his own theology—the doctrine of justification by faith alone apart from the works of the Mosaic Law. The two blocks clearly follow the laws of composition of the time, especially the *propositio/probatio* pairing (cf. *supra*):

	1:18–3:20	**3:21–4:25**
propositio	1:18	3:21-22
probatio	1:19–3:18	3:23–4:22
peroratio	3:19-20	4:23-25

Logical Progression, 1:18–3:20

One ought not to forget that Paul begins with the expectations and ideas of the Judaism of his own time. For the faithful confronting persecutions of all kinds the coming of divine justice was the object of intense expectation: God had promised to come to avenge God's own and to reward each according to his or her works, especially to punish the wicked as they deserve.

In Rom 1:19-32 Paul reviews the facts acknowledged by all and describes the situation of people who have rejected God and God's justice, making use of slogans well known from Jewish literature. From then on, beginning with Rom 2:1, he does not describe facts, but challenges, warns, and above all attempts to drive his successive interlocutors from the field, to uproot traditional ideas. Rom 1:19-32 and 2:1ff. cannot belong to the same logical unit. But someone will ask: is not Paul talking only about non-Jews (i.e., Gentiles) in these verses? No, he is not referring solely to Gentiles. Certainly the vices listed in 1:29-31 are those of which the Jews liked to accuse the uncircumcised, and Rom 2:1-5 may have in view the Greek philosophers and sages, in contrast to their teachings, but Paul deliberately omits the word! A verse like 1:23, with its obvious allusion to the golden calf (Ps 106:20), indicates instead that the apostle also, in a veiled manner, includes the Israelites of the past among the idolators. But again someone may say that the Israel of Paul's time was by no means an idolatrous nation, tightly bound as it was to fidelity to the God of the covenant. That is true, but in mentioning neither Gentiles nor

Jews and retaining a generic description ("people who . . .") Paul blocks any kind of too-hasty designation.

Apart from style and tone, another indication underscores the progress of the reasoning: the way Paul uses the adjective "all." At the very beginning of each part of his demonstration (Rom 1:18, 29) "all" describes actions, not actors: the apostle does not speak of "the ungodliness of all people," but of "all ungodliness and wickedness of those who . . . ." Taking care not to say that all people—Gentiles and/or Jews—commit injustices, Paul simply says that the wrath of God is revealed against all injustice committed by people who resist the truth; there is no hint of any knowledge of their number.

If we start from that point we can easily see how the text proceeds: first of all it describes those who do evil (1:19-31) and approve of it (1:32). But it is not a question of *all* humanity, for the next stage (2:1) indicates that others disapprove and judge the first group—while, however, they do the same evil deeds. Thus we can discern two phases: (1) all those who do injustice and approve of others who practice it, and (2) all those who criticize and judge the first lot but do the same things. The rest of the text (2:9-15) allows for a response. There will be divine punishment for all who do evil (and we know from Rom 1:24-32 that there are a certain number of these and that they already bear the marks of their punishment), and divine recompense for all who do good (are there some? Paul affirms it in the insertion at 2:14-15). But if their number does not seem important, their origin is certainly emphasized: Jews *and* non-Jews (Greeks) may belong to either category, may do good or do evil, and receive the appropriate recompense. Thus the existence of a positive category (those who do good) is not excluded; it is simply connected to divine retribution: God will give recompense (in future) to all such (whether there are any or not) because divine justice is at issue!

Beginning with Rom 2:17 a third negative group appears: Jews who preach the good but do the contrary. But we should carefully note that Paul makes no attempt to assign a number to these: nowhere in 1:18–2:29 is it said that all, without exception, have sinned, but only that all those who commit sin will, without exception, receive just punishment. The apostle even very astutely suppresses the adjective "all" within the unit about the Jews (2:17-29). Perhaps Rom 2:1 is already speaking about the Jews, because there Paul says "*whoever you are,* when you judge others. . . ." "Whoever you are," that is, as we subsequently read (v. 9) "the Jew first and also the Greek." But that is not what is important, because the progression here passes to a different level. There is a qualitative leap from 2:1 to 2:17:

	Saying	**Doing**
2:1-5	you who criticize evil	and do what is evil
2:17-24	you who preach the Good (the Law)	and do what is evil

This is a leap in awareness and therefore in ignominy, because to criticize evil and still do it is less extreme than to know the Law, the divine will in its full clarity, to preach it and glory in it, and still to contravene it. But how many Jews actually live with such a contradiction? Paul does not say: certainly the plural "you" in 2:24 describes a totality that could include everyone, but 3:3a seems to indicate, on the contrary, that only a few are unfaithful to the divine revelation. Are there not some Jews who teach the Law and keep it faithfully? A fourth, undiscoverable category? And how many pious Jews see Paul's description of the Jew in 2:17-24 as a caricature! But the apostle never once says that he is referring to *all* Jews.

Romans 3 introduces a leap that is both quantitative and qualitative: (a) it is not simply a matter of "everyone who . . ." but of "everyone" without exception (Rom 3:4, 9, 12, 19), and (b) even the pious Jews are included in the category of sinners, the wicked, those who are corrupt and deserving of divine wrath. But to do this the apostle has to invoke Scripture, the true and normative word that declares that every human being is a liar and unrighteous. The apostle cannot really refer to experience as he has up to this point with regard to those who are known not to live what they preach: how can he accuse of contradiction and hypocrisy those who are devoted to the Law and try to practice it with their whole heart, and who for that very reason cannot doubt or despair of the special mercy God has promised to the Jew who repents?

Romans 3 is a clear indication of where Paul wants to go. Having decided (in Romans 1–2) to begin his argument with the point of view of a pious Jew who awaits the manifestation of ultimate justice, the apostle manages to evoke surprise that God has not destroyed sinful humanity; God has even done the opposite by graciously offering us justification, which demands nothing of us except that we believe and accept it. Thus, in progressively placing all humanity in the same negative situation *without exception or privilege,* the apostle in no way desires to degrade creatures in order to heighten the glory of the creator, but instead to prepare for the declaration in Rom 3:21-22: the absence of differences in face of retribution permits divine justice to be extended graciously to all human beings *in the same way, through faith alone*. No one is excluded—above all, not the faithful Jew who has awaited it for such a long time!

A Closer Reading, 1:1–4:25

Address and Prologue (1:1-17)

—1-7

Address, with reference to

- the *sender* (Paul) and his qualifications (v. 1) for proclaiming the gospel of God,
- the *content* that is developed in its various christological components (vv. 2-6), and
- the *addressees* (v. 7).

—8-15

Thanksgiving. As in many of Paul's letters, this serves practically as an *exordium* (a typical *captatio benevolentiae*).

—16-17

Propositio and its *ratio* (for these terms, see above on the composition of the letter).

1:16-17

The *propositio* (i.e., the thesis to be explained and proved) in v. 16 is followed by its *ratio* (brief justification of the *propositio*) in v. 17, where each of the parts of v. 16 is reprised in the table below.

Like most Pauline *propositiones,* this one is rather elliptical; it seems deliberately formulated to raise questions: for example, why does Paul begin by speaking of shame ("I am not ashamed") and not of the work of grace? The gospel reveals God's saving power for all believers without exception, whatever their religious, cultural, or social origins. But Paul seems to maintain a precedence of the Jew over the Greek: "the Jew first and then the Greek." These are religious categories: the Jews and the others, the non-Jews, who are lumped together as "Greeks." Is there really a Jewish precedence here? And if so, in what order: the historical (because the Jews were chosen by the true God and thus knew God before the pagans did) or the qualitative (Jews are superior because they belong to the chosen people, know the divine will and are thus able to put it into practice)? Or, while respecting the sensitivity of his readers of Jewish origin, is Paul trying to defend the rights of the non-Jews (Gentiles, Greeks) who have become Christians to be full heirs of the ancestral promises of God?

What does "through faith for faith" (or, in other translations, "from faith to faith") mean? From the faith of Abraham to that of the gospel (thus Tertullian)? From the faith of the preacher to that of the hearers (Augustine)? From the faith of the beginner to that of the mature believer (Luther)? From the fidelity of God to the faith of the human being (Karl Barth)?

The quotation from Hab 2:4 can also be translated in several ways: "the one who has been justified by faith will live" (in which case the reception of justification is attributed to faith: whoever is just is so because of faith, and this is the one who will share in eternal life), or "the one who has been justified by God's fidelity will live" (giving the Greek word *pistis* the sense of fidelity, in which case it quite obviously refers to the fidelity of God; this is to insist on the fact that human justice can only come from divine justice). The phrase is deliberately ambiguous. A reader should not give a hasty answer to these

Propositio	***Ratio***
16a: I am not ashamed of the gospel; it is the power of God	17a: For in it the righteousness of God is revealed through faith for faith;
16b: for salvation to everyone who has faith, to the Jew first and also the Greek.	17b: as it is written, "The one who is righteous will live by faith."

questions, for example by referring to other Pauline letters; one must wait for Paul himself to supply the necessary precision in Romans 1–4. Readers should take care at the end of each section to see if, and how, the statements of the initial *propositio* have been justified.

Keys for Reading (1:19-32)

(a) The purpose of this passage is to establish the situation at the beginning, i.e., retribution, with the categories and points of view present in the Judaism of Paul's time, whether apocalyptic or otherwise. It is a situation in which God's faithful are being put to the test, persecuted by impious people, idolators who have forgotten God.

(b) It is necessary for the argument that humanity should be totally responsible for its actions, utterly inexcusable, *in order that divine retribution may be seen to be just.* Rom 1:19-32 repeats the same process three times, each time more explicitly:

- human action (vv. 19-23) / divine reaction (v. 24)
- human action (v. 25) / divine reaction (vv. 26-27)
- human action (v. 28a) / divine reaction (vv. 28b-31).

This logic of relationship between human action and divine reaction is only possible because the human beings described in 1:19-31 are without excuse, the very phrase that introduces the series in v. 20. Otherwise divine retribution, which expands throughout the chapter, would be flagrantly unjust. The relationship between offense and retribution thus functions solely to manifest the justice of the divine reaction to human conduct that is responsible at every point and at the same time is contradictory. Romans 1 initiates in some sense a concrete definition of wrath. It appears as negative retribution, already at work and proportional (God does not *destroy* creation, but punishes with moderation) to the repeated refusal of human beings to recognize the God who is self-manifested to them and continues to be so.

The relationship established between the rejection of God and sexual disorder is not a Pauline invention; he is taking up a biblical and Jewish *topos*.

Composition (Romans 2)

See table below. Twice the apostle challenges a person supposed to be caught up in these contradictions in order to expose them (A and A') and point out the consequences (B and B'). These parallelisms enable us better to understand the trajectory of the argumentation in Romans 2. Up to Rom 2:16 the identities of the groups remain fixed; they are not yet separated or deconstructed; later Paul will proceed to show that the existing categories of Jew and Greek are not as fixed as one might think: the real Jew is not who we suppose to be a Jew, but the Gentile whose heart is circumcised and the one who is a Jew in secret, and those who are circumcised in the flesh may be uncircumcised in their hearts. Paul deliberately establishes an intermediate stage between the idolators of Romans 1 and the unfaithful Jews of Rom 2:17-24; this enables him to enunciate the principles of divine retributive justice.

	A (2:1-8)	**A' (2:17-24)**
apostrophe	whoever you are	you, Jew
address	negative: whom do you judge? others	positive: where are you seeking glory? in yourself
contradiction	in judging others you condemn yourself; in judging, you do the same things	while teaching others you do not teach yourself; you preached against stealing, but you steal (3x)
dishonoring God	not recognizing the goodness of God	you dishonor God
use of Scripture	v. 6: allusion to Ps 61[62]:13[13]	v. 24 cites Isa 52:5
	B (2:9-16)	**B' (2:25-29)**
identity	the Jew first, and then the Greek	the visible Jew; the secret Jew
the Law	outside the Law/within the Law; doing what the Law requires	practicing and observing the Law
inscription; heart	inscribed on their hearts	circumcision of the heart, not according to the letter
what God wills	God judges secrets	praise . . . from God

Its Function in the Argument (Romans 2)

Did Paul, as is so often thought, stigmatize the basic sin of the Jews (idolatry), which thus places them in the same (hopeless) situation as that of the Gentiles? If that were the role of Romans 2 we would rightly conclude that "Paul's case for universal sinfulness, as it is stated in Rom 1:18–2:29, is not convincing; it is internally inconsistent and it rests on gross exaggeration" (E. P. Sanders, *Paul, the Law, and the Jewish People,* 125). But the apostle has never said that he is thinking here of all Jews, particularly faithful and pious Jews; if these were in view his argument would indeed miss the mark. The purpose of Romans 2 is to lead its readers to the sole criterion that determines who is righteous, that is, circumcision of the heart (which is not reserved for Jews) because, being impartial, God cannot take into account anything but that.

2:1-16: Keys for Reading

(a) Why, in Romans 1, did Paul not issue a challenge to people who do evil and are satisfied with themselves as he does in Romans 2 to those who are in conflict with themselves? Because he wants to lead his readers into the human heart, where contradictions and uncircumcision find their home; because it is circumcision of the *heart* that God favors.

(b) Paul does not say that all people are in conflict with themselves.

(c) The function of these verses is to announce the criteria on the basis of which divine retribution is and will be exercised, and then (vv. 17-29) to erase the boundaries between Jew and non-Jew in face of that same divine retribution based on works (Rom 2:6-10, 13, 15a) and impartiality (cf. Rom 2:11).

(d) At this point in the argument Paul is already engaged in a certain degree of levelling: there are not, on the one hand, some who recognize the will of God because they have the Mosaic Law, and on the other hand some who do not know it. Through their consciences human beings have an idea of justice. That point is essential to the argument because it permits Paul to affirm that circumcision of the heart is not something belonging exclusively to Jews, and thus the boundary between Jew and non-Jew is more flexible than one might think.

2:1-16: The Biblical and Jewish Background

Nothing, or almost nothing, in these verses is Pauline, and for good reason: it is by means of biblical principles, as interpreted by intertestamental Judaism, that the apostle proceeds. These principles permit him, paradoxically, to conclude to the fluidity of limits and boundaries: God does not exercise divine justice by following external categories (physical circumcision or uncircumcision) but by considering works and the circumcision of the heart.

v. 4: divine patience and mercy in light of repentance (Sir 18:10-14; Wis 11:23; 12:10, 19; 15:1; 2 Esdr 7:132-139).

v. 5a: hardness of heart (Deut 9:27; 31:27, etcetera; *1QS* 1.6; 2.14-18; *CD* 2.17-20; 3.4-12).

v. 5b: treasure in heaven as a consequence of action (*2 Esdr* 7:75-77; 8:33-36; 9:7; *2 Bar* 14:12-13; 24:1; 44:14; *PsSol* 9:5; in the NT, cf. Matt 6:19ff. and parallels).

v. 5c: "day of wrath": *Soph* 1.15, 18; 2.3; *TLev* 3:3; *2 Esdr* 7:38-44, etcetera; Rev 6:17.

v. 6: God will reward each one according to his or her works (Jer 17:9-10; Ps 61 [62]:13[12]; Prov 24:12; Job 34:11; Sir 16:14; *ʾAboth* 3.15 [in the NT, cf. Matt 16:27; Rev 2:23]; *ApAbr* 28.2. See also the Jewish texts closer to the NT era, such as Tob 4:9-11; 2 Macc 7:9; 4 Macc 17:11-12; *PsSol* 9:3-5. It should not be forgotten that those who pray in the Bible ask God to render to the wicked according to their works: Ps 27[28]:4; to avenge the faithful and reward them according to their good works. The context in Romans 1–3 is probably that of a divine justice whose clear and definitive manifestation is eagerly awaited.).

vv. 7, 10: for "glory and honor," compare the traditional formulae in Jewish liturgy adopted by the earliest Christians (1 Pet 1:7; 2 Pet 1:17; Rev 4:9-11; 5:12-13; 21:26; the pairing is frequently found in LXX and in Hellenistic literature).

v. 9a: anguish and distress (Deut 28:53ff.; Isa 8:22; in Paul, Rom 8:35; 2 Cor 6:4).

v. 11: the statement about divine impartiality recurs frequently (1 Sam 16:7; 2 Chr 19:6-7; Deut 10:17; Job 34:19; Prov 18:5; 24:23-25; 28:21; Ps 82:1-4; Mal 2:9. For the impartiality of the judge, see Isa 23:6-8; Lev 19:15; Deut 1:17; 10:17; 16:19; 28:50, etcetera The future king proclaimed by Isaiah will not judge by appearances nor on the basis of hearsay: Isa 11:3. In the deuterocanonical and pseudepigraphical books, see Sir 4:22, 27; 35:12-18; Wis 6:7; *TJob* 4:7-9; 43:13; *1 Esdr* 4:39; *Jub* 5:12-16; 21:3-5; *PsSol* 2:15-18; 2:32-35; *2 Bar* 13:8-12; 44:2-4; *Ant. Bibl.* 20:3-4; *1 Enoch* 63:8-9; in the NT, Acts 10:34; 15:8-9; Jas 2:1, 9; 1 Pet 1:17. Applied to Jesus: Matt 22:16 = Mark 12:14 = Luke 20:21. Elsewhere in Paul: Gal 2:6; Col 3:25; Eph 6:9).

We note that in and of itself the axiom of divine impartiality does not exclude different rewards and punishments for Jews and non-Jews, but it causes them to rest on a deeper religious identity defined by circumcision of the heart. Impartiality and knowledge of the heart (what is not seen) go together (cf. Rom 2:11, 16, but much earlier in 1 Sam 16:7). God thus sees both holiness and wickedness within. The axiom permits a number of different contrasts to emerge: "evident" versus "hidden," "false" versus "true." Impartiality is what distinguishes God from humans (who are incapable of impartiality and inclined to corruption), cf. 1 Sam 16:7; 2 Chr 19:6-7. Because God sees the heart (and is thus impartial), God is a just judge, assigning rewards and punishments, giving to each one according to what he or she has done (Jer 17:10; Prov 24:12). Impartiality makes God close to those who have neither protection nor status (cf. Deut 1:16-17). Divine impartiality is not the same thing as egalitarian neutrality: to reestablish justice means, first of all, to undo a wrong (independently of the intention with which it was done) and to protect the weak, those whose rights are trampled underfoot.

v. 15a: the law inscribed on our hearts. The *nomos agraphos* written on the heart is a theme well known to Stoicism and Neoplatonism. But in the rabbinic writings there is nothing about a law written on the hearts of the Gentiles; instead, the Law is written in the hearts of the Israelites according to the promises of Jer 31:33 (38:33 LXX). According to some commentaries Deut 30:14 constitutes the background of Rom 2:14-15.

v. 16: God alone knows the human heart (1 Sam 16:7; 1 Kings 8:39; Jer 11:20; 12:3; 17:10 [note the relationship between knowledge of hearts and just retribution; the same is true of Jer 20:12; Ps 7:10[9]; 16[17]:3; 43[44]:22[21]; 63 [64]:7-8[6]; 138[139]:23; Prov 15:11; 17:3; 21:2; 24:12).

2:12-16: Keys for Reading

(a) Composition (v. 12 prepares for what follows; see table below).

(b) Verses 14-15 speak of a natural revelation (ethical in nature) but the idea does not come from Paul; he is reflecting ideas expressed in the Judaism of his time (cf. Philo). Moreover, these verses are a normal outgrowth of Rom 1:20ff. (if God can be known, why not also God's will?).

(c) The category of good people has a double function:

(1) Theological: Being a just judge (cf. 2:5), God cannot render evil for good. Could a judge whose rewards and punishments were negative

	Actors	Retribution and Justice
a = v. 12a:	those who are apart from the Law	negative retribution: apart from the Law
b = v. 12b:	those who are "under the Law"	negative retribution: by the Law
B = v. 13:	those who have the Law	positive condition for retribution: following the Law
A = vv. 14-15:	those who do not have the Law	positive condition for retribution: following conscience

a priori merit the name of just? The judge must first examine the actions of those who come before him or her, who stand at the tribunal (cf. 2:6). Thus Paul is obliged to mention the category of good people in order to underscore the justice of the divine judge in pronouncing judgment and ordering its execution. What is important is not that there are at least some who do good, because even if not even one could be found that would not change the divine rule, which is to reward the good and punish the wicked. We thus take a step forward in the presentation of God, the just judge: God's justice does not consist solely in punishing people according to the degree of their refusal to acknowledge God; it acts also and above all to communicate God's own attributes (incorruptibility, glory) to those who do good.

(2) Soteriological: The existence of a group of good people (cf. 2:10) has another function, namely that of promoting the levelling of the objects of divine justice; to put it another way, to arrive at an equal justification for the Jew and the non-Jew. Is it really conceivable that Greek men could in fact be circumcised, and Jewish men uncircumcised, and that God would thus reward/punish a Jew as if he were a Gentile and a Gentile as if he were a Jew? In the positive response given in Romans 2 the apostle is not making an absolute innovation; he is adapting in his own way themes one finds in a number of Jewish authors of the period. They reflect an ongoing debate about Jewish identity. Paul thus shakes off the difference between Jew and Gentile at the very point where the Jews of his time were questioning the limits of its applicability.

The group of those who do good is thus an essential element in the argument of Rom 1:18–3:20 because it permits the levelling or calling into question of identities and, thereby, of rewards and punishments: if God is a just judge, God must consider actions without being impressed by status and the advantages or privileges that follow from it; God, who knows the hearts of all and thus is aware that, without belonging to the people of the covenant, they may still be circumcised at heart.

(d) The vocabulary of the Law and its function. This is the first time that Paul uses the word "Law" to refer to the Mosaic Law, and that Law seems to divide humanity into two parts: there are those who are "apart from the Law" (non-Jews) and those who are "subject to the Law" (Jews). Paul recalls the religious division in the world as the Jew sees it: on the one hand the people of the covenant, on the other the Gentiles. If Paul did not speak of the Mosaic Law before this it was undoubtedly because those who are not its subjects can do good and evil without knowing its precepts; it does not dictate divine retribution, whether positive or negative, for all people, but only for the Jews.

(e) At v. 13 ("the doers of the Law . . . will be justified") the apostle makes an assertion contrary to his habitual affirmations according to which it is not works of the Law that make one just (cf. 3:20 and 7:7-23). But he is not contradicting himself in any way, because in Romans 2, we must repeat, the categories he is using are not (yet) his own.

2:17-24: Jewish Identity

The apostrophe ("you, the Jew . . .") is one of several elements of the ancient diatribe that can be identified in vv. 17-24, including also such things as rebuke, indictment, and lists of vices. We can thus determine the function of this passage with assurance: Paul does not wish to offend the Jews he addresses (although, of course, he is speaking to fictional people) nor to condemn them. He makes no mention at all of future and imminent divine retribution. What, then, is his purpose? It is pedagogical. First, through the apostrophe he wants to awaken those among the Jews who have been living in contradiction to the Law so that afterward (in vv. 25-29) he can open their minds to the complexity of the categories they have supposed to be so simple and clear. Paul has thus reached the point he was aiming at, that is, the question of the status of the Jews, what constitutes their identity.

2:17-24: Keys for Reading

(a) This unit is made up of two parts, vv. 17-20 (the addressee's suppositions) and vv. 21-24 (reality, which is quite different):

α 17-18:	positive relation of Jews to God (by means of the Law)
β 19-20	positive relation of Jews to Gentiles (teaching, guidance, light)
β' 21-22:	contradiction (not teaching themselves)
α' 23-24:	contradiction (offense to God)

(b) The Mosaic Law plays a decisive role. It is not presented as a list of prohibitions, a source of fear, or an instrument of divine judgment as in Rom 2:12, but as the supreme light and goodness, the expression of the divine will—in short, as that which makes it possible for Jews to know God. It determines the vocation of a Jew, which is to obey the will of God and thus to be responsible for the rest of humanity.

(c) The category of the Jew as sinner. Paul emphasizes grave sins because they practically make the Jew who commits them a Gentile and thus a sinner. But are the accusations pertinent? Is it true that Jews have gone so far as to rob pagan temples (2:22)? Some people think that this verse should be taken in a figurative sense, and that Paul is criticizing the idolatrous attachment of Israel to the Torah. But that interpretation is without foundation. Paul alludes to real cases like that described in 2 Macc 13:6-8, where Menelaus, a Jew and even a high priest, is accused of this wicked deed. But he does not mean to say that all Jews have committed or still commit such acts: that some of them have been in that situation is eminently suited to his purpose, which is to show that Jewish identity disappears in the commission of such actions, and divine retribution takes effect as a consequence of this.

2:25-29: Boundaries are Called into Question

While vv. 17-24 insisted on the clear identity of the Jew, in vv. 25-29 Paul renders all differences and boundaries fluid. One ought not to be disturbed by the language of circumcision and uncircumcision, which marks the difference between Jews and non-Jews, and which Paul makes use of, retaining as the prophets do the idea of circumcision of the heart as a criterion of righteousness. From now on he can assert that God will reward the Greek just as the Jew and vice versa for, if the Greek is circumcised at heart and the Jew uncircumcised, God, being impartial, will treat the Jew as a Gentile and the Gentile as a Jew.

Keys for Reading (3:1-8)

(a) The end of Romans 2 could be understood as a negation of Jewish particularity. Paul rejects such an interpretation: that certain Jews may be found in the ranks of sinners (and thus of Gentiles) does not call into question the historic privileges of the Jews as a whole. For the function of the passage, see above, pp. 1559–1560.

(b) The assertion that "everyone is a liar" in v. 4 is taken from Ps 116:11, where the oppressed psalmist recalls, "I said in my consternation, everyone is a liar." This first declaration of the universality of human sin prepares for the scriptural proof in vv. 10-18. In these verses Paul comes to a turning point in his exposition: does the fact that Jews sin and lie and commit injustice imply that they are condemned by God as sinners (v. 7)? Does not the just judge have but one category, that of sinners?

(c) In v. 4 the context demands that we translate "in your judging," not "in your being judged."

(d) Two interpretations of v. 9 are possible: (1) "we" refers to Jews (as in 3:1), in which case v. 9 would be dealing with questions about the status of Jews: "are we [Jews] any better off? Not entirely. . . ." It is a coherent solution even though the verb *proechomai* does not seem to have this meaning elsewhere. Or (2) "we" refers to Paul and his argument; the verb would then have a passive sense: "Do we lose the advantage (does our argument break down)? Not at all, because we have accused everyone, Jews and Greeks, . . ." But where has he accused *everyone*? Not in Romans 2; only in Rom 3:4.

Appeal to the Authority of Scripture and Its Function (3:10-18)

(a) The biblical proof is comprised of a series of linked citations:

vv. 10-12b = Ps 14:1-3, with an accent on the universality of evil;
v. 13a = Ps 5:9 (total depravity, throat and tongue);
v. 13b = Ps 140:3 (lips)
v. 14 = Ps 10:7 (mouth);
vv. 15-17 = Isa 59:7-8 (feet, ways)
v. 18 (reprise of vv. 10-12) = Ps 36:1.

Paul begins by insisting on sin's universality (cf. "not even one" and "all" in vv. 10-12); then, in vv. 13-17, he emphasizes the fact that everything human is perverse (from top to bottom: throat, tongue, lips, mouth, feet, symbolizing speech and action).

(b) Not being God and thus not being able to see into hearts, Paul himself cannot accuse all humanity of belonging to the category of sinners.

He can only submit to the judgment of Scripture, the word of God, by choosing biblical passages (in the Greek translation) that emphasize the universal and total perversity of human beings. He thus comes to the end of his demonstration: if all without exception, Jews and non-Jews, are in the ranks of sinners and thus in danger of being destroyed, justification will be given in the same manner to all.

Keys for Reading, 3:21–4:25

Rom 1:18–3:20 has enabled Paul to dismiss the objections made to the equal status of Jew and Greek with respect to retribution. But for the apostle that conclusion is only an interim stage on the basis of which he will now return to his proposition: if there is no exception in the coming of wrath there can be none for the gift of justification.

The section extending from 3:21 to 4:25 has the same structure as the preceding one: the *propositio* (3:21-22) is followed by a series of specifications offered first of all in the form of assertions (3:22b-26) and then in the form of questions and answers (3:27-31), all of which is supported by an extensive reference to Scripture (4:1-25).

The novelty of Paul's thought is evident on the basis of Rom 3:21, in relation to the preceding development that in part textually reflects the Jewish positions. If a pious Jew sins, he or she hopes unfailingly in divine mercy. God, the just judge, is even obliged to make him or her righteous so that he or she may practice justice and equity by observing the ordinances of the Law. What would an impracticable divine law mean, unless that the legislator were unjust or powerless? The Law has its own procedures for "cleansing" (its cultic system, its required expiations): pious Jews, if they acknowledge their sin, know that they will receive pardon through sacrifices for sin and the ritual of expiation. For them the just judge was not simply someone who examines people's conduct and their hearts and punishes equitably, but also and above all one who promotes righteousness by pardoning and by sustaining in the hearts of the faithful a love for the divine Law.

In declaring that no one is justified by works of the Law (Rom 3:20) the apostle separates divine justice from law (cf. 3:21), a disjunction that creates an enormous difficulty and is insupportable for a Jew: how could God manifest divine justice without the Law, which causes people properly to recognize God's will? Has the Mosaic Law then (become) unjust in order that God may choose another means of judgment and retribution? In insisting that God has always justified by faith alone, Romans 4 indeed redoubles our astonishment: why did God reveal the Law and demand its observance? Simply so that, through it, people could recognize their injustice and sin (3:20b)? Paul is obliged to explain himself in face of that objection (cf. Rom 7:7-25). In the meantime he will show that his doctrine of justification by faith alone is in accord with the word of God.

Keys for Reading (3:21-26)

(a) The *propositio* of vv. 21-22 seems to indicate what Paul intends from this point on to make clear and to prove, that is, the justification of all humanity by faith alone without the works of the Mosaic Law. What is meant by "works of the Law"? These are the *good works required by the Law,* as in 4Q 398.14-17:

> And also we have written to you some of the works of the Torah which we think are good for you and for your people, for [we saw] in you intellect and knowledge of the Torah. Reflect on all these matters and seek from [God] so that he may support your counsel [= will] and keep far from you the evil scheming and the counsel of Belial, so that at the end of time, you may rejoice in finding that some of our words are true. And it shall be reckoned to you as in justice when you do what is upright and good before him, for your good and that of Israel. [*Source:* Florentino García Martínez, *The Dead Sea Scrolls Translated. The Qumran Texts in English,* translated by Wilfrid G. E. Watson (2nd ed. Leiden, New York, and Cologne: E. J. Brill; Grand Rapids: Eerdmans, 1996) 84–85].

(b) In these verses Paul insists on the fact that divine grace, and it alone, is the source of justification for human beings. But we find similar affirmations in the Judaism of his time. Consider, for example, 1QS 11.2-15 (especially vv. 11-14):

> As for me, if I stumble,
> the mercies of God shall be my salvation always;
> and if I fall in the sin of the flesh,
> in the justice of God, which endures eternally,
> shall my judgment be;
> if my grief commences,

> he will free my soul from the pit
> and make my steps steady on the path;
> he will draw me near in his mercies,
> and by kindnesses set in motion my judgment;
> he will judge me in the justice of his truth,
> and in his plentiful goodness
> always atone for all my sins. . . .
> [*Source:* Ibid., 18-19]

What is unique to Paul is the separation he makes between faith and (works of the) Mosaic Law.

(c) Faith in Christ or the fidelity of Christ? Paul repeats several times that the justification of sinners is accomplished *dia / ek pisteōs Christou* (or *Iēsou*), phrases that can either refer to faith in Christ or the fidelity of Christ. Both interpretations are defended today, even if those who tend to favor "fidelity of Christ" seem to have the more convincing arguments. But in the context it is difficult to see how the formulations in 3:22a and 3:26 either specify the object of faith or refer to Jesus' own fidelity. What Paul means by using these phrases in the genitive is that there is an essential connection from now on between faith in God and the coming of Jesus Christ. Since Jesus has come, died, and been raised, faith cannot be defined except as belief in the God who graciously justifies through Jesus Christ (cf. 4:25b). Faith is thus inseparable from that event because it has manifested the sovereign justice of God. In short, both *Christou* and *Iēsou* are qualitative genitives, very difficult to render in modern languages: "faith in God who is definitively self-revealed in Jesus," or perhaps "faith in the God who has pardoned [us] in Jesus Christ." We can thus see why the apostle inserts a genitive in 3:22a and 3:26. The semantic ambiguity he prefers permits him to indicate the definitively christological coloration of faith without being too precise about the subjective and objective dimensions, since from Rom 3:21 to 4:25 Paul will not have need of it for his argument.

Abraham's Justification by Faith Alone (4:1-25)

Why does Paul want to exegete Gen 15:6? To show that God always had the intention of including the Gentiles within the family of Abraham, even if he is not their ancestor according to the flesh, because God is the God of all (cf. Rom 3:27)? To show Abraham as an example of faith? What he really wants to prove is what he stated in the *propositio* in 3:21-22; in other words, that justification is by faith alone without the works of the Law. That is why we must read v. 1 thus: "What then are we to say was gained by Abraham, our ancestor according to the flesh?" For what Abraham gained by believing was righteousness, but also an incredible crowd of descendants in space and time!

If Paul has recourse to Gen 15:6 it is partly in order to situate himself in terms of the exegesis of his own time according to which God called Abraham because of his faith, that is, his works. Thus Neh 9:8 (LXX 2 Esdr 19:7-8): "you found his heart faithful before you, and made with him a covenant," as also in Sir 44:19-21. We find a tendency to interpret Gen 15:6 in light of Gen 22:17-18 because the latter text gives the reasons for the divine blessing, the numerous descendants: Abraham's obedience! Cf. 1 Macc 2:52 ("Was not Abraham found faithful when tested, and it was reckoned to him as righteousness?") See also Jub 18:15-16; 19:9; 23:10; 24:11, all texts insisting above all on Abraham's fidelity, the perfection of all his actions, his observation of the divine law. The same is true at Qumran in *CD* 3:2-3: Abraham became a friend of God because he had observed the divine commandments. The tendency is still prominent in the first rabbinic writings.

Paul does not follow that line: that is the least one can say about it. The difficulties he confronts are enormous, especially because the exegesis of his time already interpreted Gen 15:6 in light of Genesis 22 (especially vv. 17-18) by insisting on the obedience and fidelity of the patriarch, and also because the case of Abraham did not seem to admit of generalization: if his faith was counted as righteousness before his circumcision, according to the divine order in Genesis 17, had justification not become inseparable from circumcision? Abraham appeared to remain an exception. How could Paul demonstrate that his case was, on the contrary, normative, if it is true that God has always justified by faith alone, without circumcision or other works of the Law (for that does seem to be the problem)? If the word of God is to support his thesis it will have to come from the beginning, from the first book of Genesis. Now Gen 15:6 is in fact the first biblical passage that associates faith and righteousness: moreover, it is incontestable. How will the apostle proceed?

The chapter is divided into two parts:

—vv. 1-12
(key words: "be reckoned"). Here the principal and almost unique actor is Abraham. The argumentation insists on the *how* (Abraham was justified by faith alone, without works) and the *when* (he was still uncircumcised) of his justification:
- vv. 1-8
  how (key words: "works," "work")
- vv. 9-12
  when (key words: "circumcised" and "uncircumcised")

—vv. 13-25
(key words: "promise," "promised"). Here the interest shifts to the content of belief, that is, the promise of paternity to Abraham, his descendants, and the identity of his descendants (the world, many peoples)
- vv. 13-18
  (with the contrast between faith and law)
- vv. 19-25
  (Abraham's faith as type of all faith).

4:1-8

The function of vv. 1-8 is to furnish the passages of Scripture that support the thesis relative to justification by faith alone without works of the Law. Paul wants to show that the act of believing is reckoned as righteousness without being a good work calling for reward: justification is purely gratuitous.

The sharp contrasts in the *subpropositio* in 3:21-22 recur here:

"to one who works"	"to one without works" (= a believer)
"wages," "something due"	"faith" = "gratuitously"

The "wages" mentioned in relation to the works to be done emphasize the necessary connection between the work and the implied reward. Faith, however, is associated with grace and even defines the economy of grace: the act of believing is not some kind of obligation that gives one a *right* to justification or recompense. But how will the apostle show that faith and wages (or recompense) are opposites? He uses a *gezerah shawah,* literally, an "equivalent principle." It is one of the Jewish rules (attributed to Hillel) for interpreting Scripture. Two different passages from Scripture that have one or more terms in common can mutually interpret one another. Playing on the presence of the verb "to reckon," ("impute") or "to be reckoned" in Gen 15:6 and Ps 32:1-2, Paul tries to show that the act of believing "is reckoned" as righteousness, but without being considered a good work that extracts positive divine retribution, a necessary recompense. What logical connection allows Paul to interpret Gen 15:6 through Psalm 32? If forgiveness is equivalent to justification, and if forgiveness is an effect of divine graciousness, so is justification; and when Gen 15:6 says that the fact of believing was reckoned to Abraham as righteousness it is also saying that such justification is utterly gratuitous. Faith is thus not a work calling for a proportional reward, a recompense or wage. Another advantage of Psalm 32 is that it is especially effective in showing that justice has always resulted from faith alone; the psalm is about David, a subject of the Mosaic Law, who confesses that even for the subjects of that Law pardon (and therefore righteousness) is not reckoned on the basis of works, but through pure generosity. The case of Abraham is valid for everyone, Jews and non-Jews.

4:9-12

Verses 9-12 insist moreover on the fact that Abraham was reckoned as righteous in the situation described by Psalm 32, that of sinners who cannot glory in their works; for being still uncircumcised and thus still a Gentile, the patriarch belongs in that category (cf. what was said above with regard to Romans 1–2, p. 1559). This again proves that justification comes through faith alone, without works of the Law. If the patriarch was reckoned as just when he was still in the ranks of sinners that means that circumcision is not a condition *sine qua non* of justification, that it is but the *posterior* sign of a justice gratuitously received in a state of uncircumcision (v. 11), to the extent that the act of believing, the promise of posterity and the gift of justice (in Genesis 15) are in no way tied to the obligation of circumcision. This last does nothing but seal that gratuitous gift in the flesh so that it may never be forgotten.

4:13-18

Having thus showed that the righteousness bestowed on Abraham is entirely gratuitous and that it is not owing either to Abraham's good works or to his being circumcised, Paul can now consider the content of the promise in which Abraham believed. Paul shows that the act of believing, Abraham's justice, and the promise are essentially related because what Abraham was asked to believe in was his universal paternity!

Note how Paul has gotten past the objection that appeals to Genesis 17: indeed, Abraham was declared righteous for having believed in the divine word while he was still uncircumcised. But after Genesis 17 the situation was radically changed for all his descendants, beginning with Ishmael and Isaac. What Paul demonstrates here is simply that the promise is still valid today, not on the basis of Genesis 17, but because of the faith of the uncircumcised Abraham: circumcision and the Law have in no way altered the relationship among promise, faith, and gratuitous righteousness.

Verses 13-18 underscore the historical dimension of an action that is not simply a relationship between God and each individual, because to believe means to enter into a history that goes back to the beginning. Romans 4 categorically refutes everything that has been said about how Paul conceives faith: Buber was mistaken when he said that *pistis* is a Pauline creation based on Greek premises and shaped by the proclamation of Jesus' death and resurrection, and that it is opposed to biblical *emuna,* a faith that is essentially historical, founded on the great experiences of the past, an individual faith rooted in that of a whole people.

Here we can see why the apostle chose the case of Abraham, father of all believers. If there is one thing children cannot give themselves, but only receive, it is their identity as sons or daughters. They can do nothing to obtain it, but only receive it, i.e., believe that they are son or daughter. But we should also add that what is true of the children (which we are) is also true of Abraham because he received from the divine word his very identity as a father. The economy of grace in which faith thus acquires its maximum breadth is the history of a promise in the process of accomplishment, the history of an immense family, from the father to the last of the offspring as long as there are believers! Obviously the most beautiful thing is that Abraham's act of faith evokes that of the children, for he thus also receives his identity as father of all those who, "countless as the stars in the sky" (Gen 15:5) believe like him. Our act of faith thus confirms the identity of Abraham as the father of believers—in short, the fecundity of his (and every) act of faith.

4:19-22

Paul can thus enunciate some of the fundamental components of the act of believing insofar as it structures all relationships: with God, others, and the world. The act of believing permits a kind of ideal understanding of what constitutes trust: on the one hand, there is the old age of the patriarch and Sarah's sterility, on the other hand a wild promise of an immense posterity. To abandon oneself to the apparent madness of God, to a word that everything seems to make ludicrous: that was the patriarch's choice. In recalling it Paul shows how one should submit to the divine world, accepting a total dependence on it, not falling under outside control but signifying that one chooses life because only faith is fecund. At the same time, that fecundity not only authenticates the act of the believer, but is the sign of the true God, the one who gives life through faith because God loves life (cf. Rom 4:17). The act of believing reveals the graciousness, trust, and justice of a God who, as the God of all humanity, calls all to the same dignity as daughters and sons, and therefore heirs.

4:23-25

These verses recall that in Romans 4 faith—that of Abraham and of other believers after him—is not faith in Christ, but in the God who desires and gives life: the structure of the act of believing, as a reciprocal relationship between God and human beings requiring, on the human side, a complete trust in the divine word, was not changed by the coming of Christ, but rather affirmed. Continuity is decisive here because it goes hand in hand with the unity of the promise and the identity of God who is manifested in desiring and giving life.

Interpretation of the Letter of James (Romans 4)

James 2:14-26 refers to the same text (Gen 15:6) to show that justification takes place on the basis of works and not solely on the basis of faith:

> Was not our ancestor Abraham justified by works when he offered his son Isaac on the altar? [an allusion to Genesis 22]. You see that faith

> was active along with his works, and faith was brought to completion by the works. Thus the scripture was fulfilled that says, "Abraham believed God, and it was reckoned to him as righteousness," and he was called the friend of God. You see that a person is justified by works and not by faith alone (Jas 2:21-24).

Paul's and James's theses seem to be utterly opposed, but they are not. Both of them effectively assert that faith cannot fail to bear fruit: otherwise why does Paul in each of his letters exhort believers to imitate the Lord in humility, patience, and love? If the justification freely given to believers means that their whole being is transformed, it cannot help but shine forth and manifest itself in and through action. But in speaking of "works" in Romans 4 Paul is referring to those demanded by the Law, and he declares their incapacity, and thus that of the Law, to insure the pardon of sins, the gift of the Holy Spirit, and adoption as sons and daughters. For James, on the other hand, the word "works" does not refer to the Law; instead, he is talking of the actions by which baptized persons (those who according to Paul are already graciously justified by God) manifest the reality and efficacy of their faith and hence their righteousness. In short, together with other categories it envisions the same reality described by Paul in Gal 5:6, "faith working through love." There can be no doubt that there is no contradiction between the theses developed by the two apostles at the point where the confessional disputes since Luther have so often found it. Nevertheless, the fact that James and Paul do not appeal to Gen 15:6 in the same way requires that we examine the presuppositions behind each reading.

At the level of the exegetical techniques in vogue at the time, James's reading is by no means at fault because it rests on the similarities of vocabulary existing between Gen 15:5 and 22:17; if in another episode God promised Abraham descendants as numerous as the stars in the sky this was evidently for the same reason, mentioned only in 22:18, namely obedience. A *gezerah shawah* (for this term, see above at Rom 4:1-8) thus allows James to explain Gen 15:5-6 on the basis of Genesis 22. At that level the line of separation does not run between Christianity and Judaism. Paul's and James's exegeses of Gen 15:6 are completely different even though their theses are not basically opposed. Moreover, it is easy to see why they each refer to the same passage: Paul because here Scripture asserts for the first time that the act of believing can be counted as righteousness, thus indirectly confirming the thesis of justification by faith alone (without works of the Mosaic Law), and James because Gen 15:6 shows, when brought into relationship with 22:17-18, that from the beginning faith has justified by leading believers to act, or in other words to produce good works.

But what Paul underscores in Romans 4 is the relationship between faith and the gratuitousness of the gift received. Because, in Gen 15:6, Abraham believed, he received his own identity as father and, at the same time, that of his descendants, the sons and daughters to come. His and their identities were expressed in the same act of faith. That is why Paul, unlike others, does not give a privileged status to the long and continually renewed process of the act of faith, but returns to the origin, as to a fecundity that precedes us. It is that faith that has engendered us and it is by means of it that we are what we are: "faith" here should be read as the faith of Abraham but also our own, because the act of believing gives us an ancestry and attaches us to a history, the history of believers.

The Present and Future of the Baptized: Romans 5–8

Composition

a. The Function of Romans 5 in the Argument

In Romans 1–4 the development of Rom 1:18–3:20 and 3:21–4:25 constituted two stages in the same process of reasoning. The role of those two sections was to explain and confirm certain statements in the principal *propositio* (especially Rom 1:17). Having shown that there is no privilege that can be invoked in the face of divine retribution—in short, having leveled the situations of Jew and non-Jew (1:18–3:20), Paul can assert that divine justice is manifested for all, without any kind of discrimination, on the basis of faith alone, and that the same thing has for a long time been asserted by the Torah itself (3:21–4:25).

Is Romans 5 the conclusion, in a christological key, of Romans 1–4, as the "therefore" of 5:1 seems to indicate? But compared to the conclusions of other sections (8:31-39; 11:33-36) this one would be very long (ending at the earliest at

5:11). Certainly, to conclude the development of Rom 1:18–4:25 by insisting on the hope maintained in us by the work of divine justification opens the horizon toward a humanity henceforth straining toward its salvation. But that opening makes Rom 5:1-11 more an introduction than a conclusion, since the theme of hope and the future glory of the baptized will recur a number of times throughout Romans 6–8. Moreover, the connections between Romans 5 and the preceding argumentation are practically nonexistent. In fact, Rom 1:18–4:25, in a rigorous progression replete with examples, has faced the question of the "how" of justification: with or without works of the Law. That seems to be the point at which Paul wanted to arrive: to show that all humanity, Jew and Greek, received its righteousness from faith alone, and that this is in fact a fundamental characteristic of the gospel because in Jesus Christ God has definitively confirmed that faith (without the works required by the Mosaic Law) is the unique condition requisite for receiving justification. Now, in Romans 5–8, Paul drops the theme of "by faith alone" and it will not be an issue again until the end of the section, which is a further sign that Romans 5 begins a new development.

b. The Rhetorical Units, Romans 5–8

5:1-11: introduction to the section
5:12-21: preparation for the *probatio,* by a comparison *(synkrisis)* of two contrasted figures and systems: Adam and Christ, the economy of sin and that of grace
5:20-21: the comparison ends with a *propositio,* stating the questions to be explored and defined (between grace and sin, law and grace, law and sin):
- The Mosaic Law has caused sin to abound;
- Grace has abounded all the more (apart from the Law) through Jesus Christ

6:1–8:30: a series of proofs *(probatio)* in three stages:
- A. 6:1–7:6 (with a *subpropositio* in 6:1, reprised in 6:15): the baptized cannot remain in sin because they have died to sin with Christ
  - 6:1-14
  - 6:15-23
  - 7:1-6 (*subperoratio* or partial conclusion, also preparatory to the following units)
- B. 7:7-25 (with a *subpropositio* in 7:7): the Law is holy but it is at the service of sin and cannot release its subjects from their radical weakness
  - 7:7-13 (v. 13 is a transition)
  - 7:(13)14-25
- A'. 8:1-30 (*subpropositio* in 8:1): what the Law could not do, God has done in Christ. Believers have received the Spirit and, with it, adoption and inheritance.
  - 8:1-17: the gift of the Spirit and its consequences
  - 8:18-30: present sufferings and future glory

8:31-39: *peroratio* (with hymnic accents)

Compared to the preceding section where the issue was primarily *theo*logical (divine justice, its manifestation and modalities), the perspective of Romans 5–8 is dominantly *soterio*logical, because it describes the actions and especially the present and future status of the baptized. Paul no longer focuses his argument on the unique modality (faith alone without works of the Law) in which justification has always operated. Instead, he insists on the situation and possibilities—salvific, but also ethical—opened to the baptized who are now living in and with Christ.

Composition, 5:1-11

Brief introduction (vv. 1-2a): from divine activity in the past to the present situation, peace with God, followed by an inchoative statement on hope (v. 2b) preparatory to the verses that follow:

I. The circumstances and conditions of hope (vv. 3-4)

II. Hope, the reasons for hope, and the object of hope (vv. 5-10)
- v. 5a: Hope's action: it does not disappoint (this component is crucial: cf. the various allusions to "boasting" in Romans)
- v. 5b: Reason given *(ratio)* in the present tense: the love of God poured into our hearts

vv. 6-10: Explications of the *ratio*
1. vv. 6-8: God's actions for us in the *past,* an assurance for the *future*
   α. (v. 6) redemptive death (in the past)
   (vv. 7-8 = *expositio,* detailed explanation for the purpose of clarifying and emphasizing one aspect)
   β. the "how much more" of eschatological salvation (future).
2. vv. 10-11: reconciliation, the assurance of salvation:
   α. (v. 10a) death as reconciling (in the past)
   β. (v. 10b) the "how much more" of salvation and life (in the future).

Keys for Reading, 5:1-11

(a) All human beings have been graciously justified by faith. But once they have been forgiven and graced, what becomes of them? Do they change their lives? What horizons are open to them? It is to these questions that Paul responds in Romans 5, emphasizing the hope that is offered to those whom God has justified. If the argumentation of Romans 1–4 stressed *faith* as the means for obtaining justification, that in Romans 5–8 sketches the foundations and components of the *hope* that is reserved for believers. Rom 5:1-11 gives, in outline, the reasons for that hope:

(1) Reasons in the present state of our existence (v. 5): because God has sent the Holy Spirit into our hearts. (For the relationship between "love" and "Holy Spirit," see also Rom 15:30; 1 Cor 14:1; 2 Cor 6:6; Gal 5:22; Phil 2:1; Col 1:8). Is Paul alluding to the promise made by God in Ezek 36:26-27?

> A new heart I will give you, and a new spirit I will put within you; and I will remove from your body the heart of stone and give you a heart of flesh. I will put my spirit within you, and make you follow my statutes and be careful to observe my ordinances.

Such an allusion is impossible to demonstrate; on the other hand, it is certain that the image of the *Spirit poured out* comes from Joel 2:28-29.

(2) Reasons in the past: (a) Paul mentions the death of Christ for us and emphasizes that God can go no farther than this. This is the burden of the argument *a fortiori:* if in Christ God has gone to such an extreme, this must save us.

(b) Paul desires that his readers should pause at the death of Christ and the excessiveness of it (the explanation, Latin *expositio,* in vv. 7-8 has just this purpose). Christ died for (Paul does not define the sense of the preposition: "in place of"? or "on behalf of"? etcetera) the ungodly and sinners, that is, for us. Putting all people in the ranks of sinners is not in accord with Jewish nomenclature, which restricts that classification to (1) the uncircumcised, i.e., Gentiles (Greeks, Romans, barbarians) and (2) apostate Jews: cf. 1 Macc 2:44 where the context indicates that the appellation describes Jews who are sympathetic to Hellenism. The adjective "wicked" also refers to those who reject or are ignorant of the Mosaic Law, but one would never refer to those who, while committing sins, still love the Law and try to practice it as "sinners," "ungodly," or "outside the Law." Because of the preceding development (Romans 1–4) the apostle can say that all human beings are sinners without needing hereafter to prove it.

(c) Why is there so much emphasis on boasting in these verses? In vv. 2-3 the complements of the verb "to boast," that is, hope and suffering, clearly indicate that the boasting of believers (1) does not come from their own performance or brilliance, but solely from the action of God; (2) is not manifest only in happy times, but in the greatest insecurity; (3) is an essential reaction because it manifests the power of divine action and of the gospel. "Boasting" is not simply feeling pride, but speaking it out loud before others who are thus constituted witnesses of the truth of the proclamation. And boasting, which Paul contrasts with dishonor or shame (v. 5), is indispensable to the extent that it indicates an appropriation of the effects of the work of salvation: if believers cannot show themselves proud of the gospel, can it really be a witness to divine justice and mercy?

Composition and Function, 5:12-21

The passage is a simple presentation in the form of a comparison of known figures and facts, acknowledged by everyone, facts that will be useful in facing the difficulties that will follow in the course of the argumentation. The comparison is intended to put in relief the differences

	Adam—sin—death	**Christ—grace—life**
v. 15 thesis	But not like the trespass	is the free gift.
reason	For if the many died through the one man's trespass,	much more surely have the grace of God and the free gift in the grace of the one man, Jesus Christ, abounded for the many.
		16 is the free gift.
v. 16 thesis	16 And not like the effect of the one man's sin	but the free gift following many trespasses brings justification.
reason 1	For the judgment following one trespass brought condemnation,	
v. 17 reason 2	17 If, because of the one man's trespass, death exercised dominion through that one,	17 much more surely will those who receive the abundance of grace and the free gift of righteousness exercise dominion in life through the one man, Jesus Christ.
v. 18 conclusions	Therefore just as one man's trespass led to condemnation for all,	18 so one man's act of righteousness leads to justification and life for all.
v. 19 reason	19 For just as by the one man's disobedience the many were made sinners,	19 so by the one man's obedience the many will be made righteous.
vv. 20-21 contrary purposes	20 But law came in, with the result that the trespass multiplied;	20 but where sin increased, grace abounded all the more,
	21 so that, just as sin exercised dominion in death,	21 so grace might also exercise dominion through justification leading to eternal life through Jesus Christ our Lord.

between Adam and Jesus Christ and to emphasize the infinite superiority (in fact incomparable, because Paul compares what is incomparable!) of the work of grace to the effects of sin.

Paul begins the comparison (*synkrisis* in Greek) and then pauses to refine a point (vv. 13-14); he resumes the parallel in v. 15 in a regularly balanced movement that presents two economies in alternation: that of sin leading to death, and that of grace leading to life (see table above).

Note the paradoxical use of *synkrisis.* Paul begins by saying that there is no comparison (vv. 15-17) and then proceeds to compare (vv. 18-19) in order to insist on the opposition!

The contrast between one and all begins with a strong opposition (involving *negation*), issues in an explicit confrontation, this time expressed in positive terms, with a progression of causes to results.

The Difficulties in What is at Stake (5:12-21)

(a) Was Adam the sole sinner? In contrast to Jewish tradition, Paul obviously puts more emphasis on the uniqueness of the first sinner—"one" is repeated nine times in vv. 12, 15, 16, 17, 18, 19. Has he forgotten Eve, or even the sin of the angels as reported in the book of Enoch (chs. 6–36)? In speaking of the beginning, Paul takes up the biblical material, but his insistence on the "one" can only be understood in relation to what he understands of the human vocation in Jesus Christ. It is because Christ has conquered death and is the first one to be raised that he can be called the firstborn of a new humanity, justified and called to glory; it is the vastness and the extremity of the work of redemption that allows Paul to say that the effects of Adam's sin as spoken of in Scripture stand in no measurable relationship with what is henceforth graciously and definitively offered to us in Jesus. The biblical fund recalled and systematized here serves to display to advantage the grace and gift received in Jesus Christ: the ruptures of the *synkrisis* and the accumulation of Greek terms express gratuitousness and gift (grace, gracious gift, act of giving and the like appear nine times in 5:15-21) and are symptomatic in this regard. It is effectively the work of grace that has come through Jesus Christ that permits Paul to formulate in contrast what had been the situation of desolation and imprisonment within which wounded humanity was held captive and, by recalling the biblical story, to discourse on what had brought it about.

(b) Have all people always been sinners? Paul's emphasis is not on an original sin—something that did not particularly interest intertestamental Judaism—but on the fact that *all without exception* have been caught in the spiral of a death and sin that immobilizes our world: not only the people who came before the promulgation of the Mosaic Law, but also all who have come afterward, including the subjects of that Law. The passage moves toward its final affirmation: the Torah made no change in the Adamic situation, but only aggravated it. And here no Jew faithful to the Law could follow Paul because, for Judaism, it was the promulgation of the Torah that changed the fate of humanity. The assertion in Rom 5:20 also seems to run contrary to certain biblical affirmations: do not the psalmists repeatedly say that the Torah of the Lord is their light and their solace? Thus the apostle must show in the *probatio* (which he will produce in Rom 7:7-25) how the Mosaic Law, far from separating its subjects from sin, on the contrary delivers them into its power.

5:12-14: Human Death and Sin

In v. 12 we encounter the difficulty in the last proposition, which can be interpreted as relative or as subjunctive. (For the current state of the question, see Joseph A. Fitzmyer, *Romans,* 413-417.) The most common translations of vv. 12c-14 are:

> . . . so death spread to all
> a. through that Adam in whom (or "because of whom") all have sinned (relative)
> b. through the situation in which (= on the basis of which) all have sinned (relative) [NAB: "inasmuch as all sinned"]
> c. the fact being that (or "from the fact that") all have sinned (causal) [NRSV: "because all have sinned"]
> d. with the result that all have sinned (consecutive)
> . . . sin was indeed in the world before the law, but sin is not reckoned when there is no law. Yet death exercised dominion from Adam to Moses, even over those [including the first Israelites] whose sins were not like the transgression of Adam.

Interpretation (a), well known and frequently followed since Augustine, is undoubtedly the least well-founded grammatically because of the distance from the antecedent ("one man" in v. 12a). Version (b) fits very well because it is obviously fully suited to the context, that is, to the explication (or *expositio*) that immediately follows and to the Adam/Christ contrast in vv. 15-19. The context thus furnishes a clear explanation for the interpolation. It is a matter, throughout, of the difference between *sinning* and *being a sinner,* because we have already seen with respect to Romans 1–3 that sinning does not imply that one enters into the category of *sinners:* the just in the psalms confess their sin(s) but are nevertheless convinced that *God* will not allow them to fall into the ranks of sinners, those who, like the uncircumcised and apostates, respect neither God nor God's law. The difficulty to which Paul alludes in Rom 5:13-14 is this: if, without the Mosaic Law, sin could not be imputed, none of the people who came before the promulgation of that Law could be declared sinners or wicked and thus incur condemnation, separation from God, and death. Unlike his descendants, Adam violated a divine prohibition, knowing that his transgression would lead to death (Gen 3:1-3; cf. 2:16-17). Not having disobeyed a divine injunction as did Adam, breaking which would lead to death, his descendants thus did not in principle deserve that punishment. But, the apostle adds, they already found themselves in a situation of death because of Adam himself (this was also asserted by intertestamental writings): the reign of death thus precedes the sins of the children of Adam, something that obviously underscores the responsibility of the first human being with regard to the situation of all humanity after him. What Paul wants to emphasize here is that those who lived before the Mosaic Law (from Adam to Moses) are in exactly the same situation as those who lived after it.

In interpretation (c) Adam's unique responsibility would be blurred or suppressed, and the contrast in vv. 15-19 would lose its meaning. Solution (d) apparently supposes that the death Paul is speaking of is not (solely or primarily) physical: otherwise it would be the fact of death that would be the cause of individual sins, and no one has ever maintained that, Paul least of all. Rather it is a moral and spiritual death; it amounts to saying that the world was in a state of moral decomposition and that this in itself resulted in the emergence of individual sins. But how could the world have been in a state of total moral decay without the existence of sins committed by individuals? The *expositio* in vv. 13-14 does not seek to explain a consequence, but rather a universal situation that no period of history has ever escaped. We must therefore retain interpretation (b) as the best of the lot.

Keys for Reading (5:15-21)

(a) Paul and Jewish tradition. The contrasts developed in Rom 5:15-19 are not found only in Paul's writing. Compare, for example, the statement of Rabbi [José] in the midrash *Sifra Leviticus,* probably taking up an older tradition containing the same elements: (a) the first human being contrasted with those who humble themselves before God, (b) the influence of a single person on all who follow, their universal responsibility for evil and for good, and (c) the argument *a fortiori* ("how much more," "all the more rightly"):

> Rabbi [José] said: "if you want to know (what) reward (will be) given to the righteous in the future, go and learn from the first human being (that) only one commandment (one thing) was demanded of him, and he violated it; see how many deaths were decreed for the generations of generations until the end of the generations. For which is the greater measure, that of reward or that of punishment? Answer: that of reward. If the measure of punishment is less, namely so many deaths decreed for him and the generations of generations until the end of the generations, then if someone turns back from abomination and idolatry, and does penance on the day of Kippur, how much more will he transmit the divine favor for him and for the generations of generations until the end of the generations (*Sifra,* ed. Weiss, 27a, *parasha* 12 §10).

Many other intertestamental Jewish texts also underscore the decisive role played by Adam's disobedience in expanding death and the corruption of the world. They are no more interested than Paul in an original sin, but rather in its effects for humanity and the rest of creation, even if here where the influence of Adam is minimized (cf. 2 Bar [= Syr. Bar.] 54:15, 19, "each one of us is his or her own Adam"). We can also mention *2 Esdr* 3:7, 26; 4:30; 7:116-126; *2 Bar* 17:1-4; 19:8; 23:4; 48:42-43; 54:15; 56:5-6; *Jub* 3:28-30.

Just as with the figure of Adam, rabbinic Judaism also emphasizes the figure through whom the situation caused by Adam's sin is reversed. Thus in *Gen. Rabba* 14.6 Abraham is presented as the new human being who was able to repair the evil caused by Adam. The passage, which quotes a statement from the book of Joshua (14:15: "the greatest man among the Anakim") comments:

> This is Abraham. Why is he called "great"? Because he was worthy to be created before Adam, but the Holy One, blessed be his name, says: "he will break (everything) and there will be no one to repair after him, but behold, I have created the first human being, so that, if he breaks (everything) Abraham may come and repair after him.

We should also cite other midrashic passages such as *Gen. Rabba* 19.9.2; 24.5.2-3, where this time it is Israel who is the counterpart to Adam: the first disobeyed a divine command, the second loves and follows the Torah by which it has access to divine life. The Torah is the ideal antidote to Adam's sin. It is clear that Paul could only assign that role to Christ, dead, risen, and glorified, in whom the new humanity has been revealed.

(b) The contrasts and their function. The *synkrisis* or comparison is paradoxical: vv. 15-17 begin by denying that one could compare the *proton* and the *eschaton*—"but the free gift is not like the trespass" (v. 15)—and since v. 18 seems to initiate the comparison ("just as . . . so") the real purpose is to formulate a strong contrast. The negative step (vv. 15-17) functions to show that the fall (or sin) of Adam determines neither the measure nor the manner in which grace has been given. In other words, the act of salvation is not simply a contrary reaction to human disobedience; it is a matter of a totally gratuitous initiative that goes beyond the schema of disobedience and retribution (such and such a punishment for such and such a transgression). To indicate this asymmetry Paul first (v. 15) parallels elements of different nature: the human fall (Greek *paraptōma*) connotes passivity, or necessity, at least the impossibility of doing anything else, while divine grace connotes an action that is not forced, but perfectly voluntary, and is in no way proportionate to human action. Paul then emphasizes the asymmetry of the consequences (v. 16):

16b

For the judgment	following	one [trespass] brought condemnation,

16c

but the free gift	following	many [trespasses] brings justification.

The parallel "following [coming from] . . . brought/brings" is broken at the level of origins; for the second stich one expects "coming from one (human being)." But Paul's starting point is the multitude of *falls*. That rupture in the parallelism aims to make us understand that it is a free gift: (i) God has not given good for good nor punishment for evil, but has caused the wicked to be made righteous; (ii) God has not awaited this transformation in order to declare righteous each one who is transformed, but instead has brought about and effected it; (iii) God came to seek us where we are, in our sin. It is all the working of grace. Divine grace is thus very properly described as gratuitous initiative and action extended to all without exception. In v. 17 the contrast between the consequences is still stronger:

17b		
death	exercised dominion	through that one (Adam)
17e		
[they]	[will] exercise dominion in life	through the one man, Jesus Christ.

In 17e we expect "life has exercised dominion through the one man, Jesus Christ," but Paul says "[they will] exercise dominion in life through the one man, Jesus Christ," because grace, or life, does not replace death as one tyrant overthrows another and continues to oppress the subject people; the disappearance of the tyrant (death) has restored life and liberty, even power, to everyone! That is the difference: God associates human beings in God's own power and glory.

(c) By their progression, vv. 15-21 reinforce the interpretation given to v. 12c ("and so death spread to all, a situation in which [= on the basis of which] all have sinned"). In fact, from the negative or Adamic side, Paul speaks of the reign of death (vv. 15-17) before the sinful condition (vv. 18-19) and the promulgation of the Law (v. 20): confirming that it is on the basis of death that people descended from Adam have been constituted sinners. The parallelism between the two movements should be emphasized:

	vv. 12-14	**vv. 15-21**
sin of one	v. 12a	v. 15b . . .
reign of death	v. 12b	vv. 15-17
all have sinned/sinners	v. 12c	vv. 18-19
Mosaic Law	v. 13	v. 20

Verses 12-14, and particularly the *expositio* in vv. 13-14, name the different negative components by locating their diachronic relationships; from the beginning, in vv. 15-21, Paul will be able to contrast them to the work of grace that has come through the mediation of Christ. Note again in v. 19 the noun "sinners" indicating that all, without exception, were enemies of God and bound for destruction.

(d) Many commentators have seen in the formulation in v. 19b ("one man's act of righteousness leads to justification and life for all" an allusion to the last song of the suffering servant in Isaiah. But as Paul does not repeat the formulations of Isa 53:11 it is impossible to prove a direct quotation or reminiscence—which does not mean that we should necessarily exclude it.

5:20-21: The *Propositio* of the Section

(a) The comparison *(synkrisis)* concludes with a *propositio* stating the questions to be explored and explicated: between grace and sin, law and grace, law and sin. Certainly these two verses are not immediately explained in Romans 6, but they will be unfolded progressively to the point that, at the end of the section in Romans 8, one may really say that the statements in 5:20-21 have found their explication. Romans 5:20-21 is a *propositio* in the style of Rom 1:16-17.

(b) Paul's statements regarding the Mosaic Law become stronger and stronger. In Rom 2:12-14 the Law had its role for the reward of the Jew, but not for the non-Jew who is not subject to its rules—in short, its role in retribution was limited. In Rom 3:19-20 Paul recognized its decisive role in regard to the knowledge of sin, but he denied that anyone could be declared righteous by acting justly according to its instruction: the Law has no place in the process of justification (cf. also Rom 3:21-22). Romans 4:15 had gone a little farther: the Law produces wrath, that is, judgment and punishment, to the extent that its rules are almost always transgressed, and transgression of the Law is related to condemnation (cf. Deuteronomy 28–29). Now Rom 5:20 says that the Mosaic Law came *in order that* trespass might be multiplied. What Jew could accept such a statement? If the Law was promulgated it was so that the people of Israel could know the will of their God and put it into practice: how could God have given the Law in order to make sin abound? Moreover, Jews see in the

Mosaic Law a source of protection against evil and violence. Paul could not leave such propositions unexplained, as Rom 7:7-25 shows; there he reexamines the relationship between Law and sin.

The Probatio *or Nucleus of the Argument, 6:1–7:6*

Composition

How can Paul show that believers cannot remain in sin or commit sin? What argument will he give? Will he say that God does not will it? But God's will has been given to us in the Law and its requirement, "thou shalt not." Besides, we are no longer under the Law! Will he say that the baptized have been transformed by the reception of the Holy Spirit, and that the Spirit cannot cause us to desire evil? In fact Paul will proceed first to give a christological foundation for the ethical actions of the baptized: it is their union with Christ that separates them definitively from sin and turns them toward justice!

Believers cannot remain in sin because they are dead with Christ to sin and called to the service of justice. The first two units answer objections that a subject of the Torah could not fail to raise on hearing what Paul says in 5:20-21: if those who have been justified have been so without the works of the Law, does that mean that they no longer need obey any rule, that they consider the Torah of no importance? How shall they live without it, because in it God's will has been revealed? Paul must thus take his stand on the relationship between the baptized and moral action in general.

The argument develops in this way:

- 6:1-14: (*subpropositio* vv. 1-2): the baptized cannot remain in sin any longer because they are dead to sin and alive in/with Christ; emphasis on being *with Christ* (vv. 4, 5, 6, 8).
- 6:15-23: (*subpropositio* v. 15): freed from sin, the baptized do not live in a state of license, but at the service of God and of justice; the vocabulary of liberty and slavery recurs.
- 7:1-6: conclusion of the argument (vv. 1-4) and preparation for what follows (vv. 5-6).

The first two units have the same sequence.

6:1-14	**6:15-23**
What then are we to say? Should we continue in sin in order that grace may abound?	What then? Should we sin because we are not under law but under grace?
v. 2 By no means!	By no means!
v. 3 Do you not know that:	v. 16 Do you not know that
[explanations]	[explanations]
[explanations] vv. 12-13	[explanations] vv. 19bc
[reasons] v. 14	[reasons] v. 20-23

At first glance the initial questions (6:1, 15) are repeated, but that is not at all the case. First of all, one should not forget the (biblical and Jewish) difference already noted with regard to Romans 1–3 between "being a sinner," the category of those who are under the total domination of sin, and "sinning," a verb that does not necessarily imply that one is a prisoner of sin and separated from God. But besides this, the questions themselves are complementary. The first aims at the abundance of mercy already manifested in Jesus, the second at the fact that the Law cannot impose sanctions on those who are not its subjects. One could paraphrase thus: "If the grace of God has been superabundant for sinners, which we all are, why should we not remain such in order that it may continue to superabound?" (6:1); and "the Law punishes transgressions, but we are subject to a different regime, that of grace, and so our sins cannot be punished; why should we trouble ourselves not to sin?" (6:15).

Composition (6:1-14)

The *subpropositio* (vv. 1-2) is followed by a brief explanation (on the how and when of death to sin = vv. 3-4) that resumes Paul's teaching on the effects of baptism. Verse 4 states the points to be emphasized in each of the sub-units. Verses 5-10 are sharply paralleled, with vv. 5-7 emphasizing death (with Christ) to sin, and vv. 8-10 stressing life (again with Christ). (See table on next page.) Verses 12-14 merely draw the consequences of the situation of the baptized in the form of exhortations; dead to sin and living for God, they should no longer sin.

v. 4c preparing the aspect "walk in newness of life"

a = 12 Therefore, do not let sin exercise dominion in your mortal bodies, to make you obey their passions.

	v. 4a preparing the aspect "death to/with"	v. 4b preparing the aspect "life with"
a	v. 5 For if we have been united with him in a death like his, we will certainly be united with him in a resurrection like his.	v. 8 But if we have died with Christ, we believe that we will also live with him.
b	v. 6 We know that our old self was crucified with him so that . . . we might no longer be enslaved to sin.	v. 9 We know that Christ, being raised from the dead, will never die again; death no longer has dominion over him.
c	v. 7 For whoever has died is freed from sin.	v. 10 The death he died, he died to sin, once for all; but the life he lives, he lives to God.
application	v. 11 So you also must consider yourselves dead to sin	v. 11 and alive to God in Christ Jesus.

b = 13 No longer present your members to sin as instruments of wickedness.

b' = 13 but present yourselves to God as those who have been brought from death to life, and present your members to God as instruments of righteousness.

a' = 14 For sin will have no dominion over you, since you are not under law but under grace.

Keys for Reading (6:1-14)

(a) To say that the baptized cannot abide under the power of sin, that is to say, remain sinners, Paul must obviously show that they have been definitively separated from sin. But how can he show that? By invoking their interior transformation through the pouring out of the Holy Spirit in their hearts, thus reprising and enlarging the statement of Rom 5:5? Paul will do that, but not until Romans 8. The first proof, which in fact is decisive, is christologically based: in Rom 6:1-14 Paul recalls that baptism is death with Christ to sin and thus a definitive separation, as was Christ's death. Note the paradox: death is a definitive separation, but this death is positive because it is a death with Christ and it separates us from that which separates from God, namely sin.

(b) But Christ died once for all and, being raised, will not die again. Being united with him means being united to a living person, not a dead one. Then how can each baptized person die with Christ to sin if it is true that Christ dies no more? Does baptism make us contemporaries of his death on Golgotha? Yes, in the sense that this death was the liberation of the human race in all ages. But Paul also refers to the present situation of Christ who, although resurrected, remains dead to sin in the sense that he is definitively separated from it. In being united with Christ through baptism, believers thus participate in that state of separation from sin: union with the living one *par excellence* is identically a death to sin, and the "when" of that separation dates from baptism when believers receive the Spirit of filiation.

The Progress of the Argument (6:1-14)

To understand this passage it is important to see that Paul proceeds by a set of progressive refinements, for while v. 2, which is the *propositio* in this passage, clearly states the impossibility of believers' living in sin, the expression "we have died to sin" remains elliptical and requires refinement (how, when, etcetera).

(a) Verses 3-4 offer a first explanation of the "when" of death by recalling the events (it is at baptism that this death takes place) and their purpose (new life). The itinerary of death and life with Christ is stated in v. 4:

v. 4a: prepares the aspect of death to/with Christ, developed in vv. 5-7;
v. 4b: prepares the aspect of life with Christ for God, developed in vv. 8-10;
v. 4c: introduces the ethical consequences Paul will draw from this situation in vv. 12-13.

(b) After recalling the facts, Paul tries to explain v. 4 through a series of more theoretical reflections. He begins by showing more precisely how baptism has joined us to the death of Christ. For although Christ died physically on Golgotha baptism does not cause the death of those who receive it. What allows them to be declared dead with Christ? Does their immersion symbolize the burial of the baptized, and their emergence from the water the new life or birth? But even if we suppose that immersion symbolizes the death or burial of the baptized, that is not what Paul is talking about here because that symbolism says nothing about the relationship to *the death of Jesus on the cross,* and that is what is important for the apostle. The baptized person is in fact dead *with* the Lord. Why can one say that baptism is a death with Christ, even if those who receive it do not die physically? It is a similitude for the death of Christ to the extent that it separates us from sin: by being united to Christ through baptism, believers participate in *his* state of separation from sin. Baptism thus does not make sense unless it manifests what physical death represented for Jesus, that is, a death *to sin,* a total and definitive separation from the forces of evil.

One could, in fact, speak of the crucifixion and *death* of the baptized because something has really been destroyed within them as v. 6 indicates. Its composition is as follows:

We know that
a. our old self
b. was crucified with him
b'. so that might be destroyed
a'. the body of sin
and we might no longer be enslaved to sin.

Thanks to the parallelism the two expressions "old self" and "body of sin" are reciprocally explanatory and describe the human person who is or was under the domination of sin. Besides the refinements given to the image of baptism as death, v. 6 indicates the role, or rather the utility, of that death: it is the end of enslavement to sin.

But how is the death of the baptized a death *to sin*? Paul recalls a principle well known to the rabbis of his own time: "whoever has died is freed from sin." The dead are no longer tempted and no longer live in sin! The principle is taken as granted and only its fine points are discussed (does it apply if the individual did not repent before death?). We find the same kind of maxim regarding dependence on the Mosaic Law in the statement attributed to Rabbi Simeon Gamaliel (ca. 140 C.E.) in the Babylonian Talmud (151b *gem.*):

> When a man dies he is dispensed from the commandments; thus R. Johanan interpreted (Ps 88:6) "among the dead I am free": one who is dead is freed from the commandments.

Freed from the commandments, that is, from the Law, the deceased person (the baptized) is also free from faults, from transgressions, and thus from the power and domination of sin.

(c) With v. 8 Paul passes from the aspect of "death to sin" (as a separation) to that of "life for God" (v. 11b), which expresses the theological purpose of separation from sin. This "positive" aspect is important because the existence of the baptized cannot be characterized solely by separation from the power that has oppressed them. This new life is not simply that of the final resurrection; it is begun in the present (v. 11b). Certainly, although Christ has been physically raised the baptized have not yet been; nevertheless, they already live in him. The assurance the baptized have of being separated from sin thus also comes from the fact that they are united with the Risen One who has died to sin once for all. It is the resurrection of Christ that makes the separation between the baptized and sin secure and solid.

(d) The ethical consequences of vv. 12-14. By a series of imperatives, Paul invites believers to see to it that their separation from sin is manifested at the level of action. His vocabulary becomes bellicose, speaking of arming oneself for combat. This indicates, indeed, that for Paul ethics are a place of engagement in a hostile world dominated by sin, a place where the victory of Christ is also manifested and attested. Since the baptized are united to Christ they should show even in their bodies the effects of that union and thus of the definitive victory of Christ over sin. That is why Paul can say with assurance: "sin will have no dominion over you" (v. 14): if he is sure of the victory of the baptized it is because of that of Christ (vv. 9-10).

In declaring to the baptized that sin will not have dominion over them Paul certainly does not intend to say that the baptized will no longer experience weakness or imperfection, or that they will not sin any more, but that they will no longer be "in sin," prisoners of sin, or, in other words, "sinners" in the sense of the biblical and Jewish traditions mentioned in regard to Rom 3:7 and 5:8. It should be said in passing that a verse like Rom 6:14 already indicates that a person burdened by sin as in Rom 7:7-25 could not be baptized, to the extent that this passage describes a subject who is totally unable to emerge from the domination of sin. For it is precisely that which the baptized person in Romans 6 no longer is. But could we not criticize Paul for describing the baptized in ideal fashion? So many of them are still entangled in the nets of evil! For that objection, see below at Rom 8:12-17.

	Sin	Grace and Justice
6:15 hypothesis of conjunction with sin	What then? Should we sin	because we are not under law but under grace?
6:16 disjunction and distinctions	you are slaves of the one whom you obey, either of sin, which leads to death,	or of obedience, which leads to righteousness
6:17-18 proof by fact	you . . . having once been slaves of sin	having been set free from sin, [you] have become slaves of righteousness
6:19 exhortation	just as you once presented your members as slaves to impurity and to greater and greater iniquity	so now present your members as slaves to righteousness for sanctification.
6:20-23 explanation of the respective effects of each situation	When you were slaves of sin . . . 21 what advantage did you then get . . . The end of those things is death.	22 now that you have been freed from sin and enslaved to God, the advantage you get is sanctification. The end is eternal life.
	23 For the wages of sin is death,	23 but the free gift of God is eternal life in Christ Jesus our Lord.

Composition (6:15-23)

The unified structure parallels the preceding one (see table on p. 1578). The development of the thought is quite clear. (See table above.)

The key rhetorical figure is the contrast (with emphasis on incompatibility) between two superimposed levels, (1) temporal (then/now), and (2) axiological (sin + iniquity + death/righteousness + sanctification + eternal life).

Keys for Reading (6:15-23)

(a) This unit complements the preceding one; beyond liberation from sin, which constitutes an acknowledged premise, Paul now insists on moral commitment. Liberation does not imply license, but rather a change of masters, because the baptized have been placed in the exclusive service of God (just as slaves were totally dependent on their patrons for life and death) and of divine justice. The parenthesis in v. 19 ("I am speaking in human terms because of your natural limitations") indicates that the paradoxical way of describing freedom as slavery—even though slavery to justice, for how can freedom be slavery of any kind?—does not satisfy the apostle; at any rate it demonstrates the impossibility of adequately describing the status of believers in human language. The passage is more affirmative than demonstrative. The proof, in the form of an example, will be furnished in Rom 7:2-3.

(b) Far from calling the baptized to license, Paul tells them that by being in the service of justice they are moving toward *sanctification* (vv. 19c, 22). We should not underestimate his use of this term or the paradox it represents. Paul shows that ethical action makes "holy" in the sense that it allows the baptized to realize their vocation, which is holiness. Is sanctification then the effect of good works? Yes, if one immediately adds that it does not come from us and is not something owed us, but in fact the expression of a holiness we have received: the love poured into our hearts *by the Holy Spirit that has been given to us* (Rom 5:5). Even though they are not "under the [Mosaic] Law" (Rom 6:15) the baptized are not called to a lesser holiness than that to which the children of Israel were called by that same Law (cf. the frequent instances of "you shall be holy, for I the LORD your God am holy," Lev 19:2, etcetera). It is no longer the Law that defines the code of sanctity for the baptized, but the fact of being dead and alive with Christ.

Rom 7:1-6

(a) Rhetorical Status and Composition

These verses complete the argument with an example illustrating and reprising the ideas of the whole:

separation of the baptized from sin (vv. 1-14)
being alive for God and God's service alone (vv. 15-23).

At the same time, vv. 4-7 form a short peroration to the extent that they summarize the preceding argument; this is clear from the parallels between 7:5-6 and 6:20-22

Rom 6:20-22	Rom 7:5-6
When you were slaves of sin . . . what advantage did you then get . . . ?	While we were living in the flesh, . . .
The end of those things is death.	to bear fruit for death.
But now that you have been freed from sin	But now we are discharged from the law . . .
and enslaved to God, . . .	so that we are slaves . . .

The composition resembles that of the two preceding units:

- v. 1: "do you not know that" followed by a principle (cf. 6:7)
- vv. 1b-3: illustrating the principle with a casuistic example
- vv. 4-6: applying the principle to the baptized.

(b) The Value of the Example

It is intended to illustrate the principle stated in v. 1 (very close to that proposed in Rom 6:7) but the whole thing seems to limp because the principle of v. 1 applies very well to a husband, but obviously not to his widow. However, Paul is not comparing the Christians (dead to the Law) with the husband (also dead to the Law) but with the wife, who has not died! In point of fact all the examples, except that of Christ dead and risen, can only falter in describing the experience of people who have died in order to live a new and utterly different life. But while knowing that the examples will necessarily limp, Paul has decided to use them for several reasons:

- The Mosaic Law is in view because the example uses a commandment of the Decalogue (Exod 20:14; Deut 5:18). Paul can thus show how someone (while still alive) can cease to be constrained by the Mosaic Law.
- Marriage is a strong relationship, one of covenant that cannot, in principle, be dissolved except by death (Deut 22:28-29).
- In a sense the death of the husband has for his spouse the same function as that of Christ for the baptized: the widow is freed from the prohibition regarding adultery (it is no longer a matter of sin for her because her husband has died) and thus from sin, but also from the sanction (death) that is attached to it (Deut 22:22). It is the same for the baptized, who are dead (like the husband) but also alive (like the widow).
- The union of the widow with another man illustrates the union of the baptized with the risen Christ, a union that is also definitive because Christ, being raised, will never die again.

Thanks to the necessarily imperfect and *fluid* nature of the image we should avoid setting up forced analogies, e.g., wife/husband // baptized/Christ because, in the present case, the wife does not die and the husband is not resurrected.

Sin, the Law, and Those Subject to the Law (7:7-25)

The statement in Rom 5:20 regarding the Mosaic Law (that it was promulgated in order to cause sin to abound) requires refinement. Paul will now say in what way the Mosaic Law is inextricably allied to sin and at its service; as an instrument of sin it is also incapable of rescuing its subjects from the situation of death in which sin has placed them.

1. Composition

The passage can be divided into two subunits, vv. 7-12[13] and [13]14-23, each followed by an exclamation (Greek *epiphōnema*) that serves as a conclusion.

Verses 7-11 are developed in two parallel sub-units, 7-8b (knowledge of sin and the origins of concupiscence) and 8c-11 (death):

A1 = v. 7b	A2 = v. 8ab
B1 = vv. 8c-10	B2 = v. 11

followed by two consequences for the Law and its relationship to sin (vv. 12-13).

Verses 14-23 develop more or less like those preceding: (1) a double parallel movement in vv. 14-20 followed by (2) a series of consequences in vv. 21-23:

14 For we know that the law is spiritual; but I am of the flesh, sold into slavery under sin.	18a For I know that nothing good dwells within me, that is, in my flesh.
15 I do not understand my own actions. For I do not do what I want, but I do the very thing I hate.	18b I can will what is right, but I cannot do it. 19 For I do not do the good I want, but the evil

	I do not want is what I
16 Now if I do what I do not want, I agree that the law is good.	do. 20 Now if I do what I do not want,
17 But in fact it is no longer I that do it, but sin that dwells within me.	it is no longer I that do it, but sin that dwells within me.

There is a final set of parallels in vv. 21-23 (conclusion followed by a brief justification) that is logical and conceptual in nature. Paul causes the desire or will to good to alternate (in an a, a' pattern) with the execution that follows (in b, b'), beginning with two short affirmations (v. 21) that he refines more logically in vv. 22-23:

a (21) So I find it to be a law that when I want to do what is good,
b (21) evil lies close at hand.
a' (22) For I delight in the law of God in my inmost self
b' (23) but I see in my members another law at war with the law of my mind, making me captive to the law of sin that dwells in my members.

2. Development of the Argument

(a) The limits of this unit are easily determined (vv. 7-25) due to the shifting of the actors and the theme. But we should not forget that Rom 7:5-6 not only concludes the preceding unit (6:1–7:6) but also serves as a *partitio* for the following units, Rom 7:7-25 and 8:1-30:

a = v. 5: flesh, sin, law, death
b = v. 6: Spirit
β newness of the Spirit
α antiquity of the letter

———

A = 7:7-25: law, sin, death, flesh, members
B = 8:1-17: Spirit

These verses in which the contrast between "the past" (the time of submission to sin) and now (the time of the gift of the Spirit) make it obvious that Rom 7:7-25 cannot apply to the baptized unless we admit that Paul has immediately forgotten what he has just said.

(b) The argument is developed in a unit composed of two sub-units, each with a *propositio* followed by explanations or proofs:

vv. 7-13: v. 7a is the *subpropositio,* vv. 7b-12 (13) the explanations and conclusions;

vv. 13-23: v. 13bc is the *subpropositio,* vv. 14-23 the explanations.

It all concludes with a short pathetic exclamation *(epiphōnema)* in vv. 24-25 with all the characteristics of an epilogue.

(c) Problems of the argument. Verses 7-13 describe the role of the Law in the process of the subject's (spiritual) death. In v. 7 there is a clear allusion to the Mosaic Law (the last commandment of the decalogue in Exod 20:17), but is this not also an allusion to God's commandment to Adam? Some reject the idea of an allusion to the episode in Eden. It is true that "desire" (in the sense of "covet") does not appear in Genesis 2–3, but only in Ps 106:14, which also has reference to scenes from the Exodus. However, there are other lexical contacts between Genesis 2–3 and Romans 7, and they are by no means accidental. Many words from Genesis 2–3 appear here, including the verbs "to command" in Gen 2:16; 3:11, 17 (cf. the noun "commandment" in Rom 7:9-12), and "to deceive" in Gen 3:13 (cf. Rom 7:11). But does the fact of its reference to Adam give the passage a complete universality? In other words, does the "I" in Romans 7 refer to every human being? However that may be, for the moment let us notice Paul's emphasis on the gnoseological role (and competence) of the Law (in making us conscious of the evil to be avoided) and at the same time its incapacity to give its subjects the power to do what it requires: in bringing about all kinds of covetousness it is deflected from its purpose. And at that stage of the argument the Mosaic Law remains emblematic because (1) *in renewing the prohibition laid on Adam in Genesis 2 it makes all its subjects (the Jews) like to Adam, caught up in the process of concupiscence with all the known consequences,* and (2) if the Mosaic Law has such effects, no other human law can do better (and cannot evade the processes of death).

In vv. 14-23 Paul intends primarily to express the fundamental powerlessness or weakness of all those who know what they should do and desire to do it, but cannot. However, this passage raises numerous questions. According to some commentators (cf. E. P. Sanders, *Paul, the Law, and the Jewish People,* 75-81) these verses contradict what has gone before (vv. 7-13); in 7-13 the Law was the instrument of sin because it is through the Law that sin urges to transgression, while in 14-23 there is no longer any relation-

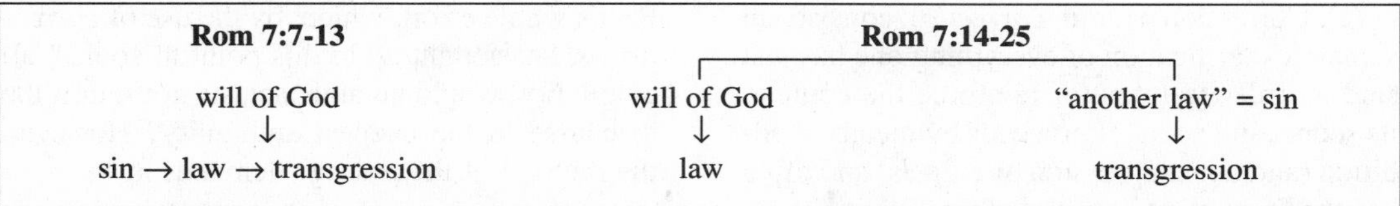

ship between the Mosaic Law and transgression. (See table above.) That is an erroneous interpretation, because Paul never speaks of transgression, disobedience, fall, or rejection: paradoxically, the text moves directly from desire to the death of the "self." Why?

(1) In this passage the Law is not what provokes transgression, but only the desire (cognitive function); it sheds light on the essentially seductive and deceitful nature of sin: at the very moment when sin makes use of the Law to seduce me, the same Law unveils its lying character. The Law does not deceive, and is not sinful in itself. (2) The passage does not emphasize transgression; on the contrary, it stresses the profound adherence of the subject to the (divine) commandment: unfortunately only at the level of will. What is emphasized is the division of the "self." (3) By not speaking of disobedience Paul at the same time eliminates the question of responsibility of the subject and sets in relief the subject's total powerlessness. (4) A final reason explaining the elimination of the responsibility of the "self" is that the true subject of evil action is the *sin* that dwells within one.

The progression of the sequence is undeniable. After recalling the use that sin makes of the holy Law (vv. 7-13) Paul describes the break brought about by the "self" manipulated by sin (vv. 14-23). Unlike vv. 7-13, vv. 14-23 speak of action, but the true subject is sin, which dwells within the "self" and prevents it from doing the good it desires. Verses 14-23 thus cannot place the reader face to face with the hypothesis of an ignorant "self." It is essential to the argument that the self knows the divine Law. The Law that in the earliest time was the occasion of the death of the "self" cannot at a later time remedy the dramatic situation: the "self" wishes to observe it but cannot.

Paul considers only the case of those who (1) know the Law (the divine will) and (2) desire to put it into practice (cf. the repetition of the verb "want" in 7:15, 16, 18, 19, 20, 21). The apostle envisages the best case. He does not exclude others (those who know the divine will and reject it; those who do not know it, etcetera) but he has in view those who could retort: "we have the Law, and it not only makes us aware of the divine will but protects us, sustains and supports our moral actions"—in short, those for whom the Law is not made use of by sin, but promotes justice. The "self" in vv. 14-25 would thus be a pious Jew. That is why some commentators on the passage see a rhetorical progression: Paul begins in vv. 7-13 with a universal situation (everyone without Christ, Jews and non-Jews) and concludes with the specific situation of the pious Jew who knows the Law and finds delight in it (vv. 14-25). But the difficulty recurs because in vv. 14-21 Paul takes up, in his own way, a *topos* that is found in Euripides' tragedy, *Medea,* and was exploited before him by many Greek and Hellenistic writers. "Passion is stronger than the decisions of my will; for mortals it is the cause of the greatest evils" (*Medea* 1077–1080). We note how Epictetus, near the end of the first century of our era, formulated the matter very much as did Paul in his letters (Epict. 2.17.18-19; 2.26.1-2):

2.17.18: I desire something and it does not happen: who is more miserable than I? I do not desire something and it happens, and who is more miserable than I? And although not desiring it, Medea kills her children.

2.26.1-2: Every sin involves a struggle because the one who sins does not desire to sin, but rather to do what is right. It is evident that the person does not do what he or she desires.

Why does Paul take up a *topos* used by pagan thinkers? Are there no biblical statements on the internal divisions of the sinner? We will see below how one should respond to these questions.

The Rhetoric of the Passage (7:7-25)

There are a number of rhetorical figures here. We will discuss only those that are most important for interpreting the passage:

(a) Correction (Latin *correctio*) consists in semantic clarification of everything one has just said in order to refine or reinforce the content, its scope, and so on; it proceeds by means of addition (and not suppression or ellipsis) and often has the form of an antithesis (not X, but Y):

Rom 7:15b (note again the synonymous expressions, alliteration [not *paranomasia*], correction used to reinforce a contrast between the verbs); see also Rom 4:4
Rom 7:17 (here in aid of a contrast of subjects)
Rom 7:19 (and by means of a contrast of verbs and adverbs)
Rom 7:20 (contrast of subjects as in v. 17).
Cf. also John 6:26, 46; 12:6; 1 John 4:10; Rom 11:11.

(b) Concession (Latin *concessio*) should not be confused with the concessive proposition. The *concessio* is not meant to correct or refine preceding propositions (as is the *correctio*), but to acknowledge the point of view (real or imaginary) of the interlocutor, e.g., "I concede this or that to you," in order to immediately show its limits. Examples of *concessio* can be found in John 8:37; 9:31.

Rom 7:14 could be rendered "certainly we know [concede] that the Law is spiritual; nevertheless, I myself am fleshly, sold to sin." That, in fact, is the point: what good does it do for the Law to be holy and spiritual if it does not change me?

(c) Antanaclasis. According to several commentators there is a fine example of antanaclasis in vv. 21-25. Antanaclasis consists in repeating the same word (here the word "Law") in different or even opposing senses. According to others the sense (here the referent) is unique and is limited to the Mosaic Law because that Law changes its role according to whether the one seeking to put it into practice is a Jew or a Christian, or again according to the part of the "I" under consideration. It is good for will and reason, but for the body, in which it arouses concupiscence, it is connected with sin; in other words the same Mosaic Law is in a sense fragmented or changes its role according to the subject or the cognitive instance. It is true that an antanaclasis in these verses gives the impression of ruining Paul's whole effort, which, by the use of *correctiones,* has sought up to this point to abolish all amgibuity: would an antanaclasis not return the discourse to the deepest ambiguity? However, the rhetoric of the passage demands it.

(1) The adjective "other" ("another law") in v. 23a favors antanaclasis, because as early as Rom 7:3-4 it has the sense of a "second" ("another" husband there evidently means a *second* husband); "another law" in v. 23 is apparently a "second law," and not the Law of God.

(2) The parallelism of vv. 21-23 (cf. table on p. 1582) shows that the law in v. 21a is subsequently described as "another law." The law that presents itself to me is not truly the one that I think I have recognized (the Law of God, which is good and holy), but the one that imprisons me, the law of sin! Thus the composition again favors antanaclasis. Verse 21 should thus be translated: "so I find it to be a law for me that when I want to do what is good it is evil that presents itself to me."

(3) The Mosaic Law cannot, in this passage, either be or appear to be a "law of sin," because the "I" *never ceases* to recognize its holiness: vv. 7-13 are essential in this respect; the *correctiones* in vv. 15b, 17, and 20 have precisely this function: they exclude all ambiguity and confusion in that regard.

(4) What is the function of the antanaclasis? As if by magic, the number of laws is multiplied: (1) the Law of God, (2) a second, probably identical with the first, to which reason assents, (3) that of sin, (4) that (of the flesh) that struggles against (1) and (2) and makes the "I" a prisoner of (3), and finally (5) the law of the Spirit (Rom 8:2). Why so many laws? To show to those (the Jews) who are convinced that they have to do with only one Law, which is holy, good, and protective, that in reality that Law paradoxically puts them in contact with many others that are quite different.

What is Being Described: Every Human Being Without Christ, Jews Alone, or Christians? (7:7-25)

The many and diverse answers can be classified under three headings:

(a) "I" represents the Christian (including Paul). In favor of that interpretation is the expression in the first person indicative present in vv. 14-25, together with the experience of many Christians who are aware of not yet being free from sin and who rightly think that the passage more or less describes their own situation.

(b) "I" represents a person without Christ (and only such a one). This interpretation rests on the dynamics of the section and the rhetorical indicators (the *partitio* in Rom 7:5-6; the *synkrisis* between Rom 7:14-25 and Rom 8:1-17; the Jewish background of the questions here raised; the Greek *topos* of contradiction between willing and doing; and the antanaclasis). But then what is the function of the *prosopopeia* (which makes the speaker someone who is absent or a being incapable of expressing all that is said in Rom 7:7-25 and, moreover, in the first person)?

(c) According to a growing number of exegetes, although Paul is not speaking here of his life as a disciple, he nevertheless evokes his past before the encounter on the Damascus road. This contradicts neither Galatians 1 nor Phil 3:6, where the apostle recalls his zeal for and fidelity to the tradition of his ancestors. Certainly Romans 7 describes an "I" incapable of observing the commandments of the Law and of doing good, but at that time Paul had no idea at all that he was in a desperate situation. He confessed his sin, his faults, he repented with a pure intention; yet at the same time he was certain that he was not included in the ranks of sinners, the impious who were outside the Law. But it is that category that is described in Romans 7, and in doing so Paul is not content to repeat the supplications of the faithful who confess their sins and implore divine mercy; he condemns a chronic and twofold weakness, that of the "I" and (worse!) that of the Law. The clear opposition between the "we" of the baptized and the "I" in Romans 7 surely indicates that the "I" is utterly isolated with no one to come to his or her aid.

But one would never find a Jew saying that the Torah leaves him or her in radical powerlessness. The speaker in Romans 7 can only be Paul the disciple of Christ, allowing Saul the subject of the Law to acknowledge that double powerlessness (of which the latter was not aware at that time). What, then, is the function of the *prosopopeia*? Why say "I" in the present tense if the situation described is that of a past that has been utterly swept away? Just because the subject of the Law, discovering the contradiction in which he or she lives, desires liberation (cf. vv. 24-25), and that desire is the unique condition for receiving it. The *prosopopeia* thus allows a situation described as desperate to be rendered no longer so.

(d) Thus Paul describes the situation of a Jew who desires to obey the divine Law. Is the rest of humanity (without Christ) excluded? Certainly not, as vv. 14-20 show, alluding to the Greek *topos* of the person who is unable to control his or her instincts. But the case of the Jew is retained because it is emblematic: the Jew cannot be ignorant of the divine Law. In other words, Paul considers the *best case,* that of a person who is entirely *aware* of the divine will contained in the Torah and *wants* to observe it. If for such a one the situation is irremediably negative it will be so for all persons without exception.

Keys for Reading (7:7-25)

The Christian interpretation of the passage. Its basis and its difficulties. As we have seen above, the Christian interpretation recommends itself for this discourse in the first person ("I") with verbs in the present tense (vv. 14-15) and for the contrast between the *interior person* (v. 22) and the *members* (v. 23), between what, for the baptized, already belongs to the eschaton and what still belongs to the old, fallen humanity: Paul (and every Christian as well) is at the same time both spiritual and fleshly. It is true that many Christians recognize themselves in the description in Rom 7:14-23 and cry out, with Rom 7:24: "Wretched man that I am! Who will rescue me from this body of death?" Undoubtedly Paul is reflecting a powerful interior tension. But the individual he describes is not merely in tension; he or she is totally abandoned to the power of sin and death, unable to do what is good. And that individual is certainly not the baptized person whom Paul has just invited, in Rom 6:12-14, 15-23, to make his or her members the instruments of righteousness, a sign that he or she has that capacity!

If the "I" of Rom 7:7-25 were the Christian, the logic of the section would leave a great deal to be desired. But if that logic is seamless from Romans 5 to 8 we must ask ourselves what is the function of Romans 7, wedged between two positive descriptions of the baptized who are in and with Christ. It appears that Rom 5:12-19 has developed a comparison between the two figures who inaugurated the two completely opposed regimes of sin leading to death, on the one hand, and grace leading to life on the other, and that their respective posterities are described in a comparable manner (technically, that of *synkrisis*) in Romans 6–8, since Adam and Christ are not contrasted except as a basis for the opposition between the old humanity (Romans 7) and the new humanity (Romans 6 and 8):

Adam	**Christ**
those without Christ (Rom 7:7-25)	those in/with Christ (Romans 6 and 8)

Paul's Assertions and Those of Judaism (7:7-25)

(a) Jewish traditions also reflected on the origins of evil or covetous desires (vv. 7-13), particularly with respect to divine retribution. See, e.g., *Apoc. Abr* 23.9-11, where the patriarch, caught up to the heavens, beholds Adam and Eve seduced by Azazel and asks:

> Eternal Mighty One, why hast thou willed that men should desire evil in their hearts? For thou art angry with what thou hast willed thyself when a man goes after the things that are of no substance in thy world. [Translation by A. Pennington in Sparks, *The Apocryphal OT.*]

On covetousness, the root of all sins and all evil, see *Apoc. Adam* 19; covetousness is the most terrible of the passions according to Philo, *Decalog*. 142. "Do not covet" summarizes all the commandments of the Torah.

(b) Regarding the contradiction between willing and doing (vv. 14-20), Jewish tradition also speaks of an evil inclination opposed to a good inclination, both of which are placed in the human heart by God (cf., e.g., *Gen. Rab*. 14.4); this does not in any way suppress free will. It may be that we find here a reminiscence (obviously with modifications required by Jewish belief) of the *topos* mentioned above (p. 1585). For Jewish tradition the Torah is an antidote that makes the believer able to resist the evil inclination. There is nothing that would allow us to say that Rom 7:7-25 represents the Jewish version of the *topos*. For the "evil inclination" in the pseudepigrapha, see *T. Reub*. 4:7; *T. Dan* 4:2; *T. Ash*. 1:3, 9; *T. Jud*. 11:1; *T. Benj*. 6:1-4.

We must immediately add that if the formulation of vv. 14-20 seems to owe a good deal to Hellenism—some have even seen the recollection of a Platonic theme in v. 15 (the human being does evil because of ignorance)—the accent is not on ignorance of values, because the "I" knows them well, but rather on ignorance of the process that impels one to act: "I do not know" or "I do not understand *what is happening*." It is true that Paul does not insist on the responsibility of the "I," and thus indirectly agrees with Platonism, but we cannot really say that he is subject to its influence.

Composition, 8:1-30

The composition is primarily argumentative in nature. Two *subpropositiones* (vv. 1-2 and 18) respectively introduce two units, vv. 1-17 and 18-30.

We should not forget that Romans 8 is the culmination of the section (see above on the composition of Romans 5–8) and recapitulates many of the themes of the preceding chapters, emphasizing the gift of the Spirit and the fact that this allows the baptized to live and to hope. It is especially important to note that the comparison between the two types of humanity continues up to 8:17:

Romans 7	**Romans 8**
indwelling of sin	indwelling of Christ and the Spirit
inability to practice the divine Law	accomplishing the commandment of the Law
living according to/in the flesh	living according to/in the Spirit
death	life
slavery	son/daughtership and inheritance

The contrast is then extended still farther in vv. 18-22 to the extent that creation is associated with the liberation of the children of God and awaits that liberation with them.

The composition can be outlined as follows:

vv. 1-17
- vv. 1-2: *subpropositio* followed by its *ratio*
- vv. 3-17: the baptized are guided by the Spirit
  - a. past: the sending of the Son and his purpose (vv. 3-4)
  - b. present: the baptized are made alive by the Spirit (vv. 5-13)
    - vv. 5-8: exposition of general principles (flesh vs. spirit)
    - vv. 9-11: application of these principles to the baptized because they

have the Spirit of life and are therefore (vv. 12-13) capable of ethical conduct that leads to life

c. the Spirit of sons/daughters and their glorification (vv. 14-17)

vv. 18-30

v. 18: *subpropositio:* the present sufferings do not detract from future glory

vv. 19-30: explanations of v. 18. Note the progression:

a. the series of groanings:
  —of creation that awaits liberation from corruption (vv. 19-22)
  —of sons and daughters (vv. 23-25)
  —of the Spirit who comes to the aid of our weakness (vv. 26-27)

b. the certainty of divine response: glorification (vv. 28-30)

vv. 31-39

peroratio for the whole section (chs. 5–8).

Keys for Reading and Questions (8:1-17)

(a) These verses confirm the interpretation given to Romans 7 (the "I" does not describe a Christian) to the extent that Paul repeats to his readers in Rom 8:5-11: "you are not in [or under the control of] the flesh; you are in the Spirit," and the Spirit will give you the power to do what is good, to carry out the will of God. Indeed, the baptized bear in their bodies the marks and wounds of sin (they cannot escape physical death: v. 10), but the Spirit who lives in them is life and the promise of resurrection: they share in the glory of Christ with whom they are now united (v. 11).

(b) The description Romans 6 and 8 give of the baptized seems unreal, too ideal to be true, because the baptized are not sinless (far from it!), and many forget the vital link that has united them with Christ. Nevertheless, Paul does not forget it, for he adds: "if you live according to the flesh, you will die." The Christian can live like a sinner and will be rewarded as such. The apostle simply emphasizes the status of the baptized and the moral attitude that should normally follow from it: how can the Spirit dwelling in them not give them power and cause them to bear spiritual fruit? The life of faith cannot fail to develop in that way if it is true that the Spirit has been poured into their hearts. And the ethical life is a necessary witness to the power of the gospel (cf. Rom 1:16).

Progress of the Argument (8:1-17)

(a) 8:1-2. The *subpropositio* and its *ratio.* "There is therefore now no condemnation for those who are in Christ Jesus" means that, not being in the ranks of sinners (in the desperate situation described in Rom 7:7-25), the baptized are unable to incur condemnation. The first reason given (called the *ratio* by the manuals of the time) is the Spirit of life who, living in and guiding believers, delivers them from that state. Paul again proceeds here by means of antanaclasis, as in 7:21-23 (q. v.).

(b) 8:3-4. First explanation of the *ratio.* We note that here again the first argument invoked is christological. It is in the excess of the event of Jesus Christ that the present situation of the baptized finds its explanation.

Verse 3 begins by recalling the paradox of a holy and good Law that is powerless. For it is just in taking our impotent flesh marked by sin (suffering, temptation, death) that the Son of God has been able to condemn sin in the very place of its domination, the flesh. As with most of his paradoxical expressions, Paul does not attempt to explain or justify what he says (was it necessary to take that route? Why the passage through the wounded flesh in order that the victory over sin be obtained in that same flesh? And so on.).

Paul does not say precisely what he means by "flesh," but obviously it represents for him the whole human person in its fragility. The expression "sinful flesh" in v. 3b does not mean that Jesus himself sinned (Rom 5:15-19 has just insisted the opposite) but that he was thoroughly and completely human, and that therefore like all human beings he suffered the consequences of sin described in Rom 5:12-19: physical testing, temptation, rejection, death. The expression "in the likeness of sinful flesh" (v. 3b) leaves no room for any kind of docetism. Paul does not mean to say that Jesus had only the appearance of a body; he wishes to emphasize, as he will do later in Phil 2:7, that the Christ was like human beings in every respect including their agonies and fragilities.

As for the expression "for sin," or "to deal with sin," in the LXX (cf. Lev 5:7, 11, and elsewhere) it describes the offering of sacrifice (or even the sacrifice itself) for sin, and some think that we should paraphrase: "God, having sent God's own son in the condition of our wounded flesh for sin, and having made of him a *sacrificial offering for sin. . . .*" It is improbable that Paul, who was well acquainted with the Greek Bible, did not consider the ambiguity of his formulation. But the syntactic arrangement does not favor such an antanaclasis (because of the "and" that places the two expressions within the same context).

After the mention of the one sent, Paul speaks of his purpose (v. 4). He does not say that God sent the Son to uphold the Law or to give it a power it had lost. The Law remains holy and good (as it always had been), but people themselves are transformed—by the work of God in Christ, and not by the Law! From the beginning, the righteousness required by the Law had been accomplished in them. Many would like to see in this verse a slightly veiled reference to Jer 31:31-33 and/or Ezekiel 36–37, and that is indeed probable.

(c) As already indicated with regard to the composition of Romans 8, v. 4 (life in the Spirit) will be expanded in three stages: vv. 5-8 are an exposition of general principles (opposition between flesh and Spirit); vv. 9-11 apply those principles to the baptized who have received the Spirit of life and are therefore capable of ethical action leading to life (vv. 12-13).

(d) The conclusion of the argument (vv. 14-17) returns to the moving force in the life of the baptized: having received the Spirit of adoption, they should act as children of God and heirs (of glory) with Christ, to the extent that they suffer with him. But why should the baptized share in the sufferings of Christ? And which sufferings are those? As so often, Paul does not explain himself, but the following verse (v. 18) gives us to understand that it is a question of the trials related to the human condition—marked by the effects of sin—that the Son of God himself underwent in this world (v. 3). The last end is *glory with* Christ: that seems to be the point at which Paul was aiming all along.

Called to Glory (8:18-30)

The "we suffer with him so that we may also be glorified with him" in v. 17 initiates the unit on the relationship between present suffering and future glory. In fact, Paul has already addressed the question of the tribulations of the baptized at the very beginning of the section (Rom 5:3) to show their usefulness, all the more because, far from extinguishing hope, they strengthen it. But here the term "sufferings" is more comprehensive: it applies to all creation (and thus to Christians) subjected to the effects of the law of sin and death. Paul multiplies terms applicable to this situation (sufferings, groaning in labor pains, patience). Everything suffers and groans, and the Spirit groans with it, awaiting the glory that is assured because promised by God to God's children: the sufferings that are the lot of all terrestrial existence cannot prevent the coming of the promised glory.

Some commentators think that in this unit the expression "all creation" applies only to human beings. In fact we should give it a maximum application because the section (Romans 5–8) uses unambiguous expressions to refer to humanity: "the many" (5:15, 19), "all [human beings]" (5:12, 18). Paul is here doing nothing more than taking up the biblical statements that already see the material universe united with the resurrection of God's elect (Isa 55:13; 65:17, 25). For Paul, as for Isaiah, the spiritual and ethical renewal of humanity cannot fail to affect the rest of creation, which is called to become a *cosmos,* a world ordered to the glory of the children of God.

The other interest of the passage comes from the way it overcomes the radical and definitive contrast (at least as described in the apocalyptic writings of the period) between this world as totally perverse and hostile to believers, moving ineluctably toward ruin, and the future world of justice and the reign of God: humanity (and the world with it) already carries within it the seeds of its redemption.

The Peroration (8:31-39)

These verses contain the two principal components of a peroration or *peroratio:* amplification (here with a pathetic character) and recapitulation (summary of the salient points of the argument). We find here forceful expression of Paul's faith and hope: in Jesus Christ, God has given us everything and in the future nothing can separate us from God.

Israel and the Nations (Romans 9–11)

The place of Romans 9–11 in the whole letter is not immediately apparent. One could leap from Rom 8:39 to 12:1 and the logic would not suffer: given the dignity of their status, the transformation of their being and the hope given them by the Father, can the baptized not deduce the conditions of their actions (Romans 12–15)? The chapters on the fate of Israel have the appearance of an excursus because they begin in an unexpected manner: the end of Romans 8 leaves no room for sadness, but opens toward hope and praise; suddenly, without transition, Paul speaks of "great sorrow and unceasing anguish" (9:2). If the connections between Romans 9–11 and the context are not fully clear, does that mean that these chapters are not by Paul or that they were written by Paul but inserted later by the apostle or one of his coworkers in this section of the epistle? It is impossible to make a compelling response. But even if these three chapters (Romans 9–11) were written after Romans 1–8 or if they were composed in other circumstances and added to the first eight chapters, their current place in the body of the letter is in any case highly significant: the very fact that the fate of Israel is treated immediately after the developed argument in Romans 5–8 on Christian existence shows that the two problems are related.

The titles suggested by various Bibles for Romans 9–11 are numerous. Some emphasize the divine initiative and its realization ("God's election of Israel [RSV, NRSV]," "Jews and Gentiles in God's plan" [Catholic Study Bible, NAB], "God's saving plan endures in spite of Israel's refusal"); others speak only of Israel, with negative connotations ("Israel's unbelief") or positive ones ("The privileges of Israel" [JB]). Still others prefer a prudent neutrality ("The situation of Israel," "Mystery of Israel," "Israel and the Gentiles"). This invites us to seek the element that Paul himself is emphasizing.

Composition, Romans 9–11

(a) A biblical model. Romans 9–11 clearly adopts the themes and movement of many collective post-exilic prayers. The most obvious parallel is certainly the prayer of Azariah in the Greek additions to the book of Daniel. There we find the three great moments that articulate the argument of Romans 9–11: (1) O Lord, you are just and mighty; all your works are great; (2) our situation is the result of our sins, because we have always been disobedient; but (3) in your mercy you cannot abandon us, you will save us (cf. the prayers in Dan 9:4-20; Bar 1:15–2:15). In Romans 9–11 the apostle begins by recalling the infallibility and justice of the divine word (Rom 9:6-29), then goes on to announce that the reason for Israel's situation comes from Israel itself, which was guilty for having rejected the righteousness of God revealed by the gospel, by Jesus Christ (9:30–10:21). He finishes by proclaiming that the situation is not definitive: far from having rejected the chosen people, God desires to save them (11:1-32). In short, the biblical foundation appears to support the tripartite division.

(b) Romans 9–11 also develops as an argument *(probatio)* in three stages, each of which elaborates and supports a thesis *(propositio):*

exordium: 9:1-5. The enigma of the situation of Israel

probatio 9:6–11:32, made up of three major units:

- A 9:6-29 (*propositio* in 9:6a: the word of God has not failed). The logic follows from the divine call, but in a somewhat paradoxical manner. Paul shows that the current situation of Israel does not result from a fault in the plan of salvation (from the beginning to the present);
- B 9:30–10:21 (*propositio* in 10:4: salvation is received through faith in Christ). The situation results from the fact that Israel preferred the Torah to Christ, because it is faith in him that brings salvation (the current situation of Israel);
- A' 11:1-32 (*propositio* in 11:1a: God has not rejected God's people). God, who has been able to profit from Israel's rejection to bring mercy to the Gentiles, will still save God's people (the future of Israel).

peroratio: 11:33-36: the unsearchable wisdom of God.

The first and last units (A and A'), which are theological in nature, recall the unfathomable logic of divine choice (9:6-29) and open to the future of salvation offered to Israel, explaining in passing the reason and function of a stumbling block that is declared to be provisional (11:1-32); as for the second unit (B), it is christological in tenor and explains the reason for the current situation of Israel: in refusing to believe in the gospel, and thus in Christ, the nation has really rejected the unique way of salvation that God desired for them and for all humanity.

If the *peroratio* does not preserve the argumentation except for the unfathomableness of divine wisdom, as powerful for drawing profit from the stumbling of the one or the other and knowing all of them, it is because the section does not insist, in the first instance, on the responsibility or rebellion of Israel: the point is *theological*. Everything in the dynamic of the argumentation leads to the final exclamation, full of astonishment and praise. One can only admire the artistry with which Paul conducts his questioning, progressively opening the field of divine mercy up to the revelation of the salvation of "all Israel." As for the theological or christological tenor of the *propositiones,* it shows that the situation is not considered, first of all, from the point of view of Israel and its rejection of the gospel, for something essential is at stake in the fate of this people: the future of the promises, the solidity of the plan of salvation, the truth and fidelity of the divine word: more than Israel, it is God who is at stake!

Divine Justice, Romans 9–11

The composition of this section shows that Paul does not emphasize, in the first place, Israel's rebellion and consequent guilt. The slow ascent to the revelation of the mystery, of the divine design, and the final exclamation in face of the unfathomable decisions of eternal wisdom: all this indicates that the point is theological. Likewise in parts A and A' in the concentric composition the theme was theological: it is a question of God, God's word, and God's justice. Paul tries here to combine realities that are apparently incompatible: justice for all and election; justice and hardening. But the apostle's explanations may seem too facile. If love and hatred, or in other words election and its opposite, occurring before any human response, underscore the free divine choice, do they not render it arbitrary and unjust? The answers Paul gives to these difficulties require careful examination.

Divine Election and Justice (9:6-29)

Composition and Argumentation

In Rom 9:6-29, the verb "call" always has God as its explicit or implicit subject: it is God, and God alone, who calls. At the same time the connotation is always positive: God calls because God loves. If the verb "call" is not sufficient to insure the thematic unity of the passage, the biblical citations do not coalesce around one single point, but two: Rom 9:6b ("not all Israelites truly belong to Israel") and 9:14 ("Is there injustice on God's part? By no means!"), each of which governs a whole series of biblical citations (vv. 7-13 and 15-29). Must one therefore divide 9:6-29 into two distinct parts and drop the hypothesis of a real literary unity?

The two theses (9:6b and 9:14) that the argumentation, in the form of a biblical construct, is meant to establish in turn depend on 9:6a, which determines the principal theme of the chapter:

v. 6a: Israel is not in its present situation because the divine word is powerless;
v. 6b: not all Israelites truly belong to Israel: there is divine election (vv. 7-13);
v. 14: God's choices are not unjust (vv. 14-29).

Verse 6a is the sole *propositio,* which initiates the first development (9:6-29) because it has all the necessary characteristics. In the first place it determines the theme to be developed: it is a matter of showing that the divine word has not failed. And the function of the whole passage is to emphasize, by employing that word itself (cf. the quotations that begin with "he says" or "it says" in vv. 15, 17, 25; "she was told" in v. 12; "Isaiah cries out" in v. 27; "Isaiah predicted" in v. 29; "this is what the promise said" in v. 9; and those that contain a term related to speech such as "call" in vv. 25 and 26) and the efficacy of that word in two time periods: Paul begins, effectively, by showing that the current situation, far from being the result of necessity or accident, is the work of the divine word itself that, in acting as it has done, does not in any way injure those whom it does not call. The unity of the passage is thus emphasized by the problem that remains a theological one from beginning (v. 6) to end (v. 29).

Chiastic Composition

A: vv. 6-9	Israel, v. 6b (2x) descendants, v. 7 (2x), v. 8	divine decisions
B: vv. 10-13	love, v. 13	
C: vv. 14-18	have pity, v. 15 (2x), vv. 16, 18 will, vv. 16, 18 (2x) power or might, v. 17 show, v. 17	

C': vv. 19-23	will, v. 22 show, v. 22 power or might, v. 22 mercy, v. 23	the question of divine justice
B': vv. 24-26	love, v. 25 (2x)	
A': vv. 27-29	Israel, v. 27 (2x) descendants, v. 29	divine decisions

Units A, B, B', and A' present divine decisions and choices in their continuity, while the two central units (C and C') consider their solid foundations using diatribe style. Note the elegance of the construction. Paul places at the center the reflection on the ways of God: it would be difficult to pose questions on divine justice on the basis of the first verses without first presenting some concrete decisions; it would be equally poor pedagogy to stop with serious questions without responding to them at length—here with the assistance of the biblical word to prove and illustrate the infallibility of the divine word.

But these chiastic parallelisms do not exclude a real rhetorical progression in the argumentation. At the temporal level Paul begins with Abraham, Isaac, then Jacob and Esau (the time of the patriarchs); he then mentions Moses and Pharaoh (the time of the Exodus), and finishes with his own era, the time of the calling of the Gentiles—and of the Jewish Christians who constitute the remnant of Israel. In a gripping foreshortening, the section thus moves from the very beginnings of Israel's history to the time of the apostle (which is already the end-time), throwing into relief the coherence of the divine word.

At the level of the actors who are not among the elect, the beginning of the section (A) simply notes that not all are children and descendants of the promise without giving this any negative connotation; however, at the end of (B) nonelection is accompanied by negative feelings: Esau is hated. (C) goes still farther in speaking of hardening (of Pharaoh), while (C') speaks of imminent destruction (of objects made of clay) and (A') ends with an allusion to destruction already accomplished (of Sodom and Gomorrah).

The theme of calling is also treated progressively. Why does the verb "call" disappear within the central units? The reason is obvious: (C) and (C') inquire about the apparent injustice of God toward those who have not been called. We could thus measure the semantic weight of the alternation of

A + B (call)
C + C' (non-call)
B' + A' (call)

Call and non-call can thus not be understood apart from each other! In (A) and (B) Paul insists on the fact that the divine call precedes any human response, positive or negative, and is not determined by it. Such affirmations cannot help raising the question of divine justice: if God hardens or hates without failing to see the consequences of a refusal or disobedience on the part of the human being, is not God unjust? No, says Paul, because God's choice is not related to human response: there would be injustice if it were a question of retribution, which always follows action as Romans 2 has emphasized. But God also calls people who do not obey God, thus manifesting the freedom of the divine call. The freedom of the creator stifles the objection of inconsistency (why does God complain about our behavior if God has determined it in advance?): what can be said in the face of divine patience?

Verses 22-23 are elliptical. What does this divine patience entail? Is it a matter of the delay of grace so that sinners may be converted? The context, however, which focuses on the freedom of the divine will in advance of any positive or negative human response, disallows that solution. Or is it that in delaying the destruction of sinners God desires to show mercy to the Gentiles? The latter hypothesis fits the passage better, for it is not interested in human responses. As for the expression "objects of wrath," the parallel expression "objects of mercy" (v. 23) demands that we understand the former to mean "objects of [the divine] wrath."

The apostle arrives at an unexpected result: "non-call" and hardening are signs of patience rather than of destruction or wrath. In short, noncalling happens in order to support God's salvific design!

9:14-24

The apostle responds to his own objections in vv. 14 and 19 by repeating, with the Judaism of his time, the answers of Scripture. These answers are not at all original, and for a reason: it is up to the word of God to show its own consistency! But the central units, (C) and (C'), do not present themselves solely as a traditional response to a total freedom of God toward creatures. Paul cannot prove the *propositio* of v. 6a by reasoning solely about the concept of Israel, showing that from the beginning Israel was not identical with the whole of the nation—a distinction that prepares for the statements about the remnant and thus about Jews who have believed the gospel. That for Paul the latter are the elect Israel, and that thus God's word has not failed, ultimately leaves untouched the problem of the gracious call of the Gentiles for which, apparently, nothing has prepared the way, and that seems to mark a clear change in the economy of salvation. We thus see the importance of v. 15, which Paul does not use solely to proclaim the sovereign freedom and justice of God. The quotation of Exod 33:19, a prophecy, proclaims the mercy in vv. 23-24, showing that the divine plan has left nothing to chance or allowed any possibility of failure: from the Exodus onward, and thus from the beginning, God has proclaimed that the divine mercy alone explains the choice of those it touches and affects. Non-calling is only provisional!

What is the meaning of Paul's statement about hatred of Esau and the hardening of Pharaoh? The question of election leaves untouched the other question of hardening: the vocabulary of hatred and hardening seems to represent Paul's customary exaggeration, which we need to reduce in order to recover the underlying idea, that is, that God did not desire a rich and powerful nation as herald of divine justice. Without doubt that is so, but the apostle did not intend merely to say that some are not chosen (speaking here of a functional election defined by a mission) even if salvation will reach them one day. Hardening also means that even creaturely resistance is foreseen and integrated into the divine plan; it does not contradict its full and definitive realization: without being denied, human freedom is found from the beginning to be placed at the service of divine glory and the salvation of all.

9:25-29

The two final units, (B') and (A'), name the objects of divine mercy. Verse 24 introduces the two series of recipients as follows:

"us whom he has called,
a. not from the Jews only,
b. but also from the Gentiles"
B' = calling of the Gentiles (vv. 25-26)
A' = calling of the Jews, the remnant (vv. 27-29).

Clearly, vv. 25-26 speak of the calling of the Gentiles and vv. 27-29 of the calling of the elect of Israel, the remnant, made up of the Jews who have accepted the gospel. But did the apostle not use the prophecy of Hosea (quoted in vv. 25-26), which obviously speaks about Israel, to describe the calling of the Gentiles? A number of indications invite us to think so. In fact, in vv. 25-26 the "you" whom God will elect or call is not specified—an astonishing silence when one considers the following verse in which, by contrast, the word "Israel" is used twice. Thus we need to search for the referent of the pronoun "you" in v. 24, where it is a question of believers who have come from Judaism and from paganism. But, one might say, if that is the case then vv. 25-26 refer to all Christians without exception, and not solely to converts from paganism. This solution in no way obviates the difficulty of the apostle's exegesis: how can he see the calling of the Gentiles prophesied in a passage of Scripture that only has the Israelites in mind? Moreover, Rom 9:6-29 as a whole forbids us to see a reference to Jewish Christians in vv. 25-26 because, in this chapter, God never turns back: the apostle does not envisage the case of a call that is put in question in order to be ratified anew. The Jewish Christians in v. 24 can thus not have belonged to the "Not-my-people" of v. 25; the phrase here must refer to the Gentiles.

But how did Paul come to use Hos 2:1b to describe the calling of the Gentiles? As Hos 1:2 tells us, "Unloved" and "Not-my-people" are the "children of prostitution," not part of the people of God, the Israel of the covenant, and their names function precisely to validate this. Their identity can thus be assimilated to that of the idolatrous pagans who are excluded from the covenant and the promises. Of course one could add that the referent remains Israel as guilty of idolatry and breaking the covenant. That is true, but the text of Hosea shows nonetheless that calling and mercy—for "Unloved" and "Not-my-people" are called; their names are changed to "Beloved" and "My people"—are not determined by fleshly descendance, but instead by the unique beneficent will of God, who purifies and bestows mercy unconditionally. Origin or descent are thus not a diriment impediment: God can call whoever God wills to enter into covenant. In this the symbolic situation in Hosea 1–2 prefigures and proclaims that of the Gentiles who are called in mercy. Status as sons and daughters (cf. "they will be called children of the living God"), which is graciously given to the Gentile nations can thus be seen as anticipated in these chapters, where divine providence and consistency are manifested. Paul's reading does not deny the literal one (with the original reference to Israel), but simply recognizes in this passage from Hosea a plan whose object and beneficiary is not Israel alone; a plan that is now realized, or better, acknowledged because it is realized.

The reading Paul gives to Hosea 2 shows the relationship and consistency between Romans 9 and Romans 4: if God justified Abraham, the sinner, while he was still uncircumcised, and if his situation prefigures that of Gentiles who are justified by faith alone, why should the situation of the two children not be a link in the series of prefigurations of justification given to all without exception?

The Remnant and Its Function (9:27-29)

Does not the final unit, A' (vv. 27-29), emphasize the non-salvation of the majority of the children of Israel, a remnant of whom, by contrast, are chosen and saved? Verses 27-29 do not in any way insist on the many children of Israel who are punished or destroyed, or on a remnant who are elect or saved, except to say that the remnant witnesses to the word of God that never fails. There is nothing at all in A' about the rejection of Israel. One even has the impression that Paul has chosen these two passages from Isaiah because they proclaim the salvation of the remnant without mentioning either punishment or any negative action of God.

9:6-29: Toward a Theology of Election

Because the divine word has not failed (v. 6a), Paul must show that the rejection of the gospel by a noteworthy portion of Israel in the name of a greater fidelity to the Mosaic covenant and the Law does not result from any kind of divine impotence.

How will Paul proceed? He will do so by restricting election, or by distinguishing between the descendants of Israel and Israel as the group of the elect. (This is why election was not listed among the privileges belonging to all the descendants of the patriarchs, the Israelites, in Rom 9:4-5a.) He will also show that this distinction between those whom Rom 11:5 counted as the remnant chosen by grace and the fleshly descendants of Abraham existed *from the beginning*.

But someone may object that the Jews themselves accept such a distinction: only the descendants of Jacob can be called children of Israel. Earlier Paul stopped the series of his own distinctions between those called and those not called with Jacob: he could not go any farther because, according to the traditions that recall the divine word, all the sons of Jacob without exception are the eponymous heads of the tribes of Israel. Nevertheless, with the aid of Isa 10:22-23 he shows that not all the descendants of the twelve sons of Jacob can be identified with the elect, who are the remnant. Here is another point that Paul has in common with his Jewish contemporaries: for the latter (and this is still true today) belonging to the chosen people can obviously not be reduced to physical descent; otherwise would they have accepted that Gentiles had, by means of circumcision and obedience to the Law, been incorporated into the people of the covenant because they believed in the God of the ancestors? But Paul undoubtedly insists, more than the Judaism of his time, on the complete gratuity of election: the principle of choice lies in God alone, and not at all in human response. This point is decisive because it permits the apostle to couple election and calling in order to apply them to the Gentiles as well, to whom the grace of God is manifested and offered through the gospel. If we do not yet find in Romans 9 a developed theology of election, it is still true that Paul wants to emphasize the theological conditions: the continuity and steadfastness of God's plan, the sovereign freedom of God's choice, its total gratuitousness. Nevertheless, in Romans 9 it is not so much election that plays a part as non-election: in raising the question of the well-foundedness of divine choice Paul can progressively lead his readers to recognize that non-election need not be forever and that it can only be understood as a departure from the merciful plan of God—a plan, because the words to Pharaoh (Exod 9:16; cf. Rom 9:17) were a prophecy indicating, again mysteriously, the paradoxical purpose of non-election.

Elsewhere in Romans, but also in other letters, the vocabulary of election is applied to Christians, whether Jewish or Gentile in origin, while in Romans 9–11 it is reserved solely for the part of Israel called the remnant (11:5). Moreover, we can see why. All the Israelites who have rejected the gospel because of the Law cannot be part of the elect Israel; if, in fact, election depends solely on the free divine initiative and cannot be called into question (for that would go against the omnipotence of the one who chooses and the infallibility of God's word), only those members of Israel can have believed in the gospel who are among the elect. If Rom 9:4-5a does not mention election among the privileges accorded to the Israelites it is thus not simply because the latter are *no longer* elect (in fact, the apostle never uses "no longer" with regard to election, because God's call is never taken back), nor solely because not all have been chosen (except the remnant), but because the development that follows in Rom 9:6-29 functions to show that the vocabulary of election needs to be completed by another, also scriptural, namely the vocabulary of calling, in order to give an account of the fullness of God's saving plan. In Rom 9:6-29, calling and election, far from being opposed, are fully complementary.

Israel and the Rejection of the Gospel (Romans 10)

Composition

Here again we find several types of composition:

A *exordium* (9:30–10:3). Paul presents the question: "why are Israel and the Gentiles in the reverse situation to what was foreseen? It is because the Israelites preferred their way of righteousness (the Mosaic Law) to that proposed by God (justification in Jesus Christ);

B thesis (*propositio,* 10:4) and explanation (*probatio,* 10:5-17) in which the key that permits us to understand the situation is presented: only faith in Christ (or in the gospel) is the way of salvation for all;

A' *peroratio* (10:18-21) returning to the situation of Israel and the Gentiles: Israel, to whom the gospel was revealed, is responsible and disobedient.

The parallels do not interrupt the progression of Paul's reasoning: the ardor with which Israel clings to its righteousness seems, however, to go hand in hand with a non-culpable ignorance (A), but it is finally judged to be disobedience and rebellion (A'). Bracketed by A and A', the central part (B), which is also the *probatio,* first presents the two contrasted types of righteousness, and then emphasizes the salvific significance of the act of faith in Jesus, its maximum extent, and finishes with the description of its origin, from the sending of the heralds of salvation to the confession of Jesus as Lord by each believer.

Christ and the Mosaic Law (10:4)

The verse could be translated: "for the end (or purpose) of the Law (is) Christ, so that (there may be) righteousness for everyone who believes." But in what sense is Christ (a) the end or (b) the purpose of the Mosaic Law?

(a) If Paul is saying that Christ puts an end to the reign of the Law, this still leaves us with a number of possible interpretations. Does he put an end to the curse or condemnation to which the Law exposes us (cf. Galatians 3; Rom 4:15)? Does he also put an end to a perverse observance of the Law because he is concerned for its true righteousness and unique merits? These two interpretations do not respect the context and have, happily, been abandoned nowadays. If Paul is speaking of the end of a flourishing regime, the end is that of the Law and not simply of a bad use of it being made by the Jews. In fact Paul's formulation is not patient of any ambiguity; he does not contrast two ways of observing the Law, but rather two economies: that of the Law and that of Faith, that of the Law and that of Christ.

(b) But the question returns: do the verse and its context not demand, in fact, that we see Jesus Christ as the purpose of the Law, the point toward which it moves, the one it proclaims and in whom it finds the accomplishment of the righteousness it promises? With the coming of Jesus Christ and the gift of the Holy Spirit, the Law's finality is accomplished. Far from being contradictory, the statements in Rom 10:5 and 10:6-8 are complementary; thus for believers adherence in heart and action to the divine will enables them to obtain salvation; "will live" in 10:5 is equivalent to "will be saved" in 10:9. But that interpretation does not really recommend itself for the preceding context (9:30–10:3) and what follows (10:5-17), neither of which combines faith in Christ with observance of the Mosaic Law.

The fact that the two citations (explicitly Lev 18:5 and implicitly Deut 30:11-14) from the Torah are prophecies does not, however, imply that Rom 10:4 sees Christ as the purpose of the Law. The preceding verse (10:3) does not trace a path leading from the Law to Christ; it simply affirms the incompatibility between two types of justice, a "special justice" (the economy of the Law for the Jew) and the "justice of God" (the economy of faith for all). A similar incompatibility requires that the Jews cease to consider the Law as a way of salvation.

Two Ways to Salvation, or Only One? (10:6-9)

Romans 4 attempted to show that the economy of faith is not an accident of history, but a constant. Still, not everything has been said. Are there not, in fact, two possible routes to the interior of the economy of faith, one for the circumcised (the Jews), and another for the uncircumcised? The first would consist in living one's faith by observing the divine will expressed in the Law transmitted by Moses, and the second of believing in Jesus Christ and becoming his disciple. Jesus Christ would thus be a substitute for the Law, a way for the Gentiles to achieve salvation by another route. Would the Jewish faith process have nothing at all to do with salvation in Jesus Christ? In Romans 10 Paul gives a negative response: everyone, Jew or non-Jew, wishing to be saved must confess Jesus Christ.

The Law does not bring salvation. Romans 10:5, which quotes Lev 18:5, and Rom 10:6-9, which alludes to Deuteronomy 30, are obviously intended to support Paul's propositions regarding the two kinds of righteousness. Paul sets forth these two types: that of the Law (followed by the Jews) and that which comes from faith in Jesus Christ (which God intends for all):

Rom 10:5 = Lev 18:5	**Rom 10:6-9 (cf. Deut 30:11-14)**
righteousness that comes from the Law	righteousness that comes from faith
written	spoken
keep the commandments	believe that Jesus is Lord
live through them	be saved

The two passages come from the Mosaic Law and show, indeed, that the latter both defines the time of the Law, indicating for its subjects what they must do to live—a regime Paul has considered as past in Romans 7–8—and at the same time announces the time of salvation through faith in Jesus Christ.

But in making Deut 30:11-14 a prophecy of righteousness through faith has Paul not deflected it from its meaning? For the passage in Deuteronomy obviously speaks of the commandments of the Law and demands that they be practiced; the ending of Deut 30:14 is omitted: "the word is . . . in your mouth, in your heart *and in your hands for you to observe.*" How can a text thus mistreated and mutilated confirm Paul's thesis? At this point, once again, his exegesis demands close and critical study. As things now stand we can only say that Paul is neither arguing nor quoting; he is simply applying the passage of Deuteronomy to the situation experienced by the group of believers to which he belongs. His exegesis of the passage reflects the same liberty as that taken by the Judaism of his era. In so doing he does not confine the Law to a bygone past, which would be the case if he had only referred to Lev 18:5, but acknowledges that it has a prophetic value: the Law itself proclaimed the mystery of faith, Jesus Christ dead and risen, through whom we are justified and through whom we will *all* be saved.

In recalling the proximity and interiority of the word of faith the apostle again emphasizes the gracious gift it expresses. Belief is not the result of an indefinite pursuit, but rather the effect of a visitation, a gift that precedes us, abides in us, and simply asks to be accepted and acknowledged.

The difficulty of the passage arises less from the manner in which Scripture is employed than from Paul's thesis, which sketches in a few traits the respective characteristics of the two righteousnesses: is the first regime (Judaism) nothing but a religion of observance? As for Christians, are they to believe and proclaim the lordship of Jesus without allowing that faith to issue in ethical action (which is precisely what Deut 30:14*b,* which Paul passes over in silence, says)? Such a contrast is nothing but caricature. The apostle paraphrases Deut 30:11-14 in order to describe the economy of faith as completely opposed to that of the Law, but in shortening it he deprives it of its aim: Deut 30:14 in fact insists, even more than Lev 18:5, on putting into practice the divine word that comes to dwell in the hearts of believers and guides their actions. If Paul thus does not forget the relationship that exists between faith and the fruits it is to give, as all his exhortations testify, why does he evade that relationship in Rom 10:6-8? If he says nothing about acts demanded of believers, that does not mean that for him faith has nothing to do with ethics and remains only an affirmation of the lips; quite the opposite. He wishes here to insist solely on the fact that the actions of believers do not determine salvation, that it is necessary always to receive (in faith) the gracious initiative of God. And if he paraphrases Deut 30:11-14 as he does, it is because the formulation of these verses prophesies the interiority of the word of faith, or in other words, the presence of Christ in every believer with his saving effects.

What Paul accuses the Jews of doing, in Rom 9:30–10:3, is seeking justification and salvation by the observance of the commandments of the Mosaic Law and not by faith in Jesus Christ. But for the faithful Jew that Law, directly revealed by God, expresses God's will for humanity and is relevant only in relation to the covenant; its observance loses all meaning if it is not guided by faith, if it is not the expression and accomplishment of faith. The Mosaic Law first of all defines religious relationships, and it is for that reason that the Jews desire to put it into practice. Was Paul entirely deceived about the role of the Law and therefore about the nature of Judaism, when he had been one of its most zealous representatives? Surely not. But he draws the consequences of his experience in Jesus Christ: if it is faith in Jesus that procures salvation (Romans 10), if the justice of God is fully manifested in Jesus and is given in his name (Rom 3:21-30), this means that believers need not be obliged to become subjects of the Mosaic Law (Jews), or in other words to obey the whole of its precepts in order to obtain salvation and life—which would be equivalent to subjection. We see thus how Romans 4 and Romans 10 complement one another: in the first development Paul presents some of the constant elements of the relationship of faith, and in the second he shows the decisive significance of the event of Jesus Christ for faith—faith in Jesus Christ, and that alone, saves. The importance of Romans 10 in the whole of the epistle thus becomes apparent: Paul here shows that to believe is not only essential for justification (Romans 4) but also for salvation.

The Salvation of Israel, Romans 11

The rhetorical composition of the section emphasizes the more and more intimate relationship established by Paul between Israel and the Gentiles. In the first part (9:6-29) there was no "horizontal" relation, except to say that some were called from the one or the other group (Rom 9:24) and if at the end of the second part (9:30–10:21) the future jealousy of Israel toward the Gentiles is scarcely evoked (10:19), in the third part (11:1-32) Paul returns more than once to the role of each group in relation to the mercy given to the other. Why does the apostle thus come to mix together, more and more, the final destiny of Israel and that of the Gentiles?

Composition

After the *propositio* in v. 1, where Paul indicates in a veiled way that God will not leave God's people far from salvation, vv. 2-10 take up the problem addressed in Rom 9:27-29: the elect remnant indeed shows that God has not rejected God's people.

vv. 2b-4 (past tense)
  a = vv. 2b-3: the wicked actions of Israel
  b = v. 4: God proclaims that a holy remnant will be preserved
vv. 5-10 (present tense)
  b' = vv. 5-6: the existence of a remnant chosen by grace
  a' = vv. 7-10: the hardening of Israel (by God)

Verse 11 marks a turning point in the discourse because in vv. 11-15 the remnant is totally absent from the argumentation. Henceforward Paul envisions the positive outcome: the admission or reintegration of hardened Israel. As for vv. 25-32, they go even farther, explicitly envisaging the salvation of all Israel. The development of the argumentation can be summarized as follows:

a. Rejection of the people (as a whole)? No, because God has maintained a remnant of Jews who believe in Jesus Christ (vv. 1-10)
b. Fall (definitive) of the others? Not at all, again because of the divine goodness and power (vv. 11-24)
c. Their hardening will end with their entry into the fullness of the Gentiles, and all Israel will thus be saved (vv. 25-32).

The Allegory of the Two Olive Trees (11:17-24)

It is fairly easy to see the point of vv. 17-24. The reasoning *a fortiori* (v. 24) helps us besides; its function is to emphasize the positive aspect of the future situation of hardened Israel. That appears to be the point on which Paul wants to insist; he does so by showing that the current estrangement of the Jews who have rejected the gospel is not at all definitive, that God is able to "reintegrate" them. But the example that is used to apply Paul's proposition seems banal. Had he never seen grafts of this type? In general the tree is wild and the graft is "noble." And yet the allegory of the two olive trees demonstrates very well the profound logic of the passage. If, in fact, God is powerful enough to accomplish the impossible, that is, to graft the Gentiles (the wild branches) into the noble and fecund root (the patriarchs), how much more can God do what is easier, to regraft the original branches! Thus we should not ask whether Paul is absolutely up to date about the laws of tree culture, for the aberrant nature of the image perfectly expresses the unfathomable character of the situation. Anyone who grafts a wild branch into a noble root would by no means expect to see good fruit on the grafted branch; but what a reasonable tree farmer avoids doing is just what God has done: God has carried out an operation contrary to nature by grafting the savage branch onto the free and noble olive tree, making the Gentiles full-fledged children of Abraham, able to bear fruit in abundance! And if God has the power to do the impossible, why deny to God the power to regraft the original branch into the holy tree? The one who can do the greater can do the less: that is the point emphasized by the argument *a fortiori* in Rom 11:24.

Are these verses polemic, and should we see here one of the reasons that would have caused Paul to write the letter? To all those in the church at Rome who came from paganism and would have had a tendency to reject the Jewish roots of their faith or to despise the Jews who had rebelled against the gospel, the apostle would be energetically recalling the gracious calling they had received and the definitive and ineradicable tie that attaches them to the blessing given to the patriarchs (cf. 11:17-21). But the dynamic of the argumentation, culminating in vv. 22-24, shows that the emphasis does not lie on some reproach by Paul on encountering Christians who do not come from Judaism, but rather on the possibility of a "reintegration" of Israel. For the purpose of vv. 17-24 is heuristic: Paul wants to make his readers understand why the reintegration of Israel may be anticipated. He sets up an imaginary interlocutor who raises an objection: has not the wild branch (the Gentiles) taken the place of the branch that was cut off (the Jews who were broken away: vv. 17-19)? To this the apostle responds, using the argument *a fortiori,* that the substitution, which after all is relative and provisional, in no ways prevents the all-powerful God from regrafting the branches that have been cut off and separated.

After recalling the existence of the holy remnant who attest that the people have not been rejected (11:2-10) Paul wanted to prepare for the prophetic proclamation of the final salvation of an Israel that has been temporarily separated (11:25-27), while affirming the possibility even of the salvation of that Israel and indicating the function of its separation (vv. 11-24). In these intermediary verses there is already a very clear affirmation that the calling of the Gentiles can only be understood in relation to Israel—the Israel that is hardened (the branches that are cut off) or the Israel of the election (the holy root).

These propositions require some explanation because, if Jesus Christ is the only thing necessary, if it is sufficient, as Romans 10 has said, to confess him in order to be saved, why can the group of believers drawn from paganism not exist without Israel? It is true that if the apostle insists in Rom 11:17-24 on the intangible tie uniting the believers who have come from paganism (whom he continues to call "the Gentiles") to the holy root, he does not explain why they cannot be detached without being immediately separated from the blessings related to the promises. One can thus return to what was said of the act of believing in Romans 4. Paul there emphasizes the tie between faith and identity, faith and salvation. Because Abraham believed, he received his proper identity as father and, at the same time, that of his descendants, the children to come. Returning to the holy root as to a fecundity that precedes us indicates that it is faith that has engendered us, given us an ancestry and, besides that, a history as believers. Christians coming from paganism are thus unable to understand and live the gracious gift given to them except by returning to the figure of Abraham and the long history of the elect people—recognizing there the paradoxical ways of divine fidelity—a people from whom the Savior took flesh and was born. If they cut themselves off from that root, if they deny it, they cut themselves off from their own past, lose their memory, the history of their calling, and thereby their identity. Does Paul even want to show the Church that it cannot exist without an Israel that has been declared unfaithful? It is impossible to know, because the distinction in Romans 9–11 between Israel and the Gentiles does not coincide with that between the Church and Israel nor that between the Church and the Gentiles.

If the Gentiles need Israel, the reverse seems equally true. In fact, Paul affirms three times that the adherence of the Gentiles to the gospel will arouse the jealousy (Greek *parazēloun:* 10:19; 11:11, 14) of Israel. One might again object that since Cain and Abel jealousy has had few positive effects; if the conversion of the Gentiles can only provoke Jewish scorn or resentment is Paul not fooling himself very much about the future? In reality he expects a positive result because for persons as zealous as observant Jews (Rom 10:2) jealousy (which is different from envy), far from paralyzing or provoking to murder, pushes toward superior achievement: why, then, should the conversion of the Gentiles to the true God, their zeal for service shown by the change in their ethical behavior, not stimulate them? If those who believe in Jesus Christ carry out the commandments to love God and neighbor, if they witness to divine mercy and the demands of biblical monotheism, is this not because the one, true God has made Godself known to them and thus allowed Godself to be known through them? Beyond the stimulating effect that the conversion of the Gentiles to the God of the promises may have, the apostle presumes that the Jews need the Church in order to recognize how divine mercy is manifested to all and definitively, without any discrimination. That is what the Church should witness, and that is what Israel should learn from it, recognizing through it how far divine tenderness extends. God's mercy extends to those who were far off and who did not know the true God (11:31); it is a mercy without conditions.

Thus the calling of the nations does not make the election of Israel (the holy root) obsolete or invalid, because it is through the Israel of the election that believers receive their memory, their history as sons and daughters, and so as heirs; at the same time, that election finds its purpose in the mercy given to all humanity: in choosing one person, one family, one people, God did not condemn or abandon the rest of humanity, but awaited another occasion to call them when the time was ripe. Divine patience and fidelity (Romans 9), the results of which are made manifest at the very end (Romans 11): the time of Pauline discourse has in some ways mimicked and even embraced it by its use of suspense, delay, and historical time.

The Salvation of Israel (11:25-32)

These verses are not content to reprise in abridged form the paradoxical logic of Romans 9–11; they go farther because they give us the final and decisive information about the future issue and reasons for Israel's being provisionally cut off. Paul has thus come progressively to the point of showing how the question of salvation cannot exclude one of the actors, either Israel or the Gentiles, because the future of each remains tied to that of the other, showing finally the whole significance of a reflection on the fate of Israel.

It is worth the effort to note how, throughout Romans 9–11, the apostle develops and modifies the themes of hardening and mercy. Thus from the beginning to the end of the section the sole cause of hardening is God, but in Romans 9 it strikes only Pharaoh, who does not belong to the chosen people, while in Romans 11 it is a major portion of Israel that is touched by it. And if in the beginning the cutting off of Pharaoh has only a theological function, at the end, in contrast, that of Israel acquires a fully salvific finality because the Gentiles have come to know the gospel as a result of Israel's defection. Romans 9:24 mentions the calling of the Gentiles without signaling what brought it about—the cutting off of Israel, evoked only on the basis of Rom 9:33—while Romans 11 explicitly ties the admission of the Gentiles to the unbelief of Israel. Another theme treated in a continuing progression is that of mercy. Romans 9:15 had effectively allowed the apostle to present the divine plan as a plan of mercy, in no way attached to any fault or sin, but mysteriously oriented to the calling of the

Gentiles (9:23-24). The last word of the section, again, is mercy (11:32), but this time relating to that which, from the human side, calls it forth, that is to say disobedience, in order, with it, to describe the whole of God's paradoxical plan.

This continuous progression does not simply authorize us to interpret Rom 9:27 and 11:25 together, but also to determine the extent of "all Israel" in 11:26. Who will be saved, only the remnant (9:27) or all Israel (11:26)? In a first period of time (Rom 9:26-29) salvation would be that of the remnant, so that the initial *propositio* (9:6a: "the word of God has not failed") would be confirmed! But that cannot be the end of the journey (Romans 11), when Paul reveals the unfathomable plan of God: all Israel will be saved! But what is meant by "all Israel"? In Romans 9–11 Paul tries to deal with the scandal of a people who awaited its Messiah and then rejected him for the sake of fidelity!—fidelity, that is, to a Torah that they consider the way God has commanded them to follow in order to receive righteousness and the promised blessing. It is thus of those Israelites that the apostle is thinking at first, and the "all Israel" of 11:26a includes both those in Rom 9:27 (the remnant, the Jews who have believed in Jesus Christ) and those in Rom 9:30–10:21 (the Jews who have rejected the gospel in the name of a total attachment to the Mosaic Law).

But if Rom 11:25-32 is the rhetorical and theological summit of the section, why is Jesus the Christ not named in it? Will he not be the savior of the Israel that has rejected the gospel? But is not the liberator of whom Rom 11:26 (quoting Isa 59:20) speaks Jesus Christ? The question returns, nevertheless: if he is the liberator in v. 26, should Paul not have named him explicitly in order to avoid any ambiguity and, above all, to emphasize his role? Undoubtedly, Rom 11:23 indicates that the hardened Jews can be regrafted into the holy root "if they do not persist in unbelief," in other words, if they believe—and that faith, according to Romans 10, cannot be anything but faith in Jesus Christ as Lord. But if Paul does not explicitly mention Jesus Christ in Rom 11:25-32 it is because, as in Romans 9, he wants first to recall the initiative of God's power: the problem is less one of mediation, as addressed in Romans 10, than of the very possibility of salvation.

Exhortations: Make Your Lives an Offering That is Pleasing to God (Romans 12–15)

Composition

A certain number of rhetorical units can be discerned (various commands having the role of *subpropositiones* are followed by explanations or justifications). The section can be divided as follows:

12:1-2: *propositio* covering all the exhortations (life as a sacrifice and spiritual worship)

12:3–13:14: life in the Church and in the world
- 12:3-16: among brothers and sisters—no pretense; mutual respect (v. 3 *subpropositio*)
- 12:17-21: with those in the world—do not avenge evil (v. 17 *subpropositio*)
- 13:1-7: with those in the world—those in authority—submission (v. 1 *subpropositio*)
- 13:8-10: among brothers and sisters—love fulfills the Law (v. 8 *subpropositio*)
- 13:11-14: eschatological orientation of Christian life

14:1–15:13: ("Welcome one another as Christ has welcomed you.")—the case of the weak
- 14:1: *subpropositio:* "welcome those who are weak in faith"
- 14:2-23: the case of the strong and the weak: various rules and principles of discernment
- 15:1-13: expansion and christological motivation
  - vv. 1-6: do not seek to please yourself; follow Christ's example
  - vv. 7-13: welcome as Christ has welcomed you

15:14-33: peroration for the entire letter.

Keys for Reading

(a) The first two verses of the section (12:1-2) are of special importance because they give the tone to the exhortations that follow: justified and graced, believers can make their whole life a sacrifice pleasing to God. But these verses also indicate that the ethical life is the effect of the redemptive work as well (the "therefore" in 12:1 recalls the *probatio*) and it should witness to the power of the gospel. The whole section thus takes up, in its own way, the declaration in 1:16 on the gospel as the power of God for the salvation of all who believe.

(b) It is common to see in Romans 14 (on the strong and the weak) one of the principal reasons for the writing of the letter to the Romans: Paul wanted to smooth out the difficulties existing between Christians of Jewish origin (the weak) and Christians of Gentile origin (the strong). But (i) that interpretation forgets that Paul avoids setting one group over against the other because these criteria are valid in different contexts, and (ii) the example is chosen because of the theme announced in the *propositio* in 1:16 (the gospel as the power of God for the salvation of all believers) to make us understand how those whom the gospel has made strong should bear the burdens of the weak (15:1) rather than despising them, thus imitating Christ who came to the rescue of our weakness. The christological argument is again decisive. The whole logic of Romans can be re-read in these verses.

(c) The exhortations in Rom 12:1–15:13 do not address the exact problems of the Romans, but all the situations that confront Christians in community and in the world: almost all the instructions are found in the earlier letters written by the apostle (particularly those to Corinth and Galatia). Paul is content to recall and develop them, emphasizing only, along the lines of his initial *propositio,* how faith should animate the work of Christians. As for the exhortations that are unique to Romans (such as that regarding submission to political authorities in Rom 13:1-7), they do not refer to difficulties peculiar to the church at Rome; Paul takes advantage of the fact that his addressees are in the capital of the empire to indicate that the field of Christian action and discernment extends even to the political, and to show how the baptized can live as full-fledged citizens wherever they are.

(d) As in his other letters Paul insists here again on humility, patience, and hospitality. The reason is christological: as those for whom Christ has been patient, whom he has received, to whom he has given an extreme example of humility, how can they not do the same in turn? Their action is definitively founded, not on external rules, but on the experience of a love received to the utmost extent.

Peroration for the Whole Letter, 15:14-33

—vv. 14-21:
Paul recalls his mission to the Gentiles in terms already used in the *exordium*;
- vv. 14-16:
two ideas (i) capacity *(dynamenoi)* of the Romans for mutual exhortation; (ii) Paul justifies his letter and its content by his vocation as apostle to the Gentiles;
- vv. 17-21
the efficacy of Paul's ministry to the Gentiles (cf. 1:16), and their obedience (cf. 1:5).

—vv. 22-29
recalling his plan to visit Rome and the reasons for the collection

—vv. 30-33
exhortations and final salutation.

Closing of the Epistolary Frame (Various Greetings and Final Acclamation), 16:1-27

BIBLIOGRAPHY

Achtemeier, Paul J. *Romans.* Interpretation. Atlanta: John Knox, 1986.

Bassler, Jouette M. *Divine Impartiality: Paul and a Theological Axiom.* SBL.DS 59. Chico: Scholars, 1982.

Brooten, Bernadette J. *Women Leaders in the Ancient Synagogue.* BJS 36. Chico: Scholars, 1982.

Cranfield, C.E.B. *A Critical and Exegetical Commentary on the Epistle to the Romans.* 2 vols. Edinburgh: T & T Clark, 1975–79.

Dunn, James D. G. *Romans.* 2 vols. WBC. Waco, Tex.: Word Books, 1988.

Fitzmyer, Joseph A. *Romans. A New Translation with Introduction and Commentary.* AB 33. Garden City, N.Y.: Doubleday, 1993.

Martin, Brice L. *Christ and the Law in Paul.* NT.S 62. Leiden and New York: Brill, 1989.

Sanders, E. P. *Paul and Palestinian Judaism: A Comparison of Patterns of Religion.* Philadelphia: Fortress, 1977.

____. *Paul, the Law and the Jewish People.* Philadelphia: Fortress, 1983.

Winninge, Mikael. *Sinners and Righteous: A Comparative Study of the Psalms of Solomon and Paul's Letters.* Stockholm: Almqvist & Wiksell, 1995.

1 Corinthians

Jan Lambrecht

Paul wrote his first letter to the Corinthians from Ephesus, most probably in the fall of 54 C.E. Like his letter to the Romans and his second to the Corinthians, the first letter to the Corinthians is both comprehensive and lengthy. Its content displays a wide range of items and the reader is immediately struck by its vehement and practical tone. At the very beginning Paul deals with a topical problem in the Christian community of Corinth: "Now I appeal to you, brothers and sisters, by the name of our Lord Jesus Christ, that all of you be in agreement and that there be no divisions among you, but that you be united in the same mind and the same purpose. For it has been reported to me by Chloe's people that there are quarrels among you . . ." (1:11-12).

The whole of this multifaceted letter is devoted to ethical and doctrinal questions that for the Christians in Corinth certainly were of immediate importance. To be sure some of them, such as meat offered to idols or extraordinary spiritual gifts, will seem less relevant to some groups of readers or in some regions. Yet where Paul speaks

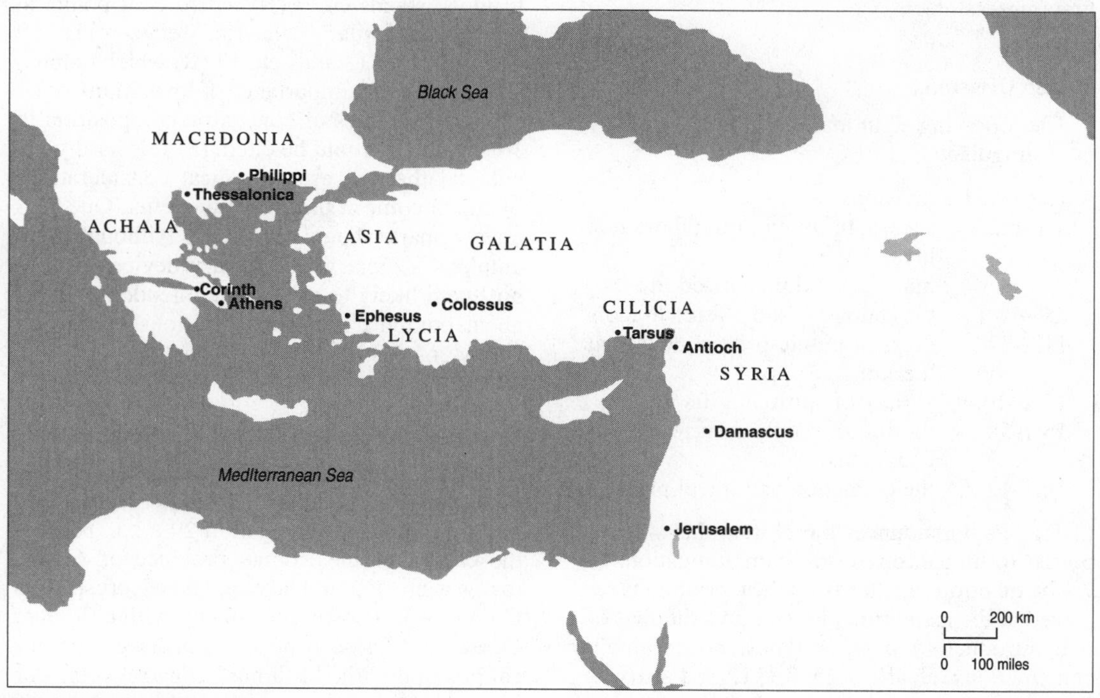

THE WORLD OF PAUL

of the central message of the gospel, Christ crucified (ch. 1), or of love as the most excellent Christian way (ch. 13), or of the Christians' future resurrection (ch. 15), Christians of all times, races, and countries cannot but listen with great attention; they should not omit personal application for their own authentic life in Christ.

Several passages of this letter are employed in the liturgies of major feasts or important celebrations of one's personal life (e.g., marriage or religious vows, funerals). Christians are still sadly divided; tensions between groups within the same Church exist; leaders continue to dispute and fight; poor Christians question the life of their rich fellow Christians: all this points to the relevance of 1 Corinthians today.

FIRST READING

1 Corinthians begins with the usual salutation (1:1-3) and thanksgiving (1:4-9). It ends with exhortations and greetings (16:13-24). Within the body of the letter very divergent materials are discussed. A strictly conceptual development does not seem to underlie the composition. There is hardly any logical progression of thought and reasoning. Paul deals successively with a variety of subjects—at least this is our first impression.

Major Divisions

The following eight major sections can easily be distinguished:

1:10–4:21	divisions
5:1–6:20	a case of immorality; lawsuits; laxity
7:1-40	marriage and unmarried life
8:1–11:1	the eating of food offered to idols
11:2-34	dress at public prayer; abuses at the Lord's Supper
12:1–14:40	variety of spiritual gifts
15:1-58	the future bodily resurrection of Christians
16:1-12	the collection and travel plans

In 1:11 Paul announces a first item that was reported to him through oral communication. In 7:1 he mentions a letter from the Corinthians received at the same time; he employs the first of five introductory *peri de* ("now concerning") constructions (cf. also 7:25; 8:1; 12:1; and 16:1). One might therefore be tempted to distinguish a twofold division: in chs. 1–6 Paul answers messages that have reached him by word of mouth (the scandals); in chs. 7–15 (and 16:1-4?) he answers questions posed by correspondence (more theological difficulties). But in Greek literature the use of "concerning" does not necessarily point to writing and we have no certainty at all about the exact contents of the oral reports (cf. 11:18: "I hear") or of the letter.

The thematic diversity and the presence of some tensions hardly constitute sufficient ground to doubt that 1 Corinthians is a single letter. Partition proposals are not convincing. The distinctive vocabulary, images, and *topoi* throughout the whole of the writing are a strong argument for the compositional integrity and unity of the letter. Moreover, its authenticity has never been disputed.

With regard to the composition of 1 Corinthians three matters should be noted. (1) There seems to be some coherence of subject matter and analogy of theme within four major blocks: chs. 1–4 (divisions), chs. 5–7 (sexual life), chs. 8–14 (matters in connection with worship), and ch. 15 (resurrection). (2) The position of ch. 9 as well as that of ch. 13 reveals Paul's fondness for the concentric A–B–A' construction. Between chs. 8 (A) and 10 (A'), both treating food offered to idols, stands ch. 9 (B) where Paul points to his own exemplary behavior. Between chs. 12 (A) and 14 (A') stands ch. 13 (B) which emphasizes the overall importance of love. Many other (minor) examples of concentric composition in 1 Corinthians could be cited. (3) It is hardly accidental that the eschatological considerations of ch. 15 come at the end of the letter. One negative remark should be added. Although Paul employs a great many literary devices it does not seem likely to me that he intended to bring about complex rhetorical divisions within the "body" of this letter (= 1:10–16:12).

Corinth and Paul's Visits

Corinth, devastated by the Romans in 146 B.C.E., was refounded as a Roman colony in 44 B.C.E. by Julius Caesar and in 29 B.C.E. became the capital of the Roman province of Achaia that was erected in that year. "New" prosperous Corinth was a cosmopolitan city with a Roman, Greek, and Oriental population. Its geographical position at the "isthmus," a narrow corridor between the Peloponnesus and the northern remainder of Greece, enabled it to function as a link between North and South and, through its ports at Lechaeum and Cenchreae, also between the West (the Gulf of Corinth) and the East (the Aegean Sea). Old Corinth had an immoral reputation. New Corinth was no doubt characterized by cultural and religious syncretism. Many authors, however, consider it little better and little worse than similar ports or cities of those days.

Paul's first visit took place during the course of his second missionary journey and is recorded in Acts 18:1-18. In Corinth Paul lived and worked with the Jewish couple Aquila and Priscilla and preached to the local Jews in the synagogue. After the arrival of his companions Silas and Timothy (and perhaps the brothers from Macedonia who brought with them financial aid, cf. Phil 4:10-20 and 2 Cor 11:9) he devoted more of his time to proclaiming the word. It was only after his rejection by the Jews that he went over to the house of Titius Justus, "a worshiper of God," and more specifically addressed the Gentiles. Paul's first visit meant the foundation of the Christian community in that city (cf. 3:6: "I planted, Apollos watered, but God gave the growth" and see also 2 Cor 10:14: "we were the first to come all the way to you with the good news of Christ"). Paul stayed in Corinth a year and six months, most probably from the end of 49 to the middle of 51. From 1 Cor 1:26-29 ("Consider your own call, brothers and sisters: not many of you were wise by human standards, not many were powerful, not many were of noble birth") we must conclude that most members of the community were poor although some may have been rather wealthy and not without power. This church cannot have been very numerous—a total of two hundred has been suggested. The majority of Christians in Corinth were probably of Gentile origin.

Possible evidence for one later visit to Corinth comes from Acts 20:1-3. Upon leaving Ephesus—after a long stay there during his third missionary journey—Paul set out for Macedonia and Greece where he stayed for three months. While this passage does not mention Corinth by name it is almost certain that Paul would have paid a visit to the Corinthian community. This visit, however, is not his second but his third visit. Between the visit described in Acts 18 and that suggested by Acts 20 there must have been an intervening visit the existence of which has to be postulated in view of some data in 2 Corinthians. We can assume that Paul's first visit of eighteen months was a successful and happy one in which the community grew in faith and strength. In 2 Cor 1:23–2:1; 12:14 and 13:1-2 we find references to a "painful" visit (a past, second one) and to a future "third" visit: "This is the third time I am coming to you. . . . I warned those who sinned previously and all the others, and I warn them now while absent, as I did when present on my second visit, that if I come again, I will not be lenient" (13:1-2).

Paul's Corinthian Correspondence

In the canon we have two letters to the Corinthians. There is, however, evidence that strongly suggests the existence of at least two other letters of Paul to this community. See 1 Cor 5:9: "I wrote to you in my letter not to associate with sexually immoral persons." This must be a reference to a lost letter that Paul had written before our 1 Corinthians; that lost writing is now commonly called the "previous" letter. Second Corinthians 2:3-4 points to a "severe" or "painful, sorrowful" letter that can hardly be identified with 1 Corinthians: "I wrote to you out of much distress and anguish of heart and with many tears. . . ." This letter, then, falls between 1 and 2 Corinthians and must have been the third letter of Paul to the church at Corinth. While biblical scholars more or less agree that the first letter is lost in its entirety there is still an ongoing debate as to what became of the third letter. Some say—and probably rightly so—that it is totally lost as well, while others claim that it has been incorporated, either wholly or in part, into 2 Corinthians (e.g., chs. 10–13).

Visits and letters fit into the following diagram (dates are probable):

First visit (49–51: eighteen months)
- A. Previous letter (53)
- B. 1 Corinthians (spring 54; cf. 16:8)

Second brief but painful visit (54)
- C. Severe letter (54)
- D. 2 Corinthians (fall 54)

Third visit (54–55: three months, in Corinth?)

What factors provided the occasion for Paul to write 1 Corinthians? First of all there were some visitors from Corinth in Ephesus: ". . . it has been reported to me by Chloe's people that there are quarrels among you . . ." (1:11). Was this information also the reason for Paul's sending Timothy to Corinth (see 4:17 and 16:10-11)? Moreover, from 7:1 we learn that the Christians in Corinth have written a letter: "Now concerning the matters about which you wrote. . . ." According to ch. 16 there were in Ephesus besides Chloe's people also Apollos, a Jew from Alexandria who had been at Corinth, and other Corinthians who visited Paul at Ephesus: "I rejoice at the coming of Stephanas and Fortunatus and Achaicus, because they have made up for your absence; for they refreshed my spirit as well as yours" (16:17-18). Thus it would seem that questions in the letter and disturbing news coming from a number of visitors forced Paul to write the letter that is called 1 Corinthians.

Christianity in Corinth

Can we have an idea of the spiritual and moral situation of the Corinthians? First Corinthians is primarily devoted to emphasizing the unity in diversity that must prevail within the Christian community. Yet the root of the problem is not factionalism as such. The manifold and quite different dangers the Christians face appear to find their common origin in the difficulty of living a truly Christian life in a Hellenistic pagan milieu. Paul seems to be concerned with the surfacing of a Gnostic-like element in the community. With their wisdom speculations and enthusiasm some members were likely to claim an unconditional moral freedom or, quite the opposite, some practiced an exaggerated sexual asceticism. May not the highly emotional spiritual manifestations during public worship be linked to a still persisting influence of pagan cults? Furthermore dualistic Greek philosophy does not allow for a bodily resurrection. It is not easy to discern whether some abuses affected the whole community and others only part of it, and whether or how the various positions on issues pointed to farther on in the letter are to be assigned to the specific factions mentioned in chs. 1–4.

Although Paul's arguments in dealing with the difficulties are mostly theological and christological, the problems in Corinth concern above all the ethical behavior of the Christians. Therefore 1 Corinthians should in the first place be read as a hortatory letter. Its style is mainly "deliberative." It would seem that in Corinth the apostolic authority of Paul has been attacked; several passages of the letter possess an apologetic tone.

Brief History of Reception and Interpretation

After the letter to the Romans that to the Corinthians has the richest history of reception among the Pauline letters. Until the Reformation 1 Corinthians was as important as Romans. It has been affirmed that the East preached the Paul of 1 and 2 Corinthians, the West the Paul of Romans.

The so-called first letter of Clement, sent in the last decade of the first century from the church in Rome to that in Corinth, refers explicitly to 1 Corinthians and uses its teaching against the revolt in Corinth. In the beginning of the second century both the letters of Ignatius and the letter (or two letters) of Polycarp attest their acquaintance with 1 Corinthians. Marcion and the Gnostics used the letter. The same applies to Irenaeus.

The first author to write a commentary on 1 Corinthians seems to have been Origen, yet only substantial fragments have been preserved. In the Greek Church the most extensive and probably the most valuable commentary (especially from a pastoral point of view) is found in the series of forty-four homilies of John Chrysostom. Many Latin Fathers used 1 Corinthians extensively, Augustine in particular. Several scholastic theologians commented on this letter. It is said that Thomas Aquinas' substantial and valuable commentaries on Paul's epistles (including 1 Corinthians) have not been sufficiently studied either from the point of view of the history of exegesis or from that of his theological teaching.

Erasmus and the French humanist Faber Stapulensis commented on all the Pauline epistles. Among the Reformers Luther did not leave us a commentary on 1 Corinthians though his interpretation of its relevant texts had a great influence on his teaching on the Eucharist. We have commentaries on 1 Corinthians by Zwingli, Melanchthon, and Calvin.

Topics in 1 Corinthians that received special attention in the Christian tradition are, for example, the unity of the Church, the Eucharist, the gifts of the Spirit, the preeminent position of charity, the resurrection of Christ and that of Christians, and the relationship between the reign of Christ and that of the Father.

SECOND READING

Salutation and Thanksgiving: 1:1-3, 4-9

Paul begins 1 Corinthians, as he does his other letters, with a salutation that indicates both writers and addressees and contains the expected greeting. Just as in most of his letters this salutation is followed by a thanksgiving to God that presents the reason for Paul's gratitude. Still a number of specific items in 1:1-9 cannot help but strike the reader.

In these nine verses Paul explicitly mentions no less than nine times the name Jesus Christ (or Christ Jesus, or Jesus, or Christ). He is our Lord. Moreover, God (our Father: v. 3) is mentioned four times. Paul alone is not the sender of the letter. "Our brother Sosthenes" (v. 1) joins him but Paul points only to himself as an apostle by the will of God. Of course before writing the letter he was already an apostle, but the expression "called to be an apostle" (v. 1) implies that he remains such, just as the Corinthian Christians are already sanctified in Christ Jesus yet are also continually "called to be saints" (v. 2). Those Christians together form the particular church of God in Corinth and are the main addressees. Paul, however, simultaneously thinks of all Christians: "all those who in every place call on the name of our Lord Jesus Christ, both their Lord and ours" (v. 2). One should realize the ease with which Paul has replaced reference to God (cf. Joel 2:32: "everyone who calls on the name of the LORD shall be saved") in this universalistic expression by "the name of our Lord Jesus Christ." A similar operation takes place in v. 8: the OT "day of the LORD" (cf. for example Amos 5:18) has become "the day of our Lord Jesus Christ." Already in the greeting of v. 3 God and Christ are closely connected: "from God our Father and the Lord Jesus Christ." The greeting itself, "grace . . . and peace," is the Pauline equivalent of Jewish ("peace") or Hellenistic ("rejoicing") expressions.

"I give thanks to my God always for you because of the grace of God that has been given you in Christ Jesus" (v. 4). In his thanksgiving Paul very much emphasizes the abundance of grace, that is, the spiritual riches and gifts the Christians in Corinth have received. They are lacking in nothing either in speech or in knowledge. (An important theme of the letter is thus announced.) The testimony that was borne to Christ in preaching has been strengthened in them. Because of these past gifts they continue now to live in the fellowship of Christ. In v. 8 the moral aspect comes to the forefront for a moment: they must be "blameless" on the day of judgment. But the hortatory tone is indirect: Christians can be sure that Christ will also strengthen (same verb as in v. 6) them to the end, and above all God by whom they were called is faithful. Paul is convinced that "the revealing" of Christ (v. 7), his parousia, is not far away. In Christian life past, present, and future are linked.

Quarreling and Divisions in the Congregation: 1:10–4:16

After the salutation and thanksgiving Paul immediately begins to warn the Corinthian Christians against the present divisions within their community. This harmful situation provides Paul with the occasion to reflect on what it means to be an apostle as well as to develop his insights into the gospel message. There is, however, a particular center of interest in these chapters. According to Paul the contentions are rooted in a self-sufficient mentality, a pseudo-wisdom that rejects the word of the cross. Paul attacks that mentality and preaches the "foolishness of God," the true wisdom.

In this first major section of the letter five units can be distinguished: 1:10-17 (quarrels in Corinth), 1:18–2:5 (the message of the cross), 2:6-16 (God's wisdom), 3:1–4:5 (Paul and Apollos), and 4:6-16 (Paul's example and plans).

Quarrels in Corinth (1:10-17)

In this first unit Paul opens with a strong appeal against factionalism ("by the name of our Lord Jesus Christ") as well as a plea for complete harmony of mind and opinion (v. 10). This exhortation is needed because there is rivalry. There are parties. In vv. 13-17 Paul immediately argues against division: Is Christ divided? Paul shifts to autobiographical language. He, Paul, was not crucified for the Corinthians. Moreover as far as he remembers he baptized very few people (Crispus—cf. Acts 18:8—and Gaius; also the household of Stephanas). This intentional mode of action is doubly motivated, first negatively in function of the divisions ("so that no one can say . . ." v. 15), then positively: Christ sent him not to baptize but to proclaim the gospel. Paul adds that his preaching did not occur with "eloquent wisdom, so that the cross of Christ might not be emptied of its power" (v. 17). These qualifications introduce the addressees to Paul's remarkable consideration of the core of the gospel.

Paul's style is lively: twice "brothers and sisters" (v. 10 and, with "my," v. 11), three incisive questions in v. 13, and an apparent self-correction in v. 16. But what do we know about the divisions? Were there actually four parties or is the fourth clause in v. 12 ("I belong to Christ") the reaction of those who reject divisions? Can the remaining three groups (cf. 3:22) be thus characterized: Paul as the founder of the community and preacher of a law-free gospel, Apollos (cf. Acts 18:24-28) as an attractive teacher because of his more hellenized Christian "wisdom," and Cephas—was he ever in Corinth?—as the person to whom Judaizing Christians refer? Some think that Paul's insistence on baptism in vv. 13-16 suggests that the person who has been baptizing was considered the leader of a group, but this is far from certain. Others (as early as Chrysostom) are of the opinion that throughout chs. 1–4 Paul was attacking in a covert way the wisdom teachers and the strife they caused, but that the four parties as such did not really exist (see 4:6).

Paul's minimal baptismal activity softens the radical construction "not . . . but" in v. 17: it can perhaps be understood as "not so much . . . as. . . ." The second half of v. 17 reminds us of the fact that the manner of proclamation (its eloquent form) has an impact on the content. A showy presentation may empty and nullify the message of the cross, but does the expression "with eloquent wisdom" point to rhetorical skills alone?

Christ Crucified (1:18–2:5)

God decided to save those who believe through the foolishness of the cross: foolishness to those who are perishing, but the power of God to those who are being saved. This second unit can be divided into three subdivisions: (a) a general exposition of the message about the cross (1:18-25), (b) an application to the Corinthians (1:26-31), and (c) a second application to Paul himself (2:1-5). In (a) and (c) we meet the expression "Christ crucified" (1:23) and the slightly different phrase "Jesus Christ and him crucified" (2:2). For the mention of Christ in (b) see 1:30: the Corinthians are "in Christ Jesus." Each of the three subdivisions stresses God's initiative: see 1:20-21; 1:27-31; and 2:5. The first subdivision motivates the opening sentence with a quotation from Isa 29:14; the second concludes the rejection of mere human boasting with an abbreviation of Jer 9:22-23. In the whole unit Paul again uses sharp questions but also antitheses, especially those of foolish/wise and weak/strong. The unit begins and ends with the opposition between human folly (or wisdom) and God's power (what God has done in Christ): compare 1:18 with 2:5.

In 1:18-25 it strikes the reader that the antithesis of human foolishness and God's wisdom (manifest in creation) is very much emphasized more than the other antithesis (weak/strong) and that quite unexpectedly in vv. 22-24 Paul not only speaks of Greeks (= Gentiles) and their wisdom but also of Jews and their demand for signs: Christ crucified is a stumbling block to Jews and foolishness to Gentiles, but for those who are called (cf. 1:2), both Jews and Greeks, Christ is "the power of God and the wisdom of God." The language in v. 25 is utterly paradoxical.

In reading 1:26-31 special attention should be given to the salient threefold "God chose" (vv. 27-28) and the addition of a third antithesis, that between "noble birth" and "low [birth]." In v. 28 Paul expands this third opposition: "what is low and despised in the world, things that are not." Instead of repeating "to shame" (twice in v. 27) he now writes "to reduce to nothing things that are" and appends a second purpose clause that contains his important theme: "so that no one might boast in the presence of God" (v. 29; see also the free quotation in v. 31). In v. 30 it is stated that Christians have their new existence in Christ Jesus who became for them "wisdom from God." The central idea of wisdom is thus personified. It is, moreover, explained by means of three more terms: Christ-wisdom is for Christians "righteousness and sanctification and redemption."

For the third subdivision (2:1-5) variant readings of two verses must be mentioned: 2:1 "mystery" or "testimony" and 2:4 "with plausible words of wisdom" or, among other readings, "the persuasiveness of wisdom." A choice is difficult but the alternative readings do not really affect the train of thought. Paul here recalls autobiographically his timid mien in Corinth and his style of proclamation. Again we have the opposition between human weakness and the power of God, between rhetorical and/or philosophical wisdom and the foolishness of Christ crucified. At the end, in 2:5, the apostle points to the aim behind his singular comportment: the faith of the Corinthians must rest "not on human wisdom but on the power of God."

A Wisdom Revealed by the Spirit (2:6-16)

"Yet among the mature we do speak wisdom . . ." (2:6). It would seem that with the category of the "mature" (or "perfect") and the verb "we speak" Paul points to a wisdom, that is, a deeper knowledge and more profound insight, that probably contains more than the bare facts of the proclamation. Paul speaks of this wisdom as a "mystery" since from eternity it has been hidden and foreordained to be revealed. Moreover, the rulers of this age have not understood it. There probably is a caesura after v. 8; if so vv. 9-10a could constitute one sentence: "*What* no eye has seen . . . , *what* God has prepared for those who love him, *these things* God has revealed to us through the Spirit." In vv. 10-16 the Spirit comes to the fore. Paul (and the Corinthian Christians) received that Spirit from God. It is by words taught by the Spirit that Paul can communicate and interpret wisdom to those who are spiritual. Those who are spiritual can discern all things.

In this unit Paul employs apocalyptic language. He also formulates general anthropological principles (see vv. 10b-11 and vv. 14-16a). Several oppositions appear: the wisdom of this age versus the wisdom of God; the spirit of the world versus the Spirit of God; those who are *psychikoi* ("unspiritual") versus those who are *pneumatikoi* (spiritual).

Exegetes hesitate in their explanation of "the rulers of this age" of vv. 6 and 8. Are these rulers human authorities or cosmic, demonic powers?—or both, in the sense that demons work on earth through human authorities? The first proposal may be the best. These rulers crucified "the Lord of glory;" they are doomed to destruction and are already in the process of being brought to nothing. "It is written" in v. 9 introduces a scriptural quotation, yet no such OT text can be found. What Paul writes here is a loose combination of various OT phrases. Did that combination perhaps already exist before him? The anthropology on which Paul appears to depend in vv. 10-16 views the human person as consisting of body (not mentioned in this passage), soul, and spirit (or mind). God reveals through the divine Spirit; Christians have received the Spirit of God. In v. 14 people without the Spirit are called *psychikoi* (although according to v. 11a they have a human spirit). The Spirit searches the depth of God and causes those who are spiritual to understand and discern all things spiritually; they themselves are to be judged by no one (v. 15 is not a Corinthian slogan but expresses Paul's conviction).

We Christians possess "the mind of Christ" (v. 16; cf. the reference to Christ at the end of v. 8). In v. 16 Paul wants his readers to understand the quotation from Isa 40:13—where, of course, "Lord" originally is God—christologically. According to Paul those who are spiritual should be convinced of that distinctively rich possession.

Paul and Apollos (3:1–4:5)

There is a break at 3:1. Paul very emphatically uses the first person singular and addresses the Corinthians as "brothers and sisters." He denies that they are spiritual people: the expression "as infants" stands in contrast to the term "mature" (or "perfect") of 2:6. The contrast between "milk" and "solid food" in 3:2 confirms that the "wisdom" within 2:6-16 contains more than the initial proclamation.

We may consider the lengthy passage 3:1–4:5 as one unit. To elucidate its line of thought we can distinguish four subdivisions: (a) The fact that among the Corinthians there is jealousy and factionalism proves that they are not yet mature and/or perfect (3:1-4); (b) in 3:5-17 Paul explains what God's servants are and what is their responsibility, employing two metaphors: the community as God's field (vv. 6-9ab) and as God's building (vv. 9c-17). In this second subdivision the eschatological outcome is broadly treated; the idea of judgment is dominant. In (c) beginning at 3:18 it is not certain that Paul again has in mind the behavior of the Corinthians themselves, but this is clearly the case in vv. 21-23. However, the new start in 3:18 ("do not deceive yourselves"), together with the resumption of the vocabulary of foolishness and wisdom in vv. 18-20 and that of boasting in v. 21, seem to indicate that 3:18-23 belongs together. After the solemn conclusion of 3:22-23, the fourth subdivision (d) 4:1-5 presents itself as an application (see the first word in 4:1: *houtōs*, "think of us *in this way*, as servants of Christ and stewards of God's mysteries"). Yet in 4:2-5 Paul again reflects on what is required of a servant of Christ; moreover in vv. 3-4 his reflection takes on a highly personal accent.

The tone in 3:1-4 is distinctly unfriendly. Paul reprimands the Corinthians: "as people of the flesh, as infants" (the addition "in Christ" is somewhat surprising) they are not ready for solid food; by their quarreling they are behaving not in a spiritual but rather in a merely human way (or in a sinful way?). Only two parties are mentioned (that of Paul and that of Apollos, v. 4; cf. also v. 5). We are led to ask whether Paul has been the apostle with a rather straightforward elementary proclamation and Apollos the more sophisticated Hellenistic wisdom preacher.

Although in vv. 5-7 Paul explains that in relation to God the servants are nothing (God alone gives the growth), in v. 9 he stresses—not without some pride, it would seem—the identity of these servants as God's coworkers. It must strike the readers that in vv. 10-11 the same idea as in "I planted" (v. 6) is elaborated with the construction metaphor: "According to the grace of God given to me, like a skilled master builder I laid a foundation . . . . no one can lay any foundation other than the one that has been laid; that foundation is Jesus Christ." It is not impossible that Paul is thinking of the party of Peter (not mentioned here, but see v. 22). Some even detect a polemical note: as opposed to Peter, the rock *(petra)* upon which the Church is built, we have Paul who in Corinth laid the foundation *(themelion)*. But all this is rather speculative. In the same subdivision Paul expands on the responsibility of fellow workers; he employs the topic of proportional reward (see vv. 8 and 14) and even more that of judgment. With its testing fire the Day of the Lord will disclose the quality of one's work. There is here no reference to purgatory (as was often thought). While in v. 15 the worker is still saved, in v. 17 God will destroy this worker if God destroys the building. The building—the community—is a holy temple since God's Spirit dwells within (vv. 16-17).

In 3:18-23 Paul clearly addresses the Corinthians themselves and warns them against the wisdom of this world. He grounds the warning by means of two quotations from Scripture (Job 5:12-13 [cf. Rom 11:35] and Ps 94:11). While in 1:29, 31 boasting about oneself was rejected, in 3:21 it is boasting about the heads of the parties, the human leaders, that is forbidden. Paul motivates this in an impressive way: all things belong to Christians; they do not belong to the leaders. Whether Paul or Apollos or Cephas or the world, life and death, present and future: all things belong to Christians, but in turn Christians belong to Christ and—just as Paul will indicate with an analogous theocentric emphasis in 15:28—Christ belongs to God.

From 4:1-5 and more specifically from the first person singular in vv. 3-4 we may probably conclude that Paul is defending himself against the Corinthians' criticism. In the final analysis what counts, he says, is trustworthiness. Paul as servant of Christ and steward of God's mysteries will be judged not by humans before the time but by Christ at his parousia; he will receive his commendation from God.

Paul's Example and Plans (4:6-21)

It would seem that vv. 6-21 belong together and form the last unit of this first major section. The expression "for your benefit" *(di' hymas)* of v. 6 sets the tone: the Corinthians should learn from the example of the ministers. In this unit we distinguish two subdivisions, vv. 6-13 and vv. 14-21. In vv. 6-13 Paul contrasts community and apostles, puffed up Christians and despised apostles. Immediately afterward in vv. 14-21 he pleads with the Corinthians, his "beloved children" *(tekna mou agapēta)*. He urges them to become imitators of him. For this reason he is sending Timothy who will remind them of his preaching, and he also announces his own coming.

Verses 6-8 begin with *tauta de, adelphoi*. If one takes the verb *meteschēmatisa* in its normal meaning, the literal translation of v. 6a is: "Now, brothers [and sisters], I *have transformed* these things (= probably 3:5–4:5, or 1:10–4:5) to myself and Apollos because of you." In what has gone before, then, Paul apparently speaks of the parties and their so-called leaders, yet these parties do not really exist; they are but a covert allusion to the wisdom-teachers and the division they brought about in the Corinthian congregation (so, more or less, already Chrysostom).

However, the common understanding of the verb in v. 6a is "to apply" (cf. already Origen). According to this more probable interpretation "all this" in v. 6 points to the general principle that a servant of Christ is but a slave whose work will be judged (3:5-15) and who is required to be found trustworthy (4:2). Paul has presented Apollos and himself as examples of this principle; he "has applied" the principle to them for the benefit of the Corinthian Christians: they should learn from their ministers' place in God's plan that boasting on behalf of one servant at the expense of another does not make sense. Yet vv. 7-8 no longer explicitly mention boasting about others. Paul attacks the self-satisfied, self-centered mentality of the Corinthians. In v. 7 he asks pertinent questions about the origin of what they possess. In v. 8, with penetrating irony and sarcasm, he ridicules their feelings of over-realized superiority. At the end of v. 8 it would appear that the opposite conclusion to that of v. 6 is reached. The apostle is no longer the example for the community; no, the community is the ideal for the apostle! (In v. 6 one clause remains obscure: that you may learn by us "not beyond what is written." Was this a well-known saying in Corinth? Is it an appeal to moderation or to a basic fidelity to Scripture? Or is the clause, after all, a gloss?)

Verses 9-13 provide us with the true, realistic picture of apostolic existence. Verse 9 and v. 13b frame and summarize Paul's depiction of what the apostles are. Both these verses say that the apostles have become a spectacle to the world, despised by all. Whereas in v. 9 this miserable condition is ascribed to God's action, in v. 13b it simply appears the result of human treatment. In v. 10 Paul contrasts the apostles and the Corinthians: "We are fools . . . you are wise. . . ." Verses 11-13a constitute one of the well-known lists of tribulations: Paul depicts the apostolic sufferings, dangers, and trials. The style of vv. 12b-13a again becomes antithetical: "when reviled, we bless. . . ." Does "we labor" in v. 12a point to Paul's apostolic care of other Christians and the added participle "working" to the way he supports himself, or are the two verbs referring to the same physical efforts?

In vv. 14-17 Paul switches from severe attack to tender pleading. The affectionate tone is achieved by the first person singular as well as by the wording ("my beloved children"), the imagery ("I became your father through the gospel") and the considerate pleading itself ("not . . . to make you ashamed, but to admonish you"). From this first person singular it also becomes evident that in vv. 9-13 Paul was thinking above all of his own apostolic lifestyle, not that of the apostles generally. Then in v. 16 Paul presents himself explicitly as an example. The Corinthians must imitate his conduct and behavior (cf. 11:1: "be imitators of me, as I am of Christ"). In v. 17 Paul connects the sending of Timothy, his beloved and faithful child in Christ, with his plea: "for this reason I sent you. . . ." Timothy will remind the Corinthians of Paul's ways in Christ as Paul teaches them everywhere in every church. Notwithstanding the verb "to teach," Paul by "my ways in Christ" probably means not only his spoken message but also his apostolic conduct as it is depicted in vv. 9-13.

The manner in which he announces his own going to Corinth in vv. 18-21 presumably reveals that some Corinthians misinterpreted Paul's absence as lack of courage. The language is again severe and, moreover, not without threat against some arrogant Christians. By employing the verb "to become inflated/arrogant" (vv. 18-19) and combining "word" and "power" (v. 20) Paul returns to themes and vocabulary that were prominent at the beginning of the section (1:18–2:5). The very end of this paragraph, with its double question, is rather abrupt: "What would you prefer? Am I to come to you with a stick, or with love in a spirit of gentleness?"

Immorality, Lawsuits, Immorality: 5:1–6:20

There can be no doubt that with 5:1 a new section begins. Paul mentions the report (by word of mouth or by letter?) of a case of sexual immorality in Corinth. Although there is no strict unity of content in chapters 5 and 6 it would seem that Paul has organized his material in a concentric way: A (immorality, 5:1-13), B (pagan courts, 6:1-11), A' (immorality, 6:12-20). There is not only a certain correspondence of theme between A and A' but also in both units the presence of terminology referring to immorality (*porneia,* 5:1 and 6:13, 18; *porneuō,* 6:18; *pornos* and *pornē,* 5:9, 10, 11 and 6:9, 15, 16). Furthermore, just as in 5:5 (A) the "flesh" is handed over to Satan for destruction, so also in 6:13 (A') it is said that God will destroy the "stomach" whereas according to 6:13-15 (B) God will raise the "body." Finally, in both A and A' the Christians' belonging to Christ is emphasized: see 5:4-7 and 6:13-17.

Nevertheless, the cyclical structure is far from perfect. Within A we quite suddenly have a reference to a previous letter whose interdiction of association with immoral people has been misinterpreted. In B Paul moves from lawsuits to evildoing in general. In A' laxity is discussed but, unlike in A, a specific case is not dealt with. On the other hand a particular case appears to be the occasion for the discussion in B and, moreover, both A and B possess a similar list of vices (see 5:11 and 6:9-10). A stylistic characteristic of the two chapters may be mentioned: Paul employs the expression "do you not know" seven times (see 5:6; 6:2, 3, 9, 15, 16, 17). The last clause "therefore glorify God in your body" (6:20b) concludes the section. In chapter 7 another theme, marriage and unmarried life, is treated.

A Case of Sexual Immorality (5:1-13)

In this first unit it is stated five times, either explicitly or metaphorically, that the person who lives a sexually immoral life with the wife of his father must be removed from the Christian community: see vv. 2 (remove), 5 (hand over to Satan), 7 (clean out the old leaven), 11 (do not associate or even eat with him), 13b (drive out). Within the whole of this passage the wicked person is never out of sight. Paul is at the same time angry that in such a context the Corinthian Christians are still arrogant and boasting (see vv. 2 and 6a, the same vocabulary as in chs. 1–4). The unity of this passage is slightly damaged by the "excursus" of vv. 9-11, not so much because of the mention of a previous letter and its injunction not to associate with sexually immoral people as because of the broadening of the immorality category: see v. 10 and above all the long list of evil people in v. 11.

Every detail in this unit is not equally clear in grammar or content. In vv. 1-2 it is generally assumed that the wife of the father is the stepmother of the sinner. The "so that" at the beginning of v. 2b probably introduces a purpose clause ("so that he who has done this would have been removed from among you"). Some, however, take the final construction as the equivalent of an imperative ("let him who has done this be removed . . .").

It would seem that grammatically vv. 4-5 explain the content of the judgment that Paul has already reached in v. 3. In the name of the Lord Jesus the Corinthians should assemble, together with the spirit of the absent Paul (for the use of "spirit" in an anthropological sense, cf. 2:11-12), in the presence also of the power of Jesus, and they must deliver such a man to Satan. What Paul actually writes in this letter will count as his vote when read during that meeting. The content of v. 5 betrays a strange dualistic view. In this view people who stay within the Christian community are protected against evil influences. However when a person is "excommunicated" he or she is exposed to the harmful, deadly sphere of Satan. The handing over is certainly a punishment. Yet according to Paul the final aim is positive: it is only the "flesh" that will be destroyed (which does not necessarily imply physical death); the "spirit" must be saved. Is this spirit the human person insofar as it is spirit or rather the indwelling Spirit together with that person?

The metaphorical language in vv. 6-8 alludes to the regulations of the Passover meal. Yeast or leaven is here a negative symbol for malice and evil. Christians have to be unleavened bread—that is, sincere and truthful. This symbolism is unexpectedly reinforced through the identification in v. 7: our paschal lamb, Christ, has been sacrificed. Christians have to be pure since they belong to Christ.

With "I wrote . . . now I am writing" in vv. 9 and 11 Paul twice refers to his earlier letter and the prohibition against associating with immoral people. In v. 10 he clarifies what he did not mean: contact with the non-Christian evil people of this world, since then Christians would have to leave this world altogether. In v. 11 he goes on to explain what he did mean: association with people who are called Christians but in fact appear to be sinners. In v. 11 Paul is visibly in a rhetorical mood and presents—as Stoic philosophers also do—a long list of examples; at the end he becomes more explicit: even eating with such Christians who live in sin is not permitted.

Verses 12-13 still motivate what Paul writes in vv. 9-11. Now the insiders are opposed to the outsiders (= the non-Christians). It is God's privilege, not that of the Christians, to judge those outside. Must we understand the second question (v. 12b) as a commandment (you have to judge those inside—and therefore drive out the wicked person, v. 13b), or as pointing to evident behavior (you are, of course, judging those inside)? The wrongdoer of v. 13b is presumably not to be taken generally; with this term Paul seems to refer back to the concrete sinner mentioned in v. 1.

Lawsuits Among Christians (6:1-11)

It is quite possible that by "when any of you has a grievance against another" in v. 1 Paul alludes to a specific case, yet in vv. 2-8 he applies the matter of lawsuits to the whole community. There is a second shift in vv. 9-11; here the topic is no longer lawsuits but wrongdoing as such. The language in this unit is emotional, lively, and direct: three times "do you not know?" plus nine or ten indignant questions. Rebuke, command or counsel, and motivation are mingled in this unit. One could however summarize Paul's reasoning as follows (albeit in a different order). The Corinthians at one time were notorious wrongdoers. Through baptism they have been justified and are now saints. As saints they will participate in the judgment of the world and the angels. Because of all this, wrongdoing among them is no longer allowed (on penalty of exclusion from God's reign). More particularly defrauding fellow believers cannot be accepted. It would be better to be defrauded. If, after all, there are lawsuits, the advice is not to go to pagan courts but to appoint Christian judges.

In v. 1 Paul calls the pagan judges "the unrighteous" (in contrast to "the saints"). From v. 6 ("unbelievers") it is clear that by this term he does not qualify their judgments or their behavior but points to their non-Christian status. The same terminology is employed differently in vv. 8-9. Must we take the main verb in v. 4 (*kathizete*: "appoint") as an ironical imperative and "those who have no standing in the church" as despised Christians (but this does not fit in well with v. 5), or should we consider the sentence as a statement with "those who have no standing in the church" pointing to the pagan judges? Paul's remark, "I say this to your shame" (v. 5), is somewhat surprising after 4:14 ("I am not writing this to make you ashamed").

Paul does not employ the expression "kingdom of God" very often. It was included in the saying in 4:20; we meet it here again twice (vv. 9 and 10). Just as with the saying in 4:20, the statement of v. 9 is fundamental: "wrongdoers will not inherit the kingdom of God." In v. 10 Paul repeats this truth and expands the term "wrongdoers" by means of a list containing ten specifications (an expansion of the list in 5:11 with the nouns in the plural). In v. 11 we have an allusion to baptism ("you were washed"). For Paul there is probably little or no difference between the two verbs that explain this washing: "you were sanctified, you were justified." Did a trinitarian baptismal formula already exist? One is led to think so through the reading of the end of v. 11: "in the name of the Lord Jesus Christ and in the Spirit of our God."

Flee Fornication (6:12-20)

In 6:12-20 (A') Paul comes back to the theme of sexual immortality (cf. ch. 5, A) and applies a number of general considerations. Three subdivisions can be distinguished in this unit. In vv. 12-14 (a) it would seem that Paul begins a fictive dialogue and answers two slogans brought forward in Corinth against his doctrine: "all things are lawful for me"; "food is meant for the stomach and the stomach for food." The dialogue continues (b) with two questions and a strong negation in v. 15, and with a question and clarifications in vv. 16-17 (see the twofold introduction "do you not know" in v. 15 and v. 16). In vv. 18-20 (c) Paul exhorts the Corinthians to flee fornication and to honor God with their bodies. The last clause "glorify God in your body" (v. 20b) forms an inclusion with the exhortation at the beginning: "shun fornication" (v. 18a). The basic argument in this whole unit is that Christians, because they belong to Christ, cannot tolerate sexual immorality.

We may quote the less literal NEB translation of vv. 12-13:

> "I am free to do anything," you say. Yes, but not everything is for my good. No doubt I am free to do anything, but I for one will not let anything make free with me. "Food is for the belly and the belly for food," you say. True; and one day God will put an end to both. But it is not true that the body is for lust; it is for the Lord.

The additions "You say," "yes," and "true" underline Paul's reactions. In this translation the first slogan is repeated as part of Paul's answer ("no doubt I am free to do anything") and the word-play *moi exestin exousiasthēsomai* is preserved by "I am *free*—I will not let anything make *free* with me." We should also pay attention to Paul's parallel statement in v. 14: God raised the Lord and will raise us too through divine power. Because our bodies are for the Lord, belong to the Lord and are thus members of the Lord, we can be convinced that God, having already raised Christ (past), will raise us as well (future). Flesh, stomach, and food will be destroyed; the body, however—that is, the whole human person—will be raised.

In vv. 15-17 Paul first states that the bodies of Christians are members of Christ; one cannot take the members of Christ and make them members of a prostitute (v. 15). Then in a chiastic way, beginning with the prostitute, he explains: any man who joins himself to a prostitute becomes one body (with her) and those who join themselves to the Lord form one spirit (with him) (vv. 16-17). The Greek articular participle *ho kollōmenos* is realistic language: "the one who clings to"; most probably Paul therefore avoids a too-realistic "body" in the Christ parallel and writes "spirit." The Genesis quotation in v. 16b functions strangely as a proof text for condemning the physical union between man and prostitute.

Paul's reasoning in v. 18 is not completely clear. Why is every (other) sin outside the body and why does fornication alone sin against the body itself? Still one understands what Paul means: in sexual immorality more than in other sins the entire person—especially his or her body!— is involved. Whereas in 3:16 the whole community is called "God's temple" (in which God's Spirit dwells), in 6:19 it is the body of the individual Christian that is "a temple of the Holy Spirit" (this Spirit is within the Christian). Christians have this Spirit from God and are thus possessed by the Spirit, with the consequence that they are no longer their own. The motivating clause "for you were bought with a price" of v. 20a discreetly yet unmistakably alludes to Christ's bloody sacrifice on the cross.

Married and Unmarried Life: 7:1-40

In 7:1a Paul introduces the next topic with a *peri de* construction: "Now concerning the matters about which you wrote." The *peri de* construction will occur again in 7:25; 8:1; 12:1; 16:1 and 2. The issues in ch. 7 were brought forward in a letter; the formula itself, however, does not automatically point to a letter. It is possible but not at all certain that in 7:1b Paul quotes a sentence (an ascetic slogan) from that letter: "It is well for a man not to touch a woman." He may already be expressing by it his own opinion and preference (cf. v. 7a). At any rate it is fairly certain that in ch. 7 Paul deals with more details of married and unmarried life than the Corinthians' letter was asking about, although one can hardly expect to derive from this chapter a complete and balanced treatise on sexuality and marriage. Two specific factors no doubt influenced and, to a certain extent, "biased" Paul's presentation. First, in Corinth there seem to have existed simultaneously a certain freedom as well as a certain asceticism regarding sexuality and marriage, to both of which Paul must react. Second, it is clear that Paul is convinced that the end of the world is not far away; this causes him to relativize earthly values, particularly that of marriage.

A strict division within this lengthy chapter is not easily decided upon. We distinguish eight units: (a) vv. 1-7 (conjugal rights); (b) vv. 8-16 (marriage and divorce); (c) vv. 17-24 (permanence of situation); (d) vv. 25-28 (the case of virgins); (e) vv. 29-31 (the shortness of the time); (f) vv. 32-35 (undivided interests); (g) vv. 36-38 (a specific case); (h) vv. 39-40 (the husband's death). We shall see that units (c) and (e) broaden the horizon; they offer more general considerations.

In v. 23 Paul repeats what he already had said in 6:20a: "You were bought with a price." At the end of 6:19 we have: "you are not your own." A related idea recurs in 7:4: "the wife does not have authority over her own body . . . ; likewise the husband does not have authority over his own body. . . ." The verb employed twice in 7:4 is *exousiazō;* it is also found in 6:12. From these linguistic details it would seem that one can safely conclude that Paul wrote (i.e., dictated) ch. 7 not long after chs. 5–6.

Conjugal Rights (7:1-7)

What is the line of thought in this first unit? Whether v. 1b contains a Corinthian slogan or Paul's own preferential position (as we tend to assume), in either case v. 2 provides a correction that, however, does not yet react to the central point of v. 1b but gives the framework of the discussion: because of much immorality marriage—that is, monogamous marriage—should be the rule among the Corinthian Christians. In vv. 3-4 Paul emphasizes that neither husband nor wife can refuse conjugal rights to the partner. Neither of them can claim his/her body as his/her own. In v. 5 after the summarizing injunction ("do not deprive one another") a clearly defined exception is mentioned, namely for prayer. Verse 6—"this" refers to what immediately precedes—states that the exception and the conditions surrounding it are but a concession, not a command. It would seem that with v. 7 Paul comes back to the beginning: he expresses a second time his preference for celibate life (cf. v. 1b) and then, by way of necessary addition, he admits that each person has his or her own gift from God.

Even if we assume that in v. 1b we may read Paul's own view, the clause still testifies to a tendency to sexual asceticism among some Corinthians. By its wording the verse reminds us of Gen 2:18 that, however, states almost the opposite: "It is not good that the man should be alone." It cannot escape one's notice that in vv. 2-6 Paul considers wife and husband as equals. The chiastic parallelism in vv. 3-4 underscores this. One also admires Paul's careful procedure in v. 5: before the exception can be admitted there has to be mutual agreement; abstention is justified only for a set time and only for prayer; afterward they have to come together again. Moreover, Paul adds in v. 6 that the whole matter is but a concession, not at all a command. The clause at the end of v. 5 runs counter to the modern positive evaluation of marriage and sexual life. Of course for married people temptation is hardly the main motive to "come together," but the clause "so that Satan may not tempt you because of your lack of self-control" points back to v. 2 ("because of cases of sexual immorality"); in both clauses Paul appears to speak in a realistic, forthright way.

Marriage and Divorce (7:8-16)

This unit has three subdivisions, each introduced by a mention of a category of people: "the unmarried and the widows" (vv. 8-9), "the married" (vv. 10-11), and "the rest (= those in mixed marriages)" (vv. 12-16). With regard to the first category, as in v. 1b Paul expresses his preference in v. 8: "I say that it is well for them to remain unmarried as I am," but again as in what follows v. 2 a qualification is added: in case of lack of self-control they should marry. For the second category Paul quotes the command of the Lord not to separate or divorce. He adds in v. 11a his own casuistic ruling: if a wife has separated, let her remain single or else be reconciled to her husband. For the third category Paul presents his own opinion; he does not simply repeat a saying of the Lord. One should not divorce the unbelieving partner if he or she consents to continue the marriage.

From v. 8 alone it is not clear whether Paul identifies himself as "unmarried" or as "widower," but in light of v. 7 (and perhaps of v. 1b) it is most probable that Paul was and remained single. The language in v. 9 is again realistic. The verb "to burn" here means "to burn with desire, to be aflame with passion," not "to burn in hell."

Through the parallel constructions in vv. 10-11 and also in vv. 12-16 the equality between wife and husband comes once more to the forefront. Although the vocabulary is slightly different one is reminded in vv. 10 and 11b of the synoptic saying of Jesus on divorce (see Mark 10:11-12 and par.). The Catholic Church refers to v. 11a for its ruling on irreparably broken marriages: though separated they must remain unmarried. Some exegetes, however, remark that in v. 11a Paul probably addresses only the partner who took the initiative of divorcing. Then the question arises: what about the other partner after separation or divorce? One must also bear in mind that it is by no means easy to reconstruct the original Jesus saying(s) or to pass judgment on the pastoral attempts by which already the New Testament itself and later Church traditions, as well as different separated churches, were and are applying Jesus' radical position.

Paul's directives for mixed marriages in vv. 12-16 avoid extreme steps; he takes a middle course. In v. 14 the terms "unclean" and "holy" are contrasted. One has the impression that these terms here point, as it were, to a substance that can be transmitted or a sphere in which one dwells. It is therefore not certain that Paul's reasoning will easily carry conviction. Something magical clings to it. In vv. 15-16 new, supplementary arguments are brought forward. Christians are called to live in peace; after all, the Christian partner does not know whether the unbelieving and disagreeing partner will be saved through a continued marriage. As is well known, this third subdivision provided the Catholic Church with the so-called *privilegium Paulinum*. Two final notes: in v. 15 a strongly attested variant reading has "called us" instead of "called you," and some exegetes defend a positive translation for v. 16, one with a missionary sense: "wife, for all you know, you might save your husband . . ." [thus NRSV], but both grammar and context do not favor such an understanding.

Personal Call and Permanence of Situation (7:17-24)

One is called by God in a given situation or status. According to 7:17-24 Christians should not change their state. In v. 17 Paul formulates the principle in a general way but he has in view in the first place married and unmarried people. Within this unit, however, two other applications of the principle are suggested: circumcised/uncircumcised (vv. 18-19) and slave/free (vv. 21-23). The parallel vv. 20 and 24 respectively form the conclusion of each application. We spontaneously think of Gal 3:28: "There is no longer Jew or Greek, there is no longer slave or free, there is no longer male and female; for all of you are one in Christ Jesus." However, the accent on permanence is not present in Gal 3:28, and in 1 Cor 7:17 Paul is thinking concretely of the married and unmarried state of "male and female."

The idea of v. 7 is taken up and expanded in v. 17: as one is called, so should one live. We note the parallelism in v. 17 between "the Lord" who apportions and "God" who calls. Paul stresses that the rules given in vv. 12-16—and for that matter in the whole chapter—are in agreement with his teaching in other churches. Verse 19 functions as the motivation for v. 18: do not care about change in your state for "circumcision is nothing, and uncircumcision is nothing"; what matters is to keep "the commandments of God." The last expression sounds strange for all who know how Paul emphasized in Galatians and Romans that justification occurs "not by the works of the law." Perhaps Paul speaks in v. 19 of the commandments as they are manifest in the Law without specific attention to this (later?) controversy. Yet in view of 9:21 (see also 12:13) it is possible that for Paul those commandments are "the law of Christ" (Gal 6:2; cf. Gal 5:6: "For in Christ Jesus neither circumcision nor uncircumcision counts for anything; the only thing that counts is faith working through love," and 6:15: "a new creation").

How is v. 21b to be understood? Should the slave seize the opportunity to become free, or should the slave rather remain a slave and lead that life in a Christian way? Grammar ("even if," "rather") as well as context plead, it would seem, for the second alternative although some exegetes still defend the first. In vv. 22-23 a new contrast appears: freedom and slavery take on a metaphorical sense that provides a play on words. A Christian slave is a freed person belonging to Christ. Because the Christians were bought at a price (cf. 6:20) they are now slaves of Christ; they should not become slaves of human masters.

The Case of "Virgins" (7:25-28)

In v. 25 Paul explicitly states that he has no command from the Lord concerning *(peri de)* "virgins" (*parthenos:* virgin, [unmarried] girl [cf. v. 34], unmarried woman) yet he gives his opinion "as one who by the Lord's mercy is trustworthy." The wording of v. 26 is somewhat irregular because of the repetition of "(it is) well," although with another construction. Moreover there appears to be a broadening in the train of thought. Paul first writes: I think this (that is, to be and to remain a virgin) is good in view of the impending (or present) distress, but then he resumes: it is well for all (*anthrōpos,* man and woman alike) to remain as they are (cf. vv. 17-24). In vv. 27-28a Paul then uses the second person singular and addresses only men: if you are bound to a wife, do not seek to be free; if you are free from a wife, do not seek marriage, but if you marry you do not sin. In v. 28b he comes back to the virgin: if she marries she does not sin. But in v. 28c he again thinks of all those who marry, men and women: they will have to endure hardships that Paul would like to spare them. Already in v. 26, and here at the end of v. 28, a new motivation against seeking marriage is brought forward: the present eschatological distress and the greater troubles thereof for those who are married.

The Shortness of the Time (7:29-30)

With "I mean, brothers and sisters" Paul stresses the nearness of the end and draws from it, not without insistence, a practical conclusion: Christians must cultivate an attitude of eschatological restraint. Verse 29b ("the appointed time has grown short") corresponds with v. 31b ("the present form of this world is passing away"):

two brief thesis-like statements with a related content. Within this frame and after the first contextual concretization (those who have wives) Paul gives four more examples: those who mourn, those who rejoice, those who buy, and those who use the riches of the world. Each time a reservation is made. They should act "as if" they do not have wives, they do not mourn. . . . We reflect: the end of the age has not yet come; earthly values should therefore be more appreciated; yet although Paul's conviction has proved erroneous the passing character of our individual lives recommends restraint.

Undivided Interest (7:32-35)

Paul returns to the theme of the married and the unmarried. His statement in v. 32a is radical: I want you to be free from anxieties. But he has to explain what he means. In vv. 32b-34 the reference to the unmarried man is balanced by that to the husband, and that to the unmarried woman (and virgin) by that to the wife: on the one hand there is a single mind, a complete devotion to the Lord; on the other there is a double concern and there are divided interests (the partner and the Lord). In the lengthy sentence of v. 35 Paul, as it were, excuses himself and stresses his genuine intention, his loving care. Again we must point out that what Paul says in this unit about the complete devotion of the unmarried as well as the concerns of those married will hardly be accepted today without serious qualification.

A Specific Case (7:36-38)

No agreement exists about the identity of the two persons spoken of in this case. Four proposals can be listed: father and daughter, master and female slave, a man and a "spiritual" sister, engaged man and "virgin." It would seem that the last proposal is the most probable. The interpretation of terms and expressions differs with each choice. "It is no sin" of v. 36 recalls the similar statement in v. 28 (twice). As in v. 5 Paul is very careful in bringing forward the circumstances and conditions for the alternative decisions in vv. 36 and 37. In v. 38b Paul once more (see vv. 1b, 7, 8, 26, and above all vv. 32-35) manifests his preference: "he who refrains from marriage will do better."

The Husband's Death (7:39-40)

The wives receive Paul's last counsel. If the husband dies, a wife is free to marry in the Lord anyone she wishes. Paul again makes known his preference: she will be more blessed if she remains a widow. In a self-conscious, perhaps somewhat playful mood he adds: at least, that is my opinion, and I think that I too have the Spirit of God. This is the end of this lengthy, multifaceted, if not systematic treatment.

Meat Offered to Idols: 8:1–11:1

The fourth major section, like the third introduced by a *peri de* ("now concerning"), deals with meat sacrificed to idols: it contains three chapters. The question was probably raised in the same letter that appears behind all this: A (ch. 8), B (ch. 9) and A' (ch. 10). Between units A and A', which both treat the issue itself, unit B (Paul's renunciation as example) is inserted. Yet regarding structure three notes must be added. (1) Very early (cf. 8:13) Paul uses the first person singular; this verse prepares for ch. 9. (2) Next to the positive example of Paul there is in 10:1-13 the negative, monitory example of Israel in the desert; one could therefore maintain that the B part consists of the whole of 9:1–10:13. (3) At the very end of the whole exposé, in 10:33–11:1, Paul again employs the autobiographical first person singular and calls for imitation.

Paul's basic position in this section is that Christians, because they know that idols do not exist (8:4-6), are free to eat sacrificed meat (8:9; 10:29). Yet no matter how much knowledge and freedom are justly valued, love of the weak fellow believers may require a renunciation of rights (8:7-13; 10:28). As a matter of fact Paul deals with a double danger, not only the danger of lack of love through the contempt of the scrupulous Christian, but also that of idolatry. True, idols are nothing, but demons do really exist, and participation in the pagan cult constitutes idolatry—that is, communication with demons (10:14, 19-20).

Eating meat is also a topic in Romans 14–15 although it is not clear that meat offered to idols is meant there. Yet since in Romans 14 as in 1 Corinthians 8 the "weak" believers are mentioned and since Romans was written in Corinth there may well be some connection between Romans 14–15 and 1 Corinthians 8–10.

Knowledge and Love (8:1-13)

In this first unit Paul's reasoning passes through three steps. First he contrasts knowledge and love (vv. 1-3). Then he emphasizes the nonexistence of idols as well as the existence of only one God and one Lord (vv. 4-6). Each of these subdivisions is introduced by a similar clause with "concerning," "food offered/sacrificed to idols," and "we know." The longer third division (vv. 7-13) deals with the avoidance of scandal. The weak believers who do not possess sufficient knowledge can be brought to fall by those who do possess knowledge and sit at table in an idol's temple.

It is not certain that "all of us possess knowledge" (v. 1a) is a Corinthian slogan. It could already be the beginning of Paul's answer to a difficulty that the letter explains and that we can no longer exactly reconstruct. That all of us "know" is admitted by Paul, but he immediately adds: "knowledge puffs up, but love builds up" (v. 1b). He further qualifies the Christians' knowing: that partial knowledge is not what it claims to be (v. 2). Over against this rather severe language Paul sets a reassuring statement: if Christians really love God they can be sure that this is known by God (v. 3). The logic in v. 3 surprises the reader. Why does Paul not say "one who loves God really knows God," or "one who loves God is loved by God"? No doubt Paul's style is calculated for effect.

Verses 4-6 deal with knowledge and the certainty of faith. It was not clear in v. 1a nor is it certain in v. 4 that Corinthian slogans are being cited. What is stated in v. 4 is what Paul fully admits. It already is part of his reaction: idols have no real existence; there is but one God. As in vv. 1c-3 Paul qualifies his reaction in the long sentence making up vv. 5-6. Grammatically speaking v. 5a is a concessive clause: there may be so-called gods; but in v. 5b Paul corrects what could be seen as a hesitation and adds: as indeed there are many gods and many lords. These gods and lords are, of course, not the idols; they are really-existing demons (see 10:20-21). The addition of "lords" in v. 5 prepares for the naming of the "Lord, Jesus Christ" in the following verse. Verse 6 contains the main clause. Paul here uses and combines traditional formulae from the creed or the baptismal confession. The parallel between "one God, the Father" and "one Lord, Jesus Christ" is striking. Christ is proclaimed as the preexistent mediator of all things in creation as well as the mediator for "us [Christians]" in redemption. Three times in v. 6 the first person plural is employed.

The line of thought in vv. 7-13 is somewhat contorted. Moreover, there is a grammatical unevenness in the use of persons. In v. 7 Paul mentions the lack of knowledge on the part of some Christians and explains what it is: they (third person plural) eat sacrificed food while considering it consecrated and contaminated, so that their weak conscience is defiled. In v. 8 he reminds himself and his readers (first person plural) that food as such has neither moral nor religious relevance. In v. 9 then the warning is given: take care that you (second person plural) do not become a stumbling block to the weak believers. Paul explains in v. 10 how this could occur. A case is brought forward (in the second person singular): on the one hand there is your behavior (sitting at table in a temple eating hall) and on the other the sin of the weak believer (following the example against his or her own conscience). In v. 11 Paul points to the consequence: the loss of the weak believer "by your knowledge" (still second person singular); Paul adds that for that believer Christ died. Then in v. 12 the implication is drawn: you sin (again second person plural) not only against your brothers and sisters but also against Christ. Verse 13 is a conclusion that reminds us of v. 9. Paul formulates a resolution: if food is a cause of falling I will never eat meat (first person singular) "so that I may not cause one of them to fall." In the whole unit the term "love" (of neighbor) is not mentioned, but abandoning one's right, giving up one's freedom, and adapting to the situation of another is certainly proof of authentic love.

Paul Defends Himself (9:1-18)

At first sight ch. 9 looks like an interruption or a digression, yet its function within the argument is to provide an example that can be compared with the renunciation that is asked from the "knowing" Corinthians. In Corinth Paul preached the gospel free of charge; he renounced his right to get a living by it. On the basis of content we distinguish two subdivisions, each introduced by the term "free": vv. 1-18 (self-defense) and v. 19-27 (adaptation and personal salvation). In presenting himself as an example Paul offers a number of considerations that could be considered as deviating somewhat from the proper subject: the reasons in favor of living by the gospel (vv. 7-14), boasting and reward (vv. 15-18), the way Paul becomes all things to all (vv. 19-23), and the strict discipline Paul imposes on himself in order not to be disqualified at the end (vv. 24-27). One probably asks: does Paul in what appears to be a very personal self-defense still have in view one of the concrete problems of the letter—that is, meat offered to idols?

The fact that Paul in this context has to defend his apostolate (vv. 1-2) informs us that his refusal of financial support from the Corinthians was not appreciated by all of them ("those who would examine" him, v. 3); this refusal must have been used against his claim to be a true apostle. Paul explicitly announces his defense in v. 3. By means of questions and a great many arguments (vv. 4-14) he first emphasizes that accepting a living is an apostolic right. Not to make use of this right, however, is his boast and a reward that is not to be taken away from him (vv. 15-18).

By stating in v. 1a (in a rhetorical question!) that he is free, Paul asserts that he too as an apostle possesses knowledge and rights. His apostleship is grounded in the appearance of the risen Lord. Moreover, the very existence of the Corinthian church is the seal of his apostleship, a sign that confirms its authenticity (vv. 1b-2).

In asking the three questions of vv. 4-6 Paul deals with the same apostolic "right": food and drink, (material) support of the wife who accompanies the apostle, no need to work for a living. Verse 7 illustrates this right with three examples from secular life: serving in the army, planting a vineyard, and tending a flock. "Sister" in apposition to "wife" (v. 4) means a wife who is a Christian. By the expression "the other apostles" (v. 5) Paul makes clear that he considers himself their equal; he mentions the "brothers of the Lord" and Cephas: all married, all traveling with their wives. In v. 6 Paul names his former companion Barnabas who like himself was working for a living.

In vv. 8-10 Paul explains how the Law confirms this evident right. He quotes the example of the treading oxen from Deut 25:4. Scripture is written not for animals but for our sake. Two new illustrations are then given: those who plow the fields and thresh the grain must have a share in the crop. In v. 11 the application is made, but Paul mentions a difference: since we apostles are showing among you spiritual goods we certainly can claim material benefits. Moreover in v. 12 Paul reflects upon a second difference, that between the other apostles and himself. As founder of the Corinthian church he possesses this right of support more than the others. Yet he gives up that right and endures many tribulations "rather than put an obstacle in the way of the gospel." This last clause recalls 8:13 ("so that I may not cause one of them to fall"), but now the missionary intention is underscored.

In vv. 13-14 new arguments in favor of support are adduced: Temple service and even a command of the Lord ("those who proclaim the gospel should get their living by the gospel"), although in v. 15 Paul repeats that he has given up this right. There should, however, be no misunderstanding. He does not write this so that his situation should be changed. No, he would rather die than . . . . The sentence is interrupted. Paul begins anew: "nobody will deprive me of my ground for boasting." Verses 16-18 then explain that for Paul preaching the gospel is rooted in his call; it is a necessity, not a ground for boasting. The only "meritorious" thing he can do is proclaim the gospel free of charge. This is his boast and paradoxically his reward is to have no reward. The verb *katachraomai* ("to make full use of") in the last clause of v. 18 may be employed purposely to indicate that while in Corinth Paul received partial support from the Macedonians.

Adaptation and Personal Salvation (9:19-27)

Verses 19-23 and 24-27 may be taken together although they are quite different. In the first part Paul deals with his own missionary adaptation to specific situations; in the second he speaks in hortatory language regarding the Christian life and his own life. Yet v. 23b, the end of the first subdivision, constitutes a transition to the second: Paul thinks of his own salvation. Final salvation is the theme of vv. 24-27. Moreover, what Paul states positively in v. 23b (that I may share in the blessings of the gospel) he expresses negatively in v. 27b (lest . . . I myself should be disqualified). One should also notice that the idea of "slavery" in v. 19 (lit.: "I have enslaved myself") is taken up in v. 27 (lit.: "I lead my body into slavery").

The structure of vv. 19-23 is very ingenious. Verse 19 corresponds to v. 22b and together they form an inclusion: see "all" in both verses and compare "that I might win more of them" (v. 19) with "that I might by all means save some" (v. 22b). Verse 19 announces Paul's main thesis of missionary adjustment: although I am free from all I have made myself a slave of all, that I might win more. Four concretizations follow and are elaborated: Jews, those under the Law, those outside the Law, and the weak (vv. 20-22). The repetition of "those under the law" after "Jews" surprises somewhat (basically these are the same group!) but we must pay due attention to the typically Pauline added correction: "though I myself am not under the law." A similarly important correction is also present in the clause: "though I am not free from God's law but am under Christ's law" (v. 21). The mention of "the weak," the fourth concretization, demonstrates that Paul has not forgotten the topic of the whole section (see the use of this term in ch. 8). Another remarkable stylistic characteristic is the presence of seven purpose clauses: the first five with the missionary verb "to win," the sixth with the more theological verb "to save." The seventh and last purpose clause ends on a sudden shift. The missionary aim is still explicit in v. 23a ("I do it all for the sake of the gospel"), but then in v. 23b Paul thinks of his own destiny, his participation in the blessings of the gospel.

The desire for participation makes Paul aware that final salvation will not be so easy. The body has to be disciplined; self-control is needed. Two athletic metaphors are employed in vv. 24-27: running and boxing. The Corinthians must have been familiar with them since the Isthmian games took place in their region. From the second person plural in v. 24 ("do you not know. . . . Run in such a way that you may win [the prize]") Paul changes in v. 25 to the third person singular and plural and then, at the end of the verse, to the first person plural ("but we [to receive] an imperishable [wreath]") and in vv. 26-27 to the autobiographical first person singular. In ch. 10, however, he will return to his addressees by means of the second plural and an example taken from Israel's past. With "so that after proclaiming to others I myself should not be disqualified" the long self-defensive digression, the example of Paul, ends rather strangely.

Israel in the Desert (10:1-13)

In the first half of ch. 10 (= A') Paul pays attention to the dangers that threaten the Christians, especially the "knowing" among them. Only in 10:23 does he return to the theme dealt with in ch. 8 (= A). Paul begins the chapter with a midrash on the negative example of the ancestors of Israel in the desert. This passage consists of three subdivisions: vv. 1-5 (the narrative), vv. 6-11 (the exhortation), and vv. 12-13 (the conclusion).

"I do not want you to be unaware, brothers and sisters" (v. 1a) is the introductory clause. Paul's extremely free presentation of the desert events in vv. 1b-4—a combination of different data from Exodus—is guided by his typological sacramental interpretation. Cloud and sea are taken together and refer to baptism. Manna and water out of the rock are linked and refer to the Eucharist. According to a Jewish legend the rock followed the Israelites on their way in the desert. Paul identifies it with Christ. Five times "all" is emphasized: all Israelites experienced the same miracles. "Nevertheless, God was not pleased with most of them, and they were struck down in the wilderness" (v. 5).

Verse 6 corresponds to v. 11; both verses frame the middle part. Twice it is explicitly stated that the past desert events are "examples for us," that is, prefigurations of what we today confront; they were written down to instruct us "on whom the ends of the ages have come" (11b). The Christians are the eschatological generation who should not "desire evil as they did" (v. 6b). In vv. 7-10 four specific warnings are given: no idolatry, no immorality, no testing of God, no complaint or grumbling. Each warning (except the first, the only one with an OT quotation, Exod 32:6) consists of three clauses: the negative exhortation, the comparison with the sinful behavior of some of the desert generation, and their punishment and destruction.

Paul's main fear with regard to the Corinthian Christians is their (probably sacramental) over-confidence: "So if you think you are standing, watch out that you do not fall" (v. 12). He ends the passage, however, on a reassuring note: the testing does not exceed human proportions. God is a faithful God who will not let you be tested beyond your strength. "With the testing he will also provide the way out so that you may be able to endure it" (last clause of v. 13). The whole of v. 13 may consist of an already traditional formula.

No Partnership with Demons (10:14-22)

"Therefore, my dear friends, flee from the worship of idols" (v. 14; cf. 6:18a: "shun fornication"). Only twice in this letter (and in the whole NT) does *dioper*—"therefore"—occur; for the warm "my dear friends" (or: "my beloved") see also 4:14 and 15:58. In this introductory sentence there is obviously a great insistence. The connection with the preceding passage is evident not only through "therefore" but also through the warning itself (see "idolatry" in v. 7) and further in vv. 16-17 through the reflection upon the Eucharist (see vv. 3-4). Three times Paul appeals to the judgment of the Corinthians who are addressed as sensible, reasonable people: v. 15 ("judge for yourselves what I say"); v. 18 ("consider the people of Israel"); and v. 19 ("what do I imply then?"). They must consider and compare the Eucharist, the Jewish sacrifices, and pagan worship. What is going on in these rites?

The basic concept Paul brings forward here is participation, partnership through sharing in worship. Partaking creates communion either with Christ (and other Christians) or with demons. A compromise is impossible. Just as he did in 8:4-5, so also in 10:19 Paul stresses the nonexistence of idols. Still, although the pagan gods are but demons, demons really exist. The final questions in v. 22a contain a serious warning: we should not provoke God by idolatrous behavior. "Are we stronger than [God]?" in v. 22b reminds the Corinthians of 4:10b: "we are weak, but you are strong."

One should note the parallel constructions in vv. 16 and 21. Moreover, in both verses the cup is mentioned first and then the bread or table. This inversion is conditioned by the continuation in v. 17 with a reflection on the "one bread." In vv. 16-17 Paul probably employs an already more or less fixed traditional explanation of the Eucharistic words.

Personal Freedom and Care for the Others (10:23–11:1)

This last unit is clearly a conclusion of the whole of chs. 8–10. Verses 23-24 and 32-33 form an *inclusio* for the unit: compare their content and also the wording (beneficial; not seeking one's own advantage but that of the other/the many). Verse 23 repeats a saying (a slogan in Corinth?) we already know from 6:12. Paul's comment pleads for consideration for the scrupulous believers, yet in what follows he also strongly emphasizes the freedom of those who possess knowledge and judge correctly. Two situations are brought forward: one buys food (v. 25), and one is invited for a meal by an unbeliever (in his home? v. 27). Twice the principle is clearly stated: "eat . . . without raising any question on the ground of conscience." Verse 26 adduces a citation from Ps 24:1 as motivation. In vv. 28-29a Paul deals with the possible exception: your action scandalizes the conscience of either the unbeliever or weak believer. But in vv. 29b-30 Paul, employing the first person singular, again reflects upon Christian freedom and defends it against the objections of the weak. Then vv. 31-32 beautifully conclude with a generalization: "So, whether you eat or drink, or whatever you do, do everything for the glory of God. Give no offense to Jews or to Greeks or to the church of God." This is the double rule: glorify God (cf. 6:20b) in freedom, yet give no offense to the other! It should be noted that in v. 32 Paul as if by accident speaks of "the church of God" (= the Christians) as a "third race" next to the Jews and Greeks.

In 10:33–11:1 there is a somewhat surprising addition. Paul comes back to his own behavior as depicted in ch. 9; he expresses once more his missionary consideration for "[the] many, so that they may be saved" (v. 33; cf. the end of 9:22). His appeal is daring, almost provocative: "Be imitators of me, as I am of Christ" (11:1). We met the first part of this appeal in 4:16 (cf. Gal 4:12; Phil 3:17; 1 Thess 1:6; 2:14).

In this fourth major section (meat offered to idols) the "knowledge" of the mature Christians is fully recognized but it has to give way to love for the weak neighbor. Love is more important: it builds up.

Abuses at the Christian Meetings: 11:2-34

The fifth major section consists of two units that Paul introduces with the same verb epainoμ ("I commend you," v. 2; "I do not commend you," v. 17; cf. v. 22). Each of the units mentions the "traditions just as I handed them on to you" (see v. 2; cf. v. 23). In both of them Paul deals with abuses. Women pray and prophesy with their heads unveiled (vv. 2-16); well-off Christians eat and drink greedily at the Lord's Supper, separate themselves from the have-nots and humiliate them (vv. 17-34). It can be asked whether both these abuses—and not only the second (see "I hear" in v. 18)—were reported to Paul orally. In ch. 11 Paul discusses these abuses; he reprimands and argues; he gives clear directions so that the wrong practices will disappear.

Women with Unveiled Heads (11:2-16)

The introductory v. 2 must be considered as a *captatio benevolentiae*. The whole unit looks very much like a treatise but because of the greater emphasis on the right comportment of women one feels that Paul intends to deal with a specific abuse. From v. 16 ("if anyone is disposed to be contentious") we learn that not all Corinthians agreed with Paul's reasoning; some seem to have defended and justified the behavior of these women. The positive v. 2 corresponds to a certain extent with the rather negative v. 16 at the end in that both verses refer to tradition/customs. We propose three subdivisions with three distinct arguments: vv. 3-6 (what the given order of authority implies), vv. 7-12 (what creation involves), and vv. 13-15 (what nature teaches). In this passage Paul deals with behavior during public worship including loud prayer and prophecy (vv. 4-5). In the praise of v. 2 there is already an implicit exhortation: remembering Paul must include maintaining the tradition he delivered (v. 2).

In a first reasoning (vv. 3-6: I want you to understand) the recurring word is "head." There is a play on the word since it is employed in a physical and a metaphorical sense: head (of a body) and source or authority. In v. 3 the line is ascending: woman, man, Christ, and God. It is the order that goes back to creation. But the first member takes into account redemption as well: "the head of every man is Christ." Two symmetrical sentences follow in vv. 4-5a: man and women, head covered and head uncovered during prayer or prophecy, and in both cases disgrace. Verses 5b-6 show the problem at Corinth: women are not wearing a veil.

The second subdivision (vv. 7-12) uses the creation narrative of Genesis 2. Man is created by God, woman is taken from man; man, not woman, is directly "the image and reflection of God" (v. 7). In ascending line the order is: woman, man, God (see v. 12). Christ is not mentioned here. The thematic word is "reflection" (or "glory"). In vv. 8-9 Paul elaborates this basic insight and in v. 10 applies it to the veil, yet in v. 11 (and v. 12) a correction is inserted: woman and man are equal (cf. ch. 7!); they need each other. Although the reference is still the creation story—and not the "new creation" as, for example, in Gal 3:28—a christological element is introduced in v. 11: "in the Lord." The interpretation of v. 10 remains uncertain. Perhaps we should understand it as follows: a woman ought to have (a sign of) authority (= a veil) on her head; the veil manifests that she is under the authority of her husband. (Some would argue it is a sign of her authority to speak publicly in the assembly.) The expression "because of the angels" may point either to the presence (in worship) of angels who require decent conduct, or to angels who like those of Genesis 6 could be tempted through women's improper behavior.

The third argument (vv. 13-15) is taken from nature. In v. 13 Paul interrupts his reasoning and appeals to the Corinthians: "judge for yourselves"; judge from what is "proper for a woman." Man (disgraceful long hair) is put over against woman (long hair that is her "glory" and functions for her as a veil) (vv. 14-15). A few exegetes try to find in these verses a confirmation for the improbable hypothesis that in the whole unit Paul does not deal with veiled and unveiled heads but with bound and unbound hair (and—some say—with homosexual tendencies).

After the three arguments—all connected to the order that according to Paul and his contemporaries the Creator determined—v. 16 refers to Paul's apostolic authority and the customs in the other churches. Reading this verse one has the impression that Paul becomes somewhat nervous and wants to stop the discussion and that, moreover, he is not all too certain of his own argument. There is no reason, however, for denying this passage to Paul. Modern readers cannot accept that "woman" is not like "man" a direct image of God (see Gen 1:26-27) nor will they take for granted customs or conventions that are clearly time-conditioned or culture-bound. The questions, however, remain: to what degree does equality between the sexes involve uniformity, and to what degree does sexual difference imply diversification in function and responsibility?

Factions at the Lord's Supper (11:17-34)

The second unit also consists of three subdivisions: vv. 17-22 (abuses); vv. 23-26 (institution narrative); and vv. 27-34 (needed examination). In the first subdivision the unacceptable situation is explained; in the second Paul refers back to the origin of the Lord's Supper; in the third he gives directions to redress the situation. The practical suggestions at the end of the passage in vv. 33-34a are already implicit in the questions of v. 22. The verb "to come together" that occurs in v. 33 as well as in v. 34 is also used at the beginning of the pericope in vv. 17, 18, and 20; it thus frames the passage.

The main reason why Paul cannot commend the Corinthians is already indicated in v. 17: when they come together it is not for the better but for the worse. A more general explanation is given in vv. 18-19, a concretization in vv. 20-21. After "to begin with" (v. 18) one expects "second," but only in v. 34b does Paul say "about the other things I will give instructions when I come." Verses 18-19 mention divisions and factions. Paul does not necessarily believe all that is reported but part of it must be true. He reflects on the sad situation: there must be factions, but one positive factor is that those who are genuine will thus be recognized. Verses 20-21 present an account of the disorder in detail. The rich arrive first and start the meal; when the poor arrive little is left. The rich eat their "own supper" (*idion deipnon;* the expression clashes with *kyriakon deipnon,* "the Lord's supper," just mentioned). Verse 22 proposes four incisive questions. The first contains a suggestion: why not eat and drink at home (which implies a separation of the common meal and the Eucharist proper)? In the second question Paul uses the expression "church of God" (cf. v. 16, but in the plural; see also 1:1; 10:32; 14:19; 15:9). Contempt, humiliation, lack of love of the poor falsify the Lord's supper. The last two questions follow: "What should I say to you? Should I commend you? In this matter I do not commend you!"

"For I received from the Lord what I also handed on to you, that . . ." (v. 23). By its position at the beginning of the sentence the "I" *(egō)* is emphasized. "To receive" and "to hand on" are the technical terms for passing on tradition that are also found in rabbinic literature. "From the Lord" must be interpreted to mean that what is handed on goes back to the earthly Jesus through faithfully delivered tradition. The report itself (vv. 23b-26) is in many respects close to that of Luke (22:15-20) and different from that of Mark (14:22-25; cf. Matt 26:26-29). The following Pauline features should be noticed: "for you" (v. 24), the double remembrance clause (vv. 24 and 25), the "the new covenant in my blood" (v. 25). "Blood" certainly refers to Jesus' death on the cross, yet because of the parallelism with bread = body in v. 24 (and also because of 10:16) the wine in the cup is identified with Jesus' blood. "After supper" (v. 25) reminds us of the fact that Jesus' bread gesture took place at the beginning of the meal, but his "eucharistic" words over the wine after the meal. In v. 26 the three time dimensions are brought together in an impressive way: the reference to Jesus' death (past), the repetition of the rite as long as history lasts (present), the expectation of Jesus' parousia (future).

Verses 27-34 contain the conclusion and application: "therefore" (v. 27). Paul begins with a serious warning against unworthy behavior that profanes the body and blood of the Lord. Christians must examine themselves. Not discerning that body brings condemnation. In vv. 29-34 there is a sophisticated play on words: the English vocabulary "judge, discern, condemn; judgment, condemnation" goes back to terms that all possess the Greek root *krin.* In vv. 27-32 Paul offers more general considerations. Verse 30 strikes us by its almost magical sacramental realism; it would seem that vv. 31-32 are intended as a kind of correction: ". . . we are disciplined so that we may not be condemned along with the world." Then in vv. 33-34a Paul returns to the situation at Corinth, the abuses that must be removed: "so then, my brothers and sisters, when you come together to eat, wait for one another. If you are hungry, eat at home. . . ." He will give instructions on other matters at his coming (v. 34b).

Paul had already referred to the Lord's supper in 10:3-4 as well as 10:16-17. This third time the treatment is thorough and extensive. The texts witness to sacramental realism; the Eucharist is more than a simple memorial. In each of them Paul stresses that participation (*koinōnia,* 10:16) cannot go together with wrongdoing, be it idolatry or despising the poor fellow Christian. Sacramental life demands religious and ethical behavior. One pauses and cannot but regret deeply the schisms and disunity, past and present, among the followers of Christ. Through the Eucharist Christians are anchored in the oldest tradition and obey the command of the Lord himself. Moreover, the words of institution put us in the midst of salvation history and bring us back to the OT (cf. Exod 24:8; Jer 31:31; and perhaps also Isaiah 53).

Variety of Spiritual Gifts: 12:1–14:40

The sixth major section of 1 Corinthians deals with the *pneumatika,* the gifts of the Holy Spirit (see 12:1 and 14:1). The section is introduced by *peri de* ("now concerning") and "brothers and sisters." Most exegetes accept within this long passage the presence of another A-B-A' structure. Chapter 12 deals with diversity of gifts within the one body of Christ in a rather general way (A); with its focus on love as the most eminent way ch. 13 interrupts the line of thought (B); ch. 14 returns to the spiritual gifts, and here Paul provides specific, practical directives (A'). "Strive for the greater gifts" (12:31a) corresponds with 14:1b ("strive for the spiritual gifts, and especially that you may prophesy"), just as 12:31b ("and I will show you a still more excellent way") does with 14:1a ("pursue love"). These chiastic sentences, 12:31 and 14:1, frame chapter 13 (B). Of course the contents differ.

This section is rather similar to the fourth (chs. 8–10; meat offered to idols) in its concentric structure, its length, and the use of the first person singular in the B-unit—that is, in the way Paul refers to himself. The reference to "idols" in 12:2 may not be accidental.

What is the structure of chapter 12 (= A)? Verse 1 announces the topic; in vv. 2-3 a basic principle is enunciated; v. 31 is a transition to what follows. The remainder of this first unit, vv. 4-30, consists of three subdivisions: vv. 4-11 (diversity in unity), vv. 12-26 (diversity in a physical body), and vv. 27-30 (diversity in the body that is the Church). The third subdivision corresponds to the first. In both the plural "charisms" occurs twice (see vv. 4, 9 and vv. 28, 30; cf. also v. 31); in both the variety of gifts is highlighted; moreover, several gifts that are mentioned in the first subdivision reappear in the third (prophecy, miracles, healings, tongues, interpretation of the tongues).

Diversity in Unity (12:1-11)

Paul does not want the Corinthians to remain uninformed concerning spiritual gifts (v. 1). The grammatical construction reminds the Gentile Christians of their pagan practices; the present context suggests that enthusiastic, ecstatic rites and cultic meetings are referred to. Verse 3 is difficult to interpret. We may conjecture that an opposition between the earthly Jesus and the risen Christ has been put forward. The Spirit does not allow the rejection of the earthly Jesus, and the same Spirit assures the validity of the confession that the risen Jesus is "Lord." There probably existed in Corinth a wrong view on Jesus Christ that was connected with the heathen past of these Christians (v. 2). All this remains vague and uncertain. More can hardly be said.

The main stress in vv. 4-11 lies on the existence of a great diversity of gifts that have the same origin. "The Spirit" is a strongly emphasized and often repeated term in these verses. In the threefold almost perfectly symmetrical composition of vv. 4-6 the variety of gifts, services, and activities and their common "trinitarian" origin in the same Spirit, the same Lord, and the same God are affirmed. Of God it is said by way of climax that God activates all activities in all Christians (v. 6). Then in v. 7 it is stated that to each the manifestation of the Spirit—that is, the manifestation of one's gifts—is given for the benefit of the whole community, for the common good. This is worked out by an enumeration in vv. 8-10: the utterance of wisdom and of knowledge are mentioned first, then three miraculous gifts—wonder-working faith, healings, and mighty works—finally prophecy and its discernment, as well as tongues and their interpretation (or translation into intelligible language). It is not by accident that the gift of tongues—so highly desired in Corinth—stands, together with the interpretation of them, in the last position. Verse 11 summarizes the whole development: The same Spirit activates all (cf. v. 6: God); this Spirit "varies" or "allots" at will (cf. "varieties," the very term that is used three times at the beginning of vv. 4, 5, and 6); each receives the appropriate gift (cf. v. 7 and vv. 8-10).

Diversity in the Body (12:12-26)

In the second subdivision the comparison of the Church with a human body is broadly worked out. In v. 12 there is the construction "just as . . . so." Its first part is long, the second (lit.: "so Christ") is extremely terse. The emphasis lies on unity: just as the body is one and has many members *but* all the members, though many, are one body, so it is with Christ. In v. 13 the Christ/Church part of v. 12 is explained: note the ecclesiological use of body and the reference to baptism and perhaps also to the Eucharist ("we were all made to drink of one Spirit"). Jews/Greeks and slaves/free are mentioned, not male/female. Verse 14 then stresses the diversity.

In vv. 15-21 this is elaborated. One member needs the other. We notice that according to v. 18 God the creator acted freely (the same idea as in v. 11 with reference to the Spirit) and that in v. 20 the unity of the body is again underscored. In vv. 22-25 a shift has taken place: it is God's will (v. 24) that the weak and inferior members be taken care of, that there be no discord in the body. The tone is decidedly parenetical. Verse 26 concludes beautifully: "If one member suffers, all suffer together with it; if one member is honored, all rejoice together with it."

In vv. 12-26 Paul employs an image that must have been well known in Corinth. In his description of the body he certainly already has in mind the reality to which the image points.

Diversity in the Church (12:27-31)

In the third subdivision the diversity is again stressed together with the unequal value of the gifts. With "you are the body of Christ and individually members" (v. 27; cf. vv. 12-13) the application begins. The list in v. 28 is irregular: first three categories of persons, then five gifts or functions. The concept "church" is no longer strictly local since the apostles possess more than local authority. What is striking in this list is the numbering (first, second, third) and moreover that "offices" of apostle, prophet, and teacher are included in a list of spiritual gifts. However some of the gifts themselves are just functions: forms of assistance, forms of leadership. In the questions of vv. 29-30 these two "gifts" of assistance and leadership are missing but another is added: interpretation of tongues (cf. the end of v. 10). As in v. 10 tongues and the interpretation of them occupy the last position in vv. 28 and 30. Paul argues against overestimation of this gift.

Verse 31a-b should not be separated. Verse 31b appears as an afterthought, somewhat a correction of v. 31a: strive (imperative!) for the greater gifts, yet I will still show you a way beyond compare. "Greater" supposes an evaluation of gifts such as is already suggested by the numbering in v. 28. Love, however, is strictly speaking not a "gift."

The Most Eminent Way (13:1-13)

There is a change of style at the beginning of ch. 13 (= B). Rhetorical analysis notes that the deliberative genre of ch. 12 yields here to the demonstrative genre. The subject matter, too, clearly indicates that this unit is a digression. Yet this "excursus" is not conceived as a self-contained hymn on love. It functions within the flow of thought of the whole section. The connection with ch. 12 is manifest. "Tongues" of 13:1 is taken up from 12:28, 30, and "prophetic powers" of 13:2 from 12:28, 29. Chapter 13 contains three subdivisions. Verses 1-3 emphasize that love is the condition without which no gift is of any value to us; love is indispensable. Verses 4-7 depict the qualities of love positively and negatively. Verses 8-13 constitute the longest subdivision and explain how love, unlike the gifts, never ends; love is permanent. One easily detects the concentric character of ch. 13. The second subdivision forms the center (b) and is completely devoted to love; the first and third subdivisions (a and a') contrast the spiritual gifts with love.

a. The Indispensability of Love, 13:1-3

The three long tripartite sentences each consist of a double protasis and an apodosis: (1) "If I" + verb(s), (2) "but [if I] do not have love," (3) a conclusive clause: "I am a noisy gong or a clanging cymbal," "I am nothing," "I gain nothing." This threefold repetition is impressive. In this subdivision Paul uses the first person singular. It is ordinarily taken in a general rather than a strictly autobiographical sense, yet these verses may be more self-referential, more pointed toward Paul's own apostolic experiences and more anchored in his own behavior than many are willing to accept.

In vv. 1-3 five "charisms" are mentioned, it would seem in an ascending order of importance. "Tongues," the least important, comes first (v. 1). The comparison with the loud accompaniment in pagan worship reveals Paul's rather derogatory attitude toward this charism. In v. 2 mysteries and knowledge may belong to "prophecy"; "faith" is here the wonder-working charism. This faith is more than prophecy, and prophecy more than tongues (cf. 14:1 and 5). Then in v. 3 Paul refers to even greater charisms: the most generous "giving away of all possessions" to assist others and the apostolically motivated "handing over of the body." The text here is uncertain. It remains difficult to choose between the two readings: I deliver my body to be burned *(kauthēsōmai)* or, more probably, I deliver my body (for example, to hardships and suffering) so that I may boast *(kauchēsōmai).*

b. Description of Love (13:4-7)

Love is characterized by means of fifteen verbs. The original Greek in this subdivision manifests a delicate style as well as a sophisticated structure. At the beginning, in v. 4a, there is a chiasm (lit.: love is patient, kind is love) and at the end in v. 7 we have the fourfold repetition of "all" (love bears, believes, hopes, and endures all things). In the middle love is further characterized by a series of seven negative verbs (vv. 4b-5) relieved by an antithetical construction (v. 6: love "does not rejoice in wrongdoing, but rejoices in the truth").

The structure itself is subservient to the thought. After the repeated statements in vv. 1-3 that notwithstanding extraordinary gifts and personal endeavor a person without love is nothing, Paul depicts the nature of that love. We may assume that in vv. 4-7 Paul is referring both to himself and to the Corinthians. Paul's personal exemplary life as well as the harmful attitudes of the Corinthians seem to have entered into this positive and negative characterization of love.

c. The Permanence of Love (13:8-13)

In the third subdivision Paul emphasizes that love is permanent. Verses 8b-12 are framed by v. 8a and v. 13, both containing the noun "love": faith, hope, and love remain, love is the greatest, love never ends.

Verse 8 assumes that just like prophecies, tongues, and knowledge, love is present in Christian life. The difference, however, is that love will never end. In view of the three future tenses within v. 8 one rightly also assumes a future nuance in the present tense "ends." The antithetical situation between love and the gifts requires such an understanding. In vv. 9-10 the phrase "in part" is now clearly opposed to "what is complete." Paul wants to work out and explain what is implied in v. 8, yet we cannot avoid the impression that a shift occurs. While according to v. 8 prophecies, tongues, and knowledge will simply disappear, in vv. 9-10 prophesying and knowing will rather be completed; only their partial character will disappear. We notice that the gift of tongues is no longer spoken of. One should also pay attention to the sudden appearance of the first person plural in v. 9. Verse 10 injects a rather abstract reflection on the disappearance of what is partial when completion comes. The literal translation of v. 10a should use a *futurum exactum:* after the complete "will have come"; v. 10b follows: (then) the partial will disappear.

Verse 11 contains an analogy wherein infancy and adulthood are contrasted. Paul reflects on his own past; he now employs the autobiographical (at the same time typical) first person singular. The first half of v. 11 means: during the period "when I was a child" I was speaking, thinking, and reasoning as a child. The nuance of "when" in the second half is not exactly the same as in the first: "when I became an adult," then, at that moment, I put an end to childish ways.

In v. 12 Paul returns to the situation of the Christians (first person plural) before death that stands in sharp contrast to the future completion, the resurrection of life. He explains and applies the analogy. The two halves of the verse are parallel. Face-to-face vision and full knowledge correspond to each other. Two metaphors are used: mirror and riddle. Does Paul mean (only) indirect or, more probably, (also) unclear and indistinct seeing over against "face-to-face" vision? Then in the second half, employing the first person singular, Paul again refers to partial knowledge that is opposed to future, perfect knowledge. The perfection is indicated by the compound verb *epiginōskō* and compared with the way he himself has been known (by God; cf. a similar passive form in 8:3). The shift noted in v. 9 continues. Knowledge does not simply disappear; it is brought to perfection. The progressive narrowing of focus also continues: from three gifts in v. 8 to two in v. 9 to one (knowledge) in v. 12. One rightly wonders whether the partial knowledge in v. 12 is still simply the charism of vv. 2 and 8-9. In vv. 8-12 two negative characteristics of the gifts are indicated: they will end; they are partial, imperfect.

With v. 13 Paul brings the argument to its conclusion. This verse is loaded with difficulties. The two main interpretations are the following: (1) So then (a logical *nuni*) faith, hope, and love have no end; all three of them will last and remain for ever. But love is the greatest. This additional note, however, in no way denies the eschatological permanence of faith and hope. (2) In v. 13a Paul does not speak of the eschaton but of present-life realities: faith, hope, and love that are essential in each Christian existence (a temporal *nuni,* "now"). In v. 13b Paul states that love is greatest of these three. Why? Of course because of love's preeminent, irreplaceable role in Christian life on earth; but also because of love's unique eschatological nature, its eternal permanence. For Paul (see 2 Cor 5:7 and Rom 8:24) faith and hope will no longer have a role in the eschaton. In 1 Cor 13:13a Paul most probably deals with the present-day Christian life (second option). Not all Christians are equipped with extraordinary gifts, but in their lives there must be and is the abiding presence of faith, hope, and love. Faith and hope, however, will pass away and be replaced by sight and fulfillment. Only eschatological love will remain forever; it will never end.

Does Paul mean love of God or love of neighbor? Although in v. 12 the term "love" is not mentioned we cannot but assume that the face-to-face vision and perfect knowledge include love. In this verse future seeing and knowing of God are spoken of, but love of God is likewise intended. Yet one must remember that in vv. 4-7 it is primarily love of neighbor that Paul depicts: this love is practiced during present life on earth. Love of neighbor is also meant in v. 13a. However since in this last clause Paul, with faith and hope, refers to believing and hoping in God (and Christ), the third term of the triad, love, cannot but participate in that God-ward direction. Apparently for Paul daily love of neighbor constitutes the only way to attaining authentic, eschatologically enduring love of God.

In vv. 4-7 love is personified. In v. 9 and v. 12a Paul uses the first person plural but by the first person singular in vv. 1-3, 11, 12b he most probably refers primarily to himself. What Paul says about love in 1 Corinthians 13 was for himself both a program to be executed and a final goal to be attained.

In ch. 13 God is not explicitly named, nor is Christ. In a certain sense this chapter is "anthropological," different from the more ecclesiological ch. 12. Love consists in what is required from each Christian individually, daily and concretely. However, to go that "more excellent way," *via maxime vialis* (Bengel) will of course not be possible without God's grace and the Spirit of Christ.

Prophecy versus Tongues (14:1-25)

The exhortation of 14:1 brings the reader back to the central matter of the section: "Pursue love and strive for the spiritual gifts, and especially that you may prophesy." The third and last unit, chapter 14 (= A'), contains reasoned directives. Through the whole unit the focus is on "tongues" and "prophecy." The manifestation of charisms must occur in good and decent order and above all to the edification of the Church (for the "building up" vocabulary see the verb in vv. 4 and 17 and the noun in vv. 3, 5, 12, 26). The unit contains two subdivisions: vv. 1-25 (prophecy versus tongues) and vv. 26-40 (practical directives). The interruption at v. 26 ("What should be done then, my friends?") marks the caesura. Within the first subdivision we successively deal with vv. 1-5 (contrasting tongues and prophecy), vv. 6-19 (speaking in tongues calls for interpretation) and vv. 20-25 (tongues and prophecy differ for believers and unbelievers).

Paul esteems all spiritual gifts but already in v. 1 one feels his preference for prophecy. In vv. 2-4 tongues and prophecy are contrasted. The addressees are different: God and oneself for tongues; the others, the Church, for prophecy. Paul's major concern is the upbuilding of the Church (see the end of both v. 4 and v. 5). Tongues cannot be understood by the community, but through intelligible prophecy the faithful are encouraged and consoled. In v. 5 Paul repeats that prophecy is better "unless," he adds, "someone interprets." This clause will be worked out in the following verses.

Without interpretation speaking in tongues is unintelligible, sterile, unproductive. The result will be frustration, "speaking into the air" (v. 9); there will be no profit for others (v. 6), no edification of the Church (v. 12; cf. vv. 4 and 5), no instruction of others (v. 19). One will be a foreigner (*barbaros,* v. 11). Paul wants his readers to see this. In vv. 6-19 he stresses that speaking in tongues should be completed by interpretation. It should be made intelligible by revelation or plain knowledge, prophecy, teaching (v. 6). To explain what he means he employs a number of comparisons (flute, harp, tuba, human speech, sound, vv. 7-11) and he distinguishes between praying, singing praise, or saying a blessing with the (ecstatic, unintelligible) spirit alone and the same activities where the (intelligible) "mind" is also present (vv. 14-19).

Paul's exposé here is very lively and versatile. He appeals to his hearers; they should apply what he says to themselves (second person plural in vv. 9 and 12). He also uses the objective third person singular and turns to the exemplary first person singular in vv. 6, 11 and 14-15. The second person singular suddenly appears in vv. 16-17 (here a participating "outsider" who is not yet a Christian is brought in). In vv. 18-19 the "I" comes back again but is now decidedly self-referential: Paul himself speaks in tongues more than all Corinthians, "nevertheless, in church I would rather speak five words with my mind, in order to instruct others also, than ten thousand words in a tongue" (v. 19). Without doubt the interpretation of tongues is needed.

The address "brothers and sisters" and the exhortation in v. 20 constitute an interruption and a new beginning. The Corinthians will have grasped Paul's barely hidden criticism of their childish preference for tongues. However, the train of thought in vv. 21-25 is difficult to follow. The quotation in v. 21 from Isa 28:11-12 originally pointed to unbelieving Israel and the punishing intervention of the Assyrians who spoke an unintelligible language: "yet even then they (= the Israelites) will not listen to me." Paul, however, has unbelieving Gentiles in mind. In v. 22 he applies the Scripture text to tongues and prophecies. One wonders whether in his general statement *sēmeion* still contains the nuance of a punishing and hardening sign that v. 21 seems to require. Perhaps we should understand this verse in a quite simple way: tongues are not meant for believers but for unbelievers, prophecy not for unbelievers but for believers. In v. 23 the "outsider" of vv. 16-17 reappears together with the unbeliever. When all Christians in church speak in tongues there is no profit for these visitors; it seems to them to be madness (v. 23). By prophecy, however, the unbeliever and the outsider are brought to insight into their distinct states; these persons recognize that God is really among the Christians (vv. 24-25). The passage now receives a missionary bent. Contrary to what is said in v. 22, prophecy is useful for the unbelievers as well!

Practical Directives (14:26-40)

In the second subdivision three clusters of verses, 26-33a, 33b-36, and 37-40 should be treated in succession. In v. 26 Paul expresses his agreement about the diversity of charisms in actual worship but the all-important rule is repeated: "let all things be done for building up." Tongues and prophecy are then dealt with separately. To a certain extent the guidelines are the same: small number (two, at most three) and order. Interpretation must be added to tongues; otherwise "let them be silent in church and speak to themselves and to God" (v. 28; cf. vv. 2 and 4). For prophecy evaluation is needed as well as respect for the other who might receive a revelation during the meeting. The prophets must remain in control of their prophetic activity (v. 32). Verse 33a ("for God is a God not of disorder but of peace") motivates what precedes but at the same time widens the horizon and, together with the clause at the end of v. 26, frames the passage.

Most probably v. 33b belongs to the sentence in v. 34. "As in all the churches of the saints" is Paul's answer to an opposition in Corinth to which v. 36 also seems to refer. In vv. 34-35 three injunctions are given to the women: silence, subordination, and receiving explanation at home. Each is motivated by a clause that follows. Data regarding vv. 33b-36 make it appear that they are an insertion. The injunction to be silent during worship does not fit with what Paul apparently takes for granted in 11:5 (prophesying women). One asks what the topic is doing in this context. Some manuscripts (the Western family) transpose vv. 34-35 after v. 40. Is the whole passage (or part of it, vv. 34-35) therefore a post-Pauline intrusion? However, this is subject to doubt for many features connect it with the preceding context (vv. 26-33a). First there is the vocabulary: to be silent, to speak, to be subordinated, to learn, "in church," God. The content of v. 36 is related to that of v. 37, and subordination is also assumed in 11:3. Is it therefore perhaps better to assume the authenticity of the passage and duly recognize the existing tension? It must be said that in this case a choice between what is genuinely Pauline and what is interpolation remains difficult. A third proposal looks farfetched: to take vv. 34-35 as the option of certain people in Corinth and v. 36 as Paul's rebuttal. Of course, as with some other biblical texts, a modern approach to such a theme can hardly avoid *Sachkritik* (criticism of the content itself).

In vv. 37-40 Paul brings the unit, and with it the entire section, to a close. He once again focuses on the spiritual gifts. From vv. 37-38—as already from v. 36—one gets the impression that Paul has to fight against people who disagree. He grounds his authority in that of Christ ("a command of the Lord," v. 37, text-critically the best reading). Whoever does not acknowledge what Paul has written in this section will be rejected (by God: v. 38 employs a *passivum divinum*). In v. 39 prophecy and tongues reappear; one also notes once more Paul's well-known preference for prophecy; yet since tongues are also a spiritual gift speaking in tongues should not be forbidden. The final injunction (v. 40) takes up the idea more or less present in v. 33a; it constitutes a major criterion for community gatherings: "all things should be done decently and in order."

At the end of this lengthy section the reader is invited to reflect on the almost complete absence of the spiritual gifts in the great churches of our day, on Paul's plea for intelligibility as well as care for the building up of the community, and on the central and indispensable place of love.

The Resurrection: 15:1-58

Although 1 Corinthians 15 does not begin with *peri de* ("now concerning") it is apparent that the chapter constitutes a well delineated whole. There is a solemn new beginning in v. 1 ("now I would remind you, brothers and sisters . . .") while the parenetical v. 58 is without any doubt a conclusion. The subject matter treated in this section clearly differs from that in chs. 12–14 and that of ch. 16. The unifying factor, in terms of content, is the resurrection.

A threefold division is suggested by the caesurae in v. 12 and v. 35. The first unit (vv. 1-11) deals with the resurrection and appearances of Christ; the second and third units (vv. 12-34 and 35-58) treat the resurrection of believers. In v. 12 the particle *that* occurs twice: "that" there is a resurrection of the dead is proved by the fact "that" Jesus is risen from the dead. From v. 35 onward the *how* of the bodily resurrection is dealt with: see the double question in this verse: "how" are the dead raised and "with what kind of body" do they come? Moreover, these two units conclude with an exhortation in the second person plural (vv. 33-34 and v. 58).

The Resurrection and Appearances of Christ (15:1-11)

To focus on the main argument of 1 Corinthians 15 and situate the function of vv. 1-11 within the chapter one has to pay special attention to v. 12b: some Corinthians say that there is no resurrection of the dead. That is the issue. The disproof of this heretical opinion is what Paul is aiming at in the chapter. Verses 1-11 are written within the framework of such a refutation. Three affirmations—or perhaps better, concerns—control Paul's line of thought in these verses.

First of all, in vv. 1-3a as well an in v. 11 Paul stresses his thesis: that is, the preaching of the same gospel, the basic elements of which he cites in vv. 3b-5. The sameness of the gospel is indicated, as it were, vertically by reference to the delivering and receiving of the tradition in vv. 1-3a (for the terminology, cf. 11:23) as well as horizontally by the emphasis on the common gospel in v. 11 ("whether then it was I or they, so we proclaim and so you have come to believe"). Within that tradition Christ's resurrection is central. This appears clearly not only from vv. 5-8 (witnesses) but also from v. 12a ("now if Christ is proclaimed as raised from the dead, how can some of you say . . ."). This commonly held belief in the past resurrection of Christ is the starting point and ground of the argument about the future resurrection of Christians.

A second emphasis concerns the reality of Christ's resurrection. We find this unmistakably behind vv. 5-8. If that event were not real, if it had not occurred, how could Paul use it in his reasoning? We may regard the list in vv. 6-8 (or 5b-8) as an expansion of v. 5 (or 5a). All appearances of the risen Christ mentioned in vv. 5-8 establish and validate what is said in v. 4b: Christ is risen.

The third idea or assertion is rather a digression found in vv. 9-10. Paul may be the last and least apostle but qualitatively he is a true apostle. Already in v. 8 he writes "last of all, as to one untimely born, he appeared also to me." In vv. 9-10 Paul explains that emphasis. He admits his unworthiness (v. 9) but he also stresses his work, harder than that of the others; God's grace toward him was not in vain (v. 10).

There is a consensus concerning the traditional character of vv. 3b-5. The extent and vocabulary of the confessional formula, however, are disputed; "to the twelve" (v. 5b) probably still belongs to it. The tradition is very old. Its provenance may be Antioch; some postulate Damascus or even Jerusalem. The pre-Pauline statement consists of four clauses; the first (death) and third (resurrection) are long, the second (burial) and fourth (appearances) brief. It would seem that the burial and appearances confirm, as it were "prove" the reality of the saving events of Jesus' death and resurrection. Thus to the basic original antithetical elements "Christ died and rose [or was raised]" burial and appearances have been added. Further added material includes the soteriological expression "[died] for our sins," the twofold "in accordance with the scriptures" (with probable reference to Isaiah 53 in v. 3b and perhaps to Hos 6:2 in v. 4b) and the time indication "on the third day" (probably pointing not to an exact date but to God's saving intervention "quickly"). The traditional creedal formula "Christ died for our sins in accordance with the scriptures" (v. 3b) cannot but remind us of what Jesus said at the Last Supper: "This is my body that is for you" and "this cup is the new covenant in my blood" (11:24 and cf. Matt 20:28; Mark 10:45: "The Son of Man came . . . to give his life a ransom for many"). As elsewhere in his letters Paul refers to Christ's sacrificial death for our sins (cf. for example Gal 1:3-4 and Rom 3:24-26).

In vv. 6-8 Paul expands the list of witnesses by means of several "then's" (*eita* or *epeita,* already in v. 5b) and by "last of all." Verses 5-8 provide an impressive list. The data of vv. 6a and 7 are also traditional but Paul himself is probably responsible for the wording and structure. This applies above all to v. 7 which is parallel to v. 5: James and all the apostles, Peter and the twelve. For Paul the number of apostles is greater than twelve (it includes, for example, James and Barnabas) yet "all" and "last of all" betray that in his opinion the number is closed. It is possible that the mention of James points to his authority in Jerusalem after Peter had left the city. "Christ appeared to . . ." may have functioned as a legitimating formula. Such authentication, however, could not have possessed any value if the authenticity of the appearance was in doubt. Verse 6b is striking in this regard. Paul seems to say: if you do not believe me you can ask those who are still alive. The apologetic, humble, but at the same time self-conscious tone of vv. 9-10 should not go unnoticed.

One question remains. Was the resurrection of Christ accepted by all the Corinthians? Most exegetes are rather firm in assuming that it was, yet several details in the text seem to reveal that some Corinthians are not so sure. "I would remind you" (v. 1); "if you hold firmly to the message that I proclaimed to you" and "unless you have come to believe in vain" (v. 2); "we proclaim" (v. 11, present tense) over against "you have come to believe" (v. 11, aorist): all these clauses or phrases seem to hint at the presence of doubt concerning Christ's resurrection as well. The list of eyewitnesses may have been intended precisely to remove that doubt.

The "That" of Our Future Bodily Resurrection (15:12-34)

In the second unit vv. 20-28 are usually regarded as the central subdivision. Verses 12-19 and 29-32 correspond to each other in structure and content, so that the unit presents a concentric structure with a parenetic conclusion (vv. 33-34).

In vv. 12-19 Paul draws out the implications of a supposed denial of the resurrection. For this argument he uses a series of interrelated conditional sentences that may be summarized as follows: (1) an indignant question (v. 12); (2) negative hypothesis and consequences (vv. 13-15 and 16-18); (3) a concluding conditional period (v. 19). The indignant question constitutes the first conditional period (v. 12). Paul's indignation indicates that in his opinion the *protasis* implies the resurrection of the dead. We can reconstruct his profound conviction in positive form: If Christ is risen *(protasis)* there is of course also a resurrection of the dead *(apodosis).* Already in vv. 12-19 (as in vv. 20-22) Paul sees Christ's resurrection as the basis for the future resurrection of Christians. In two parallel steps (vv. 13-15 and 16-18) Paul then argues that denial of the resurrection of the dead involves denial of the resurrection of Christ (vv. 13 and 16), and that such denial has negative consequences for Paul and the apostles (the kerygma they preach is in vain, v. 14b; they are false witnesses of God, v. 15), for the Corinthians still alive (their faith is in vain, vv. 14c and 17b; they are still in their sins, v. 17c), and for the dead (they have perished, v 18). Then in v. 19 Paul concludes his series of periods. If hope is confined to this life, then we (Paul and all Corinthians?) are the most pitiable of people.

Verses 20-28 contain two steps, each with thesis and explanation (vv. 20-22 and 23-28). Christ is referred to as the first fruits of those who have fallen asleep. This statement or thesis (v. 20) is then explained. Christ is compared with Adam. Both represent a temporal and causal beginning: Adam of death for all men and women, Christ of life and resurrection for all Christians (vv. 21-22). In v. 20 the term "first fruits" points to a temporal sequence (first of a series) as well as to a causal relation between the first and the others. The idea of causality is then emphasized in vv. 21-22: by a human being came the death, by a human being comes the resurrection; in Christ shall all be made alive.

The idea of sequence is taken up in vv. 23-28 which also open with a thesis. There will be an order and different groups: (1) Christ is the first who is already risen; (2) at his parousia those who belong to him will rise; (3) then comes the end *(telos),* when Christ hands over the kingdom to God after having overthrown all inimical powers (vv. 23-24). The second and third stages are then further explained. Christ must reign until all his enemies, death included, are put under his feet. Finally the Son himself will be subjected to God in order that God may be everything in every one (or: in all things, vv. 25-28). In Paul's vision there will be no messianic reign on earth between Christ's parousia and the last judgment. Pauousia and judgment coincide. The two psalm verses that are employed must have been very familiar to the early Christians. In v. 25 Paul thoroughly rewrites Ps 110:1. The major change is the christological transposition. The subject of "until he has put . . ." is no longer God but Christ. Furthermore sitting at the right hand of God in heaven (an idea present in the same verse of the psalm) is interpreted by Paul as Christ's active reigning on earth. From the resurrection onward Christ is reigning and the purpose of this rule is the subjection of all enemies. Death is included; personified death is the last enemy (v. 26). The destruction of death is resurrection. In v. 27a Paul quotes Ps 8:7. Some commentators hold that once more a transposition should be assumed. In the psalm it was God who subjected all things under the feet of "humanity" in general. For Paul it would be Christ who subjects all things under his own feet. In v. 28 Paul returns to his theocentric vision of the end of history. The Son himself will be subjected to the Father. The ultimate aim is "that God may be all in all."

Although in a less regular manner Paul employs the same style of reasoning in vv. 29-32 as in vv. 12-19: *protasis* ("if the dead are not raised," vv. 29b and 32c) and *apodosis* (the remaining clauses). It strikes the reader that Christ's resurrection is no longer mentioned. Paul now links the implications immediately to the denial of the resurrection of the dead. This is probably the reason why the type of implication is also different. In vv. 14-15 and 17-18 kerygma, faith, witnessing, and forgiveness of sins were dealt with; here the meaninglessness of Christian practice and apostolic dedication if there is no resurrection is brought to the fore. In v. 29 Paul probably refers to an unknown custom among the Corinthians. Some ask for a second baptism for the benefit of a dead pagan relative or friend. Paul does not judge this custom; he only employs it in his argumentation. In vv. 30-32 Paul writes autobiographically. Of course the "fight with wild animals" in Ephesus (v. 32) is metaphorically intended. Notice should be taken of the citation of Isa 22:13 at the end of v. 32.

In vv. 33-34 the Corinthians are addressed in the second person plural. The parenetic tone is sharp and polemical. In v. 33b a sentence of the Attic poet Menander is quoted. The last clause of v. 34 ("I say this to your shame") repeats what Paul wrote in 6:5 (cf. 4:14). "Some" in v. 34 recalls the beginning of the unit (v. 12: "some" of you say that there is no resurrection of the dead). A majority of exegetes assume that these Corinthians did not reject the immortality of the soul but only the future resurrection of the body. However, due attention should be given to vv. 29-32 and 33-34. It seems at least possible that according to Paul some Christians in Corinth denied all life after death.

The "How" of Our Future Bodily Resurrection (15:35-58)

Between the introductory questions of v. 35 and the parenetic conclusion (v. 58) the third unit can be divided into three subdivisions that appear concentrically arranged: vv. 36-44a (change), vv. 44b-49 (the Adam-Christ typology), and vv. 50-57 (change). The unit deals with the "how" of bodily resurrection. The second question of v. 35 concretizes the first.

In the first subdivision (vv. 36-44a) three steps are taken. Can the possibility of change and transformation be shown? Paul first relates an analogy from nature (vv. 36-38), then he comments on the different types of bodies (vv. 39-41), and finally he applies this to the resurrection of the dead (vv. 42-44a). In the first step he appeals to features of common experience: the buried seed and its new body. In the second step he stresses the differing shapes of "flesh"—here the term is neutral—and the variety of terrestrial and celestial bodies as well as their difference in splendor. The application follows in the third step. As with the seed, there is a sowing (dying) and raising of human bodies, and as there is a multiplicity of bodies and of their splendor in the cosmological order there is also a difference in splendor between earthly and heavenly human bodies. The earthly body is sown in perishability, dishonor, and weakness; the future body will be raised in imperishability, glory, and power. This leads Paul to the climax of the argumentation: "It is sown a physical body, it is raised a spiritual body" (v. 44a).

In vv. 44b-49 Paul's argument takes a turn. He now appeals to the authority of Scripture. The conditional period of v. 44b draws the conclusion from vv. 42-44a and clearly expresses Paul's conviction. On the basis of Gen 2:7 an Adam–Christ typology (cf. vv. 21-22) is developed in vv. 45-47 and then applied to believers in vv. 48-49. In v. 45 the general statement of v. 44b is concretized by means of the two Adams. In v. 46 the sequence is emphasized: the spiritual does not come first but the physical (differently from Philo's comment on Genesis 1 and 2). In v. 47 the origin of both men is indicated: from earth, from heaven. Verse 48 shows how the two figures determine the identity of the people they include. Verse 49 then says: As we (Christians) have borne the image of the man of dust, so we shall also bear the image of the man of heaven.

Within the third subdivision (vv. 50-57) we distinguish two steps: vv. 50-53 and vv. 54-57. In vv. 50-53 Paul first draws attention to the importance of the principle he is about to give: the opposition between the earthly person, living or dead, who is called "flesh and blood" as well as "corruption" and the reign of God characterized by incorruption. What is finite, fragile, and corruptible cannot inherit what is incorruptible. A turn of thought occurs in v. 51; a "mystery" is announced. Paul now focuses his attention more directly (and personally) on the time of the parousia. He expects to be among those who are still alive, but everyone, living and dead, must be changed. In v. 52ab he quickly adds a few details borrowed from apocalyptic imagery: the change will be instantaneous; it will be an end-time event (for the imagery, cf. 1 Thess 4:16). Still focusing on the parousia, Paul in v. 52cd distinguishes between the resurrection in imperishability of the dead and the transformation of the living. In v. 53 he resorts to a new image, that of clothing (cf. 2 Cor 5:2-4) to explain the transformation (of all) in yet another way.

In vv. 54-57 Paul further reflects on transformation. When the indispensable clothing process will have taken place the Scriptures that announce the destruction of death will be fulfilled.

"The saying that is written" introduces a combined quotation; in v. 54 Paul adapts Isa 25:8 and in v. 55 he radically reinterprets Hos 13:14 by giving that text a positive orientation. The expression "the sting of death" requires comment; it is provided in two laconic, typically Pauline statements on the relationship between death, sin, and law (v. 56). The annihilation of death is nothing other than the divine victory given to all Christians through Jesus Christ (v. 57). Verse 58 is the conclusion of vv. 50-57 as well as of the whole chapter: "Therefore, my beloved, be steadfast, immovable, always excelling in the work of the Lord, because you know that in the Lord your labor is not in vain."

A few more notes regarding the third unit should be added. The expression "as he has chosen" in v. 38 is also used in 12:18 for God's organization of the body. The celestial bodies in vv. 41-42 seem to be living beings. The bringing together of bodily and spiritual elements in v. 44 (= "a spiritual body," a body under the domination of the spirit) must have shocked the Corinthians. In v. 45b one expects "living spirit" rather than "living being"; Paul, however, daringly writes that the last Adam became a "life-giving spirit." The Adam-Christ typology is developed by means of the Jewish concept of corporate personality. In v. 48 there are still two separate groups (those of the earth, or dust, and those of heaven). In v. 49, however, only one class of people remains: Christians. They *have borne* (aorist) the image of the earthly man, they *will bear* (future) the image of the heavenly man. "Mystery" in v. 51 points to a secret truth about what will occur and be revealed in the eschaton. The term *kenos* in v. 58 (their labor will not be "in vain") occurs twice in v. 14; the same idea is present in v. 2 (unless you have come to believe "in vain," but employing a different Greek term).

An overall treatment of Paul's view of the future resurrection of believers must of course study passages such as 1 Thess 4:13-18; 2 Cor 5:1-11; and Phil 3:21. Already in 1 Cor 6:14 Paul wrote: "God raised the Lord and will also raise us by his power." It is clear that here, as well as in 15:22b-23, 49, 51-57, Paul does not think of a "general" resurrection but of that of "those who belong to Christ" (v. 23). Bodily resurrection means eschatological redemption of the whole human person, body and soul. Do many Christians today not repeat what some Corinthians said: "there is no resurrection of the dead" (v. 12)? Yet this Pauline (and genuinely Christian) hope is as central to our faith as the belief in Christ's sacrificial death for our sins (cf. vv. 3b-4).

The Collection and Travel Plans: 16:1-12

The division of the rather brief eighth section is easily provided: vv. 1-4 (the collection for the saints) and vv. 5-12 (the travel plans of Paul, Timothy, and Apollos). The section is framed by *peri de* ("now concerning") at the beginning in v. 1 and a last time in v. 12 at the end.

The collection is a free gift (see the word *charis* in v. 3). The "saints" are the poor of Jerusalem. To be sure, the gift is meant as a material help for them, but in Paul's opinion the collection should confirm and seal the communion between the Gentile Christians and the Jewish Christians, and also between the diaspora and the center. In a practical manner Paul indicates the way it must be organized. The expression "the first day of every week" (v. 2) already witnesses to the existence of the Christians' distinctive day of the week, the day of the Lord, our Sunday. One notices Paul's prudential planning for the transfer of the money to Jerusalem: people approved by the community of Corinth, letters that should facilitate hospitality in places on the way and in Jerusalem, and the possibility that he himself would become the leader of that mission. Paul wants to avoid any suspicion whatsoever of mismanagement in financial matters.

Macedonia, Corinth, and Ephesus are mentioned in vv. 5-12. Paul plans only to pass through Macedonia but to remain longer, perhaps even spend the winter, in Corinth. The "now" in v. 7 may contain a reference to Paul's second brief and painful visit of Corinth. For the time being, that is, "until Pentecost" (v. 8) he will stay in Ephesus. "A wide door for effective work" is open there but (lit. "and") there are also adversaries (v. 9). One feels Paul's unrelenting apostolic spirit. Paul is fond of the verb *energeō* and its derivatives (here the adjective *energēs;* cf. for example Gal 5:6: faith "made effective" through love). As in 4:17 Paul pleads for his beloved Timothy in vv. 10-11. He uses a language of loving concern; the Corinthians should not despise him. With regard to Apollos (v. 12) we may ask whether his clear decision not to return to Corinth at present is not motivated by his refusal to encourage the Apollos faction through his presence in Corinth. We may also ask whether Paul's emphasis on his urging Apollos to return is not a reaction to what is said in Corinth, namely that Apollos' absence is due to Paul's scheming.

Final Exhortations and Greetings: 16:13-24

In this last section we have Paul's final exhortation (vv. 13-14 and 15-18) as well as the greetings and his handwritten wishes (vv. 19-20 and 21-24).

The five imperatives in vv. 13-14 express an exhortation to eschatological vigilance, to strength and perseverance. In vv. 15-18 there is a special appeal regarding the household of Stephanas. The sentence in vv. 15-16 appears to be interrupted: "Now, brothers and sisters . . . I urge you": the *hina*-clause of v. 16 should be connected with this verb (for the construction cf. v. 12 and 1:10). In the rest of v. 15 Paul remembers who these people are and what they have done. Therefore they—and all similar fellow workers—should be duly appreciated by the Corinthians and their leadership accepted (vv. 16 and 18b). In vv. 17-18a Paul reflects on what the visit of Stephanas, Fortunatus, and Achaicus has meant to him.

In vv. 19-20 greetings are sent from the churches of the province of Asia, from Aquila and Prisca (who in Ephesus, as in Rome and Corinth, open their house for a "church"), and from all the Christians. The Corinthians in turn should greet "one another with a holy kiss." Then at the end (vv. 21-24) Paul writes his greetings and wishes in his own hand. Verse 22 contains the ultimately decisive rule of love of the Lord. The formula *"marana tha"* is in this context no doubt a wish; it could be and has later been read as *"maran atha"* which means "the Lord has come." The whole of v. 22 may have its origin in the celebration of the Lord's supper (cf. 11:27-32). Verse 23 reminds us of the salutation in 1:3. Paul concludes his letter in an affectionate tone: "My love be with all of you in Christ Jesus" (v. 24).

BIBLIOGRAPHY

Commentaries

Barrett, Charles Kingsley. *A Commentary on the First Epistle to the Corinthians.* BNTC. London: Adam and Charles Black, 1968.

Conzelmann, Hans. *1 Corinthians.* Hermeneia. Philadelphia: Fortress, 1975.

Fee, Gordon D. *The First Epistle to the Corinthians.* NIC.NT. Grand Rapids: Eerdmans, 1987.

Robertson, Archibald, and Alfred Plummer. *First Corinthians.* ICC. 2nd ed. Edinburgh: T & T Clark, 1914.

Snyder, Graydon F. *First Corinthians: A Faith Community Commentary.* Macon, Ga.: Mercer University Press, 1992.

Talbert, Charles. *Reading Corinthians: A Literary and Theological Commentary on 1 and 2 Corinthians.* New York: Crossroad, 1987.

Watson, Nigel. *The First Epistle to the Corinthians.* Epworth Commentaries. London: Epworth, 1992.

Monographs

Brown, Alexandra. *The Cross and Human Transformation: Paul's Apocalyptic Word in 1 Corinthians.* Minneapolis: Fortress, 1995.

Hurd, John C. *The Origin of I Corinthians.* London: SPCK, 1965.

Marshall, Peter. *Enmity in Corinth: Social Conventions in Paul's Relations with the Corinthians.* WUNT II, 23. Tübingen: Mohr, 1987.

Mitchell, Margaret Mary. *Paul and the Rhetoric of Reconciliation: An Exegetical Investigation of the Language and Composition of 1 Corinthians.* 1st American ed. Louisville: Westminster/John Knox, 1993.

Murphy-O'Connor, Jerome. *St. Paul's Corinth: Texts and Archaeology.* GNS 6. Wilmington, Del.: Michael Glazier, 1983.

Ramsaran, Rollin. *Liberating Words: Paul's Use of Rhetorical Maxims in 1 Corinthians 1–10.* SBL.DS 68. Chico: Scholars, 1985.

Theissen, Gerd. *The Social Setting of Pauline Christianity: Essays on Corinth.* Edinburgh: T & T Clark, 1982.

Yeo, Khiok-Khng. *Rhetorical Interaction in 1 Corinthians 8 and 10: A Formal Analysis with Preliminary Suggestions for a Chinese, Cross-Cultural Hermeneutic.* Leiden and New York: Brill, 1995.

2 Corinthians

Jorge Sanchez-Bosch

FIRST READING

First and Second Corinthians were clearly addressed to the same community. Second Corinthians was written shortly after First Corinthians. From 1 Corinthians (see commentary thereon) we can learn much about the Corinthian community, its evangelization, its diversity, and some of its problems.

If 1 Corinthians may be considered the most eloquent description of the actual life of a community during the first Christian generation, our letter is without a shadow of a doubt the most intimate account of Paul's personality and his deep-rooted sense of his vocation as an apostle of Christ. Second Corinthians enables one to enter deeply into the conscience of Paul. It shows in a special way how devoted the apostle could be to a person who lived on this earth (being poor, meek, and gentle, faithful to God and human beings, afflicted and put to death), but whom he had never met on this earth. Paul measures his inner feelings and his actions by this heroic figure and rejects (or tries to reject) everything that is not "according to the Lord." That brings him into conflict with himself because he feels ever so strongly the demands of his mission, which he is not able to fulfill in the "meek and gentle" way his Lord would have used.

At the same time the letter shows the extraordinary capacity God had granted to Paul for bringing God's light to a world dominated by "another god" (or many other gods) and for shepherding the people who once believed in Christ but were often in danger of wandering from him. In a theoretical and practical way the apostle shows us his "weapons": looking deep into the soul of each person, trusting him or her, and then, at the deepest level of his soul, speaking to his or her conscience. Neither human "prestige" nor diplomacy were considered. His only "technique" was to be more "in Christ" than others were so that Christ himself might speak through him.

Second Corinthians is not in fact the second letter written by the apostle to that community. Our 1 Corinthians itself (5:9) alludes to a previous letter. Critical exegesis strongly suggests that at least in the first nine chapters our letter is not even the third letter Paul wrote to the Corinthians. It was preceded by a "tearful letter" alluded to in 2 Cor 2:3-4, 9; 7:12, dealing with very severe problems Paul had to work out with his Corinthian faithful.

Second Corinthians begins as a letter of reconciliation and develops into a laudatory discourse about the apostolic mission itself (mainly from 3:1 to 6:10). The kernel of the discourse is the vision of apostolic mission as a participation in the illuminating power of God (4:1-6), which is not obscured by the fact that "we have this treasure in clay jars" (vv. 7-12).

Following two minor sections about the collection being organized for the brothers and sisters in Jerusalem (chs. 8 and 9) the last four chapters of the letter (chs. 10–14) take the form of an extremely personal apology of Paul in which the apostle defends his position even if he is going to be taken for a "fool" (see especially 11:1–12:10). The kernel of this second discourse is a "list of adventures" (11:22-33) that marks the difference between Paul and any of his potential opponents.

Many readers may ask if Paul is not going too far in his boasting. The apostle himself was anxious about that possibility. But at least he had very worthy excuses: he was stating only the truth; he was not boasting of his own merits but of the work of God's grace; and this boasting had been made absolutely necessary in face of the dissension created by other people.

I. Circumstances of the Letter

The Crisis in Corinth

We know that 1 Corinthians was occasioned by bad news Paul had received from Corinth and questions the Corinthians had posed to him. This might have given him moments of concern but it did not represent a tragedy: he knew what the starting point was for many of their lives (1 Cor 6:9-11) and at the same time he saw how the witness of Christ affirmed itself among them (1 Cor 1:5-8). The divisions into groups obscured the sense of community experienced by the faithful as the one Church of Christ (1 Cor 11:22) but did not disrupt it: all the faithful kept meeting together (1 Cor 11:17-18, 20, 33; 14:23, 26). The conduct of the incestuous man would have been unacceptable even to pagans (1 Cor 5:1) but the apostle was sure that the "old yeast . . . of malice and evil" would be expelled and make possible a new Passover celebration (1 Cor 5:7-8).

But in a short time, almost certainly less than two years after the writing of 1 Corinthians, the apostle was the object of three virtually simultaneous (and perhaps coordinated) attacks: in Corinth, in Galatia, and in Philippi. We learn something of the last two from the introductions to the respective letters (Galatians and Philippians). As for the Corinthian crisis, which is the best attested, it appears that Paul paid a second visit to Corinth, even though Acts does not mention it, and that he was not well received. We do not know whether Timothy or others had informed Paul beforehand. From 2 Cor 2:1 we can infer rather that the apostle was already "sad" as he undertook this trip. In Corinth he met somebody who grieved (2:5) and offended him (7:12). It seems that Paul was not willing to respond face to face to the offenders but that later he wrote a letter "with many tears" to the community (2:3-4, 9; 7:8, 12: the so called "intermediate" letter written between the first and the second). This hypothesis of an "intermediate" visit and an "intermediate" letter compels us to read 2 Corinthians not as an explanation of 1 Corinthians but as a response to new facts.

It is still possible to find commentaries or interpretations, for the most part older works, that understand all the above texts directly in light of 1 Corinthians: the visit of 2 Cor 2:1 would refer to the same evangelization mentioned in 1 Cor 2:3 where Paul was "in weakness and in fear and in much trembling"; the letter referred to in 2 Cor 2:3-4, 9; 7:8, 12 would be 1 Corinthians, mainly because of the incestuous man (5:1), identified as such with the one who caused him pain (2 Cor 2:5) and wronged him (7:12).

It is impossible for us to imagine the evangelization of Corinth, the mission during which Paul brought them the "Good News," as a visit made "in pain." It is even more difficult to read 1 Corinthians as a letter written "out of much distress and anguish of heart and with many tears" (2 Cor 2:4). Furthermore, in 2 Cor 2:5 and 7:12 we see the prestige of Paul and his position in the community much more at stake than would be the case in a dispute over incest. We must therefore read 2 Corinthians in the light of 2 Corinthians itself.

"The one who did the wrong" (2 Cor 7:12) may have been a member of the community but the crisis had been provoked by a group of Judeo-Christians who came from abroad to take over the community. Instead of finding a clear rebuke from the Corinthians they were accepted and even "tolerated" by them (see 2 Cor 11:4, 20) though they behaved in a somewhat tyrannical way (v. 20).

We infer the Jewish origin of this group from 2 Cor 11:22. Sometimes Paul seems to accept their "belonging to Christ" (10:7) and being "ministers of Christ" (11:23). But between these verses he denies them any credibility, calling them "false apostles," "deceitful workers," "ministers of Satan" who "disguis[e] themselves as apostles of Christ" and "ministers of righteousness" (11:13, 15).

Except for these apparently contradictory texts we find only indirect references to his opponents. We can assume with almost complete certitude that they are the "some" who arrive with letters of recommendation (3:1), and the "many" who are "peddlers of God's word" (2:17) and even "falsify" it (4:2). They are dealing with the same word of God that Paul deals with, but not in the same way. This would exclude (though not all commentators agree) their identification with the unbelievers of 2:14-15; 3:14-15; 4:3-4.

Other references to his opponents can be found in 10:12-15: they are surely those "who commend themselves" (v. 12) but indirectly the apostle probably refers to them as those who "boast beyond limits" (v. 13), "overstepping [their] limits" (v. 14, on the lines of 3:1). They are those who "boast beyond limits . . . in the labors of others" (v. 15), people who enter another person's field when the fruits are ripe.

It is clear that his opponents could not boast of more apostolic work (see 10:13-16) or of more "battle scars" than Paul (see 11:23b-29), but is not so evident that they enjoyed more "visions and revelations" (see 12:1) or more "signs and wonders and mighty works" (12:12) than he did. In general Paul's words do not demonstrate that they are "Gnostics" or followers of a wonder-working "divine man." Not every word Paul uses in his own defense should be understood as a reflection of the accusations directed against him or of the "theology" of his opponents.

Nowhere do these opponents require others to be circumcised. The reference to "another gospel" (11:4; cf. Gal 1:6-7) and the words: "when somebody makes slaves of you" (11:20; cf. Gal 2:4-5) are not clear statements, but conditional phrases, possibly highly rhetorical. In no case should reference to "another Jesus," "a different spirit" and "a different gospel" (11:4) lead us to the conclusion that they were not preaching about Jesus of Nazareth and the Spirit and gospel that originated in him.

The only thing that is clear is that these people wanted to discredit Paul with petty quibbles: whether he had to visit them twice or only once (1:15-17); whether his letters were harsher than his personal presence (10:10); whether he did not accept money from his converts while others did (11:7); whether he took money from other communities but not from this one (11:9, 11; 12:13). Personally his opponents had nothing that might make them superior to Paul. Their strength, unlike Paul's, depended on the letters of recommendation they offered (3:1). We do not know who was supposed to be recommending them or whether the letters were true or false. We are inclined to think that in one way or another Paul's opponents involved the great Jerusalem apostles in their campaign, saying: "there is no comparison between this apostle of yours and the great Jerusalem apostles" with whom they were well acquainted. In this sense we can understand the two texts in which the apostle says that he does not feel being "less" than the great apostles (11:5; 12:11: the qualification "super-apostles" is not necessarily pejorative). At this stage of evangelization no one in the newly converted world had any authority to stand before (let alone in the way of) a man who had worked as much as Paul except those who were apostles before him (see Gal 1:17-18).

At the same time we do not believe that those who were apostles before him in fact promoted or approved of the campaign against Paul. The decisive consideration from a historical point of view is the fact that the crisis is occurring simultaneously with a great collection on behalf of the Jerusalem community. It is unlikely that the pillars of the church in Jerusalem would have requested help while declaring war on him; it is even less likely that Paul would have organized the collection if he thought the Jerusalem apostles were ready to destroy a project of which they had approved only two or three years earlier (Gal 2:6-9).

In Galatians 2 we distinguish between the "pillars" of the Church who gave Paul and Barnabas the right hand of fellowship (vv. 6, 9) and the "false believers secretly brought in" (v. 4) who opposed them. The latter could have organized the Galatian campaign but on coming to Corinth they may have discovered that to require circumcision was asking too much to begin with, and thus decided to speak only of the "true" Jesus, the "true" gospel (see 4:11) and the "true" apostles (see 11:5; 12:11). The important thing for the moment was to get rid of Paul. The rest would come later.

Immediate Occasion of the Letter

The crisis, as such, is the immediate occasion of the "tearful letter," lost in theory but possibly corresponding, as we will discuss below, to 2 Corinthians 10–13. Our "2 Corinthians," at least in its first chapters, reflects a more or less complete resolution of the same crisis and seems to presuppose a few specific events subsequent to the "tearful letter." Among these was the fear of death from which the apostle had been liberated shortly before (2 Cor 1:8-10). This "fear" could also have included a few months of imprisonment. It is possible that once Paul was liberated from prison he was asked to leave the city (see Acts 16:36-39). He might have understood also that other people (if we read Phil 1:14-18 into the Ephesian situation) would have been able to take care of the churches of Asia. We possess two fairly coincident descriptions of his plans at this time. According to Acts (19:21-22) "Paul resolved . . . to go through Macedonia and Achaia, and then to go on to Jerusalem. . . . So he sent two of his helpers, Timothy and Erastus, to Macedonia, while he himself stayed for some time longer in Asia." According to 2 Cor 1:15-16 this was not his original plan: he had already wanted to come to Corinth twice (before and after Macedonia) and then travel to Judea.

The fact that there are no doubts about the journey to Judea demonstrates that the weekly collection of money for the community of Jerusalem proceeded rather well, if we consider 1 Cor 16:3-4 (see v. 3: "If it seems advisable that I should go also, they will accompany me"). Probably the counsel that it was "advisable" for him to travel with them to Jerusalem came from Macedonia more than from Achaia, but also from Achaia if what Paul later told the Macedonians ("Achaia has been ready since last year; and your zeal has stirred up most of them," 2 Cor 9:2) was not a pure lie (we do not exclude a certain exaggeration).

Certainly if the apostle had the thought of granting a "double benefit" to Corinth it was because at that moment he was sure of their support (2 Cor 1:15, "Since I was sure of this . . ."). The crisis initiated later was overcome or reinitiated before Paul could keep his promises. He did not want another personal confrontation (according to v. 23, "to spare you"), and sent them Titus.

Meanwhile he went to Troas, but anxiety (and bad news) drew Paul from Troas and made him go to Macedonia (2:12-13). In Macedonia Paul received some good news, thanks to the fine diplomacy of Titus (7:5-7, 13). The time again came to send Titus—always so eager (8:16-17)—together with another mysterious brother (8:18) to definitively prepare the collection because the apostle does not want it being taken in his presence (1 Cor 16:2). These are the circumstances of 2 Corinthians, or at least of its first seven chapters.

If 2 Corinthians were in fact only one letter it would be easy to describe where it was composed and its relative chronology: written from Macedonia after the arrival of Titus, as the collection was in its final stages, close to the winter the apostle spent "in Greece" (see Acts 20:1-3) before he went to Jerusalem. According to the most widely accepted chronology this corresponds to the "summer" of 57 C.E. The difficult thing, we repeat, is to know whether the whole letter proceeds from the same situation. In this sense 2 Corinthians may include different parts written before or after the first seven chapters: but that is not a long time, because the whole crisis did not last more than two years.

II. Major Literary Divisions

Second Corinthians is in the view of all scholars a rather complicated construction. From the point of view of its stylistic construction, without presupposing (nor excluding) from the start that they are really different letters (that is, sent at different moments), we will speak of several "letters."

Some of them are relatively easy to distinguish: for instance the division between chs. 8 and 9. Both have similar contents (exhortation concerning the collection) but ch. 9 seems to ignore what has been said in ch. 8: "Now it is not necessary for me to write you about the ministry to the saints . . ." (v. 1), alluding to 1 Cor 16:1 but ignoring the preceding twenty-four verses. At the same time it would be logical that at the end of the letter Paul should mention the collection, as he does in 1 Cor 16:1-4 and Rom 15:26-28. Therefore it would be stylistically acceptable to locate ch. 8 in the same letter as chs. 1–7, but this is not so for ch. 9 because of its beginning and the repetition of the same contents. It seems even less likely that after a long speech about the collection Paul would again start a long polemic lasting four chapters. That is why we will speak of chs. 10–13 provisionally as from another letter. We will distinguish therefore:

A. The letter of reconciliation (chs. 1 to 7);
B. First note about the collection (ch. 8);
C. Second note about the collection (ch. 9);
D. Paul's apology (chs. 10–13).

On the other hand there are so many linguistic and historical connections within the different parts of 2 Corinthians that it would not be logical to treat the different parts in absolute isolation (due also to the lack of unity within the many "partitions"). Therefore we study the letter as it is, observing the differences in level where we find them but not regarding as definitive any conclusions we may reach in our discussion of the unity of the letter.

Further divisions within letters B, C, and D create no problems for scholars and can be discussed directly in our second reading, but the same cannot be said of letter A. In the first seven chapters it is easy, after the address (1:1-2) and the *exordium* (1:3-7) to distinguish between an eminently narrative portion at the beginning and end of the "letter" (1:8–2:13 and 7:5-16) and a central and much more "argumentative" portion. The delimitation of "portions" can be placed provisionally at the end of 2:13 and the beginning of 7:5 because the first text ends with the words: "I went to Macedonia" and the second begins: "when we came into Macedonia." Between the two the story of his travels seems to have been forgotten, with the exception of 2:14-17 and 6:11-13; 7:2-4, amplifying the two narrative "portions."

At 3:1 begins a series of "self-commendations" by the apostle that, as we will see, continues over four chapters to 6:4-10, where the phrase "we have commended ourselves" is determined by two dozen circumstantial complements. Between these two points we see an argumentative section about the commendations of the apostle.

The subsequent material is more complicated because of a strange note between 6:14 and 7:1. If we consider this section as something different we will see that what we read in 6:11-13 as well as what we read in 7:2-4 can be taken as a good example of what happened to Paul on his arrival at Macedonia (7:5). Taking the text as we have it we can append 6:11-13 and 7:2-4 to the note about separation (6:14–7:1), as constructing a transition to the second narrative portion (7:5-16).

Without rejecting mutual relationships among them we will divide this first "letter" into four parts:

I. Epistolary prologue (1:1-7)
II. First narrative section (1:8–2:17)
III. The apostle's "commendations" (3:1–6:10)
IV. Transition (6:11–7:4)
V. Second narrative section (7:5-16)

In fact the number of scholars who consider 6:14–7:1 as authentic and rightly placed is increasing. These are open questions we will discuss immediately.

III. The Composition of 2 Corinthians

To say that these different portions, or at least some of them, are in fact different letters is to pass from a literary analysis to a historical statement. At this point opinions are less in agreement, but we must face the question at least for the sake of understanding other people's opinions.

The tendency to distinguish several letters in 2 Corinthians began more than two hundred years ago and still continues. Most of the problems have been mentioned above in the discussion of the major divisions of the letter. Using the same terminology we will try to answer three questions: whether "letter" A, the letter of reconciliation (chs. 1 to 7), is a unit or a composite of two or three letters; whether either of the "letters" B and C, the two notes about the collection (chs. 8–9), was appended to "letter" A or whether they were independent; and whether "letter" D, Paul's apology (chs. 10–13), was an independent letter, and if so whether D was prior or subsequent to A.

The Letter of Reconciliation (2 Corinthians 1–7)

The unity of the first seven chapters has in its favor the beginning and end of the letter: from the salutation (1:1-2) and the *exordium* (1:3-7) it moves on to news about afflictions recently suffered (1:8-11) and praise for the mutual understanding between the apostle and his community (1:12-14), with a smooth transition to the narrative about the satisfactory solution to the crisis (1:15–2:13), a subject continued in 7:5-16. But the problem arises precisely from the mutual attraction between 2:13 and 7:5 (departing for Macedonia, arriving in Macedonia). Many authors would assign the text between these two verses to another letter, stressing the controversial points contained in the remaining discourse and referring them to another moment in the crisis.

However, as I have said and the commentary seems to substantiate, 2:14-17 appears closely related to 2:13, while 6:11-13; 7:2-4 (leaving aside the contested fragment 6:14–7:1) seem to be closely connected to 7:5, forming a transition only the apostle himself could have written. So in my opinion chs. 1 to 7, except for the contested fragment, were sent as a single letter. My only reservation is that 3:1–6:10 (the apostle's "commendations") could have been taken from a preexisting sermon written by Paul and adapted subsequently to the present circumstances.

The complete unity of the seven chapters seems to be broken only by the disputed fragment 6:14–7:1. Some authors contest its authenticity, while for others it might be a fragment from the "very first" letter the apostle sent to Corinth (see 1 Cor 5:9). I do not favor assuming its spurious character nor do I see it as belonging to the "very first" letter. In fact the problem in the lost letter was the lack of morality, and here we have idolatry and lack of faith. However in prophetic tradition idolatry is often regarded as immorality, and immorality as idolatry. In my opinion these verses may belong to a speech against falling back into idolatry (see 1 Cor 10:14) and could have been included here by later ecclesiastics who had heretics in mind, identifying the opponents of Paul with the nonbelievers alluded to in the letter (2:15-16; 4:3-4). This, however, does not fit with my reconstruction of the facts.

The Two Notes on the Collection (2 Corinthians 8–9)

We have mentioned a few reasons for dividing chs. 8 and 9: their similar content (exhortation about the collection) and the fact that ch. 9 seems to ignore what has been said in ch. 8—". . . about the ministry to the saints . . ." (v. 1), alluding to 1 Cor 16:1, but as if the preceding twenty-four verses had not discussed the same subject.

Some scholars insist on the unity of these two chapters, but many more would do so if chs. 10–13 did not present still greater difficulties. Once we have accepted these last four chapters as being "somewhat different" we are then ready to accept arguments about the chapter that precedes them.

Chapter 9 could be part of a letter sent before, also from Macedonia (v. 2). In the midst of the crisis, as a sort of test and without mentioning any problems, Paul would have sent a letter to the churches of Achaia reminding them of their commitment to the church in Jerusalem. This would be high strategy, inviting his friends to enter into action.

Paul's Apology (2 Corinthians 10–13)

Chapters 10–13 form a unit we could call "Paul and his opponents." The difficulty is to fit them in with ch. 7, as well as with 8 and 9, which have a kind of conclusive character. The opinion has been often repeated that these chapters are the "tearful letter" spoken of in 2:4. This, however, is not a unanimous opinion because, among other things, in the context of 2:3-9 and 7:12 (both of which mention the same letter) the accent is on the offense inflicted by a member of the community, while chs. 10–13 concentrate on opponents who have come from abroad (see 11:4, 13-15, 22-23). Thus it should be considered a "second tearful letter" or we should look for another solution.

It is certainly difficult to measure the "tearfulness" of a piece of writing, but it is hard for us to attribute so many tears to 2 Corinthians 10–13 where the apostle begins with the language of a victorious general (10:3-6) and where he "boasts" so loudly (10:8, 13, 15-17; 11:12, 16, 18, 30; 12:1, 5-6, 9; see 11:10, 17). On the other hand I think that 10:9-11 refers to the "tearful letter" as having been "weighty and strong." If these chapters really mention that letter they cannot belong to it. We would say the same about the mention of Titus (12:18), whose visit takes place after that letter.

The history that follows (see Rom 15:23, 25-28) unfolds on the lines of reconciliation announced in chs. 1–8: Paul goes to Corinth, stays there for three months (Acts 20:2-3), takes the collection and departs for Jerusalem with the idea that this chapter of his life has ended happily. This would play against the possibility that the reconciliation could have been countered by a revival of the crisis. It is possible that Paul's letter asking for more money after the reconciliation encouraged his enemies to new opposition in which they enjoyed some success and provoked the attack we read about in chs. 10–13, but this time the apostle does not renounce his visit: he is ready to be as "weighty and strong" when present as he was in the "tearful letter" (10:6, 9-11; 12:20-21; 13:1-2, 10). Either through this last letter or through his personal work Paul in all likelihood obtained a full settlement, as we assume from the continuation of the story.

IV. The Letter in the Life of the Church

Our letter has strongly served, perhaps more than the book of Acts, to underscore the heroic dimensions of the figure of the apostle (especially 11:23-27), together with the ardor of his pastoral worries (11:28-29), according to the motto we read in 5:14: "the love of Christ urges us on." The doubts the apostle expresses about his own behavior (see 11:17, 23) did not cause any blame to fall on him: they were interpreted ironically (see 10:12), given that his behavior was fully justified by the need to defend a good cause (see 5:13; 12:5).

The whole of Christian doctrine has found confirmation along with brilliant formulations in 2 Corinthians. The Christ's earthly figure in Christian consciousness also owes something to 2 Corinthians, which stresses "the meekness and gentleness of Christ" (10:1), he being God's unchangeable "amen" to the promises (1:19-20) for those "anointed" by the Spirit (1:21-22). Tradition also mediates the letter's new formulations describing Christ's death: "crucified in weakness" (13:4), "For our sake [God] made him to be sin" (5:21), as well as the very graphic expressions about Christian and apostolic participation in the sufferings and death of Christ: "the sufferings of Christ are abundant for us" (1:5); "carrying in the body the death of Jesus" (4:10); "one has died for all; therefore all have died" (5:14). Even the word *mortificatio* used by the Vulgate in 4:10 has given a name to ascetic praxis.

The Church has no doubts that Christ's affliction and death are only temporary and that his glory shines through our sufferings in this earthly life. As for 2 Corinthians, tradition finds this idea expressed in the "triumphal procession" of Christ communicated to the world (2:14) and in the comparison between Moses and the ministers of the new covenant, so favorable to the latter (3:8-11). The same text opens the way to a progressive "transformation" of believers (the Church Fathers will say "divinization"). The "visions and revelations" of Paul and his mystical ascent to the third heaven (12:2-4) have also been fully incorporated by Christian mystics.

As for the idea of God's fatherlike attitude toward us (6:18), the relationship between God's being "Father of mercies" and "Father of our Lord Jesus Christ" (1:3) was never questioned. In ancient times the idea of God making an exception with God's own Son was inconceivable: Christ being made "sin" for us (5:21) was interpreted by many (Augustine, Cyril of Alexandria, Ambrosiaster, Thomas) as "sacrifice for sin," by others, in conjunction with Gal 3:13, as his "being treated" as a sinner but not because of the anger of God. This theory was initiated by Anselm of Canterbury to speak of God's need for "satisfaction," thus contributing to a more tragic image of God.

The blessing of 13:13 has always been clearly understood in a Trinitarian sense, and this Trinitarian faith has not been disturbed by the famous phrase about "the Lord" being "the Spirit" (v. 17a): the latter was not understood as a confusion of the Son with the Holy Spirit but as a statement of the Spirit's divine character *(et in Spiritum Sanctum Dominum)*. Perhaps this is not the correct interpretation of this text but it corresponds to the principle of not destroying a theology based on the whole of the NT because of one text.

Some symbols used in this letter have a special influence in the sacramental and liturgical life of the Church. These include "illumination" (4:4), "anointing," "seal," and "pledge" (1:21-22). The splendor of many Christian rites refers to the idea of matching Moses' splendor (3:7-11), and processions with an abundant use of incense have to do with the idea of the triumphal procession of Christ in which his fragrance spreads abroad (2:14-15).

As for the theology of the ministry, 2 Corinthians offers its special contribution in stressing a specific participation of ministers in the sufferings of Christ (see 4:12; 13:3-4), whereby a minister is a believer (4:13) with a special assignment (10:13). Catholic and Orthodox traditions with their sense of apostolic succession have insisted on this very last point, while Protestants with their *theologia crucis* and priesthood of the laity insisted more on humility and equality.

SECOND READING

The Letter of Reconciliation: 2 Corinthians 1–7

Epistolary Prologue (1:1-7)

(1) The *address* (1:1-2), somewhat expanded, is very similar to that of 1 Corinthians: Paul describes himself again as an apostle by the will of God (v. 1a); he also describes the Corinthian church as "the church of God" and "the saints," and Timothy (no mention of Sosthenes) as "brother" (v. 1b); he adds no other names, but includes "all the saints throughout Achaia" (thus including Athens at least); the salutation (v. 2) is exactly the same as in 1 Corinthians.

(2) The *exordium* (1:3-7) also takes the form of a thanksgiving (more like a blessing) but concentrates on the affliction and the comfort Paul has experienced instead of mentioning the manifold grace the community has received (perhaps because he cannot praise them in all respects). Defining God as "the Father of our Lord Jesus Christ" (v. 3; see 11:31; Rom 15:6), Paul stresses the uniqueness of Christ's sonship (see the solemnity of "the Son of God, Jesus Christ" in v. 19) and the importance of this revelation for our idea of God who as a result appears much more as a "Father of mercies." As such God has comforted Paul in his affliction so that he in turn might comfort others (v. 4), partaking of the mission of the Son: both affliction and comfort are "Christ's" (v. 5; see Col 1:24) and are for the good of the community (v. 6) as are Christ's sufferings and glory. So in a nearly poetic tone and in the form of a prayer Paul has vindicated his position at the side of Christ and the Father, even underlining his part in Christ's sufferings. He can only express the hope that the faithful will participate in both aspects of the mystery (v. 7).

First Narrative Section (1:8–2:17)

A narrative section begins at 1:8 ("We do not want you to be unaware, brothers and sisters . . .") and pauses at the end of v. 11 with a rather solemn phrase. There follows a reflection (v. 12: "Indeed, this is our boast . . .") related not to what preceded but to what follows. The story resumes at v. 15 ("Since I was sure of this, I wanted to come to you first . . .") but it adopts an increasingly reflective intensity to the point of needing a pause at the end of v. 21. Moreover v. 23 has something of the character of a new beginning ("But I call on God as witness against me . . ."). The story follows in a more or less continuous manner up to 2:11, which also seems to need a pause. The new beginning is provided by a change of scene ("When I came to Troas . . ." in v. 12). The story ends for the moment at v. 13 and will resume at 7:5, but as we mentioned, the reflection that follows seems to connect with what has been said as well as with 1:12-14.

In the first story (1:8-11) Paul describes somewhat obscurely the affliction (see v. 4) from which he has been liberated in Asia (the Ephesus region): he even despaired of living (v. 8), sensing that a death sentence had been passed on him (v. 9a). We do not believe this refers to a real judicial process, but to preventive detention that may have lasted for several months. The fear of a possible death sentence brings him closer to the mystery of Christ: not only the binomial suffering–consolation (as in 1:5) but also death–resurrection (1:9b), a liberation he has often experienced (1:10; see 4:11-12; 11:23). The help of the faithful (1:11; see 1:7) enters forcefully into the story in view of the next reflection and the remaining story.

"We have behaved in the world with frankness (1:12) Paul "boasts," with an assurance only a good conscience can give. He alludes for the first time to his opponents, who must conceal their inner soul beneath external arguments (see commentary to 5:12). The proofs of his transparency (even today's readers can confirm this!) are his letters, opening the apostle's soul and not signifying more than they say (1:13a). He hopes that most of his converts (the words "in part" refer to a minority of opponents) will know it in any circumstance because they know him (1:13b-14a). Others may be convinced by the fact that they will need each other before Christ's tribunal (1:14b; see 5:10). "I hope" and "in part," in vv. 13-14 sound like last minute additions to the phrase but are fully justified by the rest of the letter.

The second story begins with an explanation of Paul's change of plans (1:15-22). He had promised them a double visit (1:15) before and after going to Macedonia (1:16). He would have done that if Achaia (including Corinth) had been in fact ready with the collection (9:2): he thought that in this manner he could impress the Macedonians more. His change of plans was interpreted as frivolity or selfishness (literally, acting "according to the flesh": v. 17) or as favoritism toward the other region (see 11:11; 12:13-15). He denies this for he can identify himself with every aspect of the work of Christ. His word is not "yes and no" (1:18). Like the word of Christ he and his companions preach (1:19) it is a "yes," an "amen" to the promises of God (1:20). The apostle confirms this identification, playing with the word "Christ" (which means "anointed") and referring to Christ's "anointing" by the Spirit (1:21-22).

The change of plans came from his remembering an unpleasant experience (1:23–2:11). Paul had to "spare" his faithful (1:23) because they are not his personal property (1:24). Let us reconstruct the sequence of events. Once he went to them in sadness (2:1: somebody may have warned him) and somebody offended him in public (2:5). Following the visit he wrote a very sad letter assuring them of his love (2:4) and expecting from them a demonstration of their obedience (2:9). As long as the demonstration did not arrive he postponed the planned visit, for he did not desire a repetition of what had happened from those who were his unique joy (2:2-3). Anticipating the end of the story, Paul says that now things have changed: the majority (2:6; see v. 5: "to some extent . . . all of you") have shown with a clear reproach their adherence to Paul and this may have touched the same person who had offended him. The apostle forgives this person (2:10) and exhorts his friends to a similar forgiveness (2:7a, 8) lest this sadness (2:7b) carry the offender into the arms of Satan (2:11; see 11:14). This could mean that the real promoters of the crisis were still active.

Returning to the crisis he tells of his journey to Troas and Macedonia (2:12-13). In Troas Paul had a certain apostolic success (2:12) but the anxiety of not finding Titus there compelled him to depart for Macedonia (2:13). If the "affliction" in Asia (1:8-9) involved an imprisonment we can imagine that he may have been released and then invited to leave town. So he went to Troas simply to "do something"; there, although he was full of anxiety, he enjoyed an apostolic success.

Second reflection: God bears us in triumph (2:14-17). As at Troas the gospel continues its triumphal journey despite persecutions (2:14). Paul is associated with this triumph as a fragrance to its origin (2:15); therefore we fail to see here the emphasis on his humiliation (as the comparison with Col 2:15 might suggest) but instead on his being a coworker of Christ (as in 1:5 with Christ's afflictions and 1:18-22 with Christ's word and "anointing"). This fragrance can be deadly for unbelievers who persecute it (2:15b, 16a). His opponents, in my opinion, are not mentioned until a new question is raised: "Who is sufficient for these things?" (2:16b). Someone who "peddles" the word of God (2:17a) will not be capable of the ministry because such a one's personal interests will obscure the pure shining light of Christ (see 4:4). The necessary purity is expressed here with four attributes: sincerity, being in Christ, being sent from God, and standing in God's presence (2:17b).

The Apostle's Recommendations (3:1–6:10)

A new subject starts at 3:1 in the sense that the idea of self-commendation, provoked by the recommendation letters the "opponents" have put forward continues, as we will see, as the frame of the discourse (see 4:2; 5:12; 6:4). The word "again" presupposes something previous: it could refer to his presenting himself as associated with Christ or with God (see 1:5, 12, 18-21) but it touches especially the rude confrontation with the opponents put forward in 2:17. In any case it is right to take the preceding verses as a kind of transition to the following discourse.

Up to the end of 6:10 the argumentation has these opponents in view in a polemic way but abstains from making specific allusions to the problems of the apostle with the Corinthians. The address in 6:11 is very solemn (it is the only time we read the word "Corinthians" in all the letters). It induces us to place there the beginning of a new section that we call "transition."

The "discourse" itself could be divided as follows:

1. *Exordium:* we do not need recommendations (3:1-3)
2. *Propositio:* our ministry comes from God (3:4-6)
3. Historical argument: the comparison with Moses (3:7-18)
    a. Two levels of splendor (3:7-11)
    b. Two different behaviors (3:12-18)
4. Theological argument (4:1–5:10)

   a. A ministry of pure light (4:2-6)
   b. Contained in earthen lamps (4:7-12)
   c. Therefore we are courageous (4:13-15)
   d. To the end of our days (4:16–5:10)
5. Christological argument
   a. Christ compels us (5:11-15)
   b. Christ is present in us (5:16-21)
   c. Because we are similar to him (6:1-10)

1. Exordium: *We Do Not Need Recommendations, 3:1-3*

Paul dislikes a personal confrontation even though now and again he will have to engage in it (see 2:17; 4:2; 5:12; 11:12-15, 18, 21-23; 12:11). That explains the rather nervous tone of 3:1. He also dislikes being recommended by other people: in his view the very need for human recommendations disqualifies those who seek them (v. 1b). He is simply happy at being recommended by God and by the signs of God's presence, just like his faithful, who are an open letter written in the heart (3:2) by the Spirit (not with ink or on stone tablets). With a bold turn the apostle has passed from the letters of recommendation to the law written in the heart according to Jeremiah (Jer 31:31, 33) and Ezekiel (Ezek 11:19; 36:26). The implicit argument is: "In the hearts of my faithful you may discover that the new covenant is at work, and so I am its minister" (see 3:3: "prepared by us").

2. Propositio: *Our Ministry Comes from God, 3:4-6*

What Paul claims is to have Christ and God on his side (3:4). He ought to be accepted because he is a "competent" (3:5a, as in 2:16; see in 3:5b, 6, the substantive and the verb "to make competent") minister of the new covenant, but that is God's work, not his own (3:5). The emphasis on God's action was precisely a sign of the new covenant (3:6a) according to Jeremiah and Ezekiel: God had to write the divine Law in their hearts because by themselves they were incapable of fulfilling the Law of Moses. In this sense Paul can say that the letter (of the Law) kills because it is incapable of doing what the Spirit does: give life (3:6b; see John 6:63).

3. Historical Argument: The Comparison with Moses, 3:7-18

Elaborating on these prophetic texts, Paul has spoken of "hearts" (3:2-3; see 1:22), of "the Spirit" (3:3, 6; see 1:22), of "stone tablets" (3:3), the "new covenant" (3:6), and the mediation of "ministers" (3:3, 6). Now he comes to the comparison between ministers: Moses and the apostle.

a. Two Levels of Splendor (3:7-11)

The main argument is clear: if someone who brings about death can be enveloped with splendor (3:7), much more so the one who brings life (3:8). The splendor of the first will be irrelevant compared with that of the second (3:10). Verse 9 repeats the argument, putting condemnation–justification in place of death–Spirit. Verse 11 stresses the fact that, as mentioned at the end of v. 7, Moses' splendor was passing away. To understand this we may refer to Ezekiel and to other letters of Paul: the Law of Moses came from God (see Rom 7:12, 14, 22, 25; 8:7) but, because of the "stone hearts" of human beings (Ezek 11:19; 36:26) it was unable to obtain salvation (see Gal 3:21, 24; Rom 7:14-25; 8:6-7). The ministry of Moses brought only death (3:7; see v. 6b); nevertheless it was full of splendor because of its divine origin. The book of Exodus does not say that Moses' splendor was passing away: the statements in 2 Cor 3:7, 11 may refer to some tradition about the veil of Moses (see below at 3:12) or to the fact that the old covenant had to give way to the new (see Gal 3:19; 4:2; Heb 8:13).

b. Two Different Behaviors (3:12-18)

The "hope" of not passing away eternally is only alluded to: it will be widely expressed in the central section (4:16–5:10). Now it is important to see that this hope gives the apostle a boldness (3:12) Moses did not have: Moses used to put a veil on his face so that people could not notice that the splendor was fading (v. 13: because he had ceased looking to the Lord?—see v. 16). Hence Paul concludes that the minds of the people were hardened (v. 14a), as if they had a veil on their faces (v. 15: "over their minds"). It is unlikely that someone at that time would refer to a book or series of books as "the Old Testament," but Paul says it indirectly: "when they hear the reading of the old covenant" (v. 14b; similar to v. 15a, "whenever Moses is read"). Christ, he adds, removes the veil (v. 14c), for "when one turns to the Lord, the veil is removed" (3:16). Verse 16, I believe, refers to

Moses, the verb being in the singular, while vv. 13-15 have the plural; the quotation of Exod 34:34 is also clear enough. We understand that Paul is referring to this text when he says: "the Lord" *(here)* is "the Spirit" (3:17a), having in mind the contrast with the "letter" (3:6), from which we understand that where the Spirit of the Lord is, there is freedom (3:17b), that is, "boldness," the behavior of free persons, not of slaves.

Other commentaries see in this verse a certain confusion between "the Lord" (the heavenly Christ) and "the Spirit," a view that is not confirmed, in my opinion, by other texts of the same apostle. For us Paul's "Lord" is simply "Jesus" (see 4:14; 11:31) or "Jesus Christ" (see 1:2-3, 14; 4:5; 8:9; 13:13).

Paul's boldness is expressed, then, as looking (rather than reflecting) with uncovered face to the mirror (which is Christ) and being transformed from one degree of glory to another into the same image (3:18; also Christ, according to 4:4).

4. Theological Argument, 4:1–5:10

After this somehow narrative argument Paul arrives at the depth of the thesis enunciated in 3:4-6. Verse 1 condenses all its themes: The ministry announced in 3:6 is now developed in 4:2-6; "by God's mercy" makes a special reference to 3:5 ("from God" and "not from us") and is developed in vv. 7-12; "we do not lose heart," corresponding to the "confidence" of 3:4, is expressed in vv. 13-15 and expanded in 4:16–5:10.

a. A Ministry of Pure Light (4:2-6)

With his opponents in view the apostle insists on rejecting every concealment due to shame, craftiness, or "falsification" of the word (4:2a). Perhaps his opponents intended to make the gospel more palatable by adapting it to the wishes of its listeners, but Paul will recommend himself only by a manifestation of the truth, which touches the consciences (see 1:12; 5:11) of those who are in the presence of God (4:2b). The objection arises that this strategy may prevent many people from accepting the gospel, but the apostle responds that those persons are not from God (4:3; see 2:15; 1 Cor 1:18; 2 Thess 2:10); another "god" has prevented them from seeing the splendor of the gospel of Christ, who is the image of God (4:4; see Col 1:15). If Paul has to preach Jesus Christ as the Lord he should forget himself and adopt the style of Christ as "slave" (4:5; see 1:24; 1 Cor 3:5, 21-23). If Christ is the image of God, creator of the light, his ministry can only be pure communication of his splendor (4:6).

b. Contained in Earthen Lamps (4:7-12)

Next Paul presents the other side of the coin: as he is only an earthen pot (4:7a) it is clear that the power to convert people comes from God and not from his ministry (4:7b; see 3:5; 12:9-10). There it shines through the image of an "earthen pot" called Jesus Christ, in whom the power of God has been shown in a special way (see 1:5, 9; 13:4; 1 Cor 1:22-25). The following four contrapositions are not perfect from a philological point of view: the meaning is that the apostle, as Christ, has been afflicted, perplexed, persecuted, and struck down, but only in a certain sense (4:8-9). He has carried everywhere the death of Christ (4:10a; see v. 11a: "we are always being given up to death for Jesus' sake") in his body (v. 10b, d; see v. 11d: "in our mortal flesh"), in order that the life of Jesus may be shown in it as it was in his resurrection (4:10c, 11c). As for the future life, every Christian participates in the same hope, but Paul, as apostle, participates more in Jesus' death (4:12: as Christ's death has communicated life; see 13:4; 1 Cor 4:9).

c. Therefore We are Courageous (4:13-15)

The courage announced in 4:1c is expressed in 4:16a as a conclusion of these three verses. Here it appears in the words of the psalmist: "I believed, and so I spoke" (v. 13), that is to say, "I have the courage. . . ." Paul repeats the reason: the one who has raised Jesus will raise us and will present us to you (v. 14); hence we will not need any recommendations. But in response to his personal faith he is working for others in order that grace and thanksgiving (of the majority) may abound for the glory of God (v. 15).

d. To the End of Our Days (4:16–5:10)

Underlying Paul's courage (4:16a) we find the idea that within the vase there is the treasure (see 4:7). In what follows he develops this idea under the Hellenistic distinction between "the outer and the inner nature" (4:16b), adding that visible things are passing away but the invisible are eternal (4:18). He implies, however, against Greek thinking, that "the outer nature" plays a decisive role in that renewal: a slight affliction achieves (in a superlative way) a great *weight* of glory (4:17; is there an allusion to the fact that *kabod* in Hebrew also means "weight" or was Paul thinking only of the specific weight of gold?).

The reference is amplified and becomes general in the next five verses: Paul compares the body to a nomad's tent (5:1a—like the ones he made!), rather uncomfortable in comparison with the eternal palace not made by human hands (see Mark 14:58) that he has (note the present tense!) in heaven (5:1b). But he would not like to spend even one night in the open air; he would instead prefer that the palace itself cover the tent (5:2, 4a) or that the tent grow into a palace (5:4b). He compares not wanting to leave the tent with not wanting to go naked (5:3), and thus he has switched from the image of the house to that of clothes.

Verses 5-6a, as a brief pause, return to the style of the previous paragraphs: this desire comes from God who gave us the pledge of the Spirit (5:5; see 1:22; Eph 1:14) and we have the courage (see 5:8; 7:16; 10:1-2) for it. But vv. 6b-10 resume the general reflection: living in the body takes us far from the Lord (5:6b, 8; see Phil 1:23) because we walk by faith and not by sight (5:7; see 4:18; Rom 8:24-25). But if our concern is to please God (5:9; see Phil 1:20-24) we shall see how important before the tribunal of Christ is that which we have accomplished with our bodies (5:10; the "vessel" of 4:7!). This may not be directly controversial or apologetic but it explains how Paul lives in the presence of God (see 1:12; 2:17; 3:18; 4:2), as he will soon stress.

5. Christological Argument, 5:11–6:10

In ch. 4 Paul could not mention the "clay jars" (4:7) without alluding to the "earthly Christ" (4:10-12). In this third argumentative block he speaks more directly of Christ as the driving force of his life.

a. Christ Compels Us (5:11-15)

This section begins by recapitulating the reasons that have moved Paul to speak: the apostle dislikes an explicit self-commendation (5:12a; see 3:4; 4:5; 10:12, 18; 12:11) but the outsiders (especially his opponents) need to be convinced in that way (5:11b) and Paul supplies the arguments for it (5:12b). These people are described (5:12c) as those who boast "in outward appearance," that is, in external proofs (such as letters of recommendation: 3:1), leaving aside the conscience. Paul would like to boast without words (5:12d: "in the heart"; see "heart" in 1:22; 3:2-3; 4:6), in a dialogue between consciences, as he is transparent to God (5:11c; see 1:12; 4:2). The controversial way is in itself a madness (5:13a; see 11:1–12:11), but necessary for the sake of God; at the same time he has to temper himself, so as not to shock them (5:13b). Another interpretation of this v. 13 would be: "my ecstasies regard only God; speaking to you, I am reasonable" (in the light of 12:1-5; 1 Cor 14:2, 4, 15-19).

The love by which Christ died for all compels him to madness (5:14a, b, 15a). As a person who has assimilated the death of Christ (see 1:9-10; 4:10-12; 11:23) he cannot take care of his reputation; he can no longer live for himself (5:14c, 15b). Of course these two verses have also a general validity: Christ's death calls to identification with it, as is made explicit in baptism (see Rom 6:3-6) and Eucharist (1 Cor 10:16-17; 11:26).

b. Christ is Present in Us (5:16-21)

Without a break the text goes on to talk positively (death is not everything!) of the work of Christ in Paul and the role Christ has entrusted to him. In view of his relationship with other people Paul says that it cannot be guided by simple human calculations (5:16a; see 1:17; 10:2-3), those that once caused him to err about Christ (5:16b). Most interpreters agree that Paul does not say that he had known Christ according to the flesh (that is, in his earthly existence) but rather that he had an according-to-the-flesh knowledge of Christ (that is, he was not aware of his divine nature).

The true Christ represents the beginning of a new creation (5:17; see Gal 6:15; Eph 2:10, 15; 4:24), because God reconciled "us" to Godself through Christ and entrusted to "us" the ministry of reconciliation (5:18). The simply reconciled (first "us") are generalized as "the world" in 5:19a, but the "ministry" (second "us") is spoken of in terms of a very specific function: "ambassadors" (5:20a) of "the word" (5:19c) "through" whom God exhorts (5:20b) and who speak "on behalf of Christ" (5:20a, c). If we interpret "the righteousness of God" in Rom 1:17; 3:21-22, 25-26 as God's redeeming act we will also be able to see in 2 Cor 5:21c the agents of reconciliation (second "us") becoming "the righteousness of God."

The reconciliation itself is expressed as "not counting their trespasses against them" (5:19b; see Rom 4:8), which belongs to the normal language of forgiveness. But the work of Christ is expressed also in a paradox as "For our sake [God] made him to be sin who knew no sin" (5:21a). The first part stands on a firm NT tradition (John 8:46; Heb 4:15; 1 Pet 2:22; 1 John 3:5). As for the second, there is in my opinion one interpretation that does not fit the context: God "discharging" divine anger in Jesus (because God is active in reconciling). As a way for understanding this verse we mention the fact that the Hebrew word for "sin" *(ʾasham)* means also "sacrifice for sin," and this word is found in Isa 53:10, a text normally applied to Christ.

c. Because We are Similar to Him (6:1-10)

The brief pause is marked by the solemnity of 5:21, by the practical content of what follows, and by the initial participle, a construction that has already signaled other pauses (3:12; 4:1, 7, 13, 16; 5:6, 11). But the argument continues. The "ministers of reconciliation" again occupy the foreground: as coworkers (of God: 6:1; see 5:20) they honor their ministry, avoiding criticism (6:3; see 5:13b) and recommending themselves (in a favorable sense as in 3:1; 4:2; 5:12) as ministers of God (6:4a). In a sort of parenthesis 6:2 gives an example of a "word" of reconciliation: a biblical quotation together with its application to the present.

In a second list of "adventures" (after 4:8-11) the apostle enumerates the reasons for recommending himself. They appear in the form of simple circumstances ("in . . ." 18 times: 6:4b-7b), double circumstances ("through . . . and . . ." 3 times: 6:7c-8b), and comparisons ("as . . . but . . ." 7 times: 6:8c-10). Let us synthesize them according to the meaning: some are occurrences in a proper sense: hardships, afflictions, calamities, privations, beatings, prison, riots, fatigue, sleepless nights, hunger (6:4d-5); then follow "balanced" adversities: honor and dishonor, ill repute and good repute (6:8a, b) as well as apparent adversities: we are treated as impostors, unknown, punished, dying, sorrowful, poor, people who have nothing—but by deeper analysis the contrary is found to be true (6:8c-10). In other sentences Paul refers to virtues: great endurance (6:4c), purity, knowledge, patience, kindness (6:6a, d), genuine love (6:6f). He enumerates also the "weapons" (see 10:4) of his fight: holiness of spirit (6:6e), truthful speech, the power of God, the weapons—defensive and offensive—of righteousness (6:7). So the discourse with which Paul has begun distancing himself from self-commendation ends with another kind of self-commendation stressing transparency and humiliation, by which he is assimilated to Christ and so is made participant in God's commendation.

Transition (6:11–7:4)

1. A Warm Invitation

As we have said, 6:11-13 and 7:2-4 can be read as a good illustration of what happened to Paul on his arrival in Macedonia (7:5) as well as a *peroratio* following the *argumentatio* unfolded from 3:1 forward. The address in 6:11 is very solemn (it is the only time we read the word "Corinthians" in all the letters) and does not seem justified from the context. The addressees appeared first in 3:1 as *being* Paul's letter, indirectly in 4:2, and directly in 5:11 as "consciences" to which the apostle is transparent, then in 5:12 as people who will have to boast for Paul, in 5:13 as people to whom he should be reasonable, and finally in 5:20 and 6:1-2 as generally invited to "reconcile" with God. But 6:11 has in view another kind of reconciliation: that of some beloved children (6:13) in Christ, whose faith did not fail (1:24), with their father in Christ; the rift has occurred because of a lack of communication (as happens today between parents and their children). Paul has opened his mouth and heart to them (6:11a,b; see 1:4, 6; 7:6, 7, 13), but they close themselves through no fault of the apostle (6:12).

The same exhortation to "open wide" their hearts (6:13) comes again in 7:2, together with the assurance that Paul is innocent (he neither did wrong, nor corrupted, nor defrauded) and did not condemn them, but kept them in his heart (7:3; see 3:2; 4:12).

Immediately, as proper in a sudden reconciliation, he proclaims his complete unity with his people: they give him courage (see 3:12) and occasion for boasting (see 1:14), consolation (see 7:6, 7, 13) and joy (7:4; see 2:2-3).

2. Against Idolatry

Between these two brief sections closely linked with the Corinthian situation we find the contested fragment 6:14–7:1. The condition for keeping it here is the belief that it is an excursus in which Paul, with extreme exaggeration, exhorts the faithful to remain in communion (see 6:14) with him as the true minister of the new covenant.

We can observe that the "unbelievers" (6:14-15) have already appeared in 4:4 (see 2:15-16) and that "Beliar" (6:15), under the name of Satan, appears in 11:14. But it is also clear that the people referred to in the last text "disguise themselves as apostles of Christ" (11:13), which is not the case with the "idols" (6:16). So we must say at least that in its literal sense the fragment does not fit the context. At the same time it probably does not belong to the letter mentioned in 1 Cor 5:9 either, where the problem is immorality and not idolatry. As an exhortation against not falling back into idolatry (see 1 Cor 10:14) the text can be easily understood and has sufficient Pauline characteristics to be taken as authentic.

After the proposition of not being "mismatched" with unbelievers (6:14a; see Gal 5:1) the text by means of five questions proclaims the incompatibility between righteousness, light, Christ, believers, and the temple of God on the one side and, on the other, lawlessness, darkness, Beliar, unbelievers, and idols (6:14b-16a; cf. 4:4; 11:13-15). The central statement about being the temple of God (v. 16b) also has its clear parallels in 1 Cor 3:16; 6:19. Then after a proof from Scripture (6:16c-18) the passages ends with an exhortation to purify oneself completely (flesh and spirit) of any stain and to achieve perfect holiness (7:1), confirming that one's body is the temple of God (see 6:19).

Second Narrative Section (7:5-16)

Verse 5 takes up the story apparently abandoned in 2:13. As a matter of fact the reconciliation has been already expressed in 2:5-11 and proclaimed in 7:4. Now Paul tells how it happened: in the midst of his struggles and fears (7:5) the coming of Titus comforted him (7:6), telling him of their longing, their sorrow, and their zeal (to put things right, defending him: v. 7). In v. 8 Paul mentions again the sadness he had caused them with his letter (see 2:4), a "godly grief" for repentance and salvation (7:9-10; see 2:7.11) that provoked a very favorable disposition toward him (v. 11b). Now he confesses their innocence in that matter (v. 11c), a point for him much more relevant than the offense or the offender (7:12; see 2:5, 9).

The next four verses (7:13b-16) express the same feelings from the point of view of Titus. Paul certainly has a debt of thanks to his coworker but the fragment may have another function: to prepare for the following chapter about the collection, in which he also mentions Titus (8:6, 16, 23) as well as his boasting about the Corinthians that ought not to be disappointed (8:24, as above, 7:14-16).

First Note on the Collection: 2 Corinthians 8

As we have said, the different origin of the two chapters on the collection for the church in Jerusalem can be inferred from the fact that both say essentially the same thing but, surprisingly, 9:1 begins as if it were not preceded by twenty-four verses on the same subject. It has been observed also that while, of these two, only ch. 8 speaks of Titus (8:6, 16, 23), only ch. 9 speaks of "Achaia" (9:2). These are the only indications of a different setting for the two chapters.

In ch. 8 it is easy to distinguish certain stages in the argument even if the syntactical marks are not always well placed. The chapter begins by speaking, perhaps with exaggeration, of the example of the Macedonians (vv. 1-5): though living in severe affliction and extreme poverty they abounded in joy, simplicity, and generosity beyond their abilities and comfort (vv. 2-4a). The collection is spoken of only with the dignifying names of grace, sharing, and ministry (v. 4b) because of what it represents: the Macedonians had delivered themselves to the Lord and to the apostle (v. 5).

Next (8:6-8) Paul proposes a similar attitude to the Corinthians: they should abound in the same "grace" (v. 6), as also in faith, speech, knowledge, eagerness, and love for him (v. 7). Their sincerity is put to the test by the diligence shown by others (v. 8).

Verse 9 gives the theological argument: Jesus Christ, being rich, has made himself poor so that by his poverty we might become rich (v. 9; here "grace" or "generosity" means something more than the collection). If everyone knew that Jesus was sociologically poor from his birth they could also understand that as Son of God (1:19) he had been "rich" before his birth. This does not deny his subsequent commitment to the poor.

Verses 10-12 give the practical argument ("I am giving my advice"): act according to the willingness you have shown (v. 10) because good intentions are not enough to please God (vv. 11-12). Against the possible objection that they might become poor the apostle offers a fundamental principle (try only to establish a fair balance: v. 13) and proves it by Scripture (v. 15, quoting Exod 16:18 about the manna). The question is: who will dare to say (and practice!) this nowadays with respect to the Third World?

After a short transition ("thanks be to God . . ." v. 16) Paul recapitulates the story of Titus (8:16-17, 23a) and introduces another brother, recommended and commissioned by the churches, who will accompany him (vv. 18-19a). His going personally has to do with the almost liturgical sense of the collection ("administering this grace for the glory of the Lord"); it must also be a sign of his "goodwill" toward Jerusalem (v. 19b), a sign that the Corinthians may need as much as the community in Jerusalem (v. 23), a proof of their love and of Paul's boasting (v. 24).

Second Note on the Collection: 2 Corinthians 9

The second note has a similar structure. It begins with a typical epistolary introduction to the argument ("about the ministry . . ." v. 1), including an explicit reference to "writing." There follows a short narrative (9:2-4) about the example the Macedonians have received from Achaia (see 8:1-6) and the mission of the brothers in that region (9:3-4; see 8:18-19, 22): they "*pre*-ceded" Paul for the sake of "*pre*-paring" what has been "*pro*-mised" (v. 5a: three Greek verbs with *pro*).

The theological argument extends to 9:11, speaking of "bounty" (vv. 5-6) instead of "grace" (as in 8:4, 6-7, 19). With three texts from Scripture (v. 7: Prov 11:24 LXX; v. 9: Ps 111:9 LXX; v. 10: Isa 55:10) Paul argues that God expects joyful generosity (v. 7) and will respond with even more generosity. In v. 10 appears the word for "becoming rich," reminding us of 8:9. Paul twice says that this collection will produce "thanksgiving to God" (9:11-12) precisely in Jerusalem, where it will plead for the legitimacy of their loyalty to the gospel (v. 13) and will transform itself into prayer for them (v. 14). According to his goals he has also qualified the collection as a ministry (9:1, 12-13; see 8:4, 19-20) and a "liturgy" (9:12a; see Rom 15:27). The little discourse ends in a pure expression of thanksgiving (v. 15).

Paul's Apology: 2 Corinthians 10–13

Chapters 10–13 comprise a discourse of four chapters. Paul is not only its author but also its subject (see "I" in 10:1; 11:16, 18, 21-23, 29; 12:11, 13, 15-16, 20; "we" either meaning or including Paul in 10:7, 13; 11:12, 21; 4:6, 7a, 7b, 9). It is not difficult to imagine these chapters as a letter (probably it was one, as we have said) in which after an address that has been lost comes an *exordium* in loftier tones: "I myself, Paul . . ." (10:1; see Gal 1:6). The *exordium* ends as it began, referring to both his absence and his presence (10:1, 11)

In the center of this discourse we find a section that is clearly distinguished: the "fool's speech" *(Narrenrede).* It is clear where it begins (11:1: "I wish you would bear with me in a little foolishness") and where it announces its end (12:11: "I have been a fool!"), though until 12:13, it continues with a concentrated recapitulation of what has been said (compare 12:11a with 11:5-6; 12:12a with 11:23-33; 12:11b with 12:1-4; 12:13 with 11:7-12).

Following that "fool's speech" we come to two epistolary finales beginning with the phrase: "I am coming to you for the third time" (12:14 and 13:1).

The "fool's speech" logically constitutes the *argumentatio* of the discourse. The remaining piece (10:12-18) is expected to play the role of a *propositio.* It fulfills this role brilliantly in the form of five contrapositions ("not . . . but . . ." in 10:12, 13, 14, 15, 18), commenting on the biblical principle: "Let the one who boasts, boast in the Lord" (10:17). Curiously, the last of those contrapositions ("it is not those who commend themselves that are approved, but those whom the Lord commends," v. 18) also fits in with the discourse between 3:1 and 6:10 (see "commend ourselves" in 3:1; 4:2; 5:12; 6:4).

Thus we have:

1. *Exordium* (10:1-11)
2. *Propositio:* Commended by the Lord (10:12-18)
3. *Argumentatio:* The "fool's speech" (11:1–12:13)
4. First epistolary finale (12:14-21)
5. Second epistolary finale (13:1-13).

Some of those sections will require a further division, which will be duly given.

1. Exordium *(10:1-11)*

The chapter starts as if it were the exhortative part of a letter (v. 1a; see Rom 12:1a), but immediately becomes an apology. Even while recalling the "gentleness and kindness" of (the earthly) Christ (v. 1b) Paul is putting his weakness in a favorable light. At the beginning and end of this *exordium* the apostle refers five times (vv. 1c, 2, 9-11) to the contrast between his humble visit and his bold letter, alluding most probably to the "intermediate" visit in which he tolerated an offense (see 2:5, 10; 7:12) without giving a sharp response, which he later did in a letter (see 2:4; 7:8, 12).

It was to spare them (see 1:23) that he demeaned himself. If they now force him to it he is ready to act very boldly (v. 2a; see 1 Cor 4:21) against those who say he acts "according to human standards" (v. 2b; 1:17; 5:16), that is, for the sake of human respect. These chapters show a special boldness, attacking his opponents from the very beginning.

Paul refers to his mission in general, distinguishing between living *in* the flesh (see 4:11) and acting (fighting!) *according to* the flesh (10:3); he describes his weapons (10:4a; see 6:7) and speaks of evangelization in terms of "destroying strongholds" (10:4b-5a; see 2:14; 4:6 where he speaks also from the "knowledge of God"). But, he adds, with the same weapons he is ready to punish the disobedience of the opponents, aided by the obedience of the majority of his faithful (10:6).

After a breathing pause (required by the solemnity of the last phrases) the apostle compares himself to his opponents: he first asks that his audience consider what is self-evident (10:7a) and allegedly he is modest: he is *also* Christ's (10:7b; see 11:13, 23). The second is a loftier, more specific boast (10:8a; see "boasting" above at 1:12, 14; 5:12; 7:4, 14; 8:24; 9:3) with no less assurance (10:8d; see 7:14; 9:4): the authority the Lord gave him can also be used for exacting obedience (10:8; see 13:10).

2. Propositio: *Commended by the Lord (10:12-18)*

The *propositio* begins with an irony: the apostle would not have the boldness to compare himself with others (10:12a—yet he does dare! —see above at 2:17; 3:1; 4:2; 5:12; 10:7-8, but more is to come). Next the text presents a series of five negative phrases followed by adversatives ("not . . . but . . .": 10:12-15, 18; see 10:16). In the first part of each phrase we can see an allusion to things the opponents are doing *and Paul is not;* in the second part we see a description of what Paul does, except for the first contraposition if we take as authentic the words in the transition between vv. 12 and 13: "they do not show good sense. We, however, . . ." But it is also a text-critical alternative to suppress those words, thus restoring the parallelism. Against the majority of manuscript witnesses and modern scholars we tend to remove these words: without them the phrase is too bold to be invented by anyone else (and introduced where it structurally fits in so well). In this case the meaning would be that Paul finds in himself (not by comparison with others) the measure of his position (10:12b; see Gal 6:4).

Leaving this question aside, what Paul does not do is commend himself for his own sake (10:12a, 18a; see 3:4; 5:12a), boasting without measure (10:13a), overstepping his limits as one who cannot reach them (10:14a), boasting about the work of others (10:15a), of things done by or attributed to others (10:16b). According to the second part of the comparisons what Paul does do is to boast, within the field God has assigned him (10:13b), of having arrived with the gospel *before* others (10:14b; see 1 Cor 4:15), and if things proceed favorably in this region he hopes to preach the gospel beyond them, evangelizing elsewhere (10:15b-16a; see Rom 15:20, 23-24).

For the apostle all this has a name: to "boast *in the Lord*" (10:17) because he understands that none of these advantages over his opponents are his work (see 3:3, 5; 6:7; 10:4; 1 Cor 15:10), but he is boasting only of what Christ has worked through him (see Rom 15:17-18), that is to say, of God's commendation (10:18b). According to the abovementioned critical alternative this has another name: to measure himself by himself and compare himself with himself in the sense of leaving others (see the description of the "others" in 10:15-16) aside.

3. Argumentatio: *"The Fool's Speech" (11:1–12:13)*

This section of forty-six verses can be divided as follows:

a. The reasons for Paul's foolishness (11:1-6)
b. The apostle's financial independence (11:7-12)
c. Emissaries of Satan (11:13-15)
d. Second reflection on foolishness (11:16-20)
e. "Catalogue of adventures" (11:21-29)
f. A special "adventure" (11:30-32)
g. The visions and revelations (12:1-10)
h. Concluding reflection (12:11-13)

a. The Reasons for Paul's Foolishness, 11:1-6

Paul starts with a rather mild qualification of his attitude: "a little foolishness," hoping that the faithful will be able to put up with it (11:1). In any case we must not confuse this "foolishness" with the "foolishness of our proclamation" in 1 Cor 1:21; see 1 Cor 1:18, 23, 25, 27), by which Paul is a "fool for the sake of Christ" (1 Cor 4:10). The Greek words employed here *(afrōn, afrosunē)* never have a positive meaning in the NT (see Rom 2:20; 1 Cor 15:36; Eph 5:17; 1 Pet 2:15).

This "foolishness" can be explained as zeal of God (v. 2a; see 5:13), like the zeal of a father who must assure the virginity of the daughter he gives in marriage (v. 2b; here: to Christ) and fears the astuteness of the Adversary (v. 3).

The next three verses are full of irony, as appropriate to a "fool's speech," but we do not know to what degree each verse means what it says because Paul's irony may in fact be very serious (as it is in 1 Cor 4:9-13). In my opinion v. 4 should be taken as highly ironic, v. 5 as almost unironic, and v. 6 as only half ironic. For other commentators v. 4 is not nearly as ironic while v. 6 is absolutely ironic.

The general sense of v. 4 is clear: if they put up with anybody preaching anything, they should also put up with him! (see vv. 19-20). The problem is the sense in which the opponents speak of "another Jesus, a different gospel, a different spirit." If it were really so Paul would not have written 10:7 and 11:13, 23. But the text has a conditional phrase, perhaps retorting to the argument that he, Paul, is not reflecting the true image of Jesus they know better from Palestine.

In 11:5 as in 12:11 Paul asserts that he is not inferior to the "super" apostles. That could be "super" irony referring to those cited below in 11:13-15. Some others, and myself, understand it on the lines of Gal 1:17; 1 Cor 15:9-10, responding to the objection that a newcomer to Christianity cannot be compared with the "highest" apostles of Jerusalem. Paul could also recognize sincerely that he is not brilliant in words (11:6a; see 10:10; 1 Cor 2:4), at least according to the professional standards of his time. But he could stress his knowledge (11:6b; see 2:14; 4:6; 10:5) and his total transparency (11:6c; see 1:12-14; 5:11).

b. The Apostle's Financial Independence, 11:7-12

Paul takes as an offense the fact that they have interpreted badly a gesture so important for him as his financial independence (see 1 Thess 2:9; 1 Cor 9:15-18): he uses very strong, nearly aggressive, expressions: "to commit sin" (v. 7), "to humble himself" (v. 7), "to rob" (v. 8), "support" (v. 8), "to burden" (v. 9), "to silence" (v. 10), "to deny" (v. 12). His swearing is also very strong ("As the truth of Christ is in me": v. 10; "God knows!": v. 11) and so are his repetitions: "I proclaimed God's good news" (in Greek: *euaggelion euēggelisamēn:* v. 7), "I refrained and will continue to refrain" (v. 9), "what I do I will also continue to do, in order to deny an opportunity to those who want an opportunity" (v. 12). In the bipolar humiliation–exaltation (v. 7a) they should have seen the image of Christ (see 8:9; Phil 2:8) and also the internal coherence of giving God's gift gratis (v. 7b; see 1 Cor 9:18). The problem is that he took money from others (vv. 8-9) and his renunciation of that right has been taken as a sign of lesser love (v. 10; see 12:13); so has his not coming twice to them (1:15-17). But he insists on his general point of not being a burden to them (v. 9b; see 1 Thess 2:9), with more reason now because he has to break the plans of those who want him to be like them (v. 12).

c. Emissaries of Satan, 11:13-15

With stronger phrases Paul discharges his anger at those who have discredited him: they disguise themselves falsely as apostles of Christ (v. 12) and ministers of righteousness (v. 15; see 3:9; 5:21; 6:7), just as Satan transforms himself into an angel of light (v. 14). The problem remains, in this rhetorical and ironical context, to understand what they really were and what they really pretended to be. Elsewhere Paul does not deny their being "Christ's" (10:7) and "ministers of Christ" (11:23) and the only specific accusation we hear against them is that of "peddling" (2:17) or "falsifying" the word of God (4:2), that is, transmitting it with insufficient purity. But it was the fact that they did not recognize Paul's apostolic character that earned them classification as "false messengers" ("pseudo-apostles" in a generic sense, as in 8:23; Phil 2:25). Another question is whether they pretended to be "apostles" in the specific sense we find in 1 Cor 15:7, 9; Gal 1:17, 19. We doubt it strongly.

d. Second Reflection About Foolishness, 11:16-20

Precisely because he understands that he has gone too far in his criticism the apostle returns to the subject of "foolishness" without stating it categorically: "let no one think that I am . . ." (11:16a), "accept me as . . ." (v. 16b), "as a fool . . . (v. 17b). He confesses some foolishness in the sense that he is not speaking "with the Lord's authority" (v. 17a; see 10:1; Rom 12:14, 17; 1 Thess 5:15), but a situation has been created (see 5:12; 11:12) to which he cannot respond without boasting (v. 17b). At any rate there is a difference: the others boast "according to human standards" (v. 18a); Paul only boasts (v. 18b; see 1:12, 17; 5:16; 10:2-3). It is easier to understand why he accuses them of boasting "according to human standards": they boasted in "the labors of others" (10:14-16), they denigrated him with futile arguments (11:7, 12), they were arrogant (vv. 19-20). It is not so easy to understand why he accuses himself of not speaking "with the Lord's authority." Here the comparison with the "meekness and gentleness" of (the earthly) Christ (10:1) should have a decisive weight. In that sense we observe that this kind of confession used to come after a direct attack by his opponents (see 11:1 after 10:18; 11:16 after 11:13-15; 11:21, 23b in the following catalogue; also 5:13 after 5:12). He would like to speak without words (see 5:12) or to speak only for himself, but his congregations seem to understand only the language of comparison. The next two verses put that in a sarcastic way: they are so "wise" (v. 19; see v. 4), that they will follow only the foolish who humiliate them in every way (v. 20).

e. "Catalogue of Adventures," 11:21-29

After a compendious introduction (v. 21) the catalogue proceeds without a break from v. 22 to v. 29. Between v. 23b and v. 29 it becomes a compact explanation of v. 23a ("Are they ministers of Christ? . . . I am a better one!"). This part of the "catalogue" is in clear parallelism with 6:4-10; 4:7-12 and 1 Cor 4:9-13. On the other hand v. 23a belongs to a series in which the apostle claims to be also a Hebrew, Israelite, and descendant of Abraham (v. 22).

The self-accusation of "dishonor," "weakness" (v. 21a), and "foolishness" (v. 21c) cannot apply only to v. 22 (his Jewish condition; see Rom 11:1-2 more than Phil 3:7-8), because the strongest phrase ("I am talking like a madman," v. 23b) refers to a fact that is substantial for his self-understanding: he is a minister of Christ. The only painful thing for Paul can be, therefore, the comparison with others ("whatever anyone dares to boast of," v. 21b).

As for the specific "adventures" we observe that in 6:5 we find the three first with the same words ("labors, imprisonments, floggings," v. 23c, d, e) plus two others that we find below in v. 27 ("sleepless nights, hunger"). In 1 Cor 4:11, by means of the respective derived verbs, we find the rest of v. 27 ("toil and hardship . . . hungry and thirsty, . . . cold and naked"); a more curious thing is that the "often near death" of v. 23 appears in singular form in 1:10 and 4:12, in a similar form in 4:10, and in the formula "as though sentenced to death" in 1 Cor 4:9.

Moreover our text adds some very specific autobiographical notes: judicial punishments of five sets of thirty-nine lashes from the Jews (v. 24) plus three other flagellations and a lapidation (v. 25b); on water three shipwrecks, one of which lasted more than twenty-four hours (v. 25c, d), dangers in rivers (v. 26b), dangers in the sea (v. 26h); on earth frequent journeys (v. 26a), dangers from bandits (v. 26c), dangers in the city and in the wilderness (v. 26f, g); from the ill-will of other persons, dangers from those of his nation (v. 26d; see v. 24), from the Gentiles (v. 26e), and from false brothers and sisters (v. 26i). More relevant for him is a less spectacular "adventure" that goes on within his soul (v. 28a): anxiety for all his churches (v. 28b), by which he sees the problems of everyone as his own problems (v. 29).

A key to understanding the whole speech lies in the fact that here Paul does not cite any virtues (as he did in 6:4c, 6a, d, f). The sense can be that here the apostle is not exalting his own work in any way, but rather God's protection (which implies his recommendation: see 10:18). In vv. 28-29 he shows how he loves them "with the compassion of Jesus Christ" (Phil 1:8), how he has engendered them as a true father (1 Cor 4:15) and is constantly engendering them again (Gal 4:19). As associated with Christ he can also claim his commendation.

f. A Special "Adventure," 11:30-32

The final anecdote (vv. 32-33), confirmed by a solemn oath (v. 31), is placed under the sign of weakness (v. 30)—not, certainly, moral weakness, but the disgrace of having been forced to flee and also the weakness of ridicule (escaping in a basket! v. 32), as when a non-professional is forced to act in the theater (see 1 Cor 4:9-10). At the same time he stresses God's protection (v. 33) as in the preceding verses.

The subject of the "apostolic weakness" that in my opinion begins here will be developed in 12:5-10. Let me say only that weakness is not considered for its own sake: it is the way the apostle "brings about" all over the world the death of Christ (see 5:10). That is to say: his weakness is *Christ's* as much as his afflictions (see 1:5). Therefore it represents also a divine commendation (see 10:18).

g. The Visions and Revelations, 12:1-10

Before entering into the subject the letter gives a very brief reflection on his boasting: it is necessary to boast (12:1a; cf. 11:30; 12:2-3, 17), even if not beneficial (12:1b; we understand "beneficial" as in 8:10; 1 Cor 6:12; 10:23; 12:7).

Then he tells just one story: a Christian (vv. 2a, 3a), fourteen years ago (v. 2b), perhaps in a spiritual way (vv. 2c, d, 3b, c), was caught up to the third heaven (v. 2e), that is to say Paradise (v. 4a), and heard secret words nobody is allowed to pronounce (v. 4b, c). Maybe Paul has been accused of not being "spiritual" at all (see 1 Cor 2:13, 15; Gal 6:1); maybe the opponents have claimed higher revelations and displayed them openly. But we must not take that for certain. His reasoning can be: if one is not allowed to tell what has been revealed to him it is better if he does not speak at all of having received a revelation.

He boasts about "such a one" (v. 5a) as if it were not himself because that was a pure work of God. But "on his own behalf" (v. 5b; cf. 3:4; 5:12a; 11:12a, 18a), he adds, he will boast only about his weaknesses (v. 5c; see 11:30) for he wishes to be considered only in view of what everybody sees in him (v. 6c; see 10:7) or hears from him (v. 6d; see v. 11 and 5:12). That is not a clear-cut definition because everyone sees in him and hears from him many things that are not weakness (for instance his apostolic successes). The meaning may be that his weak appearance, as a sign of God's power and the presence of Christ (see 4:7-12), belongs essentially to his apostolic ministry: he may not "compensate" this image by adding some marvelous legend. But in v. 6a, b in a kind of parenthesis he expresses himself as if he wanted to deny everything he had said before: his boasting would never be foolish because he would speak the truth (on the lines of 10:8, but in spite of 11:1, 17, 21). That is to say: a "fool" for God's sake (5:13) is not a fool at all.

Immediately Paul takes up the subject of weakness (here physical: in 11:32-33 it was "social") and begins also with an anecdote: a "thorn in the flesh" humiliated him (12:7) and he asked to be liberated from it (12:8) but the Lord told him to be content with divine grace (12:9a; see 1:12; 4:15; 6:1), for God's power shows itself in a weak subject (12:9b; see 4:7; 6:7). Here "Satan" functions as does "temptation" in Gal 4:13. So with most interpreters we may see the same illness (called also "weakness" in Gal 4:12) referred to in both texts.

The conclusion is general and stresses the same principle: Paul does not like weakness for what it is, but for what it brings: the power of Christ indwelling in him (12:9c, d, 10). Preparing for the end of the speech he adds to weakness insults, hardships, persecutions, and calamities sustained for the sake of Christ (v. 10a, on the lines of vv. 11:22b-30 and parallels).

h. Concluding Reflection, 12:11-13

The subject of foolishness is now summed up in one verse: Paul has been forced to be foolish because his people failed to recommend him (v. 11c; see 6d; 5:12). Then he recalls the other themes of the speech. The comparison with the super-apostles (v. 11c; see 11:5-6) takes a sincerely humble tone: "even though I am nothing" (v. 11d; see 1 Cor 15:9-10).

God's commendation takes here the form of "signs of a true apostle" (v. 12a; see 11:22a). They are summed up as patience (v. 12b; see 11:22b-29, and the same word in 1:6; 6:4), and "signs and wonders and mighty works" (v. 12c), which until now he has not included (see only 12:1-4, 6b). The problem of his financial independence has grieved them more than he ever thought (v. 13a; see 11:11). He repeats his general principle of not being a burden to them (v. 13b; see 11:9) and apologizes for having shown a preference to others (v. 13c; see 11:7).

4. First Epistolary Finale (12:14-21)

The announcement of the next visit (12:14) signals the end of the letter. As the theme of this first finale we have again his financial independence (vv. 14-18), a qualification of the letter (v. 19), and the preparation for the visit (vv. 20-21).

The underestimation the Corinthians feel in comparison to the Macedonians forces Paul to a dramatic expression of his love (vv. 14-15; again 11:11) but he is not going to change his policy because he knows the positive effect it has (some people will call that "craftiness": v. 16; see 4:2; 11:3). In the same defense he includes Titus and the other brother he sent to them (vv. 17-18a; see 8:16-19, 22-23; 9:5). Paul denies his letter is (pure) apologetics (v. 19a), for it is written before God (v. 19b, repeating 2:17) and for the sake of building them up (v. 19c; see 10:8; 13:10). As for the visit, he expresses the fear that he will still find discord (v. 20b) but also moral disorder (v. 21). That would grieve him (v. 21a; see 2:5-6; 7:12), in which case he would be forced again to grieve many (v. 21b, c; 2:1-4; 7:8f-9).

5. Second Epistolary Finale (13:1-13)

The second finale begins with another announcement of the next visit (v. 1a) and contains two other fragments about it (vv. 1b-2, 10), a last defense of his position (vv. 3-4 as a statement; vv. 5-9 as a personal address). The letter ends with a general exhortation (v. 11), general greetings (v. 12) and a benediction (v. 13).

This conclusion takes up what we called the *exordium* of this letter: the apostle will not be ashamed in his next visit to them (vv. 1b, 2; see 10:1-2, 6). Playing on the contrast between his weakness (as absent) and his strength (as present) he gives us a theological pearl (vv. 3-4): they question the solidity (that is, "approval"; see 10:18) of Christ's speaking in him (v. 3a) because they feel strong and see his weakness (v. 3b; see 1 Cor 4:10). The reason is that Paul as apostle has to participate much more in Christ's weakness (v. 4c; see 11:30; 12:5, 9, 10), that is to say in his cross, from which Christ himself receives his power (v. 4a, b; see 4:10-12). So Paul, strengthened by Christ, will be ever strong in their favor (v. 4d).

Verses 5-9 apply this principle in the form of a personal address, playing on this "solidity" or "approval": maybe you will not be (v. 5) and I will (v. 6), even if I would be ready to be disapproved for the sake of not doing wrong to you. Paul's constant plea for sincerity and transparency receives here its final expression: he cannot do anything against the truth (v. 8; see 4:2; 6:7; 7:14). The same is true of the contrast between their strength and Paul's weakness (v. 9; see v. 11; 12:9-10; 1 Cor 1:10; 1 Thess 3:10). Verse 10 refers again to the visit and his acting during it as boldly as in his letter (v. 10a, b) according to the authority God gave him for edification and not for destruction (v. 10c, d; see v. 19c; 10:8).

The very last exhortation (v. 11) refers to community life in terms that are new in this letter: encourage one another (see 1 Thess 4:18; 5:11), agree with one another (see Rom 12:16; 15:5), live in peace (see 1 Thess 5:13; Rom 12:18). The mutual greeting (v. 12), including a kiss (see Rom 16:16; 1 Cor 16:20; 1 Thess 5:26) could not be more general.

The final benediction (v. 13) is the last pearl: grace, love and communion can form only one higher reality, as it is with the Lord Jesus Christ (see 8:9; Rom 16:20, 24; 1 Cor 16:23; Gal 1:6; 6:18), God the Father (see v. 11; Rom 5:5, 8; 8:39) and the Holy Spirit. The "communion" of the Spirit is a new formulation that synthesizes many things (see 1:22; 3:3, 6, 8, 17-18; 4:13; 5:5; 6:6; 11:4; 12:18).

BIBLIOGRAPHY

Barrett, Charles Kingsley. *A Commentary on the Second Epistle to the Corinthians.* New York: Harper & Row, 1973.

Barnett, Paul. *The Second Epistle to the Corinthians.* NIC.NT. Grand Rapids: Eerdmans, 1997.

Becker, J. Christiaan. *Suffering and Hope: The Biblical Vision and the Human Predicament.* Philadelphia: Fortress, 1987.

Belleville, Linda L. *Reflections of Glory. Paul's Polemical Use of the Moses-Doxa Tradition in 2 Corinthians 3,1-18.* Sheffield: JSOT Press, 1991.

Bieringer, Reimund, and Jan Lambrecht. *Studies in 2 Corinthians.* Leuven: Leuven University Press/ Peeters, 1994.

Furnish, Victor P. *II Corinthians.* AB 32A. Garden City, N.Y.: Doubleday, 1984.

Kistemaker, Simon J. *New Testament Commentary: Exposition of the Second Epistle to the Corinthians.* Grand Rapids: Baker Book House, 1997.

Murphy-O'Connor, Jerome. *The Theology of the Second Letter to the Corinthians.* Cambridge: Cambridge University Press, 1991.

Spencer, Aida Besançon. *Paul's Literary Style. A Stylistic and Historical Comparison of 2 Cor 11,16–12,3 and Rom 8,9-39.* Jackson, Miss.: Evangelical Theological Society, 1984.

Sumney, Jerry L. *Identifying Paul's Opponents: The Question of Method in 2 Corinthians.* JSNT.S 40. Sheffield: Sheffield Academic Press, 1990.

Thrall, Margaret E. *A Critical and Exegetical Commentary on the Second Epistle to the Corinthians.* Edinburgh: T & T Clark, 1994.

Watson, Nigel. *The Second Epistle to the Corinthians.* Epworth Commentaries. London: Epworth Press, 1993.

Witherington, Ben III. *Conflict and Community in Corinth: A Socio-Rhetorical Commentary on 1 and 2 Corinthians.* Grand Rapids: Eerdmans, 1995.

Young, Frances, and David F. Ford. *Meaning and Truth in 2 Corinthians.* Grand Rapids: Eerdmans, 1988.

Galatians

Elsa Tamez

The letter to the Galatians is one of the most important documents of the first century for our knowledge of the history of the newborn Church and of Christian thought in general. Because of the important theological themes treated in it the letter becomes a source, rich in meaning, to be read and re-read in light of new realities. In addition we come to know some of the history of the internal struggles among Christians at the time of Paul. To live out of the freedom with which Christ has made us free and not to let ourselves be oppressed (5:1) is the central challenge of this letter for readers of all centuries. Galatians 3:28 is one of the most powerful theological discourses for affirming the equality of women on all levels within the Church and in society.

FIRST READING

In a first reading of the letter the reader perceives a serious conflict among the Galatians, the apostle, and a group of Judeo-Christians who were trying to modify the gospel proclaimed by Paul. The rhetorical style allows one to observe an author ostensibly disturbed and bothered by that situation. In the central part of the letter, in the midst of the argumentation, Paul elaborates some fundamental theological elements in relation to the liberating work of Jesus Christ. Linked to that task are the themes of justification by faith and not by Law and the gift of the Spirit that brings to birth the new life in Christ as manifest in the practice of justice. Grace and freedom summarize the good news announced by Paul to those communities in Galatia who had lived under fear, whether because of the dictates of the cosmic order that were part of their religious beliefs or because of the political and economic situation of the Roman Empire. Would they be capable of turning back now because of the dictates of the Mosaic Law?

General Character of the Book

Literary Genre

Galatians is an apologetic type of letter, common in the Greco-Roman world. The language is laden with emotional overtones. Its style is rhetorical and for that reason has as its function to persuade its readers. In this particular case Paul as author wants to make clear that the gospel he presents is true. Polarization is part of this style. It is very important to take into account the rhetorical style of the letter so as not to oversimplify the position of Paul regarding the Jewish Law and accuse him of being anti-Semitic due to his violent declarations against the Mosaic Law and male circumcision.

General Structure of the Letter

If this letter is assumed to be an apologia in the form of a letter the structure is easily perceptible.

Prescript (1:1-5): Greeting and Paul's introduction to the community
Exordium or Introduction (1:6-10)
Narratio or Statement of Facts (1:11–2:14)
    The call of God (1:11–2:14)
        The Assembly at Jerusalem (2:1-10)
        The conflict in Antioch (2:11-14)

Propositio or Proposition (2:15-21)
  The gospel of Paul
Probatio or Proofs (3:1–4:31)
  The experience of the Galatians' receiving new life (3:1-5)
  The faith experience of Abraham (3:6-14)
  The promise over and above the Law (3:15-18)
  The role of the Law (3:19-25)
  Those clothed with Christ are freed from enslaving laws (3:26–4:11)
  Good memories of friendship between the Galatians and Paul (4:12-20)
  Inheritors of a lineage of freeborn children: Sarah and Hagar (4:21-31)
Exhortatio or Exhortation (5:1–6:10)
  The manifestation of freedom in the practice of justice (5:1-12)
  Living according to the freedom appointed by the Spirit (5:13–6:10)
Postscript or Conclusion (6:11-18)
  The most important element is the new creation

Authorship, Audience, and Date of the Letter

Paul is the undisputed author of the letter to the Galatians. A scribe wrote it down since it is clearly stated at the end of the letter that Paul wrote that section with his own hand in large letters (6:11). His intention is to call his readers to attend to a situation that was quite delicate for he feared that all his work among the Galatians would be cast aside (4:11).

Throughout the letter we are assured that the ones addressed were non-Jewish converts to Christianity. Since the letter reflects good rhetorical usage it can be assumed that within the Galatian Christian communities there were members of the middle class who were educated within the Greek culture. These were very probably merchants, artisans, and war veterans although there were also poor slaves as well as poor free persons and freed slaves. The relationship between the Galatians and Paul had been excellent, as he himself testifies. Because of an illness Paul had stayed in Galatia where the people welcomed him with arms open to him and to his gospel (4:13, 14). At the time of his writing this letter, however, that friendship is endangered (4:14, 20) since other missionaries have brought in another gospel that has ensnared the communities of Galatians. It is impossible to identify with precision the adversaries about whom Paul writes; we have only his description. Very probably they were Judeo-Christian missionaries who had arrived after Paul and who were preaching circumcision and the fulfillment of the Law in addition to faith in Christ as necessary for salvation.

With regard to the geographical identification of the original communities who received this letter the debate continues to this day. For a long time scholars have discussed whether Paul refers to the Galatians from central Anatolia (North Galatian theory) or to the Roman province of Galatia (South Galatian theory). Cities such as Lystra, Derbe, and Iconium were part of this province. According to the book of Acts Paul preached the gospel in these cities on his so-called first missionary journey. The problem is that the inhabitants of those cities are never referred to as Galatians; that name is used to refer to the inhabitants of the Anatolian plateau. On the other hand Luke does not mention the founding of communities of Galatians in the book of the Acts, but he does mention in Acts 16:6 and 18:23 that Paul went to the region of Galatia and Phrygia. Is it possible that Luke was not acquainted with the churches of that region? Although we find pros and cons for both hypotheses, it seems that the majority of studies support the North Galatian theory, that is, that Paul is referring to the Galatians from central Anatolia (present-day Turkey).

The date is also a controversial topic. The letter tends to be placed between 50 and 57 C.E. It is believed that Paul wrote this letter during his stay in Ephesus or Corinth, as is noted in the itinerary given in the Acts of the Apostles. In any case it is before the letter to the Romans (57 C.E.).

Recommendations for a First Reading of the Letter

This epistle ought to be read as a letter; that is to say, it must be read as a whole, at one sitting. In that way one can observe the message of the gospel in the midst of situations full of passion and dynamism. The great theological affirmations take on life and new meanings each time they are situated in particular historical situations.

Since the letter is full of subordinate clauses that allude to different themes related to the central problem it is important to go deeply into the text as an impartial reader and to make an effort to grasp the situation that generated the letter in the first century. One will need to recognize the profile of Paul and that of the opponents described by Paul as well as the experience of the Galatians in the face of the two messages received. After that, without losing sight of the rhetorical style of the letter, the reader may ask the following: What is it that led Paul to take such a strong position against his opponents even to the point of condemning them on two occasions? Is he merely defending his authority as an apostle? What is the centrality of Paul's gospel and why does he defend it against storm and sea? What is at work within the life of the Christian communities of Galatia? Recalling these questions and the historical context can deepen one's understanding of the text.

Contexts for Interpretation

Historical Context

This letter was written toward the middle of the first century (50–57 C.E.). At that moment absolute power was in the hands of the Roman emperor, Claudius (41-54) or Nero (under his tutors Seneca and Burrus since Nero assumed full power some years later when he came of age). The Roman empire is well known for its system of bondage, for its army, and for its system of laws. Galatia had suffered the burden of obedience to the empire. For example, the constant passage of military troops was devastating. In the reign of Trajan the province was obliged to answer to the demands of the army during its passage through its lands; the Galatians had to collaborate financially with the governing force of the province in order to bear the economic burden of the soldiery. On the other hand the sale of slaves was common in Galatia and throughout the history of the province brought in abundant mercenary gain.

In Galatia the economy depended more on cattle raising than on agriculture since the earth was not very fertile for crops. Large plots of land belonged to the city residents while the peasants lived in miserable conditions. Commerce and artisanal work were abundant in the cities. A middle sector of the population prospered economically and attained access to Greek culture. Nevertheless, a large part of the people remained marginalized: the slaves, humble artisans, and laborers. The events of daily life with its existing discriminations and oppression were present to the very people who were reading Paul's message about slavery and freedom. Thus the letter must not be reduced to the theme of conflict over the Mosaic Law and circumcision. This is merely the point of departure leading to the analysis of some new dimensions of human existence such as race, social class, and ethnic groups.

Paul knew both the Roman and the Jewish worlds very well. According to the book of Acts he was a Roman citizen and also a Pharisee. For the sake of the gospel he had suffered Roman flagellation as well as the Jewish punishment of forty lashes minus one (2 Cor 11:24). He knew what it meant to be subject to the Mosaic Law. His zeal for fulfilling the Law had brought him to the point even of committing injustices, believing that in so doing, he was accomplishing the will of God. In addition he was conscious of the fact that this Law excluded non-Jews and discriminated against the sick and the ignorant. He also knew the Roman law that established social distinctions among citizens, the free, the rich and poor, the liberated, slaves and transients; he knew that it did not tolerate transgressions that threatened the stability of the empire. He observed a society based on merit in which power, money, and nobility counted above all. People who did not have these means were not counted worthy. The message that the grace of God welcomes all persons without their having to deny their humanity if they lacked such merits turns out to be more powerful when placed in this context of exaggerated stratification.

Throughout the letter one perceives a historical, ecclesial process. At that time there were certain theological and ecclesial bases established in the formation of Christianity. There was a variety of theological approaches in the diverse communities (Johannine, Pauline, Petrine, etcetera); some groups were more allied with Jewish traditions (the Law and circumcision) and there were sectors more free of those traditions. Apparently there was no clarity about whether or not Christianity formed part of Judaism or whether it was the confession of a distinct faith. In any case Paul's position tended more toward the foundation of a new community of faith.

Paul reluctantly announced the good news of Jesus Christ, and although he suffered for it, it is very probable that the theology of the cross and resurrection strengthened his faith. The marks of Jesus on the body of Paul (Gal 6:17) are perhaps the apostle's floggings mentioned in 2 Cor 11:23-27, signs proving his faith in Christ. At the same time they manifest the intolerance of a regime threatened by the message about an innocent crucified one who invites all people to new life and freedom without distinctions and without enslaving submission (Gal 3:28) common in this urban society. Paul without ceasing to be a Jew believes that his culture ought not to be imposed on the identity of other cultures, especially with respect to elements that invite subjection. At the same time he criticizes those aspects of Galatian culture that lead along the path to slavery (Gal 4:9). It is then from this insignificant body, persecuted, tortured, and criticized that the call comes so strongly to live the justice of God in freedom.

The Purpose of the Letter

The primary intention of the author is to persuade his readers not to go backwards by submitting themselves to new requirements for belonging to the people of God. They had already been welcomed by God through grace; that is to say, they had been justified by faith and not by the works of the Law. To submit themselves to circumcision and to the observance of certain days would be equivalent to returning to the slavery of various elements in the world and living in terror. On receiving the gift of the Spirit they could live out of Christian freedom while practicing justice as free sons and daughters of God.

To substantiate his position he uses four arguments and an exhortation. (1) Paul has the authority of an apostle who was chosen by God. The gospel he proclaims to them is of divine origin. Besides, the people in Jerusalem had already accepted his ministry among the non-Jews. (2) The justice of God does not proceed from the Law, but rather from faith in Jesus Christ. God chooses by faith; there is no need for recourse to any other means. (3) The justice of God is for everyone, Jews and non-Jews. Ever since the time of Abraham, who acted out of faith, the non-Jewish nations had been blessed by God in accordance with the promise that was fulfilled in Jesus Christ. (4) Through the Spirit they are called sons and daughters of God, able to call God their Father. They are children of the free woman, according to the allegory of Sarah and Hagar. In the exhortation Paul makes the people see that it is the Spirit who drives them to practice justice (they do not need an external law). If they have been re-created in Christ they no longer live according to their instincts or according to the flesh.

Canonical Context

The canonicity of the letter to the Galatians has never presented problems. Its interpretation, however, as with the letter to the Romans, has been a source of controversy since earliest times. That the letter was well received is obvious from the fact that as early as the end of the second century there were lists of letters in which the letter to the Galatians appeared. The epistle is cited by name or by its themes from the year 175. Polycarp and Clement of Alexandria allude to it or cite it. Irenaeus mentions it frequently. Origen dealt with it in his commentaries as did Marcion, Jerome, and Pelagius. Finally, during the patristic period more commentaries were dedicated to the letter to the Galatians than to any other letter of Paul. Tertullian, Marcion, the Gnostics, Origen, and others of divergent opinions all based their positions on the same Pauline sources.

It is known that for Luther in the sixteenth century the letter to the Galatians was fundamental to interpreting the situation of his time and launching the Protestant Reformation. Luther called it "my Catherine." (Catherine was his wife.) Finally the letter has been a light in conflict situations within the Church as well as outside of it. The themes of freedom and faith, the Spirit and ethics, the Gospel and the Law all lend themselves to being updated in each situation in which Christian liberty and the practice of justice may be threatened.

Relationship to Other Biblical Texts

Genesis and other books of the Hebrew Scriptures. Paul uses the Scriptures in order to give greater credence to his arguments. For him the promises of God to his ancestors as recorded in the Scriptures are fulfilled in the coming of Jesus Christ, the Messiah and Son of God. From the time when Paul assumed a ministry among the non-Jews one of his objectives was to make them see that they were not to be simply fearful of God but that they also had the right to participate fully in the promises of God to Abraham. In addition in citing the text of Genesis 15 he was led to affirm that they are children and descendants of Abraham through the mediation of Christ (Gal 3:6-18) in spite of their not having been circumcised. In Gal 4:22-31 he takes up the story of Hagar and Sarah from Genesis 16 and 21. He allegorizes it in order to stress the fact that from the beginning the people were called to freedom since they were born of the lineage of the promise and not in agreement with a physical order occurring within the Jewish racial system. Other scriptural texts within this letter include the Sinai tradition (3:19-25), the commandment to love (5:14; Lev 19:18), and the impartiality of God.

The letter to the Romans written by Paul about the year 57 C.E. evokes the same themes, but since the situation was distinct the themes appear to be developed with more calm, depth, and coherence. In Romans Paul elaborates his thought with respect to sin and the role of the Jews as the chosen ones (Romans 9–11); he also expresses himself in more diplomatic language. The central theme of the letter to the Romans is the justice of God that is revealed to all, Jews and non-Jews alike, while in Galatians Paul alludes more to the freedom that obtains by virtue of his having accented the justice of God.

The Letter of James. It seems that toward the end of the first century the theme of justification by faith had been changed into a slogan that was being badly interpreted. Some thought that upon believing they were justified by faith and not through works, and that consequently they were exempt from any commitment whatsoever to the practice of justice. The letter of James deals directly with that problem even to the point of citing the same source that Paul used, that is, the justification of Abraham. "Faith without works is dead" declared James in order to demonstrate that if there is no solidarity with the orphans, widows, or poor, the status of the justified is in question (Jas 2:1-26). Thus without any effort to find agreement between James and Paul we can affirm with the same radicality that for Paul also there is no justification if faith is not shown in love (5:6). What is important is that new creation that alone produces the fruits of the Spirit (Galatians 5–6).

Liturgical Contexts

In this brief letter we find liturgical phrases used in hymns and creeds referring to God (1:1-3; 4:6; 3:20 and others) or to Christ (1:1, 4; 2:20; 3:13); a doxology in 1:5; blessings in 6:16, 18; Christological titles such as Lord (1:3) or Son of God (2:20). The well-known text from Gal 3:26-28 is a pre-Pauline baptismal formula. Likewise we find a list of vices and virtues in Gal 5:19-23.

Parts of this letter are read on three occasions of the liturgical year, in the first and second periods of Ordinary Time. On the first of January, the feast of Mary, the Mother of God, we read 4:4-7 in order to recall that Jesus was born of a woman under the Law to rescue us from the Law and call us to be adopted sons and daughters. On June 29, the feast of St. Peter and St. Paul, we read 1:11-20 to remember when these apostles were known in Jerusalem. Finally the letter is read between October 3 and 12 to recall the grace of God, the new life in Christ, and faith united with Christian commitment.

SECOND READING

Prescript: Greeting: 1:1-5

The mention of the name of the sender (among others), the recipients, and a blessing are common elements in the letters of Paul. These appear here also. Nevertheless, from the greeting itself the reader notices that the correspondence is about a rather delicate topic. In v. 1 Paul introduces himself with the title of apostle. The apostle was a delegate or ambassador with all official powers. By adding that he was so named by Jesus Christ directly, and not by human authority, he already hints at the principal issues that generated this letter. On the one hand Paul defends his apostolic authority that was being questioned; on the other, because he was chosen by God directly and not by human intervention he puts himself indirectly into the controversy over grace and law.

The ancient formula that alludes to expiation ("who gave himself for our sins") and the following phrase ("to set us free from the present evil age") allow us a glimpse of Pauline theology, centered on the death and resurrection (v. 1) of Jesus for the liberation of those who choose that same life of faith. From the opening of the letter Paul reminds his addressees that they have been set free from the oppressive world in which they lived and continue to live. Obviously it is not a matter of isolating them from the world but of their taking on freedom as subjects in an alienated world. The verb "to free or liberate" carries with it as proof the Exodus event. Both past and present freedom bring this greeting to a conclusion with a song of praise to God.

Exordium or Introduction: 1:6-10

Paul comes sharply to the point. He skips the customary praises to the communities because of their growth in faith and instead reproaches them for having let themselves be influenced so rapidly by those who have distorted the gospel, the good news of Jesus Christ. They had been so enthusiastic about their new life in Christ (3:3-5) that it seems incredible to Paul that they have forgotten that experience. He does not indicate here the nature of the misrepresentation that his opponents ("some who are confusing you," v. 7) have given to the message of the gospel. He merely distinguishes the difference between them and their counterparts, namely the Galatians who had turned to God after being called by pure grace (v. 6). The situation is so critical that Paul twice curses anyone (including himself, his own people, or even an angel) who perverts the gospel previously proclaimed by him (vv. 8-9). The curse here denotes an absolute condemnation. Paul believes it important to clarify the fact that his open attitude toward non-Jews is not due to his wanting to please everyone as some may possibly have thought, but rather, because he was following the will of God since he was now God's servant.

New Life, Recounted: 1:11–2:14

The Call of God (1:11-24)

What proves the veracity of the message is not so much the discourse itself but the change in people's lives. Paul, before describing his gospel, tells the story of his life. Throughout the narration one observes simultaneously something of his theology and also the conflictual situation. Three elements stand out in this testimonial section.

(1) Paul underlines the truth that his gospel comes from God without any human mediation. It is so important for him to clarify that truth that he points out twice that it is not of human origin (v. 11) and twice he writes that the gospel or the Son was revealed to him, whether by Jesus Christ (v. 11) or by God (v. 15). With that certitude Paul for now does not see himself obligated to render an account to the authorities at Jerusalem (although they were the most revered among the apostles). Having been converted to the call of God to announce his Son among the non-Jews (v. 16), Paul continues on his mission. His expanding the understanding of "messiah" to "Son of God" universalizes the Good News.

(2) Paul gives an account of his conversion (vv. 13-16). No matter how many times he may affirm the fact that his authority comes from above, if that new life is not observed in daily living his discourse would have no backing. Paul's conversion was radical. From being a persecutor, destroyer, and accomplice in killings (Acts 8:1) for a cause he thought was just according to the tradition of his ancestors, he changed to being a proclaimer of the good news of faith to both Jews and non-Jews. Because of that radical change the persecuted communities of Judea rejoiced (1:24). His fervent zeal for the Law had converted him into a violent destroyer. Paul understood what it meant to submit to the Law. When obedience to the Law is observed blindly there is no room for grace and one runs the danger of losing its original meaning.

(3) The third element (observable in v. 18) can indicate two situations depending upon two distinct perspectives: that of Paul and that of the Galatians. According to his own testimony he does not scorn the authority of Jerusalem. Although he was called by grace (v. 15) from his mother's womb, as were some of the prophets, after staying a certain length of time in Arabia and Damascus he wanted to meet Peter. (One wonders what they might have spoken about during those fifteen days of being together.) He sought contact with the other apostles as well. We do not know why he only saw James. Fourteen years later he returned to Jerusalem to be acknowledged again by the hierarchy of the Christian community (2:1-10). From the perspective of the Galatians Paul wanted to make

his readers see that his gospel was legitimate in the eyes of God and in the minds of the Church authorities in Jerusalem. The importance of this last insight throws into relief the solemn oath in 1:20. Paul does not want to enter into conflict with the hierarchy except when that authority acts ambiguously as compared with the liberty of the gospel. This autobiographical fragment offers very valid data on the course of his development as an apostle.

The Meeting at Jerusalem (2:1-10)

The second visit to Jerusalem clearly demonstrates to the Galatians and to the group of opponents who had infiltrated themselves into the community that the apostolate of Paul among the non-Jews had been recognized by the authorities at Jerusalem during a celebrated reunion. After so many years of experience as an apostle in various regions of the Roman empire Paul felt the need to go to Jerusalem in order to clarify some points about his work among the non-Jews. He says that he was motivated by a revelation (v. 2). By that time the gospel had already spread to several communities outside Jerusalem, after which there was unleashed in Jerusalem a persecution during which Stephen was martyred (Acts 8:1). Obviously one of the first discussions had to be focused on male circumcision. For followers of Judaism it was natural that the newly converted non-Jewish men would follow the Judaic tradition and the observance of the Law. It was impossible to live together amicably without the rites of purification. Paul, on the other hand, affirms that the God of grace received everyone through the mediation of Jesus Christ without the necessity of fulfilling other requirements. This discussion must surely have developed into a grave problem that then needed to be discussed in a council. Acts 15 records that assembly with certain distinct facts. Paul attended it, accompanied by Barnabas and Titus. According to Luke, Barnabas had looked for Paul in Tarsus to bring him to Antioch (Acts 11:25) and perhaps it was he who introduced Paul to the authorities in Jerusalem (Acts 9:27). Titus was a converted Greek, an uncircumcised coworker with Paul (v. 3). According to Paul, upon explaining the content of his gospel to the authorities (James, Cephas, and John) he was able to convince them of the authenticity of his ministry. Without imposing anything on his converts (v. 6), that is to say neither circumcision nor obedience to the Law, they recognized his charism for proclaiming the Good News to non-Jews. One concrete proof of the agreement was that they did not oblige him to circumcise Titus (v. 3). In a final agreement sealed with a handshake as a sign of their unity the tasks were divided: Paul would busy himself with the non-Jews and the apostles from Jerusalem with the Jews, but both had the obligation of declaring solidarity with the poor of Jerusalem (2:10). The fact that Paul mentions only that task as his own ("ours") does not overrule the commitment of those in Jerusalem for the poor. According to Luke's account certain norms related to foods (Acts 15:29) were imposed on the non-Jewish converts, but in Galatians Paul does not allude to this requirement.

Paul accomplished his objective in Jerusalem, but not all difficulties were resolved. He had to stay firm in the face of some "false believers" who had infiltrated their way into the community (v. 4) and who were not in agreement with his gospel because they looked unfavorably on the abandonment of the Law and circumcision. Paul uses strong words against them: they came to "spy on the freedom we have in Christ Jesus, so that they might enslave us" (v. 4). In this section Paul recognizes James, Cephas, and John as notable and respectable pillars of the community but he declares himself equal to them in power. Since the authority of these apostles was recognized among the Christian communities within and outside of Jerusalem Paul perhaps saw a danger in canonizing the leaders. For that reason he relativizes their power and affirms the fact that God shows no partiality to persons (v. 6). The fact that in vv. 7 and 8 only the name of Peter is mentioned (curiously enough he is not called Cephas as he is elsewhere) and that Paul puts himself on the same level, invoking the authority of God for both of them, indicates that there was general recognition of the authority of Peter among Christians. Paul claims for himself a similar authority, not for any personal prestige but because before God there is neither Jew nor Greek, slave nor free, no male and female (3:28). The Galatians could be at peace: the gospel they had heard from Paul was legitimate because it was of divine origin and the pillars of the Church had approved it in the Jerusalem assembly.

The responsibility to remember the poor (v. 10) appears as an insignificant appendage but in reality it is not so. Solidarity with the poor is one of the marks of the new life in Christ. The importance Paul affords to it in his other letters proves that he made an effort to fulfill that commitment (2 Corinthians 8, 9). As a result of the Jesus movement the marginalized (the poor, women, the sick) have come to Jerusalem. It is probable that the various famines that were suffered in that time aggravated the situation to the utmost. For that reason the Christian communities of the different cities of the empire, even those composed of members of modest resources such as the Thessalonians, had to share with their poor brothers and sisters in Jerusalem. Concrete examples of solidarity did not enter into the discussion of the assembly. Many times, in spite of doctrinal differences, agreements were reached in commitment to the needy. Paul affirms on two occasions that the important truth is not circumcision or uncircumcision, but faith working through love (5:6).

The Conflict in Antioch (2:11-14)

Notwithstanding the agreement achieved at the assembly in Jerusalem, difficulties continued among the Christians of Jewish traditions and the non-Jews free of the observance of the Law. Paul recalls the incident at Antioch between himself and Cephas (Peter). Now there was question of the possibility of Jews and non-Jews eating together. Since within the proclamation of the Good News there was no partiality shown to persons Paul considered it incorrect not to share bread. This sharing of bread included the eucharistic meals. Peter had dared to share the meal with non-Jews, a great piece of audacity for a Jew, but he retreated when some conservatives with a modicum of authority arrived (were they sent by James or were they his collaborators?). Why did Peter retract? What did he fear? Perhaps he was not sure of acting correctly when he looked beyond his Jewish traditions. In any case the attitude of a person as important as Peter jeopardized the advances made in living with non-Jews since even Barnabas let himself be convinced by the idea. Even worse, it could happen that the non-Jewish Christians would feel obligated to follow the Law in order to be considered on the same level as the Jews. That would mean the rejection of the gift of freedom. For that reason Paul publicly censured the attitude of Peter. In his mind Peter was not proceeding in the truth of the gospel that includes the risk of sharing bread with everyone, freely and without prejudice. The letter challenges us even today to free ourselves of the limitations of distinct ecclesial traditions in order to share the Supper of the Lord.

Galatians 2:11-14 offers no direct justification for today's "open communion" policy in certain Christian denominations. Nonetheless, it serves to point up the sin of division within the body of Christ and separation between members of that body at the Lord's table.

As early as the middle of the second century Justin the Martyr declared: "No one may share the Eucharist with us unless he or she believes that what we teach is true, unless he or she is washed clean in the regenerating waters of baptism for the remission of sins, and unless he or she lives in accordance with the principles given us by Christ" (*Apol. 1,* 66). The Catholic and Orthodox churches have always considered the Eucharist the sign of full unity in faith and charity. For this reason neither of them allows "open communion." This situation is no less painful for Catholics and Orthodox than it is for Protestant Christians and is a powerful incentive for all Christians to pray and work for full ecclesial and eucharistic communion among all Christians. At this point in history, however, "open communion" between Protestants and Catholics would create the false impression that we have already achieved a sufficient unity of faith and such an impression would weaken our ecumenical efforts.

In the Catholic Church the local bishop may make exceptions in particular cases when serious pastoral need warrants it and those who ask for eucharistic communion believe in the real presence of Christ and repent of their sins out of love for God. Protestant Christians share with Roman Catholics a common baptism and the basics of Christian faith. Such an exceptional eucharistic sharing may intensify the search for full unity in faith and love in the one Church of Christ (cf. *CCC* 1398-1401).

The Thesis: Justification is by Faith and Not by the Works of the Law (2:15-21)

In this pericope Paul defines his gospel and presents the central thesis of the letter. In the brief chiasm of v. 16 the proposition of justification by faith is outlined:

A. Human beings are not justified by works of the Law
  B. but by faith in Jesus Christ
    C. We also have believed in Christ Jesus
  B'. so as to be justified by faith in Christ
A'. and not by works of the Law because no one will be justified by works of the Law.

Paul underlines here the fact that the Galatians have already believed in Christ Jesus and therefore have been justified. They have, then, been freed from the Law. The term "to justify" is not used widely in our day, but if it is related to such terms as "justice," "just," "injustice," it is easier to perceive its meaning. To be justified by faith means that human beings can achieve justice (i.e., be just and be declared just by God) independent of the Law (Rom 3:21). God through the liberating life of Jesus Christ receives them by divine grace and transforms them into new subjects capable of practicing justice. They can do this guided by their own renewed consciousness in Christ and not by the dictates of the Law, thanks to the gift of the Spirit (Gal 3:5; Rom 8:6).

Paul probably came to perceive the problem of the Law through his own experience. He as a Pharisee zealously followed the Law and violently persecuted the faithful. When it was revealed to him that the Crucified One had been raised from the dead by God (Gal 1:1) he realized that God had made Godself one with the Crucified and that on the other hand Roman law had condemned one who was innocent and Jewish Law had condemned the Son of God (3:13). Justice (2:21) cannot come from the Law since the Law does not give life (3:21). Paul relativizes the Law, recognizing its limitations and accepting the regimen of faith. Upon discovering the dimension of faith he universalizes the Good News. All can acquire the justice of God (Rom 3:22): Jews, Greeks, women, men, slaves, and masters. Justification by faith and not by Law is a proclamation of good news for the Galatians for a number of reasons. From the religious point of view they are elevated to the same level as the Jews and are freed from fear of the cosmic order (4:8, 9). From the perspective of their stratified and discriminatory society they can consider themselves worthy persons without need of merits since they are received by the grace of God. Faith in Jesus Christ (2:16) is the key to accessing the gift of justification. Traditionally this phrase is translated as "faith in Jesus Christ." Nevertheless, it can also be translated as "the faith of Jesus Christ." That is, the faith that Jesus lived, faithful to the Father, is the same faith that makes justification possible. Romans 5:18 and 19 refers to Jesus' work of justice and obedience through which came the justification that gives life (Rom 5:18) and the belief that all are constituted just (Rom 5:19). To believe in that event (2:16) and to believe that God resurrected the Crucified One (Rom 4:25) leads to justification. Therefore the non-Jews are not the only sinners; neither are the Jews (2:17, Romans 1–2). The function of law (whether that be the Torah, Roman law, or all kinds of customs and institutional logic) makes one see the need to transcend that law and look for another logic. For Paul it is a matter of the logic of faith, of the Spirit, of God, or of love.

Orienting oneself by that logic, one lives for God and not for the Law. This means that one acts as Christ acted, since it is Christ who lives within a person (2:20). These persons no longer act selfishly in accord with their own interests but are motivated by the mutually binding love of Christ. If Christ died to reveal the grace of God and the impotence of the Law (Rom 8:3) one should not receive the grace of God in vain (Gal 2:21; 2 Cor 6:1). The faith of Christ is received by acting always as he does. Paul preaches the kerygma not only in word but also with his own body (2:20; 6:17).

Probatio or Proofs: 3:1–4:31

Chapters 3 and 4 fashion the arguments Paul uses to prove his thesis as laid out in 2:15-21. He uses three kinds of argument: his own experience (3:1-5), the Scriptures (3:6-14; 4:21-31) and examples taken from daily life (3:15; 4:1-2). In 4:12-20 he evokes his good relationship with the Galatians. The apostle's plan is to convince the Galatians with his arguments that they have already been justified by faith, blessed by God, made heirs of a lineage of free persons, and all of that independent of the Law. Consequently to submit to the Law again would be equivalent to taking a step backward on history's path toward liberation in Christ.

Why Go Backward After the Experience of New Life? (3:1-5)

The argument from change in one's own life is fundamental; it is worth more than any ratiocination. Paul and the Galatians know very well what has happened in the communities after having heard the gospel of Jesus, the crucified Messiah. They received the Spirit, "experienced great things" (he does not explain the nature of these experiences) and even performed miracles. But they ought to remember that fulfillment of the Law was never given as the condition for receiving the Spirit and that nevertheless they were living a full and meaningful life. The opponents had to be excellent and sophisticated preachers to fascinate those who were supposedly firm in the faith.

On two occasions Paul calls the Galatians foolish and leads them by way of rhetorical questions to reflect on their past and present lives. He wants to make them see the absurdity of listening to those who preach fulfillment of the Law and circumcision. If they began so well with the Spirit (3:3) and if they continue experiencing the Spirit in their lives (3:5) they are indeed foolish if they believe in any other discourse that ends by subjecting them to the Law (3:3). In an ironic statement Paul contrasts the Spirit and the flesh. Flesh can be a direct allusion to circumcision or it can be thought of as describing a rather inferior concept of life, or it may be that which is contrary to the Spirit (cf. Rom 8:6). Perhaps one can begin with the flesh and end with the Spirit (as a total change of life takes place) but never the reverse.

Abraham's Experience of Faith (3:6-14)

Paul has recourse to Scripture to legitimize his position. Possibly the text about Abraham as well as the one about Hagar and Sarah (4:22-31) formed a part of the arguments of his opponents. Obligated as he was to refer to these passages in his responses, Paul boldly reinterpreted them. One does not find texts in the Hebrew Scriptures that contrast faith and Law but they appear intimately related to one another (cf. Sir 44:19-21; 1 Macc 2:50-52). Paul as a student of the Law must surely have known the promises made to the Israelites who obeyed the Law, namely life and blessing, and that disobedience carried with it death and a curse (Deut 30:15-20). How was it possible to make a change of interpretation so radical as to arrive at the point of setting faith and the Law in opposition? Perhaps the concrete experience of life led him to consider the negative side of the Law when instead of being written in hearts it was petrified in traditions and institutions. Roman law condemns an innocent man on the cross; Jewish Law curses the one hung on the wood, none other than Jesus, the very giver of life. Paul himself in his zeal for the Law arrested innocent people and approved of the stoning of Stephen. So it would seem that justice could not proceed from the Law (3:21).

Paul picks up the story of Abraham again to testify to the fact that it was faith (and not the Law) that credited him with being just before God (3:6). This gives him a basis for affirming that the true descendants of Abraham are those who like him act in faith, and not simply those who are bound to him by racial ties. With this argument one can include those peoples excluded by the Law. They attain the divine blessing inasmuch as they are received by God for having the same attitude of faith as had Abraham. No people needs to feel either superior or inferior to another.

Verses 10-12 seek to persuade the reader of the seriousness of the problems connected with the Law. Paul compares obedience to the Law to a dead-end street. The Law itself claims that the one who fulfills the entire Law is saved and comes into life (3:12) but whoever does not fulfill the Law is cursed (3:10). Paul's warning implies not only one's inability to fulfill the entire Law but the state of slavery, fear, and dehumanization that those persons experience who try to fulfill the requirements of the Law. He does not want anyone to think that he invalidates the Scriptures. For that reason he recalls the text of Habakkuk (Gal 3:11). When it seemed that everything was lost, that soon the small nation of Judah would be invaded by the powerful empire of Babylonia, Habakkuk affirmed with hope: "the one who is righteous will live by faith." The path of faith is the one that carries and strengthens life.

Galatians 3:13 introduces the messiah (Christ) as the liberator from that slavery. The redemptive work of Jesus Christ alludes to the ransom of the slaves of that time in order to free them. The difference with the liberation of Jesus Christ is that payment for freedom does not come from outside but from the handing over of his life and submission to condemnation itself (3:13). This fact is, for Paul, a public demonstration of the uselessness of the Mosaic Law. In cursing the one hanged on wood the Law cursed the Son of God, and this would necessarily have been a scandal for Paul.

Galatians 3:14 makes it clear that in Christ the promise of God to Abraham is fulfilled, namely that the nations would be blessed. Likewise in this text the question posed in v. 5 is answered: the Galatians have received the promised Spirit not through the Law but through faith.

The Law Does Not Nullify the Promise (3:15-18)

In this section it is stated that the nations are heirs to the promises of the God of Abraham. Paul gives three reasons: (1) the promises came before the Law (vv. 15, 17); (2) the offspring to whom the promise in Genesis 15 alludes is not the innumerable descendants bound to Abraham by the flesh but rather Christ (v. 16); and (3) the inheritance proceeds from the direct promise of God to Abraham and not by decree nor by a determinant of the Jewish Law (v. 18). The key word "promise" occurs eight times in ch. 3. The promise is not only superior to the Law but determines the application of the Law.

In order to lay the basis for the first point Paul uses a comparison from the legal system. Just as a well-written will or testament cannot be annulled or changed, so the promise of God to Abraham cannot be annulled by the Law that came after the promise. Will and promise are considered synonyms. The reference to four hundred thirty years is a direct allusion to Exod 12:40 in agreement with the LXX; it is the estimate of years during which the Israelites (Hebrews) stayed in Egypt and Canaan. According to the laws of Greece and Rome wills could be changed by the testators at any time. For that reason if Paul chose this example it could be that he had in mind that only God had the power to change the divine will and testament.

To solidify the second argument Paul reads the collective noun "offspring" in the singular. This exegesis seems strange to us perhaps, but it is not uncommon to find this procedure in rabbinical exegesis where a small fact or piece of information sometimes serves as the basis for an entire argument. On the other hand the belief that Christ was the seed of Abraham formed part of the pre-Pauline tradition. Finally, Paul wants to exclude the traditional Jewish interpretation (descendants by reason of race) and affirm Christ as the offspring par excellence: that is, through him all believers in Christ are the true descendants of Abraham (by virtue of the promise). God, not the Law, is the subject of that promise, and because God is the actor the promise happens in accordance with the order of grace (the third reason). The promise is the inheritance/blessing for all nations.

The Role of the Law (3:19-25)

After all that Paul has said about the Law the recipients of the letter would have had to ask themselves what its function could have been. Here Paul tries to respond. The Law appears in history because of the transgressions of human beings (v. 19) and their need for a disciplinarian (v. 24). It establishes a manner of measuring the time prior to and following the arrival of faith, or rather of Christ. The time following his arrival is qualitatively superior and marks the end of the former era, that of the Law. Paul insists on the inferiority of the Law as compared with Christ and faith by exposing its negative function. The Law appears not to give life or produce justice, but to be the cause of human sinfulness; it was not given directly by God who had given Abraham the promise but was promulgated by angels and through a mediator (Moses). Although in the Hebrew Scriptures the narratives about the revelation of the Torah do not describe the presence of angels on Sinai it seems that in Judaism that tradition existed and was viewed quite positively. Paul, however, objects to it for that very reason; Gal 3:20 reenforces the idea that the Law is inferior precisely because it comes through mediators.

Verse 21 is crucial to understanding that Paul's attitude to the Law is not arbitrary. He reaffirms the fact that the Law is incapable of giving life. Before, we had said that he draws that conclusion from his own experience. He would not be against the Law if it really were to bring new life. After all is said and done what matters is to discover the source of justice. For Paul justice proceeds from Christ, the source of life. Christ had to come because the Law did not give life. To the contrary, it excludes the "nations"; it subjects or imprisons those who are under the Law (3:23), and it functions as a disciplinarian to punish the one who transgresses its commands. In antiquity the disciplinarian was not the teacher but the slave who accompanied the student to and from school. His job was to protect him on the road and make sure that he learned good manners. It seems that the meaning of a disciplinarian for Paul was related to severity, punishment, and hard discipline. He considers that time one of enslavement, imprisonment (3:23), and submission to sin (3:22). The Law was applicable until the arrival of the offspring to whom the promise was made (3:19) and until the promise was handed on to those who believed in Jesus Christ (3:22)—whether Jew or Gentile—until such time as the faith was to be revealed (3:23) and believers were justified by that faith (3:24). Once the faith had arrived neither prisons nor disciplinarians nor possibilities of being excluded had any reason for being (3:25).

From Slavery to Life as Free Sons and Daughters: The Banishment of All Discrimination (3:26–4:11)

The movement in this section throws into relief the specific condition of being a son or daughter of God. Such a condition is made reality by accepting Christ (3:26), through baptism (3:27), and through one's having been liberated from the Law, thanks to the Son of God (4:5).

The core of the entire argumentation of chs. 3 and 4 is contained in 3:26-28. Here Paul clearly describes the message of liberation for the Galatians and for the other nations. Also there appears here the only reference to baptism. If Paul mentions it, it is because he wants to remind the Galatians of the meaning of the new creation to which they now belong. The text (vv. 26-29) alludes to the new reality of those who have been clothed in Christ, that is to say, those who have assumed his life and work and act like Christ. There is agreement among the commentaries that 3:26-28 is part of a pre-Pauline baptismal formula. Paul cites it in order to affirm the novelty of a new society without discrimination. In the dimension of faith no one is either superior or inferior to anyone else. The formula is radical if read within the context of a Greco-Roman society that was highly stratified and meritocratic, and in a Jewish society that considered itself superior to other nations by virtue of its having the Torah. What is radical about the affirmation is that it touches not only ethnic and religious elements but also social and cultural ones. In a society devoted to patriarchy and servitude to hear that there is no longer slave nor free or that there is equality between man and woman is to welcome the utopian society, the dream and goal of all the marginalized and unjustly treated. With good reason women participated in the Jesus movement and in the first Christian communities. What would the Galatian women think of the return to circumcision as a prerequisite for salvation? They would probably feel that they themselves were the first victims of discrimination under the Law and circumcision. Paul has to stress the fact in 3:29—after the baptismal fragment—that if the Galatians already belong to Christ, they are also descendants of Abraham and heirs according to the promise.

To be called a child of God is to be considered a worthy person. The emperors had themselves called sons of God and thus attributed to themselves divine prerogatives. The Jews also considered themselves children of God because of the covenant of God with this people. Paul here makes it very clear that divine filiation occurs through faith in Christ Jesus. The particular christological event that makes filiation possible is developed in 4:4-5 which deals with the maximum solidarity of God in the Son who assumes history in all its human dimension: he was born of a woman and born under the Law. Liberation happens from below and consists of abolishing slavery to the Law, thus making children who were previously enslaved free sons and daughters.

Those freed from the Law now have a voice. Whereas before the Law had taken possession of them and imposed its way on them, now they have become persons, actors with their own voices who cry out "Abba, Father." God instilled the Spirit of the Son in them and made them heirs by divine grace (4:7).

Perhaps the Galatians did not know what it meant to be subject to the Jewish Law. In 4:8, 9 Paul reminds them of their former life when they did not know Christ. They lived subject to "the weak and beggarly elemental spirits" (4:9), possibly what they considered to be cosmic powers that directed their lives for them. Paul categorizes these as weak and of little value. To follow the observance of certain days, months, and years of the calendar would be equivalent to turning back, to allowing oneself to be enslaved by idols, to losing the status of being a worthy person, a free child of God. The fear Paul expresses in 4:11 allows the Galatians to see that they are on the point of abandoning the gospel of freedom or that they have already been convinced in many aspects by their opponents. In 5:10, however, he is more optimistic.

Good Memories of Friendship (4:12-20)

The argument from friendship was common in Hellenistic rhetoric; Paul uses it in this part of the letter. He changes the tone of the prior paragraphs and calls forth, with great brotherly feeling, former good relationships with the Galatian communities. The Galatians had received him with open arms when he was with them. Even when because of his illness they could have cast him aside, considering his sickness a work of the devil (according to the customs of the times), they received him as an angel and even as Christ himself (4:14). We do not know what illness Paul suffered (it may have been epilepsy or malaria or a malady of the eyes). His recent converts, as Paul perceived it, showed themselves disposed to offer him even their most valued possession if that were necessary.

Paul uses the image of a mother to show the Galatians his profound affection and concern. In 4:12 he asks them to reciprocate with a similar feeling. He speaks the truth in all frankness as would a mother and not an enemy. He advises them with maternal zeal concerning their enemies. These enemies are not who they appear to be; rather they are seeking to divide the Galatians from the Christian community to which they belong, thus enticing them to follow their way (in founding another community?) (4:17). Paul even feels that he is giving them birth, that the image of Christ is still in the process of formation, and he recommends that they be faithful and persevering not only when he is with them but also when he is absent (4:18). With maternal love he addresses them as "my little children" (4:19). He sees himself as a nagging mother who no longer knows what to do with her children since she cannot convince them with her words (4:20). For that reason he wants to be with them so that the tone of his voice and his gestures might help to solidify his written words and convince them of the grave danger to which they are exposed.

Heirs of a Lineage of Free Persons (4:21-31)

Paul returns to theological argument, interpreting his last written passage in such a way as to underline the status of liberty already acquired by the Galatians who received the faith. It is very probable that the stories of Hagar and Sarah were frequently cited by the opponents to prove that the true heirs of the promise were the Jews descended from Isaac, son of the promise. The nations, if they desired to be heirs of Abraham, would have to fulfill the Law and be circumcised. The text if read literally is obvious and convincing. It argues more for the position of the adversaries. For that reason Paul sees himself obligated to respond by using the same texts from Scripture but employing a hermeneutical process that leads to a total inversion of the literal reading. Paul allegorizes the text, or rather warns that it deals with a typology and reads it as such. He directs his words especially to those who want to subject themselves to the Law (v. 21).

The allusion is to Genesis 16 and 21. Hagar and Sarah, spouses of Abraham, one free and the other slave, each had a son by Abraham. The mothers of these children are interpreted as mother foundresses of two peoples, one of free lineage (that of Sarah) and the other of a slave (that of Hagar). Paul and his opponents overlook the fact that in that time the son of a slave woman was considered free if such were the condition of the father. Ishmael and Isaac, therefore, were both free, but this reality is not important since the reading of the Scripture is not based on historical persons but on the typology represented. What is up for discussion is the true line of Abraham, the heirs to the promise. Paul wants to demonstrate that they are the ones who are in Christ and are not subject to the Law, that is to say, the Gentiles and the Jewish Christians freed from the Law.

The line of Hagar is marked by servitude because her son is born normally in obedience to the laws of nature. Hagar is fecund and gives birth to Abraham's son. Sarah, on the other hand, is sterile and is blessed with a son at an unexpected time by means of the promise. It is the promise, grace, that points to the status of Sarah's freedom.

The inverted interpretation appears clearer when a geographical location is given to the origin of the covenants, since each son represents a covenant. The covenant proceeding from present-day Jerusalem is the covenant from Mount Sinai where the Law of Moses was given. The world represented is the true slave, and its descendants live in slavery. Readers will understand that these are the Jewish followers of the Law, those who believe themselves to be the true descendants of Abraham and Sarah. For Paul they are the ones who belong to the world represented by Hagar, the former slave.

According to 4:26 the truly free world is the one proceeding from Jerusalem above. This term was familiar to readers who understood this Jerusalem to be of divine origin, a universal city to which belong all the races who receive the faith. It is not reduced to the Church of the Gentiles but includes all peoples including the Jewish Christians free from the Law. It is a question of the covenant that engenders free sons and daughters. Thus the true descendants of Sarah are not the Jews who are subject to the Law but the nations free from the Law.

Galatians 4:27 is a reference to Isa 54:1. Why does Paul choose this text? Sarah was sterile, but she was married and was not abandoned. Surely Paul wants to emphasize the preference God has for the excluded (C. K. Barrett, "The Allegory of Abraham, Sarah, and Hagar"). The marginalization of Sarah comes from her being sterile, yet God blesses her. Hagar, according to Genesis 21, is the socially marginalized and abandoned one; God blesses her in the desert. In Galatia the point of discussion is the exclusion and marginalization of nations on the part of the Jews because of the Law. In the Genesis account Sarah would be the ancestor of the Jews and Hagar of the foreign nations. Thus a coherent reading from Paul's point of argumentation would be that the Jews, blood descendants of Sarah, should be considered the "spiritual descendants" of Hagar in her status as slave, while the "spiritual descendants" of Sarah, the free woman, would be the descendants of Hagar, that is, the Gentiles, the true heirs of the promise. Galatians 4:28 makes that explicit.

Verses 29 and 30 allow one to see the tension between the Judaizers and the Gentiles. It is not the Gentiles who pursue the Jews but the reverse. Paul shows himself firm with the Jews. In Romans 9–11 he will review this posture. In Gal 4:30 he apparently proposes that the Jews should have the same attitude toward the nations, but if so he is arguing contrary to his own stance against the exclusiveness of the Law. What we can perhaps say here is that in the new life in Christ there is no place for slavery. All those who are in Christ are free because all are one in Christ. Galatians 4:31 not only synthesizes this last argument but summarizes all the arguments developed in chs. 3 and 4; at the same time it introduces the call to freedom that will be treated in the next chapter.

Exhortation: 5:1–6:10

Freedom as Shown in the Practice of Justice (5:1-12)

Justification by faith called forth a new identity in the Christians: they are now righteous and free. Paul authoritatively exhorts the Galatians (5:1) to live in accord with that identity and remain firm. Verse 1 is emphatic. The purpose of freedom in Christ does not consist in merely changing masters but in living the gift of freedom. To return to circumcision would be to submit to the Law, the equivalent not only of falling into slavery but also of separating oneself from Christ (5:4). The discussion is not centered in a simple ritual: circumcision versus non-circumcision. That would be the least of the issues; rather it is a question of two distinct ways of seeing and acting in the world. For that reason the fundamental opposition is between the justice sought in fulfillment of the Law and the justice caused by God in the innocent crucified one, that is to say, in the order of the Spirit and faith. The first enslaves, terrorizes, and condemns; it is of the order of the flesh and for that reason activity is centered in personal interests. On the other hand the other type of justice frees, produces life, and saves. Its concrete manifestation is communitarian and disinterested love (5:6). This happens because the justice of Christ is born of grace.

Verse 6 is fundamental for preventing a misunderstanding of justification by faith in the sense of passivity, disjoined from the practice of justice. The new identity of the justified and liberated is visible only through the works of love.

James is right in affirming that faith without works is dead. Paul would agree with James, as is evidenced in 5:6.

Galatians 5:7-12 alludes to the opponents. The apostle is more optimistic in 5:10 than in 4:20 with respect to the Galatians. The text indicates that the future of the Galatians is still not decided with reference to the proposals of the opponents. According to 5:11 it seems that the adversaries argued that Paul was still preaching circumcision (might this be due to the case of Timothy as described in Acts 16:3?). Paul denies it since if he had preached circumcision he would no longer be suffering persecution and the cross would stop being a scandal. Circumcision conferred security and privileges in Jewish society and also in Roman society during the first years of the empire.

The author is sarcastic in 5:12, most probably because he is making an indirect reference to the castration practiced within the cult of Cybele, the most important goddess of Galatia.

Living the Freedom Directed by the Spirit (5:13–6:10)

The new identity of those in Christ demands concrete manifestation of their being free sons and daughters. Liberty is a gift that is evident before God and society. For that reason, in this section Paul exhorts and advises the Galatians concerning how they are to live ethically responsible lives. He contrasts spirit and flesh as two opposing forces. The flesh has various connotations: in some contexts it means simply "the human being" (1:16; 2:16; 4:13); in others it is a question of a power that pulls a human being toward action in violation of his or her will (5:17). Paul exhorts them not to abuse their freedom since that might give opportunity to the flesh to lead them along ways contrary to the Spirit. It seems that living freely and not being subject to the Law implies having the option either of letting oneself be consumed by the flesh or of manifesting the fruit of the Spirit. But paradoxically if one opts for the first choice one loses freedom. The basic preoccupation of Paul and the Galatians is how to maintain liberty without having a law direct one's behavior by means of precepts. This was possibly a serious problem in the community and the preaching of the opponents (Christ *and* the Law) resolved the dilemma. For Paul it is possible to conduct oneself rightly without the Torah when persons act out of love. The free love of God is reproduced in the free love of the Christian communities for their neighbors. It is the love of one's neighbor as a fruit of the Spirit. What the Law asks becomes a renewed obligation and responsibility; what is born of the Spirit becomes the natural way of acting. If Paul mentions the Torah in 5:14 it is in order to assure the Galatians of the fact that liberty is manifested responsibly in accord with the logic of love. The call to liberty leads necessarily to mutual service (5:13).

The actions and attitudes described in 5:19-23 will have to be considered beyond a simple listing of vices and virtues; they are the intrinsic, visible consequences of two opposing forms of life orientation. While the negatives are deliberate actions of the flesh (v. 19), the positives refer to the fruit of the Spirit (5:22). It is notable that love heads the list in vv. 22-23. Although the tendencies of the flesh do not disappear in human beings Paul recalls that the flesh with its desires and passions has been crucified together with Christ. There is no reason to fear. The Spirit, if followed, will prevail over the power of the flesh. Paul closes the exhortation with concrete advice for the communities in which he underlines the importance of doing good (6:1-10); he repeats common phrases and proverbs from Judaic and Hellenistic culture.

Conclusion: 6:11-18

The Importance of the New Creation

Paul summarizes his letter while continuing the polemic against the opponents (6:12, 13). He writes the last lines with his own hand. This by no means unusual custom was used to legitimize a document. What was new was that he used large letters so as to attract attention. Three aspects stand out in the summary: the imposition of circumcision (6:12) as the concrete problem in which the community was embroiled, the new creation (6:15) as the basic focus in any discussion on law and faith, and the marks of Jesus on the body of Paul (6:17) giving him the authority to proclaim the gospel of the cross. These are the products of his call to be an apostle (cf. 2 Cor 11:23-29) but they are marks quite different from those imposed in the rite of circumcision.

We find two very brief blessings, one in 6:16, the traditional Jewish blessing directed in this case to the "Israel of God," the whole people of the new creation that does not discriminate between Gentiles and Jews. At the end (6:18) Paul repeats a blessing that was perhaps well known since it is somewhat foreign to his vocabulary.

Galatians 6:10 echoes what was contained in 5:6. The repetition indicates that the most important issue surrounding circumcision and faith, the Law and grace, is visible manifestation in the actions and attitudes of persons, that is, through an active faith that works on behalf of love or the new creation, two sides of the same coin. That is the characteristic of those who live Christian freedom.

BIBLIOGRAPHY

Barrett, Charles Kingsley. "The Allegory of Abraham, Sarah, and Hagar in the Argument of Galatians." London: SPCK, 1982.

Betz, Hans Dieter. *Galatians.* Hermeneia. Philadelphia: Fortress, 1979.

Boucher, Madeleine. "Some Unexplored Parallels to I Cor 11:11-12 and Gal 3:28: The New Testament on the Role of Women," *CBQ* 31 (1969) 50–58.

Buckel, John. *Free to Love: Paul's Defense of Christian Liberty in Galatians.* Louvain: Peeters, 1993.

Burton, Ernest DeWitt. *A Critical and Exegetical Commentary on the Epistle to the Galatians.* ICC. Edinburgh: T & T Clark, 1921; repr. 1977.

Cousar, Charles B. *Galatians.* Atlanta: John Knox, 1982.

Dunn, James D. G. *The Theology of Paul's Letter to the Galatians.* Cambridge: Cambridge University Press, 1993.

Gaventa, Beverly Roberts. "The Maternity of Paul: An Exegetical Study of Galatians 4:19," in Robert Fortna and Beverly Roberts Gaventa, eds., *The Conversation Continues: Studies in Paul and John in Honor of J. Louis Martyn* (Nashville: Abingdon, 1990) 189–201.

Lührmann, Dieter. *Galatians.* Minneapolis: Fortress, 1992.

Matera, Frank J. *Galatians.* SP 9. Collegeville: The Liturgical Press, 1992.

Morris, Leon. *Galatians: Paul's Charter of Christian Freedom.* Leicester: InterVarsity Press, 1996.

Osiek, Carolyn. *Galatians.* NTMes 12. Wilmington, Del.: Michael Glazier, 1980.

Tarazi, Paul Nadim. *Galatians: A Commentary.* Crestwood, N.Y.: St. Vladimir's Seminary Press, 1994.

Ziesler, John. *The Epistle to the Galatians.* London: Epworth Press, 1992.

Ephesians

Margaret Y. MacDonald

Ephesians, to be truly appreciated, should be read aloud. This NT work is replete with the language of prayer, worship, and celebration. It moves the listener with passages that sound like rousing sermons and others resembling majestic hymns. It is an excellent text for illustrating the close connection between NT texts and the worshiping assembly. The NT Greek word *ekklēsia,* commonly translated as "church," in fact has the literal meaning of assembly. It is a word that occurs frequently in Ephesians. But unlike the usage in other Pauline writings that often use the word to refer to gatherings that took place in private homes (house-churches), the *ekklēsia* of Ephesians is always a wider-than-local phenomenon. Of all Pauline works it is Ephesians that demonstrates the greatest interest in a universal Church.

In Ephesians the apostle is intent on encouraging unity. This unity should begin with the home, the place for nurturing family relations and, in the early Church, the physical space where church meetings occur. Unity should extend to include various cultural groups in the Church; the historical context of Ephesians leads to a special interest in the breaking down of barriers between Jewish Christians and those from Gentile backgrounds. The concern with unity even takes on cosmic proportions in this work: unity is created by Christ filling the world with salvific power. By drawing on such powerful images as the harmony of Christ's body and the intimacy shared by husband and wife in Christ, Ephesians has succeeded in calling for harmony with language that has had a timeless appeal and has seemed relevant in a variety of situations. Its importance for ecumenical discussions within modern Christianity and in dialogues between Christianity and other religions is unmistakable.

FIRST READING

I. General Character

Ephesians presents interpreters with many puzzles. The influence of liturgical forms has seemed to some to be so great as to lead to the conclusion that the document is closer in shape to a liturgical tract than to a letter. Its authorship by the apostle Paul has been disputed. The association of the work with Ephesus has been questioned on the basis of the manuscript evidence. Thus a first reading of Ephesians should include consideration of several important issues related to the general character of the book.

1. Literary Genre

If one compares Ephesians to the other Pauline epistles it quickly becomes apparent that Ephesians lacks references to the particular community concerns that are so obvious, for example, in the Corinthian correspondence. The tone of the letter leads to a feeling of greater distance between the apostle and congregation than is usually the case, and the customary references and greetings to members of the community (cf. Romans 16) are virtually absent (6:21). It is by no means easy to discern the specific situation that inspired the letter. The manuscript tradition even raises questions about whether the work was actually intended for the Ephesians: the words "in Ephesus" (1:1) are missing from some ancient manuscripts. The superscription "To the Ephesians" was not part of the original document, with definite proof for the superscription coming from the latter part of the second century. The difficulty of the work being addressed to the church in Ephesus was noted early in Church history in the period of the Church Fathers. One theory that has gained considerable support is that Ephesians is an encyclical designed to reach several churches. The NT itself offers other examples of such documents. The first letter of Peter is intended for a number of congregations in Asia Minor (1 Pet 1:1). Revelation also seems to have been composed with an audience of several churches in mind (Rev 1:4). If the letter to the Ephesians was indeed intended for a broad audience this would go some way to explain the tenor of the work.

The lack of reference to specific Church matters, coupled with the liturgical-catechetical style, has led some biblical scholars to suggest the work may in fact be essentially a liturgical tract or a sermon that is merely cast in the form of a letter. The first three chapters have been viewed by some as having the overall framework of a long thanksgiving. However in many respects Ephesians does keep to the usual form of Paul's letters. It contains the usual salutation (1:1-2) and conclusion, including a blessing (6:21-24). While it occurs somewhat later than usual, Ephesians has the customary thanksgiving for good conduct of the faithful (1:15-17). In keeping with the pattern in some of the other letters a section of ethical exhortation (4:1–6:20) follows a doctrinal or theological section (1:3–3:21—although in Ephesians this section is heavily influenced by liturgical forms). Thus it is probably best to think of the work as a letter that has been greatly influenced by the patterns of worship in the Church. [See the article "Letters in the New Testament."] It offers testimony to the importance of rituals to the process of articulating the religious beliefs of the first Christians and as a locus of religious experience. Moreover, while it is difficult to derive direct information about community problems in the letter we should not assume a lack of interest in pastoral affairs. There is much in the long ethical exhortations to suggest that the work was inspired by great concern for the shape of daily life in the churches.

The various sections of Ephesians are held together by the common theme of unity. In order to understand how this theme functions to integrate the work one should begin by reading the whole of Ephesians. To gain a full appreciation of the profound nature of the reflection, however, one should then study closely one of the great "unity" texts in Ephesians such as Eph 2:11-22 or Eph 5:21-33.

Outline

I. Salutation: address and greeting (1:1-2)
II. Part 1: Christ, the Church, and the revelation of God's plan (1:3–3:21)
  1. Blessing (1:3-14)
  2. Thanksgiving and prayer (1:15-23)
  3. Consequences of life together with Christ (2:1-10)
  4. Unity of Jews and Gentiles created by Christ (2:11-22)
  5. Paul's mission and the revelation of God's plan for the universe (3:1-13)
  6. Prayer and doxology (3:14-21)
III. Part 2: Ethical Exhortations (4:1–6:20)
  1. Many gifts but one body (4:1-16)
  2. Life as children of God and the rejection of the conduct of non-believers (4:17–5:20)
  3. The household code (5:21–6:9)
  4. Christian commitment and the necessity of doing battle with evil (6:10-20)
IV. Conclusion: personal matters and blessing (6:21-24).

2. Authorship

Although its authorship was not disputed in the early Church, since the eighteenth century much of the scholarly discussion about Ephesians has been concerned with the question of authenticity—whether the work was actually composed by the apostle Paul. Unfortunately this preoccupation has sometimes led to the neglect of other important features of the text. Authors who argue that Ephesians was written by the apostle Paul understand the work to have been composed late in the Apostle's career, from prison, probably in Rome (cf. Acts 28:16-31). Differences between Ephesians and other Pauline letters are explained largely in terms of changes in Paul's thought and style. Authors who argue that Ephesians is pseudonymous have based their case on a number of linguistic, stylistic, and theological features. The many literary parallels between Ephesians and other letters in the Pauline corpus have been judged to be especially significant. The very close relationship between Colossians (a letter that is also considered by some to be deutero-Pauline) and Ephesians has made it seem probable that the author of Ephesians had access to this epistle in composing the work either in textual form or by memory (e.g., Eph 6:21-22; Col 4:7-8; Eph 2:5 = Col 2:13). Scholars have suggested that Ephesians reflects the efforts of an author in the generation that followed the disappearance of the apostle to repeat Pauline tradition, thereby arguing that the acceptance of pseudonymity sheds light on the purpose of the work. It appears that a majority of biblical scholars now consider Ephesians to be deutero-Pauline, but debate continues. For example, commentators such as C. L. Mitton (1951) and Rudolf Schnackenburg (1982) have favored deutero-Pauline authorship but F. F. Bruce (1984) and Markus Barth (1974) have argued for Pauline authorship.

The practice of writing pseudonymously, that is, writing in the name of one's teacher in order to allow the teacher to speak to a new situation, was widespread in the ancient world. It is not at all appropriate to think of such efforts as forgery or misrepresentation in the modern sense. Indications that Ephesians reflects a new situation in Pauline churches in comparison to the challenges faced by the first generation of believers have been interpreted as a sign of deutero-Pauline authorship. For example the use of the household code (which draws upon the moral traditions of household management that were common in both Jewish and pagan literature) points to the need for more clearly articulated authority structures in the household than are present in the uncontested letters (5:21–6:9). Such rule-like statements are also found in writings that are often dated from the later decades of the first century to the middle of the second century C.E.: Colossians (3:18–4:1), 1 Peter (2:13–3:7), the Pastoral Epistles (1 Tim 2:8-15; 3:4; 6:1-2; Titus 2:1-10; 3:1), the writings of the Apostolic Fathers (Ignatius, *Poly.* 4:1–5:1; Polycarp, *Phil.* 4:2–6:1). The need for more clearly defined authority structures in light of the disappearance of the apostle and the challenges created by growth and the passage of time may also be reflected in the evolution of the symbol of the body of Christ one detects in Ephesians. As in Colossians, in Ephesians the body of Christ is equated explicitly with the Church and Christ is presented as its head. Rather than be carried to and fro "by every wind of doctrine" and by the "deceitful scheming" of cunning teachers, the community is to "grow up in every way into him who is the head, into Christ" (4:14-15). A new stage of Church development where problems of governance are emerging may also be reflected in the manner in which the Church is presented as "the household of God, built upon the foundation of the apostles and prophets, with Christ Jesus himself as the cornerstone" (2:19-20). The perspective is one of a "built-up" Church looking back to its origins. The work reflects a need to be clear about the boundaries of the Church and secure reliable tradition. In response to a changed situation texts such as Eph 2:11-22 and 4:1-16 appear to offer a summary of Pauline teaching; drawing on such Pauline themes as "the breaking down of barriers between Jew and Gentile in the church" and "the many gifts that make up the one body," they communicate Pauline exhortation in a manner that may speak to a variety of communal circumstances.

Some have found it useful to understand Ephesians in light of the existence of a Pauline school. Pauline Christianity was clearly a communal enterprise with the apostle conducting his work in association with numerous fellow workers and local leaders. It may well have seemed natural for close associates of Paul to continue to bring his teaching to bear upon the changed realities of Church life that accompanied the death of the earliest witnesses and authorities. Already in the NT period there are signs that the Apostle's teaching was subject to a variety of interpretations and this created considerable controversy (2 Pet 3:15-16). The attempt to present an adequate summary of Paul's teaching and to offer the Apostle's direction seemed so central to the work's purpose according to E. J. Goodspeed (1933) that he put forward the theory that the author of Ephesians was the collector of Paul's letters and that Ephesians was written as a general letter to provide an introduction to the corpus of Pauline writings. While such a theory is impossible to prove, many scholars have since accepted the general correctness of the idea that Ephesians sprang from a relationship with the

Pauline corpus and from an intentional effort to offer a guide to the Pauline message for a new generation. This would have interesting implications for the shape of the NT canon; it means that a work that may have been intended largely as a guide to the Pauline tradition was included in the NT canon itself.

3. Use of Tradition and Canonical Intertextuality

In the past the reliance on tradition in Ephesians was sometimes judged by Protestant commentators as the sign of an emerging "early catholicism" that was intent on making a particular message normative, emphasizing Church structure and authority and leaving increasingly less room for innovative interpretation. However most interpreters today, with a greater knowledge of sociological realities, understand the focus and reliance on tradition in Ephesians in light of the ongoing process of institutionalization. For example the correlations of Ephesians with Colossians and other Pauline epistles, as well as with Acts and 1 Peter, point to the fact that the first generation of Christians left behind an initial body of tradition as a guide for the community. The transfer of a legacy to a new generation created the need for the protection, communication, and interpretation of time-honored teachings of the earliest witnesses. In Ephesians this need seems to manifest itself especially in a concern for unity and an interest in ecclesiology.

While it clearly has its own particular interests and themes, Ephesians is to a certain extent a masterful synthesis of traditional elements. Liturgical traditions, scriptural influences, and Pauline themes are woven together in texts calling for unity in community life. Ephesians does not contain many scriptural quotations (exceptional citations are in 4:8; 5:31), but it does include many scriptural allusions indicating a thorough knowledge of Jewish Scripture. The exhortation concerning marriage in 5:21-33, for example, contains an explicit reference to Gen 2:24 where husband and wife are described as becoming one flesh (5:31), but the text also includes an allusion to a ritual bath of purification undertaken by women before the marriage ceremony that becomes symbolically juxtaposed with the Christian rite of baptism (5:26-27). Moreover, the bridegroom-bride imagery used in Hosea and elsewhere to refer to YHWH's relationship to Israel forms an essential part of the background of Eph 5:21-33 where marriage is described as a reflection of the relationship between Christ and the Church. In considering the relationship between Ephesians and Jewish literature it is also important to note that scholars have explored similarities between the language of Ephesians and the Qumran material.

In Ephesians Pauline themes are sometimes expanded to include ideas that are rooted in the context of a transition of the Pauline churches beyond the first generation. In Eph 2:11-22, for example, Paul's vision of the unity of Jew and Gentile in the Church, which is tied to specific historical struggles, becomes a depiction of the reconciliation of Gentile and Jew in cosmic terms and the vehicle for communicating the harmony that Christ has created in the Church and in the universe. Ephesians may lack the blazes of innovation that one detects in Paul's epistle to the Galatians where we find Paul's impassioned plea for Gentiles to be accepted into the Church without being required to accept those aspects of the Jewish Law that traditionally separated Jew from Gentile. Instead Ephesians is more meditative and reflective. It calls for harmony by looking to the foundations of the tradition and by reminding believers of the experiences that led them into the Church: the hearing of the word and baptism. The members of the community are frequently called to remember: "In him you also, when you had heard the word of the truth, the gospel of your salvation, and had believed in him, were marked with the seal of the promised Holy Spirit; this is the pledge of our inheritance toward redemption as God's own people, to the praise of his glory" (1:13-14).

II. Original Historical Context

Those who argue that Paul wrote Ephesians understand both Colossians and Ephesians to have been composed at about the same time, late in the Apostle's career (about 63 C.E.). However, if Ephesians is deutero-Pauline the use of the uncontested Pauline letters and Colossians by its author suggests a date in the later decades of the first century C.E. (80–90 C.E.). The use of Jewish Scripture and the interest in clarifying the relationship of the Gentile Church to Israel are among the factors that have often led to the conclusion that the author was a Jewish Christian member of the Pauline churches. The work seems to have been destined to reach several congregations. The manuscript evidence makes it impossible to be certain that Ephesians was actually intended for Ephesus but the traditional association of the document with Ephesus may point to the importance of the church there among the churches that received the letter. The close association of Colossians with Ephesians has also led to the suggestion that Ephesians may have been intended for Colossae, Laodicea (cf. Col 4:16), and other neighboring congregations in the Lycus Valley and elsewhere in Asia.

In discussing the new challenges created by the disappearance of the apostle Paul for his communities we have been considering the general Church situation underlying Ephesians. It is by no means easy to discern the specific realities in the Church that inspired the consistent celebrations of, and pleas for, unity that permeate the text, but biblical scholars have turned most frequently to Eph 2:11-22 in the hope of shedding light on the communal context. Commentators have sometimes understood this to be a teaching directed at Gentile Christians who were in danger of divorcing themselves from their Jewish origins. There is no reference to a specific conflict but throughout the passage the author reminds the Gentile believers of their past alienation from Israel and their present adoption as fellow citizens (2:12, 19). In speaking of Christ the author of Ephesians states: "he is our peace; in his flesh he has made both groups into one and has broken down the dividing wall, that is, the hostility between us" (2:14). The text leaps off the page with its power to address a variety of pastoral situations ranging from interpersonal conflict to racial tension to ecumenical debate.

The presentation of the accomplished unity of Jews and Gentiles is a truly remarkable feature of Ephesians. Gentiles are presented as joint heirs, members of the same body and joint sharers of the promise in Christ Jesus through the gospel; this joining together is described as the mystery of Christ (3:3-6). But they are reminded with language of reconciliation of the gracious action of God in Christ that allowed them to become members of the commonwealth of Israel (2:13-18). In the shadow of Auschwitz it is impossible to repeat too often the Jewish heritage of early Christianity and the dangers of Gentile Christians forgetting their origins.

Behind Eph 2:11-22 may lie tensions between a Gentile majority and a Jewish minority in the Church. The intent of the author is perhaps to call for respect for Jewish Christians and Jewish origins. Assuming that Ephesians comes from the period of 80–90 C.E. the situation in the Church is quite different from the period during which Paul conducted his ministry. The acceptance of Gentiles into the Church is no longer an issue of contention. Instead a Gentile majority is instructed to remember its estrangement from Israel and ultimate incorporation as a joint heir to the promises made to Israel. Moreover the issue of how Jews and Gentiles should live together may still require attention. In other NT works that probably come from the same period the problems of a mixed community of Jews and Gentiles also emerge. It has been argued that the story of the development of the Church in the Acts of the Apostles addressed the needs of a mixed community of Jews and Gentiles. The consistent interest in table-fellowship, for example, has been understood in that light (cf. Acts 10:1–11:18; 15:20, 29; 16:14-15, 25-34; 18:7-11; 27:33-8). The presentation of Paul's missionary enterprise in which a pattern emerges so clearly—first to the Jews and then to the Gentiles (Acts 13:46; 18:6; 28:28)—in all likelihood is designed to communicate the important role played by Israel in God's plan of salvation. Similarly in 1 Peter there are repeated reminders of former Gentile isolation from the people of God (1 Pet 1:14, 18; 2:10; 4:2-4).

Although it is impossible to arrive at precise conclusions about the historical context of Ephesians, comparison with other NT writings that appear to come from the complex period following the disappearance of the earliest apostolic authorities is useful in understanding the general situation of Ephesians. This was a period with great potential for intra- and inter-group conflict. The growing separation between Judaism and the early Church and the concomitant development of early Christianity as a distinct entity required theological explanation. The death of the earliest apostles and witnesses, the growth of the community, and the passage of time created something of a crisis of governance calling for clarity with respect to tradition, leadership, and authority. Various permutations of the Christian message arose. Some commentators have interpreted the similarities between ideas found in Colossians and Ephesians and the terminology of later Gnostic systems either as evidence for the influence of Gnosticism or as an early attempt by Church members to distance themselves from Gnostic teachings. In the face of several challenges Ephesians emerges to encourage cohesion in community life at all levels (e.g., 2:11-22; 4:3-6, 15-16; 5:21-33). Unity is central in exhortations dealing with home life and pastoral affairs but is also central in theological concepts describing the nature of the universe. Ephesians describes the cosmic significance of Christ (1:20-23) and the Church clearly has a universal mission (3:9-10). Christ's headship extends over all and his body fills all: "he has put all things under his feet and has made him the head over all things for the church, which is his body, the fullness of him who fills all in all" (1:22-3).

III. History of Reception

Many of the "universalistic" ideas in Ephesians have had a great influence on the development of Christian thought. The attempt to describe how Christ orders and unites the cosmos leads to a focus on divine election: "just as he chose us in Christ before the foundation of the world to be holy and blameless before him in love. He destined us for adoption as his children through Jesus Christ" (1:4-5). Among the Church Fathers the view that salvation proceeds entirely from God was held in balance with the notion that humanity is called to cooperate with divine initiative. For example Eph 1:4-14 is understood by Chrysostom as a testimony to the fact that it is God who makes saints but Christians must also remain holy (Homily on Ephesians, NPNF 13.51), but the same text played an important role in Calvin's controversial doctrine of predestination and the ensuing debates. The tendency to speak in cosmic and eternal terms can also be seen in Eph 1:10 which speaks of "a plan for the fullness of time, to gather up all things in him, things in heaven and things on earth." The Greek term *anakephalaiōsis* ("a summing up or gathering together") which the Latin Fathers translated as *recapitulatio* contributed to the development of the doctrine of recapitulation. Irenaeus was especially influential in the development of this concept that he understood as referring to both a restoration of fallen humanity to God through the obedience of Christ and a "summing up" in the Incarnation of all previous revelations of God (*Adv. Haer.* ANF 1.330; 1.442–4433; 1.548). The fact that the notion of recapitulation appears in the documents of the Second Vatican Council is a testimony to the continuing influence of Ephesians in attempts to understand how Christ renews the world. In the Pastoral Constitution on the Church in the Modern World *(Gaudium et Spes)* the Word of God is described as entering the world as a real human being, making the world his own and gathering it together in himself. This entry into the world leads to the revelation that God is love and thus points the way to human perfection and the transformation of the world (Austin Flannery, ed., *Vatican Council II. Constitutions, Decrees, Declarations* [Northport, N.Y.: Costello, 1996] 203).

Ephesians 5:21-33 has also been very influential in Christian thought and practice. The fact that Ignatius of Antioch referred to Eph 5:21-33 in about 110 C.E. offers an indication of the power of these verses to address community life and also provides evidence for knowledge of Ephesians early in Church history (Ignatius, Letter to Polycarp 5:1-2). It is interesting that within the context of exhorting husbands and wives (drawing upon the Ephesian notion of Christ's love for the Church being reflected in human marriage, cf. Eph 5:25, 29) Ignatius turns his attention to the celibate members of the community, warning them not to boast of their continence. Ignatius' use of Ephesians points to the potential of human marriage to mirror Christ's relationship with the Church but also to act as a model for Christian commitment whether it be lived as husband and wife or as a celibate believer. Among the Church Fathers as a whole, however, special attention was paid to Eph 5:31-32 where Gen 2:24 is cited and marriage and/or the union between Christ and the Church is described as a "great mystery." These verses also figured prominently in the developments that eventually led to the designation of marriage as a sacrament in the Roman Catholic tradition.

In general, of all of the Pauline letters Ephesians displays the greatest interest in ecclesiology. There are many similarities between Colossians and Ephesians, but the focus of Colossians is on Christology while Ephesians concentrates on ecclesiology. There is, however, a repeated emphasis throughout Ephesians on the intimate, physical connection between Christ and the Church. The use made of Ephesians in Avery Dulles' discussion of the Church as mystery (*Models of the Church* [New York: Doubleday, 1987] 17–18, 74) is an example of how this NT work remains fundamental to modern ecclesiology. It should probably always figure prominently in ecclesiological debate for ecumenism. During periods when interest in ecumenism might be waning it boldly confronts its readers with the idea of one Church: one Lord, one faith, one baptism (4:5).

SECOND READING

I. Salutation: Address and Greeting: 1:1-2

The salutation follows the usual pattern of Paul's letters. Some list Paul and other fellow workers as senders but Ephesians, like Romans, names only Paul as the sender. Insistence on the apostolic authority and teaching of Paul may well be integral to the purpose of the letter (see comment, 3:1-13).

The apostle greets the "saints" who are said to be "also faithful in Christ Jesus." The notion of "saints" has a broad meaning in the NT, referring to all believers who are part of the holy people of God. The usage is very much in keeping with the OT notions of being set apart as God's people and of "covenant faithfulness." Faith in Christ Jesus is the core of the identity of the addressees as saints. In fact Ephesians includes several references to the saints (e.g., 1:15, 18; 3:8; 4:12). As is made clear in 1:18 this term extends beyond an understanding of the identity of believers in the present to include the promise of future fulfillment—the hope to which believers have been called, "the riches of his glorious inheritance among the saints."

Paul often refers to the saints in particular geographic locations such as "all the saints throughout Achaia" (2 Cor 1:1) or "the saints in Christ Jesus who are in Philippi" (Phil 1:1). Because of the variations in the manuscript tradition, however, it is impossible to arrive at precise conclusions about the geographical specificity of the address in Ephesians. In some ancient manuscripts the words "in Ephesus" are missing, leading to the widespread conclusion that the work was intended for several church communities probably including Ephesus. (See First Reading I. 1.) This explains why some biblical translations omit these words from 1:1, choosing instead to present an alternate reading in the notes. But the difficulty of pinning Ephesians down to one place is in keeping with the universalistic perspective of the work as a whole. Ephesians calls for cosmic harmony, Church unity, and inclusiveness.

II. Part 1: Christ, the Church, and the Revelation of God's Plan: 1:3–3:21

1. Blessing (1:3-14)

The blessing in 1:3-14 calls to mind the opening of 2 Corinthians and of 1 Peter. It repeats many of the notions found in Colossians and its language has been judged to be in keeping with Jewish and early Christian prayers and liturgical rites. Scholars have also found comparison of Ephesians to the Qumran literature to be helpful in uncovering the importance of the ritual setting of this NT work. The content of vv.13-14 in particular has been instrumental in the development of the theory that 1:3-14 may reflect a benediction before baptism. It has even been suggested that an appreciation of the liturgical form 1:3-14 unlocks the purpose of Ephesians as a whole: recalling the implications of baptism for new converts.

The Greek text of 1:3-14 functions as a unit without any formal stop. The concepts are sometimes loosely connected to one another but their effectiveness in communicating central ideas is clearly apparent when the verses are proclaimed aloud. One can feel the congregation being reminded of God's gracious act of salvation with language that evokes the emotional aspect of Christian commitment as strongly as it announces Christian doctrines.

Commentators have been intrigued by the distinction made between "we" and "you" in 1:11-14. While it may represent an effort to distinguish the recipients of the work from Christians in general, it has most often been read in terms of the contrast between the Jewish Christians (including Paul) who first believed and the Gentile Christians who also believed. This would fit very well with 2:11-22 which seeks to remind Gentile members of the Jewish origins of the

Church and may function to protect a Jewish minority in the Church.

Believers are said to have been blessed by God "in Christ" (1:3). Being in Christ is a notion that occurs often in these verses and elsewhere in Ephesians. Throughout the work there is great emphasis on Christ as the agent through whom God carries out the divine plan. Hence one might tend to understand the use of the expression "in Christ" in Ephesians as referring to Christ as the instrument of salvation as opposed to the more common Pauline notion of incorporation into Christ. However, believers have also been blessed with "every spiritual blessing in the heavenly places." It is difficult to be precise about the meaning here but it is clear that believers already share in the salvation found in heavenly places (cf. 1:20; 2:6; 3:10; 6:12). In 2:6 God is said to have raised believers up with Christ and to have made them sit with him "in the heavenly places in Christ Jesus." An important concept in Ephesians is that Christ brings heaven and earth together and the Church, his body, fills this new cosmological order. The creation of new space, new world, and new cosmos is central to this NT writing. Thus, it is best to understand the use of "in Christ" in Ephesians as referring both to the instrument of God's salvation and to the process of incorporation of believers into a new sacred body.

The focus on the participation of believers in God's pre-ordained plan of salvation is unmistakable in these verses (especially 1:4-5) and it is not surprising that they have figured in theories of predestination. (See First Reading III.) However, the focus on divine election here should be held in balance with other NT texts where humanity is clearly called upon to cooperate with divine initiative. Moreover, while Ephesians stresses the present shape of redemption (e.g., 2:6), salvation also has a future dimension. The Holy Spirit is a seal received during baptism that guarantees inheritance until possession of it is acquired (1:13-14; 4:30; cf. 2 Cor 1:21-22). Ephesians is by no means uninterested in history, as the image of Christ breaking down the wall of hostility between Jews and Gentiles makes clear (Eph 2:14). The ethical exhortations in the second half of the book announce important ethical responsibilities that accompany Christian commitment and culminate in a call to stand ready for a day of judgment (6:13). In general the focus on divine election in Ephesians should be understood as emerging from the desire to describe how Christ orders and unites the cosmos.

The revelation of God's plan for the universe is described as a making known of the "mystery of his will" (1:9). The NT use of the Greek term for mystery or secret *(mystērion)* is rooted in Jewish eschatology: God will make known the contents of divine mysteries at the end of this age. A distinctive feature of the use of the term "mystery" in Ephesians is its close association with ecclesiology (cf. 3:4-6; 5:32). In 1:3-14 the mystery that is revealed is God's plan for the fullness of time: to sum up all things in Christ, things in heaven and things on earth (1:10). The Church is fundamental to God's designs; the Church is Christ's body, the fullness of him who fills all in all (1:23). The mystery of God's will for the universe is made known to believers in "all wisdom and insight" (1:8). This is in keeping with the Hebrew Bible where wisdom is a divine quality associated with creation. The audience is called to reflect on the grandeur of God's plan. In a contemporary setting the blessing is a particularly apt invitation to give praise for God's bounty and to contemplate Christian responsibility for the globe and the universe.

2. Thanksgiving and Prayer (1:15-23)

The brief thanksgiving in 1:15-16 (closely resembling Phlm 4-5; Col 1:3-4) quickly moves into a prayer for spiritual wisdom and revealed knowledge in 1:17-19 (cf. Phlm 6-7; Col 1: 9-10). The hope that one is to come to know centers around the heavenly enthronement of Christ (1:20-23). The Christ event is described in majestic terms in Ephesians. Christ's power is beyond measure and reaches into infinity. With echoes from Ps 110:1 and Ps 8:6 Christ is described as sitting at the right hand of God in the heavenly places, as having power over all, and as having put all things under his feet.

It is interesting to note how the Pauline symbol of the body of Christ is employed to reinforce the notion of Christ's authority. In Paul's earlier letters the body of Christ is used as a metaphor for the Church community in order to call for harmony and to stress the intimate relationship between believers and Christ as members of his body. But in Colossians and Ephesians the symbol has been expanded and this is sometimes judged as an example of a transformed theology that is most easily explained by the argument of deutero-Pauline authorship. (See First Reading I. 2.) Christ is now the head while the members of the Church make up his body (1:22; 4:4, 15; 5:23). Christ is not only the head of the Church but also head over all things (1:22). The encouragement of unity is a priority in Ephesians and the strong assertion of authority implied by calling Christ the head of the body clearly functions to instill cohesion.

The connection between Christ and the Church in Ephesians is sometimes so close as to suggest a complete merger of the Church with Christ's divinity. The Church is much more than an earthly community; it is a heavenly reality with cosmic dimensions. It is not surprising that Ephesians has been central to the development of the ecclesiological concept of the Church as the "mystical communion"—a powerful metaphor for community identity and purpose. But as modern ecclesiologists point out, such language is not without its limits. It can lead to an unhealthy divinization of the Church and should be balanced with alternate understandings of the Church such as "herald of the good news" and "suffering servant."

3. Consequences of Life Together with Christ (2:1-10)

Although the notion of a "universal church" is introduced in 1:22-23 and figures prominently again in 2:11-22, 2:1-10 returns to the question of how God's plan for the salvation of the world is worked out through Christ. The first three verses explain the nature of past alienation and existence without Christ. The Gentile recipients of the work are described as once having been dead through trespasses and sin. The course of this world is said to be dominated by the devil (cf. 6:11-12), who is described as the "ruler of the power of the air." Ephesians reflects ancient astronomical ideas according to which the air was thought to be an intermediate realm between the earthly and the heavenly—a realm inhabited by various cosmic powers (stars, spiritual forces, demons, even angels).

The world without Christ, the present course of history, and even the cosmos itself are sometimes described in very pessimistic terms in Ephesians. The language is sometimes dark and ominous. Evil has an ethical dimension in the work but Ephesians also reflects an awareness of evil as a power that transcends the ethical patterns of everyday interaction. Spiritual forces of evil even impinge on heavenly places. Believers must be ready to do battle with the "cosmic powers of this present darkness" (6:12).

In these verses believers are set apart from nonbelievers in a manner that would make many modern Christians uncomfortable. As they sought to create an alternate existence in tiny household communities NT Christians seem to have had a profound sense of an evil world around them and of their past alienation and sinfulness. The language they used to communicate the great transformation that occurs in Christ incorporated apocalyptic imagery that sometimes presents matters in dualistic and uncompromising terms. Modern readers must hold concepts such as those found in 2:1-3 and 6:10-17 in balance with other notions in Ephesians such as God's ability to unite all in Christ (e.g., 1:23) and the presentation of salvation as transcending all human differences (e.g., 2:11-22). While it requires great sensitivity, it is nevertheless important not to stare past the strong depictions of evil in Ephesians. When we consider such environmental tragedies as the burning of the rain forest or tragedies of war such as Hiroshima, descriptions of evil of a cosmic magnitude have loud modern resonances.

It is also important to note that in 2:1-10 the description of the dire state of life in the absence of Christ and humanity's utter helplessness (2:1-3) serves to prepare the way for the bold proclamation that believers have been raised up with Christ and are seated with him in heavenly places (2:4-6). Both Colossians and Ephesians display considerable interest in cosmic powers and heavenly mysteries. In fact there are indications in Colossians that some Church members felt that ascetic practices such as fasting allowed them to gain control over cosmic powers and might even lead to visions of heavenly mysteries (e.g., Col 2:18). Such a strong statement of believers' present access to the full magnitude of salvation as is found in Eph 2:10 renders such measures futile.

Ephesians 2:8-10 has been called the most concise summary of Pauline theology in the NT. Terms such as "faith," "gift," "works," and "boast" are central to Paul's message. The opposition between faith and works is especially well known. However, in comparing this text to Paul's use of the dichotomy in earlier works one can detect a significant difference. In Galatians, for example, this language is linked to Paul's struggle to ensure that Gentiles can enter the Church without adopting those works of the Law that traditionally separated Jew from Gentile such as male circumcision and food laws. The painful struggles of Galatians seem at some distance from the perspective of Ephesians. While in Galatians Paul is clearly concerned with the significance of the works of the Jewish Law (e.g., Gal 2:16; 3:12) in Eph 2:9-10 the reference is simply to "works." Here one finds a straightforward statement that seems to flow naturally from the focus on God's sovereignty in chs.1–2: Faith in Christ is a gift and is not by human accomplishment. Good works flow naturally from God's choosing to save us.

The faith/works language in Eph 2:9-10 has an objective quality; it has more to do with a general Christian attitude than with a particular community problem. This language has no doubt been very useful in leading people to meditate on the essence of salvation: God's free gift. Yet the broad scope of the language in this text calls to mind a recent caution that has emerged from scholarship on Paul's letters. It is clear that Paul's main purpose in using the language was to illustrate that the center of salvation was no longer works of the Jewish Law but was now faith in Christ. He was calling believers to transfer into the body of Christ. He was not trying to make the point that a "legalistic" or "merit-seeking" attitude among Jews prevented their access to salvation (i.e., that they did not recognize the giftedness of God's covenant). Commentators on the Pauline texts that include the faith/works opposition must take care that they do not inadvertently misrepresent either the Jewish attitude toward the Law or Paul's understanding of it (See E. P. Sanders, *Paul, the Law, and the Jewish People*. Philadelphia: Fortress, 1983).

4. Unity of Jews and Gentiles Created by Christ (2:11-22)

This section explains how God's plan for the universe is worked out through Christ in the historical realm. Yet while the historical happening of the unity of Jew and Gentile in the Church is given prominence, the cosmological, trans-historical perspective of Ephesians remains in evidence. Ephesians 2:11-22 can speak to a variety of contemporary problems and Church situations where there is a need for healing, reconciliation, or unity.

Ephesians 2:11-22 has been central to discussions of the communal setting of the work. Especially because of the explicit reference to the recipients being at one time Gentiles in the flesh (2:11) and the repeated remembrances of past alienation from the people of God, commentators have understood this teaching as directed at Gentile Christians who were in danger of neglecting their Jewish origins. Scholars have speculated that Eph 2:11-22 was precipitated by tensions between a growing Gentile majority and a Jewish minority in the Church. While there is clearly a great concern in the text for the origins of the Church lying in Israel, there is no specific reference to a conflict in the Church at the time of the composition of Ephesians. Those who believe that such a conflict existed base their case on comparison to such works as Acts and 1 Peter, which have much in common with Ephesians, and on a general understanding of the social context of NT works. (See First Reading II.)

Jewish ideas and institutions underlie this text. The distinction between Jew and Gentile is described in a manner that recognizes the importance of circumcision as a sign of Jewish identity in the Greco-Roman world (2:11). The Gentiles are described as once having been alienated from the commonwealth of Israel; they were excluded from the people of God (2:12). The text goes on to explain that this is no longer the case (cf. 2:19). There is a sense in which Israel here is a metaphor for a recreated, unified entity brought about through Christ's agency. In contrast to Romans 9–11, Eph 2:11-22 does not consider the situation of Jews who are not part of the Church. Most today would be reluctant simply to appropriate language of Jewish nationhood for describing Church identity. Interpreters must recognize that the language of Ephesians is rooted in the desire to communicate the Jewish origins of the Church and the transformation of the people of God through Christ, but they must also remain sensitive to the reality of the historical Israel existing apart from the Church.

The text reflects an awareness of a hostility that once existed between Jews and Gentiles as social groups. With echoes of Isa 52:7 and 57:19 Christ is described as proclaiming peace to those who were far off (Gentiles) and to those who were near (Jews: 2:17, cf. 2:13-14). The reference to Christ breaking down the dividing wall in Eph 2:14 is especially dramatic. It is most likely a reference to the partition that separated the Gentiles from the inner court of the Jerusalem Temple. If Ephesians was composed after the destruction of the Temple in 70 C.E. the reference to the breaking down of the wall may have seemed especially significant to its first recipients. This text offers a good example of the power of the imagery of Ephesians to transcend its historical referents: walls mean barriers in most social contexts. As was so vividly illustrated in relation to the Berlin wall a few years ago, the tearing down of a wall can function as profound sign of reconciliation and unity.

The new unity created by the blood of Christ (2:13) where Jews and Gentiles are now one (2:14) is the Church. Although the word *ekklēsia* (church) does not appear in 2:11-22, the Church is referred to metaphorically in 2:19-22 as the household of God, the holy temple, and the body of Christ (implicitly; cf. 2:16). The typical Pauline notion of the Church as body is here fused with the idea of the Church as building (cf. 1 Cor 3:16-17). New Testament works and contemporary Jewish literature make it clear that the Jewish Temple exercised a profound influence on the religious imagination in the first century C.E.—an influence that was by no means limited to contemplation of the magnitude of the building. The use of the temple metaphor in Pauline literature is in keeping with the Qumran community's understanding of itself as God's temple. Composed well before buildings were erected specifically to accommodate church meetings, Ephesians reminds its audience that it is the community of "flesh and blood" believers that is the dwelling place for God.

Ephesians describes the household of God as constructed upon a living foundation of apostles and prophets with Christ as the cornerstone. Although some scholars have seen here a reference to OT prophets, most commentators believe that early Church prophets (cf. 3:5; 4:11) are primarily in view. Ephesians 2:20 may reflect an awareness of the need for the Church to be anchored in a tradition. The process of construction depends on Christ first and foremost but it also requires the apostles and prophets for viability in order that the Church may grow into a holy temple that incorporates the believers (the living stones). The picture presented is one of harmonious growth. It is impossible to be in any way precise with respect to numbers, but growth must have been an important aspect of the experience of early Christians who were intent on making known God's wisdom to the farthest corners of the universe (cf. 3:9-10). It is also interesting to reflect on how the experience of believers meeting in private homes (house-churches) was related to their understanding of the Church as the household of God. Early Christians drew upon the intimacy of family life to communicate the nature of their relationship to God (cf. 5:1) and their relationships with each other (cf. 5:21–6:9; 6:21).

5. Paul's Mission and the Revelation of God's Plan for the Universe (3:1-13)

In these verses the role of Paul's apostleship in God's plan for the universe is explained. Ephesians 3:1 reads somewhat like an interrupted thought that is resumed in the prayer of Eph 3:14-19. The interruption gives pause for consideration of Paul's mission and authority as an apostle. This section acts as an important bridge between the remembrance of Gentile alienation and subsequent salvation throughout chs. 1–3 and the ethical exhortations that begin in ch. 4. It is Paul the apostle, the revealer of the mystery of Christ (3:4), who has unquestionable authority to call believers to lead a life worthy of their calling (4:1).

If Ephesians is deutero-Pauline, reinforcement of Paul's authority is especially important. As the Church struggled to continue after the death of the earliest authorities and witnesses it was important to hear the reliable voices of apostolic teachers. If Ephesians was composed by Paul the absence of the apostle is still an important feature of the backdrop of the work, for Paul is in prison (Eph 3:1; cf. 4:1). Two features of Paul's apostleship that receive special attention in the later Pauline works are featured in this text. First Paul is the "redeemed persecutor." Paul's involvement in the persecution of the Church before he became an apostle seems to have led some to question his authority. The fact that he did not know the historical Jesus and based his apostleship on claims of having received a special revelation of the resurrected Christ (cf. 3:3) probably also contributed to credibility problems. Paul, however, used these concerns with status to communicate the true nature of his apostleship. In 1 Cor 15:9, for example, Paul refers to himself as the "least of the apostles." Similarly, in Eph 3:8 Paul is called "least of the saints." Since "saints" is a general word for believers here (see comment on 1:1-2) the solidarity between Paul and the recipients is no doubt reinforced. One might even say that the text reflects a reversal of hierarchical patterns of leadership since Paul, the apostle, is the least of all the saints!

Another important feature of Paul's apostleship in Eph 3:1-13 is his suffering. Imprisonment clearly implies suffering (3:1; 4:1) and suffering is a sign of true apostleship (cf. 1 Cor 4:9-13; 2 Cor 11:23-33). But in Ephesians Paul's sufferings are described as the believers' glory—they are central to the success of the Gentile mission in the world (3:13). While at first glance they may seem to represent an unhealthy glorification of suffering, Paul's comments are clearly meant to encourage when believers might otherwise lose hope in a world that imprisons apostles. Without a doubt the presentation of the suffering apostle in Ephesians implies a reversal of the normal standards of progress.

While Paul's authority is central in Eph 3:1-13, his mission is one shared with other apostles and prophets and with the whole Church. In Eph 3:2-3 Paul's apostleship is described as rooted in the fact that the mystery of Christ was made known to him by revelation (on mystery see comment on 1:3-14). But in Eph 3:5 this mystery is also said to have been revealed to the apostles and prophets. Similarly according to Eph 3:9 Paul's mission is to make everyone see "the plan of the mystery hidden for ages in God." But according to Eph 3:10 the wisdom of God is made known to the rulers and authorities in heavenly places through the Church. Paul's role and apostolic authority are linked to the mission and apostolic authority of the Church. Like Paul the Church is presented as having an evangelical mission. The "rulers and authorities" are malevolent forces that have been subdued through Christ's dominion (cf. 1:20-23; 2:1-10), and the Church is depicted as playing a vital role in this cosmic transformation. The picture of the Church revealed by Ephesians is multi-faceted. Many texts disclose the image of the Church as "mystical communion" (see comment on 1:15-23), but in Eph 3:1-13 the Church acts as herald of the good news.

Perhaps the most concise expression of the Christian message in Ephesians is found in 3:6. The content of the gospel, described as a mystery that was not previously known to humankind (cf. 1 Pet 1:10-12), is as follows: "the Gentiles have become fellow heirs, members of the same body, and sharers in the promise in Christ Jesus through the gospel." The emphasis on the equal participation and joining together of Jew and Gentile in the Church is weakened somewhat by the English translation. In Greek the same prefix *syn* (together) is attached to the three nouns (co-heirs, co-members, co-sharers). In the twentieth century, at a great distance from the events that led to the birth of the Church, it may seem difficult to appreciate the deep religious significance that early Christians attached to the unity of Jew and Gentile in one body, but Eph 3:6 can nevertheless speak to any context; it recalls that the breaking down of barriers and the coming together of peoples is at the very heart of Christianity's purpose in the world. Moreover throughout ch. 3 one finds the suggestion that this "mystery" must be contemplated in great depth (Eph 3:8-9, 18-19) before one can grasp what is required for daily life (chs. 4–6).

6. Prayer and Doxology (3:14-21)

Ephesians 3:14-19 is a prayer of adoration and intercession (cf. Eph 1:15-20). At 3:14 the thought that was interrupted at Eph 3:1 is taken up again. The verse contains a fascinating play on words that English translations do not always make clear. The Greek word often translated as family here *(patria)* derives from the word for Father *(pater)*. The family is so important to God's plan for the world that its very name derives from God's identity as Father. The reference to naming may also recall the importance of naming in the Hebrew Bible as an act that establishes God's dominion (Ps 147:4; Isa 40:26; Gen 2:19-20). When the recipients of Ephesians heard of families taking their name from God they must not only have thought of their own families but also of the household churches that resembled the extended families of the Roman world. The link between God, house, and house-church is made especially clear by Eph 5:21–6:9 where the foundational relationship of the family—marriage—is presented as reflecting the relationship of Christ to the Church.

Ephesians 3:14-19 offers a good example of the meditative quality of Ephesians—a work that is particularly well suited for prayer and liturgical celebrations. It pays attention to the inner being, calling for God to strengthen believers with God's power through the divine Spirit (3:16) and speaking of Christ dwelling in the hearts of believers through faith (3:17). Ephesians 3:14-21 cannot be pressed too hard for doctrinal clarity, however. The prayer for comprehension of "the breadth and length and height and depth" may refer either to the extent of Christ's love or to the magnitude of God's plan for the universe. Faith, love, and knowledge are interwoven themes in these verses, but knowledge involves an awareness that the love of Christ surpasses human knowledge (3:19) and a sensitivity to the limits of human comprehension (3:20).

Ephesians 3:20-21 serves as a conclusion to the first part of Ephesians (the doctrinal section). It is a celebration of the glory of God and the power of God to transform the lives of believers. It resembles the doxology of Rom 16:25-27, but in keeping with the ecclesiological interests of the work as a whole it explicitly calls for God to be glorified in the Church.

III. Part 2: Ethical Exhortations: 4:1–6:20

1. Many Gifts but One Body (4:1-16)

The importance of unification in God's plan for the world is stressed throughout the first three chapters of Ephesians and the last four chapters offer practical recommendations for living in a way that mirrors God's plan. With a tone that communicates his authority as the suffering apostle Paul calls the addressees to lead a life worthy of the calling in which they have been called (4:1). This is a life that is worthy of the gospel they have received, a gospel proclaiming the momentous event of the Gentiles joining with the Jews to become members of the same body (3:6). Aggression, division, and arrogance are foreign to a community characterized by love and defined by the bonds of peace (4:2-3). With poetic beauty the author of Ephesians sustains this vision of Church life by repeating the terms "one" and "all": oneness and fullness flow from the one God who has dominion over the universe (4:4-6).

There is an unusual reference to Ps 68:18 in Eph 4:8. The psalm has been altered to read "he (Christ) gave gifts" instead of "you (God) received gifts." This alteration is in keeping with rabbinic Jewish traditions that understood the passage as referring to Moses ascending Mount Sinai and subsequently giving the Jewish Law to the people. The Psalm is interpreted here as referring to Christ, perhaps understood as the new Moses. The comments on Ps 68:18 in Eph 4:9-10 describe Christ as the one who not only ascended but also descended into the lower parts of the earth. It is not certain whether this descent refers simply to the incarnation or to a descent into Hades (the abode of the dead; cf. Acts 2:27, 31). Despite the interpretative difficulties, however, the main point is clear. Specifically the aim is to emphasize Christ's initiative in the giving of gifts and more broadly to relate leadership in the community to divine initiative.

Although Ephesians is unique in stressing Christ's initiative in the giving of gifts, in many respects this passage resembles Rom 12:5-8 and 1 Cor 12:27-28. The gifts empower the ministers and edify the whole body (4:11-12). The ministerial roles described in Eph 4:11 focus on the roles of teaching and evangelizing. Even the role of pastor may well be connected to teaching. In Acts 20:28 the related verb "to shepherd" is listed as a duty of the elders who must protect the community from false teachers (Acts 20:29-31). Similarly in Eph 4:14 the community is called to hold firm against the unsettling winds of false doctrines. There is no doubt that Church leadership is understood as integral to community harmony in Ephesians. Nevertheless there is no specific attention given here to a hierarchy of Church offices nor to hierarchical relations between ministers and those they serve; rather the vision is more symbiotic with ministers taking their part in the integrated whole of the body of Christ (4:15-16).

2. Life as Children of God and the Rejection of the Conduct of Nonbelievers (4:17–5:20)

The call for believers no longer to live as the Gentiles live is in keeping with Jewish tendencies to distinguish their way of life from the moral conduct of non-Jews (4:17-19). As part of their means for preserving their identity in the Roman world Jews had characteristic ways of describing the pagan world. Idolatry and sexual immorality were especially frequently cited as vices. Early Christians relied heavily on Jewish teaching for their ethical exhortations and the importance of this influence can be seen throughout 4:17–5:20. The Gentiles that are in view, however, obviously exclude Gentile members of the Church. In fact the term "Gentile" essentially functions as a label for all those unbelievers who are outside the Church and "alienated from the life of God." This alienation manifests itself through sinful comportment.

As in many NT texts we find here a very sharp, uncompromising distinction being made between those inside the Church and those outside (see comment on 2:1-10). The language of light and darkness to convey ethics is reminiscent of the Qumran literature. It is important to recognize, however, that the association of unbelief with disobedience and darkness in Ephesians serves as the antithesis of the proclamation of the perfected creation that occurs through Christ (4:20-24). Moreover, NT authors constantly felt bound to encourage recipients to dissociate themselves from past ways of life and associations, including religious associations. Membership in the Church required exclusive commitment. Some scholars have detected in Ephesians what they believe to be the beginning of an apologetic tendency that became more pronounced in the second century C.E.: the need to dissociate Christianity from other religious groups judged by the Romans to be suspicious (see comment on 5:21–6:9). Cults such as those of the god Dionysus and the goddess Isis were often viewed as contributing to the corruption of women and encouraging sexual immorality as well as general disorder and debauchery. It is possible that the warning against drunkenness coupled with the call for appropriate worship in the Spirit in Eph 5:18-19 is in response to such perceptions (cf. 1 Cor 14:23-25). While the notion that God brings to light what others try to keep secret is found in Jewish and early Christian texts (e.g., 1 Cor 4:5), it is also possible that in the context of Ephesians the reference to secrecy (Eph 5:12) alludes to the Roman perception that illegitimate religious groups were secretive, holding clandestine initiations at night.

The reference to the putting off of one's old nature in Eph 4:22-25 is probably an allusion to baptism. The ritual of baptism was understood as a type of participation in the death and resurrection of Christ (cf. Rom 6:1-14; Col 3:9-10). There is good reason to believe early Church members symbolized their new identity in baptism through the removing of old garments and the putting on of new clothes. The experience of baptism is central in Ephesians (cf. 1:11-14; 2:1-6; 4:4-6, 30; 5:25-27). Remembrances of baptism (a transforming event) play a key role in the encouragement of Christian behavior. The call for believers to come into the light culminates in a proclamation of a saying probably taken from an early Christian baptismal hymn: "Sleeper, awake! Rise from the dead, and Christ will shine on you."

For the most part the virtues and vices listed in this passage have a timeless significance for setting the standards for Christian churches. The warning that believers should not grieve the Spirit of God (4:30) is especially intriguing for it suggests that they may offend the holy presence that dwells within individuals and indeed within the whole community (cf. Eph 2:20-22; on the "seal" see comment on 1:3-14). The call for Church members to forgive one another as God in Christ has forgiven them (4:32) and to live in love as Christ loved (5:2) offers a very good illustration of the conviction that one senses in the transition from the doctrinal section of chs. 1–3 to the ethical exhortations in chs. 4–6, and at various junctures throughout Ephesians: What God has accomplished through Christ makes behavior in the "likeness of God" (Eph 4:24; 5:1) possible. Divine initiative should be reflected in Christian behavior.

3. The Household Code (5:21–6:9)

Like Col 3:18–4:1, Eph 5:21–6:9 is an example of a type of ethical teaching, the household code, found in the NT and early Christian literature. (See First Reading I. 2.) The distinctive feature of the Ephesian household code is the long treatment of marriage that incorporates reflections about the relationship between Christ and the Church. This text contains many beautiful thoughts and profound insights, but it is also a text that alarms modern congregations and requires informed and sensitive interpretation. It is a very good text for illustrating the importance of examining the NT in its own social context. The indebtedness to patterns of life in the Roman Empire is made clear, for example, by the acceptance of the viability of the institution of slavery—something considered abhorrent in modern times. Discussion of Ephesians offers an opportunity for demonstrating the dangers of using certain NT verses to justify behavior in a modern setting involving domination, exploitation, racism, or sexism and not in keeping with the broad meaning of the gospel message.

The household code with its rules governing three pairs of relationships (wives and husbands; children and fathers; slaves and masters) is a Christian adaptation of ethical teaching propounded by ancient philosophers and moralists from the time of Aristotle onward. The influence of the standard teaching on household management also appears in some Jewish writings that come from the same period as the NT, including the works of Philo of Alexandria and Josephus. In the face of strained relations with Greco-Roman society Jewish authors sought to underline the stability of the Jewish household. Commentators have understood a similar purpose to be operative in NT household codes. Because of the common belief that illegitimate religious groups fostered immorality and corrupted women it would follow naturally that apologetic efforts would focus on the marriage relationship (see comment on 4:17–5:20).

In keeping with the common patterns of the day Ephesians supports the existence of hierarchical relations between members of the household but qualifies the "superior/subordinate" relationship with ethical demands that moderate the traditional emphasis on the householder as "ruler": husbands are to love their wives (Eph 5:25). Fathers are not to provoke their children to anger (Eph 6:4). Masters are to stop threatening their slaves (Eph 6:9). It is also important to note that these relations are understood as having a new meaning in Christ. That this new meaning involves the very essence of human interaction is made clear at the outset and at the end of these ethical exhortations. Ephesians 5:21 qualifies the whole passage by calling for the mutual submission of members to one another and hence in a sense reverses the typical patterns of interaction in the household. Ephesians 6:9 relativizes the power of the heads of households by reminding them of the ultimate equality of all before God. Yet it is impossible to avoid the conclusion that Eph 5:21–6:9 calls for the daily lives of slaves, wives, and children to involve subordination to those who have authority over them. Modern readers often ask why the profound sense among New Testament Christians that Christ had transformed the world did not lead to complete transformation of the social order. The best answer to this question seems to be that it was not seen as wise or practical to do so. Some commentators go so far as to say that given a first-century social setting and worldview it would not even have been possible to do so. Although the Pauline letters often call believers apart from the nonbelievers, they frequently accept existing social arrangements in the process of evangelizing the urban world of the Greco-Roman city. Moreover, Paul seems to have been concerned that sudden changes in life or status could cause anxiety and disorder in the fledgling community (1 Corinthians 7). Recognition of this pastoral approach suggests that one could maintain the general view of relationships governed by mutual submission and deference to God's ultimate authority in Ephesians while at the same time allowing for relationships to work themselves out practically in a far different way than was common in the first century C.E.

The use of the husband/wife // Christ/Church metaphor in Ephesians serves a dual purpose. First it helps to explain the character and significance of marriage in the Church. Second, it allows the author of Ephesians to develop further the theological reflection on the nature of the Church (a constant preoccupation throughout the work). The metaphor draws its origins from the use of marriage as a metaphor for God's relationship with Israel throughout the book of Hosea and elsewhere in the Hebrew Bible (cf. Ezek 16:8-14). References and allusions to Hebrew Scripture occur throughout this text, infusing the metaphor with deeper levels of meaning linking marriage with Church life. The commandment to love one's neighbor as oneself in

Lev 19:18 underlies the exhortations in Eph 5:28-30 and serves to communicate both the care and respect one should have for one's spouse and the nature of Christ's love for the Church. Genesis 2:24, which describes man and woman becoming one flesh, is cited in Eph 5:31 to shed light on the mysterious union between Christ and the Church and to place marriage unquestionably within God's plan for the universe (on "mystery" see the comment on 1:3-14). In Eph 5:25-27 the preparation of a Jewish woman for her marriage involving a ritual bath is juxtaposed with the ritual of baptism ("washing of water by the word") to communicate the sanctity both of matrimony and of a Church made ready for Christ.

Nevertheless the use of marriage as a metaphor for the relationship between divinity and humanity is not without its limits. The problem lies in the fact that it is the husband who is seen to represent God or Christ and the woman who is the reflection of the human community (Church or Israel). The marriage metaphor should never be taken, however, as a statement of male impunity in the face of female fallibility. Such interpretations are in fact precluded in the text of Ephesians itself not only by the call for mutual submission in Eph 5:21, but also by the simple fact that both husbands and wives are part of the Church and ultimately subject to Christ. Moreover it is important to recognize that biblical metaphors are not exhaustive and must be explored in relation to other metaphors. In Ephesians other metaphors such as "holy temple" or "household of God" are used to express the relationship between Christ and community (Eph 2:19-22). This is not to suggest, however, that Eph 5:21–6:9 has nothing to say to modern marriages or to the modern Church. It is the most important text in the NT on the sanctity of marriage and should play a part in discussions on topics ranging from Christian commitment to the value placed on family life in both Church and society. This text reveals that marriage can serve as a reflection of the relationship that is the very foundation of Christianity: the union between Christ and the community. Marriage can serve as the ultimate model of self-giving love and the ultimate sign of God's dealings with the world. [See the excursus "The New Testament Household Codes" in the commentary on Colossians.]

4. Christian Commitment and the Necessity of Doing Battle with Evil (6:10-20)

The conclusion to the ethical exhortations in Ephesians is expressed in very strong terms. Christians must pray, stand alert, and be ready to do battle with the evil forces around them. Christ is the head over all things (1:22) and Church members have experienced salvation (2:8), but Christian existence is not yet free from the experience of evil. This text has nothing to do, however, with the taking up of arms on earth (cf. 2 Cor 10:4); the battle involves a spiritual warfare against the wiles of the devil and the malevolent cosmic forces that penetrate even the heavenly places (see comment on 2:1-10). The reference to "God's armor" is in keeping with OT ideas (Isa 11:5; 59:16-17). Paul drew upon such notions elsewhere (e.g., Rom 13:11-14; 1 Thess 5:1-11). Military might was strongly evident in the Roman world and thus earthly weapons and shields could serve as symbols of the kind of power that was required to fight evil. It is interesting to note that the picture presented is of a soldier waiting attentively, not of a soldier provoking aggression. Protection comes in the form of Christian attributes.

The image of the ambassador in chains who nevertheless must speak in Eph 6:18-20 holds out the promise that earthly evils will not thwart the Christian mission. Even when he is in prison Paul's mission is "to make known with boldness the mystery of the gospel" (6:19).

IV. Conclusion: Personal Matters and Blessing: 6:21-24

The information about the role of Tychicus closely resembles Col 4:7-8 and some scholars take this relationship to be an especially strong indication of dependence on Colossians on the part of the author of Ephesians. Such arguments figure prominently in theories about the deutero-Pauline authorship of Ephesians. Tychicus is the only individual mentioned in Ephesians. He is presented here as the bearer of the letter who will also bring oral reports concerning Paul to the community. He may well exhort the community himself for he is being sent to encourage their hearts. Paul's fellow workers probably played a vital role in instructing communities and maintaining links between them during Paul's imprisonment and even after his death.

Deutero-Pauline authorship is often explained as a natural extension of the work of these co-workers. (See First Reading I. 2.)

The blessing is typical of Paul's letters with the exception of the last phrase. Believers are described in a striking way as those "who have an undying love for our Lord Jesus Christ" (6:24).

BIBLIOGRAPHY

Major Commentaries on Ephesians Include:

Barth, Markus. *Ephesians.* 2 vols. AB 34, 34A. Garden City, N.Y.: Doubleday, 1974.

Bruce, F. F. *The Epistles to the Colossians, to Philemon, and to the Ephesians.* Grand Rapids: Eerdmans, 1984.

Mitton, C. Leslie. *Ephesians.* NCBC. London: Marshall, Morgan and Scott, 1973.

Useful Article-Length Commentaries Include:

Dahls, N. A. "Ephesians" *Harper's Bible Commentary,* ed. James L. Mays. San Francisco: Harper & Row, 1988, 1212–1219.

Johnson, E. Elizabeth. "Ephesians," *The Women's Bible Commentary,* eds. Carol A. Newsom and Sharon H. Ringe. Louisville: Westminster/John Knox, 1992, 338–342.

Kobelski, Paul J. "The Letter to the Ephesians" *The New Jerome Biblical Commentary,* ed. Raymond E. Brown et al. Englewood Cliffs, N.J.: Prentice Hall, 1990, 883–890.

In addition to the works of Dahl and Johnson cited above the following works were written for a broad audience and would be especially well suited to ministerial purposes:

Patzia, A. G. *Colossians, Philemon, Ephesians.* A Good News Commentary. San Francisco: Harper & Row, 1984.

Stockhausen, Carol L. *Letters in the Pauline Tradition. Ephesians, Colossians, 1 Timothy, 2 Timothy, and Titus.* Message of Biblical Spirituality. Wilmington, Del.: Michael Glazier, 1989.

Taylor, W. F., and J.H.P. Reumann. *Ephesians, Colossians.* Augsburg Commentary on the New Testament. Minneapolis: Augsburg, 1985.

For Further Information on Specific Themes:

Ecclesiology

Dulles, Avery. *Models of the Church.* New York: Doubleday, 1987.

Household Ethics

Balch, David L. "Household Codes" in David E. Aune, ed., *Greco-Roman Literature and the NT: Selected Forms and Genres.* Atlanta: Scholars, 1988, 25–50.

Social Setting

MacDonald, Margaret Y. *The Pauline Churches: A Socio-Historical Study of Institutionalization in the Pauline and Deutero-Pauline Writings.* Cambridge: Cambridge University Press, 1988.

Philippians

Pedro Ortiz

FIRST READING

The City of Philippi

Philippi was situated in the eastern part of Macedonia (the northern part of present-day Greece). In the Acts of the Apostles (16:6-40) Luke tells how in the course of their missionary journey and after many diverse happenings Paul, Silas, and Timothy arrived at Philippi, the city privileged to be the first European city evangelized by Paul. Paul's second visit to Macedonia (which included Philippi) is mentioned in 1 Cor 16:5; 2 Cor 2:13; 7:5; Acts 19:21; 20:1-6. He was on his third missionary journey.

Authenticity and Literary Unity Within the Letter

It is generally accepted today that this letter to the Philippians is an authentic Pauline letter. The vocabulary, style, themes, and historical situation, as well as external testimony (manuscripts plus the confirmation of Polycarp, Irenaeus, and the entire ancient tradition) corroborate its authenticity. On the other hand, in recent times diverse hypotheses have been presented to explain some literary as well as contextual problems such as changes of theme and of tone, especially in 3:2–4:1. These have raised doubt about the literary unity of the letter, that is, whether or not the actual letter could be a combination of two or more letters of Paul written at different times and in different situations. However, the great diversity in the reconstructions proposed shows that the standards of judgment are in large part subjective. On the other hand many authors, even while recognizing the difficulty of coordinating logically and historically all the elements of the letter into a perfect unity, positively defend the literary unity of the entire letter (see the article by David E. Garland cited in the bibliography).

For purposes of this study we will analyze the letter in the form in which it has been handed down to us from earliest times, that is, as a unit.

Place and Date of Writing

It is clear that when Paul wrote this letter he was in prison (Phil 1:7, 13, 14, 17). Traditional interpretation understands the mention of "the imperial guard" (1:13) and "the emperor's household" (4:22) as references to Paul's imprisonment in Rome (cf. Acts 28:16-31). However, some authors have proposed Caesarea (Acts 23:23–26:32) while others think the more likely place for the letter's composition was Ephesus (Acts 19:1–20:1). The latter hypothesis has in its favor the fact that Ephesus is closer to Philippi and that there was therefore opportunity for greater and more frequent exchange between Paul and this community such as the letter intimates.

For the moment none of the proposed locations can be considered definitive. In 2 Cor 6:5; 11:23 Paul speaks of various imprisonments without being specific. We cannot know with absolute certitude in which city Paul was prisoner while writing the letter to the Philippians, nor is it possible to establish the precise date on which the letter was written.

Philippians in the Exegetical and Theological Tradition

John Chrysostom left us a complete series of homilies on all the Pauline epistles, among them a set of fifteen commenting in detail on Philippians. From Severian of Gabala we have only fragments. Theodore of Mopsuestia's commentary is extant in its complete form only in an early Latin translation but we have numerous fragments of the Greek original. Theodoret of Cyrus's brief commentaries on all the Pauline epistles, including Philippians, are preserved in the original Greek. From among the Greek writers of the later patristic or Byzantine period we have commentaries or fragments of commentaries by John of Damascus and Photius of Constantinople, Oecumenius of Tricca (tenth century), Theophylact (eleventh century), and Euthymius Zigabenus (early twelfth century).

The first Latin patristic author who commented on the Pauline epistles is Marius Victorinus. The writer called "Ambrosiaster" (an unknown author of the fourth century whose works have been falsely attributed to St. Ambrose) has left us commentaries on all the Pauline epistles including Philippians. So did Pelagius, whose commentaries antedate his controversies with Augustine. In the Syrian church Ephraim (ca. 306–373) commented on all the Pauline epistles; these commentaries have been preserved in Armenian translations and indirectly also in Latin.

Some of the major medieval authors who commented on the Pauline epistles were Hugh of St. Victor, Peter Lombard, Thomas Aquinas, and Dionysius the Carthusian (d. 1471). Among the Protestant Reformers John Calvin published commentaries on all the Pauline epistles (Strasbourg, 1539). Catholic commentators of the sixteenth and early seventeenth centuries include Cajetan (= Thomas de Vio), whose commentary on the Pauline epistles was published in Rome in 1529, and Cornelius de Lapide (Antwerp, 1614).

SECOND READING

Greeting: 1:1-2

Timothy, Paul's companion at the time (cf. 2:19-23) and an acquaintance of the Philippians (cf. Acts 16), is included in the greeting. It is interesting to notice that among those receiving this letter the religious directors of the Christian community (the bishops and deacons) are expressly mentioned. It is the earliest mention in the Christian Scriptures of these responsibilities. Cf. also Acts 20:28; 1 Tim 3:1-13; Titus 1:5-9.

Paul's Prayer of Thanksgiving: 1:3-11

After the greeting Paul (following a general custom) adds a prayer of thanksgiving. He begins (1:3-6) by giving thanks to God for the solidarity the Philippians have shown with him in his apostolic work, a solidarity born of their participation in the same faith in Christ and the same Spirit (2:1) and concretely manifested in the help they have given Paul in his moments of need (cf. 4:14). Paul does not hide the sentiments of intimate affection he feels toward the entire community of Philippi (1:7-8); now that he is a prisoner he feels in a special way that they are associated with him and his work in their sending him Epaphroditus to help him and serve him in his need. In exchange for that Paul asks God (1:9-11) that the love they already have may grow more and more and that it may be enriched with the intimate knowledge of God and the capacity to discern and choose always what is best. Thus they will be kept pure in a world in which evil prevails, and when the Lord comes for the eschatological judgment he will find them irreproachable, producing a harvest of righteousness, that is, the good works they have accomplished thanks to the help of Christ Jesus and all redounding to the glory and praise of God.

Personal News: 1:12-26

The body of the letter begins on a personal note. Before anything else Paul refers to his situation (1:12-14). He is a prisoner for having served Christ in a city where there was a praetorium (the palace of the Roman authority or a Roman military barracks); his legal process is on course and has served to make his cause better known. Indeed, the preachers, far from being frightened by Paul's imprisonment, have been motivated to preach the gospel with even greater courage.

In 1:15-18a the labor of preachers is mentioned, setting up against each other two types of motivation, some proceeding from good intentions, others from twisted intentions. It is not entirely clear who those are who allow themselves to be moved by a spirit of envy or rivalry;

perhaps this refers to those who want to found rival communities not subject to the authority of Paul. Since it is not probable that they will teach a gospel different from the Pauline gospel Paul is comforted in thinking that at least Christ is being proclaimed.

Paul again speaks of his personal circumstances in 1:18a-20. He knows that his good Philippian friends are praying for him and that Jesus Christ will help him with his Spirit, so that whatever happens will be for his salvation (an allusion to Job 13:16 LXX). Although he is going to appear before the judgment of the Roman authorities he knows that he will not be put to shame. Whether he lives or dies, in him the greatness of Christ will be manifest.

In greater detail now Paul refers to his indifference to the results of his trial (1:21-24). The alternatives are to continue living or to die. Both possibilities present a positive aspect. The statement "to me, living is Christ" has an active meaning in this context; that is, for me to continue living is to have the opportunity of working for Christ. Likewise death—though apparently, total loss—would be gain for Paul since in this way he would win Christ forever.

While in other Pauline letters the hope is centered especially in being alive at the moment of the *parousia* (cf. 1 Thess 4:15-17) or in the idea of the resurrection for those who may have died (cf. 1 Thess 4:14; 1 Corinthians 15), here Paul expresses the certain knowledge that his death will permit him to be with Christ forever. This perspective does not in any way deny the others. Philippians 1:6, 10; 2:16; 4:5 express the hope that the Lord will come soon, and in 3:11 Paul speaks of the resurrection of the dead. From a purely personal point of view Paul would prefer to go, that is, to die in order to be with Christ. But in considering apostolic needs he sees that it is more important for him to continue living. Finally (1:25-26), with the conviction that God wants him to continue working for the good of the community, he expresses confidence that God will grant him this life for the joy of the Philippians.

An Exhortation to Remain Firm in the Faith: 1:27-30

Paul immediately directs an exhortation to the community encouraging it to live a life worthy of the gospel of Christ. He does not know whether he will be able to go personally to visit them, but above all he wants to know that the Christians of Philippi will "stand firm in one spirit" (or "in the only Spirit"). Their struggle for the faith of the gospel ought to make them be of "one mind" (literally "one soul") without allowing themselves to be intimidated in any way by their adversaries. Everything seems to indicate that we are dealing with the hostility that a Christian community had to suffer from a pagan majority who neither understood nor accepted their way of life (a hostility similar to that mentioned in 1 Thess 2:14). In that kind of a situation unity of spirit is particularly necessary (a theme that reoccurs in 2:2; 4:2). This steadiness and unanimity in the struggle, which can only be obtained by the grace of God, will be the sure sign of salvation for the community and perdition for its enemies.

Not only is believing in Christ a grace of God; suffering for him is also a privilege that manifests a special election of God (cf. 2 Cor 12:10; Acts 5:41). Christians participate in the same struggle in which Paul is actually engaged, although in a distinct manner. Paul is in prison for his missionary activity; the Christians of Philippi suffer vexations for their Christian faith.

Exhortation to Live in Harmony and Selflessness: 2:1-18

Paul speaks now in an especially solemn tone as he introduces the most important section of the letter. It contains a very urgent exhortation and is inspired by a singularly pressing motivation: the example of Christ (exemplified in the christological hymn). The section is divided into three parts: 2:1-6, 6-11, 12-18.

(1) The exhortation (2:1-5) begins with four premises expressed in Greek only by a series of conditional substantives, a fact that lends itself to diverse interpretations that appear in the different verbs supplied by the translations. These may well be conditions that are real for Paul. The first premise can be translated "if there is any encouragement in Christ," referring to the mission Christ has confided to him. The second premise is founded on the love that unites Paul with the community and allows him to direct these heartfelt words to them: "[if there is] any consolation from love." The third premise is that he and they

"share" in the same Spirit (1 Cor 12:13; Eph 4:4), while the fourth speaks of "compassion and sympathy," qualities proper to God but to us also, virtues in which the believer can participate.

Since those conditions are real Paul can exhort the Philippians to live in harmony and humility. In four sentences he expresses the same basic ideal: harmony in community relationships. This is the central focus of the exhortation, and the community of Philippi obviously needed that encouragement (see 4:2). In endeavoring to have that harmony they will make Paul's joy complete.

To this exhortation one further aspect is added: that of humility. It is expressed first in a negative form (avoid doing anything out of selfish ambition or conceit), and then in a positive form: humble yourselves, prefer others to oneself, do not seek personal advantage but rather the interests of the others (cf. Rom 15:1-4; 1 Cor 10:24).

The first part of the exhortation ends with a christological motivation; here also the form is so concise that it is capable of diverse interpretations. The readers are encouraged to adopt "with one another" or "among themselves" a distinctive attitude (that includes thoughts and decisions). The attitude is designated, in Pauline terminology, as "in Christ Jesus." This can be understood either in an exemplary sense (to have the attitude that Christ Jesus already had) or in the sense of union with Christ (to have the attitude that anyone united with Christ Jesus ought to have). In summary—since immediately afterward Paul speaks of the humiliation suffered by Christ—it is clear that Christ is the model for the attitude the Christian ought to have by reason of being a Christian and being united to Christ.

(2) The christological hymn is the most famous passage in the letter. There is an immense literature dedicated to this passage (see especially the work of Ralph P. Martin cited in the bibliography). It is generally accepted that this text has a poetic form manifested in the rhythm, the parallelism, the contrasts, and the solemn tone. It is customarily designated a "hymn." Although there are other possible analyses it seems preferable to distinguish two stanzas: (1) in 2:6-8 (the humiliation of Christ) and (2) in 2:9-11 (the exaltation of Christ). The first stanza is subdivided in turn into two units or half-stanzas: (A) 2:6-7ab; (B) 2:7cd-8.

First Stanza: Humiliation (2:6-8)

Half-stanza A (2:6-7ab). The first sentence states the point of departure of the humiliation of Christ: his being in the condition of God (literally "being in the form of God"). The most appropriate interpretation of the word "form" is in the sense of "condition," that is, a manner of being that manifests what one really is. The ancient Christian tradition rightly saw in this sentence an affirmation of the divinity of Christ: he was God, and being God he could reveal himself as such. Using this word in basically the same sense Paul speaks of "being conformed" in texts like Rom 8:29 and Phil 3:21. On the other hand the same idea appears in the following line as "equality with God." Being in that condition, however, he did not take advantage of that equality with God (literally "he did not regard equality with God as something to be exploited"). Being equal to God means substantially the same as being in the condition of God and refers not only to the divine being of the Son of God but also to the glorious condition he could claim as God.

In v. 7 appears the main verb: "he emptied himself." It is used here in an absolute sense, without specifying any object; it is equivalent to "he humbled himself completely." It can also be understood to mean "he relinquished something he had," and in this case it can only be that of which he did not take advantage: being equal to God, the glorious condition belonging to his divine nature.

"Taking the condition of a slave": with the word "slave" the hymn seeks to express a concrete form of becoming human: his total renunciation of honors, power, riches, the ultimate humiliation that would lead to a most ignominious death. "The condition (literally 'the form') of a slave" is in contrast to the proclamation of Jesus as Lord in the second half of the hymn. As in 2 Cor 8:9, here Paul refers to the incarnation not in a general way, but in the concrete and particular way it happened. The obedience to which more precise reference will be made in the second half-stanza is already insinuated here.

Half-stanza B (2:7cd) reaffirms the human condition of Jesus in two sentences that translate literally into "made in the likeness of the human being, having appeared in external countenance as an ordinary man. Paul wants to express in these sentences that Christ became equal to all people; he took on the human manner of being and living. His humiliation reached the extreme: he "became obedient to the point of death—even death on a cross." The text exalts the free nature of this action: he humbled himself by becoming obedient. Death on the cross is the supreme expression of humiliation, especially for Roman citizens: it was a death proper for slaves and foreigners.

Second Stanza: Exaltation (2:9-11)

The second stanza begins with the word "therefore" and the change of subject is notorious: "God" and, at the end of the sentence, "every tongue." The exaltation of Christ appears to be God's response to the humiliation freely chosen by Christ. The action of God is described with two verbs; in the first place "God . . . highly exalted him." (See also John 3:14; 8:28; 12:32; Acts 2:33; 5:31.) The second aspect of the exaltation is "and [God] gave him the name that is above every name." Exaltation is now symbolized by the giving of a name, not a personal name, Jesus, which he already had in his humiliation, but a "title" to express the new state in which Christ now finds himself. That "title" expresses the new reality of Christ glorified, a state which places him above all other beings. That title will be explained in v. 11.

The conferring of that title is not realized in the intimacy of God, but instead publicly "so that at the name of Jesus every knee should bend, in heaven and on earth and under the earth, and every tongue should confess that Jesus Christ is Lord, to the glory of God the Father." All rational creatures, angels, humans, and beings in Sheol offer him this gesture of adoration. The language used is without doubt a reminder of Isa 45:23 where YHWH is acclaimed as the only God, the only one who can save: "To me every knee shall bow, every tongue shall swear."

The object of that recognition is "that Jesus Christ is Lord." Lord *(kyrios)* is the title given to Jesus in his glorification, a title that expresses the sovereignty of Jesus. It is more than an honorary title since it recalls the characteristic title of God in the Bible. This recognition is given "to the glory of God the Father," who is the author of Christ's exaltation. It is not a matter of Christ now taking the place of the Father. God the Father continues to be the beginning and end of all things (cf. Rom 11:36).

The hymn presents this exaltation of Christ as something already accomplished. For Paul the decisive event that is set over against the death of Christ is his resurrection (cf. Rom 4:25; 6:3-5, 9-10; 1 Cor 15:20-28; Eph 1:19-20; Col 1:18). Although Paul does not ordinarily refer to the resurrection with the verb "exalt" (as it is used in Acts 2:33; 5:31), one can surmise that in the mind of Paul the exaltation does coincide with the resurrection of Christ.

Origin of the Hymn

Many modern authors believe Paul has incorporated into his letter, with some modifications, a preexistent text—that is, a pre-Pauline hymn. Nevertheless, nothing more than the possibility of this can be verified, and it must be borne in mind that if Paul incorporated such a text in his letter he made it his own; he appropriated as his own all the affirmations of the hymn.

Conceptual Background of the Hymn

Various proposals have been made to explain the conceptual background of the hymn: (1) typology: Adam as type of Christ (cf. Rom 5:12-21; 1 Cor 15:22, 45); (2) Isaiah's figure of the servant of YHWH (cf. Isa 53:1-12); (3) Gnostic or Hellenistic myths. However, it cannot be demonstrated that there was a literary precedent that supposedly influenced in any certain way the total hymn contained in Philippians. At most we can speak of partial coincidences. Instead the hymn takes its departure from concepts known in the Hebrew and Christian Scriptures, especially belief in the death and resurrection of Jesus, a certain and primitive element throughout all of Christian tradition. To present the death of the Messiah, and even more so, death on the cross, as humiliation is natural (cf. 1 Cor 1:23). In 2 Cor 8:9, Gal 2:20, and Eph 5:2 the idea of Christ's voluntary handing over of himself to death appears again. On the one hand, to see the resurrection as exaltation is equally natural (cf. Isa 52:13; Rom 1:4; 1 Cor 15:43; Acts 2:32-33). The idea of preexistence is not exclusive to this hymn. It is found at least implicitly in Rom 8:3; Gal 4:4; 2 Cor 8:9, and explicitly in Col 1:15-17; John 1:1-18; 1:30; 8:58; Heb 1:1-14. It must be kept in relationship with the concept of

Jesus as Son of God in a special and proper sense, a fact that is rooted in the very experience of Jesus (Mark 14:36 *"abba").* On the other hand, the schema "voluntary humiliation—exaltation" appears elsewhere in the Bible (cf. Sir 3:17-24; Matt 23:12; Luke 14:11; 18:14).

The proclamation of Jesus as Lord is equally well recognized in the early Church as has already been indicated. The universal lordship of Christ can be found in many passages of the Christian Scriptures (cf. Matt 28:18; Acts 2:34-36; 1 Cor 15:23-28; Rev 1:5; 19:16). These elements known throughout the tradition of the early Church have been gathered into a single poetic composition in order to express the mystery of the humiliation of Christ that led him to death on the cross and to his exaltation in the resurrection.

The use and interpretation of Phil 2:5-11 has by far transcended the limits of commentaries on Philippians as a whole. It seems to have been quoted for the first time by the letter of the communities of Lyons and Vienne (preserved in Eusebius, *Hs. Eccl.* 5.1) and applied to the attitude of the Christian martyrs. The first author who used it frequently was Origen, who interpreted it mostly as speaking of the self-humiliation of the preexistent Son by his becoming human (connecting in this text the *morphē doulou* with the *doulos* of Isa 49:3). The text acquired special importance in the Arian controversies of the fourth century. The Arians used especially the second part of the hymn (Phil 2:9-11) as a proof of the inferiority of the nature of the Son in relation to the Father, although they also interpreted the *morphē theou* in the sense of an inferior God. The defenders of Nicene orthodoxy, especially Athanasius and Gregory of Nyssa, insisted on the full divinity and humanity of Christ; both also pointed out the soteriological significance of the exaltation of Christ as to his humanity. John Chrysostom dedicated two of his homilies (6 and 7; *PG* 62, 217–238) to our text, giving it a very detailed and balanced interpretation. The hymn again played an important role in the christological controversies of the fifth century. The Nestorian tendency was to emphasize the distinction of two natures; Cyril of Alexandria, who quoted our text over a hundred times in his works, recognized the distinction of natures but insisted on the unity of the ultimate subject, the person of the Son.

Among Latin theologians Ambroisaster and Pelagius are the only patristic authors who, consciously departing from the preceding tradition, understood the subject of Phil 2:6-11 to be the human Christ, although without denying Christ's divinity. It is interesting to note that Luther, though firmly holding the traditional doctrine on the Son's eternal divinity, interpreted Phil 2:6-11 as "describing the attitude of the incarnate earthly Christ." (Paul Althaus, *The Theology of Martin Luther* [Philadelphia: Fortress, 1966] 194–196). According to Althaus "Luther's interpretation is followed by Calvin, by the older Lutheran exegetes until J. A. Bengel, also by modern exegetes, e.g., A. Schlatter, and by dogmaticians such as A. Ritschl and Werner Elert."

The Conclusion to the Exhortation: 2:12-18

(3) Paul continues his exhortation, presenting it at first under the aspect of obedience to the practical exigencies of the faith that he had stressed. For Paul, salvation is at one and the same time something freely received from God (Rom 1:16; Phil 1:28; Eph 2:8) and something that human beings must actively carry out, not by their own strength but because God makes it possible for them to do so. Paul recommends that all be done "without murmuring and arguing," thus alluding to the murmuring of the people of Israel in the desert (Exod 16:2) when they failed to trust in the providence and power of God. The reference to "a crooked and perverse generation" (v. 15) is taken from Deut 32:5, characterizing that incredulous people. Here, however, reference is made rather to the pagan society in the midst of which the Christians find themselves. If they remain faithful to the word that gave them life (that is, the gospel), they will keep themselves irreproachable and pure. The contrast between the Christians and the pagans is illustrated with the image of stars that shine in the darkness (cf. Rom 13:12; 2 Cor 6:14; 1 Thess 5:4-5). Thus they will appear as "children of God without blemish." Here the ethical aspect of being children and heirs is emphasized (cf. Eph 5:1).

That kind of conduct will complete the joy of Paul on the day of Christ's second coming since he will see that his work has not been in vain. Here he again considers the possibility of having to die beforehand (cf. 1:20-26), and he compares his death to a libation. Libations (of wine, oil, or water) were used as much in Israel's sacrifices (cf. Num 15:1-13) as in pagan sacrifices. The faith of the Philippians is also compared to a sacrifice and an oblation. Paul speaks of joy. The motive for his joy is his seeing the solid, efficacious faith of the Philippians even though he may have to die.

Personal Information: 2:19–3:1a

This section refers to some personal matters in his relationship with the Philippians: first the sending of Timothy to Philippi (2:19-23) and the return of Epaphroditus to whom the Philippians had given responsibility for helping Paul (2:24-30). It seems that v. 3:1a ought to be considered the conclusion of the entire section. Others, however, prefer to join it to what follows.

A Serious Warning: 3:1b–4:1

Section 3:1b–4:1 is different from the former section and also from the one to follow by virtue of its theme and its tone. From personal notices related to his intention of sending Timothy and Epaphroditus to Philippi Paul goes into a polemic against those who teach doctrines contrary to those he preached. Some interpret these changes as a sign that here we really have a fragment of another letter (see Introduction).

The section presents an overall unity. It can be subdivided into four smaller units according to themes that relate to one another:

1. The Values upon Which the Adversaries Insist (3:1-6)

The polemic begins with very hard words: "Beware of the dogs, beware of the evil workers, beware of those who mutilate the flesh!" The three sentences refer to the same persons. The metaphor of the "dogs" is harsh; it points to dangerous and despicable beings (cf. Matt 7:6; Rev 22:15). Mutilation is a pejorative term referring to circumcision. The second characteristic appears in the comparison "it is we who are the circumcision [i.e., the true Israelites]." Their adversaries say that in order to enjoy the privileges of Israel and the promises made by God to the chosen people they must practice circumcision (cf. Acts 15:1).

Just as the adversaries were described with three sentences, now three verbs characterize the Christians:

"We . . . worship in the Spirit of God." Paul recognizes that one of the privileges of Israel was to "worship" (Rom 9:4), but in Rom 12:1 he holds that the Christian cult is a spiritual one through which the entire person is offered as a sacrifice to God. (Cf. also John 4:23-24.)

"We . . . boast in Christ Jesus." In contrast to circumcision, the glory of those in the Church is rooted in their relationship with Christ Jesus. (See also 1 Cor 1:30-31; 2 Cor 10:17.)

"We have no confidence in the flesh" (that is, in human signs). Such "human signs" are the prerogatives of any kind belonging to an authentic Jew, whether racial, physical, or even religious, as Paul begins to enumerate them. Paul could also appeal to those signs as a Jew:

"circumcised on the eighth day." (Cf. Gen 17:12.)

"a member of the people of Israel": that is to say Paul is a true Israelite, not a Greek converted to the Jewish religion. (Cf. 2 Cor 11:22.)

"of the tribe of Benjamin": from which Paul probably derived his Hebrew name, Saul, in remembrance of King Saul, who was of the tribe of Benjamin (1 Sam 9:1-2; cf. also Rom 11:1).

"a Hebrew born of Hebrews": Paul emphasizes the preservation of the country's traditions such as its language, customs, and religion. (Cf. 1 Cor 11:22.)

"as to the law, a Pharisee": Paul mentions this fact only in this reference, but cf. Acts 23:6; 26:5.

"as to zeal, a persecutor of the church": mentioned also in 1 Cor 15:9 and Gal 1:13, 23.

"as to righteousness under the law, blameless": Paul lived his Israelite faith sincerely and fully; he did not become a Christian because he felt incapable of fulfilling the Law or because of some moral or religious crisis.

2. Christ, the Central Value for Paul (3:7-11)

Paul's encounter with Christ completely changed his scale of values. All that was to his advantage before now means nothing to him. The knowledge of Christ (that includes the decision to live for him and to love him) relativizes everything else. Here he reveals his own personal experience; in Rom 9:4-5 he speaks of those privileges in a more objective form.

One of the central themes for Paul is "justice." According to his former understanding justice is based on the fulfillment of the Law, which indicated some token of merit that a person could present to God, but in accepting Christ the believer is incorporated into him. So it is no longer a matter of being able to present merits to God but of accepting the action of God, who through Christ and through faith puts us at peace with God. The initiative proceeds from God and the means is our relationship with Christ, expressed in the term "faith," which is not only a theoretical acceptance of truths but the complete offering of the total person to God because of having accepted Christ.

In v. 10 Paul speaks again of solidarity with Christ, using the term, "to know him," which implies here the experiencing of all his saving power. That participation in the salvific power of Christ is made explicit as a participation in his death and resurrection. The sufferings of the apostle are a participation in the death of Christ, but Paul (and every Christian) also participates in the power of Christ's resurrection, which permits them to stand firm until they arrive at full participation in the resurrection of Christ with their own resurrection from the dead (cf. Phil 3:21; Rom 8:17; 1 Cor 15:20-22; 2 Cor 1:5-7).

3. Opposing Ideas of Perfection (3:12-16)

One may suppose that the adversaries of Paul in Philippi had certain ideas about perfection that Paul rejects here. He insists that he has not yet reached perfection, expressing this idea through the metaphor of a race in a stadium. He has still not reached his goal. The goal Paul desires and struggles to reach is the full and final possession of Christ. Even though he has already entered into a true solidarity with him through baptism and faith (cf. Rom 6:2-11; Gal 3:27) the perfect possession of Christ has not yet been realized (Phil 1:23). Although the image of the race symbolizes human effort, again he insists on the fact that the initiative is from God through the mediation of Christ: he refers to "the heavenly call of God in Christ Jesus."

In v. 15 Paul seems to contradict what he had said in the previous verse. He includes himself among the "mature" (cf. also 1 Cor 2:6), which is the correct understanding of this word (as opposed to "beginners") (as in 1 Cor 14:20). Besides, Paul gives the reader to understand that some in the community have already accepted the point of view that he criticizes but nevertheless expresses the certainty that the Lord will make them see things with clarity. Finally, in v. 16, he returns to the metaphor of the race: what is most important is that one continue running without deviating from the path.

Philippians 3:12-14, especially the phrase "forgetting what lies behind and straining forward to what lies ahead" has been exceptionally influential in the Christian tradition as a description of the ideal of spiritual progress. Clement of Alexandria quotes Phil 2:12-13 in order to present Paul as an example in this sense (*Paedagogus* 6). Origen uses it quite often in texts on spiritual progress. It is found several times in the works of Basil of Caesarea and is one of the central texts of Gregory of Nyssa's spiritual theology, which insists on continuous growth in partaking of God (for this Jean Danielou coined the French term *epectase* from the Greek *epekteinomenos* in Phil 3:13). John Chrysostom, in his *Hom. 2. de laudibus S. Pauli* (*PG* 50, 477–480), found also in the present Roman Catholic Liturgy of the Hours (second reading for the feast of the Conversion of St. Paul, January 25) uses this text to characterize Paul: "He summed up his attitude in the words: 'I forget what is behind and push on to what lies ahead.'" In Latin patristic literature the text has special importance in the works of Augustine; it is found also in Gregory the Great and is later one of the most frequently used Pauline texts in the spiritual theology of Bernard of Clairvaux. A more complete history of its use and interpretation in Christian literature would be a fascinating enterprise.

4. Exhortation to Follow the Example of Paul (3:17–4:1)

The final part of this controversial section is an exhortation. Before everything else Paul invites his readers to follow his example and that of the others who are following him. The Christian faith includes solidarity with Christ, and that solidarity with him includes reproducing in oneself the death of Christ, participation in his sufferings. Paul's adversaries apparently defend a triumphalistic understanding of the faith and manifest that understanding in their conduct.

Now a second invective against the adversaries appears in four sentences. The first advances the conviction that "their end is destruction," eternal perdition (Rom 9:22; Phil 1:28). "Their god is the belly" has been interpreted in many ways: (a) they think of nothing but eating; (b) they think only of sensual pleasures; (c) they are only preoccupied with laws concerning food (cf. Rom 14:17); (d) they worry only about themselves (they are egoists); (e) they are only concerned about material and physical realities (related to the signs mentioned earlier in vv. 2-5). A similar sentence appears in Rom 16:18: "such people does not serve our Lord Christ, but rather their own appetites." However, the meaning of this passage in Romans is not any more clear than the one in Philippians. At any rate the text characterizes the opponents' preoccupation with physical issues or questions possibly related to the content of the following two invectives. "Their glory is in their shame" is a clear reference to circumcision. "Their minds are set on earthly things," that is, titles or signs based on physical realities such as circumcision, the physical sign of one's belonging to the people of Israel.

After this characterization of his adversaries Paul lays out his teaching in a positive form. Christians are citizens of heaven. In contrast to the triumphalistic ideas of his adversaries he insists on the fact that we are still pilgrims (cf. 2 Cor 5:6; see also Heb 13:14; 1 Pet 2:11) and that our true value lies not within the material and human realm but in the spiritual and divine order of things. His reference to our awaiting the *parousia* (v. 20) appears here as well as in many other Pauline letters (Phil 1:6, 10; 1 Cor 1:8; 2 Cor 5:10; 1 Thess 1:10). Christ will carry to completion the work of salvation.

Paul presents this work of salvation under the aspect of the transformation of the poor mortal body (that is, the entire human person) in which Christ communicates to human beings his own glory, making them like himself in his own body. It is a matter of full and perfect solidarity with the glorified Christ, already begun in baptism (cf. Rom 8:29; Phil 3:10). Christ will cause that transformation by virtue of the power he has to subject all things to his dominion (an allusion to Ps 8:7[6] LXX, also cited in 1 Cor 15:25-27; Eph 1:22; Heb 2:8). The polemic ends with a reaffirmation of the cordial relationship between Paul and the community—they are his joy and crown (cf. also 2 Cor 1:14; Phil 2:16)—and with an invitation to remain steadfast in the Lord, which is to say united to the Lord Jesus, faithful to him, and at the same time grateful for his help in remaining so.

The Adversaries of Philippians 3

To which adversaries is Paul referring in Philippians 3? The most that we can do is gather the data that appears clearly in Philippians. These adversaries insist on the value of circumcision in order to be able to enjoy the privileges given by God to Israel; they understand this belonging to Israel as being founded in physical signs, probably aspects proper to Israelite worship and the observance of the Law (but we cannot be precise about which aspects or the extent to which they are to be carried out). Finally, they do not credit any importance to the death of Christ on the cross; they consider themselves perfect, probably because of their fulfilling the Law. Because of ideas of this kind we ought to categorize these opponents as among the Christian "Judaizers" (possibly of Jewish origin) who insist on the Jewish roots of the Christian community and the permanent and universal validity of the Law.

A New Exhortation to Harmony: 4:2-9

The theme and tone change again from those in ch. 3 and the themes of chs. 1 and 2 reappear.

In vv. 2 and 3 Paul addresses two women from the community whom we know only by their names, Euodia and Syntyche. They, together with Clement and other coworkers, had helped Paul when he was preaching the gospel. He considers them his companions who have struggled beside him in the work of spreading the gospel. For some reason the peace between them has been threatened. Paul exhorts them to live in harmony.

Then he addresses an unidentified person (the Greek word *syzygos* can be taken as a common noun [= companion] or as a proper name [= Syzygos] asking that he help Euodia and Syntyche to restore the lost harmony between them. The names of all the coworkers are contained in the book of life (cf. Dan 12:1; Ps 69:28[29]; Rev 3:5).

In vv. 4-7 we find an exhortation centered on the themes of joy and peace. The theme of joy is recurrent in Philippians (1:4, 18, 25; 2:2, 17, 18, 28, 29; 3:1; 4:1, 4, 10). The Lord is the motive and guarantee of our joy. This joy ought to be shown to everyone under the guise of kindness and equanimity. Paul does not lose sight of the theme of the *parousia* (cf. 3:20), but neither is the *parousia* a reason for anxiety to the believer. Peace will be God's gift for Christians in spite of all their anguish and concerns.

A more general exhortation follows (vv. 8-9) and expands into an enumeration of values that all Christians will appreciate. We have one of those catalogues frequently found in the Christian Scriptures (cf. Gal 5:22-23; Col 3:12; 1 Tim 6:11; 2 Tim 2:22, 24-25; 1 Pet 3:8-9; 2 Pet 1:5-7). Here Paul uses terms and concepts frequently found in Stoic philosophy. There are acts of human behavior that even the Greek philosophers recognized as commendable, a fact that ought to make them respectable even to outsiders (cf. v. 5). Finally Paul recommends that the Philippians uphold the teachings he had given them in word and example. He concludes the exhortation by assuring them that the God of peace will be with them (cf. Rom 15:33; 2 Cor 13:11).

Gratitude for the Offering: 4:10-20

This section (4:10-20) has a clear thematic unity that distinguishes it from the former section but relates it to 2:25. The theme is unique: gratitude for the help sent to Paul by the Philippians as well as some marginal commentary. Although Paul had learned how to be satisfied in all circumstances he is grateful for help received. Here he uses again a concept typical of Stoic philosophy: sufficiency. He knows how to live in poverty and in abundance. For these philosophers that virtue frequently carried with it a touch of proud self-sufficiency. For Paul, on the other hand, this "sufficiency" is founded on the help of the Lord who gives him strength (cf. 2 Cor 12:9-10).

Paul expresses his gratitude clearly in vv. 14-20. The Philippians jointly shared with Paul in his need. When he left Macedonia on his missionary trip (cf. Acts 17–18) the Philippians initiated an exchange of goods with Paul. Later, while he was in Thessalonica, they had sent him help more than once. What the Philippians sent was beneficial on another level. Paul points out to them that their gift merits the spiritual gifts that Paul communicates to them (cf. Rom 15:27). The formula "I have received" (= "I acknowledge the receipt of") gives an official character to his gratitude, but Paul rounds off his reference to the generosity of the Philippians with the term "sacrifice." He compares the Philippians' gift to a fragrant offering, a sacrifice God is pleased to accept (cf. Lev 1:9). Christian gratitude includes a petition to God that God reward generously those who have given gifts, bestowing on them a participation in the divine glory through Jesus Christ. The section ends with a doxology (v. 20).

Farewell: 4:21-23

The greeting is brief and does not mention any of the persons addressed in particular. It includes everyone. Neither does it mention any of those who are with Paul at the moment; rather it includes greetings to all the faithful of the church "especially those of the emperor's household," that is to say the personnel at his service. The mention of the emperor's household does not indicate for certain that the letter was written in Rome since there were persons in the service of the emperor outside of Rome. The concluding formula is typically Christian and is an exact duplicate of the one in Philemon 25.

BIBLIOGRAPHY

Bruce, Frederick Fyvie. *Philippians.* Peabody, Mass.: Hendrickson, 1993.

Fee, Gordon D. *Paul's Letter to the Philippians.* Grand Rapids: Eerdmans, 1995.

Garland, David E. "The Composition and Unity of Philippians: Some Neglected Literary Factors," *NT* 27 (1985) 141–173.

Marshall, I. Howard. *The Epistle to the Philippians.* Epworth Commentaries. London: Epworth Press, 1991.

Thielman, Frank. *Philippians.* Grand Rapids: Zondervan, 1995.

Witherington, Ben III. *Friendship and Finances in Philippi.* Valley Forge: Trinity Press International, 1994.

Colossians

César Alejandro Mora Paz

FIRST READING

The Community at Colossae

Colossae was a city in Phrygia in Asia Minor, in the valley of the Lycus River (from the Greek *lykus* = wolf). An important city in the fifth and fourth centuries B.C.E., it was probably destroyed by an earthquake around 60–61 C.E. since that earthquake destroyed Laodicea, a city very close by. Pliny does not even mention it in the year 70 and there is no report of its being rebuilt. It probably continued to survive for a few years in a process of extinction. The inhabitants of Colossae were Phrygians, Greeks, and Jews. According to the letter to the Colossians (1:21, 27; 2:13) the community consisted especially of former pagans. However, without the presence of Jews it would have been impossible for the letter's writer to speak of circumcision, the Sabbath, new moons, and some other features of Jewish religious life. The community may have been founded by Epaphras (Col 1:7; 4:12).

Authenticity

Many scholars have voiced their opinion against the authenticity of Colossians as a Pauline letter, basing their choice especially on questions of theology, vocabulary, style, and situation that are reflected in the letter. Still others have declared themselves in favor of its authenticity. The latter explain the differences of style and vocabulary by the apostle's recent sufferings (Lohmeyer) or posit that Paul was using the vocabulary of the "heretics" he was attacking in the letter or that the apostle had entrusted the writing to a "secretary." In addition it is pointed out that many Pauline elements are present even though not with the same intensity as in the other, certainly authentic letters.

We do not think this is the proper place to resolve this much-debated question but we do see that this letter maintains and expands Paul's christological and ecclesiastical reflections. It is difficult to understand Colossians if we are not familiar with the other Pauline letters. In this sense we consider Colossians as heir to the best Pauline tradition. Therefore a knowledge of the Pauline literature gives us a good basis for interpretation. We must also attempt to reconstruct the communicative situation of the Church in which the letter was written on the basis of the text itself.

Purpose and Genre

The most often mentioned purpose of the letter is to fight a certain "heresy" that some have attempted to reconstruct on the basis of the letter itself. Which one was it? We want to make three specific points on this subject. First: it is evident, especially in 2:6-23, that with his arguments and recommendations the author of Colossians has one or several errors in mind. Second: it is not possible on the basis of the studies thus far conducted to detect clearly what is the concrete teaching in question. Some think of Gnostic ideas or a certain "philosophy" in relation to

Greek philosophy or elements of mystery religions. Others insist on the syncretism of the Colossians' heresy. Third: I do not think that we are necessarily dealing with actual heretics or a single heresy in Colossians. It is essential to reconsider the argumentative techniques used there. This "letter" is conditioned by the author's rhetorical techniques, which are in agreement with Paul's style. This is the case also with Philemon and Galatians. Jean-Noël Aletti's literary analysis in his commentary on Colossians (and see his essay on the letter to the Romans in this book) furnishes a model for rhetorical analysis: in Colossians there is a *partitio* in 1:21-23 listing the themes to be developed: (a) the work of Christ for the holiness of believers (vv. 21-22), (b) fidelity to the gospel as proclaimed (v. 23), and (c) the proclamation of this gospel by Paul (v. 23). This is what the author of the letter wants to inculcate or "prove." In fact, in the *probatio* (1:24–4:1) these elements are considered albeit in the opposite order (see below). If we accept this rhetorical *partitio* we will have to accept that it is what determines the argumentation and the very selection of the arguments. The rhetorical literary genre in Colossians is deliberative (persuasive, oriented to the future): the text wants to show the essential components of Christian life. This is the point of view from which we should read Colossians rather than focusing our attention on identifying an alleged and very specific heresy.

This is confirmed by the fact that in the thanksgiving (with its introductory function: 1:3-8) the alleged components of the heresy are not mentioned. As in Romans 11:18-24 the author anticipates readers' objections, their "temptations" and their possible ways of conceiving Christianity. In view of the author's passionate words it is completely acceptable to suppose that there were real errors but we are not necessarily dealing with a single "sect." The description may already be stereotypical in function of the teaching. If Paul is the one who is debating with his disciple, the editor would have had to be someone else who wrote the letter before or after the apostle's death. Some have thought of Timothy. This would explain the aspects of continuity and discontinuity of the letter. What was said before makes us think of a circular rather than a normal letter in which concrete circumstances are definitive.

Place and Time of Composition

This involves problems that have not yet been solved. Let us look at two possibilities. On the premise that Paul is the author of Colossians three places and dates have been suggested: Ephesus (54–57 C.E.), Caesarea (58–60 C.E.), and Rome (61–63 C.E.). Ephesus would better explain Epaphras' coming and going and Onesimus' return. However, since the theology of the letter does not agree with that of Galatians and 1 Corinthians, which Paul wrote from that city, we prefer not to opt for Ephesus. We also reject Caesarea since the collaborators Paul gathers around him are more plausible in Rome than in Caesarea. The freedom Paul enjoys (Col 4:3) does not seem possible in Ephesus. Colossians and Philemon are well suited to Paul's benign imprisonment in Rome. The greatest difficulty is the distance from Phrygia and the fact that this presumes that Paul has abandoned or delayed his journey to Spain. In that case the supposition of Epaphras' or Onesimus' journey would be equally difficult. Still, it is the place that best corresponds to the theology of Colossians which assumes a few years distance with regard to the major letters.

Colossians and the Pauline Epistles

In Colossians there are themes characteristic of the letters that were definitely written by Paul: for example Christ is the Son in whom believers have redemption (1:13-14; cf. Rom 3:24 and 1 Cor 1:30) and inheritance (cf. 3:24 and 1:12); Christ liberates from the Law of Moses (2:14; cf. Gal 4:4); believers were buried with Christ in baptism (2:12; cf. Rom 6:4); Christ is seated at the right hand of the Father (3:1; cf. Rom 8:34); there are two kingdoms, one of light and one of darkness, and a transference from one to the other (cf. 1 Thess 5:4-5; Rom 13:12 and elsewhere). The theme of the Church as the body of Christ is not unusual in authentic Pauline literature even though Christ is not mentioned there as the head in view of the objective of the texts (cf. 1 Cor 12:12-27; Rom 12:4-5). We even find terms and expressions that we could classify as being typically Pauline. Some authors think that these terms could be explained by the author's knowledge of a first collection of letters from Paul, but in Colossians there is no description of offices or structures in the Church either, as is the case in the Pastoral Letters which are probably of a later date. Paul calls himself an apostle (1:1); Epaphras and Tychicus are called "ministers" (1:7, 23; 4:7). There is, therefore, a certain approximation to the Pauline ecclesial situation.

Colossians and Philemon

Several elements in Colossians parallel Philemon: Paul appears as the co-author with Timothy (cf. 2 Cor 1:1; Phil 1:1; 1 Thess 1:1); in 4:18 Paul verifies writing in his own hand as in Philemon 19 (cf. 1 Cor 16:21; Gal 6:11). The list of collaborators who are with Paul is also similar in both letters (cf. also 2 Tim 4:10-12). Tychicus may be missing in Philemon because he is the bearer of the letter to the Colossians (cf. 4:7) and Onesimus' traveling companion. Thus of the collaborators who are with Paul in Colossians only Jesus called Justus is missing in Philemon, but he may also be mentioned in Philemon if the punctuation is read differently: "Epaphras, my fellow prisoner in Christ, Jesus . . ." (Phlm 23). With regard to the addressees, Apphia and Philemon do not appear in Colossians and Nympha is missing from Philemon. Thus everything seems to indicate that Colossians and Philemon are letters from the same period. However, we have seen that Philemon, Apphia, and Onesimus may have been from Laodicea like Archippus (4:17). In that case the term "brothers and sisters" would be used in a broader sense because of the proximity of Laodicea and the "letter to Laodicea" would be the letter to Philemon, written shortly before Colossians (cf. 4:16). There also exists the possibility that Colossians may have been "modeled" on Philemon, like the Pastoral Letters, highlighting some aspects of Paul as a "martyr."

Ephesians and Colossians

From a literary viewpoint Ephesians is dependent on Colossians which it knows but does not follow to the letter. It does take up many themes and words but few sentences or long sequences. Some scholars have thought that Ephesians may not depend directly on Colossians but rather on hymnic, liturgical, and catechetical traditions that could have been used independently in each letter. However this supposition makes it difficult to explain the stylistic contacts and the emphasis on these contacts in Ephesians with regard to Colossians. The author of Ephesians takes a good deal of liberty with the text of Colossians: he summarizes, expands, develops what is implicit, often showing a theological and stylistic development with regard to the other letter. In so doing the author reveals a profound knowledge of Pauline theology. Among scholars the view that Ephesians is Deutero-Pauline predominates although it is not a universally accepted theory.

Colossians in the Life of the Church

This letter caught the attention of the best commentators right from the beginning. Among them we can mention John Chrysostom, John of Damascus, Theodoret, Cassiodorus, Peter Lombard, Thomas Aquinas, Hugo Grotius, and John Calvin. The christological hymn of 1:15-20 has been especially controversial since the days of Justin and Irenaeus. Christ is the *prōtotokos,* the "firstborn." (Firstborn in terms of dignity? order of birth? pre-existing?) If "firstborn," does this refer to the incarnate or the pre-existing Word? There has also been considerable discussion about whether 1:16 deals with "the first creation" (in accord with the Wisdom literature) or with the "new creation" (Theodoret) in relation to redemption. Throughout the history of the Church there has been extensive speculation on the scope of 1:2: the reconciliation of "all things" in Christ. There have been attempts to expand Christ's action to all of creation (if so in what sense?) or else faith and obedience have been underscored, limiting the concept of "universe." From the Reformation until the present there have been especially heated discussions attempting to clarify questions concerning the universality of Christ's work and recently questions also linked to ecological and political themes.

The moral or ethical aspect of the letter should also be mentioned. The "household rules" or "household code" of Col 3:18–4:1 have been a focus of reflection from the time of Alexander until our own era. There have been interpretations stressing the letter's support for the status quo and also in the more objective line pointing out Christ's influence on believers' lives in terms of "daily life." We are trying to offer the readers of our commentary elements to help them discern in these matters.

In the liturgy we read Colossians on weekdays in Ordinary Time (Weeks Twenty-two and Twenty-three, on the 15th to 18th Sundays in Ordinary Time (Year C), on the feast of Christ the King (Year C), Easter Sunday, May 1, in the Common of Pastors, and at religious professions, as well as in the liturgies for Christian unity, the Name of Jesus, thanksgiving, and in the rites of penance (1:12-14; 3:1-5, 9, 11; 3:8-10, 12-17), the anointing of the sick (1:22-29), the baptism of adults (3:9-17) and marriage (3:12-17).

The Colombian liturgy by Pedro Ortiz, S.J., has done an excellent translation of this letter. We would also recommend the *Biblia de América* (Casa de la Biblia de Madrid) and the *Biblia de Estudio* (SBU) for Latin American readers. The *Biblia del Peregrino* (L. Alonso-Schökel) is recommended for people with more literary preparation.

Literary Structure of the Letter

Although other authors (including Paul Lamarche and Michael Wolter) had already taken seriously the influence of rhetoric in Colossians the most accurate recent commentary seems to be that of Aletti. Like Aletti we think a *partitio* in 1:21-23 is decisive for the structure. Thus the structure is as follows:

Epistolary Setting: 1:1-2 (initial greeting)
Rhetorical Composition: *Exordium* (1:3-23), with hymnic developments that would include a *partitio* we will discuss
Thanksgiving (1:3-8)
Prayer (1:9-14)
Hymnic development (1:15-20)
The *partitio* (1:21-23)
- a. What Christ does for the holiness of believers (vv. 21-22)
- b. Fidelity to the gospel received (v. 23)
- c. The gospel proclaimed by Paul (v. 23)

The *probatio* (1:24–4:1) takes up the same themes in reverse order:
- c. Paul's struggling to proclaim the gospel (1:24–2:5)
- b. Fidelity to the gospel received (2:6-23). Verses 20-23 could serve as a *subperoratio*.
- a. The holiness of believers (3:1–4:1)

The *peroratio* (final exhortations with a peroratory function: 4:2-6)
Return to the epistolary setting: 4:7-18

SECOND READING

Opening (Epistolary Setting): 1:1-2

Paul usually starts his letters by mentioning his ministry as an apostle (2 Cor 1:1; Gal 1:1). He is "an apostle of Christ Jesus," thus indicating the source and objective of his activity according to the commentary of John Chrysostom who alludes to the "heresy" of Colossae. The "saints" are set apart by God for God. "Saints" also describes the assembly of the Israelites (cf. Exod 19:6; Lev 11:44). The Qumran monks called themselves "saints" and this is what Paul calls Christians (Rom 1:7). "In Christ" means that Christ is the one who initiates and completes salvation (Rom 5:2). The Hebrew "peace" *(shalōm)* is the synthesis of all that is good (cf. 2 Sam 18:28; Ps 37:11). It is an eschatological messianic blessing (Isa 11:1-11; 52:7). We are all destined to have peace in Jesus Christ.

Exordium, Part One: Thanksgiving: 1:3-8

"Thanksgiving" is an element of Greco-Roman epistolography that Paul christianized. In the thanksgiving he states the themes he is going to present and sets the tone for the letter. In Col 1:9-14 Paul mentions the basic components of Christian life: faith, hope, love, good deeds, genuine wisdom, patience, joy.

1:3: The thought seems to parallel John 20:17, "my Father and your Father, my God and your God" (cf. Eph 1:3).

1:4-5: Faith, hope, and love form a typical triad in Paul (1 Cor 13:13; 1 Thess 1:3). Faith is surrender to Christ (Rom 1:5) and it works through love (Gal 5:6; Phlm 4-6). Colossians 1:3-4 presents hope in an objective sense ("the hope laid up for you," cf. Rom 8:24-25).

1:6: "In the whole world" refers to the eschatological promises of universal salvation (Rom 1:16; Isa 66:20); this leads to the schema of revelation: the silent, hidden "mystery" now revealed to the Gentiles by God's command. For "bearing fruit and growing" cf. Matt 13:8, 32 // Mark 4:8, 38 // Luke 8:8, 13:19.

Exordium, Part Two: Intercession: 1:9-14

The intercession of the letter prolongs the introductory functions of giving thanks (1:3-8) as it does in Philemon 4-6.

1:9: With "knowledge . . . wisdom and understanding" (cf. 1:6, 9, 10; 2:2; 3:10: *epignōsis, sophia,* and *synesis*). Colossians is referring to the practical knowledge leading to following the will of God (Ps 143:10; Jer 5:5; Sir 17:7; 1 Cor 2:14-15).

1:10: This verse confirms that 1:9 is dealing with practical knowledge leading to "walking" (1 Thess 4:1; Rom 8:4) so as to be pleasing to the Lord and bear fruit in every good work (2 Cor 10:15).

1:11: Christians will certainly encounter difficulties on this journey; they need perseverance (Rom 2:7; 5:4) and patience (Gal 5:22; 1 Cor 13:4) but they will receive this strength from God (Rom 4:20; Luke 1:51; John 15:5-6).

1:12-14: Verse 12 insists on giving thanks to God with joy, which is a fruit of the Spirit (Gal 5:22) and evokes the time of the addressees' conversion (cf. Acts 26:18). "Sharing in the inheritance" reminds us of the "inheritance" the faithful will receive (an eschatological expression: Col 3:24; Dan 12:13), an inheritance that is the Lord himself (Ps 16:5 [15:5]). The expression *en tō photi* ("in the light") reminds us of a vocabulary of "conversion," as in 1 Thess 5:4-5; Eph 5:8; 1 Pet 2:9; cf. John 1:1-18. "Light" and "darkness" form part of the Qumran vocabulary and indicate the dominion of sin and injustice (Belial) on one hand and the followers of the Holy One (God) on the other hand. In Christ we have redemption (Rom 3:24-26; 5:9; 1 Pet 1:18-19) and the remission of sins (Matt 26:28; Heb 9:22; 10:18). We have to infer that vv. 12-14 are already a transition to the hymn (vv. 15-20).

Exordium, Part Three: The Hymn: 1:15-20

1:1-14: The hymn is identifiable as a unit by its literary genre, the parallelisms, the repetitions, and the non-Pauline vocabulary. The usual view is that it is not the work of the author of the letter. The theme is Christ's mediation *(en, dia,* and *pro).* Nevertheless the subject of the whole hymn is the incarnate and redeeming Son (1:14: verbs in the present tense; cf. Heb 1:2-4; John 1:1-18). Before and also after the hymn its content is applied to the community ("He has rescued us . . . and transferred us": cf. 1:13, 14, 21). Some think this means that reconciliation here should not be understood in a cosmic context but already refers to the community. Christ is "the head of the body, the church" (cf. 2:18). However, we should not forget that through men and women (because they are the centers of creation according to the Judeo-Christian tradition) the elements of nature are called to be reconciled among themselves and with humankind. With this background Colossians points to the universal and definitive outreach of the Christ event and the need to proclaim it everywhere. Behind Col 1:16 can also be the awareness that as centers of creation men and women are "groaning in labor pains" (Rom 8:18-25). The author of Colossians may have been familiar with these Pauline traditions and developed what was present in them in germ. In fact this reconciliation will only be perfect at the end (1 Cor 15:24-28; Rom 8:19-23).

Some look for the background of the hymn in Hellenistic Judaism: in the Jewish liturgy of the Day of Atonement or in the myth of archetypal human beings. With Aletti we think there is no concrete indication of this in the hymn. Instead one should speak of a general influence of the theme of wisdom in Colossians.

1:15-18: The entire hymn focuses on the relation of Christ to the powers: Colossians should be read in the light of this concern. Christ is neither the image of God because he is visible nor because of traits he has in common with the Father such as incorruptibility, but because of his active participation in the work of creation in line with the Wisdom writings (cf. Prov 8:22-31; Sir 24:3-9). Philo of Alexandria defends the invisibility of the *logos* as the image of God (cf. also 2 Cor 4:4). The *prōtotokos* ("firstborn") has been interpreted as "begotten before all things," "beloved" (cf. Ps 89:27[28]; Exod 4:22; Jer 31:9; Sir 36:11). It is difficult to be more specific. In any case it is a title of preeminence and anteriority (cf. vv. 15-17): "all things have been created through him and for him" (cf. Heb 1:6); "he himself is before all things, and in him all things hold together." It is evident that the Word cannot be placed on the same level as creatures. In their struggle against the Arians the Fathers of the Church state that generation befits the Son while creation is fitting for creatures. Even as a human being he is the "firstborn" not in terms of time but in terms of dignity (Anselm, Jerome). Thrones, dominions, rulers, and powers are mentioned. There is a reference to powers that might compete with the Word: they are possible rivals of the Son. Christ is the *kephalē* (head) of the body of the Church. This is not Philo's idea of the *logos* as the head of the universe. It is simply the Semitic concept of *roʾsh:* the first, the one in charge. The Church is the body (rather than *his* body as in Eph 1:23 and Col 1:24). The Church has to recognize the absolute lordship of Christ who is *archē* ("beginning"), the name Philo gives to wisdom and to the *logos*. If *archē* has no article it is an "attribute" like *prōtotokos* ("firstborn"). These can be taken as parallels and synonyms (cf. Deut 21:17).

1:19-20: The verb "to dwell" evokes the narrative about "the glory of the Lord" in the OT (cf. Heb 2:9; 1 Kings 8:27, Ps 68:16 [67:17 LXX]). Some have argued about the meaning of *plērōma* ("fullness") in 1:19. It is not a Gnostic use of the word since there is a clear reference to the OT world. This meaning is explained in 2:9: "For in him the whole fullness of deity dwells bodily"—that is to say, the Son has always been God and the incarnation has not changed anything. Peace comes through the blood of Christ on the cross. According to some authors the reference is to universal, eschatological peace (Isa 9:5-6; Mic 5:4) through the paschal mystery. As a matter of fact the emphasis appears to be on Christ's universal mediation. The powers cannot reestablish peace between God and humankind.

Partitio (Announcing the Themes): 1:21-23

The delimitation of this passage does not seem to be a problem. It has been called: "application and transition." There is an obvious change of style and language. The style is now direct and conversational. (For questions of structure see the Introduction above.) After mentioning the former situation of sin (1:21) the author indicates the present transformation (1:22) and the way to continue in this positive situation (1:23).

1:21: Before the Colossians were "estranged and hostile." In the OT this is said of idolaters (Ezek 14:5) and the wicked (Ps 58:3); cf. Rom 5:10.

1:22: "He has reconciled" us: the subject is God as in 1:19. The expression "in his fleshly body" refers to the human part of Christ that is suffering (cf. Sir 23:16-17), that is, the suffering humanity of Christ. The idea is taken from 1:20. "So as to present you" *(parastēsai)* has sacrificial (presentation of the sacrifice, cf. Rom 12:1; Lev 16:7) and legal connotations (presenting someone to the court, cf. 1 Cor 8:8), but it does not necessarily deal with the final judgment.

1:23: The attitudes of being steadfast in the faith and in hope are presented with two images of believers as living foundations of God's temple (cf. 2:7; 1 Cor 3:10-17; 1 Pet 2:4-8) with parallels in Qumran. In Col 1:5, 23, 27, hope indicates the very content of the gospel. This gospel has been proclaimed to "every creature," thus showing its universality and credibility. Paul is its *diakonos* ("servant"), 1 Cor 3:5.

What follows in 1:24–4:1 is a section resembling a *probatio.* (Remember that in the present *probatio* the elements of the *partitio* are used in inverse order, C → B → A. See "Structure of the Letter" above.)

Paul's Struggle to Proclaim the Gospel: 1:24–2:5 (= C)

Paul's sufferings are a living proof (a kind of *narratio*) of the value of the message he is proclaiming. Here it is relevant to note the many terms referring to "knowledge" including *phaneroō* and *gnōrizō*. However, we do not find typical apocalyptic terms *(apokalyptein, apokalypsis)* such as are present in Eph 3:5.

1:24: "And in my flesh I am completing what is lacking in Christ's afflictions *(tōn thlipseōn)* for the sake of his body, that is, the church." The author is not saying that something is lacking in Christ's afflictions to save humankind or that Christ has not suffered enough. The mediation of Christ is perfect (cf. Col 1:19-20, 22; 2:9-10, 13-14; 3:1). Some commentators think that these afflictions of Christ are only incomplete in terms of their application to people of all times (subjective redemption). Following Thomas Aquinas, other commentators say that one has to be conformed to the head who is Christ: just as Christ endured what he had to suffer in accordance with the Father's designs (John 17:4; 19:30) so his members must share in his afflictions until the plan of God is fulfilled and in this way they will also share in his glory (Rom 8:17, 29). Without denying this others add that "completing what is lacking in Christ's afflictions" means feeling associated in the apostolic works of Jesus in his mortal life by continuing his work for the sake of the Church. Moreover, because of his culture Paul considered himself in continuity with Christ, one with the Master, just as in his time the person sent *(shalīah* in Hebrew) was one with the sender. It has been noted that Paul calls "Christ's afflictions in my flesh" his own activity reproducing that of Christ in proclaiming the gospel, a laborious and tiring activity that is always for the sake of the Church. In fact *thlipsis* ("affliction") is never used to refer to Christ's redemptive passion but rather applies to the hardships of evangelical proclamation (Rom 5:3; 8:35; 2 Cor 1:4, 8; 2:4; 4:17; 6:4; 7:4). Christians are mystical images of the physical Christ. The genitive in the phrase "Christ's afflictions" would be a "genitive of similarity" or, as González Ruiz suggests, a "mystical genitive." The interpretations of John Chrysostom, Jerome, and Theodoret seem to go along this line. There may also be an apocalyptic influence in the formulation (cf. Matt 24:8; Acts 14:22; 1 Tim 4:1). Similar comments may be made concerning the use of *agōnizomai* and *agōn* ("struggling," "struggle" in 2:1; cf. 1 Thess 2:2; Phil 1:30).

1:25: The term *oikonomia* in Colossians is equivalent to "office" (1 Cor 9:17; 4:1-5; cf. Luke 16:2). The objective of this ministry is "to make the word of God fully known" (cf. 1:9, 25; 4:4; Rom 15:19).

1:26: Here *mystērion* ("mystery") replaces *logos* ("word") or *euangelion* ("good news"). It manifests the unfathomable newness of Christ. If the background may have been apocalyptic (cf. Dan 2:18-19, 27-30), in contact with the terminology of mysteries, this apocalyptic vein has been transformed in Colossians.

1:27: This verse develops the theme of the content of the *mystērion.* The mystery is not only Christ but also the plan of God who wanted Christ to be proclaimed among the Gentiles (Col 1:27; Rom 9:23-24; 16:25-26).

1:28: The verb "to proclaim" can be almost a technical term for the early preaching (cf. 1 Cor 9:14; Acts 17:3, 23). The *mystērion* is prolonged in the apostle's activity.

1:29: The verb *kopiō* ("I toil and struggle") indicates Paul's labors for the good of the community (1 Thess 5:12; 1 Cor 16:16; Rom 16:6; cf. Col 1:24).

2:1-5: These verses mark the beginning of the transition to the direct confrontation with Colossae's errors. Concerning *agōn* ("struggling") see the commentary on 1:24. We find the repetition of the themes of love (cf. 1:4; 2:2), understanding, wisdom and knowledge (cf. 1:6, 9, 10; 2:2; 3:10 and commentary on 1:9), of the mystery of God (cf. 1:26) and the faith of the community (1:4, 23). Verse 3 refers us to Romans 11:33. In the context the Greek concept of *pithanologia* ("plausible arguments," 2:4) is negative. It refers to "sophism," "deceptive plausible arguments."

Fidelity to the Gospel: 2:6-23 (B)

The purpose of this section is to point out the contradiction of those in Colossae who pretend to become humble but instead despise others, those who think they are controlling the flesh with their practices but do not succeed. The only appropriate behavior is to be in union with the head.

2:6: In the *homologoumena* (the letters generally acknowledged as coming from Paul: Romans, 1–2 Corinthians, Galatians, Philippians, 1 Thessalonians, Philemon), in speaking of receiving Christ *(paralambanein)* the author is dealing with faith according to tradition (cf. Gal 1:9-12) that is being rooted in a person (cf. Gal 2:17-21). Only in this passage and in Eph 3:11 is Christ given the complete name of *Christon Iēsoun ton kyrion* (Christ Jesus the Lord). This may be an ancient profession of faith (cf. Acts 2:36). "Walk in him" is referring to the journey in an ethical sense (Rom 6:4; cf. John 8:12; 14:6, "I am the way"; Acts 19:23).

2:7: In biblical tradition rooting and building up are found as images of life (cf. Isa 11:1) that are taken up by 1 Cor 3:10-11 and Rom 15:12. In the present case "rooted" and "built up" are parallel and converge on "walking" according to Christ.

2:8: Here the injunction is to beware of deceit, which is compared with enslaving captivity. "Philosophy" (a hapax legomenon [= single occurrence] in the NT) followed by a parallel ("empty deceit") indicates what is involved, that is, false doctrines that are deceptive and empty.

2:9: "For in him the whole fullness of deity dwells bodily *(sōmatikōs).*" Some have understood *sōmatikōs* as "bodily" (*sōma* = body, an idea found in John 1:14) or "really" by opposing "body" to "shadow" (Augustine, Cyril; cf. 2:17). Jerome translated it as "completely" or "fully" (cf. 1:19). This is the meaning required by v. 10. It is also required by the situation the letter is addressing, namely the superiority of the saving mediation of Christ.

2:10: "You have come to fullness in him (as opposed to other powers)": cf. Eph 1:13; 3:19; Col 1:19; Eph 1:21-23.

2:11: The term "putting off the body of the flesh" refers to circumcision in a metaphorical sense inherited from the OT (Deut 10:16; cf. Rom 2:28-29). This is achieved through baptism (v. 12; cf. 3:9; Romans 6 and 8). The "putting off" *(apekdysei)* may allude to the rite of baptism (cf. Gal 3:27) or even to the rites of the mysteries though this is not the relevant focus but rather the proximate literary context. It is not a matter of stripping off a small piece of skin but instead the "old self" or "the mortal body," in other words the self under the dominion of sin (cf. 2:15 and 3:9; Rom 6:3-11; Eph 4:22).

2:12: "Raised with" expresses the identification of the Christian with the resurrection of Christ in baptism (cf. 1:29; 2:12; Rom 6:4). All of this takes place "through faith in the power of God." This insistence on the power of God has the objective of counteracting the attention given to other powers in Colossae.

2:13: "The uncircumcision of your flesh" may be a metaphor (cf. Eph 2:1-5).

2:14: "God erased the record of our trespasses." This record is the *cheirographon* ("manuscript," "autograph," "record") that Christ erased by "nailing it to the cross," an allusion to his redemptive death (Rom 3:24-25). This is obviously a metaphor. Many think that it deals with the cancellation of the old Law that would keep us in servitude and could lead to death (cf. Rom 5:20-21; 7:5-13; 1 Cor 15:56; Gal 5:1). There is something special that connects the *dogmata* (clauses or precepts) of the *cheirographon* with the angelic powers. In the angelology of the time the angels wrote down the sins of humankind in a book. This could explain the origin of an excessive power conceded to angels among the teachers of Colossae. Angelic powers would be in charge of having practices scrupulously observed and punishing those who refuse them (cf. Gal 3:19).

2:15: All angelic powers have been stripped of their dominion over human beings (their power to punish). All angelic powers appear in Christ's royal retinue.

2:16: "Therefore do not let anyone condemn you in matters of food and drink." There may be a Judaic background (cf. Hos 2:13) or a mixture of religious elements here. Such practices were also used in other religions.

2:17: All the mentioned practices are a shadow of eschatological, definitive realities (Heb 10:1). Reality, what is immortal, comes from Christ.

2:18: "Do not let anyone disqualify you." The author is using metaphorical language. We must not lose the prize of the race (cf. 1 Cor 9:24; Phil 3:14). The term *tapeinophrosynē* signifies "humility" (fasting, deprivation, etcetera are practices promoting it: cf. 2:23). Some think that the reference to a possible "worship of angels" *(threskeia tōn angellōn)* by the Colossians could indicate worshiping angels. There are some testimonies (cf. Rev 19:10; 22:8-9). But there are Jewish texts that because of their literary and religious context suggest that believers were joining the angels' worship of God. Here it would be an erroneous worship of God, the kind of worship that exaggerates the power of angels. This is also indicated by the logic of the context. The participle *embateuōn* (dwelling in, entering into) was the technical term to indicate the "entrance" into the mysteries. Here it has a negative connotation of presumption or obsession. The teachers at Colossae are "puffed up" (cf. 1 Cor 4:6, 18; 8:1; 5:2), perhaps some kind of "initiates." Their minds are set "on the flesh" (cf. Rom 8:7).

2:19: In fact the Colossae teachers despise the head, Christ, and their preaching does not accord him the place he should have. Christ's place is not only one of preeminence but is also a source of life "by its ligaments and sinews."

2:20: "With Christ you died to the elemental spirits of the universe" (cf. commentary on 2:8, 14). What is at stake here is also the freedom of believers. This freedom cannot be lived as if believers' lives were determined by their former way of doing things to which they have died. That would be unworthy of Christians.

2:21: "Do not handle, do not taste, do not touch" (cf. Lev 11:24; Exod 19:12). These are questions of legal purity. Some think they are also restrictions of a sexual type (cf. 1 Tim 4:3). It is possible, given what is said in the following verse, but it is not certain.

2:22: "All these regulations refer to things that perish with use." This sentence situates us in God's plan. All created things are destined to be consumed, to be used by men and women (cf. Gen 1:31, "God saw that everything was very good"). Therefore what the Colossae teachers are saying is human teaching (quoting Isa 29:13; cf. Matt 15:9 // Mark 7:7).

2:23: These practices of "humility" and "severe treatment of the body" have only an appearance of wisdom and they are of no value *(timē)*. Some think that the term *timē* may contain a reference to mystery religion, that is, election and deification. Paradoxically they only serve to satisfy the flesh.

The Holiness of Believers: 3:1–4:1 (A)

The composition of this passage is as follows: (1) vv. 3:1-4: motivations with a kind of *partitio:* (a) Seek the things that are above (vv. 1-2), (b) not things that are on earth (vv. 2-4); (2) The parts previously announced are taken up in inverse order: (b) vv. 5-9: exhortations to put the old self and its motivations to death, (a) vv. 9-17: exhortations to live the newness of Christ and its prolongation in family life (household code: 3:18–4:1).

3:1: "So" indicates that acting ethically depends on the believer's situation described in ch. 2 (see 2:1, 6, 12, 20; cf. 1:9-11, 21-23). "The things that are above" are in the heavenly world (John 8:23; Phil 3:14, and elsewhere).

3:2: The author adds the antithesis of "the things that are above," namely "the things that are on earth" or disorderly passions.

3:3: This verse presents an antithesis: you have died (Greek aorist)/your life is hidden (perfect tense). Having died (Romans 6) one lives a new life that is described in ch. 2 ("through faith," cf. Gal 2:17-21).

3:4: Being revealed with Christ in glory will happen at the *parousia*. The eschatology of the letter is not yet truly "realized" but is mystical and metaphorical. The identification with Christ that started with baptism will have no end and it takes place in three decisive moments: death, resurrection, and glorification. In Colossians the Pauline eschatology has not really changed; it is only another way of presenting Christian life.

3:5: "Put to death . . . whatever in you is earthly." There are similar warnings in Rom 6:11; 8:13. With regard to this there is a paradox in Colossians, namely, what has already been accomplished in baptism is still a task that remains to be done (cf. 3:1-4) although we are not told why. In fact it is another way of presenting the paradox "already but not yet" that characterizes the Reign of God that is among us though it has not yet come to its fullness. What is the meaning of "whatever in you is earthly?" It may be a metonymy as in Rom 6:13, 19; 7:5, 23.

3:6: Paul frequently ends a list of vices with a mention of the divine judgment of justice (*orgē;* cf. 1 Thess 1:10; 2:16). This is the case in 1 Thess 4:3-6; 1 Cor 5:10-13; 6:9; Rom 1:18-32.

3:7: An application to believers' lives is sought ("you . . . you . . ."). As to *peripatein* (to walk), *halakh* in Hebrew, cf. 1:10. The Colossians lived in this condition and they were "dead in trespasses" (cf. 2:13; Eph 2:1-10). Following this way brings life.

3:8: "But now you must get rid of all such things." Positive attitudes, taken from the Pauline baptismal exhortations, are recommended (Rom 13:12; cf. 1:21; Eph 4:22; 1 Pet 2:1). This is not to say that the affirmations of 1:3-8 and 3:7 are false but that vices are a constant temptation.

3:9a: "Do not lie to one another." Because of the imperative this first part of v. 9 belongs to the previous section. Just as God cannot lie, so Christians should not lie (cf. Heb 6:18; Gal 1:20; 2 Cor 11:31; Rom 9:1).

3:9b: The second part of v. 9 returns to the christological theme abandoned in 3:5. Verses 9-11 provide the motivation for the preceding exhortations (vv. 5-9) and those that follow (vv. 12-17).

3:10: Clothing ourselves with Christ is a Pauline image (cf. Rom 13:12, 14; Gal 3:27; 1 Cor 5:7; 2 Cor 4:16; 5:17) and it has its roots in the OT. For example 1 Thess 5:8 evokes Isa 59:17; this means abandoning old practices and living one's life according to Christ.

3:11: "There is no longer Greek and Jew . . . ." Some think that Colossians is suggesting that social differences ought to disappear in the Church. This is an anachronism since at the time people were not thinking about a classless society. What is at stake is to deduce the consequences of faith in Christ Jesus for a better coexistence in society. The consequences, which the Church's social teaching has been inferring from the evangelical message, are in the Bible as seeds but time was needed for their formulation because human processes are slow. If we compare this with Gal 3:28, in Colossians the concept of the absence of religious discrimination becomes sharper, moving from Jews to Greeks, from Greeks to barbarians, and from barbarians to the most abject, the Scythians who "are slightly better than wild beasts" (Josephus).

3:12: "Clothe yourselves with compassion" (cf. 1 Pet 3:8; Eph 4:32 and the *Testaments of the Twelve Patriarchs*). Israelites were called "holy and beloved." The author sees the Church as the new Israel. This newness must be reflected in our relationships with one another; five virtues are mentioned.

3:13: "Bear with one another . . . forgive each other." This verse contains its own motivation: "just as the Lord has forgiven you."

3:14: Love "binds everything together in perfect harmony" *(syndesmos tēs teleiotētos)*. This may be a genitive of quality (binding in perfect harmony) or objective (the bond whose objective is perfection). We may choose to opt for the second meaning, which gives the ultimate reason of the Christian task.

3:15: "And let the peace of Christ rule in your hearts." See the commentary on 1:2 and Rom 15:13.

3:16: See the commentary on 1:12. Since in Colossae not every teaching is sound (as, for example, the heretics' teaching) the author gives qualifying christological indications: goodness, peace . . . (cf. 1:9-11; 3:1-4). The exhortations are taking the liturgy into account as can be seen in the choice of words: "psalms, hymns, and spiritual songs." The exhortations also reinforce mutual responsibility ("one another").

3:17: Christians proclaim the mediation of Christ by giving thanks to God through him in their own lives, which must become an ongoing thanksgiving. "Do everything in the name of the Lord Jesus" is a christological principle that implies the presence of Christ with all his power (cf. 1 Cor 5:4; 6:11; Acts 3:6; 2 Thess 3:6).

Household Code: 3:18–4:1

In reading these exhortations we must keep in mind that belonging to different social strata was not yet challenging the baptized of Colossae. Family codes belong to an ethical subgenre going back to Aristotle. Stoics were also teaching them. They are the literary model for the corresponding codes in the NT. They might have been widespread in early Christianity but they have a motivation different from those of the pagan codes. Here we are not dealing with the harmony of the *polis* (the city or state) but rather with christological and theological reasons. From now on everything must be done in the Lord (Christ: cf. Eph 5:21-33). There may be some apologetic elements in these exhortations: the intention of making early Christianity acceptable and eliminating one of the first accusations against it, namely its being anarchical. Naturally the pastors of early Christianity were not attempting to "baptize" the structures and adhere to them unconditionally. Behind these codes we do recognize a certain patriarchal order (even prevailing in Roman law). Only the first conclusions are deduced on the basis of Christ's message. We see that this code is in some way an extraneous segment that differs from vv. 6-17. We observe that the author of Colossians inherited rather than formulated this code.

3:18: "Be subject to your husbands" *(hypotasesthai)*. There is a difference between asking women simply to be subjects and asking them to accept an existing order. They are not asked to be subjects like children or slaves *(hypakouein)* but to be subject as the Son is subject to the Father (1 Cor 11:3; 15:28). This is the way citizens are subject to authorities (Rom 13:1), and this should be "as is fitting *(hōs anēken)* in the Lord." Custom and tradition are most reliable in order to know "what is fitting." Love *(agapē)* is recommended to men to regulate the scale of social ethics. This is not superiority associated with arrogance but instead humility and love that must dictate the behavior of the baptized.

3:20: Obedience is pleasing to the Lord (cf. 2 Cor 5:9; Rom 12:1; 14:18, Phil 4:18; Eph 5:10). Here in Colossians the expression *en kyriō* (in the Lord) would mean what is acceptable within a human group, the Church. This admonition follows the line of the previous ones; it is a matter of Christian wisdom.

3:21: As in the case of spouses, so the admonition to fathers and children in their behavior toward superiors is "human." Because at times education is very hard, fathers are asked to be understanding and humane lest children become timid and lose heart.

3:22: Slaves who have already embraced Christianity must obey their masters, not in order

THE NEW TESTAMENT HOUSEHOLD CODES

The household codes of the New Testament continue to cause trouble and consternation in today's Church, particularly to the extent that interpreters want to suggest that they represent some kind of positive and lasting will of God about the subordination of wives to husbands. (The same interpreters will with total inconsistency pass over in silence slaves and masters in the same text.) The fact that the wife-husband relationship in the texts now gets the most attention is simply an indication that gender roles are in transition in our own society. Because these texts cause so many problems today it is difficult for modern readers to appreciate the ways in which in their own context, while reinforcing the prevalent hierarchical view of society, they yet took significant steps forward. A sound method of biblical interpretation challenges us to do the same.

It has been demonstrated by David Balch ("Household Codes," in David E. Aune, ed., *Greco-Roman Literature and the New Testament* [Atlanta: Scholars Press, 1988] 25–50) that the household code as a literary topos has its origins in the Hellenistic discussion of household management, based largely on Aristotle. However these Hellenistic guides to the well-managed household are purely patriarchal in both conception and form, that is, they envision the male householder as husband, father, and master with sole authority not only to rule but also to teach those subject to him how they are to behave as subordinate members of the household. Their instruction is addressed only to him. We have examples of an adaptation of this form in the NT in the Pastoral Epistles, where the literary genre of personal letter requires that the author instruct the male authority figure Timothy or Titus how he is to teach others to conduct themselves as Christians (1 Tim 2:1–3:13; 5:4-17; 6:1-2, 17-19; Titus 1:6-9; 2:1-10; 3:1-2). Compare *1 Clem.* 1.3 where the recipients of the letter are envisioned as the males of the community even though the letter is addressed to the whole church at Corinth, for they are commended among other things for having taught wives to be submissive to their husbands.

The household codes of Ephesians and Colossians are quite different in two respects: they address directly all parties involved and they address the subordinate member of each pair first. It is not "Husbands, teach your wives to be submissive," and so on, but "Wives, be submissive to your husbands," and of course the Ephesians code prefaces everything with the ideal of mutual submission as to Christ (5:21). Second, wives, children, and slaves are addressed before husbands, parents, and masters. Both of these elements are innovations in the Christian formulations. They can only indicate a distinctive approach to the treatment of baptized individuals in subordinate social positions as persons in their own right. Rather than being considered merely members of a household whose principal function is to reflect the honor of the householder, wives, adult children, and slaves are granted a dignity and autonomy that they lack in previous discussions of household management. Meanwhile those who fear that Christians will be accused of undermining the social order are assured that the patriarchal system remains intact.

We know from passages like 1 Cor 7:12-16, 21-22 and 1 Pet 3:1-2 that wives and slaves were admitted to baptism independently of their husbands and owners and that even if the husbands or owners became Christian, the wives, children, and slaves did not necessarily follow but could make their own decisions. Similarly synoptic passages like Matt 8:21-22; 10:37; 19:27-29 and parallels that seem to encourage abandonment of family ties in favor of discipleship may echo the experience of Christian family members, especially adult children, whose parents do not approve of their choice but whose authority they are bound to respect. This Christian practice of admitting individuals independently of their patriarchal authority, a practice that Christians shared with Jews and some of the unofficial popular religious cults, was one of the things that made them suspect: they were undermining established social order.

Thus while the authors of the household codes felt it necessary—or perhaps even wanted—to reinforce the essentially patriarchal structure of the household, at the same time they did what none before them had done by acknowledging the personal dignity of all concerned, directly addressing each group as full members of the community. By doing that they moved a familiar piece of their culture toward greater human freedom and dignity for all. The best way to be faithful to their method and intention is to continue taking further steps along the same way.

—*Carolyn Osiek*

to be seen (Theodoret). In speaking of seeking "to please" their masters the author is referring to an OT concept (cf. Eph 6:6): they do not follow God's authority but human authority instead. To this the author opposes wholehearted obedience. The required attitude does not show partiality (cf. v. 25). All have to be pleasing to the Lord; masters and slaves are serving the same Lord.

3:23: Now the slaves are asked to obey "wholeheartedly." The recommendation is similar to 3:17 (cf. Matt 22:37 // Mark 12:30 // Luke

10:27; Prov 11:17 LXX). "As done for the Lord" indicates the motivation here.

3:24: In this text the promised reward is expressed in terms of "inheritance" (cf. 1:5, 27; 3:1-4). "Serve" parallels "[do it] wholeheartedly" of v. 23. "The Lord" continues to refer to Jesus.

3:25: "For the wrongdoer will be paid back for whatever wrong has been done." Since the admonitions to masters begin only in 4:1, in 3:24 the author is still referring to slaves as the addressees of his admonition.

4:1: Masters are advised to treat their slaves justly and fairly. This is part of popular philosophical teaching. However, there is a new dimension here: masters are accountable to the Lord. They are not ordered to liberate the slaves but they are forbidden any excess of their use of authority. In this regard the posture of the letter to Philemon goes farther in its negative expression toward slavery even though we cannot affirm with certainty that Paul is asking for the emancipation of the slave Onesimus. [See commentary on Philemon.]

Final Exhortations with a Perorative Function: 4:2-6

In this section the author returns to the major themes of the letter: (a) The reference to prayer and thanksgiving ties in with the rest of the letter and above all with Col 3:16-25; (b) The mention of prison refers to the struggle cited in 1:24–2:5; (c) "That I may reveal . . . as I should" links with 2:6-23. Therefore it is a kind of epilogue. At the same time the baptized are to conduct themselves "wisely toward outsiders." There are two basic themes: a being firm and behaving "wisely toward outsiders" but with graciousness and discretion. We find analogous exhortations in 1 Thess 5:12-22; Gal 5:26–6:6; and Phil 4:8-13.

The Epistolary Setting Once Again: 4:7-18

The list of Paul's collaborators in Colossians coincides rather closely with the list in Philemon (cf. the Introduction above). Both seem to be reproduced by 2 Tim 4:10-12. Tychicus (cf. Acts 20:4) is from Asia and the presumed bearer of the letter, along with Onesimus, for whom cf. the letter to Philemon. This verse suggests that Onesimus is from Colossae (or Laodicea); see the Introduction. Aristarchus is Paul's fellow-prisoner: cf. Acts 19:29; 20:4; 27:2; Philemon 24. Mark: cf. Acts 12:12-25; 13:13; 15:37, 39; Philemon 24. It is the only time that Jesus called Justus is mentioned. Epaphras: the evangelizer of the Colossians; cf. 1:7; Philemon 23 (mentioned there as a fellow-prisoner as Aristarchus is now). Luke: the physician; cf. Philemon 24. Demas: we know very little about him; cf. Philemon 24. Archippus: cf. Philemon 2. "I, Paul, write this greeting with my own hand": cf. 1 Cor 16:21; this was a Greco–Latin epistolary custom. Tychicus does not appear in Philemon and neither do Nympha and Jesus. In turn Philemon and Apphia are not mentioned in Colossians.

We know the names of at least sixteen of Paul's coworkers. It is interesting to observe his organizational ability. Alone he could not have carried out the enormous work he accomplished. The secret was his having collaborators. Why did Paul always have coworkers? One first explanation could be his decisive personality and his passion for his ideal, Jesus Christ. Another explanation might be the type of communities he founded. We might categorize them as "missionary." He took this model of community from Antioch, the church that sent him on his first missionary journey. Paul created in his communities an awareness that faith was not a treasure that could be hidden; it had to be shared. Paul always asked for temporary assistants, paid for by these communities, to help him in spreading the gospel. At times, as in the case of Philippi, a real bond of brotherly and sisterly love was established between the apostle and the community.

BIBLIOGRAPHY

Aletti, Jean-Noël. *Saint Paul: Épître aux Colossiens.* Paris: Gabalda, 1993.

Bruce, F. F. "Commentary on the Epistle to the Colossians," in E. K. Simpson and F. F. Bruce, eds., *Commentary on the Epistles to the Ephesians and the Colossians.* 9th ed. Grand Rapids: Eerdmans, 1977.

González Ruiz, J. M. *San Pablo. Cartas de la cautividad.* Rome: Marova, 1956.

Horgan, Maurya P. "The Letter to the Colossians," *New Jerome Biblical Commentary.* Englewood Cliffs, N.J.: Prentice-Hall, 1990, 876–882.

Lamarche, Paul. "Structure de l'épître aux Colossiens," *Bib.* 56 (1975) 453–463.

Lightfoot, J. B. *Saint Paul's Epistles to the Colossians and to Philemon.* London: Macmillan, 1879.

Lohmeyer, Ernst. *Die Briefe an die Philipper, Kolosser, und an Philemon.* Göttingen: Vandenhoeck & Ruprecht, 1956.

Lohse, Eduard. *Colossians and Philemon.* Hermeneia. 3rd ed. Philadelphia: Fortress, 1982.

McDonald, H. Dermot. *Commentary on Colossians and Philemon.* Waco, Tex.: Word Books, 1980.

Moule, C.F.D. *The Epistles of Paul the Apostle to the Colossians and to Philemon.* Cambridge: Cambridge University Press, 1957.

O'Brien, P. T. *Colossians, Philemon.* WBC 44. Waco, Tex.: Word Books, 1982.

Pfitzner, John C. *Chi Rho Commentary on Colossians and Philemon.* Adelaide: Lutheran Publishing House, 1983.

Wall, Robert W. *Colossians and Philemon.* Leicester: InterVarsity Press, 1993.

Wolter, Michael. *Der Brief an die Kolosser, Der Brief an Philemon.* ÖTK NT 12. Gütersloh: Gerd Mohn, 1993.

Yates, Roy. *The Epistle to the Colossians.* Epworth Commentaries. London: Epworth Press, 1993.

1 Thessalonians

George M. Soares-Prabhu

FIRST READING

A first reading of Paul's first letter to the Thessalonians will probably leave the reader dissatisfied. Not only is the letter (like all Paul's letters) sometimes irritatingly obscure, but it seems to have little of interest to say to us today. Its exhortations are much too general to be useful and its theology focuses on a problem (the *parousia*) that is not pressing for most of us. The letter has been accepted as a genuine Pauline letter from the beginning (it figures in our earliest list of canonical books, the late-second-century Muratorian Canon) but it has never been very popular in the preaching of the Church. There is no certain reference to 1 Thessalonians in the Apostolic Fathers or the Apologist, but we find it quoted extensively in Irenaeus (ca. 202) and Clement of Alexandria (ca. 211). We know from Jerome that Origen wrote a commentary in three volumes on the letter (ca. 254), but this has not survived. The earliest commentary we possess is that of John Chrysostom (407) given in a series of eleven homilies he preached in Constantinople.

Nevertheless, the letter is important because it is the first of Paul's letters and possibly the earliest Christian writing that we have. It illuminates the early stages of Paul's theology and missionary praxis and allows us a glimpse into the life of a very early Christian community, struggling (as we do today) to live out its faith in the hostile atmosphere of a "pagan" culture. That is why the letter is of growing interest to scholars today.

The authenticity of the letter (its Pauline authorship) has never been in doubt and its integrity is generally accepted. Attempts to show that the letter is a compilation of two originally separate letters or that parts of it (5:1-11 and especially 2:13-16) are later additions have not been convincing. The letter makes good sense as it stands and there really are no serious grounds for doubting its unity or its integrity.

How, Where, and When the Letter Was Written

The circumstances under which the letter was written are fairly clear, especially if indications in the letter itself are supplemented by data from Acts. The latter should be used with caution because what it tells us about Paul's ministry in Thessalonica (Acts 17:1-10) is not meant to be a complete, historically accurate report of what Paul did. It is a reconstruction made by the author of Acts from traditions available to him according to a standard scheme he follows. As everywhere, Paul preaches in a synagogue (Acts 17:2). He succeeds in converting a few Jews but many Gentiles friendly to Judaism, largely of the upper classes (Acts 17:4). His success arouses the anger of Jews who instigate trouble and drive him out of the city on unsubstantiated charges of political subversion (Acts 17:5-10).

This standard Lukan picture of Paul's ministry in Thessalonica does not quite agree with what Paul tells us in his own letter, which has obviously been written for a community of predominantly, if not exclusively, Gentile converts

(1:9) who by and large are artisans or laborers earning their living by manual work (4:11). They have been converted not through preaching in the synagogue (about which the letter says nothing) but through Paul's proclamation of the gospel carried out while he was working at his trade (2:9). Their conversion implies a much longer stay than the three or four weeks (three Sabbaths) allowed by Acts (Acts 17:2), for the dynamic community to which Paul writes, the one that has remained so firm under persecution (3:1-6), the one whose constancy has become an inspiration to Christians throughout Greece (1:7), could scarcely have been formed in so short a time.

Allowing for these differences, which derive from the different purposes of the two writings, the information given by Paul in 1 Thessalonians fits quite well with the overall picture of Paul's ministry that Acts provides. By supplementing what Paul says in his letter with a judicious use of Acts we can, therefore, reconstruct the following plausible and generally accepted scenario for the origin of the letter:

Paul, with Silvanus (called Silas in Acts) and presumably also Timothy (mentioned later in Acts 17:14), visits Thessalonica (the modern Saloniki), an important city situated on the Via Egnatia, the main West–East artery of the Roman empire, during his so-called second missionary journey. The group comes to Thessalonica from Philippi where they have been mistreated and driven out for disturbing the peace (1 Thess 2:2; Acts 16:11–17:1). Paul's mission in Thessalonica, lasting presumably several months, is forcibly disrupted. He is forced to leave his fledgling community (1 Thess 2:17; Acts 17:10, and move on to Athens (Acts 17:15). Frustrated several times in his desire to revisit his Thessalonian converts (2:18), Paul sends Timothy who has joined him in Athens (while not explicitly stated this seems to be implied in Acts 17:15-16) to encourage and sustain them in the persecution they are suffering (3:1-2). Timothy brings news of the community to Paul who has now moved on to Corinth (Acts 18:5). His report is the occasion for Paul to write this letter, which he sends through Timothy to Thessalonica to be read aloud to the Christian community there (5:27). Since Paul's stay in Corinth can be dated quite precisely by the reference in Acts 18:12 to Gallio who, according to an inscription found in Delphi, was proconsul of Achaia in 51/52 or 52/53 C.E., 1 Thessalonians was probably written at Corinth around 50 C.E., a few months after the founding of the community.

Form and Function of the Letter

The reader of 1 Thessalonians is moved by its warm, personal, and communicative tone. The letter abounds in first- and second-person pronouns ("we," "you," "ours," "yours"), in forms of direct address ("brothers and sisters" is found ten times in the letter), in parenthetical observations that invite the participation of the readers/listeners ("you know," "you remember," "you are witness"), in repeated assurances that they are in fact doing what Paul is telling them (4:1; 4:10; 5:11), in explicit declarations of affection (1:8; 2:19-20; 3:12), and in expressions of gratitude for the outstanding Christian life of the newly founded community (1:2-10; 2:13-16; 3:9-10). Yet the letter is more than an act of friendly communication. Paul reminds his readers of what he had been to them and attempts through his letter to recreate this helping pastoral relationship. His primary purpose is to encourage this group of new Christians who are living out their faith in the hostile climate of a large Hellenistic city and suffering persecution from their fellow citizens because of it (1:6; 3:3-4) and who are experiencing stress within the community, possibly because of moral failings (4:3-8) and certainly because of wrong ideas about the future coming of the Lord (4:13–5:11).

To help this community Paul offers encouragement, instruction, and advice using the familiar form of the Greek letter and probably also the devices of traditional Greek rhetoric, but he does this in a highly creative way. The newness of the Christian experience that Paul brings breaks through traditional forms and creates (as all such experiences do) a new language. First Thessalonians witnesses to the emergence of a new literary form, the "apostolic letter," which along with the "gospel" (also a new creation) will become one of the dominant forms of NT literature. In it the framework of a private letter, traditional literary forms, and conventional modes of persuasion are creatively adapted for pastoral use.

Because Paul is writing a letter he must obviously follow the form of a Greek letter in its broad outline. Like every such letter 1 Thessalonians has a letter-opening (1:1), a letter-body (1:2–5:24), and a letter-closing (5:25-28), but apart from this the letter is structured not by the compulsions of any epistolary or rhetorical genre but by Paul's pastoral concerns. These concerns are twofold. Paul wants (1) to encourage the community by reestablishing affective ties with them, and (2) to instruct them regarding some specific problems he has heard about. His letter therefore falls into two parts corresponding to these two concerns. A first part (1:2–3:13), dominated by the theme of the grateful remembrance of his dealings with the Thessalonians, responds to the first of these concerns. A second part (4:1–5:24), containing exhortations and instructions, responds to the second. Each of these parts is further subdivided into clearly defined sections according to the outline given below. The outline will be justified and further elaborated in the second reading of the letter, where individual sections will be discussed.

Outline of 1 Thessalonians

A Letter Opening (1:1): Salutation and greeting
B. Body of the Letter (1:2–5:24)
- 1. Grateful Remembrance (1:2–3:13)
    - a. Thanksgiving for the Christian life of the Thessalonians (1:2-10)
    - b. Paul's apologia for his Thessalonian mission (2:1-12)
    - c. Thanksgiving for the Thessalonians' reception of the gospel (2:13-16)
    - d. Paul's apologia for delaying his visit (2:17–3:8)
    - e. Thanksgiving for the joy he has received from the Thessalonians (3:9-10)
    - f. Concluding prayer (3:11-13)
- 2. Exhortation and Instruction (4:1–5:24)
    - a. Exhortation on moral issues (4:1-12)
    - b. Clarifications about the *parousia* (4:13–5:11)
    - c. Exhortation about life in the community (5:12-24)

C. Letter Closing (5:25-28): Final Greetings

SECOND READING

In commenting on the units of the letter I shall follow the outline given above. The translation I have used is that of the NRSV. In a letter like ours, whose Greek original (as in all Paul's letters) is often ambiguous because it contains unwieldy sentences that can be broken up in different ways, any translation is necessarily an interpretation. The translator must continually choose one out of several possible ways of reading the text. The NRSV offers, on the whole, a sound interpretation.

Paul's thought in 1 Thessalonians, as a first reading of the letter will have shown, is often difficult to follow. This is so not only because his apocalyptic worldview is different from ours, but because his way of writing or speaking (the letter may have been dictated to a secretary) is conversational rather than academic. His rhetoric is often overloaded, repetitive, and prone to digression. Paul writes movingly, but seldom clearly. The primary purpose of this commentary is to make his meaning clear.

The Letter Opening: 1:1

Paul begins the letter, as he always does, with addresses and a greeting ("grace and peace"). Both are very simple, reduced to their minimal formulation, so that the letter opening in 1 Thessalonians is the shortest we know of in the Pauline letters. In it Paul does not call himself an "apostle" as he does elsewhere (except in 2 Thessalonians, Philippians, and Philemon). He associates Silvanus and Timothy with himself as co-authors of the letter on an apparently equal basis. The consistent use of the first person plural throughout the letter (except in rare moments of emotional emphasis as in 2:18; 3:5; 5:27) shows that this association is not just a formal gesture. Unlike Acts, which tends to focus sharply on Paul alone (almost as if he were some kind of missionary Rambo), Paul's own letters show how much his mission owes to unsung, often native, collaborators.

I: Grateful Remembrance: 1:2–3:13

The specific shape of the letter becomes clear in the thanksgiving report that, as in all Paul's letters except Galatians, follows the initial salutation. The thanksgiving here is particularly impressive. It sets the tone for the first half of the letter (1:2–3:13), as exhortation and instruction will set the tone for the second (4:1–5:24). This can be seen from the structure of this first part given below. Three explicit reports of thanksgiving frame Paul's apologia for his mission in Thessalonica and its sequel. Both thanksgiving and apologia look back to events that precede the sending of the letter. They are an exercise in remembering (1:3) and reminding (2:9; 3:6) through which Paul establishes common ground with his readers in order to explain himself and encourage them.

Part I: 1:2–3:13

a. Thanksgiving for the Christian life of the Thessalonians (1:2-10)
  b. Paul's defense of his Thessalonian mission (2:1-12)
a'. Thanksgiving for the reception of the gospel (2:13-16)
  b'. Paul's defense of his delay in visiting (2:17–3:8)
a". Thanksgiving for the joy the Thessalonians have brought him (3:9-10)

Concluding prayer (3:11-13)

Thanksgiving for the Christian Life of the Thessalonians (1:2-10)

The thanksgiving with which Paul begins is better organized than a first reading might suggest. Its somewhat involved argument can be sorted out as follows:

(1) The starting point of Paul's comprehensive ("for all of you") and ongoing ("always") gratitude to God is his recollection of the profoundly Christian life of his converts. Their life is an active expression of the basic Christian virtues of faith, love, and hope (1:3). This familiar triad is for Paul an indivisible unity (1 Thess 5:8; 1 Cor 13:13; Col 1:4-5) so that "work of faith," "labor of love," and "steadfastness of hope" do not define three separate sets of activities belonging to different areas of life but indicate the qualities of commitment, concern, and constancy that mark the total life of this new Christian community.

(2) This Christian life is not the result of human achievement but of divine grace. It is possible only because the Thessalonian converts have been chosen by God (1:4). We have here a first affirmation of the absolute gratuity of salvation, which Paul will later in a narrower and more juridical context defend as "justification by faith" (Rom 3:21-26; Gal 2:16; Phil 3:9). The basic perspectives of classic Pauline theology are already discernible in his first letter.

(3) The election of the Thessalonians was evident from the way in which the gospel was both proclaimed to and received by them. These two dimensions of the initial preaching, proclamation and reception, are central to this first part of Paul's letter. Paul continually returns to them, both as reasons for thanksgiving and as grounds for his defense. The reason for this is that both the way in which the gospel was proclaimed by Paul (with intense conviction and a power to transform others) and the way it was received by the Thessalonians (with joy in spite of persecution) witnessed to the working of the Spirit (1:5-6).

(4) In receiving the word in this way (with joy in suffering) the first Christians of Thessalonica became imitators of Paul and through him of Jesus (1:6). This has made them exemplars and missionaries to their fellow Christians throughout Greece (1:7-8), so that these Christians too speak out of the two basic aspects of the initial mission (its proclamation and its reception) that Paul has mentioned. They speak of Paul's visit to Thessalonica and of the conversion of the Thessalonians that followed it (1:9-10).

(5) To describe this conversion Paul uses a traditional Jewish formula for the conversion of Gentiles ("to turn from [dead] idols to serve the living God"), and then expands this by a reference to their hope in Jesus. Because he has been raised from the dead Jesus will come to save them from "the wrath" (that is from God's judgment) that is (soon) to come (1:9-10). Through this dense theological formula Paul leads his thanksgiving to what is going to be one of the major preoccupations of the letter, the coming of our Lord Jesus Christ at the end of time (2:19; 3:13; 4:15; 5:23).

Paul's Defense of His Mission in Thessalonica (2:1-12)

The tone of the letter now changes from thanksgiving to apologia, but its topic remains the same. Paul continues to reflect on the beginning of the Christian community in Thessalonica, with its two dimensions of the proclamation of the gospel and its reception (1:5-6). Here he takes up the first of these (proclamation), leaving the second (reception) for the section that follows (2:13-16). This proclamation, Paul insists, was wholly disinterested. It was not motivated by any desire for honor or money but by a sense of vocation and a concern for his converts. He demonstrates this in two steps, each with a distinctive introduction. The first of these (2:1-8) stresses his disinterest, the second (2:9-12) his concern.

Paul's Apologia: 2:1-12

Part 1 (2:1-8)

Paul's proclamation was disinterested
"You yourselves know, brothers and sisters . . ." (v. 1)

- it was undertaken in spite of previous and continuing opposition (vv. 1-2)
- it was undertaken not out of impure motives but out of responsibility for a mission entrusted by God (vv. 3-4)
- it was undertaken not out of greed for honor or money but out of concern for the Thessalonians (vv. 5-8)

Part 2 (2:9-12)

Paul showed concern for his converts
"You remember, brothers and sisters . . ." (v. 9)

- by working for his living to avoid being a burden to them (v. 9)
- by being upright and blameless in his conduct toward them (v. 10)
- by his parental concern for them (vv. 11-12)

The completely disinterested character of Paul's mission is explicitly asserted in the first part of his apologia (2:1-8) in a series of antithetical (not this . . . but that) propositions (vv. 3-4, 5-8). It is implied in the second part (2:9-12) where Paul shows how his deep concern for his converts had led him to forego the community support due to him as an apostle (v. 6) and work hard at a trade for his living (v. 9). We get here a fascinating glimpse of Paul proclaiming the gospel while laboring in his workshop, and moving images of his great love for his converts for whom he is both a nursing mother (v. 7) and a caring father who encourages and instructs them (v. 11).

Because the language of this apologia is very similar to that used by contemporary Cynic philosophers it is not clear whether Paul aims at rebutting real accusations made against him by dissident groups within the community or by Jews or Gentiles outside it, or whether he is merely using a conventional form to win over his listeners and communicate to them the true nature of his missionary praxis. Possibly he had both objectives in mind, for while there is little evidence of serious dissidence in the Thessalonian community the fact of Paul's untimely departure (2:17) and his failure to return (2:18) would have left him open to charges of indifference, especially by the unconverted fellow citizens of the Thessalonians who were persecuting them (2:14). At the same time Paul uses the apology (as no Cynic text does) to express his incomparably close relationship to his converts. He and his companions are ready to give them not only the gospel but themselves (2:8). It is in this powerful affirmation of pastoral concern that the real focus of the apologia lies.

Thanksgiving for the Reception of the Gospel (2:13-16)

The thanksgiving of 1:2 is repeated in 2:13 in almost the same words, but it now focuses more sharply on how the Thessalonians have received the gospel as God's life-giving word and how they have done this while being persecuted by their compatriots, just as the first Christian communities in Judea had been persecuted by their fellow Jews (2:14). Note that in the NRSV's over-literal translation of 2:14b ("you suffered the same things from your own compatriots as they did from the Jews") the "they" does not refer to "your compatriots" but to the preceding "churches of God . . . in Judea." Paul is not saying that the Gentiles who were persecuting the Thessalonian Christians had themselves been persecuted by Jews from Judea; as is clear from the Greek text he is comparing the persecution of the Thessalonians by their compatriots to the persecution of the Judean churches by the Jews. The NIV puts it well: "You suffered from your own countrymen the same things those churches suffered from the Jews."

This section thus takes up the second element of the initial missionary event (proclamation–reception) as 2:1-12 developed the first. It fits in well, therefore, with the movement of Paul's thought and also with the structure of the first part of the letter with its alternating episodes of thanksgiving and apologia (see the outline of 1 Thessalonians above). Yet many scholars today would see 2:13-16 as a later addition to the letter made by a Christian polemicist after the fall of Jerusalem in 70 C.E., some twenty years after the letter was written. There are two main reasons for this. The text (1) contains a strident attack against the Jews (2:15-16) quite unlike anything else written by Paul, who elsewhere shows no anti-Jewish prejudice but rather a passionate concern for his people (see especially Romans 9–11), and (2) it speaks of a definite punishment ("God's wrath") meted out to the Jews (2:16), which is best referred to the fall of Jerusalem.

The first difficulty is lessened by omitting what has been called "the anti-Semitic comma" that most English versions insert between verses 14 and 15 and making a more rigorous translation of the verses. They would then read: "You suffered the same things from your compatriots as they [the Christian communities in Judea] did from those Jews who killed the Lord, that is, Jesus, and his prophets." The "Jews" here are not to be understood as the whole Jewish people, accused of killing Jesus and the OT prophets. This was a later Christian charge (see Matt 23:29-37; Acts 7:52) based on an inner-Jewish tradition articulated, for instance, in Neh 9:26. Instead Paul is here thinking only of those Jews who have been responsible for the death of Jesus and have continued to oppose and hinder the Christian mission. He is reacting emotionally to the persecution he and his fellow Christians have experienced, not making a well-thought-out theological judgment on Judaism. The reference to "God's wrath" too could well be not so much a reference to any completed event (such as the destruction of Jerusalem) as to the impending judgment Paul sees looming over those who have rejected God's grace. Understood in this way the verses could well go back to Paul.

Of course Paul's language here is surprisingly violent, but its violence is matched by the severity of his (rarely noticed) anti-Gentile bias, shown in such breathtaking generalizations as that the Gentiles are all "driven by lustful passion" (4:5), "do not know God" (4:5), and "have no hope" (4:13) and by the ferocity of his attacks on the Christian teachers who oppose him (2 Cor 11:13-15; Gal 2:4). What we have in 2:13-16, then, is not an expression of anti-Judaism but a somewhat extreme example of Paul's polemical language. This language is, as always, exaggerated. Its exaggeration here is a result of (1) Paul's own emotional reaction to persecution, (2) his bipolar apocalyptic perspective that divides the world sharply into the persecuted righteous (the Lord, the prophets, the Thessalonian Christians) on the one hand and the evil persecutors (the Jew and Gentile Thessalonian compatriots) on the other, and (3) the situation of the community that, as a persecuted minority under considerable social pressure to conform to the Gentile society around it, needs to be stirred to an aggressive stance in order to survive. Paul's language is not unlike the violent language of Christian missionaries, warning their converts against the satanic forces at work in the "pagan" religions they have left! Problems arise when these emotionally loaded polemical utterances are taken out of context and read (as commentators have been reading 1 Thess 2:13-16) as if they were sober statements of timeless theological truth.

Paul's Apologia for His Delay in Returning (2:17–3:13)

Paul now moves back from thanksgiving to apologia and from his initial proclamation of the gospel to the Thessalonians (2:1-12) to what happened after he had been forced to leave them. Impeded in his desire to visit his Thessalonian converts for various unspecified reasons, behind which he sees the working of a supernatural power, Satan (2:17-20), Paul sends Timothy to strengthen them in their trials (3:1-5). Two parallel notices of Timothy's sending (vv. 1-3a and v. 5) frame a short, typically Pauline digression about the necessity of persecution in Christian life (vv. 3b-4). Paul does not develop this theme here, but elsewhere in his letters shows that he understood such persecution to be both an expression of the suffering of the righteous that apocalyptic theology expected in the last days (Matt 24:9a; 10:17-20 // Mark 13:9-13 // Luke 21:12-15) as well as a sharing in the passion of Jesus (Matt 16:24 // Mark 8:34 // Luke 9:23; 2 Cor 1:5; Phil 3:10; Col 1:24). The very casualness with which he introduces it here shows how much this theme of persecution was an indispensable part of his teaching.

Timothy's return (3:6-8), highlights the striking reciprocity between Paul's attitude toward his converts and theirs to him. The Thessalonians keep a happy memory of Paul (3:6) as Paul does of them (1:3); they too wish to see Paul (3:6) as Paul wants to see them (2:17); Timothy's return comforts Paul in his afflictions (3:7) much as he had hoped his sending of Timothy would comfort them in theirs (3:2-3).

2:17–3:13	
a. 2:17-20: Paul's desire to visit the Thessalonians	
b. 3:1-8: Timothy's visit	Desire to meet: 2:17-18 = 3:10-13
—the sending of Timothy (vv. 1-5)	Joy: 2:19-20 = 3:9
—the return of Timothy (vv. 6-8)	*Parousia:* 2:19 = 3:13
a'. 3:9-13: Paul's continuing desire to visit	
—shown in thanksgiving (vv. 9-10)	
—shown in prayer (vv. 11-13)	

The news Timothy brings elicits from Paul thanksgiving and petition (3:9-13). He thanks God for the joy he has received from the Thessalonians (vv. 9-10) and prays both for their spiritual growth (vv. 11-13) and the realization of his great desire to see them again (vv. 10-11).

The whole section (2:17–3:13) has a concentric structure. Timothy's visit (3:1-8) is framed by two descriptions of Paul's eager desire to visit the Thessalonians (2:17-20 and 3:9-13) which share the common themes of a reciprocal desire to meet, joy, and the *parousia* of the Lord. The structure is indicated in the table at the top of this page, in which the inset gives the themes common to the framing passages 2:17-20 (a) and 3:9-13 (a'), where these themes are found.

What unifies the whole of this first part of the letter (1:2–3:13) is Paul's desire to be with his greatly loved (2:8; 3:12) and persecuted (1:6; 3:3) Thessalonians as a supportive and encouraging presence. This desire leads him to send them a letter through an emissary, Timothy, with the implied promise of a personal visit. It is widely believed that these three elements are the components of a form that has been called the "apostolic *parousia,*" which Paul uses elsewhere in his letters (Rom 15:14-33; 1 Cor 4:14-21; Phil 2:19-24) to assert his apostolic authority. It is possible that these themes used for the first time in 1 Thessalonians were later developed by Paul into a fixed form for the assertion of apostolic authority, but this is not how they are used here. The consciousness of apostolic authority plays no part in 1 Thessalonians as the opening address of the letter indicates. If Paul writes so vehemently and at such length of his desire to be with his Thessalonians it is not to assert his authority but to renew his close and affectionate pastoral relationship with them. Earlier letters must not be interpreted in the light of later developments of Paul's language and thought. One should therefore be wary of speaking, as some authors do, of an "apostolic apology" in 1 Thess 2:1-12 or an "apostolic *parousia*" in 2:17–3:13.

II: Instruction and Exhortation 4:1–5:24

Paul's grateful remembrance of his Thessalonian mission (1:2–3:13) leads to a series of instructions to the community he has founded (4:1–5:24). The focus of the letter shifts from the past to the future, its tone from thanksgiving to exhortation. The instructions Paul gives are occasioned by the report Timothy has brought (orally or possibly by letter) about the specific concerns of the young church. Paul responds to these not by giving ad hoc solutions but by reminding his readers of the principles of Christian living he has already taught them.

Paul, moreover, treats the specific issues Timothy reports as part of his more basic concern for the spiritual growth of the community. This second part of the letter therefore frames Paul's answers to the specific questions about the *parousia* posed by the Thessalonians with general exhortations to growth in Christian life and community. (See table below.)

4:1–5:24	
a. 4:1-12: Exhortation to spiritual growth	ask/urge: 4:1, 10 = 5:12, 14
b. 4:13–5:11: Clarifications about the *parousia*	will of God: 4:3 = 5:18
a'. 5:12-24: Exhortations on community life	sanctification: 4:3 = 5:23

Growth in Christian Life (4:1-12)

The first of these units is clearly divided into an introduction followed by two parts. The introduction (4:1-2) is an appeal to grow "more and more" in a life pleasing to God. The force of the appeal, which uses a formula of polite demand (the so-called *parakalō* formula) familiar in private and official letters of the time ("we ask and urge you"), falls somewhere between an injunction and a request; its tone is that of a caring parent rather than of an authority-conscious official. The Thessalonians are urged to grow in a life pleasing to God by following the instructions Paul has already given them. What such a life means is now spelled out in the two parts that follow.

The first part (4:3-8), which is centered on the key word "sanctification" (4:3), gives a negative paraphrase of Paul's exhortation, for sanctification is described as abstaining from sexual immorality by "each one [i.e., each man]" "acquiring or possessing *(ktasthai)* his own vessel *(skeuos)*" (4:4). Since "vessel" is sometimes used in Jewish writings both for one's body and for a man's wife this can be read as a recommendation to control one's sexuality, or for men to marry and remain sexually faithful to their wives. However we interpret the text, the point Paul is making is clear. Christians are to lead a life of sexual restraint and fidelity in a world of immoral and godless Gentiles (4:5).

Is this lesson on sexuality carried over into the second element of sanctification that Paul speaks about now (4:6)? When Paul tells us that we are not to "wrong or exploit" a fellow Christian is he thinking of adultery, through which we do injustice to a brother or sister "in this matter" (so the NRSV) or has he now shifted to a new area of morality and is he warning against cheating "in business" (a possible translation of the underlying Greek, *en tō pragmati*)? The Greek verbs Paul uses *(hyperbainein* and *pleonektein)* suggest economic rather than sexual wrongdoing, so it is likely that Paul has here turned away from sexual to business morality. He is warning not against adultery but against greed and dishonesty in trade. (See table at top of next column.)

4:1-8

Introduction (vv. 1-2): grow more and more
Part 1 (vv. 3-8): True Holiness
- principle: God's will is your sanctification (v. 3a) that is to be shown by:
  1. abstaining from sexual immorality (vv. 3b-5)
  2. abstaining from dishonesty in trade (v. 6)
- Conclusion: God has called us to sanctity (v. 7)
  Therefore to reject Paul's instructions is to reject God (v. 8)

Sexual immorality and greed always figure in the traditional Jewish lists of vices that Paul uses in his letters (Rom 1:29-31; 1 Cor 6:9-10) and together offer a traditional framework for the ethical behavior of Christians converted from paganism. This first part of the exhortation, then, probably does not have in mind specific failings of the Thessalonians. It offers a warning against possible dangers to Christian life in any pagan society—not least in ours. The warning is grounded in God's call to sanctity with the divine sanction this implies (4:7-8).

The second part of Paul's exhortation (4:9-12) is a positive admonition focused on "love of the brothers and sisters" (4:9). We are to please God "more and more" (4:1) by loving one another "more and more" (4:10).

4:9-12

Part 2: True Love (vv. 9-12)
- principle: you have been taught by God to love one another (v. 9)
- conclusion: grow more and more in love (v. 10)
  1. by living quietly
  2. by minding your own affairs
  3. by working with your hands (v. 11)
- motivation: so that
  1. you make a good impression on those outside
  2. you are not dependent on anyone (v. 12)

The Thessalonians have been imbued with this love by the spirit given to them by God (4:8) and have demonstrated it (we are not told how) not only within their own community but outside it as well (4:9-10). They are to grow in this love by living quietly, minding their own business, and engaging as Paul himself had done (2:9) in productive manual labor (4:11). This odd combination of demands cannot have come from any traditional code. Paul is clearly addressing a concrete situation of inner community unrest and is probably thinking of the "unruly" (*ataktoi,* translated as "idlers" by the NRSV) of 5:14.

Who exactly these are is not clear, though the general concerns of the letter suggest that they may have been (like the "idlers" and "busybodies" of a later time mentioned in 2 Thess 3:6-12) people whose excitement at the imminent coming of Christ led them to neglect their work and busy themselves with communicating their fervor to others. Paul rebukes them gently (contrast 2 Thess 3:6-12), urging the community to become (as any mission community should) edifying and self-sufficient (4:12).

Clarification About the Parousia (4:13–5:11)

Paul now moves on to answer the two questions about the *parousia* that have been sent to him by the agitated Thessalonians. The first (4:13-18) is about the situation of the members of the community who have died since their conversion. Their death disturbs the community not because they have not been told about the resurrection of the dead or because (like some Christians in Corinth later on) they do not believe in bodily resurrection, but because they share with some contemporary apocalyptic writings the belief that when God comes in judgment "those who are left will be more blessed than those who have died" (4 Ezra 13:24). They believe, then, that their dead will in some way be disadvantaged at the *parousia,* possibly because they think resurrection will take place after the *parousia,* so that the dead will not witness the coming of the Lord and be with him when he comes. Paul offers the troubled Thessalonians a double reassurance.

4:13-18

The Thessalonians need not grieve about those who have died (v. 13).

1. The resurrection of Jesus guarantees the gathering together of all Christians at the *parousia.*
2. A word of the Lord offers a description of the *parousia* in which the dead are not disadvantaged (vv. 15-17)

The Thessalonians must encourage one another with this message (v. 18)

Paul first appeals to the resurrection of Jesus (4:14). Expanding a traditional credal formula he argues that because Jesus died and rose again, therefore (not "even so" as in NRSV) God will make the dead participants in the *parousia* (4:14). The resurrection of Jesus is proposed here not as a paradigm for the resurrection of Christians (as in 1 Corinthians 15) but as the basis of God's action in bringing all Christians, even those who have died, to be "with Jesus" at the *parousia.*

This reassurance is confirmed by an appeal to a word of the Lord (4:15-17). No such saying is found in the gospels; indeed, its stereotyped apocalyptic language makes it unlikely that it could have been uttered by Jesus at all. It is most likely an oracle of an apocalyptically-minded early Christian prophet, current in the early Church as a word of the (risen) Lord. Paul introduces this saying with an introductory comment that gives what he believes to be its essential point (4:15b) and adds a summarizing conclusion (4:17a). The word itself (4:16-17a) gives a scenario of the *parousia* that confirms what Paul has been saying. It is only after the dead have been raised that the saved (all of them) will be taken up together to meet the Lord who has come. Those who survive to the *parousia* (Paul includes himself among them) will not be in any privileged position.

The scenario proposed for the last days is taken from a particular way of looking at reality (apocalyptic) that is quite foreign to us today. It must not be read as a literal description of what will happen at the end of the world; rather it uses the beliefs and imagery of its time to describe God's decisive irruption into history—that by its nature is beyond "name and form." What the passage is really affirming is that because of the death and resurrection of Jesus all Christians faithful to him will be "with him" (4:17; 5:10) when he comes.

This discussion about the *parousia* leads to a second question (5:1-11) about "the times and the seasons" (5:1), a technical term for the time of the *parousia* and the events associated with it (Acts 1:7). Paul is obviously replying to a question put by the Thessalonians asking for more precise information about the timing of the *parousia* than he had given them (5:2), but he has in fact no more information to give. He offers instead an exhortation to vigilance, using traditions about the *parousia* some of which are echoed in the gospels. The traditions are elaborated into an argument that (as in 1:2-10) is quite tortuous. We can make some sense of it by reading it as follows:

(1) The coming of the "day of the Lord" (an OT prophetic term for God's judgment applied here to the *parousia* of Jesus) is to be sudden and unpredictable, like "a thief in the night" (5:2). By using this familiar NT image for the coming of the Lord (Matt 24:43-44 // Luke 12:39-40; 2 Pet 3:10; Rev 3:3; 16:15) whose wide attestation suggests that it goes back to Jesus himself, Paul answers a question about the "when" of the *parousia* by telling us about its "how." Whenever the *parousia* comes (and neither Jesus nor Paul claims to know just when, though both appear to believe that it will be soon) it will come suddenly, without warning (like birth pangs) breaking in inescapably when least expected (5:3; see Matt 24:37-39 // Luke 17:26-30).

(2) If this situation of impending judgment poses a threat to those outside the community who place their security in the world of *Pax Romana* (5:3) and live in spiritual darkness it will not disturb Christians. Because they are "children of the light and children of the day" (that is, because they belong to the new age and are leading lives pleasing to God) they will not be taken by surprise by the day of the Lord (5:4-5a).

(3) But for this to happen they, and indeed all Christians (for Paul shifts to the first person, "we," as he begins the exhortation of 5:5b-8) must continue to be (spiritually) alert and sober, not (spiritually) drowsy or drunk, as those who live in the dark night (that is, outside the light of Christ) will be (5b-7). They must do this by arming themselves with the three virtues constitutive of their Christian life (5:8), to whose conspicuous presence in their lives Paul drew explicit attention in the beginning of his letter (1:3).

(4) Their hope, given an emphatic final position in Paul's listing, is justified because God has destined them for the salvation prepared through Jesus, who died "for us" (Rom 5:8; cf. 1 Cor 11:24). That is why everyone whether "awake" (alive) or "asleep" (dead) at the *parousia* will live with him (5:9-10).

By this play on the words awake/asleep, which describe the moral condition of the Thessalonians in the present in vv. 6-8 and their eschatological situation at the *parousia* in v. 10, Paul brings us back to the question with which the section began (4:13). He has answered the question and taken away the anxiety that lies behind it by pointing out that because the salvation wrought by Jesus is already a reality in their lives (as a dialectic of God's grace and human response) it really does not matter to Christians when the *parousia* comes. Whenever it comes, whether they are dead or alive, it will come not as judgment but as grace. So the Thessalonians can encourage one another (5:11) as they were invited to do at the end of the previous section also (4:18), for this is the ultimate purpose of Paul's exhortation.

Exhortation on Community Life (5:12-24)

Paul now winds up his letter as usual with an exhortation on community life. This has two clearly defined parts: a set of admonitions (5:12-22) is followed by a concluding prayer (5:23-24). The admonitions are very general and so do not necessarily have specific failings of the Thessalonian community in view. We find the same kind of advice in other letters of Paul. Still, the way in which topics have been selected and arranged may hint at some of the problems that are troubling the community, for though seemingly unrelated to one another the admonitions fit into a pattern that gives the concluding section of the letter the following outline:

5:12-24

1. Admonitions (vv. 12-22)
   a. on community relationships (vv. 12-15)
   b. on personal attitudes (vv. 16-18)
   c. on spiritual gifts (vv. 19-22)
2. Prayer (vv. 23-24)
   a. May God sanctify you wholly (v. 23a)
   b. May you be kept wholly blameless at the *parousia* by God (v. 23b)
   c. God will do this because God is faithful (v. 24)

As always in his letters Paul attaches importance to inner community harmony. The Thessalonians are to be at peace among themselves (5:13). They will achieve this by (1) showing esteem for those exercising leadership in the community, in which an incipient ministry of pastoral care without clearly labeled offices (contrast. Phil 1:1) is clearly emerging (5:12), and (2) by treating with appropriate concern all those in the community who are marginalized or troublesome (5:14-15). Three groups are mentioned: the unruly or idle (the Greek word *ataktoi* could mean either) who are probably the objects of the admonitions in 4:13–5:1, the fainthearted *(oligopsychoi)* who may be those whom

Paul reassures about the fate of the dead and the time of the *parousia* in 4:13–5:11, and the weak *(asthenoi)* who, it has been suggested (not very convincingly), are the ones prone to the immorality prohibited in 4:3-8. However these groups are identified, the point Paul is making is clear. All of the marginalized in the community (like "the little ones" of Matt 18:10-14) are to be treated with patience. Indeed the community is to strive ardently (the "seek" of the NRSV is much too weak a translation of the Greek *diōkete*) to do good not only to those in the community but to all (5:15). The absolute universality of Christian love is clearly affirmed, but (as in 3:12) not without a note of special concern for those in the community.

As for their personal lives the Thessalonians are exhorted to pray for an abiding attitude of joy, prayerfulness, and thanksgiving (5:16-18), for this is willed by God, as was their sanctification (4:3), of which these are the positive notes. Spiritual gifts *(charismata),* and especially prophecy are not to be suppressed in the community, but to be discerned (5:19-22). This standard Pauline advice is given a special nuance here. The emphasis is not on controlling the gifts (as in Corinth) but on not suppressing them. The community seems to have been suspicious of such gifts. It was hardly the enthusiastic, millenarian community some scholars imagine it to have been.

The exhortation concludes (as did the first part of the letter in 3:11-13) with a prayer for the total sanctification of the Thessalonians so that they may be wholly blameless at the *parousia* (5:23-24). The prayer is remarkable for its description of the human person in terms of the Greek categories of spirit, soul, and body that Paul (who uses them nowhere else) has probably taken from popular usage, and for its reference to the *parousia* (5:23). Clearly in spite of the relatively little space explicitly given to it the theme of the *parousia* dominates the letter from beginning to end. The prayer ends with the confident assertion that what has been prayed for will be granted (5:24) because (a favorite theme of Paul) the God who has called them to the Christian faith is faithful (1 Cor 1:9).

Letter Closure: 5:25-28

The letter closes, as is usual with Paul, with specific requests (5:25-27) and a final greeting matching the one in the prescript (5:28). Of the three requests Paul makes, two (to pray for him and to greet the community) are found in his other letters (Rom 15:30; 1 Cor 16:20; 2 Cor 13:12; Phil 4:21). The third is unusual. The people to whom the letter has been sent (the pastoral ministers of the church?) are "solemnly commanded" to have the letter read aloud to the whole community (5:27). Was there a suspicion that the letter would not be so read and its message not communicated? We have no way of telling. What we do know is that the letter was not suppressed. We may presume that it was read out to the church of the Thessalonians and to the (many?) illiterate in it. It has continued to be read to Christian communities down the ages (text becoming word) right up to our own. Amid the anxieties of daily living and in face of the absurdity of death it continues to bring the powerful assurance that the God of peace "has called us to be with Jesus." "The one who calls you is faithful: God will do this" (5:24).

BIBLIOGRAPHY

Best, Ernest. *The First and Second Epistles to the Thessalonians.* BNTC. London: Black, 1972.

Bruce, F. F. *1 & 2 Thessalonians.* WBC 45. Waco, Tex.: Word Books, 1982.

Collins, Raymond F. *Studies on the First Letter to the Thessalonians.* BEThL 66. Louvain: Louvain University Press, 1984.

Collins, Raymond F., ed. *The Thessalonian Correspondence.* BEThL 87. Louvain: Louvain University Press, 1990.

Frame, James Everett. *A Critical and Exegetical Commentary on the Epistles of St. Paul to the Thessalonians.* ICC. Edinburgh: T & T Clark, 1912.

Jewett, Robert. *The Thessalonian Correspondence: Pauline Rhetoric and Millenarian Piety.* Philadelphia: Fortress, 1986.

Malherbe, Abraham J. *Paul and the Thessalonians: The Philosophic Tradition of Pastoral Care.* Philadelphia: Fortress, 1987.

Marshall, I. Howard. *1 and 2 Thessalonians.* NCeB. Grand Rapids: Eerdmans, 1983.

Schleuter, Carol J. *Filling up the Measure: Polemic Hyperbole in 1 Thessalonians 2:14-16.* JSNT.S 98. Sheffield: JSOT Press, 1994.

Wanamaker, Charles A. *The Epistles to the Thessalonians: A Commentary on the Greek Text.* NIGTC. Grand Rapids: Eerdmans, 1990.

2 Thessalonians

George M. Soares-Prabhu

FIRST READING

Anyone reading quickly through 1 and 2 Thessalonians at a stretch gets the impression that the second letter is a sort of postscript to the first. It seems to have been written by Paul soon after his first letter in order to correct some Thessalonian ideas about the eschatological "day of the Lord" (2:2), the central theme of 2 Thessalonians. The attempt of 2 Thessalonians to correct misunderstandings about the "day of the Lord" must have followed very soon after 1 Thessalonians was written, for Silvanus, mentioned along with Timothy as a co-author of the letter (2 Thess 1:1) appears to have been with Paul (if Acts is to be trusted) only during the so-called second missionary journey (Acts 15:40–18:5). Besides this, 2 Thessalonians has the same overall outline as 1 Thessalonians and echoes its language to a quite unusual degree. It would seem, then, to have been written to the church of the Thessalonians when Paul was still full of his first letter to them.

Who Wrote 2 Thessalonians?

This is how 2 Thessalonians has been traditionally understood and is still understood by many scholars today, but there is a growing trend in current scholarship that sees the letter differently. Second Thessalonians is increasingly taken to be a pseudonymous letter, that is, a letter written not by Paul but by an unknown author writing much later (when Paul's letters had already become a recognized part of the early Christian tradition) who to add authority to his writing uses Paul's name and took 1 Thessalonians as his model.

There are several convergent arguments in favor of this. Though they cannot be discussed in detail in a short commentary like this one, the following gives some idea of the kind of arguments involved.

(1) While the overall vocabulary, theology, and style of the two letters are really quite different, parts of 2 Thessalonians echo 1 Thessalonians so closely (compare, for instance, 2 Thess 3:8 with 1 Thess 2:9) that it is impossible to escape the impression that one letter has been copied by the other. The kind of verbal similarity that we find here (and nowhere else in Paul!) is much too close to be explained by supposing that Paul is simply repeating from memory expressions he had used in the first letter written shortly before. There is clearly some sort of literary dependence between the two letters and this is best explained by supposing that a later anonymous author has used 1 Thessalonians as a model for his pseudonymous letter to add verisimilitude to its claim to be a letter from Paul.

(2) The two letters to the Thessalonians do not quite agree in their eschatology. The first looks forward to a *parousia* that will come so suddenly as to be wholly unpredictable (1 Thess 5:1-3). The second gives us an apocalyptic time table (2 Thess 2:1-8) from which the arrival of the *parousia* can be known because it is preceded by observable events.

(3) The repeated insistence of 2 Thessalonians on the importance of tradition (2:15; 3:6) and its

consistent use of "the Lord" (= Jesus) in expressions where 1 Thessalonians (and other Pauline letters) say "God" (compare 2 Thess 2:13 with 1 Thess 1:4; 2 Thess 3:3 with 1 Cor 1:9 and 1 Thess 5:24; 2 Thess 3:16 with 1 Thess 5:23) also suggest that the letter belongs to a period later than that of the genuine letters of Paul. This usage reflects a time when a high christology had developed and apostolic presence had been replaced by "tradition."

(4) The tone of the two letters is very different. The first letter is warm and personal (1 Thess 1:8; 3:8-10), full of precise reminiscences of Paul's founding mission in Thessalonica (1 Thess 1:3; 2:5-12) and repeated references to his desire to see his converts again (2:17; 3:6, 10). The second is on the whole impersonal and didactic, conspicuously lacking in such concrete references to the past except when it recalls past teaching (2 Thess 2:5).

(5) The two letters differ in style. The first is Pauline in its wording. As in the other genuine letters of Paul, its grammatical structure is simple: expressions are coordinated rather than subordinated to one another, it abounds in antithetical (not this . . . but that) constructions (1 Thess 2:3-4, 6-7, 13, 17; 4:7; 5:6, 9), and it shows a particular fondness for triads (1 Thess 1:3, 5; 2:3, 10, 12, 19; 4:16; 5:14, 16-18). Second Thessalonians, on the other hand, like the deutero-Pauline letters to the Colossians and the Ephesians, has a complex structure of subordinate, embedded clauses (cf. especially 2 Thess 1:3-12); it prefers the synonymous parallelism typical of Jewish writing to the antithetical parallels that Paul likes (note the many synonymous parallels in 2 Thess 1:6-12; 2:8-9, 13-17; 3:1-5, and the rare antitheses in 2:12 and 3:5).

These stylistic differences are decisive, for the style betrays the person. The mind behind the bubbling, emotionally loaded, grammatically simple, and sharply dialectical language of 1 Thessalonians is different from the one we meet in the cool, didactic, grammatically involved, repetitive Jewish language of 2 Thessalonians in which a rather monotonous parallelism replaces the vivid antitheses that are so characteristic of Paul's thinking and style. It is doubtful whether the two letters could have been written by the same person.

Second Thessalonians, then, is probably a pseudonymous letter written by an anonymous author in the name of Paul some time after his death to offer an appropriate interpretation of Paul's tradition for a new time. Like the other deutero-Pauline letters, 2 Thessalonians was probably written after the death of Paul, somewhere toward the end of the first century when various competing interpretations of Paul's theology were beginning to take shape. There is no way of fixing its date, its recipients, or the place of its writing more precisely. It was written to a severely persecuted community (1:4, 6, 7) sometime between the death of Paul (ca. 62 C.E.) and about 110 C.E., when Polycarp of Smyrna (d. 155 C.E.) and probably Ignatius of Antioch (d. ca. 110 C.E.) refer to it.

SECOND THESSALONIANS AS
A PSEUDONYMOUS LETTER

It is important to know that pseudonymity would have meant something very different in the world of Paul than what a literary forgery would mean today. The world in which Paul lived did not value private property or "intellectual rights" the way our capitalist society does. Individuals were not as individualistic as they are in Western society today. People experienced themselves, as they still do in most parts of the Third World, as members of a community, with a strong sense of belonging. Teachers lived on in their works. The interpretation of these works by a disciple for later generations could legitimately be made in the teacher's name. The tradition, not the person, mattered.

This attitude permeates the whole of the NT. An allegorizing interpretation of the parable of the sower by an early Christian scribe is unabashedly attributed to Jesus in the synoptic gospels (Matt 13:18-23 // Mark 4:13-20 // Luke 8:11-15), as are many sayings of early Christian prophets who claim to be speaking in the name of the risen Lord. The pseudonymity of NT letters is analogous to this. Paul lives on in his tradition. The authors of the deutero-Pauline letters (the Pastorals, very probably Ephesians, and probably 2 Thessalonians too), writing in the spirit of Paul, would have felt authorized to use his name and claim his authority for the writings through which they were attempting to adapt the Pauline tradition to new situations—even appealing, if necessary, to a "forged" signature as in 2 Thess 3:17 or Col 4:18.

Why was 2 Thessalonians Written?

Why was this pseudonymous letter written? Its intention is clearly set out in the opening verses of the body of the letter (2:1-2) that announce the subject of the letter and its purpose. The letter has been written to correct a wrong idea that "the day of the Lord is already here," a misapprehension that may have been occasioned by a prophetic utterance in the community ("by spirit"), by some non-ecstatic teaching ("by word"), or by a letter "as though from us" (2:2).

It is not easy to decipher the obscure language of 2 Thess 2:2. The "as though from us" could refer to all three terms of the preceding clause (spirit, word, letter), but probably refers only to the last. The author excludes every possible valid basis for this wrong understanding of the *parousia,* whether it is within the community ("spirit," "word"), or outside it ("a letter as though from us"). The "letter as though from us" could stand for a forged Pauline letter, real or surmised, or even for a genuine letter (such as 1 Thessalonians) that had been misunderstood. The original Greek admits of either meaning. Whatever the author had in mind, what he wants to say is clear: any letter allegedly from Paul that seems to support the error he is correcting is either forged or has been misunderstood.

Second Thessalonians thus has a primarily pastoral intent of addressing a specific problem that had arisen in the Thessalonian community. The author of 2 Thessalonians addresses this situation by speaking of eschatological events that must happen before the arrival of the *parousia,* which is still in the future. The Thessalonians should thus continue to live in vigilance and hope for this future day (cf. 1 Thess 5:1-11).

What has been the Significance of 2 Thessalonians?

Second Thessalonians has contributed significantly to the development of a curious but enduring theme of Christian eschatology, the coming of an antichrist figure known as the "man of lawlessness" or "lawless one" mentioned in 2 Thess 2:3, 8, 9. Second Thessalonians is unique in depicting this specific figure who is described as opposing God in the last days. The lawless one is an agent of Satan in the world who will exalt himself in a God-like fashion and bring about apostasy through deception and signs and wonders (2:3-4, 9-10). Reference to the "lawless one" in 2 Thessalonians reflects a belief widespread in Jewish apocalyptic, that the cosmic conflict between God and Satan would culminate in the last days with the appearance of a satanic figure who would claim divine worship and cause a massive apostasy among the faithful (*2 Bar.* 36–40; 4 Ezra 5; *TMos* 8). The lawless one in 2 Thessalonians also recalls many related figures in the NT. In the letters of John we meet the "antichrist" (1 John 2:18, 22; 4:3; 2 John 7), in the synoptic apocalypse "false Christs" (Matt 24:24 // Mark 13:22), and in the book of Revelation the "beast rising out of the sea" (Rev 13:1-10). All refer to a similar apocalyptic figure of the end-time anti-Messiah but they understand it in different ways. In most of the NT texts, and especially in 1 and 2 John, the antichrist is a Christian teacher, a false prophet propagating erroneous teachings about Jesus (1 John 2:22; 4:3; 2 John 7; 2 Pet 2:1; Matt 24:5 // Mark 13:6 // Luke 21:8; Matt 24:24 // Mark 13:22). In the book of Revelation the beast from the sea (representing the Roman empire) is an anti-God figure that claims divine worship and persecutes those who refuse to worship it (Rev 13:1-10). Both these aspects of "false prophet" and "anti-God" seem to meet in the "lawless one" of 2 Thessalonians, a satanic figure deliberately contrasted with the risen Lord (see on 2:3-12 below).

In the early Church these different images of the antichrist were consolidated into a confused, imprecise picture of the end-time "enemy." With the conversion of Constantine this enemy was no longer identified with the oppressive Roman empire, but with the political or religious opponents of the now-united Church and state, to whom the image, now detached from its original apocalyptic context, could be applied at will. Individual popes unworthy of their office, like John XII (935–963) or secular rulers opposed to the papacy like Frederick Barbarossa (1155–1190) were identified as the antichrist. Eventually Martin Luther, taking up a suggestion made by the followers of the twelfth-century Cistercian mystic Joachim of Fiore (1130–1201), went a step farther and identified the antichrist with the papacy itself. In the heated polemic of the Reformation this identification acquired confessional status and became part of the creed of some of the Reformed churches. It is found, for instance, in the Westminster Confession of Faith (1646) which holds that "The Pope of Rome . . . is that Antichrist, that man of sin, and son of perdition, that exalteth himself in the Church, against

Christ and all that is called God" (25.6). Nothing could show more clearly the danger of reading an apocalyptic text like 2 Thessalonians without an awareness of its historical context and without distinguishing the teaching of the letter from the obsolete forms in which it is expressed.

This commentary will try, therefore, to understand the proper meaning of this short but extraordinarily difficult text by reading it carefully in its historical context. Such a reading will show us that the letter has a well-defined structure that, while following the general outline of a Greek letter with its letter opening, body, and letter closing, imposes on that outline an elaborate multi-layered concentric pattern of its own. The basic structure of the letter is shown in the outline given below. Its further elaboration will be indicated in the commentary that follows.

Outline of 2 Thessalonians

1. Letter opening (1:1-2): Salutation and greeting
2. Body of the letter (1:3–3:16)
   - A. Introductory thanksgiving (1:3-12)
     - a. Thanksgiving for growth in Christian life amid persecution (1:3-4)
     - b. Instruction on the righteous judgment of God (1:5-10)
     - a'. Prayer report about fulfillment of Christian life (1:11-12)
   - B. Central theme: The day of the Lord (2:1-17)
     - a. Exhortation against anxiety caused by wrong idea of *parousia* (2:1-2)
     - b. Instruction on what must precede the *parousia* (2:3-12)
     - a'. Thanksgiving and prayer for comfort and strength (2:13-17)
   - A'. Concluding exhortation (3:1-16)
     - a. Exhortation to pray concluding with wish-prayer (3:1-5)
     - b. Instruction on how to deal with the troublemakers (3:6-15)
     - a'. Exhortation to do good concluding with wish-prayer (3:16)
3. Letter closing (3:17-18)
   - a. Authenticating signature (3:17)
   - b. Final greeting (3:18)

The letter has been carefully structured into a series of concentric circles centering around the teaching on the *parousia* in 2:3-12. This is clearly the thematic focus of the letter. In the document as a whole the letter opening (1:1-2) and letter closing (3:16-18), with their parallel greetings, frame the body of the letter (1:3–3:16). The body again has three concentrically arranged parts (A–B–A'), each concluding with a wish-prayer. The introductory thanksgiving (1:3-12) resembles the concluding exhortation (3:1-16) in its stress on prayer and thanksgiving. Together they frame the central part (2:1-17), an instruction on the day of the Lord that develops the basic theme of the letter. Each of these three parts is again concentrically structured (a–b–a'). In each thanksgiving, exhortation or wish-prayer again frames a central section of instruction. The instruction in each of the three parts is further structured concentrically, as the commentary that follows will show.

SECOND READING

The letter opening is so similar to that of 1 Thessalonians that it needs no further explanation. The commentary will therefore begin with the body of the letter, focusing in each of its three parts on the central section in which the teaching of the letter is developed. It will conclude with a few observations on the letter's conclusion.

Introductory Thanksgiving: 1:3-12

The introductory thanksgiving (1:3-12) is, in the original Greek, a single convoluted sentence that modern-language translations (like the NRSV which is followed here) are forced to break up into smaller units to make it intelligible. The sentence begins with a thanksgiving for the Christian life of the readers (1:3-4) and ends with a wish-prayer that this life may be fulfilled by God (1:11-12). In between there is a concentric reflection on the just judgment of God (1:5-10), markedly different in content and style from the thanksgiving and prayer that precede and follow. The section, then, has a two-tier concentric structure, indicated in the outline below.

2 Thess 1:3-12

A. Thanksgiving for growth in Christian life (vv. 3-4)

B. Instruction on God's righteous judgment (vv. 5-10)

a. God afflicts the oppressor and gives relief to the oppressed (vv. 5-7a)
b. at the *PAROUSIA* of the Lord Jesus (vv. 7b-8a)
a'. where Jesus inflicts vengeance on unbelievers and is glorified by believers (vv. 8b-10)

A'. Wish-prayer for fulfillment in Christian life (vv. 11-12)

Both the opening thanksgiving and the concluding wish-prayer are curiously impersonal. They lack the specific detail (fond reminiscences of Paul's stay at Thessalonica as in 1 Thess 1:3; 2:8-12, or repeated mention of his ardent desire to visit its Christian community again, as in 1 Thess 2:17; 3:6, 10) that gives life to the prayer and thanksgiving of 1 Thessalonians. Instead God is thanked in rather stilted liturgical language ("we must always give thanks . . . as is right") for the growth that is taking place in the vertical ("faith") and horizontal ("love") dimensions of the Christian life of the readers (1:3). Such growth is particularly commendable because it occurs in a situation of repeated ("all") and still continuing ("you are enduring") persecution in which faith shows itself as fidelity, and hope as steadfastness (1:4).

The reflection on the judgment of God (1:5-10) that intrudes between the prayer and the thanksgiving is the thematic center of the section and introduces what is to be the main theme of the letter, the day of the Lord (1:7-8). It begins with surprising abruptness: "This is evidence of the righteous judgment of God." (1:5). What this means is that the steadfastness of the Christians in the "persecutions and the afflictions" they have endured (1:4) is a guarantee of their salvation in the judgment that is soon to come (1:5), for here God will reverse an unjust world order by afflicting those who unjustly oppress the community and setting free from their unjust suffering those whom they oppress (1:6-7).

This apocalyptic reversal (cf. Luke 1:52; 6:20-27; 16:25) will take place at the *parousia* of the Lord, described here in the stock images of Christian apocalyptic (1:7-8). Christ will come *from* heaven, *with* his angels *in* a flame of fire to "inflict vengeance," that is, to execute God's retributive judgment on the unjust and the just (1:6-7). The passage thus centers on the *parousia* of the Lord (vv. 7-8) and so prepares for the discussion of the day of the Lord that follows in ch. 2.

Central Theme: The Day of the Lord: 2:1-17

The chapter that follows (2:1-17) is the central section of the letter, in which its aim is stated and its basic thesis developed. Like the other sections it has an elaborate concentric structure. Exhortation and thanksgiving (A–A') frame the central instruction of the letter (B), which is itself formulated concentrically (a–b–a') so as to focus on the notion of the restraining power. This is the letter's most original contribution. By using it the author is able to reinterpret the traditional apocalyptic eschatology he follows and turn it into an argument against the thesis he is challenging that "the day of the Lord is already here" (2:2).

2 Thess 2:3-17

A. Exhortation against anxiety caused by a wrong idea of the *parousia* (vv. 1-2)

B. Instruction on what must precede the *parousia* (vv. 3-12)
a. The apostasy and the revelation of the "lawless one" as anti-God (vv. 3-5)
b. THE RESTRAINING POWER AND PERSON (vv. 6-7)
a'. The "lawless one" as a false prophet causing apostasy (vv. 8-12)

A'. Thanksgiving and wish-prayer for comfort and strength (vv. 13-17)

"The Day of the Lord is Already Here" (2:1-2)

As can be inferred from its opening exhortation (2:1) the letter has been written to correct the erroneous belief held by its readers that "the day of the Lord is already here" (2:1-2). It is not easy to understand what exactly this slogan could have meant. One possible way of understanding it is to suppose that its advocates were Gnostics, who believed that their experience of the risen Lord had already liberated them fully, so that no further coming of Jesus was necessary (cf. 2 Tim 2:18). Whatever the scenario, the author clearly supposes that his readers share his apocalyptic understanding according to which the *parousia* is not an inner spiritual experience but a spectacular external event that is to take place at the end of history. They differ from him not about the nature of the *parousia* but about its timing, for they believe that the *parousia* is not just imminent (a belief the author may have shared) but is already here in the sense that the series of events that will lead to the coming of the Lord has already begun. According to them, the countdown to the *parousia* had started.

The Apostasy and the Lawless One (2:3-5, 8-12)

In 2 Thess 2:3-12 the author reminds his readers of two things that must happen before the *parousia* can take place (2:3-4). The *parousia* must be preceded by the "apostasy" (a better translation here of the Greek *apostasia* than the "rebellion" of the NRSV) and by the revelation or coming of the "lawless one" *(ho anomos).* These have not yet taken place because of a mysterious restraining power or person *(to katechon* or *ho katechōn)* that holds them in check. So the day of the Lord cannot have begun.

Second Thessalonians does not describe the details of the apostasy, which is probably to be understood (as in Matt 24:10) as a massive falling away of people from God or from Christ because of persecution and the seductions of satanic power (2:3). The lawless one, on the other hand, is described in some detail. He is both an anti-God figure who will (as in Dan 8:9-12; Rev 13:1-10) set himself up in place of God and claim the worship due to God alone (2:4) and as a false, Satan-inspired prophet who, like the false prophets of the synoptic apocalypse (Matt 24:23-24 // Mark 13:22), will lead people astray through the counterfeit miracles he performs (2:9-12).

The Restraining Power or Person (2:6-7)

Between his descriptions of these two aspects of the "lawless one" the author makes his own special contribution to the eschatology of the letter. He speaks of a restraining power ("what is now restraining him"), referring to someone ("the one who now restrains") whose activity holds back the coming of the lawless one and so delays the parousia of Jesus that must follow it (2:6-7). (Although the general purport of what the author wants to tell us in 2:6-7 is clear enough his Greek text is so obscure that no two English translations render it in exactly the same way.)

The identity of this restraining power *(to katechon)* in v. 6 has been the object of speculation for centuries and possibly indicates something like an institution. Since Hippolytus of Rome (235 C.E.) it has been widely identified with the Roman empire (or even with one of its "successors" like the Catholic Church!). The empire is believed to play this role either because it is a force for order and so a bulwark against the disintegration of the last days or because it is a force of evil that must play itself out before the climax of evil, the "lawless one" can appear.

Widely popular though this political interpretation has been, especially in patristic and medieval Christianity in the West, it does not do justice to the orientation of 2 Thessalonians that, unlike the Revelation of John, shows no political interest whatever. Its understanding of the restraining power is theological, not political. The author takes up a familiar apocalyptic theme according to which the events of history take place at predetermined times fixed by God. It is God, therefore, who is responsible for the delay or the hastening (Matt 24:22 // Mark 13:20) of the end. The restraining power, then, is God's providential guidance of history, and the restrainer is best thought of as an agent through whom God acts, analogous to the angel who binds Satan for a thousand years in Revelation (Rev 20:1-3).

As long as this restraining force is allowed to function the "mystery of lawlessness" (that is, the power of evil already operating secretly in the world) is held in check and the lawless one cannot be openly revealed. But when, at the appointed time, the restraint is taken away the lawless one will appear openly and the events of the Lord's day will follow in quick succession. There will be a massive display of satanic deception leading to a great apostasy (2:9-10), then the *parousia* of the Lord and his effortless ("with the breath of his mouth") annihilation of the lawless one (2:8), and, finally the judgment that will lead to the condemnation of all those who have not accepted the gospel (2:12) and the salvation of those who have held fast to the traditions taught by Paul (2:14-15). (See table at top of next page.)

Concluding Thanksgiving and Wish-Prayer (2:13-17)

With its concluding thanksgiving and prayer (2:13-17) the letter turns again to the mode of exhortation (note the "brothers and sisters" in

The Apocalyptic Timetable of 2 Thessalonians

1>	2>	3>	4>	5>	6>	7>	8
Mystery of lawlessness	Restraining power	Removal of the restrainer	*Parousia* of the lawless one	Apostasy	*Parousia* of the Lord Jesus	Annihilation of the lawless one	Judgment
(2:7)	(2:6)	(2:7)	(2:3)	(2:9)	(2:8)	(2:8)	(2:12)

2:1 and 2:13). It contrasts the readers' salvation with the condemnation of the unbelievers that has just been described (2:12). The retributive judgment predicted in 1:5-10 is now spelled out in detail. We learn that both salvation and condemnation are the result of human effort (2:10, 12, 15), and divine predestination (2:11, 13-14) that, here as elsewhere in the NT, remain in an unresolved tension. The result of their interplay is that people are sharply divided into two groups: a small minority, those who believe in Jesus, will be saved; a vast majority, the "wicked and evil" unbelievers (3:2), will be condemned. This division is part of a long series of oppositions that shapes the apocalyptic rhetoric of the letter. (See table at bottom of this page.)

What is important in these apocalyptic oppositions is the author's pastoral intent of comforting the readers about their future destiny. This intent suggests that we do not have to read the letter's description of the day of the Lord and the events that will precede it as a literal timetable of future events. Both the diversity of apocalyptic motifs in the NT and the history of exegesis have shown the futility of trying to calculate a literal timetable of future events based on a writing such as 2 Thessalonians. Rather we must read in the text the basic reassurance given by the Bible that history will find its fulfillment, that the just will be vindicated, and that justice will ultimately prevail. In laying out the apocalyptic scenario for the reader, the author thus intends to comfort them by providing a sure hope for the future. The defeat of the lawless one is assured and eternal glory awaits the readers if they hold firm to the sure traditions taught to them.

The Concluding Exhortation: 3:1-16

The concluding section of the letter is a loose collection of exhortations (3:1-4, 13-15) and wish-prayers (3:5, 16), into which the author has inserted a strongly worded instruction on dealing with certain troublesome elements in the community (3:6-12).

2 Thess 3:1-16

a. Exhortation to pray, and wish-prayer (vv. 1-5)
b. Instruction on dealing with troublemakers (vv. 6-12)
a'. Exhortation to do good, and wish-prayer (vv. 13-16)

Opening Exhortation (3:1-5)

The opening exhortation begins with a request for prayer (3:1-2) and ends with a wish-prayer (3:5). Both contain petitions that lack reference to any specific situation (contrast Rom 15:30-32) and are formulated in the paired, parallel sets of phrases the author favors. The readers are to pray that the gospel may spread rapidly and that its preachers may not be hindered by unbelievers (3:1-2). The author prays that his readers may grow in their love of God and in their Christ-like steadfastness in persecution (3:5). Between the

Apocalyptic Oppositions in 2 Thessalonians

The mystery of lawlessness (2:7)	The restraining power (2:6)
The lawless one (2:3)	The Lord Jesus (2:8)
The *parousia* of the lawless one (2:9)	The *parousia* of the Lord (2:8)
The deception by Satan (2:9)	The sanctification by the Spirit (2:13)
A powerful delusion sent by God (2:11)	God's choice of the first fruits of salvation (2:13)
Those who refuse to love [= be committed] to the truth	Those who believe in the truth (2:10) [= the gospel] (2:13)
Those who take pleasure in unrighteousness (2:12)	Those who hold fast to traditions received (2:15)
Those who will be condemned (2:12)	Those who will obtain glory (2:14)

request for prayer and the wish-prayer the author inserts a reassurance (3:3) and an expression of confidence (3:4) that is clearly meant to prepare for the instruction that follows.

Instruction to the Community (3:6-12)

This instruction that is the structural and thematic center of section 2. A' is again formulated in the author's familiar concentric style. The author "commands" *(paraggellein)* his readers to keep away from certain troublemakers in the community (3:6), gives reasons for this command (3:7-10), and then turns to command the troublemakers themselves to work for their living (3:11-12).

2 Thess 3:6-12

a. Command to the community to keep away from troublemakers (v. 6)
b. Reasons for the command:
   1. The example given by Paul when he was with them (vv. 7-9)
   2. The command given by Paul when he was with them (v. 10)

a'. Command to the troublemakers to work for their living (vv. 11-12)

The section is thus concerned about a group of troublemakers whom the community is strictly enjoined to avoid (3:6). They are described by a rather unusual expression, *ataktōs peripatōn,* related to the term *ataktoi* used in 1 Thessalonians to describe "idlers" whom the community was earlier asked to admonish (1 Thess 5:14). Since much of this section echoes the vocabulary of 1 Thessalonians (compare v. 7 with 1 Thess 2:1; v. 10 with 1 Thess 3:4; and especially v.8 with 1 Thess 2:9) it is likely that the author has borrowed the expression "idlers" from the earlier letter. These "idlers" are members of the community who have stopped working, are living off the community, and are meddling in its affairs. This is evident (1) from the way in which the readers are referred to the counter-example of Paul's own toil and labor among them in vv. 7-9, (2) from the terse instruction given by Paul that "anyone unwilling to work should not eat" in v. 10, (3) from the elegant and witty description of the troublemakers as people who are "in no way busy" but busybodies *(periergazamenoi)* in v. 11, and (4) from the author's command to them "to do their work quietly and to earn their own living" in v. 12. We are not told why they should be behaving in this way, but given the eschatological thrust of the letter it is likely that they refuse to work because they believe that the day of the Lord has already come, putting an end to the concerns of everyday living.

Of the many arguments the author uses to get this group of idlers to work, the one that has made the deepest impression on the readers of the letter has been Paul's terse instruction: "Anyone unwilling to work should not eat" (3:10). A working-class adage is here raised to a principle of Christian ethics, possibly by linking it with Gen 3:17-19. Against the norms of Greek (and Hindu) society this affirms the religious value of manual work. Early monastic rules like those of Basil, Augustine, and Benedict, which insist on the place of work in a monk's life, and modern Christian social teaching on the importance of labor have been significantly influenced by this text.

Concluding Exhortation (3:13-16)

Like the opening exhortation in 3:1-5 which it balances (note the "brothers and sisters" in 3:1 and 3:13), the concluding part of this third section is a loose collection of exhortations and instructions. An introductory exhortation to do what is right (3:13) is followed by more specific instructions on how to deal with those who do not obey the letter (3:14-15) and a wish-prayer for peace (3:16). Once again a specific instruction is framed by general exhortation and prayer. The unrepentant among the troublemakers ("those who do not obey what we say in this letter") are to be ostracized by the community not as a measure of definitive rejection but as a means of correction. There is a suggestion here of a procedure of correction like the one outlined in Matt 18:15, which softens the unqualified rejection of the troublemakers commanded in 3:6.

Letter Conclusion: 3:17-18

The letter closing is remarkable for the extreme brevity of its concluding greeting and its insistence on what has been called its authentic signature (3:17). In several genuine letters of Paul we find a greeting in his own hand added to letters presumably dictated to a secretary (1 Cor 16:21; Gal 6:11; cf. Col 4:18), but only here are we told: "this is the mark in every letter of mine; it is the way I write" (3:17). There has been much discussion as to whether this should be taken as a sign of the authenticity of the letter (Paul himself is drawing attention to his "signature" that will distinguish this authentic letter of his from other forged letters) or as an indication of a pseudonymous author who, to establish the credibility of his composition, strongly emphasizes its authenticity. Had Paul himself written the letter this would have been, as we have seen, soon after he wrote 1 Thessalonians, his first extant letter. It is unlikely that he would have had to worry about forgeries then, nor would he have referred to "every letter" as if several letters had been written by him. The authenticating signature, then, confirms the pseudonymous character of this short, dry, difficult, yet surprisingly influential letter that continues to speak a word of hard-headed hope to us today—provided we learn to read it responsibly, paying attention to the historical situation in which it was written and the canonical context in which it has been placed.

BIBLIOGRAPHY

(See also the works on 1 and 2 Thessalonians mentioned in the bibliography on 1 Thessalonians.)

Giblin, Charles Homer. *The Threat to Faith. An Exegetical and Theological Reexamination of 2 Thessalonians 2.* AnBib 31. Rome: Pontifical Biblical Institute, 1967.

Hughes, Frank Witt. *Early Christian Rhetoric and 2 Thessalonians.* JSNT.S 30. Sheffield: JSOT Press, 1989.

Martin, D. Michael. *1, 2 Thessalonians.* NAC 33. Nashville: Broadman and Holman, 1995.

Menken, Maarten J. J. *2 Thessalonians.* New Testament Readings. London: Routledge, 1994.

Morris, Leon. *The First and Second Epistles to the Thessalonians.* Rev. ed. Grand Rapids: Eerdmans, 1991.

Richard, Earl J. *First and Second Thessalonians.* SP 11. Collegeville: The Liturgical Press, 1995.

Weiss, N. E. *Chi Rho Commentary on 1 and 2 Thessalonians.* Adelaide: Lutheran Publishing House, 1988.

Introduction to the Pastoral Epistles

Enrique Nardoni

The Pastoral Epistles (PE) are an epistolary collection of the last instructions of Paul to Titus and Timothy. They are called "pastoral" because of their practical character: they include instructions on Church discipline, appointment of officers, and combating false teachers; they aim at helping the leaders to guide the Christian communities. They were written in a time of inner crisis in the Pauline churches due to false teachers who endangered apostolic doctrine and disrupted the communities. The PE show the ability of the apostolic Church to counteract destructive forces in a new inner crisis by preserving the apostolic tradition and developing new social structures that would protect and increase Church unity.

Distinctive Features of the PE

The distinctive features of these letters are primarily their ideas of the Church and the gospel, their eschatological expectation, and their characterization of their adversaries. They conceive of the Church as the ground of truth (1 Tim 3:15) and the place where believers live (2 Tim 2:20) instead of understanding it as being born from the preaching of the gospel (1 Cor 3:11; 4:14-15) and identified with the believers (1 Cor 12:12, 27). They show a threefold ministerial structure of the Church made up of appointed officers and constituted by a board of presbyter-bishops, a presbyterial council and a body of deacons (1 Tim 3:1-13; 5:17; Titus 1:5-9), whereas the Corinthian correspondence describe the Church formed by a great variety of functions derived from the Spirit (1 Cor 12:4-30). The PE conceive the gospel as a fixed body of doctrine, a deposit (1 Tim 1:11; 2 Tim 1:10-14; 2:2; Titus 1:3). This is different from the gospel conceived as proclamation of the death and resurrection of Christ, a conception common to the authentic Pauline epistles. The PE hold an eschatological orientation but do not have the sharp tension characteristic of the authentic Pauline epistles. The PE, on the one hand, consider the present time as the fulfillment of the predictions for "the last days," but on the other hand they have a strong concern for the future generations of the Church (2 Tim 2:2). The adversaries in the PE are not the same as those of the other Pauline epistles. They are described as disrupting the community by ignoring the accepted norms of behavior in the household (1 Tim 6:3-5). What is striking in reference to the adversaries is the lack of a substantive debate; the false teachers are not confronted with the preaching about Christ as is customary in the authentic Pauline letters, but are simply refuted by reference to the traditional teaching, the "sound doctrine" from which they are said to have departed.

It is noteworthy that against the false teachers the PE insist not only on "sound doctrine," but also on respect for the order established by God in creation for nature and the household; hence the importance of *eusebeia* ("godliness") in the PE (1 Tim 2:2; 3:16; 4:7, 8; 5:4; 6:3, 5, 6, 11; 2 Tim 3:5; Titus 1:1). *Eusebeia,* in the Greco-Roman world, designated the virtue that nurtures respect toward gods and the natural order of household and city, the divinely established order, and moves people to accept subordination to the authority established in such an order. Associated with this respect for the household are references in the PE to the domestic codes, as in 1 Tim 2:9-15; 6:1-2; Titus 2:1-10. These references, however, are not unique to the PE. Such references are also found in Col 3:18–4:1; Eph 5:22–6:9; 1 Pet 2:18-37; 5:1-6. These domestic codes originated in Hellenistic thought and developed in the Greco-Roman world. They were adopted and Christianized partially for apologetic reasons, in order to refute pagan critics who claimed that Christians were immoral, and to show that Christians practiced those virtues that were highly appreciated according to Greco-Roman standards. But the use of these codes had primarily an internal function: promoting and strengthening the social bonds of the Christian household, the basic unit of Christian communities, amid the destructive forces both inside and outside the Christian body.

The Authorship of the Pastoral Epistles

The distinctive features of the PE have led a great number of scholars to regard them as pseudonymous. The concept of pseudonymity should not degrade the rank of the PE, for in the ancient Greek world pseudonymity was an accepted practice. The people of that time had neither the modern idea of copyright and its legal consequences nor an elaborated concept of what genuine authorship is. Pseudonymity was widespread especially in philosophical circles, and in Judaism during the Hellenistic and Greco-Roman periods pseudonymity was a flourishing practice. The Jewish pseudonymous writers shared the conviction that normative knowledge for the present and future was revealed in the past and kept hidden in the sacred text or in the unfolding events of sacred history. The pseudonymous writers in the apocalyptic literature, ascribed their books to a famous man of the past because they shared the conviction that such a man, now exalted in heaven, keeps molding the mind and action of the community through the authority and wisdom of his tradition. In revealing the truth for the present the Jewish pseudonymous writers did not claim the right of intellectual property because of their strong awareness of sharing "a transsubjective tradition." The Christian pseudonymous writers of the first century and first half of the second shared these presuppositions with the homologous Jewish literature, although with some differences. They believed that normative knowledge was not in the past history of Israel, but in Christ's revelation through the apostles. In addition they believed that the presence of the Spirit helped them develop Christ's teaching by applying it to new circumstances. These ideas were shared not only by the pseudonymous writers but also by the communities that accepted their writings. Within a similar framework of thought we may place the writer of the PE and the Christian community that accepted them from the very beginning. Who was the pseudonymous writer? Various names have been proposed (Luke and Polycarp, among others), but without convincing argument.

Time and Place of Composition

A comparison with the letters of Clement of Rome, who wrote to the Corinthians in 96 C.E., and Ignatius of Antioch, who arrived at Rome in 113 C.E., may help establish the time of composition, since the ministerial structure of the PE churches lies between Clement's and Ignatius' church structures. On the one hand 1 Clement (44:2, 5) shows that the bishops (in the plural) are identified with presbyters and form a collegial government; Ignatius' letters, on the other hand, witness the presence of monepiscopacy everywhere in Asia Minor. The PE show something in between. In the PE there is a threefold ministerial structure of presbyter-bishops, presbyterial council, and deacons (see 1 Tim 3:2-13; 4:14; 5:17). Therefore, it is probable that the PE were written between 1 Clement (96) and Ignatius' letters (113). The place of composition of the PE is a matter of controversy. Two places under debate are Ephesus and Rome.

The Inclusion of the Pastoral Epistles in the Canon

The earliest known witnesses of the collection of the thirteen letters of Paul (including the PE) are Irenaeus and the Muratorian Fragment in the late second century. Subsequently Tertullian refers to the thirteen letters of Paul, while Clement of Alexandria knows the collection of the fourteen Pauline letters (including Hebrews).

The Greek text of the PE has been transmitted in many Greek manuscripts since the fourth century. The absence of the PE from the Vatican Codex (B) puzzles scholars.

Regarding the canonical value of the PE there are two main positions among Protestant scholars. One is polemical and regards the PE as a distortion of true Pauline thought; hence their normative value is denied. The other is ecumenical and thinks that the PE represent one of the several viable views that the NT offers regarding the structure of the Church. Most Roman Catholic scholars, following Vatican Council II, believe that the Church is essentially both charismatic and institutional. They read the PE in continuity with the other Pauline letters, balancing the former with the latter. In doing so they emphasize that the style of authority portrayed in the PE should be animated by a spirit of service for the community and modified by a wide, active responsibility given to the faithful according to the variety of their gifts. Likewise, several of them raise the question, for ecumenical purposes, of whether the ritual of the bishop's imposition of hands that developed from the PE is the only way in which the Church can appoint sacred ministers or whether it can express in other ways its appointment or recognition.

BIBLIOGRAPHY

Barrett, Charles Kingsley. *The Pastoral Epistles in the New English Bible.* NCB. Oxford: Clarendon Press, 1963.

Bassler, Jouette M. *1 Timothy, 2 Timothy, Titus.* Nashville: Abingdon, 1996.

Boer, Martinus C. de. "Images of Paul in the Post-Apostolic Church," *CBQ* 42 (1980) 359–380.

Brown, Raymond E. *The Churches the Apostles Left Behind.* New York: Paulist, 1984.

____. *Priest and Bishop: Biblical Reflections.* Paramus, N.J.: Paulist, 1970.

Collins, Raymond F. *Letters That Paul Did Not Write: The Epistle to the Hebrews and the Pauline Pseudepigrapha.* GNS 28. Wilmington, Del.: Michael Glazier, 1988.

Davies, Margaret. *The Pastoral Epistles.* Sheffield: Sheffield Academic Press, 1996.

Fee, Gordon D. *1 and 2 Timothy, Titus.* NIBC 13. Peabody, Mass.: Hendrickson, 1984.

Fiore, Benjamin. *The Function of Personal Examples in the Socratic and Pastoral Epistles.* AnBib 105. Rome: Biblical Institute Press, 1986.

Hanson, Anthony Tyrrell. *The Pastoral Epistles.* NCBC. Grand Rapids: Eerdmans, 1982.

Johnson, Luke Timothy. *1 Timothy, 2 Timothy, Titus.* John Knox Preaching Guides. Atlanta: John Knox, 1987.

Karris, Robert J. "The Background and Significance of the Polemic of the Pastoral Epistles," *JBL* 92 (1973) 549–564.

Kidd, Reggie M. *Wealth and Beneficence in the Pastoral Epistles: A "Bourgeois" Form of Early Christianity?* Atlanta: Scholars, 1990.

Koch, Klaus. "Pseudonymous Writing," *IDBSup,* 712–714.

Köstenberger, Andreas J., ed. *Women in the Church: A Fresh Analysis of I Timothy 2:9-15.* Grand Rapids: Baker Book House, 1995.

Kroeger, Catherine, and Richard Kroeger. *I Suffer Not a Woman: Rethinking I Timothy 2:11-15 in Light of Ancient Evidence.* Grand Rapids: Baker Book House, 1992.

Meade, David G. *Pseudonymity and Canon: An Investigation into the Relationship of Authorship and Authority in Jewish and Earliest Christian Tradition.* Grand Rapids: Eerdmans, 1987.

Nardoni, Enrique. "Ministries in the New Testament," *Studia Canonica* 11 (1977) 5–36.

Towner, Philip H. *The Goal of Our Instruction: The Structure of Theology and Ethics in the Pastoral Epistles.* JSNT.S 34. Sheffield: Sheffield Academic Press, 1989.

____. *1–2 Timothy and Titus.* IVP.NT. Leicester: InterVarsity Press, 1994.

1 Timothy

Hans-Hartmut Schroeder

FIRST READING

The first and second letters to Timothy and the letter to Titus make up the group of the "Pastoral Epistles." They were written pseudonymously under the name of Paul (see the remarks below on Paul's biography and use of language) and supposedly sent to his coworkers, Timothy and Titus (cf. Acts 16; 2 Cor 2:13) and their communities in Ephesus and Crete around 100 C.E. They were conceived as a unit and, together with the letter to Philemon, they conclude the Pauline corpus in the NT canon, not only because of their brevity but because they attempt to wrap up the Pauline heritage (called "sound teaching," cf. 1 Tim 1:10) in a brief compass and hand it on to those who come after, so that they may know *how one ought to behave in the household of God* (1 Tim 3:15). That is the central theme of 1 Timothy: the doctrine of the Church. It is developed in two interlocking ways, one theological (to the extent that the Christ event constitutes the Church [3:16] and is at the same time the content of the Church's proclamation) the other ecclesiological (an order for Church communities and Church offices combined with instructions for behavior corresponding to faith). Key theological phrases, confessional formulae, and doxologies sprinkled throughout (e.g., in 1:15, 17; 2:(3-4), 5-6; 4:8b, 10b; 6:15-16) stand for Paul's gospel (1:11). The teaching of Paul thus summarized is threatened by *false teachers* (1:3b, 6-7; 4:1b-3b; 6:3-5) who are trying to draw the members of the community away from the faith.

First Timothy could be entitled "The Gospel of Paul in Conflict with False Teaching." In order to achieve victory for sound teaching the author adopts a strategy that makes it clear that we are no longer in the early period of preaching the gospel among the Gentiles, but instead in the third generation. The issue is not success against foreign, Hellenistic cults or quarrels between Jewish and Gentile Christians, but rather intra-community conflicts and the combatting of false teaching related to ideas that would later be called Gnosis. Myths and genealogies (1:4) play a role, but so do law (1:7), asceticism and virginity (4:3), and the kind of piety that aims at material gain (6:5). These are contrasted to the divine plan of salvation (1:5), the gospel entrusted to Paul (1:11) which the apostle's disciples, empowered by the presbyters' laying hands on them and by the words of prophecy (4:14; 1:18), should militantly (1:18) bring to fruition. The struggle is compared to a sea battle in which one may experience shipwreck (1:19). The battle plan or strategy for the struggle includes a proper order of worship, which involves both liturgical prayer (2:1-2) and knowing how one ought to behave in the household of God (3:15; cf. Titus 1:7).

The task of preserving community order and *sound teaching* (1:10) and causing them to prevail is fictionally bestowed by Paul himself on his "son Timothy" (1:18). Paul regards himself as a living proof of the truth of the message of salvation. He is the chief sinner to be saved (1:15).

Faith and love were given to him in Jesus Christ (1:14). Conveying that truth is the *aim of instruction* (1:5) that Timothy is commissioned to give, so that *everyone may be saved* (2:4). Every human person can contribute something to his or her salvation: *good works* (2:10; 5:25; 6:18) and the practice of piety (or "godliness"), for which both present and future life are the reward (4:8; 6:6). Timothy is to pay close attention to himself and his teaching, for "in doing this you will save both yourself and your hearers" (4:16b). Models thus play an important role: Paul is the model for all who seek eternal life (1:16). Timothy is also a model in speech, conduct, love, faith, and purity (4:12b). The members of the community should behave in like manner. Their duties are explained to them in terms of their various callings within the Church, and they are admonished to behave as befits their station. Instructions are given to individual groups: men and women at prayer (2:8-15); the bishop (3:1-7), the deacons, both male and female (3:8-13), and Timothy himself (4:6–5:2). These are followed by regulations for widows (5:3-16), the elders (5:17-22), slaves (6:1-2a), and the wealthy (6:17-19; cf. 6:7-10). The imposition of hands (4:11-16) is an important precondition for the assignment given to Timothy.

How Should We Read the Letter?

One possibly entrée into the reading of 1 Timothy could be the statements about women (2:9-15) and widows (5:3-16), which have powerfully shaped Christian images of women even to the present day. The things that are said here about women's roles are frequently cited as evidence of Paul's misogyny. Although 1 Timothy was declared to be a work of Paul and yet was shown by a number of its characteristics to have been written by an author from the third Christian generation, it would be interesting to pursue this accusation and to test whether the statements relating to this question correspond to anything in the genuine Pauline letters. We could also seek to understand whether a new situation brought the author of the Pastorals to take this position and at the same time drove him to declare his teaching to be that of Paul.

The following scenario is possible: The Pastorals were written to communities Paul had founded and to which he had, in his own time, proclaimed the definitive form of the gospel. After his death there arose the question of the way in which his gospel should be interpreted under changed historical circumstances and how it could continue to be regarded as authoritative. In particular there was the issue of distinguishing the Christian gospel from other teachings; these latter were to be opposed by *sound teaching* (1:10b). It seemed impossible to assure the authority of such teaching except by declaring it to be the teaching of Paul and binding it to the office of the presbyter or bishop—or in the present case a disciple of the apostle—who stood, with Paul, in the apostolic tradition. Thus:

1. Paul is made to appear as the writer of the letter.
2. He is depicted as having (prophetically) foreseen the future challenges that would be posed to the churches, and
3. In general he is seen to have anticipated the continuation of history.

In this way structures of community life that had developed since the death of Paul and stood the test of combat with foreign teachings were formulated as instructions from Paul and represented as his enduring legacy (until the *parousia,* 6:14).

Breaks with and differences from what Paul had said in his authentic letters resulted. The question remains whether, in spite of this, the original intention of Paul's words was retained and further developed, or whether the author's purpose was to legitimate a new concept by referring it to Paul. It becomes our task to judge whether the gospel, as transmitted to the third Christian generation, can still be regarded as authentic by us; to put it another way, can we learn something from this new interpretation of the gospel we find in the Pastorals that will help us to proclaim the gospel in our own time? Can it help us with our preaching?

In approaching the sections of text referred to above we might ask, for example, when they differ from the genuine Pauline letters, whether the social context, including the patriarchal structure of households, gave rise to a different assignment of roles to women within the Christian community. Do we have to speak of a pressure to conform that the Christian community should have resisted? Or should we instead see this as a sectarian attempt on the part of the community to distance itself from a general trend to liberalization? Is the criterion of merely trying to avoid giving offense (cf. 5:14; 3:7) in accord with the gospel? Beyond that, we should ask whether the community had been offered a critical starting point from which a different understanding of women's roles might have been derived. In any case, in 1 Timothy we encounter only a theological rationale that strengthens the primacy of the man (2:13-15). How can we deal with it?

Another example that arouses critical inquiry about the degree to which the instructions in the Pastorals aiming at institutionalization are in harmony with the gospel is the pericope about the order for prayer (2:1-7), which is prescribed as a reading for Rogation Sunday. Is the twofold division implied here both in politics (which are left to those in power) and in the private sphere of devotional practice still possible after Auschwitz? Moreover, when we refer to the instructions to slaves in 6:1-2a it is fully obvious that only a critical stance toward the text of 1 Timothy can be productive for preaching today.

Alongside these we find pericopes that, in light of the Pauline heritage, attempt to express faith and devotion in terms of contemporary understanding and current modes of expression. Here we find words like *epiphaneia, sōtēr, eusebeia,* and attributes like *sōphrōn* and *kosmios*.

It is not impossible that the formulations directed toward a *praxis pietatis* do in fact give an accurate rendering of Pauline thought, drawn from a period of imminent expectation of the *parousia,* for a later time that expected history to continue, and that they can also appear for us today as an authentic witness to Paul's thinking. This can yield a number of ideas with which we may approach a reading of 1 Timothy.

History of Interpretation

The Pastorals are in themselves a part of the history of interpretation of the Pauline letters. They are an example of the way in which texts are reinterpreted in changed historical circumstances. These letters are only one link in a chain of interpretations that, in every age, make the old matters significant for the present time. Each new interpretation is revealing of its own time as well as of the underlying text.

The interpretive history of 1 Timothy as a whole is sparse. We may mention the works of John Chrysostom, Theodore of Mopsuestia, Ambrosiaster, Pelagius, and Thomas Aquinas, as well as those of the Reformation period by Melancthon, Calvin, and Luther, J. Gerhardi and Hugo Grotius, and the nineteenth-century books of J. T. Beck and H. J. Holtzmann.

In addition, shorter portions of the text have their own history. We may mention especially their impact on church order, canon law, and ordination, as well as the questions of the role of women, slavery, and to some degree the character of law. Thus, for example, Luther interpreted 1 Tim 1:9 in the sense of *usus elenchticus:* the Law serves to confront sinners with their sinfulness. This idea continues to affect interpretations even at the present time, though not without opposition.

Or: Luther found in 1 Tim 3:2 the basic principle of the priesthood of all believers in contradistinction to a separate priestly order. For him, the only office is that of preaching; referring to 1 Tim 3:2 (cf. Titus 1:6) he connects the office of bishops to the local church (as did Jerome). This passage also served him as a basis for asserting that the bishop or pastor should be married.

More will be said about the interpretive history of individual passages in the letter as these are discussed below.

Outline

A. Introduction (1:1-20)
- Preface (1:1-2)
- Timothy's assigned duty (1:3-11)
- Paul as servant of Christ and model of the salvation of sinners (1:12-17)
- Timothy's obligation to carry out his task (1:18-20)

B. Norms for behavior in the household of God (2:1–3:16)
- Prayer during worship (2:1-7)
- Men and women at prayer (2:8-15)
- Offices of leadership (3:1-13)
- The Church as the locus of truth in the world (3:14-16)

C. Advice for Timothy (4:1–6:2)
- False teachers (4:1-5)
- Protection against false teaching (4:6-11)
- Imposition of hands and the authority of office (4:12–5:2)

The order of widows in the community (5:3-16)
The elders (5:17-25)
The slaves (6:1-2)
D. The greed of the false teachers (6:3-10)
E. Reminder of calling and acknowledgment of the duties of office (6:11-16)
F. The positive aspect of wealth (6:17-19)
G. Concluding admonition and greeting (6:20-21)

SECOND READING

Introduction: 1:1-20

1. Preface (1:1-2)

First Timothy begins with a short apostolic greeting mentioning the sender and addressee and invoking a blessing, like the prefaces of the genuine Pauline letters. Paul is introduced with the title "apostle *of Christ Jesus*" but here his apostolate is traced to God as well as to Jesus Christ. On the one hand, this characterizes Paul as *the* apostle; on the other hand, this authorization by God means that Paul's instructions and teachings are to be understood as divine instruction. The designation of God as *savior* is in harmony with Hellenistic Jewish usage, but "Christ Jesus our hope" is not a common predication. Something similar is, however, found in the Apostolic Fathers (Ign. *Eph.* 21.2: "in Jesus Christ, our common hope").

Sōtēr, with its strong Hellenistic coloring, appears frequently in the Pastorals as a predicate; both it and the verb *sōzein* are applied both to God (1 Tim 1:1; 2:3-4; 4:10; 2 Tim 1:9; Titus 2:10; 3:5) and to Christ (1 Tim 1:15; 2 Tim 1:10; Titus 1:3-4; 2:13). Titus 2:11 speaks of the *saving* grace that God has caused to appear. This has to do with the salvation of sinners (1 Tim 1:15) and of *all humanity* (1 Tim 2:4; 4:10). Christ is *sōtēr,* but at the same time the means used by God for the salvation of human beings. Thus God is the source of the will to save. The original designation of God as *sōtēr* goes back to the LXX and became current in Hellenistic Judaism. The transfer of the title to Jesus may well be connected to the influence of Hellenistic religions; in the Hellenistic Greek world it was used both in the worship of the gods and in the veneration of rulers. In the Pastorals it describes Jesus as the one who brings eschatological salvation (similar to Paul's usage in Phil 3:20).

2. Timothy's Assigned Duty (1:3-11)

The task Paul lays on his disciple, Timothy, is founded in the fact known to the author (v. 3a) that false teachers are dividing the community (v. 3b). There seem to be community members who are listening to this new teaching (1:20; 2 Tim 2:17; 4:14; 1 Tim 4:1b; 5:15; 6:21; 2 Tim 4:3-4; 3:6b; Titus 1:11b) and handing it on to others (5:13c). They appeal to so-called "myths" and otherwise undefined "genealogies" (v. 4).

Against this false teaching, the author sets up the divine *oikonomia* (household order/plan of salvation). False teaching about the Law (v. 7) is opposed by borrowing from Paul's teaching (Rom 7:1-6) that believers are freed from the Law while the vices of the godless are condemned by the Law (Rom 1:28-31). These latter act contrary to the community's teaching, which was entrusted to the apostle along with the gospel (vv. 8-11).

3. Paul as Servant of Christ and Model of the Salvation of Sinners (1:12-17)

The special service entrusted to Paul by Jesus is established, in vv. 12-17, by means of a retrospect on his past and his call (cf. Acts 9; 22; 26; 1 Cor 15:8-11; Gal 1:13-16; 2 Cor 4:1-6; Phil 3:4-11; Rom 1:1-7; Col 1:23b-29; Eph 3:1-11). The author calls him an unbeliever and blasphemer, someone with whom others who have come to believe can well identify. Thus he becomes a model and even a prototype of the sinner saved by grace (1:15-16). His example serves to solidify the truth, valid for the whole Church, that Jesus came into the world to save sinners. This establishes the authority by which Paul teaches the authentic gospel. The doxology in v. 17 and the thanksgiving to Christ Jesus in v. 12 are the frame containing Paul's being entrusted with the gospel.

The doxology in v. 17 is an expression of valedictory praise in the tradition of Hellenistic Judaism. Its content has no particular reference to what has been said before; rather, it is formulaic: recipient (in the dative), here with four Hellenistic-Jewish divine predicates + two doxological predicates + formula of eternity + Amen (cf. Rev 4:9; Jer 10:10; Tob 13:7, 11; *1 Clem.* 61.2).

4. Timothy's Obligation to Carry out His Task (1:18-20)

Now that vv. 12-17 have legitimated and authorized the one giving the assignment the author again turns, in vv. 18-20, to strengthen Timothy by reminding him, on the one hand, of his filial duty of obedience (v. 18), and on the other hand of his calling, to which he was summoned by the presbyters' laying hands on him (v. 18b; 4:14; 6:13-14). He is thus to be strengthened for the fight (v. 18c; 6:12a; cf. 2 Tim 4:7) that will result from his assignment to preach the gospel against the false teaching (v. 3). The author does not forget to warn him against the consequences that can result from a failure to do his duty (vv. 19b, 20; cf. 2 Tim 2:17; 1 Cor 5:5).

Norms for Behavior in the Household of God: 2:1–3:16

The theme of this section is: norms for behavior in the household of God (house of God = Church as bulwark of the truth, founded on the Christ-event, 3:15-16). The instructions are for the whole Church (2:4). They are intended to regulate the life of all communities, not merely that in Ephesus. These are *direct* instructions (cf. 2:1, 8, 12, etcetera), as distinct from the *mediated* directions that dominate chapter 4 and are intended for the community only via the leadership. In detail, they concern:

1. Prayer During Worship (2:1-7)

Verse 1: The section on worship begins with an injunction to pray. The importance of prayer is underscored by the sequence of four words describing different types of prayer: *deēsis* and *proseuchē* refer to common prayer in worship, while *enteuxis* and *eucharistia* (cf. 1 Tim 4:4-5) refer to grateful prayer and praise addressed to God (2:1). Special emphasis is placed on prayer for *all* people (cf. *1 Clem.* 59.4; 60.4). It appears that this universalist initiative is something new in comparison to synagogue prayer (v. 2). Moreover, prayer for pagan kings and governments (2:2) could have met with resistance in communities that had suffered from the imposition of the imperial cult. But if we take *1 Clem.* 61.1-2 as a fundamental prayer formula we can see that the communities prayed that kings should rule "with piety in peace and gentleness," to the end that people might live "a quiet and peaceable life in all godliness and dignity *(en pasē eusebeia, kai semnotēti)*" (1 Tim 2:2).

For our own part, since we also depend on just governments, this rule of prayer, rightly understood, could be agreed upon today as well. It would be a different matter if it were interpreted in the sense of Rom 13:1 as a demand for obedience and submission, as in the Third Reich when prayer for the Führer was understood as an uncritical acclamation and acknowledgment of Hitler as a God-given ruler.

The concept of *eusebeia*/godliness that appears in 2:2 and rarely elsewhere in the NT (Acts 3:12; 10:2, 7; 17:23; 2 Pet 1:3, 6-7; 2:9; 3:11) is a governing principle in the Pastorals, where it is found thirteen times (including the verb and adverbial forms). It belongs to Hellenistic ethics, where it means reverence before the realm of the divine and the rules established by the gods. In the Pastorals, *eusebeia* means the Christian way of life guided by right teaching and recognition of the truth (cf. Titus 1:1). It is true that, to the extent that it acknowledges the existing external order, it corresponds to the understanding of the pagan world outside. But according to 2 Tim 3:12 it also designates a life-praxis that is sustained in suffering and persecution, i.e., in conflict with the surrounding world. And because Jesus Christ himself is the "mystery of *eusebeia*" *(hos ephanerothē en sarki,* 3:16) it is he who sets the standard for Christian life, which is therefore a life shaped by the grace of God. Thus *eusebeia,* unlike "faith" in Paul's writings, refers to a way of life that encompasses action. In the third Christian generation, when people expected history to go on and on, Christian existence is fulfilled not only in the act of believing, but in a praxis that incorporates the whole of life.

Verses 3-4: Life in *eusebeia* is the goal of God's saving action for all humanity. It is achieved through *epignōsis alētheias* (knowledge of the truth: 2:3-4). *Epignōsis alētheias* is the concept that must be mentioned alongside *eusebeia*. It replaces what Paul called "faith." Knowledge of the truth is an understanding acceptance of *sound teaching*. It occurs when God has led people to repentance (2 Tim 2:25). But knowledge of the truth also has a practical side. It expresses itself as godliness or piety *(eusebeia).*

The liturgical hymn fragment (2:5-6a) is introduced here as a reference to the eucharistic celebration in which the community encounters the universal (cf. 6a, "for all") saving will of God. This is underscored by the emphasis on the oneness of God and Jesus.

Verse 7: To proclaim this saving act of the *one* God for all humanity is the purpose for which Paul was called. Through this empowerment the author, who identifies with Paul, acquires the authority by means of which he can give further instructions.

2. Men and Women at Prayer (2:8-15)

Prayer for everyone and *in every place* (v. 8), which is to secure a quiet and inoffensive life and thus has external effects, should correspond to a particular attitude of those who pray (first of all, the men). The thought is in the first place of the usual posture for prayer in the Hellenistic period, with uplifted arms and open hands (there is no desire to be "different"); but at the same time there is concern for internal attitudes: holy hands, without anger or argument (v. 8).

This brief instruction for the men is followed by a lengthy advisory for the women. But instead of continuing with a statement about how women should pray, the author talks about what they should wear (vv. 9-10), which in itself has nothing to do with worship. That is, when we take the verses out of context we find we are looking at a customary rule that applies to the behavior of all women, not only Christians. It is thus correct to inquire whether the author is relying on a fixed tradition (cf. 1 Pet 3:3-4), i.e., taking the viewpoint of Hellenistic-Roman ethics, which contrasted virtuous women with those who were simply concerned about their appearance. Hence it is only through *good works* (v. 10) as signs of their piety that women achieve their specifically Christian character. The fact that this (universal) regulation for women is expressed as a rule for behavior in the worship service, however, makes it clear that the Church was regarded as a public place. Hence an effort was made to see that the behavior of women in the worship service matched what was expected of women in general. This tendency to see worship in the context of the surrounding society accords also with the rule of silence (v. 11; cf. 1 Cor 14:34-35) for the woman (now in the singular!). Keeping quiet and being submissive (v. 11; 1 Pet 3:1, 5; 1 Cor 14:34) would also have corresponded, in general, to the ancient Roman ideal for women, but here it is coupled with an injunction to learn (v. 11), namely from the *man* who is assigned the task of teaching, and to teach (v. 12) the prohibition, so as not to set themselves above the man. This means that we must presume here a worship service that included didactic preaching, and no longer prophetic speech as in Corinth (1 Cor 11:5). The priority of the man is justified by the argument that Adam was made first, while the sin of transgression was first committed by Eve (vv. 13-14). This reference to Genesis 2 and 3 suggests that in the question of women's submission special weight was given to Jewish tradition (1 Cor 14:34; 1 Pet 3:5-6). But by taking on themselves the *punishment* of childbearing, women can escape the curse that rests on them since Eve's transgression, so long as they continue in faith (v. 15).

Even if we were able to understand this statement in a positive sense as anti-Gnostic and combating false teaching by affirming creation (cf. 4:3-5), it still expresses an attitude of discrimination toward women that has marked Christian understanding of women even to the present time. Verses 11-15 have been applied, frequently in combination with Gen 3:6, 16; 1 Cor 11:1-6; 14:33b-36, and Eph 5:21-24, from early patristic times to denigrate women in contrast to men and to exclude them from active service at worship. Thus, for example, Tertullian assigns women the guilt for the death of the Son of God and demands that, in consequence, they must do penance by neglecting their external appearance. According to him they are also unfit for cultic service. There are similar expressions from Epiphanius, John of Damascus, and Ambrosiaster. Augustine adopted the idea in v. 15a to show that women were created only for the purpose of procreation. Thomas Aquinas combines the assignment of that function to women with the prohibition against teaching (v. 12) "so that the souls of the men should not be led astray to sensuality." Many statements in the ancient Church and in the early Middle Ages are intended to exclude women from any active role in worship: they are not to enter the sanctuary (Council of Laodicea); they are not to sing (Pope Leo IV); they are not to speak during worship (Trullanum, 692). The Reformers held fast to the subordination of women to men as the order of creation. Luther, in spite of his affirmation of universal priesthood, refused to allow women to preach.

We know now that the picture of women presented in the Pastorals was shaped by ancient ideas of society and corresponding interpretations. Therefore it is our duty today to test such texts critically to determine how they relate to the gospel. [See the excursus "The New Testament Household Codes" in the commentary on Colossians.]

3. Offices of Leadership (3:1-13)

The third chapter is concerned with the offices of leadership: in particular, the qualifications one must possess in order to be admitted to the offices of bishop and deacon.

The word *episkopē* (3:1) appears as a technical term only here in the NT. It refers to the office of an *episkopos*. In secular Hellenistic Greek this word described someone who was in charge of something, an overseer or administrator. In the context in 1 Timothy it refers to the person in charge, the one who regulated the life of a local church community. In particular this involved presiding at the assembly for worship. As a rule this would be a house church, and there were other, similar house churches, each of which had its own *episkopos*.

We should not, therefore, think of the *episkopos* as resembling the bishop of our own time. Instead, both the Church Fathers (e.g., Jerome) and even Luther understood the *episkopos* to be the leader of a local church. It was the duty of the *episkopos* to exercise the office of preaching, that is, to lead the community through word and sacrament. The Pastorals also adopted Paul's idea of the local church, according to which the Church comes into existence through the preaching of the gospel.

Unlike *episkopos,* the word *diakonos* has a specifically Christian meaning, even though it had never figured in religious language before this time. The *diakonos* was the one who served at table. In that sense the Christian *diakonoi* probably served at the eucharistic table as well. Their *service* was related in a special way to that of Jesus.

These two offices are found in the letters of Paul (e.g., Phil 1:1), where they are closely related. The qualifications for both offices are similar (1 Tim 3:2-7 and 3:8-13). *Didache* 15.1-2 also attests the close relationship of bishops and deacons as those responsible for the worship services.

Thus in 1 Timothy as well the discussion of these offices is incorporated within the larger theme of worship: "[that] you may know how one ought to behave in the household of God" (3:15). The description of the community's place of assembly, and even the community itself as the *house* or *household* of God makes it clear that the structure of the community was similar to that of a household or family. That is why the virtues of a bishop (3:2-7) correspond to those of a good head of household (v. 4). It was not only customary for the community to assemble for worship in private houses (cf. Acts 2:46), but from the beginning the community of the faithful was structured like a family. Since in the ancient world the house as an economic unit (a place not only for living, but also for working) was the basic cell or building block of community life, the catalogue of virtues was compiled in terms of household order (3:4-5, 12; cf. the household codes in Eph 6:1-9; Col 3:1–4:1; 1 Pet 5:5). As early as Aristotle it was divided into three parts corresponding to the three types of relationships in the household: masters and slaves, husband and wife, parents and children.

Here it was a matter not only of living inoffensively, but also as models that would be attractive to the pagan world outside (vv. 7, 13). The table of duties for the bishop was directed especially to this outward aspect: because the bishop, corresponding to the father of the family, represented the community in the outside world, he must be measured by the behavioral expectations of that world. Accordingly not all the virtuous qualities mentioned here are formulated in terms of the duties of church office; instead we find concepts derived from a pre-formulated catalogue of public obligations. That is also the source of the Hellenistic terminology. Popular philosophical ethics presumed that everyone should be virtuous, regardless of profession or gender (cf. also Titus 1:7-9). But the bishop should be *above reproach* (v. 2), that is, immune to slander.

This frame encloses the other virtues demanded of the bishop, one of which is that he should be "the husband of one wife" or "married only once." This is probably not a special ethical principle for *episkopoi,* but simply forbids polygamy, which was not permitted for any Christian (Matt 5:27-32; Mark 10:6-9). The demand that he be "temperate, sensible, and respectable" (v. 2b) describes the virtuous ideal of late antiquity. In Christian usage the meaning of these concepts was altered, even within the NT. Thus for example in 1 Thess 5:6, 8 Christians are urged to "be sober" (*nēphō,* the verb) in light of the imminent end, whereas they are called to be "temperate" or "sober" (*nēphalios,* the adjective) in 1 Timothy in preserving the faith in face of the challenges of an ongoing history. *Sōphrōn* ("sensible") could be interpreted as thoughtfulness or good sense about life, while *kosmios* ("respectable") originally referred to keeping order in household and finances. The hospitality that is also demanded of the bishop (v. 2b) was regarded by Greeks and Jews as a sacred obligation. For the Jewish and Christian communities it was also connected with sheltering and caring for itinerant missionaries (Matt 10:11; Acts 16:15; 21:7, 17; 28:14). Ability to teach was especially important to this author because the teaching office, that is, the preaching of the gospel, was to be the central duty of the community leader. The expressions "not a drunkard" and "not quarrelsome" have verbal parallels in Titus 1:7, where greed is also condemned. The requirement that the bishop should not be a new convert (v. 6) was probably meant to insure that he could demonstrate stability in combating "other" teaching.

The *deacons,* who were to undergo careful testing before entering on their office (v. 10) were judged by standards similar to those for the bishop. This office could also be filled by women (v. 11). We may conclude from this that it was not a teaching office (cf. 2:12). From the command that deacons not be greedy (v. 8) we might conclude that the deacons had duties connected with money, that is, with receiving the community offering and distributing it to the poor.

4. The Church as the Locus of Truth in the World (3:14-16)

At the conclusion of the rules for the community there follows a theological foundation: "I am writing these instructions to you so that, if I am delayed, you may know how one ought to behave in the household of God" (vv. 14-15). That is, the Church should be guided by the principles established by the apostle even after his death. In this way the Church will be secured over time as the locus of truth, that is, the Christ-event. The Church is regarded as the place where, even in the course of history and in the midst of the pagan world, the revelation of God that has occurred in Christ will be preached and believed (as expressed in the Christ-hymn in v. 16b).

The *hymn* quoted in 1 Tim 3:16 is introduced by a principle universally accepted *(homologoumenōs)* by the community, that "the mystery of our religion is great." The revelation of this mystery is chanted in song: it has been revealed *(ephanerōthē),* has appeared *(ōphthē),* and consequently (as a further act of revelation) it is preached *(ekēruchthē)* among the Gentiles. In the first strophe (lines 1 and 2) we find a contrast between *sarx* and *pneuma,* with the former understood as the earthly sphere in contrast to the heavenly. The epiphany takes place in the world, in the earthly life of Jesus, and with "vindication" or "justification" *(edikaiōthē)* in the realm of the Spirit *(pneuma)* the earthly epiphany is confirmed.

In the second strophe (lines 3 and 4) *ōphthē* is to be read as a term for theophany (cf., for example, Gen 12:7; 17:1; 18:1; 26:2; Exod 3:2). The exalted Lord appears before the angels, and he will be proclaimed on earth as the one thus acknowledged in the heavenly sphere. He will, in fact, be proclaimed among the Gentiles *(ta ethnē)*—a reference to Paul's Gentile mission, but also a confirmation of Christ's claim to be ruler of the whole creation (cf. Rev 5:13-14).

The third strophe (lines 5 and 6) celebrates the result of the epiphany: the proclamation has brought about faith in the whole *kosmos* (the human world), and Christ is taken up into the *doxa* (glory) of God.

Thus the community understands itself as the one who, through the divine epiphany in Jesus Christ, has become the place of God's presence and the guarantor (*stulos,* "pillar") and bulwark *(hedraiōma)* of the truth (v. 15). (Similarly the Community Rule at Qumran, 1QS 5.5-6, speaks of the "foundation of truth . . . for the community of the eternal covenant" and "the house of truth in Israel.")

In all this the author is thinking of the concrete, worshiping community. Like Paul, he holds fast to the principle of the local church. Thus the "house" or "household" (= church) as the gathering place of the community refers both to the building itself and to the community, the *familia Dei*. Now, in following the instructions of the apostle, it has acquired established structures through liturgical prayer and offices of community leadership modeled after those of the household.

Because, as we have seen, the house was the basic unit of ancient society without which community life could not function, one might ask whether the adoption of the same structures would not have led to a situation in which it was impossible to distinguish between the political assembly and the worshiping community. In positive terms this would mean that the Christian community was oriented to the world and that Christian faith enabled them to fulfill the tasks given to human beings in this world by God the creator—or rather, to fulfill them better than human beings can do on the basis of their nature alone (cf. Titus 3:2-3).

It is difficult to say where the lines must be drawn in every case—where the adoption of socially-structured norms involves taking over structures of injustice at the same time, as in the case of the laws of slavery. Can we be content to say that Christian slaves acquired an inner freedom to go on being slaves (1 Cor 7:21-22; cf. 1 Tim 6:1-2; Titus 2:9-10), so that Christian faith found no concrete expression with regard to that question? The same would then be true in the case of the subordination of women: is the equality spoken of in Gal 3:28 only a spiritual, internal process? And does Christianity express itself outwardly in the very fact that one adopts the existing norms and structures of society without creating controversy? But we should also ask whether something that was acceptable in light of eschatological portents and in the expectation of an imminent end—namely to make no direct attempt to exercise influence to change unjust relationships—is defensible also if history is seen to be ongoing? Or, to put it the other way around, in a changed world can one cling to structures that were *at one time* accepted uncritically and under pressure to conform to the surrounding society? Can one *now* interpret them as genuinely Christian because, after all, they are in the canon of Scripture, and hold to them for supposedly theological reasons?

Advice for Timothy: 4:1–6:2

1. False Teachers (4:1-5)

True doctrine is once again outlined to distinguish it from false teaching. The former is described as prophetic prediction ("the Spirit says," v. 1), a traditional *topos* of early Christian apocalyptic prophecy (cf. Matt 24:23-24). From this we may conclude that the "prediction" of the future is really a description of current happenings (cf. 1 John 2:18; 4:1-3; 2 John 7). The accusation of hypocrisy (v. 2) is a standard motif in early Christian polemic against heretics. The false teachers' purpose is to gain power over others and make them dependent on themselves (2 Tim 3:6), or to achieve personal gain (1 Tim 6:5). The meaning of the reference to forbidding marriage (v. 3) is not clear. Refusal of certain types of food in line with ascetic inclinations is denounced as behavior that denigrates the creation (4:3).

The false teachers appear to be people who formerly belonged to the community and to some extent still operate within its sphere. They are known by name (1 Tim 1:20; 2 Tim 2:17; 4:14). They are described as wooden and earthen vessels in the household of God (2 Tim 2:20). They are interested in knowledge (*gnōsis:* 6:20). They believe that they know God (Titus 1:16), but their deeds deny it. They are counted among those who will appear "in the last days" to lead the faithful astray, and they are accused of every vice characteristic of those people (1 Tim 4:1-5; 2 Tim 3:1-5). They are ascetics and thus against marriage and certain foods (1 Tim 4:3). They deny the bodily resurrection (2 Tim 2:18). Myths and genealogies are important to them (1 Tim 1:4). They cause confusion with their questioning instead of being obedient to God (1:4; 6:4-5). They regard piety as a business, are greedy and even rapacious (cf. 2 Tim 3:6). It is difficult to identify them with any particular heretical group, even though some of these characteristics were later attributed to the Gnostics.

2. Protection Against False Teaching (4:6-11)

The following sections are characterized by direct address to and commissioning of Timothy.

The opponents appear once again as people who tell godless "old wives' tales" (v. 7), to which are contrasted the words of faith *(logoi tēs pisteōs),* good teaching *(kalē didaskalia),* and godliness *(eusebeia)* in vv. 6-7. This last appears ten times in the Pastorals: 1 Tim 2:2; 3:16; 4:7, 8; 6:3, 5, 6, 11; 2 Tim 3:5; Titus 1:1; cf. 5:4; 2 Tim 3:12; Titus 2:12.

The practice of godliness (v. 7), in contrast to asceticism and the rejection of creation, means leading a life guided by the gospel. The *value* of godliness is its promise of present and future life (v. 8). Earthly life is not devalued: in fact, it receives its strength and vitality from godliness. The godly or pious person has the promise of the lifegiving power of God even now (cf. Mark 10:29-30; Luke 18:29-30). It is true that Timothy is personally challenged to practice godliness, but the author speaks of it in general terms that apply to every Christian. This is emphasized by the use of the passive phrase "worthy of full acceptance" (v. 9). Timothy is to work and struggle so that this form of godliness, in contrast to the merely physical (prayers and) practices (*sōmatikē gymnasia,* v. 8) of the opponents, and the knowledge of the promise that godliness brings with it will come to fruition and be known to all people (v. 11). The "we" of v. 10 shows Paul including Timothy as a partner in the struggle (from earlier times, cf. Acts 16:1-3, and especially now), but it also encompasses the holders of Church offices. Their struggle is also marked by the sign of hope in God as savior of all humanity (v. 10).

3. Imposition of Hands and the Authority of Office (4:12–5:2)

The author suggests that if Timothy is thus obligated to model behavior and teaching someone might object that he is too young and despise him for that reason (v. 12). Because Paul is prevented from coming himself, and he has appointed Timothy as his representative, he takes this occasion to formulate extensive regulations for community leadership. The apostolic instruction makes it clear that it is not one's age that is decisive for the acceptance of community duties, but only the appointment to office through the laying on of hands (v. 14; cf. 1:18). Authority was now achieved through office.

The imposition of hands *(epithesis tōn cheirōn),* as in 1 Tim 4:14, is understood according to 2 Tim 1:6 as the conferral of God's gifts *(charisma),* and the effects of these gifts (cf. 2 Tim 1:7) are spirit *(pneuma),* power *(dynamis),* love *(agapē)* and self-discipline *(sōphrosynē).* According to 1 Tim 4:14 it is the elders who impose hands; in 5:22 it is Timothy himself; in Acts 6:6 and 14:23 it is the apostles—but the true giver of the gift of *charisma* is always God. It is characteristic of the Pastorals that, differently from Paul's letters (1 Cor 12:12-31; Rom 12:3-8) in which all the members of the community participated in a variety of offices, these letters speak only of a single charism of office that enables and obligates the recipient to leadership and teaching in the community. The community in turn is instructed to listen to the officeholder (i.e., to his preaching) and obey his directions.

The practice of imposition of hands goes back to the custom of laying hands on the head of the sacrificial victim (e.g., Lev 1:4; 8:18; Exod 29:15) as a ritual that transferred both power and evil or guilt. In Judaism the ritual was practiced at the installation of scribes. This practice in rabbinic circles of handing on authority from teacher to pupil was strongly oriented to the preservation of an unbroken succession.

Because the third generation already looked upon itself as a Church that would continue to exist in history, installation in office through the imposition of hands as described in the Pastorals was of ongoing significance for the Church's concept of its identity. The officeholder was the heir of the apostle and the administrator of the apostle's heritage. According to 2 Tim 2:2 he was responsible for handing on right teaching.

With the admonition not to speak harshly to an older man (1 Tim 5:1) the author takes up a theme from 4:12a. Just as the community should not despise Timothy because of his youth, he should not take his office as justification for treating an older man in a lofty manner. Timothy is, by the same token, to be a model for younger men and women of various ages (5:1, 2). Certain characteristics are mentioned that make the author's concept of office abundantly clear for us:

1. The office of leadership in the community acquires its authority solely through installation in office, which involves the laying on of hands.

2. Its central function is reading Scripture during worship, teaching (preaching), and admonition.
3. The officeholder should be a model for the community
4. He should not rule over the members of his community, but serve them.

4. The Order of Widows in the Community (5:3-16)

Three times (vv. 3, 9a, 11) the text stresses that *widows* are to be paid, *widows* should be enrolled, and younger *widows* should be rejected. These are direct instructions from the apostle to the apostolic disciple in his function as community leader. The theme is *real* (v. 3) widows. The issue is one of criteria of differentiation according to which women are to be received into the community order of widows. Since this institution has material consequences for the community, it must be determined who is truly a widow. One criterion for exclusion is the existence of the widow's own family who can shelter their mother or grandmother (v. 4). The plural of the verb "to learn" leaves it unclear whether the widows are to be received into the family to care for the children or grandchildren, or whether it is the reverse: the children are to care for their mother. However, v. 8 and the whole context seem to favor a parenetic statement directed to the widows themselves. In order to be recognized as true widows they must be alone and pious and devoted entirely to prayer (v. 5). Contrasted with real widows are those who live for pleasure (v. 6) and are not inclined to care for their families (v. 8). Theologically interesting in this connection is the establishment of a specific connection between good works and faith ("has denied the faith," v. 8).

After these considerations, conclusions are drawn in vv. 9-10 about (positive) conditions for the acceptance of widows: they should be sixty years old, married only once, having done good works for their own children as well as for strangers and the saints, helped those in need, and other good deeds. The negative catalogue in vv. 11-13 involves younger "widows" who presumably have pledged to remain unmarried, but having changed their minds now want to marry and thus are under suspicion of not being faithful to Christ, lazy, prone to gossip, and concerned with extraneous matters. These latter women should marry, bear children, and take care of their households (v. 14). An important factor in the point of view from which these recommendations are made is the public reputation of the community (v. 14c). The command to remarry should be seen against the background of what has already occurred in the community: widows who may well have been recognized as belonging to the community order of widows have gone after the devil (v. 15), that is, turned to false teaching. All this makes it clear that it is necessary to take more care of those widows as well. The women in the community who already have widows in their houses are urged to do this, with the important side effect of saving the community the cost of their support and enabling it to turn its attention to those who are real widows (v. 16).

5. The Elders (5:17-25)

In this section the author speaks of the members of the community's council of elders, using the title *presbyteroi* (elders: cf. Acts 15:6; 21:18). Some should be chosen from this group who are well equipped to fill the office of presider, that is, persons who have devoted themselves to preaching and teaching (v. 17). Their work should be compensated; this is founded (in v. 18) on a twofold citation, from Deut 25:4 (1 Cor 9:9) and the Jesus logion in Luke 10:7. Is the preaching of the gospel becoming attached to a fixed office?

While the presbyter's good work should be *paid for,* the author also recommends that there be a rule for cases in which *complaints* are raised against an elder and the possibility of guilt cannot be excluded. First he refers to the OT legal procedures in Deut 19:15 (cf. Matt 18:16). Afterward, if the fault persists, the guilty party must be admonished in the presence of others, as a deterrent (vv. 19, 20). All this must be done without prejudice or partiality (v. 21). The author also counsels Timothy not to be too hasty in installing in the preaching office a presbyter who is under suspicion (v. 22), because in such a case he will participate in the other's sin. He is to keep himself pure.

The digression in v. 23 again underscores a certain anti-ascetical "sound teaching." With the two sayings in vv. 24-25 the author on the one hand gives a reason for his advice in v. 22, while on the other hand he points to the eschatological horizon and God's final judgment, when everything that is hidden will be revealed. In this way all the Church's disciplinary actions are placed in eschatological perspective.

6. The Slaves (6:1-2)

Having dealt with the community widows and elders, the author now turns in conclusion to the slaves within the congregation, that is, slaves as a class in the community. This is not a fundamental theological evaluation of the status of a Christian as slave, as in 1 Cor 7:20; rather this is an instruction intended to assure that the community's teaching and its faith in God should not be seen by outsiders in a bad light (v. 1b). Therefore the slaves should continue to honor their own masters (as heretofore) and not misunderstand Christian solidarity in faith as if it demanded that equality be put into practice immediately. Instead they should serve their masters all the more because they are also Christians (i.e., believers, beloved, and doers of good works). Thus among one another (among the sisters and brothers) such behavior is expected that no offense will be given to those outside: in other words, the pre-Christian class divisions remain in place among Christians as well.

Slavery was a social condition without which the economy of the household was inconceivable. Christian communities were therefore far from proposing to change the existing structures of society. On the contrary, it was hoped that other people could be won over to the faith. With the phrase that closes this section, "teach and urge these duties" (v. 2b) all the instructions the author has given are confirmed as "sound teaching" (cf. v. 3).

It is obvious that we can no longer maintain this separation between faith and social responsibility. Even though the ideas of that time may also have had something to do with the status of Christians as a minority, today's Christianity cannot withdraw from its responsibility in the world.

The Greed of the False Teachers: 6:3-10

In sharp contrast to *sound* teaching, the false teachers and their doctrine are now described as *sick* or *unsound,* a sickness characterized by a love of controversy and wrangling over words. In the vice list that follows the signs and effects of this sickness are described. Concepts are chosen that characterize a ruinous situation in the community (vv. 4b, 5). The polemic culminates in the accusation of greed. The false teachers practice piety like a business, solely for the sake of profit. This was a charge against which Paul had had to defend himself (1 Thess 2:5; 2 Cor 12:16-18). Beginning with the second century it was a standard element in polemic against heretics (e.g., in the work of Irenaeus). The concrete basis for the accuracy of this charge can be found in 2 Tim 3:6-9 (cf. 1 Tim 5:13): wealthy women are said to be the entry point for the esoteric ideas of false teachers, and the latter were probably not unpaid.

The author turns from the false teachers' greed to the dangers of wealth as such. Wealth can sink *(buthizousin)* the ship of life (v. 9). This takes up the image of shipwreck of faith from 1:19, concentrated here on the danger of covetousness as the root of all evil, by means of which not a few have wandered from the faith (v. 10). The ideas of ruin (cf. 1 Thess 5:3; 2 Thess 1:9; 1 Cor 5:5) and destruction (cf. Phil 1:28; 3:19; Matt 7:13; five times in 2 Peter) point to the eschatological judgment at the end; hence it is an ultimate and final destruction. The extraordinary emphasis on covetousness above all other vices is traceable to Hellenistic influence. Dio Chrysostom calls it "the source of the greatest evil." Therefore, because the false teachers' activity in making a business of piety is connected with the vice of covetousness, those who follow them are threatened with the judgment of God at the last day. Against this background is revealed the model character of the true community leader who is content and happy with what is necessary in the way of clothing and food (vv. 6-8).

Reminder of Calling and Acknowledgment of the Duties of Office: 6:11-16

The next section is the culmination and high point toward which the letter has been moving: namely the handing over of the "sound teaching," the (Pauline) gospel, which is to be secured in authoritative form for all time through the connection of the gift of divine grace with ordained ministry. It is formally divided into three paragraphs:

1. Verses 11-12 are characterized by a number of favorite words of the author and can be regarded as his own formulation.
2. Verses 13-15a, in clear contrast to the imperative style of the preceding verses, begin in "I" form; presumably the speaker (bishop?) utters a traditional liturgical formula, or part thereof.
3. The admonition moves into a concluding doxology (vv. 15b-16).

Verses 11-12: In contrast to the vices of the false teachers, which Timothy is to shun *(pheuge),* we now find listed the virtues that the man of God (*ho anthrōpe theou;* cf. Deut 33:1; Josh 14:6; 1 Sam 9:6; 1 Kings 17:18; 2 Kings 4:7; Neh 12:24) should pursue *(diōke)*. The antithesis shun/pursue corresponds to the style of popular philosophical advice and echoes the two-ways pattern.

The combat motif reappears in v. 12, although *agōn* is more reminiscent of sporting events (cf. 1 Cor 9:24-27; Phil 3:12-15; 2 Tim 4:7). The goal of the faith-combat is eternal life (*epilabou tēs aiōniou zōēs,* v. 12). This future goal corresponds to a calling in the past *(eklēthēs)* and, connected with it, confession *(kalē homologia)* before many witnesses (v. 12). Timothy is thus reminded of a task to which he once assented. This is probably the same action to which the author referred in 1:18 and 4:14, characterized by the reading of the words of the prophets and the imposition of the presbyters' hands.

Verses 13-15a. The fact that this confession can also include suffering and persecution is brought home by reference (in the same words) to the *kalē homologia* (v. 13) of Christ Jesus under Pontius Pilate (cf. 2 Tim 2:8-10; 3:10-11).

With this reminder of his ordination and the reference to Jesus' confession Timothy is admonished, in conclusion, to fulfill his commission blamelessly *(anepilēmptos)* until the *parousia* (and not only until Paul's return as in 3:14). Now Jesus Christ himself, and not Paul, is the one who determines the time and limitations of office and its duties. There is probably not so much an idea here that Timothy himself will see the time of Jesus' epiphany as that the office of preaching is to be exercised by any and all officeholders until that final day. And insofar as it is God who brings about *(deixei)* the epiphany of Jesus in God's own time (*kairois idiois,* v. 15; cf. 2:6), it is God who determines the date.

Verses 15b-16: God's sovereignty is praised in a concluding doxology (vv. 15b-16; cf. 1:17). This is a hymnic confession made up of seven acclamations of Jewish and Hellenistic origin. God is *makarios:* blessed in divine perfection and unapproachability (cf. 1:11) and *monos dynastēs:* the sole and unlimited ruler (cf. Luke 1:52; Sir 46:5; 2 Macc 12:15; 15:4, 23). From Near Eastern court style come the predicates "king of kings" and "lord of lords" (Ezek 26:7; Dan 2:37), but they are also applied to God in the OT (e.g., Deut 10:17; Ps 136:3; cf. Rev 17:14; 19:16). Unusual, however, are the participial forms *basileuontōn* and *kyrieuontōn.* "Who alone has immortality" (v. 16) could be a polemic statement against the imperial cult. "Dwelling in unapproachable light" (cf. *1 Enoch* 14:15ff.) and the fact that "no one has ever seen or can see [God]" (cf. Exod 33:20) emphasize the heavenly glory of God. Here the word *aoratos* (invisible) of 1:17 is recalled and developed. In the concluding doxological predicates *timē* and *kratos* (cf. 1 Pet 4:11; Rev 1:6; *1 Clem.* 20.12; 61.3; *Did.* 9.4–10.5) the believer confesses the God to whom alone glory and power belong. In proper style, the doxology ends with "amen."

The Positive Aspect of Wealth: 6:17-19

The author begins another new topic, not continuing his direct address to the apostle's disciple (vv. 11-15), but adopting the form of indirect advice: "command them . . . ." However, the wealthy are not addressed as a special class within the community nor is this a continuation of the discussion of the dangers of greed on the part of ordained ministers (6:5-10). Nevertheless, this generalized warning about wealth could be a corrective in light of the pointed criticism expressed earlier, because here the author finds a positive side to it: wealth is a precondition for doing good and performing good works, and therefore is a provision for the future, that is, "the life that really is life" (vv. 18, 19).

Concluding Admonition and Greeting: 6:20-21

The final paragraph (6:20-21) summarizes the purpose of the letter very succinctly. This letter ending is unlike that in any other letter written under the name of Paul. There are no personal greetings or remarks. Even 2 Timothy (4:19-22) and Titus (3:12-15) are unlike it in this regard. It is striking that Timothy is here (v. 20) directly addressed a second time, as in the proemium (1:18). The thought has come full circle: what has been entrusted to Timothy (cf. 2 Tim 2:12, 14), namely the gospel, is to be guarded. The author warns Timothy against turning to Gnosis, which some have already professed; is this a reference to apostate community leaders (cf. 1:3; 2 Tim 4:14)? The danger is real. False teaching has already attracted followers. But although for this author it is a clear matter of either/or, the formulation "gone astray" or "missed the mark" is moderate and connected with the hope that those who have left may yet be won back (cf. 2 Tim 2:25). Thus Timothy, as the apostle's disciple and as representative of other community leaders, is once again urgently reminded, in closing, of his responsibility for right teaching and good order in the Church.

BIBLIOGRAPHY

Dibelius, Martin, and Hans Conzelmann. *Die Pastoralbriefe*. HNT. 4th ed. Tübingen: Mohr (Siebeck), 1966. ET: *The Pastoral Epistles*. Translated by Philip Buttolph and Adela Yarbro; edited by by Helmut Koester. Hermeneia. Philadelphia: Fortress, 1972.

Quinn, Jerome D. "Timothy and Titus," *ABD* 6, ed. D. N. Freedman. New York: Doubleday, 1992.

[See also the bibliography for the article "Introduction to the Pastoral Epistles."]

2 Timothy

Enrique Nardoni

FIRST READING

Second Timothy is part of an epistolary collection called "Pastoral Epistles" (see "Letters in the NT" and "Introduction to the Pastoral Epistles") although it has its own profile, for it contains Paul's epistolary testament. This feature makes the letter of special interest for the reader. In this epistle Paul on the eve of his death (2 Tim 4:6-8) bequeaths his apostolic last will to Timothy as his most beloved child and authentic heir. In preparing his bequest he reflects on his personal relationship with Timothy, mingling his own recollections with Timothy's past (1:3-6, 13; 2:2; 3:10-11, 14), and includes him in his concerns for the future (3:1-9). These recollections and concerns are parts of Paul's testament, which should be compared with other farewell words such as those of Moses (Deut 31:1-8), Joshua (Josh 23:2-16), David (1 Kings 2:1-9), Tobit (14:3-11), Jesus (Luke 22:14-38; cf. John 13–17) and Paul to the elders of Ephesus (Acts 20:18-35). These farewell discourses share a common pattern: the approaching hero's death, remembrance of the past, prophecy of the future, words of consolation, recommendations and exhortations for the successor or successors. What Paul bequeaths is his gospel and his apostolic instruction. The gospel referred to is described as a deposit *(parathēkē)* that has been entrusted by God to Paul to be preserved unchanged and that Paul in turn entrusted to Timothy. Now Paul mandates him to transmit it intact to new office-holders in the Church. The instructions are Paul's *didaskalia;* they deal with the Church's ministerial structures and contain directions to preserve the gospel and combat false teaching.

Second Timothy stands out among the Pastoral Epistles also because of its frequent reminiscences of the material of the Pauline epistles. This frequency responds to a strategy employed by the pseudonymous author (see "Introduction to the Pastoral Epistles") to adapt Pauline material for use in his own day (the adapted passages are indicated in the Second Reading). This adaptation implies an intentional continuity with the historical Paul. Even more, because this adaptation is presented as Paul's last will and testament, it makes of 2 Timothy, together with the other Pastorals, the conclusion of the collection of Pauline epistles. Although this commentary considers the Pastoral Epistles as pseudonymous, nevertheless it follows the mode of the text and keeps the pen names of Paul and Timothy as if they were the sender and receiver of the epistle.

The earliest probable evidence for 2 Timothy occurs in Polycarp's *Letter to the Philippians.* Renowned patristic commentators on 2 Timothy include John Chrysostom, Theodore of Mopsuestia, and Ambrosiaster, and its outstanding medieval exegete is Thomas Aquinas. All of them stress the personal character of this letter and Paul's example of pastoral concern for and dedication to the flock. In the present Lectionary, Year A, the second reading of the Second Sunday of Lent is 2 Timothy 1:8b-10 (on the call to suffering leading to life). The reading is addressed to catechumens and the faithful preparing to participate at, or to renew their participation in, the baptismal mystery of the paschal feast. Texts from 2 Timothy are read also in Year C and Year II. These readings are addressed to the faithful who are on the journey of faith between Pentecost and the Second Coming. In Year C four texts are from 2 Timothy: the Twenty-seventh Sunday (2 Tim 1:6-8, 13-14, on keeping the faith received); the Twenty-eighth Sunday (2 Tim 2:8-13, on suffering for the elect); the Twenty-ninth Sunday (2 Tim 3:14–4:2, on reading the Scripture and preaching the Word); and the Thirtieth Sunday (2 Tim 4:6-8, 16-18, on the faith and courage of Christ's martyrs). In the ninth week of Year II, in the daily cycle, four readings are selected from 2 Timothy, partially overlapping the abovementioned Sunday readings in Year C.

Outline

1. Greetings (1:1-2)
2. Thanksgiving and introductory instructions of Paul's last will (1:3-14)
3. Personal notes (1:15-18)
4. The body of the epistolary testament to Timothy (2:1–4:8)
   a. Paul's last will concerning the succession of teaching (2:1-7)
   b. Paul's bequest concerning his view of suffering (2:8-13)
   c. Paul's legacy on combating false teachers (2:14–3:16)
   d. Concluding words of Paul's testament (4:1-8)
5. Personal notes (4:9-18)
6. Final greetings and blessing (4:19-22).

SECOND READING

Address and Greeting: 1:1-2

While following the pattern of the Pauline epistles (see "Letters in the New Testament"), particularly that of the Pastoral Epistles, the address and greeting of 2 Timothy stress the importance of Paul's role as Christ's apostle in the fulfillment of God's plan of salvation and bring out Timothy's unique relationship to Paul: he is not only the legitimate and loyal child in faith (1 Tim 1:2; Titus 1:4), he is also his "beloved son." The emphasis on the particular relationship prepares for the role of Timothy as the legatee of Paul's testament related to matters of history of salvation.

Thanksgiving and Instructions as Introductory Part of Paul's Testament: 1:3-14

The thanksgiving (1:3-5) is extended by instructions that prepare the body of the epistolary testament (1:6-14).

(a) Faith and loyalty make Timothy a good candidate for Paul's legacy (1:3-5). In his thanksgiving Paul rejoices at the thought that Timothy shares with him the same ancestral faith and is moved by Timothy's affectionate loyalty to him. This strong ancestral faith and firm and devoted loyalty are factors that motivate Paul to make Timothy his legatee. The phrases of this thanksgiving echo the thanksgiving of Rom 1:8-11. Now Paul on the eve of his death, in the Roman jail, longs to see Timothy as formerly he had longed to see the Roman church (Rom 1:11).

(b) The powers and the model Timothy can count on (1:6-14). Timothy has been given in the ceremony of appointment, through the Pauline and presbyteral imposition of hands, the capacity of sharing Paul's authority as herald and teacher. The purpose of his appointment was to preserve and transmit untarnished the gospel and the apostolic instructions. In order to fulfill his obligations Timothy counts on two sources of power and the motivation of a model. The powers derive from the Spirit received by Paul's imposition of hands and from the gospel entrusted to him. The model is the example of Paul. Subsequently the Apostle urges his beloved son and legatee not to be ashamed of the gospel but to join Paul's suffering in order to open himself to the power of life that the gospel contains. In these verses there are adaptations of texts of other Pauline epistles. The phrase "I am not ashamed" echoes Rom 1:16 ("I am not ashamed of the gospel"). The reference to the power of the Spirit as an aid to sharing in suffering for the gospel's sake seems to be an adaptation of Romans 8:12-17. The difference is that while the latter text refers to the Spirit given to every Christian, in 2 Timothy the power of the Spirit is given to the leaders of the Church to authorize and validate their teaching and their persons as apostolic ministers (2 Tim 1:14; 2:1-2; 1 Tim 1:18). The statement about being saved "not according to our works but [by] grace" (1:9-10) rephrases Eph 2:4-8. These adaptations connect the Pastoral Epistles with the Pauline epistles and establish the continuity of Paul's teaching in new circumstances of the Church.

Personal Notes: 1:15-18

Paul's personal notes in 1:15-18 and 4:9-18 envelop the body of his testament. In 1:15-18 the apostle confides in Timothy the bitter experience of his last days: his sharing in Jesus' suffering includes abandonment by his friends in Asia at the time when he most needed them for spiritual support. All of them left him except Onesiphorus. Abandonment by his friends in this crucial time makes it all the more imperative that he bequeath his gospel and teaching to a reliable and loyal child in faith. Timothy should not be discouraged by the desertion of many but be encouraged by the good example of one motivated by his faithfulness and love of Paul.

The Body of the Epistolary Testament: 2:1–4:8

The body of the letter contains the main points of Paul's testament on behalf of Timothy.

(a) Paul's last will concerning the succession of teaching (2:1-7). Paul begins the body of the letter with the first statement of his last will to Timothy. He orders his favorite son to "entrust to faithful people who will be able to teach others" the gospel and the *didaskalia* received from the apostle. As Paul's legatee Timothy not only has to struggle to preserve intact and teach faithfully what he has received, but also to insure a succession of teaching, which implicitly includes a continuity of the legitimate teaching office. Energized by the divine grace received through Paul's imposition of hands, Timothy will be able to perform his duties that entail hardship and trial. Paul exhorts Timothy to assume full responsibility and to join him in suffering for the gospel. To this effect he employs the illustration of the athlete in 2:4-7, which echoes a similar exhortation in 1 Cor 9:24-27.

(b) Paul's bequest concerning his view of suffering (2:8-13). In the midst of the present and prospective trial and sufferings for the cause of the gospel Paul encourages and comforts Timothy. On the one hand he gives assurance that the chains of the Roman jail do not prevent the gospel from being preached. The process of revelation of the gospel continues through the Church. God is committed to it; God is the one who effects the work of salvation. On the other hand suffering and death for the gospel open the way to life by the power of Christ's resurrection. In this regard Paul quotes what is probably an early Christian hymn that says that union with Jesus' suffering will assure our partaking in his glory: "If we have died with him, we will also live with him; if we endure, we will also reign with him" (2 Tim 2:11-12). But Paul's perspective of hope and consolation goes beyond the personal benefit of the one who suffers. In the vein of 2 Cor 4:10-12 Paul extends the benefit of suffering to others, even to the whole body of believers (2 Tim 2:10). His suffering, united with Jesus', is a way of intercession for the final salvation of Christians in the communion of saints (2 Cor 1:6; 4:10-12; Col 1:24). "Death is at work in us, but life in you" (2 Cor 4:12).

(c) Paul's legacy for combating false teachers (2:14–3:16). This polemical section is parallel to 1 Tim 4:6-16. Paul refers to the basic task of the true teacher, enjoining Timothy to "[explain rightly] the words of truth" (2:15). Accordingly Timothy has to remind the teachers of this obligation, for some wrangle over words and end up ruining the faith of the listeners. Paul recognizes that the Church is a mixed body with teachers of varied quality, but he wants to assure Timothy that in spite of this the Church is stable because it is built on "God's firm foundation" (2:19), which is God's true revelation entrusted by Christ to Paul. Each trustee is responsible for the deposit received. God, however, takes care and makes it possible for the revelation to be preserved uncontaminated until the *parousia* (1:12). The officeholders, empowered by the Spirit, have an important role in this regard. It was alluded to in 1 Tim 3:15 where the Church was called "the pillar and bulwark of the truth." The "firm foundation" in 2 Tim 2:19 bears a double inscription. The first states that "the Lord knows those who are his" (2 Tim 2:19a), giving assurance that he protects those who are true believers. The second inscription calls for precautions against the false teachers enjoining one to "turn away from wickedness" (2:19b) that perverts the true doctrine.

Paul continues the metaphor of the Church as a building with the parable of the Church as a household (2:20-21). The purpose is to teach that the variable quality of ministers and the simultaneous presence of true and false teachers in the Church are part of the design of God, the owner of the household, who has a wise divine plan therein. This thought gives the assurance that everything is under God's control for the good of the elect.

Reinforcing the assurance that even in the worst situation the Church is under God's protection, the author puts into the mouth of Paul a prophecy of the last days he wishes us to understand as being fulfilled in his own time (2 Tim 3:1-9; 1 Tim 4:1-3), for the predicted deceivers are already present (2 Tim 3:6). In his prophecy Paul characterizes the humanity of the last days as massively corrupt and lists a catalogue of vices analogous to those used by Jewish writers in the intertestamental period and by Greco-Roman philosophers at large. Corrupt people have the ability to appear as if they were good practitioners, even competent teachers of true religion. Their work is dangerous because it deprives the word of God of its power. This gloomy description ends with the optimistic remark that their effect is limited (3:9).

Distinctive to 2 Timothy and to the Pastoral Epistles in general is that there is not a substantive debate in which the false teachers are confronted with the preaching about Christ. The advice is to avoid them (2 Tim 2:14, 16; 3:5; 1 Tim 6:20; Titus 3:9). Their opinions are refuted before the community by reference to the traditional teaching. Their influence is averted by holding fast to sound doctrine (3:10, 14) and by practicing virtues. This practice counteracts the bad behavior of the false teachers, according to the author's perception, and strengthens the social bonds of the members of the community as the household of God. Thus Timothy in 2:22 is encouraged to pursue "righteousness" (the ability to judge according to established norms and show correct conduct in relation to others), "faith" (reliability and loyalty), "love" (dedicated, patient, and gentle service), and "peace" (peaceful attitude toward all, generating community harmony). He is urged to endure patiently the persecutions and sufferings that are allotted to anyone who wants "to live a godly life *(eusebōs)* in Christ Jesus" (3:12). The demonstration of good works is a pivotal matter in the Pastoral Epistles; they are the hallmark of the true believers.

Along with the exhortation to hold fast to what he has received Timothy is encouraged as Paul's legatee to read the OT Scriptures with which he was made acquainted from childhood by his mother and grandmother (3:14; 1:5). Paul speaks of the reading of Scripture from the perspective of Christian faith (3:15). He invites Timothy to "reread" the OT biblical text in a Christian context, for Scripture instructs "for salvation through faith in Christ Jesus" (3:15). But he not only invites him to read the text in a new context. In reading it he has to avoid the errors of the false teachers. He must draw from the Bible an interpretation conducive to teaching, reproving, correcting, and training in righteousness (3:16). It seems logical in the thought of Paul that in order to teach correctly or behave properly in the household of God (1 Tim 3:15) Timothy has to read the OT in light of the norms of Paul's gospel and his instruction *(didaskalia)*. Second Timothy 3:16 is the first biblical text that speaks of the divine inspiration of the OT: "all scripture is inspired by God." The concept of inspiration has been pivotal in theological discussions on the sacred character of the biblical text. In the conviction of the Church divine inspiration is considered to be the basis for belief in the divine authorship of the Bible (Vatican Council II, *Dei Verbum* 11). The exhortation to Timothy to read the Scriptures seems to be an adaptation and development of what Paul had said in Rom 15:4-6: "For whatever was written in former days was written for our instruction, so that by steadfastness and by the encouragement of the scriptures we might have hope."

(d) Concluding words of Paul's testament (4:1-8). The last words of Paul's testament begin with a solemn oath followed by five imperatives in a row. The oath with the invocation of God and of Christ as the universal judge makes Paul's statement momentous and moving at the same time. There is an allusion to Christ's power over history reaching its completion in his second coming. This history under judgment gives the frame for Paul's mandate to preach the gospel as a service to the world. His mandate is designed to assure the continuity of this service until the *parousia.*

The first imperative after the oath shows the core of Paul's testament: "Proclaim the message." Paul confers on Timothy his own function as the herald of the ruler of the universe (1 Tim

2:7; 2 Tim 1:11). The proclamation must be persistent in times favorable and unfavorable, accompanied by the actions of convincing, rebuking, and encouraging. All this work must be done with patience and gentleness and must always be intended to give religious and moral instruction (4:2). Facing a hostile world, Timothy has to keep his mind under control and be persistent in accomplishing his duty as herald of the gospel (4:2-3). At the conclusion Paul shows his imperturbability in the face of death, accomplishing the ideal of a great man facing death in the Greco-Roman world. The Apostle sees his death as a sacrificial libation of his blood, a departure for the final harbor. He feels the satisfaction of an accomplished mission and an unwavering loyalty to Christ. Therefore he is fully sure of his glorious reward. The comparison of his death with a sacrificial libation and the satisfaction of a mission fulfilled echo similar phrases from Paul in Phil 2:16-17. John Chrysostom, who calls this letter "a testament of consolation," remarks that Paul, to describe his death, "uses words conducive to consolation and joy so that it is not seen as death but as a sacrifice, a pilgrimage, even a transfer to a better world" (*PG* 62.649, 651).

Personal Notes: 4:9-18

The abandonment by all his friends, his trust in God, and the quotation of Ps 22:21 (in v. 17) make Paul's suffering an imitation of Jesus' passion. In the midst of a general disloyalty, however, Paul is pleased with the loyalty of some. He already has Luke with him and now asks Timothy to come and bring Mark with him (see Col 4:10, 14; Phlm 24). Noteworthy is Paul's request concerning his parchments (leather scrolls), probably of the OT. In this regard Aquinas says: "The closer Paul was to death, the stronger he felt the need of the Scriptures" (*In Omnes S. Pauli Apostoli Epistolas Commentaria* [Turin: Marietti, 1929] 257).

Final Greetings and Blessing: 4:19-22

In the midst of his greetings to several friends in Ephesus, Paul asks Timothy for the second time to come to Rome. At the end Paul adds a plural blessing formula as he does in 1 Tim 6:21 and Titus 3:15, extending his teaching not only to the Church leaders but to all Christians ("Grace be with you *[humōn]*").

BIBLIOGRAPHY

Dibelius, Martin, and Hans Conzelmann. *The Pastoral Epistles.* Hermeneia. Philadelphia: Fortress, 1972.

Kurz, William S. "Luke 22:14-38 and Greco-Roman and Biblical Farewell Addresses," *JBL* 104 (1985) 251–268.

Quinn, Jerome D. "Timothy and Titus, Epistle to," *ABD* 6 (1993) 560–571.

[See also the bibliography for the article "Introduction to the Pastoral Epistles."]

Titus

Mark Goodwin

FIRST READING

General Character of the Book

An interpretive key for grasping Titus as a whole is that of the Church, and more particularly the Church as a visible institution in the world. The centrality of the Church in Titus is clear even though the term itself is never explicitly used in the letter. Ecclesial motifs and imagery permeate the letter and can be seen in a number of instances. For example, the letter opens by speaking of the Church as God's "elect" (1:1; cf. 2 Tim 2:10; 1 Thess 1:4); later there is a mention of the community as God's "people" redeemed by the sacrifice of Christ (2:14; see the Second Vatican Council on the people of God, *Lumen Gentium* 9–17). Another important ecclesial motif is found in the reference to baptism, which enables initiation into the people of God (3:5-6).

There are two significant ecclesial images at work in the letter that are crucial for appreciating its wider aims. They are the Church as the pillar and bulwark of truth (1 Tim 3:15) and the household of God, a Christian family managed by the bishop (1:7). It should be noted that Titus drew upon this latter image of the house/household of God without actually using the corresponding Greek term *oikos;* however the image of the Church as household is implicit in the letter. How do we know this? Titus can be read in connection with the ecclesial imagery of 1 Timothy where the household image was explicit in 3:4, 5, 15. First Timothy 3:15 is particularly significant in this regard, designating the Church as "the household of God, ... the church of the living God, the pillar and bulwark of the truth" (1 Tim 3:15).

Also, that Titus used the kind of household imagery present in 1 Timothy is suggested in Titus 1:7 and 2:1-10. The former refers to the bishop as an *oikonomos,* a household steward (cf. Luke 12:42), implying the bishop's function of managing the ecclesial household. Further there are the so-called "household rules" in Titus 2:1-10 that are paralleled by the shorter rules of 1 Tim 5:1-2. These rules reflect a popular tradition in the Greco-Roman world that defined the duties of individual members in the ancient household. Titus stands among various NT writers who took up and adapted the rules to a Christian framework: see, for example, Eph 5:22–6:9, Col 3:18-24, and 1 Pet 2:18–3:7. The Christian household rules in some cases reflect the social situation of the earliest Christian communities as house churches, e.g., 1 Cor 1:16, 16:5; Col 4:15; Acts 18:8. In other cases the rules reflect the general theological view of the church as a Christian family. In whatever way the household rules are taken in Titus 2:1-10, they nonetheless serve to continue the household motif of Titus 1:7 and reinforce the centrality of the household as an ecclesial image in Titus.

In addition to viewing the Church as the household of God, Titus also saw it as the "pillar and bulwark of the truth," a kind of fortress structure that upheld the truth of the gospel. This ecclesial image in Titus is reflected in passages that speak of "the knowledge of the truth" (Titus 1:1, 14; 1 Tim 2:4; 4:3; 6:5; 2 Tim 2:15, 18) and "sound doctrine" (Titus 1:9, 13; 2:2; 2:8; 2 Tim 1:13). Sound doctrine is understood as a kind of fixed content, the "good deposit" of teaching that is found only in the Church. What is the basis for this particular understanding of the Church? The Church is grounded on the apostolic witness of Paul and its sound teaching ultimately derives from Paul! In the Pastorals Paul is repeatedly highlighted as the foremost apostle of Jesus Christ (Titus 1:1; 1 Tim 1:1; 2 Tim 1:1) and the teacher par excellence (Titus 1:3; 1 Tim 2:7; 3:14-15; 6:3; 3:10; 2 Tim 1:11, 14). Titus 1:3 illustrates this point by presenting Paul as the apostle entrusted with the revealed "word" for preaching and teaching. It is also clear that Paul's apostolic witness could be represented in the figure of a coworker such as Titus or Timothy who served to mediate this genuine apostolic witness.

The image of the Church as fortress of divine truth was particularly useful in the Church's struggle with false teachers (1:10-16; 3:8b-11; cf. 1 Tim 1:3-7; 4:1-5; 2 Tim 3:1-9). Who were the false teachers? Based on the parallels of Titus 1:10-16 and 1 Tim 4:1-5 it has been suggested that they promoted a radical asceticism in the community that renounced the good things of creation such as food and marriage. However, despite numerous references it is not exactly clear who they were and what they taught, and it is hard to decide to what extent the polemic used against them reflects rhetorical conventions commonly used in ancient polemic. What is clear from Titus is that the false teachers taught what was contrary to divine truth and produced serious divisions within the Church (the word "heretic" in Titus 3:10 is used in the sense of someone who is "factious"). The notion of Church as a bulwark of truth could thus serve to strengthen its identity in struggles with heterodox teachers.

In summary then, Titus is a letter of pastoral exhortation that presents an image of Church more structured than the communities of Paul's genuine letters. Titus's ecclesiology is more practical and institutional, revolving around two dominant images: the Church as pillar and bulwark of truth with its teaching offices of bishops and presbyters, and the Church as a great household of God, structured so as to ensure good order in Christian life.

In terms of literary structure Titus can be divided into five major sections:

1. Apostolic Greetings (1:1-4)
2. Exhortations on Order within the Household of God (1:5–2:10)
   a. Teaching Authority within the Household: Bishop and Presbyters (1:5-9)
   b. The Church as the Fortress of Truth: Warnings about False Teachers (1:10-16)
   c. Virtuous Character and Duties within the Household (2:1-10)
3. Theological Motive: The People of God Zealous for Good Works (2:11-15)
4. Further Exhortations on Life within God's Household (3:1-15)
   a. Good Works and Relations with Non-Christians (3:1-2)
   b. Theological Motive: Baptismal Grace as the Motive for Good Works (3:3-8a)
   c. Further Warnings on "Heretics" in the Community (3:8b-11)
5. Final Greetings (3:12-15)

It will be noticed from this outline that there are two passages that stand out as hymnic or confessional formulations and provide the theological premises for the exhortations. Titus 2:11-14 refers to Christ's incarnation as the basis for the Christian life that is zealous for good works, and 3:4-7 speaks of baptism as that which transforms and motivates a life fruitful in good works. The Catholic Church has recognized the significance of these two passages by incorporating them as second readings in the Christmas Masses at midnight and dawn. In his commentary on Titus 2:11-14 Thomas Aquinas expresses well the Christmas meaning of these two passages: "In the nativity of Christ it can be said that this grace of God has appeared in a twofold manner: first, inasmuch as Christ has been given to us, which was the greatest of God's favors; and secondly, because through the Incarnation the entire human race has been enlightened."

Interpretive Contexts for Reading Titus

1. Issues of Authenticity and Canonical Context

In the canon of the NT Titus is one of thirteen letters in the Pauline letter corpus, reflecting the Church's early and long-held belief that Paul's apostolic witness is expressed in Titus. However, while the letter is explicitly attributed to Paul in 1:1-4, serious questions have been raised about

Paul's role in the composition of Titus and the other Pastorals. In certain respects Titus seems to be non-Pauline in language and thought and the letter situation does not seem to accord with facts known of Paul's life and missionary work. For example, only in Titus do we find reference to a Pauline ministry in Crete (1:5) and 2 Timothy refers to a subsequent mission of Titus in Dalmatia (2 Tim 4:10). For these reasons Titus is often considered a Pauline pseudepigraphon.

On the other hand Titus does have a strong Pauline character that cannot be denied. The letter presupposes that Titus was a coworker of Paul, reflecting the actual situation attested in Gal 2:1-3; 2 Cor 7:6-7; 8:6, 16-24; 12:18. In several places the letter to Titus uses Pauline language and ideas, as in 1:1 where the author describes the Church as "God's elect" (cf. Rom 8:33; 16:13); Titus 3:7 speaks in Pauline fashion of "having been justified" by grace (cf. Rom 3:24; 1 Cor 6:11). Viewed in this light the letter is squarely within the Pauline tradition of the early Church.

A few points can be made about Titus's biography. He first appears in Gal 2:1-3 accompanying Paul to Jerusalem; he is there described as an uncircumcised "Greek." Paul never mentions Titus's mission to Crete; however in later Christian tradition Titus was the first bishop of Crete (Eusebius, *Eccl. Hs.* 3.4). Also according to tradition Titus was buried in Crete, in the ancient capital of Gortyna, but his relics were later removed to Venice and deposited in St. Mark's cathedral. The Catholic Church commemorates Titus along with Timothy on January 26.

2. The Reception of Titus in Later Christian Tradition

In the patristic era Titus received its fair share of attention in commentaries and homilies. In the Greek-speaking East, Theodore of Mopsuestia and John Chrysostom represent the major commentators. Chrysostom's six homilies on Titus 1:5-6; 1:12-14; 2:2-5; 2:11-14, and 3:8-11 are accessible in English in Philip Schaff's *The Nicene and Post-Nicene Fathers,* vol. 13. Origen wrote a commentary on Titus that is lost except for scant references in Pamphilus's *Apologia hyper Origenous;* however there are numerous citations and allusions to Titus in Origen's works that illustrate what he considered significant in the letter, e.g., *Contra Celsum* 1.64.

In the Latin West, Jerome seems to have been the major commentator on Titus (*De Viris Illustribus* 135) although his commentary is lost; still, allusions to Titus in his other writings give some impression of his thinking: see, for example, *Contra Rufinum* 23. Although Augustine did not write commentaries on the Pastorals he did draw on Titus in several writings, especially in his polemic against the Manicheans, Donatists, and Pelagians; for example Titus 2:14 was used in his *Epistle* 93 to argue against the Donatists. Finally, Thomas Aquinas's commentary on Titus provides one of the best examples of medieval treatments of the letter.

In patristic and medieval tradition Titus had significance in three primary areas. First, Titus 1:5-9 was often used as a practical guide for ecclesiastical discipline and Church order (e.g., Tertullian, *Adversus Marcionem* 5.21); more specifically Titus 1:5-9 was often cited in discussions pertaining to the requirements and role of the bishop. Second, Titus 3:9-10 was also taken as a practical guide on how to treat heretics (e.g., Irenaeus, *Adv. Haer.* 3.3. 4 and Tertullian, *De praescriptione haereticorum* 6). Third, Titus 2:13 figured in later doctrinal development on the subject of Jesus' divinity especially among fourth and fifth century writers (e.g., Gregory of Nyssa and Theodoret of Cyrus). Also Titus 3:5-6 was often cited among patristic commentators in discussing the doctrine of baptism.

SECOND READING

Apostolic Greetings: 1:1-4

The letter begins by highlighting the apostolic origins of the exhortations that will follow. As an apostle Paul has received a divine commission and is thus entrusted with the divinely-revealed word (cf. 1 Tim 1:1; 2:7; 2 Tim 1:1). Further highlighting his authority, Paul is described as a "servant of God" in the line of Moses (Josh 1:1-2; Ps 105:26; Rev 15:3), David (Ps 89:4; 1 Kings 8:26), and the prophets (Amos 3:7; Jer 7:25; Dan 9:10). The title thus links Paul with other important figures in salvation history.

According to 1:1 Paul's divine commission was to promote the faith of the elect (cf. 2 Tim 2:10). Paul was thus commissioned to build up the Christian elect in their life as the new people of God, and such a task would be accomplished in connection with Titus, Paul's representative in Crete. Titus's special relation to Paul is evident in that he is a "loyal child in the faith," a title that stresses his faithfulness to Paul's teaching (a similar characterization is given of Timothy in 1 Tim 1:2; 2 Tim 2:2).

Exhortations on Order Within the Household of God: 1:5–2:10

Teaching Authority Within the Household: Bishop and Presbyters (1:5-9)

As part of the task of furthering the faith of the elect Titus is charged with organizing the church in Crete by appointing an "elder" or "bishop" in every town, an action that is necessary in light of the disruption caused by the false teachers (1:10-16). These Church leaders are appointed as the primary teachers in the community; their particular task is to preach sound doctrine and refute those who contradict it (1:9). Through the teaching of the elders and bishops the Church's role as pillar and bulwark of truth is exercised.

In the appointment of bishops and elders some primitive elements of Church organization are indicated. What kind of organization is envisioned here? In answering this question one should be careful not to read later ecclesiastical forms back into Titus, and it is unlikely that a monarchical episcopate (the church organized around a single bishop) is presented here even though the letter seems to point in that direction. Nor does Titus mention the three-part Church structure of bishop, presbyter, and deacon that is found in 1 Timothy, 1 Clement, and the letters of Ignatius. Titus only speaks of a bishop (always singular) and elders, omitting any mention of deacons.

Further complicating the question, in 1:5-7 the relation of the bishop and presbyters is obscured by a confusing shift in subject. There is an abrupt shift from "elders" in 1:5 to "bishop" in 1:7 with no explanation or comment. What can be concluded from this shift of subject? To many scholars it suggests that "elder" was another designation for the bishop, the two terms reflecting two functions that were similar and interchangeable in community. This conclusion is supported by the observation that presbyters (elders) and bishops are described with similar functions and attributes in 1 Tim 3:1-7; 5:19-21; Titus 1:6-9.

What is clear about Church organization in Titus is the primary teaching authority of presbyters and bishop; the Church stands as pillar and bulwark of truth concretely through the teaching of the presbyters and bishop. Further, the bishop's role of managing the community is suggested in the Greek term *episkopos,* which means overseer or steward; the bishop oversees the community. In 1:7 the bishop is described as "God's steward," implying the function of managing the ecclesial household just as does the faithful and prudent manager of Luke 12:42. On the role of the presbyter in the early Church see Acts 14:23; 20:17; 1 Pet 5:1-2; *1 Clem* 44:2, 5.

The Church as the Fortress of Truth: Warnings About False Teachers (1:10-16)

In 1:9 the presbyters and bishop are assigned the task of rebuking those who contradict sound doctrine. Who are the latter? Caution is necessary in answering this question. The author's polemic may be reflective of conventional polemical forms as opposed to the actual situation. A good example of this conventional rhetoric is found in 1:12 in the proverb quoted from the poet Epimenides, expressing the crude character of Cretans. Conceivably the polemical accusation of 1:11 could also be part of a conventional polemic concerning the motive of base gain on the part of the opponents.

Further, the author of Titus, as in the other Pastorals, gives no sustained or detailed arguments describing the teaching of the opponents. The author speaks of "myths" and Jewish teaching, which are branded as human concoctions (1:14) and contrary to the sound teaching of the community (cf. 1 Tim 1:4-11). Whoever these false teachers were and wherever they came from, they were clearly agitators who disrupted the community and thus needed to be silenced (1:11).

Virtuous Character and Duties Within the Ecclesial Household (2:1-10)

With 2:1-10 the letter returns to the image of the household, continuing the exhortations in 1:5-9. The latter passage had described the role of the bishop as the household steward and so now the exhortation turns to the other members in the household. What kind of moral character was expected of different groups within the household and what roles were they to play? In response, 2:2-10 presents household rules that provided practical guidelines on the various roles within the community. The larger aim here was to establish an ideal of orderly community life.

In the Greco-Roman era the household was a complex entity involving not only the immediate family but also servants, slaves, and tenant workers. It was thus a much more complex social unit than is typical in modern western society. A tradition of household rules had developed among the philosophers extolling the ideal of order and stability within the family. Such concerns are reflected in Plato and Aristotle who believed that the proper management of the household, usually by the father, was a matter of political and social significance. The ideal of the good citizen was founded on the household. In the NT these household rules were useful for two reasons: first they provided an ideal for social life within fledgling Christian communities whose diverse groups may have experienced some tension with one another; second, the rules may also have served the apologetic function of counteracting the suspicions of outsiders that Christians were socially or politically subversive.

Titus 2:2-10 makes its own distinctive use of household rules, adapting them to the particular needs of the community and addressing groups according to age and gender: older men, older women, younger married women, younger men. Slaves are the exception to this classificatory scheme, representing a social group all their own. Each group was exhorted to follow particular virtues and roles befitting their life in the community. However one virtue is consistently encouraged in all groups: temperance or moderation (the Greek is *sōphrosyne*). The term can be rendered in English as modesty or sensibleness, stressing the qualities of self-discipline and knowing one's limits. Among Greek philosophers this virtue was a prerequisite for citizenship in the Greek polis, designating the virtue of knowing one's place within the sociopolitical order. This virtue is applied to the four groups in 2:2, 4, 5, 6 but also recalls a virtue required of the bishop in 1:8. In a Christian framework life should be characterized by *sōphrosyne,* which meant knowing one's place in the created order and in the community, exercising moderation in all things, and avoiding the ascetic extremes of the heretics. According to 2:12 this virtue of moderate self-discipline is one that should typify the outlook of all Christians.

One other observation should be made about the household rules in 2:1-10. Modern readers of Titus may find certain exhortations difficult, especially those concerning the submissive role accorded to women (2:4-5) and the presupposition of a slave class (2:9-10). There are no easy answers to these concerns, but the following approach is sometimes taken. Modern interpreters stress the time-conditioned character of the household rules, which reflect a patriarchal structure that was common in the Greco-Roman world but nonexistent today. In this light no serious interpreter today would, for example, accept the content of Titus 2:9-10 as a divine sanction for the institution of slavery. Rather the meaning of the passage would be found in the deeper concern for stability and order in the household of God that is expressed in the use of the household codes. [See the excursus "The New Testament Household Codes" in the commentary on Colossians.]

Theological Premise: The People of God Zealous for Good Works: 2:11-15

Within the context of the letter this passage functions as a kind of mini-climax, serving to provide the christological basis for the previous exhortations. Titus 2:11-14 explains why the exhortations in 2:2-10 are consistent with sound doctrine (2:1). In his sacrificial self-giving on the cross Christ has "redeemed" a people of his own in the sense of "electing" them and forming them (1:1). This people of God was formed by Christ that they may be "purified" from wickedness and zealous for good works! (2:14). Practical and moral aspects of Church life are thus grounded in the action of Christ and more specifically, in 2:11, in the appearance of grace. According to this verse, grace "has appeared," which in Greek is cognate with the term epiphany, meaning a manifestation or appearance of deity. The appearance of grace is thus a reference to the incarnation, the first appearance of Christ, which should not be confused with Christ's future eschatological appearance in

2:13. The christological content of 2:11 thus makes the passage an appropriate reading for the Christmas Mass at midnight.

How is divine grace the foundation for a moral life in the household of God? Titus 2:12 speaks of grace "training" in the sense of education. The reference here is to the incarnate Christ's own example of upright living. The appearance of Christ has trained believers to live according to the cardinal virtues of moderation, justice, and godliness. Divine grace has thus enabled the believer to achieve a life of virtue. John Chrysostom's "First Homily on Titus" nicely summarizes this point, observing that in the letter Paul "dwells continually upon the grace of God as being a sufficient encouragement to believers to persevere in virtue." The basis for the exhortations of 2:2-10 is thus Christ's incarnation, expressed in the notion of his "appearing" as God's grace (2:11).

One other important feature of this passage is worthy of note. Titus 2:13 suggests that Jesus himself is the "great God and Savior." This is the only reference to Jesus' divinity in the Pastoral Epistles. Some translators, however, attempt to avoid this striking claim about Jesus' divinity by interpreting it as a double reference to God and Jesus; for example, the NAB reads "the appearing of the glory of our great God and of our Savior Jesus Christ," suggesting a distinction between God and Christ. However, the Greek wording of 2:13 favors a single appearance of Christ as God and Savior (cf. NRSV, "the manifestation of the glory of our great God and Savior, Jesus Christ"), and the majority of Church Fathers take this view, citing 2:13 as evidence of Jesus' divinity (e.g., Gregory of Nyssa, *Adv. Eunomium* 6).

Further Exhortations on Life Within God's Household: 3:1-15

Good Works and Relations with Non-Christians (3:1-2)

Titus 3:1-2 is a continuation of the earlier household rules established in 2:1-10, but here the topic is virtuous behavior in relation to those outside the household, that is, non-Christians. Titus 3:1-2 takes up from 2:14 the earlier motif of God's people zealous for good works and elaborates on the meaning of good works in relation to non-Christians. What constitutes a good work in the author's mind? Members of God's household are urged to submit respectfully to governmental authority (cf. Rom 13:1-7; 1 Tim 2:1-2), and in 3:2 they are to avoid quarreling and to act with gentleness and courtesy toward all people in imitation of Christ's own gentleness and meekness (as described in 2 Cor 10:1). In short, Christians should devote themselves as good citizens to the welfare of the city in a spirit of gentleness and kindness.

Theological Premise: Baptismal Grace as the Motive for Good Works (3:3-8a)

Why should members of God's household behave so kindly toward non-Christians? Titus 3:3-7 provides the theological premise for such behavior. God's gracious love manifested in the person of Christ (2:11; cf. 2 Tim 1:9-10) was offered to all who were non-Christians, including the members of God's present household. Formerly sinners themselves and characterized by a life of vice described in 3:3, the current Church members had been recipients of God's loving kindness that released them from sin. In fact 3:3-7 points to the transformation that occurred by the use of a then/now schema, contrasting the sinful pre-conversion state with the current state of salvation (cf. Eph 2:3). The temporal indicator in 3:4, "but when," points to the decisive moment when Christ appeared in the world (= the incarnation) enabling salvation through baptism. In this light 3:3-7 reflects on the status of those who have experienced the transforming power of grace made possible by the incarnation. It is thus fitting to find Titus 3:3-7 as the second reading for the dawn Mass on Christmas day in the Catholic lectionary.

It is also evident that 3:3-7 reflects an ancient liturgical setting in the Church involving baptism, as is evident from several observations. Titus 3:5-7 speaks of a "bath" or "washing" of rebirth and being "justified" by grace, language that echoes Paul's baptismal language in 1 Cor 6:11. In fact the passage presents a Trinitarian form involving the actions of God, Holy Spirit, and Jesus Christ and recalling the baptismal formula in the early Church (Matt 28:19). An indication of a liturgical setting also comes in the use of language in the first person plural, we/us, representing a dramatic shift from the previous hortatory "you" in 3:1-2; the first plural indicates the communal character of the "washing." Finally 3:4-7 is summed up in 3:8a as "a sure saying," referring to something familiar in the community, as certainly the baptismal experience would be.

How was baptism understood in Titus's community? According to 3:4-7 baptism involved the action of the Holy Spirit within us as "renewal by the Holy Spirit" (3:5). The notion of renewal points to the transformation experienced in baptism, a transformation that results in one becoming an "heir of eternal life" (3:6). These notions of baptism as rebirth and renewal are attested elsewhere in early Christianity, e.g., John 3:3, 5 and 1 Pet 1:3, 23. In the second century Justin Martyr in *Apology 1*. 61 also speaks of baptism in terms of rebirth and new creation. In baptism God acts in recreating the one baptized, transforming the sinner into an "heir of eternal life" and thus one of God's own people (2:14).

Why does Titus speak of baptism at this point in the letter? The logic here is to appeal to a common baptism as the ground for the exhortations in both 3:1-2 and 3:8-15. More specifically the primary function of this baptismal piece is to motivate the readers to good works. In fact 3:3-7 is bracketed by exhortations to good works in both 3:1 and 3:8b, thus displaying the close relation of baptism (3:4-7) to the moral life exemplified in good works (3:1, 8b). As in 2:11-14 the point is made again that Christian moral life is empowered by God's transforming grace experienced in baptism.

Further Warnings on "Heretics" in the Community (3:8b-11)

With 3:8b-11 the practical and ethical aims of the letter again become explicit. Members of God's household, transformed by divine grace, should "devote themselves to good works" that are profitable to others (3:8b). On the other hand they should avoid quarrels that are unprofitable and worthless (3:9). The exhortations here concern the practical issue of dealing with "heretics" in the community who are described as "factious," translating the Greek word *hairetikos* (3:10). The community is to take three steps in dealing with these "heretics" who agitate the community. First it should avoid foolish arguments about things pertaining to the Jewish Law, which were of particular interest to the heretics (cf. 1 Tim 1:7); next, admonitions should be issued with the pastoral aim of turning them from their error (cf. 2 Tim 2:25-26); and finally, if there is no repentance the agitators should be removed from the community.

Final Greetings: 3:12-15

In the concluding passage of 3:12-15 Paul provides personal instructions on Titus's future itinerary but again stress is given to the performance of "good works" (3:14), underlining the primarily practical concerns of the letter.

BIBLIOGRAPHY

Callan, Charles J., ed. *Sermon Matter From St. Thomas Aquinas*. St. Louis: B. Herder, 1950.

Johnson, Luke Timothy. *The Writings of the New Testament*. Philadelphia: Fortress, 1986, 402–406.

Karris, Robert J. *The Pastoral Epistles*. New Testament Message 17. Wilmington, Del.: Michael Glazier, 1984.

Knight, George W. *Commentary on the Pastoral Epistles*. NIGTC. Grand Rapids: Eerdmans, 1992.

Quinn, Jerome D. *The Letter to Titus*. AB 35. New York: Doubleday, 1990.

[See also the bibliography for the article "Introduction to the Pastoral Epistles."]

Philemon

Young Bong Kim

FIRST READING

An Invitation to Read Philemon Afresh

What do you know about the letter to Philemon? You may have heard from your university or seminary professors or introductory textbooks that a slave named Onesimus ran away from his master Philemon. You may have heard that Onesimus had stolen a sum of money from his master. You may also have heard that Paul managed to persuade Onesimus to return to his former master; Paul intended Onesimus to go back to his previous status. You may have heard that in this letter Paul entreats Philemon to accept Onesimus in spite of his wrongdoing; this letter is private correspondence between Paul and Philemon. These are the "facts" that standard textbooks tell about Philemon.

Now I invite you to read the letter afresh in order to find how many of all these standard explanations are true. Read the letter with questions; it will not take much time. Try to make your own judgment about all these matters. If you use your critical mind fully you will find that some of them are questionable. This will make a good start for our study of Philemon.

General Character of the Letter Itself

This letter is the shortest of the whole Pauline corpus. Scholars have rarely doubted Paul's authorship of this letter. Its vocabulary, style, and theology are in accord with those attested in other undisputed letters of Paul. In spite of its short length we find many of the characteristics of Paul's longer letters. The most distinctive feature of this letter is that, in contrast to other letters dealing with congregational matters, it treats a very personal one in a most skillful and comprehensive manner. It is, however, misleading to define it as a private letter. Timothy appears as a co-author (v. 1), and the greeting goes not only to three leading figures, Philemon, Apphia, and Archippus, but also to the whole congregation (v. 2). At the end farewell greetings are given from Epaphras, Mark, Aristarchus, Demas, and Luke (vv. 23-24). Furthermore Paul addresses his readers in the second person plural (vv. 22, 25). All these persons are expected to take part in the seemingly private communication between Paul and Onesimus's former owner. In this sense this intimate missive is an open letter directed toward the whole congregation. It is thus important to take into account the presence of these witnesses in reading this letter.

The reader of this letter will also benefit from reading it in relation to Colossians, especially ch. 4. Although serious scholars have disputed Pauline authorship of Colossians, we are persuaded on balance of its authenticity (see article on Colossians). Colossians contains references to some of the same names that Philemon does. Especially important are the references to Onesimus (4:9) and Archippus (4:17), who play a central role in Philemon. These references are a clear indication of the close relationship between Philemon and Colossians.

General Contexts for Interpretation

Original Historical Context

The immediate historical situation that prompted Paul to write this letter is assumed to be as follows: Paul is in prison (vv. 1, 9, 10) probably in Ephesus but possibly in Rome. He was still allowed, however, to engage in missionary work with his coworkers (Phlm 1, 22, 23; Col 4:7, 10-14). For an unspecified period of time a slave named Onesimus from the Lycus valley (Col 4:9) had been assisting Paul. In the meantime Onesimus was converted by Paul (v. 10), who very much appreciated Onesimus's work for the gospel (Phlm 10-12) and would have been glad to hold on to him as a permanent coworker (v. 13). In order to fulfill this hope, however, Paul could not but arrange for Onesimus to return to the Lycus valley where things could be worked out with his owner in a face-to-face meeting. The owner of the slave was one of Paul's partners in the Lord (vv. 17-18). Paul could ill afford to damage his apostolic credibility as a trustworthy partner in the Lord.

About the same time Paul also found the need to write to the churches of Colossae and Laodicea (Col 4:16; for the occasion, see Colossians). Paul took advantage of this situation to deal with the matter concerning Onesimus. He wrote at least three letters (Colossians, Philemon, and Laodiceans [this last has been lost]) and had Tychicus and Onesimus deliver them by hand to their proper destinations.

Canonical Context

Scholars have long wondered about the reason why such a short and seemingly private letter as Philemon came to find a place in the Christian canon. Ignatius's letter to the Ephesians may possibly offer a clue. He extols the bishop of Ephesus named Onesimus (1:1-3). Under the assumption that Onesimus the bishop of Ephesus was the same man as Onesimus the slave-helper of Paul we may make such a reconstruction as the following (see John Knox, 1959).

Onesimus the slave became a free man as the result of Paul's arrangement in this letter and returned to Ephesus to help Paul. In the following years he came to play a leading role in the churches of Ephesus, and it is plausible that the process of collecting Paul's letters started there. Inclusion of this letter in the final corpus was thus quite possibly due to Onesimus's position and role in the whole process. If this was indeed the case it will aid our understanding of the history of the reception of the text: (1) the place of writing, (2) what Paul intended by his request in the letter, (3) how the owner responded to Paul's request, and (4) how the text of the letter was preserved and how it served to help form the nucleus of the collection at an early stage in its development through the personal interest and support of an important bishop in Asia. It would also help explain how the cost of editing and making copies of these letters was met.

Canonical Intertextuality

As a part of the Christian canon Philemon works as an illustration for various teachings about master-slave relationships in the NT. While Paul did not claim to be an emancipationist he proclaimed that in principle there is no difference between master and slave in Christ (Gal 3:28). Both are equal in that they are all slaves of Christ (1 Cor 7:22a). For this reason, in the ethical admonitions Paul asks slaves and their owners to treat each other as brother and sister in Jesus Christ (Col 3:24; 4:1; cf. Eph 6:8-9; 1 Tim 6:2). Paul's advice thus implicitly prepared the way for a dissolution, if not a nullification, of the slave system by the new-making power of the Spirit.

In his letter to Philemon Paul reveals that he lived up to his teaching. According to the custom at that time Paul was entitled to exercise the full authority of a slave owner over Onesimus. He, however, refused to treat Onesimus as his slave. He called the latter "my child" (v. 10), "my very heart" (v. 12), and "a beloved brother" (v. 16). He was a man who lived as he believed.

Historical Use

Throughout the subsequent history of Christianity Philemon has experienced a strange history of interpretation. According to available ancient commentaries John Chrysostom was the first who introduced the fugitive theory (that Onesimus was a runaway slave). Before his time, when Christians were an oppressed minority, we cannot find such an interpretation. It suggests that the fugitive theory was the product of the age of the slave owning Christian society after Constantine. Such a conclusion is affirmed in the history of interpretation of the letter in the United States during the nineteenth century. The scholars supporting the slave system followed the fugitive slave theory that had become traditional since the time of Chrysostom. On the other hand, the minority supporting the abolition of slavery questioned such a theory. In their view the fugitive theory is not grounded in the text itself. It is a typical example of eisegesis. Unfortunately the legacy of Chrysostom and pro-slavery Americans has dominated most of the twentieth-century interpretation of the letter. Now it is time to change our paradigm.

The interpretation of the letter also bears on the Church's attitude toward social reform. In this context the letter again has been subjected to two opposing interpretations. These controversies center on the meaning of v. 21: "you will do even more than I say." One line of interpretation is to find here an implicit request for manumission of Onesimus and to use it as a proof-text for social reform. The other line rejects such an interpretation and argues that Paul (and thus Christianity as a whole) was indifferent to such social questions. The latter has been the majority opinion, and partly for that reason the slavery system survived a very long time even in Christian countries. This led some Christian slaves to reject Paul. As will appear below, we believe that there is a third way to bring about social reform. It is not true that Paul was indifferent to social matters. Paul, however, attempted to solve this problem in a Christian manner. Christians have their own way to deal with social problems.

SECOND READING

General Historical Background

After the first reading the careful reader may well wonder about the identity of Onesimus's owner. We suggested above that the owner lived in one of the three churches in the Lycus valley. Is he then Philemon or Archippus? The traditional and majority view has favored Philemon because he was the first named in v. 1. Paul's request in Col 4:17 ("And say to Archippus, 'See that you complete the task that you have received in the Lord'"), however, offers another way of interpretation. The only known ministry that Paul wants fulfilled that could have involved Archippus is the ministry concerning the slave owner Paul addresses in his letter to Philemon. It is thus very likely that Archippus was Onesimus's owner. Such a hypothesis explains well the order of names in Phlm 1-2. Philemon and Apphia come first probably because they were the leaders of the church, and Archippus follows as the primary addressee of this letter. Philemon and Apphia with the whole congregation were mentioned because Paul expected them to constrain Archippus to do what Paul requested in the letter. In Col 4:17 Paul asks the Colossians to use their influence with the owner in a similar manner. It is thus more reasonable to take Archippus as the slave owner. "Philemon" became the title of this letter probably because it was understood from the beginning that Paul had instructed Tychicus and Onesimus to place the letter directly in the hands of Philemon because he was the leader of the church in which the real owner worshiped. That would best explain why his name is mentioned first, and why the letter has come to be called the letter to Philemon.

Commentary

Introduction (vv. 1-3)

Paul strategically describes himself "a prisoner of Christ Jesus" (v. 1). By this description he tries to show how much he sacrifices himself for the gospel, that is, the whole of his life. He is implicitly offering here an example for Archippus to follow. It is Paul's habit to reinforce his teaching by his own example (see, for example, 1 Corinthians 8–10). Here is a lesson for pastors to bear in mind: the leader should live up to his or her teachings. By referring to others such as Timothy, Philemon, and Apphia, and to the whole church, he exerts communal pressure on Archippus to do his bidding.

Thanksgiving (vv. 4-7)

One may find a chiasm in the whole section of thanksgiving: A. "Archippus's love" (v. 5); B. "his faith" (v. 5); B'. "his fellowship of faith" (v. 6); A'. "his love" (v. 7). It becomes evident from this structure that Paul tries to put a special emphasis on Archippus's love. This "love" is for the saints. Paul here emphasizes Archippus's love for all the saints based on faith in the Lord Jesus. This stress on love well prepares the ground for Paul's following request. What Paul asks Archippus to do is render a concrete expression of his love for Paul as a partner in the Lord and for Onesimus as a brother and potential partner in the Lord. If what Paul heard about Archippus's love is true, then it should also prove to be true in the case of Onesimus.

Verse 6 because of its ambiguity demands a more detailed discussion. First, "sharing *(koinōnia)* of faith" here means participation in the common faith that demands, in Paul's understanding, participation in reciprocal community relationships. Those coming into this fellowship are to take responsibility for responding to the needs of others in the community. Second, "knowledge" *(epignōsis)* in Paul's usage means recognition of God's will effective in the conduct of the one who knows God. "Every good thing" refers to God's will. This usage occurs again in v. 14, according to which God's will for Archippus in this particular situation is to accede to Paul's request concerning Onesimus. In summary, Paul here prays that Archippus's fellowship of faith may enable him to find and accomplish God's will concerning Onesimus. According to the body of the letter God's will for Archippus is to accept Onesimus as a brother in Christ and return him to Paul as a new partner in the Lord.

Body of the Letter (vv. 8-20)

The body of the letter consists of two parts. The earlier part (vv. 8-16) carefully prepares the ground for a more direct entreaty in the later part (vv. 17-20).

Paul reveals his considerate mind in his choice of expressions in the first part. Most of them have been carefully designed to win Archippus's heart. He refers to his willingness to hold in reserve his apostolic authority (vv. 8-9) in order to get Archippus's free agreement (v. 14). He does not forget mentioning his imprisonment as an ambassador (v. 9). He describes Onesimus as his "child" (v. 10), "useful" (v. 11), his "own heart" (v. 12), a substitute for Archippus (v. 13), and a permanent brother in Christ (vv. 15-16). All these references serve to dispose Archippus to be favorable toward Paul's request on behalf of Onesimus in advance of the request itself.

Paul's rhetoric in vv. 8-9 is comparable to that in v. 19. In both places Paul mentions his status and right as an apostle and spiritual creditor of Archippus. He here wishes the latter to know how much he humbled himself in not ordering Archippus as an apostle could but appealing to him as a partner. Paul has learned such a way of humility from Jesus who, "although he existed in the form of God, emptied himself so as to become a servant and humbled himself to be obedient to the point of death, even death on a cross" (free rendering of Phil 2:6-8).

Why does Paul abruptly break the line of thought in the middle of v. 9 and mention his imprisonment as an ambassador? He already alluded to that fact in the beginning of the letter. Such repetitive references to his imprisonment play a significant role in his whole entreaty. He, who is asking Archippus to sacrifice something for the gospel, is himself sacrificing his own life for that same end. If Archippus regards Paul as a partner for Christ he should participate in Paul's suffering by sacrificing something of himself.

In v. 11 Paul describes in Onesimus's concrete example the drastic change in human existence after Christian conversion. Before conversion, that is, without Christ, Onesimus was "useless." Although Paul does not say in what sense Onesimus was useless we may well take it in general terms: human existence without Christ is for Paul basically and eventually useless. After conversion, that is, in Christ, Onesimus became a new being (2 Cor 5:17) and thus "useful" in the real sense. The best way for a human being to be truly useful is to be in Christ Jesus.

In vv. 13-14 Paul tacitly expresses his hope concerning Onesimus: to have him returned to Paul for ministry on behalf of Archippus. In order for Paul to have Onesimus back permanently Archippus should return Onesimus as virtually a freed slave, now his equal as a co-partner with Paul. While it is not explicit, this is what Paul intends to say in v. 21. We can here view the broad dynamic of Paul's missionary mode of operation. Paul was able to expedite the gospel by forming a network of partnerships in the Lord with people from radically different social classes. Since there was "neither slave nor free . . . in Christ" (Gal 3:28) Paul could make even the most socially revolutionary request of his partners in the Lord. Its implication for today's readers is clear: There still are barriers (social, racial, national, sexual, religious, etcetera) to be overcome as Christians carry forward the ministry of the gospel. For example there is a high and thick barrier between Koreans and Japanese because of the latter's past violent domination over the former. For Korean Christians this barrier is one of the most difficult to overcome in the gospel of Christ.

Paul describes the proper attitude of the Christian slave owner toward his or her fellow Christian slave in v. 16: to treat the slave as a beloved brother or sister. In canonical reading this verse works together with 1 Tim 6:2 which describes the proper attitude of the Christian slave toward the Christian owner. Both owner and slave should not forget that they are in the loving fellowship of faith as sisters and brothers in Christ. The new relationship in Christ overrides and supersedes the former relationship.

In the second part (vv. 17-20) Paul becomes more explicit in his request. First he reminds Archippus that they are in the Christian fellowship (v. 17). Archippus has been spiritually benefited by his fellowship with Paul (v. 19). Now it is Archippus's turn to give something back to Paul as a partner in that fellowship. That "something" is to accept Onesimus (v. 17) and do more than that (v. 21).

Scholars have long debated the meaning of v. 18: In what way did Onesimus do wrong to Archippus? According to the traditional fugitive slave theory Paul here refers to a sum of money that Onesimus has stolen from his owner. Our theory, however, does not presume such a situation. In connection with deciding to send Onesimus back to his owner Paul has presumably discussed the whole situation with Onesimus, wanting to anticipate any foreseeable problems. Apparently Onesimus has shared with Paul that there is a potential problem of an unsettled account, whether due to wrongdoing or not, going back to the time before Onesimus came to work with Paul. Even if Archippus is willing to accede to Paul's revolutionary request, there still remains the question of past indebtedness on the part of Onesimus. In that case, writes Paul to his long-time partner in the Lord, "charge that to my account."

The pastoral implications are to be noted. The revolutionary social consequences that result from implementing the gospel in the practical everyday life of the Church does not result in a blanket cancellation of all past obligations. In Christ we are not constrained to become less responsible for the consequences of our past actions, but more responsible. Apparently Paul realizes that any possible indebtedness on the part of Onesimus can best be handled by Paul's assuming the debt. He does not want to put Onesimus and Tychicus in the position of having to negotiate this difficult matter. Now that he knows that Onesimus has become useful Paul can confidently take on all of the past indebtedness of Onesimus providing his owner will agree to return him to Paul as a partner in the Lord.

Closing (vv. 21-25)

Here Paul gives a final, additional appeal (v. 21), a personal request (v. 22), farewell greetings from coworkers (vv. 23-24) and a blessing (v. 25). The author abruptly shifts attention from Archippus to the whole congregation in the middle of v. 22. Paul intends this letter to be read to the whole congregation, and the latter to provide witnesses of what will be happening between Archippus and Onesimus. Philemon and Apphia, who were probably the leaders of the church, were presumably expected to play the role of mediators or overseers.

We have already noted Paul's unexpressed intention in v. 21: he hopes to have Onesimus back for the service of the gospel. He also expresses his confidence about Archippus's free obedience to his appeal. He does not want to compel his partner to obey the demands of the gospel. Instead he expects Archippus's willing obedience to be evoked by his own redemptive action on behalf of Onesimus. We can see here the power of Paul's teaching: "Be imitators of me as I am of Christ" (1 Cor 4:16; 11:1; Gal 4:12; Phil 3:17; 1 Thess 1:6-7; 2:14).

Paul next mentions his plan to visit the church of which Archippus and Onesimus are members, probably that of Hierapolis (v. 22). This "travelogue" was probably intended to secure Archippus's favorable decision: "remember, I will see you soon!" This is the final constraint. Eventually all those addressed will have to face Paul in the full power of his personal presence. In light of the names of colleagues mentioned in the farewell (vv. 23-24) readers should also note how much Paul respected the network of partnerships for ministry. Those engaged in this ministry should be always open-minded toward all kinds of people, ever prepared to enter into new and more wonderful partnerships leading to ever more effective ways to expedite the gospel.

BIBLIOGRAPHY

Callahan, Allen Dwight. "Paul's Epistle to Philemon: Toward an Alternative Argumentum, *HThR* 86:4 (1993) 357–376.

____. *Embassy of Onesimus: The Letter of Paul to Philemon.* Valley Forge: Trinity Press International, 1997.

Knox, John. *Philemon Among the Letters of Paul.* Rev. ed. New York: Abingdon, 1959.

Martin, Ralph P. *Colossians and Philemon.* Grand Rapids: Eerdmans, 1985.

Moule, C.F.D. *The Epistles of Paul the Apostle to the Colossians and to Philemon.* Cambridge: Cambridge University Press, 1957.

Petersen, Norman R. *Rediscovering Paul: Philemon and the Sociology of Paul's Narrative World.* Philadelphia: Fortress, 1985.

Winter, Sara C. "Paul's Letter to Philemon," *NTS* 33 (1987) 1–15.

Hebrews

Albert Vanhoye

The letter to the Hebrews is particularly interesting from a pastoral point of view because it is a magnificent example of Christian preaching. It nourishes our faith by deepening the priestly aspect of the mystery of Christ, and as a result it calls for a new outburst of Christian life.

Getting Started

In order to get acquainted with this work we should read its first sentences (1:1-4) and immediately after that its last verses (13:22-25). The first sentence does not at all resemble the beginning of the Pauline letters. It does not name the author or the addressees and there is no greeting. This is not the beginning of a letter. It is the beautiful exordium of a sermon. In contrast, the final verses resemble the last verses of the Pauline letters: they contain some news, greetings to be passed on and received, and they conclude by wishing "grace" (cf. Rom 16:20; 1 Cor 16:23, etcetera).

What is the literary genre of the work between this beginning of a sermon and its epistolary finale? Let us read the whole text as we ask ourselves this question. We will ascertain that it is not a mixed genre as we might have expected. With the exception of a short epistolary phrase (13:19) inserted before the sermon's solemn conclusion (13:20-21) the entire body of this work belongs to the oratory genre. We do not find a single element characteristic of an epistolary situation.

We are dealing, therefore, with a fine Christian sermon composed by an itinerant apostle (in 13:17-18, we see that the author does not rank among the community "leaders" being addressed) and sent in writing to distant Christians. On that occasion a few epistolary sentences have been added. The first of these confirms that what precedes is a homily. As a matter of fact, it says: "I appeal to you, brothers and sisters, bear with [this sermon]" (13:22). Exegetes increasingly tend to identify this work as a long sermon followed by a brief message.

What is the structure of this sermon? Thomas Aquinas suggested a two-part division, the first part doctrinal (1:1–10:39) and the second moral (11:1–13:25) as in the letter to the Romans. This division is not entirely groundless but it does not take into account the presence of several exhortations in the so-called "doctrinal" part (2:1-4; 3:7–4:16; 5:11–6:12; 10:19-39). Many modern exegetes, especially in Germany, prefer a division into three parts, each combining doctrine and exhortation and dealing with three successive themes: (1) the word of God (1:1–4:13), (2) the priesthood of Christ (4:14–10:31), and (3) the Christian life (10:32–12:29). Chapter 13 is often considered an appendix. This division, satisfying at first sight, ignores the fact that the author does not wait until 4:14 to speak of Christ's priesthood. That theme is introduced as early as the end of ch. 2 (v. 17).

A methodical study of the author's literary techniques—a study whose main conclusions are now accepted by many exegetes—enables us to recognize that the sermon is divided into five parts with some of them subdivided into several sections. Each of these parts is introduced by a *propositio* (a term from ancient rhetoric meaning "announcing the subject"). It is very important to identify these *propositio* formulas with accuracy and to understand their connections in order to have a good grasp of the author's thought.

(1) According to the rules of rhetoric the first *propositio* is found at the end of the exordium. There the author declares that the "Son" (1:2) has inherited a "name . . . more excellent" than that of the angels (1:4). Thus the author announces that the theme of the first part will be the "name" the glorified Christ has from now on. In other words it will be an exposition of christology. Because this "name" involves several different aspects, a single title will not suffice to define it. A long explanation is needed. The author provides it from 1:5 to 2:18 by comparing Christ's position with that of the angels.

(2) The second *propositio* is found at the end of this first part. There the author declares that "Jesus" (2:9) was to become "a merciful and faithful [or: trustworthy] high priest" (2:17); this is a completely new theme. The second part is divided into two sections corresponding to the two attributes of the high priest: being "worthy of trust" (3:1–4:14) and "merciful" (4:15–5:10), starting with the quality announced last.

(3) We read the third *propositio* at the end of the second part. There the author proclaims that Christ (a) having been made perfect, (b) became the source of eternal salvation for all who obey him, (c) having been designated by God a high priest according to the order of Melchizedek (5:9-10). Immediately after that the author declares: "about this we have much to say . . ." (5:11), thus confirming that this will be the theme of the next part of the sermon. This third part is more important than the others. It starts with a strong call to attention (5:11–6:20) and then includes three sections of doctrinal exposition dealing with the three points mentioned in 5:9-10, beginning with the last: (c) 7:1-28, (a) 8:1–9:28, (b) 10:1-18. This part concludes with an exhortation securing the junction between the doctrine presented and the unfolding of Christian life.

(4) The fourth *propositio* is situated at the end of this exhortation. The author insists on two aspects of Christian life: the necessary "endurance" (10:36-37) and the "faith" by which the righteous live (10:38-39). The fourth part deals with these two aspects, beginning, of course, with the last: the description of the faith of the righteous people of old (11:1-40) precedes the call to endurance in trials (12:1-13).

(5) The fifth and last *propositio* is found at the end of this second section. There the author invites Christians to "make straight paths for [their] feet" (12:13). The beginning of this fifth part specifies the nature of these paths: "Pursue peace with everyone, and . . . holiness" (12:14); this is the subject of this fifth part (12:14–13:18).

The homily's solemn conclusion briefly recalls the teaching (13:20) and expresses a wish corresponding to the exhortations (13:21) before ending with a short doxology accentuated by a final "Amen." The last verses (13:22-25) in epistolary style do not belong to the sermon.

This analysis of the composition leads to the following conclusions:

(1) The author presents a *christological doctrine* in three stages:

First there is a summary of traditional christology expressed with the help of a comparison between Christ and angels. Son of God (1:5-14) and brother of human beings (2:5-18), the glorified Christ has a "name . . . more excellent" than that of the angels (1:4). His glorification (1:5-14) is the fruit of his passion (2:5-18). On the basis of this traditional christology the author establishes the shift to a priestly christology (2:17) whose general characteristics are first indicated (3:1–5:10). Christ possesses the two priestly qualifications necessary in order to exercise mediation. On the one hand, as the glorified Son he is "faithful [that is, rather "worthy of faith"] . . . in the service of [or: in relationship with] God" (2:17; 3:1-6; 4:14-15); on the other hand "in every respect [he] has been tested as we are" (4:15), and he is "merciful" (2:17) and "[able] to sympathize with our weaknesses" (4:15).

In a second exposition of priestly christology (7:1–10:18) the author brings out the specific aspects of Christ's priesthood: a different priestly order not based on genealogical succession but instead founded on "the power of an indestructible life" (7:16), a new type of sacrificial offering that has opened access to the heavenly sanctuary (8:1–9:28); perfect efficacy for the forgiveness of sins and for our sanctification (10:1-18). This second presentation strongly underlines the differences between the priesthood of Christ and the former priesthood. In the final analysis it shows that Christ alone is fully a priest.

(2) To these doctrinal expositions the author is always careful to add exhortations that in most cases have the doctrine as their foundation.

A first exhortation to "pay greater attention to what we have heard" (2:1) is based on recalling the glorification of Christ (1:5-14). A long warning against an "unbelieving heart" (3:12, 19) and "disobedience" (4:6, 11) that would prevent us from entering "God's rest" in the footsteps of Christ (cf. 4:1) is based on the qualification of Christ as a "faithful high priest" (that is, a high priest "worthy of faith"). A brief call to trust (4:16) is based on Christ's qualification as a "merciful . . . high priest" (2:17; cf. 4:15) applied to him because of his passion. Differently from the others, the long exhortation of 5:11–6:20 is not founded on the previously expressed doctrine. Instead it appears as a necessary preparation for understanding the exposition that follows: listeners are not only invited to make an effort of attention but also of conversion so that they may assimilate the substantial doctrine the author is about to present to them.

The most important exhortation (10:19-39) is based on this substantial doctrine (7:1–10:18). It invites listeners to welcome the priestly dynamism of Christ's offering in the reality of their lives by approaching God with faith, hope and love. The author builds the exhortation to endurance (12:1-13) on the extensive praise of faith (11:1-40) with its evident parenetic intention, even though it does not contain any statement of exhortation. The last part of the sermon (12:14–13:18) is entirely exhortative. It does not have a doctrinal discourse as its foundation but only brief references to the previous presentations: "Jesus, the mediator of a new covenant" (12:24; cf. 7:22; 8:6; 9:15) who "suffered . . . in order to sanctify the people by his own blood" (13:12; cf. 2:17-18; 5:8-9; 9:26; 10:10, 14). The conclusion (13:20-21) also manifests the unity between doctrine (13:20) and Christian life (13:21).

We can offer the following outline of this complex and harmonious structure:

Introduction: God spoke to us through the Son (1:1-4)

- I. Brief Exposition of Traditional Christology (1:5–2:18)
  - A. Son of God, the glorified Christ is superior to angels (1:5-14)
  - B. Brief exhortation to acknowledge his authority (2:1-4)
  - C. Christ our brother, having suffered, remains one with us (2:5-18)
- II. First Exposition of Priestly Christology in its Main Aspects (3:1–5:10)
  - A. Like Moses but even more so, Christ the high priest is worthy of faith (3:1-6)
  - B. Lengthy warning against lack of faith (3:7–4:14)
  - C. Christ is a sympathetic high priest; brief call to trust (4:15-16)
  - D. Description of this aspect of the priesthood and application to Christ (5:1-10)
- III. Second Exposition of Priestly Christology in its Specific Aspects (5:11–10:39)
  - A. Preliminary exhortation: call to attention and generosity (5:11–6:20)
  - B. A different priestly order was prefigured by Melchizedek (7:1-28)
  - C. Christ's offering belongs to a new order. It founded the new covenant and opened the way to the heavenly sanctuary (8:1–9:28)
  - D. Christ's offering is totally efficacious against sin and for sanctification (10:1-18)
  - E. Exhortation to enter into the spirit of Christ's offering with faith, hope, and love (10:19-39)
- IV. Examples of Faith and Exhortation to Necessary Endurance (11:1–12:13)
  - A. Examples of faith given by our OT ancestors (11:1-40)
  - B. Exhortation to endurance because Jesus endured the cross (12:1-13)
- V. Exhortation to Live in Holiness and Peace with Everyone (12:14–13:18)
  - A. Warning: do not be unfaithful to the grace of God (12:14-29)
  - B. Brief exhortations to mutual love, conjugal chastity, and the spirit of poverty (13:1-6)
  - C. Exhortation to preserve Christian identity: fidelity to leaders, allegiance to Jesus, offering of praise and a generous life (13:7-18)

Conclusion: May God guide you through Jesus Christ! (13:20-21)

We can tell that the author composed this homily with utmost care, paying close attention to the ministry of the word and showing sincere respect for the listeners. To produce a composition "well-told and to the point" (2 Macc 15:38) the author of Hebrews followed the biblical literary tradition and arranged the work according to the principle of concentric symmetry. As a matter of fact the five parts, each announced by a *propositio,* correspond as follows: the first (I) and the last (V) have similar length and a ternary arrangement; the second (II) and the next to last (IV) are more extensive and are divided into two related themes: to the development in part two on the "high priest [worthy] of our confession [of faith]" (3:1–4:14) accompanied by a warning against lack of faith there corresponds, in the fourth part, a complementary development on the faith of our ancestors (11:1-40). Then to the development on the "merciful high priest" formed by suffering (4:15–5:10), there again corresponds, in the fourth part, an exhortation to endure patiently the trying discipline imparted by God (12:1-13). With its three doctrinal sections (7:1–10:18) preceded and followed by an exhortation (5:11–6:20 and 10:19-39) the third part (5:11–10:39) constitutes an impressive central body. That third part itself is centered on its second expository section (8:1–9:28) which the author designates as "the main point" (8:1) of the whole. At the center of this central section (9:11) and, therefore, of the whole sermon, the author placed the name of "Christ" and his title as "high priest." The author's entire art is placed at the service of the proclamation of faith.

Original Historical Context

It is difficult to situate the letter to the Hebrews in history. The Church assures us that it is an inspired text that forms part of the Bible and communicates to us, along with the other books of the NT, the authentic revelation of Jesus Christ. But we do not know with certainty who wrote this sermon, to whom it was sent in writing, where, or when.

Pauline Origin?

The text itself contains the name of only one person alive at that time, "our brother Timothy" (13:23) and only one geographical reference about other people, "those from Italy" (13:26). The only Timothy who is mentioned elsewhere in the NT—but very often, at least twenty-three times—is a disciple of Paul who had become his fellow apostle. In 1 Thess 3:2 Paul calls him "our brother," an expression we find again in Heb 13:23. In all likelihood it is the same Timothy who is well known by the letter's addressees. This provides us with an indication about the milieu in which the sermon was composed: a Pauline group. In fact, the earliest testimonies assert the Pauline origin of this work even though they do not claim that it was written by Paul himself.

Modern exegesis has observed that the letter to the Hebrews is too different from Paul's authentic letters to be attributed to the apostle. Its style has none of Paul's impetuous spontaneity. It reveals an author who remains in the background of the work and does not claim to have any apostolic authority. The author is the very antithesis of Paul who strongly asserts his authority and willingly speaks about himself.

Author

Some modern scholars do not even accept a Pauline origin in the broad sense of the term, but this point of view is not well founded since the letter to the Hebrews is connected with the Pauline letters in very significant points. Its criticism of the old Law, in particular, is expressed very forcefully (cf. Heb 7:12, 18-19; 8:13; 10:1, 8-9), as strongly as in Galatians and Romans. On the other hand, Christ's redemptive obedience (Rom 5:19; Phil 2:8) is also found in Heb 5:8. The sacrificial presentation of the passion of Christ (Heb 9:14; 10:10) has some support in several Pauline texts (1 Cor 5:7; Rom 3:25; Eph 5:2) and other aspects of christology are the same in the letter to the Hebrews and in the captivity letters. Thus the very solid eastern tradition is confirmed: the letter to the Hebrews has a Pauline origin. Its author belonged to a Pauline apostolic group. No decisive objection allows us to exclude the possibility that this author may have been one of Paul's companions and that the work may have been approved by the apostle. It has been suggested that the final note could have been written by Paul himself. Thus he would have given support to his fellow apostle's sermon by his own authority. This is a plausible hypothesis, although it can neither be proven nor validly refuted.

Many people have attempted to identify the author of the sermon. To the names suggested in the Patristic era (Luke, Clement of Rome, Barnabas), at a later time other names have been added (Philip, Jude, Silas, Priscilla, Apollos). The candidate in the best position appears to be

Apollos because of his Jewish and Alexandrian origin, his knowledge of Scripture, his literary formation (cf. Acts 18:24-28) and his ties with Paul (1 Cor 1:12; 3:4-9; 16:12; Titus 3:13), yet the absence of any early testimony in favor of his candidacy does not allow us to go beyond a slight degree of probability.

Addressees

The only indication of a place for the work is found in the final greetings: "those from Italy" (13:24). This is much too vague. It does not allow us to draw any conclusion about the place from which the letter was sent or about where the addressees lived. According to the traditional title they were "Hebrews," but there is nothing in the text of the sermon to confirm this attribution. The author never speaks about Hebrews, Jews, or "Gentiles," but addresses Christians without being concerned about their Jewish or pagan origin.

These are not recent converts. They have been Christians for a long time (cf. 5:12). They did not know the Lord directly (2:3) and this dissuades us from attributing a Palestinian origin to them. In the early days of their conversion they endured difficulties and persecutions with generosity (10:32-34). Now, because of new difficulties, they are in danger of becoming discouraged (12:1-3). At one point in the sermon (5:11-12) the author even reproaches them for having become negligent, yet what follows discloses that this is an oratorical technique: quickly changing the tone, the author begins to praise their generosity and explains that the intent of what was just said was to stimulate them (6:9-12). The author strongly urges them to reject sin, an irreparable path to perdition (10:26-31; 12:16-17) and warns them against Judaizing positions (13:9-10).

Not one of these traits is precise enough to allow us to identify a Christian community known from other sources. They correspond to a common situation in the second half of the first century. The suggested loci are quite varied (Jerusalem, Rome, Ephesus, Corinth, Galatia, Antioch) and all of them are insufficiently founded.

Similarly, opinions about the date of the work vary greatly, ranging from 52 to 115 C.E. The development of the christology presented in the letter makes a very early date unlikely. The use of this letter by Clement of Rome (ca. 95 C.E.?) goes against proposing a very late date. The way the author speaks of the sacrifices that continue to be offered by Jewish priests leads us to think that the Temple of Jerusalem had not yet been destroyed when the sermon was written. A date just before the Jewish War (66–70 C.E.) seems plausible. The mention of Timothy also goes in that direction, as does the eastern tradition of Pauline origin.

Canonical Intertextuality

The main contribution of the letter is obviously its priestly christology. In order to renew the vital dynamism of sorely afflicted communities in danger of giving in to discouragement the author not only exhorted them and reminded them of the "basic teaching about Christ" (6:1), but also offered them a deepening of doctrine that could anchor them in their faith and strengthen their confidence and generosity.

The author chose a new theme—priesthood—that demanded serious reflection about the relation between faith in Christ and the inspired Scriptures of the OT. Christian preaching was proclaiming that Christ's paschal mystery had fulfilled the Scriptures. Although it was easy at certain points, the demonstration of this "fulfillment" did not seem possible regarding one fundamental aspect of the covenant with God, that of worship and priesthood. At first glance Christians appeared to have no priests and no sacrifices. According to the law of Moses, Jesus could not be a priest because he did not belong to the tribe of Levi. His ministry had not been priestly and his death had been the death of one cursed (cf. Gal 3:13; 2 Cor 5:21), the very opposite of a sacrifice in the ancient meaning of the term. Therefore if one essential element was missing, how could it be said that the Scriptures had been fulfilled?

This problem was even more delicate because the expectation of a priestly Messiah was present in an entire line of Jewish tradition. The Qumran writings, in particular, express this expectation (cf. 1 QS IX, 10-11, 1 QSA II, 11-12; CD XII, 23; XIX, 10; XX, 1) and so does the "Testament of the Twelve Patriarchs."

In reading Psalm 110, recognized as being messianic, the author found a solution. In the first verse of this psalm, apostolic preaching had discovered the prophetic affirmation of the glorification of Christ "seated at the right hand of

God" (cf. Acts 2:34; Rom 8:34, and elsewhere). Verse 4 contains a second divine oracle proclaiming the priestly dignity of the enthroned Messiah. Thus Scripture reveals that the Messiah (Christ) is a priest. To demonstrate this the author moves from v. 1 to v. 4 and back again (Heb 1:3, 13; 5:6, 10; 6:20; 7:11-28; 8:1; 10:12). The author accomplishes even more, submitting the priesthood and worship of Israel to a rigorous analysis by distinguishing the fundamental project, which is valid, and the way to achieve it, which is defective. Then the author shows that by his personal and existential offering Christ brought the project of priestly mediation to its successful conclusion. His offering is the only perfect sacrifice. He himself is the only priest fully approved by God. At the same time the way of understanding the priesthood and sacrifice is profoundly transformed. It is no longer a matter of rites separated from life. The sacrifice on Calvary is based on Christ's total obedience to God by way of his real life and his generous solidarity with us, even to the point of death which is thus transformed into an offering of love and the foundation of the new covenant. We can never insist enough on the fact that the letter to the Hebrews has elaborated a new concept of sacrifice based on the paschal mystery of Christ: no more animal sacrifices theoretically taken up to God by the fire of the altar; instead an offering of the person putting self at the service of divine love for the salvation of others (Heb 2:17-18; 9:14; 10:8-9).

Consequently the author's doctrine has a threefold foundation: the paschal mystery of Christ, the inspired texts of the OT, and the Christian experience of union with God thanks to the glorified Christ.

The author does not limit scriptural citations to Psalm 110, but resorts to many OT texts. These are extremely well chosen; the author fully recognizes their value in terms of divine revelation and is also keenly aware of the newness brought by Christ, a newness making the earlier institutions, sacrifices, priesthood, sanctuary, and the system of the Law obsolete. Still the author takes care to note that this newness was announced in Scripture: in its prophetic aspect the OT foretold the replacement of its own institutions (7:18-19; 8:13; 9:8; 10:8-9).

In manner of thought and expression the author is dependent on Jewish-Hellenistic formation, but here is none of the spiritualizing philosophical allegorization that Philo of Alexandria loved so much. The author remains within the perspectives of salvation history. The connections of this work with the Qumran writings do not suggest a direct relationship; they are more plausibly explained by their common roots in the Jewish traditions of the first century.

On the Christian side, in addition to the already mentioned links with some aspects of the Pauline doctrine, what has been especially observed is a close relation between Hebrews and the Hellenistic tendency represented by Stephen's discourse in Acts 7.

History of Acceptance

Although it does not contain Paul's name, from the earliest days the letter to the Hebrews was linked to the apostle by the tradition of the eastern churches. They resorted to several hypotheses to account for the differences of style. For example, Clement of Alexandria supposed that it was a Greek adaptation of a letter written in Hebrew by Paul, with Luke as the editor. Others spoke of Clement of Rome (cf. Phil 4:3). Tertullian did not hesitate to attribute this work to Barnabas.

The letter to the Hebrews is found among the Pauline letters in $\mathfrak{P}^{46}$, the oldest collection we have of these letters. It is noteworthy that instead of being at the end of the list, as it is in our present editions, it comes in the second place, just after Paul's letter to the Romans. Going back to the second century, this papyrus attests that at that time in Egypt the letter to the Hebrews was already thought to be a Pauline letter. Its place varies in other manuscripts (after 2 Corinthians or Galatians or 2 Thessalonians or Philemon).

In the western churches the absence of Paul's name at the beginning of the text caused ongoing perplexity, reinforced by controversies with some heretics. However, in the end the strength of the tradition of the eastern churches eliminated the doubts. At the end of the fourth century, when the canon of Scripture was officially established, the letter to the Hebrews was placed at the end of the list of Pauline letters. As a result of this there was no further interest in the distinction between "Pauline origin" and "Pauline authenticity." The letter was considered to have been written by Paul himself.

Among the patristic commentaries the one by John Chrysostom is the most important; it is the fruit of his pastoral ministry, based on a series of thirty-four homilies delivered in Antioch. In the Middle Ages, Thomas Aquinas wrote a commentary considered the "masterpiece of medieval exegesis," bursting with patristic references and further expanding the theological analysis of the text. At the time of the Reformation, Luther and Calvin gave very careful commentaries on the letter to the Hebrews.

Certain passages received special attention. The statement in Heb 3:2 that Jesus "was faithful to the one who appointed him" had a prominent part in the controversies of the fourth and fifth centuries because Arians used it to support their claim that the Son of God was only a created being. Interpreted in a rigoristic sense the texts of Heb 6:4-6 and 10:27 (concerning second repentance) stirred up other controversies that were revived during the Reformation. This led Luther to view the letter to the Hebrews as a composite work which, though presenting some splendid texts, also contains "straw or hay." During the first centuries ch. 7 gave rise to strange speculations about Melchizedek. Thomas Aquinas and other theologians became very interested in the definition of faith in Heb 11:1 ("the assurance of things hoped for, the conviction of things not seen").

The presence of Hebrews in the canon of the NT led to emphasis on the sacrificial understanding of the death of Jesus, something already suggested by the words of the Last Supper ("my blood of the covenant" in Matt 26:28 // Mark 14:24 // Luke 22:20 // 1 Cor 11:25) and expressed in a few Pauline texts (1 Cor 5:7; Eph 5:2). On the one hand the new notion of sacrifice elaborated by the author of Hebrews has led some to recognize a sacrificial sense in expressions that, in and of themselves, had nothing in common with the sacrifices of old ("give his life as a ransom," Matt 20:28 // Mark 10:45; "lay down his life," John 10:11, 15; "gave himself" Gal 1:4; 2:20). On the other hand, at times a superficial reading of Hebrews may have caused a retreat to earlier sacrificial notions that do not faithfully express the dynamism of the offering of Christ.

By expressing the priestly dimension of the person and of the work of Christ, Hebrews opened up perspectives that have proved to be very fruitful and have never ceased to be used for Christian thought and spirituality. The proclamation of the priesthood of Christ is already found several times in the First Letter of Clement (1 Clem. 36:1; 61:3; 64) that calls Jesus Christ "the high priest of our offerings, the defender and helper of our weakness" (36:1) and then alludes to the text of Heb 1:3-13. Church Fathers often resort to Hebrews to meditate and preach on the mystery of the passion. In addition, Hebrews' insistence on the priesthood of Christ, "mediator of a new covenant" (9:15), has brought ecclesial tradition to acknowledge that the ministers of Christ, "ministers of a new covenant" (2 Cor 3:6), share his priesthood. This doctrinal development is already present in the consecratory prayer used in Rome for the ordination of bishops at the time of Hippolytus (around the year 215 C.E.) and it was peacefully affirmed in the following centuries. In this and in many other ways the letter to the Hebrews had a profound impact on the faith and life of the Church.

Hebrews has been given an important place in Catholic liturgy. The second reading for the Mass of the feast of the Annunciation is taken from Heb 10:4-10, a text that expresses the oblational attitude of the Son of God from the first moment of the incarnation. Every year at Christmas the daytime Mass includes the proclamation of the beginning of the letter (Heb 1:1-6), which provides a profound view of Christ's divine filiation. Hebrews 2:14-18 was selected for the Mass of the Presentation of Jesus to the Temple. The text underscores Jesus' orientation to his passion out of solidarity with "the children" whom God has entrusted to him. In the Liturgy of the Hours, from the fifth Sunday of Lent to and including Holy Saturday, the Office of Readings proposes a rereading of Hebrews. The liturgy of Good Friday has us listen to the beautiful text of Heb 4:14-16; 5:7-9 on the passion and priestly compassion of Christ. The description of the priesthood given in Heb 5:1-10 is read at the ordination liturgy and also at Masses for vocations and for the election of a bishop or a pope. The Sunday Lectionary assigns a sequential reading of Hebrews for the last seven Sundays of the B cycle and several Sundays of the C cycle (from the nineteenth to the twenty-second Sunday in Ordinary Time). Hebrews has the honor of occupying the first place in the Lectionary for weekdays: from Monday of the first week to Friday of the fourth week in Ordinary Time in odd years. In this way we fully recognize the importance of this splendid text that nourishes the faith of Christians and stimulates their generosity.

Commentary on the Text

Introduction (1:1-4)

This admirably composed exordium, a single sentence in Greek, situates the entire sermon in the perspective of the word God has addressed to us. Here this word is not presented as a revelation of truths but as a means of establishing relationships between persons. Through a parallelism we are invited to compare two stages in these relationships. In the first stage, that of the OT characterized by many and fragmentary divine interventions, God took the prophets as spokespersons. In the second stage, that of God's decisive intervention in human history, God "has spoken to us by a Son" (Heb 1:2). By leaving the article out in Greek the author emphasizes the newness of the relationship that is no longer that of a mere prophet but of a "Son" and makes us expect further details that are provided at once.

All the rest of the sentence is, in fact, devoted to the Son. His present position is that of "heir of all things" (1:2; cf. Dan 7:13-14), that is to say, son and heir of David (2 Chr 17:11-14), Abraham (Gen 15:3-4), and Adam (Gen 1:26; Ps 8:5-9). This last messianic position corresponds to the initial role of the Son: he can inherit all things because God has created all things through him (Heb 1:2). Here the author embraces the sapiential tradition (Prov 8:27-31; Wis 7:21; 9:9; Sir 24:2-6) and goes beyond it. Surpassing it still further, the author defines the very being of the Son in terms of a personal relationship with God, much closer than that of Wisdom (Heb 1:3; cf. Wis 7:25-26). In fact the Son cannot be separated from the divine "glory" since he is its ongoing "radiation." The Son is not merely the manifestation of a particular attribute of God but is "the exact imprint of God's very being." Coming down from this summit to return to the connection with creation, the author declares the Son's permanent role in sustaining the universe (Heb 1:3b; verb in the present tense) and then describes the Son's historical intervention in our world (verbs in the past tense). The author evokes the two aspects of the paschal mystery in terms that discreetly prepare the priestly christology of the sermon and its reasoning based on Psalm 110. By its use of a comparison with angels to define the situation of the glorified Son the end of the sentence announces the first part of the sermon (1:5–2:18) that is going to be a presentation of traditional christology.

For centuries this magnificent text has been selected for the Mass of Christmas day. The two following verses (1:5-6) which have been added to the reading suggest an inaccurate interpretation of v. 6. In fact this verse does not deal with Jesus' humble coming into our world but rather his glorious enthronement in the "coming world" (cf. Heb 2:5).

The Son's Relationship with God (1:5-14)

First of all the author considers Christ's present position in relation to God by quoting scriptural texts read in the light of Christ's paschal glorification. In the Hebrew Bible two of these texts are applied to God (Deut 32:43 LXX; Ps 102:25-27), but their context allows us to apply them also to the risen Lord (cf. Ps 102:12-13, "but you, O Lord . . . *will rise up* . . ." [the LXX has the past tense: "have arisen"]), the one who has become the judge of the world (cf. Deut 32:41, "my hand takes hold on judgment"). The quotations are arranged in order to express three antitheses that follow in inverse order between the glorified Christ and angels: Christ—angels (1:5-6); angels—Christ (1:7-12) and Christ—angels (1:13-14). The author, a talented orator, prompts the listeners' cooperation by posing a rhetorical question dealing with biblical oracles at the beginning (1:5) and at the end (1:13). Christians have to know how to situate these oracles in the Bible and how to identify their addressee, who is not an angel but the enthroned Messiah-King.

In these oracles Christ is proclaimed Son of God (1:5; Ps 2:7; 1 Chr 17:13). Angels are to worship him (Deut 32:43 LXX) because his resurrection has made him "the firstborn" (Ps 89:27) and introduced him into "the coming world" (1:6; cf. 2:5). Angels are mutable and subordinate beings (1:7; Ps 104:4) whereas Christ is henceforth immutable and all-powerful (1:8-12; Pss 45:6-7; 102:25-27). The oracle about sitting definitively at the right hand of God applies to Christ (1:13; Ps 110:1) whereas angels are sent here and there to serve the chosen ones (1:14).

According to this passage the "name" inherited by Christ (cf. 1:4) includes, first of all, the titles of "Son of God" (1:5), "firstborn" (1:6), "God" (1:8, 9), and "Lord" (1:10). The scope of these titles is manifested in facts: the glorified Christ sits on the eternal throne and holds the divine scepter (1:8); because of his passion he received the anointing that assures his preeminence (1:9); creator of the universe, he will remain immutable when through his action everything will be transformed (1:10-12). Therefore his relationship with God could not be closer. The comparison with angels enables us to have a greater appreciation of his superior rank.

Brief Exhortation (2:1-4)

From Christ's close relationship with God the author immediately derives a consequence for Christian existence: the need to better welcome the salvation announced by the risen Lord and passed on "by those who heard him" (2:3). The comparison of the glorified Christ with angels continues: the role of angels at Sinai (cf. Deut 33:2-3 LXX; Acts 7:38, 53; Gal 3:19) provides the exhortation with an argument *a fortiori* that leads to an impressive rhetorical question ("how can we escape . . . ?"). The support given by God to evangelization by way of wonders and spiritual gifts (2:4; cf. Mark 16:17-20; Acts 5:12) reinforces the argument even more.

The Son's Relationship with Us (2:5-18)

The author moves on to the second aspect of the "name" of Christ. Contrary to the spontaneous opinion of many exegetes, the divine titles are not enough to define this name because the risen Christ is not only the Son of God. At the same time he is also a human being who is glorified because of his sufferings and his human death. From that perspective too his name is "more excellent" (*diaphorōteron,* 1:4) than the names of angels.

The author quotes and comments on Psalm 8 (Heb 2:6-9) and follows this with a theological reflection (2:10-18). Psalm 8:4-6 describes human destiny as God has planned it. The author observes that v. 6 was fulfilled to the letter in the human destiny of the Son of God. Of him and of him alone can we literally say that he was "*made lower* than the angels" because in his glory as Son he was first superior to them (cf. 1:3). By sharing "flesh and blood" (2:14) and by accepting suffering and death (2:9) he was made lower than the angels, but this lowering had as its result the paschal glorification that assures him, the glorified human being and not the angels, of all power in the coming world (2:5, 8). In this interpretation the author does not restrict the meaning of Psalm 8 to the individual case of Jesus, but on the contrary underscores that in Jesus the human vocation has been fulfilled "for everyone" (2:9).

The theological reflection continues (2:10-18) along the same lines, insisting on the necessary solidarity between the "pioneer of salvation" and the "many children" God wanted "to bring to glory" (2:10), declaring that "the one who sanctifies" and "those who are sanctified" have the same origin (2:11). If this were not the case, sanctification could not be communicated. Finally, the author emphasizes that the glorified Christ is not ashamed of calling us brothers and sisters (2:11-12), a bond willed by God (2:13) and established by the incarnation (2:14) with a view to a liberating mission whereby death is overcome by way of solidarity, even unto death (2:14-15). A first conclusion (2:16; cf. 2:5) comes back to the question of the relationship between Christ and angels to establish the distance between them once again. Christ did not come to help angels; he became part of a human family. He bears a human name, "Jesus" (2:9), and the corresponding designations "mortal" and "human being" (2:6), "pioneer of their salvation" (2:10): human beings are his "brothers and sisters" (2:11-12).

A second conclusion opens up a new perspective, that of priestly christology (2:17-18). Christ was to become a "high priest." The required condition is very surprising. In order for anyone to attain the dignity of a high priest the OT prescribed ritual ceremonies of setting apart (Exodus 28; Leviticus 8–9) and it forbade any contact with death (Lev 21:11). In contrast, the path that Christ was to follow was that of becoming like his brothers and sisters in every respect, to the point of suffering and death (Heb 2:14, 17-18).

Implicitly the author makes us understand that the Son's incomparable relationship with God in glory (1:3) did not make him a high priest. An equally close relationship with the people of God was indispensable because the priesthood is a mediatory function requiring excellent rapport between the two parties. The preexisting Son was only in relation with God. The glorified Christ possesses the necessary twofold relation in its fullness. Son of God (1:5-14) and brother of human beings (2:5-16), he is the ideal mediator.

A High Priest Worthy of Our Confession [of Faith] (3:1-6)

The author starts the work's initial exposition of christological priesthood (3:1–5:10) by inviting the audience to "consider" the first necessary qualification for exercising mediation: the high priest must be "worthy of faith" and accredited by God. Since Christians have a "heavenly calling" (3:1) they need a high priest who has this qualification. They find it in Jesus "who *is* [the Greek verb is in the present tense] faithful to [or: accredited by] the one who appointed him" (3:2). The title of "apostle" given to Jesus corresponds to that facet of the priesthood reflected in Mal 2:7. Instead of "worthy of faith," the first meaning of the Greek *pistos,* here many translations use "faithful," which is another meaning of the same word. However, this is erroneous because the author is referring to the episode in Numbers 12, where *pistos* means "worthy of faith" rather than "faithful." In response to Miriam and Aaron who contested the authority of Moses as God's spokesman (Num 12:2) God proclaims that Moses "is worthy of faith in all my house" (Num 12:7 LXX; Heb 3:5). One has to recognize the same qualification in the glorified Christ in a more excellent way since the oracle of the prophet Nathan was fulfilled in him. Nathan presented him as the future builder of the house of God (1 Chr 17:12; Heb 3:3) proclaiming his divine filiation (1 Chr 17:13; Heb 1:5; 3:6); God said: "I will *make him worthy of faith* in my house" (1 Chr 17:14 LXX; Heb 3:6). The "house" built by Christ in the paschal mystery (cf. Matt 26:61 // Mark 14:58; Matt 27:40 // Mark 15:29) is not a material temple, but "we are his house" (Heb 3:6; cf. Eph 2:21-22; 1 Pet 2:4-5) if we remain firmly united to him.

Warning Against Lack of Faith (3:7–4:13)

Christ, therefore, fully deserves our confession of faith. After the doctrinal presentation in 3:2-6 the author moves on to a long exhortation based on the inspired words (cf. 3:7) of Ps 95:7-11, which are still valid. For Christians the divine "voice" referred to in the psalm is the voice of the glorified Christ mentioned in the previous verse. In the Greek version the psalm alludes to a single episode of the Exodus, the one detailed in Numbers 13–14 and recalled in Deut 1:20-45 and Ps 106:24-26. Shortly after the Israelites left Egypt and arrived near the Promised Land, God invited them to take possession of this land. However, their explorers' report caused them to draw back and react with suspicion. God became furious and he sent the people back to the wilderness to wander for forty years.

The commentary is divided into three paragraphs whose boundaries are marked by inclusions (3:12-19; 4:1-5; 4:6-11). At the center of the first paragraph (3:15) and the last (4:7) the beginning of the quotation is repeated, and its conclusion is repeated at the center of the second paragraph (4:3).

In 3:12-19 Christians are cautioned against "unbelief" (3:12, 19, an inclusion). A parallelism is established between their situation as "partners of Christ" and the situation of the Israelites who were led by Moses. The sentences correspond to each other according to concentric symmetry (vv. 12 and 19, 13 and 17, 14 and 16). Verse 18 serves to prepare the following paragraphs.

In 4:1-5 the parallelism focuses on the good news (the verb in Greek is *evangelizein*). At the time of the Exodus the good news was: "The LORD your God has given the land to you; go up, take possession" (Deut 1:21). The Israelites did not believe it (Heb 4:2; Ps 106:24) and as a result they were not able to enter the land. The good news for us Christians is the paschal victory of Christ (Heb 4:14). If we believe this good news it allows us to enter the rest of God (4:3). A midrashic comparison between the text of Ps 95:11 and that of Gen 2:2 suggests a connection between the rest evoked in the psalm and God's own heavenly rest (Heb 4:3-5).

In 4:6-11 Christians are warned against "such a disobedience" (4:6-11, an inclusion) of God's invitation. This invitation still stands. In fact Scripture speaks of a "today" that is much later than Joshua's time. This suggests that the establishment of the people in Canaan was not their authentic entering into rest. Concerning the glorified Christ we can say that he rests from his labors as God rested after the creation (4:10; cf. 10:11-13); therefore one should make every effort to follow him in order to have a share in his rest (4:11).

As a conclusion to his commentary on the psalm the author proclaims the praise of the "word of God," emphasizing its efficacy and the formidable capacity of discernment (4:12-13).

Conclusion and Transition (4:14-16)

The conjunction "since" indicates that v. 14 concludes the section that began in 3:1. The words "high priest," "heavens," "Jesus," and "our confession" are taken up again from 3:1 and form an inclusion marking the end of the section. The title "Son of God" recalls 3:6. By presenting Jesus as the high priest glorified at the right hand of God (divine majesty is higher than the heavens: Pss 8:1; 113:4) the author recalls the doctrine presented in 3:1-6; then the lengthy exhortation (3:7-4:13) is summarized with the invitation to "hold fast to our confession." The author thus discloses its link with the doctrine: a glorified high priest, Jesus is worthy of faith for the sake of our relationship with God and we must, therefore, profess our faith in him.

Verse 15 is the answer to a possible objection, namely, whether the elevated position of the glorified Christ is an obstacle to our relationship with him since we are so weak. It would be a valid objection if Christ had broken his relationship with us when he passed through the heavens. But that is not the case. The glorified Christ remained our brother since it is by sharing our trials that he obtained his glory (4:15; cf. 2:9, 17-18). Thus he possesses the second priestly qualification. Not only is he worthy of our faith; he is also able "to sympathize with our weaknesses." Thanks to him the divine throne that frightened sinners (cf. Isa 6:1-5) has become "the throne of grace" that believers can and should approach with total trust.

A Truly Human High Priest (5:1-10)

The description of "every high priest" (5:1-4) and its application to Christ (5:5-10) correspond to the second priestly qualification (4:15). Already in the general definition of 5:1 the human aspect of the mediation is evoked twice before the brief mention of the relationship with God. Among the various possible purposes of sacrificial worship (adoration, thanksgiving, etcetera), only one is mentioned, the one that is more akin to human misery, that is, the high priest's offering "for sins." The following verses insist on the high priest's ability to relate to sinners. They are sympathetically referred to as "ignorant and wayward" (cf. Luke 23:34; Acts 3:17). The author succeeds in finding in ritual laws an attestation of the solidarity of the high priest with sinners. In fact, the Law prescribed that the high priest should first make a sin offering for himself (Lev 9:7-8; 16:6), and then for the sins of his people (Lev 9:15; 16:15). Another aspect of the high priest's humanity consisted in his being required to be humble. The episode of Korah's revolt and his punishment (Numbers 16) demonstrates that the priesthood is not a career open to ambitious people. God and God alone can confer the priesthood.

In this description the author takes care to avoid the details defined by the old ritual (Levitical origin, ritual bath, priestly vestments, anointing, animal sacrifices), keeping the description in general terms in order to be able to apply it to Christ later on. The connection between Christ and Aaron referred to here is only one of similarity. "As Aaron was, so also Christ . . . ." Commentators since Thomas Aquinas who speak of superiority are not faithful to the text. There will be a different perspective in the following part (cf. 7:11). Continuity is the first necessary link between the NT and the OT.

The application to Christ is made first with regard to humility: "Christ did not glorify himself" (5:5, a literal translation; cf. Phil 2:8). As in the case of Aaron, Christ was appointed high priest by God. Here for the first time the author introduces the scriptural proof of the doctrine to be used in ch. 7, the oracle of Psalm 110 in which God proclaims the priesthood of the Messiah-King (Heb 5:6). In the previous verse, to designate God the author uses a long periphrasis containing another oracle regarding divine filiation (Heb 5:5; Ps 2:7) already quoted at the beginning of the first part (Heb 1:5). Both of these oracles apply to Christ at the time of his paschal glorification. Filiation and priesthood are closely interrelated although they are not the same. The Son has always been Son, "the [radiation] of God's glory" (1:3). He was not always a priest, but became a high priest (cf. 2:17).

For Christ the path leading to the priesthood was a path of humility and suffering (5:7-8), a path of effective solidarity with human weakness. His priestly offering (cf. 5:1-3) consisted of "prayers and supplications" (cf. Matt 26:36-44) emerging from a situation of distress, and they were accompanied by a "loud cry" (cf. Matt 27:46-50) and "tears." In this way Christ's whole passion is presented as a priestly action that assumes human anguish in the presence of death and transforms it into an offering of prayer. This prayer was offered to God with "reverent submission" (*eulabeia* in Greek: Heb 5:7). Jesus did not pretend to impose his own will on God (cf. Matt 26:39); instead, he let his Father choose the best solution. This is the reason why he "was heard." The divine solution did not consist in preserving him from death; it transformed his sufferings and death into the instrument of definitive victory over evil and over death itself. Distorted by sin, human nature had to "learn obedience" so that it could forever be reintroduced into God's intimacy. Since Christ was "a Son," he did not need this painful learning for himself, yet he accepted it (5:7; cf. 2:17) because of his generous solidarity with us. Thus he became the "perfect" man, fully worthy of being accepted and even enthroned at God's right hand, and he did that for the sake of all since this perfection was the fruit of his complete solidarity with us. Having brought the two relationships of intimacy with God and solidarity with us that are needed in priestly mediation to their perfection, Christ "became the source of eternal salvation" and was designated by God a high priest forever as the oracle of Psalm 110 had announced.

This splendid text expresses the paschal glorification of Christ with a new depth because it shows its connection with priestly mediation, something that Christian preaching was not yet doing. The christological hymn of Phil 2:6-11, for example, does not mention this aspect. Several New Testament texts come close to it (Luke 24:46-47; Acts 5:30-31; John 20:22-23; Rom 4:25; 8:34; 1 John 2:1-2) but the letter to the Hebrews alone shows the connection in its full light.

Strong Call to Attention (5:11–6:20)

First of all the author leads us to understand that 5:9-10 has just pointed out the theme of a new part of the homily, and then proceeds to shake up the listeners by reproaching them. The author emphasizes the importance of the doctrine that is now to be presented and the necessity to make a spiritual effort rather than just an intellectual one in order to be able to assimilate it. It will not deal with a basic teaching comparable to the milk given to infants (cf. 1 Cor 3:2; 1 Pet 2:2), but with a substantial doctrine offered to those who have already made progress in Christian life.

The extremely harsh sentence of 6:4-6 has created endless discussions. It expresses a strong contrast between the abundance of the wonderful gifts that Christians have received (over twenty words) and an eventual, catastrophic fall (one single word) into apostasy. It insists on the impossibility of apostates' being restored again. Placed at the beginning of the sentence, the term "impossible" has given rise to a rigoristic interpretation that categorically excludes forgiveness for apostates. However, the sentence is actually more nuanced. It does state that apostates cannot be given a second conversion while they are crucifying the Son of God again and holding him up to contempt (Greek verbs in the present tense). As long as they reject their savior they make their salvation impossible. Is that not obvious? Nothing is said about what their situation would be if they ceased to hold the Son of God up to contempt. We can easily understand this omission, necessary in order to obtain the effect of extreme dissuasion intended by this text.

If we are to interpret this passage correctly we also have to observe that the literary unit to which it belongs encompasses vv. 4-12. At the center (6:7-8) a comparison from the rural world presents two possible outcomes, a positive one of divine blessing (vv. 6-7) and the other, a negative one of being cursed forever (v. 8). Verses 4-6 correspond to the negative possibility while vv. 9-12 refer to the positive one. Yet it is on the side of salvation that the author situates the addressees (v. 9) because they live in the love of God and in serving their neighbors (v. 10). Thus the harsh verses were only a warning aimed at preserving them from becoming sluggish and securing their perseverance in the faith (v. 12).

Abraham's perseverance is given as an encouraging example (6:13-20). God gave the patriarch the twofold support of a promise (Gen 12:1-3) and an oath (Gen 22:16-18). Christians also benefit from this twofold support, namely the promise of eternal inheritance (Heb 6:17; 9:15) and the divine oath that guarantees the priesthood of Christ (Ps 110:4; Heb 7:21-22). Their hope is therefore steadfastly anchored. It literally penetrates "the inner shrine behind the curtain" (Heb 6:19) which is the Holy of Holies, as the high priest does on the Day of Atonement (Lev 16:2, 12, 15), the curtain serving to "separate the holy place from the Holy of Holies" (Exod 26:33). For Christians, however, this does not refer to the Jerusalem Temple. Here the metaphorical expression is referring to Jesus entering "into heaven itself . . . in the presence of God" (Heb 9:24). This entering into heaven should not be understood as a personal privilege. Since it is an act of priestly mediation it opens up the path to God for every believer.

The Priesthood of Melchizedek (7:1-10)

The last words of ch. 6 take up the declaration of 5:10 where the priesthood of the Messiah-King is defined in terms of its resemblance to that of Melchizedek. What are the specific aspects of this priesthood? A reading of Gen 14:17-20 in the light of the glorified Christ will enable us to discover them. This text presents Melchizedek's titles and an account of the events (Heb 7:1-2). The author first explains the titles (7:2-3). The name and the royal title have a messianic resonance because they evoke righteousness and peace (cf. Isa 9:5-6; 11:1-9; Psalm 72). Before referring to the priestly title the author points out two surprising omissions in the biblical text: the absence of genealogy and of temporal limitations. These absences give the priesthood of Melchizedek its particular aspect, which is very different from the Levitical priesthood. The latter was strictly related to a genealogy and was limited to the duration of a human life. The absence of temporal limitations makes Melchizedek similar to God's Son who is eternal (cf. Heb 1:11-12). Thus in Genesis 14 the priesthood of Melchizedek appears with an aspect of indefinite "perpetuity," thereby prefiguring the priesthood of Christ, a "priest forever" (Ps 110:4).

Verses 4-10 focus on the facts reported in Gen 14:18-20, namely the title Melchizedek received and the blessing he gave. From this, and with rabbinical skill the author draws an argument to demonstrate Melchizedek's superiority to Levitical priests. The absence of priestly genealogy (7:6) and perpetuity (7:8) contribute to the demonstration. Thus we ascertain that even before presenting the institution of the Levitical priesthood the OT prophetically put before our eyes the image of a different and superior priesthood.

The Priesthood of the Messiah-King (7:11-28)

The prophetic scope of the account in Genesis 14 is confirmed in the oracle of Ps 110:4, which now calls for our complete attention. In the psalm God attributes to the Lord an eternal priesthood "according to the order of Melchizedek." Here the tone of the exposition becomes polemical. The author questions the value of the priestly consecration conferred on the Jewish high priests. The Greek Pentateuch calls it *teleiōsis,* the "act of making perfect" (Exod 29:22-34; Lev 8:21-33). Indeed, in order to be able to come close to God as a priest, a man had to have been "made perfect"; otherwise he would not be worthy of this ministry. But the author notes that the ritual consecration conferred "by the Levitical priesthood" did not deserve the name of *teleiōsis* because it did not make its recipient perfect and therefore did not really give access to God. If it had actually deserved its name the divine oracle would not have foreseen its being replaced by a different priesthood (Heb 7:11) not based on Levitical descent (cf. 7:3) or limited to the time span of a human life (cf. 7:3). The oracle was fulfilled in Jesus who did not belong to the tribe of Levi (7:13-14) and who, through his resurrection, possesses henceforth "an indestructible life" (7:16).

Here we have to remember that the author has already spoken of the perfection obtained by Christ (2:10; 5:9). This perfection was not sought through an ineffective ritual consecration but was the result of a divine action at work in his real life and more precisely "through sufferings" (2:10). The priestly consecration Christ received truly "made him perfect" because "he learned obedience through what he suffered" (5:8-9). This is the reason why his priesthood is real rather than merely ritual as in the case of the earlier priesthood.

It is quite remarkable that the author is not content to contest the former priesthood, but extends the challenge to the entire Mosaic Law, saying "when there is a change in the priesthood, there is necessarily a change in the law as well" (7:12). In fact the old Law was based on a special relationship between the people and God, and this relationship was maintained thanks to the priestly institution. If the nature of the institution changes, the body of the law, deprived of its basis, cannot endure and has to be replaced. Here the author vigorously reopens the Pauline polemic against the Law by using a priestly vocabulary of "perfection" instead of the juridical vocabulary of "justification" used by Paul. The author declares that the Law cannot "make perfect" (7:19; 10:1) just as Paul declared that it could not "justify" (Gal 3:11; Rom 3:20).

The author exploits the text of the psalm in all its details in order to offer a better demonstration of the superiority of Christ's priesthood. He underlines the formula of the oath guaranteeing the definitive value of the oracle (7:20-22; cf. 6:13-17). He insists on the term "forever" on which he had prepared a commentary in vv. 3, 8, and 16. A priest established "forever" does not need a substitute or a successor (7:24). Since "he always lives to make intercession" (7:25) he obviously supersedes all mortal priests.

The conclusion (7:26-28) expresses his contemplative admiration before the image of the ideal high priest (7:26). It prepares the following section by introducing the theme of sacrificial worship (7:27) and ends by summarizing the contrast between the priesthood of the Law and that of the oath. On the one hand we find mere men who were not transformed by their ritual consecration, and on the other hand a man who is also the Son of God (cf. 4:14) and who was truly "made perfect" by an existential consecration (7:28; cf. 5:8-9).

Our High Priest (8:1-2)

In referring to the high priest of Ps 110:4 just mentioned, the author proclaims exultantly, "we have such a high priest" and confirms the statement by alluding to the first verse of the same psalm, which speaks of a Lord invited to sit at the right hand of God. The gospel catechesis (Matt 22:44 // Mark 12:36 // Luke 20:42; Matt 26:64 // Mark 14:62 // Luke 22:69) and apostolic preaching (Acts 2:34-36; 1 Cor 15:25) did, in fact, teach Christians that this "Lord" is Jesus Christ, the glorified Son of God. According to the psalm this Lord is, at the same time, a priest forever. Thus Christians are invited to acknowledge that they have "such a high priest." They know it through their experience of union with God thanks to the mediation of Christ.

Having said that, the author specifies the subject of this long section (8:3–9:28) by calling our high priest "a minister in the sanctuary and the true tent that the Lord, and not any mortal, has set up" (8:2). It is a mistake to seek to identify "the sanctuary" and "the tent" on the basis of the immediate context, which refers to a tent erected by a human being (8:5). In order to obtain details on the tent set up by the Lord and the sanctuary to which it provides access one must refer to the second half of this exposition (9:11-28). The first half, in fact, only provides detailed information about the worship of the former covenant, which it subjects to sharp criticism.

The Worship of the First Covenant (8:3–9:10)

Verse 3 explains the title of "minister" given to our high priest (8:2) by recalling that sacrificial offering is a necessary function of the priesthood. However, the Greek text suggests some differences. In the case of "every high priest" the verb "to offer" is in the present tense, indicating repetition, and its objects are plural, that is, multiple external offerings. In the case of our high priest the same verb is in the aorist tense, indicating an action accomplished only once, and its object, in the singular, remains imprecise. The details will be provided in the second part (9:14, 26, 28). The author then excludes for "this priest" (Christ's name only appears from 9:11 on) a priesthood that would have left him on earth, and criticizes the earthly worship prescribed by the Law. A quotation from Exod 25:40 shows that this type of worship does not attain heavenly realities; it is only a reproduction on earth of a model that was shown to Moses on Sinai. Verse 6, which is very significant, attests to an intimate connection between worship and covenant, something the OT did not think of expressing. Jesus obtained "a more excellent ministry" because he was to establish "a better covenant."

Criticism then shifts from previous worship to the first covenant (8:7-13). To demonstrate that it was faulty the author uses Jeremiah's oracle in which God promises "a new covenant" (Jer 31:31-34). This oracle opens up wonderful perspectives of personal relationship with God and forgiveness of past faults; however, the author does not stress them but simply underlines that the reproaches expressed in the oracle manifest the imperfection of the old dispensation and that the proclamation of a "new" covenant, which is very different from the covenant of the Exodus (since God's laws will be written "on hearts," not on two stone tablets), implies the casting aside of the old covenant.

The author proceeds to describe and criticize the cultic institutions of the first covenant (9:1-10). Based on the text of the Law of Moses (Exodus 25–26; 36–37; 40), the description of the holy place (9:2-5) deals with the "tent" in the wilderness, not with the Temple of Jerusalem. It insists on the distinction between a holy place, the "first tent," and a very holy place, which is also a "tent." The description of the rituals (9:6-7) continues with this distinction and emphasizes the restrictions that limited the possibility of entering "into the second tent" (cf. Exod 30:10; Leviticus 16). In a parallel way the criticism deals first with the holy place (9:8), then with the rituals (9:9-10). Concerning the holy place, by the very precepts which the Holy Spirit had inspired, the Spirit showed that the old institution was not really the path leading to God. Theoretically it was the high priest's role to take this path and open it up to the people. However, this first tent, made by human hands, could only provide access to another humanly made tent, the second, which was not the dwelling of God. Therefore, the "way into the sanctuary" was unknown. The high priest did not take it and consequently could not open it up to the people. The same restrictions applied. The inadequate nature of the first tent was an expressive "symbol" (9:9). It showed that the old worship was at an impasse. As a matter of fact, even if he had known the true way the high priest could not have taken it because the old rites did not even provide him with that power. To be able to approach God one must have perfect integrity of conscience. The sacrifices of the OT, non-personal offerings, could not make the one offering them interiorly perfect. The old priestly worship was, therefore, ineffective and had to be replaced.

The Personal Offering of Christ (9:11-28)

The intervention of Christ in his paschal mystery solves the anguishing problem of the relationship with God since Christ replaced the old rites by efficacious means that, once for all, opened access to the divine sanctuary. Two intimately connected means are mentioned: it is "*through* [that is, by means of] the greater and perfect tent" and "*with* [that is, by means of] his own blood" that Christ "entered into the Holy Place" (9:11-12). In both cases we are dealing with metaphors. The second is easy to understand, but sometimes it is misinterpreted by imagining a heavenly rite during which Christ would have offered his own blood to God. The text does not mention a blood offering. The expression used simply means that Christ obtained his glorification in heaven by his death on the cross (cf. 2:9) since he transformed this violent death into a generous self-offering.

The much more enigmatic metaphor of "the tent" gives rise to various interpretations. In this case too, it would be a mistake to consider the tent as the vestibule of a heavenly temple of which God would only occupy the main room. However, the less simplistic cosmological interpretation, according to which the tent would represent the heavens that Christ passed through in his ascension (cf. 4:14) stumbles against one objection: according to Heb 1:10-12 and 12:26-27 the heavens form part of "this creation," whereas the tent does not. In order to solve the enigma it is better to turn to Jesus' words about the fate of the Jerusalem Temple. On the one hand Jesus foretold the destruction of the Temple (Matt 24:1-2 // Mark 13:1-2 // Luke 21:5-6), and on the other hand he announced the rebuilding in three days of another that, in Mark's words, is "not made by hands" (Mark 14:58) like the tent in Heb 9:11. John specifies that Jesus "was speaking of the temple of his body" and of his resurrection (John 2:19-22). It would be odd for the author of Hebrews to have been unaware of such an important tradition regarding the subject now at issue. Here, as in Matt 26:61-64 and Mark 14:58-62, we should note the close link between the word on the Temple and the word whereby Jesus applies to himself the oracle of Ps 110:1

about being seated at the right hand of God. As we have observed, this oracle plays an important role in Hebrews (cf. above, "Canonical Intertextuality"). It has just been evoked again at the solemn beginning of this section (8:1) immediately before the first mention of the "true tent" (8:2). This observation increases the already strong probability of a christological interpretation. In addition, this is the only interpretation that is in harmony with the close connection in 9:11-12 between "the tent" and Christ's "own blood." By saying that Christ "entered through the greater and perfect tent . . ." the author wants to confirm that it is thanks to his risen body that Christ, as a human being, was able to enter into God's intimacy. Because he was "made perfect" through his sacrifice (5:9), his glorified body is "the more perfect tent." It is also "the greater tent" because henceforth it can welcome all believers (cf. 1 Cor 12:27; Eph 4:12; Heb 3:6, 14). Christ's risen body is the first fruit of the "new creation" (cf. 2 Cor 5:17; Eph 4:24). It is "the way into the sanctuary . . . not yet disclosed" in the OT but realized and revealed in the paschal mystery, the way that leads to perfect communion with God. Christ took this way first for himself (9:11; 10:20) and at the same time he opened it up to all his brothers and sisters.

The sentence in 9:11-12 that has just been analyzed corresponds to the one in 9:7-8 since it uses the same vocabulary of local transference to present the mystery of Christ. The following sentence (9:13-14) corresponds to 9:9-10 since it uses a vocabulary of offering and of personal transformation. On the one hand the text speaks of repeated non-personal sacrifices (9:9), and on the other hand of a unique offering of the very person (9:14); on the one hand, flesh sacrifices without any influence on the worshiper's conscience (9:9), and on the other hand an offering prompted by "the eternal Spirit" and one that gives Christ's blood the power to "purify our conscience" and prepare us to worship the living God (9:14).

This twofold efficacy manifests the mediating value of the offering. Thus the author returns to the connection between worship and the covenant in the following paragraph (9:15-22) in symmetry with 8:7-13. In this explanation the author uses the common meaning of the Greek word *diathēkē,* which we translate by "covenant" in the Bible. Strictly speaking, *diathēkē* does not mean "covenant," but "disposition," and its common meaning was "last disposition," that is to say "testament" (as in "last will and testament: cf. Gal 3:15). Since it contained a promise of inheritance (Gen 15:1-8) from the beginning, the divine covenant had an aspect of testament. This aspect is reinforced in the new covenant because the latter was founded on and made definitive by the death of Jesus. The animal sacrifices offered to establish the Sinai covenant (Exod 24:5-8; Heb 9:18-21) are interpreted in that perspective, to which is later added the idea of purification with blood (9:22-23). In the case of the new covenant the necessary sacrifices had to have a greater value since the realities to be sanctified were destined for heaven, whether it is a question of Christ's humanity that had to be "made perfect" (5:9), of his message that was to become "blood that speaks" (12:24), or of a people of believers, "holy partners in a heavenly calling" (3:1).

The last verses of the exposition (9:24-28) correspond to the first (8:1-6). They specify the "sanctuary" of which Christ became "minister" (8:2). They exclude any sanctuary "made by hands," that is, built by human beings. By his sacrifice Christ entered into heaven itself in a definitive way. In consequence his offering will remain unique. Christ will return, but it will no longer be to offer himself in sacrifice. The purpose of his return will be to bring salvation (9:28).

An Efficacious Offering (10:1-18)

Returning to the polemic against the Mosaic Law (cf. 7:12, 19, 28), the author denounces the inefficacy of the sacrifices it prescribed (10:1). In their indefinite repetition the author detects a sign of their impotence (10:2). The only effect here attributed even to the most solemn ones offered "year after year" on the Day of Atonement is that they are a reminder of sins, not their remission. This bold stand contradicts the divine promise expressed in Leviticus 16:30, but the author justifies it by way of a theological idea (Heb 10:4) and, moreover, by resorting to a scriptural text that expresses God's rejection of all the old types of sacrifices (10:5-7 = Ps 40:6-8). This text from Psalm 40 is far from being the only such text in the Bible (cf. Isa 1:11-13; Jer

6:20; 7:22; Amos 5:21-25; Mic 6:6-8); it presents the added interest of bringing forth someone who, according to the Greek translation, says to God: "a body you have prepared for me" and who then offers personal obedience to replace the ritual sacrifices. Read in the light of Christ, these verses from the psalm take on a prophetic meaning. They evoke the incarnation of the Son of God (cf. Heb 2:14; Gal 4:4) and his redemptive obedience (cf. Heb 5:8-9; Phil 2:8). This is why the author puts them on Christ's lips when he came into the world (Heb 10:5). The author takes care to emphasize that according to this text Christ abolishes the worship set up by the Law and replaces it with a different type of relationship with God (10:9). The first cult was ineffective. "The offering of the body of Jesus Christ," perfect fulfillment of God's will, has been totally efficacious and has obtained our sanctification (10:10).

The following verses (10:11-14) reinforce the demonstration by expressing a contrast between the posture of the priests of the old worship, standing day after day to offer their sacrifices, and the posture of the glorified Christ sitting at the right hand of God (cf. Ps 110:1). The contrasting postures are explained by the contrasting services, namely, impotent gestures on one hand (10:11) and efficacious offering on the other (10:14).

Inspired by the Holy Spirit, the oracle from Jeremiah explicitly confirms the efficacy of the new covenant for the transformation of hearts and the forgiveness of sins (10:16-17). As a result, the former sacrifices of atonement no longer have any reason to continue (10:18).

The Priesthood of Christ and Christian Life (10:19-39)

Moving from the doctrinal presentation to the exhortation, the author enthusiastically describes the situation resulting from Christ's priestly offering (10:19-21). More privileged than the high priest of Israel (cf. 9:7), henceforth and without any time limitations Christians possess the right to enter the true sanctuary (cf. 9:24) "by the blood of Christ," that is to say, thanks to his violent death transformed into a generous offering (cf. 9:12, 14). In order to have access to the sanctuary they now have a "new and living way" that is the glorified humanity of Jesus (10:20; cf. 9:8, 11; John 14:6). Moreover, Christians have the very person of Christ, their priest, as a guide (Heb 10:21; cf. 3:1, 6; 5:10). They are invited to remain (the verbs in the present indicate this aspect) in the dispositions corresponding to the dynamism of this privileged situation: sincere faith placed in relation to baptism (10:22), unwavering hope based on the promises of a faithful God (10:23), and effective love manifested in generous deeds and regular participation in ecclesial assemblies (10:24-25). As can be seen, this exhortation does not preach moral virtues but the three theological virtues (cf. 1 Thess 1:3; 5:8; 1 Cor 13:13; Col 1:4-5) which bring us into personal relationship with God through Jesus Christ. The mention of the "Day" of the Lord that is approaching (Heb 10:25) makes the exhortation even more pressing. The author is probably alluding to the events preceding the Jewish War.

The perspective of judgment is linked to the Day of the Lord (cf. 1 Cor 4:5; 2 Cor 5:10). Here in 10:26-31 the exhortation takes on a tone of merciless severity like the parallel passage in 6:4-8. Its interpretation produced the same controversies and prompts the same remarks. In fact, we have to observe that the author evokes the hypothesis (unreal because "we" also includes the author) of a persistent situation (10:26, verb in the present) of complete rupture with the Son of God (10:29) undertaken willingly and with full knowledge (10:26). In such a case the only foreseeable outcome is obviously that of a "fearful prospect of judgment" (10:27). As in 6:4-8, nothing is said about what would happen if sinners ceased to remain obstinately in their sins. Once again this silence has an oratorical motive; in other words, the author does not want to weaken the dissuasive effect.

Here, as after 6:4-8, dissuasion is followed by words of encouragement (10:32-35). The author reminds the listeners of their first generosity. After having welcomed the light of Christ they had to put up with all sorts of sufferings that they endured valiantly. The book of Acts reports that such was the situation of many communities (Acts 8:1; 12:1; 14:22; 17:5-6; cf. 1 Thess 2:14).

The last verses (10:36-39) express first of all the need for "endurance" in order "to do the will of God." The example of Christ in his passion (10:9-10; cf. Matt 26:42) is implicitly evoked. Because of its close link with hope (cf. Rom

8:25; 15:4) Christian endurance strains toward the realization of "what was promised." Then the author cites an oracle of Habakkuk announcing the imminent arrival of "the one who is coming" (Heb 10:37; Hab 2:3 LXX; cf. Matt 11:3 // Luke 7:19). The following verse of the same oracle insists on the importance of "faith" in the lives of the righteous (Heb 10:38; Hab 2:4; Rom 1:17; Gal 3:11). This quotation allows a close union of the two themes of faith and endurance, which will be the theme of the following section (11:1–12:13).

The Faith of the Righteous in the Old Testament (11:1-40)

Seemingly academic, the definition of faith (11:1) remains very general. There is nothing specifically Christian or even religious about it. Faith is defined in terms of its effects: it assures the possession of things hoped for and the knowledge of things not seen. This objective meaning is preferable to the subjective meaning ("firm confidence" and "conviction") chosen by some translators since the word *elenchos* never has the meaning of "conviction" but only that of "proof," a "way of knowing."

The author here juxtaposes two distinct perspectives formed in the Judeo-Hellenistic tradition. One, biblical and more dynamic, connects faith with things hoped for, while the other, Hellenistic and more intellectual, is interested in faith as a source of knowledge. These two perspectives are found again in the following verses but the second is not given much attention (11:3, 6, 7). The author insists especially on the dynamism of faith and from this point of view presents a very positive image of the OT, thus compensating for the negative image presented in the second part (cf. 3:7–4:11), an image based on Psalm 95.

At first glance this magnificent fresco seems unrelated to the exposition of priestly christology that fills the preceding chapters. As a matter of fact Christ is briefly mentioned only once, in connection with Moses (11:26). However, a more attentive reading shows that the author is re-reading the OT in light of three stages of Christ's priestly mediation: sacrificial offering, welcome at the right hand of God, and efficacy for the salvation of believers. The first three examples are significant in this regard because they correspond to these three stages by successively recalling the sacrifice of Abel (11:4), Enoch being taken by God (11:5), and the building of Noah's ark "to save his household" (11:7).

In the paragraph concerning Abraham (11:8-22) the theme of sacrifice is outlined at the beginning (11:8, "Abraham obeyed," cf. 5:8) and clearly made explicit in 11:17. Welcome at the right hand of God is evoked in 11:10, 13-16. The fruitfulness of death appears in 11:12 as well as in 11:20-22. The paragraph centered on Moses (11:23-31) explicitly cites Christ and the "abuse suffered" (11:26), thereby placing Moses' history in direct relation to the sacrifice of Christ. The fruitfulness of this sacrifice is reflected in vv. 28-31 that, after recalling the Passover and the blood shed (cf. 9:14, 22), mention the first-born preserved from the plague, passing through the Red Sea, the falling walls of Jericho, and the salvation accorded to Rahab.

The impressive general picture that concludes this chapter (11:32-38) includes no perceptible allusion to the priesthood of Christ, but one can consider that the triumphs of faith evoked in 11:33-35 have a certain connection with the glorification of the Lord and that the trials valiantly endured thanks to faith (11:35-38) contain an analogy with the passion of Christ. At the center of this text the refusal to accept an earthly deliverance in order to obtain "a better resurrection" (11:35) rather clearly makes one think of Jesus' attitude with regard to his passion (cf. Matt 26:51-54). This connection is confirmed shortly after, at the beginning of the following section (12:2). The conclusion (11:39-40) indirectly alludes to the work of Christ since it emphasizes that in spite of their admirable faith the righteous people of the OT did not obtain the realization of the promise. They had to wait to be "made perfect" at the same time as Christians, thanks to Christ's "single offering" (cf. 10:14). Their example is all the more stimulating.

Endurance and Divine Instruction (12:1-13)

Nevertheless, this example receives a merely secondary role in the following exhortation (12:1-3) in which the righteous people of old are only presented as "witnesses" of the trial that Christians face and not as their models. The only model set up before the eyes of afflicted Christians is "Jesus . . . who endured the cross . . .

endured the hostility . . ." and thus obtained heavenly glory (12:2-3; cf. 10:12). The title given to Jesus, "pioneer and perfecter of our faith," recalls the close link uniting Christian endurance and faith, namely, what is at stake is persevering in the faith in spite of tribulations and persecutions (cf. 10:32-39; 1 Thess 3:2-3; 1 Pet 1:7).

The connection expressed here between Jesus and faith is open to various interpretations. The text implies that from the start to the end of his life Jesus mapped out the way of faith. Was it because he himself was the first believer? This interpretation would not be in harmony with ch. 11, which states that countless believers had opened the way of faith before Jesus' time. Besides, it is hard to imagine how the Son of God, "the radiation of God's glory" (1:3), could have been a mere believer. Therefore it seems preferable to understand that, by his glorifying passion, Jesus established the foundation that allowed believers to have access to "full assurance of faith" (10:22). From then on Jesus himself is that perfect foundation.

The remainder of the section (12:4-13) says nothing else about faith, but focuses only on the trials to be endured. A well-chosen quotation (Prov 3:11-12) presents these trials as divine instruction, a testimony of God's parental love. We should note the difference between the situation of Christ who, being Son, did not need trials (cf. 5:8) and that of Christians for whom filiation necessarily implies discipline (12:7-8). Comparisons between the instruction given by God and the kind human beings try to give help us to understand how beneficial it is to welcome divine discipline.

The exhortation ends (12:12) with an uplifting quotation from Isa 35:3 taken from a passage promising God's saving intervention. To this the author adds a piece of advice from Prov 4:26, thus introducing another theme, that of the straight paths, to prepare for the following section (12:14–13:18).

Call to Holiness in Love (12:14–13:18)

To begin this last section the author specifies that the "straight paths" (12:13) are paths of "peace with everyone" and of "sanctification" (12:14), then begins with what concerns the second point. A severely worded exhortation warns against infidelity to "the grace of God." The example of Esau's indifference serves to produce a very strong dissuasive effect (12:15-17). Then the exhortation is reinforced by a contrast (12:18-24) that prepares the argument *a fortiori* (12:25-27). To the somber evocation of the Sinai experience from which the author is careful to exclude any mention of God (12:18-21) is opposed a description of Christian initiation which is situated, on the contrary, in a serene atmosphere and a rich network of relationships between persons (12:22-24). Still, the author does not draw reassuring consequences from the spiritual superiority of this experience, insisting rather on the need to be more obedient (12:25) which has been rendered urgent by the proclamation of the final shaking of earth and heaven (12:26-27).

Nevertheless, the conclusion (12:28-29) adopts a positive perspective. By welcoming the reign of God now Christians are invited "to give thanks" to God and thus to offer God an acceptable worship with reverence and awe. In Psalm 50, God had already declared that only "a sacrifice of praise," that is to say, thanksgiving, was pleasing (Ps 50:14-15, 23).

From the worship of God the following sentence moves abruptly to "mutual love" (13:1). Thinking there was a lack of connection, many exegetes have concluded that ch. 13 did not belong to the original composition and was an addition. Such a conclusion is debatable. In fact, in the perspective of the NT authentic worship and mutual love are inseparable (cf. Matt 5:23-24; 22:39 // Mark 12:31 // Luke 10:27; 1 John 4:20-21). In 13:15-16 the author will clearly express the same viewpoint by joining the "sacrifice of praise" and "doing good" as two forms of sacrificial worship pleasing to God. Consequently there is no break in the discourse at 13:1 but only an asyndeton intended to indicate the distinction between two literary units within the same section.

In spite of the change of rhythm, this passage is carefully composed. It develops the first theme announced in 12:14, "peace with everyone," by recommending successively love, conjugal chastity, and a spirit of poverty. These brief exhortations are in groups of two, in keeping with biblical parallelism. Each of the three points has its own motivation (13:2, 4, 5) always introduced by the same Greek conjunction, *gar* ("for"). The last and more extensive motivation quotes God's words that elicit the faithful's response, also expressed by a biblical text.

The last paragraph (13:7-18) quickly touches upon many aspects of Christian life. It tends to reinforce the cohesiveness of the community. Christians are first invited to remember their initial leaders and imitate their faith (13:7). Faith looks to Jesus Christ who assures faith of his immutable support (13:8). Thus Christians should stay away from "strange teachings" (13:9) that try to impose regulations concerning food (cf. Col 2:16, 21; 1 Tim 4:3). An allusion to "those who officiate in the tent" (13:10) suggests that the author intends to fight against Judaizing propaganda (cf. 9:10). The author uses this opportunity for a last comparison between the death of Jesus "outside the city gate" (13:12) and the Israelites' sacrifices of atonement (Lev 16:27; cf. Heb 9:7, 12, 25-26) and from that draws some conclusions for Christian life, namely rejecting earthly conformism, accepting the humiliation of Christ, and striving toward the city of God. That does not mean refusing human solidarity: to the contrary, to the vertical dimension of praising God (13:15) Christian worship closely joins the horizontal dimension of generosity toward others and of solidarity (*koinōnia,* 13:16). Within the community, solidarity cannot be effective without obedience to leaders who are responsible to God for everyone's spiritual welfare (13:17). There follows a request for prayers for the author's intentions; a conviction of having a clear conscience leads the author to hope that these prayers will not be in vain (13:18; cf. Pss 34:15-16; 66:18-20; 145:18-20; John 9:31).

Final Wish (13:20-21)

The homily ends with a solemn sentence. It is not a prayer addressed to God. Instead, it is a wish for divine grace that names God in the third person as do the priestly blessing of Num 6:24-26 and other analogous texts (Ps 20:2-5; 2 Macc 1:2-5; Rom 15:5-6; 1 Thess 3:11-13). God is presented as the one who raised Jesus (cf. Rom 4:24; 8:11; 10:7) but an added clarification ("by the blood of the eternal covenant") places the resurrection in relation to the priestly christology of the sermon (cf. Heb 9:14; 10:29; 12:24). The title given to Christ, "the great shepherd of the sheep," is a transposition of his priestly titles (4:14; 10:22). The adjective "great" situates Christ above Moses (cf. 3:3-6) who is simply called "shepherd of the sheep" in Isa 63:11 (LXX).

After this mention of the doctrinal presentation, the second part of the sentence (13:21) recalls the exhortations (cf. 10:36; 12:28; 13:16) although without using a hortatory tone, instead wishing that God may accomplish this work in the lives of the faithful (cf. Ezek 36:27) through the mediation of Christ. A short doxology gives to this sentence and to the entire homily its final orientation.

Final Message Accompanying the Sermon (13:19, 22-25)

The style of these sentences is different and more familiar. "I" is used instead of "we" (contrast 2:5; 4:14-16; 6:9, 11; 13:18). The sentences correspond to an epistolary situation in which author and addressees are in widely-separated places, which is never the case in the homily. They have obviously been added either by the author or by someone else to send the homily to a distant community. The sermon is called "my word of exhortation" (13:22). The only other use of that expression in the NT (Acts 13:15) shows that it should not be taken literally (cf. Acts 13:16-41). It is evident that Hebrews 1:1–13:21 is more than a simple exhortation. It includes lengthy doctrinal discourses of considerable importance to faith and Christian life.

The mention of the liberation of Timothy implies that he had been arrested under circumstances we do not know. We do not know either where "those from Italy" were located when the message was written and when it was sent with the sermon. The hesitancy of the western Church concerning the origin of Hebrews suggests that it was probably sent to a Church of the eastern Mediterranean. We should be very grateful to these Christians for having preserved it for us.

BIBLIOGRAPHY

Attridge, Harold W. *Hebrews.* Hermeneia. Philadelphia: Fortress, 1989.

Buchanan, G. W. *To the Hebrews.* AB 36. Garden City, N.Y.: Doubleday, 1972.

DeSilva, David A. *Despising Shame: Honor Discourse and Community Maintenance in the*

Epistle to the Hebrews. SBL.DS 152. Atlanta: Scholars, 1995.

Dunnill, John. *Covenant and Sacrifice in the Letter to the Hebrews.* MSSNTS 75. Cambridge: Cambridge University Press, 1992.

Ellingworth, Paul. *The Epistle to the Hebrews. A Commentary on the Greek Text.* NIGTC. Grand Rapids: Eerdmans; Carlisle: Paternoster Press, 1993.

____. *The Epistle to the Hebrews.* Epworth Commentaries. London: Epworth Press, 1991.

Guthrie, George H. *The Structure of Hebrews: A Text-Linguistic Analysis.* NT.S 73. Leiden: Brill, 1994.

Hagner, Donald A. *Hebrews.* NIBC. Peabody, Mass.: Hendrickson, 1990.

Héring, Jean. *The Epistle to the Hebrews.* Translated by A. W. Heathcote and P. J. Allcock. London: Epworth Press, 1970.

Hughes, Graham. *Hebrews and Hermeneutics.* MSSNTS 36. Cambridge: Cambridge University Press, 1979.

Hughes, Philip E. *A Commentary on the Epistle to the Hebrews.* Grand Rapids: Eerdmans, 1977.

Hume, C. R. *Reading Through Hebrews.* London: SCM Press, 1997.

Jewett, Robert. *Letter to Pilgrims: A Commentary on the Epistle to the Hebrews.* New York: Pilgrim, 1981.

Lindars, Barnabas. *The Theology of the Letter to the Hebrews.* Cambridge: Cambridge University Press, 1991.

Lussier, Ernest. *Christ's Priesthood According to the Epistle to the Hebrews.* Collegeville: The Liturgical Press, 1975.

Moffatt, James. *A Critical and Exegetical Commentary on the Epistle to the Hebrews.* ICC. Edinburgh: T & T Clark, 1924.

Montefiore, Hugh. *A Commentary on the Epistle to the Hebrews.* HNTC. New York: Harper & Row, 1964.

Swetnam, James. *Jesus and Isaac. A Study of the Epistle to the Hebrews in the Light of the Aqedah.* AnBib 94. Rome: Biblical Institute Press, 1981.

Thompson, James. *The Beginnings of Christian Philosophy: The Epistle to the Hebrews.* CBQ.MS 13. Washington, D.C.: Catholic Biblical Association, 1982.

Vanhoye, Albert. *Old Testament Priests and the New Priest: According to the New Testament.* Translated by J. Bernard Orchard. Petersham, Mass.: St. Bede's Publications, 1986.

James

Cain Hope Felder

FIRST READING

Before Getting Started—A Word of Caution!

Bible study and the appeal to the Bible in preaching often have become either a rather dull weekly routine and esoteric survey of ancient texts or sensationalized ancient "sound bites" for a modern "pop culture." Yet God's word should never become so prosaic and banal, the victim of "hop-scotch" proof-texting. The Epistle of James offers pastors today an opportunity to reignite the burners of Christians who may be disillusioned with rhetoric about the difference that Christianity can and should make in one's life. It is a daunting but deceptive little treatise that preserves a sobering corrective for the people of God today who need some reality therapy!

This Epistle takes its name from the authority and tradition associated with the brother of Jesus. After he experienced a post-resurrection appearance of Jesus (1 Cor 15:7) the devotional life of James was forever changed. Eventually he was elevated to Chief Elder in the church of Jerusalem. In Gal 2:9 Paul includes James as one of those (along with Cephas and John) who were "pillars" of the Jerusalem church. Then in Acts 12:17, following Peter's miraculous deliverance from prison, Peter tells those who had been praying for him to report this to James who in Acts 15 presides over the Jerusalem Conference that divides a contested mission field between Peter and Paul. Luke alludes to the authority of James again in Acts 21:18.

The Epistle of James opens as if the author's identity is self-evident. Jas 1:1 begins simply with "James, a servant of God and of the Lord Jesus Christ" (similarly Jude 1:1). Directed to congregations of the Diaspora, this Epistle was penned by one who is either the Lord's brother or a devotee who invokes his name and authority. The writer uses many wise but strong moral teachings (119 imperatives). For readers today James contains a harvest of good things for those seeking an alternative to the comfortable kind of civil religion that tolerates injustices of the status quo.

An Overview: James as a Book Worthy of a Fresh Reading

In attempting to resolve the more perplexing technical dimensions of James many commentators unwittingly cause pastors and the laity alike to lose interest in its basic message and perennial significance. James's focus is on courageous, redemptive faith that can survive the manifold tests or trials that personal and community life present. Such faith produces actions that are commensurate with the level of integrity contained in one's faith beyond rhetoric and pretense. This is neither a complex nor an exclusively moral message; rather it is deeply spiritual and theological. The message becomes complex, however, when one reconsiders human tendencies to complain and even to blame God while still committing personal sins and acts of injustice against others. The observations and reprimands of James can stir something within us and prove quite refreshing. The letter causes us to reflect anew on our modern-day fondness for merely being called "Christian" without having actually to be Christian!

After considering a variety of recent proposals for the overall structure of James we suggest the following outline:

Chapter One
- 1:1 Address and Salutation
- 1:2-8 A Faith That Rejoices in Trials
- 1:9-11 A Reversal of Fortunes
- 1:12-18 A God Who Rewards Faithful Endurance
- 1:19-25 The Righteousness of God in Word and Deed
- 1:26-27 A Religion That is Personal and Social

Chapter Two
- 2:1-13 Christian Faith and Acts of Discrimination (The Manifest Inconsistency)
- 2:14-26 The Unity of Faith and Deeds (The Need for Consistency)

Chapter Three
- 3:1-12 Faithfulness Through a Disciplined Tongue
- 3:13-18 Two Kinds of Wisdom

Chapter Four
- 4:1-6 Faithlessness in the Community
- 4:7-10 Corrective Formulae—A Call to Repentance
- 4:11-12 Warnings—The Law Does Not Deal in Trifles
- 4:13-17 Cautions to Those Who Take God for Granted

Chapter Five
- 5:1-6 Final Warning to Unjust Rich Land Owners
- 5:7-12 A Word of Consolation to the Faithful
- 5:13-20 Pastoral Encouragement: The Power of Prayer and Confession

The Ancient Socio-Historical Settings

James has a vocabulary parts of which are found nowhere else in the NT such as "Father of lights" (1:17), "the implanted word"(1:21) or "the wheel of birth"(3:6). The oddity is that many of these rare NT words or phrases are found in second-century Christian and non-Christian literature. This problem disappears once one recognizes that James, like numerous other NT documents, must have originated at one point and later was edited and circulated under the name and reputation of James, chief spokesman for Jewish Christianity.

My suggestion is that the original text was a sermon by James in the months prior to his martyrdom in Jerusalem. Then one skilled in the Hellenistic idiom edited and distributed James's original sermon, now styled as an encyclical, probably in the late 80's or 90's. This missive was sent to churches of the Diaspora that were divided internally.

This was a period in which church and synagogue were moving farther apart to establish or protect their respective identities. The strategic aim of the redactor, a James devotee, was to alleviate tensions for Jewish Christians who still wanted to have things both ways, perhaps without taking either tradition seriously. Another motive seems to be to mollify Gentile Christians by intentionally downplaying cultic law. In this sense we probably have in James the last echoes of the Jewish Christianity of the first century.

Biblical Internal Literary Relationships (Canonical Intertextuality)

The Epistle of James gives one today an uncanny sense that she or he has re-entered the ethos of the synoptic tradition. James provides remarkably similar moral imperatives and wisdom teachings variously akin to those found in Jesus traditions preserved in Matthew and Luke. James also preserves imminent expectations that are congenial with a tone often sounded by the Jesus of the synoptics. Still this epistle is such an eclectic book that it has affinities with almost every segment of the biblical corpus. One speaks not so much of direct literary dependence but of a kinship through allusion and similarity of style. While one finds some basis for comparing James with parts of the Pentateuch and with parts of the OT prophetic or Wisdom literature, and while in the NT there are suggestive parallels with parts of the Pauline corpus, nonetheless James remains without biblical parallel. It offers a rare glimpse into the kind of Christianity that some think dominated the Christian movement for most of the first century.

History of Reception

James's reputation for exemplary piety was so proverbial that testimonies of praise about him extend from Josephus through Hegesippus (a second-century Church historian), Clement of Alexandria, and Origen (ca. 200 C.E.). Josephus went so far as to suggest that the fall of Jerusalem in 70 C.E. resulted from James's martyrdom. Moreover, the Gospel of Thomas (Logion 12) mentions James favorably. It is ironic that in the West the Epistle of James is otherwise scarcely mentioned before 300 C.E. (being omitted from the Muratorian Canon). Conversely the epistle gained canonical status in the Coptic Church about 300. Codex Sinaiticus from North Africa, dated c.350, includes James. It is remarkable that once James gains access to the canon it is placed right after the Acts of the Apostles and is then followed by Jude, Peter, John and Paul. As far as the Western tradition is concerned Eusebius (325 C.E.) includes James at the beginning of a list of "disputed" *(antilegomena)* NT books although he appears to accept it. The canonical list of Athanasius in 367 C.E. includes James.

For well over a thousand years James's place in the NT was secure. It fell on "hard times" again at the hands of Martin Luther who called it "a rather strawy Epistle, written by a Jew who scarcely mentions Christ" amid other uncomplimentary dogmatic observations. Without a doubt Luther's early assessment of James has dogged its modern history of interpretation. By contrast John Calvin had a much more positive understanding of James, one that was closer to Luther's later revised opinion of the book. A few years after Luther's death Calvin said that he himself was inclined "to receive it without controversy."

SECOND READING

Scholarship often has its own hidden presuppositions that are seldom admitted by the exegete. Our analytical decisions and interpretive stances invariably expose our social location and attendant middle-class biases. Pastors should not dismiss as unfounded or inept their own insights about the text drawn from community experiences and common sense. Critical scholarship should not intimidate or "lord it over" the reader (whether lay person, student, or pastor), but rather should encourage creative dialogue. It is unlikely if not unimaginable that this document was written for a completely fictitious audience. Because we are persuaded that the author/editor presupposes a real historical set of issues we encourage the modern reader to join in a creative dialogue with ancient Christians struggling with the meaning and application of their faith. It is beneficial to begin the dialogue, therefore, by reading the text itself. The commentator's most helpful role is to offer encouragement along the way.

Chapter One

Address and Salutation (1:1)

To the modern reader it may seem strange that a letter would open with one's own name as the sender, but such was common practice in antiquity for both Jewish and Hellenistic private letters. On the other hand the writer ascribes the more Semitic title "servant of God" to himself as if to hold up his Jewish credentials first. Out of the thirteen NT Epistles associated with Paul, only Titus finds its author using the title "servant of God."

A Faith That Rejoices in Trials (1:2-8)

Unlike 1 Peter, James's opening does not bring to mind religious persecution. Rather by the expression "various trials" the author means those "thousand natural shocks" or stresses incidental to daily living under difficult socio-economic circumstances. Within modern societies it is too easy for well-off Christians to forget how many fellow Christians and others face painful deprivations and homelessness. James does not minimize this pain (see 2:14-17) but opens with the reminder that struggle and pain can have a redemptive purpose.

1:2-4

The Greek word for "trial" also means testing or temptation. One should not miss the possible allusion to the elaboration of Jesus' temptations in the wilderness offered in the synoptics (Matt 4:1-11; Luke 4:1-13; compare Heb 4:15). Running through James is an implicit *imitatio Christi* like that so prominent in Matthew. The idea of rejoicing amid trials is perplexing today in a milieu that tries so desperately to anesthetize itself to all pain. Here we find time-honored coping strategies that have a spiritual objective. Notice the progression: "trials, endurance, perfection." The aim in so coping is to demonstrate "genuineness" (or "proof") of one's faith in the fundamental providence of God (cf. Matt 6:25-34). Without this the so-called believer remains immature, incomplete, and thus lacking! The idea here is akin to the higher-righteousness motif in the Sermon on the Mount (Matt 5:48).

1:5-8

The fourth segment in the thought progression now completes James's advice. He points out that when faith is lacking there is another shortcoming: one's "wisdom" is likewise deficient. Not only are these pithy notices similar to biblical Wisdom traditions but James will later explicitly admonish those who seek or profess to be "teachers" (3:1). No doubt the mention of "lacking" at the end of v. 4 led to the quick association with the idea that "wisdom" of a spiritual nature is evidently lacking. This is so because the issue here is phrased in terms of a conditional sentence; note the "if-clause" in v. 5a. Verses 12-16 below illustrate that persons known to the author have not only been complaining about trials and temptations but have also been blaming God for their condition. The author diplomatically states conditionally what he knows is the case among the nominal "believers" in his audience or readership. They are failing the test of faith because they lack spiritual wisdom. Again echoes of the Sermon on the Mount are discernible (Matt 6:24; see Jas 4:4). The similarities between Jas 1:5b and Matt 7:7-8 (Luke 11:9-10) are irrefutable; the author thus invites believers of every stripe to petition God afresh.

James 1:6-8 contrasts "asking in faith" and the act of doubting, suggesting that those who superficially or disingenuously make petitions to God are "double-minded" *(dipsychos);* this Greek expression is without parallel in the NT and not found in Christian literature prior to 70 C.E. The frequency of such rare NT expressions suggests the hand of a later editor. Notice the imagery in v. 6: "one who doubts is like a wave of the sea, driven and tossed by the wind." The graphic sea imagery occurs again in 3:4.

From the vantage point of hermeneutical application these verses frame a timeless problem for the Church. Modern materialism and consumerism often quietly or cynically mock spirituality; material self-gratification when denied only serves to occasion further doubts about God. Religion in much of Western society has become "big business." This serves to blind Christians to the opportunity of embracing a spirituality that defines one's own interests through the needs of others who in some respects may be less fortunate. James seems to offer an ancient antidote to the consequent widespread phenomenon of stress and "burn out," namely rediscovery of the kind of faith that enables one to "consider it nothing but joy" when one is faced with seemingly insurmountable trials.

A Reversal of Fortunes (1:9-11)

James harbors the fundamental belief that "the humble poor" (Greek *tapeinos,* literally "the believer who lives in humble circumstances") can claim a rich biblical legacy from a spiritual perspective. In this second subdivision the author introduces the specific theme of the fortunes of the poor and the rich against the biblical background of Hebraic *"anawim"* piety. The subject does not suddenly intrude into the text but proceeds quite naturally from the spiritual insights already underway in vv. 2-8, particularly the invitation to "ask God" or the idea of "asking on faith," that is, in prayer. The rich spiritual heritage of the humble poor who always have recourse to a God who can exalt them appears in many biblical texts, notably in the prayer of Hannah (1 Sam 2:7; Luke 1:52), in the prophetic warnings of Amos 5:11-24 or Isa 40:6-8 and 47:8-11. In such Wisdom texts as Sir 35:21-22 one encounters "the prayer of the humble *(tapeinos)* pierces the clouds, and it will not rest until it reaches its goal; it will not desist until the Most High responds and does justice for the righteous, and executes judgment," since prayer reaches the Lord who responds as an agent of justice against the proud adversaries of the humble. In Jas 4:10 the author again refers to "the humble" in an apparent allusion to Prov 3:34 (LXX). James seems quite familiar with such biblical traditions and invokes them as a dramatic reminder to poor brothers and sisters within his congregations who have resorted to despairing and complaining instead of redoubling their prayer life.

More poignant still is the way in which the motif of eschatological "role reversal" passes into the Jesus tradition of the synoptics. One thinks immediately of the Lukan beatitudes (especially Luke 6:20-25) or the parable of Lazarus and the rich man (Luke 16:19-31). It is a mistake, however, for interpreters to argue that James does not see the rich as capable of being believers. In the teachings of both Jesus and James the rich simply have some difficult questions to answer (see Matt 19:16-26; Mark 10:17-31; Luke 18:18-30). The overarching concern has to do with their behavior, personal and social, with self-deception and the deceiving of others.

A God Who Rewards Faithful Endurance (1:12-18)

This final segment of the large opening pericope returns to the subject of enduring trials and temptations as "tests" but the focus shifts from the earlier function and nature of coping strategies to the inherent rewards for faithful endurance. The section opens with a beatitude: "blessed is 'a man' who endures a trial or temptation" (here a rare instance in James of the specific Greek term for "man"). Again the masculine referent is undoubtedly used to recall implicitly the man Jesus who so endured. It is to be noticed that in Jas 2:14 James is explicit about his general concern for the welfare of men and women.

Many OT and intertestamental Wisdom texts adopt a variety of images associated with a metaphorical "crown," but rare in the Bible is "the crown of life." This phrase is, however, found in Rev 2:10. John of Patmos first, in remarks directed to the church at Smyrna in Asia Minor, prefaces his crown reference by saying in Rev 2:9 "I know your affliction and your poverty," and in v. 10 he immediately promises "the crown of life" for those who are "faithful until death." The matter is put differently in Jas 1:12b, c which indicates that "the crown of life [is] promised to those who love him." The uncertainty of the reference of "him" in this setting is relieved by another use of the stock formula "those who love him" in Jas 2:5b. In this later context James clearly speaks of God, not Jesus! The likelihood therefore is that the author means the same in the present instance (1:12c), "those who love him [God]." The theocentric perspective is entirely consistent with the Jewish Christianity of James and with an early dating for the document.

That God rewards the faithful leads James into a brief discourse concerning the unfaithful who to their peril are blaming God for the woeful condition of not being able to cope with trials and/or temptations (vv. 13-16). The author begins with observations about human responsibility for sin but the thought here is different from Paul's existential dilemma as presented by the relation between the Law and dealing with sin as found in Rom 7:14-25. James is more basic, for evidently he holds a different perspective about the Law (see 2:1-13 and 4:11-12). In this segment the undisciplined believer is accountable for being vulnerable to sinful enticements.

Often missed in the discussion of Jas 1:13-16 is the compassionate pastoral note sounded in v. 16, "do not be deceived, my beloved [brothers]." James is certainly concerned with the patterns of self-deception within the Church that obscure faithful endurance, yet it is more significant perhaps that he remains compassionate in a comprehensive pastoral manner. As upset as he seems to be with personal and social ethical lapses within the community he does not lose his religion or compromise his reputation for extraordinary righteousness by showing revulsion or bitterness. Significantly, here and elsewhere he still calls the offending believers "beloved [brothers]." He sees potential in them beyond their manifest faults.

When James in v. 16 exhorts his readers "do not be deceived" he envisions a twofold deception, one that misconstrues the human sources for sin about which he has spoken and the other having to do with the nature of God as one who rewards generously. Verses 17-18 now provide a fitting end to this passage. James's thoughts accordingly return to the subject of God's generosity (recall v. 5 above). By speaking of God as "the Father of lights" the author skillfully synthesizes three traditions related to Judaism. One readily associates this image with Gen 1:15-16 that depicts YHWH as the creator God of the heavenly "lights" (compare Ps 136:7 [LXX 137]) "[God] who made the great lights." See also Jer 4:23). Plainly the Jewish tradition represented in the Hebrew Bible lies in the background. Extra-biblical Jewish sources offer instructive parallels; for example the appellation "Father of lights" occurs in the OT pseudepigrapha (*T. Abr.* 7:60) and God is called "the Prince of Lights" in Qumran documents (*CD* 5.17-18). For James God is more than the "Father of lights," God is the giver of every good and perfect gift including the gift of salvation. The distinctive Christian nuances continue in that Jas 1:18a does not suggest that persons are created in the image of God (Gen 1:26; 5:1) or that they are just born of God (Deut 32:18). Rather he indicates that "[God] gave *us* birth"—not merely human beings, *"us,"* meaning evidently that we Christians are "brought forth" by the specific "word of truth" (i.e., the gospel) when God so willed.

By closing the entire pericope with the salvo on the distinctive gift of the Christian life (see 1:12) James reminds his readers of their original conversion. Presumably he has in view a defining moment in the history of salvation. This passage deeply impressed the Danish theologian Søren Kierkegaard. Moreover, James has now set the stage for this "word of truth" to reemerge as the saving "implanted word" in the following pericope.

The Righteousness of God in Word and Deed (1:19-25)

The customary arrangement in many investigations for the balance of ch. 1 of James is to follow Martin Dibelius in construing vv. 19-27 as a single pericope containing a series of sayings on hearing and doing. That opinion establishes the threefold wisdom-oriented saying in v. 19b ("quick to listen, slow to speak, slow to anger) as determining the basic literary character and moral content of vv. 19-27. One recent study, "Personal Speech Ethics in James," argues that the tripartite proverbial phrase not only heads the section but lends structure to it through two cautions and an advice on anger.

The thought is not in some respects very different from the observation made by Paul in 2 Cor 5:21b ("so that . . . we might become the righteousness of God") although Paul probably means a "righteousness found in God" but imparted to believers as a gift, whereas the Jewish Christian James means a standard of righteousness established by God to which the believer seeks to conform. It might be better to consider vv. 19-25 as a unit. In this case the summary function of vv. 26-27 would be clarified in stronger terms.

New Testament authors generally portray human anger as a manifestation of the "antigodly." James while sharing this view seems to extend the thought by insisting that Christian behavior should be guided by such righteousness. He implies an *imitatio Dei* (see Matt 5:44-48). A variety of Jewish traditions contain the thought that the believer can and ought to be righteous just as God is righteous (so Gen 18:19; Ps 11:7) but the determinative influence stems from Jesus traditions like Matt 5:22.

The adversative "but" (1:22) is an intentional addition to the original. The preceding passage set forth believers who were blaming God and misconstruing the nature of sin as well as of God. The "but" highlights the new subject of instructions, or more poignantly "corrections," for believers who need a tutorial on what constitutes the "righteousness of God" (v.20). Once again it seems clear that the author is reminding his congregations about the presuppositions of their baptism (see further Jas 2:7b "the sublime name invoked over you" and the baptismal formulae that follow below in 1:21 and more elaborately in 4:7-10). James has a holistic understanding of faith. Nothing short of this embraces fully his view of the righteousness of God. This righteousness coheres in a unity of speech-action and/or a unity in word-deed, actually the explicit topic of vv. 21-25. In v. 21 James begins drawing inferences from v. 20. His injunction in v. 21a ("therefore rid yourselves of all sordidness and rank growth of wickedness") simply names a wider class of evils that, like anger, do not work the righteousness of God.

By contrast readers are then enjoined to receive "with meekness the implanted word that has the power to save your souls." We are indebted to Philip Carrington for showing the similarity here and in 4:7-19 between early Christian baptismal formulae and the format of James's instruction at certain points. The "implanted word" is a synonym for "the word of truth" (1:18) and probably is the same thought that epitomizes the reference in 1:25 to "the perfect law, the law of liberty," that is, the Jewish Christian gospel.

1:22-25

The instruction to be "doers of the word" is a divine imperative for James. By adding "and not merely hearers" he wishes to make it absolutely clear that his meaning is not to be misunderstood. From James's vantage point working the righteousness of God is axiomatic for Christians who must follow the whole gospel and its moral law as found in the Jesus tradition. The sequel image of one who looks in the mirror and promptly forgets what she or he saw there is a surprising bit of humor for someone as serious as James the Just, once even called "bishop of bishops" by Clement of Alexandria or later and more startlingly called "brother of God" by Eusebius. Although funny and almost unimaginable, the simile of someone looking at one's own image in a mirror only to forget what was seen is an effective way to drive home the point to new converts that their current behavior seems analogous to just such a ridiculous (if not pathetic) circumstance. James's attitude toward the Law is similar to that of the Jesus tradition especially as found in Matthew's Sermon on the Mount, but refined by Matt 23:23 and the emphasis that Jesus placed there on "the weightier matters of the Law," namely justice, mercy, and faith. In 1:25 the author can speak of the Law as perfect or as a law of liberty, precisely because the Law has been liberated from the piety of the cultus and the attending system of comprehensive merits and guarantees. The understanding of what constitutes the righteousness of God is definitively changed with early Jewish Christianity.

A Religion That is Personal and Social (1:26-27)

The Greek word *thrēskeia* ("religion") dominates these two verses and shapes the basic concern with the outward public practice of one's faith. The term or a variant use of it appears as a catchword twice in v. 26 and once in v. 27. In Acts 26:5 it refers to Pharisaic Judaism, whereas in Wis 14:27 it is associated with the worship of idols. James employs the term in a manner akin to *1 Clem.* 62:1 as he speaks of Christianity. One must bear in mind that James has a twofold purpose in speaking now of religion. First, his aim is to describe the kind of so-called religious faith that is "worthless" (v.26) in contradistinction to a holistic faith that is "pure and undefiled"(v. 27). Second, he wants to reassert succinctly that holistic faith bespeaks a religion that involves personal conduct and appropriate discipline, and concern for the welfare of one's fellow Christian or fellow human being. Furthermore, in vv. 26-27 the author identifies two indispensable ingredients of Christianity in its best sense. For him this kind of religion, while having personal integrity, goes deeper to include actions that militate against social injustice. This seems to be, in short, what James means by a religious faith that takes its cues from discerning and replicating in one's life the very "righteousness of God." To do this one must bridle the tongue or control irresponsible speech (e.g., gossip, slander, cursing and the like) as in v. 26, and one should at the same time be concerned about the materially less fortunate or oppressed.

One should take note of the description of God as "Father" in v. 27 (see Jas 1:17), a characteristic tendency in early Christianity. The divine Father's providence would most assuredly turn to those "in distress," including orphans and widows who otherwise have no conventional earthly protector in ancient biblical settings. Thus it is best to take the specific mention of "orphans and widows" (perhaps intentionally reversing the usual OT order) as symbolic of the needy in general, because James adds the qualification "in their distress."

In a concise manner Jas 1:26-27 make explicit what for the author probably has been implicit in the document from the beginning. This would apply certainly to the preceding unit but also from the outset of his homily-epistle. Clearly his concerns are theologically rich and spiritually sensitive. It also seems evident as one scans the sequel pericopes in chs. two and three that James with this quick summation sets the stage for his teachings in those chapters that further highlight Law and wisdom respectively.

Chapter Two

Christian Faith and Acts of Discrimination (2:1-13)

Verses 1-13 represent the first of the two large units that comprise ch. 2. For present purposes it is helpful to subdivide the extended passage into two units:

2:1-7

The subject matter has already been introduced in the summary transitional pericope that immediately precedes. Now James expounds on how the standard of righteous doing applies to specific socio-economic difficulties and class conflicts within Christian communities and assemblies. The leading issue in this pericope is the blatant inconsistency of claiming to be a Christian and yet discriminating against the poor and otherwise oppressing the needy or fellow Christians of lower social class. The opening verse puts the matter plainly before the readers with a divine imperative.

The issue is directly addressed. There is no use of euphemism. One will notice in 2:1 that James refers to "our glorious Lord Jesus Christ," a highly embellished appellation for one who so seldom mentions Jesus, but it is understandable as an editorial flourish. The teaching point is thereby accentuated inasmuch as it was and remains a sad paradox that persons professing a faith about a spiritual figure raised to glory would treat so shabbily persons of lower social status in their own communities, particularly fellow believers. James (2:2-4) depicts a flagrant example of class discrimination within a congregation. This need not be construed as an exaggerated hypothetical example. To do so would make us all more comfortable with the scene. As one who has pastored and encountered similar problems I think that it is not advisable to downplay the realism of James's scene. For thousands of years problems of social class have forced people to lay aside and otherwise alter their religious practice. Further confirmation of this is evident within the history of Jewish and early Christian usage of the term "favoritism."

The example of class discrimination portrayed by Jas 2:2-4 helps one to see that James was familiar with rich and poor persons participating in the worship services. It is a popular misconception today that the early Church was only composed of poor men, women, and slaves. James highlights a real social problem among his readers and forthrightly condemns the kind of discriminating behavior that he has in view. Modern Christianity has become rather polite and genteel in middle-class Western society. In our context too a disheveled homeless individual smelling of poor hygiene would most likely be quickly and quietly ushered out of the church before the person had a chance to sit down even in the rear of the sanctuary. James's illustration in vv. 2-4 probably was searing at that time, but it remains searing today.

Both 2:1 and 2:5 open with a formulaic fraternal salutation "my brothers" (and presumably sisters as in 2:15) that contrasts ironically with the tone of righteous indignation (not anger!) that would suitably describe James's staccato of imperatives as he intensely offers counsel and gives directives about the community turmoil. In fact the fraternal salutation is one of greater endearment in v. 5 ("my beloved brothers").

An important rhetorical question ensues, one that has been mistranslated for years in my opinion. James calls attention to the so-called election or chosen status of the faithful poor. For decades scholars have found it useful to translate the Greek *tous ptōchous tō kosmō plousious en pistei* (lit. "the poor with respect to the world, rich in faith") as if somehow God has singled out only the poor to be especially "rich in faith." In English translations of this verse one routinely finds "has not God chosen the poor . . . to be rich in faith." It is unfortunate that some translators render this verse as if God has selected and expects the poor to be disproportionately "rich in faith" in comparison to those with material resources. The OT tradition of *anawim* piety that constitutes the background for the faithful poor has little to do with God's choosing poor people in any special way to be somehow more faithful because of their poverty. Rather the *anawim* or Hebraic tradition of "faithful poor" arises out of the sixth-century B.C.E. Babylonian captivity wherein the remnants of Judah were cast into impoverished slavery and in such a wretched condition had the opportunity to redouble their faith for survival. Because they deepened rather than abandoned their faith in that extreme circumstance they became God's special treasure. Yet this is a far cry from saying that the poor alone were chosen to be faithful or that only the poor will be heirs to the reign of God.

James 2:5 has for its essential intent a word of caution to members of the assembly who discriminate against the faithful poor in their midst. The text reminds those nominal Christians exhibiting class prejudice that they are oppressing a rich part of God's elect. The gospel traditions among other early Christian sources tell of the rich faith on the part of persons of relative wealth—from the women of means who help Jesus to Joseph of Arimathea. Unfortunately the problem is worse among James's communities.

James 2:6 brings out the full upbraiding of his hearers and readers for not only dishonoring "the [faithful] poor" but currying the favor of the rich. James spares no irony as he perhaps sarcastically calls attention to the specter of rich landlords dragging Church members off to court for unpaid rents. James's stern comments here show that the communities he addresses are behaving very much like the "synagogue" members in his example in vv. 2-4. This unit closes (with v. 7) with the reminder that wealthier persons, including Christians, have been known to curse the name of Jesus—that sublime name under which they were baptized—thus adding insult to injury. The situation is stark and pitiful, but is it any less realistic today?

2:8-13

These verses represent the second segment in the pericope that began with 2:1. This claim is supported by the explicit reference to "partiality: in v. 9, continuing the subject introduced in v. 1. Also it will be noticed that these verses repeatedly lift up the word "law," which is quite natural because the concern for impartiality in the assembly originated in the Bible as part of the OT social legislation (Leviticus 19 and Deuteronomy 15 are illustrative). Impartiality as a moral concern was associated with Jesus (Matt 22:15-22; Mark 12:13-17; Luke 20:20-26) who had the reputation of showing no partiality to persons based on their lofty social status. Paul shared the concern, as is clear for example in Rom 2:11 and Gal 2:6.

James 1:25 mentions "the perfect law, the law of liberty." The author uses the latter expression again in the present context (v. 12). Verse 8 provides ample caution against construing James's legal language to be vague allusions to the Torah. Nowhere else in Jewish or Christian tradition is Lev 19:18c ("You shall love your neighbor as yourself") called "the royal law." James makes an appeal to this precept through the formula "according to the scripture," meaning the OT (LXX), but he also knows that this precept rose to prominence not in the Torah but in the teachings of Jesus. The closest James comes to Law as Torah is in v. 10, but even here that sense is mitigated by Matthean Jesus tradition that says much the same (Matt 5:17-20). To a great extent James understandably respects the Law and insists on abiding especially by the moral aspects of the Decalogue. Verse 11 poses no problem either, for even Paul cites the second half of the Decalogue in similar fashion (Rom 13:9). James champions a holistic faith with strong and consistent social ethics: v. 12, "so speak and so act as those who are to be judged by the law of liberty." There is a hint here of James's imminent eschatology on which he will later elaborate (5:1-9).

The final verse (2:13) does not stand alone; it is an integral part of the pericope. Verse 13 bears directly on the topic of partiality (vv. 1, 9) and on an eschatological aspect of adherence to the moral law of the gospel. Verse 13a, "for judgment will be without mercy" gives the impression that James is concluding the pericope; instead, it begins to set forth a principle of reciprocal eschatological justice stated as a warning for those who have tended to show no mercy to their neighbors or the less fortunate. Verse 13b is rather pastoral, probably offered with the hope that offending parties will change their ways before it is too late. More fundamentally, v. 13b reminds all James's audience and readers that God's ultimate nature is to be merciful: God is the one who generously bestows "every perfect gift" (1:17).

The Unity of Faith and Deeds (2:14-26)

Few debate the integrity of these verses as a unified pericope. The key for appreciating this fact lies in James's skillful and somewhat unique usage of the noun "work" *(ergon),* otherwise widely associated in the NT with "works of the Law." James gives clear evidence in this pericope that by "works" he means two things. First, as is manifest in 2:14-17, "merciful deeds" of social concern for the less fortunate become "works" for James. They demonstrate the unified nature of one's faith by indicating that the believer takes seriously "the royal law" (2:8) as highlighted in the preceding pericope. Second, by "works" James also suggests strongly in 2:18-26 that he means acts of faith that specifically show that men and women are personally open to a new (and renewing) spiritual relationship with God. Having just raised the issue of "mercy" in 2:13 the author now typically provides a flagrant example, thereby perhaps trying to guarantee that he will not be misunderstood—even by "hearers who forget" (the image used in Jas 1:25b).

The new example in 2:14-17 is undoubtedly drawn from reports of community life experiences: this despite the rhetorical style of the diatribe with the customary imaginary interlocutor: "What good (lit. "profit") is it, my brothers [and sisters], if you say you have faith . . . ?" (see the similar use of this rhetorical device in vv.

18-20). The focus within this example is the superficiality or rhetorical pretense of faith that apparently was widespread among James's readers then as over the centuries. As with the earlier example in 2:2-4, there is an air of realism here despite the tinge of humorous caricature. The comfortable Christian has studiously learned the art of dismissing socio-economic disparities that may at times be glaring but remain unseen due to class blinders well in place. The poor, the homeless, the ex-convict, or the street beggar merely receives a perfunctory "greeting" as the Sunday-only comfortable Christian hurries by, scarcely seeing the needy "neighbor." While it is true that one can get killed trying to be the good Samaritan today, this possibility is no warrant for distancing oneself from virtually every opportunity to extend Christian mercy.

Too many Christians today have moved from a belief in justification by faith to self-justification; James was familiar with their ancient counterparts. In 2:14-17 James adopts and adapts the language of "faith-works" most probably because he had become aware of how prominent a place such language had in the missionary activity of Paul. James, like Paul in some respects, had his own tightrope to walk in Jerusalem.

2:18-26

This unit repositions the terminology of "faith-works" so that greater distance stands between it and the Law. One can only surmise that James is doing this for strategic rather than theological reasons; after all he, unlike Paul, still has to live in Jerusalem. The unit begins and ends with the explicit "faith/works" terminology and James apparently intends to clarify not only the nature of "works" described here but also to explicate the relationship between faith and works.

Verse 18 begins with another instance of the diatribe (used by Stoics and Cynics alike) wherein one debates with an imaginary interlocutor. The technique is an effective way for James to dramatize his lesson that "faith" and what he means by "works" are flip sides of the same coin; they have a symbiotic relationship but James seems to tip the balance in favor of "works." At least in this context James refers to "faith" as merely the superficial confession of a set of beliefs.

Verse 19 makes it rather plain that here (and above in vv. 14, 17) "faith" among many of his readers has been weakened or vitiated as empty rhetoric rather than being a dynamic understanding of one's total personal and social obligation to show forth "the righteousness of God" according to biblical precepts. The first tenet of Judaism as set forth in the *Shema* specifies that "God is one" (v. 19a). James's affirmation of this precept is quick, but with a proviso. Outside the context of a holistic faith even the *Shema* is devoid of meaning. Here it seems that the audience has a Hellenistic Jewish background. Nevertheless in v. 19 James promptly alludes not to another precept of Judaism but again to the Jesus tradition (most probably Matt 8:28-34; Mark 5:1-20; Luke 8:26-29) with which he also assumes his readers are familiar). Thus v. 19b: "even the demons believe—and shudder."

Another rhetorical question presents itself in v. 20, but here the author bristles, calling the imaginary interlocutor a "senseless" (lit. "empty-headed") person. The designation seems appropriate for one whom James sees as empty of works and superficial in the understanding of faith and religion. Two cogent examples follow in vv. 21-25; one involves a preeminent man of faith, the other a woman who, despite her different ethnic background and dubious social status in Jericho of old (Joshua 2), had shown so much faith that Jewish traditions over the centuries had elevated Rahab to lofty heights.

James's appeal to the example of Abraham (2:21), who noticeably is not called "our father" as is common in the NT (here he is "our ancestor"), is similar to Paul's appeal in Romans 4 in that both direct attention to Abraham as one who exhibited a righteous faith. Yet James makes the appeal to the Abraham example for entirely different reasons than the apostle Paul in Romans. There Paul uses the example to underscore the fact that the patriarch was deemed righteous by God before there was a Mosaic law or "works of the Law"; on the other hand James appeals to the Abraham example not to subvert or minimize the Law but to stress the importance of "righteous deeds" that ultimately do not depend on the Law: so v. 22 "faith was brought to completion by the works." As in 2:8 James quotes the Scripture of the early Church, the OT (here Gen 15:6 which is the same text that Paul often cited—as in Romans 4 and Galatians 3—increasing the likelihood that the author of this epistle is offering correctives not so much for Paul himself, but for Jewish Christians who have heard Paul and are twisting his teachings to suit their own dubious purposes. If this proposal is accurate it would help interpreters of James today to appreciate how rhetorically adroit and theologically astute James the Just may have been after all.

As if the foregoing were not enough, v. 24 adds the then well-known Rahab example; she had become a hero within Judaism by virtue of her elevated status in Jewish intertestamental literature. One should also recall that it is only in Matthew's infancy narrative that Rahab is included in the genealogy of Jesus. Her example of "faith and works" necessarily going together was ideal for James's bold lesson. James 2:26 is merely a refrain that reiterates the point already established in v. 17, but now the argument has been sufficiently buttressed with examples and the basic message is summarily repeated as the pericope ends.

Chapter Three

Faithfulness Through a Disciplined Tongue (3:1-12)

This pericope takes up again the topic of "personal speech ethics" that was introduced in 1:19-25 and then given wider significance in 1:26 (see our analysis of conclusions for those passages). The author redirects his concern to the contours of responsible speech and the inherent dangers of not disciplining one's tongue. James 3:1 is a sober reminder specifically to teachers in religious contexts but the stern admonition could apply to a variety of teachers at any stage of formal education. James discourages persons in his audience from aspiring to the position of "teacher," given the heavy accountability that he envisions for those who either pretend to or actually fulfill such a role. His cautions proceed evidently from the fact that the current behavior of his readers suggests that whatever teachers have been instructing in their midst, they scarcely have been effective.

The author, or here more probably editor, in commenting on the human tendency to make mistakes (3:2) makes an observation that appears to work against the ideal of striving for perfection that constitutes part of the initial thoughts that begin the epistle (1:4). The awkward concession on human imperfection suggests a different set of circumstances from the one envisioned at the outset of the document. Similarly, an abrupt shift in conceptual framework seems to be underway in the litany of images: horses (v. 3), ships (v. 4), forest fire (v. 5), the peculiar reference to "the wheel of birth" (v. 6), and the comprehensive survey of living creatures of the air, land, and sea (v. 7). All this is pressed into the service of upbraiding the community on the abuses of the tongue. One cannot but imagine that there is some compelling event or community circumstance that has erupted to justify such passion and graphic imagery. The passage, yet another diatribe, is thus riddled with such striking metaphors and illustrations from nature that the author (really editor here) seems to extend his concern beyond the protocols of personal speech ethics. Something is causing great divisions and further tensions within the communities (see 4:1-6). A disciplined tongue seems sorely needed.

Two Kinds of Wisdom (3:13-18)

This second unit in ch. 3 clarifies further James's perspective on the two types and respective functions of wisdom. On the one hand there is "wisdom from below" (mundane and carnal), elaborated in vv. 14-16; on the other hand there is "wisdom from above" (spiritual), the topic of v. 17. The progression of thought reiterates in 3:13 the need for persons to show "works" incidental to a "good life" (discussed in 2:14-26), moving toward the strategic sapiential *mashal* of 3:18. One refers to the "strategic" nature of v. 18 because it prepares the readers for what follows in 4:1-6. There one sees the terrible contrasting social conflicts and community problems where "righteousness and peace" are so absent.

James 3:13-18 looks back and reiterates the emphasis on "doing," as we discussed in connection with 1:19-25, 26-27. Not surprising is the reappearance of the word "gentleness"; in 1:21 it is the recommended attitude with which one should receive the "implanted word," whereas in this context (v. 13) "gentleness" describes the attitude in which "works" are done for a good life. If one considers James's interchangeable use of the terms humble/humility (1:9; 4:10; also cf. 1 Pet 3:8; 4:4-11) the pattern of thought on gentleness/humility is even more extensive. A contrasting paradigm on "boasting" comes into view as James excoriates believers who exhibit "bitter envy and selfish ambition" in 3:14. James's chastisement here is "do not be boastful," whereby he again raises the problem of boasting as he does paradoxically in 1:9 and 2:13 (the humble and God as the epitome of mercy have a right to "boast"), but in confronting tones in 3:14; 4:6, 16. Such patterns suggest a literary integrity and conceptual consistency for large sections of James, highlighting the possibility that 3:1-12 represents an editorial interpolation.

James has a basic interest in contrasting the "wisdom from below" with the "wisdom from above." The former causes bitter envy, selfish ambition, disorder, and wickedness of all sorts, but the latter for James is "full of mercy and good fruits" and like God is "without a trace of partiality" (vv. 16-17).

Now the climactic and strategic nature of 3:18 comes to the fore more plainly. James now speaks of "a harvest of righteousness . . . sown in peace." The saying has its parallels in the Wisdom literature (Prov 3:9; 11:22) and the NT "fruit of righteousness" in both Phil 1:11 and Heb 12:11). The agrarian James wants all the fruit, the whole harvest of righteousness "sown in peace for those who make peace." (So "blessed are the peacemakers" Matt 5:9, although Luke mentions the word "peace" more than any other gospel.)

Finally one sees the overarching constructive purpose of James's concern for a personal religion with a disciplined tongue (not a boasting, cursing, deceitful or slandering one) as well as for a social religion that in community relations works and shows forth "the righteousness of God," namely to bring peace and order to his congregations that are in utter turmoil. James 3:18 is a fitting transition to this central concern with which chapter four so graphically deals.

Chapter Four

Faithlessness in the Community (4:1-6)

This opening passage presents a horrible community situation. It would be both easy and comforting to treat such human degradation as depicted here by James as so much hyperbole and righteous indignation out of control. Polite society over the centuries has always had difficulties imagining (admitting) that so-called Christian communities could degenerate to such low levels. Polite society denies many things. The sad likelihood is that James addresses real problems that have been brought to his attention at a difficult and quite ugly phase of early Jewish Christianity. The Bible assumes authority and perennial significance not only due to its spiritual insights but also because of its realism; it is more than "historicized fiction" as too many modern Western scholars suggest.

James 4:1-6 constitutes the opening unit for this chapter even in the form-critical analysis of Martin Dibelius (although for him this is but the first unit of vv. 1-12) . The stern admonitions of these verses aim at establishing harmonious social relations within Jewish Christianity gone terribly wrong. James's strident tone should not obscure the aim and role of peacemakers (3:18), which explains his adopting warfare terminology in 4:1 as he deals forthrightly with the "conflicts and disputes" among his readers. The figurative usage of military imagery is common in NT epistles (2 Cor 7:5; Eph 6:11, 13; 2 Tim 2:23; Titus 3:9). However James applies such imagery to riotous living, fights, and pleasure-seeking impulses "at war" within individuals.

Verse 2 continues the rhetoric of violence, suggesting that extreme socio-economic disparities have caused Christians to lay aside their religious values and engage in desperate struggles between "haves and have-nots." It appears that the word "cravings" in 4:1b prompts the indictment about desire in 4:2a but James does not elaborate on this. Instead he offers a chain of indictments regarding murder, jealousy, fighting, and engaging in other conflicts, presumably because large segments of the communities are materially lacking in resources. The awkward logical sequence is not explained merely by random word association. Rather the reference to "desire" precipitates images of death already introduced in 1:15 (desire–sin–death).

One will notice that earlier (3:14-16) James condemned community strife; this allows us now to appreciate the greater specificity that he wishes to bring to the subject. If taken literally, as to an extent it should be, the situation is alarming. The indictments in 4:2 bespeak widespread disunity caused also by petty jealousies that previously featured prominently in the author's depiction of "wisdom from below" (3:15). One should note that at the root of the social turmoil are materialism and self-gratification. Again we see the interplay between the personal and social strivings that have subverted a faith and a religion that is supposed to be personal and social.

The most significant feature of 4:5-6 is the citation of Scripture in each verse, virtual prooftexts for the preceding admonitions. Still, no one can be certain about the scriptural basis for 4:5 and consequently many have offered exotic extra-canonical proposals. It may be that the author quotes a Septuagintal variant of a Wisdom text no longer extant. This might be so because James employs the formula "the Scripture says" and in such instances James and other NT authors mean what they say. The jealousy of God occupies a prominent place in the first half of the Decalogue, but beyond that James mentions the "so-called" Scripture because he wishes purposely to contrast the frightful human jealousies within the communities with the jealousy of God that seeks the salvation of their souls. One should recall the "implanted word" reference in 1:21; it is in view again here but transformed as "the spirit [God] made to dwell within" or implanted, that is, the gospel. With reference to James 4:6-10, one finds a parallel sequence in 1 Pet 5:5-9, including the quotation of Prov 3:34. Both authors are probably indebted to a common stock of parenetic tradition or the author of 1 Peter has borrowed from James (compare Jas 1:1 and 1 Pet 1:1).

Corrective Formulae—A Call to Repentance (4:7-10)

Having detailed the extensive personal and social turmoil among his readers and offered his rebuke together with an accompanying analysis of their condition, James issues a call to repentance. The formulaic framework of this call suggests a return to their original conversion and the baptismal catechism that now lies forgotten, far in the background. James speaks here as the exasperated pastor who realizes that he must start all over again! He thus issues the formal call in 4:7, "submit yourselves therefore to God. Resist the devil . . . ." The idea is to make an intentional contrast akin to that seen in 1:21 "therefore rid yourselves . . . welcome," but here stated in reverse and presenting God and the devil as opposite and mutually exclusive (as in Jas 4:4).

James's call to repentance plays itself out as a kind of antithetical parallelism:

4:8a Draw near to God	4:9a Lament
4:8b Cleanse your hands	4:9a Mourn
4:8c Purify your hearts	4:9a Weep

On the surface 4:8 is a development of 4:7a, yet 4:9a introduces the idea of judgment for those who refuse to repent. Clearly James is speaking to sinners and double-minded persons who have engaged in irresponsible speech, false values, and reprehensible behavior toward fellow Christians, including themselves. The appeal in Jas 4:10 ("Humble yourselves before the Lord, and [God] will exalt you") returns to the motif of the exaltation of the humble as seen in 1:9-11 (but here the rich are omitted for the moment). This appeal, moreover, prefigures the imminent reversal for the rich as presented in Jas 5:1-6.

Warnings—The Law Does Not Deal in Trifles (4:11-12)

James's "call to repentance" is an interim strategy; he is not finished with his survey of community problems. His thoughts turn from the severe conflicts caused by jealousies to the problem of "judging one another," meaning casting aspersions based on social class, slandering, and otherwise exercising "wrongful judgments" upon fellow Christians. James 2:2-4 again becomes the focus, here not limited to specific acts of discrimination but as a general concern. James keeps focus on the need for unity and peace, which probably explains his resumption of a discussion about aspects of a Law that "does not deal in trifles."

That James resumes a subject so fully addressed earlier is probably due to the way that he construes the issue of unrighteous judgments between believers as a major infraction of the foundational moral law of Jewish Christianity. Already in 2:10 he has established that breaking one part of the Law constitutes an infraction of the whole, and here the issue is a pattern of gross violations of "the royal law"(2:8). James moves in the same ethos as the Matthean Jesus, accentuating the twin themes of the higher righteousness and the continuing validity of the Law, particularly the moral aspects. James is absolutely silent about all features of cultic piety (perhaps purged by an editor or intentionally de-emphasized for strategic reasons).

It is easy to detect in this context a renewed accent on "doing" and the theocentric contours of James's perspective. In 4:11 importance is attached to being "doers of the law" which is reminiscent of 1:22 ("be doers of the word"). This close identification of the word with OT moral law places James with Jesus as bridges between the OT and Pauline Christianity; it is a tense, sensitive, and all the more ambiguous position for James who writes at a time of increasing problems between Jews and Gentiles. Relief is found only in repeated invocations about the nature of God. Thus in 4:12 James invokes the image and authority of God as lawgiver and judge. He frequently appeals to different aspects of God (as "Father of lights" in 1:7, as Father in 1:27, as One in 2:19, the Lord "Sabaoth" or "of hosts" in 5:4, again as judge in 5:9, as compassionate and merciful in 5:11 (compare 2:13b) and as healer in 5:15.

Cautions to Those Who Take God for Granted (4:13-17)

Customarily commentators on James regard 4:13–5:6 as a single pericope with two parallel units both introduced by the imperative formula "Come now." Certainly the tone of 4:13-17 and 5:1-6 resemble that of OT prophetic apostrophes, the first against arrogant merchants, the second against oppressive landowners. Despite this it seems better to isolate 4:13-17 from its sequel. However, the former follows naturally from the emphases on arrogant boasting and the nature of God as "lawgiver and judge," that is, on God's authority or sovereignty (4:12), while 5:6 returns to a much earlier social justice motif, the reversal of fortunes for the oppressive rich (1:9-11; compare 2:6-7).

Verses 13-17 single out Jewish Christian and possibly Jewish merchants (the distinctively Christian element is lacking here and to a slightly less extent in 5:1-6) who evidently are taking God's providence for granted. Instead of properly acknowledging the factor of divine providence such businessmen are only interested in making profits. The author speaks to many of us today! Unlike the apostrophe in 5:1-6 James does not rebuke them because of their oppressive actions; rather these merchants are upbraided for arrogance and boasting, the same subject that opens ch. 4 (see 4:6b). This is explicit in 4:61, "you boast in your arrogance; all such boasting is evil." They know what is right, but fail to do it.

Chapter Five

Final Warning to Unjust Rich Land Owners (5:1-6)

Using the same imperative formula that introduced the preceding pericope, "Come now," this new prophetic apostrophe directs attention to the unjust rich. The author thereby picks up anew the eschatological reversal motif first seen in 1:9-11. One should always be careful to assert that James does not categorically inveigh against the rich simply because they have wealth. On the contrary, he knows that there are persons of substantial means who do attend the "assemblies" (2:2-4). James's ire focuses on those wealthier Christians who lack a holistic faith. They have fraudulently held back the daily wages of the farm workers and other laborers in violation of the well-established social legislation of the Bible (notably Deut 24:14-15). Their "word" has meant nothing for they have disrespected the Word, trivializing the non-violent biblical recourse of the poor and needy in swearing an oath against them (Deuteronomy 15). In this sense 5:1-6 does more than present a new pericope; it anticipates the specific topic of "oaths" that we find in v. 12.

The features of this small unit merit further comment. First, James's apostrophe is thoroughly eschatological. Indeed, he speaks as if somehow the judgment against the unjust rich has already begun. "Your gold and silver have rusted" (5:3) is symbolic because gold does not rust and silver only tarnishes. Nevertheless the author is thinking fast and dramatizing the futility of hoarding luxuries at the expense of the needy who have the right to expect wages as promised. The prospect of the defrauded laborers and harvesters invoking divine revenge (5:4) is a profound reminder to the unjust: James views them as "demons" who now should shudder (see 2:19).

The second dimension of 5:1-6 upon which we must comment is the intriguing 5:6 "you have condemned and murdered the righteous one, who does not resist you." The great temptation would be to construe this as a cryptic allusion to the crucifixion. That is unlikely since James is theocentric rather than christocentric. Without trying to argue the point here in detail we suggest that the better guess would be that 5:6 is the editor's reference to the death of James the Righteous himself. Among the crucifixion of Jesus, the stoning of Stephen, and the stoning to death of James the record shows a profound resemblance: all innocent, all making a prophetic witness, all highly regarded by followers or numerous close associates, all killed by a sinful mob without resisting. An allusion of this sort by an editor either circulating or recirculating authentic sermonic material would have a profound effect.

A Word of Consolation to the Faithful (5:7-12)

Despite the fact that the word of the unjust landowners has meant nothing, James here reminds his readers that their word should have integrity. Everything in this new pericope culminates in 5:12. The framework for this unit is a pastoral word of consolation; the author at this point begins to close his homily-epistle. He again resumes calling the faithful among his congregation "beloved," urges patience, and reassures them of the imminent "coming of the Lord" (here possibly an allusion to the *parousia* or second coming of Christ) and rehearses several sub-themes in vv. 7-8. There the language and imagery seems decidedly Christian, but in vv. 9-11 the idiom appears to take on an equally distinctive Jewish flavor; note the reference to Job and the description of God. One needs little further confirmation that James is a preeminent document representing what was once a dominant brand of early Christianity.

Then comes the apparent main point of this section, as underscored by the author's own "above all, my beloved." James in the words and tone of the Matthean Jesus (Matt 5:33-37) emphasizes again the importance of "personal speech ethics," particularly as a matter undergirded with biblical authority (OT) and intensified in the Sermon on the Mount. Underlying much of the subject matter here is the notion of patient redemptive suffering made all the more acceptable with the foregoing assurance about the almighty God who is already moving into action on behalf of the poor and oppressed.

Overall, James's great litany of divine imperatives, Wisdom teachings, and apostrophes begins to come to an end with the simple directive of v. 12, "let your 'Yes' be yes and your 'No' be no." The heart of the sermon-epistle has been identified and it has been "heart-wrenching" as this little epistle has made its bold case for a religion that is personal and social, worthy indeed to be associated with "the righteousness of God."

Pastoral Encouragement: The Power of Prayer and Confession (5:13-20)

The last pericope in James consists of eight verses all of which represent a somewhat ironic and abrupt shift in content and style. These concluding verses have no specific final salutation nor is there even an "amen." The mood is that of the ending of an episcopal sermon; here the author is very pastoral but the impression that remains is that of a document that is incomplete for some reason. It is as if the actual ending has been lost or the sermon-epistle was suddenly halted as the author was closing. One can only speculate on the circumstances for such an ending, but it is clear that the document is closing.

Verses 13-20 mention several basic pastoral matters, namely prayer, the singing of hymns, healing, forgiveness, confession, and the restoration of lapsed or excommunicated believers. James 5:16c has become gospel for many African Americans since the American slave period: "the prayer of the righteous is powerful and effective." These are words of encouragement, consolation, and hope, yet, given the body of the document with its utter social chaos, one finds it quite difficult to comprehend how the author can now ask such questions as "Are any among you suffering?" or "Are any cheerful?" or "Are any among you sick?" The real question is, how could they not obviously be suffering or sick? How could anyone be cheerful? No, it rather appears once again that the document is a composite of edited material that has been hurriedly reworked and circulated to meet some significant crisis in first-century Jewish Christianity.

Whatever was in fact the case, one gives thanks to these "last echoes" of Jesus offered by none other than his esteemed brother, James the Righteous, who even for some of us today shows himself to be worthy of being called "bishop of bishops" for social justice in the New Testament. Amen.

BIBLIOGRAPHY

Carrington, Philip. *The Primitive Christian Catechism: A Study in the Epistles.* Cambridge: Cambridge University Press, 1949.

Daniélou, Jean. *The Theology of Jewish Christianity.* Vol. 1. Philadelphia: Westminster, 1964.

Dibelius, Martin. *James.* Hermeneia. Philadelphia: Fortress, 1976.

Felder, Cain Hope. *Troubling Biblical Waters: Race, Class, and Family.* Maryknoll, N.Y.: Orbis, 1989.

Laws, Sophie. *The Epistle of James.* HNTC. San Francisco: Harper & Row, 1981.

Martin, Ralph P. *James.* WBC. Waco, Tex.: Word Books, 1988.

Maynard-Reid, Pedrito U. *Poverty and Wealth in James.* Maryknoll, N.Y.: Orbis, 1987.

Tamez, Elsa. *The Scandalous Message of James: Faith Without Works is Dead.* New York: Crossroad, 1990.

Townsend, Michael J. *The Epistle of James.* Epworth Commentaries. London: Epworth Press, 1994.

Wall, Robert W. *Community of the Wise: The Letter of James.* Valley Forge: Trinity Press International, 1997.

1 Peter

José Cervantes Gabarrón

FIRST READING

The First Letter of Peter is excellent, as a NT writing, for enabling the readers to perceive the height of theological reflection, the spiritual depth, and the vital force of the Christian communities mentioned at the beginning of the letter as its recipients. Specialized studies done in the last thirty years have reawakened interest in the specific contributions of this letter in the fields of christology, ecclesiology, and Christian life.

We will now read a paradoxical text of this letter about the problem of suffering: 1 Pet 2:18-25. Does it not seem strange, at first glance, that the Christians are called to bear unjust suffering as if the suffering were good in itself? Does the letter invite resignation as an attitude toward suffering? What is the value of suffering in Christian life? Does the letter try to legitimize in some way the different social levels that appear in it? Does it intend to justify the submission of Christians before public institutions or people with socially dominant roles such as those of emperor, governor (2:14), master (2:18), husband (3:1), or elder (5:5)? If we continue reading the text of 1 Pet 3:8-18 we will better understand the urgent appeal that the author of the letter makes to all believers. Finally we will read in 1 Pet 4:12-19 the height of the Christian paradox: how is it possible to live joyously in the midst of suffering?

Situation and Problematic

The beginning of the letter mentions great and various regions of Asia Minor including the coastal zones of Asia, Bithynia, and Pontus and the continental zones of Galatia and Cappadocia. No city is mentioned, indicating that the evangelization referred to in the letter most probably takes place in the interior rural areas of these regions. Moreover, the letter does not address itself to individuals or particular communities but rather to Christian groups that live principally in rural towns. Those who receive the letter are probably farmers or shepherds for the most part, coming from paganism and the lower social class, people who care for and work the estates of the Roman or local upper classes. It is possible that there were also some small Christian estates in those rural populations, but their owners cannot be considered rich. There are no reliable reasons for thinking that the believers found themselves subjugated to some kind of official persecution by the authorities. The term "persecution" does not appear anywhere, but we can speak of the suffering that came from the hostile environment of the society in which they lived. This we can infer from the references to the "testing" that the Christians had to undergo (1:7; 4:12) and the insults, calumnies, and slanders (2:12; 3:9, 16; 4:4; 5:9) in which the believers found themselves implicated to the point of being mistreated and ridiculed (4:14).

Author

In the letter we find the following identification of its author: Peter, apostle of Jesus Christ (1:1), co-elder, witness of the passion of Christ and participant in the glory that is to be revealed

(5:1), by means of Silvanus his faithful brother has written this short letter (5:12) to the chosen people of Pontus, Galatia, Cappadocia, Asia, and Bithynia from Babylon (5:13) where Mark, his son, also is.

However, the identification of the author of 1 Peter with the apostle Peter is a controversial matter. The most significant arguments against authenticity are:

(1) The theological themes of 1 Peter stem from a date later than 67; therefore the apostle had already died (in 64 or 67) when the letter was written (in the decade of the 80s).

(2) The literary quality of the letter is against authenticity, for the Greek used and the literary style employed, as well as the use of the LXX, do not suit an uneducated fisherman from Galilee (cf. Acts 4:13).

(3) Silvanus's active participation in the writing of the letter is mentioned (5:12).

(4) Among those who receive the letter are the people of the regions of Galatia and Asia, Gentile churches founded by Paul and people who would be difficult for the apostle Peter to address during Paul's lifetime (cf. Gal 2:8-9).

(5) The situation of a hostile environment corresponds to the description furnished by Pliny the Younger to Trajan (c. 110).

We believe, then, that we are dealing with a pseudepigraphic writing by a responsible, educated member of the community who is familiar with the situation of the Christians and who, using the authority of Peter the apostle, addresses this circular letter to the churches of Asia Minor.

Date and Place

The time of the letter's writing can be deduced from the historical localization of the different doctrinal topics and parenetic instructions in the letter by placing emphasis on the literary and doctrinal relationships of dependence or influence of 1 Peter on other NT writings and showing its specific deficiencies as well as its contributions. First Peter has made substantial contributions to NT theology. It is an original formulation revealing its own body of thought that enriches the global message of the NT. Clear examples of this are the theme of regeneration (1:3, 23) in direct relation to the resurrection of Christ; the theme of the passion of Christ in relation to the suffering of Christians; and the extraordinary metaphor of believers (2:4-5) as transformed into living stones because united to Christ, the living stone: together they constitute a spiritual house (2:5). The unique character of 1 Peter is perceptible in its original treatment of some NT themes such as christology, since it alludes to the theology of the Suffering Servant, but with a more parenetical orientation, or also in the eschatological structure of the letter that points not to an immediate eschatology but, with greater realism, concentrates on the present life of Christians, calling them to hope, good conduct, and service to all people. Therefore the elements of christology, ecclesiology and eschatology supply good reasons for locating the date of writing within the subapostolic period, around the year 80.

As the place of composition many commentators are inclined to name Rome, concealed under the name of Babylon (5:13). However, nothing can be concluded with certainty and we are more inclined to accept the hypothesis that locates 1 Peter in some important Christian nucleus in Asia Minor.

Literary Structure

The diverse topics this letter tackles and the internal connections of the literary and theological elements within it permit us to consider 1 Peter as a convergence text drawing together different catechetical and liturgical traditions of the primitive Church.

Outline

Initial Greeting: Grace and peace to the chosen (1:1-2)

- I. Theological Prologue centered on Christ: 1:3-12
  - A. God has given us new birth through the resurrection of Jesus Christ: 1:3-5
    1. To a living hope: 1:3
    2. To an imperishable inheritance: 1:4
    3. To a salvation through faith: 1:5
  - B. The joy in the testing of faith: 1:6-9
    1. The glory in the testing of faith: 1:6-7
    2. The joy of believing in Christ and loving him: 1:8
    3. The goal of the faith is salvation: 1:9
  - C. The passion and glorification of Christ: Grace and salvation announced: 1:10-12

II. Development of the letter: 1:13–5:9
  A. Regeneration: salvation and good conduct through the resurrection of Jesus Christ: 1:13–4:11
    1. Called and reborn to a new life: 1:13–2:10
      a. Called to hope and sanctification: 1:13-21
      b. Reborn from an incorruptible seed: 1:22-25
      c. The chosen, together with the living stone, grow in salvation: 2:1-10
    2. Called to good Christian conduct: being available to all human creatures as servants of God: 2:11–3:7
      a. Availability and respect toward all human creatures for the Lord's sake: 2:11-17
      b. Availability of slaves: suffering and doing good like the suffering Christ: 2:18-25
      c. Availability and respect in marriage: 3:1-7
    1'. Called to life of doing good: 3:8-22
      b'. As inheritors of the blessing of God: 3:8-12
      a'. Suffering for doing good and righteousness in hope: 3:13-16
      c'. Suffering for doing good, as Christ did, who brings salvation through baptism: 3:17-22
    3. Double conclusion: 4:1-11
      a. The passion of Christ, source of a new Christian mentality: 4:1-6
      b. The glorification of God through love and other charisms: 4:7-11
  B. Joy and glory in the test of suffering: 4:12–5:9
    1. Joy in communion with the passion and glory of Christ: 4:12-19
    2. Particular appeals to elders and young people to obtain the glory of God: 5:1-5
    3. General appeals to humility, faith, and solidarity with those who suffer: 5:6-9
III. Theological and Doxological Epilogue
  A. God called you and will strengthen you: 5:10-11
Final Greeting: Grace and peace from those who are also chosen: 5:12-14

Content and Message

The passion of Christ in its relation to the Christian life appears to constitute the fundamental theme of this letter. The theme of suffering is the most frequent in the letter: we encounter it twelve times in verb form (to suffer) and four more times as a noun (suffering). More than twenty-five percent of the references to suffering in the NT using this terminology appear in 1 Peter. In addition the passion of Christ, expressed with a vocabulary of its own in a total of twelve references, seems to constitute the primary theme of the letter: the blood of Christ (1:2, 19) and the suffering of Christ (1:11; 4:13; 5:1) as well as the verbs "suffer" (2:20-21, 23; 3:18; 4:1) and "reject" (2:4, 7) all refer to Christ and are the fundamental core of the doctrine and parenesis of the letter.

Besides this frequent reference to the passion of Christ there is special importance in the fact that the subject of the passion of Christ appears in practically all sections of the letter as indicated by the literary structure outlined above. That is why we consider this subject the central axis of the letter. Certainly the passion of Christ is the doctrinal key to the letter at the same time that it is the most profound reason for the urgent appeal to good conduct in the midst of this world. Thus a central element in the literary structure clearly manifests the theological thought and objective of the author. The passion of Jesus Christ is the source from which flows the genuine novelty of 1 Peter in its treatment of the doctrine and parenesis of the Church in the diaspora to the people the author tries to nurture and strengthen in faith and hope in the midst of their sufferings. The christological aspects and ecclesiological considerations, like the focus and attitudes of a truly Christian life, have in the passion of Christ their ultimate origin and their own dynamism, as we will see more fully in the commentary that follows.

Literary Genre

This letter has usually been considered an urgent appeal or a writing of parenetic character, but this is not, in fact, the dominant tone in 1 Peter. The letter participates also in the genres of exposition or doctrinal teaching. In its entirety it does not allow for a clear separation of exposition and parenesis. Because both appear to be interwoven throughout, it is better to call the genre of the entire letter "foundational appeal" or "concerted appeal." This designation serves to vindicate and emphasize the doctrinal importance of this letter within the NT.

Use of the Hebrew Bible in the Letter

The author of 1 Peter has used the Greek LXX as a basis for quotation from the Scriptures of Israel, but we cannot exclude in some cases a direct relationship to the Hebrew text. After Revelation, and together with Hebrews, 1 Peter is one of the NT writings that, in proportion to its length, makes the greatest use of the OT. Above all the fact that all parts of Sacred Scripture are present in some way within the letter is significant. We recognize the influence of Genesis in allusions to Noah, Sarah, and Abraham; Exodus through the figure of the paschal lamb, the rescue of the people and the commandments of the covenant; Leviticus in the strong appeal to holiness; Psalms, Proverbs, and the prophetic literature through multiple references. Especially emphatic are quotations from the canticle of the Suffering Servant of YHWH in Isaiah 53 that are found in the central text of 1 Pet 2:22-25, and other texts from Isaiah and Hosea combined with Psalm 117 (LXX) in 1 Pet 2:4-10, as well as the extensive citations of Isa 40:6-8 in 1 Pet 1:24-25 and of Ps 33:13-17 (LXX) in 1 Pet 3:10-12. In this broad use of the OT as a literary resource the Church appears as the people of God, legitimate heirs of the promises of God to Israel from the perspective of the plan of salvation in Jesus Christ.

SECOND READING

Initial Greeting: Grace and Peace to the Chosen: 1:1-2

The author introduces himself with the name of Peter and the title "apostle," addressing this circular letter, as a responsible member of the community, to the Christians of the diaspora, inhabitants of the regions of Asia Minor that are here named. The traditional Christian greeting, "grace and peace," is trinitarian in character and emphasizes the function Christ represents for the chosen because of the mystery of his death. The statement that the addressees have been "chosen . . . to be obedient to Jesus Christ and to be sprinkled with his blood" alludes to this. Christ in his obedience, even to the spilling of his own blood, fulfills the will of the Father. Through his love for his brothers and sisters and through his spilled blood, as a just person murdered, he carries out the plan of his Father.

The obedience of Jesus Christ expresses in the first place the profound attitude with which Christ accepted and was brought to his passion and death: *because of* the obedience of Jesus Christ we have been chosen and saved. In the second place his obedience manifests the ethical dynamism into which Christians have entered: the chosen have been called to live an obedience like that of Jesus Christ, adhering to the mystery of his passion and death and taking on his attitudes.

The blood of Jesus Christ constitutes an image of the sacrificial passion and death of Jesus. However, we are not dealing with the ritualistic value of the blood but rather with the power of the spilling of blood that corresponds to an existential sacrifice, the handing over of life itself for the good of all humankind. The relationship to Exod 24:3-8 where the elements of blood, sprinkling, and obedience appear in a context of covenant, gives 1 Pet 1:2 a like orientation. Here it is a matter of the blood of the new covenant that grants to human beings the forgiveness of sins and declares that they have definitive access to God (cf. 1 Pet 3:18). Christ's wisdom and obedience are inseparable aspects of his person. The obedience of Christ, sealed with his blood, establishes the foundation of the new covenant through which humanity can enter into communion with God. On the one hand the blood of Jesus is the blood of the righteous person (3:18) violently killed; on the other hand this blood is purifying. It is the cause of salvation for the chosen and at the same time it is a call to live the sacrificial dynamism and forgiveness that, throughout the letter, will shape itself into concrete attitudes of service and availability to all people in the adverse circumstances of the Christians' suffering.

Prologue Centered on Christ: 1:3-12

In 1 Peter's theological, Christ-centered prologue (1:3-12) we find the principal themes of the letter as well as its literary key and hints of its diverse structural elements. Thus in 1:3-5 regeneration as the great original theme of 1 Peter within the NT with its aspects of living hope, imperishable inheritance, and universal salvation anticipate the structuring themes of the second part (1:13–4:11) and of sections (a) (1:13–2:10) and (a') (3:8-12). In 1:6-9 the joy at the testing of faith anticipates the theme of the second part of the letter (4:12–5:9) and the passion and glorification of Christ (1:10-12) gives us the theological key to the letter as a whole. We also find that the unifying elements of the prologue are the name of Christ, the word "salvation," and the many references to the theme of revelation.

The passion and glorification of Christ (1:11) constitute the syntactic, literary, and thematic center of the last part of the prologue (1:10-12). Both prophetic activity in the past and the preaching of the gospel in the present have as their primary objective to give witness to the passion and glorification of Christ and to announce it as the good news of salvation. The passion in its saving dimension remains prominent in the prologue thanks to its link to the constant theme of salvation (1:5, 9, 10). The passion/glorification of Christ is the concrete and culminating event in the history of salvation. In 1 Pet 1:10 salvation is the generic motif of the prophets' investigation, while in 1:11 the passion of Christ is the specific aim of their testimony, thanks to the action of the Spirit in them. Thus we can say that the core of soteriology is established by christology whose fundamental key in 1 Peter is the paschal mystery expressed in the terminology of passion and glory.

The passion of Christ has particular meaning for those to whom 1 Peter is addressed, people whose faith is being tested by suffering. The center of the prologue (1:6-9) deals with the existential paradox of joy in suffering. Thanks to the regeneration experienced in the Christian life through the resurrection of Jesus from the dead it is possible to live with the hope and promise of an eschatological salvation. In this way the correlation between the suffering of the Christians referred to in the middle of the prologue (1:6) and the passion of Christ in the final part (1:11) represents a stimulus for the Christian life, for those who face the consequences of identifying with the one they love without having seen him, and with the process of his paschal mystery.

Called to Hope and Sanctification: 1:13-21

The parenetic structure of the first section 1:13–2:10 is formed by five syntactically related imperatives (1:13, 15, 17, 22; 2:2). Hope is the principal theme of the discourse in the first literary unit (1:13-21), and the corresponding doctrinal part (1:18-21) is the foundation for the imperatives that follow (the call to be holy in 1:15 and to religiously respectable conduct in 1:17), all under the dominant theme of hope. The faithful memory of the liberating event carried out through the blood of Christ is the profound reason for the Christians' change in conduct: they pass from a life without meaning to a life of hope, and also from ignorance to holiness. The liberator is Christ and the way of liberation is the passion sealed with the spilling of his blood (1:18-19). Using the paschal typology of Exod 12:5 the letter presents the event of salvation by means of the precious blood of Christ, which pertains to a new order of values, the absolute values that suppose a new kind of salvation. In this rescue there is no exchange of perishable objects but rather the gift of precious blood. The memory of believing faith is rooted in the passion of Christ and thus also in the greatness of the event of liberation from a theological perspective. This was God's project from before the creation of the world: Jesus Christ, revealed in later times, is resurrected by God and given glory. Passion and glory are again united because they pertain to the only saving plan of the Father for the chosen. Faith in God and in the paschal mystery of Jesus Christ brings a living hope that must be shaped into a new conduct because it corresponds to regeneration through God the Father.

Reborn from an Incorruptible Seed, the Living Word: 1:22-25

In 1:23 rebirth, an original theme of 1 Peter, reappears. The mediating function that Christ's resurrection has in the rebirth of believers (1:3) is identified in this text with the living and permanent word of God (1:23) that, like the imperishable seed, expresses the origin of a new life purified by obedience for a life of mutual love (1:22). The word of God identifies itself with the message of the gospel (1:25) that, according to 1 Pet 1:11-12, is the proclamation of the passion and glorification of Christ. Thus we can deduce that the basis of rebirth is found in the mystery of Christ's passion, which embraces his suffering, death, and resurrection. The quotation from Isa 40:6-9 in 1 Pet 1:24-25 acts as a verbal line of reasoning that shows the vitality of the word of God in its regenerating potential.

The Chosen, Together with the Living Stone, Grow in Salvation: 2:1-10

The third unit (2:1-10) of this hortatory and doctrinal section describes the objective of the change of conduct and the nourishment that Christians must experience for growth into salvation (2:2). This is the reason for the appeal to believers to long for pure milk, an allusion to the living word of God (1:23). Salvation is described in words from Ps 33:9 as tasting the goodness of the Lord (cf. 2:3). Thus we approach the dominant image of this unit, the stone (2:4, 5, 6, 7, 8) especially as a christological image. After 2:3 there is an extensive theological development in which motifs, quotations, and allusions drawn from the OT are gathered, forming a doctrinally dense text of a christological and ecclesiological character. The verb "to reject" (2:4, 7) is key as a reference to the passion of Jesus Christ. The image of the rejected stone has messianic significance that detaches itself from the resonances of the OT texts expressly cited (Isa 28:16; 8:14; Ps 117:22).

However, the application of this messianic image of the Lord Jesus as a precious stone rejected stresses for us some aspects of the messiah that were avoided in the earlier traditions of the NT. The rejection of the stone in 1 Pet 2:7 implies the identification of Jesus as messiah, especially in his passion and death, which are the most concrete historic moments culminating in the rejection of the stone by the builders. The builders are the religious leaders of the people of Israel in the age of Jesus. First Peter 2:4 speaks of a more generalized rejection by human beings, but with a new aspect: they have rejected Christ, the living stone. The mystery of Christ's passion continues to be present in the story. Christians keep the mystery of the passion present in the midst of their world, continuing to grow in salvation and to construct, thanks to their priestly transformation by the Spirit, the authentic messianic Christian community called to identify itself with the paschal Christ.

The rejection of the living Christ undeniably has repercussions for Christian and ecclesial identity. Only insofar as the community contemplates and assumes the true messianic identity of Christ in his passion is it possible to experience birth to a new life and growth in salvation.

Availability and Respect Toward All Human Creatures for the Lord's Sake: 2:11-17

The central section of the letter is marked by three themes corresponding to the verbs "be available" or "make oneself a servant of" all people (2:13, 18; 3:1, 5), "do good" or "do what is right" (2:14, 15, 20; 3:6), and "suffer" (2:19, 20, 21, 23). The three verbs express very important appeals in 1 Peter. The first is also a structural verb because it determines the subdivision of this section into three units: 2:11-17, 2:18-25, and 3:1-7. The theme of the passion of Christ (2:21-25) constitutes the theological basis for this whole section since in reality the passion of Christ is the most profound reality legitimizing and giving meaning to all conduct guided by the attitude of making oneself a servant of all.

The general appeal to maintain good conduct in a pagan environment rests on the observation of a Christian who wants to be a light in the midst of this world. But good conduct in this letter does not remain undetermined or defined by abstract values. Instead, it is defined by something as concrete as the uniqueness of Jesus' own attitudes in the crucial experience of his life: his passion unto death on the cross.

Therefore this series of commands in the Petrine appeal is not about demanding the submission of someone or subjugation before something, but rather of showing service and respect toward all human creatures for the Lord's sake as a distinctive trait of Christian identity while always safeguarding the human freedom and Christian dignity of those who are, above all, servants of God (1 Pet 2:16). First Peter is about making oneself a servant of all people as a concrete expression of good Christian conduct and of love within the Gentile world, considering all others as superiors and placing oneself below them as a demonstration of great humility.

Availability of Slaves: Suffering and Doing Good Like the Suffering Christ: 2:18-25

This passage is central to the whole letter, and in it we find the true nobility of the Christian vocation expressed with clarity. Since the call to be available and to be of service to all people has no limits one must live in all circumstances and with all people (cf. 2:13), and as a consequence of this with all masters as well, including those who behave badly and those who are wicked. This is the culmination of the paradoxical Christian calling. Always to maintain oneself in this attitude of availability and service, even before those who cause unjust suffering, is the Christian vocation *par excellence,* following the example of Christ.

The indirect style of the urgent appeal to the slaves (2:18) permits us to interpret the discourse on being available in a more general sense, extending to the whole community. This community finds in the passion of Christ a model of behavior capable of giving meaning to the more important themes of this section, namely the general and particular call to serve all human creatures for the Lord's sake (2:13), the appeal to slaves to be available to their masters (2:18) and to wives to accept that of their husbands (3:1, 5), as well as the call to do good in all circumstances (2:14, 15, 20; 3:6), specifically when tested by suffering (2:19, 20, 21, 23).

This attitude of being available even in a situation of unjust suffering is valued as a grace, a gift from God, if it is accepted in virtue of the experience that one has of God and of doing good. It is not the pain in itself that constitutes a grace, but rather the suffering caused by doing what is good, or of countering evil with good just as Christ did.

In 2:21 we find a kerygmatic affirmation of great significance that expresses the concrete act and significance of the passion of the Lord: "Christ also suffered for you, leaving you an example, so that you should follow in his steps" (2:21bc). Taking up and elaborating the expressions and motifs of the fourth Suffering Servant song in Isa 53:4, 5, 6, 9, 12, the author presents in 1 Pet 2:22-25 a suffering Christ with some elements of the theology of the servant. In the foreground of the doctrinal development are the figure of Christ and the event of his passion. The verb "suffer," referring to Christ in this context, refers not only to his death but also to his passion, which may include his death but is not limited to that. The parallels to the kerygmatic formulae with the verb "die" (1 Cor 15:3 and Rom 5:8) cannot be allowed to obscure the specific content of suffering that the Petrine formulation entails.

There are two essential aspects of the passion of Christ that are intrinsically united and remain at the forefront of this central development: the uniqueness of salvation (cf. 2:21b, 24) and the example of suffering (cf. 2:21cd, 22-23). These are supported by the references to the Suffering Servant of Isaiah 53 and the motif of the shepherd in Ezek 34:16, both of which provide an exceptional presentation of the suffering of Christ in relation to doing good, since Christ suffered (2:21) without having committed any sin (2:22), without returning evil for evil (2:23), bearing us from sin to righteousness (2:24) because he is the (good) shepherd (2:25).

The christological exposition of 1 Pet 2:21-25 establishes the fundamental doctrinal core of the letter. The salvation and liberation that the messiah brings have their culminating moment in the passion of Christ. At the same time the example of Christ's suffering is the foundation of the new identity of Christians who, following the example of the Lord, are called to endure unjust suffering by doing good works and returning good for evil, thus fulfilling the will of God and at the same time experiencing God's true grace.

Availability and Respect in Marriage: 3:1-7

Far from facing an attempt to legitimize the superiority of the man with respect to the woman and the subordination of the woman with respect to the man, we find ourselves before another paradigmatic appeal to express the Christian vocation, here placing emphasis on the comparison between the dignity of the man and that of the woman and of the different behavior required of both. The adverb "equally" ("in the same way") appears in 3:1 and 3:7 and permits us to understand the availablity and mutual respect between man and woman as interchangeable and homologous elements in a relationship of reciprocal love. Just as in 1 Pet 2:13-17 availability and respect toward all human persons make up the fundamental content of the appeal, so here they are the object of the discourse on married life as well.

The woman occupies a unique place in family and Christian life. Her conduct should be exemplary. She must also be sensitive and like those who have received the grace of life so that the husband may also participate in this grace of life. The authenticity and transparency of a serving and serene heart are things that are valued in the eyes of God. These appeals in the letter plead in the first place with the women, but they are not addressed exclusively to the women; they belong to all Christians. The author breaks away from these concrete, specific, and often difficult human relationships in order to emphasize the specific behavior of believers whose lives are marked by the grace that flows from the passion of Christ. We can therefore say that after 1 Peter all Christians, men as well as women, masters as well as slaves, the young with the old, are called to maintain good conduct in service and honor toward all others, with a transparent and humble heart, capable of sacrificing themselves for the good of the rest.

Called to a Life of Doing Good as Inheritors of the Blessing of God: 3:8-12

With this pericope begins the third and last literary section of the central part of the letter. It is a general appeal addressed to everyone on the theme of doing good, and is headed by a series of adjectives and participles with imperative force regarding the internal and external relationships of the Christian community. The sharing of one common attitude is asked of all who are heirs of the blessing of God. In the fundamental criteria of conduct there must not be discrepancy among the believers. Solidarity and mutual love within the community are indispensable. Mercy and humility toward others implies, as in Phil 2:3, that one lower oneself and consider everyone as superior to oneself just as Christ did, humbling himself even to his death on the cross. But the highest point of Christian morality undoubtedly is the stance one should have before enemies, adversaries, and those who would harm one: simply to do good or, even better, to return good for evil. The harm in question is mainly the evil done with words. The letter speaks of insults, calumny, slander, lies, and deceit. Here the author argues at length, using a quotation from Ps 33:13-17 (LXX) on the same subject. The genuinely Christian response in the hostile environment within which faithful Christians now live cannot be limited to avoiding evil in word or in work (3:10-11a), but most envision a more constructive plan, one of responding by wishing good to the other (3:9b) and actually doing good (3:11b). The fundamental reason for this behavior is that the believers are inheritors of a blessing, a regenerating word of life, the word that announces birth to a new life through the resurrection of Jesus Christ from the dead. The inheritance is the pardon obtained as grace for sinners, for the unjust, and for those who insulted Jesus on the cross, to whom Jesus also responded with a blessing, wishing and granting them good.

Suffering for Doing Good and Righteousness in Hope: 3:13-16

In the context of the concrete suffering of injuries and offenses to which believers are subjected the author of 1 Peter responds with echoes of the gospel. The proclamation of blessing in 3:14 corresponds to the eighth beatitude (Matt 5:10a) and the response in 1 Pet 4:14. These texts deal with suffering or being persecuted for righteousness' sake, in other words, fidelity to good conduct consistent with the will of God even though the person knows that he or she will have to face unmerited suffering. The three principal commands in this pericope (3:14b-15) are taken almost word for word from Isa 8:12-13, which the author of the letter transforms in order to put the confession of Jesus as Lord of life at the center of this urgent appeal. This acknowledgment is an action that comes from within the person, from the human heart, but it must be openly and publicly manifested as a rational testimony to the hope that is in us.

First Peter 3:15 is about the testimonial value of hope. It is a foundational text for theology as it calls for giving reason for hope with rational words and works, with gentleness and reverence. Communion with Christ, personal love for him, and faith in him as Lord lead to a public confession of that hope by way of the word and with the light of reason (3:15b) as well as through good conduct (3:16).

Suffering for Doing Good as Christ Did Brings Salvation Through Baptism: 3:17-22

Two references to the passion of Christ in 1 Pet 3:18 lay the christological foundations for the discourse dedicated to the theme of the good. This is characteristic of the whole section (cf. 3:10, 11, 13, 16, 21), and gives theological consistency to the instructions to the suffering Christians (3:14, 17). In addition there are also doctrinal references that deepen the themes of hope and sanctification (3:15) as well as salvation, following a thematic outline similar to the one that underlies the first section of the letter (cf. 1:13, 21; 1:15-16; 2:2).

Just as in 1 Pet 2:21, in 3:18a we also perceive the saving dimension and exemplary character of the passion of Jesus Christ. The uniqueness of this saving action is implied in the expression "for sins," while its exemplary character can be deduced from the connection between 3:18 and 3:17 by means of the adverb "also" (v. 18). The suffering of Christ was *par excellence* suffering for doing good and, even more, it was the suffering of the just one that achieved the supreme good of salvation for the unjust. Christ in his passion is the savior and model for Christians; it is he who brings us to communion with God (3:18c) and who shows us the level of love to which Christians are called by the will of God: he loved even to his passion, always doing good.

The theme of Christ's suffering achieves a unique formulation in the antithetical parallelism of 3:18d: Christ, subjected by humankind, experiences a violent death; in this process he also experiences the vivifying force of the Spirit that rests on him and leads him to life and glory. This is the event that is at the origin of the salvation expressed and celebrated in the baptism of Christians (cf. 3:21) as a source for life regenerated by God in order that we may experience God's goodness, righteousness, and hope.

Another level of saving activity of the risen Christ is found in 3:19-20, where Christ addresses even the world of spirits. This text is the source of the christological theme of *descensus ad inferos,* which forms an article of the Christian creed. Leonhard Goppelt (*A Commentary on I Peter,* ed. Ferdinand Hahn; translated and augmented by John E. Alsup [Grand Rapids: Eerdmans, 1993] *ad loc*) is right in saying that the spirits are persons who have already died, not the fallen angels (cf. Gen 6:1-4). The author of the letter makes use of the mythic-apocalyptic image of the preaching of Enoch to the imprisoned spirits (*1 Enoch* 21:10) in order to present the figure of Christ not only as a second Enoch but also as a messenger and bearer of salvation. It seems that the scope of salvation present in this text transcends time, space, and the coordinates of life and death. The risen Christ is the one who was to announce a message of salvation to the sinners of the past, including those to whom part of the rabbinical tradition denied all hope of salvation (cf. m.Sanh. 10.3). The author of 1 Peter goes back to Noah—in other words, as far back as the first saving event the Bible relates—to establish a connection between definitive salvation in Christ (1 Pet 3:18) and the first saving action of God in human history (Genesis 7–8). The more traditional interpretation has understood the action of Christ as a descent into hell in the interval between his death and resurrection. However, with respect to 1 Pet 3:19 we prefer to assert, with W. Wieder, that Christ takes for himself a superhuman but not divine boundary for the purpose of announcing himself as the definitive victor over death and evil by way of his death and resurrection. This is the word of salvation that is proclaimed not only to those who receive this letter, but also to those rebels who in the past had separated themselves from God (cf. 3:19-20). Christ's patience and magnanimity await them, for he has been the foundation of salvation since the time of Noah and continues to be the saving basis for believers at the present time.

The reference to baptism in 3:21 does not try to define the word, but rather to show a dimension of interiority in it and in the saving reality it entails. Baptism is here understood as a free response of the believer to the saving action of God. A similar orientation was already present in the baptismal practices of the first half of the second century, and from these we are able to confirm this character of baptism as an obligation to God secured by an oath, as Pliny and Justin testify.

The Passion of Christ, Source of a New Christian Mentality: 4:1-6

The conclusion (4:1-11) of this first part of the central section of the letter begins with the passion of Christ: "Since therefore Christ suffered . . ." (4:1a). In a double conclusion (4:1-6, 7-11) the exposition seeks to recapitulate what was said in the earlier sections and therefore speaks of arming oneself with a mentality (4:1b) determined by the fact and significance of Christ's passion (4:1a, c). At the same time the author tries to stress the fundamental aspects of conduct coherent with the new Christian identity: leading to a sober life of prayer, mutual hospitality, service in the community, and above all a life of intense love (cf. 4:7-11).

Thus in the theology of the letter emphasis is placed on the priority of the passion of Jesus Christ. The fact of his passion (4:1a) and its essential meaning as victory over sin (4:1c) constitute the profound reason for the change in mentality and conduct that corresponds to the Christian plan of life. The exemplary character of Christ and the liberation he brings are aspects of the passion that continue to be obvious. By following the example of Jesus Christ in his passion, experiencing suffering and human rejection as Christ did, and doing good to all others, believers begin to live according to the will of God. Conscious, thanks to Christ, of the liberating event in their lives, knowing that by means of the passion their rebirth has been made possible, with the consequence that they have definitively broken with sin, Christians are continually called to relive the novelty of the grace of God in the experience of love. This love is an eminent expression of the radical transformation brought about by the Spirit in the heart of the human being, and an essential characteristic of the Christian mentality.

The Glorification of God Through Love and Other Charisms: 4:7-11

With the proclamation of the end of all things (v. 7) this second and concluding pericope of the first part begins. This verse unites, as it seems, the moral and eschatological meaning of "end": on the one hand putting an end to an earlier situation of sin and pagan style of life, but at the same time initiating an ethnic dynamism that emanates from the participation of believers in the new state of things, in life as renewed by the resurrection of Jesus Christ. There is a new mentality in those who have taken part in the passion of Christ, the action that has ended sin and inaugurated a new situation that permits living in sobriety, prayer, and intense love.

Love continues to be emphasized as an essential part of Christian conduct; this is reinforced by a quotation from Prov 10:12 from a literal translation of the Hebrew text and not from the LXX as is otherwise typical of this letter (v. 8). An interesting parallel exists between 1 Pet 4:1c and 4:8b, both of which are about victory over sin. In 4:1 Christ, by his passion, ends sin, while in 4:8b it is love that covers a multitude of sins. In virtue of this parallelism regarding sin we can understand the passion of Christ as a concrete expression of his love, and the love demanded by Christian morality as a concrete opportunity for imitating and following Jesus Christ, taking part in his passion and in the glory of God.

Joy in Communion with the Passion and Glory of Christ: 4:12-19

This section, which begins the second major part of the letter, is an urgent appeal to joy in the face of suffering (4:13). In general the theme of suffering is the dominant thread that unites the three subsections of this part (4:12–5:9), either in reference to Christians (4:15, 19; 5:9; cf. 4:12, 14; 5:8) or to Christ (4:13; 5:1) and normally carries with it the theme of glory as well (4:13, 14; 5:1, 4). The specific aspect of suffering (4:15, 19; cf. 4:12, 14) celebrated in this part, 4:12-19, is the call to joy because of solidarity with Christ in his passion: "but rejoice insofar as you are sharing Christ's sufferings" (4:13a). The considerations regarding suffering insistently invite believers to live it as authentic Christians (4:15-16), according to the will of God, trusting in God and doing good (4:19). Only from this clue is it possible to understand the mysterious paradox: joy despite suffering, joy in suffering, and joy through suffering. This consists in actually participating in the passion of Christ. First Peter does not incite merely joy, but the joy inherent in the mystery of the passion. The reason for joy is not, in this letter, the future reward of heaven or participation in the destiny of the prophets (cf. Matt 5:12; Luke 6:23), nor, of course, is it suffering in itself, but rather the personal link to Christ through identification with him in a communion of life and destiny with the coming messiah at the end of the world. First Peter presents the voluntary welcoming of this joy as a condition for reaching the great and final joy. The grace of finding this joy in the midst of suffering is owed to the presence in the believers of the vivifying Spirit of God, the Spirit of glory (cf. 4:14).

Particular Appeals to Elders and Young People: 5:1-5

The author of the letter presents himself as an elder of the community and a witness of the passion (5:1) in order to call for Christian humility, appealing to the elders (5:2-4), the young (5:5a), and all people in general (5:5b). The key personal identification to which he refers in order to speak of his responsibility in the Christian community is not the authority of his received role but rather the experience of faith from being witness to the passion of Christ. If the letter was written, as seems probable, at a time after the death of the apostle Peter it would represent the first testimony about Peter the martyr, put into written form by some elder who was Peter's disciple. By means of a pseudepigraphic writing the real author of the letter remains linked to the tradition of the martyrdom of the apostle Peter through the experience of suffering, and from this common experience he gives his writing an apostolic authority it would not have if it did not carry the name of Peter (1:1). When the author of the letter speaks of himself he does not appeal to preeminence over the rest; rather with total humility he presents himself as a fellow elder with and like the other elders, and refers to an essential experience of Christian identity: giving testimony to the passion of the Lord.

The mission of the elders is to shepherd the flock of God, but we are not told in what this shepherding consists; more insistence is placed on the manner and attitudes involved in the carrying out of this work. The triple opposition of attitudes reflected in the participles and adverbs of 5:2-3 leans toward that meaning. Opposed to the idea of an elder as an official who limits himself or herself to simply completing assigned work, the letter invites all responsible people to be free models for the flock, models of devotion, service, and generosity in opposition to the desire for profit, despotism, or the abuse of authority over members of the flock. The author also asks that the young, for their part, accept authority (5:5a) and says that all Christians must clothe themselves with reciprocal humility (5:5b), an appeal supported by an argument from Prov 3:34.

General Appeals to Humility, Faith, and Solidarity with Those Who Suffer: 5:6-9

Almost at the end of the letter this recapitulating discourse reminds us of the centers of interest that have been the focus of the letter. Humility and trust in God (cf. Ps 54:23), sobriety and vigilance, but with the firmness of faith must be the arms for confronting evil, which is represented as a roaring lion (Ps 21:14; Ezek 22:25), a figure of the enemy who harasses Christians. Solidarity with the suffering Christian community is a profound motivation for maintaining themselves firm in faith (5:9) when tribulation arrives, as in the circumstances of the hostile environment that the community of the chosen is experiencing. Is not this solidarity with the suffering of brothers and sisters one of the concrete opportunities for entering into communion with the passion of Christ? If sharing the suffering of a brother or sister is a motive for perseverance in faith (5:9), does this not mean that in such an experience there is a living out of salvation? Are we not in reality evoking the possibility of transforming "suffering" into "passion," thanks to the vivifying dynamism of the Spirit and the exemplary love of Christ? In that communion in love there certainly is an obvious indication of the definitive triumph of love over sin, of life over death, and of good over evil. Therefore all suffering, by the means in which it is shared, is a sign of communion with the passion of Christ and a primordial manifestation of the grace of God in the world.

Epilogue and Doxology: 5:10-11

The letter concludes in solemn form with a blessing and final doxology. The God of Jesus Christ who calls us to eternal glory (5:10) will give strength to Christians so that they may live through their present suffering in communion with the passion of Christ and the suffering of their brothers and sisters. This is the only access to eternal joy. In Christ there is already a complete reality, and in Christians there exists a vocation that little by little makes itself a reality. In this consists the true grace of God (5:12) to which the first letter of Peter is a precious testimony.

Final Greeting: Grace and Peace from Those Who are Also Chosen: 5:12-14

The final farewell of 1 Peter is in epistolary style. It combines references to individual persons and the circumstances of writing as well as a resumé of the primary points of content. The letter seems to be the work of an educated person in the community who uses the name of the apostle Peter (1:1) to give authority to his writing. It could be by Silvanus, the same person who physically wrote the letter. The mention of Mark and of Babylon permit the attribution of the letter to the Christian community in Rome. However, these concrete references do not establish the fact conclusively. The linking of Mark to the figure of Peter and the presence of Silvanus as the actual writer of the letter evoke the harmony of the Christian community after the first period of tension between Jewish Christian and Gentile Pauline tendencies. Those tensions were present at the Council of Jerusalem (Acts 15), at a time when Mark had separated himself from Paul (Acts 13:13; 15:37-38; Col 4:10) and Silvanus became his companion. The appearance of both of them with the apostle Peter in this letter is an appeal to the cohesion and authority of the Church.

The value of the Petrine tradition of martyrdom, a key factor in the primacy of Rome, helps to explain the pseudepigraphy of the letter. Because of the way Peter was martyred the group to whom the letter is addressed remains united with the community of the apostle Peter in Rome through communion in the passion of Christ.

The objective of the letter thus remains evident at the end. Its claim is to give testimony to the authentic grace of God and to bring that grace to life in accord with the new mentality originating in the loving and glorious passion of Christ in which all members feel that they are members of one community and co-participants in the same choice. This circular letter was intended to be read in the community during the assembly, where the kiss of mutual love was the customary greeting.

BIBLIOGRAPHY

Achtemeier, Paul J. *1 Peter.* Hermeneia. Minneapolis: Fortress, 1996.

Balch, David L. *Let Wives Be Submissive: The Domestic Code in 1 Peter.* SBL.MS 26. Chico: Scholars, 1981.

Cranfield, C.E.B. *The First Epistle of Peter.* London: SCM Press, 1950.

Davids, Peter H. *The First Epistle of Peter.* Grand Rapids: Eerdmans, 1990.

Elliott, John H. *A Home for the Homeless: A Sociological Exegesis of 1 Peter, Its Situation and Strategy.* Philadelphia: Fortress, 1981.

Goppelt, Leonhard. *A Commentary on First Peter,* ed. Ferdinand Hahn. Translated and augmented by John E. Alsup. Grand Rapids: Eerdmans, 1993.

Martin, Clarice J. "The Haustafeln (Household Codes) in African American Interpretation: 'Free Slaves' and 'Subordinate Women'" in Cain Hope Felder, ed., *Stony the Road We Trod: African American Biblical Interpretation.* Minneapolis: Fortress, 1991, 206–231.

Selwyn, Edward Gordon. *The First Epistle of St. Peter. The Greek Text with Introduction, Notes, and Essays.* 2nd ed. Grand Rapids: Baker Book House, 1947 (repr. 1981).

Senior, Donald. *1 and 2 Peter.* NTMes 20. Wilmington, Del.: Michael Glazier, 1980.

Talbert, Charles H., ed. *Perspectives on First Peter.* Macon, Ga.: Mercer University Press, 1986.

Thuren, Lauri. *The Rhetorical Strategy of 1 Peter: With Special Regard to Ambiguous Expressions.* Åbo: Åbo Academy Press, 1990.

2 Peter

Denis Farkasfalvy

FIRST READING

This book presents itself as an apostolic letter, a literary genre known to its author since it refers to "all the letters [of Paul]" (3:15-16). Its purpose is to settle matters of doctrinal controversy by the authority of the apostle Peter and thus admonish Christians against both false teachers and false teachings.

After the usual introductory greeting (1:1-2) and a section of thanksgiving (1:3-11) the authority of the apostle is established with reference to two revelatory experiences, the first concerning his imminent death (1:12-15), the second regarding his presence at the Lord's transfiguration (1:16-19). The author presents these revelations received by Peter as in continuity with the "prophetic message" of Scripture, originating in a similar divine intervention: the inspiration of the Holy Spirit (1:20-21).

The false teachers causing doctrinal confusion in the Church are presented as false prophets. The author dwells more on their moral depravity than on the particulars of their false teaching (2:1-19). They are described as Christian leaders who have fallen away from "the holy commandment that was passed on to them" (2:21).

It is, however, clear that the false teachings in question center on the *parousia* which the author treats in a somewhat wider soteriological context. After establishing the threefold basis of doctrinal truth (teachings of the prophets and apostles, the latter transmitting the teaching of Jesus; cf. 3:2) he reaffirms the traditional eschatological teaching (3:7) with some insistence on the fact that the time of the *parousia* is unknown and thus eschatological faith must result in vigilance and morally upright conduct (3:10-14).

In spite of the traditional character of the letter's eschatology the horizon within which it is framed is new. It uses Ps 90:4 to show that in God's perspective time is relativized: "with the Lord one day is like a thousand years, and a thousand years are like one day" (3:8). Also using Sir 35:19 and 1 Pet 3:20, he appeals to the power of God's patience and universal salvific will (3:9), reducing the urgency of eschatological expectations to a stricter adherence to the doctrinal tradition that claims no knowledge of the "day of the Lord" and an attitude of patient endurance. The author believes that his doctrine is consistent with what Paul taught in "all his letters," yet he immediately adds that the Pauline writings—like "the other scriptures"—are in some parts difficult to understand and therefore without proper interpretation give rise to distorted doctrines (3:15-16).

Contexts for Interpretation

Original Context

This letter presents the strongest case for pseudepigraphy in the NT. The main reasons that exclude Peter's personal authorship have been well known since the nineteenth century. They can be summarized as follows:

a. The reference to some at least initial collection of Pauline letters in 3:15, raised to the level of Scripture in 3:16;
b. The use of Jude 3-16 in 2:1-22;

c. The reference to 1 Peter as the only previous letter by Peter (3:1) and to Peter's imminent death (1:14-15): these imply the existence of two and only two authentic letters and thus manifest the intention of blocking the composition of further Petrine epistles.
d. The literary dependence of 2 Pet 1:16-18 on the canonical Greek text of the gospel of Matthew (Matt 17:4-5)

To this list one must add the results of linguistic inquiries that make it impossible to attribute 2 Peter to the author of 1 Peter and point to a second-century date of composition.

Although pseudepigraphic, the letter should not be considered an instrument of deception. It is rather the result of an effort to create a literary monument to important elements of authentic apostolic tradition: not only early Christian eschatology but also the important truth that, when rightly interpreted, the apostles Peter and Paul have delivered identical teaching.

This makes it easier to understand the author's use of the only literary genre these apostles had employed: the apostolic letter. More specifically, however, 2 Peter has the marks of the literary form called "apostolic testament." Such "testaments" are constituted in the NT by Paul's speech in Miletus (Acts 20:18-35), the last two chapters of 2 Timothy (2 Tim 3:1–4:8); the letter of Jude (vv. 3-16), the last section of Hebrews (10:19–13:22) and to some extent certain elements in the appendix of John's gospel (John 21:15-25). Frequent common features of these texts are the death of the first leaders of the Church, predictions of persecution and dissent within the Church, emphasis on the role of Scripture and reliance on tradition, a vocabulary of "remembrance" (reminding and remembering), and testimony to the value of martyrdom.

Second Peter was written with the supposition that its readers knew 1 Peter and a collection of Pauline letters. The portrayal of Peter as a privileged eyewitness of the Transfiguration, as a recipient of revelation about his imminent death (by martyrdom) and as a "brother" of the apostle Paul, "all" of whose "letters" he knows and can interpret correctly, including the "difficult passages"—all these details manifest the author's intention not only to establish parity between Peter and Paul but also to point out a significance in Peter's mission not possessed by that of Paul. The passages in Paul's letters portraying him as a "visionary" (cf. Gal 1:12, 16; 2 Cor 12:1-7) well explain the need for emphasizing Peter's visionary experiences. On the other hand, reference to the Transfiguration reminds the reader of Peter's role as one of those who accompanied Jesus in his earthly life and was privileged at that time to witness a *parousia*-like manifestation of the glorified Lord. Similarly, mentioning Peter's correct understanding of Paul's difficult passages implies the claim that he possessed a more intimate knowledge of Paul's mind than those who quote him to deride the Church's ongoing eschatological expectation.

Second Peter seems to present the doctrine of an indefinitely postponable *parousia* against those who interpreted 1 Thessalonians and other streams of Christian tradition in the sense of a quick return of the Lord (cf. Matt 10:23; Mark 9:1; John 21:23). The apostle Peter, as presented by the letter, uses his privileged association with Christ and his claim to superior knowledge to interpret Paul's letters. Moreover, he uses the fact of his imminent death to close the controversy. There is a good probability that Peter's referring to the Transfiguration makes explicit what Mark 9:1, placed before the story of the Transfiguration, only suggests: this generation of the apostles has indeed not passed away without having seen the Lord in his glory since all this had taken place "on the holy mountain" (2 Pet 1:18).

Use and Interpretation of 2 Peter

The position taken by 2 Peter on both eschatology and the joint authority of Peter and Paul has entered into the very fabric of the doctrinal synthesis that can be followed from the time of Irenaeus through Origen into the golden age of patristics (fourth and fifth centuries). Consequently the canonicity of the epistle was not the object of significant doubt or controversy. Although the Muratorian Canon may not have contained it, the probable use of the work by Irenaeus and a third-century papyrus containing both letters of Peter argue for early canonicity. The work received no special attention in the form of patristic commentaries. There is also little evidence for its importance in the major doctrinal controversies of the patristic or medieval Church.

Nevertheless, two verses obtained early attention for their doctrinal content. The first was 1:4 for its phrase: "participants of the divine nature." For its philosophical ring both Greek and Latin Fathers welcomed in it the use of the term "nature" and quoted it in the context of theological anthropology. In classical textbooks of scholastic theology it appears as a key text proving the reality of sanctifying grace. The other passage, 2 Pet 1:21, became a "classic" scriptural passage on inspiration. Its widespread use was chiefly responsible for the approach scholasticism took when using the model of prophetic inspiration for explaining scriptural inspiration in general. The fusion and confusion of the two concepts persisted until the time of Vatican II.

In the nineteenth century 2 Peter became a chief example for theories on the deceptive nature of pseudepigraphy, forcing a fading minority into desperate efforts to prove its authenticity. A more substantial argument was fought over the claim by liberal biblical theology that blamed 2 Peter for its role in distorting early Christian eschatology. Those who found the core of the "original" Christian message in the urgency of the eschatological expectation saw in 2 Peter a conclusive argument for the idea that the Church had betrayed this message by replacing ongoing eschatology with a mode of historical existence. In such a context the theory of "Frühkatholizismus" was born, identifying early forms of catholic doctrines within the last books of the NT. Protestant liberal scholars like Ernst Käsemann went so far as to demand the elimination of 2 Peter from the canon of Holy Scripture. They did not realize that 2 Peter was one of the most significant documents in the process producing the canon. Its contribution did not so much consist in its specific teaching on eschatology as in the method it followed when presenting the unity of the apostolic heritage of the Twelve and of Paul, thus preparing the Church of the NT for the challenge of Marcionism.

The liturgical books edited after Vatican II (the new *Liturgia Horarum* and Lectionary) prescribe the reading of 2 Peter more frequently in the liturgy and provide for a more abundant exposure to its doctrinal content.

General Historical Background

In view of what has been said above, the composition of 2 Peter is reasonably dated around 125 C.E. Earlier criticism often suggested a date as late as 150 or even 180, but the probable use of the work by Irenaeus as well as its apparent lack of use of the Pastorals would recommend a date not beyond the first quarter of the second century. A close dependence on 1 Peter, itself written in Rome, speaks for a Roman origin.

The letter's greeting does not designate any specific church community, yet from the hint we read in 3:1 that 1 Peter has already addressed the same Christians one can reasonably assume that its first intended readers were Christians of Asia Minor and, perhaps more broadly, all those who by the beginning of the second century knew and used 1 Peter. Nevertheless, both the reference to Paul's letters and the features of the "apostolic testaments" present in 2 Peter point to an even larger circle of intended readers. The author wants to strengthen and widen the acceptance of Peter's authority in questions of doctrine and scriptural interpretation, including the interpretation of Paul's letters. At the same time, by portraying Peter as writing "for the second time" before his death, it intends to provide closure to a Petrine "mini-corpus" as a depository of traditions tied to his name and parallel to the Pauline corpus envisaged in 2 Pet 3:15. It would therefore be a mistake to interpret the letter as containing directives only for the local churches of Asia Minor. Intentionally it addresses all Christian churches, that is, all those who need to keep in memory the "words spoken in the past by the holy prophets, and the commandment of the Lord and Savior spoken through your apostles" (3:2).

A proper interpretation of the letter must envisage also the situation in which Christianity became conscious of its historical nature, for in this writing the problem of the second coming is not dealt with as a particular tenet of the faith but as a matter determining how Christians must face the ongoing process of salvation history and confront crises and changes within and outside the Church. Rather than being a document deviating from an original belief in early *parousia* 2 Peter closes the process of revelation about the *parousia*'s unfathomable time that is not just a matter of a "postponement" but the revelation of God's sovereign rule over history, governed by the divine universal salvific will. Second Peter reveals how the death of the apostles—a topic dealt with repeatedly by the authentic letters of Paul (especially 2 Corinthians and Philippians)—was the life setting in which these truths of eschatology were revealed and stimulated a deeper understanding of Christian origins by the Church itself. Rather than being a document of a distorting "Frühkatholizismus," 2 Peter is a valuable literary witness to the formation of catholic Christianity, establishing continuity between the apostolic and the patristic Church.

SECOND READING

Greeting: 1:1-2

1:1: The best manuscripts have instead of Simon "Symeon," a form found only in Acts in an address of James (Acts 15:14). This appears to be purposely archaic, stressing Peter's Jewish identity. On the other hand "Simon Peter" is characteristically Johannine. The combination of "servant and apostle" is found not only in Paul (Rom 1:1) and the Deutero-Pauline address of Titus 1:1, but in the only verse of John that uses the term apostle: "servants are not greater than their master, nor are messengers (= *apostolos* in the Greek text) greater than the one who sent them" (John 13:16).

The addressees are those who have received "a faith as precious as ours" or faith "of equal value." The term not only reflects elevated style but an awareness of non-genuine faith in some persons who are not addressed. The faith in question comes from God's "justice" or "righteousness" in the same way the author speaks of it later in 3:13; there follows a reference to God's forbearance, a topic of all the letters of Paul (3:14-15). This indicates that 2 Peter harks back to Romans already in its address.

The phrase "our God and Savior Jesus Christ" seems to imitate Titus 1:3 where the text speaks of the *parousia* of Christ; thus only one person, Christ, is referred to, not both God the Father and the Son. The "righteousness of Christ" in this text therefore means the Savior's mercy making humans righteous, to be manifested at his coming.

1:2: The greeting "grace and peace" recurs in all Pauline letters. However, the added "be yours in abundance" makes it a copy of 1 Pet 1:2. That the abundance of these gifts results in "the knowledge of God and of Jesus our Lord" has close parallels in Colossians (1:10; 2:2) but appears to be closest to Titus 1:1. The knowledge indicated may not be all intellectual but clearly the letter is intent on doctrine and teaching, considered as the result of divine grace.

Gifts and Promises: 1:3-4

1:3: The "divine power" mentioned here has resulted in all spiritual gifts in us because of a call we received to reach God's "own glory and power," that is, to be elevated beyond the normal course of human life.

1:4: The believer escapes from the world, characterized as being under "corruption" coming from "lust." These notions come from Hellenistic philosophy and were widespread in the second century due to the popular success of Stoicism. The use of the Greek word for passion *(epithumia)* in Rom 7:7-8 might be the model for the author in describing the general human propensity toward sin. Similarly Pauline use of "corruption" (see especially Rom 8:21) shows that its usage here is not entirely innovative. Still, the expression "participants of the divine nature"—also of philosophical origin—is unparalleled in the NT. The resulting image is that of mitigated dualism: the world is under the rule of passions and is headed toward corruption, but through faith the believer escapes its power and becomes a sharer of God's "nature," a concept equivalent to the more Pauline vocabulary of "glory and power" of the previous verse. The fruition of grace is a matter of "very great promises" so that Christian existence emerges as a dynamic notion: passage from a corruptible world into the stable realm of divine nature.

The "flight from the world" underlies these notions. The concept of such a flight *(fuga mundi)* animated later monastic movements. The purpose of this flight is to share God's nature; this was called divinization in later patristic theology and mystical tradition. This verse played an important role in prompting the development of both lines of tradition.

The Path of Ascent: 1:5-8

The virtues listed here are presented as consecutive steps beginning with "faith" and ending at "love" and collectively resulting in "knowledge." This rudimentary outline of ethics contains Stoic notions and vocabulary but the vision is specifically Christian: moral progress leads from the acceptance of faith through self–disciplined behavior to brotherly love *(agapē)*. These virtues are fruits of the knowledge *(epignōsis)* of Jesus Christ, meaning inner familiarity and identification with God's self-disclosure.

Failure or Success in Reaching the Goal of Faith: 1:9-11

Refusal to move along the path described above results in blindness, characterized as being "forgetful" of purification from past sins. Perseverance on this path "confirm[s] your call and election." In these verses Christian existence appears as a precarious one, ending either in "stumbling" or entering into "the eternal kingdom of our Lord and Savior Jesus Christ." The kingdom described here is already established in glory with the Christian not yet participating in a full and final way. Similarly "call and election" are preliminary and need to be finalized and authenticated by Christian life.

Reminders of the Apostle's Imminent Departure: 1:12-15

This passage defines the literary framework of the letter, created by the author according to his understanding of Peter's position and attitude at the threshold of his death. The word "to remind" *(hypomimnēskein)* signals the author's intention of presenting a teaching already made public. The reason for committing to writing this teaching is Peter's premonition received from Christ that his death, described as "the putting off of [his] tent," is close at hand and the need to keep the memory of this teaching after his death is urgent. The language referring to the apostle's death recalls 2 Cor 5:1-4, but the statements about a frequent use of his teaching's written record registers the post-apostolic Church's awareness of its reliance on the memory of Peter.

Peter's Reliable Witness: 1:16-21

The apostle's teaching about the "power and coming" *(dynamis kai parousia)* of Christ is not based on "myths" (meaning the product of fantasy) but on his being the eyewitness of the Transfiguration. It was at that event that Peter with his companions received from the Father's words the revelation of Jesus' divine sonship. Peter's claim seems to parallel that of Paul in Gal 1:12-16. The reference to the mountain as "holy" and the twofold use of the word "glory" *(doxa)* convey the ecstatic nature of the experience. The fact that the words spoken by the heavenly voice represent a fusion of Matt 17:5 and Matt 12:18 (= Isa 42:1) and differ from Mark 9:7 (= Luke 9:35) makes a strong argument that 2 Peter is using the written gospel of Matthew.

The "prophetic message" mentioned in v. 19 may be this same message of the Transfiguration or possibly Christian prophetic utterances announcing the *parousia*. It constitutes a light shining in the darkness to facilitate keeping vigil. The image of the morning star "rising in the hearts" effectively expresses the anticipation of the *parousia* in experiences analogous to the Transfiguration. Verse 20 extends the theme of prophecy to include "[every] prophecy of Scripture." Verses 20-21 declare that the interpretation of prophecies requires the presence of the same Spirit who inspired the human beings uttering them. We have here in a nutshell the understanding of biblical inspiration and hermeneutics that was practiced by the early Church and carried through patristic and medieval times. It includes three major principles: (a) all Scripture falls under the concept of prophecy, not because of its telling about the future but because of its inspired origin; (b) the inspired words of the OT (here called "scripture") as well as those of the Christian period (here the "prophetic message" paralleled with the account of the Transfiguration, described as an anticipation of the future *parousia*) are properly interpreted only under the guidance of the Spirit; (c) the need for an interpretation assisted by the Holy Spirit points in two directions, demanding the guiding ministry of an apostolic church—someone writing in Peter's name—leading the interpreter, but also implying an encounter with the Spirit by the interpreter in a spiritual experience—an act of knowing involving all mental faculties and the freedom of the will freely responding to the word in faith.

False Prophecy and Its Condemnation: 2:1-3

These verses concisely characterize the "false prophets" and "false teachers" arising "among the people." By recalling Deut 13:1-5, v. 1 repeats the Pauline parallelism between the Church and the people of Israel wandering in the desert. Here, however, false prophets are described as operating "secretly," living immorally, motivated by greed and using deception. Their chief sin is that of "denying the Master" (v. 1); this is best understood when referred to a situation of persecution in which faithfulness is tried by external pressure to abandon the faith. A similar social setting is presupposed by the statement that these false prophets damage the reputation of Christians: because of them "the way of truth will be maligned" (v. 2).

Christ is portrayed as "the Master who bought them" (v. 1), a concise phrase that entails picturing the Christian as a slave (cf. *doulos* in 1:1) and Jesus as purchasing us by his blood. The word "master" describes him not as teacher, but as Lord and ruler *(despotēs)*. The evil fate of the false prophets is assured in two ways. Their action is self-destructive, but they are also subject to divine condemnation (v. 3). It is at this point that the author switches the topic from the *parousia* to the eschatological judgment, which is conceived as in operation "long ago" and in fact permanently operating: "their destruction is not asleep" (v. 3).

Examples of God's Judgment Active from Long Ago: 2:4-10a

2:4. The sin of the angels: The reference is to Gen 6:1-4, expanded still more by *1 Enoch*. Second Peter 2:4 does not describe this sin but seems to consider it as an archetype of grace rejected. Patristic exegesis, following the lead of Origen, has dealt with the fall of the angels as the first sin constituting hell. Although it is described in mythical language in Gen 6:1-4 as a sin of covetousness and lust, early Christian interpretation saw in it both a sin of pride and a falling away from the contemplation of God by preferring creatures to the Creator. For the author of 2 Peter it is an example of sin followed by the punishment of hell, although he considers the fallen angels kept in hell as in prison and waiting for the final judgment of the end.

2:5. The Flood: Genesis 7:21 also proves that God's tolerance of human sins is limited. The position of the Christian is like that of Noah: he or she is "a herald of righteousness" (in terms both of saving mercy and punishing judgment) and manages to be saved with seven others. This makes the number of those saved eight. The example of the fallen angels followed by that of the flood is found also in 1 Pet 3:18-20, with the number "eight" emphasized there as the figure of baptism. The Christian symbolism of the number eight, which became abundantly present in patristic literature, here refers to a new creation: the eighth day is that of the resurrection, the day following the Sabbath, which marked the end of the first creation.

2:6-10a. Sodom and Gomorrah: Besides citing here another example of God's judgment operating effectively, the author draws a parallel between Lot and the Christians, both tormented by conflicts between their conscience and the ungodly of the surrounding culture (vv. 6-8). The parallel is extended further in vv. 9-10a, for just like Lot the Christians addressed by the letter are protected against the judgment that belongs to their depraved environment immersed in lust and rebellion.

The Evil Conduct of the False Teachers: 2:10b-22

From the beginning of 2:1 the author has borrowed elements of the denunciation of the false teachers found in Jude's letter. In 2:10b-20 he follows even more closely the rhetoric of Jude 8-16.

The "glorious ones" mentioned in v. 10b are the fallen angels: their condemnation has been reserved by the faithful angels and their prince, Michael, to God alone (Jude 8-10) while the false teachers boldly denounce them. Purposely, it seems, 2 Peter keeps the reference to this issue vague and brief while expanding on the immorality of the false teachers. Compulsive animal behavior (v. 12), lack of understanding, lust and revelry (v. 13), adultery, instability and greed (v. 14) are attributed to them in egregious terms. From the scriptural comparisons used in Jude (Cain, Balaam, Koreh) 2 Peter selects only the case of Balaam, whose seductive prophecy was corrected by a donkey, a mere beast, receiving the ability to speak like a human being (cf. Num 22:28-29). The transformation of Jude's text reveals that the author of 2 Peter selects the one example involving seduction for money and the fate of a false prophet. However, he sees the need of going beyond a mere reference and explains the relevance of the case of Balaam. This seems to indicate that the goal of monetary reward involved in the activities of the false teachers is no mere literary *topos:* the persons who cause unrest among the Christians are either paid agitators or self-styled charismatic persons working for material gain.

Verse 17 is an abbreviated version of Jude 12b-13, 16, continuing with a special concern about the relapse of Christians under the influence of the false teachers, for these "entice people who have just escaped from those who live in error" (v. 18). The Pauline topic of slavery versus freedom (v. 19) harks back to Romans (8:21) and apparently also to John 8:34. Those who see the false teachers as propagandists creating social unrest among slaves and artisans in Asia Minor interpret these verses in highly political terms, but the author's concern is liberation from sin and "the defilements of the world" (v. 20) by means of "knowledge of . . . Jesus Christ." The author projects a Johannine attitude toward the mainstream of pagan society and a concept of "knowing Christ" very consistent with the first section of the letter (1:2-3, 5-6, 8).

Falling away from the faith one has once embraced is depicted in harsh terms. Most probably the author quotes Matthew's gospel (Matt 12:45) in an applied sense in v. 20. He then explains that "turning back" results in a worse condition than that of people who never converted (v. 21). In v. 22 the use of Prov 26:11 to illustrate the same truth shows an early technique of exegesis used to show the harmony of Old and New Testament texts.

Definition of Tradition: 3:1-2

Here the author assesses the role of the apostolic letters. This is supposedly his second letter, but he says that in both the first and the second (see the plural "in them" in v. 1) the faithful are admonished to "remember" *(mnēsthēnai)* the tradition they received. The source of this tradition is further described by the triplet of "holy prophets," "apostles," and "the Lord and Savior." This is a structured list that expands Jude 17 by on the one hand adding "the words [of] the holy prophets" and on the other hand articulating the role of the apostles in transmitting "the commandment" of the Lord. The term "commandment" or "precept" is not to be taken in a restrictive moral sense but, as in other early Christian sources, as synonymous with "the gospel." The importance of these two verses can be seen if we realize that in a way unique in the NT they juxtapose the two testaments but at the same time show the primacy of the Lord's teaching with regard to both "the holy prophets" and "the apostles."

Attacks on Belief in the *Parousia:* 3:3-4

Verse 3 begins to draw from the resources of sacred tradition to remedy the controversies about the *parousia.* It first assures the believers that the appearance of the false teachers, the "scoffers," is itself part of the divine plan. Their taunt about the unfulfilled "promise of his coming" makes reference to the death of "our ancestors" (v. 4), meaning the first apostolic generation (see Reicke, *Epistles* 175). The obvious connection with the beliefs described in John 21:23 (cf. also Mark 9:1; Matt 10:23; 24:34) shows that the "scoffers" debase the expectation of the *parousia* to factual elements found in early Christian eschatological expectations.

A Twofold Response: 3:5-12

Two counterarguments are presented. The first is cosmological; it is based on the first creation story (Genesis 1) and makes use also of the story of the flood (Genesis 7). As the earth made out of water by God's word was once destroyed by water, the present "heavens and earth" will end in destruction by fire on the day of judgment. In both cases God's sovereign word sets the time of punishment (3:5-7).

The second argument confronts directly the question of "delayed judgment." The author, using Ps 90:4, declares that before God the human computation of time is irrelevant: one day is like a thousand years and vice versa (v. 8). What appears to be "slow" or delayed is such only in human eyes. God, "not wanting any to perish," offers mercy in patience. Consequently God's way of reckoning time cannot undergo human scrutiny (v. 9). This reasoning is used by the author as an introduction to a *logion* of Jesus very frequently quoted in the NT: "the day of the Lord will come like a thief" (v. 10). This is the earliest datable written quotation from Jesus

(1 Thess 5:2), reported in the most widely used gospel of early Christianity (Matt 24:43), and quoted not only here, in the latest NT document, but also in the last book of the NT canon, the book of Revelation (16:15 and 3:3). Second Peter continues the quotation by further references to the end of the world by fire (vv. 10 and 12) and moral exhortations to watchfulness (v. 11). The consummation of the world in fire will be followed by the appearance of "new heavens and a new earth" (v. 13), an expression from Deutero-Isaiah used in a similar context in Rev 21:1.

Paul's Testimony on Eschatology: 3:14-16

The manifold NT parallels found for 2 Pet 3:8-13 reveal the author's intention to settle the question of the *parousia* in documented harmony with authoritative Christian sources: OT texts, the sayings of Jesus, and the book of Revelation, which Justin Martyr already quoted as the work of the apostle John (*Dialogue with Trypho* 81). Furthermore, the author emphasizes his position's agreement with his "beloved brother Paul" who possesses God-given "wisdom" (v. 15). These expressions presuppose that every Pauline source was esteemed as authoritative and inspired. Pauline theology is presented here as centered on the universality of God's plan of salvation moderated by divine "patience" (v. 15). The term *makrothumia* is found twice as a divine attribute, and only in one Pauline epistle (Rom 2:4; 9:22). The author presents a picture of Paul's theology based mainly on Romans, with its universalistic horizon emphasized both in regard to human sinfulness (chs. 1–3) and the way in which Jews and Gentiles alternate in contributing to each other's salvation (chs. 9–11).

Verse 16 contains a note about the difficulties encountered by the interpreter of Paul's letters and the fact that indeed some individuals—presumably the false teachers—have distorted Paul's teaching just as they distort other scriptural texts. In view of what we have in 2 Thessalonians these remarks most probably concern those passages of 1 Thessalonians that suggest a timely date for the *parousia* and possibly the early Gnostic interpretation of Pauline letters. The author defends the authority of the Pauline letters as equivalent to "the other scriptures." At the same time he demands that their interpretation, like that of any other Scriptures, be guarded against abuse. The norms set for interpretation could hardly mean anything different from the general norms of faith presented in 2 Pet 3:2.

Conclusion: 3:17-18

Once more the author declares that his letter forewarns the Christians about false teachers and scoffers and that such foreknowledge can protect their stability (v. 17). The final greeting (v. 18a) forms a loose inclusion with 1:1-2 by juxtaposing "grace and knowledge" and making a last reference to Christ as "Lord and Savior." The doxology again suggests dependence on Romans (16:27). The reading "to the day of eternity," which differs from Rom 16:27 but is attested by the most important witnesses and papyri, summarizes the special message of this letter, enunciated above: for God one day is equivalent to any measure of time; in fact, God's eternity is a single day. The expression "day of eternity" might be derived philologically from the Hebrew Bible's "days of eternity" *(y^{ə}mē ʿolam),* but carries in it the seed of a theology of time and eternity that could only later be exploited with the tools of Hellenistic philosophical thought.

BIBLIOGRAPHY

Boobyer, G. H. "The Indebtedness of Second Peter to 1 Peter," in Angus J. B. Higgins, ed., *New Testament Essays. Studies in Memory of Thomas Walter Manson, 1893-1958.* Manchester: University of Manchester Press, 1959, 34–53.

Danker, Frederick W. "Second Peter 1: A Solemn Decree," *CBQ* 40 (1978) 64–82.

Farkasfalvy, Denis. "Prophets and Apostles. The Conjunction of the Two Terms before Irenaeus," in W. Eugene March, ed., *Texts and Testaments. Critical Essays on the Bible and Early Church Fathers: A Volume in Honor of Stuart Dickson Currie.* San Antonio: Trinity University Press, 1980, 109–134.

_____. "The Ecclesial Setting of Pseudepigraphy in Second Peter and its Role in the Formation of the Canon," *Second Century* 5 (1985–1986) 3–29.

Farmer, William R., and Denis Farkasfalvy. *The Formation of the New Testament Canon: An Ecumenical Approach.* New York, Toronto, and Ramsey, N.J.: Paulist, 1983.

Käsemann, Ernst. "An Apology for Primitive Christian Eschatology" in idem, *Essays on New Testament*

Themes. Translated by W. J. Montague. Naperville, Ill.: Allenson, 1964, 169–196.

Neyrey, Jerome H. "The Apologetic Use of the Transfiguration in 2 Pet 1:16-21" *CBQ* 42 (1980) 504–519.

_____. "The Second Epistle of Peter," *The New Jerome Biblical Commentary*. Englewood Cliffs, N.J.: Prentice Hall, 1990, 1017–1022.

_____. *2 Peter, Jude*. AB 37C. New York: Doubleday, 1993.

1 John

Francis Martin

During the period from Christmas until the feast of the Baptism of the Lord the attention of believers is directed to the mystery of the incarnation. We look upon the figure of Jesus Christ in and through whom God is made visible. It is at this time that the Church uses the first letter of John as the first reading at the eucharistic liturgy. The aptness of this choice will become obvious to anyone who ponders this text in which the witness God bears to Godself and to God's Son is presented clearly in a "radiant vision of glory" (Preface I for Christmas). The author mediates to the audience a faith vision of Jesus Christ who is at once truly God and truly human. Just as the beauty of a statue or painting or piece of music can only be grasped by someone who truly seeks to take in the actual and concrete work of art, so the divine light becomes manifest to the one whose gaze is fixed on the concrete reality of Jesus Christ as he was in history and still is in glory.

FIRST READING

The Relation of the Letters of John and the Gospel of John

Even a cursory reading of the gospel and the letters reveals their close resemblance. The purpose of the first (and to some degree the second) letter is to set forth, explain, and defend the teaching we now find in the gospel. Most of the vocabulary divergence is explicable by the fact that a letter and a gospel are different types of literature. There are, however, some baffling differences such as the absence in the letters of the term "glory," so important in the theology of the gospel. None of the differences obliges us to posit two different authors for the works, nor do the similarities point unequivocally to a unity of author.

Neither the Gospel of John nor the letters of John name their author, though in the second and third letters the author describes himself as "the Elder" *(ho presbyteros).* In contrast the author of the book of Revelation, a work that has some relation to these other four texts, does name himself "John" (Rev 1:1, 4, 9; 22:8). No other name than John has ever been associated with these writings, but neither ancient nor modern scholarship has been consistent in identifying exactly who is meant by this "John." Irenaeus, writing his work *Against Heresies* about 180, mentions "John the disciple of the Lord" about thirty-five times as the author of the gospel and the book of Revelation and also names the same person as the author of the first letter (which included the second as well). Dionysius of Alexandria (d. ca. 264) compares the differing styles of the gospel and letters on the one hand with that of Revelation on the other. He attributes the former to John the son of Zebedee and the latter to another John called "the Elder." These and other hesitations of the early writers seem to have given way by the end of the third century to a general consensus that the gospel and letters were written by John the son of Zebedee, the apostle. Discussions about the book of Revelation were to continue for some time longer. In this commentary the author(s) of the gospel and the letters will be considered as morally one, and shall henceforth be called "John."

Original Historical Context

When we think of John we are probably to envisage an old man. He is someone who is a mystic and endowed with the authority of a prophetic teacher. He is writing to those for whom he has a pastoral care. They are scattered among various house churches, most likely in the general area of Ephesus. Some people have left their number and have joined with others in the world. They somehow deny the historical, physical reality of the appearance of the Son of God in Jesus Christ. They can see no connection between the death of Jesus and sharing in the divine life. They claim to have communion with God but they are disobedient to God's commandments, especially that of believing in Jesus and practicing mutual love (1 John 3:23).

John exhibits great tenderness for the communities for which he is responsible. He wishes to protect his "children" and "dear friends" by presenting them with the truth, the revelation of God the Father in Jesus Christ. His genuine love and concern for his people are palpable and are the fruit of his own union of love with Jesus Christ. He wishes to educate them in the nuances of spiritual life and to impart to them wisdom and discernment as protection against the enemies of their souls (world, Antichrist, devil). In these ways John is an encouragement and model for those in ministry in the modern Church.

The Pastoral and Theological Message of the Letter as a Whole

John knows that the interior act by which one yields to this truth through the witness of the Spirit is not merely a mental activity of forming ideas but a spiritual activity of laying hold of divine life. This indwelling of God's divine life in the believer through faith in Jesus Christ is for John a source of power, wisdom, and authority and leads to victory, confidence, and "overcoming." He opposes this to the theories and claims of the false teachers and lists some criteria by which these teachers and their ideas can be discerned.

In discussing this spiritual activity of laying hold of divine life John is describing revelation and its effect on the human personality. Throughout the letter there is a constant ebb and flow of attention between exterior activity (keep the commandments, confess Jesus, etcetera) and an interior dimension of life. Actually John describes two different sets of interior dynamics. The first has to do with a conscious faith awareness and an interior disposition of the will in which the believer clings to the truth and makes choices to live out his or her faith in daily situations. The chief word John uses for this activity is "know." John also speaks of "the word," "the truth," "the oil of anointing," or "the seed." These terms, particularly the last two, refer to God's act of self-revelation through the Church that takes up residence in the believer's heart. By the action of the Holy Spirit it becomes a dynamic source of energy enabling the Christian to believe and confess Jesus as the Son of God even amid difficulties, and to imitate God's love, overcoming sin and laying down his or her life for others.

The second, deeper set of interior realities is found in the depths of the person's being and has to do with what is changed when that person first accepts Jesus Christ as Lord and is born from the Spirit. It modifies the very source of the personality. The terms that John uses are: "to have" God, the Son, or life; to have "communion" with God; to be "born of God"; to be a "child" of God or simply be "of God"; and finally mutual "abiding," God in the believer and the believer in God. All these expressions are synonymous with sharing in the divine life.

For John exterior human actions are the proof of these interior realities. Claiming to share God's life while acting in a way that is opposed to God's way of acting is a lie and proves that one is not being transformed within by the active power of God's revelation whereby one "does what is true" (1:6). By arguing that the divine life and its revelation in a believer's heart always manifest themselves visibly in the person's life, John's ethical teaching is remarkable for its understanding of the work of grace in the human personality.

Historical Reception

Testimony concerning the existence of the first letter and the esteem in which it was held can be obtained from considering the use made of it by early ecclesiastical writers. The *First*

Letter of Clement (ca. 90), the letters of Ignatius (ca. 115) and the *Didache* (ca. 100) all contain language that is found as well in the letters of John. This probably reflects the fact that the language of the Johannine communities was not as exclusive or "sectarian" as some have supposed. Other writings such as the *Letter of Barnabas* (ca. 130), the *Apologies* and *Dialogue* of Justin Martyr (ca. 150), and the *Letter to Diognetus* (ca. 150?) seem to contain allusive citations to the letter itself. By the end of the second century the letter is being quoted rather frequently in both East and West. All of this tends to confirm the witness of Irenaeus who explicitly cites the letter and says that John, the disciple of the Lord, came to Asia Minor and composed writings during the time of Trajan (98–117). This dating, and the location of the place of origin as Asia Minor, correspond to the general scholarly consensus that the letters of John and at least the last level of redaction of the Gospel of John were composed in or near Ephesus about the year 100 C.E.

The author is writing from within the very heart of the Christian tradition. While he has his own disciples especially in mind he is no sectarian perpetuating a peculiar notion of the gospel. Anyone who reads this letter can experience its power to put one in contact with the lifegiving power of the cross as the Church has always preached it. It was because the Church recognized in the letter an authentic expression of its "rule of faith" that it considered it to be canonical, that is, a reliable expression of the truth of the gospel. This is also why, from at least the fourth century, it has been called a "universal" ("catholic") letter, a title that was probably then extended to the other five letters in the canon that now also bear that name.

General Structure of the Letter

Commentators have long struggled in their attempts to discern a structure in this letter. Some consider it a literary masterpiece while others despair of finding any particular order or development of thought at all. Difficulties begin with the fact that, despite the twelve or so times that the author says he is "writing" to his audience, the document bears none of the usual features of an ancient letter. There is no naming of the letter's sender and destination, there is no initial greeting and no concluding commendation. It seems obvious that the author could presume on his authority and reputation and was more intent on writing his treatise than on complying with cultural norms. The most likely hypothesis is that this "letter" was meant to be circulated among several small communities who looked to the author as an authoritative teacher, would recognize his right to address them, and already, as a result of his teaching, shared a common outlook with him.

In regard to this letter the question of structure and that of goal are intimately linked. We may do well to compare the treatise to a symphony, let us say Beethoven's Seventh or Brahms' Fourth, in which a fundamental statement is made, a "ground" is established, to be developed through variations that divide and reunite its components through several movements until what was first stated is said again only this time in different terms and with all the meaning that has accrued to the initial statement in the meanwhile. Like a symphony, the letter moves toward a climax: this is to be found in the first twelve verses of chapter 5 which take the themes of light, love, and life and link them to the historical activity of the Son of God whose power reaches us through the witness of the Holy Spirit so that "whoever has the Son has life" (1 John 5:12). To continue the analogy there are three "movements" to the letter, each repeating the basic theme while developing it through counterthemes and unexpected "harmonics."

Outline of the Letter

The Prooemium: The appearance of Life is announced in order to bring about a share in this Life (1:1-4)

The First Section: The Signs of Life (1:5–2:28)

- The announcement of the theme: God is Light (1:5)
- Two triple developments of the theme (1:6–2:11). The triple repetition of the phrase "If we say" in 1:6, 8, 10 introduces the notions of light, communion, truth, lie, sin, cleansing, Jesus, and righteous expiation (1:6–2:2). The triple formula "whoever says" in 2:4, 6, 9 introduces the notions of knowledge, commandments, truth, lie, love, light, and darkness (2:3-11)
- Two triple statements developing the theme (2:12-14)

Forgiveness, knowledge of Christ, and victory, utilizing "I am writing to you" (2:12-13)
Knowing the Father, knowledge of Christ, and victory, utilizing "I write to you" (2:14)
Love for the world leads to a share in its instability (2:15-17)
Corroborative Theme: It is the last hour (see 2:8—time of fulfillment)
The announcement of the theme (2:18)
First sign of the last hour: the antichrists (2:18-19)
Second sign of the last hour: the anointing, the knowledge of the truth—Jesus is the Christ (2:20-21)
Variation of the first sign: the antichrists deny the Son (2:22-23)
Mutual abiding and eternal life (2:24-25)
Variation of the second sign: the anointing, the new covenant, is proven true (2:26-27)
Exhortation in the light of his appearing (2:28)

The Second Section: Sharing the Justice of God (2:29–4:6)
The Theme: The Justice of God Brings New Life (2:29)
Harmonic theme: Being born of God now and when Christ appears (3:1-3)
Theme and counter-theme: Justice and sin (3:4-10)
Development of the theme: Justice is Love (3:11-22)
The message: love each other (3:11)
Two counter-themes
The hatred of Cain (3:12)
The hatred of the world (3:13)
Love and Life (3:14-15)
The revelation of love
In Christ (3:16)
In us (3:17)
The results
Possess criterion of truth (3:18)
Have assurance (3:19-20)
Prayer is heard (3:21-22)
The twofold commandment
The commandment itself: faith and love (3:23)
The fruit: mutual indwelling and the testimony of the Spirit (3:24)
Faith as part of the commandment
Do not yield to every spirit (4:1)
Confession of faith in the historical reality of God's work in Christ as the criterion of discernment (4:2-3)
Faith is greater than the world (4:4-5)
Faith recognizes the authority of the prophetic word (4:6)

The Third Section: How faith and love are integrated (4:7–5:21)
The Theme: Born of God (see 2:29)
First Development: All who love are born of God
The theme itself and its corollary, knowledge of God (4:7-8)
Harmonic theme: The source of love is God, and God's action in Christ (4:9-10)
Return to the theme: Our love for each other and its fruit: God's abiding in us (4:11-12)
Three dimensions of mutual abiding
The witness of the Spirit (4:13)
Confession of faith (4:14-15)
Abiding in love (4:16)
Love and Confidence (4:17-18; see 2:28; 3:21)
The Link between God's Historical Activity and Ours (4:19-21)
Second Development: All who believe that Jesus is the Christ are born of God
The theme itself (5:1a)
Harmonic theme: love for God and for God's children is obedience to God's commandments (5:1b-4a)
Return to the theme: faith overcomes the world (5:4b-5; see 4:1-6)
Faith means receiving life from the acts of Jesus in history
The reality of his consecration and death (5:6a)
The threefold witness: Spirit, water, and blood (5:6b-8)
The witness of God
The witness itself (5:9)
Consenting to the witness is faith (5:10)
The witness is Life (5:11-12)
The Reason for Writing: That you may know you have eternal life (5:13; see 1:4)

Coda
Confidence and Prayer
Confidence based on God's will (5:14-15)
Applied to prayer for a sinning brother or sister (5:16-17)
Three Certainties
Everyone born of God does not sin (5:18)

We are of God and the world is in the power of the evil one (5:19)
The Son of God has come and given us knowledge of the True One (5:20)
Final word: Guard yourselves against idols (5:21)

SECOND READING

The Prooemium: 1:1-4

In a typical movement John proceeds by enunciating a theme, developing a related theme, and returning to the original theme. This is usually referred to as an "ABA" structure. John begins with the one whom he has seen and touched on earth (1 John 1:1), reaches into heaven to proclaim the communion of this Son and the Father (1 John 1:2), then returns to the earthly fellowship that results from beholding the Son (1 John 1:3-4). Together these themes are a sort of "prelude" announcing all the basic statements to be orchestrated throughout the letter.

The word "beginning" (eight times in 1 John) has several connotations. Here, in usage similar to John 1:1 and 1 John 2:13, 14, it indicates that the existence of the "eternal Life that was with the Father" belongs to a realm beyond creation and time. The paradox is that this Life has become the object of sight and touch; it has entered history. The author bears witness to this to the world at large but especially to his disciples, so that they may share communion with the Father and the Son and have complete joy. This is the object of all Christian witnessing.

The First Section: 1:5–2:28

God is Light: The Theme Announced and Developed (1:5–2:11)

1:5: The "ground theme," to be developed throughout the letter, is that God (the Father) is light and there is no darkness in him at all. We should observe that the letter, in keeping with the general practice of the NT (there are about five exceptions) uses the term "God" *(theos)* to refer to the Father. Because the Son and the Spirit are what the Father is, they too are Light, yet it is important to share the perspective of our author who sees the Father revealed in the working out of his plan in Jesus Christ, his Son. It is for this reason that he insists on Jesus' sonship: if he is not Son in the full Christian understanding of the term then we do not really know the Father either, and the Father's witness to the Son is false.

In the term "light" we have, along with the term "beginning," another allusion to the opening lines of Genesis. While the word implies a fullness of beauty, wisdom, power, compassion, and holiness, a fuller understanding of what is specifically meant here is only obtained by following the teaching of the whole letter including the twofold statement (1 John 4:8, 16) that God *(theos)* is Love.

1:6–2:2: There now follows a triple antithetical development of the theme of Light, introduced each time by the phrase "If we say." The claim of communion with God not accompanied by a life that reflects God's reality is a lie. Such a person is not "doing the truth," a biblical and intertestamental expression (Neh 9:33; Tob 4:6; 1QS 8.1-2, etcetera) that has here the particular Johannine notion of interiorizing ("doing") the revelation of the Father in Jesus ("the truth") so as to make it the principle of activity (see John 3:21).

On the other hand a life lived in imitation of and obedience to *theos* manifests and secures our communion with each other (1 John 1:7). This is the fourth and last time the word "communion" will occur in the letter: it is later replaced by the notions of "abiding" and "having life." The other consequence of walking in the Light is that "the blood of Jesus his Son cleanses us from all sin," that is, his outpoured life still has the power to "purify our conscience from dead works to worship the living God" (Heb 9:14).

The other two antithetical developments concentrate on the need to accept the revelation of the Father's plan ("the truth") in order to understand our true state as sinners (1 John 1:8-9), and the power of the cleansing action of God in God's Son Jesus Christ who is called "Paraclete," "the Just One," and "the atoning sacrifice for our sins" (1 John 1:10–2:2).

2:3-11: Yet another threefold antithesis is based on the theme, enunciated in 2:3, of the knowledge of God and obedience to the commandments God gives us. We have here a clear allusion to the prophecy of Jer 31:31-34 of a new covenant to be written in the hearts of believers by the divine action. God will provide the interior principle of obedient response to the saving work realized among us, thus bringing the people to that knowledge of God that consists in experiencing the divine reality and gratefully acknowledging the personal authority of the One who has wrought salvation among us: "I will write [my law] on their hearts . . . [and] they shall all know me . . . for I will forgive their iniquity" (Jer 31:33-34). This text is never quoted in 1 John (in fact no OT text is ever explicitly cited), but its promise underlies an important dimension of the letter's teaching about the criteria for judging the presence of new life.

The criteria are applied immediately in the three antitheses. On the one hand, knowledge of God without obedience to the divine commandments is impossible as it contradicts the very nature of that knowledge as described in Jer 31:31-34. On the other hand, laying hold of God's word means allowing it to have its way with us and this in turn brings God's love to its goal within us: our obedience is the sign that we are yielding to the power of God's revelation.

The commandment to walk as Christ walked, that is, to love (1 John 2:6, 10), is not new because it was given as part of the baptismal catechesis ("the beginning"), yet it is new because Jesus' life and our present capacity to love have made "true" (1 John 2:8), that is, fulfilled Jeremiah's prophecy. Thus the final age is here: "the darkness is passing away and the true light (the life of God, 1 John 1:5) is already shining." The final antithesis (1 John 2:9-11) unites the themes of "light" and "love" and prepares for the orchestration of the theme of *agapē* (love) in the first part of both the second (1 John 3:11-22) and final (1 John 4:7-21) movements.

Address to Children, Fathers, and Young People, and a Warning About the World (2:12-17)

2:12-14: The threefold address probably refers to the whole community ("children"), the more mature members and leaders ("fathers"), and the fervent younger disciples ("young people"). There are six declarations ("I am writing" three times, and "I write *that*" three times) composed with a note of insistence:

To the whole community John first declares the forgiveness of sins "on account of his name," a baptismal allusion grounding forgiveness in the whole reality of Jesus crucified and risen (1 John 2:12). When the whole community is addressed again (1 John 2:14) John declares that they know the Father. Knowledge of God and forgiveness of sins are both promised in the prophecy of Jeremiah. To the mature members ("fathers") John twice declares that they have come to know "[the One] who is from the beginning." Knowledge of the eternal origins of Christ is what constitutes Christian maturity and authority.

The young people have conquered the evil one because of their faith (see 1 John 5:4-5). This is developed to include the notion of being strong because God's act of revelation ("the word of God") is active ("abides") in them (the conscious level of interiority).

2:15-17: The thought shifts from "the evil one" to the world. These two realities are linked in John's mind (1 John 4:4-6; 5:19; 2 John 7). For him the notion of "world" in the negative sense serves to unmask the demonic universe of refusal and rejection. The injunction not to love the world and the incompatibility established between such a love and the love brought about in us by the Father's initiative (1 John 4:10) is akin to the analysis in John's Gospel regarding the power of the love of darkness (John 3:19), of self (John 12:25), and of human glory (John 5:44; 12:43) to keep people from the truth that is God's revelation. That which is in the world is summed up by speaking of the craving of the flesh and the eyes and the arrogance that comes with possessions. This is not far from the description in Genesis of the totality of the temptation facing Eve: "[then] the woman saw that the tree was good for *food,* and that it was a delight to the *eyes,* and that the tree was to be desired to make one *wise* [or: *successful]"* (Gen 3:6). The contrast between the ephemeral nature of the world and the permanence of the one who does God's will is another expression of the common biblical teaching that evil and untruth cannot last, while the one who lays hold of God's law will have an abiding existence (see for instance Psalm 1).

The Drama of the Last Hour: The Antichrist, the Oil of Anointing, and Christ's Return (2:18-28)

The last few stanzas of the first movement pick up the recent themes of "evil" and "world" and show their dramatic interplay in the "last hour" with the previous theme of the Christian's communion with the Father and Son.

2:18-27: In a carefully crafted passage John points to the Antichrist and the oil of anointing as two signs of the last hour (see the outline). The presence of the Christ, the fulfillment of all that God promised, is already for the NT the indication that "the ends of the ages have come" (1 Cor 10:11; see 1 Pet 4:7; Heb 1:2, etcetera). John shares this view (1 John 2:8) and adds to it the sign of the Antichrist, a term he seems to have coined to allude to the notion, to be found in late Jewish writings (Dan 8:9-25; 9:25-27; 12:9-11), that a great adversary of God would arise in the last days. This expectation is reflected in 2 Thess 2:3-4 and probably in Matt 24:15, Mark 13:14, and Rev 13:1-18. The false teachers who have gone out from the communities are individually and collectively the Antichrist because what they teach corrupts the revelation of God in Christ. For John truth and falsity are not conjectures to be judged as closer and farther approximations to the Transcendent One, they are light from God and darkness from the evil one leading respectively to conscious communion with the Father and the Son or to the shadow of death.

In spite of the deception of the antichrists who have left the Christian fellowship believers can abide (remain) in the Father and the Son. The notion of communion is linked with "what you heard from the beginning," namely the baptismal cathechesis (1 John 2:24). We now understand that the "anointing" possessed by the believer is the revelation of God in Jesus Christ made a living source of knowledge and life by the action of the Holy Spirit.

2:28: Finally a new theme, that of "confidence," is sounded. It is rooted in the promise of Christ's return. The historical drama of Christians in the world will be resolved at Christ's *parousia* and the knowledge and forgiveness characteristic of the last times prophesied by Jeremiah will reach their perfection when "he appears."

The Second Section

The Theme of Justice, Its Harmonic and Its Counter-Theme (2:29–3:10)

2:29: The second "movement" advances the theme of light to that of justice or righteousness by proclaiming that since God is just those who practice justice are born of God. This is like arguing from the existence of a plant to the fact that a seed must be at its origin. The same argument, using the same phrase ("everyone who"), is later applied to love (1 John 4:7) and faith (1 John 5:1). Sharing the life of God, being "born of" God (the deepest level of interiority) manifests itself in acts of justice according to God's will, acts of love, and confession of faith (the exterior level).

3:1-3: Before passing on to consider justice by looking at the counter-theme (lawlessness: see 1 John 3:4-10) John first proposes the harmonic theme of our birth from God. He promises us an unending life of unimaginable intimacy with the Father as an alternative to the life of lawlessness.

3:4-10: The opposite of justice is sin, spoken of here as "lawlessness," rebellion against God in the eschatological hour. Sin manifests the devil as justice manifests God, but we can have confidence because the Son of God "appeared" (1 John 3:5, 8)—this term refers to his entire redemptive work—in order to destroy the devil's deeds. The believer has personal experience of this fact because the "seed of God," the word by which he or she has been begotten (see 1 Pet 1:23-25), brings the conscious interior level of a person into harmony with the will of God (1 John 3:9-10). Thus the difficult verse 3:9 becomes more understandable; as the sixth century theologian Oecumenicus wrote: "When someone who is born of God gives him- or herself over to the indwelling Christ who abides interiorly by the grace of adoption, such a person remains unreachable by sin" (*PG* 119.684).

We Know the Love: Jesus Contrasted with Cain (3:11-24)

3:11-15: This section is a full orchestration of the contrasting themes of love/light and hatred/darkness announced in 2:7-11. The message "from the beginning" that instructs the believer concerning the true identity of Jesus Christ (1 John 2:18-28) is also the message that enables us to love one another (1 John 3:11). We are then given two figures who show forth the work of hatred (Cain: 3:12-15) and love (Jesus: 3:16-22). Alluding to a notion found in the targumic interpretation of Genesis 4, John links evil works with hatred and darkness in a manner not unlike that of John 3:19-21 and then portrays the world in the role of Cain.

3:16-17: We know what love is by gazing on the act of love in which Jesus Christ died on the cross. This reveals the Father (who will be called Love in the last section) and becomes the source of the believer's activity. Just as the genuineness of faith is found in an open confession, so love's authenticity is shown in practical action. The exhortation to love in "truth and action," while it addresses this question of authenticity, also teaches that integral Christian activity proceeds from a personally appropriated knowledge of Christ's love and reveals it (compare Matt 5:16).

3:18-22: This exterior activity brought about in us by the Holy Spirit witnesses to the fact that we share God's life (the deepest level of interiority), and this reassures our hearts (the conscious level of interiority) and gives us confidence based not on our performance but on the perceived and manifested action of God in our lives.

3:23-24: Verse 23 brings together the two aspects of the message, faith and love, now described as a twofold commandment. It sums up the preceding section on love and prepares for the treatment of faith in 4:1-6. Verse 24 is also a summary. It insists once again that keeping God's commandments (cf. 1 John 2:3; 3:22) is not a human work that "earns" divine life (the deepest level of interiority), but is rather the fruit in the believer of yielding to the interior word (the conscious level of interiority) that brings the truth to action. To this is added the witness of the Spirit.

The Spirit of Truth and the Spirit of Deception (4:1-6)

As the passage in 3:11-22 took up the theme of love/hate and moved it to a new plane by personalizing it (Jesus/Cain), so 4:1-6 takes up the theme of truth/lie and links it with the Spirit of truth and the spirit of deception. The characteristic of the Spirit of truth is the confession that Jesus Christ has come in the flesh: that is, the ability to acknowledge the plan of God who has willed that the divine Son enter fully into the physical, and thus historical, dimension of humankind and work salvation *within* it. Throughout the centuries the "scandal of the incarnation" has been the stumbling block to those who seek to arrive at God by a self-reliant series of mental and moral techniques that despise the limitations of human existence and seek salvation in "knowledge." With apostolic and prophetic authority John distinguishes the Spirit of truth from the spirit of deception by saying "whoever knows God listens to us" (1 John 4:6).

The Third Section: Faith in God Who is Love: 4:7–5:21

In this third "movement" the themes of faith and love are brought into intimate relation and find their unity in the historical act of Jesus Christ that is mediated by the action of the Holy Spirit. The efficacious witness of the Spirit brings the Church into living contact with the truth: the act of love of Jesus on the cross that reveals the Father (see John 18:37; 14:31). In this final and resolving movement somber tones of darkness, hatred, deception, and Antichrist are practically absent, while only the pure light of faith and love is held up for our attention (1 John 4:7–5:12). The last nine verses are a sort of "coda" that gathers some of the themes from the letter into another unity.

Love and the Knowledge of God (4:7-12)

The "message" to love one another (1 John 3:11) is now repeated and brought to another level. First it is stated that love is "of" God, a preposition that in this letter indicates both origin and possession. This is followed by the second of the three descriptions of those who are born of God (1 John 4:7; cf. 2:29; 5:1), and to this is added the fact that this birth at the deepest level of a person's being is a matter of conscious awareness: the one born of God knows God, that is, the Father (1 John 2:14). The one who does not love never knew God (1 John 4:8) because God, the Father, is love. With this statement, repeated in 1 John 4:16, the heart of the Trinity is opened for us. The very Source of the Son and the Spirit produces them without beginning as eternal relations because he is generous love. We are brought into this space of love by our love for each other: "Love your neighbor, then look inside yourself to see whence comes this love; and there you will see, as far as you are able, God" (Augustine, *Tracts on John* 17.8 [*PL* 35.1532]).

In saying that this love "appeared" in the expiatory life, suffering, and death of Jesus (1 John 4:9) John grounds everything in the history of the Son of God. The appearance of God's love can still be experienced by those who believe the Son and love each other.

Three Dimensions of Indwelling (4:13-16)

This remarkable Trinitarian passage discusses three dimensions of the indwelling of God, a reality at the deepest level of the believer's being. The first is the criterion of that indwelling provided by the witness of the Spirit (the conscious level of interiority). The second criterion moves from this conscious awareness of what God has done in Jesus Christ to the public confession of Jesus as the Son of God (exterior). The third criterion consists in consciously knowing and believing in the Father's love, which John says is "in" us (the deepest level of interiority), and "abiding" in that love which probably describes an act of inner adherence that expresses itself in outer action.

Love and Confidence (4:17-21)

Returning now to the theme of active love as the source of confidence (see 1 John 3:19-22), John brings this into close relation with the eschatological theme of judgment. The last part of 1 John 4:17 speaks of our resemblance to Jesus (1 John 2:6; 3:3, 7, 16). Then, on the basis of God's initiative in revealing the divine love in the death of the Son, we are told that our love has to achieve an equally objective and historical existence (1 John 4:19-21). Otherwise our claim to love God belongs to the realm of lie (1 John 1:10; 2:4, 21, 22, 27) and the truth, the revelation of the Father, is not in us.

Faith and Divine Life (5:1-5)

The culminating description of the activity characteristic of one born of God is given here: "Everyone who believes that Jesus is the Christ has been born of God." By using the same terms found in 1 John 4:7, John emphasizes the intimate unity of love and faith. The faith spoken of here is not the work of flesh and blood (Matt 16:17; Mark 8:29; Luke 9:20); it is the fruit of the divine life. Believing that Jesus is the Christ means identifying him as the incarnation of God's wisdom, the unique and definitive recapitulation of all the approaches of God to humanity since creation (see 1 Pet 1:18-21). Since all who have been begotten of God, the Father, love God (1 John 4:7), we also love all those who have received the same gift as ourselves. In stating that the divine life, the *agapē* by which we love others (the deepest level of interiority), establishes itself as genuine in external actions by obedience to the Father (1 John 5:2) John applies here the criterion Jesus applies to himself in John 15:10. Then, in the only use of the noun "faith" in the Johannine gospel and letters, the power of believing is linked to the victory over darkness as in 1 John 4:1-6 (compare John 12:31; 16:33; Rev 2:7, 11, 17, 26; 3:6, 12, 21). Such an act of believing is not merely the repetition of the formula that Jesus is the Christ, the Son of God (1 John 5:5); it is a confession "that is joined to works in keeping with (God's) virtue" (Didymus the Blind, *Discourse on First John, PG* 39.1802).

God is Manifested in Jesus Christ (5:6-12)

As the author reaches the high point of his whole presentation he fixes our attention on the mystery of Jesus Christ effected in history and living on in the Church. He came "by water and blood" (1 John 5:6). That is, he was baptized, thus embracing the Father's plan that he be the Suffering Servant, and he was crucified, thus bringing the plan to its completion (John 19:30). The Elder, by alluding to the baptism of Jesus, evokes the NT tradition that at his baptism Jesus formally and publicly accepted his vocation to be the Servant in whom the Father was "well pleased" (Isa 42:1; Matt 3:17). Jesus knew that this call was his "from his mother's womb" (Isa 49:1). By coming forward and being baptized by John he declared himself in solidarity with his people who were being called to turn back to God. Sinless though he was, by this act of solidarity he became the one about whom the prophet had written: "Surely he has borne our infirmities and carried our diseases . . . he was wounded for our transgressions, crushed for our iniquities; upon him was the punishment that made us whole, and by his bruises we are healed" (Isa 53:4-5).

John may have in mind some false teachers who may have held that Jesus' teaching came from the Word who entered him at his baptism but left him at the cross. For this reason he insists on the historical reality of the baptism by which Jesus committed his whole life to the Father's plan for him; this lifelong commitment resulted finally in the historical act of love in which Jesus died. This act completes and gives full existence to the Father's redemptive plan (compare Heb 10:5-10).

Just as the whole historical mission of Jesus can be described by saying that he "came," so the continued historical work of the Spirit is described by calling the Spirit "the one that testifies." The witness of the Spirit consists in that action by which the truth of Jesus' baptism and death is brought to life within the Church through the sacraments of baptism and the Eucharist. As each believer appropriates this witness, what Jesus has done becomes *actually* for him or her the revelation of the Father. It is for this reason that the Spirit's action is called the "testimony of God" (1 John 5:9). Believing in the Son of God is an act of yielding to and moving toward the divine reality of Jesus Christ on the strength of the witnessing action of God within the believer (the conscious level of interiority). Faith is a sure sign that we possess the life that is in the Son at the deepest level of our being, and in fact this life *is* the Son (1 John 5:11-12). With this we return to the opening statement (1 John 1:2).

Concluding Lines (5:13-21)

Verse 13 sums up the argument of the letter in the terms of the last "movement." This is followed by an exhortation to prayer, particularly prayer for a member of the community whose life is not in keeping with the message heard from the beginning. John clearly distinguishes sins that are "unto death," by which he probably means a refusal to accept the whole witness of God, from those that are not "lethal." Later theology applied this distinction to other sins, calling them "forgivable" ("venial") and "lethal" ("mortal").

Verses 18-20 enunciate three certainties by way of summary. The verb used here to speak of the state of knowledge ("we know") may contain the nuance of a particular kind of faith as certitude: knowledge by experience that is confirmed by the preaching of the Church.

In the concluding line John equates false teaching with idols and warns the hearers once again to stay free of such teaching (compare 1 John 2:18-28; 4:1-6).

BIBLIOGRAPHY

Brown, Raymond E. *The Epistles of John.* AB 30. New York: Doubleday, 1983.

Law, Robert. *The Tests of Life.* 3rd ed. Grand Rapids: Baker Book House, 1979.

Martin, Francis. "The Integrity of Christian Moral Activity: The First Letter of John and *Veritatis Splendor*," *Communio* 21 (1994) 265–285.

Perkins, Pheme. *The Johannine Epistles.* NTMes 21. Rev. ed. Wilmington, Del.: Michael Glazier, 1984.

Schnackenburg, Rudolf. *The Johannine Epistles. A Commentary.* Translated by Reginald Fuller and Ilse Fuller. New York: Crossroad, 1992.

Strecker, Georg. *The Johannine Letters.* Translated by Linda M. Maloney. Hermeneia. Minneapolis: Fortress, 1996.

2 John

Francis Martin

After a long and uncertain history both of the short letters of the Elder, which are called "Second John" and "Third John" respectively, were accepted into the canon as being part of the correspondence of the author of the first letter. Their length (about that of a long postcard) and the fact that they are only represented in the liturgical readings for Year 2, Friday and Saturday of the thirty-second week, has meant that they are not as frequently meditated upon as they actually deserve. These remarks are intended to initiate the reader into some of the depth and spiritual beauty of the Second Letter of John that can be appreciated by an attentive and personal reading.

The vocabulary, outlook, and preoccupations of 2 John are so close to those of 1 John that it is practically certain that they are by the same author. Here and in 3 John the author describes himself as "the Elder," a title that needs no explanation to his audience who he can presume recognizes in him both an authentic bearer of the apostolic tradition and one endowed with particular authority in this regard. The manner in which he uses the title indicates that his role is far greater than that of being merely a member of a group of elders responsible in some way for the direction of a local church. The recipient of this letter, described as "the Elect Lady," is a local community with its own leaders that still looks to the Elder as an authoritative voice.

The thirteen verses of this short note move in a logical progression from a greeting (vv. 1-3) to a central section that treats of: (1) The importance of the relationship between the love commandment, which has its origin in the Father and its historical transmission through Jesus Christ, and "the truth," that is, the revelation, also through Jesus Christ, of the Father's identity (vv. 4-6). (2) The grave danger posed by the false teachers and their doctrine that refuses to acknowledge the human reality of Jesus Christ (vv. 7-11). Finally there is a conclusion (vv. 12-13).

In this short commentary we will follow the line of John's thought as it moves from speaking about "the truth" through a description of fidelity to the love command as "walking in the truth" to a warning about those who deny the historical reality of Jesus Christ and who thus are unfaithful to Christ's teaching in regard to the truth.

The Greeting: 2 John 1-3

John greets a local community and says that he loves this group "in the truth" (see 3 John 1) going on to say that all those "who know the truth" share his love for them because of "the truth that abides in us and will be with us forever" (vv. 1-2). He declares that "grace, mercy, and peace" (see 1 Tim 1:2; 2 Tim 1:2) coming from God the Father and from Jesus Christ the Son of the Father will also "be with us," "in truth and love." His fourfold repetition of the word "truth" sets the tone for the letter. As we saw in the first letter, John uses the word "truth" to designate the revelation of God the Father in and through the historical existence of Jesus Christ, especially the act of love in which he died, and in the transforming power by which he still lives.

Love "in the truth" is thus, for John, an efficacious share in the love of the Father that appeared in Jesus Christ, "the atoning sacrifice for our sins" (1 John 4:9-10). All who have come to know the truth manifest that fact because their lives, yielded to the power of the revelation in Jesus Christ, are characterized by *agapē*. The life of God revealed in the flesh of Christ "will be with us forever."

The Central Section, Part 1: 2 John 4-6

John frames these three verses by the notion of "walking in the truth." Jesus' life in the flesh, still existing in his risen state, is a manifestation of the Father, who is *agapē* (1 John 4:8, 16). As the believer appropriates this revelation it becomes the source of energy and life. To walk in the truth is thus to conduct oneself from and within the vital sphere of this revelation. The love commandment echoed throughout John's writings (John 13:34; 15:12, 17; 1 John 3:11, 23; 4:7) flows from this and derives its authority from the word of Jesus himself. In the first letter John describes the commandment as both "new," that is, intimately linked with the new and definitive age introduced by Jesus, and "old" in that it was prophesied beforehand. The "beginning" for each Christian is the moment when he or she first accepts the Gospel and is formed by the baptismal catechesis. As an early preacher expressed it: "[The] knowledge that Christ is the Passover lamb who was sacrificed for us should make us regard the moment of his immolation as the beginning of our lives. As far as we are concerned, Christ's immolation on our behalf takes place when we become aware of this grace and we understand the life conferred on us by this sacrifice" (Pseudo-Chrysostom, *Homily on Easter* [SC 36, 59-61]).

Love for each other, then, is what is meant by "walking in the truth," and is refracted (as through a prism) out into all the commandments we have been given. Love, which derives from the revelation of the Father, is both "singular" in that it is expressed in one command (v. 5) and "plural" in that it is obedience to all the commands of the Father (v. 6).

The Central Section, Part 2: 2 John 7-11

As John proceeds to the second part of the central section he echoes his warnings in the first letter concerning those he calls here "deceivers" (see 1 John 2:26; 3:7) and "Antichrist" (see 1 John 2:18, 22; 4:3). The heart of their deception is that they do not confess "Jesus Christ coming in the flesh." John's use of the word "coming" is broader than the "having come in the flesh" of 1 John 4:2, probably implying as well that Christ still possesses a humanity and will return as human to bring all history to a close. The most important aspect of the position of the deceivers is, however, the fact that they deny a "fleshly" existence to Jesus Christ, thus depriving his life among us of any historical reality. The consequence of this error is twofold: Christ's life and death are not a real manifestation, within the confines of history, of the love of the Father (see John 3:16), and secondly there is no obligation for Christians to imitate Jesus and give a historical dimension to their life of faith and love. Such a position denies, ultimately, the very nature of the God who has revealed Godself in Jesus Christ.

John warns his reader in words not unlike those of Paul (1 Cor 15:2, 14, 58; Gal 2:2; 3:4, etcetera) that if they lose the clarity of their faith in the historical reality of Jesus Christ, the Son of God, they will lose "what we have worked for." He further adds that anyone who seeks to go beyond what Jesus has taught in his words, his life, and his death and resurrection does not "have God." For the meaning of this phrase see the commentary on the first letter.

In terms echoed elsewhere in the NT (Matt 18:17; 1 Tim 6:3-4; Titus 3:10; Rev 2:2, etcetera) John formally forbids any contact between the members of the community and those who may "come" as wandering teachers or preachers and who are not faithful to the "teaching of Christ." While John's injunction may seem severe in our age of pluralism it is based on his love for the truth and his awareness that the human mind's capacity to retain revealed truth is fragile, endangered as it is by many forces both within and outside the person.

The Conclusion: 2 John 12-13

In terms that closely resemble the conclusion of 3 John the author expresses his desire to see the community personally and speak with them; he looks forward to the mutual joy that will be theirs on such an occasion. We may infer from such words that he does not live very far from his audience and that his visits are not an unknown event in their lives. He concludes by describing the community in which he lives as being an "elect sister," continuing the feminine metaphor he introduced at the outset of the letter.

BIBLIOGRAPHY

In addition to the works listed in connection with the first letter, see also:

Lieu, Judith. *The Second and Third Epistles of John*. Edinburgh: T & T Clark, 1986.

3 John

Francis Martin

The Third Letter of John is really a note to a certain Gaius. As with any personal communication between friends there is much that need not be said. Though we could wish for more information, enough is given us to make this short missive valuable both theologically and historically. Four individual men are mentioned: the Elder, Gaius, Diotrephes, and Demetrius. We have but scanty information about the first of these and none about the other three. There is little doubt that the Elder is the author as well of the first two letters of John though there is no way of knowing in what order the letters were written. Many efforts have been made to understand the events that gave rise to 3 John, but the hypothetical character of the reconstructions and the fact that they do not agree with each other are good indications that the allusions in the text, while meaningful to John the Elder and Gaius, give us only a sketchy notion of the conflict to which they refer. Nevertheless, the letter gives us a glimpse into the life of the early Christian communities with their itinerant preachers, their struggle to preserve the purity of the truth they had received, and the rise of factions within them.

After the opening greeting (vv. 1-2) John moves to the body of the letter (vv. 3-12) where he treats of three points in succession: (1) A commendation of Gaius, particularly because of his care for some itinerant preachers who have reported his hospitality to the community where John resides (vv. 3-8); (2) a report on the opposition of Diotrephes (vv. 9-10); (3) a testimony in favor of Demetrius (vv. 11-12). Finally, there is the conclusion of the letter (vv. 13-15).

The Greeting: 3 John 1-2

John's opening greeting is remarkable for two reasons: first, it is the shortest of any in the NT, and second, it bears a closer resemblance to the greeting common in secular letters of the time with its wish that Gaius prosper and have good health (though this is somewhat modified by mentioning the prosperity of his soul). The specifically Christian, and indeed Johannine, orientation of the greeting is contained in the remark that John loves Gaius "in the truth," a phrase we discussed in regard to 2 John.

The Body of the Letter: 3 John 3-12

In the first paragraph of the body of the letter John commends Gaius because "the brothers [NRSV: friends]" who came to John from Gaius testified to his "truth." This is further specified by twice describing Gaius as "walking in the truth," that is, living his life in the power of the revelation of the Father made by Jesus Christ, and expressing this in acts of love (1 John 3:16-18; 2 John 4-6). The occasion of John's praise of Gaius is that he received some visiting missionaries, and though they were strangers he provided for their needs, thus proving himself a "co-worker with the truth." This action of Gaius implies two things. First, he was able to discern the authenticity of the missionaries' message, that it was a share in the truth. These brothers were not like those other missionaries whom John characterizes with the terms "deceiver" and "Antichrist" (2 John 10-11). Second, Gaius came to their aid, thus loving them "in truth and action [based on the revelation of the Father]" (see 1 John 3:18).

John urges Gaius to send these missionaries "on [their way] in a manner worthy of God" (v. 6). In our own day when missionaries visit us they deserve the same honor and support granted to missionaries in the NT, including sustenance and supplies and our sincere prayers. In these ways we also become "co-workers with the truth."

We find in this paragraph a characteristic of 3 John, namely a number of "un-Johannine" terms that are found in the rest of the NT, usually in Paul, but never elsewhere in the Johannine corpus. Examples of such words are "church," "send on," "co-worker," "worthily," "for the sake of the Name" (see Acts 5:41). The abundance of such terms in this postcard-length letter is a reminder that arguments based on the presence or absence of certain vocabulary as an attempt to portray the Johannine communities as part of an isolated sect are extremely risky. When the occasion calls for it, terms common to the NT as a whole come readily to John's pen.

John deals with a certain Diotrephes in the second paragraph (vv. 9-10). He is someone known to both Gaius and John but he does not seem to be in the same group as Gaius: he is described to Gaius as someone who "likes to put himself first" (v. 9). Diotrephes' fault is twofold. First of all, he does not "accept" John—the term implies an acceptance of John's person and his doctrinal authority. Second, he does not accept "the brothers," most likely itinerant preachers, perhaps those already mentioned, whose teaching is correct. Diotrephes' authority within his group is such that he can prevent those who wish to accept these brothers [and sisters] and can even "expel them from the (house?) church" (v. 10). John presumes that his authority as a witness to the originating tradition will suffice to make a difference if he comes in person (v. 10).

In the last paragraph (vv. 11-12), John contrasts this activity of Diotrephes—which is described as "evil" and which Gaius is warned not to imitate—with that of Demetrius. John lays down this principle: "Whoever does good is from God; whoever does evil has not seen God" (v. 11). He adapts terminology found in the first letter. To be "from God" means to receive one's life from God and to belong to God. Some examples would be: all who carry out justice, who love and who believe "are born of God" (1 John 2:29; 4:7; 5:1); those born of God do not sin and have overcome the world (1 John 3:9; 5:4); again, those who confess rightly are "from God" (1 John 4:2, 4, 6). On the other hand, those who "sin"—like the one in this passage who "does evil"—have not "seen God" (1 John 3:6), that is, have not "known [God]" (1 John 3:6).

Demetrius, on the other hand, is testified to by everyone and by the truth itself: his life manifests that he is "walking in the truth" (vv. 3-4). John himself renders testimony to Demetrius and "you know that our testimony is true." This phrase bears an intriguing similarity to John 21:24 ("and we know that his testimony is true") and is not far from the remark in John 19:35 ("his testimony is true"). It is likely that such a phrase is part of the vocabulary of the Johannine group and as such it is applied to anyone who preaches the truth. Yet it is impossible to avoid the impression that in applying this expression to himself and appealing to Gaius's knowledge of the truth of his testimony John is alluding to his role as witness in the formation of the gospel.

The Conclusion: 3 John 13-15

The first line of the conclusion is very similar to 2 John 12 and may be John's usual way of ending his letters (though of course his remark to Gaius that he hopes to see him "soon" (v. 14) is dictated by the special circumstances). John concludes by wishing Gaius and those close to him that peace that is the fruit of the death and resurrection of Jesus (John 20:19, 21, 26) and, using another term with echoes of the Fourth Gospel, goes on to describe the members of his community and that of Gaius as "friends" (John 15:13-15).

This note to Gaius was brought into the canon partly on the basis of its thought and vocabulary, which served to make it "Johannine." Yet on a deeper level these few lines can form the basis of a profound reflection on the nature of Christian truth itself. This includes an understanding of the role of that truth in grounding the prophetic authority by which the Church lives as well as grasping the intimate link between the revelation of the Father as both the source and energy of love in the community, on one hand, and on the other the ability to discern the authentic message confided by Christ to his Church. These are all lessons we need in our day.

Jude

Pierre Reymond

Introduction

The little letter of Jude (25 verses) is essentially a piece of polemic: the author is primarily concerned to denounce some opponents of whom he speaks in derogatory terms and against whom he wants to put his addressees firmly on guard. The audience itself is almost impossible to identify, because the letter gives no particularities of any kind.

As for the adversaries who are the subject of the major portion of the letter, we have very little in the way of precise information about them either: the author never names them, being content to describe them with the pronoun *houtoi* ("those people" in a pejorative sense). The portrait of these false teachers generally falls within traditional lines: they are characterized by means of clichés drawn from the polemic literature of Judaism contemporary with the early Christian era. There are the usual accusations of immorality, greed, and gluttony; these people are also denounced for creating divisions within the Church, insulting the angels, denying God and Christ, and so on. Verse 19 describes them ironically as "psychics" or "worldly people," which may suggest that these opponents belonged to a precursor of Gnosticism similar to that against which Paul struggled in Corinth.

On the other hand the letter does give us some information about the life setting of its author. His milieu seems to have been very similar to the circles that had been developing apocalyptic literature since the second century B.C.E. The author even quotes a passage from the book of Enoch (in vv. 14-15) and in v. 9 he makes use of the Assumption of Moses or a similar document. This Judeo-Christian milieu also stressed the veneration of certain categories of angels (vv. 8-9). Finally, we can observe that Jude practiced a typological reading of the OT or the apocalyptic writings: thus, for example, the great condemnations of the past are seen as prefiguring the inevitable punishment of the impious of today.

The author of the letter says that he is Jude, the brother of James. The NT speaks elsewhere of James and Jude, the brothers of the Lord and also of Joses (or Joseph) and Simon (Matt 13:55; Mark 6:3). This Jude should be distinguished from Jude Thaddeus, one of the Twelve (Luke 6:16; Acts 1:13). But is he the author of the letter? It seems doubtful. There are signs that the letter is post-apostolic: in v. 3 it speaks of "the faith that was once for all entrusted to the saints," and especially in v. 17 the audience is exhorted to remember "the predictions of the apostles of our Lord Jesus Christ." The teachings of the apostles seem to be located entirely in the past. Thus this letter is probably a pseudepigraphic writing whose author calls on the spirit of Jude, the brother of the Lord. In the milieu in which the author lived Jude and his brother James enjoyed great prestige, and the traditions related to those two had authority.

This consideration leads us to suggest a relatively late date for the letter's redaction, but not too late: for one thing the letter is rooted in Judaism, and for another Jude was certainly used in the writing of 2 Peter, which was undoubtedly composed in the first quarter of the second century. We thus suggest an approximate date of 80–100 C.E. [See commentary on 2 Peter.]

Commentary

Salutation (vv. 1-2)

The sender of the letter presents himself as "brother of James," the latter being the brother of the Lord (see introduction above). James was a notable person in the early community; in referring to him the author is trying to benefit from the authority of the man he calls his brother.

The audience in turn are described in three phrases: they are "called," a popular term for believers, they are "beloved in God the Father"—the love of God is both the instrument and the purpose of the appeal addressed to human beings—and finally, they are "kept safe for Jesus Christ": they are promised eternal salvation, which will be accomplished on the Day of the Lord, and even now they are protected and maintained in the love of God.

The three terms of this salutation constitute a genuine summary of Christian existence: grounded in forgiveness ("mercy"), that is, a restored relationship with God, this life in communion with God ("peace") is always rooted more and more in "love."

Occasion and Purpose of the Letter (vv. 3-4)

The author has been forced to send his letter on "the salvation we share" earlier than he had planned. Salvation here has more than purely eschatological significance: the author speaks of an already present state in which all participate if they cling to the faith for which it is necessary to "contend." The word "faith" (here as in v. 20) has a primarily objective meaning: it is adherence to a collection of doctrinal truths that are foundational to the Christian message and the life of the Church *(fides quae creditur).* That is why the author can speak of "the faith that was once for all entrusted to the saints [i.e., the Church]." This faith, whose center is Christ, was transmitted once for all through the apostles as intermediaries (cf. v. 17).

Now we learn why the letter has been sent prematurely: certain "intruders" have entered the community and both their actions and their teaching have gravely endangered the faithful. But they were long ago "designated for this condemnation," that is, publicly accused of the serious sin of impiety. The office of public accuser is assumed by the Scriptures (or the heavenly books containing the secrets of the future: cf. Dan 7:10, and elsewhere), which predict the fate that awaits the ungodly. The ungodliness of the opponents probably consists in their pretending to be "spiritual" and taking that as a pretext for licentiousness, which (according to the author) leads them to deny God and Jesus Christ; their actions betray concretely their spiritual and theological denial.

Against the False Teachers: They are Judged in Advance, as Confirmed by Three OT Examples (vv. 5-8)

"I desire to remind you" introduces three examples from the OT. The author emphasizes the importance of memory (cf. v. 17), which consists in making real and contemporary for the believers of today what was definitively accomplished or spoken in the past. From this typological perspective the past becomes present: it remains a reservoir of usable meaning for those who remember it and thus render it contemporary.

The first example clearly refers to the deliverance from Egypt (cf. Exod 12:51). The words "afterward destroyed . . ." undoubtedly allude to the murmuring of the people and the events described in Exodus 15–33, Numbers 14 and 21, and elsewhere. In this way the author wants to show that even the saving God will not leave disbelief unpunished.

For a second example the author makes use of the Jewish traditions about the fall of the angels developed on the basis of Gen 6:1-4. The angels abandoned their duty, left God's heaven, "defiled themselves with women" (*1 Enoch* 12:3), which is why a double punishment from God fell upon them. Thus God is just, punishing those who reject the divine order even if they are celestial beings.

The second and third examples are closely related. The inhabitants of Sodom committed the same sin as the angels: they left their proper place to indulge in debauchery (cf. Gen 19:4-25). The example of the punishment of Sodom and Gomorrah was a traditional one in Jewish and Christian literature. "They . . . serve as an example": even now one can see the traces of the catastrophe that overtook them.

The author applies these three examples to those who today disturb the community by their actions and their teaching. The expression "these dreamers" characterizes their attitude and undoubtedly relates to the fact that the false teachers claim to have received extraordinary revelations. Jude then makes three serious accusations against them: they "defile the flesh" (cf. v. 4): by letting themselves be ruled by their instincts they neglect the spiritual dimension of sexual relations; they "reject authority" (literally "the lordship"), that is, God's very self; they "slander the glorious ones," apparently certain categories of angels, by pretending to spiritual sufficiency apart from them.

Against the False Teachers: The Counter-Example of Michael Condemns Their Pretensions (vv. 9-10)

Jude counters the arrogant attitude of the false teachers with the traditional example of the archangel Michael, who held back from judging or insulting the devil and left it to God to punish him: "The LORD rebuke you!" (Zech 3:2). In late Jewish texts Michael (whose name means "who is like God") is God's champion who fights against Satan and is the protector of Israel. Michael's combat with the devil was narrated in Jewish apocalyptic writings, perhaps in the Assumption of Moses, a lost fragment of which may have been preserved here. According to those traditions Satan accused Moses of being an assassin (cf. Exod 2:12) and not worthy of an honorable burial. The author uses this example to illustrate the pretensions of the opponents, who dare something Michael himself did not: to put themselves in the place of God, the sole judge.

We find here, in inverse order, the two offenses mentioned in v. 8, one spiritual (blasphemy) and one moral (living like irrational animals). In the first accusation what the author has in mind is the false wisdom of the opponents that permits them to believe themselves superior to the celestial beings, beginning with the angels. The second offense is that their pretended knowledge is in reality located at the sub-human level of irrational animals. Like the beasts they know only their instincts, particularly the sexual ones. It is through corporeal, purely natural realities that they will perish, because submission to them is a rejection of the Spirit of God.

Against the False Teachers: They are Reproducing Within the Community the Sins Previously Denounced (vv. 11-13)

Jude returns to the OT to find other examples of guilty people with whom to compare his opponents. In Judaism Cain (cf. Genesis 4) had become the type of the prideful, cynical spirit that defies God; Balaam (cf. Numbers 22–24; 2 Pet 2:15) was the type of the greedy person who would betray for the sake of money; Korah (cf. Numbers 16) was the type of one who revolts out of pride. These are the behaviors exemplified by the false teachers.

The opponents are now accused of perverting the meaning and practice of the community meals, which seem to have taken place within the scope of the eucharistic celebration and were called *agapes* (from the Greek *agapē,* love). This is the only NT text in which *agapē* is used in this precise sense (unless one accepts the variant in 2 Pet 2:13). The use of this term to describe a meal shows that the first Christians regarded the Lord's Supper as the action of the love of Christ *par excellence* inviting them to continue to act in the same way. In making these *agapes* the occasions for shameless behavior "those people" are a "scandal" or "blemish" in the community: literally they are "reefs" on which the faith and love of the faithful may be smashed.

The end of v. 12, with v. 13, intensifies the polemic by means of a series of powerful images: the metaphors of waterless clouds and dead trees ("twice dead" because they are sterile and uprooted) underscore the lack of solidity and the spiritual sterility of the opponents, who are incapable of keeping their promises. The images of v. 13, on the other hand, are more difficult to understand: the wild waves of the sea may represent the pretensions of the false teachers, leaving behind them nothing but traces of shame, like foam that, having fallen, expires on the dark silt and every kind of filth. The image of "wandering stars," finally, may relate to the planets (etymologically "wanderers"): their movements seem uncertain and irregular and they appear to be condemned to wander endlessly. So also the opponents, like wandering stars, are destined for eternal darkness.

Against the False Teachers: The Prophecy of Enoch Denounces Them (vv. 14-16)

In vv. 14-15 the author brings his long diatribe against the false teachers to an end with a quotation from the book of Enoch (1:9 in the Greek version). This apocalyptic book enjoyed great prestige in Judaism and Christianity because of the importance of the figure of the patriarch "in the seventh generation from Adam" (cf. Gen 5:3-24; 1 Chr 1:1-3; Luke 3:37). Enoch is the very example of the just person, having "walked with God" before being taken up by God without passing through death. The book is cited here as an uncontested authority and is placed on the same level as the OT prophets. In this quotation ungodliness seems to manifest itself in actions contrary to the will of God and in insolent, blasphemous words against God. It appears that the author is thinking here of the opponents' calling God's creative work into question.

In v. 16 the author returns directly to the false teachers, whom he characterizes in five ways:

(1) They are "grumblers" like the Israelites in the desert: they murmur and complain against God out of ingratitude or unbelief (cf. v. 5).

(2) They are "malcontents," complaining about God and undoubtedly attacking God's creative work (cf. v. 15) and the way God governs the world.

(3) They "indulge their own lusts" (literally "they walk according to their desires"): this accusation of immorality is a constant in Jude's polemic (cf. vv. 4, 8, 10, 18). Once again he establishes a connection between the claims of the opponents and their acts, which attest to their true enslavement to immorality.

(4) "They are bombastic in speech." They speak thoughtless words against God, blasphemous in their immoderation and pretentiousness (cf. also vv. 8, 10, 15).

(5) Finally, they "[flatter] people to their own advantage." This either means that they only pay attention to those who follow them or (and this is the preferred reading) they flatter the rich members of the community who can furnish them with material advantages.

Exhortation to the Faithful (vv. 17-23)

"But you, beloved, must remember" (cf. v. 5): this last part of the letter again seeks to establish (cf. v. 5; 2 Pet 3:1-2) the importance of memory, of remembering what has been said "before" either by the prophets (Enoch, v. 14) or the apostles (the Twelve, apparently) concerning the end of time. Remembering their words means remaining grounded in the faith transmitted by the apostles once for all (v. 3).

The apostles predicted that in the end-time "scoffers" would appear. As in the OT these mockers are proud and insensitive people who think themselves above the law; they laugh at sin and ridicule the scruples of the faithful. We note that the verb with the same root describes the mockery of the soldiers present at Jesus' passion (cf. Matt 20:19 // Mark 10:34 // Luke 18:32).

"It is these . . ." makes an explicit connection between the "scoffers" predicted by the apostles and the opponents whom Jude is denouncing. The author adds three additional qualifications:

(1) They are divisive. They are creating schisms and parties within the community, but the struggle remains internal. We may also understand this to mean that Jude is attacking the way in which the opponents "classify" (another possible meaning of the verb used here) or categorize believers. This accords well with the following phrase:

(2) They are "psychics" or "worldly people." According to the opponents there is among Christians a highest class of "pneumatics" animated by the Spirit (Greek *pneuma*), and below them a class of "psychics" who have not received the Spirit and still live as ordinary, natural beings. We find this distinction in certain Gnostic movements, but also in Paul (cf. 1 Cor 2:11-16, and elsewhere). Using his opponents' categories, Jude turns them back on the adversaries: it is they who live as "worldly people." Consequently:

(3) They are "devoid of the Spirit." They are not "pneumatics" even though they pretend to be spiritually superior to others. Ultimately they are not even Christians.

The two hortatory verses 20-21 form a unit whose radiant center is "keep yourselves in the love of God," that is, the love that God shows to human beings. We are here at the heart of the letter. In a few lines Jude describes the dynamic of the life of faith and lists its essential elements: faith, prayer, love, mercy in relation to the One who never ceases, in the triple form of Spirit, God, and the Lord Jesus Christ, an endless self-donation to human beings in order that they in turn may encounter that One as Love. This love is at the same time the foundation of all existence, presence in the Spirit, and the creator's mercy that yields "eternal life," a life entirely new.

We note at the beginning of this exhortation the repetition of an image that appears very frequently in the NT, in the construction "build yourselves up in your most holy faith" (as in v. 3 faith is taken in an objective sense). However it is Jude's original contribution to make the believers both the builders and the material of this upbuilding.

Verses 22-23 contain a number of textual variants generally falling within two readings (each with its own variations): a long version with three parts and a short version with two parts; we have chosen the latter.

First, "some who are wavering": it is urgently necessary to persuade Christians who are tempted to follow the false teachers of their error (variant: to have mercy on them); that is the only way to save them and snatch them out of the fire (of God's judgment) that threatens them if they follow the opponents.

Second, "have mercy on still others": this undoubtedly refers to the false teachers themselves and those who have declared allegiance to them. It is necessary to break with them for fear of being soiled by contact: "hating even the tunic defiled by their bodies." We may take this injunction in a symbolic sense of hating these people's way of life, or in a literal sense of not even touching the heretics' tunic. One is reminded here of the ancient idea that the clothing retains something of the power, good or evil, possessed by the person who wears it (cf., for example, Matt 9:20b-21 // Mark 5:27-30 // Luke 8:44-46). But how is it possible to "have mercy on" these people? It can only mean one thing: from a distance and in "fear" one should submit them in prayer to the mercy of God (cf. Ign. *Smyrn.* 4.1).

Concluding Doxology (vv. 24-25)

This beautiful doxology contains two elements: the acknowledgment of what God can do for God's own, and the acclamation of some of the divine qualities or attributes. God is not only able to preserve the faithful from falling, but also—and here Jude adds an important note—to prepare them for a joyous encounter with God.

Among the divine attributes to be praised a special place belongs to "the only God our Savior." This emphasis on the unity of God is not accidental: against opponents who have a tendency to devalue creation, and consequently the Creator, one must insist on the unity of God. There is only one God who is both Creator of the world and Savior of human beings. Hence the close link established by the author between the affirmation of the one God and the divine title of "Savior": God is the initiator of salvation, and it is the Christ ("through Jesus Christ our Lord") who accomplished it in history.

BIBLIOGRAPHY

Bauckham, R. J. *Jude, 2 Peter*. WBC 50. Waco, Tex.: Word Books, 1983.

____. *Jude and the Relatives of Jesus in the Early Church*. Edinburgh: T & T Clark, 1990.

Cedar, P. A. *James, 1, 2 Peter, Jude*. Communicator's Commentary 11. Waco, Tex.: Word Books, 1984.

Danker, Frederick W. *Invitation to the New Testament. Epistles IV. A Commentary on Hebrews, James, 1 and 2 Peter, 1, 2, and 3 John, and Jude*. Garden City, N.Y.: Doubleday Image, 1980.

Hamann, H. P. *Chi Rho Commentary on James and Jude*. Adelaide: Lutheran Publishing House, 1980.

Moo, Douglas J. *2 Peter and Jude*. Grand Rapids: Zondervan, 1996.

Neyrey, Jerome H. *2 Peter, Jude*. AB 37C. New York: Doubleday, 1993.

Revelation

Eduardo Arens Kuckerlkorn,
Manuel Díaz Mateos, and Tomás Kraft

When one mentions the book of Revelation one unleashes a most extraordinary variety of reactions, usually including fear, consternation, and uncertainty. This is principally due to the prejudices associated with the end of the world that have been created with respect to this book. For this very reason people generally prefer not to read it. Those who have heard or read some part of the book of Revelation tend to react by lamenting "I don't understand it," "it confuses me," or "it frightens me." And yet it is really much less "mysterious" than most people think.

The book of Revelation is for many people synonymous with calamities and the end of the world. Many fundamentalist circles are dedicated to showing how Revelation (or "the Apocalypse") supposedly reveals that the end of the world is near: "the predictions of the Apocalypse are coming true," they tell us. It is a fact that the book of Revelation is *the* fundamental text for

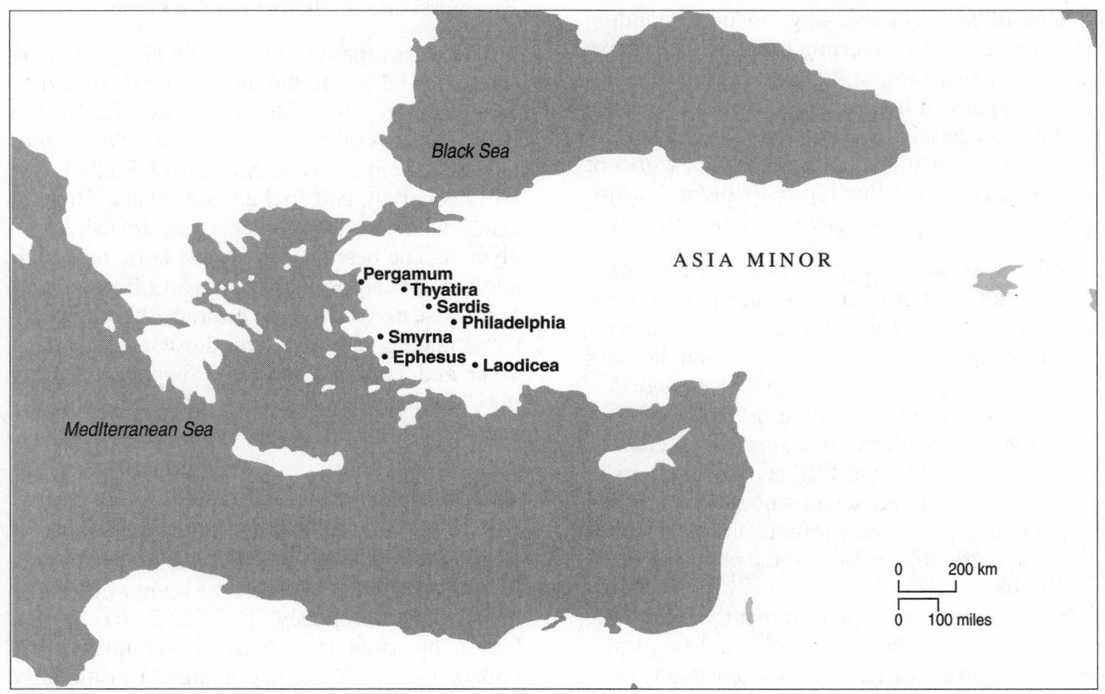

REVELATION: THE CHURCHES OF ASIA MINOR

many religious groups; despite hundreds of years difference in time and its enigmatic, esoteric appearance it has maintained its appeal fresh and intact. But is this really the subject matter and message of Revelation? To respond adequately to this question it is necessary to have a minimum of information, which the reader will find in the following section.

FIRST READING

To understand Revelation correctly one must take into account two important dimensions. One is that of form. This is a literary question and includes the genre and the type of language employed. Is the book of Revelation prophecy? Why did John use so many images, symbols, metaphors, myths, and hymns? How is the book of Revelation structured? The other dimension is that of content. Here it is a question of history: what provoked the composition of the book? In what situation did John and his community find themselves? For what reason and with what purpose was this work written?

I. General Character of the Book

Literary Genre

One of the principal keys to understanding Revelation is the determination of its literary genre: its structure, style, and distinctive content. To speak of literary genre is to speak of the author's purpose. The constellation of characteristics that Revelation shares with other works of the same genre and that typify them (and distinguish them from other genres) is the following:

- It is an eminently literary (i.e., written) work; it is not the end result of an oral tradition. A messenger orders the visionary (the author) to write down what he sees (1:3, 10, 19; 2:12; 10:4, and elsewhere).
- The message is presented in the form of visions (revelations) that disclose secrets to the elect. Otherworldly beings take part in these visions. An angel who serves as guide and interpreter has a prominent role. Heaven and earth, this world and the other are intertwined.
- The language is predominantly figurative, full of metaphors, symbols, and word pictures taken in large part from nature, numerology, astrology, and (especially) the Bible. Apocalyptic writings also intertwine myths in their symbolism.
- The work is framed within a dualistic and pessimistic vision of the world and of history; there exist only two realities—good and evil—without any middle ground possible. The world and its institutions are corrupt and are God's enemies; that is why they are hostile to God's followers. This explains the genre's violent atmosphere, which gives birth to a "new world."
- In the apocalyptic author's view history is foreordained by God. For this reason it is divided into stages; everything is rushing infallibly toward its end.
- History is interpreted in light of a predetermined conception of the supernatural world oriented toward the future. This produces ethical demands.
- There is an ardent desire that the end of history occur soon so that God's definitive reign might begin. This will happen when God conquers the forces of evil and inaugurates a world radically different from the present one. This ending of history will be preceded by catastrophes and by God's punishment, and will be followed by the universal judgment. In this final stage a messianic mediator will intervene.

The works that have this basic group of characteristics belong to the literary genre known as "apocalyptic." In addition to Revelation the Bible contains other samples of this same genre: Daniel 7–12 and several chapters of Ezekiel, Isaiah, Zechariah, and Joel among others. There is also a whole series of apocryphal Jewish apocalypses. The best known are the book of Enoch and the apocalypses of Esdras and Baruch, and now those discovered in Qumran. Other popular Christian apocalypses are those attributed to Peter and Thomas, and the "Shepherd of Hermas." In the NT Matthew 24, Mark 13, Luke 21, and 2 Thessalonians 2 are examples of this genre.

Apocalypse or Prophecy?

It is the current practice in many groups to refer to Revelation as prophecy, and this can easily lead to confusion. True, the author described his work as "prophecy" (1:3; 22:7, 10, 18-19), but in his time there was as yet no explicit understanding of literary genres. Traditionally prophecy was the communication of a message from God concerning the present and the future (without being reducible to one or the other alone). It was addressed to the Israelites who had turned their backs on God; its fundamental purpose was to call to conversion, interpreting God's will for the present time.

Unlike prophecy, which typically consists in a series of oracles delivered orally for the most part, Revelation contains a series of scenes (visions) that were communicated "visually." Thus instead of repeating the classical prophetic phrase "word of the Lord" or "thus says the Lord," John uses the refrain "and then I saw," or "he showed me." The inspiration here is visual rather than verbal. Prophecies were also occasionally presented in the form of "scenes" as the fruit of visions (cf. Amos 7–8). In the case of prophecy, however (unlike apocalyptic), images were taken from everyday life, described people who belong to our world, and had the function of calling to conversion. Not so the apocalyptic writings, which rather focused on the end of the world and the end of history (which was not a major prophetic theme). The apocalyptic writers' concern was not so much history as it was eschatology: their primary message was not one of conversion but of perseverance until the end.

In summary the book of Revelation has the *form* of an apocalypse—a genre from which it has taken a great deal—but its function and message are essentially prophetic. It speaks in God's name and is oriented principally to the Christians of those times, exhorting them to stand firm in their faith. The focus is not on the end-time but rather on the present: blessed are they who remain faithful till the end (13:10; 14:12; 16:15).

The Language Employed

One of the difficulties in understanding Revelation is the language in which it is written, so full of images and symbols that describe beings and events that are not of this world. Its language is similar to that of myths. Revelation is a sort of "reverse myth": instead of explaining the origin of things it speaks of their end. There are numerous descriptions and happenings in an unreal world (monsters, extraordinary phenomena), not to mention the obviously symbolic elements such as certain numbers and colors, which remind one of poetical expression. It is an evocative, not an abstract language; it appeals to the receiver's emotions (i.e., produces a reaction) instead of just communicating information. It is "heart-language" rather than "head-talk." The type of language used reveals the author's purpose in writing Revelation.

For one unaccustomed to apocalyptic language the question arises: how does one know if it is to be understood literally or figuratively? "If only we could discover the key to its enigmatic language"—so think many readers of Revelation—"then it would all be plain and clear." That is why there are always those who try to "decipher" the symbols of the book of Revelation, but they normally do so in relation to today's world. Four observations are necessary on this score.

First, images, metaphors, and symbols all have to do with figurative (non-literal) language. This is obvious when one notes that the numbers, colors, and many such details are used symbolically. Therefore except in those cases where it is obvious (when the author says so to the reader) we must assume that *all* language in Revelation is metaphorical—that is, non-literal.

Second, the book of Revelation is *not* written in a secret code. The images and symbols it uses were understood by the readers of its time; they were taken from the "world" of the first century C.E. If Revelation pretended to be the unveiling of something mysterious it is unthinkable that John would have expressed it in enigmatic language. Our problem in understanding its language is manifest proof that it was not written with us in mind. Of course familiarity with its principal symbols will help us to understand the work.

Frequent Symbols in Revelation

Colors

Rainbow = celestial glory (symbol of God, God's dwelling)

White = dignity ("white hair"); victory ("white garments")

Black = tragedy, fatality, death

Purple/Scarlet = pomp (imperial rank); luxury, lust

Red = violence, blood, war

Numbers

3 = totality, God (thrice holy), the Trinity—or a false (demonic) "trinity"

4 = universality (normally related to the world of nature; occurs 29 times)

7 = totality, fullness (this number occurs 54 times in the book!)

12 = perfection (generally used as a symbol of [the tribes of] Israel); in some contexts it refers to the Church [the twelve apostles; cf. 21:12-14])

Numbers (cont'd)

10 (and its multiples [thousands, myriads]) = a great many, a multitude, an immense quantity of something

Objects

wings = mobility; the capacity to be in any place
crown = kingship, sovereignty; victory
horns = power (as a personal capacity or as an institution, as kingship)
old man = wise man; (as a group they form the supreme council)
woman = [symbolizes] a nation, its people, or a city
virgin = faithful, dedicated to someone
angel = a messenger or representative of God
hybrids = weird, grotesque creatures representing evil as repugnant, ugly, abnormal and definitively not part of God's creation
stars = extraordinary, noble beings (for example angels, spirits)
name = [in Semitic languages] tantamount to the person
eyes = vision, perception ("full of eyes"/"seven eyes" = who sees [knows] everything)
clothing = a person's quality, dignity, or conduct ("wash one's clothing in the blood of the Lamb" = be purified through martyrdom in likeness to Christ)
sealed/seals = to belong to someone (as in the case of slaves); or referring to the confidentiality/secret of a document or message
book(s) = the meaning of history, of God's plan; God's message
alpha and omega = the beginning and the end: eternal
the slain lamb = Jesus as a martyr who was executed but is alive again

Third, the author used the language of imagery because it was the most appropriate for conveying the *profound meaning* of the life experiences of the author and his brothers and sisters in the faith. John used images that evoke a whole range of associations to appeal to the imagination, images that stir the emotions and moves us to act. It is something like poetic language in this respect.

Finally one must remember that the *message* is conveyed by the entire scene portrayed by the author and not by its parts in isolation. For this reason each pericope must be seen as a whole and at the same time should be understood as part of the entire work. The meaning and the fundamental message are perceived by considering the work as a whole. One might note here that it is not uncommon to hear people refer to this book as Revelations, which is not correct; the entire work is the "revelation" ("apocalypse" = unveiling) to John. It is not for nothing that Rev 1:3 declares blessed those who practice "what is written" in this prophetic message (i.e., Revelation as a whole); at the end the author warns that nothing must be added to or taken away from this "book" (22:18-19).

General Structure

In order to help the reader understand and situate the content of Revelation this exposition of its structure offers a bird's-eye view of the entire book. To be sure the author of Revelation left no architectonic blueprint of the way he would structure his work. He simply wrote it. The fundamental structure of Revelation we give here is derived from its thematic content rather than literary devices.

Outline

Presentation of the characters (ch. 1)

Critical observations made to the Church: seven letters (chs. 2–3)

First Cycle: the seven seals (chs. 4–7):
- the opening of the first six seals (ch. 6)
  - a triumphal interlude (ch. 7)

Second Cycle: the seventh seal = seven trumpets (8:1-11, 19):
- the first six trumpets resound (8:7–9:21)
  - interlude anticipating the third cycle (10:1–11:14)
- the seventh trumpet: the great victory (11:15-19)

Third Cycle: the great and definitive confrontation (ch. 12 to the end):
- presentation of characters:
  - myth of origins (12:1-18)
  - evil characters (13:1-18)
  - good characters (14:1-5)
- warnings (14:6–15:4)
- what is happening?
  - seven bowls of wrath (15:5–18:24)
    - anticipations of glory (19:1-10)
  - the end of the dragon and the two beasts (19:11–20:15)
- the grand finale: the New Jerusalem (21:1–22:5)

Epilogue: final warnings (22:6-21)

Recommendations for a First Reading of Revelation

Revelation should be read in its major sections, in its literary units, not isolating small parts, much less picking and choosing among its texts. A first reading ought to be rather simple, with no attempt to decipher or guess at the meaning of its images and symbols. It is best to adopt the attitude of one who visits an art museum: simply observe and let the pictures "hit" you. After all is said and done, what we have in Revelation is a series of scenes ("visions"). Questions will inevitably arise: what does the author intend to communicate? what is he trying to say? what situation led him to present the scene we are looking at? what sentiments or emotions does it unleash? do I fit into this picture of things? does it resemble in some way the world in which I live?

Ideally one should read the entire work continuously, just as it is, the way the first generations of Christians read it: aloud. However, one can also get a first appreciation of Revelation by reading the following chapters:

Chapter 1
Presentations and the inaugural vision: who is Lord?
Chapters 4–5
The real sovereigns and lords of the world and its history: God and the Lamb
Chapters 6–7
The first vision of the unfolding of the end of time: calamities and canticles (shadows and light)
Chapters 12–13
The principal actors
Chapters 18–19
The denouement: the decisive events
Chapter 21
Free at last! The new heavens and earth

Author and Recipients of Revelation

Revelation was written by "John"—but we are not sure exactly *which* John he was. Through detailed literary and theological analyses as well as comparisons with the other Johannine writings biblical scholars have reached a general consensus that the author of Revelation was not the same one who wrote the fourth Gospel and the letters of John. The author, who refers to himself as a prophet, not an apostle (22:7, 9, 10, 18), was undoubtedly a very important and influential person in the Church with authority to write such a work. This "John" wrote the book for the Christians of the "seven churches of Asia" (1:4, 11) for whom he was a "brother" who shared with them "in Jesus the persecution and the kingdom and the patient endurance" (1:9). He did not write it for the pagans, much less with us in mind. This should be clear from the linguistic and conceptual difficulties we have in understanding it, and it is confirmed by the author's conviction that the end was near (1:1, 3; 3:11; 12:12; and elsewhere).

II. Interpretative Contexts of the Book of Revelation

The Historical Context

One may deduce from the content of Revelation that it was written in an epoch hostile to Christianity. It was the time of a ruler with supreme powers: the Roman emperor, who in John's view merited the epithet "beast" (chs. 13 and 17), since he was responsible for the violent opposition suffered by Christians for their faith in Jesus Christ. Without needing to enter into all the historical arguments concerning the identification of the Beast as Nero, one of his successors, or Domitian, we can posit with the majority of biblical scholars that Revelation such as we have it dates from the time of Emperor Domitian (81–96 C.E.) or more precisely from the second half of his reign. The geographical context of the drama is the Roman province of Asia (now known as Asia Minor, that is, the western part of the Republic of Turkey, where the seven churches of chapters 2 and 3 and the island of Patmos are located. Ephesus appears to have been its focal point.

More specifically, the heart of the problem was the emperor's exaltation as lord of the world and of history; moreover this exaltation was expressed in a religious cult of emperor worship. Asia Minor in particular had a long tradition of offering religious cult to its kings. There were even temples constructed in honor of the emperor, that they might be venerated along with the goddess "Rome." Worthy of note is the fact that the first temple in Ephesus dedicated to an emperor was in honor of Domitian, with an enormous statue of this emperor behind the altar. It was a citizen's duty to participate in official cultic acts. Since such acts were dedicated to the emperor or the imperial deities cultic participation was an expression of loyalty; not to participate was considered a crime against the royal majesty. The emperor was the supreme authority; only the gods themselves were above him; for this reason he was considered to be close to them. To venerate him, therefore, was not merely a religious or cultic matter; it was the acknowledgment of the empire both ideologically (the empire) and in the political-economic plane (the person of the emperor). This is what we find in Revelation 13 and 18, and this is what the images of fornication, luxury, and pomp represent. One must remember that in the first century Roman empire the whole religious domain was subservient to the political arena; those who did not participate in the former ("bearing the seal") were excluded from the latter (cf. 13:17; 18:3). For Christians of that epoch it was a matter of choosing allegiances: which "lord" had priority, the Lamb or the Emperor? Thus the royal terminology was applied preferentially to God and the Lamb (and that in superlative degree), with clearly polemical overtones; thus too the abundance of liturgical references, especially hymns, which celebrate God's supremacy (4:11; 5:12; 7:12; 11:15-18, and elsewhere).

The non-participation of Christians in the imperial cult naturally would bring consequent hostility toward them on the part of the authorities. Thus it is that in Revelation we find numerous references to "persecutions." There is some discussion as to whether or not there really were what we would call "persecutions" of Christians at that time, and if so whether or not they responded to an imperial edict. Whatever the case, the Christians (and among them, John, "brother who share[s] with [them] . . . the persecution" [1:9] since he had been exiled for his Christian faith) considered them persecutions. Although neither Nero nor Domitian decreed that they themselves be adored as gods or instigated persecutions as such, the fact that these occurred (at a local or regional level) and that the imperial authority did nothing to stop them meant that the local authority "wielded all the authority of the first beast" (13:12), that is to say the ultimate responsibility was the emperor's.

Keeping this context in mind, the reader should not be surprised to find two aspects that virtually dominate the book of Revelation: the political and the social dimensions. On the one hand we find a recurring mention of kings, thrones, powers, signs of veneration, pomp, etcetera. There is a clear opposition between the Lamb that was sacrificed and the beast; between the woman (of Revelation 12) and the prostitute. John contrasted the supremacy of God and the Lamb with that of the emperor. On the other hand we have the frequent references to wars, hostilities, blood, death, and victory, which directly concern the Christians for whom Revelation was written.

In these two aspects especially Revelation presents a striking similarity to current situations. This is part of its perennial appeal: we cannot serve two "lords" at the same time. The lords of pomp, vanity, hedonism, and self-aggrandizing enrichment want to impose themselves upon our world and demand absolute obedience with violence similar to or greater than in times past. In the face of this the message of Revelation has lost nothing of its timeliness.

The Purpose of Revelation

Given the situation that brought about the composition of Revelation and for which the book was written, its purpose and message ought to be easy to discern. In the first place it exhorts Christians to remain faithful to their Lord despite all the adversities they might have to suffer. That is why it offers reasons for hope to those who are disconcerted and besieged by adversities. God is the Lord of lords and King of kings. The Lamb, the "first born of the dead" because of his fidelity to God, is in control of history. By means of hymns and triumphant portrayals John assures those who remain faithful that just as with the 144,000 and the myriads of others in heaven, they too will participate in the glory (the "wedding feast") of the Lamb in the heavenly Jerusalem.

Second, when he affirms God's justice and final victory John is warning those Christians tempted by syncretism or apostasy that one cannot serve two lords: the beast and the Lamb, the emperor with his institutions and God. By means of the calamities depicted John categorically affirms that all those who turn their backs on God are headed toward a catastrophic end. His message was therefore uncomplicated for the Christians: assured of the divine sovereignty and justice, be faithful to the Lord! Nobody, nothing will escape God's judgment! Only those who are faithful will enjoy the Lamb's marriage and the heavenly Jerusalem.

The center of attention here, rather than the calamities, is the final triumph; it is Christ and not the emperor or the Roman empire. The overall perspective is focused on the present, looking toward the future (and not on the future, looking back at the present): it is to live faithfully *today* one's commitment to Christ till the end. John's concern is for the Christians, not the Romans. Thus we see that the purpose of Revelation runs along the lines of liberation and the victory of justice. Fidelity to the Lord presupposes not only having him as one's sovereign Lord but also responding to him faithfully in one's daily life, evidenced by one's "works." Succinctly put, Revelation is a book of hope and of eschatological optimism. It is one of the clearest imaginable affirmations of the absolute sovereignty of God and of the Lamb.

Canonical Context

The fact that John's apocalypse was included in the Christian canon (not so in the case of the popular apocalypses of Peter and Thomas) and thus came to form part of the NT means that the Church recognized its inspired and inspiring value. Not only did it "speak" to society toward the end of the first century C.E.; its message also endures: stretching beyond its own historical purposes and limitations, it is the word of God for all time. (For more on the history of its acceptance as a canonical writing see below.) Its placement at the end of the canon is also significant. The internal order of NT books is thematic; it is not based on their respective dates of composition. The gospels were placed at the beginning of the NT because they expound the basis of the faith. At the end we find Revelation, in which the eschatological dimension is set forth and whose central theme is Christian hope. The Bible as we have it begins with creation and "paradise lost" and it culminates in the "re-creation" of the world ("a new heaven and a new earth") as a sort of "paradise regained."

It was on the basis of the book of Revelation that subsequent affirmations about the end of the world, judgment, and especially the final retribution were nourished. Revelation reaffirms that those who are faithful until the end will be "blessed," inscribed in the "book of life," and will enjoy the glory of God with the Lamb. Those who capitulate to "the beast," on the contrary, will end up in the "lake of fire and sulfur" (20:10). Revelation is, then, the great "manifesto" of Christian eschatological hope, of the triumph of good over evil, of God and the Lamb over the dictators of this world and their subjects, of life over death and all its signs.

Intertextual Relations

No other book of the NT can compare with Revelation in its use of the OT. In addition to dozens of OT themes, images, and reminiscences, nearly two thirds of the verses in the book of Revelation clearly allude to the OT. This was the principal source of John's literary inspiration. John intertwined this OT material in his writing without ever mentioning it explicitly; it is a sort of plagiarism. For a few eloquent examples, see the insert below. What we have here are "rereadings" of Daniel and Ezekiel, indicating that for John prophecy was a living reality, not a "museum piece," that the word of God is alive and must continue to "speak." If previously there had been an exodus from Egypt, and later an exile to Babylon, in John's time the people were living in a similar situation. If there were persecutions in the time of Antiochus, in John's time they were experiencing something similar. That is why John drank heartily from the books of Exodus and the prophets, especially Ezekiel, Zechariah, and Daniel. This manner of presenting his apocalypse, using principally prophetic material, appears normal if one takes into account that John considered himself a prophet and situated himself in continuity with classical prophecy (1:3; 10:11; 11:3; 22:7, 19).

Revelation 1:13-15	**Daniel 7 and 10**
. . . and in the midst of the lampstands I saw one like the Son of Man,	(7:13) in the night visions . . . I saw one like a human being . . . [Aramaic "son of man"]
clothed with a long robe and with a golden sash across his chest.	(10:5) clothed in linen, with a belt of gold from Uphaz around his waist.
His head and his hair were white as white wool . . .	(7:9) . . . and the hair of his head like pure wool . . .
his eyes were like a flame of fire,	(10:6) his eyes [were] like flaming torches,
his feet were like burnished bronze, refined as in a furnace, and his voice was like the sound of many waters.	his arms and legs like the gleam of burnished bronze, and the sound of his words like the roar of a multitude.

The Biblical Origin of Certain Key Themes in Revelation

Genesis 1–3:
creation, the serpent, the tree of life
Genesis 19:
Sodom punished by fire
Exodus 7–11:
Moses, the plagues
Exodus 12:
the Paschal Lamb, saving blood
Exodus 25–27:
the Temple
Leviticus 26 and Deuteronomy 28:
"all the curses in the book"; sevenfold retribution
1 Kings 17–19:
Elijah shuts up the heavens, calls down fire from heaven; great prophet
Psalm 2:
rebellion of the kings; the Messiah on Mount Zion; rod of iron
Isaiah 6:
vision of God in the Temple
Isaiah 61–62:
bride; name; marriage of God with God's people
Jeremiah 50–51:
flee Babylon; the sinful city repaid, devastated, drunk from its own cup; its sudden fall; funeral dirge for the city
Ezekiel 1–3:
theophany with lightning, four animals; throne-carriage; descriptions "like"; the seer falls to the ground, has to eat a scroll; thunder
Ezekiel 37:
resurrection of a people
Ezekiel 38–39:
Gog and Magog; plagues; change of fortune; massacre of the enemy; birds' feast
Ezekiel 40; 43; 47:
Temple measurements; its cubical structure; God's dwelling; a river of life-giving water surging from under the Temple
Daniel 7:
four animals from the ocean; ten-headed beast; the throne; the Ancient of Days with a book; Son of Man
Daniel 10:
man dressed in tunic with a golden belt
Daniel 12:
Michael; a time, times, and half a time
Joel 1–2:
locusts
Zephaniah 1:
day of the Lord, day of anguish (cf. Isaiah 2)
Zechariah 1:
riders; horses of different colors; angels; "how long?"
Zechariah 4:
the seven-branched lampstand; eyes; two anointed ones; olive trees
Zechariah 14:
battle; the glory of Jerusalem

Revelation 19:17-18	**Ezekiel 39:17-18, 20**
an angel . . . called to all the birds that fly in midheaven, "Come, gather for the great supper of God,	Speak to the birds of every kind . . . Assemble and come, gather from all around to the sacrificial feast that I am preparing for you . . .
to eat the flesh of kings, the flesh of captains, the flesh of the mighty, the flesh of horses and their riders—flesh of all . . . both small and great."	You shall eat the flesh of the mighty, and drink the blood of the princes of the earth . . . And you shall be filled at my table with horses and charioteers, with warriors and all kinds of soldiers . . .

Liturgical Contexts

The book of Revelation was composed to be read in community liturgical assemblies: "Blessed is the one who reads aloud the words of the prophecy, and blessed are those who hear" (1:3). Some scholars think that this was its real life context. Revelation also incorporates over and above the cultic imagery a series of hymns probably used in liturgical situations, and it portrays heavenly liturgies (1:12-13; 4:8; 5:8; 6:9; 7:15; 8:3-6, and elsewhere). We shall say more about the matter of the use of Revelation in modern-day liturgies of the Christian churches in the last part of this article, "The Apocalypse Through the Centuries."

III. Several Clarifications

Before undertaking the commentary on the text itself that is designed to accompany a second reading of Revelation several supplementary clarifications are in order. For many readers, the credibility of the book's literal interpretation depends precisely upon the affirmation that these were really authentic visions God gave to John so that he could transmit their message. The question, then, is not merely an "academic" one. In four different places our author mentions the state in which he had his supposed visions. In 1:10 and 4:2 he writes: "I was in the [S]pirit *(egenomēn en pneumati),*" which is to say John was absorbed by the sphere of the "spirit." We do not know to what exactly he was referring, but in 17:3 and 21:10 he says that he was "carried away *(apopherein)* in spirit." These brief descriptions indicate that John situated his visions in a sphere or domain "in the Spirit," that is to say beyond the senses. Some scholars compare this phenomenon with modern visions, others with ecstasies and trances or with mystical experiences. Were they like that?

One must take into account a series of factors. (1) What we have here is not one single vision but a long, complicated sequence of interrelated "visions." It is highly improbable that John had so many visions one after the other without ever confusing or combining them and that he would have remembered them in order unless he wrote them down right away—note that the author often speaks as if he were having the vision at the very moment of writing, as if from "within" the vision. (2) In fact John seems to have had the visions some time before, while he was on the island of Patmos, and not at the later date when he wrote Revelation, even if at times he seems to contradict himself (see 1:9-11). That is, there was a certain interval of time between the visions and the composition of Revelation. (3) The language in the entire book is predominantly figurative (metaphorical), not literal. What is more, as we have seen, Revelation is a mosaic of OT phrases, allusions, and images, and of certain myths (cf. ch. 12): that is, a literary composition with a markedly poetic character. This is not the language of a factual report or a historical chronicle. (4) If these were visions from God one would have to explain the incongruences and incoherences that are found in the work: (for example, between 1:11 and chs. 2–3; between 6:14 and 6:15; between 8:7 and 9:4). One could also mention that the presentation of a message as the product of visions may be found not only in Jewish and Christian apocryphal literature but also in pagan literature. It was a well-known literary device. Such "literary" visions are found especially in the prophetic writings (cf. Ezekiel 37), and let us not forget that the author presents himself as a prophet.

The "visions" of Revelation probably were not, therefore, visions in the literal sense. This was really a form of expression as figurative as the rest of Revelation. They *are* "visions" in the sense of profound perceptions of reality, of contemporary history such as some poets possess (which is why they too have recourse to metaphorical language). The Peruvian poet César Vallejos is a good example of this extraordinary perceptive and expressive capacity. In short, it is a question of a literary genre by means of which the author communicates his or her message, or again when the author speaks of visions this represents a literary style of communication. If John presented his message as a product of visions it was because by attributing them to God he gave to understand that his message was from God—what we would call divine inspiration.

The Composition of Revelation

Although opinions concerning the structure and process of redaction of Revelation differ greatly, a series of clues suggests that actually there were two separate "editions" of Revelation that were intertwined to form our present book. A first apocalypse would have been written in the time of the persecutions and martyrdom under Nero, which would basically cover chapters 4–11, preceded by the introduction in 1:9-20. In 8:13, after the first four trumpets, it is said that three "woes" are coming, related to "the blasts of the other trumpets that the three angels are about to blow." That is to say that the third woe should correspond to the seventh and last trumpet blast, which occurs in 11:15. With that the first version of Revelation would have closed its series of calamities. In fact, in 11:14 it is announced that "the second woe has passed. The third woe is coming very soon." Immediately afterward mention is made that the angel has sounded the seventh trumpet. The third "woe" is the judgment of the nations sung in 11:18. The final hymns (11:15-18) chant God's righteous and triumphant actions with which the divine plan culminates.

During the reign of Domitian (thirty years later) the current nucleus of Revelation (chs. 12–22) would have been composed, tying it in with the previous version and at the same time introducing the seven letters to the churches (chs. 2–3 and the introduction in 1:4-8). On this basis we may suppose that there are really two juxtaposed apocalypses that have come to form the present book. At some later time an editor or scribe "touched up" the work, adding the current "prologue" as a sort of general introduction (1:1-3) and giving it a grand ending in the rather complicated epilogue (22:9-21) so that in its present form Revelation appears as an encyclical-style letter.

All of this hypothetical redactional history deduced from a detailed examination of the text need not impede our current use of the book, however, since what was canonically accepted was the entire book as we have it (disconcerting as it sometimes is), and not the separate earlier texts in their various stages of development.

Violence in the Book of Revelation

Unquestionably a good number of passages in Revelation breathe anger; others more clearly depict violent scenes. We must not attempt to minimize or cover up this aspect of the book. In order to understand it (*not* to justify it, much less to emulate it) we must keep several things in mind.

On the one hand there are negative feelings easily understood as psychological reactions to the situation in which the author and his readers lived (a situation perceived as profoundly hostile to the Christian faith): feelings of anger, rage, frustration, and powerlessness in the face of injustices, even despair: "Sovereign Lord, holy and true, how long will it be before you judge and avenge our blood on the inhabitants of the earth?" (6:10).

On the other hand people in the Middle East are very expressive and unaccustomed to repressing their sentiments. Thus we find in Revelation typical expressions of those times that are rather foreign to our current occidental sensibilities. However, such language is not entirely new to us since it may be found also in some of Jesus' sayings (cf. Matt 22:7) and before him it was commonplace among the prophets and also in the psalms. The "day of the Lord," the day of divine judgment was traditionally awaited as a day of fierce punishment, suffering, and destruction. Again let us not forget that John took much of his inspiration from the prophets.

Asking for or awaiting divine vengeance on behalf of the faithful is at the very basis of the book of Revelation; it is a hope that, as in many psalms and prophetic books, the seer takes as already assured, trusting that God will give due answer to his prayers.

Revelation Yesterday and Today

Perhaps the most widespread opinion concerning Revelation is that it contains a series of predictions about the end of the world. It is often mentioned together with "Nostradamus" and other supposed "prophecies." The first thing to keep in mind with respect to this is that Revelation was not written with us in mind, but rather for the benefit of the Christians in Asia Minor in the latter part of the first century C.E. In the second place the author himself affirms and reaffirms that according to his convictions the Second Coming and the end of the world will occur "very shortly," "right away," "soon" (1:1, 3; 3:11; 12:12; 22:6, 7, 10, 12, 20). Clearly then, Revelation was not written thinking of readers two thousand years later. The fact is that the historical references in metaphorical language are all from John's time.

As in the case of the prophets John wrote principally for the "here and now" of his readers, for a precise moment in their historical journey. His orientation was not one of fixation on the future but rather was focused on the present and from that vantage point looked toward the future: fidelity to God at any cost was his great concern. In other words Revelation never sought to be a prediction of what would occur in the world as such, no more than the works of the prophets who preceded it; note that at no point is the author interested in signs (and much less in the exact date) of "the end." He unequivocally affirms that there *will* be an end of the world, that there will be punishments (calamities), that there will be a judgment, and that God will finally mete out justice. *How* all this is to come about is a matter of opinion. The portrayals of calamities and of the end of the world are at the service of the message: to exhort the readers to total and absolute fidelity to God. John's concern was with the present, not the future; it was about the end of the history of salvation, not the end of the cosmos.

Why, then, do we continue to read Revelation? For the same reason that we read, for example, the letters of Paul: because it contains a message that surpasses the limits of that particular historical moment. The message of Revelation continues to be as valid today as centuries ago: the reader is referred again to what was said above in the paragraph entitled "The Purpose of Revelation."

SECOND READING

I. Prologue: 1:1-8

The book of Revelation could well begin with v. 4 which reminds us of the epistolary greetings in Paul's letters. Two important things precede this greeting, however: the title and the "beatitude." These three elements (the title, the beatitude, and the greeting) set the tone of the book and introduce its content. All three seek to give encouragement and hope.

The Title (1:1-2)

"The revelation of Jesus Christ." These first three Greek words of the book are its best theological synthesis. It is a revelation (not revelations) because it unveils, uncovers, and unmasks, and in virtue of this it is a word that illuminates, gives meaning and hope when persecution is darkening the horizon. Moreover, it is a revelation *"of* Jesus Christ." This construction can be understood as a subjective genitive (i.e., something that comes from Jesus Christ; he is the instrument) or as an objective genitive (Christ himself being the content of the revelation). Although grammatically one must take it in the former sense since God gives the revelation through Jesus, theologically speaking the latter sense is primary: the revelation of a person and his salvific action in history.

This is why "what must soon take place" (1:1) is not a detailed prediction of terrifying, catastrophic events but rather the revelation of the only event that really matters: the action of God and of Christ in human history or (in other words) the victory of the Lord of life in a death-dominated history. John is servant and prophet of "all that he saw," which is nothing else than "the word of God and . . . the testimony of Jesus Christ," which is to say the word pronounced by God in Christ. Jesus Christ is the word and the faithful, credible witness of that word. Revelation, then, is a "word" full of encouragement and hope. The book is going to speak to us about the salvific word that God pronounced over our history, a word publicly proclaimed and carried out by Jesus Christ with coherence and fidelity to the point of putting his life on the line. John and his community also risked their lives on account of the same word. This is the meaning of "testimony" and is the basis for John's exhortation to resist and triumph in the midst of trials, encouraged by the example of those who "have triumphed."

The Beatitude (1:3)

This is the fruit of faithful witnessing and is the first of seven beatitudes found throughout the book (1:3; 14:13; 16:15; 19:9; 20:6; 22:7, 14). Altogether they set the tone of this book as true prophecy that invites one to hope: the book is framed in beatitudes (not curses) from beginning to end, but one needs the boldness of both prophet and witness because it is a question of loyalty and confession of faith that could result in the gift of one's very life (1:5, 9; 2:13; 3:10).

The Greeting (1:4-8)

As do the Pauline letters, this book bears the names of both sender and receiver and is not pseudonymous as is the apocalyptic literature. These are people who know each other well; together they form a close-knit group. The greeting (synthesis of the Christian "good news") comes from God who is referred to as "[the one] who is and who was and who is to come." The final clause breaks the rhythm since we would expect "he who will be," but we do not have the future tense of the verb "to be." Instead we find the present tense of the verb "to come," clearly a reference to Exod 3:14 in which God's name is revealed and its meaning is given: God's close, active presence as a liberating power for God's people. It is the mystery of God who is eternal and proximate, transcendent and the Lord of history. The same title will be given to Christ, and the expression "the one who is to come" indicates the movement of the entire book and of the whole of history. Jesus is coming, risen and victorious. That is why the book will end with the Spirit's and the Church's prayer: "Come, Lord Jesus!"

The titles given to Christ speak of his relation to the community. The first three, with the article, are grammatically linked to what was just said: the faithful witness, the firstborn, the ruler. The other three are tied to what follows ("to him be glory . . .") and express more clearly his salvific work. Christ is the authentic and trustworthy witness, the witness *par excellence*. He is the firstborn from the dead, that is to say, risen and Lord of life; he is the ruler of the kings of the earth. This last title especially invites readers to a contest because of its strongly political content. In the midst of the Roman empire in which the Christian communities resisted giving ceremonial worship to the emperor the title is a provocation because it affirms that Caesar too is subservient to the one and only supreme ruler of the kings of the earth. Affirming the victory of Christ assures the Christian's victory as well; thus one understands the repeated invitation to "conquer" directed to the Church at large (2:7, 11, 17, 26; 3:5, 12, 21).

Next the author describes three activities of Christ on behalf of his community, or more properly on behalf of humanity (cf. 1:7). This is "[he] who loves us" (in the present tense; cf. 3:9) with an ever-present love in which the author includes himself. It is a love that unites and constitutes the Church. From this love liberation springs forth: he has "freed us from our sins" (1:5). When the author speaks of the third activity of Christ who has "made us to be a kingdom, priests serving his God and Father") the grammatical structure is interrupted and an abstract noun (*basileia:* kingdom) is paired with a plural concrete noun (*hiereis:* priests). This is a clear allusion to Exod 19:6 and could be translated as "made (of) us a kingdom and priests." Christ made us a kingdom: that is to say, we participate in his triumph. Christians in the midst of the empire feel themselves strangers, unprotected and faced with the alternative: fit in or flee (the same alternative is sometimes imposed on dissidents in our days: "love it or leave it"). Their task, however, is to serve God *in* the world as its priests, that is, to be servants of God's work on behalf of the world. The priestly service of Christians does not consist in a ceremonial "ministry" or in seeking refuge in a liturgical role; rather it is a matter of putting oneself at the service of life, of being celebrants of life in contrast to the other (imperial) "cult" that is at the service of death.

"Every eye will see" this coming of the crucified one, constituted Lord of history. The author here combines phrases from Dan 7:13 and Zech 12:10. Verse 8 is an amplification of v. 4 and it is God who speaks. Since "alpha and omega" are the first and last letters of the Greek alphabet it is he too who will "have the last word" concerning human history and the powers that come to play within it. The "almighty" is coming to judge and to save. The community must interiorize this certainty, above all when the empire's power seems to be absolute.

The book's prologue is a hope-inspiring prophetic message about the coming of Christ who loves his community and saves it. He has it under his care and defends it with his power. The book will indeed be a "revelation of Jesus Christ."

II. Part One: "What is": 1:9–3:22

The whole book is a message to the Church concerning what John saw and about which he must write (22:16). It is a word trustworthy and true (22:6), since it comes from Christ, the true and faithful one (1:5 and 3:7), who is the one who ordered it to be put into writing (1:11). The message appears in the form of letters to the seven churches which are preceded by an impressive vision of the risen Christ, conqueror of death who lives and gives life forever. It is a word of encouragement to a Church which is experiencing persecution and death. We can distinguish two sections: the inaugural vision and the letters to the Churches. But it turns out that these letters form a whole with the rest of the book.

The Inaugural Vision (1:9-20)

This vision is not only the first one the author presents in his work; it is also the key to the entire book, and it continues until 22:8 which reads: "I, John, am the one who heard and saw these things." Here we have three well-distinguished moments: the presentation of the seer (1:9-11), the presentation of Christ (1:12-16), and the command to write what he sees (1:17-20).

The Presentation of the Seer, 1:9-11

The seer is a Christian well known to the community but he does not seem to include himself in their number (21:14). Rather he is a prophet, witness, and brother of theirs who shares the same experience. He is in solidarity with the Christian community and is close to them despite his exile since he shares their distress, their kingdom (that is to say, the victory) and their endurance in order to proclaim "the word of God and the testimony of Jesus" (1:9). If there exists an exterior power that exiles and separates, there is also an inner power that melds into a communion of resistance: Jesus Christ (1:9) with whom one shares the kingdom, the trials, and the firm resistance. The vision occurs on "the Lord's day" in which the triumph of Christ is celebrated, and by means of the Spirit's is clarity that makes him a prophet "for . . . upbuilding and encouragement and consolation" (1 Cor 14:3).

The Presentation of Jesus Christ, 1:12-16

What John sees is a human figure, but one that has supernatural attributes. The vision of someone "like the Son of Man" makes us think of texts like Dan 7:13 and 10:5, which the author has filled out with other OT texts in order to present the priest and king, sovereign and judge of the world. The author, faithful to his style, presents concrete characteristics (tunic, bronze feet, etcetera) where we would use abstract nouns (divinity, power, and so on). To mention only a few features of this vision: in the first place, the figure's feet appear to be "like burnished bronze, refined as in a furnace" which is a clear allusion to Nebuchadnezzar's dream interpreted in Dan 2:33-34 and in contrast to that dream. In the dream the statue had clay feet; here the feet of the figure are of bronze, symbol of stability and resistance. The empire (that of Nebuchadnezzar or any other) has clay feet. The kingdom of Christ is eternally stable.

In the second place, the most important element of the vision is that Christ appears "in the midst of the lampstands" that represent the Church, and "in his right hand he held seven stars" that are also one and the same Church (1:16, 20). The protective power of the Lord of life watches over this weak and fearful community. This God in the midst of the people recalls the promise of Lev 26:12 and anticipates the book's final vision (Rev 21:3). Why be afraid? At any rate their confidence will be strengthened in the following section.

The Command to Write Down What He Sees, 1:17-20

The seer who was capable of resisting without bending the knee before the emperor now falls down at the feet of Christ as if dead, thus acknowledging the sovereignty and divinity of the one and only Lord of history. The hand that sustains the Church (the seven stars) now rests upon John giving him security. He is told three things: "Do not be afraid; I am . . . write . . . ." The word and the gesture of touching him with the right hand strengthen the visionary's conviction of what he has experienced and desires to communicate to the Church.

"I am" is an echo of the protective presence of God both in the Old Testament and the New. The titles of Christ confirm the confidence of the seer: "the first and the last, and the living one. I was dead, and see, I am alive forever and ever; and I have the keys of Death and of Hades." The Lord of life is paradoxically one who was dead, that is to say someone very much rooted in history and its conflicts. The Church is able to confront death valiantly because it is in the hands of the Lord of life.

The command to write concerns "what you have seen." The vision is not limited to the first chapter but rather extends to the entire book, and what John saw (which will be the leading idea of the whole book) is the triumph of the Lord of life and of life itself in the tormented history of humanity.

Verse 20 serves as a transition to the following section of the seven letters to the churches. John presents the "mystery" (symbolism) of the Church in two luminous images (lampstands and stars). A symbol need not be logical; its power resides in its evocative capacity. Here both images suggest the calling and the responsibility to be Church. Caesar is not Lord of the world and of history. The Church is grasped by the powerful hand of its Lord who walks in its midst as the conqueror of death. With this certainty in its heart it will find the following section a constant invitation to "conquer."

The Seven Letters to the Seven Churches (Revelation 2–3)

These letters are not isolated elements but rather an integral part of the book, as the author will explicitly reaffirm with repeated references. There are seven of them, a number that is repeated fifty-four times altogether throughout the book. This number represents fullness and totality, thus its importance. Instead of commenting on the letters one by one we will give a structural overview.

Literary Unity with the Rest of the Book

The initial vision ends in a command: "Now write what you have seen, what is, and what is to take place after this" (1:19). The command is repeated at the beginning of each letter. The presentation of Christ to the church of Ephesus ("These are the words of him who holds the seven stars in his right hand, who walks among the seven golden lampstands") dovetails with 1:13, 16. The same thing will occur with Jesus' other titles that repeat those already given in the inaugural vision.

The rewards offered to the churches bring to mind especially the ending of the book with its mention of the "tree of life" (2:7 and 22:2), the "new Jerusalem" (3:12 and 21:2), the "second death" (2:11 and 20:6, 14), the "book of life" (3:5 and 21:27), the "morning star" (2:28 and 22:16), and the written name (3:12 and 22:4). From an editorial point of view the letters are integrated into the book, and both the book and the letters constitute the angel's testimony "for the churches" (22:16). The letters synthesize and anticipate the subsequent developments.

The Addressees of the Letters

There are seven letters and this number sets the pace of revelation in the book: seven letters, seven seals, seven trumpets, seven bowls, seven plagues. The seven letters are a sort of showpiece of the one and only face of the Church, a sort of general letter from the risen Lord to his community. At the end of each letter addressed to a given church there is an invitation to listen to "what the Spirit is saying to the churches." The entire Church is addressed in each of the letters. This general letter (the group of seven letters) precedes the rest of the book because our author's interest is not in predicting events but rather in the community's attitude in the face of the Lord's coming, which is the only event that should be discerned among the various events of human history. The verb "to come" appears in 2:5, 16, 25; 3:3, 11.

The Basic Message

The fundamental attitude that is needed when one is faced with trials (3:10) is very well summed up in "be faithful until death, and I will give you the crown of life" (2:10) or in "To the one who conquers I will give a place with me on my throne, just as I myself conquered and sat down with my Father on his throne" (3:21). The entire exhortation is therefore an invitation to conquer, to be like Antipas (2:13) or like Christ himself. The letters are part of the prophecy that is the book itself, and that is why they encourage a community living in the midst of the conflict that the book decries.

Conquering Through Resistance

It is a question of conquering through resistance with respect to exterior and interior forces. From without the Christians are seen as "suspicious" in the era of the Flavians (Vespasian, Titus, and Domitian, the last having had himself proclaimed "Lord and God") for resisting the emperor worship that flourished especially in the province of Asia. Pergamum claimed to be the center of this cult with its temple dedicated to "the divine Augustus and the goddess, Rome." The Christians because of their refusal to worship the emperor lost political and economic rights as citizens of the empire. Their unfavorable situation in the empire seemed to belie the central doctrine of their faith, that Christ has conquered and that God is the Lord. On the other hand, from within a group of Christians inclined to Gnosticism justified their moral laxity as a way of dealing with the pressures of the environment. Here we see the strength and weakness of a Church tempted by easy solutions in which either out of fear or out of a desire to "accommodate oneself" one acceded in matters of fidelity. In times of persecution or assault faithfulness and resistance define the witnesses' identity.

Christ in the Letters

The heart of the letters, and the heart of the entire vision, is Christ himself. There is a veritable agglomeration of christological titles because Christ is the principal protagonist who speaks and challenges each of the churches, saying "I know your works." The "works" refer to overall conduct, life itself, and it is praxis that reveals the truth of one's faith. It is a question of coherence between what one professes and what one lives. Christ has "eyes . . . like a flame of fire" (2:18) and judges the Church with a word that cuts like a "sharp two-edged sword" (2:12). The Church ought to discern its own works so that Christ might call them "my works" (2:26). They are the bride's wedding gown (19:8) and according to them will she be judged (22:12).

The Seven Churches

Ephesus:

"you have abandoned the love you had at first"

Smyrna:
"be faithful until death, and I will give you the crown of life"
Pergamum:
"you are holding fast to my name . . . in the days of Antipas my witness"
Thyatira:
"all the churches will know that I am the one who searches minds and hearts"
Sardis:
"cadavers of a life that never was" (César Vallejo, Peruvian poet)
Philadelphia:
"I will keep you from the hour of trial"
Laodicea:
"You say, 'I am rich,' . . . [yet] you are wretched, pitiable, poor, blind, and naked."

The Victory

Jesus Christ, the faithful and victorious witness, invites the Church to share in his victory. The one who makes the offer is someone who was slain for his fidelity but has conquered and is seated on God's throne. The time of trial is about to begin. The prizes reserved for those who "conquer" anticipate the book's ending with Paradise recovered and life in the New Jerusalem.

III. Part Two: "What Must Take Place After This" 4:1–22:5

The vision continues and in ch. 4 begins the second major part of this book concerning "what must take place after this" (4:1 and 1:19) that will be unraveled in series of seven (seven seals, seven trumpets, seven bowls), but it is a beginning that does not constitute a break with what went before because the subsequent groups of seven are tied in with the seven letters. The same voice heard in the inaugural vision is heard again (1:10 and 4:1) and John is caught up in the same Spirit in order to see visions. But above all the reward offered to the victor in the letter to Laodicea introduces us into the theme so directly that chs. 4 and 5 could be an expansion of 3:21: "To the one who conquers I will give a place with me on my throne, just as I myself conquered and sat down with my Father on his throne." The throne is the symbol of victory and of sovereignty achieved once and for all. From this throne history will be seen and judged.

The Inaugural Vision (Revelation 4–5)

The "open door [to heaven]" that John sees is a ray of light that lights up the troubled history of humankind. Invited by the voice to "come up here, and I will show you," he discovers that the One who was holding the Church in his hand holds human history in it as well. Everything that happens, according to this book, will also be a "revelation of Jesus Christ."

"Come up here, and I will show you." However, he goes up not to see the heavens but to see the earth from heaven's vantage point. What is more, the entire vision is nothing other than the reply to a clamor that rises up from the earth and with which John considers himself to be in solidarity. The elders and the creatures are holding golden bowls filled with incense, which are the prayers of the saints (5:8) and very close to the altar "the souls of those who had been slaughtered for the word of God and for the testimony they had given" (6:9) represent the cry of the shed blood that calls for justice to be done (6:10). The vision appears to belong to the royal court more than to the temple environment and has as its backdrop the imperial court and the cult in honor of the emperor, lord of the earth and of history. This information is important in order to interpret adequately the author's "liturgical code."

The vision in these two chapters is a veritable mosaic of themes and symbols not always easy to explain. However, among them four major elements emerge:

The throne in heaven and the One seated upon it (4:2-11)
The scroll sealed with seven seals (5:1-4)
The Lamb that was slain, standing erect (5:5-7)
The universal acclamation (5:8-14)

The Throne in Heaven and the One Seated upon It, 4:2-11

Of greater importance than the person, the throne is the most striking feature of this vision and a fundamental theme of the book. This throne will stand out in contrast to other thrones. The one who is seated upon it is recognized as "our Lord God" and is acclaimed as the one "who was and is and is to come" (4:8). He is seated on the throne as the Lord of life and of history and as judge of the nations. The other elements of the vision are decorative, used to highlight the majesty of the one seated upon the throne.

Masterfully combining elements taken from Isa 61:1-2, Ezek 1:26-27, Dan 7:9, and elsewhere, the author presents us with an image in which the overall picture is more important than the identification of its details. For example in the case of the twenty-four elders there may well be different levels of symbolism superimposed one upon the other; this has given rise to the most varied explanations. In Revelation, however, the number twelve and its multiples have to do with the chosen people and the twenty-four elders could be a prototype of the Church, the community of those who are victorious (dressed as they are in white robes, crowned and seated upon thrones) and who are in solidarity with the Church militant, since these elders hold the prayers of the saints in their hands (5:8). But more important than the identification of all these characters is the role they play: "they cast their crowns before the throne" (4:10), recognizing that one alone is worthy to receive "glory and honor." This is truly a polemical and *political* affirmation in that it effectively robs every earthly "throne" of its claim to dignity.

The Scroll Sealed with Seven Seals, 5:1-4

The author makes no attempt to visualize the face of the one seated upon the throne. The only anthropomorphic features upon which he fastens his gaze are a hand and a scroll "in the right hand of the one seated on the throne, written on the inside and on the back, sealed with seven seals" (5:1). To "break its seals" and "look into [the scroll]" means to gain access to history's secret meaning. Everything written in this book has absolute validity and is immutably determined; nothing can be taken away from or added to it (22:18-19). Paradoxically the wailing of the seer expresses humanity's predicament: incapable of deciphering its own history and anguished in the face of a future closed to all hope. Human destiny is in God's safekeeping and the key to understanding it is the Lamb.

The Lamb That was Slaughtered,
Standing Erect, 5:5-7

"The Lion of the tribe of Judah, the Root of David, has conquered . . . a Lamb" (5:5-6). With the joining of titles taken from Gen 49:9 and Isa 11:10 the author identifies Christ as the Messiah King who has come and "has conquered." Paradoxically, the Lion is the Lamb who stands erect—a sign of victory—but has been slain. The Passover is truly the key moment of God's action. The wounds reaffirm the Lamb's victory and speak to us of the road that leads to it. The word translated "slaughtered" is sometimes translated "sacrificed," yet his is not a cultic sacrifice but rather a secular one, a sign of solidarity with all those slain in human history. Here we encounter the scandalous paradox of the Good News proclaimed through Jesus' death and resurrection. It is a case of "victory from the underside of history," from the victims' perspective and in solidarity with them, since he himself is one of them. This is why he is able to open the scroll, unravel the meaning of history, and be personally the key to its interpretation. The Lamb, because he was slain, has the authority and the power to open up the secrets of history and to avenge all those who have been victims throughout the ages.

The Universal Acclamation, 5:8-14

The Lamb receives the scroll and by this same act receives sovereignty over the nations and control of the destiny of all peoples. But what the seer describes is not so much a liturgy as an enthronement ceremony and a taking possession of the Lamb's due authority, recognized by the four living creatures, the twenty-four elders, the thousands of angels, and the whole of creation. An immense multitude from "every tribe and language and people and nation" (5:9) joins in the new song of liberation that celebrates the Lamb's role in history.

Those who sing have been made "a kingdom and priests" (5:10) but it is not the priestly role the author emphasizes; it is the royal office, their victory, for "they will reign on earth." The originality of our author consists in associating priesthood and royalty, which is to say worship and history. The author is not thinking of sacred precincts with special ceremonies but rather of history in which the redeemed extend the victory of the Lamb. Serving their fellow human beings, contributing to the triumph of life and of Christ's reign—that will be their priestly ministry. In the end they will reign forever with neither temple nor priesthood (22:5).

The Seven Seals (6:1–8:1)

The Lamb is the point of articulation between what precedes and the opening of the seven seals that follows. The four riders (the first four seals) are those who have passed into notoriety, but all seven seals form a literary unit whose center is really in the last three, not the first four. Indeed one could say that the fifth seal is key to the scene and to the entire book since in this seal one witnesses a loud scream calling for justice to which God attends. What God does is the divine response to this outcry.

The first four seals (6:1-8)
The fifth seal (6:9-11), key element in the book, and the sixth seal (6:12-17)
The dramatic interlude (7:1-17)

The First Four Seals, 6:1-8

The scene of the four different horses, which the author has deftly and very freely constructed from texts of Ezekiel (5:12; 14:21) and Zechariah (1:8-10; 6:1-8) and allusions to contemporary historical events, is full of enigmas not easily decipherable. It is best not to lose oneself in the details and rather contemplate the grand scheme of things. The first four seals form a unity and the four riders are called forth by the four living beings that attend God's throne. Behind each of them we can discover historical references that the writer universalizes. The first rider, described as victorious, could be an invading power that endangers the security of the empire, for example the Parthians (9:13); the second rider reflects the violent atmosphere of civil wars; the third represents hunger, or more precisely the rationing of foodstuffs (putting high prices on staple products); the fourth brings out the dire effects of the previous scourges. It does not appear valid to identify the first rider with Jesus Christ (simply on the basis of the color of the horse and his victorious character: cf. 19:11) since it is he (as Lamb) who opens the seals. At any rate it is worth noting the contrast between the first rider "conquering and to conquer" (6:2) and the fourth with the ominous name "Death" (6:8). Here we have a prophetic vision of the end-time, of the judgment of God on the earth in response to the outcry that arises from the victims revealed by the opening of the fifth seal: "Sovereign Lord, holy and true, how long will it be before you judge and avenge our blood on the inhabitants of the earth?" (6:10). The reply could be a dramatization of Ezekiel's phrase: "I have now set myself against you, I will inflict punishments upon you" (Ezek 5:8, JB). Behind the Empire's apparent peace, guaranteed for all its citizens, are other forces that God controls and that destabilize the empire and pass judgment on it. The plagues sent upon the earth, not always easy to interpret, are seen by the author and by the apocalyptic tradition as warning signs of the imminent end-time and of divine judgment. The central part of the book offers us a gradual clarification of this judgment.

The Fifth Seal, Key Element in the Book, and the Sixth Seal, 6:9-11, 12-17

One of the clearest signs of the end-time is the persecution and suffering of the elect. The fifth seal speaks of this: the victims cry out. They as well as the Lamb have been slain. They are in a privileged place close to God, "under the altar" (6:9), and they issue a challenge crying out "with a loud voice: 'Sovereign Lord, holy and true, how long will it be before you judge and avenge our blood on the inhabitants of the earth?" (6:10). The unfolding of the plot of Revelation will show that God is not deaf to this outcry, and it will be made clear in the face of the empire's death-dealing capability that the Lamb is able to hear the outcry and give life. They are given white robes which constitute the first divine response to their prayers (as a guarantee of their victory) and they are invited to wait confidently (6:11). The author thus invites the readers to adopt an ethics of confidence and resistance. In the Puebla document (Third General Conference of the Latin American Episcopate, 1979) we find the following paragraphs that seem to echo the outcry of the victims in the fifth seal:

> From the depths of the countries that make up Latin America a cry is rising to heaven, growing louder and more alarming all the time. It is the cry of a suffering people who demand justice, freedom, and respect for the basic rights of human beings and peoples.
>
> A little more than ten years ago, the Medellín Conference noted this fact when it pointed out: "A muted cry wells up from millions of human beings, pleading with their pastors for a liberation that is nowhere to be found in their case" (Med-PC:2).
>
> The cry might well have seemed muted back then. Today it is loud and clear, increasing in volume and intensity, and at times full of menace (*Documento de Puebla* 87–89. IIIa Conferencia

General del Episcopado Latinoamericano. Buenos Aires: Conferencia Episcopal Argentina, 1979).

The sixth seal explicitates the wrath of the Lamb in face of the challenge issued by the victims. The powerful and striking description represents the reaction of the universe to the great "day of the Lamb" (6:17). Above all the security of the magnates (those responsible for creating the victims) is shaken in the presence of Christ's wrath. The Lamb, a peaceable creature, appears with an irresistible anger, for when injustice is tolerated indignation is called for (8:5; 11:18; 14:10; 16:19 and 19:15). Thus the sixth seal is the beginning of God's response to the outcry of the fifth seal in the face of so many lives frustrated and so much blood shed throughout history (11:18; 16:5-6; 18:24; 20:4-6). The anger expresses God's indignation in the face of evil and the divine will to intervene in order to set God's people free, even as God intervened to free the Lamb.

The Dramatic Interlude, 7:1-17

Between the sixth seal and the opening of the seventh there is a pregnant pause, a waiting period as a reply to humanity's question: "the great day of their wrath has come, and who is able to stand?" (6:17). The number of the elect is mentioned; these are they who can withstand securely, marked with the seal of the living God. "God's seal" appears to be a reference to Ezek 9:4 or to God's "passage" through Egypt respecting the houses marked with the blood of the lamb (Exod 12:13). Farther on we will be told that the mark (seal) is the very name of the Lamb and of God (14:1) and that those so marked are God's possession (14:3). The number 144,000, the result of multiplying 12 x 12 x 1,000, is a symbolic number expressing the totality and universality of salvation. It describes the fullness of the renewed Israel open to the nations.

As confirmation of this universality of the elect John sees "a great multitude that no one could count" (7:9) proclaiming salvation with a thunderous voice (7:10 and 12:10). It is truly a community without borders, made up of those "who have come out of the great ordeal" (7:14) that the seer experiences in his own flesh. Through such trials and tribulations the nuptial robes of the bride are being woven (19:7). This multitude "have washed their robes and made them white in the blood of the Lamb." They are "robed in white, with palm branches in their hands" and are "standing before the throne"—that is, all are conquerors and their victory is a participation in the victory of the Lamb they adore. Their worship is eternal, for it occurs in the presence of God who has pitched a tent in the midst of the people. In this manner John anticipates the vision of the New Jerusalem, the only difference being that in the new heavenly city there will no longer be a temple. God's people is on the march, and is guided and shepherded by the Lamb (Isa 49:10 and Psalm 23). The Lord walks ahead of his Church, guiding it to the fountain of life that is found in the company of God and of the Lamb.

The Seventh Seal: The Seven Trumpets (8:1–11:19)

The seventh seal opens a new series of seven: the seven trumpets, preceded by a transitional scene (8:3-5) that is key to understanding what follows. There is an obvious contrast between the liturgical action of offering incense (presenting prayers to God) in the midst of an impressive albeit ominous silence and the hardly liturgical gesture of the angel hurling down to earth the censer and fire from the altar, backed by peals of thunder and an earthquake. The image dovetails with that of 6:10-11 but expresses still more forcefully the divine indignation because of what is happening on earth. The trumpets are the response to the prayers of the saints and are an expression of divine anger.

The seven trumpets constitute a literary unit and each of them points toward the seventh, when the waiting period will be over and the divine plan fulfilled (10:7). It is a salvific plan inasmuch as the Messiah assumes power and begins to reign upon the earth (11:15-17); at the same time it is a plan of judgment to destroy "those who destroy the earth" (11:18). The judgment on Babylon is the best example of this (18:24). The rest of the book describes this singular happening despite the multitude of scenes the author is about to present. The section can be divided as follows:

The first four trumpets (8:7-12)
The fifth trumpet and the first "woe" (8:13–9:12)

The sixth trumpet and the second "woe" (9:13-21)
The dramatic interlude (10:1–11:14)
The seventh trumpet and the third "woe" (11:15-19)

The First Four Trumpets, 8:7-12

An angel blowing the trumpet indicates the beginning of God's judgment, still admonitory and not definitive as if still leaving time for conversion (9:20). The plagues of the first four trumpets, like the first four seals, affect humanity's environment (the earth, the sea, rivers, and stars) and have as their backdrop the plagues of Egypt, an expression of God's justice against the oppressive empire, be it that of Egypt or whichever one dominates the world scene at the moment (Exod 9:24; 10:21). Even though there is an escalation of the damage in these plagues with respect to the earlier series (a quarter in 6:8; a third here), more escapes intact than is destroyed. People are not affected: this is a warning that invites to conversion (9:20); however, as in Egypt the human heart is hardened and will not convert. This is why the four trumpets result in the anticipatory vision of the three "woes" (8:13).

The Fifth Trumpet and the First "Woe," 8:13–9:12

The fifth trumpet, which coincides with the first "woe," is inspired by Joel 1–2 and Jer 51:27. It concerns the plague of locusts, symbol of foreign invasion and military-political power. The locusts wear crowns of gold and have human faces, and are ready for battle (9:7) with chests like iron breastplates (9:9). They are merciless when it comes to violence. Their king has a name that speaks volumes: the Destroyer (9:11). But there are those who are protected by God's mark, who are tormented but not killed (9:5).

The Sixth Trumpet and the Second "Woe," 9:13-21

Unlike 7:1-3 in which the angels were held back from causing damage to the earth or the elect, here the order is given to unleash them "to kill a third of humankind" (9:15). The order issues from the altar (8:3), thus calling attention to the fact that it is God's response to the prayers of the holy ones. The Euphrates is not only geographical nomenclature for a particular river; it is above all the name of a border (Isa 8:7) and implies a threat of invasion. The Roman empire looked with horror toward the East, beyond the Euphrates, where the Parthians threatened to cause problems once again. Our author transcends them and sees them as signs of the end-time; he underlines the danger and threat, telling us the number of their cavalry: two hundred million (9:16). It is a warning that invites to repentance of idolatry, crime, injustice, and corruption.

The Dramatic Interlude, 10:1–11:14

Readers are expecting the fulfillment of the second "woe" that does not arrive until 11:14, just before the blast of the seventh trumpet. As between the sixth and seventh seals, here also the sequence of events halts so that the author may speak of something central to the book: the prophetic task and the context in which it is exercised. It turns out that chs. 10 and 11 are an amplification of the sixth trumpet, an interlude or waiting period the purpose of which is to "raise consciousness" about what is approaching and about the mission that corresponds to the witnesses. The unity of the following two scenes derives from the theme of prophetic testimony: John's testimony, that of the two witnesses, and the testimony of the entire Church.

The Prophetic Vocation (10:1-11)

An angel appears holding an open (that is, unsealed) scroll and proclaims that "there will be no more delay . . . the mystery of God will be fulfilled" (10:6-7), that God had revealed to the prophets and through the prophets. Here the issue is the character of the seer as a prophet. To be a prophet he, like Ezekiel (Ezek 2:8–3:3) must "eat the scroll" (10:9-11), and digest it, make it his own even though it embitters the entrails. He is to prophesy once more "about many peoples and nations and languages and kings" (10:11). The mention of kings suggests the context of this new prophecy: the confrontation with political "powers," a fundamental theme in the coming chapters. The presence of a prophet is dangerous for the empire and for the prophet himself because the truth disturbs and destabilizes.

The Two Witnesses (11:1-14)

If the scene of the open scroll underscores the prophetic mission toward the world ("about many peoples and nations and languages and kings"), the scene of the two witnesses (authoritative proclamation according to Deut 19:17) makes manifest the consequences of this mission for the world and for the prophet. Prophecy upsets the great empire; it is a "torment" for the inhabitants of the earth (11:10). Just as in the description of the two witnesses traits of Elijah and Moses and perhaps Peter and Paul are superimposed, in the same way in the description of the city there are certain symbols superimposed that make any effort at identification of the city useless. The city in which the prophetic activity is exercised bears a symbolic name and has features of Sodom, Egypt, Rome, and Jerusalem. But like the symbol the city is open. Its inhabitants are "inhabitants of the earth . . . members of the peoples and tribes and languages and nations" (11:9-10). It is the city where injustice, oppression, and corruption reign, a city that kills the great prophet of Jerusalem. Behind all this appears the "beast that comes up from the bottomless pit" (11:7) whose activity will be described especially in chs. 13 and 17. The entire scene is intended to be a warning to the prophetic Christian community, but just as in the case of the two witnesses Christians are also protected and after death will rise and go up to heaven in the sight of their enemies (11:11-12). Perhaps the most characteristic aspect of this scene is not the layering of symbols and references to the OT prophets but above all the references to Christ to show that his servants share the same destiny.

The Seventh Trumpet and the Third "Woe," 11:15-19

In 10:7 it is said very clearly that "in the days when the seventh angel is to blow his trumpet, the mystery of God will be fulfilled, as he announced to his servants the prophets." The Church of prophets and witnesses is already aware of the appointed time and of its mission. The last trumpet (coinciding with the third "woe") can sound, allowing the auditors to hear a grand hymn, a thanksgiving (11:17) for the victory of God, of the Lamb, and of his followers: "We give you thanks, Lord God Almighty, who are and who were, for you have taken your great power and begun to reign" (11:17). The dominion of the world has been transferred to God and to the Lamb. Note the predominance of verbs in past tenses, and that God is no longer referred to as "[the one] who is to come." God has *already* come and has begun to reign. The temple opens and the Ark of the Covenant appears: that is to say, the longed-for intimacy of God with God's people becomes a reality. The message of the rest of the book is synthesized here: the nations' anger and God's anger toward "those who destroy the earth" (11:18). The heavens are opened; the horizon brightens; hope appears.

Conflict and Victory (12:1–15:4)

The seventh trumpet ought to be the last or lead into the seven plagues that only appear in 15:7. Everything that occurs from 11:15 to that point is the seventh trumpet and the third "woe" that, albeit without a sevenfold pattern, represents a long interlude and an extension of the seventh trumpet. The blowing of the seventh trumpet is tied in with the seven bowls of plagues by the mention of the opening of "God's temple in heaven" (11:19) and the appearance of a great sign in the sky (12:1) in the beginning of this section and the appearance of "another portent in heaven, great and amazing" (15:1) to begin the following section with the repeated reference to the opening of "the temple of the tent of witness" (15:5).

Dovetailing with 10:7 in which was announced the end of the preparatory period and the consummation of God's mystery (revealed to Israel's prophets and proclaimed by the Christian prophets), the present section intends to make explicit the "eternal gospel" as good news for "those who live on the earth" (14:6). This everlasting good news has two poles: it is the proclamation of the reign of God and of the Lamb in accordance with what is expressed by the hymns interspersed in this section (12:10 and 15:3-4) and it is also a proclamation of the moment of divine judgment, of God's anger (15:1-7) that will destroy "those who destroy the earth" (11:18) according to the programmatic announcement of the seventh trumpet. Between these two poles the Christian community, persecuted for a short time (12:12, 17 and 13:7, 10), can already—in the present moment, as the first fruits of humanity (14:4)—join in and sing the new song of the redeemed of the earth (14:3), the new song of those who are victorious (15:2).

In this section we find the following scenes:

- The vision (sign) of the woman and the dragon (12:1-17)
- The vision of the two beasts (13:1-18)
- The vision of the Lamb and his companions (14:1-5)
- The vision of God's judgment: announced and imaged (14:1-20)
- Dramatic interlude before the seven plagues (15:1-4)

The Vision of the Woman and the Dragon, 12:1-17

Properly speaking the scene begins in 11:19, and starting from there we find the word "appeared" three times (11:19; 12:1, 3). The continuity with the preceding section is evident. Chapters 11–12 refer to the same period of time ("forty-two months," 11:3; 13:5 = "one thousand two hundred sixty days," 12:6). What the two witnesses went through is now the lot of the entire messianic community. It is a question of paschal time, a time of prophecy, a time for testimony, a time of trial; in ch. 12 the reason for the hostility toward the woman and her descendants will be explained. The author presents three scenes in this vision: the woman and the dragon (vv. 1-6), the battle in heaven (vv. 7-12), and once again the woman and the dragon (vv. 13-17). The key is found in the central scene in heaven, in the challenge reflected in Michael's name (etymologically "who is like God?") in the proclamation that "now have come the salvation and the power and the kingdom of our God and the authority of his Messiah" (12:10) and in the fourfold affirmation that the dragon "has been thrown down" (12:9, 10, 12, 13). This section could be entitled "the dragon vanquished." The Church faces a vanquished enemy and the Christian life, although a trial, is victory above all. It is precisely the dragon's fury in the face of defeat that unleashes the persecution against God's people, represented by the woman and her progeny.

Our author masterfully combines biblical symbols and texts (Isa 66:7, 9; 26:16-17; 54:1; Zephaniah 3; Jeremiah 31) in speaking of this woman, symbol of the people of God. Her crown of "twelve stars" could be an allusion to the twelve tribes of Israel (Gen 37:9-11). The dragon is a traditional prophetic image used to refer to Pharoah and his empire (Isa 51:9; Ezek 29:3). When it is defined as the "ancient serpent . . . the deceiver of the whole world" (12:9) and associated with the woman there is allusion made to the primeval enmity between the woman and the serpent of Gen 3:15. It is a question of the conflict between good and evil, between the serpent and Christ, but historicized in the conflict with Pharoah or the empire. The woman represents the messianic people since in Revelation there is a constant fusion of Israel and the Church. She is clothed in glory because she is already triumphant and is pregnant with life, albeit an endangered life. We have here the definitive conflict between life and death, between the woman and the dragon, between the Church and the empire. The birth pangs are the pains of the victims who by their death are born into life (12:11). The woman flees to the desert (as opposed to the city, the system), traditionally a place for refugees and those persecuted, but also the place where one experiences God's protection.

From this fusion of woman–Israel–Church the Catholic Church has gone on to see in the woman Mary the mother of Christ. This interpretation is not in the foreground, and Revelation does not speak of a historical persecution of the mother of Jesus or of her fleeing to the desert, but if we follow the symbolism of the Fourth Gospel in which the mother of Jesus is the woman as prototype of the faith community, the interpretation does not seem so strange even though it is not in the foreground and is the fruit of a typological reading of the text.

The birth of the child is his victory because immediately he is "snatched away and taken to God and to his throne" (12:5). This birth, then, is not that of Bethlehem but rather that of Easter morning and the birth pangs would refer to the passion (cf. John 16:21-22). This conception of the resurrection as a birth is confirmed by the use the NT makes of the second psalm, cited here. The child is destined "to rule all the nations with a rod of iron" (12:5). The contrast is evident: the child is "snatched away and taken to God and to his throne" (12:5), an allusion to Jesus' paschal triumph, while the dragon is "thrown down to the earth" (12:9, 10, 13) venting his rage against the woman and "the rest of her children" (12:17). This last verse is a clear reference to the messianic text of Gen 3:15. The woman's offspring—that is to say, the Church—is called to confront triumphantly the hostility of the world's deceiver, but "they have conquered him by the blood of the Lamb" (12:11). The Church is born in the victory of the Witness and the witnesses.

Many cultures and religions have used the dragon symbolism to represent obscure forces hostile to humankind. What is original in the biblical tradition and in our author's usage is that they historicize the myth; in the biblical tradition it represents the oppressive and menacing empire of Pharoah in Egypt (Ps 74:13; Ezek 29:3) or of Nebuchadnezzar (Jer 51:34). But the identification of the dragon in the text as "that ancient serpent, who is called the Devil" (12:9) requires a radicalization of viewpoint since it says in effect that the Devil is behind every oppressive empire. It cuts through to the root of evil. All Satan's fury is behind the empire that sets out to attack Christians (12:11, 17), but the Christian enters into the fray with confidence since this is the rage of one whose time is almost up, whose opportunities are running out. "They have conquered him by the blood of the Lamb and by the word of their testimony, for they did not cling to life even in the face of death" (12:11). This is a strange way to conquer, as strange as "wash[ing] their robes . . . in blood" (7:14)!

The Vision of the Two Beasts, 13:1-18

With ch. 13 two new characters enter the action; the first was already mentioned in 11:7 as "the beast that comes up from the bottomless pit." If ch. 12 celebrates the victory of God and of the Lamb, and Satan's definitive overthrow, this chapter will speak to us of Satan's desperate war against the woman's progeny (12:17) by means of his instrument, the beast that rises up out of the sea (13:1). Behind this figure there is a historical reality well known to the author and his readers: the Roman empire and its absurd pretension to divine honors ("Who is like the beast?" 13:4).

The author's prudence causes him to speak in coded language: instead of presenting persons he introduces beasts, thereby emphasizing the inhumanity of what the symbolic language hides. There is a clear reference to Daniel 7 here: the vision of the four beasts that represent four empires. But while Daniel spoke of four beasts our author concentrates in a single beast the characteristics of all four. Here we have a super-empire (ten crowns), an absolute concentration of power to the point of divinization demanding that all the inhabitants of the earth render him homage (13:8). Thus this whole passage has a strong political tone as it attempts to unmask the absurd and blasphemous ambitions of the empire.

In antithetical parallels, the author presents us this scene as a parody of the Lamb's throne. Just as the Lamb is God's instrument, so too the beast is Satan's (the dragon's) instrument. The dragon has handed over "his power and his throne and great authority" (13:2) to the beast. "One of its heads seemed to have received a death-blow" but was healed (13:3 and 12). According to 17:9 the heads are kings, and the text seems to allude to a legend very widespread in the first century C.E., especially in Asia Minor, that Nero would return from the dead *("Nero redivivus")*. This emperor, of violent temperament and the first persecutor of Christians, seems to have incarnated, better than anyone else the hostility of the empire. The description of this "beast" takes its inspiration from Dan 7:7-25 in which Antiochus IV, the prototype of persecutors of God's people, is described. It matters little whether it is a question of Antiochus, Nero, or Domitian: what is important is the imperial capacity to dispose of human lives while claiming divine status for oneself (or the empire), together with the uncanny knack of subjugating everyone to himself through the fascination of his power (13:5). With the exception of those marked (sealed) for life, who resist, "all the inhabitants of the earth" (13:8) adore the beast and it receives extraordinary powers "over every tribe and people and language and nation" and is allowed "to make war on the saints and to conquer them" (13:7) even though these latter are guaranteed enrollment in the Lamb's book of life. But this is a time of danger, a time calling for resistance and fidelity on the part of the saints (13:10), which is why we find the same warning as at the end of each letter: "let anyone who has an ear listen" (13:9).

The vision is completed with a second beast "that rose out of the earth": it is the dragon masquerading as a lamb (13:11). Just as the Lamb is at the service of God's plan, the second beast is totally at the service of the first. If the first beast represents the political and economic power of the empire, the second represents religious and ideological power, something like an "official theology" of the state. The description of this beast is not what is important, but rather what he does: he persuades the entire world and all its inhabitants to worship the first beast (13:12) and its image. Here is an excellent "Ministry of Propaganda" in support of the imperial cult's pretensions.

Just as the Lamb puts his mark on his followers and thereby protects them (7:3; 9:4; 14:1), so too the beast marks those of his group, "all, both small and great, both rich and poor, both free and slave" (13:16). This mark, an important theme in the rest of the book (14:9, 11; 16:2; 19:20; 20:4) is "on the right hand or the forehead, . . . 'the name of the beast' or the number of its name" (13:16-17). The contrast with those who "had [the Lamb's] name and his Father's name written on their foreheads" (14:1) is obvious. It is therefore a religious mark, a sign and seal of belonging, of protection. The people submit to the beast, seeking his protection. The author uses the Greek word *charagma* that was used for the emperor's seal (and not *sphragis* as in 7:3). This is the god who protects people by enslaving them. To refuse to adore him is tantamount to excluding oneself from citizenship in the empire with all its attendant privileges (including economic ones). This is why the Christians' situation is so awkward: either one enters into the game, with all the advantages it entails, or one becomes a stranger to that society and is excluded from it because one does not have the "party card" (the mark of the beast) (13:17). These are difficult times that call for faithful perseverance and standing firm in one's witness (13:10 and 12:17).

At the end of this passage the author seems to give us a key to identifying the beast when he speaks of "the number of the beast," the famous six hundred sixty-six. It is a number that suggests a name ("the name of a person") identifiable in the history of that time. The author's clue, clear enough for his contemporary readers, is not so clear to us, and has left the door wide open to all sorts of commentators' speculations concerning the beast's identity. (See the section "The Apocalypse Through the Centuries," paragraph 2, below for a list of candidates.) Let us note two things on this score.

First, the author has recourse to gemmatry, a practice common in antiquity that consists in deciphering a name codified numerically (or vice versa) since in both Hebrew and Greek the letters of the alphabet have a numerical value (neither language has separate number figures; letters do double duty as numbers). There is a well-known inscription found in the ruins of Pompey that reads: "I love the woman whose number is 545." The majority of commentators are inclined to identify the number 666 with the Hebrew letters of Nero-Caesar (*NRWN QSR: N* = 50; *R* = 200; *W* = 6; *Q* = 100, and *S* = 60). The reference would thus be to Nero, or to what he represented: the oppressive power of the Empire that persecuted Christians. It could be, therefore, a reference to Domitian as a "reincarnation" of Nero's spirit, but all of this is still no more than a hypothesis.

Perhaps for our author the very symbolism of the number was more important than the identification of the person. In the Sybilline Oracles (1. 325–331) mention is made of Jesus as the "888," and in Revelation the number seven signifies fullness. In giving the beast the number "666" the author would be denouncing its pretension of wanting to be like "777" (God). This would be a way of indicating a limited power that does not attain to perfection (777).

"Resist and stand firm" is the password (cf. 13:10). The Christians with their dogged perseverance go against the current and proclaim who is really Lord of the world, aware that they are inscribed in the book of life even if the empire does not consider them citizens. Nevertheless, is it worth all the trouble to resist, at such a high price, knowing that the beast is "allowed to make war on the saints and to conquer them" (13:7)? The visions that follow are the answer to this question.

The Vision of God's Judgment, 14:1-20

The beast "was allowed to make war on the saints and to conquer them" (13:7), but there is a word of encouragement for the persecuted community (14:12-13) presenting the model of those who have resisted and are crowned: the Lamb and his followers, "first fruits for God and the Lamb" (14:4). In this way the Christian presence in the midst of the Roman Empire is made manifest: God protects God's people. Jesus stands on Mount Zion because he has full and definitive powers; the dragon stands on the ocean sands (14:1 and 12:18). Those who belong to Christ, those who have received neither the number nor the mark of the beast, bear on their foreheads "the [Lamb's] name and his Father's name" (14:1) and sing the new song of the victorious ones.

Who are those who accompany the Lamb? The author tells us: those "who have not defiled themselves with women, for they are virgins" (14:4). He is not speaking of celibate males but rather of faithful Christians who have not succumbed to the empire's seduction (shortly hereafter the empire is described as a "prostitute"). They have not prostituted themselves, entering into the game of imperial lies; they have not capitulated to the idolatry of the beast and his power (13:4, 8, 12, 15). That is why they follow Christ in his sacrifice and in his victory. It is a matter of the new world of the elect, entrenched in fidelity and patience (14:12) but already participating in the triumph. They are with the Lamb, standing on Mount Zion, site of life's definitive triumph (cf. Isa 24:23; 25:7, 10; Joel 2:32). His presence is already an announcement of the "everlasting good news" (14:6), salvation for the chosen, but at the same time it proclaims that "the hour of his judgment has come" (14:7).

The Vision of God's Judgment: Announced and Imaged, 14:6-20

This judgment comes to point out the illusiveness of the beast's apparent victory. An angel announces: "Fallen, fallen is Babylon the great" (14:8), employing a symbolic name for Rome (16:19; 17:5; 18:2, 10, 21; 1 Pet 5:13). The judgment is also for those who venerate the beast and its image, and is "good news" for the persecuted and those who have died in the Lord and for the Lord (14:13).

The following chapters will be concerned with this judgment in its two manifestations as judgment and salvation, but a preview is given already in the double scene of 14:14-20 in the dual images of harvest and vintage. The first will be of the elect, the second of those condemned. The scene is inspired by Joel 3:12-13: "Let the nations rouse themselves, and come up to the valley of Jehoshaphat; for there I will sit to judge all the neighboring nations. Put in the sickle, for the harvest is ripe. Go in, tread, for the wine press is full. The vats overflow, for their wickedness is great."

The one who judges is "one like the Son of Man" (14:14 and Matt 24:30/Mark 13:27/Luke 21:27), that is to say, Jesus himself. It is specified that those who execute judgment come out of the temple and from the altar (14:15, 17, 18) in order to convey once again that God's judgment is the divine response to the saints' outcry (6:10 and 8:3-5). "God's wrath" is God's fury and indignation in the face of so much bloodshed "outside the city" (14:20), which is the blood of those condemned and excluded by the system, just as Christ died "outside the city gate" (Heb 13:11-12). All this blood cries out to heaven and draws down the judgment of God's wrath (18:14; cf. "ripe" for judgment in 14:15, 18). This is why Jesus himself wears a cloak stained with blood; "he will tread the wine press of the fury of the wrath of God the Almighty" (19:13, 15). The "blood flowed from the wine press, as high as a horse's bridle, for a distance of about two hundred miles" (14:20). The original text reads "one thousand six hundred stadia"—a figure that is a multiple of 4 (4 x 4 x 100), which itself represents geographic universality (the four compass points). It is a way of telling us that the judgment has acquired cosmic proportions.

Dramatic Interlude Before the Seven Plagues, 15:1-4

John sees "another portent in heaven, great and amazing" (15:1), in continuity with that of 12:1, 3. This is a key vision that both sums up and anticipates. The sign is the seven bowls through which "the wrath of God is ended" (15:1). The text will speak of them beginning in v. 5, but first of all what strikes the author is to see "those who had conquered the beast and its image and the number of its name" standing beside the sea and singing the new song of liberation. It is the song of Moses and the Lamb, that is to say the song celebrating God as liberator of all the oppressed peoples of history. This is why "all nations will come and worship before [God]," sole "king of the nations" (15:3-4), and not before the emperor. In a certain sense the hymn celebrates God's design (10:7) sung in 11:15; 12:10, and 14:4, which responds to the victims' outcry in 6:10.

The Seven Bowls of the Seven Plagues (15:5–16:21)

The Seven Plagues: Anticipatory Vision and Canticle, 15:5-8

The seven plagues are not only tied in with the seven trumpets; they also allude (as did the trumpets) to the backdrop of Revelation: the Exodus liberation. These plagues recall those of Egypt through which God carried out judgment on the power that oppressed God's people. As in the previous section, the scene begins with the opening of the heavens (15:6 and 11:19). On the other hand, the angels who execute the plagues leave from the heavenly sanctuary next to the altar from which the cries of the convicted Christians issue (6:9-10), to make clear that the current activity is also a divine response to the cry that rises up from the earth for all the blood that was shed.

The Seven Plagues: Fulfillment, 15:9–16:21

The first four angels, as in the series of trumpets, pour out their bowls one after another upon the earth, sea, rivers, and stars, no longer to kill a third of the human race, but rather *all* those who bear the mark of the beast and adore its statue (16:2). The repetition of the word "blood" is striking, for sentence has been pronounced upon all those who have shed blood (16:6); striking too is the voice that resounds from the altar proclaiming the justice of God's actions (16:7). There is an undeniable connection between the scene in 6:10 and the present one.

The intervention of the fifth angel with the fifth bowl hits the bull's eye: the beast's throne and his reign begin to totter because the sixth angel leaves the road open for an invasion that originates beyond the Euphrates, home of the Parthians, a constant threat to the empire. The dragon, the beast, and the false prophet (a new name for the second beast) are all "inspired" by the same demonic spirit and make a last desperate but futile attempt (16:13-14): they convoke all the kings for the "battle on the great day of God the Almighty" (16:14), but in the end these rebel against the empire, besieging its capital (17:15-17). The worst darkness that can come upon a human being is that of the spirit unable to recognize God's activity (16:9, 11, 21).

When the seventh bowl is poured out God personally declares the verdict, confirming what was said in 14:8: "It is done!" (16:17). The future has been decided and Babylon will have to drink "the wine-cup of the fury of [God's] wrath" (16:19). God's patience (the time for conversion) has been exhausted and the moment of judgment has arrived. Note that the author does not speak of punishment but of judgment and justice (16:7). Christians should await, in an attitude of vigilance and hope, the coming of God's justice which is salvation for God's people.

God's Justice (17:1–22:5)

Chapter 17 begins with the phrase "one of the seven angels who had the seven bowls" because what will be described next is an amplification of the seventh bowl. There are "heads and tails" to the coin of God's justice (diverse manifestations of one and the same reality): judgment and salvation. The "woman," a prophetic symbol, gives unity to the narration (cf. Jer 51:9, 13, 45; Isa 23:17; Ezekiel 22). The woman is a city or an entire people that can be either a prostitute or a spouse. Chapters 17–18 will speak to us of a prostitute (Babylon-Rome) and ch. 21 will present a spouse (Jerusalem). The intervening text of 19:1–20:15 narrates the Lamb's final victory over the beast, the dragon, and death itself. Thus we can speak of a grand finale in three scenes:

Judgment	17:1–19:10
Victory	19:11–20:15
Salvation	21:1–22:5

God's Judgment, 17:1–19:10

God's judgment is presented in two parts: the judgment of the woman (ch. 17) and the fall of the city (ch. 18). The angel shows us the "judgment of the great whore" (17:1) who has a symbolic name: "Babylon the great, mother of whores and of earth's abominations" (17:5) and is identified as "the great city that rules over the kings of the earth" (17:18). Her being seated on "seven mountains," but also on "peoples and multitudes and nations and languages" (17:9, 15) is a reference to Rome, the capital of the world, the center of economic and political power that seduces and traps everyone. What the author has in mind is not urban sexual perversion but rather the generalized corruption and the absolutizing of power that turns into idolatry. The present text is a strong political accusation. The key passages concerning this judgment are "the woman was drunk with the blood of the saints and the blood of the witnesses to Jesus" (17:6) and "in her was found the blood of prophets and of saints, and of all who have been slaughtered on earth" (18:24). The luxury and security of the state are built on crime and bloodshed. The empire's well-being has a high social cost, for it requires victims. Drunkenness and prostitution are powerful images to speak of the sin of all imperialism: insensitivity to the sufferings of the victims (because of its lust for power or pleasure) and giddiness with dominion to the point of considering itself the master of men and women. Everything had to be sacrificed before this cult, including people's lives (18:13).

"The mystery of the woman" (17:7) that the author attempts to explain is as a whole made clear but continues to be a puzzle in some of its details despite all our efforts to apply "wisdom" (17:9) to it. This is why various authors speak of different sources or stages of redaction of the text, basing their arguments on the contradictions they discover: the heads of the beast are alternately seven mountains or seven kings; the woman is seated on "many waters" which are multitudes (17:1, 15), on the beast (17:3) or on the seven mountains (17:9). The same symbolism seems to vacillate between the empire, the emperor, and the city. We believe, however, that rationality and logic are not recommended tools for understanding the text of Revelation, but rather an openness to symbolic polyvalence and to the artistic layering of different symbols by which the author presents his prophetic accusation of the idolatry of imperial power. This would seem to be the gist of the angel's explanation of "the mystery of the woman, and of the beast with seven heads and ten horns" (17:7).

In this chapter there is a virtual identification of the woman with the beast (17:8) and of this beast with the one that appeared in 13:1 with a mortal wound that had healed. Perhaps our author is alluding to the popular belief in *Nero redivivus,* according to which the return of Nero risen from the dead was expected toward the end of the first century. An allusion to this belief would also explain the peculiar description of the beast that "was, and is not, and is about to ascend" (17:8) in terms echoing the description of Jesus. The empire, incarnation of the satanic spirit of Nero, is God's rival, but in reality it is only a cheap parody of the resurrection because the beast returns only to "go to destruction" (17:8). The words of God will be fulfilled (17:17).

However the verses hardest to decipher are: "the seven heads are seven mountains . . . seven kings, of whom five have fallen, one is living, and the other has not yet come . . . . As for the beast that was and is not, it is an eighth but it belongs to the seven . . ." (17:9-11). The woman of the seven mountains is well enough known: she represents Rome as the center of the empire. The beast represents the demonic forces that drive it and is incarnated in the successive emperors. From this perspective there is a clear-cut opposition between God and the beast of whom it is affirmed three times that it "was and is not" (17:8, 11) and is about to return (intentionally contradictory) to "go to destruction" (17:8). Meanwhile God is defined as the one who "was and is" (11:17) and who remains (lives) forever. The empire, the beast, the capital city (the woman), and "her luxury" (what these symbols represent) have a limited span of life and are headed for "destruction" (17:8).

The problem that arises here is the question of the identity of the emperors to which the text alludes. All are astounded, says the angel-guide to the seer, that the beast who was and is no longer "has not yet come" and is the eighth king and at the same time one of the seven. In the paradox of the beast who was and is not but is about to come we can discover an allusion, once again, to the popular first-century legend of *Nero redivivus* according to which the world awaited the appearance of Nero risen from the dead. This incarnation of Nero is Domitian, a contemporary of the writer of Revelation. But some authors, unaware of the value of symbols and other techniques of the apocalyptic writers, question whether this could possibly be a contemporary of the seer if he spoke of the beast as one "who has not yet come." We believe that this manner of expression is a literary fiction by means of which present events are narrated as if already past or as still in the future (for example, Daniel writes as if he lived in the time of Nebuchadnezzar when actually he lived in the time of the Maccabees).

If we remember that for John the definitive overthrow of Satan occurred in the paschal event the list of emperors in the service of Satan must begin at that point, that is, starting with Augustus or Tiberius and continuing with Caligula, Claudius, Nero, Vespasian, Titus, and Domitian (skipping the three transitional kings: Galba, Otho, and Vitellius). Domitian is the eighth but also one of the seven because he is the reincarnation of Nero. The Jewish apocalypses speak a good deal about the return of Nero. The Sibylline Oracles say of him that he will be dangerous after his death since he will return and will be like God (*Sib. Or.* 5. 33–34). Christians in their relations to the empire participate in Jesus' paschal mystery, a mystery of struggle and resistance, but above all a mystery of victory.

The judgment on oppressive imperialism is made unequivocally evident in the fall of Babylon (ch. 18), narrated against the background of Ezekiel 27–28. The news is proclaimed by an angel with a powerful voice at the beginning of the chapter and another angel dramatizes it at the end of the same chapter, throwing into the ocean "a stone like a great millstone" (18:21). The lamentation sounds three times in this chapter: "Alas, alas, the great city" (18:10, 16, 19) in the mouths of kings, merchants, and seafarers, which is to say all those involved in the luxury, the commerce, and the exploitation, who "grew rich by her wealth" (18:19) and included in their merchandise not only luxury items but above all negotiated in "slaves—and human lives" (18:13). Yes, there is to be found in her the blood of "all who have been slaughtered on earth" (18:24), including the blood of the Lamb, all those assassinated by the idolatry of power and money.

Christians cannot be citizens of this city. Hence the exhortation: "Come out of her, my people, so that you do not take part in her sins" (18:4). They live in the world as strangers and outcasts because they bear neither the mark nor the name of the beast (13:17), but at the same time they are in solidarity with the victims and the victors. "For God has given judgment for you against her" (18:20).

In 19:1 there is a change of scene (to heaven) but it is the logical conclusion of the preceding judgment. The Hebrew expression "hallelujah," repeated four times (19:1, 3, 4, 6) is an invitation to "praise God," building on 18:20. The victory is sung by the celestial court and by the Church triumphant. The first "hallelujah" retrospectively sums up the judgment of Babylon. In it God not only honors the divine name with "true and just judgments" (19:2 and 16:7), but also does justice to God's servants who are asking that their blood be avenged (19:3, 6, 9; 18:20). Corruption and bloodshed are Babylon's sins. The last song points forward, inviting us to celebrate because God "reigns" (19:6 and 11:17) and "the marriage of the Lamb has come" (19:7). It is the triumph of the Messiah and of those associated with him: his people and his spouse who is clothed "with fine linen, bright and pure" (19:8) "washed in the blood of the Lamb" (7:14).

The Lamb's Victory, 19:11–20:15

The theme of judgment continues in this section (19:11; 20:4, 12, 13) and this whole part could be considered an amplification of what was said in 11:18: "the time [has come] for judging the dead, for rewarding your servants . . . and for destroying those who destroy the earth." The dominant note is certainly the Lamb's victory and his ability to conquer evil down to its roots, eliminating its causes: the beast and its false prophet, the dragon, and death itself.

Christ, Victorious Judge (19:11-16)

"Then I saw heaven opened" (19:11) is an expression of something important that is revealed—or rather some*one*. In Christ, God personally comes to earth to judge and to save (cf. Luke 3:21; John 1:51). A white horse appears—the antithesis of 6:2—and upon it Christ, victorious judge and savior, is mounted. He judges and fights for the implementation of true justice (19:11). This description builds upon the well-known ritual of Roman emperors triumphantly entering the city after their conquests. The one who is "Faithful and True" enters riding a white horse in the company of his allies (19:14). The champion of justice has a name and title that belong to him alone: "King of kings and Lord of lords" (19:16 and 17:14). His is absolute sovereignty that destroys the powerful; for this reason on his head are many crowns (19:12). From the point of view of the divinized emperor Caesar it would be a blasphemous, challenging, and provocative title.

In an unmistakable allusion to Isa 63:1 he wears a "robe dipped in blood" (19:13) because "he will tread the wine press of the fury of the wrath of God the Almighty" (19:15 and 14:20). It is a victory gained with bloodshed: the blood of his followers and his own blood since he is one of the victims immolated in the bloody history of the great imperial city. The title "Word of God" (19:13) is inspired by Wis 18:15 in a similar context of war and judgment. His triple victory is recounted in the following section with almost identical phrases (19:20; 20:10, 14).

Victory over the Beast and the False Prophet (19:17-21)

The author tells us twice more "then I saw" (19:17, 19). The first vision speaks of "the great supper of God," inspired by Ezek 39:17-22 (see the synoptic table under "First Reading"). It is a grotesque feast, the antithesis of the Lamb's banquet to which the same personalities as in 16:15 are invited to celebrate their own defeat. The second vision seems to be tied in with 16:13, 14 and concentrates on what is essential: those responsible for humanity's errors (the beast and the false prophet) who are "thrown alive into the lake of fire that burns with sulfur" (19:20).

Victory over the Dragon (20:1-10)

This is one of the most complicated and controversial passages in the entire book of Revelation, whose primary claim to fame historically is what has come to be known as "millenarianism" (see the final section of this article, "The Apocalypse Through the Centuries," for a brief historical survey of this tendency within Christianity). At the very outset, before entering into the intricacies of this polemic, let us state straightforwardly what is clearest and most fundamental in this text.

In two visions (20:1, 4) there is an affirmation of the victory over the devil who also is thrown into the lake of fire (20:10). The symbols of both visions are eloquent all by themselves. In the first vision, in contrast to 9:1-11, an angel with a key and a large chain binds and encloses the dragon that, as in 12:9, is given four names: the dragon, the ancient serpent, the Devil, and Satan. His days of activity are numbered (the "little while" of 20:3); his defeat lasts "forever and ever" (20:10 and 12:9).

The second vision presents the thrones and those who are responsible for pronouncing sentence as a response to the demands of justice in 6:9-12. From the "underside" of history, from the victims' vantage point (20:4: "those who had been beheaded for their testimony to Jesus and for the word of God") judgment is passed on the oppressive satanic power. The tables are turned and the accused and those excluded are now the judges alongside the Lamb. Those who never submitted to the emperor's cult nor bowed before his image come back to life and sit upon the thrones to judge (cf. Dan 7:22, 27). "They will be priests of God and of Christ, and they will reign with him a thousand years" (20:6). The emphasis is placed on the definitive overthrow of Satan and the victory of the saints who reign with Christ. These "thousand years" have excessively absorbed the attention of the commentators, causing them to neglect the content of these two visions. The thousand years are the duration of Satan's binding and of the saints' (martyrs') reign with Christ. To understand these thousand years in a literal sense is contrary to the spirit of Revelation, which presents other time figures on different occasions (one thousand, two hundred sixty days, one hour, etcetera). And to understand them symbolically one must take into account not only the allusions to Ezek 37:39 or Daniel 7, but also Jewish speculations on the configuration of history in seven days of a thousand years each (cf. 2 Enoch 32 or the psalmist's phrase in Ps 90:4, "a thousand years in your sight are like yesterday"; cf. 2 Pet 3:8). There was a belief among the Jews that Paradise would last a thousand years. Therefore in speaking of a thousand years our author is not making a statement about chronology; he is using a theological symbol and is speaking about the *present* already inaugurated by Christ. It is his way of presenting Jesus as the Messiah, as victor and restorer of Paradise. This allusion to Paradise is confirmed by the reference to "the ancient serpent" (20:2) and to the tree of life promised to the victors (22:2 and 2:7).

In the same symbolic vein we must understand the other affirmations concerning "the first resurrection" (20:5: nothing is said of the second resurrection) or "the second death" (2:11; 20:6, 14; and 21:8). This latter phrase is identified in the text (21:8) as the "lake of fire that burns with sulfur" into which the beast and the false prophet are thrown (19:20), that is to say, as an eternal and definitive condemnation. It also coincides with the second resurrection, the eternal and definitive one, which however is not spoken of by the author. Therefore the first death is bodily death of the martyrs who "had not worshiped the beast or its image" (20:4) and that Christians do not fear because they already live in the "first resurrection." They see contemporary events in the light of Jesus' pasch, the definitive eschatological event that broke once and for all the power of Satan and death (20:10). By their faith in Christ believers have truly passed "from death to life" (1 John 3:13) and reign with Christ (20:4, 6). Because of their victory they participate in the judgment of the world and are priests for God celebrating henceforth the triumph of life.

Victory over Death (20:11-15)

Two elements of the narrative confirm this line of interpretation for us: the expression "I saw a throne" or "I saw also" (twice) and the affirmation that "Death and Hades were thrown into the lake of fire" (20:14). The mention of the throne dovetails with 20:4 and recalls the vision of chs. 4–5. It is judgment on death and hell, avenging all those killed throughout human history. The moment has arrived when death will be "swallowed up forever" (Isa 25:7), but the judgment is not for those who are registered in the "book of life" (20:15). The old world (earth, sky, sea) disappears (20:11 and 21:1) to open the way for the new world, the work of God and the Lamb.

Salvation, or the Triumph of Life, 21:1–22:5

The woman of ch. 12 is contrasted with the prostitute of ch. 17. Here as well the bride (Jerusalem) of the present chapter represents the opposite of the whore (Babylon) of ch. 17, and both women are signs of the life that is coming to birth and establishing itself definitively. One of the seven angels who explained the mystery of the woman (17:7) and now is "one of the seven angels who had the seven bowls full of the seven last plagues" (21:9) presents the spouse of the Lamb. In both cases the seer is carried away by the Spirit (17:3 and 21:10) and the book of life is mentioned (17:8 and 21:27). The beast the woman is riding comes "from the bottomless pit" and is bound "to destruction" (17:8); the bride comes down from heaven to earth and will reign forever (21:2 and 22:5). The continuity and contrast are clearly evident. What our author has seen under different figures is the definitive triumph of life that springs from God and the Lamb. The vision concentrates and superimposes symbols and images attempting to reconstruct humanity's utopia. A clear example of what we are saying is the restoration of Paradise as an expression of people's utopian dream, but now coinciding with God's dream. The vision is constituted by three grand scenes we could entitle as follows: Everything is new (21:1-8), the new city (21:9-27), and the new Paradise (22:1-5).

Everything is New (21:1-8)

A new heaven, a new earth, a new Jerusalem; definitively "all things [are made] new" (21:5) is the joyous affirmation of having achieved the utopia (21:6). It is not John who assures us of its achievement, since he is but a witness of one who is more authoritative than he: "the Alpha and the Omega, the beginning and the end" (21:6). The old order has passed away and what is new has appeared (cf. 2 Cor 5:17).

The precise nature of this newness is explained by the voice the seer hears. First there is a "negative" description: there will be *no* death, or mourning, or wailing, or pain (21:4), and the sea (symbol of all that is agitated and unstable) no longer exists (21:1). But the reason for all this has to do with the "solidarity," the tenderness of God-with-us who came down to be with God's people, to wipe away their tears and make them children of God. Those who are thirsty and those who conquer (a phrase that recalls the end of each letter) are invited by God to drink "from the spring of the water of life" (21:6).

The New City (21:9-27)

In this second part the seer, guided by an angel, describes for us the beauty of the city-bride, having "the glory of God and a radiance like a very rare jewel" (21:11). It is not a question of reconstruction of the historical city of Jerusalem; instead we have here a symbol that transcends it, a symbol of the sharing of life among peoples, expressing thus that salvation is essentially social and communicative.

It is difficult to imagine a city that is a perfect cube, more than 9 miles high, long, and wide. These are symbols or images that evoke the invisible: beauty, graciousness, perfect stability, and the fullness of light and life because of God's presence. That is why our author does not worry about contradicting himself in affirming that the city is pure gold and at the same time that it has all kinds of gemstones. At this point there is no one who will fight for the gold, which will be put at the service of human society.

In the background we have an artistic combination of texts like Isa 60:1-2; 65:17-18 or Ezekiel 40–48, handled with a great deal of freedom. Ezekiel also describes for us the reconstruction of the city with the new, significant name of "The Lord is There" (Ezek 48:35). The city symbolism speaks of its "roots" in Israel and of a new relationship with God and among peoples. It is a question of a city with open doors where there are neither outcasts nor marginalized people; all its inhabitants have citizen status.

John is surprised by what is absent from the city, the absence of which would seem strange to any visitor: "I saw no temple in the city" (21:22). Strange and inconceivable: a city without a temple! Would it be then a profane, secular city? No; it is rather a city that has transcended the sacred-profane dichotomy (seeing certain people, places, and moments as "sacred"). *Everything* within it is sacred and consecrated by God's presence. Historically in Jerusalem the Temple separated priests from laity and drew lines of separation among the priests themselves, for only the high priest could enter into the very presence of God once a year. In this city there is no temple because God's very self has come to dwell with God's people and the entire city is a temple, which is to say, a divine presence. It is a city with a mission: to illuminate by its presence humanity's pilgrimage and quest (21:24). It is a city of light inasmuch as in it the day reigns forever and there is no need for sun or moon, because God and the Lamb are its perpetual luminaries. There is no night, which is symbol of death, shadows, and insecurity. Light and life spring forth eternally from God.

The New Paradise (22:1-5)

Fleshing out 21:6 and anticipating 22:17, the seer shows us the river of the water of life, a clear allusion to Ezek 47:1-12 (the water that sprang up from under the temple). Here there is no temple, but only the Lamb, and it is from him that the water (that is, life) flows forth. With the river of the water of life and the tree of life, life in Paradise is assured. In the book of Genesis an angel guarded access to the tree of life; here the water flows out freely to the nations and floods them with life. God in person makes "peace, like a river, to flow out" toward them (cf. Isa 66:12) and gratuitously offers them gifts out of God's sheer divine abundance (21:6 and Isa 55:1-2). Living together peacefully and enjoying a fullness of life, "they will reign forever and ever" (22:5).

Epilogue: 22:6-21

The epilogue is in strict relation to the book's introduction, thus highlighting its fundamental unity. We find the same references to the book's prophetic character, the angel, happiness, "what must soon take place" and, above all, the book's central theme: Jesus' [second] coming.

What is highlighted most of all is the purpose of this piece of writing. In the first place it was written to render testimony that its message is "trustworthy and true" (22:6). For this reason "blessed is the one who keeps the words of the prophecy of this book" (22:7). Those who testify are the angel, John, and Jesus himself (22:8, 16, 20). Second, it is intended to exhort believers to stand firm, be watchful, and resist even to the point of shedding one's blood in order to have a right to enter the city and experience the fullness of life (22:14). Christians must allow themselves to be illuminated by the "morning star" (22:16) that announces the new day of resurrection. Third, it invites one to join in the universal invocation, calling for the Lord's coming in unison with John, the Church, and the Spirit. The Lord is coming (and with him those who are victorious) to inaugurate a city full of light and life. What a beautiful utopia toward which our dark, disconcerting, inhuman history is headed!

The Book of Revelation Through the Centuries

Revelation is one of the biblical books that throughout the centuries has had the greatest impact in the diverse fields of Christian endeavor: theology, ecclesiastical order, the liturgy, the fine arts, and literary production. One can discern three major areas of influence of Revelation on the life of the Christian churches: (1) Catholic and mainline Protestant theology (especially in the fields of christology, ecclesiology, and eschatology); (2) "biblical prophecy" (as understood by the fundamentalist churches) and related communal expressions (most notably among millenarian groups), and (3) liturgy, the fine arts, music, and literature.

1. Contributions to Catholic and Protestant Theology

Revelation has contributed important accents to Christian theology, both directly through commentaries on its text that were produced in great profusion in certain epochs of Church history (the sixth century, the High Middle Ages, the Reformation era, and the twentieth century) and indirectly through its use in liturgy and the arts. Through these diverse media Revelation has contributed or enriched perspectives in christology (paschal themes: Lamb of God, blood redemption, and Jesus as protomartyr), ecclesiology (images of the Church as victorious people of God, the "white-robed army of martyrs" sealed with the Lamb's seal, the Bride of the Lamb, the New Jerusalem) and eschatology (theology of history, the relationship between the Church and the reign of God, and the nature of God's definitive reign). In the Catholic Church it contributed support to the doctrines of the communion of saints, the "last things" (death, judgment, heaven and hell), and the ascetic mystique of martyrdom. A recent example of the continuing doctrinal influence of Revelation is its contribution to the new *Catechism of the Catholic Church*" in the areas of christology (nos. 449–451), ecclesiology (nos. 775–778), and eschatology (nos. 671–677; 865; 1029; 1044–1045). In this last area the book of Revelation appears as the Church's favorite source of doctrine and preferred expression of the definitive reign of God:

> The Church will enter the glory of the kingdom only through this final Passover, when she will follow her Lord in his death and Resurrection (cf. Rev 19:1-9). The kingdom will be fulfilled, then, not by a historic triumph of the Church through a progressive ascendancy, but only by God's victory over the final unleashing of evil, which will cause his Bride to come down from heaven (cf. Rev 13:8, 20:7-10, 21:2-4) . . . [no. 677].

In this new universe, the heavenly Jerusalem, God will dwell among men and women (cf. Rev 21:5). "He will wipe every tear from their eyes. Death will be no more; mourning and crying and pain will be no more, for the first things have passed away" (Rev 21:4).

For humanity this consummation will be the final realization of the unity of the human race, which God willed from creation and of which the pilgrim Church has been "in the nature of sacrament" (cf. *LG* 1). Those who are united with Christ will form the community of the redeemed, "the holy city" of God, "the Bride, the wife of the Lamb" (Rev 21:2, 9). It will not be wounded any longer by sin, stains, self-love that destroy or wound the earthly community (cf. Rev 21:27). The beatific vision, in which God opens God's very self in an inexhaustible way to the elect, will be the ever-flowing wellspring of happiness, peace, and mutual communion [*Catechism* nos. 1044–1045].

The thirteenth chapter of Revelation (which portrays the Roman empire as the "beast") has served in diverse epochs of Church history as an antidote or counterweight to Romans 13, which if taken unilaterally could open the way to subservience and legitimation of totalitarian regimes in the name of God. A tragic example of this very thing is found in the "Book of Truth" (report of investigations into the assassination of the six Jesuits in El Salvador, November 1989), which revealed that the assassins read the thirteenth chapter of Romans the evening before their murderous action in favor of state security. What might have been the outcome if they had read instead (and understood) Revelation 13? The book of Revelation thus offers a critical perspective sorely needed for a cogent "political theology" (and a proper understanding of Church-state relations) in our time.

2. A Gold Mine of "Biblical Prophecy"

Students of "Biblical Prophecy"

Among fundamentalists Revelation has long been used as a gold mine of biblical prophecy, that is, as indispensable (and in some cases, along with Daniel, practically the only) resource material for working up end-time scenarios. This almost exclusive dependence on Revelation and Daniel constitutes a sort of "canon within the canon" for many of the more eschatological Christian denominations, which interpret Revelation literally with respect to the nature, moment, and manner of arrival of God's glorious reign. Little does it concern these groups that such interpretations are unanimously rejected by contemporary biblical scholars as projections of present-day preoccupations and mind-set upon the text. These speculations usually occur within the ideological framework of belief in "biblical prophecy" (understood uncritically, notwithstanding an eclectic use of certain exegetical data when these would seem to support their predetermined theories). This belief in the fulfillment of "biblical prophecies" (most often in the believer's lifetime) has had a long and variegated history within (and especially on the fringes of) Protestantism. Especially since the dawn of "dispensationalism" in the late nineteenth century there has been "in the air" (so to speak) the idea that God has a "master plan," a divine strategy of world government revealed long ago to the prophets (or actually to the apocalyptic writers). This conception in turn has frequently degenerated into anxious comparisons of one's current situation with "biblical truth" in an (inevitably successful) search for clues to the conclusive stages of the last and most terrifying war humanity is to know: Armageddon.

Over the centuries one of the favorite pastimes of such "students of biblical prophecy" has been trying to identify "the beast of Revelation" (equated with the Antichrist, a term found not in Revelation but rather in 1 and 2 John). Paul Boyer, in a fascinating study of apocalyptic fundamentalism, mentions the following "identifications" of the Antichrist offered by different individuals and groups in the course of Christian history (in alphabetical order): Lord Bute, Charles I, Oliver Cromwell, Moshe Dayan, Frederick II, George III, Mikhail Gorbachev, Adolf Hitler, Saddam Hussein, Juan Carlos, John F. Kennedy, Henry Kissinger, William Laud, Mohammed, Sun Myung Moon, Benito Mussolini, Napoleon Bonaparte, Ronald Reagan, Anwar Sadat, and Saladin.

The Millenarian Phenomenon

A particularly striking manifestation of this "biblical prophecy" current has been (and is) millennialism: the belief in a literal thousand-year reign of Christ together with his saints. Despite the scarcity of biblical basis for such a doctrine (explicitly found only in Rev 20:4-7) expectation of a Christian "millennium" has been extraordinarily persistent among believers ever since the beginnings of Christianity. Among the earliest Christian writers Justin Martyr, Irenaeus, and Hippolytus understood the mentioned passage literally (albeit with different shades of meaning), while Clement of Alexandria rejected such an interpretation. Tertullian and the Montanists espoused an especially precise interpretation of the millennium, even to the point of identifying the city of Pepuza as the location of Christ's reign; they were really the first millennialists in the modern sense of the word. The diversity of opinion persisted in the following centuries, with various Christian leaders (Lactantius, Victorinus of Pettau, Cerinthus) favoring diverse millennialist interpretations while Origen, Jerome, Augustine and many others battled against such ideas. (Incidentally, the support the millenarians found in Revelation for their theories seems to have been the reason why, after widespread acceptance of the book by the Christian churches for more than a hundred years, in the third century there arose discordant voices that argued against the book's inclusion in the canon.) Ever since the golden patristic era Augustine's figurative interpretation, in which the "millennium" is the chronologically indefinite reign of Christ in the Church until the end of time, has been the unofficially normative Catholic interpretation. Since then millennialism has been found principally in the other Christian confessions, and when it has sprouted in the Catholic community it generally has been discredited. In the course of this century the Catholic Church has come closest to an official condemnation of millennialism, in the decree of the Holy Office of June 21, 1944, that termed it a "dangerous doctrine" (cf. *Catechism of the Catholic Church,* nos. 676–677). Many of the Protestant reformers also categorically rejected millennialism in their respective churches: John Calvin said concerning it "the fiction is too puerile to need or to deserve refutation," and in fact Revelation is the only NT book for which he did not write a commentary.

Millennial beliefs, however, were not limited to biblical commentaries or to the opinions of Church leaders. Over the centuries end-time expectations, whether or not directly inspired by Revelation, contributed to the most diverse experiments in community living. The extraordinary opportunities offered by the New World in the sixteenth and seventeenth centuries, for example, inspired many utopian projects among both Catholics and Protestants. The best known of the former are the communitarian Santa Fe "Hospitals" of Bishop Vasco de Quiroga in Mexico, the initiatives of peaceful evangelization of Bartholomew de las Casas and the Dominicans in Central America, and the Jesuit "reductions" in South America. Among Protestants the Mayflower expedition (1620) intended to meet the Lord in the new promised land, and many of the Protestant migrations to the New World (e.g., Puritans, Moravians) had similarly apocalyptic overtones. Nevertheless few of these projects sustained by hopes of founding a new and pristine Christianity in the New World were directly or primarily inspired by the book of Revelation. There have been, however, many other Christian groups that, moved by their conviction about the proximate end of the world and conveniently ignoring passages like Matt 24:36 (par. Mark 13:32), tried to discover the date of the final encounter with Christ. The utopian attractiveness and the psychological impact of the announcement of the imminent end of the world would seem to have been decisive factors in the apparition and growth of various such Christian denominations. Among the principal ones are the Anabaptists (and other similar groups in the early years of the Protestant Reformation), the Adventists (beginning with William Miller, whose predictions of the precise date of Christ's return in glory—1843/1844—resulted in the "Great Disappointment") and the Jehovah's Witnesses (who have deftly recuperated from a whole series of unfulfilled predictions of the end of the world during the course of this century). (See chart on next page.)

Such denominations, practically defined by millennial expectation, are frequently of a sectarian nature, affirming that their group is the one and only community of salvation. On some occasions this sectarian character has had tragic results. Two examples, one from past centuries and the other from our own time, will suffice. In 1534, when the German Melchiorites led by Mathys and Bockelson took up arms to inaugurate the millennial kingdom of God, which was supposed to begin in Münster on Easter Sunday, the result was a blood bath in which all of the avid millenarians were killed. Most recently, on April 19, 1993, the world's attention was riveted upon the sectarian community at "Apocalypse Ranch" in Waco, Texas, where the majority of the members, living under the influence of David Koresh (self-designated "Lamb of God"), died in the horrible conflagration that was witnessed practically world wide through the international news media.

3. Inexhaustible Source of Symbolic and Artistic Inspiration

The most original and valuable contribution of Revelation, however, would seem to be in the area of symbolic expression (the arts in the broadest sense of the word). Even a summary investigation reveals incredible artistic-symbolic wealth in different fields—certainly with different degrees of creativity and originality, ranging from the ludicrous to masterpieces that enhance the already powerful and sublime expressiveness of Revelation. One work on the subject (see Charles Brütsch, *La Clarté de l'Apocalypse.* 6th ed. Geneva: Editions Labor et Fides, 1966) lists over one hundred fifty artistic representations of Revelation in all the graphic and plastic arts as well as some references in the areas of music and literature, principally from European sources. Let us briefly examine these separate fields.

Liturgy

The Catholic liturgy owes a great deal to the last book of the NT: in the first place its texts are used as canticles in Vespers, as readings at Mass on Sundays in Paschal time and at daily Eucharist during the last two weeks of the liturgical year. Consoling, hope-filled readings from the book of Revelation are proclaimed on All Saints' Day and are among the choices established for funeral liturgies. Moreover, the book is read in its entirety by those who pray the Liturgy of the Hours in the "Office of Readings" during the Easter season. In the Common Lectionary (which unites Catholics, Anglicans, Lutherans, and other Protestant liturgical traditions in common Sunday readings) the selection of texts from Revelation is primarily composed of hymnic materials, passing over the woeful passages like the paschal angel of doom. The Orthodox liturgy does not include readings from Revelation, perhaps due to the Oriental churches' reluctance to grant it canonical status.

Several different hermeneutical principles are discernible in the Catholic liturgical intertextuality. First of all there is the *eschatological (end-time) reading* of Revelation in the daily eucharistic readings during the last two weeks of the Church year (including significant portions of chs. 14–18); these selections accompany the Lukan apocalypse and alternate with Daniel and 1–2 Maccabees in odd-numbered years. The feast of All Saints gives an especially triumphant note to this interpretation with the reading of Revelation 7. Second, we have the *paschal reading* of Revelation in Sunday liturgies of the "C" cycle (Common Lectionary) in which mainly hymnic portions are used as a bridge between

Predictions of the End of the World
(the list is not exhaustive)

Year predicted	*Persons and Places*
c. 172	Montanus, in Phrygia
500	Hippolytus of Rome
1000	Various groups
1200 or 1260	Joachim of Fiore, writing in 1183/1184
1348, then 1349	Flagellants during the Black Death
c. 1396	Vincent Ferrer, in Spain, France, and Italy
c. 1525	Thomas Müntzer, leader of the Peasants' War in Germany
8 a.m. October 19, 1533	Michael Stiefel, friend of Martin Luther (who totally rejected his friend's millennial expectation)
1533	Melchior Hoffmann, in Strasbourg: early Anabaptists
April 5, 1534 [Easter]	Melchiorites Jan Matthys and Jan Bockelson (John of Leiden), in Münster
1588	Erasmus (predicted the fall of the papacy for this year)
1625–1626	Drabicus (fall of the papacy 1625; the millennium in 1626)
1655	Christopher Columbus
1660	Partisans of the "Fifth Monarchy," England
1663	John Toldervy, of the Quakers
1666	Agrippa d'Aubigné: Quaker leader George Fox wrote that every thunderstorm in 1666 produced expectations of the end
1688	Scottish mathematician John Napier, in a book published in 1593, which reached twenty-three editions in the seventeenth century
1697, then 1736	Cotton Mather in the United States
1715, then 1766	Astronomer and mathematician Isaac Newton in his posthumous book *Observations upon the Prophecies of Daniel, and the Apocalypse of St. John,* 1733
Christmas 1748	Frenetic mystics in Bern, Switzerland
1761–1763	Two books in United States in 1759 (Antichrist 1761; end of the world 1763)
1835, 1838, 1842, 1845	Edward Irving, in England
1843, then October 22, 1844	William Miller in the United States: the 1844 date, awaited by some 50,000 "Adventists," became their "Great Disappointment"
1892–1900	Pierre Lachèze (conversion of the Jews 1892; millennium in 1900)
1914	Charles Russell, founder of the (future) Jehovah's Witnesses, "millions now alive will never die"
1925, various later dates	J. R. Rutherford in the United States and after him Jehovah's Witnesses
1988	Edgar Whisenant (in a book that sold two million copies in 1988)
2000	Samuel Sewall, in the United States (late 1600s); Frédéric de Rougemont in nineteenth century; various apocalyptic groups in the 1990s
Other	Michael de Notredame (Nostradamus) when Good Friday falls on April 23, Easter on the 25th, and Trinity Sunday on June 24, which already occurred since his book's composition (late 1550s) in the years 1666, 1734, 1886, and 1943, and will again occur in 2038.

God did not wish to reveal the exact date of the second coming of Christ. "To prevent his disciples from asking the time of his coming, Christ said: *About that hour no one knows, neither the angels nor the Son. It is not for you to know times or moments.* He has kept those things hidden so that we may keep watch, each of us thinking that he will come in our own day. If he had revealed the time of his coming, his coming would have lost its savor: it would no longer be an object of yearning for the nations and the age in which it will be revealed. He promised that he would come but did not say when he would come, and so all generations and ages await him eagerly.

"Though the Lord has established the signs of his coming, the time of their fulfillment has not been plainly revealed. These signs have come and gone with a multiplicity of change; more than that, they are still present. His final coming is like his first. As holy men and prophets waited for him, thinking that he would reveal himself in their own day, so today each of the faithful longs to welcome him in his own day, because Christ has not made plain the day of his coming. *(continued)*

"He has not made it plain for this reason especially, that no one may think that he whose power and dominion rule all numbers and times is ruled by fate and time. He described the signs of his coming; how could what he has himself decided be hidden from him? Therefore, he used these words to increase respect for the signs of his coming, so that from that day forward all generations and ages might think that he would come again in their own day" (Office of Readings, First Thursday in Advent: commentary of St. Ephraim on Tatian's *Diatessaron*).

the historical readings of Acts and the "realized eschatology" of John's gospel. Here Revelation is used to inspire in us praise and adoration of the risen Lord present in our communal celebration of the "Lord's day." Note that the calamitous sections have been suppressed. In this way the Church highlights its positive appreciation and authentic interpretation of the book of Revelation's message to Christians: those who are faithful to God until the end will share in the glory of the Lord. Finally, in the Catholic liturgy there is the *Mariological reading* of Revelation 12 in the Mass of the Assumption of Mary and other Marian feasts (Liturgy of the Hours). This interpretation has had a tremendous impact on different areas of Catholic life: sacred art, hymnody, popular religiosity, and more, where the theme of "a woman clothed with the sun, with the moon under her feet, and on her head a crown of twelve stars" (12:1) is commonplace. Referring these diverse instances to Revelation 12 does not indicate ignorance of the mythical roots of such symbolism, but neither does the prehistory of the text exclude seeing these expressions as instances of authentic biblical interpretation (albeit recognized by Catholics as an "accommodated sense").

Above and beyond the use of specific texts from Revelation, however, the liturgy—Orthodox no less than Roman Catholic—finds itself very close to the figurative idiom of Revelation in its own ritual expressions and symbolic language that attempt to convey the ineffable. The liturgy has incorporated many motifs of Revelation in its diverse celebrations: the symbolic use of colors and clothing, silence and hymnody, Alleluia and Amen, incense, certain numbers, lamb imagery, etcetera. In some cultures it turns out that it is rather popular religiosity that is most attuned to (and most creatively reproduces) the type of symbolism used in the book of Revelation.

Graphic Arts

The graphic arts have been especially prolific in rendering scenes from Revelation both in works that represent the totality of the book and in partial representations (i.e., of certain of its aspects or themes). Among the former are found illuminated manuscripts (such as the Bamberg Apocalypse or that of Beato de Liébano), the Renaissance Flemish tapestries now in possession of the Spanish royal family, the synoptic painting of Hans Memling (Bruges, 1475–1479), the icon of the entire Apocalypse by Master Dionysius (c. 1500, in the Church of the Dormition, Moscow), and the well-known series of woodcuts by Albrecht Dürer in 1498 (whose slavishness to the letter of Revelation produced almost grotesque results even in majestic images such as the inaugural vision of 1:10-20 or the lamb that was slain in 5:6—with seven eyes and seven horns!). In the second group (representations of part of the book or of certain select images) the most popular themes seem to have been the four living creatures of Revelation 4–5, identified with the four evangelists since the time of Irenaeus (as in the magnificent cover of the "Book of Kells" or the stone sculpture in the doorway of the Chartres Cathedral), the woman and the dragon of Revelation 12 (as in the famous tapestry of Lurçat in the chapel of Assy, France) and the New Jerusalem/new Paradise (as in the unsurpassed Ghent altarpiece of Van Eyck, "The Adoration of the Lamb" c. 1432).

We could also mention here Picasso's awesome masterpiece "Guernica," which conveys on a single canvas a stunning experience of suffering, confusion, and human barbarity in war. The symbolism is different from that of Revelation, with modern technological images (bombs, electric light bulb) combined with more "natural" depictions (anguished faces, severed members and animal heads), but the genre is the same: an apparently confused, chaotic hodgepodge of symbolism that creates an effect not so much in logical, linear fashion, but by the tremendous impact of its juxtaposed representations. As in Revelation, what at first appears to be a hopeless morass of violence and destruction turns out to include a message of hope for our death-dealing world, a light held above the darkness of our times.

Sacred Music

The visions of the book of Revelation, especially the hope-filled scenes of the New Jerusalem, have inspired much of our Christian sacred music. There are many English-language hymns used by Catholics and Protestants alike that clearly allude to themes from Revelation. The majority of these hymns were originally composed in and for the churches of the Reformation, thus testifying to their continuing interest in this biblical book. Various spirituals reflect the setting of Revelation, such as "When the saints go marchin' in." In the area of orchestral and choral works we have Handel's universally acclaimed "Messiah" (mid-eighteenth century), whose "Hallelujah Chorus" is an unparalleled and enthralling interpretation of the songs of victory in Revelation 19.

Fifty years ago E. F. Scott, in an article on preaching Revelation, related a story that highlights the power of the musical "idiom" to convey the hope-filled message of this biblical book in a preaching situation:

> I listened once to an eloquent preacher who spoke on the subject of immortality. His sermon was impressive and full of weighty argument, but one could feel that the audience grew impatient. The reasoning was often hard to follow; some of it was plainly open to objection, and perhaps no one was really convinced by it. Then the service closed with the hymn "Jerusalem the Golden"—of all hymns the most fantastical, made up entirely of apocalyptic images which have long ago become meaningless. Yet in singing it the mood of the people was obviously changed. There was something in that hymn which went directly home to them. It offered no argument but simply touched a nerve, a conviction deep in every one that there is a life beyond ("The Natural Language of Religion: Apocalyptic and the Christian Message," *Interpretation* 2 [1948] 428).

Literary Production

Revelation seems never to have had the direct impact in classical literature that it had in the graphic arts and music, but its influence is nevertheless discernible. The book of Revelation influenced not a few medieval works, among them ones by Francis of Assisi and Thomas de Celano. Brütsch mentions a little-known French mystery play based on Revelation. Dante's *Divine Comedy* could be cited as an example of the formal influence of apocalyptic on Western literature, inasmuch as the "tour of heaven and hell" is a standard element in Jewish-Christian apocalyptic works (cf. the book of Enoch).

William Blake, English engraver, painter, and poet was very familiar with Revelation. He illustrated specific passages and borrowed throughout his career from its narrative and imagery. He recognized it as a dramatically unified revelation, a system at one with the rest of the Bible. Blake's works strive to reach a similarly oriented and unified vision.

Recent popular secular literature includes *The Number of the Beast* (Robert A. Heinlein, 1980). In this same vein we could mention a similar albeit much more eclectic use of apocalyptic motifs in contemporary cinema, notably "The Seventh Seal" of Ingmar Bergman and other films such as "The Omen," "Prophecy," and "Apocalypse Now." In most of these cases, however, the relation to our biblical book is really quite superficial, limited to the title or at best a few common symbols or motifs such as the famous 666. Popular religious literature of the fundamentalist sort is another matter: here explicit references to Revelation abound. In recent decades various fundamentalist books that purport to interpret Revelation for our times have made phenomenal sales in the paperback market. Among these, two simply cannot be passed over in silence: Hal Lindsey's bestseller *The Late Great Planet Earth* (1970, with twenty-eight million copies by 1990), which Boyer calls a "popularization of premillennialism" (p. 5), and Edgar Whisenant's *88 Reasons Why the Rapture Will Be in 1988,* whose two-million-copy title is self-explanatory!

In a word, here is a book that has produced incredibly diverse results: from hell-fire and brimstone harangues to utopian experiments toward a perfect society, from the most ridiculously literal representations to some of humanity's most sublime artistic masterpieces, from massacres in the name of God to the highest degree of Christian heroism in the martyrs' witness.

BIBLIOGRAPHY

Boring, M. Eugene. *Revelation.* Interpretation. Louisville: John Knox, 1989.

Boyer, Paul S. *When Time Shall Be No More: Prophecy Belief in Modern American Culture.* Cambridge, Mass.: Belknap Press of Harvard University Press, 1992.

Buchanan, George Wesley. *The Book of Revelation: Its Introduction and Prophecy.* MBC 22. Lewiston, N.Y.: Mellen Biblical Press, 1993.

Charles, Robert H. *A Critical and Exegetical Commentary on the Revelation of St. John.* 2 vols. ICC. Edinburgh: T & T Clark, 1920.

Collins, Adela Yarbro. *Crisis and Catharsis: The Power of the Apocalypse.* Philadelphia: Westminster, 1984.

Court, John M. *Revelation.* New Testament Guides. Sheffield: JSOT Press, 1994.

Giblin, Charles Homer. *The Book of Revelation: The Open Book of Prophecy.* Collegeville: The Liturgical Press, 1991.

Gunsalus González, Catherine, and Justo L. González. *Revelation.* Louisville: Westminster/John Knox, 1997.

Harrington, Wilfrid J. *Revelation.* SP 16. Collegeville: The Liturgical Press, 1993.

Malina, Bruce. *On the Genre and Message of Revelation.* Peabody, Mass.: Hendrickson, 1995.

Mazzaferri, Frederick David. *The Genre of the Book of Revelation From a Source-Critical Perspective.* BZNW 54. New York: Walter de Gruyter, 1989.

Michaels, J. Ramsey. *Interpreting the Book of Revelation.* Grand Rapids: Baker Book House, 1992.

Richard, Pablo. *Apocalypse: A People's Commentary on the Book of Revelation.* Maryknoll, N.Y.: Orbis, 1995.

Schüssler Fiorenza, Elisabeth. *Revelation. Vision of a Just World.* Proclamation Commentaries. Revised and enlarged ed. Minneapolis: Fortress, 1991.

Sweet, John. *Revelation.* Philadelphia: Trinity Press International, 1990.

Swete, Henry B. *The Apocalypse of St. John.* 3rd ed. Grand Rapids: Eerdmans, 1908.

Talbert, Charles H. *The Apocalypse: A Reading of the Revelation of John.* Louisville: Westminster/John Knox, 1994.

Thompson, Leonard L. *The Book of Revelation: Apocalypse and Empire.* New York: Oxford University Press, 1990.

Wainwright, Arthur W. *Mysterious Apocalypse: Interpreting the Book of Revelation.* Nashville: Abingdon, 1993.

Contributors

Samuel Oyin Abogunrin
Nigeria
Luke

José María Abrego, S.J.
Spain
Habakkuk

Ofoso Adutwum
Ghana
Ruth

Jean-Noël Aletti, S.J.
France
Romans

Ana Flora Anderson
Brazil
Proverbs and *Joel*

Pablo R. Andiñach
Argentina
Zechariah

Gonzalo Aranda Pérez
Spain
2 Maccabees

Eduardo Arens Kuckerlkorn, S.M.
Peru
Revelation

Olivier Artus
France
Numbers

Jesús Asurmendi Ruiz
France
Ezekiel

Santiago Ausín
Spain
Nahum

David L. Balás, O.Cist.
Hungary/United States
Patristic Exegesis of the Books of the Bible

Giuseppe Bettenzoli
Italy
Ezra–Nehemiah

Maria Clara Lucchetti Bingemer
Brazil
Jesus Christ

D. Jeffrey Bingham
United States
Patristic Exegesis of the Books of the Bible

Joseph Blenkinsopp
United Kingdom
Prophetism and Prophets

Lawrence Boadt, C.S.P.
United States
Genesis

Normand Bonneau, O.M.I.
Canada
The Bible and Liturgy

François Bovon
Switzerland
Luke: Portrait and Project and *The Canonical Structure of the New Testament: The Gospel and the Apostle*

Barbara Bozak
Canada
Jeremiah

Georg Braulik, O.S.B.
Austria
Introduction to the Deuteronomistic History

Camilla Burns, S.N.D. de N.
United States
The Use of Proverbs 8 and Other Lady Wisdom Texts in Christian Liturgy [excursus]

Antony Campbell, S.J.
Australia
1–2 Samuel and *1–2 Kings*

José Cervantes Gabarrón
Spain
1 Peter

Enzo Cortese, O.F.M.
Italy
Introduction to 1 and 2 Chronicles, Ezra–Nehemiah

John F. Craghan
United States
Exodus

Donald S. Deer
United States
How the Bible Came to Us

Daniel G. Deffenbaugh
United States
The Bible and Ecology

Manuel Díaz Mateos, S.J.
Peru
Revelation

David L. Dungan
United States
The Synoptic Problem: How Did We Get Our Gospels? and *The Bible and Ecology*

M. Timothea Elliott, R.S.M.
United States
Song of Songs

E. Earle Ellis
United States
Interpretation of the Bible Within the Bible Itself

Erik Eynikel
The Netherlands
Jonah and *Introduction* to *How Did We Get Our Bible?*

Denis Farkasfalvy, O. Cist.
Hungary/United States
2 Peter

Kathleen Farmer
United States
Psalms 42–89

William R. Farmer
United States
Introduction to *How Did We Get Our Bible?, The Historic Jesus: God's Call to Freedom Through Love,* and *The Church's Gospel Canon: Why Four and No More?*

Cain Hope Felder
United States
James

Víctor Manuel Fernandez
Argentina
Lamentations

Reginald C. Fuller
United Kingdom
The Deuterocanonical Writings

Jean Galot, S.J.
Belgium
Jesus Christ

Florentino García Martínez
Spain
Biblical Interpretation in Qumran

Timothy Gollob
United States
The Bible and the Servant–Priest–Disciple

Mark Goodwin
United States
Titus

Gilberto Gorgulho, O.P.
Brazil
Proverbs and *Joel*

Adrian Graffy
United Kingdom
Malachi

Paul D. Hanson
United States
The Intertestamental Period and the Rise of Apocalyptic

Daniel J. Harrington, S.J.
United States
Sirach

Paul Hinnebusch, O.P.
United States
The Bible in the Charismatic Movement

Jan Holman, S.V.D.
The Netherlands
Micah

Virgil Howard
United States
Mark, Introduction to *Unleashing the Power of the Bible,* and *The Bible and Preaching*

John C. Hurd
Canada
Letters in the New Testament

Humberto Jiménez G.
Colombia
1 Maccabees

Hans-Winfried Jüngling, S.J.
Germany
Psalms 1–41

Charles Kannengiesser
Canada
How has the Bible Exercised Power to Guide the Faithful in the Early History of the Church?

John Karavidopoulos
Greece
Text Criticism of the New Testament

Roch Kereszty, O. Cist.
Hungary/United States
The Eucharist in the New Testament

Young Bong Kim
South Korea
Philemon

John S. Kloppenborg
Canada
The Synoptic Problem: How Did We Get Our Gospels?

Tomás Kraft, O.P.
Peru
Revelation

André LaCocque
Belgium
Daniel and *A Guide to the Maps* and *Map Index*

Jan Lambrecht, S.J.
Belgium
1 Corinthians

Patricia LeNoir
United States
Introduction to *Unleashing the Power of the Bible*

Adrian Leske
Canada
Matthew

Armando J. Levoratti
Argentina
Leviticus, The Power of the Word of God, and *How to Interpret the Bible*

Norbert Lohfink, S.J.
Germany
Covenant [excursus]

José Loza Vera, O.P.
Mexico
Haggai

Margaret Y. MacDonald
Canada
Ephesians

Temba L. J. Mafico
Zimbabwe
Judges

Francis Martin
United States
1 John, 2 John, 3 John, Truth Told in the Bible: Biblical Poetics and the Question of Truth, and *The Bible in the Retreat Movement*

Luca Mazzinghi
Italy
1 Chronicles and *2 Chronicles*

Sean McEvenue
Canada
Truth Told in the Bible: Biblical Poetics and

the Question of Truth, Wisdom: A Way of Thinking About God, and *Violence and Evil in the Bible*

Jorge Mejía
Argentina
Antisemitism in the Bible and After and *Ecumenism*

Rui de Menezes, S.J.
India
Amos

J. Maxwell Miller
United States
Archeology and the Bible

César Alejandro Mora Paz
Mexico
Colossians

Domingo Muñoz León
Spain
Rabbinic Exegesis

Roland E. Murphy, O.Carm.
United States
Job

Jerome Murphy-O'Connor, O.P.
Ireland
The Life of Paul

Enrique Nardoni
Argentina
2 Timothy, Justice, Work and Poverty, and *Introduction to the Pastoral Epistles*

Irene Nowell, O.S.B.
United States
Tobit

Mark O'Brien, O.P.
Australia
1–2 Kings and *1–2 Samuel*

Mercy Amba Oduyoye
Ghana
Family: An African Perspective

Teresa Okure, S.H.C.J.
Nigeria
John

Pedro Ortiz, S.J.
Colombia
Philippians

Carolyn Osiek, R.S.C.J.
United States
The New Testament Household Codes [excursus]

Yuichi Osumi
Japan
Deuteronomy

Willemien Otten
The Netherlands
The Power of the Bible in the Middle Ages

Samuel Pagán
Puerto Rico
Esther

David B. Peabody
United States
Mark

Anne-Marie Pelletier
France
Isaiah

Rudolf Pesch
Germany
Peter and Paul

Albert Pietersma
Canada
How Reliable is the Text of the Bible?

Carolyn Pressler
United States
To Heal and Transform: Women's Biblical Studies

R. J. Raja, S.J.
India
Judith and *Inculturation of the Biblical Message*

Gianfranco Ravasi
Italy
Psalms 90–150

Pierre Reymond
Switzerland
Jude

Luis Heriberto Rivas
Argentina
Baruch and *Letter of Jeremiah*

Victor Salanga, S.J.
Philippines
Obadiah

Anthony J. Saldarini
United States
The Pentateuch as Torah in the Jewish Tradition

Jordi (Jorge) Sánchez-Bosch
Spain
2 Corinthians

Edesio Sánchez Cetina
Costa Rica
Joshua

Antoon Schoors
Belgium
Ecclesiastes

Hans-Harmut Schroeder
Germany
1 Timothy

Milton Schwantes
Brazil
Exodus: An Introduction

Philip L. Shuler
United States
The Meaning of the Term "Gospel" and *Genre(s) of the Gospels*

Horacio Simian-Yofre, S.J.
Argentina
Hosea, Baal, and *The Minor Prophets*

Jean-Louis Ska, S.J.
Belgium
The Pentateuch

† George Soares-Prabhu, S.J.
India
1 Thessalonians and *2 Thessalonians*

Jon Sobrino, S.J.
El Salvador
Jesus Christ and *Liberation*

Elsa Tamez
Costa Rica
Galatians

Justin Taylor, S.M.
New Zealand
Acts of the Apostles

Albert Vanhoye, S.J.
France
Hebrews

José Vílchez, S.J.
Spain
Wisdom

Benedict Thomas Viviano, O.P.
Switzerland
The Christian and the State According to the New Testament and in the Early Church and *Nationalism and Christian Faith*

Walter Vogels, M.Afr.
Belgium
Zephaniah and *The Day of YHWH* [excursus]

D. W. Waruta
Kenya
The Bible and Prayer in Africa

Frederik Wisse
Canada
The Nag Hammadi Corpus and *How Reliable is the Text of the Bible?*

Ida Zatelli
Italy
1 and 2 Chronicles, Ezra–Nehemiah

Pastoral Guide
for the Use of the Bible in Preaching

(The numeration of chapters and verses of the Old Testament follows the versification of the Hebrew text.)

Aaron, the brother of Moses and Miriam.
genealogy of Moses and Aaron: Exod 6:14-27
Moses' mouthpiece: Exod 4:14; 5:1; 7:1
priestly duties: Leviticus 8–10
in the desert: Numbers 12; 14; 17–20
buried: Deut 10:6
in the New Testament: Acts 7:40; Heb 5:4; 7:11; 9:4

Abba, the emphatic state of the Aramaic noun *ʾab,* meaning "the father," and used as a vocative ("O Father") in Mark 14:36; Gal 4:6; Rom 8:15.

Abel, second son of Adam and Eve, and brother of Cain.
murdered by Cain: Gen 4:2-25
in New Testament: Matt 23:35; Luke 11:51; Heb 11:4; 12:24

Abner, cousin of Saul (1 Sam 14:51) and Saul's army commander (2 Sam 2:8-30), treacherously slain by Joab (2 Sam 3:22-39).

Abraham, ancestor of the Hebrew and other nations (Gen 17:5); his life is recorded in Gen 12:1–25:11 and summarized in Acts 7:2-8.
genealogy of Abraham: Gen 11:25-32
as "Friend of God": 2 Chr 20:7
justified by his faith, not by his circumcision: Rom 4:1-12
model of believers: Gen 12:1-4; 15:6; 22:1-19; John 8:56; Rom 4:2; Gal 3:6; Heb 11:8-10, 17-19; Jas 2:21
embrace of Abraham: Luke 16:22
Abraham, Isaac, Jacob: Exod 3:16; 4:5; 6:3; Matt 8:11; 22:32; Mark 12:26; Luke 13:28; 20:37; Acts 3:13

Absalom, third son of David: 2 Sam 3:3.
his sister Tamar: 2 Sam 13:1
his banishment from the court, his rebellion against David, and his end: 2 Sam 13:21–19:9

Adam, the first man.
the creation of Adam: Gen 2:7
the fall: Genesis 3
Adam's two sons, Cain and Abel: Gen 4:1-2
Adam's descendants: Genesis 5
Adam and Jesus Christ: Rom 5:12-21; 1 Cor 15:22

Agabus, a Jerusalem prophet.
his prediction of a severe famine: Acts 11:27-28
his prediction of Paul's fate at Jerusalem: Acts 21:10-11

Ahab, son and successor of Omri, and seventh king of Israel. He married Jezebel, daughter of Ethbaal, king of Sidon and priest of Asherah. The prophet Elijah prophesied the fate of Ahab, his wife and the dynasty: 1 Kings 16:28–22:40.

Ananias, Greek form of Hananiah ("YHWH has dealt graciously").

1. A member of the primitive church of Jerusalem, who fell dead when his dishonesty was exposed: Acts 5:1-6
2. A follower of Jesus in Damascus: Acts 9:10-17; 22:12-16
3. Ananias son of Nedebaios who became high priest about 47 C.E.: Acts 23:2; 24:1

Andrew, the brother of Simon Peter, one of the twelve apostles: Matt 4:18 par; John 1:40-41, 44; 6:8; 12:22.

Anna, an aged widow dedicated to the Lord who witnessed the presentation of the infant Jesus in the Temple, and with prophetic insight spoke of the child to all who looked forward to the redemption of Israel: Luke 2:36-38.

Antiochus was the name of thirteen kings of the Seleucid Dynasty which after the death of Alexander the Great in 323 B.C.E. had become master of Asia Minor, Syria, and the more westerly of Alexander's eastern dominions.

1. Antiochus III the Great: Dan 11:10-19
2. Antiochus IV Epiphanes: 1 Macc 1:10–6:16; 2 Macc 4:7–9:29; Dan 11:21-45
3. Antiochus V Eupator: 1 Macc 6:17–7:4
4. Antiochus VI Dionysus: 1 Macc 11:39, 54-59; 13:31
5. Antiochus VII Sidetes: 1 Maccabees 15

Apocalyptic, *see* "The Intertestamental Period and the Rise of Apocalyptic," pp. 1206–1225.

Apollos, an Alexandrian Jew, instructed in the Way of the Lord. He combined natural gifts of eloquence with a sound knowledge of the Scriptures.
his presence in Ephesus and Corinth: Acts 18:24-28
Apollos and Paul: 1 Cor 1:12; 3:4-22; 4:6; 16:12

Aquila, a Jewish leather worker, husband of Priscilla, and friend of Paul: Acts 18:2-26; Rom 16:3; 1 Cor 16:19; 2 Tim 4:19.

Archelaus, son of Herod the Great who became ethnarch of Judea, Samaria, and Idumea when his father died in 4 B.C.E. A notoriously cruel and arbitrary ruler, whose reign was short and disastrous: Matt 2:22.

Baal, *see* "Baal," p. 1112.

Barnabas, the cognomen of Joseph, a Levite from Cyprus who became a leader in the early Church. He introduced Saul (Paul) to the Apostles in Jerusalem and worked with him on a mission tour to Cyprus and Asia Minor: Acts 4:36; 11:22-30; 13:1–15:41; 1 Cor 9:6; Gal 2:1, 9, 13; Col 4:10.

Bartholomew, one of the Twelve; his name appears only in the list of the Apostles: Matt 10:3; Mark 3:18; Luke 6:14; Acts 1:13.

Bartimaeus, a blind beggar healed by Jesus. The name means "Son of Timaeus," and may have been recorded by Mark because he was a well-known figure in the early Church: Mark 10:46-52.

Baruch, a faithful attendant on the prophet Jeremiah, who wrote his master's prophecies and read them to the people: Jer 32:12-16; 36; 43:3-7; 45:1-5.

Bathsheba, daughter of Eliam and wife of Uriah the Hittite. She was coveted and seduced by David while her husband was fighting against the Ammonites at Rabbath, east of the Jordan. After David had ordered Uriah sent into the forefront of the battle where he was killed, he married Bathsheba, and she became mother of Solomon: 2 Sam 11:3–12:25; 1 Kings 1:11-21; 2:13-25.

Blood

- as the seat of life power: Lev 17:11-14
- injunctions against consuming blood: Gen 9:4; Lev 17:10-16; 1 Sam 14:32-35; Acts 15:29
- bloodshed forbidden under penalty of death: Gen 9:5-6; Exod 20:13; 21:23; Lev 24:17; Deut 19:21; cf. Matt 5:21-26, 38-42
- the expression "flesh and blood" as a designation of human beings in their earthly life: Matt 16:17; 1 Cor 15:50; Gal 1:16; Eph 6:12; Heb 2:14
- the blood on the door posts of Hebrew houses at the night of Passover: Exod 12:7, 13
- a powerful expiatory agent, especially on the Day of Atonement: Lev 16; cf. Heb 9:7, 22
- the blood of the covenant: Exod 24:6-8; Zech 9:11; Heb 9:19-21
- the shed blood of Jesus and its atoning character: Rom 3:25; Eph 1:7; Col 1:20; 1 Pet 1:18-19; Rev 5:9
- the blood of the New Covenant poured out for the forgiveness of sin: Luke 22:20; 1 Cor 11:25; cf. Matt 26:28; Mark 14:24
- eating Jesus' flesh and drinking his blood as the means of attaining eternal life: John 6:53-58

Charisms, special gifts of the Holy Spirit given to individuals for the benefit of the whole community and for the building of the Body of Christ which is the Church.

- bestowed as an act of divine grace: Rom 12:6
- given by the same Spirit: 1 Cor 12:7, 9, 11
- in distinction from the "fruit of the Spirit," which all Christians are to manifest without variation, the "gifts of the Spirit" are understood to vary from one believer to another: 1 Cor 12:4-7; cf. 1 Pet 4:10; cf. Gal 5:22-23
- listings of the charisms: Rom 12:6-8; 1 Cor 12:8-10, 28-30; Eph 4:7-13
- their purpose is to serve the "common good": 1 Cor 12:7
- the gifts of utterance:
  - prophecy: Rom 12:6; 1 Cor 12:10, 28; cf. 14:3, 24; Eph 4:11
  - the ability to distinguish between true and false prophecy: 1 Cor 12:10; cf. 14:29-33; 1 Thess 5:19-21
  - instruction: Rom 12:7; 1 Cor 12:8
  - speaking in tongues: 1 Cor 12:10
  - the ability to interpret speaking in tongues: 1 Cor 12:10; 14:27-28
- the gifts of pastoral care:
  - apostleship: 1 Cor 12:28; Eph 4:11
  - caring for the needy: 1 Cor 12:28

performing acts of mercy: Rom 12:8; 1 Cor 12:28
administration: 1 Cor 12:28
the gifts of wonder-working faith:
healing: 1 Cor 12:9, 28
working of miracles: 1 Cor 12:10, 28

Circumcision, the removal of the foreskin (prepuce) of the male penis.
performed upon infants of eight days: Gen 17:12; 21:4; Lev 12:3; Luke 1:59; 2:21; Acts 8:8; Phil 3:5
sign of allegiance to YHWH and witness of one's adherence to the covenant: Gen 17:11
Israel's contempt for uncircumcised: Judg 14:3; 15:18; 1 Sam 14:6; 17:26; 2 Sam 1:20; Ezek 32:21-30
the real circumcision is in the heart: Lev 26:41; Deut 10:16; 30:6; John 6:10; Rom 2:25-29
the necessity of circumcision proposed by Jewish Christians: Acts 15:1
the council of Jerusalem's final decision against the necessity of circumcision for male Gentile converts: Acts 15:22-29
Abraham justified by his faith, not by his circumcision: Rom 4:1-12
both circumcised and uncircumcised accepted by God because of their faith: Rom 3:30

Covenant, *see* pp. 444–445.

David
born in Bethlehem of Judah, as the youngest son of Jesse: 1 Sam 16:11; 17:12
anointed by the prophet Samuel as king of Israel: 1 Sam 16:1-13
David and Goliath: 1 Sam 17:1-54
in the court of Saul: 1 Sam 16:14-23; 17:55–18:5
his conflict with Saul: 1 Sam 18:6-30; 19:8–10; 23:19-24; 24–26
the flight of David: 1 Sam 19:8–21:1
David among the Philistines: 1 Sam 27:1–30:31
David's elegy over Saul and Jonathan: 1 Sam 1:17-27
anointed as king of Judah: 2 Sam 2:4
anointed as king of Israel: 2 Sam 5:1-4
the capture of Jerusalem and the transfer of the Ark to the city of David: 2 Sam 5:6–6:23
the prophecy of Nathan: 2 Sam 7:1-17
David's triumph over nearly all the neighboring nations: 2 Sam 10:1–11:1; 12:26-31
David's sin and repentance 2 Sam 11:2–12:25
the story of David's family: 2 Sam 13:1–15:6
Absalom's rebellion: 2 Sam 15:7–19:40
the later years of David: 2 Sam 19:41–1 Kings 2:11

Day of YHWH, *see* "The Day of YHWH," p. 1128.

Delilah, a woman, probably Philistine, who was loved by Samson: Judg 16:1-21.

Deborah, a prophet like Miriam, Exod 15:20, and Huldah, 2 Kings 22:14. She dispensed justice in YHWH's name to the Israelites who came to her in the hill country of Ephraim, and, together with Barak, led an Israelite coalition to victory over the militarily superior Canaanite forces of Sisera by the river of Kishon, in the plain of Esdraelon: Judges 4–5.

Elijah the Tishbite, of Tishbe in Gilead, a prophet of the Lord, fighting against idolatry and injustice in the times of Ahab and Ahaziah, kings of Israel (ninth century B.C.E.).
his bold claim to be YHWH's messenger and his foretelling of the drought as a punishment for the introduction of the cult of Baal: 1 Kings 17:1

his miraculous survival during the drought: 1 Kings 17:2-16; cf. Luke 4:25-26
the contest between Elijah and the Baal prophets on Mt. Carmel: 1 Kings 18:16-40
the end of the drought: 1 Kings 18:41-46
Elijah's flight to Mt. Horeb (Mt. Sinai): 1 Kings 19:1-8
the encounter with God: 1 Kings 19:9-18
the house of Ahab doomed to death because of Naboth's murder: 1 Kings 21:17-29; cf. 2 Kings 10:17
Elisha, Elijah's servant: 1 Kings 19:19-21
Elijah's ascent to heaven living, his prophetic spirit to Elisha to continue God's work: 2 Kings 2:1-18
the eschatological return of Elijah before the great day of the Lord: Mal 4:5-6
this expectation fulfilled in John the Baptist: Matt 17:9-13; cf. Mark 9:9-13
the eulogy of Elijah in Sir 48:1-12
Elijah and Jesus: Matt 17:3; Mark 9:4; Luke 9:33

Elisha, prophet from Abel Meholah in Gilead, active for a period of some fifty years in the ninth century B.C.E.
his call: 1 Kings 19:19-21
successor of Elijah: 2 Kings 2:1-18; cf. 3:11
among the "sons of the prophets": 2 Kings 5:38; 6:1
his miracles: 2 Kings 2:19-25; 4:1–5:7
deeply involved in the politics of his day and in the affairs of the nation: 2 Kings 3:11-20; 6:8–7:20; 8:7-15; 9:1-3
his death: 2 Kings 13:10-21

Eucharist, *see* general article on pp. 215–238.

Faith, the human response to God's revelation recognized in God's word and deeds.
brought about in us by the Holy Spirit: 1 Cor 12:3; cf. Eph 2:8-9; 2 Thess 2:13
the Gospel, God's power for the salvation of everyone who has faith: Rom 1:16
the saving justice of God based on faith and addressed to faith: Rom 1:17
the obedience implicit in the act of faith: Rom 1:5; cf. 6:16; 15:18
faith comes from the hearing of the word of God: Rom 10:17; cf. Luke 8:21; 11:28; 1 Thess 2:13
faith dependent not on human wisdom but on the power of God: 1 Cor 2:5
the power of faith: Matt 17:20; Mark 11:23; Luke 17:6
faith in God: Mark 11:22; 1 Thess 1:8
faith in Jesus as the manifestation of God's power: Mark 9:23-24
Jesus as the pioneer and perfector of our faith (i.e., he who leads us in our faith and brings it to perfection): Heb 12:2
faith, unwavering reliance on God's promise: Rom 4:18; cf. Gal 5:5
faith, the anticipated and assured possession of heavenly realities: Heb 11:1
Abraham, type and father of believers: Gen 12:1-3; 15:1-6; 22:1-19; Rom 4:18-25; Heb 11:8-10, 17-19
the faith of Israel in the Lord and in his servant Moses: Exod 14:31
faith, i.e., unconditional trust in God, the only guarantee of salvation for Israel: Isa 7:9; cf. 28:16; 30:15
faith in the gospel: Mark 1:15
justification by faith and not by the works of the Law: Rom 3:21-26; Gal 3:24
faith working through love: Gal 5:6
direct references of Jesus to the faith of his audience: Matt 15:28; Mark 5:34; 10:52; cf. 2:5
the triadic formula "faith, hope, and love": 1 Cor 13:13; cf. 1 Thess 1:3; 5:8; Gal 5:5-6
faith and love: 1 Thess 3:6; 2 Thess 1:3; Phlm 5

faith and fortitude: 2 Thess 1:4
faith as source of patience and strength: Heb 11:1-40
faith in prayer: Mark 11:24
Jesus reproval of the lack of faith: Mark 4:40
little faith, i.e., faith mingled with fear and doubt: Matt 8:26; 14:31; cf. 28:17
special intense faith as a gift of the Holy Spirit (a charism): 1 Cor 12:9
faith involves progress: 1 Thess 3:10; cf. Phil 3:12-14
faith in Jesus Christ, a source of joy: 1 Pet 1:8
"the goal of your faith, that is, the salvation of your souls": 1 Pet 1:9
faith, the victory that has overcome the world: 1 John 5:4-5

Family, *see* general article on pp. 289–292.

Gethsemane (Heb. "oil press"), the site where Jesus prayed in lonely anguish before his arrest. It was on or near the Mount of Olives, but its precise location is not known: Matt 26:36; Mark 14:32.

Gospel, *see* "The Meaning of the Term 'Gospel,'" pp. 1229–1230.

Herod the Great, appointed by the Roman Senate as king of the Jews in 40 B.C.E. He fortified his realm with a string of fortresses, but his main construction was the Temple in Jerusalem, which he built on a grandiose scale (cf. Matt 24:1; Mark 13:1; Luke 21:5; John 2:20).
the birth of Jesus when Herod was king: Matt 2:1; cf. Luke 1:5
Herod and the Magi from the east: Matt 2:1-12
the massacre of the Innocents: Matt 2:13-18
his death in 4 B.C.E.: Matt 2:15, 19

Herod Antipas, son of Herod the Great and tetrarch of Galilee and Perea (4 B.C.E.–39 C.E.). The Herod most frequently mentioned in the New Testament. Both Jesus and John the Baptist were his subjects and carried out their public ministry mostly in his territories.
his relation to Herodias criticized by John the Baptist: Luke 3:19
John the Baptist decapitated by Antipas: Matt 4:1-12; Mark 6:14-29; Luke 9:9
Herod's estimation of Jesus as John the Baptist raised from the dead: Matt 14:1-2; Mark 6:14, 16; Luke 9:7, 9
Herod's desire to kill Jesus: Luke 13:31-33
Jesus' warning against "the yeast of Herod": Mark 8:15
his role in the trial of Jesus: Luke 23:6-16; Acts 4:27

Herodians, probably the supporters of the rule and policies of Herod Antipas.
together with the Pharisees opposed to Jesus: Mark 3:6
associated with the Pharisees in putting before Jesus the difficult questions regarding paying taxes to Caesar: Matt 22:15-17; Mark 12:13-15

Herodias, a granddaughter of Herod the Great and mother of Salome.
John the Baptist's criticism of the marriage between Herod Antipas and Herodias: Matt 14:3-4; Mark 6:17-20; Luke 3:19-20
Herodias's retaliation: Matt 14:6-11; Mark 6:21-28

Holy Spirit
Jesus, born by the action of the Holy Spirit in Mary: Luke 1:35; cf. Matt 1:20
the coming of the Holy Spirit upon Jesus at his baptism: Matt 3:16; Mark 1:10; Luke 3:21-22; John 1:32-33

led by the Spirit and into the desert: Matt 4:1; Mark 1:12; Luke 4:1
his return into Galilee "in the power of the Spirit": Luke 4:14
anointed with the Holy Spirit to preach good news to the poor: Luke 4:18-19; Acts 10:38; cf. Isa 61:1-2
the action of the Holy Spirit in the ministry of Jesus: Matt 12:28; John 3:34
the Holy Spirit, a source of joy: Luke 10:21; 1 Thess 1:6
Jesus, the Spirit-filled servant of the Lord: Matt 12:16-21; cf. Isa 42:1-4
Jesus, the possessor of the Spirit, which he would dispense after his glorification: John 7:37-39
the words of Jesus, Spirit and life: John 6:63
the Holy Spirit present by way of pledge and of first-fruits: Rom 8:23; 2 Cor 1:22; 5:5; Eph 1:13-14
the Holy Spirit, a gift of the heavenly Father to those who ask him: Luke 11:13
the blasphemy against the Holy Spirit: Matt 12:31-32; Mark 3:29; Luke 12:10
the promise of the Holy Spirit (the Paraclete) in the farewell discourse of Jesus: John 14:16-17, 26; 15:26; 16:7-15
the Spirit of truth coming from the Father only through Jesus: John 14:26; 15:26; 16:7
leading to the very fullness of the truth (i.e., to a fuller understanding of what Jesus revealed and taught): John 16:12
dwelling with the disciples forever: John 14:17
the primary witness to Jesus and the support of all other witnesses: John 15:26-27
the fulfillment of the promise: Jesus, as glorified Lord, bestows the Spirit: John 20:22-23
the disciples empowered by the Holy Spirit to carry out the task of witnessing to Jesus: Luke 24:47-49; Acts 1:8
the Church as a Spirit-filled community: Acts 2:1-4, 33
baptism, a source of new life through water and the Holy Spirit: John 3:3-8; Acts 2:38; 1 Cor 6:11
the Holy Spirit, received into the Christian by faith and baptism: Gal 3:2, 14; Titus 3:5; cf. Acts 11:17
the covenant of the letter that kills and the covenant of the Spirit that gives life: 2 Cor 3:6; cf. Rom 2:29; 7:6
the law of the Spirit that gives life in Christ Jesus: Rom 8:1
God has sent into our hearts the Spirit of his Son crying *Abba,* "Father!": Gal 4:6; cf. Rom 8:15-17
the spiritual person, taught by the Holy Spirit, able to evaluate the gifts of God: 1 Cor 2:10-16
the believer, a temple of God with the Spirit of God living in him/her: 1 Cor 3:16; cf. Rom 8:9
charisms, special gifts of the Spirit given to individuals for the benefit of the whole community: 1 Cor 12:4-11; Eph 4:7, 11-13
charity, the "fruit of the Spirit" flowering in all kind of virtues: Gal 5:22-23
the prayer of the Holy Spirit: Rom 8:26-27
the sword of the Spirit, that is, the word of God: Eph 6:17
the Spirit in contrast to the flesh: Rom 8:5-9; Gal 5:16-26; 3:3; cf. Matt 26:41
the Spirit must not be quenched or grieved: 1 Thess 5:19; Eph 4:30
one Body, one Spirit, on Lord, one faith, one baptism: Eph 4:4-6

Hope

YHWH, the hope of Israel: Jer 14:8; 17:13
YHWH, not only the hope of the nation but of the individual as well: Ps 71:5
hope in God's steadfast love: Ps 33:18
God, the source of Israel's true hope, because "YHWH is a rock forever": Isa 26:4; cf. Pss 18:3; 94:22
hope in the Lord and reliance on the divine promises: Ps 130:5-6
the plans of YHWH to give his people "a future and a hope": Jer 29:11; cf. 31:17

the nations waiting to be instructed by the Servant of the Lord: Isa 42:4; Matt 12:21
hope in the redemption of Israel: Luke 24:21; cf. Acts 1:6
false hope (i.e., hope in anyone or anything other than God):
the chariots and the great number of warriors: Hos 10:13
wealth: Ps 49:7; cf. Luke 12:16-21
idols: Isa 44:9-11
foreign alliances: Isa 31:1-3
hope rich with immortality: Wis 3:4
the prophetic denunciation of illusory hope: Jer 8:15; 13:16; Amos 5:20
the believer, rich in hope by the power of the Holy Spirit: Rom 15:13
the new birth into a loving hope by the resurrection of Jesus Christ: 1 Pet 1:3
hope for the resurrection: Dan 12:2-3; cf. 1 Cor 15
"Christ among you, your hope of glory": Col 1:27
hope, "a sure and steadfast anchor of the soul, a hope that enters the inner shrine where Jesus, a forerunner in our behalf, has entered": Heb 6:19-20
"our citizenship is in heaven and it is from there that we are expecting a Savior, the Lord Jesus Christ": Phil 3:20-21
"in hope we were saved": Rom 8:24
the hope of the Church, joyful even in suffering: Rom 12:12; 1 Pet 4:13
the hope of the creation: Rom 8:18-25
the triadic formula of "faith, hope, and love": 1 Cor 13:13; cf. 1 Thess 1:3; 5:8; Gal 5:5-6
Abraham's hope, contrary to all human expectation ("hoping against hope, Abraham believed"): Rom 4:18; cf. Gen 15:6; 22:1-19
the Christian community, Paul's hope "before our Lord Jesus at his coming": 1 Thess 2:19

Intercession or prayer of petition made for someone other than oneself: Acts 12:5; Phil 1:4, 19; Eph 6:18; 1 Tim 2:1.
the great intercessors:
Moses: Exod 5:22-23; 32:11-14, 30-32; Num 11:2; 12:13; 14:13-19; 16:22; 21:7-8; Deut 9:25-29; Pss 99:6; 106:23; Sir 45:3
Joshua: Josh 7:6-9
Samuel: 1 Sam 7:5-9; 12:19-25; Ps 99:6
Jeremiah: Jer 14:7-9; cf. 15:1; 2 Macc 15:14
the Servant of the Lord: Isa 53:12
Job: Job 42:8
the angels: Tob 12:12; Zech 1:12
the prophets: Amos 7:2, 5
for the dead: 2 Macc 12:38-45
Jesus, the mediator above all others: Heb 7:25; 1 John 2:1

Iota, the smallest letter of the Greek alphabet: Matt 5:18

Isaac, from the Heb. *yiṣhaq,* the abbreviation of *yiṣhaq-ʾel:* "May God smile (be favorable)!" The *Akedah Isaak* ("The binding of Isaac") is a theological motif in the later Judaism targums of Genesis 22. Isaac's willingness to be sacrificed and the exemplary faith of Abraham were seen to have atoning power for Israel.
son of Abraham and Sarah: Gen 17:17-19; 21:5-7; Matt 1:2; Luke 3:34
heir of the divine promise: Gen 17:15-22; 18:9-15; Rom 9:8-13; Heb 11:9
offered in sacrifice by his father but saved from death: Gen 22:1-19; Heb 11:17-19; Jas 2:21
as prefiguration of the freedom of the believers: Gal 4:22-31
Abraham, Isaac, Jacob: Exod 3:16; 4:5; 6:3; Matt 8:11; 22:32; Mark 12:26; Luke 13:28; 20:37; Acts 3:13

Jacob, an Old Testament patriarch, the father of the twelve sons who gave their names to the tribes of Israel.

birth and youth of Esau and Jacob: Gen 25:20-34
the blessing obtained by fraud: Gen 27:1-19
Jacob's departure to northeast and the theophany en route at Bethel: the recipient of the divine promise: Genesis 28
his arrival at Laban's home: Gen 29:1-14
his marriages to Leah and Rachel: Gen 29:15-30
Jacob's children: Gen 29:31–30:24; 35:16-18, 22-26
acquisition of herds and riches: Gen 30:25-43
Jacob's flight with his flocks, progeny, and wives: Gen 31:1–32:21
Jacob's wrestling with God and his name changed to "Israel": Gen 32:23-33
in the land of Canaan: Gen 33:1–35:29
Jacob and Joseph: Gen 37:1-11, 31-35
Jacob's journey to Egypt: Gen 46:1–47:12; cf. Exod 1:1-5
Jacob's testament: Gen 49:1-28
his death: Gen 49:29–50:14
Abraham, Isaac, Jacob: Exod 3:16; 4:5; 6:3; Matt 8:11; 22:32; Mark 12:26; Luke 13:28; 20:37; Acts 3:13

Jesus Christ, *see* general articles on pp. 242–264.

John the Baptist, or John the Baptizer, a prophet of priestly descent, the son of Zechariah and Elizabeth, and forerunner to Jesus by preparing a way for the Lord.

the birth of John the Baptist foretold: Luke 1:5-25
Jesus' relative: Luke 1:36, 39-45
his birth and circumcision: Luke 1:57-79
his hidden life in the desert: Luke 1:80
his appearance as a prophet: Matt 3:1-4; Mark 1:2-8; Luke 3:1-6
his call to repentance: Matt 3:7-12; Mark 1:4; Luke 3:7-9
denounces the illusion of those who bragged about being sons of Abraham but did not bear good fruit: Matt 3:8-9; Luke 3:8
his social message: Luke 3:10-14
the disciples of John the Baptist: Matt 9:14; 11:2; Mark 2:18; Luke 5:33; John 1:35; 3:25
the relationship between Jesus and John: Matt 3:11-12; 1:7-8; Luke 3:16-17; John 1:6-8, 19-33
as forerunner to the Messiah, John marks the division between the two great epochs of prophecy and fulfillment: Matt 11:11-13; Luke 16:16
imprisoned before the beginning of Jesus' public ministry: Matt 4:12; Mark 1:14; Luke 3:20
decapitated by Herod Antipas: Matt 14:1-12a; Mark 6:14-29
the report to Jesus of John's death: Matt 14:12b
the sayings of Jesus concerning John the Baptist: Matt 11:7-19; Luke 7:24-34; 16:16; cf. Matt 21:23-27; Mark 11:27-33; Luke 20:1-8
John's identification with Elijah: Matt 17:10-13; cf. Mark 9:11-13
further attestations to the Baptist's ministry: Acts 1:22; 10:37; 13:24
the baptism of John and the Christian baptism: Acts 18:25; 19:1-6

John Mark, traditionally identified as the author of the second Gospel.

the son of Mary of Jerusalem: Acts 12:12
cousin to Barnabas: Col 4:10
companion of Barnabas and Saul (Paul) on a journey from Antioch to Jerusalem: Acts 12:25
assistant to Barnabas and Saul (Paul) on a missionary journey: Acts 13:5
his abandonment of the mission: Acts 13:13

sailed off with Barnabas to Cyprus: Acts 15:36-40
with Paul during this captivity in Rome: Col 4:10; Phlm 24; 2 Tim 4:11
named as assistant to Peter: 1 Pet 5:13

Jonathan, the most important son of Saul, the first king of Israel, and David's bosom friend.
his military capacity: 1 Samuel 14
his deep friendship and loyalty to David: 1 Sam 18:1-4; 19:1-7; 20; 23:16-18
his death on Mt. Gilboa: 1 Sam 31:2, 6

Joseph, the name of several men in the biblical narrative, especially:
1. the oldest son of Rachel, favorite wife of the patriarch Jacob. The Joseph story in the Pentateuch constitutes a link between the traditions of the patriarchs in Genesis and the traditions about Moses in Exodus: Gen 3:22-24; 37:2-36; 39:1–48:22; 50:1-26; Exod 1:8
2. the husband of Mary and the legal father of Jesus
his Davidic descent: Matt 1:20; Luke 2:4
a craftsman (Greek *tektōn,* word usually translated "carpenter," but having a wider range of meaning, from a maker of furniture to a builder of considerable skill): Matt 13:55
being "just," Joseph had first thought of divorcing Mary when he noticed that she was pregnant: Matt 1:19
gone to Bethlehem to register there in the Roman census: Luke 2:1-4
his flight into Egypt and his return to Nazareth with the infant Jesus and his mother: Matt 2:19-23
Joseph and the loss of the twelve-year-old Jesus in the Temple: Luke 2:41-51
3. Joseph surnamed Barnabas: *see* **Barnabas** above.
4. Joseph known as Barsabbas, whose surname was Justus: Acts 1:23-26
5. Joseph of Arimathea, who buries Jesus: Matt 27:57-60; Mark 15:42-46; Luke 23:50-54; John 19:38

Joshua, originally called Hoshea and renamed by Moses: Num 13:16.
appointed by Moses to lead the battle against Amalek: Exod 17:8-13
a young man serving as Moses' assistant: Exod 33:11
one of the twelve men sent to reconnoiter the land of Canaan: Num 13:8; 14:6-10
successor of Moses: Num 27:18-23; Deut 3:28; 31:3, 7-8; 34:9
Joshua and the conquest of the Promised Land: Joshua 1–12
Joshua's prayer for Israel: Josh 7:6-9
his obedience to the Law: 1 Macc 2:55
the allotment of the Land to the tribes: Joshua 13–20
the last discourse of Joshua: Joshua 23
the great assembly at Shechem: Josh 24:1-28
Joshua's death: Josh 24:29-31; Judg 2:8-9
remembered as a great savior of the chosen people: Sir 46:1-8

Justice, *see* general article on pp. 293–297.

Kingdom of God, Greek *basileia* ("reign," "rule," "kingdom"). Matthew used the rabbinic term "reign" or "kingdom of heaven," "heaven" being circumlocution for "God" (Matt 4:17; 5:3, 10, 19-20; 7:21; 8:11; 10:7; 13:52, etc.).
the dominant motif in Jesus' preaching: Matt 4:17; Mark 1:14-15
a major turning point in salvation history, inaugurated by the arrest of John the Baptist and by the public ministry of Jesus: Mark 1:14-15a; Luke 16:16; cf. Matt 11:12-13
close at hand: Matt 3:2; 4:17; 10:7; Mark 1:15; Luke 10:9, 11
truly present in germ and now at work: Matt 12:28

Jesus' wonder-working activity as a sign and an anticipation of the full realization of the Kingdom of God: Matt 11:2-6; Luke 7:18-23
like a seed, enjoying irresistible power: Matt 18:8, 31-32; Mark 4:8, 26-29, 30-32; Luke 13:18-19
like the leaven, unpretentious in its beginnings but destined for enormous growth: Matt 13:33; Luke 13:20-21
repentance and faith as the appropriate human response to the coming of the kingdom: Matt 3:2; 4:17; Mark 1:15c
to be approached as a child: Matt 18:1-4; 19:13-14; Mark 10:13-15; Luke 18:15-17
to be sought: Matt 6:33; Luke 12:31
the eucharistic meal as an anticipation of the kingdom: Matt 26:29; Mark 14:25; Luke 22:18
the prayer for the coming of the kingdom in its fullness: Matt 6:10; Luke 11:2
the gospel of the kingdom to be proclaimed to the whole world: Matt 24:14; cf. 4:23; 9:35; 28:19
the word of the kingdom (i.e., Jesus' message): Matt 13:19
thing that can be done for the sake of the kingdom of God: Matt 19:12; Luke 18:29
the heirs of the kingdom:
the poor: Matt 5:3; Luke 6:20
those who are hungry now: Luke 6:21
those who are weeping now: Luke 6:21
the persecuted in the cause of uprighteous: Matt 5:10
the kingdom of God, justice, peace, and joy in the Holy Spirit: Rom 14:17
the reign of the Messiah: Luke 1:33; cf. Rev 20:4

Law, Heb. *Torāh* ("instruction"), a word with a broader and less strictly juridical meaning than the Greek *nomos* ("law"). It designates the revelation given to Israel by God for the regulation of its conduct.
in a broad sense, as the equivalent of the whole Old Testament: John 10:34; Rom 3:19-20; 1 Cor 14:21
the division of the Hebrew Bible into the Law, the Prophets, and the Writings: Prologue of Sirach 1, 9-10, 24-25; cf. Luke 24:44
as designation of the first five books of the Bible (the Pentateuch): 2 Macc 15:9; Matt 5:17; 7:12; Luke 2:27; 16:16-17; 24:44; Rom 3:21; Gal 4:21
given to Israel through the mediation of Moses: Ps 103:7
the glorious prerogative of Israel, given to no other nations: Ps 147:19-20; cf. Rom 9:4
the Law, a source of joy and a lamp for the feet: Pss 1; 19:7-14; 119
the priests, custodians of the *torāh:* Deut 33:10; Jer 18:18; Ezk 7:26; Hos 4:4-6
the septennial reading of the Law, at the feast of Booths: Deut 31:9-13
the authority and enduring validity of the Law and the exhortation to attend to even its least commandment: Matt 5:18-19; cf. Luke 16:17
the demands of the Old Testament and their fulfillment in the teaching of Jesus: Matt 5:17
the teaching of Jesus as the full revelation of what God intended through the Law: Matt 5:21-48
the keeping of the commandments as condition to obtain eternal life: Matt 19:16-19; Mark 10:17-19; Luke 18:18-20
Ezra, the scribe learned in the *torāh* of Moses: Ezra 7:10, Nehemiah 8
the greatest commandment of the Law: Matt 22:34-40; Mark 12:28-31; Luke 10:25-28; cf. Matt 23:23
the Law and the Prophets come to an end with John the Baptist: Luke 16:16; cf. Matt 11:12-13
the Law engraved in the conscience of those who do not know the Mosaic law: Rom 2:14-15
the Law given through Moses opposed to the grace and truth given through Jesus Christ: John 1:17
the Law written on the stone tablets at Sinai: Exod 24:12; 32:15-19; 34:1

the Law written not with ink but with the Spirit of the living God on the tablets of human hearts: 2 Cor 3:3; cf. Jer 21:33; Ezek 36:26
as expression of the will of God the Law is holy, upright, and good: Rom 7:12; 1 Tim 1:8
but it is powerless to prevent sin, because it does not give spiritual strength to transform human conduct: Rom 8:3
thus the commandment meant to bring life brought death: Rom 7:10
therefore the impious is justified not in virtue of the observance of the Law, but in virtue of the grace of God in Jesus Christ, to whom the believer is united by faith: Rom 1:17; 3:21-26; 4:25; Phil 3:8-9; Titus 3:5-7
no human being can be found upright by keeping the Law: Gal 2:16
the Spirit as the interior law of the New Testament: Rom 8:9
Jesus Christ, the end of the Law: Rom 10:4; Eph 2:14-15
the law of Christ: Gal 6:2
the law of the Spirit: Rom 8:2
the law of faith: Rom 3:27
the perfect law of freedom: John 1:25

Liberation, *see* general article on pp. 280–281.

Life

God, the Living One and the source of all life: Gen 2:7; 1 Sam 2:6; Ps 36:9; Jer 2:13; 10:10; Matt 16:16; 26:63; Acts 14:15; Heb 10:31
God, the owner of life: Ezek 18:4
all created life is fragile and perishable, however precious it might be in God's eyes: Job 7:7-10; 14:1-2; Pss 78:39; 89:46-47
life in its full sense (happiness, security, liberation): Deut 30:15; Ps 119:17; Ezek 18:32
life associated with keeping the commandments of God: Deut 30:15-20; Prov 4:4
Jesus, the Bread of life: John 6:35, 48, 51
the Resurrection and the Life: John 11:25
the Way, the Truth, and the Life: John 14:6; cf. 8:12
faith in Jesus as source of eternal life in the present and in the future: John 5:24; 6:40, 47; Rom 6:22

Light

the creation of light: Gen 1:3-4; cf. 2 Cor 4:6
as symbol of happiness, prosperity and joy: Isa 9:1-2
Matt 4:16; Luke 1:78-79
God is light: 1 John 1:5; cf. Pss 27:1; 36:9; 104:2; Isa 58:8; 60:19-20; Dan 2:22; 1 Tim 6:16; Jas 1:17
God's word, a lamp to the feet and a light to the path: Ps 119:105
the word of the prophets, a lamp for lighting a way through the dark: 2 Pet 1:19
the day of the Lord expected to be light: Zech 14:7; cf. Amos 5:18, 20
wisdom as the reflection of eternal light: Wis 7:26
the Messiah, light of the nations: Luke 2:32
Jesus, the true light: John 8:12; 9:5; 12:35, 46
believers described:
- as enlightened: Heb 6:4; 10:32
- as light of the world: Matt 5:14
- as sons of the light: John 12:36; 1 Thess 5:5
- as bright stars in the world: Phil 2:15

the light of the gospel of the glory of Christ 2 Cor 4:4
people called "out of darkness into his wonderful light": 1 Pet 2:9; cf. Col 1:13-14

the combat between light and darkness: John 1:5-7; 3:19-21; 1 John 2:8
Jesus' disciples called to bring their light to the world: Matt 5:16; cf. Luke 12:35
the light of the heavenly Jerusalem: Rev 21:23; 22:5

Love
God is love: 1 John 4:7
the universality and gratuity of God's love
for every creature: Wis 11:23; cf. Matt 5:45
for the poor and lowly: Deut 10:18
for life: Wis 11:26
for justice: Ps 37:28
the faithful love of the Lord fills the earth: Ps 37:5
God's love manifested in the election of Israel: Deut 4:37; 7:7-8; cf. Hos 11:1
God's love for God's people presented in the prophetic tradition under the traits of a conjugal love: Jer 2:1-3; Isa 54:5; Hos 2:16-18
God's passionate love rewarded only with ingratitude and unfaithfulness: Jer 2:4-13; Hos 11:1-4
God's love manifested in the sending of the Son as savior of the world: John 3:16; 1 John 4:9; cf. Rom 5:8
Jesus, the beloved Son of God: Matt 3:17; 17:5; Mark 1:11; 9:7; Luke 3:22; John 3:35; 5:20; 10:17
Christ's love for his Church: Eph 5:25; cf. Eph 5:2; cf. John 17:23; Rev 1:5
the greatest commandment of all: to love the Lord with all the heart: Deut 6:5; Matt 22:37-38; Mark 12:29-30
the new commandment: John 13:34; 1 John 2:7; 2 John 5
the love of neighbor inseparable form the love of God: Matt 22:39; Mark 12:31; Luke 10:27; 1 John 4:20-21; 5:2; cf. 2:9
love of neighbor as the fulfillment of all moral demands: Rom 13:8-10; Gal 5:14; Jas 2:8
the love of God poured into our hearts by the Holy Spirit: Rom 5:5
love linked to faith and hope, "but the greatest of these is love": 1 Cor 13:13; cf. 1 Thess 1:3; 5:8
faith working through love: Gal 5:6
love as strong as death: Song 8:6
the love of God, stronger than death: Rom 8:31-38
love of God's commandments: Ps 119:113, 127
love of God's word: Ps 119:140
Israel instructed to love the foreigner or stranger: Lev 9:34; Deut 10:9
love of one's enemies: Prov 25:21-22; Matt 5:43-48
the authority given to Peter to be exercised in the context of love: John 21:15-17
conjugal love: Gen 24:67; 29:20; Eph 5:22-23; Col 3:18-19
love within the family: Gen 22:2; 25:28; Ruth 4:13-15; Eph 6:1-4; Col 3:20-21
the Lord, bestower of wisdom on those who love him: Sir 1:10
the beloved disciple: John 19:26; 20:2; 21:7

Luke, *see* "Luke: Portrait and Project," pp. 1503–1505.

Lydia, a woman who was in the purple-dye trade, Paul's first convert in Europe (at Philippi in Macedonia): Acts 16:12-15, 40.

Martha, sister of Lazarus and Mary of Bethany, close friends and followers of Jesus: Luke 10:38-42; John 11:5, 20-27, 39; 12:2.

Mary, the Virgin
the wife of Joseph: Matt 1:18; Luke 1:27

the virginal conception announced to Joseph in a dream and to Mary by the angel Gabriel: Matt 1:18-25; Luke 1:26-38
her travel from Nazareth to Judea, to her pregnant kinswoman Elizabeth: Luke 1:39-45
Mary's hymn of praise: Luke 1:46-55
in Bethlehem at the birth of Jesus: Luke 2:1-19
the wise men from the East bringing precious gifts: Matt 2:1-13
Joseph takes Mary and Jesus to Egypt: Matt 2:13-15
settled in Nazareth: Matt 2:19-23
in the Temple for postpartum purification of the firstborn: Luke 2:21-24
the prophecy of Simeon: Luke 2:35
Jesus and his mother in the Temple: Luke 2:41-50
Mary's belief in Jesus' power at the wedding in Cana: John 2:1-11
Mary at the cross: John 19:25
Mary and the beloved disciple: John 19:26-27
at Pentecost: Acts 1:14; cf. 2:1-4

Mary of Bethany, the sister of Martha and Lazarus: Luke 10:39, 42; John 11:1, 28-31, 45; 12:1-8.

Mary, the mother of Jacob and Joseph (Joses), or "the other Mary": Matt 27:56, 61; 28:1; Mark 15:40, 47; 16:1.

Mary of Jerusalem, the mother of John Mark: Acts 12:12.

Mary Magdalene, or of Magdala, mentioned first in every listing of Jesus' female disciples.
her presence with the Twelve in Jesus' ministry in Galilee: Luke 8:1-3
among the first witnesses to his resurrection: Matt 27:56, 61; 28:1; Mark 15:40, 47; 16:1; Luke 24:10; John 19:25; 20:1, 18

Melchizedek, the king of Salem (Jerusalem) and priest of El-Elyon ("The Most High") who blessed Abraham after he defeated the four kings of the East: Gen 14:17-20.
the king of Israel as "priest for ever after the order of Melchizedek": Ps 110:4
as type of Christ, the High Priest of the New Covenant: Heb 5:6, 10; 6:20–7:25

Michael ("who-is-like-God?"), the guardian angel of the people of God: Dan 10:13, 21; 12:1; Jude 9; Rev 12:7.

Moses, Heb. *Mōshe,* a name of Egyptian origin (*mos* = "son"), the liberator and legislator of Israel.
born of an oppressed people: Exod 1:8–2:1; Acts 7:17-20
drawn from the waters: Exod 2:2-10
his genealogy: Exod 6:14-25
adopted by the Pharaoh's daughter and educated at the Egyptian court: Acts 7:21-22
forced to flee into the desert: Exod 2:11-15; Acts 7:29
refugee in Midian: Exod 2:16-22
Moses' call: Exod 3:1-12; 6:2-13; Acts 7:30-34
the divine name revealed to him: Exod 3:13-15
made acquainted with the plans of God for his mission: Exod 3:16-20; 6:26-27; cf. Ps 103:7
Moses granted miraculous powers: Exod 4:1-9; Acts 7:36
Aaron, the mouthpiece of Moses: Exod 4:10-17
his return to Egypt: Exod 4:18-23
Moses liberator of his people: Exod 7:1–15:21
mediator of God's law to the chosen people: Exod 24:12; 34:1-5; Sir 45:3-6
mediator of the covenant: Exod 19:3-8; 24:1-8

a prophet without equal: Deut 34:10-12
like every true prophet, the mouthpiece of God: Deut 18:15-20
the most faithful servant of the Lord: Num 12:7
the opposition of his people: Exod 15:23; 16:2; 17:1-3; Num 11:1-6; 14:1-4; 16; Acts 7:39
discouraged and overwhelmed by a burden too heavy for him: Num 11:14-15; cf. Exod 18:18
as exemplary for faith in God: Heb 3:2; 11:23-28
the great intercessor on behalf of his people on their journey through the desert: Exod 5:22-23; 32:11-14, 30-32; Num 11:2; 14:13-19; 16:22; 21:7; Deut 9:25-29; Pss 99:6; 106:23; Sir 45:3; Jer 15:1
the radiant face of Moses: Exod 34:29-35; 2 Cor 3:7-9
friend of God, to whom the Lord speaks face to face: Exod 12:6-8; cf. Exod 33:11
Jesus and Moses: Matt 17:3; 19:7; Mark 9:4; 10:3-4; Luke 9:30; 16:29, 31; John 1:17
the death of Moses: Deut 34:1-8

Mystery (Heb. *sôd,* Aram. *râz,* Gr. *mysterion)*
in a broad sense, something hidden, a secret: Tob 12:7, 11; Sir 27:16, 21
in mystery religions, the esoteric doctrines and rituals revealed only to initiates: Wis 12:5; 14:23
God's secrets revealed to God's servants, the prophets: Amos 3:6; cf. Num 24:4
God the Revealer of depths and mysteries ("what will happen at the end of days"): Dan 2:22, 28, 47; 4:6
the mystery of God, in which all the jewels of wisdom and knowledge are hidden: Col 2:2; cf. Rev 10:7
the mystery of God's purpose (to bring everything in the heavens and everything on earth together under Christ, as their one head): Eph 1:9-10
the mystery of Christ, unknown to humanity in previous generations, now revealed in the Spirit to his holy apostles and prophets (i.e., the salvation of the Gentiles): Eph 3:3-4; Col 1:26; 4:3; cf. Rom 16:25-26
the mystery of the gospel, of which Paul is an ambassador: Eph 6:19
the mystery of piety (i.e., Jesus Christ himself exalted at God's right hand, as Lord of the universe, after his earthly life and his crucifixion): 1 Tim 3:16
the mystery of faith: 1 Tim 3:9
the mystery of the kingdom of God (i.e., God's purposes with respect to the kingdom): Mark 4:11; cf. Matt 13:11
the mysteries of wisdom: Wis 6:22

Paul, *see* general articles on pp. 265–273.

Peace, a word with a wide range of meaning in both the Old Testament and the New Testament. The root meaning of Heb. *shalōm* ("peace") is "wholeness" or "well-being."
God, a God of peace: Rom 15:33; Phil 4:9, 1 Thess 5:23
peace, a gift of God: Lev 26:6; 1 Kings 2:33; Pss 29:11; 85:9; Isa 26:12
as a greeting and a farewell: Exod 4:18; Judg 6:23; 2 Sam 15:9; Ezra 5:7; Mark 5:34; Luke 7:50; John 20:19, 21, 26
peace in the opening greeting of the New Testament letters: Rom 1:7; 1 Cor 1:3; 2 Cor 1:2; Gal 1:3; Eph 1:2; Phil 1:2; Col 1:2; 1 Thess 1:1; 2 Thess 1:2; 1 Tim 1:2; 2 Tim 1:2; Titus 1:4; Phlm 3; 1 Pet 1:2; 2 Pet 1:2; 2 John 1:3; Jude 2; Rev 1:4
peace, the absence of strife among individuals and nations: Josh 10:1, 4; 1 Sam 7:14; Luke 14:32; cf. Rev 6:4
as opposed to war: Eccl 3:8
peace within the Christian community: Rom 12:18-19; 14:19; 1 Cor 14:33; 2 Cor 13:11; 1 Thess 5:13b
Christians should strive for peace with all people: Heb 12:14; cf. Mark 9:50

righteousness as source of peace: Isa 32:17; Pss 72:4-5; 85:11; cf. Isa 60:17; Rom 14:17; Heb 12:11; Jas 3:18
peace and prosperity: Ps 122:6-9
the Messiah, prince of peace: Isa 9:5
the covenant of peace in connection with priests: Num 25:12-13; Mal 2:4-6
the gospel of peace: Acts 10:36; Eph 6:15
Christ, our peace: Eph 2:11-18; cf. Rom 5:1; Col 1:20
the peace given by Christ: John 14:27; Col 3:15; 2 Thess 3:16
the messianic peace: Isa 2:4; 11:6-9; Mic 4:3-4

Peter (originally named Simon, son of John or Jonah), one of Jesus' twelve disciples. His Greek name *Petrus* is the translation of the Aramaic *Kefas,* which means "rock" *(petra).* That Jesus changed Simon's name to *Kefas* is well attested: Matt 10:2; Mark 3:16; Luke 6:14; John 1:42.
summoned to be a "fisher of human beings": Matt 4:18-19; Mark 1:16-17; Luke 5:1-11
his mother-in-law healed by Jesus: Matt 8:14-15; Mark 1:29-31; Luke 4:38-39
his special position among the Twelve: Matt 10:1-4; Mark 3:13-19; Luke 6:12-16
singled out, along with James and John, for special revelations of Jesus: Mark 5:37; Luke 8:51 (the healing of Jairus' daughter); Matt 17:1; Mark 9:2; Luke 9:28 (the transfiguration)
credited with special insight into Jesus' identity as God's Messiah: Matt 16:16-17; Mark 8:29; Luke 9:20; John 6:68-69
his function as the "Rock" or foundation of the building that is the Church: Matt 16:18-19
his opposition to Jesus' prediction that it is his messianic role to suffer and die: Matt 16:22-23; Mark 8:31-33
spokesman of the apostles: Matt 19:27; Mark 10:28; Luke 18:28; cf. Matt 15:15; 18:21-22
Jesus' prayer that his faith may not fail and his function in strengthening his brothers: Luke 22:32
Peter's denials of Jesus and his repentance: Matt 26:69-75; Mark 14:53-54, 66-72; Luke 22:54-62; John 18:15-18, 25-27
the first disciple to see the risen Lord: 1 Cor 15:5
the threefold protestation of love, corresponding to the threefold denial, and his mission to feed Jesus' sheep: John 21:15-17
first witness to the Easter faith: Acts 2:14-41; 3:12-26; 4:8-12; 5:29-32; 10:34-43
leader of the Church at Jerusalem: Acts 1:15-22; 5:1-11; Gal 1:18; 2:9
engaged in missionary activity among Jews and Gentiles: Acts 8:14-17; 9:32-35; 10:5-48; 11:1-18; Gal 2:7
his traveling as a missionary: 1 Cor 9:5
his prestige among the Corinthians, some of whom claimed special allegiance to him: 1 Cor 1:12; 3:22

Pilate, Pontius, Roman prefect of Judea, the fifth governor of the province and the second-longest holder of the office (26–36 C.E.).
at the time of John the Baptist's activity: Luke 3:1
his part in the trial and execution of Jesus: Matt 27:1-2, 11-26; Mark 15:1-15; Luke 23:1-25; John 18:29–19:16
in the New Testament outside the gospels: Acts 3:13; 4:27; 13:28; 1 Tim 6:13

Poverty, *see* general article on pp. 293–297.

Prayer, the act of petitioning, praising, giving thanks, or confessing to God. *See also* **Intercession**.
prayer of Christ at decisive moments:
on coming into the world: Heb 10:5

his baptism: Luke 3:21
the calling of his disciples: Luke 6:12
transfiguration: Luke 9:29
Gethsemane: Matt 26:36-46; Mark 14:32-42; Luke 22:39-45; cf. Heb 5:7
crucifixion: Matt 27:46; Mark 15:34; Luke 23:46
God addressed as Father: Matt 6:9; 11:25-26; 26:39, 42; Luke 10:21-22; 11:2; 22:42; John 17:1, 5, 11, 21, 24-25; Rom 8:15; Gal 4:6; cf. Ps 89:26
the Lord's prayer: Matt 6:9-13; Luke 11:2-4
the High Priestly prayer: John 17
prayer of Christians: Acts 1:14, 24; 2:42; 6:6; 10:4-9; 12:5; 13:2-3
prayer at meals: Matt 15:36; 26:26-27; Mark 8:6; Acts 27:35; 1 Cor 10:30
gestures of prayer:
standing: Mark 11:25; Luke 18:11
kneeling: 1 Kings 8:54; Luke 22:41; Acts 7:60; 9:40; 20:36; Phil 2:10
prostrate on the ground: Matt 26:39; Mark 14:35
with upraised hands: 1 Kings 8:22; 1 Tim 2:8
the Temple as a place of prayer: Ps 5:8; Mark 11:17; Matt 21:13; Luke 2:37; Acts 3:1
prayer for the necessities of life: Num 11:11-15; 1 Kings 8:35-40; Prov 30:7-9; Matt 6:11; Luke 11:3
for civil authorities: Ezra 6:10; 1 Tim 2:2
for all: 1 Tim 2:1
for guidance: Gen 24:12-14; Acts 1:24-25
for wisdom: 1 Kings 3:5-14; Wis 7:7; Jas 1:5-8
for deliverance from enemies: 1 Kings 8:33; 44-51; Pss 31:16; 59:1; 143:9
for forgiveness: Pss 25:11; 51; 130:1-3; 143:1-2; Matt 6:12; Luke 11:4; 18:13; 23:33; Acts 7:60
for the sick: Jas 5:13-16a
for the dead: 1 Macc 12:38-45
the prayer of the Holy Spirit: Rom 8:26-27
God's reproval of the prayer without righteousness: Isa 1:15; 59:1-3; Mic 3:4
Jesus' reproval of prayer done for the sake of ostentation: Matt 6:5-8
effective prayer: Luke 11:5-13; 18:1-8; Jas 5:16b-18
God hears the prayers of his people: 1 Kings 9:3; Ps 34:15; Matt 7:7-11; 1 John 3:22; 5:14-15
Paul's prayers for his congregations: Rom 15:13; Phil 1:9-11
his request for their intercession: Rom 15:30-32; 2 Cor 1:11; 1 Thess 5:25
prayers not always answered in the way expected: 2 Cor 12:7-9

Prophet, *see* "Prophetism and Prophets," pp. 951–956.

Redemption

YHWH, Israel's redeemer (Heb. *goʾēl,* the kinsman who had the duty of buying back an enslaved or captured relative): Pss 19:14; 69:18; 72:14; Isa 41:14; 43:14; 44:6; 47:4; 48:17
referred to the freeing of Israel from Egyptian bondage: Deut 13:6; 15:15; 24:18; Mic 6:4
referred to the return of Israel from Babylonian captivity: Isa 51:11; 52:3-9
redemption of Israel: Luke 1:68; 2:38; 24:21
redemption from sin: Ps 130:8; Isa 44:21-23
Christ, our redemption: 1 Cor 1:30
the redemption which is in Christ Jesus: Rom 3:24; Eph 1:7, 14; Col 1:14; Rev 5:9
the Christians as having been bought for a price: 1 Cor 6:20; 7:23
the Christians redeemed from their worthless manner of life by the precious blood of Christ: 1 Pet 1:18-19
the awaited redemption of the body: Rom 8:23
all creation groaning in expectation of redemption: Rom 8:19-22

Responsibility

the burden of the critical choices open to everyone: Deut 30:15-20; Sir 15:11-20; cf. Gen 2:16-17; Jas 1:13-15

the principle of collective retribution (the penalty contracted by all the members of a family or a group for the fault of one): Exod 20:5-6; Lev 4:3; Deut 5:9-10; Josh 7:1-26

the proverb about children suffering for their parents' misdeeds: Jer 31:29-30; Ezek 18:1-4

the principle of individual responsibility (each person judged on his own record): Ezek 18; Luke 16:19-26; Rom 2:5-10, 16; 1 Cor 4:5

Samson, an early Israelite hero, famous for his superhuman strength and his mighty exploits in the struggle against the Philistines. The tales present him as a Nazirite from birth, but his passion for foreign women compromised the Nazirite vow: Judges 13–16.

Saul, a Benjaminite from the mountain village of Gibeah who became Israel's first king (cf. the commentaries on 1 Samuel 9–31).

the handsome and unusually tall son of a prominent Benjaminite called Kish: 1 Sam 9:1-2
anointed by Samuel as king over Israel: 1 Sam 9:3–10:8
selected in a public lottery and acclaimed king by the people: 1 Sam 10:17-27
his kingship renewed or confirmed after his victory over the Ammonites: 1 Sam 11:14-15
his prowess as a military leader: 1 Sam 14:47-48
the war against the Philistines: 1 Sam 13:1-7; 15b-23; 14:1-23
his conflict with David: 1 Sam 18:6-30; 24:1-23; 26:1–27:1
rejected by God for disobedience to the instructions given him by Samuel: 1 Sam 15:10-35
Saul and the witch of En-Dor: 1 Sam 28:3-25
his defeat and death on Mt. Gilboa: 1 Samuel 31

Seed, the productive unit of a plant.

in contrast to trees: Gen 1:11, 12, 29
used as examples in four parables of Jesus:
- the seed and the weeds: Matt 13:24-30, 36-43
- the seed growing secretely: Mark 4:26-29
- the sower, seed, and soils: Matt 13:3-9, 18-23; Mark 4:3-9, 14-20; Luke 8:5-8, 11-15
- the mustard seed: Matt 13:31-32; Mark 4:30-32; Luke 13:18-19

Seek

God: Deut 4:29; Pss 40:16; 69:6; 105:3-4; Isa 55:6; Hos 5:6; Amos 5:4; Acts 17:27; cf. Pss 14:2; 53:2; Rom 3:11
the face of God: Ps 27:8-9
Jesus: John 6:26; 7:34-36; 13:33
the kingdom of God and God's justice: Matt 6:33; cf. Luke 12:31
the will of God: John 5:30
the things that are above: Col 3:1
peace: Ps 34:14; Heb 13:14; 1 Pet 3:11
justification in Christ: Gal 2:17
their own justice instead of submitting to the saving justice of God: Rom 10:2
death: Rev 9:6

Sin

revolt against God: Gen 3:1-7; Isa 1:2-3
transgression of God's laws: Ps 78:56; Rom 2:17-24; 5:13
unfaithfulness to God's covenant: Ps 78:10; Jer 11:10
disobedience to the Lord and forgetfulness of God's saving acts: Pss 78:11-58; 106:6-7, 13, 21-22

abandonment of the living God to follow lifeless idols: Jer 2:5, 11-12
desire "to be like God": Gen 3:5
the beginning of sin: Gen 3:1-13; Rom 5:12
sin, the sting of death: 1 Cor 15:55; cf. Wis 2:23-24
the heart as the source of sin: Jer 5:23; 17:9-10; Isa 29:13; Matt 15:18-20; Mark 7:21-22; Rom 1:29-30; cf. Ezek 36:26
the sinful condition of humanity: Ps 51:3-5; Prov 15:9; Eccl 7:20; 1 John 1:8-10
all people under the power of sin: Pss 14:1-4; 53:1-5; Rom 5:12
political and social sins: Isa 5:8; Amos 1:6, 9, 11, 13, 2:6-8; 4:1; Job 24:1-25; Eccl 5:7; Jas 5:1-6
the "unforgivable" sin against the Holy Spirit: Matt 12:31-32; Mark 3:28-29; Luke 12:10
sin implicit in the failure of a person to do right: Matt 25:41-46; Luke 16:19-21
in the failure to use God-given ability: Matt 25:24-30; Luke 19:20-26
God's eagerness to forgive sins: Ezek 18:23; Luke 15:1-32
the Servant of the Lord undergoes vicarious suffering for the sins of the people: Isa 53:4-12
repentance as the prerequisite of being forgiven: Ps 32:5; Isa 1:16-20; 57:15; Ezek 18:30-32; Joel 2:13-14; 1 John 1:9
Jesus as friend of sinners: Matt 9:10-13; Luke 15:1-2; 19:7
the remission of sins fully efficacious through Jesus' blood and by virtue of his resurrection: Acts 13:38-39; Rom 3:21-26; 4:25; 5:9; Heb 9:12-14; 1 Pet 1:18-19; 1 John 2:1-2; Rev 7:4

Solomon, also known as Jedidiah (Heb. "YHWH's beloved"), David's son by Bathsheba and his successor, who reigned for forty years (10th century B.C.E.).
his birth: 1 Sam 12:24-25
consecrated king on David's nomination: 1 Kings 1:28-40
Solomon's dream at Gibeon: 1 Kings 3:4-14; 2 Chr 1:3-12
his wisdom: 1 Kings 3:16-28; 5:9-14
the builder of the Temple: 1 Kings 5:15-38
Solomon's prayer on the feast of Dedication: 1 Kings 8:22-61
his decline: 1 Kings 11:1-40
the end of his reign: 1 Kings 11:41-43

Wisdom: *see* "Wisdom: A Way of Thinking About God," pp. 751–757.

Work: *see* general article on pp. 293–297.

Wrath, the divine reaction to human sin.
as the result of human disobedience and transgression: Num 11:1; Ps 85:3-5; Mic 7:9; Rom 1:18; 4:15; Eph 5:6; Col 3:6
even in reaction God is "slow to anger": Ps 103:8-10; Joel 2:13
Jesus' angry reaction against those who desecrated the Temple: John 2:13-17
Jesus as the one who saves us from the wrath that is coming: John 3:36; 1 Thess 1:10
now justified by the blood of Christ, much more shall we be saved by him from the wrath of God: Rom 5:9

Zipporah, one of the seven daughters of Reuel, priest of Midian (also known as Jethro).
her unexpected encounter with Moses: Exod 2:16-17
given to Moses as his wife: Exod 2:18-22
credited with saving her husband's life by circumcising her son and touching Moses with the foreskin: Exod 4:24-26
brought by Jethro to Moses when he came to meet Israel in the desert: Exod 18:2-5

Map Index

NOTE: The following Index is a repertoire of geographical place names as they appear in this Commentary, including the different maps (those inserted in the text and those grouped at the end of the volume). Not all occurrences are listed here, but only when the reader may learn something about the place mentioned. Some biblical books and their ad hoc commentaries are replete with a given place name; in such cases the Index quotes only the first occurrence of the name and adds "etc."

LINE DRAWING MAPS (IN TEXT)

SIGNATURE (COLOR) MAPS

A

B

C

OLD TESTAMENT

A

B

C

D

E

G

H

I

J

K

L

M

T

U

V

Z

NEW TESTAMENT

1. Culture and Commerce in the Ancient Near East of the First Millennium

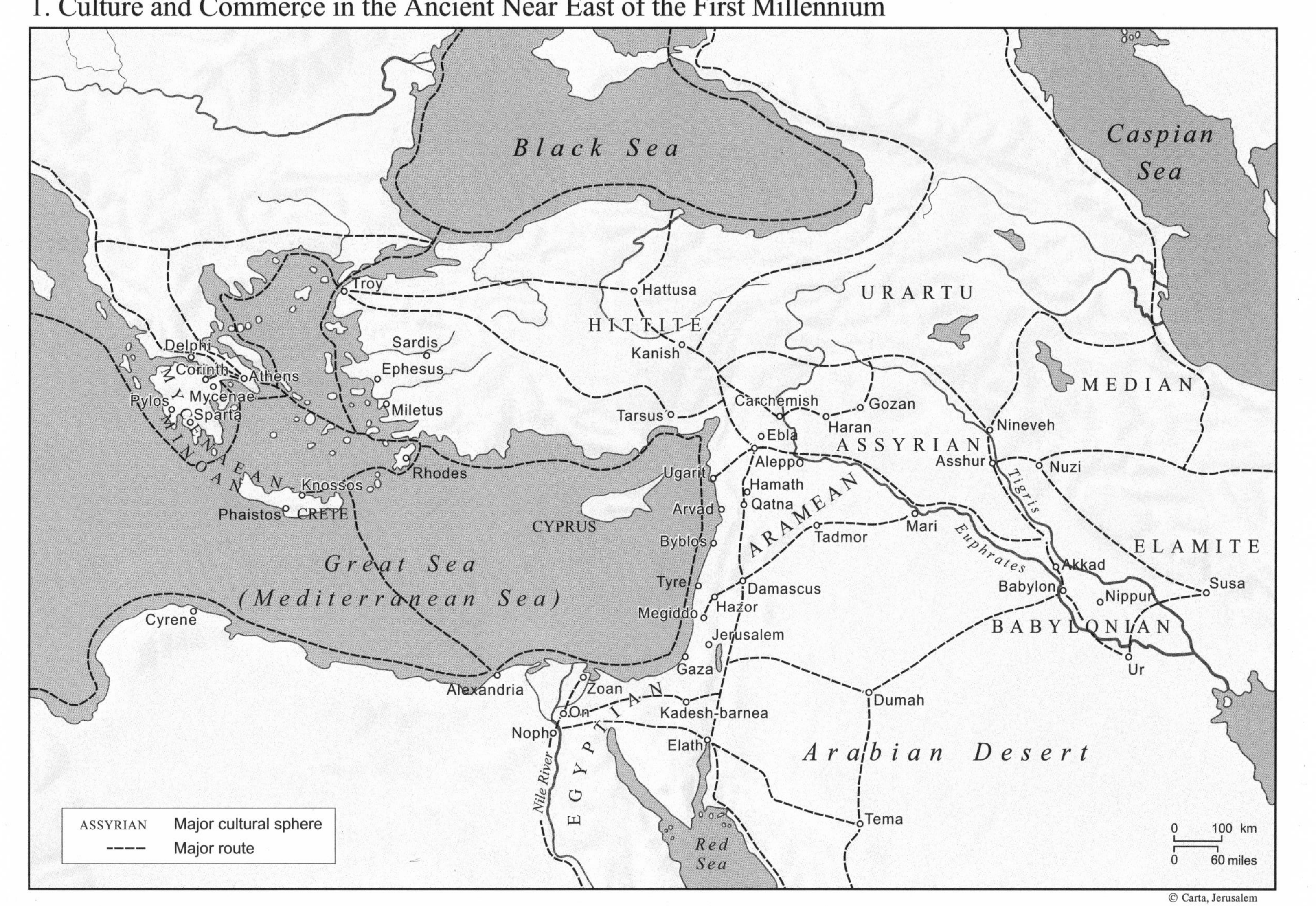

2. Palestine: Physical Geography

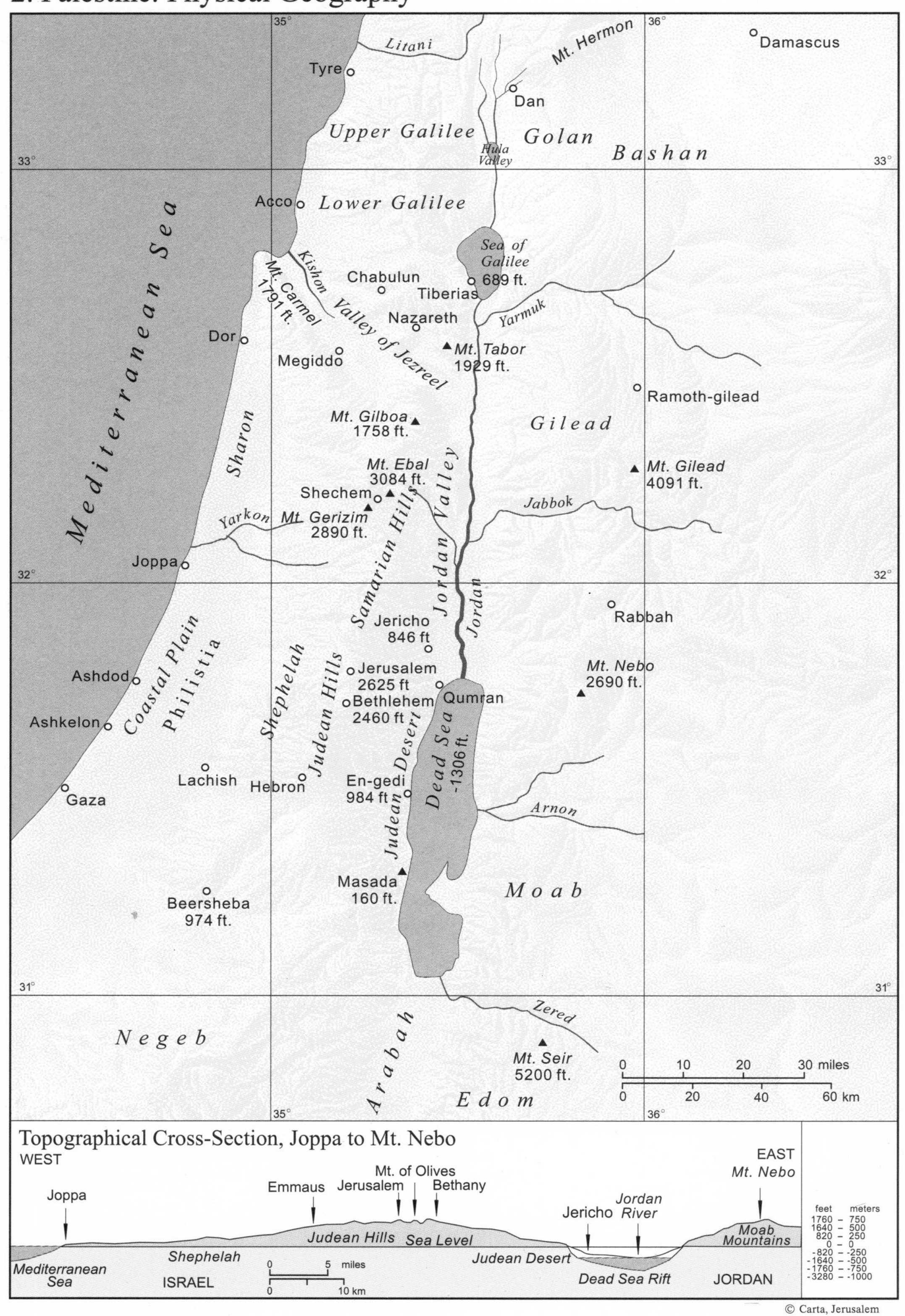

3. Abraham's Journey (2nd Millennium)

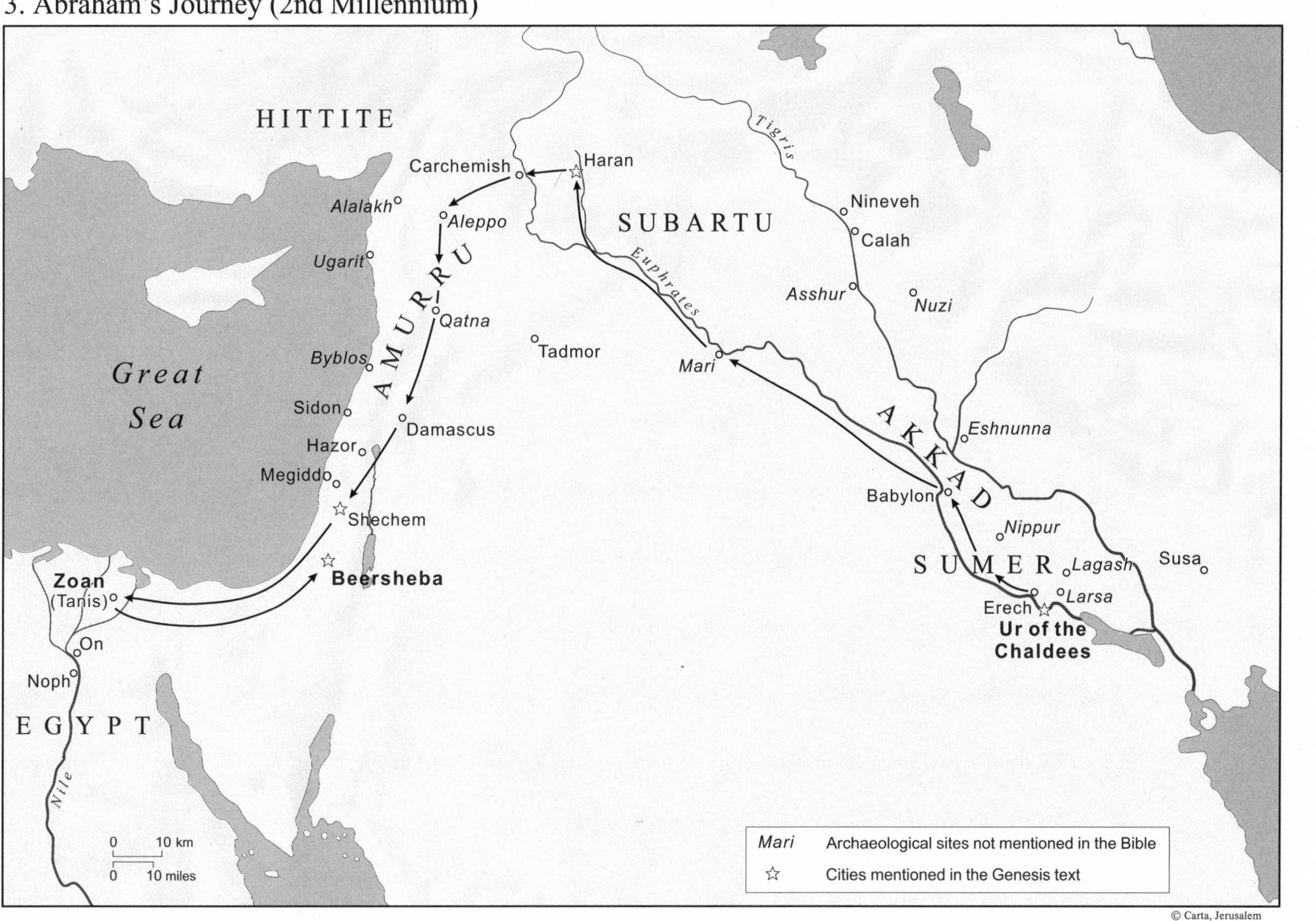

Genesis 11:31-13:1

4. The Exodus and Conquest of Canaan (13th Century)

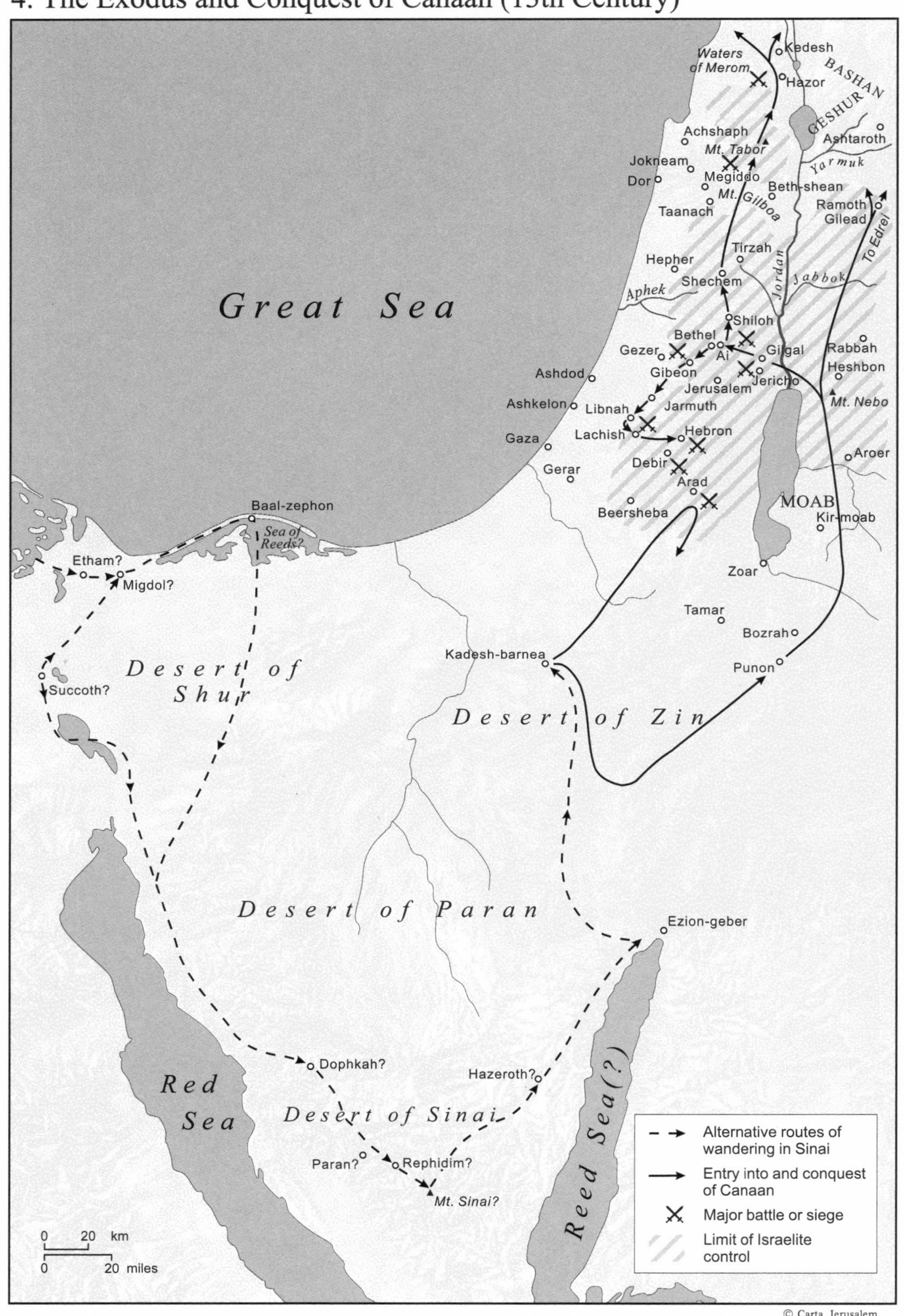

Exodus 12:37-19:2; Numbers 10:11-14:45; 20-21; 27:12-23; 31-33; Joshua 1-12; Judges 1

5. Tribal Territories of the Israelites

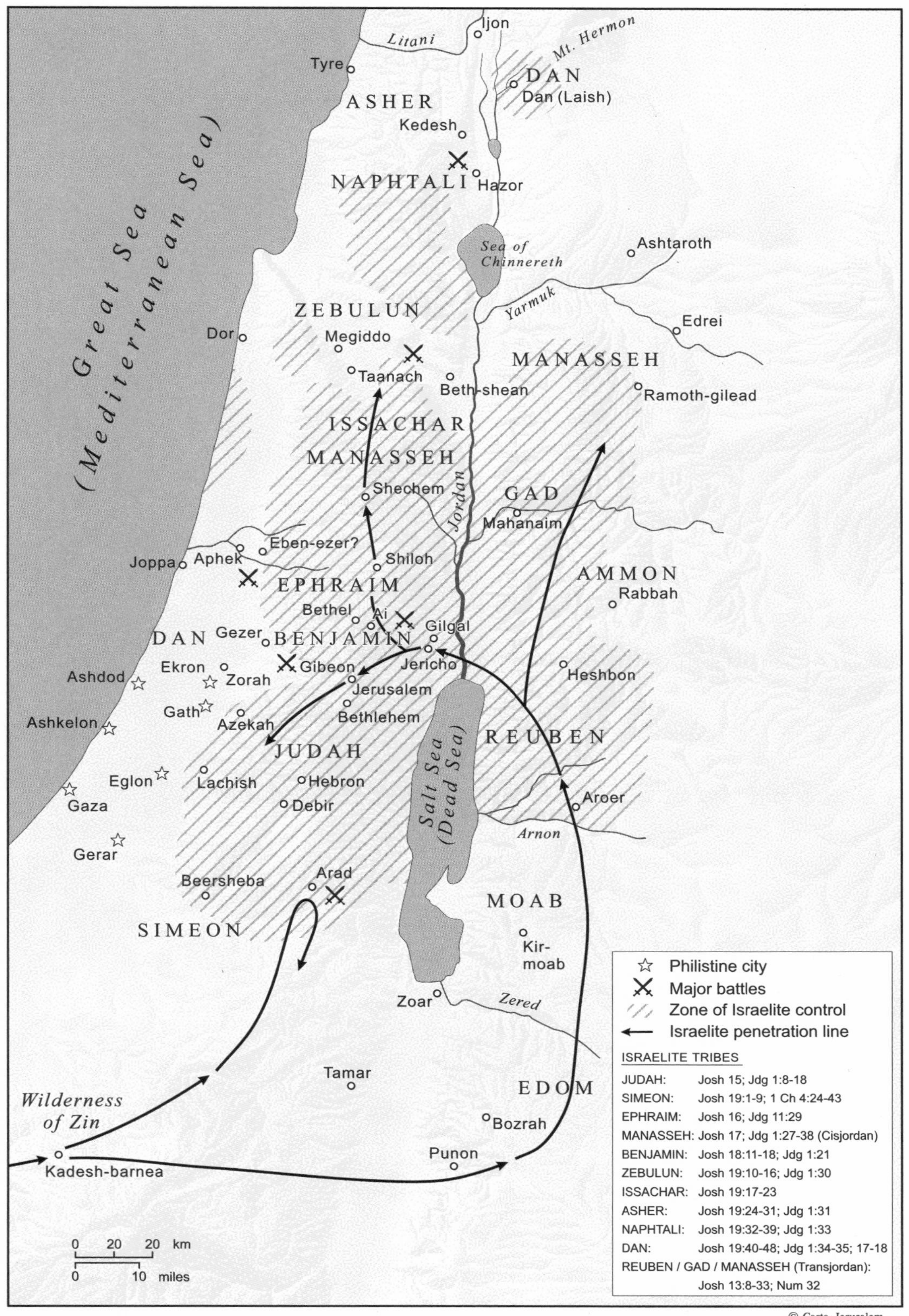

Litani
Ijon
Mt. Hermon
Tyre
DAN
Dan (Laish)
ASHER
Kedesh
NAPHTALI
Hazor
Great Sea
(Mediterranean Sea)
Sea of Chinnereth
Ashtaroth
Yarmuk
ZEBULUN
Edrei
Dor
Megiddo
MANASSEH
Taanach
Beth-shean
Ramoth-gilead
ISSACHAR
MANASSEH
Shechem
Jordan
GAD
Mahanaim
Eben-ezer?
Joppa
Aphek
Shiloh
AMMON
EPHRAIM
Rabbah
Bethel
Ai
Gilgal
DAN
Gezer
BENJAMIN
Ekron
Gibeon
Jericho
Heshbon
Ashdod
Zorah
Jerusalem
Gath
Azekah
Bethlehem
Ashkelon
JUDAH
REUBEN
Salt Sea (Dead Sea)
Eglon
Lachish
Hebron
Aroer
Gaza
Debir
Arnon
Gerar
Arad
Beersheba
MOAB
SIMEON
Kir-moab
Zoar
Zered
Tamar
EDOM
Wilderness of Zin
Bozrah
Punon
Kadesh-barnea
0 20 20 km
0 10 miles
Philistine city
Major battles
Zone of Israelite control
Israelite penetration line
ISRAELITE TRIBES
JUDAH: Josh 15; Jdg 1:8-18
SIMEON: Josh 19:1-9; 1 Ch 4:24-43
EPHRAIM: Josh 16; Jdg 11:29
MANASSEH: Josh 17; Jdg 1:27-38 (Cisjordan)
BENJAMIN: Josh 18:11-18; Jdg 1:21
ZEBULUN: Josh 19:10-16; Jdg 1:30
ISSACHAR: Josh 19:17-23
ASHER: Josh 19:24-31; Jdg 1:31
NAPHTALI: Josh 19:32-39; Jdg 1:33
DAN: Josh 19:40-48; Jdg 1:34-35; 17-18
REUBEN / GAD / MANASSEH (Transjordan): Josh 13:8-33; Num 32

6. Samuel and the Ark of the Covenant (11th Century)

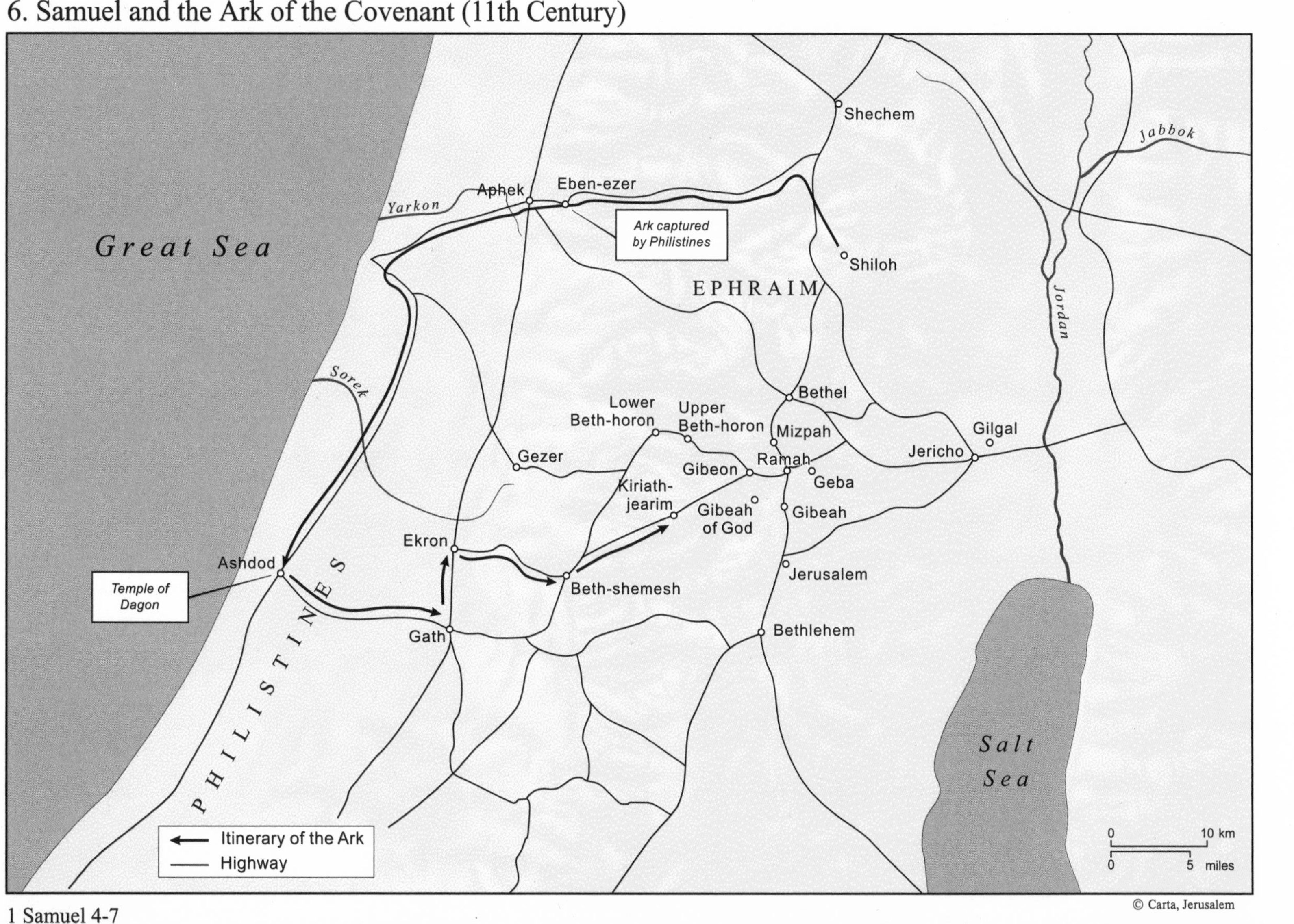

1 Samuel 4-7

7. Israel's Hegemony at the Time of David and Solomon (10th Century)

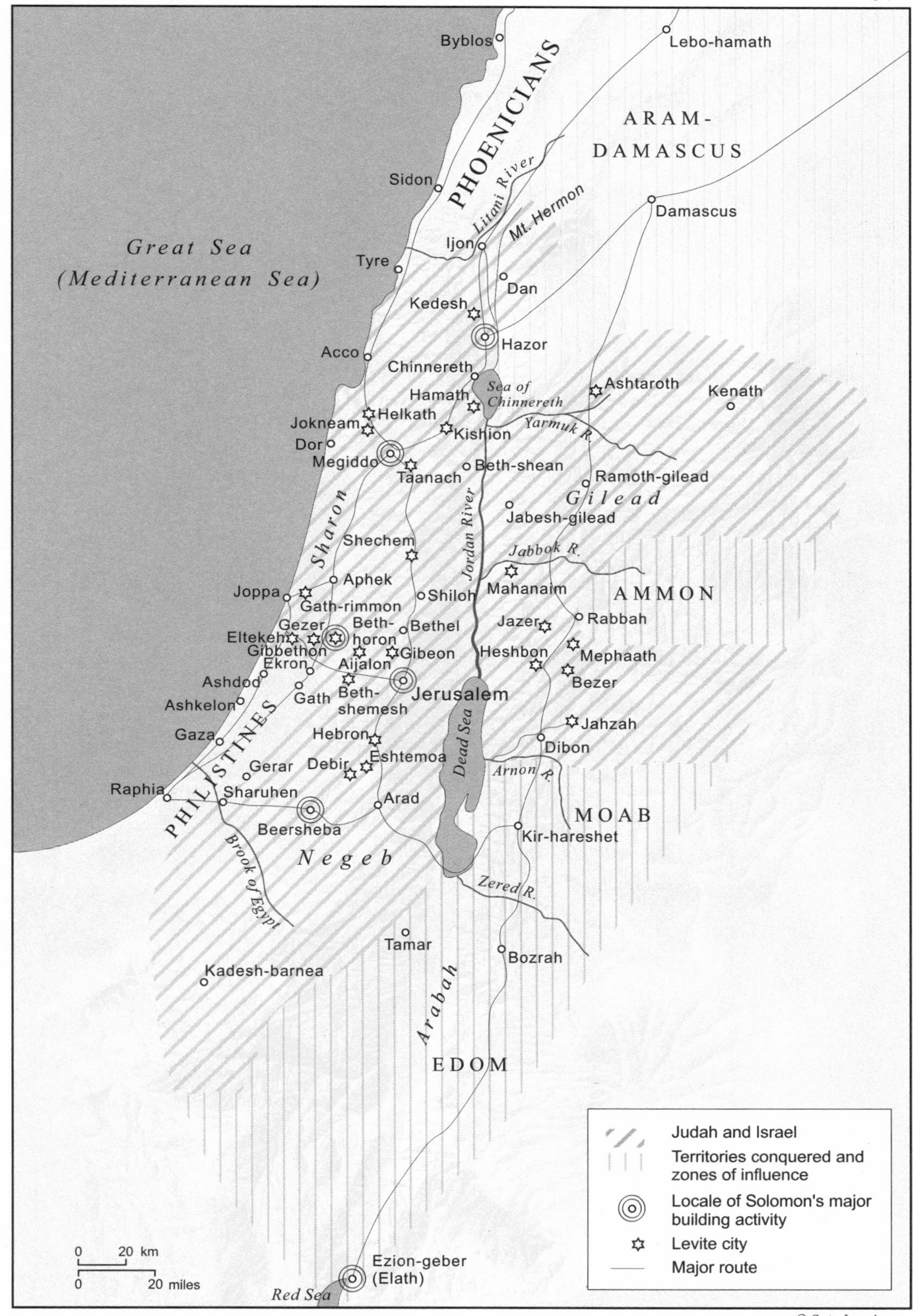
Byblos
Lebo-hamath
PHOENICIANS
ARAM-
DAMASCUS
Sidon
Litani River
Mt. Hermon
Damascus
Great Sea
(Mediterranean Sea)
Ijon
Tyre
Dan
Kedesh
Hazor
Acco
Chinnereth
Sea of Chinnereth
Hamath
Ashtaroth
Kenath
Helkath
Jokneam
Kishion
Yarmuk R.
Dor
Megiddo
Taanach
Beth-shean
Ramoth-gilead
Gilead
Sharon
Jabesh-gilead
Jordan River
Shechem
Jabbok R.
Aphek
Mahanaim
AMMON
Joppa
Shiloh
Gath-rimmon
Gezer
Beth-horon
Bethel
Jazer
Rabbah
Eltekeh
Gibbethon
Gibeon
Heshbon
Mephaath
Ekron
Aijalon
Ashdod
Bezer
Gath
Beth-shemesh
Jerusalem
Ashkelon
Gaza
PHILISTINES
Hebron
Jahzah
Dead Sea
Dibon
Debir
Eshtemoa
Gerar
Arnon R.
Raphia
Sharuhen
Arad
MOAB
Beersheba
Kir-hareshet
Negeb
Brook of Egypt
Zered R.
Tamar
Bozrah
Kadesh-barnea
Arabah
EDOM
Judah and Israel
Territories conquered and zones of influence
Locale of Solomon's major building activity
Levite city
Major route
0 20 km
0 20 miles
Ezion-geber
(Elath)
Red Sea

Genesis 15; 2 Samuel 8; 10; 19; 1 Kings 4:24

8. The Two Kingdoms at the Time of Jeroboam II (787-747)

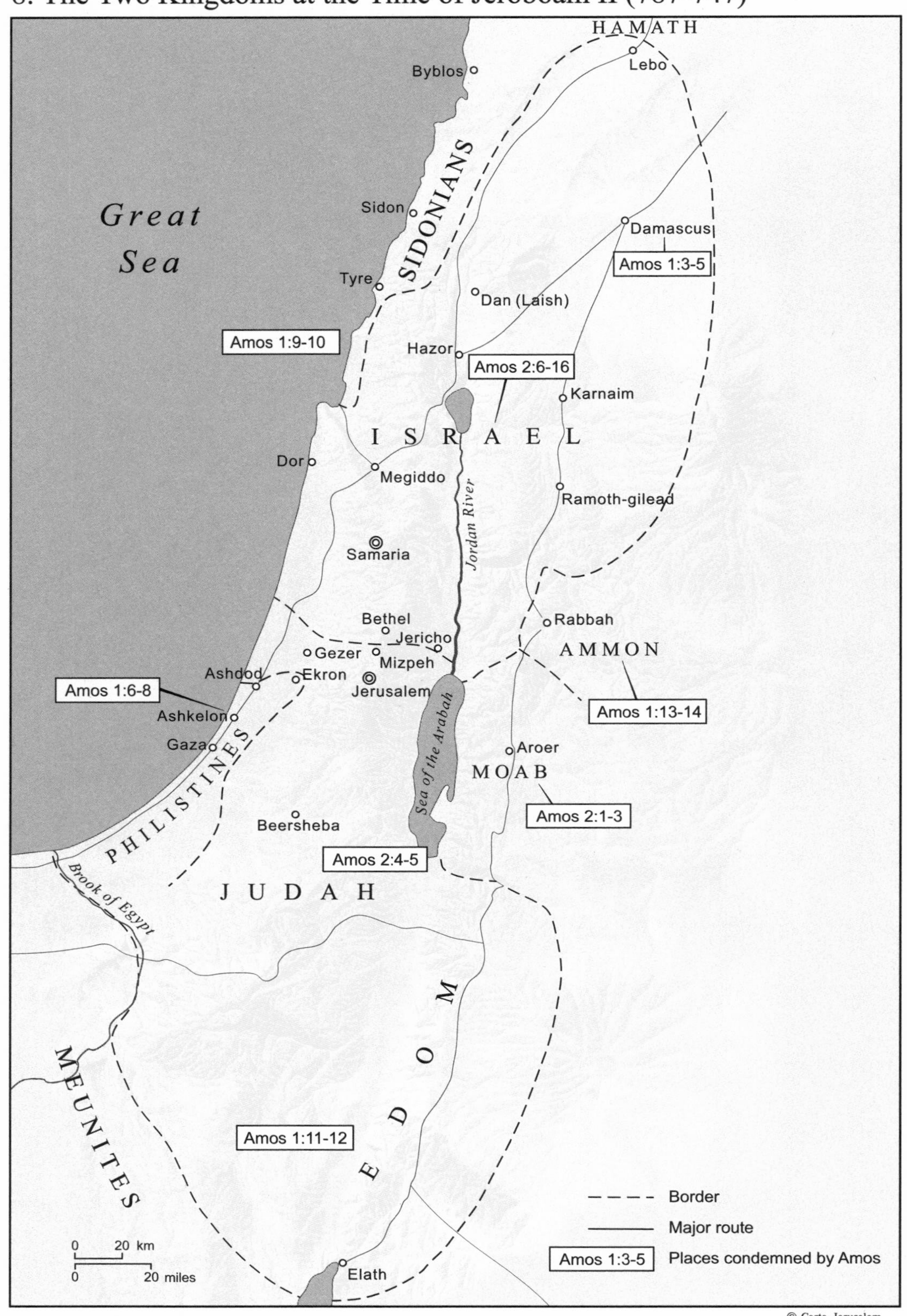

2 Kings 14:23-29; 2 Chronicles 26:7; Amos 1-2

9. The Assyrian Empire (8th Century)

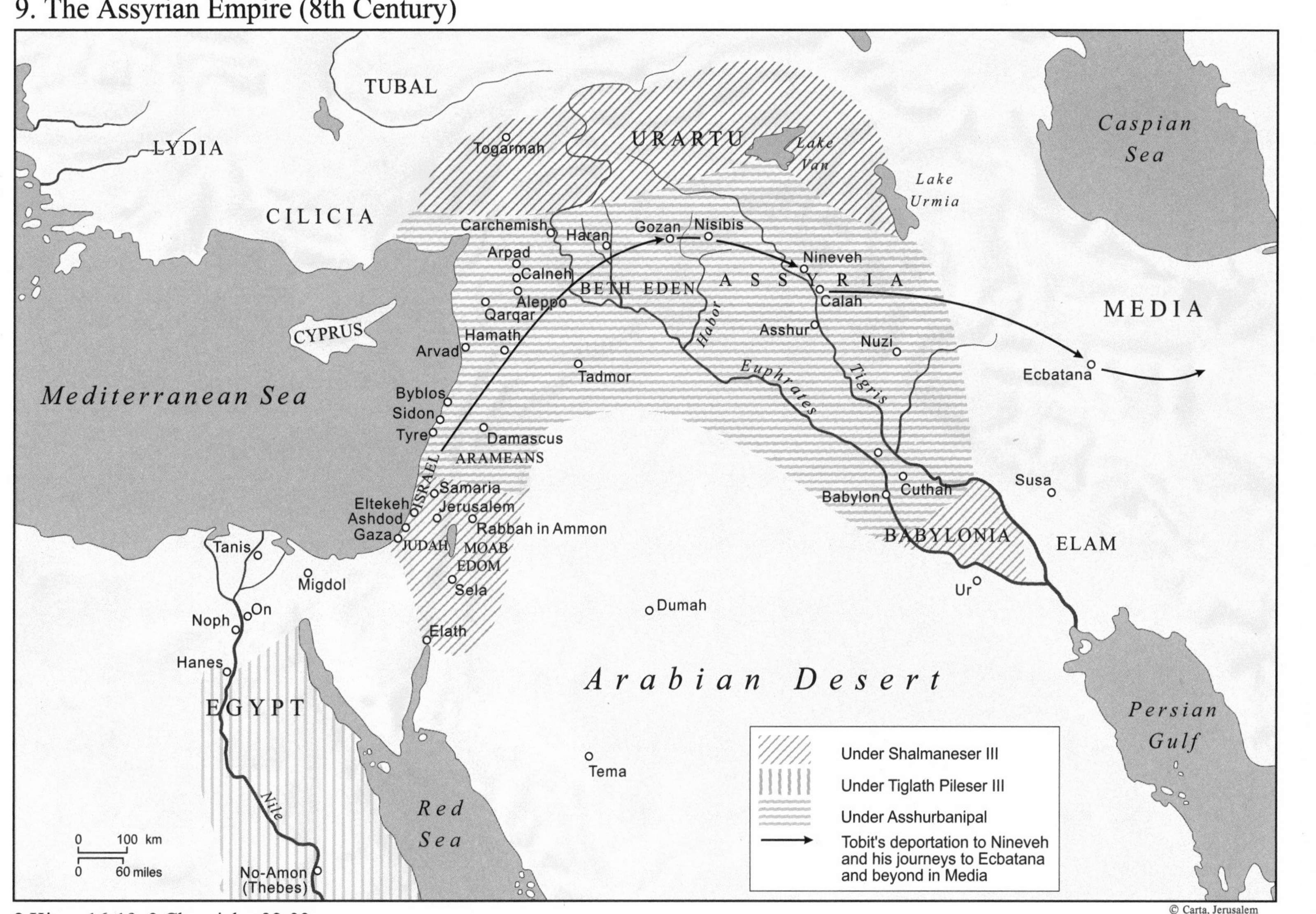

2 Kings 16-19; 2 Chronicles 32-33

10. The Babylonian Empire and the Conquest of Judah (6th Century)

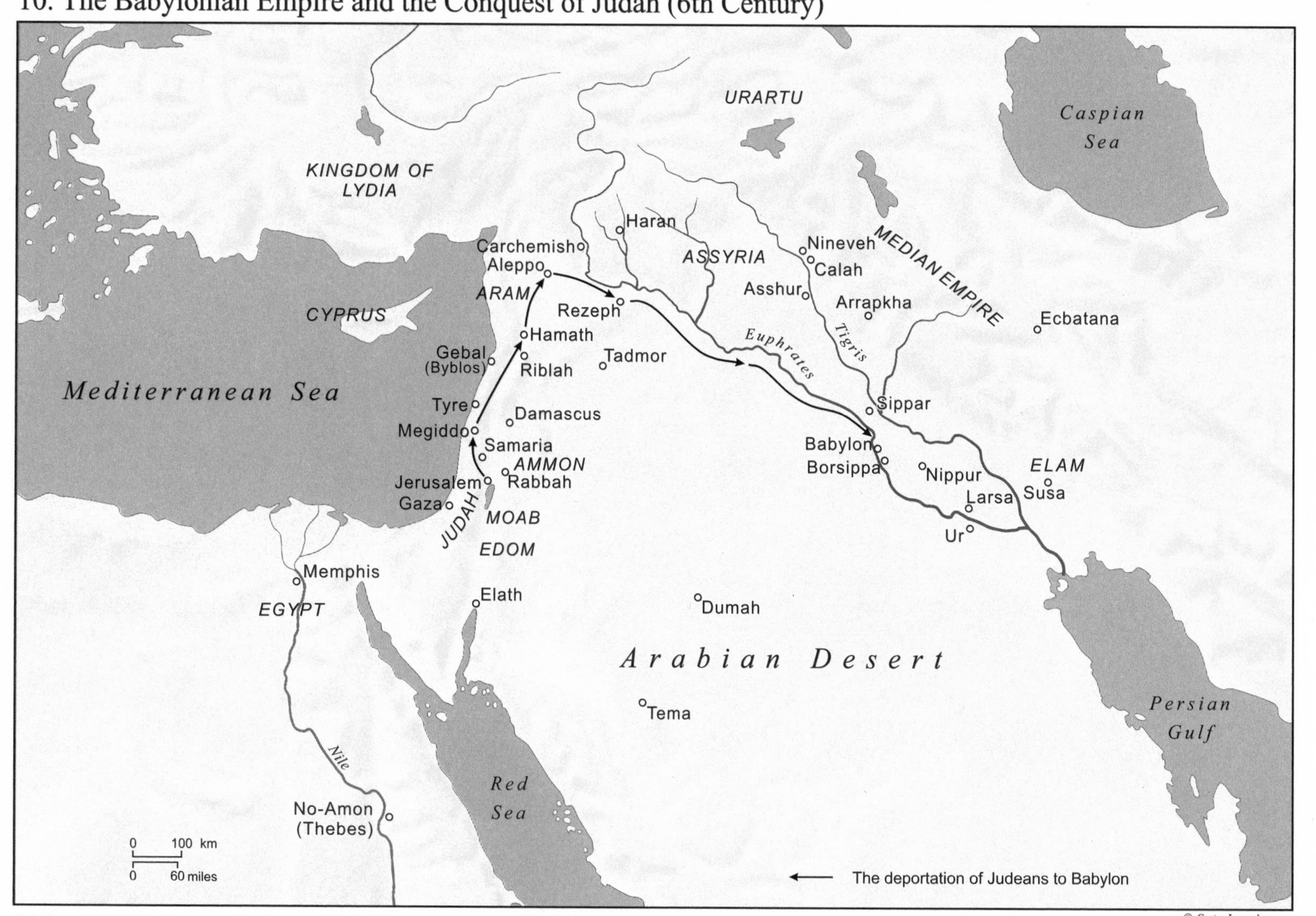

2 Kings 24-25:21; 2 Chronicles 36; Jeremiah 39

11. The Persian Empire (Time of Darius I: 522-486)

12. The World of the Greeks (Fourth Century)

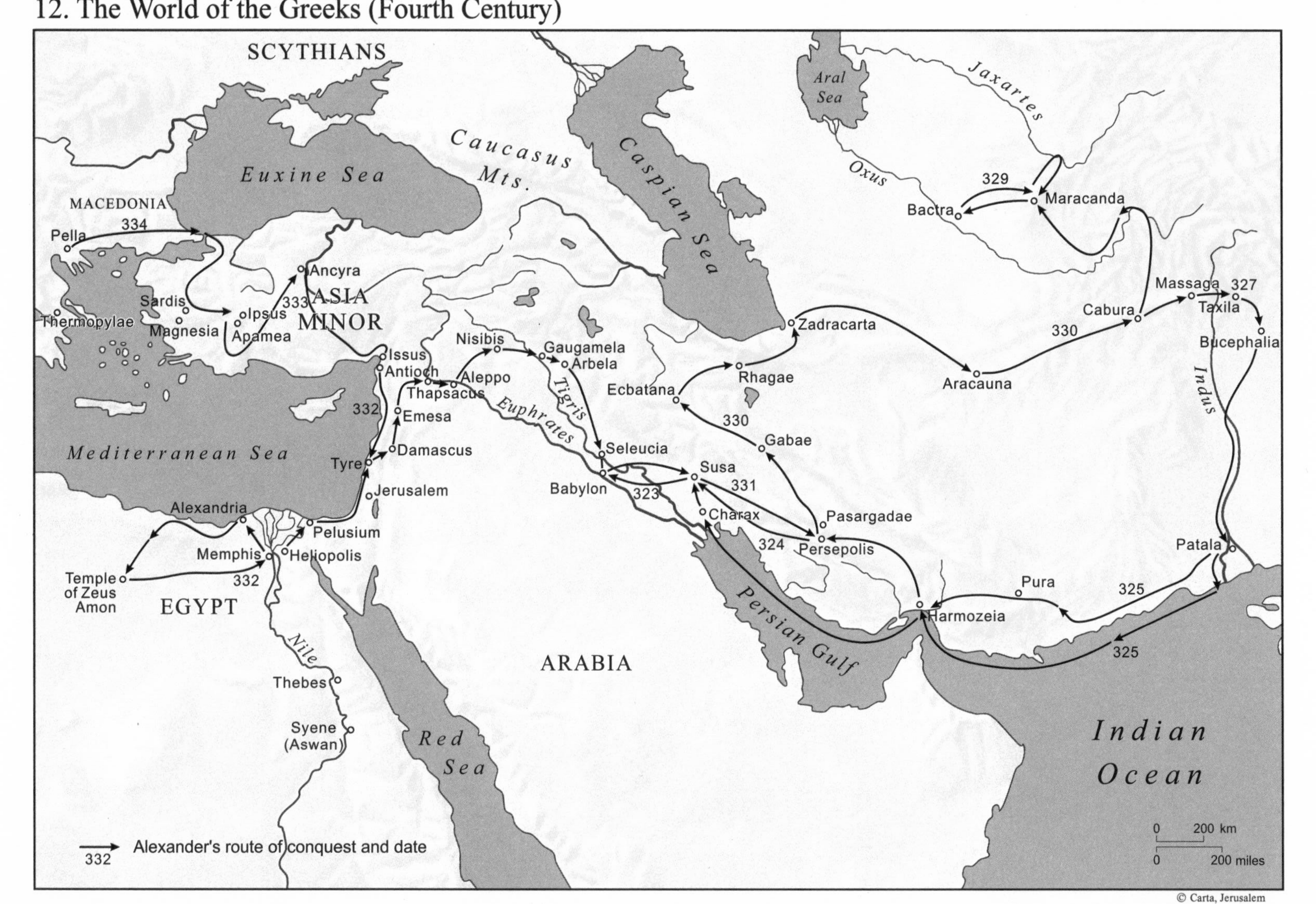

13. The Roman Empire (ca. 150 C.E.)

14. Jesus in His Land

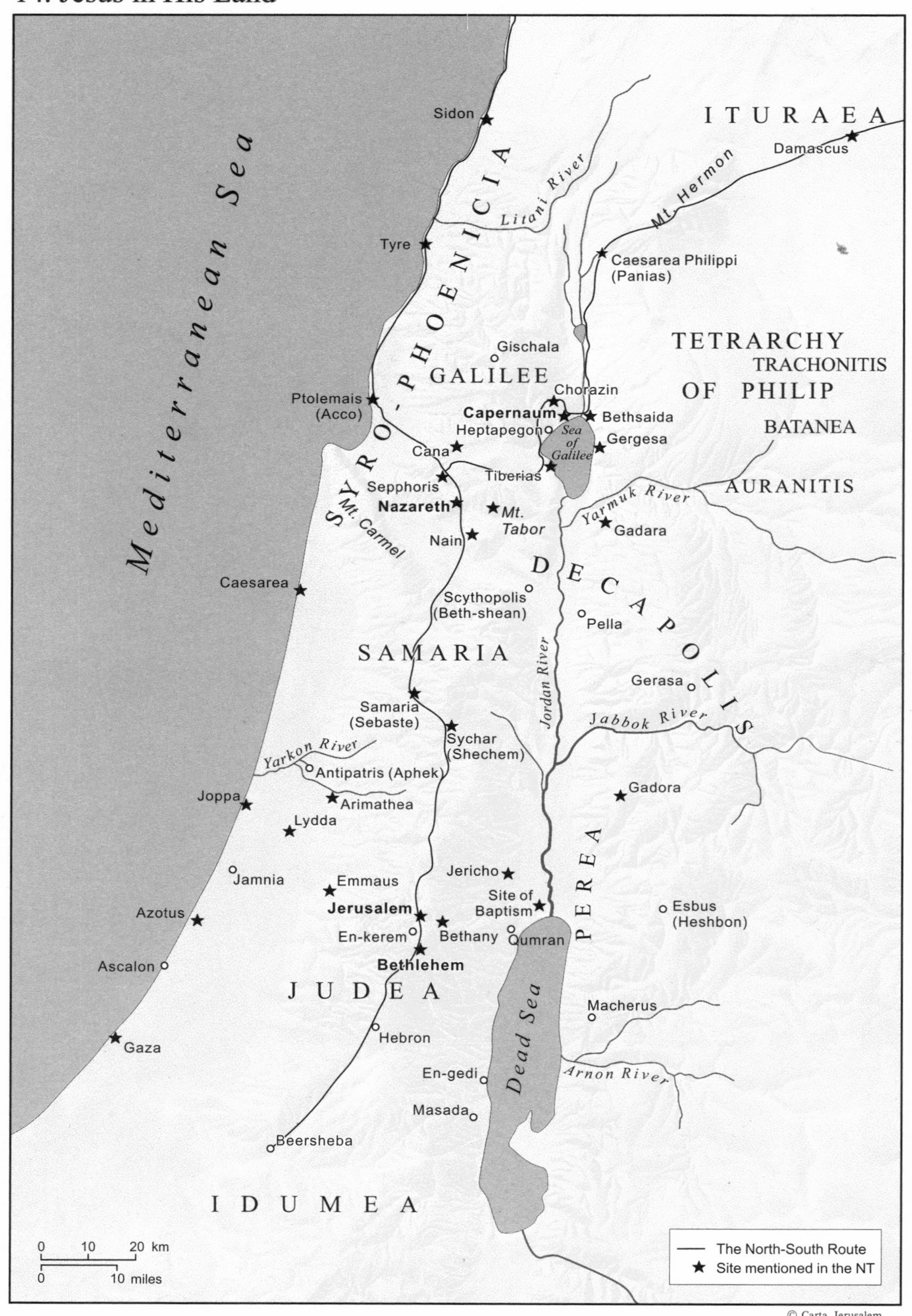

Mediterranean Sea
Sidon
ITURAEA
Damascus
Litani River
Mt. Hermon
Tyre
Caesarea Philippi
(Panias)
SYRO-PHOENICIA
Gischala
GALILEE
TETRARCHY
TRACHONITIS
OF PHILIP
Chorazin
Ptolemais
(Acco)
Capernaum
Bethsaida
Heptapegon
Sea of Galilee
BATANEA
Gergesa
Cana
Tiberias
Sepphoris
AURANITIS
Yarmuk River
Nazareth
Mt. Tabor
Mt. Carmel
Nain
Gadara
Caesarea
DECAPOLIS
Scythopolis
(Beth-shean)
Pella
SAMARIA
Jordan River
Gerasa
Samaria
(Sebaste)
Jabbok River
Sychar
(Shechem)
Yarkon River
Antipatris (Aphek)
Joppa
Gadora
Arimathea
Lydda
PEREA
Jamnia
Jericho
Emmaus
Site of
Baptism
Azotus
Jerusalem
Esbus
(Heshbon)
En-kerem
Bethany
Qumran
Ascalon
Bethlehem
JUDEA
Dead Sea
Macherus
Hebron
Gaza
En-gedi
Arnon River
Masada
Beersheba
IDUMEA
0 10 20 km
0 10 miles
The North-South Route
Site mentioned in the NT